Standard Catalog of®

World Paper Money

Specialized Issues

Edited by George S. Cuhaj

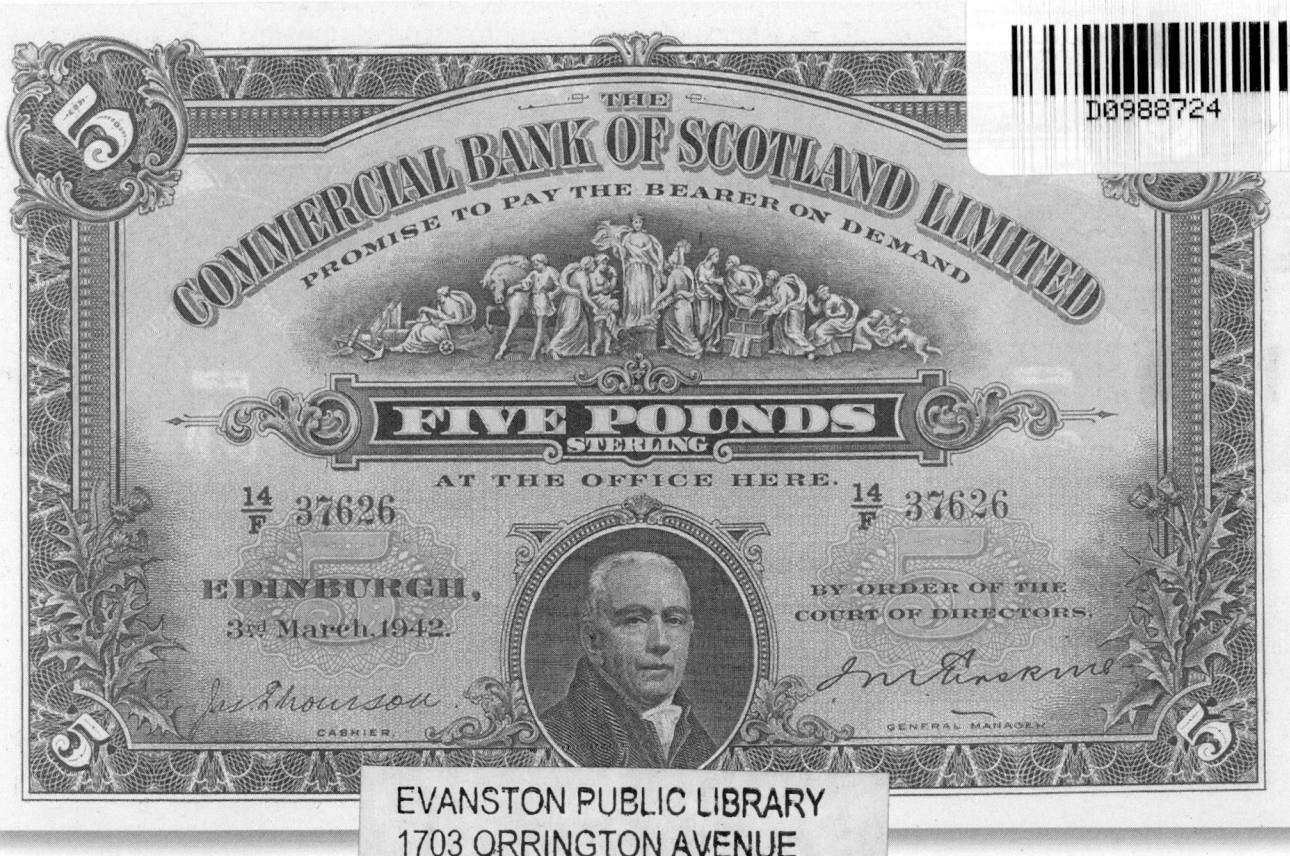

11th Edition

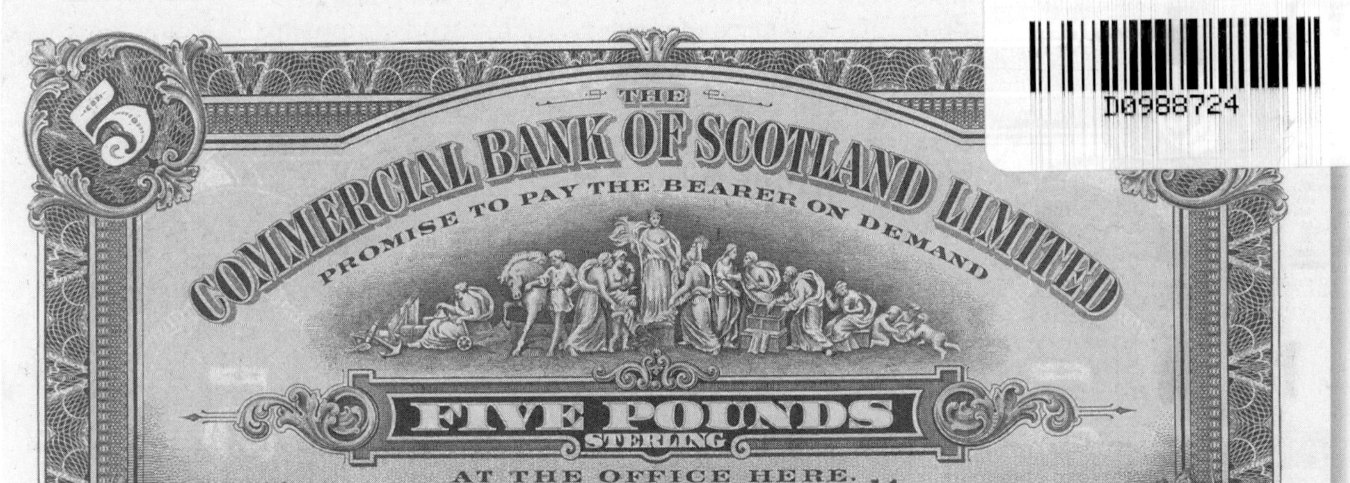

PROMISE TO PAY THE BEARER ON DEMAND
FIVE POUNDS

AT THE OFFICE HERE.
14/F 37626
14/F 37626

3rd March, 1942.
BY ORDER OF THE
COURT OF DIRECTORS.

kp The World's Authority on Paper Money

Published by

krause publications

A subsidiary of F+W Media, Inc.

700 East State Street • Iola, WI 54990-0001
715-445-2214 • 888-457-2873
www.krausebooks.com

ISSN 1538-1994
ISBN-13: 978-1-4402-0450-0
ISBN-10: 1-4402-0450-0

Designed by: Sandi Carpenter
Edited by: George Cuhaj

Printed in the United States of America

Introduction

Welcome to this 11th edition of the *Standard Catalog of World Paper Money, Specialized Issues.*

For those of you already familiar with this volume, you will be glad to see an upgrade in illustration quality. Numerous additions have been made to the text, variety listings and illustrations. Extensive specimen varieties continue to be added throughout.

This volume presents bank notes issued by states, municipalities and companies which circulated on a local or regional basis in addition to Foreign Exchange Certificates and Military Payment Certificates. Many of these notes are scarce or rare, and some only exist in proof or remainder form.

This volume is a companion to the *Standard Catalog of World Paper Money, General Issues, 1368-1960* which covers world paper money from the earliest known Chinese notes of 1368 to issues circulating in 1960, and the *Standard Catalog of World Paper Money, Modern Issues – 1961 to present.*

For the ease of identification, notes are listed under their historic country identification (British Honduras is no longer hidden within Belize). North Korea and South Korea are now under N and S respectively, not under K. Northern Ireland is under N. Please consult the country or bank issuer index.

Notes of a particular bank are listed in release date order, and then grouped in ascending denomination order. In the cases of countries where more than one issuing authority is in effect at a single time, follow the bank headings in the listings and it will become apparent if that country's listing is by date or alphabetical by issuing authority. In the cases where a country has changed from a kingdom to a republic all the banknotes of the kingdom's era would be listed before that of the republic. Please use the extensive Bank Note Issuer Index starting on page 7.

If you wish to contribute images, please contact us first and follow the guidelines as set forth in the information notices placed throughout the book. We can accept them as JPGs, and preferably on a disc, rather than as an email attachment. But please contact us first before you do a lot of work, duplicating items already in progress for inclusion in future editions.

An Invitation

Users of this catalog may find a helpful adjunct to be the Bank Note Reporter, the only monthly newspaper devoted exclusively to North American and world paper money. Each issue presents up-to-date news, feature articles and valuable information. All purchasers of this catalog are invited to subscribe to the Bank Note Reporter. Requests for a sample copy should be addressed to Bank Note Reporter, 700 East State Street, Iola, WI, 54990-0001.

Table of Contents

A review of modern paper money collecting

Paper money collecting is probably as old as paper money itself. However, this segment of the numismatic hobby did not begin to reach a popularity approaching that of coin collecting until the latter half of the 1970's. While coins and paper money are alike in that both served as legal obligations to facilitate commerce, long-time paper money enthusiasts know the similarity ends there.

Coins were historically guaranteed by the intrinsic value of their metallic content - at least until recent years when virtually all circulating coins have become little more than legal tender tokens, containing little or no precious metal - while paper money possesses a value only when it is accepted for debts or converted into bullion or precious metals. With many note issues, this conversion privilege was limited and ultimately negated by the imposition of redemption cutoff dates.

The development of widespread collector interest in paper money of most nations was inhibited by a near total absence of adequate documentation. No more than four decades ago collectors could refer to only a few catalogs and dealer price lists of limited scope, most of which were difficult to acquire, or they could build their own knowledge through personal collecting pursuits and contact with fellow collectors.

The early catalogs authored by Albert Pick chronicled issues of Europe and the Americas and were assembled as stepping-stones to the ultimate objective, which became reality with publication of the first Standard Catalog of World Paper Money in 1975. That work provided collectors with fairly complete listings and up-to-date valuations of all recorded government note issues of the 20th century, incorporating Pick's previously unpublished manuscripts on Africa, Asia and Oceania, plus many earlier issues.

The completely revised and updated 16th Edition of Volume III, Modern Issues, along with the companion 12th Edition Volume II General Issues, presents a substantial extension of the cataloging effort initiated in 1975 and revised in succeeding editions. As the most comprehensive world paper money references ever assembled, they fully document the many and varied legal tender paper currencies issued and circulated by over 380 past and current government issuing authorities of the world from 1360's to present.

Falling within the scope of this Specialized Issues volume are all state, local, municipal and company issues which circulated under auspices of recognized regional governments ands and their banking agents - thus notes which enjoyed limited circulation in their respective countries. Exceptions are the multitudinous notes of the German states and cities, especially those of the World War I and postwar period to 1923, and the vast category of Chinese local issues and similar limited-circulation issues of other countries.

George S. Cuhaj
Editor

Acknowledgements

The contributions to this catalog have been many and varied, and to recognize them all would be a volume in itself. Accordingly, we wish to acknowledge these collectors, scholars and dealers in the world paper money field, both past and present, for their specific contributions to this work through the submission of notes for illustration, improved descriptive information and market valuations.

Alex Abezgauz
Esko Ahlroth
Walter D. Allan
Jorge E. Arbelaez
Keith Austin
Cem Barlok
Adriaan C. F. Beck
Wolfgang Bertsch
Milt Blackburn
Ed Bohannon
Joseph E. Boling
Jean Bricaud
Colin R. Bruce II
Jonathan Calloway
David Carew
Arthur D. Cohen
Alan M. Cole
Scott E. Cordry
Guido Crapanzano
Ray Czahor
Michel Dufour
Wilhelm Eglseer
Esko Ekman
Guvendik Fisekcioglu
Luis H. Flores
Wolfgang A. Frick
Carl Gomez
Lee Gordon
Urs Graf
Rajni Gupta
Flemming Lynbeck Hansen
James A. Haxby
Mikhail Istomin
Sergio Jaramillo
Kishore Jhunjhunwalla
Alex Kaglyan
Josef Klaus
John Kleeberg
Wolfgang Koenig
Chester L. Krause
Samson Kim Chiu Lai
Michael Lang
Akos Ledai
Claire Lobel
Alan Luedeking
Ma Tok Wo
John T. Martin
Martin MacDevitt
Rolf Marklin
Ian A. Marshall
John T. Martin
Arthur C. Matz
Leo May
Ali Mehilba
Donald Medcalf
William Myers
Michael Morris
Arthur H. Morowitz
Jon Morowitz
Richard Murdoch
David Murphy
Tanju Mutlu
Colin Narbeth
Eric P. Newman
Antonio E. Pedraza
Juan Pena
A.A.C. de Albergaria Pinheiro
Tony Pisciotta
Laurence Pope
Rick Ponterio
Miguel A. Pratt-Myans
Michel Prieur
Nazir Rahemtulla
Kavan Ratnatunga
Rudolph Richter
Alistair Robb
Kerry Rodgers
William M. Rosenblum
Alan Sadd
Karl Saethre
Wolfgang Schuster
Timothy R.G. Sear
David Seelyee
Joel Shafer
Brian A. Silsbee
Ladislav Sin
Gary Snover
Mauricio Soto
Lee Shin Song
Jimmie C. Steelman
Jeremy Steinberg
Mel Steinberg
Tim Steiner
Alim A. Sumana
Imre Szatmari
Steven Tan
Mark Tomasko
Anthony Tumonis
Jan Vandersande
Michael Vort-Ronald
Ludek Vostal
Evangelos Vyzas
Trevor Wilkin
Heinz Wirz
Yu Jian Hua
Christof Zellweger

INSTITUTIONS AND SOCIETIES:

American Numismatic Association
American Numismatic Society
International Bank Note Society
Smithsonian Institution

Country & State Index

Bank Note Issuer Index

Numerics

A

B

C

D

E

F

G

H

I

M

N

O

P

T

U

V

W

Y

Z

Standard International Numeral Systems

Prepared especially for the ***Standard Catalog of World Paper Money***© 2009 by Krause Publications

Western	0	½	1	2	3	4	5	6	7	8	9	10	50	100	500	1000
Roman			I	II	III	IV	V	VI	VII	VIII	IX	X	L	C	D	M
Arabic-Turkish	٠	١/٢	١	٢	٣	٤	٥	٦	٧	٨	٩	١٠	٥٠	١٠٠	٥٠٠	١٠٠٠
Malay-Persian	٠	١/٢	١	٢	٣	۴	۵	٦ or ۶	٧	٨	٩	١٠	۵٠	١٠٠	۵٠٠	١٠٠٠
Eastern Arabic	०	१/२	۱	۲	۳	۴	۵	۶	۷	۸	۹	۱०	۵०	۱००	۵००	۱०००
Hyderabad Arabic	٥	١/٢	١	٢	٣	٤	٥	٦	٧	٨	٩	١٠	٥٠	١٠٠	٥٠٠	١٠٠٠
Indian (Sanskrit)	०	१/२	१	२	३	४	५	६	७	८	९	१०	५०	१००	५००	१०००
Assamese	০	১/২	১	২	৩	৪	৫	৬	৭	৮	৯	১০	৫০	১০০	৫০০	১০০০
Bengali	০	১/২	১	২	৩	৪	৫	৬	৭	৮	৯	১০	৫০	১০০	৫০০	১০০০
Gujarati	૦	૧/૨	૧	૨	૩	૪	૫	૬	૭	૮	૯	૧૦	૫૦	૧૦૦	૫૦૦	૧૦૦૦
Kutch	०	१/२	१	२	३	४	५	६	७	८	९	१०	५०	१००	५००	१०००
Devavnagri	०	१/२	१	२	३	४	५	६ or ६	७	८	९ or ९	१०	५०	१००	५००	१०००
Nepalese	०	१/२	१	२	३	४	५	६	७	८	९	१०	५०	१००	५००	१०००
Tibetan	༠	༡/༢	༡	༢	༣	༤	༥	༦	༧	༨	༩	༡༠	༥༠	༡༠༠	༥༠༠	༡༠༠༠
Mongolian	᠐	᠑/᠒	᠑	᠒	᠓	᠔	᠕	᠖	᠗	᠘	᠙	᠑᠐	᠕᠐	᠑᠐᠐	᠕᠐᠐	᠑᠐᠐᠐
Burmese	၀	၁/၂	၁	၂	၃	၄	၅	၆	၇	၈	၉	၁၀	၅၀	၁၀၀	၅၀၀	၁၀၀၀
Thai-Lao	๐	๑/๒	๑	๒	๓	๔	๕	๖	๗	๘	๙	๑๐	๕๐	๑๐๐	๕๐๐	๑๐๐๐
Lao-Laotian	໐		໑	໒	໓	໔	໕	໖	໗	໘	໙	໑໐				
Javanese	꧐		꧑	꧒	꧓	꧔	꧕	꧖	꧗	꧘	꧙	꧑꧐	꧕꧐	꧑꧐꧐	꧕꧐꧐	꧑꧐꧐꧐
Ordinary Chinese Japanese-Korean	零	半	一	二	三	四	五	六	七	八	九	十	十五	百	百五	千
Official Chinese			壹	貳	叁	肆	伍	陸	柒	捌	玖	拾	拾伍	佰	佰伍	仟
Commercial Chinese			〡	〢	〣	〤	〥	〦	〧	〨	〩	十	〥十	〡百	〥百	〡千
Korean		반	일	이	삼	사	오	육	칠	팔	구	십	오십	백	오백	천
Georgian			ა	ბ	გ	დ	ე	ვ	ზ	ჱ	თ	ი	ნ	რ	ფ	ჩ
			11 ია	20 კ	30 ლ	40 მ	60 ჲ	70 ო	80 პ	90 ჟ	200 ს	300 ტ	400 უ	600 ქ	700 ღ	800 ყ
Ethiopian	◆		፩	፪	፫	፬	፭	፮	፯	፰	፱	፲	፶	፻	፭፻	፲፻
				20 ፳	30 ፴	40 ፵	60 ፷	70 ፸	80 ፹	90 ፺						
Hebrew			א	ב	ג	ד	ה	ו	ז	ח	ט	י	נ	ק	תק	
				20 כ	30 ל	40 מ	60 ס	70 ע	80 פ	90 צ	200 ר	300 ש	400 ת	600 תר	700 תש	800 תת
Greek			Α	Β	Γ	Δ	Ε	Τ	Ζ	Η	Θ	Ι	Ν	Ρ	Φ	Α
				20 Κ	30 Λ	40 Μ	60 Ξ	70 Ο	80 Π		200 Σ	300 Τ	400 Υ	600 Χ	700 Ψ	800 Ω

Foreign Exchange Table

The latest foreign exchange rates below apply to trade with banks in the country of origin. The left column shows the number of units per U.S. dollar at the official rate. The right column shows the number of units per dollar at the free market rate.

COUNTRY	Official #/$	Market #/$
Afghanistan (New Afghani)	.52	–
Albania (Lek)	102	–
Algeria (Dinar)	.72	–
Andorra uses Euro	.788	–
Angola (Readjust Kwanza)	.75	–
Anguilla uses E.C. Dollar	2.7	–
Antigua uses E.C. Dollar	2.7	–
Argentina (Peso)	3.63	–
Armenia (Dram)	.359	–
Aruba (Florin)	1.79	–
Australia (Dollar)	1.55	–
Austria (Euro)	.788	–
Azerbaijan (New Manat)	.81	–
Bahamas (Dollar)	1.0	–
Bahrain Is. (Dinar)	.377	–
Bangladesh (Taka)	.69	
Barbados (Dollar)	2.0	–
Belarus (Ruble)	2,870	–
Belgium (Euro)	.788	–
Belize (Dollar)	1.95	–
Benin uses CFA Franc West	.517	–
Bermuda (Dollar)	1.0	–
Bhutan (Ngultrum)	.51	–
Bolivia (Boliviano)	7.02	–
Bosnia-Herzegovina (Conv. marka)	1.54	–
Botswana (Pula)	8.28	–
British Virgin Islands uses U.S. Dollar	1.0	–
Brazil (Real)	2.37	–
Brunei (Dollar)	1.54	–
Bulgaria (Lev)	1.54	–
Burkina Faso uses CFA Fr. West	.517	–
Burma (Kyat)	6.43	1,250
Burundi (Franc)	1,234	–
Cambodia (Riel)	4,124	–
Cameroon uses CFA Franc Central	.517	–
Canada (Dollar)	1.28	–
Cape Verde (Escudo)	.87	–
Cayman Islands (Dollar)	0.82	–
Central African Rep.	.517	–
CFA Franc Central	.517	–
CFA Franc West	.517	–
CFP Franc	.94	–
Chad uses CFA Franc Central	.517	–
Chile (Peso)	.607	–
China, P.R. (Renminbi Yuan)	6.84	–
Colombia (Peso)	2,549	–
Comoros (Franc)	.388	–
Congo uses CFA Franc Central	.517	–
Congo-Dem.Rep. (Congolese Franc)	.774	–
Cook Islands (Dollar)	1.99	–
Costa Rica (Colon)	.566	–
Croatia (Kuna)	5.85	–
Cuba (Peso)	1.00	27.00
Cyprus (Euro)	.788	–
Czech Republic (Koruna)	21.7	–
Denmark (Danish Krone)	5.87	–
Djibouti (Franc)	.177	–
Dominica uses E.C. Dollar	2.7	–
Dominican Republic (Peso)	35.4	–
East Caribbean (Dollar)	2.7	–
Ecuador (U.S. Dollar)	1.00	–
Egypt (Pound)	5.59	–
El Salvador (U.S. Dollar)	1.00	–
Equatorial Guinea uses CFA Franc Central	.517	–
Eritrea (Nafka)	.15	–
Estonia (Kroon)	12.3	–
Ethiopia (Birr)	11.1	–
Euro	.788	–
Falkland Is. (Pound)	.709	–
Faroe Islands (Krona)	5.87	–
Fiji Islands (Dollar)	1.88	–
Finland (Euro)	.788	–
France (Euro)	.788	–
French Polynesia uses CFP Franc	.94	–
Gabon (CFA Franc)	.517	–
Gambia (Dalasi)	.26	–
Georgia (Lari)	1.69	–
Germany (Euro)	.788	–
Ghana (New Cedi)	1.39	–
Gibraltar (Pound)	.709	–
Greece (Euro)	.788	–
Greenland uses Danish Krone	5.87	–
Grenada uses E.C. Dollar	2.7	–
Guatemala (Quetzal)	8.01	–
Guernsey uses Sterling Pound	.709	–
Guinea Bissau (CFA Franc)	.517	–
Guinea Conakry (Franc)	4,955	–
Guyana (Dollar)	.204	–
Haiti (Gourde)	39.7	–
Honduras (Lempira)	18.88	–
Hong Kong (Dollar)	7.75	–
Hungary (Forint)	.240	–
Iceland (Krona)	.112	–
India (Rupee)	51.7	–
Indonesia (Rupiah)	12,010	–
Iran (Rial)	9,916	–
Iraq (Dinar)	1,169	–
Ireland (Euro)	.788	–
Isle of Man uses Sterling Pound	.709	–
Israel (New Sheqalim)	4.24	–
Italy (Euro)	.788	–
Ivory Coast uses CFA Franc West	.517	–
Jamaica (Dollar)	.88	–
Japan (Yen)	.97	–
Jersey uses Sterling Pound	.709	–
Jordan (Dinar)	.71	–
Kazakhstan (Tenge)	.150	–
Kenya (Shilling)	79.8	–
Kiribati uses Australian Dollar	1.55	–
Korea-PDR (Won)	2.2	142
Korea-Rep. (Won)	1,543	–
Kuwait (Dinar)	.29	–
Kyrgyzstan (Som)	.41	–
Laos (Kip)	8,568	–
Latvia (Lats)	.558	–
Lebanon (Pound)	1,503	–
Lesotho (Maloti)	10.4	–
Liberia (Dollar)	.65	–
Libya (Dinar)	1.32	–
Liechtenstein uses Swiss Franc	1.15	–
Lithuania (Litas)	2.72	–
Luxembourg (Euro)	.788	–
Macao (Pataca)	7.98	–
Macedonia (New Denar)	.48	–
Madagascar (Franc)	1,975	–
Malawi (Kwacha)	.140	–
Malaysia (Ringgit)	3.71	–
Maldives (Rufiya)	12.8	–
Mali uses CFA Franc West	.517	–
Malta (Euro)	.788	–
Marshall Islands uses U.S.Dollar	1.00	–
Mauritania (Ouguiya)	.263	–
Mauritius (Rupee)	.34	–
Mexico (Peso)	15.2	–
Moldova (Leu)	10.7	–
Monaco uses Euro	.788	–
Mongolia (Tugrik)	1,570	–
Montenegro uses Euro	.788	–
Montserrat uses E.C. Dollar	2.7	–
Morocco (Dirham)	8.72	–
Mozambique (New Metical)	27.25	–
Namibia (Rand)	10.41	–
Nauru uses Australian Dollar	1.55	–
Nepal (Rupee)	82.7	–
Netherlands (Euro)	.788	–
Netherlands Antilles (Gulden)	1.79	–
New Caledonia uses CFP Franc	.94	–
New Zealand (Dollar)	1.99	–
Nicaragua (Cordoba Oro)	.20	–
Niger uses CFA Franc West	.517	–
Nigeria (Naira)	.147	–
Northern Ireland uses Sterling Pound	.709	–
Norway (Krone)	7.04	–
Oman (Rial)	.385	–
Pakistan (Rupee)	.80	–
Palau uses U.S.Dollar	1.00	–
Panama (Balboa) uses U.S.Dollar	1.00	–
Papua New Guinea (Kina)	2.83	–
Paraguay (Guarani)	5,135	–
Peru (Nuevo Sol)	3.2	–
Philippines (Peso)	.48	–
Poland (Zloty)	3.7	–
Portugal (Euro)	.788	–
Qatar (Riyal)	3.64	–
Romania (New Leu)	3.38	–
Russia (Ruble)	.36	–
Rwanda (Franc)	.568	–
St. Helena (Pound)	.709	–
St. Kitts uses E.C. Dollar	2.7	–
St. Lucia uses E.C. Dollar	2.7	–
St. Vincent uses E.C. Dollar	2.7	–
San Marino uses Euro	.788	–
Sao Tome e Principe (Dobra)	17,474	–
Saudi Arabia (Riyal)	3.75	–
Scotland uses Sterling Pound	.709	–
Senegal uses CFA Franc West	.517	–
Serbia (Dinar)	74.9	–
Seychelles (Rupee)	16.77	–
Sierra Leone (Leone)	3,087	–
Singapore (Dollar)	1.5	–
Slovakia (Sk. Koruna)	23.7	–
Slovenia (Euro)	.788	–
Solomon Islands (Dollar)	8.11	–
Somalia (Shilling)	1,415	–
Somaliland (Somali Shilling)	1,800	4,000
South Africa (Rand)	10.4	–
Spain (Euro)	.788	–
Sri Lanka (Rupee)	.114	–
Sudan (Pound)	2.3	–
Surinam (Dollar)	2.74	–
Swaziland (Lilangeni)	10.4	–
Sweden (Krona)	9.18	–
Switzerland (Franc)	1.15	–
Syria (Pound)	.47	–
Taiwan (NT Dollar)	34.7	–
Tajikistan (Somoni)	3.74	–
Tanzania (Shilling)	1,304	–
Thailand (Baht)	.36	–
Togo uses CFA Franc West	.517	–
Tonga (Pa'anga)	2.24	–
Transdniestra (Ruble)	–	–
Trinidad & Tobago (Dollar)	6.26	–
Tunisia (Dinar)	1.45	–
Turkey (New Lira)	1.78	–
Turkmenistan (Manat)	14,250	–
Turks & Caicos uses U.S. Dollar	1.00	–
Tuvalu uses Australian Dollar	1.56	–
Uganda (Shilling)	2,000	–
Ukraine (Hryvnia)	7.85	–
United Arab Emirates (Dirham)	3.67	–
United Kingdom (Sterling Pound)	.709	–
Uruguay (Peso Uruguayo)	23.9	–
Uzbekistan (Sum)	1,413	–
Vanuatu (Vatu)	.120	–
Vatican City uses Euro	.788	–
Venezuela (New Bolivar)	2.15	5.7
Vietnam (Dong)	17,481	–
Western Samoa (Tala)	3.07	–
Yemen (Rial)	.200	–
Zambia (Kwacha)	5,540	–
Zimbabwe (Dollar)	–	–

How To Use This Catalog

Catalog listings consist of all regular and provisional notes attaining wide circulation in their respective countries for the period covered. Notes have been listed under the historical country name. Thus Dahomey is not under Benin, as had been the case in some past catalogs. The listings continue to be grouped by issue range rather than by denomination, andthe listing format should make the bank name, issue dates as well as catalog numbers and denominations easier to locate. These improvements have been made to make the catalog as easy to use as possible for you.

The editors and publisher make no claim to absolute completeness, just as they acknowledge that some errors and pricing inequities will appear. Correspondence is invited with interested persons who have notes previously unlisted or who have information to enhance the presentation of existing listings in succeeding editions of this catalog.

Catalog Format

Listings proceed generally according to the following sequence: country, geographic or political, chronology, bank name and sometimes alphabetically or by date of first note issue. Release within the bank, most often in date order, but sometimes by printer first.

Catalog number — The basic reference number at the beginning of each listing for each note. For this Modern Issues volume the regular listings require no prefix letters except when 'a' or 'b' appear within the catalog number as a suffix or variety letter. (Military and Regional prefixes are explained later in this section.)

Denomination — the value as shown on the note, in western numerals. When denominations are only spelled out, consult the numerics chart.

Date — the actual issue date as printed on the note in day-month-year order. Where more than one date appears on a note, only the latest is used. Where the note has no date, the designation ND is used, followed by a year date in parentheses when it is known. If a note is dated by the law or decree of authorization, the date appears with an L or D.

Descriptions of the note are broken up into one or more items as follows:

Color — the main color(s) of the face, and the underprint are given first. If the colors of the back are different, then they follow the face design description.

Design — The identification and location of the main design elements if known. Back design elements identified if known.

Printer — often a local printer has the name shown in full. Abbreviations are used for the most prolific printers. Refer to the list of printer abbreviations elsewhere in this introduction.

Valuations — are generally given under the grade headings of Good, Fine and Extremely Fine for early notes; and Very Good, Very Fine and Uncirculated for the later issues. Listings that do not follow these two patterns are clearly indicated. UNC followed by a value is used usually for specimens and proofs when lower grade headings are used for a particular series of issued notes.

Catalog suffix letters

A catalog number followed by a capital 'A', 'B' or 'C' indicated the incorporation of a listing as required by type or date it may indicate newly discovered lower or higher denominations to a series which needed to be fit into long standing listings. Listings of notes for regional circulation are distinguished from regular national issues with the prefix letter 'R'; military issues use a 'M' prefix; foreign exchange certificates are assigned a 'FX' prefix. Varieties, specific date or signature listings are shown with small letters 'a' following a number within their respective entries. Some standard variety letters include: 'ct' for color trials, 'p' for proof notes, 'r' for remainder notes, 's' for specimen notes and 'x' for errors.

Denominations

The denomination as indicated on many notes issued by a string of countries stretching from eastern Asia, through western Asia and on across northern Africa, often appears only in unfamiliar non-Western numeral styles. With the listings that follow, denominations are always indicated in Western numerals.

A comprehensive chart keying Western numerals to their non-Western counterparts is included elsewhere in this introduction as an aid to the identification of note types. This compilation features not only the basic numeral systems such as Arabic, Japanese and Indian, but also the more restricted systems such as Burmese, Ethiopian, Siamese, Tibetan, Hebrew, Mongolian and Korean. Additionally, the list includes other localized variations that have been applied to some paper money issues.

In consulting the numeral systems chart to determine the denomination of a note, one should remember that the actual numerals styles employed in any given area, or at a particular time, may vary significantly from these basic representations. Such variations can be deceptive to the untrained eye, just as variations from Western numeral styles can prove deceptive to individuals not acquainted with the particular style employed.

Dates and Date Listing Policy

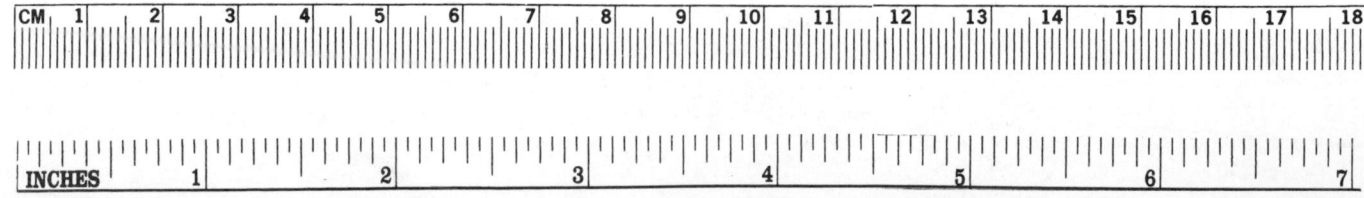

In previous editions of this work it was the goal to provide a sampling of the many date varieties that were believed to exist. In recent times, as particular dates (and usually signature combinations) were known to be scarcer, that particular series was expanded to include listings of individual dates. At times this idea has been fully incorporated, but with some series it is not practicable, especially when just about every day in a given month could have been an issue date for the notes.

Accordingly, where it seems justifiable that date spans can be realistically filled with individual dates, this has been done. In order to accommodate the many new dates, the idea of providing variety letters to break them up into narrower spans of years has been used. If it appears that there are too many dates for a series, with no major differences in value, then a general inclusive date span is used (beginning and ending) and individual dates within this span are not shown.

For those notes showing only a general date span, the only important dates become those that expand the range of years, months or days earlier or later. But even they would have no impact on the values shown.

Because a specific date is not listed does not necessarily mean it is rare. It may be just that it has not been reported. Those date varieties known to be scarcer are cataloged separately. Newly reported dates in a wide variety of listings are constantly being reported. This indicates that research into the whole area is very active, and a steady flow of new dates is fully expected upon publication of this edition.

Valuations

Valuations are given for most notes in three grades. Earlier issues are usually valued in the grade headings of Good, Fine and Extremely Fine; later issues take the grade headings of Very Good, Very Fine and Uncirculated. While it is true that some early notes cannot be valued in Extremely Fine and some later notes have no premium value in Very Good, it is felt that this coverage provides the best uniformity of value data to the collecting community. There are exceptional cases where headings are adjusted for either single notes or a series that really needs special treatment.

Valuations are determined generally from a consensus of individuals submitting prices for evaluation. Some notes have NO values; this does not necessarily mean they are expensive or even rare, but it shows that no pricing information was forthcoming. A number of notes have a 'Rare' designation, and no values. Such notes are generally not available on the market, and when they do appear the price is a matter between buyer and seller. No book can provide guidance in these instances except to indicate rarity.

Valuations used in this book are based on the IBNS grading standards and are stated in U.S. dollars. They serve only as aids in evaluating paper money since actual market conditions throughout the worldwide collector community are constantly changing. In addition, particularly choice examples of many issues listed often bring higher premiums than values listed. Users should remember that a catalog such as this is only a guide to values.

FV (for Face Value) is used as a value designation on new issues as well as older but still redeemable legal tender notes in lower conditions. FV may appear in one or both condition columns before Uncirculated, depending on the relative age and availability of the note in question. Some non-current notes which are still exchangeable carry FV designations.

Collection care

The proper preservation of a collection should be of paramount importance to all in the hobby - dealers, collectors and scholars. Only a person who has housed notes in a manner giving pleasure to him or herself and others will keep alive the pleasure of collecting for future generations. The same applies to the way of housing as to the choice of the collecting specialty: it is chiefly a question of what most pleases the individual collector.

Arrangement and sorting of a collection is most certainly a basic requirement. Storing the notes in safe paper envelopes and filing boxes should, perhaps, be considered only when building a new section of a collection, for accommodating varieties or for reasons of saving space when the collection has grown quickly.

Many paper money collections are probably housed in some form of plastic-pocketed album, which are today manufactured in many different sizes and styles to accommodate many types of world paper money. Because the number of bank note collectors has grown continually over the past thirty-five years, some specialty manufacturers of albums have developed a paper money selection. The notes, housed in clear plastic pockets, individually or in groups, can be viewed and exchanged without difficulty. These albums are not cheap, but the notes displayed in this manner do make a lasting impression on the viewer.

A word of concern: certain types of plastic and all vinyl used for housing notes may cause notes to become brittle over time, or cause an irreversible and harmful transfer of oils from the vinyl onto the bank notes.

The high demand for quality that stamp collectors make on their products cannot be transferred to the paper money collecting fraternity. A postage stamp is intended for a single use, then is relegated to a collection. With paper money, it is nearly impossible to acquire uncirculated specimens from a number of countries because of export laws or internal bank procedures. Bends from excessive counting, or even staple holes, are commonplace. Once acquiring a circulated note, the collector must endeavor to maintain its state of preservation.

The fact that there is a classification and value difference between notes with greater use or even damage is a matter of course. It is part of the opinion and personal taste of the individual collector to decide what is considered worthy of collecting and what to pay for such items.

For the purposed of strengthening and mending torn paper money, under no circumstances should one use plain cellophane tape or a similar material. These tapes warp easily, with sealing marks forming at the edges, and the tape frequently discolors. Only with the greatest of difficulty (and often not at all) can these tapes be removed, and damage to the note or the printing is almost unavoidable. The best material for mending tears is an archival tape recommended for the treatment and repair of documents.

There are collectors who, with great skill, remove unsightly spots, repair badly damaged notes, replace missing pieces and otherwise restore or clean a note. There is a question of morality by tampering with a note to improve its condition, either by repairing, starching, ironing, pressing or other methods to possibly deceive a potential future buyer. Such a question must, in the final analysis, be left to the individual collector.

IBNS GRADING STANDARDS FOR WORLD PAPER MONEY

The following introduction and Grading Guide is the result of work prepared under the guidance of the Grading Committee of the International Bank Note Society (IBNS). It has been adopted as the official grading standards of that society.

Introduction

Grading is the most controversial component of paper money collecting today. Small differences in grade can mean significant Vdifferences in value. The process of grading is so subjective and dependent on external influences such as lighting, that even a very experienced individual may well grade the same note differently on separate occasions.

To facilitate communication between sellers and buyers, it is essential that grading terms and their meanings be as standardized and as widely used as possible. This standardization should reflect common usage as much as practicable. One difficulty with grading is that even the actual grades themselves are not used everywhere by everyone. For example, in Europe the grade 'About Uncirculated' (AU) is not in general use, yet in North America it is widespread. The European term 'Good VF' may roughly correspond to what individuals in North America call 'Extremely Fine' (EF).

The grades and definitions as set forth below cannot reconcile all the various systems and grading terminology variants. Rather, the attempt is made here to try and diminish the controversy with some common-sense grades and definitions that aim to give more precise meaning to the grading language of paper money.

How to look at a banknote

In order to ascertain the grade of a note, it is essential to examine it out of a holder and under a good light. Move the note around so that light bounces off of it at different angles. Try holding the note obliquely, so the note is even with your eye as you look up at the light. Hard-to-see folds or slight creases will show up under such examination. Some individuals also lightly feel along the surface of the note to detect creasing.

Cleaning, Washing, Pressing of Banknotes

a) Cleaning, washing or pressing paper money is generally harmful and reduces both the grade and the value of a note. At the very least, a washed or pressed note may lose its original sheen and its surface may become lifeless and dull. The defects a note had, such as folds and creases, may not necessarily be completely eliminated and their telltale marks can be detected under a good light. Carelessly washed notes may also have white streaks where the folds or creases were (or still are).

b) Processing of a note which started out as Extremely Fine will automatically reduce it at least one full grade.

Unnatural Defects

Glue, tape or pencil marks may sometimes be successfuly removed. While such removal will leave a cleaned surface, it will improve the overall appearance of the note without concealing any of its defects. Under such circumstances, the grade of that note may also be improved.

The words "pinholes", "staple holes", "trimmed", "graffiti", "writing on face", "tape marks" etc. should always be added to the description of a note. It is realized that certain countries routinely staple their notes together in groups before issue. In such cases, the description can include a comment such as "usual staple holes" or something similar. After all, not everyone knows that certain notes cannot be found otherwise.

The major point of this section is that one cannot lower the overall grade of a note with defects simply because of the defects. The value will reflect the lowered worth of a defective note, but the description must always include the specific defects.

GRADING

Definitions of Terms

UNCIRCULATED: A perfectly preserved note, never mishandled by the issuing authority, a bank teller, the public or a collector.

Paper is clean and firm, without discoloration. Corners are sharp and square without any evidence of rounding. (Rounded corners are often a tell-tale sign of a cleaned or "doctored" note.)

NOTE: Some note issues are most often available with slight evidence of very light counting folds which do not "break" the paper. Also, French-printed notes usually have a slight ripple in the paper. Many collectors and dealers refer to such notes as AU-UNC.

ABOUT UNCIRCULATED: A virtually perfect note, with some minor handling. May show very slight evidence of bank counting folds at a corner or one light fold through the center, but not both. An AU note canot be creased, a crease being a hard fold which has usually "broken" the surface of the note.

Paper is clean and bright with original sheen. Corners are not rounded.

NOTE: Europeans will refer to an About Uncirculated or AU note as "EF-Unc" or as just "EF". The Extremely Fine note described below will often be referred to as "GVF" or "Good Very Fine".

EXTREMELY FINE: A very attractive note, with light handling. May have a maximum of three light folds or one strong crease.

Paper is clean and firm, without discoloration. Corners are sharp and square without any evidence of rounding. (Rounded corners are often a tell-tale sign of a cleaned or "doctored" note.)

VERY FINE: An attractive note, but with more evidence of handling and wear. May have several folds both vertically and horizontally.

Paper may have minimal dirt, or possible color smudging. Paper itself is still relatively crisp and not floppy.

There are no tears into the border area, although the edges do how slight wear. Corners also show wear but not full rounding.

FINE: A note that shows consideralble circulation, with many lds, creases and wrinkling.

Paper is not excessively dirty but may have some softness.

Edges may show much handling, with minor tears in the bor-er area. Tears may not extend into the design. There will be no enter hole because of excessive folding.

Colors are clear but not very bright. A staple hole or two ould would not be considered unusual wear in a Fine note. verall appearance is still on the desirable side.

VERY GOOD: A well used note, abused but still intact.

Corners may have much wear and rounding, tiny nicks, tears ay extend into the design, some discoloration may be prsent, taining may have occurred, and a small hole may sometimes be een at center from excessive folding.

Staple and pinholes are usually present, and the note itself is uite limp but NO pieces of the note can be missing. A note in VG ondition may still have an overall not unattractive appearance.

GOOD: A well worn and heavily used note. Normal damage rom prolonged circulation will include strong multiple folds and reases, stains, pinholes and/or staple holes, dirt, discoloration, dge tears, center hole, rounded corners and an overall unattrac-ive appearance. No large pieces of the note may be missing. raffiti is commonly seen on notes in G condition.

FAIR: A totally limp, dirty and very well used note. Larger ieces may be half torn off or missing besides the defects men-ioned under the Good category. Tears will be larger, obscured ortions of the note will be bigger.

POOR: A "rag" with severe damage because of wear, staining, ieces missing, graffiti, larger holes. May have tape holding ieces of the note together. Trimming may have taken place to emove rough edges. A Poor note is desiralble only as a "filler" or vhen such a note is the only one known of that particular issue.

A word on crimps to otherwise uncirculated notes.

Due to inclusion of wide security foils, crimps appear at the top and bottom edge during production or counting. Thus notes which are uncirculated have a crimp. Examples without these crimps are beginning to command a premium.

International Bank Note Society

The International Bank Note Society (IBNS) was formed in 1961 to promote the collecting of world paper money. A membership of almost 2,000 in over 100 nations around the globe draws on the services of the Society for advancing their knowledge and collections.

The benefits of the society include the quarterly IBNS Journal featuring learned writings on the notes of the world, their history, artistry and technical background. Additionally each member receives a directory, which lists the membership by name as well as geographic location. Collector specialties are also given. The Society also conducts auctions that all members may participate in.

The greatest benefit of IBNS membership is the ability to correspond with other members around the world for purposes exchanging notes, information and assistance with research projects. The web page for the IBNS is www.theibns.org.

Application for Membership in the International Bank Note Society

Name: ______________________________

Address: ______________________________

City: ______________________________

Province/State: ______________________________

Postal/Zip Code: ______________________________

Country: ______________________________

Telephone: ______________________________

E-mail: ______________________________

Collecting Interest: ______________________________

Do you wish your postal address to be displayed in the Membership Directory?

❑ Yes ❑ No

Do you wish your e-mail address to be displayed in the Membership Directory?

❑ Yes ❑ No

Do you wish your e-mail address to appear on the IBNS web site?

❑ Yes ❑ No

Type of Membership

Individual:	❑ $US33.00	❑ £16.50	❑ A$41.25
Family:	❑ $US41.00	❑ £20.50	❑ A$51.25
Junior:	❑ $US16.50	❑ £8.25	❑ A$20.65

Mail to the appropriate member of the Secretarial team:

The General Secretary:	Clive Rice, 25 Copse Side, Godalming, Surrey GU7 3RU, United Kingdom
Assistant Secretary:	Brian Giese, PO Box 081643, Racine, WI 53408, USA.
Assistant Secretary:	Johnathan Lalas, 30 Radburn Road, Hebersham, NSW 2770, Australia

STANDARD INTERNATIONAL GRADING TERMINOLOGY AND ABBREVIATIONS

U.S. and ENGLISH SPEAKING LANDS	UNCIRCULATED	EXTREMELY FINE	VERY FINE	FINE	VERY GOOD	GOOD	POOR
Abbreviation	UNC	EF or XF	VF	FF	VG	G	PR
BRAZIL	(1) DW	(3) S	(5) MBC	(7) BC	(8)	(9) R	UTGeG
DENMARK	O	01	1+	1	1÷	2	3
FINLAND	0	01	1+	1	1?	2	3
FRANCE	NEUF	SUP	TTB or TB	TB or TB	B	TBC	BC
GERMANY	KFR	II / VZGL	III / SS	IV / S	V / S.g.E.	VI / G.e.	G.e.s.
ITALY	FdS	SPL	BB	MB	B	M	—
JAPAN	未使用	極美品	美品	並品	—	—	—
NETHERLANDS	FDC	Pr.	Z.F.	Fr.	Z.g.	G	—
NORWAY	0	01	1+	1	1÷	2	3
PORTUGAL	Novo	Soberbo	Muito bo	—	—	—	—
SPAIN	Lujo	SC, IC or EBC	MBC	BC	—	RC	MC
SWEDEN	0	01	1+	1	1?	2	—

BRAZIL

FE — Flor de Estampa
S — Soberba
MBC — Muito Bem Conservada
BC — Bem Conservada
R — Regular
UTGeG — Um Tanto Gasto e Gasto

DENMARK

O — Uncirkuleret
01 — Meget Paent Eksemplar
1+ — Paent Eksemplar
1 — Acceptabelt Eksemplar
1 —Noget Slidt Eksemplar
2 — Darlight Eksemplar
3 — Meget Darlight Eskemplar

FINLAND

00 — Kiitolyonti
0 — Lyontiveres
01 — Erittain Hyva
1+ — Hyva
1? — Keikko
3 — Huono

FRANCE

NEUF — New
SUP — Superbe
TTB — Tres Tres Beau
TB — Tres Beau
B — Beau
TBC — Tres Bien Conserve
BC — Bien Conserve

GERMANY

VZGL — Vorzüglich
SS — Sehr schön
S — Schön
S.g.E. — Sehr gut erhalten
G.e. — Gut erhalten
G.e.S. — Gering erhalten
Schlect

ITALY

Fds — Fior di Stampa
SPL — Splendid
BB — Bellissimo
MB — Molto Bello
B — Bello
M — Mediocre

JAPAN

未使用 — Mishiyo
極美品 — Goku Bihin
美品 — Bihin
並品 — Futuhin

NETHERLANDS

Pr. — Prachtig
Z.F. — Zeer Fraai
Fr. — Fraai
Z.g. — Zeer Goed
G — Good

NORWAY

0 — Usirkuleret eks
01 — Meget pent eks
1+ — Pent eks
1 — Fullgodt eks
1- — Ikke Fullgodt eks
2 — Darlig eks

ROMANIA

NC — Necirculata (UNC)
FF — Foarte Frumoasa (VF)
F — Frumoasa (F)
FBC — Foarte Bine Conservata (VG)
BC — Bine Conservata (G)
M — Mediocru Conservata (POOR)
Schlecht
— Goed

SPAIN

EBC — Extraordinariamente Bien Conservada
SC — Sin Circular
IC — Incirculante
MBC — Muy Bien Conservada
BC — Bien Conservada
RC — Regular Conservada
MC — Mala Conservada

SWEDEN

0 — Ocirkulerat
01 — Mycket Vackert
1+ — Vackert
1 — Fullgott
1? — Ej Fullgott
2 — Dalight

Dating

Determining the date of issue of a note is a basic consider-tion of attribution. As the reading of dates is subject not only to ie vagaries of numeric styling, but to variations in dating roots aused by the observation of differing religious eras or regal eriods from country to country, making this determination can ometimes be quite difficult. Most countries outside the North frican and Oriental spheres rely on Western date numerals and ie Christian (AD) reckoning, although in a few instances note ating has been tied to the year of a reign or government.

Countries of the Arabic sphere generally date their issues to ie Muslim calendar that commenced on July 16, 622 AD when ie prophet Mohammed fled from Mecca to Medina. As this cal-ndar is reckoned by the lunar year of 354, its is about three per-ent (precisely 3.3 percent) shorter than the Christian year. A onversion formula requires you to subtract that percent from ie AH date, and then add 621 to gain the AD date.

A degree of confusion arises here because the Muslim calen-ar is not always based on the lunar year (AH). Afghanistan and ran (Persia) used a calendar based on a solar year (SH) intro-uced around 1920. These dates can be converted to AD by sim-ly adding 621. In 1976, Iran implemented a solar calendar ased on the founding of the Iranian monarchy in 559 BC. The rst year observed on this new system was 2535(MS) which ommenced on March 20, 1976.

Several different eras of reckoning, including the Christian AD) and Muslim (AH), have been used to date paper money f the Indian subcontinent. The two basic systems are the ikrama Samvat (VS) era that dates from October 18, 58 BC,. nd the Saka (SE) era, the origin of which is reckoned from /larch 3, 78 AD.

Dating according to both eras appears on notes of several ative states and countries of the area.

Thailand (Siam) has observed three different eras for dating. he most predominant is the Buddhist (BE) era originating in 543 3C. Next is the Bangkok or Ratanakosind-sok (RS) era dating rom 1781 AD (and consisting of only 3 numerals), followed by he Chula-Sakarat (CS) era dating from 638 AD, with the latter lso observed in Burma.

Other calendars include that of the Ethiopian (EE) era that commenced 7 years, 8 months after AD dating, and that of the Hebrew nation beginning on October 7, 3761 BC. Korea claims a lating from 2333 BC which is acknowledged on some note ssues.

The following table indicates the years dating from the various eras that correspond to 2007 by Christian (AD) calendar reckon-ing. It must be remembered that there are overlaps between the eras in some instances:

Christian Era (AD)	—	2008
Mohammedan era (AH)	—	AH1429
Solar year (SH)	—	SH1387
Monarchic Solar era (MS)	—	MS2567
Vikrama Samvat era (VS)	—	SE2065
Saka era (SE)	—	Saka 1930
Buddhist era (BE)	—	BE2551
Bangkok era (RS)	—	RS227
Chula-Sakarat era (CS)	—	CS1370
Ethiopian era (EE)	—	EE2000
Jewish era	—	5768
Korean era	—	4341

Paper money of Oriental origin - principally Japan, Korea, China, Turkestan and Tibet - generally date to the year of the gov-ernment, dynastic, regnal or cyclical eras, with the dates indi-cated in Oriental characters usually reading from right to left. In recent years some dating has been according to the Christian cal-endar and in Western numerals reading from left to right.

More detailed guides to the application of the less prevalent dating systems than those described, and others of strictly local nature, along with the numeral designations employed, are pre-sented in conjunction with the appropriate listings.

Some notes carry dating according to both the locally observed and Christian eras. This is particularly true in the Arabic sphere, where the Muslim date may be indicated in Arabic numerals and the Christian date in Western numerals.

In general the date actually shown on a given paper money issue is indicated in some manner. Notes issued by special Law or Decree will have L or D preceding the date. Dates listed within parentheses may differ from the date appearing on the note; they have been documented by other means. Undated notes are listed with ND, followed by a year only when the year of actual issue is known.

Timing differentials between the 354-day Muslim and the 365-day Christian year cause situations whereby notes bearing dates of both eras have two date combinations that may overlap from one or the other calendar system.

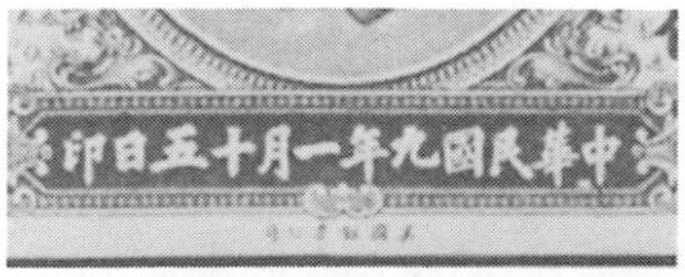

China - Republic 9th year, 1st month, 15th day (15.1.1920), read r. to l.

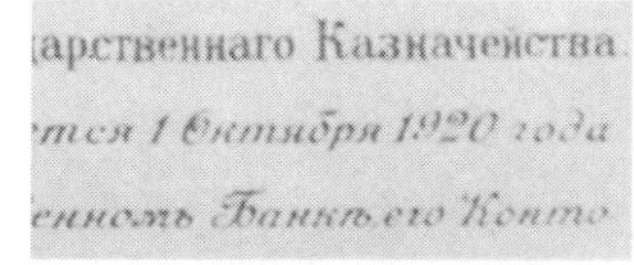
Russia-1 October 1920

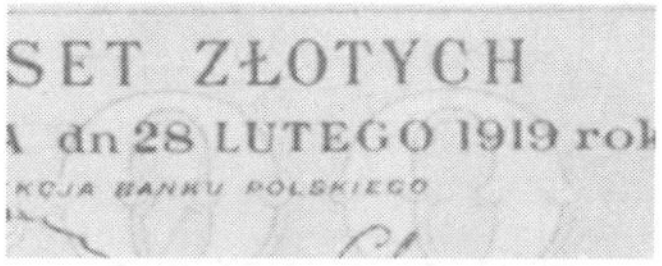

Poland - 28 February 1919

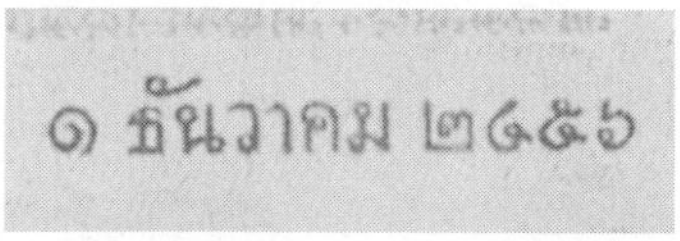
Thailand (Siam) - 1 December 2456

Israel - 1973, 5733

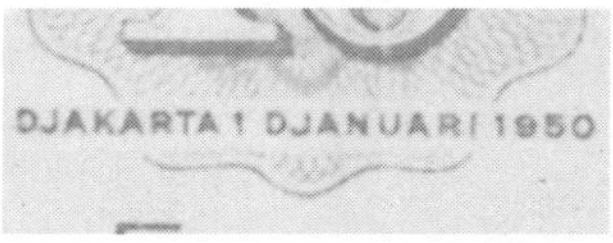

Indonesia - 1 January 1950

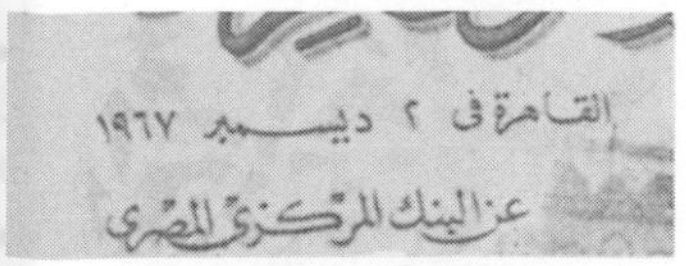
Egypt - 1967 December 2

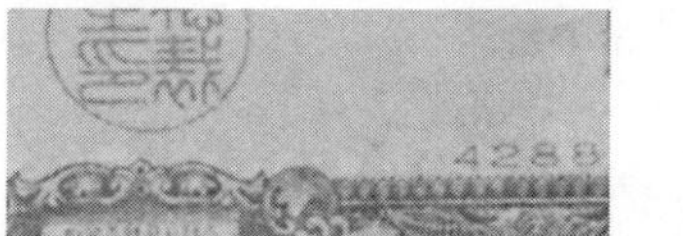
Korea - 4288 (1955)

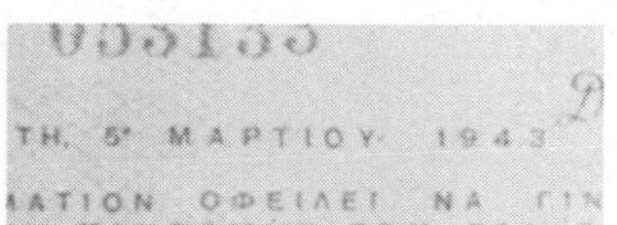
Greece - 5 March 1943

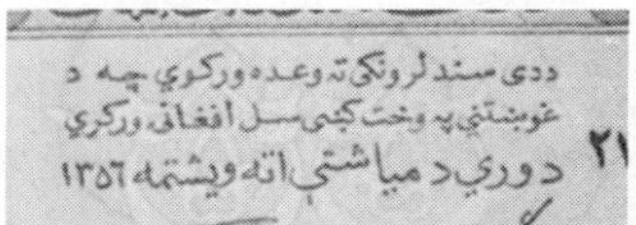
Afghanistan - Solar Year 1356

Bank Note Printers

Printers' names, abbreviations or monograms will usually appear as part of the frame design or below it on face and/or back. In some instances the engraver's name may also appear in a similar location on a note. The following abbreviations identify printers for many of the notes listed in this volume:

ABNC	American Bank Note Company (USA)
BABN(C)	British American Bank Note Co., Ltd. (Canada)
B&S	Bouligny & Schmidt (Mexico)
BDDK	Bunddesdruckerei (Germany)
BEPP	Bureau of Engraving & Printing, Peking (China)
BF	Banque de France (France)
BFL	Barclay & Fry, Ltd. (England)
BWC	Bradbury, Wilkinson & Co. (England)
CABB	Compania Americana de Billetes de Banco (ANBC)
CBC	Columbian Banknote Co. (US)
CBNC	Canadian Bank Note Company (Canada)
CC	Ciccone Calcografica S.A. (Italy)
CCBB	Compania Columbiana de Billetes de Banco (CBC)
CdM-	Casa de Moeda (Brazil)
CdM-	Casa de Moeda (Argentina, Chile, etc.)
CHB	Chung Hua Book Co. (China)
CMN	Casa de Moneda de la Nacion (Argentina)
CMPA	Commercial Press (China)
CNBB	Compania Nacional de billetes de Banco (NBNC)
CONB	Continental Bank Note Company (US)
CPF	Central Printing Factory (China)
CSABB	Compania Sud/Americana de billetes de Banco (Argentina)
CS&E	Charles Skipper & East (England)
DLR or (T)DLR	De La Rue (England)
DTB	Dah Tung Book Co., and Ta Tung Printing (China)
E&C	Evans & Cogswell (CSA)
EAW	E.A. Wright (US)
FLBN	Franklin-Lee Bank Note Company (US)
FNMT	Fabrica Nacional de Moneda y Timbre (Spain)
G&D	Giesecke & Devrient (Germany)
HBNC	Hamilton Bank Note Company (USA)
HKB	Hong Kong Banknote (Hong Kong)
HKP	Hong Kong Printing Press (Hong Kong)
H&L	Hoyer & Ludwig, Richmond, Virginia (CSA)
HLBNC	Homer Lee Bank Note Co. (US)
H&S	Harrison & Sons, Ltd. (England)
IBB	Imprenta de Billetes-Bogota (Colombia)
IBSFB	Imprenta de Billetes-Santa Fe de Bogota (Colombia)
IBNC	International Bank Note Company (US)
JBNC	Jeffries Bank Note Company (US)
JEZ	Joh, Enschede en Zonen (Netherlands)
K&B	Keatinge & Ball (CSA)
KBNC	Kendall Bank Note Company, New York (USA)
LN	Litographia Nacional (Colombia)
NAL	Nissen & Arnold (England)
NBNC	National Bank Note Company (US)
OCV	Officina Carte-Valori (Italy)
OBDI	Officina Della Banca D'Italia (Italy)
OFZ	Orell Füssli, Zurich (Switzerland)
P&B	Perkins & Bacon (England)
PBC	Perkins, Bacon & Co. (England)
PB&P	Perkins, Bacon & Petch (England)
SBNC	Security Banknote Company (US)
TDLR or (T)DLR	Thomas De La Rue (England)
UPC	Union Printing Co., Ltd. (China)
UPP	Union Publishers & Printers Fed. Inc. (China)
USBNC	United States Banknote Corp. (US)
WDBN	Western District Banknote Fed. Inc.
W&S	Waterlow & Sons Ltd. (England)
WPCo	Watson Printing Co. (China)
WWS	W.W. Sprague & Co. Ltd. (England)

Specimen Notes

To familiarize private banks, central banks, law enforcement agencies and treasuries around the world with newly issued currency, many nations provide special "Specimen" examples of their notes. Specimens are actual bank notes, complete with dummy or all zero serial numbers and signatures bearing the overprinted and/or perforated word "SPECIMEN" in the language of the country of origin itself or where the notes were printed.

Some countries have made specimen notes available for sale to collectors. These include Cuba, Czechoslovakia, Poland and Slovakia after World War II and a special set of four denominations of Jamaica notes bearing red matched star serial numbers. Also, in 1978, the Franklin Mint made available to collectors specimen notes from 15 nations, bearing matching serial numbers and a Maltese cross device used as a prefix. Several other countries have also participated in making specimen notes available to collectors at times.

Aside from these collectors issues, specimen notes may sometimes comand higher prices than regular issue notes of the same type, even though there are far fewer collectors of specimens. In some cases, notably older issues in high denominations, specimens may be the only form of such notes available to collectors today. Specimen notes are not legal tender or redeemable, thus have no real "face value".

The most unusual forms of specimens were produced by Waterlow and Sons. They printed special off colored notes for salesman's sample books adding the word SPECIMEN and their seal.

Some examples of how the word "SPECIMEN" is represented in other languages or on notes of other countries follow:

AMOSTRA: Brazil
CAMPIONE: Italy
CONTOH: Malaysia
EKSEMPLAAR: South Africa
ESPÉCIME: Portugal and Colonies
ESPECIMEN: Various Spanish-speaking nations
GIAY MAU: Vietnam
MINTA: Hungary
MODELO: Brazil
MODEL: Albania
MUSTER: Austria, Germany
MUESTRA: Various Spanish-speaking nations
NUMUNDEDIR GECMEZ: Turkey
ORNEKTIR GECMEZ: Turkey
ОБРАЗЕЦ or ОБРАЗЕЦЪ Bulgaria, Russia, U.S.S.R.
PARAUGS: Latvia
PROFTRYK: Sweden
UZORAK: Croatia
WZOR: Poland
ЗАГВАР: Mongolia

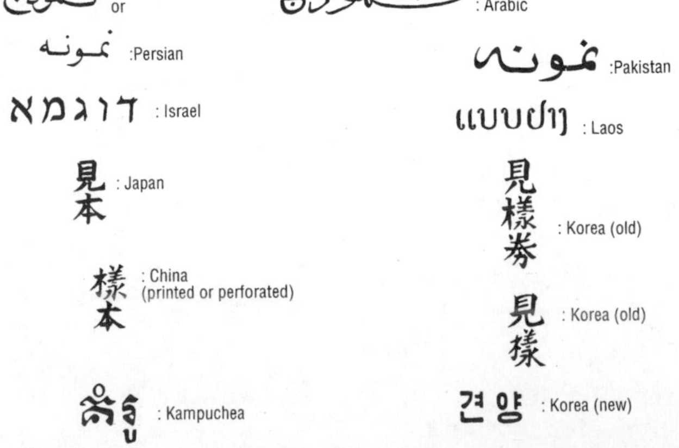

The Republic of Albania, a Balkan republic bounded by the rump Yugoslav state of Montenegro and Serbia, Macedonia, Greece and the Adriatic Sea, has an area of 11,100 sq. mi. (28,748 sq. km.) and a population of 3.5 million. Capital: Tirana. The country is mostly agricultural, although recent progress has been made in the manufacturing and mining sectors. Petroleum, chrome, iron, copper, cotton textiles, tobacco and wood products are exported.

Since it had been part of the Greek and Roman Empires, little is known of the early history of Albania. After the disintegration of the Roman Empire, Albania was overrun by Goths, Byzantines, Venetians and Turks. Skanderbeg, the national hero, resisted the Turks and established an independent Albania in 1443, but in 1468 the country again fell to the Turks and remained part of the Ottoman Empire for more than 400 years.

Independence was re-established by revolt in 1912, and the present borders established in 1913 by a conference of European powers which, in 1914, placed Prince William of Wied on the throne; popular discontent forced his abdication within months. In 1920, following World War I occupancy by several nations, a republic was set up. Ahmet Zogu seized the presidency in 1925, and in 1928 proclaimed himself king with the title of Zog I. King Zog fled when Italy occupied Albania in 1939 and enthroned King Victor Emanuel of Italy. Upon the surrender of Italy to the Allies in 1943, German troops occupied the country. They withdrew in 1944, and communist partisans seized power, naming Gen. Enver Hoxha provisional president. In 1946, following a victory by the communist front in the 1945 elections, a new constitution modeled on that of the USSR was adopted. In accordance with the constitution of Dec. 28, 1976, the official name of Albania was changed from the People's Republic of Albania to the People's Socialist Republic of Albania. A general strike by trade unions in 1991 forced the communist government to resign. A new government was elected in March 1992. In 1997 Albania had a major financial crisis which caused civil disturbances and the fall of the administration.

MONETARY SYSTEM

1 Franc = 100 Centimes
1 Skender = 100 Qint

Regional - Berat

Bashkia e Beratit

1925 Issue

		Good	Fine	XF
S101	**50 Qindtar** 19.12.1925. Rare.	—	—	—

Dhoma Tregetare e Beratit

1924 Issue

		Good	Fine	XF
S102	**0.50 Lirë Italiane** May 1924. Red on yellow underprint. Dancing crowned Liberty. Back: Oval handstamp.			
	a. Issued note. Rare.	—	—	—
	r. Unissued remainder without signature or oval hand stamp.	—	Unc	200.

		VG	VF	UNC
S103	**1 Lirë Italiane** 1924. Black on red underprint. Dancing crowned Liberty. Back: Oval handstamp.			
	a. April 1924. Rare.	—	—	—
	b. May 1924. Rare.	—	—	—
	r1. As a. Unissued remainder without signature or oval hand stamp.	—	—	200.
	r2. As b. Unissued remainder without signature or oval hand stamp.	—	—	200.

Regional - Elbasan

Bashkia e Elbasanit

1924-25 Issue

		Good	Fine	XF
S111	**0.10 Franga Argjent** 1924-25. Black on red underprint. Double-headed eagle. At least two perforated margins. Back: Black circular double-headed eagle hand stamp with imprint: *Bashkija e Elbasanit.*			
	a. 1.6.1924. Rare.	—	—	—
	b. 1.4.1925. Rare.	—	—	—
S112	**0.20 Franga Argjent** 1.4.1925. Red on gray underprint. Double-headed eagle in red. At least two perforated margins. Back: Circular double-headed eagle hand stamp with imprint: *Bashkija e Elbasanit.* Rare.	—	—	—
S113	**0.40 Franga Argjent** 1.4.1925. Red on black underprint. Double-headed eagle in red. Circular double-headed eagle hand stamp with imprint: *Bashkija e Elbasanit.* At least two perforated margins. Rare.	—	—	—

Regional - Fier

Fier

1921, ND Issue

		Good	Fine	XF
S121	**1 Lira** 1921. Rare.	—	—	—
S122	**0.50 Qind Kart** ND. Rare.	—	—	—
S123	**1 Frank Kart** ND. Rare.	—	—	—

Regional - Gjirokastër

Bashki e Gjirokastres

ca 1920 Issue

		Good	Fine	XF
S131	**0.50 Franga Kart** ND. Black. Back: Circular double-headed eagle hand stamp. Rare.	—	—	—

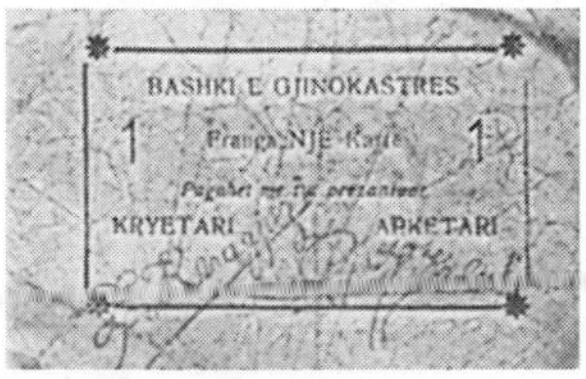

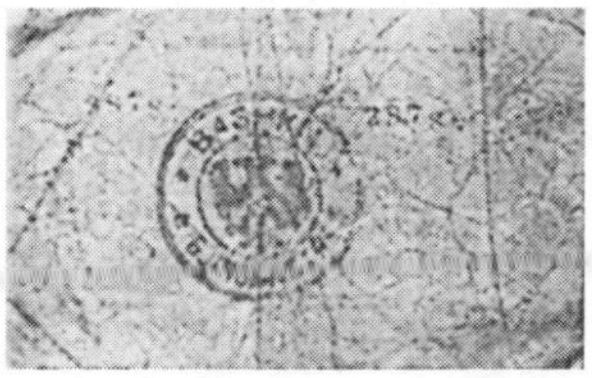

		Good	Fine	XF
S132	**1 Franga Karte** ND. Black. Back: Circular double-headed eagle hand stamp. Rare.	—	—	—
S133	**2 Franga Karte** ND. Black. Back: Circular double-headed eagle hand stamp. Rare.	—	—	—

Regional - Korçë

Shqipërië Vetqeveritare - Korçë

1917 Series A

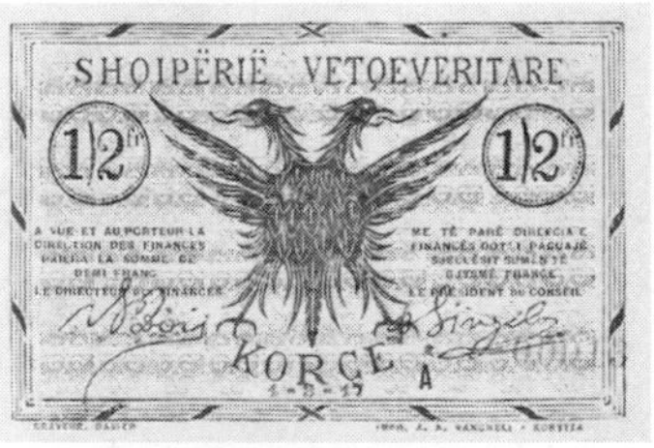

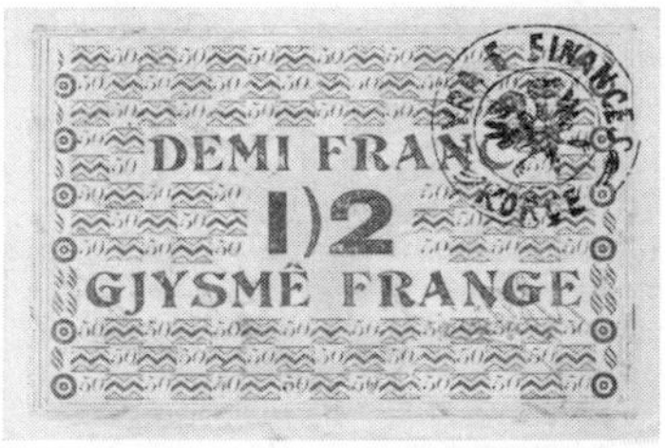

		VG	VF	UNC
S141	**1/2 Franc** 1.3.1917. Brown on aqua underprint. Title: *SHQIPËRIË VETQEVERITARE / KORÇË.* Double-headed eagle at center. Back: Aqua. Circular purple hand stamp at right. Printer: A. A. Vangheli-Korytza.			
	a. Blue serial #. Violet hand samp on back.	15.00	50.00	120.

		VG	VF	UNC
S142	**1 Franc** 1.3.1917. Black on brown-orange underprint. Title: *SHQIPËRIË VETQEVERITARE / KORÇË.* Double-headed eagle at center. Back: Brown. Printer: A. A. Vangheli-Korytza.			
	a. Blue serial #. Black hand stamp on back.	20.00	50.00	100.
	b. Blue serial #. Violet hand stamp on back.	20.00	50.00	100.
	r. As b. Remainder. Black overprint: *Anulé* on back.	—	—	—

1917 Series B

		VG	VF	UNC
S143	**1/2 Franc** 25.3.1917. Brown on aqua underprint. Title: *SHQIPËRIË VETQEVERITARE / KORÇË.* Double headed eagle at center. Back: Aqua. Circular purple handstamp at right.			
	a. Violet serial #. Violet hand stamp on back.	25.00	75.00	160.
	r. As b. Remainder. Black overprint: *Anulé* on back.	—	—	—

S144 1 Franc	VG	VF	UNC
25.3.1917. Black on brown-orange underprint. Title: *SHQIPËRIË VETQEVERITARE / KORÇË*. Double headed eagle at center. Back: Brown. Circular purple handstamp at right.			
a. Violet serial #. Violet hand stamp on back.	25.00	75.00	160.
r. As a. Remainder. Blue overprint: *Anulé* on back.	—	—	—

1917 Series C

S145 1/2 Franc	VG	VF	UNC
10.10.1917. Title: *REPUBLIKA SHQIPETARE / KORCE.* Double-headed eagle at center.			
a. Black serial #. Blue hand stamp on back.	25.00	60.00	150.
b. Black serial #. Black hand stamp on back.	25.00	60.00	150.
c. Black serial #. Red hand stamp on back.	25.00	60.00	150.
r. Like c. Remainder. Black overprint: *Anulé* on back.	—	—	—

S146 1 Franc	VG	VF	UNC
10.10.1917. Title: *REPUBLIKA SHQIPETARË / KORÇË.* Double-headed eagle at center.			
a. Violet serial #. Blue hand stamp on back.	30.00	75.00	175.
b. Violet serial #. Black hand stamp on back.	25.00	60.00	150.
c. Black serial #. Blue hand stamp on back.	20.00	50.00	125.
d. Black serial #. Black hand stamp on back.	25.00	60.00	150.
r. As d. Remainder. Blue overprint: *Anulé* on back.	—	—	—

1918 Series A

S147 0.50 Franc	VG	VF	UNC
1.11.1918. Dark green and dark blue. Back: Dark green. Town view.			
a. Violet serial #. Red circular hand stamp at upper right.	20.00	50.00	120.

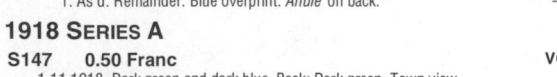

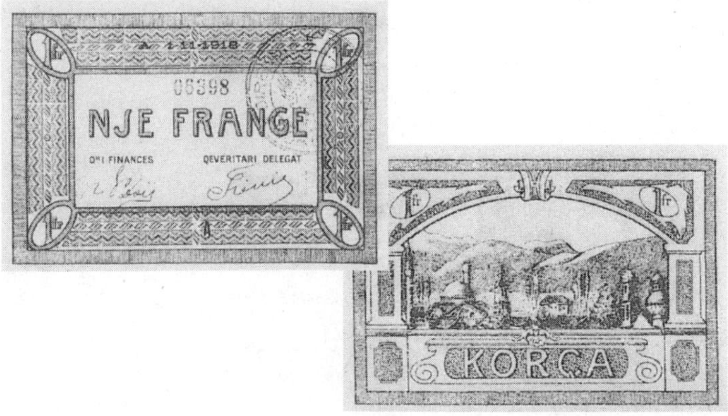

S148 1 Franc	VG	VF	UNC
1.11.1918. Red-brown and dark blue. Back: Red-brown. Town view.			
a. Violet serial #. Violet hand stamp at upper right.	25.00	60.00	130.
b. Black serial #. Violet hand stamp at upper right.	25.00	60.00	130.

1918 Series B

S149 0.50 Franc	VG	VF	UNC
1.12.1918. Dark green and dark blue. Back: Town view.			
a. Violet serial #. Red hand stamp at upper right.	30.00	75.00	175.
b. Black serial #. Red hand stamp at upper right.	30.00	75.00	175.

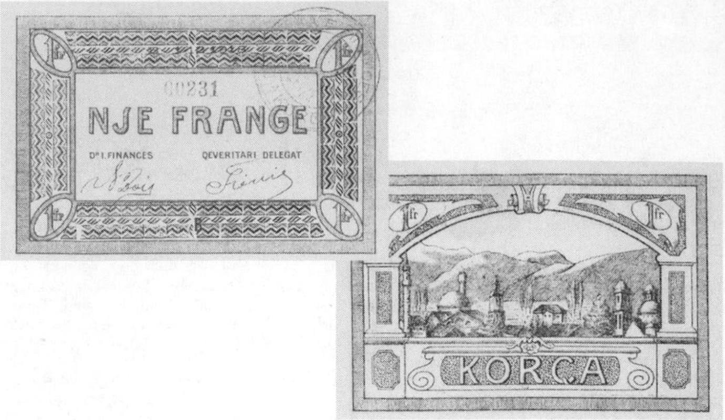

S150 1 Franc	VG	VF	UNC
1.12.1918.Red-brown and dark blue. Back: Town view.			
a. Violet serial #. Violet hand stamp at upper right.	30.00	75.00	175.
b. Violet serial #. Red hand stamp at upper right.	30.00	75.00	175.
c. Black serial #. Violet hand stamp at upper right.	30.00	75.00	175.

1918 Series C

S151 0.50 Franc	VG	VF	UNC
10.12.1918. Dark green and dark blue. Back: Town view.			
a. Violet serial #. Red hand stamp at upper right.	40.00	80.00	200.

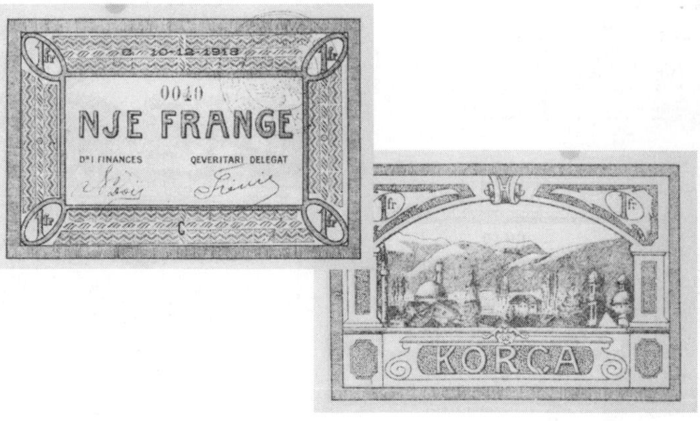

S152 1 Franc	VG	VF	UNC
10.12.1918. Red-brown and dark blue. Back: Town view.			
a. Violet serial #. Violet hand stamp at upper right.	50.00	100.	250.
b. Black serial #. Violet hand stamp at upper right.	50.00	100.	250.

Territoire de Koritza - Korçë

1920 Issue

S153 0.50 Centimes	VG	VF	UNC
March 1920. Black. Title: *TERRITOIRE DE KORITZA* monochrome, circular hand stamp: *Commandement Militaire de Korytza-Armee d'Orient.* Circular hand stamp: *Direksiae Finances-Korçë* Back: Circular hand stamp: *Direksiae Finances-Korce.* Paper: Brown.	10.00	30.00	70.00

S154 1 Franc	VG	VF	UNC
March 1920. Black. Title: *TERRITOIRE DE KORITZA* monochrome, circular hand stamp: *Commandement Militaire de Korytza-Armee d'Orient.* Circular hand stamp: *Direksiae Finances-Korçë* Back: Circular hand stamp: *Direksiae Finances-Korce.* Paper: Red.	10.00	30.00	70.00

1921 First Issue

S155 1/2 Skender	VG	VF	UNC
1.8.1921. Dark brown and red on yellow underprint. Skanderbeg at left. Title: *KATUNDAR'I E KORÇËS.*			
a. Issued note.	75.00	160.	350.
r. Remainder without serial #.	—	Unc	175.

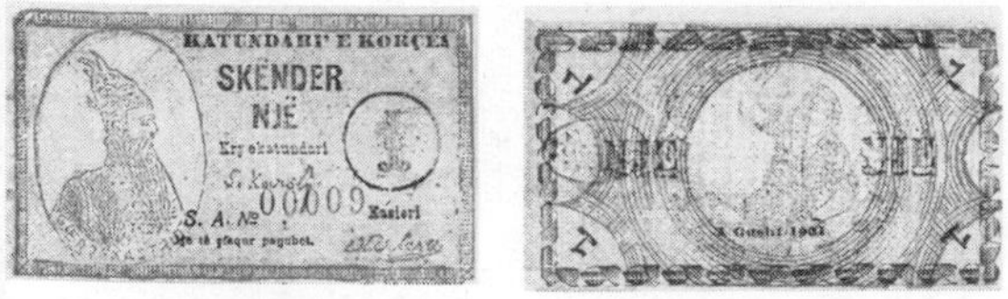

		VG	VF	UNC
S156	**1 Skender** 1.8.1921. Red and black on green underprint. Skanderbeg at left. Title: *KATUNDAR'I E KORÇËS.*	50.00	80.00	250.
S157	**2 Skender** 1.8.1921. Red and olive green on yellow underprint. Skanderbeg at left.	100.	350.	750.

1921 Second Issue

		VG	VF	UNC
S158	**25 Qint** 9.11.1921. Farmer plowing. Title: *KATUNDARI E KORÇËS.* Back: Skanderbeg on horseback.			
	a. Olive green frame underprint.	60.00	140.	275.
	b. Dark green frame underprint.	50.00	120.	250.

		VG	VF	UNC
S159	**50 Qint** 1.11.1921. Red brown underprint. Farmer plowing. Title: *KATUNDARI E KORÇËS.* Back: Skanderbeg on horseback.	55.00	120.	250.

		VG	VF	UNC
S160	**1 Skender** 9.11.1921. Dark green underprint. Farmer plowing. Title: *KATUNDARI E KORÇËS.* Circular stamp at upper right. Back: Skanderbeg on horseback.	40.00	100.	225.

		VG	VF	UNC
S161	**20 Skender** 9.11.1921. Yellow. Farmer plowing. Title: *KATUNDARI E KORÇËS.* Circular stamp at upper right. Back: Skanderbeg on horseback.	300.	750.	1250.

#161 Celebrates the fixation of Albanian boundaries.

1923 Issue

		VG	VF	UNC
S162	**0.10 Franga Argjent** 1.1.1923. Dark blue on dark brown underprint. Title: *BASHKIJAE KORÇËS.* Back: Dark blue double-headed eagle and red circular hand stamp. Has at least two perforated margins.	50.00	150.	350.

#161 celebrates the fixation of Albanian boundaries.

		VG	VF	UNC
S163	**0.25 Fr. Arg.** 1.1.1923. Red and green. Title: *BASHKIJAE KORÇËS.* Back: Double-headed eagle. Has at least two perforated margins.	40.00	125.	300.

Regional - Shkodër

Sigurim Arke - Shkodres Permbe

1920 Issue

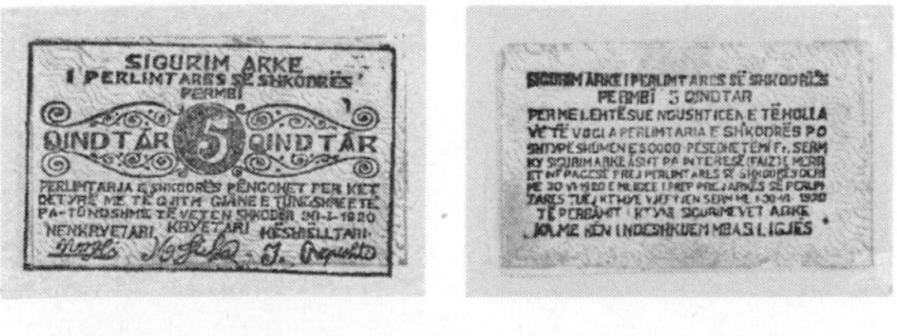

		VG	VF	UNC
S171	**5 Qindtar** 30.1.1920. Black on red underprint. Title: *SIGURIM ARKE I PERLIMT ARES SE SHKODRES PERMBI.* Paper: Brown.	15.00	35.00	75.00

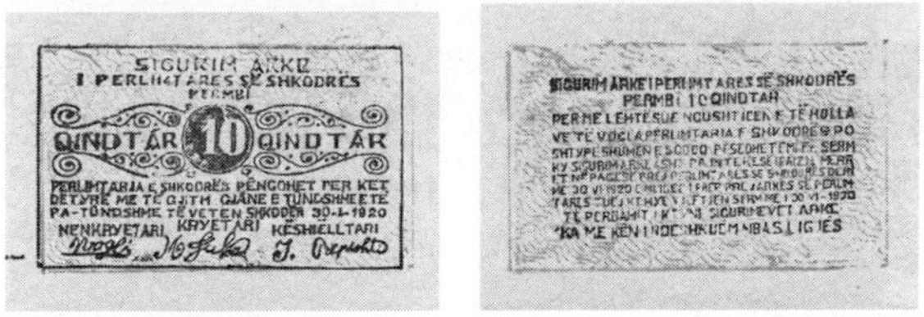

		VG	VF	UNC
S172	**10 Qindtar** 30.1.1920. Black on red underprint. Title: *SIGURIM ARKE I PERLIMT ARES SE SHKODRES PERMBI.* Paper: Brown.	15.00	35.00	75.00

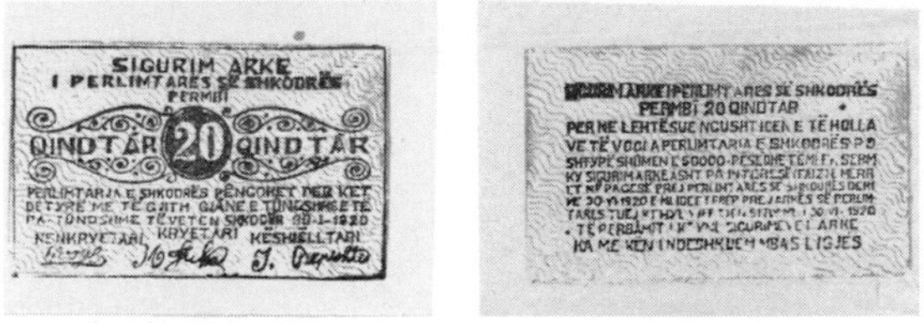

		VG	VF	UNC
S173	**20 Qindtar** 30.1.1920. Black on red underprint. Title: *SIGURIM ARKE I PERLIMT ARES SE SHKODRES PERMBI.* Paper: Brown.	15.00	35.00	75.00
S174	**50 Qindtar** 30.1.1920. Black on red underprint. Title: *SIGURIM ARKE I PERLIMT ARES SE SHKODRES PERMBI.* Paper: Brown. Reported not confirmed.	—	—	—

Regional - Vlorë

Bashkia e Vlorës

1924 Series A

		Good	Fine	XF
S181	**10 Qindtar** 1.5.1924. Title: *BASHKIA E VLORËS.* Double-headed eagle at center in underprint. Rare.	—	—	—

		Good	Fine	XF
S182	**25 Qindtar** 1.5.1924. Title: *BASHKIA E VLORËS.* Double-headed eagle at center in underprint. Rare.	—	—	—

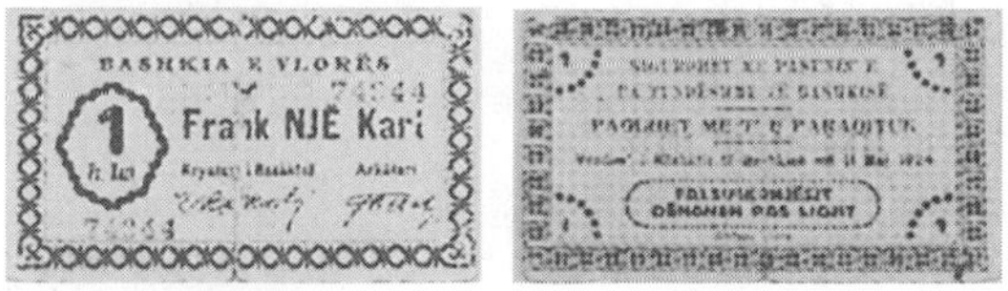

		Good	Fine	XF
S183	**1 Frank Kart** 11.5.1924. Black on orange underprint. Title: *BASHKIA E VLORËS.* Double-headed eagle at center in underprint. Rare.	—	—	—

1924 Series B

		Good	Fine	XF
S184	**1 Frank Kart** 11.5.1924. Brown and red on gray underprint. Title: *BASHKIA E VLORËS.* Portrait man at left.	125.	300.	625.

		Good	Fine	XF
S185	**2 Frank Kart** 11.5.1924. Blue and brown on green underprint. Title: *BASHKIA E VLORËS.* Portrait man at left. Rare.	—	—	—

1924 Series C

		Good	Fine	XF
S186	**1 Frank Kart** 11.5.1924. Portrait man at left.	125.	250.	600.
S187	**2 Frank Kart** 11.5.1924. Portrait man at left. Rare.	—	—	—

The items formerly listed as siege notes of East Pasha are really fiscal stamps and not banknotes, therefore they will no longer be listed here.

Foreign Exchange Certificates

Banka e Shtetit Shqiptar

1950 Issue

		VG	VF	UNC
FX1	**5 Lek** July 1950. Black on orange underprint. Back: Orange.	—	—	—

1953 Issue

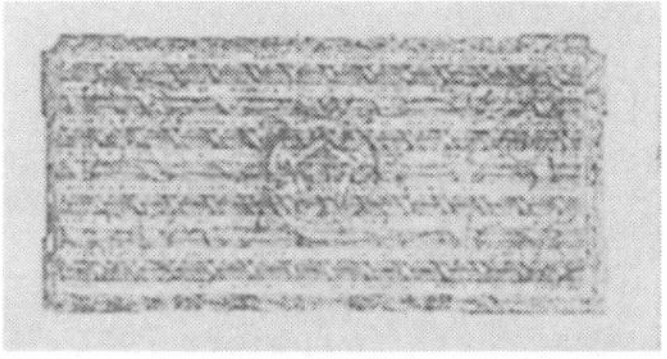

		VG	VF	UNC
FX4	**1 Lek** 1953. Brown and red on multicolor underprint. Arms at right. Back: Brown-orange and purple on yellow underprint. Bank seal at center.	—	—	3.00
FX5	**5 Lek** 1953. Green and red on multicolor underprint. Arms at right. Back: Green and purple on multicolor underprint. Bank seal at center.	—	—	3.50
FX6	**10 Lek** 1953. Purple and red on multicolor underprint. Arms at right. Back: Purple on multicolor underprint. Bank seal at center.	—	—	4.00

		VG	VF	UNC
FX7	**50 Lek** 1953. Black and red on yellow underprint. Arms at right. Back: Green on orange and yellow underprint. Bank seal at center.	—	—	5.00
FX8	**100 Lek** 1953. Brown, purple and red on yellow underprint. Arms at right. Back: Purple on red and yellow underprint. Bank seal at center.	—	—	7.50
FX9	**500 Lek** 1953. Grayish green and red on multicolor underprint. Arms at right. Back: Red on yellow underprint. Bank seal at center.	—	—	10.00

Note: A hoard of about 70-80 sets of FX4-FX9 came on the market in the late 1990s.

1956 Issue

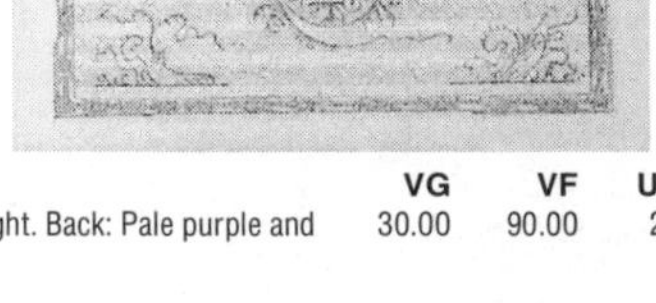

		VG	VF	UNC
FX10	**1/2 Lek** 1956. Gray on red-orange underprint. Arms at right. Back: Pale purple and multicolor. Bank seal at center.	30.00	90.00	200.

1965 Issue

		VG	VF	UNC
FX21	**.05 Lek** 1965. Deep blue-green on pink and pale yellow-orange underprint. Arms at right. Back: Bank arms at center.	—	—	50.00
FX22	**.10 Lek** 1965. Deep olive-brown on pink and pale blue underprint. Arms at right. Back: Bank arms at center.	—	—	50.00

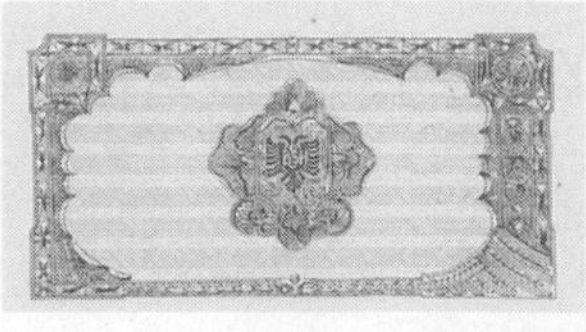

		VG	VF	UNC
FX23	**1/2 Lek** 1965. Deep purple on pink and lilac underprint. Arms at right. Back: Bank arms at center.	—	—	50.00

		VG	VF	UNC
FX24	**1 Lek** 1965. Blackish green on pale yellow and pale yellow-orange underprint. Arms at right. Back: Bank arms at center.	—	—	50.00

		VG	VF	UNC
FX25	**5 Lek** 1965. Blue-black on pale yellow-green underprint. Arms at right. Back: Bank arms at center.	—	—	125.

		VG	VF	UNC
FX26	**10 Lek** 1965. Blue-green on pale yellow and pale grayish green underprint. Arms at right. Back: Bank arms at center.	—	—	125.

		VG	VF	UNC
FX27	**50 Lek** 1965. Deep red-brown on pink and pale yellow underprint. Arms at right. Back: Bank arms at center.	—	—	125.

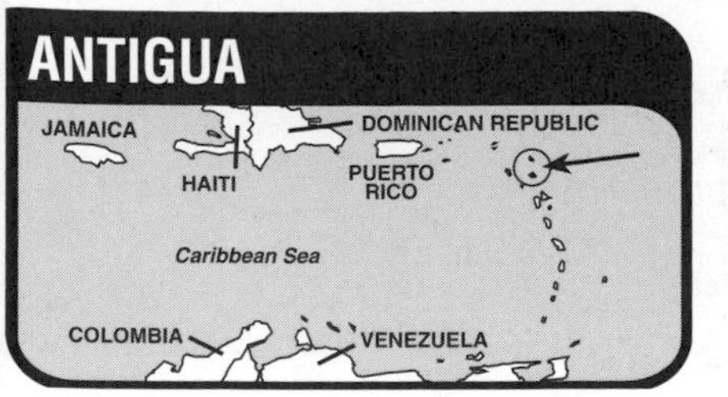

The Associated State of Antigua, located on the eastern edge of the Leeward Islands in the Caribbean Sea, has an area of 171 sq.mi. (442 sq. km). Capital: St. John's. Antigua and its dependencies, Barbuda and Redonda, comprised a presidency of the Leeward Islands.

Antigua was discovered by Columbus in 1493, settled by the British in 1632, occupied by the French in 1666, and ceded to Britain in 1667.

RULERS:

British

MONETARY SYSTEM:

1 British West Indies Dollar = 4 Shillings - 2 Pence
5 British West Indies Dollars = 1 Pound - 10 Pence

NOTE: For later issues see British East Caribbean Territories in Vol. 2 and East Caribbean States in Vol. 3.

British Administration

Barclays Bank (Dominion, Colonial and Overseas)

1926 Provisional Issue

S105 5 Dollars	Good	Fine	XF
1926. Black on pink and green underprint. Arms at center. Rare.	—	—	—

1937 Provisional Issue

S108 5 Dollars	Good	Fine	XF
1937-40. Purple on multicolor underprint. Arms at right. Office of issue: Bridgetown, Barbados. Overprint: *ISSUED AT ANTIGUA BRANCH.* Printer: BWC.			
a. 1.5.1937.	250.	850.	1750.
b. 1.3.1939.	225.	750.	1500.
c. 1.3.1940.	200.	700.	1400.

Colonial Bank

1900 Issue

S112 5 Dollars	Good	Fine	XF
To 1926. Arms at upper center. Printer: P&B. Reported not confirmed.	—	—	—

Royal Bank of Canada

1913 Provisional Issue

S115 5 Dollars	VG	VF	UNC
2.1.1913. Black on green underprint. Portrait C. E. Neill at left, arms at center, portrait H. S. Holt at right. Back: Green. Royal crest at center. Overprint: Blue; *ANTIGUA* at left and right, *PAYABLE AT ST. JOHN'S ANTIGUA* at left center. Printer: ABNC.			
a. Issued note		—	
p. Proof.		—	550.
s. Specimen.		—	2250.

1920 Regular Issue

S116 5 Dollars = 1 Pound 10 Pence	Good	Fine	XF
2.1.1920. Black on green underprint. Steamship at center. Back: Green. Royal crest at center. Printer: ABNC.			
a. Issued note.	400.	1250.	—
p. Proof.			

1938 Issue

S117 5 Dollars = 1 Pound 10 Pence	Good	Fine	XF
3.1.1938. Black on green underprint. Steamship at center. Similar to #S116 but reduced size. Printer: CBNC.			
a. Issued note.	250.	750.	—
p. Proof.			

The Argentine Republic, located in South America, has an area of 2.76 million sq. km. and a population of 40.48 million. Capital: Buenos Aires. Its varied topography ranges from the subtropical lowlands of the north to the towering Andean Mountains in the west and the windswept Patagonian steppe in the south. The rolling, fertile pampas of central Argentina are ideal for agriculture and grazing, and support most of the republic's population. Meat packing, flour milling, textiles, sugar refining and dairy products are the principal industries. Oil is found in Patagonia, but most of the mineral requirements must be imported.

In 1816, the United Provinces of the Rio Plata declared their independence from Spain. After Bolivia, Paraguay, and Uruguay went their separate ways, the area that remained became Argentina. The country's population and culture were heavily shaped by immigrants from throughout Europe, but most particularly Italy and Spain, which provided the largest percentage of newcomers from 1860 to 1930. Up until about the mid-20th century, much of Argentina's history was dominated by periods of internal political conflict between Federalists and Unitarians and between civilian and military factions. After World War II, an era of Peronist authoritarian rule and interference in subsequent governments was followed by a military junta that took power in 1976. Democracy returned in 1983, and has persisted despite numerous challenges, the most formidable of which was a severe economic crisis in 2001-02 that led to violent public protests and the resignation of several interim presidents. The economy has recovered strongly since bottoming out in 2002.

MONETARY SYSTEM:

1 Peso (m/n) = 100 Centavos to 1970
1 'New' Peso (Ley 18.188) = 100 'Old' Pesos (m/n), 1970-83
1 Peso Argentino = 10,000 Pesos, (Ley 18.188) 1983-85
1 Austral = 100 Centavos = 1000 Pesos Argentinos, 1985-92
1 Peso = 10,000 Australes, 1992-
1 Peso = 8 Reales = 100 Centavos
1 Peso = 8 Reales = 100 Centavos

REPLACEMENT NOTES:

#260d onward: R prefix before serial #.

ARRANGEMENT

Listings for Argentina are divided into six major sections. The first contains early government, government-controlled institutions and banks for the period 1820-1864. The second contains such notes issued between 1865 and 1903. Presented at the beginning of each of these sections are government or Treasury issues, followed by bank issues according to the headings found on the notes. The third section consists of notes falling under a National Bank system called *Bancos Nacionales Garantidos,* first issued in 1888. The fourth lists earlier provincial issues, and the fifth lists all regional and private bank issues in alphabetical sequence. The sixth lists all later provincial issues, from 1890 to 2002.

The following chart indicates the contents of each of these six major sections:

Section I, 1820-64

GOVERNMENT

Government of the Province of Buenos Aires

Customs Notes of 1820-1821 .... #S101-S120
Provincia de Buenos Aires, 1823. .... #121-S123

Argentine Confederation

Treasury Notes, 1853-1854. .... #S151-S166
Customs Bonds-Gobierno Nacional, 1855-1859 .... #S170-S172, S181-S211

República Argentina

Treasury Notes, 1860-61 .... #S216-S231

EARLY BANCOS

Banco de Buenos Ayres, 1822-1829. .... #S301-S336
Banco Nacional, 1826 .... #S337-S359
Banco Nacional de las Provincias Unidas del Rio de la Plata, 1829-1840 .... #S360-S376
Casa de Moneda - notes titled *La Provincia de Buenos Aires,* 1841-1851 .... #S377-S401
Banco y Casa de Moneda - notes titled
La Provincia de Buenos Aires, 1853-1854. .... #S402-S414
- as above, notes titled *El Estado de Buenos Aires,* 1856-1858 .... #S415-S435
- as above, in its own name 1864 .... #S441-S450

Section II, 1865-1903

TREASURY

Treasury Bills, 1876. .... #S461-S464
Bonos de Tesoro, Provincia de Buenos Aires, 1880 .... #S464A-S464C
Treasury Notes, 1890 .... #S465-S466

BANKS

Banco de la Provincia de Buenos Aires, 1865, 1869-1891 .... #S467-S470, S500-S579
- as above, notes titled *La Provincia de Buenos Aires,* 1867, 1869. .... #S471-S499
Banco Británico de la América del Sud, 1894 .... #S601
Banco Hipotecario de la Provincia de Buenos Aires, 1891 .... #S611-S632
Banco Nacional, 1873-1883. .... #S641-S720
Banco Provincial de Córdoba, 1873-1891 .... #S721-S757
Banco Provincial de Entre-Rios, 1885. .... #S760-S772
Banco Provincial de Salta, 1884-1903. .... #S786-S797
Banco Provincial de Santa Fé, 1874-1882 .... #S798-S835
Banco Provincial de Tucumán, 1888. .... #S841-S846

Section III, 1888

BANCOS NACIONALES GARANTIDOS

Banco Alemán Transatlántico .... #S1008

SECTION I

Early Forerunners of Paper Money, 1813-18

Several kinds of paper issues took place shortly after Argentinian independence, but these did not constitute true paper money. They represented loans to the government, and could serve in only a very limited capacity as payment for customs or certain debts.

GOVERNMENT

GOVERNMENT OF THE PROVINCE OF BUENOS AIRES

1820 CUSTOMS NOTES FIRST ISSUE

#S101-S106 legend in circular design: *PROVINCIA DE BUENOS-AYRES*. Text on notes: *PAPEL VILLETE O AMORTIZAVLE* above *VALE POR...* line. Issued under Decrees of 27 May and 29 November 1820. Several watermark varieties. Circle with oval hand stamp of arms and text at upper center. Printed signature.

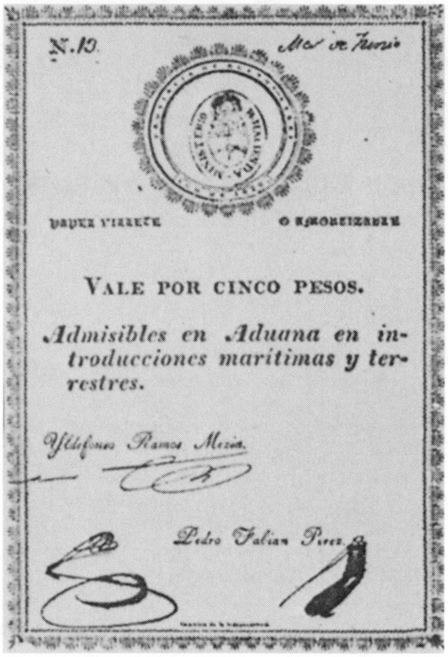

		Good	Fine	XF
S101	**5 Pesos** 1820. Black. Printed signature. Paper: White.	250.	500.	900.
S102	**10 Pesos** 1820. Black. Printed signature. Paper: White.	250.	500.	900.
S103	**20 Pesos** 1820. Black. Printed signature. Paper: White.	250.	500.	900.
S104	**40 Pesos** 1820. Black. Printed signature. Paper: White.	275.	750.	1200.
S105	**50 Pesos** 1820. Black. Printed signature. Paper: White.	250.	500.	900.
S106	**100 Pesos** 1820. Black. Printed signature. Paper: White.	250.	500.	900.

1820 CUSTOMS NOTES SECOND ISSUE

		Good	Fine	XF
S107	**5 Pesos** 1820. Handwritten signature.	200.	500.	900.
S108	**10 Pesos** 1820. Handwritten signature.	200.	500.	900.
S109	**20 Pesos** 1820. Handwritten signature.	200.	500.	900.
S110	**40 Pesos** 1820. Handwritten signature.	250.	500.	900.
S111	**50 Pesos** 1820. Handwritten signature.	200.	500.	900.
S112	**100 Pesos** 1820. Handwritten signature.	200.	500.	900.
S113	**100 Pesos** 1821. Handwritten signature.	200.	500.	900.

1820; 1821 CUSTOMS NOTES THIRD ISSUE

#S114-S120 legend in circular design: *PAPEL MONEDA DE LA PROVINCIA DE BUENOS-AYRES*. Without text: *PAPEL VILLETE ...* above *VALE ...* line. Similar to previous issue.

		Good	Fine	XF
S114	**10 Pesos** 1820. Handwritten signature.	250.	500.	900.
S115	**20 Pesos** 1820. Handwritten signature.	250.	500.	900.
S116	**100 Pesos** 1820. Printed signature.	250.	500.	900.
S117	**100 Pesos** 1820. Handwritten signature.	250.	500.	900.
S118	**10 Pesos** 1821. Handwritten signature.	250.	500.	900.
S119	**20 Pesos** 1821. Handwritten signature.	250.	500.	900.
S120	**100 Pesos** 1821. Handwritten signature.	250.	500.	900.

PROVINCIA DE BUENOS AIRES

1823 ISSUE

#S121-S123 issued by the government of the Province in 1823. Payable in metallic money.

	Good	Fine	XF
S121 1 Peso 1823. Black. Circle with text and value at center.	200.	500.	900.

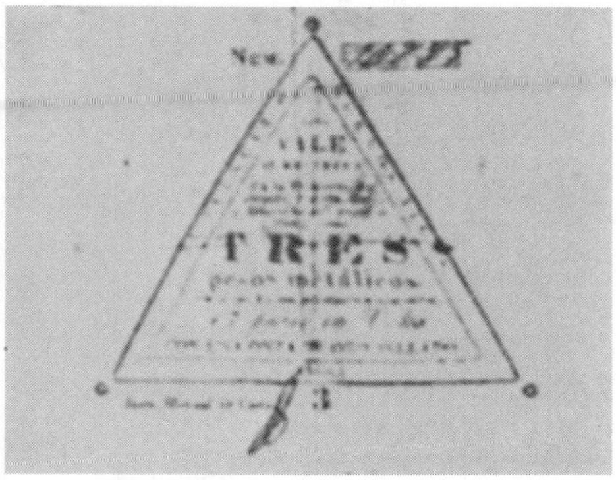

	Good	Fine	XF
S122 3 Pesos 1823. Black. Triangle with text and value at center. Rare.	—	—	—
S123 5 Pesos 1823. Black. Pentagon with text and value at center. Rare.	—	—	—

ARGENTINE CONFEDERATION

1853-54 ND TREASURY NOTES ISSUE

#S151-S154 authorized by decree of January 30, 1854 while the government was waiting for copper coins to arrive from Europe.

	Good	Fine	XF
S151 1/2 Real Reported not confirmed.	—	—	—

	Good	Fine	XF
S152 1 Real ND. Black. Ram at bottom center. Uniface. Rare.	—	—	—
S153 2 Reales ND. Reported not confirmed.	—	—	—
S154 4 Reales ND. Reported not confirmed.	—	—	—

ADMINISTRACIÓN DE HACIENDA Y CREDITO

1853 ND TREASURY NOTES

#S155-S159 Issue controlled by the *Administración de Hacienda y Credito.*

	Good	Fine	XF
S155 1 Peso 9 December 1853 (handwritten). Black. Horse at bottom center. Uniface. Squarish format.	100.	275.	600.
S156 5 Pesos 9 December 1853 (handwritten). Black. Horses and cow at top center, clasped hands at bottom center. Uniface.	150.	400.	850.

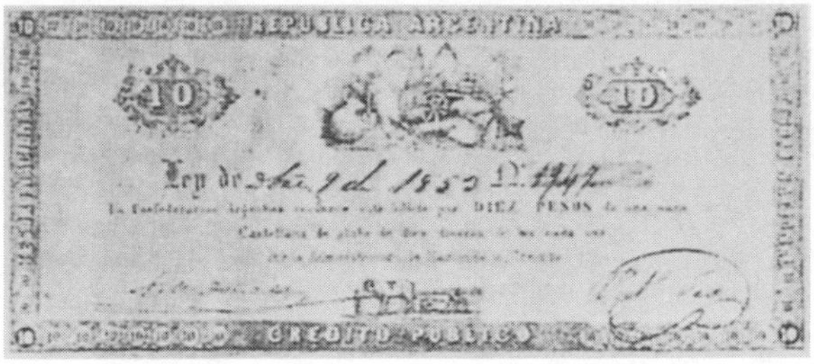

	Good	Fine	XF
S157 10 Pesos 9 December 1853 (handwritten). Black. Cows, plants and bales at top center, cow at bottom center. Uniface.	250.	550.	1100.
S158 20 Pesos 9 December 1853 (handwritten). Black. Uniface. Reported not confirmed.	—	—	—
S159 50 Pesos 9 December 1853 (handwritten). Black. Uniface. Reported not confirmed.	—	—	—
S160 100 Pesos 9 December 1853 (handwritten). Black. Uniface. Reported not confirmed.	—	—	—

185X ND TREASURY NOTES

	Good	Fine	XF
S161 1 Peso 185x. Black. Farm tools at upper center. Printer: PBC. Specimen. Rare.	—	—	—

	Good	Fine	XF
S162 5 Pesos 185x. Black. Allegorical figures at upper center. Printer: PBC. Specimen. Rare.	—	—	—

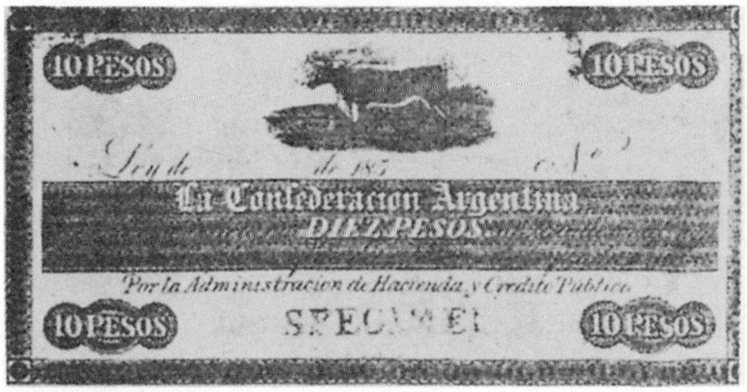

	Good	Fine	XF
S163 10 Pesos 185x. Black. Bull at upper center. Printer: PBC. Specimen. Rare.	—	—	—
S164 20 Pesos 185x. Black. Printer: PBC. Reported not confirmed.	—	—	—

	Good	Fine	XF
S165 50 Pesos 185x. Black. Allegory of Commerce at upper center. Printer: PBC. Specimen. Rare.	—	—	—
S166 100 Pesos 185x. Black. Printer: PBC. Reported not confirmed.	—	—	—

CUSTOM BONDS - GOBIERNO NACIONAL

DECRETO DE 15 DE NOVIEMBRE DE 1855

	Good	Fine	XF
S170 10 Pesos D.1855. Rare.	—	—	—

		Good	Fine	XF
S171	**100 Pesos**			
	D.1855. Rare.	—	—	—
S172	**200 Pesos**			
	D.1855. Rare.	—	—	—

Decreto de 7 de Mayo de 1857

#S181-S184 Various handwritten dates in 1857. Interest payable at 1% per month.

		Good	Fine	XF
S181	**10 Pesos**			
	1857. Handwritten. Black. Uniface. Interest payable at 1% per month.	25.00	75.00	150.
S182	**20 Pesos**			
	1857. Handwritten. Black. Uniface. Interest payable at 1% per month.	25.00	75.00	150.
S183	**50 Pesos**			
	1857. Handwritten. Black. Uniface. Interest payable at 1% per month.	25.00	75.00	150.

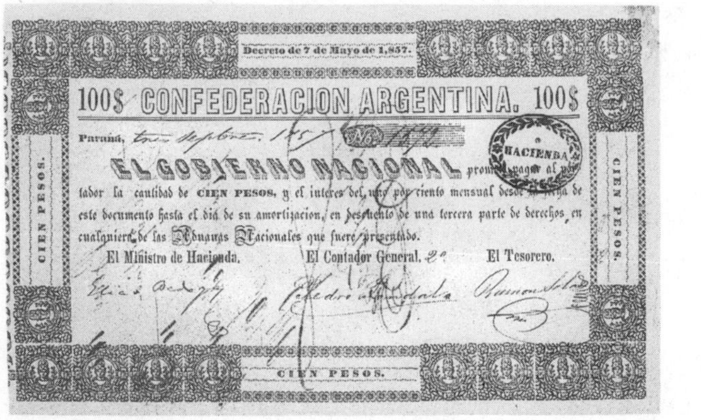

		Good	Fine	XF
S184	**100 Pesos**			
	1857. Black. 20 tiny portrait medalets make up part of border design. Uniface. Interest payable at 1% per month.	25.00	75.00	150.

Decretos de 7 de Mayo y 5 de Junio 1857

#S185-S188 like previous issue. Various handwritten dates into 1859. Interest payable at 2% per month.

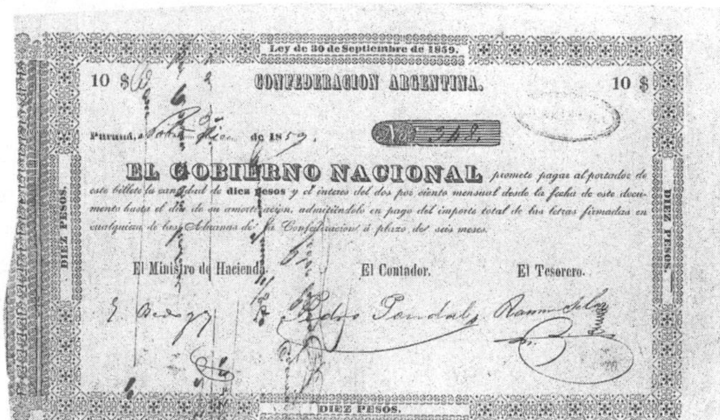

		Good	Fine	XF
S185	**10 Pesos**			
	1857-59. Handwritten. Black. Uniface. Interest payable at 2% per month.			
	a. Issued note.	25.00	75.00	150.
	x. Error with *descento* in text.	40.00	100.	200.

Decretos de 7 de Mayo y 5 de Junio 1857

		Good	Fine	XF
S186	**20 Pesos**			
	1857-59. Handwritten. Black. Uniface. Interest payable at 2% per month.	25.00	75.00	150.

Custom Bonds - Gobierno Nacional

Decretos de 7 de Mayo y 5 de Junio 1857

#S185-S188 like previous issue. Various handwritten dates into 1859. Interest payable at 2% per month.

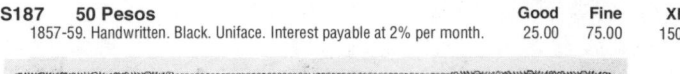

		Good	Fine	XF
S187	**50 Pesos**			
	1857-59. Handwritten. Black. Uniface. Interest payable at 2% per month.	25.00	75.00	150.

		Good	Fine	XF
S188	**100 Pesos**			
	1857-59. Black. Similar to #S184, but only 18 portrait medalets in border design. Uniface. Interest payable at 2% per month.	25.00	75.00	150.

1857 First Issue

#S189-S191 payable from October 1, 1857.

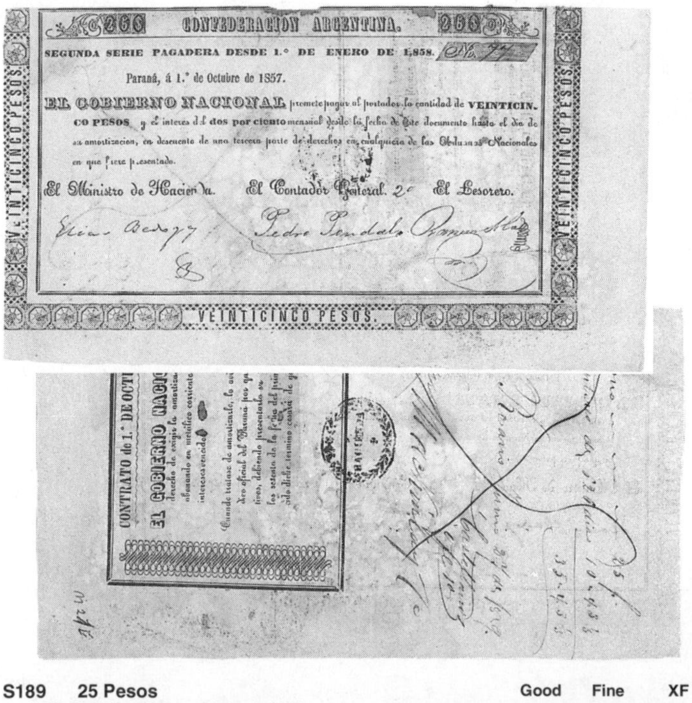

		Good	Fine	XF
S189	**25 Pesos**			
	1857. Black. Payable from October 1, 1857.	—	—	—

		Good	Fine	XF
S190	**50 Pesos** 1857. Black. Payable from October 1, 1857.	—	—	—

		Good	Fine	XF
S191	**200 Pesos** 1857. Black. Payable from October 1, 1857.	25.00	75.00	150.

1857 Second Issue

#S192-S195 payable from January 1, 1858.

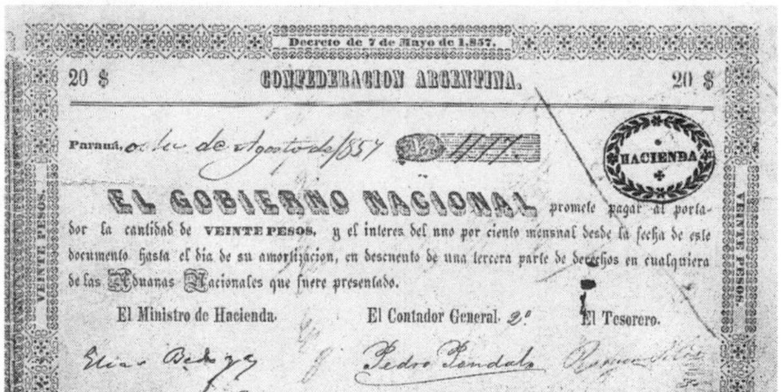

		Good	Fine	XF
S192	**20 Pesos** 1857. Black. Payable from January 1, 1858.	25.00	75.00	150.

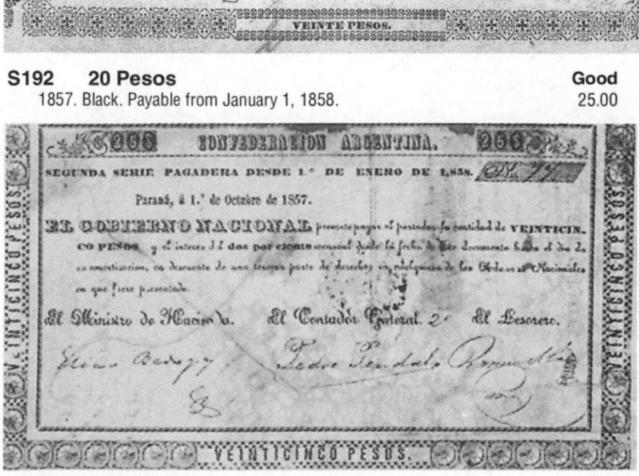

		Good	Fine	XF
S193	**25 Pesos** 1857. Black. Payable from January 1, 1858.	25.00	75.00	150.
S194	**50 Pesos** 1857. Black. Payable from January 1, 1858.	25.00	75.00	150.
S195	**200 Pesos** 1857. Black. Payable from January 1, 1858.	25.00	75.00	150.

1857 Third Issue

#S196-S198 payable from January 1, 1859.

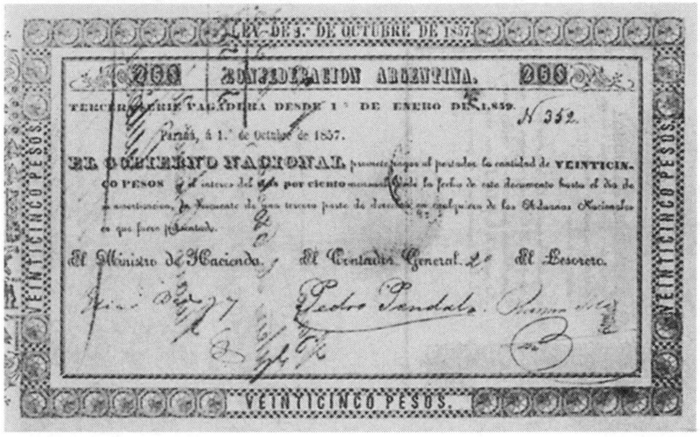

		Good	Fine	XF
S196	**25 Pesos** 1857. Black. Payable from January 1, 1859.	25.00	75.00	150.
S197	**50 Pesos** 1857. Black. Payable from January 1, 1859.	25.00	75.00	150.
S198	**200 Pesos** 1857. Black. Payable from January 1, 1859.	25.00	75.00	150.

1859 Issue

#S201-S203 black. Uniface. Issued in 1859 to help finance the war between the Confederation and the State of Buenos Aires. No law or contract is shown. Various handwritten dates in 1859.

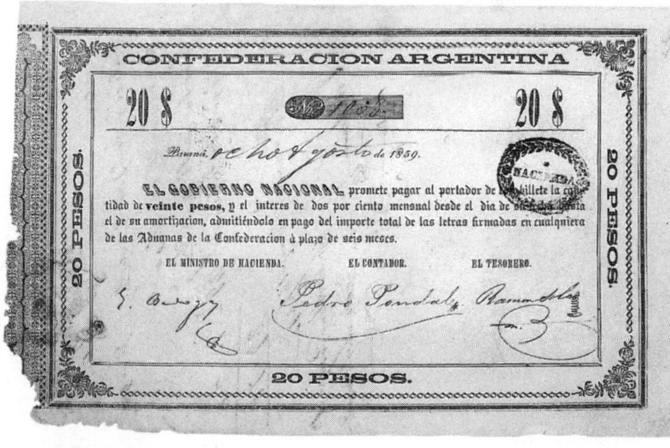

		Good	Fine	XF
S201	**20 Pesos** 1859. Handwritten. Black. Uniface.	25.00	75.00	150.

		Good	Fine	XF
S202	**50 Pesos** 1859. Handwritten. Black. Uniface.	25.00	75.00	150.

S203 100 Pesos

	Good	Fine	XF
1859. Handwritten. Black. Uniface.	25.00	75.00	150.

Contrato de 10 de Mayo de 1859

#S204-S206 Interest was set at 1-1/2% per month.

S204 100 Pesos

	Good	Fine	XF
1859. Black. Uniface. Interest was set at 1-1/2% per month.	25.00	75.00	150.

S205 200 Pesos

	Good	Fine	XF
1859. Black. Uniface. Interest was set at 1-1/2% per month.	25.00	75.00	150.

S206 500 Pesos

	Good	Fine	XF
1859. Black. Border design like #S188 and #S211. Uniface. Interest was set at 1-1/2% per month.	50.00	100.	225.

Ley Septiembre 29 de 1859

S207 Various Amounts

	Good	Fine	XF
1859. Black. Uniface. Interest rate was 6% annually. Rare.	—	—	—

Ley de 30 de Septiembre de 1859

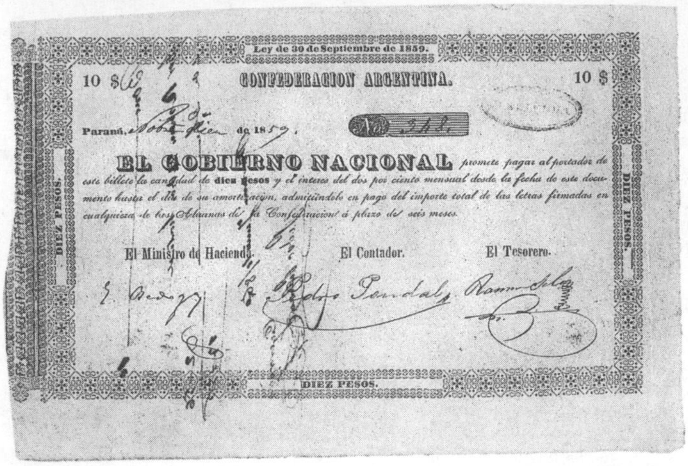

S208 10 Pesos

	Good	Fine	XF
1859. Handwritten. Black. Uniface. Interest rate was 2% per month.	25.00	75.00	150.

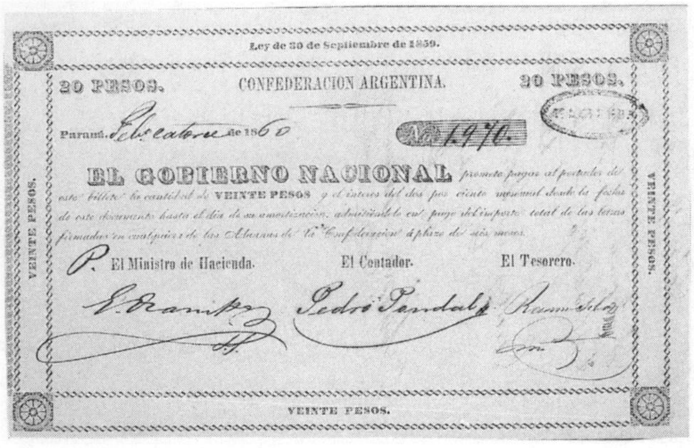

S209 20 Pesos

	Good	Fine	XF
1859. Black. Uniface. Interest rate was 2% per month.	25.00	75.00	150.

S210 50 Pesos

	Good	Fine	XF
1859. Black. Uniface. Interest rate was 2% per month.	25.00	75.00	150.

SENDING SCANNED IMAGES BY E-MAIL

We have been receiving an ever-increasing flow of scanned images from sources world wide. Unfortunately, many of these scans could not be used due to the type of scan, or simple incompatibility with our systems. We appreciate the effort it takes to produce these images and accuracy they add to the catalog listings.

Here are a few simple instructions to follow when producing these scans. We encourage you to continue sending new images or upgrades to those currently illustrated and please do not hesitate to ask questions about this process.

- Scan all images within a resolution of 300 dpi.
- Size setting should be at 100%
- Please include in the e-mail the actual size of the image in millimeters height x width
- Scan in true 4-color
- Save images as jpeg and name in such a way which clearly indentifies the country of the note and catalog number
- Do not compress files
- Please e-mail with a request to confirm receipt of the attachment
- Please send multiple images on a disc if available
- Please send images to: george.cuhaj@fwmedia.com

		Good	Fine	XF
S211	**100 Pesos** 1859. Black. Similar to #S188. Uniface. Interest rate was 2% per month.	25.00	75.00	150.

República Argentina

In October of 1860, the Argentine Confederation adopted the name REPUBLICA ARGENTINA. For a time that year, the war between the Confederation and Buenos Aires ceased and the two were joined. But by June 1861 relations between them had ruptured once again, and fighting began in earnest. The final defeat of Buenos Aires by the Confederation in September, 1861, brought about unification and the end of the Confederation.

Treasury

Ley de 1 de Octubre de 1860

#S216-S223 various handwritten dates in 1860 and 1861. Most have blue overprint: *PAGADO No.* in oval on face or back.

		Good	Fine	XF
S216	**1/2 Peso** 1860-61. Overprint: Blue;*PAGADO No.* in oval on face or back. Reported not confirmed.	—	—	—
S217	**1 Peso** 1860-61. Overprint: Blue; *PAGADO No.* in oval on face or back. Reported not confirmed.	—	—	—
S218	**2 Pesos** 1860-61. Overprint: Blue; *PAGADO No.* in oval on face or back. Reported not confirmed.	—	—	—

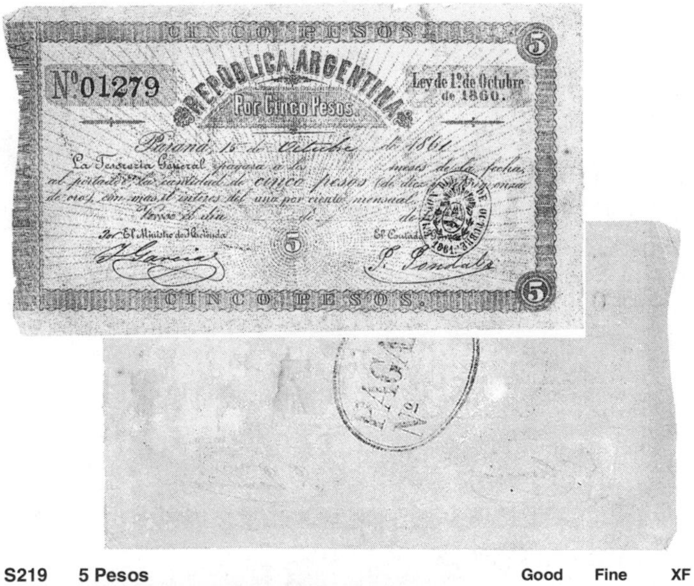

		Good	Fine	XF
S219	**5 Pesos** 1860-61. Overprint: Blue; *PAGADO No.* on face or back. Rare.	—	—	—

		Good	Fine	XF
S220	**10 Pesos** 1860-61. Black. Denomination in oval at upper center. Overprint: Blue; *PAGADO No.* in oval on face or back. Paper: Green.	40.00	100.	200.

		Good	Fine	XF
S221	**20 Pesos** 1860-61. Black. Arms at upper center. Overprint: Blue; *PAGADO No.* in oval on face or back. Paper: Greenish yellow.			
	a. Issued note.	40.00	100.	200.
	b. Oval hand stamp: *PAGADO*.	25.00	75.00	150.

		Good	Fine	XF
S222	**50 Pesos** 1860-61. Black. Seated woman in oval at left. Overprint: Blue; *PAGADO No.*in oval on face or back. Paper: Light tan.			
	a. Issued note.	40.00	100.	200.
	b. Oval hand stamp: *PAGADO*.	25.00	75.00	150.

		Good	Fine	XF
S223	**100 Pesos** 1860-61. Black and pink. Seated allegorical man with bales at center. Overprint: Blue; *PAGADO No.* in oval on face or back.	40.00	100.	200.

Ley de 1 de Octubre de 1860; 1861 Issue

#S224-S231 like previous issue but blue oval ovpt: *EMISION DE 15 DE OCTUBRE 1861* at r. Handwritten date 15 Octubre 1861. Oval hand stamped seal.

		Good	Fine	XF
S224	**1/2 Peso** 15.10.1861. Handwritten date. Black. Oval hand stamped seal. Overprint: Blue oval *EMISION DE 15 DE OCTUBRE 1861* at right.	50.00	125.	225.

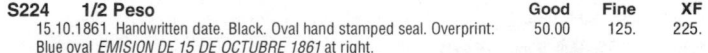

	Good	Fine	XF
S225 1 Peso			
15.10.1861. Handwritten date. Brown-violet. Oval hand stamped seal. Overprint: Blue oval *EMISION DE 15 DE OCTUBRE 1861* at right.			
a. Issued note.	75.00	150.	250.
b. Oval hand stamp: *PAGADO*.	60.00	125.	225.
S226 2 Pesos			
15.10.1861. Handwritten date. Blue. Oval hand stamped seal. Overprint: Blue oval *EMISION DE 15 DE OCTUBRE 1861* at right.	60.00	125.	225.

	Good	Fine	XF
S227 5 Pesos			
15.10.1861. Handwritten date. Orange. Oval hand stamped seal. Overprint: Blue oval *EMISION DE 15 DE OCTUBRE 1861* at right.	60.00	125.	225.
S228 10 Pesos			
15.10.1861. Handwritten date. Oval hand stamped seal. LIke #S220. Overprint: Blue oval *EMISION DE 15 DE OCTUBRE 1861* at right.	60.00	125.	225.
S229 20 Pesos			
15.10.1861. Handwritten date. Oval hand stamped seal. Overprint: Blue oval *EMISION DE 15 DE OCTUBRE 1861* at right.	60.00	125.	225.
S230 50 Pesos			
15.10.1861. Handwritten date. Oval hand stamped seal. Overprint: Blue oval *EMISION DE 15 DE OCTUBRE 1861* at right.	75.00	150.	—
S231 100 Pesos			
15.10.1861. Handwritten date. Uniface. Oval hand stamped seal. Overprint: Blue oval *EMISION DE 15 DE OCTUBRE 1861* at right. Watermark: Denomination and bank crest.	125.	—	—

Banco de Buenos-Ayres

1822 First Issue

Consisted of a form on which the various specified denominations were written. Practically the entire issue was redeemed and no original examples are known. Reprints of the blank form were made by the Compania Sud-Americana de Billetes de Banco around 1900.

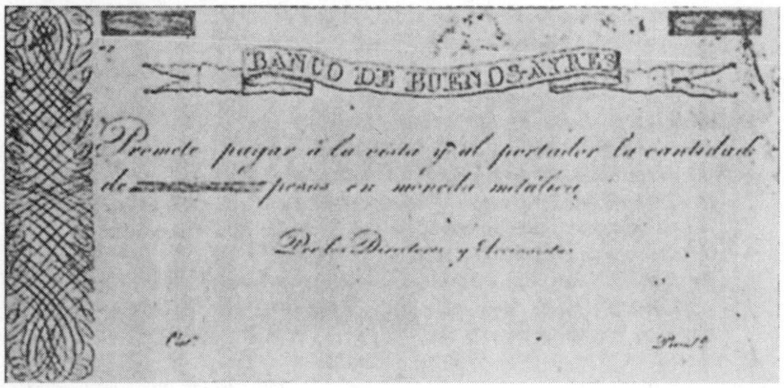

	Good	Fine	XF
S301 20 Pesos			
ND (1822). Black. Uniface.	—	—	—
S302 50 Pesos			
ND (1822). Black. Uniface.	—	—	—
S303 100 Pesos			
ND (1822). Black. Uniface.	—	—	—
S304 200 Pesos			
ND (1822). Black. Uniface.	—	—	—
S305 500 Pesos			
ND (1822). Black. Uniface.	—	—	—
S306 1000 Pesos			
ND (1822). Black. Uniface.	—	—	—

June 1823 Second Issue

Consisted of 2 emissions separately designed and dated.

	Good	Fine	XF
S307 1 Peso			
9.6.1823. Black. Uniface. One bank seal (rayed sun in circle) at left. Rare.	—	—	—

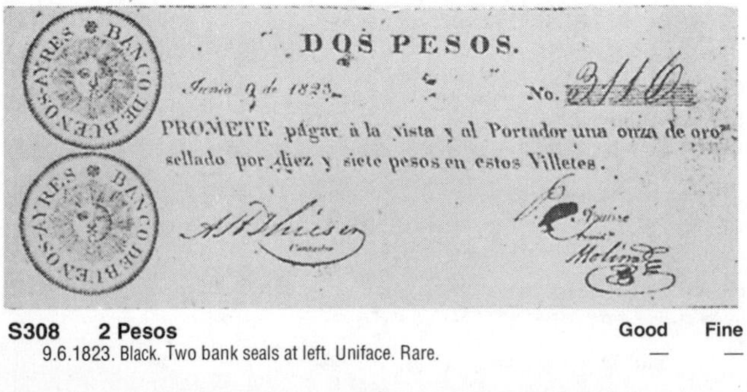

	Good	Fine	XF
S308 2 Pesos			
9.6.1823. Black. Two bank seals at left. Uniface. Rare.	—	—	—

Nov. 1823 "Second" Issue

	Good	Fine	XF
S309 1 Peso			
20.11.1823. Black. Uniface. One bank seal at center, heavy border. Rare.	—	—	—

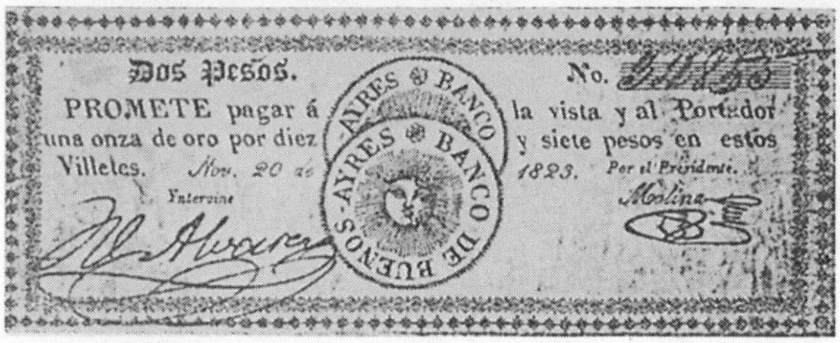

	Good	Fine	XF
S310 2 Pesos			
20.11.1823. Black. Uniface. Two bank seals, one partly over the other, at center. Rare.	—	—	—

1823-24 Third Issue

	Good	Fine	XF
S311 1 Peso			
ND. Black. National arms at top center. Hand signature V. Alvarez. Uniface. Paper: Rose. Printer: London. Rare.	—	—	—

NOTE: For 1 Peso notes like #S311 but w/different sign., see #S320.

	Good	Fine	XF
S312 5 Pesos			
1823-24. Black. Arms at left. Uniface. Paper: White. Printer: London. Rare.	—	—	—

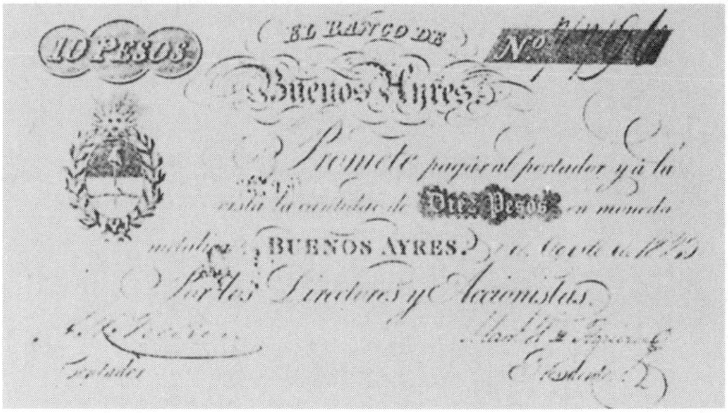

	Good	Fine	XF
S313 10 Pesos			
1823-24. Black. Arms at left. Uniface. Paper: White. Printer: London. Rare.	—	—	—
S314 20 Pesos			
1823-24. Black. Arms at left. Uniface. Paper: White. Printer: London. Rare.	—	—	—
S315 50 Pesos			
1823-24. Black. Arms at left. Uniface. Paper: White. Printer: London. Rare.	—	—	—
S316 100 Pesos			
1823-24. Black. Arms at left. Uniface. Paper: White. Printer: London. Rare.	—	—	—

NOTE: For notes like #S312-S313 and S315-316 but dated in 1826, see #S321-S324.

#S317-S319 *Deleted.*

1826 Third Issue (Continuation)

The Banco de las Provincias Unidas del Rio de la Plata was formed on January 28, 1826. It was to take over the issuance of bank notes from the Banco de Buenos-Ayres. The first issue of this newly created bank consisted of notes printed from plates for the Third Issue of the Banco de Buenos-Ayres.

	Good	Fine	XF
S320 1 Peso			
ND. Black. National arms at top center. Uniface. Printer: Printed in London.			
a. Rose paper.	225.	500.	1250.
b. White paper.	225.	500.	1250.

		Good	Fine	XF
S321	**5 Pesos** 1826. Handwritten date. Arms at left. Rare.	—	—	—
S322	**10 Pesos** 1826. Handwritten date. Arms at left. Rare.	—	—	—
S323	**50 Pesos** 1826. Handwritten date. Arms at left. Rare.	—	—	—
S324	**100 Pesos** 1826. Handwritten date. Arms at left. Rare.	—	—	—

#S325-S327 *Deleted.*

1827 Fourth Issue

#S328-S336 carry the name of Banco de Buenos-Ayres but were issued by the Banco Nacional. Notes had been ordered by the former in 1825 but because of a Brazilian blockade they were not delivered until March 1827. Black on thin white paper. Uniface. Printer: Fairman, Draper, Underwood and Co., Philadelphia. Some notes later reprinted from the same plates in Buenos Aires on thicker paper. Notes hand dated from 1827-28 or 1829. Reprints of all values except the 1 Peso were made by the Compania Sud-Americana de Billetes de Banco around 1900.

		Good	Fine	XF
S328	**1 Peso** 1827-29. Black. Portrait Simon Bolívar at left, allegorical figures at center, portrait George Washington at right. Paper: Thin, white. Printer: Fairman, Draper, Underwood and Co., Philadelphia.			
	a. Issued note.	175.	500.	950.
	r. Unsigned remainder.	—	—	—

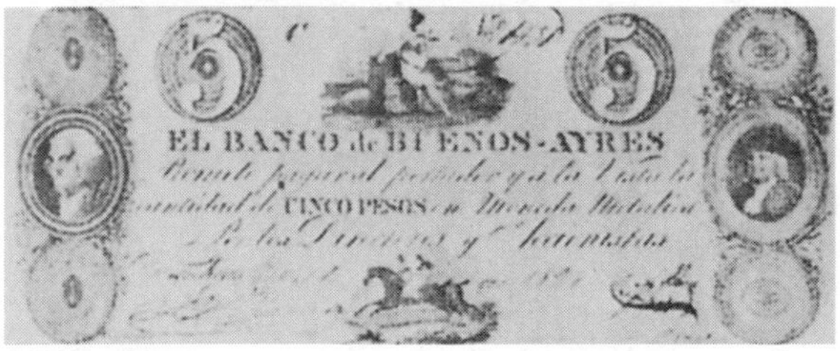

		Good	Fine	XF
S329	**5 Pesos** 1827-28. Black. Portrait Benjamin Franklin at left, allegorical woman at upper center, two horseback riders at bottom center, portrait W. Penn at right. Uniface. Paper: Thin, white. Printer: Fairman, Draper, Underwood and Co., Philadelphia.	—	—	—
S330	**10 Pesos** 1827-28. Black. Eagle with shield at center, portrait Simon Bolívar at upper right, portrait George Washington at lower right. Paper: Thin, white. Printer: Fairman, Draper, Underwood and Co., Philadelphia. Rare.	—	—	—

		Good	Fine	XF
S331	**20 Pesos** 1827-28. Black. Portrait Simon Bolívar at left, beehive at center, portrait George Washington at upper right. Uniface. Paper: Thin, white. Printer: Fairman, Draper, Underwood and Co., Philadelphia. Rare.	—	—	—
S332	**50 Pesos** 1827-28. Black. Portrait Simon Bolívar at upper left, George Washington at lower left, allegorical figures and denomination at center. Paper: Thin, white. Printer: Fairman, Draper, Underwood and Co., Philadelphia. Rare.	—	—	—

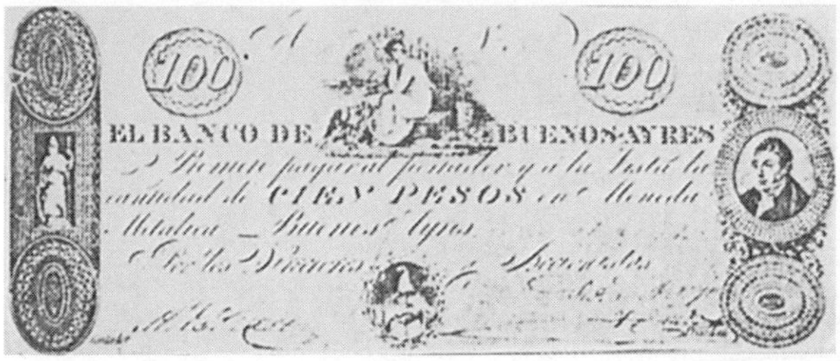

		Good	Fine	XF
S333	**100 Pesos** 1827-28. Black. Standing woman at left, allegorical woman at center, man at right. Uniface. Paper: Thin, white. Printer: Fairman, Draper, Underwood and Co., Philadelphia. Rare.	—	—	—

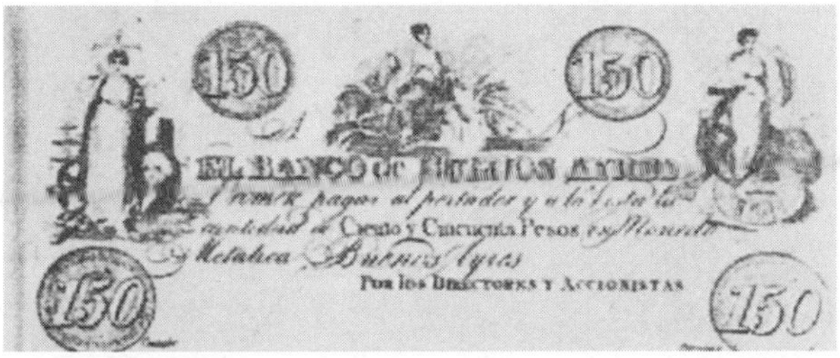

		Good	Fine	XF
S334	**150 Pesos** 1827-29. Black. Standing woman near portrait George Washington at left, allegorical women at center and right. Uniface. Paper: Thin, white. Printer: Fairman, Draper, Underwood and Co., Philadelphia. Rare.	—	—	—

		Good	Fine	XF
S335	**500 Pesos** 1827-29. Black. Allegorical woman with bales at center. Uniface. Paper: Thin, white. Printer: Fairman, Draper, Underwood and Co., Philadelphia. Rare.	—	—	—
S336	**1000 Pesos** 1827-29. Black. Allegorical woman with two children at left, eagle at center, woman standing with scale at right. Uniface. Paper: Thin, white. Printer: Fairman, Draper, Underwood and Co., Philadelphia.			
	a. Reported, not confirmed.	—	—	—
	x. Reprint.	—	Unc	20.00

Banco Nacional

1826 1 Peso Issues

Notes with the "short form" bank name were first issued in 1826, though the notes bore no date. Two distinct types were made, and both were marked for issue in Buenos Aires or Provincia Oriental (later to become Uruguay).

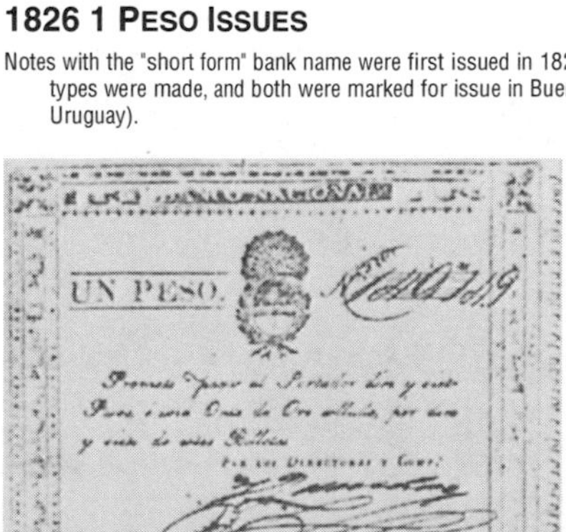

		Good	Fine	XF
S337	**1 Peso** ND (1826). Black. Square format. Text: *CAJA DE* at lower left. (without any indication of circulating area). Uniface. Arms at center.	—	—	—
S338	**1 Peso** ND (1826). Black. Arms at center. Uniface. Square format. Text: *CAJA DE* printed and *B.A.* (for Buenos Aires) filled in by hand at lower left.	—	—	—

	Good	Fine	XF
S339 1 Peso			
ND (1926). Black. Square format. Text: *CAJA DE P.O.* (for Provincia Oriental) at lower left. Arms at center. Uniface.	—	—	—
S340 1 Peso			
ND (1826). Black. Rectangular format. Printed *CAJA DE B. A. (for Buenos Aires)* at lower left. Arms at center. Uniface.	—	—	—

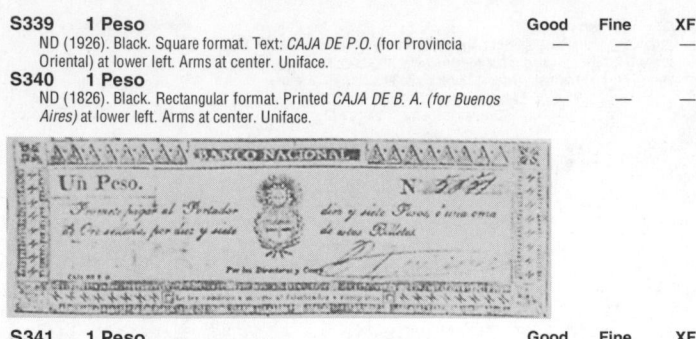

	Good	Fine	XF
S341 1 Peso			
ND (1826). Black. Rectangular format. Printed text: *CAJA DE P.O. (for Provincia Oriental)* at lower left. Arms at center. Uniface.	—	—	—

1826 Fractional Issue

Issued in 1826 and 1827 without numerals, sign. or date. Printed in sheets of 32 subjects. Various colors are are known. Denominations are in parts of a Real. Corners are decorated with flowers, leaves or other design elements.

	Good	Fine	XF
S342 10 Decimos			
ND. Black, green or red-orange. Rare.	—	—	—

	Good	Fine	XF
S343 20 Decimos			
ND. Orange or brown. Leaves in corners. Rare.	—	—	—
S344 20 Decimos			
ND. Blue, ochre or green. Pointed arches in corners. Rare.	—	—	—

1826 "Whole Denomination" Issues

Two distinct issues were made during 1826. The first had the heading *BANCO NACIONAL,* and the second *EL BANCO NACIONAL.* Notes were hand dated 12.2.1826, 15.7.1826, or 1.12.1826. All are very rare or no longer known as original notes. Reprints (in both colors, red and black) were made by the Compania Sud-Americana de Billetes de Banco around 1900.

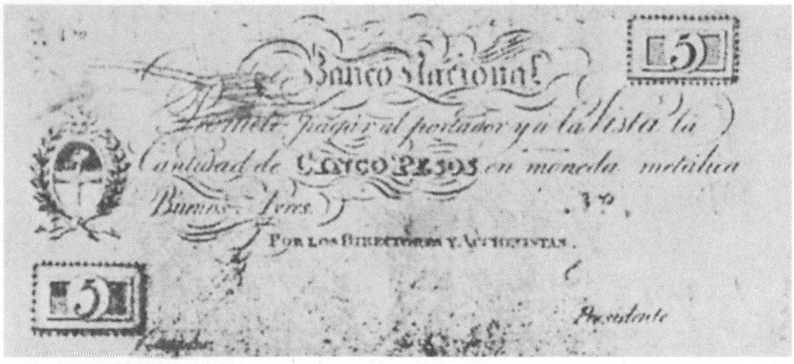

	Good	Fine	XF
S345 5 Pesos			
1826. Black. *BANCO NACIONAL.* National arms at left. Uniface. Rare.	—	—	—
S346 10 Pesos			
1826. Black. *BANCO NACIONAL.* National arms at left. Uniface. Reported not confirmed.	—	—	—
S347 20 Pesos			
1826. Black. *BANCO NACIONAL.* National Arms at left. Uniface.			
a. Rare.	—	—	—
x. Reprint.	—	Unc	15.00

	Good	Fine	XF
S348 50 Pesos			
1826. Black. *BANCO NACIONAL.* National arms at center. Uniface. Rare.	—	—	—
S349 100 Pesos			
1826. Black. *BANCO NACIONAL.* National arms at center. Uniface. Rare.	—	—	—
S350 5 Pesos			
1826. Red. *BANCO NACIONAL.* Uniface.			
a. Rare.	—	—	—
x. Reprint.	—	Unc	20.00
S351 10 Pesos			
1826. Red. *BANCO NACIONAL.* Uniface. Reported not confirmed.	—	—	—
S352 20 Pesos			
1826. Red. *BANCO NACIONAL.* Uniface.			
a. Rare.	—	—	—
x. Reprint.	—	Unc	20.00
S353 50 Pesos			
1826. *BANCO NACIONAL.* Uniface.			
a. Rare.	—	—	—
x. Reprint.	—	Unc	20.00
S354 100 Pesos			
1826. Red. *BANCO NACIONAL.* Uniface. Rare.	—	—	—
S355 10 Pesos			
1826. Red. *EL BANCO NACIONAL.* Arms at center. Uniface. Reported not confirmed.	—	—	—
S356 20 Pesos			
1826. Red. *EL BANCO NACIONAL.* Arms at center. Uniface. Reported not confirmed.	—	—	—
S357 50 Pesos			
1826. Black. *EL BANCO NACIONAL.* Arms at center. Uniface.			
a. Rare.	—	—	—
x. Reprint.	—	Unc	20.00
S358 100 Pesos			
1826. Black. *EL BANCO NACIONAL.* Arms at center. Uniface.			
a. Rare.	—	—	—
x. Reprint.	—	Unc	10.00

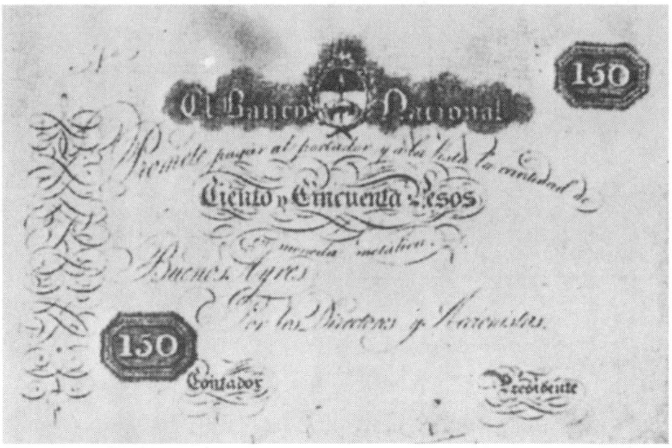

	Good	Fine	XF
S359 150 Pesos			
1826. Black. *EL BANCO NACIONAL.* Arms at center. Uniface.			
a. Rare.	—	—	—
x. Reprint.	—	—	—

Banco Nacional de las Provincias Unidas del Rio de la Plata

1829 Issue

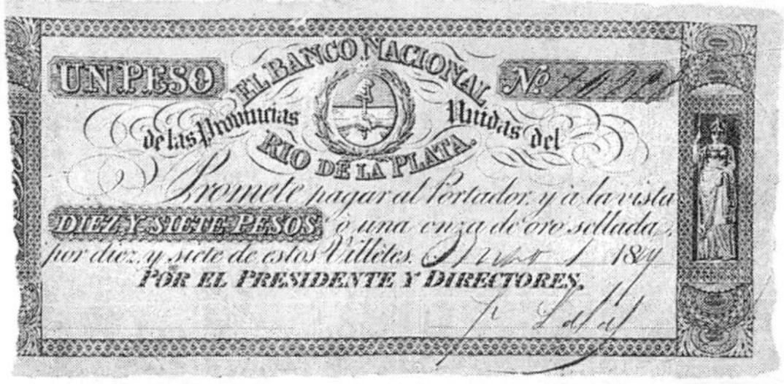

	Good	Fine	XF
S360 1 Peso			
1.3.1829; 1.9.1829; 12.2.1830. Black. Arms at center. Standing woman at right. Uniface. Printer: Perkins and Heath, London (without imprint).			
a. Red paper.	100.	225.	550.
b. 1.9.1829. White paper.	100.	225.	550.

NOTE: The 1830 date is very rare.

	Good	Fine	XF
S361 5 Pesos			
1.3.1829; 1.9.1829. Black. Uniface. Arms at left, three allegorical women seated at upper center. Text at bottom: *POR EL PRESIDENTE Y DIRECTORES.* Paper: Light blue. Printer: Perkins and Heath, London (without imprint).	—	—	—
S362 10 Pesos			
1.3.1829; 1.9.1829. Arms at left, three allegorical women seated at upper center. Bottom text: *POR EL PRESIDENTE Y DIRECTORES.* Paper: Green. Printer: Perkins and Heath, London (without imprint). Uniface. Rare.	—	—	—
S363 20 Pesos			
1.3.1829; 1.9.1829. Black. Arms at left, three allegorical women seated at upper center. Bottom text: *POR EL PRESIDENTE Y DIRECTORES.* Paper: Yellow. Printer: Perkins and Heath, London (without imprint). Uniface. Rare.	—	—	—
S364 50 Pesos			
1.3.1829; 1.9.1829. Black. Uniface. Text at bottom reads: *POR LOS DIRECTORES Y ACCIONISTAS.* Three allegorical women at left, arms at center. Paper: White. Printer: Perkins and Heath, London (without imprint). Rare.	—	—	—
S365 100 Pesos			
1.3.1829; 1.9.1829. Black. Uniface. Arms at left, three allegorical women seated at upper center. Text at bottom reads: *POR LOS DIRECTORES Y ACCIONISTAS.* Paper: White. Printer: Perkins and Heath, London (without imprint). Rare.	—	—	—
S366 200 Pesos			
1.3.1829; 1.9.1829. Black. Uniface. Arms at left, three allegorical women seated at upper center. Text at bottom reads: *POR LOS DIRECTORES Y ACCIONISTAS.* Paper: White. Printer: Perkins and Heath, London (without imprint). Rare.	—	—	—
S367 500 Pesos			
1.3.1829. Black. Uniface. Arms at center. Text at bottom reads: *POR LOS DIRECTORES Y ACCIONISTAS.* Paper: White. Printer: Perkins and HEath, London (without imprint). Rare.	—	—	—

1834 Renovacion Transitional Issue

Starting in 1834 the Banco Nacional reissued some of the lower denominations of the previous issue. Higher values as well as certain lower value notes were not issues of the Banco Nacional but were instead under the control of the newly formed Casa de Moneda. Such notes are so indicated in the listings. The Casa de Moneda was created by decree on May 30, 1836.

	Good	Fine	XF
S368 1 Peso			
1834-38. Arms at center. Standing woman at right. *RENOVACION 1834* twice on face in small circles at left and right. Uniface.			
a. 29.8.1834. Serial #1 to 418,000. Banco Nacional.	100.	250.	750.
b. 29.8.1834. Serial #418,001 to 1,000,000. Casa de Moneda.	50.00	125.	300.
c. 8.12.1838. 1,443,000 notes issued by Casa de Moneda.	25.00	100.	250.

	Good	Fine	XF
S369 5 Pesos			
29.8.1834. Black. Arms at left, three allegorical women seated at upper center. Text at bottom: *POR EL PRESIDENTE Y DIRECTORES. RENOVACION 1834* printed twice at bottom left and right beneath curved lines. Paper: White.			
a. Serial #1 to 115,000. Banco Nacional.	300.	750.	—
b. Serial #115,001 to 278,000. Casa de Moneda.	150.	500.	—
S370 5 Pesos			
8.12.1838. Arms at left, three allegorical women seated at upper center. Text at bottom: *POR EL PRESIDENTE Y DIRECTORES. RENOVACION 1834* printed twice at bottom left and right beneath curved lines. Paper: Red. Printer: CdM-A 416,000 notes issued. Rare.	—	—	—
S371 10 Pesos			
1834-38. Arms at left, three allegorical women seated at upper center. Text at bottom: *POR EL PRESIDENTE Y DIRECTORES. RENOVACION 1834* printed twice at bottom left and right beneath curved lines. Paper: White.			
a. 29.8.1834. Serial #1 to 49,000. Banco Nacional. Rare.	—	—	—
b. 29.8.1834. Serial #49,001 to 246,000. Casa de Moneda.	200.	650.	—
c. 8.12.1838. 349 notes issued by Casa de Moneda. Rare.	—	—	—
S372 20 Pesos			
1834-38. Arms at left, three allegorical women seated at upper center. Text at bottom: *POR EL PRESIDENTE Y DIRECTORES. RENOVACION 1834* printed twice at bottom left and right beneath curved lines. Paper: White.			
a. 29.8.1834. Serial #1 to 39,000. Banco Nacional. Rare.	—	—	—
b. 29.8.1834. Serial #39,001 to 125,000. Casa de Moneda.	250.	750.	—
c. 8.12.1838. 38,000 notes issued by Casa de Moneda.	225.	550.	—

	Good	Fine	XF
S373 50 Pesos			
1829-38. Arms at left, three allegorical women seated at upper center. Text at bottom: *POR EL PRESIDENTE Y DIRECTORES. RENOVACION 1834* printed twice at bottom left and right beneath curved lines. Paper: White. Printer: CdM-A			
a. 1.9.1829. Serial #1 to 20,000.	250.	750.	—
b. 29.8.1834. Serial #20,001 to 30,000.	250.	750.	—
c. 8.12.1838. 103,000 notes issued.	250.	750.	—
S374 100 Pesos			
1.9.1829; 29.8.1834. Arms at left, three allegorical women seated at upper center. Text at bottom: *POR EL PRESIDENTE Y DIRECTORES. RENOVACION 1834* printed twice at bottom left and right beneath curved lines. Paper: White. Printer: CdM-A Rare.	—	—	—

NOTE: 57,000 notes dated 1.9.1829; 39,000 dated 29.8.1834.

	Good	Fine	XF
S375 200 Pesos			
29.8.1834; 8.12.1838. Arms at left, three allegorical women seated at upper center. Text at bottom: *POR EL PRESIDENTE Y DIRECTORES. RENOVACION 1834* printed twice at bottom left and right beneath curved lines. Paper: White. Printer: CdM-A Rare.	—	—	—

NOTE: 19,165 notes dated 29.8.1834; 37,000 dated 8.12.1838.

	Good	Fine	XF
S376 500 Pesos			
8.12.1838; 28.3.1840. Arms at left, three allegorical women seated at upper center. Text at bottom: *POR EL PRESIDENTE Y DIRECTORES. RENOVACION 1834* printed twice at bottom left and right beneath curved lines. Paper: White. Printer: CdM-A 44,000 notes issued. Rare.	—	—	—

Casa de Moneda

1841 Issue

Each denomination has a different date in 1841. The year date is sometimes printed in full, or the last 1 or 2 numerals may be handwritten.

S377 1 Peso	Good	Fine	XF
1.1.1841. Black. Allegorical women with shields at center. Uniface. Handwritten signature. Printer: PBP.			
a. *1841* fully printed. Orange paper.	30.00	125.	250.
b. *1841* fully printed. Pinkish purple paper. Without imprint.	30.00	125.	250.
c. *184* printed. Orange paper. With imprint.	30.00	125.	250.
d. *184* printed. Pinkish purple paper.	30.00	125.	250.
s. Specimen.	—	—	—

S378 5 Pesos	Good	Fine	XF
1.2.1841. Fully printed. Black. Rheas at center. Paper: Orange. Printer: PBP.			
a. Issued note.	75.00	175.	400.
s. Specimen.	—	—	—

S379 10 Pesos	Good	Fine	XF
1.3.1841. Cow and sheep at center. *Viva LA Federacion!* at top. Paper: Orange. Printer: Wilson & Sons, London.			
a. Year *1841* fully printed.	125.	400.	—
b. Only *184* of year printed.	125.	400.	—

S380 20 Pesos	Good	Fine	XF
1.4.1841. Horse at lower center. *Viva La Federacion!* at top. Paper: Orange. Printer: Wilson & Sons, London.			
a. *1841* fully printed.	—	—	—
b. *184* printed.	—	—	—
s. Specimen.	—	—	—

S381 50 Pesos	Good	Fine	XF
1.5.1841. Cows at center. *18* printed. *Viva La Federacion!* at top. Paper: Orange. Printer: Wilson & Sons, London.	—	—	—

S382 100 Pesos	Good	Fine	XF
1.6.1841. Municipal Council building at center. *18* printed. *Viva La Federacion!* at top. Paper: Orange. Printer: Wilson & Sons, London.	—	—	—

S383 200 Pesos			
1.7.1841. View of Buenos Aires at center. *1841* fully printed. *Viva La Federacion!* Paper: Pinkish purple. Printer: Wilson & Sons, London. Rare.	—	—	—

1844 Issues

#S384-S387 2-line political heading at top: *VIVA LA CONFEDERACION ARGENTINA! MUERAN LOS SALVAGES UNITARIOS!* Printer: plates by PB&P; notes printed in Buenos Aires.

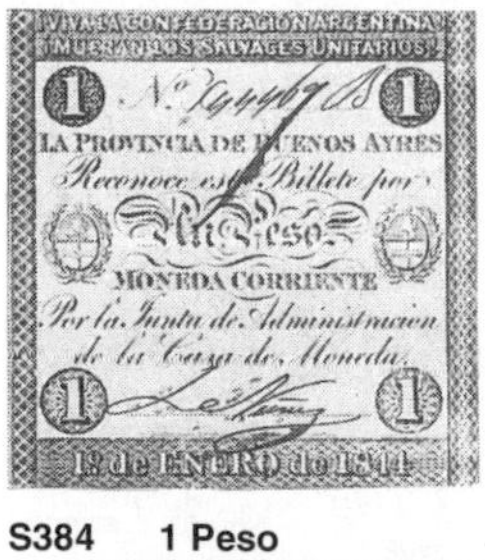

S384 1 Peso	Good	Fine	XF
1.1.1844. Orange. Arms at left and right. Square format. Uniface. Two line political heading at top. Printer: PB&P.			
a. Yellow paper.	20.00	60.00	125.
b. Textured or plain white paper.	40.00	100.	250.
c. Light blue paper.	75.00	150.	400.

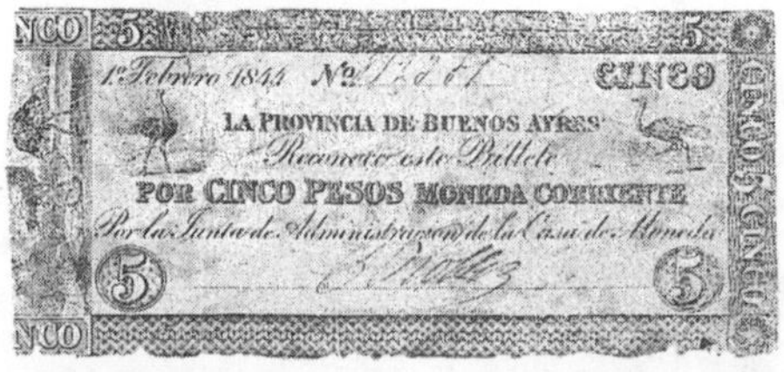

S385 5 Pesos	Good	Fine	XF
1.2.1844. Orange. Ostriches at left border and at left and right. Signature. Uniface. Two line political heading at top. Printer: PB&P.			

	Good	Fine	XF
a. Yellow paper.	50.00	125.	225.
b. Textured or plain white paper.	75.00	150.	300.
c. Two hand signatures (first 29,000 issued).	75.00	150.	300.

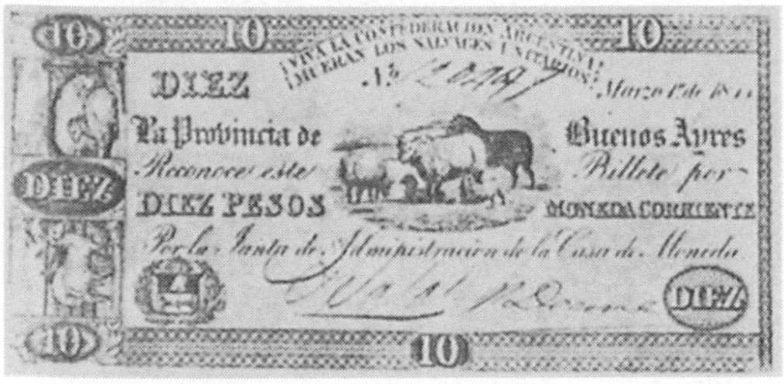

S386 10 Pesos

1.3.1844. Orange. Sheep at left border, arms at lower left, sheep and horse at center. Uniface. Two line political heading at top. Printer: PB&P.

	Good	Fine	XF
a. Yellow paper.	250.	600.	—
b. Textured or plain white paper.	300.	650.	—

S387 20 Pesos

1.4.1844. Orange. Two horses at bottom left and right. Uniface. Two line political heading at top. Printer: PB&P.

	Good	Fine	XF
a. Yellow paper.	300.	650.	—
b. Textured white paper.	350.	750.	—

#S388-S391 black. Like #S384-S387. White paper except for some of #S388 printed on yellow paper.

S388 1 Peso

1.1.1844. Black. Arms at left and right. Square format. Two line political heading at top.

	Good	Fine	XF
a. Yellow paper.	50.00	125.	300.
b. White paper.	25.00	75.00	175.

S389 5 Pesos

	Good	Fine	XF
1.2.1844. Black. Ostriches at left border and at left and right.Two line political heading at top. Paper: White.	100.	175.	500.

S390 10 Pesos

	Good	Fine	XF
1.3.1844. Black. Sheep at left border, arms at lower left, sheep and horse at center. Two line political heading at top. Paper: White.	—	—	—

S391 20 Pesos

	Good	Fine	XF
1.4.1844. Black. Two horses at bottom left and right. Two line political heading at top. Paper: White.	—	—	—

NOTE: For notes similar to #S388-S391 but w/o political headings at top, see #S402-S406.

1845-47 Issues

Higher values were issued to supplement those of lower value issued earlier.

#S392-S394 and S396 Printing plates by PB&P. #S395 Printing plates by Wilson & Sons. All notes were printed locally in Buenos Aires.

S392 50 Pesos

	Good	Fine	XF
1.5.1845. Black. Cow at upper left, bull and cow at center, cow at upper right. Uniface. Paper: Yellow. Printer: Locally on plated supplied by PB&P. Rare.	—	—	—

S393 50 Pesos

	Good	Fine	XF
1.5.1845. Black. Cow at upper left, bull and cow at center, cow at upper right. Uniface. Paper: White. Printer: Locally on plated supplied by PB&P. Rare.	—	—	—

S394 100 Pesos

1.6.1845. Black. Municipal Council building at center. Uniface. Paper: Yellow. Printer: Locally on plated supplied by PB&P.

	Good	Fine	XF
a. Background lines *CIEN PESOS* repeated many times. Rare.	—	—	—
b. Background of parallel lines without words. Rare.	—	—	—

NOTE: For issue similar to #S394 but without political headings at top, see #S408.

S395 500 Pesos

1.9.1845. Black. Ships at center, allegorical women standing at left and right. Paper: Yellow. Printer: Locally on plated supplied by Wilson & Sons.

	Good	Fine	XF
a. *184* of date printed (first 498 notes). Reported not confirmed.	—	—	—
b. Entire date printed. Rare.	—	—	—

S396 1000 Pesos

Sept.1847. Orange. Standing allegorical woman with anchor at center. Two line political heading at top. Paper: White. Printer: Locally on plated supplied by PB&P.

	Good	Fine	XF
a. Numerals of serial # printed. Rare.	—	—	—
b. Numerals entered by hand. Reported not confirmed.	—	—	—

NOTE: For issue similar to #S396b but w/o political headings at top, see #S412.

1848-51 Issues

#S397-S399 Printer: plates, PB&P. Printed in Buenos Aires.

S397 50 Pesos

	Good	Fine	XF
1.10.1848. Black. Bull at center. Uniface. Paper: White. Printer: Locally on plated supplied by PB&P. Rare.	—	—	—

S398 100 Pesos

	Good	Fine	XF
1.11.1848. Black. Allegorical woman seated in oval at center, ship in background. Uniface. Paper: White. Printer: Locally on plated supplied by PB&P. Rare.	—	—	—

S399 200 Pesos

	Good	Fine	XF
1.7.1848. Black. City view of Buenos Aires at center. Uniface. Paper: White. Printer: Locally on plated supplied by PB&P. Rare.	—	—	—

NOTE: For notes similar to #S397-S399 but w/o political headings at top, see #S407, S409 and S410.

S400 500 Pesos

1.8.1849. City view of Buenos Aires, Mercury flying above. Printer: Locally on plated supplied by PB&P.

	Good	Fine	XF
a. Red. Reported not confirmed.	—	—	—
b. Black. Reported not confirmed.	—	—	—
r. Reprint done ca. 1900 from original plates.	—	—	—

S401 500 Pesos

	Good	Fine	XF
1.12.1851. Red. Seated allegorical woman, two children and shields at center. Paper: White. Printer: Locally on plated supplied by PB&P. Rare.	—	—	—

NOTE: For note similar to #S401 but without political headings at top, see #S411.

Banco y Casa de Moneda

1854 ND Issues

#S402-S412 with old dates 1844-51, political headings obliterated or erased.

	Good	Fine	XF
S402 1 Peso ND (1854 - old date 1.1.1844). Arms at left and right. Like #S388 but only the second political heading erased (error?).	75.00	150.	300.

	Good	Fine	XF
S403 1 Peso Arms at left and right. Like #S388 but both political headings obliterated.			
a. Both headings erased completely.	25.00	75.00	150.
b. Both headings crossed out by overprint.	25.00	75.00	150.
S404 5 Pesos ND (1854 - old date 1.2.1844). Ostriches at left border and at left and right. Like #S389 but both political headings crossed out by overprint.	75.00	175.	—

	Good	Fine	XF
S405 10 Pesos ND (1854 - old date 1.3.1844). Sheep at left border, arms at lower left, sheep and horse at center. Like #S390 but both political headings crossed out by overprint.	100.	225.	—
S406 20 Pesos ND (1854 - old date 1.4.1844). Two horses at bottom left and right. Like #S391 but both political headings crossed out by overprint.	150.	450.	—
S407 50 Pesos ND (1854 - old date 1.10.1848). Bull at center. Like #S397 but both political headings erased completely. Rare.	—	—	—
S408 100 Pesos ND (1854 - old date 1.6.1845). Municipal Council building at center. Like #S394 but both political headings crossed out by overprint. Reported not confirmed.	—	—	—
S409 100 Pesos ND (1854 - old date 1.11.1848). Allegorical woman seated in oval at center, ship in background. Like #S398 but both political headings erased completely. Rare.	—	—	—
S410 200 Pesos ND (1854 - old date 1.7.1848). View of Buenos Aires city at center.Like #S399 but both political headings crossed out by overprint. Rare.	—	—	—
S411 500 Pesos ND (1854 - old date 1.12.1851). Seated allegorical woman, two children and shields at center. Like #S401 but both political headings erased completely.			
a. Issued note. Rare.	—	—	—
r. Repritn in red.	—	—	—
S412 1000 Pesos ND (1854 - old date 9.1847). Like #S396b but both political headings erased completely.			
a. Issued note. Reported not confirmed.	—	—	—
r. Reprint in red.	—	—	—

La Provincia De Buenos Aires

1853 Issue

A plate was prepared by PB&P for a proposed 1853 issue of what would have been the first Argentine 5000 Pesos note. It was lost en route to Buenos Aires. Specimens may exist.

	Good	Fine	XF
S413 5000 Pesos 1.3.1853. Reported not confirmed.	—	—	—

1854 Issue

	Good	Fine	XF
S414 200 Pesos 1.1.1854. Black. City view of Buenos Aires at center. Uniface. Printer: BWC. Specimen. Rare.	—	—	—

El Estado De Buenos Ayres

1856 Issue

#S415-S425 dated except for #S423. Printer: plates by Pickett London (w/o imprint except for #S424 and S425). Notes printed in Buenos Aires.

	Good	Fine	XF
S415 1 Peso 1.5.1856. Black. Arms at center. Uniface. Printer: Pickett London (without imprint).	40.00	75.00	175.

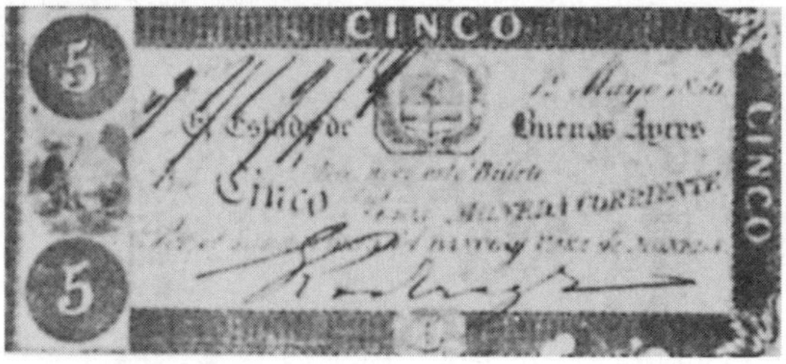

	Good	Fine	XF
S416 5 Pesos 1.5.1856. Black. Shepherd and sheep at left, arms at center. Uniface. Printer: Pickett London (without imprint).			
a. One signature.	50.00	150.	350.
b. Two signatures.	50.00	150.	350.

	Good	Fine	XF
S417 10 Pesos 1.5.1856. Black. Allegorical woman standing at left, arms at upper left, farm tools at center. Uniface. Printer: Pickett London (without imprint).			
a. 1 signature	50.00	150.	350.
b. 2 signature	100.	225.	500.

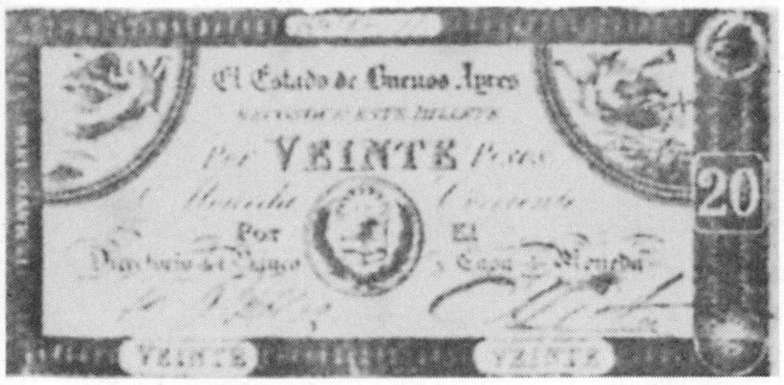

S418 20 Pesos	Good	Fine	XF
1.5.1856. Black. Allegory of Victory at upper left, arms at center, flying Mercury at upper right. Liberty cap in upper right corner. Uniface. Printer: Pickett London (without imprint).	—	—	—

S419 50 Pesos	Good	Fine	XF
1.5.1856. Black. Arms at upper left, caduceus with sword at center. Liberty cap at lower right. Uniface. Printer: Pickett London (without imprint). Rare.	—	—	—

S420 100 Pesos	Good	Fine	XF
1.5.1856. Black. Train and boats at left, arms at upper right. Uniface. Printer: Pickett London (without imprint). Rare.	—	—	—
S421 200 Pesos			
1.5.1856. Black. Mercury flying over bundles and ship at center, arms at right. Uniface. Printer: Pickett London (without imprint). Rare.	—	—	—

S422 500 Pesos	Good	Fine	XF
1.5.1856. Black. Arms at upper left, Greek soldier carrying sheep at center, Liberty cap at upper right. Uniface. Printer: Pickett London (without imprint). Rare.	—	—	—
S423 1000 Pesos			
ND (1.5.1856). Black. Arms and kangaroo at left, llama at right. Uniface. Printer: Pickett London.			
a. Issued note. Rare.	—	—	—
r. Reprint made in 1900 by the CSABB in Buenos Aires.	—	—	—

S424 5000 Pesos	Good	Fine	XF
1.5.1856. Black. Allegorical woman with staff at left, Neptune riding chariot at right. Printer: Pickett London. Rare. Uniface.	—	—	—
S425 5000 Pesos			
1.5.1856. Black. Allegorical woman with staff at left, Neptune riding chariot at right. Back: Blue. *BANCO Y CASA DE MONEDA DE BUENOS AIRES.* Printer: Pickett London. Rare. Uniface.	—	—	—

NOTE: #S425 is the first Argentine note to have printing on the back.

1857 Issue

Several higher values were reissued beginning in 1857. All backs are printed in different colors but with the same design as the face.

#S426-S428 printer: plates by PBC. Notes printed in Buenos Aires.

S426 500 Pesos	Good	Fine	XF
1.8.1857. Black. Farm tools at left, Neptune with seahorses at center, beehive at right. Back: Red. Printer: locally on plates by PBC. Rare.	—	—	—

NOTE: Beware of good quality counterfeits.

S427 1000 Pesos	Good	Fine	XF
1.8.1857. Black. Allegorical woman with plants and farm tools at center, arms at lower center. Back: Green. Printer: locally on plates by PBC.			
a. Handwritten serial # (1857-65). Rare.	—	—	—
b. Printed serial # (1866-67). Blue *1000* added on back. Rare.	—	—	—

S428 5000 Pesos	Good	Fine	XF
1.8.1857. Black. Neptune in chariot at upper center, arms below. Back: Blue. Printer: locally on plates by PBC.			
a. Handwritten serial # (1857-64). Rare.	—	—	—
b. Printed serial # (1865-67). Rare.	—	—	—

1858 Issue

#S429-S435 Printer: plates by PBC. Notes printed in Buenos Aires.

S429 1 Peso	Good	Fine	XF
25.5.1858. Black. Arms at center. Uniface. Paper: White. Printer: locally on plates by PBC.			
a. Issued note.	25.00	75.00	150.
s. Specimen.	—	—	—

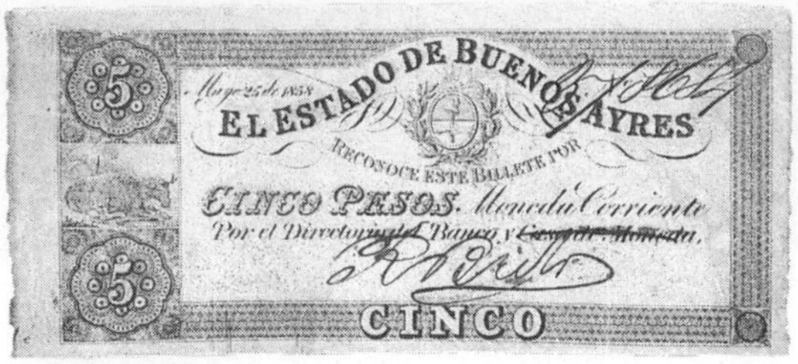

S430 5 Pesos

25.5.1858. Black. Cow at left. Arms at center. Uniface. Paper: White. Printer: locally on plates by PBC.

	Good	Fine	XF
a. Issued note.	25.00	75.00	150.
s. Specimen.	—	—	—

S431 10 Pesos

	Good	Fine	XF
25.5.1858. Black. Cows at left and right. Arms at center. Uniface. Paper: White. Printer: locally on plates by PBC.	40.00	125.	275.

S432 20 Pesos

	Good	Fine	XF
25.5.1858. Black. Sheep at left and right. Arms at center. Uniface. Paper: White. Printer: locally on plates by PBC.	100.	225.	600.

S433 50 Pesos

	Good	Fine	XF
25.5.1858. Black. Allegory with three women at left and right. Arms at center with cannon and flags. Uniface. Paper: White. Printer: locally on plates by PBC.	—	—	—

S434 100 Pesos

	Good	Fine	XF
25.5.1858. Black. Farm tools, sheep and ship at left. Arms at center with cannon and flags. Uniface. Paper: White. Printer: locally on plates by PBC.	—	—	—

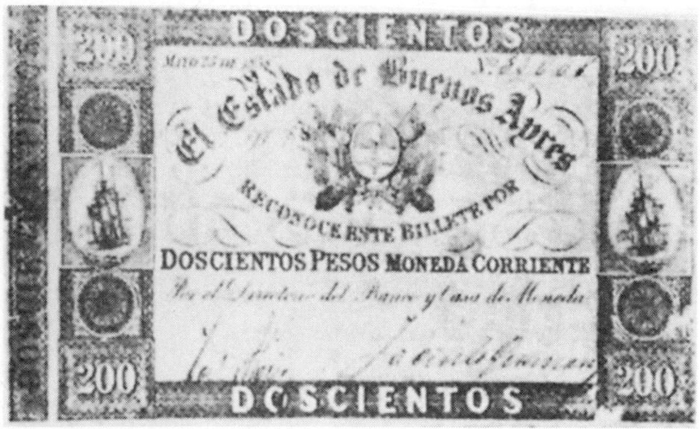

S435 200 Pesos

	Good	Fine	XF
25.5.1858. Black. Sailing ship at left and right. Arms at center with cannon and flags. Uniface. Paper: White. Printer: locally on plates by PBC. Rare.	—	—	—

1864 Transitional Issue

The 1864 issue was the only one to carry the name *EL BANCO Y CASA DE MONEDA DE BUENOS AYRES* as the main heading. However, by that time the issuing institution was the Banco de la Provincia de Buenos Aires. This bank name was applied to the backs of all notes from 20 to 200 Pesos. Plans called for values of 500, 1000 and 5000 Pesos to be part of this issue but they were never released. Prints using original artwork were made in 1969.

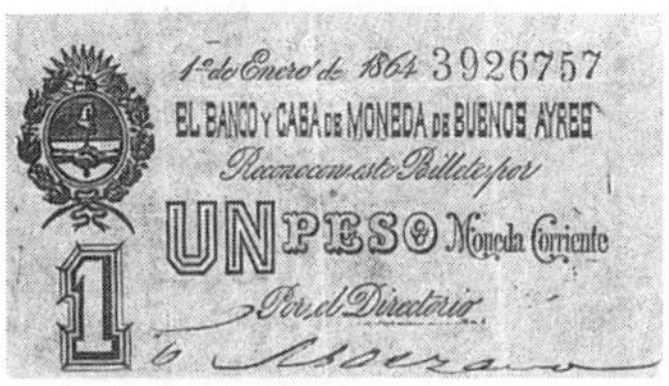

S441 1 Peso

1.1.1864. Black. Arms at upper left. Uniface.

	Good	Fine	XF
a. Green paper.	20.00	75.00	150.
b. Tan paper.	15.00	50.00	125.

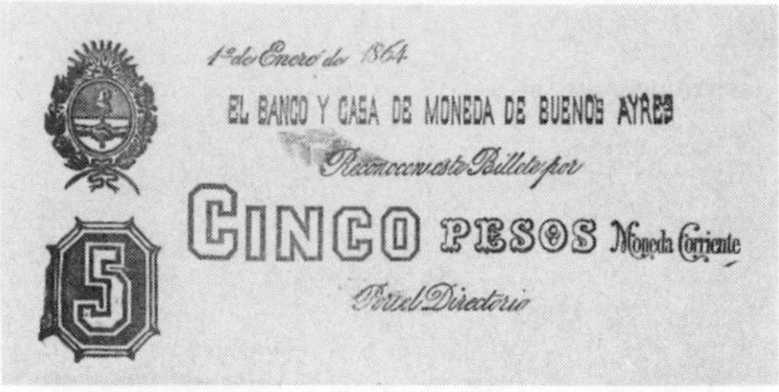

S442 5 Pesos

	Good	Fine	XF
1.1.1864. Black. Arms at upper left. Uniface. Paper: Green.	25.00	75.00	175.

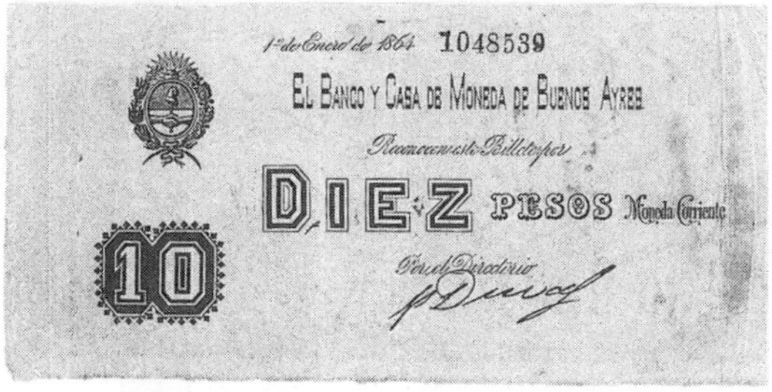

S443 10 Pesos

	Good	Fine	XF
1.1.1864. Black. Arms at upper left. Uniface. Paper: Blue.	25.00	100.	225.

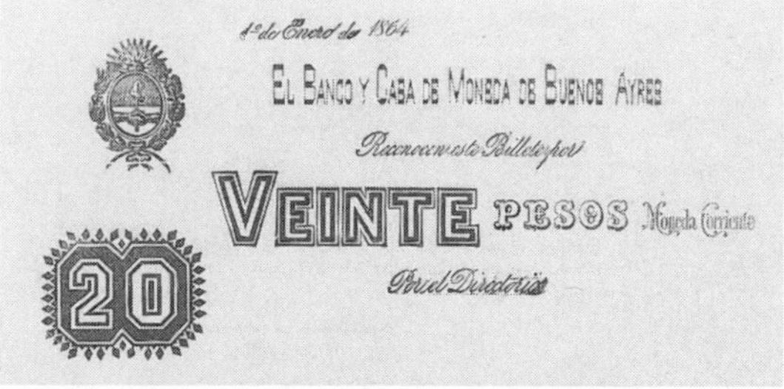

S444 20 Pesos

	Good	Fine	XF
1.1.1864. Black. Arms at upper left. Back: Green. Bank name. Paper: Pinkish violet.	40.00	125.	250.

S445 50 Pesos

	Good	Fine	XF
1.1.1864. Black. Horse and cow at left and center right. Arms at upper left with cannon and flags. Back: Bank name. Paper: Salmon.	—	—	—

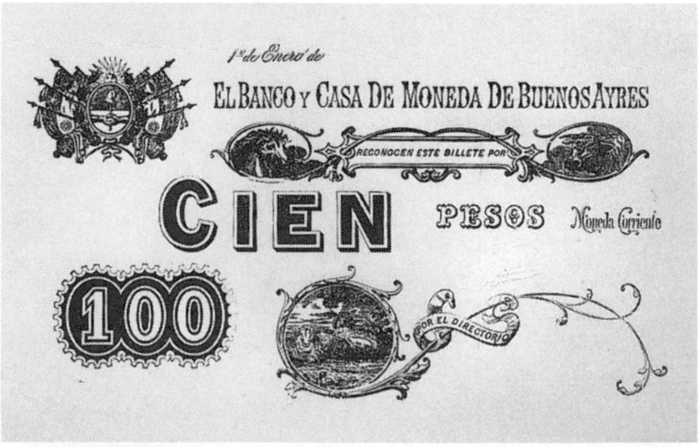

S446 100 Pesos

1.1.1864. Black. Horse and cow at left and center right. Sheep in circle at bottom center. Arms at upper left with cannon and flags. Back: Black. Bank name.

	Good	Fine	XF
a. Rose paper.	—	—	—
b. White paper.	—	—	—

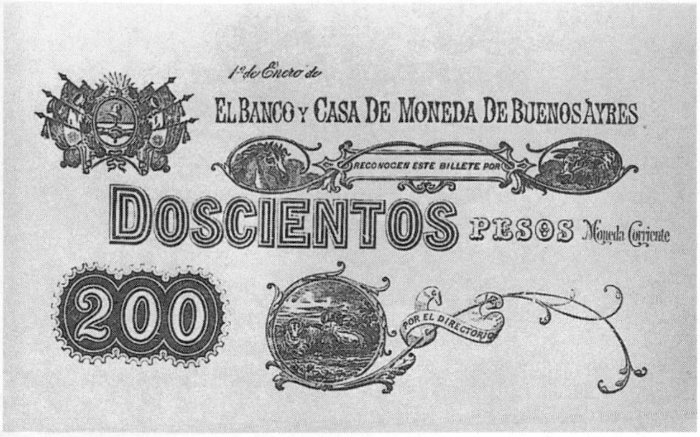

		Good	Fine	XF
S447	**200 Pesos** 1.1.1864. Black. Horse and cow at left and center right. Sheep in circle at bottom center. Arms at upper left with cannon and flags. Back: Maroon.			
	a. Blue-violet paper.	—	—	—
	b. White paper.	—	—	—
S448	**500 Pesos** 1.1.(1864). Black. Horse and cow at left and center right. Sheep in circle at bottom center. Arms at upper left with cannon and flags. Bull at lower center. Paper: Olive or white. Reprint only.	—	—	—

		Good	Fine	XF
S449	**1000 Pesos** 1.1.1864. Black. Horse and cow at left and center right. Sheep in circle at bottom center. Arms at upper left with cannons and flags.Three horse heads at lower center. Paper: Orange. Reprint.	—	—	—
S450	**5000 Pesos** 1.1.1864. Black. Horse and cow at left and center right. Sheep in circle at bottom center. Arms at upper left with cannons and flags.Three horse heads at lower center. Paper: Yellow. Reprint only.	—	—	—

Section II

Treasury

Ley de 10 de Octobre de 1876 Treasury Bill Issue

The inconvertibility of notes into specie which began in 1876 started a monetary crisis in Argentina. The government then issued Customs Notes very similar in characteristics to the Customs Notes used in 1820-21.

		Good	Fine	XF
S461	**50 Pesos Fuertes** ND (1876). Black and light green. Arms with cannon anf flags at center. Series A. Back: Light green. Two allegorical figures. Printer: Alberto Larsen Bs.As. Rare.	—	—	—

		Good	Fine	XF
S462	**100 Pesos Fuertes** ND (1876). Black, maroon and green. Allegorical women at left and right. Series B. Back: Maroon. Arms twice. Rare.	—	—	—
S463	**50 Pesos** ND (1876). Blue. Arms surrounded by 14 provincial arms at center. Back: Arms at left center. Printer: Guillermo Kraft Bs. As. Rare.	—	—	—

		Good	Fine	XF
S464	**100 Pesos** ND (1876). Ochre. Arms surrounded by 14 provincial arms at center. Back: Maroon. Arms at left center. Printer: Guillermo Kraft Bs. As. Rare.	—	—	—

Bonos del Tesoro, Provincia de Buenos Ayres

		Good	Fine	XF
S464A	**500 Pesos** L.1880. Black on brown underprint. Sailor at left, agriculture at center, and soldier at right. Back: Brown. Founders of Banco de la Provincia de Aires at center. Printer: ABNC. 38 interest coupons attached. Specimen.	—	—	—
S464B	**1000 Pesos** L.1880. Black on green underprint. Sailor at left, agriculture at center, and soldier at right. Back: Brown. Founders of Banco de la Provincia de Aires at center. Printer: ABNC. 38 interest coupons attached. Specimen.	—	—	—
S464C	**5000 Pesos** L.1880. Black on blue underprint. Sailor at left, agriculture at center, and soldier at right. Back: Brown. Founders of Banco de la Provincia de Buenos Aires at center. Printer: ABNC. 38 interest coupons attached. Specimen.	—	—	—

1890 Treasury Notes Issue

These notes were issued by the Treasury through the Caja de Conversion. They were equal in value to notes issued by the Bancos Nacionales Garantidos (see later section).

#S465-S466 issued w/red seal like Bancos Nacionales Garantidos. Printer: BWC (w/o imprint).

		Good	Fine	XF
S465	**50 Pesos** 15.9.1890. Black on green underprint. Dr. J. Celman at left, allegorical man with trident at right, arms at center. Printer: BWC (without imprint). Issued with red seal like Bancos Nacionales Garantidos. Reported not confirmed.	—	—	—

		Good	Fine	XF
S466	**500 Pesos** 15.9.1890. Black on light blue and brown underprint. Allegorical woman with portrait General M. Belgrano at left, arms at center. Back: Blue. Allegorical woman with arms at center. Printer: BWC. Issued with red seal like Bancos Nacionales Garantidos.	—	—	—

Banco de la Provincia de Buenos Aires

1865 Issue

#S467-S470 Redeemable in gold and worth more than the regular circulating currency.

S467 20 Pesos Fuertes	Good	Fine	XF
1.7.1865. Black and green. Liberty and Mercury at left, arms at center.			
a. Issued note. Rare.	—	—	—
b. Reprint. Uniface. (1975).	—	—	—

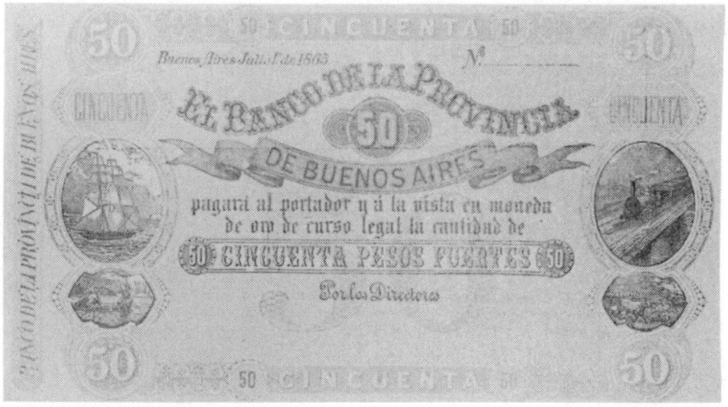

S468 50 Pesos Fuertes	Good	Fine	XF
1.7.1865. Black, maroon and green. Sailing ship at left, train at right. Back: Black and green.			
a. Issued note. Rare.	—	—	—
b. Reprint. Uniface. (1975).	—	—	—

S469 200 Pesos Fuertes	Good	Fine	XF
1.7.1865. Black, green and salmon. Lighthouse at left, arms at upper left and lower right, allegorical woman with agricultural plants at center.			
a. Issued note. Rare.	—	—	—
b. Reprint (1975).	—	—	—
p. Proof.	—	—	—

S470 500 Pesos Fuertes	Good	Fine	XF
1.7.1865. Black, maroon and orange. Liberty at left, arms at center, Justice at right.			
a. Issue note. Rare.	—	—	—
r. Reprint.	—	—	—

La Provincia de Buenos Ayres

1867 Issue

An issue in regular currency (not Pesos Fuertes) was prepared in 1867.

S471 1 Peso	Good	Fine	XF
1.4.1867. Black. Ram at center. Uniface. Printer: BWC (without imprint).	20.00	50.00	125.

S472 5 Pesos	Good	Fine	XF
1.4.1867. Black. Dog at left and right. Uniface. Printer: BWC (without imprint).	25.00	75.00	150.

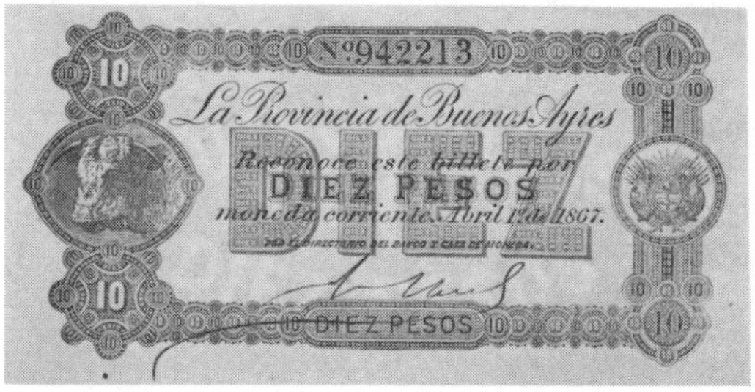

S473 10 Pesos	Good	Fine	XF
1.4.1867. Black on blue underprint. Cow at left, arms atright. Printer: BWC (without imprint). Uniface.	50.00	125.	250.

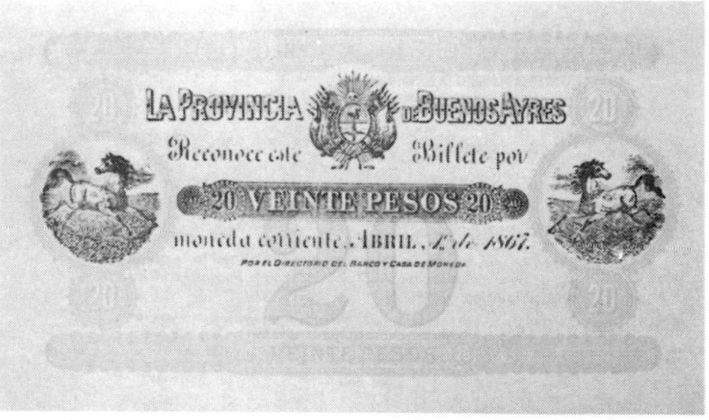

S474 20 Pesos	Good	Fine	XF
1.4.1867. Black on green underprint. Horse at left and right, arms at upper center. Uniface. Printer: BWC (without imprint).	75.00	175.	350.

ILLUSTRATIONS

Illustrations of bank notes used throughout this catalog are 42% of the actual size.

S475 50 Pesos

	Good	Fine	XF
1.4.1867. Black on green underprint. Rider on horseback with lasso at left. Uniface. Printer: BWC.	300.	550.	—

S476 100 Pesos

	Good	Fine	XF
1.4.1867. Black on rose underprint. Portrait woman at center. Back: Rose. Printer: BWC (without imprint).	300.	550.	—

S477 200 Pesos

	Good	Fine	XF
1.4.1867. Black on blue underprint. Portrait seated woman at left, arms at right. Back: Blue. Printer: BWC. Rare.	—	—	—

S478 500 Pesos

	Good	Fine	XF
1.4.1867. Black on green underprint. Arms at left and right, standing woman and sheep at center. Back: Gray. Printer: BWC (without imprint). Rare.	—	—	—

S479 1000 Pesos

	Good	Fine	XF
1.4.1867. Black on green and salmon underprint. Woman with shovel at left, flags above, arms at right. Back: Green and salmon. Printer: BWC. Rare.	—	—	—

S480 5000 Pesos

	Good	Fine	XF
1.4.1867. Black on maroon, blue and salmon underprint. Standing woman with sheaf and sickle at left. Back: Blue and salmon. Rare.	—	—	—

1869 Issue

#S481-S499 printer: ABNC. Imprint in Spanish: *Compania Americana de Billetes de Banco, Nueva York* except on #S490, S495 and S496.

S481 1 Peso

	Good	Fine	XF
1.1.1869. Black. Woman at lower left and right, ram and ewes at upper center. Uniface. Printer: ABNC in Spanish.			
a. Handwritten signature (1870-75). Red or blue serial #.	10.00	25.00	60.00
b. Printed signature (1877-83).	10.00	25.00	60.00

S482 5 Pesos

	Good	Fine	XF
1.1.1869 (1869-76). Handwritten. Black. Seated man at lower left and right, bull at top center. Uniface. Printer: ABNC in Spanish.	15.00	40.00	100.

S483 5 Pesos

	Good	Fine	XF
1.1.1869 (1876-83). Black on light blue and salmon underprint. Seated man at lower left and right, bull at top center. Uniface. Printer: ABNC in Spanish.			
a. Handwritten signature (1876-77).	10.00	40.00	100.
b. Printed signature (1877-83).	10.00	40.00	100.

S484 10 Pesos

	Good	Fine	XF
1.1.1869 (1870-76). Handwritten. Black on light blue underprint. H. F. Varela at lower left, horse at upper center, portrait woman at lower right. With *DIEZ. Uniface.* Printer: ABNC in Spanish.	10.00	40.00	150.

S485 10 Pesos

	Good	Fine	XF
1.1.1869 (1876-83). Black on blue and ochre underprint. H. F. Varela at lower left, horse at upper center, portrait woman at lower right. With *X.* Uniface. Printer: ABNC in Spanish.			
a. Handwritten signature (1876-77).	10.00	40.00	125.
b. Printed signature, red or blue serial # (1877-83).	10.00	40.00	125.

S486 20 Pesos

	Good	Fine	XF
1.1.1869 (1869-74). Black on green underprint and back numerals. Seated allegorical woman at lower left and right, Gen. J. Lavalle at center. Handwritten signature. Printer: ABNC in Spanish.	20.00	100.	300.

S487 20 Pesos

	Good	Fine	XF
1.1.1869 (1874-83). Black on green and salmon underprint. Seated allegorical woman at lower left and right, Gen. J. Lavalle at center. Imprint in Spanish. Uniface. Printer: ABNC.			
a. Handwritten signature (1874-77).	10.00	100.	300.
b. Printed signature (1877-83).	10.00	100.	300.
p. Proof.	—	—	—
s. Specimen.	—	—	—

S488 50 Pesos — Good | Fine | XF

1.1.1869 (1869-74). Black on rose underprint. Back numerals. *L 50 L* protector in underprint. "Gaucho with Guitar" at lower left, two allegorical women at upper center, Gen G. de las Heras at lower right. Handwritten signature. Printer: ABNC.

	Good	Fine	XF
a. Issued note.	100.	500.	—
p. Proof.	—	—	—

S489 50 Pesos — Good | Fine | XF

1.1.1869 (1874-77). Black on green and maroon underprint. "Gaucho with Guitar" at lower left, two allegorical women at upper center, General G. de las Heras at lower right. *CINCUENTA* protector in underprint. Uniface. Printer: ABNC. — 150. | 500. | —

S490 50 Pesos — Good | Fine | XF

1.1.1869 (1877-83). Black on green and brown underprint. "Gaucho with Guitar" at lower left, "Bachus" at center, General de las Heras at lower right. Printed signature. Uniface. Printer: ABNC.

	Good	Fine	XF
a. Issued note.	150.	500.	—
s. Specimen.	—	—	—

S491 100 Pesos — Good | Fine | XF

1.1.1869 (1869-76). Black on ochre underprint. Woman seated at lower left, two allegorical women at upper center, General J. M. Paz at lower right. Handwritten signature. Uniface. Printer: ABNC.

	Good	Fine	XF
a. Issued note.	150.	500.	—
p. Proof.	—	—	—
s. Specimen.	—	—	—

S492 100 Pesos

1.1.1869 (1876-83). Black on green and salmon underprint. Woman seated at lower left, two allegorical women at upper center, Gen. J. M. Paz at lower right. Handwritten signature. Printer: ABNC. Uniface.

	Good	Fine	XF
a. Handwritten signature (1876-77)	200.	600.	—
b. Printed signature (1877-83).	200.	600.	—

S493 200 Pesos

1.1.1869 (1869-76). Black on ochre underprint. General C. M. de Alvear at left, "Corral" at center, Pallas Athena at right. Handwritten signature. Back: Orange. Printer: ABNC.

	Good	Fine	XF
a. Issued note.	—	—	—
p. Proof.	—	—	—

S494 200 Pesos — Good | Fine | XF

1.1.1869 (1876-77). Black on brownish red and light blue underprint. Gen. C. M. de Alvear at left, "Corral" at center, Pallas Athena at right. Handwritten signature. Printer: ABNC. — — | — | —

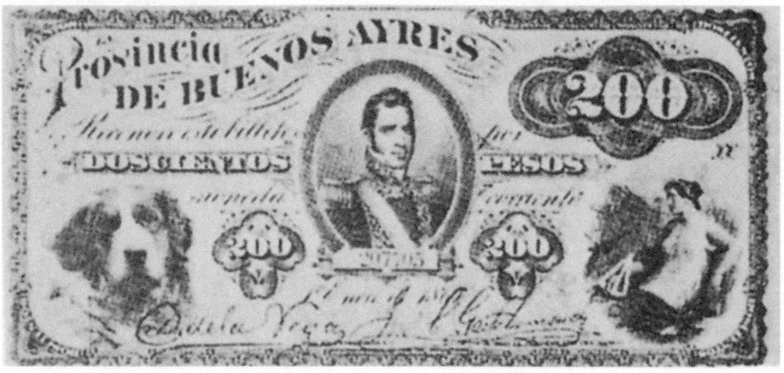

S495 200 Pesos — Good | Fine | XF

1.1.1869 (1877-83). Black on green underprint. "Dog's Head" at lower left, portrait General C. M. Alvear at center, seated female with sextant "Navigation" at right. Printed signature. Back: Red and blue. Printer: ABNC. — — | — | —

S496 200 Pesos — Good | Fine | XF

1.1.1869 (1879-83). Black on green underprint. Man shearing sheep ("So. American Sheep Shearing") at left, portrait General C. M. Alvear at center, "Navigation" at right. Printed signature. Printer: ABNC. — — | — | —

S497 500 Pesos — Good | Fine | XF

1.1.1869 (1869-83). Black on red underprint. Slaughterhouse "Saladero" at upper left, Gen. J. M. de Pueyrredon at lower right. Handwritten signature. Back: Red. Printer: ABNC. — — | — | —

S498 1000 Pesos

1.1.1869 (1869-83). Black on light blue underprint. Navigator at left, ship at center, Adm. G. Brown at right. Handwritten signature. Back: Light blue. Printer: ABNC.

	Good	Fine	XF
a. Issued note. Rare.	—	—	—
p. Proof.	—	—	—

S499 5000 Pesos

1.1.1869 (1869-83). Black on green underprint. Horses at upper left, Dr. D. Sarsfield at lower left, child head at center right, seated allegorical woman by large globe at lower right. Handwritten signature. Back: Green. Printer: ABNC. Rare.

	Good	Fine	XF
	—	—	—

El Banco de la Provincia de Buenos Aires

1869 Issue

This issue consists of notes in Centesimos Fuertes and Pesos Fuertes. Lower values (#S500-S504) use the spelling AYRES; #S505-S511 use the form AIRES in the title. Imprint appears in English on #S500-S504, in English and Spanish on #S510, and in Spanish on #S505-S509, and S511. In 1876 some notes of all denominations were revalidated; these are cataloged as a separate group.

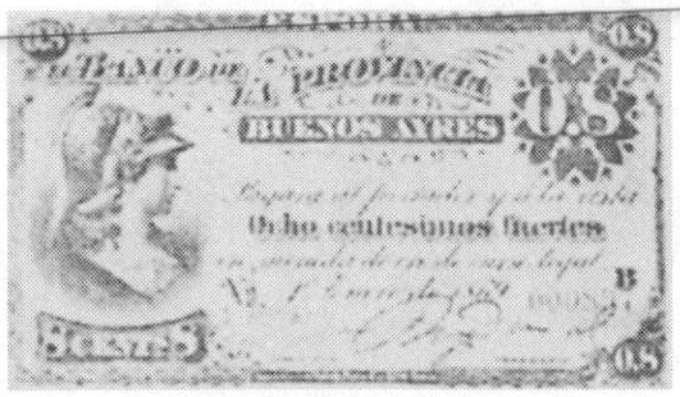

S500 8 Centesimos Fuertes

1.1.1869. Black on ochre underprint. Helmeted female ("Minerva No. 2") at left. Handwritten signature. Back: Orange. Small bust of Athena at center.

	Good	Fine	XF
a. 2 signature.	20.00	50.00	150.
b. 1 signature.	10.00	40.00	100.

S501 10 Centesimos Fuertes

1.1.1869. Black on green underprint. "Mercury" at right. Handwritten signature. Back: Green. Portrait Indian woman ("Chola") at center.

	Good	Fine	XF
a. Issued note, 2 signature.	40.00	125.	350.
b. Issued note, 1 signature.	20.00	75.00	200.
r. Unsigned remainder.	—	—	—

S502 16 Centesimos Fuertes

1.1.1869. Black on red-orange underprint. Col. L. Argerich at center. Handwritten signature. Back: Red-orange. Steam locomotive at center.

	Good	Fine	XF
a. 2 signature.	50.00	125.	325.
b. 1 signature.	50.00	125.	325.

S503 20 Centesimos Fuertes

1.1.1869. Black on gray-brown underprint. Girl ("Nathalie") at left. Handwritten signature. Back: Brown. Dog on safe at center.

	Good	Fine	XF
	50.00	125.	325.

S504 40 Centesimos Fuertes

1.1.1869. Black on light blue underprint. Young woman ("Fannie") at center. Handwritten signature. Back: Blue. Steamship at lower center.

	Good	Fine	XF
a. 2 signature.	50.00	125.	325.
b. 1 signature.	50.00	125.	325.

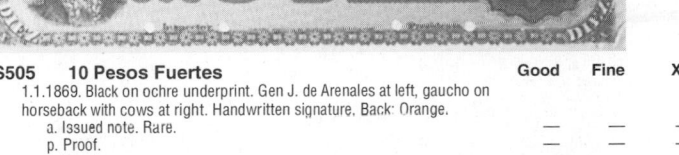

S505 10 Pesos Fuertes

1.1.1869. Black on ochre underprint. Gen J. de Arenales at left, gaucho on horseback with cows at right. Handwritten signature. Back: Orange.

	Good	Fine	XF
a. Issued note. Rare.	—	—	—
p. Proof.	—	—	—
s. Specimen.	—	—	—

S506 20 Pesos Fuertes

1.1.1869. Black on ochre underprint. Allegorical woman and child at lower left, wagon train ("S.A. Ox Train") at center, Dr. M. Moreno at lower right. Handwritten signature. Back: Brown.

	Good	Fine	XF
a. Issued note. Rare.	—	—	—
s. Specimen overprint: *MUESTRA*.	—	—	—

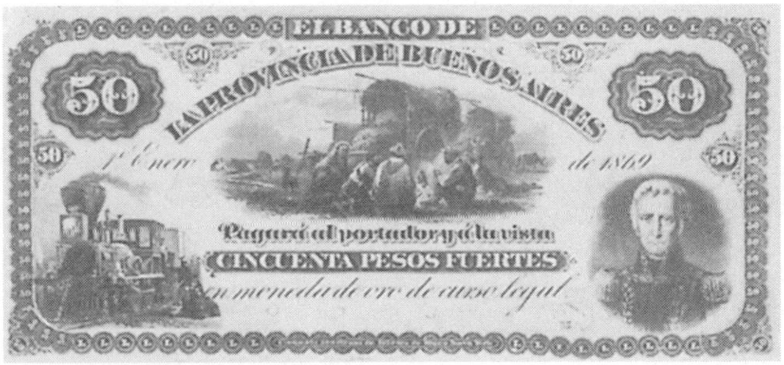

S507 50 Pesos Fuertes

1.1.1869. Black on red-orange underprint. Steam locomotive at left, wagons and campfire ("Camping on the Pampa") at center, Col. C. Saavedra at right. Handwritten signature. Back: Red.

	Good	Fine	XF
a. Issued note. Rare.	—	—	—
p. Proof.	—	—	—

S508 100 Pesos Fuertes

1.1.1869. Black on green underprint. Dr. B. Rivadavia at lower left, gaucho with horse ("Gaucha and Horse") at center, allegorical woman at lower right. Handwritten signature. Back: Green. Rare.

	Good	Fine	XF
	—	—	—

S509 200 Pesos Fuertes

1.1.1869. Black on purple-rose underprint. Gen. M. Belgrano at lower left, steam passenger train at upper center, allegory of Industry at right. Handwritten signature.

	Good	Fine	XF
a. Issued note. Rare.	—	—	—
p. Proof.	—	—	—
s. Specimen with or without overprint: *MUESTRA.*	—	—	—

S510 200 Pesos Fuertes

	Good	Fine	XF
1.1.1869. Black on green underprint. Gen M. Belgrano at left, sailing ship ("City of Tokio") at center, allegorical woman and child at right. Handwritten signature Back brown; cattle and sheep. Specimen overprint: *MUESTRA.* Rare.	—	—	—

S511 500 Pesos Fuertes

	Good	Fine	XF
1.1.1869. Black on light blue underprint. Allegorical woman at left, man, dog and woman pounding corn ("Gaucho and Girl") at center, Gen. J. de San Martin at right. Handwritten signature. Back: Blue. Specimen overprint: *MUESTRA.*	—	—	—

Ley de 25 Septiembre de 1876 Provisional Issue

#S512-S523 overprint: *LEY DE 25 SETBRE. (25.9) 1876* in circular seal on face.

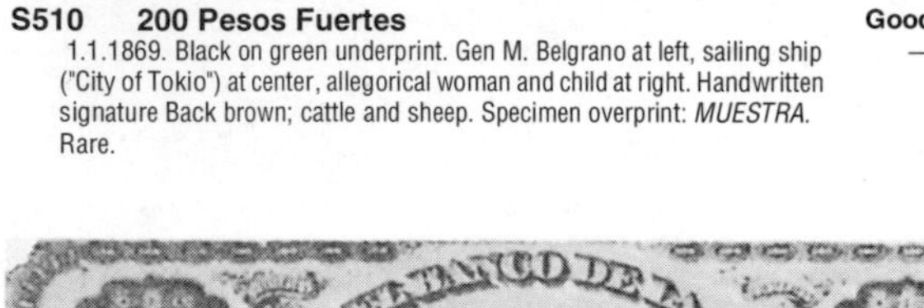

S512 8 Centesimos Fuertes

ND (- old date 1.1.1869). Black on ochre underprint. Overprint: *LEY DE 25 SETBRE. (25.9) 1876* in circular seal on face of #S500.

	Good	Fine	XF
a. 1 handwritten signature.	10.00	40.00	125.
b. 1 printed signature.	10.00	40.00	125.

S513 10 Centesimos Fuertes

ND (-old date 1.1.1869). Black on green underprint. Overprint: *LEY DE 25 SETBRE. (25.9) 1876* in circular seal on face of #S501.

	Good	Fine	XF
a. 1 handwritten signature.	15.00	60.00	175.
b. 1 printed signature.	15.00	60.00	175.

S514 16 Centesimos Fuertes

ND (-old date 1.1.1869). Black on gray-brown underprint. Overprint: *LEY DE 25 SETBRE. (25.9) 1876* in circular seal on face of #S502.

	Good	Fine	XF
a. 1 handwritten signature.	25.00	75.00	225.
b. 1 printed signature.	25.00	75.00	225.

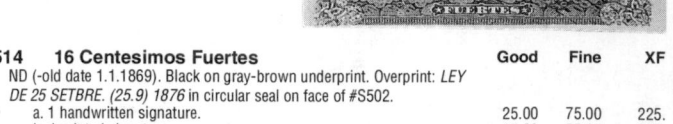

S515 20 Centesimos Fuertes

ND (-old date 1.1.1869). Black on ochre underprint. Overprint: *LEY DE 25 SETBRE. (25.9) 1876* in circular seal on face of #S503.

	Good	Fine	XF
a. 1 handwritten signature.	50.00	125.	300.
b. 1 printed signature.	25.00	75.00	225.

S516 40 Centesimos Fuertes

ND (-old date 1.1.1869). Black on light blue underprint. Overprint: *LEY DE 25 SETBRE. (25.9) 1876* in circular seal on face of #S504.

	Good	Fine	XF
a. 1 handwritten signature.	50.00	125.	300.
b. 1 printed signature.	50.00	125.	300.

S517 10 Pesos Fuertes

ND (-old date 1.1.1869). Black on ochre underprint. Overprint: *LEY DE 25 SETBRE. (25.9) 1876* in circular seal on face of #S505.

	Good	Fine	XF
a. 2 handwritten signature. Rare.	—	—	—
b. 2 printed signature. Rare.	—	—	—

	Good	Fine	XF
S518 20 Pesos Fuertes ND (-old date 1.1.1869). Black on ochre underprint. 2 handwritten signatures. Overprint: *LEY DE 25 SETBRE. (25.9) 1876* in circular seal on face of #S506. Rare.	—	—	—
S519 50 Pesos Fuertes ND (-old date 1.1.1869). Black on red-orange underprint. 2 handwritten signatures. Overprint: *LEY DE 25 SETBRE. (25.9) 1876* in circular seal on face of #S507. Rare.	—	—	—
S520 100 Pesos Fuertes ND (-old date 1.1.1869). Black on green underprint. 2 handwritten signatures. Overprint: *LEY DE 25 SETBRE. (25.9) 1876* in circular seal on face of #S508. Rare.	—	—	—
S521 200 Pesos Fuertes ND (-old date 1.1.1869). Black on purple-rose underprint. 2 handwritten signatures. Overprint: *LEY DE 25 SETBRE. (25.9) 1876* in circular seal on face of #S509. Rare.	—	—	—
S522 200 Pesos Fuertes ND (-old date 1.1.1869). Black on green underprint. 2 handwritten signatures. Overprint: *LEY DE 25 SETBRE. (25.9) 1876* in circular seal on face of #S510. Rare.	—	—	—
S523 500 Pesos Fuertes ND (-old date 1.1.1869). Black on pale blue underprint. 2 handwritten signatures. Overprint: *LEY DE 25 SETBRE. (25.9) 1876* in circular seal on face of #S511. Reported not confirmed.	—	—	—

1871 Issue

The 1871 emission was prepared in order to fill in several denominations not included in the previous issue. The notes were issued from 1876 to 1883. Printer ABNC.

NOTE: Some 1 and 4 Pesos were ovpt. in 1876.

	Good	Fine	XF
S524 1 Peso Fuerte 1.1.1871. Black on ochre underprint. Sailor at lower left, Gen. M. Pinto at center, peasant woman at right. Back: Brown. Printer: ABNC.			
a. Handwritten signature.	50.00	150.	400.
b. Printed signature.	75.00	200.	450.
p. Proof.	—	Unc	400.
S525 2 Pesos Fuertes 1.1.1871. Black on green underprint. Brigadier Gen. M. Rodriguez at left, dog head ("Ceasar") at center. Handwritten signature. Back: Dark brown. Printer: ABNC.			
a. Issued note.	200.	650.	—
p. Proof.	—	Unc	1000.
S526 4 Pesos Fuertes 1.1.1871. Black on light blue underprint. Horses at left, Dr. M. Garcia at right. Back: Blue.			
a. Handwritten signature.	150.	425.	—
b. Printed signature.	150.	425.	—

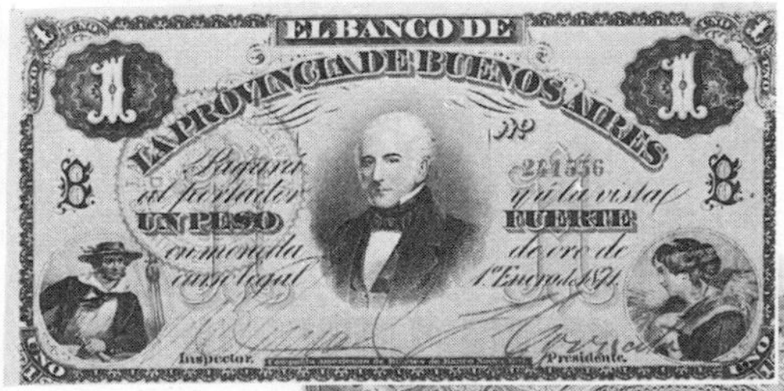

	Good	Fine	XF
S527 1 Peso Fuerte ND (- old date 1.1.1871). Overprint: *LEY DE 25 SETBRE 1876* in seal on face of #S524.			
a. Handwritten signature.	75.00	200.	500.
b. Printed signature.	75.00	200.	500.

	Good	Fine	XF
S528 4 Pesos Fuertes ND (- old date 1.1.1871). Overprint: *LEY DE 25 SETBRE 1876* in seal on face of #S526.			
a. Handwritten signature.	150.	500.	—
b. Printed signature.	150.	500.	—
s. Specimen.	—	—	—

1881 Issue

	Good	Fine	XF
S529 5 Pesos Fuertes 14.1.1881. Black on multicolor underprint. Gaucho riding horseback ("Gaucho on the Pampa") at left, portrait Dr. A. Alsina at center, woman seated at right. Back: Dark brown. Steam passenger train at station. Specimen (not issued).	—	—	—

Ley 8 Noviembre de 1881; 1883 Issue

This issue was originally backed by gold, but in 1885 a law was passed stopping any convertibility of paper money. Some denominations were ovpt. showing this law.

	Good	Fine	XF
S530 8 Centesimos Oro 1.1.1883. Helmeted femele ("Minerva No. 2") at left, Dr. N. Avellaneda at right. Uniface. Printer: ABNC.			
s. Specimen.	—	Unc	400.

	Good	Fine	XF
S531 10 Centesimos Oro 1.1.1883. Dr. D. Sarmiento at left, "Mercury" at right. Uniface. Printer: ABNC. Specimen. Not issued.	—	Unc	550.

S532 16 Centesimos Oro

	Good	Fine	XF
1.1.1883. Gen. B. Mitre at left, Col. L. Argerich at right. Uniface. Printer: ABNC. Specimen. Not issued.	—	Unc	750.

S533 20 Centesimos Oro

	Good	Fine	XF
1.1.1883. Girl ("Nathalie") at left, Dr. S. Derqui at right. Uniface. Printer: ABNC. Specimen. Not issued.	—	Unc	900.

S534 40 Centesimos Oro

	Good	Fine	XF
1.1.1883. Young woman ("Fannie") at left, Justice J. Urquiza at right. Uniface. Printer: ABNC. Not issued.			
p. Proof.	—	Unc	1250.
s. Specimen.	—	—	—

S535 1 Peso Oro

	Good	Fine	XF
1.1.1883. Black on maroon underprint. Gen. M. Rodriguez at left, farm tools at center, Gen. M. Pinto at right. Uniface. Printed signature. Printer: ABNC.			
a. 1 signature.	50.00	225.	600.
b. 2 signature.	75.00	250.	700.
p. Proof.	—	Unc	900.
s. Specimen.	—	—	—

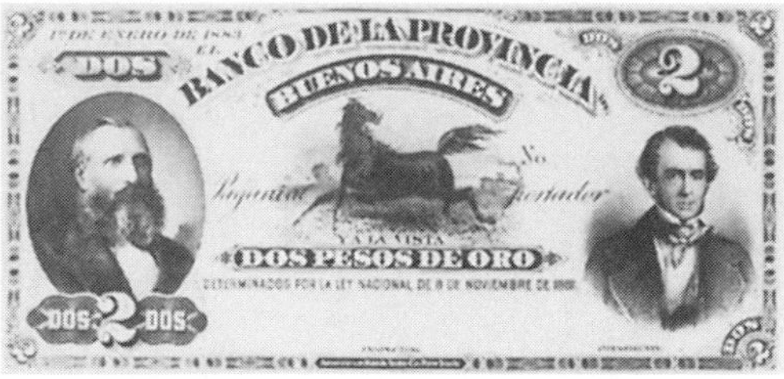

S536 2 Pesos Oro

	Good	Fine	XF
1.1.1883. Black on rose underprint. A. Alsina at left, horse at center, F. Varela at right. Uniface. Printed signature. Printer: ABNC.			
a. 1 signature.	150.	500.	—
b. 2 signature.	150.	500.	—
p. Proof.	—	Unc	1000.
s. Specimen.	—	—	—

S537 4 Pesos Oro

	Good	Fine	XF
1.1.1883. Black on cream underprint. Dr. M. Alberti at left, cow at center, J. Castelli at right. Uniface. 2 printed signatures. Printer: ABNC.			
a. Issued note.	175.	550.	—
p. Proof.	—	Unc	1250.
s. Specimen.	—	—	—

S538 5 Pesos Oro

	Good	Fine	XF
1.1.1883. Black on green underprint. Gen. J. Lavalle at left, ram at center, Gen. J. M. Paz at right. Uniface. 2 printed signatures. Printer: ABNC.			
a. Issued note.	150.	550.	—
p. Proof.	—	Unc	1400.
s. Specimen.	—	—	—

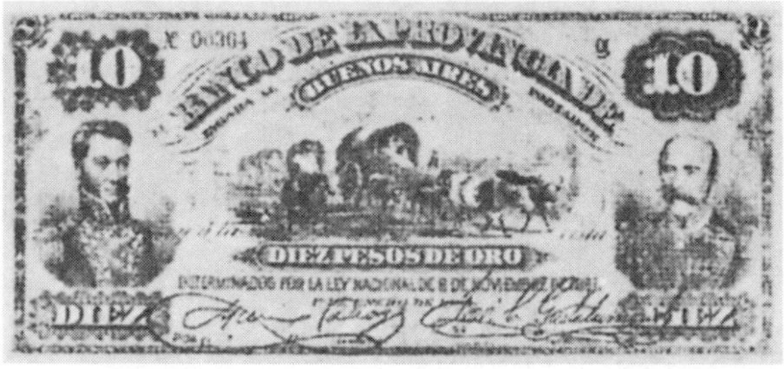

S539 10 Pesos Oro

	Good	Fine	XF
1.1.1883. Black on light blue underprint. Gen. J. A. de Arenales at left, wagon train ("S.A. Ox Train") at center, Gen. G. Las Heras at right. 2 printed signatures. Back: Maroon. Printer: ABNC.			
a. Issued note.	175.	650.	—
p. Proof.	—	Unc	1750.
s. Specimen.	—	—	—

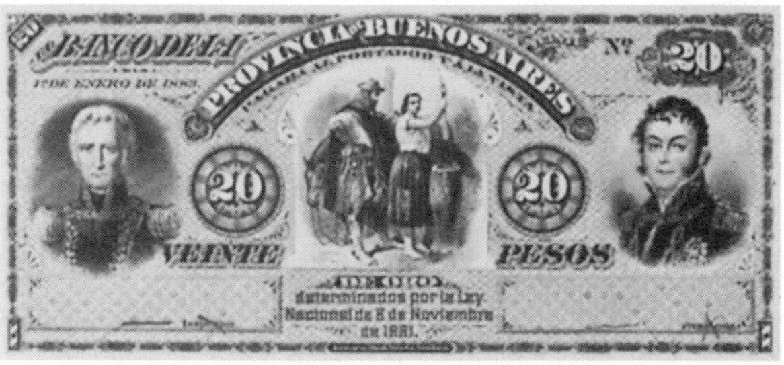

S540 20 Pesos Oro

	Good	Fine	XF
1.1.1883. Black on rose underprint. Col. C. Saavedra at left, man and woman ("Gaucho & Girl No. 2") at center, Gen J. M. de Pueyrredon at right. 2 printed signatures. Back: Maroon-bronze. Printer: ABNC.			
a. Issued note.	—	—	—
p. Proof.	—	Unc	2250.
s. Face on light brown underprint. Back brown. Specimen.	—	—	—

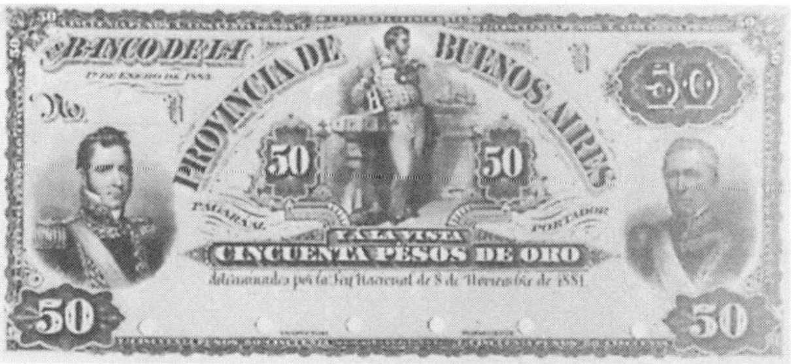

S541 50 Pesos Oro

	Good	Fine	XF
1.1.1883. Black on cream underprint. Gen. C. de Alvear at left, navigator at center, Adm. G. Brown at right. Back: Orange. Printer: ABNC.			
a. Issued note.	—	—	—
p. Proof.	—	—	—
s. Specimen.	—	—	—

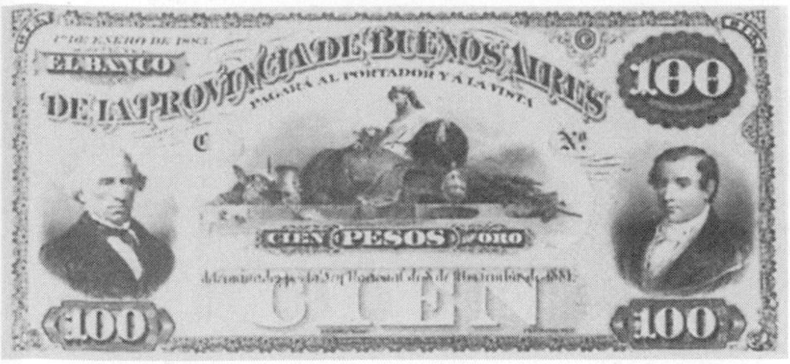

S542 100 Pesos Oro — Good | Fine | XF

1.1.1883. Black on rose underprint. D. Sarsfield at left, reclining allegorical woman (L'Orient) at center, M. Moreno at right. 2 printed signatures. Back: Rose. Train. Printer: ABNC.

	Good	Fine	XF
a. Issued note.	—	—	—
p. Proof.	—	—	—
s. Specimen.	—	—	—

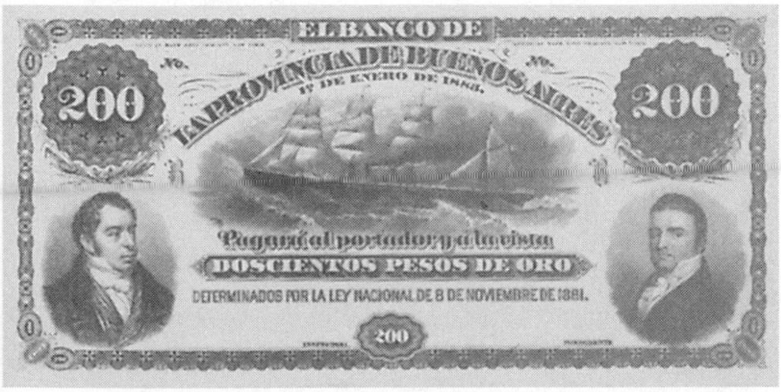

S543 200 Pesos Oro — Good | Fine | XF

1.1.1883. Black on light blue underprint. B. Rivadavia at lower left, sailing ship ("City of Tokio") at center, M. Garcia at lower right. Back: Blue. Bank founders at center. Printer: ABNC.

	Good	Fine	XF
a. Issued note.	—	—	
p. Proof.	—	Unc	4000.

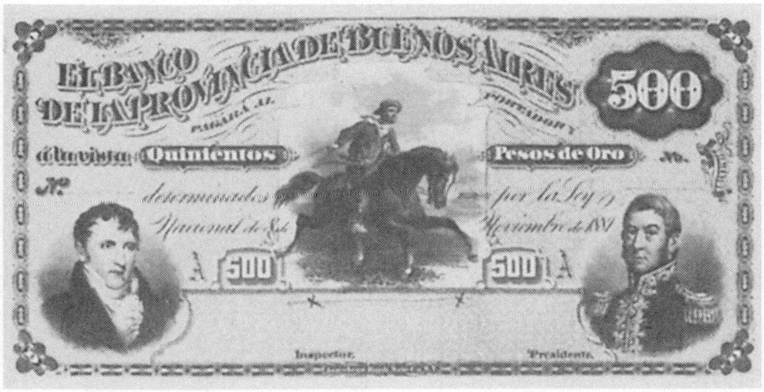

S544 500 Pesos Oro — Good | Fine | XF

1.1.1883. Black on green underprint. Gen M. Belgrano at lower left, gaucho on horseback ("Gaucho Lassoing") at center, J. de San Martin at lower right. Back: Green. Allegory of the Republic at center. Printer: ABNC.

	Good	Fine	XF
p. Proof. ND.	—	—	—
s. Specimen. 1.1.1883.	—	—	—

1885 Provisional Issue

#S545-S553 ovpt: *LEY 14 OCTUBRE 1885 GOBIERNO NACIONAL / INTERVENCION* in circle on face.

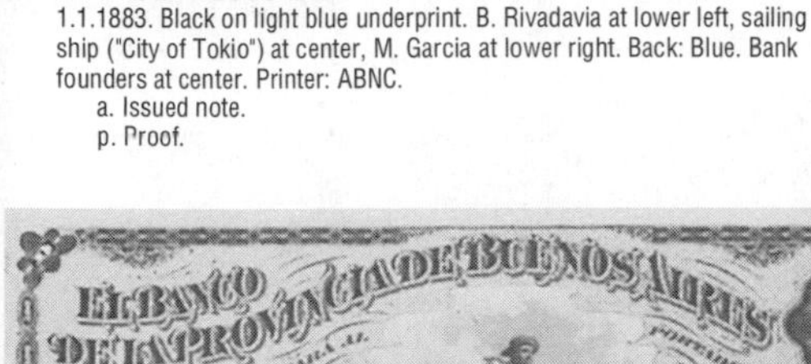

S545 1 Peso Oro — Good | Fine | XF

ND (- old date 1.1.1883). Black on maroon underprint. Overprint: *LEY 14 OCTUBRE 1885 GOBIERNO NACIONAL/INTERVENCION* in circle on face of #S535.

	Good	Fine	XF
a. 1 signature.	50.00	200.	450.
b. 2 signature. Reported not confirmed.	—	—	—

S546 2 Pesos Oro — Good | Fine | XF

ND (-old date 1.1.1883). Black on rose underprint. Overprint: *LEY 14 OCTUBRE 1885 GOBIERNO NACIONAL/INTERVENCION* in circle on face of #S536.

	Good	Fine	XF
a. 1 signature.	150.	500.	—
b. 2 signature.	150.	500.	—

	Good	Fine	XF
S547 4 Pesos Oro ND (-old date 1.1.1883). Black on cream underprint. Overprint: *LEY 14 OCTUBRE 1885 GOBIERNO NACIONAL/INTERVENCION* in circle on face of #S537.	150.	500.	—
S548 5 Pesos Oro ND (-old date 1.1.1883). Black on green underprint. Overprint: *LEY 14 OCTUBRE 1885 GOBIERNO NACIONAL/INTERVENCION* in circle on face of #S538.	150.	500.	—
S549 10 Pesos Oro ND (-old date 1.1.1883). Overprint: *LEY 14 OCTUBRE 1885 GOBIERNO NACIONAL/INTERVENCION* in circle on face of #S539.	200.	—	—
S550 20 Pesos Oro ND (-old date 1.1.1883). Black on rose underprint. Overprint: *LEY 14 OCTUBRE 1885 GOBIERNO NACIONAL/INTERVENCION* in circle on face of #S540.	225.	—	—
S551 50 Pesos Oro ND (-old date 1.1.1883.). Black on cream underprint. Overprint: *LEY 14 OCTUBRE 1885 GOBIERNO NACIONAL/INTERVENCION* in circle on face of #S541.	275.	—	—
S552 100 Pesos Oro ND (-old date 1.1.1883). Black on rose underprint. Overprint: *LEY 14 OCTUBRE 1885 GOBIERNO NACIONAL/INTERVENCION* in circle on face of #S542.	300.	—	—
S553 200 Pesos Oro ND (-old date 1.1.1883). Black on light blue underprint. Overprint: *LEY 14 OCTUBRE 1885 GOBIERNO NACIONAL/INTERVENCION* in circle on face of #S543.	375.	—	—

Ley de 5 de Noviembre de 1881; 1885 Regular Issue

The purpose of the 1885 issue was to replace earlier notes with denominations in *PESOS DE ORO* to notes in Pesos but in *Moneda Nacional Oro.* All issued notes of this issue carry the 1885 circular overprint in circle on face. All backs have bank name.

S561 1 Peso — Good | Fine | XF

1.1.1885. Black on salmon and green underprint. Gen. M. Rodriguez at left, llamas at center, Gen. M. Pinto at right. Back: Blue. Bank name. Printer: ABNC.

	Good	Fine	XF
a. Issued note.	75.00	150.	450.
s. Specimen.	—	—	—

S562 2 Pesos — Good | Fine | XF

1.1.1885. Black on ochre and green underprint. A. Alsina at left, horse at center, F. Varela at right. Uniface. Back: Green. Bank name. Printer: ABNC.

	Good	Fine	XF
a. Issued note.	150.	500.	—
s. Specimen.	—	—	—

S563 5 Pesos

1.1.1885. Black on rose and green underprint. Cows at center. Back: Maroon. Bank name. Printer: ABNC.

	Good	Fine	XF
a. Issued note.	150.	550.	—
s. Specimen.	—	—	—

S564 10 Pesos

1.1.1885. Black on maroon and light blue underprint. Gen. J. A. de Arenales at left, wagon train ("S.A. Ox Train") at center, Gen. G. Las Heras at right. Back: Green. Bank name. Printer: ABNC.

	Good	Fine	XF
a. Issued note.	300.	1000.	—
s. Specimen.	—	—	—

S565 20 Pesos

1.1.1885. Black on maroon and light blue underprint. Back: Maroon. Bank name. Printer: ABNC.

	Good	Fine	XF
a. Issued note.	350.	1100.	—
s. Specimen.	—	—	—

S566 50 Pesos

1.1.1885. Black on orange, ochre and rose underprint. Back: Maroon. Bank name. Printer: ABNC.

	Good	Fine	XF
a. Issued note.	400.	1250.	—
s. Specimen.	—	—	—

S567 100 Pesos

1.1.1885. Black on cream, blue and light blue underprint. Back: Blue and black. Farmers herding cattle and sheep at center. Bank name. Printer: ABNC.

	Good	Fine	XF
a. Issued note.	500.	1500.	—
s. Specimen.	—	—	—

S568 200 Pesos

1.1.1885. Black on maroon, green and bronze underprint. Back: Maroon and black. Bank name. Printer: ABNC.

	Good	Fine	XF
a. Issued note.	650.	1750.	—
s. Specimen.	—	—	—

S569 500 Pesos

1.1.1885. Black on red, green and maroon underprint. Back: Red and black. Men and horses at left. Bank name. Printer: ABNC.

	Good	Fine	XF
a. Issued note. Rare.	—	—	—
p. Proof.	—	—	—
s. Specimen.	—	—	—

NOTE: #S569a is known from a single example with signature and circular overprint in the Banco de la Provincia museum in Buenos Aires.

1891 Certificados de Deposito Issue

This issue consisted of money substitutes needed because of a political and monetary crisis occurring in 1890. First printings of the 1 and 5 Pesos did not carry the title: *CERTIFICADO DE DEPOSITO* and were not issued. Printer: Talleres del Museo de La Plata. All notes except the 1 Peso (#S571 and S573) carry this imprint on the back.

All noted under Law of 7 August 1891.

S571 1 Peso

L.1891. Blue on ochre and violet underprint. Arms at left, Mercury and woman in chariot with lions at right. Back: Gray. Allegorical group at center. Rare.

	Good	Fine	XF
	—	—	—

S572 5 Pesos

L.1891. Black. Arms at upper left, cows at lower left, seated woman at right. Face proof only.

	Good	Fine	XF
	—	—	—

S573 1 Peso

L.1891. Arms at left, Mercury and woman in chariot with lions at right. Text:*CERTIFICADO DE DEPOSITO*. Back: Allegorical group at center.

	Good	Fine	XF
a. Issued note.	15.00	40.00	100.
b. Punched hole cancelled.	—	Unc	10.00

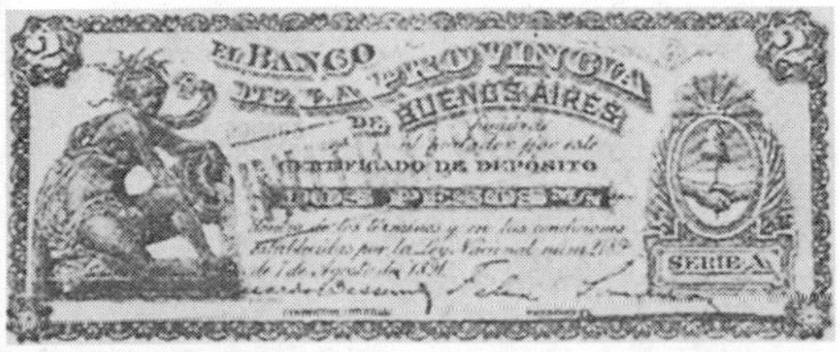

S574 2 Pesos

L.1891. Black on light blue and ochre underprint. Indian pouring water from jug at left, arms at right. Text:*CERTIFICADO DE DEPOSITO*. Back: Green. Animals, grain, peasants and carts. Rare.

	Good	Fine	XF
	—	—	—

S575 5 Pesos

L.1891. Black on ochre and light blue underprint. Arms at upper left, cow at lower left, peasant carrying grain at right. Text:*CERTIFICADO DE DEPOSITO*. Back: Blue and green. Manager, woman and cows.

	Good	Fine	XF
a. Issued note.	40.00	80.00	150.
b. Punched hole cancelled.	—	Unc	40.00
r. Remainder without signature	—	Unc	150.

S576 10 Pesos

L.1891. Black on salmon and green underprint. Portrait Liberty at left, arms at right. Text:*CERTIFICADO DEPOSITO*. Back: Gray and maroon. Horse head at left and right. Rare.

	Good	Fine	XF
	—	—	—

S577 50 Pesos

L.1891. Black on green and maroon underprint. Sailing ship at left, arms at center, allegorical man at right. Text:*CERTIFICADO DEPOSITO*. Back: Green. Three cows. Rare.

	Good	Fine	XF
	—	—	—

S578 100 Pesos

L.1891. Black on maroon and cream underprint. Ox-cart at left, arms at right. Text:*CERTIFICADO DE DEPOSITO*. Back: Light blue, gray and black. Horses. Rare.

	Good	Fine	XF
	—	—	—

S579 500 Pesos

L.1891. Black on blue-gray and ivory underprint. Arms at lower left, field workers at upper right. Text:*CERTIFICADO DE DEPOSITO*. Back: Blue-gray and black. Rare.

	Good	Fine	XF
	—	—	—

A word on date ranges

Often date ranges or specific dates are listed. These have been observed or reported by our contributors. If a note is outside the published range, it only means that it is a newly reported date, and not necessarily worthy of a premium value.

Banco Británico de la América del Sud

1888 Conformes por Oro Issue

This issue took place from 1888 to 1897; notes were hand dated. Only one denomination is presently known, and in a single example.

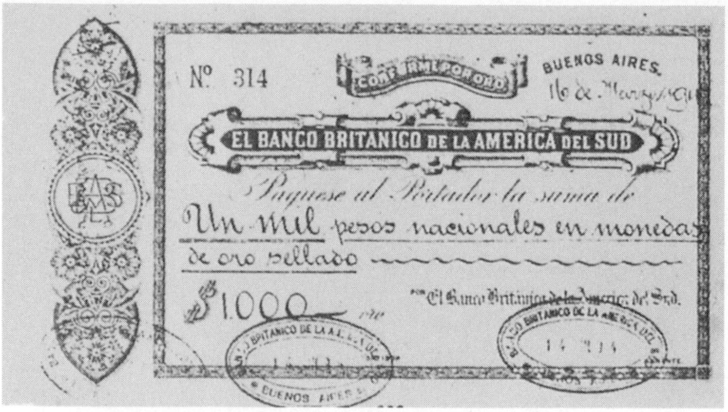

S601 1000 Pesos	Good	Fine	XF
16.3.1894. Hand dated. Black on rose underprint. Handwritten signature. Back: Rose. Rare.	—	—	—

Banco Hipotecario de la Provincia de Buenos Aires

Ley de 14 de Julio de 1891

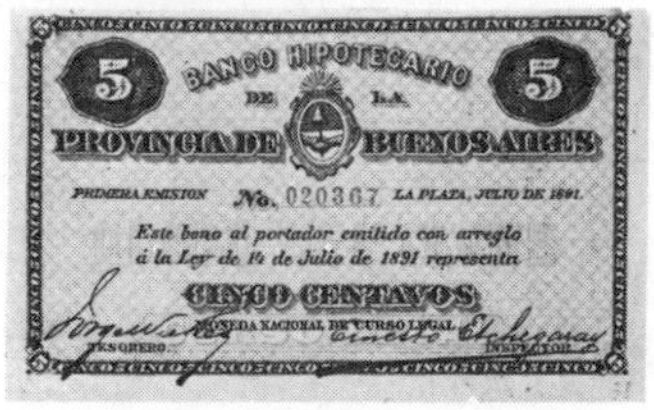

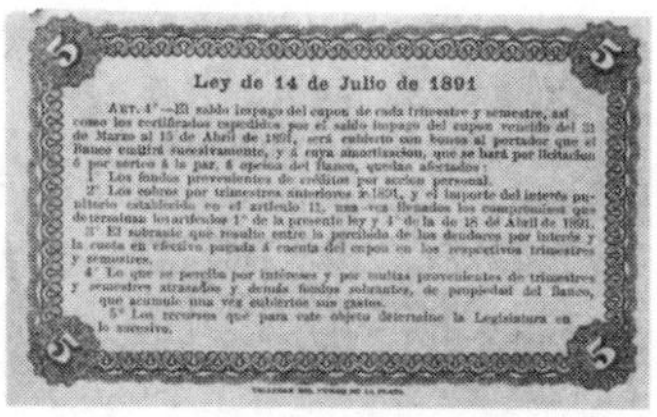

S611 5 Centavos	Good	Fine	XF
7.1891. Black on sepia underprint. Arms at upper center. Text: *MONEDA NACIONAL DE CURSO LEGAL*. Back: Maroon. Legal text. Printer: Talleres del Museo de La Plata.	10.00	25.00	50.00
S612 10 Centavos			
7.1891. Text: *MONEDA NACIONAL DE CURSO LEGAL*. Arms. Back: Legal text. Printer: Talleres del Museo de La Plata. Reported not confirmed.	—	—	—

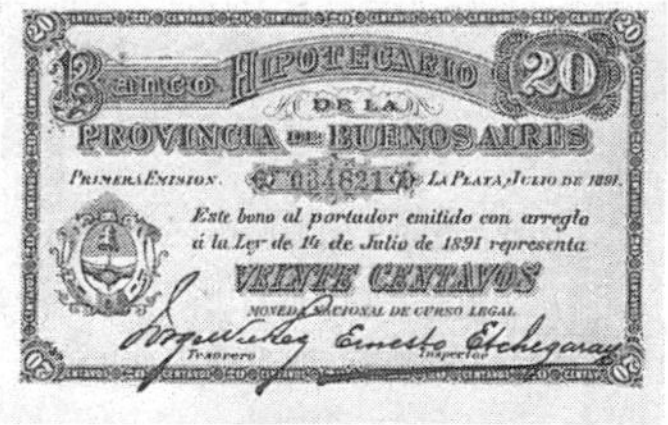

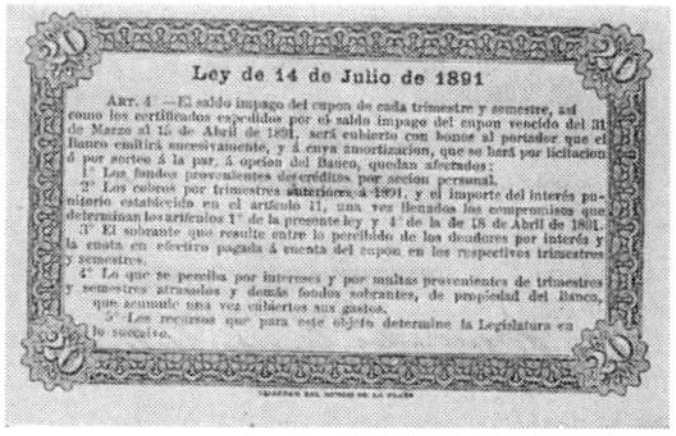

S613 20 Centavos	Good	Fine	XF
7.1891. Black on rose underprint. Text: *MONEDA NACIONAL DE CURSO LEGAL*. Arms at left. Back: Orange. Legal text. Printer: Talleres del Museo de La Plata.	10.00	25.00	50.00

S614 50 Centavos	Good	Fine	XF
7.1891. Black on light blue underprint. Text: *MONEDA NACIONAL DE CURSO LEGAL*. Arms at upper center. Back: Green. Legal text. Printer: Talleres del Museo de La Plata.	15.00	30.00	75.00

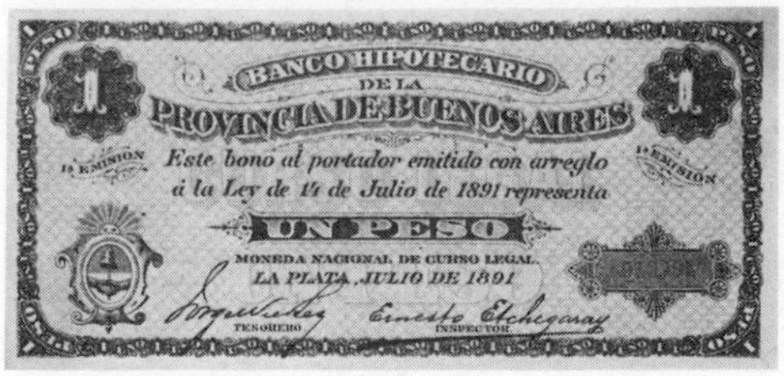

S615 1 Peso	Good	Fine	XF
7.1891. Black on dull maroon underprint. Text: *MONEDA NACIONAL DE CURSO LEGAL*. Arms at lower left. Back: Dull maroon. Legal text. Printer: Talleres del Museo de La Plata.	15.00	30.00	75.00
S616 2 Pesos			
7.1891. Black on ochre underprint. Text: *MONEDA NACIONAL DE CURSO LEGAL*. Arms at center. Back: Maroon. Legal text. Printer: Talleres del Museo de La Plata.	40.00	80.00	200.

S617 5 Pesos	Good	Fine	XF
7.1891. Black on light blue underprint. Text: *MONEDA NACIONAL DE CURSO LEGAL*. Arms at center. Back: Orange. Legal text. Printer: Talleres del Museo de La Plata.	20.00	50.00	150.
S618 10 Pesos			
7.1891. Black on ochre underprint. Text: *MONEDA NACIONAL DE CURSO LEGAL*. Arms at center. Back: Maroon. Legal text. Printer: Talleres del Museo de La Plata.	40.00	80.00	200.
S619 20 Pesos			
7.1891. Black on blue-green underprint. Text: *MONEDA NACIONAL DE CURSO LEGAL*. Arms at left. Back: Green. Legal text. Printer: Talleres del Museo de La Plata.	20.00	50.00	150.
S620 50 Pesos			
7.1891. Black on beige and light blue underprint. Text: *MONEDA NACIONAL DE CURSO LEGAL*. Arms at right. Back: Blue. Legal text. Printer: Talleres del Museo de La Plata.	40.00	90.00	225.

S621 100 Pesos	Good	Fine	XF
7.1891. Black on maroon and light blue underprint. Text: *MONEDA NACIONAL DE CURSO LEGAL*. Arms at right. Back: Blue. Legal text. Printer: Talleres del Museo de La Plata.	75.00	125.	300.

	Description	Good	Fine	XF
S622	**200 Pesos** 7.1891. Black on green underprint. Text: *MONEDA NACIONAL DE CURSO LEGAL.* Arms at center. Back: Sepia. Legal text. Printer: Talleres del Museo de La Plata. Rare.	—	—	—
S623	**500 Pesos** 7.1891. Black on green and ochre underprint. Text: *MONEDA NACIONAL DE CURSO LEGAL.* Arms at center. Back: Blue. Legal text. Printer: Talleres del Museo de La Plata.	75.00	200.	400.

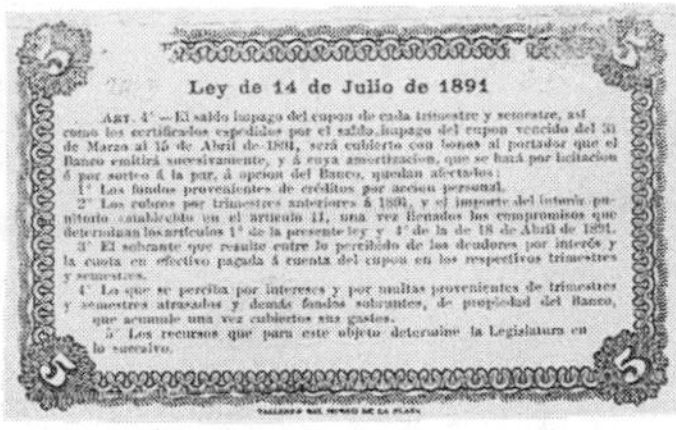

	Description	Good	Fine	XF
S624	**5 Centavos** 7.1891. Black on sepia underprint. Arms at upper center. Text: *MONEDA NACIONAL ORO SELLADO.* Back: Maroon. Legal text. Printer: Talleres del Museo de La Plata. Specimen.	15.00	40.00	75.00
S625	**10 Centavos** 7.1891. Text: *MONEDA NACIONAL ORO SELLADO.* Back: Legal text. Printer: Talleres del Museo de La Plata. Specimen. Reported not confirmed.	—	—	—
S626	**20 Centavos** 7.1891. Black on rose underprint. Text: *MONEDA NACIONAL ORO SELLADO.* Arms at left. Back: Orange. Legal text. Printer: Talleres del Museo de La Plata. Specimen.	15.00	40.00	75.00
S627	**50 Centavos** 7.1891. Black on light blue underprint. Text: *MONEDA NACIONAL ORO SELLADO.* Arms at upper center. Back: Green. Legal text. Printer: Talleres del Museo de La Plata. Specimen.	25.00	50.00	100.
S628	**1 Peso** 7.1891. Black on blue underprint. Text: *MONEDA NACIONAL ORO SELLADO.* Arms at lower left. Back: Legal text. Printer: Talleres del Museo de La Plata. Specimen.	25.00	50.00	125.
S629	**5 Pesos** 7.1891. Black on green underprint. Text: *MONEDA NACIONAL ORO SELLADO.* Arms at center. Back: Legal text. Printer: Talleres del Museo de La Plata. Specimen.	25.00	50.00	125.
S630	**10 Pesos** 7.1891. Black on green underprint. Text: *MONEDA NACIONAL ORO SELLADO.* Arms at center. Back: Legal text. Printer: Talleres del Museo de La Plata. Specimen.	75.00	175.	400.
S631	**20 Pesos** 7.1891. Black on maroon underprint. Text: *MONEDA NACIONAL ORO SELLADO.* Arms at left. Back: Legal text. Printer: Talleres del Museo de La Plata. Specimen.	40.00	75.00	150.
S632	**50 Pesos** 7.1891. Text: MONEDA NACIONAL ORO SELLADO. Arms at right. Back: Legal text. Printer: Talleres del Museo de La Plata. Reported not confirmed. Specimen.	—	—	—

Banco Nacional

1873 Issue

The 1873 dated issue was large and with many variations. It consisted of 19 different denominations of notes which come with or without overprints and stampings from different branches of issue. The varieties break down into 4 major face and 3 back variants. Various combinations of faces and backs are shown for each note. Faces are indicated by numbers and backs with capital letters according to the following descriptions:

Faces:

1. As printed, w/o revalidation or ovpt.
2. Vertical ovpt: *Ley de 24 Octubre 1876.*
3. Ovpt: *Ley... 1876* plus sign. *Delgado Gerente* underneath.
4. Ovpt: *Moneda Nacional Oro Ley de 5 Noviembre 1881* in oval, plus lg. capital letter (A-V) which may indicate branch office. (Specific designations of letter to branch office are not known.)

	Description	Good	Fine	XF
S641	**4 Centavos Fuertes** 1.8.1873. Black on green underprint. Dog and safe at upper center, arms below. Uniface.			
	a. Face 1, back A.	15.00	40.00	75.00
	b. Face 1, back C.	20.00	50.00	100.
	c. Face 2, back A.	20.00	50.00	100.
	d. Face 2, back B.	20.00	50.00	100.
	e. Face 2, back C.	20.00	50.00	100.
	f. Face 3, back A.	20.00	50.00	100.
	g. Face 3, back B.	15.00	40.00	75.00
	h. Face 3, back C.	15.00	40.00	75.00
	s. Specimen.	—	—	—

	Description	Good	Fine	XF
S642	**5 Centavos Fuertes** 1.8.1873. Black on blue underprint. Arms at center. Uniface.			
	a. Face 1, back A.	15.00	40.00	75.00
	b. Face 1, back C.	15.00	40.00	75.00
	c. Face 2, back A.	15.00	40.00	75.00
	d. Face 2, back B.	15.00	40.00	75.00
	e. Face 2, back C.	15.00	40.00	75.00
	f. Face 3, back A.	15.00	40.00	75.00
	g. Face 3, back B.	15.00	40.00	75.00
	h. Face 3, back C.	15.00	40.00	75.00
	s. Specimen.	—	—	—

	Description	Good	Fine	XF
S643	**10 Centavos Fuertes** 1.8.1873. Black on ochre underprint. Arms at center. Uniface.			
	a. Face 1, back A.	20.00	40.00	80.00
	b. Face 1, back C.	25.00	50.00	100.
	c. Face 2, back A.	40.00	60.00	125.
	d. Face 2, back B.	40.00	60.00	125.
	e. Face 2, back C.	40.00	60.00	125.
	f. Face 3, back A.	40.00	60.00	125.
	g. Face 3, back B.	40.00	60.00	125.
	h. Face 3, back C.	25.00	75.00	150.
	s. Specimen.	—	—	—

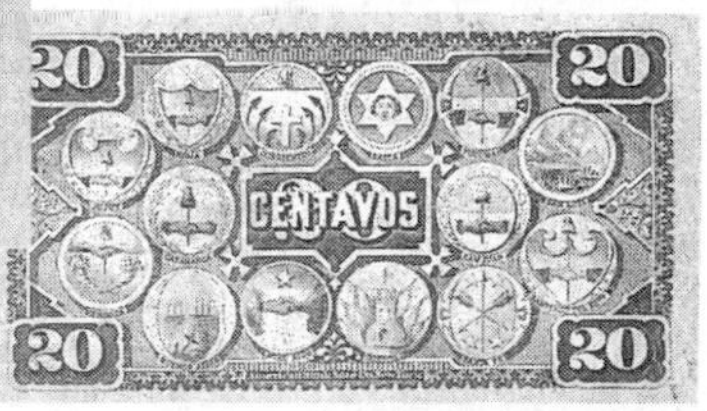

	Description	Good	Fine	XF
S644	**20 Centavos Fuertes** 1.8.1873. Black. Gaucho on horseback herding cows at center, arms below. Back: Blue. Arms of the 14 provinces of the Republic.			
	a. Face 1, back A.	25.00	50.00	150.
	b. Face 1, back C.	25.00	50.00	150.
	c. Face 2, back A.	40.00	75.00	200.
	d. Face 2, back B.	40.00	75.00	200.
	e. Face 2, back C.	40.00	75.00	200.
	f. Face 3, back A.	40.00	75.00	200.
	g. Face 3, back B.	40.00	75.00	200.
	h. Face 3, back C.	25.00	50.00	150.

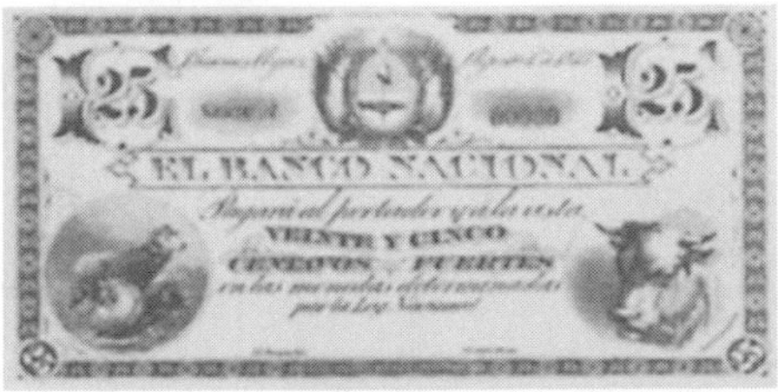

	Description	Good	Fine	XF
S645	**25 Centavos Fuertes** 1.8.1873. Black. Sheep at lower left, arms at upper center, cow at lower right. Back: Red. Arms of the 14 provinces of the Republic.			
	p. Proof.	—	—	—
	r. Remainder. Without signature.	200.	600.	—
	s. Specimen.	—	—	—

NOTE: It appears likely that #S645 was never signed or issued because of the disappearance of a box containing them and some 50 Centavos notes at the customs office. No issued examples are presently known.

S646 40 Centavos Fuertes

1.8.1873. Black on ochre underprint. Allegorical woman at left and right. Back: Green. Arms of the 14 provinces of the Republic.

	Good	Fine	XF
a. Face 1, back A.	40.00	75.00	200.
b. Face 1, back C.	40.00	75.00	200.
c. Face 2, back A.	50.00	100.	250.
d. Face 2, back B.	50.00	100.	250.
e. Face 2, back C.	50.00	100.	250.
f. Face 3, back A.	50.00	100.	250.
g. Face 3, back B.	50.00	100.	250.
h. Face 3, back C.	40.00	75.00	200.
p. Proof.	—	—	—

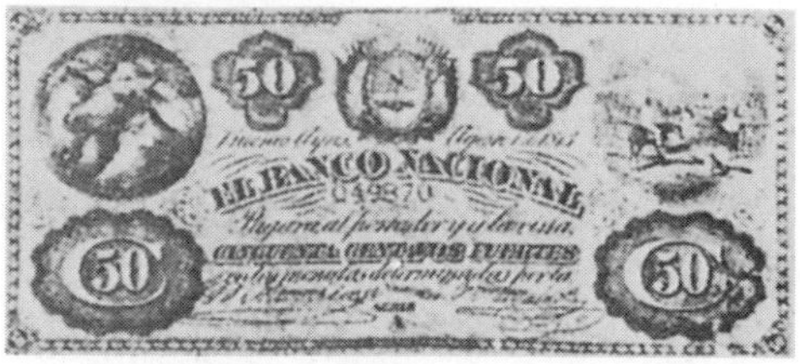

S647 50 Centavos Fuertes

1.8.1873. Black. Horses at left, arms at center, farmer scene at right. Back: Green. Arms of the 14 provinces of the Republic.

	Good	Fine	XF
a. Face 1, back A.	175.	750.	—
p. Proof.	—	—	—
s. Specimen.	—	—	—

NOTE: Very few of #S647 was signed and released (see NOTE following #S645).

S648 75 Centavos Fuertes

1.8.1873. Black on ochre underprint. Ostriches running at lower left, arms at center, portrait J. M. de. Pueyrredon at lower right. Back: Brown. Arms of the 14 provinces of the Republic.

	Good	Fine	XF
a. Face 1, back A. Reported not confirmed.	—	—	—
b. Face 1, back C.	75.00	200.	600.
c. Face 2, back A.	75.00	200.	600.
d. Face 2, back B.	80.00	225.	650.
e. Face 2, back C.	75.00	200.	600.
f. Face 3, back A.	80.00	225.	650.
g. Face 3, back B.	75.00	200.	600.
h. Face 3, back C.	75.00	200.	600.
p. Proof.	—	—	—
s. Specimen.	—	—	—

NOTE: An issue of 75 Centavos notes printed by Guillermo Kraft, Bs. As. requires conformation.

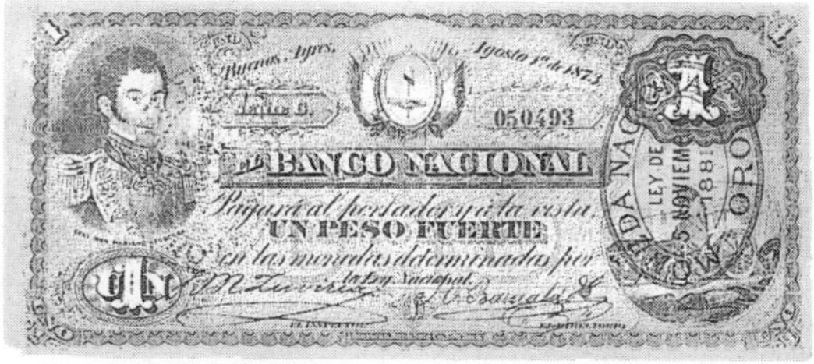

S649 1 Peso Fuerte

1.8.1873. Black on salmon underprint. General M. Necochea at left, arms at center, ox-cart at right. Back: Brown. Arms of the 14 provinces of the Republic.

	Good	Fine	XF
a. Face 1, back A.	90.00	250.	650.
b. Face 1, back C.	90.00	250.	650.
c. Face 2, back A.	90.00	250.	650.
d. Face 2, back B.	90.00	250.	650.
e. Face 2, back C.	90.00	250.	650.
f. Face 3, back A.	90.00	250.	650.
g. Face 3, back B.	90.00	250.	650.
h. Face 3, back C.	90.00	250.	650.
i. Face 4, back A. Blue or red overprint.	90.00	250.	650.
p. Proof.	—	—	—
s. Specimen.	—	—	—

S650 2 Pesos Fuertes

1.8.1873. Black on rose and green underprint. Train at upper left. center, arms at center, train at upper center right, Dr. A. Saenz at lower right. Back: Blue. Arms of the 14 provinces of the Republic.

	Good	Fine	XF
a. Face 1, back A.	100.	300.	700.
b. Face 1, back C.	100.	300.	700.
c. Face 2, back A.	100.	300.	700.
d. Face 2, back B.	100.	300.	700.
e. Face 2, back C.	100.	300.	700.
f. Face 3, back A.	100.	300.	700.
g. Face 3, back B.	100.	300.	700.
h. Face 3, back C.	100.	300.	700.
i. Face 4, back A. Blue or red overprint.	100.	300.	700.
p. Proof.	—	—	—
s. Specimen.	—	—	—

S651 3 Pesos Fuertes

1.8.1873. Black on sepia and light green underprint. Arms at left, allegorical woman ("Commerce") at center, portrait B. Rivadavia at right. Back: Yellow-brown. Arms of the 14 provinces of the Republic.

	Good	Fine	XF
a. Face 1, back C.	300.	750.	—
p. Proof.	—	Unc	850.
s. Specimen.	—	—	—

S652 5 Pesos Fuertes

1.8.1873. Black on light blue and ochre underprint. Ship at upper left, arms at center, ship at upper right, Dean Funes at lower right. Back: Violet. Arms of the 14 provinces of the Republic.

	Good	Fine	XF
a. Face 1, back A. Rare.	—	—	—
b. Face 1, back C. Rare.	—	—	—
c. Face 2, back A. Rare.	—	—	—
d. Face 2, back B. Rare.	—	—	—
e. Face 2, back C. Rare.	—	—	—
f. Face 3, back A. Rare.	—	—	—
g. Face 3, back B. Rare.	—	—	—
h. Face 3, back C. Rare.	—	—	—
p. Proof.	—	Unc	1000.
s. Specimen.	—	—	—

S653 10 Pesos Fuertes

1.8.1873. Black on blue-green underprint. Arms at lower left, woman with sheep at center, Gen. A. Balcerce at lower right. Back: Brown. Arms of the 14 provinces of the Republic.

	Good	Fine	XF
a. Face 1, back A. Rare.	—	—	—
b. Face 1, back C. Rare.	—	—	—
c. Face 2, back A. Rare.	—	—	—
d. Face 2, back B. Rare.	—	—	—
e. Face 2, back C. Rare.	—	—	—
f. Face 3, back A. Rare.	—	—	—
g. Face 3, back B. Rare.	—	—	—
h. Face 3, back C. Rare.	—	—	—

S654 15 Pesos Fuertes

1.8.1873. Black on green underprint. Portrait woman ("Spanish Girl") at lower left, arms at center, portrait Gen. M. Rodriguez at lower right. Back: Green. Arms of the 14 provinces of the Republic.

	Good	Fine	XF
a. Face 1, back C. Reported not confirmed.	—	—	—
p. Proof.	—	Unc	850.
s. Specimen with or without overprint: *SPECIMEN.*	—	—	—

S655 20 Pesos Fuertes

1.8.1873. Black on brown underprint. N. Pena at left, sailor at center, arms at right. Back: Blue. Arms of the 14 provinces of the Republic.

	Good	Fine	XF
a. Face 1, back A. Rare.	—	—	—
b. Face 1, back C. Rare.	—	—	—
c. Face 2, back A. Rare.	—	—	—
d. Face 2, back B. Rare.	—	—	—
e. Face 2, back C. Rare.	—	—	—
f. Face 3, back A. Rare.	—	—	—
g. Face 3, back B. Rare.	—	—	—
h. Face 3, back C. Rare.	—	—	—
p. Proof.	—	—	—
s. Specimen.	—	—	—

S656 50 Pesos Fuertes

1.8.1873. Black on green underprint. Allegory of Work at left, arms at center, Fray J. de ro at right. Back: Brown. Arms of the 14 provinces of the Republic.

	Good	Fine	XF
a. Face 1, back A. Rare.	—	—	—
b. Face 1, back C. Rare.	—	—	—
c. Face 2, back A. Rare.	—	—	—
d. Face 2, back B. Rare.	—	—	—
e. Face 2, back C. Rare.	—	—	—
f. Face 3, back A. Rare.	—	—	—
g. Face 3, back B. Rare.	—	—	—
h. Face 3, back C. Rare.	—	—	—
p. Proof.	—	—	—
s. Specimen.	—	—	—

S657 100 Pesos Fuertes

1.8.1873. Black on ochre underprint. Allegory of Sciences at left, arms at center, Gen. M. Rodriguez at right. Back: Black and green. 14 provincial flags and national arms.

	Good	Fine	XF
a. Issued note. Reported not confirmed.	—	—	—
p. Proof.	—	—	—
s. Specimen.	—	—	—

S658 200 Pesos Fuertes

1.8.1873. Black on ochre underprint. Allegorical woman and child at left, J. Paso at center, arms at right. Back: Black and ochre. 14 provincial flags and national arms.

	Good	Fine	XF
a. Issued note. Reported not confirmed.	—	—	—
p. Proof.	—	—	—
s. Specimen.	—	—	—

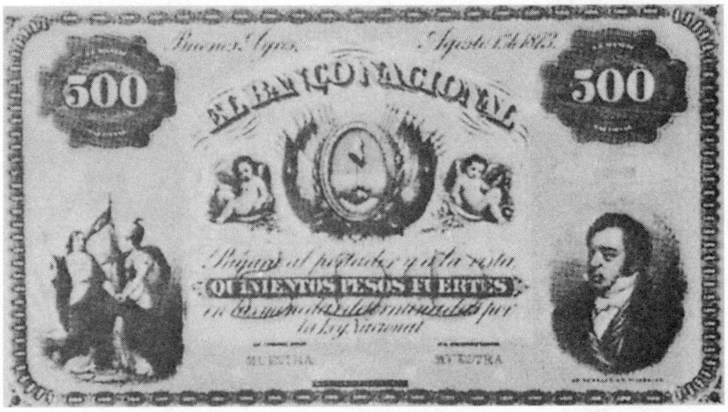

S659 500 Pesos Fuertes

1.8.1873. Black on violet underprint. Two women with flag at left, arms flanked by cherubs at center, Dr. B. Rivadavia at lower right. Back: Black and dark brown. 14 provincial flags and national arms.

	Good	Fine	XF
a. Issued note. Reported not confirmed.	—	—	—
p. Proof.	—	—	—
s. Specimen.	—	—	—

1879 Issue

#S661-S664 vertical ovpt: *Ley de 24 Octubre 1876* and sign. *Delgado gerente* underneath at l. These special denominations were made to facilitate the exchange of notes denominated in Reales Bolivianos. 4-1/2 Centavos = 1/2 Real, 9 Centavos = 1 Real, 18 Centavos = 2 Reales, and 36 Centavos = 4 Reales Bolivianos. Printer: Guillermo Kraft, Bueno Aires.

Backs come either w/o branch office stamping or w/such stamping and date *1879.* Additionally, some notes w/branch office indicated on back will have sign. of branch manager added. Branches which stamped some of these notes are as follows:

Catamarca	Gualeguaychú	Salta
Concepción del Uruguay	Jujuy	San Juan
Concordia	La Rioja	San Luís
Córdoba	Mendoza	Santiago del Estero
Corrientes	Paraná	Tucuman
Gualeguay	Rosario	

S661 4-1/2 Centavos Fuertes

2.1.1879. Black on light blue underprint. Arms at center. Uniface. *Delgado gerente* signature underneath overprint at left. Overprint: Red, vertical: *Ley de 24 Octubre 1876.* Printer: Guillermo Kraft, Bueno Aires.

	Good	Fine	XF
a. Without branch office stamping on back.	25.00	50.00	100.
b. Branch office and date *1879* stamped on back.	35.00	65.00	125.

S662 9 Centavos Fuertes

2.1.1879. Black on light green underprint. Girl and dog at center. *Delgado gerente* signature underneath overprint at left. Back: Brown. Overprint: Red, vertical: *Ley de 24 Octubre 1876.* Printer: Guillermo Kraft, Bueno Aires.

	Good	Fine	XF
a. Without branch office stamping on back.	40.00	75.00	135.
b. Branch office and date *1879* stamped on back.	40.00	75.00	140.

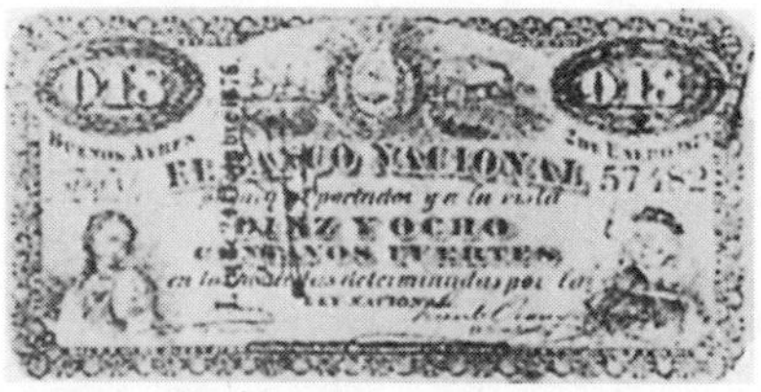

S663 18 Centavos Fuertes

2.1.1879. Black on ochre underprint. Girl at left, ship, arms and train at center, boy at right. *Delgado gerente* signature underneath overprint at left. Back: Ochre. 14 provincial arms. Overprint: Dark blue, vertical: *Ley de Octubre 1876.* Printer: Guillermo Kraft, Bueno Aires.

	Good	Fine	XF
a. Without branch office stamping on back.	125.	225.	425.
b. Branch office and date *1879* stamped on back.	125.	225.	425.

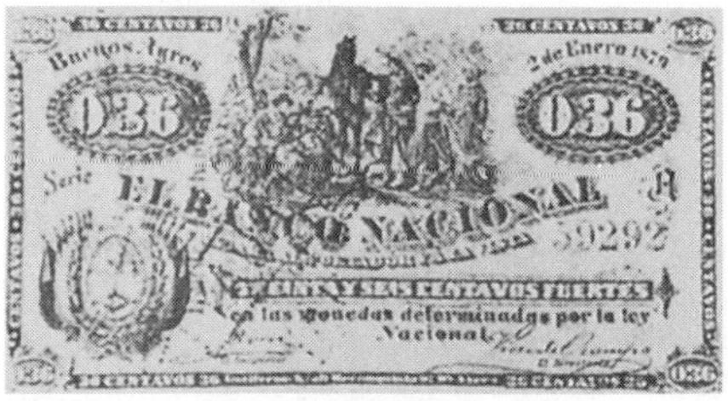

S664 36 Centavos Fuertes

2.1.1879. Black on salmon underprint. Arms at lower left, gauchos and horse at center. *Delgado gerente* signature underneath overprint at left. Back: Blue. 14 provincial arms. Overprint: Red, vertical: *Ley de 24 Octubre 1876.* Printer: Guillermo Kraft, Bueno Aires.

	Good	Fine	XF
a. Without branch office stamping on back.	100.	175.	400.
b. Branch office and date *1879* stamped on back.	100.	175.	400.

1880 First Issue

These were made to circulate in the northern provinces. Once again, their purpose was to facilitate the exchange of notes denominated in Pesos Bolivianos and fractions thereof. Each note had text stating its equivalent in *Chirolas* of specified value. The value of a *Chirola* fluctuated with the price of silver on the international market. It was also affected by the silver content in the Bolivian coinage.

Two issues of Centavos/Chirolas notes were made, and both are dated 1.3.1880. The difference is the stated value of the Chirola, the first being @ 14 centavos and the second @ 16 centavos. Printer: Guillermo Kraft, Buenos Aires.

All notes except #S668 have the same vertical ovpt: *1876.* and sign. as the previous

S665 14 Centavos Fuertes = 1 Chirola

1.3.1880. Black on violet underprint. Girl at left, arms at upper right. *Delgado gerente* signature underneath overprint. at left. Back: Light gray. Overprint: Red, vertical: *Ley de 24 Octubre 1876.* Printer: Guillermo Kraft, Buenos Aires.

	Good	Fine	XF
a. Without branch office stamping on back.	175.	500.	—
b. With branch office and date *1879* stamped on back.	175.	500.	—

S666 28 Centavos Fuertes = 2 Chirolas

1.3.1880. Black on brown-orange underprint. Gaucho on horseback at left, arms at lower center, seated Liberty at right. *Delgado gerente* signature underneath overprint at left. Back: Green. Overprint: Red, vertical: *Ley de Octubre 1876.* Printer: Guillermo Kraft, Bueno Aires.

	Good	Fine	XF
a. Without branch office stamping on back.	175.	500.	—
b. With branch office and date *1879* stamped on back.	175.	500.	—

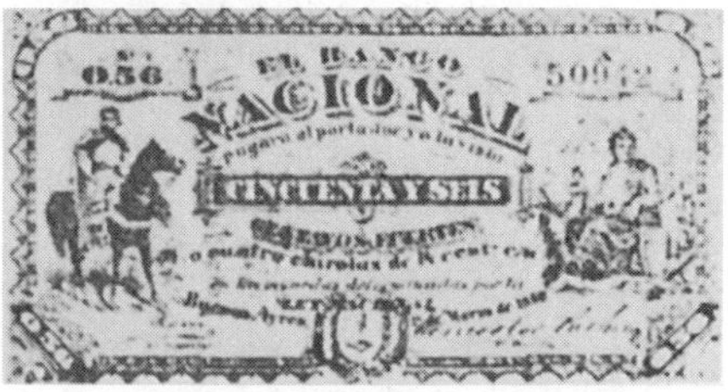

S667 56 Centavos Fuertes = 4 Chirolas

1.3.1880. Black on brown-orange underprint. Gaucho on horseback at left, arms at lower center, seated Liberty at right. *Delgado gerente* signature underneath overprint at left. Back: Green. Overprint: Red, vertical: *Ley de 24 Octubre 1876.* Printer: Guillermo Kraft, Buenos Aires.

	Good	Fine	XF
a. Without branch office stamping on back.	175.	500.	—
b. With branch office and date *1879* stamped on back.	175.	500.	—

S668 5 Pesos-60 Centavos Fuertes = 40 Chirolas

1.3.1880. Black on ochre underprint. Arms, gaucho and cows at left without vertical overprint. Back: Green. Arms.

	Good	Fine	XF
a. Without branch office stamping on back. Rare.	—	—	—
b. With branch office and date *1879* stamped on back. Rare.	—	—	—

1880 Second Issue

#S669-S671 Chirola = 16 Centavos Fuertes.

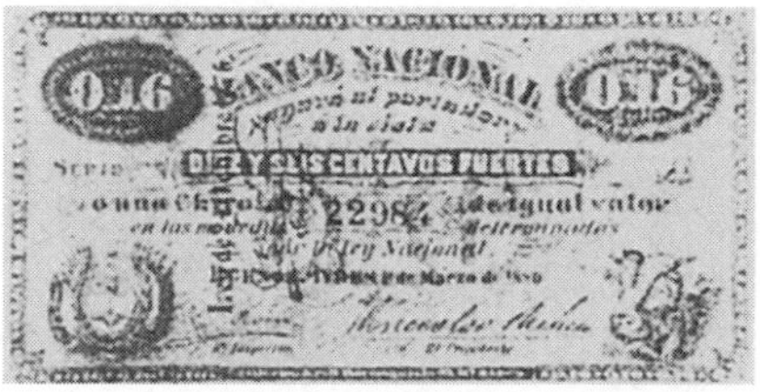

S669 16 Centavos Fuertes = 1 Chirola

1.3.1880. Black on maroon underprint. Arms at lower left, cow's head at lower right. Back: Maroon. Overprint: Dark blue, vertical.

	Good	Fine	XF
a. Without branch office stamping on back.	175.	500.	—
b. With branch office and date *1879* stamped on back.	175.	500.	—

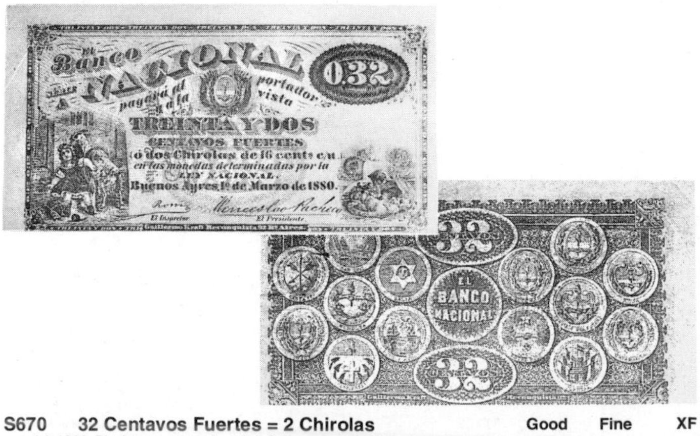

S670 32 Centavos Fuertes = 2 Chirolas

1.3.1880. Black on green underprint. Baby and goat at left, arms at center, domestic animals at right. Back: Light brown. Overprint: Red, vertical.

	Good	Fine	XF
a. Without branch office stamping on back.	175.	500.	—
b. With branch office and date *1879* stamped on back.	175.	500.	—

S671 64 Centavos Fuertes = 4 Chirolas	Good	Fine	XF
1.3.1880. Black on rose underprint. Arms at left, sailing ship in storm at center. Back: Maroon. Overprint: Blue or black, vertical.			
a. Without branch office stamping on back.	200.	600.	—
b. With branch office and date *1879* stamped on back.	200.	600.	—

1883 First Issue

#S676-S684 may have large capital letter from A to V possibly indicating branch office. The exact designation of letter to office is not known. Also a reissue of these notes (#S685-S693) took place w/circular revalidation overprint: *GOBIERNO NACIONAL-INTERVENCION* around *Ley 14 de Octubre de 1885* (similar to #S545-S553). Printer: ABNC.

S676 1 Peso	Good	Fine	XF
1.1.1883. Black on orange underprint. Portrait woman at left, reclining allegorical woman and globe ("Science") at center, Gen. M. Rodriguez at right. Back: Orange. Printer: ABNC.			
a. Issued note.	75.00	200.	425.
p. Proof.	—	Unc	600.
s. Specimen.	—	—	—

S677 2 Pesos	Good	Fine	XF
1.1.1883. Black on ochre underprint. Woman ("Industry") at left, portrait B. Rivadavia upper center, female head ("America") at lower right. Back: Brownish maroon. Printer: ABNC.			
a. Issued note.	125.	300.	750.
p. Proof. Back brown.	—	Unc	1000.
s. Specimen.	—	—	—

S678 5 Pesos	Good	Fine	XF
1.1.1883. Black on blue-green underprint. Gen. R. Pena at upper left, two cherubs at center, standing woman ("Commerce") at right. Back: Blue-green. Printer: ABNC.			
a. Issued note.	125.	400.	1000.
p. Proof. Back green.	—	Unc	1000.
s. Specimen.	—	—	—

S679 10 Pesos	Good	Fine	XF
1.1.1883. Black on deep rose underprint. Portrait woman's head at left and right, J. A. Roca at center. Back: Deep rose. Arms with flags and cannon. Printer: ABNC.			
a. Issued note.	200.	—	—
p. Proof.	—	—	—
s. Specimen.	—	—	—

S680 20 Pesos	Good	Fine	XF
1.1.1883. Black on light green underprint. Allegorical woman with staff, bird and plants ("The Tropics") at center, Dean Funes at lower right. Back: Grayish green. Printer: ABNC.			
a. Issued note.	250.	—	—
p. Proof.	—	—	—
s. Specimen.	—	—	—

S681 50 Pesos	Good	Fine	XF
1.1.1883. Black on rose underprint. Cherub ("Abundance") at left, farm implements at center M. Gonzalez B. facing left at right. Back: Rose. Printer: ABNC.			
p. Proof.	—	—	—
s. Specimen.	—	—	—

S682 100 Pesos	Good	Fine	XF
1.1.1883. Black on pink underprint. Two allegorical women ("Commerce & Agriculture") overlooking ships at left, J. J. Paso at right. Back: Black and violet. Flowers. Printer: ABNC.			
p. Proof.	—	—	—
s. Specimen.	—	—	—

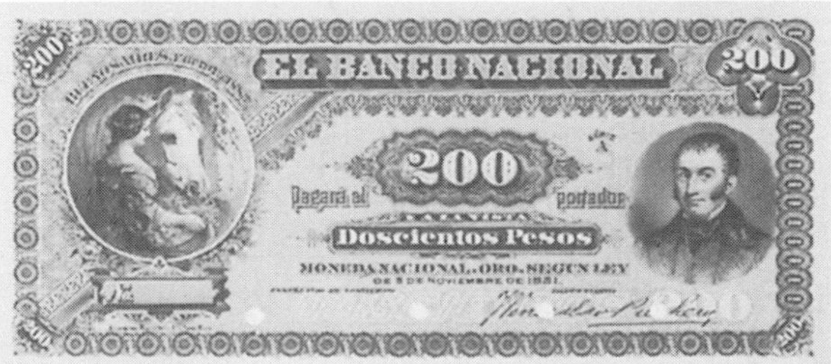

S683 200 Pesos	Good	Fine	XF
1.1.1883. Black on ochre underprint. Woman and horse at left, A. P. Saenz at right. Back: Black and maroon. Two allegorical women at center. Printer: ABNC.			
p. Proof. Back brown.	—	Unc	1500.
s. Specimen.	—	—	—

S684 500 Pesos — Good / Fine / XF

1.1.1883. Black on green and rose underprint. Arms at lower left, woman reclining ("Literature No. 2") at upper center, Gen. J. de San Martín at lower right. Back: Black and orange. Woman in oval at center. Printer: ABNC. Specimen. — — / — / —

1885 First Provisional Issue

#S685-S693 with circular revalidation overprint: *1885* on face.

		Good	Fine	XF
S685	**1 Peso** ND (- old date 1.1.1883). Black on orange underprint. Overprint: Circular revalidation *1885* on face of #s676.	50.00	200.	550.
S686	**2 Pesos** ND (- old date 1.1.1883). Black on ochre underprint. Overprint: Circular revalidation *1885* on face of #S677	125.	300.	900.
S687	**5 Pesos** ND (- old date 1.1.1883). Black on blue-green underprint. Overprint: Circular revalidation *1885* on face of #S678.	125.	400.	1250.
S688	**10 Pesos** ND (- old date 1.1.1883). Black on deep rose underprint. Overprint: Circular revalidation *1885* on face of #S679.	175.	—	—
S689	**20 Pesos** ND (- old date 1.1.1883). Black on green underprint. Overprint: Circular revalidation *1885* on face of #S680.	250.	—	—
S690	**50 Pesos** ND (- old date 1.1.1883). Black on rose underprint. Overprint: Circular revalidation *1885* on face of #S681.	—	—	—
S691	**100 Pesos** ND (- old date 1.1.1883). Black on pink underprint. Overprint: Circular revalidation *1885* on face of #S682.	—	—	—
S692	**200 Pesos** ND (- old date 1.1.1883). Black on ochre underprint. Overprint: Circular revalidation *1885* on face of #S683. Reported not confirmed.	—	—	—
S693	**500 Pesos** ND (- old date 1.1.1883). Black on green and rose underprint. Overprint: Circular revalidation *1885* on face of #S684.	—	—	—

1883 Second Issue

#S694-S703 were also reissued w/circular revalidation ovpt: *1885* (#S704-S713) similar to the 1883 First Issue w/arms at ctr. Printer: BWC.

S694 1 Peso — Good / Fine / XF

1.1.1883. Black on green underprint. Arms at center. Sailor at left, Gen. M. Rodriguez at right. Back: Rose and green. Head of Liberty. Printer: BWC. — 50.00 / 125. / 400.

S695 2 Pesos — Good / Fine / XF

1.1.1883. Black on green underprint. Arms at center. Mercury with caduceus at left, Dr. B. Rivadavia at right. Back: Rose, green and violet. Head of Liberty with Phrygian cap. Printer: BWC.

- a. Issued note. — 125. / 350. / 900.
- p. Proof. — — / — / —

S696 5 Pesos — Good / Fine / XF

1.1.1883. Black on rose underprint. Arms at center. Gen. R. Pena at left, cows at right. Back: Rose. Head of Liberty with Phrygian cap. Printer: BWC.

- a. Issued note. — 125. / 300. / 750.
- p. Proof. — — / — / —

		Good	Fine	XF
S697	**10 Pesos** 1.1.1883. Black on green and light blue underprint. Arms at center. Liberty standing at left, President J. A. Roca at right. Back: Green. 14 provincial arms. Printer: BWC. Rare.	—	—	—
S698	**10 Pesos** 1.1.1883. Black on yellow and light blue underprint. Arms at center. Generally similar to #S697 but many plate differences. Back: Light green. 14 provincial arms. Printer: BWC. Rare.	—	—	—
S699	**20 Pesos** 1.1.1883. Black on green and light blue underprint. Arms at center. Standing Liberty at left, Dean Funes at right. Back: Brown. Woman's head. Printer: BWC. Rare.	—	—	—
S700	**50 Pesos** 1.1.1883. Black on ochre and rose underprint. Arms at center. Group of four people at left, Gen. A. Balcarce at right. Back: Light blue. Printer: BWC. Rare.	—	—	—

S701 100 Pesos — Good / Fine / XF

1.1.1883. Black on ochre underprint. Arms at center. Liberty at left, J. J. Paso at right. Back: Rose. Printer: BWC. Rare. — — / — / —

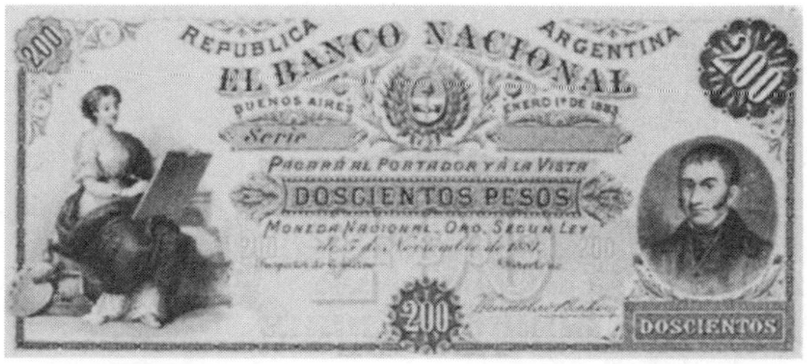

		Good	Fine	XF
S702	**200 Pesos** 1.1.1883. Black on green underprint. Arms at center. Allegory of Art at left, A. P. Saenz at right. Back: Black, brown and blue. Hay wagon at center. Printer: BWC. Specimen. Rare.	—	—	—
S703	**500 Pesos** 1.1.1883. Black on green and ochre underprint. Arms at center. Gen J. de San Martín at right, allegory of Painting at left. Back: Green. Printer: BWC. Specimen. Rare.	—	—	—

1885 Second Provisional Issue

#S704-S713 with circular revalidation ovpt: *1885* on face.

	Good	Fine	XF
S704 1 Peso ND (- old date 1.1.1883). Black on green underprint. Arms at center. Overprint: Circular revalidation *1885* on face of #S694.	75.00	150.	450.
S705 2 Pesos ND (- old date 1.1.1883). Black on green underprint. Arms at center. Overprint: Circular revalidation *1885* on #S695.	125.	300.	750.

	Good	Fine	XF
S706 5 Pesos ND (- old date 1.1.1883). Black on rose underprint. Arms at center. Overprint: Circular revalidation *1885* on #S696.	125.	400.	900.
S707 10 Pesos ND (- old date 1.1.1883). Black on green underprint. Arms at center. Overprint: Circular revalidation *1885* on face of #S697. Rare.	—	—	—

	Good	Fine	XF
S708 10 Pesos ND (-old date 1.1.1883). Black on yellow and light blue underprint. Arms at center. Overprint: Circular revalidation *1885* on face of #S698. Rare.	—	—	—
S709 20 Pesos ND (- old date 1.1.1883). Black on green and light blue underprint. Arms at center. Overprint: Circular revalidation *1885* on face of #S699. Rare.	—	—	—
S710 50 Pesos ND (- old date 1.1.1883). Black on ochre and rose underprint. Arms at center. Overprint: Circular revalidation *1882* on face of #S700. Rare.	—	—	—
S711 100 Pesos ND (- old date 1.1.1883). Black on ochre underprint. Arms at center. Overprint: Circular revalidation *1885* on face of #S701. Rare.	—	—	—
S712 200 Pesos ND (- old date 1.1.1883). Black on green underprint. Arms at center. Overprint: Circular revalidation *1885* on face of #S702. Reported not confirmed.	—	—	—
S713 500 Pesos ND (- old date 1.1.1883). Black on green and ochre underprint. Arms at center. Overprint: Circular revalidation *1855* on face of #S703. Reported not confirmed.	—	—	—

1883 Third Issue

A third issue was prepared for this bank, but apparently not placed into circulation. All known examples are either specimens or proofs. All faces have the shorter version of the bank name. All backs carry the long version. Printer: ABNC.

	Good	Fine	XF
S715 2 Pesos 1.1.1883. Black on blue and light orange underprint. Arms at left, Dr. B. Rivadavia at right. Back: Deep blue. Large numeral at center. Printer: ABNC. Specimen without serial #.	—	—	—

	Good	Fine	XF
S716 5 Pesos 1.1.1883. Black on green, brown and light red underprint. Col. Borrego at left, "Raphael's "Angel" at center, arms at right. Back: Brown. Printer: ABNC. Specimen without serial #.	—	—	—

	Good	Fine	XF
S717 10 Pesos 1.1.1883. Black on green and brown underprint. "Justice" seated at left, arms at center, J. A. Roca in uniform at right. Back: Deep green. Printer: ABNC. Specimen without serial #.	—	—	—

	Good	Fine	XF
S718 20 Pesos 1.1.1883. Black on multicolor underprint. Arms at left, allegorical woman ("Repose") at center, man at right. Printer: ABNC. Specimen.	—	—	—
S720 500 Pesos 1.1.1883. Back: Mules going down mountain trail ("Mule Train No. 2") at right. Printer: ABNC. Proof.	—	—	—

Banco Provincial de Córdoba

1873 First Issue

S721 1/2 Real Boliviano	Good	Fine	XF
27.3.1873. Green. Portrait woman at left, bird at right. Back: Head at left and right. Printer: BWC.			
a. Without overprint on back.	125.	400.	—
b. With overprint: *INSPECCION DE BANCOS* on back.	125.	400.	—

S722 1 Real Boliviano	Good	Fine	XF
27.3.1873. Green. Woman and chipmunk at left. Back: Head at left and right. Printer: BWC.			
a. Without overprint.	125.	400.	—
b. With overprint: *INSPECCION DE BANCOS* on back.	125.	400.	—
S723 2 Reales Bolivianos			
27.3.1873. Black on brown underprint. Dog. Printer: BWC.			
a. Without overprint.	175.	—	—
b. With overprint: *INSPECCION DE BANCOS* on back.	175.	—	—
S724 4 Reales Bolivianos			
27.3.1873. Black. Arms at lower left, galloping horse at center. Printer: BWC.			
a. Without overprint.	175.	—	—
b. With overprint: *INSPECCION DE BANCOS* on back.	175.	—	—

S725 1 Peso Boliviano	Good	Fine	XF
27.3.1873. Black. Reclining allegorical woman at upper center, woman's head at upper right. Uniface. Printer: Lit. S. Martin, Buenos aires.			
a. Without overprint.	125.	300.	—
b. With overprint: *INSPECCION DE BANCOS* on back.	125.	300.	—
S726 5 Pesos Bolivianos			
27.3.1873. Black on rose underprint. Gaucho. Printer: Lit. S. Martin, Buenos Aires.			
a. Without overprint.	—	—	—
b. With overprint: *INSPECCION DE BANCOS* on back.	—	—	—
S727 10 Pesos Bolivianos			
27.3.1873. Black. Printer: Lit. S. Martin, Buenos Aires.			
a. Without overprint.	—	—	—
b. With overprint: *INSPECCION DE BANCOS* on back.	—	—	—

1873 Second Issue

#S728 and S729 printer: Lit. S. Martín.

S728 50 Centavos	Good	Fine	XF
27.3.1873. Sheep. Printer: Lit. S. Martin.			
a. Without overprint.	—	—	—
b. With overprint: *INSPECCION DE BANCOS or BOLNOS* on back.	—	—	—
S729 1 Peso			
27.3.1873. Black on green underprint. Allegorical group. Printer: Lit. S. Martin.			
a. Without overprint.	—	—	—
b. With overprint: *INSPECCION DE BANCOS or BOLNOS* on back.	—	—	—

NOTE: #S728 and S729 come with or without overprint: *INSPECCION DE BANCOS or BOLNOS* on back.

1873 Third Issue

S730 1 Peso Fuerte	Good	Fine	XF
27.3.1873. Allegorical group.	—	—	—

1881 First Issue

Two different issues were made in 1881 for this bank. The first was locally printed, and the second was produced in England.

S731 1 Peso	Good	Fine	XF
1.1.1881. Printer: Mackern & McLean, Buenos Aires. Reported not confirmed.	—	—	—
S732 5 Pesos			
1.1.1881. Printer: Mackern & McLean, Buenos Aires. Reported not confirmed.	—	—	—

S733 10 Pesos	Good	Fine	XF
1.1.1881. Black with rose *10.* Dean G. Funes at left, provincial cathedral at right. Printer: Mackern & McLean, Buenos Aires.			
a. Without overprint.	125.	400.	—
b. Overprint: *Ley 14 Octubre 1885.*	125.	400.	—
S734 20 Pesos			
1.1.1881. Printer: Mackern & McLean, Buenos Aires. Reported not confirmed.	—	—	—

S735 50 Pesos	Good	Fine	XF
1.1.1881. Black with rose *50.* Portrait Gen. J. Paz at left, train, arms and wagons at center right. Back: Green. Liberty. Printer: Mackern & McLean, Buenos Aires.			
a. Without overprint.	250.	700.	—
b. Overprint: *Ley 14 Octubre 1885.*	250.	700.	—

1881 Second Issue

S736 1 Peso	Good	Fine	XF
1.1.1881. Black on gray underprint. Six people at lower left, man watching girl pounding corn at center. Back: Orange. Printer: W&S.			
a. Without overprint.	125.	250.	—
b. Overprint: *Ley 14 Octubre 1885.*	125.	250.	—

S737 5 Pesos	Good	Fine	XF
1.1.1881. Black on gray and brown underprint. Portrait M. Fragueiro at left, gaucho on horseback at right. Back: Blue. Printer: W&S.			
a. Without overprint.	175.	500.	—
b. Overprint: *Ley 14 Octubre 1885.*	175.	500.	—

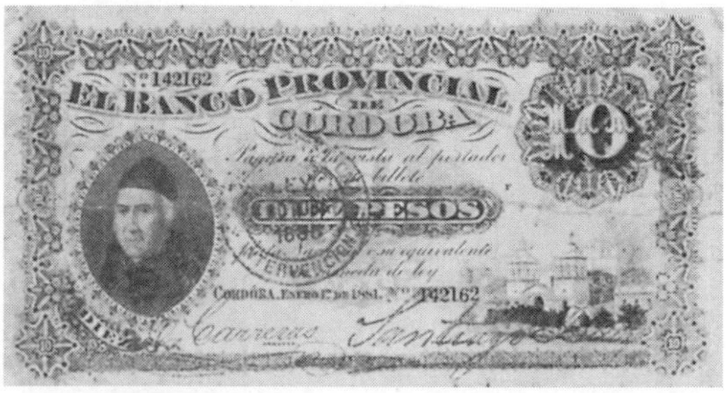

S738 10 Pesos	Good	Fine	XF
1.1.1881. Black on light blue underprint. Dean G. Funes at left, provincial cathedral at right. Back: Brown. Arms at upper center. Printer: W&S.			
a. Without overprint.	—	—	—
b. Overprint: *Ley 14 Octubre 1885.*	200.	650.	—
S739 20 Pesos			
1.1.1881. Printer: W&S. Reported not confirmed.	—	—	—
S740 50 Pesos			
1.1.1881. Printer: W&S. Reported not confirmed.	—	—	—

1889 Issue

Bonos

Circulating bonds issued by the *Sección Hipotecaria Agricola e Industrial* of the bank.

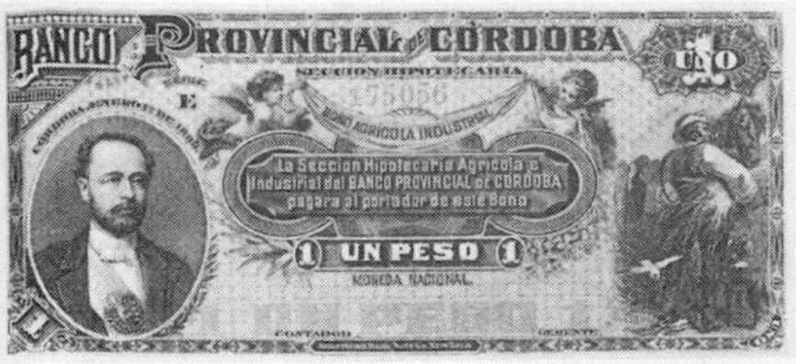

S741 1 Peso	Good	Fine	XF
1.1.1889. Black on green underprint. Portrait J. Ceilman at lower left, cherubs at center, farmer and horse at right. Back: Green. Building at center. Printer: ABNC.			
a. Issued note.	60.00	100.	200.
s. Specimen.	—	—	—

S742 5 Pesos	Good	Fine	XF
1.1.1889. Black on yellow and brown underprint. Portrait D. Sarsfield at left, seated allegorical woman with gear and tools at right. Back: Brown. Structure with two tall pillars at center. Printer: ABNC.	60.00	125.	300.

S743 10 Pesos	Good	Fine	XF
1.1.1889. Black on blue and yellow underprint. Statue of Freedom at left, Gen. J. M. Paz at right. Back: Blue. Government building at center. Printer: ABNC.	75.00	200.	—

S744 20 Pesos	Good	Fine	XF
1.1.1889. Black on orange and yellow underprint. M. Fraguiero at lower left, seated allegorical woman with pitcher ("Naiad") at right. Back: Scene with bridge and mountains at center. Printer: ABNC.			
p1. Proof. Back orange.	—	Unc	750.
p2. Proof. Back green.	—	Unc	750.
r. Remainder.	175.	500.	—

1891 Issue

	Good	Fine	XF
S755 50 Pesos			
20.4.1891 (handwritten date). Arms at left. Uniface. Printer: La Minerva, Córdoba. Rare.	—	—	—
S756 100 Pesos			
20.4.1891. Arms at left. Uniface. Printer: La Minerva, Córdoba. Rare.	—	—	—
S757 200 Pesos			
20.4.1891. Arms at left. Uniface. Printer: La Minerva, Cordoba. Rare.	—	—	—

Banco Provincial de Entre-Ríos

First Issue - Series A

#S761-S766 text with incorrect date: *8 de Noviembre de 1881.*

S760 1 Peso	Good	Fine	XF
1.4.1885. Black on red-orange underprint. Two allegorical figures at lower left, portrait Gen. E. Racedo at upper center, steam train at lower right. Back: Maroon. Provincial arms.			
a. Issued note.	75.00	200.	—
s. Specimen overprint: *MUESTRA.*	—	—	—

S761 1 Peso	Good	Fine	XF
1.4.1885. Gen. E. Racedo at lower left, provincial arms at upper center, steam train at lower right. Text with incorrect date: *8 de Noviembre de 1881.* Printer: La Union de Stiller y Laass, Buenos Aires.			
a. Issued note.	—	—	—
s. Specimen.	—	—	—

S762 2 Pesos	Good	Fine	XF
1.4.1885. Black on light blue underprint. Text with incorrect date: *8 de Noviembre de 1881.* Portrait A. Crespo at left, farm implements and plants at center right. Back: Blue-green. Arms. Printer: La Union de Stiller y Laass, Buenos Aires.			
a. Issued note.	125.	400.	—
s. Specimen overprint: *MUESTRA.*	—	—	—

S763 5 Pesos	Good	Fine	XF
1.4.1885. Black on blue-green underprint. Gen. J. de Urquiza at lower left, arms at center, view of Paraná at lower right. Text with incorrect date: *8 de Noviembre de 1881.* Back: Blue. Liberty. Printer: La Union de Stiller y Laass, Buenos Aires.			
a. Issued note.	200.	600.	—
s. Specimen overprint: *MUESTRA.*	—	—	—

S764 10 Pesos	Good	Fine	XF
1.4.1885. Black. Text with incorrect date: *8 de Noviembre de 1881.* Cows at lower left, portrait Gen. L. Sola at upper center, horses at right. Printer: La Union de Stiller y Laass, Buenos Aires.			
a. Issued note. Rare.	—	—	—
s. Specimen overprint: *MUESTRA.*	—	—	—
S765 20 Pesos			
1.4.1885. Black on ochre underprint. Text with incorrect date: *8 de Noviembre de 1881.* Gen. E. Racedo as an old man.			
a. Issued note. Rare.	—	—	—
s. Specimen overprint: *MUESTRA.*	—	—	—
S766 50 Pesos			
1.4.1885. Text with incorrect date: *8 de Noviembre de 1881.* Printer: La Union de Stiller y Laass, Buenos Aires. Reported not confirmed.	—	—	—

Second Issue - Series B

#S767-S772 text with corrected date: *5 de noviembre de 1881.* With circular 1885 revalidation overprint on face.

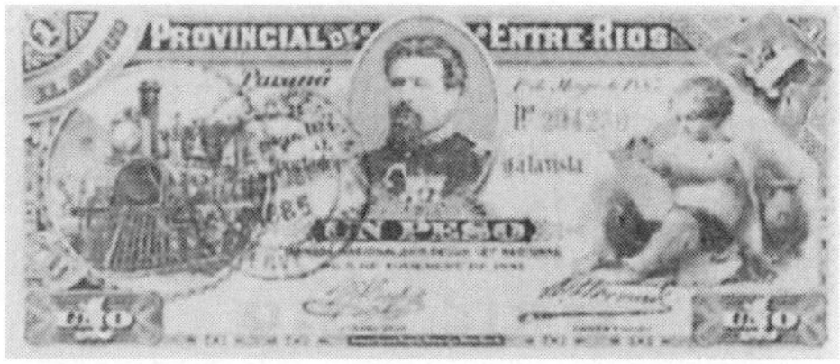

S767 1 Peso	Good	Fine	XF
1.5.1885. Black on rose and green underprint. Steam train at left, portrait Gen. E. Racedo at top center, young allegorical figure at right. Corrected date: *5 de noviembre de 1881.* Back: Green. Provincial arms. Overprint: With circular 1885 revalidation on face. Printer: ABNC.			
a. Issued note.	50.00	125.	400.
s. Specimen.	—	—	—

S768 2 Pesos	Good	Fine	XF
1.5.1885. Black on ochre and green underprint. Corrected date: *5 de noviembre de 1881.* A. Crespo at center, allegory of Farming at right. Back: Red. Arms at center. Overprint: With circular 1885 revalidation on face. Printer: ABNC.			
a. Issued note.	125.	425.	—
s. Specimen.	—	—	—

S769 5 Pesos	Good	Fine	XF
1.5.1885. Black on green and rose underprint. Corrected date: *5 de noviembre de 1881.* Provincial arms and allegory of Navigation at left, J. de Urquiza at right. Back: Maroon. Liberty. Overprint: With circular 1885 revalidation on face. Printer: ABNC.			
a. Issued note.	200.	600.	—
s. Specimen.	—	—	—

S770 10 Pesos	Good	Fine	XF
1.5.1885. Black on blue and orange underprint. Corrected date: *5 de noviembre de 1881.* Gaucho herding cows at left, "Raphael's Angel No. 2" at upper center right, portrait Gen. L. Sola at right. Back: Blue. Arms at center. Overprint: With circular 1885 revalidation on face. Printer: ABNC.			
a. Issued note.	250.	—	—
p. Proof.	—	—	—
s. Specimen.	—	—	—

S771 20 Pesos	Good	Fine	XF
1.5.1885. Black on pink and green underprint. Corrected date: *5 de noviembre de 1881.* Gen. L. Mansilla at left, "Raphael's Angel" at center, open law book at right. Back: Brown. Arms at center. Overprint: With circular 1885 revalidation on face. Printer: ABNC. Proof.	—	—	—
S772 50 Pesos			
1.5.1885. Corrected date: *5 de noviembre de 1881.* Overprint: With circular 1885 revalidation on face. Printer: ABNC. Reported not confirmed.	—	—	—

Banco Provincial de Salta

1884 Issue

#S786-S789 w/ovpt: *Ley 14 Octubre 1885* on face.

S786 1 Peso	Good	Fine	XF
1.1.1884. Black on green underprint. Cow and ram at center. Back: Green. Overprint: *Ley 14 Octubre 1885* on face. Printer: G&D.			
a. Issued note.	100.	300.	—
b. Cancelled, perforated: *PAGADO.*	125.	350.	—

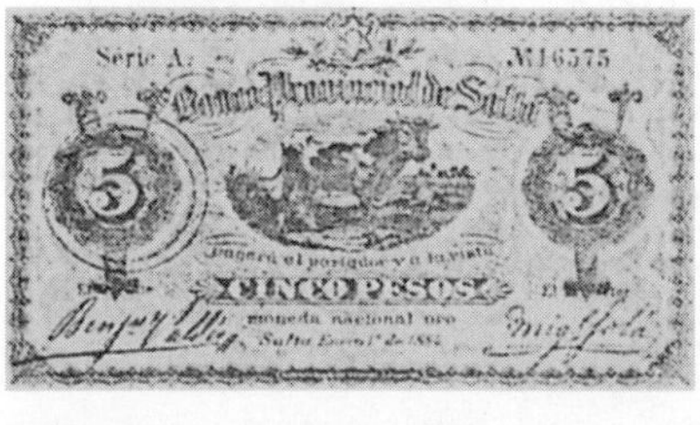

S787 5 Pesos — Good 250. | Fine 750. | XF —
1.1.1884. Black on rose and light blue underprint. Cows at center. Back: Red. Overprint: *Ley 14 Octubre 1885* on face. Printer: G&D.

S788 10 Pesos — Good — | Fine — | XF —
1.1.1884. Man with horse at right. Overprint: *Ley 14 Octubre 1885* on face. Printer: G&D. Proof.

S789 20 Pesos — Good — | Fine — | XF —
1.1.1884. Overprint: *Ley 14 Octubre 1885* on face. Printer: G&D. Reported not confirmed.

#S791-S794 not assigned.

Ley de Octubre 30 de 1891; 1899 Issue

S796 1 Peso — Good 40.00 | Fine 85.00 | XF 200.
25.7.1899. Black on brown underprint. Gen. A. de Arenales at left, provincial arms at upper center. Back: Orange. Cow's head at left and right, plantation and field at center.

1903, 1907 Renovacion Provisional Issue

S797 1 Peso — Good 75.00 | Fine 150. | XF 300.
1903 (- old date 25.7.1899). Overprint: Black; *RENOVACION AÑO 1903* on back of #S796.

S797A 1 Peso — Good 75.00 | Fine 150. | XF 300.
1907 (-old date 25.7.1899). Overprint: Black; *RENOVACION ANO 1907* on back of #S796.

Banco Provincial de Santa Fé

1874 First Issue

S798 5 Centavos Fuertes — Good — | Fine — | XF —
1.9.1874. BlaCK. Sheep at lower left, arms at upper center. Printer: Litografia E. Fleuti, Rosario.

S799 10 Centavos Fuertes — Good — | Fine — | XF —
1.9.1874. Blue. Arms at top center, deer at right. Printer: Litografia E. Fleuti, Rosario.

S800 20 Centavos Fuertes — Good — | Fine — | XF —
1.9.1874. Blue. Horse at left, arms at top center. Printer: Litografia E. Fleuti, Rosario.

S801 37-1/2 Centavos Fuertes — Good — | Fine — | XF —
1.9.1874. Arms at top center, cow at right. Printer: Litografia E. Fleuti, Rosario.

S802 1 Peso Fuerte — Good — | Fine — | XF —
1.9.1874. Black on green underprint. Plowman at right. Printer: Litografia E. Fleuti, Rosario.

1874 Second Issue

S804 1 Real Plata Boliviana — Good 50.00 | Fine 100. | XF 200.
1.11.1874. Black. Horses at lower left, provincial arms at center. Rosario issue. Uniface. Printer: *Lito E. Fleuti Rosario.*

S805 1 Real Boliviano — Good — | Fine — | XF —
1.11.1874. Horses at lower left, provincial arms at center. Santa Fe issue. Uniface. Paper: Rose. Printer: *Lito E. Fleuti Rosario.*

S806 4 Reales Bolivianos — Good — | Fine — | XF —
1.11.1874. Black. Arms at center, puma at right. Rosario issue.

S807 4 Reales Bolivianos — Good — | Fine — | XF —
1.11.1874. Black. Arms at center, puma at right. Paper: Rose. Santa Fe issue.

1874 Second Issue

S808 1 Peso Boliviano — Good — | Fine — | XF —
1.11.1874. Black on yellow-ochre paper. Farmer plowing with oxen at left, arms at top center. Back: Brown. Rosario issue.

S809 1 Peso Boliviano — Good — | Fine — | XF —
1.11.1874. Black on green underprint. Farmer plowing with oxen at left, arms at top center. Back: Blue. Santa Fe issue.

S810 10 Pesos Bolivianos — Good — | Fine — | XF —
1.11.1874. Black. Steam train at upper left, arms at top center, ship at right. Rosario issue.

S811 10 Pesos Bolivianos — Good — | Fine — | XF —
1.11.1874. Black on yellow underprint. Steam train at upper left, arms at top center, ship at right. Back: Violet. Santa Fe issue.

1875 First Issue

S811A 50 Centavos Plata Boliviana — Good — | Fine — | XF —
1.1.1875. Black on salmon underprint. Provincial arms at lower left, horse at upper center, child at lower right. Series A; B. Printer: ABNC. Rosario issue.

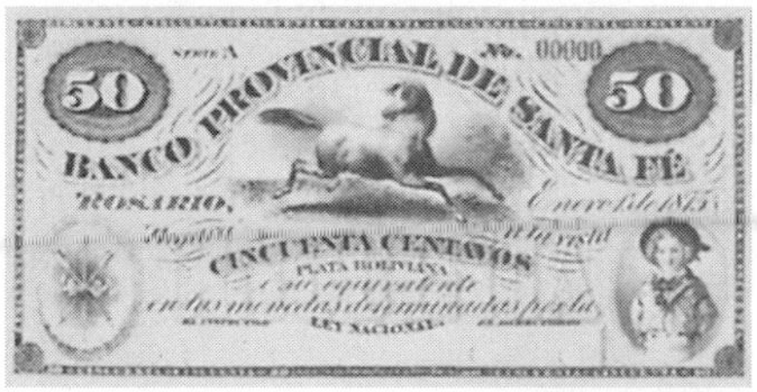

S812 50 Centavos Plata Boliviana
1.1.1875. Black on yellow underprint. Provincial arms at lower left, horse at upper center, child at lower right. Series A; B. Printer: ABNC. Santa Fe issue.

	Good	Fine	XF
a. Issued note.	200.	600.	—
p. Proof.	—	—	—
s. Specimen.	—	—	—

S813 1 Peso Plata Boliviana — Good — | Fine — | XF —
1.1.1875. Black on green underprint. Portrait child at left, farmer with horse plowing at center, provincial arms at right. Series A; B. Back: Green. Printer: ABNC. Rosario issue.

S814 1 Peso Plata Boliviana — Good — | Fine — | XF —
1.1.1875. Black on orange underprint. Farmer with pig at left, steam tractor at center, provincial arms at right. Series A; B. Back: Orange. Printer: ABNC. Santa Fe issue.

S814A 5 Pesos Plata Boliviana — Good — | Fine — | XF —
1.1.1875. Black on orange underprint. Farmer with pig at left, steam tractor at center, provincial arms at right. Back: Orange. Printer: ABNC. Rosario issue. Proof.

S815 5 Pesos Plata Boliviana	Good	Fine	XF
1.1.1875. Black on green underprint. Farmer with pig at left, steam tractor at center, provincial arms at right. Series A; B. Printer: ABNC. Santa Fe issue.	—	—	—

S816 10 Pesos Plata Boliviana	Good	Fine	XF
1.1.1875. Black on green underprint. Provincial arms at left, gaucho and ostrich at center, J. B. Alberdi at right. Series A; B. Back: Green. Printer: ABNC. Rosario issue.	—	—	—

S817 20 Pesos Plata Boliviana	Good	Fine	XF
1.1.1875. Sheep at lower left, seated allegorical woman at center, General E. Lopez at lower right. Series A. Back: Brown. Steam locomotive at center. Printer: ABNC. Rosario issue.	—	—	—
S818 50 Pesos Plata Boliviana			
1.1.1875. Black on maroon underprint. Dog at left, gauchos roping steer at upper center, G. Urquiza at right. Series A. Back: Maroon. Cow's head at center. Printer: ABNC. Rosario issue.	—	—	—

1875 Second Issue

S819 1/2 Real Plata Boliviana	Good	Fine	XF
1.1.1875. Provincial arms at left, Liberty at right. Printer: E. Fleuti or D. Boldt.			
a. Handwritten signature. Black serial #.	—	—	—
b. Stamped signature, black or red serial #.	—	—	—

S820 1 Real Plata Boliviana	Good	Fine	XF
1875 (1.11.1874). Black. Horses at lower left, provincial arms at center. Like #S804 but slightly narrower shield of arms, ornament added to left of *SERIE UNA* at top, and imprint changed to *Lito A Vapor Fleuti Rosari* Printer: E. Fleuti or D. Boldt.	60.00	150.	500.

S821 10 Pesos Plata Boliviana	Good	Fine	XF
1.1.1875. Black on green underprint. Provincial arms at upper left, vaqueros driving cattle at upper center, dog with pheasant at lower right. Back: Green. Printer: Fleuti, Rosario.			
a. Issued note.	125.	250.	750.
r. Remainder.	—	—	—

1875 Third Issue

#S822-S824 are dated 1875 but were actually contracted for and issued in 1881.

S822 1 Peso Plata Boliviana	Good	Fine	XF
1.1.1875. Black on blue underprint. Portrait child at left, farmer with horse plowing at center, provincial arms at right. Series C. Back: Blue. Printer: A. Pech, Buenos Aires. Rosario issue.	125.	500.	—
S823 1 1/2 Pesos = 12 Reales Plata Boliviana			
1.1.1875. Child at left, cattle at center, provincial arms at right. Series A. Printer: A. Pech, Buenos Aires. Rosario issue. Specimen.	—	—	—
S824 2 Pesos Plata Boliviana			
1.1.1875. Black on brown underprint. Provincial arms at left, seated woman at center, dog at right. Series A. Back: Brown. Printer: A. Pech, Buenos Aires. Rosario issue.			
a. Issued note.	—	—	—
b. Stamped: *SUCURSAL* 4 times on back (for Santa Fé).	—	—	—

NOTE: #S822-S824 were stamped w/designation for Santa Fé as needed, on the back.

1881 Issue

S825 1 Real Plata Boliviana	Good	Fine	XF
1.1.1881. Black. Standing woman with basket and cornucopia at left, provincial arms at lower right. Uniface. Printer: Fleuti (Rosario).	125.	250.	—

1882 Issue

All notes of this issue are dated at Rosario but some notes destined for Santa Fe have that city name in red overprint on face. Issues for Rosario and Santa Fé come without or with overprint: *Ley 14 Octubre 1885.*

S826 1 Peso

1.1.1882. Black on light brown underprint. Provincial arms at left, vaqueros driving cattle at center, portrait girl at right. Back: Brown. Printer: ABNC. Issued at Rosario.

	Good	Fine	XF
a. Without overprint.	100.	225.	—
b. Overprint: *Ley 14 Octubre 1885.*	100.	225.	—

S827 1 1/2 Pesos

1.1.1882. Black on green underprint. Provincial arms at left, horse and dogs at center, gaucho at right. Back: Green. Printer: ABNC.

	Good	Fine	XF
a. Without overprint.	150.	400.	—
b. Overprint: *Ley 14 Octubre 1885.*	125.	500.	—

S828 5 Pesos

1.1.1882. Black on blue underprint. Gaucho at lower left, factory at center, provincial arms at right. Back: Blue. Printer: ABNC. Issued at Rosario.

	Good	Fine	XF
a. Without overprint.	250.	650.	—
b. Overprint: *Ley 14 Octubre 1885.*	250.	650.	—
s. Specimen.	—	—	—

S829 10 Pesos

1.1.1882. Black on rose underprint. J. B. Alberdi at left, gaucho on horseback, Indian on food, and animals a Back: Red. Printer: ABNC. Issued at Rosario.

	Good	Fine	XF
a. Without overprint.	250.	750.	—
b. Overprint: *Ley 14 Octubre 1885.*	250.	750.	—
p. Proof back, green.	—	—	—

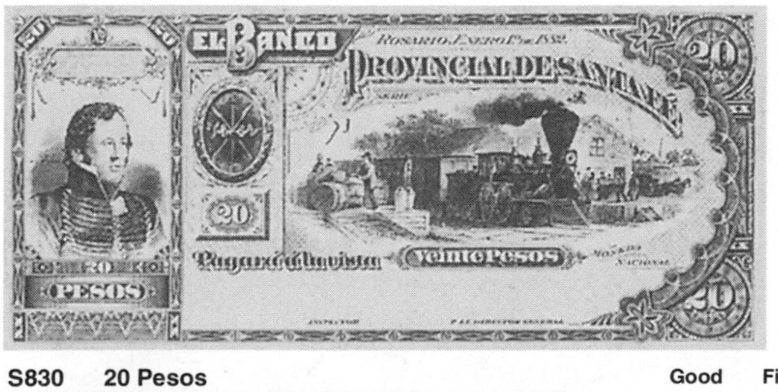

S830 20 Pesos

1.1.1882. Black on ochre underprint. Portrait Gen. E. Lopez at left, provincial arms at left center, steam freight train at center right. Back: Ochre. Printer: ABNC. Issued at Rosario.

	Good	Fine	XF
a. Without overprint. Rare.	—	—	—
b. Overprint: *Ley 14 Octubre 1885.* Rare.	—	—	—
s. Specimen.	—	—	—

S830A 50 Pesos

1.1.1882. Black on orange underprint. Provincial arms and allegorical woman with scales at left, portrait Urquiza at right. Series A. Back: Orange. Printer: ABNC. Proof.

Good	Fine	XF
—	—	—

S830C 200 Pesos

1.1.1882. Black on dark brown underprint. Seated allegorical woman at left, Raphael's Angel at upper center, provincial arms at right. Series A. Back: Dark brown. Seated allegorical woman with sheep at center. Printer: ABNC. Proof.

Good	Fine	XF
—	—	—

S830D 500 Pesos

1.1.1882. Black on brown underprint. Seated allegorical woman ("Literature No. 2") at left, and upper center, griffin at left and right of provincial arms at bottom center, men in harbor scene at right. Series A. Back: Brown. Horse at center. Printer: ABNC. Proof.

Good	Fine	XF
—	—	—

S831 1 Peso

1.1.1882. Black on light brown underprint. Provincial arms at left, vaqueros driving cattle at center, portrait girl at right. Back: Brown. Overprint: Red *Santa Fe* on face.

	Good	Fine	XF
a. Without overprint.	100.	200.	—
b. Overprint: *Ley 14 Octubre 1885.*	100.	200.	—

S832 1 1/2 Pesos

1.1.1882. Black on green underprint. Provincial arms at left, horse and dogs at center, gaucho at right. Back: Green. Overprint: Red *Santa Fe* on face.

Good	Fine	XF
—	—	—

S833 5 Pesos

1.1.1882. Black on blue underprint. Gaucho at lower left, factory at center, provincial arms at right. Back: Blue. Overprint: Red *Santa Fe* on face. Printer: ABNC.

	Good	Fine	XF
a. Without overprint.	250.	600.	—
b. Overprint: *Ley 14 Octubre 1885.*	250.	600.	—

S834 10 Pesos

1.1.1882. Black on rose underprint. J.B. Alberdi at left, gaucho on horseback, Indian on food, and animals at center, provincial arms at right. Back: Red. Overprint: Red *Santa Fe* on face.

	Good	Fine	XF
a. Without overprint.	300.	750.	—
b. Overprint: *Ley 14 Octubre 1885.*	300.	750.	—

S835 20 Pesos

1.1.1882. Black on ochre underprint. Portrait Gen. E. Lopez at left, provincial arms at left center, steam freight train at center right. Back: Ochre. Overprint: Red *Santa Fe* on face.

	Good	Fine	XF
a. Without overprint. Rare.	—	—	—
b. Overprint: *Ley 14 Octubre 1885.* Rare.	—	—	—

A WORD ON DATE RANGES

Often date ranges or specific dates are listed. These have been observed or reported by our contributors. If a note is outside the published range, it only means that it is a newly reported date, and not necessarily worthy of a premium value.

Banco Provincial de Tucumán

1888 Issue

#S841-S846 all come with overprint: *Ley 14 Octubre 1885* on face.

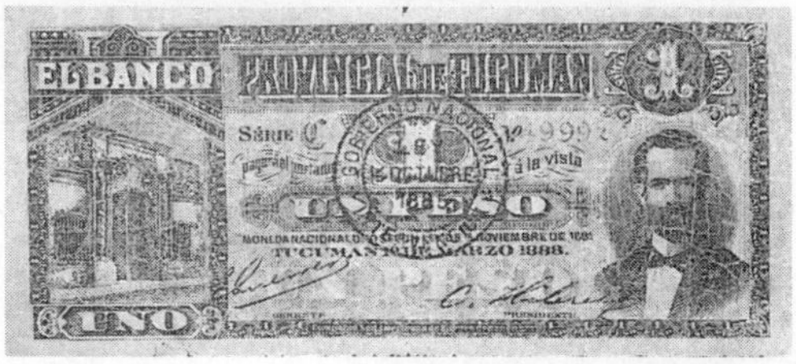

		Good	Fine	XF
S841	**1 Peso** 1.3.1888. Black on ochre underprint. House of Tucumán at left, Gov. L. Quinteros at lower right. Back: Maroon. Overprint: *Ley 14 Octubre 1885* on face. Printer: CSABB, Buenos Aires.	75.00	250.	600.

		Good	Fine	XF
S842	**2 Pesos** 1.3.1888. Black on rose underprint. Gov. Col. M. Paz at upper center. Back: Red. Overprint: *Ley 14 Octubre 1885* on face. Printer: CSABB, Buenos Aires.	125.	500.	—
S843	**5 Pesos** 1.3.1888. J. B. Alberdi at left, steam train at center. Overprint: *Ley 14 Octubre 1885* on face. Printer: CSABB, Buenos Aires.	—	—	—

		Good	Fine	XF
S844	**10 Pesos** 1.3.1888. Black on ochre and light blue underprint. N. Avellaneda at left, steam train leaving tunnel at center. Overprint: *Ley 14 Octubre 1885* on face. Printer: CSABB, Buenos Aires.	—	—	—

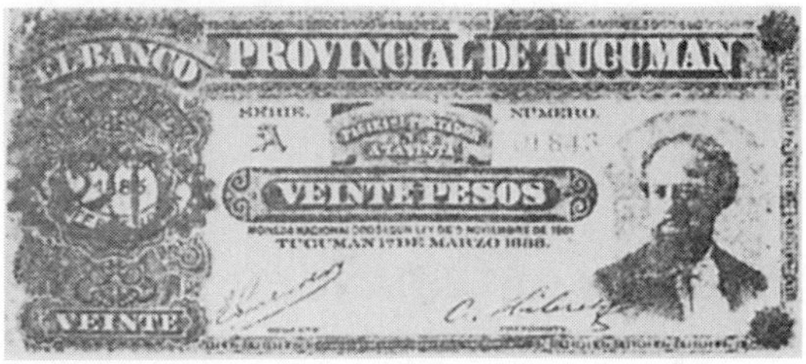

		Good	Fine	XF
S845	**20 Pesos** 1.3.1888. Man at lower right. Overprint: *Ley 14 Octubre 1885* on face. Printer: CSABB, Buenos Aires.	—	—	—
S846	**50 Pesos** 1.3.1888. Overprint: *Ley 14 Octubre 1885* on face. Reported not confirmed.	—	—	—

Section III

Bancos Nacionales Garantidos

(Guaranteed National Banks)

In a further effort at unifying the currency, Argentina passed a law on November 3, 1887, stating that any corporation or society with capital of 250,000 pesos in national money could function as a bank and issue notes guaranteed by national public funds. Such notes would be legal in all parts of the country.

Not all denominations were printed by all banks participating. In a few instances notes were prepared for issue but withheld from circulation and later destroyed. All notes of any given denomination were uniform except for bank name and series designation. Printer: BWC.

Descriptions of each denomination are given below:

1 PESO 1.1.1888. Black on pink unpt. Portr. Adm. G. Brown at l., arms at ctr., 3 cherubs at r. Back rose; allegory of Arts and Sciences.

2 PESOS 1.1.1888. Black on grayish brown unpt. 2 cherubs and anchor at l., arms at upper ctr., portr. Gen. C. de Alvear at r. Back maroon; allegory of Commerce.

5 PESOS 1.1.1888. Black on green and rose unpt. Portr. Dr. D. Sarsfield and allegorical woman at l., arms at ctr. Back green; allegory of Science.

10 PESOS 1.1.1888. Black on blue unpt. Portr. Dr. J. Roca at l., arms at ctr., cherub and cow at r. Back blue; fruit gathering.

20 PESOS 1.1.1888. Black on brown and yellow unpt. Portr. Dr. W. Pacheco at l., arms at upper ctr., winged Victory and cherubs at r. Back maroon; vaqueros roping cattle.

50 PESOS 1.1.1888. Black on blue and yellow unpt. Arms at ctr., portr. Dr. M. Celman and mythological figure w/trident at r. Back green; ranch working.

100 PESOS 1.1.1888. Black on sepia unpt. Portr. Dr. M. Moreno at l., arms at upper ctr., allegorical woman at r. Back maroon; teaching Indians.

200 PESOS 1.1.1888. Black on sepia unpt. Allegorical winged woman at l., arms at upper ctr., Portr. Dr. B. Rivadavia at r. Back maroon; horses.

500 PESOS 1.1.1888. Black on m/c unpt. Portr. Gen. J. de San Martin and allagory of Victory w/2 angels at l., arms at str. Back green; allegory of Agriculture and 3 children.

Because of various financial conditions, occurrences and crises, various issues were overprinted with revalidations at certain times. All known ovpt. are listed under their respective banks. The ovpts. appear as follows:

Ley 6 Setiembre 1890

Ley 16 Octubre 1891

Ley 29 Octubre de 1891
(used only on #S1098)

Ley 8 Enero de 1894

Ley 20 de Setiembre de 1897

NOTE: Only those notes w/o any of these ovpt. are issues of the Bancos. All ovpt. notes are in reality issues of the Caja de Conversion.

Banco Alemán Transatlántico

Series 010

		Good	Fine	XF
S1008	**200 Pesos** 1.1.1888. Rare.	—	—	—

Banco Británico de la América del Sud
Series 024

S1020 1000 Pesos	Good	Fine	XF
1.1.1888. Rare.	—	—	—

NOTE: A single example is known of #S1020 and it has only 1 sign. A total of 250 notes of this issue were made.

Banco Buenos Aires
Series 013

S1024 10 Pesos	Good	Fine	XF
1.1.1888. Rare.	—	—	—

S1026 50 Pesos	Good	Fine	XF
1.1.1888. Rare.	—	—	—
S1027 1000 Pesos			
1.1.1888. Rare.	—	—	—

Banco Carabassa
Series ?

S1040 1000 Pesos	Good	Fine	XF
1.1.1888.	—	—	—

NOTE: #S1040 was prepared for issue but not released. All were later destroyed.

Banco Constructor de la Plata
Series ?

S1041 1 Peso	Good	Fine	XF
1.1.1888.	—	—	—
S1043 5 Pesos			
1.1.1888.	—	—	—

NOTE: #S1041 and S1043 were prepared for issue but not released. All were later destroyed.

Banco Frances del Rio de la Plata
Series 020

S1057 100 Pesos	Good	Fine	XF
1.1.1888.	—	—	—

NOTE: #S1057 was prepared for issue but not released. All were later destroyed.

Banco Inglés de Rio de Janeiro
Series 017

S1063 5 Pesos	Good	Fine	XF
1.1.1888.	—	—	—
S1064 10 Pesos			
1.1.1888.	—	—	—
S1065 20 Pesos			
1.1.1888.	—	—	—

NOTE: #S1063-S1065 were prepared for issue but not released. All were later destroyed.

Banco de Italia y Rio de la Plata
Series 017

S1078 200 Pesos	Good	Fine	XF
1.1.1888.	—	—	—

NOTE: #S1078 was prepared for issue but not released. All were later destroyed.

Banco Londres y Rio de la Plata
Series ?

S1090 1000 Pesos	Good	Fine	XF
1.1.1888. Not released and later destroyed.	—	—	—

Banco Nacional
Series 001

S1091 1 Peso	Good	Fine	XF
1.1.1888.			
a. Without overprint.	20.00	50.00	150.
b. Overprint: *Ley 8.1.1894.*	20.00	50.00	150.
c. Overprint: *Ley 20.9.1897.*	20.00	50.00	150.

S1092 2 Pesos	Good	Fine	XF
1.1.1888.			
a. Without overprint.	25.00	75.00	200.
b. Overprint: *Ley 16.10.1891.*	40.00	100.	250.
c. Overprint: *Ley 8.1.1894.*	25.00	75.00	200.

S1093 5 Pesos	Good	Fine	XF
1.1.1888.			
a. Without overprint.	40.00	100.	250.
b. Overprint: *Ley 6.9.1890.*	50.00	125.	300.
c. Overprint: *Ley 16.10.1891.*	50.00	125.	300.
d. Overprint: *Ley 8.1.1894.*	40.00	100.	250.

S1094 10 Pesos	Good	Fine	XF
1.1.1888.			
a. Without overprint.	50.00	150.	325.
b. Overprint: *Ley 6.9.1890.*	75.00	200.	450.
c. Overprint:*Ley 16.10.1891.*	75.00	200.	450.
d. Overprint:*Ley 8.1.1894.*	50.00	150.	325.
S1095 20 Pesos			
1.1.1888.			
a. Without overprint.	100.	350.	—
b. Overprint: *Ley 6.9.1890.*	125.	400.	—

S1096 50 Pesos	Good	Fine	XF
1.1.1888.			
a. Without overprint.	200.	600.	—
b. Overprint: *Ley 6.9.1890.*	250.	800.	—

S1097 100 Pesos	Good	Fine	XF
1.1.1888.			
a. Without overprint.	250.	1000.	—
b. Overprint: *Ley 6.9.1890.*	300.	1100.	—
c. Overprint: *Ley 16.10.1891.*	350.	1250.	—
d. Overprint: *Ley 8.1.1894.*	350.	1250.	—

S1098 200 Pesos	Good	Fine	XF
1.1.1888.			
a. Without overprint.	—	—	—
b. Overprint: *Ley 6.9.1890.*	—	—	—
c. Overprint: *Ley 16.10.1891.*	—	—	—
d. Overprint: *Ley 29.10.1891.*	—	—	—
s. Specimen.	—	—	—

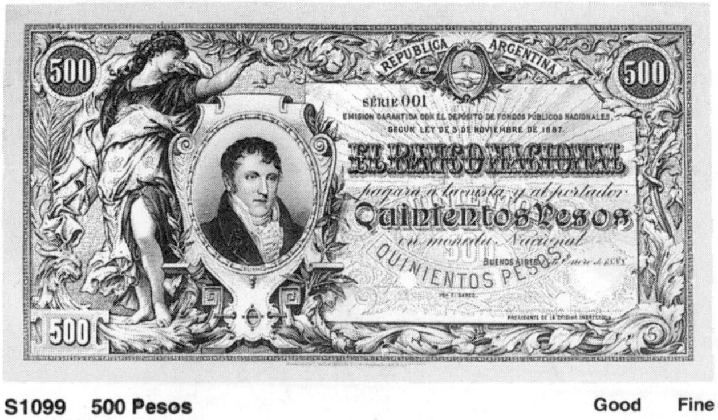

S1099 500 Pesos	Good	Fine	XF
1.1.1888.			
a. Without overprint.	—	—	—
b. Overprint: *Ley 6.9.1890.*	—	—	—
c. Overprint: *Ley 16.10.1891.*	—	—	—

S1100 1000 Pesos	Good	Fine	XF
1.1.1888.			
a. Without overprint.	—	—	—
b. Overprint: *Ley 6.9.1890.*	—	—	—
c. Overprint: *Ley 16.10.1891.*	—	—	—

Banco de la Provincia de Buenos Aires

Series 002

	Good	Fine	XF
S1101 1 Peso			
1.1.1888.			
a. Without overprint.	25.00	75.00	125.
b. Overprint: *Ley 8.1.1894.*	40.00	80.00	150.
S1102 2 Pesos			
1.1.1888.			
a. Without overprint.	25.00	75.00	125.
b. Overprint: *Ley 16.10.1891.*	40.00	80.00	150.
c. Overprint: *Ley 8.1.1894.*	25.00	75.00	125.
S1103 5 Pesos			
1.1.1888.			
a. Without overprint.	50.00	100.	250.
b. Overprint: *Ley 6.9.1890.*	75.00	175.	400.
c. Overprint: *Ley 16.10.1891.*	75.00	175.	400.
S1104 10 Pesos			
1.1.1888.			
a. Without overprint.	125.	225.	550.
b. Overprint:*Ley 6.9.1890.*	125.	225.	550.
c. Overprint:*Ley 16.10.1891*	150.	275.	750.
S1105 20 Pesos			
1.1.1888.			
a. Without overprint.	125.	350.	1250.
b. Overprint:*Ley 6.9.1890.*	125.	350.	1250.

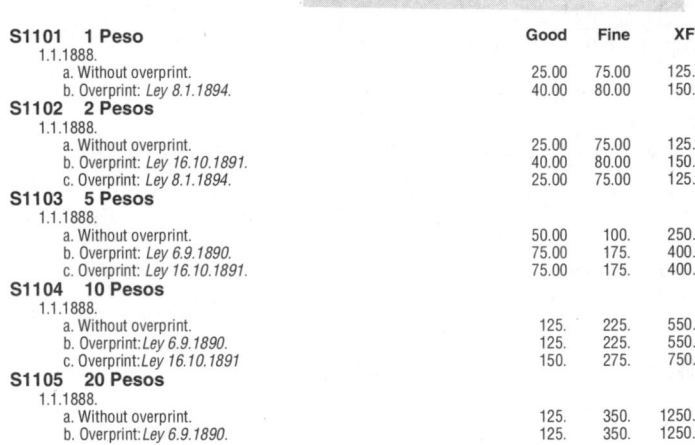

S1106 50 Pesos	Good	Fine	XF
1.1.1888.			
a. Without overprint.	250.	900.	—
b. Overprint: *Ley 6.9.1890.*	300.	1000.	—

S1107 100 Pesos	Good	Fine	XF
1.1.1888.			
a. Without overprint.	300.	1000.	—
b. Overprint: *Ley 6.9.1890.*	350.	1250.	—

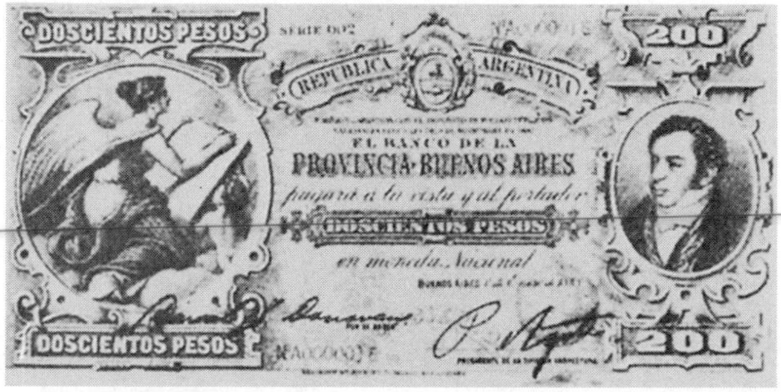

S1108 200 Pesos	Good	Fine	XF
1.1.1888.			
a. Without overprint.	—	—	—
b. Overprint: *Ley 6.9.1890.*	—	—	—

S1109 500 Pesos	Good	Fine	XF
1.1.1888.			
a. Issue note.	—	—	—
b. Reprint. Advertisement on back.	—	—	—

Banco Provincial de Catamarca

Series 014

	Good	Fine	XF
S1111 1 Peso			
1.1.1888.			
a. Without overprint.	25.00	60.00	125.
b. Overprint: *Ley 20.9.1897.*	40.00	75.00	150.
S1112 2 Pesos			
1.1.1888.			
a. Without overprint.	75.00	125.	300.
b. Overprint: *Ley 8.1.1894.*	50.00	100.	225.
S1113 5 Pesos			
1.1.1888.			
a. Without overprint.	100.	200.	400.
b. Overprint: *Ley 16.10.1891.*	125.	250.	600.
S1114 10 Pesos			
1.1.1888.	175.	400.	850.
S1115 20 Pesos			
1.1.1888.	200.	600.	—
S1116 50 Pesos			
1.1.1888.	—	—	—

Banco Provincial de Córdoba

Series 004

S1121 1 Peso	Good	Fine	XF
1.1.1888.			
a. Without overprint.	25.00	75.00	150.
b. Overprint: *Ley 8.1.1894.*	25.00	75.00	150.

S1122 2 Pesos	Good	Fine	XF
1.1.1888.			
a. Without overprint.	25.00	75.00	150.
b. Overprint: *Ley 16.10.1891.*	50.00	100.	225.
c. Overprint: *Ley 8.1.1894.*	25.00	75.00	150.

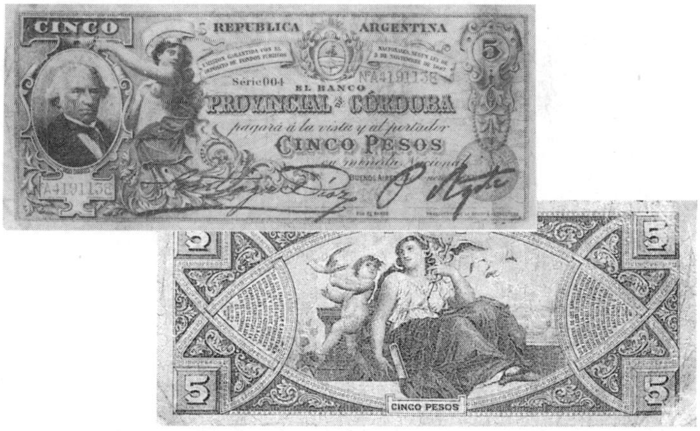

	Good	Fine	XF
S1123 5 Pesos			
1.1.1888.			
a. Without overprint.	50.00	125.	275.
b. Overprint: *Ley 6.9.1890.*	75.00	150.	300.
c. Overprint: *Ley 16.10.1891.*	85.00	175.	350.
S1124 10 Pesos			
1.1.1888.			
a. Without overprint.	150.	300.	650.
b. Overprint: *Ley 16.10.1891.*	200.	350.	750.

	Good	Fine	XF
S1125 20 Pesos			
1.1.1888.	250.	425.	—
S1126 50 Pesos			
1.1.1888.	—	—	—
S1127 100 Pesos			
1.1.1888.	—	—	—
S1128 200 Pesos			
1.1.1888.	—	—	—
S1129 500 Pesos			
1.1.1888.	—	—	—

Banco Provincial de Corrientes

Series 015

	Good	Fine	XF
S1131 1 Peso			
1.1.1888.			
a. Without overprint.	25.00	75.00	150.
b. Overprint: *Ley 8.1.1894.* Reported not confirmed.	—	—	—
c. Overprint: *Ley 20.9.1897.*	20.00	50.00	125.
S1132 2 Pesos			
1.1.1888.			
a. Without overprint.	50.00	125.	250.
b. Overprint: *Ley 16.10.1891.*	75.00	150.	350.
c. Overprint: *Ley 8.1.1894.*	40.00	75.00	175.
S1133 5 Pesos			
1.1.1888.	75.00	150.	400.
S1134 10 Pesos			
1.1.1888.	175.	400.	750.
S1135 20 Pesos			
1.1.1888.	200.	500.	—
S1136 50 Pesos			
1.1.1888.	—	—	—
S1137 100 Pesos			
1.1.1888.	—	—	—

Banco Provincial de Entre Rios

Series 005

	Good	Fine	XF
S1141 1 Peso			
1.1.1888.			
a. Without overprint.	10.00	40.00	125.
b. Overprint: Ley 8.1.1894.	10.00	40.00	125.
c. Overprint: Ley 20.9.1897.	25.00	75.00	150.
S1142 2 Pesos			
1.1.1888.			
a. Without overprint.	40.00	100.	200.
b. Overprint: *Ley 16.10.1891.*	75.00	150.	325.
c. Overprint: *Ley 8.1.1894.*	25.00	75.00	150.
S1143 5 Pesos			
1.1.1888.	75.00	150.	350.
S1144 10 Pesos			
1.1.1888.	100.	200.	450.
S1145 20 Pesos			
1.1.1888.	175.	350.	—
S1146 50 Pesos			
1.1.1888.	—	—	—

Banco Provincial de La Rioja

Series 012

	Good	Fine	XF
S1151 1 Peso			
1.1.1888.			
a. Without overprint.	25.00	75.00	150.
b. Overprint: *Ley 8.1.1894.*	25.00	75.00	150.
S1152 2 Pesos			
1.1.1888.			
a. Without overprint.	40.00	80.00	150.
b. Overprint: *Ley 16.10.1891.*	50.00	100.	200.
c. Overprint: *Ley 8.1.1894.*	25.00	75.00	150.
S1153 5 Pesos			
1.1.1888.	75.00	150.	300.
S1154 10 Pesos			
1.1.1888.			
a. Without overprint.	175.	300.	650.
b. Overprint: *Ley 6.9.1890.*	200.	350.	700.

	Good	Fine	XF
S1155 20 Pesos			
1.1.1888.	250.	550.	—
S1156 50 Pesos			
1.1.1888.	—	—	—
S1157 100 Pesos			
1.1.1888.	—	—	—

Banco de la Provincia de Mendoza

Series 008

	Good	Fine	XF
S1161 1 Peso			
1.1.1888.			
a. Without overprint.	25.00	75.00	150.
b. Overprint: *Ley 20.9.1897.*	25.00	75.00	150.
S1162 2 Pesos			
1.1.1888.			
a. Without overprint.	40.00	100.	200.
b. Overprint: *Ley 6.9.1890.*	100.	200.	400.
c. Overprint: *Ley 8.1.1894.*	100.	200.	400.
S1163 5 Pesos			
1.1.1888.			
a. Without overprint.	100.	200.	400.
b. Overprint: *Ley 6.9.1890.*	125.	250.	600.
S1164 10 Pesos			
1.1.1888.			
a. Without overprint.	100.	225.	550.
b. Overprint: *Ley 6.9.1890.*	175.	350.	—
c. Overprint: *Ley 16.10.1891.*	175.	350.	—
S1165 20 Pesos			
1.1.1888.			
a. Without overprint.	200.	425.	—
b. Overprint: *Ley 6.9.1890.*	200.	450.	—

Banco Provincial de Salta
Series 006

	Good	Fine	XF
S1171 1 Peso			
1.1.1888.			
a. Without overprint.	25.00	50.00	125.
b. Overprint: *Ley 8.1.1894.*	25.00	50.00	125.
c. Overprint: *Ley 20.9.1897.*	25.00	50.00	125.
S1172 2 Pesos			
1.1.1888.			
a. Without overprint.	40.00	75.00	150.
b. Overprint: *Ley 16.10.1891.*	50.00	100.	275.
c. Overprint: *Ley 8.1.1894.*	40.00	75.00	150.
S1173 5 Pesos			
1.1.1888.	75.00	125.	300.
S1174 10 Pesos			
1.1.1888.	100.	200.	400.
S1175 20 Pesos			
1.1.1888.	175.	400.	—

Banco Provincial de San Juan
Series 011

	Good	Fine	XF
S1181 1 Peso			
1.1.1888.			
a. Without overprint.	25.00	75.00	150.
b. Overprint: *Ley 8.1.1894.*	25.00	75.00	150.
c. Overprint: *Ley 20.9.1897.*	40.00	75.00	175.
S1182 2 Pesos			
1.1.1888.			
a. Without overprint.	40.00	100.	200.
b. Overprint: *Ley 16.10.1891.*	50.00	125.	275.
c. Overprint: *Ley 8.1.1894.*	40.00	75.00	225.
S1183 5 Pesos			
1.1.1888.			
a. Without overprint.	100.	200.	400.
b. Overprint: *Ley 6.9.1890.*	100.	200.	425.
S1184 10 Pesos			
1.1.1888.			
a. Without overprint.	175.	300.	650.
b. Overprint: *Ley 6.9.1890.*	175.	325.	700.
c. Overprint: *Ley 16.10.1891.*	225.	600.	—
S1185 20 Pesos			
1.1.1888.	225.	600.	—
S1186 50 Pesos			
1.1.1888.			
a. Without overprint.	—	—	—
b. Overprint: *Ley 6.9.1890.*	—	—	—

Banco Provincial de Santa Fé
Series 003

	Good	Fine	XF
S1191 1 Peso			
1.1.1888.			
a. Without overprint.	25.00	75.00	150.
b. Overprint: *Ley 20.9.1897.*	20.00	50.00	125.

	Good	Fine	XF
S1192 2 Pesos			
1.1.1888.			
a. Without overprint.	25.00	75.00	150.
b. Overprint: *Ley 8.1.1894.*	40.00	75.00	150.
S1193 5 Pesos			
1.1.1888.	50.00	125.	350.

	Good	Fine	XF
S1194 10 Pesos			
1.1.1888.			
a. Without overprint.	75.00	200.	500.
b. Overprint: *Ley 16.10.1891.*	100.	225.	500.
S1195 20 Pesos			
1.1.1888.	200.	400.	—
S1196 50 Pesos			
1.1.1888.			
a. Without overprint.	—	—	—
b. Overprint: *Ley 6.9.1890.*	—	—	—
S1197 100 Pesos			
1.1.1888.	—	—	—
S1198 200 Pesos			
1.1.1888.	—	—	—
S1199 500 Pesos			
1.1.1888.	—	—	—
S1200 1000 Pesos			
1.1.1888.	—	—	—

Banco de la Provincia de Santiago del Estero
Series 009

	Good	Fine	XF
S1201 1 Peso			
1.1.1888.			
a. Without overprint.	40.00	75.00	150.
b. Overprint: *Ley 8.1.1894.*	40.00	75.00	150.

	Good	Fine	XF
S1202 2 Pesos			
1.1.1888.			
a. Without overprint.	50.00	100.	175.
b. Overprint: *Ley 16.10.1891.*	50.00	125.	275.
c. Overprint: *Ley 8.1.1894.*	40.00	75.00	150.
S1203 5 Pesos			
1.1.1888.			
a. Without overprint.	100.	225.	550.
b. Overprint: *Ley 6.9.1890.*	125.	250.	600.
S1204 10 Pesos			
1.1.1888.	200.	425.	—
S1205 20 Pesos			
1.1.1888.	350.	650.	—
S1206 50 Pesos			
1.1.1888.	—	—	—
S1207 100 Pesos			
1.1.1888.	—	—	—

Banco Provincial de Tucumán

Series 007

	Good	Fine	XF
S1211 1 Peso			
1.1.1888.			
a. Without overprint.	25.00	75.00	150.
b. Overprint: *Ley 20.9.1897.*	40.00	75.00	150.

	Good	Fine	XF
S1212 2 Pesos			
1.1.1888.			
a. Without overprint.	40.00	75.00	150.
b. Overprint: *Ley 8.1.1894.*	40.00	100.	200.
S1213 5 Pesos			
1.1.1888.	75.00	175.	400.
S1214 10 Pesos			
1.1.1888.			
a. Without overprint.	125.	250.	600.
b. Overprint: *Ley 6.9.1890.*	150.	300.	650.
S1215 20 Pesos			
1.1.1888.	200.	400.	—
S1216 50 Pesos			
1.1.1888.	—	—	—

Banco de San Luis

Series 016

	Good	Fine	XF
S1221 1 Peso			
1.1.1888.			
a. Without overprint.	40.00	100.	200.
b. Overprint: *Ley 8.1.1894.*	40.00	100.	200.
S1222 2 Pesos			
1.1.1888.			
a. Without overprint.	75.00	150.	300.
b. Overprint: *Ley 16.10.1891.*	100.	200.	500.
c. Overprint: *Ley 8.1.1894.*	75.00	150.	350.
S1223 5 Pesos			
1.1.1888.	100.	300.	800.
S1224 10 Pesos			
1.1.1888.	200.	350.	900.
S1225 20 Pesos			
1.1.1888.	300.	750.	—
S1226 50 Pesos			
1.1.1888.	—	—	—

Nuevo Banco Italiano

Series ?

	Good	Fine	XF
S1236 50 Pesos			
1.1.1888.	—	—	—
S1237 100 Pesos			
1.1.1888.	—	—	—

NOTE: #S1236 and S1237 were prepared for issue but not released. All were later destroyed.

Section IV

PROVINCIAL

Province of Catamarca

1849 Issue

	Good	Fine	XF
S1251 1 Real			
June 1849. Black. Arms at right. With text: *Mueran los salvajes Unitarios* at left.	—	—	—

Province of Córdoba

1829 Issue

	Good	Fine	XF
S1263 10 Pesos			
1829. Black. Handwritten signature.	—	—	—

NOTE: Issues for 1853 and 1858 require conformation.

Province of Corrientes

1826 Issue

	Good	Fine	XF
S1281 1 Peso			
30.5.1826.	—	—	—

1827 Issue

	Good	Fine	XF
S1291 1 Peso			
29.5.1827.	—	—	—
S1292 2 Pesos			
29.5.1827.	—	—	—

1841 Treasury Notes Issue

	Good	Fine	XF
S1301 1 Peso			
23.7.1841. .	—	—	—
S1302 5 Pesos			
23.7.1841.	—	—	—
S1304 20 Pesos			
23.7.1841.	—	—	—

1843 Issue

	Good	Fine	XF
S1311 1 Peso			
1843. Black. Back: Without date stamping.	—	—	—
S1312 1 Peso			
1843. Back: Date stamping: *1843*	—	—	—
S1313 1 Peso			
1843. Stamped arms at center. Longer text than on #S1311. Back: Date stamping: *1843.*	—	—	—

1852 Issue

	Good	Fine	XF
S1321 1 Real 1852. Black. Goat at upper left and right, stamped arms at center. Text: *VIVA LA CONFEDERACION.*	—	—	—

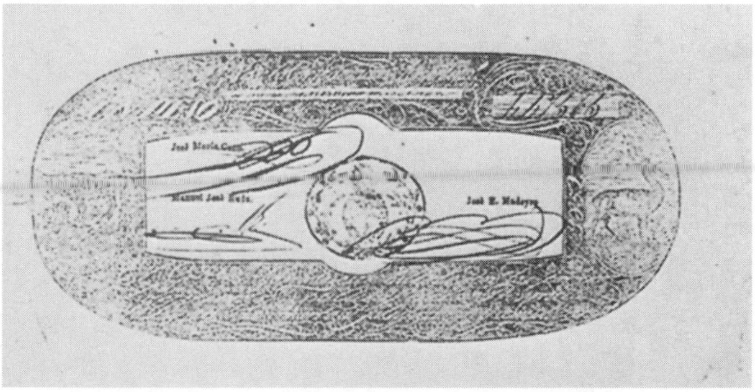

	Good	Fine	XF
S1324 1 Peso 1852. Black. Calf at left, deer at right. Text: *VIVA LA CONFEDERACION.*	—	—	—
S1325 5 Pesos 1852. Black. Horse and ship. Text: *VIVA LA CONFEDERACION.*	—	—	—

1857 Issue

	Good	Fine	XF
S1335 5 Pesos 1857. Black. Eagle and Ceres head.	—	—	—
S1336 10 Pesos 1857. Black.	—	—	—

1861 Issue

	Good	Fine	XF
S1344 4 Reales 1861. Black. Issued for the Casa de Moneda and Banco de la Provincia de Corrientes.	—	—	—

	Good	Fine	XF
S1345 1 Peso 1861. Arms at top center. Issued for the Junta de Administración de la Casa de Moneda.	—	—	—
S1348 20 Pesos 1861. Issued for the Junta de Administración de la Casa de Moneda.	—	—	—

NOTE: An 1865 dated issue requires confirmation.

Province of Entre-Rios

1826 Issue

	Good	Fine	XF
S1361 1 Real 11.10.1826. Rare.	—	—	—

1868 Issue

	Good	Fine	XF
S1366 2 Pesos 1868.	—	—	—

1876 Issue

#S1374-S1375 issued at Concepción del Uruguay.

	Good	Fine	XF
S1372 10 Centavos 1.3.1876. Black. Girl at left.	—	—	—
S1373 20 Centavos 1.3.1876. Black. Shield at upper left, male portrait at lower left.	—	—	—

	Good	Fine	XF
S1374 50 Centavos 1.3.1876. Brown and black. Portrait woman's head at left and right. Uniface. Printer: Lit. San Martín.	—	—	—

	Good	Fine	XF
S1375 1 Peso Fuerte 1.3.1876. Black. Cat's head at upper left, arms at lower center, star with value at upper right. Back: Blue. Printer: Lit. San Martín.	—	—	—

Province of Mendoza

Law of 21.6.1839

	Good	Fine	XF
S1381 1/4 Real ND.	—	—	—

Province of San Luis

1871 Issue

	Good	Fine	XF
S1394 4 Reales 27.9.1871. Red-orange.	—	—	—
S1395 1 Peso 27.9.1871.	—	—	—
S1396 5 Pesos 27.9.1871.	—	—	—

Province of Santa Fé

Law of 23.8.1823

	Good	Fine	XF
S1401 1 Peso = 8 Reales	—	—	—
S1402 2 Pesos 1 Real = 17 Reales	—	—	—
S1403 4 Pesos 2 Reales = 34 Reales	—	—	—

Province of Santiago del Estero

1870 Issue

	Good	Fine	XF
S1411 50 Pesos 5.83.1870.	—	—	—

1876 Issue

	Good	Fine	XF
S1416 5 Centavos Fuertes 30.9.1876. Uniface. Paper: Blue-green. Printer: G. Kraft.	75.00	150.	—
S1418 20 Centavos Fuertes 30.9.1876. Black. Jaguars at upper center. Uniface. Printer: G. Kraft.	100.	225.	—

	Good	Fine	XF
S1420 1 Peso Fuerte 30.9.1876. Blue. Dog at top center. Uniface. Paper: Buff. Printer: G. Kraft.	100.	225.	—

	Good	Fine	XF
S1421 5 Pesos Fuertes 1876. Red-orange. Group of people at center.	—	—	—

Section V

Regional and Private Banks

Banco Argentino

1871-73 Concordia Issues

	Good	Fine	XF
S1451 1/2 Real Plata Boliviana 187x. Black. Dog's head at center. Uniface. Paper: Green paper.	40.00	125.	—

#S1456-S1463 back green. Printer: ABNC.

	Good	Fine	XF
S1456 1/2 Real Plata Boliviana 187x, 1871, 1873. Black on green underprint. Back: Green. Printer: ABNC.	25.00	100.	—
S1457 1 Real Plata Boliviana 1871, 1873. Black on green underprint. Back: Green. Printer: ABNC.	25.00	100.	—

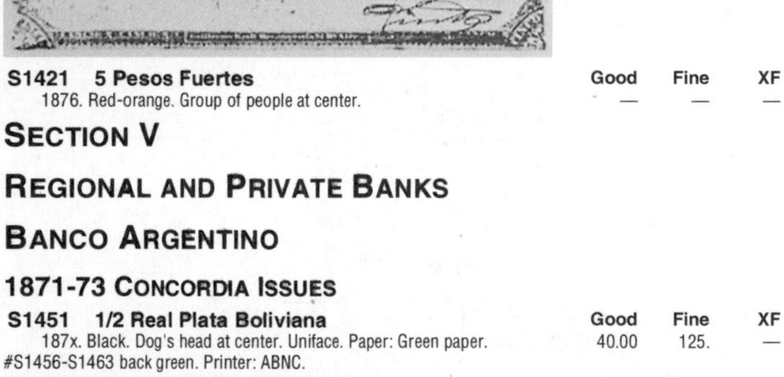

	Good	Fine	XF
S1458 4 Reales Plata Boliviana 1.7.1873. Black on blue underprint. Back: Green. Printer: ABNC.	40.00	125.	—
S1459 1 Peso Plata Boliviana 1.7.1873. Black on green underprint. Back: Green. Printer: ABNC.	40.00	125.	—
S1460 5 Pesos Plata Boliviana 1.7.1873. Black on blue underprint. Back: Green. Printer: ABNC.	25.00	125.	—

	Good	Fine	XF
S1461 10 Pesos Plata Boliviana 1.7.1873. Black on green underprint. Back: Green. Printer: ABNC.	25.00	100.	200.

	Good	Fine	XF
S1463 50 Pesos Plata Boliviana 1.7.1873. Black on green underprint. Back: Green. Printer: ABNC.	40.00	125.	—

Concordia ND Provisional Issue

	Good	Fine	XF
S1466 50 Centavos Fuertes ND (- old date 1.5.1866). Black. Overprint: Vertical *CONCORDIA* at left center on #S1530. Paper: Salmon. Rosario issues overprint: *CONCORDIA*.	40.00	125.	—
S1467 1 Peso Fuerte ND (- old date 1.12.1866). Black. Overprint: Vertical *CONCORDIA* at left and center right on #S1531. Paper: Blue. Rosario issues overprint: *CONCORDIA*.	40.00	125.	—

1871-73 Córdoba Issues

	Good	Fine	XF
S1471 1/2 Real Plata Boliviana 187x. Dog. (Not issued).	40.00	125.	—

	Good	Fine	XF
S1472 1 Real Plata Boliviana 187x. Black. Horse's head at upper left. (Not issued).	25.00	100.	200.
S1473 1/2 Real Plata Boliviana 1871. Woman's head.	40.00	100.	—
S1476 1/2 Real Plata Boliviana 187x; 1872; 1873. Black on brown underprint. Back: Orange. Printer: ABNC.	25.00	75.00	—

	Good	Fine	XF
S1477 1 Real Plata Boliviana 187x; 1872; 1873. Black on brown underprint. Back: Orange. Printer: ABNC.	25.00	75.00	—
S1478 1 Real Plata Boliviana 1.7.1873. Printer: ABNC.	—	—	—
S1479 1 Peso Plata Boliviana 1.7.1873. Black on brown underprint. Back: Gold. Printer: ABNC.	40.00	125.	250.

	Good	Fine	XF
S1481 10 Pesos Plata Boliviana 1.7.1873. Black on gold underprint. Back: Gold. Printer: ABNC.	25.00	75.00	150.
S1482 20 Pesos Plata Boliviana 1.7.1873. Black on brown underprint. Back: Orange. Printer: ABNC.	40.00	150.	—
S1483 50 Pesos Plata Boliviana 1.7.1873. Black on brown underprint. Back: Gold. Printer: ABNC.	40.00	150.	—

1873 Córdoba Peso Fuerte Issue

	Good	Fine	XF
S1486 50 Centavos Fuertes 1.7.1873. Rooster at center.	40.00	150.	—

Gualeguay ND Provisional Issue

	Good	Fine	XF
S1488 1 Peso ND (- old date 1.9.1866). Black. Three winged figures at upper center. Uniface. Overprint: *GUALEGUAY* at upper center. Printer: A. Larsch.	—	—	—

1873 Paraná Plata Boliviana Issues

	Good	Fine	XF
S1491 1/2 Real Plata Boliviana 187x. Gray and black. Dog's head at center. Uniface.	40.00	100.	200.
S1496 1/2 Real Plata Boliviana 1.7.1873. Black on orange underprint. Back: Red. Printer: ABNC.	40.00	100.	—
S1497 1 Real Plata Boliviana 1.7.1873. Black on rose underprint. Back: Red. Printer: ABNC.	—	—	—

	Good	Fine	XF
S1498 4 Reales Plata Boliviana 1.7.1873. Black on red underprint. Back: Red. Printer: ABNC.	40.00	125.	—
S1499 1 Peso Plata Boliviana 1866, 1.7.1873. Black on red underprint. Back: Red. Printer: ABNC.	40.00	125.	—
S1501 10 Pesos Plata Boliviana 1.7.1873. Black on red underprint. Back: Red. Printer: ABNC.	—	—	—

	Good	Fine	XF
S1502 20 Pesos Plata Boliviana 1.7.1873. Allegorical woman ("Fortune") seated at upper left, steam train at passenger station at upper center right. Back: Red. Printer: ABNC.	—	—	—

	Good	Fine	XF
S1503 50 Pesos Plata Boliviana 1.7.1873. Black on rose underprint. Woman ("The Bride") at lower left, sheep at upper center, woman ("Florence") at lower right. Back: Red. Printer: ABNC.	—	—	—

1873 Paraná Peso Fuerte Issue

	Good	Fine	XF
S1506 50 Centavos Fuertes 1.7.1873.	—	—	—

Paraná ND Provisional Issues

#S1511-S1514 are Rosario notes w/ovpt: *PARANÁ*.

	Good	Fine	XF
S1511 5 Pesos ND (- old date 1866). Overprint: *PARANA*. Rosario note.	—	—	—
S1512 10 Pesos ND (- old date 1872). Overprint: *PARANA*. Rosario note.	—	—	—

	Good	Fine	XF
S1513 10 Pesos ND (- old date 13.7.1872). Black on red underprint. Portrait seated woman at left, train vertically at right. Uniface. Overprint: *PARAN<A/>* twice, at left and center right. Printer: Lit. Alb. Larsch, Buenos Aires.	—	—	—
S1514 20 Pesos ND (- old date 1866).	—	—	—

Rosario Issues

1866-72 Issues

	Good	Fine	XF
S1516 1/2 Real Plata Boliviana 1.1.1867. Black. Ram at upper center. Uniface. Printer: Lito. C. Held, Rosario.	—	—	—
S1517 1/2 Real Plata Boliviana 1.7.1869. Uniface. Printer: Lito. C. Held, Rosario. Unsigned remainder.	—	—	—
S1518 1 Peso Plata Boliviana 1.7.1869. Black. Uniface. Printer: Lito. C. Held, Rosario.	25.00	75.00	150.
S1519 1 Real Plata Boliviana 187x. Black on purple paper. Horse head at upper left. Uniface. Printer: Lito. C. Held, Rosario.	—	—	—

1869-1873 Issue

	Good	Fine	XF
S1521 1/2 Real Plata Boliviana 1869; 1871; 1873. Black on blue underprint. Printer: ABNC.	40.00	100.	—
S1522 1 Real Plata Boliviana 187x; 1871; 1873. Black on blue underprint. Printer: ABNC.	40.00	100.	—
S1523 4 Reales Plata Boliviana 1.7.1867; 1.12.1868. Black. Uniface. Printer: ABNC.	40.00	100.	—

#S1524 *Deleted*. See #S1531.

	Good	Fine	XF
S1525 1 Peso Plata Boliviana 1.7.1873. Black. Like #S1524. Printer: ABNC.	25.00	75.00	125.

	Good	Fine	XF
S1526 5 Pesos Plata Boliviana 1.9.1866; 1.11.1866. Printer: ABNC.			
a. Black on light orange paper. Back green.	40.00	125.	250.
b. 1.11.1866. Black on brown underprint. White paper.	50.00	150.	300.

	Good	Fine	XF
S1527 10 Pesos Plata Boliviana 1866; 1872; 1873. Black. Printer: ABNC.	40.00	150.	300.
S1529 50 Pesos Plata Boliviana 1866; 1873. Black. Paper: Green. Printer: ABNC.	100.	225.	—

1866; 1867 Rosario Peso Fuerte Issue

	Good	Fine	XF
S1530 50 Centavos Fuertes 1.5.1866; 1.6.1866; 2.7.1866; 18.1866. Black. Paper: Peach.	40.00	100.	—
S1531 1 Peso Fuerte 1.11.1867-1.7.1868. Black. Back: Brown. Paper: Blue.	40.00	125.	—

	Good	Fine	XF
S1532 2 Pesos Fuertes 1866; 1.1.1867. Black. Back: Red. Paper: Yellow.	75.00	175.	—

	Good	Fine	XF
S1534 20 Pesos Fuertes 1866; 1873. Black.	75.00	175.	—

187x Santa Fé Issue

	Good	Fine	XF
S1536 1/2 Real Plata Boliviana 187x. Blue. Dog's head at center. Uniface.	40.00	100.	200.

NOTE: Higher denominations for this reseries require confirmation.

Santa Fé ND Provisional Issue

#S1543-S1545 Rosario issue w/ovpt: *SANTA FÉ*.

	Good	Fine	XF
S1543 2 Pesos Fuertes ND (- old date 1.9.1866). Rosario issue. Overprint: Vertical: *SANTA FE* twice at left and center right on #S1532.	150.	400.	—
S1545 10 Pesos Fuertes ND (- old date 1.10.1866). Rosario issue. Back: Blue. Overprint: Blue *SANTA FE* vertically on #S1527.	—	—	—

NOTE: Other values with overprint: *SANTA FE* require confirmation.

Banco J. Benites e Hijo

1867 Issue

	Good	Fine	XF
S1551 1/2 Real Boliviano 1.1.1867. Black. Standing woman and two cherubs at left. Uniface. Paper: Yellow. Printer: Lit. San Martín.	75.00	200.	—
S1552 1 Real Boliviano 1.1.1867. Black. Three cherubs and numeral at left. Uniface. Paper: Dark green. Printer: Lit. San Martín.	100.	225.	—

	Good	Fine	XF
S1553 2 Reales Bolivianos 1.1.1867. Black and gray. Justice seated at left, dog and lock box at upper center. Uniface. Printer: Lit. San Martín.	125.	275.	—

	Good	Fine	XF
S1556 1 Peso Moneda Boliviana 15.10.1867. Black on brown underprint. Portrait girl and birds at lower left, vaqueros roping cattle at center, portrait girl with rabbits at lower right. Back: Green. Printer: ABNC.	75.00	225.	—

	Good	Fine	XF
S1557 5 Pesos Moneda Boliviana 15.10.1867. Black on red underprint. Man at lower left, gauchos at top center, seated women at lower right. Back: Gold. Printer: ABNC.			
a. Issued note.	75.00	225.	—
b. overprint: *GUALEGUAY*.	—	—	—

	Good	Fine	XF
S1559 20 Pesos Moneda Boliviana 15.10.1867. Black on green underprint. Allegorical woman reclining on bales at lower left, woman with pigeon at center, allegorical woman reclining with shield at lower right. Back: Red-orange. Printer: ABNC.			
a. Issued note.	75.00	250.	—
p. Proof.	—	—	—
S1560 50 Pesos Moneda Boliviana 15.10.1868. Black on green underprint. Allegorical woman standing at left, man at upper center, woodsman ("The Ship Carpenter") at right. Back: Blue. Printer: ABNC.	—	—	—

1868 Issue

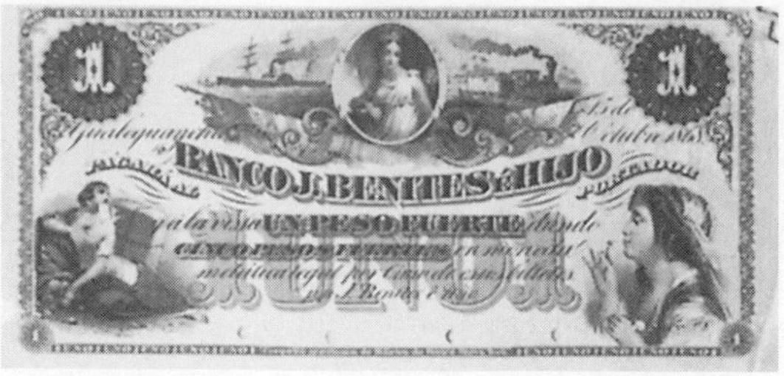

S1562 1 Peso Fuerte	Good	Fine	XF
15.10.1868. Black on orange underprint. Allegorical woman seated at left, ship and steam passenger train flanking portrait woman at upper center, woman at lower right. Back: Green. Printer: ABNC. Proof.	—	—	—

S1563 5 Pesos Fuertes	Good	Fine	XF
15.10.1868. Black on blue underprint. Man at left, three allegorical women at center, woman with bird at right. Back: Green. Printer: ABNC. Proof.	—	—	—
S1564 20 Pesos Fuertes			
15.10.1868. Black on brown underprint. Man at left, modes of transportation at center, young girl at right. Back: Green. Printer: ABNC. Archive copy.	—	—	—

S1565 100 Pesos Fuertes	Good	Fine	XF
15.10.1867. Black on orange underprint. Portrait woman at lower left, allegorical woman with sheep at upper center, cattle at lower right. Back: Brown. Printer: ABNC. Proof.	—	—	—

Banco del Chaco

1884 Issue

S1566 1 Peso	Good	Fine	XF
1.10.1884. Black on red and green underprint. Portrait woman at center between dog's head at left, cow's head at right. Back: Green and red. Printer: BWC.	40.00	100.	200.

Banco Comercial de Corrientes

1867 Issue

#S1571-S1577 with stamped and hand signature.

S1571 6 1/4 Centesimos	Good	Fine	XF
1.2.1867. Black. Rooster at upper center. Uniface. Paper: Blue. Printer: Lit. San Martín.			
a. Issued note.	25.00	75.00	—
r. Unsigned remainder with counterfoil.	—	—	—

S1572 12 1/2 Centesimos	Good	Fine	XF
1.2.1867. Black. Dog at upper center facing right. Uniface. Paper: Yellow. Printer: Lit. Alb. Larsch, Buenos Aires.			
a. Issued note.	40.00	100.	200.
r. Unsigned remainder with counterfoil.	—	—	—

S1573 25 Centesimos	Good	Fine	XF
1.2.1867. Black on gray underprint. Jaguar at upper center facing right. Uniface. Printer: Lit. Alb. Larsch, Buenos Aires.	50.00	100.	—
S1574 50 Centesimos			
1.2.1867. Black. Swan at upper center. Uniface. Paper: Yellowish brown. Printer: Lit. Alb. Larsch, Buenos Aires.	75.00	—	—

S1575 1 Peso Fuerte	Good	Fine	XF
1.2.1867. Black on brown underprint. Horse galloping at upper center facing left. Printer: Lit. Alb. Larsch, Buenos Aires.			
a. Issued note.	75.00	150.	—
r1. Unsigned remainder with counterfoil.	—	50.00	100.
r2. Unsigned remainder without counterfoil.	—	25.00	50.00

S1576 5 Pesos Fuertes	Good	Fine	XF
1.2.1867. Black on brown underprint. Viking at left, bull at upper center. Uniface. Printer: Lit. Alb. Larsch, Buenos Aires.			
a. Issued note.	75.00	150.	—
r1. Unsigned remainder with counterfoil.	—	—	—
r2. Unsigned remainder without counterfoil.	—	—	—

S1577 10 Pesos Fuertes	Good	Fine	XF
1.2.1867. Black on orange underprint. Liberty head at lower left, cows at top center, dog on safe at lower right. Uniface. Printer: Lit. San Martín.			
a. Issued note.	225.	—	—
r1. Unsigned remainder with counterfoil.	—	—	—
r2. Unsigned remainder without counterfoil.	—	—	—

1868 Issue

S1581 12 1/2 Centesimos	Good	Fine	XF
ND. Black on gray underprint. Dog at upper center facing left. Stamped signature.	50.00	150.	—

S1582 25 Centesimos	Good	Fine	XF
1.3.1868. Black on gray underprint. Jaguar at upper center facing left. Stamped signature.	50.00	150.	—

S1583 50 Centesimos	Good	Fine	XF
1.3.1868. Black. Cow at upper center. Stamped signature.	75.00	175.	—

S1584 1 Peso Fuerte	Good	Fine	XF
1.3.1868. Black on brown underprint. Seated allegorical woman with child at lower left, cow's head at upper center right. Stamped signature.	100.	200.	—

Banco Comercial de Santa Fé

1867 Issue

S1590 1 Peso Plata Boliviana	Good	Fine	XF
1.5.1867. Black. Cherub with chickens at lower left, villagers at upper center. Paper: Rose. Printer: Lit. San Martín, Bs As.	—	—	—

1869 Issue

S1593 4 Reales Plata Boliviana	Good	Fine	XF
2.1.1869. Black on green underprint. Girl's head ("Autumn") at upper center. Printer: ABNC.			
a. Issued note.	50.00	175.	—
s. Specimen.	—	—	—

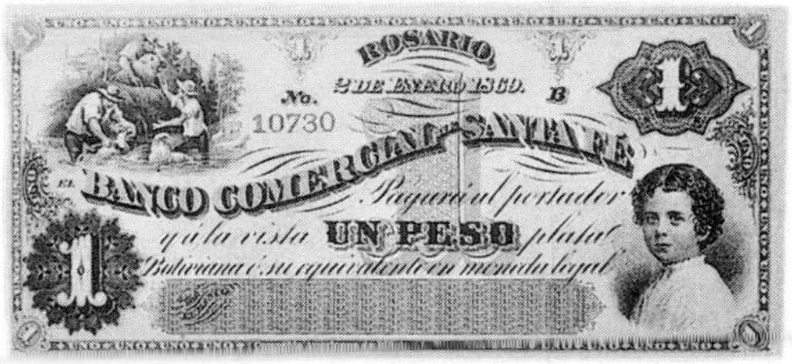

S1594 1 Peso Plata Boliviana	Good	Fine	XF
2.1.1869. Black on orange underprint. Men shearing sheep at upper left, young girl ("Chloe") at lower right. Printer: ABNC.			
a. Issued note.	50.00	175.	—
r. Unsigned remainder.	—	40.00	100.
s. Specimen.	—	—	—

S1595 5 Pesos Plata Boliviana	Good	Fine	XF
2.1.1869. Black on green underprint. Anchor and boxes at left, galloping horse at center, young boy at right. Back: Brown. Printer: ABNC.	100.	225.	—

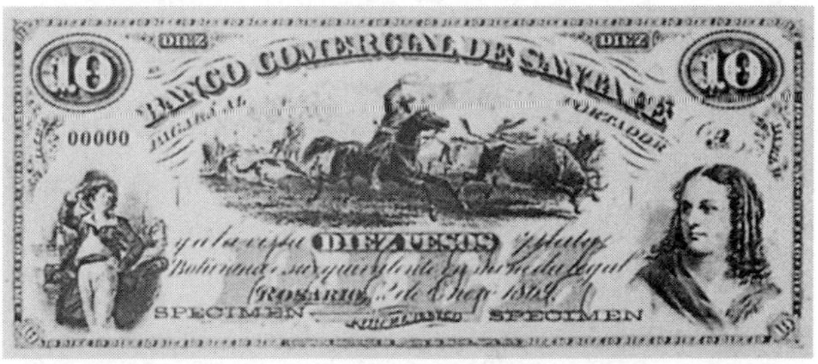

S1596 10 Pesos Plata Boliviana	Good	Fine	XF
2.1.1869. Black on brown underprint. Young sailor at lower left, gauchos roping cattle at upper center, young woman at lower right. Back: Brown. Printer: ABNC. Specimen.	—	—	—

S1597 20 Pesos Plata Boliviana	Good	Fine	XF
2.1.1869. Black on orange underprint. Gaucho at lower left, cow's head at center, man at right. Back: Brown. Printer: ABNC. Specimen.	—	—	—

S1598 50 Pesos Plata Boliviana	Good	Fine	XF
2.1.1869. Black on blue or green underprint. Horse with children at lower left, woman with marine implements at center, cow at lower right. Printer: ABNC. Specimen.	—	—	—

Banco del Comercio

1869 Issue

		Good	Fine	XF
S1601	**1/2 Real** 1.7.1869. Red or brown serial #.	—	—	—
S1604	**4 Reales** 1.7.1869. Black. Man standing with numeral at left. Printer: Local print.	—	—	—

		Good	Fine	XF
S1606	**5 Pesos Bolivianos** 1.7.1869. Black on blue underprint. Man and boy at lower left, seated allegorical woman at upper center, two sailors, one with spyglass ("Looking Out") at lower right. Back: Red. Printer: ABNC.			
	a. Issued note.	—	—	—
	r. Unsigned remainder.	75.00	200.	—
	s. Specimen.	—	—	—

		Good	Fine	XF
S1607	**10 Pesos Bolivianos** 1.7.1869. Black on brown underprint. Farmer and sheep at lower left, seated woman at upper center, child ("Chloe") at lower right. Back: Green. Portrait woman's head at each corner. Printer: ABNC.			
	a. Issued note.	—	—	—
	r. Unsigned remainder.	75.00	200.	—

		Good	Fine	XF
S1608	**20 Pesos Bolivianos** 1.7.1869. Black on red-brown underprint. Sailor at lower left, monument at top center, anchor at lower right. Back: Brown. Printer: ABNC.			
	a. Issued note.	—	—	—
	r. Unsigned remainder.	75.00	200.	—
	s. Specimen.	—	—	—

Banco de Consignaciones de Frutos del País

1890s Issue

		Good	Fine	XF
S1610	**100 Pesos** 189x. Man at left.	—	—	—

Banco de Corrientes

1873 Issue

		Good	Fine	XF
S1611	**6 1/4 Centavos Fuertes** 15.3.1873. Black. Heron. Paper: Rose. Printer: Guillermo Kraft, Buenos Aires.	—	—	—
S1612	**12 1/2 Centavos Fuertes** 15.3.1873. Black on ochre underprint. Deer. Printer: Guillermo Kraft, Buenos Aires.	—	—	—
S1613	**25 Centavos Fuertes** 15.3.1873. Black on lilac underprint. Puma group. Printer: Guillermo Kraft, Buenos Aires.	—	—	—

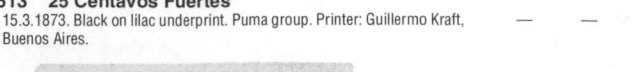

		Good	Fine	XF
S1614	**50 Centavos Fuertes** 15.3.1873. Green. Ostrich at left. Printer: Guillermo Kraft, Buenos Aires.	75.00	200.	—
S1615	**1 Peso Fuerte** 15.3.1873. Black on pink underprint. Dog at upper center. Printer: Guillermo Kraft, Buenos Aires.	—	—	—

		Good	Fine	XF
S1616	**5 Pesos Fuertes** 15.3.1873. Black on orange underprint. Bull at lower left. Back: Green. Printer: Guillermo Kraft, Buenos Aires.	125.	250.	—

		Good	Fine	XF
S1617	**10 Pesos Fuertes** 15.3.1873. Black on blue underprint. Horse at upper left. Back: Red. Printer: Guillermo Kraft, Buenos Aires.	—	—	—
S1620	**100 Pesos Fuertes** 15.3.1873. Black on green and yellow underprint. Gauchos. Printer: Guillermo Kraft, Buenos Aires. Rare.	—	—	—

NOTE: An 1876 issue needs to be confirmed.

Banco de Cuyo

1868 Mendoza Issue

S1628 20 Pesos Plata Boliviana | Good — | Fine — | XF —
1.7.1868. Black. Mountains and sailing ship at left and right center, allegorical woman at left and right.

1892 San Juan Issue

S1631 10 Centavos | Good — | Fine — | XF —
15.7.1892.

S1633 50 Centavos | Good — | Fine — | XF —
15.7.1892. Brown-yellow. Man at left.

18xx Issue

S1636 5 Centavos Fuertes | Good — | Fine — | XF —
18xx. Black. Plant at top center, armadillo at right. Series C. Uniface. Printer: BWC. Proof.

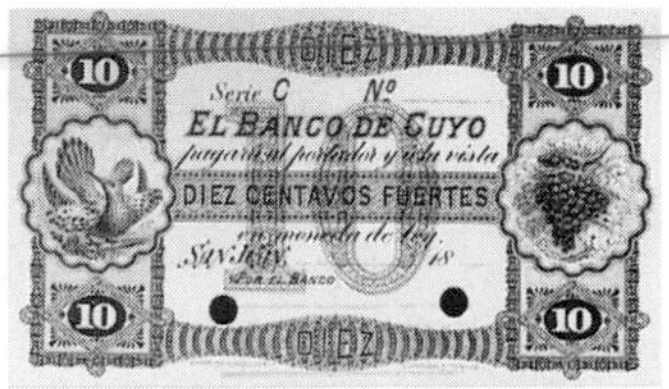

S1637 10 Centavos Fuertes | Good — | Fine — | XF —
18xx. Black. Bird at left, grapes at right. Series C. Uniface. Printer: BWC. Proof.

S1638 20 Centavos Fuertes | Good — | Fine — | XF —
18xx. Black on green underprint. Woman's head at left. Series C. Uniface. Printer: BWC. Proof.

S1639 50 Centavos Fuertes | Good — | Fine — | XF —
18xx. Black on blue underprint. Woman's head at upper left. Series C. Uniface. Printer: BWC. Proof.

S1640 1 Peso Fuerte | Good — | Fine — | XF —
18xx. Black on lilac underprint. Woman's head at upper left, young goat at lower left. Series C. Uniface. Printer: BWC. Proof.

S1641 5 Pesos Fuertes | Good — | Fine — | XF —
18xx. Black on red, orange and green underprint. Woman's head at left, gaucho herding cattle at upper center. Series C. Back: Brown and blue. Head at left and right. Printer: BWC. Proof.

S1642 10 Pesos Fuertes | Good — | Fine — | XF —
18xx. Black on orange, lilac and green underprint. Woman's head at left, pathway and mountains at upper center. Series C. Uniface. Back: Green, blue and brown. Proof.

S1642A 20 Pesos Fuertes | Good — | Fine — | XF —
18xx. Black. Series C. Printer: BWC. Proof.

S1643 50 Pesos Fuertes | Good — | Fine — | XF —
18xx. Black on red and green underprint. Woman's head at left, longhorn steers at center. Back: Violet and green. Printer: BWC. Proof.

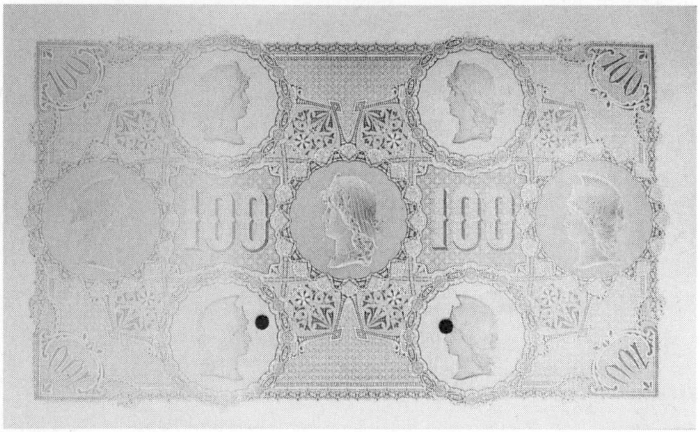

S1644 100 Pesos Fuertes	Good	Fine	XF
18xx. Black on pink and green underprint. Woman's head at left, pack mules at right. Series C. Back: Orange and green. Seven heads. Printer: BWC. Proof.	—	—	—

Banco Entre-Riano

1864 Issue

S1651 5 Centavos	Good	Fine	XF
15.3.1864. Black. Animal at center.			
a. Issued note.	75.00	225.	—
b. Overprint: *GUALEGUAY.*	—	—	—

S1652 10 Centavos	Good	Fine	XF
15.3.1864. Black. Ostrich at top center. Paper: Blue.			
a. Issued note.	75.00	225.	—
b. Overprint: *GUALEGUAY.*	—	—	—
S1653 20 Centavos			
15.3.1864. Cow's head at left. Printer: Lit. Megey, Williams, Montevideo.	—	—	—

S1655 1 Peso Fuerte	Good	Fine	XF
15.3.1864. Black on green underprint. Dog walking right vertically at left. Uniface. Printer: Lit. Mege y Williams, Montevideo.			
a. Issued note.	—	—	—
b. Overprint: *GUALEGUAY.*	—	—	—

1866 Issue

S1657 1 Real Boliviano	Good	Fine	XF
15.5.1866. Black. Pampas cat at center.			
a. Issued note.	75.00	225.	—
b. Overprint: *CONCORDIA* on back.	—	—	—

1870 Issue

S1661 1 Peso Moneda Boliviana	Good	Fine	XF
1.6.1870. Black. Seated woman ("Industry") at left, farmers herding animals at center, boat at right. Back: Brown. Cow head at upper left and right. Printer: CNBB.			
a. Issued note.	100.	325.	—
b. Overprint: *CONCORDIA.*	—	—	—

S1662 5 Pesos Moneda Boliviana	Good	Fine	XF
1.6.1870. Black. Man at lower left, men and horses ("Horse Fair") at center, woman with barrels and sheaves at lower right. Back: Green. Horse ("My Horse") at center. Printer: CNBB. Proof.	—	—	—

S1663 10 Pesos Moneda Boliviana — Good | Fine | XF

1.6.1870. Black. Standing Liberty at left, two seated allegorical women with scales and flags at center, woman at right. Back: Red. Basket of fruit at left, basket of corn at right. Printer: CNBB.

	Good	Fine	XF
a. Issued note.	100.	325.	—
b. Overprint: *CONCORDIA.*	—	—	—
c. Overprint: *VICTORIA.*	—	—	—

	Good	Fine	XF
S1664 20 Pesos Moneda Boliviana 1.6.1870. Black. Mercury at lower left, three seated figures overlooking troops ("Pro Patria Armatus") at center, standing woman ("Commerce") at right. Back: Blue. Woman and child at lower center. Printer: CNBB.	—	—	—
S1665 100 Pesos Moneda Boliviana 1.6.1870. Black. Urquiza at upper center, standing allegorical woman at lower left, standing Liberty with staff at lower right. Back: Black and gold. Cannon, anchor and other implements at center. Printer: CNBB. Proof.	—	—	—

1872 Issue

S1666 1/2 Real Boliviano — Good | Fine | XF

8.1.1872. Black. Rooster at upper left. Paper: Blue. Printer: Lit. San Martín.<

	Good	Fine	XF
a. Issued note.	100.	250.	—
b. Overprint: *VICTORIA* on back.	—	—	—

S1668 2 Reales Boliviano — Good | Fine | XF

8.1.1872. Black. Puma at upper center. Paper: Yellow. Printer: Lit. San Martín.<

	Good	Fine	XF
a. Issued note.	100.	250.	—
b. Overprint:*VICTORIA* on back.	—	—	—

Banco Hipotecario de la Provincia de Córdoba

ND Issue

	Good	Fine	XF
S1671 1 Decimo ND. Rose and blue underprint. Arms.	—	—	—
S1672 10 Centavos Pesos Bolivianos ND. Black on brown underprint. Arms; V. Sobremonte.	—	—	—

Banco Hipotecario de las Provincias Ligadas del Norte

1841 Issue

In 1841 several provinces formed what was called the Coalition of the North, and a bank was established to issue notes for circulation in the member provinces. They were Catamarca, Jujuy, La Rioja, Salta and Tucumán.

	Good	Fine	XF
S1679 1 Real 9.3.1841. Black. Stamping *RECURSO* in brown at left.	—	—	—
S1680 2 Reales 9.3.1841. Black. Stamping *RECURSO* in brown at left. Back: Green.	—	—	—
S1681 4 Reales 9.3.1841. Stamping *RECURSO* in red-orange. Text states that 10% interest was to be paid after termination of the war.	—	—	—

	Good	Fine	XF
S1682 1 Peso 9.3.1841. Stamping *RECURSO* in brown. Text states that 10% interest was to be paid after termination of the war.	—	—	—
S1683 1 Peso 1841. Black. Woman at center. Without stamping.	—	—	—

Banco Industrial de la Provincia de La Rioja

1884 Issue

	Good	Fine	XF
S1691 1 Peso 1884.	—	—	—
S1692 2 Pesos 1884.	—	—	—
S1693 5 Pesos 1884.	—	—	—
S1694 10 Pesos 1884.	—	—	—
S1695 20 Pesos 1884.	—	—	—

Banco del Litoral

1871-75 Issues

	Good	Fine	XF
S1701 1/2 Real Plata Boliviana 1.2.1875. Black. Animals at lower left. Printer: Lit. Fleuti, Rosario.	—	—	—

	Good	Fine	XF
S1702 1 Real Plata Boliviana 21.7.1871. Black. Uniface.	75.00	250.	—
S1703 1 Real Plata Boliviana 1.1.1874. Swans at center right.	75.00	250.	—
S1704 1 Real Plata Boliviana 1.10.1875. Black. Swans at right. Uniface. Paper: Orange.	—	—	—
S1705 4 Reales Plata Boliviana 21.7.1871. Black. Man at left, dog and safe at center, girl at right.	—	—	—
S1706 1 Peso Plata Boliviana 1.7.1874. Black on green paper. Allegory of Navigation seated on bale leaning on anchor at left, allegory of Industry with wheel seated at right. Series C Back: Purple. Horse head at left and right. Overprint: *VICTORIA* at right. Printer: Fleuti.	—	—	—

Provisional ND Issue

#S1711-S1715 values in Pesos Fuertes ovpt. on Plata Boliviana notes.

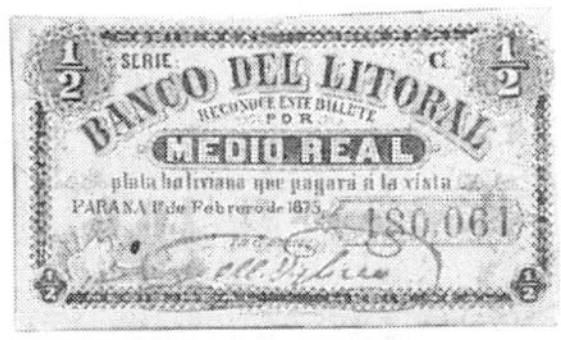

	Good	Fine	XF
S1711 4 1/2 Centavos on 1/2 Real ND (- old date 1.2.1875). Overprint: With purple overprint stamped across face on #S1701.	75.00	225.	—

	Good	Fine	XF
S1712 9 Centavos on 1 Real ND (- old date 1.10.1875). Overprint: With purple overprint stamped across face on #S1703.	75.00	225.	—

S1714 37 1/2 Centavos on 4 Reales	Good	Fine	XF
ND (- old date 21.7.1871). Overprint: With red overprint on #S1705.			
a. Issued note.	100.	250.	—
b. Overprint: *VICTORIA*.	—	—	—

S1715 75 Centavos on 1 Peso	Good	Fine	XF
ND (- old date 1.7.1874). Overprint: Overprint on #S1706.	—	—	—

Ley de 24 de Octubre de 1876; 1880 Issue

S1718 4-1/2 Centavos	Good	Fine	XF
31.12.1880. Portrait dog's head facing right at center. Series A. Printer: E. Fleuti.	—	—	—

Banco de Londres y Rio de la Plata

Córdoba Issues

S1721 1/2 Real Moneda Boliviana	Good	Fine	XF
15.11.1869. Black. Steam locomotive at center. Uniface. Printer: BWC.	25.00	75.00	—
S1722 1 Real Moneda Boliviana			
15.11.1869. Black. Dog's head at left. Paper: Yellow. Printer: BWC.	40.00	100.	—
S1723 1 Real Moneda Boliviana			
1869. Black on brown underprint. Horse. Printer: BWC.	50.00	125.	—

S1724 2 Reales Moneda Boliviana	Good	Fine	XF
15.11.1869. Black. Rooster at upper left. Printer: BWC.	50.00	125.	—
S1725 4 Reales Moneda Boliviana			
1869. Black. Sheep. Printer: BWC.	75.00	150.	—

S1726 1 Peso Moneda Boliviana	Good	Fine	XF
15.11.1869. Black on brown underprint. Horse's head at left. Printer: BWC.	75.00	150.	—
S1727 10 Pesos Moneda Boliviana			
15.11.1869. Printer: BWC.	—	—	—
S1728 20 Pesos Moneda Boliviana			
15.11.1869. Printer: BWC.	—	—	—
S1729 50 Pesos Moneda Boliviana			
15.11.1869. Printer: BWC.	—	—	—

NOTE: With or without: *INSPECCION DE BANCOS* on back.

Rosario Issues

1866-69 Issues

S1731 1 Real Plata Boliviana	Good	Fine	XF
15.9.1866. Black. Uniface.	50.00	125.	—

S1732 1 1/2 Reales Plata Boliviana	Good	Fine	XF
15.9.1866. Black. Uniface.	75.00	150.	—

S1734 4 Reales Plata Boliviana	Good	Fine	XF
1.1.1867. Black on gray underprint. Goat's head at center. Uniface.	100.	225.	—
S1735 1 Peso Moneda Boliviana			
15.11.1869. Man at center. Uniface.	—	—	—
S1737 10 Pesos Plata Boliviana			
15.9.1866. Man at top center. Uniface.	—	—	—
S1738 10 Pesos Plata Boliviana			
15.11.1869. Uniface.	—	—	—
S1738A 20 Pesos Plata Boliviana			
15.11.1869. Uniface.	—	—	—
S1739 50 Pesos Plata Boliviana			
15.11.1869. Cherub at left, man at top center. Uniface.	—	—	—

1866 Issue

S1739A 25 Centavos	Good	Fine	XF
1.7.1866. Black. Condor at left.	75.00	200.	—

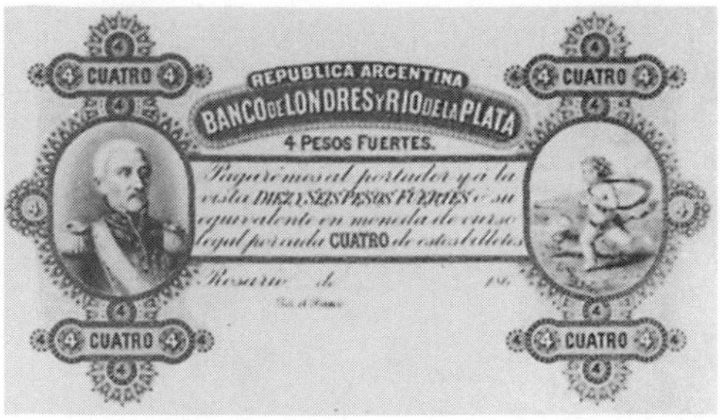

	Good	Fine	XF
S1739E 4 Pesos Fuertes 186x. Portrait Belgrano at left, cherub at right. Uniface.	—	—	—

	Good	Fine	XF
S1740 50 Pesos Fuertes 15.9.1866. Portrait Belgrano at left, cherub at right.	—	—	—

1871 Issue

	Good	Fine	XF
S1741 10 Pesos 10.11.1871.	—	—	—
S1742 20 Pesos 10.11.1871.	—	—	—
S1743 50 Pesos 10.11.1871.	—	—	—

1872-74 Issue

	Good	Fine	XF
S1744 1/2 Real 25.9.1872. Arms at right.	—	—	—
S1745 10 Pesos Fuertes 1.6.1874. Belgrano at left.	—	—	—

Banco Mauá & Cia.

1865 Issue

	Good	Fine	XF
S1745A 5 Centavos 1.7.1865. Black. Printer: Lito left. Therier, Rosario.	—	—	—

1867 Peso Boliviano Issue

#S1746 and S1747 printer: ABNC.

	Good	Fine	XF
S1746 1 Peso Plata Boliviana 2.1.1867. Black on green underprint. Printer: ABNC.			
a. Issued note.	100.	200.	—
p. Proof.	—	—	—

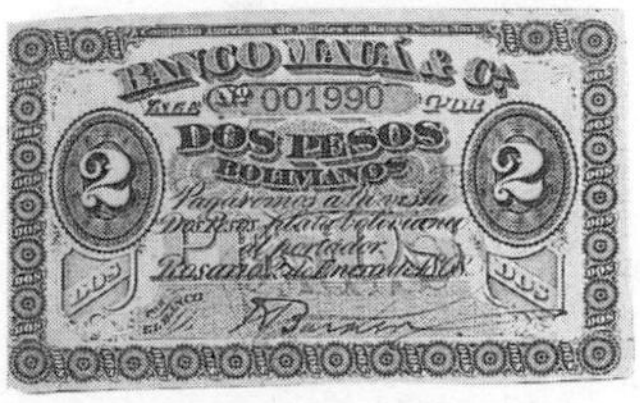

	Good	Fine	XF
S1747 2 Pesos Plata Boliviana 2.1.1867. Black on green underprint. Printer: ABNC.			
a. Issued note.	125.	250.	—
p. Proof.	—	—	—
s. Specimen. Overprint: *MUESTRA.*	—	—	—

1860's Peso Fuerte Issue

	Good	Fine	XF
S1747C 20 Centesimos Fuertes 186x. Portrait man at left, gaucho on horseback at top center right. Series B.	—	—	—

Banco Mendez Hermanos y Cia.

Provisional Issue

#S1747E-S1747G w/ovpt new bank name on notes of the Banco Muñoz & Rodriguez & Ca.

	Good	Fine	XF
S1747E 1 Peso Overprint: On #S1761.	—	—	—
S1747F 5 Pesos Overprint: On #S1762.	—	—	—
S1747G 10 Pesos Overprint: On #S1763.	—	—	—

Regular Issue

#S1747K-S1747M issued 1886-88. Possibly also issued w/1885 circular stamping.

	Good	Fine	XF
S1747K 1 Peso 188x.	—	—	—
S1747L 5 Pesos 188x.	—	—	—
S1747M 10 Pesos 188x.	—	—	—

Banco de Mendoza

1876; 1877 Issue

#S1748-S1755 printer: H. Simon.

	Good	Fine	XF
S1748 1/2 Real Moneda Boliviana 1.1.1877. Blue. Helmeted Athena at left. Series A. Printer: H. Simon.			
a. Issued note.	—	—	—
r. Unsigned remainder.	—	—	—

	Good	Fine	XF
S1749 1 Real Moneda Boliviana 1.1.1876; 1.1.1877. Black. Gaucho on horseback roping cattle at center. Series B. Printer: H. Simon.			
a. Issued note.	—	—	—
r. Unsigned remainder.	—	—	—

	Good	Fine	XF
S1750 2 Reales Moneda Boliviana 1.1.1876; 1.1.1877. Brown. Seated allegorical woman and child at left. Uniface. Series C. Printer: H. Simon.			
a. Issued note.	—	—	—
r. Unsigned remainder.	—	—	—
s. Specimen.	—	—	—

	Good	Fine	XF
S1751 4 Reales Moneda Boliviana			
1.1.1876; 1.1.1877. Black on green underprint. Gaucho standing with horse and dog at center. Series D. Printer: H. Simon.			
a. Issued note.	—	—	—
r. Unsigned remainder.	—	—	—
S1752 1 Peso Boliviano			
1.1.1877. Black on blue underprint. Back: Blue. Printer: H. Simon.			
a. Issued note.	—	—	—
r. Unsigned remainder.	—	—	—

	Good	Fine	XF
S1753 5 Pesos Bolivianos			
1.1.1877. Black on green underprint. Building, people at upper center. Printer: H. Simon.			
a. Issued note.	—	—	—
r. Unsigned remainder.	—	—	—
S1755 20 Pesos Bolivianos			
1.1.1877. Printer: H. Simon. Rare.	—	—	—

1877 Issue

	Good	Fine	XF
S1756 1 Peso Moneda Boliviana			
ca. 1877. Hand dated. Printer: CNBB.	—	—	—

	Good	Fine	XF
S1757 5 Pesos Moneda Boliviana			
ca. 1877. Hand dated. Brown on rose underprint. Military encampment at center, steam passenger train crossing stone arch bridge with cattle below in stream at lower left, woman at lower right. Printer: CNBB.			
r. Unsigned remainder.	—	—	—
s. Specimen, punched hole cancelled.	—	—	—
S1758 10 Pesos Moneda Boliviana			
ca. 1877. Hand dated. Printer: CNBB.	—	—	—

Banco Muñoz & Rodriguez & Ca.

1883 First Issue

	Good	Fine	XF
S1760 7 Pesos			
1.6.1883. Allegory of the Republic at left, arms at right.	—	—	—

1883 Second Issue

	Good	Fine	XF
S1761 1 Peso			
30.6.1883. Black on brown underprint. Portrait girl and dog at left, allegorical woman at center, Gen. J. de San Martín at right. Series A. Back: Brown. Printer: ABNC.			
a. Issued note.	—	—	—
s. Specimen.	—	—	—

	Good	Fine	XF
S1762 5 Pesos			
30.6.1883. Black on rose underprint. Portrait girl with rabbits at left, two farmers with horse plowing at center, B. Rivadavia at right. Series A. Back: Rose. Printer: ABNC.			
p. Proof without underprint.	—	—	—
s. Specimen.	—	—	—

	Good	Fine	XF
S1763 10 Pesos			
30.6.1883. Black on blue underprint. Portrait Christopher Columbus at left, steam passenger train at center, Gen. Belgrano at right. Series A. Back: Blue. Printer: ABNC.			
p. Proof.	—	—	—
s. Specimen.	—	—	—

NOTE: It is reported that #S1761-S1763 may also have overprint. w/1855 circular stamping. Also, these notes are reported overprint. w/earlier bank name *Banco Mendez Hermanos y Cia.* on face and back. The Banco Muñoz & Rodriguez & Ca. became absorbed by the Banco Provincial de Tucumán listed earlier (see #S841-S846).

(Banco) Oxandaburu y Garvino

1867 Issue

	VG	VF	UNC
S1771 1/2 Real Boliviano			
1.12.1867. Black. Gaucho on horseback with bull at left. Bank name with *GARVINO*. Uniface. Printer: Lit. San Martín.			
a. Issued note.	7.50	20.00	40.00
r. Unsigned remainder.	—	—	15.00
S1772 1 Real Boliviano			
1.12.1867. Black. Bank name with *GARVINO*. Paper: Blue. Printer: Lit. San Martín.			
a. Issued note.	—	—	—
r. Unsigned remainder.	—	—	—

	VG	VF	UNC
S1774 4 Reales Bolivianos			
1.12.1867. Light red. Bull's head at center. Bank name with *GARVINO*. Printer: Lit. San Martín.			
a. Issued note.	—	—	—
r. Unsigned remainder.	—	—	25.00

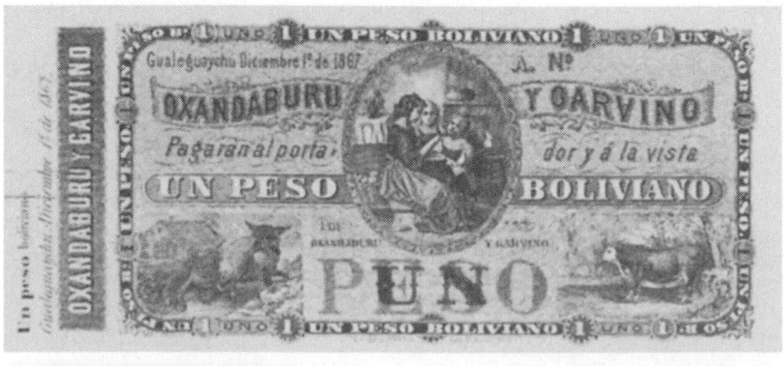

	VG	VF	UNC
S1775 1 Peso Boliviano			
1.12.1867. Black on red underprint. Fox stealing a duck at lower left, portrait woman with two children at center, bull at lower right. Bank name with *GARVINO*. Printer: Lit. San Martín.			
a. Issued note. Rare.	—	—	—
r. Unsigned remainder with counterfoil.	—	—	—

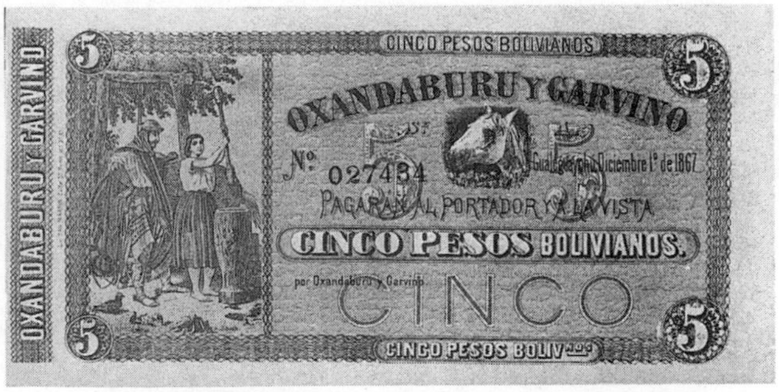

S1776 5 Pesos Bolivianos

1.12.1867. Brown on red-violet and rose underprint. Gaucho and woman at left, horse's head at center. Bank name with *GARVINO*. Printer: Lit. San Martín.

	VG	VF	UNC
a. Issued note.	—	500.	—
b. Unsigned remainder.	—	10.00	25.00

S1778 20 Pesos Bolivianos

1.12.1867. Red on green underprint. Two gauchos and woman at center. Bank name with *GARVINO*. Back: Brown. Printer: Lit. San Martín. Unsigned remainder.

VG	VF	UNC
—	—	25.00

Banco Oxandaburu y Garbino

1869 Peso Boliviana Issue

S1781 4 Reales Bolivianos

2.1.1869. Black on brown underprint. Dog's head ("Ceasar") at center. Uniface. Bank name with *GARBINO*. Printer: ABNC.

	VG	VF	UNC
a. Issued note.	100.	350.	—
r. Unsigned remainder.	—	—	10.00

S1782 1 Peso Boliviana

2.1.1869. Black on green underprint. Girl at lower left, "cow and calf" at center, seated woman and child at lower right. Uniface. Bank name with *GARBINO*. Printer: ABNC.

	VG	VF	UNC
a. Issued note.	—	—	—
r. Unsigned remainder.	—	—	15.00

S1783 5 Pesos Bolivianos

2.1.1869. Black on green underprint. Seated allegorical woman with sickle and sheaf at lower left, workers, men on horseback at center, sailor at lower right. Bank name with *GABRINO*. Back: Brwon. Printer: ABNC.

	VG	VF	UNC
a. Issued note.	—	—	—
r. Unsigned remainder.	—	—	20.00

S1784 10 Pesos Bolivianos

2.1.1869. Black on red underprint. Gaucho seated at lower left, man watching woman mashing corn ("Gauch and Girl No. 2") at center, 3 horse heads ("Pharaoh's Horses") at lower right. Bank name with *GARBINO*. Back: Brown. Printer: ABNC.

	VG	VF	UNC
a. Issued note.	—	—	—
r. Unsigned remainder.	—	—	25.00

S1785 20 Pesos Bolivianos

2.1.1869. Black on red underprint. Gaucho at left, wagons in camp at center, woman at right. Bank name with *GARBINO*. Back: Brown. Printer: ABNC. Rare.

VG	VF	UNC
—	—	—

1869 Peso Fuerte Issue

S1791 1 Peso Fuerte

2.1.1869. Black on blue underprint. Girl at lower left, horse's head ("My Horse") at center, anchor at lower right. Uniface. Bank name with *GABRINO*. Printer: ABNC. Unsigned remainder.

VG	VF	UNC
—	—	25.00

S1792 5 Pesos Fuertes	VG	VF	UNC
2.1.1869. Black on green underprint. Girl at lower left and right, dog on safe ("On the Watch") at upper left center. Bank name with *GABRINO*. Back: Green. Printer: ABNC. Unsigned remainder.	—	—	25.00

S1794 200 Pesos Fuertes	VG	VF	UNC
2.1.1869. Black on red-brown underprint. Gauchos and carriage at center. Bank name with *GABRINO*. Back: Red-brown. Printer: ABNC. Unsigned remainder.	—	—	25.00

Banco Domingo Garbino

Provisional ND Issue

#S1801-S1806 w/red vertical ovpt: *BANCO DOMINGO GARBINO* on face of Banco Oxandaburu y Garbino issues.

S1801 4 Reales	VG	VF	UNC
ND (- old date 2.1.1869). Handwritten signature. Overprint: Red and vertical; *BANCO DOMINGO GARBINO* on face of #S1781. Rare.	—	—	—

S1802 1 Peso	VG	VF	UNC
ND (- old date 2.1.1869). Handwritten signature. Overprint: Red and vertical; *BANCO DOMINGO GARBINO* on face of #S1791.	7.50	15.00	30.00

S1803 5 Pesos	VG	VF	UNC
ND (- old date 2.1.1869). Handwritten signature. Overprint: Red and vertical; *BANCO DOMINGO GARBINO* on face of #S1792.	25.00	40.00	100.

S1804 10 Pesos	VG	VF	UNC
ND (- old date 2.1.1869). Handwritten signature. Overprint: Red and vertical; *BANCO DOMINGO GARBINO* on face of #S1784.	100.	250.	—

S1805 20 Pesos	VG	VF	UNC
ND (- old date 2.1.1869). Handwritten signature. Overprint: Red and vertical; *BANCO DOMINGO GARBINO* on face of #S1785.	75.00	225.	—

S1806 20 Pesos	VG	VF	UNC
ND (- old date 2.1.1869). Handwritten signature. Overprint: Red and vertical; *BANCO DOMINGO GARBINO* on face of #S1794.	100.	250.	—

Banco Paraná

1868 ND; 1868-69 Issues

S1811 1/2 Real Boliviano	Good	Fine	XF
1.4.1868. Blue. Rooster at upper center. Back: Branch name in oval stamping. Printer: Lit. San Martín.			
a. Issued note.	5.00	10.00	—
b. Hand stamped: *LA PAZ*.	—	—	—
c. Hand stamped: *VICTORIA*.	—	—	—
d. Hand stamped: *1869* in oval.	—	—	—

S1812 1 Real Boliviano	Good	Fine	XF
1.4.1868. Red. Dog's head at left, dog facing right at center. Back: Branch name in oval stamping. Printer: Lit. San Martín.			
a. Issued note.	5.00	15.00	—
b. Hand stamped: *LA PAZ*.	—	—	—
c. Hand stamped: *VICTORIA*.	—	—	—
d. Hand stamped: *1869* in oval.	—	—	—

S1813 2 Reales Bolivianos	Good	Fine	XF
1.4.1869. Purple. Standing allegorical woman at left, puma at lower right. Back: Branch name in oval stamping. Printer: Lit. San Martín.			
a. Issued note.	5.00	25.00	—
b. Hand stamped: *LA PAZ*.	—	—	—
c. Hand stamped: *VICTORIA*.	—	—	—
d. Hand stamped: *1869* in oval.	—	—	—

S1814 4 Reales Bolivianos

1.4.1868. Brown. Ram at lower left, portrait boy with sheep at upper center. Back: Branch name in oval stamping. Printer: Lit. San Martín.

	Good	Fine	XF
a. Issued note.	5.00	25.00	—
b. Hand stamped: *LA PAZ.*	—	—	—
c. Hand stamped: *VICTORIA.*	—	—	—
d. Hand stamped: *1869* in oval.	—	—	—

S1815 1 Peso Boliviano

ND (1868). Black and green. Seated woman with anchor at loading dock at lower left, two horses at center, man with horse and child at lower right. Series A. Back: Branch name in oval stamping. Printer: Lit. San Martín.

	Good	Fine	XF
a. Issued note.	7.50	25.00	—
b. Hand stamped: *LA PAZ.*	—	—	—
c. Hand stamped: *VICTORIA.*	—	—	—
d. Hand stamped: *1869* in oval.	—	—	—

S1816 1 Peso Boliviano

ND (1868). Black and red. Seated woman with anchor at loading dock at lower left, two horses at center, man with horse and child at lower right. *Se. A.* Back: Branch name in oval stamping. Printer: Lit. San Martín.

	Good	Fine	XF
a. Issued note.	7.50	25.00	—
b. Hand stamped: *LA PAZ.*	—	—	—
c. Hand stamped: *VICTORIA.*	—	—	—
d. Hand stamped: *1869* in oval.	—	—	—

S1817 5 Pesos Moneda Boliviana

1.4.1868. Purple on green underprint. Bull at lower left. Back: Branch name in oval stamping. Printer: Lit. San Martín.

	Good	Fine	XF
a. Issued note.	10.00	40.00	—
b. Hand stamped: *LA PAZ.*	—	—	—
c. Hand stamped: *VICTORIA.*	—	—	—
d. Hand stamped: *1869* in oval.	—	—	—

S1818 10 Pesos Plata Boliviana

1.4.1868. Black on tan underprint. Seated allegorical woman with shield and sailing ships at upper center, arms below. Back: Animals and old train at center. Branch name in oval stamping. Printer: Lit. San Martín.

	Good	Fine	XF
a. Issued note.	75.00	125.	—
b. Hand stamped: *LA PAZ.*	—	—	—
c. Hand stamped: *VICTORIA.*	—	—	—
d. Hand stamped: *1869* in oval.	—	—	—

S1819 20 Pesos Moneda Boliviana

1.4.1868. Black on blue-gray underprint. Cherubs at lower left and right, paddlewheel steamer at upper center. Back: Brown. Sailing ship at center, small head of Mercury at right. Branch name in oval stamping. Printer: Lit. San Martín.

	Good	Fine	XF
a. Issued note.	15.00	75.00	—
b. Hand stamped: *LA PAZ.*	—	—	—
c. Hand stamped: *VICTORIA.*	—	—	—
d. Hand stamped: *1869* in oval.	—	—	—

Banco Rio Cuarto

1874 Issue

	Good	Fine	XF
S1821 1/2 Real Boliviana 1.4.1874. Woman at left.	—	—	—
S1822 1 Real Boliviana 1.4.1874. Woman.	—	—	—
S1823 2 Reales Boliviana 1.4.1874. Woman.	—	—	—

S1825 1 Peso Boliviana

1.4.1874. Black on blue and green underprint. Portrait woman at upper left, allegorical woman reclining with scroll at center, man and sheep at lower right. Back: Green. Printer: ABNC. Rare.

Good	Fine	XF
—	—	—

S1826 5 Pesos Bolivianas

1.4.1874. Black on brown underprint. Stag head ("Monarch") at upper left, man in canoe at center, woman ("May") at lower right. Back: Brown. Printer: CNBB. Proof.

Good	Fine	XF
—	—	—

A word on date ranges

Often date ranges or specific dates are listed. These have been observed or reported by our contributors. If a note is outside the published range, it only means that it is a newly reported date, and not necessarily worthy of a premium value.

Banco del Rio de la Plata

1868 First Issue

		Good	Fine	XF
S1831	**1/2 Real Plata Boliviana**			
	3.10.1868. Brown. Horse's head at upper center.			
	a. Issued note.	75.00	250.	—
	b. Overprint: *CONCEPCION DEL URUGUAY.*	—	—	—
S1832	**1 Peso Plata Boliviana**			
	3.10.1868. Black. Cow's head at upper center.			
	a. Issued note.	75.00	250.	—
	b. Overprint: *CONCEPCION DEL URUGUAY.*	—	—	—

		Good	Fine	XF
S1833	**2 Reales Plata Boliviana**			
	3.10.1868. Black. Goat's head at upper center. Printer: Lito. Hongsfeld, Buenos Aires.			
	a. Issued note.	75.00	250.	—
	b. Overprint: *CONCEPCION DEL URUGUAY.*	—	—	—
S1834	**4 Reales Plata Boliviana**			
	3.10.1868. Black. Portrait Liberty at left.	75.00	250.	—

		Good	Fine	XF
S1835	**1 Peso Plata Boliviana**			
	3.10.1868. Black on violet paper. Woman standing at center with sheep. Printer: Lit. San Martín.			
	a. Issued note.	75.00	250.	—
	b. Overprint: *CONCEPCION DEL URUGUAY.*	—	—	—

		Good	Fine	XF
S1836	**2 Pesos Plata Boliviana**			
	3.10.1868. Black on violet paper. Dog on safe at upper center. Printer: Lit. San Martín.			
	a. Issued note.	75.00	250.	—
	b. Overprint: *CONCEPCION DEL URUGUAY.*	—	—	—

		Good	Fine	XF
S1837	**5 Pesos Plata Boliviana**			
	3.10.1868. Black and dull red on yellow paper. Portrait seated allegorical woman with scales at left.			
	a. Issued note.	75.00	250.	—
	b. Overprint: *CONCEPCION DEL URUGUAY.*	—	—	—
S1838	**10 Pesos Plata Boliviana**			
	3.10.1868. Black, green and rose. Woman standing at left. Paper: Orange.			
	a. Issued note.	—	—	—
	b. Overprint: *CONCEPCION DEL URUGUAY.*	—	—	—

1868 Second Issue

		Good	Fine	XF
S1843	**1 Peso Plata Boliviano**			
	28.9.1868. Black on orange underprint. Uniface. Printer: Lit. Mege y Willems, Montevideo.	75.00	250.	—

1869 Issue

		Good	Fine	XF
S1848	**5 Pesos Moneda Boliviana**			
	9.1.1869. Black on brown underprint. Uniface. Paper: Dark blue. Printer: Lit. San Martín.	100.	300.	—

Banco (del) Rosario de Santa Fé

1865-69 Issues

		Good	Fine	XF
S1851	**1 Real Plata Boliviana**			
	1.10.1869. Black on light yellow underprint. Heading with *DEL*. Uniface. Printer: Lit. C. Heid, Rosario.			
	a. Stamped signature.	75.00	200.	—
	b. Handwritten signature.	—	—	—
S1853	**1 Peso Plata Boliviana**			
	1865-67. Angels at top center. Printer: Lit. C. Heid, Rosario.	—	—	—

S1854 1 Peso Plata Boliviana	Good	Fine	XF
1.10.1869. Black. Gauchos at top center. Printer: Lit. C. Heid, Rosario.			
a. Stamped signature.	75.00	200.	—
b. Handwritten signature.	100.	300.	—

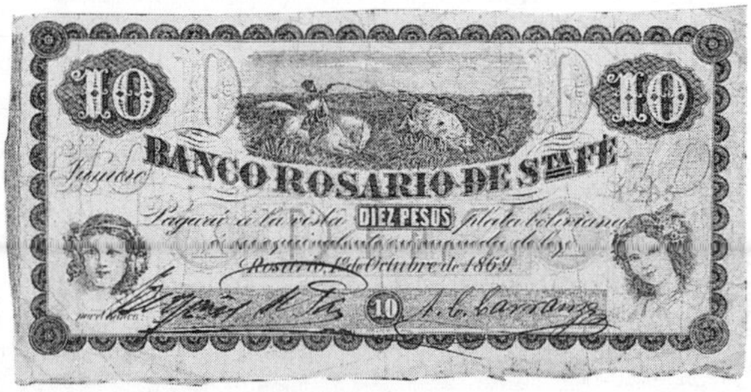

S1856 10 Pesos Plata Boliviana	Good	Fine	XF
1.10.1869. Black on red underprint. Girl's head at lower left and lower right, gaucho roping cattle at top center. Printer: Lit. C. Heid, Rosario.			
a. Stamped signature. Red or brown serial #.	—	—	—
b. Handwritten signature. Green or blue serial #.	—	—	—

Banco de San Juan

1860s San Juan, Catamarca and Tucumán Issue

S1860 2 Reales	Good	Fine	XF
186x. Printer: G. Kraft, Bs. As.	—	—	—

1870s Catamarca Issue

S1862 1 Peso Boliviano	VG	VF	UNC
187x. Black and red on green underprint. Horses at center. Back: Blue. Printer: Guillermo Kraft. Proof stamped *MUESTRA*.		—	500.

1873 San Juan Peso Plata Boliviana Issue

S1864 4 Reales Plata Boliviana	Good	Fine	XF
1.7.1873.	—	—	—

S1873 1 Peso Plata Boliviana	Good	Fine	XF
18xx. Black on green underprint. Woman holding spool of yarn at left. Uniface. Series C. Proof.	—	—	—

1876 San Juan Peso Fuerte Issue

S1876 5 Centavos Fuertes	Good	Fine	XF
3.1.1876. Black. Portrait woman at left. Series D. Printer: BWC. Proof. Uniface.	—	—	—
S1877 10 Centavos Fuertes			
3.1.1876. Series D. Printer: BWC. Proof.	—	—	—
S1878 20 Centavos Fuertes			
3.1.1876. Series D. Printer: BWC. Proof.	—	—	—

S1880 1 Peso Fuerte	Good	Fine	XF
3.1.1876. Black on green underprint. Bird at left. Series D. Back: Red, green and tan. Two heads. Printer: BWC.	—	—	—
S1881 5 Pesos Fuertes			
18xx. Series D. Printer: BWC.	—	—	—
S1882 10 Pesos Fuertes			
18xx. Series D. Printer: BWC.	—	—	—

S1883 20 Pesos Fuertes	Good	Fine	XF
18xx. Black on orange underprint. Cow's head, allegorical woman's head and shield at upper right. Series D. Back: Red and green. Six heads of Liberty. Printer: BWC.	—	—	—
S1884 50 Pesos Fuertes			
187x. Black on yellow underprint. Gathering of people at lower left. Series A. Printer: G. Kraft, Bs. As.	—	—	—

1874-76 Tucumán Peso Boliviana Issue

S1886 5 Centavos Moneda Boliviana	Good	Fine	XF
(ca.1874). Specimen.	—	—	—
S1887 1 Real Moneda Boliviana			
1876.	—	—	—
S1888 1 1/2 Reales Moneda Boliviana			
1876.	—	—	—
S1891 1 Peso Moneda Boliviana			
1.7.1874. Seal of branch at San Juan.	—	—	—

1876 Tucumán Peso Fuerte Issue

S1892 10 Centavos Fuertes	Good	Fine	XF
3.1.1876. Black. Paper: Green.	—	—	—
S1896 60 Centavos Fuertes			
1.10.1878. Payable in national money or 4 chirolas of 15 centavos each in Bolivian money.	—	—	—
S1897 1 Peso Fuerte			
(ca. 1876).	—	—	—
S1900 20 Pesos Fuertes			
(ca. 1876).	—	—	—

Banco de San Luis

1894 Issue

S1901 1 Peso	Good	Fine	XF
17.3.1894. Green.	—	—	—

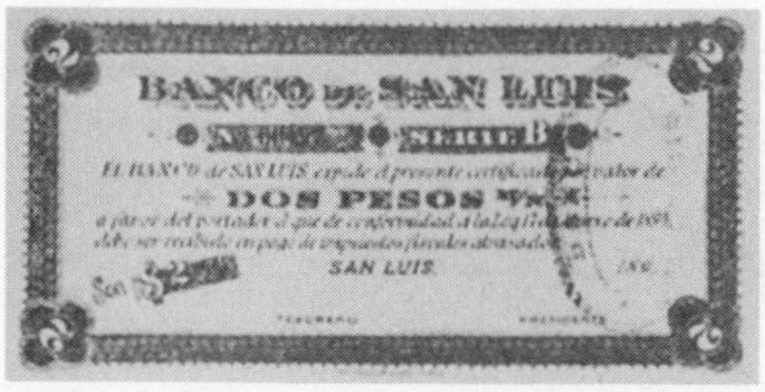

S1902 2 Pesos	Good	Fine	XF
17.3.1894. Black on gold underprint. Series B. Back: Green.	—	—	—

S1904 10 Pesos	Good	Fine	XF
17.3.1894. Black on gold underprint. Series D. Back: Blue.	—	—	—

Banco Solanas & Cia.

1874 Issue

S1912 1 Real Plata Boliviana	Good	Fine	XF
1.8.1874. Green and black. Ram at center. Uniface. Printer: A. Godel. Unsigned remainder.	—	—	—

S1913 2 Reales Plata Boliviana	Good	Fine	XF
1.8.1874. Blue and black. Bull at center. Uniface. Printer: A. Godel. Unsigned remainder.	—	—	—

S1915 1 Peso Boliviano	Good	Fine	XF
1.8.1874. Brown and black. Allegorical woman at left, gaucho on horseback chasing ostriches at center right. Back: Gray. Printer: A. Godel. Unsigned remainder.	—	—	—

S1916 5 Pesos Moneda Boliviana	Good	Fine	XF
1.8.1874. Black on brown underprint. Three allegorical women at left, sheep under trees at upper center, allegorical woman at right. Back: Brown. Printer: ABNC. Proof.	—	—	—

S1918 20 Pesos Moneda Boliviana	Good	Fine	XF
1.8.1874. Black on brown underprint. Woman, ducks and horse at left, dog on safe at center, two allegorical women with sailing ships behind at right. Back: Brown. Printer: ABNC. Proof.	—	—	—

Banco de Victoria

1873 Issue

S1923 1 Peso	Good	Fine	XF
1.4.1873. Black. Man at left. Rare.	—	—	—

Caja de Ahorros de Rosario

1870 Issue

S1931 1 Real Boliviana	Good	Fine	XF
1870.	—	—	—

Credito Popular

1906 Bono de Credito Issue

S1944 5 Pesos	Good	Fine	XF
8.6.1906. Black on brown underprint. Standing allegorical woman and cherub at left. Back: Blue-black.	50.00	250.	—

Credito Territorial

1877 Issue

S1951 1 Peso Fuerte	Good	Fine	XF
June 1877. Black on salmon underprint. Arms at upper center, steam train at lower center. Overprint: *Law 5.6.1879* on back. Printer: Lit. San Martín, Buenos Aires. Rare.	—	—	—

Credito Territorial de Santa Fé

Law of 28.9.1869

S1958 1 Real Plata Boliviana	Good	Fine	XF
1.1.1870. Black. Large ornate *"1"* in underprint at center. Printer: C. [-], Rosario.	—	—	—

S1963 1 Peso Plata Boliviana	Good	Fine	XF
ND (ca. 1869). Black and orange. Woman's head at left, galloping horse at upper center facing left. Uniface. Printer: Lit. San Martín. Rare.	—	—	—

Daniel Gonzalez y Compa.

1860s Issue

Issued in the Province of Mendoza. The firm operated from 1866 to 1879.

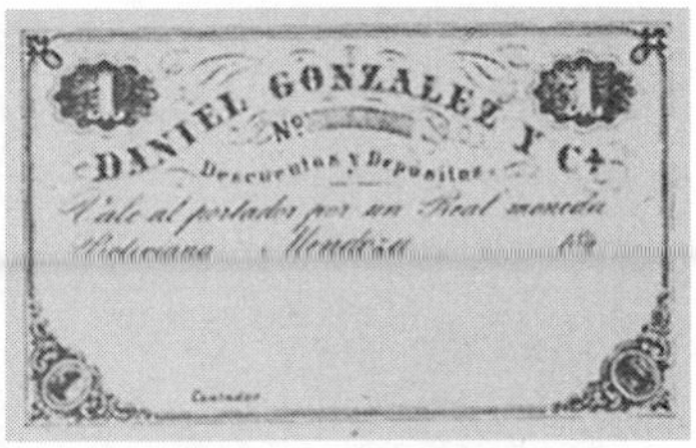

S1971 1 Real Moneda Boliviana	Good	Fine	XF
186x. Uniface.			
a. Light green without watermark.	—	—	—
b. Light green with watermark.	—	—	—
c. Dark green without watermark.	—	—	—
d. Dark green with watermark.	—	—	—
S1972 2 Reales Moneda Boliviana			
186x. Red-orange. Uniface.			
a. Without watermark.	—	—	—
b. With watermark.	—	—	—

S1974 1 Peso Plata Boliviana	Good	Fine	XF
1.3.1866; 1.9.1868. Black on green underprint. Condor at center with wings spread across face. Back: Red-brown. Printer: ABNC.			
a. Black on green underprint and border. Issued note.	—	—	—
p. Black on orange underprint and border. Proof.	—	—	—

S1975 5 Pesos Plata Boliviana	Good	Fine	XF
186x. Black on blue underprint. Young girl's head at lower left. ("Isabella") and lower right. ("Autumn"), Agriculture at upper center. Back: Blue. Printer: ABNC. Proof.	—	—	—

S1976 10 Pesos Plata Boliviana	Good	Fine	XF
186x. Black. Girl at lower left, gauchos herding cattle at center, young woman ("Florence") at lower right. Back: Brown. Printer: ABNC.			
p1. Brown underprint. Face proof.	—	—	—
p2. Red-orange underprint. Face proof.	—	—	—

Miguel Lanieri

1871 Issues

S1982 4 Reales Bolivianos	Good	Fine	XF
1.11.1871. Black. Cow's head at center, boat at upper right. Uniface. Back: Stamped with issuer's name and design in oval.	75.00	250.	—

S1983 4 Reales Bolivianos	Good	Fine	XF
1.11.1871. Black. Dog's head at left, ship at center. Back: Blue. Stamped with issuer's name and design in oval.	75.00	250.	—

S1983A 1 Peso Boliviano	Good	Fine	XF
1.11.1871. Black.. Indian seated at lower left, steamship at top center. Back: Stamped with issuer's name and design in oval.	—	—	—

Otero y Cia.

1867 Issue

	Good	Fine	XF
S1984 1/2 Real Plata Boliviana 31.11.1867.	—	—	—
S1985 1 Real Plata Boliviana 1.6.1867; 31.11.1867.	—	—	—
S1986 2 Reales Plata Boliviana 1.6.1867; 31.11.1867.	—	—	—
S1987 4 Reales Plata Boliviana 1.6.1867; 31.11.1867.	—	—	—
S1988 1 Peso Plata Boliviana 31.11.1867.	—	—	—
S1989 5 Pesos Plata Boliviana 31.11.1867.	—	—	—
S1990 10 Pesos Plata Boliviana 31.11.1867.	—	—	—

1868 Issue

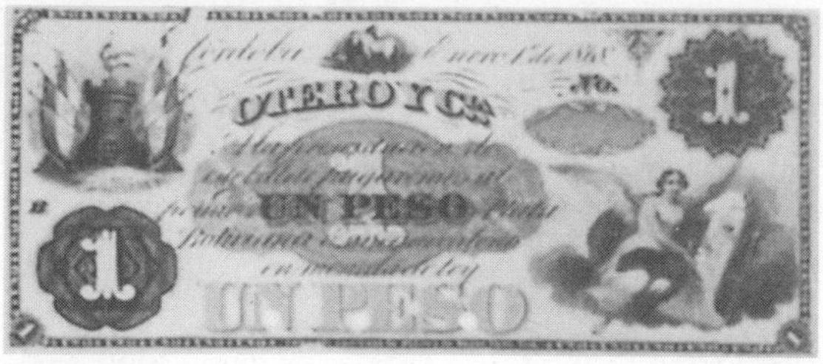

	Good	Fine	XF
S1991 1 Peso Plata Boliviana 1.1.1868. Black on orange underprint. Arms of Córdoba at upper left, horses at upper center, winged allegorical woman with numeral *1* at lower right. Printer: ABNC. Proof.	—	—	—

	Good	Fine	XF
S1992 5 Pesos Plata Boliviana 1.1.1868. Black on red-orange underprint. Girl's head at upper left, five cherubs with numeral *5* at center, arms of Córdoba at lower right. Printer: ABNC.			
p. Proof.	—	—	—
s. Specimen.	—	—	—

	Good	Fine	XF
S1993 10 Pesos Bolivianos 1.1.1868. Black on green underprint. Girl tending cows at upper left, two horse's heads ("Stable Window") at upper center right, man smoking at lower right. Printer: ABNC. Proof.	—	—	—

1869 Issue

	Good	Fine	XF
S1996 1/2 Real Plata Boliviana 1.4.1869. Black. Text across. Proof.	—	—	—

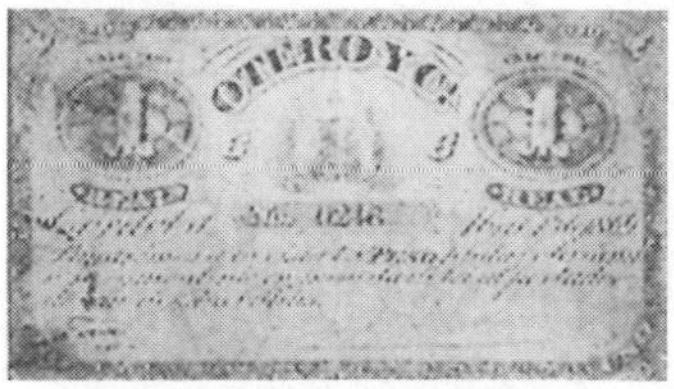

	Good	Fine	XF
S1997 1 Real Plata Boliviana 1.4.1869. Black. Arms of Córdoba at center. Uniface.	75.00	150.	—

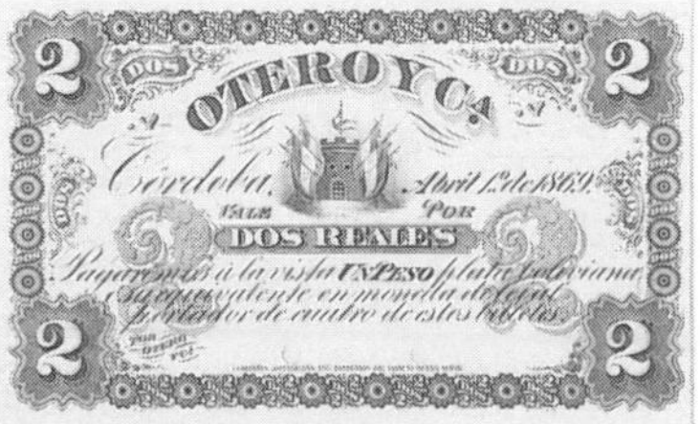

	Good	Fine	XF
S1998 2 Reales Plata Boliviana 1.4.1869. Black. Arms of Córdoba at upper center. Proof.	—	—	—
S1998A 4 Reales Plata Boliviana 1.4.1869.	—	—	—

1872 Issue

	Good	Fine	XF
S1999 4 Reales Plata Boliviana 1.1.1872. Portrait girl at lower left and lower right, arms of Córdoba at center. Proof.	—	—	—

Banco Otero y Cia.

1880 Issue

	Good	Fine	XF
S2001 1 Peso Plata 2.1.1880. Black on green underprint. Portrait Gen. M. Paz at left. Printer: BWC.	—	—	—
S2002 5 Pesos Plata 2.1.1880. Black on carmine underprint. Gauchos. Portrait Gen. M. Paz at left. Printer: BWC.	—	—	—
S2003 10 Pesos Plata 2.1.1880. Black. Portrait Gen. M. Paz at left. Printer: BWC.	—	—	—

	VG	VF	UNC
S2004 20 Pesos Plata 2.1.1880. Black. Man watching woman mashing corn at right. Male portrait at left. portrait Gen. M. Paz at left. Printer: BWC. Proof.	—	—	400.

Section VI

Provincial

Province of Corrientes

Billetes de Tesoreria ND Issue

<RLS>Ley Promulgada El 16 De Noviembre de 1891

	Good	Fine	XF
S2015 5 Pesos L.1891. Black on brown underprint. Provincial arms at left. Back: Blue. Farmer and dog at left. Printer: CSABB.	25.00	75.00	150.

Province of Jujuy

1903; 1905 Obligaciones de Tesoreria Issue

S2021 5 Centavos — Good 10.00 | Fine 40.00 | XF 100.
1.1.1903. Black on brown underprint. Provincial arms at left. Back: Brown. Printer: CSABB.

S2022 10 Centavos — Good 25.00 | Fine 50.00 | XF 125.
1.1.1903. Black on light green underprint. Provincial arms at upper left. Printer: CSABB.

S2023 50 Centavos — Good 25.00 | Fine 50.00 | XF 125.
1.1.1903. Black on light brown underprint. Provincial arms at upper center. Printer: CSABB.

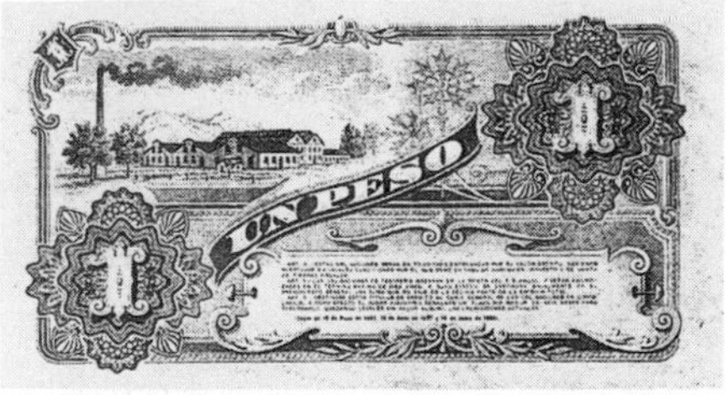

S2024 1 Peso — Good 20.00 | Fine 40.00 | XF 100.
16.6.1905. Red. Provincial arms at left, steam train emerging from tunnel at right. Back: Red and green. Plantation at left. Printer: CSABB.

Leyes 529 & 530 de 20.4.1928; 1928 Issue

S2025 20 Centavos — Good — | Fine — | XF —
L.1928. Black on blue-gray underprint.

1932 Titulos de Crédito Interno Issue

S2035 1 Peso — Good 40.00 | Fine 75.00 | XF 125.
8.11.1932. Black on red-brown underprint. Provincial arms at upper left. Series A. Back: Red.

Province of Mendoza

Ley del 28 de Noviembre de 1892; 1893 Issue

S2042 10 Centavos — Good 10.00 | Fine 25.00 | XF 75.00
1.1.1893. Black on green underprint. Arms at lower left. Series D. Back: Blue. Printer: J. Peuser, Buenos Aires.

S2044 50 Centavos
1.1.1893. Series C. Printer: J. Peuser, Buenos Aires.
- a. Issued note. — — —
- s. Specimen overprint: *MUESTRA.* — — —

	Good	Fine	XF
S2045 1 Peso			
1.1.1893. Arms at top center. Series A. Printer: J. Peuser, Buenos Aires.			
a. Issued note.	10.00	25.00	75.00
s. Specimen overprint: *MUESTRA.*	—	—	—
S2046 5 Pesos			
1.1.1893. Series B. Printer: J. Peuser, Buenos Aires.			
a. Issued note.	—	—	—
s. Specimen overprint: *MUESTRA.*	—	—	—

Ley 28.11.1892 y 25.4.1895; 1893 Issue

	Good	Fine	XF
S2051 1 Peso			
1.1.1893. Series A. Printer: CSABB.			
a. Issued note.	—	—	—
s. Specimen overprint: *MUESTRA.*	—	—	—
S2052 5 Pesos			
1.1.1893. Series B. Printer: CSABB.			
a. Issued note.	—	—	—
s. Specimen overprint: *MUESTRA.*	—	—	—

Ley de 25 de Abril de 1895; 1897 Issue

	Good	Fine	XF
S2056 1 Peso			
Nov. 1897. Series E. Printer: J. Peuser, Buenos Aires.			
a. Issued note.	—	—	—
s. Specimen overprint: *MUESTRA.*	—	—	—

	Good	Fine	XF
S2057 5 Pesos			
Nov. 1897. Black on gold underprint. Arms at left. Series F. Back: Aqueduct. Printer: J. Peuser, Buenos Aires.			
a. Issued note.	25.00	50.00	100.
s. Specimen overprint: *MUESTRA.*	—	—	—

Ley No. 74; 1898 Issue

	Good	Fine	XF
S2059 1 Peso			
May 1898. Black on green underprint. Series 1. Printer: J. Peuser.			
a. Issued note.	—	—	—
s. Specimen overprint: *MUESTRA.*	—	—	—
S2060 5 Pesos			
May 1898. Series 2. Printer: J. Peuser.			
a. Issued note.	—	—	—
s. Specimen overprint: *MUESTRA.*	—	—	—

Ley del 25 de Abril de 1895; 1899 Issue

S2065 1 Peso	Good	Fine	XF
1.12.1899. Arms at lower left. Series E. Back: Mercury with caduceus at right. Printer: CSABB.			
a. Issued note.	20.00	40.00	100.
s. Specimen overprint: *MUESTRA*.	—	—	—

S2066 5 Pesos			
1.12.1899. Series F. Printer: CSABB.			
a. Issued note.	—	—	—
s. Specimen overprint: *MUESTRA*.	—	—	—

Ley No. 210 del 22 de Junio de 1901; First Issue

S2075 1 Peso	Good	Fine	XF
June 1901. Black on green and orange underprint. Arms at top center. Series B; C. Back: Blue. Athena at right. Printer: CSABB.	10.00	25.00	75.00

S2075A 5 Pesos			
June 1901. Woman seated near barrels at left, arms at right. Series A. Back: Mountains. Printer: CSABB.			
a. Issued note.	—	—	—
s. Specimen overprint: *MUESTRA*.	—	—	—

1901 Second Issue

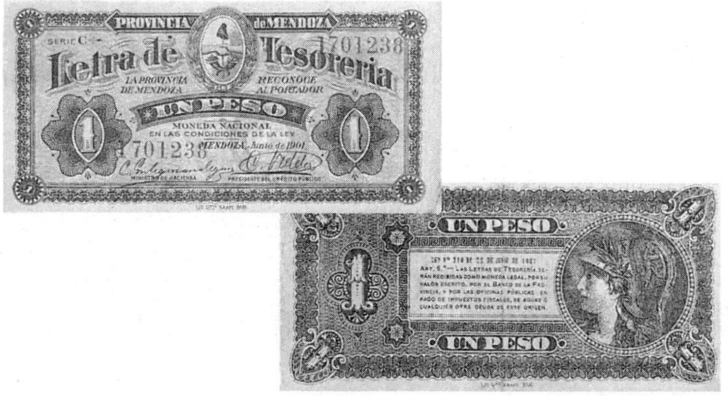

S2076 1 Peso	Good	Fine	XF
June 1901. Black on blue and orange underprint. Arms at top center. Series C. Printer: G. Kraft, Buenos Aires.			
a. Issued note.	10.00	25.00	75.00
s. Specimen overprint: *MUESTRA*.	—	—	—

S2077 5 Pesos			
June 1901. Series B. Printer: G. Kraft, Buenos Aires.	—	—	—

Ley No. 645; 1914 Issues

S2081 50 Centavos	Good	Fine	XF
December 1914. Black and brown on tan underprint. Liberty head at upper left, arms at lower right. Series A. Back: Orange-brown. Overprint: Circular *POR CANJE* on face. Printer: Guillermo Kraft, Buenos Aires.			
a. Issued note.	10.00	40.00	100.
s. Specimen overprint: *MUESTRA*.	—	—	—

S2082 50 Centavos	Good	Fine	XF
December 1914. Back: 2 signatures. Overprint: Black *POR CANJE 1918* Printer: Guillermo Kraft, Buenos Aires.	15.00	40.00	100.

S2083 50 Centavos	Good	Fine	XF
December 1914. Brown, green and black. Series B; C. Back: Green. Girl at center. Overprint: Black *CANJE* twice. Printer: Guillermo Kraft, Buenos Aires.	10.00	25.00	75.00

S2084 50 Centavos	Good	Fine	XF
December 1914. Blue and dark green. Arms at left, portrait woman at lower right. Series A-P. Printer: Guillermo Kraft, Buenos Aires.			
a. Issued note.	15.00	40.00	100.
s. Specimen.	—	—	—

S2085 1 Peso			
December 1914. Black on blue and orange underprint. Arms at top center. Series A. Back: Text. Printer: Guillermo Kraft, Buenos Aires.	10.00	25.00	75.00

S2086 1 Peso	Good	Fine	XF
December 1914. Arms at top center. Back: 2 signatures. Overprint: Black *POR CANJE 1918*. Printer: Guillermo Kraft, Buens Aires.			
a. Issued note.	10.00	20.00	50.00
s. Specimen.	—	—	—

S2087 1 Peso	Good	Fine	XF
December 1914. Black and violet on peach underprint. Arms at center. Series B; C. Back: Red. Black *CANJE* twice. Printer: Guillermo Kraft, Buenos Aires.	10.00	25.00	75.00

S2088 1 Peso	Good	Fine	XF
December 1914. Black and red on olive underprint. Standing Justice at left, winged allegorical man at right. Series A-P. Back: Brown. Monument at center. Printer: Guillermo Kraft, Buenos Aires.			
a. Issued note.	10.00	25.00	75.00
s. Specimen.	—	—	—
S2088A 5 Pesos			
December 1914. Series A. Printer: Guillermo Kraft, Buenos Aires.	—	—	—
S2089 5 Pesos			
December 1914. Allegorical woman reclining by barrels at left, arms at right. Series B. Back: Mountains. Overprint: *CANJE* twice. Printer: Guillermo Kraft, Buenos Aires.	20.00	60.00	125.

S2090 5 Pesos	Good	Fine	XF
December 1914. Black and green. Seated allegorical woman flanking child at center. Series A-P. Back: Woman. Printer: Guillermo Kraft, Buenos Aires.			
a. Issued note.	20.00	60.00	125.
s. Specimen.	—	—	—
S2091 10 Pesos			
December 1914. Grayish green on light gray underprint. Seated woman and globe at center. Series A-P. Back: Blue. Building and hills. Printer: Guillermo Kraft, Buenos Aires.			
a. Issued note.	40.00	100.	—
s. Specimen.	—	—	—

S2092 20 Pesos	Good	Fine	XF
December 1914. Allegorical woman reclining by barrels at left, arms at right. Series A-P. Back: Mountains at center. Printer: Guillermo Kraft, Buenos Aires.			
a. Issued note.	—	—	—
s. Specimen.	—	—	—
S2092A 20 Pesos			
December 1914. Series A-P. Back: *POR CANJE (1923-24)*. Printer: Guillermo Kraft, Buenos Aires.	—	—	—

S2093 50 Pesos	Good	Fine	XF
December 1914. Black on yellow-green underprint. Liberty at center, arms above. Series A-P. Back: Brown-violet. Overprint: *POR CANJE (1923-24)*. Printer: Guillermo Kraft, Buenos Aires.			
a. Issued note.	—	—	—
s. Specimen.	—	—	—

S2094 100 Pesos	Good	Fine	XF
December 1914. Allegorical woman reclining by barrels at left, arms at right. Series A; B. Back: Allegorical woman seated, child standing at center. Printer: Guillermo Kraft, Buenos Aires.			
a. Issued note.	—	—	—
s. Specimen.	—	—	—

S2094A 100 Pesos	Good	Fine	XF
December 1914. Green on yellow underprint. Arms at lower center. Series A-P. Back: *POR CANJE (1923-24)* Printer: Guillermo Kraft, Buenos Aires.			
a. Issued note.	—	—	—
s. Specimen, punched hole cancelled.	—	—	—
S2095 500 Pesos			
December 1914. Black and green on gray underprint. Series A-R. Back: Red.			
a. Issued note.	—	—	—
s. Specimen.	—	—	—

	Good	Fine	XF
S2095A 500 Pesos December 1914. Justice with sword and balance scales at center. Series A-P. Back: Two children with produce at center. Overprint: *POR CANJE* (1923-24).	—	—	—
S2095B 1000 Pesos December 1914. Series A.	—	—	—

Ley No. 650; 1914 Issue

	Good	Fine	XF
S2095C 1 Peso December 1914. Brown-orange. Series A. Printer: Guillermo Kraft, Buenos Aires.	—	—	—
S2095D 5 Pesos December 1914. Black on green underprint. Series A. Printer: Guillermo Kraft, Buenos Aires.	—	—	—
S2095E 10 Pesos December 1914. Black on red underprint. Series A; B. Printer: Guillermo Kraft, Buenos Aires.	—	—	—
S2095F 20 Pesos December 1914. Black and violet on yellow underprint. Series A; B. Printer: Guillermo Kraft, Buenos Aires.	—	—	—
S2095G 50 Pesos December 1914. Black and brown on brown underprint. Reclining figure with implements at left, arms at right. Series A. Printer: Guillermo Kraft, Buenos Aires.	—	—	—

Decreto de 26 de Octobre de 1923

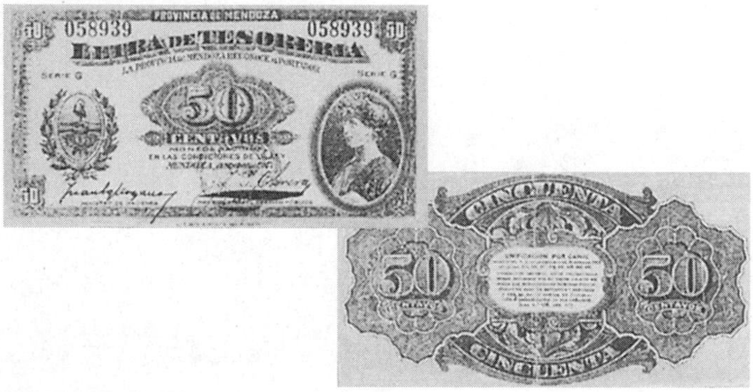

	Good	Fine	XF
S2096 50 Centavos D.1923. Arms at left, portrait woman at lower right. Back: Decree date.	—	—	—

	Good	Fine	XF
S2096A 1 Peso D.1923. Like #S2088. Back: Decree date.	—	—	—

1908 Crédito y Habilitación Industrial Issue

	Good	Fine	XF
S2096F 1 Peso May 1908. Black on green underprint. Arms at upper center. Series A. Back: Allegory of Industry seated at upper center. Overprint: Circular *CREDITO PUBLICO MENDOZA* on front. Square *HABILITADA-Leyes 389 y 437* on back. Printer: CSABB.	—	—	—
S2096G 5 Pesos May 1908. Overprint: Square *HABILITADA -Leyes 389 y 437* on back. Reported not confirmed.	—	—	—
S2096H 20 Pesos May 1908. Overprint: Square *HABILITADA-Leyes 389 y 437* on back. Reported not confirmed.	—	—	—

Province of Salta

1891 Provincial Issue

	Good	Fine	XF
S2097 1 Peso 30.10.1891. Multicolor. Portrait Gen. R. Alvarado at lower left, allegorical woman with sheep at lower right. Series A. Back: Blue. Printer: ABNC. Specimen handstamped: *MUESTRA.*	—	—	—

	Good	Fine	XF
S2098 2 Pesos 30.10.1891. Multicolor. Portrait Dr. Pedro J. Frías at left, woman with cornucopia at right. Series B. Back: Brown. Specimen handstamped: *MUESTRA.*	—	—	—

	Good	Fine	XF
S2099 5 Pesos 30.10.1891. Multicolor. Portrait Gen. E. Frías at left, soldiers on horseback at right. Series C. Back: Green. Specimen handstamped: *MUESTRA.*	—	—	—

	Good	Fine	XF
S2100 10 Pesos 30.10.1891. Multicolor. Portrait Gen. M. Guemes at left, monument of allegorical woman with flag at right. Series D. Back: Red-brown. Specimen handstamped: *MUESTRA.*	—	—	—

Obligaciones de la Provincia; 1907 Issue

	Good	Fine	XF
S2101 1 Peso 30.4.1907. Black on orange underprint. Gen. A. de Apenales at left.	20.00	50.00	125.

1916 Issue

	Good	Fine	XF
S2111 1 Peso 31.8.1916. Black on brown underprint. Small head in star at center. Back: Brown. Cow's head at center. Printer: CSABB.	20.00	50.00	100.
S2112 2 Pesos 31.8.1916. Black on green underprint.	25.00	65.00	125.

1921 Issue

S2121 1 Peso
30.9.1921. Green. Back: Provincial arms at center. Overprint: Red, circular: *EMISION 30 SETIEMBRE 1921 SERIE D* at lower right.

Good	Fine	XF
20.00	50.00	100.

Laws of 20.7.1921, 5.6.1922 and 30.9.1922; 1927 Issue

S2131 1 Peso
6.1927. Portrait Gen. Guemes at left. Round hand stamp: *EMISION DE JUNIO AÑO 1927* at lower center. Back: Chilean railroad at center, provincial arms at right on back. Printer: Peuser.

Good	Fine	XF
25.00	65.00	125.

Laws of 30.9.1922 and 24.1.1928; 1928 Issue

S2136 1 Peso
3.1928. Black on blue underprint. Circular red hand stamp at top center: *EMISION DE MARZO ANO 1928.* Back: Blue. Printer: Peuser.

Good	Fine	XF
20.00	50.00	100.

S2137 2 Pesos
3.1928. Black on red underprint. Circular red hand stamp at top center:*EMISION DE MARZO ANO 1928.* Back: Red. Printer: Peuser.

Good	Fine	XF
25.00	65.00	125.

1931 Renovacion Provisional Issue

S2139 1 Peso
10.1931. Black on blue underprint. Like #S2136 but red circular emission date stamping at upper center on face. Overprint: *RENOVACION 1931* in rectangular box at upper center on back.

Good	Fine	XF
—	—	—

Laws of 5.6.1922, 30.9.1922, 24.1.1928 and 20.10.1932

S2141 1 Peso
L.1932. Black on green underprint. Circular red hand stamp at top center: *EMISION DE MARZO ANO 1928.* Back: Green.

Good	Fine	XF
20.00	40.00	100.

1933 Issue

S2142 1 Peso
1.1933. Black on blue underprint. Red circular emission date stamping at center. Like #2136.

Good	Fine	XF
—	—	—

S2143 2 Pesos
1.1933. Red circular emission date stamping at center. Like #2136.

Good	Fine	XF
—	—	—

Province of San Juan

Ley de 15 de Julio de 1893 Letras de Tesoreria Issue

Treasury Letters of Credit

S2151 1 Peso
31.12.1896. Black on brown underprint. Arms at left. Series G. Back: Brown. Grinder at upper center. Overprint: Black, square; *CREDITO PUBLICO / RENOVACION / SAN JUAN* at center. Printer: CSABB.

Good	Fine	XF
20.00	40.00	100.

Ley de 25 de Julio de 1894

S2155 50 Pesos
L. 1894. Black on green underprint. Portrait Laprida at left, arms at right. Series E. Printer: CSABB.

Good	Fine	XF
—	—	—

Ley de 17 de Enero de de 1898; 1899 Issue

S2161 5 Centavos
15.5.1899. Black on green underprint. Arms at left. Series D. Back: Blue. Printer: CSABB.

Good	Fine	XF
20.00	40.00	100.

S2162 10 Centavos
15.5.1899. Black on brown underprint. Arms at left. Series C. Back: Brown. Printer: CSABB.

Good	Fine	XF
20.00	40.00	100.

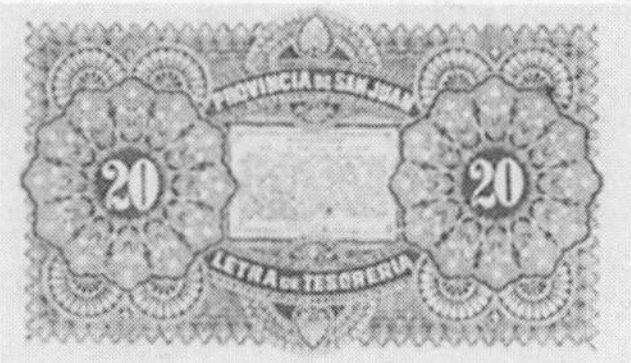

		Good	Fine	XF
S2163	**20 Centavos** 15.5.1899. Black on light green underprint. Arms at right. Series B. Back: Olive-gray. Printer: CSABB.	25.00	50.00	125.

Ley de 17 de Enero de de 1898; 1909 Issue

		Good	Fine	XF
S2174	**50 Centavos** 1.7.1909. Black on brown underprint. Printer: CSABB.	20.00	40.00	100.

		Good	Fine	XF
S2175	**1 Peso** 1.7.1909. Black on green underprint. Arms at left. Series D. Back: Green. Girl and grapes at center. Printer: CSABB.			
	a. Issued note.	20.00	40.00	100.
	b. Red stamping in rectangle on face: *Credito Público / Renovación.*	—	—	—
S2177	**5 Pesos** 1.7.1909. Black on light brown underprint. Back: Brown. Two standing women at right. Overprint: Red; *CREDITO PUBLICO / RENOVACION* across face. Printer: G. Kraft, BsAires.	—	—	—
S2178	**10 Pesos** 1.7.1909. Black on brown underprint. O. Rawson at left, arms at center. Overprint: Red, diagonal; *CREDITO PUBLICO / RENOVACION.*	—	—	—
S2179	**20 Pesos** 1.7.1909. Portrait Sarmiento. Series A.	—	—	—

Ley de 30 de Junio de 1923

		Good	Fine	XF
S2184	**50 Centavos** 1.9.1923. Black on brown underprint. Arms at center. Series A. Back: Green. Printer: Peuser, Buenos Aires.	20.00	40.00	100.

		Good	Fine	XF
S2185	**1 Peso** 1.9.1923. Black on green underprint. Arms at center. Series B. Back: Blue. Printer: Peuser, Buenos AIres.	20.00	40.00	100.
S2187	**5 Pesos** 1.9.1923. Black on light brown underprint. Arms at center. Series D. Back: Light violet. Printer: Peuser, Buenos Aires.	40.00	100.	—
S2188	**10 Pesos** 1.9.1923. Black on ochre underprint. Arms at center. Series A. Back: Black and violet. Printer: Peuser, Buenos Aires.	40.00	100.	—

Ley de 20 de Diciembre 1893; Obligaciones del Monte de Piedad 1894-95 Issue

Obligations of the National Pawn Shop

		Good	Fine	XF
S2191	**5 Centavos** 30.1.1894. Black on light brown underprint. Arms at left. Signature at center right. Series 4. Back: Brown. Printer: CSABB.	20.00	40.00	100.

		Good	Fine	XF
S2192	**5 Centavos** 30.9.1895. Similar to #S191 but signature at left center. Series 4. Back: Like #S191, but different text. Printer: CSABB.	20.00	40.00	100.
S2193	**10 Centavos** 30.9.1895. Black on green underprint. Arms at left. Series 3. Back: Green. Printer: CSABB.	20.00	40.00	100.

		Good	Fine	XF
S2194	**20 Centavos** 30.9.1895. Black on brown underprint. Arms at lower right. Series 2. Back: Brown. Printer: CSABB.	20.00	40.00	100.

Province of Santa Fé

1890 Billetes de Tesoreria Issue

Treasury Bills

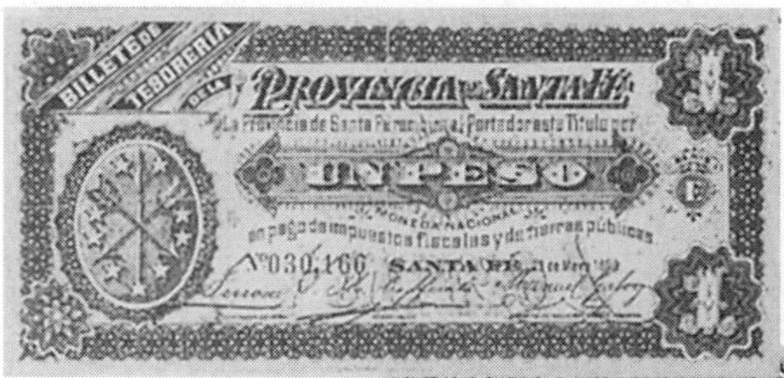

		Good	Fine	XF
S2214	**1 Peso** 23.5.1890. Black on orange underprint. Provincial arms at lower left. Series E. Printer: CSABB.	—	—	—

		Good	Fine	XF
S2215	**2 Pesos** 23.5.1890. Provincial arms at upper right. Series F. Back: Farmer with dog at center. Printer: CSABB.	—	—	—

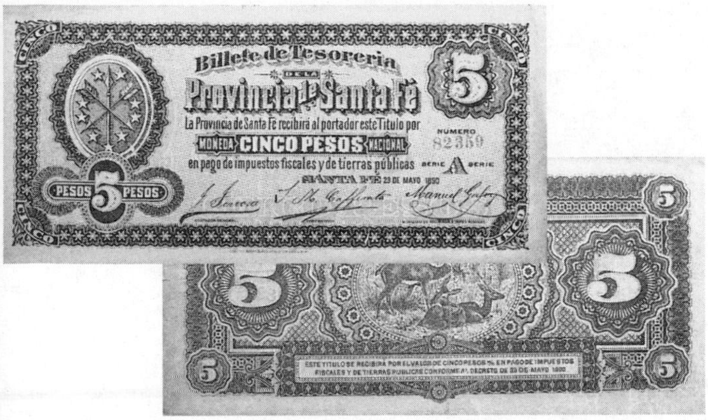

S2216 5 Pesos	Good	Fine	XF
23.5.1890. Black on green underprint. Provincial arms at upper left. Series A. Back: Green. Deer at center. Printer: CSABB.	50.00	150.	—

S2217 10 Pesos	Good	Fine	XF
23.5.1890. Black on blue underprint. Provincial arms at left. Series B. Back: Blue. Eagle at center. Printer: CSABB.	50.00	150.	—

Province of Santiago del Estero

Ley 17.4.1891 Titulo de Credito Issue

S2221 1 Peso	Good	Fine	XF
L.1891. Black on brown underprint. Arms at lower left. Back: Blue. Printer: CSABB.	100.	300.	—

Province of Tucumán

Ley 30.3.1900 Letras de Tesoreria Issue

Treasury Letters of Credit

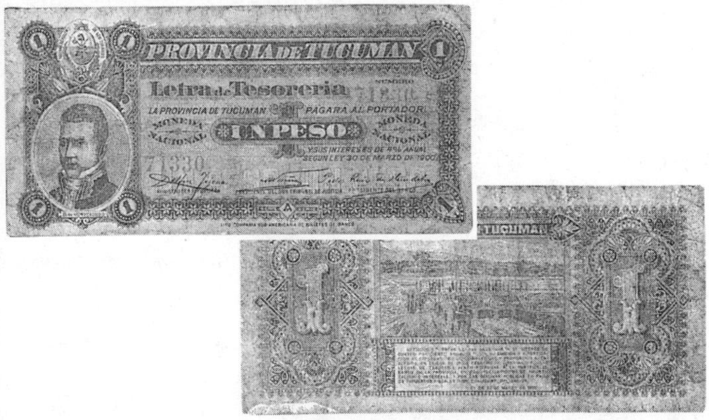

S2235 1 Peso	Good	Fine	XF
ND. Black on brown underprint. Portrait B. de Monteagudo at left, arms above. Series A. Back: Brown. Field scene at center. Printer: CSABB.	20.00	50.00	125.

S2236 2 Pesos	Good	Fine	XF
L.1900. Black on brown underprint. Portrait Alberdi at left. Back: Brown. Tunnels under river at center. Printer: CSABB.	—	—	—

Ley de 12 de Julio de 1915 Titulos de Deuda Pública, Bonos de Fomento Issue

Certificates of Public Debt, Development Bonds

S2245 1 Peso	Good	Fine	XF
1.11.1915. Black on green underprint. Arms at upper center. Series A; D; F; H. Back: Brown. Building at top. Printer: CSABB. Vertical format.	20.00	50.00	125.

S2246 2 Pesos	Good	Fine	XF
1.11.1915. Printer: CSABB. Vertical format.	—	—	—

Ley del 1920

#S2247 and S2248 rectangular ovpt: *Emision de Canje Año 1920* on back.

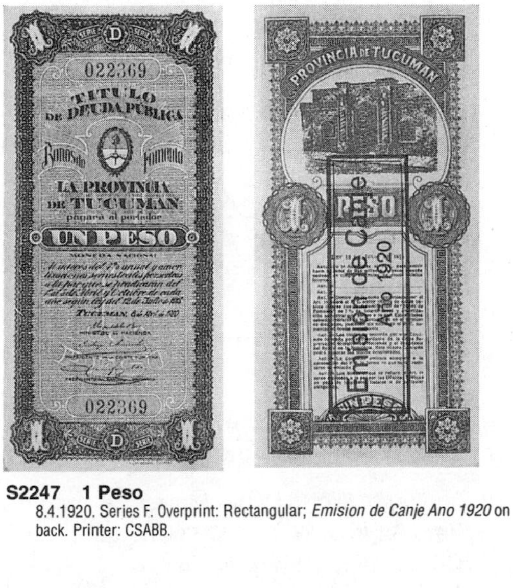

S2247 1 Peso	Good	Fine	XF
8.4.1920. Series F. Overprint: Rectangular; *Emision de Canje Ano 1920* on back. Printer: CSABB.	—	—	—

		Good	Fine	XF
S2248	**2 Pesos** 8.4.1920. Similar to #S2246. Overprint: Rectangular; *Emision de Canje Ano 1920* on back. Printer: CSABB.	20.00	50.00	125.
S2249	**2 Pesos** 1923 (- old date 1920). 1923 date. Overprint: 1923 date on back.	40.00	75.00	150.

Provincial Bonos, 1985-2002

Province of Buenos Aires

Ley No. 12.727; ND Issue

		VG	VF	UNC
S2310	**1 Peso** ND. Riogo Rocha at right. Back: Text, building. Printer: Ciccone.	1.00	2.00	5.00

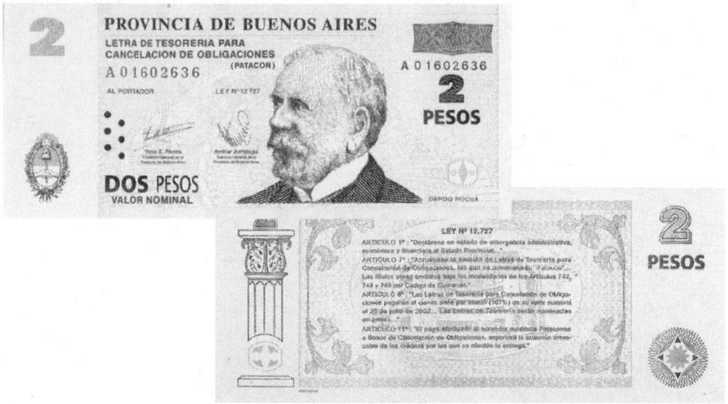

		VG	VF	UNC
S2311	**2 Pesos** ND. Riogo Rocha at right. Back: Text, building. Printer: Ciccone.	1.00	4.00	10.00

NOTICE

Readers with unlisted dates, signature varieties, etc., are invited to submit photocopies or scans of their notes to:

Standard Catalog of World Paper Money,
700 East State St. Iola, WI 54990-0001,
E-Mail: george.cuhaj@fwmedia.com.

		VG	VF	UNC
S2312	**5 Pesos** ND. Riogo Rocha at right. Back: Text, building. Printer: Ciccone.	2.00	6.00	15.00

		VG	VF	UNC
S2313	**10 Pesos** ND. Riogo Rocha at right. Back: Text, building. Printer: Ciccone.	3.00	8.00	20.00

		VG	VF	UNC
S2314	**20 Pesos** ND. Rioga Rocha at right. Back: Text, building. Printer: Ciccone.	5.00	10.00	30.00

Province of Catamarca

Ley 4748 (exp. date 30.11.1998) - Titulo Publico al Portador; 1993 ND Issue

		VG	VF	UNC
S2351	**1 Peso** ND (1993). Dark blue-gray on light blue and multicolor underprint. Mountain highway at center right. Serie A. Arms at upper right. Back: Dark blue-gray text. Printer: Ciccone.	.30	.60	3.00

S2352 5 Pesos	VG	VF	UNC
ND (1993). Green on light blue and multicolor underprint. Barn at center right. Arms at upper right. Serie A. Back: Green text. Printer: Ciccone.	1.00	2.00	10.00

S2353 10 Pesos	VG	VF	UNC
ND (1993). Dark brown on pink and multicolor underprint. Cathedral at center right. Arms at upper right. Serie A. Back: Dark brown text. Printer: Ciccone.	2.00	4.00	20.00

2002 ND Issue

	VG	VF	UNC
S2354 1 Peso ND (2001). Blue and violet. Mountain highway at left center. Serie B. Back: Violet and ochre. Printer: CdM-A.	1.00	2.00	5.00
S2355 5 Pesos ND (2001). Series C. Printer: CdM-A.	2.00	6.00	15.00
S2356 10 Pesos ND (2001). Serie C. Printer: CdM-A.	4.00	10.00	25.00

Province of Cordoba

Ley 8472 (exp. date 1.8.97); ND Issue

	VG	VF	UNC
S2375 5 Pesos 1.8.1995. Black on light green underprint. Provincial arms at upper left, interest coupons at right. Serie A. Back: Text.	1.00	5.00	12.00
S2376 10 Pesos 1.8.1995. Provincial arms at upper left, interest coupons at right. Serie A. Back: Text.	4.00	10.00	25.00

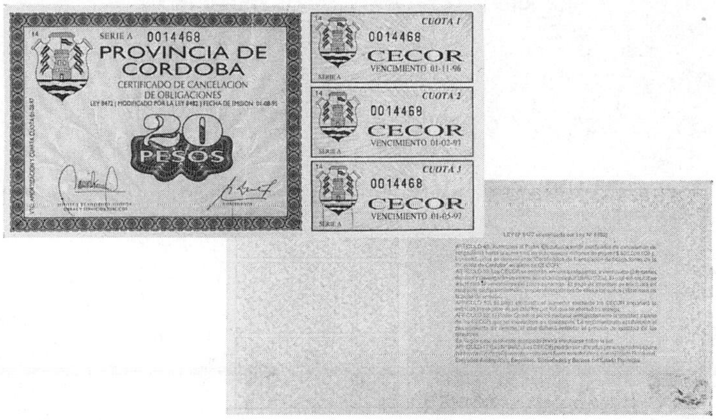

S2377 20 Pesos	VG	VF	UNC
1.8.1995. Provincial arms at upper left, interest coupons at right. Back: Text.	4.00	20.00	45.00

S2378 50 Pesos	VG	VF	UNC
1.8.1995. Provincial arms at upper left, interest coupons at right. Back: Text.	8.00	40.00	100.

Ley 8472 (exp. date 1.1.98); ND Issue

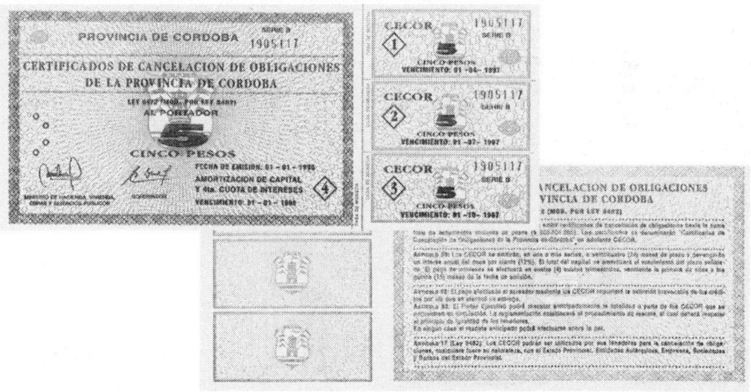

	VG	VF	UNC
S2379 5 Pesos 1.1.1996.	1.00	3.00	10.00
S2380 10 Pesos 1.1.1998. Serie B.	2.00	10.00	25.00

S2381 20 Pesos	VG	VF	UNC
1.1.1996. Serie B.	4.00	20.00	45.00

Decreto No. 2600/01 (exp. date 31.10.2004); ND Issue

		VG	VF	UNC
S2382	**5 Pesos** ND (2002). Cabildo Historico de Cordoba at right. Back: Text.	1.00	5.00	15.00

Province of Corrientes

Ley No. 1/99 (exp. date 17.11.2000); ND Issue

		VG	VF	UNC
S2390	**2 Pesos** 17.1.2000. Blue and red on multicolor underprint. National coat of arms at right, provincial map at center. Serie A. Back: Text. Printer: CdM-A.	1.00	2.00	5.00

		VG	VF	UNC
S2391	**5 Pesos** 17.1.2000. National coat of arms at right, provincial map at center. Serie A. Back: Text. Printer: CdM-A.	2.00	4.00	12.00

		VG	VF	UNC
S2392	**10 Pesos** 17.1.2000. Purple and green on multicolor underprint. National coat of arms at right, provincial map at center. Serie A. Back: Text. Printer: CdM-A.	2.00	4.00	12.00

Ley No. 1/99 (exp. date 31.1.2002); ND Issue

		VG	VF	UNC
S2393	**2 Pesos** 1.8.2000. Provincial coat of arms at right, map at center. Back: Text. Printer: CdM-A.	1.00	2.00	5.00
S2394	**5 Pesos** 1.8.2000. Gray and brown on multicolor underprint. Provincial coat of arms at right, map at center. Serie B. Back: Text. Printer: CdM-A.	2.00	4.00	10.00
S2395	**10 Pesos** 31.1.2002. Provincial coat of arms at right, map at center. Back: Text. Printer: CdM-A.	3.00	6.00	15.00

Province of Formosa

Ley 9/95; ND Issue

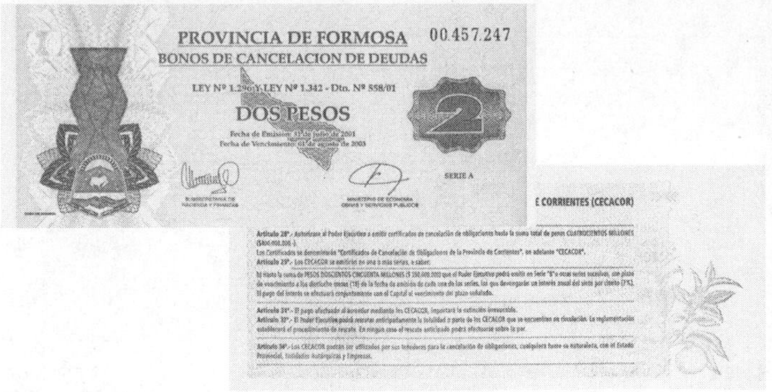

		VG	VF	UNC
S2399	**2 Pesos** ND(1995). Map at center. Back: Text.	1.00	2.00	5.00

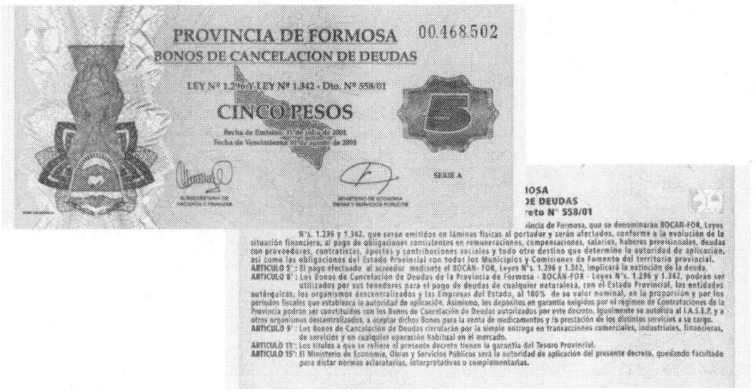

		VG	VF	UNC
S2399A	**5 Pesos** ND(1995). Map at center. Back: Text.	1.00	4.00	10.00

Province of Jujuy

Titulo Publico al Portador Issues

Ley No. 4248 (exp. date 31.12.1988)

		VG	VF	UNC
S2401	**10 Centavos** ND (1986). Brown on orange-brown and multicolor underprint. Military formation at center. Back: Light red text. Printer: Ciccone.	.05	.10	.50

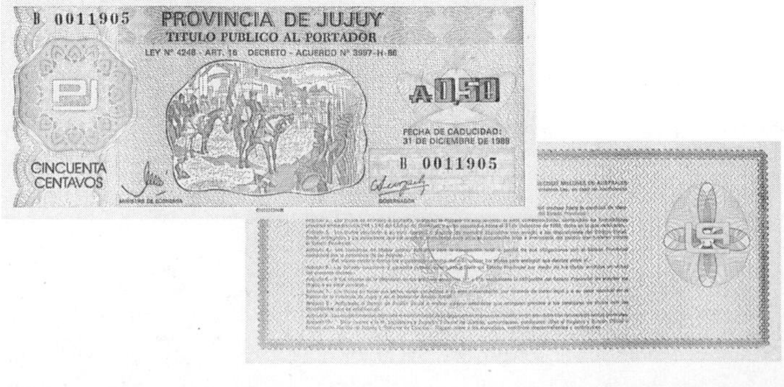

S2402 50 Centavos | VG .10 | VF .20 | UNC .75
ND (1986). Brown on blue and multicolor underprint. Military formation at center. Back: Violet text. Printer: Ciccone.

S2403 1 Austral | VG .10 | VF .25 | UNC 1.00
ND (1986). Blue on aqua and multicolor underprint. Military formation at center. Back: Lilac text. Printer: Ciccone.

S2404 5 Australes | VG .15 | VF .35 | UNC 1.60
ND (1986). Brown on pink and multicolor underprint. Military formation at center. Back: Tan text. Printer: Ciccone.

S2405 10 Australes | VG .20 | VF .50 | UNC 2.25
ND (1986). Deep blue on light blue and multicolor underprint. Military formation at center. Back: Aqua text. Printer: Ciccone.

S2406 50 Australes | VG .30 | VF .80 | UNC 4.00
ND. Green. Military formation at left, arms in underprint at center right. Printer: CdM.

Ley No. 4434/89 (Exp. date 31.12.1989); ND Issue

S2407 100 Australes | VG .40 | VF 1.00 | UNC 5.00
ND. Pink on light blue and multicolor underprint. Military formation at center. Printer: Ciccone.

Ley No. 1422 (Exp. date 1.10.1990); ND Issue

S2408 50 Australes | VG .25 | VF .75 | UNC 3.50
ND. Green. Military formation at left, arms in underprint at center right. Like #S2406. Printer: CdM-A

Ley No. 4439 (Exp. date 31.12.1991); ND Issue

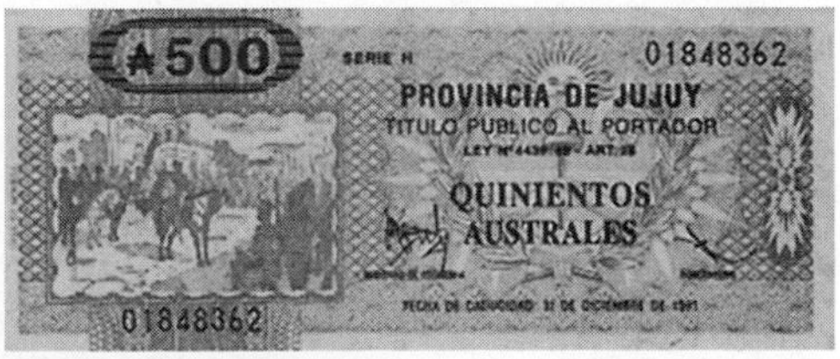

S2409 500 Australes | VG .10 | VF .25 | UNC 1.25
ND. Black text on pink, tan and multicolor underprint. Military formation at center. Back: Text. Printer: Ciccone.

S2410 1000 Australes | VG .20 | VF .50 | UNC 2.50
ND. Lilac. Military formation at center. Back: Text. Printer: Ciccone.

Ley No. 4488 (Exp. date 31.12.1991); ND Issue

S2411 1000 Australes | VG .20 | VF .50 | UNC 2.00
ND. Lilac. Military formation at center. Back: Text. Printer: Ciccone.

Ley No. 4499 (Exp. date 31.12.1990); ND Issue

S2412 5000 Australes | VG .50 | VF 1.25 | UNC 6.50
ND. Light blue. Military formation at center. Back: Text. Printer: Ciccone.

Ley No. 4516/90 (Exp. date 31.12.1991); ND Issue

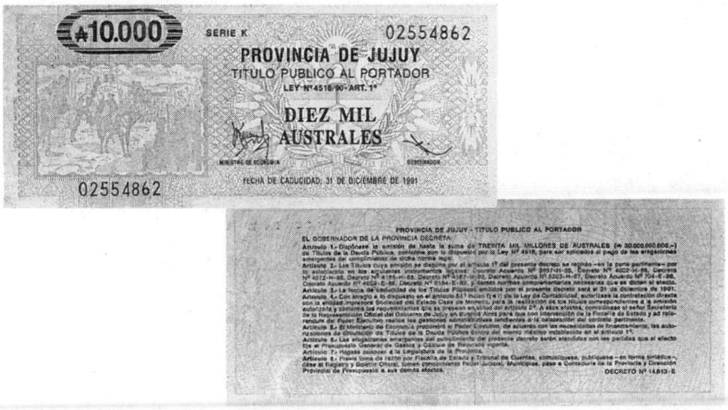

S2413 10,000 Australes | VG 1.00 | VF 2.50 | UNC 10.00
ND. Military formation at left. Back: Text. Printer: Ciccone.

Ley No. 4824 (Exp. date 1.4.2007); ND Issue

S2414 1 Peso | VG 1.00 | VF 2.00 | UNC 4.00
ND. Municipal building at right. Back: Text. Printer: Ciccone.

Province of La Rioja

Ley No. 4534 - Bono Cancelacion de Deuda; 1986 ND Issue

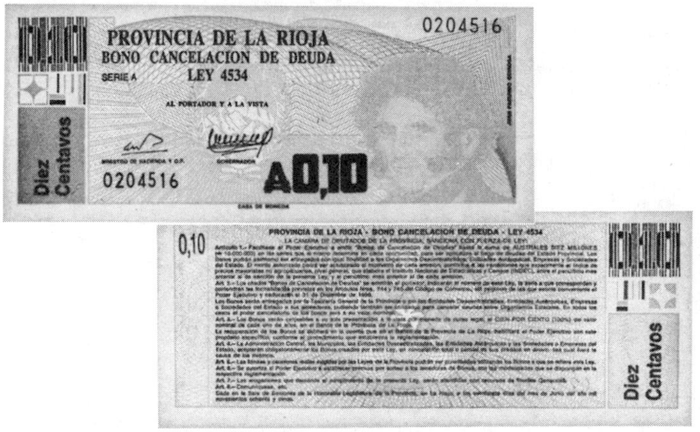

S2501 10 Centavos | VG .05 | VF .10 | UNC .50
ND (1986). Orange with dark brown text on multicolor underprint. Portrait of J. Facundo Quiroga at right. Provincial arms at center. Printer: CdM-A.

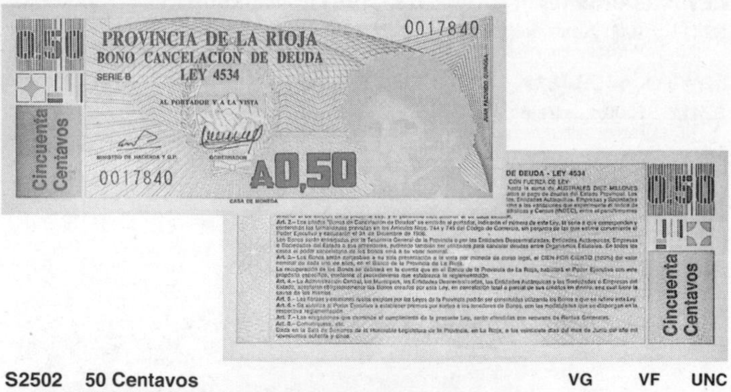

S2502 50 Centavos	VG	VF	UNC
ND (1986). Purple. Portrait of J. Facundo Quiroga at right. Provincial arms at center. Printer: CdM-A.	.10	.20	.75

S2503 1 Austral	VG	VF	UNC
(1986). ND. Green. Portrait of J. Facundo Quiroga at right. Provincial arms at center. Printer: CdM-A.			
a. *Un Austral* written out above denomination at lower center.	.10	.30	1.25
b. Without *Un Austral* above donomination at lower center.	.10	.25	1.00

S2504 5 Australes	VG	VF	UNC
ND (1986). Brown. Portrait of J. Facundo Quiroga at right. Provincial arms at center. Printer: CdM-A.	.15	.35	1.50

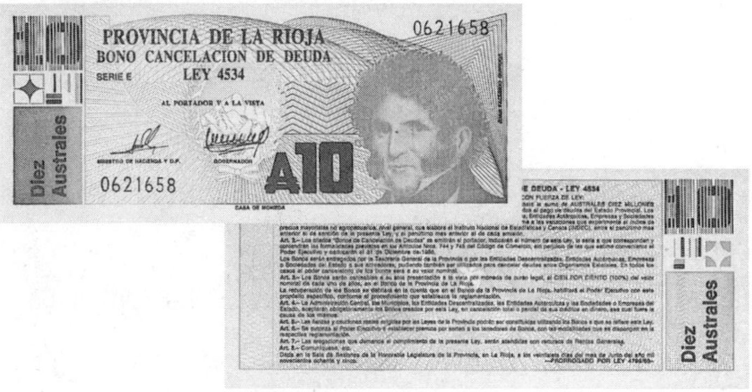

S2505 10 Australes	VG	VF	UNC
ND (1986). Black text on blue and multicolor underprint. Portrait of J. Facundo Quiroga at right. Provincial arms at center. Back: Dark blue text. Printer: CdM-A.	.20	.50	2.25

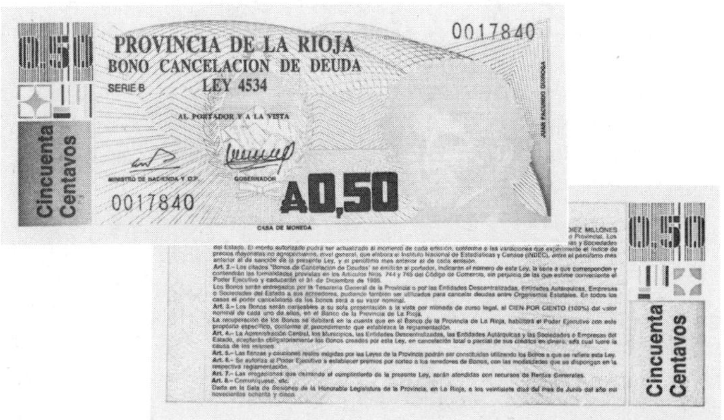

S2506 50 Australes	VG	VF	UNC
ND. Purple. Portrait of J. Facundo Quiroga at right. Provincial arms at center. Printer: CdM-A.	.25	.75	3.50

S2507 100 Australes	VG	VF	UNC
ND. Red and black on multicolor underprint. Portrait of J. Facundo Quiroga at right. Provincial arms at center. Printer: CdM-A.	.25	1.00	5.00

Province of Mendoza

Certificados de Cancelacion de Obligaciones

Ley 8472 (modified by Law 8482)

1995 Issue

S2521 5 Pesos	Good	Fine	XF
1.8.1995. Arms at upper left.	—	—	—

1996 Issue

S2531 5 Pesos	Good	Fine	XF
1.1.1996. Arms at center.	—	—	—

Province of Rio Negro

Decreto Ley 9.95

S2550 1 Peso	VG	VF	UNC
ND. Arms at left. Back: Text. Printer: CdM-A.	1.00	2.00	5.00

S2551 2 Pesos	VG	VF	UNC
ND. Arms at left. Back: Text. Printer: CdM-A.	1.00	3.00	8.00

S2552 5 Pesos	VG	VF	UNC
ND. Arms at left. Back: Text. Printer: CdM-A.	2.00	4.00	12.00

Province of Salta

Ley No. 6228 - Bono de Cancelacion de Deuda;

1985 ND Issue

S2601 50 Pesos Argentinos	VG	VF	UNC
ND (1985). Provincial arms at upper left. Redeemable 31.12.1987. Printer: CdM-A. (Not issued).	.15	.50	2.00

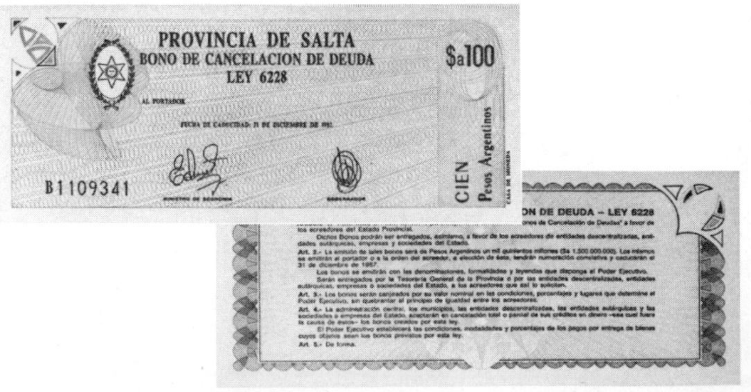

S2602 100 Pesos Argentinos	VG	VF	UNC
ND (1985). Black on green, blue and multicolor. Provincial arms at upper left. Redeemable 31.12.1987. Printer: CdM-A.	.20	.50	2.50

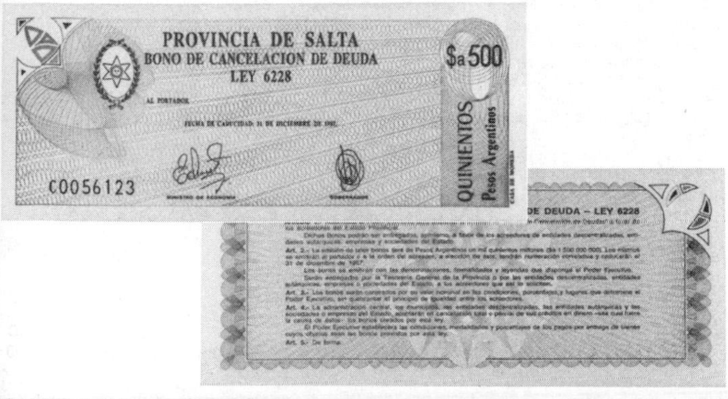

S2603 500 Pesos Argentinos	VG	VF	UNC
ND (1985). Black on ochre, orange and multicolor. Provincial arms at upper left. Redeemable 31.12.1987.	.25	.75	3.50

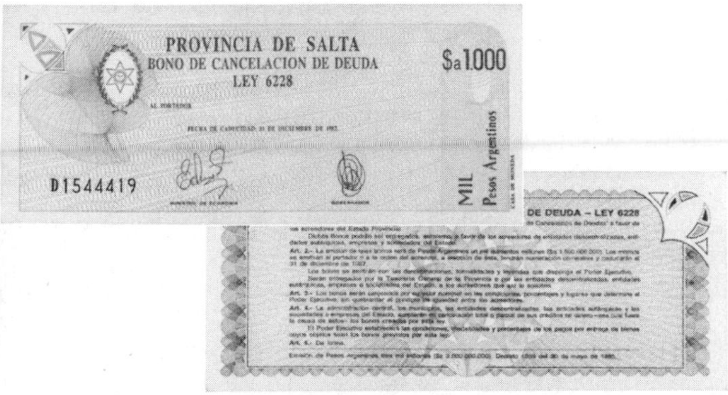

S2604 1000 Pesos Argentinos	VG	VF	UNC
ND (1985). Black on pink, light blue and multicolor. Provincial arms at upper left. Redeemable 31.12.1987. Printer: CdM-A.			
a. Bottom line of text on back ends without *DECRETO...*	.25	1.00	5.00
b. Bottom line ends: *Decreto 1059 del 30 de Mayo de 1985.*	.50	1.25	6.00

S2605 5000 Pesos Argentinos	VG	VF	UNC
ND (1985). Black on blue, light blue and multicolor. Provincial arms at upper left. Redeemable 31.12.1987. Printer: CdM-A.			
a. Bottom line of text on back ends without *DECRETO...*	.50	1.50	7.00
b. Botton line ends: *DECRETO 1059 del 30 Mayo de 1985.*	.50	1.75	8.50

1986 ND Provisional Issue

Currency Reform

1 Austral = 1,000 Pesos Argentinos

#S2606-S2608 brownish black ovpt. new denomination at r. on similar notes like #S2603-S2605 but bottom line of text on back ends w/ *Decreto 1605 del 15 de Agosto de 1985.*

S2606 50 Centavos on 500 Pesos Argentinos	VG	VF	UNC
ND (1986). Black on ochre, orange and multicolor. Back: Text. Overprint: On #S2603.	.10	.20	.75

S2607 1 Austral on 1000 Pesos Argentinos	VG	VF	UNC
ND (1986). Black on pink, light blue and multicolor. Back: Text. Overprint: On #S2604.	.10	.25	1.00

S2608 5 Australes on 5000 Pesos Argentinos	VG	VF	UNC
ND (1986). Black on blue, light blue and multicolor. Back: Text. Overprint: On #2605.	.15	.25	1.50

Ley 6628; 1986 ND Issue

S2611 50 Centavos	VG	VF	UNC
ND (1986). Dark brown on multicolor underprint. Provincial arms at upper left. Back: Bottom line of text on back ends: *Decreto 2248 del 18 de Noviembre de 1985.* Printer: CdM-A.	.05	.10	.25

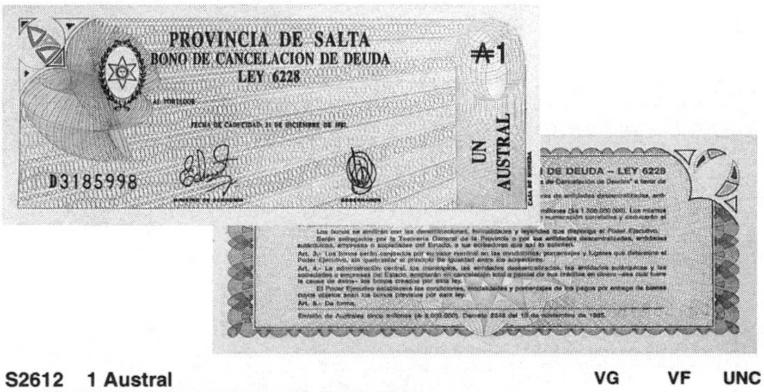

S2612 1 Austral	VG	VF	UNC
ND (1986). Provincial arms at upper left. Printer: CdM-A.			
a. Bottom line of text on back ends: *Decreto 2248 del 16 de Noviembre de 1985.*	.05	.10	.35
b. Bottom line ends: *Decreto 1984/86.*	.05	.10	.25
c. Bottom line ends: *Decreto 245/87.*	.05	.10	.25
d. Bottom line ends: *Decreto 949/87.*	.05	.10	.25
e. Bottom line ends: *Decreto 1520/87.*	.05	.10	.25

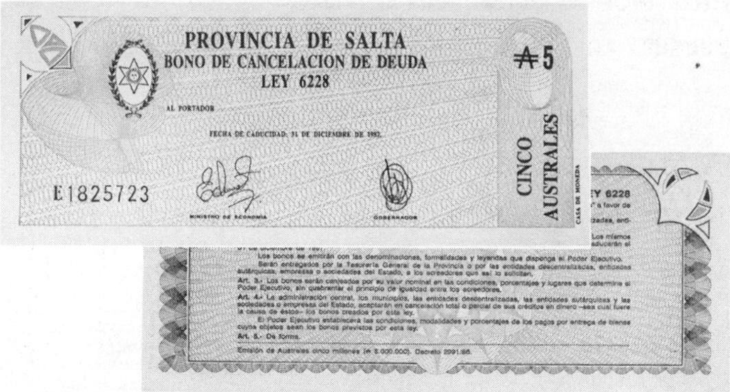

S2613 5 Australes	VG	VF	UNC
ND (1986). Dark brown on multicolor underprint. Provincial arms at upper left. Printer: CdM-A.			
a. Bottom line of text on back ends: *Decreto 2248 del 16 de Noviembre de 1985.*	.10	.20	.50
b. Bottom line on back ends: *Decreto 1984/86.*	.05	.15	.40
c. Bottom line ends: *Decreto 2291/86.*	.05	.15	.40
d. Bottom line ends: *Decreto 245/87.*	.05	.15	.40
e. Bottom line ends: *Decreto 949/87.*	.05	.15	.40
f. Bottom line ends: *Decreto 1520/87.*	.05	.15	.40
g. Bottom line ends: *Decreto 2292/87.*	.05	.15	.40

Leyes No. 6228-6495 (Redeemable 31.10.1991)

S2621 10 Australes	VG	VF	UNC
ND. Black on violet, pale olive-green and multicolor underprint. Provincial arms at upper left, geometric design at right. Back: Text. Printer: CdM-A.			
a. Bottom line of text on back ends: *Decreto 359.88.*	.05	.10	.35
b. Bottom line ends: *Decreto 1556/88 del 01/09/88.*	.05	.10	.35

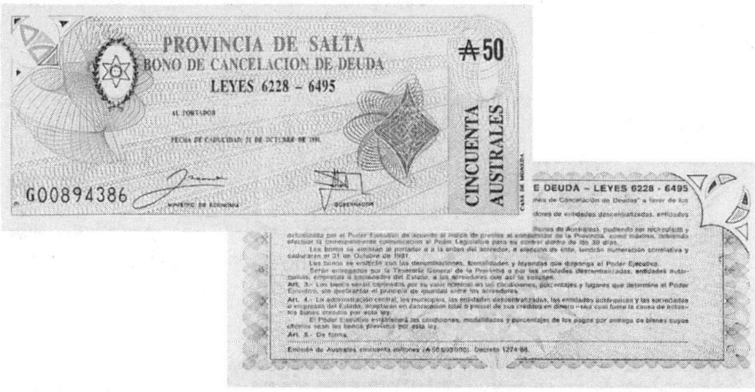

S2622 50 Australes	VG	VF	UNC
ND. Red and black on lilac and multicolor underprint. Provincial arms at upper left, geometric design at right. Back: Bottom line of text on back ends: *Decreto 1274/88.* Printer: CdM-A.	.05	.15	.50

S2623 100 Australes	VG	VF	UNC
ND. Dark olive-green on pale green and multicolor underprint. Provincial arms at upper left, geometric design at right. Back: Text. Printer: CdM-A.			
a. Bottom line of text on back ends: *Decreto 1895/88 del 05/10/88.*	.10	.20	.75
b. Bottom line ends: *Decreto 28/89.*	.10	.20	.75
c. Bottom line ends: *Decreto 887/89 del 31/05/89.*	.10	.20	.75
d. Bottom line ends: *Decreto 1161/89.*	.10	.20	.75

S2624 500 Australes	VG	VF	UNC
ND. Brown, olive-gray and black on lilac and multicolor underprint. Provincial arms at upper left geometric design at right. Back: Text. Printer: CdM-A.			
a. Bottom line of text on back ends: *Decreto 1161/89.*	.10	.25	1.00
b. Bottom line ends: *Decreto 1420 del 31 de Julio de 1989.*	.10	.25	1.00

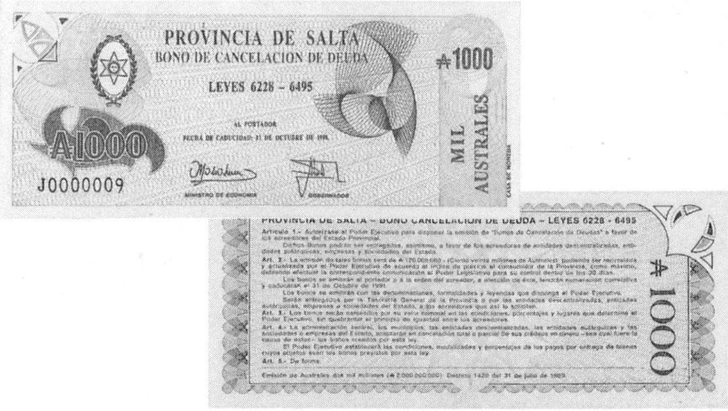

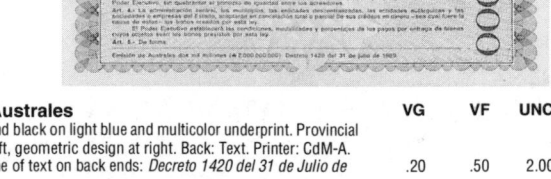

S2625 1000 Australes	VG	VF	UNC
ND. Blue-gray and black on light blue and multicolor underprint. Provincial arms at upper left, geometric design at right. Back: Text. Printer: CdM-A.			
a. Bottom line of text on back ends: *Decreto 1420 del 31 de Julio de 1989.*	.20	.50	2.00
b. Bottom line ends: *Decreto 1624 del 26 de Septiembre de 1989.*	.20	.50	2.00
c. Bottom line ends: *Decreto 2075 del 12 de Diciembre de 1989.*	.20	.50	2.00

S2626 5000 Australes	VG	VF	UNC
ND. Brownish black and violet on multicolor underprint. Provincial arms at upper left, geometric design at right. Back: Text. Printer: CdM-A.			
a. Bottom line of text on back ends: *Decreto 35 del 8 de Enero de 1990.*	.50	1.25	6.50
b. Bottom line ends: *Decreto 277 del 23 de Febrero de 1990.*	.50	1.25	6.50

#S2627 and S2628 replacement notes: Serial # prefix *L99* and *M99.*

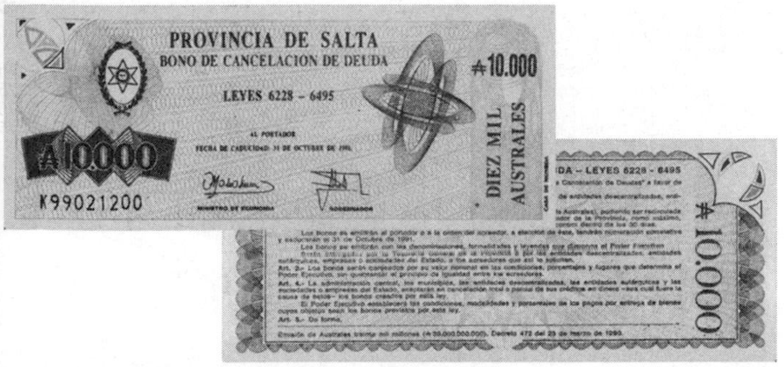

S2627 10,000 Australes	VG	VF	UNC
ND. Brownish-black on multicolor underprint. Provincial arms at upper left, geometric design at right. Back: Text.			
a. Bottom line of text on back ends: *Decreto 277 del 23 de Febrero de 1990.*	1.00	2.50	12.50
b. Bottom line ends: *Decreto 472 del 23 de Marzo de 1990.*	1.00	2.50	12.50
c. Bottom line ends: *Decreto 858 del 18 Mayo de 1990.*	1.00	2.50	12.50
d. Bottom line ends: *Decreto 2620/90.*	1.00	2.50	12.50

Replacement notes: Serial number prefix *L99* and *M99*.

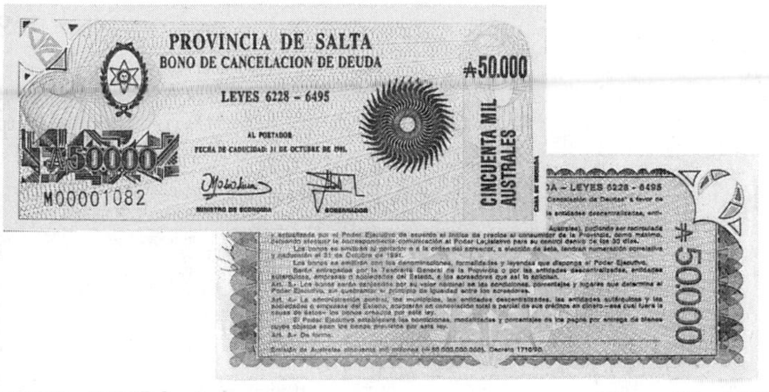

S2628 50,000 Australes	VG	VF	UNC
ND (1990-91). Brownish black on multicolor underprint. Provincial arms at upper left, geometric design at right. Back: Text.			
a. Bottom line of text on back ends: *Decreto 1710/90.*	3.50	12.50	50.00
b. Bottom line ends: *Decreto 2620/90.*	3.50	12.50	50.00
c. Bottom line ends: *Decreto 628/91.*	3.50	12.50	50.00

Replacement notes: Serial number prefix *L99* and *M99*.

Leyes No. 6228-6623; 1991 ND Issue

#S2629 and S2630 replacement notes serial # prefix *L99* and *M99*.

NOTE: #S2629-S2630a redeemable 31.10.1991.

NOTE: #S2630b redeemable 31.03.1992.

S2629 10,000 Australes	Good	Fine	XF
ND (1991). Brownish black on multicolor underprint. Serial # prefix L99 and M99. Back: Bottom line of text on back ends: *Decreto 702/91*. Replacement note.	1.00	2.50	12.50

S2630 50,000 Australes	VG	VF	UNC
ND (1991). Brownish black on multicolor underprint. Serial # prefix L99 and M99. Replacement note.			
a. Bottom line of text on back ends: *Decreto 702/91.*	3.50	12.50	50.00
b. Bottom line ends: *Decreto 1039/91 y 1133/91.*	3.50	12.50	50.00

Province of San Juan

Decreto Acuerdo No 0059/95 (Exp. date 31.7.1995)

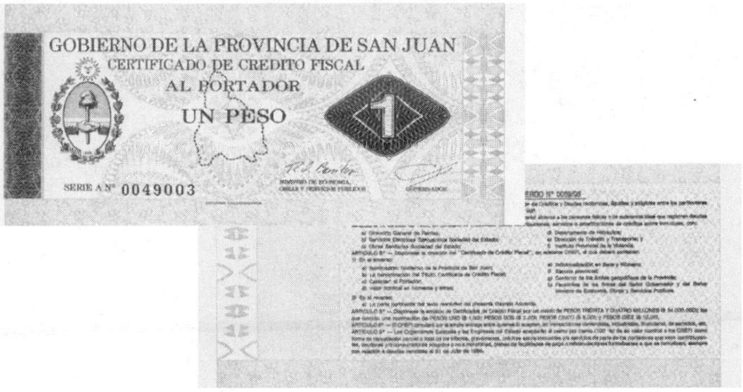

S2651 1 Peso	VG	VF	UNC
ND (1995). Deep blue-violet and red on multicolor underprint. Arms at left. Watermark: Design. Printer: Ciccone Calcografica.	.25	1.25	3.50

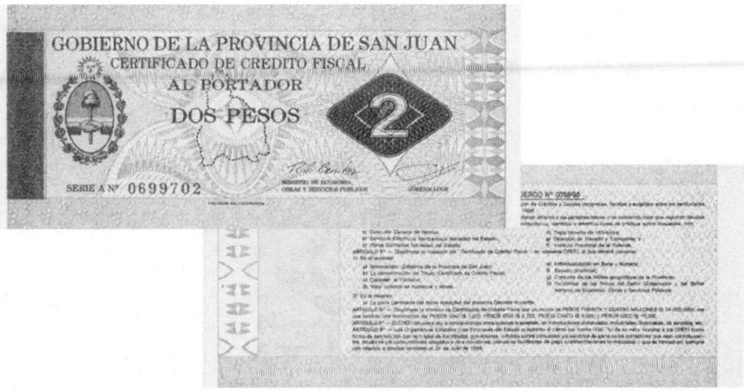

S2652 2 Pesos	VG	VF	UNC
ND (1995). Blue and red on multicolor underprint. Arms at left. Watermark: Design. Printer: Ciccone Calcografica.	.50	3.00	6.00

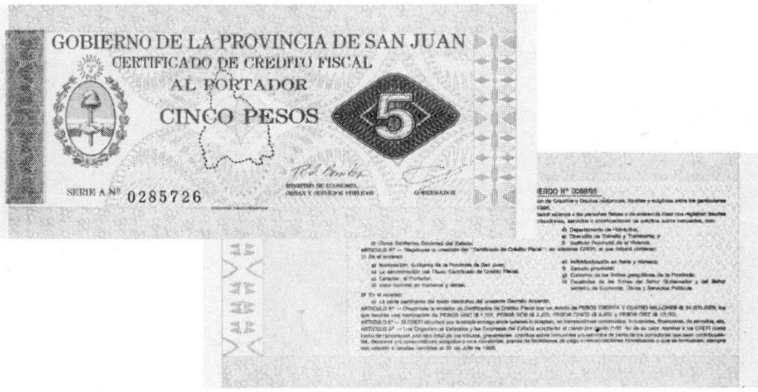

S2653 5 Pesos	VG	VF	UNC
ND (1995). Dark green and deep red on multicolor underprint. Arms at left. Watermark: Design. Printer: Ciccone Calcografica.	1.00	6.00	12.50
S2654 10 Pesos			
ND (1995). Brown-violet and deep blue-green on multicolor underprint. Arms at left. Watermark: Design. Printer: Ciccone Calcografica.	2.00	12.00	25.00

PROVINCE OF TUCUMÁN

BONO DE CANCELACION DE DEUDAS

LEY NO. 5728 (EXP. DATE30.11.1987; 1985 ISSUE

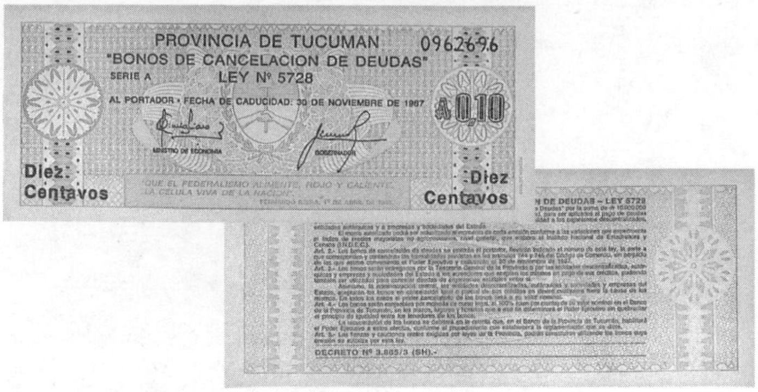

S2701 10 Centavos VG VF UNC
1.4.1985. Dark brown text on pink, green and multicolor underprint. Arms at center in underprint. Three line legend at bottom center. Back: Red-brown text Printer: CdM-A.

	VG	VF	UNC
a. Bottom line of text on back without *Decreto.*	.05	.15	.50
b. Bottom line of text on back with *Decreto* and number.	.05	.15	.50

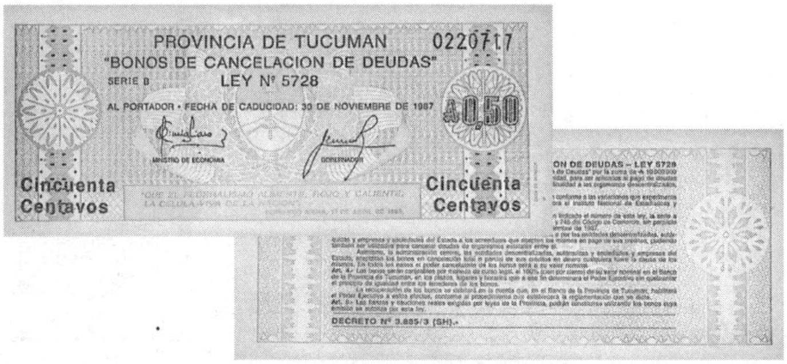

S2702 50 Centavos

	VG	VF	UNC
1.4.1985. Dark brown on lilac and multicolor underprint. Arms at center in underprint. Three line legend at bottom center. Back: Violet text. Printer: CdM-A.	.10	.20	.75

S2703 1 Austral

	VG	VF	UNC
1.4.1985. Dark brown text on lilac and multicolor underprint. Arms at center in underprint. Three line legend at bottom center. Back: Red-brown text. Printer: CdM-A.	.10	.25	1.00

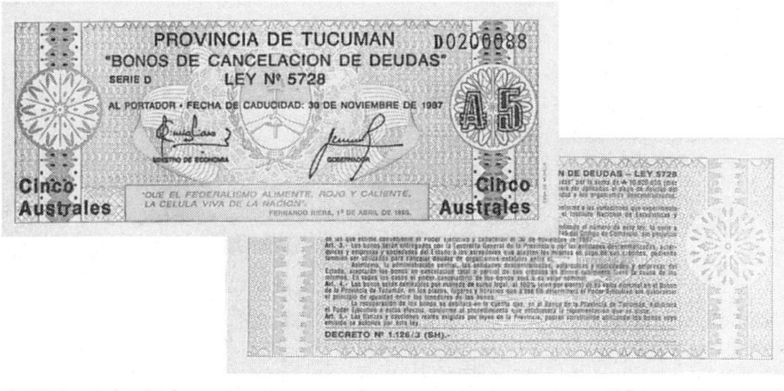

S2704 5 Australes VG VF UNC
1.4.1985. Dark brown text on lilac and multicolor underprint. Arms at center in underprint. Three line legend at bottom center. Printer: CdM-A.

	VG	VF	UNC
a. Bottom line of text on back without *Decreto.*	.10	.25	1.50
b. Bottom line of text on back with *Decreto* and number.	.10	.25	1.25

S2705 10 Australes VG VF UNC
1.4.1985. Light blue, pink and multicolor underprint. Arms at center in underprint. Three line legend at bottom center. Printer: CdM-A.

	VG	VF	UNC
a. Bottom line of text on back without *Decreto.*	.15	.50	2.25
b. Bottom line of text on back with *Decreto* and number.	.15	.50	1.75

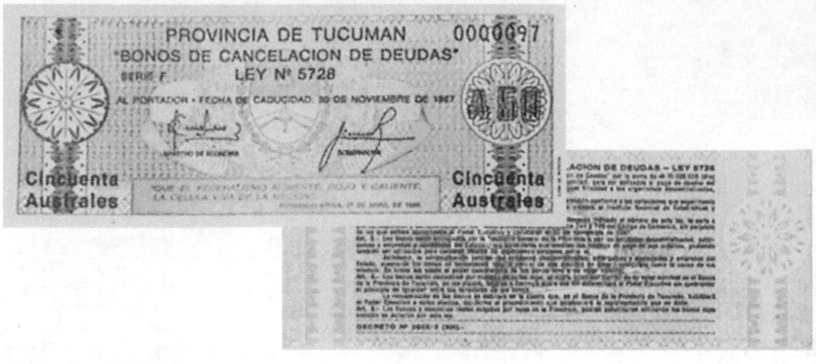

S2706 50 Australes

	VG	VF	UNC
1.4.1985. Dark brown text on lilac and multicolor underprint. Arms at center in underprint. Three line legend at bottom center. Printer: CdM-A.	.15	.50	2.50

LEY NO. 5728 (EXP. DATE 30.11.1991); ND ISSUE

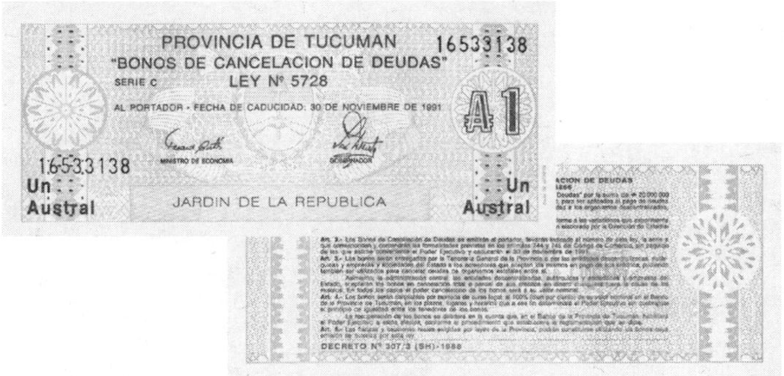

S2711 1 Austral VG VF UNC
ND. Green. Arms at center in underprint. Three line legend at bottom center. Printer: CdM-A.

	VG	VF	UNC
a. No text at bottom center.	.05	.10	.35
b. *JARDIN DE LA REPÚBLICA* at bottom center.	.05	.10	.25

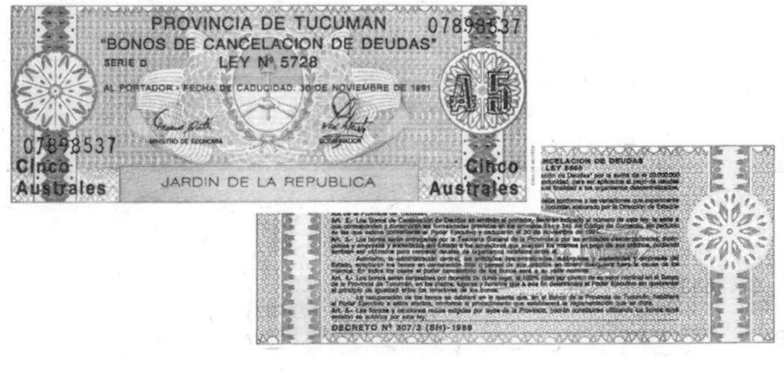

S2712 5 Australes VG VF UNC
ND. Pink. Arms at center in underprint. Three line legend at bottom center. Printer: CdM-A.

	VG	VF	UNC
a. No text at bottom center.	.05	.15	.50
b. *JARDIN DE LA REPÚBLICA* at bottom center.	.05	.15	.50

S2713 10 Australes
ND. Light blue. Arms at center in underprint. Three line legend at bottom center. Printer: CdM-A.

	VG	VF	UNC
a. No text at bottom center.	.10	.20	.50
b. *JARDIN DE LA REPÚBLICA* at bottom center.	.10	.20	.50

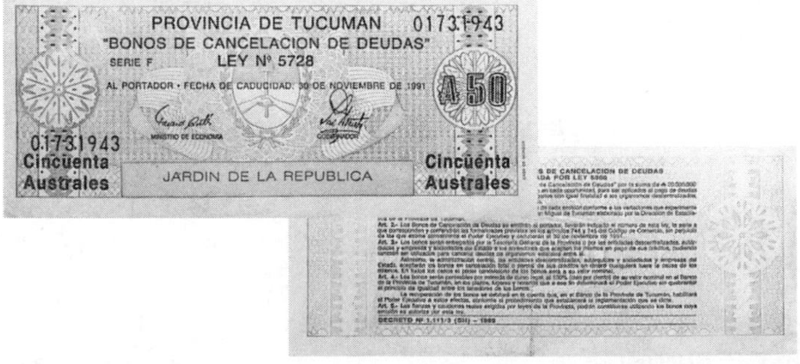

S2714 50 Australes

	VG	VF	UNC
ND. Black text on lilac and tan underprint. *JARDIN DE LA REPÚBLICA* at bottom center. Printer: CdM-A.	.10	.20	.75

#S2715-S2719 house of Tucumán at ctr., arms at r.

S2715 100 Australes

	VG	VF	UNC
ND. Red-violet, black and multicolor. House of Tucumán at center. Arms at right.	.10	.25	1.00

S2716 500 Australes

	VG	VF	UNC
Nd. Light blue. House of Tucumán at center. Arms at right. Series H.	.20	.50	2.00

S2717 5000 Australes

	VG	VF	UNC
ND. Black on light green and multicolor underprint. House of Tucumán at center. Arms at right. Series I.	.50	1.50	6.50

S2718 10,000 Australes

	VG	VF	UNC
ND. Black on light reddish brown and multicolor underprint. House of Tucumán at center. Arms at right. Series J.	1.00	2.50	12.50

S2719 50,000 Australes

	VG	VF	UNC
ND (1990). Black text on light red-violet and multicolor underprint. House of Tucumán at center. Arms at right. Back: Dark blue-green text on light blue and multicolor underprint. Watermark: Multiple oval arms. Printer: CdM-A.	1.00	2.50	12.50

Ley No. 5728 (exp. date 30.11.1995); ND Issue

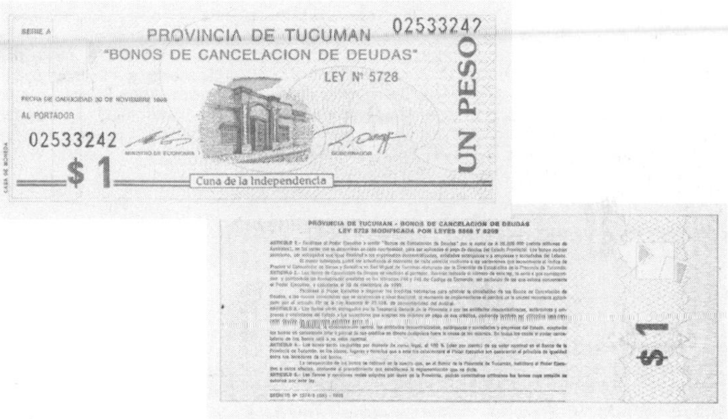

S2720 1 Peso

	VG	VF	UNC
ND. House of Tucuman at center. Back: Text. Printer: CdM-A.	1.00	4.00	10.00

Ley No. 5728 (exp. date 31.12.2003); ND Issue

	VG	VF	UNC
S2721 2 Pesos			
ND. House of Tucuman at right. Back: Text. Printer: Ciccone Calcografica.	1.00	2.00	5.00
S2722 5 Pesos			
ND. House of Tucuman at right. Back: Text. Printer: Ciccone Calcografica.	1.00	4.00	10.00
S2723 10 Pesos			
ND. House of Tucuman at right. Back: Text. Printer: Ciccone Calcografica.	4.00	10.00	20.00

AUSTRALIA

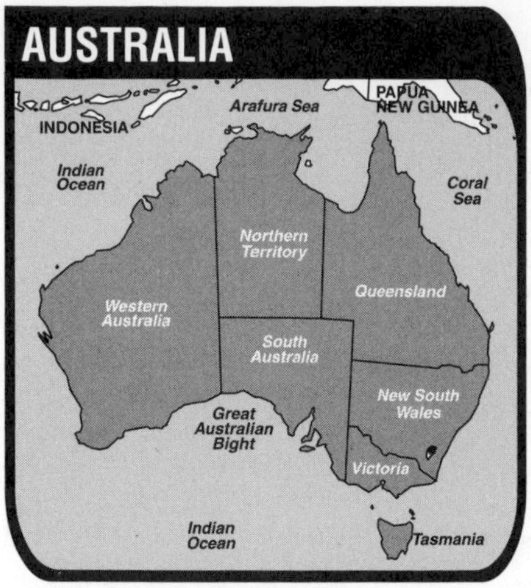

The Commonwealth of Australia, the smallest continent and largest island in the world, is located south of Indonesia between the Indian and Pacific oceans. It has an area of 7.68 million sq. km. and a population of 21 million. Capital: Canberra. Due to its early and sustained isolation, Australia is the habitat of such curious and unique fauna as the kangaroo, koala, platypus, wombat and barking lizard. The continent possesses extensive mineral deposits, the most important of which are gold, coal, silver, nickel, uranium, lead and zinc. Livestock raising, mining and manufacturing are the principal industries. Chief exports are wool, meat, wheat, iron ore, coal and nonferrous metals.

Aboriginal settlers arrived on the continent from Southeast Asia about 40,000 years before the first Europeans began exploration in the 17th century. No formal territorial claims were made until 1770, when Capt. James Cook took possession in the name of Great Britain. Six colonies were created in the late 18th and 19th centuries; they federated and became the Commonwealth of Australia in 1901. The new country took advantage of its natural resources to rapidly develop agricultural and manufacturing industries and to make a major contribution to the British effort in World Wars I and II. In recent decades, Australia has transformed itself into an internationally competitive, advanced market economy. It boasted one of the OECD's fastest growing economies during the 1990s, a performance due in large part to economic reforms adopted in the 1980s. Long-term concerns include climate-change issues such as the depletion of the ozone layer and more frequent droughts, and management and conservation of coastal areas, especially the Great Barrier Reef.

RULERS:

British

MONETARY SYSTEM:

1 Shilling = 12 Pence
1 Pound = 20 Shillings = 2 Dollars
1 Pound = 20 Shillings; to 1966
1 Dollar = 100 Cents, 1966-

PRIVATE BANKS

Although prolific in number of issues, few notes of the early banks have survived or have been accurately recorded except for the very late issues ca. 1910 bearing the superscribed ovpt: *AUSTRALIAN NOTE*. The pioneer work in this field is *Australian Bank Notes 1817-1963* by G.W. Tomlinson published in 1963. The latest reference work is *Banks of Issue in Australia* by Michael P. Vort-Ronald published in 1982. The following listing of banks of issue is taken from the latter reference.

BANKS OF ISSUE	HEAD OFFICE	DATES
Australian and European Bank Limited	Melbourne	1874-1879
Australian Banking Company Limited	Sydney	1886-1891
Australian Bank of Commerce Limited	Sydney	1910-1931
Australian Joint Stock Bank Limited	Sydney	1853-1910
Bank of Adelaide	Adelaide ***	1865-1980
Bank of Australasia ***	London	1835-1951
Bank of Australia	Sydney	1826-1843
Bank of Newcastle	Newcastle	1828-1829
Bank of New South Wales ***	Sydney	1817-1982
Bank of New Zealand	Wellington	1861-
Bank of North Queensland Limited	Brisbane	1888-1917
Bank of Parramatta **	Parramatta	1830's
Bank of Queensland Limited	London	1863-1866
Bank of South Australia Limited	London	1836-1892
Bank of Tasmania	Launceston	1853-1885
Bank of Van Diemen's Land Limited	Hobart	1823-1891
Bank of Victoria Limited ***	Melbourne	1853-1927
Bank of Western Australia	Perth	1837-1841
Bathurst Bank	Bathurst	1835-1840
City Bank of Sydney ***	Sydney	1863-1918
City of Melbourne Bank Limited	Melbourne	1873-1895
Colonial Bank	Hobart	1840-1843
Colonial Bank of Australasia Limited	Melbourne	1856-1918
Commercial Bank of Australia Limited ***	Melbourne	1866-1982
Commercial Bank of South Australia	Adelaide	1878-1886
Commercial Bank of Tasmania Limited ***	Hobart	1829-1921
Commercial Banking Company of Sydney Limited ***	Sydney	1834-1982
Cornwall Bank	Launceston	1828-1835
Derwent Bank	Hobart	1827-1849
English, Scottish & Australian (Chartered) Bank Limited	London	1852-1970
Excelsior Bank *	Sydney	1880-1893
Federal Bank of Australia Limited	Melbourne	1881-1893
London Bank of Australia Limited ***	London	1852-1921
Mercantile Bank of Australia	Melbourne	1885-1892
Mercantile Bank of Sydney	Sydney	1869-1892
Metropolitan Bank Limited	Melbourne	1888-1891
National Bank of Australasia Limited ***	Melbourne	1858-1982
National Bank of Tasmania Limited	Launceston	1885-1918
New South Wales Government	Sydney	1893
Oriental Bank Corporation	London	1851-1884
Port Phillip Bank	Melbourne	1839-1843
Producers' Bank, Sydney **	Sydney	1851-1861?
Provincial and Suburban Bank Limited	Melbourne	1872-1879
Queensland Government	Brisbane	1866-1869
Queensland Government ***	Brisbane	1893-1910
Queensland National Bank Limited	Brisbane	1872-1948
Royal Bank of Australia (Boyd's)	London	1840-1850
Royal Bank of Australia Limited ***	Melbourne	1888-1927
Royal Bank of Queensland Limited	Brisbane	1885-1917
Sydney & County Bank Limited	Sydney	1881-1882
Sydney Bank **	Sydney	1826
Sydney Banking Company	Sydney	1839-1843
Sydney Deposit Bank	Sydney	1885-1892
Tamar Bank	Launceston	1834-1838
Tasmanian Bank	Hobart	1826-1829
Town and Country Bank	Adelaide	1881-1886
Union Bank of Australia Limited ***	London	1837-1951
Waterloo Company	Sydney	1822-1834
Western Australian Bank ***	Perth	1841-1927

Many of the above banks issued notes at branch offices and some were located in other states.

* A bank which had not become a bank of issue, but whose note forms have been observed.

** Not regarded as a legitimate or genuine bank, or bank of issue.

*** Various notes issued by fifteen banks and the Queensland Government (marked "****" in the listing of private banks) were used by the Australian Government from 1910-1914. These superscribed notes were vertically ovpt: *AUSTRALIAN NOTE* and include a promise to pay in gold, with the date *1st December 1910*. For further details and illustrations see Vol. 2.

BRITISH ADMINISTRATION

GOVERNMENT OF NEW SOUTH WALES

1893 ND TREASURY ISSUE

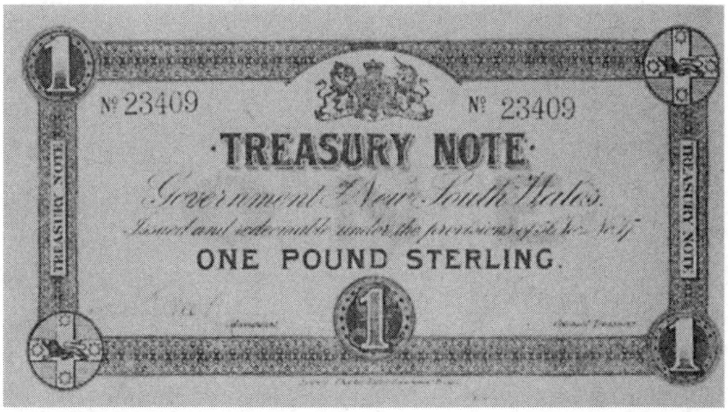

		Good	Fine	XF
S1001 1 Pound ND (1893). Black. Arms at top center.		—	—	—

NOTE: Aug. 1990 Spink auction, $10,500 in VF.

		Good	Fine	XF
S1002 5 Pounds ND (1893). Arms at top center. Back: Brown.		—	Unc	16,500.
S1003 10 Pounds ND (1893). Yellow. Arms at top center.		—	Unc	17,000.
S1004 20 Pounds ND (1893). Green. Arms at top center.		—	Unc	18,000.
S1005 50 Pounds ND (1893). Light blue. Arms at top center.		—	Unc	20,000.

QUEENSLAND

1866 TREASURY ISSUE

		Good	Fine	XF
S1006 1 Pound 1.11.1866. Light blue. Medallic portrait of Queen Victoria at upper center. Back: Violet.		—	—	—
S1007 5 Pounds 1866. Pink. Medallic portrait of Queen Victoria at upper center. Back: Brown.		—	—	—

1893 Superscribed Issue

Ovpt: *GOVERNMENT OF QUEENSLAND/TREASURY NOTE* payable on demand on face or back on issues of eight different private banks.

	Good	Fine	XF
S1008 1 Pound 2.6.1893 Overprint: *GOVERNMENT OF QUEENSLAND/TREASURY NOTE.* Overprint on Australia Joint Stock Bank. Rare.	—	—	—
S1009 5 Pounds 2.6.1893. Overprint: *GOVERNMENT OF QUEENSLAND/TREASURY NOTE.* Overprint on Australia Joint Stack Bank. Rare.	—	—	—
S1010 10 Pounds 2.6.1893. Overprint: *GOVERNMENT OF QUEENSLAND/TREASURY NOTE.* Overprint on Australia Joint Stock Bank.	—	—	—
S1011 20 Pounds 2.6.1893. Overprint: *GOVERNMENT OF QUEENSLAND/TREASURY NOTE.* Overprint on Australia Joint Stock Bank. Rare.	—	—	—

#S1012-S1015 Ovpt. on Bank of Australasia.

	Good	Fine	XF
S1012 1 Pound 2.6.1893. Overprint: *GOVERNMENT OF QUEENSLAND/TREASURY NOTE.* Overprint on Bank of Australia. Rare.	—	—	—
S1013 5 Pounds 2.6.1893. Overprint: *GOVERNMENT OF QUEENSLAND/TREASURY NOTE.* Overprint on Bank of Australasia. Rare.	—	—	—
S1014 10 Pounds 2.6.1893. Overprint: *GOVERNMENT OF QUEENSLAND/TREASURY NOTE.* Overprint on Bank of Australia. Rare.	—	—	—
S1015 50 Pounds 1893. Overprint: *GOVERNMENT OF QUEENSLAND/TREASURY NOTE.* Overprint on Bank of Australia. Rare.	—	—	—

#S1016-S1019 Ovpt. on Bank of New South Wales.

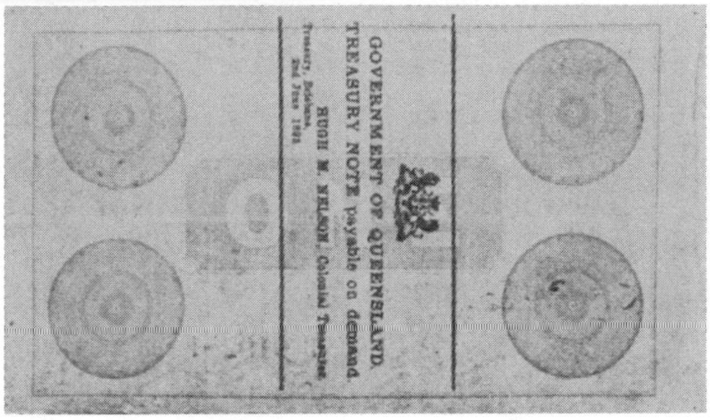

	Good	Fine	XF
S1016 1 Pound 2.6.1893. Overprint: *GOVERNMENT OF QUEENSLAND/TREASURY NOTE.* Overprint on Bank of New South Wales. Rare.	—	—	—
S1017 5 Pounds 2.6.1893. Overprint: *GOVERNMENT OF QUEENSLAND/TREASURY NOTE.* Overprint on Bank of New South Wales. Rare.	—	—	—
S1018 10 Pounds 2.6.1893. Overprint: *GOVERNMENT OF QUEENSLAND/TREASURY NOTE.* Overprint on Bank of New South Wales. Rare.	—	—	—
S1019 20 Pounds 2.6.1893. Overprint: *GOVERNMENT OF QUEENSLAND/TREASURY NOTE.* Overprint on Bank of New South Wales. Rare.	—	—	—

#S1020-S1023 Ovpt. on Bank of North Queensland.

	Good	Fine	XF
S1020 1 Pound 2.6.1893. Overprint: *GOVERNMENT OF QUEENSLAND/TREASURY NOTE.* Overprint on Bank of North Queensland. Rare.	—	—	—
S1021 5 Pounds 2.6.1893. Overprint: *GOVERNMENT OF QUEENSLAND/TREASURY NOTE.* Overprint on Bank of North Queensland. Rare.	—	—	—
S1022 10 Pounds 2.6.1893. Overprint: *GOVERNMENT OF QUEENSLAND/TREASURY NOTE.* Overprint on Bank of North Queensland. Rare.	—	—	—
S1023 20 Pounds 2.6.1893. Overprint: *GOVERNMENT OF QUEENSLAND/TREASURY NOTE.* Overprint on Bank of New Queensland. Rare.	—	—	—

#S1024-S1027 Ovpt. on Commercial Banking Co. of Sydney.

	Good	Fine	XF
S1024 1 Pound 2.6.1893. Overprint: *GOVERNMENT OF QUEENSLAND/TREASURY NOTE.* Overprint on Commercial Banking Co. of Sydney. Rare.	—	—	—
S1025 5 Pounds 2.6.1893. Overprint: *GOVERNMENT OF QUEENSLAND/TREASURY NOTE.* Overprint on Commercial Banking Co. of Sydney. Rare.	—	—	—
S1026 10 Pounds 2.6.1893. Overprint: *GOVERNMENT OF QUEENSLAND/TREASURY NOTE.* Overprint on Commercial Banking Co. of Sydney. Rare.	—	—	—
S1027 20 Pounds 2.6.1893. Overprint: *GOVERNMENT OF QUEENSLAND/TREASURY NOTE.* Overprint on Commercial Banking Co. of Sydney. Rare.	—	—	—

#S1028-S1031 Ovpt. on Queensland National Bank.

	Good	Fine	XF
S1028 1 Pound 2.6.1893. Overprint: *GOVERNMENT OF QUEENSLAND/TREASURY NOTE.* Overprint on Queensland National Bank. Rare.	—	—	—
S1029 5 Pounds 2.6.1893. Overprint: *GOVERNMENT OF QUEENSLAND/TREASURY NOTE.* Overprint on Queensland National Bank. Rare.	—	—	—
S1030 10 Pounds 2.6.1893. Overprint: *GOVERNMENT OF QUEENSLAND/TREASURY NOTE.* Overprint on Queensland National Bank. Rare.	—	—	—
S1031 20 Pounds 2.6.1893. Overprint: *GOVERNMENT OF QUEENSLAND/TREASURY NOTE.* Overprint on Queensland National Bank. Rare.	—	—	—

#S1032-S1035 Ovpt. on Royal Bank of Queensland.

	Good	Fine	XF
S1032 1 Pound 2.6.1893. Overprint: *GOVERNMENT OF QUEENSLAND/TREASURY NOTE.* Overprint on Royal Bank of Queensland. Rare.	—	—	—
S1033 5 Pounds 2.6.1893. Overprint: *GOVERNMENT OF QUEENSLAND/TREASURY NOTE.* Overprint on Royal Bank of Queensland. Rare.	—	—	—
S1034 10 Pounds 2.6.1893. Overprint: *GOVERNMENT OF QUEENSLAND/TREASURY NOTE.* Overprint on Royal Bank of Queensland. Rare.	—	—	—
S1035 20 Pounds 2.6.1893. Overprint: *GOVERNMENT OF QUEENSLAND/TREASURY NOTE.* Overprint on Royal Bank of Queensland. Rare.	—	—	—

#S1036-S1039 Ovpt. on Union Bank of Australia.

	Good	Fine	XF
S1036 1 Pound 2.6.1893. Overprint: *GOVERNMENT OF QUEENSLAND/TREASURY NOTE.* Overprint on Union Bank of Australia. Rare.	—	—	—
S1037 5 Pounds 2.6.1893. Overprint: *GOVERNMENT OF QUEENSLAND/TREASURY NOTE.* Overprint on Union Bank of Australia. Rare.	—	—	—
S1038 10 Pounds 2.6.1893. Overprint: *GOVERNMENT OF QUEENSLAND/TREASURY NOTE.* Overprint on Union Bank of Australia. Rare.	—	—	—
S1039 20 Pounds 2.6.1893. Overprint: *GOVERNMENT OF QUEENSLAND/TREASURY NOTE.* Overprint on Union Bank of Australia. Rare.	—	—	—

1893; 1899 Brisbane Regular Issue

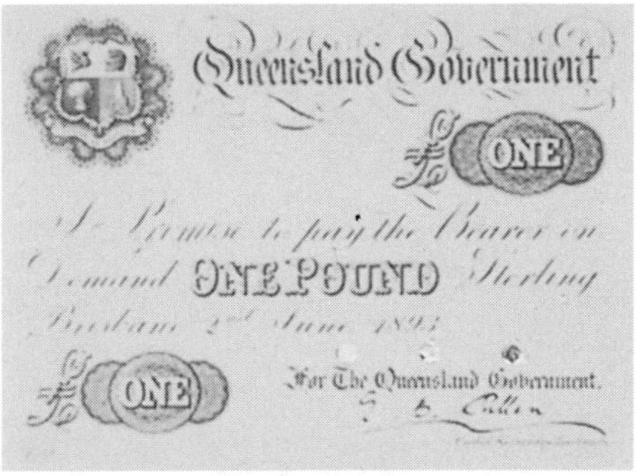

	Good	Fine	XF
S1040 1 Pound 2.6.1893. Black and green. Arms at upper left.	—	—	—

A WORD ON DATE RANGES

Often date ranges or specific dates are listed. These have been observed or reported by our contributors. If a note is outside the published range, it only means that it is a newly reported date, and not necessarily worthy of a premium value.

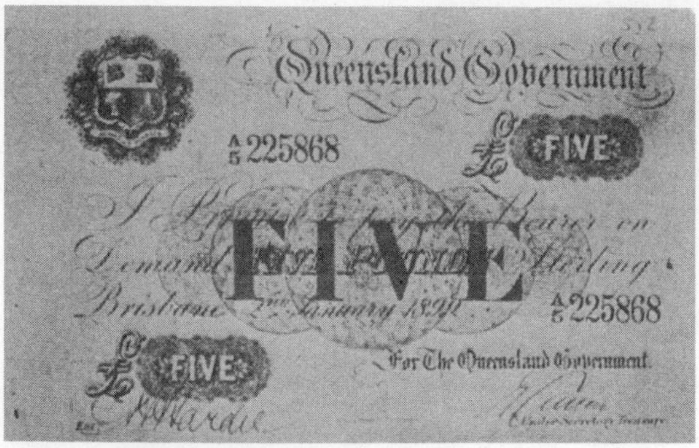

	Good	Fine	XF
S1041 5 Pounds 2.1.1899; 2.1.1902; 1.7.1903. Black and green. Arms at upper left.	—	—	—
S1042 10 Pounds 1893-99. Arms at upper left.	—	—	—
S1043 20 Pounds 1893-99. Arms at upper left.	—	—	—

1905 Issue

	Good	Fine	XF
S1044 1 Pound 1906-10. Black on gree underprint. Arms at upper left. Back: Blue.	—	—	—
S1045 5 Pounds 1906-10. Black on pink underprint. Arms at upper left. Back: Brown.	—	—	—
S1046 10 Pounds 1906-10. Arms at upper left.	—	—	—
S1047 20 Pounds 1906-10. Arms at upper left.	—	—	—

The Republic of Austria, a parliamentary democracy located in mountainous central Europe, has an area of 32,374 sq. mi. (83,849 sq. km.). Capital: Vienna.

The territories later to be known as Austria were overun in pre-Roman times by various tribes, including the Celts. Upon the fall of the Roman Empire, the country became a margravate of Charlemagne's Empire. Ottokar, King of Bohemia, gained possession in 1252, only to lose the territory to Rudolf of Habsburg in 1276. Thereafter, until World War I, the story of Austria was that of the ruling Habsburgs, German emperors from 1438-1806. From 1815-1867 it was a member of the "Deutsche Bund" (German Union).

During World War I, the Austro-Hungarian Empire was one of the Central Powers with Germany, Bulgaria and Turkey. At the end of the war, the Empire was dismembered and Austria established as an independent republic.

RULERS:

Maria Theresa, 1740-1780
Joseph II, jointly with his Mother, 1765-1780, alone, 1780-1790
Leopold II, 1790-1792
Franz II (I), 1792-1835 (as Franz II, 1792-1806), (as Franz I, 1806-1835)
Ferdinand I, 1835-1848
Franz Joseph, 1848-1916
Karl I, 1916-1918

MONETARY SYSTEM:

1 Krone = 100 Heller 1892-1924

Banks

Wiener Commissions Bank

1888 Cassa-Scheine - Interest Bearing Notes Issue

	Good	Fine	XF
S56 1000 Gulden 12.1.(?) 1888/7x. Seated allegorical figures at left and right.	—	—	—

Regional - Federal States, 1918-23; 1945

Banks:

Kärten (Carinthia)

Kärnten (Carinthia)

1918 Issue

	VG	VF	UNC
S101 10 Kronen 11.11.1918. Black. Uniface proof of face. Back: Arms at center.	1.50	7.50	35.00
S102 10 Kronen 11.11.1918. Orange. Back: Arms at center. Uniface proof of face or back.	.50	2.00	7.50

	VG	VF	UNC
S103 20 Kronen 11.11.1918. Blue. Printed on both sides, with serial #. Back: Arms at center. (Not issued).	1.00	5.00	15.00

S104 100 Kronen VG VF UNC
11.11.1918. Black. Back: Arms at center. Uniface proof of face. 5.00 20.00 50.00

S105 100 Kronen
11.11.1918. Orange. Back: Arms at center.
- a. Uniface proof of face or back. 2.00 5.00 12.50
- b. Proof of both sides. 4.00 10.00 25.00

1920 Issue

S106 10 Heller VG VF UNC
1.3.1920. Black and red on light brown underprint. .10 .20 .50

S107 20 Heller VG VF UNC
1.3.1920. Black and blue on light brown underprint. .10 .20 .50

S108 50 Heller VG VF UNC
1.3.1920. Black and green on light brown underprint. .10 .20 .50

1945 Reichsgau Kärnten Issue

S108A 50 Reichsmark VG VF UNC
15.4.1945. Purple. Uniface. Paper: Off-white. Issued during the last weeks of WWII. 50.00 150. 325.

NOTE: #S108A was issued during the last weeks of WWII.

Niederösterreich (Lower Austria)

May 1920 Issue

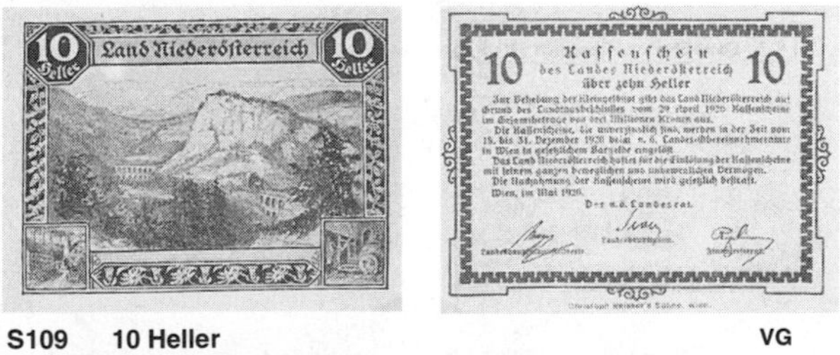

S109 10 Heller VG VF UNC
May 1920. Dark green. Mountain scene with Semmering railway bridge.
- a. Issued note. .10 .20 .50
- p. Uniface proof of back, picture dark green. 1.00 5.00 10.00

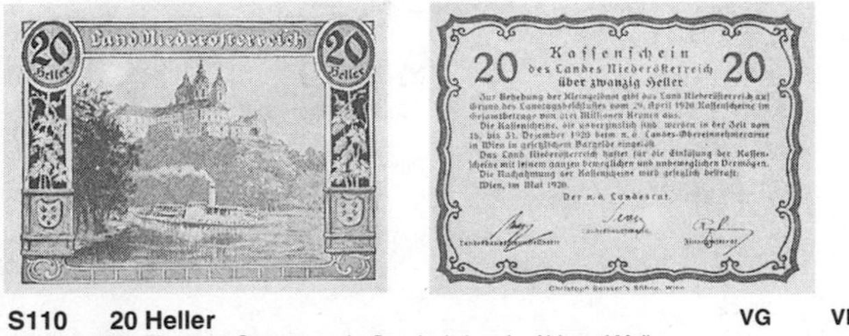

S110 20 Heller VG VF UNC
May 1920. Blue-gray. Steamer on the Danube below the Abbey of Melk.
- a. Issued note. .10 .20 .50
- p. Uniface proof of back, picture dark green. 1.00 5.00 10.00

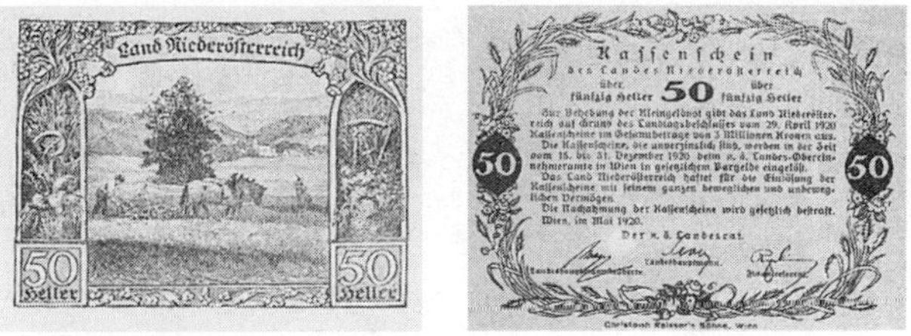

S111 50 Heller VG VF UNC
May 1920. Brown. Farmer plowing with horses.
- a. Issued note. .10 .20 .50
- p. Uniface proof of back, picture dark green. 1.00 5.00 10.00

July 1920 Issue

S112 10 Heller VG VF UNC
July 1920. Green to dark green. Farmer's wife with cows.
- a. *II. AUFLAGE* (2nd issue). .10 .20 .50
- b. Uniface proof on orange, green, red-brown, blue or lilac tinted paper. 3.00 10.00 17.50
- x. Error, picture on both sides (one inverted). 3.00 10.00 17.50

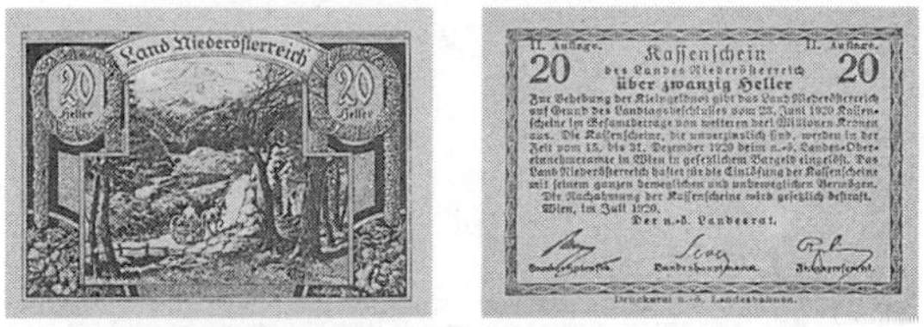

S113 20 Heller VG VF UNC
July 1920. Blue to dark blue. Landscape with horse-drawn cart.
- a. *II. AUFLAGE* (2nd issue). .10 .20 .50
- p. Uniface proof on white, brown, red-brown or lilac tinted paper. 4.00 12.00 20.00
- x1. Error, picture on both sides. 4.00 12.00 20.00
- x2. Error, mountains missing. .50 1.50 3.00

S114 50 Heller VG VF UNC
July 1920. Brown. Castle at center.
- a. *II, AUFLAGE* (2nd issue). .10 .20 .50
- p. Uniface proof on green, blue, red-brown or lilac tinted paper. 2.00 9.00 15.00
- x1. Error, picture on both sides, brown (back inverted). 4.00 10.00 17.50
- x2. Error, picture on both sides, light blue (proof print). 3.00 9.00 15.00

Oberösterreich (Upper Austria)

1920-21 Issues

S115 20 Heller VG VF UNC
1.3.1920. Back: Arms at center.
- a. Blue-green on white paper. .10 .20 .50
- b. Green-blue on bluish paper. .10 .20 .50
- c. Blue on gray paper. 1.00 2.25 3.00
- d. Violet. .25 1.00 1.50
- p1. Green. Proof. 4.00 10.00 15.00
- p2. Brown. Proof. 5.00 12.00 17.50
- p3. Black. Uniface proof of face or back. — Unc 20.00

S116 50 Heller
1.3.1920.
- a. Dark brown. .10 .20 .50
- b. Red. .10 .20 .50

S117 10 Heller
1.6.1920. Uniface.
- a. Pink. .10 .20 .50
- b. Gray-violet. .10 .20 .50

S118 80 Heller
21.6.1920. Red and gray. .10 .20 .50

S119 10 Heller

	VG	VF	UNC
1921.			
a. Red.	.05	.10	.25
b. Green.	.05	.10	.25
c. Orange.	.10	.25	1.00
d. Brown.	.05	.10	.25
e. Blue.	.05	.10	.25

S120 20 Heller

	VG	VF	UNC
1921. Village at upper left. Back: Rural views.			
a. Brown.	.05	.10	.25
b. Violet.	.05	.10	.25
c. Black.	.05	.10	.25
d. Green.	.05	.10	.25
x. Error, different picture of Steyr with fountain on back. Printed in nine different colors. Value for each.	10.00	30.00	50.00

S121 50 Heller

	VG	VF	UNC
1.2.1921. Orange.	.10	.20	.50

Österreich ob der Enns (Austria above the Enns)

1918 Issue

	VG	VF	UNC
S122 5 Kronen			
30.11.1918. Brown on green.	1.00	5.00	10.00
S123 10 Kronen			
30.11.1918. Green on blue-gray.	2.00	7.50	17.50
S124 20 Heller			
30.11.1918. Blue on gray-brown.	3.00	10.00	25.00

S125 50 Kronen

	VG	VF	UNC
30.11.1918. Brown on light brown.	4.00	20.00	50.00

Salzburg

1919 Issues

S126 10 Heller

	VG	VF	UNC
1.10.1919. Blue on green. Uniface.			
a. Issued note.	.10	.20	.50
b. Error, without underprint.	.50	3.00	5.00

S127 20 Heller

	VG	VF	UNC
1.10.1919. Black on yellow. Uniface.	.10	.20	.50

S128 50 Heller

	VG	VF	UNC
1.10.1919. Blue on pink. Uniface.			
a. Issued note.	.10	.20	.50
p. Black. 90 x 60mm. Proof.	—	—	35.00
x. Error, without underprint.	1.00	3.00	4.50

1920 Issue

S129 10 Heller

	VG	VF	UNC
May 1920. Black and red. Salzburg town view ca. 1500. Back: Bishop's hat above two shields.			
a. Issued note.	.10	.20	.50
x1. Error, face without red printing.	.50	3.00	4.50
x2. Error, back without red printing.	.50	3.00	4.50

S130 20 Heller

	VG	VF	UNC
May 1920. Black and red. Salzburg town view ca. 1600. Back: Bishop's hat above two sheilds.			
a. Issued note.	.10	.20	.50
x1. Error, face without red printing.	.50	3.00	4.50
x2. Error, back without red printing.	.50	3.00	4.50

S131 50 Heller

	VG	VF	UNC
May 1920. Black and red. Salzburg town view ca. 1700. Back: Archbishop's hat above oval shield.			
a. Issued note.	.10	.20	.50
x1. Error, face without red printing.	.50	3.00	4.50
x2. Error, back without red printing.	.50	3.00	4.50

1921 Issues

S132 5 Kronen

	VG	VF	UNC
1921. Crowned shield at center. Back: Mirabell Palace. (Not issued).			
a. Face brown on red-brown underprint. Picture on back brown. Printer's name at center. With and without serial #.	.50	3.50	7.50
b. Like "a" but printer and designer's name at left and right.	.50	4.50	10.00
c. Like "a" but without printer's name, and picture on back in lilac.	1.00	5.00	12.50
d. Printing on face brown on green underprint.	4.00	15.00	22.50

S133	20 Kronen	VG	VF	UNC
	1921. Crowned shield at center. Back: Summer Riding School in Salzburg. (Not issued).			
	a. Face brown on red-brown underprint. Back brown. Printer at center. With and without serial #.	1.00	3.50	7.50
	b. Like 'a' but printer and designer names at left and right.	1.00	3.50	7.50
	c. Like 'a' but without printer's name. Picture on back in lilac.	2.00	5.00	10.00
	d. Printing on face brown on green underprint.	10.00	15.00	22.50

S134	20 Kronen	VG	VF	UNC
	1921. Crowned shield at center. Back: Residence in Salzburg.			
	a. Face brown on red-brown underprint. Picture on back brown. Printer name at center. With and without serial #.	1.00	3.50	7.50
	b. Like 'a' but printer and designer's name at left and right.	1.00	4.50	10.00
	c. Like 'a' but without printer name. Back picture in lilac.	2.00	6.00	15.00
	d. Face brown on green underprint.	10.00	15.00	22.50

NOTE: Other varieties of #S132-S134 were printed, most exist as unfinished pieces.

Steiermark (Styria)

1919 Issue

S135	10 Heller	VG	VF	UNC
	17.10.1919. Blue on tan underprint.	.10	.20	.50

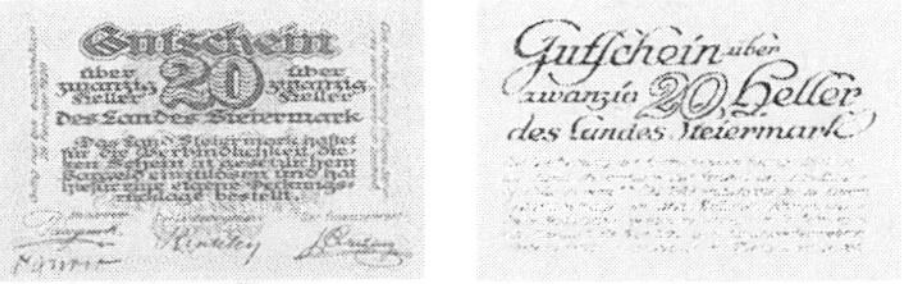

S136	20 Heller	VG	VF	UNC
	17.10.1919. Green on yellow-green underprint.	.10	.20	.50
S137	50 Heller			
	17.10.1919. Red-brown on gray-green underprint.	.10	.20	.50

S138	50 Heller	VG	VF	UNC
	17.10.1919. Red-brown. *II AUFLAGE* (2nd issue).			
	a. Blue underprint.	.10	.20	.50
	b. Green underprint.	.10	.20	.50
	c. Yellow-brown underprint.	.10	.20	.50
	d. Pink underprint.	.10	.20	.50

Tirol (Tyrol)

1919 Issue

#S139-S141 imperial eagle at ctr. on back.

S139	10 Heller	VG	VF	UNC
	1.9.1919. Orange. Back: Imperial eagle at center.	.10	.20	.50

S140	20 Heller	VG	VF	UNC
	1.9.1919. Gray. Back: Imperial eagle at center.	.10	.20	.50

S141	50 Heller	VG	VF	UNC
	1.9.1919. Green. Back: Imperial eagle at center.	.10	.20	.50

1920 Issue

S142	10 Heller	VG	VF	UNC
	1.10.1920. Back: Imperial eagle at center.	.10	.20	.50

S143	20 Heller	VG	VF	UNC
	1.10.1920. Brown. Back: Imperial eagle at center.	.10	.20	.50

S144	50 Heller	VG	VF	UNC
	1.10.1920. Blue. Back: Imperial eagle at center.	.10	.20	.50

Vorarlberg

1919 Issue

S145	10 Heller	VG	VF	UNC
	1.10.1919. Green. Back: Shield at center.	.10	.20	.50

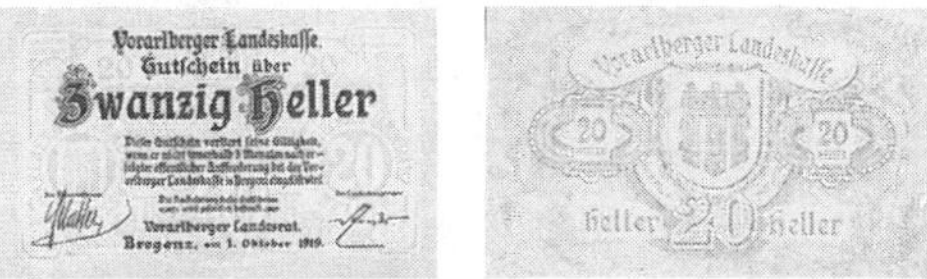

S146	20 Heller	VG	VF	UNC
	1.10.1919. Light brown. Back: Shield at center.	.10	.20	.50

S147 50 Heller	VG	VF	UNC
1.10.1919. Blue.	.10	.20	.50

1921 Issue

S148 50 Heller	VG	VF	UNC
1.5.1921. Shield at upper center. Back: Feldkirch Katzeturm (cat's tower) at left center.			
a. Brown.	.10	.30	.75
b. Violet.	.10	.30	.75
c. Brown. Card stock.	—	—	15.00
d. Violet. Card stock.	—	—	15.00
x1. Brown. Error, back inverted.	2.00	5.00	10.00
x2. Violet. Error, back inverted.	2.00	5.00	10.00

Donaustaat (Danube State)

1923-37 Lottery Tickets

S151 10	VG	VF	UNC
ND. Green and red-brown. Girl's head at right.			
a. Unfinished note.	—	—	.75
b. With lottery overprint.	2.00	5.00	10.00

S152 20	VG	VF	UNC
ND. Green and violet. Girl's head at right.			
a. Unfinished note.	—	—	60.00
b. With lottery overprint.	1.00	3.00	5.00

S153 50	VG	VF	UNC
ND. Blue and violet. Woman's head at right. Back: Blue and brown.			
a. Unfinished note.	—	—	60.00
b. With lottery overprint.	2.00	5.00	10.00

S154 100	VG	VF	UNC
ND. Blue and brown. Woman's head at right. Back: Blue and gray-green.			
a. Unfinished note.	—	—	75.00
b. With lottery overprint.	2.00	5.00	10.00

S155 1000	VG	VF	UNC
ND. Green and blue. Girl's head at right. Back: Blue and red-brown.			
a. Unfinished note.	—	—	100.
b. With lottery overprint.	2.00	5.00	10.00

S156 10,000	VG	VF	UNC
ND. Red, brown and olive. Back: Blue, lilac, violet and olive. Heads of eleven children.			
a. Unfinished note.	—	—	60.00
b. With lottery overprint.	2.00	7.50	20.00

NOTE: Many lottery text varieties and stampings exist. Illustrated pieces are only examples.

BARBADOS

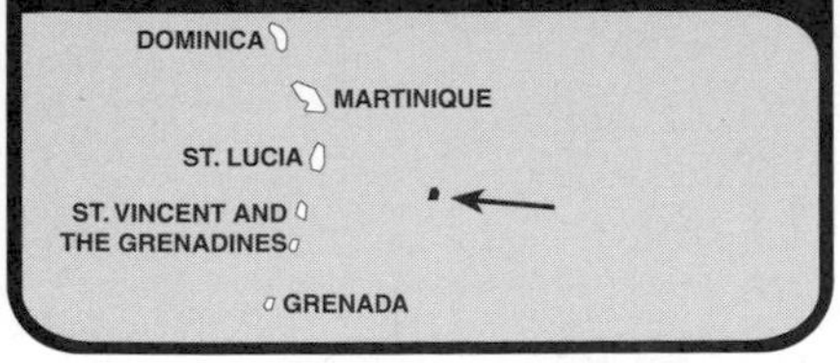

Barbados, an independent state within the British Commonwealth, is located in the Windward Islands east of St. Vincent. The coral island has an area of 431 sq. km and a population of 281,900. Capital: Bridgetown. The island was uninhabited when first settled by the British in 1627. Slaves worked the sugar plantations established on the island until 1834 when slavery was abolished. The economy remained heavily dependent on sugar, rum, and molasses production through most of the 20th century. The gradual introduction of social and political reforms in the 1940s and 1950s led to complete independence from the UK in 1966. In the 1990s, tourism and manufacturing surpassed the sugar industry in economic importance.

RULERS:

British to 1966

MONETARY SYSTEM:

1 Dollar = 100 Cents, 1950-
1 British West Indies Dollar = 4 Shillings - 2 Pence
5 British West Indies Dollars = 1 Pound - 10 Pence

British Administration

Barclays Bank (Dominion, Colonial and Overseas)

1922 Issue

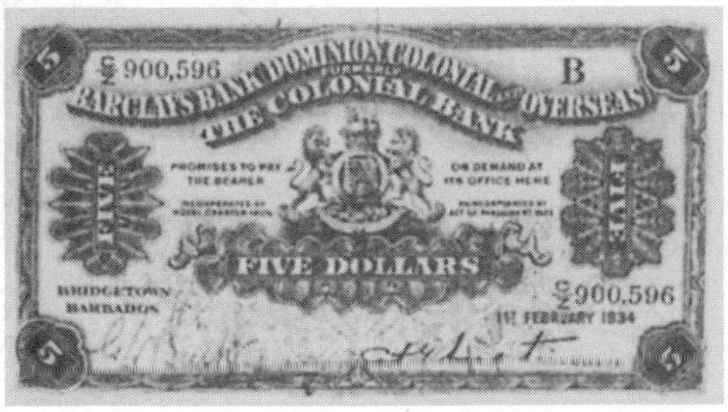

	Good	Fine	XF
S101 5 Dollars 1922; 1.9.1926; 1.2.1934. Black on pink and blue-green underprint. Arms at center. Back: Green. Overprint: Large *B* at upper right. Printer: BWC.	500.	1000.	—
S102 20 Dollars 1922; 1926. Arms at center. Overprint: Large *B* at upper right. Printer: BWC. Rare.	—	—	—

	Good	Fine	XF
S103 100 Dollars 1922; 1926; 1933; 1935. Arms at center. Overprint: Large *B* at upper right. Printer: BWC.			
a. Issued note. 1922; 1926. Rare.	—	—	—
r. Remainder perforated: *CANCELLED*. 31.3.1933; 1.1.1935.	—	Unc	2500.

1937 Issue

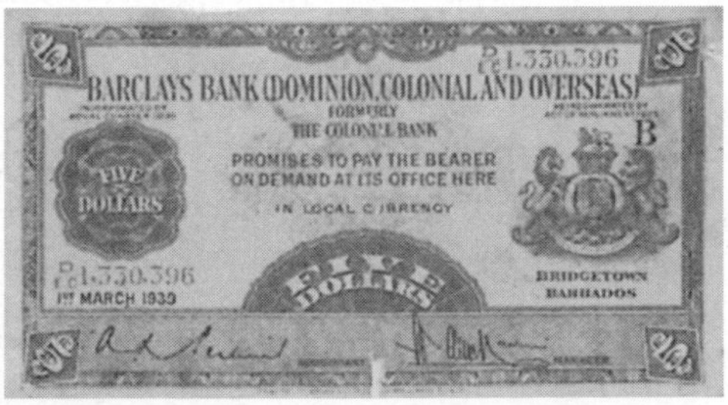

	Good	Fine	XF
S111 5 Dollars 1937-49. Purple on multicolor underprint. Arms at right. Overprint: Large *B* at upper right. Printer: BWC.			
a. Signature titles: *ACCOUNTANT* and *MANAGER*. 1.3.1937-1.3.1940.	250.	500.	1000.
b. Signature titles: *ASSISTANT MANAGER* and *MANAGER*. 1.10.1949.	300.	750.	1500.
s. Specimen. 1.5.1937.	—	Unc	1000.
S112 20 Dollars 1.1.1937; 1.3.1940. Brown. Arms at right. Overprint: Large *B* at upper right.	500.	1650.	—
S113 100 Dollars 1.1.1937; 1.3.1940. Green. Arms at right. Overprint: Large *B* at upper right. Rare.	—	—	—

NOTE: Also issued with various branch office overprint.

Canadian Bank of Commerce

1922 Issue

	Good	Fine	XF
S120 5 Dollars 2.1.1922. Black on green and red-orange underprint. Seated woman with rudder and jug ("Naiad") at center. Back: Orange. Mercury and allegorical woman flanking bank arms at center. Overprint: Black vertical *BARBADOS* at left and right. Printer: ABNC.	300.	750.	—
S121 5 Dollars 2.1.1922. Black on green and red-orange underprint. Seated woman with rudder and jug ("Naiad") at center. Overprint: Black vertical *BARBADOS* at left and right. Printer: CBNC.	300.	750.	—
S122 20 Dollars 2.1.1922; 1.7.1940. Black on red-brown and green underprint. Seated woman and globe at center. Back: Blue. Mercury and allegorical woman flanking bank arms at center. Overprint: Black vertical *BARBADOS* at left and right. Printer: CBNC.	1000.	2000.	—
S123 100 Dollars 2.1.1922. Black on blue and olive underprint. Seated woman with book and lamp at left center. Back: Brown. Mercury and allegorical woman flanking bank arms at center. Overprint: Black vertical *BARBADOS* at left and right. Printer: CNBC. Rare.	—	—	—

NOTE: A similar issue of #S123 was made for Trinidad.

1940 Issue

	Good	Fine	XF
S131 5 Dollars 1.7.1940. Black on green and red-orange underprint. Allegorical group at center. Back: Orange. Printer: CBNC.	200.	750.	1400.

NOTE: Design of #S131 is similar to a regular Canadian issue made by this bank, though color and wording on the face distinguish it from the actual Canadian counterpart.

Colonial Bank

1882 Issue

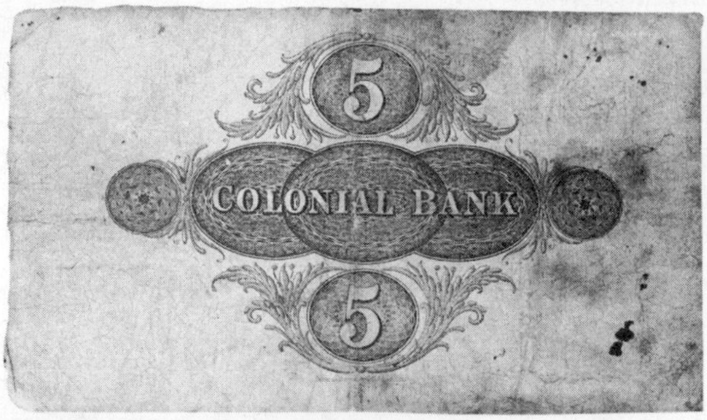

	Good	Fine	XF
S141 5 Dollars 1.7.1882; 1.6.1907; 1.6.1912. Black with reddish-brown underprint. Arms at upper center, *B* in circle at upper left and right. Back: Green. Printer: P&B. Rare.	—	—	—

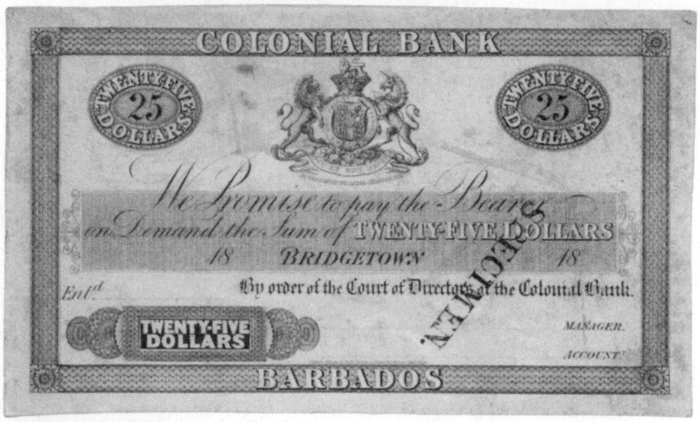

	Good	Fine	XF
S143 25 Dollar 18xx. Black. Royal Arms at top center. Printer: PB&P. Proof. Handstamped *SPECIMEN*. Uniface.	—	—	—

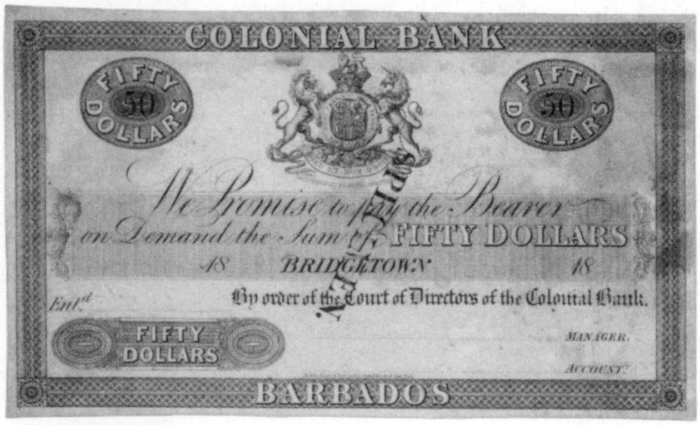

	Good	Fine	XF
S144 50 Dollars 18xx. Black. Royal Arms at top center. Printer: PB&P. Proof. Handstamped *SPECIMEN*. Uniface.	—	—	—

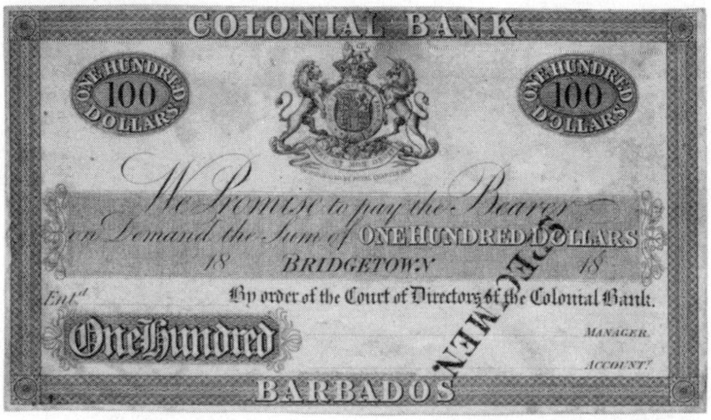

	Good	Fine	XF
s145 100 Dollars 18xx. Black. Royal Arms at top center. Printer: PB&P. Proof. Handstamped *SPECIMEN*. Uniface.	—	—	—

1918 Issue

	Good	Fine	XF
S151 5 Dollars 1918; 1919. Black on orange underprint. Arms at upper center. Back: Green. Overprint: Large *B* at upper right. Printer: PBC.			
a. Issued note. 1.1.1918.	1500.	—	—
s. Specimen perforated: *CANCELLED*. 1.7.1919.	—	Unc	4000.
S152 20 Dollars 191x. Arms at upper center. Overprint: Large *B* at upper right. Printer: PBC. Rare.	—	—	—
S153 100 Dollars 191x. Arms at upper center. Overprint: Large *B* at upper right. Printer: PBC. Rare.	—	—	—

NOTE: #S152 and S153 are reported to have dates to 1920, but no specifics are known.

Royal Bank of Canada

1909 Provisional Issue

	Good	Fine	XF
S161 5 Dollars 2.1.1909. Black on green and yellow underprint. Overprint: Vertical *BARBADOS* at left and right. Smaller vertical *PAYABLE AT BRIDGETOWN, BARBADOS* Printer: ABNC. Overprint on Canada #S1371.	750.	2250.	—
S162 20 Dollars 2.1.1909. Black on blue and yellow underprint. Overprint: Vertical *BARBADOS* at left and right. Smaller vertical *PAYABLE AT BRIDGETOWN, BARBADOS* Printer: ABNC. Overprint on Canada #S1375b. Rare.	—	—	—
S163 100 Dollars 2.1.1909. Black on red-orange underprint. Overprint: Vertical *BARBADOS* at left and right. Smaller vertical *PAYABLE AT BRIDGETOWN, BARBADOS* Printer: ABNC. Overprint on Canada #S1377.			
a. Issued note. Rare.	—	—	—
s. Specimen.	—	—	—

Sending Scanned Images by e-mail

We have been receiving an ever-increasing flow of scanned images from sources world wide. Unfortunately, many of these scans could not be used due to the type of scan, or simple incompatibility with our systems. We appreciate the effort it takes to produce these images and accuracy they add to the catalog listings.

Here are a few simple instructions to follow when producing these scans. We encourage you to continue sending new images or upgrades to those currently illustrated and please do not hesitate to ask questions about this process.

- Scan all images within a resolution of 300 dpi.
- Size setting should be at 100%
- Please include in the e-mail the actual size of the image in millimeters height x width
- Scan in true 4-color
- Save images as jpeg and name in such a way which clearly indentifies the country of the note and catalog number
- Do not compress files
- Please e-mail with a request to confirm receipt of the attachment
- Please send multiple images on a disc if available
- Please send images to: george.cuhaj@fwmedia.com

1920 Issue

Designed specifically for circulation in the West Indies. Large size notes.

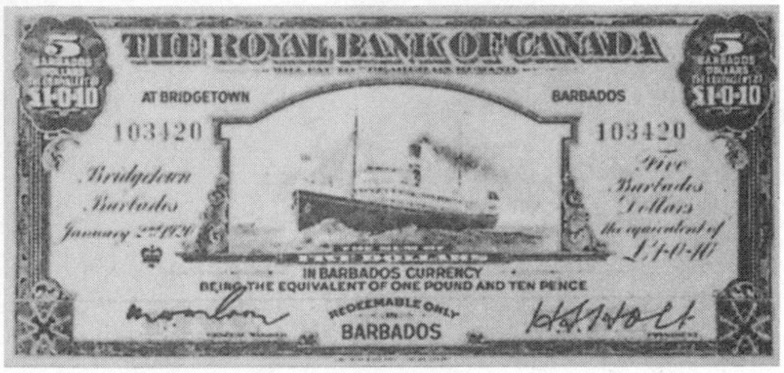

	Good	Fine	XF
S171 5 Dollars = 1 Pound 10 Pence 2.1.1920. Black on green underprint. Passenger steamship at center. Back: Green. Crowned supported arms at center. Printer: ABNC.	500.	1250.	—
S172 20 Dollars = 4 Pounds 3 Shillings 4 Pence 2.1.1920. Black on blue underprint. Sugar cane harvesting at center. Back: Blue. Crowned supported arms at center. Printer: ABNC. Rare.	—	—	—
S173 100 Dollars = 20 Pounds 16 Shillings 8 Pence 2.1.1920. Black on orange underprint. Seated woman with island behind. Back: Orange. Crowned supported arms at center. Printer: ABNC. Rare.	—	—	—

1938 Issue

#S181 and S182 Reduced size.

	Good	Fine	XF
S181 5 Dollars = 1 Pound 10 Pence 3.1.1938. Black on green underprint. Passenger steamship at center. Back: Green. Crowned supported arms at center. Printer: CBNC.	250.	600.	1250.
S182 20 Dollars = 4 Pounds 3 Shillings 4 Pence 3.1.1938. Black on orange underprint. Ox cart at center. Back: Rose. Crowned supported arms at center. Printer: CBNC.	1000.	2250.	—

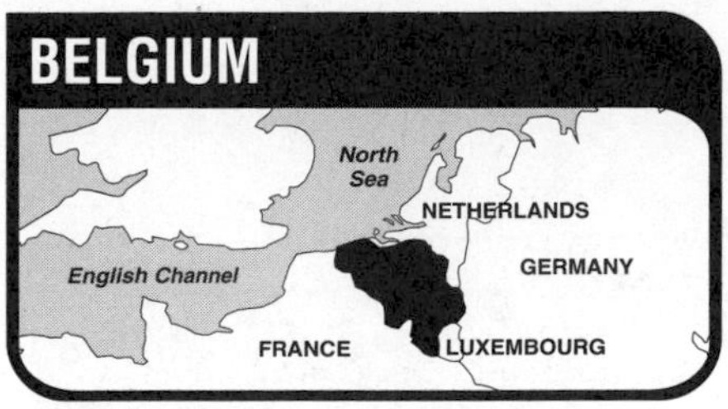

The Kingdom of Belgium, a constitutional monarchy in northwest Europe, has an area of 30,528 sq. km. and a population of 10.40 million, chiefly Dutch-speaking Flemish and French-speaking Walloons. Capital: Brussels. Agriculture, dairy farming, and the processing of raw materials for re-export are the principal industries. "Beurs voor Diamant" in Antwerp is the world's largest diamond trading center. Iron and steel, machinery, motor vehicles, chemicals, textile yarns and fabrics comprise the principal exports.

Belgium became independent from the Netherlands in 1830; it was occupied by Germany during World Wars I and II. The country prospered in the past half century as a modern, technologically advanced European state and member of NATO and the EU. Tensions between the Dutch-speaking Flemings of the north and the French-speaking Walloons of the south have led in recent years to constitutional amendments granting these regions formal recognition and autonomy.

RULERS:

Leopold I, 1831-1865
Leopold II, 1865-1909
Albert I, 1909-34
Leopold III, 1934-51
Baudouin I, 1952-93
Albert II, 1993-

MONETARY SYSTEM:

1 Franc = 100 Centimes to 2001
1 Belga = 5 Francs
1 Euro = 100 Cents, 2002-

Military Occupation of Germany

Armée Belge - Belgisch Leger

Military Payment Certificates

#M1-M8 issued under the authority of the Ministry of Defense for Belgian troops stationed in Germany after World War II.

M1 1 Franc	Good	Fine	XF
1.8.1946. Green and blue.			
a. Serial # prefix *A*.	3.00	10.00	30.00
b. Serial # prefix *B*.	20.00	50.00	100.
s. Specimen.	—	Unc	150.

M2 2 Francs	Good	Fine	XF
1.8.1946. Green and violet.			
a. Issued note.	3.00	30.00	80.00
s. Specimen.	—	Unc	150.

M3 5 Francs	Good	Fine	XF
1.8.1946. Green and red.			
a. Serial # prefix *A*.	3.00	32.50	85.00
b. Serial # prefix *B*.	50.00	100.	200.
s. Specimen.	—	Unc	150.

M4 10 Francs	Good	Fine	XF
1.8.1946. Brown and blue.			
a. Issued note.	10.00	50.00	130.
s. Specimen.	—	Unc	150.

M5 **20 Francs**

	Good	Fine	XF
1.8.1946. Brown and green.			
a. Issued note.	15.00	65.00	200.
s. Specimen.	—	Unc	150.

M6 **50 Francs**

	Good	Fine	XF
1.8.1946. Brown and red.			
a. Issued note.	30.00	125.	325.
s. Specimen.	—	Unc	300.

M7 **100 Francs**

	Good	Fine	XF
1.8.1946. Gray-blue and violet.			
a. Issued note.	100.	400.	700.
s. Specimen.	—	Unc	500.

M8 **500 Francs**

	Good	Fine	XF
1.8.1946. Gray-blue and green.			
a. Issued note.	500.	1250.	—
s. Specimen.	—	Unc	1500.

The Republic of Bolivia, a landlocked country in west central South America, has an area of 1,098,580 sq. km. and a population of 9.25 million. Capitals: La Paz (administrative); Sucre (constitutional). Mining is the principal industry and tin the most important metal. Minerals, petroleum, natural gas, cotton and coffee are exported.

Bolivia, named after independence fighter Simon Bolivar, broke away from Spanish rule in 1825; much of its subsequent history has consisted of a series of nearly 200 coups and countercoups. Democratic civilian rule was established in 1982, but leaders have faced difficult problems of deep-seated poverty, social unrest, and illegal drug production. In December 2005, Bolivians elected Movement Toward Socialism leader Evo Morales president - by the widest margin of any leader since the restoration of civilian rule in 1982 - after he ran on a promise to change the country's traditional political class and empower the nation's poor majority. However, since taking office, his controversial strategies have exacerbated racial and economic tensions between the Amerindian populations of the Andean west and the non-indigenous communities of the eastern lowlands.

RULERS:

Spanish to 1825

MONETARY SYSTEM:

1 Boliviano = 100 (Centavos) to 1965
1 Bolivar = 100 Centavos, 1945-1962
1 Peso Boliviano = 100 Centavos, 1962-1987
1 Boliviano = 100 Centavos, 1987-

SPECIMEN NOTES:

All *SPECIMEN, MUESTRA, MUESTRA SIN VALOR* and *ESPECIMEN* notes always have serial #'s of zero.

BANKS

Banco Agricola . . . . . #S101-S106
Banco Boliviano . . . . . #S111-S116
Banco de Bolivia y Londres . . . . . #S121-S126
Banco del Comercio . . . . . #S131-S136
Banco Francisco Argandoña . . . . . #S141-S150
Banco Industrial de La Paz . . . . . #S151-S156
Banco Industrial . . . . . #S161-S166
Banco Mercantil . . . . . #S171-S177
Banco Nacional de Bolivia . . . . . #S181-S217
Banco Potosí . . . . . #S221-S236

REPUBLIC

BANCO AGRICOLA

1903 ISSUE

S101 **1 Boliviano**

	Good	Fine	XF
22.11.1903. Black on light brown and rose underprint. Building at left, allegorical woman with sickle and sheaf at right. Back: Brown. Farmers loading wagon at center. Printer: BWC.			
a. Series E-K.	75.00	125.	500.
s. Specimen. Uniface.	—	—	—

S102 5 Bolivianos	Good	Fine	XF
22.11.1903. Black on light brown and rose underprint. Sheep grazing on hillside at center, bank at lower right. Back: Blue. Oxen driven wagon at center. Printer: BWC.			
a. Series B.	150.	300.	—
s. Specimen. Uniface.	—	—	—

S103 10 Bolivianos	Good	Fine	XF
22.11.1903. Black on multicolor underprint. Winged man with rake at left, sheep behind portrait Simon Bolívar at lower right. Printer: BWC.			
a. Issued note.	—	—	—
s. Specimen. Uniface.	—	Unc	350.

S104 20 Bolivianos	Good	Fine	XF
22.11.1903. Black on multicolor underprint. Bank at left, farm woman with bucket on shoulder and cattle at right. Back: Sheep at center. Printer: BWC.			
a. Issued note.	—	—	—
s. Specimen. Uniface.	—	Unc	500.

S105 50 Bolivianos	Good	Fine	XF
22.11.1903. Black on red and multicolor underprint. Woman with basket on head and holding sickle at left, bank at center. Back: Green. Bull, cow and calf at center. Printer: BWC.			
a. Issued note. Rare.	—	—	—
s. Specimen. Uniface.	—	—	—

S106 100 Bolivianos			
22.11.1903. Black and red on multicolor underprint. Woman with basket on head and holding sickle at left, bank at center. Back: Green. Bull, cow and calf at center. Printer: BWC. Reported not confirmed.	—	—	—

Banco Boliviano

1868 Issue

S111 1 Peso Fuerte	Good	Fine	XF
6.11.1868. Black on dark green underprint. Seated allegorical women at left and right of shield with arms, condor above. Series C. Back: Green. Printer: CNBB.	—	—	—

NOTE: For provisional issue overprint. new bank name see #S181.

S112 5 Pesos Fuertes			
18xx (ca.1868). Black on brown underprint. Three allegorical women with bust of Gen. A. J. de Sucre at center. Back: Brown. Proof.	—	—	—

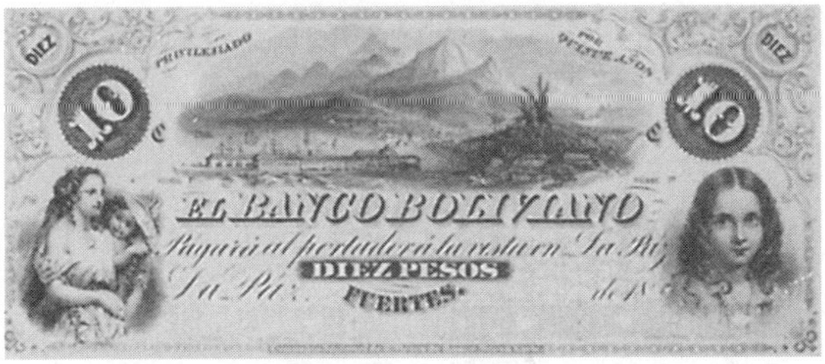

S113 10 Pesos Fuertes	Good	Fine	XF
18xx (ca.1868). Black on orange underprint. Two allegorical young girls ("Summer") at bottom left, mountain scene ("Inter-Ocean Rail Road") at center, young girl ("Mary") at bottom right. Back: Orange.	—	—	—

S114 20 Pesos Fuertes	Good	Fine	XF
18xx (ca.1868). Black on blue underprint. Spaniard ("Columbus") at left, men and horses ("Horse Fair") at center, allegorical woman with flowers ("May") at lower right. Back: Blue. Proof.	—	—	—

S115 50 Pesos Fuertes	Good	Fine	XF
19.10.1868. Black on red-orange underprint. Cotton boll at left. Female seated with scales ("Justice") at upper center, portrait woman at right. Back: Red-orange.			
a. Issued note. Rare.	—	—	—
p. Proof.	—	—	—

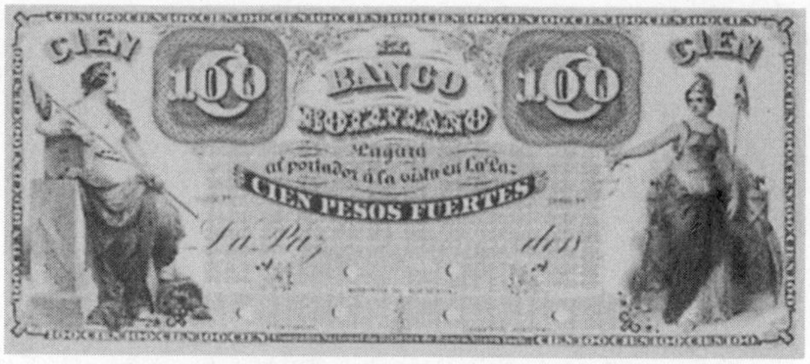

S116 100 Pesos Fuertes

	Good	Fine	XF
18xx (ca.1868). Black on green underprint. Standing females left and right, ("Liberty" at left and "Constitution" at right.) Back: Green. Proof.	—	—	—

Banco de Bolivia y Londres

1909 Issue

	Good	Fine	XF
S121 1 Boliviano 1.2.1909. Black on yellow-red underprint. Portrait Sra. Argandoña (La Princesa de la Glorieta) at center. Series A. Signature varieties. Back: Green. Two Indians and burro at center. Printer: W&S.	100.	250.	600.
S122 5 Bolivianos 1.2.1909. Signature varieties. Printer: W&S.	—	—	—

	Good	Fine	XF
S123 10 Bolivianos 1.2.1909. Black on yellow and violet underprint. Portrait Sra. Argandoña (La Princesa de la Glorieta) at left, llamas in pasture at right. Series A. Signature varieties. Back: Dark green. Printer: W&S. Rare.	—	—	—
S124 20 Bolivianos 1.2.1909. Signature varieties. Printer: W&S. Rare.	—	—	—
S125 50 Bolivianos 1.2.1909. Signature varieties. Printer: W&S. Rare.	—	—	—
S126 100 Bolivianos 1.2.1909. Signature varieties. Printer: W&S.	—	—	—

NOTE: For notes of this bank overprint: *Banco de la Nación Boliviana*, see #96-101 in Vol. 2.

Banco del Comercio

1900 Issue

	Good	Fine	XF
S131 1 Boliviano 1.1.1900. Black on green and pink underprint. Two miners standing at left, portrait Simon Bolívar at right. Series A. Signature varieties. Back: Blue. Arms at center. Printer: BWC.	10.00	25.00	100.

	Good	Fine	XF
S132 5 Bolivianos 1.1.1900. Black on green and blue underprint. Allegorical woman and child at left, portrait Gen. A. Nariño at lower right. Signature varieties. Series A. Back: Green. Arms aon back. Printer: BWC.	40.00	125.	300.

	Good	Fine	XF
S133 10 Bolivianos 1.1.1900. Black on pink and green underprint. Woman seated at left, portrait Christopher Columbus at lower right. Signature varieties. Series A. Back: Red. Arms at center. Printer: BWC.	75.00	250.	1000.
S134 20 Bolivianos 1.1.1900. Black on blue and pink underprint. Portrait helmeted Minerva at lower left, allegory of Art seated at right. Signature varieties. Series A. Back: Purple. Arms at center. Printer: BWC.	200.	650.	—

	Good	Fine	XF
S135 50 Bolivianos 1.1.1900. Black on orange and green underprint. Llamas in Potosí street at left, Mercury seated at right. Signature varieties. Series A. Back: Brown. Arms at center. Printer: W&S.	250.	800.	—
S136 100 Bolivianos 1.1.1900. Signature varieties. Series A. Back: Arms at center. Printer: W&S. Reported not confirmed.	—	—	—

Banco Francisco Argandoña

1893 Issue

	Good	Fine	XF
S141 1 Boliviano 1.7.1893. Black on pale blue and yellow-orange underprint. Portrait Francisco Argandoña as a young man at left, child with pick at right. Series left. Back: Green. Two seated allegorical women flanking arms at center. Printer: BWC.	250.	800.	—

S142 5 Bolivianos

	Good	Fine	XF
1.7.1893. Black on blue and red underprint. Portrait Francisco Argandoña as a young man at left with cherub at left, arms at upper center right. Back: Dark brown. Castillo de la Glorieta at Sucre at center. Printer: BWC.	125.	300.	—

S143 10 Bolivianos

	Good	Fine	XF
1.7.1893. Black on grayish violet and orange underprint. Two cherubs holding portrait Francisco Argandoña as a young man at left, arms at upper center, bull's head at lower right. Series A; B. Back: Red. Printer: BWC. Rare.			

S144 20 Bolivianos

	Good	Fine	XF
1.7.1893. Black on pale green and orange underprint. Portrait Francisco Argandoña as a young man at left, arms at upper center, two allegorical women with easel and lyre at right. Back: Blue and dark blue. Castillo de la Glorieta at Sucre at center. Printer: BWC.			
p. Proof.	—	Unc	450.
s1. Specimen perforated: *SPECIMEN/BW&Co/LONDON.*	—	Unc	500.
s2. Specimen perforated: *SPECIMEN.*	—	Unc	500.

#S144A *Deleted.* See #S144.

S145 50 Bolivianos

	Good	Fine	XF
1.7.1893. Black on brown and orange underprint. Portrait Francisco Argandoña as a young man at left, stylized plant at left, arms at upper center. Back: Orange. Cattle drinking at pond. Printer: BWC.			
p. Unfinished proof.	—	—	—
s. Specimen perforated: *SPECIMEN.*	—	Unc	750.

S146 100 Bolivianos

	Good	Fine	XF
1.7.1893. Black on green and red underprint. Portrait Francisco Argandoña as a young man at left, arms at upper center, Clotilde Urioste Velasco (Mrs. F. Argandoña) seated at lower right. Back: Dark brown. Arms at left, reclining allegorical woman on clouds at center, legend at right. Printer: BWC.			
p. Proof.	—	Unc	450.
s. Specimen perforated: *SPECIMEN.*	—	Unc	750.

NOTE: 500 Bolivianos denomination for this bank required confirmation.

1898 Issue

S147 1 Boliviano

	Good	Fine	XF
1898; 1909. Black on red and lilac underprint. Two seated allegorical women flanking arms at center. Older portrait Argandona with coat at left. Printer: BWC.			
a. Series B-Z. 1.1.1898.	75.00	150.	—
b. Series CC-FF. 1.1.1909.	40.00	75.00	200.

S148 5 Bolivianos	Good	Fine	XF
1.1.1898. Dark gray on pale green underprint. Argandona with coat at left. Back: Dark brown. Building at center. Printer: BWC.	75.00	150.	—

1905 Issue

S149 5 Bolivianos	Good	Fine	XF
1.1.1905. Black on pink, lilac and light blue underprint. Mercury with Argandoña portrait at left, arms at upper center, Mrs. Argandoña with allegory Fame at right. Series A-G. Larger size. Back: Blue. Printer: BWC.	50.00	125.	400.

Note: Beware quality contemporary counterfeits.

1907 Issue

S150 5 Bolivianos	Good	Fine	XF
1.1.1907. Black on light green, brown, red, light blue and yellow underprint. Mercury with Argandoña portrait at left, arms at upper center, Mrs. Argandoña with allegory Fame at right. Series A-G. Back: Blue. Printer: BWC.	50.00	125.	400.

Banco Industrial de La Paz

1900 Issue

S151 1 Boliviano	Good	Fine	XF
1900; 1905. Black on yellow underprint. Two Indian women and children at left. Signature varieties. Back: Olive. Helmeted arms of La Paz at center. Printer: ABNC.			
a. Series A-G. 1.6.1900.	100.	225.	600.
b. 1.1.1905.	125.	250.	600.
p. Proof.	—	Unc	250.
s. Specimen. 1.6.1900.	—	Unc	250.

S152 5 Bolivianos	Good	Fine	XF
1900; 1905. Black on yellow and red-orange underprint. Man on horseback leading pack animals, Indian with rifle at right. Signature varieties. Back: Red-orange. Helmeted arms of La Paz at center. Printer: ABNC.			
a. Series A. 1.6.1900.	150.	350.	—
b. Series B. 1.1.1905.	150.	400.	—
s. Specimen. 1.6.1900.	—	Unc	250.
S152A 5 Bolivianos			
1.1.1905. Black on yellow and red-orange underprint. Man on horseback leading pack animals, Indian with rifle at right. Like #S152 but *DE LA PAZ* crossed out. Signature varieties. Back: Red-orange. *DE LA PAZ* crossed out. Helmeted arms of La Paz at center. Printer: ABNC.	—	—	—

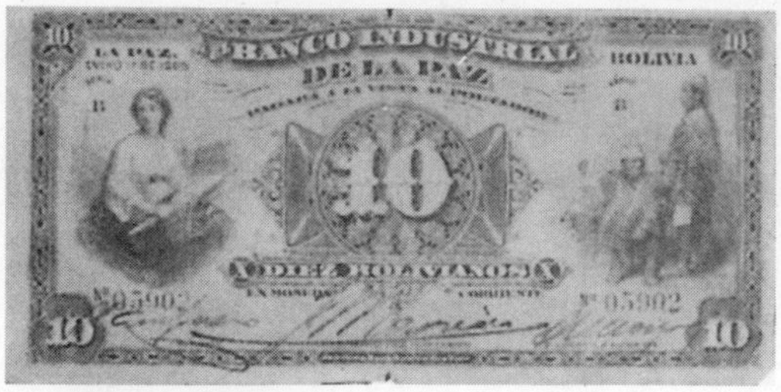

S153 10 Bolivianos	Good	Fine	XF
1.6.1900; 1.1.1905 Black on yellow and brown underprint. Woman holding yarn ("Industry") at left, two Indians at right. Signature varieties. Back: Brown. Helmeted arms of La Paz at center. Printer: ABNC.			
a. 1.6.1900. Rare.	—	—	—
b. Series B. 1.1.1905. Rare.	—	—	—
p. Proof.	—	Unc	1250.
s. Specimen. 1.6.1900.	—	Unc	450.

S154 20 Bolivianos	Good	Fine	XF
1.6.1900. Black on green and yellow underprint. Two allegorical women with barrels and other commodities at left. Signature varieties. Back: Green. Helmeted arms of La Paz at center. Printer: ABNC. Proof or specimen.	—	Unc	1250.

S155 50 Bolivianos	Good	Fine	XF
1.6.1900. Black on olive-green and yellow underprint. Three Indians at center. Signature varieties. Back: Blue. Helmeted arms of La Paz at center. Printer: ABNC. Proof or specimen.	—	Unc	1250.

S156 100 Bolivianos	Good	Fine	XF
1.6.1900. Black on orange and yellow underprint. Allegorical woman with globe and cherub at center. Signature varieties. Back: Red. Helmeted arms of La Paz at center. Printer: ABNC. Proof or specimen.	—	Unc	350.

Banco Industrial

1906; 1907 Issue

S161 1 Boliviano	Good	Fine	XF
1906; 1907. Black on yellow underprint. Two Indian women and children at left. Signature varieties. Back: Dark brown. Printer: ABNC.			
a. Series H-P. 1.1.1906.	50.00	125.	300.
b. 1.1.1907.	50.00	125.	350.
p. Proof.	—	Unc	900.

S162 5 Bolivianos	Good	Fine	XF
1.1.1907. Black on yellow and red-orange underprint. Horseback rider roping horse at left, standing figure at right. Signature varieties. Back: Red-orange. Printer: W&S.	75.00	250.	750.
S163 10 Bolivianos			
1.1.1907. Group of people. Signature varieties. Printer: ABNC. Rare.	—	—	—
S164 20 Bolivianos			
1.1.1906. Signature varieties. Printer: ABNC. Reported not confirmed.	—	—	—
S165 50 Bolivianos			
1.1.1906. Signature varieties. Printer: ABNC. Reported not confirmed.	—	—	—
S166 100 Bolivianos			
1.1.1906. Signature varieties. Printer: ABNC. Reported not confirmed.	—	—	—

Banco Mercantil

1906 Issue

S171 1 Boliviano	Good	Fine	XF
1906; 1911. Black on green underprint. Girl at left, arms at right. Signature varieties. Back: Back olive or lighter green. Building and farm animals at center. Printer: ABNC.			
a. Series C-O. 1.7.1906.	50.00	125.	250.
b. Series R-Y. 1.7.1911.	75.00	150.	350.
p. Proof.	—	Unc	800.

#S172 *Deleted.* See #S173.

S173 5 Bolivianos	Good	Fine	XF
1906; 1911. Black on yellow, brown and yellow-green underprint. Miners at center. Signature varieties. Back: Brown. Arms with church and monument in circle with Potosí mountain at center. Printer: ABNC.			
a. Series A-D. 1.7.1906.	100.	200.	400.
b. Series D-G. 1.7.1911.	75.00	150.	300.
p. Proof.	—	Unc	1000.

S174 10 Bolivianos	Good	Fine	XF
1906; 1911. Black on red-orange and yellow underprint. People including mother and child, and hut at center. Clock tower and building at center. Signature varieties. Back: Red-orange. Printer: ABNC.			
a. Series A; B. 1.7.1906.	125.	400.	—
b. Series B. 1.7.1911.	125.	400.	—

S175 20 Bolivianos	Good	Fine	XF
1.7.1906. Black on green and yellow underprint. Three allegorical figures at center. Signature varieties. Back: Blue. Plaza of Cochabamba at center. Printer: ABNC.			
a. Issued note.	500.	1100.	—
p. Proof.	—	Unc	1750.

S176 50 Bolivianos	Good	Fine	XF
1.7.1906. Black on brown underprint. Two young girls at center. Signature varieties. Back: Brown. Viaduct with mountain in background. Printer: ABNC.			
p. Proof.	—	—	—
r. Remainder. Numbered, without signature.	—	—	—
s. Specimen.	—	—	—

S177 100 Bolivianos	Good	Fine	XF
19xx. Black on orange and yellow underprint. Young woman at left. Signature varieties. Back: Red. Manufacturing scene at center. Printer: ABNC.			
a. Issued note.	—	—	—
p. Proof.	—	—	—
s. Specimen.	—	—	—

Banco Nacional de Bolivia

1872 Provisional Issue

#S181 w/ovpt. new bank name on notes of the Banco Boliviano.

S181 1 Peso	Good	Fine	XF
1.8.1872. Series D. Overprint: *BANCO NACIONAL DE BOLIVIA* across center on face and back on #S111.	300.	850.	—

NOTE: Higher values require confirmation.

1873 Cobija Issue

#S184-S189 were payable in Cobija or Valparaiso (now within Chile as a result of the War of the Pacific, 1879).

S184 1 Boliviano	Good	Fine	XF
17.2.1873. Black on dark brown underprint. Like #S191, but with different text at center. Back: Brown. Printer: ABNC.			
a. Issued note. Rare.	—	—	—
p1. Proof. Orange underprint, back orange.	—	Unc	500.
p2. Proof. Red overprint: *EMISION DEL LITORAL* across lower center.	—	—	—

S185 5 Bolivianos	Good	Fine	XF
187x (ca.1873). Black. Like #S192, but with different text at center. Printer: ABNC.			
p1. Proof. Blue underprint. Back blue.	—	Unc	500.
p2. Uniface proof. Green underprint.	—	—	—

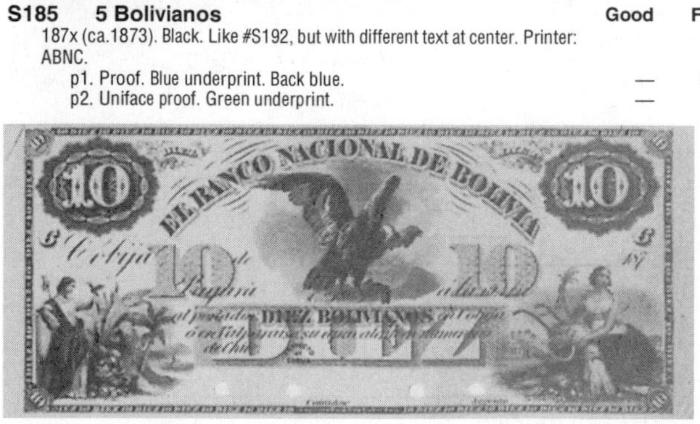

S186 10 Bolivianos	Good	Fine	XF
187x (ca.1873). Black. Like #S193, but with different text at center. Printer: ABNC.			
p1. Proof. Green underprint. Back blue.	—	Unc	500.
p2. Uniface proof. Green underprint. Red overprint: *EMISION DEL LITORAL* across lower center.	—	—	—
p3. Uniface proof. Brown underprint.	—	—	—

S187 20 Bolivianos	Good	Fine	XF
187x (ca.1873). Black on tan underprint. Sucre at lower left, Potosí city scene with mountain across upper center, seated woman with globe ("Science") at lower right. Back: Tan. Printer: ABNC. Proof.	—	Unc	600.

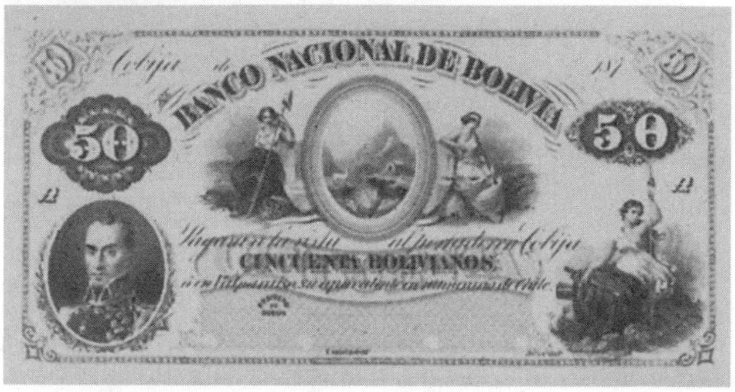

S188 50 Bolivianos	Good	Fine	XF
187x (ca.1873). Black on orange underprint. Like #S195, but different text at center. Back: Orange. Printer: ABNC. Proof.	—	Unc	600.

1873 Cobija Issue

#S184-S189 were payable in Cobija or Valparaiso (now within Chile as a result of the War of the Pacific, 1879).

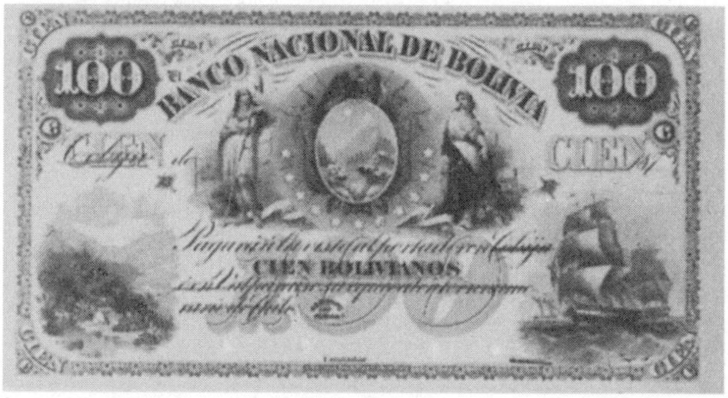

S189 100 Bolivianos	Good	Fine	XF
187x (ca.1873). Black. River and mountains at lower left, Potosí mountain scene in oval with eagle and flags flanked by two allegorical women at upper center, sailing ships at lower right. Printer: ABNC.			
p1. Proof. Deep orange underprint. Back deep orange.	—	Unc	600.
p2. Uniface proof. Brown underprint. Series C.	—	—	—

1873 La Paz Provisional Issue

S190 1 Boliviano	Good	Fine	XF
17.2.1873. Overprint: Red; handwritten: *La Paz*/Cobija on #S184. Rare.	—	—	—

1874 Antofagasta Issue

S191 1 Boliviano	Good	Fine	XF
187x (ca.1874). Black on green underprint. Man and llamas at left, mountain and town at center, man at right. Back: Green. Printer: ABNC. Payable at Antofagasta.			
a. Red overprint: *EMISION DEL LITORAL* across lower center on face and in circular form at center on back. Rare.	—	—	—
p. Proof.	—	Unc	500.
s. Specimen.	—	Unc	550.

S192 5 Bolivianos	Good	Fine	XF
187x (ca.1874). Black on red-orange underprint. Miners at lower left, Potosí mountain scene in oval flanked by two seated allegorical women at upper center, Indian woman at lower right. Back: Red-orange. Printer: ABNC. Payable at Antofagasta.			
a. Blue overprint: *EMISION DEL LITORAL* across lower center on face and in circular form at center on back.	—	—	—
p. Proof.	—	—	—
s. Specimen.	—	Unc	500.

S193 10 Bolivianos	Good	Fine	XF
187x (ca.1874). Black on orange underprint. Allegorical woman and plants at lower left, condor at upper center, Agriculture seated at lower right. Back: Orange. Printer: ABNC.			
a. Blue overprint: *EMISION DEL LITORAL* across lower center on face and in circular form at center on back. Rare.	—	—	—
p. Proof.	—	—	—
s. Specimen.	—	Unc	500.
S195 50 Bolivianos			
187x (ca.1874). Black on blue underprint. Bolívar at lower left, Potosí mountain scene in oval flanked by two seated allegorical women at upper center, seated allegorical woman with pole and cap at lower right. Back: Blue. Printer: ABNC. Proof. Payable at Antofagasta.	—	—	—

1875 La Paz Issue

S197 20 Centavos	Good	Fine	XF
1.11.1875. Black on green underprint. Potosí mountain scene in oval at center. Back: Green. Value at center. Printer: ABNC.			
a. Issued note. Rare.	—	—	—
p. Uniface proof.	—	Unc	275.
s. Specimen overprint: *MUESTRA* or *SPECIMEN*, punched hole cancelled. Series A.	—	Unc	400.

S198 40 Centavos	Good	Fine	XF
1.11.1875. Black on orange underprint. "Raphael's Angel" at center. Back: Orange. Value at center. Printer: ABNC.			
a. Issued note. Rare.	—	—	—
p. Proof.	—	Unc	500.
s. Specimen overprint: *MUESTRA*, punched hole cancelled.	—	Unc	500.

1877 Sucre Issue

S199 1 Boliviano	Good	Fine	XF
1.1.1877. Black on red and green underprint. Mountain and city of Potosí at center. Back: Brown. Indian with llamas at left, Indian at right. Printer: ABNC.			
a. Issued note.	125.	250.	750.
p. Proof.	—	—	—
s. Specimen.	—	—	—

S200 5 Bolivianos	Good	Fine	XF
1.1.1877. Black on light blue and tan underprint. Similar to #S185 and #S192, but with major plate changes. Series A. Back: Blue. Printer: ABNC.			
a. Issued note.	—	—	—
p. Proof.	—	Unc	750.
s. Specimen.	—	—	—

S201 10 Bolivianos	Good	Fine	XF
1.1.1877. Black on red and green underprint. Allegorical woman at left and right of bank at center. Series A. Back: Green. Printer: ABNC.			
p. Proof.	—	Unc	1250.
s. Specimen.	—	—	—

S202 20 Bolivianos	Good	Fine	XF
1.1.1877. Black on orange underprint. Similar to #S187, but with major plate changes. Back: Black and orange. Indian with llamas at center. Printer: ABNC.			
p. Proof.	—	Unc	1750.
s. Specimen. Series A.	—	—	—

S203 50 Bolivianos	Good	Fine	XF
1.1.1877. Black on red-orange underprint. Similar to #S188 and #S195, but with major plate changes. Series A. Back: Black and red-orange. Mule team in mountains at center. Proof.	—	Unc	2000.

S204 100 Bolivianos	Good	Fine	XF
1.1.1877. Black on magenta underprint. Indian woman and Potosí mountain scene in oval at left, clock tower and monument at center, sailing ships at right. Series A. Back: Black and magenta. Men and horses at center. Printer: ABNC. Proof.	—	Unc	2250.

1882-83 Sucre Issue

S205 1 Boliviano	Good	Fine	XF
1.1.1883. Black on green and red underprint. Condor at upper center, portrait S. Bolívar at lower right. Back: Brown. Reclining allegorical woman at center. Printer: ABNC.			
a. Issued note. Series A1-R1.	25.00	50.00	150.
p. Proof. Series AA.	—	—	—
s. Specimen. Series S1; T1; DD.	—	—	—

S206 5 Bolivianos	Good	Fine	XF
1.1.1883. Black on orange and blue underprint. Justice at left, two allegorical women paying homage to bust of A. J. de Sucre at center, two men at right. Back: Blue. Seated Justice allegory with condor at center. Printer: ABNC.			
a. Series B.	125.	400.	—
p. Proof. Series B.	—	Unc	600.
s. Specimen. Series B1.	—	—	—

NOTE: Many quality counterfeits (including the illustrated note) of #S206 exist.

S207 10 Bolivianos	Good	Fine	XF
1.1.1883. Black on green and red underprint. Allegorical woman ("Fortune") at left, men and llamas at center, allegorical woman ("Tropics No. 3") at right. Series B. Back: Green. Allegorical woman feeding condor at center. Printer: ABNC. Proof.	—	Unc	1250.

S208 20 Bolivianos	Good	Fine	XF
1.1.1883. Black on brown and red underprint. Reclining woman ("The Siesta") at left. center, two young girls at right. Back: Black and brown. Allegorical woman with child and globe at center. Printer: ABNC.			
a. Issued note.	—	—	—
p. Proof.	—	Unc	750.
s. Specimen.	—	—	—

S209 50 Bolivianos	Good	Fine	XF
1.1.1883. Black on red-orange underprint. Indian woman at left, seated allegorical woman with globe ("La Critique") at center, portrait Sucre at right. Back: Black and red-orange. Reclining allegorical woman with ancient oil lamp at center. Printer: ABNC.			
p. Proof.	—	Unc	800.
s. Specimen, punched hole cancelled.	—	—	—

S210 100 Bolivianos

1.1.1882; 1.1.1883. Black on orange underprint. "Reception of Columbus" at left, allegorical woman with pitcher ("Naiad") at center right. Back: Orange and black. Standing Liberty with shield and faces at center. Printer: ABNC.

	Good	Fine	XF
p. Proof.	—	Unc	1200.
s. Specimen.	—	—	—

NOTE: The 1882 date of #S210 was prepared in error according to ABNC records.

1892-94 ISSUE

S211 1 Boliviano

1892; 1894. Black on yellow and orange underprint. Miners at lower left, helmeted female head ("Minerva No. 3") at center. Back: Brown-orange. Young woman and sheep at center. Printer: ABNC.

	Good	Fine	XF
a. Serial # at lower left and upper right. 1.1.1892. Series L-Z; AA-HH.	25.00	50.00	150.
b. Serial # at upper left and right. 1.1.1892. Series II-ZZ; A1-L1.	25.00	50.00	150.
c. 1.1.1894. Reported not confirmed.	—	—	—
p. Proof.	—	Unc	650.
s. Specimen. As a. Series A.	—	—	—

S212 5 Bolivianos

1.1.1892. Black on green and yellow underprint. Horse at left, seated woman with two children ("Peace") at right. Back: Dark brown. Seated woman with sheaf and two sheep at center.

	Good	Fine	XF
a. Issued note.	75.00	150.	350.
p. Proof.	—	Unc	850.

S213 10 Bolivianos

1.1.1894. Black on blue and yellow underprint. Man with oxen plowing at center, seated woman at right. Back: Green. Woman, child and cows at center. Printer: ABNC.

	Good	Fine	XF
a. Issued note.	125.	250.	500.
p. Proof.	—	—	—

NOTE: Higher denominations require confirmation.

1904 ISSUE

S214 5 Bolivianos

1.1.1904. Black on peach and light green underprint. Portrait Simon Bolívar at top center. Series A; B. Back: Brown. Girl at center. Printer: BWC.

	Good	Fine	XF
a. Issued note.	250.	750.	—
s. Specimen perforated: *CANCELLED*.	—	—	—

S215 10 Bolivianos

1.1.1904. Printer: BWC.

	Good	Fine	XF
	—	—	—

NOTE: Higher denominations require confirmation.

1910 ISSUE

S217 20 Bolivianos

1910. Black on brown and multicolor underprint. Allegorical woman ("Study") seated at left. Back: Portrait allegorical woman at center.

	Good	Fine	XF
a. Issued note. Rare.	—	—	—
p. Proof.	—	Unc	1750.

BANCO POTOSÍ

1887 ISSUE

S221 1 Boliviano

1.1.1887. Black on green and pink underprint. Seated allegorical woman leaning on trunk ("Industry") at left, A. Ballivian at right. Back: Brown. People in village square at center. Printer: ABNC.

	Good	Fine	XF
a. Issued note. Red serial #. Series A-O.	25.00	50.00	125.
b. Issued note. Black serial #. Series P-W.	25.00	50.00	125.
r. Remainder.	—	Unc	75.00
s. Specimen. Series A; I; P.	—	Unc	150.

S222 5 Bolivianos
1.1.1887. Black on blue and orange underprint. Arms at left, steam freight train at center, child writing at lower right. Back: Blue. Justice seated at center. Printer: ABNC.

	Good	Fine	XF
a. Issued note.	75.00	150.	500.
s. Specimen.	—	Unc	175.

S223 10 Bolivianos
1.1.1887. Black on rose and green underprint. Ox-drawn cart at center, seated Justice at right. Back: Green. Allegorical woman ("Arts") at center. Printer: ABNC.

	Good	Fine	XF
a. Issued note.	125.	275.	—
s. Specimen.	—	Unc	200.

S224 20 Bolivianos
1.1.1887. Black on red and ochre underprint. Woman in hammock ("La Siesta") at left, allegorical woman at right. Back: Brown and black. Group of angels and fish at center. Printer: ABNC.

	Good	Fine	XF
a. Issued note.	250.	600.	—
s. Specimen.	—	Unc	250.

S225 50 Bolivianos
1.1.1887. Black on multicolor underprint. Woman emptying pitcher ("Rebecca") at left, men with llamas at center, portrait Gen. A. Nariño at right. Back: Orange and black. Condor at center. Printer: ABNC.

	Good	Fine	XF
a. Issued note. Rare.	—	—	—
s. Specimen.	—	—	—

S226 100 Bolivianos
1.1.1887. Black on orange and gray underprint. Scene of Potosí at center, portrait Simon Bolívar at upper right. Back: Orange and black. Miners at center. Printer: ABNC.

	Good	Fine	XF
p. Proof.	—	—	—
s. Specimen.	—	—	—

1894 Issue

S231 1 Boliviano
1.1.1894. Black on pink, orange, and green underprint. Kneeling child at left, portrait Gen A. Nariño at right. Back: Dark brown on yellow underprint. Indians and llamas at center. Printer: BWC. Unsigned remainders.

Good	Fine	XF
—	Unc	50.00

NOTE: A hoard of uncirculated remainders of #S231 numbering in the thousands was located during 1984.

S232 5 Bolivianos

1.1.1894. Black on light blue and yellow underprint. Arms at left, steam locomotive at upper center, cupid painting at right. Back: Blue on yellow underprint. Allegorical woman at center. Printer: BWC.

	Good	Fine	XF
	125.	200.	400.

S233 10 Bolivianos

1.1.1894. Black on pale green and red-orange underprint. Ox-drawn cart at upper center, allegorical woman with musical instruments at right. Back: Deep green. Allegory of Culture. Printer: BWC.

	Good	Fine	XF
p. Proof.	—	—	—
s. Specimen.	—	—	—

S234 20 Bolivianos

1.1.1894. Black on tan and red-orange underprint. Woman with sheep at left, portrait helmeted Roman warrior at right. Back: Brown and black. Cherubs on dock at center. Printer: BWC.

	Good	Fine	XF
p. Proof.	—	—	—
s. Specimen.	—	—	—

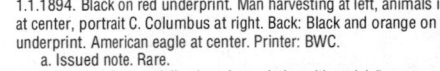

S235 50 Bolivianos

1.1.1894. Black on red underprint. Man harvesting at left, animals in town at center, portrait C. Columbus at right. Back: Black and orange on yellow underprint. American eagle at center. Printer: BWC.

	Good	Fine	XF
a. Issued note. Rare.	—	—	—
r. Unsigned or partially signed remainder with serial #.	—	Unc	1250.
s. Uniface specimen with or without perforated: *SPECIMEN* without serial #.	—	—	—

S236 100 Bolivianos

1.1.1894. Black on orange underprint. Potosí at center, portrait S. Bolívar at upper right. Back: Orange and black. Mine opening with donkey drawn ore car and miners at center. Printer: BWC.

	Good	Fine	XF
a. Black on orange underprint. Rare.	—	—	—
r. Unsigned remainder without serial #.	—	—	—
s. Uniface specimen with or without perforated: *SPECIMEN* without serial #. Purple on yellow-green underprint.	—	—	—

The Republic of Bosnia-Herzegovina borders Croatia to the north and west, Serbia to the east and Montenegro in the southeast with only 12.4 miles of coastline. The total land area is 51,209 sq. km. It has a population of 4.59 million. Capital: Sarajevo. Electricity, mining and agriculture are leading industries.

Bosnia and Herzegovina's declaration of sovereignty in October 1991 was followed by a declaration of independence from the former Yugoslavia on 3 March 1992 after a referendum boycotted by ethnic Serbs. The Bosnian Serbs - supported by neighboring Serbia and Montenegro - responded with armed resistance aimed at partitioning the republic along ethnic lines and joining Serb-held areas to form a "Greater Serbia." In March 1994, Bosniaks and Croats reduced the number of warring factions from three to two by signing an agreement creating a joint Bosniak/Croat Federation of Bosnia and Herzegovina. On 21 November 1995, in Dayton, Ohio, the warring parties initialed a peace agreement that brought to a halt three years of interethnic civil strife (the final agreement was signed in Paris on 14 December 1995). The Dayton Peace Accords retained Bosnia and Herzegovina's international boundaries and created a joint multi-ethnic and democratic government charged with conducting foreign, diplomatic, and fiscal policy. Also recognized was a second tier of government comprised of two entities roughly equal in size: the Bosniak/Croat Federation of Bosnia and Herzegovina and the Bosnian Serb-led Republika Srpska (RS). The Federation and RS governments were charged with overseeing most government functions. The Office of the High Representative (OHR) was established to oversee the implementation of the civilian aspects of the agreement. In 1995-96, a NATO-led international peacekeeping force (IFOR) of 60,000 troops served in Bosnia to implement and monitor the military aspects of the agreement. IFOR was succeeded by a smaller, NATO-led Stabilization Force (SFOR) whose mission was to deter renewed hostilities. European Union peacekeeping troops (EUFOR) replaced SFOR in December 2004; their mission is to maintain peace and stability throughout the country. EUFOR's mission changed from peacekeeping to civil policing in October 2007, with its presence reduced from nearly 7,000 to 2,500 troops.

RULERS:

Ottoman, until 1878
Austrian, 1878-1918
Yugoslavian, 1918-1941

MONETARY SYSTEM:

1 Dinar = 100 Para 1992-1998
1 Convertible Marka = 1 Deutschemark
1 Convertible Marka = 100 Convertible Pfeniga, 1998-

PARTISAN - WWII

DECREE 15.1.1943; NARODNOG OSLOBODENJA ISSUE

NATIONAL BONDS

S134 100 Dinara = 100 Kuna	Good	Fine	XF
D. 1943. Brown, red and light blue. Star in sprays with long ribbons with text: *SMRT FASIZMO-SLOBODA NARODU* at upper center. Series BH and I/V.	150.	350.	—

ZEMALJSKO ANTIFASISTICKO VIJECE BOSNE I HERCEGOVINE

BOSNIA AND HERZEGOVINA ANTI-FASCIST AUTHORITY

DECREE 15.1.1943; NARODNOG OSLOBODENJA ISSUE

NATIONAL BONDS

S135 500 Dinara = 500 Kuna	Good	Fine	XF
D. 1943. Brown, red and light blue. Star in sprays with long ribbons with text: *SMRT FASIZMO-SLOBODA NARODU* at upper center. Series BH and I/V.	150.	350.	—

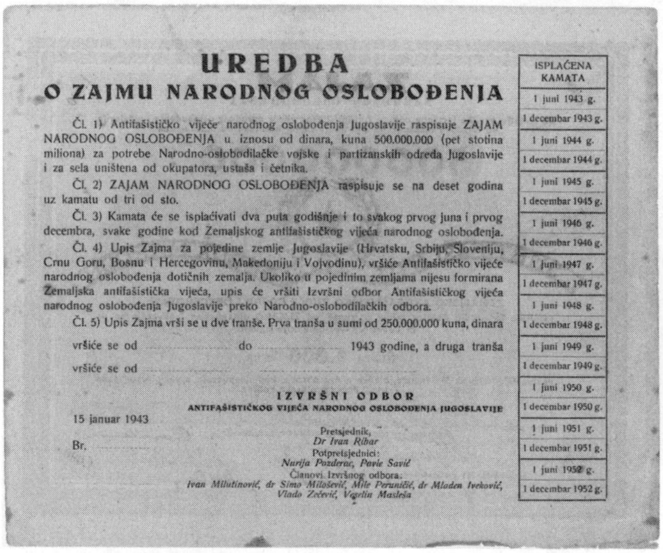

UREDBA
O ZAJMU NARODNOG OSLOBOĐENJA

Čl. 1) Antifašističko vijeće narodnog oslobođenja Jugoslavije raspisuje ZAJAM NARODNOG OSLOBOĐENJA u iznosu od dinara, kuna 500.000.000 (pet stotina miliona) za potrebe Narodno-oslobodilačke vojske i partizanskih odreda Jugoslavije i za sela uništena od okupatora, ustaša i četnika.

Čl. 2) ZAJAM NARODNOG OSLOBOĐENJA raspisuje se na deset godina uz kamatu od tri od sto.

Čl. 3) Kamata će se isplaćivati dva puta godišnje i to svakog prvog juna i prvog decembra, svake godine kod Zemaljskog antifašističkog vijeća narodnog oslobođenja.

Čl. 4) Upis Zajma za pojedine zemlje Jugoslavije (Hrvatsku, Srbiju, Sloveniju, Crnu Goru, Bosnu i Hercegovinu, Makedoniju i Vojvodinu), vršiće Antifašističko vijeće narodnog oslobođenja dotičnih zemalja. Ukoliko u pojedinim zemljama nijesu formirana Zemaljska antifašistička vijeća, upis će vršiti Izvršni odbor Antifašističkog vijeća narodnog oslobođenja Jugoslavije preko Narodno-oslobodilačkih odbora.

Čl. 5) Upis Zajma vrši se u dve tranše. Prva tranša u sumi od 250.000.000 kuna, dinara vršiće se od .... do .... 1943 godine, a druga tranša vršiće se od ....

IZVRŠNI ODBOR
ANTIFAŠISTIČKOG VIJEĆA NARODNOG OSLOBOĐENJA JUGOSLAVIJE

15 januar 1943

Br. ....

Pretsjednik,
Dr Ivan Ribar
Potpretsjednici:
Nurija Pozderac, Pavle Savić
Članovi Izvršnog odbora:
Ivan Milutinović, dr Simo Milošević, Mile Peruničić, dr Mladen Iveković, Vlado Zečević, Veselin Masleša

ISPLAĆENA KAMATA
1 juni 1943 g.
1 decembar 1943 g.
1 juni 1944 g.
1 decembar 1944 g.
1 juni 1945 g.
1 decembar 1945 g.
1 juni 1946 g.
1 decembar 1946 g.
1 juni 1947 g.
1 decembar 1947 g.
1 juni 1948 g.
1 decembar 1948 g.
1 juni 1949 g.
1 decembar 1949 g.
1 juni 1950 g.
1 decembar 1950 g.
1 juni 1951 g.
1 decembar 1951 g.
1 juni 1952 g.
1 decembar 1952 g.

S136 1000 Dinara = 1000 Kuna	Good	Fine	XF
D.1943. Brown, red and light blue. Twelve stylized soldiers in attack ranks in underprint. Star in sprays with long ribbons with text: *SMRT FASIZMO-SLOBODA NARODU* at upper center. Series BH and I/V.	150.	350.	—
S137 5000 Dinara = 5000 Kuna			
D.1943. Brown, red and light blue. Star in sprays with long ribbons with text: *SMRT FASIZMO-SLOBODA NARODU* at upper center. Series BH and I/V.	150.	350.	—
S138 10,000 Dinara = 10,000 Kuna			
D.1943. Brown, red and light blue. Star in sprays with long ribbons with text: *SMRT FASIZMO-SLOBODA NARODU* at upper center. Series BH and I/V.	150.	350.	—

The Federative Republic of Brazil, which comprises half the continent of South America, is the only Latin American country deriving its culture and language from Portugal. It has an area of 8,511,965 sq. km. and a population of 196.34 million. Capital: Brasília.

Following three centuries under the rule of Portugal, Brazil became an independent nation in 1822 and a republic in 1889. By far the largest and most populous country in South America, Brazil overcame more than half a century of military intervention in the governance of the country when in 1985 the military regime peacefully ceded power to civilian rulers. Brazil continues to pursue industrial and agricultural growth and development of its interior. Exploiting vast natural resources and a large labor pool, it is today South America's leading economic power and a regional leader. Highly unequal income distribution and crime remain pressing problems.

RULERS:

Pedro II, 1831-1889

ARRANGEMENT

Listings for Brazil in this volume are divided into six major sections. The first contains provincial notes for the period 1808 to 1857. The second contains notes titled *Banco do Brazil* (actually from three separate banks with this name), issued from 1808 to 1890. The third lists issues from banks under the Empire, from 1850 to 1885. The fourth is a listing of regional issues from 1892 to 1897. Fifth is another section on bank issues, this time under the Republic, from 1889 to 1893. The sixth section is comprised of later regional issues from 1924 to 1966.

The following chart indicates specific contents of each of these sections:

Section I, 1808-1857

PROVINCIAL ISSUES

Bahia, 1828 . . . . . . #S101-S104
Ceará, 1857 . . . . . . #S111
Minas Geraes, 1808-1818 . . . . . . #S121-S145
República Rio Grandense, 1838 . . . . . . #S151

Section II, 1808-1890

BANCO DO BRAZIL

First Banco do Brazil, 1808-1829 . . . . . . #S171-S224
Second Banco do Brazil, 1851-1853 . . . . . . #S227-S229
Third Banco do Brazil, 1853-1890 . . . . . . #S231-S358

Section III, 1850-1885

BANK ISSUES EMPIRE

Banco da Bahia, 1858-1860 . . . . . . #S381-S390
Banco Commercial e Agricola, 1858-1859 . . . . . . #S401-S419
Banco Commercial da Bahia, 1850 . . . . . . #S421
Banco Commercial do Maranhão, 1854 . . . . . . #S424
Banco do Maranhão, 1857-1885 . . . . . . #S425-S430
Banco do Rio Grande do Sul, 1859 . . . . . . #S436
Banco Rural e Hypothecario, 1859 . . . . . . #S441-S443
Novo Banco de Pernambuco, 1858 . . . . . . #S447-S450

Section IV, 1892-1897

REGIONAL ISSUES

Alagoas, 1895 . . . . . . #S471-S473
Amazonas, 1892 . . . . . . #S477-S478
Maranhão, 1894 . . . . . . #S481
Pernambuco, 1895-1898 . . . . . . #S486-S498
Rio Grande do Norte, 1897 . . . . . . #S501-S506
Sergipe, 1897 . . . . . . #S511-S515

Section V, 1889-1893

BANK ISSUES REPUBLIC

Banco da Bahia, 1890 . . . . . . #S521-S522
Banco do Brazil, 1890 . . . . . . #S526-S535
Banco do Café, 1890 . . . . . . #S541-S542
Banco de Crédito Popular do Brazil, 1891-1892 . . . . . . #S546-S555
Banco Emissor da Bahia, 1890 . . . . . . #S561-S566
Banco Emissor do Norte, 1890 . . . . . . #S571-S580
Banco Emissor de Pernambuco, 1890 . . . . . . #S581-S586
Banco Emissor do Sul, 1890 . . . . . . #S591-S593
Banco dos Estados Unidos do Brazil, 1890 . . . . . . #S596-S607B
Banco Industrial dos Estados do Sul, 1891 . . . . . . #S608-S609
Banco Mercantil de Santos, 1890 . . . . . . #S611-S616
Banco Nacional do Brazil no Rio de Janeiro, 1890 . . . . . . #S621-S630
Banco da República dos Estados Unidos do Brazil, 1889-1891 . . . . . . #S631-S650
Banco da República do Brazil, 1893 . . . . . . #S656-S680
Banco de São Paulo, 1889 . . . . . . #S681-S683
Banco Sul Americano de Pernambuco, 1890 . . . . . . #S686-S689
Banco Uniao Ibero Americano, 1891 . . . . . . #S691
Banco Uniao de São Paulo, 1890 . . . . . . #S693-S711

Section VI, 1924-1966

REGIONAL ISSUES

Minas Geraes, 1930 . . . . . . #S751-S764
Rio Grande do Sul, 1930-1934, 1959-1966 . . . . . . #S771-S854
São Paulo, 1932 . . . . . . #S861-S876
Revolution Issue, 1924 . . . . . . #S881

SECTION I, 1808-57

EMPIRE - PROVINCIAL ISSUES

PROVINCIA DA BAHIA

LAW OF 27.11.1827 / DECREE OF 24.12.1827; 1828 ISSUE

	Good	Fine	XF
S101 10 Mil Reis 1828. Black. Imperial arms at upper center. Uniface. Rare.	—	—	—
S102 25 Mil Reis 1828. Black. Imperial arms at upper center. Uniface. Rare.	—	—	—
S103 50 Mil Reis 1828. Black. Imperial arms at upper center. Uniface. Rare.	—	—	—

	Good	Fine	XF
S104 100 Mil Reis 1828. Black. Imperial arms at upper center. Uniface. Rare.	—	—	—

NOTE: A second issue consisting of the same denominations requires confirmation.

PROVINCIA DO CEARÁ

1857 TREASURY NOTES ISSUE

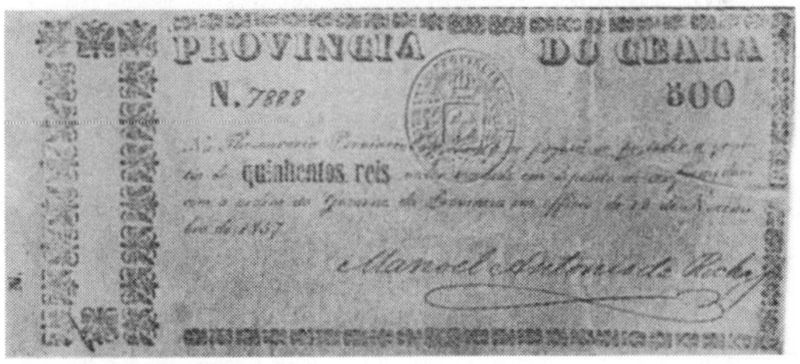

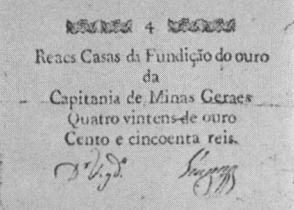

	Good	Fine	XF
S111 500 Reis 12.11.1857. Black. Embossed oval provincial arms at upper center. Rare.	—	—	—

CAPITANIA DE MINAS GERAES

1808 ND GOLD EXCHANGE NOTES ISSUE

	Good	Fine	XF
S121 37 1/2 Reis = 1 Vintem de Ouro ND (1808). Black. Denomination at top between two ornaments. Uniface. Rare.	—	—	—
S122 75 Reis = 2 Vintens de Ouro ND (1808). Black. Denomination at top between two ornaments. Uniface. Rare.	—	—	—

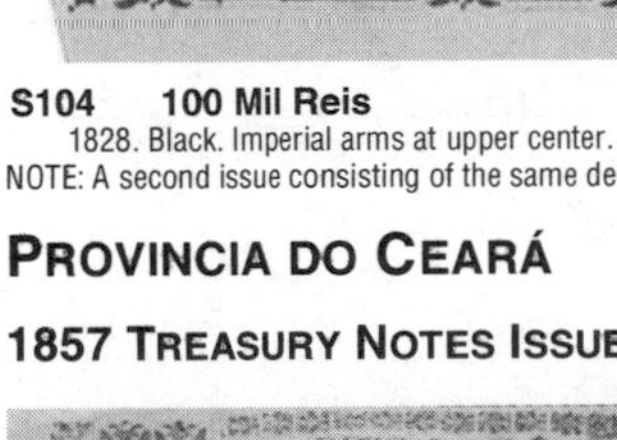

	Good	Fine	XF
S123 150 Reis = 4 Vintens de Ouro ND (1808). Black. Denomination at top between two ornaments. Uniface. Rare.	—	—	—
S124 300 Reis = 8 Vintens de Ouro ND (1808). Black. Denomination at top between two ornaments. Uniface. Rare.	—	—	—
S125 450 Reis = 12 Vintens de Ouro ND (1808). Black. Denomination at top between two ornaments. Uniface. Rare.	—	—	—
S126 600 Reis = 16 Vintens de Ouro ND (1808). Black. Denomination at top between two ornaments. Uniface. Rare.	—	—	—

1809 ND Issue

		Good	Fine	XF
S131	**37 1/2 Reis = 1 Vintem de Ouro** ND (1809). Black. Crowned arms of Portugal in half wreath at upper center. Uniface. Rare.	—	—	—
S132	**75 Reis = 2 Vintens de Ouro** ND (1809). Black. Crowned arms of Portugal in half wreath at upper center. Uniface. Rare.	—	—	—
S133	**150 Reis = 4 Vintens de Ouro** ND (1809). Black. Crowned arms of Portugal in half wreath at upper center. Uniface. Rare.	—	—	—
S134	**300 Reis = 8 Vintens de Ouro** ND (1809). Black. Crowned arms of Portugal in half wreath at upper center. Uniface. Rare.	—	—	—
S135	**450 Reis = 12 Vintens de Ouro** ND (1809). Black. Crowned arms of Portugal in half wreath at upper center. Uniface. Rare.	—	—	—

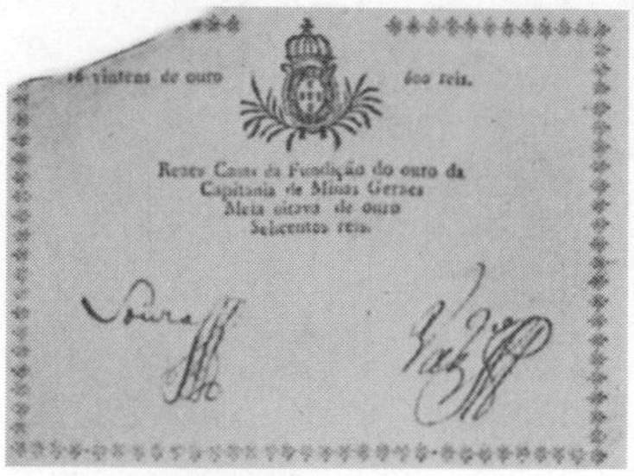

		Good	Fine	XF
S136	**600 Reis = 16 Vintens de Ouro** ND (1809). Black. Crowned arms of Portugal in half wreath at upper center. Uniface. Rare.	—	—	—

1818 ND Issue

Printed in 1818 at Rio de Janeiro but apparently not issued as no examples in issued form are known.

		Good	Fine	XF
S141	**37 1/2 Reis = 1 Vintem de Ouro** (ca.1818).	—	—	—
S142	**75 Reis = 2 Vintens de Ouro** (ca.1818).	—	—	—
S143	**150 Reis = 4 Vintens de Ouro** (ca.1818).	—	—	—
S144	**300 Reis = 8 Vintens de Ouro** (ca.1818).	—	—	—
S145	**450 Reis = 12 Vintens de Ouro** (ca.1818).	—	—	—

NOTE: The 600 Reis denomination was not printed as part of this issue.

República Rio-Grandense, 1835-1845

1838 Conhecimientos Issue

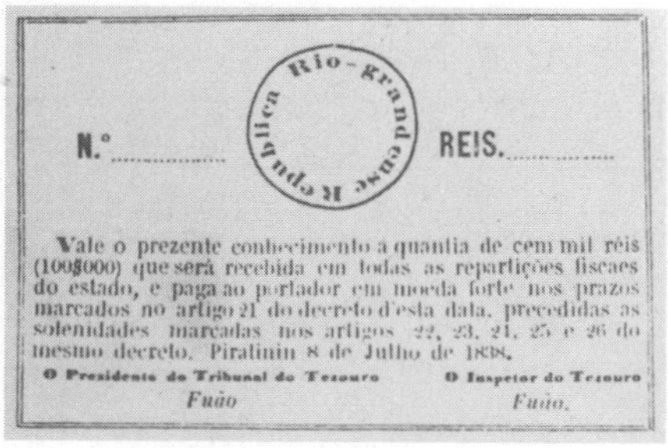
Republica Rio-grandense

N.º .... REIS. ....

Vale o prezente conhecimento a quantia de cem mil réis (100$000) que será recebida em todas as repartições fiscaes do estado, e paga ao portador em moeda forte nos prazos marcados no artigo 21 do decreto d'esta data, precedidas as solenidades marcadas nos artigos 22, 23, 24, 25 e 26 do mesmo decreto. Piratinin 8 de Julho de 1838.

O Presidente do Tribunal do Tezouro — Fulão

O Inspetor do Tezouro — Fulão.

		Good	Fine	XF
S151	**100 Reis** 6.7.1838. Black. Rare.	—	—	—

Section II, 1808-90

Banco do Brazil - During the 19th century there were three separate institutions established with the same bank name. The first came in 1808 by royal letter. It issued banknotes up to the time of its closing in 1829. A second bank (Banco do Brazil no Rio de Janeiro) was formed in 1851 by the Viscount of Mauá. Several notes from this bank are reported, not confirmed (see listing).

The Banco do Brazil no Rio de Janeiro merged with the Banco Commercial no Rio de Janeiro in 1853 to form the #S302-S304 overprint: *CAIXA FILIAL DO OURO PRETO* on face of Banco do Brazil issues.

Banco do Brazil (First)

1810-13 Issue

		Good	Fine	XF
S171	**4 Mil Reis** ND (1813-29). Black. Neptune reclining, water jug at upper left. Uniface. Rare.	—	—	—
S172	**6 Mil Reis** ND (1813-29). Black. Neptune reclining, water jug at upper left. Uniface. Rare.	—	—	—
S173	**8 Mil Reis** ND (1913-29). Black. Neptune reclining, water jug at upper left. Uniface. Rare.	—	—	—
S174	**10 Mil Reis** ND (1813-29). Black. Neptune reclining, water jug at upper left. Uniface. Rare.	—	—	—
S175	**12 Mil Reis** ND (1813-29). Black. Neptune reclining, water jug at upper left. Uniface. Rare.	—	—	—
S176	**20 Mil Reis** ND (1813-29). Black. Neptune reclining, water jug at upper left. Uniface. Rare.	—	—	—
S177	**30 Mil Reis** ND (1810-29). Black. Neptune reclining, water jug at upper left. Uniface. Rare.	—	—	—

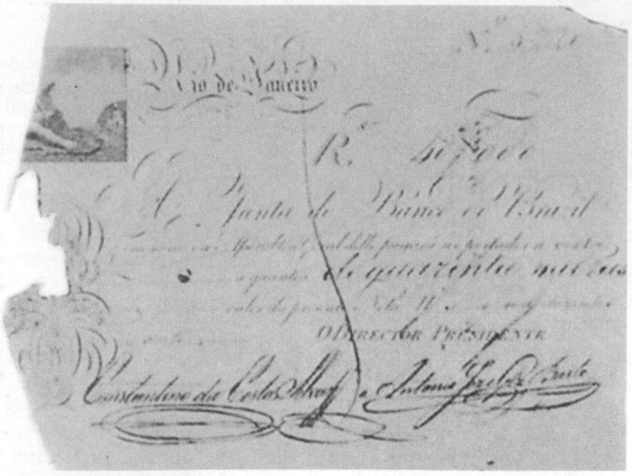

		Good	Fine	XF
S178	**40 Mil Reis** ND (1810-29). Black. Neptune reclining, water jug at upper left. Uniface. Rare.	—	—	—
S179	**50 Mil Reis** ND (1810-29). Black. Neptune reclining, water jug at upper left. Uniface. Rare.	—	—	—
S180	**60 Mil Reis** ND (1810-29). Black. Neptune reclining, water jug at upper left. Uniface. Rare.	—	—	—
S181	**70 Mil Reis** ND (1810-29). Black. Neptune reclining, water jug at upper left. Uniface. Rare.	—	—	—
S182	**80 Mil Reis** ND (1810-29). Black. Neptune reclining, water jug at upper left. Uniface. Rare.	—	—	—
S183	**90 Mil Reis** ND (1810-29). Black. Neptune reclining, water jug at upper left. Uniface. Rare.	—	—	—
S184	**100 Mil Reis** ND (1810-29). Black. Neptune reclining, water jug at upper left. Uniface. Value in shaded area at center right. Rare.	—	—	—
S185	**100 Mil Reis** ND (1810-29). Black. Neptune reclining, water jug at upper left. Uniface. Value in open area at center right. Rare.	—	—	—
S186	**200 Mil Reis** ND (1810-29). Black. Neptune reclining, water jug at upper left. Uniface. Rare.	—	—	—
S187	**300 Mil Reis** ND (1810-29). Black. Neptune reclining, water jug at upper left. Uniface. Rare.	—	—	—
S188	**400 Mil Reis** ND (1810-29). Black. Neptune reclining, water jug at upper left. Uniface. Rare.	—	—	—

NOTE: Higher values of this issue require confirmation.

Decree of 4.7.1828

		Good	Fine	XF
S201	**1 Mil Reis** 1828-29. Filled in by hand. Black. Allegorical figures and ship at upper center. Uniface. Rare.	—	—	—

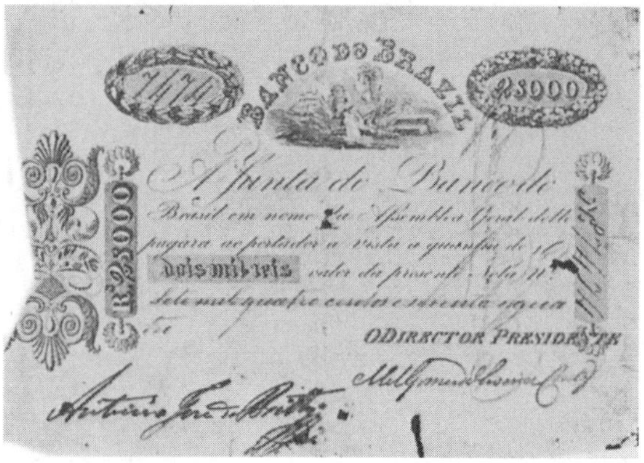

		Good	Fine	XF
S202	**2 Mil Reis** 1828-29. Filled in by hand. Black. Allegorical figures and ship at upper center. Uniface. Rare.	—	—	—

Decree of 23.9.1829

		Good	Fine	XF
S206	**1 Mil Reis** 1829-33. Hand dated. Black. Allegorical figures at left center and right. Uniface. Back: Four portraits in circles. Printer: Perkins and Heath or Perkins and Bacon. Rare.	—	—	—
S207	**2 Mil Reis** 1829-30. Hand dated. Black. Allegorical figures at left center and right. Uniface. Back: Four portraits in circles. Printer: Perkins and Heath or Perkins and Bacon. Rare.	—	—	—
S208	**4 Mil Reis** 1829-30. Hand dated. Black. Allegorical figures at left center and right. Uniface. Back: Four portraits in circles. Printer: Perkins and Heath or Perkins and Bacon. Rare.	—	—	—
S209	**6 Mil Reis** 1829-30. Hand dated. Black. Allegorical figures at left center and right. Uniface. Back: Four portraits in circles. Printer: Perkins & Heath orPerkins & Bacon. Rare.	—	—	—
S210	**8 Mil Reis** 1829-30. Hand dated. Black. Allegorical figures at left center and right. Uniface. Back: Four portraits in circles. Printer: Perkins & Heath or Perkins & Bacon. Rare.	—	—	—

		Good	Fine	XF
S211	**10 Mil Reis** 1829-30. Hand dated. Black. Allegorical figures at left center and right. Uniface. Back: Four portraits in circles. Printer: Perkins & Heath and Perkins & Bacon. Rare.	—	—	—
S212	**12 Mil Reis** 1829-30. Hand dated. Black. Allegorical figures at left center and right. Uniface. Back: Four portraits in circles. Printer: Perkins & Heath and Perkins & Bacon. Rare.	—	—	—
S213	**20 Mil Reis** 1829-30. Hand dated. Black. Allegorical figures at left center and right. Uniface. Back: For portraits in circles. Printer: Perkins & Heath and Perkins & Bacon. Rare.	—	—	—

		Good	Fine	XF
S214	**30 Mil Reis** 1829-30. Hand dated. Black. Allegorical figures at left center and right. Uniface. Back: Four portraits in circles. Printer: Perkins & Heath and Perkins & Bacon. Rare.	—	—	—
S215	**40 Mil Reis** 1829-30. Hand dated. Black. Allegorical figures at left center and right. Uniface. Back: Four portraits in circles. Printer: Perkins & Heath and Perkins & Bacon. Rare.	—	—	—
S216	**50 Mil Reis** 1829-30. Hand dated. Black. Allegorical figures at left center and right. Uniface. Back: Four portraits in circles. Printer: Perkins & Heath and Perkins & Bacon. Rare.	—	—	—
S217	**60 Mil Reis** 1829-30. Blue. Allegorical figures at left center and right. Uniface. Back: Four portraits in circles. Printer: Perkins & Heath and Perkins & Bacon. Rare.	—	—	—
S218	**70 Mil Reis** 1829-30. Hand dated. Gray. Allegorical figures at left center and right. Uniface. Back: Four portraits in circles. Printer: Perkins & Heath and Perkins & Bacon. Rare.	—	—	—
S219	**80 Mil Reis** 1829-30. Hand dated. Yellow. Allegorical figures at left center and right. Uniface. Back: Four portraits in circles. Printer: Perkins & Heath and Perkins & Bacon. Rare.	—	—	—
S220	**90 Mil Reis** 1829-30. Hand dated. Blue. Allegorical figures at left center and right. Uniface. Back: Four portraits in circles. Printer: Perkins & Heath and Perkins & Bacon. Rare.	—	—	—
S221	**100 Mil Reis** 1829-30. Hand dated. Sepia. Allegorical figues at left center and right. Uniface. Back: Four portraits in circles. Printer: Perkins & Heath and Perkins & Bacon. Rare.	—	—	—
S222	**200 Mil Reis** 1829-30. Hand dated. Green. Allegorical figures at left center and right. Uniface. Back: Four portraits in circles. Printer: Perkins & Heath and Perkins & Bacon. Rare.	—	—	—
S223	**300 Mil Reis** 1829-30. Hand dated. Green. Allegorical figures at left center and right. Uniface. Back: Four portraits in circles. Printer: Perkins & Heath and Perkins & Bacon. Rare.	—	—	—
S224	**400 Mil Reis** 1829-30. Hand dated. Green. Allegorical figures at left center and right. Uniface. Back: Four portraits in circles. Printer: Perkins & Heath and Perkins & Bacon. Rare.	—	—	—

Banco do Brazil no Rio de Janeiro (Second)

1851 ND Issue

		Good	Fine	XF
S227	**200 Mil Reis** ND. Issued at Rio de Janeiro. Reported not confirmed.	—	—	—
S228	**100 Mil Reis** ND. Issued at São Paulo. Reported not confirmed.	—	—	—
S229	**100 Mil Reis** ND. Issued at São Pedro de Rio Grande do Sul. Reported not confirmed.	—	—	—

Banco do Brazil (Third)

Decree of 31.8.1853 (1853-54)

		Good	Fine	XF
S231	**20 Mil Reis** ND (1854-55). Black. View of naval arsenal at center. Uniface. Printer: CMRJ. Rare.	—	—	—
S232	**30 Mil Reis** ND (1853-55). Black. Gaucho at center. Uniface. Printer: CMRJ. Rare.	—	—	—
S233	**50 Mil Reis** ND (1854-55). Black. Indian woman in hammock at center. Uniface. Printer: CMRJ. Rare.	—	—	—

		Good	Fine	XF
S234	**100 Mil Reis** ND (1854-55). Black. Manned rowboat, two swans at center. Uniface. Printer: CMRJ. Rare.	—	—	—

		Good	Fine	XF
S235	**200 Mil Reis** ND (1854-55). Black. Reclining sailor at center. Uniface. Printer: CMRJ. Rare.	—	—	—

		Good	Fine	XF
S236	**500 Mil Reis** ND (1854-55). Black. Standing woman at left and right, allegory of Abundance at upper center. Uniface. Printer: CMRJ. Rare.	—	—	—

1856-57 ND First Issue

	Good	Fine	XF
S241 20 Mil Reis ND (1856). Black. View of Rio de Janeiro at upper center. Uniface. Rare.	—	—	—
S242 30 Mil Reis ND (1856). Black. Different view of Rio de Janeiro at upper center. Uniface. Paper: Rose. Rare.	—	—	—
S243 50 Mil Reis ND (1857). Black. Allegory of Abundance at upper center. Uniface. Rare.	—	—	—
S244 100 Mil Reis ND (1856). Black. City of Santos at upper center. Uniface. Paper: Yellow. Rare.	—	—	—

	Good	Fine	XF
S245 200 Mil Reis ND (1856). Black. Shore of Icarai at upper center. Uniface. Paper: Green.			
a. Issued note. Rare.	—	—	—
b. Cancelled, perforated: *SEM VALOR.*	—	—	—

1856 ND Second Issue

	Good	Fine	XF
S246 20 Mil Reis ND (1856). Black. Different view of Rio de Janeiro at upper center. Uniface.	50.00	125.	300.
S247 50 Mil Reis ND (1856). Black. Scene of Rio de Janeiro at center. Uniface. Paper: Green. Rare.	—	—	—

A WORD ON DATE RANGES

Often date ranges or specific dates are listed. These have been observed or reported by our contributors. If a note is outside the published range, it only means that it is a newly reported date, and not necessarily worthy of a premium value.

1857 ND Issue

	Good	Fine	XF
S248 20 Mil Reis ND (1857-60). Black and green on brown underprint. Liberty standing with flag at left, coffee worker at right. Back: Green. Printer: BWC. Rare.	—	—	—

1860's ND Issue

	Good	Fine	XF
S251 25 Mil Reis ND. Black and red. Two sailors dockside with sailing ship at anchor at lower left, St. Sebastian and allegory of Transport at top center, portrait C. Columbus at lower right. Back: Red. Printer: ABNC.			
a. Issued note. Rare.	—	—	—
p. Proof.	—	—	—
s. Specimen.	—	—	—

	Good	Fine	XF
S252 30 Mil Reis ND. Black and brown. St. Sebastian at lower left, horse at top center, seated allegorical woman ("Fortune") at lower right. Back: Brown. Printer: ABNC.			
a. Issued note. Rare.	—	—	—
p. Proof.	—	—	—
s. Specimen.	—	—	—

	Good	Fine	XF
S253 50 Mil Reis ND. Black and green. St. Sebastian at lower left, explorer landing at upper center, portrait girl with pups at lower right. Back: Green. Printer: ABNC.			
a. Issued note. Rare.	—	—	—
p. Proof.	—	—	—
s. Specimen.	—	—	—

S254 100 Mil Reis	Good	Fine	XF
ND. Black and blue. St. Sebastian at lower left, steam passenger train at upper center, allegory of Justice at lower right. Back: Blue. Printer: ABNC.			
a. Issued note. Rare.	—	—	—
p. Proof.	—	—	—
s. Specimen.	—	—	—

S255 200 Mil Reis	Good	Fine	XF
ND. Black and yellow underprint. Seated woman at lower left, seated female ("The Tropics") at top center, St. Sebastian at lower right. Back: Red. Steam passenger train at station at upper center. Printer: ABNC.			
a. Issued note. Rare.	—	—	—
p. Proof.	—	—	—
s. Specimen.	—	—	—

S256 500 Mil Reis	Good	Fine	XF
ND. Black and orange. Portrait Liberty at lower left, St. Sebastian and field workers at upper center, portrait woman at lower right. Back: Orange. Sailor in oval at center. Printer: ABNC.			
a. Issued note. Rare.	—	—	—
p. Proof.	—	—	—
s. Specimen.	—	—	—

NOTE: #S254, S255 and S256 were reissued in 1890 with sign. of A. A. Vieira da Costa. For a listing of those notes and a new issue of 1890 by the Banco do Brazil see #S526-S528, and S531-S535.

Bahia

1856 ND Issue

	Good	Fine	XF
S261 10 Mil Reis ND (1856). Black. View of Bahia at upper center. Uniface. Paper: White. Printer: Bradbury and Evans. Rare.	—	—	—
S262 20 Mil Reis ND (1856). Black. View of Bahia at upper center. Uniface. Paper: Red. Printer: Bradbury and Evans. Rare.	—	—	—
S263 50 Mil Reis ND (1856). Black. View of Bahia at upper center. Uniface. Paper: Yellow. Printer: Bradbury and Evans. Rare.	—	—	—
S264 100 Mil Reis ND (1856). Black. View of Bahia at upper center. Uniface. Paper: Green. Printer: Bradbury and Evans. Rare.	—	—	—
S265 200 Mil Reis ND (1856). Black. View of Bahia at upper center. Uniface. Paper: Light brown. Printer: Bradbury and Evans. Rare.	—	—	—
S266 500 Mil Reis ND (1856). Black. View of Bahia at upper center. Uniface. Paper: Rose. Printer: Bradbury and Evans. Rare.	—	—	—

NOTE: A second issue consisting of 10, 20, 50, 100 and 200 Mil Reis requires conformation.

Maranhão

1856 ND Issue

	Good	Fine	XF
S276 10 Mil Reis ND (1856). Black. Allegory of Commerce with Brazilian flag at upper center. Uniface. Paper: Red. Printer: Knowles and Foster (without imprint). Rare.	—	—	—
S277 20 Mil Reis ND (1856). Black. Allegory of Commerce with Brazilian flag at upper center. Uniface. Paper: Green. Printer: Knowles and Foster (without imprint). Rare.	—	—	—

	Good	Fine	XF
S278 50 Mil Reis ND (1856). Black. Allegory of Commerce with Brazilian flag at upper center. Uniface. Paper: Green. Printer: Knowles and Foster (without imprint). Rare.	—	—	—
S279 100 Mil Reis ND (1856). Black. Allegory of Commerce with Brazilian flag at upper center. Uniface. Paper: Brown. Printer: Knowles and Foster. Rare.	—	—	—
S280 200 Mil Reis ND (1856). Black. Allegory of Commerce with Brazilian flag at upper center. Uniface. Paper: White. Printer: Knowles and Foster (without imprint). Rare.	—	—	—

NOTE: A second issue consisting of 10, 20, 50, 100 and 200 Mil Reis notes require confirmation.

Ouro Preto

1856 ND Issue

S291 10 Mil Reis — Good / Fine / XF
ND (1856). Black. Beehive at upper center. Uniface. This is a special design for branch issues. Rare. — — —

S292 20 Mil Reis
ND (1856). Black. Overprint: *CAIXA FILIAL DO OURO PRETO* on face of #S231. Rare. — — —

S293 30 Mil Reis
ND (1856). Black. Overprint: *CAIXA FILIAL DO OURO PRETO* on face of #S232. Rare. — — —

S294 50 Mil Reis
ND (1856). Black. Overprint: *CAIXA FILIAL DO OURO PRETO* on face of #S233. Rare. — — —

S295 100 Mil Reis
ND (1856). Black. Overprint: *CAIXA FILIAL DO OURO PRETO* on face of #S234. Rare. — — —

S296 200 Mil Reis
ND (1856). Black. Overprint: *CAIXA FILIAL DO OURO PRETO* on face of #S235. Rare. — — —

1857 ND Issue

#S302-S304 overprint: *CAIXA FILIAL DO OURO PRETO* on face of Banco do Brazil issues.

S301 20 Mil Reis — Good / Fine / XF
ND (1857). Black. Shoreline of Botafogo at center. Uniface. Printer: Knowles & Foster (without imprint). This is a special design for this issue. Rare. — — —

#S302-S304 ovpt: *CAIXA FILIAL DO OURO PRETO* on face of Banco do Brazil issues.

S302 50 Mil Reis — Good / Fine / XF
ND (1857). Black. Overprint: *CAIXA FILIAL DO OURO PRETO* on face of #S243. Rare. — — —

S303 100 Mil Reis — Good / Fine / XF
ND (1857). Black. Overprint: *CAIXA FILIAL DO OURO PRETO* on face of #S244. Rare. — — —

S304 200 Mil Reis — Good / Fine / XF
ND (1857). Black. Overprint: *CAIXA FILIAL DO OURO PRETO* on face of #S245. Rare. — — —

NOTE: Two other issues (10, 20 and 30 Mil Reis, and 20 and 50 Mil Reis) for this branch require confirmation.

Pará

1856 ND First Issue

S311 10 Mil Reis — Good / Fine / XF
ND (1856). Black. Woman with globe and plants at upper center. Uniface. Paper: Yellow. Printer: Knowles & Foster (without imprint). Rare. — — —

S312 20 Mil Reis
ND (1856). Black. Woman with globe and plants at upper center. Uniface. Paper: Green. Printer: Knowles & Foster (without imprint). Rare. — — —

S313 50 Mil Reis
ND (1856). Black. Woman with globe and plants at upper center. Uniface. Paper: Yellow. Printer: Knowles & Foster (without imprint). Rare. — — —

S314 100 Mil Reis
ND (1856). Black. Woman with globe and plants at upper center. Uniface. Paper: Gray. Printer: Knowles & Foster (without imprint). Rare. — — —

S315 200 Mil Reis — Good / Fine / XF
ND (1856). Black. Woman with globe and plants at upper center. Uniface. Paper: Red. Printer: Knowles & Foster (without imprint). Rare. — — —

1856 ND Second Issue

S316 10 Mil Reis — Good / Fine / XF
ND (1856). Black. Woman with globe at upper center. Uniface. Paper: Green. Printer: Knowles & Foster (without imprint). Rare. — — —

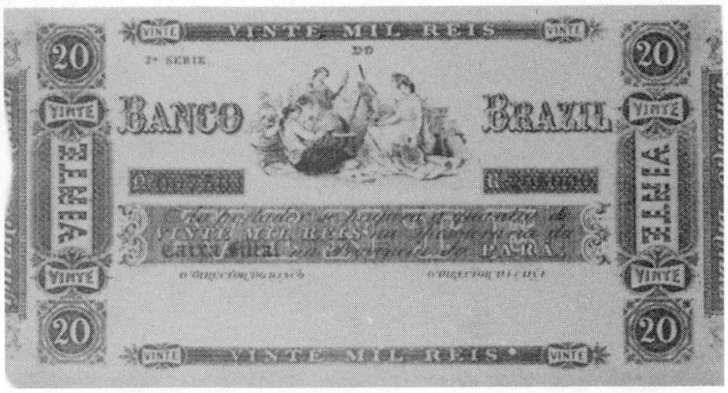

		Good	Fine	XF
S317	**20 Mil Reis** ND (1856). Black. Allegory of Arts at upper center. Uniface. Paper: Rose. Printer: Knowles & Foster (without imprint). Rare.	—	—	—

		Good	Fine	XF
S318	**50 Mil Reis** ND (1856). Black. Horses galloping at upper center. Uniface. Paper: Red. Printer: Knowles & Foster (without imprint). Rare.	—	—	—
S319	**100 Mil Reis** ND. Black. Uniface. Printer: Knowles & Foster (without imprint). Reported not confirmed.	—	—	—
S320	**200 Mil Reis** ND. Black. Uniface. Printer: Knowles & Foster (without imprint). Reported not confirmed.	—	—	—

Pernambuco

1856 ND First Issue

		Good	Fine	XF
S321	**10 Mil Reis** ND (1856). Black. View of Recife at upper center. Uniface. Paper: White. Printer: Bradbury & Evans (without imprint). Rare.	—	—	—
S322	**20 Mil Reis** ND (1856). Black. View of Recife at upper center. Uniface. Paper: Gray. Printer: Bradbury & Evans (without imprint). Rare.	—	—	—

		Good	Fine	XF
S323	**50 Mil Reis** ND (1856). Black. View of Recife at upper center. Uniface. Paper: Rose. Printer: Bradbury & Evans (without imprint). Rare.	—	—	—
S324	**100 Mil Reis** ND (1856). Black. View of Recife at upper center. Uniface. Paper: Yellow. Printer: Bradbury & Evans (without imprint). Rare.	—	—	—
S325	**200 Mil Reis** ND (1856). Black. View of Recife at upper center. Uniface. Paper: Green. Printer: Bradbury & Evans (without imprint). Rare.	—	—	—
S326	**500 Mil Reis** ND (1856). Black. View of Recife at upper center. Uniface. Paper: Brown. Printer: Bradbury & Evans (without imprint). Rare.	—	—	—

1856 ND Second Issue

		Good	Fine	XF
S327	**10 Mil Reis** ND (1856). Black. Sailboat at left and right, city view of Recife at upper center. Uniface. Printer: Knowles & Foster (without imprint). Rare.	—	—	—

		Good	Fine	XF
S328	**50 Mil Reis** ND (1856). Black. View of Recife with bridge at upper center. Uniface. Paper: Yellow. Printer: Knowles & Foster (without imprint). Rare.	—	—	—

NOTE: 20, 100 and 200 Mil Reis notes for the Second Issue require confirmation.

Rio Grande do Sul

1856 ND First Issue

		Good	Fine	XF
S331	**10 Mil Reis** ND (1856). Black. Woman with globe and plants at upper center. Uniface. Paper: Green. Printer: Knowles & Foster (without imprint). Rare.	—	—	—

		Good	Fine	XF
S332	**20 Mil Reis** ND (1856). Black. Woman with globe and plants at upper center. Uniface. Paper: Brown. Printer: Knowles & Foster (without imprint). Rare.	—	—	—
S333	**50 Mil Reis** ND (1856). Black. Woman with globe and plants at upper center. Uniface. Paper: Gray. Printer: Knowles & Foster (without imprint). Rare.	—	—	—
S334	**100 Mil Reis** ND (1856). Black. Woman with globe and plants at upper center. Uniface. Paper: Rose. Printer: Knowles & Foster (without imprint). Rare.	—	—	—
S335	**200 Mil Reis** ND (1856). Black. Woman with globe and plants at upper center. Uniface. Paper: Yellow. Printer: Knowles & Foster (without imprint). Rare.	—	—	—

1856 ND Second Issue

S338 50 Mil Reis Good Fine XF
ND (1856). Black. Ox-cart and palm at left and right, horses galloping at upper center. Uniface. Paper: Green. Printer: Knowles & Foster (without imprint). Rare. — — —

NOTE: 10 and 20 Mil Reis notes for the Second Issue require confirmation.

1860 ND Issue

S340 100 Mil Reis Good Fine XF
ND (ca.1860). Black. Small buildings at left and right, gaucho roping longhorn steers at upper center. Printer: Bradbury & Evans. Proof. — — —

São Paulo

1856 ND First Issue

S341 10 Mil Reis Good Fine XF
ND (1856). Black. Beehive at upper center. Uniface. This is a special design for branch issues. Rare. — — —

S342 20 Mil Reis
ND (1856). Black. Overprint: *CAIXA FILIAL DE S. PAULO* on face of #S231. Rare. — — —

S343 30 Mil Reis
ND (1856). Black. Overprint: *CAIXA FILIAL DE S. PAULO* on face of #S232. Rare. — — —

S344 50 Mil Reis Good Fine XF
ND (1856). Black. Overprint: *CAIXA FILIAL DE S. PAULO* on face of #S233. Rare. — — —

S345 100 Mil Reis
ND (1856). Black. Overprint: *CAIXA FILIAL DE S. PAULO* on face of #S234. Rare. — — —

S346 500 Mil Reis
ND (1856). Black. Overprint: *CAIXA FILIAL DE S. PAULO* on face of #S236. Rare. — — —

1856 ND Second Issue

S347 50 Mil Reis Good Fine XF
ND (1856). Rare. — — —

1856 ND Third Issue

S348 10 Mil Reis Good Fine XF
ND (1856). Black. Woman with globe and plants at upper center. Uniface. Paper: Yellow. Printer: Knowles & Foster (without imprint). Rare. — — —

1856 ND Fourth Issue

S351 10 Mil Reis Good Fine XF
ND (1856). Black. View of Santos at center. Uniface. Printer: Knowles & Foster (without imprint). Special design for this issue. Rare. — — —

S352 20 Mil Reis
ND (1856). Black. Overprint: *CAIXA FILIAL DE S. PAULO* on #S241. Rare. — — —

S353 30 Mil Reis Good Fine XF
ND (1856). Black. Overprint: *CAIXA FILIAL DE S. PAULO* on #S242. Rare. — — —

S354 50 Mil Reis
ND (1856). Black. Overprint: *CAIXA FILIAL DE S. PAULO* on #S243. Rare. — — —

S355 100 Mil Reis Good Fine XF
ND (1856). Black. Overprint: *CAIXA FILIAL DE S. PAULO* on #S244. Rare. — — —

S356 200 Mil Reis
ND (1856). Black. Overprint: *CAIXA FILIAL DE S. PAULO* on #S245. Rare. — — —

1856 ND Fifth Issue

S357 20 Mil Reis Good Fine XF
ND (1856). Reported not confirmed. — — —

S358 50 Mil Reis	Good	Fine	XF
ND (1856). Black. Overprint: *CAIXA FILIAL DE S. PAULO* on #S247. Rare.	—	—	—

Section III, 1850-85

Empire Bank Issues

Banco da Bahia

1858 ND Issue

S381 10 Mil Reis	Good	Fine	XF
ND (1858). Black. Sailing ship at left, group of allegorical women and children at top center. Series 1. Uniface. Printer: Knowles & Foster (without imprint). Rare.	—	—	—

S382 20 Mil Reis	Good	Fine	XF
ND (1858). Black. Dock workers at upper center. Series 1. Uniface. Printer: Knowles & Foster (without imprint). Rare.	—	—	—

S383 25 Mil Reis	Good	Fine	XF
ND (1858). Black. Mule train at upper center. Series 2. Uniface. Printer: Knowles & Foster (without imprint). Rare.	—	—	—

S384 50 Mil Reis			
ND (1858). Black. Man riding mule at upper center. Series 1. Uniface. Paper: White. Printer: Knowles & Foster (without imprint). Rare.	—	—	—

S385 100 Mil Reis	Good	Fine	XF
ND (1858). Black. Ox-cart in rural scene at upper center. Uniface. Printer: Knowles & Foster (without imprint). Rare.	—	—	—

S386 200 Mil Reis			
ND (1858). Black. Uniface. Printer: Knowles & Foster (without imprint). Reported not confirmed.	—	—	—

1860's ND Issue

S387 25 Mil Reis	Good	Fine	XF
ND (ca. 1860). Black, green and rose. Mule train at upper center. Series 3 or 4. Back: Green and rose. Paper: Gray. Tinted.	125.	250.	400.

S388 50 Mil Reis	Good	Fine	XF
ND (ca. 1860). Black, green and rose. Man riding mule at upper center. Series 2, 3 or 4. Back: Green and rose. Paper: Pink. Tinted.	125.	250.	400.

S389 100 Mil Reis	Good	Fine	XF
ND (ca. 1860). Black and green. Ox-cart in rural scene at upper center. Series 3 or 4. Back: Green. Paper: Yellow. Rare.	—	—	—

S390 200 Mil Reis			
ND (ca. 1860). Reported not confirmed.	—	—	—

Banco Commercial e Agricola

1858 ND First Issue

S401 20 Mil Reis

ND (1858). Black. Village scene at upper center. Sailing ships at left. Uniface. Paper: Blue. Printer: CMRJ. Rare.

Good	Fine	XF
—	—	—

S402 30 Mil Reis

ND (1858). Cow at upper center. Sailing ships at left. Uniface. Paper: Lilac. Printer: CMRJ. Rare.

Good	Fine	XF
—	—	—

S403 50 Mil Reis

ND (1858). Mercury seated at upper center. Sailing ships at left. Uniface. Paper: White. Printer: CMRJ. Rare.

Good	Fine	XF
—	—	—

NOTE: Higher values of 100, 200, 500 Mil Reis require confirmation.

1858 ND Second Issue

S411 20 Mil Reis

ND (1858). Black. Seated allegorical woman at upper center. Uniface. Paper: Blue. Printer: PBC. Rare.

Good	Fine	XF
—	—	—

S412 30 Mil Reis

ND (1858). Black. Allegory of Abundance at upper center. Uniface. Paper: White. Printer: PBC. Rare.

Good	Fine	XF
—	—	—

S413 50 Mil Reis

ND (1858). Black. Discovery of Brazil at upper center. Uniface. Paper: White. Printer: PBC. Rare.

S414 100 Mil Reis

ND (1858). Black. Three allegorical women (Arts) at upper center. Uniface. Paper: White. Printer: PBC. Rare.

S415 200 Mil Reis

ND (1858). Black. Seated woman at upper center. Uniface. Paper: White. Printer: PBC. Rare.

	Good	Fine	XF
S413	—	—	—
S414	—	—	—
S415	—	—	—

S416 500 Mil Reis

ND (1858). Black. Standing woman at upper center. Uniface. Paper: White. Printer: PBC. Rare.

Good	Fine	XF
—	—	—

CAMPOS

1859 ND ISSUE

		Good	Fine	XF
S418	**10 Mil Reis** ND (1859). Black. Two seated women at upper center. Uniface. Paper: Rose. Printer: PBC. Rare.	—	—	—

VASSOURAS

1858 ND ISSUE

		Good	Fine	XF
S419	**10 Mil Reis** ND (1858). Black. Two seated women at upper center. Uniface. Paper: Blue. Printer: PBC. Rare.	—	—	—

NOTE: Values of 20, 30, 50, and 100 Mil Reis for this issue require confirmation.

BANCO COMMERCIAL DA BAHIA

1850 ISSUE

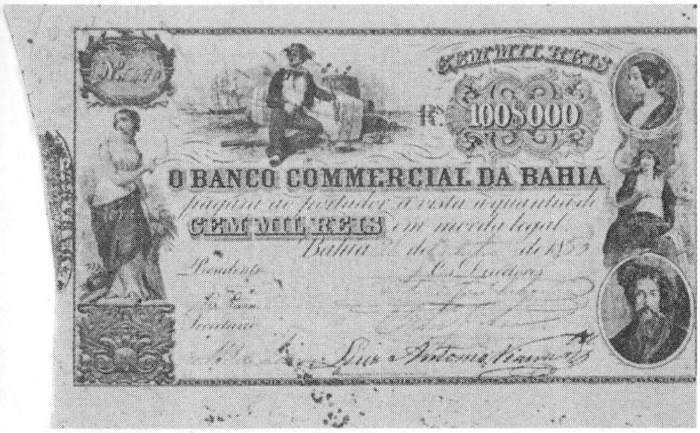

		Good	Fine	XF
S421	**100 Mil Reis** 26.10.1850 (date filled in by hand). Black. Standing allegorical woman with sickle at left, seated man with bales at upper left center, portrait woman at right, allegorical woman below, portrait man at bottom. Uniface. Printer: TCC. Rare.	—	—	—

BANCO COMMERCIAL DO MARANHÃO

DECREE OF 24 MARCH 1849; 1854 ISSUE

		Good	Fine	XF
S424	**100 Mil Reis** 1.4.1854 (date filled in by hand). Black. Uniface. Rare.	—	—	—

NOTE: Values of 5, 10, 20, and 50 Mil Reis for this issue require confirmation.

BANCO DO MARANHÃO

DECREE OF 25.11.1857

		Good	Fine	XF
S425	**20 Mil Reis** D.1857. Deep aqua on gray underprint. Uniface.	—	—	—

NOTE: Values of 10, 25, 50, 100, 200 and 500 Mil Reis require confirmation.

DECREE OF 25.11.1857 / DECISION OF 9.7.1885

		Good	Fine	XF
S427	**25 Mil Reis** ND (1885). Black. Mercury seated at left. Uniface. Printer: BWC. Reported not confirmed.	—	—	—

		Good	Fine	XF
S428	**50 Mil Reis** ND (1885). Black and green on yellow underprint. Mercury seated at left. Uniface. Printer: BWC. Rare.	—	—	—
S429	**100 Mil Reis** ND (1885). Black and red. Mercury seated at left. Uniface. Printer: BWC. Rare.	—	—	—
S430	**200 Mil Reis** ND (1885). Black and blue. Mercury seated at left. Uniface. Printer: BWC. Rare.	—	—	—

Banco do Rio Grande do Sul

1859 ND Issue

	Good	Fine	XF
S436 10 Mil Reis ND (1859). Black. Mercury in allegory of Commerce at center. Uniface. Printer: Knowles & Foster (without imprint).			
a. White paper.	—	—	—
b. Yellow paper.	—	—	—
c. Green paper.	—	—	—
d. Blue paper.	—	—	—

Banco Rural e Hypothecario

1859 ND Issue

	Good	Fine	XF
S441 20 Mil Reis ND (1859). Black. Seated allegorical woman at upper center. Uniface. Paper: Blue. Printer: PBC. Rare.	—	—	—
S442 30 Mil Reis ND (1859). Black. Neptune and two seahorses at upper center. Uniface. Printer: PBC. Rare.	—	—	—
S443 50 Mil Reis ND (1859). Black. Standing allegorical woman at upper center. Uniface. Printer: PBC. Rare.	—	—	—

NOTE: Additional values for this issue require confirmation.

Novo Banco de Pernambuco

1858 ND Issue

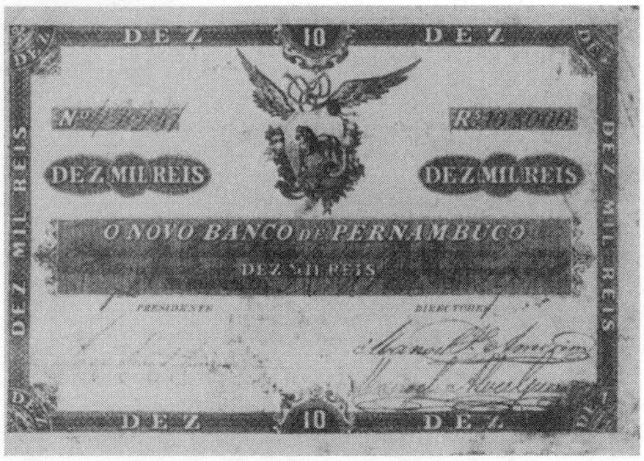

	Good	Fine	XF
S447 10 Mil Reis ND (1858). Black. Winged arms with horse at upper center. Uniface. Printer: Knowles & Foster (without imprint). Rare.	—	—	—

	Good	Fine	XF
S448 20 Mil Reis ND (1858). Black. Winged arms with three bunches of grapes at upper center. Uniface. Printer: Knowles & Foster (without imprint). Rare.	—	—	—
S450 100 Mil Reis ND (1858). Black. Uniface. Printer: Knowles & Foster (without imprint). Specimen.	—	Unc	300.

NOTE: Additional values for this issue require confirmation.

Section IV, 1892-97

Republic Regional Issues

Apólices do Estado/Securities of the State

Law of 5.8.1895

	Good	Fine	XF
S471 100 Reis L.1895. Blue on green underprint. State arms at left. Back: Blue. Woman at center.	15.00	50.00	100.
S472 200 Reis L.1895. Black on rose underprint. State arms at left. Back: Black. Woman at center.	25.00	50.00	100.
S473 500 Reis L.1895. Coral on green underprint. State arms at left. Back: Coral. Woman at center.	25.00	50.00	125.

Titulos de Divida/Titles of Debt

Law of 15.12.1891; 1892 ND Issue

	Good	Fine	XF
S477 2 Mil Reis ND (1892). Reported not confirmed.	—	—	—
S478 5 Mil Reis ND (1892). Reported not confirmed.	—	—	—

Titulos de Divida ao Portador

Titles of Debt to the Bearer

Law of 25.6.1894

	Good	Fine	XF
S481 10 Mil Reis L.1894. Black.	100.	200.	—

Apólices da Divida Pública

Securities of the Public Debt

Law of 22.6.1895

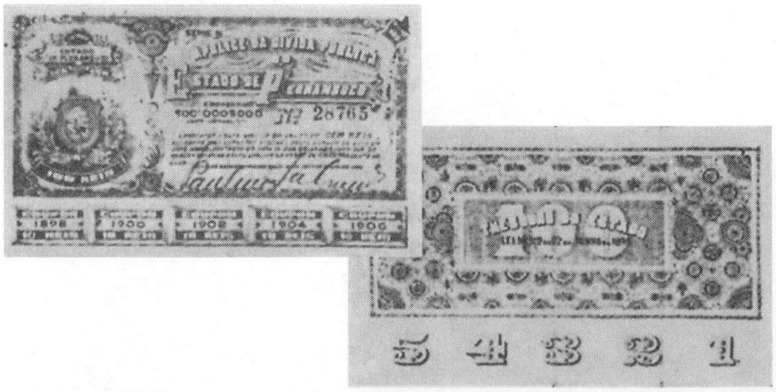

	Good	Fine	XF
S486 100 Reis L.1895. Blue-black on orange underprint. Back: Blue-black. Printer: Recife.	7.50	20.00	50.00
S487 200 Reis L.1895. Red on red-brown underprint. Back: Red-brown. Printer: Recife.	7.50	25.00	75.00
S488 500 Reis L.1895. Dull green on brown underprint. Back: Dark green. Printer: Recife.	7.50	25.00	75.00

Law of 19.11.1896; 1897 Issue

	Good	Fine	XF
S491 50 Mil Reis 4.1.1897. Black and blue. Back: Light blue. Printer: Recife.	—	—	—
S492 100 Mil Reis 1897. Printer: Recife. Reported not confirmed.	—	—	—

Law of 30.6.1898

	Good	Fine	XF
S496 100 Reis L.1898. Green underprint. Printer: Barbosa Primo & Ca., Recife.	10.00	25.00	75.00
S497 200 Reis L.1898. Red on red-brown underprint. Back: Red-brown. Printer: Barbosa Primo & Ca., Recife.	15.00	50.00	100.
S498 500 Reis L.1898. Dull green on brown underprint. Back: Dark green. Printer: Barbosa Primo & Ca., Recife.	20.00	75.00	125.

Law of 15.12.1896; 1897 ND Issue

	Good	Fine	XF
S501 100 Reis ND (1897). Blue-green. Dog at lower left. Printer: J.E. Purcell, Recife.	—	—	—
S502 200 Reis ND (1897). Red-brown. Lion at left. Printer: J.E. Purcell, Recife.	—	—	—
S503 500 Reis ND (1897). Black on green underprint. Woman with sheaf and sickle at left, conch shell at right. Back: Dark brown. Printer: J.E. Purcell, Recife.			
a. Issued note.	—	—	—
b. Unsigned remainder.	—	—	—

	Good	Fine	XF
S505 5 Mil Reis ND (1897). Black and orange. Indian wearing feathered headdress at left. Back: Violet. Printer: J.E. Purcell, Recife.	—	—	—

	Good	Fine	XF
S506 10 Mil Reis ND (1897). Black. Young girl at left. Back: Coral. Printer: J.E. Purcell, Recife.	—	—	—

Apólices do Estado/Securities of the State

Law of 27.2.1897

	Good	Fine	XF
S511 100 Reis L.1897. Dark brown and green. State arms at left. (Man with hot air balloon and basket). Back: Brown. Printer: J.E. Purcell, Recife.	—	—	—

	Good	Fine	XF
S512 200 Reis L.1897. Light and dark coral. State arms at left. (Man with hot air balloon and basket). Back: Blue. Printer: J.E. Purcell, Recife.	—	—	—
S513 500 Reis L.1897. Orange and blue. State arms at left. (Man with hot air balloon and basket). Back: Blue. Printer: J.E. Purcell, Recife.	—	—	—
S514 1 Mil Reis L.1897. Brown and red. State arms at left. (Man with hot air balloon and basket). Back: Brown. Printer: J.E. Purcell, Recife.	—	—	—
S515 5 Mil Reis L.1897. Violet and green. State arms at left. (Man with hot air balloon and basket). Printer: J.E. Purcell, Recife.	—	—	—

Section V, 1889-93

Republic - Bank Issues

Banco da Bahia

1890 ND Provisional Issue

#S521 and S522 overprint new bank name on Imperial Treasury Notes.

	Good	Fine	XF
S521 50 Mil Reis ND (1890). Black on orange yellow underprint. Overprint on Estampa 6, #A263 in Vol. 2. Rare	—	—	—
S522 100 Mil Reis ND (1890). Black on red and green underprint. Overprint on Estampa 5, #A247 in Vol. 2. Rare.	—	—	—

Banco do Brazil

Reissue

	Good	Fine	XF
S525 50 Mil Reis ND (1890). St. Sebastian at lower left, explorer landing at upper center, portrait girl with pups at lower right. Proof.	—	—	—
S526 100 Mil Reis ND (1890). St. Sebastian at lower left, steam passenger train at upper center, allegory of Justice at lower right. Signature of Anto. Arnaldo Vieira da Costa.	225.	—	—
S527 200 Mil Reis ND (1890). Seated woman at lower left, seated female ("The Tropics") at top center, St. Sebastian at lower right. Signature of Anto. Arnalda Vieira da Costa.	300.	—	—
S528 500 Mil Reis ND (1890). Portrait Liberty at lower left, St. Sebastian and field workers at upper center, portrait woman at lower right. Signature of Anto. Arnaldo Vieira da Costa.	400.	—	—

Law of 24.11.1888 / Decree of 8.3.1890

S531 10 Mil Reis — Good | Fine | XF

ND (1890). Black on orange and yellow underprint. Two seated allegorical women ("Commerce and Agriculture") and ("Government and Justice") at left and right, two cherubs at center. Back: Black and orange. Reclining woman with lamp ("Literature") at center. Printer: ABNC.

	Good	Fine	XF
p. Proof.	—	Unc	2250.
s. Specimen. Rare.	—	—	—

S532 20 Mil Reis — Good | Fine | XF

ND (1890). Black on blue and multicolor underprint. Portrait two heads ("The Reapers No. 3") at upper left, seated female ("Mechanics") at upper right. with condor between above bank title. Back: Sepia. Lions ("Lions at Home") at center. Printer: ABNC.

	Good	Fine	XF
p. Proof.	—	Unc	2250.
s. Specimen. Rare.	—	—	—

	Good	Fine	XF
S533 50 Mil Reis ND (1890). Black on multicolor underprint. Portrait woman between two seated women at left, bull's head at lower right. Back: Blue. Woman at center. Printer: W&S. Specimen. Rare.	—	—	—
S534 200 Mil Reis ND (1890). Black on multicolor underprint. Standing woman at left, woman at center, allegory of Commerce at right. Back: Sepia. Rural scene at center. Printer: W&S. Specimen. Rare.	—	—	—
S535 500 Mil Reis ND (1890). Black on multicolor underprint. Woman at left, ship at center, standing woman at right. Back: Sepia. Woman at center. Printer: W&S. Specimen. Rare.	—	—	—

Banco do Café

Decrees of 19.1.1890 and 3.5.1890

	Good	Fine	XF
S541 100 Mil Reis D. 1890. Green on lilac underprint. Shield between two reclining allegorical women at center. Back: Lilac. Squares showing months and value. Printer: ABNC. Unsigned remainder with serial #.	—	Unc	25.00

	Good	Fine	XF
S542 500 Mil Reis ND (1890). Purple on olive-brown underprint. Shield between two reclining allegorical women at center. Printer: ABNC. Proof.	—	Unc	250.

Banco de Crédito Popular do Brazil

Decree of 14.11.1890; 1891 ND Provisional Issue

#S546-S550 overprint new bank name on notes of the Banco dos Estados Unidos do Brazil.

	Good	Fine	XF
S546 5 Mil Reis ND (1891). Black on multicolor underprint. New bank name on #S601. Printer: G&D and Laemmert & Co. Rare.	—	—	—
S547 20 Mil Reis ND (1891). Black on orange, brown and multicolor underprint. Overprint: New bank name on #S603. Printer: G&D and Laemmert & Co. Rare.	—	—	—
S548 100 Mil Reis ND (1891). Overprint: New bank name on #S605. Printer: G&D and Laemmert & Co. Reported not confirmed.	—	—	—
S549 200 Mil Reis ND (1891). Black on brown and multicolor underprint. Overprint: New bank name on #S606. Printer: G&D and Laemmert & Co. Rare.	—	—	—

	Good	Fine	XF
S550 500 Mil Reis ND (1891). Black on brown and yellow underprint. Overprint: New bank name on #S607. Printer: G&D and Laemmert & Co. Rare.	—	—	—

Decrees of 8.3.1890 and 14.11.1890; 1891-92 ND Issue

S550A 1 Mil Reis — Good | Fine | XF

ND (ca.1891). Black on brown underprint. Steam passenger train at center. Back: Dark brown. Allegorical woman with coins, scale and safe at center. Printer: ABNC.

	Good	Fine	XF
p. Proof	—	—	—
s. Specimen.	—	—	—
S550B 2 Mil Reis ND (ca.1891). Black on green underprint. Steam train at left and right, two children reading at center. Back: Green. Woman at left. Printer: ABNC. Proof.	—	—	—

	Good	Fine	XF
S551 5 Mil Reis ND (1892). Black on rose underprint. Seated allegorical woman with flowers ("Rose") at left, woman and child at right. Back: Sepia. Woman at center. Printer: ABNC. Proof.	—	—	—
S551A 10 Mil Reis ND (ca.1891). Black on olive-green and yellow underprint. Justice at left, street scene with tree and mountain behind at right. Back: Olive-green. Printer: ABNC. Proof.	—	—	—

S551B 20 Mil Reis — Good | Fine | XF

ND (ca. 1891). Black on orange and yellow underprint. Portrait girl ("Spanish Girl") at left, Indian woman seated in small boat ("La Verdulera") at right. Back: Orange. Printer: ABNC.

	Good	Fine	XF
p. Proof.	—	—	—
s. Specimen.	—	—	—

NOTICE

Readers with unlisted dates, signature varieties, etc., are invited to submit photocopies or scans of their notes to:
Standard Catalog of World Paper Money,
700 East State St. Iola, WI 54990-0001,
E-Mail: george.cuhaj@fwmedia.com.

S552 50 Mil Reis — Good | Fine | XF

ND (1892). Black on yellow and brown underprint. Basket and tree at left, woman seated ("Agriculture") at right. Back: Red-brown. Printer: ABNC.

	Good	Fine	XF
p. Proof.	—	—	—
s. Specimen.	—	—	—

S553 100 Mil Reis	Good	Fine	XF
ND (1892). Black on yellow and purple underprint. Lion's head ("Lion's Head - Rosa Benheur") at left, reclining woman ("The Siesta") at right. Back: Red-brown. Rural scene with sheep at center. Printer: ABNC. Proof.	—	—	—

S554 200 Mil Reis	Good	Fine	XF
ND (ca.1891). Black on orange and yellow underprint. Allegory of Electricity at left, equestrians, oxen teams and train at right. Back: Orange. Miners at center. Printer: ABNC. Proof.	—	—	—

S555 500 Mil Reis — Good | Fine | XF

ND (ca.1891). Black on blue and yellow underprint. Allegorical woman with book and globe ("La Critique") at upper left, young girl ("The Brunette") at upper right. Back: Blue and black. Allegorical woman at right. Printer: ABNC.

	Good	Fine	XF
p. Proof.	—	—	—
s. Specimen.	—	—	—

Banco Emissor da Bahia

1890 ND Provisional Issue

#S561-S564 overprint new bank name on Imperial Treasury Notes.

S561 10 Mil Reis	Good	Fine	XF
ND (1890). Black on green and orange underprint. Overprint: On Estampa 8, #A262 in Vol. 2. Rare.	—	—	—

S562 20 Mil Reis	Good	Fine	XF
ND (1890). Black on orange and green underprint. Overprint: On Estampa 8, #A263 in Vol. 2. Rare.	—	—	—

S563 50 Mil Reis	Good	Fine	XF
ND (1890). Black on orange and yellow underprint. Overprint: On Estampa 6, #A253 in Vol. 2. Rare.	—	—	—
S564 100 Mil Reis			
ND (1890). Black on red and yellow underprint. Overprint: On Estampa 5, #A247 in Vol. 2. Rare.	—	—	—

1892 ND Issue

S565 10 Mil Reis — Good | Fine | XF

ND (ca.1892). Black on blue and yellow underprint. Two standing allegorical women ("North and South") at right. Back: Blue. Printer: ABNC.

	Good	Fine	XF
p. Proof.	—	—	—
s. Specimen.	—	—	—

S565A 20 Mil Reis	Good	Fine	XF
ND (ca.1892). Black on brown and yellow underprint. Standing Liberty at center. Back: Brown. Printer: ABNC. Proof.	—	—	—

S565B 50 Mil Reis	Good	Fine	XF
ND (ca.1892). Black on orange and yellow underprint. Reclining allegorical woman with flag, lion and sailing ship in background at left. Back: Orange. Printer: ABNC. Proof.	—	—	—

Decrees of 17.1.1890 and 12.5.1890

S566 100 Mil Reis — Good / Fine / XF

ND (1890). Black on light blue and rose underprint. Seated woman at left, cupid and constellation at right. Back: Dark brown. Bank at center. Printer: CMRJ. (Not issued). Rare. — — —

Banco Emissor do Norte

1890 ND Provisional Issue

#S571-S573 overprint new bank name on Imperial Treasury Notes.

S571 10 Mil Reis — Good / Fine / XF

ND (1890). Black on green and orange underprint. Overprint: On Estampa 8, #A262 in Vol. 2. Rare. — — —

S572 50 Mil Reis

ND (1890). Black on orange and yellow underprint. Overprint: On Estampa 6, #A253 in Vol. 2. Rare. — — —

S573 100 Mil Reis

ND (1890). Black on red and green underprint. Overprint: On Estampa 5, #A247 in Vol. 2. Rare. — — —

Decrees of 8.3.1890 and 19.6.1890

S576 10 Mil Reis — Good / Fine / XF

ND. Black on multicolor underprint. Two allegorical women seated at left, national arms at right. Back: Red. Ornate building at center. Printer: ABNC. Specimen. — — —

S577 20 Mil Reis — Good / Fine / XF

ND. Black on blue and yellow underprint. Minerva at left, two seated allegorical women flanking national arms at center, palm at right. Back: Blue. Palm-lined street with bank at left. Printer: ABNC. Proof. — — —

S578 50 Mil Reis — Good / Fine / XF

ND. Black on green and yellow underprint. Justice at left, national arms at left center, railroad workers and steam passenger train at right. Back: Green. Bank at center. Printer: ABNC. Specimen. — — —

S579 100 Mil Reis — Good / Fine / XF

ND. Black on yellow and orange underprint. National arms at center, seated female ("Naiad") at right. Back: Brick red. Bank at center right. Printer: ABNC.

p. Proof. — — —

s. Specimen. — — —

Decree 19.6.1890

S580 10 Mil Reis — Good / Fine / XF

D.1890. Black on blue and yellow underprint. Two standing allegorical women at right. Back: Green. Proof. — — —

Banco Emissor de Pernambuco

1890 ND Provisional Issue

#S581-S582 overprint new bank name on Imperial Treasury Notes.

S581 100 Mil Reis — Good / Fine / XF

ND (1890). Black on red and green underprint. Overprint: On Estampa 5, #A247 in Vol. 2. Rare. — — —

S582 200 Mil Reis

ND (1890). Black on blue and yellow underprint. Overprint: On Estampa 6, #A254 in Vol. 2. Rare. — — —

Decrees of 8.3.1890 and 18.10.1890

S586 100 Mil Reis — Good / Fine / XF

ND. Black on ochre underprint. Dog's head at left, reclining allegorical woman at right. Estampa 1, Series 1. Back: Sepia. Entrance to port of Recife at center. Printer: Companhia de Artes Graphicas do Brazil. (Not issued). Rare. — — —

Banco Emissor do Sul

1890 ND Provisional Issue

#S591-S593 overprint new bank name on Imperial Treasury Notes.

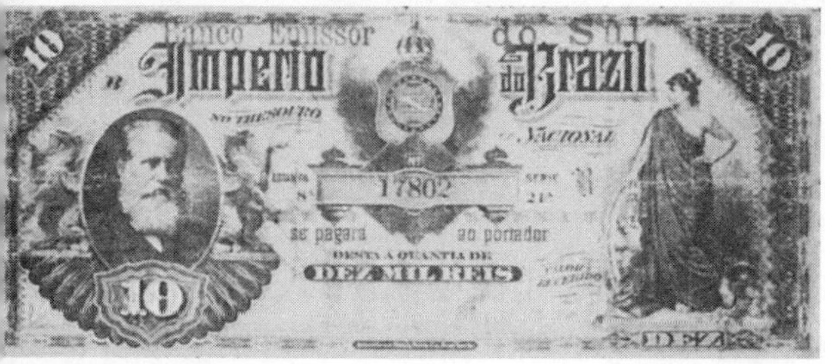

	Good	Fine	XF
S591 10 Mil Reis ND (1890). Black on green and orange underprint. Overprint: On Estampa 8, #A262 in Vol. 2. Rare.	—	—	—
S592 50 Mil Reis ND (1890). Black on orange and green underprint. Overprint: On Estampa 6, #A253 in Vol. 2. Rare.	—	—	—
S593 100 Mil Reis ND (1890). Black on red and green underprint. Overprint: On Estampa 5, #A247 in Vol. 2. Rare.	—	—	—

Banco dos Estados Unidos do Brazil

1890 ND Provisional Issue

#S596-S599 overprint new bank name on Imperial Treasury Notes.

	Good	Fine	XF
S596 10 Mil Reis ND (1890). Black on green and orange underprint. Overprint: Red; on Estampa 8, #A262 in Vol. 2. Rare.	—	—	—
S597 20 Mil Reis ND (1890). Black on orange and green underprint. Overprint: Wine; on Estampa 8, #A263 in Vol. 2. Rare.	—	—	—
S598 50 Mil Reis ND (1890). Black on orange and yellow underprint. Overprint: Light blue; on Estampa 6, #A250 in Vol. 2. Rare.	—	—	—

	Good	Fine	XF
S599 200 Mil Reis ND (1890). Black on blue and yellow underprint. Overprint: Red; on Estampa 6, #A254 in Vol. 2. Rare.	—	—	—

Decrees of 17.1.1890 and 8.3.1890

#S607-S607B like later Banco da República dos Estados Unidos issue for #S607A and S607B.

	Good	Fine	XF
S601 5 Mil Reis ND (1890). Black on multicolor underprint. Standing woman and national arms at center. Back: Green. National arms at center. Printer: G&D and Laemmert & CO. (Not issued). Rare.	—	—	—

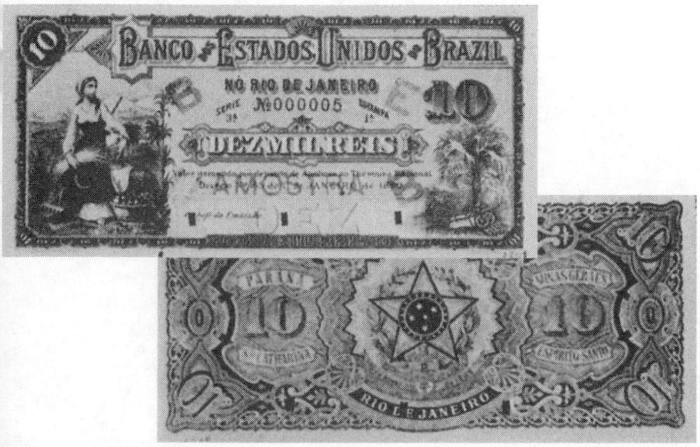

	Good	Fine	XF
S602 10 Mil Reis ND (1890). Black on rose. Standing allegory of Agriculture at left, palm tree at right. Back: Multicolor. Arms at center. Printer: G&D and Laemmert & Co.			
a. Overprint: *CIRCULA EM TODOS OS ESTADOS DA REPUBLICA* on back. Rare.	—	—	—
b. Overprint: *PAGAVEL EM OURO NOS TERMOS DO DECRETO no. 253, DE 8 DE MARCO DE 1890* on face.	—	—	—

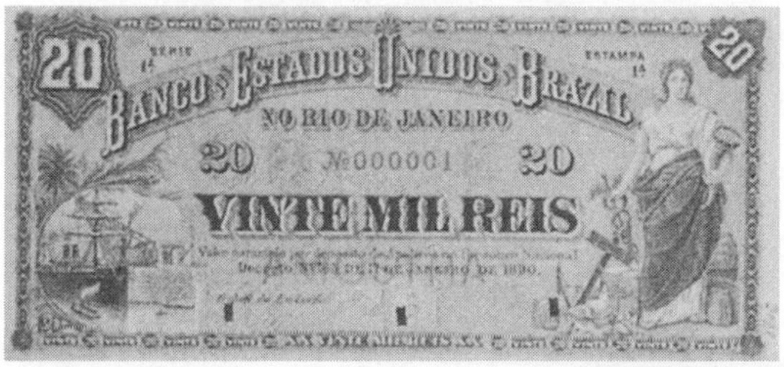

	Good	Fine	XF
S603 20 Mil Reis ND (1890). Black on orange, brown and multicolor underprint. Sailing ship in port at lower left, standing allegory of Navigation at right. Back: Blue and orange. Arms at center. Printer: G&D and Laemmert & Co. (Not issued). Rare.	—	—	—
S604 50 Mil Reis ND (1890). Black on multicolor underprint. Woman at left, ship and steam train at right. Back: Multicolor. Arms at center. Printer: G&D and Laemmert & Co. (Not issued). Rare.	—	—	—
S605 100 Mil Reis ND. Printer: G&D and Laemmert & Co. Reported not confirmed.	—	—	—

	Good	Fine	XF
S606 200 Mil Reis ND (1890). Black on brown and multicolor underprint. Liberty within coffee plant sprays at center. Back: Multicolor. Arms. Printer: G&D and Laemmert & Co. (Not issued). Rare.	—	—	—

	Good	Fine	XF
S607 30 Mil Reis ND (ca.1890). Black on brown and yellow underprint. Woman at left, steam powered ship in rough seas at left center, girl smelling flowers ("Innocence") at right. Back: Dark brown. Printer: ABNC. Proof. (Not issued).	—	—	—

	Good	Fine	XF
S607A 50 Mil Reis ND (ca.1890). Black on green underprint. Allegorical woman leaning on anchor ("Hope") at left, reclining woman ("La Siesta") at right. Printer: ABNC. (Not issued).			
p. Proof.	—	—	—
s. Specimen.	—	—	—

S607B 500 Mil Reis — Good | Fine | XF

ND (1890). Black on green and yellow underprint. Sailing ship at left, woman seated at center, standing woman at right. Printer: ABNC. Proof. (Not issued). — — —

Banco Industrial dos Estados do Sul

1891 Issue

S608 10 Mil Reis — Good | Fine | XF

1.10.1891. Black and gray. Steam passenger train at upper center. Back: Red-brown. List of encashment values and dates. Printer: Companhia Editora Fluminense Rio de Janeiro. Rare. — — —

S609 10 Mil Reis

1.10.1891. Black and gray. Steam passenger train at upper center. Without imprint at bottom. Rare. — — —

Banco Mercantil de Santos

Law of 24.11.1888 / Decree of 8.3.1890

S611 10 Mil Reis — Good | Fine | XF

ND. Black on yellow and ochre underprint. Two seated allegorical women ("Commerce and Agriculture") and ("Government and Justice") at left and right. Two cherubs at center. Printer: ABNC. (Not issued).

p. Proof. — — —

s. Specimen. — — —

S612 20 Mil Reis — Good | Fine | XF

ND. Black on yellow and ochre underprint Portrait two heads ("The Reapers No. 3") at upper left, seates female ("Mechanics") at upper right with condor between above bank title. Back: Sepia. Lions ("Lions at Home") at center. Printer: ABNC. (Not issued).

p. Proof. — — —

s. Specimen. — — —

S613 50 Mil Reis — Good | Fine | XF

ND. Black on multicolor underprint. Portrait woman between two seated women at left, bull's head at lower right. Back: Woman at center. Printer: W&S. (Not issued). Rare. — — —

S614 100 Mil Reis

ND. Black on yellow and blue underprint. Woman at left, three allegorical women at center, coffee workers at right. Back: Blue. Steer's head at center. Printer: W&S. (Not issued). Rare. — — —

S615 200 Mil Reis

ND. Black on multicolor underprint. Standing woman at left, woman at center, allegory of Commerce at right. Back: Rural scene at center. Printer: W&S. (Not issued). Rare. — — —

S616 500 Mil Reis

ND. Black on multicolor underprint. Woman at left, ship at center, standing woman at right. Back: Sepia. Woman at center. Printer: W&S. (Not issued). Rare. — — —

Banco Nacional do Brazil no Rio de Janeiro

1890 ND Provisional Issue

#S621-S624 overprint new bank name and other inscription on Imperial Treasury Notes. Overprint work printed by Laemmert & Co.

S621 10 Mil Reis — Good | Fine | XF

ND (1890). Black on orange and green underprint. On Estampa 7, #A258 in Vol. 2. Rare. — — —

S622 100 Mil Reis — Good | Fine | XF

ND (1890). Black on red and green underprint. Overprint: On Estampa 5, #A247 in Vol. 2. Rare. — — —

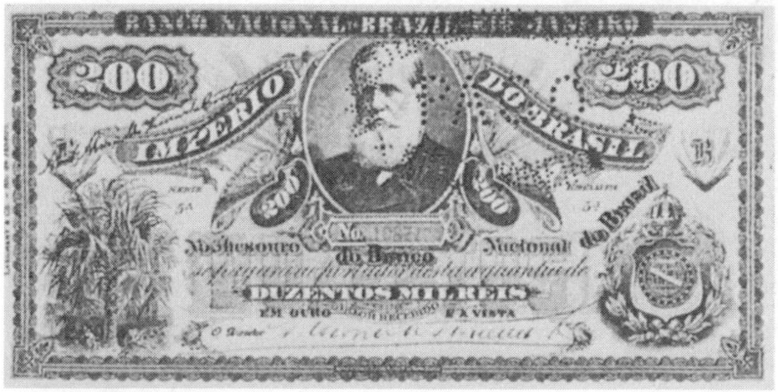

S623 200 Mil Reis — Good | Fine | XF

ND (1890). Black on red and blue underprint. Overprint: On Estampa 5, #A248 in Vol. 2. Rare. — — —

S624 500 Mil Reis — Good | Fine | XF

ND (1890). Black on orange and blue underprint. Overprint: On Estampa 5, #A249 in Vol. 2. Rare. — — —

Law of 24.11.1888 / Decree of 8.3.1890

10
BANCO NACIONAL DO BRAZIL
10
RIO DE JANEIRO
DEZ MIL REIS
DEZ MIL REIS
10
10

S625 10 Mil Reis

ND (1890). Black on orange and yellow underprint. Two seated allegorical women ("Commerce and Agriculture") and ("Government and Justice") at left and right, two cherubs at center. Printer: ABNC.

	Good	Fine	XF
p. Proof.	—	—	—
s. Specimen.	—	—	—

S626 20 Mil Reis

ND (1890). Black on blue and multicolor underprint. Portrait two heads ("The Reapers No. 3") at upper left, seated female ("Mechanics") at upper right. with condor between above bank title. Printer: ABNC.

	Good	Fine	XF
p. Proof.	—	—	—
s. Specimen.	—	—	—

S627 30 Mil Reis

ND (1890). Black on orange underprint. Woman at left, steam passenger train and mountains at right. Back: Dark brown. Printer: W&S. (Not issued). Rare.

Good	Fine	XF
—	—	—

S628 100 Mil Reis

ND (1890). Black on yellow and blue underprint. Woman at left, three allegorical women at center, coffee workers at right. Printer: W&S. Rare.

Good	Fine	XF
—	—	—

S629 200 Mil Reis

ND (1890). Black on multicolor underprint. Standing woman at left, woman at center, allegory of Commerce at right. Printer: W&S. Rare.

Good	Fine	XF
—	—	—

S630 500 Mil Reis

ND (1890). Black on multicolor underprint. Woman at left, ship at center, standing woman at right. Printer: W&S. Rare.

Good	Fine	XF
—	—	—

Banco da República dos Estados Unidos do Brazil

1891 ND Provisional Issues

#S631-S634 black overprint new bank name on notes of the Banco Nacional do Brazil.

S631 20 Mil Reis

ND (1891). Black on blue and multicolor underprint. Overprint: New bank name in circle around vignette at left, on #S626. Rare.

Good	Fine	XF
—	—	—

S632 100 Mil Reis

ND (1891). Black on yellow and blue underprint. Overprint: New bank name on #S628. Rare.

Good	Fine	XF
—	—	—

S633 200 Mil Reis

ND (1891). Black on multicolor underprint. Overprint: New bank name on #S629. Rare.

Good	Fine	XF
—	—	—

S634 500 Mil Reis	Good	Fine	XF
ND (1891). Black on multicolor underprint. Overprint: New bank name on #S630. Rare.	—	—	—

S635 500 Mil Reis			
ND (1891). Overprint: New bank name on #S607B. Rare.	—	—	—

Decrees of 14.1.1889 and 7.12.1889

S637 500 Mil Reis	Good	Fine	XF
ND. Black on green and yellow underprint. Woman's head over standing sailor at left, mint building at left center, standing female with spear & shield at lower right. Back: Deep red and black. Girl at left. Printer: Cia. de Billetes de Banco, F. Rieusset. Specimen.	—	—	—

NOTE: #S637 is most likely a design done on speculation for an issue which never gained approval. The authorization decrees noted on the design are not referenced in official documents. However is certainly is very similar to the 200 Mil Reis note #S644.

Decrees of 17.1.1890 and 7.12.1890

S641 10 Mil Reis	Good	Fine	XF
ND (1891). Black on yellow and blue underprint. Two standing allegorical women ("North and South") at right. Serial #1 to 85,712. Back: Blue. Printer: ABNC.			
a. Issued note.	125.	300.	—
p. Proof.	—	Unc	900.
r. Remainder, punched hole cancelled.	—	—	—

NOTE: Higher serial # of #S641 were issued by the Banco da República do Brazil before its own notes were ready. See #S656.

S642 20 Mil Reis	Good	Fine	XF
ND (1891). Black on yellow underprint. Woman leaning on shield on pedestal between flags at center. Series 1. Serial #1-100,000. Back: Sepia. Printer: ABNC. Rare.	—	—	—

NOTE: #S642 design as Series 2 is an issue of the Banco da República do Brazil. See #S657.

S643 50 Mil Reis	Good	Fine	XF
ND (1891). Black on orange and yellow underprint. Seated allegorical woman with flag, lion and sailing ship in background at left. Serial #1 to 79,000. Back: Orange. Printer: ABNC.			
a. Issued note. Rare.	—	—	—
p. Proof.	—	—	—

NOTE: Higher serial # of #S643 were issued by the Banco da República do Brazil before its own notes were ready. See #S658.

S644 200 Mil Reis	Good	Fine	XF
ND (1891). Black on green underprint. Woman's head over standing sailor at left, mint building at left center, standing female with spear & shield at lower right. Serial #1 to 70,500. Rare.	—	—	—

NOTE: Higher serial # of #S44 were issued by the Banco da República do Brazil before its own notes were ready. See #S659.

Decree of 8.3.1890

S645 10 Mil Reis	Good	Fine	XF
ND (1891). Black on multicolor underprint. Standing allegory of Agriculture at left, palm tree at right. Serial #1 to 78,680. Printer: G&D.			
a. Issued note. Rare.	—	—	—
b. Punched hole cancelled, hand stamped: *AMOSTRA*.	—	—	—

Decree of 7.12.1890

S646 30 Mil Reis	Good	Fine	XF
ND (1891) Black on multicolor underprint. Two seated allegorical figures at center.Serial #1 to 58,668. Back: Multicolor. Printer: G&D.			
a. Issued note. Rare.	—	—	—
b. Punched hole cancelled, hand stamped: *AMOSTRA*.	—	—	—

S647 50 Mil Reis	Good	Fine	XF
ND (1891). Black on green underprint. Allegorical woman leaning on anchor ("Hope") at left, reclining woman ("La Siesta") at right. Serial #1 to 100,000 in First Series, 1 to 13,000 in Second Series. Back: Blue. Printer: ABNC.			
a. Issued note. Rare.	—	—	—
p. Proof.	—	—	—
s. Specimen.	—	—	—

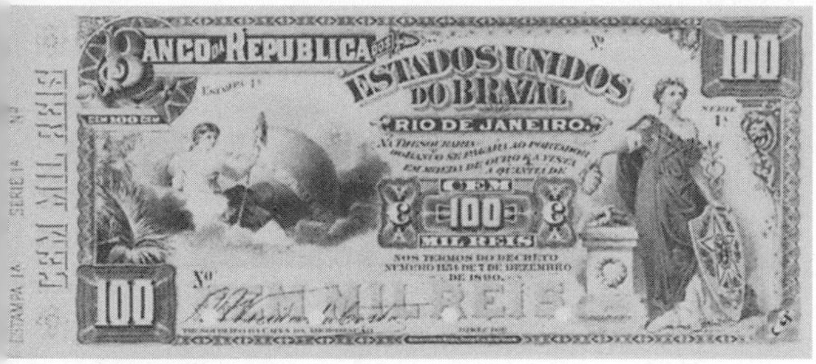

S648 100 Mil Reis

ND (1891). Black on yellow and ochre underprint. Reclining allegorical woman with Liberty pole and globe at left, standing allegorical woman with pedestal and shield with arms at right. Back: Sepia. National arms at center. Serial #1 to 43,000. Printer: ABNC.

	Good	Fine	XF
a. Issued note. Rare.	—	—	—
p. Proof.	—	—	—
s. Specimen.	—	—	—

S640 200 Mil Reis

ND (1891). Black on orange and yellow underprint. Steam passenger train at left, two standing allegorical women at right. Back: Black and orange. Palace in Rio de Janeiro at center. Serial #1 to 17,000. Printer: ABNC.

	Good	Fine	XF
a. Issued note. Rare.	—	—	—
b. Cancelled, hand stamped: *AMOSTRA*.	—	—	—
s. Specimen.	—	—	—

S650 500 Mil Reis

ND (1891). Black on green and yellow underprint. Sailing ship at left, woman seated at center, standing woman at right. Back: Black and green. Docks and arsenal at Rio de Janeiro at center. Serial #1 to 69,000. Printer: ABNC.

	Good	Fine	XF
a. Issued note. Rare.	—	—	—
s. Specimen.	—	—	—

NOTE: For a reissue of notes #S645-S650 with higher serial #, see Banco da República do Brazil, #S661-S666.

NOTE: Values of 50 and 100 Mil Reis under a decree of 1892 require confirmation.

Banco da República do Brazil

1893 ND First Emergency Issue

#S656-S659 is an emergency reissue of notes of the Banco da República dos Estados Unidos do Brazil. #S641-S644. #S656, S658 and S659 have higher serial #, #S657 is a different series.

	Good	Fine	XF
S656 10 Mil Reis ND (1893). Two standing allegorical women ("North and South") at right. Serial #85,713to 99,423. Printer: ABNC. Rare.	—	—	—
S657 20 Mil Reis ND (1893). Woman leaning on shield on pedestal between flags at center. Series 2 and serial #1 to 8000. Printer: ABNC. Rare.	—	—	—
S658 50 Mil Reis ND (1893). Seated allegorical woman with flag, lion and sailing ship in background at left. Serial #79001 to 87000. Printer: ABNC. Rare.	—	—	—
S659 200 Mil Reis ND (1893). Woman's head over standing sailor at left, mint building at left. center, standing female with spear & shield at lower right. Serial #70,501 to 74,000. Rare.	—	—	—

1893 ND Second Emergency Issue

#S661-S666 is an emergency reissue of notes of the Banco da República dos Estados Unidos do Brazil, S645-S650.

	Good	Fine	XF
S661 10 Mil Reis ND (1893). Standing allegory of Agriculture at left, palm tree at right. Serial #78,681 to 100,000 in First series and 1 to 15,247 in Second series. Rare.	—	—	—
S662 30 Mil Reis ND (1893). Two seated allegorical figures at center. Serial #58,669 to 65,000. Rare.	—	—	—
S663 50 Mil Reis ND (1893). Allegorical woman leaning on anchor ("Hope") at left, reclining woman ("La Siesta") at right. Serial #13,001 to 24,000. Second series. Rare.	—	—	—
S664 100 Mil Reis Reclining allegorical woman with Liberty pole and globe at left, standing allegorical woman with pedestal and shield with arms at right. Serial #43,001 to 92,500. Rare.	—	—	—
S665 200 Mil Reis ND (1893). Steam passenger train at left, two standing allegorical women at right. Serial #17,001 to 21,000. Rare.	—	—	—

S666 500 Mil Reis

ND (1893). Sailing ship at left, woman seated at center, standing woman at right. Serial #69,001 to 71,004.

	Good	Fine	XF
a. Issued note. Rare.	—	—	—
r. Remainder cancelled, hand stamped: *AMOSTRA*.	—	—	—

Decree of 17.12.1892; 1893 ND Issue

S671 10 Mil Reis

ND (1893). Black on brown, blue and multicolor underprint. Star around Liberty at left, seated woman at right. Back: Brown and light blue. Arms at right. Printer: G&D and Laemmert & Co.

	Good	Fine	XF
a. Issued note. Rare.	—	—	—
s. Specimen overprint and perforated: *AMOSTRA*. Rare.	—	—	—
S672 50 Mil Reis ND (1893). Black on green and multicolor underprint. Woman in profile at left, sailing ship near lighthouse at right. Back: Multicolor. Arms at left center. Printer: G&D and Laemmert Co. Rare.	—	—	—

Law of 23.9.1893

		Good	Fine	XF
S674	**10 Mil Reis** ND (1893). Star around Liberty at left, seated woman at right. Printer: G&D and Laemmert & Co. Rare.	—	—	—

		Good	Fine	XF
S675	**20 Mil Reis** ND (1893). Black on light blue and multicolor underprint. Seated Justice with shield of arms at right. Back: Blue and orange. Arms at right. Printer: G&D and Laemmert & Co. Rare.	—	—	—

		Good	Fine	XF
S676	**30 Mil Reis** ND (1893). Black on red, light blue and multicolor underprint. Palm and sailing ship at lower left, seated allegory of Industry and Commerce at right. Back: Red, blue and multicolor. Arms at left. Printer: G&D and Laemmert & Co. Rare.	—	—	—

		Good	Fine	XF
S677	**50 Mil Reis** ND (1893). Woman in profile at left, sailing ship near lighthouse at right. Printer: G&D and Laemmert & Co. Rare.	—	—	—

		Good	Fine	XF
S678	**100 Mil Reis** ND (1893). Black on multicolor underprint. Reclining allegorical woman at lower left and right, portrait woman's head in profile at upper center. Back: Black and rose. View of the port at Rio de Janeiro at center. Printer: G&D and Laemmert & Co. Rare.	—	—	—

		Good	Fine	XF
S679	**200 Mil Reis** ND (1893). Black on multicolor underprint. Arms at left. center, two allegorical women and shield with arms at right. Back: Black and green. View of loading area on docks at Rio de Janeiro. Printer: G&D and Laemmert & Co. Rare.	—	—	—

		Good	Fine	XF
S680	**500 Mil Reis** ND (1893). Black on multicolor underprint. Eagle between reclining Minerva and Neptune at center. Lighthouse, globe and anchor at lower right. Back: Black and rosse. Sailing ships at anchor in port of Rio de Janeiro. Printer: G&D and Laemmert & Co. Rare.	—	—	—

Banco de São Paulo

1889 ND Provisional Issue

#S681-S683 overprint: new bank name and other details on Imperial Treasury Notes. Overprint work printed by Laemmert & Co.

		Good	Fine	XF
S681	**10 Mil Reis** ND (1889). Black on orange and green underprint. Overprint: On Estampa 7, #A258 in Vol. 2. Rare.	—	—	—

		Good	Fine	XF
S682	**100 Mil Reis** ND (1889). Black on red and green underprint. Overprint: On Estampa 5, #A247 in Vol. 2. Rare.	—	—	—

		Good	Fine	XF
S683	**500 Mil Reis** ND (1889). Black on orange and blue underprint. Overprint: On Estampa 5, #A249 in Vol. 2. Rare.	—	—	—

Banco Sul Americano de Pernambuco

Decrees of 17.1.1890 and 7.3.1890

S686-S689 No notes of this bank were released to circulation.

S686 10 Mil Reis — Good — Fine — XF
ND. Black on multicolor underprint. Sailing ships at port of Recife at left, two sailors at right. Back: Purple. Printer: ABNC. (Not issued). Rare. — — —

S687 20 Mil Reis
ND. Black on multicolor underprint. Back: Blue. Printer: ABNC. (Not issued). Rare. — — —

NOTE: The face design for #S687 is not known.

S688 50 Mil Reis — Good — Fine — XF
ND. Black on multicolor underprint. Portrait woman between two reclining allegorical women at left center, Mercury seated at right. Back: Green. Printer: ABNC. (Not issued). Rare. — — —

S689 200 Mil Reis — Good — Fine — XF
ND. Black on multicolor underprint. Seated woman at left. center, sailor at center right, two standing allegorical women at right. Back: Yellow. Printer: ABNC. (Not issued). Rare. — — —

Banco União Ibero Americano

1891 Obrigacoes (Obligations) Issue

S691 20 Mil Reis — Good — Fine — XF
8.7.1891. Blue and red. Three allegorical women and two shields with arms at upper left. Back: Red-brown. Table of redemption dates and values. Rare. — — —

Banco União de São Paulo

Decree of 17.1.1890; First Issue

S693 100 Mil Reis — Good — Fine — XF
ND (1890). Black on green underprint. Reclining Indian with lion at left, sailing ships at port of Santos at upper center. Back: Green. National arms at center. Printer: Laemmert and Co. and G&D. Rare. — — —

S694 200 Mil Reis
ND (1890). Black on rose underprint. Reclining Indian with lion at left, sailing ships at port of Santos at upper center. Back: Sepia. Printer: Laemmert & Co. and G&D. Rare. — — —

Decree of 8.3.1890; First Issue

S694A 500 Mil Reis — Good — Fine — XF
ND (1890). Black on green underprint. Seated woman with shield of arms at left. Back: National arms at center. Rare. — — —

Decree of 8.3.1890; Second Issue

S695 10 Mil Reis — Good — Fine — XF
ND (1890). Black on sepia and multicolor underprint. Allegorical figure of Electricity at left, steam passenger train at lower right. Back: Sepia, orange and multicolor. National arms at center. Printer: Laemmert & Co. and G&D.
- a. Issued note. Rare. — — —
- r. Remainder punched hole cancelled, hand stamped: *AMOSTRA*. — — —

S696 20 Mil Reis
ND (1890). Allegorical figure of Electricity at left, steam passenger train at lower right. Back: National arms at center. Printer: Laemmert & Co. and G&D. Rare. — — —

S697 50 Mil Reis
ND (1890). Allegorical figure of Electricity at left, steam passenger train at lower right. Back: National arms at center. Printer: Leammert & Co. and G&D. Rare. — — —

		Good	Fine	XF
S698	**100 Mil Reis** ND (1890). Black on lilac and multicolor underprint. Standing allegorical woman and cupid at left, Mercury in circle at lower right. Back: Brown and multicolor. National arms at center. Printer: Laemmert & Co. and G&D.			
	a. Issued note. Rare.	—	—	—
	r. Remainder punched hole cancelled, hand stamped: *AMOSTRA.*	—	—	—
S699	**200 Mil Reis** ND (1890). Black on lilac and multicolor underprint. Standing allegorical woman and cupid at left, Mercury in circle at lower right. Back: Brown and multicolor. National arms at center. Printer: Laemmert & Co. and G&D. Rare.	—	—	—
S700	**500 Mil Reis** Black on lilac and multicolor underprint. Standing allegorical woman and cupid at left, Mercury in circle at lower right. Back: Brown and multicolor. National arms at center. Printer: Laemmert & Co. and G&D. Rare.	—	—	—

Decree of 8.3.1890; Third Issue

		Good	Fine	XF
S705	**10 Mil Reis** ND (ca.1892). Black on green and yellow underprint. Seated allegorical woman with marine implements at left, cherub ("Abundance") at right. Back: Green. Printer: ABNC. Not issued.			
	p. Proof.	—	—	—
	s. Specimen.	—	—	—

		Good	Fine	XF
S706	**20 Mil Reis** ND (ca.1892). Black on orange and yellow underprint. Cherub at lower left, seated allegorical woman with eagle at left center. Back: Orange or green. Printer: ABNC. Not issued.			
	p. Proof.	—	—	—
	s. Specimen.	—	—	—

		Good	Fine	XF
S707	**30 Mil Reis** ND (ca.1892). Black on brown and yellow underprint. Woman at left ("Vertumna") and seated woman ("Virgin del Sol") at right. Back: Brown or green. Bust of allegorical woman at left and center right. Printer: ABNC.			
	p. Proof.	—	—	—
	s. Specimen.	—	—	—

		Good	Fine	XF
S708	**50 Mil Reis** ND (ca.1892). Black on blue and yellow underprint. Cherub representing Electricity at left, cherub ("Raphael's Angel") at center, woman with quill pen ("Trade") at right. Back: Blue or green. Cherub's head at top center. Printer: ABNC.			
	p. Proof.	—	—	—
	s. Specimen.	—	—	—

		Good	Fine	XF
S709	**100 Mil Reis** ND (ca.1892). Black on orange and yellow underprint. Miner at left and right, two men conversing at center. Back: Red or green. Printer: ABNC. Not issued.			
	p. Proof.	—	—	—
	s. Specimen.	—	—	—

		Good	Fine	XF
S710	**200 Mil Reis** ND (ca.1892). Black on orange and yellow underprint. Plant at lower left, dog at upper left, allegorical woman and child ("Cupid Disarmed") at center, allegorical woman at right. Back: Orange or green. Young girl ("Helen") at center. Printer: ABNC. Not issued.			
	p. Proof.	—	—	—
	s. Specimen.	—	—	—

		Good	Fine	XF
S711	**500 Mil Reis**			
	ND (ca.1892). Black on olive-green and yellow underprint. Standing allegorical woman with scales at left, oxen team pulling wagon at center right. Back: Olive or green. Steam train and cowboys on horseback at right. Printer: ABNC. Not issued.			
	p. Proof.	—	—	—
	s. Specimen.	—	—	—

SECTION VI, 1924-66

PROVINCIAL ISSUES

OBRIGACOES DO THESOURO DO ESTADO

OBLIGATIONS OF THE TREASURY OF THE STATE

LAW OF 16.10.1930

		Good	Fine	XF
S751	**5 Mil Reis**			
	L. 1930. Black-green on tan underprint. Back: Green. Printer: Imp. Official do Estado de Minas.	25.00	75.00	150.

NOTE: Values of 10, 20, 50, 100, 200, 500 Mil Reis and 1 Conto de Reis require confirmation.

PREVIDENCIA DOS SERVIDORES DO ESTADO DE MINAS GERAES

1930 ISSUE

		Good	Fine	XF
S761	**2 Mil Reis**			
	21.10.1930. Brown and pink on pink underprint. Back: Gray.	20.00	50.00	110.

		Good	Fine	XF
S762	**5 Mil Reis**			
	20.10.1930. Brown and orange on orange underprint. Back: Gray.	20.00	50.00	110.

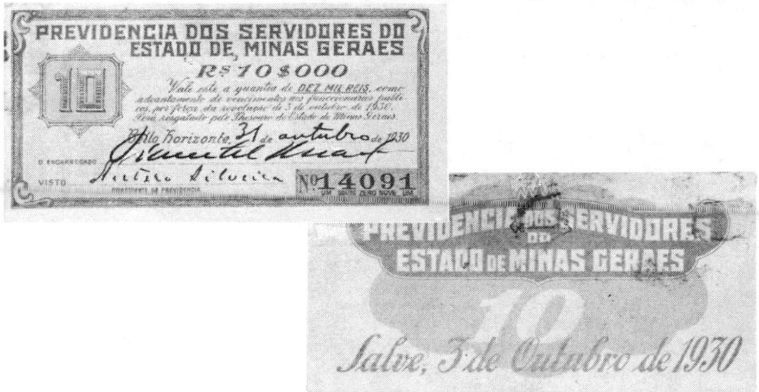

		Good	Fine	XF
S763	**10 Mil Reis**			
	31.10.1930. Brown and gray on gray underprint. Back: Gray.	25.00	75.00	150.
S764	**20 Mil Reis**			
	31.10.1930. Brown and light pink on light pink underprint. Back: Gray.	25.00	75.00	150.

THESOURO DO ESTADO

TREASURY OF THE STATE

1930 ISSUE - SERIES A

		Good	Fine	XF
S771	**5 Mil Reis**			
	31.10.1930. Black and red on multicolor underprint. Arms at right. Back: Dull red. Printer: Lith. da Livraria do Globo, Porto Algre.	25.00	75.00	150.
S772	**10 Mil Reis**			
	31.10.1930. Black and red on multicolor underprint. Arms at right. Back: Blue. Printer: Lith. da Livraria do Globo, Porto Algre.	25.00	75.00	150.
S773	**20 Mil Reis**			
	31.10.1930. Black and red on multicolor underprint. Arms at right. Back: Violet. Printer: Lith. da Livraria do Globo, Porto Algre.	25.00	75.00	150.
S774	**50 Mil Reis**			
	31.10.1930. Black and red on multicolor underprint. Arms at right. Back: Yellow. Printer: Lith. da Livraria do Globo, Porto Algre.	27.50	100.	200.

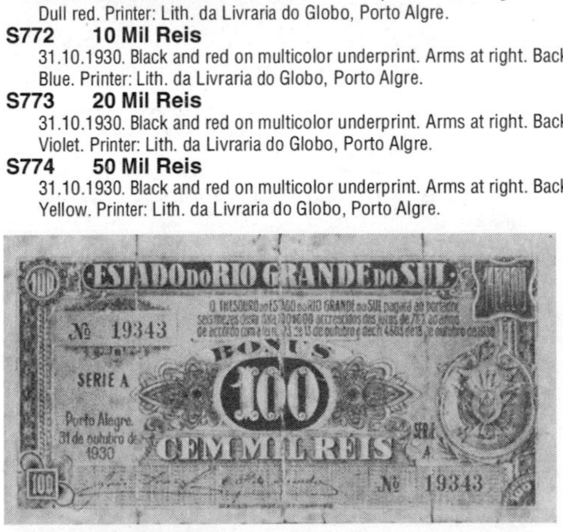

		Good	Fine	XF
S775	**100 Mil Reis**			
	31.10.1930. Black and red on multicolor underprint. Arms at right. Back: Green. Printer: Lith. da Livraria do Globo, Porto Algre.	50.00	100.	250.
S776	**200 Mil Reis**			
	31.10.1930. Black and red on multicolor underprint. Arms at right. Printer: Lith. da Livraria do Globo, Porto Algre.	75.00	150.	300.
S777	**500 Mil Reis**			
	31.10.1930. Black and red on multicolor underprint. Arms at right. Printer: Lith. da Livraria do Globo, Porto Algre.	100.	200.	350.

1931 Issue - Series B

		Good	Fine	XF
S781	**5 Mil Reis** 1.5.1931. Dark blue-gray on olive underprint. Portrait O. Aranha at left. Back: Dark blue. State Treasury. Printer: Lith. da Livraria do Globo, Porto Algre.	25.00	50.00	125.
S782	**10 Mil Reis** 1.5.1931. Black on blue underprint. Portrait G. Vargas at left. Back: Green. State Treasury. Printer: Lith. da Livraria do Globo, Porto Algre.	50.00	75.00	150.
S783	**20 Mil Reis** 1.5.1931. Black on rose underprint. Portrait A. Brasil at left. Back: Red. State Treasury. Printer: Lith. da Livraria do Globo, Porto Algre.	50.00	100.	200.
S784	**50 Mil Reis** 1.5.1931. Black on green and multicolor underprint. Portrait B. de Medeiros at left. Back: Dark violet. State Treasury. Printer: Lith. da Livraria do Globo, Porto Algre.	50.00	100.	200.
S785	**100 Mil Reis** 1.5.1931. Black on multicolor underprint. Portrait S. Martins at left. Back: State Treasury. Printer: Lith. da Livraria do Globo, Porto Algre.	75.00	125.	250.
S786	**200 Mil Reis** 1.5.1931. Black on multicolor underprint. Portrait J. de Castilhos at left. Back: StateTreasury. Printer: Lith. da Livraria do Globo, Porto Algre.	75.00	125.	250.
S787	**500 Mil Reis** 1.5.1931. Black on multicolor underprint. Portrait P. Machado at left. Back: State Treasury. Printer: Lith. da Livraria do Globo, Porto Algre.	100.	200.	350.

NOTE: Values for a 1931 Issue - Series C require confirmation.

1932 Issue - Series D

		Good	Fine	XF
S791	**5 Mil Reis** 1.5.1932. Black on rose and multicolor underprint. Portrait O. Aranha at left. Back: Red-brown. Printer: Lith. da Livraria do Globo, Porto Algre.	25.00	50.00	100.

		Good	Fine	XF
S792	**10 Mil Reis** 1.5.1932. Black on brown, green and multicolor underprint. Portrait G. Vargas at left. Back: Olive. Printer: Lith. da Livraria do Globo, Porto Algre.	25.00	50.00	125.

		Good	Fine	XF
S793	**20 Mil Reis** 1.5.1932. Black on blue, yellow and multicolor underprint. Portrait A. Brasil at left. Back: Red. Printer: Lith. da Livraria do Globo, Porto Algre.	50.00	100.	200.
S794	**50 Mil Reis** 1.5.1932. Black on multicolor underprint. Portrait B. de Medeiros at left. Back: Dark blue. Printer: Lith. da Livraria do Globo, Porto Algre.	50.00	100.	225.
S795	**100 Mil Reis** 1.5.1932. Black on multicolor underprint. Portrait S. Martins at left. Back: Wine. Printer: Lith. da Livraria do Globo, Porto Algre.	75.00	125.	275.

		Good	Fine	XF
S796	**200 Mil Reis** 1.5.1932. Black on multicolor underprint. Portrait J. de Castihos at left. Back: Blue. Printer: Lith. da Livraria do Globo, Porto Algre.	100.	150.	300.
S797	**500 Mil Reis** 1.5.1932. Black on multicolor underprint. Portrait P. Machado at left. Back: Dark violet. Printer: Lith. da Livraria do Globo, Porto Algre.	100.	175.	400.

1933 Issue - Series E

		Good	Fine	XF
S801	**5 Mil Reis** 1.5.1933. Blue on multicolor underprint. Portrait O. Aranha at left. Back: Dark blue. Printer: Lith. da Livraria do Globo, Porto Algre.	25.00	50.00	125.
S802	**10 Mil Reis** 1.5.1933. Blue on multicolor underprint. Portrait G. Vargas at left. Back: Violet. Printer: Lith. da Livraria do Globo, Porto Algre.	25.00	50.00	125.
S803	**20 Mil Reis** 1.5.1933. Violet on multicolor underprint. Portrait A. Brasil at left. Back: Light brown. Printer: Lith. da Livraria do Globo, Porto Algre.	50.00	100.	200.
S804	**50 Mil Reis** 1.5.1933. Black on multicolor underprint. Portrait B. de Medeiros at left. Back: Wine. Printer: Lith. da Livraria do Globo, Porto Algre.	50.00	100.	250.
S805	**100 Mil Reis** 1.5.1933. Black on multicolor underprint. Portrait S. Martins at left. Back: Dark red. Printer: Lith. da Livraria do Globo, Porto Algre.	75.00	125.	300.
S806	**200 Mil Reis** 1.5.1933. Black on multicolor underprint. Portrait J. de Castihos at left. Back: Red-brown. Printer: Lith. da Livraria do Globo, Porto Algre.	75.00	125.	275.
S807	**500 Mil Reis** 1.5.1933. Black on multicolor underprint. Portrait P. Machado at left. Back: Green. Printer: Lith. da Livraria do Globo, Porto Algre.	100.	175.	375.

1934 Issue - Series F

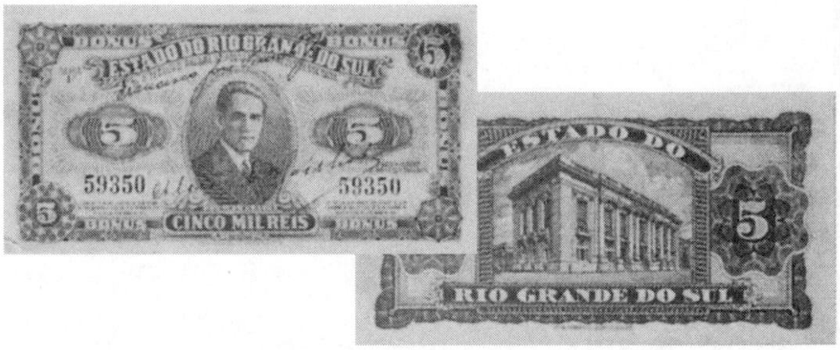

		Good	Fine	XF
S811	**5 Mil Reis** 1.5.1934. Black on green and multicolor underprint. Portrait O. Aranha at center. Back: Violet. Palace of Piratini. Printer: Lith. da Livraria do Globo, Porto Algre.	25.00	50.00	125.
S812	**10 Mil Reis** 1.5.1934. Black on multicolor underprint. Portrait G. Vargas at center. Back: Olive. Palace of Piratini. Printer: Lith. da Livraria do Globo, Porto Algre.	50.00	75.00	200.
S813	**20 Mil Reis** 1.5.1934. Black on multicolor underprint. Portrait A. Brasil at center. Back: Light brown. Palace of Piratini. Printer: Lith. da Livraria do Globo, Porto Algre.	50.00	75.00	200.
S814	**50 Mil Reis** 1.5.1934. Black on orange and multicolor underprint. Portrait B. de Medeiros at center. Back: Brown. Palace of Piratini. Printer: Lith. da Livraria do Globo, Porto Algre.	75.00	125.	250.
S815	**100 Mil Reis** 1.5.1934. Black on multicolor underprint. Portrait S. Martins at center. Back: Dark red. Palace of Piratini. Printer: Lith. da Livraria do Globo, Porto Algre.	75.00	125.	250.
S816	**200 Mil Reis** 1.5.1934. Black on multicolor underprint. Portrait J. de Castihos at center. Back: Blue. Palace of Piratini. Printer: Lith. da Livraria do Globo, Porto Algre.	75.00	125.	275.
S817	**500 Mil Reis** 1.5.1934. Black on multicolor underprint. Portrait P. Machado at center. Back: Palace of Piratini. Printer: Lith. da Livraria do Globo, Porto Algre.	100.	200.	400.

Letras do Tesouro

Treasury Letters

Law of 30.7.1959; 1960-63 Issue

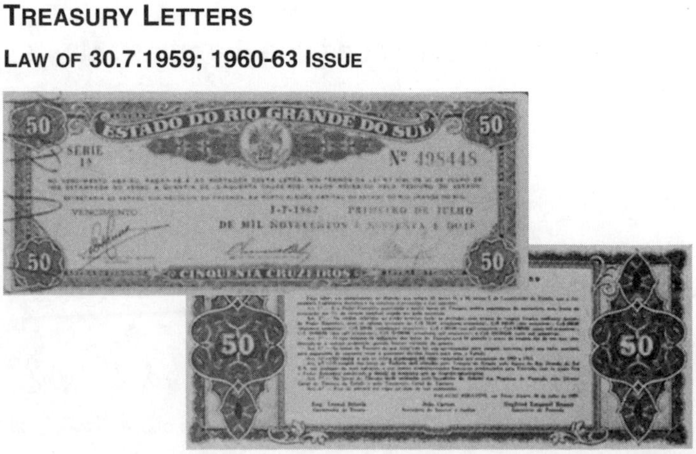

	Good	Fine	XF
S821 50 Cruzeiros 1962-66. Green. Arms of the old Republica Rio Grandense of 1835 at top center. Printer: Lit. Globo S. A.-P. Alegre.			
a. Small date: 15.1.1960; 1.7.1962.	25.00	50.00	125.
b. Large date: 25.4.1966.	25.00	50.00	125.
S822 100 Cruzeiros 14.1.1963; 29.1.1963; 3.2.1963. Blue on gray underprint. Arms of the old Republica Rio Grandense of 1835 at top center. Printer: Lit. Globo S. A.-P. Alegre.	25.00	50.00	125.
S823 200 Cruzeiros 10.2.1960; 25.4.1966. Green and pink. Arms of the old Republica Rio Grandense of 1835 at top center. Printer: Lit. Globo S. A.-P. Alegre.	—	—	—
S824 500 Cruzeiros (ca.1962). Brown. Arms of the old Republica Rio Grandense of 1835 at top center. Printer: Lit. Globo S. A.-P. Alegre.	—	—	—
S825 1000 Cruzeiros (ca.1962). Green and cream. Arms of the old Republica Rio Grandense of 1835 at top center. Value expressed as *1 MIL CRUZEIROS*. Printer: Lit. Globo S. A.-P. Alegre.	—	—	—
S826 1000 Cruzeiros (ca.1962). Dark green and light yellow. Arms of the old Republica Rio Grandense of 1835 at top center. Value expressed as *1000 CRUZEIROS*. Printer: Lit. Globo S. A.-P. Alegre.	—	—	—
S827 5000 Cruzeiros (ca.1962). Brown and green. Arms of the old Republica Rio Grandense of 1835 at top center. Printer: Lit. Globo S. A.-P. Alegre.	—	—	—

	Good	Fine	XF
S828 10,000 Cruzeiros (ca.1962). Dark and light green. Arms of the old Republica Rio Grandense of 1835 at top center. Printer: Lit. Globo S. A.-P. Alegre.	—	—	—
S829 50,000 Cruzeiros (ca.1962). Sepia and yellow. Arms of the old Republica Rio Grandense of 1835 at top center. Printer: Lit. Globo S. A.-P. Alegre.	—	—	—
S830 100,000 Cruzeiros (ca.1962). Dark brown and yellow. Arms of the old Republica Rio Grandense of 1835 at top center. Printer: Lit. Globo S. A.-P. Alegre.	—	—	—

Law of 30.7.1959 / Decree of 31.8.1961

#S844-S849 similar to previous issue but red ovpt: *LEGALIDADE* and black ovpt. of decree date on face.

	Good	Fine	XF
S844 500 Cruzeiros D. 1961. Brown on gray underprint. Arms of the old Republica Rio Grandense of 1835 at top center. Overprint: Red; *LEGALIDADE*. Black overprint of decree date on face. Printer: TDLR, S.A.	25.00	50.00	125.
S845 1000 Cruzeiros D.1961. Blue on gray underprint. Arms of the old Republica Rio Grandense of 1835 at top center. Value expressed as *1 MIL CRUZEIROS*. Overprint: Red; *LEGALIDADE*. Black overprint of decree date on face. Printer: TDLR, S.A.	25.00	50.00	125.
S846 5000 Cruzeiros D.1961. Brown and green. Arms of the old Republica Rio Grandense of 1835 at top center. Overprint: Red; *LEGALIDADE*. Black overprint of decree date on face. Printer: TDLR, S.A.	—	—	—
S847 10,000 Cruzeiros D.1961. Dark and light green. Arms of the old Republica Rio Grandense of 1835 at top center. Overprint: Red; *LEGALIDADE*. Black overprint of decree date on face. Printer: TDLR, S.A.	—	—	—
S848 50,000 Cruzeiros D.1961. Sepia and yellow. Arms of the old Republica Rio Grandense of 1835 at top center. Overprint: Red; *LEGALIDADE*. Black overprint of decree date on face. Printer: TDLR, S.A.	—	—	—
S849 100,000 Cruzeiros D.1961. Dark brown and yellow. Arms of the old Republica Rio Grandense of 1835 at top center. Overprint: Red; *LEGALIDADE*. Black overprint of decree date on face. Printer: TDLR, S.A.	—	—	—

Law of 6.12.1965 / Decree of 21.12.1965; 1966 Issue

	Good	Fine	XF
S851 5000 Cruzeiros (ca.1966). Brown and green. Arms of the old Republica Rio Grandense of 1835 at top center. Printer: Lit. Globo S.A.-P. Alegre.	—	—	—
S852 10,000 Cruzeiros 23.9.1966. Dark and light green. Arms of the old Republica Rio Grandense of 1835 at top center. Printer: Lit. Globo S.A.-P. Alegre.	—	—	—
S853 50,000 Cruzeiros (ca.1966). Sepia and yellow. Arms of the old Republica Rio Grandense of 1835 at top center. Printer: Lit. Globo S.A.-P. Alegre.	—	—	—
S854 100,000 Cruzeiros (ca.1966). Dark brown and yellow. Arms of the old Republica Rio Grandense of 1835 at top center. Printer: Lit. Globo S.A.-P. Alegre.	—	—	—

Bonus do Thesouro

Bonds of the Treasury

Decree of 14.7.1932; First Issue

#S861-S865 imprint: (Weiszflog Irmaos Incorporada) S. Paulo-Rio-Cayeiras.

	Good	Fine	XF
S861 5 Mil Reis D.1932. Dark blue on orange underprint. Portrait D. J. Velho at center. Back: Brown. Printer: *Comp. Melmoramentos de São Paulo*			
a. Without imprint.	25.00	50.00	125.
b. With imprint.	20.00	40.00	100.

	Good	Fine	XF
S862 10 Mil Reis D.1932. Olive. Portrait D.J. Velho at center. Back: Green. Printer: *Comp. Melmoramentos de São Paulo*	50.00	100.	175.
S863 20 Mil Reis D.1932. Blue and light brown. Portrait D.J. Velho at center. Back: Orange. Printer: *Comp. Melmoramentos de São Paulo*	50.00	100.	200.
S864 50 Mil Reis D.1932. Blue and violet. Portrait D.J. Velho at center. Back: Green. Printer: *Comp. Melmoramentos de São Paulo*	75.00	150.	300.

	Good	Fine	XF
S865 100 Mil Reis D.1932. Black on multicolor underprint. Portrait F. D. Paes Leme at center. Back: Blue-green. Printer: *Comp. Melmoramentos de São Paulo*	75.00	150.	350.

Decree of 14.7.1932; Second Issue

It is reported that the Second Issue was in circulation only 3 days, then withdrawn.

	Good	Fine	XF
S871 5 Mil Reis D.1932. Blue on orange underprint. Portrait A. Barroso at right. Back: Brown. Printer: TDLR, S.A.	—	—	—

	Good	Fine	XF
S872 10 Mil Reis D.1932. Blue. Portrait Marques de Tamandare at right. Back: Yellow. Printer: TDLR, S.A.	—	—	—
S873 20 Mil Reis D.1932. Blue-green on orange underprint. Gen. Osorio at right. Back: Green on rose underprint. Coffee gathering at center. Printer: TDLR, S.A.	—	—	—

S874 50 Mil Reis

	Good	Fine	XF
D.1932. Blue on orange underprint. Portrait Marshal F. Peixoto at upper center. Back: Blue on orange underprint. Printer: TDLR, S.A.	—	—	—

S875 100 Mil Reis

	Good	Fine	XF
D.1932. Blue on brown underprint. Duke of Caxias at left. Back: Blue on yellow underprint. Printer: TDLR, S.A.	—	—	—

S876 200 Mil Reis

	Good	Fine	XF
D.1932. Blue on orange underprint. Portrait right. Barbosa at upper center. Back: Green on orange underprint. Printer: TDLR, S.A.	—	—	—

Revolution 1924

O Governo Revolucionario do Brazil

Revolutionary Government

1924 Issue

S881 5 Mil Reis

	Good	Fine	XF
5.7.1924. Dark blue. Justice at center. Paper: Pale pink, tinted.			
a. Finished note.	125.	300.	—
b. Unfinished note.	—	—	—

NOTE: Most of the printing of #S881 was not finished or issued.

BRITISH VIRGIN ISLANDS

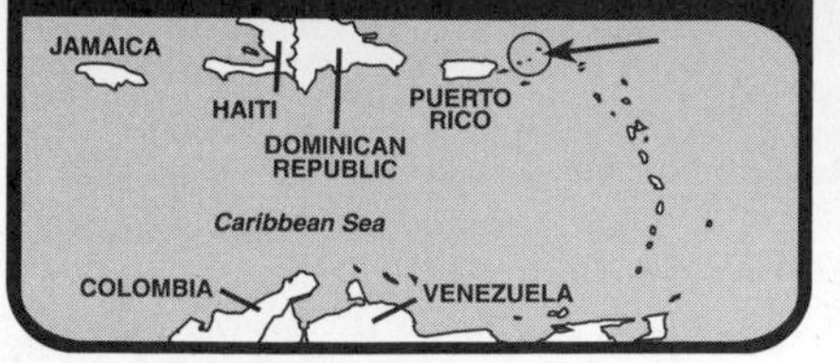

The Colony of the Virgin Islands, a British colony situated in the Caribbean Sea northeast of Puerto Rico and west of the Leeward Islands, has an area of 153 sq. km. and a population of 24,040. Capital: Road Town. The principal islands of the 36-island group are Tortola, Virgin Gorda, Anegada, and Jost Van Dyke.

First inhabited by Arawak and later by Carib Indians, the Virgin Islands were settled by the Dutch in 1648 and then annexed by the English in 1672. The islands were part of the British colony of the Leeward Islands from 1872-1960; they were granted autonomy in 1967. The economy is closely tied to the larger and more populous US Virgin Islands to the west.

RULERS:
British

MONETARY SYSTEM
1 Shilling = 12 Pence
1 Pound = 20 Shillings

British Administration

Government of the British Virgin Islands

1921 Issue

	Good	Fine	XF
S101 2 Shillings-6 Pence (ca. 1931). Reported not confirmed.	—	—	—
S102 5 Shillings (ca. 1931). Rare.	—	—	—
S103 10 Shillings (ca. 1931). Rare.	—	—	—

NOTE: The above issue was reported in the mid 1960s, but requires confirmation.

The Republic of Bulgaria (formerly the Peoples Republic of Bulgaria), a Balkan country on the Black Sea in southeastern Europe, has an area of 110,910 sq. km. and a population of 7.26 million. Capital: Sofia. Agriculture remains a key component of the economy but industrialization, particularly heavy industry, has been emphasized since the late 1940's. Machinery, tobacco and cigarettes, wines and spirits, clothing and metals are the chief exports.

The Bulgars, a Central Asian Turkic tribe, merged with the local Slavic inhabitants in the late 7th century to form the first Bulgarian state. In succeeding centuries, Bulgaria struggled with the Byzantine Empire to assert its place in the Balkans, but by the end of the 14th century the country was overrun by the Ottoman Turks. Northern Bulgaria attained autonomy in 1878 and all of Bulgaria became independent from the Ottoman Empire in 1908. Having fought on the losing side in both World Wars, Bulgaria fell within the Soviet sphere of influence and became a People's Republic in 1946. Communist domination ended in 1990, when Bulgaria held its first multiparty election since World War II and began the contentious process of moving toward political democracy and a market economy while combating inflation, unemployment, corruption, and crime. The country joined NATO in 2004 and the EU in 2007.

RULERS:

Alexander I, 1879-1886
Ferdinand I, as Prince, 1887-1908
Ferdinand I, as King, 1908-1918
Boris III, 1918-1943
Simeon II, 1943-1946

MONETARY SYSTEM:

1 Lev LHV = 100 Stotinki STOTINKI until 1999
1 Lev = 1,000 "Old" Lev, 1999
Silver Lev = Lev Srebro
Gold Lev = Lev Zlato

ALLIES & BULGARIAN ADMINISTRATION

THRACE-INTERALLIEE

1919 PROVISIONAL ISSUE

#S101-S114 Bulgarian National Bank notes w/Thrace Internationale adhesive stamp and embossed oval seal w/*THRACE-INTERALLIEE.*

ADHESIVE REVENUE STAMP VARIETIES:

Type A - Black on blue paper.
Type B - Black on white paper.

	Good	Fine	XF
S101 1 Lev Srebro ND (1919-20). Adhesive stamp Type A and embossed seal on back of #14 (Vol. 2).	—	—	—
S102 2 Leva Srebro ND (1919-20). Adhesive stamp Type A and embossed seal on back of #15 (Vol. 2).	—	—	—
S105 5 Leva Srebro ND (1919-20). Adhesive stamp Type B and embossed seal on back of #16 (Vol. 2).	—	—	—
S106 5 Leva Srebrni ND (1919-20). Adhesive stamp Type B and embossed seal on back of #21 (Vol. 2).	—	—	—

	Good	Fine	XF
S107 10 Leva Srebro ND (1919-20). Adhesive stamp Type B and embossed seal on face of #17 (Vol. 2).	—	—	—
S108 10 Leva Zlatni ND (1919-20). Adhesive stamp Type B and embossed seal on back of #22a (Vol. 2).	—	—	—

	Good	Fine	XF
S109 20 Leva Zlato ND (1919-20). Adhesive stamp Type A and embossed seal on back of #18 (Vol. 2).	—	—	—
S110 20 Leva Zlatni ND (1919-20). Adhesive stamp Type A and embossed seal on back of #23 (Vol. 2).	—	—	—
S111 50 Leva Zlato ND (1919-20). Adhesive stamp Type A and embossed seal on back of #19 (Vol. 2).	—	—	—

	Good	Fine	XF
S112 50 Leva Zlatni ND (1919-20). Adhesive stamp Type A and embossed seal on back of #24 (Vol. 2).	—	—	—
S113 100 Leva Zlato ND (1919-20). Adhesive stamp Type B and embossed seal on back of #20 (Vol. 2).	—	—	—
S114 100 Leva Zlatni ND (1919-20). Adhesive stamp Type B and embossed seal on back of #25 (Vol. 2).	—	—	—

NOTE: Higher denominations may exist.

NOTE: Apparently for a period of about six months, beginning in late 1919 until May 1920 (the end of Thrace Interallie) special revalidated notes of 1903, 1916, and 1917 were placed in circulation. No official documentation has been uncovered to this date for this particular series. Some authorities believe the entire issue to be spurious.

FOREIGN EXCHANGE CERTIFICATES

CORECOM

1966 ND ISSUE

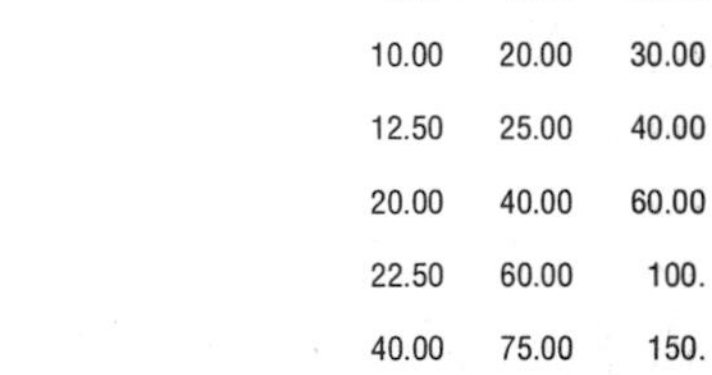

	VG	VF	UNC
FX1 1 Lev ND (1966). Light brown on yellow underprint.	3.00	10.00	15.00
FX2 2 Leva ND (1966). Light brown on yellow underprint.	5.00	12.50	20.00
FX3 5 Leva ND (1966). Light brown on yellow underprint.	10.00	20.00	30.00
FX4 10 Leva ND (1966). Light brown on yellow underprint.	12.50	25.00	40.00
FX5 20 Leva ND (1966). Light brown on yellow underprint.	20.00	40.00	60.00
FX6 50 Leva ND (1966). Light brown on yellow underprint.	22.50	60.00	100.
FX7 100 Leva ND)1966). Light brown on yellow underprint.	40.00	75.00	150.

1968 ND ISSUE

	VG	VF	UNC
FX8 1 Lev ND (1968). Brown on light green underprint.	3.00	10.00	15.00
FX9 2 Leva ND (1968). Brown on light green underprint.	5.00	12.50	20.00

		VG	VF	UNC
FX10	**5 Leva** ND (1968). Brown on light green underprint.	7.50	15.00	25.00
FX11	**10 Leva** ND (1968). Brown on light green underprint.	10.00	20.00	30.00
FX12	**20 Leva** ND (1968). Brown on light green underprint.	15.00	30.00	40.00
FX13	**50 Leva** ND (1968). Brown on light green underprint.	22.50	50.00	80.00
FX14	**100 Leva** ND (1968). Brown on light green underprint.	30.00	60.00	100.

1975 ND Issue

		VG	VF	UNC
FX14A	**.05 Lev** ND (1975).	2.00	5.00	9.00

		VG	VF	UNC
FX15	**1 Lev** ND (1975). Brown on light pink underprint.	3.00	6.00	10.00
FX16	**2 Leva** ND (1975).	5.00	10.00	15.00

		VG	VF	UNC
FX17	**5 Leva** ND (1975).	7.50	12.50	20.00
FX18	**10 Leva** ND (1975).	10.00	20.00	30.00
FX19	**20 Leva** ND (1975).	15.00	30.00	40.00
FX20	**50 Leva** ND (1975).	20.00	40.00	60.00
FX21	**100 Leva** ND (1975).	22.50	50.00	80.00

1978 ND Issue

		VG	VF	UNC
FX22	**1 Lev** ND (1978). Red on light blue underprint. Watermark: Wavy lines.	1.00	3.00	5.00
FX23	**2 Leva** ND (1978). Watermark: Wavy lines.	2.00	5.00	10.00
FX24	**5 Leva** ND (1978). Watermark: Wavy lines.	3.00	7.50	15.00
FX25	**10 Leva** ND (1978). Watermark: Wavy lines.	7.50	12.50	20.00
FX26	**20 Leva** ND (1978). Watermark: Wavy lines.	15.00	30.00	40.00
FX27	**50 Leva** ND (1978). Wavy lines.	30.00	40.00	50.00
FX28	**100 Leva** ND (1978). Watermark: Wavy lines.	35.00	50.00	60.00

Bulgarian National Bank

1981 Issue

		VG	VF	UNC
FX29	**1 Lev** 1981. Light brown on pale red underprint. Watermark: BNB in oval, repeated. a. Issued note. s. Specimen.	 1.00 —	 3.00 —	 5.00 —

		VG	VF	UNC
FX30	**2 Leva** 1981. Watermark: BNB in oval, repeated. a. Issued note. s. Specimen.	 2.00 —	 5.00 —	 10.00 —
FX31	**5 Leva** 1981. Green-blue on yellow underprint. Watermark: BNB in oval, repeated. a. Issued note. s. Specimen.	 3.00 —	 8.00 —	 15.00 —
FX32	**10 Leva** 1981. Watermark: BNB in oval, repeated. a. Issued note. s. Specimen.	 5.00 —	 12.50 —	 20.00 —
FX33	**20 Leva** 1981. Watermark: BNB in oval, repeated.	15.00	30.00	40.00
FX34	**50 Leva** 1981. Watermark: BNB in oval, repeated.	25.00	50.00	80.00
FX35	**100 Leva** 1981. Watermark: BNB in oval, repeated.	30.00	100.	125.

1986 Issue

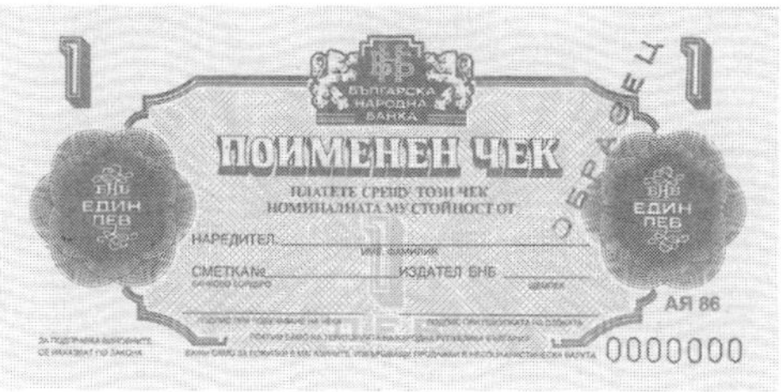

		VG	VF	UNC
FX36	**1 Lev** (19)86. Red on ochre underprint. a. Issued note. s. Specimen.	 1.00 —	 3.00 —	 5.00 —

		VG	VF	UNC
FX37	**2 Leva** (19)86. Blue on grey underprint. a. Issued note. s. Specimen.	 2.00 —	 6.00 —	 10.00 —

FX38 5 Leva	VG	VF	UNC
(19)86.			
a. Issued note.	3.00	7.50	15.00
s. Specimen.	—	—	—

FX39 10 Leva	VG	VF	UNC
(19)86.			
a. Issued note.	5.00	12.50	20.00
s. Specimen.	—	—	—

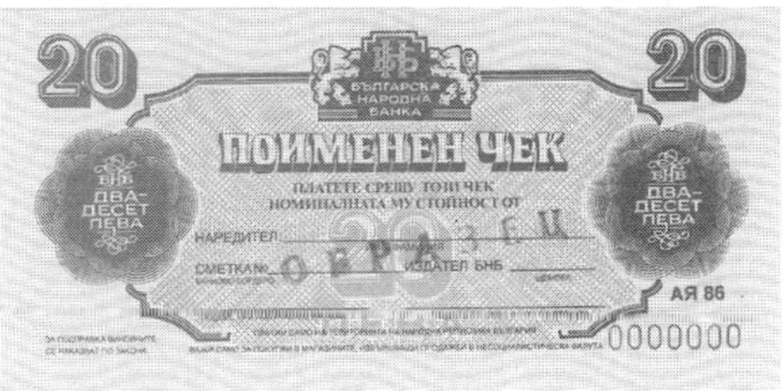

FX40 20 Leva	VG	VF	UNC
(19)86.			
a. Issued note.	10.00	20.00	30.00
s. Specimen.	—	—	—
FX41 50 Leva			
(19)86.	20.00	35.00	50.00
FX42 100 Leva			
(19)86. Olive on light brown underprint.	30.00	50.00	100.

Note: A 1988 dated issue requires confirmation.

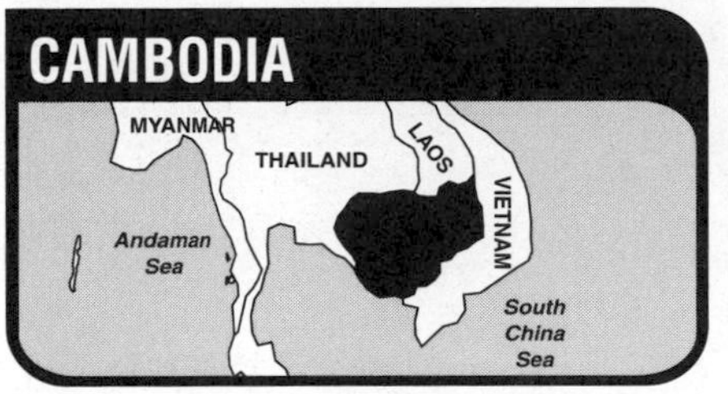

Cambodia, formerly known as Democratic Kampuchea and the Khmer Republic, a land of paddy fields and forest-clad hills located on the Indo-Chinese peninsula fronting on the Gulf of Thailand, has an area of 181,040 sq. km. and a population of 14.24 million. Capital: Phnom Penh. Agriculture is the basis of the economy, with rice the chief crop. Native industries include cattle breeding, weaving and rice milling. Rubber, cattle, corn, and timber are exported.

Most Cambodians consider themselves to be Khmers, descendants of the Angkor Empire that extended over much of Southeast Asia and reached its zenith between the 10th and 13th centuries. Attacks by the Thai and Cham (from present-day Vietnam) weakened the empire, ushering in a long period of decline. The king placed the country under French protection in 1863 and it became part of French Indochina in 1887. Following Japanese occupation in World War II, Cambodia gained full independence from France in 1953. In April 1975, after a five-year struggle, Communist Khmer Rouge forces captured Phnom Penh and evacuated all cities and towns. At least 1.5 million Cambodians died from execution, forced hardships, or starvation during the Khmer Rouge regime under Pol Pot. A December 1978 Vietnamese invasion drove the Khmer Rouge into the countryside, began a 10-year Vietnamese occupation, and touched off almost 13 years of civil war. The 1991 Paris Peace Accords mandated democratic elections and a ceasefire, which was not fully respected by the Khmer Rouge. UN-sponsored elections in 1993 helped restore some semblance of normalcy under a coalition government. Factional fighting in 1997 ended the first coalition government, but a second round of national elections in 1998 led to the formation of another coalition government and renewed political stability. The remaining elements of the Khmer Rouge surrendered in early 1999. Some of the remaining Khmer Rouge leaders are awaiting trial by a UN-sponsored tribunal for crimes against humanity. Elections in July 2003 were relatively peaceful, but it took one year of negotiations between contending political parties before a coalition government was formed. In October 2004, King Sihanouk abdicated the throne due to illness and his son, Prince Norodom Sihamoni, was selected to succeed him. Local elections were held in Cambodia in April 2007, and there was little in the way of pre-election violence that preceded prior elections. National elections are scheduled for July 2008.

Foreign Exchange Certificates

Ministere du Tourisme du Cambodge

1960's Bon Touristique Issue

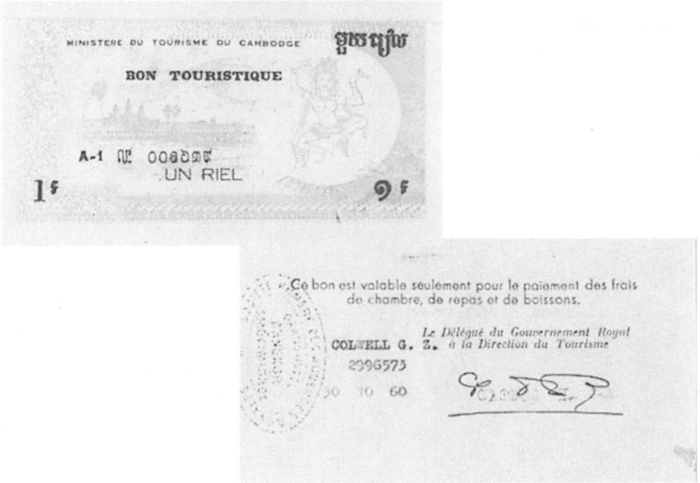

FX1 1 Riel	VG	VF	UNC
ca. 1960's. Pink and tan. Black text, shoreline at left center, royal dancer at right. Back: Black text, perforated along left edge.	25.00	60.00	125.

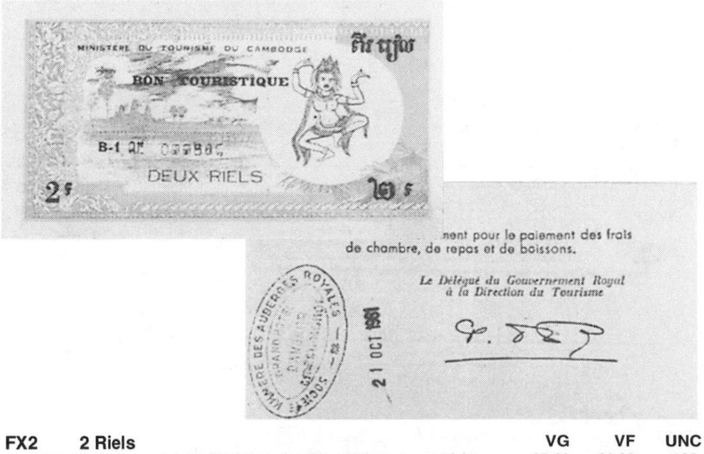

FX2 2 Riels	VG	VF	UNC
1961. Light green and violet. Black text, shoreline at left center, royal dancer at right. Back: Black text, perforated along left edge.	25.00	60.00	125.

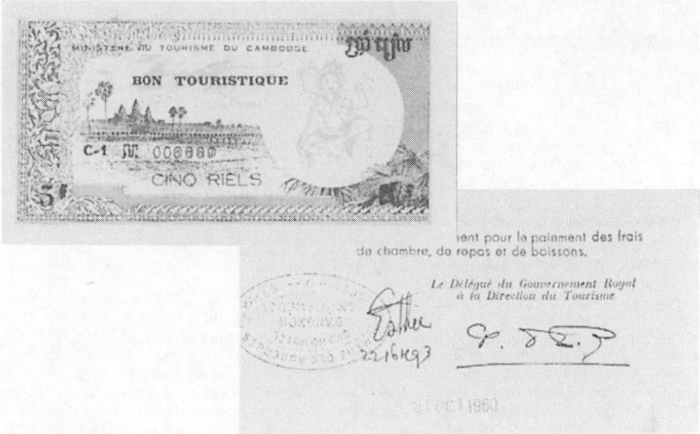

		VG	VF	UNC
FX3	**5 Riels** ca. 1960's. Dark purple and orange. Black text, shoreline at left center,royal dancer at right. Back: Black text, perforated along left edge. .	25.00	60.00	125.
FX4	**10 Riels** ca. 1960's. Yellow and light green. Black text,shoreline at left center, royal dancer at right. Back: Black text, perforated along left edge.	25.00	60.00	125.
FX5	**20 Riels** ca. 1960's. Brown and pale green. Black text, shoreline at left center, royal dancer at right. Back: Black text, perforated along left edge.	25.00	60.00	125.

REGIONAL

KHMER ROUGE INFLUENCE

1993 ND ISSUE

		VG	VF	UNC
R1	**5 Riels** ND (1993-99). Multicolor. Children harvesting vegetables at center, temple carvings at left and right, Signature of President Khiew Samphan. Back: Caravan of ox carts at center, temple carvings at left.	.50	3.00	10.00

		VG	VF	UNC
R2	**10 Riels** ND (1993-99). Multicolor. Village at center right, temple carvings at left and right, signature of Presedent Khieu Samphan. Back: Fishing village, boats at center, temple carvings at left and right.	.50	3.00	10.00

		VG	VF	UNC
R3	**20 Riels** ND (1993-99). Multicolor. Villagers leading cattle along road at center, temple carvings at left and right, signature of President Khieu Samphan. Back: Street scene at center, temple carvings at left and right.	1.00	4.00	15.00

		VG	VF	UNC
R4	**50 Riels** ND (1993-99). Multicolor. Planting rice at center Ox-drawn carts at left center, signature of President Khieu Samphan. Back: Temple carvings at left and right.	1.00	4.00	15.00

		VG	VF	UNC
R5	**100 Riels** ND (1993-99). Multicolor. Field workers at center, temple carvings at left, signature of President Khieu Samphan. Back: Temples of Angkor Wat at center, temple carvings at left and right.	2.00	10.00	55.00

SENDING SCANNED IMAGES BY E-MAIL

We have been receiving an ever-increasing flow of scanned images from sources world wide. Unfortunately, many of these scans could not be used due to the type of scan, or simple incompatibility with our systems. We appreciate the effort it takes to produce these images and accuracy they add to the catalog listings.

Here are a few simple instructions to follow when producing these scans. We encourage you to continue sending new images or upgrades to those currently illustrated and please do not hesitate to ask questions about this process.

- Scan all images within a resolution of 300 dpi.
- Size setting should be at 100%
- Please include in the e-mail the actual size of the image in millimeters height x width
- Scan in true 4-color
- Save images as jpeg and name in such a way which clearly indentifies the country of the note and catalog number
- Do not compress files
- Please e-mail with a request to confirm receipt of the attachment
- Please send multiple images on a disc if available
- Please send images to: george.cuhaj@fwmedia.com

CANADA

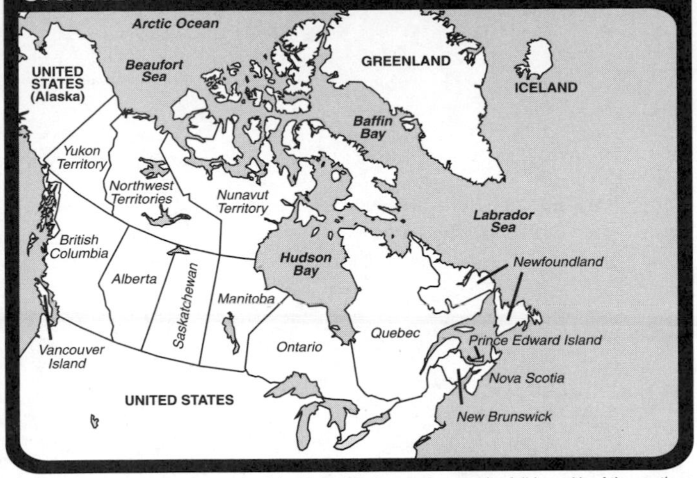

Canada is located to the north of the United States, and spans the full breadth of the northern portion of North America from Atlantic to Pacific oceans, except for the State of Alaska. It has a total area of 9,984,670 sq. km. and a population of 33.21 million. Capital: Ottawa.

A land of vast distances and rich natural resources, Canada became a self-governing dominion in 1867 while retaining ties to the British crown. Economically and technologically the nation has developed in parallel with the US, its neighbor to the south across an unfortified border. Canada faces the political challenges of meeting public demands for quality improvements in health care and education services, as well as responding to separatist concerns in predominantly francophone Quebec. Canada also aims to develop its diverse energy resources while maintaining its commitment to the environment.

RULERS:

French 1534-1763
British 1763-

MONETARY SYSTEM:

French:
12 Deniers = 1 Sou (sols)
20 Sous or Sols = 1 Livre Coloniale
1 Liard = 3 Deniers
1 Ecu = 6 Livres
1 Louis D'or = 4 Ecus

English:
4 Farthings = 1 Penny
12 Pence = 1 Shilling
20 Shillings = 1 Pound

Canadian Decimal Currency
100 Cents = 1 Dollar

ARRANGEMENT

Canada listings in this volume include sections covering French colonial issues, Provincial (British) issues, Chartered Bank issues (including Hudsons Bay Company), and Spurious and Expired banks. The following outline indicates exact location of the various issuers by catalog number.

FRENCH COLONIAL

Playing Card Money - New France 1685-1728
Card Money 1729-1757 .... #S101-S108
Ordonnances or Treasury Notes 1753-1769 .... #S111-S117

BRITISH COLONIAL

British Army

British Army Bill 1813-1815 .... #S118A-S120

PROVINCIAL ISSUES

British Columbia .... #S126-S128
Nova Scotia .... #S132-S140
Ontario .... #S141-S143
Prince Edward Island .... #S144-S157
Province of Canada .... #S161-S176

CHARTERED BANKS

Bank of British Columbia .... #S201-S219
Bank of British North America .... #S221-S435
Bank of Hamilton .... #S441-S468
Bank of Montreal .... #S471-S564
Bank of New Brunswick .... #S571-S599
Bank of Nova Scotia .... #S601-S633
Bank of Ottawa .... #S636-S664
Bank of Toronto .... #S666-S693
Bank of Vancouver .... #S696-S700
Bank of Yarmouth .... #S701-S704
Banque Canadienne Nationale .... #S706-S717
Banque d'Hochelaga .... #S721-S815
Banque Internationale du Canada .... #S816-S818
Banque Jacques Cartier .... #S821-S837
Banque Nationale .... #S841-S875
Bank of the People .... #S875A-S875E
Banque du Peuple .... #S876-S909
Banque Provinciale du Canada .... #S911-S922
Banque de St. Hyacinthe .... #S924-S929
Banque de St. Jean .... #S931-S935
Banque Ville Marie .... #S936-S946
Barclays Bank (Canada) .... #S947-S951
Canadian Bank of Commerce .... #S952-S972
City Bank .... #S972A-S972C
Commercial Bank of Canada .... #S973-S996
Commercial Bank of Manitoba .... #S997-S1000
Commercial Bank of the Midland District .... #S1000A-S1000W
Commercial Bank of Windsor .... #S1001-S1004
Crown Bank of Canada .... #S1006-S1009
Dominion Bank .... #S1011-S1036
Eastern Townships Bank .... #S1041-S1057
Exchange Bank of Yarmouth .... #S1058-S1060
Farmers Bank of Canada .... #S1061-S1065
Gore Bank .... #S1066-S1069
Halifax Banking Company .... #S1070-S1086
Home Bank of Canada .... #S1087-S1091
Hudsons Bay Company .... #S1095-S1121
Imperial Bank of Canada .... #S1122-S1145H
Merchants Bank of Canada .... #S1146-S1173
Merchants' Bank of Halifax .... #S1174-S1189
Merchants Bank of Prince Edward Island .... #S1191-S1196
Metropolitan Bank .... #S1197-S1201
Molsons Bank .... #S1202-S1243
Montreal Bank .... #S1243A-S1243K
Niagara District Bank .... #S1243L-S1243V
Northern Bank .... #S1244-S1247
Northern Crown Bank .... #S1248-S1251
Ontario Bank .... #S1252-S1286
Peoples Bank of Halifax .... #S1287-S1290
Peoples Bank of New Brunswick .... #S1291-S1302
Quebec Bank .... #S1306-S1368
Royal Bank of Canada .... #S1369-S1394
St. Lawrence Bank .... #S1395-S1399
St. Stephens Bank .... #S1400-S1430
Sovereign Bank of Canada .... #S1431-S1434
Standard Bank of Canada .... #S1435-S1447
Sterling Bank of Canada .... #S1448-S1453
Summerside Bank of Prince Edward Island .... #S1454-S1465
Traders Bank of Canada .... #S1466-S1482
Union Bank of Canada .... #S1483-S1507
Union Bank of Halifax .... #S1511-S1521
Union Bank of Lower Canada .... #S1521A-S1521J
Union Bank of Prince Edward Island .... #S1522-S1533
United Empire Bank of Canada .... #S1534-S1535
Western Bank of Canada .... #S1536-S1538
Weyburn Security Bank .... #S1539-S1541

SPURIOUS OR EXPIRED BANKS

The following notes are irredeemable.
Bank of Acadia .... #S1542-S1545
Accommodation Bank .... #S1546-S1547
Agricultural Bank, Montreal .... #S1548-S1550
Agricultural Bank, Toronto .... #S1551-S1564
Arman's Bank .... #S1565-S1567
Banque De Boucherville .... #S1568
Bank of Brantford .... #S1569-S1576
British Canadian Bank .... #S1577-S1578
Canada Bank, Montreal .... #S1579-S1580
Canada Bank, Toronto .... #S1581-S1583
Bank of Canada, Montreal .... #S1584-S1595
Banque Canadienne .... #S1596-S1599
Central Bank of Canada .... #S1600-S1602
Central Bank of New Brunswick .... #S1603-S1617
Charlotte County Bank .... #S1618-S1622
Bank of Charlottetown .... #S1623-S1625
City Bank, Banque de la Cité .... #S1626-S1656
City Bank of Montreal .... #S1656A
Bank of Clifton .... #S1657-S1665
Colonial Bank of Canada .... #S1666-S1680
Colonial Bank of Chatham .... #S1681-S1683
Commercial Bank, Brockville .... #S1684-S1685
Commercial Bank, Kingston, U.C. .... #S1686-S1689
Commercial Bank, Montreal, L.C. .... #S1689A-S1689C
Commercial Bank of Fort Erie, U.C. .... #S1690-S1696
Commercial Bank of Montreal, L.C. .... #S1697-S1702
Commercial Bank of New Brunswick .... #S1703-S1720
Commercial Branch Bank of Canada, Collingwood, C.W. .... #S1721-S1722
Consolidated Bank of Canada, Montreal .... #S1723-S1728
Bank of the County of Elgin, St. Thomas, C.W. .... #S1729-S1732
Eastern Bank of Canada, St. John, N.B. .... #S1733-S1734
Exchange Bank, Quebec, L.C. .... #S1735
Exchange Bank of Canada, Montreal, L.C. .... #S1736-S1742
Exchange Bank of Canada, Windsor .... #S1743
Exchange Bank of Toronto, U.C. .... #S1744-S1747
Exchange Bank Company of Chippewa, U.C. .... #S1748-S1749
Farmer's Bank, Toronto, U.C. .... #S1750
Farmers' Bank of Malden, U.C. .... #S1751-S1753
Farmer's Joint Stock Banking Co., Toronto, U.C. .... #S1754-S1769
Farmers J.S. Banking Co., Toronto, U.C. .... #S1770
Farmers Bank of Rustico. P.E.I. .... #S1771-S1776
Farmers Bank of St. Johns, L.C. .... #S1777-S1781
Federal Bank of Canada, Toronto .... #S1782-S1788
Bank of Fredericton, N.B. .... #S1789-S1793
Free Holders Bank of the Midland District, Bath, U.C. .... #S1794-S1795
Goderich Bank, U.C. .... #S1796-S1797
Gore Bank of Hamilton, U.C. .... #S1798-S1800
Hart's Bank, Three Rivers, L.C. .... #S1801-S1807
Henry's Bank, L.C. .... #S1808-S1813
International Bank of Canada, Toronto, C.W. .... #S1814-S1828
Kingston Bank, L.C. .... #S1829
Bank of Liverpool, N.S. .... #S1830-S1833
Bank of London in Canada .... #S1834-S1838
Lower Canada Bank, Montreal, L.C. .... #S1839-S1841

Bank of Lower Canada, Quebec, L.C. .... #S1842-S1846
MacDonald & Co., Victoria, B.C. .... #S1847-S1852
Maritime Bank of the Dominion of Canada, St. Johns, N.B. .... #S1853-S1859
Mechanics Bank, Montreal, L.C. .... #S1860-S1862
Mechanics Bank, Montreal, C.E. .... #S1863-S1865
Mechanics Bank of Saint John's, L.C. .... #S1866-S1874
Mercantile Banking Corporation, Halifax, N.S. .... #S1875
Merchants Bank, Montreal, C.E. .... #S1875A-S1875I
Merchants Bank, Toronto, U.C. .... #S1876-S1879
Merchants Exchange Bank, Goderich, C.W. .... #S1880
Metropolitan Bank, Montreal .... #S1881-S1885
Montreal Bank, C.W. .... #S1886
Newcastle Banking Company, Amherst, U.C. .... #S1887-S1888
New Castle District Loan Company, Peterborough, U.C. .... #S1889-S1892
Niagara Suspension Bridge Bank, Queenston, U.C. .... #S1893-S1908
Bank of Ottawa (Banque de Ottawa), Montreal, L.C. .... #S1909-S1914
Phenix Bank, Phillipsburg, L.C. .... #S1915-S1918
Pictou Bank, N.S. .... #S1919-S1921
Bank of Prince Edward Island, Charlottetown .... #S1922-S1933
Provincial Bank, London .... #S1934-S1935
Provincial Bank of Canada, Stanstead, C.E. .... #S1936-S1938
Bank of Quebec, Lower Canada .... #S1939
Royal Canadian Bank, Toronto, C.W. .... #S1940-S1952
Saint Francis Bank, Stanstead, C.E. .... #S1953-S1954
Banque St. Jean Baptiste, Montreal. .... #S1955-S1957
St. Lawrence Bank & Lumber Co., Malbaie, L.C. .... #S1958-S1959
St. Stephens Joint Stock Banking Comp'y .... #S1959A
Bank of Saskatchewan, Moose Jaw .... #S1960-S1962
Stadacona Bank, Quebec City .... #S1963-S1966
Tattersall Bank, Montreal, L.C. .... #S1967
Union Bank, Montreal, L.C. .... #S1968-S1988
Union Bank of Montreal, L.C. .... #S1989-1990
Bank of Upper Canada, Kingston, U.C. .... #S1991-S1996
Bank of Upper Canada, York, U.C. .... #S1997-S2037
Bank of Western Canada, Clifton, C.W. .... #S2038-S2041
Westmorland Bank of New Brunswick, Bend of the Petticodiac .... #S2042-S2050
Zimmerman Bank, Elgin, C.W. .... #S2051-S2076

French Administration

New France

Card Money, 1729-57

Pieces of plain cardboard with signature of Governor and Intendant, also their seals.

	Good	Fine	XF
S101 7 Sols-6 Deniers 1749. Rare.	—	—	—

	Good	Fine	XF
S102 15 Sols 1749; 1757. Rare.	—	—	—
S103 20 Sols 1734. Rare.	—	—	—

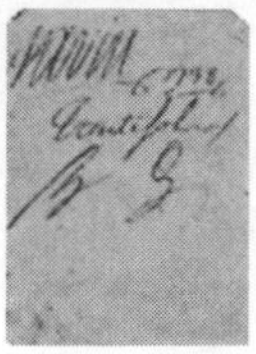

	Good	Fine	XF
S104 30 Sols 1733; 1738; 1752; 1757. Rare.	—	—	—
S105 3 Livres 1742; 1747; 1749. Rare.	—	—	—

	Good	Fine	XF
S106 6 Livres 1729; 1735; 1749. Rare.	—	—	—

	Good	Fine	XF
S107 12 Livres 1729-49. Rare.	—	—	—

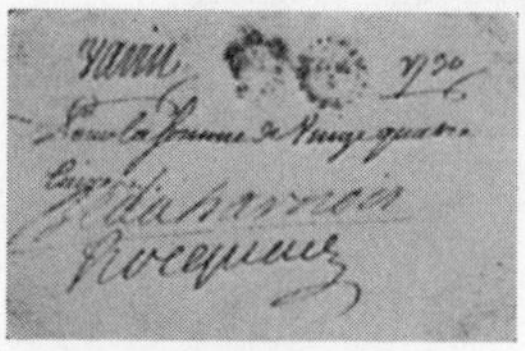

	Good	Fine	XF
S108 24 Livres 1729-49. Rare.	—	—	—

Ordonnances or Treasury Notes, 1753-60

Treasury notes were issued to supplement card money.

	Good	Fine	XF
S111 20 Sols 1754; 1757-59.			
a. Issued note. Rare.	—	—	—
p. Proof.	—	Unc	1250.

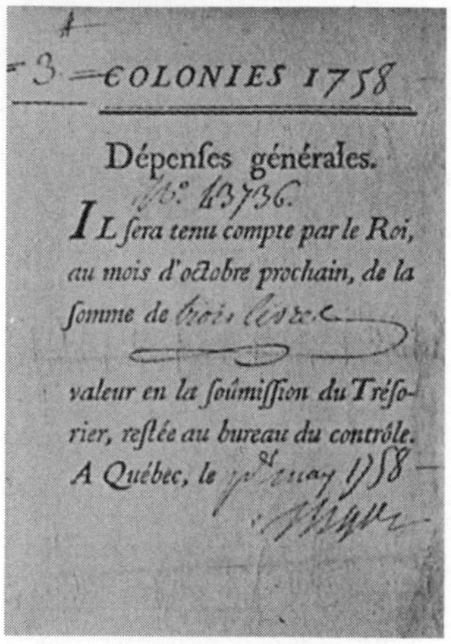

3 COLONIES 1758

Dépenses générales.

No. 13736.

IL sera tenu compte par le Roi, au mois d'octobre prochain, de la somme de trois livres

valeur en la soumission du Trésorier, restée au bureau du contrôle.

A Québec, le 1758

	Good	Fine	XF
S112 3 Livres 1756; 1758; 1760. Black. Rare.	—	—	—

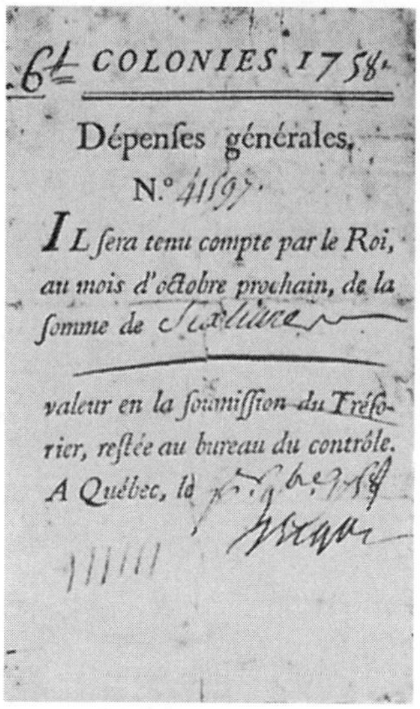

6 COLONIES 1758.

Dépenses générales.

N.° 41597.

IL sera tenu compte par le Roi, au mois d'octobre prochain, de la somme de six livres

valeur en la soumission du Trésorier, restée au bureau du contrôle.

A Québec, le

	Good	Fine	XF
S113 6 Livres 1758; 1759. Black. Rare.	—	—	—
S114 12 Livres 1757-59. Black. Rare.	—	—	—
S115 24 Livres 1756. Black. Rare.	—	—	—

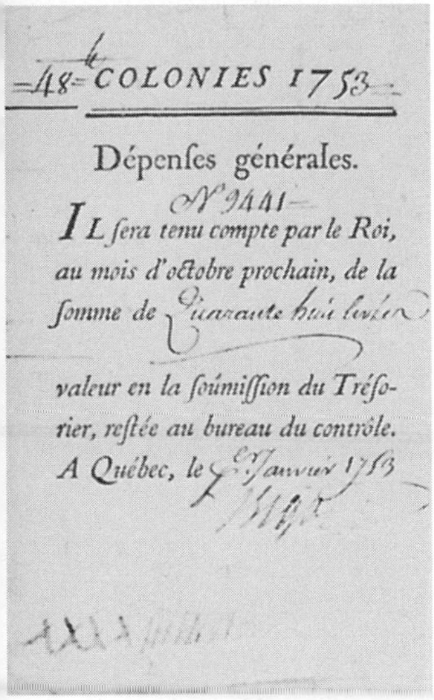

	Good	Fine	XF
S116 48 Livres			
1753; 1758. Black. Rare.	—	—	—
S117 96 Livres			
1757; 1759. Black.			
a. Issued note. Rare.	—	—	—
p. Proof.	—	Unc	1500.

British Administration

British Army

1813 First Army Bill Issue

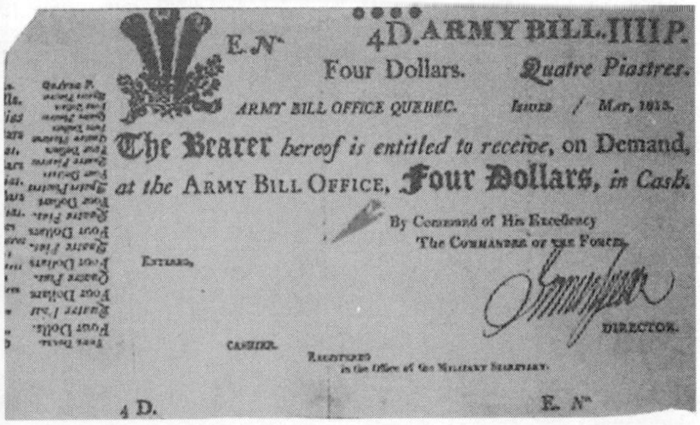

	Good	Fine	XF
S118A 4 Dollars			
May and June 1813. Black. Plumes at upper left. Rare.	—	—	—

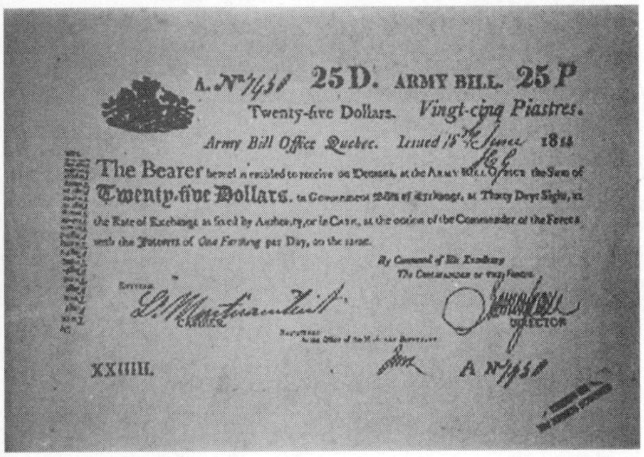

	Good	Fine	XF
S118B 25 Dollars			
15.6.1813; 17.4.1813. Black. Rare.	—	—	—
S118C 50 Dollars			
ca.1813. Black. Rare.	—	—	—
S118D 100 Dollars			
ca.1813. Black. Rare.	—	—	—
S118E 400 Dollars			
ca.1813. Black. Rare.	—	—	—

1813 Second Army Bill Issue

	Good	Fine	XF
S119A 1 Dollar			
ca.1813-14. Black. Rare.	—	—	—
S119B 2 Dollars			
ca.1813-14. Reported not confirmed.	—	—	—
S119C 8 Dollars			
ca.1813-14. Reported not confirmed.	—	—	—
S119D 10 Dollars			
ca.1813-14. Reported not confirmed.	—	—	—
S119E 12 Dollars			
ca.1813-14. Reported not confirmed.	—	—	—
S119F 16 Dollars			
ca.1813-14. Reported not confirmed.	—	—	—
S119G 20 Dollars			
ca.1813-14. Reported not confirmed.	—	—	—

1814 Army Bill Issue

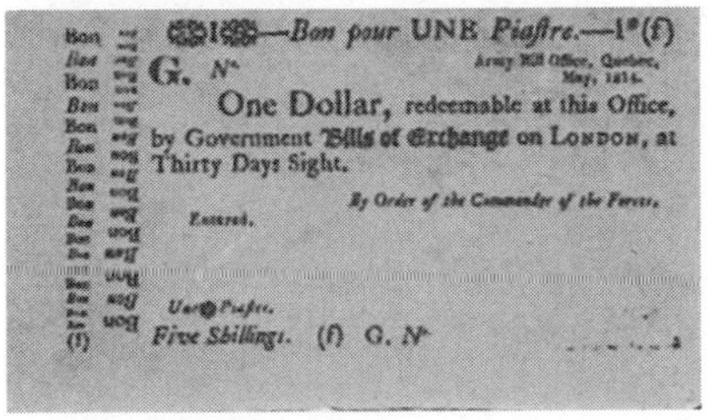

	Good	Fine	XF
S120A 1 Dollar = 1 Piastre = 5 Shillings			
March or May 1814. Black.			
a. Issued note. Rare.	—	—	—
r. Remainder.	—	—	800.

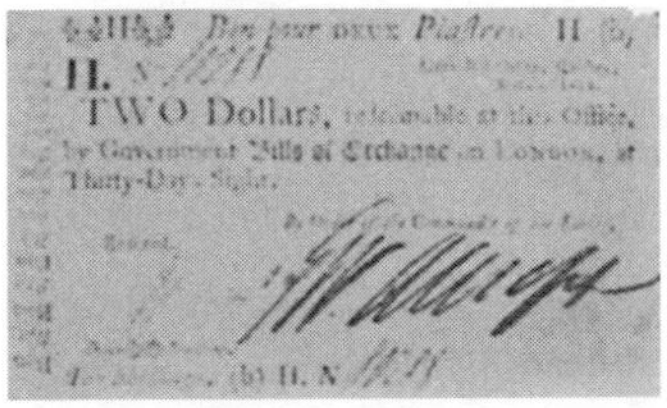

	Good	Fine	XF
S120B 2 Dollars = 2 Piastres = 10 Shillings			
March 1814. Black.			
a. Issued note. Rare.	—	—	—
r. Remainder.	—	—	800.

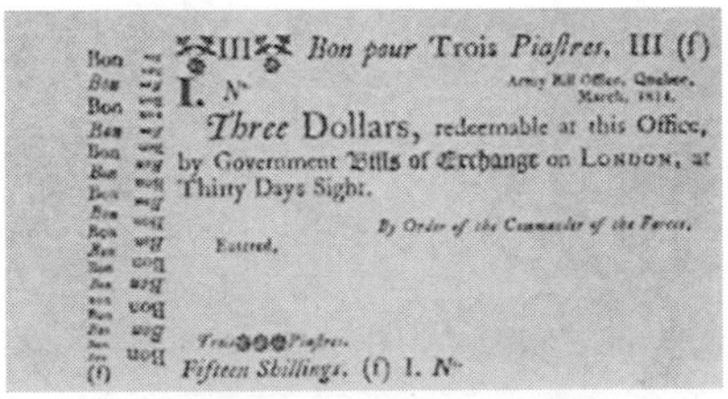

	Good	Fine	XF
S120C 3 Dollars = 3 Piastres-15 Shillings			
March 1814. Black.			
a. Issued note. Rare.	—	—	—
r. Remainder.	—	—	800.

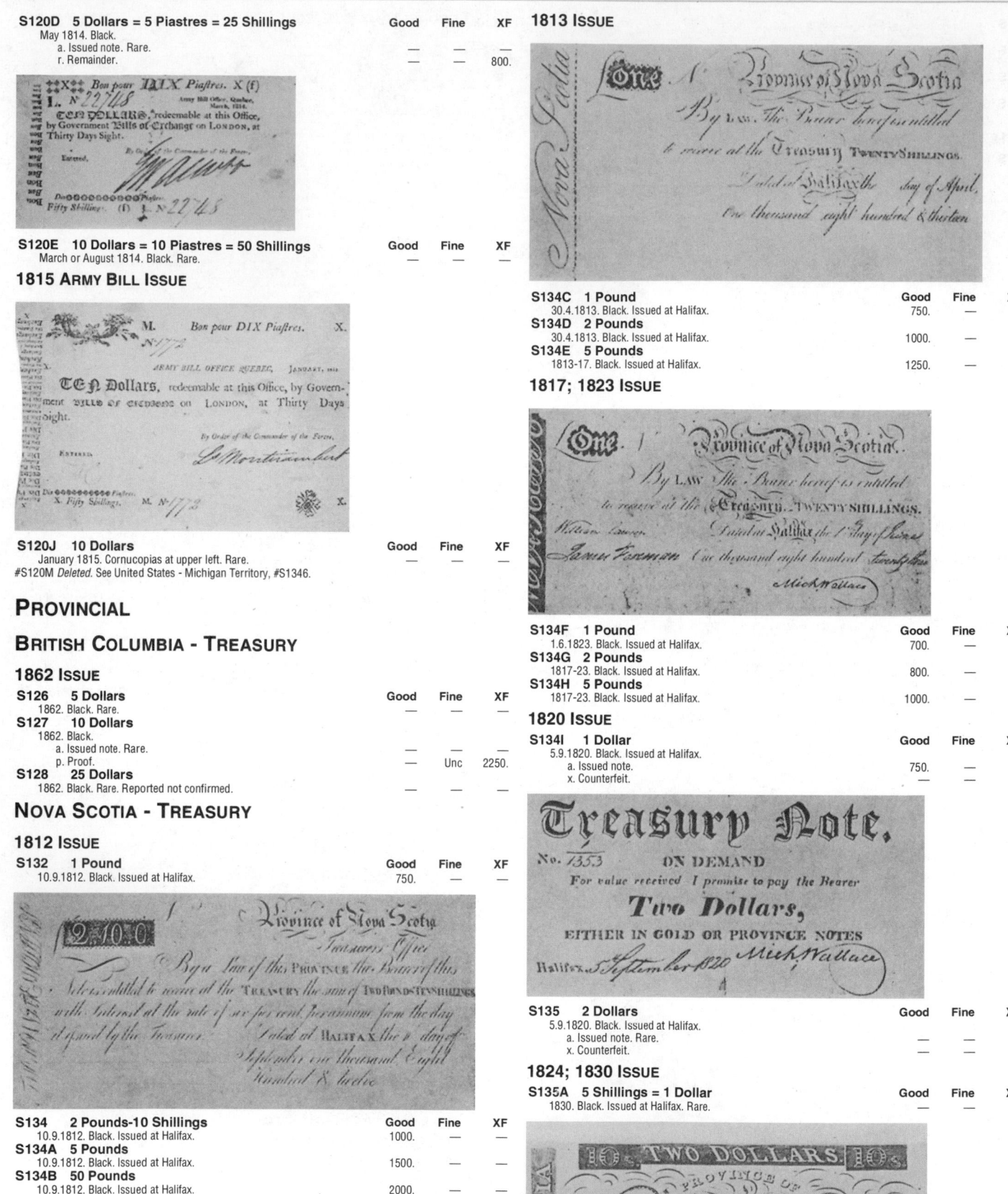

	Good	Fine	XF
S120D 5 Dollars = 5 Piastres = 25 Shillings May 1814. Black.			
a. Issued note. Rare.	—	—	—
r. Remainder.	—	—	800.

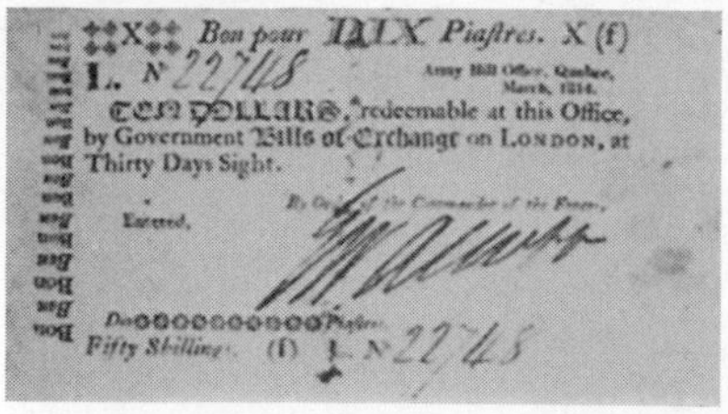

	Good	Fine	XF
S120E 10 Dollars = 10 Piastres = 50 Shillings March or August 1814. Black. Rare.	—	—	—

1815 Army Bill Issue

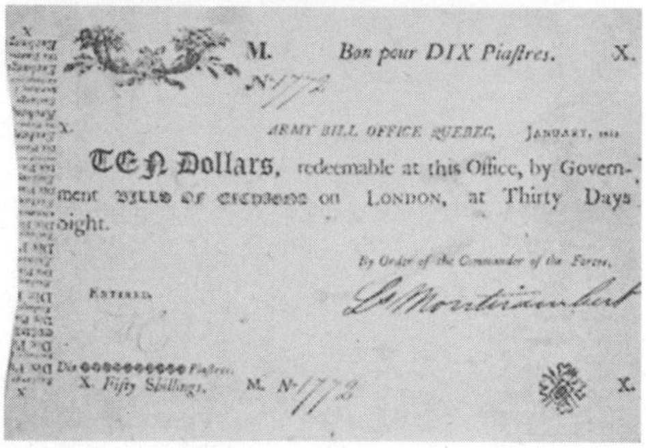

	Good	Fine	XF
S120J 10 Dollars January 1815. Cornucopias at upper left. Rare.	—	—	—

#S120M *Deleted.* See United States - Michigan Territory, #S1346.

Provincial

British Columbia - Treasury

1862 Issue

	Good	Fine	XF
S126 5 Dollars 1862. Black. Rare.	—	—	—
S127 10 Dollars 1862. Black.			
a. Issued note. Rare.	—	—	—
p. Proof.	—	Unc	2250.
S128 25 Dollars 1862. Black. Rare. Reported not confirmed.	—	—	—

Nova Scotia - Treasury

1812 Issue

	Good	Fine	XF
S132 1 Pound 10.9.1812. Black. Issued at Halifax.	750.	—	—

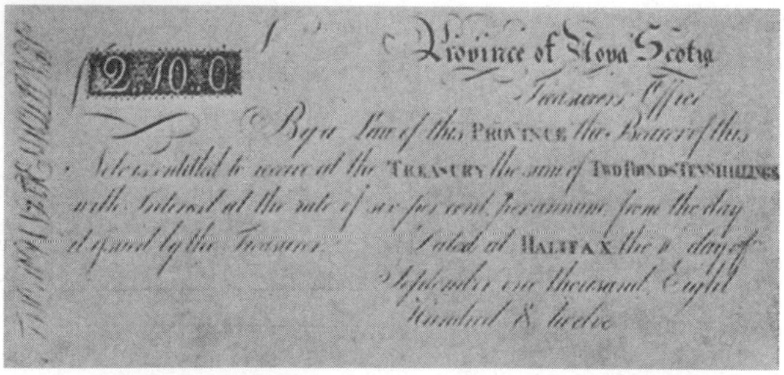

	Good	Fine	XF
S134 2 Pounds-10 Shillings 10.9.1812. Black. Issued at Halifax.	1000.	—	—
S134A 5 Pounds 10.9.1812. Black. Issued at Halifax.	1500.	—	—
S134B 50 Pounds 10.9.1812. Black. Issued at Halifax.	2000.	—	—

1813 Issue

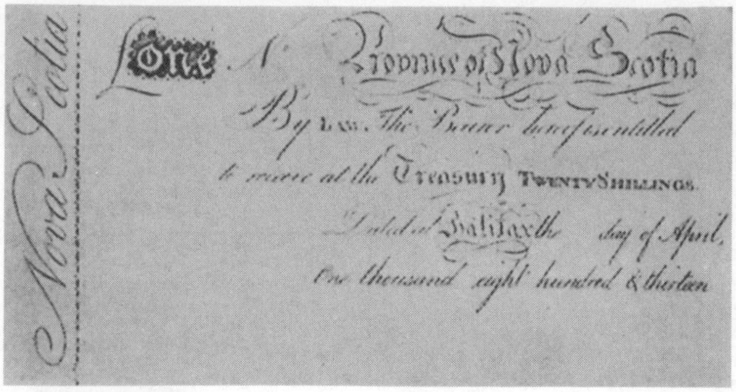

	Good	Fine	XF
S134C 1 Pound 30.4.1813. Black. Issued at Halifax.	750.	—	—
S134D 2 Pounds 30.4.1813. Black. Issued at Halifax.	1000.	—	—
S134E 5 Pounds 1813-17. Black. Issued at Halifax.	1250.	—	—

1817; 1823 Issue

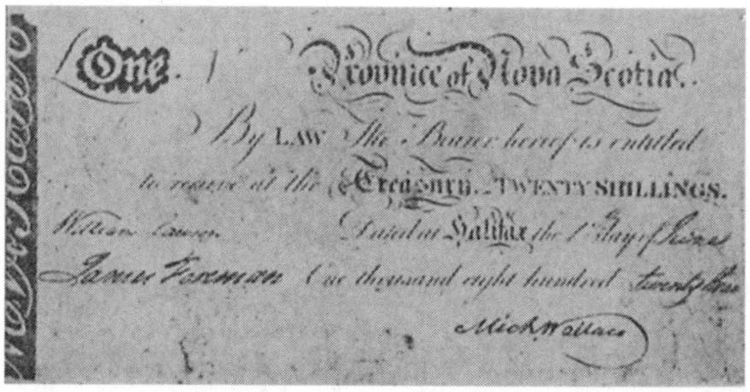

	Good	Fine	XF
S134F 1 Pound 1.6.1823. Black. Issued at Halifax.	700.	—	—
S134G 2 Pounds 1817-23. Black. Issued at Halifax.	800.	—	—
S134H 5 Pounds 1817-23. Black. Issued at Halifax.	1000.	—	—

1820 Issue

	Good	Fine	XF
S134I 1 Dollar 5.9.1820. Black. Issued at Halifax.			
a. Issued note.	750.	—	—
x. Counterfeit.	—	—	—

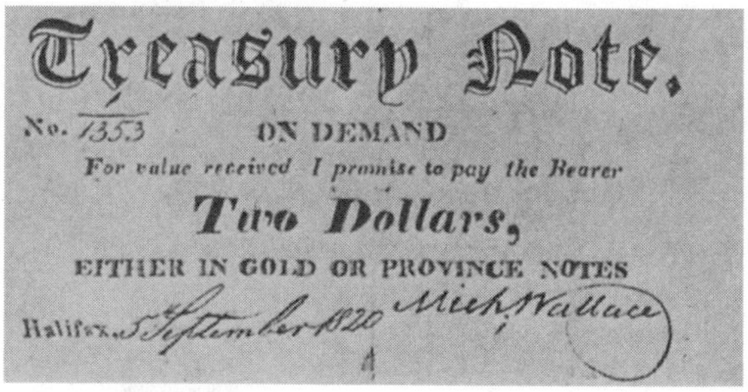

	Good	Fine	XF
S135 2 Dollars 5.9.1820. Black. Issued at Halifax.			
a. Issued note. Rare.	—	—	—
x. Counterfeit.	—	—	—

1824; 1830 Issue

	Good	Fine	XF
S135A 5 Shillings = 1 Dollar 1830. Black. Issued at Halifax. Rare.	—	—	—

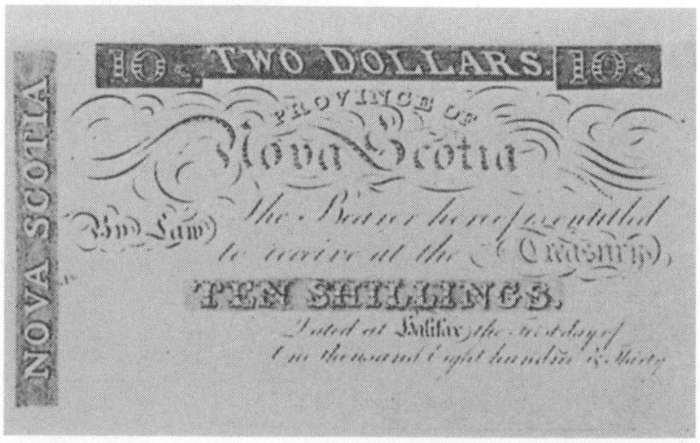

		Good	Fine	XF
S136	**10 Shillings = 2 Dollars** 1830. Black. Issued at Halifax. Rare.	—	—	—
S137	**1 Pound** 1824-. Black. Issued at Halifax. Rare.	—	—	—
S137A	**2 Pounds** 1824-. Black. Issued at Halifax. Rare.	—	—	—
S137B	**5 Pounds** 1824-. Black. Issued at Halifax. Rare.	—	—	—

1825; 1828 Issue

		Good	Fine	XF
S138	**1 Pound** 1.8.1825. Black. Printer: Peter Maverick of New York. Lithographic issue. Rare.	—	—	—

		Good	Fine	XF
S138D	**20 Shillings = 1 Pound** 1828; 1.6.1829; 1.3.1832. Black. Printer: Peter Maverick of New York. Lithographic issue. Rare.	—	—	—

1838 Issue

		Good	Fine	XF
S138E	**1 Pound** 1838. Black. Printer: RW&H. Rare.	—	—	—

1848 Issue

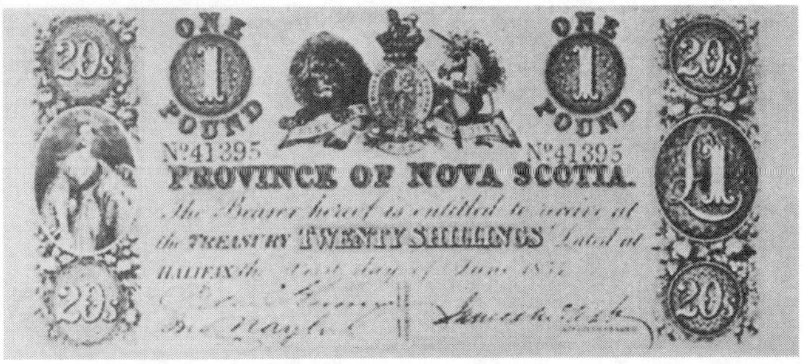

		Good	Fine	XF
S139	**1 Pound = 20 Shillings** 1.5.1848; 1.6.1853; 1.6.1854. Black. Portrait Queen Victoria at left, supported royal arms at upper center. Handwritten or printed serial #. Printer: PB&P.	150.	525.	1750.

1861 Issue

		Good	Fine	XF
S140	**5 Dollars** 1.6.1861; 1.5.1865; 1.5.1866; 1.8.1866. Black on green underprint. Portrait Queen Victoria at lower left, kneeling Indian at right of shield at upper center, portrait Prince Albert at lower right. Back: Orange. St. George slaying dragon at center. Printer: ABNC.	175.	625.	2250.

Ontario - Provisional Government of Upper Canada

1837 Issues

		Good	Fine	XF
S141	**1 Dollar** 27.12.1837. Black. Paper: Blue tint. Rare.	—	—	—
S142	**2 Dollars** 27.12.1837. Black. Paper: Blue tint.	850.	—	—
S143	**10 Dollars** 27.12.1837. Black. Large letters. Paper: Blue tint.	1000.	—	—
S143A	**10 Dollars** 27.12.1837. Black. Small letters. Paper: Blue tint.	1000.	—	—

Island of Saint John - Treasury

1790 Issue

		Good	Fine	XF
S144	**1 Shilling** 20.11.1790. Black. Uniface.	300.	1000.	2500.
		Good	Fine	XF
S145	**1 Shilling-6 Pence** 20.11.1790. Black. Uniface.	300.	1000.	2500.
S146	**2 Shillings-6 Pence** 20.11.1790. Black. Uniface.	300.	1000.	2500.
S147	**5 Shillings** 20.11.1790. Black. Uniface.	300.	1000.	2500.
S148	**10 Shillings** 20.11.1790. Black. Uniface.	300.	1000.	2500.
S149	**20 Shillings** 20.11.1790. Black. Uniface.	300.	1000.	2500.
S150	**40 Shillings** 20.11.1790. Black. Uniface.	300.	1000.	2500.

Prince Edward Island - Treasury

1848-58 Issue

		Good	Fine	XF
S151	**5 Shillings** 1855; 1866. Black. Sailing ship at top center, seal on ice at upper right. Supported royal arms at top center. Uniface.	300.	1000.	3000.
S152	**10 Shillings** 1855; 1866. Black. Farmer plowing with horses at upper center, ship building at upper right. Supported royal arms at top center. Uniface.	250.	1000.	3000.

		Good	Fine	XF
S153	**1 Pound** 1848; 9.3.1870. Black. Farmer raking straw at lower left, sheaf of wheat at right. Supported royal arms at top center. Uniface.	300.	1000.	3750.
S154	**2 Pounds** 23.7.1858. Black. Provincial Provincial Legislature building at top center. Supported royal arms at top center. Uniface.	300.	1000.	3750.
S155	**5 Pounds** 1858. Black. Provincial Seal at upper center. Supported royal arms at top center. Uniface.	300.	1000.	3750.

1872 Issue

		Good	Fine	XF
S156	**10 Dollars** 1872. Black on green underprint. Prince Arthur at lower left, seated Britannia at lower right. Supported royal arms at top center. Uniface. Back: Green. Printer: BABNC.	500.	1500.	5000.
S157	**20 Dollars** 1872. Black. Plow at lower left, sailors with sailing ship in background at lower right. Supported royal arms at center. Back: Green. Printer: BABNC.	500.	1500.	5000.

NOTE: For other bank issues refer to Canada - "Chartered" or "Spurious & Expired" bank listings.

Province of Canada - Provincial Debentures

185x Issue

		Good	Fine	XF
S161	**1 Dollar = 5 Shillings** 185x. Black with red *ONE* protector. Seated female with farm tools at top center. Uniface. Printer: RW&H. Proof.	—	Unc	800.
S162	**2 Dollars = 10 Shillings** 185x. Black with red *TWO* protector. Two seated females at top center. Uniface. Printer: RW&H. Proof.	—	Unc	800.
S162A	**5 Dollars = 1 Pound-5 Shillings** 185x. Black with red *FIVE* protector. Three cherubs and two seated allegorical women with ornate *5* at top center. Uniface. Printer: RW&H.	—	Unc	800.
S163	**10 Dollars = 2 Pounds-10 Shillings** 185x. Black. Britannia and arms at top center. Uniface. Printer: RW&H. Proof.	—	Unc	800.
S164	**20 Dollars = 5 Pounds** 185x. Black. Supported royal arms at top center. Uniface. Printer: RW&H. Proof.	—	Unc	800.

NOTE: Do not confuse the rare Provincial Debentures with the more commonly available County Debentures 1850-54 of similar design issued by the Municipal Council at Brockville.

1849-62 Provisional Issue

#S171-S176 Bank of Montreal notes issued at various offices between 1849-62 with green or blue overprint: *PROVINCIAL NOTE / LEGAL TENDER* and vertical overprint: *PAYABLE IN...* Several different issues were overprint, but only in the listed denominations. All are very rare.

		Good	Fine	XF
S171	**4 Dollars** 1852-59.			
	a. Overprint: *PAYABLE IN MONTREAL.* Rare.	—	—	—
	b. Overprint: *PAYABLE IN TORONTO.* Rare.	—	—	—
S172	**5 Dollars** 1844-59.			
	a. Overprint: *PAYABLE IN MONTREAL.* Rare.	—	—	—
	b. Overprint: *PAYABLE IN TORONTO.* Rare.	—	—	—
S173	**10 Dollars** 1842-59.			
	a. Overprint: *PAYABLE IN MONTREAL.* Rare.	—	—	—
	b. Overprint: *PAYABLE IN TORONTO.* Rare.	—	—	—

		Good	Fine	XF
S174	**20 Dollars**			
	18xx.			
	a. Overprint: *PAYABLE IN MONTREAL.* Rare.	—	—	—
	b. Overprint: *PAYABLE IN TORONTO.* Rare.	—	—	—
S175	**50 Dollars**			
	18xx.			
	a. Overprint: *PAYABLE IN MONTREAL.* Rare.	—	—	—
	b. Overprint: *PAYABLE IN TORONTO.* Rare.	—	—	—
S176	**100 Dollars**			
	1861.			
	a. Overprint: *PAYABLE IN MONTREAL.* Rare.	—	—	—
	b. Overprint: *PAYABLE IN TORONTO.* Rare.	—	—	—

NOTE: For Province of Canada regular issue see Vol. 2, #A26-A33.

PRIVATE AND CHARTERED BANKS

BANK OF BRITISH COLUMBIA 1862-94

1862-63 ISSUE

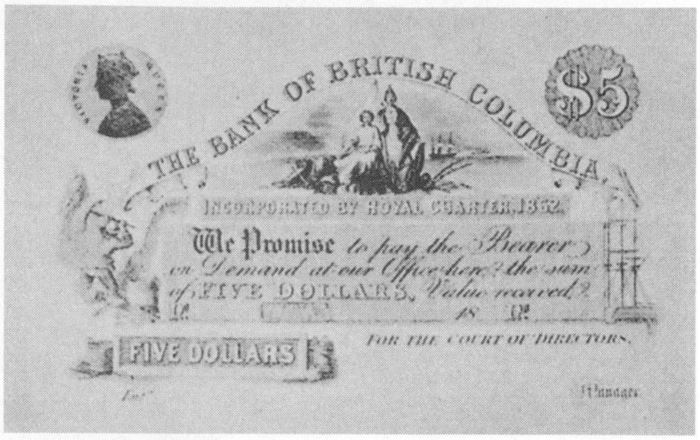

		Good	Fine	XF
S201	**5 Dollars**			
	28.11.1862-6.1.1863. Black on blue underprint. Miner with pickaxe at left. Coin portrait Queen Victoria at upper left, standing Britannia with seated woman at upper center. Printer: Rixon & Arnold.			
	a. With *VICTORIA* after left hand serial #.	—	—	—
	b. Without *VICTORIA* after left hand serial #.	—	—	—
S202	**20 Dollars**			
	28.11.1862. Black on blue underprint. Miner pouring ore at left. Coin portrait Queen Victoria at upper left, standing Britannia with seated woman at upper center. Printer: Rixon & Arnold.	—	—	—

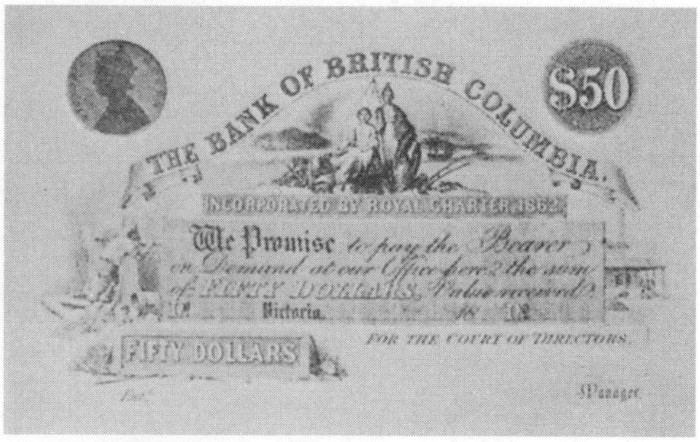

		Good	Fine	XF
S203	**50 Dollars**			
	28.11.1862. Black on blue underprint. Miner at crank at left. Coin portrait Queen Victoria at upper left, standing Britannia with seated woman at upper center. Printer: Rixon & Arnold.	—	—	—
S204	**100 Dollars**			
	6.1.1863. Black on blue underprint. Miner with sledge hammer at left. Coin portrait Queen Victoria at upper left, standing Britannia with seated woman at upper center. Printer: Rixon & Arnold.	—	—	—

NOTE: All issued notes of #S204 were redeemed.

1863-75 ISSUE

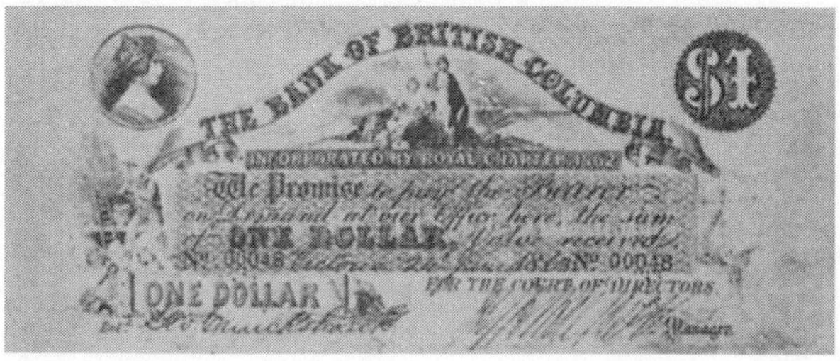

		VG	VF	UNC
S206	**1 Dollar**			
	24.6.1863; 30.6.1863. Black on blue underprint. Various portrait frame with Queen Victoria at upper left, standing Britannia with seated woman at upper center. Printer: Wm. Brown & Co.	3000.	4500.	—

		Good	Fine	XF
S207	**5 Dollars**			
	31.3.1864. Black on blue underprint. Various portrait frame with Queen Victoria at upper left, standing Britannia with seated woman at upper center. Printer: Wm. Brown & Co.	—	—	—
S208	**10 Dollars**			
	15.5.1873. Black oin blue underprint. Various portrait frame with Queen Victoria at upper left, standing Britannia with seated woman at upper center. Printer: Wm. Brown & Co.	—	—	—
S209	**20 Dollars**			
	23.5.1875. Black on blue underprint. Various portrait frame with Queen Victoria at upper left, standing Britannia with seated woman at upper center. Printer: Wm. Brown & Co.	—	—	—
S210	**50 Dollars**			
	23.5.1875. Black on blue underprint. Various portrait frame with Queen Victoria at upper left, standing Britannia with seated woman at upper center.	—	—	—

1879 ISSUE

		Good	Fine	XF
S211	**5 Dollars**			
	1.6.1879. Black. Sailing ship at lower left, coin portrait Queen Victoria at upper center, mine head at lower right. Back: Green. Printer: Wm. Brown & Co. Rare.	—	—	—

		Good	Fine	XF
S212	**10 Dollars**			
	1.6.1879. Black. Sailing ship at lower left, coin portrait Queen Victoria at upper center, mine head at lower right. Back: Green. Printer: WM. Brown & Co. Rare.	—	—	—
S213	**20 Dollars**			
	1.6.1879. Black. Sailing ship at lower left, coin portrait Queen Victoria at upper center, mine head at lower right. Back: Green. Printer: WM. Brown & Co. Rare.	—	—	—
S214	**50 Dollars**			
	1.6.1879. Black. Sailing ship at lower left, coin portrait Queen Victoria at upper center, mine head at lower right. Back: Green. Printer: Wm. Brown & Co. Rare.	—	—	—
S215	**100 Dollars**			
	1.6.1879. Black. Sailing ship at lower left, coin portrait Queen Victoria at upper center, mine head at lower right. Back: Green. Printer: Wm. Brown & Co. Rare.	—	—	—

1894 ISSUE

		Good	Fine	XF
S216	**5 Dollars**			
	1.1.1894. Black on yellow and green underprint. Standing Britannia with seated woman at upper center. Back: Green. Serial # printed in very large red numerals. Printer: ABNC.			
	a. Issued note. Rare.	—	—	—
	p. Face and back proofs.	—	Unc	1250.
	s. Specimen.	—	Unc	1500.

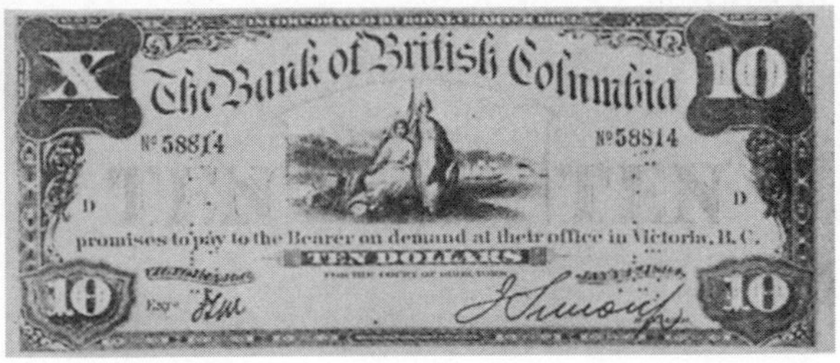

S217 10 Dollars	Good	Fine	XF
1.1.1894. Black on yellow and blue underprint. Standing Britannia with seated woman at upper center. Back: Blue. Serial # printed in very large red numerals. Printer: ABNC.			
a. Issued note. Rare.	—	—	—
p. Face and back proofs.	—	Unc	1250.
s. Specimen.	—	Unc	1500.

S218 20 Dollars	Good	Fine	XF
1.1.1894. Black on yellow and brown underprint. Miners at upper center. Back: Dark brown. Serial # printed in very large red numerals. Printer: ABNC.			
a. Issued note. Rare.	—	—	—
p. Face and back proofs.	—	Unc	1250.
s. Specimen.	—	Unc	1500.

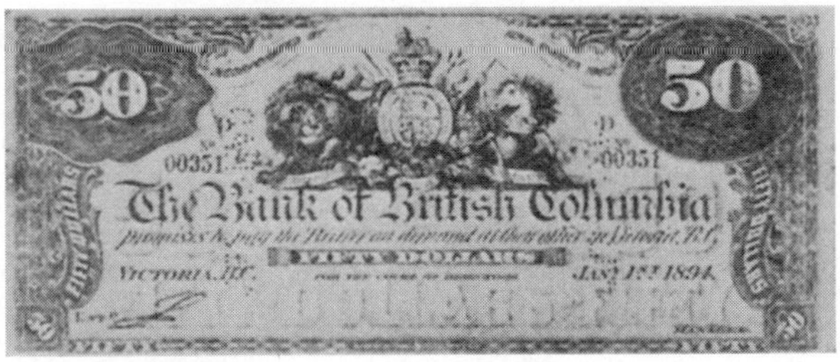

S219 50 Dollars	Good	Fine	XF
1.1.1894. Black on yellow and deep red underprint. Supported royal arms at top center. Back: Brownish red. Serial # printed in very large red numerals. Printer: ABNC.			
a. Issued note. Rare.	—	—	—
p. Face and back proofs.	—	Unc	1250.
s. Specimen.	—	Unc	1500.

Bank of British North America

Brantford

1852-53 Issue

	Good	Fine	XF
S221 4 Dollars = 1 Pound 1.7.1853. Black. Standing Britannia with shield at left, reclining allegory at upper center, seated allegory Commerce at right. Uniface. Printer: PB&P. Proof.	—	Unc	400.
S222 5 Dollars = 1 Pound-5 Shillings 5.7.1852. Black. Green underprint. Sheep and plough at left. Uniface. Printer: PB&P.	150.	600.	—

1871 Issue

	VG	VF	UNC
S226 5 Dollars 29.11.1871. Black. Britannia at lower left. Queen Victoria at lower right. Uniface. Supported royal arms at center. Printer: PBC.	350.	600.	—
S227 10 Dollars 31.1.1871. Black. Supported royal arms at center. Uniface. Printer: PBC. Proof.	—	—	300.
S228 20 Dollars 31.1.1871. Black. Supported royal arms at center. Uniface. Printer: PBC. Proof.	—	—	400.

Canada - East

1852 Issue

	VG	VF	UNC
S231 1 Dollar = 5 Shillings 1.12.1852. Black with red numeral protector. Uniface. Printer: PBC.			
a. Montreal.	500.	1000.	—
b. Quebec. Reported not confirmed.	—	—	—
S232 2 Dollars = 10 Shillings 1.12.1852. Black with red numeral protector. Uniface. Printer: PBC.			
a. Montreal. Black overprint: *BYTOWN* at center.	500.	1000.	—
b. Quebec.	500.	1000.	—

1856 Issue

	VG	VF	UNC
S236 1 Dollar = 5 Shillings 1.1.1856. Black with blue protector on coins. Uniface. Printer: PBC.			
a. Montreal. Blue overprint: *OTTAWA* at center and ends.	500.	1000.	—
b. Quebec. Red overprint: *PAYABLE IN OTTAWA.*	500.	1000.	—
S237 2 Dollars = 10 Shillings 1.1.1856. Black with blue word protector on coins. Uniface. Printer: PBC.			
a. Montreal. Blue overprint: *OTTAWA* at center and ends.	500.	1000.	—
b. Quebec.	500.	1000.	—

Canada - West

1852 Issue

S241 1 Dollar = 5 Shillings	Good	Fine	XF
1.12.1852. Black. Uniface. Printer: PBC.			
a. Brantford.	300.	900.	—
b. Hamilton. Blue numeral on face.	200.	600.	—
c. Blue word on face.	200.	600.	—
d. Toronto. Red numeral on face.	300.	900.	—

1856 Issue

	Good	Fine	XF
S246 1 Dollar = 5 Shillings 1.1.1856. Black with blue word protector. Uniface. Printer: PBC.			
a. Brantford.	300.	900.	—
b. Hamilton.	200.	600.	—
c. Kingston.	200.	600.	—
d. London.	200.	600.	—
e. Toronto.	200.	600.	—
S247 2 Dollars = 10 Shillings 1.1.1856. Black with blue word protector. *2* at upper left and right. Uniface. Printer: PBC.			
a. Brantford.	300.	900.	—
b. Hamilton.	200.	600.	—
c. Kingston.	200.	600.	—
d. Toronto.	200.	600.	—

S248 2 Dollars = 10 Shillings	Good	Fine	XF
ND. Black with blue word protector. Text: *TEN SHILLINGS* at upper left. Uniface. Printer: PBC.			
a. Kingston. Proof.	—	Unc	350.
b. Toronto. Proof.	—	Unc	350.

Fredericton

1847 Issue

	Good	Fine	XF
S251 4 Dollars = 1 Pound 1.9.1847. Black. Britannia at left, beehive at upper center, reclining allegory Commerce at right, supported royal arms at bottom center. Uniface. Printer: PB&P. Proof.	—	Unc	2000.

Halifax

1838 Issue

	Good	Fine	XF
S256 5 Pounds ND (1838). Black. Bank crest at upper center. Uniface. Printer: PB&P. Proof.	—	Unc	500.
S257 7 Pounds-10 Shillings ND (1838). Black. Bank crest at upper center. Uniface. Printer: PB&P. Proof.	—	Unc	500.

1841-72 Issue

	Good	Fine	XF
S259 5 Pounds 18xx. Black. Printer: PBC. Proof.	—	Unc	800.

1865-74 Issue

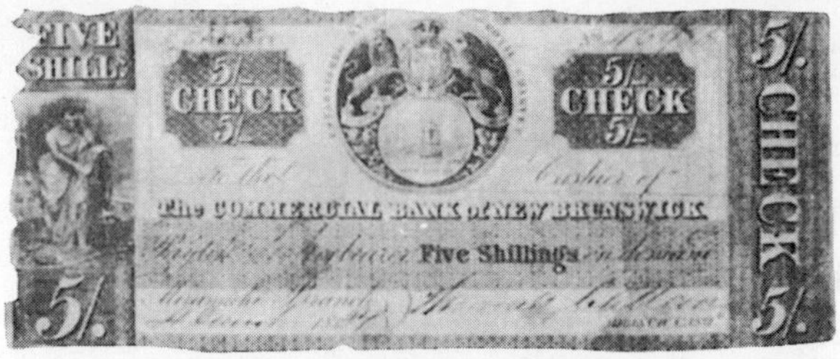

		VG	VF	UNC
S261	**4 Dollars** 1872; 1.12.1874. Balck with green word protector. Uniface. Printer: PBC. Proof.	—	Unc	350.
S262	**5 Dollars** 1870-74. Black with green word protector. Uniface. Printer: PBC.			
	a. Red overprint: *HALIFAX* at left and right and text overprint: *PAYABLE IN DOMINION CURRENCY* across top. 1.7.1871.	600.	1200.	—
	p. Proof. 1.7.1870; 2.1.1871; 1.11.1871; 1.12.1874.	—	Unc	350.
S263	**10 Dollars** 1.7.1870; 1.7.1871; 1.12.1874. Black with green word protector. Uniface. Printer: PBC. Proof.	—	Unc	350.

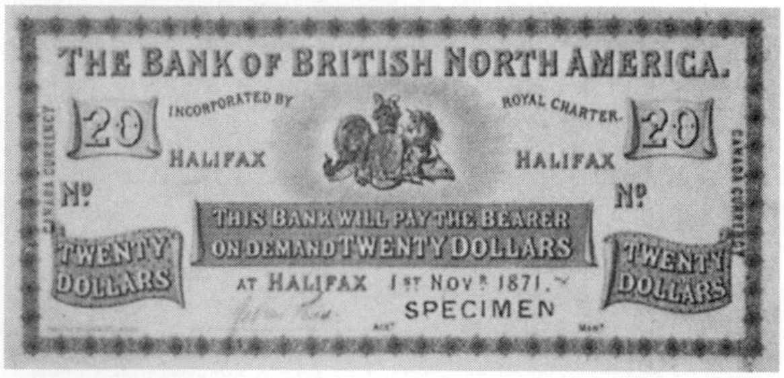

		Good	Fine	XF
S264	**20 Dollars** 24.5.1865; 1.11.1871. Black with green word protector. Supported royal arms at upper center. Uniface. Printer: PBC. Proof.	—	Unc	350.

#S266-S267 *Deleted*. See #S283-S284.

Hamilton

1845-56 Issue

		Good	Fine	XF
S271	**4 Dollars = 1 Pound** 1845-55. Black. Uniface. Printer: PBC.			
	a. 1.11.1845.	200.	600.	—
	b. Green word on face and back. 1.11.1852.	200.	600.	—
	c. Blue word on face with blue overprint: *PARIS*. 1.5.1855.	200.	600.	—
S272	**5 Dollars = 1 Pound-5 Shillings** 1.11.1845; 1.5.1855. Black. Blue word. Uniface. Printer: PBC.	200.	600.	—
S273	**10 Dollars = 2 Pounds-10 Shillings** 1.5.1853. Black. Blue word. Uniface. Printer: PBC.	225.	650.	—
S274	**50 Dollars = 12 Pounds-10 Shillings** 1.3.1856. Black. Blue word. Uniface. Printer: PBC. Proof.	—	Unc	350.

1874-75 Issue

		Good	Fine	XF
S275	**5 Dollars** 1.6.1874; 1.5.1875. Black. Supported royal arms. Uniface. Printer: PBC. Proof.	—	Unc	225.

		VG	VF	UNC
S275A	**10 Dollars** 1.6.1874. Black. Supported royal arms. Uniface. Printer: PBC. Proof.	425.	850.	—

Hamilton / Brantford Agency

1852 Issue

		Good	Fine	XF
S276	**5 Dollars = 25 Shillings** 1.3.1852. Black. Bank crest at left, beehive at upper center, sheep and plow at right, small supported royal arms at bottom center. Uniface. Printer: PBC.	200.	600.	—

Hamilton / Dundas Agency

1852-53 Issue

		Good	Fine	XF
S280	**4 Dollars = 1 Pound** 18xx. Black. Small supported royal arms at bottom center. Uniface. Printer: PBC. Proof.	—	Unc	400.
S281	**5 Dollars = 1 Pound-5 Shillings** 1.3.1852; 1.3.1856. Black. Britannia at left, allegory Commerce in crowned ornate frame at right. Small supported royal arms at bottom center. Uniface. Printer: PBC. Proof.	—	Unc	350.
S282	**10 Dollars = 2 Pounds-10 Shillings** 2.2.1853. Black. Sheep and plow at left, cherubs at upper center, Indian camp at right. Small supported royal arms at bottom center. Uniface. Printer: PBC. Proof.	—	Unc	400.

Hamilton / Simcoe Agency

1845 Issue

		Good	Fine	XF
S283	**4 Dollars = 1 Pound** 1845-48. Black. Seated allegory Agriculture at left, reclining allegorical woman at upper center, seated allegorical woman at right. Small supported royal arms at bottom center. Uniface. Printer: PBC.			
	a. 1.1.1845.	200.	600.	—
	p. 1.1.1848. Proof.	—	Unc	300.
S284	**5 Dollars = 1 Pound-5 Shillings** 1.1.1848. Black. Small supported royal arms at bottom center. Uniface. Printer: PBC. Proof.	—	Unc	300.

#S286 and S287 *Deleted*. See #S275-S275A.

Kingston

1840s-1853 Issue

		Good	Fine	XF
S291	**4 Dollars** 184x-1853. Black. Seated Indian at Commerce at upper center, seated woman at right. Uniface. Printer: PBC.			
	a. 1.2.1852.	200.	650.	—
	c. Green underprint. 1.7.1853.	200.	650.	—
	p. Proof. 184x.	—	Unc	300.
	r. Remainder. 1.7.1853.	—	Unc	300.
S292	**5 Dollars** 184x-1852. Black. Queen Victoria, allegorical women, Indian. Uniface. Printer: PBC.			
	a. 4.8.1852.	200.	650.	—
	p. Proof. 184x.	—	Unc	300.
S293	**10 Dollars** 184x. Harbor scene, allegorical women, bank crest. Proof.	—	Unc	325.

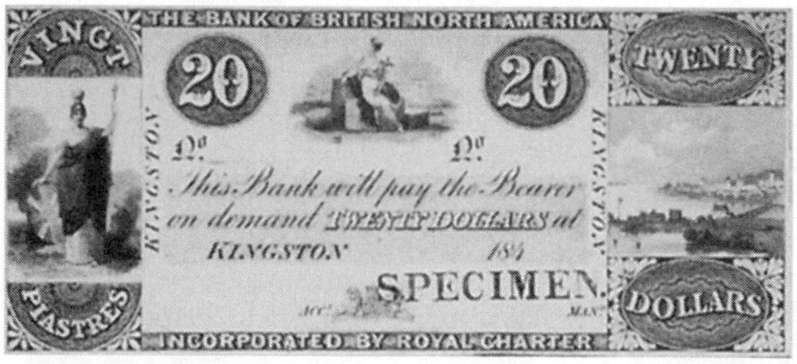

		Good	Fine	XF
S294	**20 Dollars** Black. Britannia at left, Commerce seated at upper center, harbor scene at right. Uniface. Printer: PBC. Proof.	—	Unc	400.
S295	**50 Dollars** 184x. Black. Commerce, Britannia, Agriculture. Uniface. Printer: PBC. Proof.	—	Unc	475.

1872; 1875 Issue

		VG	VF	UNC
S296	**4 Dollars** 4.5.1872. Black. Justice at left, supported royal arms at center, woman with sheaf and sickle at right. Uniface. Printer: PBC.	425.	850.	—

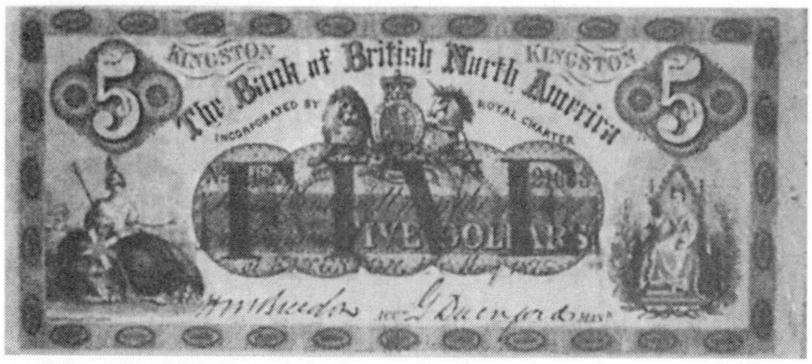

		Good	Fine	XF
S297	**5 Dollars** 1.5.1875. Black. Britannia seated at left, supported royal arms at upper center, Victoria seated at right. Uniface. Printer: PBC.			
	p. Proof.	—	Unc	225.
	x. Counterfeit with engraved signature	—	—	—
S298	**10 Dollars** 6.5.1872. Black. Supported royal arms at upper center. Uniface. Printer: PBC. Proof.	—	Unc	245.

London

1854-56 Issue

		Good	Fine	XF
S301	**4 Dollars = 1 Pound** 1854-56. Black with blue word protector. Seated Britannia with lion at left, bank crest at center, seated allegory Justice at right. Uniface. Supported royal arms at bottom center. Printer: PBC.			
	a. Red overprint: *NAPANEE*. 1.1.1856.	200.	650.	—
	p. Proof. 1.3.1854.	—	Unc	150.
S302	**5 Dollars = 25 Shillings** 1.3.1854. Black with blue word protector. Sheep and plow at left, three seated allegories at upper center, seated Britannia at right. Uniface. Supported royal arms at bottom center. Printer: PBC.	200.	650.	—
S303	**10 Dollars = 50 Shillings** 1.3.1854. Black with blue word protector. Agriculture, seated Agriculture, seated woman with harp. Supported royal arms at bottom center. Uniface. Printer: PBC. Proof.	—	Unc	175.

1866-75 Issue

S305 4 Dollars — Good — Fine — XF
3.8.1875. Black. Justice at left, supported royal arms at center, woman with sheaf and sickle at right. Uniface. Printer: PBC. Proof. — Unc 275.

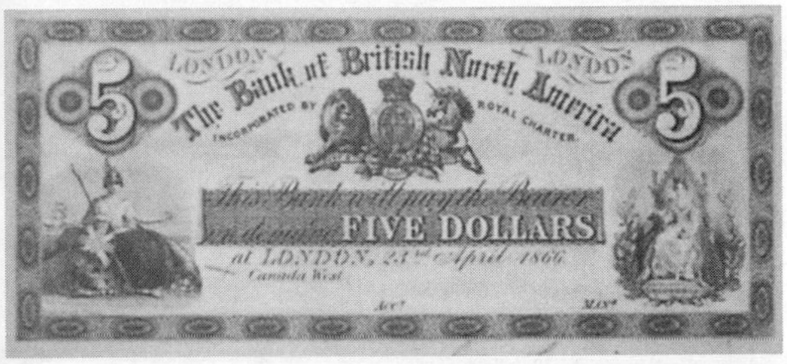

S306 5 Dollars — VG — VF — UNC
1866-75. Black. Britannia seated at left, supported royal arms at upper center, Victoria seated at right. Uniface. Printer: PBC.
- a. 3.8.1875. — 350. 625. —
- p1. Proof. 23.4.1866. — — Unc 225.
- p2. Proof. 1.8.1872. — — Unc 225.

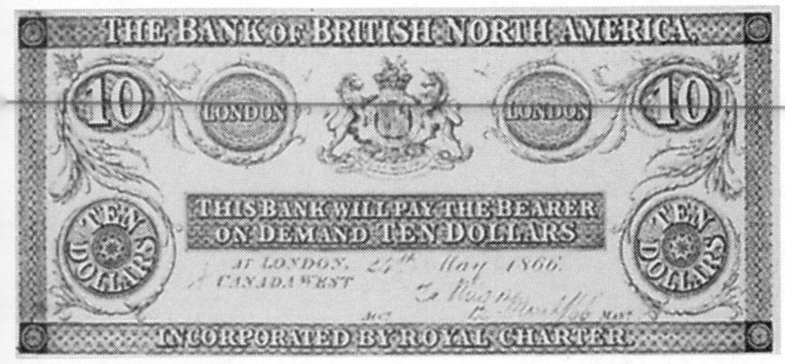

S307 10 Dollars — Good — Fine — XF
24.5.1866. Black. Supported royal arms at upper center. Uniface. Printer: PBC. Proof. — — Unc 250.

S308 20 Dollars
3.8.1875. Black. Supported royal arms at upper center. Uniface. Printer: PBC. Proof. — — Unc 325.

Montreal

1838 Issue

S311 1 Dollar — Good — Fine — XF
1.9.1838. Black. Bank crest at center. Uniface. Printer: PBC. — 125. 400. 1100.

S312 10 Dollars
18xx. Black. Bank crest at center. Uniface. Printer: PBC. Proof. — — Unc 400.

S313 50 Dollars
ND (1838). Black. Bank crest at center. Uniface. Printer: PBC. Proof. — — Unc 400.

1841-54 Issue

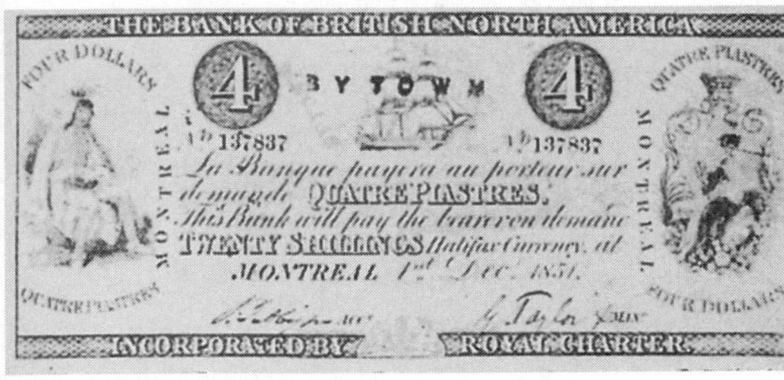

S316 4 Dollars = 20 Shillings — Good — Fine — XF
1841-52. Black. Seated Indian at left, sailing ship at upper center, seated allegory Commerce in crowned ornate frame at right. Small supported royal arms at bottom center. Uniface. Printer: PBC.
- a. Black and red overprint: *BYTOWN* and *PARIS*. 1.1.1841-1.1.1847. — 200. 650. —
- b. Black and red overprint: *BYTOWN* and *PARIS*. 1.12.1851. — 200. 650. —
- c. Green word on face and black. Black and red overprint: *BYTOWN* and *PARIS*. 1.12.1852. — — — —

S317 5 Dollars = 1 Pound-5 Shillings
1841-54. Black. Brock's monument at left, sailing ship upper center, seated Queen Victoria at right. Small supported royal arms at bottom center. Uniface. Printer: PBC.
- a. 1.1.1841. — 200. 650. —
- b. Green word on face and back. 21.1.1854. — 200. 650. —

S318 10 Dollars = 2 Pounds-10 Shillings
184x. Black. Indian camp at left, allegory Commerce at upper center, harbor scene at right. Small supported royal arms at bottom center. Uniface. Printer: PBC. — — Unc 250.

S319 20 Dollars = 5 Pounds
184x. Black. View of Montreal at left, three allegorical women at upper center, monument and houses at right. Small supported royal arms at bottom center. Uniface. Printer: PBC. Proof. — — Unc 275.

S320 50 Dollars = 12 Pounds-10 Shillings
184x. Black. Bank crest at left, steamship at upper center, monument and houses in Montreal at right. Small supported royal arms at bottom center. Uniface. Printer: PBC. Proof. — — Unc 300.

1865-73 Issue

S321 4 Dollars — VG — VF — UNC
1.12.1873. Black. Uniface. Printer: PBC. — 425. 850. —

S322 5 Dollars — Good — Fine — XF
1.8.1870; 8.4.1872. Black. Seated Britannia at lower left, supported royal arms at upper center, Queen Victoria on throne at lower right. Uniface. Printer: PBC. Proof. — — Unc 200.

S323 10 Dollars — VG — VF — UNC
1865-70. Black. Supported royal arms at upper center. Uniface. Printer: PBC.
- a. 1.8.1870. — 425. 850. —
- p. Proof. 30.11.1865. — — — 250.

S324 20 Dollars
1.12.1865. Black. Sheep, beehive and tools at upper center. Uniface. Printer: PBC. Proof. — — — 300.

S325 50 Dollars
1.1.1866. Black. Standing woman with lute at left, supported royal arms at upper center, seated allegorical woman at right. Uniface. Printer: PBC. Proof. — — — 325.

Ottawa

1863-73 Issue

S326 4 Dollars — VG — VF — UNC
1871-73. Black. Portrait seated Justice at lower left, supported arms at upper center, portrait woman lower right. Uniface. Printer: PBC.
- a. Blue overprint: *ARNPRIOR* at left and right. 1.12.1873. — 425. 850. —
- p. Proof. 1.12.1871. — — — 275.

S327 5 Dollars
10.8.1866; 31.1.1871; 1.5.1872. Black. Uniface. Printer: PBC. Proof. — — — 225.

S328 10 Dollars
1.9.1865; 31.1.1871. Black. Uniface. Printer: PBC. Proof. — — — 250.

S329 20 Dollars
31.1.1871. Black. Supported royal arms. Uniface. Printer: PBC. Proof. — — — 325.

Quebec

1838 Issue

S331 1 Dollar — Good — Fine — XF
1.9.1838. Black. Bank crest at upper center. Uniface. Printer: PB&P. — 125. 450. 750.

S332 10 Dollars
18xx. Black. Bank crest at upper center. Uniface. Printer: PB&P. Proof. — — Unc 600.

1841-53 Issue

S336 4 Dollars = 20 Shillings — Good — Fine — XF
1.1.1853. Black. Seated allegory Commerce in crowned ornate frame at left, seated Indian at right. Small supported royal arms at bottom center. Uniface. Printer: PB&P.
- a. Issued note. — 200. 600. —
- p. Proof. 18xx. — — Unc 150.

S337 5 Dollars = 1 Pound-5 Shillings
1.1.1841. Black. Seated Queen Victoria at left, seated allegorical woman with sickle at right. Small supported royal arms at bottom center. Uniface. Printer: PB&P. — 200. 600. —

S338 10 Dollars = 2 Pounds-10 Shillings
1.1.1841. Black. Sheep and plow at left, sailing ship at right. Small supported royal arms at bottom center. Uniface. Printer: PB&P. — 200. 600. —

1871 Issue

S341 4 Dollars — Good — Fine — XF
22.11.1871. Black. Small supported royal arms at bottom center. Uniface. Printer: PBC. — 200. 550. —

St. John, New Brunswick

1837 Issue

S346 1 Dollar = 5 Shillings — Good — Fine — XF
1.7.1837. Black. Bank crest at upper center. Uniface. Printer: PB&P. — 200. 650. —

S347 2 Dollars = 10 Shillings
ND (1837). Black. Bank crest at upper center. Uniface. Printer: PB&P. Proof. — — Unc 350.

1853-71 Issue

S351 1 Dollar = 5 Shillings — VG — VF — UNC
1854-62. Black with green word protector. Seated Justice at left, bank crest at upper center, seated Commerce with lute at right. Small supported royal arms at bottom center. Uniface. Printer: PBC.
- a. Issued note. 1.12.1859; 1.12.1862. — 425. 900. —
- p. Proof. 2.1.1854. — — — 350.

	VG	VF	UNC
S352 2 Dollars = 10 Shillings			
1.2.1854. Black with green word protector. Seated Britannia at left, small seated allegory Commerce at upper center, Commerce, Britannia and Agriculture in circles at right. Small supported royal arms at bottom center. Uniface. Printer: PBC.	425.	900.	—
S353 4 Dollars = 1 Pound			
1.1.1853; 1.2.1871. Black with green word protector. Bank crest at left, sailing ship at upper center, standing allegorical woman with anchor by beehive at right. Small supported royal arms at bottom center. Uniface. Printer: PBC. Proof.	—	—	350.

NOTE: Counterfeit dated 1846 exists.

	VG	VF	UNC
S354 5 Dollars = 1 Pound-5 Shillings			
1862; 1869. Black with green word protector. Bank crest at left, sailing ship at upper center, standing allegorical woman with anchor by beehive at right. Small supported royal arms at bottom center. Uniface. Overprint: Red: *V V*. Printer: PBC.			
a. Issued note. 1.12.1862.	425.	900.	—
p. Proof. 1.9.1869.	—	—	350.
S355 20 Dollars = 5 Pounds			
18xx. Black with green word protector. Portrait Queen Victoria at left, two allegorical women at upper center, reclining allegorical woman with sailing ship in background at right. Small supported royal arms at bottom center. Uniface. Printer: PBC. Proof.	—	—	350.
S356 40 Dollars = 10 Pounds			
18xx. Black with green word protector. Portrait Queen Victoria at left, bank crest at upper center. Small supported royal arms at bottom center. Uniface. Printer: PBC. Proof.	—	—	350.

1866; 1868 Issue

	VG	VF	UNC
S361 1 Dollar			
31.8.1866; 1.12.1868. Black with green word protector. Without frame. Back: Black with green word protector. Overprint: Red *S*. Printer: PBC.	500.	1000.	—
S362 2 Dollars			
1.12.1868. Black with green word protector. Without frame. Back: Black with green word protector. Overprint: Red *S*. Printer: PBC.	500.	1000.	—

1866-72 Issue

	VG	VF	UNC
S366 4 Dollars			
1871-72. Black. Uniface. Printer: PBC.			
a. Blue overprint: *FREDERICTON* at left and right and blue overprint: *MONCTON* across center 31.5.1872.	600.	1400.	—
p. Proof. 31.5.1871.	—	—	350.
S367 5 Dollars			
1.5.1871; 1.5.1872. Black. Uniface. Printer: PBC. Proof.	—	—	265.
S368 10 Dollars			
1.1.1870; 18.6.1872. Black. Uniface. Printer: PBC. Proof.	—	—	300.
S369 20 Dollars			
29.4.1871; 29.4.1872. Black. Supported royal arms. Uniface. Printer: PBC. Proof.	—	—	325.
S370 50 Dollars			
1.9.1866; 1.1.1870. Black. Uniface. Printer: PBC. Proof.	—	—	350.

St. John, Newfoundland

1837-47 Issue

	Good	Fine	XF
S371 1 Pound			
20.3.1837. Black. Bank crest at upper center. Uniface. Printer: PB&P.	450.	1400.	—
S372 5 Pounds			
1.7.1847. Black. Bank crest at upper center. Uniface. Printer: PB&P. Proof.	—	Unc	425.

St. Stephen

1872 Issue

	Good	Fine	XF
S376 4 Dollars = 1 Pound			
12.8.1872. Black. Bank crest at left, sailing ship at upper center, standing allegorical woman with anchor by beehive at right, small supported royal arms at bottom center. Uniface. Printer: PBC. Proof.	—	Unc	350.

Toronto

1840s Dollar Issue

	Good	Fine	XF
S381 4 Dollars			
184x. Black. Uniface. Printer: PBC. Proof.	—	Unc	275.
S382 5 Dollars			
184x. Black. Uniface. Printer: PBC. Proof.	—	Unc	275.
S383 10 Dollars			
184x. Black. Uniface. Printer: PBC. Proof.	—	Unc	275.
S384 20 Dollars			
184x. Black. Uniface. Printer: PBC. Proof.	—	Unc	275.
S385 50 Dollars			
184x. Black. Uniface. Printer: PBC. Proof.	—	Unc	275.

1846-65 Dollar / Pound Issue

	VG	VF	UNC
S386 4 Dollars = 1 Pound			
1846-52. Seated Commerce at left, bank crest at right. Printer: PBC.			
a. 1.11.1852.	425.	850.	—
p. Proof. 1.1.1846.	—	—	250.

	VG	VF	UNC
S387 5 Dollars = 1 Pound-5 Shillings = 25 Shillings			
1.1.1846. Mountains, village at left, seated Commerce in crowned ornate frame at right. Printer: PBC.	—	—	250.
S387A 5 Dollars = 25 Shillings			
4.1.1865. Mountains, village at left, seated Commerce in crowned ornate frame at right. Printer: PBC. Proof.	—	—	280.
S388 10 Dollars = 50 Shillings			
1864. Printer: PBC.	425.	850.	—

1864-71 Issue

	VG	VF	UNC
S390 3 Dollars			
8.12.1871. Black. Seated Justice at lower left, supported royal arms at upper center, allegorical woman with sheaf and sickle at lower right. Uniface. Printer: PBC.			
a. Issued note.	—	—	—
p. Proof.	—	—	275.
S391 5 Dollars			
1865-71. Black. Seated Britannia with lion at lower left, supported royal arms at upper center, seated Queen Victoria at lower right. Uniface. Printer: PBC.			
a. Blue vertical overprint: *DUNNVILLE* at left and right 4.1.1865.	325.	700.	—
p. Proof. 31.1.1871.	—	—	225.
S392 10 Dollars			
1864-71. Black. Supported royal arms at upper center. Uniface. Printer: PBC.			
a. 23.4.1864.	425.	850.	—
p. Proof. 1.1.1871.	—	—	250.
S393 20 Dollars			
31.1.1871. Black. Supported royal arms at upper center. Uniface. Printer: PBC. Proof.	—	—	250.

Victoria

1859-67 Issue

	Good	Fine	XF
S396 1 Dollar			
1859-67. Black with green word protector. Portrait Queen Victoria at lower left, seated Britannia at upper center. Without frame. Uniface. Back: Black with green word protector. Printer: PBC.			
a. 1.12.1859.	100.	250.	—
p1. Proof. 18xx.	—	Unc	350.
p2. Proof. 2.12.1867.	—	Unc	350.
s. Specimen. 1.12.1859.	—	Unc	200.
S397 2 Dollars			
2.1.1860. Black with gree word protector. Seated Indian at left, seated Commerce at upper center, standing Britannia with shield at right. Without frame. Uniface. Back: Black with green word protector. Printer: PBC. Proof.			
a. Issued note.	—	—	—
p. Proof.	—	Unc	200.

1859-68 Issue

	Good	Fine	XF
S401 5 Dollars			
1859-67. Black. Seated Britannia with lion at lower left, supported royal arms at upper center, seated Queen Victoria at lower right. Uniface. Printer: PBC.			
a. Issued note. 1859.	—	—	—
p. Proof. 23.4.1867.	—	Unc	250.
s. Specimen. 27.9.1859.	—	Unc	650.
S402 10 Dollars			
1860-67. Black. Supported royal arms at upper center. Uniface. Printer: PBC.			
a. Issued note. 3.2.1860.	—	—	—
p. Proof. 23.4.1867; 16.10.1873.	—	Unc	250.
s. Specimen. 3.2.1860.	—	Unc	250.
S403 20 Dollars			
5.3.1860. Black. Sheep, beehive and tools at upper center. Uniface. Printer: PBC. Specimen.			
a. Issued note. 5.3.1860.	—	—	—
s. Specimen. 1.1.1868.	—	Unc	650.
S404 20 Dollars			
1.1.1868. Black. Supported royal at upper center. Uniface. Printer: PBC. Proof.	—	Unc	250.

1861-72 Issue

	Good	Fine	XF
S406 100 Dollars			
1861-72. Black. Cherubs at lower left and lower right, supported royal arms at center. Branch name to be filled in. Uniface. Printer: PBC.			
a. 1.8.1861; 15.8.1865.	—	Unc	475.
b. 5.9.1861; 22.1.1871.	—	Unc	475.
p1. Proof. 22.11.1866.	—	Unc	275.
p2. Proof. 15.4.1872.	—	Unc	300.
s. Specimen. 15.8.1861.	—	Unc	500.
S407 500 Dollars			
1.8.1861; 15.8.1861; 5.9.1961. Black. Seated allegory with caduceus at left and right, supported royal arms at center. Branch name to be filled in. Uniface. Printer: PBC. Proof.	—	Unc	850.

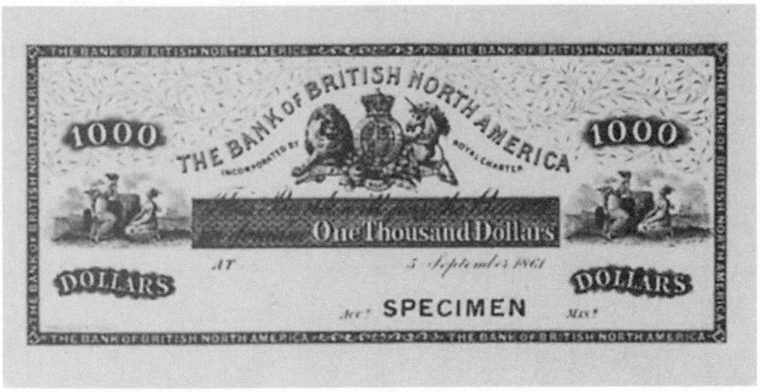

S408 1000 Dollars	Good	Fine	XF
1.8.1861; 15.8.1861; 5.9.1861. Black. Seated and kneeling allegorical woman at left and right, supported royal arms at upper center. Branch name to be filled in. Uniface. Printer: PBC. Proof.	—	Unc	1250.

MONTREAL

1876-77 ISSUE

	VG	VF	UNC
S411 4 Dollars 3.7.1877. Black on green underprint. Seated Britannia with lion at lower left, supported royal arms at center, seated Queen Victoria at lower right. Signature varieties. Back: Green. Printer: BABNC.	700.	1750.	—
S412 5 Dollars 3.7.1877. Black on green underprint. Seated Britannia with lion at lower left, supported royal arms at center, seated Queen Victoria at lower right. Signature varieties. Back: Green. Printer: BABNC.	350.	700.	—

NOTE: Counterfeits abundant.

	VG	VF	UNC
S413 10 Dollars 1876-77. Seated Britannia with lion at lower left, supported royal arms at center, seated Queen Victoria at lower right. Signature varieties. Back: Green. Printer: BABNC.			
a. Black on green underprint. 3.7.1877.	500.	1000.	—
b. Blue on reddish brown underprint. 3.7.1877.	550.	1250.	—
p. Proof. 1.7.1876.	—	—	350.
S414 20 Dollars 3.7.1877. Black on green underprint. Seated Britannia with lion at lower left, supported royal arms at center, seated Queen Victoria at lower right. Signature varieties. Back: Green. Printer: BABNC.	500.	1000.	—
S415 50 Dollars 3.7.1877. Black on greenunderprint. Seated Britannia with lion at lower left, supported royal arms at center, seated Queen Victoria at lower right. Signature varieties. Back: Green. Printer: BABNC.	1250.	2500.	—
S416 100 Dollars 3.7.1877. Black on green underprint. Seated Britannia with lion at lower left, supported royal arms at center, seated Queen Victoria at lower right. Signature varieties. Back: Green. Printer: BABNC.	1250.	2500.	—

1884 ISSUE

S421 5 Dollars	VG	VF	UNC
1.5.1884. Blue on orange underprint. Portrait elderly Queen Victoria at center. Back: Black. Printer: PBC.	1250.	2500.	—

1886; 1889 ISSUE

S426 5 Dollars	Good	Fine	XF
28.5.1886. Black on green underprint. Portrait Prince of Wales at lower left, bank crest at center, portrait elderly Queen Victoria at lower right. Signature varieties. Back: Green. Bank crest at center. Printer: BABNC.			
a. Handsigned at right.	25.00	100.	250.
b. Printed signature at right.	25.00	100.	250.

S427 10 Dollars	Good	Fine	XF
3.7.1889. Black on green underprint. Portrait elderly Queen Victoria at center. Signature varieties. Back: Green. Bank crest at center. Printer: BABNC.			
a. Handsigned at right.	50.00	200.	400.
b. Printed signature at right.	50.00	200.	400.

1911 ISSUE

S431 5 Dollars	Good	Fine	XF
3.7.1911. Black on green underprint. Royal crest at left, portrait King George V at lower center, Canadian crest at right. Signature varieties. Back: Green. Large bank arms at center. Printer: W&S.			
a. Signature Stikeman at right.	75.00	300.	600.
b. Signature Mackenzie at right.	75.00	300.	600.

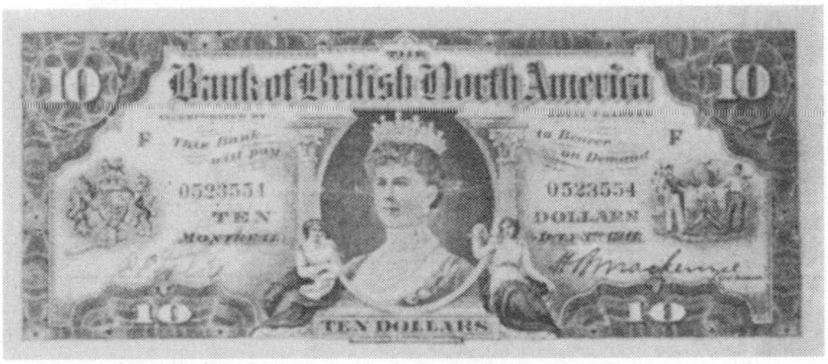

S432 10 Dollars	Good	Fine	XF
3.7.1911. Black on blue-green underprint. Supported royal arms at left, portrait Queen Mary at center, bank crest at right. Signature varieties. Back: Blue. Large bank arms at center. Printer: W&S.			
a. Signature Stikeman at right.	75.00	300.	600.
b. Signature Mackenzie at right.	75.00	300.	600.

	Good	Fine	XF
S433 20 Dollars 3.7.1911. Black on red-orange underprint. Royal crest at left, portrait King Edward VII at center, Canadian crest at right. Signature varieties. Back: Carmine. Large bank arms at center. Printer: W&S.			
a. Signature Mackenzie at right.	450.	900.	—
s. Signature Stikeman at right. Specimen.	—	Unc	500.
S434 50 Dollars 3.7.1911. Black on lilac underprint. Portrait Queen Alexandra at bottom center. Signature varieties. Back: Purple. Large bank arms at center. Printer: W&S.			
a. Signature Mackenzie at right.	450.	900.	—
s1. Signature Stikeman at right. Specimen.	—	Unc	500.
s2. Signature Mackenzie at right. Specimen.	—	Unc	500.
S435 100 Dollars 3.7.1911. Orange. Royal crest at left, portrait Queen Victoria at center, bank crest at right. Signature varieties. Back: Brown. Large bank arms at center. Printer: W&S.			
a. Signature Mackenzie at right.	650.	1500.	—
s. Signature Mackenzie at right. Specimen.	—	Unc	750.

NOTE: Specimen notes from salesman's sample books exist in other colors than noted above.

Bank of Hamilton

1872-73 Issue

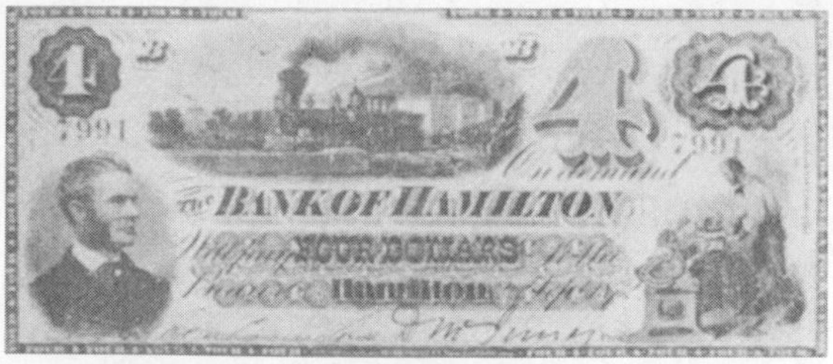

		VG	VF	UNC
S441	**4 Dollars** 1.9.1872; 2.9.1872. Black on green underprint. D. McInnes at lower left, steam passenger train at top left center, machinist at lathe at lower right. Back: Green. Hamilton City crest at center. Printer: BABNC.	1250.	2500.	—
S442	**5 Dollars** 1.9.1872; 2.9.1872. Black on green underprint. D. McInnes at lower left, blacksmith and woman with Large ornate *5* at right. Back: Green. Hamilton City crest at center. Printer: BABNC.	1250.	2500.	—
S443	**10 Dollars** 1.9.1872; 2.9.1872. Black on green underprint. Two allegorical women seated with Large ornate *X* at left, D. McInnes at upper center right. Back: Green. Hamilton City crest at center. Printer: BABNC.	1250.	2500.	—
S444	**20 Dollars** 2.1.1873. Black on green underprint. D. McInnes at left, seated allegorical woman at right. Back: Green. Hamilton City crest at center. Printer: BABNC. Proof.	—	—	500.
S445	**50 Dollars** 2.1.1873. Black on green underprint. D. McInnes at upper left, milkmaid with cows at lower right. Back: Green. Hamilton City crest at center. Printer: BABNC. Proof.	—	—	500.
S446	**100 Dollars** 2.1.1873. Black on green underprint. D. McInnes at upper center. Back: Green. Hamilton City crest at center. Printer: BABNC. Proof.	—	—	500.

1887 Issue

		VG	VF	UNC
S447	**5 Dollars** 1.3.1887. Black on green underprint. J. Stuart at left, workers, factories at right. Back: Green. Hamilton City crest at center. Printer: BABNC. Proof.	—	—	500.

		VG	VF	UNC
S448	**5 Dollars** 1.12.1887. Black. Portrait J. Stuart at left, view overlooking Hamilton at center. Back: Green. Hamilton City crest at center. Printer: CABNC.			
	a. Issued note with ochre underprint.	1250.	2500.	—
	p1. Face proof with blue underprint.	—	—	500.
	p2. Face proof with green underprint.	—	—	500.
	p3. Back proof blue.	—	—	—

1892 Issue

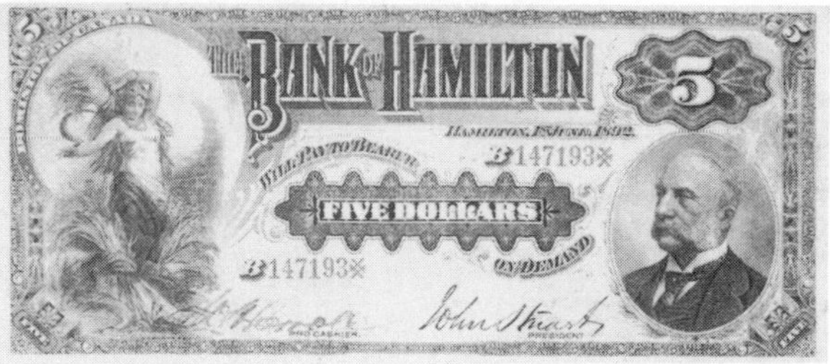

		Good	Fine	XF
S451	**5 Dollars** 1.6.1892. Black on green underprint. Agriculture at left, portrait J. Stuart at lower right. Back: Green. Head office building at center. Printer: Western Bank Note Co., Chicago.	300.	600.	1000.
S452	**10 Dollars** 1.6.1892. Black on green underprint. Horseshoe and Niagara Falls at upper center, Commerce at right. Back: Red-brown. Head office building at center. Printer: Western Bank Note Co., Chicago.	125.	500.	—

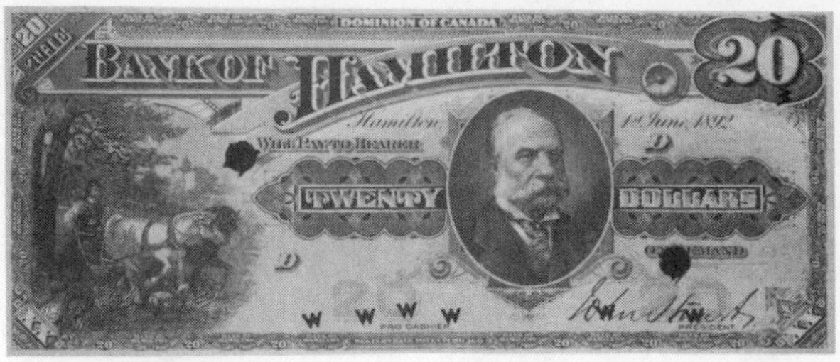

		Good	Fine	XF
S453	**20 Dollars** 1.6.1892. Black on ochre underprint. Farmer plowing with horses at lower left, portrait J. Stuart at center right. Back: Brown. Stag's head at center. Printer: Western Bank Note Co., Chicago. Proof, punched hole cancelled.	—	Unc	650.
S454	**50 Dollars** 1.6.1892. Black on olive-green underprint. Portrait J. Stuart at upper left, tugboat at center. Back: Olive-green. Indians hunting buffalo at center. Printer: Western Bank Note Co., Chicago. Specimen.	—	Unc	1000.
S455	**100 Dollars** 1.6.1892. Black on red-brown underprint. Steam passenger train at left center, J. Stuart at lower right. Back: Dull red. Printer: Western Bank Note Co., Chicago. Specimen.	—	Unc	1000.

1904 Issue

		VG	VF	UNC
S456	**5 Dollars** 2.1.1904. Black on green underprint. Seated Queen Alexandra with cherubs at left. Back: Green. Printer: Western Bank Note Company, Chicago.	450.	—	—
S457	**10 Dollars** 2.1.1904. Black on orange underprint. Seated Queen Alexandra with cherubs at left center. Back: Orange. Printer: Western Bank Note Company, Chicago.	1000.	—	—
S458	**20 Dollars** 2.1.1904. Black on olive underprint. King Edward VII at lower center. Back: Brown. Printer: Western Bank Note Company, Chicago.	1250.	—	—
S459	**50 Dollars** 2.1.1904. Black on blue underprint. Seated Queen Alexandra with cherubs at lower right. Back: Blue. Printer: Western Bank Note Company, Chicago.	2000.	—	—
S460	**100 Dollars** 2.1.1904. Brown. King Edward VII at lower left. Printer: Western Bank Note Company, Chicago.	3250.	—	—

1909-14 Issue

#S461-S465 red ovpt: *E E* or *S S* on 1909 issue; *C C* or *E E* on 1914 issue.

		Good	Fine	XF
S461	**5 Dollars** 1909; 1914. Black on green underprint. Reclining Britannia, Agriculture and Industry at center. Back: Green. Overprint: Red: *E E* or *S S* on 1909 issue; *C C* or *E E* on 1914 issue. Printer: ABNC.			
	a. 1.6.1909.	50.00	150.	400.
	b. 1.6.1914.	25.00	100.	250.

		Good	Fine	XF
S462	**10 Dollars** 1.6.1909; 1.6.1914. Black on brown and yellow underprint. Seated allegorical woman between agriculture and industrial backgrounds at left center. Back: Brown. Overprint: Red: *E E* or *S S* on 1909 issue; *C C* or *E E* on 1914 issue. Printer: ABNC.	50.00	175.	500.
S463	**20 Dollars** 1909; 1914. Black on blue underprint. Reclining Britannia as #S461 at center right. Back: Slate gray. Overprint: Red: *E E* or *S S* on 1909 issue; *C C* or *E E* on 1914 issue. Printer: ABNC.			
	a. 1.6.1914.	75.00	300.	—
	s. Specimen. 1.6.1909.	—	Unc	550.

		Good	Fine	XF
S464	**50 Dollars** 1909-14. Black on red underprint. Seated allegorical woman as at #S462 at center. Back: Red-orange. Bust of woman at center. Overprint: Red: *E E* or *S S* on 1909 issue; *C C* or *E E* on 1914 issue. Printer: ABNC.			
	a. 1.6.1914.	125.	525.	—
	p. Proof. 1.6.1909.	—	Unc	350.
S465	**100 Dollars** 1.6.1909; 1.6.1914. Black on olive-green underprint. Reclining Britannia as #S461 at left center. Overprint: Red: *E E* or *S S* on 1909 issue; *C C* or *E E* on 1914 issue. Printer: ABNC.	425.	1750.	—

1922 Jubilee Issue

#S466-S468, 50th Anniversary of the Bank

		Good	Fine	XF
S466	**5 Dollars** 1.3.1922. Black on green underprint. Reclining Britannia as #S461 at center. Back: Green. Printer: ABNC.	125.	525.	1250.
S467	**10 Dollars** 1.3.1922. Black on orange underprint. Seated allegorical woman as #S462 at center. Back: Orange. Printer: ABNC.	125.	400.	1000.

		Good	Fine	XF
S468	**25 Dollars** 1.3.1922. Black on multicolor underprint. Two allegorical women at left. Back: Purple. Printer: ABNC.			
	a. Issued note.	750.	2500.	4500.
	p. Face and back proofs.	—	Unc	1250.

NOTE: While #S466-S468 constitute the 1922 Jubilee issue, only #S468 shows commemorative text *JUBILEE ISSUE* on face.

Bank of Montreal

1820s Issue

		Good	Fine	XF
S471	**1 Dollar** 1.8.1823-1.5.1825. Black. Seated Britannia, sailing ship at upper center. Uniface. Printer: Graphic.	400.	1250.	—
S472	**2 Dollars** 1.12.1826. Black. Seated Britannia and Indian at upper center. Uniface. Printer: Graphic.	400.	1250.	—
S473	**5 Dollars** 18xx. Black. Seated woman and sailing ship at upper center. Uniface. Printer: Graphic. Proof.	—	Unc	500.

1830-35 Issue

		Good	Fine	XF
S474	**1 Dollar** 1.7.1831. Black. Indian with ornate *ONE* at top center above child's head. Sir W. Raleigh at right. Uniface. Signature varieties. Printer: Fairman, Draper and Underwood.			
	a. *MONTREAL* at lower right.	400.	1250.	—
	b. Text: *PAYABLE AT QUEBEC* at top.	400.	1250.	—
S474A	**2 Dollars = 10 Shillings** 1.6.183x. Black. Woman in ornate *Z* at upper center, two coins below, standing Justice at upper right. Text: *PAYABLE AT QUEBEC*. Uniface. Signature varieties. Printer: Fairman, Draper and Underwood. Proof.	—	Unc	500.
S474B	**5 Dollars = 1 Pound-5 Shillings** 1.6.183x. Black. Portrait C. Columbus at left, two allegorical women, child and eagle in ornate *5* at upper center, bird below. Text: *PAYABLE AT QUEBEC*. Uniface. Signature varieties. Printer: Fairman, Draper and Underwood. Proof.	—	Unc	500.
S475	**10 Dollars = 2 Pounds-10 Shillings** 1.6.1835. Black. Seated allegorical woman at upper center, man's head in circular frame below, ornate 10's in all four corners. Uniface. Signature varieties. Printer: Fairman, Draper and Underwood.			
	a. *MONTREAL* at lower left.	400.	1250.	—
	b. Text: *PAYABLE AT QUEBEC* at top.	400.	1250.	—

1835-37 Issue

		Good	Fine	XF
S476	**1 Dollar = 5 Shillings** 1.1.1835-1.1.1837. Black. Two with livestock at left, portrait King William IV at upper center, St. George slaying dragon at upper right. Uniface. Signature varieties. Printer: RWH & C.			
	a. *MONTREAL* engraved. Black stamp: *PAYABLE AT QUEBEC*.	300.	1000.	—
	b. Stamp: *PAYABLE AT QUEBEC*. 18xx.	300.	1000.	—
	c. Text: *PAYABLE AT QUEBEC* engraved. 18xx.	300.	1000.	—
S477	**2 Dollars = 10 Shillings** 3.6.1837. Black. Indian woman at upper left, sailing ships at upper center, Indian brave aiming bow and arrow at upper right. Uniface. Signature varieties. Printer: RWH & C.			
	a. *MONTREAL* engraved. Black stamp: *PAYABLE AT AT QUEBEC*.	300.	1000.	—
	b. Stamp: *PAYABLE AT QUEBEC*. 18xx.	300.	1000.	—
	c. Text: *PAYABLE AT QUEBEC* engraved. 18xx.	300.	1250.	—
S478	**5 Dollars = 1 Pound-5 Shillings** 18xx. Black. Reclining Greek god by fountain at center above lion on crown. *MONTREAL* engraved. Uniface. Signature varieties. Printer: RWH & C. Proof.	—	Unc	500.
S479	**10 Dollars = 2 Pounds-10 Shillings** 18xx. Black. Sailing ships at upper and lower left, griffin, allegorical man and woman at center *MONTREAL* engraved. Uniface. Signature varieties. Printer: RWH & C. Proof.	—	Unc	500.
S480	**20 Dollars = 5 Pounds** 18xx. Black. Seated Indian at left, seated woman with crowned shield at upper center, Justice at right. *MONTREAL* engraved. Uniface. Signature varieties. Printer: RWH & C. Proof.	—	Unc	500.
S481	**50 Dollars = 12 Pounds-10 Shillings** 18xx. Black. *MONTREAL* engraved. Uniface. Signature varieties. Printer: RWH & C. Proof.	—	Unc	500.
S482	**100 Dollars = 25 Pounds** 18xx. Black. Female in chariot drawn by lions at top center, Commerce at lower left and right. *MONTREAL* engraved. Uniface. Signature varieties. Printer: RWH & C. Proof.	—	Unc	500.

1842-49 Issues

		Good	Fine	XF
S483	**1 Dollar = 5 Shillings** 1842-49. Black. Bison at top center, plants at right. Small "dog and safe" vignette at bottom center. Uniface. Signature varieties.			
	a. 1847.	300.	1000.	—
	b. Red handstamp: *BELLEVILLE*. Printer: RWH & Co. 2.8.1842.	300.	1000.	—
	c. Red handstamp: *BELLEVILLE*. Printers: Danforth, Underwood, New York and Underwood, Bald, Spencer, Hufty, New York. 2.8.1843-2.8.1847.	350.	1250.	—
	d. Fully engraved date. Red overprint: *BROCKMAN, BYTOWN, HAMILTON, LONDON*, and *ST. THOMAS*. Red word on face and back. Printer: RWH & E. 1.5.1849.	—	—	—
	p. Partially engraved date. Printer: RW & H. Proof. 2.4.184x.	—	Unc	600.
S484	**2 Dollars = 10 Shillings** 1847-49. Black. Seated Mercury with lion at top center. Small "dog and safe" vignette at bottom center. Uniface. Signature varieties.			
	a. 1847.	300.	1000.	—
	b. Red handstamped: *BELLEVILLE*. Printers: Danforth, Underwood, New York and Underwood, Bald, Spencer, Hufty, New York. 2.8.1843-2.8.1847.	350.	1250.	—
	c. Fully engraved date. Red overprint: *BROCKVILLE, BYTOWN, HAMILTON, LONDON*, and *ST. THOMAS*. Red word on face and back. Printer: RWH & E. 1.5.1849.	350.	1250.	—
	p1. Partially engraved date. Printer: RWH & E. Proof. 2.4.184x.	—	Unc	600.
	p2. Red handstamped: *BELLEVILLE*. Printer: RWH & C. Proof. 2.8.184x.	—	Unc	600.
S485	**5 Dollars = 1 Pound-5 Shillings** 1842-49. Black. Plants at left, royal crest at center, plants at right. Small "dog and safe" vignette at bottom center. Uniface. Signature varieties.			
	a. 1843-47.	300.	1000.	—
	b. Red handstamped: *BELLEVILLE*. Printers: Danforth, Underwood, New York and Underwood, Bald, Spencer, Hufty, New York. 2.8.1843-2.8.1847.	350.	1250.	—
	c. Fully engraved date. Red overprint: *BROCKVILLE, BYTOWN, HAMILTON, LONDON*, and *ST. THOMAS*. Red word on face and back. Printer: RWH & E. 1.5.1849.	300.	1000.	—
	p1. Partially engraved date. Printer: RW & H. Proof. 2.4.184x.	—	Unc	600.
	p2. Red handstamped: *BELLEVILLE*. Printer: RWH & E. Proof. 2.8.184x.	—	Unc	600.
S486	**10 Dollars = 2 Pounds-10 Shillings** 1842-49. Black. Woman at upper left, seated Indian at top center, plants at right. Small "dog and safe" vignette at bottom center. Uniface. Signature varieties.			
	a. Red handstamped: *BELLEVILLE*. Printers: Danforth, Underwood, New York and Underwood, Bald, Spencer, Hufty, New York. 2.8.1843-2.8.1847.	—	—	—
	b. Red handstamped: *BELLEVILLE*. Printer: RWH & Co. 2.8.1842.	250.	900.	—
	c. Fully engraved date. Red overprint: *BROCKVILLE, BYTOWN, HAMILTON, LONDON*, and *ST. THOMAS*. Red word protector on face and back. Printer: RWH & E. 1.5.1849.	300.	1000.	—
	p. Partially engraved date. Printer: RW & H. Proof. 2.4.184x.	—	Unc	600.

1844-61 Issue

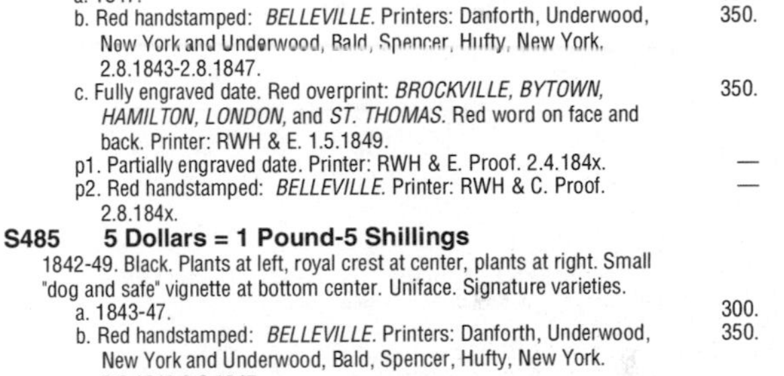

		Good	Fine	XF
S487	**1 Dollar = 5 Shillings** 1846-49. Black. Standing woman in ornate outlined 1 at left and right, sailing ships in harbor at upper center. Montreal arms at bottom center. Uniface. Signature varieties.			
	a. Quebec. Red numeral protector on face and back. 1.5.1846.	200.	800.	—
	b. Montreal. Red word protector on face and back. Fully engraved date. 1.1.1849.	200.	750.	—
	c. Quebec. Red word protector on face and back. Fully engraved date. 1.1.1849.	150.	600.	—

	Good	Fine	XF
d. Hamilton. Green word protector on face and back. Red overprint: *BRANTFORD.* Fully engraved date. Printers: RWH & E and ABNC. 1.1.1849.	225.	500.	—
e. Montreal. Green word protector on face and back. Green overprint: *LONDON* and blue handstamped: *S* handstamp. Fully engraved date. Printers: RWH & E and ABNC. 1.1.1849.	250.	500.	—
f. Quebec. Green word protector on face and back. Fully engraved date. Printers: RWH & E and ABNC. 1.1.1849.	150.	600.	—
g. Toronto. Green word protector on face and back. Fully engraved date. Red overprint: *BRANTFORD* and *COBOURG.* Printer: RWH & E and ABNC. 1.1.1849.	175.	625.	—
h. Montreal. Partially engraved date. Printer: RWH & C. 18xx.	125.	500.	—
p. As h. Proof.	—	Unc	600.

S488 2 Dollars = 10 Shillings

1846-49. Black. Standing woman in ornate outlined *2* at left and right. Ornate *2* between seated Britannia and standing Justice at upper center. Montreal arms at bottom center. Uniface. Signature varietie

	Good	Fine	XF
a. Quebec. Red numeral protector on face and back. 1.5.1846.	250.	750.	—
b. Montreal. Red word protector on face and back. 1.1.1849.	250.	750.	—
c. Cobourg. Green word protector on face and back. Red overprint: *LINDSAY.* Fully engraved date. Printers: RWH & E and ABNC. 1.1.1849.	150.	600.	—
d. Montreal. Green word protector on face and back. Fully engraved date. Printers: RWH & E and ABNC. 1.1.1849.	150.	600.	—
e. Quebec. Green word protector on face and back. Fully engraved date. Printers: RWH & E and ABNC. 1.1.1849.	150.	600.	—
f. Toronto. Red overprint: *SIMCOE.* Green word protector on face and back. Fully engraved date. Printers: RWH & E and ABNC. 1.1.1849.	150.	600.	—
p. Montreal. Partially engraved date. Printer: RWH & Co. Proof. 18xx.	—	Unc	500.

S489 3 Dollars = 15 Shillings

1844. Black. Standing woman in ornate outlined *3* at left and right, floating allegorical woman with crest at upper center. Montreal arms at bottom center. Uniface. Signature varieties.

	Good	Fine	XF
a. Montreal. Partially engraved date. Printer: RWH & C. 1.1.1844.	750.	2500.	—
b. Quebec. 1.5.1844.	750.	2500.	—

	Good	Fine	XF
S490 4 Dollars = 1 Pound 18xx. Partially engraved. Standing Britannia in ornate outlined *4* at left, supported royal arms at top center, standing Justice in ornate outlined *4* at right. Montreal arms at bottom center. Uniface. Signature va Printer: RWH & C. Proof.	—	Unc	500.
S491 5 Dollars = 1 Pound-5 Shillings 1.1.1844. Partially engraved. Black. Red numeral protector. Young woman at lower left and right, woman seated in ornate *V* at center. Montreal arms at bottom center. Uniface. Signature varieties. Back: Red numeral protector. Printer: RWH & C. Proof.	250.	1000.	—

S492 10 Dollars = 2 Pounds-10 Shillings

1846.52. Black. Seated woman at lower left and right, two women seated in ornate *X* at center. Montreal arms at bottom center. Uniface. Signature varieties.

	Good	Fine	XF
a. Montreal. Partially engraved date. Blue overprint: *T T* and green *M M.* Green word protector on face and back. Printer: RWH & C. 1.1.1849.	250.	1000.	—
b. Quebec. 1.5.1846-1.5.1852.	250.	1000.	—

	Good	Fine	XF
S493 20 Dollars = 5 Pounds 18xx. Partially engraved. Black. Standing Indian with drawn bow at left, deer at upper center, Indian princess at right. Montreal arms at bottom center. Uniface. Signature varieties. Printer: RWH & Co. Proof.	—	Unc	500.
S494 50 Dollars = 1 Pound-10 Shillings 18xx. Partially engraved. Black. Victoria at left, sailing ship at center, Prince Consort at right. Montreal arms at bottom center. Uniface. Signature varieties. Printer: RWH & C. Proof.	—	Unc	500.
S495 100 Dollars = 25 Pounds 1.8.1861. Partially engraved. Green word protector. Standing Justice at left, seated Victoria at upper center, seated Commerce at right. Montreal arms at bottom center. Uniface. Signature varieties. Back: Green word protector. Printer: RWH & C.	300.	1250.	—

1851-53 Issue

Type I: W/denomination panel at lower l.

Type II: W/additional *ONE, 2, 5* or *10* numeral protectors behind denomination panel at lower l.

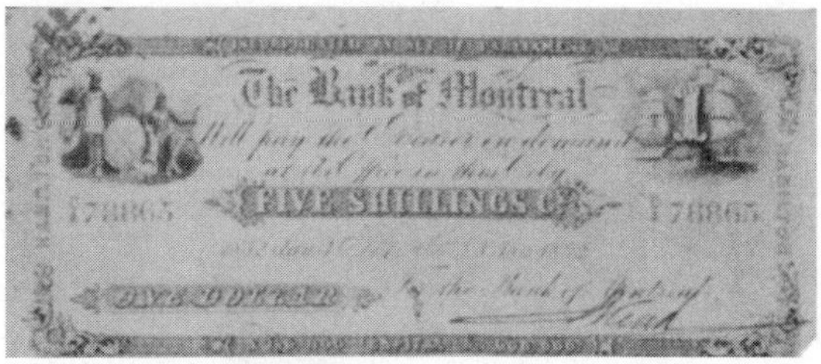

S496 1 Dollar = 5 Shillings

1852. Black. Sailing ships at upper right. Bank crest, two Indians with shield at upper left. Uniface. Signature and overprint varieties. Printer: PBC.

	Good	Fine	XF
a. Type I: Montreal-Montreal. 1.1.1852.	250.	850.	—
b. Type I: Toronto-Kingston. 6.6.1852.	250.	850.	—
c. Type II: Montreal-Montreal. 1.1.1852.	250.	850.	—

S497 2 Dollars = 10 Shillings

1851-1852. Black. Commerce at upper right. Bank crest, two Indians with shield at upper left. Uniface. Signature and overprint varieties. Printer: PBC.

	Good	Fine	XF
a. Type I: LONDON/Montreal-Montreal. 1.3.1852.	250.	850.	—
b. Type I: Toronto-Bytown. 5.3.1852.	250.	850.	—
c. Type I: Toronto-Hamilton. 3.1.1852.	300.	900.	—
d. Type I: Toronto-Toronto. 1.1.1851.	—	Unc	800.
e. Type II: 1852.	250.	850.	—
f. Type III: Large green *TWO* in underprint. LONDON/Montreal-Montreal. 1.3.1852.	300.	900.	—

S498 4 Dollars = 20 Shillings

1851-52. Black. Abundance at upper right. Bank crest, two Indians with shield at upper left. Uniface. Signature and overprint varieties. Printer: PBC.

	Good	Fine	XF
a. Type I: Toronto-Toronto. 1.7.1851.	—	Unc	500.
b. Type I: THREE RIVERS/Montreal-Montreal. 1.4.1852.	350.	1100.	—
c. Type II: 1852.	350.	1100.	—

S499 5 Dollars = 25 Shillings

3.4.1852-1.3.1853. Black. Indians horseback at upper right. Bank crest, two Indians with shield at upper left. Uniface. Signature and overprint varieties. Printer: PBC.

	Good	Fine	XF
a. Type I: Quebec-Quebec. 3.4.1852; 1.3.1853.	200.	750.	—
b. Type II: 1852-53.	200.	750.	—

S500 10 Dollars = 50 Shillings

1852. Black. Paddle wheel steamboat at upper right. Bank crest, two Indians with shield at upper left. Uniface. Signature and overprint varieties. Printer: PBC.

	Good	Fine	XF
a. Type I: Toronto-Bytown. 5.5.1852.	350.	1100.	—
b. Type II: Toronto-London. 5.5.1852.	350.	1100.	—

1853-57 Issues

S501 1 Dollar

1853-57. Black. Portrait Queen Victoria at lower right. Bank crest at upper left. Signature varieties. Back: Blue. Printer: Toppan, Carpenter, Casilear & Co.

	Good	Fine	XF
a. *GODERICH* engraved. Red overprint: *LONDON* in date. Green *BRANTFORD* overprint 1.8.1856.	300.	650.	—
b. *PICTON* engraved. Red overprint: *KINGSTON* in date. 1.8.1856.	250.	650.	—
c. *WHITBY* engraved. Red overprint: *BOWMANVILLE* in date. 1.8.1856.	250.	650.	—
d. *WOODSTOCK* engraved. Red overprint: *LONDON* in date. 1.8.1856.	250.	650.	—
e. *BROCKVILLE* engraved. Red overprint: *BROCKVILLE* in date. 2.1.1857; 2.2.1857.	250.	650.	—
f. *LONDON* engraved. Red overprint: *LONDON* in date. *T T* at top. 2.1.1857; 2.2.1857.	250.	650.	—
g. *OTTAWA* engraved. Red overprint: *OTTAWA* in date. 2.1.1857; 2.2.1857.	250.	650.	—
h. *PORT HOPE* engraved. Red overprint: *COBOURG* in date with additional red overprint: *LINDSAY.* 2.1.1857; 2.2.1857.	250.	650.	—
p. *MONTREAL* engraved. Face proof.	—	Unc	500.
r. *TORONTO* engraved. Red overprint: *TORONTO* in date. Remainder. 1.2.1853.	—	—	—

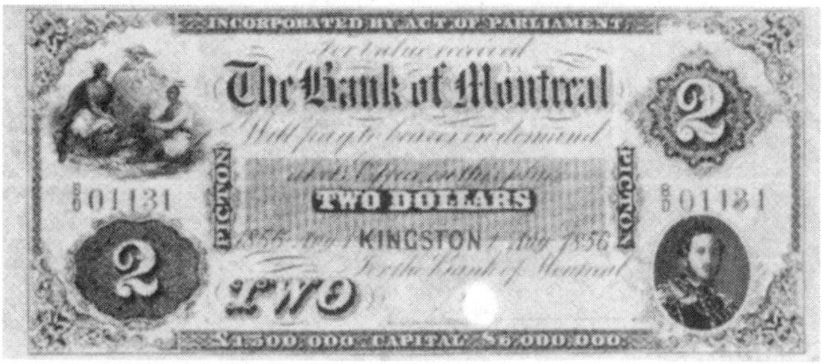

S502 2 Dollars

1856-57. Black. Portrait Prince Consort at lower right. Bank crest at upper left. Signature varieties. Back: Blue. Printer: Toppan, Carpenter, Casilear & Co.

	Good	Fine	XF
a. *LONDON* engraved. Red overprint: *LONDON* in date. *T T* at top. 1.8.1856.	250.	650.	—
b. *PERTH* engraved. Red overprint: *OTTAWA* in date. 1.8.1856.	250.	650.	—
c. *PICTON* engraved. Red overprint: *KINGSTON* in date. 1.8.1856.	250.	650.	—
d. *SIMCOE* engraved. Red overprint: *BRANTFORD* in date. 1.8.1856.	250.	650.	—
e. *OTTAWA* engraved. Red overprint: *OTTAWA* in date. 2.1.1857; 2.2.1857.	250.	650.	—
p. *QUEBEC* engraved. Face proof.	—	Unc	350.

NOTE: All notes dated 1858 or 1864 are counterfeits.

1859 Issue

S503 1 Dollar

3.1.1859. Black on green underprint. Bank crest at upper center portrait Queen Victoria at lower left, reclining allegory Ceres with produce at lower right. Plain or fully tinted large numerals. Signature varieties. Back: Printed backs-green. St. George and dragon at center. Overprint: Branch names across center in red or blue. Printer: RWH&E and ABNC.

	VG	VF	UNC
a. Printed back.	750.	1500.	—
b. Uniface.	700.	1250.	—

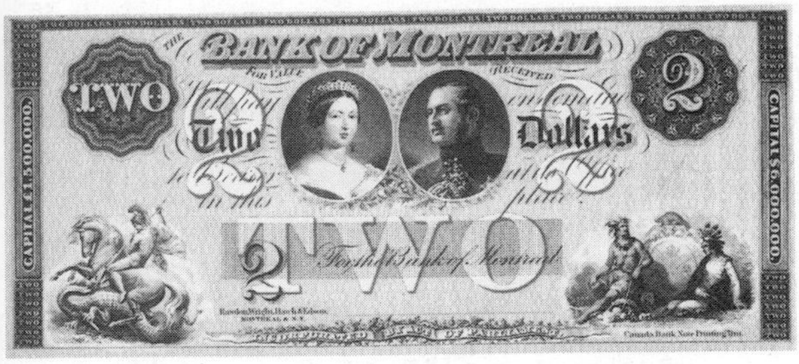

		VG	VF	UNC
S504	**2 Dollars**			

3.1.1859. Black on green underprint. Portrait Queen Victoria and Prince Albert at upper center, St. George slaying dragon at lower left, bank crest at lower right. Plain or fully tinted large numerals. Signature varieties. Back: Printed backs-green. St. George abd dragon at center. Overprint: Branch name across center in red or blue. Printer: RWH&E and ABNC.

	VG	VF	UNC
a. Printed back.	750.	1500.	—
b. Uniface.	700.	1250.	—

S505 4 Dollars
3.1.1859. Black on green underprint. Portrait Wellington at upper center, bank crest at lower left, reclining Britannia at lower right. Plain or fully tinted large numerals. Signature varieties. Back: Printed backs-green. St. George and dragon at center. Overprint: Branch name across center in red or blue. Printer: RWH&E and ABNC.

	VG	VF	UNC
a. Printed back.	750.	1500.	—
b. Uniface.	700.	1250.	

S506 5 Dollars
3.1.1859. Black on green underprint. Head office facade at upper center, bank crest at lower left, seated blacksmith at lower right. Plain or fully tinted large numerals. Signature varieties. Back: Printed backs-green. St. George and dragon at center. Overprint: Branch name across center in red or blue. Printer: RWH&E and ABNC.

	VG	VF	UNC
a. Printed back.	750.	1500.	—
b. Uniface.	700.	1250.	—

S507 10 Dollars
3.1.1859. Black on green underprint. Portrait right. Peel at upper center, reclining allegorical woman at lower left, bank crest at lower right. Plain or fully tinted large numerals. Signature varieties. Back: Printed backs-green. St. George and dragon at center. Overprint: Branch name across center in red or blue. Printer: RWH&E and ABNC. — 750. 1500. —

1862 Issue

	Good	Fine	XF
S508 1 Dollar 1.8.1862. Black on green underprint. Bank crest at upper center. Portrait Queen Victoria at lower left, reclining allegory Ceres with produce at lower right. Branch name in red or blue. Uniface. Signature varieties. Printer: ABNC.	250.	600.	1250.
S508A 2 Dollars 1.8.1862. Black on green underprint. Portrait queen Victoria and Prince Albert at upper center, St. George slaying dragon at lower left, bank crest at lower right. Branch name in red or blue. Uniface. Signature varieties. Printer: ABNC.	500.	1250.	3000.
S509 5 Dollars 1.8.1862. Black on green underprint. Angular view of head office facade at upper center, bank crest at lower left, seated blacksmith at lower right. Branch name in red or blue. Uniface. Signature varieties. Printer: ABNC.	500.	1250.	3000.
S510 10 Dollars 1.8.1862. Black on green underprint. Portrait right. Peel at upper center, reclining allegorical woman at lower left, bank crest at lower right. Branch name in red or blue. Uniface. Signature varieties. Printer: ABNC.	400.	1000.	2500.

NOTE: All notes dated 1858 or 1864 are counterfeits.

1871 Issue

	Good	Fine	XF
S511 4 Dollars 6.2.1871. Black on green underprint. Woman and cherubs with ornate *4* at center, right. B. Angus at lower left, E. H. King at lower right. Back: Green. St. George slaying dragon at center. Signature varieties. Printer: BABNC.	400.	1250.	—

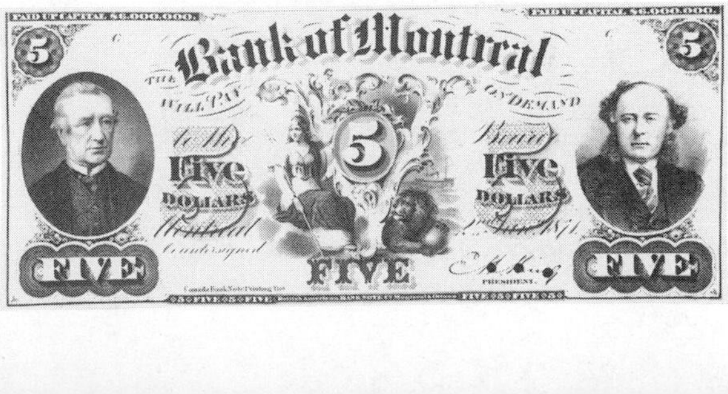

	Good	Fine	XF
S512 5 Dollars 2.1.1871. Black on green underprint. Seated Britannia with lion, ornate *V* with *5* at center, portrait T. Ryan at left, portrait E. H. King at right. Signature varieties. Back: Green. St. George slaying dragon at center. Printer: BABNC.	400.	1250.	—
S513 10 Dollars 1.3.1871. Black on green underprint. Cherubs with ornate *X* at center, portrait T. Ryan at lower left, portrait E. H. King at lower right. Signature varieties. Back: Green. St. George slaying dragon at center. Printer: BABNC.	450.	1500.	—
S514 20 Dollars 3.3.1871. Black on green underprint. E. H. King at center. Signature varieties. Back: Green. St. George slaying dragon at center. Printer: BABNC.	600.	1750.	—
S515 50 Dollars 5.5.1871. Black on green underprint. Allegorical woman seated on Large ornate *L* at center, right B. Angus at lower left, E. H. King at lower right. Signature varieties. Back: Green. St. George slaying dragon at center. Printer: BABNC.	600.	1750.	—
S516 100 Dollars 6.6.1871. Black on green underprint. Justice seated within Large ornate *C* at center, right B. Angus at left, E. H. King at right. Signature varieties. Back: Green. St. George slaying dragon at center. Printer: BABNC.	600.	1750.	—

1882 Issue

	Good	Fine	XF
S517 5 Dollars 2.1.1882. Black on green underprint. Britannia with lion, Large ornate *V* with *5* at center, portrait W. J. Buchanan at lower left, portrait C. F. Smithers at lower right. Signature varieites. Back: Green. St. George slaying dragon at center. Printer: BABNC.	600.	1750.	—

	Good	Fine	XF
S518 10 Dollars 2.1.1882. Black on green underprint. Cherubs with Large ornate *X* at center, portrait Dr. G. W. Campbell at lower left, portrait C. F. Smithers at lower right. Signature varieties. Back: Green. St. George slaying dragon at center. Printer: BABNC.	600.	1750.	—
S519 20 Dollars 2.1.1882. Black on green underprint. Portrait C. F. Smithers at center. Signature varieties. Back: Green. St. George slaying dragon at center. Printer: BABNC.	750.	2000.	—

1888 Issue

	Good	Fine	XF
S520 5 Dollars 2.1.1888. Black on green underprint. Britannia with lion, Large ornate *V* with *5* at center, W. J. Buchanan at lower left, D. Smith at lower right. Signature varieties. Back: Green. Printer: BABNC.	450.	1500.	—
S521 10 Dollars 2.1.1888. Black on green underprint. Cherubs with Large ornate *X* at center, portrait G. Drummond at lower left, D. Smith at lower right. Signature varieties. Back: Green. Printer: BABNC.	500.	1500.	—

1891 Issue

S522 5 Dollars
2.1.1891. Black on green underprint. Bank crest at center. Signature varieties. Back: Green. E. Clouston at lower left, Toronto Branch office building at center. Printer: ABNC.

	VG	VF	UNC
a. Issued note.	1000.	2250.	—
s. Specimen.	—	—	—

S523 10 Dollars

2.1.1891. Black on green underprint. G. Drummond at lower left, D. Smith at lower right. Bank crest at center. Signature varieties. Back: Green. Montreal Head Office building at center. Printer: ABNC.

	VG	VF	UNC
a. Issued note.	1250.	2500.	—
s. Specimen.	—	—	—

S524 20 Dollars

2.1.1891. Black on green underprint. E. Clouston at left, D. Smith at right. Bank crest at center. Signature varieties. Back: Green. Montreal Head Office building at center. Printer: ABNC.

	VG	VF	UNC
a. Issued note.	1250.	2500.	—
s. Specimen.	—	—	—

S525 50 Dollars

2.1.1891. Black on green underprint. Large script "£" at center, G. Drummond at lower left, D. Smith at lower right. Signature varieties. Back: Green. Printer: ABNC.

	VG	VF	UNC
a. Issued note.	1250.	2500.	—
s. Specimen.	—	—	—

1892 Issue

		VG	VF	UNC
S526	**50 Dollars** 2.1.1892. Black on green underprint. Portrait E. S. Clouston at left, portrait D. Smith at center, bank crest at lower right. Signature varieties. Back: Green. Montreal Head Office building at center. Printer: CBNC.	1750.	3250.	—
S527	**100 Dollars** 2.1.1892. Black on green underprint. E. S. Clouston at upper left, bank crest at center, D. Smith at lower right. Signature varieties. Back: Green. Montreal Head Office building at left. Printer: CBNC.	1750.	3250.	—

1895 Issue

		VG	VF	UNC
S528	**5 Dollars** 2.1.1895. Black on green underprint. E. S. Clouston at lower left, bank crest at upper center, D. Smith at lower right. Signature varieties. Back: Green. Tornonto Branch Office building at center. Printer: BABNC.	250.	750.	—
S529	**10 Dollars** 2.1.1895. Black on green underprint. Bank crest at upper left. over D. Smith, G. Drummond at lower right. Signature varieties. Back: Green. Montreal Head Office building at center. Printer: BABNC.	1000.	2000.	—
S530	**20 Dollars** 2.1.1895. Black on green underprint. D. Smith at lower left, bank crest at center, E. S. Clouston at lower right. Signature varieties. Back: Green. Montreal Head Office building at center. Printer: BABNC.	1000.	2000.	—

1903 Issue

S531 50 Dollars

2.1.1903. Black, orange and green. Portrait D. Smith at left, bank crest at upper center, portrait G. Drummund at right. Signature varieties. "Double Size." Back: Black and green. Montreal Head Office building at left, Toronto branch building at right. Printer: W&S.

	VG	VF	UNC
a. Issued note.	4500.	10,000.	—
s. Specimen perforated: *SPECIMEN.*	—	—	—

S532 100 Dollars

2.1.1903. Black, gold and rose. Portrait D. Smith at left, bank crest at top center, portrait G. Drummund at right. Signature varieties. "Double Size." Back: Black and green. Montreal Head Office building at center. Printer: W&S.

	VG	VF	UNC
a. Issued note.	5000.	12,500.	—
s. Specimen perforated: *SPECIMEN.*	—	—	—

1904 Issue

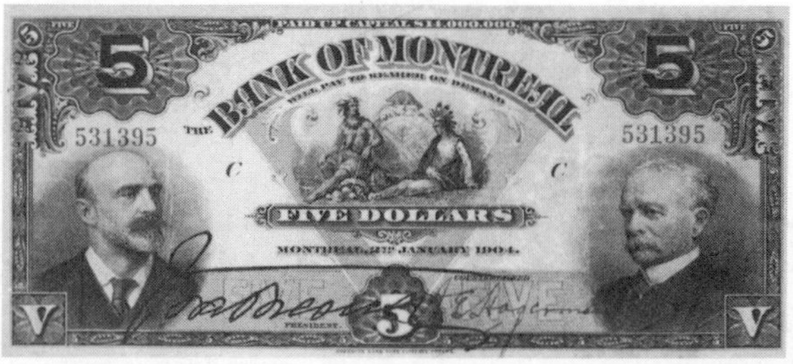

S533 5 Dollars

2.1.1904. Black on olive-green underprint. E. S. Clouston lower left, bank crest at upper center, G. Drummond at lower right. Signature varieties. Back: Green. Montreal Head Office building at center. Printer: ABNC.

VG	VF	UNC
100.	250.	750.

S534 10 Dollars

2.1.1904. Black on olive-green underprint. E. S. Clouston at left, bank crest at bottom center, D. Smith at right. Signature varieties. Back: Green. Toronto Bank Branch Office building at center. Printer: ABNC.

	VG	VF	UNC
a. Issued note.	125.	300.	850.
s. Specimen.	—	—	—

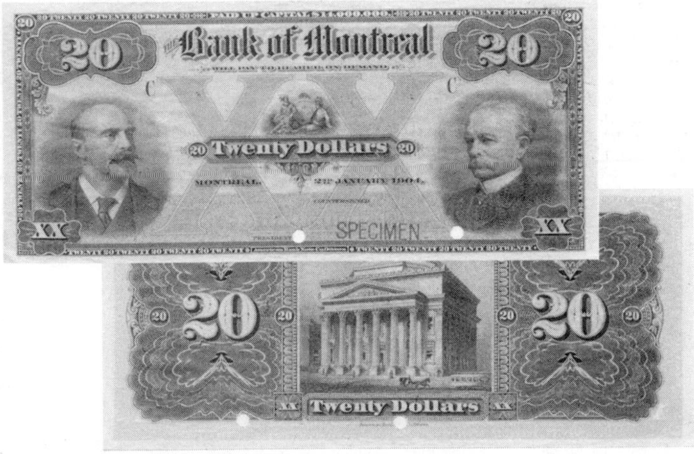

S535 20 Dollars

2.1.1904. Black on olive-green underprint. Portrait E. S. Clouston at lower left, bank crest at center, portrait G. Drummond at lower right. Signature varieties. Back: Green. Montreal Head Office building at center. Printer: ABNC.

	VG	VF	UNC
a. Issued note.	125.	300.	850.
s. Specimen.	—	—	—

1911 Issue

	VG	VF	UNC
S536 5 Dollars 3.1.1911. Black on olive-green underprint. E. S. Clouston at lower left, bank crest at upper center, R. B. Angus at lower right. Signature varieties. Back: Olive-green. Montreal Head Office building at center. Printer: ABNC.	150.	350.	1000.
S537 20 Dollars 3.1.1911. Black on olive-green underprint. E. S. Clouston at lower left, bank crest at upper center, R. B. Angus at lower right. Signature varieties. Back: Green. Printer: ABNC.	200.	400.	1100.

1912 Issue

	VG	VF	UNC
S538 5 Dollars 3.9.1912. Black on olive-green underprint. V. Meredith at lower left, bank crest at upper center, right. B. Angus at lower right. Signature varieties. Back: Green. Montreal Head Office building at center. Printer: ABNC.	150.	350.	1000.
S539 10 Dollars 3.9.1912. Black on olive-green underprint. V. Meredith at left, bank crest at bottom center, D. Smith at right. Signature varieties. Back: Green. Toronto Branch Office building at center. Printer: ABNC.	200.	400.	1250.
S540 20 Dollars 3.9.1912. Black on olive-green underprint. V. Meredith at lower left, bank crest at upper center, right. B. Angus at lower right. Signature varieties. Back: Green. Montreal Head Office building at center. Printer: ABNC.	300.	600.	1500.
S541 50 Dollars 3.9.1912. Black on olive-green underprint. V. Meredith at left, bank crest at bottom center, D. Smith at right. Signature varieties. Back: Green. Printer: ABNC.	300.	600.	—
S542 100 Dollars 3.9.1912. Black on olive-green underprint. V. Meredith at lower left, bank crest at upper center, right. B. Angus at lower right. Signature varieties. Back: Montreal Head Office building at center. Printer: ABNC.	300.	600.	—

1914 Issue

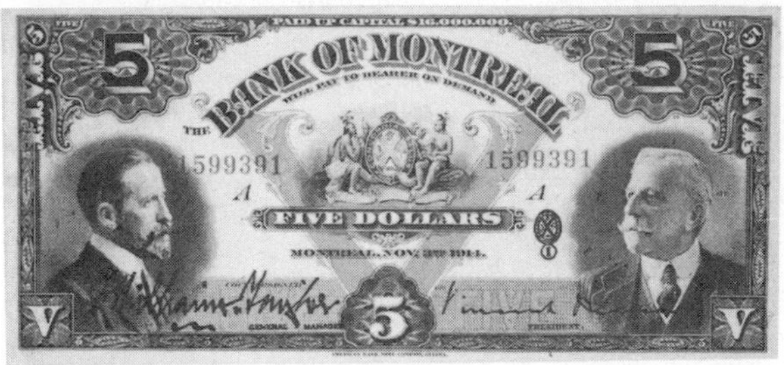

	VG	VF	UNC
S543 5 Dollars 3.11.1914. Black on olive-green underprint. Sir F. Williams-Taylor at lower left, bank crest at center, V. Meredeith at lower right. Signature varieties. Back: Green. Montreal Head Office building at center. Printer: ABNC.	25.00	50.00	150.
S544 10 Dollars 3.11.1914. Black on olive-green underprint. Sir F. Williams-Taylor at lower left, bank crest at center, V. Meredith at lower right. Signature varieties. Back: Green. Toronto Branch Office building at center. Printer: ABNC.	25.00	50.00	150.
S545 20 Dollars 3.11.1914. Black on olive-green underprint. Sir F. Williams-Taylor at lower left, bank crest at center, V. Meredeith at lower right. Signature varieties. Back: Green. Montreal Head Office building at center. Printer: ABNC.	50.00	100.	300.
S546 50 Dollars 3.11.1914. Black on olive-green underprint. Sir F. Williams-Taylor at lower left, bank crest at center, V. Meredeith at lower right. Signature varieties. Back: Green. Toronto Branch Office at center. Printer: ABNC.	200.	400.	1250.
S547 100 Dollars 3.11.1914. Black on olive-green underprint. Sir F. Williams-Taylor at lower left, bank crest at center, V. Meredeith at lower right. Signature varieties. Back: Green. Montreal Head Office building at center. Printer: ABNC.	250.	500.	1500.

1923 Issue

S548 5 Dollars

2.1.1923. Black on olive-green underprint. Sir F. Williams-Taylor at lower left, bank crest at lower center, V. Meredeith at lower right. Back: Green. Montreal Head Office building. Printer: CBNC.

	VG	VF	UNC
a. Issued note.	25.00	50.00	150.
s. Specimen.	—	—	—

S549 10 Dollars

2.1.1923. Black on olive-green underprint. Sir F. Williams-Taylor at lower left, bank crest at lower center, V. Meredeith at lower right. Back: Green. Toronto Branch Office building at center.

	VG	VF	UNC
a. Issued note.	25.00	50.00	150.
s. Specimen.	—	—	—

S550 20 Dollars	VG	VF	UNC
2.1.1923. Black on olive-green underprint. Sir F. Williams-Taylor at lower left, bank crest at lower center, V. Meredith at lower right. Back: Green. Montreal Head Office building at center. Printer: CBNC.			
a. Issued note.	25.00	50.00	200.
s. Specimen.	—	—	—
S551 50 Dollars			
2.1.1923. Black on olive-green underprint. Sir F. Williams-Taylor at lower left, bank crest at lower center, V. Meredith at lower right. Back: Green. Toronto Branch Office building at center. Printer: CBNC.	150.	400.	1250.

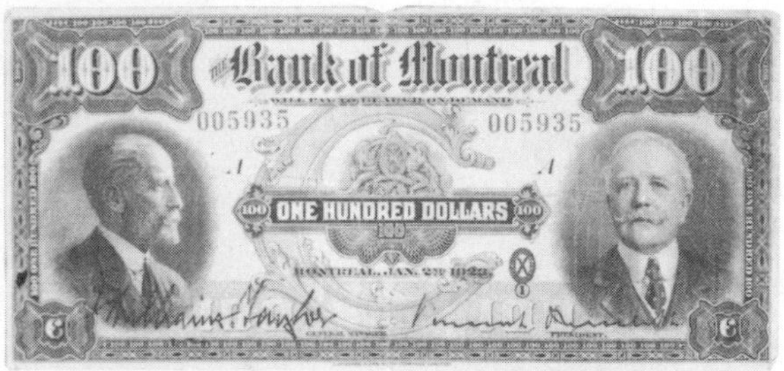

S552 100 Dollars	VG	VF	UNC
2.1.1923. Black on olive-green underprint. Sir F. Williams-Taylor at lower left, bank crest at lower center, V. Meredith at lower right. Back: Green. Montreal Head Office building at center. Printer: CBNC.	150.	400.	1250.

1931 Issue

S553 5 Dollars	VG	VF	UNC
2.1.1931. Black on olive-green underprint. W. A. Bog at lower left, bank crest at upper center, C. B. Gordon at lower right. Signature varieties. Back: Green. Montreal Head Office building at center. Printer: CBNC.	25.00	50.00	150.

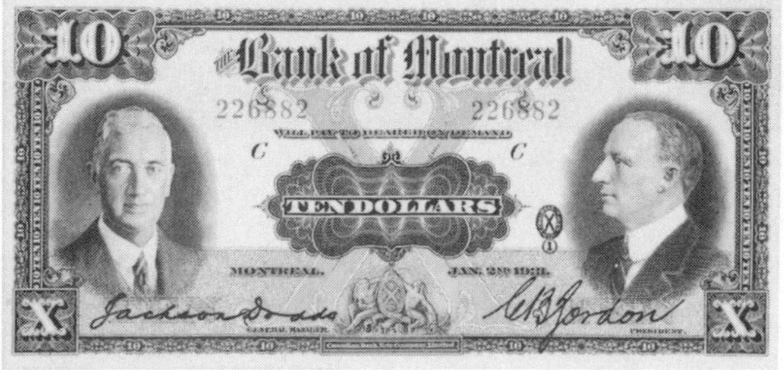

S554 10 Dollars	VG	VF	UNC
2.1.1931. Black on olive-green underprint. J. Dodds at left, bank crest at bottom center, C. B. Gordon at right. Signature varieties. Back: Green. Toronto Branch Office building at center. Printer: CBNC.	25.00	50.00	150.
S555 20 Dollars			
2.1.1931. J. Dodds at left, bank crest at upper center, C. B. Gordon at right. Signature varieties. Back: Green. Montreal Head Office building at center. Printer: CBNC.	300.	850.	1750.

S556 50 Dollars	VG	VF	UNC
2.1.1931. Black on olive-green underprint. J. Dodds at left, bank crest at bottom center, C. B. Gordon at right. Signature varieties. Back: Green. Toronto Branch Office building at center. Printer: CBNC.	100.	200.	750.
S557 100 Dollars			
2.1.1931. W. A. Bog at lower left, bank crest at upper center, C. B. Gordon at lower right. Back: Green. Montreal Head Office building at center. Printer: CBNC.	100.	225.	800.

1935 Issue

S558 5 Dollars	VG	VF	UNC
2.1.1935. Black olive-green underprint. W. A. Bog at lower left, bank crest at upper center, C. B. Gordon at lower right. Signature varieties. Back: Green. Montreal Head Office building at center. Printer: CBNC. Reduced size.			
a. Signature W. A. Bog and C. B. Gordon.	25.00	50.00	150.
b. Signature J. Dodds and C. B. Gordon.	25.00	50.00	150.

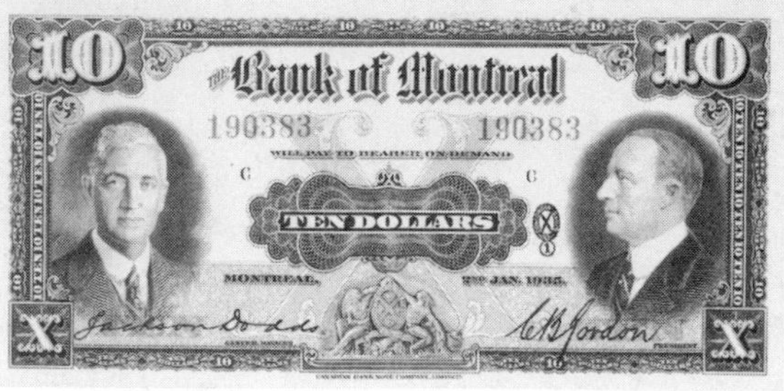

S559 10 Dollars	VG	VF	UNC
2.1.1935. Black olive-green underprint. J. Dodds at left, bank crest at bottom center, C. B. Gordon at right. Signature varieties. Back: Green. Toronto Branch Office building at center. Printer: CBNC. Reduced size.			
a. Signature W. A. Bog and C. B. Gordon.	25.00	50.00	150.
b. Signature J. Dodds and C. B. Gordon.	25.00	50.00	150.
S560 20 Dollars			
2.1.1935. Black olive-green underprint. J. Dodds at left, bank crest at upper center, C. B. Gordon at right. Signature varieties. Back: Green. Montreal Head Office building at center. Printer: CBNC. Reduced size.			
a. Signature W. A. Bog and C. B. Gordon.	25.00	50.00	150.
b. Signature J. Dodds and C. B. Gordon.	25.00	50.00	150.

1938 Issue

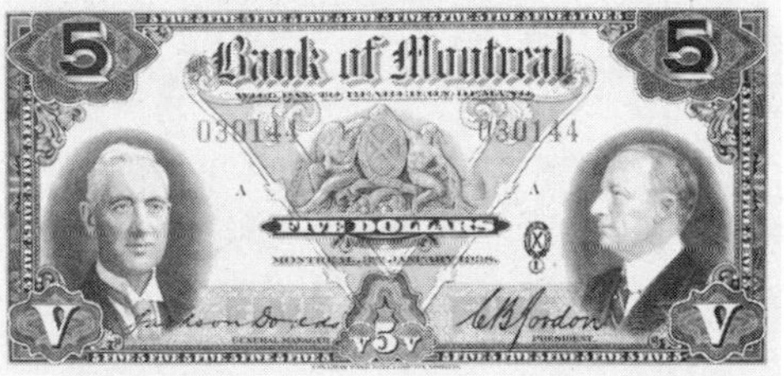

S561 5 Dollars	VG	VF	UNC
3.1.1938. Black on olive-green underprint. J. Dodds at lower left, bank crest at upper center, C. B. Gordon at lower right. Signature varieties. Back: Green. Montreal Head Office building. Printer: CBNC.			
a. Signature J. Dodds and C. B. Gordon.	25.00	50.00	150.
b. Signature G. W. Spinney and C. B. Gordon.	25.00	50.00	150.

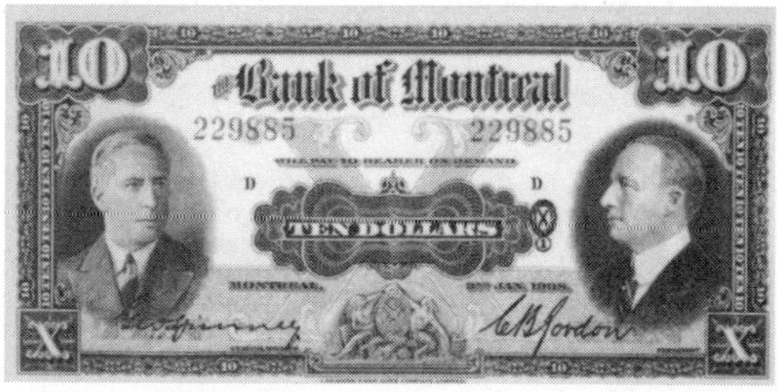

S562 10 Dollars	VG	VF	UNC
3.1.1938. Black on olive-green underprint. G. W. Spinney at left, bank crest at bottom center, C. B. Gordon at right. Signature varieties. Back: Green. Toronto Branch Office. Printer: CBNC.			
a. Signature J. Dodds and C. B. Gordon.	25.00	50.00	150.
b. Signature G. W. Spinney and C. B. Gordon.	25.00	50.00	150.
S563 20 Dollars			
3.1.1938. Black on olive-green underprint. G. W. Spinney at left, bank crest at bottom center, C. B. Gordon at right. Back: Green. Montreal Head Office building. Printer: CBNC.			
a. Signature J. Dodds and C. B. Gordon.	25.00	50.00	150.
b. Signature G. W. Spinney and C. B. Gordon.	25.00	50.00	150.

1942 Issue

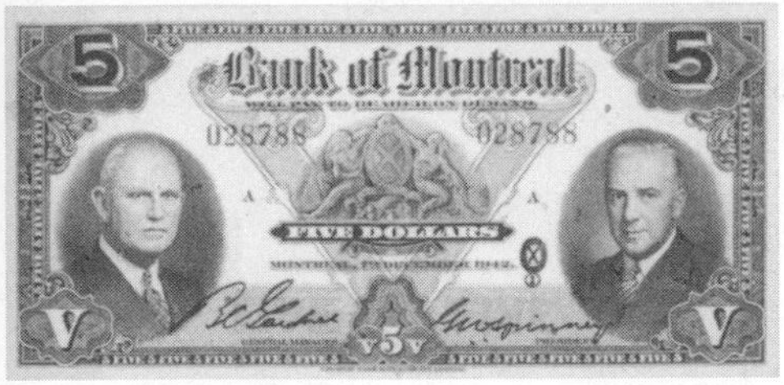

		VG	VF	UNC
S564	**5 Dollars** 7.12.1942. Black on olive-green underprint. B. C. Gardner at lower left, bank crest at upper center, G. W. Spinney at lower right. Back: Green. Montreal Head Office building. Printer: CBNC.	25.00	50.00	150.

Bank of New Brunswick 1820-1906

1820-32 Issue

		Good	Fine	XF
S571	**5 Shillings** 26.12.1820. Black on green underprint. Standing Britannia at left, cherubs and women around seated Britannia at top center, two cherubs, cask and bale at lower center. Back: Blue. 2 women's heads at upper and lower left and right, two cherubs, cask and bale at upper and lower cen Printer: Perkins, Fairman & Heath. 185 x 100mm.	400.	1250.	—
S572	**1 Pound** 1.1.1831. Black. Standing Britannia at left, cherubs and women around seated Britannia at top center, two cherubs, cask and bale at lower center. Back: Blue. 2 women's heads at upper and lower left and right, two cherubs, cask and bale at upper and lower cen Printer: Perkins, Fairman & Heath. 185 x 100mm.	400.	1250.	
S573	**2 Pounds** 1.12.1832. Black. Standing Britannia at left, cherubs and women around seated Britannia at top center, two cherubs, cask and bale at lower center. Back: Blue. 2 women's heads at upper and lower left and right, two cherubs, cask and bale at upper and lower cen Printer: Perkins, Fairman & Heath. 185 x 100mm.	400.	1250.	—
S574	**10 Pounds** 18xx. Black. Standing Britannia at left, cherubs and women around seated Britannia at top center, two cherubs, cask and bale at lower center. Back: Blue. 2 women's heads at upper and lower left and right, two cherubs, cask and bale at upper and lower cen Printer: Perkins, Fairman & Heath. Proof. 185 x 100mm.	—	Unc	500.

1838-59 Issues

		Good	Fine	XF
S575	**5 Shillings** 1.6.1849-1.10.1856. Standing Britannia at left, cherubs and women around Britannia at center, two cherubs, cask and bale at lower center. Back: 2 women's heads at upper and lower left and right, 2 cherubs, cask and bale at upper and lower cente Printer: New England Bank Note Co. 170 x 72mm.	400.	1250.	—
S575A	**5 Shillings** 1.12.1858; 1.10.1859. Standing Britannia at left, cherubs and women around Britannia at center, two cherubs, cask and bale at lower center. Back: 2 women's heads at upper and lower left and right, 2 cherubs, cask and bale at upper and lower cente Overprint: Red, *ONE DOLLAR*. Printer: New England Bank NOte Co. Reduced size, 170 x 72mm.	400.	1250.	—
S576	**1 Pound** 1.10.1845-1.7.1852. Standing Britannia at left, cherubs and women around Britannia at center, two cherubs, cask and bale at lower center. Back: 2 women's heads at upper and lower left and right, 2 cherubs, cask and bale at upper and lower cente Printer: New England Bank Note Co. 170 x 72mm.	400.	1250.	—
S577	**2 Pounds** 18xx. Standing Britannia at left, cherubs and women around Britannia at center, two cherubs, cask and bale at lower center. Back: 2 women's heads at upper and lower left and right, 2 cherubs, cask and bale at upper and lower cente Printer: New England Bank Note Co. Proof. 170 x 72mm.	—	Unc	500.
S578	**5 Pounds** 14.9.1838. Standing Britannia at left, cherubs and women around Britannia at center, two cherubs, cask and bale at lower center. Back: 2 women's heads at upper and lower left and right, 2 cherubs, cask and bale at upper and lower cente Printer: New England Bank Note Co. 170 x 72mm.	50.00	150.	—

Known examples of apparently issued notes of #S578 are counterfeits. Genuine examples are found in sheets of proof notes.

		Good	Fine	XF
S579	**10 Pounds** 18xx. Standing Britannia at left, cherubs and women around Britannia at center, two cherubs, cask and bale at lower center. Back: 2 women's heads at upper and lower left and right, 2 cherubs, cask and bale at upper and lower cente Printer: New England Bank Note Co. Proof. 170 x 72mm.	—	Unc	300.
S580	**25 Pounds** 1.11.1860. Standing Britannia at left, cherubs and women around Britannia at center, two cherubs, cask and bale at lower center. Back: 2 women's heads at upper and lower left and right, 2 cherubs, cask and bale at upper and lower cente Printer: New England Bank Note Co. 170 x 72mm.	600.	2000.	—

1860-84 Issue

		Good	Fine	XF
S581	**1 Dollar** 1.11.1860; 1.7.1863; 1.9.1868. Standing Britannia at left, cherubs and women around Britannia at center, two cherubs, cask and bale at lower center. Back: 2 women's heads at upper and lower left and right, 2 cherubs, cask and bale at upper and lower cente Printer: ABNC.	500.	1500.	—
S582	**2 Dollars** 1.9.1868. Standing Britannia at left, cherubs and women around Britannia at center, two cherubs, cask and bale at lower center. Back: 2 women's heads at upper and lower left and right, 2 cherubs, cask and bale at upper and lower cente Printer: ABNC. Proof.	—	Unc	500.
S583	**5 Dollars** 1860-84. Standing Britannia at left, cherubs and women around Britannia at center, two cherubs, cask and bale at lower center. Back: 2 women's heads at upper and lower left and right, 2 cherubs, cask and bale at upper and lower cente Printer: ABNC.			
	a. 1.11.1860; 1.7.1863; 1.9.1868.	500.	1500.	—
	p. Proof. 1.1.1884.	—	Unc	500.
S584	**10 Dollars** 1860-80. Standing Britannia at left, cherubs and women around Britannia at center, two cherubs, cask and bale at lower center. Back: 2 women's heads at upper and lower left and right, 2 cherubs, cask and bale at upper and lower cente Printer: ABNC.			
	a. 1.11.1860.	500.	1500.	—
	p. Proof. 1.7.1880.	—	Unc	500.

		Good	Fine	XF
S585	**20 Dollars** 1.11.1860; 1.9.1868. Standing Britannia at left, cherubs and women around Britannia at center, two cherubs, cask and bale at lower center. 2 signature varieties. Back: 2 women's heads at upper and lower left and right, 2 cherubs, cask and bale at upper and lower cente Printer: ABNC.	600.	1750.	—
S586	**50 Dollars** 1.11.1860. Standing Britannia at left, cherubs and women around Britannia at center, two cherubs, cask and bale at lower center. Back: 2 women's heads at upper and lower left and right, 2 cherubs, cask and bale at upper and lower cente Printer: ABNC.	600.	1750.	—
S587	**100 Dollars** 1.11.1860. Standing Britannia at left, cherubs and women around Britannia at center, two cherubs, cask and bale at lower center. Back: 2 women's heads at upper and lower left and right, 2 cherubs, cask and bale at upper and lower cente Printer: ABNC.	600.	1750.	—

1892 Issues

		VG	VF	UNC
S591	**5 Dollars** 25.3.1892. Black on green and yellow underprint. J. S. Lewin at lower left, bank crest at lower right. Women and cherubs around seated Britannia at center. Back: Blue.			
	a. Issued note.	1250.	2500.	—
	s. Specimen.	—	—	—
S592	**5 Dollars** 25.3.1892. Black on green and yellow underprint. J. S. Lewin at lower left, bank crest at lower right. Women and cherubs around seated Britannia at center. Red Roman numeral *VV*. Back: Blue.	1250.	2500.	—
S593	**10 Dollars** 25.3.1892. Black on green and yellow underprint. Sailor and provincial crest at lower left, J. S. Lewin at lower right. Women and cherubs around seated Britannia at center. Back: Green.	1250.	2500.	—
S594	**10 Dollars** 25.3.1892. Black on green and yellow underprint. Sailor and provincial crest at lower left, J. S. Lewin at lower right. Women and cherubs around seated Britannia at center. Red Roman Numerals *X X*. Back: Green.	1250.	2500.	—

1903-06 Issue

		Good	Fine	XF
S596	**5 Dollars** 2.1.1904. Black on yellow-green and pink underprint. J. Manchester at lower left, suspension bridge, view of St. John at center, bank crest at lower right. Back: Bank façade at center. Printer: ABNC.			
	a. Signature title: *MANAGER* at left.	450.	1500.	—
	b. Signature title: *FOR GENERAL MANAGER* at left.	450.	1500.	—

		Good	Fine	XF
S597	**10 Dollars** 1.9.1903. Black on yellow-green and green underprint. Sailor and provincial crest at left. Britannia, women and cherubs at center, portrait J. Manchester at lower right. Back: Bank façade at center. Printer: ABNC.			
	a. Signature title: *MANAGER* at left.	450.	1500.	—
	b. Signature title: *FOR GENERAL MANAGER* at left.	450.	1500.	—
S598	**20 Dollars** 2.1.1906. Black and blue. J. Manchester at left, reclining allegorical woman with bale and casks at center, bank crest at right. Back: Bank façade at center. Printer: ABNC.			
	a. Signature title: *MANAGER* at left.	650.	2000.	—
	b. Signature title: *FOR GENERAL MANAGER* at left.	650.	2000.	—

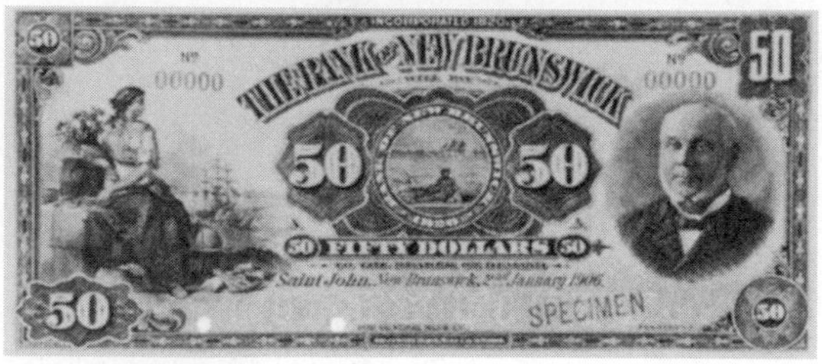

		Good	Fine	XF
S599	**50 Dollars** 2.1.1906. Black and green. Seated allegory Commerce at left, bank crest at center, J. Manchester at right. Back: Bank façade at center. Printer: ABNC.			
	a. Signature title: *MANAGER* at left.	650.	2000.	—
	b. Signature title: *FOR GENERAL MANAGER* at left.	650.	2000.	—

Bank of Nova Scotia

1832-52 Issues

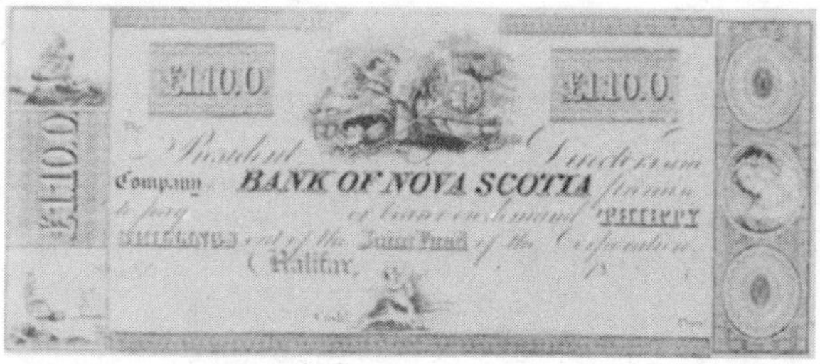

		Good	Fine	XF
S601	**1 Pound-10 Shillings** 18xx. Black. Sailing ships at top and bottom left, farm implements, produce at top center, child riding deer at bottom center, portrait Ceres at right. Proof.	—	Unc	500.
S602	**2 Pounds** 18xx. Black. Proof.	—	Unc	500.

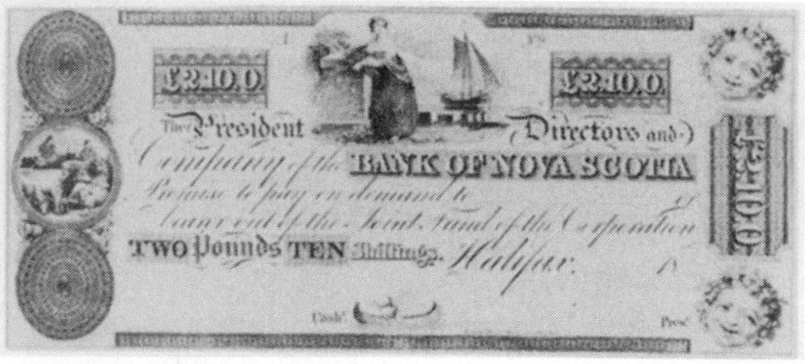

		Good	Fine	XF
S603	**2 Pounds-10 Shillings** 18xx. Black. Standing allegorical woman with sailing ship in background at upper center, man in canoe at bottom center, two men with livestock at left, cherub's face at top and bottom right. Proof.	—	Unc	500.
S604	**5 Pounds** 3.4.1837. Black. Three cherubs at top center, blacksmith at left, alchemist at right. Portrait Ceres at lower center.	600.	1750.	—
S605	**5 Pounds** 2.6.1834; 1.1.1852. Black. Three cherubs at top center, blacksmith at left, alchemist at right, horse's head at lower center.	600.	1750.	—

#S606 *Deleted*. See #S612.

		Good	Fine	XF
S607	**5 Pounds-5 Shillings** 2.5.1840. Black. St. George slaying dragon at top center, man and boy at left, sailing ship at right.	650.	2000.	—
S608	**6 Pounds** 1.7.1840. Black. Allegorical male on chariot at top center, men harvesting wheat at left, steamboat at bottom center, man on horseback and farmer at right.	650.	2000.	—
S609	**7 Pounds** 1.8.1840. Black. Halifax harbor at top center, sailor with flag at left, deer at bottom center, milkmaid at right.	650.	2000.	—
S610	**7 Pounds-10 Shillings** 1.8.1840. Black. Crest at top center, standing Justice at left, dog with key at bottom center, woman with lyre at right.	650.	2000.	—

		Good	Fine	XF
S611	**10 Pounds** 1.1.1839; 1.1.1852. Black. Portrait King William IV at left, royal arms at upper center, allegory Navigation at right.	600.	1750.	—

1864 Issue

		VG	VF	UNC
S612	**20 Dollars** 1.1.1864. Black and green. Royal arms at top center. Printer: Blades, East & Blades, London.	1500.	2500.	—

1870; 1871 Issue

		Good	Fine	XF
S616	**4 Dollars** 1.7.1870; 1.7.1871. Black on green underprint. Beehive and flowers at upper center. Printer: BABNC.			
	a. Issued note.	800.	2000.	—
	b. Red overprint: *CANADA CURRENCY* twice. 1.7.1870.	800.	2000.	—

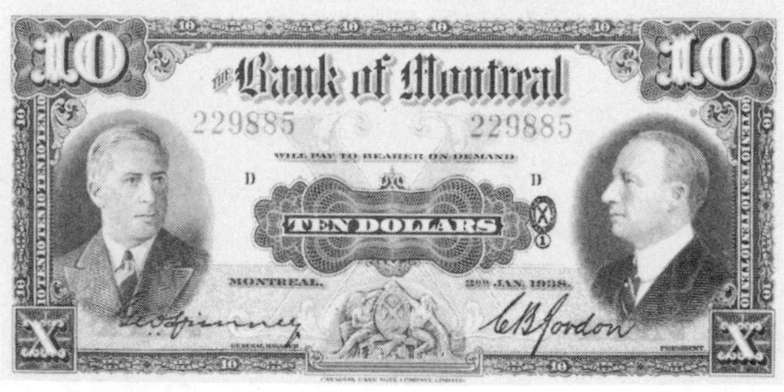

		Good	Fine	XF
S617	**5 Dollars** 1.7.1870; 1.7.1871; 2.7.1877. Black and green. St. George slaying dragon at upper center. Printer: BABNC.			
	a. Issued note.	800.	2000.	—
	b. Red overprint: *CANADA CURRENCY* twice. 1.7.1870.	800.	2000.	—
S617A	**20 Dollars** 1.7.1871; 1.1.1877. Black on green underprint. Printer: ABNC. Reported not confirmed.	—	—	—
S617B	**4 Dollars** 2.7.1877. Black on green underprint. *PROVINCE OF - NOVA SCOTIA* at top center. Printer: BABNC.	800.	2000.	—

1877 Issue

		Good	Fine	XF
S618	**5 Dollars** 2.7.1881. Black on blue underprint. Pallas at upper left, portrait J. Howe at center, bank crest at lower right. *FIVE* at lower left and right of portrait. Back: Green. Proof.	—	Unc	900.

1881-1929 Issues

		Good	Fine	XF
S618A	**5 Dollars** 2.7.1881. Pallas at upper left, portrait J. Howe at center, bank crest at lower right. Back: Brown. Printer: ABNC.			
	a. Issued note.	750.	2000.	—
	b. Red overprint: *WINNIPEG* twice.	800.	2500.	—
S618B	**5 Dollars** 2.7.1881. Black on blue, green and ochre underprint. Large curved *FIVE* under portrait. Printer: ABNC.	650.	2000.	—

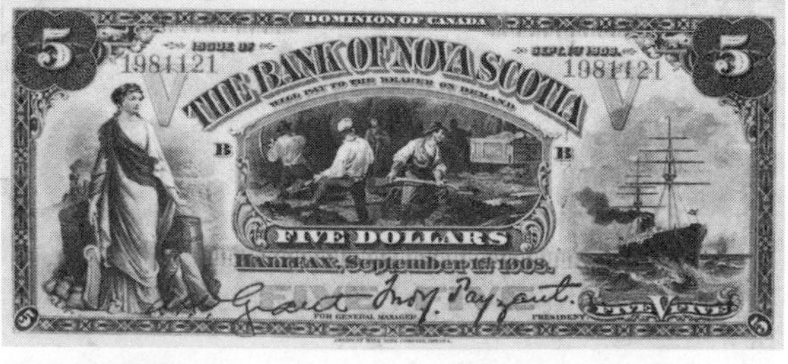

		VG	VF	UNC
S619	**5 Dollars** 1898-1908. Black on green and orange underprint. Mining scene at center, standing allegorical woman at left, steamship at right. Printer: ABNC.			
	a. With and without red overprint: *SS*. 1.6.1898.	125.	225.	—
	b. With orange Roman numerals *V*s. 1.9.1908.	50.00	125.	350.
	c. Without orange Roman numeral *V*'s at upper left and right. 1.9.1908.	75.00	150.	375.

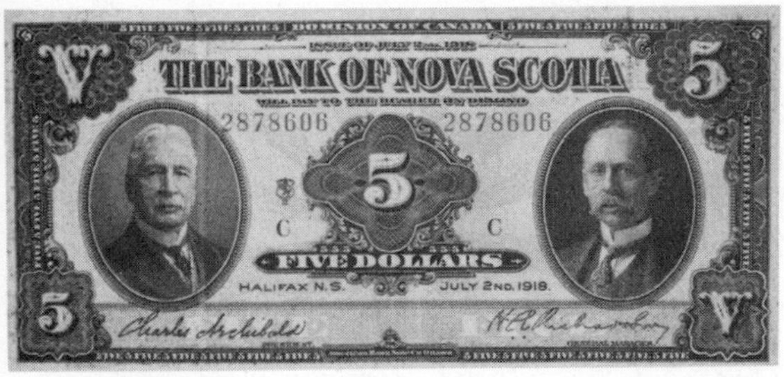

S620 5 Dollars	VG	VF	UNC
2.7.1918. Black on green underprint. Portrait J. Y. Payzant at left, portrait H. A. Richardson at right. Printer: ABNC.	50.00	100.	275.

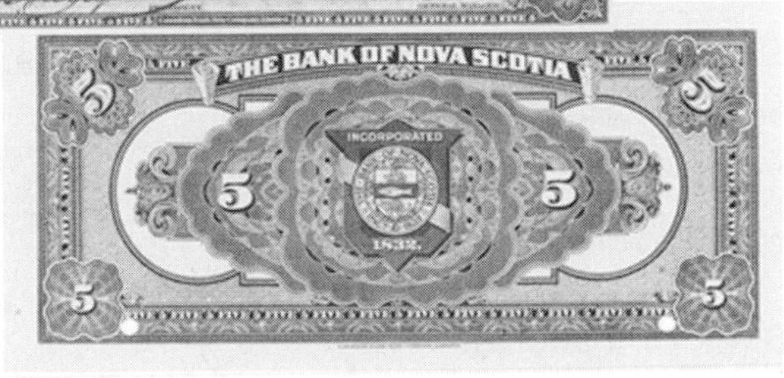

S621 5 Dollars	VG	VF	UNC
2.1.1924. Black on red and green underprint. Portrait G. S. Campbell at left, portrait J .A. McLeod at right. Printer: CBNC.			
a. Issued note.	25.00	50.00	175.
s. Specimen.	—	—	—

S622 5 Dollars	VG	VF	UNC
2.1.1929. Black on red and green underprint. Printer: CBNC.	25.00	50.00	175.

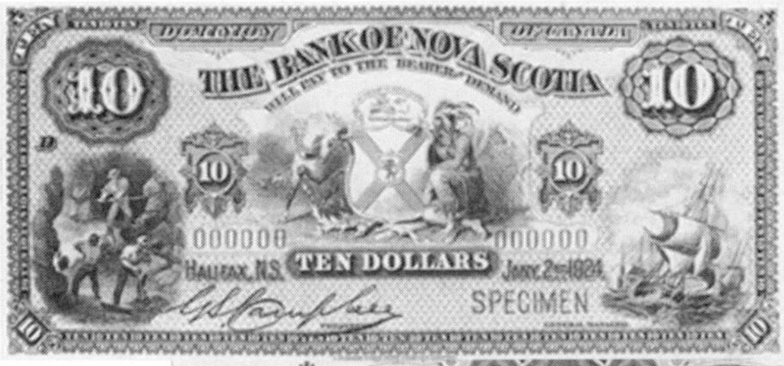

S623 10 Dollars	VG	VF	UNC
1877-1929. Black on ochre and blue underprint. Printer: ABNC or CBNC.			
a. Back green. 2.7.1877.	750.	1250.	—
b. Back green. 2.1.1903.	150.	300.	1000.
c. As b. 2.1.1917.	50.00	100.	275.
d. As b. 2.1.1919.	50.00	100.	275.
e. Back blue. 2.1.1924.	25.00	50.00	150.
f. Back gray. 2.1.1929.	25.00	50.00	150.
s. As e. Specimen.	—	—	—

#S624 *Deleted*. See #S671A.

S625 20 Dollars	VG	VF	UNC
1.1.1882. Printer: ABNC. Proof.	—	—	750.

S626 20 Dollars	VG	VF	UNC
2.7.1896. Black on pink and blue underprint. Allegorical woman, globe and cherub at center. Printer: ABNC.	1750.	4000.	—

S627 20 Dollars	VG	VF	UNC
1.11.1897. Black on yellow-green and rose underprint. Allegorical women at left and right, portrait of woman at upper center. Printer: ABNC.	1750.	4000.	—

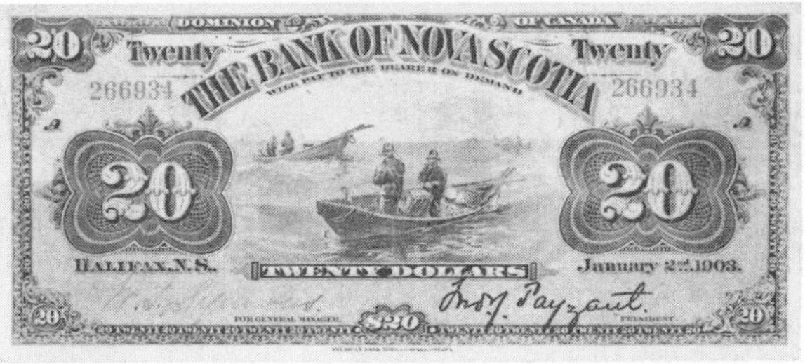

S628 20 Dollars	VG	VF	UNC
1903; 1918. Black on yellow-green and rose underprint. Fishermen in boats at center with *HALIFAX, N.S.* at lower left and date at lower right. Back: Olive. Printer: ABNC or CBNC.			
a. 2.1.1903.	200.	500.	1250.
b. 1.2.1918.	50.00	100.	500.

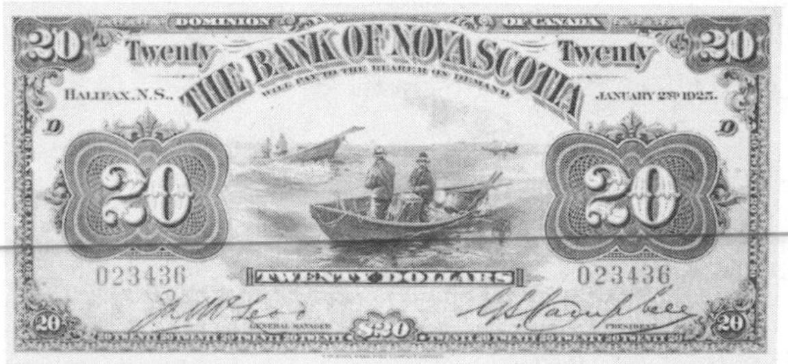

S629 20 Dollars	VG	VF	UNC
1925; 1929. *HALIFAX, N.S.* at upper left and date at upper right. Printer: ABNC or CBNC.			
a. Back green. 2.1.1925.	50.00	100.	500.
b. Back orange. 2.1.1929.	25.00	75.00	275.

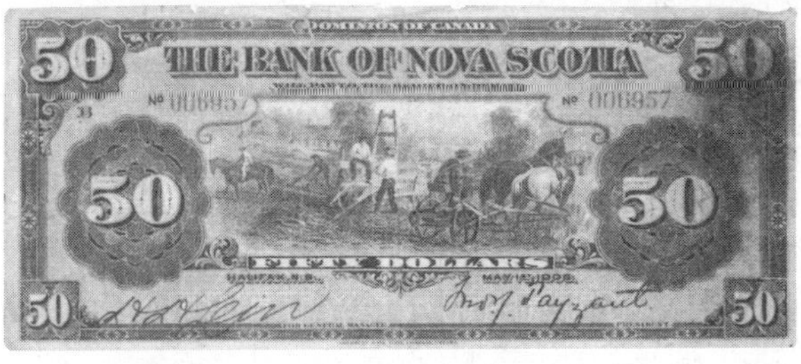

S630 50 Dollars	VG	VF	UNC
1.5.1906; 2.7.1920; 2.1.1925. Black on olive and red underprint. Threshing scene at center. Back: Slate. Printer: ABNC or CBNC.			
a. 1.5.1906.	750.	1500.	—
b. 2.7.1920.	500.	1000.	3250.
c. 2.1.1925.	500.	1000.	3250.

S631 100 Dollars	VG	VF	UNC
1899-1929. Black on yellow-green and rose underprint. Liberty seated with lion at left center, seated Art and Industry at center right. Back: Brown. Printer: ABNC or CBNC.			
a. 1.8.1899.	850.	2000.	—
b. 3.1.1911.	750.	1750.	—
c. 2.1.1919; 2.1.1925; 2.1.1929.	500.	1250.	—

1935 Issue

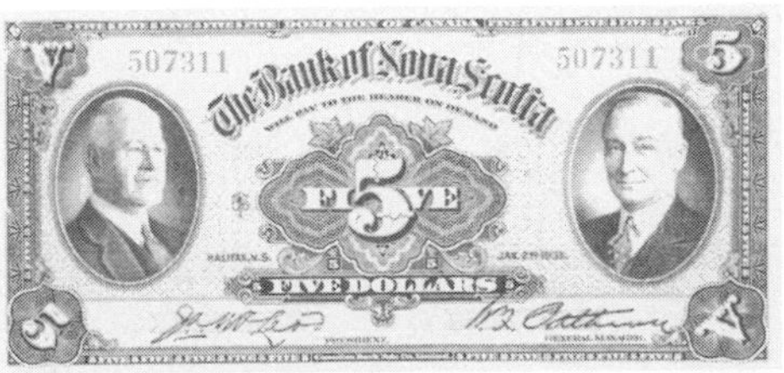

S632 5 Dollars	VG	VF	UNC
2.1.1935. Black on red and green underprint. Portrait J. A. McLeod at left, portrait H. F. Patterson at right. Back: Green. Seal at center. Printer: CBNC. Reduced size.	20.00	40.00	125.

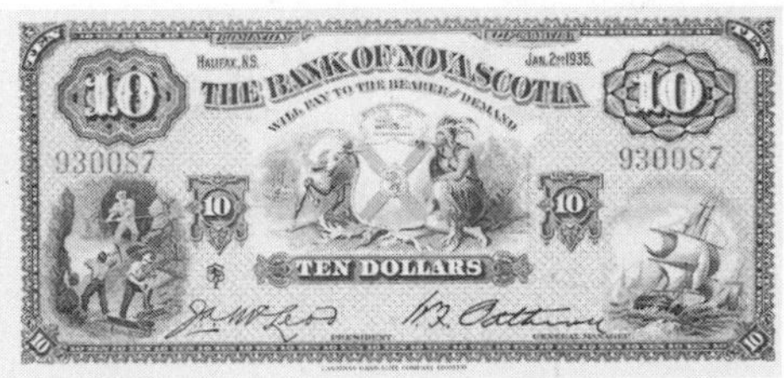

	VG	VF	UNC
S633 10 Dollars 2.1.1935. Black on ochre and blue underprint. Portrait J. A. McLeod at left, portrait H. F. Patterson at right. Back: Slate gray. Bank seal at center. Printer: CBNC. Reduced size.	25.00	50.00	150.

Bank of Ottawa

1874 Issue

	Good	Fine	XF
S636 4 Dollars 2.11.1874. Black on green underprint. G. Bryson at lower left, J. Maclaren at lower right. Crest of Ottawa at upper center. Back: Green. Printer: BABNC.	650.	1750.	—
S637 5 Dollars 2.11.1874. Black on green underprint. G. Bryson at upper left, J. Maclaren at upper right. Crest of Ottawa at upper center. Back: Green. Printer: BABNC.	600.	1600.	—
S638 10 Dollars 2.11.1874. Black on green underprint. Crest of Ottawa at upper center. Like #S636 and #S637. Back: Green. Printer: BABNC. Face proof.	—	Unc	400.

1880 Issue

	VG	VF	UNC
S641 5 Dollars 2.11.1880. Black on olive underprint. Girl with lamb at left, loggers ("Rafting") at center, woman with pen ("Trade") at right. Back: Brown. Rafting at left. Printer: ABNC.			
a. Issued note.	1250.	2250.	—
s. Specimen.	—	—	600.

	VG	VF	UNC
S642 10 Dollars 2.11.1880. Black on olive underprint. Portrait blacksmith at left, Justice with two oval shields at center, portrait sailor at right. Back: Brown. Indian maiden at center. Printer: ABNC.			
a. Issued note.	1250.	2250.	—
s. Specimen.	—	—	600.

1888-91 Issue

	VG	VF	UNC
S646 5 Dollars 2.11.1888. Black on green underprint. Lumberjack felling tree at left, cattle at center, J. Maclaren at right. Back: Green. Printer: BABNC.			
a. Issued note.	1250.	2500.	—
p. Proof.	—	—	600.
S647 10 Dollars 2.11.1888. Black on green underprint. Back: Green. J. Maclaren at center Crest at center. Printer: BABNC. Proof.	—	—	600.
S648 20 Dollars 2.11.1891. Black on green underprint. Loggers, J. Maclaren and Canal Locks No. 2 at center. Back: Green. Printer: BABNC. Proof.	—	—	600.
S649 50 Dollars 2.11.1891. Black on green underprint. Back: Green. Printer: BABNC. Proof.	—	—	750.

1895-1900 Issue

	VG	VF	UNC
S651 5 Dollars 1895; 1900. Reclining allegorical woman at center, C. Magee at left, Parliament building at right. Back: Green. Ottawa Crest at center. Printer: BABNC.			
a. Black on green underprint. 2.1.1895.	1250.	2500.	—
b. Black on ochre underprint. 1.6.1900.	1250.	2500.	—
S652 10 Dollars 1895-1900. Reclining allegorical woman at center, C. Magee at left, Parliament building at right. Back: Green. Ottawa Crest at center. Printer: BABNC.			
a. Black on green underprint. 2.1.1895.	1500.	3000.	—
b. Black on ochre underprint. 1.6.1900.	1500.	3000.	

1903 Issue

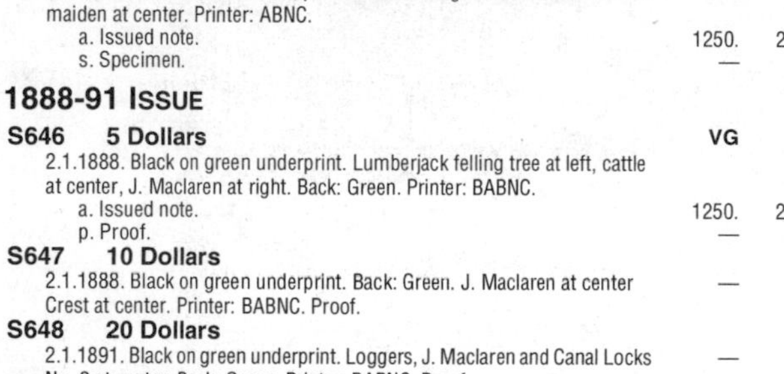

	VG	VF	UNC
S653 5 Dollars 2.1.1903. Black on ochre underprint. Steam locomotive at left, Parliament building at center right. Back: Green. Ottawa Crest at center. Printer: BABNC.			
a. Issued note.	1000.	2000.	—
p. Proof.	—	—	750.
S654 10 Dollars 2.1.1903. Black on olive underprint. Head office building at left, cattle scene at center Parliament building at right. Back: Green. Ottawa Crest at center. Printer: BABNC.			
a. Large tint.	1250.	2500.	—
b. Modified smaller tint.	1250.	2500.	—
S655 20 Dollars 2.1.1903. Black and green. Loggers, portrait G. Bryson and Canal Locks No. 2 at center. Back: Green. Ottawa Crest at center. Printer: BABNC.	1250.	2500.	—
S656 50 Dollars 2.1.1903. Black and green. Farmer with horse and dog at left, Parliament building above portrait G. Bryson at center, three horses' heads at right. Back: Green. Ottawa Crest at center. Printer: BABNC.	1250.	2250.	—

1906 Issue

	VG	VF	UNC
S657 5 Dollars 1906; 1917. Logging camp scene at center. Printer: ABNC.			
a. Black on green underprint. signature Hay at right. 1.6.1906.	600.	1250.	—
b. Black on green underprint. signature Maclaren at right.	600.	1250.	—
c. Black on yellow and green underprint. signature Maclaren at right. 1.6.1906.	600.	1250.	—
d. Black on yellow and green underprint. signature Bryson at right. 1.6.1917.	750.	1500.	—
S658 10 Dollars 1.6.1906. Dairy farm scene at center. Printer: ABNC.			
a. Black on green underprint. signature Hay at right.	600.	1250.	—
b. Black on green underprint. signature Maclaren at right.	600.	1250.	—
c. Black on yellow and green underprint. signature Maclaren at right.	600.	1250.	—

1912-13 Issues

	Good	Fine	XF
S661 5 Dollars 1.6.1912. Black on blue underprint. Logging camp scene at center. Back: Olive-green. Ottawa Crest at center. Printer: W&S.	300.	800.	1750.
S662 5 Dollars 1.9.1913. Black on blue-green and ochre underprint. Logging camp scene at center. Back: Brown. Ottawa Crest at center. Printer: W&S.	250.	600.	1250.
S663 10 Dollars 1.8.1913. Dairy farm scene at center. Back: Green. Ottawa Crest at center. Printer: ABNC.			
a. Black on green underprint.	275.	700.	—
b. Black on ochre and green underprint.	275.	700.	—
S664 10 Dollars 1.9.1913. Black on green underprint. Cattle under trees at center. Back: Green. Ottawa Crest at center. Printer: BABNC.	275.	700.	1750.

Bank of Toronto

1856-65 Province of Canada Issues

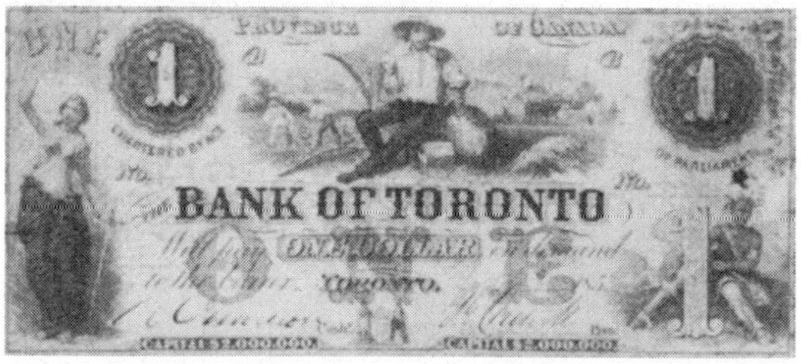

	Good	Fine	XF
S666 1 Dollar 3.7.1856. Justice at left, seated farmer at upper center, seated Indian at lower right. Small Toronto Crest at bottom center. Back: Orange. Queen Vitoria and Prince Albert medallion at center.			
a. Black with blue *ONE* protector.	450.	1250.	—
b. Black with green *ONE* protector.	450.	1250.	—
S667 1 Dollar 2.7.1859. Black with green *ONE* protector. Justice at left, seated farmer at upper center, seated Indian at lower right. Small Toronto Crest at bottom center. Back: Orange. Black with green *ONE* protector. Queen Victoria and Prince Albert medallion at center.			
a. Issued note.	150.	600.	—
b. Blue overprint: *MONTREAL* twice.	150.	600.	—
c. Red overprint: *PETERBORO* twice.	150.	600.	—
d. Blue overprint: *PORT HOPE* twice.	150.	600.	—
S668 2 Dollars 3.7.1856. Two children with sheaves at lower left, steam train and wagons at wharf at top center, allegorical woman at right. Small Toronto Crest at bottom center. Back: Orange. Queen Victoria and Prince Albert medallion at center.			
a. Black with blue *TWO* protector.	450.	1250.	—
b. Black with green *TWO* protector.	450.	1250.	—
S669 2 Dollars 2.7.1859. Black with green *TWO* protector. Two children with sheaves at lower left, steam train and wagons at wharf at top center, allegorical woman at right. Small Toronto Crest at bottom center. Back: Orange. Black with green *TWO* protector. Queen Victoria and Prince Albert medallion at center.	225.	1000.	—
S670 4 Dollars 3.7.1856. Farmer with scythe at lower left, three allegorical women at top center, Indian Chief Red Jacket at lower right. Small Toronto Crest at bottom center. Back: Orange. Queen Victoria and Prince Albert medallion at center.			
a. Black with blue *FOUR* protector.	450.	1250.	—
b. Blue overprint: *BARRIE* twice.	450.	1250.	—
c. Black with green *FOUR* protector.	450.	1250.	—

	Good	Fine	XF
S671 4 Dollars			
2.7.1859. Black with green *FOUR* protector. Farmer with scythe at lower left, three allegorical women at top center, Indian Chief Red Jacket at lower right. Uniface. Back: Orange. Black with green *FOUR* protector. Queen Victoria and Prince Albert medallion at center.			
a. Issued note.	350.	1100.	—
b. Blue overprint: *BARRIER* twice.	350.	1100.	—
c. Blue overprint: *COBOURG* twice.	350.	1100.	—
d. Blue overprint: *MONTREAL* twice.	350.	1100.	—
S672 5 Dollars			
3.7.1856. Woman at lower left, royal arms at upper center, Commerce with large *5* sideways at lower right. Small Toronto Crest at bottom center. Back: Orange. Queen Victoria and Prince Albert medallion at center.			
a. Black with blue *V - V* protector.	400.	1200.	—
b. Black with green *V - V* protector.	400.	1200.	—
S673 5 Dollars			
3.1.1857. Woman at lower left, royal arms at upper center, Commerce with large *5* sideways at lower right. Small Toronto Crest at bottom center. Back: Orange. Queen Victoria and Prince Albert medallion at center. Overprint: Blue: *COBOURG* twice. Rare.	—	—	—
S674 5 Dollars			
1859-65. Woman at lower left, royal arms at upper center, Commerce with large *5* sideways at lower right. Small Toronto Crest at bottom center. Uniface. Back: Orange. Queen Victoria and Prince Albert medallion at center.			
a. Black with green *V - V* protector on face and back. 2.7.1859.	300.	1100.	—
b. Black with blue *V - V* protector on face and back. 3.7.1865.	300.	1100.	—
S675 10 Dollars			
185x. Beaver at lower left, Toronto Crest at upper center, steam passenger train at lower right. Small Toronto Crest at bottom center. Back: Orange. Queen Victoria and Prince Albert medallion at center. Proof.	—	Unc	500.
S676 10 Dollars			
2.7.1859. Black with green *TEN* protector. Beaver at lower left, Toronto Crest at upper center, steam passenger train at lower right. Small Toronto Crest at bottom center. Uniface. Back: Black with green *TEN* protector. Queen Victoria and Prince Albert medallion at center.			
a. Issued note.	400.	1250.	—
b. Blue overprint: *COLLINGWOOD* twice.	400.	1250.	—
c. Blue overprint: *ST. CATHARINES* twice.	400.	1250.	—

1876-80 Dominion of Canada Issue

#S681-S684 *DOMINION OF CANADA* replaces *PROVINCE OF CANADA* below bank title.

	Good	Fine	XF
S681 4 Dollars			
1.1.1876. Black on green and pink underprint. Man's portrait at lower left, allegorical woman with two children at center, portrait W. Gooderham at lower right. Uniface. Printer: ABNC.			
a. Issued note.	500.	1500.	—
b. Blue overprint: *COLLINGWOOD* twice.	500.	1500.	—
c. Blue overprint: *ST. CATHARINES* twice.	500.	1500.	—

#S682-S684 back blue; Qn. Victoria and Prince Albert medallion at ctr.

	Good	Fine	XF
S682 5 Dollars			
1.7.1880. Black with green *FIVE* protector. Woman at lower left, royal arms at upper center, Commerce with lerge *5* sideways at lower right. Back: Blue. Queen Victoria and Prince Albert medallion at center. Printer: ABNC.			
a. Issued note.	500.	1500.	—
b. Blue overprint: *ST. CATHARINES* twice.	500.	1500.	—
S683 10 Dollars			
1.7.1880. Black. Beaver at lower left, Toronto Crest at upper center, steam passenger train at lower right. Back: Blue. Queen Victoria and Prince Albert medallion at center. Printer: ABNC. Proof.	—	Unc	500.
S684 20 Dollars			
1.7.1880. Black. Portrait Queen Victoria at lower left, steam passenger train at center, milkmaid by cow and calf at lower right. Back: Blue. Queen Victoria and Prince Albert medallion at center. Printer: ABNC.	—	Unc	500.

NOTE: Counterfeit notes of this issue exist w/overprint: *PETERBORO* or *PORT HOPE* but no genuine notes w/these particular overprint. are currently known.

1887-1929 Issue

	Good	Fine	XF
S686 5 Dollars			
1890-1929. Black on yellow underprint. Black with green *5* protector. Printer: ABNC or CBNC.			
a. Issued note. 1.7.1890; 1.2.1906.	250.	750.	—
b2. Overprint: *CARDINAL*. 1.7.1890.	1500.	—	—
c. Blue overprint: *COLDWATER* (Ontario). 1.7.1890. Rare.	—	—	—
d. Overprint: *CREEMORE*. 1.7.1890. Rare.	—	—	—
e. Overprint: *ELMVALE*. 1.7.1890. Rare.	—	—	—
f. Blue overprint: *GANANOQUE* (Ontario). 1.7.1890. Rare.	—	—	—
g. Overprint: *KEENE*. 1.7.1890. Rare.	—	—	—
h. Blue overprint: *LONDON*. 1.7.1890.	300.	—	—
i. Overprint: *MILLBROOK*. 1.7.1890.	300.	—	—
j. Overprint: *MONTREAL*. 1.7.1890.	300.	—	—
k. Overprint: *NIAGARA FALLS CENTRE*. 1.7.1890.	300.	—	—
l. Overprint: *OIL SPRINGS*. 1.7.1890.	300.	—	—
m. Overprint: *OMOMEE*. 1.7.1890.	300.	—	—
n. Overprint: *PETERBORO*. 1.7.1890. Rare.	—	—	—
o. Blue overprint: *POINT ST. CHARLES* (Quebec). 1.7.1890. Rare.	—	—	—
p. Overprint: *PORT HOPE*. 1.7.1890. Rare.	—	—	—
q. Overprint: *ST. CATHARINES*. 1.7.1890. Rare.	—	—	—
r. Overprint: *SUDBURY*. 1.7.1890. Rare.	—	—	—
s. Blue overprint: *VICTORIA HARBOUR* (Ontario). 1.7.1890. Rare.	—	—	—
s1. As m. Specimen.	—	—	—
t. Blue overprint: *WINNIPEG*. 1.7.1890. Rare.	—	—	—
u. Overprint: *GASPE*. 1.2.1906. Rare.	—	—	—
v. Overprint: *POINT ST. CHARLES*. 1.2.1906. Rare.	—	—	—
w. Overprint: *ST. CATHARINES*. 1.2.1906. Rare.	—	—	—
x. Overprint: *WATERLOO*. 1.2.1906. Rare.	—	—	—
y. 1.2.1911.	300.	1000.	—
z. 1.2.1912.	100.	250.	600.
aa. 1.2.1914.	100.	250.	600.
ab. 1.2.1917.	50.00	100.	300.
ac. 1.2.1923.	25.00	75.00	250.
ad. 1.10.1929.	25.00	75.00	175.

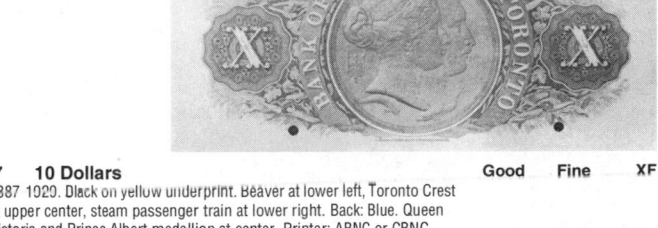

	Good	Fine	XF
S687 10 Dollars			
1887-1929. Black on yellow underprint. Beaver at lower left, Toronto Crest at upper center, steam passenger train at lower right. Back: Blue. Queen Victoria and Prince Albert medallion at center. Printer: ABNC or CBNC.			
a. 1.7.1887.	300.	750.	—
b. 1.6.1892.	200.	500.	—
c. Blue overprint: *KING STREET WEST BR.* (Toronto). 1.7.1887. Rare.	—	—	—
d. Blue overprint: *LONDON*. 1.7.1887. Rare.	—	—	—
e. Overprint: *LONDON FF*. 1.7.1887. Rare.	—	—	—
f. Overprint: *CARTWRIGHT*. 1.6.1892. Rare.	—	—	—
g. Overprint: *COPPER CLIFF*. 1.6.1892. Rare.	—	—	—
h. Overprint: *KING STREET WEST BR.* 1.6.1892. Rare.	—	—	—
i. Overprint: *LONDON*. 1.6.1892. Rare.	—	—	—
j. 1.6.1902.	200.	500.	—
k. 1.2.1906.	200.	500.	—
l. 1.2.1911.	200.	500.	—
m. 1.2.1912; 1.2.1914.	100.	250.	—
n. 1.2.1917; 1.2.1923; 1.10.1929.	50.00	100.	300.
s. Specimen.	—	—	—

	Good	Fine	XF
S688 20 Dollars			
1887-1923. Black on yellow underprint. Portrait Queen Victoria at lower left, steam passenger train at center, milkmaid by cow and calf at lower right. Back: Queen Victoria and Prince Albert medallion at center. Printer: ABNC or CBNC.			
a. 1.7.1887.	350.	1000.	—
b. Blue overprint: *PARRY SOUND*. 1.7.1887. Rare.	—	—	—
c. Blue overprint: *WINNIPEG*. 1.7.1887. Rare.	—	—	—
d. 1.2.1906; 2.2.1913.	250.	650.	—
e. 1.2.1917; 1.2.1923; 1.10.1929.	75.00	150.	500.
s. Specimen.	—	—	—

S689 50 Dollars	Good	Fine	XF
1890-1929. Black on yellow underprint. Bull's head at lower left, City Hall at center, cattle at lower right. Printer: ABNC or CBNC.			
a. 1.2.1906; 1.2.1914.	500.	1250.	—
b. 2.2.1920; 1.10.1929.	200.	500.	1250.
p. Proof. 1.7.1890; 2.2.1913.	—	Unc	350.
s. Specimen. 1.2.1906.	—	Unc	400.

1935-37 Issue

S691 5 Dollars	VG	VF	UNC
1935; 1937. Black on yellow underprint. Black with green *5* protector. Back: Queen Victoria and Prince Albert medallion at center. Printer: CBNC. Reduced size.			
a. Signature H. B. Henwood and W. G. Gooderham. 2.1.1935.	25.00	50.00	200.
b. Signature H. B. Henwood and J. R. Lamb. 2.1.1937.	25.00	50.00	200.
c. Signature F. H. Marsh and J. R. Lamb. 2.1.1937.	25.00	50.00	200.

S692 10 Dollars	VG	VF	UNC
1935; 1937. Black on yellow underprint. Beaver at lower left, Toronto Crest at upper center, steam passenger train at lower right. Printer: CBNC. Reduced size.			
a. Signature H. B. Henwood and W. G. Gooderham. 2.1.1935.	25.00	50.00	200.
b. Signature H. B. Henwood and J. R. Lamb. 2.1.1937.	25.00	50.00	200.
c. Signature F. H. Marsh and J. R. Lamb. 2.1.1937.	25.00	50.00	200.
S693 20 Dollars			
2.1.1935. Black on yellow underprint. Portrait Queen Victoria at lower left, steam passenger train at center, milkmaid by cow and calf at lower right. Back: Queen Victoria and Prince Albert medallion at center. Printer: CBNC. Reduced size.	50.00	100.	300.

Bank of Vancouver

1910 Issue

S696 5 Dollars	Good	Fine	XF
2.5.1910. Black on green and yellow-green underprint. Ships in harbor at center. Back: Green. Parliament building, Victoria. Printer: BABNC.			
a. Issued note.	2500.	7500.	—
p. Proof.	—	Unc	750.

S697 10 Dollars	Good	Fine	XF
2.5.1910. Black on green and red-brown underprint. Lumberjacks cutting down fir tree at left. Back: Brown. Parliament building, Victoria. Printer: BABNC.			
a. Issued note.	3000.	10,000.	—
p. Proof.	—	Unc	750.
S698 20 Dollars			
2.5.1910. Black on yellow-orange and red underprint. Fishermen in boats at center. Back: Red. Parliament building, Victoria. Printer: BABNC.			
a. Issued note.	3000.	10,000.	—
p. Proof.	—	Unc	750.
S699 50 Dollars			
2.5.1910. Black on blue underprint. Miners at center right. Back: Blue. Parliament building, Victoria. Printer: BABNC.	—	Unc	750.

S700 100 Dollars	Good	Fine	XF
2.5.1910. Black on olive-green underprint. Harvesting grain at center. Back: Parliament building, Victoria. Printer: BABNC. Proof.	—	Unc	750.

Bank of Yarmouth

1860 Issue

S701 20 Dollars	Good	Fine	XF
1.12.1860. Black on green underprint. Farmer planting at lower left, portrait Princess of Wales between lion and unicorn at top center, ship in dry dock at right. Back: Orange. Printer: ABNC.			
a. Issued note.	1000.	3250.	—
b. Red overprint: *CANADIAN CURRENCY*.	1000.	3250.	—

1870-91 Issue

S702 4 Dollars	Good	Fine	XF
1.7.1870. Black on green underprint. Allegorical woman at sea borne by two porpoises at left. Indian maiden at right. Signature varieties. Back: Green. Printer: BABNC.			
a. Issued note.	1000.	3250.	—
b. Red overprint: *CANADIAN CURRENCY*.	1000.	3250.	—
p. Face proof.	—	Unc	750.
S703 5 Dollars			
1870; 1891. Black on green underprint. Anchor at upper left, sailing ships at upper center, allegorical woman with flag, sailing ships in background at lower right. Signature varieties. Back: Green. Printer: BABNC.			
a. 1.7.1870.	1000.	3250.	—
b. Red overprint: *CANADIAN CURRENCY*.	1000.	3250.	—
c. 1.7.1891.	1000.	3250.	—
S704 10 Dollars			
1870; 1891. Black on green underprint. Oval portrait of Queen Victoria in "Widow's Weeds" between lion and unicorn at lower center. Signature varieties. Back: Green. Printer: BABNC.			
a. 1.7.1870.	1000.	3250.	—
b. Red overprint: *CANADIAN CURRENCY*.	1000.	3250.	—
c. 1.7.1891.	1000.	3250.	—

Banque Canadienne Nationale

1925 Issue

S706 5 Dollars	VG	VF	UNC
1.2.1925. Black on green underprint. Monument at center. Portrait J. A. Vaillancourt at left, portrait B. Leman at right. Back: Green. Provincial crests on back. Printer: CBNC.			
a. Issued note.	50.00	100.	—
s. Specimen.	—	—	—

S707 10 Dollars VG VF UNC

1.2.1925. Black on brown underprint. Monument at center. J. A. Vaillancourt at left, portrait B. Leman at right. Back: Brown. Provincial crests. Printer: CBNC.

	VG	VF	UNC
a. Issued note.	50.00	100.	—
s. Specimen.	—	—	—

S708 20 Dollars VG VF UNC

1.2.1925. Black on blue underprint. Monument at center. J. A. Vaillancourt at left, portrait B. Leman at right. Back: Blue. Provincial crests. Printer: CBNC.

	VG	VF	UNC
a. Issued note.	100.	200.	—
s. Specimen.	—	—	—

S709 50 Dollars VG VF UNC

1.2.1925. Black on olive underprint. Maisonneuve monument at center.J. A. Vaillancourt at left, portrait B. Leman at right. Back: Olive. Provincial crests. Printer: CBNC.

	VG	VF	UNC
a. Issued note.	250.	500.	—
s. Specimen.	—	—	—

	VG	VF	UNC
S710 100 Dollars 1.2.1925. Black on purple underprint. J. A. Vaillancourt at left, portrait B. Leman at right. Back: Purple. Printer: CBNC. Specimen.	350.	750.	—

1929 Issue

	VG	VF	UNC
S711 5 Dollars 1.2.1929. Black on green underprint. Monument at center. Portrait F. L. Beique at left, portrait B. Leman at right. Back: Green. Provincial crests at center. Printer: CBNC.	50.00	100.	—
S712 10 Dollars 1.2.1929. Black on brown underprint. Monument at center. Portrait F. L. Beique at left, portrait B. Leman at right. Back: Brown. Provincial crests at center. Printer: CBNC.	50.00	100.	—

	VG	VF	UNC
S713 20 Dollars 1.2.1929. Black on blue underprint. Monument at center. Portrait F. L. Beique at left, portrait B. Leman at right. Back: Blue. Provincial crests at center. Printer: CBNC.	150.	300.	—

	VG	VF	UNC
S714 50 Dollars 1.2.1929. Black on olive underprint. Maisonneuve monument at center. Portrait F. L. Beique at left, portrait B. Leman at right. Back: Olive. Provincial crests at center. Printer: CBNC.	350.	600.	—
S715 100 Dollars 1.2.1929. Black on purple underprint. Portrait F. L. Beique at left, portrait B. Leman at right. Back: Purple. Provincial crests at center. Printer: CBNC. Specimen.	—	—	750.

1935 Issue

		VG	VF	UNC
S716	**5 Dollars** 2.1.1935. Black on green underprint. Monument at center. Back: Green. Printer: CBNC. Reduced size.	25.00	50.00	175.

		VG	VF	UNC
S717	**10 Dollars** 2.1.1935. Black on brown underprint. Monument at center. Back: Brown. Printer: CBNC.	25.00	55.00	225.

Banque d'Hochelaga

1874-77 Issues

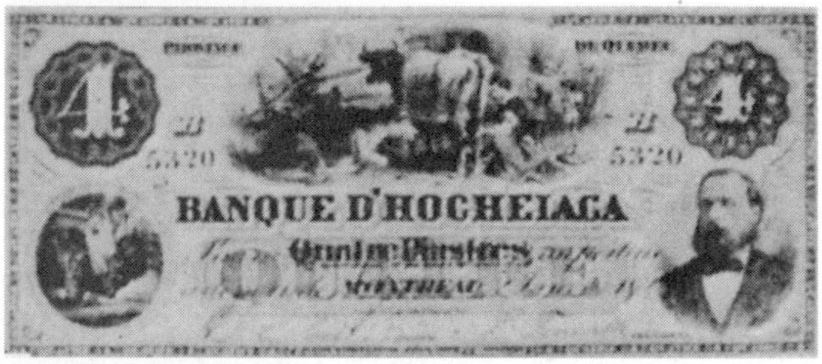

		VG	VF	UNC
S721	**4 Dollars** 2.1.1874. Black on green underprint. Three horses' heads at lower left, milkmaid with cows at top center. L. Tourville at lower right. Signature varieties. Back: Green. Printer: BABNC.	1000.	2000.	—
S722	**4 Dollars** 2.7.1877. Black on green underprint. Three horses' heads at lower left, milkmaid with cows at top center. L. Tourville at lower right. Signature varieties. Back: Green. Overprint: Blue: *TROIS-RIVIERES.* Printer: BABNC.	1000.	2000.	—
S723	**5 Dollars** 2.1.1874. Black on green underprint. Steam passenger train, ships at dockside. L. Tourville at lower right. Signature varieties. Back: Green. Printer: BABNC. Face proof.	—	—	400.
S724	**10 Dollars** 2.1.1874. Black on green underprint. Shepherd boy at left, Jacques Cartier landing at center. L. Tourville at lower right. Signature varieties. Back: Green. Printer: BABNC. Face proof.	—	—	400.
S725	**20 Dollars** 1.11.1875. Black on green underprint. Dog on strong box at lower left, woman operating telegraph at upper center. L. Tourville at lower right. Signature varieties. Back: Green. Printer: BABNC. Face proof.	—	—	400.
S726	**50 Dollars** 1.11.1875. Black on green underprint. Woman with sheaf at left, fisherman, sailing ships at center. Tourville at lower right. Signature varieties. Back: Green. Printer: BABNC. Face proof.	—	—	400.
S727	**100 Dollars** 1.11.1875. Black on green underprint. Dog by safe at lower left, sailing ships dockside, factories at upper center. L. Tourville at lower right. Signature varieties. Back: Green. Printer: BABNC. Face proof.	—	—	400.

1880 Issue

		Good	Fine	XF
S781	**5 Dollars** 1.9.1880. Black on green underprint. Queen Victoria in "Widow's Weeds" at lower right. Signature varieties. Back: Green. Printer: BABNC. Face proof.	—	—	400.
S782	**10 Dollars** 1.9.1880. Black on green underprint. Queen Victoria in "Widow's Weeds" at lower right. Signature varieties. Back: Green. Printer: BABNC. Face proof.	—	—	400.
S783	**20 Dollars** 1.9.1880. Black on green underprint. Queen Victoria in "Widow's Weeds" at lower right. Signature varieties. Back: Green. Printer: BABNC. Face proof.	—	—	400.
S784	**50 Dollars** 1.9.1880. Black on green underprint. Queen Victoria in "Widow's Weeds" at lower right. Signature varieties. Back: Green. Printer: BABNC. Face proof.	—	—	400.
S785	**100 Dollars** 1.9.1880. Black on green underprint. Queen Victoria in "Widow's Weeds" at lower right. Signature varieties. Back: Green. Printer: BABNC. Face proof.	—	—	400.

1889 Issue

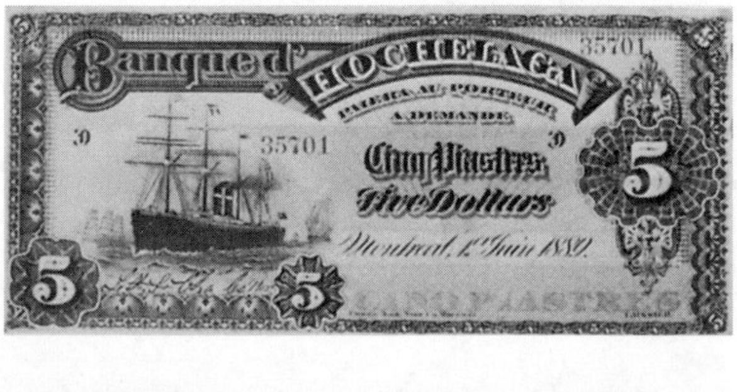

		VG	VF	UNC
S786	**5 Dollars** 1.6.1889. Black on multicolor underprint. Steam, sailing ships at left. Back: Provincial crest at center. Printer: CABNC.			
	a. Issued note.	1250.	2500.	—
	p1. Black. Proof.	—	—	300.
	p2. Black on multicolor underprint. Proof.	—	—	600.
	s. Back blue. Specimen.	—	—	800.

		Good	Fine	XF
S787	**10 Dollars** 1.6.1889. Farmers plowing with horses at left, portrait S. de Chaplain at right. Back: Provincial crest at center. Printer: CABNC.			
	p1. Black. Proof.	—	Unc	400.
	p2. Black on multicolor underprint. Proof.	—	Unc	600.
	s. Back orange. Specimen.	—	Unc	800.

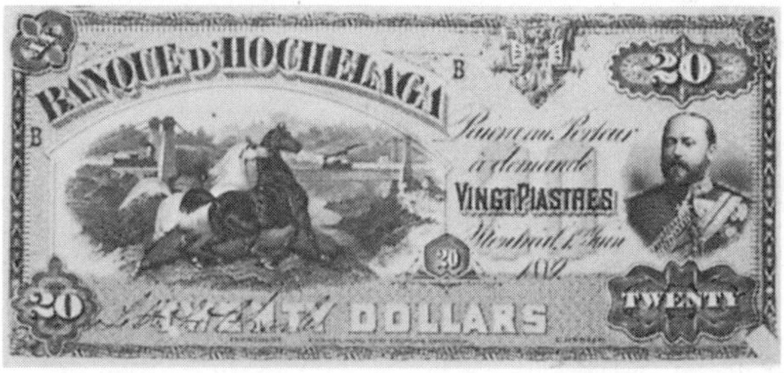

		Good	Fine	XF
S788	**20 Dollars** 1.6.1889. Horses with Roebling suspension bridge in background at left, Prince of Wales at right. Back: Provincial crest at center. Printer: CABNC.			
	p. Black on multicolor underprint. Proof.	—	Unc	600.
	s. Back green. Specimen.	—	Unc	800.

		Good	Fine	XF
S789	**50 Dollars** 1.6.1889. Prince of Wales at left, family on house raft at right. Back: Provincial crest at center. Printer: CABNC.			
	p. Black on multicolor underprint. Proof.	—	Unc	600.
	s. Back green. Specimen.	—	Unc	750.

		Good	Fine	XF
S790	**100 Dollars** 1.6.1889. Portrait S. de Champlain at upper left, Indians on bluff overlooking steam passenger train at right. Back: Provincial crest at center. Printer: CABNC.			
	p. Black on multicolor underprint. Proof.	—	Unc	600.
	s. Back green. Specimen.	—	Unc	750.

1894 Issue

		Good	Fine	XF
S791	**5 Dollars** 1.6.1894. Black on green underprint. Sailing ships in Montreal Harbor at top center. ortrait M. J. Pendergast at left, L. H. St. Charles at right. Signature varieties. Printer: BABNC. Face proof.	—	Unc	400.
S792	**10 Dollars** 1.6.1894. Black on green underprint. Cartier landing at center. Portrait M. J. Pendergast at left, L. H. St. Charles at right. Signature varieties. Printer: BABNC. Face proof.	—	Unc	400.

1898; 1907 Issue

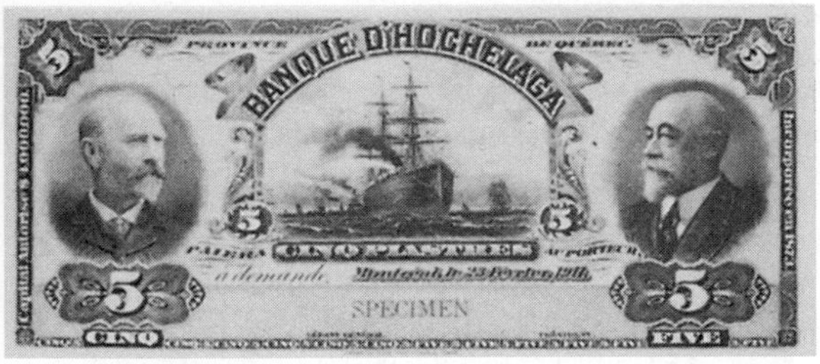

S796 5 Dollars	Good	Fine	XF
2.5.1898; 1.3.1907. Black on olive underprint. M. J. Pendergast at left, steamship at upper center, left. H. St. Charles at right. Signature varieties. Back: Green. Provincial arms at center. Printer: ABNC.	750.	2000.	—

S797 10 Dollars
1898; 1907. Black on olive underprint. Maissoneuve monument at left, portrait left. H. St. Charles at center right. Back: Carmine. Provincial arms at center. Printer: ABNC.

	Good	Fine	XF
a. Issued note. 2.5.1898.	750.	2000.	—
p1. Black. Face proof. 1.3.1907.	—	Unc	225.
p2. Black on olive underprint. Face proof. 2.5.1898; 1.3.1907.	—	Unc	400.

S798 20 Dollars
1898; 1907. Black on olive underprint. Farmer's loading hay at left. center, portrait left. H. St. Charles at right. Signature varieties. Back: Blue. Provincial arms at left. Maissoneuve monument at center right. Printor: ABNC.

	Good	Fine	XF
p1. Black. Proof. 2.5.1898; 1.3.1907.	—	Unc	225.
p2. Black on olive underprint. Proof. 2.5.1898.	—	Unc	500.

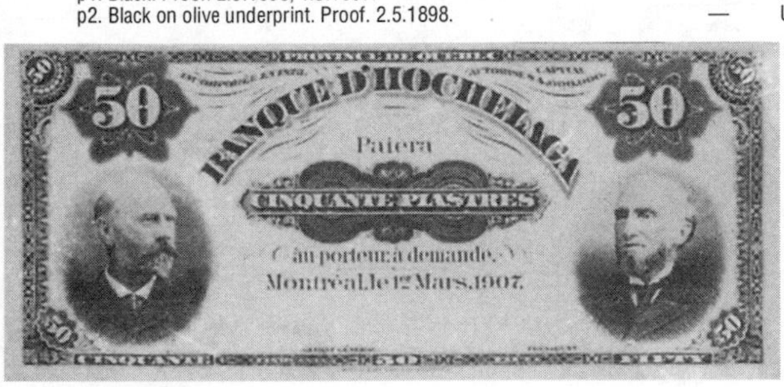

S799 50 Dollars
1898; 1907. M. J. Pendergast at lower left, left. H. St. Charles at lower right. Signature varieties. Back: Olive. Maissoneuve monument at center. Printer: ABNC.

	Good	Fine	XF
p1. Black on green and olive-green underprint. Face proof. 2.5.1898; 1.3.1907.	—	Unc	500.
p2. Black. Face proof. 1.3.1907.	—	Unc	225.

S800 100 Dollars
1898; 1907. Dock scene with ship by elevator building, left. H. St. Charles at upper right. Signature varieties. Back: Green. Maissoneuve monument at center. Printer: ABNC.

	Good	Fine	XF
p1. Black on olive underprint. Face proof. 2.5.1898; 1.3.1907.	—	Unc	500.
p2. Black. Face proof. 1.3.1907.	—	Unc	400.

1911 Issue

S801 5 Dollars
25.2.1911. M. J. Pendergast at left, steamship at upper center, left. H. St. Charles at right. Signature varieties. Back: Green. Provincial arms at center. Printer: ABNC.

	Good	Fine	XF
p. Face and back proofs.	—	Unc	250.
s. Specimen.	—	Unc	400.

S802 10 Dollars
25.2.1911. Black on olive underprint. Maissoneuve monument at left, portrait left. H. St. Charles at center right. Back: Red. Provincial arms at center. Printer: ABNC.

	Good	Fine	XF
a. Issued note.	500.	1500.	—
p. Face and back proofs.	—	Unc	300.

S803 20 Dollars	Good	Fine	XF
25.2.1911. Black on olive underprint. Farmer's loading hay at left. center, portrait left. H. St. Charles at right. Signature varieties. Back: Blue. Provincial arms at center. Printer: ABNC. Face and back proofs.	—	Unc	300.

S804 50 Dollars	Good	Fine	XF
25.2.1911. M. J. Pendergast at lower left, left. H. St. Charles at lower right. Signature varieties. Back: Olive. Arms at left, Maissoneuve monument at center. Printer: ABNC. Face and back proofs.	—	Unc	300.

S805 100 Dollars	Good	Fine	XF
25.2.1911. Dock scene with ship by elevator building, left. H. St. Charles at upper right. Signature varieties. Back: Green. Maissoneuve monument. Printer: ABNC. Face proof.	—	Unc	300.

1914 Issue

S806 5 Dollars	Good	Fine	XF
1.1.1914. Black on light blue underprint. Place d'Arms at center, Maissoneuve monument at lower right. J. A. Vaillancourt at left. Signature varieties. Back: Blue-green. Provincial arms at center. Printer: W&S.	50.00	100.	300.

S807 10 Dollars	Good	Fine	XF
1.1.1914. Black on yellow-orange underprint. Quebec City at center, Champlain monument at lower right. J. A. Vaillancourt at left. Signature varieties. Back: Yellow-brown. Provincial arms at center. Printer: W&S.	50.00	150.	350.

S808 20 Dollars	Good	Fine	XF
1.1.1914. Black on blue-green underprint. Parliament buildings at center, Jacques Cartier at right. J. A. Vaillancourt at left. Signature varieties. Back: Green. Provincial arms at center. Printer: W&S.	350.	1250.	—

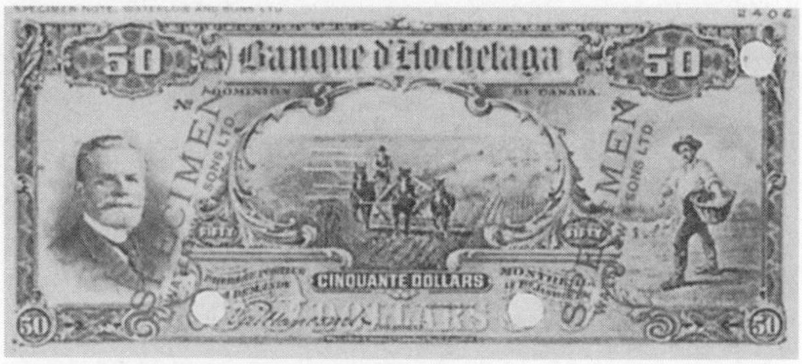

S809 50 Dollars	Good	Fine	XF
1.1.1914. Black on salmon underprint. Horse-drawn reaper in in wheat field at center, farmer broadcasting seeds at right. Signature varieties. Back: Brown. J.A. Vaillancourt at left. Printer: W&S.	350.	1250.	—

S810 100 Dollars	Good	Fine	XF
1.1.1914. Black on lilac underprint. Lake Moraine scene at center, De La Verendrye monument at lower right. J. A. Vaillancourt at left. Signature varieties. Back: Slate. Provincial arms at center. Printer: W&S.	350.	1250.	—

1917-20 Issue

S811 5 Dollars	Good	Fine	XF
2.1.1917. Black on olive underprint. Four figure statue at center. Portrait J. A. Vaillancourt at left, portrait B. Leman at right. Signature varieties. Back: Olive. Provincial arms at center. Printer: ABNC.	50.00	200.	350.

S812 10 Dollars	Good	Fine	XF
2.1.1917. Black on brown underprint. Four figure statue at center. J. A. Vaillancourt at left, portrait B. Leman at right. Signature varieties. Back: Brown. Provincial arms at center. Printer: ABNC.	50.00	200.	350.
S813 20 Dollars			
2.1.1917. Black on blue underprint. Seated allegorical woman with flag and Canadian shield of arms at center. Portrait J. A. Vaillancourt at left, portrait B. Leman at right. Signature varieties. Back: Blue. Provincial arms at center. Printer: ABNC.	150.	500.	1250.
S814 50 Dollars			
2.1.1920. Black on red underprint. Maissoneuve monument at center. Portrait J. A. Vaillancourt at left, portrait B. Leman at right. Signature varieties. Back: Red. Provincial arms at center. Printer: ABNC.	300.	1100.	—

S815 100 Dollars	Good	Fine	XF
2.1.1920. Black on purple underprint. Portrait J. A. Vaillancourt at left, portrait B. Leman at right. Signature varieties. Back: Purple. Provincial arms at center. Printer: ABNC.			
a. Issued note.	300.	1100.	—
p. Proof.	—	Unc	1500.

Banque Internationale du Canada

1911 Issue

S816 5 Dollars	Good	Fine	XF
2.10.1911. Black on green and yellow underprint. Portrait right. Forget at center. Back: Green. Bank seal with globe at center. Overprint: Red: *M M.* Blue: *QUEBEC.* Printer: ABNC.			
a. Issued note.	1250.	4250.	—
p. Proof.	—	Unc	2250.

S817 10 Dollars	Good	Fine	XF
17.10.1911. Black, orange and yellow. Portrait R. Forget at left, portrait right. Bickerdike at right. Back: Brown. Bank seal with globe at center. Overprint: Red: *M M.* Blue: *QUEBEC.* Printer: ABNC.	1250.	4250.	—
S818 20 Dollars			
17.10.1911. Black, olive and yellow. Portrait R. Forget at left, portrait right. Bickerdike at right. Back: Brown. Bank seal with globe at center. Overprint: Red: *M M.* Blue: *QUEBEC.* Printer: ABNC.	1250.	4250.	—

Banque Jacques Cartier

1862 Issue

S821 1 Dollar	Good	Fine	XF
2.1.1862. Black on green underprint. Portrait Queen Victoria at lower left, portrait right. Trudeau at lower right. J. Cartier at center. Back: Green. Printer: ABNC.	1000.	4000.	—
S822 2 Dollars			
2.1.1862. Black on green underprint. Portrait Princess Eugenie at lower left, portrait Prince of Wales at lower right. J. Cartier at center. Back: Green. Printer: ABNC.	1000.	4000.	—
S823 5 Dollars			
2.1.1862. Black on green underprint. J. Cartier at center. Back: Green. Printer: ABNC. Reported not confirmed.	—	—	—
S824 10 Dollars			
2.1.1862. Black on green underprint. J. Cartier at center. Back: Green. Printer: ABNC. Reported not confirmed.	—	—	—

1870 Issue

S826 4 Dollars	VG	VF	UNC
2.5.1870. Seated allegorical woman, sailing ships at lower left, beaver at lower right. Portrait Queen Victoria at left, portrait Prince Albert at center.			
a. Ornate black *4*'s at upper left and right.	3500.	—	—
b. Green *FOUR* over ornate black *4*'s at upper left and right.	3500.	—	—
S827 5 Dollars			
1870-80. R. Trudeau at lower left, A. Desjardins at lower right. Portrait Queen Victoria at left, portrait Prince Albert at center.			
a. 2.5.1870.	3500.	—	—
b. Blue overprint: *VICTORIAVILLE.* 1.6.1880.	3500.	—	—
S828 20 Dollars			
2.5.1870; 2.5.1871. Dog's head at lower left, blacksmith with horses at lower right. Portrait Queen Victoria at left, portrait Prince Albert at center. Face proof.	—	—	500.
S829 50 Dollars			
2.5.1870. Woman with parchment at left, woman reaping grain at right. Portrait Queen Victoria at left, portrait Prince Albert at center. Face proof.	—	—	500.
S830 10 Dollars			
2.5.1870. Queen Victoria in "Widow's Weeds" at left, anchor, barrel and bales at right. Portrait Queen Victoria at left, portrait Prince Albert at center. Face proof.	—	—	500.

1886-89 Issues

	Good	Fine	XF
S831 5 Dollars 1.6.1886. Black on green underprint. Farm family with animals at center. J. Cartier at left, bank building facade at right. Printer: CABNC. Face proof.	—	Unc	750.
S832 5 Dollars 1.6.1889. Black on blue-green and ochre underprint. Farm family with animals at center. J. Cartier at left, bank building facade at right. Printer: CABNC. Face proof.	—	Unc	750.
S833 10 Dollars 1.6.1886. Indians on bluff, steam passenger train below. J. Cartier at left, bank building facade at right. Printer: CABNC.			
a. Black on orange and blue underprint.	3250.	—	—
p. Face proof. Black on green underprint.	—	Unc	750.
S834 10 Dollars 1.6.1889. Black on blue-green and ochre underprint. Indians on bluff, steam passenger train below. J Cartier at left, bank building facade at right. Printer: CABNC.			
a. Issued note. Rare.	—	—	—
p. Face proof.	—	Unc	750.

1895 Issue

	Good	Fine	XF
S836 5 Dollars 2.1.1895. Black on green underprint. Jacques Cartier, Montreal views at center. A. L. Demontigny at lower left, A. Desjardins at lower right. Back: Green. Indian on bluff. Printer: BABNC. Face proof.	—	Unc	500.
S837 10 Dollars 2.1.1895. Black on green underprint. Jacques Cartier with shipmates at center. A. L. Demontigny at lower left, A. Desjardins at lower right. Back: Green. Indian on bluff. Printer: BABNC. Face proof.	—	Unc	500.

Banque Nationale

1860 Issue

	Good	Fine	XF
S841 1 Dollar 1860. Black on green underprint. Standing male citizen at lower left, Quebec City arms at upper center, Jacques Cartier at lower right. Signature varieties. Uniface. Printer: ABNC.			
a. Partially engraved date, handsigned sheet #. 28.4.1860.	350.	1000.	1750.
b. Engraved date, printed sheet #. 28.4.1860.	225.	700.	1200.
c. As b. 25.5.1860.	250.	750.	1250.
S842 2 Dollars 1860. Black on green underprint. 2 allegorical women at lower left, Quebec City arms at upper center, oval portrait Jacques Cartier at right. Signature varieties. Uniface. Printer: ABNC.			
a. Partially engraved date, handsigned sheet #. 28.4.1860.	600.	1000.	1750.
b. Engraved date, printed sheet #. 28.4.1860.	225.	650.	1250.
c. As b. 25.5.1860.	250.	775.	1750.
S843 5 Dollars 1860. Black on green underprint. Farm tools at lower left, farmers plowing with horses at top center, woman with cornucopia at lower right. Signature varieties. Uniface. Printer: ABNC.			
a. Partially engraved date, handsigned sheet #. 28.4.1860.	400.	1000.	2000.
b. Engraved date, printed sheet #. 28.4.1860.	250.	775.	1750.
S844 10 Dollars 1860. Black on green underprint. St. John the Baptist with lamb at lower left, steam passenger train at top center, seated Britannia with Upper Canada shield of arms at lower right. Signature varieties. Uniface. Printer: ABNC.			
a. Partially engraved date, handsigned sheet #. 28.4.1860.	400.	1000.	2000.
b. Engraved date, printed sheet #. 28.4.1860.	250.	775.	1750.

1870-71 Issue

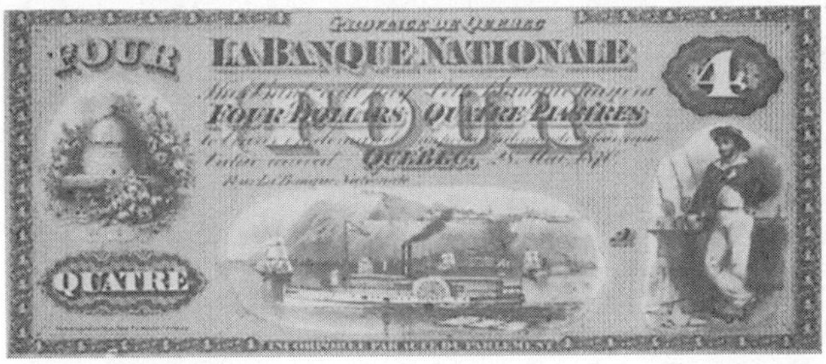

	Good	Fine	XF
S846 4 Dollars 1870-71. Black on green underprint. Beehive at upper left, paddle wheel steamboat Quebec at bottom center, sailor at lower right. Signature varieties. Back: Green. Printer: BABNC.			
a. Issued note. 28.5.1870.	250.	775.	1750.
b. Red overprint: *OTTAWA*.	250.	775.	1750.
c. Red overprint: *SHERBROOKE*.	250.	775.	1750.
s. Specimen. 28.5.1871; 2.10.1871.	—	Unc	850.
S847 6 Dollars 28.5.1870. Black on green underprint. Elderly woman teaching girl knitting at lower left, girl with cattle at top center, oval portrait S. de Champlain at lower right. Signature varieties. Back: Green. Printer: BABNC.			
a. Issued note.	1500.	5000.	—
b. Red overprint: *OTTAWA*.	1500.	5000.	—
c. Red overprint: *SHERBROOKE*.	1500.	5000.	—
S848 20 Dollars 2.10.1871. Black on green underprint. Farmer feeding horses at lower left, Quebec City arms at top center, young sailor climbing rope ladder at lower right. Signature varieties. Overprint: Black: *XX*. Printer: BABNC.	450.	1250.	3250.

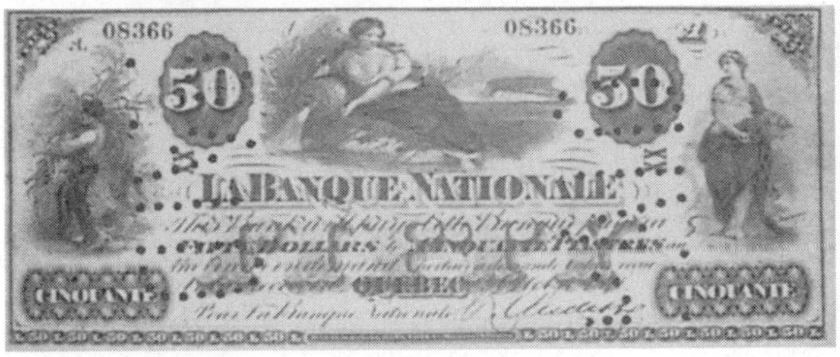

	Good	Fine	XF
S849 50 Dollars 2.10.1871. Black on green underprint. Farmer carrying cornstalks at left, reclining woman with waterjug at top center, Agriculture at right. Signature varieties. Back: Green. Overprint: Black: *XX*. Printer: BABNC.	450.	1250.	3250.
S850 100 Dollars 2.10.1871. Black on green underprint. Sailors looking to sea at top center. Back: Green. Overprint: Black: *XX*. Printer: BABNC.	450.	1250.	3250.

1873 Issue

	Good	Fine	XF
S851 5 Dollars 2.1.1873. Black on green underprint. Plow and agricultural produce at lower left, shipbuilders at upper center, seated Britannia with shield of *5* at lower right. Back: Green. Printer: BABNC.	400.	1000.	2250.
S852 10 Dollars 2.1.1873. Black on green underprint. St. John the Baptist with lamb at lower left, agricultural produce and tools at upper center, anchor at lower right. Back: Green. Printer: BABNC.	400.	1000.	2250.

1883 Issue

	VG	VF	UNC
S856 5 Dollars 1.3.1883. Black on green underprint. S. de Champlain at lower left, paddle wheel steamboat *Quebec* at upper center. J. R. Thibaudeau at lower right. Signature varieties. Back: Green. Quebec City arms at center. Overprint: Red: *A D* and blue: *P*. Printer: BABNC.	800.	1500.	—
S857 10 Dollars 1.3.1883. Black on green underprint. Jacques Cartier at left, farmer plowing with horses at upper center. J. R. Thibaudeau at lower right. Signature varieties. Back: Green. Quebec City arms at center. Overprint: Red: *A D* and blue: *P*. Printer: BABNC.	800.	1500.	—

1891 Issue

	VG	VF	UNC
S861 5 Dollars 2.1.1891. Black on green underprint. S. de Champlain at lower left, steam train at upper center. A. Gaboury at lower right. Signature varieties. Back: Green. Quebec City arms at center. Overprint: Red: *A D* and *R* or blue *P*. Printer: BABNC.	800.	1500.	—
S862 10 Dollars 2.1.1891. Black on green underprint. Jacques Cartier at lower left, farmer plowing with horses at upper center. A. Gaboury at lower right. Signature varieties. Back: Green. Quebec City arms at center. Overprint: Red: *A D* and *R* or blue *P*. Printer: BABNC.	800.	1500.	—

1897 Issue

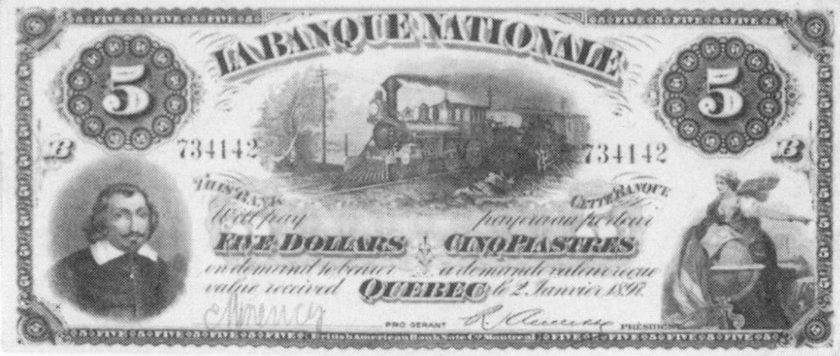

S866 5 Dollars

2.1.1897. Black on orange underprint. S. de Champlain at lower left, steam passenger train at upper center, Britannia leaning on globe, flag at lower right. Signature varieties. Back: Green. Quebec City arms at center. Printer: BABNC.

	Good	Fine	XF
a. Right hand signature title: *PRESIDENT.*	125.	300.	750.
b. Right hand signature title: *PRÉSIDENT.*	125.	300.	750.

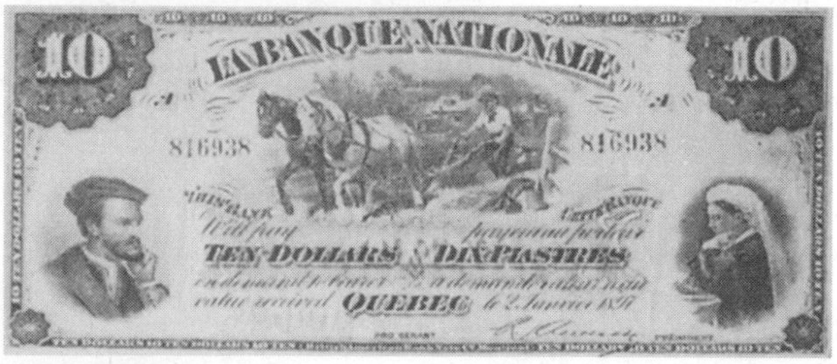

S867 10 Dollars

2.1.1897. Black on orange underprint. J. Cartier at lower left, farmer plowing with horses at upper center, Queen Victoria in "Widow's Weeds" at lower right. Signature varieties. Back: Green. Quebec City arms at center. Printer: BABNC.

	Good	Fine	XF
a. Right hand signature title: *PRESIDENT.*	150.	350.	1000.
b. Right hand signature title: *PRÉSIDENT.*	150.	350.	1000.

1922 Issue

S871 5 Dollars

2.11.1922. Black on olive underprint. Monument at left. Portrait G. E. Amyot at right. Back: Green. Quebec City arms at center. Printer: BABNC.

	VG	VF	UNC
a. Issued note.	1000.	1750.	—
s. Specimen.	—	—	300.

S872 10 Dollars

2.11.1922. Black and orange. Portrait Jacques Cartier sighting land at left. Portrait G. E. Amyot at right. Back: Green. Quebec City arms at center. Printer: BABNC.

Good	Fine	XF
—	Unc	300.

S873 20 Dollars

2.11.1922. Black and orange. Quebec Citadel at left. Portrait G. E. Amyot at right. Back: Green. Quebec City arms at center. Printer: BABNC.

	VG	VF	UNC
a. Issued note.	1500.	2750.	—
s. Specimen.	—	—	300.

S874 50 Dollars

2.11.1922. Black and brown. Portrait G. E. Amyot at center. Back: Green. Quebec City arms at center. Printer: BABNC. Specimen.

Good	Fine	XF
—	Unc	350.

S875 100 Dollars

2.11.1922. Black and brown. Portrait G. E. Amyot at right. Back: Green. Quebec arms at center. Printer: BABNC. Specimen.

Good	Fine	XF
—	Unc	400.

Bank of the People

1836-40 Issue

Good Fine XF

S875A 1 Dollar = 5 Shillings
12.10.1836. Black. Seated allegorical woman at left, sailboats in Toronto harbor at upper center, small steamboat at bottom center, seated allegorical male with chest and anchor at right. Printer: Durand, Burton & Edmonds, N. York.
a. Issued note. 800. 2000. —
p. Partially engraved date. Proof. — Unc 750.

S875B 2 Dollars = 10 Shillings
18xx. Black. Paddle wheel steamboat at left, seated allegorical woman at top center, small passenger train at bottom center. Sail boats in Toronto harbor at right. Printer: Durand, Burton & Edmonds, N. York. Proof. — Unc 750.

S875C 3 Dollars
9.10.1840. Black. Three seated allegorical women at top center. Printer: Durand, Burton & Edmonds, N. York. 900. 2250. —

S875D 4 Dollars = 20 Shillings
9.10.1840. Black. Portrait J. Fox at left, reclining Indian maiden at top center. Printer: Durand, Burton & Edmonds, N. York. 900. 2250. —

S875E 8 Dollars = 2 Pounds
8.6.1840. Black. Supported royal arms at top center, small horse's head at bottom center. Printer: Durand, Burton & Edmonds, N. York. 1750. 4250. —

S875F 10 Dollars
18xx. Black. Portrait J. Fox at left, reclining allegorical woman with lion shield and farm tools, ships in background at upper center, small crown at bottom center, standing young farm girl at right. Printer: Durand, Burton & Edmonds, N. York. Proof. — Unc 750.

Banque du Peuple

1835-36 Issue

Good Fine XF

S876 1 Dollar
11.7.1835; 2.8.1836. Black. Seated shepherd boy at left; men with cattle and sheep at upper center, small child riding deer at bottom center, cherub at right. Signature varieties. Back: Blue. Standing male citizen at center. Printer: RWH & Co. 250. 750. —

S877 2 Dollars
11.7.1835. Black. Portrait of man at left, two allegorical women at upper center, small man in canoe at bottom center, seated allegorical male at right. Signature varieties. Back: Blue. Standing male citizen at center. Printer: RWH & Co. 250. 750. —

S878 5 Dollars
1835. Black. Portrait L.-J. Papineau at left, woman in lion drawn chariot at upper center, small sailing ship at bottom center. Signature varieties. Back: Blue. Standing male citizen at center. Printer: RWH & Co.
a. Title: *Cassier* at lower left. 11.7.1835. 300. 1000. —
r. Company name at lower left. Remainder. 18xx. — Unc 750.

S879 10 Dollars
1836. Black. Sailing ship and Commerce at upper center, portrait L.-J. Papineau at right. Signature varieties. Back: Blue. Standing male citizen at center. Printer: RWH & Co.
a. Title: *Cassier* at lower left. 2.3.1836. 300. 1000. —
r. Company name at lower left. Remainder. 18xx. — Unc 750.

1838 Issue

Good Fine XF

S881 5 Dollars
1.7.1838. Black. Seated woman with lamb at left, farm family at top center, five Spanish 8 reales coins vertically at right. Back: Blue. Standing citizen at left, farmer picking corn at right. Printer: RWH & Co.
a. Printed date: 18xx. 150. 500. —
b. Printed date: 1838. 325. 1000. —

1839 Issue

Good Fine XF

S882 1 Dollar
1.10.1839. Black. Portrait Christ child at left and right, angel with shield of Britannia, cherub at upper center. Company name at lower left. Dollars only. Back: Blue. Spanish 8 Reales coin at left, Agriculture at center, standing male citizen at right. Printer: Durand & Co. 200. 750. —

S883 2 Dollars
1.10.1839. Black. Seated woman with shield at left, angel with shield of Britannia at upper center. Company name at lower left. Dollars only. Back: Blue. Two Spanish 8 reales coins at left. Printer: Durand & Co. 325. 1000. —

1845 Issue

Good Fine XF

S884 1 Dollar = 5 Shillings
1.3.1845. Black. Portrait Christ child at left and right, angel with shield of Britannia, cherub at upper center. Bilingual denominations and with *Cash* at lower left. Dollars and shillings. Printer: Durand & Co. 325. 1000. —

Good Fine XF

S885 2 Dollars = 10 Shillings
1.3.1845. Black. Seated woman with shield at left, angel with shield of Britannia at upper center. Bilingual denominations and with *Cash* at lower left. Dollars and shillings. Printer: Durand & Co. 325. 1000. —

1845-50 Issue

Good Fine XF

S886 1 Dollar = 5 Shillings
1.9.1846-1.3.1850. Black. Cooper making barrel at left, farm boy with wheat sheaf and cradle at top center, 4 cherubs with large *1* at lower right. Signature varieties. Back: Blue. Standing citizen at left and right. Overprint: Blue: *TORONTO*. Printer: TCC. 325. 1000. —

Good Fine XF

S887 2 Dollars = 10 Shillings
1.9.1846; 1.3.1850. Black. Farmer sharpening scythe at lower left, blacksmith and logger at upper center, dog at lower right. Signature varieties. Back: Blue. Standing male citizen at center. Overprint: Blue: *TORONTO*. Printer: TCC. 325. 1000. —

S888 4 Dollars = 20 Shillings
1.5.1847. Black. Seated carpenter at left, milkmaids by cows at top center right, blacksmith at right. Signature varieties. Back: Blue. Portrait of young woman at center. Overprint: Blue: *TORONTO*. Printer: TCC. 500. 1250. —

S889 5 Dollars = 1 Pound-5 Shillings
184x. Black. Seated Commerce at left, woman with sheaves in large ornate *V* at center, allegorical seated woman on globe with trumpet at right. Signature varieties. Overprint: Blue: *TORONTO*. Printer: TCC. Face proof. — Unc 500.

S890 10 Dollars = 2 Pounds-10 Shillings
184x. Black. 2 allegorical women with ornate *X* at left and right, Queen Victoria and Prince Albert with cherubs along top. Signature varieties. Overprint: Blue: *TORONTO*. Printer: TCC. Face proof. — Unc 500.

S891 20 Dollars = 5 Pounds
1.3.1845. Black. Sailor with telescope at left, small steamboat at bottom center, man plowing with horses at upper right. Signature varieties. Overprint: Blue: *TORONTO*. Printer: TCC. 500. 1250. —

S892 50 Dollars = 12 Pounds-10 Shillings
1.3.1845. Black. Canal boat at left, reclining sailor with flag, sailing ship in background at upper center, young girl's bust at bottom center, paddle wheel steamboat at right. Signature varieties. Overprint: Blue: *TORONTO*. Printer: TCC. 700. 1600. —

S893 100 Dollars = 25 Pounds
184x. Black. Portrait of woman at left, Montreal harbor at center, small shield at bottom center, portrait of woman at right. Overprint: Blue: *TORONTO*. Printer: TCC. Face proof. — Unc 500.

1854-70 Issues

Good Fine XF

S896 1 Dollar = 5 Shillings
2.5.1870. Black. Cooper making barrel at left, farm boy with wheat sheaf and cradle at top center, 4 cherubs with large *1* at lower right. Signature varieties. Green *ONE* protector. Back: Blue. Printer: TCC.
a. Inscription above signature. 250. 750. —
b. Inscription deleted. 250. 750. —

S897 2 Dollars = 10 Shillings
2.5.1870. Black. Farmer sharpening scythe at lower left, blacksmith and logger at upper center, dog at lower right. Signature varieties. Green *TWO* protector. Back: Blue. Printer: TCC. 300. 800. —

S898 4 Dollars = 20 Shillings
2.1.1854. Black. Seated carpenter at left, milkmaids by cows at top center right, blacksmith at right. Signature varieties. Green *FOUR* protector. Back: Blue. Printer: TCC. 300. 850. —

S899 4 Dollars = 20 Shillings
2.5.1870. Black on green underprint. Seated carpenter at left, milkmaids by cows at top center right, blacksmith at right. Signature varieties. Green *FOUR* protector. Back: Green. Printer: TCC and BABNC. 350. 875. —

S900 5 Dollars = 1 Pound-5 Shillings
2.5.1870. Black on green underprint. Seated Commerce at left, woman with sheaves in large ornate *V* at center, allegorical seated woman on globe with trumpet at right. Signature varieties. Back: Green. Printer: TCC. Reported not confirmed. — — —

S901 10 Dollars = 2 Pounds-10 Shillings
2.5.1870. Black on green underprint. 2 allegorical women with ornate *X* at left and right, Queen Victoria and Prince Albert with cherubs along top. Signature varieties. Back: Green. Printer: TCC. Reported not confirmed. — — —

S902 20 Dollars = 5 Pounds
2.5.1870. Black on green underprint. Sailor with telescope at left, small steamboat at bottom center, man plowing with horses at upper right. Signature varieties. Back: Green. Overprint: Red: *S* twice. Printer: TCC. 500. 1250. —

1882 Issue

	Good	Fine	XF
S903 5 Dollars = 1 Pound-5 Shillings			
2.5.1882. Black on green underprint. Signature varieties. Back: Blue. Overprint: Blue: *QUEBEC* twice. Printer: TCC and BABNC.	400.	1000.	—
S904 10 Dollars = 2 Pounds-10 Shillings			
2.5.1882. Black on green underprint. Signature varieties. Back: Blue. Overprint: Red: *D M* twice. Printer: TCC and BABNC.	400.	1000.	—

1885-92 Issue

S906 5 Dollars

1885-1892. Black on green underprint. Seated Commerce at left, woman with sheaves in large ornate *V* at center, allegorical seated woman on globe with trumpet at right. Signature varieties. Back: Blue. Printer: TCC and BABNC.

	Good	Fine	XF
a. Blue numbers. Blue overprint: *QUEBEC* twice. Printers: TCC and BABNC. 6.11.1885.	400.	1000.	—
b. As a. 2.7.1892.	400.	1000.	—
c. Red numbers. Red overprint: *S S*. Printers: TCC and CBNC. 6.11.1885.	400.	1000.	—

	Good	Fine	XF
S907 10 Dollars			
2.5.1888. Black on green underprint. 2 allegorical women with ornate *X* at left and right, Queen Victoria and Prince Albert with cherubs along top. Signature varieties. Blue numbers. Back: Blue. Printer: TCC and BABNC.	—	Unc	500.
S908 50 Dollars			
6.11.1885. Black on green underprint. Canal boat at left, reclining sailor with flag, sailing ship in background at upper center, young girl's bust at bottom center, paddle wheel steamboat at right. Signature varieties. Back: Blue.			
a. Red numbers. Printers: TCC and CABNC.	500.	1250.	—
p. Face proof. Blue numbers. Printers: TCC and BABNC.	—	Unc	500.
S909 100 Dollars			
6.11.1885. Black on green underprint. Portrait of woman at left, Montreal harbor at center, small shield at bottom center, portrait of woman at right. Signature varieties. Back: Blue.			
a. Blue numbers. Printers: TCC and BABNC.	—	Unc	500.
p. Face proof. Red numbers. Printers: TCC and CABNC.	—	Unc	500.

Banque Provinciale du Canada

1900 Issue

	Good	Fine	XF
S911 5 Dollars			
2.7.1900. Black on green underprint. Farm woman with cow and calf at lower left, lumberjack chopping tree at lower right. Supported bank crest at center. Signature varieties. Back: Green. Indians on bluff at center. Printer: BABNC.	500.	1500.	3250.
S912 10 Dollars			
2.7.1900. Black on green underprint. Two allegorical women at lower left, steamship at lower right. Supported bank crest at center. Signature varieties. Printer: BABNC.	—	Unc	500.

1907 Issue

S913 5 Dollars

1.6.1907. Steam passenger train at station at center. T. Bienvenu at lower left, H. Laporte at lower right. Signature varieties. Back: Green. Head office building façade at center. Printer: BABNC.

	VG	VF	UNC
a. Black on green underprint.	600.	1250.	—
b. Black on brown underprint. Face proof.	—	Unc	500.

	Good	Fine	XF
S914 10 Dollars			
1.6.1907. Black on green underprint. Steamboat *Montreal* at center. T. Bienvenu at lower left, H. Laporte at lower right. Signature varieties. Back: Green. Head office building façade at center. Printer: BABNC.	1000.	2250.	—

1913; 1928 Issue

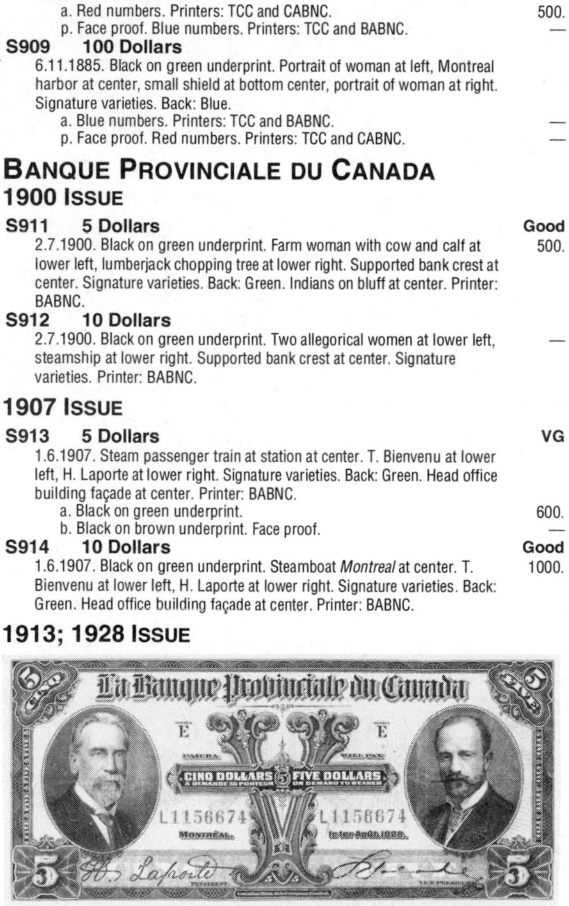

S916 5 Dollars

1913-28. Portrait H. Laporte at left or left center, portrait T. Bienvenu at right or center right. Signature varieties. Back: Green. Head office building façade at center. Printer: ABNC or CBNC.

	VG	VF	UNC
a. Black on orange and green underprint. 2.1.1913.	300.	600.	1500.
b. 31.1.1919.	200.	400.	100.
c. Black on green and yellow underprint. 31.1.1919.	75.00	150.	400.
d. 1.8.1928.	50.00	100.	300.
p. Proof.	—	Unc	600.

S917 10 Dollars

1913-28. Portrait H. Laporte at left or left center, portrait T. Bienvenu at right or center right. Signature varieties. Back: Head office building façade at center. Printer: ABNC or CBNC.

	VG	VF	UNC
a. Black on orange and yellow-green underprint. Back orange. 2.1.1913.	100.	200.	600.
b. 31.1.1919.	100.	200.	600.
c. Black on brown and yellow underprint. Back brown. 31.1.1919.	50.00	150.	400.
d. 1.8.1928.	50.00	150.	400.

	VG	VF	UNC
S918 20 Dollars			
1.8.1928. Black on blue underprint. Portrait H. Laporte at left or left center, portrait T. Bienvenu at right or center right. Signature varieties. Back: Blue. Head office building façade at center. Printer: ABNC or CBNC.	100.	200.	600.

1935 Issue

	VG	VF	UNC
S919 5 Dollars			
2.1.1935. Brown. Portrait S. J. B. Roland at center. Back: Green. Bank building at center. Printer: BABNC. Reduced size.	25.00	75.00	250.

	VG	VF	UNC
S920 10 Dollars			
2.1.1935. Black. Portrait S. J. B. Roland at center. Back: Olive-green. Bank building at center. Printer: BABNC. Reduced size.	25.00	75.00	200.

1936 Issue

S921 5 Dollars

1.9.1936. Black on yellow and blue underprint. Portrait C. A. Roy at center. Back: Bank building at center. Printer: CBNC.

	VG	VF	UNC
a. Back blue.	25.00	75.00	200.
b. Back green.	50.00	125.	300.
p. Proof.	—	—	—

S922 10 Dollars

1.9.1936. Black on yellow and orange underprint. Portrait C. A. Roy at center. Back: Bank building at center. Printer: CBNC.

	VG	VF	UNC
a. Back orange.	25.00	75.00	225.
b. Back green.	25.00	75.00	200.
p. Face proof with green tint.	—	—	—

Banque de St. Hyacinthe

1874 Issue

	Good	Fine	XF
S924 4 Dollars 2.1.1874. Black on green underprint. Farmer with cornstalks at left, shepherd boy at center, P. Bachand at right. Back: Green. Printer: BABNC. Face proof.	—	Unc	500.
S925 5 Dollars 2.1.1874. Black on green underprint. Allegorical woman at lower left, farmer watering livestock at top center, G. C. Dessaulles at lower right. Back: Green. Printer: BABNC. Face proof.	—	Unc	500.
S926 10 Dollars 2.1.1874. Black on green underprint. St. John the Baptist with lamb at lower left, farmer plowing with horses at lower center G. C. Dessaulles at lower right. Back: Green. Printer: BABNC. Face proof.	—	Unc	500.

1880-92 Issue

	VG	VF	UNC
S927 5 Dollars 1.7.1880. Black on green underprint. Allegorical woman at lower left, farmer watering livestock at top center, G. C. Dessaulles at lower right. Signature varieties. Back: Green. Printer: BABNC.	2500.	5000.	—
S928 10 Dollars 1.7.1880. Black on green underprint. John the Baptist with lamb at lower left, farmer plowing with horses at lower center. G. C. Dessaulles at lower right. Signature varieties. Back: Green. Printer: BABNC.	2500.	5000.	—
S929 20 Dollars 2.1.1892. Black on yellow-green and green underprint. Shepherdess with sheep at left, crowned Canadian arms at left center, allegorical woman at lower right. Signature varieties. Back: Brown. Printer: CBNC and BABNC.	2500.	5000.	—

Banque de St. Jean

1873-1900 Issue

	VG	VF	UNC
S931 4 Dollars 1.9.1873. Black on green underprint. Supported ornate *4* with shield at left, left. Molleur at upper center right. St. John the Baptist with lamb at right. Signature varieties. Back: Green. Printer: BABNC.	2500.	5000.	—
S932 5 Dollars 1873; 1900. Black on green underprint. L. Molleur at left, workers, factories with large ornate, *5* at top center. St. John the Baptist with lamb at right. Signature varieties. Back: Green. Printer: BABNC.			
a. 1.9.1873.	2750.	5250.	—
b. 1.4.1900.	2500.	5000.	—
S933 10 Dollars 1873; 1881. Black on green underprint. L. Molleur at upper left, two seated allegorical women with large ornate *X* at bottom center. St. John the Baptist with lamb at right. Signature varieties. Back: Green. Printer: BABNC.			
a. 1.9.1873.	2750.	5250.	—
b. 1.4.1881.	2500.	5000.	—

1906 Issue

	VG	VF	UNC
S934 5 Dollars 1.4.1906. Black on green underprint. J. Cartier at left, workers, factories with large ornate, *5* at top center. Printer: BABNC.	2500.	5000.	—
S935 10 Dollars 1.4.1906. Black on green underprint. J. Cartier at upper left, two seated allegorical women with large ornate *X* at bottom center. Printer: BABNC.	2500.	5000.	—

Banque Ville-Marie

1873-90 Issue

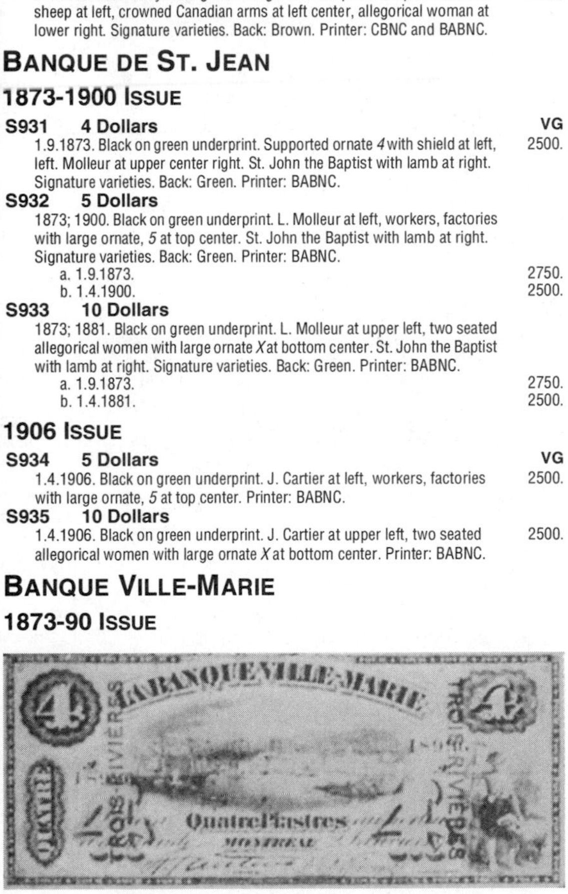

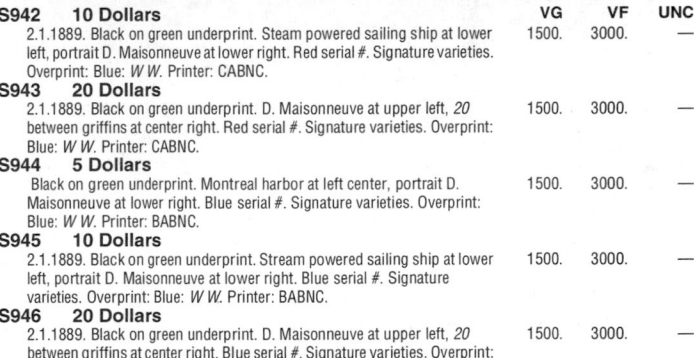

	Good	Fine	XF
S936 4 Dollars 1873-79. Black on green underprint. St. John the Baptist with lamb at lower right. Montreal harbor at upper center. Signature varieties. Back: Green. Overprint: Red: *TROIS-RIVIERES* and *SOREL*. Red *F* and blue *N N*. Printer: BABNC.			
a. Red overprint: *TROIS-RIVIERES*. 2.1.1873.	750.	2250.	—
p. Face proof. 1.8.1879.	—	Unc	500.
S937 5 Dollars 1873-85. Black on green underprint. S. de Champlain at lower left. Montreal harbor at upper center. Signature varieties. Back: Green. Overprint: Red: *TROIS-RIVIERES* and *SOREL*. Red *F* and blue *N N*. Printer: BABNC.			
a. 2.1.1873.	750.	2250.	—
b. 1.10.1885.	750.	2250.	—
p. Face proof. 1.8.1879.	—	Unc	500.
S938 10 Dollars 1873-85. Black on green underprint. Jacques Cartier shipboard sighting land at lower left. Montreal harbor at upper center. Signature varieties. Back: Green. Overprint: Red: *TROIS-RIVIERES* and *SOREL*. Red *F* and blue *N N*. Printer: BABNC.			
a. 2.1.1873.	750.	2250.	—
p. Face proof. 1.10.1885.	—	Unc	600.
S939 50 Dollars 1185-90. Black on green underprint. Young "Lucy" at lower left, St. John the Baptist with lamb at lower right. Montreal harbor at upper center. Back: Green. Overprint: Red: *TROIS-RIVIERES* and *SOREL*. Red *F* and blue *N N*. Printer: BABNC.			
a. 1.10.1885.	750.	3250.	—
p. Face proof. 1.9.1890.	—	Unc	600.

1889 Issues

	VG	VF	UNC
S941 5 Dollars 2.1.1889. Black on green underprint. Montreal harbor at left center, portrait D. Maisonneuve at lower right. Red serial #. Signature varieties. Overprint: Blue: *W W*. Printer: CABNC.	1500.	3000.	—

	VG	VF	UNC
S942 10 Dollars 2.1.1889. Black on green underprint. Steam powered sailing ship at lower left, portrait D. Maisonneuve at lower right. Red serial #. Signature varieties. Overprint: Blue: *W W*. Printer: CABNC.	1500.	3000.	—
S943 20 Dollars 2.1.1889. Black on green underprint. D. Maisonneuve at upper left, *20* between griffins at center right. Red serial #. Signature varieties. Overprint: Blue: *W W*. Printer: CABNC.	1500.	3000.	—
S944 5 Dollars Black on green underprint. Montreal harbor at left center, portrait D. Maisonneuve at lower right. Blue serial #. Signature varieties. Overprint: Blue: *W W*. Printer: BABNC.	1500.	3000.	—
S945 10 Dollars 2.1.1889. Black on green underprint. Stream powered sailing ship at lower left, portrait D. Maisonneuve at lower right. Blue serial #. Signature varieties. Overprint: Blue: *W W*. Printer: BABNC.	1500.	3000.	—
S946 20 Dollars 2.1.1889. Black on green underprint. D. Maisonneuve at upper left, *20* between griffins at center right. Blue serial #. Signature varieties. Overprint: Blue: *W W*. Printer: BABNC.	1500.	3000.	—

Barclays Bank (Canada)

1929 Issue

S947 5 Dollars	VG	VF	UNC
3.9.1929. Black on green underprint. Seated allegorical female with globe at center. Signature varieties. Back: Green. Bank building facade at center. Printer: CBNC.			
a. Signature J. R. Bruce and R. L. Bordon.	350.	700.	3000.
b. Signature F. H. Dickenson and R. L. Bordon.	350.	700.	3000.
c. Signature H. A. Stevenson and R. L. Bordon.	350.	700.	3000.
S948 10 Dollars			
3.9.1929. Black on orange underprint. Seated allegorical female with globe at center. Signature varieties. Back: Bank building facade. Printer: CBNC.			
a. Signature J. R. Bruce and R. L. Bordon.	350.	700.	3000.
b. Signature F. H. Dickenson and R. L. Bordon.	350.	700.	3000.
c. Signature H. A. Stevenson and R. L. Bordon.	350.	700.	3000.
S949 20 Dollars			
3.9.1929. Black on blue underprint. Seated allegorical female with globe at center. Signature varieties. Back: Blue. Bank building facade at center. Printer: CBNC.			
a. Signature J. R. Bruce and R. L. Bordon.	500.	1000.	2750.
b. Signature H. A. Stevenson and R. L. Bordon.	500.	1000.	2750.

1935 Issue

S950 5 Dollars	VG	VF	UNC
2.1.1935. Black on green underprint. Seated allegorical female with globe at center. Back: Green. Bank building facade at center. Printer: CBNC. Reduced size.			
a. Signature H. A. Stevenson and R. L. Bordon.	50.00	150.	600.
s. Signature H. A. Stevenson and A. A. Magee. Specimen.	—	Unc	750.

S951 10 Dollars	VG	VF	UNC
2.1.1935. Black on orange underprint. Seated allegorical female with globe at center. Back: Orange. Bank buildinf facade at center. Printer: CBNC. Reduced size.			
a. Signature H. A. Stevenson and R. L. Bordon.	50.00	150.	600.
b. Signature H. A. Stevenson and A. A. Magee.	50.00	150.	600.

Canadian Bank of Commerce

1867-71 Issue

#S952-S957 Some notes of 1867 have blue ovpt: *GUELPH, HAMILTON, LONDON* or *ST. CATHARINES*, and red ovpt: *G* with blue ovpt: *ST. CATHARINES*.

S952 1 Dollar	VG	VF	UNC
1.5.1867. Black on green underprint. Woman on shell drawn by dolphins at upper left, small woman's bust at bottom center, Indian maiden at lower right. Signature varieties. Back: Green. Printer: BABNC.	600.	1250.	—

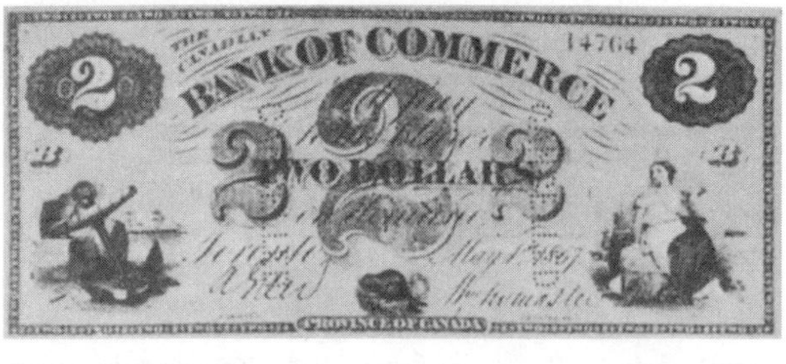

S953 2 Dollars	VG	VF	UNC
1.5.1867. Black on green underprint. Anchor, crate and barrel at lower left, small beaver at bottom center, seated allegorical woman at wharf at lower right. Signature varieties. Back: Green. Printer: BABNC.	800.	2250.	—

S954 4 Dollars	VG	VF	UNC
1.7.1870. Black on green underprint. Elderly woman teaching young girl to knit at lower left, cattle at center, beehive at lower right. Signature varieties. Back: Green. Printer: BABNC.	750.	2000.	—

S955 5 Dollars	VG	VF	UNC
1867-71. Black on green underprint. Portrait Queen Victoria in "Widow's Weeds" at center. Back: Green. Printer: BABNC.			
a. 1.5.1867.	900.	2500.	—
b. Text: *CAPITAL $4,000,000* at bottom. 1.5.1871.	900.	2500.	—
c. Text: *CAPITAL $6,000,000* at bottom. 1.5.1871.	900.	2500.	—

NOTE: #S955b counterfeits w/E. J. Smith as Cashier are abundant.

S956 10 Dollars	Good	Fine	XF
1867-71. Black on green underprint. Supported royal arms at upper center. Signature varieties. Back: Green. Printer: BABNC.			
a. 1.5.1867. Rare.	—	—	—
b. Text: *CAPITAL $4,000,000* at bottom. 1.5.1871. Rare.	—	—	—
c. Text: *CAPITAL $6,000,000* at bottom. 1.5.1871. Rare.	—	—	—

NOTE: #S956c counterfeits are abundant.

S957 50 Dollars	Good	Fine	XF
1.7.1870. Black on green underprint. Reclining allegory Intelligence at lower left, seated allegory Science with child holding torch upwards at right. Signature varieties. Back: Green. Printer: BABNC.			
a. Text: *CAPITAL $4,000,000* at bottom. Rare.	—	—	—
b. Text: *CAPITAL $6,000,000* at bottom. Rare.	—	—	—

NOTE: Only 12 examples of #S957 were outstanding in 1922.

1879; 1887 Issues

S958 5 Dollars	VG	VF	UNC
1.1.1879. Black on green underprint. Rectangular frame around portrait W. McMaster at center. Signature varieties. Back: Green. Canadian arms at center. Printer: BABNC.	2750.	—	—

S958A 5 Dollars	VG	VF	UNC
1.1.1879. Black on green underprint. Oval frame around portrait W. McMaster at center. Back: Green. Canadian arms at center. Printer: BABNC.	2750.	—	—

S959 10 Dollars	Good	Fine	XF
3.1.1887. Black on green underprint. Portrait W. McMaster at left, steam ship at center, portrait H. W. Darling at right. Signature varieties. Back: Green. Lathework, counters and bank name. Printer: BABNC.	—	—	—

NOTE: #S959 was withdrawn shortly afer issue because the green tint pattern blurred easily.

1888; 1893 Issues

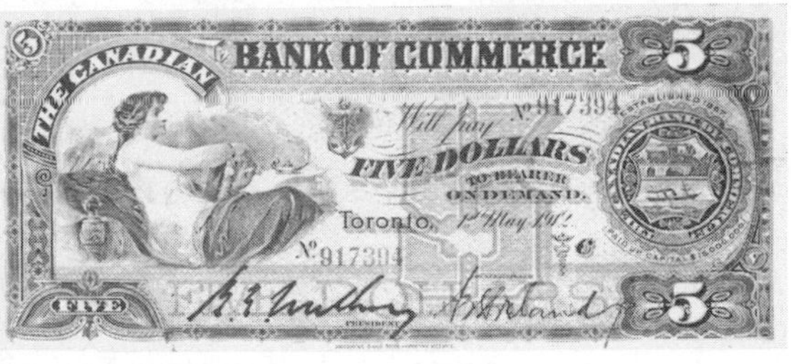

S960 5 Dollars

1888-1912. Black on orange and yellow-brown underprint. Reclining allegorical woman with lamp ("Literature") at left, bank seal at right. Signature varieties. Back: Red-brown. Printer: ABNC.

	VG	VF	UNC
a. 2.1.1888.	600.	1250.	—
b. 2.1.1892.	200.	500.	—
c. Red overprint: *D D*. 2.1.1892.	—	—	—
d. Blue, green or purple overprint: *YUKON* twice. 2.1.1892.	2500.	4250.	—
e. 2.1.1901.	200.	400.	—
f. Red overprint: *DAWSON* twice. 2.1.1901.	—	—	—
g. Withoutr Without red overprint: *E E* or *H H*. 2.1.1906.	200.	400.	—
h. 8.1.1907.	150.	300.	—
i. 1.5.1912.	150.	300.	—

S961 10 Dollars

1888-1912. Black on yellow and red underprint. Bank seal at left, cherubs around portrait of Minerva at center, seated child painting at right. Signature varieties. Back: Blue. Printer: ABNC.

	VG	VF	UNC
a. 2.1.1888.	600.	1250.	—
b. 2.1.1892.	200.	500.	—
c. Blue, green or purple overprint: *YUKON* twice. 2.1.1892.	2500.	—	—
d. 2.1.1901.	125.	250.	—
e. Red overprint: *DAWSON* twice. 2.1.1901.	—	—	—
f. 2.1.1906.	200.	500.	—
g. 8.1.1907; 1.5.1912.	150.	400.	—

S962 20 Dollars

1888-1912. Black on orange and green underprint. Reclining child with dolphin, sailing ships in background ("Off Sandy Hook") at left, bank seal at center right, seated allegorical woman with globe and urn at lower right. Signature varieties. Back: Orange. Printer: ABNC.

	VG	VF	UNC
a. 2.1.1888.	1000.	—	—
b. 2.1.1892.	1000.	—	—
c. Red, green or orange overprint: *YUKON* twice. 2.1.1892.	2500.	—	—
d. 2.1.1901.	500.	—	—
e. Brown overprint: *YUKON* twice. 2.1.1901.	2500.	—	—
f. Red or green overprint: *DAWSON* twice. 2.1.1901.	—	—	—
g. 2.1.1906.	500.	—	—
h. 8.1.1907.	500.	—	—
i. 1.5.1912.	150.	400.	—
p. Proof. 2.1.1901; 1.5.1912.	—	—	—

S963 50 Dollars

1893-1912. Black on yellow and brown underprint. Reclining allegorical woman with spilled urn and lyre ("Naiad") at center. Signature varieties. Back: Brown. Printer: ABNC.

	VG	VF	UNC
a. 3.7.1893.	1250.	—	—
b. Red, green or orange overprint: *YUKON* twice. 3.7.1893. Rare.	—	—	—
c. 2.1.1901.	1250.	—	—
d. Red or green overprint: *DAWSON* twice. 2.1.1901. Rare.	—	—	—
e. 2.1.1906.	1250.	—	—
f. 8.1.1907; 1.5.1912.	1000.	—	—
p. Proof. 2.1.1907; 1.5.1912.	—	—	—
s. Specimen. 2.1.1901; 2.1.1906; 1.5.1912.	—	—	—

S964 100 Dollars

1888-1912. Black on orange and blue underprint. Seated allegorical woman with books and globe ("La Critique") at center. Signature varieties. Back: Dark green. Printer: ABNC.

	VG	VF	UNC
a. 1.5.1912.	750.	—	—
p. Face proof. 2.1.1888; 2.1.1901; 2.1.1906; 8.1.1907.	—	—	500.
s. Specimen. 2.1.1901.	—	—	—

1917 Issues

S965 5 Dollars

2.1.1917. Black. Allegorical group of standing Agriculture, Mercury and Invention at center. Back: Olive-green. Bank seal between standing Mercury and Ceres at center. Printer: ABNC, Ottawa and CBNC.

	VG	VF	UNC
a. Red and green seal.	100.	200.	600.
b. Multicolor seal.	150.	300.	750.
s. Specimen.	—	—	—

S965A 5 Dollars

2.1.1917. Black on green and multicolor underprint. Allegorical group of standing Agriculture, Mercury and Invention at center. Back: Olive-green. Bank seal between standing Mercury and Ceres at center. Printer: ABNC, Ottawa and CBNC.

	VG	VF	UNC
a. Signature B. E. Walker and J. Aird.	50.00	125.	350.
b. Signature J. Aird and F. M. Gibson.	50.00	125.	350.
c. Signature J. Aird and S. H. Logan with title: *General Manager.*	50.00	125.	350.
d. As c, but with title: *GENERAL MANAGER.*	25.00	75.00	250.

S966 10 Dollars

2.1.1917. Black. Allegories standing Juno with bull at upper left, reclining woman at lower left center, seated women with goats at lower right, cherubs with shield with *X* at lower left and right. Multicolor se Back: Blue. Bank seal between standing Mercury and Ceres at center. Printer: ABNC, Ottawa and CBNC.

	VG	VF	UNC
a. Issued note.	100.	200.	600.
p. Proof.	—	—	650.
s. Specimen.	—	—	—

S966A 10 Dollars

2.1.1917. Black on orange and multicolor underprint. Back: Blue. Bank seal between standing Mercury and Ceres at center. Printer: ABNC, Ottawa and CBNC.

	VG	VF	UNC
a. Without imprint. Signature of B. E. Walker and J. Aird.	50.00	125.	400.
b. With imprint. Signature as a.	50.00	125.	400.
c. Signature J. Aird and C. W. Rowley with title: *General Manager.*	50.00	125.	400.
d. As c, but with title: *GENERAL MANAGER.*	50.00	125.	400.
e. Signature J. Aird and S. H. Logan with title: *General Manager.*	50.00	125.	400.
f. As e, but with title: *GENERAL MANAGER.*	50.00	125.	400.

S967 20 Dollars

2.1.1917. Black. Neptune reclining with trident at left, seated sea maidens at lower center right, seated Mercury and maiden at right. Back: Orange. Bank seal between standing Mercury and Ceres at center. Printer: ABNC, Ottawa and CBNC.

	VG	VF	UNC
a. Issued note.	100.	250.	625.
s. Specimen.	—	—	—

S967A 20 Dollars

2.1.1917. Black on yellow and multicolor underprint. Back: Orange. Bank seal between standing Mercury and Ceres at center. Printer: ABNC, Ottawa and CBNC.

	VG	VF	UNC
a. Signature B. E. Walker and J. Aird.	125.	250.	625.
b. Signature J. Aird and A. St. L. Trigge.	200.	450.	1250.
c. Signature J. Aird and S. H. Logan with title: *General Manager.*	50.00	125.	300.
d. As c, but with title: *GENERAL MANAGER.*	50.00	125.	300.

S968 50 Dollars

2.1.1917. Black. Standing Vulcan, herculean youth at left, standing herculean youths at right. Back: Brown. Bank seal between standing Mercury and Ceres at center. Printer: ABNC, Ottawa and CBNC.

	VG	VF	UNC
a. Issued note.	225.	500.	1250.
s. Specimen.	—	—	—

S968A 50 Dollars

2.1.1917. Black on olive-green and multicolor underprint. Back: Brown. Bank seal between standing Mercury and Ceres at center. Printer: ABNC, Ottawa and CBNC.

	VG	VF	UNC
a. Signature B. E. Walker and J. Aird.	150.	300.	1000.
b. Signature J. Aird and S. H. Logan.	150.	300.	1000.

S969 100 Dollars

2.1.1917. Black. Seated Mercury, standing Manufacturing at left, three seated goddesses at lower left center, standing pioneer, explorer at right. Back: Purple. Bank seal between standing Mercury and Ceres at center. Printer: ABNC, Ottawa and CBNC.

	VG	VF	UNC
a. Issued note.	150.	300.	1000.
s. Specimen.	—	—	—

1935 Issue

	VG	VF	UNC
S970 5 Dollars			
2.1.1935. Black on green and multicolor underprint. Allegorical group of standing Agriculture, Mercury and Invention at center. Back: Olive-green. Bank seal between standing Mercury and Ceres at center. Printer: CBNC. Reduced size.			
a. Signature J. Aird and S. H. Logan.	20.00	50.00	200.
b. Signature S. H. Logan and A. E. Arscott.	25.00	60.00	225.

	VG	VF	UNC
S971 10 Dollars			
2.1.1935. Black on orange and multicolor underprint. Back: Blue. Bank seal between standing Mercury and Ceres at center. Printer: CBNC.			
a. Signature J. Aird and S. H. Logan.	40.00	80.00	250.
b. Signature S. H. Logan and A. E. Arscott.	50.00	100.	275.

	VG	VF	UNC
S972 20 Dollars			
2.1.1935. Black on yellow and multicolor underprint. Back: Orange. Orange. Printer: CBNC.	50.00	100.	275.

City Bank

1836-38 Issue

	Good	Fine	XF
S972A 2 Shillings-6 Pence			
1.1.1838. Black. Steam passenger train at top center over small steamboat. Uniface. Printer: New England Bank Note Co.	650.	1750.	—

	Good	Fine	XF
S972B 5 Shillings			
16.7.1836. Black. Crest with moose supporters at top center. Uniface. Printer: New England Bank Note Co.	650.	1750.	—

	Good	Fine	XF
S972C 1 Pound			
16.7.1836. Black. Waterfront scene at top center. Uniface. Printer: New England Bank Note Co.	650.	1750.	—
S972D 5 Pounds			
18xx. Black. Town, fence and cattle at top center. Uniface. Printer: New England Bank NOte Co. Face proof.	—	Unc	750.
S972E 10 Dollars			
18xx. Black. Supported royal arms at top center. Uniface. Printer: New England Bank NOte Co. Face proof.	—	Unc	750.
S972F 20 Dollars			
18xx. Black. Military encampment at top center. Uniface. Printer: New England Bank Note Co. Face proof.	—	Unc	750.

Commercial Bank of Canada

1857 Regular Issues

	Good	Fine	XF
S973 1 Dollar			
2.1.1857. Black on yellow underprint. Seated Indian with rifle at lower left, steam passenger train in countryside at upper center, portrait Indian maiden in oval frame at right. Uniface. Printer: TCC.			
a. *BROCKVILLE* at bottom.	250.	750.	—
b. *HAMILTON* at bottom.	250.	750.	—
c. *LONDON* at bottom. Handstamp: *C* on back.	250.	750.	—
d. *TORONTO* at bottom. Black handstamp: *W*.	250.	750.	—
S974 2 Dollars			
2.1.1857. Black on yellow underprint. Chickens at lower left, cow and calf in stream at upper center, farm woman feeding chickens at lower right. Uniface. Printer: TCC.			
a. *HAMILTON* at ends.	250.	750.	—
b. *LONDON* at ends.	250.	750.	—
S975 5 Dollars			
2.1.1857. Black on yellow underprint. Surveyors at left, steam passenger train in countryside at upper center, seated man with pick and shovel at lower right. *KINGSTON* at ends. Uniface. Overprint: Red: *LONDON.* Printer: TCC.			
a. Brown back with lathework and bank name.	250.	750.	—
S976 5 Dollars			
2.1.1857. Black on yellow underprint. Surveyors at left, steam passenger train in countryside at upper center, seated man with pick and shovel at lower right. *LONDON* at ends. Uniface. Printer: TCC.			
a. Brown back with lathework and bank name.	250.	750.	—
S977 10 Dollars			
2.1.1857. Black on yellow underprint. Portrait Queen Victoria at lower left, two standing men with sailor seated on anchor at upper center, portrait Princess Eugenie at lower right. *GALT* at ends. Back: Brown. Printer: TCC.	250.	750.	—

1857 Montreal Branch Issue

	Good	Fine	XF
S978 1 Dollar			
2.1.1857. Black on yellow underprint. Standing Indian at left, seated farmer with scythe at center, farm woman with sheaf at lower right. *MONTREAL* at bottom. Uniface. Printer: TCC.	300.	900.	—
S979 2 Dollars			
2.1.1857. Black on yellow underprint. Seated Indian maiden with shield, cattle and sheep at water's edge. *MONTREAL* at ends. Uniface. Printer: TCC. Face proof.	—	Unc	500.
S980 5 Dollars			
2.1.1857. Black on yellow underprint. Portrait of C. Columbus at left, sailing ships in harbor at center, sailor with sextant at right. *MONTREAL* at ends. Back: Brown. Printer: TCC. Face proof.	—	Unc	500.
S981 10 Dollars			
2.1.1857. Black on yellow underprint. Woman, Montreal arms at left, harbor scene at center, bust of Wellington at right. *MONTREAL* at bottom. Back: Brown. Printer: TCC.	300.	900.	—
S982 100 Dollars			
2.1.1857. Black on yellow underprint. Bank building at upper center, portrait Princess Eugenie at lower right. *MONTREAL* at bottom. Back: Brown. Printer: TCC. Face proof.	—	Unc	500.
S983 1000 Dollars = 250 Pounds			
2.1.1857. Black on yellow underprint. Portrait Princess Eugenie at center. *MONTREAL* at center right. Back: Brown. Printer: TCC. Face proof.	—	Unc	750.

1857-61 Regular Issue

S986 1 Dollar	Good	Fine	XF
1860-61. Seated Indian with rifle at lower left, steam passenger train in countryside at upper center, portrait Indian maiden in oval frame at right. Uniface.			
a. *BELLEVILLE* at ends. 2.1.1860.	225.	600.	—
b. *BROCKVILLE* at ends. Black handstamp: *K.* 2.1.1860.	225.	600.	—
c. *INGERSOLL* at ends. 2.1.1860.	225.	600.	—
d. *KINGSTON* at ends. 2.1.1860.	225.	600.	—
e. *LONDON* at ends. 2.1.1860.	225.	600.	—
f. *PERTH* at ends. 2.1.1860.	225.	600.	—
g. *TORONTO* at ends. 2.1.1860.	225.	600.	—
h. *WINDSOR* at ends. 2.1.1860.	225.	600.	—
p. *KINGSTON* at ends. Proof. 2.1.1861.	—	Unc	400.

S987 2 Dollars	Good	Fine	XF
2.1.1860. Chickens at lower left, cow and calf in stream at upper center, farm woman feeding chickens at lower right. Uniface.			
a. *BELLEVILLE* at ends.	225.	600.	—
b. *HAMILTON* at ends.	225.	600.	—
c. *KINGSTON* at ends.	225.	600.	—
d. *LONDON* at ends.	225.	600.	—
e. *WINDSOR* at ends.	225.	600.	—
p1. *PORT HOPE* at ends. Proof.	—	Unc	400.
p2. *PRESCOTT* at ends. Proof.	—	Unc	400.

S988 5 Dollars	Good	Fine	XF
2.1.1860. Surveyors at left, steam passenger train in countryside at upper center, seated man with pick and shovel at lower right. *KINGSTON* at ends. Uniface.			
p1. *CHATHAM* at ends. Proof.	—	Unc	400.
p2. *KINGSTON* at ends. Proof.	—	Unc	400.

1860-62 Montreal Branch Issue

	Good	Fine	XF
S991 1 Dollar 2.1.1860. Black on green underprint. Standing Indian at left, seated farmer with scythe at center, farm woman with sheaf at lower right. *MONTREAL* at bottom. Uniface. Printer: TCC. Proof.	—	Unc	500.
S992 2 Dollars 2.1.1860. Black on green underprint. Seated Indian maiden with shield, cattle and sheep at water's edge. *MONTREAL* at bottom. Uniface. Printer: TCC. Proof.	—	Unc	500.
S993 5 Dollars 2.1.1860. Black on green underprint. Portrait of C. Columbus at left, sailing ships in harbor at center, sailor with sextant at right. *MONTREAL* at bottom. Uniface. Printer: TCC. Proof.	—	Unc	500.
S994 10 Dollars 2.1.1860. Black on green underprint. Woman, Montreal arms at left, harbor scene at center, bust of Wellington at right. *MONTREAL* at bottom. Uniface. Printer: TCC and ABNC. Proof.	—	Unc	600.
S995 100 Dollars 2.1.1862. Black on green underprint. Bank building at upper center, portrait Princess Eugenie at lower right. *MONTREAL* at bottom. Uniface. Printer: ABNC. Proof.	—	Unc	750.
S996 1000 Dollars 2.1.1860. Black on green underprint. Portrait Princess Eugenie at center. *MONTREAL* at center right. Without imprint. Uniface. Proof.	—	Unc	1000.

Commercial Bank of Manitoba

1885 Issue

	VG	VF	UNC
S997 5 Dollars 1.5.1885. Black on green underprint. Standing allegorical woman with shield at upper left, Indian camp at center, portrait Queen Victoria at right. Back: Brown. Printer: CABNC.	4000.	—	—
S998 10 Dollars 1.5.1885. Black and yellow. Standing allegorical woman with shield at upper left, farmers reaping grain at center right. Back: Green. Printer: CABNC.	4000.	—	—

1891 Issue

	VG	VF	UNC
S999 5 Dollars 2.1.1891. Black on green underprint. Horse drawn reaper at center. Head office building at lower left, D. McArthur at lower right. Signature varieties. Back: Green. Steam passenger train at station at center. Printer: BABNC.	4000.	—	—
S1000 10 Dollars 2.1.1891. Black on green underprint. Plowing with horses at center. Head office building at lower left, D. McArthur at lower right. Signature varieties. Back: Green. Crest at center. Printer: BABNC.	4000.	—	—

Commercial Bank of the Midland District

1832-35 Issue

	Good	Fine	XF
S1000A 1 Dollar = 5 Shillings 1832-33. Black. Paddle wheel steamboat at upper center, cherub face at upper and lower right. Uniface. Printer: Rawdon, Clark & Co. Proof.			
a. 1.11.1833.	500.	1750.	—
p. Proof. 2.8.1832.	—	Unc	500.
S1000B 2 Dollars = 10 Shillings 1.3.1833; 1.1.1835. Black. Woman seated at left, two allegorical women with shield with large *2* at upper center, town, harbor view sideways at right. Uniface. Printer: Rawdon, Clark & Co.	500.	1250.	—

1836 Issue

	Good	Fine	XF
S1000C 1 Dollar = 5 Shillings 1.3.1836. Black. Indian seated at left, milk maid churning butter at center, farm woman with grain at right. Uniface. Printer: RWH & E.	500.	1250.	—
S1000D 2 Dollars = 10 Shillings 1.3.1836. Black. Harbor scene at left, allegorical man by urn at center, allegorical man at upper right, allegorical woman at lower right. Uniface. Printer: RWH & E.	500.	1250.	—

1843 Issue

	Good	Fine	XF
S1000E 1 Dollar = 5 Shillings 1.7.1843. Black. Indian maiden stepping out of canoe at top center. Oval portrait Prince Consort at left, Queen Victoria at right. Uniface. Printer: RWH & C or RWH & E.	500.	1250.	—
S1000F 2 Dollars = 10 Shillings 1.7.1843. Black. Seated Britannia and Agriculture at top center. Oval portrait Prince Consort at left, Queen Victoria at right. Uniface. Printer: RWH & C or RWH & E.	500.	1250.	—
S1000G 5 Dollars = 25 Shillings 1.7.1843. Black. Two seated allegorical women with cherubs with large ornate *5* at top center. Oval portrait Prince Consort at left, Queen Victoria at right. Uniface. Printer: RWH & C or RWH & E.	500.	1250.	—
S1000H 10 Dollars = 50 Shillings 1.7.1843. Black. Portrait Queen Victoria at left. Uniface. Printer: RWH & C or RWH & E. Proof.	—	Unc	500.

1847-54 Issues

	Good	Fine	XF
S1000J 1 Dollar = 5 Shillings 1.7.1846; 1.7.1847; 1.7.1848; 1.7.1853; 1.7.1854. Black. Farmer with sickle and sheave at lower left, reclining allegorical woman with large ornate *1* at upper center, standing sailor with telescope at lower right. Uniface. Overprint: Red: *TORONTO* or *BROCKVILLE*. Printer: RWH & Co. or RWH&E.	500.	1250.	—
S1000K 2 Dollars = 10 Shillings 18xx. Black. Justice and Liberty at left, two seated allegorical women with cornucopia at top center, Agriculture and Commerce at right. Uniface. Overprint: Red: *TORONTO* or *BROCKVILLE*. Printer: RWH & Co. or RWH&E.			
a. Issued note.	500.	1250.	—
p. Proof.	—	Unc	500.
S1000L 5 Dollars = 1 Pound-5 Shillings 18xx. Black. Queen Victoria at left, Prince Consort at right. Reclining allegorical woman on large ornate *5* supported by four cherubs at top center. Uniface. Overprint: Red: *TORONTO* or *BROCKVILLE*. Printer: RWH & Co. or RWH&E. Proof.	—	Unc	500.
S1000M 10 Dollars = 2 Pounds-10 Shillings 18xx. Black. Queen Victoria at left, Prince Consort at right. Seated allegorical woman with large ornate *10* at top center. Uniface. Overprint: Red: *TORONTO* or *BROCKVILLE*. Printer: RWH & Co. or RWH&E. Proof.	—	Unc	500.

	Good	Fine	XF
S1000N 20 Dollars = 5 Pounds 18xx. Black. Queen Victoria at left, Prince Consort at right. Woman seated with large ornate *20* at top center. Uniface. Overprint: Red: *TORONTO* or *BROCKVILLE.* Printer: RWH & Co. or RWH&E. Proof.	—	Unc	600.
S1000P 50 Dollars = 12 Pounds-10 Shillings 18xx. Black. Portrait Queen Victoria on royal crest at left. Uniface. Overprint: Red: *TORONTO* or *BROCKVILLE.* Printer: RWH & Co. or RWH&E. Proof.	—	Unc	600.
S1000Q 100 Dollars = 25 Pounds 18xx. Black. Allegorical woman at top center, royal crest at right. Uniface. Overprint: Red: *TORONTO* or *BROCKVILLE.* Printer: RWH & Co. or RWH&E. Proof.	—	Unc	600.

1854 Issue

	Good	Fine	XF
S1000R 5 Dollars 18xx. Black. Mercury seated with lion at top center, portrait of woman at right. Uniface. Printer: RWH & Co. Proof.	—	Unc	500.

	VG	VF	UNC
S1000S 10 Dollars 2.1.1854. Black. Allegorical male in flight holding cornucopia spilling coins at top center right, sailing ships at lower right. Uniface. Printer: RWH & Co.	125.	200.	—

1854 Brockville Issue

	VG	VF	UNC
S1000T 4 Dollars 2.5.1854. Black. Green panel with branch name at upper left and right. Portrait of young woman lower left and at lower right, steam passenger train in countryside at top center. Printer: RWH & Co.	600.	1000.	—

1854 Hamilton Issue

	VG	VF	UNC
S1000U 4 Dollars 2.5.1854. Black. Green panel with branch name at upper left and right. Portrait of young woman lower left and at lower right, steam passenger train in countryside at top center. Uniface. Printer: RWH & Co.	600.	1000.	—

1854 London Issue

	VG	VF	UNC
S1000V 4 Dollars 2.5.1854. Black. Green panel with branch name at upper left and right. Portrait of young woman lower left and at lower right, steam passenger train in countryside at top center. Uniface. Printer: RWH & Co.	600.	1000.	—

1854 St. Catherines Issue

	VG	VF	UNC
S1000W 4 Dollars 2.5.1854. Black. Green panel with branch name at upper left and right. Portrait of young woman lower left and at lower right, steam passenger train in countryside at top center. Uniface. Printer: RWH & Co.	600.	1000.	—

1854 Toronto Issue

	Good	Fine	XF
S1000X 4 Dollars 2.5.1854. Black. Green panel with branch name at upper left and right. Portrait of young woman lower left and at lower right, steam passenger train in countryside at top center. Uniface. Printer: RWH & Co. Proof.	—	Unc	500.

Commercial Bank of Windsor

1860 Issue

	Good	Fine	XF
S1001 20 Dollars 186x. Black on green underprint. Two children holding sheaves at lower left, steam passenger train at station at upper center, standing sailor with lion at lower right. Back: Green. Printer: ABNC. Proof.	—	Unc	1000.

1870-98 Issue

	VG	VF	UNC
S1002 4 Dollars 1870-71. Black on green underprint. Reclining woman spilling water jar at bottom center, Niagara Falls in background. Back: Green. Printer: BABNC.			
a. 1.7.1871.	2750.	—	—
p. Proof. 1.9.1870.	—	—	850.
S1003 5 Dollars 1.9.1870; 1.7.1871; 1.7.1898. Black on green underprint. Back: Green. Printer: BABNC. Proof.	—	—	850.
S1003A 10 Dollars 1870-98. Black on green underprint. Back: Green. Printer: BABNC.			
a. 1.7.1871.	2750.	—	—
p. Proof. 1.9.1870; 1.7.1898.	—	—	850.

#S1004 *Deleted.* See #S1001.

Crown Bank of Canada

1904 Issue

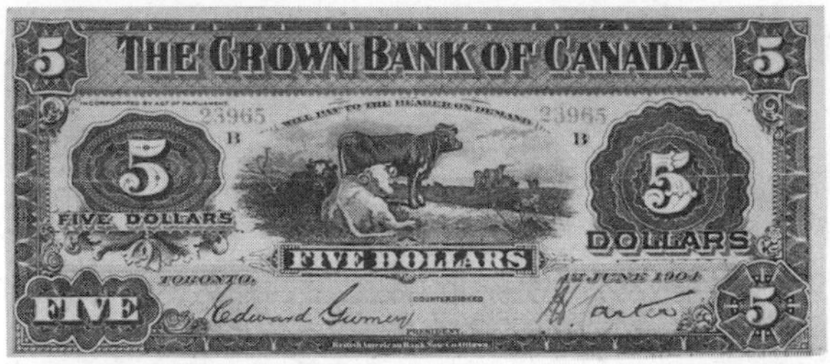

	VG	VF	UNC
S1006 5 Dollars 1.6.1904. Black on green and yellow underprint. Cattle at center. Back: Brown. Crown. Printer: BABNC.	3000.	—	—
S1007 10 Dollars 1.6.1904. Black on brown and yellow underprint. Lion on mountain at left. Back: Blue. Crown. Printer: BABNC. Face proof.	—	—	1000.
S1008 20 Dollars 1.6.1904. Black on red and blue underprint. Seated allegorical man, child and two reclining women at left center. Back: Red. Crown. Printer: BABNC. Face proof.	—	—	1000.
S1009 50 Dollars 1.6.1904. Black on red and yellow underprint. Parliament building at left center. Back: Red-brown. Crown. Printer: BABNC. Face proof.	—	—	1000.

Dominion Bank

1871-73 Issue

	VG	VF	UNC
S1011 4 Dollars 1.2.1871. Black on green underprint. Portrait Prince Arthur at lower left, farmer watering livestock at top center, seated Britannia with shield with large ornate *4* at lower right. Signature varieties. Back: Green. Printer: BABNC.	1250.	2500.	—

	VG	VF	UNC
S1012 5 Dollars 1.2.1871. Black on green underprint. Supported oval portrait of Queen Victoria in "Widow's Weeds" at center. Signature varieties. Back: Green. Printer: BABNC.	1250.	2500.	—
S1013 10 Dollars 1.5.1871. Black on green underprint. Girl at left, paddle wheel steamboat at top center, lumberjack at lower right. Signature varieties. Back: Green. Printer: BABNC.	1500.	2750.	—
S1014 20 Dollars 1.5.1871. Black on green underprint. Blacksmith shoeing horses at lower left, farm machinery at upper center, lumberjack at lower right. Signature varieties. Back: Green. Printer: BABNC.	1500.	2750.	—
S1015 50 Dollars 1.5.1871. Black on green underprint. Signature varieties. Back: Green. Printer: BABNC. Face proof.	—	—	750.
S1016 100 Dollars 1.10.1873. Black on green underprint. Reclining woman spilling water jar at center, Niagara Falls in background. Signature varieties. Back: Green. Printer: BABNC.	1250.	2500.	—

1876-88 Issue

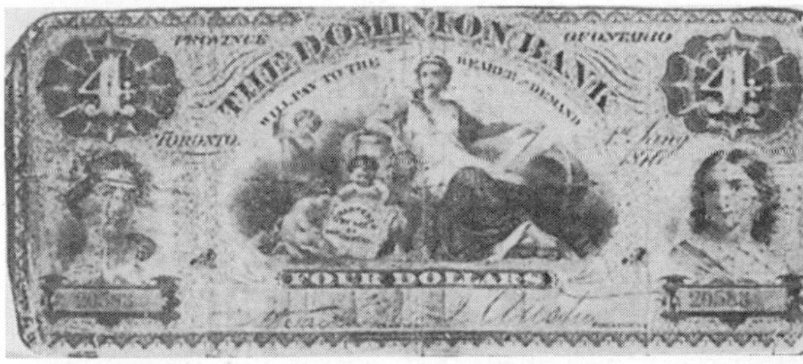

	VG	VF	UNC
S1017 4 Dollars 1.1.1876. Black on green and red underprint. Laureate woman's bust at left, seated allegorical woman with children at center, girl's bust at right. Signature varieties. Back: Brown. Printer: ABNC.	1000.	2250.	—

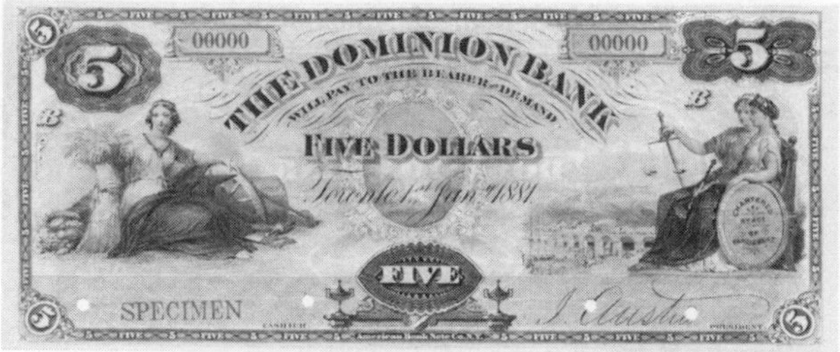

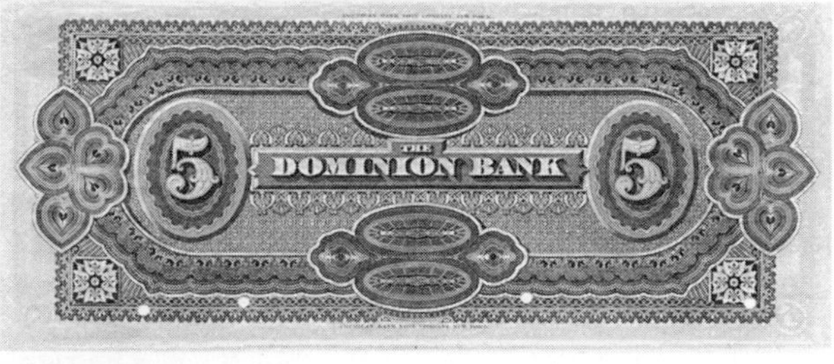

S1018 5 Dollars

1.1.1881. Black on blue underprint. Seated woman with sheaf at left, two seated allegorical women at right. Signature varieties. Back: Blue. Printer: ABNC.

	VG	VF	UNC
a. Issued note.	1000.	2250.	—
s. Specimen.	—	—	—

S1019 10 Dollars

2.1.1888. Black on brown and green underprint. Allegorical woman with fasces at left, seated allegorical women by beehive at upper center right. Signature varieties. Back: Brown. Reclining Indian at center. Printer: ABNC.

	VG	VF	UNC
a. Issued note.	1250.	2500.	—
s. Specimen.	—	—	—

S1020 50 Dollars

	VG	VF	UNC
1.7.1881. Black on green underprint. Jacques Cartier sighting land at lower left, ships dockside at top center, Queen Victoria in "Widow's Weeds" at lower right. Signature varieties. Back: Green. Printer: BABNC.	1250.	2250.	—

1891; 1898 Issue

S1021 5 Dollars

	VG	VF	UNC
1.7.1891. Black on green underprint. Lighthouse, boats at left, farmer reaping grain with horses at center, power lines and cattle at right. Back: Green. Printer: BABNC.	1000.	2000.	—

S1022 10 Dollars

	VG	VF	UNC
1.7.1898. Black on green underprint. Portrait F. Smith at lower left, cattle at center right. Back: Green. Printer: BABNC.	1250.	2250.	—

A WORD ON DATE RANGES

Often date ranges or specific dates are listed. These have been observed or reported by our contributors. If a note is outside the published range, it only means that it is a newly reported date, and not necessarily worthy of a premium value.

1896-1901 Issue

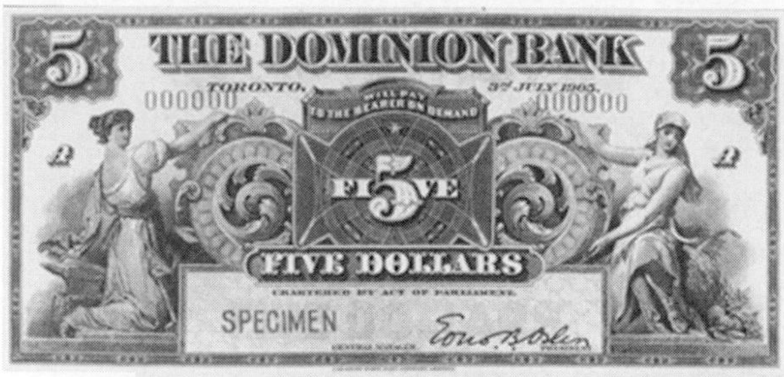

S1023 5 Dollars

1896-1925. Black on green underprint. Woman kneeling at left, woman seated at right. Back: Green. Greek god at center.

	VG	VF	UNC
a. 1.1.1896; 1.1.1898.	1000.	2000.	—
b. 2.1.1900.	1000.	2000.	—
c. 2 signature varieties. 3.7.1905.	150.	300.	—
d. 2 signature varieties. 2.1.1925.	125.	225.	750.
s1. Specimen. As a.	—	—	—
s2. Specimen. As c.	—	—	—

S1024 10 Dollars

1900-10. Black on yellow-green and green underprint. Reclining Britannia with lion at center. Back: Red, yellow-green and green. Beaver at center.

	VG	VF	UNC
a. 2.1.1900.	300.	600.	—
b. 2 signature varieties. 3.1.1910.	125.	200.	600.
s. As a. Specimen.	—	—	—

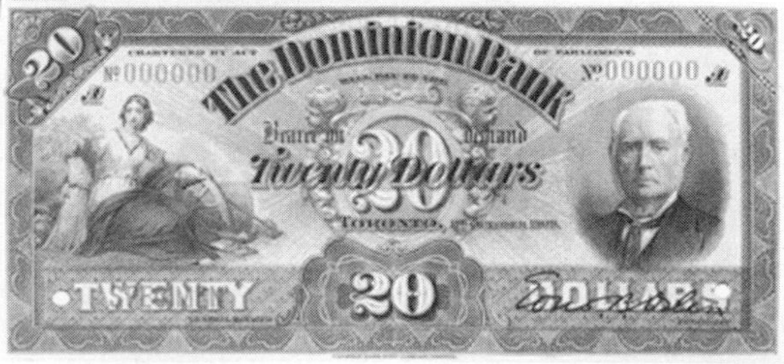

S1025 20 Dollars

1897-1925. Black on blue and yellow-green underprint. Woman with tools and sheaf at left, portrait F. Smith at right. Back: Olive-green. Greek goddess at center.

	VG	VF	UNC
a. 1.10.1897.	750.	1500.	—
b. 2 signature varieties. 1.10.1909.	150.	250.	750.
c. 2.1.1925.	100.	150.	500.
s. As b. Specimen. Overprint: *SPECIMEN*.	—	—	—

S1026 50 Dollars	VG	VF	UNC
1901; 1925. Black on brown, purple and green underprint. Beehive at left, livestock at right. Back: Multicolor. Beaver at center.			
a. 2.7.1901.	300.	600.	—
b. 2.1.1925.	200.	400.	—

1925 Issue

S1027 10 Dollars	VG	VF	UNC
2.1.1925. Black on yellow and green underprint. Reclining Britannia with lion at center. 2 signature varieties. Back: Yellow and green.			
a. Issued note.	50.00	100.	300.
s. Specimen.	—	—	—
S1027A 50 Dollars			
2.1.1925. Black on blue, olive-green and multicolor underprint. Beehive at left, livestock at right.	50.00	100.	300.

1931 Issue

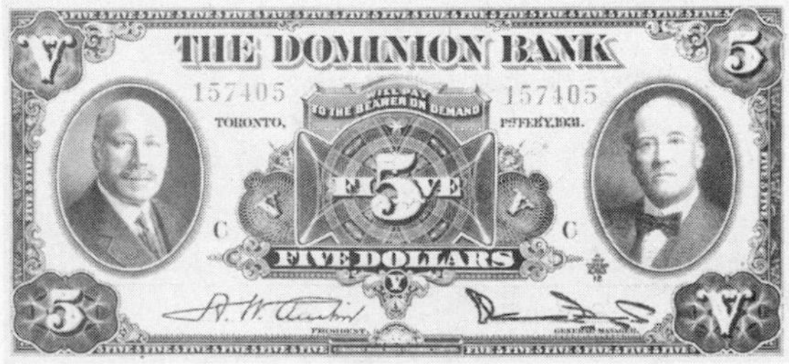

S1028 5 Dollars	VG	VF	UNC
1.2.1931. Black on blue and orange underprint. Portrait A. W. Austin at left, portrait C. A. Bogert at right. 2 signature varieties. Back: Green. Map of Canada. Printer: CBNC.	50.00	100.	300.

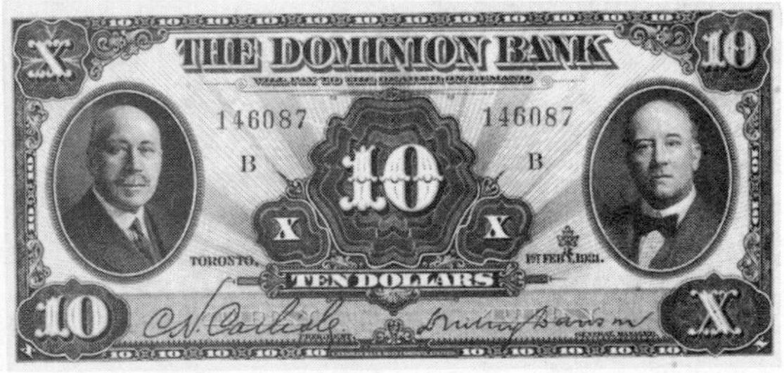

S1029 10 Dollars	VG	VF	UNC
1.2.1931. Black on blue and orange underprint. Portrait A. W. Austin at left, portrait C. A. Bogert at right. 2 signature varieties. Back: Blue. Map of Canada. Printer: CBNC.	75.00	125.	425.

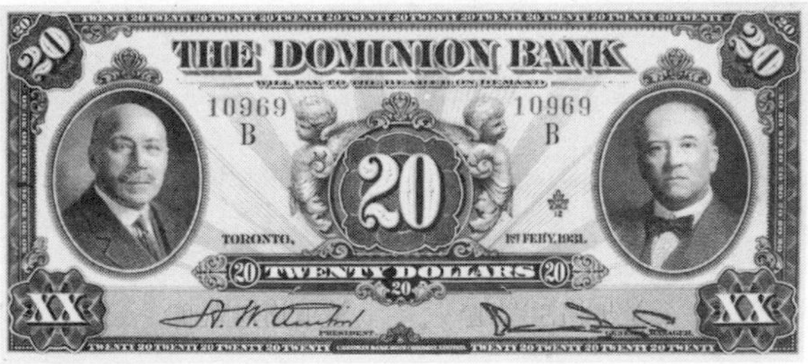

S1030 20 Dollars	VG	VF	UNC
1.2.1931. Black on purple and orange underprint. Portrait A. W. Austin at left, portrait C. A. Bogert at right. Back: Purple. Map of Canada. Printer: CBNC.	100.	200.	600.
S1031 50 Dollars			
1.2.1931. Black on yellow, pink and orange underprint. Portrait A. W. Austin at left, portrait C. A. Bogert at right. Back: Orange. Map of Canada. Printer: CBNC. Specimen.	—	—	600.
S1032 100 Dollars			
1.2.1931. Black on olive and orange underprint. Portrait A. W. Austin at left, portrait C. A. Bogert at right. Back: Red-brown. Map of Canada. Printer: CBNC.	300.	650.	—

1935 Issue

S1033 5 Dollars	VG	VF	UNC
2.1.1935. Black on green and orange underprint. Portrait D. Danson at left, portrait C. H. Carlisle at right. Back: Green. Printer: CBNC. Reduced size.	25.00	50.00	150.
S1034 10 Dollars			
2.1.1935. Black on yellow, pink and orange underprint. Portrait D. Danson at left, portrait C. H. Carlisle at right. Back: Orange. Printer: CBNC.	25.00	55.00	200.

1938 Issue

S1035 5 Dollars	VG	VF	UNC
3.1.1938. Black on orange and brown underprint. Portrait C. H. Carlisle at left, portrait R. Rae at right. Back: Brown. Printer: CBNC.	25.00	50.00	200.

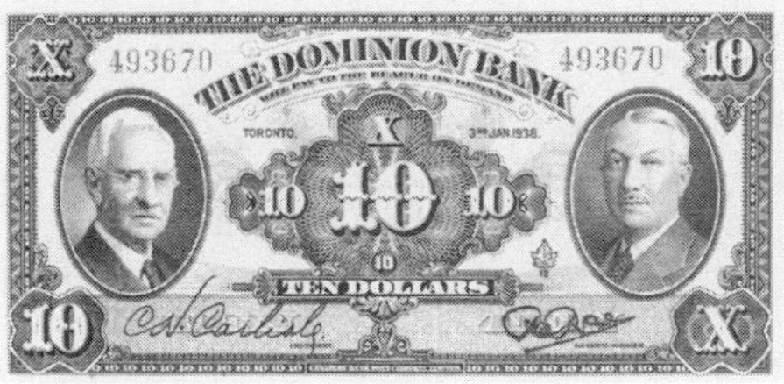

S1036 10 Dollars	VG	VF	UNC
3.1.1938. Black on blue and yellow underprint. Portrait C. H. Carlisle at left, portrait R. Rae at right. Back: Olive. Printer: CBNC.	50.00	100.	250.

Eastern Townships Bank

1859 Issue

S1041 1 Dollar	Good	Fine	XF
1.8.1859. Black on green underprint. Portrait Queen Victoria at lower left, Magog River Falls at upper center, standing Indian at upper right. Signature varieties. Printer: ABNC.			
a. Partially engraved date. Red word protector on back.	600.	2000.	—
b. Engraved date, hand signed signature of B. Pomroy at right. Red overprint: *STANBRIDGE*.	600.	2000.	—
c. As b. Red overprint: *STANSTEAD*.	600.	2000.	—
d. As b. Red overprint: *WATERLOO*.	600.	2000.	—
e. Engraved date and printed signature of B. Pomroy at right.	600.	2000.	—

S1042 2 Dollars	Good	Fine	XF
1.8.1859. Black on green underprint. Portrait Queen Victoria at lower left, cattlemen on horseback with herd at top center, portrait Prince Consort at lower right. Signature varieties. Printer: ABNC.			
a. Partially engraved date. Red word protector on back.	600.	2000.	—
b. Engraved date; hand signed signature of B. Pomroy at right. Red overprint: *STANBRIDGE*.	600.	2000.	—
c. As b. Red overprint: *STANSTEAD*.	600.	2000.	—
d. As b. Red overprint: *WATERLOO*.	600.	2000.	—
e. Engraved date and printed signature of B. Pomroy at right.	600.	2000.	—

S1043 4 Dollars	Good	Fine	XF
1859-61. Black on green underprint. Portrait Prince of Wales at lower left, Magog River Falls at upper center, portrait B. Pomroy at lower right. Signature varieties. Back: Red word protector. Printer: ABNC.			
a. Partially engraved date. Red overprint: *WATERLOO*. 1.8.1859.	600.	2000.	—
b. Engraved date; hand signed signature of B. Pomroy at right. 1.2.1861.	600.	2000.	—
c. Engraved date; printed signature of B. Pomroy at right. 1.2.1861.	600.	2000.	—

S1044 5 Dollars	Good	Fine	XF
1.8.1859. Black on green underprint. Seated allegorical woman at lower left, horse, colt and farmer at top center, farmer with scythe at lower right. Signature varieties. Printer: ABNC.			
a. Partially engraved date. Red word protector on back.	700.	2250.	—
b. Engraved date; hand signed signature of B. Pomroy at right. Red overprint: *STANBRIDGE*.	700.	2250.	—
c. As b. Red overprint: *STANSTEAD*.	700.	2250.	—
d. As b. Red overprint: *WATERLOO*.	700.	2250.	—
e. Engraved date and printed signature of B. Pomroy at right.	700.	2250.	—

S1045 10 Dollars	Good	Fine	XF
1.8.1859. Black on green underprint. Hunter with dog by campfire at lower left, reclining shepherd boy at top center, steam train at lower right. Signature varieties. Printer: ABNC.			
a. Partially engraved date. Red word protector on back.	800.	2500.	—
b. Engraved date; hand signed signature of B. Pomroy at right. Red overprint: *STANBRIDGE*.	800.	2500.	—
c. As b. Red overprint: *STANSTEAD*.	800.	2500.	—
d. As b. Red overprint: *WATERLOO*.	800.	2500.	—
e. Engraved date and printed signature of B. Pomroy at right.	800.	2500.	—

S1046 20 Dollars	Good	Fine	XF
1.8.1859. Black on green underprint. Signature varieties. Printer: ABNC.			
a. Partially engraved date. Red word protector on back.	800.	2500.	—
b. Engraved date; hand signed signature of B. Pomroy at right. Red overprint: *STANBRIDGE*.	800.	2500.	—
c. As b. Red overprint: *STANSTEAD*.	800.	2500.	—
d. As b. Red overprint: *WATERLOO*.	800.	2500.	—
e. Engraved date and printed signature of B. Pomroy at right.	800.	2500.	—

1873 Issue

S1047 4 Dollars	Good	Fine	XF
1.7.1873. Black on green underprint. Farm animals at lower left, Magog River Falls at upper center, portrait B. Pomroy at lower right. Signature varieties. Back: Green. Blacksmith shoeing horse at center. Printer: BABNC.	800.	2500.	—

S1048 5 Dollars	Good	Fine	XF
1.7.1873. Black on green underprint. Portrait William Farwell at lower left, paddle wheel steamboat at upper center, lumberjack at lower right. Signature varieties. Back: Green. Printer: BABNC.	800.	2500.	—

S1049 10 Dollars	Good	Fine	XF
1.7.1873. Black on green underprint. Portrait William Farwell at lower left, farmer watering livestock at top center, portrait B. Pomroy at lower right. Signature varieties. Back: Green. Blacksmith shoeing horse at center. Printer: BABNC.	800.	2500.	—

S1050 50 Dollars	Good	Fine	XF
1.7.1873; 1.7.1874. Black on green underprint. Steam passenger train at upper left. Portrait William Farwell at upper center right, portrait B. Pomroy at lower right. Signature varieties. Back: Green. Blacksmith shoeing horse at center. Printer: BABNC.	1000.	3000.	—

S1051 100 Dollars	Good	Fine	XF
1.7.1873; 1.7.1874. Black on green underprint. Portrait William Farwell at left, Magog River Falls at top center, portrait B. Pomroy at right. Signature varieties. Back: Green. Blacksmith shoeing horse at center. Printer: BABNC. Rare.	—	—	—

1879; 1893 Issue

S1052 4 Dollars	Good	Fine	XF
Black on green underprint. Farm animals at lower left, Magog River Falls at upper center, portr. R. W. Heneker at lower right. Signature varieties. Back: Green. Printer: BABNC.	750.	2250.	—
S1053 5 Dollars			
1879; 1902. Black on green underprint. Portrait William Farwell at lower left, paddle wheel steamboat at upper center, lumberjack at lower right. Signature varieties. Back: Green. Printer: BABNC.			
a. 1.7.1879.	750.	2250.	—
b. 2.7.1902.	500.	1750.	—

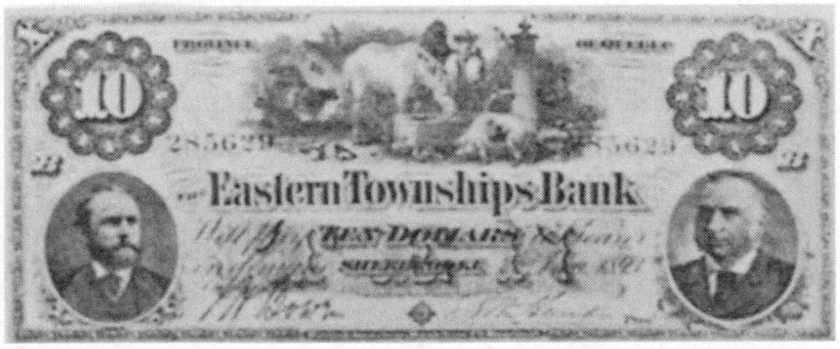

S1054 10 Dollars	Good	Fine	XF
1.7.1879; 2.1.1893. Black on green underprint. Portrait William Farwell at lower left, farmer watering livestock at top center,portrait R. W. Heneker at lower right. Signature varieties. Back: Green. Printer: BABNC.	750.	2250.	—

S1055 20 Dollars	Good	Fine	XF
2.1.1893. Black on green underprint. Cattle at left, portrait R.W. Heneker at lower right. Signature varieties. Back: Green. Bull's head at center. Printer: BABNC. Rare.	—	—	—

1906 Issue

S1056 5 Dollars	Good	Fine	XF
2.1.1906. Black on red and yellow underprint. Portrait J. Mackinnon at left, steam train in countryside at center right. Signature varieties. Back: Green on multicolor underprint. Bank crest. Printer: ABNC.	300.	1000.	2000.

S1057 10 Dollars	Good	Fine	XF
2.1.1906. Black on orange and green underprint. Portrait William Farwell at left, miners drilling at center. Signature varieties. Back: Green on multicolor underprint. Bank crest. Printer: ABNC.	300.	1000.	2000.

Exchange Bank of Yarmouth

1869; 1870 Issue

S1058 5 Dollars	VG	VF	UNC
1870-1900. Black. Sailing ships at left, sailor, man and boy on shore, fishermen in background at top center, young sailor at right. Back: Blue. Overprint: Red: *S* and *CANADIAN CURRENCY; 1800 1002* with red *S*. Printer: ABNC.			
a. Issued note. Green underprint. 1.7.1871; 1.7.1890.	3500.	—	—
b. Red-orange underprint. 1.7.1900.	3500.	—	—
p. Proof. 1.8.1870.	—	—	900.

S1059 10 Dollars	VG	VF	UNC
1870-1900. Black. Seated allegorical woman at lower left, ships, wharf scene at top center, ship's carpenter at lower right. Back: Green. Overprint: Red: *S* and *CANADIAN CURRENCY; 1890-1902* with red *S*. Printer: ABNC.			
a. Issued note. Green underprint. 1.7.1871; 1.7.1890.	3500.	—	—
b. Ochre underprint. 1.7.1900.	3500.	—	—
p. Proof. 1.8.1870.	—	—	900.
S1060 20 Dollars			
1869-1902. Black. Two sailors dockside at lower left, wharf scene, steam passenger train, wagons at top center, man mounted on horse drinking at lower right. Back: Green. Overprint: Red: *S* and *CANADIAN CURRENCY; 1890-1902* with red *S*. Printer: ABNC.			
a. Green underprint. 1.7.1871.	3500.	—	—
b. Orange underprint. 1.7.1901.	3500.	—	—
p. Blue underprint. Proof. 1.8.1869.	—	—	900.

NOTE: All the notes of the Exchange Bank of Yarmouth are extremely rare and usually are found punched hole cancelled.

Farmers Bank of Canada

1907 Issue

S1061 5 Dollars	VG	VF	UNC
2.1.1907; 1.9.1908. Black on green underprint. Farmer watering livestock at upper left. Signature varieties. Back: Green. Printer: BABNC.	2250.	—	—
S1062 10 Dollars			
2.1.1907. Black on orange underprint. Sheep grazing at upper center. Back: Green. Bull's head at center. Printer: BABNC.	3500.	—	—
S1063 25 Dollars			
1907-08. Black on gold underprint. Portrait Sir W. Laurier at left, J. P. Whitney at right. Signature varieties. Back: Gold. Printer: BABNC.			
a. 1.9.1908.	5000.	—	—
p. Face proof. 2.1.1907.	—	—	2000.
S1064 50 Dollars			
2.1.1907. Black on olive-green underprint. Farmers plowing with horses at center. Signature varieties. Back: Green. Woman with sickle in filed at center. Printer: BABNC. Face proof.	—	—	850.

S1065 100 Dollars | VG — | VF — | UNC 900.
2.1.1907. Black on red underprint. Farmer storing hay into barn at left center. Signature varieties. Back: Green. Farmer with boy sharpening tools on grindstone at left. Printer: BABNC. Face proof.

Gore Bank

1836 Issue

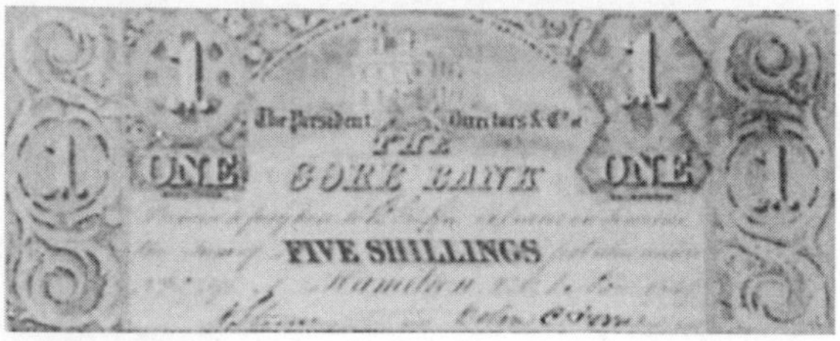

S1066 1 Dollar | VG | VF | UNC
1836-56. Black. Wentworth County Court House at top center. Uniface. Signature varieties. Printer: New England Bank Note Co.

	VG	VF	UNC
a. Partially engraved date. 6.2.1840; 1.11.1849; 1.3.1850.	850.	—	—
b. Fully engraved date. 2.9.1850; 2.6.1856.	500.	1250.	—

S1067 2 Dollars | VG | VF | UNC
1836-56. Black. Seated Britannia with lion, reclining allegorical woman, unicorn at top center. Uniface. Signature varieties. Printer: New England Bank Note Co.

	VG	VF	UNC
a. Partially engraved date. 9.12.1845.	900.	—	—
b. Fully engraved date. 2.9.1850; 2.9.1852; 2.6.1856.	500.	1250.	—

S1068 4 Dollars
1836-56. Black. Supported royal arms at top center. Uniface. Signature varieties. Printer: New England Bank Note Co.

	VG	VF	UNC
a. Partially engraved date. 7.11.1836; 7.1839; 1.3.1850.	900.	—	—
b. Fully engraved date. 2.9.1852.	600.	1100.	—

S1069 10 Dollars
1836-56. Black. Sailing ship at left, St. George slaying dragon at top center. Uniface. Signature varieties. Printer: New England Bank Note Co.

	VG	VF	UNC
a. Partially engraved date. 16.11.1836; 3.1.1839.	1000.	—	—
b. Fully engraved date. 2.9.1852.	600.	1100.	—

Halifax Banking Company

1825 Issue

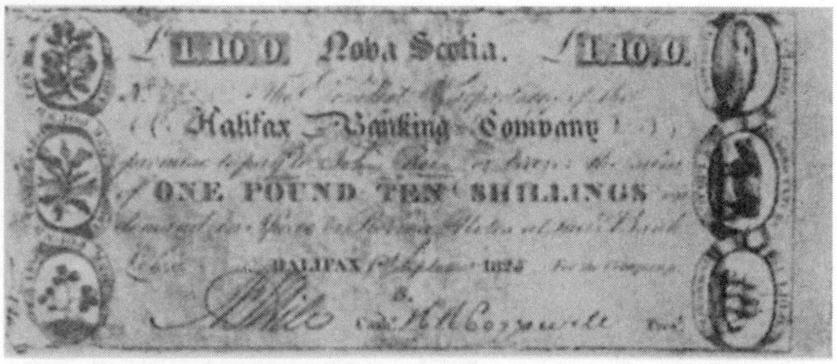

S1070 1 Pound-10 Shillings | Good 1250. | Fine 3500. | XF —
1.9.1825; 1.9.1826. Black. Uniface. Printer: Maverick.

1833 Issue

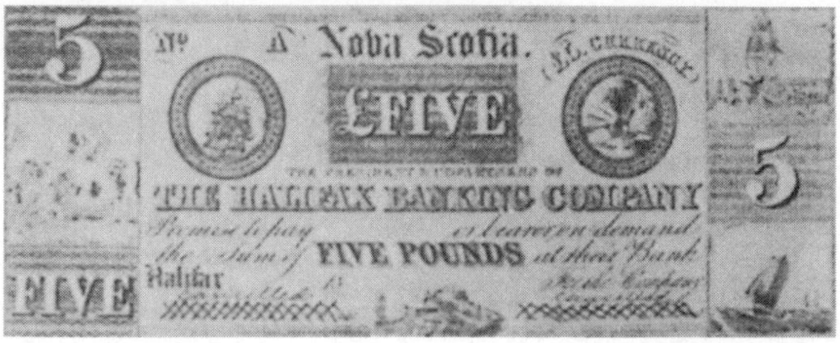

S1071 5 Pounds | Good — | Fine Unc | XF 1500.
18xx. Black on blue underprint. Cattle at left, sailing ship, cask and bales at bottom center, farm implements, sailing ship at upper left and upper right. Uniface. Printer: New England Bank Note Company, Boston.

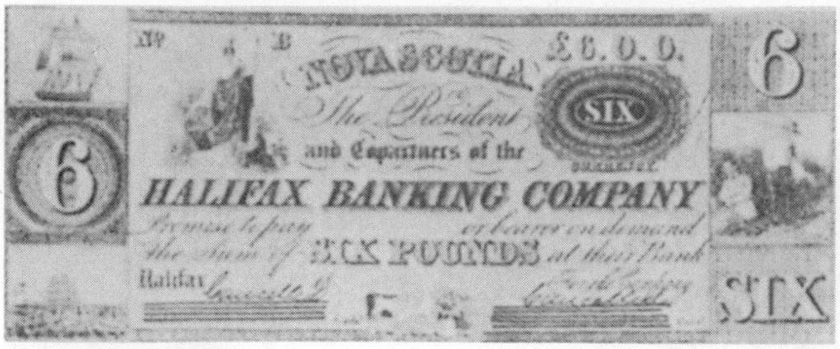

S1072 6 Pounds | Good — | Fine Unc | XF 1500.
18xx. Black on blue underprint. Sailing ships at upper left and lower right, standing Britannia at top left center, farm implements at bottom center, farmers harvesting at right. Uniface. Printer: New England Bank Note Company, Boston. Remainder.

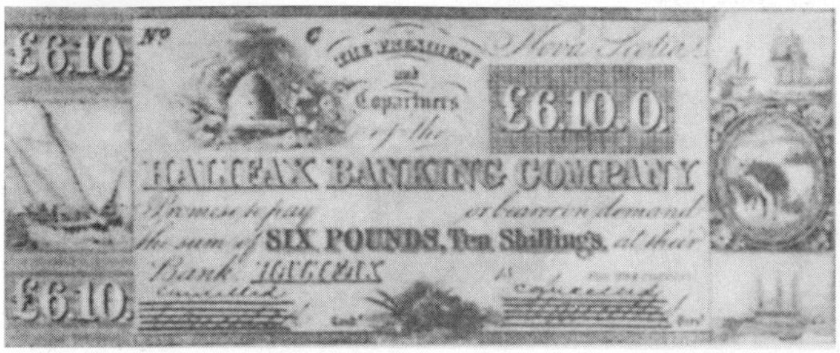

S1073 6 Pounds-10 Shillings | Good — | Fine Unc | XF 1500.
18xx. Black on blue underprint. Fishing vessel at left, beehive at upper left. center, farm tools at bottom center, whaling scene over cattle with whaling scene below at right. Uniface. Printer: New England Bank Note Company, Boston. Remainder.

S1074 7 Pounds-10 Shillings | Good — | Fine Unc | XF 1500.
18xx. Black on blue underprint. Allegorical woman at left, sailing ships at upper left center, casks and sailing ship at bottom center, cattle at right. Uniface. Printer: New England Bank Note Company, Boston. Remainder.

1863 Issue

S1075 20 Dollars | VG | VF | UNC
9.12.1863. Black on green underprint. Sailing ships in Halifax harbor at upper center. Printer: ABNC.

	VG	VF	UNC
a. Handwritten or printed serial #.	3250.	—	—
b. Red overprint: *July 1, 1871* and *CANADA CURRENCY*.	3250.	—	—

1871 Issue

S1076 20 Dollars

	VG	VF	UNC
14.9.1871. Engraved. Sailing ships in Halifax harbor at upper center. *CANADA CURRENCY* engraved. Printer: ABNC.	3250.	—	—

1872; 1880 Issue

S1077 4 Dollars

	VG	VF	UNC
1.10.1872; 1.10.1880. Black on green underprint. Sailing ships in Halifax harbor at center. Back: Green. Printer: ABNC.	3500.	—	—

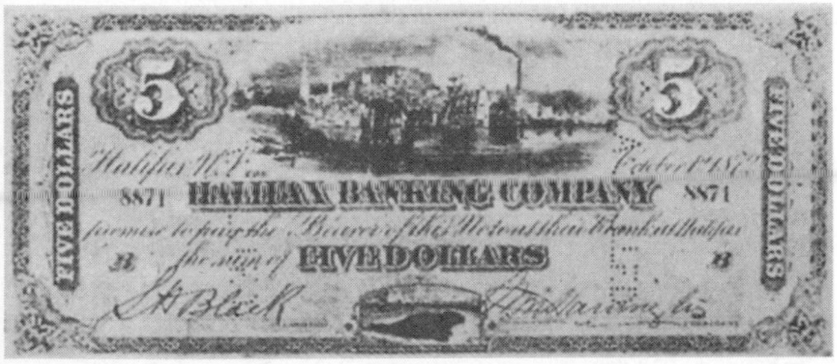

S1078 5 Dollars

1872; 1880. Black on green underprint. Sailing ships in Halifax harbor at center. Back: Green. Printer: ABNC.

	VG	VF	UNC
a. 1.10.1872; 1.10.1880.	3500.	—	—
b. Slightly modified panels, and imprint: *BABNC.* 1.10.1880.	3500.	—	—

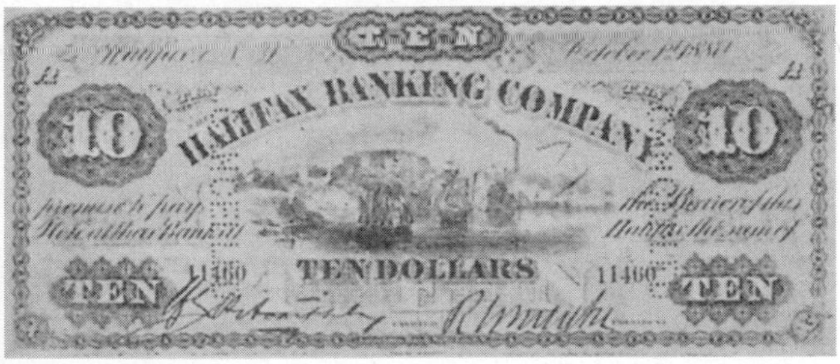

S1079 10 Dollars

1872; 1880. Black on green underprint. Sailing ships in Halifax harbor at center. Back: Green. Printer: ABNC.

	VG	VF	UNC
a. 1.10.1872; 1.10.1880.	3500.	—	—
b. Imprint: *CBNC.*1.10.1880.	3500.	—	—

S1079A 20 Dollars

	VG	VF	UNC
1.10.1880. Black on green underprint. Sailing ships in Halifax harbor. Back: Green. Printer: CBNC. Proof.	—	—	500.

1887-94 Issue

S1080 5 Dollars

1.1.1887. Black. Fishermen, fishing vessel at left, sailing ships in Halifax harbor at center. Halifax crest at right. Back: Halifax crest. Printer: CABNC.

	VG	VF	UNC
a. Green underprint. Back green.	3500.	—	—
b. Red underprint. Back brown.	3500.	—	—
p. Black underprint. Back brown. Proof.	—	—	500.

S1081 5 Dollars

	VG	VF	UNC
1.1.1894. Black on blue underprint. Fishermen, fishing vessel at left, sailing ships in Halifax harbor at center. Halifax crest at right. Imprint: *BABNC.* Back: Halifax crest. Printer: CABNC.	3500.	—	—

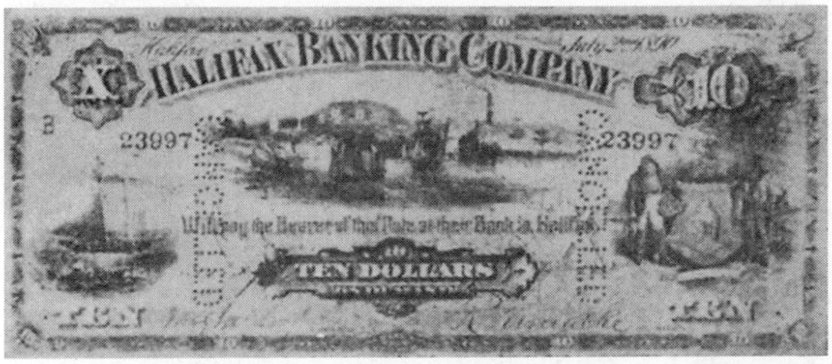

S1082 10 Dollars

	VG	VF	UNC
2.7.1890. Black on green underprint. Fishermen, fishing vessel at left, sailing ships in Halifax harbor at center. Halifax crest at right. Back: Green. Halifax crest. Printer: CABNC.	3500.	—	—

S1083 20 Dollars

	VG	VF	UNC
2.7.1890. Black on green underprint. Fishermen, fishing vessel at left, sailing ships in Halifax harbor at center. Halifax crest at right. Back: Green. Halifax crest. Printer: CABNC.	3500.	—	—

1896-98 Issue

S1083A 5 Dollars

	Good	Fine	XF
2.7.1896. Black on green underprint. H. N. Wallace at left, sailing ships in Halifax harbor at center. R. Uniake at right. Back: Green. Halifax crest at left. Printer: BABNC. Proof.	—	Unc	500.

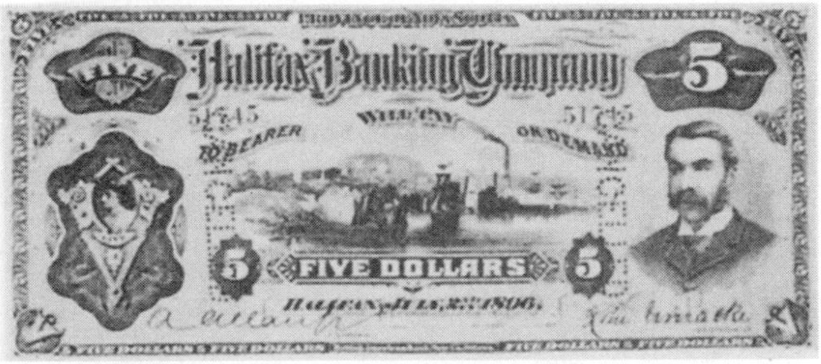

S1084 5 Dollars

	VG	VF	UNC
2.7.1896. Black on green underprint. Head of Mercury in ornate *V* at left, sailing ships in Halifax harbor at center. R. Uniake at right. Back: Green. Halifax crest at left. Printer: BABNC.	3500.	—	—

S1085 10 Dollars

	VG	VF	UNC
1.7.1898. Black on green underprint. Ocean freighter, boats at lower left. R. Uniake at right. Back: Green. Printer: BABNC.	3500.	—	—

S1086 20 Dollars	VG	VF	UNC
1.7.1898. Black on green underprint. Halifax crest at left. R. Uniake at right. Back: Green. Printer: BABNC.	3500.	—	—

Home Bank of Canada

1904-20 Issue

S1087 5 Dollars	Good	Fine	XF
1904-20. Black on red underprint. Portrait Major Gen. I. Brock at left, seated woman with sailing ships in background ("Commerce") at center right. Signature varieties. Back: Black on red, green and brown underprint. Children reading at center. Printer: ABNC.			
a. Blue overprint: *S S.* 1.3.1904.	500.	1750.	—
b. 2.3.1914.	500.	1750.	—
c. 1.3.1917.	500.	1750.	—
d. 1.3.1920.	500.	1750.	—

S1088 10 Dollars	Good	Fine	XF
1904-20. Black on green underprint. Fenian Raid monument at left, woman with farm animals at center right. Signature varieties. Back: Black on red, green and brown underprint. Children reading at center. Printer: ABNC.			
a. Red overprint: *S S.* 1.3.1904.	500.	1750.	—
b. 2.3.1914.	500.	1750.	—
c. 1.3.1917.	500.	1750.	—
d. 1.3.1920.	500.	1750.	—

S1089 20 Dollars	Good	Fine	XF
1904-20. Black on brown underprint. Riel Rebellion monument at left, agricultural scene at center right. Signature varieties. Back: Black on red, green and brown underprint. Children reading at center. Printer: ABNC.			
a. 1.3.1920.	650.	2000.	—
s. Specimen. 1.3.1904; 2.3.1914.	—	Unc	900.
S1090 50 Dollars			
1.3.1904; 2.3.1914. Black on blue underprint. Boer War monument at left, farmer with horse and children scene at center right. Signature varieties. Back: Black on red, green and brown underprint. Children reading at center. Printer: ABNC. Specimen.	—	Unc	1000.
S1091 100 Dollars			
1904-17. Black and olive. S. de Champlain monument at left, portrait of Minerva at upper center right. Signature varieties. Back: Black on red, green and brown underprint. Children reading at center. Printer: ABNC.			
a. 1.3.1917.	650.	2000.	—
p. Face proof. 2.3.1914.	—	Unc	600.
s. Specimen. 1.3.1904.	—	Unc	1000.

Hudsons Bay Company

1820-70 York Factory Issues

Notes were first dated and signed in London before being shipped to York Factory. Upon issue the notes were dated and countersigned. In the case of #S1095c, they also bear a blue machine date stamp of the Red River Settlement. London dates appear first; actual issue dates follow.

S1095 1 Shilling	Good	Fine	XF
1821-70. Blue.			
a. 1.5.1821-1.9.1833.	900.	—	—
b. 3.5.1837-4.3.1846.	—	—	—
c. 1.5.1846-1.5.1870.	600.	—	—
r. Remainder with counterfoil. 1.5.1846-1.5.18(70).	—	—	—

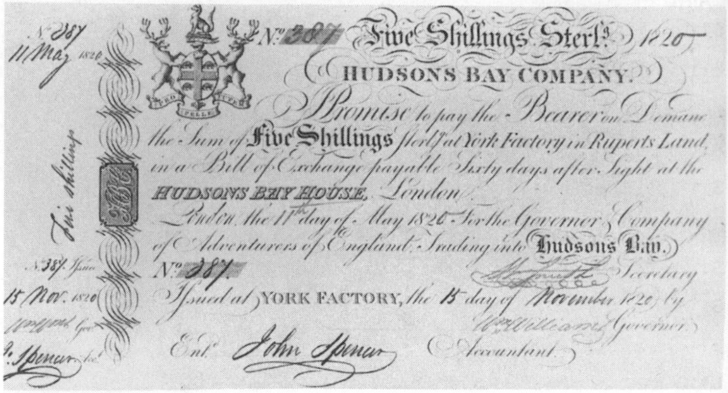

S1096 5 Shillings	Good	Fine	XF
1820-28. Black.			
a. 4.5.1820-1.9.1828.	800.	—	—
r. Remainder with counterfoil. 11.5.1820-1.6.1821.	—	—	—
S1097 5 Shillings			
1832-66. Red-brown.			
b. 27.5.1832-25.8.1840.	—	—	—
c. 1.5.1845-1.3.1866.	750.	—	—

NOTE: Later dated notes are usually found hand cancelled.

S1098 1 Pound	Good	Fine	XF
Black.			
a. 1.5.1820-1.9.1824.	800.	1500.	—
b. 1.5.1832-25.8.1832.	800.	1500.	—
c. 9.5.1832-6.7.1846.	—	—	—
d. 1.5.1850-20.10.1857.	600.	1250.	—
e. 26.7.1858-1.6.1869.	—	—	—
r1. Remainder. 4.5.1820-7.6.1821.	—	—	—
r2. Remainder with counterfoil 1.6.1870-18xx.	—	—	—
S1099 5 Pounds			
7.10.1870.	—	—	—

1870 Ft. Garry, N.W.T. Promissory Note Issue

S1100 5 Shillings	Good	Fine	XF
2.5.1870. Rare.	—	—	—
S1101 1 Pound			
2.5.1870. Rare.	—	—	—
S1102 5 Pounds			
10.5.1870. Rare.	—	—	—
S1103 10 Pounds			
16.5.1870. Rare.	—	—	—

1870 Red River Promissory Note Issue

S1104 1 Shilling	Good	Fine	XF
1870. Rare.	—	—	—

Dease Post, British Columbia Card Money Issue

S1106 25 Cents	Good	Fine	XF
ND. White. Rare.	—	—	—
S1107 50 Cents			
ND. Green. Rare.	—	—	—
S1108 1 Dollar			
ND. Red. Rare.	—	—	—
S1109 5 Dollars			
ND. Blue. Rare.	—	—	—

Fort Grahame Post Card Money Issue

S1110 25 Cents	Good	Fine	XF
ND. White. Rare.	—	—	—
S1112 1 Dollar			
ND. Red. Rare.	—	—	—
S1113 5 Dollars			
ND. Blue. Rare.	—	—	—

Laird Post Card Money Issue

	Good	Fine	XF
S1114 1 Dollar ND. Red. Rare.	—	—	—
S1115 5 Dollars ND. Blue. Rare.	—	—	—

McDames Creek Post Card Money Issue

	Good	Fine	XF
S1116 5 Dollars ND. Blue. Text reads *H.B.C. B.C. District*. Rare.	—	—	—
S1117 5 Dollars ND. Blue. Text reads *H.B.C. CASSIAR*. Rare.	—	—	—

Miscellaneous (No Post Name) Card Money Issue

	Good	Fine	XF
S1118 1 Dollar ND. Back: Red-orange. Rare.	—	—	—
S1119 5 Dollars ND. Blue. Back: Olive. Rare.	—	—	—
S1120 5 Dollars ND. Blue. Back: Dark brown.	—	—	—
S1121 10 Dollars ND. Deep red. Back: Dark brown.	—	—	—

NOTE: #S1120 and S1121 are thought to be modern fantasy reproductions.

Imperial Bank of Canada

1875-1886 Issues

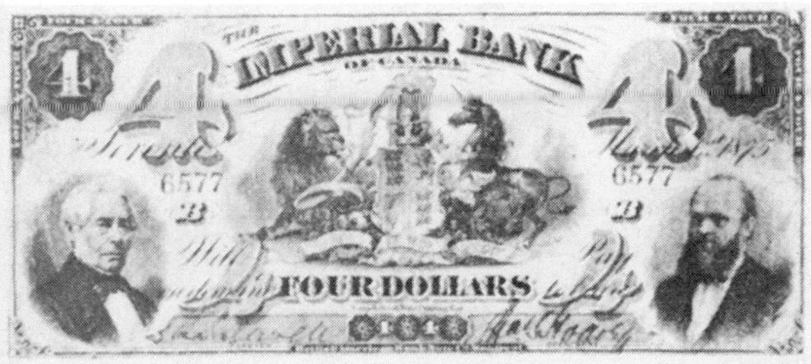

	VG	VF	UNC
S1122 4 Dollars 1.3.1875. Black on green underprint. Supported ornate *4* on royal crest at center. W. H. Merritt at left, H. S. Howland at right. Signature varieties. Overprint: Blue: *Z Z*. Printer: BABNC.	1000.	1750.	—
S1123 5 Dollars 1.3.1875. Black with green *V-FIVE-V* protector in underprint. Farmer plowing with horses at center. W. H. Merritt at left, H. S. Howland at right. Signature varieties. Overprint: Blue: *Z Z*. Printer: BABNC.	750.	1250.	—
S1124 5 Dollars 1.11.1876. Black on green underprint. Guilloche as underprint. Farmer plowing with horses at center. W. H. Merritt at left, H. S. Howland at right. Signature varieties. Printer: BABNC.	750.	1250.	—
S1125 5 Dollars 1886-96. Black on green underprint. Supported large ornate 5 and tilted royal crest at center. W. H. Merritt at left, H. S. Howland at right. Signature varieties. Printer: BABNC.			
a. 2.8.1886.	750.	1250.	—
b. 2.8.1890.	750.	1250.	—
c. Black on ochre underprint. Back orange. 1.10.1895.	850.	1500.	—
d. Black and ochre. Back orange 1.10.1896.	750.	1250.	—
S1126 10 Dollars 1.3.1875. Black on green underprint. Bank crest between lion and reclining Indian at top center. W. H. Merritt at left, H. S. Howland at right. Signature varieties. Overprint: Blue: *Z Z*. Printer: BABNC.	750.	1250.	—
S1127 20 Dollars 1876-1906. Black on green underprint. Farmer mowing with horses at left, H. S. Howland at lower right. Signature varieties. Printer: BABNC.			
a. 1.11.1876.	850.	1500.	—
b. 1.5.1906.	850.	1500.	—
S1128 50 Dollars 1.11.1876. Black on green underprint. W. H. Merritt at upper center. Signature varieties. Printer: BABNC. Face proof.	—	—	500.
S1129 100 Dollars 1.11.1876. Black on green underprint. Supported Canadian crest at upper center. Signature varieties. Printer: BABNC. Face proof.	—	—	500.

1902 Issue

	VG	VF	UNC
S1130 5 Dollars 1902-10. Black on ochre underprint. Woman by chest at left, portrait Prince Edward at top center, Canadian crest at right. Signature varieties. Back: Green. Seated woman with tablet at center. Printer: W & S.			
a. 1.10.1902; 1.5.1906.	450.	850.	—
b. 1.1.1910.	300.	625.	—

	VG	VF	UNC
S1131 10 Dollars 1902-10. Black on blue underprint. Cherubs at left and right of portrait Queen Alexandria at left, supported royal arms at upper center right. Signature varieties. Back: Yellow-brown. Seated woman with cherub at center. Printer: W & S.			
a. 1.1.1910.	275.	600.	—
s. Specimen. 1.10.1902.	—	—	750.

1902; 1907 Double Size Note Issues

	Good	Fine	XF
S1132 20 Dollars 1.10.1902. Blue on orange and violet underprint. Seated woman with child, beehive at lower left, George Vas Duke of York at upper center. Back: Red-orange. Woman with fruit basket at center. Extra large size.			
a. Issued note.	3500.	8000.	—
s. Specimen.	—	—	—

	Good	Fine	XF
S1133 50 Dollars 1902-10. Black on gold and green underprint. Queen Alexandria at center, seated allegorical woman at lower right. Back: Deep red. Standing Commerce, sailing ship in background at center. Extra large size.			
a. 2.1.1907.	3500.	8000.	—
s. Specimen. 1.10.1902.	—	Unc	3000.
S1134 100 Dollars 1.10.1902. Blue on lilac, brown and yellow underprint. King Edward VIII over steam train at left, supported ornate *100* at center, T. R. Merritt over steam ship at right. Back: Ochre. Bank building at center. Specimen.	—	Unc	3000.
S1135 100 Dollars 2.1.1907. Black on red and gold underprint. King Edward VIII over steam train at left, supported ornate *100* at center, T. R. Merritt over steam ship at right. Back: Blue. Specimen. Extra large size.	—	Unc	3000.

1915-17 Issues

	Good	Fine	XF
S1136 5 Dollars 1.10.1915. Black on yellow, green and orange underprint. Supported large ornate 5 and tilted royal crest at center. W. H. Merritt at left, H. S. Howland at right. Printer: BABNC.	150.	500.	1250.

	Good	Fine	XF
S1137 5 Dollars 1916; 1920. Black on green underprint. Supported large ornate 5 and tilted royal crest at center. W. H. Merritt at left, H. S. Howland at right. Printer: BABNC.			
a. 3.1.1916.	50.00	150.	450.
b. 2.1.1920.	50.00	150.	350.

S1138 10 Dollars	Good	Fine	XF
1915; 1920. Black on green underprint. Bank crest between lion and reclining Indian at top center. W. H. Merritt at left, H. S. Howland at right. Printer: BABNC.			
a. 1.10.1915.	50.00	150.	350.
b. 2 signature varieties. 2.1.1920.	25.00	100.	250.

S1139 20 Dollars	Good	Fine	XF
1915; 1920. Black on green underprint. Farmer mowing with horses at left, H. S. Howland at lower right. Printer: BABNC.			
a. 1.10.1915.	100.	250.	600.
b. 2.1.1920.	100.	250.	600.
S1140 50 Dollars			
2.1.1917. Black on green underprint. W. H. Merritt at upper center. Printer: BABNC.	500.	1500.	—
S1141 100 Dollars			
1917; 1920. Black on green underprint. Supported Canadian crest at upper center. Printer: BABNC.			
a. 2.1.1917.	500.	1500.	—
b. 2.1.1920.	500.	1500.	—
x. Counterfeit. 2.1.1917.	—	—	—

1923 Issue

S1142 5 Dollars	VG	VF	UNC
1.11.1923. Black on green underprint. Portrait P. Howland at left, portrait A. H. Phipps at right. 2 signature varieties. Back: Green. Lion over crown. Printer: CBNC.			
a. Issued note.	75.00	150.	500.
s. Specimen.	—	—	—

S1143 10 Dollars	VG	VF	UNC
1.11.1923. Black on blue underprint. Portrait P. Howland at left, portrait A. H. Phipps at right. 2 signature varieties. Back: Blue. Lion over crown. Printer: CBNC.			
a. Issued note.	75.00	150.	500.
s. Specimen.	—	—	—

S1144 20 Dollars	VG	VF	UNC
1.11.1923. Black on brown underprint. Portrait P. Howland at center. 2 signature varieties. Back: Brown. Lion over crown. Printer: CBNC.			
a. Issued note.	75.00	150.	500.
s. Specimen.	—	—	—

S1145 50 Dollars	VG	VF	UNC
1.11.1923. Black on orange underprint. Portrait P. Howland at right. 2 signature varieties. Back: Orange. Lion over crown. Printer: CBNC.			
a. Issued note.	200.	750.	—
s. Specimen.	—	—	—

S1145A 100 Dollars	Good	Fine	XF
1.11.1923. Black on olive-green underprint. Portrait P. Howland at left. 2 signature varieties. Back: Olive-green. Lion over crown. Printer: CBNC. Specimen.	—	Unc	900.

1933 Issue

S1145B 5 Dollars	VG	VF	UNC
1.11.1933. Black on green underprint. Portrait A. H. Phipps at left, portrait F. A. Ralph at right. Back: Green. Lion over crown. Printer: CBNC.	75.00	150.	450.
S1145C 10 Dollars			
1.11.1933. Black and blue. Portrait A. H. Phipps at left, portrait F. A. Ralph at right. Back: Blue. Lion over crown. Printer: CBNC.	100.	200.	750.

S1145D 20 Dollars	Good	Fine	XF
1.11.1933. Black and brown. Portrait A. H. Phipps at center. Back: Brown. Lion over crown. Printer: CBNC. Specimen.	—	Unc	500.

1934 Issue

S1145E 5 Dollars	VG	VF	UNC
1.11.1934. Black on green underprint. Portrait A. H. Phipps at left, portrait F. A. Ralph at right. Printer: CBNC.			
a. Signature A. H. Phipps and F. A. Ralph.	25.00	50.00	200.
b. Signature H. J. Jaffray and F. A. Ralph.	25.00	50.00	200.

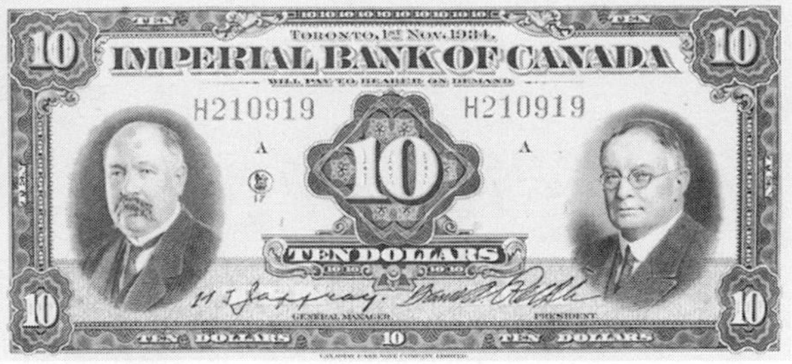

S1145F 10 Dollars	VG	VF	UNC
1.11.1934. Black on blue underprint. Portrait A. H. Phipps at left, portrait F. A. Ralph at right. Printer: CBNC.			
a. Signature A. H. Phipps and F. A. Ralph.	25.00	50.00	200.
b. Signature H. J. Jaffray and F. A. Ralph.	25.00	50.00	200.

1939 Issue

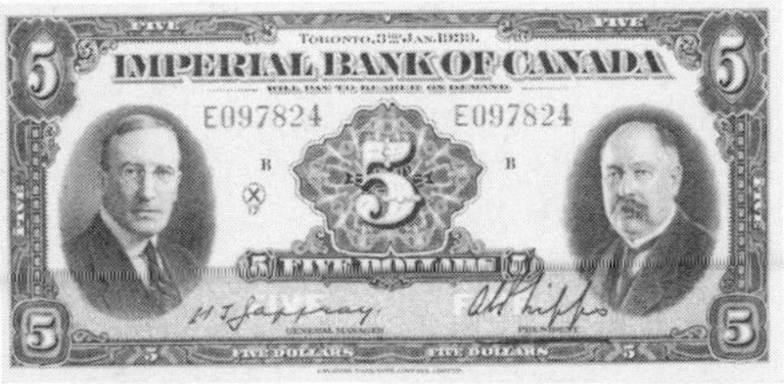

	VG	VF	UNC
S1145G 5 Dollars 3.1.1939. Black on green underprint. H. J. Jaffray at left, A. H. Phipps at right. Back: Green. Lion over crown. Reduced size.	25.00	50.00	200.
S1145H 10 Dollars 3.1.1939. Black on blue underprint. H. J. Jaffray at left, A. H. Phipps at right. Back: Blue. Lion over crown. Reduced size.	25.00	50.00	200.

Merchants Bank of Canada

1868-73 Issue

	Good	Fine	XF
S1146 1 Dollar 2.3.1868. Black on green underprint. Two sailors on wharf at lower left, steam passenger train dockside at upper center, H. Allan at lower right. Signature varieties. Back: Green. Printer: ABNC and BABNC.			
a. Issued note.	250.	750.	—
b. Blue overprint: *PERTH.*	250.	750.	—
c. Blue overprint: *TORONTO.*	250.	750.	—
S1147 2 Dollars 2.3.1868. Black on green underprint. Portrait Prince of Wales at left, sailing ship and steamboat at upper center, H. Allan at lower right. Signature varieties. Back: Green. Printer: ABNC ANd BABNC.			
a. Issued note.	250.	750.	—
b. Blue overprint: *PERTH.*	250.	750.	—
c. Blue overprint: *TORONTO.*	250.	750.	—

	Good	Fine	XF
S1148 4 Dollars 1870; 1873. Black on green underprint. Portrait Prince of Wales at lower left, cow at upper center, H. Allan at lower right. Signature varieties. Back: Green. Printer: ABNC and BABNC.			
a. 2.5.1870.	200.	600.	—
b. 2.6.1873.	200.	600.	—
S1149 5 Dollars 1868; 1873. Black on green underprint. H. Allan at lower left, reclining sailor with anchor at top center, Prince of Wales at lower right. Signature varieties. Back: Green. Printer: ABNC and BABNC.			
a. Issued note. 2.3.1868.	250.	750.	—
b. Blue overprint: *PERTH.*	250.	750.	—
c. Blue overprint: *TORONTO.*	250.	750.	—
p. Face proof. 1.8.1873.	—	Unc	600.
S1150 10 Dollars 1.8.1871. Black on green underprint. River boat pilot at lower left, head office building at center, H. Allan at lower right. Signature varieties. Back: Green. Printer: ABNC and BABNC.	500.	1250.	—
S1151 20 Dollars 1.8.1873. Black on greenunderprint. Earl of Dufferin at lower left, steam passenger train crossing stone arch bridge at center, H. Allan at lower right. Signature varieties. Back: Green. Printer: ABNC and BABNC. Face proof.	—	Unc	600.

1886 Issue

	Good	Fine	XF
S1152 5 Dollars 2.7.1886. Black on green underprint. Two sailors on wharf at lower left, steam sailing ship at top center. H. Allan at lower right. Signature varieties. Back: Green. Printer: BABNC.	150.	500.	1000.
S1153 10 Dollars 2.7.1886. Black on green underprint. River boat pilot at lower left, head office building at center, H. Allan at lower right. Signature varieties. Back: Green. Printer: BABNC.	150.	600.	1200.
S1154 50 Dollars 2.7.1886. Black on green underprint. Portrait Earl of Dufferin at left, paddle wheel steamboat *Quebec* at center. H. Allan at lower right. Signature varieties. Back: Green. Printer: BABNC. Face proof.	—	Unc	600.
S1155 100 Dollars 2.7.1886. Black on green underprint. Portrait Queen Victoria in "Widow's Weeds" at left, ship at center. H. Allan at lower right. Signature varieites. Back: Green. Printer: BABNC. Face proof.	—	Unc	600.

1900; 1903 Issue

	VG	VF	UNC
S1156 5 Dollars 1.1.1900. Black on multicolor underprint. Reclining allegorical woman holding sextant at left, clipper ships at center. 2 signature varieties. Back: Black and multicolor. Portrait gypsy woman at center. Printer: ABNC.	500.	1000.	—
S1157 10 Dollars 1.1.1900. Black on multicolor underprint. Two seated allegorical women, steam train, factories in background at center. 2 signature varieties. Back: Black on multicolor underprint. Seated Justice with reclining male and female. Printer: ABNC. Specimen.	—	—	500.
S1158 20 Dollars 2.1.1903. Black on green and orange underprint. Steer's head at left. Signature varieties. Back: Black on multicolor underprint. Bank crest at center. Printer: ABNC. Specimen.	—	—	600.
S1159 50 Dollars 2.1.1903. Black on red and olive underprint. Stag at left, young woman at right. Signature varieties. Back: Black on multicolor underprint. Bank crest at center. Printer: ABNC. Specimen.	—	—	600.

1906; 1907 Issue

	Good	Fine	XF
S1160 5 Dollars 1.2.1906. Black on green underprint. River boat pilot at lower left, steam passenger ship at top center, portrait H. Montagu Allan at lower right. Signature varieties. Back: Green. Two beavers at center. Printer: BABNC.	100.	250.	500.
S1161 10 Dollars 1.2.1906. Black on green underprint. Indian on horseback at lower left, farmer reaping with horses at center, portrait H. Montagu Allan at lower right. Signature varieties. Back: Green. Sailor with telescope at center. Printer: BABNC.	100.	250.	500.

S1162 20 Dollars — Good / Fine / XF
1.6.1907. Black on green underprint. Steer's head at left. Signature varieites. Back: Green. Sheep at pond at center. Printer: BABNC. — 200. / 600. / —

S1163 50 Dollars
1.6.1907. Black on green underprint. Stag at left, bank crest at lower right. Signature varieties. Back: Green. Printer: BABNC. — 600. / 1500. / —

S1164 100 Dollars
1.6.1907. Black on green underprint. Steam passenger ship at left, H. Montagu Allan at right. Signature varieties. Back: Green. Ancient scene with Greek woman watching youth painting jug at center. Printer: BABNC. — 600. / 1500. / —

1916 Issue

S1165 5 Dollars — Good / Fine / XF
1.2.1916. Black on green underprint. Steam passenger ship at upper center. Portrait D. C. Macrow at lower left, H. Montagu Allan at lower right. Signature varieties. Back: Green. Two beavers at center. Printer: BABNC. — 50.00 / 150. / 300.

S1166 10 Dollars — Good / Fine / XF
1.2.1916. Black on green underprint. Farmer reaping with horses at center. Portrait D. C. Macrow at lower left, H. Montagu Allan at lower right. Signature varieties. Back: Green. Sailor on watch at center. Printer: BABNC. — 50.00 / 150. / 300.

1917 Issue

S1167 5 Dollars — Good / Fine / XF
3.1.1917. Black on green underprint. Portrait H. Montagu Allan at left, voyagers loading canoes at center, portrait D. C. Macrow at right. 2 signature varieties. Back: Green. Bank crest at center. Printer: ABNC. — 200. / 600. / 1200.

S1168 10 Dollars — Good / Fine / XF
3.1.1917. Black on green underprint. Portrait H. Montagu Allan at left, ocean freighter and steam passenger train dockside at center, portrait D. C. Macrow at right. 2 signature varieties. Back: Green. Bank crest at center. Printer: ABNC. — 400. / 1200. / 2250.

S1169 20 Dollars
3.1.1917. Black on green underprint. Steer's head at left. 2 signature varieties. Back: Green. Bank crest at center. Printer: ABNC. — 400. / 1200. / 2250.

S1170 50 Dollars
3.1.1917. Black on green underprint. Stag at left, young woman ("Reverie") at right. 2 signature varieties. Back: Green. Bank crest at center. Printer: ABNC. — 400. / 1200. / 2250.

S1171 100 Dollars — Good / Fine / XF
3.1.1917. Black on green underprint. Portrait H. Montagu Allan at left, seated woman with winged wheel at center, portrait D. C. Macrow at right. 2 signature varieties. Back: Green. Bank crest at center. Printer: ABNC. — 500. / 1500. / 3250.

1919 Issue

S1172 5 Dollars — VG / VF / UNC
1.11.1919. Black on green underprint. Portrait Prince of Wales at lower center. Back: Green. Bank crest at center. Printer: ABNC. — 300. / 600. / —

S1173 10 Dollars
1.11.1919. Black on blue underprint. Portrait Sir H. Allan at center. Back: Bank crest at center. Printer: ABNC. — 500. / 1000. / —

Merchants' Bank of Halifax

1864 Issues

S1174 20 Dollars — Good / Fine / XF
31.3.1864. Black with orange *TWENTY DOLLARS* protector. Without border frames. Back: Black. Printer: Blades, East & Blades. — 1000. / 3000. / —

S1175 20 Dollars — Good / Fine / XF
1.10.1864. Black. Black with orange *TWENTY DOLLARS* protector. With border frames. Printer: Blades, East & Blades. — 1000. / 3000. / —

1869; 1870 Issue

S1175A 4 Dollars — Good / Fine / XF
1.7.1870. Black on green underprint. Steam sailing ships at left, center and at right. Overprint: Green: *CANADIAN CURRENCY, 1 JULY, 1871.* — 800. / 2750. / —

S1176 5 Dollars
1.7.1870. Black on orange underprint. Steam sailing ship at center.
- a. Issued note. — 800. / 2750. / —
- b. Green overprint: *CANADIAN CURRENCY, 1 JULY, 1871.* — 800. / 2750. / —

S1177 20 Dollars
1.10.1869. Black on orange underprint. Steam sailing ship at top center.
- a. Issued note. — 800. / 2750. / —
- b. Green overprint: *CANADIAN CURRENCY, 1 JULY, 1871.* — 800. / 2750. / —

1871-74 Issue

S1178 4 Dollars — Good / Fine / XF
1.7.1871; 1.1.1872; 1.10.1873. Black on green and orange underprint. Steam sailing ships at left, center and at right. *CANADA CURRENCY* engraved. Signature varieties. Back: Orange. Overprint: *SUMMERSIDE.* sometimes. Printer: Blades, East & Blades. — 750. / 2500. / —

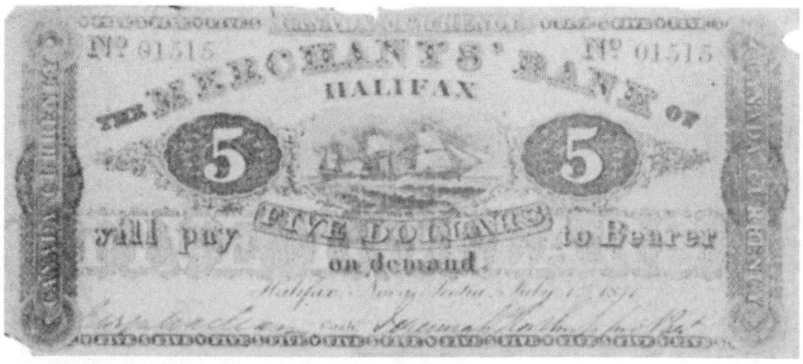

S1179 5 Dollars — Good / Fine / XF
1.7.1871; 1.1.1872; 1.10.1873. Black on orange underprint. Steam sailing ships at center. *CANADA CURRENCY* engraved. Signature varieties. Back: Green. Overprint: *SUMMERSIDE.* sometimes. Printer: Blades, East & Blades. — 750. / 2500. / —

S1180 10 Dollars
1.1.1874. Black on green and orange underprint. Steam sailing ship at upper center. *CANADA CURRENCY* engraved. Signature varieties. Back: Orange. Overprint: *SUMMERSIDE.* sometimes. Printer: Blades, East & Blades. — 900. / 3000. / —

S1181 20 Dollars	Good	Fine	XF
1.10.1873. Black on orange underprint. Steam sailing ship at top center. *CANADA CURRENCY* engraved. Signature varieties. Back: Black. Overprint: *SUMMERSIDE*. sometimes. Printer: Blades, East & Blades.	900.	3000.	—

1878; 1879 Issue

S1182 4 Dollars	Good	Fine	XF
1.1.1879. Black on yellow-green and red underprint. Sloop at lower left, steam powered sailing ships at top center, bank building at lower right. *DOMINION OF CANADA* engraved at top center. Back: Orange. Printer: Blades, East & Blades.	750.	2500.	—
S1183 10 Dollars			
1.1.1878. Black on green and orange underprint. Steam sailing ship at upper center. *DOMINION OF CANADA* engraved at top center. Back: Orange. Printer: Blades, East & Blades.	750.	2500.	—

1880; 1883 Issue

S1184 5 Dollars	VG	VF	UNC
1880-96. Black on orange and green underprint. Portrait allegorical woman ("Industry") at left, steam powered ship at center, bank building at right. Back: Brown. Printer: ABNC.			
a. 1.7.1880; 1.5.1890.	1000.	2500.	—
b. 2.1.1892.	1250.	3000.	—
p. Proof. 2.1.1896.	—	Unc	600.
s. Specimen. As a or b.	—	—	—

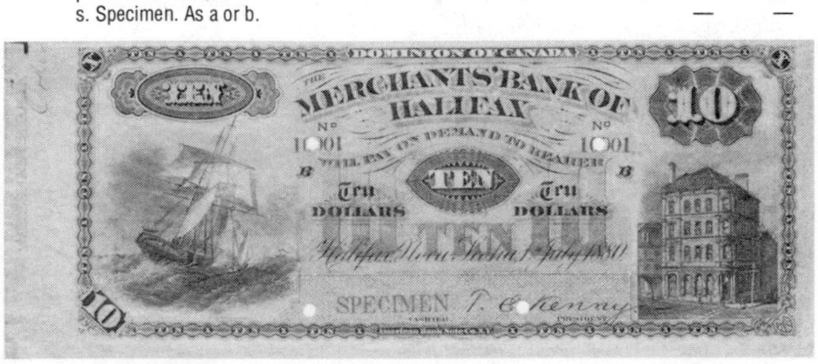

S1185 10 Dollars	VG	VF	UNC
1880-96. Black on yellow-orange and blue underprint. Sailing ship at left, bank building at lower right. Back: Green. Printer: ABNC.			
a. 2.1.1896.	600.	1750.	—
p. Proof. 1.7.1880.	—	Unc	600.
s. Specimen. 2.1.1893.	—	Unc	1000.

S1186 20 Dollars	VG	VF	UNC
1883-98. Black on blue and orange underprint. Back: Brown. Printer: ABNC.			
a. 21.1.1883.	600.	1750.	—
s. Specimen. 1.1.1898.	—	Unc	1000.

1894; 1899 Issue

S1187 5 Dollars	VG	VF	UNC
1894-99. Black on green underprint. D. H. Duncan at lower left. T. E. Kenny at right. Back: Green. Bank building at center. Printer: ABNC.			
a. 1.6.1894; 2.1.1899.	600.	1750.	—
p. Proof. 2.1.1896.	—	Unc	750.
s. Specimen. 2.1.1896.	—	—	—
S1188 50 Dollars			
18.7.1899. Black on yellow and blue underprint. Miners at upper center. T. E. Kenny at right. Back: Blue. Bank building at center. Printer: ABNC. Proof.	—	Unc	900.
S1189 100 Dollars			
3.7.1899. Black on yellow and orange underprint. Seated allegorical woman with tablet and child at left. T. E. Kenny at right. Back: Orange. Bank building at center. Printer: ABNC. Proof.	—	Unc	900.

Merchants Bank of Prince Edward Island

1871-91 Issue

S1191 1 Dollar	Good	Fine	XF
1871-89. Black on green underprint. Farmer plowing with horses at upper left, sailor on watch at lower right. Back: Green. Overprint: Red: *CANADA CURRENCY*. Printer: BABNC.			
a. Partially engraved date. 1.11.1871.	1000.	3250.	—
b. Fully engraved date. 1.9.1877.	1000.	3250.	—
c. Fully engraved date. 1.8.1889.	1000.	3250.	—

S1192 2 Dollars	Good	Fine	XF
1871; 1877. Black on green underprint. Anchor at lower left, paddle wheel steamboat at top center, three horse's heads at lower right. Back: Green. Overprint: Red: *CANADA CURRENCY*. Printer: BABNC.			
a. Partially engraved date. 1.9.1871.	1000.	3250.	—
b. Fully engraved date. 1.9.1877.	1000.	3250.	—

S1193 5 Dollars	Good	Fine	XF
1877; 1892. Black on green underprint. Young sailor climbing rope ladder at lower left, farm woman with livestock at upper center, standing allegorical woman at lower right. Back: Green. Overprint: Red: *CANADA CURRENCY*. Printer: BABNC.			
a. Fully engraved date. 1.9.1877.	1000.	3250.	—
p. Partially engraved date. Face proof. 18xx.	—	Unc	600.
s. Specimen. Fully engraved date. 1.3.1892.	—	Unc	1000.

S1194 10 Dollars	Good	Fine	XF
1891; 1892. Black on green underprint. Young woman at lower left, steam train emerging from tunnel at center, portrait Prince of Wales at lower right. Back: Green. Overprint: Red: *CANADA CURRENCY*. Printer: BABNC.			
a. Fully engraved date. 1.3.1892.	1000.	3250.	—
p. Partially engraved date. Face proof. 18xx.	—	Unc	600.
s. Specimen. Fully engraved date. 6.11.1891.	—	Unc	1000.

S1195 20 Dollars	Good	Fine	XF
1891; 1892. Black on green underprint. Portrait Queen Victoria in "Widow's Weeds" at lower center. Back: Green. Overprint: Red: *CANADA CURRENCY*. Printer: BABNC.			
p. Partially engraved date. Face proof. 18xx.	—	Unc	600.
s. Fully engraved date. Specimen. 6.11.1891; 1.3.1892.	—	Unc	1000.

1900 Issue

S1196 5 Dollars			
2.1.1900. Black on pink and green underprint. Two allegorical women at lower left, steamship at upper center, standing Indian maiden with spear at lower right. Printer: BABNC. Face proof.	—	Unc	900.

Metropolitan Bank

1902 Issue

S1197 5 Dollars	VG	VF	UNC
5.11.1902. Black on yellow and red underprint. Child standing between two reclining allegorical women at center. 3 signature varieties. Back: Green. Royal crest. Printer: ABNC.			
a. Issued note.	1750.	—	—
b. With red overprint: *S S*.	1750.	—	—
c. With red overprint: *Q Q*.	1750.	—	—

S1198 10 Dollars			
1902; 1909. Black on yellow-green and green underprint. Steam sailing ship at center. 3 signature varieties. Back: Royal crest. Printer: ABNC.			
a. 5.11.1902.	2000.	—	—
b. As a. with *S S*.	2000.	—	—
c. As a. with red overprint: *Q Q*.	2000.	—	—
d. 5.11.1909.	2000.	—	—

S1199 20 Dollars	VG	VF	UNC
1902; 1909. Black on yellow-green and green underprint. Trolley at center. Signature varieties. Back: Olive-green. Royal crest. Printer: ABNC.			
a. 5.11.1909.	2000.	—	—
s. Specimen. 5.11.1902.	—	Unc	1000.
S1200 50 Dollars			
1902; 1909. Black and brown. Steam train at station at center. Signature varieties. Back: Orange. Royal crest. Printer: ABNC.			
p. Face proof. 5.11.1909.	—	Unc	500.
s. Specimen. 5.11.1902.	—	Unc	1000.

S1201 100 Dollars	Good	Fine	XF
1902; 1912. Black, yellow-green and red. Mining scene at center. Signature varieties. Back: Gray. Royal crest. Printer: ABNC.			
s1. Specimen. 5.11.1902.	—	Unc	1000.
s2. Specimen. 5.11.1912.	—	Unc	1000.

Molsons Bank

1837 Issue

S1202 1 Dollar	Good	Fine	XF
15.9.1837. Black. Farmers with livestock at left, standing allegorical woman at center, cherub with basket at right. Back: Brown. Printer: RWH & Co. Unsigned remainder.	300.	1000.	2250.
S1203 2 Dollars			
15.9.1837. Black. Back: Brown. Printer: RWH & Co. Unsigned remainder.	300.	1000.	2250.
S1204 5 Dollars			
15.9.1837. Black. Paddle wheel steamboat at left, royal crest at upper center, seated Archimedes with globe at right. Back: Brown. Printer: RWH & Co. Unsigned remainder.	400.	1250.	2500.

1853 Issue

S1205 1 Dollar = 5 Shillings	Good	Fine	XF
1.10.1853. Black. Seated Agriculture at upper left, three ships at center, seated Commerce at upper right. Back: Brown. Overprint: Red: *PAYABLE AT MONTREAL*. Blue: *ST.C.* Printer: Toppan, Carpenter & Casillear.	300.	1000.	—

S1206 2 Dollars = 10 Shillings	Good	Fine	XF
1.10.1853. Black. Portrait Prince Consort at lower left, seated allegorical woman with farming scene in background at upper center, portrait Queen Victoria at lower right. Back: Olive. Overprint: Red: *PAYABLE AT MONTREAL*. Blue: *ST.C.* Printer: Toppan, Carpenter & Casillear.	300.	1000.	—
S1207 5 Dollars = 25 Shillings			
1.10.1853. Black. Three allegorical women with anchor at left, seated allegorical woman with cattle at upper center. Back: Brown. Overprint: Red: *PAYABLE AT MONTREAL*. Blue: *ST.C.* Printer: Toppan, Carpenter & Casillear.	350.	1250.	—
S1208 20 Dollars = 5 Pounds			
1.10.1853. Black. Standing Indian in ornate frame at left, sailing ships at top center, standing male citizen at lower right. Back: Brown. Overprint: Red: *PAYABLE AT MONTREAL*. Blue: *ST.C.* Printer: Toppan, Carpenter & Casillear. Remainder.	—	—	—
S1209 50 Dollars = 12 Pounds-10 Shillings			
1.10.1853. Black. Harvest scene at left, portrait Queen Victoria at center, steam passenger train at right. Back: Brown. Overprint: Red: *PAYABLE AT MONTREAL*. Blue: *ST.C.* Printer: Toppan, Carpenter & Casillear. Face proof.	—	Unc	500.

1855 Issues

S1210 1 Dollar = 5 Shillings	Good	Fine	XF
1.1.1855. Black. Seated Agriculture at upper left, three ships at center, seated Commerce at upper right. Engraved *Chartered by Act of Parliament*. Signature varieties. Back: Orange. Printer: Toppan, Carpenter, Casilear, Carpenter & Co. and A Montreal issue.			
a. Issued note without protector.	350.	1000.	—
b. Green *ONE* protector on face and back.	350.	1000.	—
S1211 1 Dollar = 5 Shillings			
1.10.1855. Black. Seated Agriculture at upper left, three ships at center, seated Commerce at upper right. Engraved *Chartered by Act of Parliament*. Signature varieties. Back: Blue. Printer: Toppan, Carpenter, Casilear, Carpenter & Co. and A Toronto issue.			
a. Issued note without protector.	350.	1000.	—
b. Blue overprint: *LONDON*. Green *ONE* protector on face and back.	400.	1250.	—
c. Blue overprint: *PAYABLE AT LONDON*. Green *ONE* protector.	400.	1250.	—
d. Red overprint: *PAYABLE AT MONTREAL*. Green *ONE* protector.	400.	1250.	—

S1212 2 Dollars = 10 Shillings
1.10.1855. Black. Portrait Prince Consort at lower left, seated allegorical woman with farming scene in background at upper center, portrait Queen Victoria at lower right. Engraved *Chartered by Act of Parliament.<NI* Printer: Toppan, Carpenter, Casilear, Carpenter & Co. and A Montreal issue. Face proof.

Good	Fine	XF
—	Unc	500.

S1213 4 Dollars = 1 Pound
1.10.1855. Black. Portrait of young woman at left, four cherubs without ornate *4* at center, three standing allegorical women at right. Engraved *Chartered by Act of Parliament.* Signature varieties. Back: Green. Printer: Toppan, Carpenter, Casilear, Carpenter & Co. and A Montreal issue.

	Good	Fine	XF
a. Without protector.	450.	1400.	—
b. Green *FOUR* protector on face and back.	400.	1250.	—

S1214 4 Dollars = 1 Pound
1.10.1855. Black. Portrait of young woman at left, four cherubs without ornate *4* at center, three standing allegorical women at right. Engraved *Chartered by Act of Parliament.* Signature varieties. Back: Blue. Printer: Toppan, Carpenter, Casilear, Carpenter & Co. and A Toronto issue.

	Good	Fine	XF
a. Without protector.	400.	1250.	—
b. Blue overprint: *PAYABLE AT LONDON* and green *FOUR* protector on face and back.	400.	1200.	—

S1215 5 Dollars = 25 Shillings
1.10.1855. Black. Three allegorical women with anchor at left, seated allegorical woman with cattle at upper center. Engraved *Chartered by Act of Parliament.* Signature varieties. Back: Green. Printer: Toppan, Carpenter, Casilear, Carpenter & Co. and A Montreal issue.

	Good	Fine	XF
a. Without protector.	500.	1500.	—
b. Green *FIVE* protector on face and back.	400.	1250.	—

S1216 5 Dollars = 25 Shillings
1.10.1855. Green *FIVE* protector. Three allegorical women with anchor at left, seated allegorical woman with cattle at upper center. Back: Green *FIVE* protector. Printer: Toppan, Carpenter, Casilear, Carpenter & Co. and A Toronto issue.

Good	Fine	XF
400.	1250.	—

S1217 20 Dollars = 5 Pounds
1.10.1855. Black. Standing Indian in ornate frame at left, sailing ships at top center, standing male citizen at lower right. Back: Orange. Printer: Toppan, Carpenter, Casilear, Carpenter & Co. and A Montreal issue.

	Good	Fine	XF
p1. Without underprint. Face proof.	—	Unc	500.
p2. Green underprint. Face proof	—	Unc	600.

S1218 50 Dollars = 1 Pound-10 Shillings
1.10.1855. Black. Harvest scene at left, portrait Queen Victoria at center, steam passenger train at right. Back: Orange. Printer: Toppan, Carpenter, Casilear, Carpenter & Co. and A Montreal issue.

	Good	Fine	XF
p1. Without underprint. Face proof.	—	Unc	500.
p2. Green underprint. Face proof.	—	Unc	600.

1857 Issue

S1219 1 Dollar
1.10.1857. Black on green underprint. Portrait young woman at left, reclining woman holding large ornate *1* at upper center, sailor with sextant at lower right. Back: Green. Printer: RWH & E.

Good	Fine	XF
300.	1000.	—

S1220 2 Dollars
1.10.1857. Black on green underprint. Portrait young woman at lower left, large ornate *2* between seated Britannia and Justice at upper left center, woman with sheaf and sickle in large *2* at right. Back: Green. Printer: RWH & E.

Good	Fine	XF
300.	1000.	—

1871 Issue

S1221 6 Dollars
1.11.1871. Black on green underprint. Portrait J. H. R. Molson at upper left, two beavers at lower center, portrait W. Molson at upper right. Signature varieties. Back: Green. Overprint: Blue: *TORONTO.* Printer: BABNC.

VG	VF	UNC
6500.	—	—

S1222 7 Dollars
1.11.1871. Black on green underprint. Portrait J. H. R. Molson at lower left, ship builders at center, portrait W. Molson at lower right. Signature varieties. Back: Green. Overprint: Blue: *TORONTO.* Printer: BABNC.

VG	VF	UNC
6500.	—	—

1872 Issue

S1223 4 Dollars
1872; 1875. Black on green underprint. Cherubs with large ornate *4* at upper center right. Portrait J. H. R. Molson at left, portrait W. Molson at right. Signature varieties. Back: Green. Printer: BABNC.

	Good	Fine	XF
a. 1.6.1872.	500.	1500.	—
b. 1.6.1875.	500.	1500.	—

S1224 5 Dollars
1872-1901. Black on green underprint. Portrait J. H. R. Molson at left, portrait W. Molson at right. Signature varieties. Back: Green. Printer: BABNC.

	Good	Fine	XF
a. 1.6.1880.	350.	1000.	—
b. 2.7.1890; 3.1.1893.	350.	1250.	—
c. 2.7.1898.	350.	1250.	—
d. 3.7.1899; 2.1.1900; 2.7.1901.	200.	750.	—
p. Face proof. 1.6.1872.	—	Unc	500.

S1225 10 Dollars
1872-1901. Black on green underprint. Cherubs with large ornate *X* at bottom center. Portrait J. H. R. Molson at left, portrait W. Molson at right. Signature varieties. Back: Green. Printer: BABNC.

	Good	Fine	XF
a. 1.6.1880.	400.	1250.	—
b. 2.7.1890.	350.	1000.	—
c. 2.7.1898; 3.7.1899.	300.	750.	—
d. 2.1.1900; 2.7.1901.	200.	600.	—
p. Face proof. 1.6.1872.	—	Unc	500.

1891; 1899 Issue

S1226 20 Dollars
1899; 1901. Black on green underprint. Standing Indian in ornate frame at left, sailing ships at top center, standing male citizen at lower right. Printer: BABNC.

	Good	Fine	XF
a. Issued note. 3.7.1899.	600.	1750.	—
p. Uniface proof. 1.10.1901.	—	—	—

S1226A 50 Dollars = 12 Pounds-10 Shillings
2.1.1887. Black on green underprint. Harvest scene at left, portrait Queen Victoria at center, steam passenger train at right. Printer: BABNC.

Good	Fine	XF
—	Unc	500.

S1227 50 Dollars
2.1.1891. Black on green underprint. Harvest scene at left, portrait Quenn Victoria at center, steam passenger train at right. Printer: BABNC.

Good	Fine	XF
600.	1750.	—

1903; 1904 Issue

S1228 5 Dollars
1903; 1904. Black on brown and green underprint. Woman with cherub in large ornate *5* at center. Portrait W. M. Macpherson at left, portrait W. Molson at right. Signature varieties. Back: Green. Printer: BABNC.

	VG	VF	UNC
a. 2.1.1903.	150.	500.	—
b. 2.1.1904.	150.	500.	—

S1229 10 Dollars
1903; 1904. Black on brown and green underprint. Large ornate *X* between reclining Indian and woman at center. Portrait W. M. Macpherson at left, portrait W. Molson at right. Signature varieties. Back: Green. Printer: BABNC.

	VG	VF	UNC
a. 2.1.1903.	200.	600.	—
b. 2.1.1904.	200.	600.	—

S1230 20 Dollars
2.1.1904. Black on green and orange underprint. Blacksmith at lower left, steamship *C. P. Lake* at top center, woman with flower basket at lower right. Portrai W. M. Macpherson at left, portrait W. Molson at right. Signature varieties. Back: Green. Printer: BABNC.

VG	VF	UNC
500.	1000.	2750.

1905 Issue

S1231 5 Dollars
2.10.1905. Black on brown and green underprint. Woman with cherub in large ornate *5* at center. Large ornate *V - V* in underprint. Back: Green. Printer: BABNC.

	VG	VF	UNC
a. Left hand portrait shoulders turned right.	200.	400.	—
b. Left hand portrait shoulders turned front.	150.	350.	—

S1232 10 Dollars
2.10.1905. Black on yellow and green underprint. Large ornate *X* between reclining Indian and woman at center. Large ornate *X - X* in underprint. Back: Green. Printer: BABNC.

	VG	VF	UNC
a. Left hand portrait shoulders turned right.	175.	375.	—
b. Left hand portrait shoulders turned front.	150.	350.	—

1908 Issue

S1233 5 Dollars
2.1.1908. Black on olive-green underprint. Portrait Sir W. Molson Macpherson at left, portrait W. Molson at right. Signature varieties. Back: Green. Bank crest at center. Printer: ABNC.

VG	VF	UNC
175.	375.	—

S1234 10 Dollars	VG	VF	UNC
2.1.1908. Black on olive-green underprint. Portrait Sir W. Molson Macpherson at left, portrait W. Molson at right. Signature varieties. Back: Green. Bank crest at center. Printer: ABNC.	175.	375.	—

S1241 10 Dollars	Good	Fine	XF
2.7.1918. Black on orange underprint. Portrait W. M. Macpherson at left, portrait W. Molson at right. Signature varieties. Back: Orange. Printer: ABNC.	100.	200.	500.

1912 Issue

S1235 5 Dollars	VG	VF	UNC
2.1.1912. Black on green underprint. Two beehives at left, portrait W. Molson at center, two steers at right. Signature varieties. Back: Green. Bank crest at center. Printer: W&S.	100.	250.	600.
S1236 10 Dollars			
2.1.1912. Black on lilac underprint. Steam passenger ship at left, portrait Sir W. Molson Macpherson at center, steam passenger train at right. Signature varieties. Back: Blue. Bank crest at center. Printer: W&S.	175.	375.	900.

1914 Issue

S1237 50 Dollars	Good	Fine	XF
2.1.1914. Black on green underprint. Steam locomotive at left, portrait W. Molson at center, waterfalls at right. Signature varieties. Back: Green. Bank crest. Printer: BABNC.	600.	1500.	—
S1238 100 Dollars			
2.1.1914. Black on green underprint. Portrait bearded man at center. Signature varieties. Back: Green. Bank crest. Printer: BABNC.	600.	1500.	—

1916 Issue

S1239 10 Dollars	Good	Fine	XF
3.1.1916. Black on green underprint. Riverfront factories at center, portrait Sir W. Molson Macpherson at right. Signature varieties. Back: Blue. Printer: W&S.	100.	250.	500.

1918 Issue

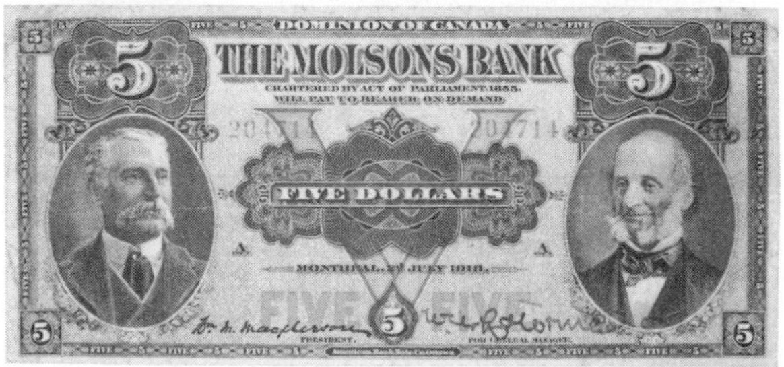

S1240 5 Dollars	Good	Fine	XF
2.7.1918. Black on green underprint. Portrait W. M. Macpherson at left, portrait W. Molson at right. Signature varieties. Back: Green. Printer: ABNC.	100.	250.	500.

1922 Issue

S1242 5 Dollars	VG	VF	UNC
3.7.1922. Black on green underprint. Portrait F. W. Molson at right. Back: Green. Bank crest at center. Printer: BABNC.	50.00	100.	400.
S1243 10 Dollars			
3.7.1922. Black on green underprint. Portrait M. Molson at center. Back: Green. Bank crest at center. Printer: BABNC.	50.00	100.	500.

Montreal Bank

1817-19 Issue

S1243A 5 Dollars	Good	Fine	XF
18xx. Black. Five coins at left, Montreal at top center. Uniface. Printer: A. Reed E. W. Con. Proof.	—	Unc	450.
S1243B 10 Dollars			
1.1.1818. Black. Five coins and Nelson's monument at left. Uniface. Printer: A. Reed E. W. Con.	500.	1500.	—
S1243C 20 Dollars			
10.10.1817; 1.1.1818. Black. Montreal harbor, sailing ships at top center. Uniface. Printer: A. Reed E. W. Con.	500.	1500.	—
S1243D 50 Dollars			
18xx. Black. Royal crest at top center. Uniface. Printer: A. Reed E. W. Con. Proof.	—	Unc	450.

1818-20 Issue

S1243E 1 Dollar	Good	Fine	XF
1.3.1819; 1.4.1819. Black. Montreal prison at top center. Uniface. Printer: Leney & Rollison.	500.	1500.	—
S1243F 2 Dollars			
1.12.1818; 1.3.1819; 1.4.1819; 5.1.1820. Black. Paddle wheel steamboat at top center. Uniface. Printer: Leney & Rollison.	500.	1500.	—

S1243G 5 Dollars	Good	Fine	XF
1.2.1819; 5.3.1819; 11.3.1819. Black. Tree and farm tools at top center. Uniface. Printer: Leney & Rollison.	500.	1500.	—

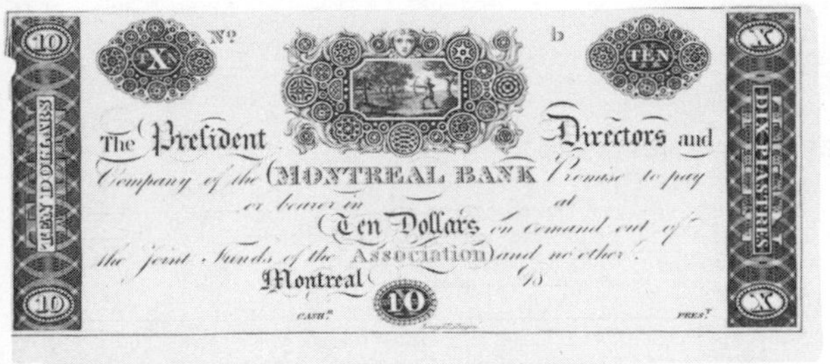

	Good	Fine	XF
S1243H 10 Dollars 1.1.1818. Black. Indian hunting in forest at top center. Uniface. Printer: Leney & Rollison.	500.	1500.	—
S1243I 100 Dollars 18xx. Black. Beehive at top center. Uniface. Printer: Leney & Rollison. Proof.	—	Unc	450.

1821-22 Issue

	Good	Fine	XF
S1243J 1 Dollar 18xx. Black. Britannia, harbor scene in background at top center. Uniface. Printer: Reed & Stiles. Proof.	—	Unc	750.

	Good	Fine	XF
S1243K 5 Dollars 2.10.1821. Black. Woman on shell drawn by sea horses at top center. Uniface. Printer: Reed & Stiles.	500.	1500.	—

1822-29 Issue

	Good	Fine	XF
S1243L 10 Dollars 1.7.1829. Black. Sailing ships at top center. Uniface. Printer: Graphic company.	500.	1500.	—
S1243M 20 Dollars 1.6.1822. Black. Seated woman with 20 at top center. Uniface. Printer: Graphic Company.	500.	1500.	—
S1243N 50 Dollars 18xx. Black. Seated Commerce at top center. Uniface. Printer: Graphic Company. Unsigned remainder.	—	—	—

	Good	Fine	XF
S1243O 100 Dollars 1.6.1822. Black. Woman seated on block with 100 at top center. Uniface. Printer: Graphic Company.	500.	1500.	—

Niagara District Bank

1854-55 Issue

	Good	Fine	XF
S1243P 1 Dollar 1854-55. Black. Milkmaid at lower left, supported royal arms at top center. Text: *Secured by Deposit of Provincial Securities.* Uniface. Printer: Danforth, Wright & Co.			
a. 1854-55.	750.	2500.	—
b. Raised to $5.	500.	1500.	—
c. Raised to $10.	500.	1500.	—
S1243Q 2 Dollars 18xx. Black. Prince Consort at left. Text: *Secured by Deposit of Provincial Securities.* Uniface. Printer: Danforth, Wright & Co. Proof.	—	Unc	650.
S1243R 5 Dollars 18xx. Black. Shipbuilding scene at left, Queen Victoria at center. Text: *Secured by Deposit of Provincial Securities.* Uniface. Printer: Danforth, Wright & Co. Proof.	—	Unc	650.

1855-62 Issue

	Good	Fine	XF
S1243S 1 Dollar = 5 Shillings 1855; 1862. Black. Horseshoe Falls at Niagara at upper left. Red word protector. Uniface. Signature varieties. Back: Red word protector. Printer: Danforth, Wright & Co. and ABNC.			
a. Without underprint. Partially engraved. 2.7.1855.	750.	1750.	—
b. Green underprint. Fully engraved date. 2.1.1862.	500.	1500.	—

	Good	Fine	XF
S1243T 2 Dollars = 10 Shillings 185x; 1862. Black. Portrait of Queen Victoria at upper left, woman kneeling viewing plaque with shipbuilding scene at bottom center, steam locomotive at lower right. Red word protector. Uniface. Signature varieties. Back: Red word protector. Printer: Danforth, Wright & Co. and ABNC.			
a. Green underprint. Fully engraved date. 2.1.1862.	500.	1500.	—
p. Without underprint. Partially engraved date. Proof. 2.7.185x.	—	Unc	650.
S1243U 4 Dollars = 20 Shillings 1855; 1862. Black. Man's portrait at lower left, paddle wheel, steamship and sailing ship at bottom center, ship in canal at lower right. Red word protector. Signature varieties. Back: Red word protector. Printer: Danforth, Wright & Co. and ABNC.			
a. Without underprint. Partially engraved date. 2.7.1855.	750.	1750.	—
b. Green underprint. Fully engraved date. 2.1.1862.	750.	1750.	—
S1243V 5 Dollars = 1 Pound-5 Shillings 185x; 1862. Black. Man's portrait at lower left, three men dock-side at bottom center. Red word protector. Uniface. Signature varieties. Back: Red word protector. Printer: Danforth, Wright & Co. and ABNC.			
a. Green underprint. Fully engraved date. 2.1.1862.	500.	1500.	—
p. Without underprint. Partially engraved date. Proof. 2.7.185x.	—	Unc	600.
S1243W 10 Dollars 18xx. Partially engraved. Black on green underprint. Sailor, woman and child at lower left, seated Justice at center, reclining woman at lower right. Uniface. Signature varieties. Printer: Danforth, Wright & Co. and ABNC. Face proof.	—	Unc	800.

1872 Issue

	Good	Fine	XF
S1243X 4 Dollars 1.7.1872. Black on green underprint. Farm girl watering cattle at top center. Portrait W. H. Merritt at left, portrait J. R. Benson at right. Back: Green. Printer: BABNC.	600.	1750.	—
S1243Y 5 Dollars 1.7.1872. Black on green underprint. Paddle wheel steamboat at top center. Portrait W. H. Merritt at left, portrait J. R. Benson at right. Back: Green. Printer: BABNC.	500.	1500.	—
S1243Z 10 Dollars 1.7.1872. Black on green underprint. Niagara Falls at bottom center. Portrait W. H. Merritt at left, portrait J. R. Benson at right. Back: Green. Printer: BABNC.	500.	1500.	—

Northern Bank

1905 Issue

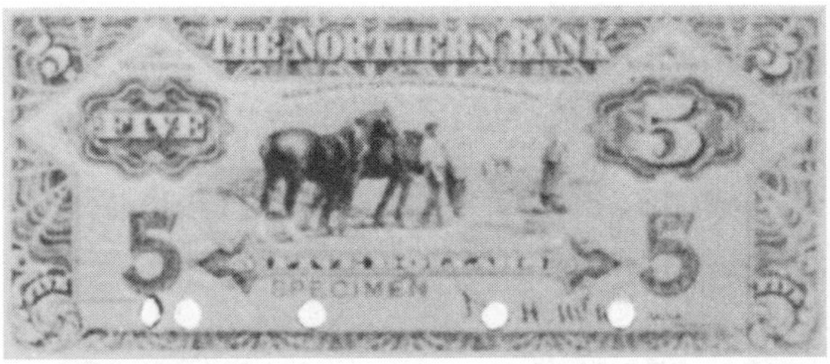

	Good	Fine	XF
S1244 5 Dollars 1.11.1905. Black on green underprint. Farmer with horses at center. Back: Green. Printer: BABNC.	1750.	6000.	—
S1245 10 Dollars 1.11.1905. Black on red-brown underprint. Farmer with horse drawn reaper at left center. Back: Green. Printer: BABNC.	1750.	6000.	—
S1246 20 Dollars 1.11.1905. Black on brown underprint. Two bison on flatland at center. Back: Green. Printer: BABNC.	1750.	6000.	—
S1247 50 Dollars 1.11.1905. Black on ochre underprint. Farm tools at lower left, farmer watering horses at center. Back: Green. Printer: BABNC. Proof.	—	Unc	1000.

The Northern Crown Bank

1908-14 Issue

S1248 5 Dollars — VG / VF / UNC
1908; 1914. Black on olive and red underprint. Farmer with horses at left center. Back: Reddish-brown. Royal crown over flower and leaves at bottom center. Printer: BABNC.

	VG	VF	UNC
a. 2.7.1908.	1250.	3000.	—
b. 2.7.1914.	1500.	3500.	—

S1249 10 Dollars
1908; 1914. Black on yellow and green underprint. Farmer with horse drawn reaper at left center. Back: Blue. Royal crown over flower and leaves at bottom center. Printer: BABNC.

	VG	VF	UNC
a. 2.7.1908.	1500.	3500.	—
b. 2.7.1914.	1500.	3500.	—

S1250 20 Dollars — VG 1750. / VF — / UNC —
2.7.1908. Black on peach and blue underprint. Bison on prairie at center. Back: Orange. Royal crown over flower and leaves at bottom center. Printer: BABNC.

S1251 50 Dollars — — / Unc / 600.
2.7.1908. Black on yellow and red underprint. Lion in mountains. Back: Purple. Royal crown over flower and leaves at bottom center. Printer: BABNC. Proof.

Ontario Bank

1857 Bowmanville Issue

S1252 1 Dollar — Good 325. / Fine 900. / XF —
15.8.1857. Black on green underprint. Agricultural produce at left, cattle at top center, shearing sheep at lower right. Signature varieties. Blue sheet number and *BOWMANVILLE* at bottom. Back: Green. Printer: RWH&E and ABNC. Red overprint: *MONTREAL* (twice) and blue overprint: *PRESCOTT, TORONTO,* (twice) or *ALEXANDRIA.*

S1253 2 Dollars — 350. / 1000. / —
15.8.1857. Black on green underprint. Standing blacksmith with sledge hammer by anvil at left, seated woman with dog by cattle at center. Blue sheet number and *BOWMANVILLE* at bottom. Signature varieties. Back: Green. Printer: RWH&E and ABNC. Red overprint: *MONTREAL* (twice) and blue overprint: *PRESCOTT, TORONTO,* (twice) or *ALEXANDRIA.*

S1254 5 Dollars — — / Unc / 500.
15.8.1857. Black on green underprint. Portrait J. Cartier at left; farmer sharpening scythe at center, bull's head at lower right. Blue sheet number and *BOWMANVILLE* at bottom. Signature varieties. Back: Green. Printer: RWH&E and ABNC. Face proof. Red overprint: *MONTREAL* (twice) and blue overprint: *PRESCOTT, TORONTO,* (twice) or *ALEXANDRIA.*

S1255 10 Dollars — — / Unc / 500.
15.8.1857. Black on green underprint. Barges at left, seated Indian and crest at center, cattle driving scene at right. Blue sheet number and *BOWMANVILLE* at bottom. Signature varieties. Back: Green. Printer: RWH&E and ABNC. Face proof. Red overprint: *MONTREAL* (twice) and blue overprint: *PRESCOTT, TORONTO,* (twice) or *ALEXANDRIA.*

1857 Montreal Issue

S1256 1 Dollar — Good 325. / Fine 900. / XF —
15.8.1857. Black on green underprint. Agricultural produce at left, cattle at top center, shearing sheep at lower right. Signature varieties. Blue sheet number and *MONTREAL* at bottom. Back: Green. Overprint: Red: *OSHAWA.* Blue: *TORONTO.* Printer: RWH&E and ABNC.

S1257 2 Dollars — 350. / 1000. / —
15.8.1857. Black on green underprint. Standing blacksmith with sledge hammer by anvil at left, seated woman with dog by cattle at center. Blue sheet number and *MONTREAL* at bottom. Signature varieties. Back: Green. Overprint: Red: *OSHAWA.* Blue: *TORONTO.* Printer: RWH&E and ABNC.

S1258 5 Dollars — — / Unc / 500.
15.8.1857. Black on green underprint. Portrait J. Cartier at left; farmer sharpening scythe at center, bull's head at lower right. Blue sheet number and *MONTREAL* at bottom. Signature varieties. Back: Green. Overprint: Red: *OSHAWA.* Blue: *TORONTO.* Printer: RWH&E and ABNC. Face proof.

S1259 10 Dollars — Good — / Fine Unc / XF 500.
15.8.1857. Black on green underprint. Barges at left, seated Indian and crest at center, cattle driving scene at right. Blue sheet number and *MONTREAL* at bottom. Signature varieties. Back: Green. Overprint: Red: *OSHAWA.* Blue: *TORONTO.* Printer: RWH&E and ABNC. Face proof.

1861 First Bowmanville Issue

S1260 1 Dollar — Good 400. / Fine 1250. / XF —
15.8.1861. Black on green underprint. Agricultural produce at left, cattle at top center, shearing sheep at lower right. Signature varieties. One red sheet number and *BOWMANVILLE* at bottom. Back: Green. Overprint: Red: *GUELPH* and *DUNDAS*> Blue: *TORONTO.* Printer: RWH&E and ABNC.

S1261 2 Dollars — 400. / 1250. / —
15.8.1861. Black on green underprint. Standing blacksmith with sledge hammer by anvil at left, seated woman with dog by cattle at center. One red sheet number and *BOWMANVILLE* at bottom. Signature varieties. Back: Green. Overprint: Red: *GUELPH* and *DUNDAS*> Blue: *TORONTO.* Printer: RWH&E and ABNC.

S1262 5 Dollars — 400. / 1250. / —
15.8.1861. Black on green underprint. Portrait J. Cartier at left; farmer sharpening scythe at center, bull's head at lower right. One red sheet number and *BOWMANVILLE* at bottom. Signature varieties. Back: Green. Overprint: Red: *GUELPH* and *DUNDAS*> Blue: *TORONTO.* Printer: RWH&E and ABNC.

S1263 10 Dollars — 400. / 1250. / —
15.8.1861. Black on green underprint. Barges at left, seated Indian and crest at center, cattle driving scene at right. One red sheet number and *BOWMANVILLE* at bottom. Signature varieties. Back: Green. Overprint: Red: *GUELPH* and *DUNDAS*> Blue: *TORONTO.* Printer: RWH&E and ABNC.

1861 Second Bowmanville Issue

S1264 1 Dollar — Good 300. / Fine 850. / XF —
15.8.1861. Black on green underprint. Agricultural produce at left, cattle at top center, shearing sheep at lower right. Two red sheet numbers and *BOWMANVILLE* at bottom. Signature varieties. Back: Green. Overprint: Blue: *HAMILTON* and *LINDSAY.* Printer: RWH&E and ABNC.

S1265 2 Dollars — 300. / 850. / —
15.8.1861. Black on green underprint. Standing blacksmith with sledge hammer by anvil at left, seated woman with dog by cattle at center. Two red sheet numbers and *BOWMANVILLE* at bottom. Signature varieties. Back: Green. Overprint: Blue: *HAMILTON* and *LINDSAY.* Printer: RWH&E and ABNC.

S1266 5 Dollars — — / Unc / 500.
15.8.1861. Black on green underprint. Portrait J. Cartier at left; farmer sharpening scythe at center, bull's head at lower right. Two red sheet numbers and *BOWMANVILLE* at bottom. Signature varieties. Back: Green. Overprint: Blue: *HAMILTON* and *LINDSAY.* Printer: RWH&E and ABNC. Face proof.

S1267 10 Dollars — — / Unc / 500.
15.8.1861. Black on green underprint. Barges at left, seated Indian and crest at center, cattle driving scene at right. Two red sheet numbers and *BOWMANVILLE* at bottom. Signature varieties. Back: Green. Overprint: Blue: *HAMILTON* and *LINDSAY.* Printer: RWH&E and ABNC. Face proof.

1861 Third Bowmanville Issue

S1268 1 Dollar — Good 300. / Fine 800. / XF —
15.8.1861. Black on green underprint. Agricultural produce at left, cattle at top center, shearing sheep at lower right. Two blue sheet numbers and *BOWMANVILLE* at bottom. Signature varieties. Back: Green. Overprint: Red: *GUELPH* and *MONTREAL.* Blue: *WHITBY.* Printer: RWH&E and ABNC.

S1269 2 Dollars — 300. / 800. / —
15.8.1861. Black on green underprint. Standing blacksmith with sledge hammer by anvil at left, seated woman with dog by cattle at center. Two blue sheet numbers and *BOWMANVILLE* at bottom. Signature varieties. Back: Green. Overprint: Red: *GUELPH* and *MONTREAL.* Blue: *WHITBY.* Printer: RWH&E and ABNC.

S1270 5 Dollars — — / Unc / 500.
15.8.1861. Black on green underprint. Portrait J. Cartier at left; farmer sharpening scythe at center, bull's head at lower right. Two blue sheets numbers and *BOWMANVILLE* at bottom. Signature varieties. Back: Green. Overprint: Red: *GUELPH* and *MONTREAL.* Blue: *WHITBY.* Printer: RWH&E and ABNC. Face proof.

S1271 10 Dollars — — / Unc / 500.
15.8.1861. Black on green underprint. Barges at left, seated Indian and crest at center, cattle driving scene at right. Two blue sheet numbers and *BOWMANVILLE* at bottom. Signature varieties. Back: Green. Overprint: Red: *GUELPH* and *MONTREAL.* Blue: *WHITBY.* Printer: RWH&E and ABNC. Face proof.

1860 Issue

S1272 20 Dollars — Good — / Fine Unc / XF 600.
3.8.1860. Black on green underprint. Young woman resting on hay at upper left, farm boy resting with sheep at upper right over portrait Prince Albert. Back: Green. Printer: ABNC. Face proof.

	Good	Fine	XF
S1273 50 Dollars 3.8.1860. Black on green underprint. Standing allegorical woman by beehive at left, portrait Prince of Wales at center, allegorical woman holding grapes and cornucopia at lower right. Back: Green. Printer: ABNC. Face proof.	—	Unc	600.
S1274 100 Dollars 3.8.1860. Black on green underprint. Portrait of the Prince of Wales at lower left, two reclining allegorical women at top center. Back: Green. Printer: ABNC. Face proof.	—	Unc	600.

1870 Issue

	VG	VF	UNC
S1275 4 Dollars 1.8.1870. Black on green underprint. Farmer plowing with horses at lower left, portrait Prince Arthur at lower right. Signature varieties. Back: Green. Overprint: Blue: *LINDSAY, PETERBORO, MONTREAL*, or *OSHAWA*. Printer: BABNC.	600.	1200.	—
S1276 5 Dollars 1.11.1870. Black on green underprint. Portrait Prince Arthur at lower left, farm woman with sickle at center, portrait young woman at lower right. Signature varieties. Back: Green. Overprint: Blue: *LINDSAY, PETERBORO, MONTREAL*, or *OSHAWA*. Printer: BABNC.	500.	1000.	—
S1277 10 Dollars 1.11.1870. Black on green underprint. Woodsman at lower left, seated girl holding scroll at lower right. Signature varieties. Back: Green. Overprint: Blue: *LINDSAY, PETERBORO, MONTREAL*, or *OSHAWA*. Printer: BABNC.	500.	1000.	—

NOTE: Counterfeits exist of #S1277.

1882 Issue

	VG	VF	UNC
S1278 5 Dollars 3.7.1882. Black on green underprint. Young woman at lower left, Indian girl with shield at center, steam train at right. Signature varieties. Back: Green. Crest at center. Printer: BABNC.	1500.	—	—
S1279 10 Dollars 3.7.1882. Black on green underprint. Portrait Prince Arthur at left, dockside scene at center, girl at right. Signature varieties. Back: Green. Printer: BABNC. Face proof.	—	Unc	500.
S1280 10 Dollars 3.7.1882. Black on green underprint. Cattle grazing at left, girl at right. Signature varieties. Back: Green. Crest at center. Printer: BABNC. Face proof.	—	Unc	500.
S1281 100 Dollars 3.7.1882. Black on green underprint. Portrait Prince of Wales at left, allegorical women at center. Back: Green. Crest at center. Printer: BABNC. Face proof.	—	Unc	500.

1888 Issue

	VG	VF	UNC
S1282 5 Dollars 1.6.1888. Black on yellow and orange underprint. Farmer haying, horses at lower left, portrait Indian brave at center, standing allegorical woman with wheel ("Fortuna") at right. Signature varieties. Back: Orange. Printer: ABNC.			
a. Issued note.	1000.	1750.	—
b. Red overprint: *1903* (twice).	1250.	2150.	—
S1283 10 Dollars 1.6.1888. Black on yellow-green and orange underprint. "Calmady children" at upper left, seated allegorical woman at center, sailor boy at upper right. Signature varieites. Back: Olive. Printer: ABNC.			
a. Issued note.	1250.	2150.	—
b. Red overprint: *1903* (twice).	1250.	2150.	—
S1284 20 Dollars 1.6.1888. Black on yellow and blue underprint. Portrait two laureate allegorical women at left, seated woman amongst sheep at center right. Signature varieties. Back: Green. Printer: ABNC. Face proof.	—	Unc	600.
S1285 50 Dollars 1.6.1888. Black on yellow-green and red underprint. Reclining woman with spilt jug at left, crouching sailor by anchor at right. Signature varieties. Back: Brown. Printer: ABNC. Face proof.	—	Unc	600.

1898 Issue

	Good	Fine	XF
S1286 5 Dollars 1.1.1898. Black on green underprint. Portrait young woman at upper left, woman and cherubs at center, bull's head at right. Signature varieties. Printer: BABNC.	750.	1600.	—

People's Bank of Halifax

1864-1903 Issue

	VG	VF	UNC
S1287 4 Dollars 1.7.1870. Black on green underprint. Seated Commerce at left, supported royal arms at lower right. Back: Green. Overprint: Red: *1871* and *CANADA CURRENCY* seal. Printer: BABNC.			
a. Issued note.	1500.	3000.	—
p. Face proof.	—	Unc	650.
S1288 5 Dollars 1870-1901. Black on green underprint. Seated woman holding trident with ship in background at lower left, horses' heads at right. Back: Green. Printer: BABNC.			
a. Red overprint: *1871* and *CANADA CURRENCY* seal.	1800.	3600.	—
b. 1.7.1882-1.10.1900.	1800.	3600.	—
c. Overall green underprint. 1.10.1901.	1800.	3600.	—
p. Face proof. 18xx.	—	Unc	650.
S1289 10 Dollars 1880-1903. Black. Woman and telegraph. Back: Green. Printer: BABNC.			
a. 1.11.1894.	2150.	4500.	—
b. Orange underprint. 1.10.1900.	2150.	4500.	—
c. 1.10.1901.	2150.	4500.	—
p1. Green underprint. Face proof. 1.9.1880.	—	Unc	650.
p2. Green underprint. Face proof. 2.7.1903.	—	Unc	650.

	VG	VF	UNC
S1290 20 Dollars 1864-1903. Black on green underprint. Portrait Princess of Wales at left, portrait Queen Victoria between reclining Indian woman and lion at center, two sailors on watch at lower right. Back: Blue. Printer: ABNC.			
a. Issued note. 1.11.1898.	2000.	3750.	—
p. Face proof. 25.5.1864; 2.7.1903.	—	Unc	600.
s. Specimen. 27.5.1870.	—	—	—

Peoples Bank of New Brunswick

1864-73 Issue

	Good	Fine	XF
S1291 1 Dollar 1.9.1864; 1.5.1867. Partially engraved. Black on green underprint. Lion with shield at center, portrait Queen Victoria at lower right. Portrait of man at lower left. Uniface. Printer: ABNC.	500.	1500.	—
S1292 2 Dollars 1873. Partially engraved. Black on green underprint. Britannia and Justice at center, portrait Queen Victoria at lower right. Portrait of man at lower left. Uniface. Printer: ABNC.	500.	1500.	—
S1293 5 Dollars 18xx. Partially engraved. Black on green underprint. Arms at center, sailboat at lower right. Portrait of man at lower left. Uniface. Printer: ABNC. Proof.	—	Unc	650.

1874; 1881 Issue

S1294 1 Dollar — VG | VF | UNC
2.1.1874; 1.12.1881. Fully engraved. Black on green underprint. Lion with shield at center, portrait Queen Victoria at lower right. Portrait of man at lower left. Uniface. Signature varieties. Back: Green. Printer: ABNC and BABNC.
- a. 2.1.1874. — 1000. | 1750. | —
- b. 1.12.1881. — 1250. | 2250. | —

S1295 2 Dollars
2.1.1874; 1.12.1881. Fully engraved. Black on green underprint. Britannia and Justice at center, portrait Queen Victoria at lower right. Signature varieties. Back: Green. Printer: ABNC and BABNC.
- a. 2.1.1874. — 1250. | 2250. | —
- b. 1.12.1881. — 800. | 1600. | —

S1295A 5 Dollars
2.1.1874. Fully engraved. Black on green underprint. Arms at center, sailboat at lower right. Signature varieties. Back: Green. Printer: ABNC and BABNC. — 1100. | 2200. | —

S1296 10 Dollars
1.12.1881. Fully engraved. Black on green underprint. Prince of Wales at lower left, seated Liberty with torch at left center, sailing ship at upper center right, portrait man at lower right. Signature varieties. Back: Green. Printer: ABNC and BABNC. — 1250. | 2250. | —

1885 Issue

S1297 1 Dollar — VG | VF | UNC
2.1.1885. Black on green underprint. Anchor at lower left, steam train at center. Portrait Queen Victoria in "Widow's Weeds" at right. Back: Green. Printer: BABNC. — 1100. | 2000. | —

S1298 5 Dollars
2.11.1885. Black on green underprint. Portrait Prince Arthur at left, sailing ship at center. Portrait Queen Victoria in "Widow's Weeds" at right. Back: Green. Printer: BABNC. — 1250. | 2500. | —

1897; 1904 Issue

S1299 5 Dollars — VG | VF | UNC
1897; 1904. Legislative building at left, A. F. Randolph at right. Signature varieties. Back: Green. Printer: BABNC.
- a. Black on red-brown underprint. 22.6.1897. — 1250. | 2500. | —
- b. Black on ochre underprint. 1.7.1904. — 1500. | 3000. | —

S1300 10 Dollars
1897; 1904. Legislative building at left, A. F. Randolph at right. Signature varieties. Back: Green. Printer: BABNC.
- a. Black on red-brown underprint. 22.6.1897. — 1500. | 3000. | —
- b. Black on ochre underprint. 1.7.1904. — 1500. | 3000. | —

1897 Issue

S1301 20 Dollars — VG | VF | UNC
22.6.1897. Black on blue underprint. Standing Justice at left, St. George slaying dragon at center, portrait Duke of Wellington at lower right. Back: Blue. Printer: ABNC and BABNC. — 1500. | 3000. | —

S1302 50 Dollars
1897; 1905. Portrait Queen Victoria at left, reclining Commerce at top center right, cattle at lower right. Printer: ABNC and BABNC.
- a. Black on green underprint. Partially engraved date, completed by red handstamp: *Nov. 2, 1905*. Back green. 6.10.1905. — 1500. | 3000. | —
- p. Black on blue underprint. Fully engraved date. Face proof. 22.6.1897. — — | Unc | 750.

#S1303-S1305 *Deleted*. See #S1936-S1938.

Québec Bank

1818 Issue

#S1306-S1310 Counterfeits exist with engraved signature and date 1 May 1819.

S1306 1 Dollar — Good | Fine | XF
1818; 1819. Black. Uniface. Printer: Maverick. — — | — | —

S1307 3 Dollars
20.10.1818. Black. Farm at upper left. Uniface. Printer: Maverick. — 750. | 1800. | —

S1308 5 Dollars
1818; 1819. Black. Uniface. Printer: Maverick. — — | — | —

S1309 10 Dollars
1818; 1819. Black. Crossed cornucopias at upper left. Uniface. Printer: Maverick. — — | — | —

S1310 100 Dollars
1818; 1819. Black. Uniface. Printer: Maverick. — — | — | —

1819 Issue

S1311 1 Dollar — Good | Fine | XF
1819-31. Black. Printer: Graphic Co. Uniface proofs. No issued notes known. — — | Unc | 750.

S1312 2 Dollars
1819-37. Black. Printer: Graphic Co. Uniface proofs. No issued notes known. — — | Unc | 650.

S1313 5 Dollars
1819-34. Black. Printer: Graphic Co. Uniface proofs. No issued notes known. — — | Unc | 650.

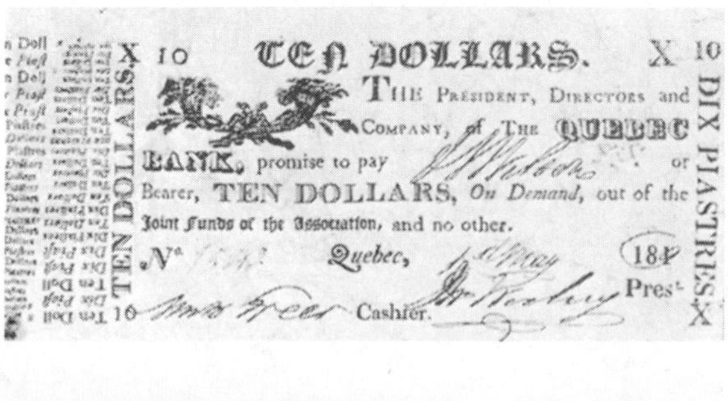

S1314 10 Dollars — Good | Fine | XF
1819-34. Black. Printer: Graphic Co. Uniface proofs. No issued notes known. — — | Unc | 650.

S1315 20 Dollars
1819-33. Black. Printer: Graphic Co. Uniface proofs. No issued notes known. Reported not confirmed. — — | — | —

S1316 50 Dollars
11819-33. Black. Printer: Graphic Co. Uniface proofs. No issued notes known. — — | Unc | 650.

S1317 100 Dollars
1819-33. Black. Printer: Graphic Co. Uniface proofs. No issued notes known. — — | Unc | 650.

1835 Issue

S1318 1 Dollar — VG | VF | UNC
1835; 1836. Black. Man with three children, seated woman with early steam passenger train in background at top center, small steamship at bottom. Signature varieties. Printer: Rawdon, Wright & Co. — 1000. | 2000. | —

S1319 5 Dollars
1.6.18xx. Black. Signature varieties. Printer: Rawdon, Wright & Co. Proof. — — | Unc | 650.

1837 Scrip Issue

S1320 6 Pence = 12 Sous — Good | Fine | XF
1.6.1837. Black. Printer: Jones. — 300. | 1000. | —

S1320A 1/4 Dollar — VG | VF | UNC
1.10.1837. Black. Cherubs at left and right of portrait woman at center, reverse of Spanish 2 reales coin at right. Uniface. Signature varieties. Printer: RWH & H. — 1000. | 1750. | —

S1320B 1/2 Dollar
1.10.1837. Black. Reverse of Spanish 4 reales coin at left, portrait woman at left and right of sailing ship over dog's head at center. Uniface. Signature varieties. Printer: RWH & H. — 1000. | 1750. | —

1837-60 Issues

S1321 1 Dollar — Good | Fine | XF
18xx. Black. Uniface. Printer: RWH & Co. Proof. — — | Unc | 500.

S1322 2 Dollars
18xx. Black. Uniface. Printer: RWH & Co. Proof. — — | Unc | 500.

S1323 2 Dollars — Good | Fine | XF
1858-59. Black. Beehive at left, supported royal arms at top center, Indian paddling canoe at lower center, standing Britannia at right. Green word protector. Uniface. Overprint: Green: *QUEBEC* and *C. E.* Printer: Harris & Sealey, New York. — 150. | 300. | —

S1324 5 Dollars
18xx. Black. Uniface. Printer: RWH & Co. Proof. — — | Unc | 500.

S1325 10 Dollars
18xx. Black. Uniface. Printer: RWH & Co. Proof. — — | Unc | 500.

S1326 20 Dollars
18xx. Black. Three allegories above ship and factory at center, sailing ship at right. Uniface. Printer: RWH & Co.
- p. Proof. — — | Unc | 500.
- r. Blue overprint: *OTTAWA* Green word protector on face. Dated with blue printed #. Unsigned remainder. 1.11.18xx. — — | — | —

S1327 50 Dollars
18xx. Black. Sailing ships, wharf scene at left, two allegories above dog by strongbox at center. Uniface. Sailing ships whaling at left. Printer: RWH & Co.
- p. Proof. — — | Unc | 500.
- r. Blue overprint: *OTTAWA*. Green word protector on face. Dated with blue printed #. Unsigned remainder. 1.11.18xx. — — | — | —

S1328 100 Dollars
18xx. Black. Seahorses pulling Neptune and woman at top center, schooner at right. Uniface. Sailing ships whaling at left. Printer: RWH & Co.
- p. Proof. — — | Unc | 500.
- r. Blue overprint: *OTTAWA*. Green word protector on face. Dated with blue printed #. Unsigned remainder. 1.11.18xx. — — | — | —

1843-65 ISSUES

	Good	Fine	XF
S1329 1 Dollar = 5 Shillings 1.11.18xx. Two allegorical women flanking shield at upper center, dog's head at lower center. Uniface. Signature varieties. Printer: RWH & C. Proof.	—	Unc	500.
S1330 1 Dollar = 5 Shillings 1.11.1855-1861. Black. Two allegorical women flanking shield at upper center, dog's head at lower center. Signature varieties. Red word protector. Blue hand stamp: *OTTAWA*. Back: Red word protector. Printer: RWH & Co.	250.	750.	1750.

	Good	Fine	XF
S1331 2 Dollars = 10 Shillings 1.11.1852-1860. Black. Standing Britannia at lower left, seated allegorical man and woman at top center, milkmaid with bucket at lower right. Uniface. Signature varieties. Printer: RWH & Co.	300.	850.	—
S1332 2 Dollars = 10 Shillings 1.11.1850. Black. Standing Britannia at lower left, seated allegorical man and woman at top center, milkmaid with bucket at lower right. Red word protector. Blue hand stamp: *OTTAWA*. Signature varieties. Back. Red word protector. Printer: RWH & Co.	350.	1000.	—
S1333 2 Dollars = 10 Shillings 1.11.1865. Black. Standing Britannia at lower left, seated allegorical man and woman at top center, milkmaid with bucket at lower right. Black text:*PAYABLE IN TORONTO at top, TORONTO at ends, and FO* Back: Green. Printer: RWH & E.			
a. Red word and green numeral protectors on face and back.	350.	1000.	—
b. Green word and green numeral protectors on face only.	350.	1000.	—
S1334 5 Dollars = 1 Pound-5 Shillings 1.11.18xx. Black. Seated woman with shield with large ornate *5* at left, two men with beehive and shield above two small ships at center, three cherubs in oval at right. Uniface. Signature varieties. Printer: RWH & Co. Proof.	—	Unc	500.
S1335 5 Dollars = 1 Pound-5 Shillings 1.11.1847; 1860-61. Black. Seated woman with shield with large ornate *5* at left, two men with beehive and shield above two small ships at center, three cherubs in oval at right. Red word protector.Blue hand stamp: *OTT* Back: Red word protector. Printer: RWH & Co.	350.	1000.	—
S1335A 10 Dollars = 2 Pounds-10 Shillings 1.11.18xx. Black. Bust of helmeted Greek soldier at left, sailing ships at center, portrait Queen Victoria at right. Signature varieties. Printer: RWH & Co. Proof.	—	Unc	500.
S1335B 10 Dollars = 2 Pounds-10 Shillings 1.11.1849. Black. Bust of helmeted Greek soldier at left, sailing ships at center, portrait Queen Victoria at right. Red word protector.Blue hand stamp: *OTTAWA*. Signature varieties. Back: Red word protector. Printer: RWH & E.	250.	1250.	—

1843-62 ISSUES

	Good	Fine	XF
S1336 1 Dollar 1.11.18xx. Black. Bust of Greek god at left, Indians hunting on horseback at top center, woman and anchor in large ornate *1* at right. Blue hand stamp: *BYTOWN*. Signature varieties. Uniface. Printer: RW & H. Proof.	—	Unc	500.
S1337 2 Dollars Black. Royal crest at top center, bust of helmeted Roman soldier at right. Blue handstamp: *BYTOWN*. Signature varieties. Uniface. Overprint: 1.11.18xx. Printer: RW&H. Proof.	—	Unc	500.
S1338 4 Dollars 1.11.18xx. Black. Bust of helmeted Roman soldier at left and right, sailing ships in harbor over mermaid at center. Blue handstamp: *BYTOWN*. Signature varieties. Uniface. Printer: RW & H. Proof.	—	Unc	500.
S1339 4 Dollars 1849-62. Black. Bust of helmeted Roman soldier at left and right, sailing ships in harbor over mermaid at center. Uniface. Signature varieties.			
a. Red word protector on face and back Printer: RWH & Co. 1.11.1849-1852.	350.	1100.	—
b. Printer: RWH & E. 1.2.1862.	325.	1000.	—

	Good	Fine	XF
S1340 5 Dollars 1852-54. Black. Man with shield at left, facing griffins at top center, portrait Queen Victoria at right. Uniface. Signature varieties.			
a. Blue hand stamp:*BYTOWN*. Printer like #S1336. 1.11.1852-1853.	350.	1100.	—
b. Printer: RWH & E. 1.2.1854.	325.	1000.	—
S1341 10 Dollars 1849-62. Black. Bust of helmeted Greek soldier at left, sailing ships at upper left center, Queen Victoria at right. Uniface. Signature varieties. Issued at Halifax.			
a. Blue handstamp: *BYTOWN*. Printer: RW & H. 1.11.1853.	350.	1100.	—
b. Red word protector on face and back. Printer: RW & H. 1.11.1849-1852.	325.	1000.	—
c. Printer: RWH & E. 1.2.1862.	325.	1000.	—

1858 SPURIOUS ISSUE

	VG	VF	UNC
S1341A 2 Dollars 1858; 1859. Black. Beehive, farm tools at left, supported royal arms at top center, standing Britannia at right. Green word protector. Uniface. Overprint: Green: *QUEBEC* and *C.E.* Printer: Harris & Sealey Engravers.	225.	500.	—

1856 ISSUE

	Good	Fine	XF
S1342 1 Dollar = 5 Shillings 185x, 1859. Anchor, barrel at left, woodsman over St. George slaying dragon at center, beehive, flowers at right. Uniface. Signature varieties. Printer: TCC.			
a. Green word protector on face. (No notes known). 2.1.185x.	—	—	—
b. Black on green underprint. 2.1.1859.	400.	1250.	—
p. Black. Proof. 2.1.185x.	—	Unc	450.

	Good	Fine	XF
S1343 4 Dollars = 1 Pound 1856-59. Men with cattle and wagons at lower left, men with cattle at lower center steam train at lower right. Uniface. Signature varieties. Printer: TCC.			
a. Black. 2.1.1856.	325.	1000.	—
b. Green word protector on face only. (No notes known). 2.1.185x.	—	—	—
c. Black on green underprint. 2.1.1859.	400.	1250.	—
S1344 10 Dollars = 2 Pounds-10 Shillings 185x, 1859. Uniface. Signature varieties. Printer: TCC.			
a. Green word protector on face only. (No notes known). 2.1.185x.	—	—	—
b. Black on green underprint. (No notes known). 2.1.1859.	—	—	—
p. Black. Proof. 2.1.185x.	—	Unc	450.

1863 ISSUE

	VG	VF	UNC
S1345 1 Dollar 2.1.1863. Black on green underprint. Portrait of sailor at left, three lumberjacks at lower right. Bank crest at upper or top center. Signature varieties. Printer: ABNC. Blue overprint: *GASPE, OTTAWA, PAYABLE IN TORONTO, ST. CATHARINES PAYABLE IN TORONTO, PAYABLE IN MONTREAL, OTTAWA PAYABLE IN MONTREAL*, or *THREE RIVERS*.	500.	1250.	—
S1346 2 Dollars 2.1.1863. Black on green underprint. Shipbuilding scene at lower left, sailing ships at lower right. Bank crest at upper or top center. Signature varieties. Printer: ABNC. Blue overprint: *GASPE, OTTAWA, PAYABLE IN TORONTO, ST. CATHARINES PAYABLE IN TORONTO, PAYABLE IN MONTREAL, OTTAWA PAYABLE IN MONTREAL*, or *THREE RIVERS*.	800.	1400.	—
S1347 4 Dollars 2.1.1863. Black on green underprint. Sailor, woman and child at lower left, seated Britannia with shield with large *4* at lower right. Bank crest at upper or top center. Signature varieties. Printer: ABNC. Blue overprint: *GASPE, OTTAWA, PAYABLE IN TORONTO, ST. CATHARINES PAYABLE IN TORONTO, PAYABLE IN MONTREAL, OTTAWA PAYABLE IN MONTREAL*, or *THREE RIVERS*.	800.	1400.	—
S1347A 4 Dollars Sailor, woman and child at lower left, seated Britannia with shield with large *4* at lower right. Large ornate *4's* at left a nd right of bank crest. Signature varieties. Overprint: Blue: *TORONTO*. Printer: ABNC.	800.	1400.	—
S1348 5 Dollars 2.1.1863. Black on green underprint. Two beavers at lower left. Seated woman with telescope at lower right. Bank crest at upper or top center. Signature varieties. Printer: ABNC. Blue overprint: *GASPE, OTTAWA, PAYABLE IN TORONTO, ST. CATHARINES PAYABLE IN TORONTO, PAYABLE IN MONTREAL, OTTAWA PAYABLE IN MONTREAL*, or *THREE RIVERS*.	1000.	2000.	—

		VG	VF	UNC
S1349	**10 Dollars**			
	2.1.1863. Black on green underprint. Reclining woman at lower left, bank crest at lower right. Signature varieties. Printer: ABNC. Blue overprint: *GASPE, OTTAWA, PAYABLE IN TORONTO, ST. CATHARINES PAYABLE IN TORONTO, PAYABLE IN MONTREAL, OTTAWA PAYABLE IN MONTREAL,* or *THREE RIVERS.*	1000.	2000.	—

1870 Issue

		VG	VF	UNC
S1350	**4 Dollars**			
	1.10.1870. Black on green underprint. Sir N. F. Belleau at lower left, bank crest at upper center, young sailor at lower right. Signature varieties. Overprint: Blue: *OTTAWA, TORONTO,* or *THREE RIVERS.* Printer: BABNC.	750.	1250.	—

1873; 1888 Issue

		VG	VF	UNC
S1351	**4 Dollars**			
	2.1.1873. Black on green underprint. Signature varieties. Overprint: Red: *A A* or blue: *B B.* Printer: ABNC and BABNC.	800.	1400.	—
S1352	**5 Dollars**			
	1873-88. Black on green underprint. Two beavers at lower left. Seated woman with telescope at lower right. Signature varieties. Printer: ABNC and BABNC.			
	a. Red overprint: *A A* or blue overprint:*B B.* 2.1.1873.	1000.	2000.	—
	b. Purple hand stamp: *D* or *B.* 3.1.1888.	1000.	2000.	—
	c. Black on brown underprint. 3.1.1888.	1250.	2250.	—
S1353	**10 Dollars**			
	3.1.1888. Black on green underprint. Reclining woman at lower left, bank crest at lower right. Purple hand stamp: *D* or *B.* Signature varieties. Overprint: Red: *A A* or blue: *B B.* Printer: ABNC and BABNC.	1250.	2250.	—

1898 Issue

		VG	VF	UNC
S1354	**5 Dollars**			
	3.1.1898. Black on green underprint. Paddle wheel steamboat and modern ship at center. Signature varieties. Back: Green. Bank crest at center. Printer: ABNC.	850.	1750.	—
S1355	**10 Dollars**			
	3.1.1898. Black on olive-green underprint. Docks at Quebec City at center. Signature varieties. Back: Blue. Bank crest at center. Printer: ABNC.	850.	1750.	—
S1356	**10 Dollars**			
	3.1.1898. Black on yellow and olive-green underprint. Docks at Quebec City at center. Signature varieties. Back: Green. Bank crest at center. Printer: ABNC.	850.	1750.	—
S1357	**20 Dollars**			
	3.1.1898. Black on yellow and olive-green underprint. Cherub on winged wheel at left, falls at right. Signature varieties. Back: Olive. Quebec City - Prescott Gate at center. Printer: ABNC.	1250.	2250.	—
S1358	**50 Dollars**			
	3.1.1898. Black on yellow and olive-green underprint. Seated woman with globe at center. Signature varieties. Back: Olive. Quebec Cty - Kent Gate at center. Printer: ABNC.	1250.	2250.	—
S1359	**100 Dollars**			
	3.1.1898. Black on yellow and olive-green underprint. Reclining woman with spear and bank crest at left center. Signature varieties. Back: Olive. Quebec City - Hope Gate at center. Printer: ABNC.	1250.	2250.	—

1901 Issue

		VG	VF	UNC
S1360	**5 Dollars**			
	2.7.1901. Black on yellow and olive underprint. Seated woman with lion and shield at center. Signature varieties. Back: Green. Bank crest at center. Printer: ABNC.	850.	1750.	—

1908; 1911 Issues

		VG	VF	UNC
S1361	**5 Dollars**			
	1.6.1908. Black on yellow and olive underprint. Seated woman with lion and shield at center. Signature varieties. Back: Green. Bank crest.. Overprint: Red: *M M.* Printer: ABNC.			
	a. Without text: *FOUNDED 1818* at top.	600.	1250.	3750.
	b. With text: *FOUNDED 1818* at top.	600.	1250.	3750.
S1362	**5 Dollars**			
	1.6.1908. Black on yellow and olive underprint. Seated woman with lion and shield at center. Without text: *FOUNDED 1818* at top. Signature varieties. Back: Green. Quebec City - Prescott Gate. Printer: ABNC.	750.	1400.	—

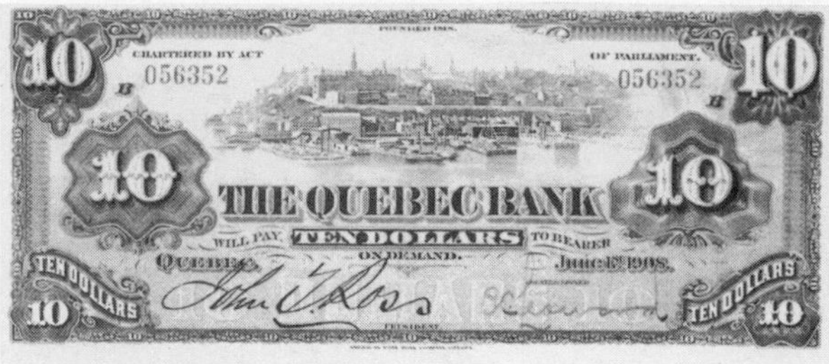

		VG	VF	UNC
S1363	**10 Dollars**			
	1.6.1908. Black on yellow and olive underprint. Docks at Quebec City at center. Signature varieties. Back: Green. Bank crest. Printer: ABNC.			
	a. Without text: *FOUNDED 1818* at top.	600.	1250.	3750.
	b. With text: *FOUNDED 1818* at top.	600.	1250.	3500.
S1364	**10 Dollars**			
	1.6.1908. Black on yellow and olive underprint. Docks at Quebec City at center. Without text: *FOUNDED 1818* at top. Signature varieties. Back: Green. Quebec City - Hope Gate. Printer: ABNC.	750.	1500.	—
S1365	**20 Dollars**			
	3.1.1911. Black on yellow and olive underprint. Cherub on winged wheel at left, falls at right.With text: *Founded 1818* at top. Signature varieties. Back: Green. Quebec City - Prescott Gate. Printer: ABNC.	1000.	2250.	—
S1366	**20 Dollars**			
	3.1.1911. Black on yellow and olive underprint. Cherub on winged wheel at left, falls at right. Signature varieties. Back: Green. Bank crest. Printer: ABNC.	1250.	2500.	—
S1367	**50 Dollars**			
	3.1.1911. Black on yellow and olive underprint. Seated woman with globe at center. With text: *Founded 1818* at top. Signature varieties. Back: Green. Quebec City - Kent Gate. Printer: ABNC.	1000.	2000.	—
S1368	**100 Dollars**			
	3.1.1911. Black on yellow and olive underprint. Reclining woman with spear and bank crest at left.With text: *Founded 1818* at top. Signature varieties. Back: Green. Quebec City - Hope Gate. Printer: ABNC.	1000.	2000.	—

Royal Bank of Canada

1901; 1909 Issue

		Good	Fine	XF
S1369	**5 Dollars**			
	2.1.1901. Black on multicolor underprint. Seated woman with two children ("Peace") at left. Signature varieties. Back: Green and multicolor. Royal crest at center. Printer: ABNC.	150.	500.	1500.
S1370	**5 Dollars**			
	2.1.1901. Black on green and yellow-green underprint. Seated woman with two children ("Peace") at left. Signature varieties. Back: Green. Royal crest at center. Printer: ABNC.	125.	250.	750.

		Good	Fine	XF
S1371	**5 Dollars**			
	2.1.1909. Black on green and yellow underprint. Seated woman with two children ("Peace") at left. Signature varieties. Back: Green. Royal crest at center. Printer: ABNC.			
	a. Black *5*'s on face.	125.	250.	750.
	b. Green *5*'s on face.	50.00	150.	300.
S1372	**10 Dollars**			
	2.1.1901. Black on multicolor underprint. Seated allegorical woman at right. Signature varieties. Back: Blue and multicolor. Royal crest at center. Printer: ABNC.	175.	600.	1200.

		Good	Fine	XF
S1373	**10 Dollars**			
	2.1.1909. Black on multicolor underprint. Seated allegorical woman at right. Signature varieties. Back: Green and multicolor. Royal crest at center. Printer: ABNC.	200.	750.	1500.
S1373A	**10 Dollars**			
	2.1.1909. 2.1.1909. Seated allegorical woman at right. Signature varieties. Back: Olive and yellow. Royal crest at center. Printer: ABNC.	125.	300.	750.

	Good	Fine	XF
S1374 20 Dollars			
2.1.1901. Black on multicolor underprint. Seated woman with lion and shield at center. Signature varieties. Back: Yellow-brown and multicolor. Royal crest at center. Printer: ABNC.			
a. Issued note.	250.	750.	1500.
p. Proof.	—	Unc	600.
S1375 20 Dollars			
2.1.1909. Black on multicolor underprint. Seated woman with lion and shield at center. Signature varieties. Back: Green and multicolor. Royal crest at center. Printer: ABNC. Specimen.	—	Unc	1250.
S1375A 20 Dollars			
2.1.1909. Black on blue and yellow underprint. Seated woman with lion and shield at center. Signature varieties. Back: Royal crest at center. Printer: ABNC.	400.	1000.	1900.
S1376 50 Dollars			
2.1.1901; 2.1.1909. Black on multicolor underprint. Steam sailing ship at right. Signature varieties. Back: Yellow-brown and multicolor. Royal crest at center. Printer: ABNC.			
p. Proof.	—	Unc	700.
s. Specimen.	—	Unc	1400.
S1377 100 Dollars			
2.1.1909. Black on red-orange underprint. Seated Commerce in oval frame at right. Signature varieties. Back: Red-orange. Royal crest at center. Printer: ABNC. Face proof.	—	Unc	700.

1913 Issue

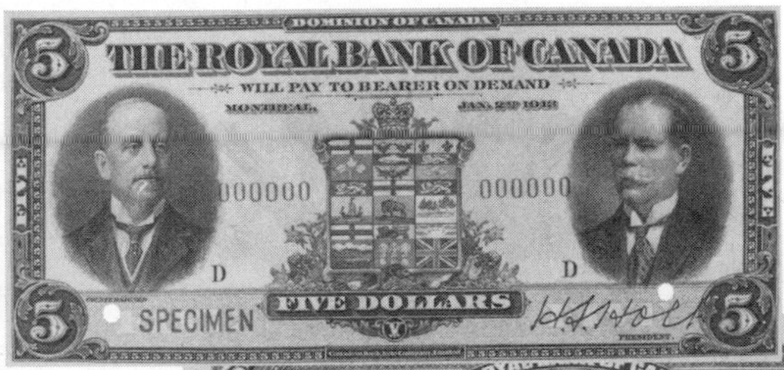

	VG	VF	UNC
S1378 5 Dollars			
2.1.1913. Black on green underprint. of E. L. Pease at left, Canadian arms at center, H. S. Holt at right. Signature varieties. Back: Green. Supported royal arms at center. Printer: ABNC or CBNC.			
a. Issued note.	75.00	200.	700.
s. Specimen.	—	—	—

	VG	VF	UNC
S1379 10 Dollars			
2.1.1913. Black on yellow-green and blue underprint. *H. M. C. S. Bellerophon* at center. Signature varieties. Back: Yellow-orange. Supported royal arms at center. Printer: ABNC or CBNC.			
a. Issued note.	75.00	250.	800.
s. Specimen.	—	—	—

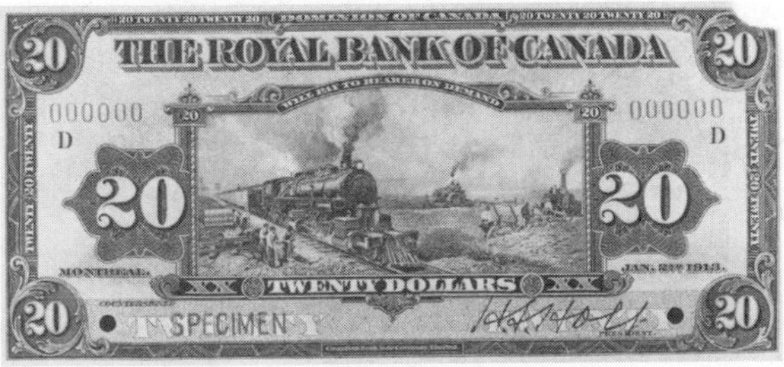

	VG	VF	UNC
S1380 20 Dollars			
2.1.1913. Black on blue underprint. Steam passenger train in prairie, steam tractors harvesting wheat at center. Signature varieties. Back: Blue. Supported royal arms at center. Printer: ABNC or CBNC.			
a. Issued note.	175.	350.	900.
s. Specimen.	—	—	—

	VG	VF	UNC
S1381 50 Dollars			
2.1.1913. Black on green and yellow underprint. E. L. Pease at left. Signature varieties. Back: Olive. Supported royal arms at center. Printer: ABNC or CBNC.			
a. Issued note.	400.	1000.	—
s. Specimen.	—	—	—

	VG	VF	UNC
S1382 100 Dollars			
2.1.1913. Black on orange and yellow-green underprint. H. S. Holt at right. Signature varieties. Back: Red. Supported royal arms at center. Printer: ABNC or CBNC.			
a. Issued note.	900.	1750.	—
s. Specimen.	—	—	—

1927 Issue

	VG	VF	UNC
S1383 5 Dollars			
3.1.1927. Black on green underprint. Canadian arms at center. C. E. Neill at left, H. S. Holt at right. Signature varieties. Back: Green. Printer: CBNC.	30.00	75.00	300.
S1384 10 Dollars			
3.1.1927. Black on orange underprint. Canadian arms at center. C. E. Neill at left, H. S. Holt at right. Signature varieties. Back: Orange. Printer: CBNC.	30.00	75.00	300.

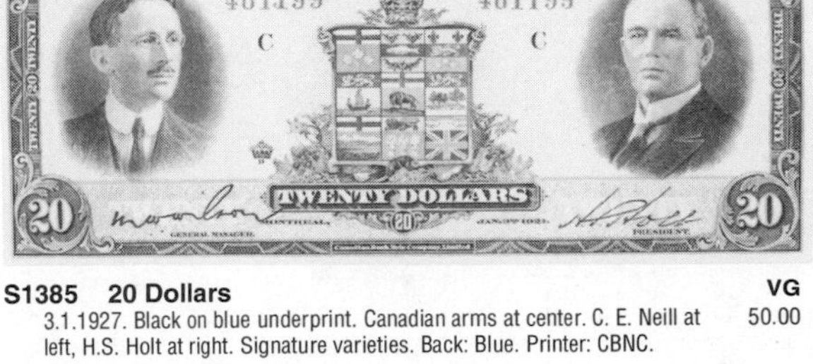

	VG	VF	UNC
S1385 20 Dollars			
3.1.1927. Black on blue underprint. Canadian arms at center. C. E. Neill at left, H.S. Holt at right. Signature varieties. Back: Blue. Printer: CBNC.	50.00	125.	400.

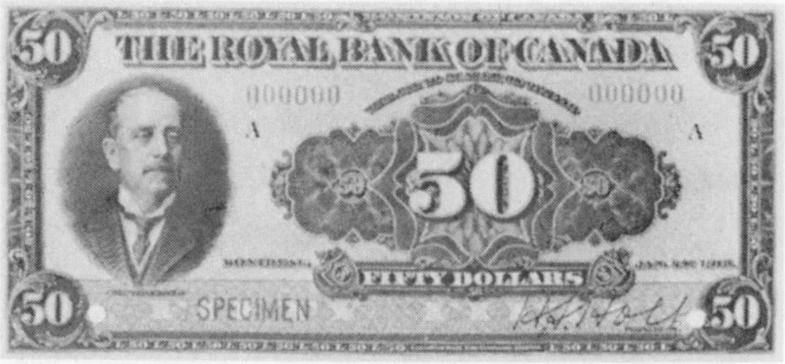

		VG	VF	UNC
S1386	**50 Dollars** 3.1.1927. Black on purple underprint. Canadian arms at center. E. L. Pease at left. Signature varieties. Back: Purple. Printer: CBNC.	150.	350.	1000.
S1387	**100 Dollars** 3.1.1927. Black on olive underprint. H. S. Holt at right. Canadian arms at center. Signature varieties. Printer: CBNC.	175.	400.	1250.

1933 Issue

		VG	VF	UNC
S1388	**5 Dollars** 3.7.1933. Black on green underprint. M. W. Wilson at left, H. Holt at right. Back: Green. Royal crest at center. Printer: CBNC.	50.00	125.	400.
S1389	**10 Dollars** 3.7.1933. Black on orange underprint. M. W. Wilson at left, H. Holt at right. Back: Orange. Royal crest at center. Printer: CBNC.	50.00	125.	400.
S1390	**20 Dollars** 3.7.1933. Black on blue underprint. M. W. Wilson at left, H. Holt at right. Back: Blue. Royal crest at center. Printer: CBNC. Specimen.	—	Unc	750.

1935 Issue

		VG	VF	UNC
S1391	**5 Dollars** 2.1.1935. Black on green underprint. M. W. Wilson at left, H. Holt at right. Back: Green. Royal arms at center. Printer: BABNC. Like #S1388 but reduced size.	25.00	50.00	150.

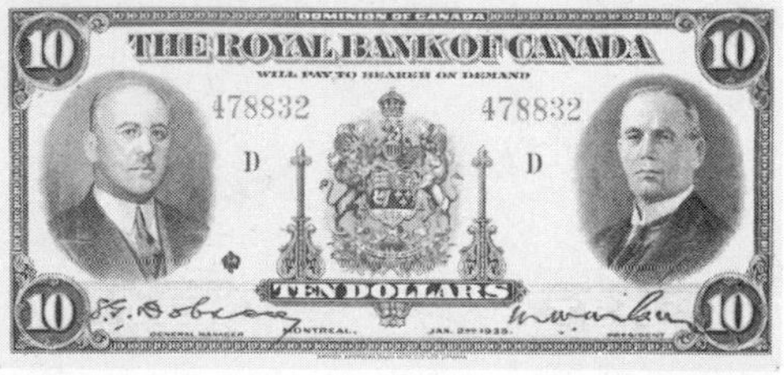

		VG	VF	UNC
S1392	**10 Dollars** 2.1.1935. Black on orange underprint. M. W. Wilson at left, H. Holt at right. Back: Orange. Royal crest at center. Printer: BABNC. Like #S1389 but reduced size.	25.00	50.00	150.

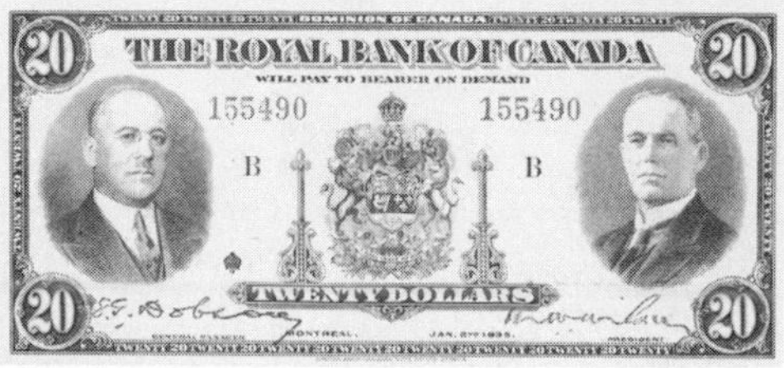

		VG	VF	UNC
S1393	**20 Dollars** 2.1.1935. Black on blue underprint. M. W. WIlson at left, H. Holt at right. Back: Blue. Royal crest at center. Printer: BABNC. Like #S1389 but reduced size.	30.00	75.00	300.

1943 Issue

		VG	VF	UNC
S1394	**5 Dollars** 2.1.1943. Black on green underprint. S. G. Dobson at left, M. Wilson at right. Back: Green. Royal crest at center. Printer: BABNC.	50.00	125.	350.

St. Lawrence Bank

1872 Issues

		Good	Fine	XF
S1395	**4 Dollars** 2.12.1872. Black on green underprint. Deer at lower left, portrait of J. C. Fitch at upper left. center, steam passenger train, ships dockside at top center right. Printer: BABNC. Face proof.	—	Unc	600.
S1396	**4 Dollars** 2.12.1872. Black on green underprint. Deer at lower left, steam passenger train, ships dockside at top center right. Printer: BABNC. Face proof.	—	Unc	600.
S1396A	**5 Dollars** 2.12.1872. Black on green underprint. Jacques Cartier sighting land at left, portrait J. C. Fitch at lower right. Printer: BABNC. Face proof.	—	Unc	600.

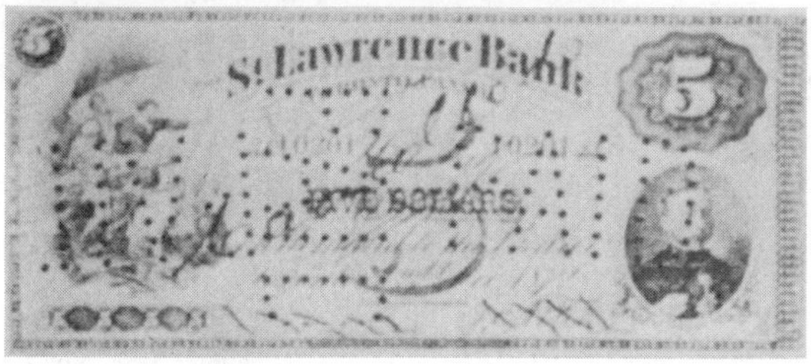

		Good	Fine	XF
S1397	**5 Dollars** 2.12.1872. Black on green underprint. Cartier sighting land at left, portrait Prince Arthur at lower right. Printer: BABNC. Face proof.	—	Unc	600.
S1398	**10 Dollars** 2.12.1872. Black on green underprint. Portrait K. F. Lockhart at upper left cherubs with large ornate *X* at lower center, portrait J. C. Fitch at upper right. Printer: BABNC. Face proof.	—	Unc	600.
S1399	**10 Dollars** 2.12.1872. Black on green underprint. Allegorical woman at upper left, denomination quilloche at upper right. Printer: BABNC. Face proof.	—	Unc	600.

St. Stephens Bank

1830s First Issue

		Good	Fine	XF
S1400	**1 Pound** 18xx. Black. Shipbuilding at left. Supported royal arms at upper center. Uniface. Printer: New England Bank Note Company. Proof.	—	Unc	500.
S1401	**5 Pounds** 18xx. Black. Standing Britannia with shield at left. Supported royal arms at upper center. Uniface. Printer: New England Bank Note Company. Proof.	—	Unc	500.
S1402	**10 Pounds** 18xx. Black. Beehive at left. Supported royal arms at upper center. Uniface. Printer: New England Bank Note Company. Proof.	—	Unc	500.

1830s Second Issue

		Good	Fine	XF
S1403	**1 Dollar** 18xx. Black. Ships at center, seated woman at right. Uniface. Printer: New England Bank Note Company. Proof.	—	Unc	500.
S1404	**2 Dollars** 1.9.1836. Black. Allegorical women at left, seated woman with produce at top center right, portrait woman at right. Uniface. Printer: New England Bank Note Company.	500.	1250.	—

1846-60 Issue

		Good	Fine	XF
S1405	**1 Dollar** 1.1.1846; 1.9.1853. Black. Sailing ships, at upper left, seated Indian woman at right. Uniface. Printer: New England Bank Note Company.	500.	1250.	—
S1406	**2 Dollars** 18xx. Black. Sailing ships at upper left, woman at well at right. Uniface. Printer: New England Bank Note Company. Proof.	—	Unc	500.
S1407	**3 Dollars** 18xx. Black. Harvesting at left, steamboat at right. Uniface. Printer: New England Bank Note Company. Proof.	—	Unc	500.

1840s Issue

		Good	Fine	XF
S1408	**1 Dollar** 18xx. Black. Sailing ships at upper left, seated Indian woman at right. With red word protector. Uniface. Back: Red word protector. (No notes known).	—	—	—
S1409	**2 Dollars** 18xx. Black. Sailing ships at upper left, woman at well at right. With red word protector. Uniface. Back: Red word protector. Remainder.	—	Unc	1000.
S1410	**3 Dollars** 18xx. Black. Harvesting at left, steamboat at right. With red word protector. Uniface. Back: Red word protector. (No notes known).	—	—	—

1852 Issue

		Good	Fine	XF
S1411	**5 Dollars** 1.6.1852. Black. Tug and sailing ships at left, two Indians near falls at center, farmer with sheaf at right. Printer: Boston Bank Note Company. Remainder.			
	p. Face proof. 18xx.	—	Unc	500.
	r. Unsigned remainder. 1.6.1852.	—	Unc	1250.
S1412	**10 Dollars** 1.6.1852; 18xx. Black. Indian in canoe at upper left center, shipbuilding at right. Printer: Boston Bank Note Company. Face proof.	—	Unc	500.

1860 Issues

	VG	VF	UNC
S1413 1 Dollar 1.7.1860. Black on green underprint. Portrait William Todd at lower left, bear attacking hunters in boat at upper center, sailor boy at lower right. Uniface. Printer: ABNC.	1100.	2250.	—
S1414 1 Dollar 1.7.1860. Black on green underprint. Portrait William Todd at lower left, bear attacking hunters in boat at upper center, sailor boy at lower right. Uniface. Back: Green. Printer: ABNC.	1100.	2250.	—

#S1415 and S1416 uniface.

	Good	Fine	XF
S1415 2 Dollars 1.7.1860. Black on green underprint. St. George slaying dragon at lower left, portrait Wmilliam Todd at lower right. Uniface. Printer: ABNC. Proof.	—	Unc	500.

	VG	VF	UNC
S1416 3 Dollars 1.7.1860. Black on green underprint. Seated allegorical woman with tablet at lower left, portrait Queen Victoria at upper center, seated Britannia with shield with large *3* at lower right. Uniface. Printer: ABNC.	1100.	2250.	—

	Good	Fine	XF
S1417 5 Dollars 1.7.1860. Black on green underprint. Two sailors on dock at lower left, lion with shield at upper center, portrait Queen Victoria at lower right. Uniface. Printer: ABNC. Proof.	—	Unc	500.
S1417A 5 Dollars 1.7.1860. Black on green underprint. Two sailors on dock at lower left, lion with shield at upper center, portrait Queen Victoria at lower right. Back: Green. Printer: ABNC.	—	Unc	500.
S1418 10 Dollars 1.7.1860. Black on green underprint. Beehive at lower left, sailor at upper center, supported royal arms at lower right. Uniface. Printer: ABNC. Proof.	—	Unc	500.
S1418A 10 Dollars 1.7.1860. Black on green underprint. Beehieve at lower left, sailor at upper center, supported royal arms at lower right. Back: Green. Printer: ABNC.	—	Unc	500.

1873-86 Issue

	Good	Fine	XF
S1419 1 Dollar 1.10.1873; 1.3.1880; 1.2.1886. Black on green underprint. Portrait William Todd at lower left, bear attacking hunters in boat at upper center, sailor boy at lower right. Uniface. Back: Green. Printer: ABNC and BABNC.	400.	1000.	—
S1420 2 Dollars 1873-86. Black on green underprint. St. George slaying dragon at lower left, portrait Wmilliam Todd at lower right. Uniface. Back: Green. Printer: ABNC and BABNC.			
a. 1.10.1873; 1.3.1880.	400.	1000.	—
b. 1.2.1886.	300.	900.	2250.

	Good	Fine	XF
S1421 3 Dollars 1.10.1873; 1.3.1880; 1.2.1886. Black on green underprint. Seated allegorical woman with tablet at lower left, portrait Queen Victoria at upper center, seated Britannia with shield with large *3* at lower right. Uniface. Back: Green. Printer: ABNC and BABNC.	300.	900.	—
S1422 5 Dollars 1.2.1886. Black on green underprint. Two sailors on dock at lower left, lion with shield at upper center, portrait Queen Victoria at lower right. Uniface. Back: Green. Printer: ABNC and BABNC.	600.	1500.	—
S1423 10 Dollars 1.2.1886. Black on green underprint. Beehive at lower left, sailor at upper center, supported royal arms at lower right. Uniface. Back: Green. Printer: ABNC and BABNC.	600.	1500.	—

1863 Issue

	Good	Fine	XF
S1424 1 Dollar 1.5.1863. Black on green underprint. Portrait W. Todd at lower left, steam passenger train at lower right. Back: Green. Payable by Z. Chipman or at Bank of New York, payable in U. S. funds.			
a. With text: *TO Z. CHIPMAN.*	600.	1500.	—
b. With text: *TO THE BANK OF NEW YORK.*	600.	1500.	—

	Good	Fine	XF
S1425 2 Dollars 1.5.1863. Black on green underprint. Portrait girl with puppies at lower left, cattle at upper center. Portrait W. Todd at lower right. Back: Green. Payable by Z. Chipman or at Bank of New York, payable in U. S. funds.			
a. With text: *TO Z. CHIPMAN.*	600.	1500.	—
b. With text: *TO THE BANK OF NEW YORK.*	600.	1500.	—

	Good	Fine	XF
S1426 3 Dollars 1.5.1863. Black on green underprint. Lumberjacks at upper left. Portrait W. Todd at lower right. Back: Green. Payable by Z. Chipman or at Bank of New York, payable in U. S. funds.			
a. With text: *TO Z. CHIPMAN.*	600.	1500.	—
b. With text: *TO THE BANK OF NEW YORK.*	600.	1500.	—

	Good	Fine	XF
S1427 5 Dollars 1.5.1863. Black on green underprint. Indians by campfire, canoe at lower left. Portrait W. Todd at lower right. Back: Green. Payable by Z. Chipman or at Bank of New York, payable in U. S. funds.			
a. With text: *TO Z. CHIPMAN.*	600.	1500.	—
b. With text: *TO THE BANK OF NEW YORK.*	600.	1500.	—

1892 Issue

	VG	VF	UNC
S1428 5 Dollars 2.1.1892; 2.1.1903. Black on green underprint. Lighthouse and ships at lower left, reclining woman at center, steam train at lower right. Back: Green. Printer: BABNC and ABNC.	1250.	2000.	—
S1429 10 Dollars 2.1.1892; 2.1.1903. Black on green underprint. Sailing ships at lower left, men unloading railroad boxcar at top center, seated Britannia with Indian girl at lower right. Back: Green. Printer: BABNC and ABNC.	1250.	2000.	—
S1430 20 Dollars 2.1.1892; 2.1.1903. Black on green underprint. Allegorical woman at left, farmer watering livestock at center, sailor at right. Back: Green. Printer: BABNC and ABNC. Face proof.	—	Unc	500.

Sovereign Bank of Canada

1902-07 Issue

		Good	Fine	XF
S1431	**5 Dollars**			
	1902-05. Black on green and yellow-green underprint. Bank seal at left, portrait King Edward VII at lower center. Signature varieties. Back: Black and multicolor. Bank crest at center. Printer: ABNC.			
	a. Red overprint: *M M.* 1.5.1902.	500.	1250.	3000.
	b. 1.5.1905.	500.	1250.	3000.
S1432	**10 Dollars**			
	1902-07. Black on red-orange and yellow-green underprint. Seated Britannia with lion and shield at center. Signature varieties. Back: Black and multicolor. Bank crest at center. Printer: ABNC.			
	a. 1.5.1905.	750.	2000.	—
	s1. Red overprint: *M.* Specimen. 1.5.1902.	—	Unc	1250.
	s2. Specimen. 1.5.1907.	—	Unc	1250.
S1433	**20 Dollars**			
	1.5.1907. Black on green underprint. Bank seal at left, portrait King Edward VII at right. Signature varieties. Back: Orange. Printer: ABNC. Specimen.	—	Unc	1000.
S1434	**50 Dollars**			
	1.5.1906; 1.5.1907. Black on blue and yellow-green underprint. Portrait King Edward VII at left. Signature varieties. Back: Green. Bank building at center. Printer: ABNC. Specimen.	—	Unc	1000.

Standard Bank of Canada

1876-81 Issue

		Good	Fine	XF
S1435	**4 Dollars**			
	1.11.1876. Black on green underprint. Portrait T. Gibbs at lower left, steam train, ships dockside at top center right. Signature varieties. Back: Green. Printer: BABNC.	600.	1750.	—
S1436	**5 Dollars**			
	1.11.1876. Black on green underprint. Jacques Cartier sighting land at left, T. Gibbs at lower right. Signature varieties. Back: Green. Printer: BABNC.	750.	2000.	—
S1437	**10 Dollars**			
	1.11.1876. Black on green underprint. Farmer haying cows at upper left, T. Gibbs at lower right. Signature varieties. Back: Green. Printer: BABNC.	750.	2000.	—
S1438	**50 Dollars**			
	1.12.1881. Black on green underprint. T. Gibbs at lower left, woman with telegraph at center. Signature varieties. Back: Green. Printer: BABNC. Face proof.	—	Unc	1000.

1890 Issue

		Good	Fine	XF
S1439	**10 Dollars**			
	1.12.1890. Black on green underprint. Farmer haying cows at upper left, T. Gibbs at lower right. Signature varieties. Back: Green. Printer: BABNC.	500.	1500.	—
S1440	**50 Dollars**			
	1.12.1890. Black on green underprint. T. Gibbs at lower left, woman with telegraph at center. Signature varieties. Back: Green. Printer: BABNC.	500.	1500.	—

1891 Issue

		Good	Fine	XF
S1441	**5 Dollars**			
	1.5.1891. Two allegorical women ("Wisdom & Strength") at left, oval portrait woman ("Innocence") at upper center, seated woman with flower basket ("Rose") at lower right. Signature varieties. Back: Bank seal at left, standing Justice with royal shield at center. Printer: ABNC.			
	a. Black on yellow and blue underprint. Back brown.	500.	1500.	—
	b. Black on yellow and green underprint. Back green.	500.	1500.	—
	c. Black on yellow and red underprint. Back green.	500.	1500.	—
	d. Black on yellow and red underprint. Back red.	200.	750.	1500.
	s. Specimen.	—	—	—

1900 Issue

		Good	Fine	XF
S1442	**10 Dollars**			
	1.5.1900. Black on gold underprint. Farmer haying cows at upper left, W. Cowan at lower right. Signature varieties. Back: Green. Printer: BABNC.	300.	900.	2000.

1914 Issue

		Good	Fine	XF
S1443	**5 Dollars**			
	1914-19. Black on orange underprint. Portrait laureate allegorical woman at center. Signature varieties. Back: Green. Bank crest at center. Printer: ABNC.			
	a. 2.1.1914; 2.1.1918.	125.	250.	—
	b. 2.1.1919.	50.00	125.	350.
	s. As b. Specimen.	—	—	—
S1444	**10 Dollars**			
	1914-19. Black on olive underprint. Portrait W. F. Cowan at center. Signature varieties. Back: Brown. Bank crest at center. Printer: ABNC.			
	a. 2.1.1914; 2.1.1918.	125.	400.	1000.
	b. 2.1.1919.	125.	400.	1000.

		Good	Fine	XF
S1445	**20 Dollars**			
	1914-19. Black on green underprint. Portrait two allegorical women at center. Signature varieties. Back: Olive. Bank crest at center. Printer: ABNC.			
	a. 2.1.1914; 2.1.1918.	200.	600.	1500.
	b. 2.1.1919.	250.	750.	1750.

		Good	Fine	XF
S1446	**100 Dollars**			
	1914-18. Black on yellow-brown underprint. Portrait W. F. Cowan at center. Signature varieties. Back: Brown-violet. Bank crest at center. Printer: ABNC.			
	a. 2.1.1914.	600.	1750.	—
	b. 2.1.1918. Proof	—	Unc	600.

1924 Issue

	Good	Fine	XF
S1447 10 Dollars 2.1.1924. Seated Britannia at lower center, statues of Industry at left, Agriculture at right. Back: Green. Printer: BABNC.			
a. Black on yellow-brown underprint.	75.00	225.	500.
b. Black on yellow-orange underprint.	50.00	150.	300.

Sterling Bank of Canada

1906 Issue

	Good	Fine	XF
S1448 5 Dollars 25.4.1906. Black on green underprint. Steam ships, sailboats at upper center. Signature varieties. Back: Green. Royal crest at center. Printer: BABNC.	350.	1000.	2000.
S1449 10 Dollars 25.4.1906. Black on yellow and yellow-orange underprint. Seated woman with flag at left. Signature varieties. Back: Green. Seated Britannia at center, Printer: BABNC.	250.	650.	1200.
S1450 20 Dollars 25.4.1906. Black on green underprint. Lion and lioness at right. Signature varieties. Back: Green. Printer: BABNC.	750.	2500.	—
S1451 50 Dollars 25.4.1906. Black on blue underprint. Allegorical woman with shield, Parliament building in background at center. Signature varieties. Back: Green. Printer: BABNC. Face proof.	—	Unc	750.

1914 Issue

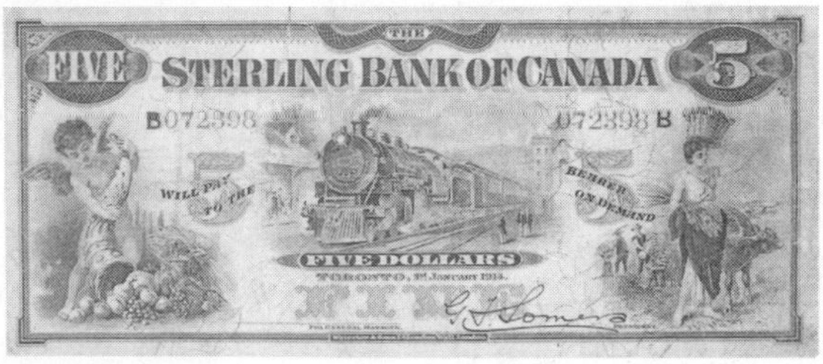

	VG	VF	UNC
S1452 5 Dollars 1.1.1914. Black on yellow underprint. Cherub emptying cornucopia at lower left, steam passenger train at center, farmers harvesting, woman with basket on head at lower right. Signature varieties. Back: Orange-red. Portrait Princess Patricia of Connaught at center. Printer: W&S.	500.	1000.	2750.

1921 Issue

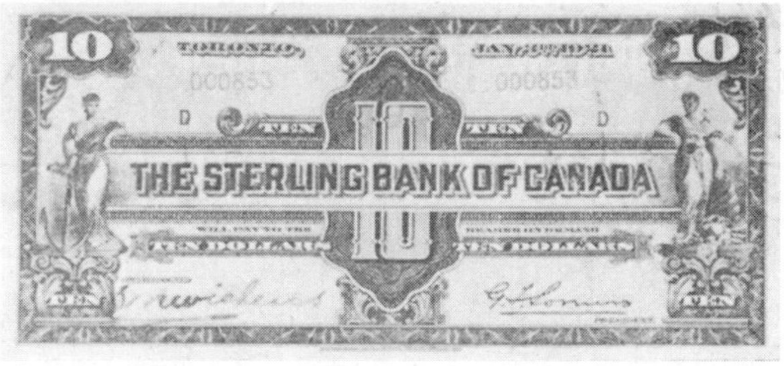

	VG	VF	UNC
S1453 10 Dollars 3.1.1921. Black on gold underprint. Standing allegorical woman with anchor at left, standing allegorical woman with cornucopia at right. Signature varieties. Back: Blue. Large *10* between Indian and woodsman at center. Printer: BABNC.	650.	1250.	—

Summerside Bank of Prince Edward Island

1866 Issue

	Good	Fine	XF
S1454 1 Dollar = 4 Shillings-2 Pence 2.4.1866. Partially engraved. Black. Three children with colt at lower left, farmer by milkmaid milking cow at center, boy with sheep at lower right. Back: Brown. Printer: ABNC.	1000.	3000.	—
S1455 2 Dollars = 8 Shillings-4 Pence 18xx. Partially engraved. Black. Shipbuilding at lower left, royal crest at center, dog by safe at lower right. Back: Brown. Printer: ABNC. Face proof.	—	Unc	1000.
S1456 8 Dollars = 33 Shillings-4 Pence 22.1.1866. PArtially engraved. Black. Cooper making barrels at lower left, sailing ships at upper center, sailing ships at lower right. Back: Brown. Printer: ABNC.	—	—	—

1872 Issue

	Good	Fine	XF
S1457 1 Dollar 1.2.1872. Fully engraved. Black. Three children with colt at lower left, farmer by milkmaid milking cow at center, boy with sheep at lower right. Green word protector. Back: Brown. Green word protector. Printer: ABNC.			
a. Issued note without red overprint.	2000.	6000.	—
b. Red overprint: *CANADA CURRENCY* at both ends.	2000.	6000.	—
S1459 2 Dollars 1.2.1872. Fully engraved. Black. Shipbuilding at lower left, royal crest at center, dog by safe at lower right. Green word protector. Back: Brown. Green word protector. Printer: ABNC.	2000.	6000.	—
S1460 5 Dollars 1.2.1872. Fully engraved. Black. Sailor with lion, bales and flag at lower left, paddle wheel steamer at upper center. Seated Britannia with shield with large *5* at lower right. Green word protector. Back: Brown. Green word protector. Printer: ABNC.	2500.	6500.	—
S1461 10 Dollars 1.2.1872. Fully engraved. Black. Cooper making barrels at lower left, sailing ships at upper center, sailing ships at lower right. Green word protector. Back: Brown. Green word protector. Printer: ABNC.	2500.	6500.	—

1884-1900 Issues

	Good	Fine	XF
S1462 1 Dollar 1.12.1884. Black on green underprint. Farm girl with cow and calf at lower left, boy watering horse ("Drinking at the Brook") at center, sailors on lookout ("Looking Out") lower right. Back: Green. Printer: BABNC.	2000.	6000.	—
S1463 1 Dollar 1.12.1884. Black on green underprint. Farm girl with cow and calf at lower left, boy watering horse ("Drinking at the Brook") at center, sailors on lookout ("Looking Out") lower right. Uniface. Printer: BABNC.	2000.	6000.	—
S1464 5 Dollars 1.7.1891. Black on green underprint. Farm tools at lower left, fishermen and boats at upper center, seated Britannia with shield with large *5* at lower right. Back: Green. Three horses' heads at left. Printer: BABNC. Face proof.	—	Unc	1000.
S1465 10 Dollars 1.9.1900. Black on green underprint. Seated woman with cornucopia at lower left, sheep grazing at upper center, steamships at right. Back: Green. Printer: BABNC. Face proof.	—	Unc	1000.

Traders Bank of Canada

1885; 1886 Issue

	Good	Fine	XF
S1466 5 Dollars 2.7.1885. Black on green underprint. Farmer with cattle at center. Portrait of H. S. Strathy at left, portrait A. Manning at right. Signature varieties. Back: Green. Printer: BABNC. Face proof.	—	Unc	600.
S1467 10 Dollars 2.7.1885. Black on green underprint. Allegorical figures with large ornate *X* at lower center. Portrait of H. S. Strathy at left, portrait A. Manning at right. Signature varieties. Back: Green. Printer: BABNC. Face proof.	—	Unc	600.
S1468 50 Dollars 1.3.1886. Black on green underprint. Allegorical women with globe at center. Portrait of H. S. Strathy at left, portrait A. Manning at right. Signature varieties. Back: Green. Printer: BABNC. Face proof.	—	Unc	600.
S1469 100 Dollars 1.3.1886. Black on green underprint. Ships dockside at center. Portrait of H. S. Strathy at left, portrait A. Manning at right. Signature varieties. Back: Green. Printer: BABNC. Face proof.	—	Unc	600.

1890; 1903 Issue

	Good	Fine	XF
S1470 5 Dollars 2.1.1893. Black on green underprint. Farmer with cattle at center. Portrait of H. S. Strathy at left, portrait W. Bell at right. Signature varieties. Back: Green. Printer: BABNC.	300.	1000.	2250.
S1471 20 Dollars 2.1.1890. Black on green underprint. Portrait H. S. Strathy at left, seated allegorical woman with machinery at center, W. Bell at right. Signature varieties. Back: Green. Printer: BABNC. Proof with face and back on one card.	—	Unc	600.

NOTICE

Readers with unlisted dates, signature varieties, etc., are invited to submit photocopies or scans of their notes to:
Standard Catalog of World Paper Money,
700 East State St. Iola, WI 54990-0001,
E-Mail: george.cuhaj@fwmedia.com.

1897; 1907 Issue

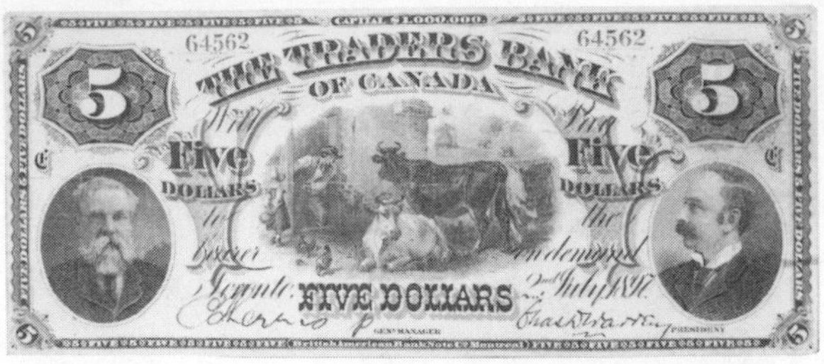

		VG	VF	UNC
S1472 5 Dollars	2.1.1897; 2.7.1897; 1.11.1907. Black on green underprint. Farmer with cattle at center. Portrait of H. S. Strathy at lower left, portrait C. D. Warren at lower right. Signature varieties. Printer: BABNC.	450.	900.	2500.
S1473 10 Dollars	2.1.1897; 2.7.1897; 1.11.1907. Black on green underprint. Allegorical figures with large ornate *X* at lower center. Portrait of H. S. Strathy at lower left, portrait C. D. Warren at lower right. Signature varieties. Printer: BABNC.	600.	1250.	—

Catalog #	Description	Good	Fine	XF
S1474 20 Dollars	1.11.1907. Black on green underprint. Portrait H. S. Strathy at left, seated allegorical woman with machinery at center, C. D. Warren at lower right. Signature varieties. Printer: BABNC. Face proof.	—	Unc	500.
S1475 50 Dollars	2.1.1897; 2.7.1897. Black on green underprint. Allegorical women with globe at center. Portrait of H. S. Strathy at lower left, portrait C. D. Warren at lower right. Signature varieties. Printer: BABNC. Face proof.	—	Unc	500.
S1476 100 Dollars	2.1.1897. Black on green underprint. Ships dockside at center. Portrait of H. S. Strathy at lower left, portrait C. D. Warren at lower right. Signature varieties. Printer: BABNC. Face proof.	—	Unc	500.

1909 Issue

Catalog #	Description	Good	Fine	XF
S1477 5 Dollars	2.1.1909. Black on yellow and green underprint. Sailing ships dockside at center. Signature varieties. Back: Green. Bank building at center. Printer: ABNC and BABNC. Face proof.	—	Unc	500.

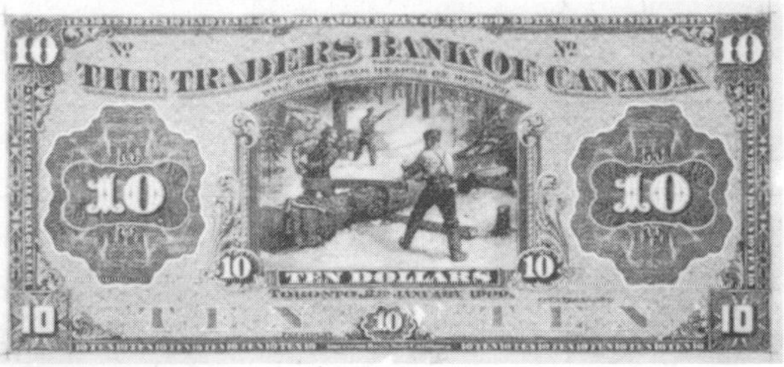

Catalog #	Description	Good	Fine	XF
S1478 10 Dollars	2.1.1909. Black on multicolor underprint. Woodsmen cutting logs at center. Signature varieties. Back: Green, red and brown. Bank building at center. Printer: ABNC and BABNC.	500.	1500.	4500.
S1479 20 Dollars	2.1.1909. Black on multicolor underprint. Steam passenger train at station at center. Signature varieties. Back: Brown, green and red. Bank building at center. Printer: ABNC or BABNC. Face proof.	—	Unc	500.
S1480 50 Dollars	2.1.1909. Black on multicolor underprint. Sailing ship in stormy sea at center. Signature varieties. Back: Blue, brown and purple. Bank building at center. Printer: ABNC and BABNC. Face proof.	—	Unc	500.
S1481 100 Dollars	2.1.1909. Black on multicolor underprint. Cowboy rounding up cattle at center. Signature varieties. Back: Orange and multicolor. Bank building at center. Printer: ABNC and BABNC. Face proof.	—	Unc	500.

1910 Issue

Catalog #	Description	Good	Fine	XF
S1482 5 Dollars	1.11.1910. Black on red, green and purple underprint. Farmer reaping grain with horses at center. Signature varieties. Back: Olive on blue and brown underprint. Bank building at center. Printer: ABNC.	500.	1500.	3000.

Union Bank of Canada

1886 Issue

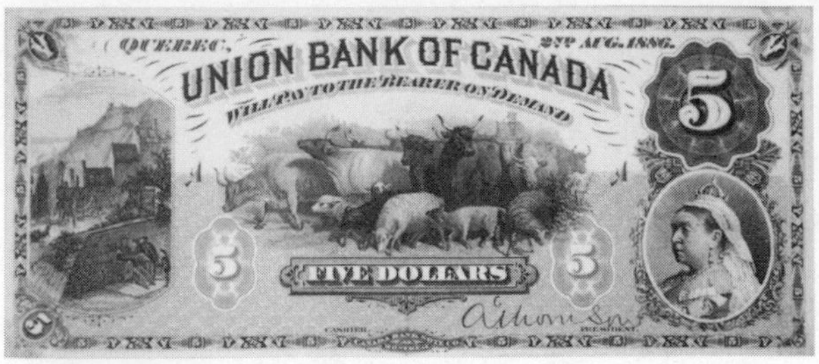

Catalog #	Description	Good	Fine	XF
S1483 5 Dollars	2.8.1886. Black on ochre underprint. Hillside village scene at left, livestock at center, portrait Queen Victoria at lower right. Signature varieties. Back: Green. Facing griffins at left and right. Printer: Canada Bank Note Co. Face proof.	500.	1500.	—
S1484 10 Dollars	2.8.1886. Black on ochre underprint. Quebec Citadel at left, farmer reaping grain with horses at center, portrait Queen Victoria at lower right. Signature varieties. Back: Blue. Facing griffins at left and right. Printer: Canada Bank Note Co.	500.	1500.	—
S1485 20 Dollars	2.8.1886. Black on red-orange underprint. Farmers plowing with horses at center. Signature varieties. Back: Brown. Printer: Canada Bank Note Co. Face proof.	—	Unc	500.
S1486 50 Dollars	2.8.1886. Black on red-orange underprint. Raphael's "angel" (without wings) at lower left, Quebec Citadel at right. Slgnature varieties. Back: Brown. Printer: Canada Bank NOte Co. Face proof.	—	Unc	500.
S1487 100 Dollars	2.8.1886. Black on red-orange underprint. Standing allegorical woman at left and at right. Signature varieties. Back: Brown. Printer: Canada Bank Note Co. Face proof.	—	Unc	500.

1893 Issue

Catalog #	Description	Good	Fine	XF
S1488 5 Dollars	1.6.1893. Black on green underprint. Sailing ship at lower left. Bank crest at center, portrait A. Thomson at lower right. Signature varieties. Printer: BABNC.	200.	650.	1500.
S1489 10 Dollars	1.6.1893. Black on green underprint. Farm tools at lower left. Bank crest at center, portrait A. Thomson at lower right. Signature varieties. Printer: BABNC.	200.	650.	1500.
S1490 20 Dollars	1.6.1893. Black on green underprint. Three horse heads at left. Bank crest at center, portrait A. Thomson at lower right. Signature varieties. Printer: BABNC. Face proof.	—	Unc	600.
S1491 50 Dollars	1.6.1893. Black on green underprint. Bank crest at center, portrait A. Thomson at lower right. Signature varieties. Printer: BABNC. Face proof.	—	Unc	600.
S1492 100 Dollars	1.6.1893. Black on green underprint. Bank crest at center, portrait A. Thomson at lower right. Signature varieties. Printer: BABNC. Face proof.	—	Unc	600.

1903; 1907 Quebec Branch Issue

Catalog #	Description	Good	Fine	XF
S1493 5 Dollars	1903-07. Black on multicolor underprint. Farmers harvesting with horse drawn reapers at center. Signature varieties. Back: Bank crest at center. Printer: ABNC.			
	a. 1.6.1903. Red serial #.	250.	750.	1500.
	b. 1.6.1903. Blue serial #.	250.	750.	1500.
S1493A 5 Dollars	1.6.1907. Black on various shades of green underprint. Farmers harvesting with horse drawn reapers at center. Signature varieties. Back: Bank crest at center. Printer: ABNC.	150.	450.	900.
S1494 10 Dollars	1.6.1903; 1.6.1907. Black on multicolor underprint. Cowboy roping steer at center. Signature varieties. Back: Bank crest at center. Printer: ABNC.	300.	1000.	2000.

1912 Winnipeg Issue

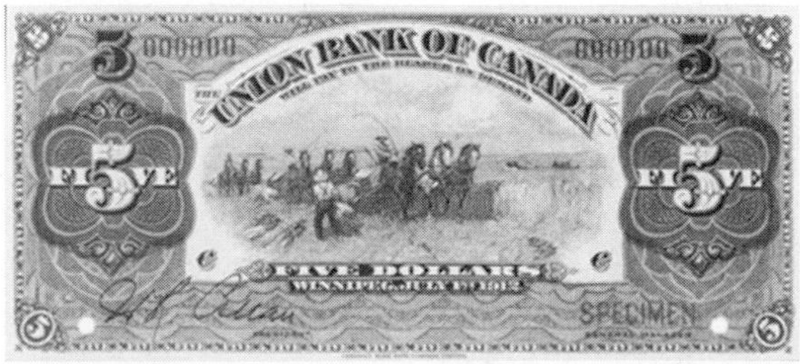

		VG	VF	UNC
S1495 5 Dollars	1.7.1912. Farmers harvesting with horse drawn reapers at center. Signature varieties. Printer: ABNC or CBNC.			
	a. Black on multicolor underprint.	125.	250.	600.
	b. Black on dark green and multicolor underprint. Left hand signature J. Galight. Blue overprint: *NORTHWEST TERRITORIES.*	1250.	2500.	—

VG VF UNC

c. Black on dark green and multicolor underprint. Left hand signature W. R. Allan. Without overprint.	100.	250.	600.
s. Specimen.	—	—	—

S1496 10 Dollars	VG	VF	UNC
1.7.1912. Black on multicolor underprint. Cowboy roping steer at center. Signature varieties. Printer: ABNC or CBNC.			
a. Issued note.	100.	250.	600.
s. Specimen.	—	—	—

1907 Quebec Issue

	Good	Fine	XF
S1497 20 Dollars 1.6.1907. Black on green underprint. Farmers plowing with horses at center. Back: Brown. Printer: BABNC. Face proof.	—	Unc	500.
S1498 50 Dollars 1.6.1907. Black on green underprint. Young girl with feather at lower left, Quebec Citadel at right. Back: Brown. Printer: BABNC. Face proof.	—	Unc	500.
S1499 100 Dollars 1.6.1907. Black on green underprint. Standing allegorical woman at left and at right. Back: Brown. Printer: BABNC. Face proof.	—	Unc	500.

1912 Winnipeg Issue

	VG	VF	UNC
S1500 20 Dollars 1.7.1912. Black on green underprint. Farmers plowing with horses at center. Back: Green.	600.	1250.	—
S1501 50 Dollars 1.7.1912. Black on green underprint. Young girl with feather at lower left, Quebec Citadel at right. Back: Green.	850.	1750.	—
S1502 5 Dollars 1.7.1912. Black on green underprint. Standing allegorical woman at left and at right. Back: Green.	1250.	2250.	—

Quebec

1921 Issue

S1503 5 Dollars	Good	Fine	XF
1.7.1921. Black on multicolor underprint. Portrait J. W. Hamilton at left, portrait W. R. Allan at right. Back: Green. Printer: ABNC.			
a. Issued note.	125.	400.	900.
p. Face proof.	—	Unc	500.

S1504 10 Dollars	Good	Fine	XF
1.7.1921. Black on multicolor underprint. Portrait J. W. Hamilton at left, portrait W. R. Allan at right. Back: Red. Printer: ABNC.			
a. Issued note.	75.00	200.	500.
p. Face proof.	—	Unc	500.
S1505 20 Dollars 1.7.1921. Black on multicolor underprint. Portrait J. W. Hamilton at left, portrait W. R. Allan at right. Back: Blue. Printer: ABNC.			
p. Face proof.	—	Unc	500.
s. Specimen.	—	Unc	900.
S1506 50 Dollars 1.7.1921. Black on multicolor underprint. Portrait J. W. Hamilton at left, portrait W. R. Allan at right. Back: Brown. Printer: ABNC.			
p. Face proof.	—	Unc	500.
s. Specimen.	—	Unc	900.
S1507 100 Dollars 1.7.1921. Black on multicolor underprint. Portrait J. W. Hamilton at left, portrait W. R. Allan at right. Back: Olive. Printer: ABNC.			
p. Face proof.	—	Unc	500.
s. Specimen.	—	Unc	900.

Union Bank of Halifax

1861 Issue

S1511 5 Dollars	Good	Fine	XF
1.9.1861; 18.9.1861. Black. Cargo at upper and lower left, two seated allegorical woman at top center with small portrait Queen Victoria below. Red word protector. Back: Red-brown. Medallic portrait Queen Victoria and Prince Albert at center. Printer: REH & E.	1250.	3500.	—

1870 Issue

	Good	Fine	XF
S1514 4 Dollars 1.6.1870. Black on green underprint. Farmer plowing with horses at top center, small flower below. Back: Green. Printer: BABNC. Face proof.	—	Unc	600.
S1515 5 Dollars 1.6.1870. Black on green underprint. Bank building at top center, small flower below. Back: Green. Printer: BABNC. Face proof.	—	Unc	500.

1871; 1904 Issues

	Good	Fine	XF
S1516 4 Dollars 1.7.1871. Black on green underprint. Steam sailing ship at upper left, dog's head at lower right. Back: Green. Printer: BABNC. Face proof.	—	Unc	500.

S1517 5 Dollars	Good	Fine	XF
1871-1909. Black on green underprint. Bank building at center. Back: Green. Fishermen at center. Printer: BABNC.			
a. 1.7.1886; 1.5.1909.	1250.	3500.	—
p. Face proof. 1.7.1871; 1.7.1882; 1.4.1900.	—	Unc	500.
S1518 10 Dollars 1871-1900. Supported royal arms at upper center. Back: Fishermen at center. Printer: BABNC.			
a. Black on ochre underprint. 1.4.1900.	1000.	3250.	—
p1. Black on green underprint. Face proof. 1.7.1871.	—	Unc	500.
p2. As a. Face proof.	—	Unc	500.
S1519 20 Dollars 1871-1900. Seated woman on deck at lower left, fishermen shipboard at center, anchor at lower right. Back: Boy with fish and dog at center. Printer: BABNC.			
p1. Black on green underprint. Face proof. 1.7.1871.	—	Unc	500.
p2. Black on ochre underprint. Face proof. 1.4.1900.	—	Unc	600.
S1520 50 Dollars 1.9.1904. Black on blue underprint. Lighthouse view in Trinidad at left, Indian and sailor with shield at center right. Printer: BABNC.	—	Unc	500.
S1521 100 Dollars 1.9.1904. Black on brown underprint. Fisherman and wife looking at ocean, portrait of sailor at center right. Printer: BABNC.	—	Unc	600.

Union Bank of Lower Canada

1866 Issue

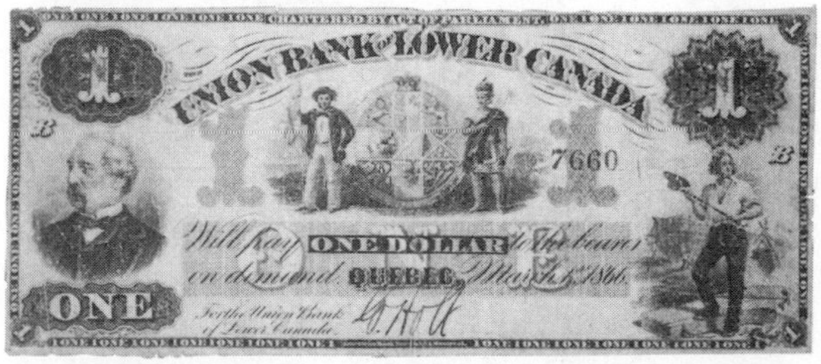

S1521A 1 Dollar	Good	Fine	XF
1.3.1866. Man at left, shipbuilder with broadaxe at lower right. Signature varieties. Printer: ABNC.			
a. Black on green underprint. with green word protectors and numeral. Large red overprint: *S S*, blue overprint: *OTTAWA* or *MONTREAL* twice.	500.	1250.	—
b. Black with green word protector. Large red overprint: *S S*, also with blue overprint: *THREE RIVERS* twice.	500.	1500.	—

S1521B 2 Dollars

1.3.1866. Anchor at lower left, man at right. Signature varieties. Printer: ABNC.

	Good	Fine	XF
a. Black on green underprint. with green word and numeral protectors. Large red overprint: *S S*, blue overprint: *OTTAWA* or *MONTREAL*. twice.	750.	2250.	—
b. Black with green word protector on face. Large red overprint: *S S*, also with blue overprint: *THREE RIVERS* twice.	600.	1500.	—

S1521C 4 Dollars

	Good	Fine	XF
1.3.1866. Black on green underprint. Green word and numeral protectors. Sailors dock side at lower left, man at lower right. Signature varieties. Overprint: Large red: *S S*, blue: *OTTAWA* or *MONTREAL* twice. Printer: ABNC.	750.	2250.	—

S1521D 5 Dollars

	Good	Fine	XF
1.3.1866. Black on green underprint. Green word and numeral protectors. Man at left, sailors on lookout at lower right. Signature varieties. Overprint: Large red: *S S*, blue: *OTTAWA* or *MONTREAL* twice. Printer: ABNC.	750.	2250.	—

1870-71 Issue

#S1521E-S1521J Red ovpt: *MONTREAL* twice.

S1521E 4 Dollars

	Good	Fine	XF
1.9.1870. Black on green underprint. Portrait Queen Victoria at lower left, sailors dockside at lower right. Canadian arms between man with flag and Indian at center. Signature varieties. Back: Green. Overprint: Red: *MONTREAL* twice. Printer: BABNC.	600.	1500.	—

S1521F 5 Dollars

	Good	Fine	XF
1.8.1871. Black on green underprint. Sailors on lookout at lower left, woman supported by two porpoises at lower right. Canadian arms between man with flag and Indian at center. Signature varieties. Back: Green. Overprint: Red: *MONTREAL* twice. Printer: BABNC.	600.	1500.	—

S1521G 10 Dollars

	Good	Fine	XF
1.12.1872. Black on green underprint. Seated allegorical woman with flag dockside at lower left, sailor boy climbing rope ladder at lower right. Canadian arms between man with flag and Indian at center. Signature varieties. Back: Green. Overprint: Red: *MONTREAL* twice. Printer: BABNC. Face proof.	—	Unc	600.

S1521H 20 Dollars

	Good	Fine	XF
1.9.1870. Black on green underprint. Canadian arms between man with flag and Indian at center. Signature varieties. Back: Green. Overprint: Red: *MONTREAL* twice. Printer: BABNC.	500.	1500.	—

S1521I 50 Dollars

	Good	Fine	XF
1.12.1871. Black on green underprint. Canadian arms between man with flag and Indian at center. Signature varieties. Back: Green. Overprint: Red: *MONTREAL* twice. Printer: BABNC. Face proof.	—	Unc	500.

S1521J 100 Dollars

	Good	Fine	XF
1.12.1871. Black on green underprint. Canadian arms between man with flag and Indian at center. Signature varieties. Back: Green. Overprint: Red: *MONTREAL* twice. Printer: BABNC. Face proof.	—	Unc	500.

Union Bank of Prince Edward Island

1864-65 Issue

S1522 1 Dollar = 4 Shillings-2 Pence

	Good	Fine	XF
18xx. Partially engraved. Black with green word protector. Sailors dockside at lower left, lion with shield at center, seated woman with sheep at lower right. Back: Black with green word protector. Printer: ABNC. Face proof.	—	Unc	2500.

S1523 2 Dollars = 8 Shillings-4 Pence

	Good	Fine	XF
1.6.1864. Partially engraved. Black with green *TWO DOLLARS* protector. Two children with sheaves at lower left, supported royal arms at center, sailor at lower right. Back: Black with green *TWO DOLLARS* protector. Printer: ABNC.	1000.	2750.	—

S1524 5 Dollars = 20 Shillings-10 Pence

	Good	Fine	XF
2.1.1865. Partially engraved. Black with green *5 FIVE 5* protector. St. George slaying dragon at lower left, seated milkmaid with cows at upper center, steam sailing ship at lower right. Back: Black with green *5 FIVE 5* protector. Printer: ABNC.	1000.	2750.	—

S1525 20 Dollars = 4 Pounds-3 Shillings-4 Pence

18xx. Partially engraved. Black with green word protector. Portrait Princess of Wales at lower left, P.E.I. arms at top center, Prince of Wales at lower right. Back: Black with green word protector. Printer: ABNC.

	Good	Fine	XF
a. Issued note.	1500.	4000.	—
p. Face proof.	—	Unc	900.

1872 Issue

S1526 1 Dollar

1.1.1872. Fully engraved. Black. Sailors dockside at lower left, lion with shield at center, seated woman with sheep at lower right. Green word protector. Back: Green word protector. Printer: ABNC.

	Good	Fine	XF
a. Issued note without overprint.	750.	2250.	—
b. Red overprint: *CANADA CURRENCY* twice.	750.	2250.	—

#S1527 *Deleted*. See #S1526b.

S1528 2 Dollars

	Good	Fine	XF
1.1.1872. Fully engraved. Black. Two children with sheaves at lower left, supported royal arms at center, sailor at lower right. Green word protector. Back: Green word protector. Printer: ABNC.	750.	2250.	—

S1529 5 Dollars

	Good	Fine	XF
1.1.1872. Fully engraved. Black. St. George slaying dragon at lower left, seated milkmaid with cows at upper center, steam sailing ship at lower right. Green word protector. Back: Green word protector. Printer: ABNC. Face proof.	—	Unc	600.

S1530 20 Dollars

1.1.1872. Fully engraved. Black. Portrait Princess of Wales at lower left, P.E.I. arms at top center, Prince of Wales at lower right. Green word protector. Back: Green word protector. Printer: ABNC.

	Good	Fine	XF
a. Issued note.	900.	2750.	—
p. Face proof.	—	Unc	900.

1875 Issue

S1531 1 Dollar

	Good	Fine	XF
1.3.1875. Black on green underprint. Codfish at lower left, steam locomotive at center, seals at lower right. Overprint: *U* upper left, *B* upper right. Printer: BABNC.	600.	1750.	—

S1532 2 Dollars

1875-77. Black on green underprint. River pilot at lower left, dog on strong box at upper center, woman with sheaf at lower right. Overprint: *U* upper left, *B* upper right. Printer: BABNC.

	Good	Fine	XF
a. 1.3.1875.	900.	2500.	—
p. Face proof. 1877.	—	Unc	500.

S1533 5 Dollars

1875-77. Black on green underprint. St. George slaying dragon at lower left, farm tools and produce at upper center, seated allegorical woman with telescope at lower right. Overprint: *U* upper left, *B* upper right. Printer: BABNC.

	Good	Fine	XF
a. 1.3.1875.	900.	2500.	—
p. Face proof. 1877.	—	Unc	500.

ILLUSTRATIONS

Illustrations of bank notes used throughout this catalog are 42% of the actual size.

United Empire Bank of Canada

1906 Issue

		Good	Fine	XF
S1534 5 Dollars	1.8.1906. Black on green underprint. Seated Britannia between two world globes at center. Signature varieties. Back: Green. Printer: ABNC.	2000.	5750.	—

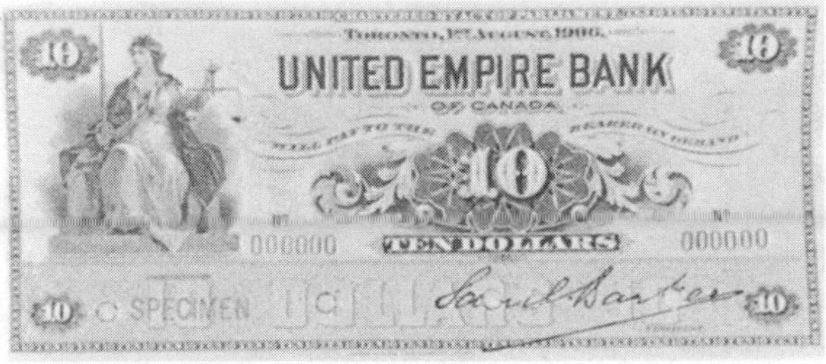

		Good	Fine	XF
S1535 10 Dollars	1.8.1906. Black on yellow-green underprint. Seated Justice at upper left. Signature varieties. Back: Blue. Two beavers at center. Printer: ABNC.	2000.	5750.	—

Western Bank of Canada

1882; 1890 Issue

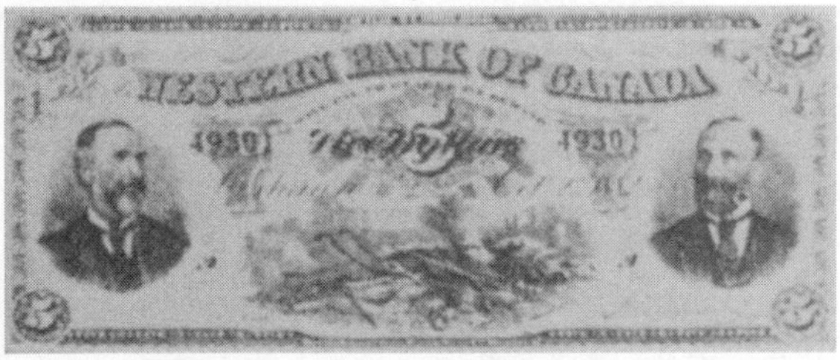

		Good	Fine	XF
S1536 5 Dollars	2.10.1882. Black on green underprint. Farm tools and produce at bottom center. R. S. Hamlin at left, J. Cowan at right. Signature varieties. Printer: BABNC.	750.	2250.	—
S1537 10 Dollars	2.10.1882. Black on green underprint. Shepherdess with sheep at center. R. S. Hamlin at left, J. Cowan at right. Signature varieties. Printer: BABNC.	850.	2500.	—
S1538 20 Dollars	2.7.1890. Black on green underprint. Seated Ceres with cornucopia at center. R. S. Hamlin at left, J. Cowan at right. Signature varieties. Printer: BABNC.	1000.	3000.	—

Weyburn Security Bank

1911 Issue

		Good	Fine	XF
S1539 5 Dollars	3.1.1911. Black on green underprint. Steam passenger train at depot at center. Signature varieties. Back: Green. Printer: ABNC or CBNC.	350.	1000.	2000.
S1540 10 Dollars	3.1.1.1911. Black on yellow-green underprint. Seated allegorical figures at left center and center right. Signature varieties. Back: Green. Printer: ABNC or CBNC.	400.	1250.	2500.

		Good	Fine	XF
S1541 20 Dollars	3.1.1911. Black on orange underprint. Oval portrait woman at center supported by two cherubs. Signature varieties. Back: Orange. Printer: ABNC or CBNC.	—	—	—

Spurious and Expired Banks

The Bank of Acadia

1872 Issue

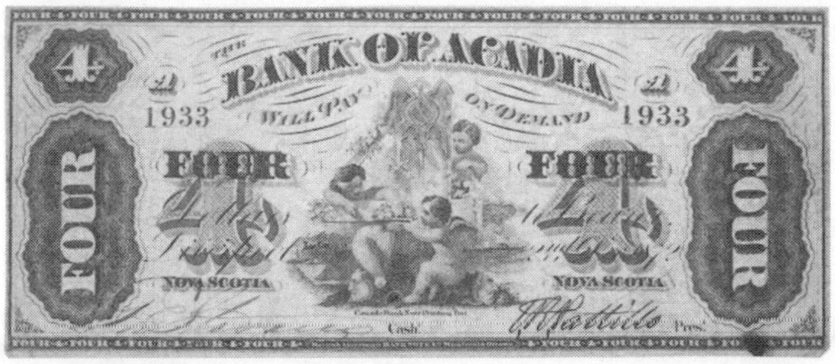

		Good	Fine	XF
S1542 4 Dollars	2.12.1872. Black on green underprint. Cherubs with large ornate *4* at center. Uniface. Printer: BABNC.	200.	500.	1250.
S1543 5 Dollars	2.12.1872. Black on green underprint. Sailing ships at upper left center. Uniface. Printer: BABNC.	250.	600.	1500.
S1544 10 Dollars	2.12.1872. Black on green underprint. Cherubs with large ornate *X* at center. Uniface. Printer: BABNC.	250.	600.	1500.
S1545 20 Dollars	2.12.1872. Black on green underprint. Sailing ship at upper left, paddle wheel steamboat at lower center. Printer: BABNC.	900.	2500.	—

The Accommodation Bank

1837 Spurious Issue

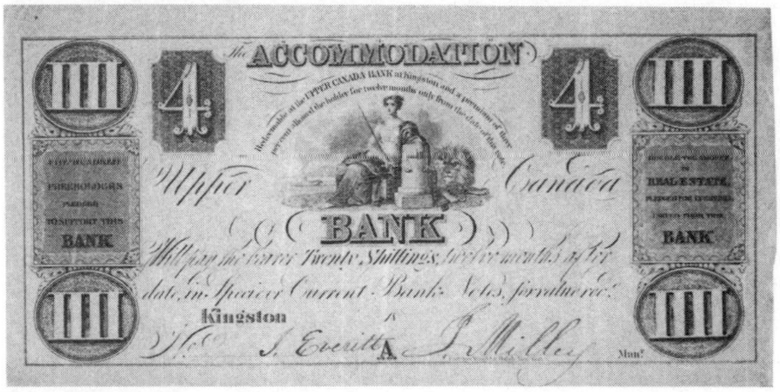

		Good	Fine	XF
S1546 4 Dollars = 20 Shillings	18(37). Black. Seated Justice with lion at center. Uniface. Printer: RWH & Co. Without redeemable clause above Justice. Unsigned remainder without serial # or date.	100.	250.	600.
S1547 4 Dollars = 20 Shillings	18(37). Black. Seated Justice with lion at center. Uniface. Printer: RWH & Co. With redeemable clause above Justice.			
	a. Completed note.	300.	750.	1500.
	r. Remainder without serial # or date.	100.	250.	600.

The Agricultural Bank (Montreal, L.C.)

1841 Issue

		VG	VF	UNC
S1548 1 Dollar	1841-46. Black. Standing Indian at left, farmer plowing with oxen at top center, standing allegorical female at right. Uniface. Printer: Burton and Gurley.	300.	600.	

		VG	VF	UNC
S1549 2 Dollars	1841-46. Black. Farmer with grain by tree at left, seated Agriculture at top center, standing allegorical helmeted woman at right. Uniface. Printer: Burton and Gurley.	300.	600.	—

S1550 3 Dollars	VG	VF	UNC
1841-46. Black. Farm woman with rake at left, seated Agriculture with shield at top center, farmer plowing with oxen at right. Printer: Burton and Gurley.	500.	1000.	—

THE AGRICULTURAL BANK

1834 ISSUE

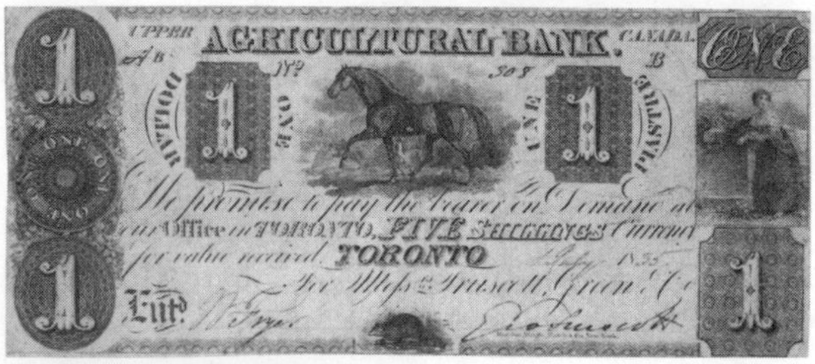

S1551 1 Dollar = 5 Shillings	VG	VF	UNC
1.4.1834; 1.7.1835. Black. Horse at upper center, woman holding sheaf of grain at right. Uniface. Printer: RWH & Co.	40.00	125.	300.

S1552 2 Dollars = 10 Shillings	VG	VF	UNC
8.8.1834-21.9.1937. Black. Farmers with livestock at left and right, beehive, cornucopia, sheaf of grain and spinning wheel at upper center. Uniface. Printer: RWH & Co.			
a. Without clause: *One year after date.*	40.00	125.	300.
b. With additional clause: *One year after date* under Large *2*'s (21.9.1837).	40.00	125.	300.

S1553 4 Dollars = 20 Shillings	VG	VF	UNC
1.4.1833-1.3.1837. Black. Plow at left, seated allegorical woman and Indian holding shield at upper center, sheaf of grain at right. Uniface. Printer: RWH & Co.			
a. Without clause: *One year after date.*	100.	225.	600.
b. With additional clause: *One year after date* (1.3.1837).	100.	225.	600.

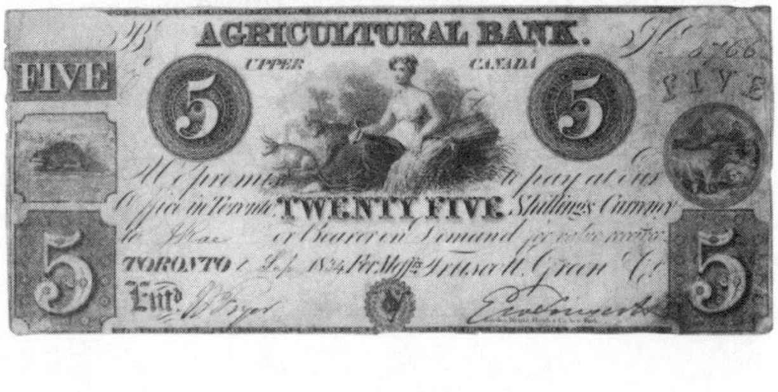

S1554 5 Dollars = 25 Shillings	VG	VF	UNC
8.8.1834-1.12.1834. Black. Beaver at left, seated Agriculture at center, farmer with livestock at right. Uniface. Printer: RWH & Co.	75.00	175.	500.

S1555 10 Dollars = 50 Shillings	VG	VF	UNC
1.1.1834-1.1.1835. Black. Farmers harvesting grain at upper center, portrait King William IV at right. Uniface. Printer: RWH & Co.	500.	1250.	—

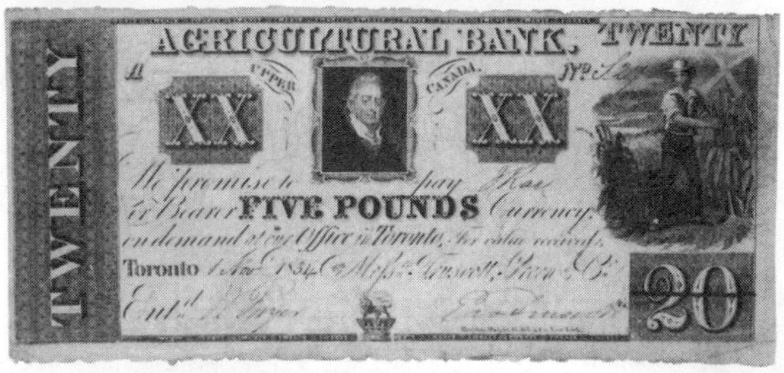

S1556 20 Dollars = 5 Pounds	Good	Fine	XF
1.9.1834; 1.11.1834. Black. Portrait King William IV at upper center, farmer picking corn at upper right. Uniface. Printer: RWH & Co.	600.	1500.	—

1835 ISSUE

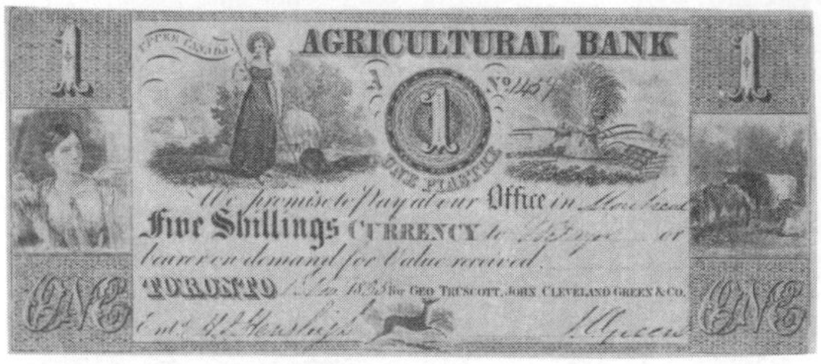

S1557 1 Dollar = 5 Shillings	VG	VF	UNC
1.10.1835; 1.11.1835; 1.12.1835; 1.1.1836. Black. Portrait girl at left, farm woman raking hay at upper left center, sheaf of grain and plow at upper center right, cattle at right, small deer at bottom center. Uniface. Printer: New England Bank Note Comp., Boston. Text: *FOR GEO. TRUSCOTT* engraved at bottom. Hand stamped black: B, red C or black H.	20.00	50.00	175.

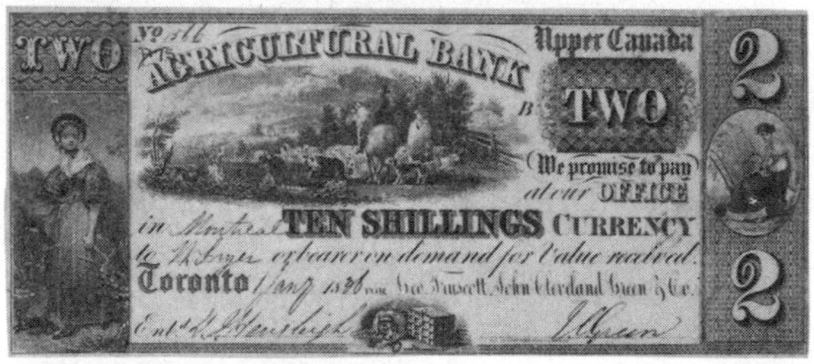

S1558 2 Dollars = 10 Shillings	VG	VF	UNC
1.10.1835-1.1.1836. Black. Milkmaid at left, men with cattle, horse and dog at upper left center, farm woman with sickle at right, small strong box at bottom center. Uniface. Printer: New England Bank Note Comp., Boston. Text: *FOR GEO. TRUSCOTT* engraved at bottom. Hand stamped black: B, red C or black H.	20.00	50.00	175.

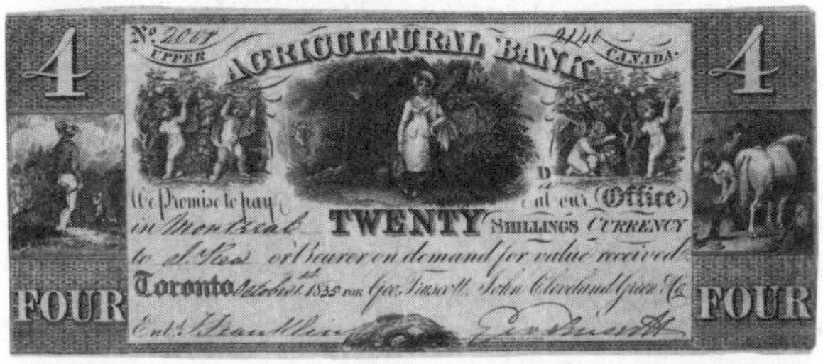

S1559 4 Dollars = 20 Shillings	VG	VF	UNC
1.10.1835-1.11.1836. Black. Boy raking at left, milkmaid between cherubs at center, blacksmith shoeing horse at right, farm produce at bottom center. Uniface. Printer: New England Bank Note Comp., Boston. Text: *FOR GEO. TRUSCOTT* engraved at bottom. Hand stamped black: B, red C or black H.	50.00	100.	250.

S1560 5 Dollars = 25 Shillings

	VG	VF	UNC
1.10.1835-1.1.1836. Black. Female group with seated helmeted Britannia at left, farmers harvesting at upper center, seated Britannia at right, produce at bottom center. Uniface. Printer: New England Bank Note Comp., Boston.	20.00	50.00	175.

1837 Issue

#S1561-S1565 w/ *THE* added to bank name.

S1561 1 Dollar = 5 Shillings

	VG	VF	UNC
1.10.1837. Black. Portrait girl at left, farm woman raking hay at upper left center, sheaf of grain and plow at upper center right, cattle at right, small deer at bottom center. Uniface.	15.00	35.00	100.

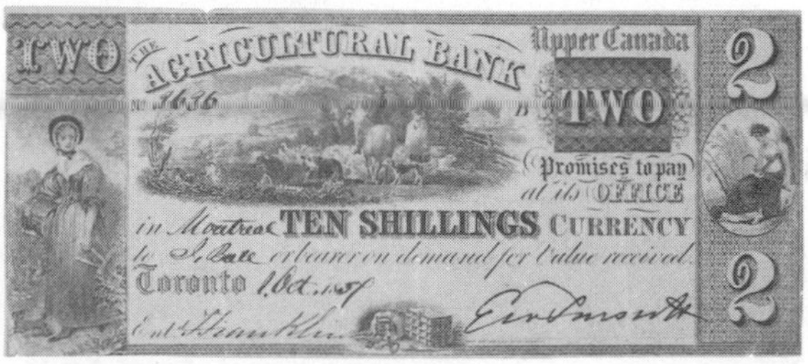

S1562 2 Dollars = 10 Shillings

	VG	VF	UNC
1.10.1837. Black. Milkmaid at left, men with cattle, horse and dog at upper left center, farm woman with sickle at right, small strong box at bottom center. Uniface.	15.00	35.00	100.

S1563 4 Dollars = 20 Shillings

	VG	VF	UNC
1.10.1837. Black. Boy raking at left, milkmaid between cherubs at center, blacksmith shoeing horse at right, farm produce at bottom center. Uniface.	35.00	75.00	125.

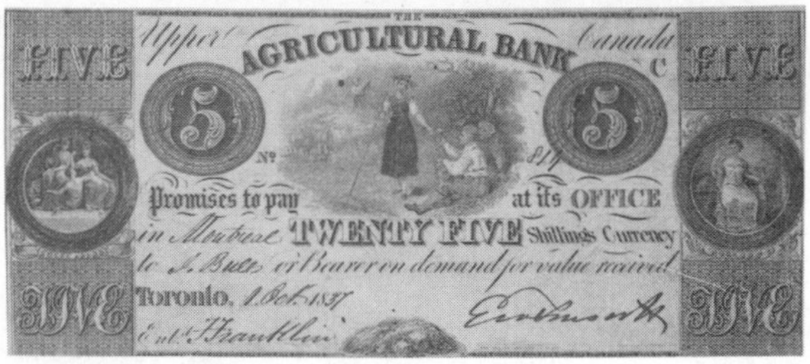

S1564 5 Dollars = 25 Shillings

	VG	VF	UNC
1.10.1837. Black. Female group with seated helmeted Britannia at left, farmers harvesting at upper center, seated Britannia at right, produce at bottom center. Uniface.	15.00	35.00	100.

Arman's Bank

1837 Issue

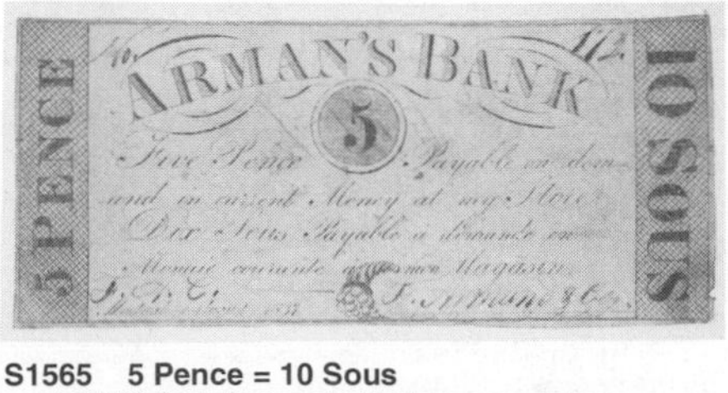

S1565 5 Pence = 10 Sous

	Good	Fine	XF
1.8.1837. Black. Cornucopia at bottom center. Uniface.	150.	500.	—

S1566 10 Pence = 20 Sous

	Good	Fine	XF
1.8.1837. Black. Cornucopia at bottom center. Uniface.	150.	500.	—

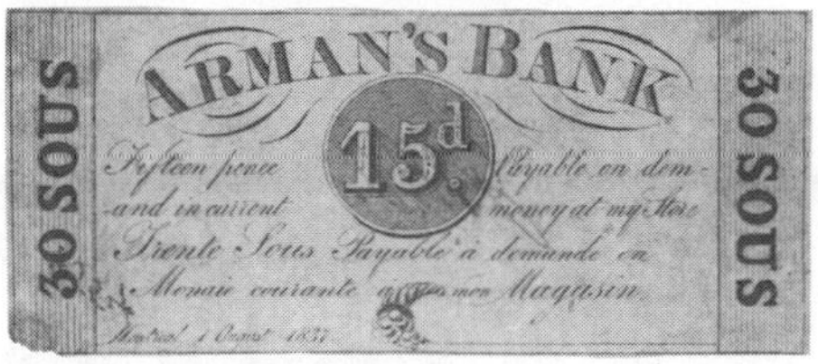

S1567 15 Pence = 30 Sous

	Good	Fine	XF
1.8.1837. Black. Cornucopia at bottom center. Uniface.	150.	500.	—

Banque de Boucherville

1830s Issue

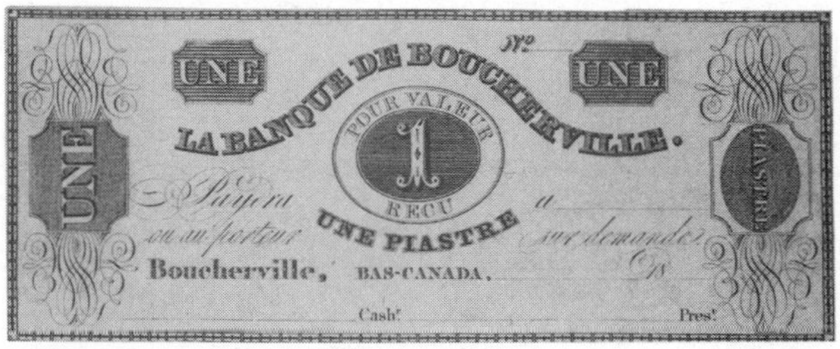

S1568 1 Piastre

	VG	VF	UNC
18xx. Black. Uniface. Printer: Bourne Sc. Unsigned remainder.	30.00	100.	200.

Bank of Brantford

1859 Issue

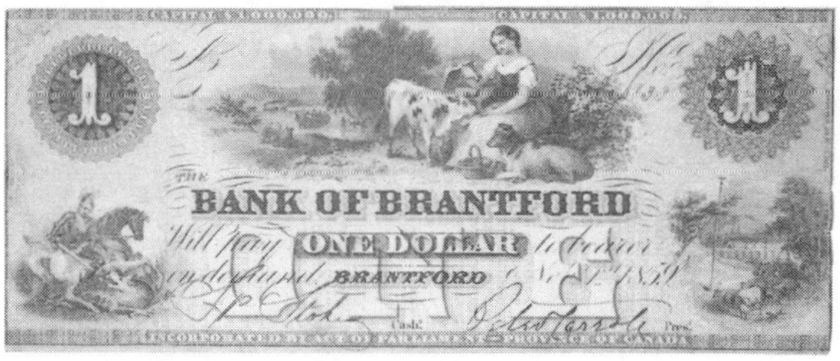

S1569 1 Dollar

	VG	VF	UNC
1.11.1859. Black on green underprint. St. George slaying dragon at lower left, farm girl with calves at upper center, cattle at lower right. Uniface. Printer: ABNC.			
a. Partially engraved date.	40.00	80.00	200.
b. Engraved date.	40.00	80.00	200.
c. Blue overprint: *Issued.../Honiton 1st May, 1862* and *CARROLE* on #S1569a.	50.00	100.	250.
d. Overprint as c. but with *KINGSMILL*.	75.00	125.	250.

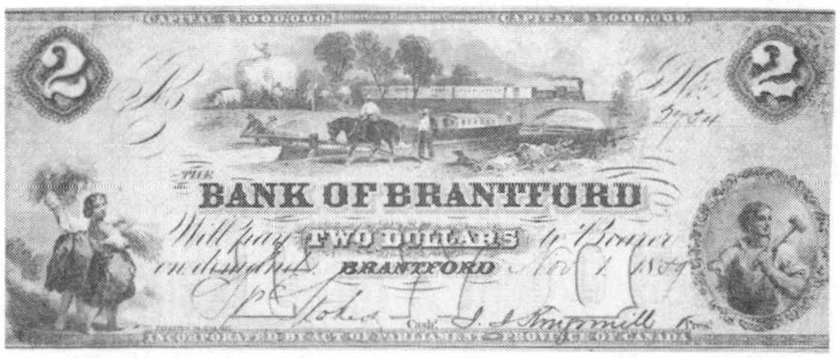

S1570 2 Dollars

	VG	VF	UNC
1.11.1859. Black on green underprint. Two young girls with sheaves of grain at lower left, boat in locks, steam passenger train in background at upper center, blacksmith with hammer at lower right. Uniface. Printer: ABNC.			
a. Partially engraved date.	50.00	100.	200.
b. Engraved date.	50.00	100.	200.
c. Blue overprint: *Issued.../Honiton, 1st May, 1862* on #S1570b.	50.00	100.	200.
d. Purple overprint as c, but with *Westbrook.*	75.00	200.	350.

S1571 4 Dollars	VG	VF	UNC
1.11.1859. Black on green underprint. Portrait Lord Elgin at lower left, mill along canal at top center, portrait young girl at lower right. Uniface. Printer: ABNC.			
a. Partially engraved date.	75.00	200.	350.
b. Engraved date.	75.00	200.	350.
c. Blue overprint: *Issued.../Honiton, 1st May, 1862* on #S1571b.	75.00	200.	350.
d. Purple overprint as c, but with *Westbrook*.	100.	275.	—

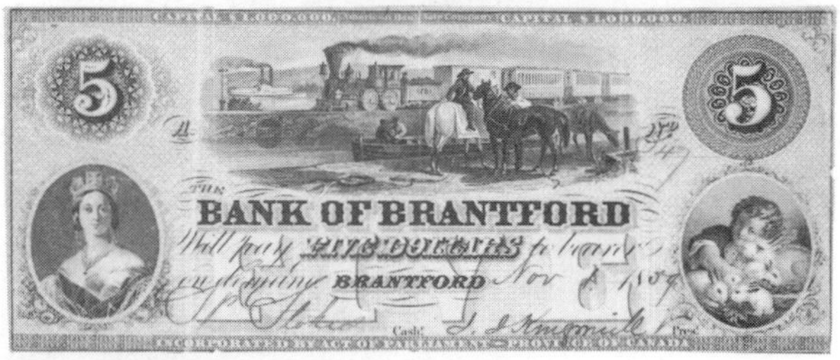

S1572 5 Dollars	VG	VF	UNC
1.11.1859. Black on green underprint. Portrait Queen Victoria at lower left, steam passenger train, boats and horses at top center, portrait child with rabbits at lower right. Uniface. Printer: ABNC.			
a. Partially engraved date.	20.00	50.00	150.
b. Engraved date.	20.00	50.00	150.
c. Blue overprint: *Issued.../Honiton, 1st May, 1862* on #S1572b.	25.00	75.00	200.
d. Purple overprint as c, but with *Westbrook*.	75.00	150.	—

1859 Sault Ste. Marie Branch Issue

	Good	Fine	XF
S1573 1 Dollar 1.11.1859. Engraved. Black on red underprint. St. George slaying dragon at lower left, farm girl with calves at upper center, cattle at lower right. Uniface. Printer: ABNC. Unsigned remainder.	—	Unc	125.
S1574 2 Dollars 1.11.1859. Engraved. Black on red underprint. Two young girls with sheaves of grain at lower left, boat in locks, steam passenger train in background at upper center, blacksmith with hammer at lower right. Uniface. Printer: ABNC. Unsigned remainder.	—	Unc	200.
S1575 4 Dollars 1.11.1859. Engraved. Black on red underprint. Portrait Lord Elgin at lower left, mill along canal at top center, portrait young girl at lower right. Uniface. Printer: ABNC. Unsigned remainder.	—	Unc	250.
S1576 5 Dollars 1.11.1859. Engraved. Black on red underprint. Portrait Queen Victoria at lower left, steam passenger train, boats and horses at top center, portrait child with rabbits at lower right. Uniface. Printer: ABNC. Unsigned remainder.	—	Unc	125.

British Canadian Bank

1884 Issue

S1577 5 Dollars	Good	Fine	XF
15.9.1884. Black on green underprint. Steam train, ships dockside at left. Back: Green. Printer: BABNC. Face proof.	—	Unc	1000.

S1578 10 Dollars	Good	Fine	XF
15.9.1884. Black on green underprint. Portrait Queen Victoria at upper left, seated Britannia with lion and child at lower right. Back: Green. Printer: BABNC. Face proof.	—	Unc	1000.

Canada Bank

1790s Issue

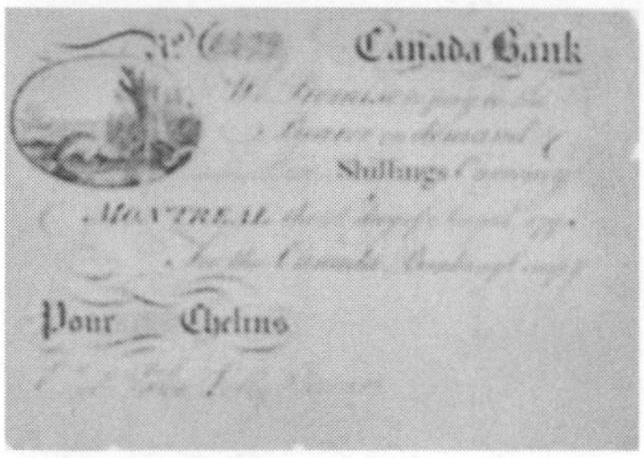

	Good	Fine	XF
S1579 5 Shillings 10.8.1792. Handwritten. Black. Beaver by tree stump with sailing ship in background at upper left. Uniface. Printer: Albby Sc., London.			
a. Issued note.	300.	900.	2500.
r. Unsigned remainder. 179x.	200.	750.	1750.
S1580 Pounds(s) 179x. Handwritten. Black. Beaver by tree stump with sailing ship in background at upper left. Uniface. Printer: Albby Sc., London. Unsigned remainder.	400.	1250.	3250.

Canada Bank, The

1855 Issue

	Good	Fine	XF
S1580A 1 Dollar 1.11.1855. Black. Portrait Queen Victoria at lower left, Falls at Niagara at upper center right, portrait Prince Albert at lower right. Uniface. Printer: Danforth, Wright & Co. Face proof.	—	Unc	1000.
S1581 1 Dollar = 5 Shillings 1.11.1855. Black. Portrait Queen Victoria at lower left, Roebling Bridge at upper center right, portrait Prince Albert at lower right. Uniface. Printer: Danforth, Wright & Co. Face proof.	—	Unc	1000.

	Good	Fine	XF
S1582 2 Dollars = 10 Shillings 1.11.1855. Black. Woman with sickle at left, royal crest at center. Uniface. Printer: Danforth, Wright & Co. Face proof.	—	Unc	1000.
S1583 5 Dollars = 1 Pound-5 Shillings 1.11.1855. Black. Cattle watering in pond at center. Uniface. Printer: Danforth, Wright & Co. Face proof.	—	Unc	1000.

Bank of Canada

1818-22 Issue

S1584 1 Dollar	Good	Fine	XF
1.8.1818; 6.11.1819. Partially engraved. Black. Seated Goddess of Plenty with cornucopia and Large *1* at top center, agricultural tools at bottom center. Uniface. Printer: Reed.	125.	400.	1150.

	Good	Fine	XF
S1585 2 Dollars 1.2.1822. Partially engraved. Black. Seated allegorical woman with cornucopia and Large *2* at top center, agricultural tools at bottom center. Uniface. Printer: Reed.	20.00	75.00	250.
S1586 10 Dollars 18xx. Partially engraved. Black. Hillside citadel and town at top center. Prince of Wales crest at bottom center. Uniface. Printer: Reed. Proof.	—	Unc	500.
S1587 50 Dollars 25.8.1818. Partially engraved. Black. Supported royal arms at upper center, small beaver at bottom center. Uniface. Printer: Reed.	100.	500.	1150.

S1588 100 Dollars	Good	Fine	XF
18xx. Partially engraved. Black. Supported royal arms at upper center, small sailing ship at bottom center. Uniface. Printer: Reed. Proof.	—	Unc	500.

1820s Issue

No.	Denomination / Description	Good	Fine	XF
S1589	**2 Dollars** 18xx. Seated female holding sword and Large *2* at top center, small sailing ship at bottom center. Curved *AT THE MECHANICS BANK IN THE CITY OF N. YORK* above vignette. Proof.	—	Unc	500.
S1590	**5 Dollars** 18xx. Female afloat holding Large *5* at upper center. Small paddle wheel steamboat at bottom center. Curved *AT THE MECHANICS BANK IN THE CITY OF N. YORK* above vignette. Proof.	—	Unc	500.
S1591	**20 Dollars** 18xx. Supported royal arms at upper center, small shield at bottom center. Curved *AT THE MECHANICS BANK IN THE CITY OF N. YORK* above vignette. Proof.	—	Unc	500.

1818 Issue

No.	Denomination / Description	Good	Fine	XF
S1591A	**1 Dollar** 1.10.1818. Engraved. Black. Couple in horse-drawn sleigh at upper center. Uniface. Printer: Graphic.	100.	300.	750.
S1592	**2 Dollars** 1.10.1818. Engraved. Black. Seated woman with sickle at top center, two coins at bottom center. Uniface. Printer: Graphic.	100.	300.	750.
S1593	**5 Dollars** 1.10.1818; 6.1.1820; 4.6.1823. Engraved. Black. Seated Indian with lion at top center, five coins at bottom center, *V* in guilloche at upper left, *5* at upper right. Uniface. Printer: Graphic.	100.	300.	750.

1818 New York City Branch Issue

No.	Denomination / Description	Good	Fine	XF
S1593A	**1 Dollar** 1.10.1818. Engraved. Black. Couple in horse-drawn sleigh at upper center. Uniface. *MECHANICS BANK.*	100.	300.	750.
S1593C	**3 Dollars** 1.10.1818. Engraved. Black. Boat, seated native and man at top center. *MECHANICS BANK.*	100.	300.	750.
S1593E	**5 Dollars** 1820-23. Partially engraved without payee's name. Black. Seated Indian with lion at top center, five coins at bottom center, *5* in guilloche at upper left, *V* at upper right. *MECHANICS BANK.*	100.	300.	750.
S1593G	**10 Dollars** 1.10.1818. Engraved. Black. Sailing ship, three seated allegorical persons at top center. *MECHANICS BANK.*	100.	300.	750.

1822 Issue

No.	Denomination / Description	Good	Fine	XF
S1594	**1 Dollar** 1.1.1822. Engraved. Black. Coin of King George IV at top center. Uniface. Printer: Graphic.	100.	300.	750.

No.	Denomination / Description	Good	Fine	XF
S1595	**2 Dollars** 1.1.1822. Engraved. Black. Two coins of King George IV at top center. Uniface. Printer: Graphic.	100.	300.	750.

Banque Canadienne

1836 Issue

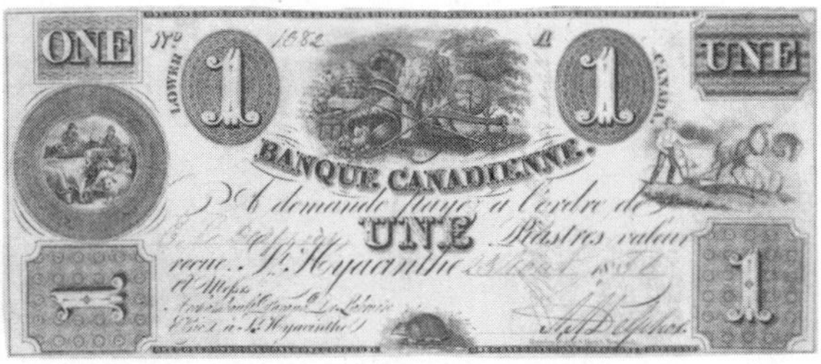

		VG	VF	UNC
S1596	**1 Dollar = 1 Piastre** 23.8.1836. Handwritten. Black. Men with livestock at left, cornucopia, sheaf of grain and spinning wheel at top center, farmer plowing with horse at right. Back: Blue-green. Printer: RWH & Co.	200.	450.	—
S1597	**2 Dollars = 2 Piastres** 23.8.1836. Handwritten. Black. Standing Britannia with anchor at upper left, seated female, cattle and sheaves at upper center. Back: Blue-green. Printer: RWH & Co.	200.	450.	—
S1598	**5 Dollars = 5 Piastres** 23.8.1836. Handwritten. Black. Indian shooting bow and arrow at upper left, sailing ship at upper center, sailing ship, steam passenger train (sideways) at right. Back: Green. Printer: RWH & Co.	300.	750.	—

		VG	VF	UNC
S1599	**10 Dollars = 10 Piastres = 2 Pounds-10 Shillings** 23.8.1836. Handwritten. Black. Portrait King William IV at left, steam passenger train, produce, tools and waterfall at top center, beehive at right, small man in canoe at bottom center. Back: Green. Printer: RWH & Co.	300.	750.	—

Central Bank of Canada

1884; 1887 Issue

		VG	VF	UNC
S1600	**5 Dollars** 1.1.1884. Black on green underprint. Allegorical female with cherubs at right. D. Blain at left. Back: Green. Horses at trough. Printer: BABNC.	500.	1150.	—
S1601	**10 Dollars** 1.1.1884. Black on green underprint. Man plowing with horses at right. D. Blain at left. Back: Green. Printer: BABNC.	625.	1250.	—
S1602	**50 Dollars** 3.1.1887. Black on green underprint. A. A. Allen at lower right. D. Blain at left. Printer: BABNC. Face proof.	—	Unc	500.

Central Bank of New Brunswick

1847; 1851 Issue

No.	Denomination / Description	Good	Fine	XF
S1603	**5 Shillings** 1.11.1847. Blue. Blacksmith at anvil at left, seated Justice at top center, cargo and ships below. Back: Gray.	550.	1750.	—
S1604	**1 Pound** 1.5.1847. Black. Indian seated with rifle at left, supported royal arms at top center, small paddle wheel steamboat below.	500.	1500.	—
S1604A	**1 Pound** 1.10.1847. Blue. Indian seated with rifle at left, supported royal arms at top center, small paddle wheel steamboat below. Back: Gray.	500.	1500.	—
S1605	**5 Pounds** 1.5.1847. Black. Portrait King William IV at left, St. George slaying dragon at top center. Back: Blue.	500.	1500.	—
S1605A	**5 Pounds** 2.1.1851; 1.11.1857. Blue. Portrait King William IV at left, St. George slaying dragon at top center. Back: Gray.	500.	1500.	—

1847 Issue

No.	Denomination / Description	Good	Fine	XF
S1605B	**1 Dollar = 5 Shillings** 10.11.1847. Blue. Blacksmith at anvil at left, seated Justice at top center, cargo and ships below. Back: Green.	600.	1750.	—

1852-53 Issue

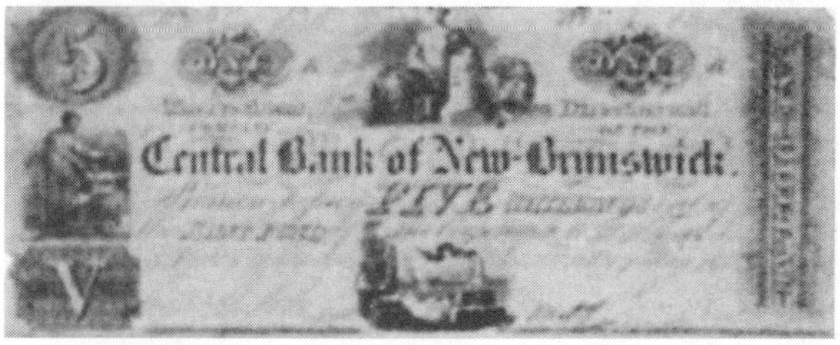

No.	Denomination / Description	Good	Fine	XF
S1606	**1 Dollar = 5 Shillings** 1.10.1852; 1.5.1853. Blue. Blacksmith at anvil at left, seated Justice at top center, cargo and ships below. Back: Orange.	500.	1500.	—
S1607	**1 Pound** 18xx. Blue. Indian seated with rifle at left, supported royal arms at top center, small paddle wheel steamboat below. Back: Orange.	500.	1500.	—
S1608	**5 Pounds** 1.5.1853. Blue. Portrait King William IV at left, St. George slaying dragon at top center. Back: Orange.	500.	1500.	—

1856-57 Issue

No.	Denomination / Description	Good	Fine	XF
S1609	**1 Dollar = 5 Shillings** Black. Blacksmith at anvil at left, seated Justice at top center, cargo and ships below. Uniface.	500.	1500.	—
S1610	**1 Pound** 1.8.1857; 1.10.1857. Black. Indian seated with rifle at left, supported royal arms at top center, small paddle wheel steamboat below. Uniface.	500.	1500.	—
S1611	**5 Pounds** 18xx. Black. Portrait King William IV at left, St. George slaying dragon at top center. Uniface. Proof.	—	Unc	1000.

1860 Issue

No.	Denomination / Description	Good	Fine	XF
S1612	**1 Dollar** 1.11.1860. Black on green underprint. Portrait man at lower left, lion with shield at upper center, portrait Queen Victoria at lower right. Uniface.	500.	1500.	—

	Good	Fine	XF
S1613 2 Dollars 1.11.1860. Black on green underprint. Portrait man at lower left, two allegorical females with large *2* at center, portrait Queen Victoria at lower right. Uniface.	500.	1500.	—
S1614 3 Dollars 1.11.1860. Black on green underprint. Portrait Prince of Wales at lower left, allegorical female at left, sailing ship at upper center right, portrait man at right. Uniface.	1500.	3250.	—
S1615 5 Dollars 1.11.1860. Black on green underprint. Portrait man at lower left, supported royal arms at top center, sailboat at lower right. Uniface. Face proof.	—	Unc	1000.
S1616 20 Dollars 18xx. Black on green underprint. Standing Justice at left, St. George slaying dragon at center, portrait Duke of Wellington at lower right. Green *TWENTY* protector. Uniface.			
p. Green. Curved outline *TWENTY*. Face proof.	—	Unc	1000.
r. Unsigned remainder.	750.	—	—
S1617 50 Pounds 18xx. Black on green underprint. Portrait Queen Victoria at left, reclining Goddess of Plenty with sailing ship in background at top center, steam passenger train on viaduct at lower right. Uniface.	—	Unc	1000.

Charlotte County Bank

1852-59 Issue

	VG	VF	UNC
S1618 5 Shillings 12.9.1853-26.8.1856. Partially engraved. Black. Standing Britannia at left. Navigation reclining at shoreline at top and bottom center. Back: Red-brown. Printer: Perkins and Heath.	1000.	—	—
S1619 1 Pound 1.9.1852; 8.11.1859. Partially engraved. Black. Standing Britannia at left. Navigation reclining at shoreline at top and bottom center. Back: Red-brown. Red-brown. Printer: Perkins and Heath.	1000.	—	—
S1620 3 Pounds 1.9.1852. Partially engraved. Black. Standing Britannia at left. Navigation reclining at shoreline at top and bottom center. Back: Red-brown. Printer: Perkins and Heath.	1500.	—	—

	Good	Fine	XF
S1621 5 Pounds 18xx. Partially engraved. Black. Standing Britannia at left. Navigation reclining at shoreline at top and bottom center. Back: Red-brown. Printer: Perkins and Heath. Face proof.	—	Unc	750.
S1622 10 Pounds 18xx. Partially engraved. Black. Standing Britannia at left. Navigation reclining at shoreline at top and bottom center. Back: Red-brown. Printer: Perkins and Heath. Face proof.	—	Unc	750.

Bank of Charlottetown

1850s Issue

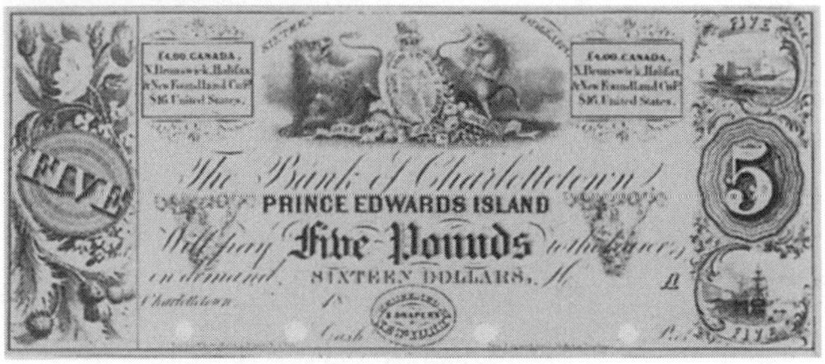

	Good	Fine	XF
S1623 5 Pounds = 16 Dollars 66 Cents 18xx. Black. Roses, shamrocks and thistles at left, supported royal arms at upper center, sailing ship at upper and lower right. Uniface. Printer: RWH&E and New England Banknote Co.			
p1. With *Payable at S. Draper's New York;* With 3 denomination: P.E.I.- *5 Pounds;* Canada - *4 Pounds.* U.S. - *SIXTEEN DOLLARS.* Proof.	—	Unc	1000.
p2. With *Redeemed at S. Draper's New York and at Wm. Elliott & Cos. British Consulate Boston;* With 3 denominations: P.E.I. - *5 Pounds;* Canada - *4.3.4. Pounds;* U.S. - *SIXTEEN DOLLARS, 66 CENTS.* Proof.	—	Unc	1000.

1852 Issue

	Good	Fine	XF
S1623A 1 Dollar 1.5.1852. Black. Seated Britannia with shield at top center. Roses, shamrocks and thistle at left, sailing at upper and lower right. Uniface. Printer: RWH&E and New England Banknote Co. Proof.	—	Unc	1000.

	VG	VF	UNC
S1624 2 Dollars 1.5.1852. Black. Reclining sailor with sailing ship in background at top center. Roses, shamrocks abd thistle at left, sailing ship at upper and lower right. Uniface. Printer: RWH&E and New England Bank Note Co.	2250.	—	—

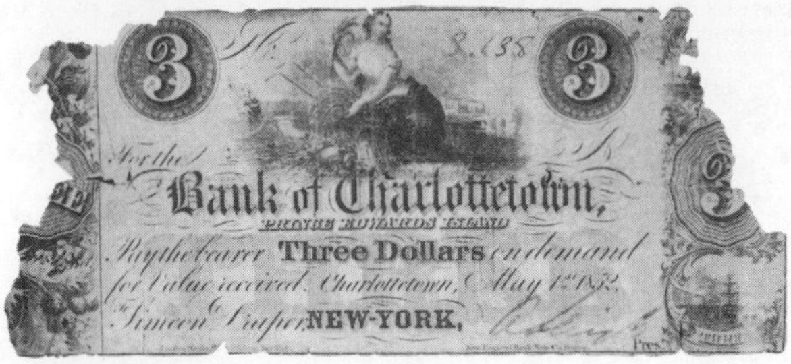

	VG	VF	UNC
S1625 3 Dollars 1.5.1852. Black. Seated Agriculture at top center. Roses, shamrocks and thistle at left, sailing ship at upper and lower right. Uniface. Printer: RWH&E and New England Bank Note Co.	3500.	—	—

The City Bank / La Banque de la Cité

Montreal

1833-40 Issue

	Good	Fine	XF
S1626 1 Dollar = 1 Piastre 10.10.1833. Black. Portrait King William IV at left, Indian shooting bow and arrow at center. Back: Red: *CITY BANK/MONTREAL* between identical standing woman at left and at right. Overprint: Large; red:*EASTERN TOWNSHIPS.* Printer: RWH & Co.	500.	1250.	—

	Good	Fine	XF
S1627 2 Dollars = 2 Piastres 18xx. Black. Indian in canoe at upper center, portrait King William IV at lower right. Overprint: Large, red:*EASTERN TOWNSHIPS.* Printer: RWH & Co. Proof.	—	Unc	500.

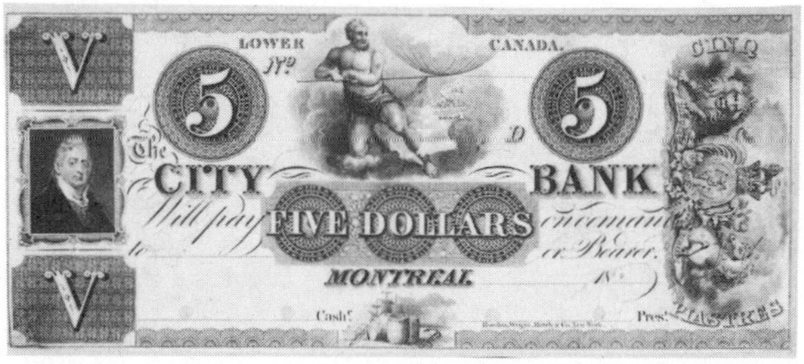

	Good	Fine	XF
S1628 5 Dollars 18xx. Black. Portrait King William IV at left, seated Archimedes moving the earth at top center, supported royal arms (sideways) at right. Overprint: Large; red:*EASTERN TOWNSHIPS.* Printer: RWH & Co. Face proof.	—	Unc	500.
S1629 10 Dollars 18xx. Black. Portrait King William IV at left, supported royal arms at upper center, woman with sheaf of wheat at right, small steamboat at bottom center. Overprint: Large; red:*EASTERN TOWNSHIPS.* Printer: RWH & Co.			
p. Face proof.	—	Unc	500.
x. Counterfeit.	50.00	150.	—

NOTE: Counterfeits exist with text: *OF PARLIAMENT* below portrait of King William IV in military dress at left.

S1630 20 Dollars — Good: — | Fine: Unc | XF: 650.
18xx. Black. Portrait King William IV between lion and unicorn at upper center. Overprint: Large; red:*EASTERN TOWNSHIPS*. Printer: RWH & Co. Face proof.

S1631 100 Dollars — Good: — | Fine: Unc | XF: 650.
18xx. Black. Portrait King William IV at top center St. George slaying dragon at left and right. Overprint: Large; red:*EASTERN TOWNSHIPS*. Printer: RWH & Co. Face proof.

1851-53 Issue

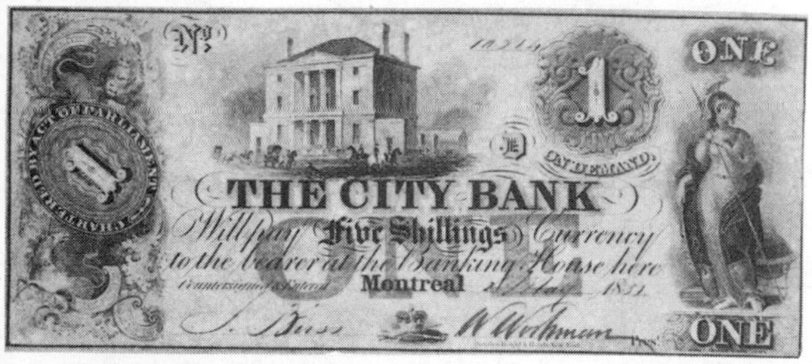

S1632 1 Dollar = 5 Shillings — Good: 500. | Fine: 1500. | XF: —
1.5.1851; 2.5.1851. Black. Counter with lion and unicorn (sideways) at left, bank building at upper left center, standing Britannia at right. Uniface. Red word protector on face and back.

S1632A 2 Dollars = 10 Shillings — Good: — | Fine: Unc | XF: 500.
18xx. Black. Uniface. Bank building. Red word protector on face and back. Proof.

S1633 4 Dollars = 1 Pound — Good: 400. | Fine: 1400. | XF: —
1.2.1853. Black. Portrait Queen Victoria at left, bank building at top center. Uniface.

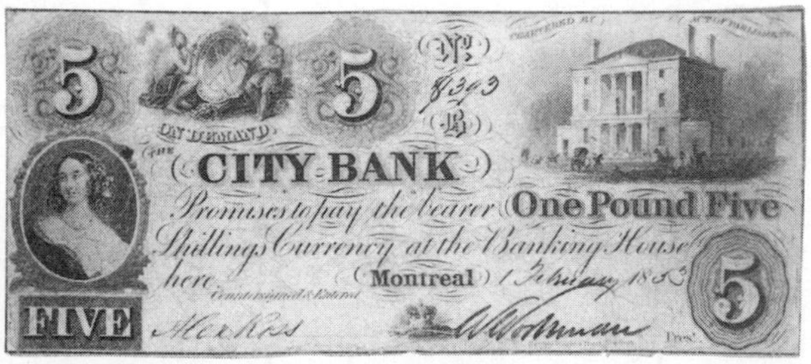

S1634 5 Dollars = 1 Pound-5 Shillings — Good: 400. | Fine: 1400. | XF: —
1.2.1853. Black. Female portrait at left, two Indians holding shield at upper left, bank building at upper right. Uniface.

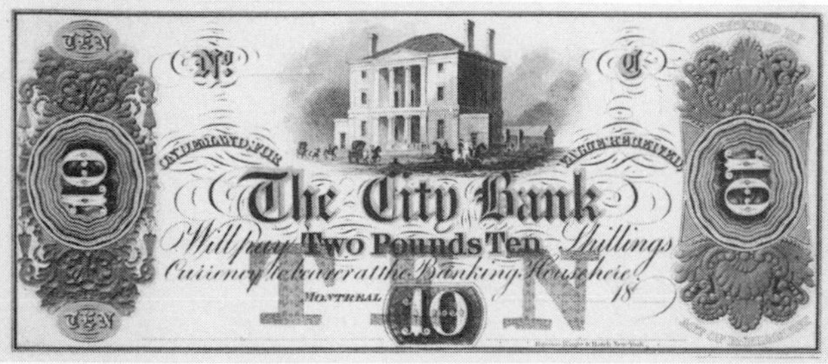

S1635 10 Dollars = 2 Pounds-10 Shillings — Good: — | Fine: Unc | XF: 500.
18xx. Black. Bank building at top center. Uniface. Red word protector on face and back. Proof.

S1635A 20 Dollars = 5 Pounds — Good: — | Fine: Unc | XF: 600.
18xx. Black. Woman at left, bank building at center. Uniface. Red word protector on face and back. Proof.

S1636 50 Dollars = 12 Pounds-10 Shillings — Good: — | Fine: Unc | XF: 600.
18xx. Black. Bank building at center. Uniface. Red word protector on face and back. Proof.

S1637 100 Dollars = 25 Pounds — Good: — | Fine: Unc | XF: 600.
18xx. Black. Portrait Prince Albert at left, bank building at center, portrait Queen Victoria at right. Uniface. Red word protector on face and back. Proof.

Toronto

1850-54 Issue

S1638 1 Dollar — Good: 250. | Fine: 750. | XF: —
1.10.1850-2.10.1865. Black. Seated Liberty with shield at top center, portrait Queen Victoria at right. Uniface. Printer: RWH & Co. and RWH&E.

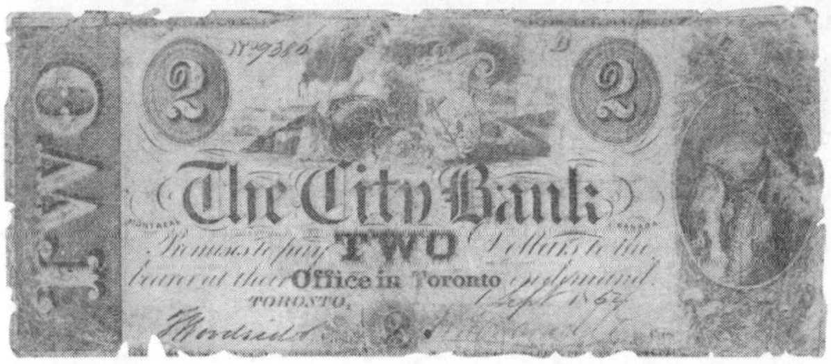

S1639 2 Dollars — Good: 500. | Fine: 1250. | XF: —
31.12.1852; 1.9.1854; 1.8.1856. Black. Seated Navigation with shield at top center, portrait Queen Victoria at right. Uniface. Printer: RWH & Co. and RWH&E.

S1640 5 Dollars — Good: 500. | Fine: 1250. | XF: —
31.12.1852. Black. Supported royal arms (sideways) at left, Archimedes moving the earth at top center, portrait King William IV at right. Uniface. Printer: RWH & Co. and RWH&E.

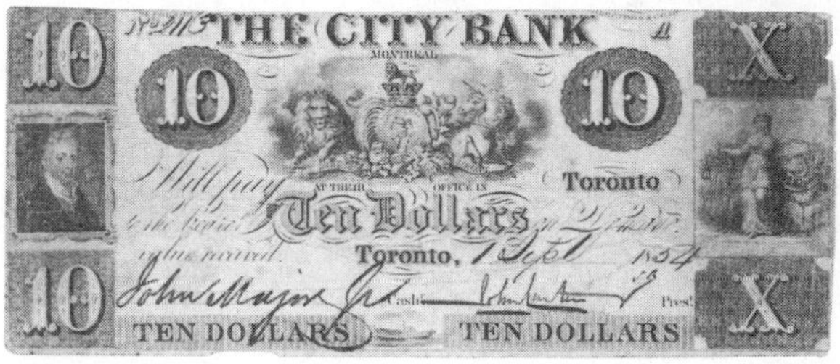

S1641 10 Dollars — Good: 500. | Fine: 1250. | XF: —
1.9.1854. Black. Portrait King William IV at left, supported royal arms at upper center, standing Justice at right. Uniface. Printer: RWH & Co. and RWH&E.

S1642 20 Dollars — Good: — | Fine: Unc | XF: 750.
18xx. Black. Allegorical female left, portrait King William IV at center. Uniface. Printer: RWH & Co. and RWH&E. Face proof.

QUEBEC

1850s ISSUE

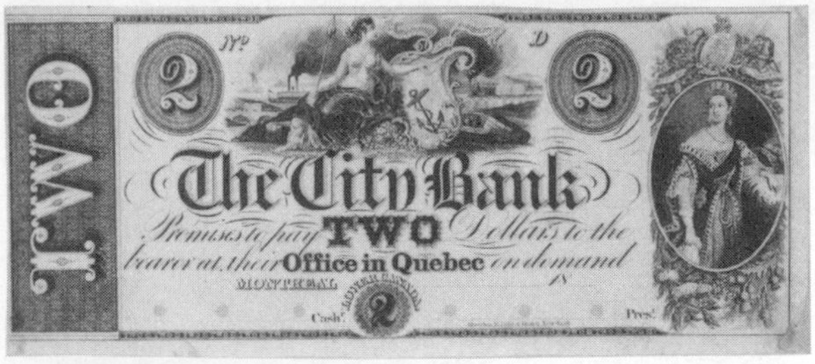

		Good	Fine	XF
S1643	**2 Dollars** 18xx. Black. Seated Navigation with shield at top center, portrait Queen Victoria at right. Uniface. Printer: RWH & Co. Proof.	—	Unc	600.
S1644	**4 Dollars = 1 Pound** 18xx. Black. Portrait Queen Victoria at left, bank building at top center. Red word protector. Uniface. Printer: RWH & Co. Proof.	—	Unc	600.

1857 FIRST ISSUE

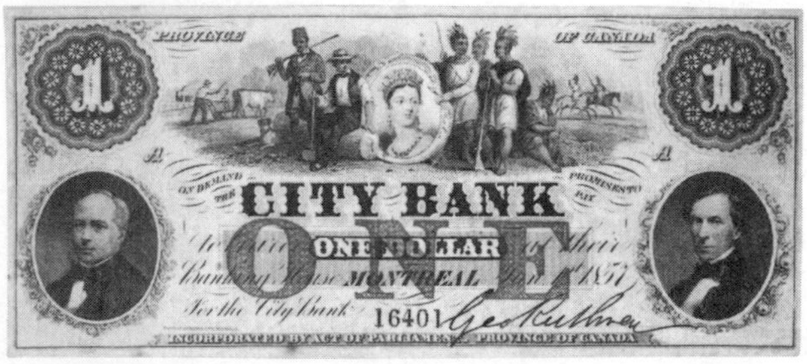

		Good	Fine	XF
S1645	**1 Dollar** 1.1.1857. Black. Settlers and Indians holding frame portrait Queen Victoria at center. Portrait man at left and right. Green word protector. Blue hand stamp:*MINES*. Back: Orange. *CITY BANK MONTREAL*. Green word protector. Overprint: Blue:*TORONTO*. Printer: TCC, Montreal.	125.	350.	—

		Good	Fine	XF
S1646	**2 Dollars** 1.1.1857. Black. Ships and boats in harbor at bottom center. Portrait man at left and right. Green word protector. Blue hand stamp:*MINES*. Back: Orange. *CITY BANK MONTREAL*. Green word protector. Overprint: Blue: *TORONTO*. Printer: TCC, Montreal.	125.	350.	—

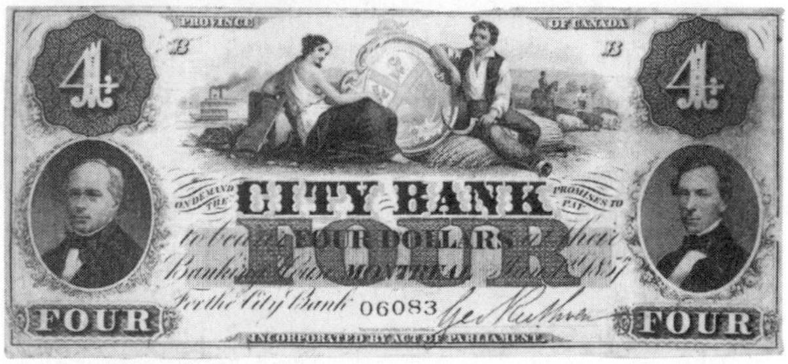

		Good	Fine	XF
S1647	**4 Dollars** 1.1.1857. Black. Reclining Commerce and farmer seated holding shield at top center. Portrait man at left and right. Green word protector. Blue hand stamp: *MINES*. Back: Orange. *CITY BANK MONTREAL*. Green word protector. Overprint: *TORONTO*. Printer: TCC, Montreal.			
	a. Issued note without overprint.	300.	750.	—
	b. Blue overprint: *MINES*.	—	—	—
	c. Blue overprint: *TORONTO*.	—	—	—

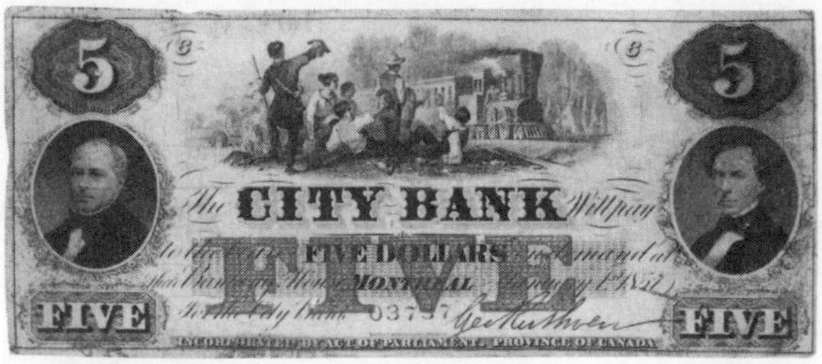

		Good	Fine	XF
S1648	**5 Dollars** 1.1.1857. Black. Farmers waving at steam passenger train at top center. Portrait man at left and right. Green word protector. Blue hand stamp: *MINES* Back: Orange. *CITY BANK MONTREAL*. Green word protector. Overprint: Blue: *TORONTO*. Printer: TCC, Montreal.	200.	750.	—

		Good	Fine	XF
S1649	**10 Dollars** 1.1.1857. Black. St. George slaying a dragon at top center. Portrait man at left and right. Green word protector. Blue hand stamp: *MINES*. Back: Orange. *CITY BANK MONTREAL*. Green word protector. Overprint: Blue: *TORONTO*. Printer: TCC, Montreal.	400.	1000.	—
S1649A	**20 Dollars** 1.1.1857. Black. Livestock by stream at center. Portrait man at left and right. Green word protector. Blue hand stamp: *MINES*. Back: Orange. *CITY BANK MONTREAL*. Green word protector. Overprint: Blue: *TORONTO*. Printer: TCC, Montreal.	400.	1000.	—

1857 SECOND ISSUE

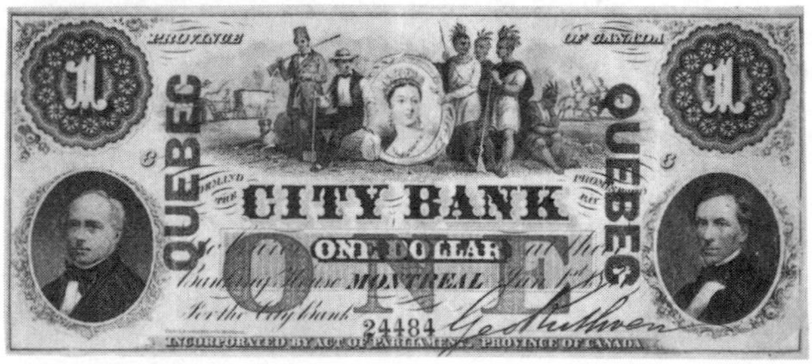

		Good	Fine	XF
S1650	**1 Dollar** 1.1.1857. Black. Green word protector. Uniface. Overprint: Blue: *QUEBEC* or *TORONTO*. Printer: TCC, Montreal.			
	a. Issued note without overprint.	125.	400.	—
	b. Blue overprint: *QUEBEC*.	—	—	—
S1651	**2 Dollars** 1.1.1857. Black. Ships and boats in harbor at bottom center. Portrait man at left and right. Green word protector. Uniface. Overprint: Blue: *QUEBEC* or *TORONTO*. Printer: TCC, Montreal.	150.	500.	—

		Good	Fine	XF
S1652	**4 Dollars** 1.1.1857. Black. Reclining Commerce and farmer seated holding shield at top center. Portrait man at left and right. Uniface. Green word protector. Overprint: Blue: *QUEBEC* or *TORONTO*. Printer: TCC, Montreal.	150.	500.	—
S1653	**5 Dollars** 1.1.1857. Black. Farmers waving at steam passenger train at top center. Portrait man at left and right. Uniface. Green word protector. Overprint: Blue: *QUEBEC* or *TORONTO*. Printer: TCC. Montrreal.	150.	500.	—
S1654	**10 Dollars** 1.1.1857. Black. St. George slaying a dragon at top center. Portrait man at left and right. Green word protector. Uniface. Overprint: Blue: *QUEBEC* or *TORONTO*. Printer: TCC, Montreal.	200.	750.	—

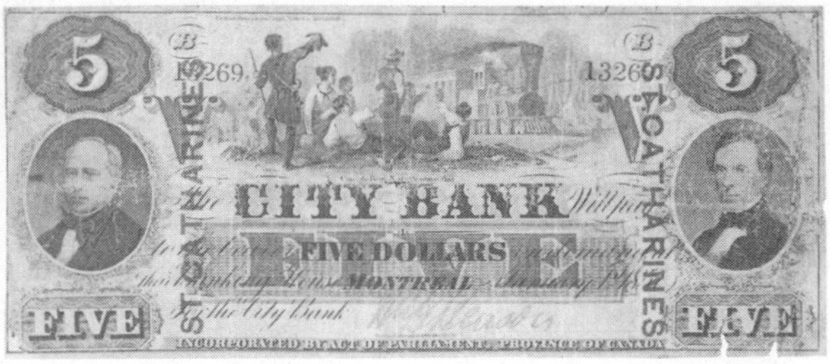

S1655 5 Dollars

1.1.1857. Black on green underprint. Green *W* and panel added to *FIVE.* Back: Green. *CITY BANK MONTREAL.* Overprint: Red: *ST. CATHARINES.* Printer: TCC and BABNC.

Good	Fine	XF
200.	750.	—

1857 Spurious Issue

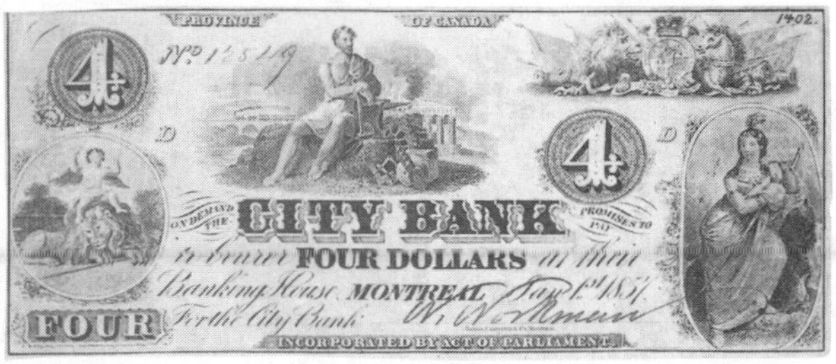

S1656 4 Dollars

1.1.1857. Black. Portrait cherub with lion at left, seated blacksmith at top center, supported royal arms at upper right above portrait Indian princess at lower right. Uniface. Printer: TCC.

VG	VF	UNC
150.	500.	—

City Bank of Montreal

1861 Spurious Issue

S1656A 5 Dollars

9.2.1861. Orange-brown. Farm family at left, Cornelia Jocelyn at lower right. Uniface. Printer: Jocelyn, Draper, Welsh & Co. and ABNC.

Good	Fine	XF
125.	350.	—

NOTE: Altered from a Colonial Bank of Canada issue.

Bank of Clifton

1859 First Issue

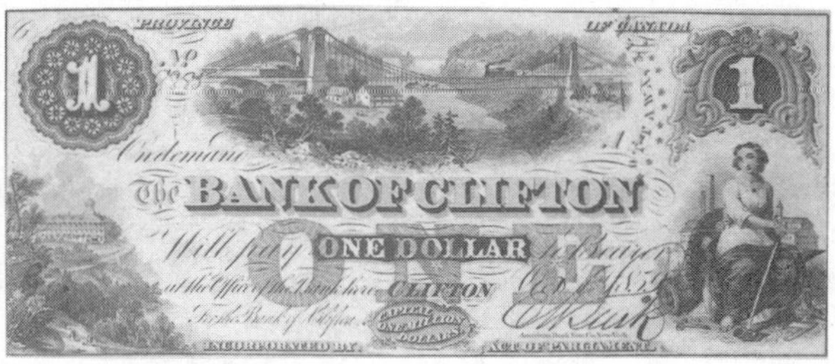

S1657 1 Dollar

1.10.1859; 1.11.1859. Partially engraved. Black. Clifton House hotel at lower left, seated Industry at lower right. Roebling bridge at Niagara Falls top center. Red word protector. Uniface. Back: Red word protector. Printer: ABNC.

VG	VF	UNC
30.00	75.00	175.

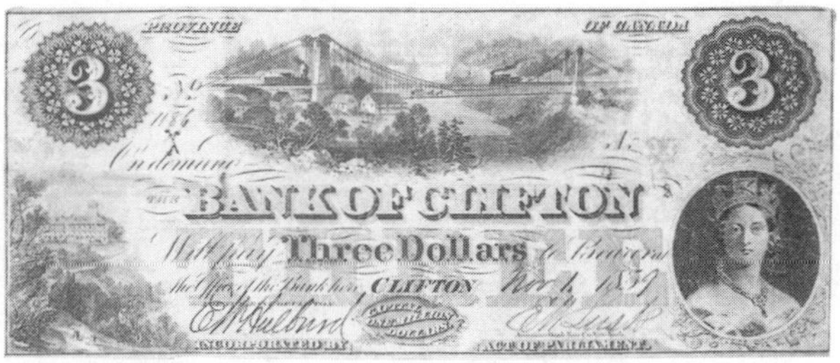

S1658 3 Dollars

1.10.1859; 1.11.1859. Partially engraved. Black. Clifton House hotel at lower left, portrait Queen Victoria at lower right. Roebling bridge at Niagara Falls top center. Red word protector. Uniface. Back: Red word protector. Printer: ABNC.

VG	VF	UNC
50.00	125.	300.

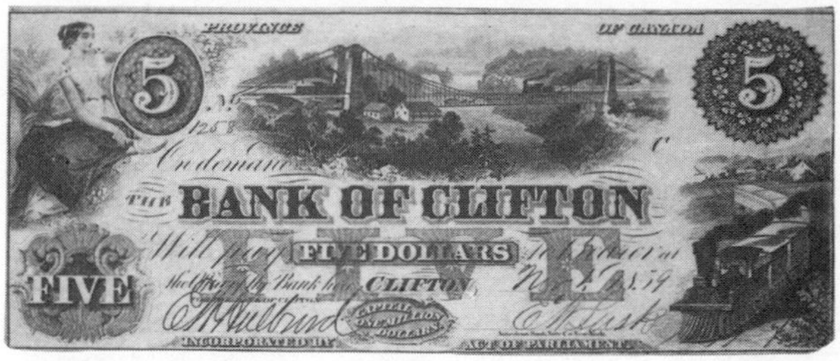

S1659 5 Dollars

1.10.1859; 1.11.1859. Partially engraved. Black. Seated farm woman with sickle at upper left, steam passenger train at lower right. Roebling bridge at Niagara Falls top center. Red word protector. Uniface. Back: Red word protector. Printer: ABNC.

VG	VF	UNC
40.00	75.00	175.

1859 Second Issue

S1660 1 Dollar

1.10.1859. Fully engraved. Black. Clifton House hotel at lower left, seated Industry at lower right. Red word protector.Text:*FOR GEO. TRUSCOTT* engraved at bottom. Hand stamped black: B, red C or black H. Back: Red word protector. Overprint: Curved, black: *OTTAWA, ILL.* and stars. Printer: New England Bank Note Comp., Boston.

VG	VF	UNC
25.00	50.00	150.

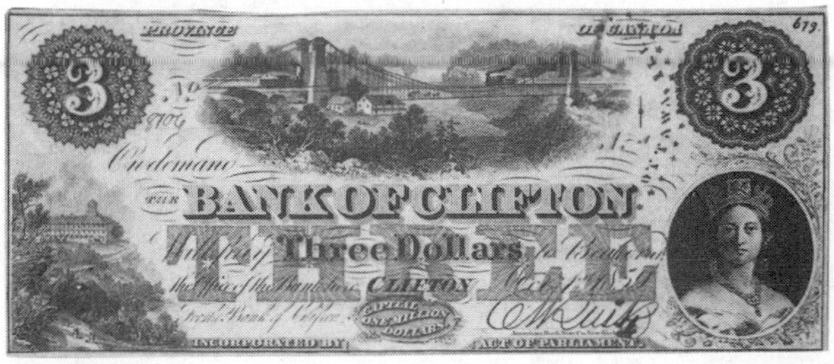

S1661 3 Dollars

1.10.1859. Fully engraved. Clifton House hotel at lower left, portrait Queen Victoria at lower right. Red word protector. Back: Red word protector. Overprint: Curved, Black: *OTTAWA, ILL.* and stars.

VG	VF	UNC
75.00	125.	250.

S1662 5 Dollars

1.10.1859. Fully engraved. Black. Seated farm woman with sickle at upper left, steam passenger train at lower right. Red word protector. Back: Red word protector. Overprint: Curved, black: *OTTAWA, ILL.* and stars.

VG	VF	UNC
25.00	50.00	150.

1860 Issue

Overprint Varieties.

Blue oval ovpt: *Sassenberg & Co., Buenos Ayres.*

Black ovpts: *Redeemed by Frederick Lau & Co. Bankers, 162 Fulton St. N.Y. at 3/4 per cent; Redeemable in Chicago at the office of Chadwick & Co.; Redeemable in bankable funds at the office of Chadwick & Co. 5 Clark Street under the - house Chicago, Ill. Blue hand stamp: 3.*

S1663 1 Dollar

1860-61. Black on red underprint. St. George slaying dragon at center. Uniface. Printer: NYBNC.

	VG	VF	UNC
a. 1.9.1860.	25.00	50.00	150.
b. 1.9.1861.	20.00	40.00	100.

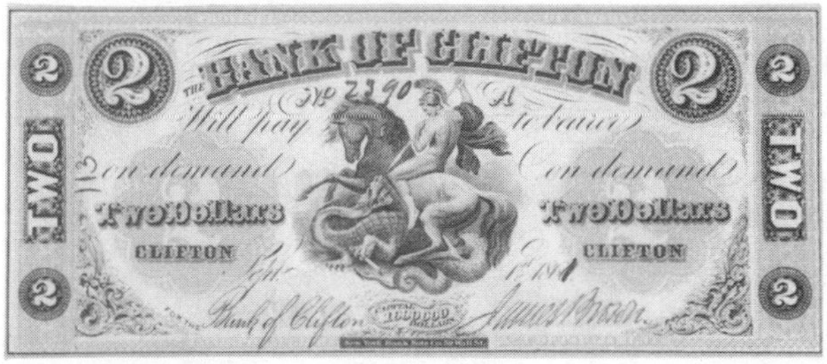

S1664 2 Dollars

1860-61. Black on red underprint. St. George slaying dragon at center. Uniface. Printer: NYBNC.

	VG	VF	UNC
a. 1.9.1860.	25.00	50.00	150.
b. 1.9.1861.	25.00	50.00	150.

S1665 5 Dollars	VG	VF	UNC
1860-61. Black on red underprint. St. George slaying dragon at center. Uniface. Printer: NYBNC.			
a. 1.9.1860.	25.00	50.00	150.
b. 1.9.1861.	20.00	40.00	100.

NOTE: 1861 variety with handwritten *1* engraved *0* in date for all denominations.

Colonial Bank of Canada

1859 First Issue

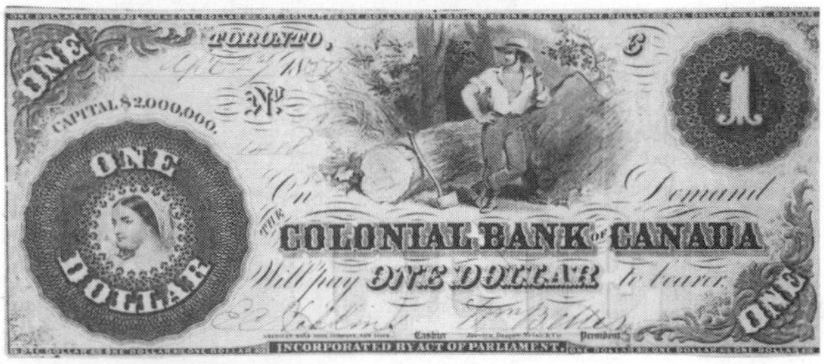

S1666 1 Dollar	VG	VF	UNC
4.4.1859-8.7.1859. Black on orange-brown underprint. Portrait woman at lower left, lumberjack at top center. 2 signatures. Uniface. Various hand stamped letters and numbers are encountered. Printer: Jocelyn, Draper, Welch & Co. and ABNC.	25.00	50.00	150.

S1667 2 Dollars	VG	VF	UNC
4.4.1859-14.7.1859. Black on orange-brown underprint. Indians on bluff at upper left, young woman at right. 2 signatures. Uniface. Various hand stamped letters and numbers are encountered. Printer: Jocelyn, Draper, Welch & Co. and ABNC.	25.00	50.00	150.

S1668 3 Dollars	VG	VF	UNC
4.4.1859-6.7.1859. Black on orange-brown underprint. St. George slaying dragon at lower left, three allegorical women at top center, C. Jocelyn at lower right. 2 signatures. Uniface. Various hand stamped letters and numbers are encountered. Printer: Jocelyn, Draper, Welch & Co. and ABNC.	75.00	150.	400.

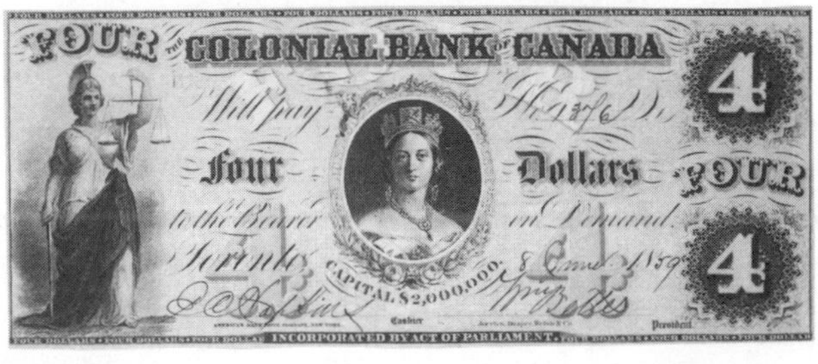

S1669 4 Dollars	VG	VF	UNC
4.4.1859-24.6.1859. Black on orange-brown underprint. Standing Justice at left, portrait Queen Victoria at center. 2 signatures. Uniface. Various hand stamped letters and numbers are encountered. Printer: Jocelyn, Draper, Welch & Co. And ABNC.	75.00	150.	400.

S1670 5 Dollars	VG	VF	UNC
4.4.1859-4.7.1859. Black on orange-brown underprint. Farm family under tree at lower left, C. Jocelyn at lower right. 2 signatures. Uniface. Various hand stamped letters and numbers are encountered. Printer: Jocelyn, Draper, Welch & Co. and ABNC.	25.00	50.00	150.

S1671 10 Dollars	VG	VF	UNC
4.4.1859; 1.5.1859. Black on orange-brown underprint. Steam passenger train at station at upper left, Indian maiden at lower right. 2 signatures. Uniface. Various hand stamped letters and numbers are encountered. Printer: Jocelyn, Draper, Welch & Co. and ABNC.	75.00	150.	400.

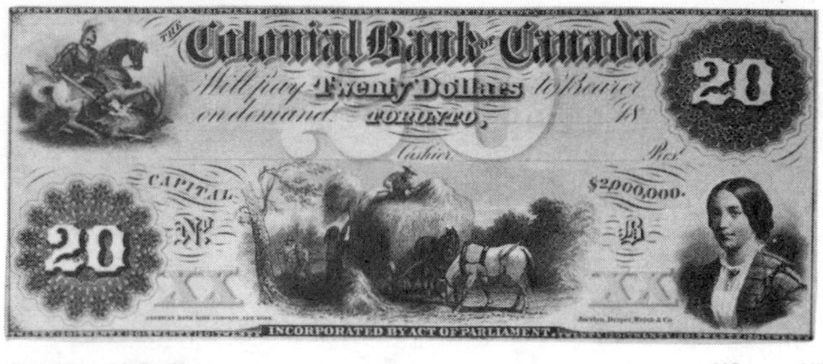

S1672 20 Dollars	VG	VF	UNC
2.5.1859; 4.8.1859. Black on orange-brown underprint. St. George slaying dragon at upper left, farmers hay at center, C. Jocelyn at lower right. 2 signatures. Uniface. Various hand stamped letters and numbers are encountered. Printer: Jocelyn, Draper, Welch & Co. and ABNC.			
a. Issued note.	1000.	2500.	—
r. Unsigned remainder.	500.	1000.	—

S1673 50 Dollars	VG	VF	UNC
2.5.1859; 4.8.1859. Black on orange-brown underprint. St. George slaying dragon at lower left, sailing ships at top center, C. Jocelyn at lower right. 2 signatures. Uniface. Various hand stamped letters and numbers are encountered. Printer: Jocelyn, Draper, Welch & Co. and ABNC.			
a. Issued note.	600.	1150.	—
r. Unsigned remainder.	200.	400.	—

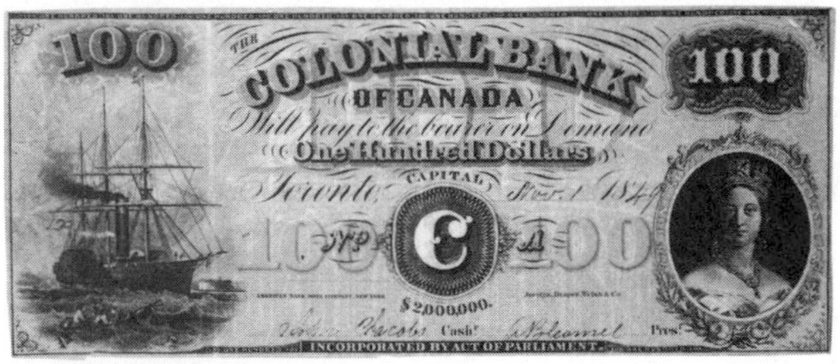

S1674 100 Dollars	VG	VF	UNC
2.5.1859; 4.8.1859. Black on orange-brown underprint. Paddle wheel steamship at left, portrait Queen Victoria at lower right. 2 signatures. Uniface. Various hand stamped letters and numbers are encountered. Printer: Jocelyn, Draper, Welch & Co. and ABNC.			
a. Issued note.	600.	1150.	—
r. Unsigned remainder.	200.	400.	—

1859 Second Issue

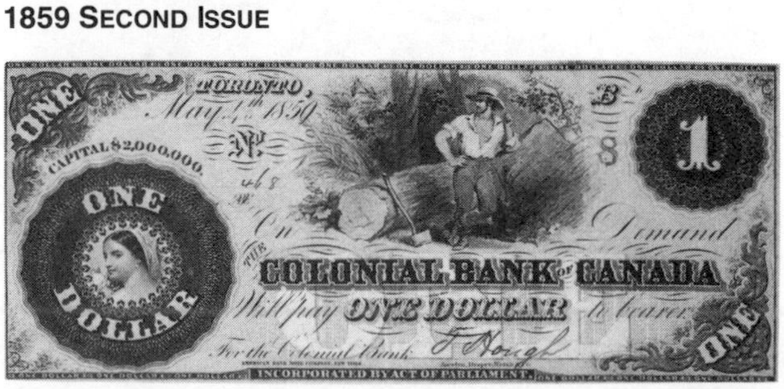

S1675 1 Dollar — VG 25.00, VF 75.00, UNC 150.
4.5.1859. Black on pink underprint. Portrait woman at lower left, lumberjack at top center. Text: *For the Colonial Bank* with 1 signature. Various hand stamped letters and numbers are encountered. Uniface. Printer: Jocelyn, Draper, Welch & Co. and ABNC monogram.

S1676 2 Dollars — VG 125., VF 250., UNC 750.
4.5.1859. Black on pink underprint. Indians on bluff at upper left, young woman at right. Text: *For the Colonial Bank* with 1 signature. Various hand stamped letters and numbers are encountered. Uniface. Printer: Jocelyn, Draper, Welch & Co. and ABNC monogram.

S1677 3 Dollars — VG 75.00, VF 150., UNC 300.
4.5.1859. Black on pink underprint. St. George slaying dragon at lower left, three allegorical women at top center, C. Jocelyn at lower right. Text: *For the Colonial Bank* with 1 signature. Various hand stamped letters and numbers Printer: Jocelyn, Draper, Welch & Co. and ABNC monogram.

S1678 4 Dollars — VG 75.00, VF 150., UNC 300.
4.5.1859. Black on pink underprint. Standing Justice at left, portrait Queen Victoria at center. Text: *For the Colonial Bank* with 1 signature. Various hand stamped letters and numbers are encountered. Uniface. Printer: Jocelyn, Draper, Welch & Co. and ABNC monogram.

S1679 5 Dollars — VG 25.00, VF 75.00, UNC 150.
4.5.1859. Black on pink underprint. Farm family under tree at lower left, C. Jocelyn at lower right. Text: *For the Colonial Bank* with 1 signature. Various hand stamped letters and numbers are encountered. Uniface. Printer: Jocelyn, Draper, Welch & Co. and ABNC monogram.

S1680 10 Dollars — VG 75.00, VF 150., UNC 500.
20.10.1859. Black on pink underprint. Steam passenger train at station at upper left, Indian maiden at lower right. Text: *For the Colonial Bank* with 1 signature. Various hand stamped letters and numbers are encountered. Uniface. Printer: Jocelyn, Draper, Welch & Co. and ABNC monogram.

Colonial Bank of Chatham

1837 Issue

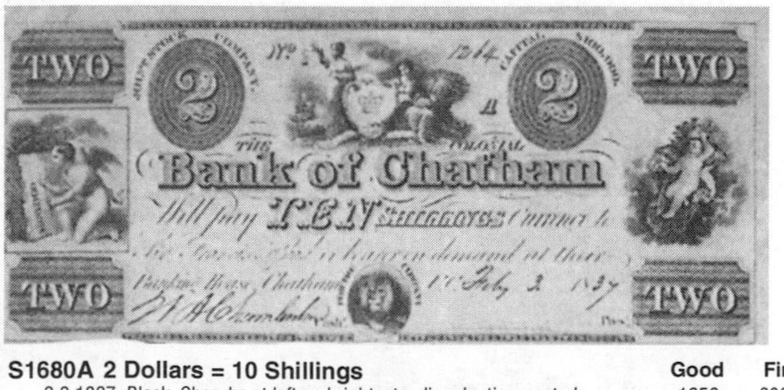

S1680A 2 Dollars = 10 Shillings — Good 1250., Fine 3000., XF —
3.2.1837. Black. Cherubs at left and right, standing Justice, seated Agriculture by arms at upper center, lion head at bottom center. Small crouching lion at bottom center. Uniface. Printer: RWH & Co.

S1681 3 Dollars = 15 Shillings — Good 1250., Fine 3000., XF —
3.2.1837. Black. Seated Justice at top center, portrait Indian chief at upper right. Small crouching lion at bottom center. Uniface. Printer: RWH & Co.

S1682 5 Dollars = 25 Shillings — Good 1250., Fine 3000., XF —
3.2.1837. Black. Supported royal arms at top center, portrait King William IV at right. Small crouching lion at bottom center. Uniface. Printer: RWH & Co.

S1683 10 Dollars = 50 Shillings — Good 1250., Fine 3000., XF —
3.2.1837. Black. Britannia in chariot drawn by lions at center, standing farm woman at right. Small crouching lion at bottom center. Uniface. Printer: RWH & Co.

Commercial Bank (Brockville, U.C.)

1834-36 Issue

S1684 5 Dollars = 25 Shillings — VG 1250., VF —, UNC —
3.11.1836. Black. Seated allegorical man with spilt urn at upper center, sailing ship at lower right, cargo and sailing ship at bottom center, sailing ship at lower right. Text: *For messrs. Sims, Colburn and Co.* Printer: Burton and Edmonds. Uniface.

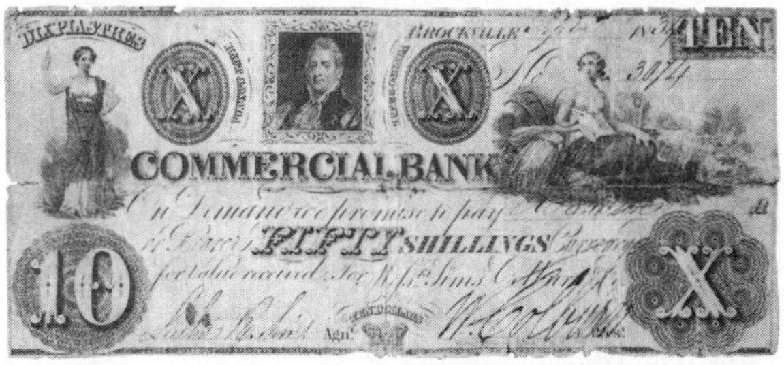

S1685 10 Dollars = 50 Shillings — VG 1250., VF —, UNC —
2.9.1834. Black. Standing Liberty at upper left, portrait King William IV at upper left. center, seated Agriculture at upper right. Text: *For Messrs. Sims, Colburn and Co.* Printer: Burton and Edmonds. Uniface.

A WORD ON DATE RANGES

Often date ranges or specific dates are listed. These have been observed or reported by our contributors. If a note is outside the published range, it only means that it is a newly reported date, and not necessarily worthy of a premium value.

Commercial Bank (Kingston, U.C.)

1837 First Spurious Issue

S1686 1 Dollar	Good	Fine	XF
18.7.1837. Black. Portrait George Washington at left, seated Mercury with sailing ship in background at top center, portrait Benjamin Franklin at right, Indian in canoe at bottom center. Uniface. Printer: Jas. Harris, N.Y. Text: *for the Foreign and Domestic Exchange Company.* Handwritten: *Commercial* and *Kingston.*	400.	1250.	—

S1687 2 Dollars = 10 Shillings	Good	Fine	XF
30.7.1837. Black. Grain sheaves at left, standing Agriculture with grain at top center, floral design with counter at right. Printer: Jas. Harris, N.Y. Text: *for the Foreign and Domestic Exchange Company.* Handwritten: *Commercial* and *Kingston.*	400.	1250.	—

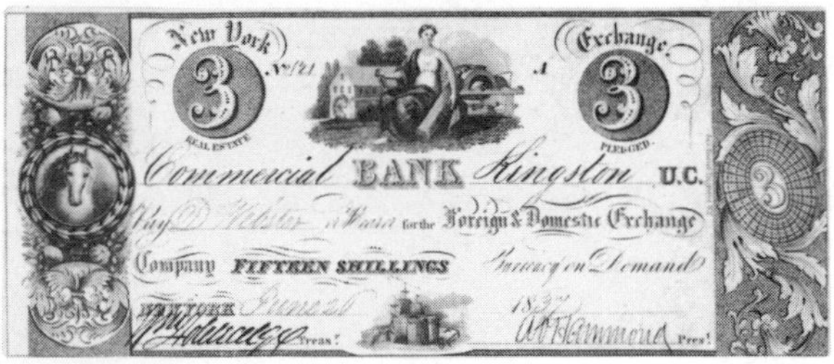

S1688 3 Dollars = 15 Shillings	Good	Fine	XF
21.6.1837; 26.6.1837. Black. Horse's head at left, seated woman with mill in background at top center, cargo and sailing ship at bottom center, floral design with counter at right. Printer: Jas. Harris, N.Y. Text: *for the Foreign and Domestic Exchange Company.* Handwritten: *Commercial* and *Kingston.*	400.	1250.	—

1837 Second Spurious Issue

S1689 1 Dollar	Good	Fine	XF
25.7.1837. Black. Horse's head at left, seated woman with mill in background at top center, cargo and sailing ship at bottom center, floral design with counter at right. Uniface. Printer: Jas. Harris, N.Y. Text: *for the Foreign and Domestic Exchange Company. COMMERICAL* and *KINGSTON* engraved.	400.	1250.	—

Commercial Bank (Montreal, L.C.)

1837 Issue

	Good	Fine	XF
S1689A 3 Dollars 1837. Black. Dock scene at left, blacksmith and two women at top center, woman with wheat at right. Uniface. Printer: RW&H. Reported not confirmed.	—	—	—
S1689B 5 Dollars 1837. Black. Youth at left, seated woman at center, blacksmith at right. Uniface. Printer: RW&H. Reported not confirmed.	—	—	—
S1689C 10 Dollars 1.6.1837. Black. Seated woman with shield at left, blacksmith and two women at top center, cherub with stone slab at right, small crouching lion at bottom center. Uniface. Printer: RW&H.	50.00	150.	300.

Commercial Bank of Fort Erie, U.C.

1837 Spurious Issue

#S1690-S1696 Encountered with various spurious signatures and dates in 1850s.

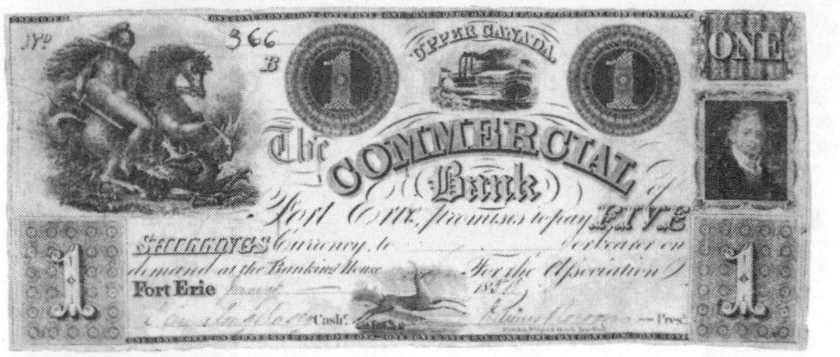

S1690 1 Dollar	VG	VF	UNC
10.1.1837. Black. St. George slaying dragon at upper left, steamship at upper center right, portrait King William IV at right, small deer at bottom center. Uniface. Printer: RWH & Co.	150.	300.	—

S1691 2 Dollars	VG	VF	UNC
10.1.1837. Black. St. George slaying dragon at upper left, supported royal arms at upper center right, small steam passenger train at bottom center. Uniface. Printer: RWH & Co.	150.	300.	—

S1692 3 Dollars	VG	VF	UNC
10.1.1837. Black. Standing Britannia at upper left, farmers sowing seed and cultivating with horses at upper left center, St. George slaying dragon at upper right, small steamboat at bottom center. Uniface. Printer: RWH & Co. Unsigned remainder.	250.	500.	—

S1693 4 Dollars	VG	VF	UNC
20.7.1836; 20.1.1837. Black. Supported royal arms at top center, farmers havesting wheat at right, small steamboat at bottom center. Uniface. Printer: RWH & Co.	200.	400.	—

S1694 5 Dollars

	VG	VF	UNC
20.7.1836; 20.1.1837; 20.8.1837. Black. Portrait King William IV at upper left. center, St. George slaying dragon at upper right, small beaver at bottom center. Uniface. Printer: RWH & Co.	1250.	250.	—

S1695 10 Dollars

	VG	VF	UNC
18xx. Black. Supported royal arms at top center, cherub at right, small dog's head at bottom center. Uniface. Printer: RWH & Co. Unsigned remainder.	400.	750.	—

S1696 20 Dollars

	VG	VF	UNC
18xx. Black. Two allegorical women seated with sailing ships in background at upper center, supported royal arms turned sideways at right, small dog's head at bottom center. Printer: RWH & Co. Unsigned remainder.	400.	750.	—

Commercial Bank of Montreal, L.C.

1835 Issue

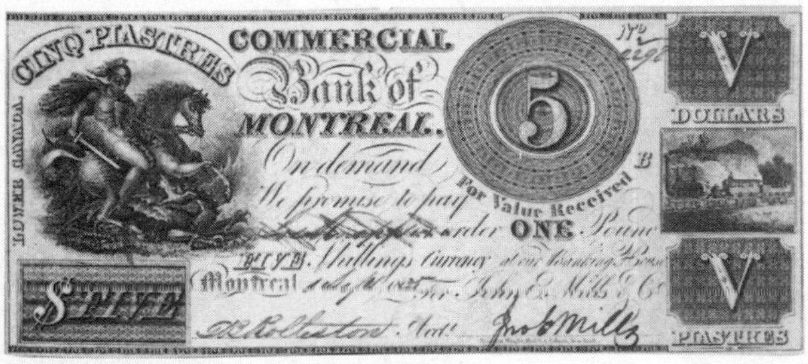

S1697 5 Dollars = 1 Pound-5 Shillings

	Good	Fine	XF
21.8.1835; 1.9.1835. Black. St. George slaying a dragon at left, steam passenger train at right. Uniface. Printer: RWH&E.	400.	1000.	—

S1698 10 Dollars = 2 Pounds-10 Shillings

	Good	Fine	XF
21.8.1835; 1.9.1835. Black. Indian maiden at upper left, early steam passenger train at right. Uniface. Printer: RWH&E. Proof.	400.	1000.	—

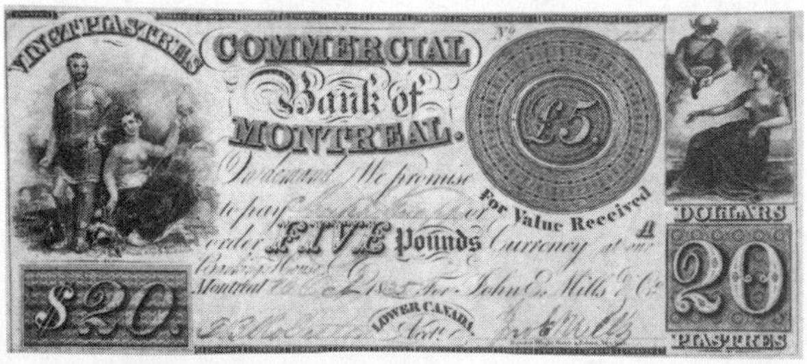

S1699 20 Dollars = 5 Pounds

	Good	Fine	XF
10.10.1835. Black. Standing allegorical vulcan standing by seated allegorical woman at upper left, allegorical man presenting offering to seated woman at right. Uniface. Printer: RWH&E.	500.	1150.	—

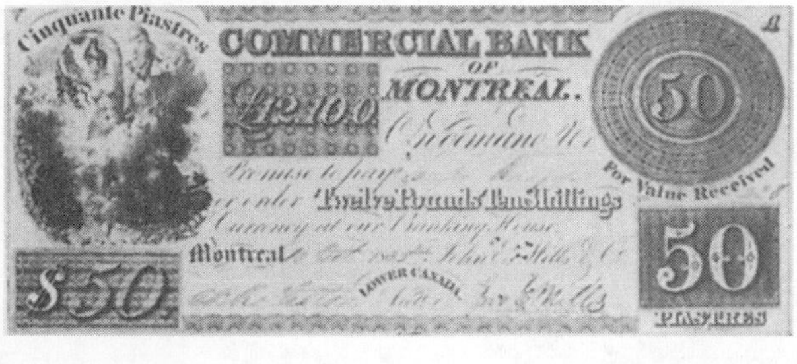

S1700 50 Dollars = 12 Pounds-10 Shillings

	Good	Fine	XF
10.10.1835. Black. Allegorical nude woman and cherub with serpents below at upper left. Uniface. Printer: RWH&E.	400.	1100.	—

1836 Issue

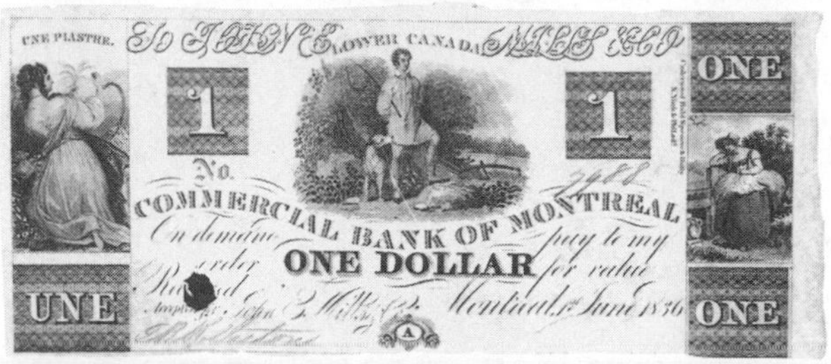

S1701 1 Dollar = 1 Piastre

	Good	Fine	XF
1.6.1836. Black. Farm woman with sickle at left, young man with dog at upper center, farm woman with sheaves of grain at right. Uniface. Printer: Underwood, Bald, Spencer & Huffy. Unissued remainders.	250.	900.	—

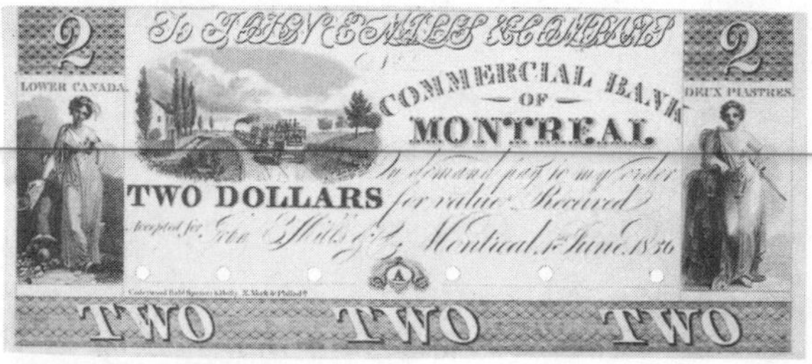

S1702 2 Dollars = 2 Piastres

	Good	Fine	XF
1.6.1836. Black. Woman with cornucopia at left, steam passenger train passing by houses at upper left center, standing Justice at right. Uniface. Printer: Underwood, Bald, Spencer & Huffy. Unissued remainders.	350.	1000.	—

Commercial Bank of New Brunswick

Fredericton

1800s Issue

		Good	Fine	XF
S1703	**1 Pound** 18xx. Sailing ships at left. Face proof.	—	Unc	650.

#S1704 and S1705 small lion on crown at bottom ctr.

		Good	Fine	XF
S1704	**2 Pounds** 18xx. Sailing ships at left. Small lion on crown at bottom center. Face proof.	—	Unc	650.
S1705	**5 Pounds** 18xx. Standing Britannia with shield at left. Small lion on crown at bottom center. Face proof.	—	Unc	650.

Miramichi

1837 Issue

		Good	Fine	XF
S1706	**5 Shillings** 4.12.1837. Allegorical woman at left.	400.	1250.	—
S1707	**7 Shillings-6 Pence** 4.12.1837. Allegorical woman with lyre and cornucopia at left.	400.	1250.	—

St. John

1850s Issue

S1708 5 Shillings

	Good	Fine	XF
18xx. Black. Sailing ships by lighthouse at left, two farmers harvesting grain at right. Supported royal arms above sailing ship medal at top center. Back: Green. Sailing ships at left and right. Small lion on crown at bottom center. Printer: New England Bank Note Company. Face proof.	—	Unc	450.

S1709 1 Pound

1.6.1850; 1.7.1852; 1.6.1853; 1.11.1853. Black. Ship, cargo and fasces at left. Supported royal arms above sailing ship medal at top center. Back: Green. Small lion on crown at bottom center. Printer: New England Bank Note Company.

	Good	Fine	XF
a. Issued note.	500.	1250.	—
p. Face proof.	—	Unc	900.

		Good	Fine	XF
S1710	**2 Pounds** 18xx. Black. Sailing ships at left. Supported royal arms above sailing ship medalat top center. Back: Green. Small lion on crown at bottom center. Printer: New England Bank Note Company. Face proof.	—	Unc	750.
S1711	**5 Pounds** 1.6.1853. Black. Seated Britannia at left. Supported royal arms above sailing ship medal at top center. Back: Green. Small lion on crown at bottom center. Printer: New England Bank Note Company.			
	a. Issued note.	400.	1150.	—
	p. Face proof.	—	Unc	900.
S1712	**10 Pounds** 18xx. Black. Sailing ship at left. Supported royal arms above sailing ship medal at top center. Back: Green. Small lion on crown at bottom center. Printer: New England Bank Note Company. Face proof.	—	Unc	650.
S1713	**25 Pounds** 18xx. Black. Sailing ships at left. Supported royal arms above sailing ship medal at top center. Back: Green. Small lion on crown at bottom center. Printer: New England Bank Note Company. Face proof.	—	Unc	750.

1860 Issue

		Good	Fine	XF
S1714	**1 Dollar = 5 Shillings** 1.11.1860. Black on green underprint. Sailing ship at left. Back: Green. Printer: ABNC.			
	a. Issued note.	150.	650.	1250.
	p. Face proof.	—	Unc	900.
S1715	**2 Dollars = 10 Shillings** 1.11.1860. Black on green underprint. Shipbuilding at right. Back: Green. Printer: ABNC.			
	a. Issued note.	250.	800.	1250.
	p. Face proof.	—	Unc	800.
S1716	**4 Dollars = 1 Pound** 1.11.1860. Black on green underprint. Ship, cargo and faces at left. Back: Green. Printer: ABNC.			
	a. Issued note.	250.	800.	1300.
	p. Face proof.	—	Unc	900.
S1717	**8 Dollars = 2 Pounds** 1.11.1860. Black on green underprint. Young girl with basket of flowers at lower right. Back: Green. Printer: ABNC. Face proof.	—	Unc	1000.
S1718	**20 Dollars = 5 Pounds** 1.11.1860. Black on green underprint. Ship at lower left, pilot at ship's wheel at lower right. Back: Green. Printer: ABNC. Face proof.	—	Unc	500.
S1719	**50 Dollars = 12 Pounds-10 Shillings** 1.11.1860. Black on green underprint. Seated allegorical woman at lower right. Back: Green. Printer: ABNC. Face proof.	—	Unc	500.
S1720	**100 Dollars = 25 Pounds** 1.11.1860. Black on green underprint. Fisherman on schooner at lower right. Back: Green. Printer: ABNC.	—	Unc	500.

Commercial Branch Bank of Canada, Collingwood, P.C.

1861 Spurious Issue

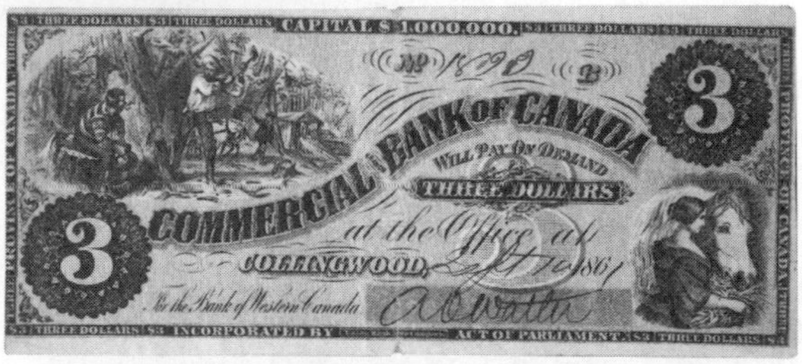

		VG	VF	UNC
S1721	**3 Dollars** 10.9.1861. Black on green underprint. Lumberjacks at upper left, woman feeding horse at lower right. Printer: Union Bank Note Company.	300.	600.	—

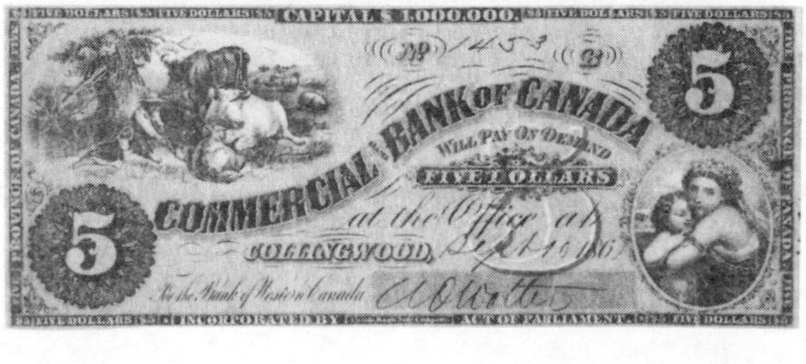

		VG	VF	UNC
S1722	**5 Dollars** 10.9.1861; 10.7.1862. Black on green underprint. Farmer and child seated under tree with cattle at upper left, woman hugging child at lower right. Printer: Union Bank Note Company.	350.	750.	—

The Consolidated Bank of Canada

1876 Issue

#S1723-S1728 Additional blue ovpts: *SEAFORTH* and *SHERBROOKE* reported.

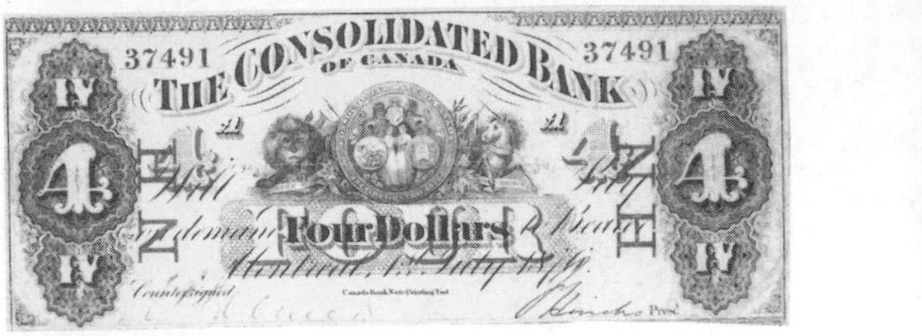

		VG	VF	UNC
S1723	**4 Dollars** 1.7.1876. Black on green underprint. Supported bank crest at upper center. Back: Green. Shield at left and another at right. Printer: BABNC.			
	a. Issued note without overprint	400.	900.	—
	b. With blue overprint: *B-B.*	400.	900.	—
	c. With blue overprint: *C-C.*	400.	900.	—
	d. With blue overprint: *D-D.*	400.	900.	—
	e. With blue overprint: *N-N.*	400.	900.	—
	f. With vertical blue overprint: *NH-NH.*	400.	900.	—
	g. With vertical blue overprint: *BELLEVILLE*	400.	900.	—
	h. With vertical blue overprint: *GALT* twice.	400.	900.	—
	i. With vertical blue overprint: *HAMILTON* twice.	400.	900.	—
	j. With vertical blue overprint: *ST. CATHARINES* twice.	400.	900.	—

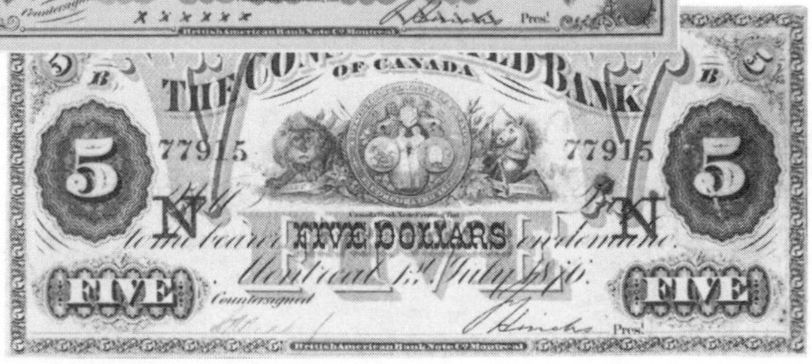

		VG	VF	UNC
S1724	**5 Dollars** 1.7.1876. Black on green underprint. Supported bank crest at upper center. Back: Green. Shield at left and another at right. Printer: BABNC.			
	a. Issued note without overprint.	200.	500.	—
	b. With blue overprint: *N N.*	200.	400.	—
	c. With vertical blue overprint: *GALT* twice.	200.	400.	—

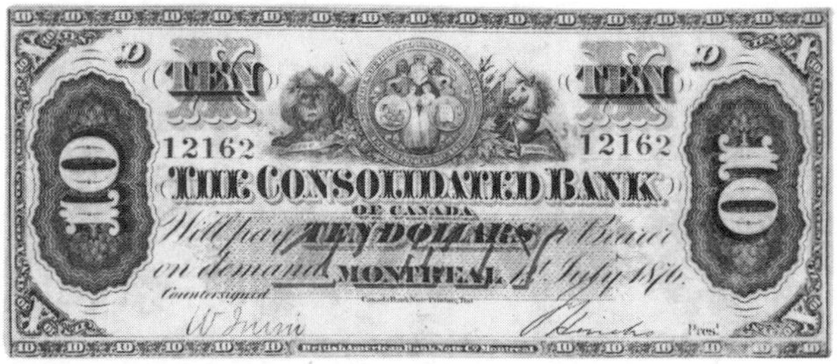

		VG	VF	UNC
S1725	**10 Dollars** 1.7.1876. Black on green underprint. Supported bank crest at upper center. Back: Green. Shield at left and another at right. Printer: BABNC.	200.	400.	—

S1726 20 Dollars	VG	VF	UNC
1.7.1876. Black on green underprint. Supported bank crest at upper center. Back: Green. Shield at left and another at right. Printer: BABNC.			
a. Issued note.	900.	2000.	—
p. Face proof.	—	Unc	600.

S1727 50 Dollars	Good	Fine	XF
1.7.1876. Black on green underprint. Supported bank crest at upper center. Back: Green. Shield at left and another at right. Printer: BABNC. Face proof.	—	Unc	600.

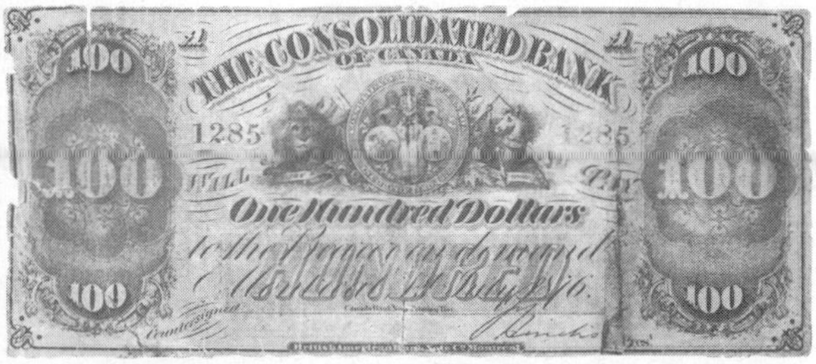

S1728 100 Dollars	VG	VF	UNC
1.7.1876. Black on green underprint. Supported bank crest at upper center. Back: Green. Shield at left and another at right. Printer: BABNC.	900.	2000.	—

The Bank of the County of Elgin

1856-57 Issue

#S1729-S1732 Also encountered cut cancelled w/lower r. hand sign. removed.

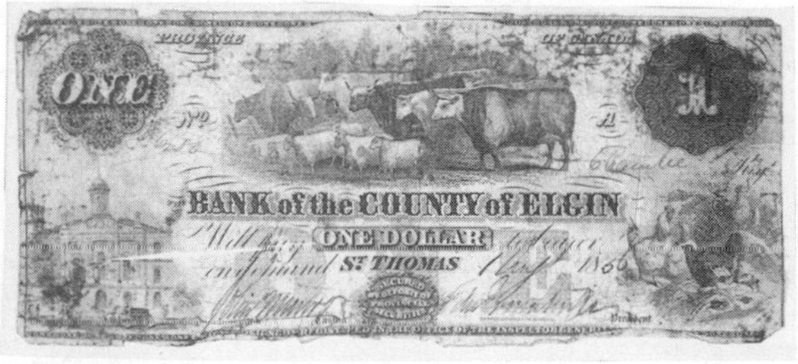

S1729 1 Dollar	Good	Fine	XF
1.7.1856; 1.8.1856; 1.9.1856. Black. Bank building at lower left, farmer driving livestock at top center, rooster with hens and chicks at lower right. Uniface. Red word protector. Back: Red word protector. Printer: TCC.			
a. Issued note.	600.	1500.	—
b. Cut cancelled.	400.	1000.	—

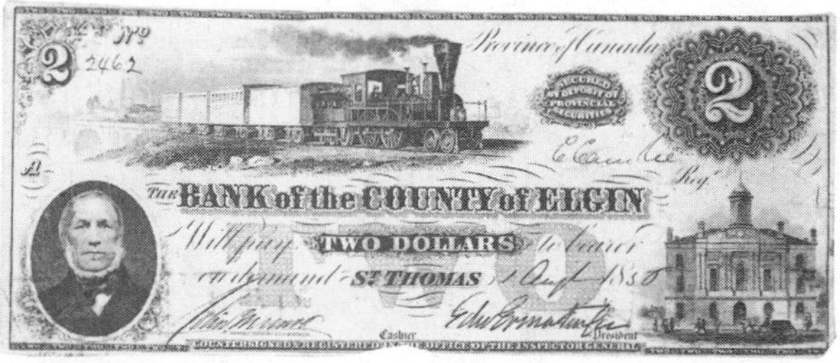

S1730 2 Dollars	Good	Fine	XF
1.8.1856; 31.1.1857. Black. Portrait E. Ermatinger at lower left, steam passenger train at top left center. Uniface. Red word protector. Bank building at lower right. Back: Red word protector. Printer: TCC.			
a. Issued note.	650.	1750.	—
b. Cut cancelled.	500.	1500.	—

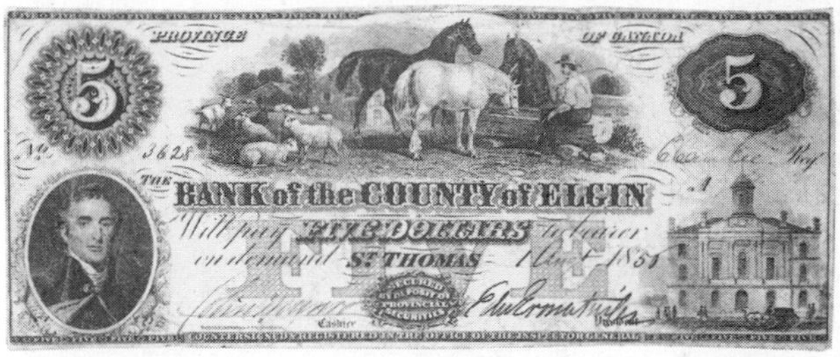

S1731 5 Dollars	Good	Fine	XF
25.6.1856; 1.8.1856. Black. Portrait Duke of Wellington at lower left, farmer with livestock at top center. Uniface. Red word protector. Bank building at lower right. Back: Red word protector. Printer: TCC.			
a. Issued note.	800.	2000.	—
b. Cut cancelled.	600.	1500.	—

S1732 10 Dollars	Good	Fine	XF
1.8.1856. Black. Portrait E. Ermatinger at lower left, farm family watching steam passenger train at top center. Uniface. Red word protector. Bank building at lower right. Back: Red word protector. Printer: TCC.			
a. Issued note.	750.	2500.	—
b. Cut cancelled.	500.	1250.	—

Eastern Bank of Canada

1929 Issue

S1733 5 Dollars	Good	Fine	XF
15.5.1929. Black on green underprint. Ship and steam train at dockside at center. Back: Orange. Bank seal at center. Printer: CNBC. Proof.	—	Unc	800.

S1734 10 Dollars	Good	Fine	XF
15.5.1929. Black on brown underprint. Allegorical woman reclining at center. Back: Brown. Bank seal at center. Printer: CNBC. Proof.	—	Unc	800.

The Exchange Bank, Quebec, L.C.

1839; 1844 Issue

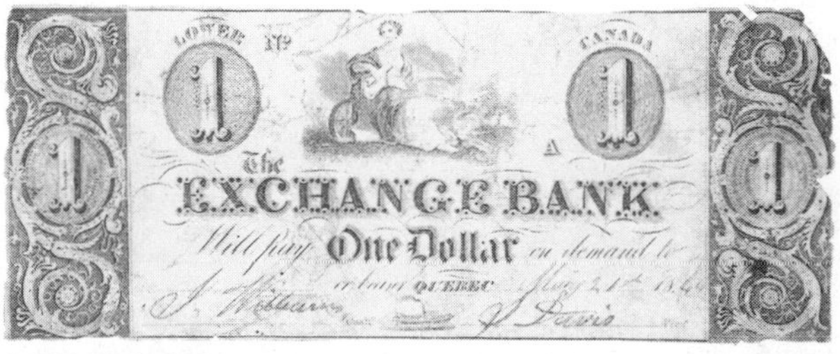

S1735 1 Dollar	VG	VF	UNC
1839; 1844. Black. Reclining allegorical woman at top center. Uniface.			
a. 29.9.1839.	1500.	—	—
b. 21.5.1844.	1500.	—	—

The Exchange Bank of Canada

1872-73 Issue

#S1736-S1742 Additional overprints: Blue *EXTER, X* over *BRUSSELS:* purple C.

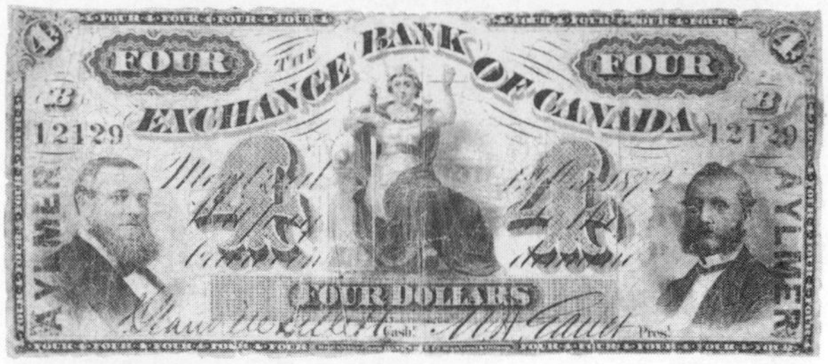

S1736 4 Dollars

1.10.1872; 1.11.1872. Black on green underprint. Seated Justice at center. T. Caverhill at left, M. H. Gault at right. Back: Green. Beehive and flowers at center. Overprint: Blue *EXTER, X* over *BRUSSELS:* purple C.

	Good	Fine	XF
a. Issued note without overprint.	300.	900.	—
b. Vertical blue overprint: *AYLMER* twice.	300.	900.	—
c. Vertical blue overprint: *BRUSSELS* twice.	300.	900.	—
d. Vertical blue overprint: *HAMILTON* twice.	300.	900.	—

S1737 5 Dollars

1.10.1872; 1.11.1872. Black on green underprint. Seated Industry at center right. T. Caverhill at left, M. H. Gault at right. Back: Green. Beehive and flowers at center. Overprint: Blue *EXTER, X* over *BRUSSELS:* purple C.

	Good	Fine	XF
a. Issued note without overprint.	300.	900.	—
b. Vertical blue overprint: *AYLMER* twice.	300.	900.	—
c. Vertical blue overprint: *BRUSSELS* twice.	300.	900.	—
d. Vertical blue overprint: *HAMILTON* twice.	300.	900.	—
e. Vertical blue overprint: *PARKHILL* twice.	300.	900.	—
f. Large overprint: *L-L.*	300.	900.	—

S1738 6 Dollars

1.10.1872; 1.11.1872. Black on green underprint. Paddle wheel steamboat at upper center. T. Caverhill at left, M. H. Gault at right. Back: Green. Beehive and flowers at center. Overprint: Blue *EXTER, X* over *BRUSSELS:* purple C.

	VG	VF	UNC
a. Issued note without overprint.	3500.	—	—
b. Vertical blue overprint: *VALLEYFIELD* twice.	3500.	—	—

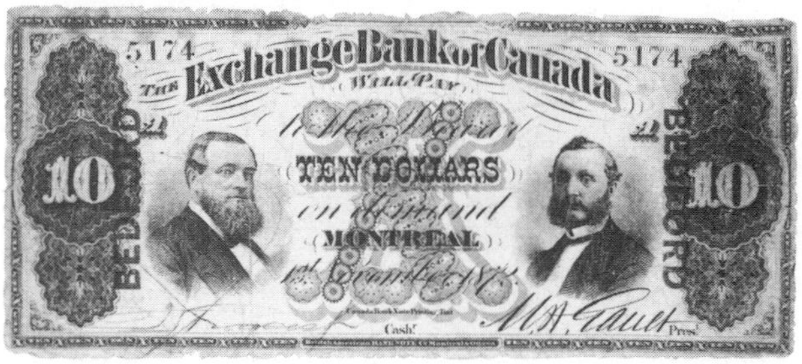

S1739 10 Dollars

1.10.1872; 1.11.1872. Black on green underprint. Large *X* in underprint at center. T. Caverhill at left, M. H. Gault at right. Back: Green. Beehives and flowers at center. Overprint: Blue *EXTER, X* over *BRUSSELS:* purple C.

	Good	Fine	XF
a. Issued note without overprint.	600.	1750.	—
b. Vertical blue overprint: *ALYMER* twice.	600.	1750.	—
c. Vertical blue overprint: *BEDFORD* twice.	600.	1750.	—
d. Vertical blue overprint: *HAMILTON* twice.	600.	1750.	—

S1740 25 Dollars

1.10.1872; 1.11.1872. Black on green underprint. Trade and Transportation at center. T. Caverhill at left, M. H. Gault at right. Back: Green. Beehive and flowers at center. Overprint: Blue *EXTER, X* over *BRUSSELS:* purple C. Face proof.

Good	Fine	XF
—	Unc	1750.

S1741 50 Dollars

2.1.1873. Black on green underprint. T. Caverhill at left, M. H. Gault at right. Back: Green. Beehive and flowers at center. Overprint: Blue *EXTER, X* over *BRUSSELS:* purple C. Face proof.

Good	Fine	XF
—	Unc	750.

S1742 100 Dollars

2.1.1873. Black on green underprint. Reclining allegorical woman with split water jug at top center. T. Caverhill at left, M. H. Gault at right. Back: Green. Beehive and flowers at center. Overprint: Blue *EXTER, X* over *BRUSSELS:* purple C. Face proof.

Good	Fine	XF
—	Unc	750.

The Exchange Bank of Canada, Windsor, Ontario

1864 Issue

S1743 1 Dollar

8.6.1864. Black. Standing Britannia at lower left, early steam passenger train at center, supported royal arms at right. Uniface.

Good	Fine	XF
300.	750.	—

The Exchange Bank of Toronto, U.C.

1855 Issue

S1744 1 Dollar

1.5.1855. Black. Stag at left of seated Indian with Large *1* at upper center, farmer with sheaf and sickle at lower right. Crest at left. Uniface. Printer: RWH&E. Unsigned remainders.

VG	VF	UNC
25.00	75.00	200.

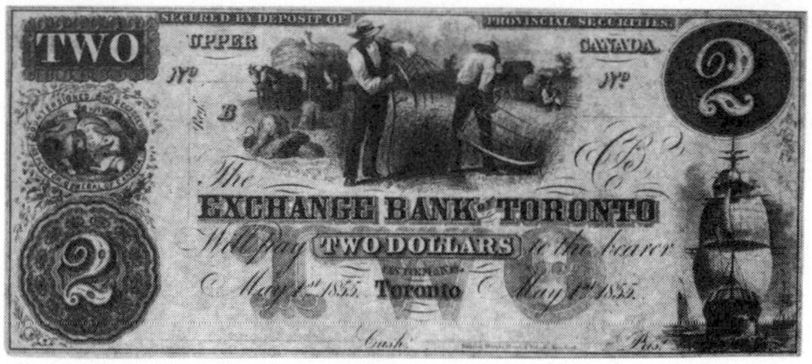

S1745 2 Dollars

1.5.1855. Black. Farmer's harvesting grain with cradles at upper center, sailing ship at lower right. Crest at left. Uniface. Printer: RWH&E. Unsigned remainders.

VG	VF	UNC
25.00	75.00	200.

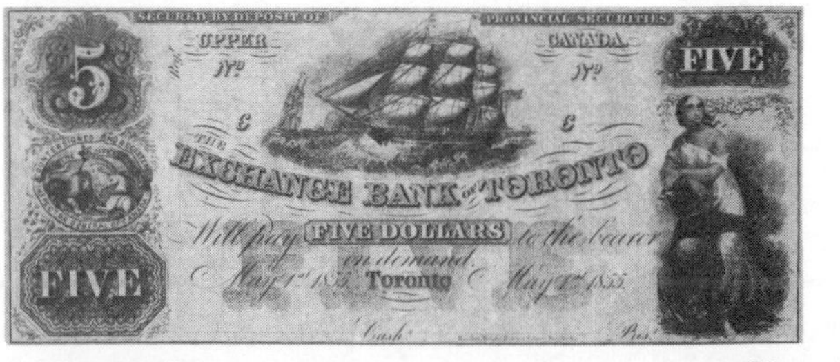

S1746 5 Dollars

1.5.1855. Black. Sailing ship at top center, standing Navigation at lower right. Crest at left. Uniface. Printer: RWH&E. Unsigned remainders.

VG	VF	UNC
25.00	75.00	200.

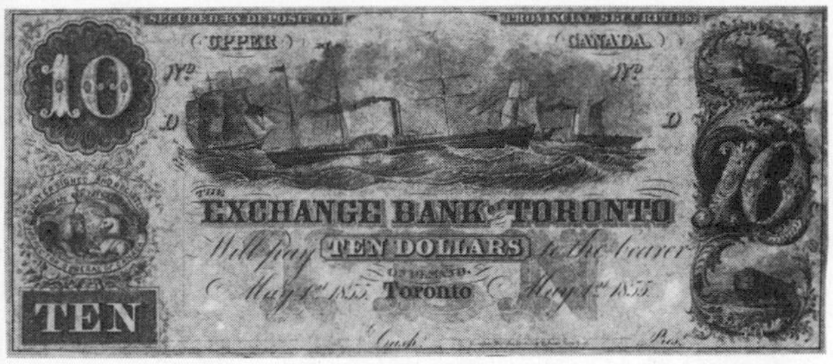

S1747 10 Dollars	VG	VF	UNC
1.5.1855. Black. Various ships at upper center, deer at upper right, bison at lower right. Crest at left. Uniface. Printer: RWH&E. Unsigned remainders.	25.00	75.00	200.

The Exchange Bank Company of Chippewa, U.C.

1837 Spurious Issue

S1748 5 Dollars	Good	Fine	XF
2.1.1837. Black. Produce and farm implements at top center, Indian at right, beaver at bottom center. Uniface. Printer: RWH & Co.			
a. Issued note.	500.	1250.	—
r. Remainder without serial #. 18xx.	500.	1250.	—

S1749 10 Dollars	Good	Fine	XF
18xx. Black. Livestock at top center, Seated Commerce at right, small steamboat at bottom center. Uniface. Printer: RWH & Co.			
r. Remainder without serial #.	500.	1250.	—

The Farmer's Bank, Toronto, U.C.

1843 Spurious Issue

S1750 5 Dollars = 1 Pound-5 Shillings	VG	VF	UNC
3.8.1843. Black. Plow at left, kneeling cherub writing on stone slab at top center, woman with bow at right. *New York - Exchange* at top border. Uniface. Printer: SC N.Y.	900.	—	—

Farmers' Bank of Malden

1800s Issue

S1751 1 Dollar = 5 Shillings	Good	Fine	XF
18xx. Black. Steamboat at left, rural scene at upper center, Indian maiden at right. Uniface. Printer: Draper, Toppan, Longacre & Co. Proof.	—	Unc	1000.

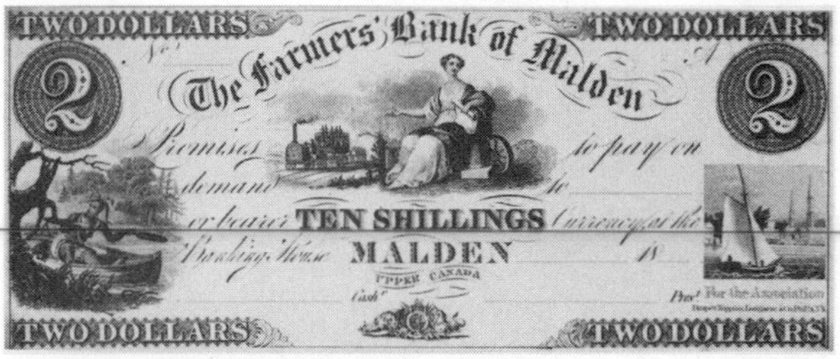

S1752 2 Dollars = 10 Shillings	Good	Fine	XF
18xx. Black. Indian in canoe at lower left, seated allegorical woman with early steam passenger train in background at upper center, sailboat at lower right. Uniface. Printer: Draper, Toppan, Longacre & Co. Proof.	—	Unc	1000.
S1753 3 Dollars = 15 Shillings			
18xx. Black. Man seated with flag at lower left, livestock at upper center, farm woman with sheaf and sickle at upper right. Uniface. Printer: Draper, Toppan, Longacre & Co. Proof.	—	Unc	1000.

Farmer's Joint Stock Banking Co.

1835-37 Issues

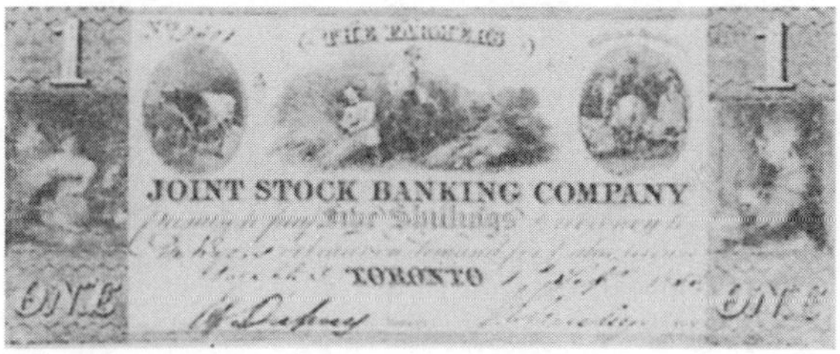

S1754 1 Dollar = 5 Shillings	Good	Fine	XF
1.9.1835. Black. Seated allegorical woman at left, farmers harvesting grain between cattle and man on horseback by man with dog at upper center, woman at lower right. Uniface. Printer: NEBNC, Boston.	150.	450.	—
S1755 2 Dollars = 10 Shillings			
11.9.1837. Black. Ship, cargo and fasces at left, seated woman with haying in background at upper left center, standing Britannia with shield at lower right. Uniface. Printer: NEBNC, Boston.	150.	450.	—
S1756 4 Dollars = 1 Pound			
18xx. Black. Indian at left, woman with sheaf and dog at top center, seated Britannia at lower right. Uniface. Printer: NEBNC, Boston.			
a. Issued note.	100.	300.	—
p. Face proof.	—	Unc	500.

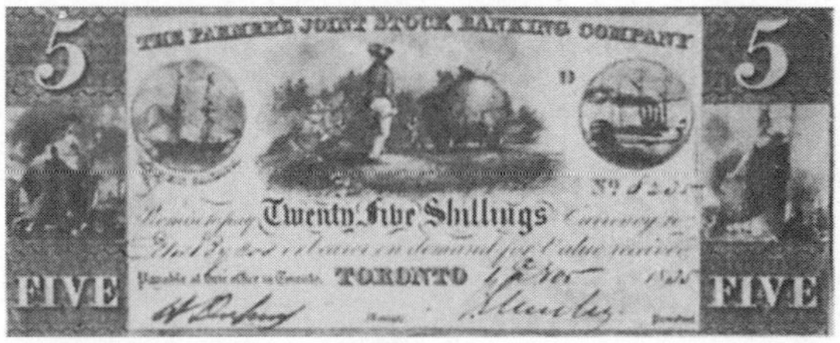

S1757 5 Dollars = 25 Shillings	Good	Fine	XF
1.11.1835. Black. Abundance at left, farmers loading hay wagon between ships at upper center, standing Britannia with shield at right. Uniface. Printer: NEBNC, Boston.	150.	450.	—

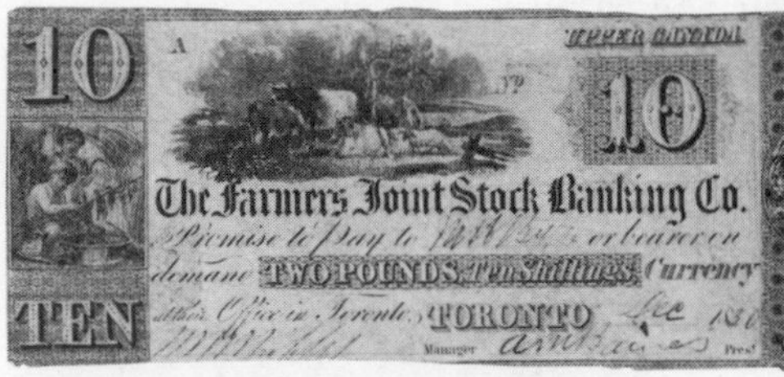

	Good	Fine	XF
S1758 10 Dollars = 2 Pounds-10 Shillings December 1835. Black. Two cherubs picking grapes at left, livestock at top left center, beehive at right. Uniface. Printer: NEBNC, Boston.	150.	450.	—
S1759 50 Dollars = 12 Pounds-10 Shillings 18xx. Black. Woman with flowers, farmers planting at left, maids by cows at center, sheaf at right. Uniface. Printer: NEBNC, Boston. Proof.	—	Unc	450.

Green Bay, Wisconsin

1849 Issue

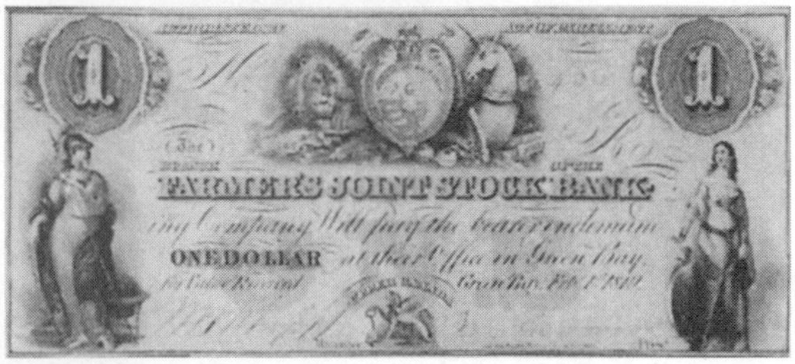

	VG	VF	UNC
S1760 1 Dollar 1.2.1849. Black. Standing Britannia at lower left, supported royal arms at top center, young woman at lower right, small griffin with key at bottom center. Uniface. Lion and unicorn supporters at top center. Printer: RWH&E. *THE BRANCH OF* and *Office in Green Bay, Wisconsin* engraved.	1750.	—	—

	VG	VF	UNC
S1761 2 Dollars 1.2.1849. Blacksmith by anvil at lower left, supported portrait Prince Consort at top center, standing Navigation at lower right, small supported royal arms at bottom center. Lion and unicorn supporter Printer: RWH&E. *THE BRANCH OF* and *Office in Green Bay, Wisconsin* engraved.	1750.	—	—

	VG	VF	UNC
S1762 5 Dollars 1.2.1849. Black. Standing Britannia and Justice at lower left, supported portrait of Queen Victoria at top center, Minerva standing by seated Prosperity at lower right, small crown on swords at bottom center. Uniface. Printer: RWH&E. *THE BRANCH OF* and *Office in Green Bay, Wisconsin* engraved.	1750.	—	—

NOTICE

Readers with unlisted dates, signature varieties, etc., are invited to submit photocopies or scans of their notes to: Standard Catalog of World Paper Money, 700 East State St. Iola, WI 54990-0001, E-Mail: george.cuhaj@fwmedia.com.

Toronto

1849 First Issue

#S1763-1765 also w/red ovpt: *KINGSTON*, various letters and numerical handstamps.

	VG	VF	UNC
S1763 1 Dollar = 5 Shillings 1.2.1849. Standing Britannia at lower left, supported royal arms at top center, young woman at lower right, small griffin with key at bottom center. Lion and unicorn supporters at top center. Overprint: Red; *KINGSTON.* Printer: RWH&E. Various letters and numerical handstamps.	40.00	75.00	200.

	VG	VF	UNC
S1764 2 Dollars = 10 Shillings 1.2.1849. Blacksmith by anvil at lower left, supported portrait of the Prince Consort at top center, standing Navigation at lower right, small supported royal arms at bottom center. Lion and unicorn supporters Overprint: Red; *KINGSTON.* Printer: RWH&E. Various letters and numerical handstamps.	40.00	75.00	200.

	VG	VF	UNC
S1765 5 Dollars = 25 Shillings 1.2.1849. Standing Britannia and Justice at lower left, supported portrait of Queen Victoria at top center, Minerva standing by seated Prosperity at lower right, small crown on swords at bottom center. Lion and Overprint: Red; *KINGSTON.* Printer: RWH&E. Various letters and numerical handstamps.	40.00	75.00	200.

1849 Second Issue

	VG	VF	UNC
S1766 1 Dollar 1.2.1849. Black. Standing Britannia at lower left, supported royal arms at top center, young woman at lower right, small griffin with key at bottom center. Lion and unicorn supporters at top center. Red word protector Printer: RWH&E. Uniface.	25.00	50.00	125.

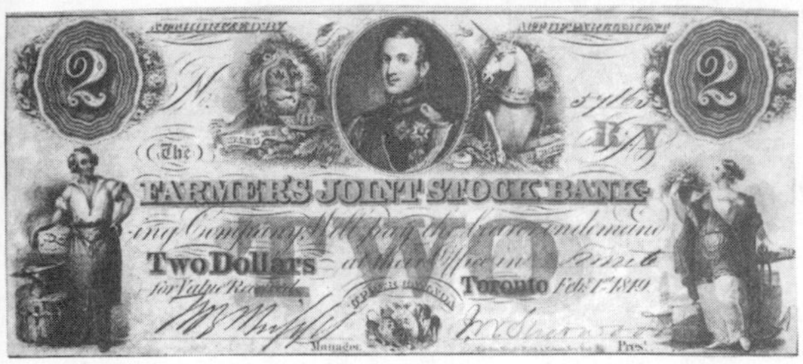

S1767 2 Dollars

1.2.1849. Black. Blacksmith by anvil at lower left, supported portrait Prince Consort at top center, standing Navigation at lower right, small supported royal arms at bottom center. Lion and unicorn supporter. Red wor Printer: RWH&E. Uniface.

VG	VF	UNC
25.00	50.00	125.

S1768 3 Dollars

1.2.1849. Black. Standing Britannia and Justice at lower left, Neptune and Liberty in chariot at top center, blacksmith, seaman and farmer with Large ornate *3* at lower right. Red word protector. Printer: RWH&E. Uniface.

VG	VF	UNC
50.00	100.	200.

S1769 5 Dollars

1.2.1849. Black. Standing Britannia and Justice at lower left, supported portrait of Queen Victoria at top center, Minerva standing by seated Prosperity at lower right, small crown on swords at bottom center. red word Printer: RWH&E.

VG	VF	UNC
25.00	50.00	125.

Farmers J.S. Banking Co., Toronto, U.C.

1800s Spurious Issue

S1770 10 Dollars = 10 Piastres

18xx. Black. Portrait J. Fox at left, seated woman holding lion shield at upper center, woman in grain field at right. Uniface. Printer: Casilear, Durand, Burton & Edmonds. Unsigned remainder.

	Good	Fine	XF
a. Printed date: 18xx.	—	Unc	200.
b. Printed date: 1849.	—	Unc	250.

Farmers Bank of Rustico, P.E.I.

1864 Issue

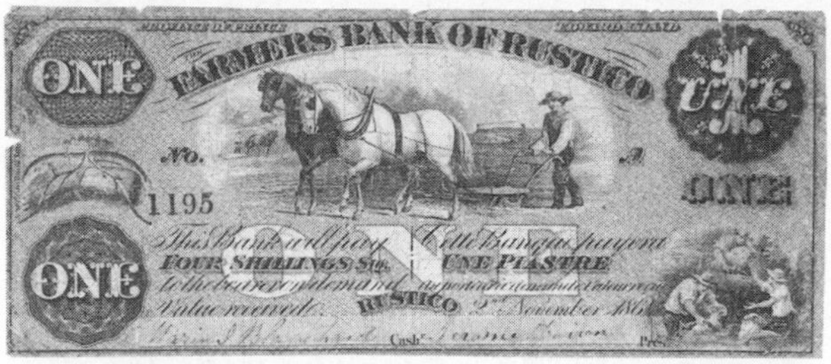

S1771 4 Shillings = 1 Piastre

2.11.1864. Black on green underprint. Two scythes on sheaf of wheat at left, farmer plowing with two horses at upper center, three men shearing sheep at lower right. Uniface. Printer: ABNC.

VG	VF	UNC
2000.	—	—

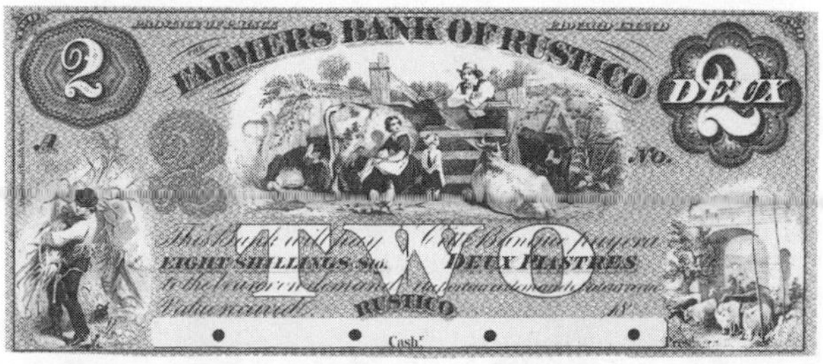

S1772 8 Shillings = 2 Piastres

2.11.1864. Black on green underprint. Farm boy carrying cornstalks at lower left, farm family with cattle and hen with chicks at upper center, driving cattle below railroad bridge at lower right. Uniface. Printer: ABNC. Proof.

Good	Fine	XF
—	Unc	900.

S1773 1 Pound = 5 Piastras

2.11.1864. Black on green underprint. Chickens at upper left, farmer watering livestock at top center, milkmaid by livestock at lower right. Uniface. Printer: ABNC. Proof.

Good	Fine	XF
—	Unc	900.

1872 Issue

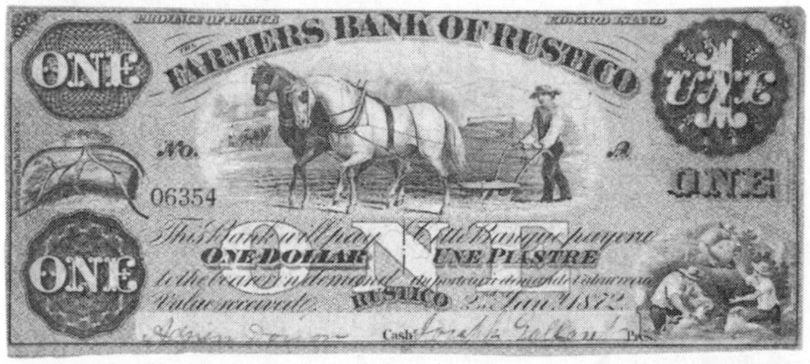

S1774 1 Dollar = 1 Piastre

2.1.1872. Black on green underprint. Two scythes on sheaf of wheat at left, farmer plowing with two horses at upper center, three men shearing sheep at lower right. Uniface. Printer: ABNC, BABNC.

VG	VF	UNC
1500.	—	—

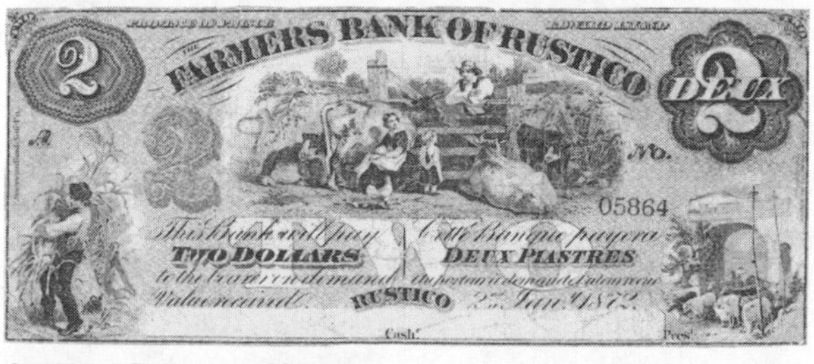

S1775 2 Dollars = 2 Piastres

2.1.1872. Black on green underprint. Farm boy carrying cornstalks at lower left, farm family with cattle and hen with chicks at upper center, driving cattle below railroad bridge at lower right. Uniface. Printer: ABNC, BABNC.

VG	VF	UNC
1750.	—	—

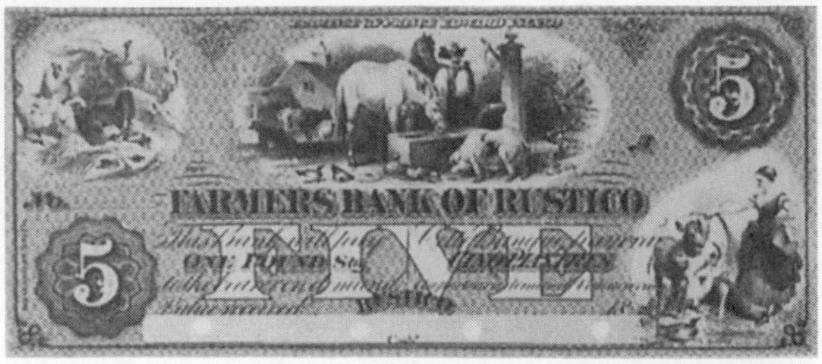

S1776 5 Dollars = 5 Piastres	VG	VF	UNC
2.1.1872. Black on green underprint. Chickens at upper left, farmer watering livestock at top center, milkmaid by livestock at lower right. Uniface. Printer: ABNC, BABNC.	2000.	—	—

Farmers Bank of St. Johns, L.C.

1837 Issue

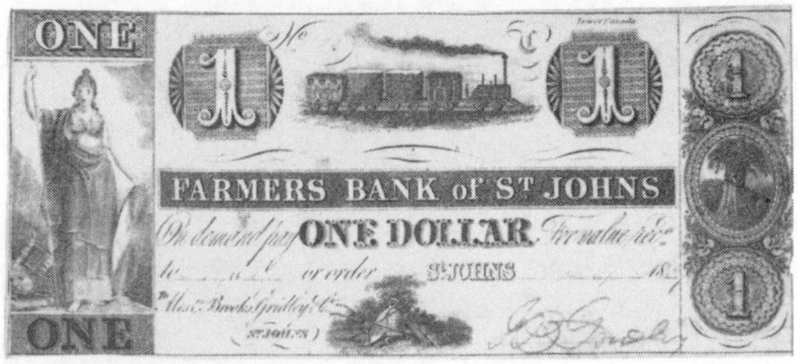

S1777 1 Dollar	VG	VF	UNC
4.12.1837; 5.12.1837. Black. Standing Britannia at left, early steam passenger train at top center, sheaf of grain at right, small farm implements at bottom center. Uniface.	650.	—	—

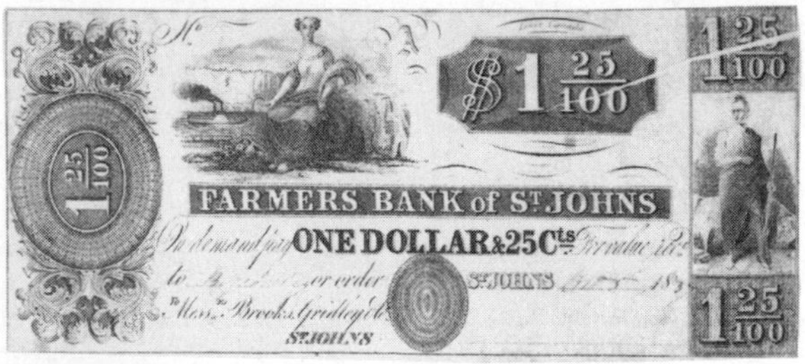

S1778 1 Dollar 25 Cents	VG	VF	UNC
5.12.1837. Black. Seated Agriculture with steamboat in background at upper left center, standing Indian brave with rifle at right. Uniface.	1250.	—	—
S1778A 1 Dollar 50 Cents 5.12.1837. Black. Seated allegorical women at lower left, seated woman with Indian brave with rifle at center, farmer plowing with horses at right. Uniface.	1250.	—	—

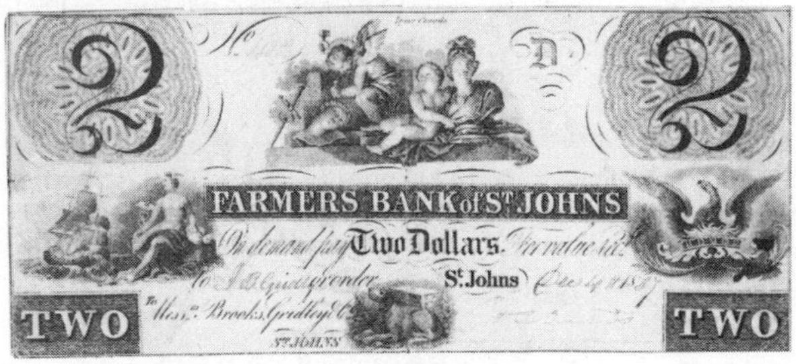

S1779 2 Dollars	VG	VF	UNC
4.12.1837. Black. Seated Mercury by shoreline with sailing ship in background at left, cherubs sculpting busts at top center, Phoenix at lower right, small dog lying by strongbox at bottom center. Uniface.	650.	—	—

1838 Issue

S1779A 3 Dollars	VG	VF	UNC
18xx. Black. Standing Indian woman with bow & arrow at left, man standing with papers, building in background at center, seated Indian with plaque at right. Uniface. Printer: Lowe.	—	—	400.

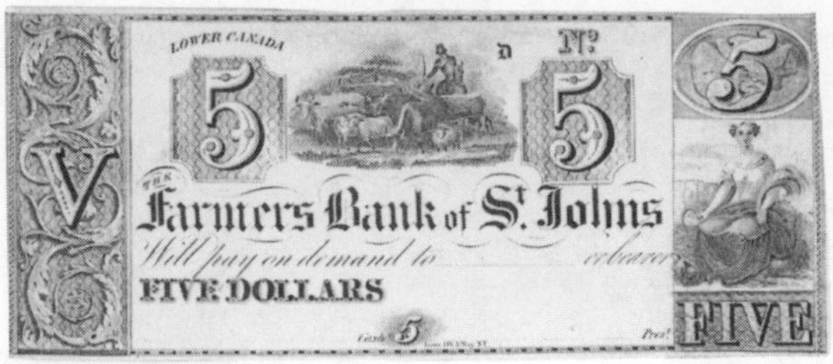

S1780 5 Dollars	VG	VF	UNC
21.5.1838. Black. Farmer with livestock at top center, seated Agriculture with sheaf and sickle at right. Uniface. Printer: Lowe.			
a. Issued note.	500.	—	—
r. Unsigned remainder.	—	—	400.
S1781 10 Dollars 18xx. Black. Farmer plowing with horses at top center, seated allegorical man at right. Uniface. Printer: Lowe. Unsigned remainder.	—	—	400.

Federal Bank of Canada, Toronto

1874-82 Issue

S1782 4 Dollars	Good	Fine	XF
1.7.1874. Black on green underprint. Cherubs with ornate *4* at center. H.S. Strathey at lower left, N. Alexandra at lower right. Back: Green. Printer: BABNC.	200.	650.	—

S1783 5 Dollars	Good	Fine	XF
1.7.1874. Black on green underprint. Blacksmiths by anvil, ornate *5* with factories in background at center. H.S. Strathey at lower left, N. Alexandra at lower right. Back: Green. Printer: BABNC.	175.	500.	—

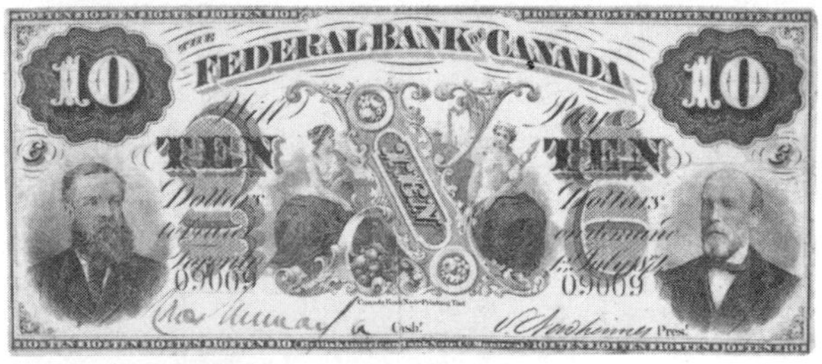

S1784 10 Dollars	Good	Fine	XF
1.7.1874; 1.1.1877. Black on green underprint. Two allegorical women seated by ornate *X* with factories in background. H.S. Strathey at lower left, N. Alexandra at lower right. Back: Green. Printer: BABNC.	200.	650.	—
S1785 50 Dollars 1.1.1877. Black on green underprint. Steam passenger train at station at center. H.S. Strathey at lower left, N. Alexandra at lower right. Back: Green. Printer: BABNC. Face proof.	—	Unc	600.
S1786 100 Dollars 1.9.1882. Black on green underprint. Canadian arms at center. H.S> Strathey at lower left, N. Alexander at lower right. Back: Green. Printer: BABNC. Face proof.	—	Unc	600.

1884 Issue

		Good	Fine	XF
S1787	**5 Dollars** 1.1.1884. Black on green underprint. Blacksmiths by anvil, ornate *5* with factories in background at center. H.S. Strathey at lower left, N. Alexandra at lower right. Back: Gree. Printer: BABNC. Face proof.	—	Unc	650.
S1788	**10 Dollars** 1.1.1884. Black on green underprint. Two allegorical women seated by ornate *X* with factories in background. H.S. Strathey at lower left, N. Alexandra at lower right. Back: Green. Printer: BABNC. Face proof.	—	Unc	650.

Bank of Fredericton, N.B.

1837-38 Issue

		VG	VF	UNC
S1789	**5 Shillings** 8.5.1837. Black. Seated girl with sheaf at left, paddle wheel steamboat and sailboats at top center, seated Indian brave at right. Back: Blue. Printer: NEBNC.	1750.	—	—

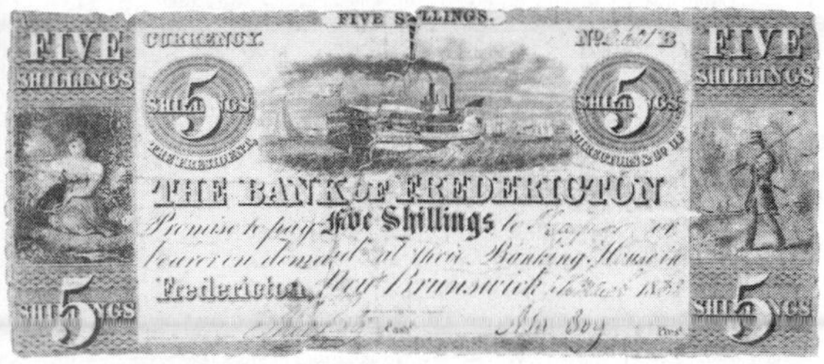

		VG	VF	UNC
S1790	**5 Shillings** 6.3.1838. Black. Seated girl with sheaf at left, paddle wheel steamboat and sailboats at top center, hunter at right. Back: Blue. Printer: NEBNC.	1750.	—	—
S1791	**10 Shillings** 18xx. Black. Blacksmith at left, sailing ships at top left center, lion and shield at right Printer: NEBNC. Proof.	—	—	900.
S1792	**1 Pound** 18xx. Two farmers harvesting grain at left, farmer sowing seed with horses in background at top center. Printer: NEBNC. Proof.	—	—	900.
S1793	**5 Pounds** 18xx. Black. Seated Justice at left, farmer by horseman and livestock at top center. Printer: NEBNC. Proof.	—	—	900.

Free Holders Bank of the Midland District

1800s Issue

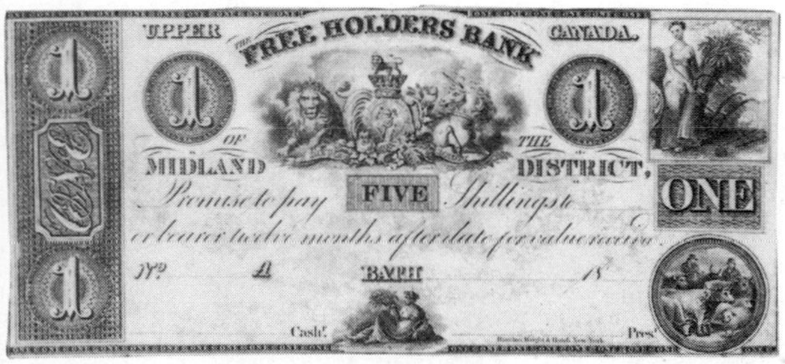

		VG	VF	UNC
S1794	**1 Dollar = 5 Shillings** 18xx. Black. Supported royal arms at top center, woman with sheaf at upper right, farmers with livestock at lower right, small reclining Agriculture with sheaf and sickle at bottom center. Uniface. Printer: RWH & Co. Unsigned remainder.	750.	—	—

		VG	VF	UNC
S1795	**5 Dollars = 25 Shillings** 18xx. Black. Beehive, cornucopia, produce, sheaf and spinning wheel at top center, small child riding deer at bottom center. Uniface. Printer: RWH & Co. Unsigned remainders.	750.	—	—

Goderich Bank, U.C.

1834 Issue

		Good	Fine	XF
S1796	**1 Dollar = 5 Shillings** 12.9.1834. Black. Uniface. Printer: C. P. Harrison.	500.	—	—

		Good	Fine	XF
S1797	**2 Dollars = 10 Shillings** 12.9.1834. Black. Lion (sideways) at left, seated Mercury by cargo with sailing ships in background at upper left. Uniface. Printer: C. P. Harrison.	500.	—	—

Gore Bank of Hamilton, U.C.

1800s Spurious Issue

		Good	Fine	XF
S1798	**10 Dollars** 18xx. Black. Portrait J. Fox at left, seated woman with lion shield at upper center, young woman with sheaf at right. Uniface. Printer: Casilear, Durand, Burton & Edmonds. Unsigned remainders.	—	—	—

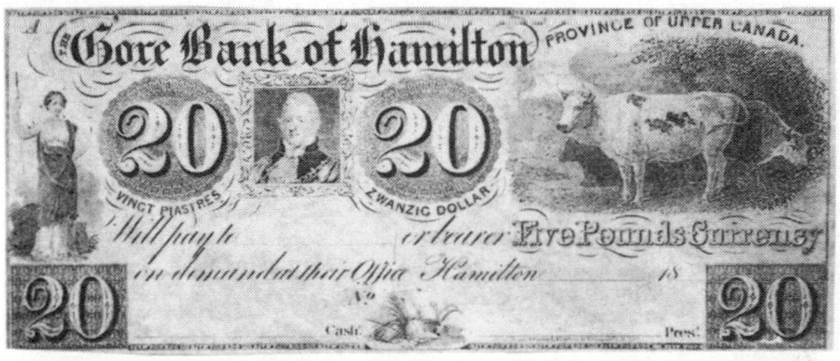

		Good	Fine	XF
S1799	**20 Dollars** 18xx. Black. Allegorical woman with shield and spear at left, portrait King William IV at upper left center, steers at upper right. Uniface. Printer: Casilear, Durand, Burton & Edmonds. Unsigned remainder.	—	—	—

		Good	Fine	XF
S1800	**50 Dollars** 18xx. Black. Identical allegorical woman at left and at right, supported portrait of King William IV at top center. Uniface. Printer: Casilear, Durand, Burton & Edmonds. Unsigned remainder.	—	—	—

Hart's Bank

1837 Issue

		VG	VF	UNC
S1801	**5 Pence = 10 Sous** 1.10.1837. Black. Uniface. Printer: Bourne. Unsigned remainder.	25.00	75.00	200.
S1802	**10 Pence = 20 Sous** 1.10.1837. Black. Uniface. Printer: Bourne. Unsigned remainder.	25.00	75.00	200.
S1803	**20 Pence = 40 Sous** 1.10.1837. Black. Uniface. Printer: Bourne. Unsigned remainder.	25.00	75.00	200.
S1804	**2 Shillings-6 Pence = 60 Sous** 1.10.1837. Black. Man smoking pipe at right. Uniface. Printer: Bourne. Unsigned remainder.	25.00	75.00	225.

1838 Issue

S1805 1 Dollar	VG	VF	UNC
28.7.1838. Black. Paddle wheel steamboat (sideways) at left, seated Indian maiden at right, small steamboat at bottom center. Two people in horse drawn sleigh at upper left center. Back: Orange. Two men portrait (sideways). Printer: Bourne.			
a. Issued note.	600.	—	—
rp. Uniface reprint.	—	—	150.

S1806 3 Dollars	VG	VF	UNC
20.8.1838. Black. Seated Indian maiden at left, couple in horse drawn sleigh at top center, small ship, casks at bottom center. Two people in horse drawn sleigh at upper left center. Back: Orange. Two men portrait (sideways). Printer: Bourne.			
a. Issued note.	600.	—	—
rp. Uniface reprint.	—	—	25.00

S1807 5 Dollars	Good	Fine	XF
18xx. Black. Seated Indian maiden at left, couple in horse drawn sleigh at top center, small ship, casks at bottom center. Two people in horse drawn sleigh at upper left center. Back: Orange. Two men portrait (sideways). Printer: Bourne. Uniface reprint.	—	Unc	250.

Henry's Bank, L.C.

La Prairie

1837 Issue

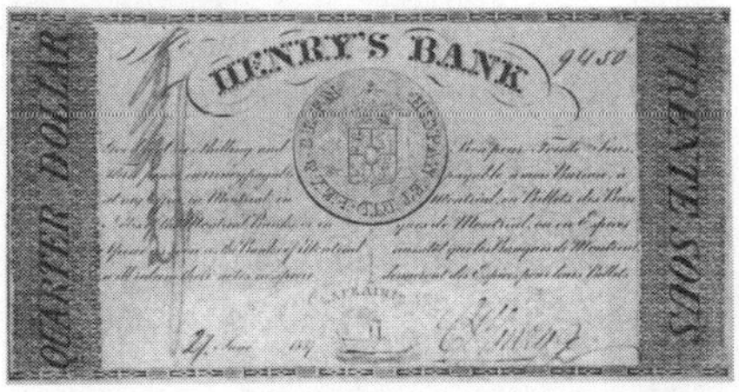

S1808 1/4 Dollar = 1 Shilling-3 Pence = 30 Sous	VG	VF	UNC
27.6.1837. Black. Reverse of Mexican two reales coin at upper center. Uniface.			
a. Issued note.	25.00	75.00	250.
rp. Reprint.	—	—	25.00

S1809 1/2 Dollar = 2 Shillings-6 Pence = 1 Ecu	VG	VF	UNC
27.6.1837. Black. Obverse of Spanish Colonial coin of Charles IV at upper center. Uniface.			
a. Issued note.	25.00	75.00	250.
rp. Reprint.	—	—	25.00

1837 Issue

S1810 1 Dollar	VG	VF	UNC
19.6.1837; 27.6.1837. Black. Identical standing allegorical woman at left and at right, seated with anchor at upper center, small steamboat at bottom center. Uniface. Printer: Burton, Gurley & Edmunds, N. Y.	50.00	100.	300.

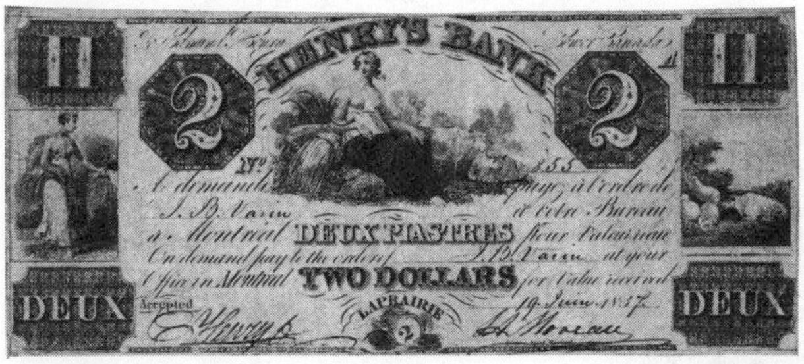

S1811 2 Dollars	VG	VF	UNC
19.6.1837; 27.6.1837. Black. Woman with sheaf at left, seated woman with sheaf by cattle at upper center, cow and sheep at right, small shield with *2* at bottom center. Uniface. Printer: Burton, Gurley & Edmunds, N. Y.	50.00	100.	300.

Montreal

1837 Issue

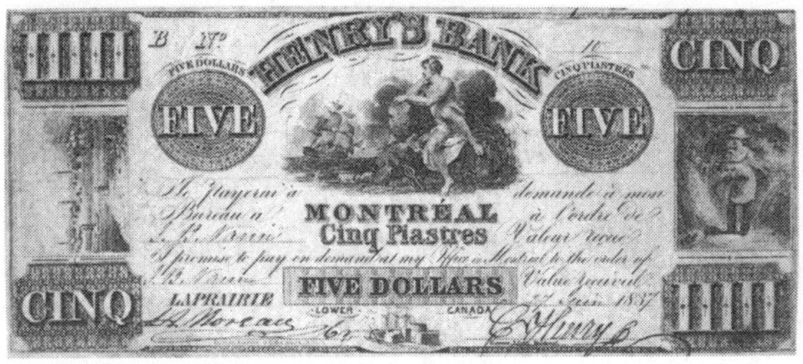

S1812 5 Dollars	Good	Fine	XF
27.6.1837. Village coastal view tipped sideways at left, seated allegorical male by shoreline with sailing ship in background at upper center, farmer with sheaf at right, small ship, casks at bottom center. Printer: Burton, Gurley & Edmunds, N. Y.	100.	200.	400.

S1813 10 Dollars	Good	Fine	XF
27.6.1837. Allegorical woman with eagle at upper center, small shield with *X* at bottom center. Printer: Burton, Gurley & Edmunds, N. Y.	125.	250.	500.

International Bank of Canada

1858 First Issue

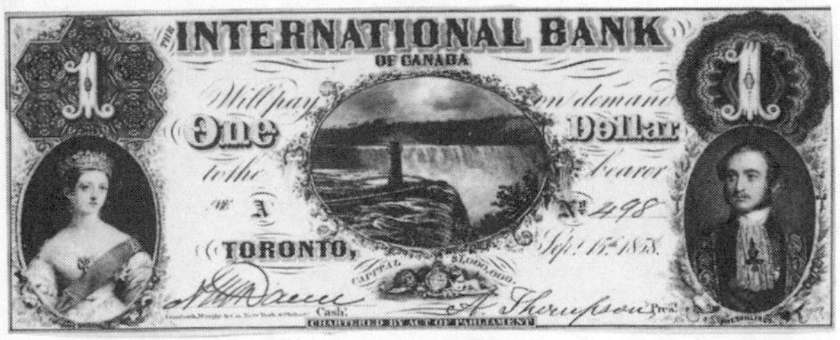

S1814 1 Dollar

15.9.1858. Black. Portrait Queen Victoria at lower left, Niagara and Horseshoe Falls at center, portrait of the Prince Consort at lower right. Uniface. Two signatures. Printer: Danforth, Wright & Co., New York and Philadelphia.

	VG	VF	UNC
a. Issued note.	100.	200.	500.
r. Remainder.	—	Unc	250.

S1815 1 Dollar

15.9.1858. Black. Portrait Queen Victoria at lower left, Roebling Suspension Bridge at Niagara Falls center, portrait of the Prince Consort at lower right. Uniface. Two signatures. Printer: Danforth, Wright & Co., New York and Philadelphia.

	VG	VF	UNC
a. Issued note.	100.	175.	550.
r. Remainder.	—	Unc	250.

S1816 2 Dollars

15.9.1858. Black. Allegorical woman at upper left, supported royal arms at top center right. Uniface. 2 signatures. Printer: Danforth, Wright & Co., New York and Philadelphia.

	VG	VF	UNC
a. Issued note.	100.	200.	550.
r. Remainder.	—	—	250.

S1817 5 Dollars

15.9.1858. Black. Small supported royal arms at left, cattle watering along river at center. 2 signatures. Uniface. Printer: Danforth, Wright & Co., New York and Philadelphia.

	VG	VF	UNC
a. Issued note.	100.	200.	600.
r. Remainder.	—	—	275.

S1818 1 Dollar

15.9.1858. Black. Portrait Queen Victoria at lower left, Niagara and Horseshoe Falls at center, portrait of the Prince Consort at lower right. Uniface. Two signatures. Red *1 1* protector. Printer: Danforth, Wright & Co., New York and Philadelphia.

	VG	VF	UNC
a. Issued note.	100.	200.	750.
r. Remainder.	—	—	275.

S1819 1 Dollar

15.9.1858. Black. Portrait Queen Victoria at lower left, Roebling Suspension Bridge at Niagara Falls center, portrait of the Prince Consort at lower right. Uniface. Two signatures. Red *ONE* protector. Printer: Danforth, Wright & Co., New York and Philaelphia.

	VG	VF	UNC
a. Issued note.	100.	200.	750.
r. Remainder.	—	—	275.

S1820 2 Dollars

15.9.1858. Black. Allegorical woman at upper left, supported royal arms at top center right. Uniface. 2 signatures. Red *TWO* protector. Printer: Danforth, Wright & Co., New York and Philadelphia.

	VG	VF	UNC
a. Issued note.	100.	200.	750.
r. Remainder.	—	—	275.

S1821 5 Dollars

15.9.1858. Black. Small supported royal arms at left, cattle watering along river at center. 2 signatures. Uniface. Red *FIVE* protector. Printer: Danforth, Wright & CO., New York and Philadelphia.

	VG	VF	UNC
a. Issued note.	100.	200.	750.
r. Remainder.	—	—	275.

1858 Second Issue

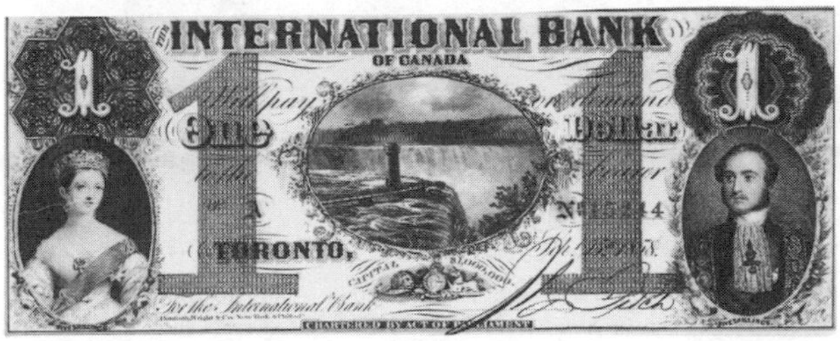

S1822 1 Dollar

15.9.1858. Black. Portrait Queen Victoria at lower left, Niagara and Horseshoe Falls at center, portrait of the Prince Consort at lower right. 1 signature. Uniface. Printer. Danforth, Wright & Co., New York and Philadelphia.

	VG	VF	UNC
a. Green protector. Blue serial #. Signature J. H. Markell.	25.00	75.00	200.
b. Red serial #. Signature J. C. Fitch.	20.00	50.00	100.
c. Brown protector. Blue serial #. Signature J. H. Markell.	25.00	75.00	200.
d. Red serial #. Signature J. H. Markell.	25.00	75.00	200.
e. Signature J. C. Fitch.	20.00	50.00	125.
f. Red protector. Small blue serial #. Signature J. H. Markell.	20.00	50.00	125.
g. Small blue serial #. Signature J. C. Fitch.	25.00	75.00	150.
h. Large blue serial #. Signature J. C. Fitch.	20.00	50.00	100.
i. Ochre protector. Red serial #. Signature J. H. Markell.	40.00	100.	225.
j. Signature J. C. Fitch.	40.00	75.00	200.
k. Small blue serial #. Signature J. C. Fitch.	25.00	50.00	150.
l. Large blue serial #. Signature J. C. Fitch.	40.00	75.00	200.
m. Blue protector. Red serial #. Signature J. H. Markell.	40.00	75.00	200.
n. Signature J. C. Fitch.	20.00	50.00	125.

S1823 1 Dollar

15.9.1858. Like #S1815.

	VG	VF	UNC
a. Green protector. Blue serial 1. Signature J. H. Markell.	40.00	75.00	200.
b. Red serial #. Signature J. C. Fitch.	25.00	50.00	125.
c. Brown protector. Blue serial #. Signature J. H. Markell.	40.00	75.00	150.
d. Red serial #. Signature J. H. Markell.	50.00	100.	200.
e. Signature J. C. Fitch.	20.00	40.00	75.00
f. Red protector. Small blue serial #. Signature J. H. Markell.	40.00	75.00	150.
g. Sm. blue serial #. Signature J. C. Fitch.	40.00	75.00	175.
h. Large blue serial #. Signature J. C. Fitch.	20.00	40.00	75.00
i. Ochre protector. Red serial #. Signature J. H. Markell.	40.00	75.00	225.
j. Signature J. C. Fitch.	40.00	75.00	225.
k. Small blue serial #. Signature J. C. Fitch.	25.00	50.00	125.
l. Large blue serial #. Signature J. C. Fitch.	40.00	75.00	225.
m. Blue protector. Red serial #. Signature J. H. Markell.	40.00	75.00	225.
n. Signature J. C. Fitch.	20.00	40.00	100.

S1824 2 Dollars

15.9.1858. Black. Allegorical woman at upper left, supported royal arms at top center right. 1 signature. Uniface.

	VG	VF	UNC
a. Green protector. Blue serial #. Signature J. H. Markell.	40.00	75.00	225.
b. Red serial #. Signature J. C. Fitch.	25.00	50.00	125.
c. Brown protector. Blue serial #. Signature J. H. Markell.	40.00	75.00	150.
d. Red serial #. Signature J. H. Markell.	40.00	75.00	175.
e. Signature J. C. Fitch.	20.00	40.00	75.00
f. Red protector. Small blue serial #. Signature J. H. Markell.	40.00	75.00	175.
g. Small blue serial #. Signature J. C. Fitch.	40.00	75.00	175.
h. Large blue serial #. Signature J. C. Fitch.	20.00	40.00	75.00

	VG	VF	UNC
i. Ochre protector. Red serial #. Signature J. H. Markell.	40.00	75.00	225.
j. Signature J. C. Fitch.	40.00	75.00	225.
k. Small blue serial #. Signature J. C. Fitch.	25.00	50.00	125.
l. Large blue serial #. Signature J. C. Fitch.	40.00	75.00	200.
m. Blue protector. Red serial #. Signature J. H. Markell.	40.00	75.00	200.
n. Signature J. C. Fitch.	25.00	50.00	125.

S1825 5 Dollars

15.9.1858. Black. Small supported royal arms at left, cattle watering along river at center. 1 signature. Uniface.

	VG	VF	UNC
a. Green protector. Blue serial #. Signature J. H. Markell.	40.00	75.00	200.
b. Red serial #. Signature J. C. Fitch.	20.00	40.00	75.00
c. Brown protector. Blue serial #. Signature J. H. Markell	25.00	50.00	125.
d. Red serial #. Signature J. H. Markell.	40.00	75.00	200.
e. Signature J. C. Fitch.	20.00	40.00	75.00
f. Red protector. Small blue serial #. signature J. H. Markell.	40.00	75.00	150.
g. Small blue serial #. Signature J. C. Fitch.	20.00	40.00	75.00
h. Large blue serial #. Signature J. C. Fitch.	20.00	40.00	75.00
i. Ochre protector. Red serial #. Signature J. H. Markell.	40.00	75.00	200.
j. Signature J. C. Fitch.	40.00	75.00	200.
k. Small blue serial #. Signature J. C. Fitch.	25.00	50.00	125.
l. Large blue serial #. Signature J. C. Fitch.	40.00	75.00	200.
m. Blue protector. Red serial #. Signature J. H. Markell.	40.00	75.00	200.
n. Signature J. C. Fitch.	25.00	50.00	125.

1859 Issue

S1826 10 Dollars	VG	VF	UNC
1.6.1859. Crests, crown on book at left, town along river, boat at top center, portrait Queen Victoria at lower right. Back: Green. Black with green word or number protector. Printer: ABNC.	125.	250.	750.

S1827 20 Dollars	VG	VF	UNC
1.6.1859. Beavers at lower left, paddle wheel steamboat at top center, youthful Prince of Wales at lower right. Back: Green. Black with green word or number protector. Printer: ABNC.	500.	900.	—

S1828 50 Dollars	VG	VF	UNC
1.6.1859. Navigation at lower left, buffalo hunting at top center, seated Britannia with arms of Canada at lower right. Back: Green. Black with green word or number protector. Printer: ABNC.	100.	200.	650.

Kingston Bank

1837 Spurious Issue

S1829 5 Dollars

1837; 12.10.1841; 3.8.1843. Black. Seated allegorical woman at left, cattle, plow and early steam passenger train at top center right, cornucopia, caduceus and chest with ships in background at bottom center. Uniface.

	VG	VF	UNC
a. Fully signed. 1837.	125.	300.	—
r. Remainder. 1837; 1841; 1843.	125.	350.	—

NOTE: #S1829 exists with an additional overprint: *New York Safety Fund* to infer being an issue of the Kingston Bank in New York.

Bank of Liverpool

1871 Issue

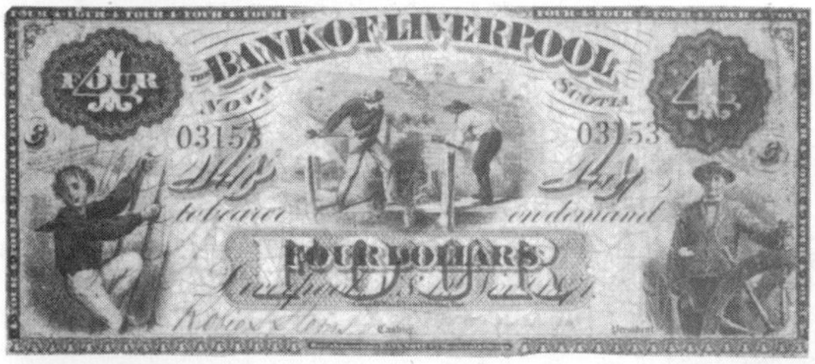

S1830 4 Dollars	Good	Fine	XF
1.11.1871. Black on green underprint. Young sailor climbing ship's rigging at lower left, shipbuilders at upper center, pilot at ship's wheel at lower right. 3 signature varieties. Back: Green. Printer: BABNC.	500.	1400.	—

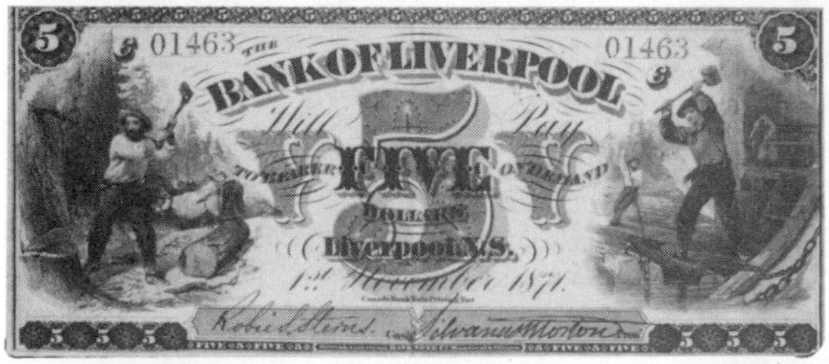

S1831 5 Dollars	Good	Fine	XF
1.11.1871. Black on green underprint. Lumberjack felling tree at left, splitting logs at right. 3 signature varieties. Back: Green. Printer: BABNC.	450.	1250.	—

S1832 10 Dollars	Good	Fine	XF
1.11.1871. Black on green underprint. Agriculture at left, fishing ships at top center, sailor at lower right. 3 signature varieties. Back: Green. Printer: BABNC.	600.	1750.	—

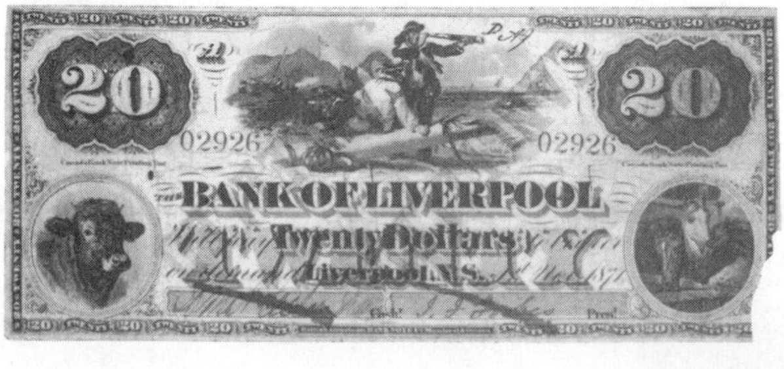

S1833 20 Dollars	Good	Fine	XF
1.11.1871. Black on green underprint. Bull's head at lower left, shipwrecked sailors at top center, three horses' heads at lower right. 3 signature varieties. Back: Green. Printer: BABNC.	750.	2500.	—

Bank of London in Canada

1883 Issue

S1834 5 Dollars	Good	Fine	XF
1.12.1883. Black on green underprint. Farm tools and produce at left, H. Taylor at center, dog on strongbox at right. Back: Green. Printer: BABNC.			
a. Issued note.	800.	3250.	—
r. Remainder unsigned at right with 2 cut *PAID* cancellations.	—	—	—

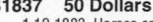

S1835 10 Dollars	Good	Fine	XF
1.12.1883. Black on green underprint. H. Taylor at lower left, allegorical woman with flowers at lower right. Back: Green. Printer: BABNC.			
a. Issued note.	1400.	4250.	—
r. Remainder unsigned at right with 2 cut *PAID* cancellations.	—	—	—

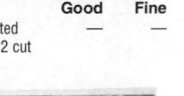

S1836 20 Dollars	Good	Fine	XF
1.12.1883. Black on green underprint. Allegorical woman with cornstalks at left, H. Taylor at center Remainder unsigned at right with two cut *PAID* cancellations. Back: Green. Printer: BABNC.	—	—	—

S1837 50 Dollars	Good	Fine	XF
1.12.1883. Horses and pigeons at left, H. Taylor at center right, seated allegorical woman at lower right. Remainder unsigned at right. with 2 cut *PAID* cancellations.	—	—	—

S1838 100 Dollars	Good	Fine	XF
1.12.1883. Black on green underprint. Cows at left, H. Taylor at center, woman operating telegraph at right. Remainder unsigned at right with two cut *PAID* cancellations. Back: Green. Printer: BABNC.	—	—	—

Lower Canada Bank

1837 Spurious Issue

S1839 1 Dollar	Good	Fine	XF
18xx. Black. Hercules wrestling lion at top center, woman with sheaves at upper right. Sea creatures at upper and lower left, small clasped hands at bottom center. Uniface. Printer: RWH & Co.			
a. Issued note.	225.	500.	—
p. Proof.	—	Unc	3500.

S1840 2 Dollars	Good	Fine	XF
4.11.1837. Black. Allegorical man slaying dragon at top center, allegorical man and woman with coins at right. Sea creatures at upper and lower left, small clasped hands at bottom center. Uniface. Printer: RWH & Co.	225.	750.	—

S1841 3 Dollars	Good	Fine	XF
18xx. Black. Seated Homer at top center, cherub with basket of fruit at right. Sea creatures at upper and lower left, small clasped hands at bottom center. Uniface. Printer: RWH & Co. Proof.	—	Unc	400.

Bank of Lower Canada

1839-51 Issue

S1842 1 Dollar	VG	VF	UNC
1839-51. Black. Beehive and farm tools at left, supported royal arms at top center *D. Birdsey* omitted. Uniface. Standing Britannia at right. Various dates 1839-51 and signature of questionable authenticity. Sm Printer: Harris & Sealey, N. York.			
b. Without *D. Birdsey.*	200.	400.	600.
p. With *A. Messrs. D. Birdsey & Cie* engraved at lower left Proof.	—	Unc	400.

S1843 2 Dollars	VG	VF	UNC
1839-51. Black. Beehive and farm tools at left, supported royal arms at top center *D. Birdsey* omitted. Uniface. Standing Britannia at right. Various dates 1839-51 and signature of questionable authenticity. Sm Printer: Harris & Sealey, N. York.	200.	400.	—

S1844 3 Dollars	VG	VF	UNC
Black. Small supported arms at left, seated allegorical man giving key to kneeling man, Minerva at top center. Small Indian in canoe at bottom center. Uniface. Printer: Harris & Sealey, N. York.	225.	—	—

S1845 5 Dollars	VG	VF	UNC
1839-51. Black. Indian brave at upper left, two trains at dockside at upper center right. Supported royal arms at bottom center. Uniface. Printer: Harris & Sealey, N. York.	225.	400.	750.

S1846 10 Dollars	VG	VF	UNC
1839-51. Black. Seated Mercury with sailing ship in background at top center. Supported royal arms at bottom center. Uniface. Printer: Harris & Sealey, N. York.	300.	500.	900.

MACDONALD & CO.

1863 ISSUE

S1847 1 Dollar	VG	VF	UNC
6.9.1863. Black. Indian maiden facing left at lower left, supported royal arms at top center, Indian brave facing with arm raised at lower right. Uniface. Printer: Britton & Co., S.F.	125.	300.	—

S1848 5 Dollars	VG	VF	UNC
6.9.1863. Black. Indian maiden facing left at lower left, supported royal arms at top center, Indian brave facing with arm raised at lower right. Uniface. Printer: Britton & Co., S.F.	200.	350.	—

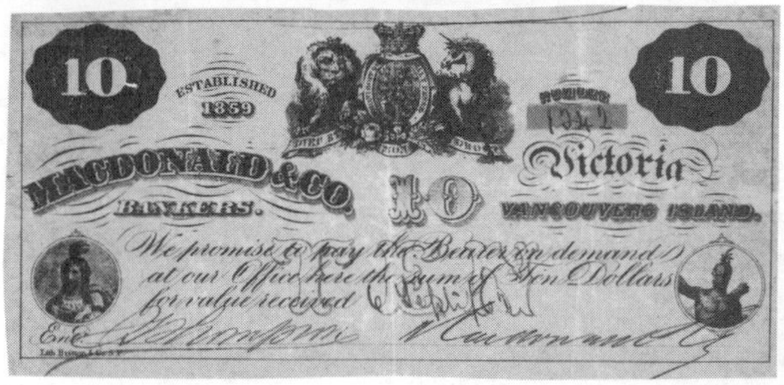

S1849 10 Dollars	VG	VF	UNC
6.9.1863. Black. Indian maiden facing left at lower left, supported royal arms at top center, Indian brave facing with arm raised at lower right. Uniface. Printer: Britton & Co., S.F.	250.	500.	—
S1850 1 Dollar			
6.9.1863. Black. Indian maiden facing right at lower left and Indian brave facing left with arm down at lower right. Remainder.	500.	900.	—

S1851 5 Dollars	VG	VF	UNC
6.9.1863. Black. Indian maiden facing right at lower left and Indian brave facing left with arm down at lower right.	500.	900.	—
S1852 10 Dollars			
6.9.1863. Black. Indian maiden facing right at lower left and Indian brave facing left with arm down at lower right. Reported not confirmed.	—	—	—

MARITIME BANK OF THE DOMINION OF CANADA

1873; 1875 ISSUE

S1853 4 Dollars	VG	VF	UNC
2.1.1873. Black on green underprint. J. Domville at lower left, sailing ship at center, J. H. R. Rowley at lower right. 2 signature varieties. Back: Green. Anchor, barrels and bale. Printer: BABNC.	3500.	—	—

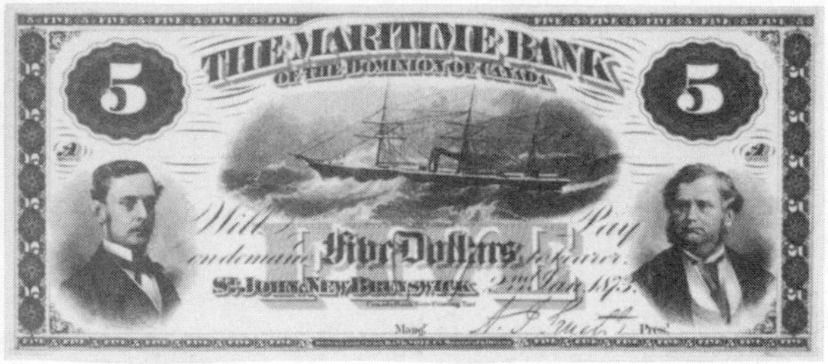

S1854 5 Dollars	Good	Fine	XF
2.1.1873. Black on green underprint. J. Domville at lower left, steam sailing ship at center, J. H. R. Rowley at lower right. 2 signature varieties. Back: Green. Anchor, barrels and bale. Printer: BABNC. Face proof.	—	Unc	750.

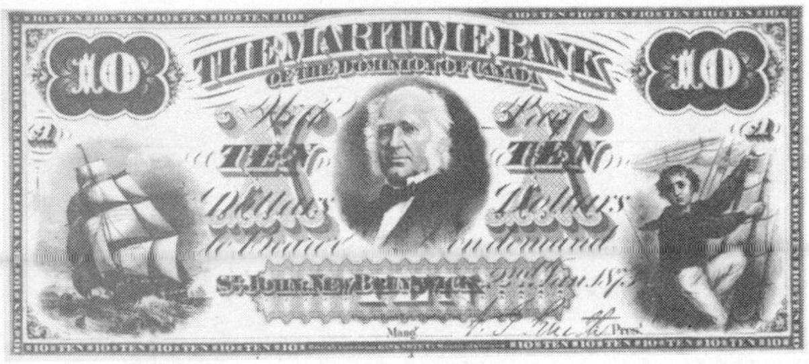

S1855 10 Dollars	Good	Fine	XF
2.1.1873. Black on green underprint. Sailing ship at lower left, J. Robertson at center, young sailor climbing ship's rigging at lower right. 2 signature varieties. Back: Green. Anchor, barrels and bale. Printer: BABNC. Face proof.	—	Unc	750.
S1856 50 Dollars			
1.6.1875. Black on green underprint. Major Gen. J. W. Domville at left, supported Great Seal of Canada at center, J. Domville at right. 2 signature varieties. Back: Green. Anchor, barrels and bale. Printer: BABNC. Face proof.	—	Unc	750.

1881; 1882 Issue

S1857 5 Dollars	VG	VF	UNC
3.10.1881. Black on green underprint. Sailor at lower left, sailing ship at dockside at center, seated woman with telescope by Large ornate *5* at lower right. Back: Green. Anchor, barrels and bale.			
a. Without overprint	2000.	—	—
b. overprint: Large red *V*.	2250.	—	—

S1858 10 Dollars	VG	VF	UNC
3.10.1881. Black on green underprint. Sailing ship at lower left, portrait Queen Victoria at center, young sailor climbing ship's rigging at lower right. Back: Green. Anchor, barrels and bales.	2500.	—	—
S1859 20 Dollars			
1.1.1882. Black on green underprint. Dock scene at left, steamship at center, allegorical woman with flag and bale at right. Back: Green. Anchor, barrels and bale. Face proof.	—	Unc	750.

Mechanics Bank, Montreal

1837 Spurious Issue

S1860 3 Dollars	Good	Fine	XF
1.6.1837. Black. Dock scene, steamboat at left, blacksmith at anvil with two women at top center, woman with wheat at right. Uniface. Printer: RWH & Co.	50.00	150.	450.

S1861 5 Dollars	Good	Fine	XF
1.5.1837; 1.6.1837. Black. Seated youth with tools at left, seated woman leaning on Large gear at top center, blacksmith at anvil at right. Uniface. Printer: RWH & Co.	40.00	125.	300.

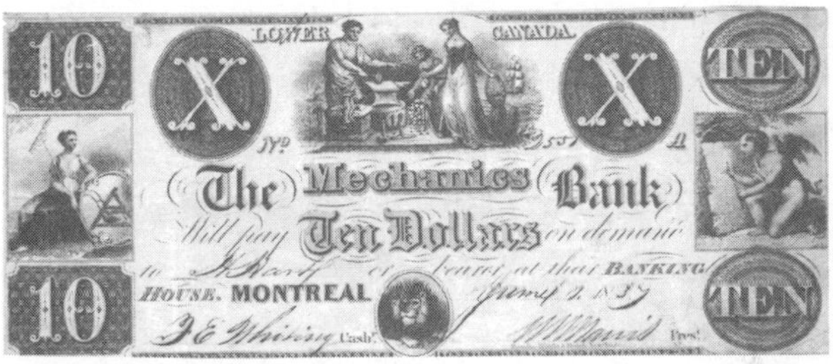

S1862 10 Dollars	Good	Fine	XF
1.5.1837; 1.6.1837. Black. Seated woman with rake at left, blacksmith at anvil with two women at top center, cherub kneeling inscribing stone at right. Uniface. Printer: RWH & Co.	40.00	125.	300.

Mechanics Bank, Montreal, C.E.

1872 Issue

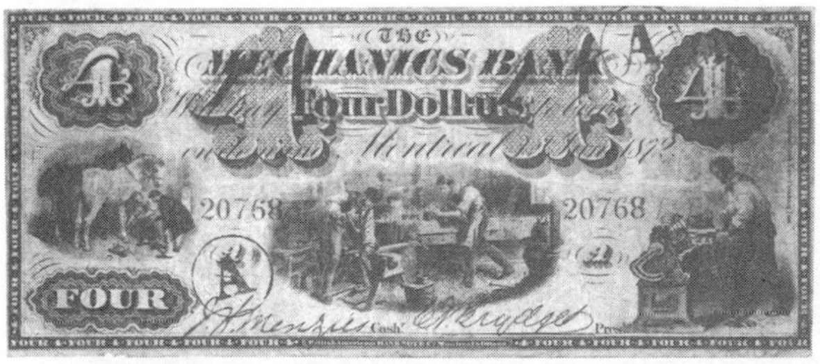

S1863 4 Dollars	VG	VF	UNC
1.6.1872. Black on green underprint. Blacksmith with man and two horses at left, carpenters at bottom center, machinist at lower right. Signature varieties. Back: Blue-green. Printer: BABNC.			
a. Purple hand stamp: circled *A*.	125.	250.	—
b. Blue overprint: *A-A*.	125.	250.	—
c. Blue overprint: *B-B*.	125.	250.	—
d. Blue overprint: *L- L*.	125.	250.	—
e. Vertical blue overprint: *ALEXANDRIA* twice.	125.	250.	—
f. Vertical blue overprint: *BEAUHARNOIS* twice.	125.	250.	—

S1864 5 Dollars	VG	VF	UNC
1.6.1872. Black on green underprint. Farmer watering livestock at upper left, stonecutters at lower right. Signature varieties. Back: Blue-green. Printer: BABNC.			
a. Purple hand stamp: circled *A-A*.	100.	200.	—
b. Blue overprint: *A-A*.	100.	200.	—
c. Vertical blue overprint: *ALEXANDRIA* twice.	100.	200.	—
d. Vertical blue overprint: *BEAUHARNOIS* twice.	100.	200.	—

S1865 10 Dollars	VG	VF	UNC
1.6.1872. Black on green underprint. Livestock at lower left, blacksmith shoeing horse at center, arm with hammer at lower right. Signature varieties. Printer: BABNC.	400.	800.	—

Mechanics Bank of St. John's, L.C.

1837 First Spurious Issue

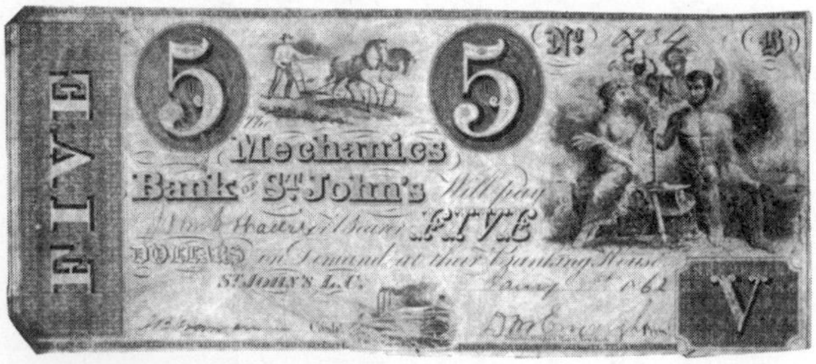

S1866 5 Dollars	Good	Fine	XF
20.5.1837. Black. Man plowing with horses at upper left center, standing Mercury behind seated allegorical man and woman at upper right. Uniface. Printer: RWH & Co.	100.	250.	750.

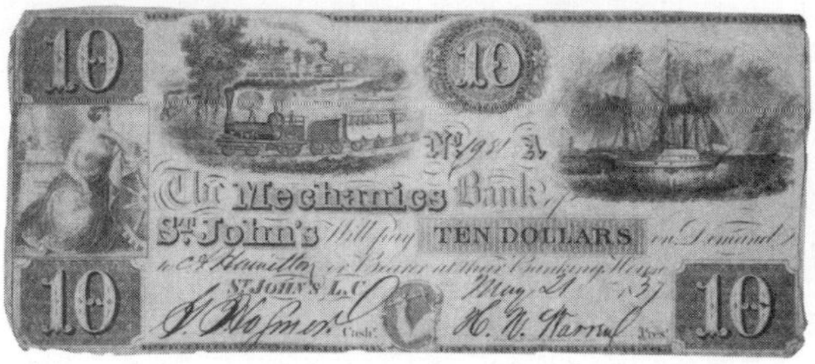

S1867 10 Dollars	Good	Fine	XF
20.5.1837; 21.5.1837. Black. Seated woman leaning on gear at left, steam passenger trains along river at top left center, sailing ships at upper right. Uniface. Printer: RWH & Co.	200.	400.	900.
S1868 20 Dollars			
20.5.1837. Black. Blacksmith at left, paddle wheel steamship at top center, allegorical woman at right. Uniface. Printer: RWH & Co.	200.	400.	900.

1837 Second Spurious Issue

S1869 1 Dollar	Good	Fine	XF
18xx. Black. Seated woman leaning against gear at left, steam passenger trains along river at top center, seated young man with tools at right. Uniface. A. Messrs. H.N. Warren & Cie a St. John's engraved at lower Printer: RWH & Co.			
a. Issued note.	—	—	—
r. Unsigned remainder.	50.00	150.	—

S1870 2 Dollars	Good	Fine	XF
1.7.1837; 29.11.1837. Black. Woman with wheat sheaf at left, blacksmith at anvil with two women at top center, farmer harvesting wheat with scythe at right. Uniface. Printer: RWH & Co.	50.00	150.	—

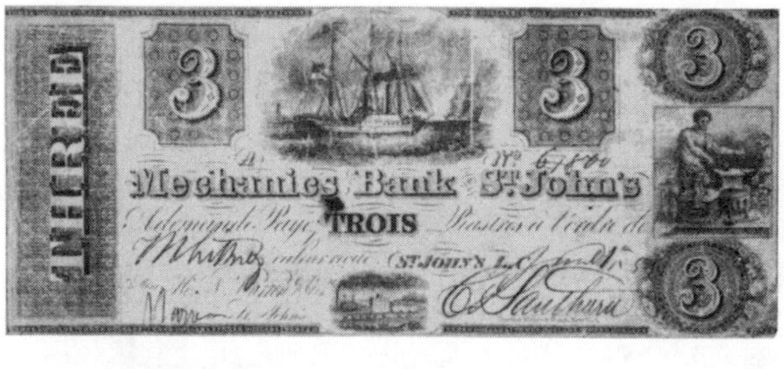

S1871 3 Dollars	Good	Fine	XF
18xx. Black. Paddle wheel steamship at top center, blacksmith at anvil at right. Uniface. Printer: RWH & Co. Unsigned remainder.	75.00	200.	—

NOTE: #S1869-1871 are encountered with various spurious dates and signatures.

1837 Third Spurious Issue

#S1872-S1874 like #S1869-1871. *A Messrs. T. H. Perry & Cie a St. John's* engraved at lower l. hand sign. T. H. Perry & Cia vertically.

S1872 1 Dollar	Good	Fine	XF
29.11.1837. Black. Seated woman leaning against gear at left, steam passenger trains along river at top center, seated young man with tools at right. Uniface. Printer: RWH & Co.	50.00	150.	—
S1873 2 Dollars			
18xx. Black. Woman with wheat sheaf at left, blacksmith at anvil with two women at top center, farmer harvesting wheat with scythe at right. Printer: RWH & Co. Unsigned remainder.	50.00	150.	—

S1874 3 Dollars	Good	Fine	XF
29.11.1837. Black. Woman with wheat sheaf at left, blacksmith at anvil with two women at top center, farmer harvesting wheat with scythe at right. Printer: RWH & Co.	75.00	200.	—

Mercantile Banking Corporation

1878 Issue

S1875 10 Dollars	Good	Fine	XF
1.1.1878. Black. Sailing ship at center. Uniface. Printer: Chas. Skipper & East. Face proof.	—	Unc	1100.

Merchants Bank, Montreal, L.C.

1840s ND Issue

	Good	Fine	XF
S1875A 5 Dollars 18xx. Commerce, anchor, ship at upper center, child with deer at right.	150.	500.	—
S1875B 10 Dollars 18xx. Commerce, ship at upper center, woman in waves at right. Reported not confirmed.	—	—	—
S1875C 20 Dollars 18xx. Commerce, ship at upper center, dock scene at right. Reported not confirmed.	—	—	—

Merchants Bank, C.E.

1864 Issue

	Good	Fine	XF
S1875D 1 Dollar 1.6.1864. Black on green underprint. Sailors dockside at lower left, train and wagons at wharf at center, portrait H. Allan at right. Printer: ABNC.			
a. Issued note.	550.	1000.	—
p. Proof.	—	—	—
S1875E 2 Dollars 1.6.1864. Black on green underprint. Portrait Prince of Wales at left, steamships and sailing ships at center, portrait H. Allan at right. Printer: ABNC.			
a. Issues note.	550.	1000.	—
p. Proof.	—	—	—

	Good	Fine	XF
S1875F 5 Dollars 1.6.1864. Black on green underprint. Sailor with anchor at upper center, Prince of Wales as a small boy at lower right. Portrait H. Allan at lower left. Printer: ABNC.			
a. Issued note.	600.	1200.	—
p. Proof.	—	—	—
S1875G 10 Dollars 1.6.1864. Black on green underprint. Train, men and cattle at center, sailor with telescope at lower right. Portrait H. Allan at lower left. Printer: ABNC.			
a. Issued note.	900.	1500.	—
p. Proof.	—	—	—
S1875H 50 Dollars 1.6.1864. Black on green underprint. Paddle wheel steamer at center right. Portrait H. Allan at lower left. Printer: ABNC. Proof.	—	Unc	1000.
S1875I 100 Dollars 1.6.1864. Black on green underprint. Paddle wheel steamer at center, dog at lower right. Portrait H. Allan at lower left. Printer: ABNC. Proof.	—	Unc	1000.

Merchants Bank, Toronto, U.C.

1836; 1837 Spurious Issue

S1876 1 Dollar	Good	Fine	XF
1836-37. Black. Allegorical woman at upper left, portrait of cherub at upper left center, three allegorical women at upper right center, portrait of young woman at lower right, small sailing ships at bottom center. U Printer: Terry, Pelton & Co.			
a. Issued note. 5.12.1836; 1.6.1837; 14.6.1837.	100.	300.	—
r. Unsigned remainder. 18xx.	—	Unc	750.

S1877 2 Dollars	Good	Fine	XF
1.6.1837; 4.7.1837. Black. Sailing ship and tugboat at left, two allegorical women at top center, portrait of young woman at lower right, small eagle at bottom center. Uniface. Printer: Terry, Pelton & Co.			
a. Issued note.	100.	300.	—
r. Unsigned remainder. 18xx.	—	Unc	750.

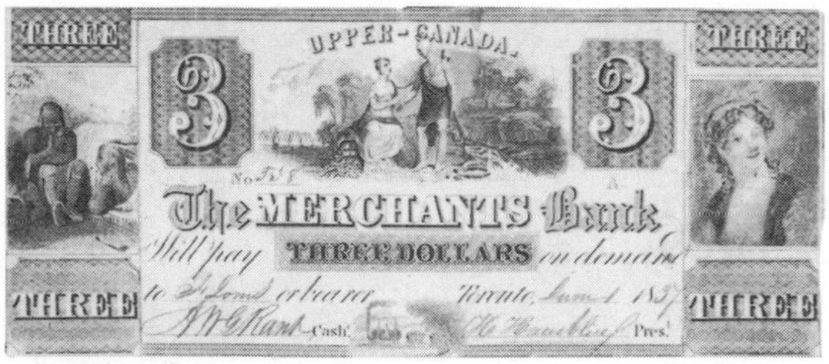

S1878 3 Dollars	Good	Fine	XF
1.6.1837. Black. Two Indians reclining at left, seated woman by Indian brave at upper center, portrait of young woman at right, small early steam passenger train at bottom center. Uniface. Printer: Terry, Pelton & Co.			
a. Issued note.	100.	350.	—
r. Unsigned remainder. 18xx.	—	Unc	750.

S1879 5 Dollars	Good	Fine	XF
1.6.1837; 4.7.1837. Black. Seated woman by Indian brave at left, dock scene at top center, small crest between men at bottom center. Uniface. Printer: Terry, Pelton & Co.	300.	900.	—

Merchants Exchange Bank, Goderich, C.W.

1853 Spurious Issue

S1880 1 Dollar	Good	Fine	XF
1.1.1853. Black. Eagle and shield at left, Agriculture and Justice with eagle and shield at upper center, sailing ship at lower right. Uniface. Printer: Wellstood, Hanks, Hay and Whiting.	500.	1250.	—

Metropolitan Bank

1872 Issue

	VG	VF	UNC
S1881 4 Dollars 1.2.1872. Black on green underprint. Supported shield at upper center. Portrait M. Cuvellier at lower left, portrait H. Starnes at lower right. Back: Green. Printer: BABNC.	2000.	—	—

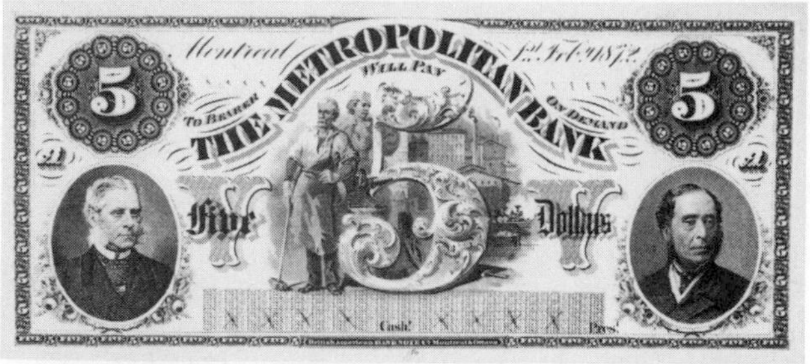

	VG	VF	UNC
S1882 5 Dollars 1.2.1872. Black on green underprint. Two blacksmiths with Large ornate *5* at center. Portrait M. Cuvellier at lower left, portrait H. Starnes at lower right. Back: Green. Overprint: Red:*OB*. Printer: BABNC.	2000.	—	—

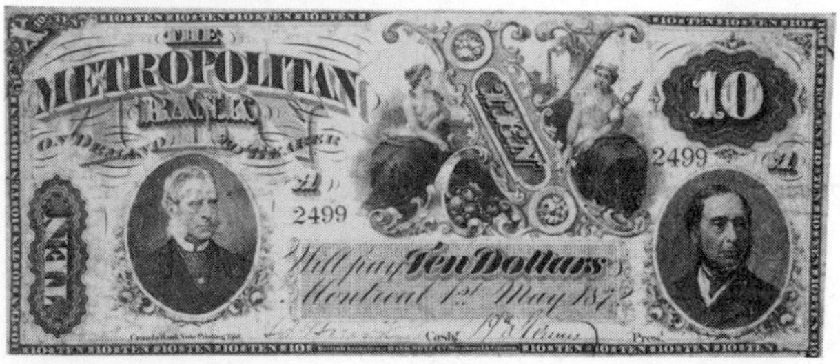

	VG	VF	UNC
S1883 10 Dollars 1.5.1872. Black on green underprint. Two allegorical women seated with Large ornate *X* at top center right. Portrait M. Cuvellier at lower left, portrait H. Starnes at lower right. Back: Green. Printer: BABNC.	2000.	—	—
S1884 50 Dollars 1.5.1872. Black on green underprint. Portrait M. Cuvellier at lower left, portrait H. Starnes at lower right. Back: Gree. Printer: BABNC. Face proof.	—	Unc	650.
S1885 100 Dollars 1.5.1872. Black on green underprint. Portrait M. Cuvellier at lower left, portrait H. Starnes at lower right. Back: Green. Printer: BABNC. Face proof.	—	Unc	650.

Montreal Bank, C.W.

1848 Spurious Issue

	VG	VF	UNC
S1886 5 Dollars 10.10.1848; 1.4.1853. Black. Farmer with livestock at left paddle wheel steamboat at upper right. Uniface.	300.	600.	—

Newcastle Banking Company

1836 Issue

	Good	Fine	XF
S1886A 1 Dollar = 5 Shillings 20.1.1836. Black. Sheaves of wheat, plow and cattle at upper center. Uniface.	150.	400.	900.

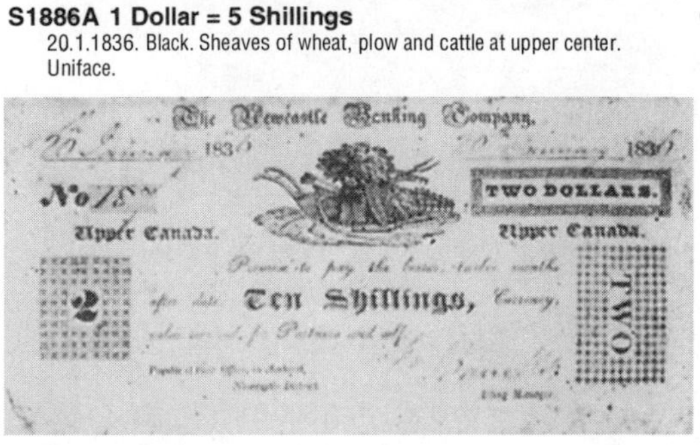

	Good	Fine	XF
S1887 2 Dollars = 10 Shillings 20.1.1836; 15.2.1836. Black. Sheaves of wheat and farm tools at upper center. Uniface.	150.	400.	900.

	Good	Fine	XF
S1888 4 Dollars = 20 Shillings 20.1.1836; 15.2.1836. Black. Seated Agriculture with farm tools and produce at upper center. Uniface.	200.	500.	1250.

New Castle District Loan Company, Peterborough, U.C.

1836 Issue

	Good	Fine	XF
S1889 1 Dollar = 5 Shillings 18xx. Black. Naval commander at upper left, seated Abundance with sheaf and cattle in background at center, standing Navigation at right, small beaver at bottom center. Printer: RWH & Co. Unsigned remainder.	100.	300.	—

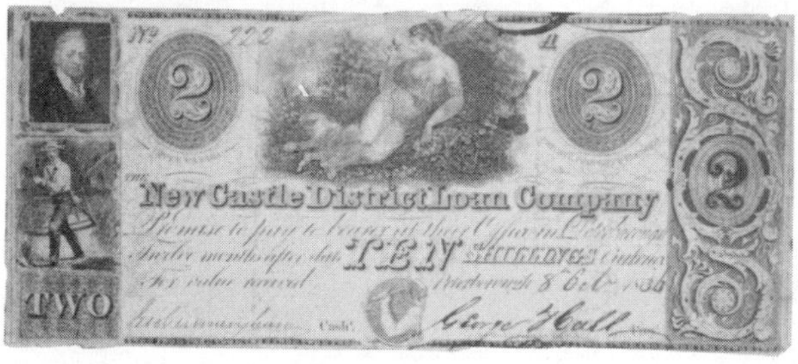

	Good	Fine	XF
S1890 2 Dollars = 10 Shillings 27.8.1836; 8.10.1836. Black. Portrait King William IV at upper left, man with cradle in grain below, reclining woman at top center, small arm with hammer at bottom center. Uniface. Printer: RWH & Co.			
a. Issued note.	100.	300.	—
r. Unsigned remainder. 18xx.	100.	325.	750.

	Good	Fine	XF
S1891 4 Dollars = 20 Shillings = 1 Pound 15.2.1836-27.8.1836. Black. Two men with livestock at left, supported portrait King William IV at upper center, blacksmith at right, small ship, cask at bottom center. Uniface. Printer: RWH & Co.	75.00	150.	450.

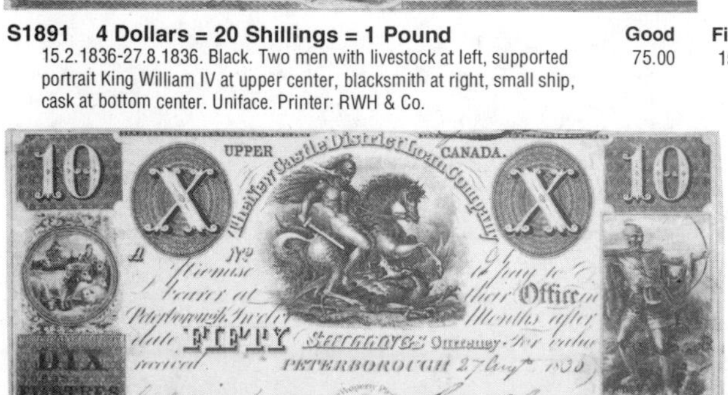

S1892 10 Dollars = 50 Shillings	Good	Fine	XF
6.8.1836; 27.8.1836. Black. Two men with livestock at left, St. George slaying dragon at upper center, Indian brave with drawn bow at lower right, small paddle wheel steamboat at bottom center. Uniface. Printer: RWH & Co.	75.00	150.	450.

Niagara Suspension Bridge Bank, Queenston, U.C.

1836 Issue

S1893 1 Dollar = 5 Shillings	Good	Fine	XF
18xx. Black. St. George slaying dragon at upper left, portrait King William IV at right, mythical Niagara suspension bridge at top left center or center right. Uniface. Printer: RWH & Co.	50.00	150.	—

#S1894-S1895A black. Uniface. W/handwritten text: *PAYABLE AT THE BANK* along bridge vignette.

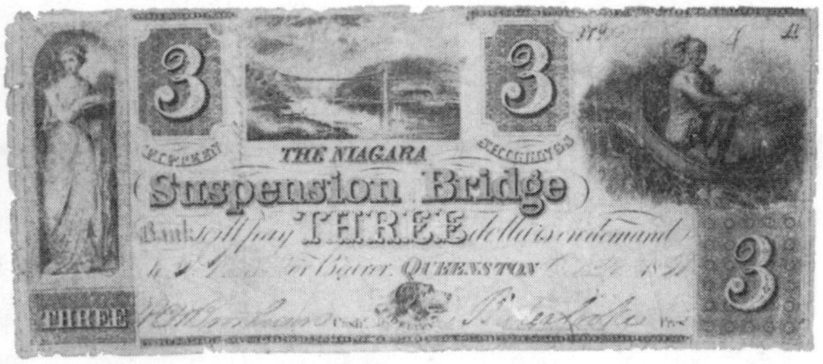

S1894 3 Dollars = 15 Shillings	Good	Fine	XF
20.12.1836; 1839. Black. Standing Navigation at left, Indian brave paddling canoe at upper right, dog's head at bottom center. Mythical Niagara suspension bridge at top left center or center right. Handwritten text: *PAYABL* Uniface.	75.00	225.	—
S1895 5 Dollars = 25 Shillings			
18xx. Black. Standing Indian brave with drawn bow at upper right, paddle wheel steamboat at bottom center, mythical Niagara suspension bridge at top left center or center right with handwritten text: *PAYABLE AT* Uniface.	50.00	150.	—

1837-39 Issue

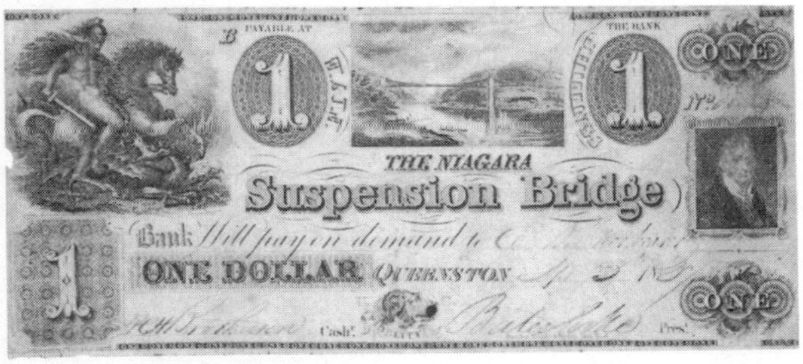

S1896 1 Dollar = 5 Shillings	Good	Fine	XF
3.4.1837. Black. St. George slaying dragon at upper left, portrait King William IV at right, mythical Niagara suspension bridge at top left center or center right, engraved text: *PAYABLE AT THE BANK* along uppe Uniface.	50.00	100.	—
S1897 3 Dollars = 15 Shillings			
18xx. Black. Standing Navigation at left, Indian brave paddling canoe at upper right, dog's head at bottom center, mythical Niagara suspension bridge at top left center or center right. Uniface.	50.00	100.	—
S1898 5 Dollars = 25 Shillings			
20.7.1839. Black. Standing Indian brave with drawn bow at upper right, paddle wheel steamboat at bottom center. mythical Niagara suspension bridge at top left center or center right. Uniface.	50.00	100.	—

1840 Issue

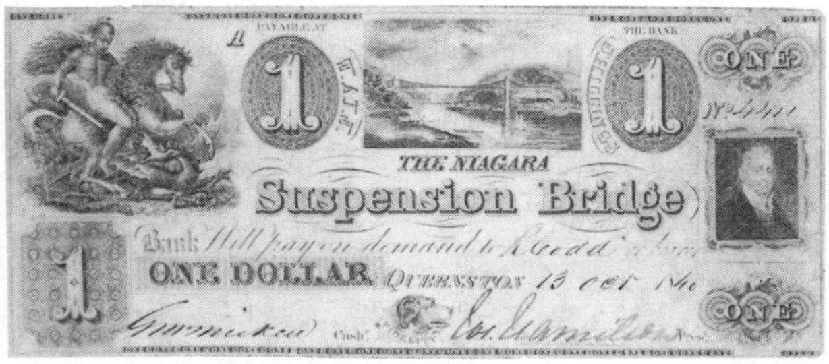

S1899 1 Dollar = 5 Shillings	VG	VF	UNC
13.10.1840. Black. St. George slaying dragon at upper left, portrait King William IV at right, mythical Niagara suspension bridge at top left center or center right. Back: Orange. Uniface.	50.00	150.	—

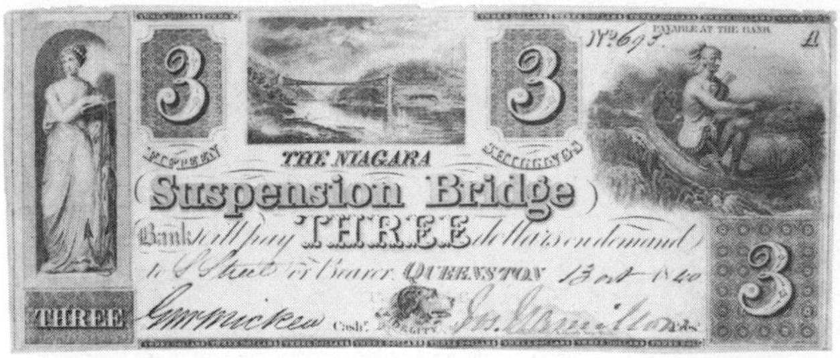

S1900 3 Dollars = 15 Shillings	VG	VF	UNC
13.10.1840. Black. Standing Navigation at left, Indian brave paddling canoe at upper right, dog's head at bottom center, mythical Niagara suspension bridge at top left center or center right. Back: Orange. Uniface.	75.00	200.	—

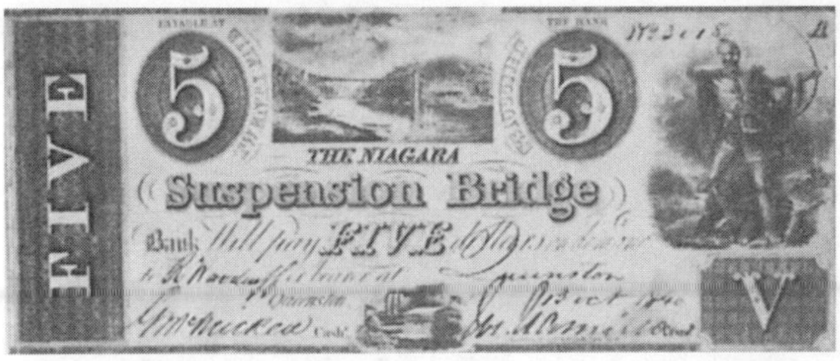

S1901 5 Dollars = 25 Shillings	VG	VF	UNC
13.10.1840. Black. With small *Queenston* to left. of paddle wheel steamboat at bottom center, *U.C.* at right, mythical Niagara suspension bridge at top left center or center right. Back: Orange. Uniface.	50.00	150.	—

1841 Issues

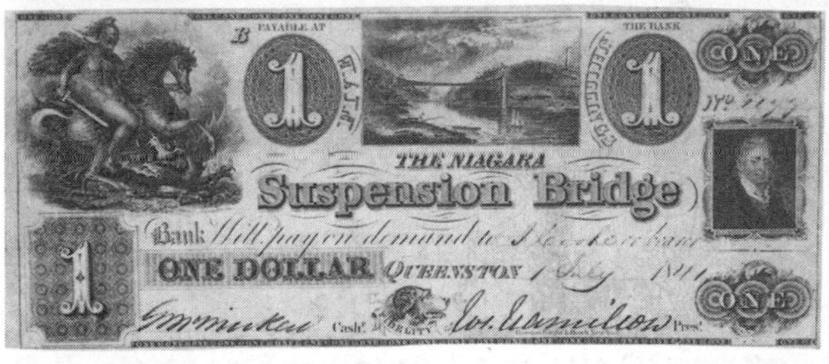

S1902 1 Dollar = 5 Shillings	VG	VF	UNC
1.7.1841. Black. St. George slaying dragon at upper left, portrait King William IV at right, mythical Niagara suspension bridge at top left center or center right. Back: Orange. Uniface.	50.00	175.	—

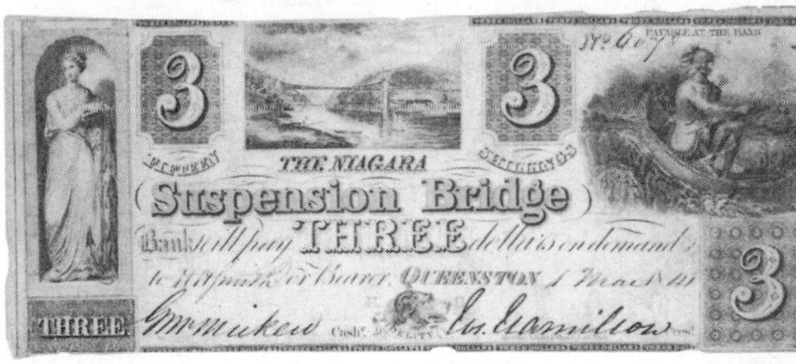

S1903 3 Dollars = 15 Shillings	VG	VF	UNC
1.3.1841; 1.5.1841; 1.7.1841. Black. Standing Navigation at left, Indian brave paddling canoe at upper right, dog's head at bottom center, mythical Niagara suspension bridge at top left center or center right. Uniface.	75.00	200.	—

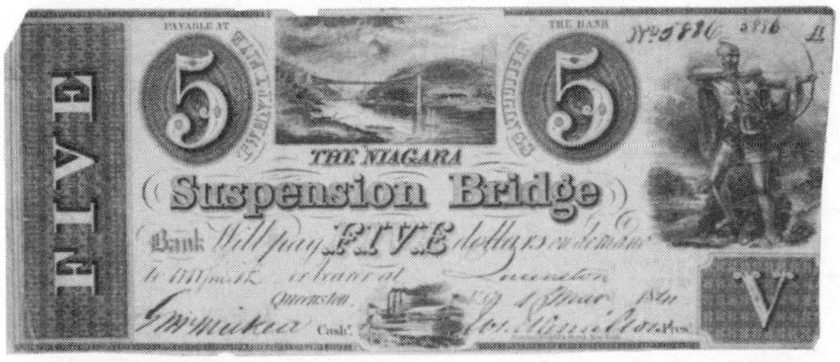

S1904 5 Dollars = 25 Shillings	VG	VF	UNC
1841. Black. Standing Indian brave with drawn bow at upper right, paddle wheel steamboat at bottom center,mythical Niagara suspension bridge at top left center or center right. Uniface.			
a. *QUEENSTON* above ship at bottom; *U.* at left, *C.* at right.	100.	300.	—
b. 1.3.1841; 1.5.1841; 1.7.1841. *Queenston* at left of ship at bottom; *U.C.* at right.	50.00	150.	—
c. *QUEENSTON* above ship at bottom; *UPPER CANADA.*	250.	600.	—
r. As a. Remainder. 18xx.	100.	200.	—

S1905 10 Dollars = 50 Shillings VG VF UNC

4.1.1841. Black. Mythical Niagara Suspension Bridge at top left center, St. George slaying dragon at upper right, *U.C.* at bottom center. Uniface.

	VG	VF	UNC
a. Issued note.	250.	450.	—
r. Remainder.	100.	225.	—

S1906 10 Dollars = 50 Shillings

4.1.1841. Black. Mythical Niagara Suspension Bridge at top left center, St. George slaying dragon at upper right, *U.C.* at bottom center. *UPPER CANADA* at bottom center. Uniface.

	VG	VF	UNC
a. Issued note.	150.	400.	—
r. Remainder.	100.	225.	—

S1907 20 Dollars = 5 Pounds VG VF UNC

4.1.1841. Black. Mythical Niagara Suspension Bridge at lower left, goddess rising from water at top left center, Greek god reclining by fountain with bathers at upper right, *U.C.* at bottom center. Uniface.

	VG	VF	UNC
a. Issued note.	200.	500.	—
r. Remainder.	200.	500.	—

S1908 20 Dollars = 5 Pounds

4.1.1841. Black. Mythical Niagara Suspension Bridge at top left center, St. George slaying dragon at upper right, *U.C.* at bottom center. *UPPER CANADA* at bottom center. Uniface.

	VG	VF	UNC
a. Issued note.	200.	500.	—
r. Remainder.	175.	450.	—

Bank of Ottawa (Banque de Ottawa) Montreal, L.C.

1837 First Spurious Issue

S1909 5 Dollars	Good	Fine	XF
15.4.1837; 15.5.1837. Black. Royal crest with lion and unicorn at top center, portrait King William IV at right, small horse's head at bottom center. Back: Blue. Printer: Burton, Gurley, Edmonds, New York.	200.	600.	—

1837 Second Spurious Issue

S1910 1 Dollar	Good	Fine	XF
10.8.1837; 11.10.1837. Black. Standing woman pouring wine at upper left, three allegorical women seated at top, helmeted allegorical woman with eagle at upper right, small crown at bottom center. Engraved text: *Accepted for MESS* Back: Blue.	200.	600.	—

S1911 5 Dollars = 1 Pound-5 Shillings	Good	Fine	XF
18xx. Black. Indian maiden reclining at top center, portrait King William IV at right. Engraved text: *Accepted for MESSRS. JOSEPH C. FRINK & CO.* at bottom left center. Back: Blue. Printer: Burton, Gurley, Edmonds, New York. Remainder.	200.	600.	—

1837 Third Spurious Issue

S1911A 1 Dollar	Good	Fine	XF
18.5.1837 Like #S1910 but *Accepted for D. F. Merril & Co.* at lower right. Printer: Burton, Gurley, Edmonds, New York.	—	—	—

1837 Fourth Spurious Issue

S1912 1 Dollar	Good	Fine	XF
1.11.1837. Black. Like #S1910 but *Accepted for D. F. Merril & Co.* at lower right. Printer: Burton, Gurley, Edmonds, New York.	200.	600.	—

S1913 3 Dollars	Good	Fine	XF
4.1.1838. Black. Standing allegorical woman with foot on globe at left, mill at top center, bust of young woman at right, small horse head at bottom center. Uniface. With engraved *Accepted for__* at bottom left or right. *SECURED BY REAL ESTATE* hand stamp.	300.	750.	—

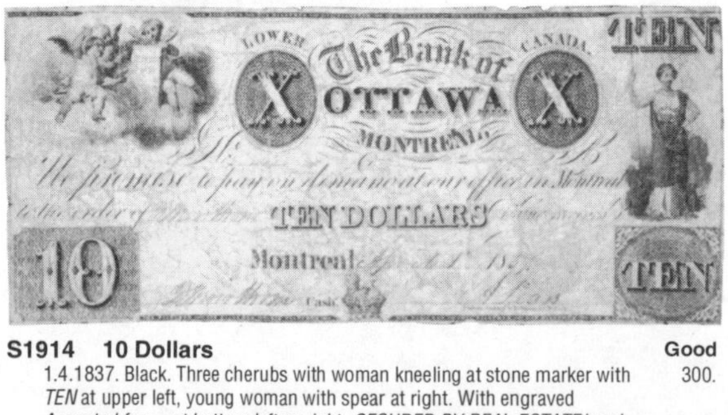

S1914 10 Dollars	Good	Fine	XF
1.4.1837. Black. Three cherubs with woman kneeling at stone marker with *TEN* at upper left, young woman with spear at right. With engraved *Accepted for __* at bottom left or right. *SECURED BY REAL ESTATE* hand stamp.	300.	750.	—

Phenix Bank, Phillipsburg, L.C.

1837 Spurious Issue

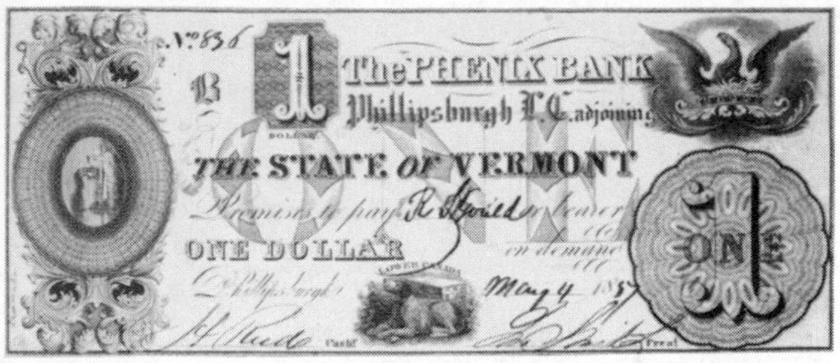

S1915 1 Dollar	VG	VF	UNC
4.5.1837. Black. Paddle wheel steamboat (sideways) at left, Phoenix at upper right, small dog lying by strongbox at bottom center with adjoining text: *THE STATE OF VERMONT* at center. Uniface. Printer: Jas Harris.	500.	1000.	—

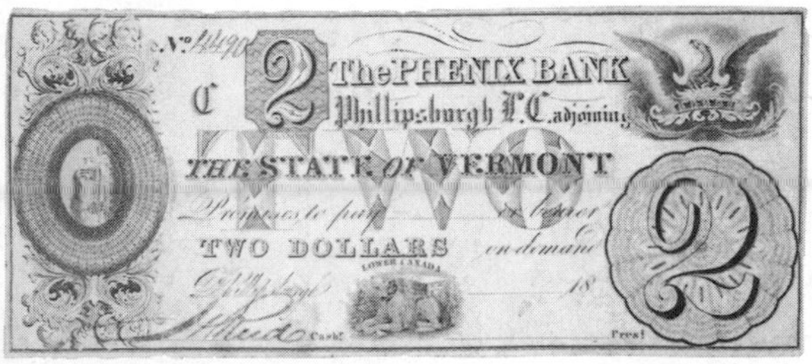

S1916 2 Dollars	VG	VF	UNC
18xx. Black. Paddle wheel steamboat (sideways) at left, Phoenix at upper right, small dog lying by strongbox at bottom center with adjoining text: *THE STATE OF VERMONT* at center. Uniface. Printer: Jas Harris. Remainder.	650.	1250.	—

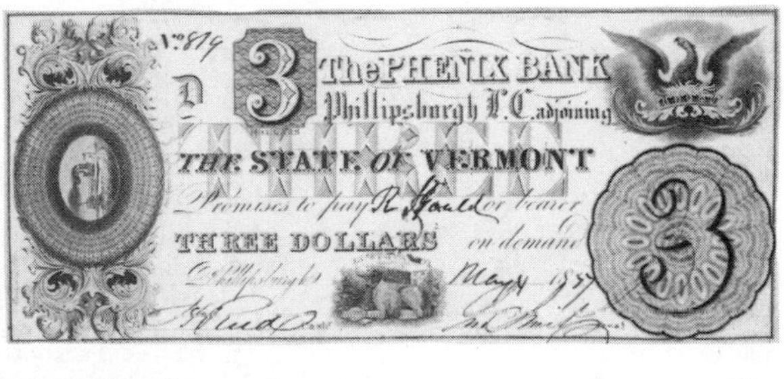

S1917 3 Dollars	VG	VF	UNC
4.5.1837. Black. Paddle wheel steamboat (sideways) at left, Phoenix at upper right, small dog lying by strongbox at bottom center with adjoining text: *THE STATE OF VERMONT* at center. Uniface. Printer: Jas Harris.	750.	1500.	—

1841 Spurious Issue

S1918 1 Dollar = 5 Shillings	VG	VF	UNC
8.10.1841. Black. Paddle wheel steamboat (sideways) at left, Phoenix at upper right, small dog lying by strongbox at bottom center with adjoining text: *THE STATE OF VERMONT* at center. Uniface. Printer: Jas Harris.	650.	1250.	—

Pictou Bank

1874 Issue

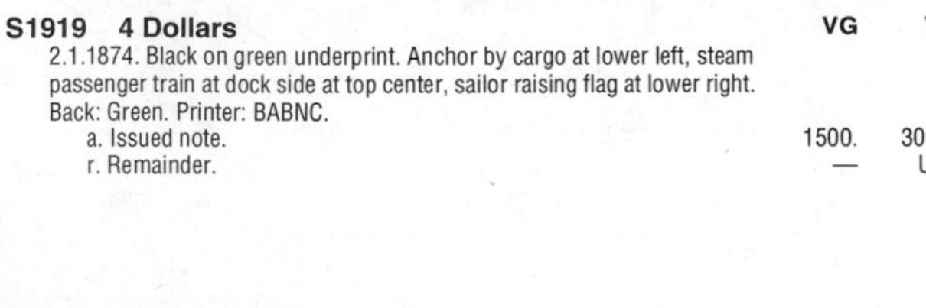

S1919 4 Dollars	VG	VF	UNC
2.1.1874. Black on green underprint. Anchor by cargo at lower left, steam passenger train at dock side at top center, sailor raising flag at lower right. Back: Green. Printer: BABNC.			
a. Issued note.	1500.	3000.	—
r. Remainder.	—	Unc	1250.

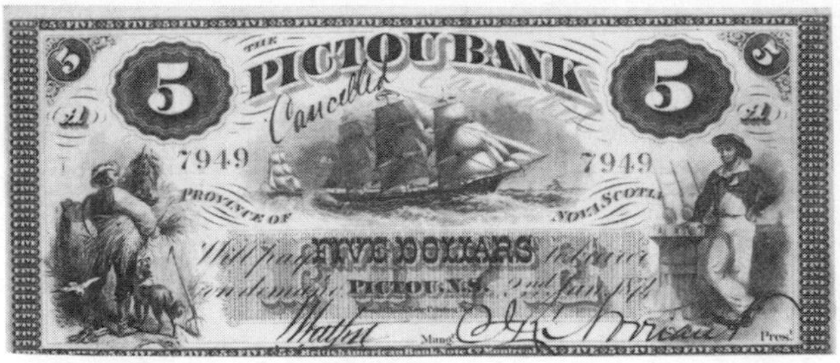

S1920 5 Dollars	VG	VF	UNC
1874; 1882. Black on green underprint. Farmer with dog feeding horse grain at lower left, sailing ships at upper center, standing sailor at lower right. Back: Green. Printer: BABNC.			
a. Issued note. 2.1.1874.	1250.	2500.	—
r. Remainder.	—	Unc	750.

S1921 10 Dollars	VG	VF	UNC
1874; 1882. Black on green underprint. Miners at top left center, sailing ships at lower right. Printer: BABNC.			
a. Issued note. 2.1.1882.	1250.	2500.	—
p. Face proof. 2.1.1874.	—	Unc	500.
r1. Remainder. 2.1.1874.	—	Unc	1250.
r2. Remainder. 2.1.1882.	—	Unc	1000.

Bank of Prince Edward Island

1856 Issue

S1922 5 Shillings	Good	Fine	XF
18.8.1856; 7.4.1857. Black. Sailing ship at left, seated woman with dog and cattle at top center. Uniface. Printer: NEBNC and RWH&E.	300.	1000.	—

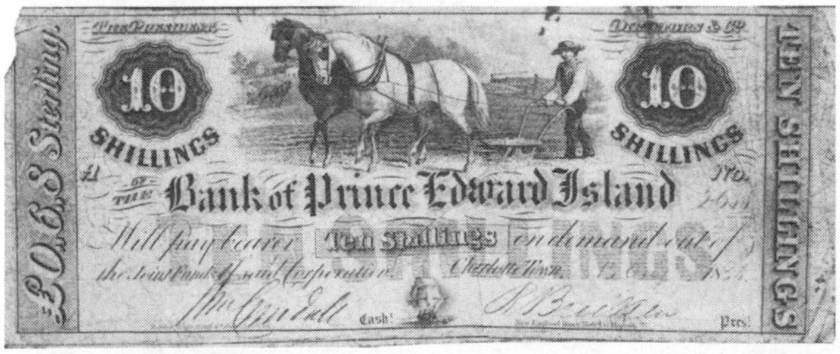

S1923 10 Shillings	Good	Fine	XF
13.8.1856; 7.4.1857. Black. Farmer plowing with horses at top center. Uniface. Printer: NEBNC and RWH&E.	400.	1250.	—

S1924 1 Pound	Good	Fine	XF
18.8.1856; 1.1.1857. Black. Seated Agriculture, sheaf with sailing ship in background at top center. Uniface. Printer: NEBNC and RWH&E.	500.	1500.	—

S1925 5 Pounds	Good	Fine	XF
13.8.1856. Black. Portrait Queen Victoria at upper left, suppored royal arms at top center, portrait of the Prince Consort at upper right. Uniface. Printer: NEBNC and RWH&E.	750.	2250.	—

1859 Issue

S1926 2 Pounds	Good	Fine	XF
1.1.1859; 1.12.1863. Black on green underprint. Sailing ship at left, seated woman with dog and cattle at top center. Uniface. Printer: ABNC monogram added.	400.	1200.	—
S1927 10 Shillings 1.1.1859; 2.1.1860; 1.1.1862. Black. Farmer plowing with horses at top center. Uniface. Printer: ABNC monogram added.	400.	1200.	—

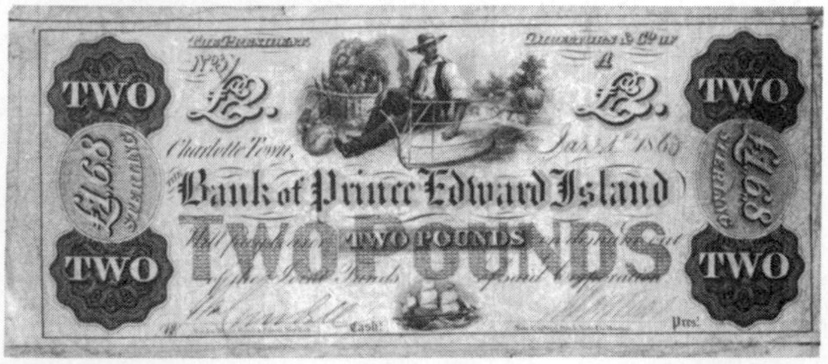

S1928 2 Pounds	Good	Fine	XF
1.1.1859; 1.1.1863. Black. Farmer seated with produce at top center. Uniface. Printer: ABNC monogram added.	400.	1200.	—

1872 Issue

S1929 1 Dollar	VG	VF	UNC
1.1.1872; 1.1.1877. Black on green underprint. Farm woman harvesting grain with sickle at center. Back: Green. Printer: BABNC.			
a. 1.1.1872.	100.	300.	1000.
b. Vertical red overprint: *CANADA CURRENCY* twice on #S1929a.	100.	300.	1000.
c. 1.1.1877.	75.00	200.	600.
d. Vertical red overprint: *CANADA CURRENCY* twice on #S1929c.	75.00	200.	650.

S1930 2 Dollars	VG	VF	UNC
1.1.1872; 1.1.1877. Black on green underprint. Anchor by cargo at lower left, horse watering in stream ("Drinking at the Brook") at upper center, cattle at lower right. Uniface. Back: Green. Printer: BABNC.			
a. 1.1.1872.	100.	300.	1000.
b. Vertical red overprint: *CANADA CURRENCY* twice on #S1930a.	125.	250.	800.
c. 1.1.1877.	75.00	150.	500.
d. Vertical red overprint: *CANADA CURRENCY* twice on #S1930c.	75.00	150.	500.

S1931 5 Dollars	VG	VF	UNC
1.1.1872; 1.1.1877. Black on green underprint. Farmer watering livestock at top center, young woman's head at bottom center. Back: Green. Printer: BABNC.			
a. 1.1.1872.	400.	750.	2500.
b. Vertical red overprint: *CANADA CURRENCY* twice on #S1931a.	400.	750.	2500.
c. 1.1.1877.	300.	600.	1750.
d. Vertical red overprint: *CANADA CURRENCY* twice on #S1931c.	300.	600.	1750.

S1932 10 Dollars	VG	VF	UNC
1.1.1872. Black on green underprint. Sailor at bottom left, fishing boats at top center, beehive at lower right. Back: Green. Printer: BABNC.			
a. Issued note.	175.	300.	750.
r. Remainder with 1 signature	100.	250.	600.

S1933 20 Dollars	VG	VF	UNC
1.1.1872. Black on green underprint. Portrait Queen Victoria at upper left, seated woman with trident ship in dry dock in background at top center, portrait of the Prince of Wales at upper right. Back: Green. Printer: BABNC.			
a. Issued note.	150.	275.	700.
r. Remainder with 1 signature	150.	275.	700.

Provincial Bank

1884 Issue

S1934 5 Dollars	VG	VF	UNC
1.8.1884. Black on green underprint. Lord Dufferin at left, farmer watering livestock at center, barge in locks at right. Back: Green. Printer: BABNC. Face proof.	—	—	750.
S1935 10 Dollars 1.8.1884. Black on green underprint. Lord Dufferin at left, farm scene at center, beavers at right. Back: Green. Printer: BABNC. Face proof.	—	—	750.

Provincial Bank of Canada

1856 Issue

S1936 1 Dollar	VG	VF	UNC
1.4.1856. Black. Supported royal arms at center. Red numeral protector. Uniface. Small supported royal arms at left. Back: Red numeral protector. Printer: Danforth Wright & Co.	500.	1000.	—

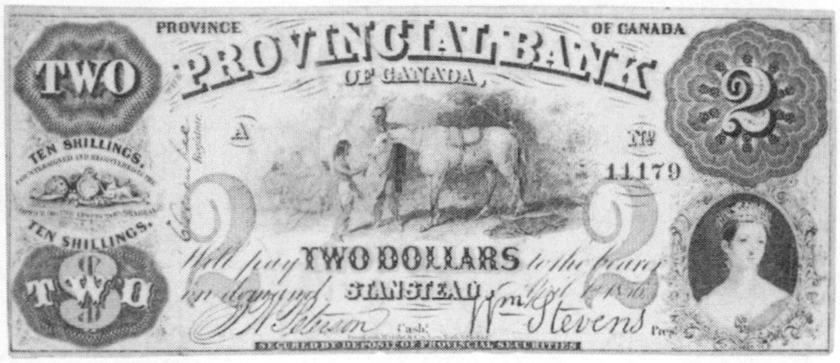

S1937 2 Dollars	VG	VF	UNC
1.4.1856. Black. Indians with horse at center, portrait Queen Victoria at lower right. Red numeral protector. Uniface. Small supported royal arms at left. Back: Red numeral protector. Printer: Danforth Wright & Co.	450.	900.	—

S1938 5 Dollars	VG	VF	UNC
1.4.1856. Black. Indian family overlooking factories at lower left, portrait of the Prince Consort at bottom center right. Red Roman numeral protector. Uniface. Back: Red Roman numeral protector. Printer: Danforth Wright & Co.	600.	1250.	—

Bank of Québec, Lower Canada

1841 Spurious Issue

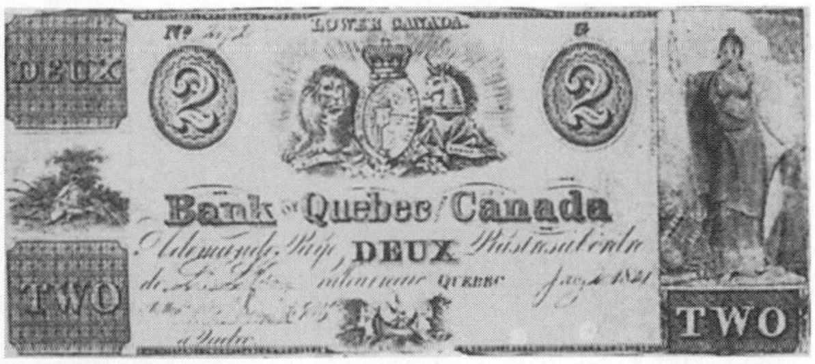

S1939 2 Piastres	VG	VF	UNC
2.1.1841. Black. Beehive and farm implements at left, supported royal arms at upper center, standing Britannia at right. Uniface. Printer: Harris & Sealey. Remainder.	400.	750.	—

Royal Canadian Bank

1865 First Issue

S1940 1 Dollar	VG	VF	UNC
4.7.1865. Partially engraved. Black on green underprint. Portrait Duke of Wellington at lower left, standing sailor at lower right. Supported bank seal at upper center. Black K hand stamp: *K*. Back: Brwon. Overprint: Red: *C*. Printer: ABNC.	750.	1500.	—

S1941 2 Dollars	VG	VF	UNC
4.7.1865. Partially engraved. Black on green underprint. Portrait Prince of Wales at lower left, reclining farm woman with basket of produce at lower right. Supported bank seal at upper center. Black K hand stamp: *K*. Back: Brown. Overprint: Red: *C*. Printer: ABNC.	750.	1500.	—
S1942 5 Dollars			
4.7.1865. Partially engraved. Black on green underprint. Princess of Wales at lower left, woman seated with telescope at lower right. Supported bank seal at upper center. Black K hand stamp: *K*. Back: Brown. Overprint: Red: *C*. Printer: ABNC. Face proof.	—	Unc	500.
S1943 10 Dollars			
4.7.1865. Partially engraved. Black on green underprint. Portrait Queen Victoria at lower left, woman with scale and sword on dock at lower right. Supported bank seal at upper center. Black K hand stamp: *K*. Back: Brown. Overprint: Red: *C*. Printer: ABNC. Face proof.	—	Unc	500.

1865 Second Issue

S1943A 1 Dollar	VG	VF	UNC
26.7.1865. Portrait Duke of Wellington at lower left, standing sailor at lower right. Supported bank seal at upper center. Black K hand stamp: *K*.			
a. Blue serial #.	900.	1750.	—
b. Red serial #.	900.	1750.	—
c. Vertical red overprint: *COBOURG* twice.	900.	1750.	—
d. Blue overprint: *T-T*.	900.	1750.	—

S1944 2 Dollars	VG	VF	UNC
26.7.1865. Portrait of the Prince of Wales at lower left, reclining farm woman with basket of produce at lower right.			
a. Blue serial #.	900.	1750.	—
b. Red serial #.	900.	1750.	—
c. Vertical red overprint: *PARIS* twice.	750.	1500.	—
S1944A 5 Dollars			
26.7.1865. Princess of Wales at lower left, woman seated with telescope at lower right.			
a. Blue serial #.	1250.	2250.	—
b. Blue overprint: *OTTAWA*.	900.	1750.	—
c. Blue overprint: *T T*.	900.	2000.	—

1865 Third Issue

S1944B 2 Dollars	VG	VF	UNC
26.7.1865. Black on green underprint. Prince Albert at lower left, farmer at lower right. Supported bank seal at upper center. Back: Green. Printer: CONB.			
a. With text: *AT ITS BANKING HOUSE IN TORONTO* above bank seal.	1000.	2250.	—
b. With text: *AT ITS AGENCY IN MONTREAL* above bank seal. Reported not confirmed.	—	—	—

1865 Second Issue

S1945 5 Dollars	VG	VF	UNC
26.7.1865. Young woman at lower left, Indian on horseback at lower right.			
a. With text: *AT ITS BANKING HOUSE IN TORONTO* above bank seal.	1150.	2250.	—
b. With text: *AT ITS AGENCY IN MONTREAL* above bank seal.	900.	2000.	—
c. Blue overprint: *T-T*.	900.	2000.	—

S1946 10 Dollars — VG | VF | UNC

26.7.1865. Portrait Queen Victoria at lower left, Indian brave at lower right.

	VG	VF	UNC
a. With text: *AT ITS BANKING HOUSE IN TORONTO* above bank seal. Reported not confirmed.	—	—	—
s. With text: *AT ITS AGENCY IN MONTREAL* above bank seal. Specimen.	—	—	1000.

1870 Issue

S1947 4 Dollars

1.7.1870. Black on green underprint. Two sailors at dock side at lower left, supported bank crest at upper center, beaver on shoreline at lower right. 1 serial #. Back: Green. Printer: BABNC.

	VG	VF	UNC
a. Issued note.	900.	1750.	—
b. Vertical blue overprint: *Montreal* twice.	900.	1750.	—
c. Black hand stamp: *A.*	750.	1500.	—

S1947A 4 Dollars

	VG	VF	UNC
1.7.1870. Black on green underprint. Like #S1947 but with Large *4* at upper left and at upper right. 2 serial #. Back: Green. Printer: BABNC.	900.	1750.	—

S1948 5 Dollars

	VG	VF	UNC
1.7.1872. Black on green underprint. Portrait T. McCracken at lower left, supported bank crest at top left center. Back: Green. Printer: BABNC.	1150.	2250.	—

S1949 10 Dollars

1.1.1872. Black on green underprint. Supported bank crest at upper left, portrait J. Crawford at lower right. Back: Green. Printer: BABNC.

	VG	VF	UNC
a. Issued note without overprint.	1250.	2500.	—
b. Vertical red overprint: *BELLEVILLE* twice and *CONSOLIDATED BANK/OF CANADA.*	1250.	2500.	—

S1950 20 Dollars

	VG	VF	UNC
2.10.1871. Black on green underprint. Allegorical woman at left, supported bank crest at center, sailor at right. Back: Green. Printer: BABNC. Face proof.	—	—	500.

S1951 50 Dollars

	VG	VF	UNC
2.10.1871. Black on green underprint. Supported bank crest at center. Back: Green. Printer: BABNC. Face proof.	—	—	500.

S1952 100 Dollars

	VG	VF	UNC
2.10.1871. Black on green underprint. Supported bank crest at center. Back: Green. Printer: BABNC. Face proof.	—	—	500.

Saint Francis Bank

1850 Issue

	VG	VF	UNC
S1953 5 Dollars 185x. Black on red underprint. Portrait Indian brave seated at left, supported portrait Queen Victoria at top center, portrait of the Prince Consort at lower right. Back: Blue. Printer: RWH & Co. Face proof.	—	—	800.
S1954 10 Dollars 185x. Black on red underprint. Anchor by cargo at left, St. George slaying dragon at top center, portrait Queen Victoria at lower right. Back: Blue. Printer: RWH & Co. Face proof.	—	—	800.

Banque St. Jean Baptiste

1875 Issue

	VG	VF	UNC
S1955 4 Dollars 24.6.1875. Black on green underprint. Man at left, St. John the Baptist with lamb at center, right. A. R. Hubert at right. Back: Green. Printer: BABNC. Face proof.	—	—	600.

	VG	VF	UNC
S1956 5 Dollars 24.6.1875. Black on green underprint. Allegorical woman reclining at lower left, St. John the Baptist seated by lamb at center, right. A. R. Hubert at lower right. Back: Green. Printer: BABNC. Face proof.	—	—	800.
S1957 10 Dollars 24.6.1875. Black on green underprint. St. John the Baptist seated by lamb at center, right. A. R. Hubert at right. Back: Green. Printer: BABNC. Face proof.	—	—	800.

St. Lawrence Bank & Lumber Co.

1837 Spurious Issue

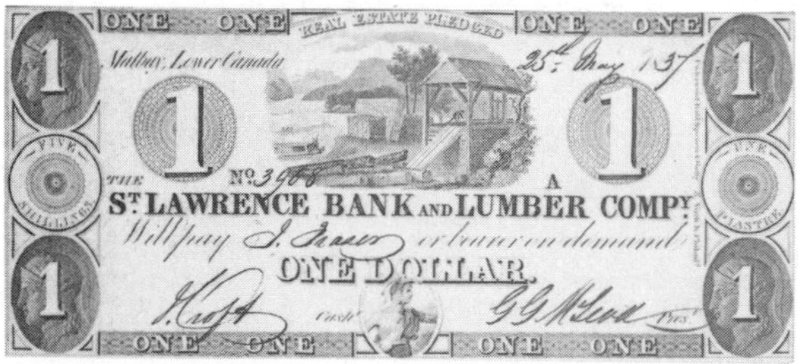

	VG	VF	UNC
S1958 1 Dollar 25.5.1837. Black. Identical Roman bust in all corners, sawmill at top center, Indian at bottom center. Uniface. Printer: Underwood, Bald, Spencer & Huffy.	25.00	50.00	150.

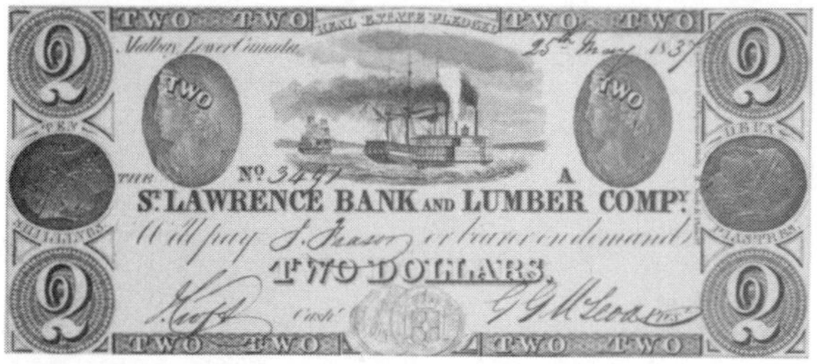

	VG	VF	UNC
S1959 2 Dollars 25.5.1837. Black. Identical Roman busts (sideways) at left and right, ferry St. Lawrence and two sailing ships between identical Roman busts at center, two Spanish 8 Reales coins at bottom center. Uniface. Printer: Underwood, Bald, Spencer & Huffy.	25.00	50.00	150.

St. Stephens Joint Stock Banking Co.

1840s Issue

	VG	VF	UNC
S1959A 3 Dollars 18xx. Black. Man at lower left, sailing ships at upper left center, steamboat and sailboat at lower right. Uniface. Printer: NEBNC. Remainder.	3000.	—	—

Bank of Saskatchewan

1913 Issue

		VG	VF	UNC
S1960 5 Dollars	1.5.1913. Black on yellow and dark green underprint. Steam passenger train approaching farmer cultivating with tractor at center. Back: Green. Allegorical woman with sheaf and sickle at center. Printer: ABNC. Face proof.	—	—	1000.

		VG	VF	UNC
S1961 10 Dollars	1.5.1913. Black on brown and yellow underprint. Steam passenger train approaching railroad construction at center. Back: Green. Printer: ABNC. Face proof.	—	—	1000.

		VG	VF	UNC
S1962 20 Dollars	1.5.1913. Black on red and yellow underprint. Steam freight trains at grain storage facility at center. Back: Green. Steam threshing at center. Printer: ABNC. Face proof.	—	—	1000.

Stadacona Bank

1874 Issue

		Good	Fine	XF
S1963 4 Dollars	2.4.1874. Black on green underprint. Sailing ship at lower left, supported royal arms at top center, portrait A. Joseph at lower right. Back: Green. Printer: BABNC.			
	a. Issued note without overprint	600.	1800.	—
	b. Red overprint: *L-L.*	600.	1800.	—
	c. Red overprint: *P-P.*	600.	1800.	—
	d. Vertical red overprint: *ST. SAVEUR* twice.	600.	1800.	—
S1964 5 Dollars	2.4.1874. Black on green underprint. S. de Champlain at lower left, steamboat at Québec at center, A. Joseph at lower right. Back: Green. Overprint: Red:*E-E.* Printer: BABNC.	900.	2250.	—

		VG	VF	UNC
S1965 6 Dollars	2.4.1874. Black on green underprint. Steam passenger train at upper left, A. Joseph at lower right. Back: Green. Printer: BABNC. Face proof.		—	1200.

		Good	Fine	XF
S1966 10 Dollars	2.4.1874. Black on green underprint. J. Cartier at lower left, A. Joseph at lower right. Back: Green. Overprint: Red vertical: *FRASERVILLE* twice. Printer: BABNC.	850.	2000.	—

Tattersall Bank, Montreal, L.C.

1830 Issue

		Good	Fine	XF
S1967 ***Deleted.***	(Advertising note.)	—	—	—

Union Bank

1838 First Issue

		Good	Fine	XF
S1968 1 Dollar	14.7.1838; 1.8.1838. Black. Woman posing in art studio at top center, small anchor, ship and caduceus at bottom center. Uniface. Printer: Burton & Gurley.	75.00	225.	—

		Good	Fine	XF
S1969 2 Dollars	14.7.1838. Black. Seated Mercury with sailing ship in background at top center, small road and sign post at bottom center. Uniface. Printer: Burton & Gurley.	75.00	225.	—
S1970 5 Dollars	14.7.1838. Black. Seated woman by Indian brave at top center, small crown at bottom center. Uniface. Printer: Burton & Gurley.	100.	300.	—

1838 Second Issue

		Good	Fine	XF
S1971 1 Dollar	1.8.1838. Black. Woman posing in art studio at top center, small anchor, ship and caduceus at bottom center. Uniface. Back: Green. Printer: Burton & Gurley.	100.	300.	—
S1972 2 Dollars	1.8.1838. Black. Seated Mercury with sailing ship in background at top center, small road and sign post at bottom center. Uniface. Back: Green. Printer: Burton & Gurley.	100.	300.	—

		Good	Fine	XF
S1973 5 Dollars	1.8.1838. Black. Seated woman by Indian brave at top center, small crown at bottom center. Uniface. Printer: Burton & Gurley.	100.	300.	—

1838 Third Issue

#S1974-S1976 like #S1971-S1973 but back blue.

	Good	Fine	XF
S1974 1 Dollar 1.8.1838. Black. Woman posing in art studio at top center, small anchor, ship and caduceus at bottom center. Uniface. Back: Blue. Printer: Burton & Gurley.	100.	300.	—
S1975 2 Dollars 1.8.1838. Black. Seated Mercury with sailing ship in background at top center, small road and sign post at bottom center. Uniface. Back: Blue. Printer: Burton & Gurley.	100.	300.	—
S1976 5 Dollars 1.8.1838. Black. Seated woman by Indian brave at top center, small crown at bottom center. Uniface. Back: Blue. Printer: Burton & Gurley.	100.	400.	—

1838 Fourth Issue

	Good	Fine	XF
S1977 1 Dollar 1.8.1838. Black. Indian hunting buffalo at top center, Indian with drawn bow at right, small portrait blacksmith at bottom center. Back: Red-brown. Printer: RWH & Co.	50.00	150.	—

	Good	Fine	XF
S1978 2 Dollars 1.8.1838. Black. Indian paddling canoe at top center, woman with sheaf of wheat at right, clasped hands in spray at bottom. Back: Red-brown. Printer: RWH & Co.	50.00	150.	—

	Good	Fine	XF
S1979 3 Dollars 1.8.1838. Black. Seated allegorical woman surrounded by cherubs in clouds at top center, standing Indian maiden at upper right, small early steam passenger train at bottom center. Back: Red-brown. Printer: RWH & Co.	100.	200.	—

1838 Fifth Issue

	Good	Fine	XF
S1980 1 Dollar 1.8.1838. Black. Indian hunting buffalo at top center, Indian with drawn bow at right, small portrait blacksmith at bottom center. Back: Orange. Printer: RWH & Co.	100.	200.	—
S1981 2 Dollars 1.8.1838. Black. Indian paddling canoe at top center, woman with sheaf of wheat at right, clasped hands in spray at bottom. Back: Orange. Printer: RWH & Co.	75.00	150.	—
S1982 3 Dollars 1.8.1838. Black. Seated allegorical woman surrounded by cherubs in clouds at top center, standing Indian maiden at upper right, small early steam passenger train at bottom center. Back: Orange. Printer: RWH & Co.			
a. Issued note.	75.00	175.	—
r. Unsigned remainder. 18xx.	—	Unc	800.

	Good	Fine	XF
S1983 5 Dollars 1.8.1838. Black. Train at center, farmer with implements, beehive and cornucopia at right. Back: Orange. Printer: RWH & Co.			
a. Issued note.	75.00	150.	—
r. Unsigned remainder.	—	Unc	600.

	Good	Fine	XF
S1984 10 Dollars 18xx. Black. Steam passenger train and cargo at left, seated Indian brave overlooking ruins of Jamestown at top center right, small griffin with key at bottom center. Back: Orange. Printer: RWH & Co. Unsigned remainder.	150.	400.	900.

	Good	Fine	XF
S1985 20 Dollars 18xx. Black. Woman kneeling at left, steam passenger train at dockside at top center, allegorical woman at right. Back: Orange. Printer: RWH & Co. Unsigned remainder.	125.	400.	750.

1838 Sixth Issue

	Good	Fine	XF
S1986 1 Dollar 1.8.1838. Black. Indian hunting buffalo at top center, Indian with drawn bow at right, small portrait blacksmith at bottom center. Back: Blue. Printer: RWH & Co.	50.00	100.	—
S1987 2 Dollars 1.8.1838. Black. Indian paddling canoe at top center, woman with sheaf of wheat at right, clasped hands in spray at bottom. Back: Blue. Printer: RWH & Co.	50.00	100.	—
S1988 3 Dollars 1.8.1838. Black. Seated allegorical woman surrounded by cherubs in clouds at top center, standing Indian maiden at upper right, small early steam passenger train at bottom center. Back: Blue. Printer: RWH & Co.	75.00	150.	—
S1988A 5 Dollars 1.8.1838. Black. Back: Blue. Printer: RWH & Co.	100.	300.	—

Union Bank of Montreal

1840 Issue

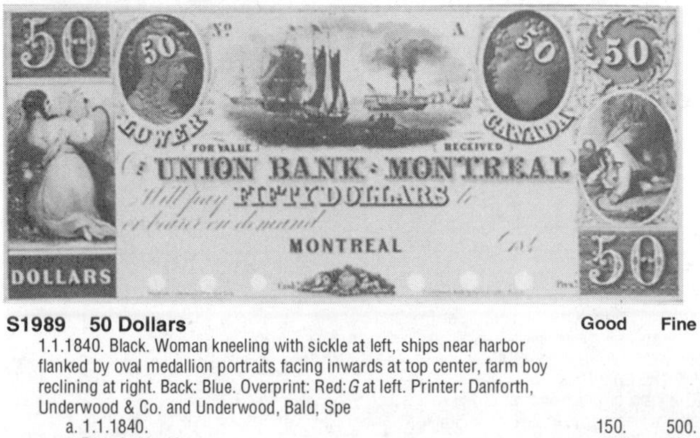

	Good	Fine	XF
S1989 50 Dollars 1.1.1840. Black. Woman kneeling with sickle at left, ships near harbor flanked by oval medallion portraits facing inwards at top center, farm boy reclining at right. Back: Blue. Overprint: Red: *G* at left. Printer: Danforth, Underwood & Co. and Underwood, Bald, Spe			
a. 1.1.1840.	150.	500.	1250.
r. Remainder. 18xx.	—	Unc	800.

1840 Dollar / Pound Issue

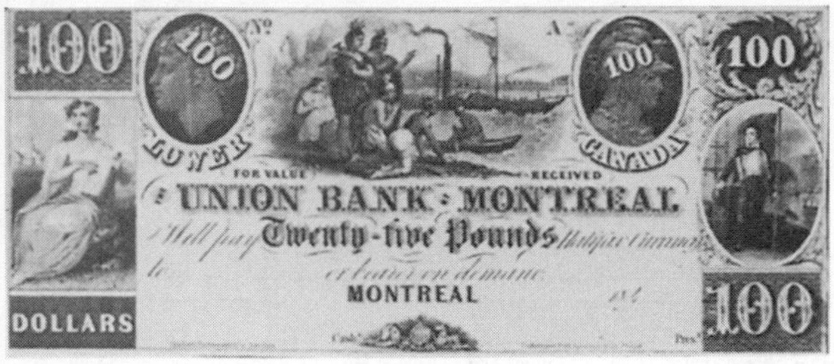

S1990 100 Dollars = 25 Pounds	Good	Fine	XF
1.1.1840. Black. Seated woman with book at left, Indians along shoreline with steamship in background flanked by oval medallion portraits facing outwards at top center, portrait young man with flag at right. Back: Blue. Overprint: Red: *G* at left. Printer: Danforth, Underwood & Co. and Underwood, Bald, Spe	150.	500.	1250.

Bank of Upper Canada, Kingston, U.C.

1819; 1820 Issue

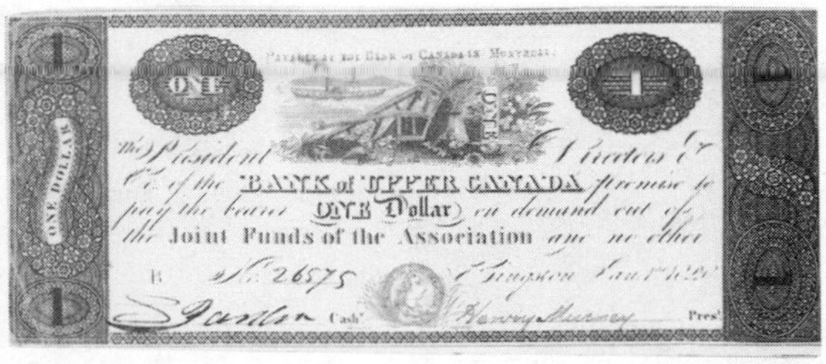

S1991 1 Dollar	Good	Fine	XF
1.5.1819; 1.1.1820. Black. Plow and sheaf with paddle wheel steamboat in background at top center, coin at bottom center. Uniface. Overprint: Black: *Payable at the Bank of Canada in Montreal.* Printer: Graphic.			
a. Partially engraved date. 29.3.1819; 1.5.1819.	100.	300.	—
b. Engraved date. 1.1.1820.	50.00	125.	350.

S1992 2 Dollars	VG	VF	UNC
1.5.1819; 1.1.1820. Black. Seated Justice with trident at top center, two coins at bottom center. Uniface. Back: Graphic. Overprint: Black: *Payable at the Bank of Canada in Montreal.*			
a. Partially engraved date. 1.5.1819.	125.	250.	—
b. Engraved date. 1.1.1820.	50.00	125.	300.

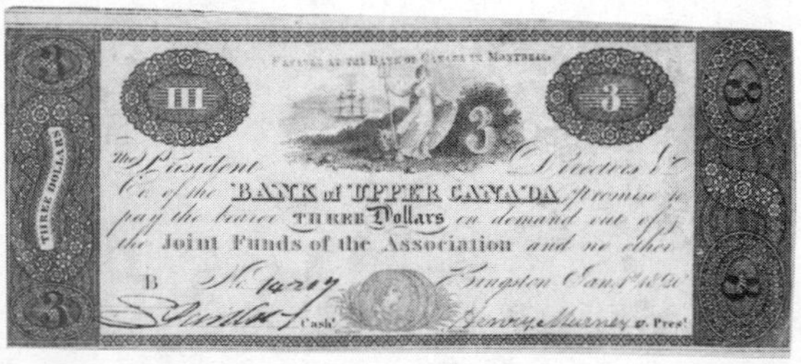

S1993 3 Dollars	VG	VF	UNC
1.1.1820. Black. Standing Britannia with sailing ship in background at top center, three coins at bottom center. Uniface. Overprint: Black: *Payable at the Bank of Canada in Montreal.* Printer: Graphic.	75.00	150.	400.

S1994 5 Dollars	Good	Fine	XF
1819-22. Black. Fort, shipbuilding along shoreline at upper right, five coins at bottom center. Overprint: Black: *Payable at the Bank of Canada in Montreal.* Printer: Graphic.			
a. Partially engraved date. 4.4.1822; 1.5.1822; 3.6.1822.	50.00	200.	350.
b. As a. 18xx.	—	—	200.

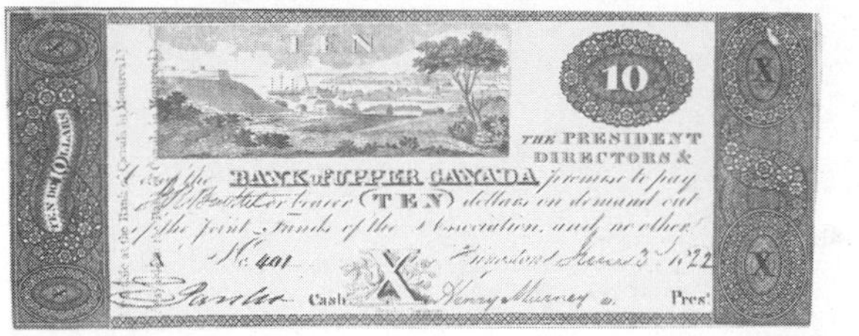

S1995 10 Dollars	Good	Fine	XF
1819-22. Black. Fort above Kingston Harbor at upper left center. Uniface. Overprint: Black: *Payable at the Bank of Canada in Montreal.* Printer: Graphic.			
a. Partially engraved date. 4.4.1819; 1.5.1819; 3.6.1822.	40.00	100.	225.
b. As d. 18xx.	—	—	150.

1820 Issue

S1996 6 Pence	Good	Fine	XF
23.8.1820. Black. Seated Britannia at upper left. Uniface.	400.	1500.	—

Bank of Upper Canada, York, U. C.

1826-30 Issues

S1997 1 Dollar = 5 Shillings	VG	VF	UNC
7.3.1829; 19.3.1831. Black. Seated Britannia with steamboat and beehive in background at top center, value at bottom center. Uniface. Printer: Graphic.	350.	700.	—

S1998 2 Dollars = 10 Shillings	VG	VF	UNC
3.8.1827. Black. Harbor view, lighthouse at top center, two coins at bottom center. Uniface. Printer: Graphic.	450.	800.	—

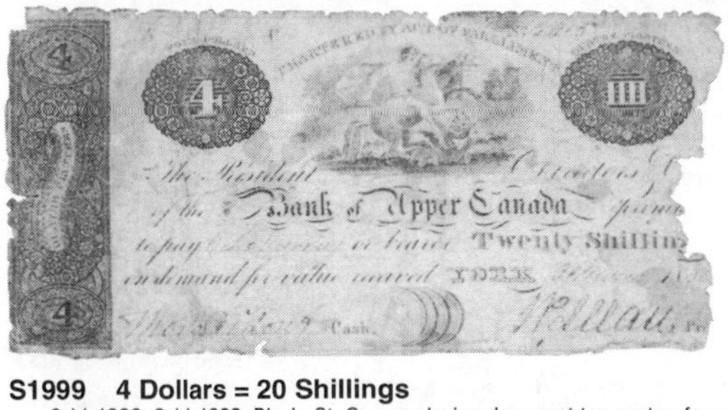

S1999 4 Dollars = 20 Shillings	VG	VF	UNC
3.11.1830; 2.11.1832. Black. St. George slaying dragon at top center, four coins at bottom center. Uniface. Printer: Graphic.	550.	1000.	—

S2000 5 Dollars = 25 Shillings	VG	VF	UNC
1826-32. Black. View of York, lighthouse at top center with text: *FIVE DOLLARS - CINQUE PIASTRES* above counters at upper left and right. Uniface. Printer: Graphic.			
a. 2.8.1826; 3.1.1827; 9.1.1830.	500.	900.	—
b. 19.9.1832.	550.	1000.	—

S2000A 5 Dollars = 25 Shillings	VG	VF	UNC
19.9.1832. Black. View of York, lighthouse at top center with text *FIVE DOLLARS - CINQUE PIASTRES* below counters at upper left and right. Uniface. Printer: Graphic.	500.	900.	—

S2001 10 Dollars = 50 Shillings	VG	VF	UNC
1.11.1830. Black. Harbor scene at top center. Uniface. Printer: Graphic.	550.	1000.	—

1836-38 Issues

S2002 1 Dollar	Good	Fine	XF
18xx. Black. Seated Justice at left, Neptune in horse drawn chariot and winged woman at top center, oval portrait Indian at bottom center. Uniface. Text: *Payable at Toronto.* Printer: RWH & Co. or RWH&E. Proof.	—	Unc	450.

S2003 2 Dollars | VG 600. | VF 1100. | UNC —

6.11.1836. Black. Standing Navigation at left, Indian brave with drawn bow at upper center, allegorical woman at right, small bison at bottom center. Uniface. Text: *Payable at Toronto.* Printer: RWH & Co. or RWH&E.

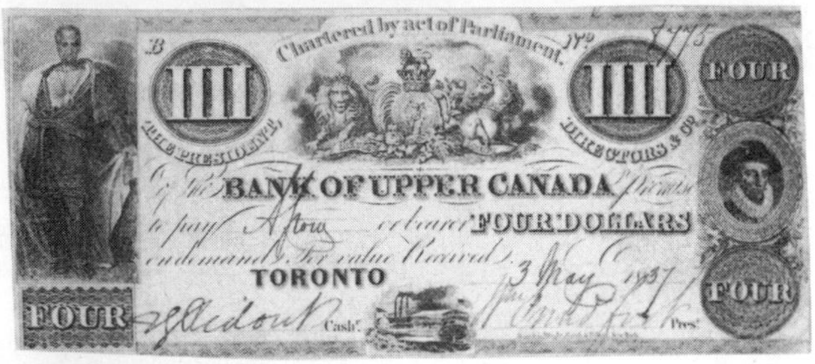

S2004 4 Dollars | VG 600. | VF 1100. | UNC —

3.5.1837. Black. Standing Indian "Red Jacket" at upper left, supported royal arms at upper center, portrait Sir Walter Raleigh at right. Uniface. Text: *Payable at Toronto.* Printer: RWH & Co. or RWH&E.

S2005 5 Dollars | Good — | Fine Unc | XF 400.

18xx. Black. Three seated allegorical women at left, Neptune with woman in horse drawn shell at top center, standing Britannia holding anchor at upper right, small sailing ship at bottom center. Uniface. Text: Printer: RWH & Co. or RWH&E.

S2006 10 Dollars | VG 600. | VF 1100. | UNC —

1.1.1838. Black. Two seated allegorical women with sailing ship in background, Neptune with woman in horse drawn shell at top center, portrait cherub at right, small sailing ship at bottom center. Uniface. Text: *Pa* Printer: RWH & Co. or RWH&E.

#S2007-S2009 obelisk at r.

S2007 20 Dollars | Good — | Fine Unc | XF 450.

18xx. Black. Griffin and three allegorical women at top center, small griffin with key at bottom center. Uniface. Text: *Payable at Toronto.* Obelisk at right. Printer: RWH & Co. or RWH&E. Proof.

S2008 50 Dollars | Good — | Fine Unc | XF 500.

18xx. Black. Portrait cherub at left, steam train at dock side at top center. Uniface. Text: *Payable at Toronto.* Obelisk at right. Printer: RWH & Co. or RWH&E. Proof.

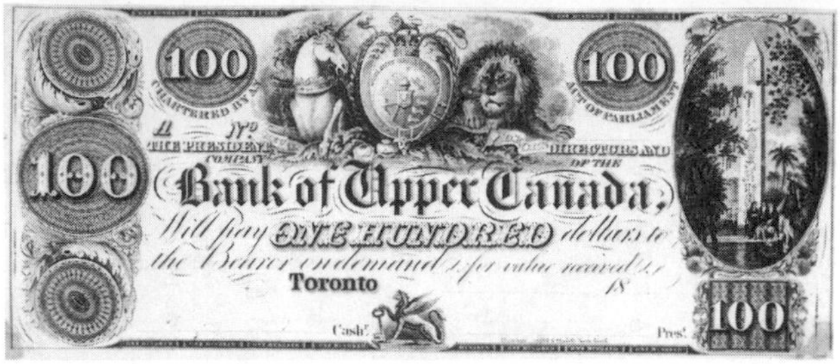

S2009 100 Dollars | Good — | Fine Unc | XF 500.

18xx. Black. Supported royal arms at top center. Uniface. Text: *Payable at Toronto.* Obelisk at right. Printer: RWH & Co. or RWH&E. Proof.

1849-51 Issues

S2010 1 Dollar = 5 Shillings | VG 600. | VF 1200. | UNC —

1.9.1849. Black. Lion at left, seated Commerce with ornate *1* at top center, woman with dog and *1* at right. Small St. George slaying dragon at bottom center. Toronto. Red word protector. Uniface. Back: Red word protector. Printer: RWH & Co.

S2011 2 Dollars = 10 Shillings | — | Unc | 450.

18xx. Black. Seated Agriculture at left, two griffins facing with *2* between at center, portrait woman at right. Small St. George slaying dragon at bottom center. Toronto. Red word protector. Uniface. Back: Red word protector. Printer: RWH & Co.

S2012 4 Dollars = 1 Pound | VG 600. | VF 1200. | UNC —

1.11.1851; 5.8.1852; 7.11.1856. Black. Portrait Queen Victoria at left, seated Britannia by lion at top center, seated Agriculture at right. Small St. George slaying dragon at bottom center. Toronto. Red word protector. Uniface. Printer: RWH & Co.

S2013 5 Dollars = 1 Pound-5 Shillings | VG 600. | VF 1200. | UNC —

9.10.1849. Black. Portrait Queen Victoria at left, lion and shield at top center, portrait of the Prince Consort at right. Small St. George slaying dragon at bottom center. Toronto. Red word protector. Uniface. Back: Red word protector. Printer: RWH & Co.

S2014 10 Dollars = 2 Pounds-10 Shillings | 600. | 1200. | —

18xx. Black. Young woman with wheat stalks at left, seated woman with harp and sheaf at top center, standing Britannia at right. Small St. George slaying dragon at bottom. Toronto. Red word protector. Uniface. Back: Red word protector. Printer: RWH & Co.

S2015 20 Dollars = 5 Pounds | Good — | Fine Unc | XF 450.

18xx. Black. Griffin at lower left, seated Mercury and woman with caduceus at top center, Britannia at lower right. Small St. George slaying dragon at bottom center. Toronto. Red word protector. Uniface. Back: Red word protector. Printer: RWH & Co. Proof.

	Good	Fine	XF
S2016 50 Dollars = 12 Pounds-10 Shillings			
18xx. Black. Seated Agriculture at lower left, seated Abundance between lion and unicorn at top center, seated Britannia at lower right. Small St. George slaying dragon at bottom center. Toronto. Red word protecto Back: Red word protector. Printer: RWH & Co. Proof.	—	Unc	450.
S2017 100 Dollars = 25 Pounds			
18xx. Black. Portrait seated Queen Victoria at lower left, supported portrait Queen Victoria at top center, medallion portrait archaic male soldier at lower right. Small St. George slaying dragon at bottom center. Back: Red word protector. Printer: RWH & Co. Proof.	—	Unc	450.

1851-57 Issues

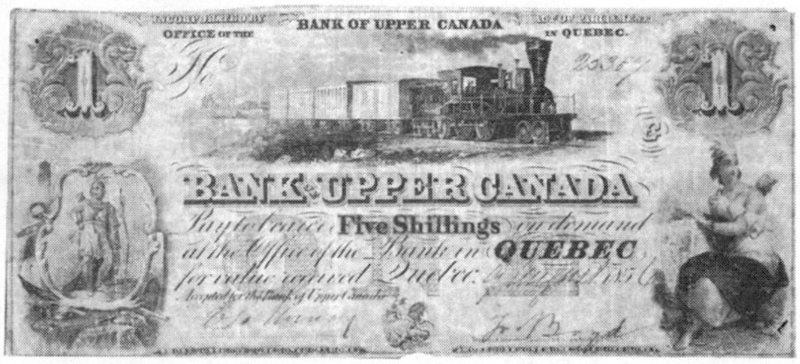

S2018 1 Dollar = 5 Shillings	VG	VF	UNC
2.1.1851-18.5.1857. Black. Ornate frame with Indian brave at lower left, steam passenger train at top center, seated Indian maiden with shield at lower right. Blue word. Uniface. Printer: TCC.			
a. Kingston. 6.1.1851.	600.	1200.	—
b. Montreal. 2.1.1851.	600.	1200.	—
c. Quebec. 2.5.1854-18.5.1857.	500.	1000.	—

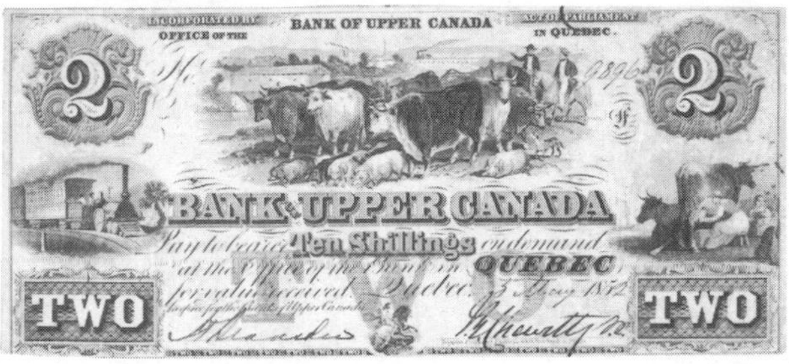

S2019 2 Dollars = 10 Shillings	VG	VF	UNC
2.1.1851-7.11.1856. Early steam passenger train at left, two herdsmen on horseback driving livestock at top center, two milkmaids milking cows at right. Uniface. Printer: TCC.			
a. Brockville. 9.1.1851.	500.	1000.	—
b. Quebec. 5.5.1852-7.11.1856.	550.	1150.	—
p. Montreal. Proof. 185x.	—	Unc	450.

S2020 5 Dollars = 1 Pound-5 Shillings	VG	VF	UNC
9.5.1857. Black. Horse galloping at left, supported portrait Queen Victoria at upper center, dog lying by strongbox at right. Uniface. Printer: TCC.			
a. Quebec. 9.5.1857.	550.	1150.	—
p. Montreal. Proof. 185x.	—	Unc	450.

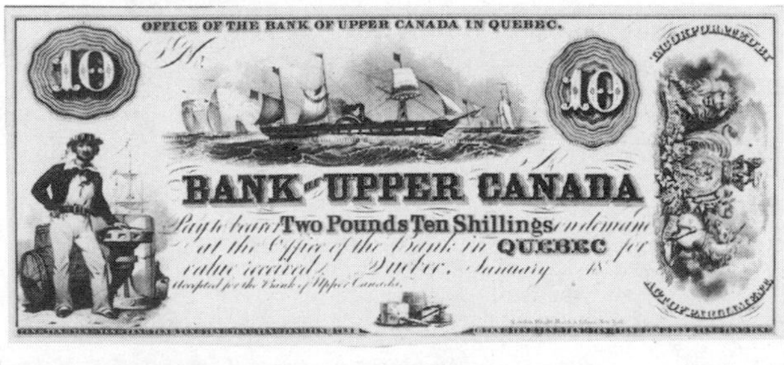

S2021 10 Dollars = 2 Pounds-10 Shillings	Good	Fine	XF
Jan. 18xx. Black. Standing sailor at lower left, paddle wheel steam sailing ship at top center. Supported royal arms (sideways) at right. Uniface. Printer: RWH & Co.			
p1. Montreal. Proof.	—	Unc	500.
p2. Quebec. Proof.	—	Unc	500.

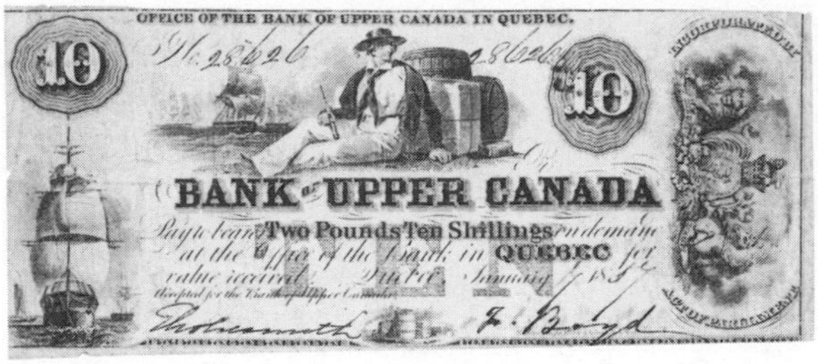

S2022 10 Dollars = 2 Pounds-10 Shillings	VG	VF	UNC
7.1.1857. Black. Three ships under full sail at lower left, seated sailor by cargo with sailing ship in background at top center. Supported royal arms (sideways) at right. Uniface. Printer: RWH & Co.			
a. Quebec. 7.1.1857.	650.	1400.	—
p. Montreal. Proof. Jan. 185x.	—	Unc	500.

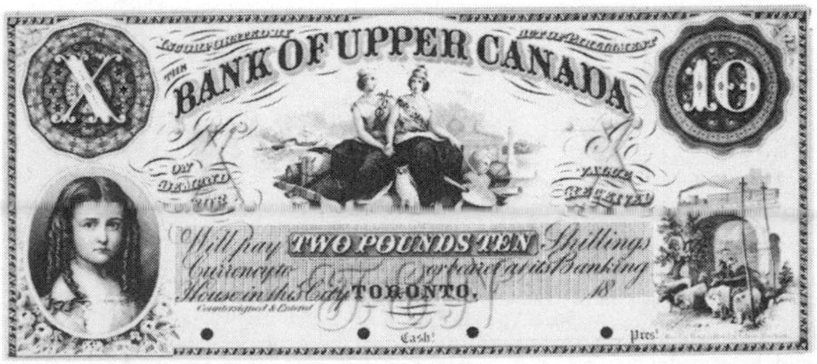

	Good	Fine	XF
S2023 10 Dollars = 2 Pounds-10 Shillings			
18xx. Black on brown-orange underprint. Young girl at lower left, seated Commerce and Britannia at upper center, herdsmen driving cattle under bridge at lower right. Toronto. Printer: RWH&E. Proof.	—	Unc	600.
S2024 10 Dollars = 2 Pounds-10 Shillings			
18xx. Black on green underprint. Young girl at lower left, seated Commerce and Britannia at upper center, herdsmen driving cattle under bridge at lower right. Toronto. Printer: RWH&E. Proof.	—	Unc	600.

1859 Issue

S2025 1 Dollar	VG	VF	UNC
1.7.1859-2.7.1859. Black on green underprint. Seated Justice at lower left, St. George slaying dragon at upper center, seated Britannia with crest of Upper Canada at lower right. 2 signatures. Back: Green. Overprint: Various numerical and branch. Printer: RWH&E and ABNC.			
a. Montreal. 1.7.1859.	550.	1000.	—
b. Quebec. 1.7.1859.	600.	1200.	—
c. Toronto. 1.7.1859. 18xx.	600.	1200.	—
d. Toronto. 2.7.1859.	600.	1200.	—

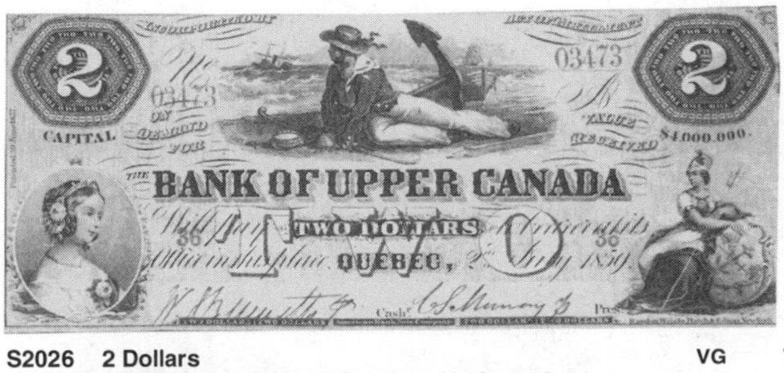

S2026 2 Dollars	VG	VF	UNC
2.7.1859. Black on green underprint. Portrait youthful Queen Victoria at lower left, sailor reclining by anchor with ships and boat in background at top center, seated Britannia with crest of Upper Canada at lower right. 2 signatures. Back: Green. Overprint: Various numerical and branch. Printer: RWH&E and ABNC.			
a. Montreal. 2.7.1859.	600.	1200.	—
b. Quebec. 2.7.1859.	600.	1200.	—
c. Toronto. 2.7.1859.	600.	1200.	—
p. Toronto. Proof. 18xx.	—	Unc	450.

S2027 4 Dollars

4.7.1859. Black on green underprint. Young woman with cornucopia at lower left, two allegorical women seated with three shields at upper center, blacksmith seated at lower right. 2 signatures. Back: Green. Overprint: Various numerical and branch. Printer: RWH&E and ABNC.

	VG	VF	UNC
a. Toronto. 4.7.1859.	600.	1200.	—
p. Toronto. Proof. 18xx.	—	Unc	500.

S2028 5 Dollars

5.7.1859. Black on green underprint. Standing sailor at lower left, two allegorical women seated with three shields at top center, portrait of the Prince of Wales at lower right. 2 signatures. Back: Green. Overprint: Various numerical and branch. Printer: RWH&E and ABNC.

	VG	VF	UNC
a. Montreal. 5.7.1859.	600.	1200.	—
b. Quebec. 5.7.1859.	600.	1200.	—
c. Toronto. 5.7.1859/18xx.	600.	1200.	—
d. Toronto. 5.7.1859.	600.	1200.	—

S2029 10 Dollars

6.7.1859. Black on green underprint. Youthful portrait Queen Victoria at lower left, two allegorical women seated with three shields at top center, seated Britannia with crest of Upper Canada at lower right. 2 signatures. Back: Green. Overprint: Various numerical and branch. Printer: RWH&E and ABNC.

	VG	VF	UNC
a. Montreal. 6.7.1859.	600.	1200.	—
b. Quebec. 6.7.1859.	600.	1200.	—
c. Toronto. 6.7.1859.	600.	1200.	—
p. Toronto. Proof. 18xx.	—	Unc	500.

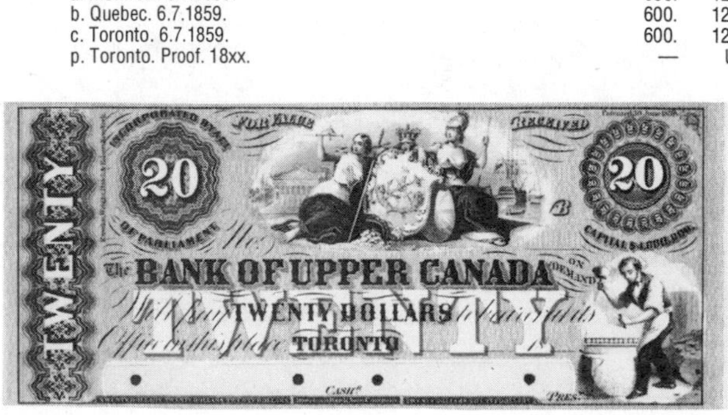

S2030 20 Dollars

	VG	VF	UNC
18xx; 8.7.1859. Black on green underprint. Seated Justice and Britannia with crest of Upper Canada at top center right, stone mason at lower right. Toronto. 2 signatures. Back: Green. Overprint: Various numerical and branch. Printer: RWH&E and ABNC. Proof.	—	—	500.

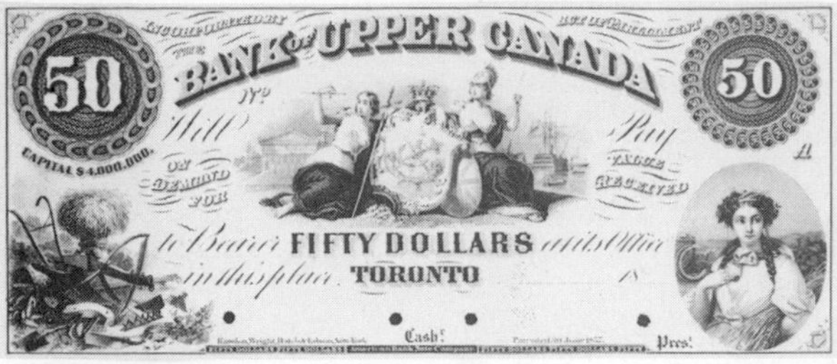

S2031 50 Dollars

	VG	VF	UNC
18xx; 8.7.1859. Black on green underprint. Farm implements at lower left, seated Justice and Britannia with crest of Upper Canada at upper center, woman with sheaf and sickle at lower right. Toronto. 2 signatures. Back: Green. Overprint: Various numerical and branch. Printer: RWH&E and ABNC. Proof.	—	—	500.

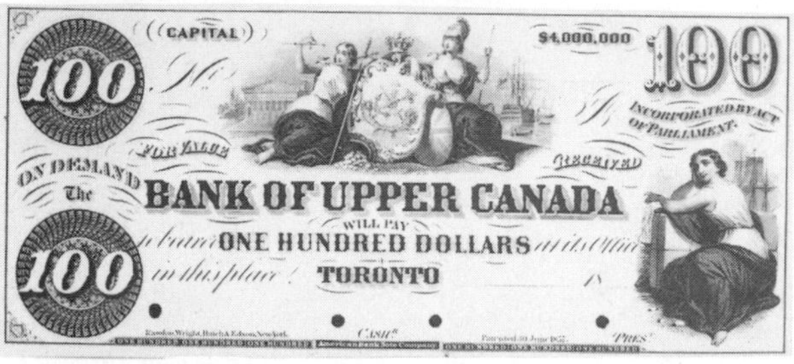

S2032 100 Dollars

	VG	VF	UNC
18xx; 9.7.1859. Black on green underprint. Seated Justice and Britannia with crest of Upper Canada at top center, seated woman by bale at lower right. Toronto. 2 signatures. Back: Green. Overprint: Various numerical and branch. Printer: RWH&E and ABNC. Proof.	—	—	500.

1861 Issue

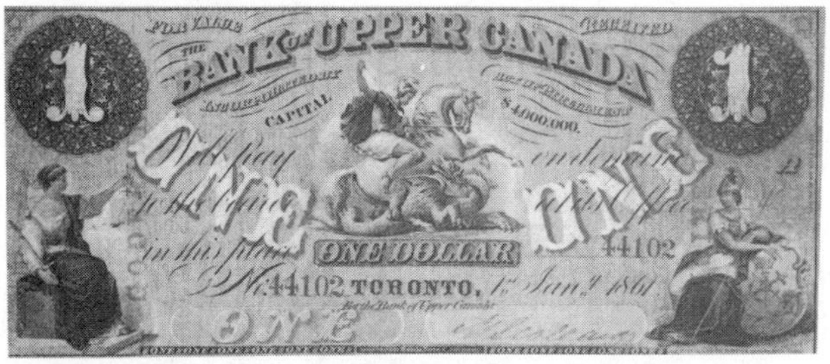

S2033 1 Dollar

	VG	VF	UNC
1.1.1861. Black on green underprint. Seated Justice at lower left, St. George slaying dragon at upper center, seated Britannia with crest of Upper Canada at lower right. 1 signature. Toronto. Back: Green. Overprint: Various branch name, with or without numbers in red or black. Printer: RWH&E and ABNC.	400.	800.	—

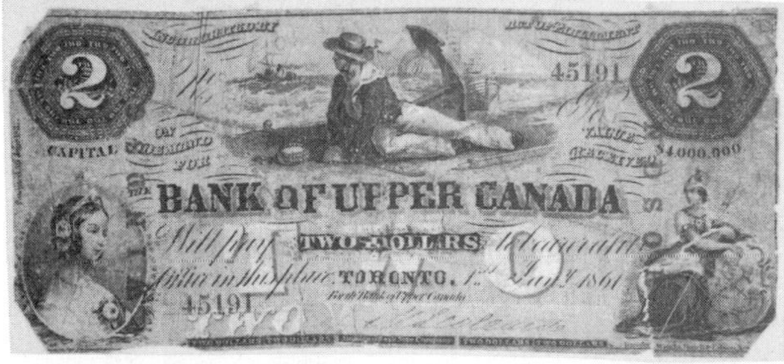

S2034 2 Dollars

	VG	VF	UNC
1.1.1861. Black on green underprint. Portrait youthful Queen Victoria at lower left, sailor reclining by anchor with ships and boat in background at top center, seated Britannia with crest of Upper Canada at lower right. 1 signature. Tor Back: Green. Overprint: Various branch name with or without numbers in red or black. Printer: RWH&E and ABNC.	500.	1000.	—

S2035 4 Dollars VG VF UNC

1.1.1861. Black on green underprint. Young woman with cornucopia at lower left, two allegorical women seated with three shields at upper center, blacksmith seated at lower right. 1 signature. Toronto. Back: Green. Overprint: Various branch name with or without numbers in red or black. Printer: RWH&E and ABNC. 500. 1000. —

S2036 5 Dollars VG VF UNC

1.1.1861. Black on green underprint. Standing sailor at lower left, two allegorical women seated with three shields at top center, portrait of the Prince of Wales at lower right. 1 signature. Toronto. Back: Green. Overprint: Various branch name with or without numbers in red or black. Printer: RWH&E and ABNC. 400. 800. —

S2037 10 Dollars VG VF UNC

1.1.1861. Black on green underprint. Youthful portrait Queen Victoria at lower left, two allegorical women seated with three shields at top center, seated Britannia with crest of Upper Canada at lower right. 1 signature. Toronto. Back: Green. Overprint: Various branch name with or without numbers in red or black. Printer: RWH&E and ABNC. 500. 1000. —

Bank of Western Canada

1859 Issue

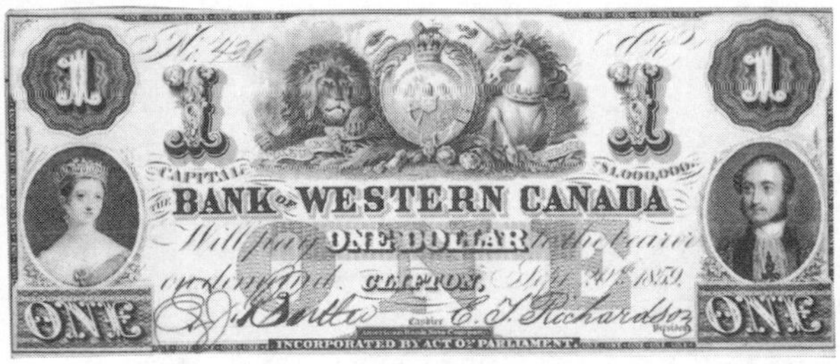

S2038 1 Dollar VG VF UNC

20.9.1859. Black on red underprint. Portrait Queen Victoria at lower left, supported royal arms at top center, portrait of the Prince Consort at lower right. Red word protector. Black hand stamps: X, SW and O. Uniface. Back: Red word protector. Printer: ABNC.

a. Right hand signature G. McMicken. 300. 600. —

b. Right hand signature E. J. Richardson. 50.00 100. 300.

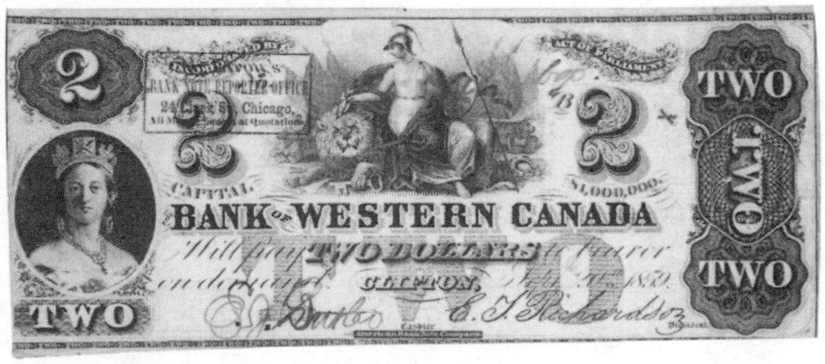

S2039 2 Dollars VG VF UNC

20.9.1859. Black on red underprint. Portrait Queen Victoria at lower left, seated Britannia by lion at top center. Red word protector. Black hand stamps: X, SW and O. Uniface. Back: Red word protector. Printer: ABNC.

a. Right hand signature G. McMicken. 300. 600. —

b. Right hand signature E. J. Richardson. 50.00 100. 300.

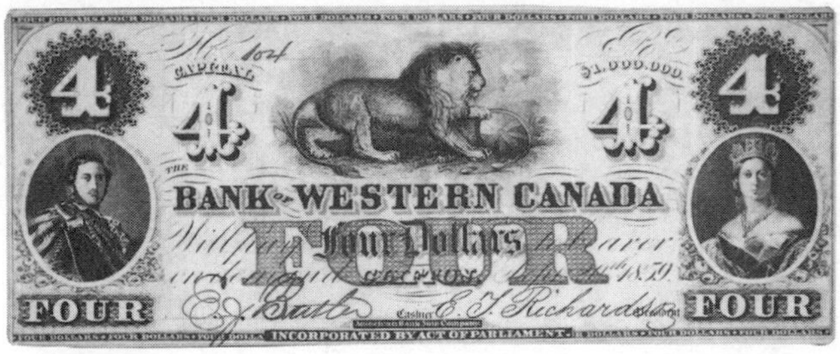

S2040 4 Dollars VG VF UNC

20.9.1859. Black on red underprint. Portrait of the Prince Consort at lower left, lion with shield at top center, portrait Queen Victoria at lower right. Word protector. Black hand stamps: X, SW, and O. Uniface. Back: Word protector. Printer: ABNC.

a. Right signature G. McMicken. 350. 700. —

b. Right signature E. J. Richardson. 50.00 100. 300.

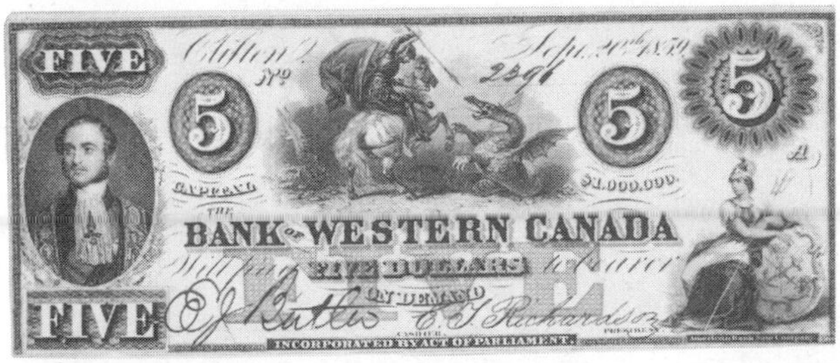

S2041 5 Dollars VG VF UNC

20.9.1859. Black on red underprint. Portrait of the Prince Consort at left, St. George slaying dragon at top center, seated Britannia with crest of Upper Canada at lower right. Red protector. Black hand stamps: X, SW and O. Uniface. Back: Red protector. Printer: ABNC.

a. Right hand signature G. McMicken. 350. 700. —

b. Right hand signature E. J. Richardson. 50.00 100. 300.

Westmorland Bank of New Brunswick

Bend of Petticodiac

1854-59 Issue

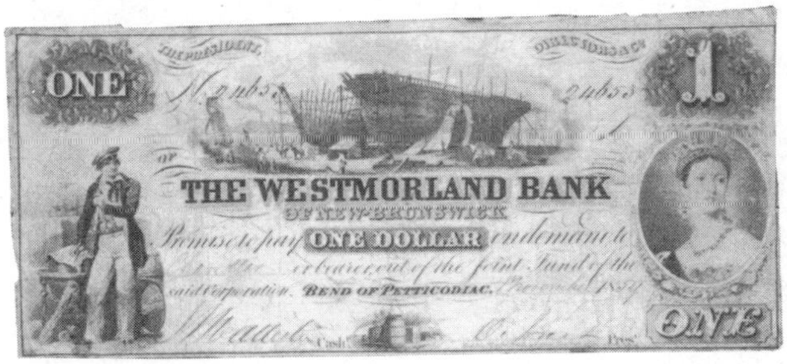

S2042 1 Dollar VG VF UNC

1.5.1854-1.11.1859. Black. Standing sailor at lower left, shipbuilding at top center, portrait Queen Victoria at right, small cask at bottom center. Bend of the Petticodiac. Uniface. Printer: RWH&E.

a. Left hand signature J. Johnson. 1.5.1854. 350. 700. —

b. Left hand signature J. McAllister. 350. 700. —

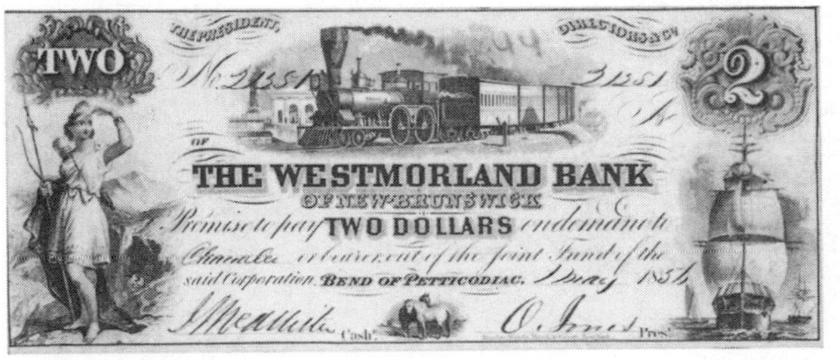

S2043 2 Dollars VG VF UNC

1.5.1854-1.11.1859. Black. Indian maiden with spear at lower left, steam passenger train at top center, three ships under full sail at lower right, two small horses at bottom center. Bend of the Petticodiac. Uniface. Printer: RWH&E.

a. Left hand signature J. Johnson. 1.5.1854. 400. 800. —

b. Left hand signature J. McAllister. 400. 800. —

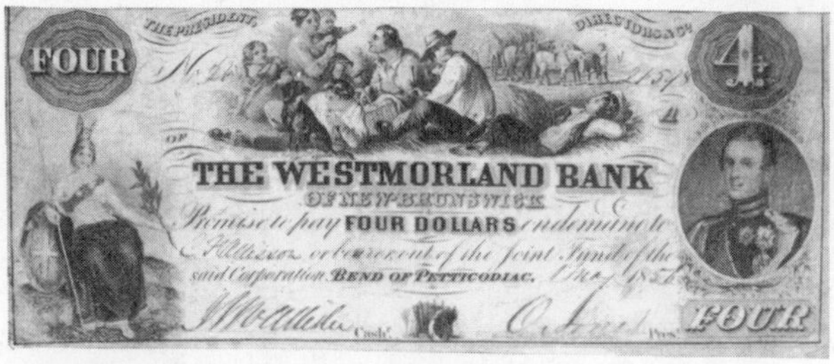

S2044 4 Dollars	VG	VF	UNC
1.5.1854-1.11.1859. Black. Seated Britannia with shield at lower left, farm family with horsedrawn hay wagon in background at top center, portrait of the Prince Consort at right, small shipbuilding at bottom center. Bend of the Printer: RWH&E.			
a. Left hand signature J. Johnson. 1.5.1854.	350.	700.	—
b. Left hand signature J. McAllister.	350.	700.	—

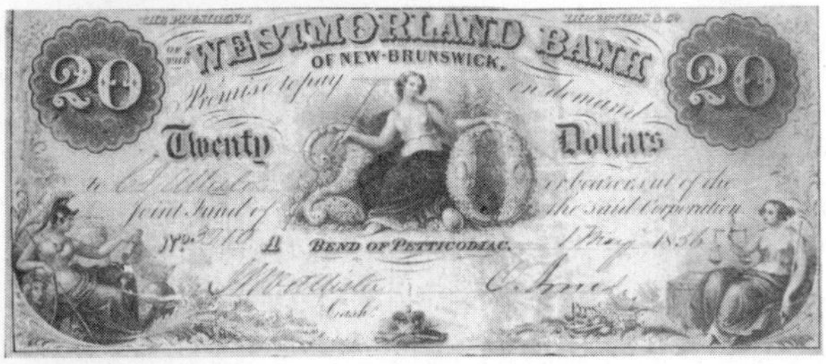

S2045 20 Dollars	VG	VF	UNC
1.5.1854-1.11.1859. Black. Seated Britannia with shield at lower left, woman with rake and ornate *20* at upper center, seated Justice at lower right, small swords, crown on cushion at bottom center. 2 signature varieties. Printer: RWH&E.	3750.	—	—
S2046 40 Dollars			
18xx. Black. Young woman at lower left, seated Justice and Britannia with royal crest at upper center, two women at lower right, small shipbuilding at bottom center. Bend of the Petticodiac. Uniface. Printer: RWH&E. Proof.	—	—	2000.

Moncton

1861 Issue

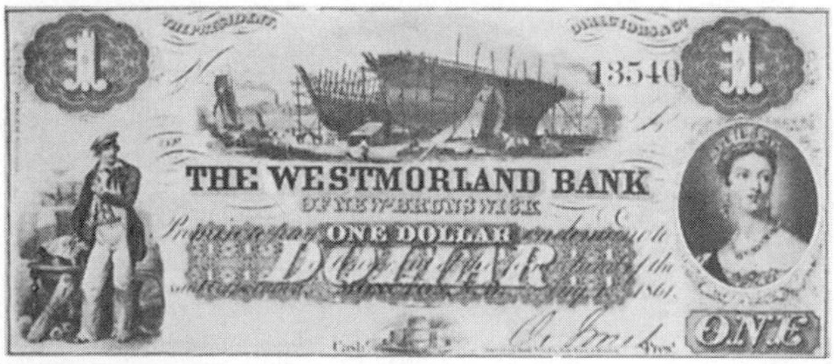

S2047 1 Dollar	VG	VF	UNC
1.8.1861. Black on green underprint. Standing sailor at lower left, shipbuilding at top center, portrait Queen Victoria at right, small cask at bottom center. Back: Blue. Printer: RWH&E and ABNC.			
a. Left hand signature J. McAllister.	50.00	100.	500.
b. Left hand signature W. C. Jones.	50.00	100.	500.
c. Left hand signature J. S. Trites.	50.00	100.	500.
r. Unsigned remainder.	—	—	400.

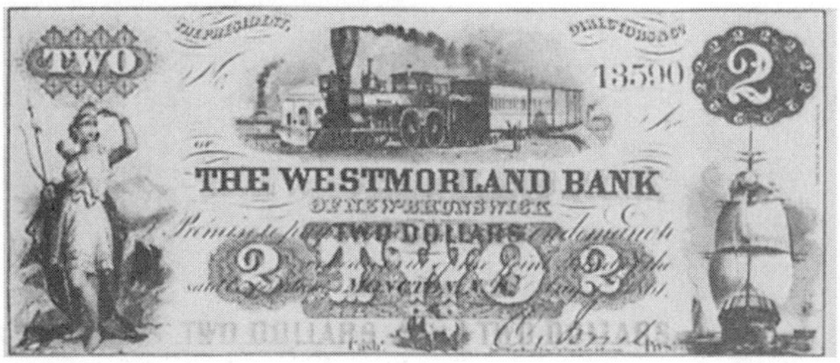

S2048 2 Dollars	VG	VF	UNC
1.8.1861. Black on green underprint. Indian maiden with spear at lower left, steam passenger train at top center, three ships under full sail at lower right, two small horses at bottom center. Back: Blue. Printer: RWH&E and ABNC.			
a. Left hand signature J. McAllister.	50.00	100.	200.
b. Left hand signature W. C. Jones.	50.00	100.	200.
c. Left hand signature J. S. Trites.	50.00	100.	200.
r. Unsigned remainder.	—	—	250.

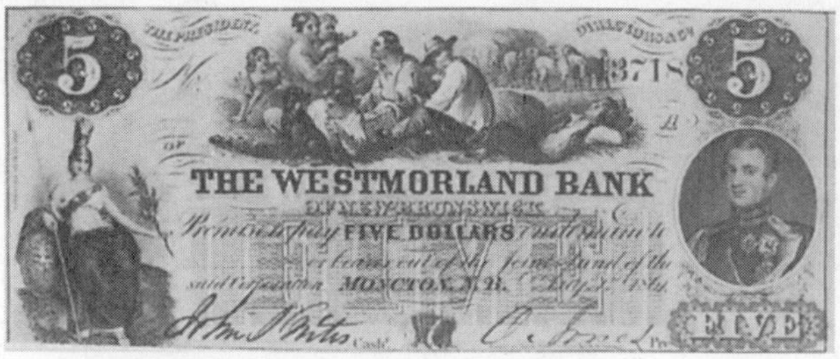

S2049 5 Dollars	VG	VF	UNC
1.8.1861. Black on green underprint. Seated Britannia with shield at lower left, farm family with horsedrawn hay wagon in background at top center, portrait of the Prince Consort at right, small shipbuilding at bottom center. Back: Blue. Printer: RWH&E and ABNC.			
a. Left hand signature J. McAllister.	50.00	100.	250.
b. Left hand signature W. C. Jones.	50.00	100.	250.
c. Left hand signature J. S. Trites.	50.00	100.	250.
r. Unsigned remainder.	—	—	250.
S2050 20 Dollars			
1.8.1861. Black on green underprint. Seated Britannia with shield at lower left, woman with rake and ornate *20* at upper center, seated Justice at lower right, small swords, crown on cushion at bottom center. Back: Blue. Printer: RWH & E and ABNC.	2500.	—	—

Zimmerman Bank

Elgin

1854-55 Issue

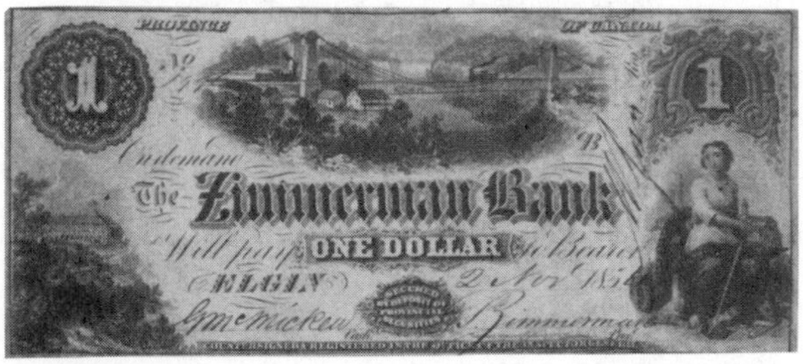

S2051 1 Dollar	VG	VF	UNC
2.11.1854. Black. Clifton House at lower left, Roebling Suspension Bridge at Niagara at top center, seated Industry at lower right. *ELGIN* at lower left. Uniface. Printer: Toppan, Carpenter, Casilear & Co.	400.	750.	—
S2052 3 Dollars			
185x. Black. Roebling Suspension Bridge at Niagara at upper center, Clifton House at lower left, portrait Queen Victoria at lower right. *ELGIN* at lower left. Uniface. Printer: Toppan, Carpenter, Casilear & Co. Proof.	—	—	450.

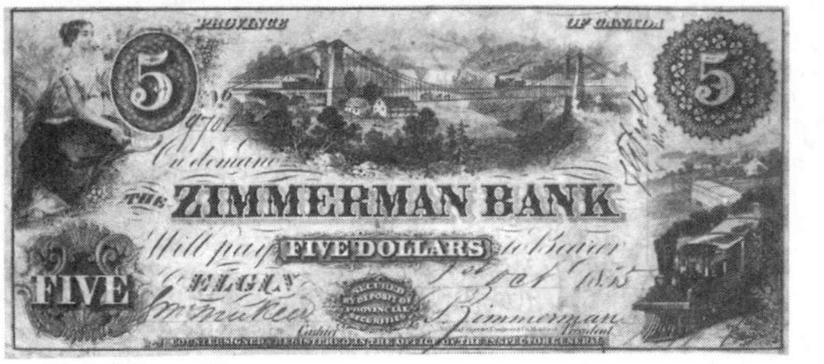

S2053 5 Dollars	VG	VF	UNC
1.10.1855. Black. Seated allegorical woman at upper left, Roebling Suspension Bridge at Niagara at top center right, steam passenger train at lower right. *ELGIN* at lower left. Uniface. Printer: Toppan, Carpenter, Casilear & Co.	400.	650.	—
S2054 10 Dollars			
185x. Black. Roebling Suspension Bridge at Niagara at top left, portrait of the Prince Consort at top center right, woman with sheaf at lower right. *ELGIN* at lower left. Uniface. Printer: Toppan, Carpenter, Casilear & Co.	—	—	400.
S2055 20 Dollars			
185x. Black. Clifton House at lower left, Roebling Suspension Bridge at Niagara at upper center, woman with telescope at lower right. *ELGIN* at lower left. Printer: Toppan, Carpenter, Casilear & Co. Proof.	—	—	400.

1856 Issue

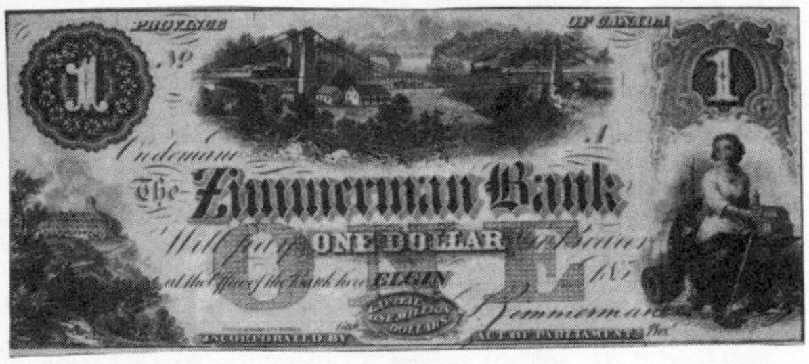

S2056 1 Dollar

7.6.1856; 1.12.1856. Black. Roebling Suspension Bridge at Niagara at upper center, Clifton House at lower left, seated Industry at lower right. *ELGIN* at lower center. Red word protector. Uniface. Back: Red word protector. Printer: Toppan, Carpenter, Casilear & Co.

	VG	VF	UNC
a. Engraved date 185x. Retrograde protector on back.	125.	250.	600.
b. Normal protector on back.	125.	250.	600.
c. Engraved date 1856. Retrograde protector on back.	225.	450.	—
d. Normal protector on back.	225.	450.	—

S2057 3 Dollars

185x. Black. Roebling Suspension Bridge at Niagara at upper center, Clifton House at lower left, portrait Queen Victoria at lower right. *ELGIN* at lower center. Red word protector. Uniface. Back: Red word protector. Printer: Toppan, Carpenter, Casilear & Co. Remaindor.

	VG	VF	UNC
a. Engraved date 185x. Retrograde protector on back.	150.	300.	900.
b. As #S2057a but with normal protector on back.	150.	300.	900.
c. Engraved date 1856. Retrograde protector on back.	300.	600.	—
d. As #S2057c but with normal protector on back.	300.	600.	—

S2058 5 Dollars

7.7.1856. Black. Seated allegorical woman at upper right, Roebling Suspension Bridge at Niagara at upper center, steam passenger train at lower right. *ELGIN* at lower center. Red word protector. Uniface. Back: Red word protector. Printer: Toppan, Carpenter, Casilear & Co.

	VG	VF	UNC
a. Engraved date 185x. Retrograde protector on back.	125.	250.	600.
b. As #S2058a but with normal protector on back.	125.	250.	600.
c. Engraved date 1856. Retrograde protector on back.	225.	500.	—
d. As #S2058c but with normal protector on back.	225.	500.	—

S2058A 10 Dollars

7.6.1856; 1.12.1856. Black. Roebling Suspension Bridge at Niagara at left, portrait of the Prince Consort at center, woman with sheaf at right. *ELGIN* at lower center. Red word protector. Uniface. Back: Red word protector. Printer: Toppan, Carpenter, Casilear & Co.

	VG	VF	UNC
a. Engraved date 185x. Retrograde protector on back. Reported not confirmed.	—	—	—
b. As #S2058a but with normal protector on back. Reported not confirmed.	—	—	—
c. Engraved date 1856. Retrograde protector on back.	500.	900.	—
d. As #S2058c but with normal protector on back. Reported not confirmed.	—	—	—

1850s First Issue

	Good	Fine	XF
S2059 1 Dollar 185x. Black. Roebling Suspension Bridge at Niagara at upper center, Clifton House at lower left, seated Industry at lower right. Blue word protector. Uniface. Printer: Toppan, Carpenter, Casilear & Co. Remainder.	50.00	100.	250.
S2060 3 Dollars 185x. Black. Roebling Suspension Bridge at Niagara at upper center, Clifton House at lower left, portrait Queen Victoria at lower right. Blue word protector. Uniface. Printer: Toppan, Carpenter, Casilear & Co. Remainder.	50.00	100.	250.
S2061 5 Dollars 185x. Black. Seated allegorical woman at upper right, Roebling Suspension Bridge at Niagara at upper center, steam passenger train at lower right. Blue word protector. Uniface. Printer: Toppan, Carpenter, Casilear & Co. Remainder.	50.00	100.	350.

1850s Second Issue

	Good	Fine	XF
S2062 1 Dollar 185x. Black. Roebling Suspension Bridge at Niagara at upper center, Clifton House at lower left, seated Industry at lower right. Red numerical protector underprint. Uniface.	50.00	125.	300.
S2063 3 Dollars 185x. Black. Roebling Suspension Bridge at Niagara at upper center, Clifton House at lower left, portrait Queen Victoria at lower right. Red numerical protector underprint. Uniface. Remainder.	75.00	175.	350.

S2064 5 Dollars

1856. Black. Roebling Suspension Bridge at Niagara at upper center, seated allegorical woman at upper left, steam passenger train at lower right. Red numerical protector underprint. Uniface.

	Good	Fine	XF
a. Engraved date 185x.	50.00	125.	300.
b. Engraved date 1856.	100.	300.	—

	Good	Fine	XF
S2065 10 Dollars 185x. Roebling Suspension Bridge at Niagara at top left, portrait of the Prince Consort at top center right, woman with sheaf at lower right. Red numerical protector underprint. Uniface. Remainder.	100.	300.	—

	Good	Fine	XF
S2066 20 Dollars 185x. Black. Clifton House at lower left, Roebling Suspension Bridge at Niagara at upper center, woman with telescope at lower right. Red numerical protector underprint. Uniface. Remainder.	100.	300.	600.

1850s Third Issue

S2067 1 Dollar

185x. Black. Roebling Suspension Bridge at Niagara at upper center, Clifton House at lower left, seated Industry at lower right. Blue numerical protector. Uniface. Remainder.

	Good	Fine	XF
a. Engraved date 185x.	25.00	50.00	125.
b. Engraved date 1856.	100.	300.	—

	Good	Fine	XF
S2068 3 Dollars 185x. Black. Roebling Suspension Bridge at Niagara at upper center, Clifton House at lower left, portrait Queen Victoria at lower right. Blue numerical protector. Uniface. Remainder.	75.00	150.	300.
S2069 5 Dollars 185x. Black. Roebling Suspension Bridge at Niagara at upper center, seated allegorical woman at upper left, steam passenger train at lower right. Blue numerical protector. Uniface. Remainder.	25.00	75.00	125.

S2070 10 Dollars | Good 25.00 | Fine 75.00 | XF 175.
185x. Black. Roebling Suspension Bridge at Niagara at top left, portrait of the Prince Consort at top center right, woman with sheaf at lower right. Blue numerical protector. Uniface. Remainder.

S2071 20 Dollars | Good 25.00 | Fine 75.00 | XF 175.
185x. Black. Clifton House at lower left, Roebling Suspension Bridge at Niagara at upper center, woman with telescope at lower right. Blue numerical protector. Uniface. Remainder.

CLIFTON

1850S ISSUE

S2072 1 Dollar | VG 50.00 | VF 100. | UNC 300.
185x. Black. Roebling Suspension Bridge at Niagara at upper center, Clifton House at lower left, seated Industry at lower right. Red word protector. *CLIFTON* at lower center. Remainder.

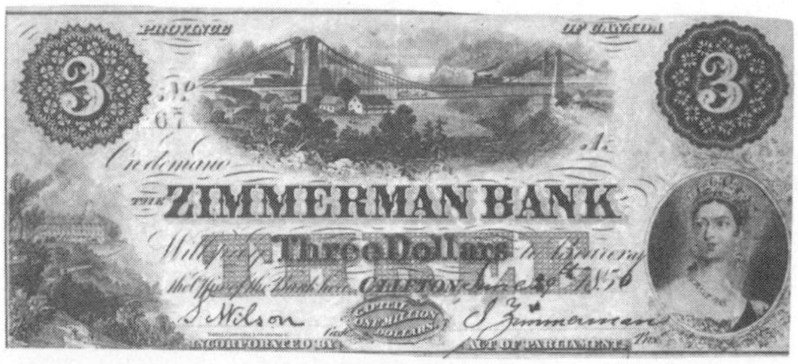

S2073 3 Dollars | VG 50.00 | VF 100. | UNC 300.
185x. Black. Roebling Suspension Bridge at Niagara at upper center, Clifton House at lower left, portrait Queen Victoria at lower right. Red word protector. *CLIFTON* at lower center. Remainder.

S2074 5 Dollars | VG 50.00 | VF 100. | UNC 300.
185x. Black. Roebling Suspension Bridge at Niagara at upper center, seated allegorical woman at upper left, steam passenger train at lower right. Red word protector. *CLIFTON* at lower center. Remainder

S2075 10 Dollars | VG 150. | VF 300. | UNC —
Black. Roebling Suspension Bridge at Niagara at top left, portrait of the Prince Consort at top center right, woman with sheaf at lower right. Red word protector. *CLIFTON* at lower center. Remainder.

S2076 20 Dollars | VG 150. | VF 300. | UNC —
185x. Black. Clifton House at lower left, Roebling Suspension Bridge at Niagara at upper center, woman with telescope at lower right. Red word protector. *CLIFTON* at lower center. Remainder.

The Republic of Chile, a ribbonlike country on the Pacific coast of southern South America, has an area of 756,950 sq. km. and a population of 16.45 million. Capital: Santiago. Copper, of which Chile has about 25 percent of the world's reserves, has accounted for a major portion of Chile's export earnings in recent years. Other important exports are iron ore, iodine, fruit and nitrate of soda.

Prior to the coming of the Spanish in the 16th century, northern Chile was under Inca rule while Araucanian Indians (also known as Mapuches) inhabited central and southern Chile. Although Chile declared its independence in 1810, decisive victory over the Spanish was not achieved until 1818. In the War of the Pacific (1879-83), Chile defeated Peru and Bolivia and won its present northern regions. It was not until the 1880s that the Araucanian Indians were completely subjugated. A three-year-old Marxist government of Salvador Allende was overthrown in 1973 by a military coup led by Augusto Pinochet, who ruled until a freely elected president was installed in 1990. Sound economic policies, maintained consistently since the 1980s, have contributed to steady growth, reduced poverty rates by over half, and have helped secure the country's commitment to democratic and representative government. Chile has increasingly assumed regional and international leadership roles befitting its status as a stable, democratic nation.

MONETARY SYSTEM:

1 Peso = 100 Centavos
1 Condor = 100 Centavos = 10 Pesos to 1960
1 Escudo = 100 Centesimos, 1960-75
1 Peso = 100 "old" Escudos, 1975-

PROVINCIAL

Province of Valdivia . . . . #S101-S102

COMMERCIAL BANKS

Banco Agricola . . . . #S106-S112
Banco de Ahorros y Préstamos . . . . #S115-S116
Banco de la Alianza . . . . #S118-S128
Banco de Arauco . . . . #S130
Banco de José Bunster. . . . . #S131-S134
Banco de Caupolican . . . . #S136-S139
Banco de Chile . . . . #S145-S147
Banco Comercial de Chile . . . . #S151-S163
Banco de Concepción. . . . . #S166-S182
Banco Consolidado de Chile. . . . . #S186-S191
Banco Constructor Hipotecario. . . . . #S198
Banco Crédito Unido. . . . . #S208-S211
Banco de Curicó . . . . #S218-S220
Banco de A. Edwards y Ca. . . . . #S231-S248
Banco de Escobar, Ossa y Ca.. . . . . #S253-S257
Banco de Llanquihue . . . . #S263
Banco de D. Matte y Ca.. . . . . #S278-S281
Banco de Matte, Mac-Clure i Ca. . . . . #S283
Banco de Melipilla. . . . . #S296-S299
Banco Mobiliario . . . . #S306-S312
Banco de Montenegro I Ca. . . . . #S313-S314
Banco Nacional de Chile. . . . . #S316-S338
Banco del Ñuble . . . . #S344-S346
Banco de Ossa y Ca. . . . . #S351-S358
Banco del Pobre . . . . #S361-S364
Banco Popular Hipotecario . . . . #S379
Banco de Rere . . . . #S388-S389
Banco San Fernando . . . . #S397-S400
Banco de Santiago . . . . #S411-S417
Banco de la Serena . . . . #S418
Banco Sud-Americano . . . . #S421
Banco del Sur . . . . #426-S432
Banco de Talca . . . . #S439-S443
Banco Banco de Tarapacá y Londres. . . . . #S447-S455
Banco de la Union. . . . . #S460-S467
Banco de Valparaiso. . . . . #S477-S512

Note: Certain listings encompassing issues circulated by provincial, state and commercial banking authorities are contained in Volume 1.

Validation Handstamps: The Regional and Republic issues are found w/ or w/o various combinations of round validation handstamps. Type I: *DIRECCION DEL TESORO-SANTIAGO* around National Arms (lg. and sm. size). Type II: *DIRECCION DE CONTABILIDAD-SANTIAGO* around plumed shield on open book. Type III: *SUPERINTENDENCIA DE LA CASA DE MONEDA* around screwpress/SANTIAGO. Type IV: *CONTADURIA MAYOR* around plumed shield on open book.

Province of Valdivia

Tesoreria y Aduana Unidas Valdivia

United Treasury and Customs

1840-44 Issue

S101 4 Reales
1840-44. Black. Value printed at center and handwritten at lower right. 2 signatures. Two oval monogram seals and two official seals inscribed for the issuing authority. Treasury seal at top center. Back: Treasury seal at top center.

Good	Fine	XF
400.	1000.	—

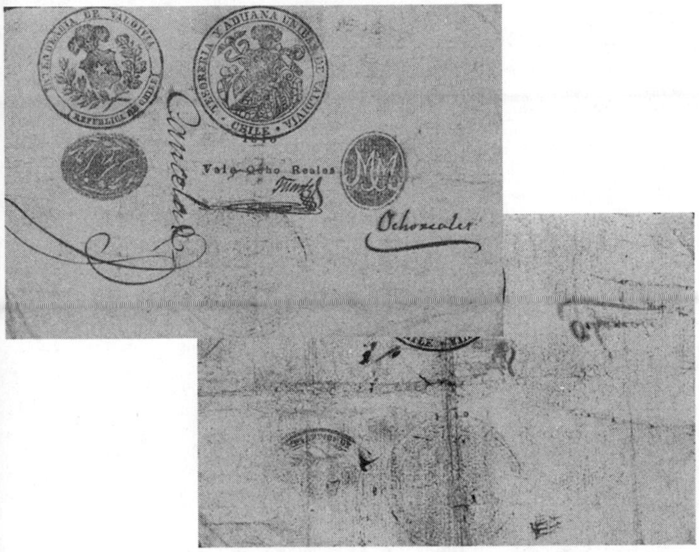

S102 8 Reales
1840-44. Black. Value printed at center and handwritten at lower right. 2 signatures. Two oval monogram seals and two official seals inscribed for the issuing authority. Treasury seal at top center. Back: Treasury seal at top center.

Good	Fine	XF
400.	1000.	—

Commercial Banks

Banco Agricola

1869-93 Issue

S106 1 Peso
7.3.1887. Black on orange and red underprint. Girl at left, allegory of Agriculture at center, woman with produce at right. Back: Brown. Printer: CABB (ABNC). Rare.

Good	Fine	XF
—	—	—

S108 5 Pesos
(ca.1870). Back: Brown or gray. Printer: CABB (ABNC). Proof.

Good	Fine	XF
—	—	—

S109 10 Pesos
18xx. Black on blue underprint. Farmer carrying hay for horse at left, cattle at center. Back: Green or orange. Printer: CABB (ABNC). Proof.

Good	Fine	XF
—	—	—

S110 20 Pesos
1869. Black on brown underprint. Two allegorical children at bottom left, allegorical woman with harvest at center, child with rabbits at lower right. Back: Red-orange. Printer: CABB (ABNC). Proof.

Good	Fine	XF
—	—	—

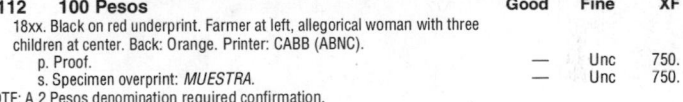

S111 50 Pesos
20.4.1893. Black on blue underprint. Cherubs at left and right, farmers loading ox-cart at upper center. Back: Green. Printer: CABB (ABNC). Rare.

Good	Fine	XF
—	—	—

S112 100 Pesos
18xx. Black on red underprint. Farmer at left, allegorical woman with three children at center. Back: Orange. Printer: CABB (ABNC).

	Good	Fine	XF
p. Proof.	—	Unc	750.
s. Specimen overprint: *MUESTRA*.	—	Unc	750.

NOTE: A 2 Pesos denomination required confirmation.

Banco de Ahorros y Préstamos

1893 Issue

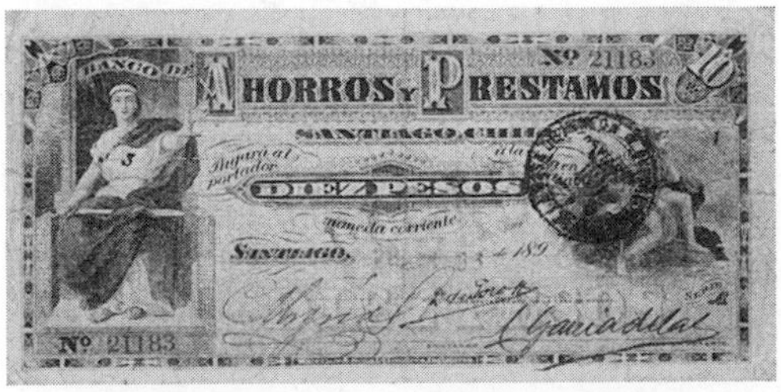

S115 10 Pesos
1893. Black on yellow underprint. Seated woman with sword at left, seated Mercury at right. Back: Green. Helmeted head at center. Printer: W&S.

Good	Fine	XF
150.	500.	—

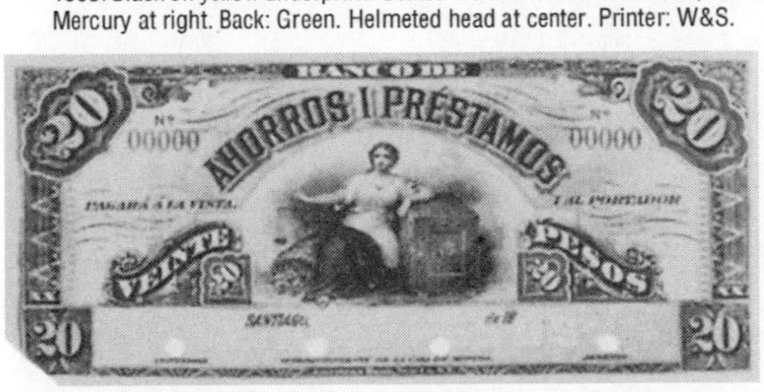

S116 20 Pesos
18xx. Black on orange and blue underprint. Woman seated with scale, coins and safe at center. Back: Orange. Young girl's head at center. Printer: ABNC.

Good	Fine	XF
—	—	—

NOTE: Additional denominations require confirmation.

Banco de la Alianza

1870's Provisional Issue

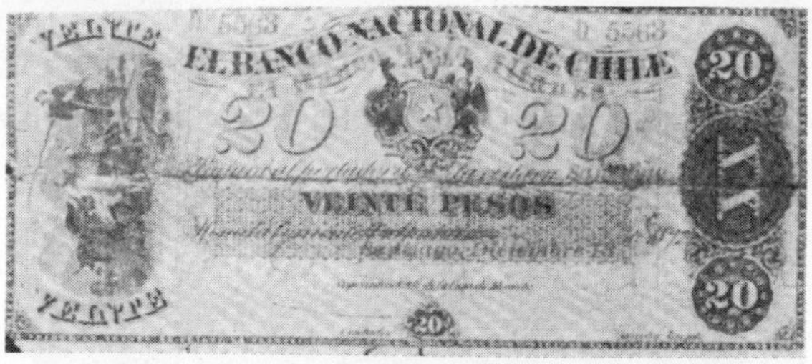

	Good	Fine	XF
S118 20 Pesos ND (- old date 1872). Black on orange underprint. Man plowing with oxen at left (sideways), arms at center. Back: Green. Overprint: On #S320. Rare.	—	—	—

1874-77 Regular Issue

	Good	Fine	XF
S121 1 Peso 1877. Black on tan underprint. Arms at lower left, palace at center, female head ("Star of Empire") at lower right. Back: Green. Printer: ABNC.	150.	600.	—

	Good	Fine	XF
S122 5 Pesos 1876-77. Black on orange underprint. Condor at left, arms at center, girl at right. Back: Green. Printer: ABNC.	—	—	—

	Good	Fine	XF
S123 10 Pesos 1874 (hand dated). Black on green underprint. Girl at lower left, condor at upper center, arms at lower right. Back: Green. Printer: ABNC.	—	—	—

1878; 1879 Issue

	Good	Fine	XF
S126 1 Peso 3.1.1879. Black on green and peach underprint. Bull's head at left, female head ("America") at center, arms at right. Back: Brown. Woman at center. Printer: ABNC.			
a. Issued note.	150.	600.	—
s. Specimen.	—	Unc	1000.

	Good	Fine	XF
S127 5 Pesos 18xx (ca.1878). Black on green and orange underprint. Child at lower left, arms at center, horse at lower right. Back: Brown. Girl at center. Printer: ABNC.			
p. Proof.	—	—	—
s. Specimen.	—	—	—
S128 10 Pesos 2.1.1878. Black on green and red-brown underprint. Valdivia at lower left, condor at center, arms at lower right. Back: Brown. Valdivia overprint showing guarantee and inconvertibility according at law, and signature of Mint Su Printer: ABNC.	350.	—	—

Banco de Arauco

1870's Issue

	Good	Fine	XF
S130 20 Pesos 18xx. Black on green and yellow underprint. Portrait woman with book ("Literature No. 2") at left center, portrait man at right. Back: Dark brown. Printer: ABNC.			
p. Proof.	—	Unc	1000.
s. Specimen.	—	Unc	1250.

Banco de José Bunster

1882 Issue

	Good	Fine	XF
S131 1 Peso 18xx (ca. 1882-98). Black on yellow underprint. Woman leaning on wheel ("Fortune") at left, "Raphael's Angel" at upper center, portrait man at right. Back: Brown. Printer: ABNC. Proof.	—	Unc	2500.

NOTE: #S131 is known as an issued note only with overprint: *EMISION FISCAL* and is listed in Vol. 2, #27A.

S132 5 Pesos — Good: — | Fine: Unc | XF: 2000.
18xx. Black on green underprint. Portrait man at left, galloping horse at center, seated allegorical woman ("Plenty") at right. Back: Green. Printer: ABNC. Proof.

S133 10 Pesos — Good: — | Fine: Unc | XF: 2750.
18xx. Black on salmon underprint. Child with sheep at right, man at center, two allegorical women at right. Back: Orange. Printer: ABNC. Proof.

	Good	Fine	XF
S134 20 Pesos 18xx (ca.1882-98). Black on orange and yellow underprint. Bridges at left center, portrait woman at right. Back: Brown. Three children looking at book at center. Printer: ABNC. Proof.	—	Unc	2750.

Banco de Caupolican

1884 Issue

	Good	Fine	XF
S136 1 Peso 2.7.1884. Black on green underprint. Woman at left, reclining woman with globe ("Science") at right. Back: Brown. Printer: ABNC.			
a. Issued note.	250.	650.	—
p. Proof. 18xx.	—	—	—

	Good	Fine	XF
S137 5 Pesos ND. Black on orange underprint. Farm animals at left, North American Indian head at center. Back: Blue. Printer: ABNC. Specimen.	—	—	—

	Good	Fine	XF
S139 20 Pesos 18xx. Black on orange underprint. Reclining allegorical woman ("L'Orient") at center. Back: Green. Plants at right. Printer: ABNC.			
r. Unsigned remainder.	25.00	40.00	100.
s. Specimen.	—	—	—

Banco de Chile

1894-96 Issue

	Good	Fine	XF
S145 20 Pesos ND (ca.1894). Black on green and yellow underprint. Bridges at left and right, arms at center. Back: Brown. Valdivia at center. Printer: ABNC. Issued at Valparaiso.			
a. Issued note. Rare.	—	—	—
s. Specimen.	—	—	—

	Good	Fine	XF
S146 50 Pesos ND (ca.1896). Black on green and yellow underprint. Allegorical woman at left and right of arms at center. Printer: ABNC. Issued at Valparaiso.			
p. Proof.	—	—	—
s. Specimen.	—	—	—
S147 100 Pesos ND (ca.1896). Black on pink, yellow and orange underprint. Allegorical woman at left and right of arms at center. Printer: ABNC. Proof. Issued at Valparaiso.	—	—	—

Banco Comercial de Chile

1890's Issue

	Good	Fine	XF
S151 1 Peso (ca.1890). Black on yellow and pink underprint. Woman with basket on head at left, arms at right. Back: Green. Condor at center. Overprint: *EMISION FISCAL*. Printer: W&S.	—	—	—
S152 2 Pesos (ca.1890). Black on green and pink underprint. Arms at left, seated woman with bales at center. Back: Red-brown. Woman at center. Overprint: *EMISION FISCAL*. Printer: W&S.	—	—	—

#S151 and S152 are known issued only with overprint: *EMISION FISCAL* and are listed in Vol.2, #30 and 31.

	Good	Fine	XF
S153 5 Pesos 18xx. Young girl at left, arms at center right. Salesman's sample book. Printer: W&S. Specimen.	—	Unc	300.
S154 10 Pesos 1890. Black on green and orange underprint. Arms at upper left, woman reclining with shield and caduceus at center right. Back: Red-brown. Printer: W&S.	—	—	—

	Good	Fine	XF
S156 50 Pesos 18xx. Three allegorical women at center. Printer: W&S. Proof.	—	—	—

1893 Issue

	Good	Fine	XF
S160 10 Pesos 8.6.1893. Black on green and rose underprint. Liberty at left, railroad bridge at center, arms at right. Series B. Back: Ox-cart. Printer: BWC.	—	—	—

NOTE: #S160 with overprint: *EMISION FISCAL* is listed in Vol. 2, #32.

	Good	Fine	XF
S161 20 Pesos 8.6.1893. Liberty and arms. Railroad bridge at center. Printer: BWC. Specimen.	—	—	—
S162 50 Pesos 8.6.1893. Liberty and arms. Railroad bridge at center. Printer: BWC. Specimen.	—	—	—

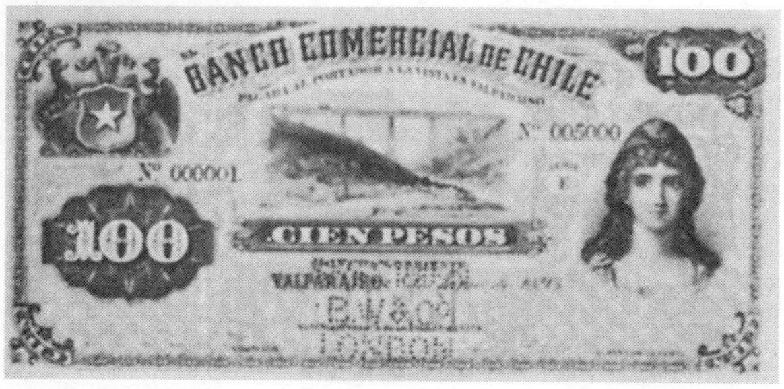

	Good	Fine	XF
S163 100 Pesos 8.6.1893. Liberty and arms. Railraod bridge at center. Series E. Printer: BWC. Specimen perforated *CANCELLED B.W. & Co.*	—	—	—

Banco de Concepción

1870's Issue

	Good	Fine	XF
S166 1 Peso 18xx (ca.1872). Black on green underprint. Woman with water jug at left, Gen. Freire at center, farmers harvesting grapes at right. Printer: CABB (ABNC).			
a. Back green.	—	—	—
b. Back orange.	—	—	—

	Good	Fine	XF
S168 5 Pesos 18xx (ca.1872). Black on orange underprint. Ox team pulling hay wagon with farmers at left, young girl at upper center, Gen. Freire at right. Back: Brown. Printer: CABB (ABNC). Proof.	—	—	—

	Good	Fine	XF
S169 10 Pesos 18xx (ca.1872). Black on brown underprint. Portrait Gen. Freire at upper left, ox team and wagon at center, woman's head ("The Bride") at lower right. Printer: CABB (ABNC). Proof.	—	—	—

	Good	Fine	XF
S170 20 Pesos 18xx (ca.1872). Black on brown or blue underprint. Two girls at lower left, Gen. Freire at upper center, anchor at lower right. Back: Brown. Printer: CABB (ABNC). Face proof.	—	—	—
S172 100 Pesos 18xx (ca.1872). Black on violet underprint. Gen. Freire at left, waterfalls and volcano scene at center, beehive at lower right. Back: Light orange. Printer: CABB (ABNC). Archive copy.	—	—	—

1880's Issue

	Good	Fine	XF
S176 1 Peso 2.1.1885. Black on green and multicolor underprint. Reclining allegorical woman with globe ("Science") at left, portrait Pinto at right. Back: Red-brown. Standing Indian at center. Printer: ABNC.			
a. Issued note.	200.	400.	—
r. Unsigned remainder.	—	Unc	75.00
s. Specimen.	—	Unc	300.

NOTE: #S176 with overprint: *EMISION FISCAL* is listed in Vol. 2, #34.

	Good	Fine	XF
S178 5 Pesos Jan. 18xx. Black on blue and orange underprint. Cherubs at left and right of monument at center. Back: Green. Horses at center. Printer: ABNC. Specimen.	—	—	—
S179 10 Pesos Jan. 18xx. Black on blue and orange underprint. Train station at center. Back: Blue. Allegorical woman (Concepción) at center. Printer: ABNC. Specimen.	—	—	—

S180 20 Pesos

2.7.1xxx (ca.1883). Black on orange and yellow underprint. Monument at left, women at left and right. of value at center. Back: Red-orange. Woman ("Zella") at center. Printer: ABNC.

	Good	Fine	XF
r. Unsigned remainder.	—	Unc	125.
s. Specimen.	—	Unc	300.

S182 100 Pesos

18xx (ca.1884). Black on orange and multicolor underprint. Rail yard and town in background at right. Back: Deep red. Two allegorical women. Printer: ABNC.

	Good	Fine	XF
p. Proof.	—	—	—
s. Specimen.	—	—	—

Banco Consolidado de Chile

1877 Issue

S186 1 Peso

	Good	Fine	XF
3.1.1877. Black on blue and orange underprint. Liberty at left, "Raphael's Angel" at center, two children holding scroll at right. Back: Blue. Commerce at center. Printer: ABNC.	—	—	—

S187 2 Pesos

3.1.1877. Black on green and brown underprint. Helmeted female head ("Minerva No. 2") at left, Mercury at right, two cherubs with scroll at bottom center. Back: Blue. Workers at center. Printer: ABNC.

	Good	Fine	XF
a. Issued note.	—	—	—
s. Specimen.	—	Unc	350.

S188 5 Pesos

3.1.1877. Black on blue and yellow underprint. Allegorical woman with cherub at left, winged cherubs with flowers and horn at center, cherubs with scroll at right. Back: Blue. Farmers and horses at center. Printer: ABNC.

	Good	Fine	XF
a. Issued note.	—	—	—
s. Specimen.	—	Unc	350.

S189 10 Pesos

3.1.1877. Black on orange and green underprint. Condor at lower left, seated allegorical woman with two cherubs ("Plenty No. 2") at center, two cherubs with scroll at lower right. Back: Blue. Train at center. Printer: ABNC.

	Good	Fine	XF
p. Proof.	—	—	—
s. Specimen.	—	Unc	400.

S190 50 Pesos

ND (1877). Black on green and orange underprint. Allegorical woman at left, woman with bales at center, cherubs with scroll at right. Back: Blue. Farmers plowing with oxen at center. Printer: ABNC.

	Good	Fine	XF
p. Proof.	—	—	—
s. Specimen.	—	Unc	400.

S191 100 Pesos

ND (1877). Black on blue and orange underprint. Woman seated at left, cherub ("Bachus") at center, cherubs with scroll at right. Back: Blue. Sheep and steer at center. Printer: ABNC.

	Good	Fine	XF
p. Proof.	—	—	—
s. Specimen.	—	Unc	500.

Banco Constructor Hipotecario

1894 Issue

S198 10 Pesos

	Good	Fine	XF
14.11.1894. Black on yellow and pink underprint. Liberty head at lower left, building at center, arms at lower right. Back: Green. Standing woman at center. Printer: W & S. Salesman's sample book specimen.	—	Unc	125.

NOTE: For #S198 with circular overprint: *BANCO POPULAR HIPOTECARIO* on back, see #S379.

Banco Crédito Unido

1889-94 Issue

S208 10 Pesos

28.4.1889; 17.6.1889; 12.6.1894. Black on green and yellow underprint. Portrait uniformed man at left, galloping horse at center, monument at right. Back: Green. Printer: ABNC.

	Good	Fine	XF
a. Issued note.	200.	400.	—
p. Proof.	—	—	—

S211 100 Pesos	Good	Fine	XF
ND. Black on orange and yellow underprint. Man at left, portrait girl at center, equestrian statue at right. Back: Orange. Proof.	—	—	—

NOTE: Other denominations require confirmation.

Banco de Curicó

1882 Issue

S218 5 Pesos	Good	Fine	XF
18xx (ca.1882). Black on green and peach underprint. Portrait Comandante E. Ramirez in uniform at center. Back: Brown. Christopher Columbus sighting land at center. Printer: ABNC. Specimen.	—	Unc	350.

NOTE: #S218 is known issued only withoverprint: *EMISION FISCAL* and is listed in Vol. 2, #35.

S219 10 Pesos	Good	Fine	XF
18xx (ca.1882). Black on pink underprint. Portrait Capt. A. Prat at left, two ships in battle at right. Back: Brown. Printer: ABNC. Proof.	—	—	—

S220 20 Pesos	Good	Fine	XF
18xx (ca.1882). Black on blue and yellow underprint. Woman with sheaf ("The Reaper") at left, portrait Capt. A. Prat at left. center, bank above arms at lower right. Back: Brown. Two ships engaged in warfare. Printer: ABNC.			
r. Unsigned remainder.	—	Unc	40.00
s. Specimen.	—	—	—

Banco de A. Edwards y Ca.

1871; 1872 Issues

S231 1 Peso	Good	Fine	XF
1.7.1871. Black. Railroad through mountains at center. Back: Bank names and *UN PESO* four times in blue. Printer: William Brown & Co., London. Rare.	—	—	—

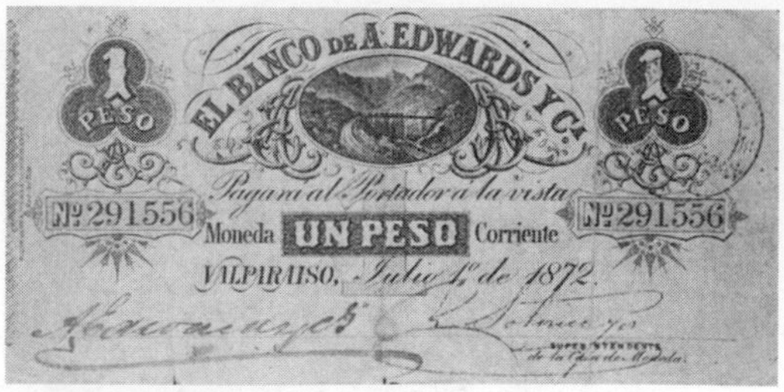

S232 1 Peso	Good	Fine	XF
1.7.1872. Black. Railroad through mountains at center. Back: *1-UN PESO-1*. Printer: William Brown & Co., London. Rare.	—	—	—

1876-79 Issues

S236 1 Peso	Good	Fine	XF
3.1.1878. Black on blue underprint. Portrait girl at upper left, arms at lower right. Back: Blue. Two portraits at center. Printer: BWC.	75.00	150.	500.

S237 1 Peso	Good	Fine	XF
1.7.1879. Black on green underprint. Portrait girl at upper left, arms at lower right. Back: Blue. Two portraits at center. Printer: BWC.	50.00	125.	400.

S238 2 Pesos	Good	Fine	XF
1.1.1878. Black on pink underprint. Portrait woman at left. Back: Pink. Printer: BWC.	125.	500.	—

S239 5 Pesos	Good	Fine	XF
1876; 1877. Black on orange and blue underprint. Portrait woman at left, cherub with sextant in sailboat at right. Back: Green, red and brown. Printer: BWC.			
a. Issued note. 3.1.1876; 3.1.1877.	150.	500.	—
r. Unsigned remainder. 3.1.1877.	—	Unc	125.

S240 10 Pesos	Good	Fine	XF
3.1.1876; 3.1.1877. Black on green and orange underprint. Portrait woman at left, cherub with plow at right. Back: Green. Printer: BWC.	150.	500.	—

S243 100 Pesos			
3.1.1876. Woman at left, cherubs at right. Printer: BWC. Specimen.	—	—	—

1890's Issue

		Good	Fine	XF
S246	**1 Pound Sterling** 189x. Portrait man at left, arms at lower right. Printer: BWC. Not issued.	—	—	—
S247	**5 Pounds Sterling** 189x. Printer: BWC. Not issued. Reported not confirmed.	—	—	—

		Good	Fine	XF
S248	**10 Pounds Sterling** 189x. Portrait man at left, arms at lower right. Printer: BWC. Not issued.	—	—	—

Banco de Escobar, Ossa y Ca.

1887 Issue

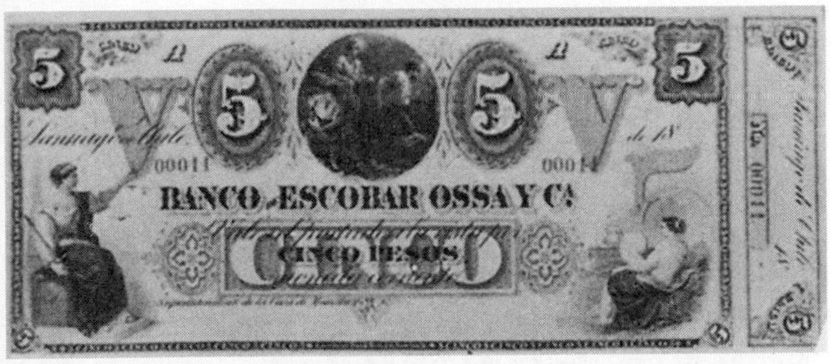

		Good	Fine	XF
S253	**5 Pesos** 1.1.1887. Black on blue underprint. Seated woman with sword at left, miners at center, woman and shoreline ("Sea Side) at right. Back: Blue. Printer: ABNC. Unsigned remainder.	—	—	—

		Good	Fine	XF
S254	**10 Pesos** 18xx. Black on brown underprint. Boy ("Oscar") at left, girl miners at center. Back: Brown. Printer: ABNC.			
	p. Proof.	—	Unc	500.
	r. Unsigned remainder.	—	—	—
S255	**20 Pesos** 18xx. Black on rose-pink underprint. Standing woman at left, miners at upper center, girl at right. Back: Rose. Printer: ABNC.	—	—	—

NOTE: #S254 and S255 were illegally overprint: *EMISION FISCAL* and are listed in Vol. 2, #38 and 39. Both are known issued with these spuriously applied overprint.

		Good	Fine	XF
S256	**50 Pesos** 18xx (ca.1872). Black on green underprint. Girls at lower left and right, miners digging at top center. Back: Green. Printer: ABNC.	—	—	—

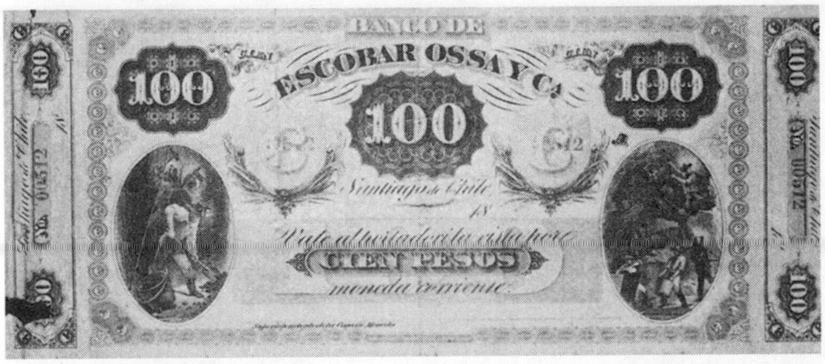

		Good	Fine	XF
S257	**100 Pesos** 18xx (ca.1872). Black on red-brown underprint. Miners at lower left and right. Back: Red-brown. Printer: ABNC.			
	r. Unsigned remainder.	—	—	—
	s. Specimen.	—	—	—

Banco de Llanquihue

1870's Issue

		Good	Fine	XF
S263	**10 Pesos** 18xx. Standing allegorical woman with sickle at center. Printer: W & S. Salesman's sample book specimen. Rare.	—	—	—

NOTE: Other denominations are reported, not confirmed.

Banco de D. Matte y Ca.

Provisional Issue

		Good	Fine	XF
S271	**1 Peso** Reported not confirmed.	—	—	—

1888; 1889 Regular Issue

		Good	Fine	XF
S278	**10 Pesos** 18xx (ca.1888). Black on yellow and green underprint. Farmer harvesting corn at left, girl and dog at right. ("The Pets"). Back: Pinkish red. Printer: ABNC.			
	a. Issued note. Rare.	—	—	—
	p. Proof.	—	Unc	2000.

NOTE: #S278 with overprint: *EMISION FISCAL* is listed in Vol. 2, #32.

S279 20 Pesos

18xx (ca.1888). Black on yellow and orange underprint. Female ("Strength") at left, allegorical woman and produce at top center, woman and grapes at right. Back: Red-brown. Printer: ABNC.

	Good	Fine	XF
p. Proof.	—	Unc	1250.
r. Remainder.	—	—	—
s. Specimen.	—	Unc	1500.

S280 50 Pesos

18xx (ca.1888). Black on blue and yellow underprint. Boy and wheat at left, Liberty and Justice at left and right of man with boy and pack horse at center, girl with flowers at right. Back: Green. Printer: ABNC.

	Good	Fine	XF
a. Issued note. Rare.	—	—	—
p. Proof.	—	Unc	1500.

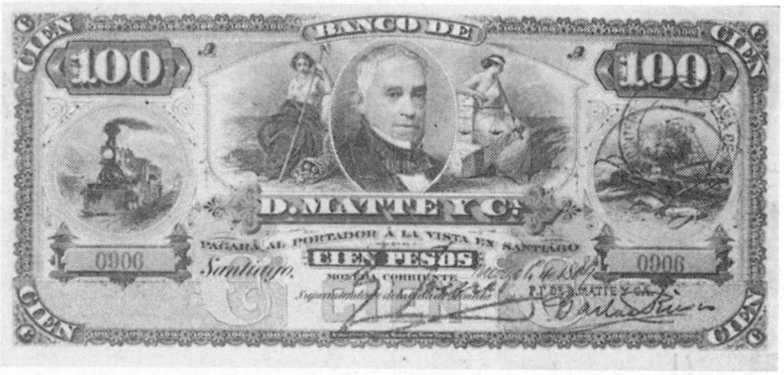

S281 100 Pesos

1.3.1889. Black on green and yellow underprint. Train at left, Liberty and Justice to left and right of portrait Montt at top center, farm tools and grain at right. Back: Olive. Printer: ABNC.

	Good	Fine	XF
a. Issued note. Rare.	—	—	—
p. Proof.	—	Unc	1750.

Banco de Matte, Mac-Clure i Ca.

1875 Issue

S283 1 Peso

	Good	Fine	XF
(ca.1875). Blue. Gathering hay at left, man at center, ships at right. Paper: Violet. Printer: William Brown & Co.	—	—	—

NOTE: #S283 is known issued only with overprint: *EMISION FISCAL* and is listed in Vol. 2, #41.

Banco de Melipilla

1879-87 Issue

S296 1 Peso

18xx (ca.1879). Black on tan underprint. Girl with sheep at left, roundup of horses at center, girl with quill pen ("Trade") at right. Back: Blue-green. Woman and child at center. Printer: ABNC.

	Good	Fine	XF
p. Proof.	—	—	—
r. Remainder.	—	Unc	125.

S297 5 Pesos

	Good	Fine	XF
(ca.1887). Black on tan underprint. Seated girl ("Lucy's Pets") at left, gathering hay at center ducks at right. Back: Blue-green. Seated woman. Printer: ABNC. Proof.	—	—	—

NOTE: #S297 w/overprint: *EMISION FISCAL* is listed in Vol. 2, #42.

S298 10 Pesos

	Good	Fine	XF
20.12.1887. Beehives at left, reclining woman with jug ("Naiad") at center, farm animals at right. Back: Blue. Farm implements at center. Printer: ABNC. Rare.	—	—	—

S299 20 Pesos

18xx (ca.1887). Black on red underprint. Griffins at lower left and right, Justice with money chest and cornucopia at center. Series C. Back: Red-orange. Allegorical woman with sheep at center. Printer: ABNC.

	Good	Fine	XF
a. Issued note. Rare.	—	—	—
r. Unsigned remainder.	—	—	—

Banco Mobiliario

1870-95 Issue

S306 1 Peso

2.1.187x. Black on green and gold underprint. Two women at lower left, boy at center, woman at lower right. Back: Brown. Printer: ABNC.

	Good	Fine	XF
a. Issued note.	150.	500.	—
s. Specimen.	—	—	—

NOTE: #S306 and S308 with overprint: *EMISION FISCAL* are listed in Vol. 2, #34 and 34A.

S307 5 Pesos

	Good	Fine	XF
2.1.18xx. Black. Woman reclining on sheaf at B., young girl at right. Back: Green. Printer: ABNC. Archive copy.	—	Unc	3500.

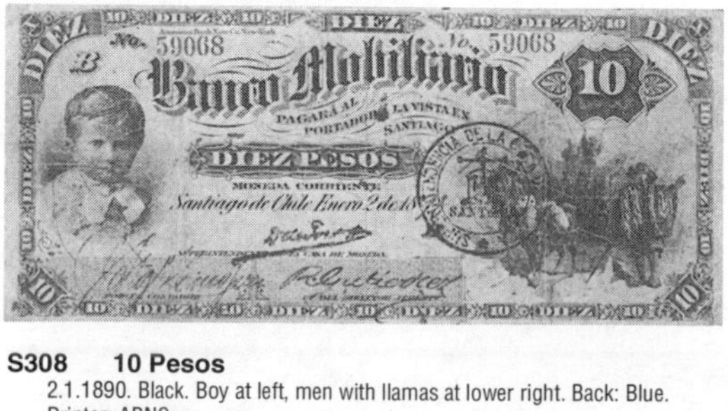

S308 10 Pesos

2.1.1890. Black. Boy at left, men with llamas at lower right. Back: Blue. Printer: ABNC.

	Good	Fine	XF
a. Issued note. Rare.	—	—	—
p. Proof	—	Unc	2500.
s. Specimen.	—	—	—

NOTE: #S306 and S308 with overprint: *EMISION FISCAL* are listed in Vol. 2, #34 and 34A.

Catalog	Description	Good	Fine	XF
S309 20 Pesos	2.1.18xx (ca.1895). Black on yellow and purple underprint. Athena at lower left, condor at upper center, men with llamas at lower right. Back: Purple. Printer: ABNC. Proof.	—	Unc	2000.
S310 50 Pesos	ND (ca.1870). Black on brown underprint. Condor at left, allegorical woman at right. Back: Brown. Printer: ABNC. Archive copy.	—	—	—
S310A 50 Pesos	18xx (ca.1895). Black on brown and yellow underprint. Similar to #S310, but differnet design above bank name at upper center. Printer: ABNC. Archive copy.	—	—	—

Catalog	Description	Good	Fine	XF
S311 100 Pesos	18xx. Girl at lower left, condor at upper center, girl ("Chloe") at lower right. Printer: ABNC. Specimen.	—	Unc	1750.
S312 500 Pesos	ND (18xx). Printer: ABNC.	—	—	—

Banco de Montenegro I Ca.

1869 Issue

Catalog	Description	Good	Fine	XF
S313 1 Peso	Jan. 18xx (Feb. 1869). Black on brown underprint. Sailors with bales at lower left, reclining allegorical woman at center, B. O'Higgins at right. Back: Blue-gray. Printer: ABNC. Proof.	—	—	—
S314 5 Pesos	18xx. Black. Printer: ABNC. Proof.	—	—	—

Banco Nacional de Chile

1872-77 Issue

Catalog	Description	Good	Fine	XF
S316 1 Peso	3.6.1872. Black on brown underprint. Arms at lower left, man at center, female head ("Star of Empire") lower right. Back: Green. Printer: CABB (ABNC).	200.	500.	—

Catalog	Description	Good	Fine	XF
S318 5 Pesos	2.1.1877. Black on yellow underprint. Condor at left, arms at center, girl at right. Back: Green. Printer: CABB (ABNC).	200.	500.	—

NOTE: #S318 and S319 like Banco de la Alianza notes #S122 and S123.

Catalog	Description	Good	Fine	XF
S319 10 Pesos	2.2.1876. Black. Girl at lower left, condor at upper center, arms at lower right. Back: Green. Printer: CABB (ABNC).			
	a. Issued note. Rare.	—	—	—
	p. Proof. 18xx.	—	—	—

NOTE: #S318 and S319 like Banco de la Alianza notes #S122 and S123.

Catalog	Description	Good	Fine	XF
S320 20 Pesos	13.12.1872. Black on orange underprint. Man plowing with oxen at left (sideways), arms at center. Back: Green. Printer: CABB (ABNC).			
	a. Issued note. Rare.	—	—	—
	p. Proof. 18xx.	—	—	—
S322 100 Pesos	18xx (ca.1865). Black on green underprint. Oxen team at left, arms at center. Proof.	—	—	—

1870's Issue

Catalog	Description	Good	Fine	XF
S325 1 Peso	2.1.187x (ca.1873). Black on brown underprint. Arms at lower left, palace at center, Liberty at lower right. Back: Green. Proof.	—	—	—

NOTE: #S325 is like Banco de la Alianza note #S121.

1878 Issue

Catalog	Description	Good	Fine	XF
S331 1 Peso	3.1.1878; 3.1.1887; 3.1.1888. Black on green and peach underprint. Bull's head at left, Valdivia at center, arms at right. Back: Brown. Valdivia at center. Printer: ABNC.	100.	250.	—

NOTE: #S331 and S333 like Banco de la Alianza notes #S126 and S127.

Catalog	Description	Good	Fine	XF
S332 2 Pesos	3.1.1878; 3.1.1888. Black on red-brown and green underprint. Valdivia at left, arms at center, girl with flowers at right. Back: Brown. Valdivia at center. Printer: ABNC.	100.	250.	—
S333 5 Pesos	(ca.1879). Black on green and orange underprint. Valdivia at lower left, arms at center, head at right. Back: Brown. Valdivia at left. Printer: ABNC.	—	—	—

NOTE: #S331-S333 with overprint: *EMISION FISCAL* are listed in Vol. 2, #45-47.

		Good	Fine	XF
S334	**10 Pesos** (ca.1879). Black on green and brown underprint. Valdivia at lower left, condor at upper center, arms at right. Back: Brown. Valdivia at center. Printer: ABNC.	—	—	—

NOTE: #S334 like Banco de la Alianza note #S128.

		Good	Fine	XF
S335	**20 Pesos** 18xx. Black on green and orange underprint. Man plowing with oxen at left (sideways), arms at center, portrait Valdivia at lower right. Back: Brown. Condor at center. Printer: ABNC.			
	p. Proof.	—	—	—
	s. Specimen.	—	—	—
S336	**50 Pesos** 3.1.18xx. Black on blue and orange underprint. Valdivia at left, farmers plowing with oxen at center, arms at right. Back: Brown. Valdivia at center. Printer: ABNC. Specimen.	—	—	—

		Good	Fine	XF
S337	**100 Pesos** 3.1.18xx. Black on blue and orange underprint. Valdivia at lower left center, wagon drawn by oxen at center, arms at lower right. Back: Brown. Valdivia at center. Printer: ABNC. Specimen.	—	—	—

		Good	Fine	XF
S338	**500 Pesos** 3.1.18xx (ca.1879). Black on green and yellow underprint. Portrait Valdivia at left, cherub at upper center, allegorical woman with hammer and anvil at upper right, arms at lower right. Back: Brown. Valdivia at left, cattle watering in pond. Printer: ABNC.			
	p. Proof.	—	Unc	1750.
	s. Specimen.	—	—	—

Banco del Ñuble

1885-90 Issue

		Good	Fine	XF
S344	**10 Pesos** 1.5.1885; 1.5.1890. Black on yellow and green underprint. Woman with child, calf and cows at left center. Back: Brown. Woman with sheaf at center. Printer: CABB (ABNC).	125.	250.	500.
S345	**20 Pesos** 18xx (ca.1888). Black on orange, pink and yellow underprint. Farmer with team of oxen plowing field at center. Back: Cow at left. Printer: CABB (ABNC).			
	p. Proof. Back orange.	—	—	—
	s. Specimen. Back blue.	—	Unc	3000.

		Good	Fine	XF
S346	**20 Pesos** ND. Overprint: Silver: *20-XX-VEINTE* on #S344. Printer: CABB (ABNC).	—	—	—

Banco de Ossa y Ca.

1860's Issue

		Good	Fine	XF
S351	**5 Pesos** Jan. 186x. Allegory of Navigation at lower left, man at upper center, allegorical woman with trident at lower right. Printer: ABNC. Proof.	—	—	—
S352	**10 Pesos** Jan. 186x. Mercury at left, allegory of Navigation reclining at upper center, man at lower right. Printer: ABNC. Specimen.	—	—	—

		Good	Fine	XF
S353	**20 Pesos** 1.186x. Black on orange underprint. Portrait woman with rabbit at left, Paddle wheel steamship at center, portrait man at right. Back: Dark brown. Printer: ABNC.			
	p. Proof.	—	—	—
	s. Specimen.	—	—	—
S354	**50 Pesos** Jan. 186x. Liberty and Minerva at lower left, dog on strongbox at upper center, man at lower right. Printer: ABNC. Specimen.	—	—	—

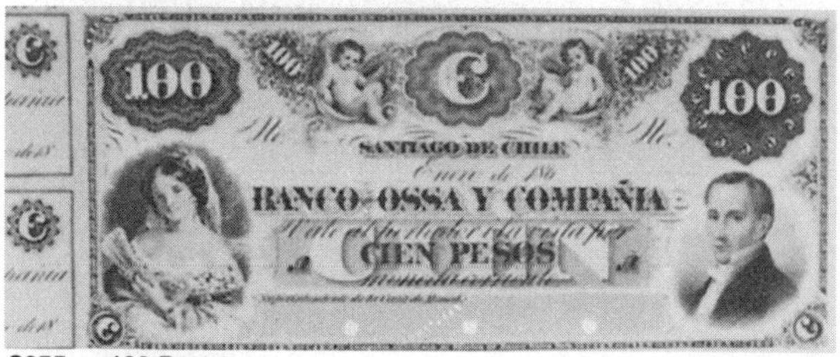

		Good	Fine	XF
S355	**100 Pesos** Jan. 186x. Woman at lower left, cherubs at upper center, man at lower right. Printer: ABNC. Proof.	—	—	—

Banco del Pobre

1876-78 Issue

S361 1 Peso	Good	Fine	XF
7.8.1877. Black and brown. Standing female and pedestal ("Liberty") at left, three children reading ("The Young Students") at center, star in wreath at right. Back: Green. Printer: CNBB (NBNC).			
a. Issued note.	—	—	—
r. 187x. Remainder with counterfoil. Series A; B.	—	Unc	50.00

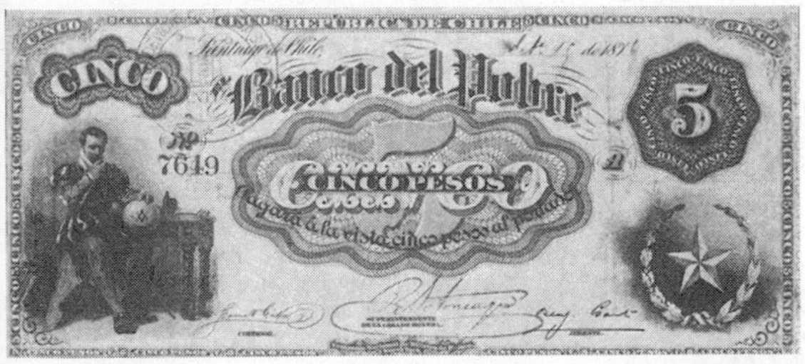

S362 5 Pesos	Good	Fine	XF
16.9.1876. Black, brown and yellow. Man seated with globe ("Columbus") at left, star in wreath at lower right. Back: Green. Printer: CNBB (NBNC).			
a. Issued note.	—	—	—
r. Remainder.	—	Unc	50.00

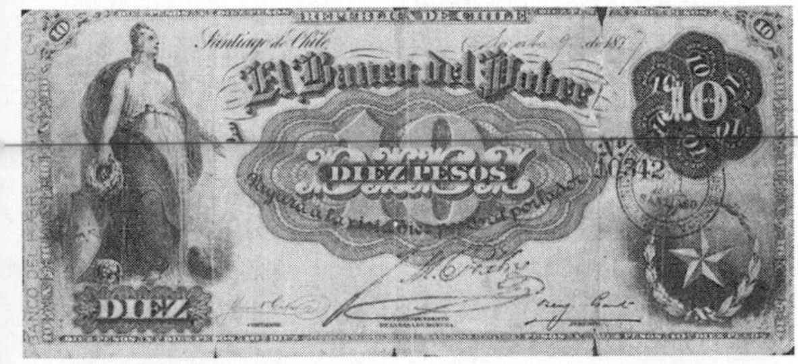

S363 10 Pesos	Good	Fine	XF
9.8.1877. Black, brown and yellow. Liberty standing at left, star in wreath at right. Back: Green. Printer: CNBB (NBNC).			
a. Issued note.	—	—	—
r. Remainder.	—	Unc	50.00
S364 20 Pesos (ca.1878). Black. Steam passenger train at upper left, Liberty at center right. Printer: CNBB (NBNC). Rare.	—	—	—

Banco Popular Hipotecario

1894 Provisional Issue

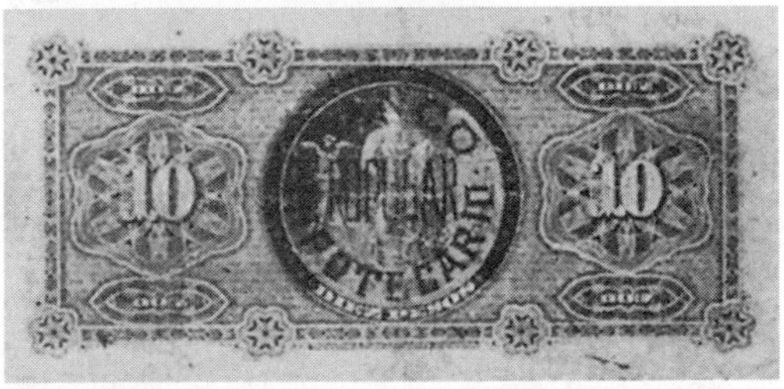

S379 10 Pesos	Good	Fine	XF
14.11.1894. Overprint on Banco Constructor Hipotecario, #S198 with old name barred out on face. Back: Circular overprint with new bank name at center. Rare.	—	—	—

Banco de Rere

1890 Issue

S388 10 Pesos	Good	Fine	XF
189x. Black on yellow underprint. Minerva standing at left, man plowing with oxen at center. Series A. Back: Blue. Printer: W&S. Unsigned remainder.	—	—	—

S389 20 Pesos	Good	Fine	XF
189x. Black on light brown underprint. Steam passenger train at upper left, helmeted woman at center right. Printer: W&S. Unsigned remainder.	—	Unc	500.

Banco San Fernando

1891-99 Issue

S397 5 Pesos	Good	Fine	XF
18xx (16.5.1899). Black on green underprint. Indian woman seated at left, horse's head ("My Horse") at right. Back: Green. Printer: ABNC.	—	—	—

S398 10 Pesos	Good	Fine	XF
1891. Ducks at left, seated Agriculture at center right. Printer: ABNC.			
a. Issued note.	—	—	—
s. Specimen. Back green.	—	—	—

S399 **20 Pesos**	Good	Fine	XF
18xx. Black on tan underprint. Agricultural tools at top center, seated women by globe ("Allegory") at lower right. Back: Brown. Printer: ABNC.	—	—	—

S400 **50 Pesos**	Good	Fine	XF
18xx (4.4.1891). Black on gold underprint. Liberty and Justice seated with shield at center. Back: Brown. Printer: ABNC.	—	—	—

NOTE: Some authorities believe that all notes from this bank which appear to be in issued condition are in reality fraudulently dated and signed. The same is true for any notes w/overprint: *EMISION FISCAL* as listed in Vol. 2, #50.

Banco de Santiago

1883-86 Issue

S411 **1 Peso**	Good	Fine	XF
25.2.1886. Black on brown underprint. Woman with fasces and portrait Tocornal at upper left, cherub at upper right. Vertical. Back: Brown. Sailing ship *Esmeralda* at center. Horizontal. Printer: CABB (ABNC).			
a. Issued note.	—	—	—
p. Proof.	—	Unc	1250.
s. Specimen with counterfoil.	—	Unc	1750.

NOTE: #S411 with overprint: *EMISION FISCAL* is listed in Vol. 2, #51.

S414 **10 Pesos**	Good	Fine	XF
20.10.1883. Black on salmon underprint. Standing woman at left holding man's portrait; woman and children at lower right. Vertical. Back: Green. Horizontal. Printer: CABB (ABNC).			
a. Issued note.	—	—	—
s. Specimen with counterfoil.	—	Unc	1250.

S415 **20 Pesos**	Good	Fine	XF
25.2.1886. Black on blue underprint. Child at center. Vertical. Back: Blue. Horizontal. Printer: CABB (ABNC).			
a. Issued note with red overprint: *27.7.1986* date over old date.	150.	400.	—
p. Proof.	—	Unc	1750.
s. Specimen with counterfoil.	—	Unc	1250.

S417 **100 Pesos**	Good	Fine	XF
ND (ca.1884). Black on green underprint. Standing woman at left holding man's portrait; woman and children at lower right. Vertical. Back: Orange. Horizontal. Printer: CABB (ABNC).			
p. Proof.	—	—	—
s. Specimen with counterfoil.	—	Unc	2250.

Banco de la Serena

1891 Issue

S418 **10 Pesos**	Good	Fine	XF
189x (ca.1891). Black on green and yellow underprint. Condor with wings spread at upper left, miners at right. Back: Green. Allegorical woman with farm implements at center. Printer: ABNC.			
p. Proof.	—	Unc	2500.
s. Specimen.	—	—	—

NOTICE

Readers with unlisted dates, signature varieties, etc., are invited to submit photocopies or scans of their notes to: Standard Catalog of World Paper Money, 700 East State St. Iola, WI 54990-0001, E-Mail: george.cuhaj@fwmedia.com.

Banco Sud-Americano

1873 Issue

	Good	Fine	XF
S421 1 Peso 16.4.1873. Black and brown. Seated woman and shield at top center. Back: Brown. Mercury standing on globe at center. Printer: CNBB (NBNC).	150.	400.	—

NOTE: Additional denominations require confirmation.

Banco del Sur

1870 Issue

	Good	Fine	XF
S426 1 Peso 18xx (ca.1870). Black on green underprint. Woman with water jug at left, Gen. Freire at center, farmers harvesting grapes at right. Back: Orange. Printer: ABNC.	—	—	—

	Good	Fine	XF
S428 5 Pesos 18xx (ca.1870). Black on red-orange underprint. Ox team pulling hay wagon with farmers at left, young girl at upper center, Gen. Freire at right. Back: Green. Printer: ABNC. Proof.	—	—	—
S429 10 Pesos 18xx (ca.1870). Black on brown underprint. Portrait Gen. Freire at upper left, ox team and wagon at center, woman's head ("The Bride") at lower right. Back: Blue. Printer: ABNC.	—	—	—
S430 20 Pesos 18xx (ca.1870). Black on orange underprint. Two girls at lower left, Gen. Freire at upper center, anchor at lower right. Printer: ABNC. Proof.	—	—	—
S432 100 Pesos 18xx (ca.1870). Gen. Freire at left, waterfalls and volcano scene at center, beehive at lower right. Archive copy.	—	—	—

COMPANION CATALOGS

Volume 2 - General Issues, 1368-1960
Volume 3 - Modern Issues, 1961- present

The Companion Catalogs in the Standard Catalog of World Paper Money series include: The General Issues volume which lists national notes dated and used, before 1960. It is updated periodically, now in it's 12th edition. The Modern Issues Book includes national notes issued since 1961, and is updated annually. Inquiries about the availability of both these volumes are invited to contact F+W Publications, 700 East State Street, Iola, WI 54990-0001. You may visit our website at: www.shopnumismaster.com.

Banco de Talca

1885-88 Issue

	Good	Fine	XF
S439 5 Pesos 18xx (ca.1885). Black on blue and orange underprint. Portrait man at left, allegorical woman with staff at right. Mountain at upper center right. Back: Blue. Printer: ABNC.			
p. Proof.	—	Unc	1250.
s. Specimen.	—	—	—

	Good	Fine	XF
S440 10 Pesos 18xx (ca. 1885). Black on green and orange underprint. Man at left, village market scene at right. Mountain at upper center right. Back: Green. Printer: ABNC.			
p. Proof.	—	Unc	1500.
s. Specimen.	—	Unc	3000.

	Good	Fine	XF
S441 20 Pesos 18xx (ca.1888). Black on orange and yellow-green underprint. Portrait two women at upper left, portrait man at lower right. Mountain at upper center right. Back: Red-brown. Printer: ABNC.			
a. Issued note.	—	—	—
p. Proof.	—	Unc	2000.
s. Specimen.	—	Unc	3000.

	Good	Fine	XF
S443 100 Pesos 18xx (ca.1885). Black on brown, blue and orange underprint. Portrait man at left, allegorical woman ("Justice") at right holding scales. Mountain at upper center right. Back: Orange. Printer: ABNC.			
p. Proof.	—	—	—
s. Specimen.	—	—	—

Banco de Tarapaca y Londres

Iquique

1891 Issue

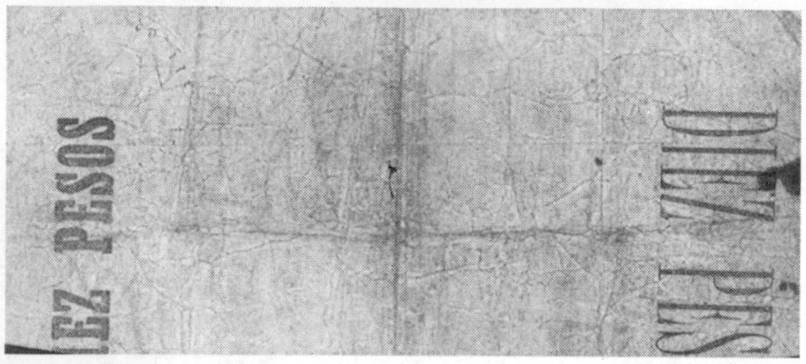

S447 10 Pesos — Good — Fine — XF
21.3.1891. Red-orange. Bank arms at center. Back: Value vertically in blue letters. Printer: R. Bini, Iquique. — — —

NOTE: #S447 was overprinted for acceptance without endorsement at the named bank or the Banco de Valparaiso.

Pisagua

1891 Issue

S453 5 Pesos — Good — Fine — XF
20.5.1891. Red-orange bank arms at center. Paper: Off-white. Printer: R. Bini, Iquique. Unsigned remainder. — — —

S454 10 Pesos — Good — Fine — XF
20.5.1891. Red-orange bank arms at center. Paper: Off-white. Printer: R. Bini, Iquique. Unsigned remainder. — — —

S455 20 Pesos
20.5.1891. Red-orange bank arms at center. Paper: Off-white. Printer: R. Bini, Iquique. Unsigned remainder. — — —

Banco de la Union

1870's Provisional Issue

S460 1 Peso — Good — Fine — XF
ND (- old date Jan. 18xx). Black and silver overprint of new bank name on #S313. Back: Solid black circular overprint at center. Remainder. — — —

1881 Issue

S462 2 Pesos — Good — Fine — XF
18xx. Black on brown and green underprint. Boy seated with dog at left, chickens at right. Back: Brown. Printer: CABB (ABNC). — — —

S463 5 Pesos — Good — Fine — XF
31.7.1878. Black on blue and orange underprint. B. O'Higgins at lower left, dog's head ("Ceasar") at center, allegorical woman at lower right. Back: Brown. Printer: CABB (ABNC).
- a. Issued note. — — —
- s. Specimen. — — —

S464 10 Pesos — Good — Fine — XF
1.1.1881. Black on blue and orange underprint. B. O'Higgins at upper left, angelic trumpeter with globe at upper center, anchor at lower right. Back: Orange. Printer: CABB (ABNC). Proof. — Unc 1750.

S465 20 Pesos — Good — Fine — XF
18xx. Black on green and orange underprint. Girl and dog at left, two horses at center, B. O'Higgins at right. Back: Orange-brown. Printer: CABB (ABNC). Specimen. — — —

S466 50 Pesos — Good — Fine — XF
18xx. Black on green and gold underprint. Woman with scroll ("History") at left. B. O'Higgins at center, seated woman with bale at right. Back: Light orange. Printer: CABB (ABNC). Specimen. — — —

S467 100 Pesos

18xx. Black on green and red underprint. Seated allegorical woman in tropical garden ("Tropics No. 2") at center. Back: Blue. Printer: CABB (ABNC). Specimen.

Good	Fine	XF
—	—	—

Banco de Valparaiso

1870 Issue

S477 1 Peso

18xx. Black. National arms at top center. Proof.

Good	Fine	XF
—	Unc	600.

S478 5 Pesos

1.4.1870. Blue. National arms at top center. Rare.

Good	Fine	XF
—	—	—

1876-77 Issue

S486 1 Peso

3.1.1876. Black and orange. Bank at upper center. Back: Green. Mercury standing on globe. Printer: CNBB (NBNC).

Good	Fine	XF
125.	500.	—

S487 2 Pesos

3.1.1876. Black and blue. Building at upper center. Back: Blue. Mercury standing on globe. Printer: CNBB (NBNC).

Good	Fine	XF
150.	600.	—

S488 5 Pesos

3.1.1876. Black and green. Girl seated with sheep, coastline at left, steam passenger train at right in background at top center. Back: Green. Mercury standing on globe. Printer: CNBB (NBNC).

Good	Fine	XF
—	—	—

S489 10 Pesos

2.7.1877. Black on green underprint. Dog's head ("Ceasar") at upper left, allegorical woman at left and right of shield at center right. Back: Black on green underprint. Two allegorical figures at center. Printer: ABNC.

	Good	Fine	XF
p. Proof.	—	—	—
s. Specimen.	—	—	—

S490 20 Pesos

2.7.1877. Black on salmon and green underprint. Dog's head ("Ceasar") at upper left, allegorical woman at left and right of shield at center right. Back: Black on orange underprint. Printer: ABNC. Archive copy.

Good	Fine	XF
—	—	—

S491 50 Pesos

2.7.1877. Black on blue and orange underprint. Allegorical woman with shield and eagle at center. Back: Black on blue-green underprint. Allegorical woman with bird at center. Printer: ABNC. Proof.

Good	Fine	XF
—	—	—

S492 100 Pesos

2.7.1877. Black on green and orange underprint. Seated allegorical woman, cherubs and Chilean arms at center, portrait woman with tiara at right. Back. Black and green. Liberty standing at center. Specimen.

Good	Fine	XF
—	—	—

1881 Issue

S498 5 Pesos

8.1.1881. Black on blue and orange underprint. Woman holding faces with child ("Prosperity") at left, two young cherubs at top center, two cherubs with shield at lower right. Back: Blue. Farmers working at center.

Good	Fine	XF
—	—	—

1891 Issues

S511 5 Pesos

30.3.1891; 15.5.1891. Blue. Circular bank arms at center. Uniface. Printer: R. Bini, Iquique. Issued at Pisagua.

Good	Fine	XF
—	—	—

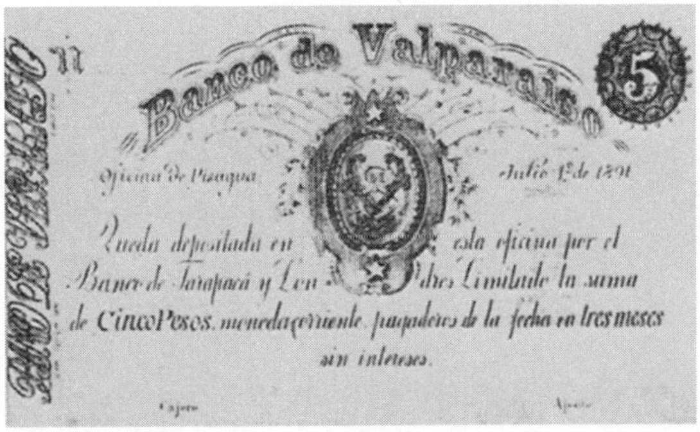

S512 5 Pesos

1.7.1891. Black. Different oval arms at center. Uniface. Printer: R. Bini, Iquique. Issued at Pisagua.

Good	Fine	XF
—	—	—

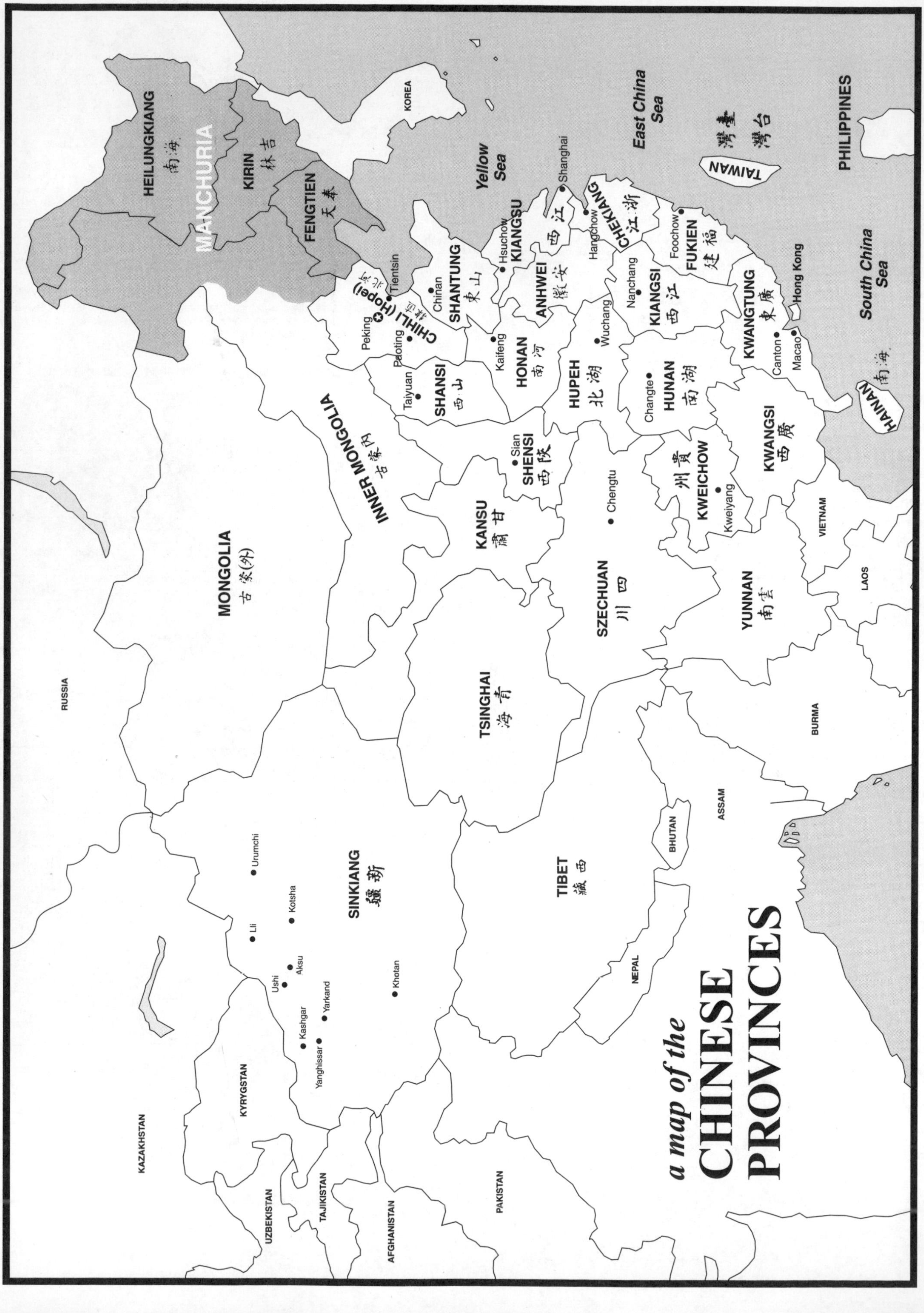
a map of the
CHINESE
PROVINCES
MANCHURIA
HEILUNGKIANG
KIRIN
FENGTIEN
KOREA
Yellow Sea
East China Sea
South China Sea
PHILIPPINES
TAIWAN
HAINAN
CHIHLI (Hopei)
Peking
Tientsin
Paoting
SHANTUNG
Chinan
KIANGSU
Hsuchow
Shanghai
CHEKIANG
Hangchow
ANHWEI
FUKIEN
Foochow
KIANGSI
Nanchang
HONAN
Kaifeng
SHANSI
Taiyuan
HUPEH
Wuchang
HUNAN
Changte
KWANGTUNG
Canton
Hong Kong
Macao
KWANGSI
KWEICHOW
Kweiyang
SHENSI
Sian
KANSU
INNER MONGOLIA
MONGOLIA
SZECHUAN
Chengtu
YUNNAN
VIETNAM
LAOS
BURMA
TSINGHAI
TIBET
BHUTAN
ASSAM
NEPAL
SINKIANG
Urumchi
Kotsha
Li
Aksu
Ushi
Khotan
Yarkand
Kashgar
Yanghissar
RUSSIA
KAZAKHSTAN
KYRYGSTAN
UZBEKISTAN
TAJIKISTAN
AFGHANISTAN
PAKISTAN

CHINA (Chung Kuo) 中國

China's ancient civilization began in the Huang Ho basin about 1500 BC. The warring feudal states comprising early China were first united under Emperor Ch'in Shih Huang Ti (246-210 BC) who gave China its name and first central government. Subsequent dynasties alternated brilliant cultural achievements with internal disorder until the Empire was brought down by the revolution of 1911, and the Republic of China installed in its place. Chinese culture attained a pre-eminence in art, literature and philosophy, but a traditional backwardness in industry and administration ill prepared China for the demands of 19th century Western expansionism which exposed it to military and political humiliations, and mandated a drastic revision of political practice in order to secure an accommodation with the modern world.

The Republic of 1911 barely survived the stress of World War I, and was subsequently all but shattered by the rise of nationalism and the emergence of the Chinese Communist movement. Moscow, which practiced a policy of cooperation between Communists and other parties in movements for national liberation, sought to establish an entente between the Chinese Communist Party and the Kuomintang (National People's Party) of Sun Yat-sen. The ensuing cooperation was based on little more than the hope each had of using the other.

An increasingly uneasy association between the Kuomintang and the Chinese Communist Party developed and continued until April 12, 1927, when Chiang Kai-shek, Sun Yat-sen's political heir, instituted a bloody purge to stamp out the Communists within the Kuomintang and the government and virtually paralyzed their ranks throughout China. Some time after the mid-1927 purges, the Chinese Communist Party turned to armed force to resist Chiang Kai-shek and during the period of 1930-34 acquired control over large parts of Kiangsi, Fukien, Hunan and Hupeh. The Nationalist Nanking government responded with a series of campaigns against the Soviet power bases and, by October 1934, succeeded in driving the remnants of the Communist army to a refuge in Shensi Province.

Subsequently, the Communists under the leadership of Mao Tse-tung defeated the Nationalists and on September 21, 1949 formally established the Peoples Republic.

EMPERORS:

TE TSUNG 德宗

Reign title: Kuang Hsu 光緒 1875-1908, Years 1-34

宣統帝 HSUAN T'UNG TI
遜帝 (Hsun Ti)

Reign title: Hsuan T'ung 宣統 1908-1911

YUAN SHIH-KAI

Proposed reign title: Hung Hsien 憲洪 Dec. 15, 1915-March 21, 1916.

MONETARY SYSTEM:

Cash Coin System
1 Tael = 800-1600 Cash*

***NOTE: In theory, 1000 cash were equal to a tael of silver, but in actuality the rate varied from time to time and from place to place.**

Dollar System
1 Cent (fen, hsien) = 10 Cash (wen)
1 Chiao (hao) = 10 Cents
1 Dollar (yuan) = 100 Cents

Tael System
1 Fen (candareen) = 10 Li
1 Ch'ien (mace) = 10 Fen
1 Liang (tael) = 10 Ch'ien (mace)

MONETARY UNITS:

The dating and following charts have been adapted from *Chinese Banknotes* by Ward Smith and Brian Matravers. Calligraphy in special instances by Marian C. Smith.

Dollar Amounts		
Dollar *(Yuan)*	元 or 員	圓 or 圜
Half Dollar *(Pan Yuan)*	圓半	
50¢ *(Chiao/Hao)*	角伍	毫伍
10¢ *(Chiao/Hao)*	角壹	毫壹
1¢ *(Fen/Hsien)*	分壹	仙壹

Tael Amounts	
Tael *(Liang)*	兩
Half Tael *(Pan Liang)*	兩半
5 Mace *(Wu Ch'ien)*	錢伍
1 Mace *(1 Ch'ien)*	錢壹
Ku Ping *(Tael)**	平庫

Copper and Cash Coin Amounts			
Copper *(Mei)*	枚	String *(Tiao)*	吊
Cash *(Wen)*	文	String *(Tiao)*	弔
String *(Kuan)*	貫	String *(Ch'uan)*	串

Common Prefixes			
Copper *(T'ung)*	銅	"Small money"	洋小
Silver *(Yin)*	銀	"Big money"	洋大
Gold *(Chin)*	金	"Big money"	洋英

ARRANGEMENT

FOREIGN BANK ISSUES .... #S97-S757

The foreign bank issues are listed in a normal alphabetic listing of note issuing authority. The notes usually bear the Chinese text on one side and the respective English, Russian, or other foreign text on the opposite side.

This includes a full listing of the foreign note issuers complete with romanizations of and including the Chinese text as found on the notes. If a particular bank changed its name through the years, the successive note issues will be found listed under the new bank name.

The branch office overprints are mentioned under each each bank's entry and are illustrated throughout the listings as the bank office changes.

PROVINCIAL BANK ISSUES .... #S802-S3041

The Provincial Bank issues are listed alphabetically, using romanizations of the principal issuer's name in Chinese and, in addition, the various English names known to have been used for note issues.

COMMUNIST BANK ISSUES .... #S3050-S3781

The Communist Bank issues are listed alphabetically, using romanizations of the principal issuer's name in Chinese and, in addition, the various English names known to have been used for note issues.

MILITARY ISSUES .... #S3791-S3960

The Military issues are listed alphabetically, using romanizations of the principal issuer's name in Chinese and, in addition, the various English names known to have been used for note issues.

NUMERICAL CHARACTERS

NUMERALS

NUMBER	CONVENTIONAL		FORMAL		COMMERCIAL
1	一 正 元		壹 弌		〡
2	二		弍 貳		〢
3	三		叁 弎		〣
4	四		肆		〤
5	五		伍		〥
6	六		陸		〦
7	七		柒		〧
8	八		捌		〨
9	九		玖		〩
10	十		拾 什		十
20	十二 or 廿		拾貳 念		〢十
25	五十二 or 五廿		伍拾貳		〢十〥
30	十三 or 卅		拾叁		〣十
100	百一		佰壹		〡百
1,000	千一		仟壹		〡千
10,000	萬一		萬壹		〡万
100,000	萬十	億一 (old)	萬拾	億壹	十万
1,000,000	萬百一	億一 (new)	萬佰壹		〡百万

DATING:

Prior to the Republican era, Chinese notes were usually dated in reference to the year of reign of the current emperor. To arrive at the corresponding AD date, subtract one year from the year *(nien)* and add this number to the emperor's accession year.

YEARS OF THE REPUBLIC

Years of the Republic

Year		AD	Year		AD	Year		AD	Year		AD
1	一	= 1912	11	一十	= 1922	21	一十二	= 1932	31	一十三	= 1942
2	二	= 1913	12	二十	= 1923	21	二十二	= 1933	32	二十三	= 1943
3	三	= 1914	13	三十	= 1924	23	三十二	= 1934	33	三十三	= 1944
4	四	= 1915	14	四十	= 1925	24	四十二	= 1935	34	四十三	= 1945
5	五	= 1916	15	五十	= 1926	25	五十二	= 1936	35	五十三	= 1946
6	六	= 1917	16	六十	= 1927	26	六十二	= 1927	36	六十三	= 1947
7	七	= 1918	17	七十	= 1928	27	七十二	= 1938	37	七十三	= 1948
8	八	= 1919	18	八十	= 1929	28	八十二	= 1939	38	八十三	= 1949
9	九	= 1920	19	九十	= 1930	29	九十二	= 1940	39	九十三	= 1950
10	十	= 1921	20	十二	= 1931	30	十三	= 1941	40	十四	= 1951

NOTE: Chinese dates are normally read from right to left, except for the modern issues of the People's Republic of China from 1953 where the Western date is read from left to right.

CYCLICAL DATING:

Another method of dating is a 60-year, repeating cycle, outlined in the table below. The date is shown by the combination of two characters, the first of the top row and the second from the column at left. In this catalog, when a cyclical date is used, the abbreviation CD appears before the AD date.

This chart has been adapted from *Chinese Banknotes* by Ward Smith and Brian Matravers. Calligraphy by Marian C. Smith.

	庚	辛	壬	癸	甲	乙	丙	丁	戊	己
戌	1850 1910		1862 1922		1874 1934		1886 1946		1838 1898	
亥		1851 1911		1863 1923		1875 1935		1887 1947		1839 1899
子	1840 1900		1852 1912		1864 1924		1876 1936		1888 1948	
丑		1841 1901		1853 1913		1865 1925		1877 1937		1889 1949
寅	1830 1890		1842 1902		1854 1914		1866 1926		1878 1938	
卯		1831 1891		1843 1903		1855 1915		1867 1927		1879 1939
辰	1880 1940		1832 1892		1844 1904		1856 1916		1868 1928	
巳		1881 1941		1833 1893		1845 1905		1857 1917		1869 1929
午	1870 1930		1882 1942		1834 1894		1846 1906		1858 1918	
未		1871 1931		1883 1943		1835 1895		1847 1907		1859 1919
申	1860 1920		1872 1932		1884 1944		1836 1896		1848 1908	
酉		1861 1921		1873 1933		1885 1945		1837 1897		1849 1909

PORTRAIT ABBREVIATIONS:

SYS = Sun Yat-sen, 1867-1925
President of Canton Government
1917-25

CKS = Chiang Kai-shek, 1886-1975
President in Nanking, 1927-31
Head of Formosa Government, 1949-75

NOTE: Because of the frequency of the above appearing in listings of Chinese notes their initials are used only in reference to their portraits.

PRINTERS ABBREVIATIONS

ABNC - American Bank Note Co. .... 鈔美
BEPK - Bureau of Engraving & Printing, Yung Heng, Kirin .... 部政財
BEPP - Bureau of Engraving & Printing .... 書印衡永
BWC - Bradbury, Wilkinson & Co. .... Not used
CCLA - Ch'ing Lien, Changsha .... 蓮青
CEPA - China Engraving & Printing .... 版凹華中
CHBA - Chung Hua Book Co. .... 局書華中
CHCC - Ch'ien Chen Chi, Sian .... 集振乾
CHCP - Chao Hsiang Color .... 刷色祥兆
CMPA - Commercial Press .... 務商
CNPC - Ch'u Nan Printing Co. .... 南楚
CPFA - Central Printing Factory .... 廠製印央中
CPFT - Central Printing Factory, Taipei .... 北台
CPOF - Changsha Printing Office .... 刷印沙長
DOFS - Dept. of Finance, Sinkiang .... 廳政財
FRBC - First Republican Book .... 一第國民
HHEC - Hsin Hua, Hong Kong .... 華新
HKCL - Hsingkuo Co., Ltd. .... 國興
HKPA - Hong Kong Printing Press .... 字印港香
HODP - Hunan Official Document .... 紙官南湖
HSPS - Hsieh Shun, Shanghai .... 順協
HWPO - Han Wen, Shanghai .... 文漢
ILBC - I Lin Book, Sian .... 林藝
IPCL - International Printing Co., Ltd. .... 文蘇
IYPC - I Yang, Changsha .... 陽宜
JIPB - Japan Govt. Printing .... 局刷印(府政)
MLTA - Mo Lin T'ang, Pinkiang .... 堂林墨
NWE&PF - Northwest Engraving & Printing Factory .... 北西
PHCF - Pai Hua Chou Feng, Nanking .... 豐州花百
PYOG - Peiyang Official Gazette .... 報官洋北
PYPO - Peiyang Printing Office .... 刷印洋北
SASO - Shensi Army Service Office .... 軍陸西陝
SHPC - Shanghai Printing Co. .... 刷印海上
SOPO - Shantung Official .... 刷印官東山
STPO - Shantung Printing Office .... 刷印東山
TCPL - Tung Chi, Liaoning .... 記東
TTBC - Ta Tung (Dah Tung) Printing (Several branch plants) .... 局書東大
TWCC - Ts'ai Wen, Tsitsihar .... 文杉
TYPC - Ta Yeh (Dah Yip) Co. (Several branches) .... 司公業大
WHPP - Wu Han Book Co. .... 書印漢武
W&S - Waterlow & Sons, Ltd. .... 路德華國英
WTBC - Wen T'ung Book, Kiukiang .... 通文
YHBA - Yung Heng Book Co. .... 書印衡永
YMSO - Yunnan Military Supply .... 雷軍南雲
YOPO - Yunnan Official Printing .... 印官南雲
YSCL - Yue Sheng & Co., Ltd. .... 興裕

PLACE NAMES

The following list is designed for users unfamiliar with written Chinese who wish to check place names appearing on notes, usually as overprints. For this reason, the arrangement is based on the number of strokes in the first character, normally found at the right or top. This is a selected list. Some obscure locations have been omitted.

English names are a mixture of popular names or variants thereon, which appear on notes, and Wade-Giles romanizations for places which lack well established English names.

Chinese place names tend to be simple descriptive terms relating to a geographical feature, e.g., "north of the lake" (Hupei), "southern capital" (Nanking) or "on the sea" (Shanghai). Most provincial names show this characteristic. In the latter case, many are paired, which has the disadvantage to the western eye and ear of making them look and sound much the same. Hunan-Hupei, Honan-Hopei, Kwangtung-Kwangsi, Kiangsu-Kiangsi (plus Kiangnan on older notes) and Shantung-Shansi are not difficult to confuse. The most serious problem, however, is Shansi-Shensi. Here, the last characters are the same rather than the first but the first characters, if pronounced correctly, differ only in tone. Even the meanings are close, Shansi, literally, is "mountains west," while Shensi is "mountain passes west," although the first character in this instance is not often used in this meaning. The difference in English spelling is generally accepted convention. Chinese find no difficulty in keeping the two separated because the tonal difference is sufficient in the spoken language and written forms for the first characters are totally dissimilar.

Westerners who might be tempted to consider these or other problems in terminology as resulting from mysterious oriental mental processes should first appraise their own place names, which are rarely as logical or as simple. Inconsistent spellings of place names in romanization too, are primarily western rather than Chinese errors. If confusion does arise, the reasons are complex, and, in any event, no satisfactory solution has yet been found.

Kiukiang, Kiangsi	江九
Pa Pu, Kwangsi	步八
Szechuan (alt)	川
Ch'uan Sha, Kiangsi	沙川
Ch'uan K'ang, Szechuan	康川
Shansi	西山
Shantung	東山
Shanhaikuan Chihli/Hopei	關海山
Shanghai, Kiangcu	海上
Shang Jao, Kiangsi	饒上
Ta T'ung Shansi	同大
Ta Cheng Chihli/Hopei	城大
Ta Ch'en Fukien	陳大
Dairen, Liaoning	連大
Honan (alt)	州中
China (alt)	華中
China	國中
Newchwang Liaoning	莊牛
Niu T'ou Chihli/Hopei	頭牛
T'ai Ku Shansi	谷太
T'ai Yuan, Shansi	原太
Tientsin, Chihli/Hopei	津天
Wen An, Chihli/Hope	安文
Wu Ch'ang, Kirin	常五
Cheng yang, Honan	陽正
Tibet	藏西
Hsien Yu, Fukien	遊仙
Kansu	肅甘
Paotow, Suiyuan	頭包
Peiping, Chihli/Hopei	平北
Peking, Chihli/Hopei	京北
Pakhoi, Kwangtung	海北
Shih I, Chihli/Hopei	邑石
Shihkiachwang, Chihli/Hopei	莊家石
Szechuan	川四
T'ai T'ou Chihli/Hopei	頭台
Taiwan (alt)	灣台
Yung Ch'ing, Chihli/Hopei	清永
Yung Ning, Chihli/Hopei	寧永
Anhwei	徽安
Chengtu, Szechuan	都成
Kirin	林吉
Chi Hsien, Chihli/Hopei	縣吉

Kiangsi	西江
Kiangnan	南江
Kiangsu	蘇江
Sian, Shensi	安西
Sikang	康西
Ili, Sinkiang	犁伊
Swatow, Kwangtung	頭汕
Tulunnoerh, Chahar	倫多
Ch'ih Feng, Johol	峯赤
Hsin Tien, Chihli/Hopei	店辛
Li Chia K'ou, Kwangsi	口家李
Sha P'ing, Shansi	坪沙
Kiangsu (al (literary)	吳
Changsha, Hunan	沙長
Changchun, Kirin	春長
Ch'ang Cheng (Great Wall)	城長
Ch'ang Li, Chihli/Hopei	棠昌
Chihli	隸直
Quemoy (Kinmen) Fukien	門金
Peking/Peiping, Chihli/Hopei	京兆
Tsingtao, Shantung	島青
Chinghai (or Tsinghai)	海青
Fengtien	天奉
Feng Hsin, Kiangsi	新奉
Fou Cheng, Chihli/Hopei	城阜
Hangchow, Chekiang	州杭
Hopei	北河
Honan	南河
Ho Chien, Chihli/Hopei	間河
Hulun, Heilungkiang	倫呼
Kunming, Yunnan	明昆
Manchuria	省三東
Manchuria (alt.)	九北東
Wu Ning, Szechuan	寧武
Wu Han, Hupei	漢武
Yenan Shensi	安延
Chekiang	江浙
Chien Ch'ang, Kiangsi	昌建
Chien Yang, Kiangsu	陽建
Chungking, Szechuan	慶重
Harbin, Heilungkiang	賓爾哈
Hsin An, Chihli/Hopei	安信
Kuling, Kiangsi	嶺牯

Liuchow, Kwangsi	州柳
Nan Chiang, Szechuan	江南
Nanchang, Kiangsi	昌南
Nanking, Kiangsu	京南
Nan Kuan Chen, Chihli/Hopei	鎮關南
Nan Hsiung, Kwangtung	雄南
Nanning, Kwangsi	(寗)寧南
Paoting, Chihli/Hopei	定保
T'ai An, Shantung	安泰
Tihua, Sinkiang	化廸
Weihaiwei, Shantung	衛海威
Shansi (literary)	(晉)晋
Chin Tz'u Shansi	祠晋
Shensi (Literary)	秦
Chinwangtao, Shantung	島皇秦
Haikow Kwangtung	口海
Hailar, Heilungkiang	爾拉海
Hainan, Kwangtung	南海
Hong Kong	港香
Hsuchow, Kiangsu	州徐
Kwangsi (literary)	桂
Kweilin, Kwangsi	林桂
Urga, Mongolia	倫庫
Matsu, Fukien	祖馬
Ma T'ou Chen Shantung	鎮頭馬
Hupei (literary)	鄂
P'u T'ien Fukien	田莆
Shensi	西陝
Tongshan, Chihli/Hopei	山唐
T'ao Yuan Hunan	源桃
Chefoo, Shantung	台烟
Kalgan, Chihli/Hopei	口家張
Ch'ang Te, Hunan	德常
Tsingkiangpu, Kiangsu	浦江清
Ch'ung Ming, Kiangsu	明崇
Huai Hai, Kiangsu	海淮
Kuo Hsien, Shansi	縣崞
Liao Cheng, Shantung	城聊
Pi'ng Hsien, Kiangsi	縣萍
Pukow, Kiangsu	口浦
Mukden, Liaoning	京盛
Su Hsien, Anhwei	縣宿

Ts'ao Ts'un, Shantung	村曹
T'ung Cheng, Hopei	城通
Wuchow, Kwangsi	州梧
Yeh Hsien, Shantung	縣掖
Chi Ning, Chahar	寧集
Chingtechen, Kiangsi	鎮德景
Hei Ho, Heilungkiang	河黑
Heilungkiang	江龍黑
Hunan (literary)	湘
Hupei	北湖
Hunan	南湖
Anhwei (literary)	皖
Kaifeng, Honan	封開
Kweichow	州貴
Kweiyang, Kwangsi	陽貴
Lung Ch'ang Szechuan	昌隆
Ningpo, Chekiang	波寗
Sheng Fang Chihli/Hopei	芳勝
Wusih, Kiangsu	錫無
Yu Tz'u, Shansi	次榆
Kwangtung/ Kwangsi (lit)	粵
Yunnan	南雲
Fu An, Fukien	安福
Foochow, Fukien	州福
Fu I, Fukien	邑福
Fukien	建福
Fu Ch'ing, Fukien	清福
Amoy, Fukien	門厦
Sinkiang	疆新
Jui Ch'ang Kiangsi	昌瑞
Fukien (literary)	閩
P'eng Lai, Shantung	萊蓬
Po Hai, Chihli/Hopei	海渤
Suiyuan	遠綏
Tan Hsien, Shantung	縣單
Yangchow, Kiangsu	州楊
Chefoo (alt) Shantung	台煙
Chahar	爾哈察
Chao Hsien, Chihli/Hopei	縣趙
Chia Ting, Kiangsu	定嘉
Hankow, Hupei	口漢
Ningpo (alt) Chekiang	波寧
Ninghsia	夏寧

Pinkiang, Heilungkiang	江賓
Shou Kuang, Shantung	光壽
Tainan, Taiwan	南臺
Taiwan (alt)	灣臺
Yunnan	滇
Chengchow, Honan	州鄭
Jehol	河熱
Kuang An Chen Chihli/Hopei	鎮安廣
Kwangsi	西廣
Canton, Kwangtung	州廣
Kwangtung	東廣
Manchukuo	國洲滿
Manchouli, Heilungkiang	里洲滿
Shantung (literary)	魯
Hopei (literary)	冀
Kweichow (literary)	黔
Chui Tzu Shan, Jehol	山字錐
Liaoning (al	東遼
Liaoning	寧遼
Lungkow, Shantung	口龍
Lungchow, Kwangsi	州龍
Mongolia	古蒙
Meng Chiang (Mongolia)	疆蒙
Honan (literary)	豫
Macao	門澳
Chinan (Tsinan) Shantung	南濟
Yingkow, Liaoning	口營
Chenkiang, Kiangsu	江鎮
Fengchen, Suiyuan	鎮豐
Li Chiang Chihli/Hopei	港鯉
Kuantung, Liaoning	東關
Lanchow, Kansu	州蘭
Kansu (literary)	隴
Kiangsu (literary)	蘇
Soochow, Kiangsu	州蘇
Su Ch'ao Chen Honan	鎮橋蘇
Hsien Hsien Chihli/Hopei	縣獻
Lu Hsien Szechuan	縣瀘
Pa Hsien Chihli / Hopei	縣霸
Li Hsien Chihli / Hopei	縣蠡
Kiangsi (literary)	贛
Watlam, Kwangsi	林鬱
Yungtsun	遵永

The above chart listings are taken from "CHINESE BANKNOTES" by Ward D. Smith and Brian Matravers (published 1970).

FOREIGN BANKS

With the passage of the Age of Discovery it became apparent that the products of the East were very desirable in Europe. The British in India, the Dutch and Portuguese in the East Indies were the leaders in developing the trade of the area.

With the Portuguese settlement at Macao in 1557 the potential for developing the China trade came closer to reality. Because of the isolationist policy of the reigning dynasty in China it was to be many years before the European powers could gain a viable foothold for trade in China. The product that was to provide the opportunity for further exploitation was to be opium. The British developed a very lucrative trade in opium from India into China sponsored by the East India Co. Opium was illegal inside China but was brough in through smuggling and official connivance.

The Treaty of Nanking, signed August 29, 1842, was to open the China trade by having as one of its terms the opening of the ports of Amoy, Canton, Foochow, Ningpo and Shanghai to foreign trade and residence. The Treaty Ports, as these were called, were the stepping stones upon which general trade was developed. By 1911 there were 50 ports opened for trade in China.

With the development of Western trade in China it was thought necessary by the traders to establish Western banking. The first Western bank in China was a branch of the Commercial Bank of India in Canton in 1851 and later in Shanghai in 1855.

The ceding of Hong Kong to Great Britain in 1842 also provided a base for European banking practices. The Bank of Western India established a branch there in 1842.

Various banks of British background dominated the banking scene in China for most of the 50 years following the treaty of Nanking. Then came a German bank in 1889, a Russian bank in 1895, a Japanese bank in 1898, a U.S. bank in 1902, a French bank in 1902, a Belgian bank in 1903 and a Dutch bank in 1904. All of these banks were note issuers at one or more branches. The notes were issued to encourage doing business with that bank in the area represented. The banknotes circulated in direct competition with the regular Chinese issues of the period.

The foreign banks also provided loans for the Chinese government (both for the empire and later for the new republic). Many of these loans were very substantial amounts and required more than one of the foreign banks to accommodate the amount.

The notes of the foreign banks circulated until World War II and a number of these banks still maintain offices in Hong Kong.

American Oriental Banking Corporation
(American Oriental Bank of Shanghai)
#S97-S103

上海美豐銀行
Shang Hai Mei Feng Yin Hang

(American Oriental Bank of Tientsin)
#S105

天津美豐銀行
T'ien Ching Mei Feng Yin Hang

American Oriental Bank of Fukien
#S106-S109

福建美豐銀行
Fu Chien Mei Feng Yin Hang

American Oriental Bank of Szechuen
#S110-S110B

四川美豐銀行
Szu Ch'uan Mei Feng Yin Hang

Asia Banking Corporation
#S113-S117

美國友華銀行
Mei Kuo Yu Hua Yin Hang

Asiatic Banking Corporation
#S117A-S117B

上海利彰銀行
Shang Hai Li Chang Yin Hang

Asiatic Commercial Bank, Ltd.
#S118-S120

美華銀行
Mei Hua Yin Hang

Banque Belge Pour L'Etranger
#S123-S149

華比銀行
Hua Pi Yin Hang

British and Belgian Industrial Bank of China
#S150-S151

英比實業銀行
Ying Pi Shih Yeh Yin Hang

Bank of Canton, Ltd. (Eng)
#S152-S153N

廣東銀行有限公司
Kuang Tung Yin Hang Yu Hsien Kung Szu

Chartered Bank of India, Australia & China
#S154-S222

印度新金山中國匯理銀行
Yin Tu Hsin Chin Shan Chung Kuo Hui Li Yin Hang

印度新金山中國麥加利銀行
Yin Tu Hsin Chin Shan Chung Kuo Mai Chia Li Yin Hang

Chartered Mercantile Bank of India, London & China
#S223-S225C

上海有利銀行
Shang Hai Yu Li Yin Hang

China Specie Bank, Ltd.
#S228-S228D

中華國寶銀行
Chung Hua Kuo Pao Yin Hang

Chinese-American Bank of Commerce
#S230-S245

中華懋業銀行
Chung Hua Mou Yeh Yin Hang

Chinese Engineering & Mining Company Limited
#S246-S247A

開平礦務有限公司
K'ai P'ing K'uang Wu Yu Hsien Kung Szu

Chinese Italian Banking Corporation
#S248-S257

震義銀行
Chen I Yin Hang

Comptoir D' Escompte de Paris
#S257B

Not Available
Shang Hai Fa Lan Hsi Yin Hang

Credit Commercial Sino-Francaise
#S258-S260

中法振業銀行
Chung Fa Chen Yeh Yin Hang

Deutsch-Asiatische Bank
#S261-S303

德華銀行
Te Hua Yin Hang

Bank of East Asia Ltd.
#S303A-S303E

東亞銀行
Tung Ya Yin Hang

Exchange Bank of China
#S303J-S310

中華匯業銀行
Chung Hua Hui Yeh Yin Hang

Hong Kong & Shanghai Banking Corporation
Hong Kong & Shanghai Banking Company, Limited
#S311-S383

英商香港上海匯豐
Hsiang K'ang Shang Hai Hui Li Yin Hang

Industrial and Commercial Bank Ltd.
#S383A-S383I

工商銀行
Kung Shang Yin Hang

Banque Industrielle de Chine
#S384-S400

中法實業銀行
Chung Fa Shih Yeh Yin Hang

International Banking Corporation
#S401-S434

美商花旗銀行
Mei Shang Hua Ch'i Yin Hang

Banque de L'Indochine
#S436-S438

東方匯理銀行
Tung Fang Hui Li Yin Hang

Mercantile Bank of India Limited
#S441-S446

有利銀行
Yu Li Yin Hang

National Bank of China Limited
#S446B

香港中華匯理銀行
Hsiang K'ang Chung Hua Hui Li Yin Hang

National Commercial and Savings Bank, Ltd.
#S447-S456

香港國民商業儲蓄銀行
Hsiang K'ang Kuo Min Shang Yeh Ch'u Hsu Yin Hang

Netherlands Trading Society
#S457-S461

上海和囒銀行
Shang Hai Ho Lan Yin Hang

Oriental Bank Corporation
#S463-S463D

東藩匯理銀行
Tung Fan Hui Lu Yin Hang

Russo-Asiatic Bank, 1910-26
(РУССКО-АЗIАТСКI(БАНКЪ)
#S465-S502

俄商道勝銀行
O Shang Tao Sheng Yin Hang

Russo-Chinese Bank, 1895-10
(Banque Russo-Chinoise, РУССКО- КИТАЙСКIЙ БАНКЪ)
#S503-S554

華俄道勝銀行
Hua O Tao Sheng Yin Hang

Sino-Belgian Bank, 1902-20
(Banque Sino-Belge)
#S555-S574

華比銀行
Hua Pi Yin Hang

Sino-Scandinavian Bank
#S581-S600

華威銀行
Hua Wei Yin Hang

Bank of Taiwan
Bank of Taiwan, Limited
#S601-S634

臺灣銀行
T'ai Wan Yin Hang

Yokohama Specie Bank, Limited
#S635-S757

橫濱正金銀行
Heng Pin Cheng Chin Yin Hang

Foreign Banks

American Oriental Banking Corporation

American Oriental Bank of Shanghai

行銀豐美海上
Shang Hai Mei Feng Yin Hang

Shanghai Branch

1919 Issue

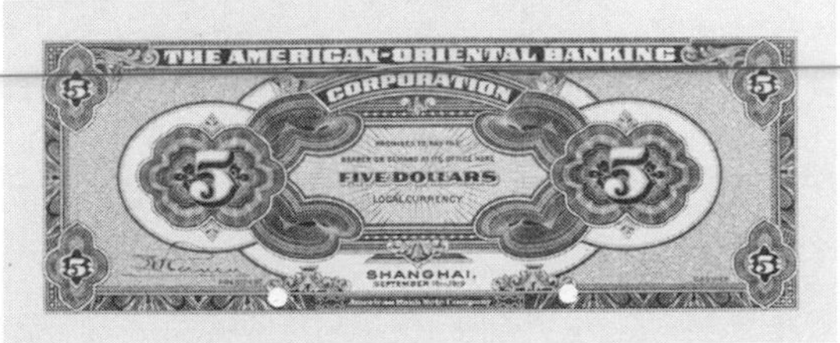

	Good	Fine	XF
S97 5 Dollars 16.9.1919. Dark green on blue and multicolor underprint. Ship, pagoda in background in circle at center. Printer: ABNC. Specimen. *(S/M #S53-0.3).*	—	Unc	850.
S98 10 Dollars 16.9.1919. Dark blue on brown and multicolor underprint. Ship, pagoda in background in circle at center. Printer: ABNC. Specimen. *(S/M #S53-0.3).*	—	Unc	1000.

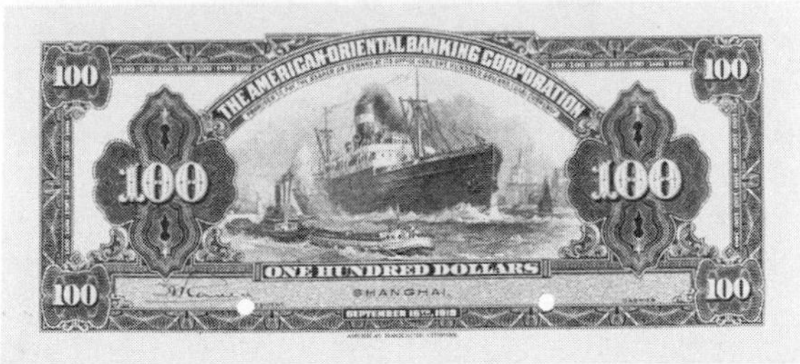

	Good	Fine	XF
S100 100 Dollars 16.9.1919. Dark brown on green and multicolor underprint. Ship, pagoda in background in circle at center. Back: Freighter, tug with barge, sailboats and ferry in harbor. Printer: ABNC. Specimen. *(S/M #S53-0.5).*	—	Unc	2250.

1924 Issue

	Good	Fine	XF
S101 1 Dollar 1924. Ship, pagoda in background in circle at center. Printer: ABNC. *(S/M #S53-1).*	150.	500.	—
S102 5 Dollars 1924. Ship, pagoda in background at center. Printer: ABNC. *(S/M #S53-2).*			
a. Issued note.	300.	750.	—
p. Proof.	—	Unc	500.
s. Specimen.	—	Unc	750.
S103 10 Dollars 1924. Ship, pagoda in background in circle at center. Printer: ABNC. *(S/M #S53-4).* Reported not confirmed.	—	—	—

American Oriental Bank of Tientsin

行銀豐美津天
T'ien Ching Mei Feng Yin Hang

Tientsin Branch

1924 Issue

	Good	Fine	XF
S105 5 Dollars 16.9.1924. Black on multicolor underprint. Back: Orange. Printer: ABNC. *(S/M #T127-).*			
a. Issued note.	—	—	—
p. Proof.	—	Unc	600.
s. Specimen.	—	Unc	750.

American Oriental Bank of Fukien

行銀豐美建福
Fu Chien Mei Feng Yin Hang

Foochow Branch 州福

1922 Dai Fook Issue

	Good	Fine	XF
S106 1 Dollar 16.9.1922. Blue. *(S/M #F26-12).*	—	—	—
S106A 5 Dollars 16.9.1922. Blue. *(S/M #F26-12).*	—	—	—

	Good	Fine	XF
S106B 10 Dollars 16.9.1922. Olive-green. Hand stamped: *SAMPLE. (S/M #F26-13).*	—	—	—

1922 Issue

	Good	Fine	XF
S107 1 Dollar 16.9.1922. Green on multicolor underprint. Ship, pagoda in background in circle at center. Printer: ABNC. *(S/M #F26-1).*			
a. Issued note.	15.00	60.00	125.
p. Proof.	—	Unc	300.
s. Specimen.	—	Unc	200.
S108 5 Dollars 16.9.1922. Brown on multicolor underprint. Ship, pagoda in background in circle at center. Printer: ABNC. *(S/M #F26-2).*	175.	400.	600.

S109 10 Dollars	Good	Fine	XF
6.9.1922. Brown on multicolor underprint. Ship, pagoda in background in circle at center. Printer: ABNC. *(S/M #F26-3).*			
a. Issued note.	225.	500.	1250.
p. Proof.	—	Unc	450.
s. Specimen.	—	Unc	750.

American Oriental Bank of Szechuen

四川美豐銀行

Szu Ch'uan Mei Feng Yin Hang

Chungking Branch 重慶

1922 Issue

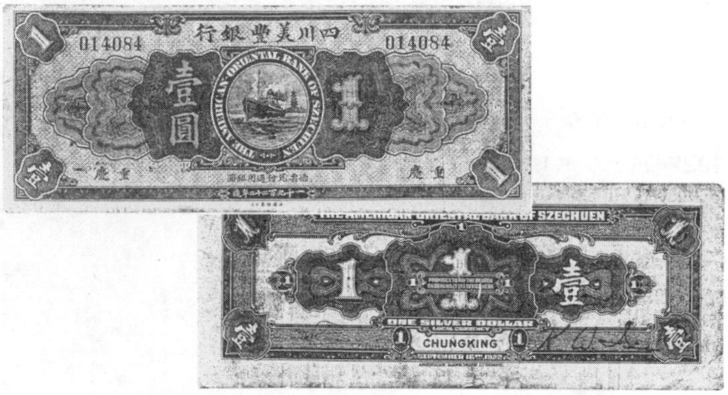

S110 1 Dollar	Good	Fine	XF
16.9.1922. Blue and gray on multicolor underprint. Pagoda in background in circle at center. Back: Brown. Printer: ABNC. *(S/M #S101-1).*			
a. Issued note.	250.	750.	—
p. Proof.	—	Unc	400.
s. Specimen.	—	Unc	650.
S110A 5 Dollars			
16.9.1922. Ship, pagoda in background in circle at center. Printer: ABNC. *(S/M #S101-2).*	400.	1000.	—
S110B 10 Dollars			
16.9.1922. Blue on multicolor underprint. Ship, pagoda in background in circle at center. Back: Orange. Printer: ABNC. *(S/M #S101-3).*			
a. Issued note.	—	—	—
p. Proof.	—	Unc	400.
s. Specimen.	—	Unc	600.

Asia Banking Corporation

美國友華銀行

Mei Kuo Yu Hua Yin Hang

1918 Issue

S111 1 Dollar	Good	Fine	XF
1918. Dark green on multicolor underprint. Camel caravan along Great Wall at center. Back: Bank seal at center. Printer: ABNC.			
a. *CHANGSHA. (S/M #Y35-1a).*	400.	1000.	—
b. *SHANGHAI. (S/M #Y35-1d).*	500.	1200.	—
c. *TIENTSIN. (S/M #Y35-1e).*	500.	1200.	—
s1. *CHANGSHA.* Specimen. *(S/M #Y35-1a).*	—	Unc	400.
s2. *PEKING.* Specimen. *(S/M #Y35-1c).*	—	Unc	400.
s3. *SHANGHAI.* Specimen. *(S/M #Y35-1d).*	—	Unc	400.
s4. *TIENTSIN.* Specimen. *(S/M #Y35-1e).*	—	Unc	400.

S112 5 Dollars	Good	Fine	XF
1918. Dark blue on multicolor underprint. Camel caravan along Great Wall at center. Back: Bank seal at center. Printer: ABNC.			
a. *PEKING. (S/M #Y35-2c).* Rare.	—	—	—
b. *SHANGHAI. (S/M #Y35-2d).* Reported not confirmed.	—	—	—
s1. *HANKOW.* Specimen. *(S/M #Y35-2b).*	—	Unc	450.
s2. *PEKING.* Specimen. *(S/M #Y35-2c).*	—	Unc	450.
s3. *TIENTSIN.* Specimen. *(S/M #Y35-2e).*	—	Unc	450.

S113 10 Dollars	Good	Fine	XF
1918. Olive-brown on multicolor underprint. Camel caravan along Great Wall at center. Back: Bank seal at center. Printer: ABNC.			
a. *PEKING. (S/M #Y35-3c).* Rare.	—	—	—
b. *SHANGHAI. (S/M #Y35-3d).* Reported not confirmed.	—	—	—
c. *TIENTSIN. (S/M #Y35-3e).*	650.	1750.	—
s1. *PEKING.* Specimen. *(S/M #Y35-3c).*	—	Unc	500.
s2. *TIENTSIN.* Specimen. *(S/M #Y35-3e).*	—	Unc	500.

S114 20 Dollars	Good	Fine	XF
1918. Dark brown on multicolor underprint. Camel caravan along Great Wall at center. Back: Bank seal at center. Printer: ABNC.			
p. Without branch name. Proof. *(S/M #Y35-).*	—	Unc	500.
s1. *PEKING.* Specimen. *(S/M #Y35-).*	—	—	—
s2. *SHANGHAI.* Specimen. *(S/M #Y35-).*	—	Unc	500.

S115 50 Dollars	Good	Fine	XF
1918. Black on multicolor underprint. Camel caravan along Great Wall at center. Back: Bank seal at center. Printer: ABNC.			
p. Without branch name. Proof. *(S/M #Y35-).*	—	Unc	500.
s1. *PEKING.* Specimen. *(S/M #Y35-4c).*	—	Unc	600.
s2. *SHANGHAI.* Specimen. *(S/M #Y35-4d).*	—	Unc	500.
s3. *TIENTSIN.* Specimen. *(S/M #Y35-4e).*	—	Unc	600.

S116 100 Dollars	Good	Fine	XF
1918. Orange on multicolor underprint. Camel caravan along Great Wall at center. Back: Bank seal at center.			
a. *SHANGHAI. (S/M #Y35-5d).* Reported not confirmed.	—	—	—
p. Without branch name. Proof. *(S/M #Y35-).*	—	Unc	600.
s1. *PEKING.* Specimen. *(S/M #Y35-5c).*	—	Unc	750.
s2. *TIENTSIN.* Specimen. *(S/M #Y35-5e).*	—	Unc	750.

#S117 *Deleted.* See #S116.

Asiatic Banking Corporation

行銀彰利海上

Shang Hai Li Chang Yin Hang

Shanghai Branch 海上

1800's Issue

S117A 10 Taels	Good	Fine	XF
18xx. Uniface. Bank seal at upper center. Printer: Smith Elder & Co., Engravers, London. Proof. *(S/M #-).*	—	Unc	3000.

S117B 25 Taels	Good	Fine	XF
18xx. Uniface. Bank seal at upper center. Printer: Smith Elder & Co., Engravers, London. Proof. *(S/M #-).*	—	Unc	4000.

Asiatic Commercial Bank, Ltd.

行銀華美

Mei Hua Yin Hang

1926 Issue

S118 1 Dollar	Good	Fine	XF
1926. Green and multicolor. Back: Orange. Printer: CHB. *(S/M #M7-1).*	600.	1000.	—

S120 10 Dollars	Good	Fine	XF
1926. Green and multicolor. Vessel at center. Back: Orange. Printer: CHB. *(S/M #M7-3).*	1250.	2500.	—

Banque Belge Pour L'Etranger, Sociéte Anonyme, 1913-35 (Banque Sino-Belge)

行銀比華

Hua Pi Yin Hang

Hankow Branch 口漢

1921 Issue

S123 1 Dollar = 1 Piastre	Good	Fine	XF
1.7.1921. Ship dockside at center. Back: Arms at center. Printer: ABNC. *(S/M #H185-1c).*	150.	400.	—

S124 5 Dollars = 5 Piastres

	Good	Fine	XF
1.7.1921. Olive-green on multicolor underprint. Ship dockside at center. Back: Arms at center. Printer: ABNC. *(S/M #H185-2c).*	200.	500.	1000.

S125 10 Dollars = 10 Piastres

	Good	Fine	XF
1.7.1921. Deep gray on multicolor underprint. Ship dockside at center. Back: Arms at center. Printer: ABNC. *(S/M #H185-3c).*	250.	600.	1250.

S126 50 Dollars = 50 Piastres

	Good	Fine	XF
1.7.1921. Orange on multicolor underprint. Ship dockside at center. Back: Arms at center. Printer: ABNC. *(S/M #H185-4c).* Rare.	—	—	—

S127 100 Dollars = 100 Piastres

	Good	Fine	XF
1.7.1921. Ship dockside at center. Back: Arms at center. Printer: ABNC. *(S/M #H185-5c).* Reported not confirmed.	—	—	—

PEKING BRANCH 京北

1921 ISSUE

S128 5 Dollars = 5 Piastres

	Good	Fine	XF
1.7.1921. Green on multicolor underprint. Ship dockside at center. Punched hole cancelled with hand stamp: *SPECIMEN.* Back: Arms at center. Printer: ABNC. *(S/M #H185-2d).*	—	—	—

S129 10 Dollars = 10 Piastres

	Good	Fine	XF
1.7.1921. Yellow-orange on multicolor underprint. Ship dockside at center. Punched hole cancelled with hand stamp: *SPECIMEN.* Back: Arms at center. Printer: ABNC. *(S/M #H185-3d).*	—	—	—

S129A 50 Dollars = 50 Piastres

	Good	Fine	XF
1.7.1921. Light blue on multicolor underprint. Ship dockside at center. Punched hole cancelled with hand stamp: *SPECIMEN.* Back: Arms at center. Printer: ABNC. *(S/M #H185-4d).*	—	—	—

SHANGHAI BRANCH 海上

1913 MEXICAN DOLLAR PROVISIONAL ISSUE

	Good	Fine	XF
S130 5 Mexican Dollars 1913 (-old date 15.7.1912). New Bank name overprint at top margin on #S567. Printer: G&D, Leipzig. *(S/M #H185-)*. Rare.	—	—	—

1921 REGULAR ISSUE

	Good	Fine	XF
S135 1 Dollar = 1 Piastre 1.7.1921. Ship dockside at center. Printer: ABNC. *(S/M #H185-1a)*.	300.	650.	1250.
S136 5 Dollars = 5 Piastres 1.7.1921. Red and multicolor. Ship dockside at center. Printer: ABNC. *(S/M #H185 -2a)*.	500.	800.	—

	Good	Fine	XF
S137 10 Dollars = 10 Piastres 1.7.1921. Ship dockside at center. Printer: ABNC. *(S/M #H185-3a)*.	400.	800.	—
S138 50 Dollars = 50 Piastres 1.7.1921. Ship dockside at center. Printer: ABNC. *(S/M #H185-4a)*. Rare.	—	—	—
S139 100 Dollars = 100 Piastres 1.7.1921. Ship dockside at center. Printer: ABNC. *(S/M #H185-5a)*. Rare.	—	—	—

TIENTSIN BRANCH 津天

1912 LOCAL DOLLAR ISSUE

	Good	Fine	XF
S142 5 Dollars 30.4.1913. Brown and blue. Port scene along bottom. Uniface. Printer: G&D, Leipzig. Specimen. *(S/M #H185 -)*.	—	—	—

1921 LOCAL DOLLAR/PIASTRE ISSUE

	Good	Fine	XF
S145 1 Dollar = 1 Piastre 1.7.1921. Ship at center. Printer: ABNC. *(S/M #H185-1b)*.	300.	600.	—
S146 5 Dollars = 5 Piastres 1.7.1921. Blue and multicolor. Ship at center. Printer: ABNC. *(S/M #H185-2b)*.	300.	600.	—
S147 10 Dollars = 10 Piastres 1.7.1921. Ship at center. Printer: ABNC. *(S/M #H185-3b)*.	400.	800.	—
S148 50 Dollars = 50 Piastres 1.7.1921. Orange and multicolor. Ship at center. Printer: ABNC. *(S/M #H185-4b)*.	800.	1750.	—
S149 100 Dollars = 100 Piastres 1.7.1921. Ship at center. Printer: ABNC. *(S/M #H185-5b)*.	1000.	2250.	—

BRITISH AND BELGIAN INDUSTRIAL BANK OF CHINA

英比實業銀行
Ying Pi Shih Yeh Yin Hang

CHANGSHA BRANCH 沙長

1913 ISSUE

	Good	Fine	XF
S150 5 Taels 22.8.1913. Brown on yellow underprint. Back: Blue and orange. Remainder. *(S/M #Y12-1)*.	—	—	—

NOTE: Crude forgeries exist of #S150.

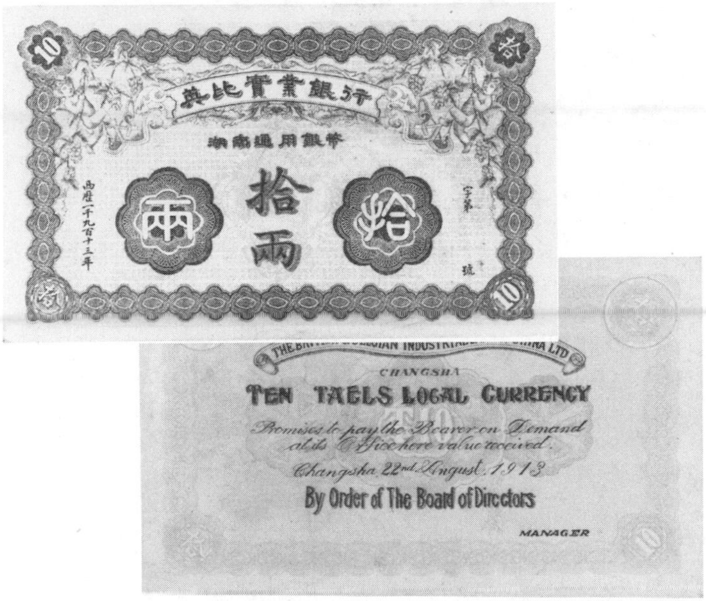

	Good	Fine	XF
S151 10 Taels 22.8.1913. Remainder. *(S/M #Y12-2)*. Rare.	—	—	—

BANK OF CANTON LIMITED

司公限有行銀東廣
Kuang Tung Yin Hang Yu Hsien Kung Szu

HANKOW BRANCH 口漢

1922 ISSUE

	Good	Fine	XF
S152 1 Dollar 1.7.1922. Green on multicolor underprint. Shanghai Bund (riverfront) at center. Back: Blue. View of Hong Kong Island at center. Printer: ABNC. *(S/M #K63-21)*.	600.	1250.	—
S152A 5 Dollars 1.7.1922. Shanghai Bund (riverfront) at center. Back: View of Hong Kong Island at center. Printer: ABNC. Proof. *(S/M #K63-22)*.	—	—	—
S152B 10 Dollars 1.7.1922. Shanghai Bund (riverfront) at center. Back: View of Hong Kong Island at center. Printer: ABNC. Proof. *(S/M #K63-23)*.	—	—	—
S152C 50 Dollars 1.7.1922. Shanghai Bund (riverfront) at center. Back: View of Hong Kong Island at center. Printer: ABNC. Proof. *(S/M #K63-24)*.	—	—	—
S152D 100 Dollars 1.7.1922. Shanghai Bund (riverfront) at center. Back: View of Hong Kong Island at center. Printer: ABNC. Proof. *(S/M #K63-25)*.	—	—	—

Shanghai Branch 海上

1917 Issue

	Good	Fine	XF
S153 1 Dollar 1.7.1917. Shanghai Bund (riverfront) at center. Back: View of Hong Kong Island at center. Printer: ABNC. Proof. *(S/M #K63-1)*.	—	—	—

	Good	Fine	XF
S153A 5 Dollars 1.7.1917. Black on multicolor underprint. Shanghai Bund (riverfront) at center. Back: Green. View of Hong Kong Island at center. Printer: ABNC. *(S/M #K63-2)*.	—	—	—

	Good	Fine	XF
S153B 10 Dollars 1.7.1917. Black on multicolor underprint. Shanghai Bund (riverfront) at center. Back: Blue. View of Hong Kong Island at center. Printer: ABNC. *(S/M #K63-3)*.	—	—	—

	Good	Fine	XF
S153C 50 Dollars 1.7.1917. Black on multicolor underprint. Back brown. *(S/M #K63-4)*.	—	—	—

	Good	Fine	XF
S153D 100 Dollars 1.7.1917. Shanghai Bund (riverfront) at center. Back: View of Hong Kong Island at center. Printer: ABNC. Proof. *(S/M #K63-5)*.	—	—	—
S153E 500 Dollars 1.7.1917. Shanghai Bund (riverfront) at center. Back: View of Hong Kong Island at center. Printer: ABNC. Proof. *(S/M #K63-6)*.	—	—	—

1920 Issue

	Good	Fine	XF
S153F 1 Dollar 1.1.1920. Dark gray on red and green underprint. *(S/M #63-11)*.	500.	1000.	—

Swatow Branch

1922 Issue

	VG	VF	UNC
S153J 1 Dollar 1.7.1922. *(S/M #K63-31)*. Specimen.		—	750.
S153K 5 Dollars 1.7.1922. *(S/M #K63-32)*. Specimen.	—	—	—
S153L 10 Dollars 1.7.1922. *(S/M #K63-33)*.	—	—	—
S153M 50 Dollars 1.7.1922. *(S/M #K63-34)*.	—	—	—
S153N 100 Dollars 1.7.1922. *(S/M #K63-35)*.	—	—	—

Chartered Bank of India, Australia & China

行銀理滙國中山金新度印
Yin Tu Hsin Chin Shan Chung Kuo Hui Li Yin Hang

行銀利加參國中山金新度印
Yin Tu Hsin Chin Shan Chung Kuo Mai Chia Li Yin Hang

Hankow Branch 口漢

1900 Issue

	Good	Fine	XF
S154 1 Dollar 1900-15. Red underprint. Supported royal arms at top center. Printer: WWS. *(S/M #Y11-20a)*. Rare.	—	—	—
S155 5 Dollars 1900-15. Supported royal arms at top center. Printer: WWS. *(S/M #Y11-21a)*. Rare.	—	—	—
S156 10 Dollars 1900-15. Supported royal arms at top center. Printer: WWS. *(S/M #Y11-22a)*. Rare.	—	—	—

1915; 1924 Issue

		Good	Fine	XF
S159	**5 Dollars** 1.3.1924. Green with large red *FIVE* protector. Supported royal arms at center. Printer: W&S. *(S/M #Y11-30a).*	150.	300.	—

		Good	Fine	XF
S160	**10 Dollars** 31.3.1924. Dark red with large blue *TEN* protector. Supported royal arms at center. Back: Dark red and black. Bank at center. Printer: W&S. *(S/M #Y11-31a).*	150.	300.	—

		Good	Fine	XF
S161	**50 Dollars** 1.5.1924. Dark blue. Supported royal arms at center. Printer: W&S. *(S/M #Y11-32a).*	800.	1750.	—
S162	**100 Dollars** 1915-30. Supported royal arms at center. Printer: W&S. *(S/M #Y11-33a).*	1000.	2250.	—

#S165-S174 *Deleted.*

Shanghai Branch 海上

1863; 1874 Issue

		Good	Fine	XF
S175	**1 Dollar** 1863-74. Printer: WWS. *(S/M #Y11-1).* Rare.	—	—	—
S176	**5 Dollars** 1863-74. Gray. Printer: WWS. *(S/M #Y11-2).* Rare.	—	—	—
S177	**10 Dollars** 1863-74. Printer: WWS. *(S/M #Y11-3).* Rare.	—	—	—
S178	**25 Dollars** 1863-74. Printer: WWS. *(S/M #Y11-4).* Rare.	—	—	—

1881; 1885 Issue

		Good	Fine	XF
S181	**1 Dollar** 1.3.1881; 17.11.1892. Printer: WWS. *(S/M #Y11-10).*	400.	1200.	—
S182	**5 Dollars** 1885-99. Printer: WWS. *(S/M #Y11-11).* Rare.	—	—	—
S183	**10 Dollars** 1885-99. Printer: WWS. *(S/M #Y11-12).* Rare.	—	—	—

1911-22 Issue

		Good	Fine	XF
S184	**5 Dollars** 20.1.1914-1.10.1927. Blue on green and red underprint. Supported royal arms at top center. Printer: WWS. *(S/M #Y11-30c).*	150.	350.	1000.

		Good	Fine	XF
S185	**10 Dollars** 29.5.1913; 30.5.1918. Red and violet with large purple *TEN* protector. Supported royal arms at top center. Back: Green. Printer: WWS. *(S/M #Y11-31c).*	150.	350.	1000.
S185A	**10 Dollars** 2.5.1921; 1.9.1922; 2.5.1927; 1.10.1929. Supported royal arms at top center. Back: Red-orange. Printer: WWS. *(S/M #Y11-31c).*	150.	350.	1000.

S186 50 Dollars — Good / Fine / XF

1916; 1921; 1927. Orange and green. Supported royal arms at top center. Back: Green. Printer: WWS. *(S/M #Y11-32c).*

	Good	Fine	XF
a. 26.6.1916. Handstamped date.	1000.	1750.	—
b. 1.6.1921; 2.5.1927. Printed date.	600.	1250.	—

S187 100 Dollars — Good / Fine / XF

30.12.1911; 21.4.1914; 1.9.1922. Blue and red on pink and purple underprint. Supported royal arms at top center. Back: Green. Printer: WWS. *(S/M #Y11-33c).* — Good 1000. Fine 2250. XF —

1930's Issue

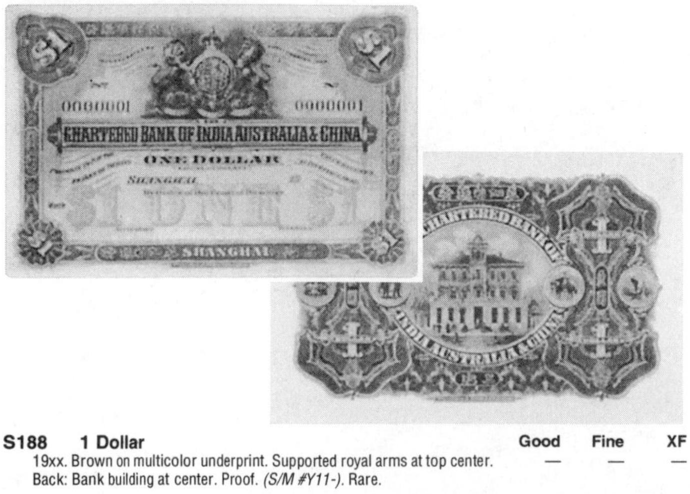

S188 1 Dollar — Good / Fine / XF

19xx. Brown on multicolor underprint. Supported royal arms at top center. Back: Bank building at center. Proof. *(S/M #Y11-).* Rare. — Good — Fine — XF —

1898-1911 Mexican Dollar Issue

S191 1 Mexican Dollar — Good / Fine / XF

1898-1913. Black on pink underprint. Supported royal arms at upper center. Signature varieties. Back: Green. Printer: WWS. *(S/M #Y11-).*

	Good	Fine	XF
a. 15.8.1898; 11.5.1899.	300.	750.	1500.
b. 13.4.1907; 22.5.1911; 22.7.1911; 14.5.1913; 19.6.1914.	225.	500.	1000.

S192 5 Mexican Dollars — Good / Fine / XF

23.11.1900-2.4.1912. Green and red. Supported royal arms at upper center. Signature varieties. Back: Green. Printer: WWS. *(S/M #Y11-).* — Good 750. Fine 1500. XF 3000.

S193 10 Mexican Dollars — Good / Fine / XF

1.6.1897; 1.11.1901; 1.6.1904; 8.4.1907. Red and purple. Supported royal arms at upper center. Signature varieties. Back: Green. Printer: WWS. *(S/M #Y11-).* — Good 750. Fine 1500. XF 3000.

S194 50 Mexican Dollars

30.12.1911. Orange on red underprint with ochre word protector. Supported royal arms at upper center. Signature varieties. Printer: WWS. *(S/M #Y11-).* Rare. — Good — Fine — XF —

S194A 100 Mexican Dollars	Good	Fine	XF
1.11.1901; 30.12.1911. Purple on pink underprint. Supported royal arms at upper center. Signature varieties. Printer: WWS. *(S/M #Y11-).*	—	—	—

1800's Tael Issue

S195 5 Taels	Good	Fine	XF
18xx. Brown. Supported royal arms at upper center. Printer: Batho & Co., London. *(S/M #Y11-).*			
a. Issued note. Rare.	—	—	—
p. Proof.	—	—	—
S195A 10 Taels			
18xx. Blue. Supported royal arms at upper center. Printer: Batho & Co., London. *(S/M #Y11-).*			
a. Issued note. Rare.		—	—
p. Proof.	—	—	—
r. Remainder.	—	—	—
S195B 25 Taels			
18xx. Black. Supported royal arms at upper center. Printer: Batho & Co., London. Proof. *(S/M #Y11-).* Rare.	—	—	—

S195C 50 Taels	Good	Fine	XF
18xx. Gray-green. Supported royal arms at upper center. Printer: Batho & Co., London. Proof. *(S/M #Y11-).* Rare.	—	—	—

1885-1911 Issue

S196 5 Taels	Good	Fine	XF
14.12.1910; 26.1.1916. Supported royal arms at upper center. Printer: WWS. *(S/M #Y11-).*	750.	1500.	—

S197 10 Taels	Good	Fine	XF
1.1.1885; 31.10.1911. Deep blue on light blue with red *TEN.* protector. Supported royal arms at upper center. Back: Green. Printer: WWS. *(S/M #Y11-).*	1000.	2000.	—

S198 50 Taels	Good	Fine	XF
28.10.1911/18xx. Green with purple *FIFTY* protector. Supported royal arms at upper center. Back: Green. Printer: WWS. *(S/M #Y11-).* Rare.	—	—	—
S199 100 Taels			
19xx. Supported royal arms at upper center. Printer: WWS. *(S/M #Y11-).*	—	—	—
S200 500 Taels			
19xx. Supported royal arms at upper center. Printer: WWS. *(S/M #Y11-).*	—	—	—

Tientsin Branch 津天

1917-29 Issues

S200A 1 Dollar	Good	Fine	XF
19xx. Supported royal arms at top center. Bank name repeated in underprint. Back: Brown. Printer: WWS. Proof. *(S/M Y11-).*	—	—	—
S201 5 Dollars			
1.10.1925; 1.7.1926. Green and blue. Supported royal arms at top center. Bank name repeated in underprint. Back: Green. Printer: WWS. *(S/M #Y11-30d).*	400.	800.	—
S202 5 Dollars			
2.5.1927; 1.10.1927. Green and blue. Supported royal arms at top center. Bank name repeated in underprint. Back: Blue. Printer: WWS. *(S/M #Y11-30d).*	300.	750.	—

S202A 10 Dollars

	Good	Fine	XF
19xx. Brown with curved purple word protector. Supported royal arms at top center. Bank name repeated in underprint. Printer: WWS. Unsigned remainder. *(S/M #Y11-).*	—	—	—

S203 10 Dollars

	Good	Fine	XF
1917; 1926; 1928. Purple and red. Supported royal arms at top center. Bank name repeated in underprint. Printer: WWS. *(S/M #Y11-31d).*			
a. Issued note. 1.7.1926; 2.1.1928.	250.	750.	—
r. Remainder perforated: *CANCELLED*. 1.7.1917; 1.7.1926.	—	Unc	1250.

S204 25 Dollars

	Good	Fine	XF
1.8.1917. Olive-green and red-orange on pink underprint. Supported royal arms at top center. Bank name repeated in underprint. Printer: WWS. Remainder perforated: *CANCELLED. (S/M #Y11-).*	—	Unc	1500.

NOTICE

Readers with unlisted dates, signature varieties, etc.,
are invited to submit photocopies or scans of their notes to:
Standard Catalog of World Paper Money,
700 East State St. Iola, WI 54990-0001,
E-Mail: george.cuhaj@fwmedia.com.

S205 50 Dollars

	Good	Fine	XF
1.10.1929. Supported royal arms at top center. Bank name repeated in underprint. Printer: WWS. *(S/M#Y11-).*	—	—	—

S206 100 Dollars

	Good	Fine	XF
1.10.1925. Red and black with large violet numeral protector. Supported royal arms at top center. Bank name repeated in underprint. Printer: WWS. Perforated: *CANCELLED. (S/M #Y11-33d).*	—	—	—

S207 100 Dollars

	Good	Fine	XF
1.10.1929. Red-orange and orange with large violet numeral protector. *(S/M #Y11-33d).*	750.	2250.	—

1920's Issue

S208 5 Dollars

	Good	Fine	XF
19xx. Green and blue. Supported royal arms at upper center above bank monogram in chain link sunburst underprint. Printer: WWS. Proof. *(S/M #Y11-).*	—	Unc	1500.

S209 10 Dollars

	Good	Fine	XF
19xx. Brown and blue. Supported royal arms at upper center above bank monogram in chain link sunburst underprint. Printer: WWS. Proof. *(S/M #Y11-).*	—	Unc	1500.

S210 50 Dollars

	Good	Fine	XF
19xx. Black and green. Supported royal arms at upper center above bank monogram in chain link sunburst underprint. Printer: WWS. Proof. *(S/M#Y11-).*	—	Unc	1750.

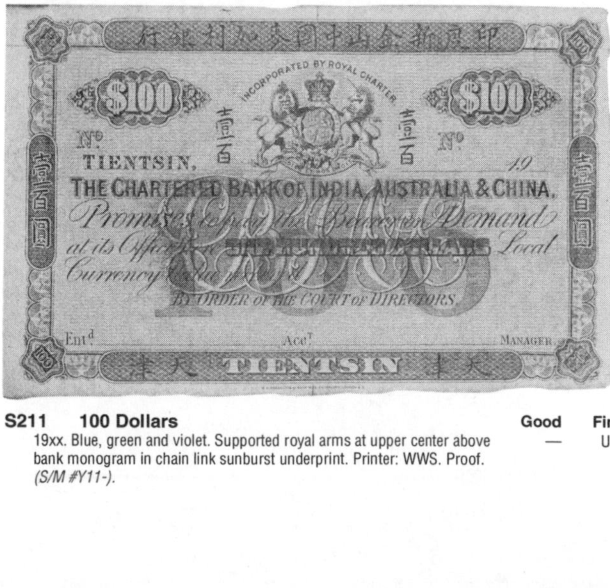

S211 100 Dollars

	Good	Fine	XF
19xx. Blue, green and violet. Supported royal arms at upper center above bank monogram in chain link sunburst underprint. Printer: WWS. Proof. *(S/M #Y11-).*	—	Unc	2000.

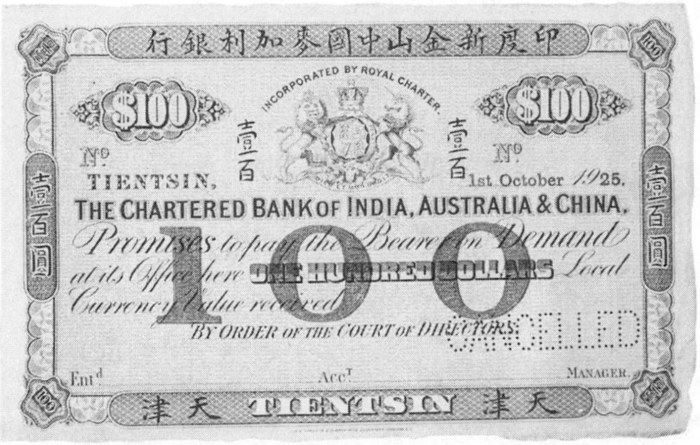

S213 100 Dollars

19xx. Sunburst underprint. Supported royal arms at upper center above bank monogram in chain link sunburst underprint. Printer: WWS. Proof. Perforated: *CANCELLED*. *(S/M #Y11-)*.

Good	Fine	XF
—	Unc	2000.

1930 Issue

S215 5 Dollars

12.6.1930. Purple and light brown. Helmeted Minerva at left, arms at center. Supported royal arms at upper center. Back: Junk at center. Printer: W&S. *(S/M #Y11-)*.

Good	Fine	XF
150.	500.	1000.

ILLUSTRATIONS

Illustrations of bank notes used throughout this catalog are 42% of the actual size.

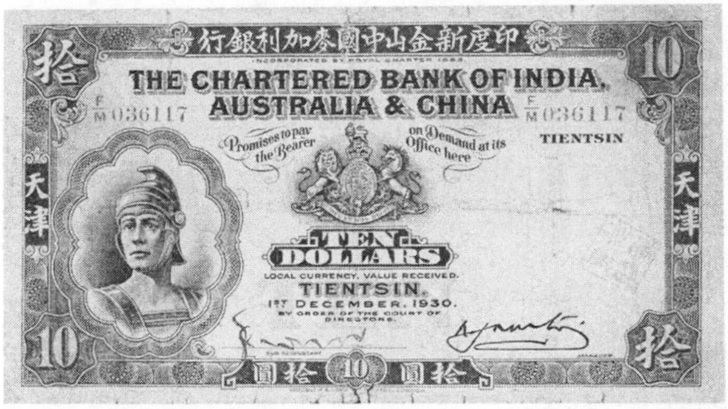

S216 10 Dollars

1.12.1930. Blue and black on yellow underprint. Supported royal arms at upper center.Portrait young helmeted Roman soldier at lower left, supported royal arms at center. Back: Junk at center right. Printer: W&S. *(S/M #Y11-)*.

Good	Fine	XF
250.	600.	1250.

S220 500 Dollars

1.1.1930. Brown and black with blue *500* at lower center. Old helmeted Roman soldier at lower left. Supported royal arms at upper center. Back: Brown. River boat at bottom center. Printer: W&S. Specimen. *(S/M #Y11-)*. Rare.

Good	Fine	XF
—	—	—

1900's "Hongping" Tael Issue

S221 5 Hongping Taels

19xx. Rose and green. Supported royal arms at top center. Bankname repeated in underprint. Printer: WWS. Proof. *(S/M #Y11-)*.

S222 10 Hongping Taels

19xx. Supported royal arms at top center. Bank names repeated in underprint. Printer: WWS. *(S/M #Y11-)*. Reported not confirmed.

	Good	Fine	XF
S221	—	Unc	1500.
S222	—	—	—

Chartered Mercantile Bank of India, London & China

上海有利銀行
Shang Hai Yu Li Yin Hang

Hankow Branch 漢口

1800s Tael Issue

	Good	Fine	XF
S223 5 Taels 18xx. *(S/M #S54-).*	—	—	—
S223A 10 Taels 18xx. *(S/M #S54-).*	—	—	—
S223B 50 Taels 18xx. *(S/M #S54-).*	—	—	—
S223C 100 Taels 18xx. *(S/M #S54-).*	—	—	—

Shanghai Branch 上海

1800s Tael Issue

	Good	Fine	XF
S224 5 Taels 18xx. Supported royal arms at upper center. *(S/M #S54-).*	—	—	—
S224A 10 Taels 18xx. *(S/M #S54-).*	—	—	—
S224B 25 Taels 18xx. *(S/M #S54-).*	—	—	—
S224C 50 Taels 18xx. *(S/M #S54-).*	—	—	—
S224D 100 Taels 18xx. *(S/M #S54-).*	—	—	—

	Good	Fine	XF
S224F 1000 Taels 18xx. Seated Britannia, lion, shield, anchor at upper center. *(S/M #S54-).*	—	—	—

1881 Mexican Dollar Issue

	Good	Fine	XF
S225 1 Mexican Dollar 1.3.1881. Red-orange with large ornate blue word protector. Supported royal arms at upper center. Printer: PB&C. *(S/M #S54-).* Rare.	—	—	—
S225A 5 Mexican Dollars 18xx. *(S/M #S54-).*	—	—	—
S225B 10 Mexican Dollars 18xx. *(S/M #S54-).*	—	—	—
S225C 50 Mexican Dollars 18xx. *(S/M #S54-).*	—	—	—

China Specie Bank, Ltd.

中華國寶銀行
Chung Hua Kuo Pao Yin Hang

1922 Issue

	Good	Fine	XF
S228 1 Dollar Oct. 1922. Dark olive-green on multicolor underprint. Cash coin at center. Back: Black. Steam passenger train, livestock, and windmills at center. Printer: ABNC. Proof. *Shanghai. (S/M #C261.5-1).*	—	—	—

	Good	Fine	XF
S228A 5 Dollars Oct. 1922. Blue on multicolor underprint. 5-cash coins. Back: Red-orange. Steam passenger train, livestock, and windmills at center. Printer: ABNC. Proof. *Shanghai. (S/M #C261.5-2).*	—	—	—

#S228B-S228D 10-cash coins on face.

	Good	Fine	XF
S228B 10 Dollars Oct. 1922. Brown on multicolor underprint. 10-cash coins. Back: Blue. Steam passenger train, livestock, and windmills at center. Printer: ABNC. Proof. *Shanghai. (S/M #C261.5-3).*	—	—	—
S228C 50 Dollars Oct. 1922. Orange on multicolor underprint. 10-cash coins. Back: Green. Steam passenger train, livestock, and windmills at center. Printer: ABNC. Proof. *Shanghai. (S/M #C261.5-4).*	—	—	—
S228D 100 Dollars Oct. 1922. Purple on multicolor underprint. 10-cash coins. Back: Black. Steam passenger train, livestock, and windmills at center. Printer: ABNC. Proof. *Shanghai. (S/M #C261.5-5).*	—	—	—

Chinese American Bank of Commerce

中華懋業銀行
Chung Hua Mou Yeh Yin Hang

1920 First Issue

S230 1 Dollar	Good	Fine	XF
15.7.1920. Black on multicolor underprint. Shield in floral spray at left, Statue of Liberty in circular frame at right. Back: Green. Printer: ABNC.			
a. *HANKOW. (S/M #C271-1a).*	150.	500.	1000.
s1. *PEKING.* Specimen, punched hole cancelled. *(S/M #C271-1c).*	—	—	—
s2. *TIENTSIN.* Specimen, punched hole cancelled. *(S/M #C271-1b).*	—	—	—
s3. Without branch name. Specimen. *(S/M #C271-1).*	—	Unc	650.

S231 5 Dollars	Good	Fine	XF
15.7.1920. Black on multicolor underprint. Shield in floral spray at left, Statue of Liberty in circular frame at right. Back: Green. Printer: ABNC.			
a. *HARBIN. (S/M #C271-3.5b).*	—	—	—
s1. *HARBIN.* Specimen, Punch hole cancelled. *(S/M #C271-3.5b).*	—	—	—
s2. *PEKING.* Specimen, punched hole cancelled. *(S/M #C271-3.5c).*	—	—	—
s3. *TIENTSIN.* Specimen, punched hole cancelled. *(S/M #C271-3f).*	—	—	—
s4. Without branch name. Specimen. *(S/M #C271-3.5).*	—	Unc	750.

S232 10 Dollars	Good	Fine	XF
15.7.1920. Black on multicolor underprint. Shield in floral spray at left, Statue of Liberty in circular frame at center. Back: Green. Printer: ABNC.			
a. *PEKING. (S/M #C271.5c).*	600.	1200.	2500.
b. *SHANGHAI. (S/M #C271-4d).*	600.	1200.	2500.
s1. *PEKING.* Specimen. *(S/M #C271-5c).*	—	—	—
s2. *SHANGHAI.* Specimen. *(S/M #C271-4d)*	—	Unc	750.
s3. *TIENTSIN.* Specimen, punched hole cancelled. *(S/M #C271-5f).*	—	—	—
s4. Without branch name. *(S/M #C271-5).*	—	Unc	750.

S233 50 Dollars	Good	Fine	XF
15.7.1920. Black on multicolor underprint. Without branch name. Shield in floral spray at left, Statue of Liberty in circular frame at right. Back: Green. Printer: ABNC. Specimen. *(S/M #C271-7).*	—	Unc	1000.

S234 100 Dollars	Good	Fine	XF
15.7.1920. Black on multicolor underprint. Without branch name. Shield in floral spray at left, Statue of Liberty in circular frame at center. Back: Green. Printer: ABNC. Specimen. *(S/M #C271-8).*	—	Unc	1250.

1920 Second Issue

S235 1 Dollar	Good	Fine	XF
15.7.1920. Blue on multicolor underprint. Statue of Liberty in oval frame in floral spray at right.			
a. *HANKOW. (S/M #C271-2a).*	500.	1250.	—
b. *PEKING. (S/M #C271-2c).*	400.	1100.	2250.
c. *SHANGHAI. (S/M #C271-2d).*	400.	1100.	2250.
d. Like #S235a but back red. *SHANTUNG. (S/M #C271-2e).*	600.	1250.	2500.
s1. *TIENTSIN.* Specimen, punched hole cancelled. *(S/M #C271-2f).*	—	—	—
s2. Without branch name. Specimen. *(S/M #C271-2).*	—	Unc	750.

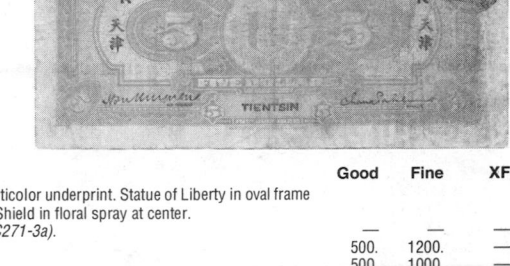

S236 5 Dollars	Good	Fine	XF
15.7.1920. Brown on multicolor underprint. Statue of Liberty in oval frame at center. Back: Orange. Shield in floral spray at center.			
a. *HANKOW. (S/M #C271-3a).*	—	—	—
b. *SHANGHAI.*	500.	1200.	—
c. *TIENTSIN.*	500.	1000.	—
s1. *PEKING.* Specimen. *(S/M #C271-3d).*	—	—	—
s2. *SHANGHAI.* Specimen. *(S/M #C271-3d).*	—	Unc	500.
s3. *TIENTSIN.* Specimen, punched hole cancelled. *(S/M #C271-3f).*	—	—	—
s4. Without branch name. Specimen. *(S/M #C271-3).*	—	—	—

#S238 Deleted. See #S232-236.

Chinese Engineering and Mining Co.

開平礦務有限公司
K'ai P'ing K'uang Wu Yu Hsien Kung Szu

1902 Issue

S246 1 Dollar	Good	Fine	XF
1.3.1902. Black on green and yellow underprint. Navigastion seated with anchor at center with pagoda and junks in background. *Tongshan. (S/M #K1-1).*	125.	300.	—

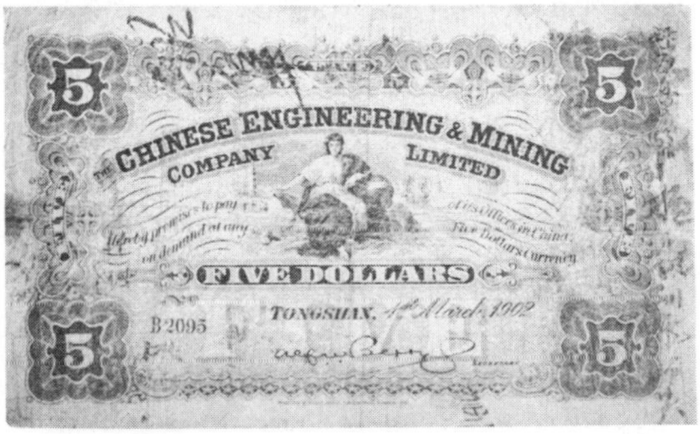

S247 5 Dollars	Good	Fine	XF
1.3.1902. Black on green and yellow underprint. Navigation seated with anchor at center with pagoda and junks in background. *Tongshan. (S/M #K1-2).*	—	—	—

S247A 10 Dollars	Good	Fine	XF
1.3.1902. Black on green and yellow underprint. Navigation seated with anchor at center with pagoda and junks in background. *Tongshan. (S/M #K1-3).*			
a. Issued note.	—	—	—
r. Remainder.	—	—	—

Chinese Italian Banking Corporation

震義銀行
Chen I Yin Hang

1921 Issue

S248 1 Yüan	Good	Fine	XF
1.4.1921. Purple. Inland marina at center. Without signature or serial #. *(S/M #C36-).*			
r1. Unsigned remainder with serial #.	—	—	—
r2. Unsigned remainder without serial #.	—	—	—

	Good	Fine	XF
S249 5 Yüan 1.4.1921. Inland marina at center. Without signature or serial #. *(S/M #C36-)*. Rare.	—	—	—
S250 10 Yüan 1.4.1921. Inland marina at center. Without signature or serial #. *(S/M #C36-)*. Rare.	—	—	—

	VG	VF	UNC
S253 1 Yüan 15.9.1921. Green on multicolor underprint. Bridge at center. Remainder without signature or branch office designation. Back: Orange. Printer: ABNC. *(S/M #C36-1)*.	10.00	25.00	75.00

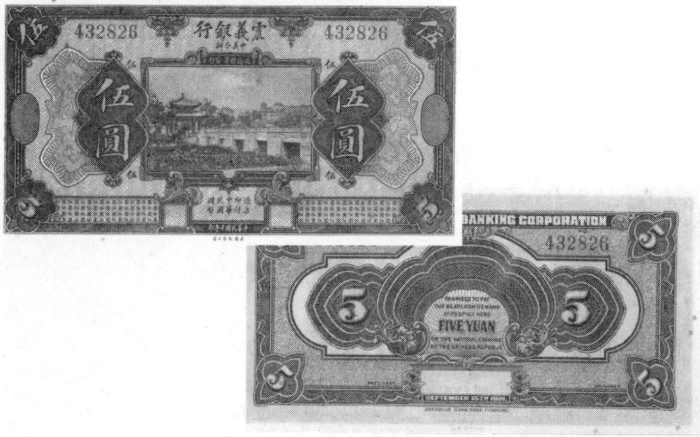

	VG	VF	UNC
S254 5 Yüan 15.9.1921. Brown on multicolor underprint. Bridge at center. Remainder without signature or branch office designation. Back: Dark green. Printer: ABNC. *(S/M #C36-2)*.	10.00	25.00	75.00
S255 10 Yüan 15.9.1921. Blue on multicolor underprint. Bridge at center. Remainder without signature or branch office designation. Back: Red-brown. Printer: ABNC. *(S/M #C36-3)*.	10.00	25.00	75.00
S256 50 Yüan 15.9.1921. Black on multicolor underprint. Bridge at center. Remainder without signature or branch office designation. Back: Purple. Printer: ABNC. *(S/M #C36-4)*.	50.00	125.	350.
S257 100 Yüan 15.9.1921. Violet on multicolor underprint. Bridge at center. Remainder without signature or branch office designation. Printer: ABNC. *(S/M #C36-5)*.	750.	1250.	3000.

Comptoir D'Escompte de Paris

Shang Hai Fa Lan Hsi Yin Hang

1866 Issue

	Good	Fine	XF
S257B 5 Taels 10.2.1866. Liberty seated between French and Colonial shields at upper center.	—	—	—

Credit Commercial Sino-Francais

中法振業銀行
Chung Fa Chen Yeh Yin Hang

Peking Branch 北京

1923 Issue

	Good	Fine	XF
S258 1 Yüan 1.8.1923. Violet on multicolor underprint. Tower at center. Printer: BEPP. *(S/M #C253-1)*.	100.	300.	900.

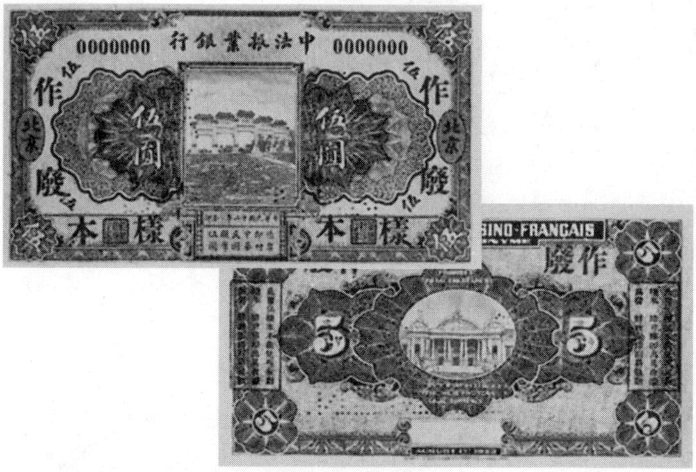

	Good	Fine	XF
S259 5 Yüan 1.8.1923. Blue on multicolor underprint. Gateway at center. Printer: BEPP. *(S/M #C253-2)*.			
a. Issued note.	200.	500.	1000.
s. Back without *PEKING*. Specimen.	—	Unc	600.

	Good	Fine	XF
S260 10 Yüan 1.8.1923. Brown on multicolor underprint. City gate at center. Back: Arch of Triumph at center. Printer: BEPP. *(S/M #C253-3)*.			
a. Issued note.	200.	500.	1200.
s1. Back with *PEKING*. Specimen.	—	Unc	600.
s2. Back without *PEKING*. Specimen.	—	Unc	400.

Deutsch-Asiatische Bank

行銀華德
Te Hua Yin Hang

Hankow Branch 口漢

1907 Dollar Issue

		Good	Fine	XF
S261	**1 Dollar** 1.3.1907. Blue on rose underprint. Eagle arms at upper left, facing Chinese dragons at lower left, Germania with shield and spear at right. Watermark: G&D. Printer: G&D. *(S/M #T101 -1a).*			
	a. Issued note.	1000.	2250.	—
	s. Specimen.	—	Unc	3000.
S262	**5 Dollars** 1.3.1907. Dark green on pale purple underprint. Eagle arms at upper left, facing Chinese dragons at lower left, Germania with shield and spear at right. Watermark: G&D. Printer: G&D. *(S/M #T101-2a).*			
	a. Issued note.	1200.	2750.	—
	s. Specimen.	—	Unc	3000.
S263	**10 Dollars** 1.3.1907. Brown on blue underprint. Eagle arms at upper left, facing Chinese dragons at lower left, Germania with shield and spear at right. Watermark: G&D. Printer: G&D. *(S/M #T101-3a).*			
	a. Issued note.	1200.	2750.	—
	s. Specimen.	—	Unc	3000.
S264	**25 Dollars** 1.3.1907. Green on rose underprint. Eagle arms at upper left, facing Chinese dragons at lower left, Germania with shield and spear at right. Watermark: G&D. Printer: G&D. Specimen. *(S/M #T101-4a).*	—	Unc	3000.
S265	**50 Dollars** 1.3.1907. Purple on gray underprint. Eagle arms at upper left, facing Chinese dragons at lower left, Germania with shield and spear at right. Watermark: G&D. Printer: G&D. Specimen. *(S/M #T101-5a).*	—	Unc	3000.

1907 Tael Issue

		Good	Fine	XF
S268	**1 Tael** 1.3.1907. Gray on yellow underprint. Specimen. *(S/M #T101-10a).*	—	Unc	3000.
S269	**5 Taels** 1.3.1907. Brown on green underprint. Specimen. *(S/M #T101-11a).*	—	Unc	3000.
S270	**10 Taels** 1.3.1907. Blue on light brown underprint. Specimen. *(S/M #T101-12a).*	—	Unc	3000.
S271	**20 Taels** 1.3.1907. Purple on blue-violet underprint. Specimen. *(S/M #T101-13a).*	—	Unc	3000.

Peking Branch 京北

1907; 1914 Dollar Issue

		Good	Fine	XF
S272	**1 Dollar** 1.3.1907. Blue on rose underprint. Eagle arms at upper left, facing Chinese dragons at lower left, Germania with shield and spear at right. Watermark: G&D. Printer: G&D. Specimen. *(S/M #T101 -1b).*	—	Unc	2500.
S273	**5 Dollars** 1.3.1907. Dark green on pale purple underprint. Eagle arms at upper left, facing Chinese dragons at lower left, Germania with shield and spear at right. Watermark: G&D. Printer: G&D. Specimen. *(S/M #T101-2b).*	—	Unc	3000.
S274	**10 Dollars** 1.3.1907. Brown on blue underprint. Eagle arms at upper left, facing Chinese dragons at lower left, Germania with shield and spear at right. Watermark: G&D. Printer: G&D. Specimen. *(S/M #T101-3b).*	—	Unc	3000.
S275	**25 Dollars** 1.3.1907. Green on rose underprint. Eagle arms at upper left, facing Chinese dragons at lower left, Germania with shield and spear at right. Watermark: G&D. Printer: G&D. Specimen. *(S/M #T101-4b).*	—	Unc	3000.
S276	**50 Dollars** 1.3.1907. Purple on gray underprint. Eagle arms at upper left, facing Chinese dragons at lower left, Germania with shield and spear at right. Watermark: G&D. Printer: G&D. Specimen. *(S/M #T101-5b).*	—	Unc	3000.
S277	**100 Dollars** 1.7.1914. Red on violet underprint. Eagle arms at upper left, facing Chinese dragons at lower left, Germania with shield and spear at right. Back: Red and blue. Watermark: G&D. Printer: G&D. Remainder. *(S/M #T101-24).*	—	Unc	2500.

1907 Tael Issue

		Good	Fine	XF
S279	**1 Tael** 1.3.1907. Gray on yellow underprint. Specimen. *(S/M #T101-10b).*	—	Unc	3000.

		Good	Fine	XF
S280	**5 Taels** 1.3.1907. Brown on green underprint. Remainder. *(S/M #T101-11b).*	—	Unc	2000.
S281	**10 Taels** 1.3.1907. Blue on light brown underprint. *(S/M #T101-12b).*	—	Unc	3000.
S282	**20 Taels** 1.3.1907. Purple on violet-blue underprint. *(S/M #T101-13b).*	—	Unc	2750.

Shanghai Branch 海上

1907; 1914 Dollar Issue

		Good	Fine	XF
S283	**1 Dollar** 1.3.1907. Blue on rose underprint. Eagle arms at upper left, facing Chinese dragons at lower left, Germania with shield and spear at right. Watermark: G&D. Printer: G&D. *(S/M #T101 -1c).*			
	a. Issued note.	1200.	3000.	—
	s. Specimen.	—	Unc	3500.
S284	**5 Dollars** 1.3.1907. Dark green on pale purple underprint. Eagle arms at upper left, facing Chinese dragons at lower left, Germania with shield and spear at right. Watermark: G&D. Printer: G&D. *(S/M #T101-2c).*			
	a. Issued note.	1250.	3000.	—
	s. Specimen.	—	Unc	3500.
S285	**10 Dollars** 1.3.1907. Brown on blue underprint. Eagle arms at upper left, facing Chinese dragons at lower left, Germania with shield and spear at right. Watermark: G&D. Printer: G&D. *(S/M #T101-3c).*			
	a. Issued note.	1500.	4000.	—
	s. Specimen.	—	Unc	3500.
S286	**25 Dollars** 1.3.1907. Green on rose underprint. Eagle arms at upper left, facing Chinese dragons at lower left, Germania with shield and spear at right. Watermark: G&D. Printer: G&D. Specimen. *(S/M #T101-4c).*	—	Unc	3500.
S287	**50 Dollars** 1.3.1907. Purple on gray underprint. Eagle arms at upper left, facing Chinese dragons at lower left, Germania with shield and spear at right. Watermark: G&D. Printer: G&D. Specimen. *(S/M #T101-5c).*	—	Unc	3500.

		Good	Fine	XF
S288	**200 Dollars** 1.7.1914. Black on red underprint. Eagle arms at upper left, facing Chinese dragons at lower left, Germania with shield and spear at right. Watermark: G&D. Printer: G&D. Remainder. *(S/M #T101-26b).*	—	Unc	3000.

1907 Tael Issue

		Good	Fine	XF
S289	**1 Tael** 1.3.1907. Gray on yellow underprint. Watermark: G&D. Printer: G&D. Specimen. *(S/M #T101-10c).*	—	Unc	3500.
S290	**5 Taels** 1.3.1907. Brown on green. Specimen. *(S/M #T101-11c).*	—	Unc	3500.
S291	**10 Taels** 1.3.1907. Blue on light blue. Specimen. *(S/M #T101-12c).*	—	Unc	3750.
S292	**20 Taels** 1.3.1907. Purple on blue-violet underprint. Specimen. *(S/M #T101-13c).*	—	Unc	3750.

Tientsin Branch 津天

1907 Dollar Issue

		Good	Fine	XF
S293	**1 Dollar**			
	1.3.1907. Blue on rose underprint. Eagle arms at upper left, facing Chinese dragons at lower left, Germania with shield and spear at right. Watermark: G&D. Printer: G&D. *(S/M #T101 -1d).*			
	a. Issued note.	1000.	2250.	—
	s. Specimen.	—	Unc	2500.
S294	**5 Dollars**			
	1.3.1907. Dark green on pale purple underprint. Eagle arms at upper left, facing Chinese dragons at lower left, Germania with shield and spear at right. Watermark: G&D. Printer: G&D. *(S/M #T101-2d).*			
	a. Issued note.	1000.	2250.	—
	s. Specimen.	—	Unc	2500.

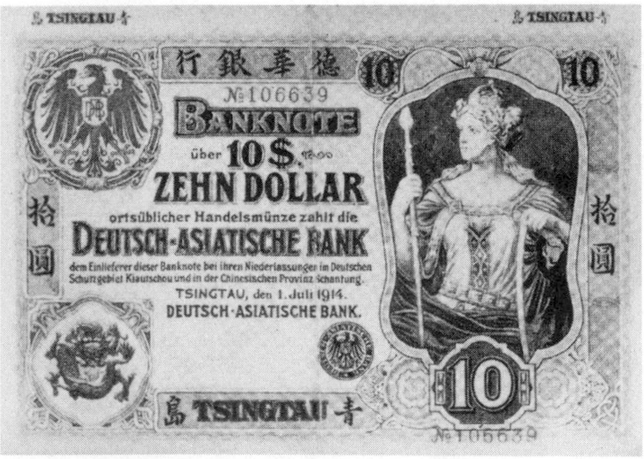

		Good	Fine	XF
S295	**10 Dollars**			
	1.3.1907. Brown on blue underprint. Eagle arms at upper left, facing Chinese dragons at lower left, Germania with shield and spear at right. Watermark: G&D. Printer: G&D. *(S/M #T101-3d).*			
	a. Issued note.	1200.	2750.	—
	s. Specimen.	—	Unc	2500.
S296	**25 Dollars**			
	1.3.1907. Green on rose underprint. Eagle arms at upper left, facing Chinese dragons at lower left, Germania with shield and spear at right. Watermark: G&D. Printer: G&D. *(S/M #T101-4d).*			
	a. Isssued note.	2000.	4000.	—
	s. Specimen.	—	Unc	2500.
S297	**50 Dollars**			
	1.3.1907. Purple on gray underprint. Eagle arms at upper left, facing Chinese dragons at lower left, Germania with shield and spear at right. Watermark: G&D. Printer: G&D. Specimen. *(S/M #T101-5d).*	—	Unc	2500.

1907 Tael Issue

		Good	Fine	XF
S300	**1 Tael**			
	1.3.1907. Gray on yellow underprint. Specimen. *(S/M #T101-10d).*	—	Unc	2500.
S301	**5 Taels**			
	1.3.1907. Brown on green underprint. Specimen. *(S/M #T101-11d).*	—	Unc	2500.
S302	**10 Taels**			
	1.3.1907. Blue on light brown underprint. Specimen. *(S/M #T101-12d).*	—	Unc	2750.
S303	**20 Taels**			
	1.3.1907. Purple on blue-violet underprint. Specimen. *(S/M #T101-13d).*	—	Unc	2750.

Tsingtao Branch

Refer to Kiachou listings in Vol. 2.

Bank of East Asia Ltd.

行銀亞東
Tung Ya Yin Hang

Shanghai Branch 海上

1924 Issue

		Good	Fine	XF
S303A	**1 Dollar**			
	1.1.1924. Brown on orange-brown underprint. Shanghai street scene at center. Back: Brown. East Asia Bank building in Hong Kong at center. Printer: W&S. Specimen. *(S/M #T220.5-11).*	—	Unc	2000.

		Good	Fine	XF
S303B	**5 Dollars**			
	1.1.1924. Orange on light green underprint. Shanghai street scene at center. Back: Orange. East Asia Bank building in Hong Kong at center. Printer: W&S. Specimen. *(S/M #T220.5-12).*	—	Unc	2500.

		Good	Fine	XF
S303C	**10 Dollars**			
	1.1.1924. Dark green with black text on light orange underprint. Shanghai street scene at center. Back: Dark green. East Asia Bank building in Hong Kong at center. Printer: W&S. Specimen. *(S/M #T220.5-13).*	—	Unc	3500.

	Good	Fine	XF
S303D 50 Dollars			
1.1.1924. Red with black text on lilac and light green underprint. Shanghai street scene at center. Back: Red. East Asia Bank building in Hong Kong at center. Printer: W&S. *(S/M #T220.5-14)*.			
s1. 3 punched holes with 1 red overprint: *SPECIMEN* on face and 2 on back.	—	Unc	6000.
s2. 5 punched holes with red and 1 dark blue-black overprint: *SPECIMEN* on face and 2 dark blue-black overprint: *SPECIMEN* on back.	—	Unc	6000.

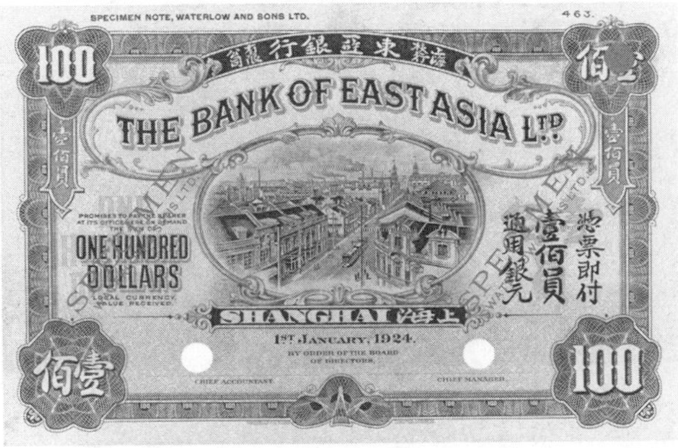

	Good	Fine	XF
S303E 100 Dollars			
1.1.1924. Dark green and black on red underprint. Shanghai street scene at center. Back: Dark green. East Asia Bank building in Hong Kong at center. Printer: W&S. Specimen. *(S/M #T220.5-15)*.	—	Unc	7500.

Exchange Bank of China

中華匯業銀行

Chung Hua Hui Yeh Yin Hang

Peking Branch 北京

1920 Issue

	Good	Fine	XF
S303J 1 Dollar			
1.1.1920. Fortress gate at center. Printer: BEPP. Specimen. *(S/M #C256-1a)*.	—	Unc	500.
S303K 5 Yüan			
1.1.1920. Mauve. Fortress gate at center. Printer: BEPP.	—	—	—
S303L 10 Dollars			
1.1.1920. Brown. Fortress gate at center. Printer: BEPP. Specimen. *(S/M #C256-3a)*.	—	Unc	600.

	Good	Fine	XF
S303M 50 Dollars			
1.1.1920. Fortress gate at center. Printer: BEPP. Specimen. *(S/M #C256-4a)*.	—	Unc	600.
S303N 100 Dollars			
1.1.1920. Fortress gate at center. Printer: BEPP. Specimen. *(S/M #C256-5a)*.	—	Unc	750.

Tientsin Branch 天津

1920 Issue

	VG	VF	UNC
S304 1 Dollar			
1.1.1920. Brown. Gate fortress at center. Printer: BEPP. *(S/M #C256-1b)*.			
a. Issued note.	40.00	100.	250.
b. Overprint: *M; P; P* with *Yu* and *37; T* or *T* with *Ta* and *35*.	40.00	100.	250.
r. Unsigned remainder.	—	Unc	125.

	VG	VF	UNC
S305 5 Dollars			
1.1.1920. Red. Gate fortress at center. Printer: BEPP. *(S/M #C256-2b)*.			
a. Issued note.	50.00	150.	300.
b. Overprint: *M; P; T; T* with *Hsiang* or *34*.	40.00	100.	200.
r. Unsigned remainder.	—	Unc	125.
s. Uniface specimens.	—	Unc	200.

S306 10 Dollars

	VG	VF	UNC
1.1.1920. Blue. Gate fortress at center. Printer: BEPP. *(S/M #C256-3b).*			
a. Issued note.	75.00	200.	400.
b. overprint: *M; P; T; T* with *Hsiang, T* with *Piao; T'ung; 33; 38; TBJ* monogram.	50.00	150.	300.
r. Unsigned remainder.	—	Unc	150.
s. Uniface specimens.	—	Unc	200.

S307 50 Dollars

	Good	Fine	XF
1.1.1920. Violet. Gate fortress at center. Overprint: M P or T. Printer: BEPP. Specimen. *(S/M #C256-4b).*	—	Unc	400.

S308 100 Dollars

	Good	Fine	XF
1.1.1920. Brown. Gate fortress at center. Printer: BEPP. Specimen. *(S/M #C256-5b).*	—	Unc	500.

1928 Issue

S309 10 Cents

	VG	VF	UNC
1.5.1928. Green. Steamship at center. Printer: BEPP. *(S/M #C256-10).*			
a. Overprint: *M.*	20.00	75.00	150.
b. Overprint: *P.*	20.00	75.00	150.
c. Overprint: *T.*	20.00	75.00	150.

S310 20 Cents

	VG	VF	UNC
1.5.1928. Brown. Steamship at center. Printer: BEPP. *(S/M #C256-11).*			
a. Overprint: *M.*	25.00	75.00	150.
b. Overprint: *P.*	25.00	75.00	150.
c. Overprint: *T.*	25.00	75.00	150.
r. Remainder.	—	Unc	150.

Hong Kong & Shanghai Banking Company, Limited

Hong Kong & Shanghai Banking Corp.

香港上海滙理銀行

Hsiang K'ang Shang Hai Hui Li Yin Hang

Amoy Branch 厦門

1886 Issue

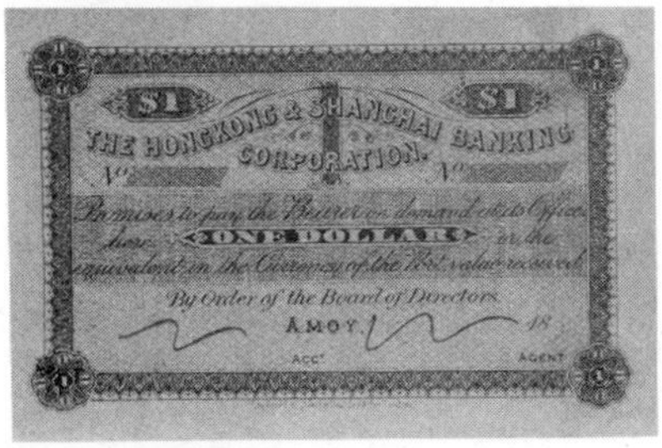

	Good	Fine	XF
S311 1 Dollar 1.1.1886. Brown and blue-green. Printer: BFLT. *(S/M #Y13-20).*	600.	1500.	—
S312 5 Dollars 1886-1904. Printer: BFLT. *(S/M #Y13-21).* Rare.	—	—	—
S313 10 Dollars 1886-1904. Printer: BFLT. *(S/M #Y13-22).* Rare.	—	—	—

Chefoo Branch 烟台

1922 Issue

S315 1 Dollar

	Good	Fine	XF
1.9.1922. Arms at left, bank building at center. Printer: TDLR. *(S/M #Y13-).*			
a. Issued note.	750.	1750.	—
s. Specimen.	—	Unc	750.

	Good	Fine	XF
S316 5 Dollars 1.9.1922. Arms at left, woman making lace at right. Printer: TDLR. *(S/M #Y13-).*			
a. Issued note.	750.	2000.	—
s. Specimen.	—	Unc	900.
S317 10 Dollars 1.9.1922. Blue, green and yellow. Woman making lace at upper left, arms at upper center right. Printer: TDLR. *(S/M #Y13-).*			
a. Issued note.	900.	2250.	—
s. Specimen.	—	Unc	1000.

Foochow Branch

1884 Provisional Issue

#S320-S325 overprint 6 Chinese characters in red on each side of supported bank arms and *BRANCH OFFICE OF THE BANK IN FOOCHOW* on Hong Kong notes. (See Vol. 2).

	Good	Fine	XF
S320 1 Dollar (ca.1884). Printer: Ashby & Co. *(S/M #Y13-)*. Reported not confirmed.	—	—	—

	Good	Fine	XF
S321 5 Dollars (ca.1884). Printer: Ashby & Co. *(S/M #Y13-)*.			
r. Unissed remainder.	—	—	—
S322 10 Dollars (ca.1884). Printer: Ashby & Co. *(S/M #Y13-)*. Reported not confirmed.	—	—	—

	Good	Fine	XF
S323 25 Dollars 1.12.1884. Green and red. Overprint: On Hon KLong #121. Printer: Ashby & Co. *(S/M #Y13-)*. Rare.	—	—	—
S324 50 Dollars 1.1.1884. Overprint: On Hong Kong #127. Printer: Ashby & Co. *(S/M #Y13-)*.	—	—	—
S325 100 Dollars (ca.1884). Printer: Ashby & Co. *(S/M #Y13-)*. Reported not confirmed.	—	—	—

1886-90's Regular Issue

	Good	Fine	XF
S326 1 Dollar 1.6.1886. Purple on red underprint. Back: Queen Victoria. Printer: BWC. *(S/M #Y13-)*.	1250.	2500.	—

	Good	Fine	XF
S331 5 Dollars 188x. Green and red. Arms at top center. Printer: BFLT. Unissued remainder. *(S/M #Y13-)*. Rare.	—	—	—
S333 25 Dollars 189x. Red-orange and green. Back: Red-orange. Arms at center. Printer: BFLT. Remainder, perforated: *CANCELLED*. *(S/M #Y13-)*. Rare.	—	—	—

Hankow Branch 口漢

1921 Issue

	Good	Fine	XF
S336 5 Dollars 1.5.1921. Blue on multicolor underprint. Pagoda at left, rocks in ocean at right. Back: Bank building at center. Printer: BWC. *(S/M #Y13-)*.	1000.	2250.	—
S337 10 Dollars 1.5.1921. Green on multicolor underprint. Pagoda at left, rocks in ocean at right. Back: Blue. Bank building at center. Printer: BWC. *(S/M #Y13-)*.			
a. Issued note. Rare.	—	—	—
s. Specimen.	—	Unc	500.
S338 50 Dollars 1.5.1921. Pagoda at left, rocks in ocean at right. Back: Bank building at center. Printer: BWC. Specimen. *(S/M #Y13-)*.	—	Unc	600.

S339 **100 Dollars**	Good	Fine	XF
1.5.1921. Brown and black on multicolor underprint. Pagoda at left, rocks in ocean at right. Back: Bank building at center. Printer: BWC. Specimen. *(S/M #Y13-).*	—	Unc	750.

1870's Tael Issue

S339A **1 Tael**	Good	Fine	XF
18xx. Black. Printer: BFL. Proof. *(S/M #Y13-).*	—	—	—

S339B **5 Taels**	Good	Fine	XF
18xx. Dark green and green on pink underprint. Printer: BFL. Specimen. *(S/M #Y13-).*	—	—	—

S339C **10 Taels**	Good	Fine	XF
18xx. Dark blue and blue on yellow-orange underprint. Printer: BFL. Specimen. *(S/M #Y13-).*	—	—	—

Peking Branch 京北

1907 Issue

S339D **5 Dollars**	Good	Fine	XF
1.6.1907. Blue and black on orange underprint. Seated cherub with cornucopia at lower left, bridge, landscape at upper center, bank arms at lower right. Printer: W&S. Rare.	—	—	—

1922 Issue

S340 **5 Dollars**	Good	Fine	XF
1.1.1922. Blue and yellow. Seated cherub with cornucopia at lower left, bridge, landscape at upper center, bank arms at lower right. Printer: W&S. *(S/M #Y13-).*			
a. Issued note	800.	2250.	—
s. Specimen.	—	Unc	1000.

S341 **10 Dollars**	Good	Fine	XF
1.1.1922. Olive and black. Man carrying water at lower left, bank arms at upper center, villagers at lower right. Printer: W&S. *(S/M #Y13-).*			
a. Issued note.	1250.	3000.	—
s. Specimen.	—	Unc	1250.

S342 **50 Dollars**	Good	Fine	XF
1.1.1922. Brown and yellow. Landscape at left, bank arms at top center, man plowing with ox at right. Printer: W&S. Specimen. *(S/M #Y13-).*	—	Unc	1750.

SENDING SCANNED IMAGES BY E-MAIL

We have been receiving an ever-increasing flow of scanned images from sources world wide. Unfortunately, many of these scans could not be used due to the type of scan, or simple incompatibility with our systems. We appreciate the effort it takes to produce these images and accuracy they add to the catalog listings.

Here are a few simple instructions to follow when producing these scans. We encourage you to continue sending new images or upgrades to those currently illustrated and please do not hesitate to ask questions about this process.

- Scan all images within a resolution of 300 dpi.
- Size setting should be at 100%
- Please include in the e-mail the actual size of the image in millimeters height x width
- Scan in true 4-color
- Save images as jpeg and name in such a way which clearly indentifies the country of the note and catalog number
- Do not compress files
- Please e-mail with a request to confirm receipt of the attachment
- Please send multiple images on a disc if available
- Please send images to: george.cuhaj@fwmedia.com

		Good	Fine	XF
S343	**100 Dollars** 1.1.1922. Bank arms at upper left, building at bottom center. Printer: W&S. Specimen. *(S/M #Y13-)*.	—	Unc	2500.

SHANGHAI BRANCH 上海

1900-23 DOLLAR LOCAL CURRENCY ISSUES

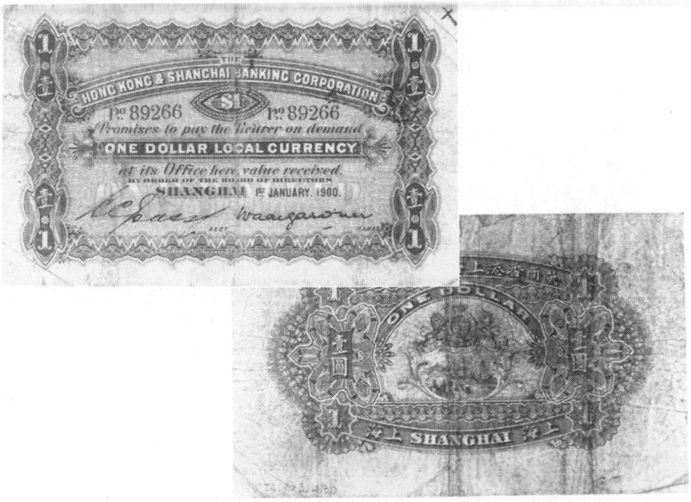

		Good	Fine	XF
S350	**1 Dollar** 1.1.1900. Blue on red underprint. Printer: BWC. *(S/M #Y13-)*.	400.	800.	—

#S351-S353 bank arms at upper or top ctr.

		Good	Fine	XF
S351	**5 Dollars** 1.1.1900; 1.1.1902. Blue and red. *FIVE* in underprint. at center. Bank arms at upper or top center. Printer: BWC. *(S/M #Y13-)*.	350.	900.	2500.

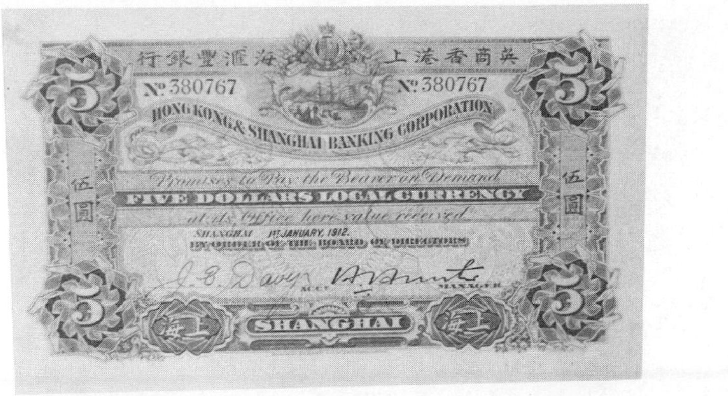

		Good	Fine	XF
S352	**5 Dollars** 1.7.1904-1.1.1912. Blue on yellow underprint. Bank arms at upper or top center. Back: Dark red. Printer: BWC. *(S/M #Y13-31)*.	200.	500.	—
S352A	**5 Dollars** 1.3.1914-24.7.1920. Blue on yellow underprint. Bank arms at upper or top center. Back: Maroon. Printer: BWC. *(S/M #Y13-31)*.	250.	600.	1000.

		Good	Fine	XF
S353	**5 Dollars** 1.3.1923. Blue on multicolor underprint. *FIVE* in underprint. at lower center. Bank arms at upper or top center. Printer: BWC. *(S/M #Y13-40)*.	150.	3000.	—

		Good	Fine	XF
S355	**10 Dollars** 1.1.1900; 1.1.1902. Green and red. Back: Children. Printer: BWC. *(S/M #Y13-)*.	400.	1000.	—

#S356 *Deleted.*

		Good	Fine	XF
S357	**10 Dollars** 1.7.1904-15.6.1913. Green on multicolor underprint. Without *TEN* in underprint. Back: Red. Printer: BWC. *(S/M #Y13-32)*.	125.	600.	1200.
S357A	**10 Dollars** 1.3.1914-24.7.1920. Green on multicolor underprint. Without *TEN* in underprint. Back: Maroon. Printer: BWC. *(S/M #Y13-32)*.	125.	600.	1200.

S358	**10 Dollars**	Good	Fine	XF
	1.9.1923. Light green on multicolor underprint. *TEN* in underprint at lower center. Printer: BWC. *(S/M #Y13-41).*	125.	600.	1200.

#S360-S364 printer: BWC.

S360	**10 Dollars**			
	(ca.1904). Red on multicolor underprint. Back: Red. Printer: BWC. *(S/M #Y13-33).* Reported not confirmed.	—	—	—

S361	**50 Dollars**	Good	Fine	XF
	28.4.1914-24.7.1920. Red on multicolor underprint. Minerva seated with globe and shield at center. Back: Maroon. Printer: BWC. *(S/M #Y13-33).*	600.	1500.	—
S362	**50 Dollars**			
	1.9.1923. *FIFTY* in underprint at lower center. Printer: BWC. Specimen. *(S/M #Y13-42).*	—	Unc	1750.

S363	**100 Dollars**	Good	Fine	XF
	4.12.1911-3.9.1919. Dark brown on multicolor underprint. Back: Red. Printer: BWC. *(S/M #Y13-34).*	600.	1500.	—

S363A	**100 Dollars**	Good	Fine	XF
	24.7.1920. Dark brown on multicolor underprint. Back: Maroon. Printer: BWC. *(S/M #Y13-34).*	600.	1500.	—

S363B	**100 Dollars**	Good	Fine	XF
	19xx. Brown on light green underprint. *ONE HUNDRED* in underprint at lower center. Back: Red-orange. Allegorical woman seated. Printer: BWC. Specimen. *(S/M #Y13-).*	—	Unc	2000.

S364	**100 Dollars**	Good	Fine	XF
	1.9.1923. Smaller outlined *ONE HUNDRED* in underprint at lower center. Printer: BWC. Specimen. *(S/M #Y13-43).*	—	Unc	1750.

1924 Dollar Issue

S365	**5 Dollars**	Good	Fine	XF
	1.1.1924. Black and brown on pale orange and light green underprint. Similar to #S359. Back: Bank building at center. Printer: W&S. *(S/M #Y13-).*			
	a. Issued note.	500.	1000.	—
	s. Specimen.	—	Unc	600.

NOTICE

Readers with unlisted dates, signature varieties, etc., are invited to submit photocopies or scans of their notes to:

Standard Catalog of World Paper Money,
700 East State St. Iola, WI 54990-0001,
E-Mail: george.cuhaj@fwmedia.com.

S365A 10 Dollars

	Good	Fine	XF
1.1.1924. Green on multicolor underprint. *TEN* in underprint at lower center. Back: Bank building at center. *(S/M #Y13-).*	150.	500.	1000.

1884-97 Mexican Dollar First Issue

S366 1 Mexican Dollar

	Good	Fine	XF
1.9.1884; 1.1.1885; 25.4.1892. Blue on red underprint. Bank arms at upper center. Back: Red. Arms at center. Printer: BFLT. *(S/M #Y13-10).*	800.	2500.	—

~~#S366A *Deleted*. See #S369.~~

S367 5 Mexican Dollars

	VG	VF	UNC
1.11.1890-1.3.1897. Brown on light blue underprint. Bank arms at upper center. Back: Arms at center. Printer: BFLT. *(S/M #Y13-11).*	1250.	3000.	—

S368 10 Mexican Dollars

	VG	VF	UNC
29.1.1897; 30.1.1897; 5.2.1897; 1.3.1897. Handwritten or printed. Dark olive-green on red underprint. Back: Red-orange. Printer: BFLT. *(S/M #Y13-12).*	1500.	4000.	—

A WORD ON DATE RANGES

Often date ranges or specific dates are listed. These have been observed or reported by our contributors. If a note is outside the published range, it only means that it is a newly reported date, and not necessarily worthy of a premium value.

S368A 50 Mexican Dollars

	Good	Fine	XF
18xx. Brown-orange on light green underprint. Bank arms at upper center. Back: Brown-orange. Arms at center. Printer: BFLT. Specimen perforated: *CANCELLED. (S/M #Y13-).*	—	Unc	1500.

S368B 100 Mexican Dollars

	Good	Fine	XF
18xx. Without imprint. Bank arms at upper center. Back: Arms at center. Printer: BFLT. Proof. *(S/M #Y13-).*	—	—	—

1892 Mexican Dollar Second Issue

S369 1 Mexican Dollar

	VG	VF	UNC
1.9.1893; 4.1.1897; 1.3.1897; 1.1.1900. Engraved. Blue on red-orange underprint. Back: Red-orange with arms at center. Printer: BFlight. *(S/M #Y13-10).*	1000.	1750.	—

1874; 1875 Tael Issue

		Good	Fine	XF
S372 1 Tael	24.9.1874; 1.6.1888. Gray and blue. Arms at upper center. Back: Purple. Printer: Ashby & Co. *(S/M #Y13-1).*	600.	3000.	—
S373 5 Taels	(ca.1875-99). Printer: Ashby & Co. *(S/M #Y13-2).*	1250.	4000.	—
S374 10 Taels	(ca.1875-99). Printer: Ashby & Co. *(S/M #Y13-3).* Rare.	—	—	—
S375 50 Taels	(ca.1875-99). Printer: Ashby & Co. *(S/M #Y13-4).* Reported not confirmed.	—	—	—
S376 100 Taels	(ca.1875-99). Printer: Ashby & Co. *(S/M #Y13-5).* Reported not confirmed.	—	—	—

Tientsin Branch 津天

1901 Dollar Issue

S378 5 Dollars | Good 750. | Fine 2000. | XF —
1.11.1901. Brown and blue-green. Arms at upper center. Back: Bank arms at center. Printer: BFlight. *(S/M #Y13 -).*

1880's Mexican Dollar Issue

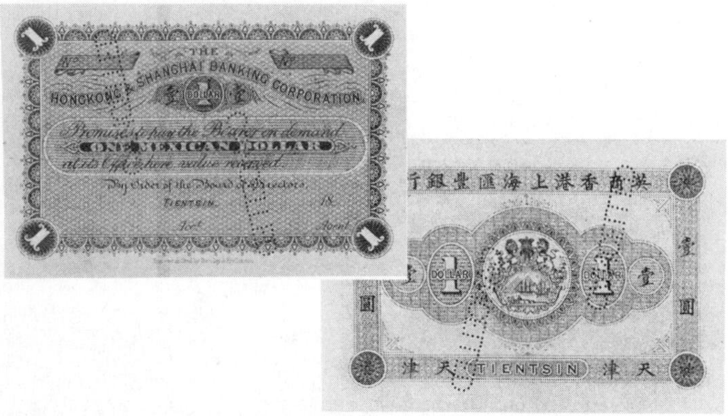

S379 1 Mexican Dollar | Good — | Fine Unc | XF 2000.
18xx. Brown on light blue underprint. Arms at upper center. Back: Red-orange. Bank arms at center. Printer: BFLT. Unsigned remainders perforated: *CANCELLED.*

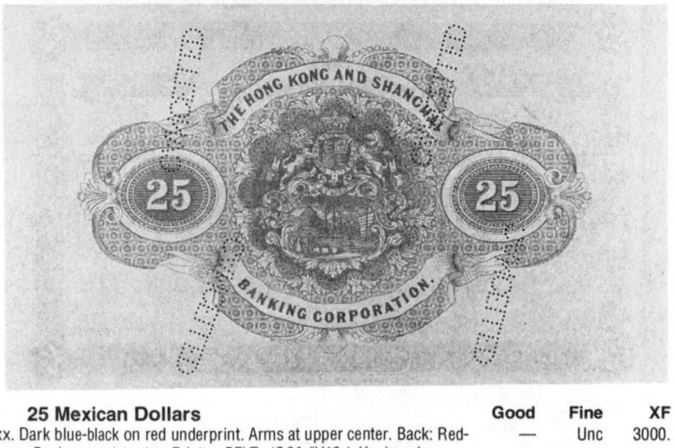

S380 25 Mexican Dollars | Good — | Fine Unc | XF 3000.
18xx. Dark blue-black on red underprint. Arms at upper center. Back: Red-orange. Bank arms at center. Printer: BFLT. *(S/M #Y13-).* Unsigned remainders perforated: *CANCELLED.*

S380A 50 Mexican Dollars | Good — | Fine Unc | XF 5000.
18xx. Red-orange on olive-green underprint. Arms at upper center. Back: Red-orange. Bank arms at center. Printer: BFLT. *(S/M #Y13-).* Unsigned remainders perforated: *CANCELLED.*

1907 Dollar Issue

S381 5 Dollars | Good 900. | Fine 2000. | XF —
1.6.1907. Red and yellow. Arms at left, city gate at upper center, cherub at right. Back: Black and red. Printer: W&S. *(S/M #Y13-).*

1920 Issue

S382 5 Dollars | VG 750. | VF 1500. | UNC —
1.1.1920. Back: Brown and green. *(S/M #Y13-).*

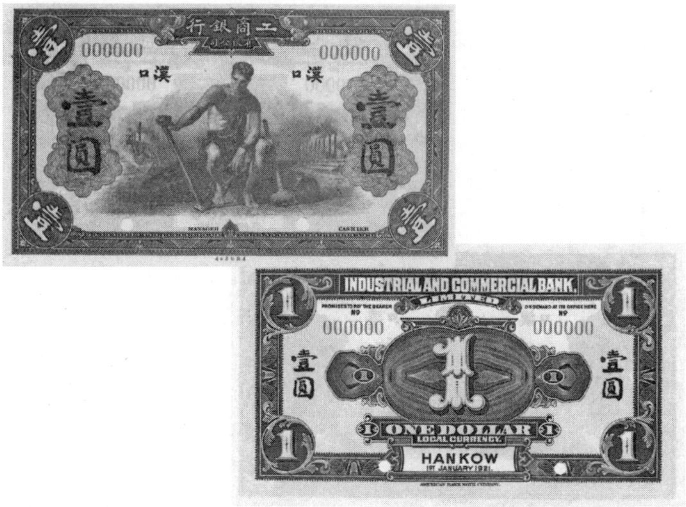

S383 10 Dollars | VG 1000. | VF 2500. | UNC —
1.1.1920. Boy seated with tablet at left, city gate at center, arms at right. *(S/M #Y13-).*

Industrial and Commercial Bank Ltd.

行銀商工
Kung Shang Yin Hang

Hankow Branch 口漢

1921 Issue

S383A 1 Dollar

	Good	Fine	XF
1.1.1921. Dark blue and multicolor. Printer: ABNC. *(S/M #K92-1a).*			
a. Issued note.	—	—	—
s. Specimen.	—	Unc	750.

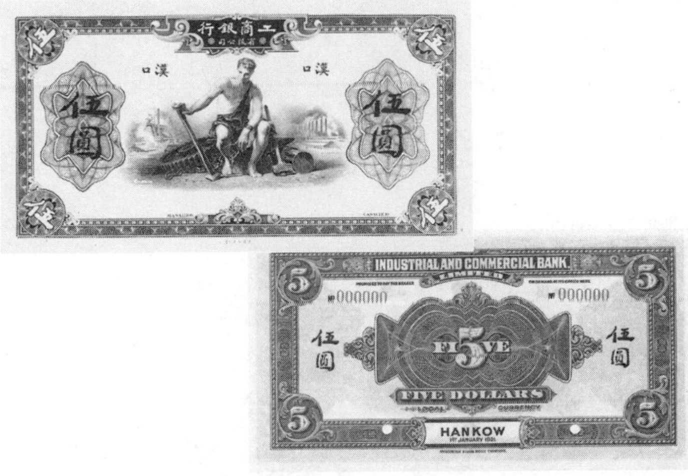

S383B 5 Dollars

	Good	Fine	XF
1.1.1921. Printer: ABNC. Specimen. *(S/M #K92-2a).*	—	Unc	800.

S383C 10 Dollars

	Good	Fine	XF
1.1.1921. Printer: ABNC. Specimen. *(S/M #K92-3a).*	—	Unc	1000.

Shanghai Branch 海上

1921 Issue

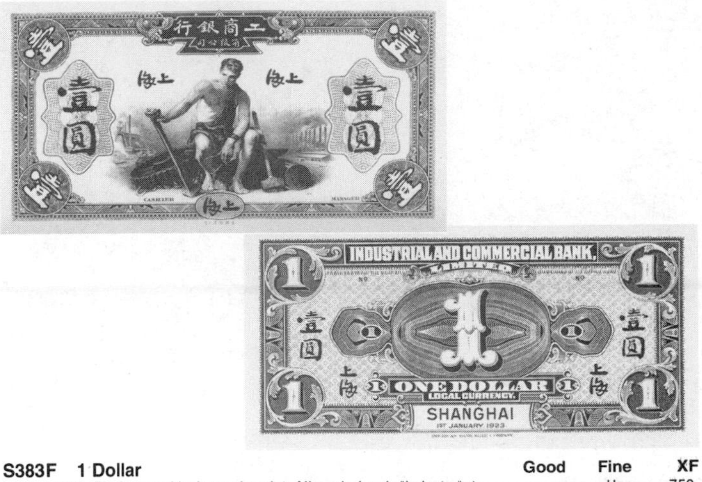

S383F 1 Dollar

	Good	Fine	XF
1.1.1921. Black on multicolor underprint. Allegorical male "Inductry" at center. Printer: ABNC. Specimen. *(S/M #K92-1b).*		Unc	750.

S383G 5 Dollars

	Good	Fine	XF
1.1.1921. Brown on multicolor underprint. Allegorical male "Industry" at center. Printer: ABNC. Specimen. *(S/M #K92-2b).*	—	Unc	800.

S383H 10 Dollars

	Good	Fine	XF
1.1.1921. Blue on multicolor underprint. Allegorical male "Industry" at center. Printer: ABNC. Specimen. *(S/M #K92-3b).*	—	Unc	1000.

		Good	Fine	XF
S383I	**50 Dollars**			
	1.1.1921. Red on multicolor underprint. Allegorical male "Industry" at center. Printer: ABNC. Specimen. *(S/M #K92-4b).*	—	Unc	1200.

Banque Industrielle de Chine

中法實業銀行
Chung Fa Shih Yeh Yin Hang

Canton Branch 廣州

1914 Issue

		Good	Fine	XF
S384	**1 Dollar**			
	1914. Printer: BWC. Specimen perforated: *CANCELLED. (S/M #C254-1-).*	—	Unc	2500.
S384A	**5 Dollars**			
	1914. Printer: BWC. Specimen perforated: *CANCELLED. (S/M #C254-2-).*	—	Unc	3500.
S384C	**50 Dollars**			
	1914. Printer: BWC. Specimen perforated: *CANCELLED. (S/M #C254-4-).*	—	Unc	6000.
S384D	**100 Dollars**			
	1914. Printer: BWC. Specimen perforated: *CANCELLED. (S/M #C254-5-).*	—	Unc	7500.

Hankow Branch 漢口

1920 Issue

		Good	Fine	XF
S385	**1 Dollar**			
	14.7.1920. Dark blue on multicolor underprint. Printer: BWC. *(S/M #C254-1-).*			
	a. Issued note.	—	—	—
	s. Specimen perforated: *CANCELLED.*	—	Unc	1500.
S385A	**5 Dollars**			
	14.7.1920. Dark blue on multicolor underprint. Back: Temple of Heaven at left. Printer: BWC. *(S/M #C254-).*	—	—	—

		VG	VF	UNC
S386	**10 Dollars**			
	14.7.1920. Back: City gate at right. *(S/M #C254-).*	1000.	2250.	—
S386A	**50 Dollars**			
	14.7.1920. Printer: BWC. Specimen perforated: *CANCELLED. (S/M #C254-4-).*	—	Unc	1750.
S386C	**500 Dollars**			
	14.7.1920. Printer: BWC. Specimen perforated: *CANCELLED. (S/M #C254-6-).*	—	Unc	2000.

Mukden Branch 盛京

1920 Issue

		Good	Fine	XF
S388	**50 Dollars**			
	1920. Two chinze at bottom. Printer: BWC. Specimen perforated: *CANCELLED. (S/M #C254-4-).*	—	Unc	2250.
S388B	**100 Dollars**			
	1920. Printer: BWC. Specimen perforated: *CANCELLED. (S/M #C254-5-).*	—	Unc	2500.

Peking Branch 北京

1914-15 Issue

		VG	VF	UNC
S389	**1 Dollar**			
	5.8.1915. Dark blue on multicolor underprint. Chinze at lower left and lower right. Back: City gate at top center. Printer: BWC. *(S/M #C254-1a).*	500.	1250.	—

		VG	VF	UNC
S390	**5 Dollars**			
	5.8.1915. Dark blue on multicolor underprint. Back: Temple of Heaven at left. Printer: BWC. *(S/M #C254-2a).*	600.	1500.	—
S391	**10 Dollars**			
	1914-15. Black on multicolor underprint. Back: City gate at right. Printer: BWC. *(S/M #C254-3a).*			
	a. Issued note.	—	—	—
	s. Specimen.	—	Unc	750.

		Good	Fine	XF
S392	**50 Dollars**			
	1914. Back: Pagoda at left. Printer: BWC. *(S/M #C254-4a)*.			
	a. Issued note.	—	—	—
	r. Remainder perforated: *CANCELLED*.		—	1500.
	s. Specimen.		—	1500.

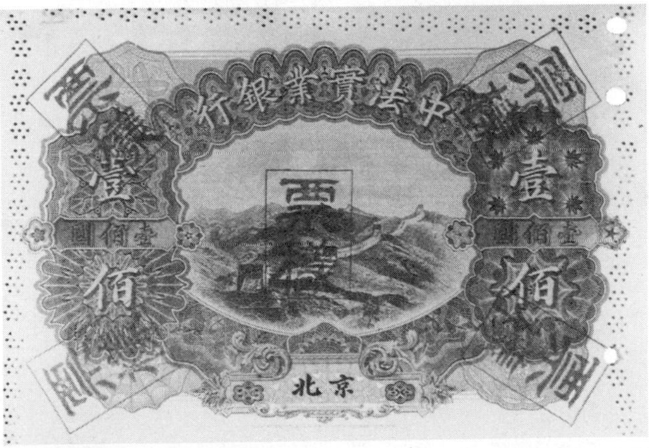

		VG	VF	UNC
S393	**100 Dollars**			
	5.8.1915. Back: Great Wall at center. Printer: BWC. S/M #C254-5a).			
	a. Issued note.		—	1750.
	s. Specimen.	—	—	—
S394	**500 Dollars**			
	1914. Printer: BWC. Specimen. *(S/M #C254-6b)*.		—	1750.

Shanghai Branch 海上

1914-16 Issue

		VG	VF	UNC
S395	**1 Dollar**			
	1.10.1915. Dark blue on multicolor underprint. Chinze at lower left and right. Printer: BWC. *(S/M #C254-1c)*.	600.	1500.	—
S396	**5 Dollars**			
	1.10.1915. Dark blue on multicolor underprint. Printer: BWC. *(S/M #C254-2c)*.			
	a. Issued note.	600.	1500.	—
	s. Specimen perforated: *CANCELLED*.	—	—	1500.

		VG	VF	UNC
S397	**10 Dollars**			
	2.10.1915. Black on multicolor underprint. Two chinze at bottom center. Printer: BWC. *(S/M #C254-3b)*.	1000.	2000.	—
S397A	**50 Dollars**			
	1914. Printer: BWC. Specimen. *(S/M #C254-4c)*.	—	—	1750.
S397B	**100 Dollars**			
	1914. Printer: BWC. Specimen. *(S/M #C254-5c)*.	—	—	2000.
S397C	**500 Dollars**			
	1914. Printer: BWC. Specimen. *(S/M #C254-6c)*.	—	—	2250.

Swatow Branch 頭汕

1914-20 Provisional Issue

#S397D-S397G ovpt: *SWATOW MEXICAN DOLLARS, SWATOW/SHANGHAI*. Ovpt: *Lung Yin* and *Swatow/Shanghai* on back.

		VG	VF	UNC
S397D	**1 Dollar**			
	1.10.1914. Value at left and right. Back: Overprint: *Lung Yin* and *Swatow/Shanghai*. Overprint: *SWATOW MEXICAN DOLLARS, SWATOW / SHANGHAI*. Printer: BWC.			
	a. Issued note.	750.	2000.	—
	s. Specimen. Perforated: *CANCELLED*. *(S/M #C254-1d)*.	—	—	1500.

		Good	Fine	XF
S397E	**5 Dollars** Value at left and right. Back: Temple of Heaven at left. Overprint: *Lung Yin* and *Swatow/Shanghai*. Overprint: *SWATOW MEXICAN DOLLARS, SWATOW / SHANGHAI*. Printer: BWC.	1200.	3250.	—

		VG	VF	UNC
S397F	**10 Dollars** 1.10.1915. Back: Overprint: *Lung Yin* and *Swatow/Shanghai*. Overprint: *SWATOW MEXICAN DOLLARS, SWATOW / SHANGHAI*. Printer: BWC. *(S/M #C254-3d)*.			
	a. Issued note.	750.	2250.	—
	s. Specimen perforated: *CANCELLED*.	—	—	1750.
S397G	**50 Dollars** 1920. Back: Overprint: *Lung Yin* and *Swatow/Shanghai*. Overprint: *SWATOW MEXICAN DOLLARS, SWATOW / SHANGHAI*. Printer: BWC. Specimen perforated: *CANCELLED*. *(S/M #C254-4d)*.	—	—	2250.

Tientsin Branch 津天

1914-15 Issue

		VG	VF	UNC
S398	**1 Dollar** 1914-15. Blue and multicolor. Chinze and value at ends. *(S/M #C254-1b)*.	600.	1250.	—

		VG	VF	UNC
S399	**5 Dollars** 1914. Value at ends. Specimen perforated: *CANCELLED*. *(S/M #C254-2b)*.	—	—	1250.
S400	**10 Dollars** 1914-15. Red. Specimen. *(S/M #C254-3b)*.	—	—	1500.
S400A	**50 Dollars** 1914. Specimen. *(S/M #C254-4b)*.	—	—	1750.
S400B	**100 Dollars** 1914. Specimen. *(S/M #C254-5b)*.	—	—	2000.

		VG	VF	UNC
S400C	**500 Dollars** 1914. Chinze and value at lower left and lower right. Specimen. *(S/M #C254-6b)*.	—	—	3000.

International Banking Corporation

行銀旗花商美
Mei Shang Hua Ch'i Yin Hang

Canton Branch 東廣

1909 Issue

		VG	VF	UNC
S401	**1 Dollar** 1.1.1909. Brown on multicolor underprint. Eagle on building pediment between two globes at center. Back: Eagle on building pediment between two globes at center. Printer: ABNC. *Kuangtung. (S/M #M10-10)*.	750.	2250.	—
S402	**5 Dollars** 1.1.1909. Green on multicolor underprint. Eagle on building pediment between two globes at center. Back: Eagle on building pediment between two globes at center. Printer: ABNC. Specimen. *Kuangtung. (S/M #M10-11)*.	—	—	1750.
S403	**10 Dollars** 1.1.1909. Blue on multicolor underprint. Eagle on building pediment between two globes at center. Back: Eagle on building pediment between two globes at center. Printer: ABNC. Specimen. *Kuangtung. (S/M #M10-12)*.	—	—	1750.
S404	**50 Dollars** 1.1.1909. Gray on multicolor underprint. Eagle on building pediment between two globes at center. Back: Eagle on building pediment between two globes at center. Printer: ABNC. Specimen. *Kuangtung. (S/M #M10-13)*.	—	—	2500.

		VG	VF	UNC
S405	**100 Dollars** 1.1.1909. Violet on multicolor underprint. Eagle on building pediment between two globes at center. Back: Eagle on building pediment between two globes at center. Printer: ABNC. Specimen. *Kuangtung. (S/M #M10-14)*.	—	—	3500.

Hankow Branch 口漢

1918 Issue

		VG	VF	UNC
S406	**1 Dollar** 1.7.1918. Eagle on building pediment between two globes. Back: Eagle on building pediment between two globes. Printer: ABNC. *(S/M #M10-40a)*.	125.	300.	—

		VG	VF	UNC
S407	**5 Dollars**			
	1.7.1918. Olive and multicolor. Eagle on building pediment between two globes. Back: Eagle on building pediment between two globes. Printer: ABNC. *(S/M #M10-41a).*	200.	600.	—
S408	**10 Dollars**			
	1.7.1918. Gray and multicolor. Eagle on building pediment between two globes. Back: Eagle on building pediment between two globes. Printer: ABNC. *(S/M #M10-42a).*	200.	600.	—
S409	**50 Dollars**			
	1.7.1918. Black and multicolor. Eagle on building pediment between two globes. Back: Eagle on building pediment between two globes. Printer: ABNC. *(S/M #M10-43a).*	600.	1500.	—
S410	**100 Dollars**			
	1.7.1918. Eagle on building pediment between two globes. Back: Eagle on building pediment between two globes. Printer: ABNC. *(S/M #M10-44a).*	750.	1750.	—

1919 Issue

		VG	VF	UNC
S411	**1 Dollar**			
	1.7.1919. Eagle on building pediment between two globes at center. Back: Eagle on building pediment between two globes at center. Printer: ABNC. *(S/M #M10-50d).*	100.	225.	—

Peking Branch 京北

1910 Issue

		VG	VF	UNC
S412	**1 Dollar**			
	1.1.1910. Eagle on building pediment between two globes. Back: Eagle on building pediment between two globes. Printer: ABNC. *(S/M #M10-20).*	125.	300.	—
S413	**5 Dollars**			
	1.1.1910. Black on multicolor underprint. Eagle on building pediment between two globes. Back: Eagle on building pediment between two globes. Printer: ABNC. *(S/M #M10-21).*	200.	600.	—

		VG	VF	UNC
S414	**10 Dollars**			
	1.1.1910. Black on multicolor underprint. Eagle on building pediment between two globes. Back: Eagle on building pediment between two globes. Printer: ABNC. *(S/M #M10-22).*	125.	325.	—
S415	**50 Dollars**			
	1.1.1910. Eagle on building pediment between two globes. Back: Eagle on building pediment between two globes. Printer: ABNC. Specimen. *(S/M #M10-23).*		—	1500.
S416	**100 Dollars**			
	1.1.1910. Eagle on building pediment between two globes. Back: Eagle on building pediment between two globes. Printer: ABNC. Specimen. *(S/M #M10-24).*		—	1750.

1917 Issue

		VG	VF	UNC
S416D	**50 Dollars**			
	1.1.1917. Black on multicolor underprint. Eagle on building pediment between two globes at center. Back: Eagle on building pediment between two globes at center. Printer: ABNC. *(S/M #M10-).*	—	—	—

1919 Issue

		VG	VF	UNC
S417	**1 Dollar**			
	1.7.1919. Black on multicolor underprint. Eagle on building pediment between two globes at center. Back: Eagle on building pediment between two globes at center. *(S/M #M10-50c).*	100.	300.	600.

Shanghai Branch 海上

1905 Dollar Issue

		VG	VF	UNC
S418	**1 Dollar**			
	1.1.1905. *(S/M #M10-1).*	75.00	200.	500.
S419	**5 Dollars**			
	1.1.1905. Green on multicolor underprint. *(S/M #M10-2).*			
	a. Issued note.	100.	300.	750.
	p. Proof.	—	—	750.
	s. Specimen.	—	—	600.
S420	**10 Dollars**			
	1.1.1905. Brown on multicolor underprint. *(S/M #M10-3).*			
	a. Issued note.	125.	500.	1250.
	p. Proof.	—	—	1000.
	s. Specimen.	—	—	750.
S421	**50 Dollars**			
	1.1.1905. *(S/M #M10-4).*	—	—	—

		VG	VF	UNC
S422	**100 Dollars**			
	1.1.1905. Blue on multicolor underprint. Eagle on building pediment between two globes at left. Printer: ABNC. *(S/M #M10 -5).*			
	a. Issued note.	—	—	—
	p. Proof.	—	—	2250.
	s. Specimen.	—	—	2000.

1919 Issue

		VG	VF	UNC
S423	**1 Dollar**			
	1.7.1919. Orange on multicolor underprint. Eagle on building pediment between two globes at center. 2 signature varieties. Back: Eagle on building pediment between two globes at center. *(S/M #M10-50a).*			
	a. Issued note.	75.00	150.	300.
	p. Proof.	—	—	250.
	s. Specimen.	—	—	250.

1918 Tael Issue

		VG	VF	UNC
S424	**1 Tael**			
	1.1.1918. Orange on multicolor underprint. Eagle on building pediment between two globes. Back: Eagle on building pediment between two globes. Printer: ABNC. *(S/M #M10-30).*	—	—	—

		VG	VF	UNC
S425	**5 Taels** 1.1.1918. Black and gray on multicolor underprint. Eagle on building pediment between two globes. Back: Eagle on building pediment between two globes. Printer: ABNC. *(S/M #M10-31).*			
	a. Issued note.	—	—	—
	p. Proof.	—	—	2000.
	s. Specimen.	—	—	1500.
S426	**10 Taels** 1.1.1918. Eagle on building pediment between two globes. Back: Eagle on building pediment between two globes. Printer: ABNC. *(S/M #M10-32).*			
	p. Proof.	—	—	2000.
	s. Specimen.	—	—	1250.
S427	**50 Taels** 1.1.1918. Eagle on building pediment between two globes. Back: Eagle on building pediment between two globes. Printer: ABNC. *(S/M #M10-33).*	—	—	—
S428	**100 Taels** 1.1.1918. Black and gray on multicolor underprint. Eagle on building pediment between two globes. Back: Brown. Eagle on building pediment between two globes. Printer: ABNC. *(S/M #M10-34).*			
	p. Proof.	—	—	3000.
	s. Specimen.	—	—	2500.

Tientsin Branch 津天

1918 Issue

		VG	VF	UNC
S429	**1 Dollar** 1.7.1918. Eagle on building pediment between two globes. Back: Eagle on building pediment between two globes. Printer: ABNC. *(S/M #M10-40b).*	100.	200.	400.
S430	**5 Dollars** 1.7.1918. Olive on multicolor underprint. Eagle on building pediment between two globes. Back: Orange. Eagle on building pediment between two globes. Printer: ABNC. *(S/M #M10-41b).*	200.	500.	—

		VG	VF	UNC
S431	**10 Dollars** 1.7.1918. Black and multicolor. Eagle on building pediment between two globes. Back: Eagle on building pediment between two globes. Printer: ABNC. *(S/M #M10-42b).*	200.	500.	—
S432	**50 Dollars** 1.7.1918. Black and multicolor. Eagle on building pediment between two globes. Back: Eagle on building pediment between two globes. Printer: ABNC. *(S/M #M10-43b).*	—	—	—
S433	**100 Dollars** 1.7.1918. Eagle on building pediment between two globes. Back: Eagle on building pediment between two globes. Printer: ABNC. *(S/M #M10-44b).*	—	—	—

1919 Issue

		VG	VF	UNC
S434	**1 Dollar** 1.7.1919. Black and multicolor. Eagle on building pediment between two globes. Back: Eagle on building pediment between two globes. Printer: ABNC. *(S/M #M10-50b).*	100.	200.	400.

Banque de l'Indochine

行銀理滙方東
Tung Fang Hui Li Yin Hang

Canton Shameen Branch 面沙東廣

Decrets des 21.1.1875, 20.2.1888 et 16.5.1900

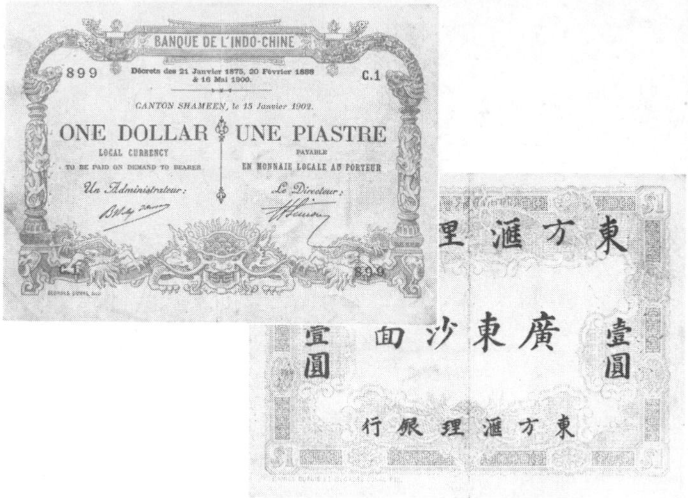

		Good	Fine	XF
S436	**1 Dollar = 1 Piastre** 15.1.1902. Red and green. Dragon border. Back: Black text on yellow. *(S/M #T204-1).* Rare.	—	—	—
S437	**5 Dollars = 5 Piastres** 1902. Red and green. Neptune reclining holding trident at at lower left. Back: Yellow with black text. *(S/M #T204-2).* Rare.	—	—	—
S438	**10 Dollars = 10 Piastres** 1902. Red and green. Elephant columns at left and right. Two reclining women with ox at left, tiger at right at lower border. Back: Yellow with black text. *(S/M #T204-3).* Rare.	—	—	—
S439	**100 Dollars = 100 Piastres** 1901. Red and green. Vasco da Gama at left, sailing ships at lower center, man with paddle at right. Back: Yellow with black text. Specimen. *(S/M #T204-4).* Rare.	—	—	—

Shanghai Branch 海上

Decrets des 21.1.1875, 20.2.1988 et 16.5.1900

		Good	Fine	XF
S440	**1 Dollar = 1 Piastre** 15.1.1902. Red with black text. Dragon border. *(S/M #T204-).* Rare.	—	—	—
S440A	**5 Dollars = 5 Piastres** 1902. Red with black text. Neptune reclining trident at lower left. Back: Orange with black text. *(S/M #T204-).* Rare.	—	—	—
S440B	**10 Dollars = 10 Piastres** 1902. Red with black text. Elephant columns at left and right. Two reclining women with ox at left, tiger at right at lower border. *(S/M #T204-).* Rare.	—	—	—
S440C	**100 Dollars = 100 Piastres** 1901. Red with black text. Vasco da Gama at left, sailing ships at lower center, man with paddle at right. Specimen. *(S/M #T204).* Rare.	—	—	—

Mercantile Bank of India Limited

行銀利有
Yu Li Yin Hang

1916 Issue

		VG	VF	UNC
S441	**1 Dollar** c.1916. Yellow. Back: Green. Portrait Mercury at center. Printer: W&S. *(S/M #S54-1).*	300.	1000.	2250.

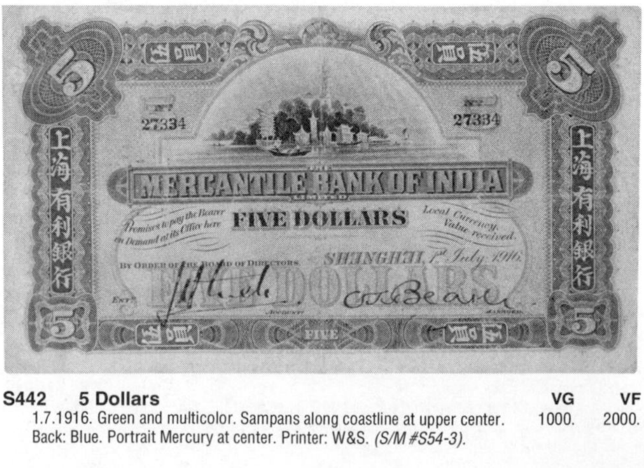

		VG	VF	UNC
S442	**5 Dollars** 1.7.1916. Green and multicolor. Sampans along coastline at upper center. Back: Blue. Portrait Mercury at center. Printer: W&S. *(S/M #S54-3).*	1000.	2000.	—

THE MERCANTILE BANK OF INDIA LIMITED
DOLLARS
10

S443 10 Dollars

1.7.1916. Brown and black on multicolor underprint. Landscape of multiple arch bridge and mountains at center. Back: Brown. Portrait Mercury at center. Printer: W&S. *(S/M #S54-4).*

VG	VF	UNC
1000.	2000.	—

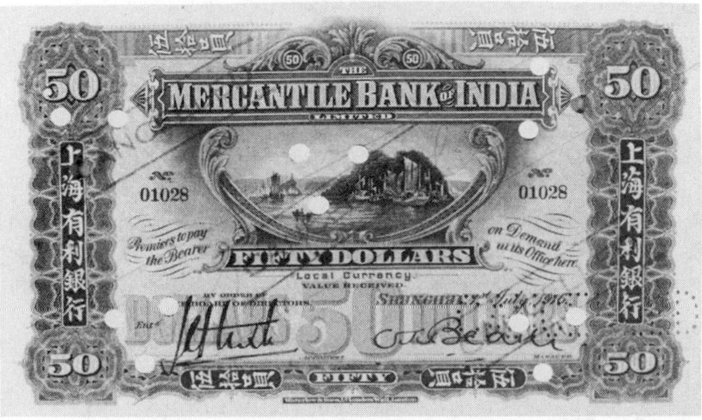

S444 50 Dollars

1.7.1916. Sampans along coastline at center. Back: Portrait Mercury at center. Printer: W&S. *Cancelled. (S/M #S54-5).*

VG	VF	UNC
—	—	3500.

S445 100 Dollars

1.7.1916. Shoreline, mountains in background at center. Back: Portrait Mercury at center. Printer: W&S. *Cancelled. (S/M #S54-6).*

VG	VF	UNC
—	—	4000.

1924 Issue

S446 1 Dollar

1.7.1924. Black and multicolor. Sampan near coastline at center. Back: Orange. Printer: BWC. *(S/M #S54-2).*

VG	VF	UNC
300.	750.	2000.

National Bank of China

行銀理滙華中港香

Hsiang K'ang Chung Hua Hui Li Yin Hang

Amoy Branch 門厦

1890s Issue

S446B 5 Dollars

189x. Red-brown with black text on yellow underprint. Arms at center. Printer: W&S. Remainder. *(S/M #H97-2b).* Rare.

VG	VF	UNC
—	—	—

National Commercial and Savings Bank, Ltd.

行銀蓄儲業商民國港香

Hsiang K'ang Kuo Min Shang Yeh Ch'u Hsu Yin Hang

Hankow Branch 口漢

1924 Issue

S447 1 Dollar

1.12.1924. Blue and multicolor. Great Wall at center. Back: Two globes at center. Printer: ABNC. *(S/M #H100-1b).*

	VG	VF	UNC
a. Issued note.	500.	1000.	2250.
b. Repaired, joined with mismatched serial #.	125.	300.	—
s. Specimen.	—	—	—

	VG	VF	UNC
S448 5 Dollars			
1.12.1924. Blue and multicolor. Great Wall at center. Back: Two globes at center. Printer: ABNC. *(S/M #H100-2b).*			
a. Issued note.	350.	800.	1500.
b. Repaired, joined with mismatched serial #.	125.	300.	—
S449 10 Dollars			
1.12.1924. Brown and multicolor. Great Wall at center. Back: Two globes at center. Printer: ABNC. *(S/M #H100-3b).*			
a. Issued note.	400.	1000.	2250.
b. Repaired, joined with mismatched serial #.	250.	500.	—
S450 50 Dollars			
1.12.1924. Green and multicolor. Great Wall at center. Back: Two globes at center. Printer: ABNC. *(S/M #H100-4b).*			
a. Issued note.	750.	1500.	4000.
b. Repaired, joined with mismatched serial #.	500.	1250.	—
S451 100 Dollars			
1.12.1924. Red and multicolor. Great Wall at center. Back: Two globes at center. Printer: ABNC. *(S/M #H100-5b).*			
a. Issued note.	1000.	2500.	6000.
b. Repaired, joined with mismatched serial #.	600.	1500.	—

Shanghai Branch 海上

1924 Issue

	VG	VF	UNC
S452 1 Dollar			
1.12.1924. Blue and multicolor. Great Wall at center. Back: Two globes at center. Printer: ABNC. *(S/M #H100-1a).*			
a. Issued note.	250.	600.	1250.
b. Repaired, joined with mismatched serial #.	100.	200.	—

	VG	VF	UNC
S453 5 Dollars			
1.12.1924. Blue and multicolor. Great Wall at center. Back: Two globes at center. Printer: ABNC. *(S/M #H100-2a).*			
a. Issued note.	250.	500.	1000.
b. Repaired, joined with mismatched serial #.	100.	200.	—
S454 10 Dollars			
1.12.1924. Brown and multicolor. Great Wall at center. Back: Two globes at center. Printer: ABNC. *(S/M #H100-3a).*			
a. Issued note.	300.	850.	1500.
b. Repaired, joined with mismatched serial #.	125.	350.	—
S455 50 Dollars			
1.12.1924. Green and multicolor. Great Wall at center. Back: Two globes at center. Printer: ABNC. *(S/M #H100-4a).*			
a. Issued note.	600.	1200.	2500.
b. Repaired, joined with mismatched serial #.	300.	750.	—
S456 100 Dollars			
1.12.1924. Red and multicolor. Great Wall at center. Back: Two globes at center. Printer: ABNC. *(S/M #H100-5a).*			
a. Issued note.	800.	1750.	3500.
b. Repaired, joined with mismatched serial #.	400.	800.	—

Netherlands Trading Society

行銀蘭和海上
Shang Hai Ho Lan Yin Hang

1909 Issue

	VG	VF	UNC
S457 1 Dollar			
1.1.1909. Printer: BWC. *(S/M #S51-1).*	—	—	—

	VG	VF	UNC
S458 5 Dollars			
1.1.1909. Blue on violet and green underprint. Back: Medieval oriental warrior at center above arch bridge. Printer: BWC. *(S/M #S51-2).*	1200.	2750.	5500.
S459 10 Dollars			
1.1.1909. Red. Back: Medieval oriental warrior at center above arch bridge. Printer: BWC. *(S/M #S51-3).*	1200.	2750.	5500.

1922 Issue

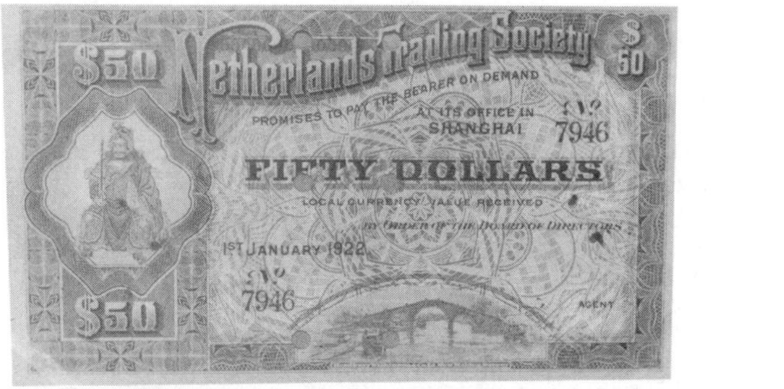

	VG	VF	UNC
S460 50 Dollars			
1.1.1922. Multicolor. Back: Medieval oriental warrior at left. Printer: BWC. *(S/M #S51-).*			
a. Issued note. Rare.	—	—	—
s. Specimen.	—	—	3000.

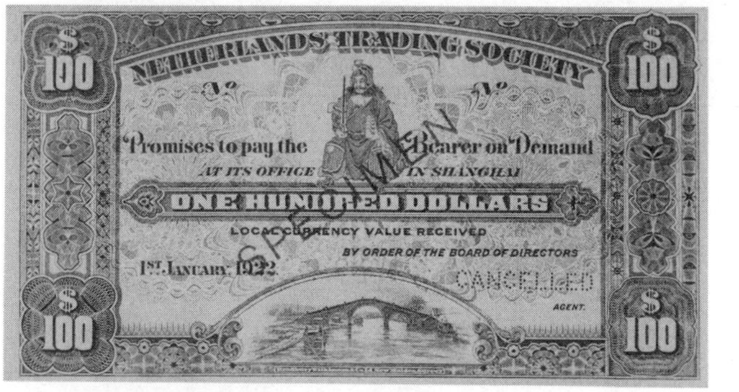

	VG	VF	UNC
S461 100 Dollars			
1.1.1922. Violet, blue and yellow. Medieval warrior at top center, bridge below. Back: Deep brown, tan and blue. Arms at top center with lion at left and right. Printer: BWC. *(S/M #S51-).*			
a. Issued note. Rare.	—	—	—
s. Specimen.	—	—	3500.

Oriental Bank Corporation

行銀理滙藩東
Tung Fan Hui Li Yin Hang

1865 Issue

	Good	Fine	XF
S463 5 Taels			
1865. Supported arms at upper center. Payable in sycee (silver ingots). Specimen. *(S/M #T203-).*	—	—	—

	Good	Fine	XF
S463A 10 Taels 1865. Supported arms at upper center. Payable in sycee (silver ingots). Specimen. *(S/M #T203-).*	—	—	—
S463B 50 Taels 1865. Supported arms at upper center. Payable in sycee (silver ingots). Specimen. *(S/M #T203-).*	—	—	—
S463C 100 Taels 1865. Supported arms at upper center. Payable in sycee (silver ingots). Specimen. *(S/M #T203-).*	—	—	—

	Good	Fine	XF
S463D 500 Taels 2.1.1865. Supported arms at upper center. Payable in sycee (silver ingots). Specimen. *(S/M #T203-).*	—	—	—

Russo-Asiatic Bank, 1900-26

РУССКО-АЗІАТСКІИ БАНКЪ

行銀勝道商俄

O Hua (and Hua O) Tao Sheng Yin Hang

Harbin Branch 賓爾哈

1910 Provisional Issue

#S465-S467 overprint denomination, new bank name and new office of issue on Tientsin Hong Ping Hua Pao Tael issue.

	Good	Fine	XF
S465 50 Dollars ND (1910). Overprint: On #S549. Printer: BWC. *(S/M #O5-).*	1000.	2500.	—
	VG	**VF**	**UNC**
S466 100 Dollars ND (1910). Overprint: On #S553. Printer: BWC. *(S/M #O5-).*	1750.	4000.	12,500.
S467 500 Dollars ND (1910). Overprint: On #S554. Printer: BWC. *(S/M #O5-).* Rare.	—	—	—

1917 Issue

	VG	VF	UNC
S473 50 Kopeks ND (1917). Green and orange. Steam passenger train at left. Printer: ABNC. Issued about 1917 in Harbin for use by the Chinese Eastern Railway. *(S/M #O5-100).*			
a. Issued note.	5.00	15.00	50.00
p. Proof.	—	—	200.
s. Specimen.	—	—	300.
S474 1 Ruble ND (1917). Orange-brown and multicolor. Back: Brown. Steam passenger train at center. Printer: ABNC. Issued about 1917 in Harbin for use by the Chinese Eastern Railway. *(S/M #O5-101).*			
a. Issued note.	5.00	15.00	50.00
p. Proof.	—	—	200.
s. Specimen.	—	—	300.

	VG	VF	UNC
S475 3 Rubles ND (1917). Green and multicolor. Back: Green. Steam passenger train at center. Printer: ABNC. Issued about 1917 in Harbin for use by the Chinese Eastern Railway. *(S/M #O5-102).*			
a. Issued note.	5.00	15.00	50.00
p. Proof.	—	—	200.
s. Specimen.	—	—	300.
S476 10 Rubles ND (1917). Brown-orange and multicolor. Back: Red. Steam passenger train at center. Printer: ABNC. Issued about 1917 in Harbin for use by the Chinese Eastern Railway. *(S/M #O5-103).*			
a. Issue note.	10.00	25.00	75.00
p. Proof.	—	—	225.
s. Specimen.	—	—	350.

#S477 Deleted.

	VG	VF	UNC
S478 100 Rubles ND (1917). Tan, green, and multicolor. Back: Brown. Steam passenger train at center. Printer: ABNC. Issued about 1917 in Harbin for use by the Chinese Eastern Railway. *(S/M #O5-105).*			
a. Issued note.	100.	200.	400.
p. Proof.	—	—	750.
s. Specimen.	—	—	500.

Kuld'sha, Chuguchak & Kashgar Branch

1913-17 Issue

	Good	Fine	XF
S479 1 Gold Fen 1913-17. Blue on brown and green underprint. Dragon at left, center and right. Back: Black on green and brown underprint. Dragon at bottom center. Printer: BWC. *(S/M #05-50).*	500.	1000.	—

	Good	Fine	XF
S480 2 Gold Fen 1913-17. Blue on multicolor underprint. Dragon at left, center and right. Back: Black on light green and pale lilac underprint. Dragon at bottom center. Printer: BWC. *(S/M #05-51).*	500.	1250.	—
S481 10 Gold Fen = 1 Mace 1913-24.7.1918. Blue on multicolor underprint. Dragon at left, center and right. Back: Black on blue and gold underprint. Dragon at bottom center. Printer: BWC. *(S/M #05-52).*			
a. Issued note.	750.	1750.	—
s. Specimen.	—	—	—

	Good	Fine	XF
S482 50 Gold Fen = 5 Mace 1913-17. Dragon at left, center and right. Back: Dragon at bottom center. Printer: BWC. Specimen. *(S/M #05-53).* Rare.	—	—	—
S483 100 Gold Fen = 10 Mace 1913-17. Dragon at left, center and right. Back: Dragon at bottom center. Printer: BWC. Specimen. *(S/M #05-54).* Rare.	—	—	—

NOTE: One gold-based cent (fen) equalled 25 silver-based cents.

Newchwang Branch 壯牛

1910 Provisional Issue

#S484 and S484A overprint new branch office name in English.

	Good	Fine	XF
S484 1 Dollar ND (ca. 1910 -old date 1/14.3.1907). Overprint: On #S517. *(S/M #05-).*	—	—	—

NOTE: No known surviving examples.

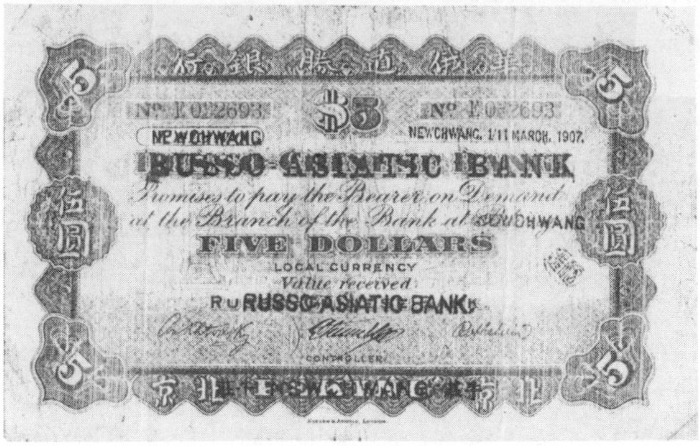

	Good	Fine	XF
S484A 5 Dollars ND (ca.1910 -old date 1/14.3.1907). Overprint: On #S518. *(S/M #05-).* Rare.	—	—	—

NOTE: See also #S517 and S518.

Shanghai Branch 海上

1914 Local Dollar Currency Issue

	Good	Fine	XF
S485 1 Dollar 1/14.1.1914. Black and red. Facing dragons at left and right. With *SHANGHAI 1/14 JANUARY* or 1/14 JULY 1914 hand stamped in lower margin. Back: Bank building at lower center. Printer: BWC. *(S/M #05-80).*	400.	800.	2000.
S486 5 Dollars 1/14.1.1914. Black on multicolor underprint. Facing dragons at left and right. With *SHANGHAI 1/14 JANUARY* or *1/14 JULY 1914* hand stamped in lower margin. Back: Bank building at lower center. Printer: BWC. *(S/M #05-81).*	500.	1000.	—
S487 10 Dollars 1914. Black on multicolor underprint. Facing dragons at left and right. With *SHANGHAI 1/14 JANUARY* or *1/14 JULY 1914* hand stamped in lower margin. Printer: BWC. *(S/M #05-82).*	—	—	—

		Good	Fine	XF
S488	**50 Dollars** 1914. Black on multicolor underprint. Facing dragons at left and right. With *SHANGHAI 1/14 JANUARY* or *1/14 JULY 1914* hand stamped in lower margin. Back: Bank building at lower center. Printer: BWC. *(S/M #O5-83).*	—	—	—
S489	**100 Dollars** 1914. Black on multicolor underprint. Facing dragons at left and right.With *SHANGHAI 1/14 JANUARY* or *1/14 JULY 1914* hand stamped in lower margin. Back: Bank building at lower center. Printer: BWC. *(S/M #O5-84a).*	—	—	—

1914 Mexican Dollar Issue

		Good	Fine	XF
S490	**1 Mexican Dollar** 1914. Printer: ABNC. Specimen. *(S/M #O5-60).*	—	—	—
S491	**5 Mexican Dollars** 1914. Printer: ABNC. Specimen. *(S/M #O5-61).*	—	—	—
S492	**10 Mexican Dollars** 1914. Printer: ABNC. Specimen. *(S/M #O5-62).*	—	—	—

		Good	Fine	XF
S493	**50 Mexican Dollars** 1914. Printer: ABNC. Specimen. *(S/M #O5-63).*	—	—	—
S494	**100 Mexican Dollars** 1914. Printer: ABNC. Specimen. *(S/M #O5-64.*	—	—	—

#S495-S499 *Deleted.*

Tientsin Branch 津天

1917 Issue

		Good	Fine	XF
S502	**10 Dollars** 19.1.1917. Red-orange. Printer: Nissen & Arnold, London. *(S/M #O5-).* Rare.	—	—	—

Russo-Chinese Bank, 1895-1910

РУССКО-КИТАЙСКІЙ БАНКЪ

行銀勝道俄華

Huo O Tao Sheng Yin Hang

1898 Issue

		Good	Fine	XF
S503	**100 Cash** CD1898. Brown. Medieval characters in frame. Blue hand stamped seals. Uniface. *(S/M #O5-3).*	—	—	—
S504	**300 Cash** CD1898. Blue. Medieval characters in frame. Red hand stamped seals. Uniface. *(S/M #O5-5).*	1250.	3000.	—

1898 Kuping Tael Issue

		Good	Fine	XF
S506	**1 Kuping Tael** CD1898. *(S/M #O5-10).*	—	—	—

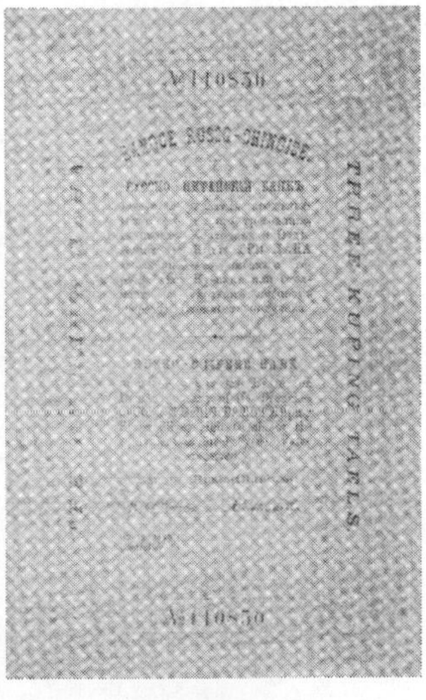

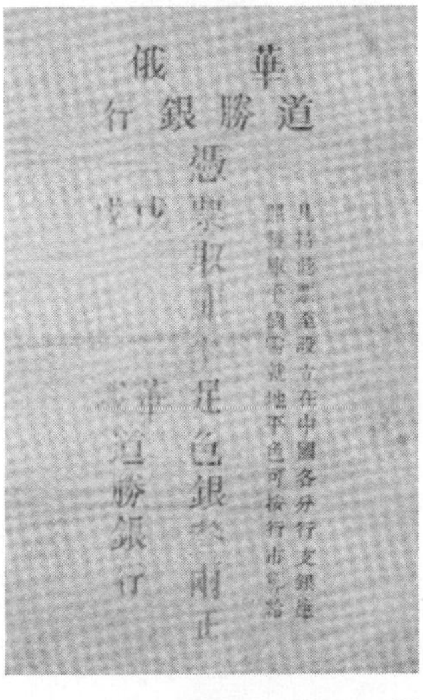

		Good	Fine	XF
S507	**3 Kuping Taels** CD1898. *(S/M #O5-11)*	1000.	2500.	—
S508	**5 Kuping Taels** CD1898. *(S/M #O5-12).*	1000.	2500.	—

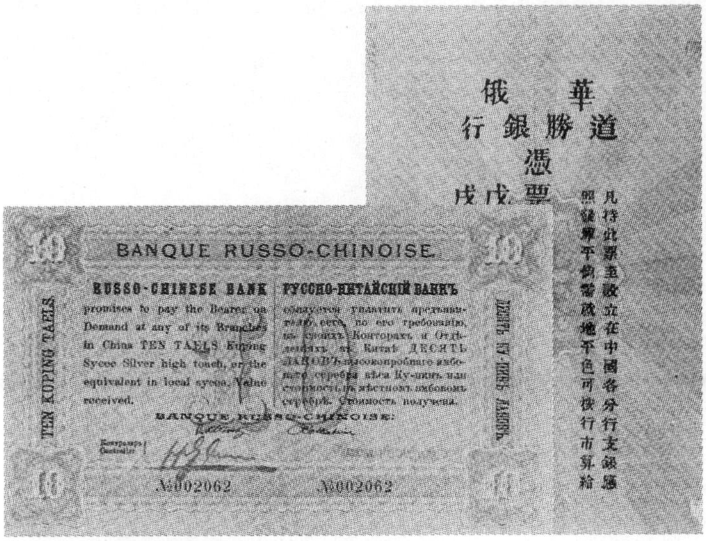

		Good	Fine	XF
S509	**10 Kuping Taels** CD1898. *(S/M #O5-13).* Rare.	—	—	—
S510	**50 Kuping Taels** CD1898. *(S/M #O5-14).* Rare.	—	—	—
S511	**100 Kuping Taels** CD1898. *(S/M #O5-15).* Rare.	—	—	—

Hankow Branch 口漢

1914 Issue

		Good	Fine	XF
S512	**1 Dollar** 6.6.1914. Overprint: On #S546. *(S/M #O5-).* Rare.	—	—	—

Newchwang Branch 莊牛

1907 Provisional Issue

#S517 and S518 overprint new branch office name in English.

	Good	Fine	XF
S517 1 Dollar			
1/14.3.1907. Overprint: On #S522. *(S/M #05-)*. Rare.	—	—	—
S518 5 Dollars			
1/14.3.1907. Overprint: On #S523. *(S/M #05-)*. Rare.	—	—	—

NOTE: See also #S484 and S484A.

Peking Branch 京北

1903-14 Issue

	Good	Fine	XF
S522 1 Dollar			
(ca. 1903-14). Printer: Nissen & Arnold, London. *(S/M #05-)*.	600.	—	—
S523 5 Dollars			
1/14.9.1903. Orange on yellow underprint. Printer: Nissen & Arnold, London. *(S/M #05-)*. Rare.	—	—	—
S524 10 Dollars			
1/14.9.1903. Orange on green underprint. Printer: Nissen & Arnold, London. Rare.	—	—	—

1907 Chingping Tsuyin Tael Issue

	Good	Fine	XF
S531 1 Tael			
Yr. 33 (1907). Blue, brown and multicolor. Printer: BWC. *(S/M #05-20)*.			
a. Issued note.	1500.	4500.	—
s. Specimen.	—	Unc	2000.
S532 5 Taels			
Yr. 33 (1907). Printer: BWC. Specimen. *(S/M #05-21)*. Rare.	—	—	—
S533 10 Taels			
Yr. 33 (1907). Printer: BWC. Specimen. *(S/M #05-22)*. Rare.	—	—	—

	Good	Fine	XF
S534 50 Taels			
Yr. 33 (1907). Printer: BWC. Specimen. *(S/M #05-23)*. Rare.	—	—	—
S535 100 Taels			
Yr. 33 (1907). Printer: BWC. Specimen. *(S/M #05-24)*. Rare.	—	—	—

Shanghai Branch 海上

1901; 1902 Mexican Dollar Issue

#S536-S540 specimen ovpt. or perforated: ОБРАЗЕЦЪ.

	Good	Fine	XF
S536 1 Mexican Dollar			
1/14.3.1902; 1/14.8.1901. Brown and multicolor. *(S/M #05-1)*.			
a. Issued note.	600.	1750.	—
s. Specimen: overprint or perforated: ОБРАЗЕЦЪ.	—	Unc	1250.
S537 5 Mexican Dollars			
(ca. 1901). Grayish green on multicolor underprint. *(S/M #05-)*			
a. Issued note.	800.	2250.	—
s. Specimen: overprint or perforated: ОБРАЗЕЦЪ.	—	Unc	1250.
S538 10 Mexican Dollars			
(ca. 1901). Specimen. *(S/M #05)*.			
s. Specimen: overprint or perforated: ОБРАЗЕЦЪ.	—	Unc	1250.
S539 50 Mexican Dollars			
(ca. 1901). Specimen. *(S/M #05-)*.			
s. Specimen: overprint or perforated: ОБРАЗЕЦЪ.	—	Unc	1250.

	Good	Fine	XF
S540 100 Mexican Dollars			
(ca. 1901). Specimen. *(S/M #05-)*.			
s. Specimen: overprint or perforated: ОБРАЗЕЦЪ.	—	Unc	1250.

1909 Issue

		Good	Fine	XF
S541	**1 Mexican Dollar** 14.8.1909. Black, pink and blue. Facing dragons at top left and right. Back: Bank building at bottom center. Printer: BWC. *(S/M #O5-40).*	600.	1800.	—
S542	**5 Mexican Dollars** 1909. Brown and multicolor. Facing dragons at left and right. Back: Facing dragons at left and right, bank building at bottom center. Printer: BWC.			
	a. Issued note.	750.	2000.	—
	s. Specimen perforated: *SPECIMEN. (S/M #O5-41).*	—	Unc	2250.
S543	**10 Mexican Dollars** 1909. Violet and multicolor. Facing dragons at left and right. Back: Facing dragons at left and right, bank building at bottom center. Printer: BWC. Specimen. Perforated *SPECIMEN. (S/M #O5-42).*	—	Unc	2250.

		Good	Fine	XF
S544	**50 Mexican Dollars** 1909. Brown and multicolor. Facing dragons at top left and right. Back: Bank building at bottom center. Printer: BWC. Specimen. Perforated *SPECIMEN. (S/M #O5-43).*	—	Unc	3000.
S545	**100 Mexican Dollars** 1909. Green and multicolor. Facing dragons at left and right. Back: Facing dragons at left and right, bank building at bottom center. Printer: BWC. Specimen. Perforated *SPECIMEN. (S/M #O5-44).*	—	Unc	4000.

Tientsin Branch 津天

1907 Dollar Issue

		Good	Fine	XF
S546	**1 Dollar** (ca. 1907-14). Printer: Nissen & Arnold, London. *(S/M #O5-).*	—	—	—
S548	**10 Dollars** 1/14.9.1903. Red on green underprint. Rare.	—	—	—

1907 Hong Ping Hua Pao Tael Issue

		VG	VF	UNC
S549	**1 Tael** Yr. 33 (1907). Red and multicolor. Dragon at center, facing dragons at left and right. Back: Bank building at center. Printer: BWC. *(S/M #O5-30).*			
	a. Issued note.	1000.	2000.	—
	s. Specimen.		—	2000.
S550	**5 Taels** Yr. 33 (1907). Green. Dragon at center, facing dragons at left and right. Back: Bank building at center. Printer: BWC. Specimen. *(S/M #O5-31).*		—	2500.
S551	**10 Taels** Yr. 33 (1907). Dragon at center, facing dragons at left and right. Back: Bank building at center. Printer: BWC. Specimen. *(S/M #O5-32).*		—	3000.
S552	**50 Taels** Yr. 33 (1907). Dragon at center, facing dragons at left and right. Back: Bank building at center. Printer: BWC. Specimen. *(S/M #O5-33).*		—	4000.

		VG	VF	UNC
S553	**100 Taels** Yr. 33 (1907). Dragon at center, facing dragons at left and right. Back: Bank building at center. Printer: BWC. Specimen. *(S/M #O5-34).*		—	5000.
S554	**500 Taels** Yr. 33 (1907). Specimen. Rare.	—	—	—

Banque Sino-Belge, 1902-20

行銀比華
Hua Pi Yin Hang

Hankow Branch 口漢

1902-08 Issue

		Good	Fine	XF
S555	**1 Dollar** 1902-08. *(S/M #H190-1c).* Reported not confirmed.	—	—	—
S556	**5 Dollars** 1902-08. Orange and green. *(S/M #H190-2c).* Rare.	—	—	—
S557	**10 Dollars** 1902-08. Blue and rose. *(S/M #H190-3c).* Rare.	—	—	—
S558	**50 Dollars** 1902-08. *(S/M #H190-4c).* Reported not confirmed.	—	—	—

Shanghai Branch 海上

1902-08 Issue

		Good	Fine	XF
S561	**1 Dollar** 1902-08. *(S/M #H190-1a).* Rare.	—	—	—
S562	**5 Dollars** 1902-08. Orange and green. *(S/M #H190-2a).* Rare.	—	—	—
S563	**10 Dollars** 1902-08. Blue and rose. *(S/M #H190-3a).* Rare.	—	—	—
S564	**50 Dollars** 1902-08. *(S/M #H190-4a).*	2000.	—	—

1908-12 Mexican Dollar Issue

		Good	Fine	XF
S567	**5 Mexican Dollars** 1.7.1908; 15.7.1912. Red and green. Printer: GD. *(S/M #H190-).*	2500.	6000.	—

NOTE: The overprint: *BANK BELGE POUR L'ETRANGER* in upper right margin was applied separately at a later date to #S567. Refer to #S130.

		Good	Fine	XF
S568	**10 Mexican Dollars** 1.7.1908; 15.7.1912. Printer: GD. *(S/M #H190-).* Rare.	—	—	—

Tientsin Branch 津天

1902-08 Issue

		Good	Fine	XF
S571	**1 Dollar** 1902-08. *(S/M #H190-1b).* Rare.	—	—	—
S572	**5 Dollars** 1902-04. *(S/M #H190-2b).* Rare.	—	—	—
S573	**10 Dollars** 1902-04. *(S/M #H190-3b).* Rare.	—	—	—
S574	**50 Dollars** 1902-04. *(S/M #H190-4b).* Rare.	—	—	—

Sino-Scandinavian Bank

行銀威華
Hua Wei Yin Hang

Ch'ang Li Branch 黎昌

1922 Provisional Issues

		VG	VF	UNC
S580	**1 Yüan** 1.2.1922. Green. High arch bridge at center. Back: Viking ship at center. Overprint: On #S585. *(S/M #H192-2c).*	25.00	50.00	100.
S581	**5 Yüan** 1.2.1922. Brown. Overprint: On #S587. *(S/M #H192-4b).*	15.00	25.00	50.00

		VG	VF	UNC
S582	**10 Yüan** 1.2.1922. Blue-black and rule. Hillside temple at lake. Back: Viking ship at center. *(S/M #H192-5c).*			
	a. Overprint on #S588. *(S/M #H192-).*	15.00	25.00	50.00
	b. Overprint on #S590C. *(S/M #H192-).*	15.00	25.00	50.00

		VG	VF	UNC
S583	**10 Yüan** 1.2.1922. Blue and multicolor. Overprint: On #S589A. *(S/M #H192-6c).*	15.00	25.00	50.00

Chinwangtao Branch 島皇秦

1926 Issue

		VG	VF	UNC
S583B	**16 Copper Coins** 1926. Purple on orange underprint. Woocha tea house, bridge at left. Back: Great Wall at center. Printer: BEPP. *(S/M #H192-20b).*	150.	400.	—
S583C	**20 Coppers** 1926. Brown on orange underprint. Woocha tea house, bridge at center. Back: Great Wall at center. Printer: BEPP.	300.	750.	—
S584	**30 Copper Coins** 1926. Purple and green. Woocha tea house, bridge at center. Back: Great Wall at center. Printer: BEPP. *(S/M #H192-21).*	100.	225.	500.

		VG	VF	UNC
S584A	**48 Copper Coins** 1926. Red on pale green underprint. Woocha tea house, bridge at center. Back: Great Wall at center. Printer: BEPP. *(S/M #H192-23b).*	300.	850.	—
S584B	**50 Copper Coins** 1926. Violet on brown underprint. Woocha tea house, bridge at center. Back: Violet on pink underprint. Great Wall at center. Printer: BEPP. *(S/M #H192-23.5).*	—	—	—

		VG	VF	UNC
S584C	**80 Copper Coins** 1926. Unmarked and unsigned. Remainder.	250.	500.	—

Peking Branch 京北

1922 Issues

		VG	VF	UNC
S585	**1 Yüan** 1.2.1922. Green. Stone arch bridge at center. Back: Viking ship at center. Printer: BEPP. *(S/M #H192-2a).*	50.00	100.	250.
S586	**1 Yüan** 1.2.1922. Green and multicolor. Stone arch bridge at center. Back: Viking bridge at center. Printer: BEPP. *(S/M #H192-1a).*			
	a. Issued note.	50.00	100.	250.
	b. With additional numerical overprint: *10.*	75.00	150.	300.
S587	**5 Yüan** 1.2.1922. Brown. Hillside pagoda, shoreline at center. Back: Viking ship at center. Printer: BEPP. *(S/M #H192-4a).*	75.00	150.	300.

		VG	VF	UNC
S588	**10 Yüan** 1.2.1922. Blue-black and multicolor. Hillside pagoda, shoreline at center. Back: Viking ship at center. Printer: BEPP. *(S/M #H192-6a).*	50.00	100.	225.

1922 Provisional Issue

		VG	VF	UNC
S589	**1 Yüan** 1.2.1922. Green and multicolor. Overprint: On #S591. *(S/M #H192-1c).*	25.00	50.00	125.
S589A	**10 Yüan** 1.2.1922. Blue-black and multicolor. Overprint: On #S594. *(S/M #H192-5b).*	15.00	40.00	100.

Suiyuan Branch 遠綏

1922 Provisional Issue

		VG	VF	UNC
S590	**1 Yüan** 1.2.1922. Green. Place name below serial number. Overprint: Suiyuan overprint with rosettes, *YUNGCHI CURRENCY* across lower center on face on #S585. *(S/M #H192-2b).*	25.00	50.00	125.
S590A	**5 Yüan** 1.2.1922. Brown. Place name below serial number. Overprint: Suiyuan overprint with rosettes, *YUNGCHI CURRENCY* across lower center on face on #S587. *(S/M #H192-4c).*	25.00	50.00	125.
S590B	**10 Yüan** 1.2.1922. Blue-black and multicolor. Place name below serial number. Overprint: Suiyuan overprint with rosettes, *YUNGCHI CURRENCY* across lower center on face on #S588. *(S/M #H192-6-).*	25.00	50.00	125.

1922 Issue

		VG	VF	UNC
S590C	**10 Yüan** 1.2.1922. Blue-black and multicolor. Place name below serial number. Overprint: Suiyuan overprint with rosettes, *YUNGCHI CURRENCY* across lower center on face. *(S/M #H192-6).*	—	—	—

Tientsin Branch 津天

1922 Issue

		VG	VF	UNC
S591	**1 Yüan** 1.2.1922. Green and multicolor. *(S/M #H192-1b).*	50.00	100.	250.

		VG	VF	UNC
S592	**5 Yüan** 1.2.1922. Brown and multicolor. *(S/M #H192-5a).*			
	a. Issued note.	10.00	25.00	50.00
	b. With various Chinese control character overprint at upper left and right on face.	10.00	25.00	50.00
S593	**10 Yüan** 1.2.1922. Blue-black and multicolor. Coastline at center. *(S/M #H192-6b).*			
	a. Issued note.	10.00	25.00	50.00
	b. With various Chinese control character overprint at upper left and right on face.	10.00	25.00	50.00
S594	**10 Yüan** 1.2.1922. Blue-black and multicolor. Overprint: On #S588. *(S/M #H192-6b).*	10.00	25.00	50.00

1925 Issue

		VG	VF	UNC
S595	**10 Cents** 1.10.1925. Green. Bridge at left. Back: Orange. Printer: BEPP. *(S/M #H192-10).*	15.00	25.00	50.00
S595A	**10 Cents** 1.10.1925. Bridge at left. Back: Dark red with different signature variety at right. *(S/M #H192-).*	15.00	25.00	50.00

		VG	VF	UNC
S596	**20 Cents** 1.10.1925. Orange. Bridge at left. Printer: BEPP. *(S/M #H192-11).*	25.00	50.00	100.

Yungchi Branch

1925 Provisional Issue

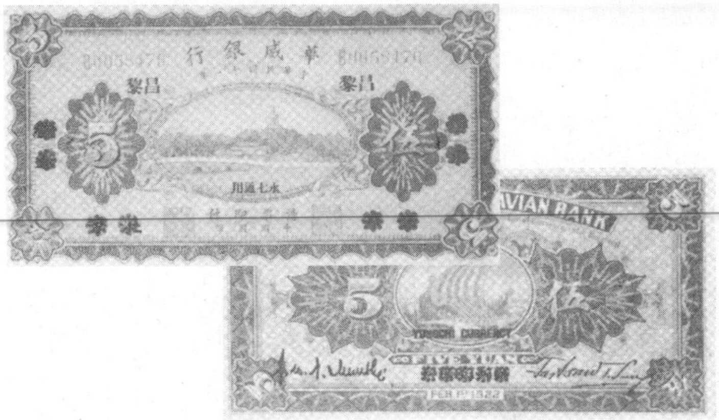

		VG	VF	UNC
S596A	**5 Yüan** 1.10.1925. Overprint: On #S590A. *(S/M #H192-).*	—	—	—

Yungtsun Branch 遵永

1926 Issue

		VG	VF	UNC
S597	**16 Copper Coins** 1926. Blue and orange. Back: Great Wall at center. Printer: BEPP. *(S/M #H192-20).*	50.00	100.	250.
S597A	**30 Copper Coins** 1926. Buildings, bridge at center. Back: Great Wall at center. Printer: BEPP. *(S/M #H192-).*	50.00	100.	250.

		VG	VF	UNC
S598	**32 Copper Coins** 1926. Green and brown. Bridge at right. Back: Great Wall at center. Printer: BEPP. Remainder. *(S/M #H192-22).*	75.00	150.	300.

		VG	VF	UNC
S599	**48 Copper Coins** 1926. Red on pale green underprint. Woocha tea house, bridge at center. Back: Great Wall at center. Remainder without serial #. *(S/M #H192-23a).*	100.	200.	350.
S600	**80 Copper Coins** 1926. Back: Great Wall at center. Printer: BEPP. *(S/M #H192-24).*	50.00	100.	400.

Bank of Taiwan (Limited)

行銀灣台

T'ai Wan Yin Hang

Amoy Branch 門厦

1905-09 Provisional Issue

#S601-S604 withdrawn silver certificates hand stamped for Amoy Branch. See Vol. 2.

	Good	Fine	XF
S601 1 Yen 10.1.1905. Hand stamped on #907. *(S/M #T71-1).* Rare.	—	—	—
S602 5 Yen 10.1.1905. Hand stamped on #908. *(S/M #T71-2).* Rare.	—	—	—
S603 10 Yen Nov. 1906. Hand stamped on #909. *(S/M #T71-12).* Rare.	—	—	—
S604 50 Yen Jan. 1909. Hand stamped on #910. *(S/M #T71-23).* Rare.	—	—	—

Canton Branch

1911 "Local Currency" Issue

	Good	Fine	XF
S604A 1 Yen 1.7.1911. Two dragons at top center. *Kuangtung. (S/M #T71-).*	—	—	—

Foochow Branch 州福

1906 Issue

	Good	Fine	XF
S605 1 Dollar 7.3.1906. Specimen, punched hole cancelled. *(S/M #T71-10).* Rare.	—	—	—
S606 5 Dollars 7.3.1906. Specimen, punched hole cancelled. *(S/M #T71-11).* Rare.	—	—	—

	Good	Fine	XF
S607 1 Dollar Oct. 1906. Specimen, punched hole cancelled. *(S/M #T71-).*	—	Unc	6000.
S608 5 Dollars Oct. 1906. Specimen, punched hole cancelled. *(S/M #T71-).* Rare.	—	—	—

1914 Issue

	Good	Fine	XF
S609 10 Dollars April 1914. Specimen, punched hole cancelled. *(S/M #T71-53).* Rare.	—	—	—
S610 10 Dollars 1.8.1914. Specimen, punched hole cancelled. *(S/M #T71-54).* Rare.	—	—	—
S611 50 Dollars 1.8.1914. Specimen, punched hole cancelled. *(S/M #T71-55).* Rare.	—	—	—

1916 Issue

	Good	Fine	XF
S612 50 Dollars Jan. 1916. Specimen, punched hole cancelled. *(S/M #T71-67).* Rare.	—	—	—

Hankow Branch 口漢

1915-18 Issue

	Good	Fine	XF
S613 1 Dollar 1.5.1915. Specimen. *(S/M #T71-60).* Rare.	—	—	—

	Good	Fine	XF
S614 5 Dollars 1.9.1917. Specimen. *(S/M #T71-61).* Rare.	—	—	—
S615 10 Dollars 1.4.1918. Specimen. *(S/M #T71-62).* Rare.	—	—	—

Kiukiang Branch 江九

1913 Issue

	Good	Fine	XF
S616 1 Dollar 4.6.1913. Specimen. *(S/M #T71-44).* Rare.	—	—	—
S617 5 Dollars July 1913. Specimen. *(S/M #T71-45).* Rare.	—	—	—
S618 10 Dollars July 1913. Specimen. *(S/M #T71-46).* Rare.	—	—	—

1914 Issue

	Good	Fine	XF
S619 1 Dollar Feb. 1914. Specimen. *(S/M #T71-50).* Rare.	—	—	—
S620 5 Dollars Feb. 1914. Specimen. *(S/M #T71-51).* Rare.	—	—	—
S621 10 Dollars Feb. 1914. Specimen. *(S/M #T71-52).* Rare.	—	—	—

Shanghai Branch 海上

1915 Issue

	Good	Fine	XF
S622 1 Dollar 1.12.1915. Specimen. *(S/M #T71-).* Rare.	—	—	—
S623 5 Dollars 1.12.1915. Specimen. *(S/M #T71-).* Rare.	—	—	—
S624 10 Dollars 1.12.1915. Specimen. *(S/M #T71-).* Rare.	—	—	—

1916-17 "Local Currency" Issue

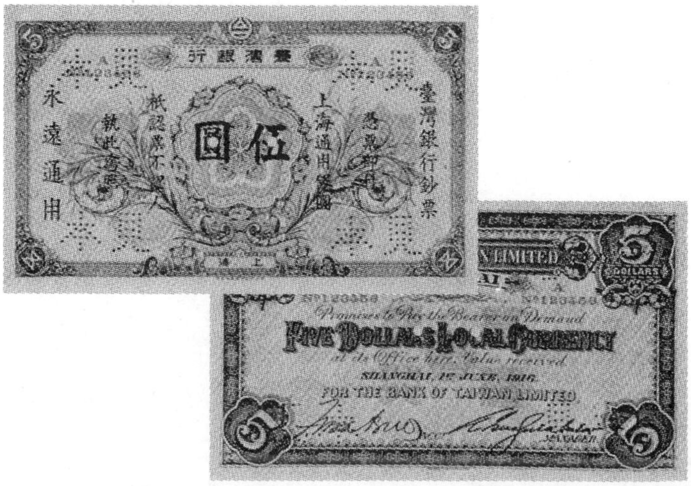

	Good	Fine	XF
S625 5 Dollars 1.6.1916. Specimen. *(S/M #T71-65).* Rare.	—	—	—
S626 10 Dollars 1.11.1917. Specimen. *(S/M #T71-66).* Rare.	—	—	—

Swatow Branch 頭汕

1908 Issue

		Good	Fine	XF
S627	**1 Dollar** 4.1.1908. Specimen. *(S/M #T71-20).* Rare.	—	—	—
S628	**5 Dollars** 4.1.1908. Specimen. *(S/M #T71-21).* Rare.	—	—	—
S629	**10 Dollars** 4.1.1908. Specimen. *(S/M #T71-22).* Rare.	—	—	—

1911 Issue

		Good	Fine	XF
S630	**5 Dollars** 1.10.1911. Specimen. *(S/M #T71-41).* Rare.	—	—	—
S631	**10 Dollars** 1.11.1911. Specimen. *(S/M #T71-42).* Rare.	—	—	—
S632	**50 Dollars** Dec. 1911. Specimen. *(S/M #T71-43).* Rare.	—	—	—
S633	**50 Dollars** 1.12.1911. Specimen. *(S/M #T71-33)* Rare.	—	—	—

1912 Issue

		Good	Fine	XF
S634	**1 Dollar** 1.3.1912. Specimen. *(S/M #T71 40).* Rare.	—	—	—

Yokohama Specie Bank, Limited

行銀金正濱橫

Heng Pin Cheng Chin Yin Hang

Tsinan (Chinan) Branch 南濟

1920 Issue

		Good	Fine	XF
S635	**1 Dollar** 15.1.1920. Green and black. *(S/M #H31-125a).* Rare.	—	—	—
S636	**5 Dollars** 15.1.1920. Violet and black. *(S/M #H31-126a).* Rare.	—	—	—

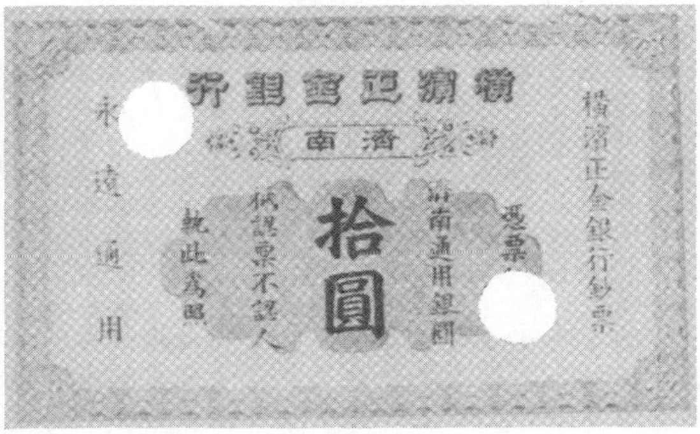

		Good	Fine	XF
S637	**10 Dollars** 15.1.1920. Green and black. 107 x 173mm. *(S/M #H31-127a).* Rare.	—	—	—

Dairen Branch 連大

1913 Issue

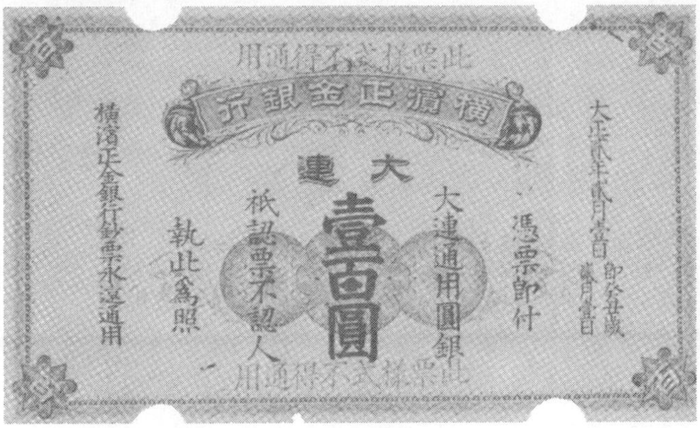

		Good	Fine	XF
S644	**100 Dollars** 1.2.1913. Violet and black. *(S/M #H31-76).* Rare.	—	—	—

1913 Gold Yen Issue

		Good	Fine	XF
S645	**1 Gold Yen** ND (1913). Brown and black. *(S/M #H31-71).* Rare.	—	—	—

		Good	Fine	XF
S646	**5 Gold Yen** ND (1913). Brown and green. *(S/M #H31-73).* Rare.	—	—	—
S647	**10 Gold Yen** ND (1913). Violet and black. *(S/M #H31-75).* Rare.	—	—	—

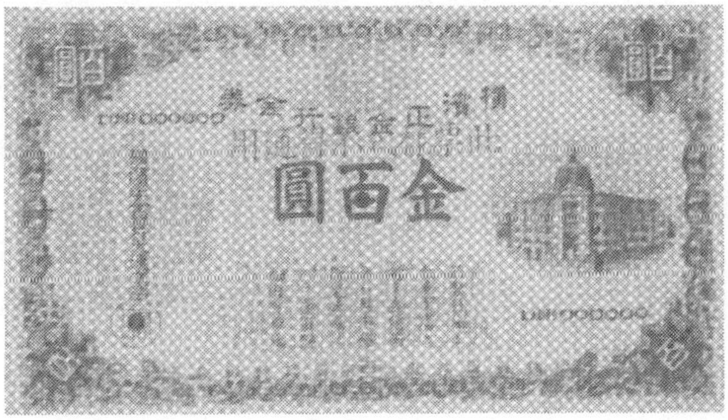

		Good	Fine	XF
S648	**100 Gold Yen** ND (1915). Blue, gold and black. *(S/M #H31-103).* Rare.	—	—	—

1918 ND Issue

		Good	Fine	XF
S652	**10 Sen** ND (1918). Blue on brown underprint. Bank building at right. Back: Green with black text. *(S/M #H31-130a).*	350.	800.	2000.
S653	**50 Sen** ND (1918). Brown, green and black. Bank building at right. *(S/M #H31-131a).* Rare.	—	—	—

1918 Dollar Local Currency Issues

		Good	Fine	XF
S654	**100 Dollars** 25.12.1918. Violet and black. Serial # at upper left and upper right. *(S/M #H31-).* Rare.	—	—	—
S655	**100 Dollars** 25.12.1918 (1925). Violet and black. Serial # at upper left and lower right. *(S/M #H31-).* Rare.	—	—	—

1927 ND Provisional Issues

		Good	Fine	XF
S656	**100 Dollars** ND (1927 -old date 1.6.1927). Overprint: On Peking #S704. *(S/M #H31-).* Rare.	—	—	—

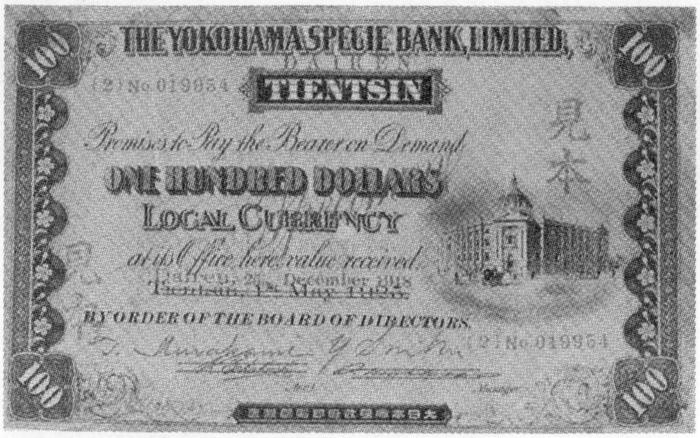

	Good	Fine	XF
S657 100 Dollars ND (1926 -old date 1.5.1925). Overprint: On Tientsin #S731. *(S/M #H31-)*. Rare.	—	—	—
S658 100 Dollars ND (1926 -old date 1.8.1917). Overprint: On #S745. *(S/M #H31-)*. Rare.	—	—	—

1930 Regular Issue

	Good	Fine	XF
S659 1 Dollar 1.4.1930. Brown and black. *(S/M #H31-)*.	600.	1200.	2400.
S660 5 Dollars 1.4.1930. Slate and black. *(S/M #H31 -)*. Rare.	—	—	—
S661 10 Dollars 1.4.1930. Gold and black. *(S/M #H31 -)*. Rare.	—	—	—

Hankow Branch 口漢

1917 Dollar Local Currency Issue

	Good	Fine	XF
S662 1 Dollar 1.10.1917. Blue and black. Back: Blue and yellow. *(S/M #H31-125b)*.	300.	600.	1000.
S663 5 Dollars 1.10.1917. Olive-green and black. Back: Brown. *(S/M #H31-126b)*. Rare.	—	—	—

	Good	Fine	XF
S664 10 Dollars 1.10.1917. Green. Bank building at lower center. Back: Brown and orange-yellow. *(S/M #H31-127b)*.	1500.	4000.	—
S665 100 Dollars 1.10.1917. Brown and yellow. Bank building at right. Back: Green and black. *(S/M #H31-128b)*. Rare.	—	—	—

Harbin Branch 濱爾哈

1921 Dollar Local Currency Provisional Issue

	Good	Fine	XF
S666 1 Dollar 1.5.1921. Overprint: On Tsinan #S635. *(S/M #H31-)*. Rare.	—	—	—

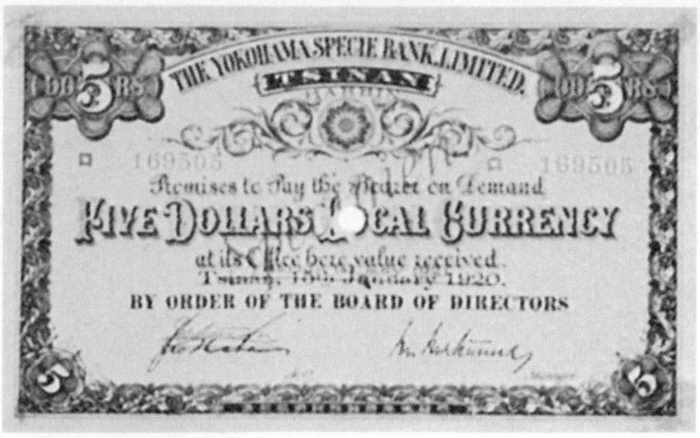

	Good	Fine	XF
S667 5 Dollars 1.5.1921. Overprint: On Tsinan #S636. *(S/M #H31-)*. Rare.	—	—	—
S668 10 Dollars 1.5.1921. Overprint: On Tsinan #S637. *(S/M #H31-)*. Rare.	—	—	—
S669 50 Dollars 1.5.1921. Overprint: On Shanghai #S715. *(S/M #H31-)*. Rare.	—	—	—
S670 100 Dollars 1.5.1921. Overprint: On Shanghai #S716. *(S/M #H31-)*. Rare.	—	—	—

1921 Regular Issue

	Good	Fine	XF
S671 1 Dollar 15.12.1921. Gray and black. *(S/M #H31-)*. Rare.	—	—	—
S672 5 Dollars 15.12.1921. Gray and black. *(S/M #H31-)*. Rare.	—	—	—

	Good	Fine	XF
S673 10 Dollars 15.12.1921. Gray and black. *(S/M #H31-)*. Rare.	—	—	—
S674 100 Dollars 15.12.1921. Green and black. *(S/M #H31-)*. Rare.	—	—	—

Newchwang Branch 莊牛

1902 Newchang Tael Issue

	Good	Fine	XF
S675 1 Tael 1.7.1902. Gold and black. *(S/M #H31-10a)*. Rare.	—	—	—
S676 5 Taels 1.7.1902. Green and black. *(S/M #H31-11a)*. Rare.	—	—	—

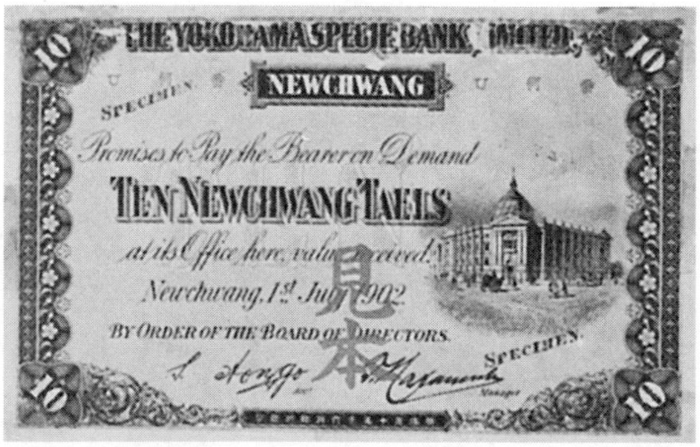

	Good	Fine	XF
S677 10 Taels 1.7.1902. Blue and black. *(S/M #H31-12a)*. Rare.	—	—	—
S678 50 Taels 1.7.1902. Brown and black. *(S/M #H31-13a)*. Rare.	—	—	—
S679 100 Taels 1.7.1902. Violet and black. *(S/M #H31-14a)*. Rare.	—	—	—

1902 Small Silver Coin Issue

	Good	Fine	XF
S680 1 Dollar 1.7.1902. Light green and black. Three large characters in oval on each side. *(S/M #H31-30)*. Rare.	—	—	—

	Good	Fine	XF
S681 5 Dollars 1.7.1902. Light green and black. Three large characters in oval on each side. *(S/M #H31-33).* Rare.	—	—	—
S682 10 Dollars 1.7.1902. Light green and black. Three large characters in oval on each side. *(S/M #H31-36).* Rare.	—	—	—

1902 Dollar Local Currency Issue

	Good	Fine	XF
S683 1 Dollar 1.7.1902. Black and brown. Western serial #. Back: Western serial #. *(S/M #H31-).* Rare.	—	—	—
S684 5 Dollars 1.7.1902. Black and blue. Western serial #. Back: Western serial #. *(S/M #H31-).* Rare.	—	—	—
S685 10 Dollars 1.7.1902. Black and yellow. Western serial #. Back: Western serial #. *(S/M #H31-).* Rare.	—	—	—
S686 1 Dollar 1.7.1902. Red and black. Chinese serial #. Back: Western serial #. *(S/M #H31-).*			
a. Issued note.	300.	750.	1500.
b. With overprint: OR *IN TIENTSIN.* Specimen. Rare.	—	—	—
S687 5 Dollars 1.7.1902. Purple and black. Chinese serial #. Back: Western serial #. *(S/M #H31-).*			
a. Issued note.	750.	1500.	—
b. With overprint: OR *IN TIENTSIN.* Specimen. Rare.	—	—	—

	Good	Fine	XF
S688 10 Dollars 1.7.1902. Black and gold. Chinese serial #. Back: Two dragons at top center below bank name. Western serial #. *(S/M #H31-).*	750.	1500.	—

#S690-S692 *Deleted.* See #S686a and S687a.

Peking Branch 京北

1910 Dollar Local Currency Issue

	Good	Fine	XF
S695 1 Dollar 15.8.1910. Green and black. *(S/M #H31-60).* Rare.	—	—	—
S696 5 Dollars 15.8.1910. Red-brown and black. *(S/M #H31-61).* Rare.	—	—	—
S697 10 Dollars 15.8.1910. Red-brown and black. *(S/M #H31-62).* Rare.	—	—	—

	Good	Fine	XF
S698 50 Dollars 15.8.1910. Olive-green and black. Back: Two dragons at top center below bank name. *(S/M #H31-63).* Rare.	—	—	—

1920-27 Issue

	Good	Fine	XF
S700 1 Dollar 15.7.1920. Green and black. *(S/M #H31-).*	600.	1200.	—
S702 10 Dollars 15.7.1920. Brown and black. *(S/M #H31-).*	1000.	2000.	—
S703 50 Dollars 15.12.1921. Green and black. *(S/M #H31-).* Rare.	—	—	—
S704 100 Dollars 1.6.1927. Orange and black. *(S/M #H31-).* Rare.	—	—	—

Shanghai Branch 海上

1902; 1907 Dollar Local Currency Issue

	Good	Fine	XF
S705 1 Dollar 10.9.1902. Brown and black. Back: Two dragons at top center below bank name. *(S/M #H31-32c).*	400.	800.	—
S706 5 Dollars 10.9.1902. Violet and black. *(S/M #H31-35c).*	600.	1200.	—
S707 10 Dollars 10.9.1902. Gold and black. *(S/M #H31-38c).* Rare.	—	—	—
S708 50 Dollars 1.5.1907 (1909). Olive-green and black. *(S/M #H31-50).* Rare.	—	—	—
S709 100 Dollars 1.5.1907 (1909). Blue and black. *(S/M #H31-51).* Rare.	—	—	—

1914 Issue

	Good	Fine	XF
S711 10 Dollars 1.7.1914. Purple, orange and black. *(S/M #H31-80).* Rare.	—	—	—

1918 Issue

	Good	Fine	XF
S713 5 Dollars 15.6.1918. Violet and black. *(S/M #H31-140).* Rare.	—	—	—
S714 10 Dollars 15.6.1918. Purple and orange. *(S/M #H31-141).* Rare.	—	—	—
S715 50 Dollars 15.6.1918. Olive-green and black. *(S/M #H31-142).* Rare.	—	—	—
S716 100 Dollars 15.6.1918. Blue and black. *(S/M #H31-143).* Rare.	—	—	—

Tientsin Branch 津天

1902 Dollar Local Currency Issue

		Good	Fine	XF
S718	**1 Dollar** 1.7.1902. Red-brown and black. *(S/M #H31-32d).*	400.	800.	1750.
S719	**5 Dollars** 1.7.1902. Violet and black. *(S/M #H31-35d).* Rare.	—	—	—
S720	**10 Dollars** 1.7.1902. Gold and black. *(S/M #H31-38d).* Rare.	—	—	—

1918 Issue

		Good	Fine	XF
S721	**1 Dollar** 15.6.1918. Brown and black. *(S/M #H31-).*	250.	600.	—
S722	**5 Dollars** 15.6.1918. Blue and black. Back: Two dragons at top center below bank name. *(S/M #H31-).* Rare.	—	—	—
S723	**10 Dollars** 15.6.1918. Tan and black. *(S/M #H31-).* Rare.	—	—	—
S725	**100 Dollars** 1.3.1918. Green and black. *(S/M #H31-).* Rare.	—	—	—

1925 Issue

		Good	Fine	XF
S731	**100 Dollars** 1.5.1925. Green and black. Signature varieties. *(S/M #H31-).* Rare.	—	—	—

1902 Tael Issue

		Good	Fine	XF
S732	**5 Taels** 1.7.1902. Green and black. *(S/M #H31-11b).* Rare.	—	—	—
S733	**10 Taels** 1.7.1902. Blue and black. *(S/M #H31-12b).* Rare.	—	—	—
S734	**50 Taels** 1.7.1902. Brown and black. *(S/M #H31-13b).* Rare.	—	—	—

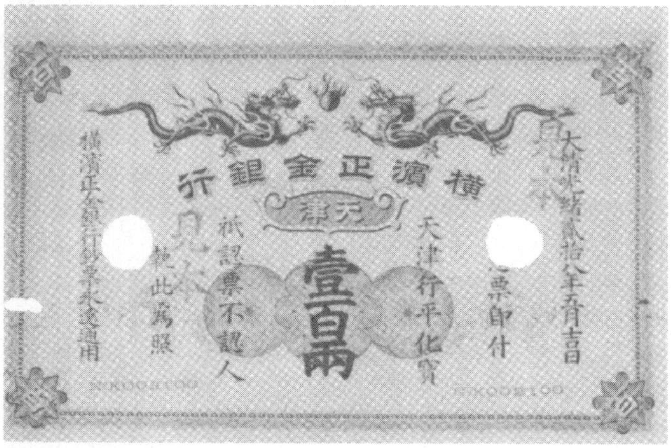

		Good	Fine	XF
S735	**100 Taels** 1.7.1902. Red-brown and black. Two dragons at top center. *(S/M #H31-14b).* Rare.	—	—	—

1937 Provisional Issue

		Good	Fine	XF
S736	**1 Dollar** 1.4.1937. Overprint: On Tsingtao #S757. *(S/M #H31-).* Rare.	—	—	—
S737	**5 Dollars** 1.4.1937. Overprint: On Tsingtao #S742. *(S/M #H31-).* Rare.	—	—	—

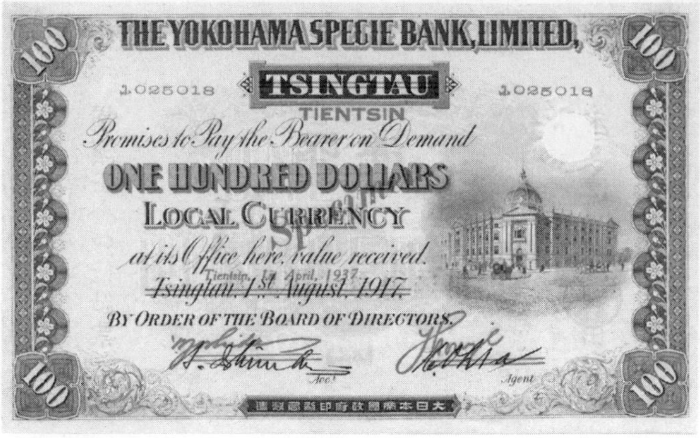

		Good	Fine	XF
S740	**100 Dollars** 1.4.1937. Overprint: On #S745. *(S/M #H31-).* Rare.	—	—	—

Tsingtao Branch 島青

1915; 1917 Dollar Local Currency Issue

		Good	Fine	XF
S741	**1 Dollar** 1.10.1915. Gray and black. *(S/M #H31-100).* Rare.	—	—	—
S742	**5 Dollars** 1.10.1915. Orange and black. Back: Two dragons at top center under bank name *(S/M #H31-101).* Rare.	—	—	—

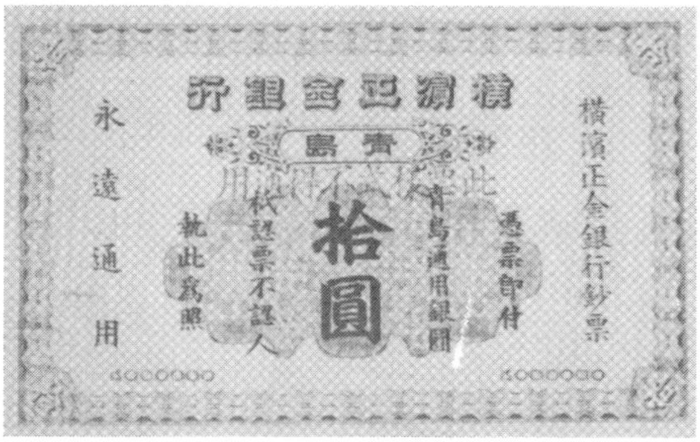

		Good	Fine	XF
S743	**10 Dollars** 1.10.1915. Slate gray and black. *(S/M #H31-102).* Rare.	—	—	—
S745	**100 Dollars** 1.8.1917. Red-brown and black. *(S/M #H31-144).* Rare.	—	—	—

1918 Issue

		Good	Fine	XF
S746	**1 Dollar** 15.6.1918. Gray and black. *(S/M #H31-).* Rare.	—	—	—

1918 ND Issue

		Good	Fine	XF
S750	**10 Sen** ND (1918). Blue and brown. Bank building at center. *(S/M #H31-130b).*			
	a. Agency period. (Block #1-1000).	250.	700.	1300.
	b. Branch period. (Block #1001-).	300.	750.	1500.
S751	**50 Sen** ND (1918). Green and brown. *(S/M #H31-131b).*	400.	800.	1750.

1921 Issue

		Good	Fine	XF
S752	**1 Dollar** 15.12.1921. Black and violet. *(S/M #H31-).*	—	—	—

1922 Issue

		Good	Fine	XF
S753	**1 Dollar** 1.6.1922. Black and violet. *(S/M #H31-).* Rare.	—	—	—

1924 Issue

		Good	Fine	XF
S757	**1 Dollar** 15.11.1924. Black and violet. Serial # varieties. Back: Two dragons under bank name at top center. *(S/M #H31-150).* Rare.	—	—	—

#S758 and S759 *Deleted.*

PROVINCIAL BANKS

Some of the provincial bank note issuing authorities were originally established during the reigns of the last two Chinese emperors prior to the establishment of the new republic. As such they continued doing business as normal with notes circulating alongside those of the foreign banks, the various early military issues which were mainly overprinted notes of provincial authorities, and the rush of the endless local issuers during the next two decades of most major cities.

In some case the old imperial notes were reissued with current years of the republic overprinted over the past emperor's name and year of reign.

The following listings, based on Ward Smith's writings, are inclusive of provincial issuers and the occasional municipal or local government issuer whose notes circulated beyond its local boundaries.

BankofAnhweiProvincialGovernment #S802	號銀省徽安 *An Hui Sheng Yin Hao*
Anhwei Regional Bank #S805-S815	行銀方地徽安 *An Hui Ti Fang Yin Hang*
Anhwei Yu Huan Bank #S819-855	局錢官皖裕徽安 *An Hui Yü Huan Kuan Chi'lien Chü*
Tsihar Hsing Yeh Bank #S825-S855	行銀業興爾哈察 *Ch'a Ha Erh Hsing Yeh Yin Hang*
Charhar Commercial Bank #S855E-S857B	局錢業商爾哈察 *Ch'a Ha Erh Shang Yeh Ch'ien Chu*
Changsha Bank #S858-S860	行銀沙長 *Ch'ang Sha Yin Hang*
Chekiang Provincial Bank #S863-S869	行銀省江浙 *Che Chiang Sheng Yin Hang*
Chekiang Provincial Bank #S871-S893	行銀方地江浙 *Che Chiang Ti Fang Yin Hang*
Kirin Government Bank #S895	局錢官林吉 *Chi Lin Kuan Ch'ien Chü*
Kirin Yung Heng Provincial Bank Yung Heng Provincial Bank of Kirin #S901-S1081F	局錢銀官衡永林吉 *Chi Lin Yung Heng Kuan Yin Ch'ien Chü*
Reconstruction Bank of Kiangsi #S1082A-S1082H	行銀設建西江 *Chiang Hsi Chien She Yin Hang*
Kiangse Government Bank #S1082L-S1085H	*Chian Hsi Kuan Yin Ch'ing Tsung Hao*
Public Bank of Kiangse #S1086-S1089	行銀立公西江 *Chiang Hsi Kung Li Yin Hang*
Kiangsi Provincial Bank #S1089C-S1089E	行銀省西江 *Chiang Hsi Sheng Yin Hang*
Kiangsi Regional Bank #S1090-S1093	行銀方地西江 *Chiang Hsi Ti Fang Yin Hang*
Kiangsi Finance Bureau #S1093D-S1096	廳政財西江 *Chiang Hsi Ts'ai Cheng T'ing*
Bank of Kiangsi #S1097-S1119	行銀西江 *Chiang Hsi Yin Hang*
Yu Ming Bank of Kiangsi #S1125-S1160	行銀民裕西江 *Chiang Hsi Yü Min Yin Hang*
Kiangnan Yu-Ning Government Bank Yu Ning Imperial Bank #S1161-S1180	票鈔元局錢銀官寧裕 *Yü Ning Kuan Yin Ch'ien Chü Yüan Ch'ao P'iao*
Kiangnam Yü Su Silver Currency Bureau #S1183-S1185	局錢銀官寧裕南江 *Chiang Nan Yü Su Kuan Yin Ch'ien Chü*
Kiang Shun Gobernment Bank #S1188	號銀官省江 *Chiang Sheng Kuan Yin Hao*
Kiangsu Famers Bank Kingsu Farmers Bank #S1191-S1205	行銀民農省蘇江 *Shiang Su Sheng Nung Min Yin Hang*
Kiangsu Province #S1208-S1213	券換兌省蘇江 *Chiang Su Sheng Tui Huan Ch'üan*
Nanking Exchange Office of the Financial Department, Kiangsu #S1215-S1217	處換兌京政司南財蘇江 *Chiang Su Ts'ai Cheng Szu Nan Ching Tui Huan Ch'üan*
Kiangsu Finance Department #S1220-S1224	廳政財蘇江 *Chiang Su Ts'ai Cheng T'ing*
Kiangsu Bank #S1226-S1227	行銀蘇江 *Chiang Su Yin Hang*
Yue Soo Imperial Bank #S1228-S1234	局錢銀官蘇裕蘇江 *Chiang Su Yü Su Kuan Yin Ch'ien Chü*
Chihli Provincial Treasury #S1238-S1243	券換兌庫金省隸直 *Chih Li Sheng Chin K'u tui Huan Ch'üan*
Chihli Province #S1247-S1252	券通流期定庫省隸直 *Shih Li Sheng K'u ting Ch'i Liu T'ung Ch'üan*
Provincial Bank of Chihli #S1254-S1290	局錢官省隸直 *Chih Li Sheng Kuan Ch'ien Chü* 行銀省隸直 *Chih Li Sheng Yin Hang*
Bank of Local Railways of Shansi and Suiyüan #S1291-S1301	號銀路鐵方地綏晋 *Chin Sui Ti Fang T'ieh Lu Yin Hao*
Tsingtao City Agricultural and Industrial Bank #S1302-S1302C	行銀工農市島青 *Ch'ing Tao Shih Nung Kung Yin Hang*
Tsingtao (Regional) city Bank #S1302D-S1302L	行銀方地島青 *Ch'ing Tao Ti Fang Yin Hang*
Fengtien Industrial Bank Hsin Yieh Bank Shing Yeh Bank Mukden Bank of Industrial Development Fentin Hsing Yeh Bank #S1303-S1325	行銀業興天奉 *Feng T'ien Hsing Yeh Yin Hang*
Hua Feng Official Currency Bureau #S1327-S1329	號銀官豐華天奉 *Feng T'ien Hua Feng Kuan Yin Hao*
Fengtien Official Currency Bureau #S1330-S1354	號銀官天奉 *Feng T'ien Kuan Yin Hao*
Fengtien Public Exchange Bank Kung Tsi Bank of Fengtien #S1355-S1380	號錢市平濟公天奉 *Feng T'ien Kung Chi P'ing Shih Ch'ien Hao*
Fengtien Agricultural and Industrial Bank #S1383-S1393	行銀總業農天奉 *Feng T'ien Nung Yeh Tsung Yin Hang*
Fukien Provincial Bank #S1395-S1431	行銀省建福 *Fu Chien Sheng Yin Hang*
Fukien Bank #S1435-S1440	行銀建福 *Fu Chien Yin Hang*
Fu Lung Bank #S1443-S1447	行銀隴富 *Fu Luang Yin Hang*
Hainan Bank #S1451-S1459	行銀南海 *Nai Nan Yin Hang*
Hio Lung Kiang Government Bank #S1461-S1515	號銀官江龍黑 *Hei Lung Chiang Kuan Yin Hao*
Kwang Sing Company/Heilungchiang Kuang Hsin Syndicate of Heilungkiang #S1521-S1619G	司公信廣 *Kuang Hsin Kung Szu* 江龍黑 *Hei Lung Chiang*
Provincial Bank of Heilungkiang #S1621-S1627	號銀官省江龍黑 *Hei Lung Chiang Sheng Kuan Yin Hao*
Amoor Government Bank #S1631-S1653	號銀省江龍黑 *Hei Lung Chiang Kuan Yin Hao* 券元銀小 *Hsiao Yin Yüan Ch'üan*

Provincial Bank of Honan
#S1661-S1693
行銀省南河
Ho Nan Sheng Yin Hang

Bank of Honan Province
Yü Ch'üan Bank of Honan
#S1691-S1700
局錢銀官泉豫南河
Ho Nan Yü Ch'üan Kuan Yin Ch'ien Chü

Hopei Province
#S1708
券通流時臨縣冀/省北河
Ho Pei Sheng/Chi Hsien Lin Shih Liu T'ung Chüan

Ho Pei Metropolitan Bank
#S1709-S1710B
局錢銀北河
Ho Pei Yin Ch'ien Chü

Bank of Hopei
#S1711-S1735
行銀北河
Ho Pei Yin Hang

Khotan District Administration
#S1737
印長政行區闐和
Ho Tien Ch'ü Hang Cheng Chang Yin

Khotan Administration Gobernment Head Public Office
#S1738
Not Available
Ho T'ien Hsing Cheng Ch'ang Kung Shu Yin Liu(?) T'ung

Sikang Provincial Bank
#S1739-S1740
行銀省康西
Hsi K'ang Sheng Yin Hang

Subtreasury of Sinkiang - Official Note
#S1742
票官庫藩疆新
Hsin Chiang Fan k'u Kuan P'iao

Main Official Currency Bureau of Sinkiang
#S1732A-S1742B
局總錢官疆新
Hsin Chiang Kuan Ch'ien Tsung Chü

Sinkiang Commercial and Industrial Bank
#S1743-S1778
行銀業商疆新
Hsin Chiang Shang Yeh Hin Hang

Industrial and Commercial Bank of Sinkiang, Ili Branch
#S1778A-S1778H
票財行分梨伊行銀業商疆新
Hsin Chiang Shang Yeh Yin Hang I Li Len Hang Ts'ai P'ioa

Sinkiang Sub-prefecture Administration Finance Department Treasury - Official Note
#S1779-S1780F
票官庫廳政財府政省疆新
Hsin Chiang Sheng Cheng Fu Ts'ai Cheng T'ing Ku Kuan P'iao

Sinkiang Province
#S1781-S1783
券庫金省疆新
Hsin Chiang Sheng Chin K'u Ch'üan

Sinkiang Provincial Bank
#S1786-S1807
行銀省疆新
Hsin Chiang Sheng Yin Hang

Treasury Department of Sinkiang - Official Note
#S1808
票官庫司疆新
Hsin Chiang Szu K'u Kuan P'iao

Provincial Treasury of Sinkiang - Official Note
#S1809-S1810
票官庫廳疆新
Hsin Chiang T'ing K'u Kuan P'iao

Sinkiang Finance Department Treasury
#S1811-S1882
票官庫廳政財府政省疆新
Hsin Chiang/Ts'ai Cheng Ting K'u Kuan P'iao

Monetary Bureau of Government Suchow
#S1891A-S1891C
局錢官市平州徐
Hsü Chou P'ing Shih Kuan Ch'ien Chü

Hulunpeierh Official Currency Bureau
#S1892A-S1892M
局錢商官爾貝倫呼
Hu Lun Pei Erh Kuan Shang Ch'ien Chü

Official Mint Hunan
Hunan Government Bank
#S1893-S1930
局錢官南湖
Hu Nan Kuan Ch'ien Chü

Hunan Provincial Treasury
#S1936-S1948
廳政財省南湖
Hu Nan Sheng Ts'ai Cheng Ting

Hunan Provincial Bank
Provincial Bank of Hunan
#S1951-S1994
行銀省南湖
Hu Nan Sheng Yin Hang

Hunan Indusrial Bank
#S1996-S2011
行銀業實南湖
Hu Nan Shih Yeh Yin Hang

Hunan Treasury
#S2016-S2020
券証庫金利有期定南湖
Hu Nan Ting Ch'i Yu Li Chin K'u Cheng Ch'üan

Hunan Bank
Hunan Provincial Bank
#S2022-S2078
行銀南湖
Hu Nan Yin Hang

Hupeh Government Cash Bank
Hupeh Provincial Bank
#S2081-S2098
局錢官北湖
Hu Pei Kuan Ch'ien Chü

Hupeh Provincial Bank
#S2101-S2124
行銀省北湖
Hu Pei Sheng Yin Hang

Hupeh Government Mint
#S2126-S2144
局元銀北湖
Hu Pei yin Yüan Chü

Ili Official Currency Bureau
#S2145-S2153
局錢官犁伊
I Li Kuan Ch'ien Chü
局總錢官犁伊
I Li Kuan Ch'ien Tsung Chü

Hsing Yeh Bank of Jehol
Industrial Development Bank of Jehol
#S2155-S2222
行銀業興河熱
Je Ho Hsing Yeh Yin Hang
行銀業興
Hsing Yeh Yin Hang

Kan Sen Bank of Kiangsi
Provincial Bank of Kiangsi
#S2223-S2236
行銀省贛
Kan Sheng Yin Hang

Monetary Bureau of Government Kansu
#S2237-S2245
局錢官市平(省)肅甘
Kan Su (Sheng) P'ing Shih Kuan Ch'ien Chü

Kansu Provincial Bank
#S2246
局錢官市平(省)肅甘
Kan Su (Sheng) P'ing Shih Kuan Ch'ien Chü

Canton Municipal Bank
#S2251-S2285
行銀立市市州廣
Kuang Chou Shih Shih Li Yin Hang

Kwangsi Official Currency Bureau
#S2287-S2292
號錢銀官西廣
Kuang Hsi Kuan Yin Ch'ien Hao

Kwangsi Farmers Bank
#S2295-S2296
行銀民農西廣
Ku7ang Hsi Nung Min Yin Hang

Kwangsi Provincial Treasury Notes
#S2301-S2309
(券)庫金省西廣
Kuang Hsi Sheng Chin K'u (Ch'üan)

Kwangsi Provincial Government
#S2311-S2315
券通流幣輔省西廣
Kuang Hsi Sheng Fu Pi Liu T'ung Ch'üan

Provincial Bank of Kwangsi (or Kwangse)
#S2318-S2342
行銀省西廣
Kuang Hsi Sheng Yin Hang

Kwangsi Bank
#S2343-S2382
行銀西廣
Kuang Hsi Yin Hang

Kwangtung Currency Bureau
#S2385-S2394
局錢東廣
Kuang Tung Ch'ien Chü

Provincial Bank of Kwangtung Province
#S2395-S2408
行銀省東廣
Kuang Tung Sheng Yin Hang Tui Huan Ch'üan

Kwangtung Provincial Bank
#S2411-S2459
行銀省東廣
Kuang Tung Sheng Yin Hang

Kweichow Provincial Government General Treasury
#S2460-S2460C
庫金總府政省州貴
Kuei Chou Sheng Cheng Fu Tsung Chin K'u

Provincial Bank of Kweichow
#S2461-S2463
行銀省州貴
Kuei Chou Sheng Yin Hang

Kweichow Bank
Kueichow Bank
Bank of Kweichow
#S2465-S2484
行銀州貴
Kuei Chou Yin Hang

Ninghsia Provincial Bank
#S2488-S2489
行銀省夏寧
Ning Hsia Sheng Yin Hang

Hunan Pao Hsing Mineral Bank
Hunan Pow Shing Mining Bank
#S2490-S2490G
行銀業鑛興寶
Pao Hsing Kuang Yeh Yin Hang

Altai District
#S2490J-S2490L
券銀用通泰爾阿
O Erh T'ai T'ung Yung Yin Ch'uan

Peiping Municipal Bank
#S2491-S2501
行銀市平北
Pei P'ing Shih Yin Hang

Pei Yang Kin Fu Bank
#S2505
號銀武經洋北
Pei Yang Ching Wu Yin Hao

Commercial Guarantee Bank of Chihli
#S2509-S2518
行銀商保洋北
Pei Yang Pao Shang Yin Hang

Peiyang Tientsin Bank
#S2521-S2530
行銀津天洋北
Pei Yang T'ien Ching Yin Hang

Peiyang Currency Bureau
#S2531
局元銀洋北
Pei Yang Yin Yüan Chü

Frontier Bank
#S2535-S2585
行銀業邊
Pien Yeh Yin Hang

Market Stabilization Currency Bureau
#S2589-S2590
局錢官市平
P'ing Shih Kuan Ch'ien Chü

Shan Hsi Zing Fun Bank
#S2593-S2598
行銀豐秦西陝
Shan Hsi Ch'in Feng Yin Hang

Fu Ching Chien Chü/Shensi
Fu Ching Bank of Shensi
Fu Ching Bank
#S2601-S2618
局錢秦富西陝
Shan Hsi Fu Ch'in Ch'ien Chüan
行銀秦富西陝
Shan Hsi Fu Ch'in Yin Hang

Shansi Provincial Railway
#S2624
處事辦合聯行兩鐵省省西山
Shan Hsi Sheng Sheng T'ien Liang Hang Lian Ho Pan Shih Ch'u

Shanse Provincial Bank
Shansi Provincial Bank
#S2625-S2680
行銀省西山
Shan Hsi Sheng Yin Hang

Provincial Bank of Shensi
#S2681-S2693
行銀省西陝
Shan Hsi Sheng Yin Hang

Bank of Shansi
#S2694
券通流 行銀西陝
Shan Hsi Yin Hang Liu T'ung Ch'üan

Shantung Commercial Bank
#S2695-S2700
行銀業商東山
Shan Tung Shang Yeh Yin Hang

Shan Tung Exchange Bureau
#S2703-S2713
局換錢官市平東山
Shan Tung P'ing Shih Kuan Ch'ien Tsung Chü

Shantung Provincial Treasury
#S2715-S2720
券庫金省東山
Shan Tung Sheng Chin K'u Ch'üan

Shantung Provincial Treasury
#S2723-S2725
券庫省東山
Shan Tung Sheng K'u Ch'üan

Shantung min Sheng Bank
#S2731-S2742
行銀生民省東山
Shan Tung Sheng Min Sheng Yin Hang

Provincia Bank of Shantung
#S2745-S2763
行銀省東山
Shan Tung Sheng Yin Hang

Shan Tung Bank
Bank of Shantung
#S2765-S2772
行銀東山
Shan Tung Yin Hang

Suiyuan Provincial Bank
#S2774-S2802
局錢官市平遠綏
Sui Yüan P'ing Shih Kuan Ch'ien Chü

Szechuan Provincial Bank
#S2804-S2808
局錢官川四
Szu Ch'uan Kuan Ch'ien Chü

Szechuan Official Bank
#S2811-S2815
局銀官川四
Szu Ch'uan Kuan Yin Hao
號銀官川四
Szu Ch'uan Kuan Hao

Szechuan Provincial Government
#S2816-S2817
券庫設建府政省川四
Szu Ch'uan Sheng Cheng Fu Chien She K'u Ch'üan

Szechuan Provincial Bank
#S2819-S2824
行銀省川四
Szu Ch'uan Sheng Yin Hang

Szechuan Province
#S2827-S2829
券換兌川四
Szu Ch'uan Tui Huan Ch'üan

Szechuan Cooper Currency Bureau
#S2830=-S2832
局元銅/川四
Szu Ch'uan/T'ung Yüan Chü

Tihua Official Currency Bureau
#S2835-S2841
局錢官化廸
Ti Hua Kuan Ch'ien Chü

Tientsin Bank
#S2843
行銀津天
T'ien Ching Yin Hao

Bureau of Finance Ching Hai
Maintenance Note
#S2845-S2850
券持維廳政財
Ts'ai Cheng T'ing Wei Ch'ih Ch'üan

Fukien South - Eastern Bank
#S2851-S2853
建福/行銀南東
Tung Nan Yin Hang/Fu Chien

Provincial Bank of the Three Eastern Provinces
Bank of Manchuria
Provincial Bank of Manchuria
Eastern Provincial Bank
Toong San Sang Government Bank
#S2854-S2965
行銀省三東
Tung San Sheng Yin Hang
行銀官省三東
Tung San Sheng Kuan Yin Hang
號銀官省三東
Tung San Sheng Kuan Yin Hao
券兌 號銀官省三東
Tung San Sheng Kuan Yin Hui Tui Ch'üan

Provincial Bank of Honan
#S2971-s2985
局錢銀官泉豫
Yü Ch'Van Kuan Yin Ch'ien Chü

Yu Sien Bank
Yü Hsiang Bank
#S2988-S2994
行銀湘裕
Yün Hsiang Yin Hang

New Fu-Tien Bank
#S2996-S3004
行銀新滇富南雲
Yün Nan Fu T'ien Hsin Yin Hang

Fu-tien Bank
Yunnan "Fu-Tien" Bank
Yunnan "Futten" Bank
#S3009-S3023
行銀滇富南雲
Yün Nan Fu T'ien Yin Hang
行銀滇富
Fu T'ien Yin Hang

Yunnan Official Currency Bureau
#S3023E
局錢官南雲
Yün Nan Kuan Ch'ien Chü

Yunnan Provincial Bank
#S3024-S3031D
票本額定圓銀行銀省南雲
Yün Nan Sheng Yin Hang Yin Yüan Ting O Pen Piao

Bank of Territorial Developement of Yunan
#S3033-S3037
行銀邊殖辦合商官南雲
Yün Nan Kuan Shang Ho Ban Chih Pien Yin Hang

Islamic Republic of Turkestan
United Islamic Republic of East Turkestan
Revolutionary or Supreme Government #S3039-S3041

Islamic Republic of East Turkestan
#S3045-S3046

OVERPRINTS:

The various city or regional overprints are easily noted, being normally two or three Chinese characters usually in two or more places on a note and sometimes found in English on the other side of the note.

Various single Chinese control characters were applied, and appear in two or more places on a note. Sometimes western numerals were utilized and appear in circles, or outlined squares, etc.

The most frequently encountered overprint in the Three Eastern Provinces and Manchurian series is a four Chinese character overprint in a 21mm square outline. This *Official Controller's Seal* overprint supervised the amount of issue of certain banks and guaranteed the notes.

In certain cases we find available an original printers' specimen, an issued note, an issued note with the official overprint along with a "local" specimen of a circulated note bearing normal serial numbers. The purpose of this overprint at present eludes the authors at this writing.

NOTE: Catalog # in () are in reference to *CHINESE BANKNOTES* by Ward Smith and Brian Matravers, 1970, Shirjieh Publishers, Menlo Park, California.

Bank of Anhwei Provincial Government

安徽省銀號
An Hui Sheng Yin Hao

1925 Issue

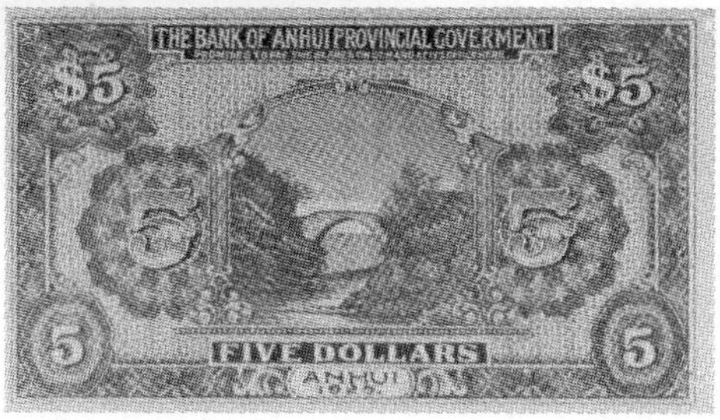

		VG	VF	UNC
S802	**5 Dollars** 1925. Red and yellow. Industrial waterfront at left, train at right. Back: Red. Arch bridge at center. *(S/M #A4-1).*	250.	600.	—
S803	**10 Dollars** 1925. Green on rose underprint. Train at left. Building and boat at right. Back: Bridge at center.	200.	500.	

Anhwei Regional Bank

安徽地方銀行
An Hui Ti Fang Yin Hang

1937 Issue

		VG	VF	UNC
S804	**1 Fen** ND (ca. 1937). Red. 2 signature varieties. Printer: TTBC. *(S/M #A5-0.5).*	5.00	10.00	40.00

		VG	VF	UNC
S805	**5 Fen** ND (ca. 1937). Brown. 2 signature varieties. Back: Red. Printer: TTBC. *(S/M #A5-1).*	5.00	10.00	40.00

		VG	VF	UNC
S806	**1 Chiao** ND (ca. 1937). Red. Tree at center. Back: Multicolor. Printer: TTBC. *(S/M #A5-2).*	5.00	10.00	40.00

		VG	VF	UNC
S807	**2 Chiao** ND (ca. 1937). Blue. Tree at center. Back: Multicolor. Printer: TTBC. *(S/M #A5-3).*	5.00	15.00	50.00

		VG	VF	UNC
S808	**5 Chiao** ND (ca. 1937). Violet. Landscape at center. Back: Green and multicolor. Printer: TTBC. *(S/M #A5-4).*	25.00	50.00	100.
S810	**1 Yüan** 1939. Red. Tree at left. 2 signature varieties. Back: Red. Printer: TTBC. *(S/M #A5-10).*	20.00	40.00	75.00

#S813-S815 printer: CHBA.

		VG	VF	UNC
S813	**1 Chiao** ND. Red. Pagoda at center. Back: Multicolor. Printer: CHBA. *(S/M #A5-20).*	5.00	10.00	40.00

		VG	VF	UNC
S814	**2 Chiao** ND. Blue. Pagoda at center. Back: Green. Printer: CHBA. *(S/M #A5-21).*	5.00	10.00	40.00

		VG	VF	UNC
S815	**5 Chiao** ND. Violet. Tree at center. Back: Multicolor. Printer: CHBA. *(S/M #A5-22).*	25.00	50.00	100.

Anhwei Yu Huan Bank

安徽裕皖官錢局
An Hui Yü Huan Kuan Ch'ien Chü

1907 Dollar Issue

		Good	Fine	XF
S819	**1 Dollar** 1907. Blue and yellow. Facing dragons in top and bottom border, dragon dollar at left and right of center. Back: Brown. Black text. Printer: CMPA. *(S/M #A6-1).*	50.00	150.	300.

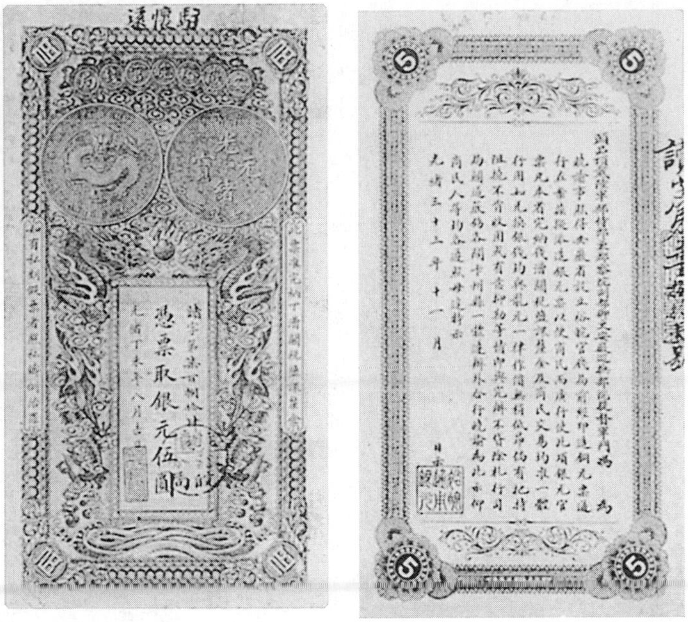

		Good	Fine	XF
S820	**5 Dollars** 1907. Black and brown on blue underprint. Dragon dollar above facing dragons at left and right. Back: Brown. Black text. Printer: CMPA. *(S/M #A6-2).*	200.	500.	900.

1909 Cash Issue

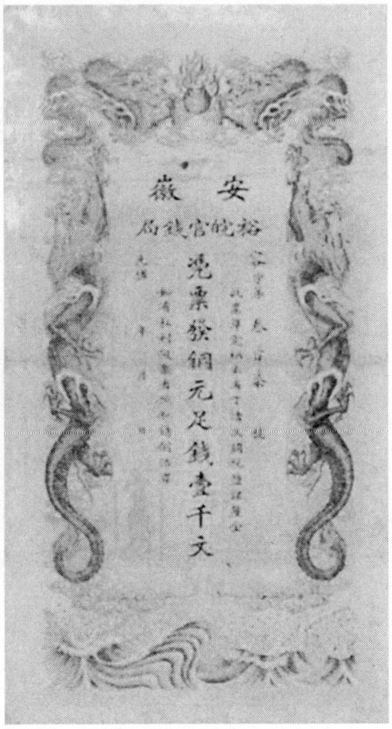

		Good	Fine	XF
S823	**1000 Cash** ND (ca. 1909). Blue and yellow. Facing dragons in upper border, waves at bottom. Back: Green. *(S/M #A6-10).*	75.00	225.	500.

> **A WORD ON DATE RANGES**
>
> Often date ranges or specific dates are listed. These have been observed or reported by our contributors. If a note is outside the published range, it only means that it is a newly reported date, and not necessarily worthy of a premium value.

Tsihar Hsing Yeh Bank

行銀業興爾哈察

Ch'a Ha Erh Hsing Yeh Yin Hang

1920 Dollar Issue

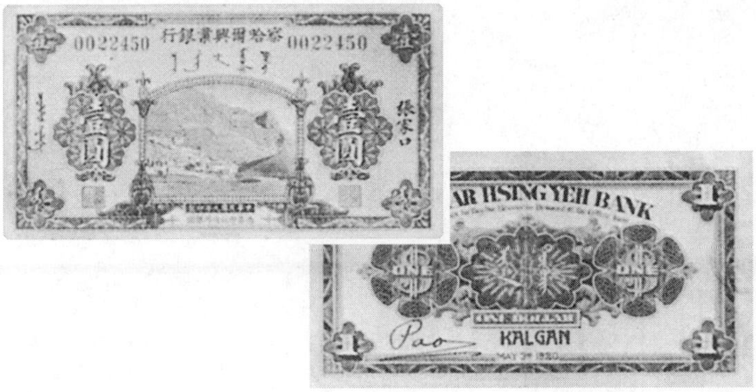

		VG	VF	UNC
S825	**1 Dollar** 3.5.1920. Green. Mountain village at center. *Kalgan* vertically in Manchu at left, Chinese at right. Back: Green. Printer: BEPP. *(S/M #C1-1).*	125.	250.	—
S825A	**20 Cash** 1920. Purple. Mountain village at center. *Kalgan* vertically in Manchu at left, Chinese at right. Overprint: *PEKING* on *KALGAN.*	125.	400.	—

		VG	VF	UNC
S826	**1 Dollar** 3.5.1920. Green. Mountain village at center. *Kalgan* vertically in Manchu at left, Chinese at right. Back: Green. *(S/M #C1-1).*			
	a. With *Kalgan* in Chinese horizontally below vertical Chinese at left and right.	125.	400.	—
	b. With *Kalgan* in Chinese below serial # at upper left and right.	125.	400.	—

#S829 *Deleted.* See #S833.

		VG	VF	UNC
S831	**10 Coppers** 1921. Green. Farm scene at right. Back: Brown. *Kalgan. (S/M #C1-).*	125.	400.	—

		VG	VF	UNC
S832	**20 Coppers** 1.6.1921; 1.6.1924. Yellow. Farm scene at right. Back: Blue. *KALGAN. (S/M #C1-11).*	125.	400.	—

1921 Copper Coin Issue

	VG	VF	UNC
S833 100 Coppers 1.6.1921. Yellow. Village at left. Back: Orange. *KALGAN. (S/M #C1-).*	200.	500.	—

1924 Dollar Issue

	VG	VF	UNC
S835 10 Cents 1924. Brown and blue. Hilltop pagoda, shoreline at center. Back: Violet. Printer: BEPP.			
a. *KALGAN. (S/M #C1-20a).*	50.00	175.	—
b. *PEKING. (S/M #C1-20b).*	50.00	175.	—
c. *TULONNOERH. (S/M #C1-20c).*	50.00	175.	—
d. *KALGAN* with additional square seal. *(S/M #C1-20d).*	50.00	175.	—

	VG	VF	UNC
S836 20 Cents 1924. Purple, brown and orange. Village at center. Back: Gray. Printer: BEPP.			
a. *KALGAN. (S/M #C1-21a).*	50.00	175.	—
b. *PEKING. (S/M #C1-21b).*	50.00	175.	—
c. *TULONNOERH. (S/M #C1-21c).*	50.00	175.	—
d. *KALGAN* with additional square red seal. *(S/M #C1-21d).*	50.00	175.	—

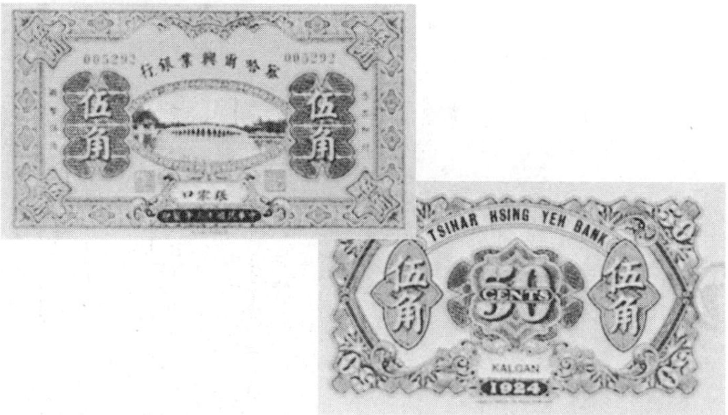

	VG	VF	UNC
S837 50 Cents 1924. Blue and brown. Bridge at center. Back: Brown. Printer: BEPP.			
a. *KALGAN. (S/M #C1-22a).*	100.	250.	—
b. *PEKING. (S/M #C1-22b).*	75.00	250.	—
c. *TULONNOERH. (S/M #C1-22c).*	75.00	250.	—

NOTE: For #S835-S837 with additional overprint, see Military-Bank of the Northwest #S3861-S3863.

1925 Copper Coin Issue

	VG	VF	UNC
S841 10 Coppers 1925. Green. Back: Blue. Printer: BEPP. *(S/M #C1-30).*	90.00	300.	—
S842 20 Coppers 1925. Brown. Back: Blue. Printer: BEPP. *S/M #C1-31).*	90.00	300.	—
S843 40 Coppers 1925. Brown. Back: Violet. Printer: BEPP. *(S/M #C1-32).*	90.00	300.	—
S844 100 Coppers 1925. Brown. Back: Red. Printer: BEPP. *(S/M #C1-33).*	90.00	300.	—

1926 Copper Coin Issue

	VG	VF	UNC
S847 10 Coppers 1926. Black. Mountain village at center. Back: Orange and blue. Printer: BEPP. *PEKING. (S/M #C1-40).*	90.00	300.	—

	VG	VF	UNC
S848 20 Coppers 1926. Brown on light blue underprint. Mountain village at center. Back: Brown. Printer: BEPP. *Peking/KALGAN.*			
a. Signature Pao Lien. *(S/M #C1-41a).*	50.00	200.	—
b. Signature Li En Ching. *(S/M #C1-41b).*	50.00	200.	—
r. Remainder. *(S/M #C1-41c).*	—	—	200.
S849 50 Coppers 1926. Green and yellow. Mountain village at center. Back: Green. Printer: BEPP. *(S/M #C1-42).*	90.00	300.	—

	VG	VF	UNC
S850 100 Coppers 1926. Red and green. Mountain village at center. Back: Red. Printer: BEPP. *PEKING / KALGAN. (S/M #C1-).*	100.	325.	—

1927 Issue

	VG	VF	UNC
S853 1 Dollar 1.11.1927. Green and multicolor. Pagoda on lakeside at center. Back: Green. Printer: BEPP.			
a. *KALGAN. (S/M #C1-50b).*	75.00	250.	600.
b. *PEKING. (S/M #C1-50).*	75.00	250.	600.
r. Remainder. *(S/M #C1-).*	—	100.	350.
S854 5 Dollars 1.11.1927. Orange and multicolor. Pagoda at lakeside at center. Back: Orange. Printer: BEPP.			
a. *PEKING. (S/M #C1-51).*	75.00	200.	600.
r. Remainder. *(S/M #C1-).*	—	125.	300.
S855 10 Dollars 1.11.1927. Tower at center. Printer: BEPP. *(S/M #C1-).* Reported not confirmed.	—	—	—

CHARHAR COMMERCIAL BANK

局錢業商爾哈察
Ch'a Ha Erh Shang Yeh Ch'ien Chu

1933 ISSUE

		VG	VF	UNC
S855D	**10 Coppers** Yr. 22 (1933). Blue. *Kalgan.*		—	

		VG	VF	UNC
S855E	**20 Coppers** Yr.22 (1933). Brown. Hillside building at center. *Kalgan. (S/M #C3-0.2).*	25.00	75.00	250.
S855F	**100 Coppers** Yr.22 (1933). Blue. Hillside building at center. *Kalgan. (S/M #C3-0.5).*	50.00	100.	275.
S856	**1 Chiao** Yr. 22 (1933). Blue-gray. Printer: BEPP. *Kalgan. (S/M #C3-0.7).*	—	—	—
S856A	**2 Chiao** Yr. 22 (1933). Red. Printer: BEPP. *Kalgan. (S/M #C3-0.8).*	—	—	—

		VG	VF	UNC
S856B	**1 Yüan** 1.12.1933. Brown. Junks in harbor at center right. Back: Brown. Hilltop temple at center. Printer: BEPP.			
	a. *Kalgan. (S/M #C3-1a).*	10.00	25.00	50.00
	b. *Peiping/Tientsin and various control numbers. (S/M #C3-1b).*	25.00	50.00	150.
	c. Without overprint on face or back. Kalgan.	25.00	50.00	150.

		VG	VF	UNC
S856C	**5 Yüan** 1.12.1933. Printer: BEPP.			
	a. *Kalgan. (S/M #C3-2a).*	10.00	25.00	50.00
	b. *Peiping/Tientsin and various control numbers. (S/M #C3-2b).*	25.00	75.00	225.
S856D	**10 Yüan** 1.12.1933. Purple on yellow underprint. Back: Green. Printer: BEPP.			
	a. *Kalgan. (S/M #C3-3a).*	10.00	25.00	75.00
	b. *Peiping/Tientsin. (S/M #C3-3b).*	—	—	—

1935 ISSUE

		VG	VF	UNC
S856G	**30 Coppers** Yr. 24 (1935). Green. Hillside building at center. *Kalgan. (S/M #C3-6).*	50.00	100.	200.
S856H	**40 Coppers** Yr. 24 (1935). Dark brown. Hillside building at center. *Kalgan. (S/M #C3-7).*	—	—	—

		VG	VF	UNC
S857A	**10 Cents** 1935. Brown. Hillside view at center right. Back: Steam ore train at center. Printer: BEPP. *Kalgan. (S/M #C3-10).*	5.00	10.00	25.00
S857B	**20 Cents** 1935. Green. Hillside view at center right. Back: Steam ore train at center. Printer: BEPP. *Kalgan. (S/M #C3-11).*	10.00	25.00	50.00

CHANGSHA BANK

行銀沙長
Ch'ang Sha Yin Hang

1928 ISSUE

#S858-S860 various control # overprint.

		VG	VF	UNC
S858	**1 Dollar** 1.1.1928. Purple on multicolor underprint. Back: Purple. Printer: ABNC. *HUNAN. (S/M #C14-1).*	150.	400.	—
S859	**5 Dollars** 1.1.1928. Green on multicolor underprint. Pavilion at center. Back: Green. Printer: ABNC. *HUNAN. (S/M #C14-2).*	125.	300.	—
S860	**10 Dollars** 1.1.1928. Brown on multicolor underprint. Modern building at center. Back: Brown. Printer: ABNC. *HUNAN. (S/M #C14-3).*	175.	500.	—

NOTE: For #S858-S860 with additional overprint, see Hunan Provincial Bank #S1951-S1953.

CHEKIANG PROVINCIAL BANK

行銀省江浙
Che Chiang Sheng Yin Hang

1949 SILVER DOLLAR ISSUE

		VG	VF	UNC
S863	**10 Cents** Yr. 38 (1949). Blue. Pagoda at left. Back: Blue. Printer: CPFT. *(S/M #C24-1).*	25.00	75.00	300.
S864	**20 Cents** Yr. 38 (1949). Orange. Printer: CPFT. *(S/M #C24-2).*	25.00	75.00	30.00
S865	**50 Cents** Yr. 38 (1949). Printer: CPFT. *(S/M #C24-3).*	40.00	100.	—

		VG	VF	UNC
S866	**1 Dollar** Yr. 38 (1949). Red. Pagoda at left, SYS dollar at right. Back: Red. Sampan dollar at center. Printer: CPFT. *(S/M #C24-10).*	10.00	25.00	50.00
S867	**5 Dollars** Yr. 38 (1949). Green. Printer: CPFT. *(S/M #C24-11).*	75.00	150.	—

1950 SILVER DOLLAR ISSUE

		VG	VF	UNC
S869	**5 Dollars** Yr. 39 (1950). Green. SYS at lower right. Back: Pagoda at lower right. *(S/M #C24-15).*	75.00	150.	300.

Chekiang Provincial Bank

浙 江 地 方 銀 行

Che Chiang Ti Fang Yin Hang

1932 Issue

S871 10 Cents — VG 20.00 | VF 40.00 | UNC 175.
1932. Green. Pavilion and pagoda at left, gateway at right. Back: Brown. Printer: CEPA. *HANGCHOW. (S/M #C26-1).*

S872 20 Cents — VG 40.00 | VF 100. | UNC 225.
1932. Blue. Pavillion and pagoda at left, gateway at right. Back: Green. Printer: CEPA. *HANGCHOW. (S/M #C26-2).*

S874 1 Dollar — VG 40.00 | VF 100. | UNC —
1932. Dark green on multicolor underprint. Building on hillside at center. Back: Blue. Printer: CEPA. *HANGCHOW. (S/M #C26-10).*

S875 5 Dollars — VG 75.00 | VF 200. | UNC —
1932. Blue on multicolor underprint. Pagoda at center. Back: Green. Printer: CEPA. *HANGCHOW. (S/M #C26-11).*

S876 10 Dollars — VG 100. | VF 250. | UNC —
1932. Violet on multicolor underprint. Lakeside pavilion at center. Back: Orange. Printer: CEPA. *HANGCHOW. (S/M #C26-12).*

1936 Issue

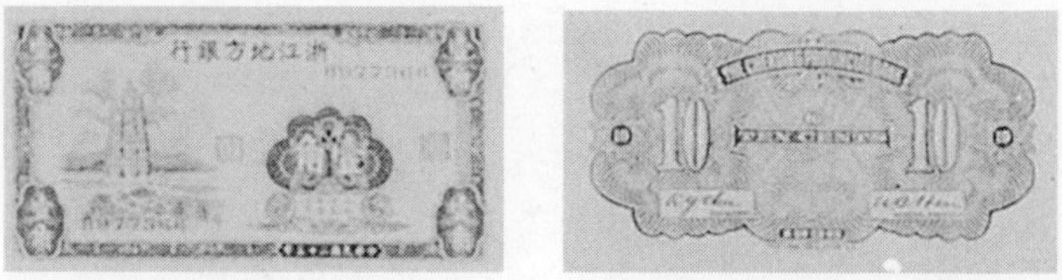

S877 10 Cents — VG 5.00 | VF 10.00 | UNC 25.00
1936. Green. Pagoda at left. Back: Multicolor. Printer: TTBC. *(S/M #C26-20).*

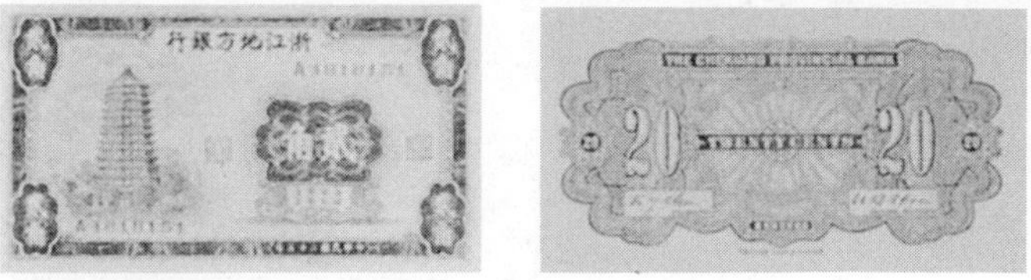

S878 20 Cents — VG 5.00 | VF 10.00 | UNC 25.00
1936. Blue. Pagoda at left. Back: Multicolor. Printer: TTBC. *(S/M #C26-21).*

S879 50 Cents — VG 5.00 | VF 10.00 | UNC 25.00
1936. Red. Pavilion at left. Back: Multicolor. Printer: TTBC. *(S/M #C26-22).*

1938 ND First Issue

		VG	VF	UNC
S880	**1 Cent** ND (ca. 1938). Blue. Back: Green. *(S/M #C26-30).*	2.50	5.00	10.00
S881	**2 Cents** ND (ca. 1938). Green. Back: Blue. *(S/M #C26-31).*	2.50	5.00	15.00
S882	**5 Cents** ND (ca. 1938). Red. Back: Blue. *(S/M #C26-33).*	2.50	5.00	15.00

1938 ND Second Issue

		VG	VF	UNC
S883	**1 Cent** ND (ca. 1938). Green. Back: Blue. *(S/M #C26-).*	5.00	10.00	30.00
S884	**2 Cents** ND (ca. 1938). Blue. Back: Light olive-green. *(S/M #C26-32).*	5.00	10.00	30.00
S885	**5 Cents** ND (ca. 1938). Red. *(S/M #C26-34).*	5.00	10.00	30.00

1939 Issue

S888 1 Yüan — VG 5.00 | VF 10.00 | UNC 30.00
1939. Blue and yellow. Pavilion at left. Back: Blue. Printer: TTBC. *(S/M #C26-40).*

1941 Issue

		VG	VF	UNC
S893	**1 Yüan** 1941. Blue. Pavillion at left. Back: Green and multicolor. Printer: TTBC. *(S/M #C26-50).*	5.00	10.00	30.00

Kirin Government Bank

吉林官錢局
Chi Lin Kuan Ch'ien Chü

1907-09 Issue

		VG	VF	UNC
S895	**1 Dollar** ND (ca. 1907-09). Black. Dragons at at upper left and right. Vertical format. Uniface. *(S/M #C71-1).*	400.	800.	—

Kirin Yung Heng Provincial Bank
Yung Heng Provincial Bank of Kirin

吉林永衡官銀錢局
Chi Lin Yung Heng Kuan Yin Ch'ien Chü

1898 Issue

		VG	VF	UNC
S901	**1 Tiao** Yr. 24 (1898). *(S/M #C76-0.1).* Reported not confirmed.	—	—	—

1902 Issue

		VG	VF	UNC
S911	**1 Tiao** Yr. 28 (1902). *(S/M #C76-0.2).* Reported not confirmed.	—	—	—

1904 Issue

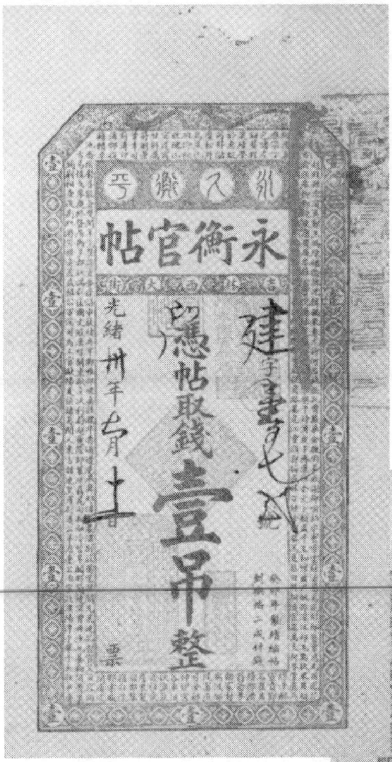

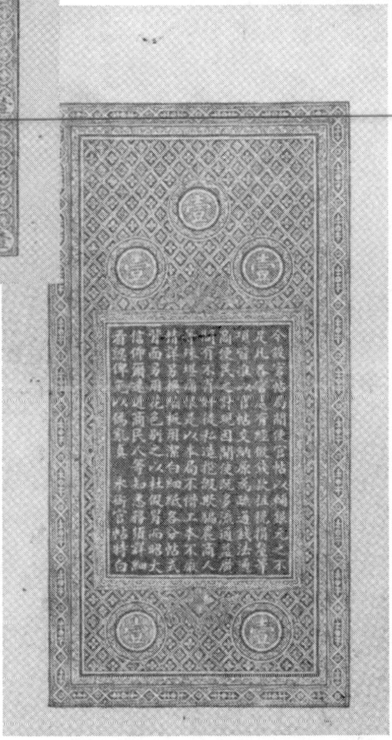

		VG	VF	UNC
S921	**1 Tiao** Yr. 30 (1904). Black. Vertical format. Back: Gray. *(S/M #C76-0.3).*	175.	500.	—

#S922 *Deleted.* See #S921.

1905 Issue

		VG	VF	UNC
S934	**10 Tiao** Yr. 31 (1905). *(S/M #C76-0.5).*	250.	600.	—
S935	**50 Tiao** Yr. 31 (1905). *(S/M #C76-0.6).* Reported not confirmed.	—	—	—

1906 Issue

		VG	VF	UNC
S941	**1 Tiao** Yr. 32 (1906). *(S/M #C76-0.7).*	175.	500.	—
S942	**2 Tiao** Yr. 32 (1906). *(S/M #C76-0.8).*	175.	500.	—

1907 Issue

		VG	VF	UNC
S951	**1 Tiao** Yr. 33 (1907). *(S/M #C76-).* Reported not confirmed.	—	—	—

1908 Issue

		VG	VF	UNC
S961	**1 Tiao** Yr. 34 (1908). Black. *(S/M #C76-1).*	300.	750.	—
S962	**2 Tiao** Yr. 34 (1908). *(S/M #C76-2).*	300.	750.	—
S963	**3 Tiao** Yr. 34 (1908). *(S/M #C76-3).*	400.	800.	—
S964	**5 Tiao** Yr. 34 (1908). *(S/M #C76-4).*	400.	800.	—
S965	**10 Tiao** Yr. 34 (1908). *(S/M #C76-5).*	500.	1000.	—
S966	**50 Tiao** Yr. 34 (1908). *(S/M #C76-6).*	500.	1000.	—
S967	**100 Tiao** Yr. 34 (1908). *(S/M #C76-7).* Reported not confirmed.	—	—	—

1911 Issue

#S968-S974 issued in the year of the Emperor Hsuan T'ung.

		VG	VF	UNC
S968	**1 Tiao** Yr. 3 (1911). Black with red seals. Back: Red. *(S/M #C76-10).*	150.	400.	—
S969	**2 Tiao** Yr. 3 (1911). *(S/M #C76-11).*	150.	400.	—
S970	**3 Tiao** Yr. 3 (1911). *(S/M #C76-12).*	200.	500.	—
S971	**5 Tiao** Yr. 3 (1911). *(S/M #C76-13).*	175.	450.	—
S972	**10 Tiao** Yr. 3 (1911). *(S/M #C76-14).*	200.	500.	—
S973	**50 Tiao** Yr. 3 (1911). *(S/M #C76-15).* Reported not confirmed.	—	—	—
S974	**100 Tiao** Yr. 3 (1911). *(S/M #C76-).* Reported not confirmed.	—	—	—

1913 Issue

		VG	VF	UNC
S976	**2 Tiao** 1913. *(S/M #C76-21).*	150.	300.	—
S977	**3 Tiao** 1913. *(S/M #C76-22).*	150.	400.	—
S978	**5 Tiao** (ca. 1913). *(S/M #C76-23).*	150.	400.	—
S979	**10 Tiao** (ca. 1913). *(S/M #C76-24).*	150.	400.	—
S980	**50 Tiao** (ca. 1913). *(S/M #C76-25).*	—	—	—
S981	**100 Tiao** (ca. 1913). *(S/M #C76-26).*	—	—	—

1916-17 Provisional Issue

#S981A Overprint: *Chung Hua Min Kuo* over *Hsuan T'ung* on #S968.

		VG	VF	UNC
S981A	**1 Tiao** 1916-17. Vertical format. Overprint: *Chung Hua Min Kuo* over *Hsuan T'ung* on #S968. Issued in the year of the Republic. *(S/M #C76-20).*	20.00	50.00	125.

1917-18 Issue

#S982-S988 issued in the year of the Republic. Overprint: Red seals.

		VG	VF	UNC
S982	**1 Tiao** 1917-18. Overprint: Red seals. Printer: BEPK. *(S/M #C76-30).*	20.00	50.00	125.
S983	**2 Tiao** 1916-17. Overprint: Red seals. Printer: BEPK. *(S/M #C76-31).*	40.00	75.00	—
S984	**3 Tiao** 1916-17. Overprint: Red seals. Printer: BEPK. *(S/M #C76-32).*	40.00	75.00	—
S985	**5 Tiao** 1917-18. Dark green with black text. Back: Yellow-orange. Overprint: Red seals. Printer: BEPK. *(S/M #C76-33).*	20.00	50.00	—

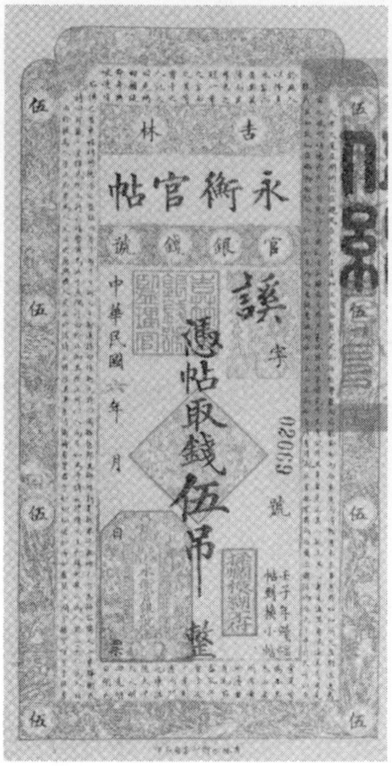

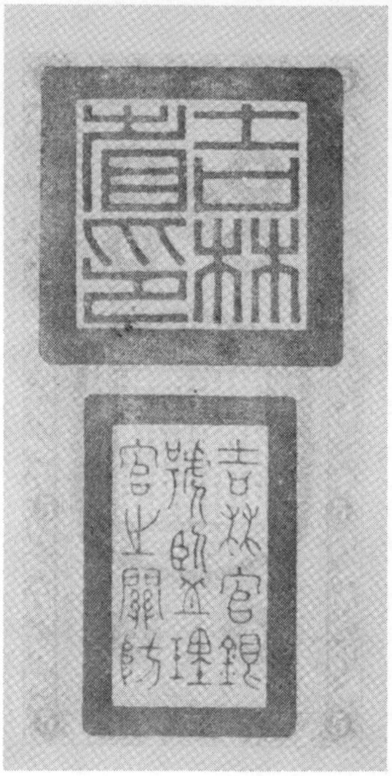

		VG	VF	UNC
S986	**10 Tiao** 1916-17. Yellow orange with black text. Vertical format. Back: Blue and green. Overprint: Red seals. Printer: BEPK. *(S/M #C76-34).*	10.00	25.00	—
S987	**50 Tiao** 1916-17. Overprint: Red seals. Printer: BEPK. *(S/M #C76-35).*	40.00	75.00	—
S988	**100 Tiao** 1916-18. Overprint: Red seals. Printer: BEPK. *(S/M #C76-36).*	—	—	—

1917 "Big Money" Issue

		Good	Fine	XF
S989	**1 Dollar** 1917. Printer: BEPK. *(S/M #C76-40).*	—	—	—
S990	**3 Dollars** 1917. Printer: BEPK. *(S/M #C76-41).*	—	—	—

NOTE: For #S990 w/additional overprint. see Frontier Bank #S2549.

		Good	Fine	XF
S991	**5 Dollars** 1917. Printer: BEPK. *(S/M #C76-).*	—	—	—
S992	**10 Dollars** 1917. Printer: BEPK. *(S/M #C76-).*	—	—	—

1917 "Small Money" Issue

		Good	Fine	XF
S994	**1 Yüan** 1917. Printer: BEPK. *(S/M #C76-42).*	—	—	—

		Good	Fine	XF
S995	**3 Yüan** 1917. Printer: BEPK. *(S/M #C76-43).*	—	—	—
S996	**5 Yüan** 1917. Printer: BEPK. *(S/M #C76-44).*	—	—	—
S997	**10 Yüan** 1917. Printer: BEPK. *(S/M #C76-45).*	—	—	—
S998	**50 Yüan** 1917. Printer: BEPK. *(S/M #C76-46).*	—	—	—

1918 Tiao Issue

		VG	VF	UNC
S1003	**100 Tiao** 1918. Red. Back: Green. Printer: BEPK. *(S/M #C76-50).*	75.00	150.	—

1918 First "Small Money" Issue

		VG	VF	UNC
S1005	**5 Cents** 1918. Blue-green. Back: Black. *(S/M #C76-).*	50.00	125.	—
S1006	**10 Cents** 1918. Blue-green. Back: Black. Printer: BEPK. *(S/M #C76-60).*			
	a. Issued note.	5.00	15.00	40.00
	s. Specimen.	—	—	100.

		VG	VF	UNC
S1007	**20 Cents** 1918. Violet and green. Building at center. Back: Green. Printer: BEPK. *(S/M #C76-62).*	20.00	50.00	100.

NOTE: For #S1006 and S1007 with additional overprint, see Frontier Bank #S2545 and S2546.

		VG	VF	UNC
S1008	**50 Cents** 1918. Blue and orange. Gateway at left. Back: Orange. Printer: BEPK. *(S/M #C76-64).*	25.00	60.00	125.

1918 Second "Small Money" Issue

		VG	VF	UNC
S1009	**1 Chiao** 1918. Black and green. Without imprint. Back: Olive. Buildings at center. *(S/M #C76-61).*	40.00	100.	250.

NOTE: For #S1009 with additional overprint, see Frontier Bank #S2544.

		VG	VF	UNC
S1010	**2 Chiao** 1918. Violet. Without imprint. *(S/M #C76-63).*	100.	225.	400.
S1011	**5 Chiao** 1918. Blue. Without imprint. Back: Red. *(S/M #C76-65).*	100.	225.	400.
S1012	**1 Yüan** 1918. Without imprint. *(S/M #C76-72).*	125.	300.	600.
S1013	**5 Yüan** 1918. Without imprint. *(S/M #C76-75).*	125.	300.	600.
S1014	**10 Yüan** 1918. Without imprint. *(S/M #C76-82).*	150.	400.	800.
S1015	**50 Yüan** 1918. Without imprint. *(S/M #C76-83).*	150.	400.	800.

1918 Dollar Issue

		VG	VF	UNC
S1017	**1 Dollar** 1918. Blue and green. Sampans at center. Back: Orange. Printer: BEPA. *(S/M #C76-71).* Payment: *IN SUBSIDIARY COINS.*	100.	225.	400.
S1018	**5 Dollars** 1918. Brown and blue. Back: Green. Printer: BEPA. *(S/M #C76-74).* Payment: *IN SUBSIDIARY COINS.*	125.	300.	600.
S1019	**10 Dollars** 1918. Blue. Back: Brown. Printer: BEPA. *(S/M #C76-81).* Payment: *IN SUBSIDIARY COINS.*	150.	400.	—

1918 "Big Money" Issue

		VG	VF	UNC
S1020	**1 Dollar** 1918. Green. Deer by woods at river's edge at center. Back: Blue. Printer: BEPA. *(S/M #C76-70).*			
	a. Issued note.	50.00	125.	250.
	s. Specimen.	—	—	350.
S1021	**5 Dollars** 1918. Printer: BEPA. *(S/M #C76-73).*	75.00	200.	—
S1022	**10 Dollars** 1918. Printer: BEPA. *(S/M #C76-80).*	150.	350.	—

1920 Tiao Issue

		VG	VF	UNC
S1023	**1 Tiao** 1920. Printer: YHBA. *(S/M #C76-90).*	40.00	125.	—
S1024	**2 Tiao** 1920. Printer: YHBA. *(S/M #C76-91).*	50.00	150.	—
S1025	**3 Tiao** 1920. Printer: YHBA. *(S/M #C76-92).*	50.00	150.	—

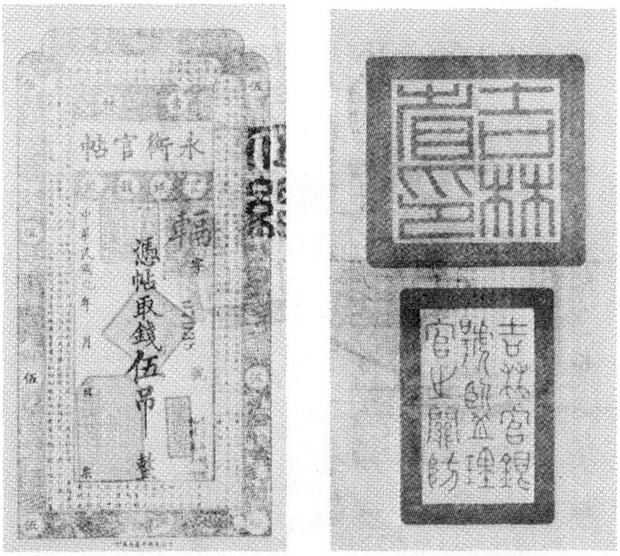

		VG	VF	UNC
S1026	**5 Tiao** 1920. Vertical format. Printer: YHBA. *(S/M #C76-93).*	40.00	125.	—
S1027	**10 Tiao** 1920. Printer: YHBA. *(S/M #C76-94).*	40.00	125.	—
S1028	**50 Tiao** 1920. Printer: YHBA. *(S/M #C76-95).*	40.00	125.	—
S1029	**100 Tiao** 1920. Red. Back: Green. Printer: YHBA. *(S/M #C76-96).*	40.00	125.	—
S1030	**100 Tiao** 1920. Orange. Back: Green. Printer: KOPB. *(S/M #C76-97).*	40.00	125.	—

1921 Dollar Issue

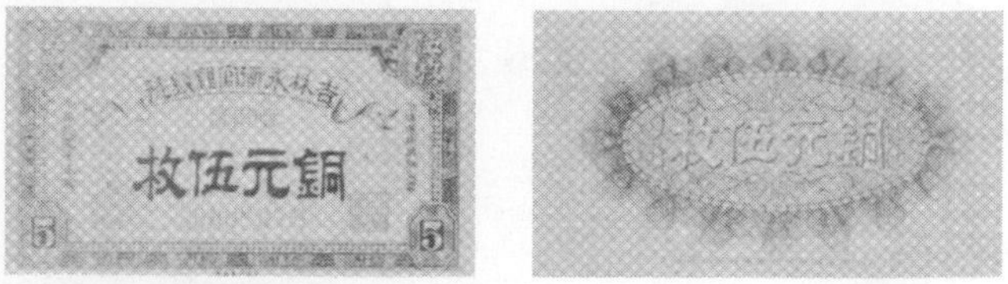

		VG	VF	UNC
S1031	**5 Coppers** 1921. Printer: BEPK. *Harbin. (S/M #C76-).*	25.00	75.00	—
S1032	**10 Coppers** 1921. Printer: BEPK. *Harbin. (S/M #C76-).*	25.00	75.00	—
S1033	**20 Coppers** 1921. Printer: BEPK. *Harbin. (S/M #C76-).*	25.00	75.00	—
S1034	**50 Coppers** 1921. Printer: BEPK. *Harbin. (S/M #C76-).*	25.00	75.00	—
S1035	**100 Coppers** 1921. Dark brown on light green underprint. Great Wall at left. Back: Black. Printer: BEPK. *Harbin. (S/M #C76-).*	25.00	75.00	—
S1036	**5 Cents** 1921. Printer: BEPK. *Harbin. (S/M #C76-).*	20.00	60.00	—
S1037	**10 Cents** 1921. Printer: BEPK. *Harbin. (S/M #C76-).*	20.00	60.00	—
S1038	**20 Cents** 1921. Printer: BEPK. *Harbin. (S/M #C76-).*	20.00	60.00	—
S1039	**1 Dollar** 1921. Printer: BEPK. *Harbin. (S/M #C76-).*	20.00	60.00	—
S1040	**5 Dollars** 1921. Printer: BEPK. *Harbin. (S/M #C76-).*	20.00	60.00	—
S1041	**10 Dollars** 1921. Printer: BEPK. *Harbin. (S/M #C76-).*	20.00	60.00	—

1923 "Big Money" Issues

		VG	VF	UNC
S1044	**5 Cents** 1923. Blue-black on light green underprint. Village wall at left. Back: Dark blue-green. Printer: BEPP. *HARBIN. (S/M #C76-9.9).*	75.00	225.	—
S1045	**10 Cents** 1923. Dark blue on light blue underprint. Steam passenger train at left. Back: Dark blue. Printer: BEPP. *(S/M #C76-100).*	75.00	225.	—

		VG	VF	UNC
S1046	**20 Cents** 1923. Dark blue on light orange underprint. Steamship, boats at left. Back: Purple. Printer: BEPP. *HARBIN. (S/M #C76-101).*			
	a. Issued note.	75.00	225.	—
	s. Specimen.	—	—	300.

NOTE: For #S1045 and S1046 with additional overprint, see Frontier Bank #S2556 and S2557.

		VG	VF	UNC
S1048	**1 Dollar** 1923. Printer: BEPP. *HARBIN. (S/M #C76-110).*	250.	500.	—
S1049	**5 Dollars** 1923. Printer: BEPP. *HARBIN. (S/M #C76-112).*	200.	400.	—
S1050	**10 Dollars** 1923. Printer: BEPP. *HARBIN. (S/M #C76-114).*	75.00	225.	—

#S1051-S1053 *Harbin* with additional red 4 Chinese character government overprint.

		VG	VF	UNC
S1051	**1 Dollar** 1.12.1923. Orange and multicolor. Back: Brown. Overprint: *Harbin* with additional red 4 Chinese character government overprint. Printer: ABNC. *(S/M #C76-111).*	150.	350.	—

		VG	VF	UNC
S1052	**5 Dollars** 1.12.1923. Green and multicolor. Pavilion at center. Back: Orange. Overprint: *Harbin* with additional red 4 Chinese character government overprint. Printer: ABNC. *(S/M #C76-113).*	100.	225.	—
S1053	**10 Dollars** 1.12.1923. Violet and multicolor. Back: Green. Overprint: *Harbin* with additional red 4 Chinese character government overprint. Printer: ABNC. *(S/M #C76-115).*			
	a. Issued note.	25.00	50.00	100.
	b. Cancelled.	—	—	80.00

NOTE: For #S1051-S1053 with additional overprint, see Frontier Bank #S2559-S2561.

1925 Issue

		VG	VF	UNC
S1055	**5 Dollars** 1.9.1925. Green on multicolor underprint. Monument at right. Back: Green. Printer: Ministry of Finance. Specimen. *(S/M #C76-119).*	—	—	300.
S1056	**10 Dollars** 1925. Olive-green on yellow underprint. Temple of Divine Light at right. Back: Blue. Printer: Ministry of Finance. Specimen. *(S/M #C76120).*	—	—	300.

1926 "Small Money" Issue

		VG	VF	UNC
S1058	**10 Cents** 1926. Printer: YHBA. *(S/M #C76-122).*	75.00	150.	—
S1059	**20 Cents** 1926. Printer: YHBA. *(S/M #C76-124).*	75.00	150.	—
S1060	**50 Cents** 1926. Printer: YHBA. *(S/M #C76-126).*	100.	200.	—
S1061	**1 Dollar** 1926. Printer: YHBA. *(S/M #C76-130).*	100.	200.	—

1926 "Big Money" Issue

		VG	VF	UNC
S1062	**5 Cents** 1926. Green and red. Farmer seated by cattle at center. Back: Green. Printer: BEPK. *(S/M #C76-120).*	75.00	150.	—

S1063 10 Cents | VG 75.00 | VF 150. | UNC —
1926. Red and yellow. Battleship and dirigible at right. Back: Red. Printer: BEPK. *(S/M #C76-121).*

S1064 20 Cents | VG 50.00 | VF 125. | UNC —
1926. Red and yellow. Tower gate at left. Back: Red. Printer: BEPK. *(S/M #C76-123).*

S1065 50 Cents | VG 25.00 | VF 50.00 | UNC 150.
1926. Brown and red. Pavilion at center. Back: Brown. Printer: BEPK. *(S/M #C76-125).*

	VG	VF	UNC
S1066 1 Dollar 1926. Black and multicolor. House at left. Back: Black. Printer: ABNC. *(S/M #C76-131).*	75.00	225.	400.
S1067 5 Dollars 1926. Blue and multicolor. House at right. Back: Blue. Printer: ABNC. *(S/M #C76-132).*	125.	300.	600.
S1068 10 Dollars 1926. Green and multicolor. Back: Green. Printer: ABNC. *(S/M #C76-133).*	100.	200.	400.

1928 Provisional Tiao Issue

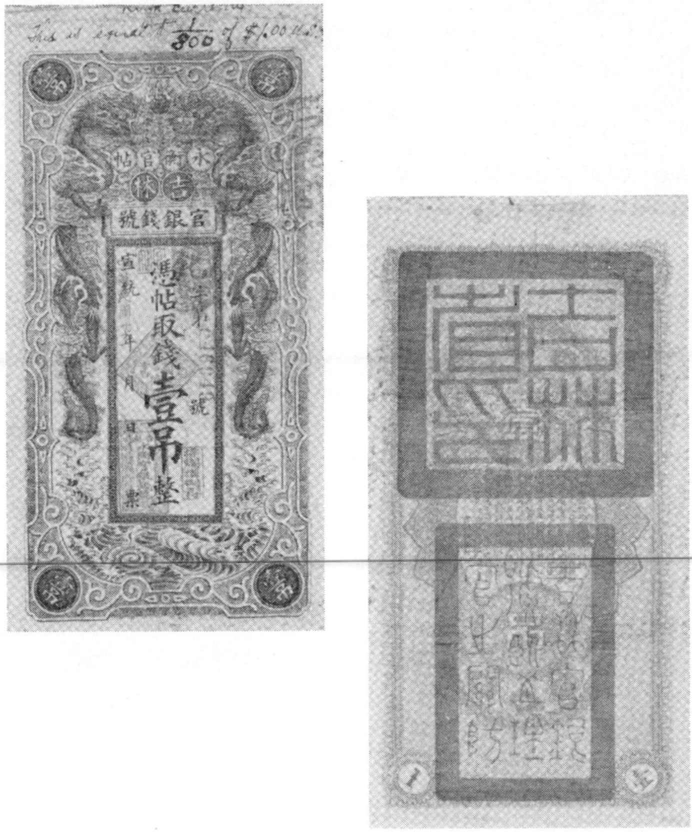

S1071 1 Tiao | VG 25.00 | VF 75.00 | UNC 200.
1928. Black. Overprint: On #S968. *(S/M #C76-140).*

1928 Regular Tiao Issue

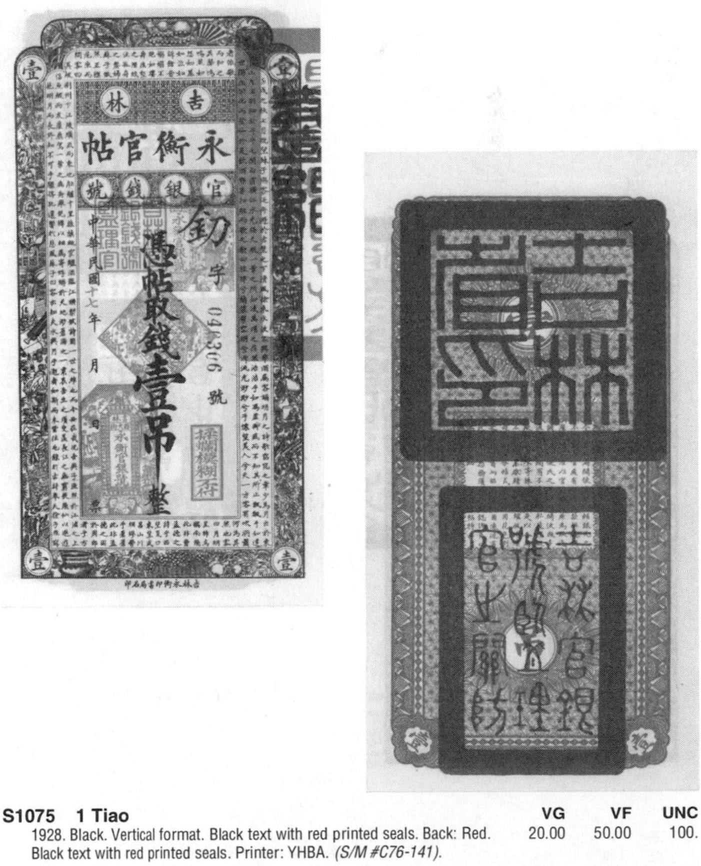

S1075 1 Tiao | VG 20.00 | VF 50.00 | UNC 100.
1928. Black. Vertical format. Black text with red printed seals. Back: Red. Black text with red printed seals. Printer: YHBA. *(S/M #C76-141).*

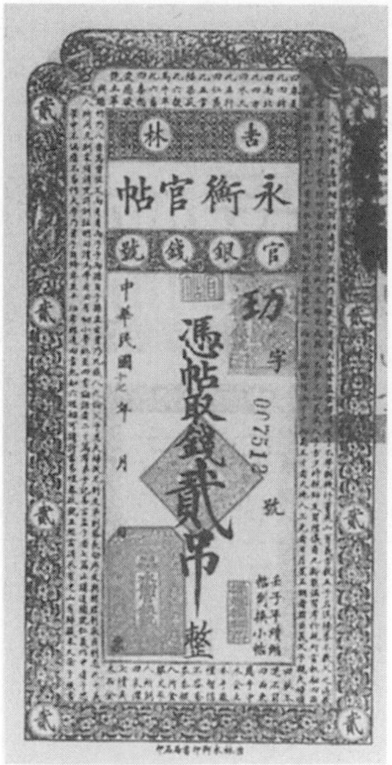

S1076 2 Tiao

1928. Black. Black text with red printed seals. Back: Red. Black text with red printed seals. Printer: YHBA. *(S/M #C76-142).*

VG	VF	UNC
20.00	60.00	125.

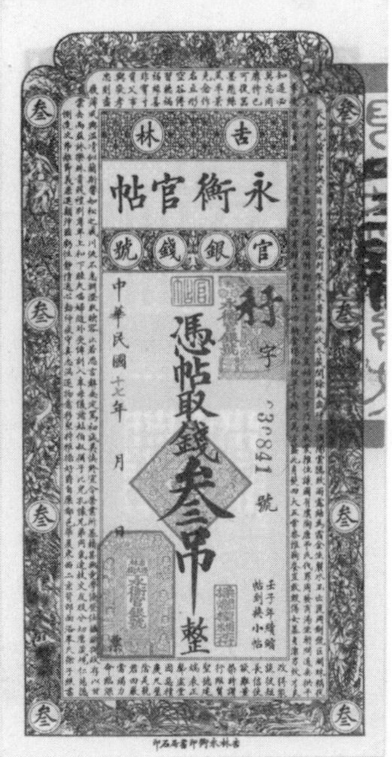

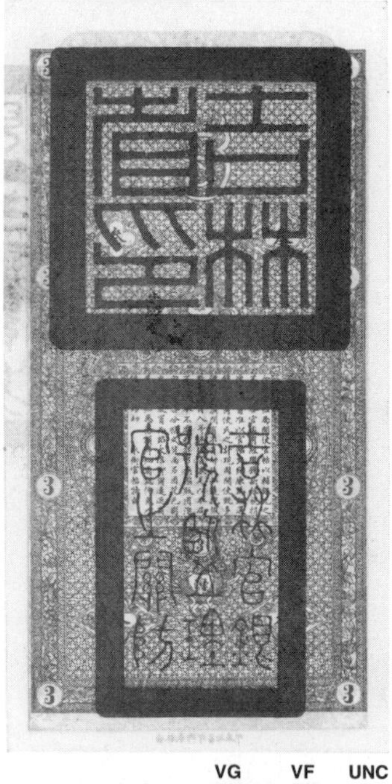

S1077 3 Tiao

1928. Black. Black text with red printed seals. Back: Red. Black text with red printed seals. Printer: YHBA. *(S/M #C76-143).*

VG	VF	UNC
20.00	60.00	125.

S1078 4 Tiao

1928. Black text with red printed seals. Back: Black text with red printed seals. Printer: YHBA. *(S/M #C76-144).* Reported not confirmed.

VG	VF	UNC
50.00	100.	200.

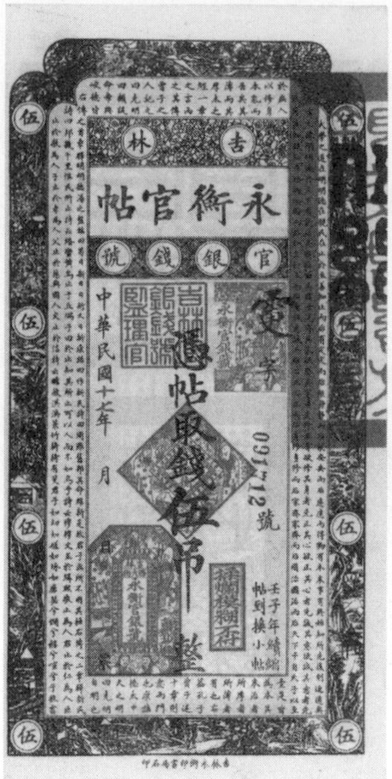

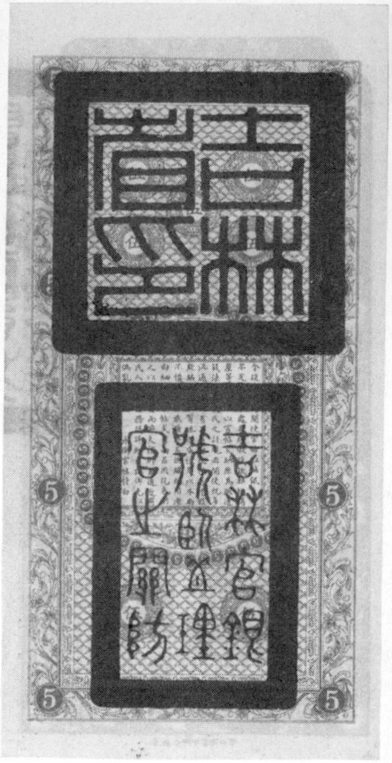

S1079 5 Tiao

1928. Dark green. Black text with red seals. Back: Orange. Black text with red seals. Printer: YHBA. *(S/M #C76-145).*

	VG	VF	UNC
a. Red seals.	20.00	60.00	125.
b. Orange seals on face.	20.00	60.00	125.

S1080 10 Tiao

1928. Orange. Black text with red seals. Back: Green. Two men carrying a canoe at bottom center. Vertical format. Black text with red seals. Printer: YHBA. *(S/M #C76-146).*

VG	VF	UNC
20.00	60.00	125.

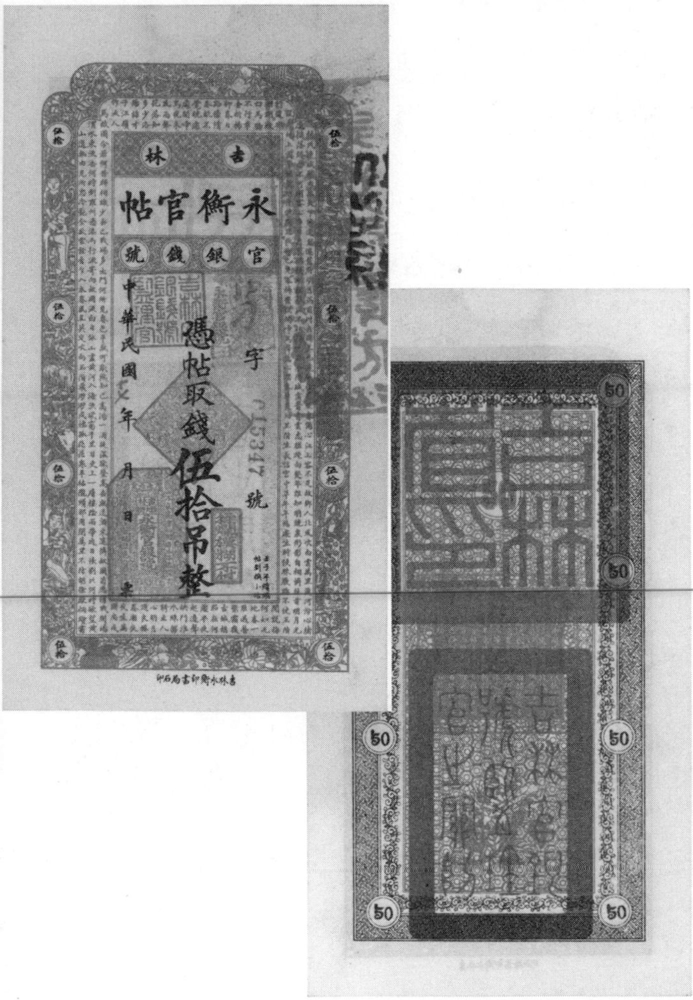

S1081 50 Tiao

	VG	VF	UNC
1928. Red. Black text with red seals. Back: Blue. Black text with red seals. Printer: YHBA. *(S/M #C76-147).*	20.00	60.00	125.

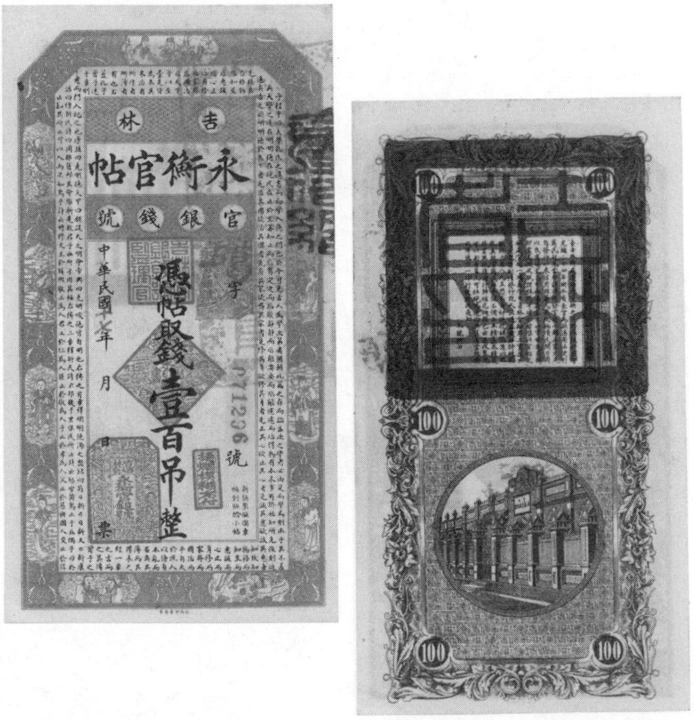

S1081A 100 Tiao

	VG	VF	UNC
1928. Orange. Ornamental fence with building in background. Vertical format. Black text with red printed seals. Back: Green. Black text with red printed seals. Printer: YHBA. *(S/M #C76-148).*	20.00	60.00	125.

1932 "Big Money" Issue

S1081F 5 Dollars

	VG	VF	UNC
Yr. 21 (1932). Red-brown. Black text with red printed seals. Back: Black text with red printed seals. Printer: YHBA. *(S/M #C76-160).*	100.	250.	500.

Reconstruction Bank of Kiangsi

江西建設銀行

Chiang Hsi Chien She Yin Hang

1932 Issue

#S1082 *Deleted.* See #S1081A.

S1082A 10 Coppers

1932. Red on green underprint. Fortress at center. Back: Blue. Steam passenger train at center. *(S/M #C90-0.1).*

	VG	VF	UNC
a. Issued note.	20.00	40.00	75.00
b. *Chiuchiang. (S/M #C90-0.1a).*	20.00	60.00	—
c. *Chian. (S/M #C90-0.1b).*	20.00	60.00	—
d. *Linch'uan. (S/M #C90-0.1c).*	20.00	60.00	—

1939 Issue

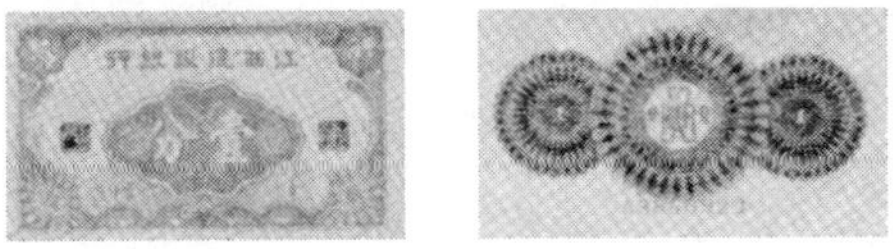

	VG	VF	UNC
S1082B 1 Cent			
ND (1939). Red. Back: Black. Ancient shoe cast coin at center. *(S/M #C90-0.5).*	20.00	60.00	—
S1082C 2 Cents			
ND (1939). *(S/M #C90-0.6).*	20.00	60.00	—
S1082D 5 Cents			
ND (1939). Red. Back: Blue. *(S/M #C90-1).*	10.00	25.00	—
S1082E 10 Cents			
1939. Blue. *(S/M #C90-10).*	10.00	25.00	—

S1082F 20 Cents

	VG	VF	UNC
1939. Blue. Great Wall at right. Back: Blue and brown. *(S/M #C90-11).*	25.00	75.00	—

	VG	VF	UNC
S1082G 50 Cents			
1939. Red. Building at center. Back: Automobile at center. *(S/M #C90-12).*	25.00	75.00	—
S1082H 50 Cents			
1939. Red. Radio towers at right. *(S/M #C90-13).*	25.00	75.00	—

Kiangse Government Bank

Chiang Hsi Kuan Yin Ch'ien Tsung Hao

1907 Cash Issue

S1082L 1000 Cash

	VG	VF	UNC
ND (ca. 1907). Dark blue and red. Dragon at top, facing dragons at left and right. Back: Red with black text. *(S/M #C94-0.4).*	200.	400.	—

1907 Dollar Issue

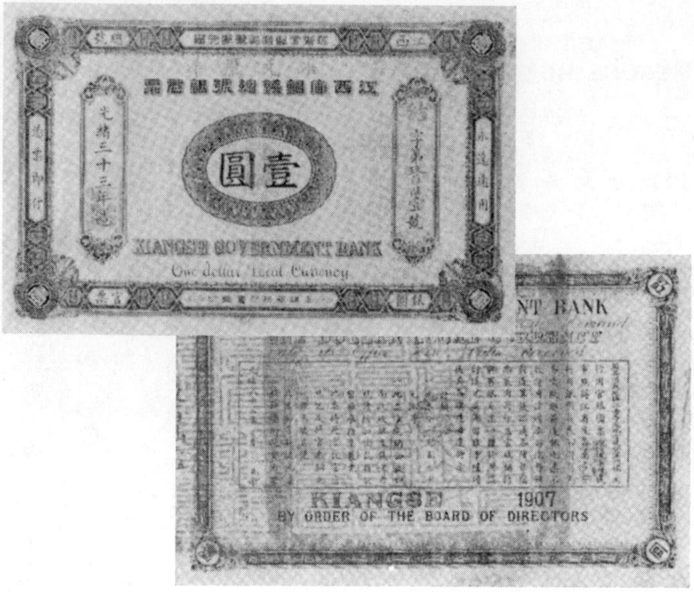

		VG	VF	UNC
S1083	**1 Dollar**			
	Yr. 33 (1907). Black and blue. Back: Black with red seal. Printer: CMPA. *(S/M #C94-1)*.	225.	600.	—
S1084	**5 Dollars**			
	Yr. 33 (1907). Black and blue. Back: Black with red seal. Printer: CMPA. *(S/M #C94-2)*. Reported not confirmed.	225.	600.	—

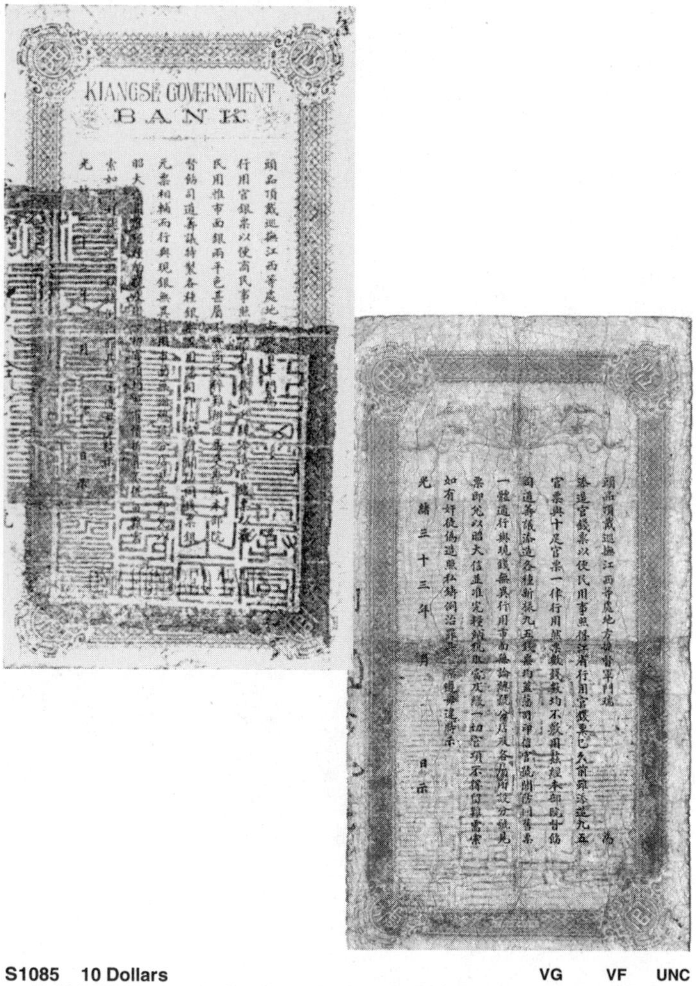

		VG	VF	UNC
S1085	**10 Dollars**			
	Yr. 33 (1907). Black and blue. Back: Black with red seal. Printer: CMPA. *(S/M #C94-3)*.	400.	800.	—

1907 Tael Issue

		VG	VF	UNC
S1085H	**100 Taels**			
	Yr. 33 (1907). Gray-black. Facing dragons at upper left and right. Vertical format. *(S/M #C94-15)*.	450.	900.	—

NOTE: "Chinese Banknotes" had titles switched in error for S/M #C94 and C95.

Public Bank of Kiangsi

江西公立銀行
Chiang Hsi Kung Li Yin Hang

1905-07 Issue

		VG	VF	UNC
S1086	**1000 Cash**			
	Yr. 31 (1905). *(S/M #C95-1)*.	300.	750.	—
S1088	**1 Tael**			
	Yr. 33 (1907). *(S/M #C95-11)*. Reported not confirmed.	—	—	—
S1089	**100 Taels**			
	Yr. 33 (1907). *(S/M #C95-17)*. Reported not confirmed.	—	—	—

Kiangsi Provincial Bank

江西省銀行
Chiang Hsi Sheng Yin Hang

1949 Issue

		VG	VF	UNC
S1089C	**10 Cents**			
	July 1949. Dark Blue. *(S/M #C98-3)*.			
	a. Issued note.	5.00	25.00	75.00
	s. Specimen.	5.00	25.00	75.00
S1089D	**20 Cents**			
	July 1949. Brown-violet. *(S/M #C98-4)*.	5.00	25.00	75.00

		VG	VF	UNC
S1089E	**50 Cents**			
	July 1949. Red. Specimen. *(S/M #C98-5)*.	—	—	225.

Kiangsi Regional Bank

江西地方銀行
Chiang Hsi Ti Fang Yin Hang

ND Provisional Issue

#S1090-S1093 overprint new bank name on issues of Kan Sen Bank of Kiangsi.

		VG	VF	UNC
S1090	**10 Coppers**			
	ND (- old date 1925). Overprint: On #S2227A. *(S/M #C100-1)*.	150.	350.	—
S1091	**1 Dollar**			
	ND (- old date 1924). Overprint: On #S2225. *(S/M #C100-10)*. Reported not confirmed.	200.	400.	—
S1092	**5 Dollars**			
	ND (- old date 1924). Overprint: On #S2226. *(S/M #C100-11)*.	125.	250.	—

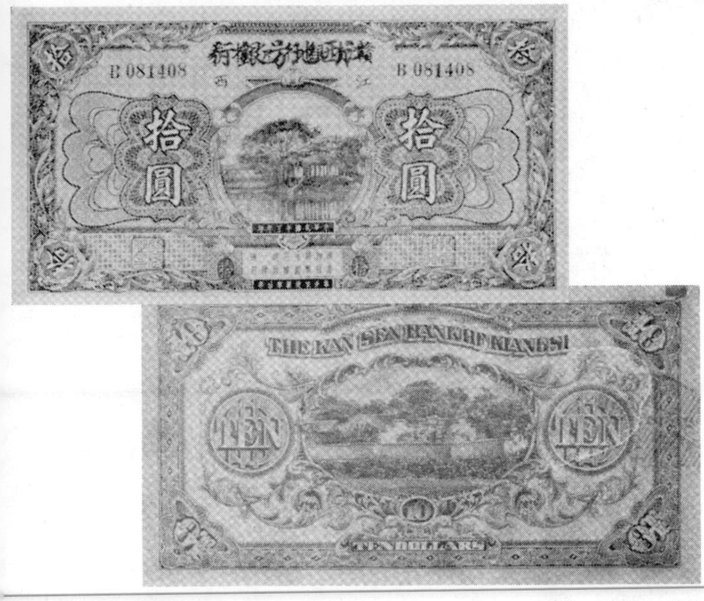

		VG	VF	UNC
S1093	**10 Dollars** ND (- old date 1924). Overprint: On #S2227. *(S/M #C100-12).*	150.	300.	—

Kiangsi Finance Bureau

江西財政廳

Chiang Hsi Ts'ai Cheng T'ing

1924 Issue

		VG	VF	UNC
S1093C	**1/2 Dollar** ND (1924). Brown on light blue underprint. Shoreline house at center. Back: Red.	225.	450.	—

		VG	VF	UNC
S1093D	**1 Yüan** 1.9. Yr. 13 (1924). Blue on purple underprint. Shoreline house at center. Back: Purple. Text. *(S/M #C101-0.5).*	100.	250.	—

1926/27 Issue

		VG	VF	UNC
S1094	**1 Yüan** Yr.15/16 (1926/27). Green and red. Pavilion at center. *(S/M #C101-1).*	150.	450.	—
S1095	**5 Yüan** Yr. 15/16 (1926/27). *(S/M #C101-2).* Reported not confirmed.	—	—	—
S1096	**10 Yüan** Yr. 15/16 (1926/27). *(S/M #C101-3).* Reported not confirmed.	—	—	—

Bank of Kiangsi

江西銀行

Chiang Hsi Yin Hang

ND Issue

		VG	VF	UNC
S1097	**1 Dollar** ND. Orange and multicolor. Back: Brown. Printer: CCCA. *(S/M #C102-1).*	75.00	150.	—

NOTE: For #S1097 with additional overprint which was issued by the quasi-national Central Bank of China, see #181A, Vol. 2.

		VG	VF	UNC
S1098	**5 Dollars** ND. Green on multicolor underprint. Back: Blue. Printer: CCCA. *(S/M #C102-2).*	225.	600.	—
S1099	**10 Dollars** ND. Blue and multicolor. Back: Green. Printer: CCCA. *(S/M #C102-3).*	75.00	225.	—

1916 Dollar Issue

		VG	VF	UNC
S1100	**1 Dollar** 1916. Red and blue. Back: Blue and yellow. Printer: PHCF. *(S/M #C102-10).*	75.00	175.	—

		VG	VF	UNC
S1101	**5 Dollars** 1916. Green and orange. Pavilion at left, tower at right. Back: Red and blue. Village along shoreline at center. Printer: PHCF. *(S/M #C102-11).*	50.00	100.	300.

		VG	VF	UNC
S1102	**10 Dollars** 1916. Orange and multicolor. Tower at left and right. Back: Blue and yellow. Printer: CMPA. *(S/M #C102-12).*	75.00	150.	400.

1919 Copper Coin Issue

		VG	VF	UNC
S1105	**10 Coppers** 1919. Blue and yellow. Back: Green. *KIUKIANG. (S/M #C102-20).*	75.00	225.	—

		VG	VF	UNC
S1108	**100 Coppers**			
	1919. Blue and yellow. Pavilion, trees at right. Back: Maroon. *(S/M #C102-23).*	100.	300.	—

1926 Copper Coin Issue

		VG	VF	UNC
S1115	**10 Coppers**			
	1926. *(S/M #C102-31).*	75.00	225.	500.

		VG	VF	UNC
S1119	**100 Coppers**			
	1926. Blue. Building at center. Back: Brown. *Kiangsi. (S/M #C102-35).*	75.00	225.	500.

Yu Ming Bank of Kiangsi

江西裕民銀行
Chiang Hsi Yü Min Yin Hang

1929 Copper Coin Issue

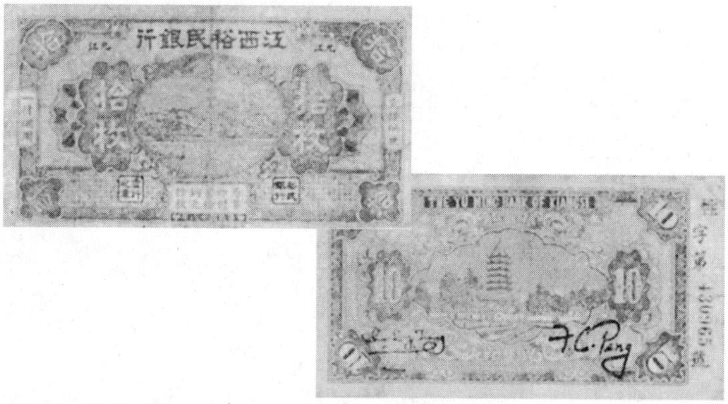

		VG	VF	UNC
S1121	**10 Coppers**			
	1929. Dark blue on green underprint. Hillside village at center. Back: Olive-green. Pagoda.			
	a. *Chiuchiang. (S/M #C103-0.5a.).*	75.00	225.	—
	b. *Chian. (S/M #C103-0.5b).*	75.00	225.	—
S1124	**100 Coppers**			
	1929. Brown. Back: Red. *(S/M #C103-0.9).*	75.00	225.	—

ND Dollar Issue

		VG	VF	UNC
S1125	**1 Cent**			
	ND. Back: Multicolor. Printer: TTBC. *(S/M #C103-1).*	10.00	25.00	50.00
S1126	**5 Cents**	VG	VF	UNC
	ND. Blue. Back: Red. Printer: TTBC. *(S/M #C103-2).*	10.00	25.00	75.00

1932 Copper Coin Issue

		VG	VF	UNC
S1129	**10 Coppers**			
	1932. Blue and green. House on rock formation surrounded by water at left. Back: Orange. House by bridge at center. *(S/M #C103-10).*	10.00	25.00	75.00
S1130	**10 Coppers**			
	1932. Red. House on rock formation surrounded by water at left. Back: Blue. House by bridge at center. *Kian. (S/M #C103-11).*	10.00	25.00	75.00
S1131	**10 Coppers**			
	1932. Blue and yellow. House on rock formation surrounded by water at left. Back: Red. House by bridge at center. *(S/M #C103-12).*	10.00	25.00	75.00
S1132	**100 Coppers**			
	1932. Blue and yellow. *Kewu. (S/M #C103-15).*	10.00	25.00	80.00

1933 Dollar Issue

		VG	VF	UNC
S1133	**20 Cents**			
	1933. Red. Pagoda, shoreline at right. Back: Brown. Additional Chinese control characters. Printer: TTBC. *(S/M #C103-20).*	10.00	25.00	80.00

		VG	VF	UNC
S1134	**50 Cents**			
	1933. Deep blue. Pavilion at center. 2 signature varieties. Back: Red. Printer: TTBC.			
	a. Issued note. *(S/M #C103-21a).*	5.00	20.00	50.00
	b. As a. Additional overprint.: *Chian* with control character *Wo. (S/M #C103-21b).*	10.00	25.00	75.00
	c. *Ji An. (S/M #C103-21c).*	10.00	25.00	75.00
	d. *Chinchiang. (S/M #C103-21d).*	10.00	25.00	75.00
	e. *Chiatsu. (S/M #C103-21e).*	10.00	25.00	75.00
	f. *Shanghai* (blocked out with black overprint.). *(S/M #C103-21f).*	10.00	25.00	75.00
	g. *Jui Jiang*	10.00	25.00	75.00
	h. *Xiu Jiang.*	10.00	25.00	75.00
	i. *Yu Da.*	10.00	25.00	75.00
	j. *Fu Zhou.*	10.00	25.00	75.00
	k. Cancellation overprint on *Ji An.*	10.00	25.00	75.00
	l. *He Kon.*	10.00	25.00	75.00
	m. *Yi Chun.*	10.00	25.00	75.00
	n. *Yu Shan.*	10.00	25.00	75.00

		VG	VF	UNC
S1135	**1 Dollar**			
	1933. Red. Hillside pagoda at left center. Back: Brown. Printer: TTBC. *(S/M #C103-30).*	25.00	50.00	—
S1136	**5 Dollars**			
	1933. Green. Hillside pagoda at left center. Back: Orange. Printer: TTBC. *(S/M #C103-31).*	125.	400.	—
S1137	**10 Dollars**			
	1933. Green. Back: Violet. Printer: TTBC. *(S/M #C103-32).*	125.	400.	—

1934; 1935 Issue

		VG	VF	UNC
S1138	**10 Cents**			
	1934. Brown. Buildings, trees at upper center. Overprint: *Kanchow.* Printer: TTBC. *Kanchow. (S/M #C103-39).*	50.00	100.	—

	VG	VF	UNC
S1139 10 Cents 1934. Orange. Island at upper center. 2 signature varieties. Vertical format. Back: Blue. Printer: TTBC.			
a. Issued note. *(S/M #C103-40a).*	25.00	50.00	100.
b. With additional Chinese control characters. *(S/M #103-40b).*	25.00	50.00	100.
S1140 20 Cents 1934. Orange. Back: Light brown. Printer: TTBC. *(S/M #C103-41).*	10.00	25.00	50.00

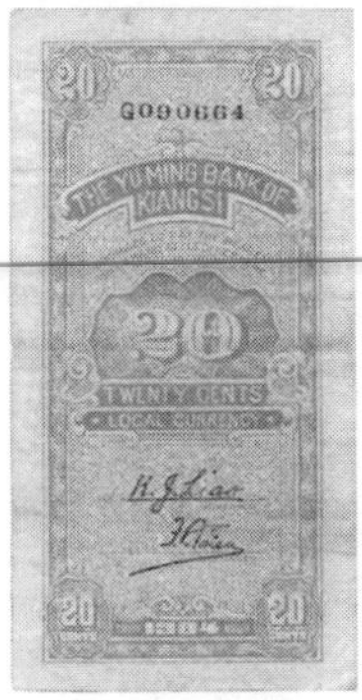

	VG	VF	UNC
S1141 20 Cents 1934. Dark green. Building, trees at upper center. Overprint: *Kanchow.* (S/M #C103-42)	125.	250.	—

	VG	VF	UNC
S1143 50 Cents 1935. Red. Tower at upper center. Vertical format. Back: Green. *Kanchou.* *(S/M #C103-45).*	20.00	50.00	125.

1935 Provisional Issue

	VG	VF	UNC
S1146 50 Cents 1935. Red. Back: Green. Overprint: *Changed to 5 Chiao note* on #S1143. *(S/M #C103-46).*	20.00	50.00	125.

1938 Issue

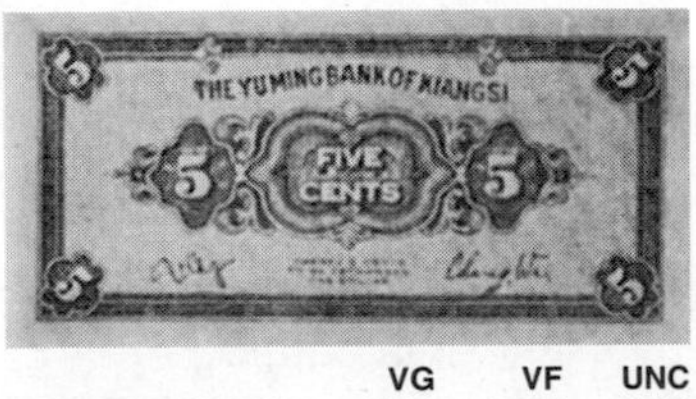

	VG	VF	UNC
S1151 5 Cents 1938. Red. Sailboats at left, towers at right. Printer: TTBC. *(S/M #C103-50).*	10.00	25.00	75.00

NOTE: Additional denominations require confirmation.

1945 Issue

	VG	VF	UNC
S1158 100 Dollars 1945. Violet. Gazebo at left. Back: Red. *(S/M #C103-70).*	100.	300.	—
S1159 200 Dollars 1945. Violet. Pagoda at center. Back: Red. *(S/M #C103-71).*	125.	350.	—
S1160 400 Dollars 1945. Violet. Back: Violet.			
a. Issued note. *(S/M #C103-72a).*	150.	400.	—
b. *Nanchang.* *(S/M #C103-72b).*	150.	450.	—
s. Specimen.	—	—	500.

Kiangnan Yu-Ning Government Bank
Yu Ning Imperial Bank

江南裕寧官銀錢局

Chiang Nan/Yü Ning Kuan Yin Ch'ien Chü (Yüan Ch'ao P'iao)

1903 Cash Issue

	VG	VF	UNC
S1161 1 Ch'uan Yr. 29 (1903). Green, blue and red. Dragons in frame. Vertical format. Back: Black. Red seals. *(S/M #C107-1).*	125.	350.	—
S1162 1 Ch'uan Yr. 29 (1903). Green and multicolor. Back: Red. Red seals. *(S/M #C107-2).*	150.	400.	—
S1163 100 Cash Yr. 29 (1903). Green and multicolor. Back: Red. *(S/M #C107-3).*	200.	500.	—
S1166 1000 Cash (ca. 1903). *(S/M #C107-).*	250.	600.	—

1905 Silver Dollar Issue

	VG	VF	UNC
S1168 1 Dollar Yr. 31 (1905). Black and multicolor. Back: Red and black. Printer: HWPO. *(S/M #C107-10).*	500.	1250.	—

	VG	VF	UNC
S1169 5 Dollars Yr. 31 (1905). Black and red. Facing dragons at center. Back: Red and yellow. Dragon dollar at left and right. Printer: HWPO. *(S/M #C107-11).*	750.	1750.	—
S1170 10 Dollars Yr. 31 (1905). Black and red on multicolor underprint. Back: Facing dragons at center between dragon dollar (obverse and reverse). Printer: HWPO. *(S/M #C107-12).*	1000.	2500.	—

1907 Copper Coin Issues

	VG	VF	UNC
S1172 10 Coppers March Yr. 33 (1907). Brown and blue. Small facing dragons at top. Back: Red. Large facing dragons with waves below. Printer: CMPA. *(S/M #C107-20).*	225.	500.	—
S1172A 20 Coppers March Yr. 33 (1907). Dark blue on ochre underprint. Small facing dragons at top. Back: Green and black. Large facing dragons with waves below. Printer: CMPA. *(S/M #C107-20A).*	225.	500.	—

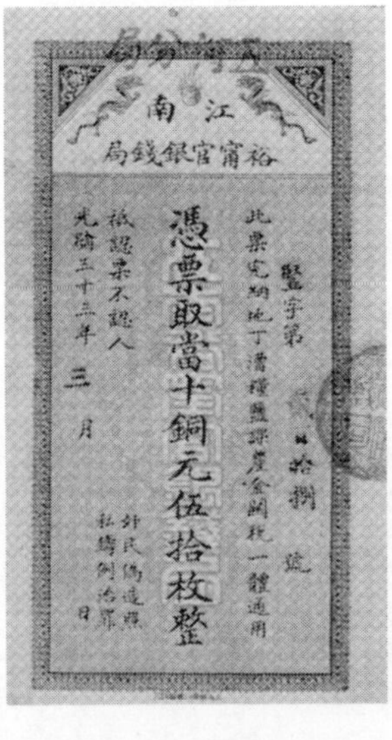

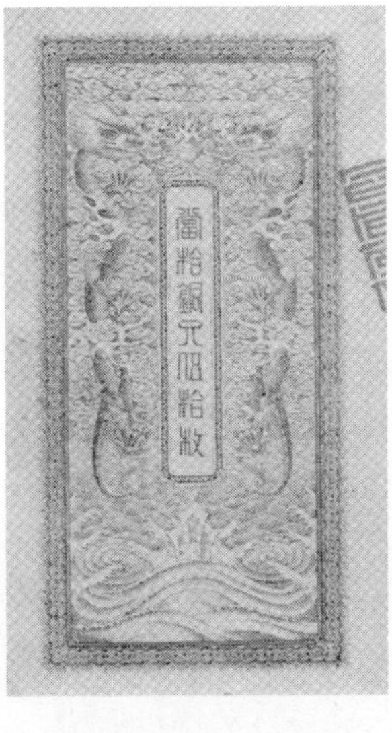

	VG	VF	UNC
S1173 50 Coppers			
March Yr. 33 (1907). Blue-green on tan underprint. Vertical format. Small facing dragons at top. Back: Blue. Large facing dragons with waves below. Printer: CMPA. *(S/M #C107-21).*	150.	400.	—

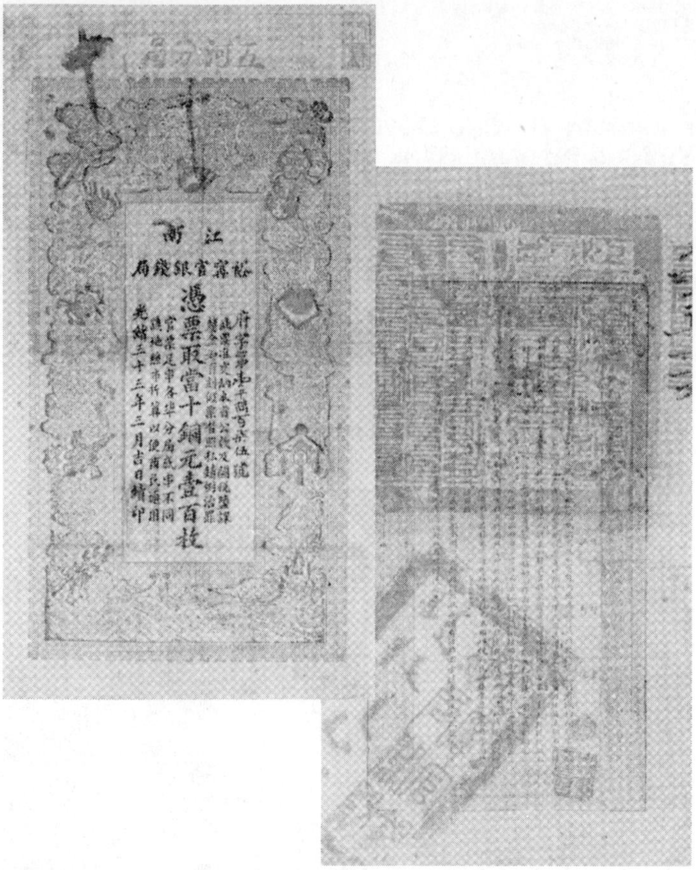

	VG	VF	UNC
S1174 100 Coppers			
1.3. Yr. 33 (1907). Green and multicolor. Facing dragons in frame. Vertical format. Back: Black. Red seals. Printer: CMPA. *(S/M #C107-23).*	100.	225.	—

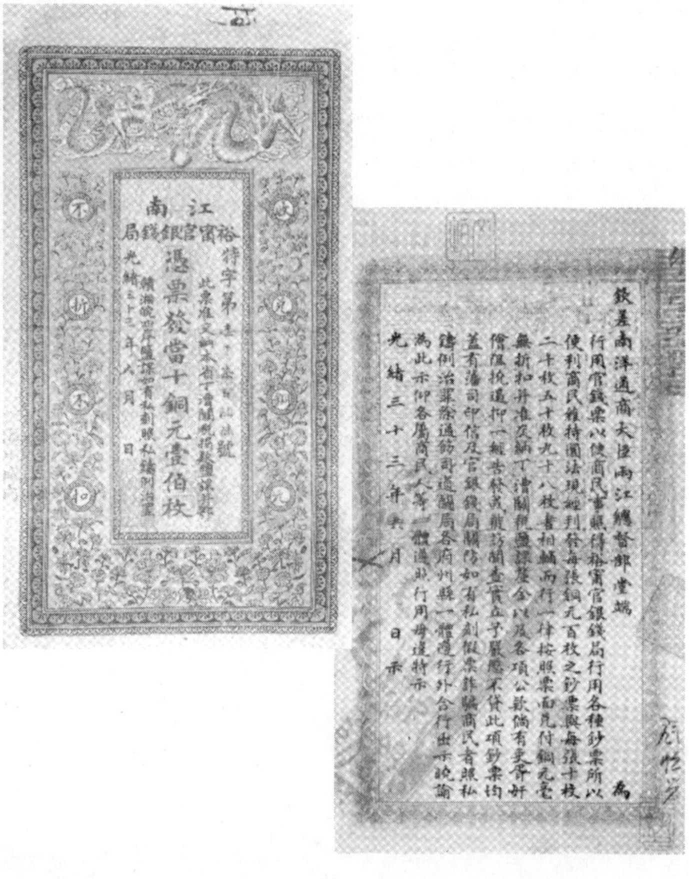

	VG	VF	UNC
S1175 100 Coppers			
June Yr. 33 (1907). Red and multicolor. Dragon at top. Vertical format. Back: Red.			
a. Issued note. *(S/M #C107-22a).*	100.	225.	—
b. *Ch'eng Yang. (S/M #C107-22b).*	200.	425.	—

1907 First Silver Dollar Issue

	VG	VF	UNC
S1177 1 Dollar			
1.7.1907. Purple and blue. Facing dragons at center. Back: Brown and blue. Portrait viceroy at center between dragon dollar obverse and reverse. Printer: HWPO.			
a. *Shanghai (S/M #C107-30a).*	600.	1500.	—
b. *Nanking. (S/M #C107-30b).*	600.	1500.	—
c. *Chiuchiang. (S/M #C107-30c).*	600.	1500.	—
d. *Nanking/Chiuchiang. (S/M #C107-30d).*	600.	1500.	—
S1178 5 Dollars			
1.7.1907. Blue and yellow. Facing dragons at center. Back: Blue and yellow. Portrait viceroy at center between dragon dollar obverse and reverse. Printer: HWPO.			
a. *Shanghai. (S/M #C107-31a).*	800.	2250.	—
b. *Nanking. (S/M #C107-31b).*	800.	2250.	—
c. *Ch'ing Chiang. (S/M #C107-31c).*	800.	2250.	—
d. *Ch'ing Chiang/Nanking. (S/M #C107-).*	800.	2250.	—
S1179 10 Dollars			
1.7.1907. Facing dragons at center. Back: Portrait viceroy at center between dragon dollar obverse and reverse. Printer: HWPO. *(S/M #C107-32).*			
a. *T'ungchow.*	1000.	3000.	—
b. *Nanking.*	900.	2500.	—

1907 Second Silver Dollar Issue

	VG	VF	UNC
S1180 1 Dollar			
1.7.1907. Silver dragon dollar. Back: Silver dragon dollar. 4 Chinese characters at left and crossed flags at right.			
a. *Shanghai. (S/M #C107-30a).*	900.	2500.	—
b. *Nanking. (S/M #C107-30b).*	900.	2500.	—
c. *Kiukiang. (S/M #C107-30c).*	900.	2500.	—
d. *Nanking/Shanghai. (S/M #C107-30d).*	900.	2500.	—
e. *Ch'ing Chiang/Nanking. (S/M #C107-30e).*	900.	2500.	—
f. *Kiukiang/Nanking. (S/M #C107-30f).*	900.	2500.	—
g. *Kiukiang/Nanking/Shanghai. (S/M #C107-30g).*	900.	2500.	—

Kiangnan Yü Su Silver Currency Bureau

局钱銀官寧裕南江

Chiang Nan/Yü Su Kuan Yin Ch'ien Chü

1903 Cash Issue

	VG	VF	UNC
S1183 100 Cash			
Yr. 29 (1903). Red. Back: Black. *Kiangnan/Kiangsu. (S/M #C110-1).*	250.	600.	—
S1184 500 Cash			
Yr. 29 (1903). Green. Back: Green. *Kiangnan/Kiangsu. (S/M #C110-2).*	300.	750.	—

ILLUSTRATIONS

Illustrations of bank notes used throughout this catalog are 42% of the actual size.

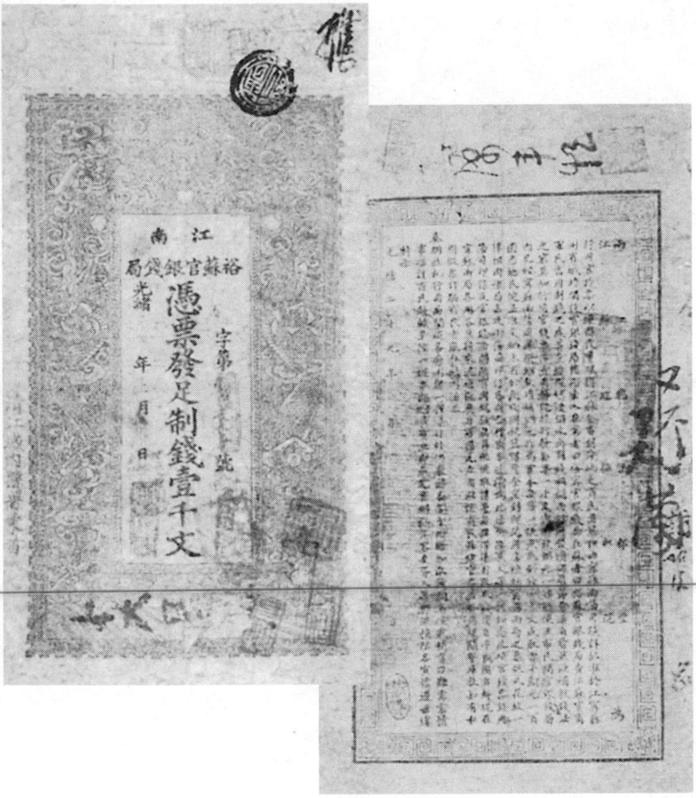

S1185 1000 Cash

	VG	VF	UNC
Yr. 29 (1903); Yr. 30 (1904). Red with black text. Facing dragons in frame. Back: Black. *Kiangnan/Kiangsu*. Vertical format. *(S/M #C110-3)*.	225.	650.	—

Kiang Shun Government Bank

江省官銀號
Chiang Sheng Kuan Yin Hao

1909 Issue

S1188 500 Cents

	VG	VF	UNC
1909. Unissued remainder. *(S/M #C111-20)*.	200.	400.	—

Kiangsu Farmers Bank
Kingsu Farmers Bank

江蘇省農民銀行
Chiang Su Sheng Nung Min Yin Hang

1933 Provisional Issue

#S1191-S1193 overprint on Government of Suchow - Monetary Bureau issue.

S1191 10 Cents

	VG	VF	UNC
1933. Verical format. Overprint: On #S1891A. *(S/M #C115-1)*. Reported not confirmed.	—	—	—

S1192 20 Cents

	VG	VF	UNC
1933. Dark blue. Vertical format. Overprint: On #S1891B. *(S/M #C115-2)*.			
a. Issued note.	25.00	50.00	—
b. With additional overprint Chinese control character.	25.00	50.00	—

S1193 50 Cents

	VG	VF	UNC
1933. Vertical format. Overprint: On #S1891C. *(S/M #C115-3)*.	25.00	50.00	—

1936 Issues

S1194 10 Cents

	VG	VF	UNC
1936. Red. Pavillion with pagoda in background. Back: Green. Printer: TYPC.			
a. Issued note. *(S/M #C115-10a)*.	10.00	40.00	100.
b. Overprint: *Su*. *(S/M #C115-10b)*.	20.00	40.00	100.

S1195 20 Cents

	VG	VF	UNC
1936. Blue. Pavillion with pagoda in background. Back: Brown. Printer: TYPC.			
a. Issued note. *(S/M #C115-11a)*.	20.00	40.00	100.
b. Overprint: *SG SU*. *(S/M #C115-11b)*.	25.00	50.00	125.

		VG	VF	UNC
S1196 50 Cents	1936. Pavillion with pagoda in background. Printer: YSCL. *(S/M #C115-).*	25.00	50.00	125.
S1198 50 Cents	1936. Brown. Pavillion with pagoda in background. Back: Violet. Printer: TTBC. *(S/M #C115-12).*	20.00	40.00	100.

1939 Issue

		VG	VF	UNC
S1200 1 Yüan	1939. Red. Pavilion with pagoda in background at right, Chinese character signature at right. Printer: TTBC. *(S/M #C115-20).*			
	a. Chinese signature at right.	40.00	75.00	150.
	b. Chinese signature seal at right.	40.00	75.00	150.

1940 Issue

		VG	VF	UNC
S1202 1 Yüan	1940. Green. Farmer plowing with oxen at upper center. Back: Brown. Pavilion with pagoda in background at right. Printer: YSCL. *(S/M #C115-30).*	40.00	75.00	150.

1941 Issues

		VG	VF	UNC
S1203 50 Cents	1941. Brown-violet. Temple at upper center. Back: Green. Printer: Sin Kee Printing Co. *(S/M #C115-38).*	40.00	75.00	150.

		VG	VF	UNC
S1203A 1 Yüan	1941. Gray-green. Hillside village at center. Back: Olive-green. Trees with house in background at left center. *(S/M #C115-39).*	40.00	75.00	150.
S1203B 1 Yüan	1941. Dark green. Hillside temple complex at center. Back dull brown; farmer plowing with ox at center *(S/M #C115-39.5)*	50.00	100.	200.
S1203B 1 Yüan	1941. Dark green. Hillside temple complex at center. Back: Dull brown. Peasant plowing with ox, at center. Printer: Sinkee Printing Co. *(S/M #C115-39.5).*	50.00	100.	200.

		VG	VF	UNC
S1204 1 Yüan	1941. Green. Pagoda at center. Printer: TTBC. *(SM #C115-40).*	25.00	50.00	100.
S1205 5 Yüan	1941. Red. Back: Green. Printer: SHPC. *(S/M #C115-41).*	50.00	150.	300.

Kiangsu Province

江蘇省兌換券
Chiang Su Sheng Tui Huan Ch'üan

ND Exchange Notes Issue

		Good	Fine	XF
S1208 1 Yüan	ND. Brownish pink and turquoise. *(S/M #C116-1).* Back yellow with large red seal.	75.00	150.	500.

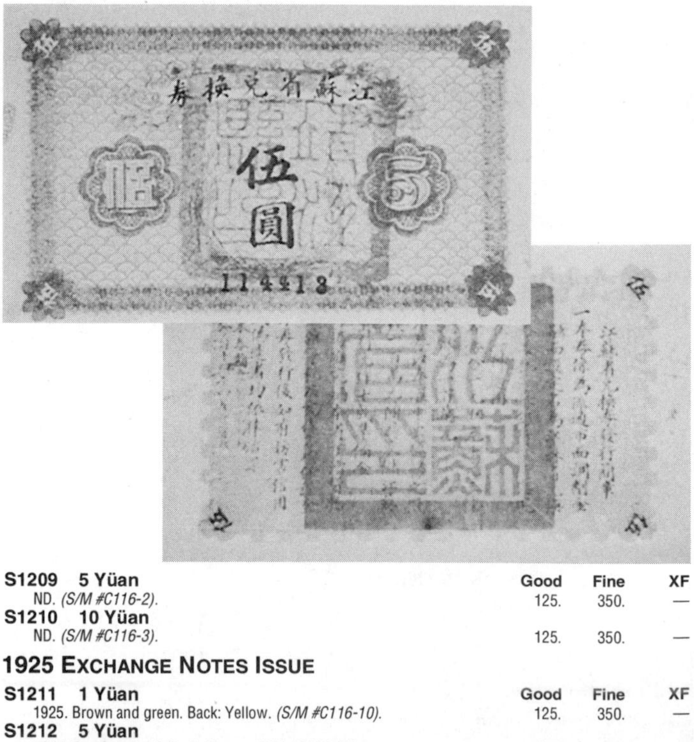

		Good	Fine	XF
S1209 5 Yüan	ND. *(S/M #C116-2).*	125.	350.	—
S1210 10 Yüan	ND. *(S/M #C116-3).*	125.	350.	—

1925 Exchange Notes Issue

		Good	Fine	XF
S1211 1 Yüan	1925. Brown and green. Back: Yellow. *(S/M #C116-10).*	125.	350.	—
S1212 5 Yüan	1925. Green and red. Back: Green. *(S/M #C116-11).*	125.	350.	—
S1213 10 Yüan	1925. Blue and green. Back: Green. *(S/M #C116-12).*	125.	350.	—

Nanking Exchange Office of the Financial Department, Kiangsu

江蘇財南司政京兌換處
Chiang Su Ts'ai Cheng Szu Nan Ching Tui Huan Ch'üan

1912 Issue

#S1215-S1217 surviving copies are usually encountered cut diagonally and the halves have been taped back together. Whole uncut notes command a considerable premium.

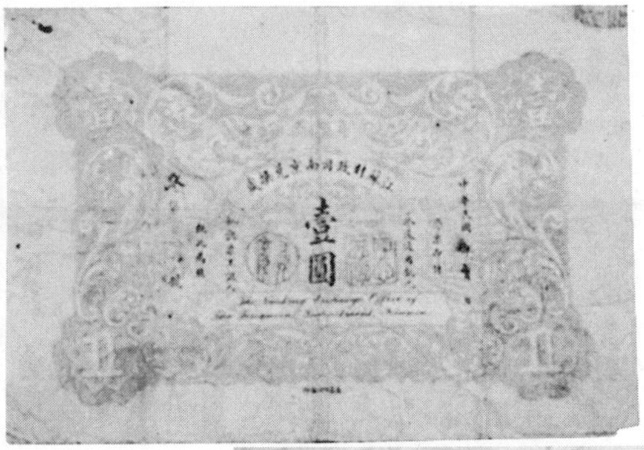

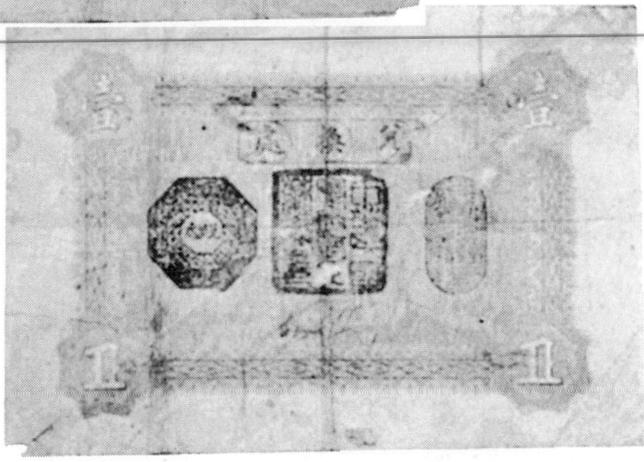

	Good	Fine	XF
S1215 1 Yüan 1912. Green on orange underprint. Back: Lilac. *(S/M #C118-1).*	450.	1250.	—
S1216 5 Yüan 1912. Beige on yellow underprint. Back: Yellow. *(S/M #C118-2).*	450.	1250.	—
S1217 10 Yüan 1912. *(S/M #C118-3).*	450.	1250.	—

Kiangsu Finance Department

江蘇財政廳
Chiang Su Ts'ai Cheng T'ing

1939 Copper Coin Issue

	Good	Fine	XF
S1220 1 Copper 1939. Red. Pagoda at left. *(S/M #C120-1).*	20.00	40.00	100.
S1221 5 Coppers 1939. Brown. *(S/M #C120-2).*	10.00	20.00	50.00

	Good	Fine	XF
S1222 10 Coppers 1939. Olive-green. Pagodas at right. *(S/M #C120-3).*	10.00	20.00	50.00

	Good	Fine	XF
S1223 15 Coppers 1939. Brown. House at left. *(S/M #C120-4).*	25.00	50.00	110.
S1224 30 Coppers 1939. Blue. House with pagoda in background at right. *(S/M C120-5).*	25.00	50.00	150.

Kiangsu Bank

江 蘇 銀 行
Chiang Su Yin Hang

1913 Issue

	Good	Fine	XF
S1226 1 Dollar 1.6.1913. Specimen. *(S/M #C121-1).*	—	Unc	1000.

1913 Issue

	VG	VF	UNC
S1226A 5 Dollars 1.6.1913. Lions supporting globe. Back: People near pagoda and bridge. Printer: BWC. Specimen. *(S/M #C121-2).*		—	1000.
S1226B 10 Dollars 1.6.1913. Lions supporting globe. Back: People near pagoda and bridge. Printer: BWC. Specimen. *(S/M #C121-3).*		—	1500.

1927 Issue

	Good	Fine	XF
S1227 1 Dollar 1927. *(S/M #C121-10).* Reported not confirmed.	—	—	—
S1227A 5 Dollars 1927. *(S/M #C121-11).* Reported not confirmed.	—	—	—
S1227B 10 Dollars 1927. *(S/M #C121-12).* Reported not confirmed.	—	—	—

Yue Soo Imperial Bank

江蘇裕蘇官銀錢局
Chiang Su Yü Su Kuan Yin Ch'ien Chü

1906 Silver Dollar Issue

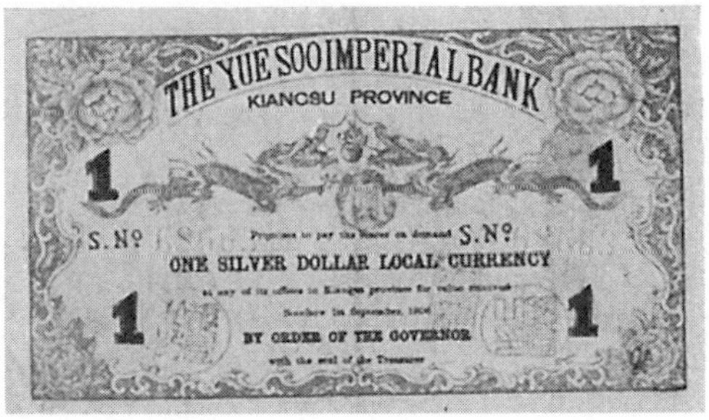

	Good	Fine	XF
S1228 1 Dollar 1.9.1906. Green and red. Man at center right. *Soochow.* Back: Green and yellow. Two dragons facing at upper center. Printer: HWPO. *(S/M #C122-1).*	750.	3000.	—
S1229 5 Dollars 1.9.1906. *Soochow.* Printer: HWPO. *(S/M #C122-2).*	—	—	—
S1230 10 Dollars 1.9.1906. Green and red. *Soochow.* Back: Green and yellow. Printer: HWPO. *(S/M #C122-3).*	900.	3250.	—

1908 Silver Dollar Issue

#S1232-S1235 Most notes encountered have been repaired after 2 corners were severed when cancelled.

	Good	Fine	XF
S1232 1 Dollar 1.9.1908. Brown and green. *Soochow.* Back: Black and violet. Facing dragons at center. Printer: IPCL. *(S/M #C122-10).*			
a. Issued note.	350.	900.	—
b. Clipped or repaired cancelled note.	250.	600.	—

	Good	Fine	XF
S1233 5 Dollars			
1.9.1908. Brown and green. *Soochow.* Back: Black and violet. Facing dragons at center. *(S/M #C122-11).*			
a. Issued note.	500.	1500.	—
b. Clipped or repaired cancelled note.	350.	900.	—
S1234 10 Dollars			
1.9.1908. *Soochow.* Back: Facing dragons at center. *(S/M #C122-12).*			
a. Issued note.	—	—	—
b. Clipped or repaired cancelled note.	300.	900.	—

CHIHLI PROVINCE

直隸省金庫兌換券

Chih Li Sheng Chin K'u Tui Huan Ch'ü

1924 TREASURY EXCHANGE NOTES ISSUE

	Good	Fine	XF
S1238 1 Dollar			
1924. *(S/M #C160-1).* Reported not confirmed.	—	—	—
S1239 5 Dollars			
1924. *(S/M #C160-2).* Reported not confirmed.	—	—	—
S1240 10 Dollars			
1924. *(S/M #C160-3).* Reported not confirmed.	—	—	—

1928 TREASURY EXCHANGE NOTES ISSUE

	Good	Fine	XF
S1241 1 Yüan			
1928. Orange. Bridge at center. Printer: BEPP. *(S/M #C160-10).*			
a. Issued note.	50.00	125.	300.
r. Remainder.	—	Unc	200.
S1242 5 Yüan			
1928. Green. Printer: BEPP. *(S/M #C160-11).*			
a. Issued note.	60.00	200.	500.
r. Remainder.	—	Unc	350.
S1243 10 Yüan			
1928. Blue. Printer: BEPP. *(S/M #C160-12).*			
a. Issued note.	100.	300.	650.
r. Remainder.	—	Unc	400.

CHIHLI PROVINCE

直隸省庫定期流通券

Chih Li Sheng K'u Ting Ch'i Liu T'ung Ch'ü

1926 TERM CIRCULATING NOTES ISSUE

	Good	Fine	XF
S1247 10 Cents			
1926. Green. *(S/M #C162-1).*	80.00	225.	450.
S1248 20 Cents			
1926. Brown. *(S/M #C162-2).*	80.00	225.	450.

#S1251 and S1252 printer: SOPO.

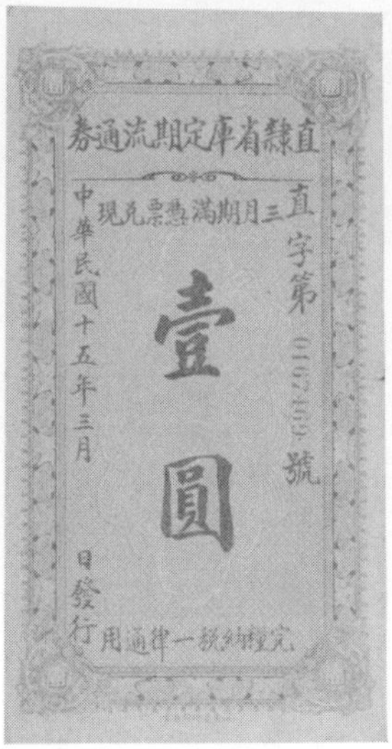

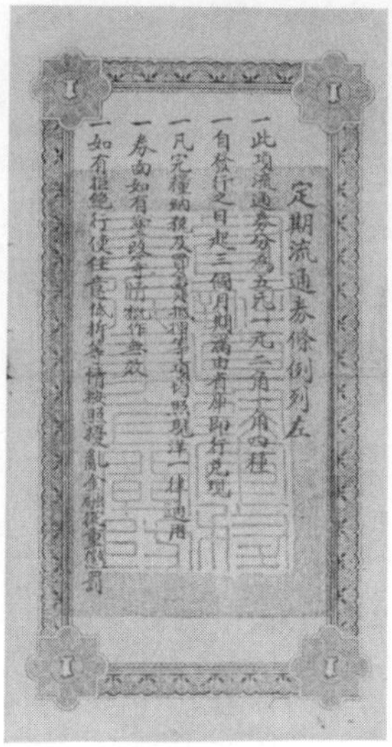

	VG	VF	UNC
S1251 1 Yüan			
March 1926. Brown-violet on green underprint. Vertical format. Back: Brown-violet. Printer: SOPO. *(S/M #C162-10).*			
a. Issued note.	150.	350.	—
r. Remainder.	—	—	150.
S1252 5 Yüan			
March 1926. Blue and violet. Vertical format. Back: Blue and red. Printer: SOPO. *(S/M #C162-11).*	125.	300.	—

PROVINCIAL BANK OF CHIHLI

直隸省官錢局

Chi Li Sheng Kuan Ch'ien Chü

直隸省銀行

Chih Li Sheng Yin Hang

1916 CASH ISSUE

	VG	VF	UNC
S1254 200 Cash			
1916. Blue and multicolor. Back: Brown and yellow. *Tientsin.* *(S/M #C163-1).*	150.	350.	—

1916 PROVISIONAL DOLLAR ISSUE

#S1257-S1260 overprint new bank name on Peiyang Tientsin Bank issue.

	VG	VF	UNC
S1257 1 Dollar			
1916. Brown on multicolor underprint. Overprint: On #S2526. *(S/M #C163-5).*	—	—	—

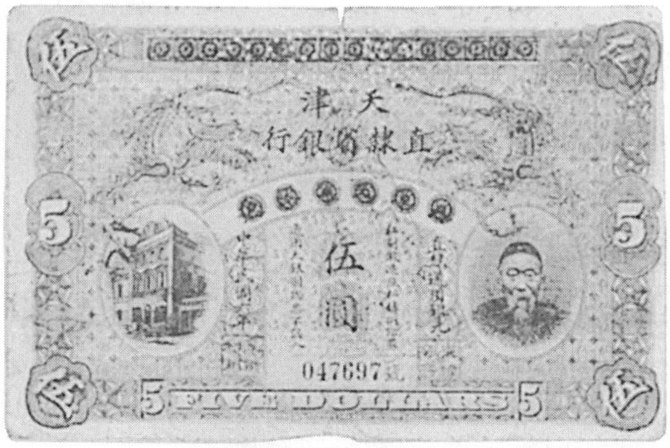

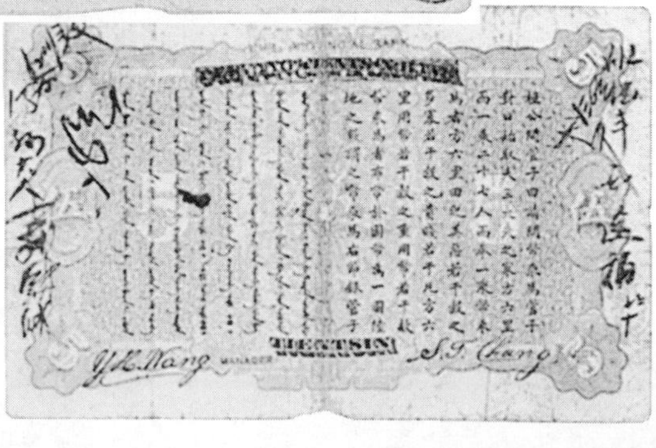

	VG	VF	UNC
S1258 5 Dollars			
1916. Chinese character pinhole cancellation perforations. Overprint: On #2528. *(S/M #C163-6).*	—	—	—

S1259 50 Dollars	VG	VF	UNC
1916. Overprint: On #S2529a. Remainder. *(S/M #C163-9).*	1250.	4000.	—

S1260 100 Dollars	VG	VF	UNC
1916. Overprint: On #S2530. Remainder. *(S/M #C163-10).*	—	—	—

1920 Dollar Issue

S1263 1 Dollar	VG	VF	UNC
1.12.1920. Black on dark green and multicolor underprint. House at center. *Tientsin.* Back: Dark green. Printer: ABNC.			
a. Signature Chen-Wang with English titles. *(S/M #C163-20b).*	15.00	50.00	125.
b. Signature Ma-Chang without English titles. *(S/M #C163-20a).*	10.00	30.00	75.00
c. Signature Wang-Wang. *(S/M #C163-20c).*	15.00	50.00	125.
d. With additional Chinese character control overprint.	10.00	30.00	75.00

S1264 5 Dollars	VG	VF	UNC
1.12.1920. Black on dark blue underprint. House at center. *Tientsin.* Back: Dark blue. Printer: ABNC.			
a. Signature Chen-Wang with English titles. *(S/M #C163-21b).*	20.00	50.00	125.
b. Signature Ma-Chang without English titles. *(S/M #C163-21a).*	15.00	50.00	125.
c. Signature Wang-Wang. *(S/M #C163-21c).*	25.00	75.00	150.

S1265 10 Dollars	VG	VF	UNC
1.12.1920. Black on multicolor underprint. House at center. *Tientsin.* Back: Brown. Printer: ABNC.			
a. Signature Chen-Wang with English titles. *(S/M #C163-22b).*	25.00	75.00	150.
b. Signature Ma-Chang without English titles. *(S/M #C163-22a).*	20.00	50.00	125.
c. Signature Wang-Wang. *(S/M #C163-22c).*	25.00	75.00	150.

1921 Copper Coin Issue

S1268 5 Coppers	VG	VF	UNC
1921. Brown and blue. Black text. *Tientsin.* Back: Green. Modern building at center. *(S/M #C163-30).*	50.00	125.	250.

S1269 10 Coppers	VG	VF	UNC
1921. Brown and green. Black text. *Tientsin.* Back: Green. Modern building at center. *(S/M #C163-31).*	50.00	125.	250.

S1270 20 Coppers	VG	VF	UNC
1921. Violet and yellow. Large hand stamped signature seal overprint. *Tientsin.* Black text. Back: Green. Modern building at center. *(S/M #C163-32).*			
a. Issued note.	75.00	150.	450.
b. With 2 signature seals on back.	75.00	150.	—

S1271 50 Coppers	VG	VF	UNC
1921. Violet and orange. Black text. *Tientsin.* Back: Green. Modern building at center. *(S/M #C163-33).*	100.	200.	—

1923 Issue

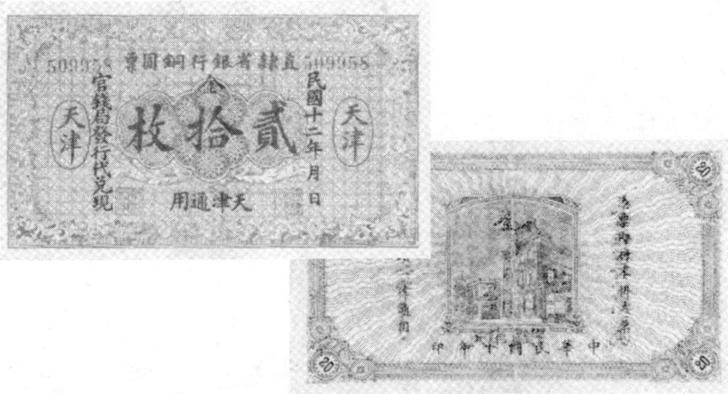

S1271A 20 Coppers	VG	VF	UNC
1923. Brown-violet on blue underprint. Back: Dark green. *Tientsin. (S/M #C163-38).*	150.	300.	—

S1271C 100 Coppers	VG	VF	UNC
1923. Purple on light green underprint. Temple at center. Back: Green. Temple at center. *YUNG TSUN.*	—	—	—

1924 Copper Coin Issue

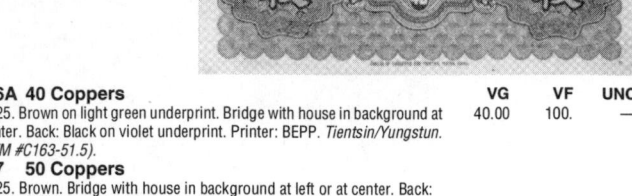

S1272 10 Coppers	VG	VF	UNC
1924. Blue on orange underprint. Bridge with house in background at center. Back: Orange and brown. Printer: BEPP.			
a. *Tientsin* with vertical Chinese 10 characters overprint at left and right. *(S/M #C163-40c).*	25.00	75.00	—
b. *Tientsin* with vertical Chinese 5 characters overprint at left and right. *(S/M #C163-40b).*	25.00	75.00	—
c. *Tientsin/Peking* with vertical Chinese 5 characters overprint at left and right. *(S/M #C163-40a).*	25.00	75.00	—
d. *Paoting. (S/M #C163-d).*	40.00	100.	—
e. *Paoting/Tientsin. (S/M #C163-e).*	40.00	100.	—

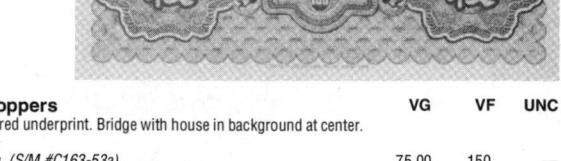

S1273 20 Coppers	VG	VF	UNC
1924. Violet and green. Bridge with house in background at center. Back: Green and black. Overprint: 10 vertical Chinese characters at left and right. Printer: BEPP.			
a. *Peking. (S/M #C163-41a).*	25.00	75.00	—
b. *Tientsin/Peking. (S/M #C163-41b).*	40.00	100.	—
S1274 40 Coppers			
1924. Brown and green. Bridge with house in background at center. Back: Violet. Printer: BEPP. *Tientsin. (S/M #C163-42).*	40.00	100.	—
S1274A 50 Coppers			
1924. Bridge with house in background at center. Printer: BEPP. *Peking. (S/M #C163-43).*	40.00	100.	—

1925 Copper Coin Issue

S1275 10 Coppers			
1925. Bridge with house in background at left. Printer: BEPP. *(S/M #C163-50).* Reported not confirmed.	—	—	—

S1276 20 Coppers	VG	VF	UNC
1925. Violet and blue. Bridge with house in background at left or at center. Back: Black and green. Printer: BEPP.			
a. *Tientsin. (S/M #C163-51b).*	25.00	75.00	—
b. *Tientsin/Peking. (S/M #C163-51a).*	75.00	150.	—

S1276A 40 Coppers	VG	VF	UNC
1925. Brown on light green underprint. Bridge with house in background at center. Back: Black on violet underprint. Printer: BEPP. *Tientsin/Yungstun. (S/M #C163-51.5).*	40.00	100.	—
S1277 50 Coppers			
1925. Brown. Bridge with house in background at left or at center. Back: Green and black. Printer: BEPP.			
a. *Tientsin. (S/M #C163-52a).*	40.00	100.	—
b. *Yungtsun. (S/M #C163-52b).*	40.00	100.	—

S1278 100 Coppers	VG	VF	UNC
1925. Green on red underprint. Bridge with house in background at center. Printer: BEPP.			
a. *Yungtsun. (S/M #C163-53a).*	75.00	150.	—
b. *Tientsin/Yungtsun. (S/M #C163-53b).*	75.00	150.	—

1926 Issues

S1279 10 Coppers	VG	VF	UNC
1926. Bridge with house in background at center. Printer: BEPP. *(S/M #C163-60).*			
a. *TIENTSIN.*	75.00	150.	—
b. *HSUCHOW / TIENTSIN.*	40.00	100.	—
S1280 20 Coppers			
1926. Violet and green. Back: Black and green. Printer: BEPP. *Tientsin. (S/M #C163-62).*	40.00	100.	—

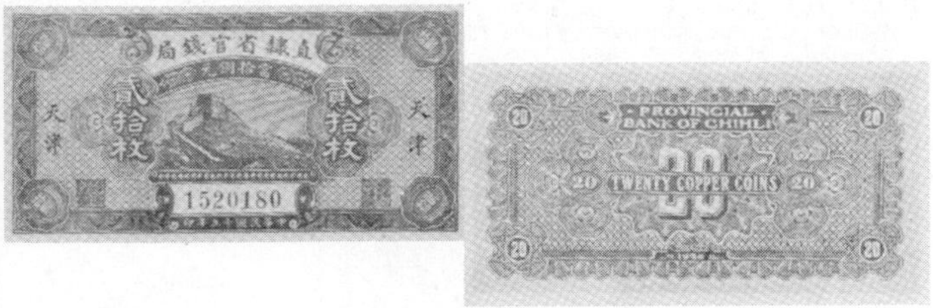

S1282 20 Coppers	VG	VF	UNC
1926. Brown on violet and gray-green underprint. Great Wall at center. Back: Gray-green on brown underprint. Printer: BEPP. *Tientsin. (S/M #C163-61).*	5.00	10.00	25.00

	VG	VF	UNC
S1285 10 Cents			
1926. Violet on brown and gray-green underprint. Great Wall at right. *Tientsin.* Back: Brown on gray-green underprint. *(S/M #C163-70).*	3.00	7.50	20.00
S1286 20 Cents			
1926. Blue-green on brown and violet underprint. Great Wall at right. *Tientsin.* Back: Violet on blue-green underprint. *(S/M #C163-71).*	3.00	7.50	20.00

NOTE: For #S1285 and S1286 with additional rectangular overprint. see Military - Chihli Provincial #S3803 and S3804.

S1288 1 Yüan	VG	VF	UNC
1.10.1926. Violet and multicolor. City gate at center. Back: Violet. Printer: BEPA.			
a. *TIENTSIN. (S/M #C163-80a).*	7.50	15.00	40.00
b. *HSUCHOwith TIENTSIN. (S/M #C163-80b).*	40.00	100.	250.

S1289 5 Yüan	VG	VF	UNC
1.10.1926. Blue-gray and multicolor. City gate at center. Back: Blue-gray. Printer: BEPA.			
a. *TIENTSIN. (S/M #C163-81a).*	15.00	40.00	75.00
b. *HSUCHOW. (S/M #C163-81b).*	75.00	150.	400.
c. *HSCHOwith TIENTSIN.*	25.00	75.00	150.

S1290 10 Yüan	VG	VF	UNC
1.10.1926. Red and multicolor. City gate at center. Back: Red. Printer: BEPA.			
a. *TIENTSIN. (S/M #C163-82a).*	20.00	40.00	100.
b. *HSUCHOW. (S/M #C163-82b).*	75.00	150.	400.
c. *HSUCHOwith TIENTSIN. (S/M #C163-82c).*	75.00	150.	400.

NOTE: For #S1288-S1290 with additional red rectangular overprint see Military - Chihli Provincial #S3805-S3807.

Bank of Local Railways of Shansi and Suiyüan

晉綏地方鐵路銀號

Chin Sui Ti Fang T'ieh Lu Yin Hao

1934 Issue

	VG	VF	UNC
S1291 1 Chiao = 10 Cents			
1934. Deep olive-green. Steam passenger train at right. Back: Brown. Printer: BEPP.			
a. *Kiaocheng. (S/M #C180-1a).*	20.00	40.00	100.
b. *TAIYUAN. (S/M #C180-1b).*	5.00	10.00	25.00
c. *Yutze.*	20.00	40.00	100.
S1292 2 Chiao = 20 Cents			
1934. Dark blue. Steam passenger train at right. Printer: BEPP. *Taiyuan. (S/M #C180-2).*	20.00	40.00	100.
S1293 5 Chiao = 50 Cents			
1934. Violet. Steam passenger train at right. Back: Violet. Printer: BEPP. *(S/M #C180-3).* (Not issued).	—	—	150.

Claimed by some authorities to have been planned but never issued.

	VG	VF	UNC
S1294 1 Yüan			
1.7.1934. Purple on yellow underprint. Steam passenger train at right. Back: Purple. Printer: BEPP.			
a. *HUNGCHUNG. (S/M #C180-10a).*	50.00	125.	250.
b. *SINHSIEN. (S/M #C180-10b).*	50.00	125.	250.
c. *TAIYUAN. (S/M #C180-10c).*	10.00	25.00	50.00
d. *YUTZE. (S/M #C180-10d).*	50.00	125.	250.
e. *KIAOCHENG. (S/M #C180-10e).*	50.00	125.	250.
f. *PINGYAO. (S/M #C180-10f).*	50.00	125.	250.
g. *YUCI. (S/M #C180-10g).*	40.00	75.00	175.
h. *HUNGTUNG.*	50.00	125.	250.
r. Remainder without signature, serial # or place name.	—	—	150.
S1295 5 Yüan			
1934. Olive-green. Staem passenger train at right. Printer: BEPP.			
a. *Taiyuan. (S/M #C180-11a).*	20.00	40.00	75.00
b. *Yuci. (S/M #C180-11b).*	25.00	50.00	100.
S1296 10 Yüan			
1934. Brown. Steam passenger train at right. Printer: BEPP. *Taiyuan. (S/M #C180-12).*	40.00	100.	200.

1936 Issue

	VG	VF	UNC
S1297 10 Cents			
1936. Green. Printer: NWPF. *(S/M #C180-20).* (Not issued).	50.00	125.	250.

Claimed by some authorities to have been planned but never issued.

	VG	VF	UNC
S1298 20 Cents			
1936. Brown. Steam passenger train at center. Printer: NWPF. *(S/M #C180-21).*	50.00	125.	250.

S1299 50 Cents	VG	VF	UNC
1936. Blue. Steam passenger train at right. Back: Red. Printer: NWPF. *(S/M #C180-22).*	5.00	15.00	50.00

S1300 1 Yüan			
1936. Brown on ochre underprint. Steam passenger train at right. Printer: NWPF.			
a. Issued note. *(S/M #C180-23a).*	7.50	35.00	70.00
b. With 2 additional black vertical Chinese 4 character overprints at left and right. *(S/M #C180-23b).*	25.00	50.00	100.

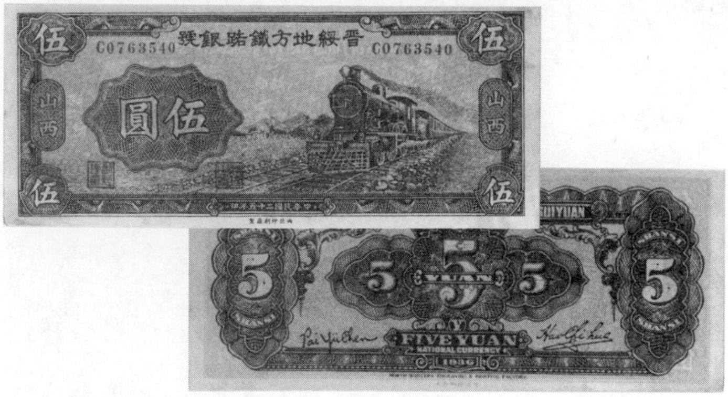

S1301 5 Yüan	VG	VF	UNC
1936. Dark brown-violet on light blue and orange underprint. Steam passenger train at right. Back: Dark brown on pale green underprint. Printer: NWPF. *Shansi.*			
a. Issued note. *(S/M #C180-24a).*	5.00	15.00	50.00
b. With 2 additional black vertical Chinese 4 character overprints at left and right. *(S/M #C180-24b).*	40.00	100.	200.

Tsingtao City Agricultural and Industrial Bank

青島市農工銀行

Ch'ing Tao Shih Nung Kung Yin Hang

1933 ND Provisional Copper Coin Issue

#S1302-S1302C overprint new bank name on Tsingtao City Bank - Tsingtao Regional Bank.

S1302 10 Coppers	VG	VF	UNC
ND (1933 - old date 1924). Overprint: On #S1302D. *(S/M #C195-1).*	50.00	125.	250.
S1302A 30 Coppers			
ND (1933 - old date 1924). Overprint: On #S1302E. *(S/M #C195-).*	75.00	200.	—

S1302B 50 Coppers	VG	VF	UNC
ND (1933 - old date 1924). Overprint: On #S1302F. *(S/M #C195-).*	100.	250.	—
S1302C 100 Coppers			
ND (1933 - old date 1924). Overprint: On #S1302G. *(S/M #C195-2).*	100.	250.	—

Tsingtao City Bank
Tsingtao Regional Bank

青島地方銀行

Ch'ing Tao Ti Fang Yin Hang

1924 Issue

S1302D 10 Coppers	VG	VF	UNC
1924. Large building at center. Printer: BEPP. *(S/M #C196-1).*	100.	250.	—
S1302E 30 Coppers			
1924. Large building at center. Printer: BEPP. *(S/M #C196-1.3).*	100.	250.	—

S1302F 50 Coppers	VG	VF	UNC
1924. Green on yellow underprint. Large building at center. Back: Green on ochre underprint. Printer: BEPP. *(S/M #C196-1.5).*	100.	250.	—
S1302G 100 Coppers			
1924. Large building at center. Printer: BEPP. *(S/M #C196-2).*	100.	250.	—

S1302J 1 Yüan	VG	VF	UNC
15.4.1924 Monument at center. Printer: BEPP. Specimen. *(S/M #C196-10).*	—	—	400.
S1302K 5 Yüan			
15.4.1924. Monument at center. Printer: BEPP. Specimen. *(S/M #C196-11).*	—	—	500.
S1302L 10 Yüan			
15.4.1924. Monument at center. Printer: BEPP. Specimen. *(S/M #C196-12).*	—	—	600.

NOTE: For #S1302J-S1302L with overprint: *SHANTUNG* see Provincial Bank of Shantung #S2745-S2747.

Fengtien Industrial Bank
Hsin Yieh Bank
Shing Yeh Bank
Mukden Bank of Industrial Development
Fentien Hsing Yng Yeh Bank

奉天興業銀行

Feng T'ien Hsing Yeh Yin Hang

1913 First Issue

S1303 1 Dollar	VG	VF	UNC
1913. Printer: PYOG. *(S/M #F7-1).*	150.	600.	—
S1304 5 Dollars			
1913. Printer: PYOG. *(S/M #F7-2).*	300.	750.	—

S1305 10 Dollars	VG	VF	UNC
1913. Back: Building at left and right. Printer: PYOG. *(S/M #F7-3).*	300.	750.	—

1913 Second Issue

S1307 1 Dollar	VG	VF	UNC
1913. Printer: ABNC. *(S/M #F7-10).*	—	—	—
S1308 5 Dollars			
1913. Printer: ABNC. *(S/M #F7-11).*	—	—	—
S1309 10 Dollars			
1913. Printer: ABNC. *(S/M #F7-12).*	—	—	—

1914 Issue

	VG	VF	UNC
S1311 1 Dollar 1914. Printer: PYPO. *(S/M #F7-20).*	125.	275.	—
S1312 5 Dollars 1914. Printer: PYPO. *(S/M #F7-21).*	100.	225.	—
S1313 10 Dollars 1914. Printer: PYPO. *(S/M #F7-22).*	125.	275.	—

1915 Issue

	VG	VF	UNC
S1315 1 Dollar 1915. Waterfront at left and right. Back: Street scene at center. *(S/M #F7-).*	225.	650.	—

1917 Issue

	VG	VF	UNC
S1320 1 Dollar 1917, 1918. House amidst trees at center. *(S/M #F7-30).*			
a. 1917. Black on multicolor underprint.	200.	500.	—
b. 1918. Green on multicolor underprint.	200.	500.	—
S1321 5 Dollars 1917. *(S/M #F7-31).*	200.	500.	—

	VG	VF	UNC
S1322 10 Dollars 1917. *(S/M #F7-32).*	300.	650.	—

1918; 1919 Bond Issue

	VG	VF	UNC
S1323 1 Dollar 1918; 1919; 1920. Black. Pavilion at right. Back: Green on multicolor underprint. Printer: ABNC. *(S/M #F7-40).*			
a. Issued note.	200.	500.	—
s1. Color trial. Black. Multicolor back.	—	—	750.
s2. Specimen. Green. Multicolor back.	—	—	750.

	VG	VF	UNC
S1324 5 Dollars 1918. Orange. Tower at left. Back: Brown. Printer: ABNC. *(S/M #F7-41).*			
a. Issued note.	200.	600.	—
s1. Black. Multicolor back.	—	—	750.
s2. Green. Multicolor back.	—	—	750.

	VG	VF	UNC
S1325 10 Dollars 1918. Green. Back: Brown. Printer: ABNC. *(SM #F7-42).*			
a. Issued note.	350.	800.	—
s1. Specimen. Black. Multicolor back.	—	—	750.
s2. Specimen. Green. Multicolor back.	—	—	750.

#S1326 *Deleted*. See #S1323.

Hua Feng Official Currency Bureau

奉天華豐官銀號

Feng T'ien Hua Feng Kuan Yin Hao

1905 Issue

	Good	Fine	XF
S1327 1 Dollar Yr. 31 (1905). Printer: PYOG. *(S/M #F8-1).*	300.	900.	—
S1328 5 Dollars Yr. 31 (1905). Printer: PYOG. *(S/M #F8-2).*	500.	1200.	—
S1329 2 Dollars Yr. 31 (1905). Printer: PYOG. *(S/M #F8-3).*	600.	1400.	—

Fengtien Official Currency Bureau

奉天官銀號

Feng T'ien Kuan Yin Hao

1905 Dollar Issue

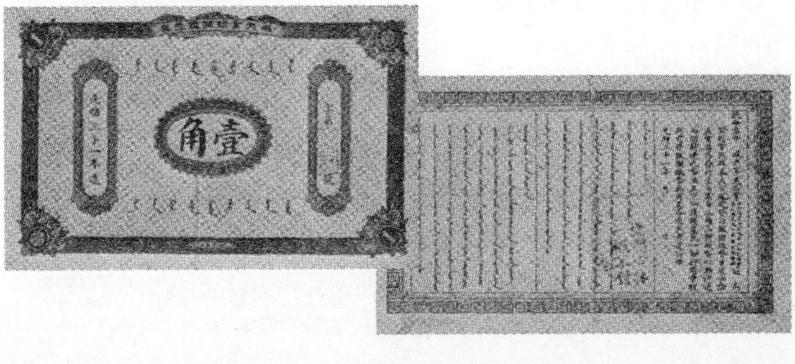

	Good	Fine	XF
S1330 10 Cents Yr. 31 (1905). Green. Back: Orange. Printer: PYOG. *(S/M #F10-1).*	250.	750.	—
S1331 20 Cents Yr. 31 (1905). Printer: PYOG. *(S/M #F10-2).*	250.	750.	—

	Good	Fine	XF
S1332 50 Cents Yr. 31 (1905). Green. Back: Orange. Printer: PYOG. *(S/M #F10-3).*	300.	800.	—
S1333 100 Cents Yr. 31 (1905). Printer: PYOG. *(S/M #F10-4).*	350.	900.	—
S1335 1 Dollar Yr. 31 (1905). Printer: PYOG. *(S/M #F10-10)*	450.	1100.	—
S1336 5 Dollars Yr. 31 (1905). Green. Back: Orange. Printer: PYOG. *(S/M #F10-11).*	450.	1100.	—
S1337 10 Dollars Yr. 31 (1905). Printer: PYOG. *(S/M #F10-12)*	600.	1500.	—

#S1337A and S1338 *Deleted.* See #S1353 and S1354.

1905 Tiao Issue

	Good	Fine	XF
S1338 1 Tiao Yr. 31 (1905). Printer: PYOG. (S/M #F10-). Rare.	—	—	—
S1339 2 Tiao Yr. 31 (1905). Printer: PYOG. (S/M #F10-). Rare.	—	—	—
S1340 3 Tiao Yr. 31 (1905). Printer: PYOG. (S/M #F10-). Rare.	—	—	—
S1341 4 Tiao Yr. 31 (1905). Printer: PYOG. (S/M #F10-). Rare.	—	—	—
S1342 5 Tiao Yr. 31 (1905). Printer: PYOG. (S/M #F10-). Rare.	—	—	—
S1343 6 Tiao Yr. 31 (1905). Printer: PYOG. (S/M #F10-). Rare.	—	—	—
S1344 7 Tiao Yr. 31 (1905). Printer: PYOG. (S/M #F10-). Rare.	—	—	—
S1345 8 Tiao Yr. 31 (1905). Printer: PYOG. (S/M #F10-). Rare.	—	—	—
S1346 10 Tiao Yr. 31 (1905). Vertical format. (S/M #F10-). Rare.	—	—	—
S1347 15 Tiao Yr. 31 (1905). (S/M #F10-). Rare.	—	—	—
S1348 20 Tiao Yr. 31 (1905). (S/M #F10-). Rare.	—	—	—
S1349 25 Tiao Yr. 31 (1905). (S/M #F10-).	—	—	—
S1350 30 Tiao Yr. 31 (1905). (S/M #F10-).	—	—	—
S1351 40 Tiao Yr. 31 (1905). (S/M #F10-).	—	—	—
S1352 50 Tiao Yr. 31 (1905). (S/M #F10-).	—	—	—
S1352A 60 Tiao Yr. 31 (1905). (S/M #F10-).	—	—	—
S1352B 70 Tiao Yr. 31 (1905). (S/M #F10-).	—	—	—
S1352C 100 Tiao Yr. 31 (1905). (S/M #F10-).	—	—	—

1906 Dollar Issue

	Good	Fine	XF
S1353 100 Cents Yr. 32 (1906). *(S/M #F10-).*	400.	1200.	—
S1354 10 Dollars Yr. 32 (1906). *(S/M #F10-).*	500.	1500.	—

NOTE: For previously listed 1908 Issue, #S1339-S1345, see #S2854-S2854F.

Fengtien Public Exchange Bank
Kung Tsi Bank of Fengtien

奉天公濟平市錢號

Feng T'ien Kung Chi P'ing Shih Ch'ien Hao

1918 Copper Coin Issues

	VG	VF	UNC
S1355 5 Coppers 1918. Green and yellow. Back: Green. *(S/M #F12-1).*	25.00	50.00	125.

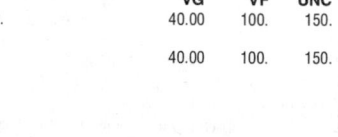

	VG	VF	UNC
S1356 10 Coppers 1918. Dark blue on yellow underprint. *(S/M #F12-2).*	40.00	100.	150.
S1357 20 Coppers 1918. *(S/M #F12-3).*	40.00	100.	150.

	VG	VF	UNC
S1358 50 Coppers 1918. Blue and tan. Back: Gray. *(S/M #F12-4).*	40.00	100.	150.

	VG	VF	UNC
S1358A 50 Coppers 1918. Black and gray. Bridge at left. Back: Orange. Printer: BEPP. *(S/M #F12-).*	40.00	100.	150.
S1359 100 Coppers 1918. *(S/M #F12-5).*	50.00	125.	250.

1922 Copper Coin Issues

	VG	VF	UNC
S1360 5 Coppers 1922. *(S/M #F12-10).*	20.00	40.00	100.

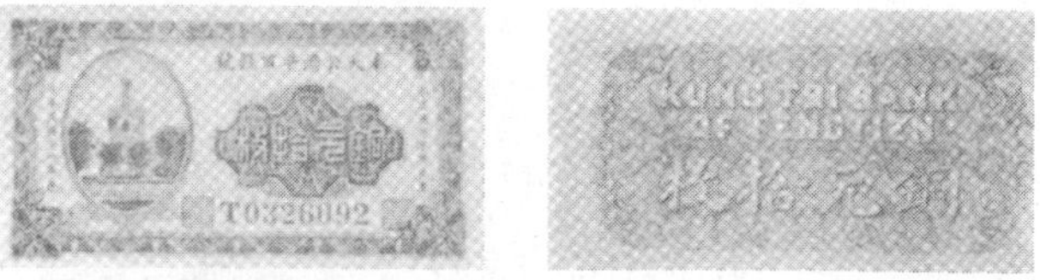

	VG	VF	UNC
S1361 10 Coppers 1922. Brown. Tower at left. Back: Blue. *(S/M #F12-11).*	15.00	30.00	75.00

	VG	VF	UNC
S1362 20 Coppers 1922. Green. City tower gate at left. Back: Red. *(S/M #F12-12).*	10.00	20.00	40.00

		VG	VF	UNC
S1363 50 Coppers	1922. Brown. Back: Orange. *(S/M #F12-13).*			
	a. Issued note.	15.00	30.00	75.00
	s. Specimen.		—	300.
S1364 100 Coppers	1922. Blue. Back: Green. *(S/M #F12-14).*	25.00	50.00	100.

		VG	VF	UNC
S1365 100 Coppers	1922. Black. City fortress gate at left. Back: Green. Engraved. *(S/M #F12-15).*	25.00	50.00	100.

		VG	VF	UNC
S1370 100 Coppers	1922. Dark gray-green. City fortress gate at left. Back: Green. Lithograph. *(S/M #F12-).*	5.00	10.00	25.00

1923 Copper Coin Issue

		Good	Fine	XF
S1371 5 Coppers	1923. *(S/M #F12-20).*	10.00	25.00	75.00
S1372 10 Coppers	1923. *(S/M #F12-21).*	20.00	40.00	100.
S1373 20 Coppers	1923. *(S/M #F12-22).*	20.00	40.00	100.
S1374 50 Coppers	1923. *(S/M #F12-23).*	20.00	40.00	100.
S1375 100 Coppers	1923. *(S/M #F12-24).*	20.00	40.00	100.

1924 Copper Coin Issue

		Good	Fine	XF
S1376 5 Coppers	1924. *(S/M #F12-30).*	10.00	25.00	75.00

		Good	Fine	XF
S1377 10 Coppers	1924. Brown-violet. Back: Blue. *(S/M #F12-31).*	5.00	15.00	30.00
S1378 20 Coppers	1924. *(S/M #F12-32).*	25.00	50.00	100.
S1379 50 Coppers	1924. *(S/M #F12-33).*	25.00	50.00	100.
S1380 100 Coppers	1924. *(S/M #F12-34).*	25.00	50.00	100.

Fengtien Agricultural and Industrial Bank

行銀總業農天奉

Feng T'ien Nung Yeh Tsung Yin Hang

1911 Issue

		Good	Fine	XF
S1383 50 Cents	1911. Printer: PYOG. *(S/M #F15-1).*	75.00	150.	275.
S1384 1 Yüan	1911. Red. Back: Green.	75.00	150.	275.

1912 Issue

		Good	Fine	XF
S1388 1 Dollar	1912. Red and green. Printer: PYOG. *(S/M #F15-10).*	75.00	150.	275.
S1389 5 Dollars	1912. Printer: PYOG. *(S/M #F15-11).*	100.	250.	—
S1390 10 Dollars	1912. Printer: PYOG. *(S/M #F15-12).*	125.	300.	—
S1391 1 Dollar	ND. *(S/M #F15-20).* Reported not confirmed.	—	—	—
S1392 5 Dollars	ND. *(S/M #F15-21).* Reported not confirmed.	—	—	—
S1393 10 Dollars	ND. Printer: PYOG. *(S/M #F15-22).* Reported not confirmed.	—	—	—

Fukien Provincial Bank

行銀省建福

Fu Chien Sheng Yin Hang

1925 Issue

		Good	Fine	XF
S1395 1 Yüan	1925. Pavilion at center. *Fuchien. (S/M #F27-1).*	125.	300.	—
S1396 5 Yüan	1925. Red and green. Back: Brown and red. *(S/M #F27-2).*	125.	300.	—
S1397 10 Yüan	1925. *(S/M #F27-3).*	150.	350.	—

1926 Issue

		Good	Fine	XF
S1399 1 Chiao	1926. Red and yellow. *(S/M #F27-5).*	50.00	100.	—

1935 Issues

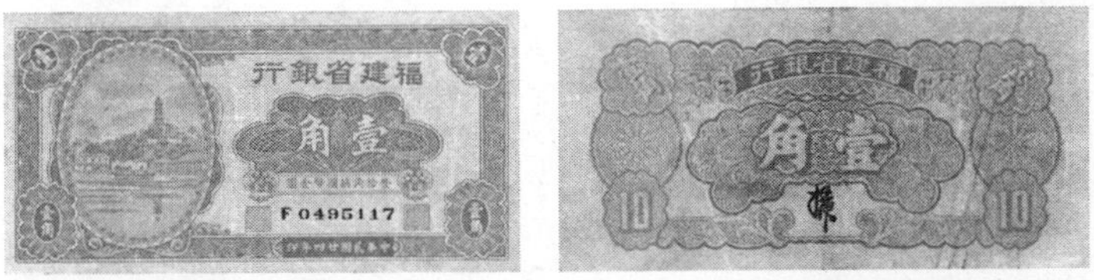

		Good	Fine	XF
S1403 1 Chiao	1935. Red. Shoreline with hilltop pagoda in background at left. Back: Multicolor. *(S/M #F27-10).*	15.00	40.00	—

		Good	Fine	XF
S1404 1 Chiao	1935. Red and yellow. *(S/M #F27-10.5).*	25.00	50.00	—
S1405 2 Chiao	1935. Red. Back: Blue. *(S/M #F27-11).*	35.00	75.00	—

S1406 2 Chiao	Good	Fine	XF
1935. Blue and green. Village with hilltop pagoda in background at right. *(S/M #F27-11.5).*	25.00	50.00	—

S1407 5 Chiao			
1935. Violet. Houses at left. Back: Blue and multicolor. *(S/M #F27-12).*	20.00	40.00	—

S1407A 5 Chiao	Good	Fine	XF
1935. Green. Shoreline village with hilltop pagoda in background, rural building at right. Back: Large *50* at upper left and right. *(S/M #F27-13).*	25.00	65.00	—

S1408 5 Chiao			
1935. Blue. Village at left. with pagoda in background, pavilion at right. Back: Blue. *(S/M #F27-14).*	20.00	40.00	—

1936 Issue

S1409 2 Chiao	Good	Fine	XF
1936. Green. Back: Red on multicolor underprint. *(S/M #F27-20).*	25.00	50.00	—

S1410 5 Chiao			
1936. Orange. Back: Multicolor. *(S/M #F27-21).*	20.00	40.00	—

1937 Issue

S1412 1 Chiao	Good	Fine	XF
1937. Red. Boat near island with house and tower at left center. Back: Orange and red. *(S/M #F27-30).*	10.00	25.00	65.00

1938-39 Issue

S1415 1 Fen	Good	Fine	XF
1938. Red and blue. Boat near island with house and tower at left center. Back: Red. *(S/M #F27-40).*	3.00	10.00	25.00

S1416 5 Fen			
1938. Green. Boat near island with house and tower at left center. Back: Purple. *(S/M #F27-41).*	5.00	15.00	30.00

S1420 1 Yüan	Good	Fine	XF
1939. Red. Bridge at right. Back: Brown. *(S/M #F27-50).*	5.00	15.00	30.00

1940-41 Issue

S1423 1 Fen	Good	Fine	XF
1940. Boat near island with house and tower at left. *(S/M #F27-60).*	5.00	15.00	30.00

S1424 5 Fen	Good	Fine	XF
1940. Green. Boat near island with house and tower at left center. Back: Purple. *(S/M #F27-61).*	4.00	10.00	25.00

S1427 2 Chiao	Good	Fine	XF
1941. Brown. Bridge at right. Back: Brown. *(S/M #F27-70).*	7.50	25.00	50.00

S1428 5 Chiao	Good	Fine	XF
1941. Red. Bridge at right. Back: Brown. *(S/M #F27-71).*	10.00	25.00	50.00

1949 Issue

S1430 5 Fen	Good	Fine	XF
1949. *(S/M #F27-79).*	10.00	25.00	60.00

S1431 1 Chiao			
1949. *(S/M #F27-80).*	7.50	25.00	50.00

S1433 5 Chiao			
1949. Red on light orange underprint. Modern building at left. Back: Green. *(S/M #F27-85).*	15.00	35.00	125.

FUKIEN BANK

行銀建福
Fu Chien Yin Hang

ND FIRST DOLLAR ISSUE

	Good	Fine	XF
S1435 1 Dollar ND (1915). Blue and multicolor. Village with mountains in background at center. Back: Blue. Memorial. *AMOY*. Printer: ABNC. *AMOY*. *(S/M #F31-1)*.	75.00	150.	—
S1436 5 Dollars ND (1915). Green and multicolor. Back: Green. Memorial. *AMOY*. Printer: ABNC. *AMOY*. *(S/M #F31-2)*.	75.00	200.	—

	Good	Fine	XF
S1437 10 Dollars ND (1915). Black and brown on yellow underprint. Back: Brown on yellow underprint. Memorial. *AMOY*. *(S/M #F31-3)*.	75.00	200.	—

ND SECOND DOLLAR ISSUE

	Good	Fine	XF
S1439 5 Dollars ND. Gateways, large tree at lower center.			
a. *AMOY*. *(S/M #F31-12a)*.	75.00	200.	—
b. *PAILOU*. *(S/M #F31-12b)*.	150.	350.	—

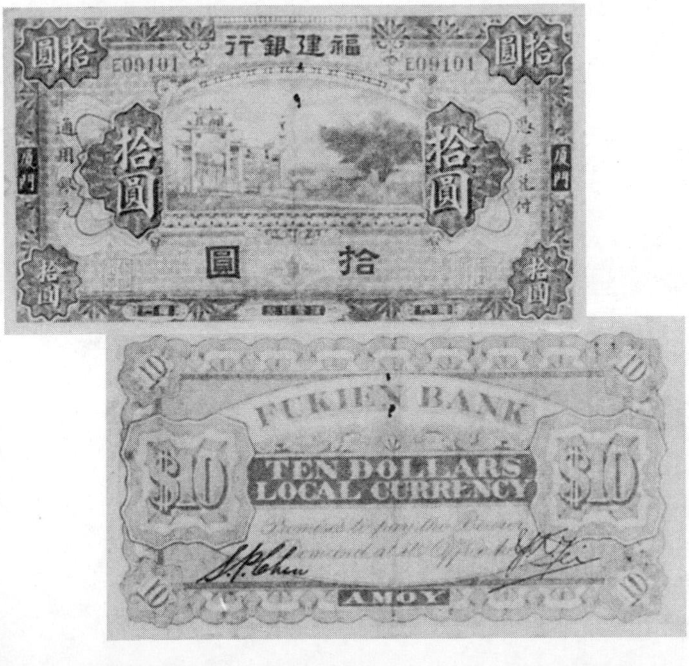

	Good	Fine	XF
S1440 10 Dollars ND. Gateway at center.			
a. *AMOY*. *(S/M #F31-13a)*.	100.	350.	—
b. *PAILOU*. *(S/M #F31-13b)*.	150.	450.	—

FU LUNG BANK

行銀隴富
Fu Lung Yin Hang

ND PROVISIONAL ISSUE

#S1443-S1447 overprint new bank name on Bank of the Northwest (Military issue).

	Good	Fine	XF
S1443 10 Cents ND (- old date 1928). Blue on multicolor underprint. Overprint: On #S3885B. *(Kansu)*. *(S/M #F44-1)*.	25.00	55.00	—
S1444 20 Cents ND (- old date 1928). Red on multicolor underprint. Overprint: On #S3886E. *(Kansu)*. *(S/M #F44-2)*.	50.00	125.	—
S1445 1 Dollar ND (- old date 1928). Brown. Overprint: #S3887C. *(Kansu)*. *(S/M #F44-10)*.	75.00	200.	—
S1446 5 Dollars ND (- old date 1928). Deep green. Overprint: #S3888 *(S/M #F44-11)*.	75.00	200.	—
S1447 10 Dollars ND (- old date 1928). Red-brown. Overprint: #S3889. *(S/M #F44-12)*.	125.	250.	—

HAINAN BANK

行 銀 南 海
Hai Nan Yin Hang

1949 ISSUE

	Good	Fine	XF
S1451 1 Cent 1949. Uniface. Printer: HKPA. *(S/M #H3-1)*. Reported not confirmed.	—	—	—

	VG	VF	UNC
S1452 2 Cents 1949. Brown. Uniface. Printer: HKPA. *(S/M #H3-2)*.	.05	.15	.50

	VG	VF	UNC
S1453 5 Cents 1949. Red on tan underprint. Uniface. Printer: HKPA. *(S/M #H3-3)*.	.05	.15	.50

	VG	VF	UNC
S1454 10 Cents 1949. Printer: HKPA. *(S/M #H3-4)*. Reported not confirmed.	—	—	—

	VG	VF	UNC
S1455 20 Cents 1949. Green. Back: Palm trees, islands at center. Printer: HKPA. *(S/M #H3-5)*.	.05	.25	.75

	VG	VF	UNC
S1456 50 Cents 1949. Maroon on light blue underprint. Back: Dark blue. Junk at center. Printer: HKPA. *(S/M #H3-6)*.	.10	.25	1.00

		VG	VF	UNC
S1457	**1 Yüan** 1949. Brown-violet on light green underprint. Back: Brown-violet. Palm trees, junks and islands at left and right. Printer: HKPA. *(S/M #H3-10).*	15.00	50.00	125.
S1458	**5 Yüan** 1949. Green on orange underprint. Printer: HKPA. *(S/M #H3-11).* Reported not confirmed.	—	—	—

		VG	VF	UNC
S1459	**10 Yüan** 1949. Black on lilac underprint. Back: Red-violet. Junk at center. Printer: HKPA. *(S/M #H3-12).*	40.00	100.	275.

HIO LUNG KIANG GOVERNMENT BANK

號銀官江龍黑
Hei Lung Chiang Kuan Yin Hao

1909 "SMALL MONEY" ISSUE

#S1461-S1465 issued in the first year of the Emperor Hsuan T'ung with western date 1909 on back.

		VG	VF	UNC
S1461	**10 Cents** 1909. Printer: PYOG. *(S/M #H6-1).*	150.	400.	—
S1462	**20 Cents** 1909. Printer: PYOG. *(S/M #H6-2).*	150.	400.	—
S1463	**50 Cents** 1909. Printer: PYOG. *(S/M #H6-3).*	100.	225.	—

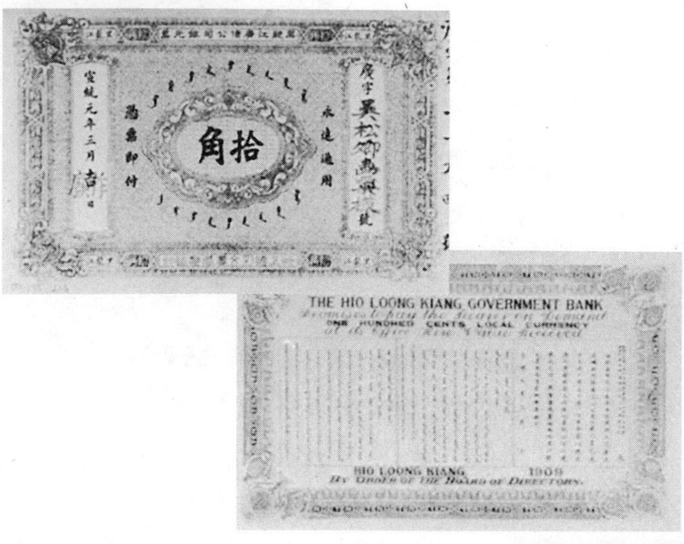

		VG	VF	UNC
S1464	**100 Cents** 1909. Printer: PYOG. *(S/M #H6-4).*	225.	500.	—

1908 COPPER COIN ISSUE

		VG	VF	UNC
S1465	**5 Coppers** 1908. Printer: PYOG. *(S/M #H6-10).*	—	—	—

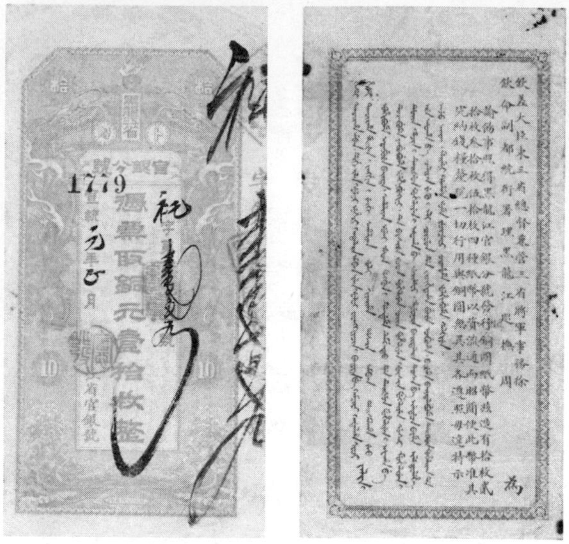

		VG	VF	UNC
S1466	**10 Coppers** 1908. Orange. Printer: PYOG. *(S/M #H6-11).*	150.	400.	—
S1467	**20 Coppers** 1908. Printer: PYOG. *(S/M #H6-12).*	—	—	—
S1468	**30 Coppers** 1908. Printer: PYOG. *(S/M #H6-13).*	—	—	—
S1469	**50 Coppers** 1908. Printer: PYOG. *(S/M #H6-14).*	175.	450.	—
S1470	**100 Coppers** 1908. Printer: PYOG. *(S/M #H6-15).*	—	—	—
S1471	**200 Coppers** 1908. Printer: PYOG. *(S/M #H6-16).*	—	—	—
S1472	**500 Coppers** 1908. Printer: PYOG. *(S/M #H6-17).*	—	—	—
S1473	**1000 Coppers** 1908. Printer: PYOG. *(S/M #H6-18).*	—	—	—

1913 COPPER COIN ISSUE

		VG	VF	UNC
S1474	**5 Coppers** Jan. 1913. Black. Back: Red. *(S/M #H6-20).*	150.	350.	—

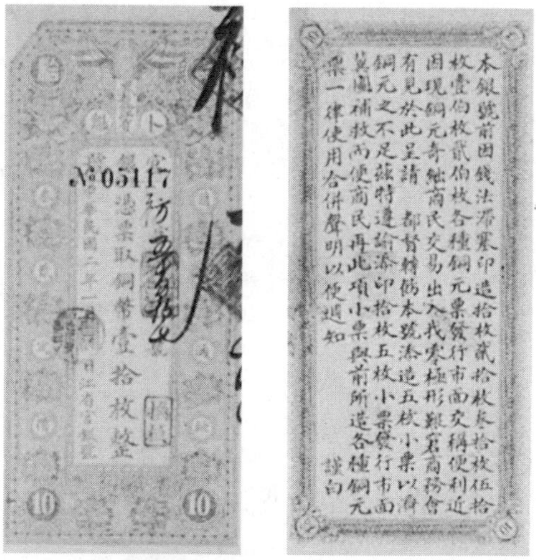

		VG	VF	UNC
S1475	**10 Coppers** Jan. 1913. Orange. Vertical format. Back: Olive-green. *(S/M #H6-21).*	75.00	250.	—
S1476	**20 Coppers** 1913. *(S/M #H6-22).*	—	—	—
S1477	**30 Coppers** 1913. *(S/M #H6-23).*	—	—	—
S1478	**50 Coppers** 1913. *(S/M #H6-24).*	—	—	—
S1479	**100 Coppers** 1913. *(S/M #H6-25).*	—	—	—
S1480	**200 Coppers** 1913. *(S/M #H6-26).*	—	—	—
S1481	**500 Coppers** 1913. Violet and green. *(S/M #H6-27).*	—	—	—
S1482	**1000 Coppers** 1913. *(S/M #H6-28).*	—	—	—

S1483-S1488 *Deleted.* See #S1629-S1634.

1914 "Small Money" Issue

		VG	VF	UNC
S1489	**10 Cents** 1914. *(S/M #H6-40).*	—	—	—
S1490	**20 Cents** 1914. *(S/M #H6-41).*	—	—	—
S1491	**50 Cents** 1914. *(S/M #H6-42).*	—	—	—
S1492	**100 Cents** 1914. *(S/M #H6-43).*	—	—	—

NOTE: #S1489-S1492 probably another Amoor Government issue.

#S1495-S1500 *Deleted.* See #S1636-S1639B.

#S1501-S1503 *Deleted.* See #S1639C-S1639E.

#S1505-S1508 *Deleted.* See #S1641-S1645.

1918 Tiao Issue

		VG	VF	UNC
S1511	**15 Tiao** 1918. *(S/M #H6-).*	—	—	—

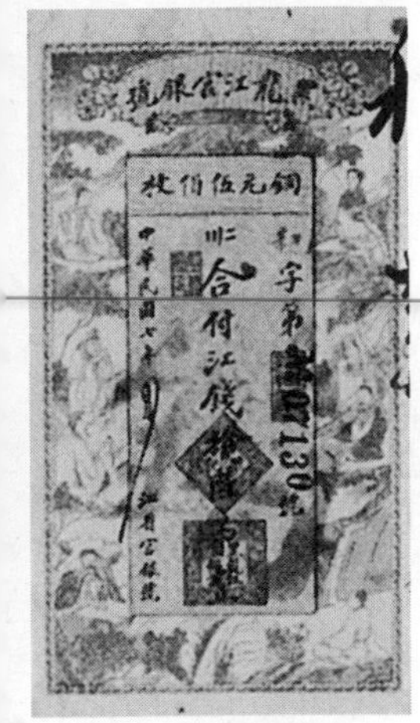

		VG	VF	UNC
S1512	**16 Tiao = 500 Coppers** 1918. Black text on purple and green underprint. People around border. Vertical format. Back: Red-orange. Fortress gateway at center. *(S/M #H6-80).*	—	—	—
S1513	**32 Tiao = 1000 Coppers** July 1918. Black text. Dark blue-green on yellow-orange underprint. Back: Green. *(S/M #H6-80.5).*	250.	—	—
S1515	**50 Tiao** 1918. *(S/M #H6-81).* Reported not confirmed.	—	—	—

Kwang Sing Company / Heilungchiang Kuang Hsin Syndicate of Heilungkiang

廣信公司
Kuang Hsin Kung Szu

黑龍江廣信公司
Hei Lung Chiang Kuang Hsin Kung Szu

1904 Tiao Issue

		VG	VF	UNC
S1521	**1 Tiao** Yr. 30 (1904). *(S/M #H7-1).*	175.	500.	—
S1522	**2 Tiao** Yr. 30 (1904). *(S/M #H7-2).*	200.	525.	—
S1523	**3 Tiao** Yr. 30 (1904). *(S/M #H7-3).*	225.	550.	—
S1524	**5 Tiao** Yr. 30 (1904). *(S/M #H7-4).*	225.	550.	—
S1525	**10 Tiao** Yr. 30 (1904). *(S/M #H7-5).*	250.	600.	—
S1527	**100 Tiao** Yr. 30 (1904). *(S/M #H7-6).*	250.	600.	—

1904 Tael Issue

		VG	VF	UNC
S1529	**1 Tael** Yr. 30 (1904). *(S/M #H7-10).*	325.	750.	—
S1530	**2 Taels** Yr. 30 (1904). *(S/M #H7-11).*	400.	1000.	—
S1531	**3 Taels** Yr. 30 (1904). *(S/M #H7-12).*	450.	1100.	—
S1532	**5 Taels** Yr. 30 (1904). *(S/M #H7-13).*	650.	1400.	—
S1533	**10 Taels** Yr. 30 (1904). *(S/M #H7-14).*	—	—	—
S1534	**30 Taels** Yr. 30 (1904). *(S/M #H7-15).*	—	—	—
S1536	**50 Taels** Yr. 30 (1904). *(S/M #H7-16).*	—	—	—

1906 Tiao Issue

		VG	VF	UNC
S1536F	**10 Tiao** Yr. 32 (1906). Orange and black. *(S/M #H7-16.9).*	—	—	—

1907 Tiao Issue

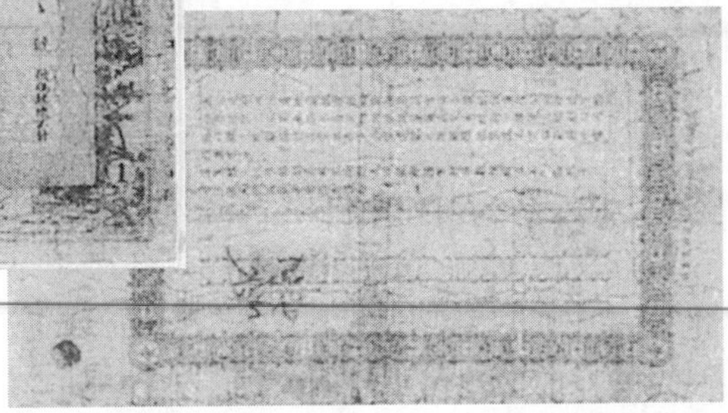

		VG	VF	UNC
S1537	**1 Tiao** Yr. 33 (1907). Red and green. Trees and people in frame border. Back: Red. *(S/M #H7-17).*	200.	600.	—
S1538	**5 Tiao** Yr. 33 (1907). Purple and black. Two dragons. *(S/M #H7-17.1).*	—	—	—
S1539	**10 Tiao** Yr. 33 (1907). Red and black. Two dragons. *(S/M #H7-17.2).*	—	—	—
S1539A	**50 Tiao** Yr. 33 (1907). Green and orange. *(S/M #H7-17.3).*	—	—	—

1908 Tiao Issue

		VG	VF	UNC
S1540	**1 Tiao** Yr. 34 (1908). Green and red. *(S/M #H7-17.6).*	—	—	—

1909 Tiao Issue

		VG	VF	UNC
S1540F	**5 Tiao** Yr. 35 (1909). Purple and black. Two dragons. *(S/M #H7-17.8).*	—	—	—

1915 Tiao Issue

		VG	VF	UNC
S1541	**5 Tiao** 1915. Violet and black. *(S/M #H7-18).*	100.	300.	—

1916 Tiao Issue

		VG	VF	UNC
S1544	**1 Tiao** 1916. Red and green. *(S/M #H7-19).*	100.	300.	—
S1545	**2 Tiao** 1916. Red and blue. *(S/M #H7-19.5).*	—	—	—

1918 Tiao Issue

		VG	VF	UNC
S1550	**1 Tiao** 1918. *(S/M #H7-).*	75.00	200.	—

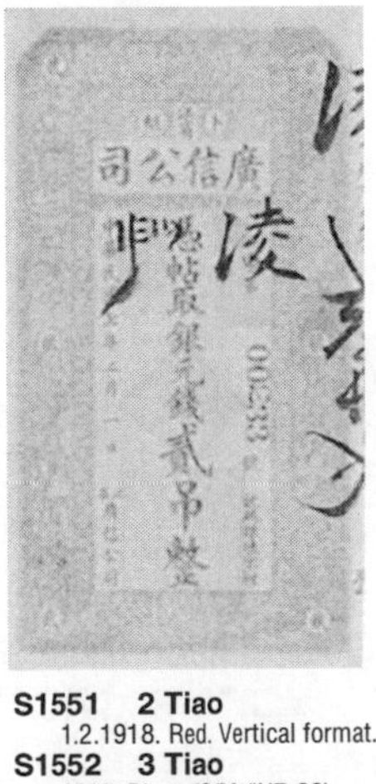

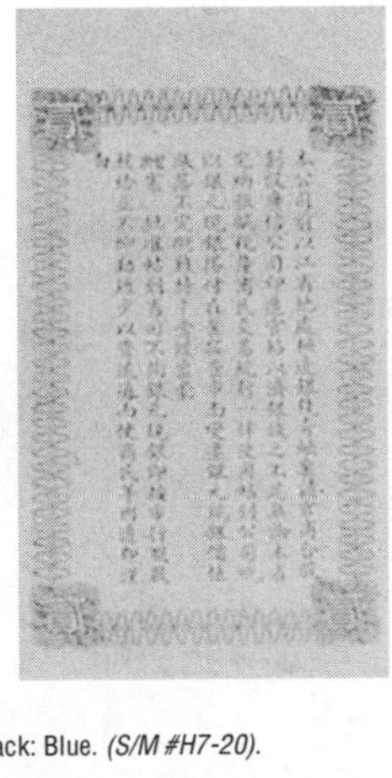

		VG	VF	UNC
S1551	**2 Tiao** 1.2.1918. Red. Vertical format. Back: Blue. *(S/M #H7-20).*	125.	275.	—
S1552	**3 Tiao** 1918. Blue. *(S/M #H7-22).*	100.	275.	—
S1553	**5 Tiao** 1918. *(S/M #H7-23).*	100.	275.	—
S1554	**10 Tiao** 1918. Red. *(S/M #H7-24).*	100.	275.	—
S1555	**100 Tiao** 1918. Red, blue and black. Back: Red. *(S/M #H7-28).*	125.	350.	—

1919 Tiao Issue

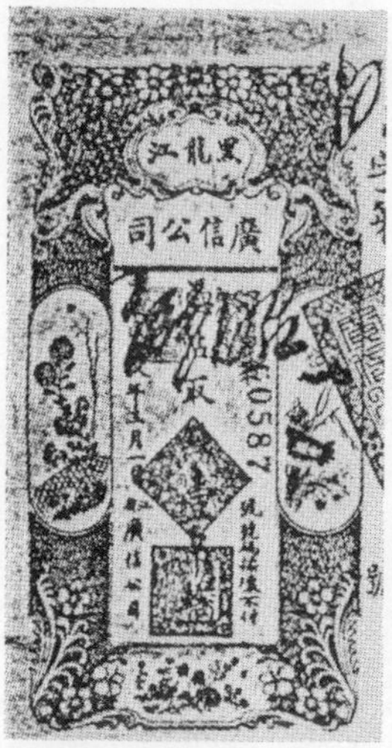
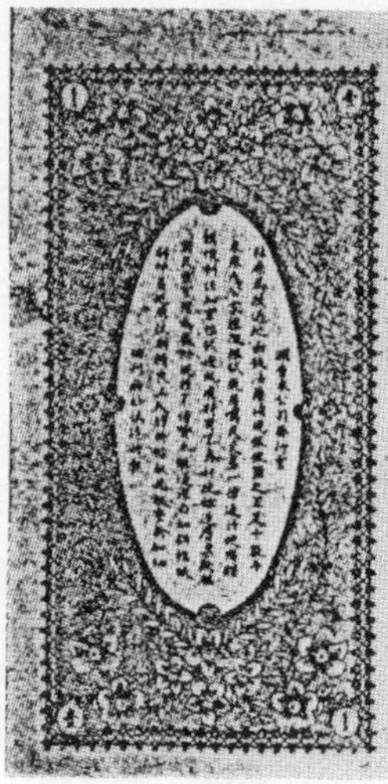

	VG	VF	UNC
S1559 1 Tiao			
1.3.1919. Green. Vertical format. Back: Red. *(S/M #H7-30).*	50.00	150.	—
S1560 2 Tiao			
1919. Red. Back: Blue. *(S/M #H7-31).*	75.00	200.	—
S1561 3 Tiao			
1919. Blue. Back: Green. *(S/M #H7-32).*	75.00	200.	—

	VG	VF	UNC
S1562 5 Tiao			
1919. Violet. Man at left, woman at right. Vertical format. Back: Green. *(S/M #H7-33).*	50.00	150.	—
S1563 10 Tiao			
1919. Orange. Back: Violet. *(S/M #H7-34).*	50.00	150.	—

1919 ND "Small Money" Issue

	VG	VF	UNC
S1565 10 Cents			
ND (1919). Violet and blue. *(S/M #H7-35).*	50.00	150.	—
S1566 20 Cents			
ND (1919). Green and violet. *(S/M #H7-36).*	50.00	150.	—

1919 "Big Money" Issue

	VG	VF	UNC
S1568 1 Dollar			
1919. Blue and violet. Printer: BEPP. *(S/M #H7-37).*	75.00	200.	—
S1569 5 Dollars			
1919. Green. Printer: BEPP. *(37.5).*	100.	250.	—
S1570 10 Dollars			
1919. Brown. Printer: BEPP. *(S/M #H7-38).*	75.00	250.	—
S1570A 10 Dollars			
1919. Green. Printer: BEPP. *(S/M #H7-).*	75.00	250.	—

1919 Harbin Branch Issue

	VG	VF	UNC
S1571 1 Dollar			
1919. Brown. *(S/M #H7-).* Specimen.	—	—	500.
S1571A 5 Dollars			
1919. Orange. *(S/M #H7-).* Specimen.	—	—	500.
S1571B 10 Dollars			
1919. Brown. *(S/M #H7-).* Specimen.	—	—	500.

1920 "Small Money" Issues

	VG	VF	UNC
S1572 10 Cents			
1920. Violet and blue. *(S/M #H7-39).*	25.00	75.00	—
S1575 10 Cents			
1920. Green. Back: Orange and green. Printer: BEPP.			
a. *Heiho. (S/M #H7-40a).*	125.	275.	—
b. *Hulun. (S/M #H7-40b).*	125.	350.	—
S1576 20 Cents			
1920. Green. Village at center. Back: Orange and green. Printer: BEPP.			
a. *Heiho. (S/M #H7-41a).*	100.	275.	—
b. *Hulun. (S/M #H7-41b).*	100.	275.	—

	VG	VF	UNC
S1577 50 Cents			
1920. Green. Fortress towers at center. Back: Dark brown on yellow-green and orange underprint. Printer: BEPP.			
a. *Heiho. (S/M #H7-42a).*	125.	375.	—
b. *Hulun. (S/M #H7-42b).*	125.	375.	—

1920 Tiao Issue

	VG	VF	UNC
S1579 1 Tiao			
1920. Red and green. *(S/M #H7-43).*	75.00	225.	—

1921 Tiao Issue

	VG	VF	UNC
S1582 50 Tiao			
1921. Green and red. *(S/M #H7-44).*	100.	300.	—
S1583 100 Tiao			
1921. Blue and violet. *(S/M #H7-46).*	100.	300.	—
S1584 100 Tiao			
1921. Red and black. *(S/M #H7-47).*	100.	300.	—

	VG	VF	UNC
S1585 100 Tiao			
1921. Blue and red. Vertical format. *(S/M #H7-48).*	100.	300.	—

1922 Tiao Issue

	VG	VF	UNC
S1590 50 Tiao 1.1.1922. Green and red. Uniface. Vertical format. *(S/M #H7-50).*			
a. Issued note.	100.	300.	—
b. Cancelled.	25.00	75.00	225.

1924 Tiao Issue

	VG	VF	UNC
S1596 100 Tiao 1922. Maroon, red, blue, and black. Like #S1555. Back: Red. *(S/M #H7-60).*	40.00	125.	—

1924 "Big Money" Issue

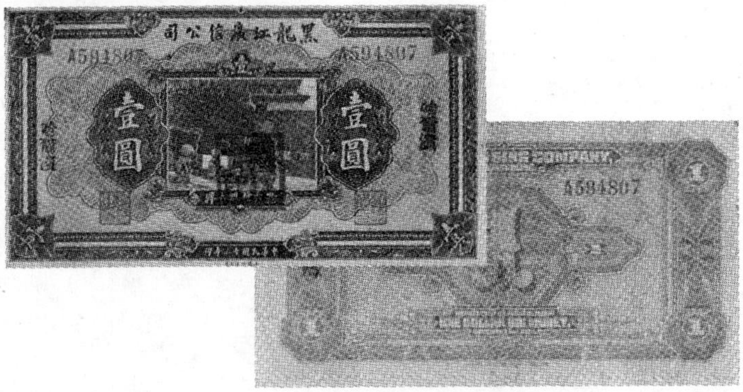

	VG	VF	UNC
S1601 1 Dollar 1.11.1924. Black and multicolor. Statues of lions with city tower gate in background at center. Back: Orange. Printer: ABNC. *(S/M #H7-71a).*			
a. *Harbin. (S/M #H7-71b).*	100.	300.	—
b. *Harbin* with otfficial Chinese 4 character overprint. *(S/M #H7-71c).*	100.	300.	—
S1602 5 Dollars 1.11.1924. Brown and multicolor. Statues of lions with city tower gate in background at center. Back: Green. Printer: ABNC. *(S/M #H7-73a).*			
a. *Harbin. (S/M #H7-73b).*	75.00	200.	—
b. *Harbin* with otfficial Chinese 4 character overprint. *(S/M #H7-73c).*	75.00	200.	—

	VG	VF	UNC
S1603 10 Dollars 1.11.1924. Red and multicolor. Statues of lions with city tower gate in background at center. Back: Blue. Printer: ABNC. *(S/M #H7-75a).*			
a. *Harbin. (S/M #H7-75b).*	50.00	150.	—
b. *Harbin* with otfficial Chinese 4 character overprint. *(S/M #H7-75c).*	50.00	150.	—
c. Without place name. *(S/M #H7-75-75d).*	40.00	125.	—

1924 Dollar Bond Issue

	VG	VF	UNC
S1604 1 Dollar 1.12.1924. Green and multicolor. Hillside shrine at center. Back: Green. Printer: ABNC. *(S/M #H7-70).*	75.00	250.	—
S1605 5 Dollars 1.12.1924. Black and multicolor. Hillside shrine at center. Back: Orange. Printer: ABNC. *(S/M #H7-72).*	125.	300.	—

	VG	VF	UNC
S1606 10 Dollars 1.12.1924. Olive-green and multicolor. Hillside shrine at center. Back: Olive. Printer: ABNC. *(S/M #H7-74).*	125.	300.	—

1925 Tiao Issue

	VG	VF	UNC
S1610 20 Tiao 1925. Brown. Back: Green. *(S/M #H7-80).*	50.00	150.	—

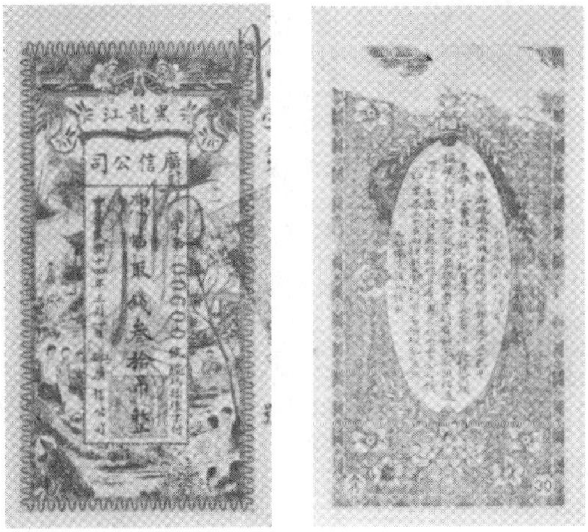

	VG	VF	UNC
S1611 30 Tiao 1.3.1925. Black. Vertical format. Back: Violet. *(S/M #H7-81).*	75.00	250.	—

#S1613 *Deleted. See #S1619G.*

1925 Dollar Issue

	VG	VF	UNC
S1614 1 Dollar 1925. Brown on multicolor underprint. With 10 Chinese characters "1 Yuan equals 12 Chiao" blackened. Printer: ABNC. *(S/M #H7-93).*	—	—	—
S1614B 10 Dollars 1925. Green on multicolor underprint. With 10 Chinese characters "1 Yuan equals 12 Chiao" blackened. Printer: ABNC. *(S/M #H7-95).*	—	—	—

1926 "Big Money" Issue

	VG	VF	UNC
S1615 10 Dollars 1926. Dark brown on multicolor underprint. Hillside shrine at center. Specimen. *(S/M #H7-96).*	50.00	150.	300.

1929 "Small Money" Issue

S1616 10 Cents	VG	VF	UNC
1929. Orange. Buildings at left. Back: Blue. (S/M #H7-100).			
a. *Harbin.*	50.00	150.	—
b. As a. With otfficial Chinese 4 character overprint.	50.00	150.	—
s. Specimen.	—	—	300.

S1617 20 Cents	VG	VF	UNC
1929. Violet. Back: Blue. *(S/M #H7-101).*			
a. *Harbin.*	50.00	150.	—
s1. Specimen.	—	—	300.
s2. As b. With otfficial Chinese 4 character overprint Specimen.	—	—	350.

S1618 50 Cents	VG	VF	UNC
1929. Blue and green. Back: Violet. *(S/M #H7-102).*			
a. *Harbin.*	50.00	125.	—
b. As a. With otfficial Chinese 4 character overprint.	50.00	125.	—
s. Specimen.	—	—	350.

1929 Tiao Issue

	VG	VF	UNC
S1619B 5 Tiao 1929. Violet. Birds, ship and steam train. *(S/M #H7-103).*	100.	300.	—
S1619D 20 Tiao 1929. Brown. *(S/M #H7-105).*	100.	300.	—
S1619E 30 Tiao 1929. Blue and violet. Back: Red. *(S/M #H7-106).*	100.	300.	—

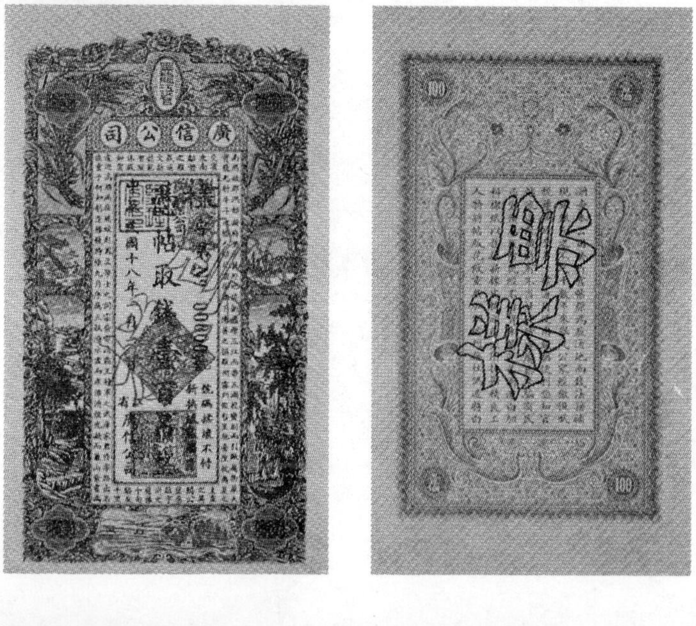

S1619G 100 Tiao	VG	VF	UNC
1.1.1929. Blue and violet. Bird, rural view in left frame panels and deer, rural view in right frame panels. Vertical format. Back: Red. *(S/M #H7-90).*			
a. Issued note.	50.00	125.	200.
s. Specimen.	—	—	300.

Provincial Bank of Heilungkiang

黑龍江省官銀號

Hei Lung Chiang Sheng Kuan Yin Hao

1929 Issue

	VG	VF	UNC
S1621 10 Cents 1929. Printer: TWCC. *(S/M #H11-1).* Reported not confirmed.	—	—	—
S1622 20 Cents 1929. Printer: TWCC. *(S/M #H11-2).* Reported not confirmed.	—	—	—
S1623 50 Cents 1929. Printer: TWCC. *(S/M #H11-3).* Reported not confirmed.	—	—	—

1931 Issue

	VG	VF	UNC
S1624 1 Yüan 1.6.1931. Brown. Forest at left, steam train at right. Printer: BEPP. Specimen. *(S/M #H11-10).*	—	—	400.
S1625 5 Yüan 1.6.1931. Forest at left, steam train at right. Printer: BEPP. Specimen. *(S/M #H11-11).*	—	—	400.
S1626 10 Yüan 1.6.1931. Forest at left, steam train at right. Printer: BEPP. Specimen. *(S/M #H11-12).*	—	—	400.
S1627 100 Yüan 1.6.1931. Forest at left, steam train at right. Printer: BEPP. Specimen. *(S/M #H11-14).*	—	—	400.

Amoor Government Bank

黑龍江官銀號小銀元券

Hei Lung Chiang Kuan Yin Hao Hsiao Yin Yüan Ch'üan

1913 Issue

	VG	VF	UNC
S1629 1 Chiao = 10 Cents 1913. Printer: FRBC. *(S/M #H6-30).*	—	—	—
S1630 2 Chiao = 20 Cents 1913. Printer: FRBC. *(S/M #H6-31).*	—	—	—

#S1631 *Deleted.* See #S1633.

	VG	VF	UNC
S1632 10 Chiao = 100 Cents 1913. Printer: FRBC. *(S/M #H6-33).*	—	—	—
S1633 50 Chiao = 500 Cents 1913. Lions facing globe at upper center. Back: Lions facing globe at upper center. Printer: FRBC. *(S/M #H6-34).*	400.	—	—
S1634 100 Chiao = 1000 Cents 1913. Printer: FRBC. *(S/M #H6-35).*	—	—	—

NOTE: #S1629-S1634 were listed in *Chinese Banknotes* under Hio Lung Kiang Government Bank.

1915 Manchurian Issue

	VG	VF	UNC
S1636 10 Cents 1.12.1915. Black and green on light orange underprint. Building at center. Back: Blue. *(S/M #H6-50).*	250.	650.	—

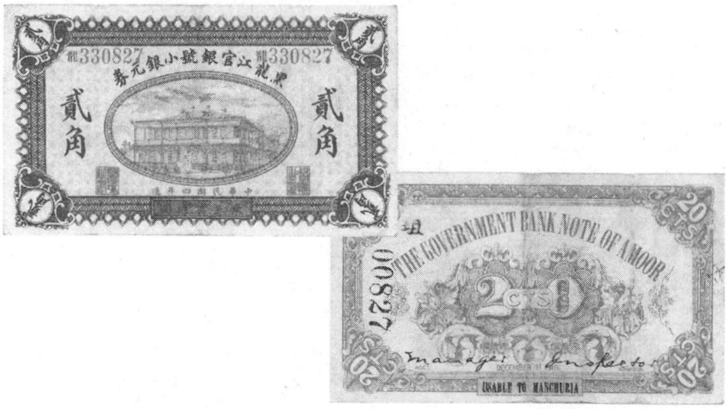

	VG	VF	UNC
S1637 20 Cents 1.12.1915. Blue and multicolor. Back: Text: *USABLE IN MANCHURIA* at bottom center. *(S/M #H6-51).*	350.	750.	—
S1638 50 Cents 1.12.1915. Green, yellow, and blue. Park scene at center. Back: Purple. Text: *USABLE IN MANCHURIA* at bottom center. *(S/M #H6-52).*	350.	750.	—
S1639 100 Cents 1.12.1915. *(S/M #H6-53 and H12-1).*	350.	800.	—
S1639A 500 Cents 1.12.1915. *(S/M #H6-54).*	—	—	—
S1639B 1000 Cents 1.12.1915. *(S/M #H6-55).*	—	—	—
S1639C 1 Dollar 1915. *(S/M #H6-60).* Reported not confirmed.	—	—	—
S1639D 5 Dollars 1915. *(S/M #H6-61).* Reported not confirmed.	—	—	—
S1639E 10 Dollars 1915. *(S/M #H6-62).* Reported not confirmed.	—	—	—

NOTE: #S1636-S1639E were listed in *Chinese Banknotes* under Hio Lung Kiang Government Bank.

1916 Issue

		VG	VF	UNC
S1641 10 Cents	1916. Green and yellow. Back: Violet. Flowers. *(S/M #H6-70 and H12-10).*	125.	350.	—
S1642 20 Cents	1916. Back: Flowers. *(S/M #H6-71 and H12-11).*	200.	500.	—

		VG	VF	UNC
S1643 50 Cents	1916. Violet and green. *(S/M #H6-72).*	400.	800.	—

		VG	VF	UNC
S1645 10 Chiao	1916. Blue on yellow underprint. Lions supporting globe at upper center. Back: Black on tan underprint. Tower gate at center. *(S/M #H6-73).*	600.	1000.	—

		VG	VF	UNC
S1646 50 Chiao	1916. Blue on yellow underprint. Lions supporting globe at upper center. Back: Black on rose underprint. *(S/M #H6-74).*	250.	600.	—

#S1641-S1645 were listed in *Chinese Banknotes* under Hio Lung Kiang Government Bank.

1917 Issue

		VG	VF	UNC
S1648 1 Dollar	1917. *(S/M #H12-20).*	300.	750.	—
S1649 5 Dollars	1917. *(S/M #H12-21).*	400.	800.	—

1918 Issue

		VG	VF	UNC
S1649A 600 Coppers	1918. Blue-gray. People, bridge in ornate border. Back: Brown. Tower gate. *(S/M #H12-28).*	325.	750.	—
S1650 1000 Coppers	1918. *(S/M #H12-30).*	400.	1100.	—
S1651 50 Chiao = 500 Cents	1918. *(S/M #H12-35).* Reported not confirmed.	—	—	—

1919 Issue

		VG	VF	UNC
S1653 50 Chiao = 500 Cents	1919. Lions facing globe at upper center. Back: Lions facing globe at upper center. *(S/M #H12-42).*	500.	1100.	—

Amoy Industrial Bank

1940s Issue

		VG	VF	UNC
S1655 1 Cent	ca.1940. Red. Pagoda at left.	5.00	25.00	50.00
S1656 5 Cents	ca.1940. Green. Pagoda at left.	5.00	25.00	50.00
S1657 10 Cents	ca.1940. Green. Pagoda at left.	10.00	40.00	125.
S1657A 20 Cents	ca. 1940. Pagoda at left.	40.00	100.	200.
S1658 50 Cents	ca.1940. Blue. Pagoda at right.	40.00	100.	200.

Provincial Bank of Honan

行銀省南河
Ho Nan Sheng Yin Hang

行銀南河
Ho Nan Yin Hang

1921 Issue

		Good	Fine	XF
S1661 10 Coppers	1921. Blue and brown. *(S/M #H62-0.2).*	100.	250.	—
S1662 20 Coppers	1921. *(S/M #H62-0.3).*	100.	250.	—
S1665 1 Yüan	1921. *(S/M #H62-).*	125.	300.	—

NOTE: For earlier issues see Provincial Bank of Honan #S2971-S2985 and for similar issues see #S1695, S1700 and S1706.

1922 Issue

		Good	Fine	XF
S1669 10 Coppers	1.8.1922. Blue on tan underprint. Back: Blue and black. Printer: BEPP. *(S/M #H62-0.6).*	100.	250.	—
S1670 20 Coppers	1.8.1922. Green on tan underprint. Back: Green and black. Printer: BEPP. *(S/M #H62-0.7).*	100.	250.	—
S1671 50 Coppers	1.8.1922. Violet on pink underprint. Back: Violet and light blue. Printer: BEPP. *(S/M #H62-0.8).*	150.	350.	—

NOTE: For #S1669-S1671 with 10 Chinese characters overprint see #S1704-S1706.

		Good	Fine	XF
S1673 1 Yüan	15.7.1922. Blue. Back: Blue and multicolor. Printer: BEPP. *(S/M #H62-1).*	40.00	125.	300.
S1674 5 Yüan	15.7.1922. Orange. Back: Dark red. Printer: BEPP. *(S/M #H62-2).*	75.00	200.	600.
S1675 10 Yüan	15.7.1922. Green. Back: Green and multicolor. Printer: BEPP. *(S/M #H62-3).*	100.	300.	800.

1923 Issues

		Good	Fine	XF
S1676 10 Coppers	1923. Blue. Pagoda at left, building at right. Back: Dark brown. *(S/M #H62-8).*	20.00	75.00	150.
S1677 10 Coppers	1923. Blue. Pagoda at left, building at right. Back: Orange. *(S/M #H62-9).*	20.00	75.00	150.

		Good	Fine	XF
S1679 20 Coppers	1923. Green. Pagoda at left, building at right. Back: Olive. *(S/M #H62-10).*			
	a. Issued note.	20.00	75.00	150.
	b. overprint: *I.*	20.00	75.00	150.
S1680 20 Coppers	1923. Gray and blue. Pagoda at left, building at right. *(S/M #H62-10.5).*	20.00	75.00	150.
S1681 20 Coppers	1923. Green and gray. Pagoda at left, building at right. *(S/M #H62-10.7).*	20.00	75.00	150.
S1682 50 Coppers	1923. Brown on pink underprint. Pagoda at left, building at right. Back: Red. *(S/M #H62-11).*			
	a. Issued note.	5.00	20.00	50.00
	b. Control letters overprint: *GG; HH; OO; QQ; RR; SS; UU.*	5.00	20.00	50.00
S1683 50 Coppers	1923. Brown on pink underprint. Pagoda at left, building at right. Back: Red. *(S/M #H62-15).*	10.00	25.00	100.
S1685 100 Coppers	1923. Orange and multicolor. Pagoda at left, building at right. Back: Orange. Shrine at center.			
	a. Issued note. *(S/M #H62-20c).*	10.00	25.00	75.00
	b. *Honan. (S/M #H62-20a).*	20.00	50.00	125.
	c. *Tientsin. (S/M #H62-20b).*	20.00	50.00	150.
	r. Remainder without serial #. *(S/M #H62-20-d).*	—	Unc	75.00

S1688 1 Dollar	Good	Fine	XF
15.7.1923. Red on multicolor underprint. Shrine at center. Back: Brown-orange. Printer: BEPP.			
a. Issued note. *(S/M #H62-20c).*	5.00	20.00	50.00
b. *HONAN. (S/M #H62-20a).*	10.00	20.00	75.00
c. *TIENTSIN. (S/M #H62-20b).*	20.00	50.00	150.
d. *Hupei. (S/M #H62-20d).*	50.00	150.	—
e. *Paotowith HONAN. (S/M #H62-20e).*	50.00	150.	—
f. *PEKING. (SM #H62-20f).*	20.00	50.00	150.
g. *CHENGCHOW.*	25.00	75.00	—
r. Remainder without place name. *(S/M #H62-20g).*	—	Unc	75.00
S1688A 1 Dollar			
15.7.1923. Brown. Shrine at center. Back: Dark brown. Printer: BEPP. *HONAN,* with place name *DABAO* on both sides.	—	—	—
S1689 5 Dollars			
15.7.1923. Green on multicolor underprint. Shrine at right. Back: Brown. Printer: BEPP.			
a. Issued note. *(S/M #H62-21c).*	10.00	40.00	100.
b. *HONAN. (S/M #H62-21a).*	10.00	40.00	100.
c. *TIENTSIN. (S/M #H62-21b).*	15.00	50.00	125.
d. *CHENGCHOW. (S/M #H62-21f).*	50.00	150.	400.
e. *PEKING. (S/M #H62-21e).*	40.00	125.	300.
r. Remainder without place name. *(S/M #H62-21g).*	—	Unc	100.
S1690 10 Dollars			
15.7.1923. Violet and multicolor. Shrine at left. Back: Green. Printer: BEPP.			
a. Issued note. *(S/M #H62-22c).*	20.00	50.00	150.
b. *HONAN. (S/M #H62-22a).*	20.00	50.00	150.
c. *TIENTSIN. (S/M #H62-22b).*	15.00	40.00	100.
d. *CHENGCHOW. (S/M #H62-22f).*	50.00	175.	350.
e. *PEKING. (S/M #H62-22e).*	50.00	125.	250.
r. Remainder without place name. *(S/M #H62-22-g).*	—	Unc	125.

NOTE: For #S1688-S1690 with large red seal overprint. on back see Military - Honan Province #S3858-S3860.

Bank of Honan Province
Yü Ch'üan Bank of Honan

局錢銀官泉豫南河
Ho Nan Yü Ch'üan Kuan Yin Ch'ien Chü

1916 Copper Coin Issue

S1691 50 Coppers	Good	Fine	XF
1916. Brown on yellow underprint. Tower at center. Back: Brown. *HONAN. (SM #H62.5-3).*	175.	500.	—

1916 Dollar Issue

S1695 10 Dollars	Good	Fine	XF
1.6.1916. Green on brown underprint. Tower at left, pagoda at right. Back: Shrine at center. *HONAN. (S/M #H62.5-8).*	225.	600.	—

NOTE: For earlier listings see Provincial Bank of Honan #S2971-S2985 and #S1661-S1690.

1922 Issues

S1700 100 Cents	Good	Fine	XF
1.3.1922. Blue on yellow-green underprint. Old Chinese man at center. Back: Red and black. Printer: BEPP. *(S/M #H62.5-15).*	125.	300.	—
S1701 100 Cents			
1.3.1922. Blue on yellow-green. Old Chinese man at center. Back: Orange and black. *(S/M #H62.5-16).*	100.	275.	—

ND Provisional Issue

#S1704-S1706 with additional Chinese 10 character bank name overprint

S1704 10 Coppers	Good	Fine	XF
ND (- old date 1.8.1922). Blue on tan underprint. Old Chinese man at center. Overprint: On #S1669. *(S/M #H62.5-20).*	100.	275.	—
S1705 20 Coppers			
ND (- old date 1.8.1922). Green on tan underprint. Old Chinese man at center. Overprint: On #S1670. *(S/M #H62.5-21).*	125.	275.	—
S1706 50 Coppers			
ND (- old date 1.8.1922). Violet on pink underprint. Old Chinese man at center. Overprint: On #S1671. *(S/M #62.5-33).*	125.	275.	—

Hopei Province

券通流時臨縣冀／省北河
Ho Pei Sheng/Chi Hsien Lin Shih Liu T'ung Chüan

1938 Temporary Circulating Note Issue

S1708 1 Chiao = 10 Cents	VG	VF	UNC
1938. Green. Mythical animals and gazebo at left. Back: Red. *(SM #H62.7-11).*	25.00	50.00	150.
S1708A 2 Chiao = 20 Cents			
1938. Dark blue. 17-arch bridge, palace ground, statue of animal at right. Back: Brown. *(S/M #62.7-12).*	75.00	225.	450.
S1708C 1 Yüan			
1938. Brown on pale blue underprint. Gazebo, house at left, 17-arch bridge, palace grounds, statue of animal at right. Back: Sailing vessels. (S/M #H62.7-14).	100.	250.	550.

Ho Pei Metropolitan Bank

局錢銀北河
Ho Pei Yin Ch'ien Chü

1929 Issue

S1709 20 Coppers	VG	VF	UNC
1929. Dark blue on pink underprint. *Pei P'ing.* Back: Dark blue. Printer: BEPP. *(S/M #H63-1).*	10.00	25.00	100.
S1709A 40 Coppers			
1929. Red brown on blue underprint. *Pei P'ing.* Back: Red brown. Printer: BEPP. *(S/M #H63-2).*	10.00	25.00	100.

1931 Issue

S1709D 20 Coppers	VG	VF	UNC
1931. Red-brown on pale blue underprint. Pagoda at center. Back: Red-brown. *(S/M #H63-5).*	10.00	25.00	100.
S1709G 100 Coppers			
1931. Brown on yellow. Back: Brown. Specimen, perforated.	—	—	300.

1933 Issue

S1709I 20 Coppers	VG	VF	UNC
1933. Black on pink underprint. Tea house behind bridge at center. *Pei P'ing.* Back: Black. Printer: Bepp. *(S/M #H63-9).*	20.00	50.00	150.
S1709J 40 Coppers			
1933. Purple on green underprint. *Pei P'ing.* Back: Purple. Printer: BEPP. *(S/M #H63-10).*	10.00	25.00	100.
S1709K 60 Coppers			
1933. *Pei P'ing.* Printer: BEPP. *(S/M #H63-11).*	20.00	50.00	150.

1934 Issue

S1709M 50 Coppers	VG	VF	UNC
1934. Red on yellow underprint. *Bei Ping.*	10.00	25.00	75.00
S1709N 60 Coppers			
1934. *(S/M #H63-14).*	20.00	50.00	150.

1935 Issue

S1710C 20 Coppers	VG	VF	UNC
1935. Black on pink underprint. *Pei P'ing.* Printer: BEPP. *(S/M #H63-16).*	10.00	25.00	75.00

1936 Issue

S1710D 10 Coppers	VG	VF	UNC
1936. Purple on yellow underprint. Tea house behind bridge at center. *Pei P'ing.* Back: Purple. Printer: BEPP. *(S/M #H63-20).*	7.50	20.00	60.00
S1710E 20 Coppers			
1936. Dark blue on pink underprint. *Pei P'ing.* Back: Black. Printer: BEPP. *(S/M #H63-21).*	7.50	20.00	60.00
S1710F 40 Coppers			
1936. Brown. *Pei P'ing.* Printer: BEPP. *(S/M #H63-22).*	7.50	20.00	60.00

1938 Issue

S1710J 4 Coppers	VG	VF	UNC
1938. Dark green. Tea house behind bridge at center. Vertical format. Printer: PYPO. *(S/M #H63-30).*	7.50	20.00	50.00
S1710K 6 Coppers			
1938. Brown. Tea house behind bridge at center. Vertical format. Printer: PYPO. *(S/M #H63-31).*	20.00	40.00	100.

	VG	VF	UNC
S1710L 8 Coppers			
1938. *(S/M #H63-32).* Reported not confirmed.	—	—	—
S1710M 20 Coppers			
1938. Dark blue on pink underprint. Back: Dark blue. *(S/M #H63-35).*	25.00	50.00	150.
S1710N 40 Coppers			
1938. Brown. *(S/M #H63-36).*	20.00	40.00	100.
S1710O 1 Yüan			
1938. Brown on light green underprint.	10.00	25.00	50.00

Bank of Hopei
Provincial Bank of Hopei

河北銀行
Ho Pei Yin Hang

河北省銀行
Ho Pei Sheng Yin Hang

1929 Issue

	Good	Fine	XF
S1711 10 Cents			
1.6.1929. Brown. Trees, house along shoreline at center. Back: Dark brown. Printer: BEPP. *(S/M #H64-1).*			
a. *Peiping.* With English title under signature. *(S/M #H64-1a).*	15.00	40.00	100.
b. *Peiping.* Without English signature titles. *(S/M #H64-1b).*	15.00	40.00	100.
c. *Tientsin.* With English title under signature. *(S/M #H64-1c).*	15.00	40.00	100.
d. *Tientsin.* Without English signature titles. *(S/M #64-1d).*	15.00	40.00	100.
S1712 20 Cents			
1.6.1929. Blue. Hut at left. Back: Black. Printer: BEPP.			
a. *Peiping. (S/M #H64-2a).*	15.00	40.00	100.
b. *Tientsin. (S/M #H64-2b)*	15.00	40.00	100.
r. Unsigned remainders. *(S/M #H64-2c).*	—	Unc	100.

1930 Issue

	Good	Fine	XF
S1715 1 Yüan			
1.5.1930. Brown. Great Wall at center. *Pei P'ing.* Printer: BEPP. *(S/M #H64-5).*	75.00	225.	450.

	Good	Fine	XF
S1715A 5 Yüan			
5.1.1930. Brown. Building at center. *Peiping.*	150.	400.	750.

1932 Copper Coin Issue

	Good	Fine	XF
S1716 10 Coppers			
1.10.1932. Olive-green. Hillside pagoda at left. *TIENTSIN.* Printer: BEPP. *(S/M #H64-8).*	30.00	100.	300.
S1717 20 Coppers			
1.10.1932. Orange-brown. Hillside pagoda at left. *TIENTSIN.* Printer: BEPP. *(S/M #H64-9).*	30.00	100.	300.
S1718 40 Coppers			
1.10.1932. Black and blue. Hillside pagoda at left. *TIENTSIN.* Back: Black. Printer: BEPP. *(S/M #H64-10).*	50.00	150.	400.
S1719 60 Coppers			
1.10.1932. Blue. Hillside pagoda at left. *TIENTSIN.* Printer: BEPP. *(S/M #H64-11).*	75.00	200.	500.
S1720 100 Coppers			
1.10.1932. Red. Hillside pagoda at left. *TIENTSIN.* Printer: BEPP. *(S/M #H64-12).*	75.00	200.	500.

1933 Issue

	Good	Fine	XF
S1723 1 Yüan			
1.7.1933. Black on multicolor underprint. Pagoda at left. *TIENTSIN.* Back: Green. Printer: W&S. *(S/M #H64-20).*			
a. Issued note.	50.00	150.	400.
b. Issued note with black numerical overprint.	50.00	150.	400.
S1724 5 Yüan			
1.7.1933. Brown on multicolor underprint. Pagoda at left. *TIENTSIN.* Back: Violet. Printer: W&S. *(S/M #H64-21).*			
a. Issued note. *(S/M #H64-21a).*	30.00	75.00	200.
b. With black numerical overprint on both sides. (S/M #H64-21b).	30.00	75.00	200.
c. With black numerical and dark blue letter overprint: *g.* on face. *(S/M #H64-21c).*	30.00	75.00	200.
d. With green numerical overprint: *34. (S/M #H64-21d).*	30.00	75.00	200.
S1725 10 Yüan			
1.7.1933. Rose on multicolor underprint. Pagoda at left. Back: Rose.			
a. Issued note. *(S/M #H64-22a).*	40.00	100.	250.
b. With black numeral overprint on both sides. *(S/M #H64-22b).*	40.00	100.	250.
c. With green numerical overprint on both sides. *(S/M #C64-22c).*	40.00	100.	250.
d. As c. with additional blue overprint letter *g* on face. (S/M #H64-22d).	40.00	100.	250.

1934 Issue

	Good	Fine	XF
S1726 10 Cents			
1934. Blue. *TIENTSIN.* Printer: BEPP. *(S/M #H64-30).*	40.00	100.	250.
S1727 20 Cents			
1934. Brown. *TIENTSIN.* Printer: BEPP. *(S/M #H64-31).*	40.00	100.	250.
S1728 50 Cents			
1934. Green. *TIENTSIN.* Printer: BEPP. *(S/M #H64-32).*	20.00	75.00	150.
S1729 1 Yüan			
1934. Orange and black. Summer palace above shoreline at left. *TIENTSIN.* Back: Orange. Printer: BEPP. *(S/M #H64-40).*	10.00	20.00	75.00

	Good	Fine	XF
S1730 2 Yüan			
1934. Green. Summer palace above shoreline. *TIENTSIN.* Printer: BEPP.			
a. Issued note. *(S/M #H64-41a).*	15.00	50.00	100.
b. With additional numerical overprint 215 seen. *(S/M #H64-41b).*	20.00	75.00	150.
c. With additional Chinese character overprint.	40.00	100.	200.

	Good	Fine	XF
S1731 5 Yüan			
1934. Red. Summer palace above shoreline at left. *TIENTSIN.* Printer: BEPP.			
a. Issued note. *(S/M #H64-42a).*	20.00	75.00	150.
b. Numerical overprint on face only.	20.00	75.00	150.
c. Numerical overprint on face and back.	20.00	75.00	150.
d. HC overprint on face and back.	20.00	75.00	150.
e. Chinese character overprint on face and back.	20.00	75.00	150.
S1732 10 Yüan			
1934. Brown on light blue underprint. Summer palace at center. *TIENSTIN.* Printer: BEPP.			
a. Issued note. *(S/M #H64-43a).*	40.00	125.	225.
b. With additional numerical overprint. *(S/M #H64-43b).*	40.00	125.	225.
c. With additional Chinese character overprint. *(S/M #H64-43c).*	60.00	150.	300.

1940 Issue

	Good	Fine	XF
S1735 50 Cents			
1940. Red. Back: Blue. *(S/M #H64-50).*	25.00	75.00	150.

Khotan District Administration

和闐區行政長印
Ho Tien Ch'ü Hang Cheng Chang Yin

1935-36 Issue

	Good	Fine	XF
S1737 3 Taels			
1935-36. Black text on red underprint. Back: Large red hand stamped seal. *(S/M #H65.5-13).*	15.00	40.00	75.00

Khotan Administration Government Head Public Office

Ho T'ien Hsing Cheng Ch'ang Kung Shu Yin Liu Chao Piao T'ung

1935 Issue

	Good	Fine	XF
S1738 1 Tael			
1934; 1935; 1936. Black text on pink underprint. Violet rectangular hand stamp. Back: Purple. Black text and large red hand stamped seal. *(S/M #H65.7-11)*.	25.00	75.00	150.
S1738A 100 Cash			
1934.	25.00	75.00	150.

Sikang Provincial Bank

行銀省康西

Hsi K'ang Sheng Yin Hang

1939 Issue

	Good	Fine	XF
S1739 1/2 Yüan			
1939. Red on orange and blue underprint. Mountain scene at left. Back: Tibetan headings. Printer: BEPP. *(S/M #H75-1)*.	125.	250.	900.
S1740 1 Yüan			
1939. Green on light green underprint. Mountain fortress at center. Back: Blue on orange underprint. Printer: BEPP. *(S/M #H75-10)*.	150.	450.	1250.
S1741 5 Yüan			
1939. *(S/M #H75-12)*.	400.	900.	1750.

Subtreasury of Sinkiang - Official Note

票官庫藩疆新

Hsin Chiang Fan k'u Kuan P'iao

	Good	Fine	XF
S1742 400 Cash			
1912. Multicolor. 2 dragons. Vertical format. Back: Chinese and Turki text on back. (S/M #-).	—	—	—

Main Official Currency Bureau of Sinkiang

局總錢官疆新

Hsin Chiang Kuan Ch'ien Tsung Chu

1908 Issue

	Good	Fine	XF
S1742A 400 Cash			
CD 1908. Multicolor. Dragons. Vertical format, 130 x 260mm. Back: Chinese and Turki text. *(S/M #-)*.	—	—	—

1909 Issue

	Good	Fine	XF
S1742B 400 Cash			
1909. Multicolor. Dragons. Vertical format, 130 x 260mm. Back: Chinese and Turki text. *(S/M #-)*.	—	—	—

Sinkiang Commercial and Industrial Bank

行銀業商疆新

Hsin Chiang Shang Yeh Yin Hang

1939 Issue

	Good	Fine	XF
S1743 1 Fen			
1939. Olive-green. Back: Green. *(S/M #H123-1)*.	10.00	25.00	75.00
S1744 3 Fen			
1939. Blue. Back: Green. *(S/M #H123-2)*.	10.00	25.00	75.00
S1745 5 Fen			
1939. Red-orange. *(S/M #H123-3)*.			
a. Two black letters before serial #.	10.00	25.00	75.00
b. No letters, but *No.* before serial #.	10.00	25.00	75.00
S1746 1 Chiao			
1939. Green. Rural scene at right. *(S/M #H123-4)*.			
a. Black signature. 2 varieties.	7.50	20.00	50.00
b. Green signature.	7.50	20.00	50.00
S1747 2 Chiao			
1939. Violet. City shops at right. Three signature varieties.			
a. Black signature. 2 varieties. *(S/M #H123-5)*.	7.50	20.00	50.00
b. Purple signature.	10.00	25.00	80.00
S1748 5 Chiao			
1939. Brown. Tower at left. Black signature 3 signature varieties. Back: Red-brown. *(S/M #H123-6)*.			
a. Black signature. 2 varieties.	10.00	25.00	80.00
b. Brown signature.	10.00	25.00	80.00
S1749 1 Yüan			
1939. Red. *(S/M #H123-10)*.	25.00	60.00	150.
S1750 3 Yüan			
1939. Green. Radio transmitting building at center. *(S/M #H123-11)*.	75.00	250.	500.
S1751 5 Yüan			
1939. Orange. Square Chinese signature in red. Back: Orange. *(S/M #H123-12)*.	40.00	125.	250.
S1752 10 Yüan			
1939. *(S/M #H123-13)*. Reported not confirmed.	—	—	—
S1753 50 Yüan			
1939. Brown and green. Men fishing at left, rural shoreline at right. Back: Brown. Shepherd and sheep at center. *(S/M #H123-14)*.	40.00	75.00	225.
S1754 100 Yüan			
1939. Red. Woman weaving at left, men farming at right. Back: Violet. Offshore house at center. *(S/M #H123-15)*.	40.00	75.00	225.

1940 Issue

	Good	Fine	XF
S1758 10 Yüan			
1940. Red. Factory at center. Back: Black signature. *(S/M #H123-20)*.			
a. Short signature on left.	25.00	60.00	200.
b. Larger signature on left.	25.00	60.00	200.
c. As b. but two black letters in front of serial #.	40.00	75.00	225.

1943-45 Issue

	Good	Fine	XF
S1761 1 Yüan			
1943. Red. *(S/M #H123-30)*.	40.00	75.00	225.
S1762 5 Yüan			
1943. Green. Back: Red. *(S/M #H123-31)*.	40.00	100.	250.
S1763 10 Yüan			
1943. Blue. Car and truck in city street at center. Back: Rural house at center. *(S/M #H123-32)*.	40.00	150.	300.

1945 Issue

	Good	Fine	XF
S1765 200 Yüan			
1945. Violet. Portrait SYS at left. 2 signature varieties. Back: Red. Bridge over wooded stream at center. *(S/M #H123-40)*.	15.00	40.00	100.

1946 Issue

	Good	Fine	XF
S1768 100 Yüan			
1946. Red. Weaving at left, farming right. Back violet. *(S/M #H123-50)*.	40.00	100.	250.
S1769 500 Yüan			
1946. Brown. Portrait SYS at left. Back: Green. Bank building at center. *(S/M #H123-51)*.	20.00	40.00	100.

1947 Issue

	Good	Fine	XF
S1771 2000 Yüan			
1947. Red and blue. SYS at left. Back: Red. Harvesting grain with tractor at right. *(S/M #H123-60)*.	20.00	75.00	200.
S1772 5000 Yüan			
1947. Blue on red underprint. SYS at left. Back: Blue. Factories at right. *(S/M #H12361)*.	20.00	75.00	200.

#S1773 and S1774 SYS at upper ctr. Bank bldg. at upper ctr. on back. Vertical format.

	Good	Fine	XF
S1773 10,000 Yüan			
1947. Brown. SYS at upper center. Vertical format. Back: Bank building at upper center. *(S/M #H123-62)*.	50.00	125.	300.
S1774 20,000 Yüan			
1947. Blue-green and yellow. SYS at upper center. Vertical format. Back: Blue. Bank building at upper center. *(S/M #H123-63)*.	20.00	75.00	200.

1948 Issue

	Good	Fine	XF
S1776 100,000 Yüan			
1948. Red and yellow. SYS at left. Back: Red. Airplane above steam train passing through hills at right. *(S/M #H123-70)*.	50.00	125.	300.
S1777 200,000 Yüan			
1948. Violet and red. Harvesting grain with tractor at right. SYS at left. Back: Violet. *(S/M #H123-71)*.	20.00	75.00	200.
S1778 500,000 Yüan			
1948. Green. SYS at left. Similar to #S1774. *(S/M #H123-72)*.	20.00	75.00	200.

Industrial and Commercial Bank of Sinkiang, Ili Branch

票財行分梨伊行銀業商疆新

Hsin Chiang Shang Yeh Yin Hang I Li Fen Hang Ts'ai P'iao

1947 Issue

	VG	VF	UNC
S1778A 2000 Dollars			
1947. Purple. Grain mill and electric power station of Ining. Chinese bank name. Back: Blue.	500.	1000.	2500.
S1778B 2500 Dollars			
1947. Red. Emin Pagoda of Turpan, farmer with grapes. Chinese bank name. Back: Black.			
a. Without AH date.	400.	750.	2000.
b. AH1366.	400.	750.	2000.
S1778C 3000 Dollars			
1947. Dark brown. Ili Branch of the Commercial and Industrial Bank at center. Chinese bank name. Back: Black.	400.	800.	2000.

1948 Issues

	VG	VF	UNC
S1778D 100 Dollars 1948. Violet. Turkish text: *yüz = 100* at center. Back: Black.	250.	500.	1000.
S1778E 300 Dollars 1948. Purple. Turkish value: *300* at center. Back: Red.	500.	1000.	2500.
S1778F 300 Dollars 1948. Deep violet. Turkish value *300* at center. Back: Black.	500.	1000.	2500.
S1778G 500 Dollars 1948. Purple. Turkish. Vertical format. Back: Green.	550.	1100.	2750.
S1778H 1000 Dollars 1948. Red. Turkish building at center. Back: Black.	550.	1100.	2750.

Sinkiang Sub-Prefecture Administration Finance Department Treasury - Official Note

票官庫廳政財府政省疆新

Hsin Chiang Sheng Cheng Fu Ts'ai Cheng Ting K'u Kuan Piao

1932 Issue

	Good	Fine	XF
S1779 3 Taels 1932. Burgundy. Back: Blue- green. Buildings at center. *Kashgar* and *Khotan*. (S/M #H123.5-9).	50.00	150.	500.

	Good	Fine	XF
S1780 5 Taels 1932. Blue on yellow underprint. Red text. 177 x 103mm. Back: Back brown and dark blue on light gren underprint. Snow capped mountains at center. *Kashgar* and *Khotan*. *(S/M #H123.5-10).*	25.00	50.00	100.
S1780A 50 Taels 1932. Red. *(S/M #H123.5-18).*	50.00	150.	300.

#S1780B *Deleted.* See #S1780F.

1934; 1935 Issues

	Good	Fine	XF
S1780C 3 Taels 1934. *Kashgar* and *Khotan. (S/M #H123.5-22).*	50.00	150.	300.
S1780D 5 Taels 1934; 1936. Floral branches in borders. *Kashgar* and *Khotan. (S/M #H123.5-23).*	100.	250.	600.
S1780F 50 Taels 1934-36. Pale olive-green with black text. Back: Blue-gray. *Kashgar* and *Khotan. (S/M #H123.5-25).*	100.	250.	600.

Sinkiang Province

券庫金省疆新

Hsin Chiang Sheng Chin K'u Ch'üan

1931 Treasury Note Issue

	Good	Fine	XF
S1781 2 Ch'ien 1931. Brown and green. Back: Green. Printer: BEPP. *(S/M #H124-1).*	150.	450.	1000.
S1782 5 Ch'ien 1931. Orange and green. Back: Blue. Printer: BEPP. *(S/M #H124-2).*	150.	450.	1000.
S1783 1 Tael 1931. Orange and green. Back: Green. Printer: BEPP. *(S/M #H124-3).*	200.	600.	1250.

Sinkiang Provincial Bank

行銀省疆新

Hsin Chiang Sheng Yin Hang

1948 Yüan Issue

	Good	Fine	XF
S1786 1,000,000 Yüan 1948. Red. Portrait SYS at upper center. Vertical format. Back: Violet. Bank building at upper center. *(S/M #H125-1).*	25.00	75.00	150.
S1787 3,000,000 Yüan 1948. Blue. Back: Violet. *(S/M #H125-2).*	25.00	75.00	150.
S1788 6,000,000 Yüan 1948. Dark blue, yellow and red. SYS at left. Back: Olive. Bank building at center. *(S/M #H125-3).*	25.00	75.00	150.
S1789 10,000,000 Yüan 1948. Reported not confirmed.	—	—	—

1949 Gold Yüan Issue

1 Gold Yüan = 600,000 *Fa Pi* Yüan

	Good	Fine	XF
S1790 30,000,000 Yüan = 50 Gold Yüan 1949. Brown and red. Portrait SYS at center right. Back: Brown. Bank building at center. *(S/M #H125-10).*	50.00	150.	300.
S1791 60,000,000 Yüan = 10 Gold Yüan 1949. Violet and red. Portrait SYS at right. Back: Red. Bank building at left. *(S/M #H125-11).*	25.00	100.	250.
S1793 300,000,000 Yüan = 500 Gold Yüan 1949. *(S/M #H125-12).* Reported not confirmed.	—	—	—
S1794 600,000,000 Yüan = 1,000 Gold Yüan 1949. Red and blue. SYS at left. Back: Blue. *(S/M #H125-13).*	40.00	125.	275.
S1796 3,000,000,000 Yüan = 5,000 Gold Yüan 1949. Dark brown and red. Portrait SYS at lower center. Back: Bank building at right. *(S/M #H125-14).*	125.	250.	550.
S1797 6,000,000,000 Yüan = 10,000 Gold Yüan 1949. Purple and green. Portrait SYS at lower left. Back: Violet. Bank building at right. *(S/M #H125-15).*	150.	300.	700.

1949; 1950 Silver Yüan Issue

	Good	Fine	XF
S1798 1 Fen 1949. Blue. Trees, hills at center center. (S/M #H125-19).	25.00	75.00	200.
S1799 5 Fen 1949. Violet. *(S/M #H125-20).*	40.00	100.	225.
S1800 1 Chiao = 10 Cents 1949. Red. Landscape, mountain at center. *(S/M #H125-21).*	40.00	100.	225.
S1801 2 Chiao = 20 Cents 1949. Violet. Landscape, mountains. *(S/M #H125-22).*	40.00	100.	225.

	Good	Fine	XF
S1802 5 Chiao = 50 Cents 1949.	75.00	150.	350.
S1803 1 Silver Yüan 1949. Blue. Farming with horses at left and right. Back: Pine trees, mountains at lower left center. *(S/M #H125-30).*	40.00	100.	225.
S1806 10 Silver Yüan 1950. Farming at left and right. *(S/M #H125-35).*	50.00	125.	275.
S1807 10 Silver Yüan 1950. Steam passenger train at left, ship at right. *(S/M #H125-36).*	75.00	150.	350.

Treasury Dept. of Sinkiang - Official Note

票官庫司疆新

Hsin Chiang Szu K'u Kuan P'iao

1913 Issue

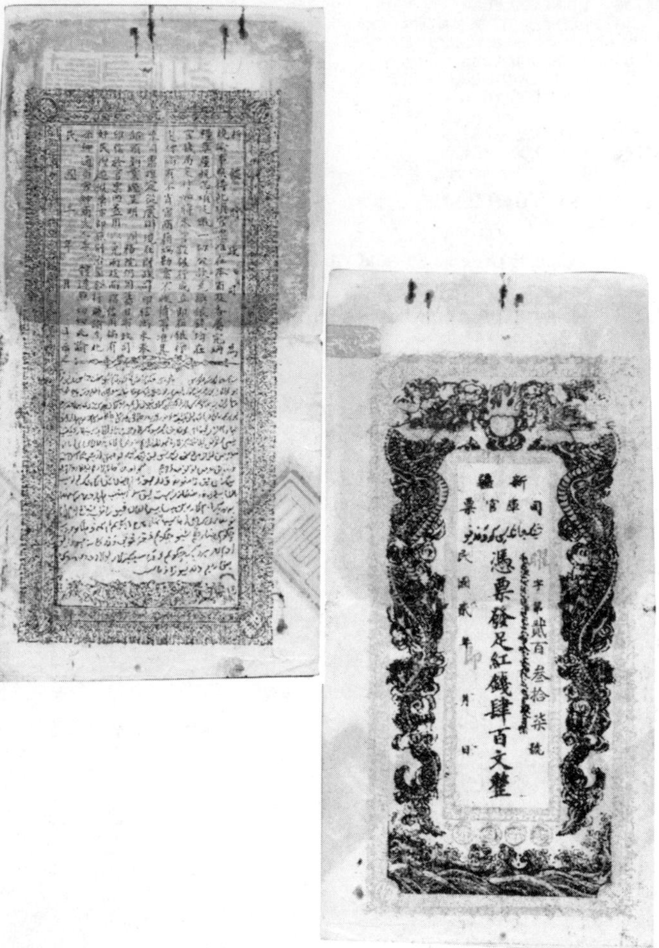

		Good	Fine	XF
S1808	**400 Cash** 1913. Multicolor. Two dragons. Vertical format. Back: Chinese and Turki text. *(S/M #-).*	200.	600.	1250.

Provincial Treasury of Sinkiang - Official Note

票官庫廳疆新

Hsin Chiang T'ing K'u Kuan P'iao

1914; 1915 Issue

		Good	Fine	XF
S1809	**100 Cash** Yr. 3 (1914). Red and black. Chinze at left and right holding two crossed striped flags. Back: Chinese and Turki text. Printed in Tihua. *(S/M #-).*	225.	650.	1400.
S1809A	**100 Cash** Yr. 4 (1915). Red and black. Chinze at left and right holding two crossed striped flags. Back: Chinese and Turki text. *(S/M #-).*	225.	650.	1400.
S1810	**400 Cash** Yr. 4 (1915). Blue, black and yellow. Two dragons. Vertical format. Back: Chinese and Turki text. *(S/M #-).*	225.	650.	1400.

Sinkiang Provincial Government Finance Department Treasury

票官庫廳政財府政省疆新

Hsin Chiang/Ts'ai Cheng T'ing K'u Kuan P'iao

1917 Issue

		Good	Fine	XF
S1811	**400 Cash** Yr. 6 (1917). Blue and yellow. Back: Green and orange. Printer: BEPP. *(S/M #H126-1).*	25.00	75.00	175.

1919 Issue

		Good	Fine	XF
S1815	**100 Cash** Yr. 8 (1919). Yellow. Back: Black. Printer: BEPP. *(S/M #H126-10).*	20.00	50.00	100.
S1817	**400 Cash** Yr. 8 (1919). Blue. Back: Black. Printer: BEPP. *(S/M #H126-11).*	40.00	100.	225.

1920 Issue

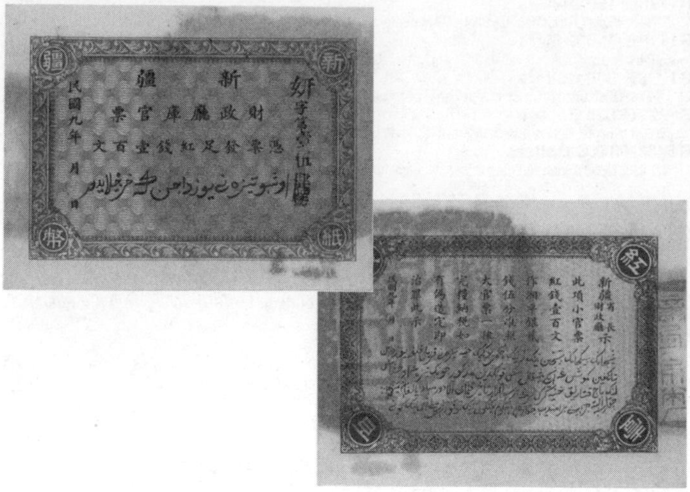

		Good	Fine	XF
S1820	**100 Cash** Yr. 9 (1920). Green and black on red underprint. Back: Black and blue on yellow underprint. *(S/M #H126-20).*	25.00	75.00	175.
S1822	**400 Cash** Yr. 9 (1920). Green on pink underprint with black text. Vertical format. Back: Blue on deep yellow underprint. Printer: BEPP. *(S/M #H126-22).*			
	a. Olive-green. Frame of good print quality.	20.00	50.00	125.
	b. Bright green. Frame of poor print quality.	20.00	50.00	125.

1921 Issue

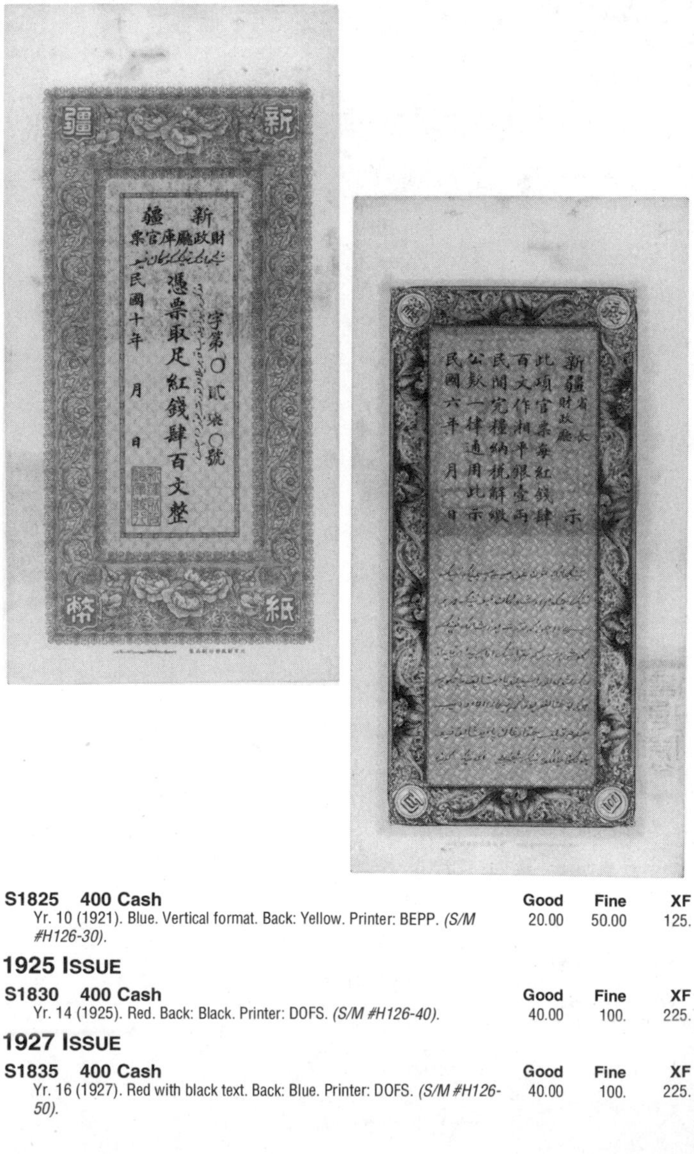

		Good	Fine	XF
S1825	**400 Cash** Yr. 10 (1921). Blue. Vertical format. Back: Yellow. Printer: BEPP. *(S/M #H126-30).*	20.00	50.00	125.

1925 Issue

		Good	Fine	XF
S1830	**400 Cash** Yr. 14 (1925). Red. Back: Black. Printer: DOFS. *(S/M #H126-40).*	40.00	100.	225.

1927 Issue

		Good	Fine	XF
S1835	**400 Cash** Yr. 16 (1927). Red with black text. Back: Blue. Printer: DOFS. *(S/M #H126-50).*	40.00	100.	225.

1928 Issue

		Good	Fine	XF
S1840	**400 Cash** Yr. 17 (1928). Red with black text. Back: Blue. Black text. Printer: DOFS. *(S/M #H126-60).*	20.00	50.00	125.

1930 Issue

		Good	Fine	XF
S1844	**400 Cash** Yr. 19 (1930). Red floral border with black text. Back: Blue. Cockerals in border with black text. *(S/M #H126-62).*	40.00	100.	225.
S1845	**400 Cash** Yr. 19 (1930). Deep blue-green on pink underprint with black text. Vertical format. *(S/M #H126-65).*	20.00	50.00	125.

1931 Issue

		Good	Fine	XF
S1850	**400 Cash** Yr. 20 (1931). Red with black text. Vertical format. Back: Blue with black text. Cockerals in border with black text. Printer: DOFS. *(S/M #H126-70).*	20.00	50.00	125.

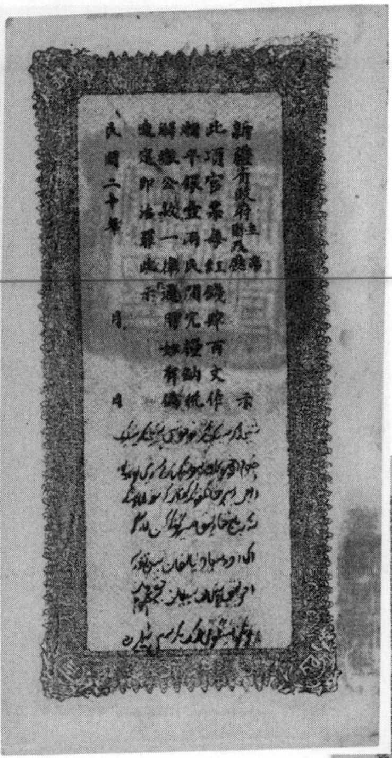

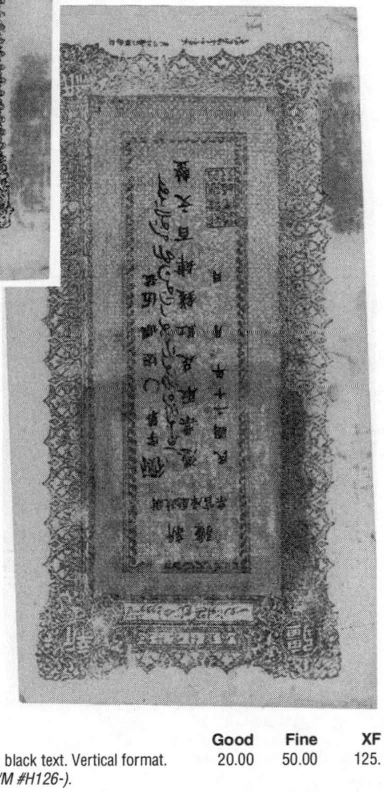

		Good	Fine	XF
S1851	**400 Cash** Yr. 20 (1931). Green on red underprint with black text. Vertical format. Back: Blue on yellow-orange underprint. *(S/M #H126-).*	20.00	50.00	125.

1932 Issue

		Good	Fine	XF
S1856	**100 Cash** Yr. 21 (1932). Blue. Vertical format. Back: Violet. Printer: DOFS. *(S/M #H126-80).*	40.00	100.	225.
S1857	**100 Cash** Yr. 21 (1932). Brown. Back: Green. *(S/M #H126-80.5).*	10.00	30.00	75.00
S1858	**400 Cash** Yr. 21 (1932). Red. Back: Black. Printer: DOFS. *(S/M #H126-81).*	40.00	100.	225.
S1859	**400 Cash** Yr. 21 (1932). Gray and yellow. Back: Violet and green. Printer: BEPP. *(S/M #H126-82).*	40.00	100.	225.
S1863	**2000 Cash** Yr. 21 (1932). Violet and green. Back: Violet and green. Printer: BEPP. *(S/M #H126-83).*	50.00	125.	275.
S1864	**4000 Cash** Yr. 21 (1932). Violet and blue. Back: Brown and yellow. Printer: BEPP. *(S/M #H126-84).*	50.00	125.	275.

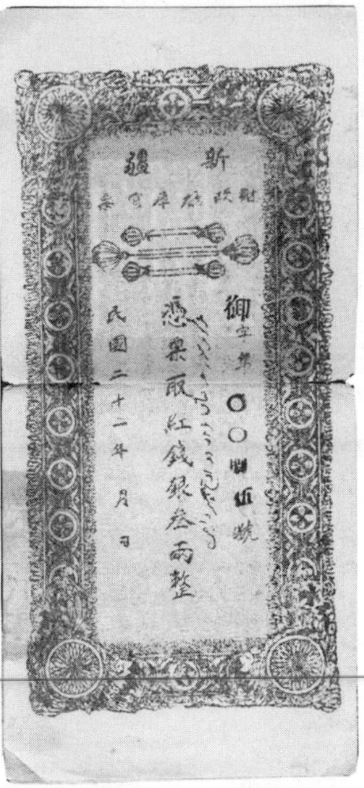

		Good	Fine	XF
S1868	**3 Taels** Yr. 21 (1932). Reddish brown on green underprint. Circles in border. Back: Deep blue with black text. Printer: BEPP. *(S/M #H126-90).*	40.00	100.	225.
S1869	**5 Taels** Yr. 21 (1932). Blue. Vertical format. Back: Black. Printer: BEPP. *(S/M #H126-91).*	20.00	50.00	125.
S1870	**10 Taels** Yr. 21 (1932). Dark blue and green. Back: Light green. Printer: BEPP. *(S/M #H126-92).*	50.00	125.	275.

1933 Issue

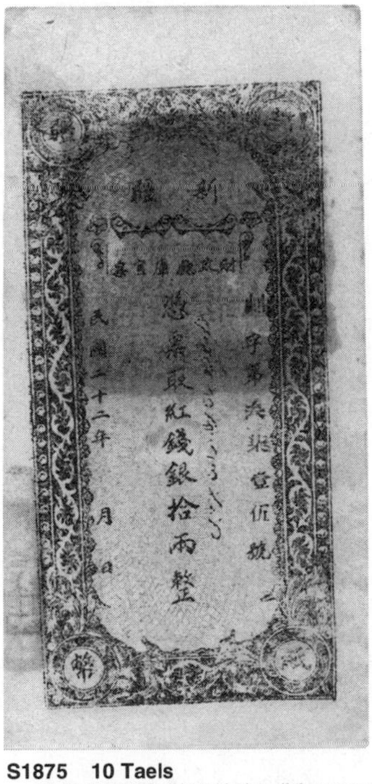

		Good	Fine	XF
S1875	**10 Taels** Yr. 22 (1933). Dark blue-black on light green underprint. Vertical format. Back: Green on yellow-orange underprint. *(S/M #H126-95).*	20.00	50.00	125.
S1876	**50 Taels** Yr. 22 (1933). *(S/M #H126-99).*	75.00	150.	350.

#S1879 *Deleted.* See #S1779.

1934 Issue

		Good	Fine	XF
S1880	**5 Taels** Yr. 23 (1934). *(S/M #H126.5-12).*	75.00	150.	350.
S1881	**10 Taels** Yr. 23 (1934). Red with black text. Vertical format. Back: Blue-gray. *(S/M #H126.5-13).*	100.	225.	500.
S1882	**50 Taels** Yr. 23 (1934). *(S/M #H126.5-15).*	125.	300.	750.

#S1886 *Deleted.* See #S1780B.

Sunning Railway Co., Ltd.

Hsin Ning T'ien Lu Kung Szu

#S1888-S1890 *Deleted.* (Local issue).

Monetary Bureau of Government Suchow

局錢官市平州徐

Hsü Chou P'ing Shih Kuan Ch'ien Chü

1933 Issue

	Good	Fine	XF
S1891A 10 Cents			
1933. Red. Building with pagoda in background at top center. Back: Green. Overprint: Various numerical and Chinese character. Printer: TTBC. *(S/M #H155-1).*			
a. Issued note.	25.00	50.00	125.
b. With additional control overprint: *32; 60; Ho; Su.*	40.00	100.	225.

	Good	Fine	XF
S1891B 20 Cents			
1933. Blue. Building with pagoda in background at top center. Back: Brown. Overprint: Various numerical and Chinese character. Printer: TTBC. *(S/M #H155-2).*			
a. Issued note.	40.00	100.	225.
b. With additional control overprint: *25; 46; 61.*	40.00	100.	225.
S1891C 50 Cents			
1933. Brown. Building with pagoda in background at top center. Back: Violet. Overprint: Various numerical and Chinese character. Printer: TTBC. *(S/M #H155-3).*	50.00	125.	275.

NOTE: For #S1891A-S1891C with solid bar overprint see #S1191-S1193.

Hulunpeierh Official Currency Bureau

局錢商官爾貝倫呼

Hu Lun Pei Erh Kuan Shang Ch'ien Chü

1918 Issue

	Good	Fine	XF
S1892A 5 Chiao			
1918. Green. *Heilungkiang.* Back: Orange. Printer: MLTA. *(S/M #H157-1).*	50.00	125.	275.
S1892B 1 Yüan			
1918. Violet and yellow. *Heilungkiang.* Back: Brown. Printer: MLTA. *(S/M #H157-10).*	75.00	150.	350.
S1892C 3 Yüan			
1918. Green and yellow. *Heilungkiang.* Back: Brown. Printer: MLTA. *(S/M #H157-11).*	100.	225.	500.
S1892D 5 Yüan			
1918. Blue and green. *Heilungkiang.* Printer: MLCA. *(S/M #H157-12).*	100.	225.	500.
S1892E 10 Yüan			
1918. Orange and red. *Heilungkiang.* Back: Orange. Printer: MLCA. *(S/M #H157-13).*	125.	275.	600.
S1892F 25 Yüan			
1918. Blue and yellow. *Heilungkiang.* Back: Violet and green. Printer: MLCA. *(S/M #H157-14).*	150.	350.	750.

1919 Issue

	Good	Fine	XF
S1892G 5 Chiao			
1919. Black and orange. *Heilungkiang.* Printer: MLCA. *(S/M #H157-20).*	40.00	100.	225.
S1892H 1 Yüan			
1919. Brown on yellow-green underprint. *Heilungkiang.* Bridge over river at center. Back: Brown. Printer: MLCA. *(S/M #H157-30).*	50.00	125.	250.
S1892I 3 Yüan			
1919. Black and yellow. *Heilungkiang.* Printer: MLCA. *(S/M #H157-31).*			
a. Red serial #.	125.	275.	625.
b. Black serial #.	125.	275.	625.
S1892J 5 Yüan			
July 1919. Dark blue on light blue underprint. *Heilungkiang.* Hillside pagoda at center. Back: Dark blue on light olive-green underprint. Printer: MLCA. *(S/M #H157-32).*	50.00	125.	275.
S1892K 10 Yüan			
1919. Orange. *Heilungkiang.* Back: Orange and green. Printer: MLCA. *(S/M #H157-33).*	75.00	175.	350.
S1892L 25 Yüan			
1919. Blue and red. *Heilungkiang.* Back: Violet and blue. Shrines at center. Printer: MLCA. *(S/M #H157-34).*	125.	275.	625.
S1892M 100 Yüan			
1919. Olive-gray on orange underprint. *Heilungkiang.* Back: Red on light green underprint. Printer: MLCA. *(S/M #H157-35).*	250.	550.	1250.

Official Mint Hunan
Hunan Government Bank

局錢官南湖

Hu Nan Kuan Ch'ien Chü

1903 Issue

	Good	Fine	XF
S1893 1 Ch'uan			
Yr. 29 (1903). Brown and green. *(S/M #H161-0.1).*	125.	275.	625.

1904 Issue

	Good	Fine	XF
S1895 1 Ch'uan			
CD 1904. Purple and yellow. Without rectangular frames. Facing dragons at upper left and right, waves at bottom. *(S/M #H61-0.2).*	175.	400.	900.
S1896 1 Ch'uan			
CD 1904. Brown and blue. With rectangular frames. Japanese imprint. Facing dragons at upper left and right, waves at bottom. *(S/M #H161-0.3).*	150.	350.	800.

	Good	Fine	XF
S1898 1 Dollar			
Yr. 30 (1904). Blue and red. Facing dragons at upper left and right, waves at bottom. *(S/M #H161-0.4).*	450.	1000.	2250.
S1899 1 Dollar			
Yr. 30 (1904). Blue and green. Facing dragons at upper left and right, waves at bottom. *(S/M #H161-0.5).*	150.	350.	800.
S1903 100 Dollars			
Yr. 30 (1904). Facing dragons at upper left and right, waves at bottom. *(S/M #H161-1).* Reported not confirmed.	—	—	—
S1904 1 Tael			
Yr. 30 (1904). Black and green. Facing dragons at upper left and right, waves at bottom. *(S/M #H161-4).*	100.	225.	500.

1906 Issue

	Good	Fine	XF
S1907 100 Coppers			
Yr. 32 (1906). Brown and green. Facing dragons at upper left and right, waves at bottom. *(S/M #H161-6).*	150.	350.	750.
S1910 1 Ch'uan			
Yr. 32 (1906). Brown and black. Facing dragons at upper left and right, waves at bottom. Back: Orange. *(S/M #H161-10).*	200.	450.	1000.
S1913 1 Tael			
CD 1906. Facing dragons at upper left and right, waves at bottom. Vertical format. *(S/M #H161-20).*	100.	225.	500.
S1914 5 Taels			
Yr. 32 (1906). Blue and black. Facing dragons at upper left and right, waves at bottom. Printer: PYOP.			
a. Issued note. *(S/M #H161-22).*	50.00	125.	275.
x. *TEALS* error. *(S/M #H161-21).*	75.00	175.	350.

1908 Issue

	Good	Fine	XF
S1917 50 Coppers			
Yr. 34 (1908). Printer: CMPA. *(S/M #H161-39).*	100.	225.	500.
S1918 100 Coppers			
Yr. 34 (1908). Blue and gray on yellow underprint. Facing dragons at upper left and right, house at left, road to factory at right.			
a. Issued note.	125.	250.	550.
r. Remainder with perforation and hand stamped cancellation. *(S/M #H161-40).*	—	Unc	250.
S1919 500 Coppers			
Yr. 34 (1908). Printer: CMPA. *(S/M #H161-).*	125.	250.	550.

Cat. #	Denomination / Description	Good	Fine	XF
S1920	**1000 Coppers** Yr. 34 (1908). Printer: CMPA. *(S/M #H161-)*.	150.	300.	600.
S1923	**1 Dollar** Yr. 34 (1908). Blue. Back: Orange. *(S/M #H161-50)*.	50.00	150.	350.
S1926	**1 Tael** Yr. 34 (1908). Black and blue. Dragons facing at top over house at left, road to factory at right. Back: Brown and red. Printer: CMPA. *(S/M #H161-60)*.	75.00	175.	375.

Many quality Uncirculated and XF counterfeits exist in the trade.

Cat. #	Denomination / Description	Good	Fine	XF
S1927	**5 Taels** Yr. 34 (1908). Violet and yellow. Dragons facing at top over house at left, road to factory at right. Back: Blue and red. Printer: CMPA. *(S/M #H161-61)*.	250.	600.	1250.

1909 Issue

Cat. #	Denomination / Description	Good	Fine	XF
S1929	**1 Tael** 1909. *(S/M #H161-70)*. Reported not confirmed.	—	—	—
S1930	**5 Taels** 1909. *(S/M #H161-71)*. Reported not confirmed.	—	—	—

Hunan Provincial Treasury

湖南省財政廳

Hu Nan Sheng Ts'ai Cheng T'ing

1920 Issues

Cat. #	Denomination / Description	Good	Fine	XF
S1936	**1 Dollar** 1920. Brown. Bearer bond type. Back: Brown and red. Printer: HODP. *(S/M #H163-1)*.	100.	225.	500.
S1937	**1 Dollar** 1920. Blue and green. Bearer bond type. Back: Green and red. Printer: HODP. *(S/M #H163-2)*.	100.	225.	500.
S1938	**5 Dollars** 1920. Brown. Bearer bond type. Back: Orange and red. Printer: HODP. *(S/M #H163-3)*.	100.	225.	500.
S1939	**5 Dollars** 1920. Brown and green. Bearer bond type. Back: Blue and red. Printer: HODP. *(S/M #H163-4)*.	100.	225.	500.
S1940	**10 Dollars** 1920. Green. Bearer bond type. Back: Brown and red. Printer: HODP. *(S/M #H163-5)*.	100.	225.	500.

1926 Issue

Cat. #	Denomination / Description	Good	Fine	XF
S1943	**1 Dollar** 1926. *(S/M #H163-10)*. Reported not confirmed.	—	—	—

1936 Issue

Cat. #	Denomination / Description	Good	Fine	XF
S1948	**10 Silver Yüan** 1936. *(S/M #H163-)*. Reported not confirmed.	—	—	—

Hunan Provincial Bank
Provincial Bank of Hunan

湖南省銀行

Hu Nan Sheng Yin Hang

ND Provisional Issue

#S1951-S1953 overprint on Changsha Bank.

Cat. #	Denomination / Description	Good	Fine	XF
S1951	**1 Yüan** ND (- old date 1.1.1928). Overprint: On #S858. *(S/M #H164-1)*.			
	a. With Chinese 5 character overprint and Chinese signature.	40.00	100.	225.
	b. With Chinese 13 character overprint and English signature.	75.00	150.	350.
S1952	**5 Yüan** ND (- old date 1.1.1928). Overprint: On #S859. *(S/M #H164-2)*.			
	a. Chinese signature.	150.	300.	650.
	b. With 13 character overprint and English signature and additional Chinese character control overprint.	150.	300.	650.
S1953	**10 Yüan** ND (-old date 1.1.1928). Chinese signature. Overprint: On #S860. *(S/M #H164-3)*.	125.	250.	550.

1930 Issue

Cat. #	Denomination / Description	Good	Fine	XF
S1956	**10 Cents** 1930. Green. Building at center. *(S/M #H164-6)*.	75.00	150.	350.
S1957	**20 Cents** 1930. Purple. Bank building at upper center. Vertical format. Back: Gazebo at upper center. *(S/M #H164-7)*.	75.00	150.	350.
S1958	**50 Cents** 1930. Red. Bank building at center. *(S/M #H164-8)*.	100.	225.	500.

1932 Issue

Cat. #	Denomination / Description	Good	Fine	XF
S1960	**200 Cash** 1932. Green. Back: Red and blue. Printer: TTBC. *(S/M #H164-10)*.	100.	225.	500.

1935 Issue

Cat. #	Denomination / Description	Good	Fine	XF
S1965	**200 Cash** 1935. Green. Printer: TTGL. *(S/M #H164-15)*.	100.	225.	500.
S1970	**50 Cents** 1935. Green and yellow. Back: Orange. Printer: CPOF. *(S/M #H164-20)*.	75.00	150.	350.

1936 Issue

Cat. #	Denomination / Description	Good	Fine	XF
S1975	**200 Cash** Green. Building at center. Back: Multicolor. *(S/M #H164-29)*.	40.00	100.	225.
S1976	**300 Cash** 1936. Dark brown. Building with tower at upper center. Vertical format. Back: Red. *(S/M #H164-30)*.	50.00	125.	275.
S1978	**1000 Cash** 1936. Red on pink underprint. Palace at upper center. *(S/M #H164-32)*.	40.00	100.	225.
S1980	**10 Cents** 1936. Green. *(S/M #H164-35)*.	50.00	125.	275.
S1981	**20 Cents** 1936. Green. Bank building at upper center. Vertical format. Back: Gazebo at upper center. *(S/M #H164-36)*.	75.00	150.	350.
S1982	**50 Cents** 1936. Purple. Building at left. Back: Orange. *(S/M #H164-37)*.	40.00	100.	225.

1937 Issue

		VG	VF	UNC
S1984	**5 Cents** 1937. Violet. Building at left. Back: Orange. Printer: CMPA. *(S/M #H164-40)*.	10.00	25.00	75.00

1938 Issue

		VG	VF	UNC
S1987	**2 Cents** 1938. Orange. Rural house at center. Back: Dark green. Printer: CMPA. *(S/M #H164-50)*.	10.00	25.00	75.00
S1988	**3 Cents** 1938. Red. Back: Blue. Printer: CMPA. *(S/M #H164-51)*.	10.00	25.00	75.00
S1989	**10 Cents** 1938. Blue. Shelter at lower right. Back: Orange and brown. Printer: CMPA. *(S/M #H164-52)*.	5.00	15.00	45.00
S1990	**20 Cents** 1938. Green. Back: Brown. Printer: CMPA. *(S/M #H164-53)*.	20.00	40.00	100.
S1991	**50 Cents** 1938. Brown. Railway girder bridge at center. Back: Green and blue. Printer: CMPA. *(S/M #H164-54)*.	20.00	50.00	125.

1940 Issue

		VG	VF	UNC
S1992	**10 Cents** 1940. Blue. Pavilion at left. Back: Brown and blue. Printer: CMPA. *(S/M #H164 60)*.	10.00	25.00	50.00
S1993	**20 Cents** 1940. Violet. Palace garden at left. Back: Green and multicolor. Printer: CMPA. *(S/M #H164-61)*.	7.50	15.00	45.00

		VG	VF	UNC
S1994	**50 Cents** 1940. Red. Fortress gate at left. Back: Orange, dark olive-green and dark blue. Printer: CMPA. *(S/M #H164-62)*.			
	a. Issued note.	20.00	50.00	125.
	s1. Specimen. Red Chinese character overprint on back. Without serial # or signature seals.		—	300.
	s2. Specimen. dark blue Chinese character overprint on face. With serial #.		—	300.

1949 Issue

		VG	VF	UNC
S1994C	**10 Cents** 1949. Gray. SYS at left. Back: Brown. Printer: CHB. *(S/M #H164-68)*.	15.00	45.00	100.
S1994D	**20 Cents** 1949. Building at left. *(S/M #H164-69)*.	25.00	75.00	150.
S1995	**50 Cents** 1949. Red-violet. SYS at center. Printer: CHB. *(S/M #H164-70)*.	15.00	45.00	100.

Hunan Industrial Bank

湖南實業銀行

Hu Nan Shih Yeh Yin Hang

1912 Tael Issue

Cat. #	Denomination / Description	Good	Fine	XF
S1996	**1 Tael** 1912. Green and orange. Back: Black. Printer: CNPC. *(S/M #H165-1)*.	300.	750.	—
S1997	**5 Taels** 1912. Modern office building at left, rural view with mountains at right. Printer: CNPC. *(S/M #H165-2)*.	300.	750.	—

1912 Copper Coin Issue

Cat. #	Denomination / Description	Good	Fine	XF
S1998	**100 Coppers** 1912. Blue. Back: Green. *(S/M #H165-)*.	100.	250.	—

1912 Yüan Issue

Cat. #	Denomination / Description	Good	Fine	XF
S1998E	**1 Yüan** 1912. *(S/M #H165-)*.	100.	250.	—

1913 Issue

	Good	Fine	XF
S1999 20 Coppers 1913. Brown and yellow. Back: Olive. Sailing ship at center. *(S/M #H165-10).*	100.	250.	—
S2000 30 Coppers 1913. Green and yellow. *HUNAN. (S/M #H165-).*	100.	250.	—
S2002 100 Coppers 1913. Blue on light green underprint. Back: Blue-green.	125.	250.	—

1916 Copper Coin Issues

	Good	Fine	XF
S2005 100 Coppers 1916. Black and orange. Bearded man at left, pagoda at right. Back: Orange. Cattle at center. *Changsha. (S/M #H165-20).*	75.00	225.	—
S2006 100 Coppers 1916. Blue and green. Bearded man at left, pagoda at right. Back: Orange. Cattle at center. *(S/M #H165-21).*	125.	250.	—

1916 Yüan Issue

	Good	Fine	XF
S2008 1 Dollar 1916. Green. Back: Brown. *Changsha. (S/M #H165-30).*	100.	225.	—

1917 Copper Coin Issue

	Good	Fine	XF
S2011 200 Coppers 1917. Countryside at left, house at right. Back: House by shoreline at center. *(S/M #H165-).*	150.	350.	—

Hunan Treasury

湖南定期有利金庫証券
Hu Nan Ting Ch'i Yu Li Chin K'u Cheng Chüan

1920 Interest-Bearing Term Certificates Issues

	VG	VF	UNC
S2016 1 Yüan 15.2.1920. Blue and green. Back: Green and red. Printer: HODP. *(S/M #H166-1).*	50.00	100.	250.
S2017 1 Yüan 1920. Brown. Back: Brown and red. Printer: HODP. *(S/M #H166-2).*	75.00	150.	300.

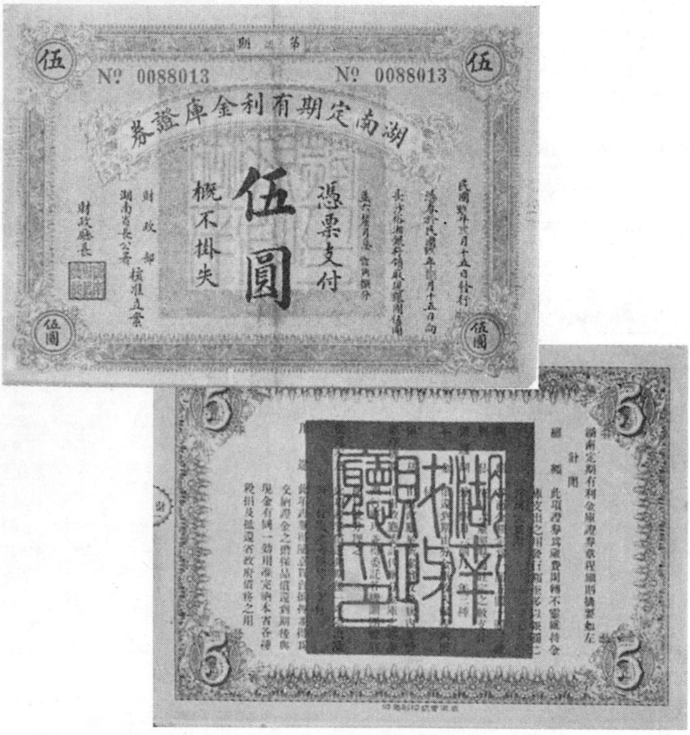

	VG	VF	UNC
S2018 5 Yüan 15.2.1920. Brown and green. Back: Blue and red. Printer: HODP. *(S/M #H166-3).*	75.00	150.	300.
S2019 5 Yüan 1920. Violet and yellow. Back: Orange and red. Printer: HODP. *(S/M #H166-4).*	100.	200.	400.
S2020 10 Yüan 1920. Green. Back: Brown and red. Printer: HODP. *(S/M #H166-5).*	200.	400.	800.

Hunan Bank
Hunan Provincial Bank

湖南銀行
Hu Nan Yin Hang

1912 Copper Coin Issue

	Good	Fine	XF
S2022 20 Coppers Jan. 1912. *(S/M #H167-0.7).*	40.00	100.	225.
S2022A 30 Coppers 1912. Violet on ochre underprint. Back: Blue. *(S/M #H167-0.8).*	75.00	150.	300.

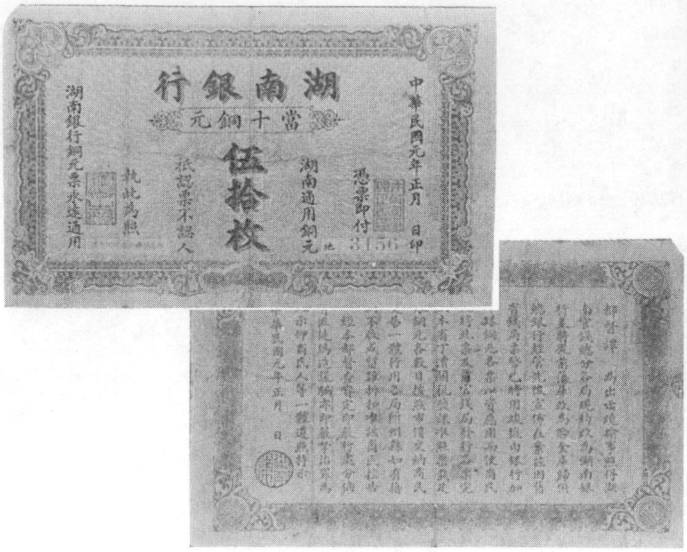

	Good	Fine	XF
S2023 50 Coppers Jan. 1912. Green and yellow. Back: Violet. Printer: SHBC. *(S/M #H167-1).*	50.00	125.	250.

	Good	Fine	XF
S2027 100 Coppers 1.1.1912. Green, black and brown. Facing peacocks at upper left and right. Back: Gray-green. *(S/M #H167-2).*	25.00	60.00	100.

1912 Yüan Issue

	Good	Fine	XF
S2029 1 Yüan 1912. Brown and multicolor. Back: Brown. *(S/M #H167-10).*	25.00	60.00	100.
S2030 5 Yüan 1912. Brown and multicolor. Back: Brown. *(S/M #H167-11).*	75.00	150.	325.
S2031 10 Yüan 1912. Brown and multicolor. Back: Brown. *(S/M #H167-12).*	75.00	150.	325.

1912 Tael Issue

	Good	Fine	XF
S2032 1 Tael 1.1.1912. Violet, black and brown. Facing peacocks at upper left and upper right. Back: Violet. *(S/M #H167-20).*	25.00	50.00	125.

	Good	Fine	XF
S2033 5 Taels 1.1.1912 Violet and black. Facing peacocks at upper left and right. Back: Violet. *(S/M #H167-21).*	75.00	150.	325.
S2034 10 Taels 1.1.1912. Violet and black. Facing peacocks at upper left and right. Back: Violet. *(S/M #H167-22).*	150.	300.	600.

1913 Copper Coin Issues

		Good	Fine	XF
S2035 10 Coppers	1913. Brown on tan underprint. Black text. Back: Black on orange. Large red circular seal.	50.00	125.	250.
S2036 20 Coppers	1913. Green and yellow. Black text. Back: Blue. Large red circular seal. Printer: CMPA. *(S/M #H167-30).*	25.00	50.00	100.
S2037 30 Coppers	1913. Brown on yellow underprint. Black text. Back: Blue. Large red circular seal. Printer: TYPC. *(S/M #H167-31).*	25.00	50.00	100.
S2039 100 Coppers	1913. Blue on yellow underprint. Black text. Back: Green. Large red circular seal. Printer: CMPA. *(S/M #H167-32).*	25.00	50.00	100.

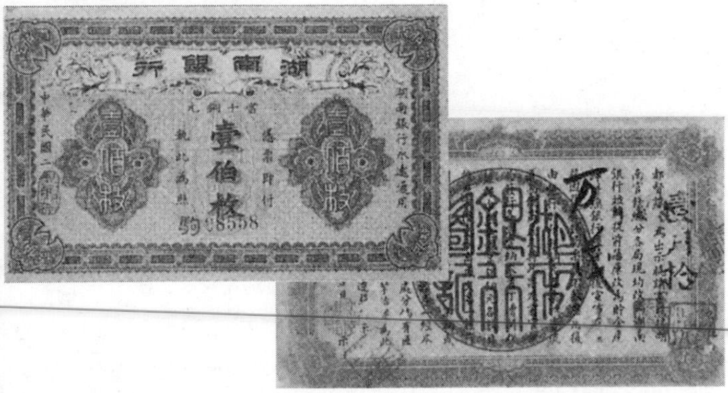

		Good	Fine	XF
S2040 100 Coppers	1913. Blue on yellow-orange underprint. Black text. Back: Olive-green. Large red circular seal. *(S/M #H167-33).*	25.00	50.00	100.
S2041 100 Coppers	1913. Dark blue on pink underprint. Black text. Back: Brown-violet. Large red circular seal. *(S/M #H167-34).*	40.00	100.	225.

1914 Copper Coin Issue

		Good	Fine	XF
S2042 30 Coppers	1914. Brown and green. *(S/M #H167-37).*	50.00	125.	250.

1915 Copper Coin Issue

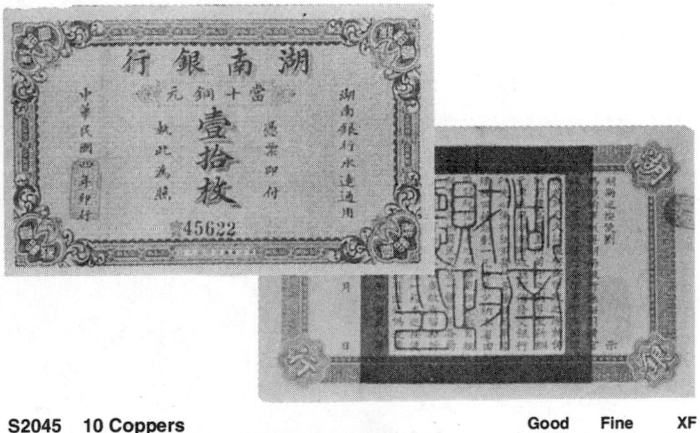

		Good	Fine	XF
S2045 10 Coppers	1915. Blue and red. Back: Green. Printer: CCLA. *(S/M #H167-40).*	20.00	40.00	100.
S2046 20 Coppers	1915. Green and orange. Back: Violet. Printer: CCLA. *(S/M #H167-41).*	25.00	50.00	100.

		Good	Fine	XF
S2047 30 Coppers	1915. Red and blue. Back: Brown. Printer: CCLA. *(S/M #H167-42).*	40.00	100.	225.
S2048 50 Coppers	1915. Red and green. Back: Blue. Printer: CCLA. *(S/M #H167-43).*	50.00	125.	250.

		Good	Fine	XF
S2050 100 Coppers	1.4.1915. Green. House at left, road to walled city at right. Back: Brown and multicolor. Printer: ABNC. *(S/M #H167-44).*	20.00	40.00	100.
S2053 10 Cents	1915. Brown and green. *(S/M #H167-47).*	20.00	40.00	100.

1917 Copper Coin Issues

		Good	Fine	XF
S2056 10 Coppers	1.1.1917. Blue and red. Temple at left, road to walled city at right. Back: Olive. Bank building at center. Printer: CMPA. *Changsha. (S/M #H167-50).*	20.00	40.00	100.
S2057 20 Coppers	1.1.1917. Blue and brown. Temple at left, road to walled city at right. Back: Brown. Bank building at center. Printer: CMPA. *Changsha. (S/M #H167-51).*	25.00	75.00	175.

		Good	Fine	XF
S2058 30 Coppers	1.1.1917. Green and red. Temple at left, road to walled city at right. Back: Brown and blue. Bank building at center. Printer: CMPA. *Changsha. (S/M #H167-52).*	25.00	75.00	175.
S2059 50 Coppers	1.1.1917. Black and yellow. Temple at left, road to walled city at right. Back: Brown and green. Bank building at center. Printer: CMPA. *Changsha. (S/M #H167-53).*	25.00	75.00	175.
S2060 100 Coppers	1.1.1917. Brown and blue. Temple at left, road to walled city at right. Back: Green and yellow. Bank building at center. Printer: CMPA. *Changsha. (S/M #H167-54).*	20.00	40.00	100.
S2061 100 Coppers	1917. Green and orange. Uniface. *Hankow. (S/M #H167-55).*	25.00	75.00	175.

1918 Copper Coin Issue

		Good	Fine	XF
S2065 10 Coppers	1918. Brown and green. Back: Blue and yellow. *(S/M #H167-60).*	75.00	150.	300.

1918 Dollar Issue

		Good	Fine	XF
S2067 50 Cents	1918. Green on orange underprint. Building at center. Back: Blue. *(S/M #H167-69).*	150.	450.	—
S2068 1 Dollar	1918. Green and yellow. Back: Green. *(S/M #H167-70).*	125.	400.	—
S2069 5 Dollars	1918. Gray and green. *(S/M #H167-71).*	150.	450.	—

ND Dollar Issue

		Good	Fine	XF
S2073 1 Dollar	ND. Green on violet underprint. Shrine at center. Back: Brown. Printer: BEPP. *HANKOW. (S/M #H167-76).*	200.	500.	—

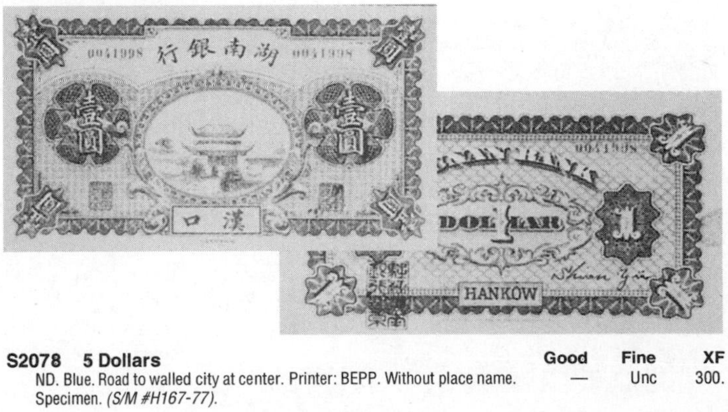

		Good	Fine	XF
S2078 5 Dollars	ND. Blue. Road to walled city at center. Printer: BEPP. Without place name. Specimen. *(S/M #H167-77).*	—	Unc	300.

Hupeh Government Cash Bank
Hupeh Provincial Bank

局錢官北湖
Hu Pei Kuan Ch'ien Chü

1896 Issue

	Good	Fine	XF
S2081 1000 Cash Yr. 22 (1896). Light blue with black text and red seals. Facing dragons at left and right. Vertical format. *(S/M #H171-0.5).*	200.	500.	—

1899 Issue

	Good	Fine	XF
S2085 1 Ch'uan Yr. 25 (1899); Yr. 26 (1900). Blue and yellow. Back: Brown. *(S/M #H171-1).*			
a. Handwritten date. Yr. 25 (1899).	350.	800.	—
b. Printed date. Yr. 26 (1900).	300.	700.	—

1904 Issue

	Good	Fine	XF
S2090 1 Yüan Yr. 30 (1904). Black and green. Dragons facing at upper left and right. Vertical format. Back: Orange. *S/M #H171-10).*	200.	500.	—
S2091 5 Yüan Yr. 30 (1904). *(S/M #H171-11).* Reported not confirmed.	—	—	—

1904 Tael Issue

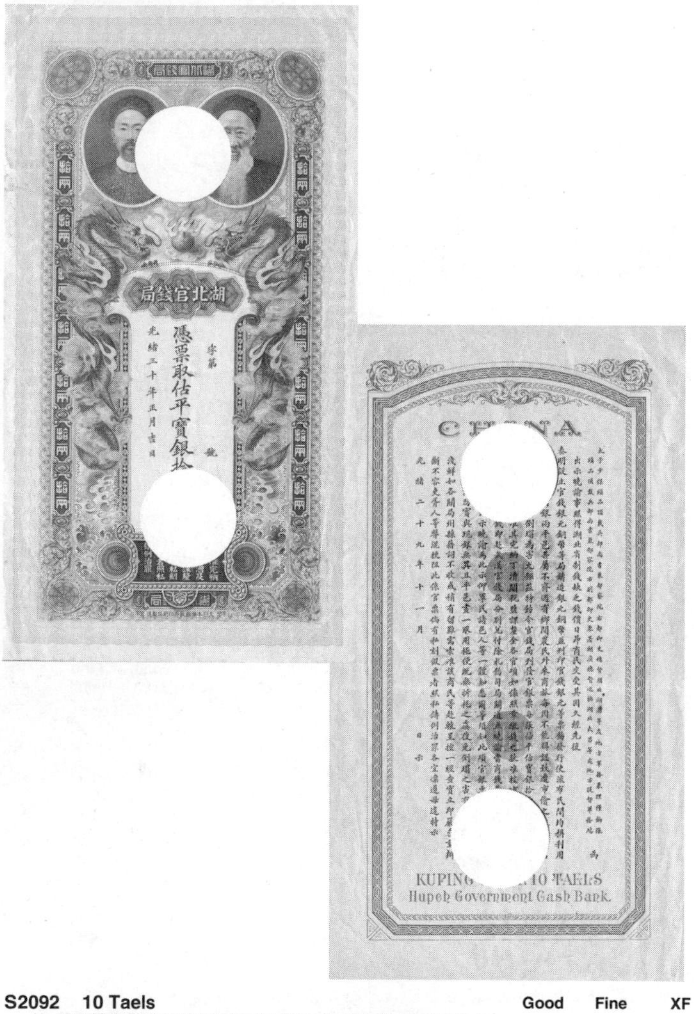

	Good	Fine	XF
S2092 10 Taels Yr. 30 (1904). Black on pink underprint. Two male portrait above two facing dragons. Vertical format. Back: Black text on pink underprint. *(S/M #H171-15).*			
a. Issued note.	—	—	—
r. Remainder. 2 large punch hole cancelations.	—	Unc	400.

1906 Issue

	Good	Fine	XF
S2093 1 Ch'uan Yr. 32 (1906)/Yr. 25. Green and yellow. Two facing dragons. Back: Orange. *(S/M #H171-17).*	—	—	—

1908 Issue

	Good	Fine	XF
S2094 1 Ch'uan Yr. 34 (1908)/Yr. 25. Green and yellow. Back: Orange. *(S/M #H171-20).*	100.	300.	—

1914 Issue

	Good	Fine	XF
S2098 100 Coppers 1914. Green and black. House at left, tower at right. Back: Green. Red seal. *(S/M #H171-30).*	7.50	20.00	75.00

Hupeh Provincial Bank

行銀省北湖
Hu Pei Sheng Yin Hang

1928 Issue

	Good	Fine	XF
S2101 1 Chiao = 10 Cents 1928. Dark blue. Pagoda at upper center. 3 signature varieties. Vertical format. Back: Orange. Printer: WHPP. *(S/M #H173-10).*	15.00	25.00	75.00
S2102 2 Chiao = 20 Cents 1928. Red. Tower at center. 2 signature varieties. Back: Brown. Printer: CCCA. *(S/M #H173-11).*	20.00	40.00	100.
S2103 5 Chiao = 50 Cents 1928. Green. Pagoda at left. Printer: WHPP. *(S/M #H173-12).*	45.00	150.	—

1929 Issue

	Good	Fine	XF
S2104 1 Yüan 1929. Violet and multicolor. Pagoda at right. Back: Blue. Printer: ABNC. *Hankow (S/M #H173-20).*			
a. Issued note.	75.00	150.	500.
p. Proof.	—	Unc	350.
S2105 5 Yüan 1929. Green and multicolor. Pagoda at center. Back: Orange. Printer: ABNC. *Hankow (S/M #H173-21a).*			
a. Issued note.	75.00	200.	500.
p. Proof.	—	Unc	400.
S2106 10 Yüan 1929. Red and multicolor. Pagoda at left. Back: Violet. Printer: ABNC. *Hankow (S/M #H173-22a).*			
a. Issued note.	125.	275.	600.
p. Proof.	—	Unc	450.

NOTE: For #S2104-S2106 with additional overprint, see Agricultural Bank of the Four Provinces, #A88-A90 and Farmers Bank of China #466-468, Vol. 2.

1932 Issue

	Good	Fine	XF
S2108 5 Chiao = 50 Cents 1932. Green. Pagoda at left. Back: Shoreline at center. Printer: CCCA. *HANKOW. (S/M #H17-30).*	20.00	50.00	125.

1936 Issue

	Good	Fine	XF
S2110 1 Chiao = 10 Cents 1936. Blue. Tower at center. Back: Green and orange. Printer: TYPC. *(S/M #H173-40).*	10.00	40.00	100.
S2112 5 Chiao = 50 Cents 1936. Blue. Waterfront building at center. Back: Green. Gateway at center. Printer: TYPC. *(S/M #H173-41).*	10.00	40.00	100.

1940 Issue

	Good	Fine	XF
S2115 5 Cents 1940. Orange. *(S/M #H173-50).*	25.00	75.00	150.

	Good	Fine	XF
S2119 1 Yüan 1940. Black on pink underprint. Tower gate at center. Back: Black on yellow-green underprint. *(S/M #H173-55).*	50.00	150.	500.

1941 Issue

	Good	Fine	XF
S2122 1 Yüan 1941. Olive. Printer: TTBC. *(S/M #H173-60).*	20.00	75.00	175.
S2123 5 Yüan 1941. Blue and yellow. Tower at center. Back: Blue. Printer: TTBC. *(S/M #H173-61).*	20.00	75.00	175.
S2124 10 Yüan 1941. Green. Printer: TTBC. *(S/M #H173-62).*	20.00	75.00	175.

Hupeh Government Mint

局元銀北湖
Hu Pei Yin Yüan Chü

1894 Issue

	Good	Fine	XF
S2126 1 Tiao Yr. 20 (1894). *(S/M #H175-1).*	275.	600.	1250.
S2127 5 Tiao Yr. 20 (1894). *(S/M #H175-2).*	275.	600.	1250.
S2128 10 Tiao Yr. 20 (1894). *(S/M #H175-3).*	350.	800.	1500.
S2130 1 Tael Yr. 20 (1894). *(S/M #H175-10.*	400.	900.	1750.

No.	Description	Good	Fine	XF
S2131 3 Taels	Yr. 20 (1894). *(S/M #H175-11.*	500.	1200.	—
S2132 5 Taels	Yr. 20 (1894). *(S/M #H175-12.*	550.	1300.	—
S2133 10 Taels	Yr. 20 (1894). *(S/M #H175-13.*	650.	1500.	—

1899 Issue

		VG	VF	UNC
S2135 1 Dollar = 7 Mace 2 Candareens	Yr. 25 (1899). Green and multicolor. Facing dragons holding obverse and reverse of silver dragon dollar at upper left and right. Vertical format. Back: Orange. Black text. *(S/M #H175-20).*	600.	1500.	—
S2136 5 Dollars	Yr. 25 (1899). *(S/M #H175-21).*	550.	1300.	—
S2137 10 Dollars	Yr. 25 (1899). *(S/M #H175-22).*	750.	1750.	—

1900 Issue

		VG	VF	UNC
S2139 1 Dollar	Yr. 26 (1900). *(S/M #H175-30).*	450.	1250.	—
S2140 5 Dollars	Yr. 26 (1900). *(S/M #H175-31).*	450.	1250.	—
S2141 10 Dollars	Yr. 26 (1900). *(S/M #H175-32).*	600.	1500.	—

1909 Issue

		VG	VF	UNC
S2142 1 Dollar	1909. *(S/M #H175-40).*	450.	1250.	—
S2143 5 Dollars	1000. *(S/M #H175-41)*	350.	1000.	—
S2144 10 Dollars	1909. *(S/M #H175-42).*	500.	1250.	—

Ili Official Currency Bureau

局錢官犂伊
I Li Kuan Ch'ien Tsung Chü

局總錢官犂伊
I Li Kuan Ch'ien Chü

1899 Issue

		VG	VF	UNC
S2145 200 Cash	Yr. 25 (1899). Cloth. *(S/M #I21.5-3).*	—	—	—
S2145A 300 Cash	Yr. 25 (1899). Cloth. *(S/M #I21.5-4).*	—	—	—
S2145B 500 Cash	Yr. 25 (1899). Cloth. *(S/M #I21.5-5).*	—	—	—

No.	Description	Good	Fine	XF
S2145C 1000 Cash	Yr. 25 (1899). Vertical format. Uniface. *(S/M #I21.5-6).*	—	—	—

1909 Issue

No.	Description	Good	Fine	XF
S2149 1000 Cash	Yr. 1 (1909). Blue and black. Dragons facing at upper left and right. Vertical format. Back: Brown. Printer: PYOG. *(S/M #I22-1).*	300.	750.	—
S2150 2000 Cash	Yr. 1 (1909). Printer: PYOG. *(S/M #I22-2).*	400.	850.	—

1914 Issue

No.	Description	Good	Fine	XF
S2152 200 Cash	1/1/1914. Black and green. Facing Chinze at top and bottom. Uniface. Vertical format. *(S/M #I22-12).*	—	—	—

1917 Issue

No.	Description	Good	Fine	XF
S2153 5 Ch'ien	1917. Cloth. Vertical format. *(S/M #I21.5-15).*	250.	700.	—

Hsing Yeh Bank of Jehol
Industrial Development Bank of Jehol

行銀業興河熱
Je Ho Hsing Yeh Yin Hang

行銀業興
Hsing Yeh Yin Hang

ND Issue

No.	Description	Good	Fine	XF
S2155 10 Coppers	ND. Olive. *(S/M #J1-0.5).*	100.	225.	—
S2155A 50 Coppers	ND. Brown. Temple at center. Back: Landscape with pagoda at center. *(S/M#J1-0.6).*	75.00	150.	—
S2156 20 Coppers	ND. Dark green. Temple at center. Back: Landscape with pagoda at center. *(S/M #J1-1).*	100.	250.	—
S2158 100 Coppers	ND. Gray. Temple at center. Back: Gray. Landscape with pagoda at center. *(S/M #J1-2).*	100.	250.	—

1918; 1919 Issue

No.	Description	Good	Fine	XF
S2160 10 Cents	1918. *(S/M #J1-10).* Reported not confirmed.	—	—	—
S2161 20 Cents	1918. *(S/M #J1-11).* Reported not confirmed.	—	—	—
S2162 30 Cents	1918. Purple and black on brown underprint. Temple at center. Back: Brown and blue. City gate at center.	125.	300.	—
S2163 40 Cents	1918. *(S/M #J1-13).* Reported not confirmed.	—	—	—
S2164 50 Cents	1918. *(S/M #J1-14).* Reported not confirmed.	—	—	—
S2165 1 Dollar	1919. *(S/M #J1-20).* Reported not confirmed.	—	—	—
S2166 5 Dollars	1919. *(S/M #J1-21).* Reported not confirmed.	—	—	—
S2167 10 Dollars	1919. *(S/M #J1-22).* Reported not confirmed.	—	—	—

1920 Issues

No.	Description	Good	Fine	XF
S2168 1 Dollar	1920. Green. House at center. Back: Orange. Buildings at center with text: *EXCHANGE NOTE* at right. Printer: BEPP.			
	a. *Chao Yang. (S/M #J1-30a).*	100.	300.	—
	b. *Chao Yang/Tientsin. (S/M #J1-30b).*	100.	300.	—
	c. *Chih Feng (Hsien). (S/M #J1-30c).*	100.	300.	—
	d. *Chih Feng/Tientsin. (S/M #J1-30n).*	100.	300.	—
	e. *Ching P'eng. (S/M #J1-30d).*	100.	300.	—
	f. *Chui Tzu Shan. (S/M #J1-30e).*	100.	300.	—
	g. *JEHOL. (S/M #J1-30f).*	100.	300.	—
	h. *JEHOL - Payable in Fengtien. (S/M #J1-30g).*	100.	300.	—
	i. *K'ai Lu. (S/M #J1-30h).*	100.	300.	—
	j. *Ling Yuan. (S/M #J1-30i).*	100.	300.	—
	k. *Ling Yuan/Tientsin. (S/M #J1-30j).*	100.	300.	—
	l. *Lung Hua. (S/M #J1-30k).*	100.	300.	—
	m. *P'ing Ch'uan. (S/M #J1-30l).*	100.	300.	—
	n. *P'ing Ch'uan/Tientsin. (S/M #J1-30m).*	100.	300.	—
	o. *Tientsin. (S/M #J1-30o).*	100.	300.	—
S2169 1 Dollar	1920. Blue and black. Buildings at center with text: *EXCHANGE NOTE* at right. Back: Green. Printer: BEPP. *JEHOL. (S/M #J1-31).*	40.00	100.	—
S2170 5 Dollars	1920. Orange. Back: Brown. Printer: BEPP. *JEHOL/Fengtien. (S/M #J1-32).*	75.00	225.	—

No.	Description	Good	Fine	XF
S2171 5 Dollars	1920. Brown. Buildings at center with text: *EXCHANGE NOTE* at right. Back: Orange. Printer: BEPP.			
	a. *Chih Feng (Hsien). (S/M J1-33c).*	50.00	150.	—
	b. *JEHOL. (S/M #J1-33f).*	25.00	75.00	—
	c. *K'ai Lu. (S/M #J1-33h).*	50.00	150.	—
S2172 10 Dollars	1920. Brown. Buildings at center with text: *EXCHANGE NOTE* at right. Back: Violet. Printer: BEPP.			
	a. *JEHOL. (S/M #J1-34f).*	20.00	60.00	—
	b. *Chih Feng/Tientsin. (S/M #J1-34n).*	75.00	150.	—
	c. *P'ing Ch'uan/Tientsin. (S/M #J1-34m).*	75.00	150.	—
	d. *P'ing Ch'uan/JEHOL. (S/M #J1-33p).*	75.00	150.	—

1921 Copper Coin Issue

No.	Description	Good	Fine	XF
S2174 10 Coppers	ND (1921). Olive-green with back text. Hillside fortress at center. Back: Pagoda in trees at center. Printer: BEPA. *(S/M #J1-40).*	40.00	100.	400.
S2174A 10 Coppers	ND (1921). Orange with black text. *Copper coin exchange money* in Chinese text. Temple at center. Back: Orange. Pagoda and trees. Printer: BEPA. *Chao yang. (S/M #J1-40.5).*	40.00	100.	400.
S2175 20 Coppers	ND (1921). Orange with black text. Hillside fortress at center. Back: Pagoda in trees at center. Printer: BEPA. *(S/M #J1-41).*	40.00	100.	—

S2175A 20 Coppers

ND (1921). Dark green with black text. Chinese text: *Copper Coin Exchange Money* at lower center panel. Hillside fortress at center. Back: Pagoda in trees at center. Overprint: *chao Yang*. Printer: BEPA.

	Good	Fine	XF
a. *Chao Yang. (S/M #J1-41.5).*	50.00	125.	—
b. *Ch'üan. (S/M #J1-41.5a).*	40.00	125.	—

S2176 50 Coppers

	Good	Fine	XF
ND (1921). Brown with black text. Hillside fortress at center. Back: Pagoda in trees at center. Printer: BEPA. *(S/M #J1-42).*	40.00	125.	—

S2177 100 Coppers

	Good	Fine	XF
ND (1921). Olive-green with black text. Hillside fortress at center. Back: Pagoda in trees at center. Printer: BEPA. *(S/M #J1-43).*	25.00	60.00	—

S2177A 100 Coppers

ND (1921). Brown with black text. Building at center. Chinese text *Copper coin exchange money* at front lower center. *Chao Yang* stamped on front center. Back: Brown.

	Good	Fine	XF
a. Issued note. *(S/M #J1-43.5a).*	25.00	60.00	—
b. With Chinese character overprint: *Chao Yang. (S/M #J1-43.5b).*	40.00	125.	—

S2177B 200 Coppers

	Good	Fine	XF
ND (1921). Dark blue with black text. Hilltop fortress at center. *(S/M #J1-43.7).*	75.00	200.	—

S2178 500 Coppers

	Good	Fine	XF
ND (1921). *(S/M #J1-44).*	100.	300.	—

1922 Issue

S2179 1 Yüan

	VG	VF	UNC
1922. Printer: BEPP. Specimen. *(S/M #J1-50).*		—	500.

S2180 5 Yüan

	VG	VF	UNC
1922. Printer: BEPP. Specimen. *S/M #J1-51).*		—	500.

S2181 10 Yüan

	VG	VF	UNC
1922. Printer: BEPP. Specimen. *(S/M #J1-52).*		—	500.

1923 Issue

S2183 1 Yüan

1.6.1923. Red. Great Wall at center. Printer: BEPP.

	Good	Fine	XF
a. *CHENG TE FU. (S/M #J1-60a).*	75.00	200.	—
b. *KIEN P'ING HSIEN. (S/M #J1-60b).*	75.00	200.	—
c. *CH'IH FENG HSIEN. (S/M #J1-60c).*	75.00	200.	—
d. *FENG NING. (S/M #J1-60d).*	75.00	200.	—
e. *LINGYUAN. (S/M #J1-60e).*	75.00	200.	—
f. *LUNG HUA. (S/M #J1-60f).*	75.00	200.	—
g. *P'ING CH'UAN. (S/M #J1-60g).*	75.00	200.	—
h. *SUI TUNG HSIEN. (S/M #J1-60h).*	75.00	200.	—
i. *WEI CH'ANG. (S/M #J1-60i).*	75.00	200.	—

S2184 5 Yüan

1.6.1923. Green. Great wall at center. Printer: BEPP.

	Good	Fine	XF
a. *KIEN P'ING HSIEN. (S/M #J1-61a).*	75.00	200.	—
b. *FENG NING. (S/M #J1-61b).*	75.00	200.	—
c. *CHAO YANG FU. (S/M #J1-61c).*	75.00	200.	—
d. *CHING P'ENG. (S/M #J1-61 d).*	75.00	200.	—
e. *FU HSING HSIEN. (S/M #J1-61e).*	75.00	200.	—
f. *LUAN PING. (S/M #J1-61f).*	75.00	200.	—
g. *LING SE. (S/M #J1-61g).*	75.00	200.	—
h. *KAI LU. (S/M #J1-61h).*	75.00	200.	—
i. *CH'IH FENG HSIEN. (S/M #J1-61i).*	75.00	200.	—

S2185 10 Yüan

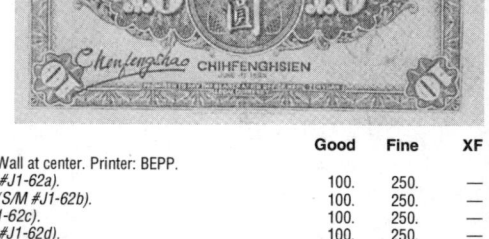

1.6.1923. Dark blue. Great Wall at center. Printer: BEPP.

	Good	Fine	XF
a. *CHENGTEHFU. (S/M #J1-62a).*	100.	250.	—
b. *CH'IH FENG HSIEN. (S/M #J1-62b).*	100.	250.	—
c. *LINGYUAN. (S/M #J1-62c).*	100.	250.	—
d. *PING CH'UAN. (S/M #J1-62d).*	100.	250.	—
e. *WEI CH'ANG. (S/M #J1-62e).*	100.	250.	—
f. *CHAO YANG FU. (S/M #J1-62f).*	100.	250.	—
g. *FU HSING HSIEN. (S/M #H1-62g).*	100.	250.	—
h. *LING SE. (S/M #J1-62h).*	100.	250.	—
i. *KIEN P'ING HSIEN. (S/M #J1-62i).*	100.	250.	—

1925 Issue

S2186 1 Yüan

1925. Violet. Great Wall at center. Printer: BEPP.

	Good	Fine	XF
a. Signature P. C. Kao. *S/M #J1-70a).*	25.00	75.00	225.
b. Signature Y. F. Wang. *(S/M #J1-70b).*	25.00	75.00	225.

S2187 5 Yüan

1925. Yellow. Great Wall at center. Printer: BEPP.

	Good	Fine	XF
a. Signature P. C. Kao. *(S/M #J1-71a).*	25.00	75.00	225.
b. Signature Y. F. Wang. *(S/M #J1-71b).*	25.00	75.00	225.

S2188 10 Yüan	Good	Fine	XF
1925. Green. Great Wall at center. Printer: BEPP. Like #S2187.			
a. Signature P. C. Kao. *(S/M #J1-72a).*	20.00	40.00	125.
b. Signature Y. F. Wang. *(S/M #J1-72b).*	20.00	40.00	125.

1926 Issue

	Good	Fine	XF
S2189 1 Yüan 1.9.1926. Green on multicolor underprint. Building at left. Printer: BEPP. *(S/M #J1-73).*	100.	250.	—
S2190 5 Yüan 1.9.1926. Blue on multicolor underprint. Printer: BEPP. *(S/M #J1-74).*	125.	300.	—

1927 Issue

	Good	Fine	XF
S2191 10 Cents 1.4.1927. Black and yellow. Cottage at center. *(S/M #J1-76).*	75.00	225.	—
S2191A 20 Cents 1.4.1927. Blue on yellow underprint.	75.00	225.	—
S2191B 50 Cents Violet.	25.00	75.00	—

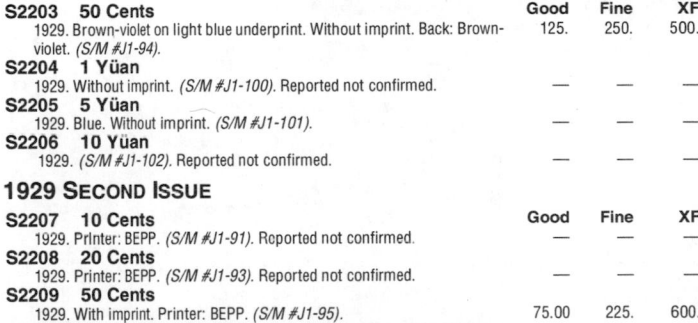

	Good	Fine	XF
S2191C 5 Dollars 1.11.1927. Orange on multicolor underprint. Gazebo, man in boat at center. *PEKING S/M #J1-77j.*	40.00	100.	225.

1928 Issue

	Good	Fine	XF
S2193 10 Cents 1928. Orange and gray. Printer: BEPP. *(S/M #J1-78).*	40.00	100.	225.
S2197 1 Yüan 1928. Printer: BEPP. *(S/M #J1-80).* Reported not confirmed.	—	—	—
S2198 5 Yüan 1928. Printer: BEPP. *(S/M #J1-81).* Reported not confirmed.	—	—	—
S2199 10 Yüan 1928. Printer: BEPP. *(S/M #J1-82).* Reported not confirmed.	—	—	—

1929 First Issue

	Good	Fine	XF
S2201 10 Cents 1929. Green and red. House at center. Without imprint. Back: Green. *(S/M #J1-90).*	75.00	200.	400.

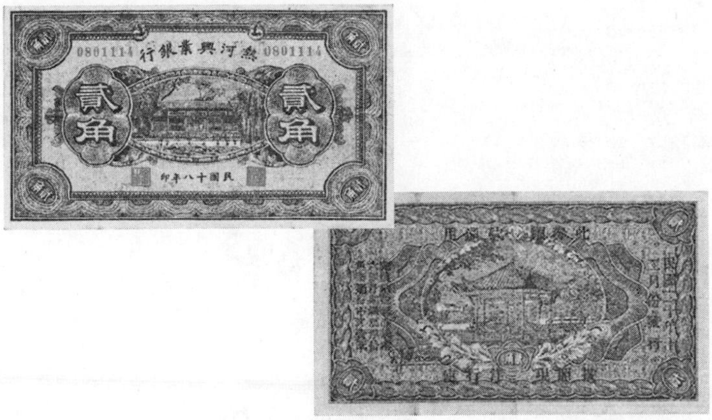

	Good	Fine	XF
S2202 20 Cents 1929. Dark blue on light green underprint. Without imprint. Back: Dark blue. *(S/M #J1-92).*	125.	250.	500.

	Good	Fine	XF
S2203 50 Cents 1929. Brown-violet on light blue underprint. Without imprint. Back: Brown-violet. *(S/M #J1-94).*	125.	250.	500.
S2204 1 Yüan 1929. Without imprint. *(S/M #J1-100).* Reported not confirmed.	—	—	—
S2205 5 Yüan 1929. Blue. Without imprint. *(S/M #J1-101).*	—	—	—
S2206 10 Yüan 1929. *(S/M #J1-102).* Reported not confirmed.	—	—	—

1929 Second Issue

	Good	Fine	XF
S2207 10 Cents 1929. Printer: BEPP. *(S/M #J1-91).* Reported not confirmed.	—	—	—
S2208 20 Cents 1929. Printer: BEPP. *(S/M #J1-93).* Reported not confirmed.	—	—	—
S2209 50 Cents 1929. With imprint. Printer: BEPP. *(S/M #J1-95).*	75.00	225.	600.

	Good	Fine	XF
S2211 5 Yüan 1.7.1929. Blue. Printer: BEPP. *(S/M #J1-97).*	125.	250.	650.
S2211A 10 Dollars or Yüan 7.1.1929. Red. Printer: BEPP.	175.	350.	750.

1930 Issue

	Good	Fine	XF
S2212 10 Cents 1930. Red. Waterfront buildings at left and right. Printer: BEPP. *(S/M #J1-108).*	40.00	100.	250.
S2212A 20 Cents 1930. Purple. Waterfront buildings at left and right. Printer: BEPP. *(S/M #J1-109).*	75.00	175.	325.
S2213 50 Cents 1930. Printer: BEPP. *(S/M #J1-110).*	100.	225.	375.
S2214 1 Yüan 1930. Printer: BEPP. *(S/M #J1-120).* Reported not confirmed.	—	—	—

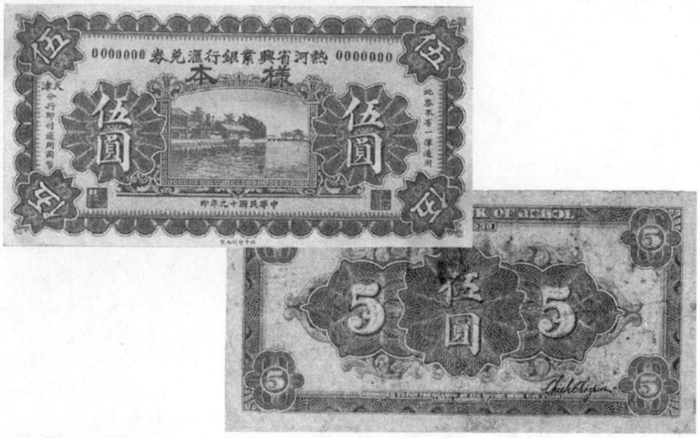

	Good	Fine	XF
S2215 5 Yüan 1930. Orange. Printer: BEPP. Specimen. *(S/M #J1-121).*	—	Unc	350.

	Good	Fine	XF
S2216 10 Yüan 1930. Blue. Printer: BEPP. *(S/M #J1-122).*	75.00	200.	350.

1931 Issue

	Good	Fine	XF
S2217 10 Cents 1931. Green and red. House at center. Back: Green. Printer: BEPP. *(S/M #J1-130).*	100.	225.	375.
S2218 20 Cents 1931. Printer: BEPP. *(S/M #J1-131).* Reported not confirmed.	—	—	—
S2219 50 Cents 1931. Printer: BEPP. *(S/M #J1-132).* Reported not confirmed.	—	—	—

	Good	Fine	XF
S2220 1 Yüan 1931. Green. Printer: BEPP. *(S/M #J1-140).*	75.00	200.	350.
S2221 5 Yüan 1931. Printer: BEPP. *(S/M #J1-141).* Reported not confirmed.	—	—	—
S2222 10 Yüan 1931. Printer: BEPP. *(S/M #J1-142).* Reported not confirmed.	—	—	—

Kan Sen Bank of Kiangsi
Provincial Bank of Kiangsi

贛省銀行
Kan Sheng Yin Hang

1912 Issue

	Good	Fine	XF
S2223 100 Cents 1912. Black and yellow. Facing dragons at top. Vertical format. Back: Shoreline at center. *Kiangsi. (S/M #K2-0.3).*	225.	500.	—

1923; 1924 Issue

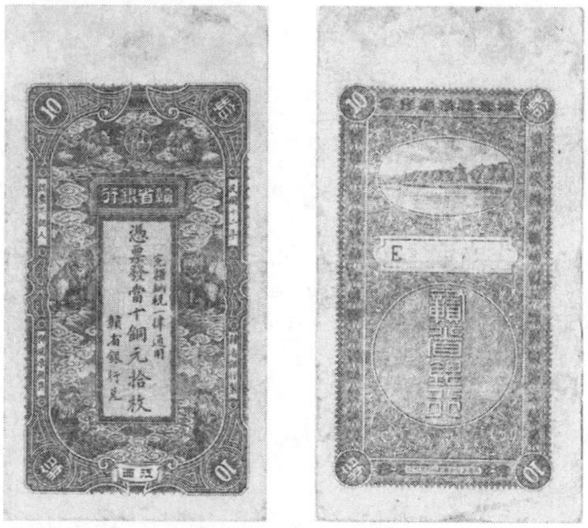

	Good	Fine	XF
S2224 10 Cents 1923. Orange. Facing dragons at top. Vertical format. *Kiangsi. (S/M #K2-0.6).*	200.	475.	—
S2225 1 Dollar 1924. Black on tan and multicolor underprint. Gazebo, house along shoreline. Back: Brown. Village within wall at center. *(S/M #K2-1).*	100.	225.	—
S2226 5 Dollars 1924. Violet on multicolor underprint. Gazebo, house along shoreline. Back: Red. Village within wall at center. *(S/M #K2-2).*	150.	325.	—

	Good	Fine	XF
S2227 10 Dollars 1924. Green on multicolor underprint. Gazebo, house along shoreline. Back: Orange. Village within wall at center. *(S/M #K2-3).*	75.00	175.	—

NOTE: #S2225-S2227 with additional overprint, see Kiangsi Regional Bank #S1090-S1093.

1925 Issue

	Good	Fine	XF
S2227A 10 Coppers 1925. *(S/M #K2-5).*	40.00	100.	—

	Good	Fine	XF
S2228 10 Cents 1924. Red and green. Pavilion in park at center. Back: Brown and yellow. *Nanchang. (S/M #K2-101).*	75.00	150.	—

	Good	Fine	XF
S2231 1 Dollar ND. Green and multicolor. Back: Brown. *Nanchang. (S/M #K2-20).*	125.	300.	—
S2232 5 Dollars ND. *Nanchang. (S/M #K2-21).*	150.	325.	—

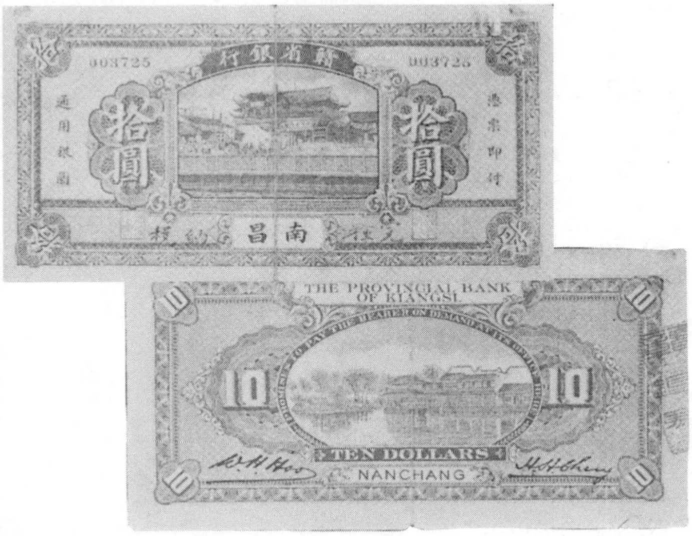

	Good	Fine	XF
S2233 10 Dollars ND. Violet and multicolor. Houses at center. Back: Green. Houses along shoreline at center. *Nanchang. (S/M #K2-22).*	150.	325.	—

1926 Issue

	Good	Fine	XF
S2234 1 Dollar 1926. *(S/M #K2-30).* Reported not confirmed.	—	—	—
S2235 5 Dollars 1926. *(S/M #K2-31).* Reported not confirmed.	—	—	—
S2236 10 Dollars 1926. *(S/M #K2-32).* Reported not confirmed.	—	—	—

Monetary Bureau of Government Kansu

甘肅(省)平市官錢局

Kan Su (Sheng) P'ing Shih Kuan Ch'ien Chü

1928 ND Issue

	Good	Fine	XF
S2237 10 Coppers ND (1928). *(S/M #K11-0.1).*	—	—	—

1932 ND Issue

	Good	Fine	XF
S2237D 10 Coppers ND (1932). Green. Buildings, mountains at center. *(S/M #K11-0.2).*	—	—	—
S2237E 20 Coppers ND (1932). Blue. Back: Orange. *(S/M #K11-0.3).*	50.00	150.	—
S2237F 50 Coppers ND (1932). *(S/M #K11-0.4).*	—	—	—

1932 Issue

	Good	Fine	XF
S2238 50 Coppers 1932. Temple at center. *KANSU. (S/M #K11-0.5).*	40.00	100.	—

1935 Issue

	Good	Fine	XF
S2240 20 Coppers 1935. Blue and yellow. Back: Blue. Printer: TTBC. *Kansu Province. (S/M #K11-1).*	40.00	100.	325.
S2245 50 Cents 1935. Red. Arch bridge at left, bridge to city at right. Back: Dark green. *KANSU. (S/M #K11-10).*	20.00	50.00	—

Kansu Provincial Bank

甘肅(省)平市官錢局

Kan Su (Sheng) P'ing Shih Kuan Ch'ien Chü

1935 Issue

	Good	Fine	XF
S2246 50 Cents 1935. Brown. Water wheels at center. Back: Blue. Printer: TTBC. *(S/M #K11-11).*	20.00	50.00	—

Canton Municipal Bank

廣州市市立銀行

Kuang Chou Shih Shih Li Yin Hang

1928 Issue

	Good	Fine	XF
S2253 10 Cents (1 Hao) 1.12.1928. Blue and red. Vertical format. Arms at center. Back: Red. SYS at upper center.			
a. Chinese signature on back.	50.00	125.	—
b. Red signature over black signature.	50.00	125.	—

#S2254 Deleted.

	Good	Fine	XF
S2255 50 Cents			
1.12.1928. Green and red. Arms at center. Back: SYS at upper center.	—	—	—

1929-32 Dollar Issue

	Good	Fine	XF
S2256 1 Dollar			
1931-32. Red orange and green. Vertical. Back: Orange. Horizontal. SYS at center. Printer: W&S.			
a. 1.10.1931.	25.00	80.00	—
b. 15.3.1932; 10.4.1932.	20.00	50.00	—
S2257 5 Dollars			
1929; 1931. Red and multicolor. Vertical. Back: Green. Horizontal. SYS at center. Printer: ABNC.			
a. 1.9.1929.	75.00	175.	—
b. 1.7.1931.	75.00	175.	—
S2258 10 Dollars			
1929; 1931. Blue and multicolor. Vertical. Back: Brown. Horizontal. SYS at center. Printer: ABNC.			
a. 1.9.1929.	100.	225.	—
b. 1.7.1931.	75.00	225.	—
S2259 50 Dollars			
1929; 1931. Violet and multicolor. Vertical. Back: Orange. Horizontal. SYS at center. Printer: ABNC.			
a. 1.9.1929.	—	—	—
b. 1.7.1931.	175.	350.	—

1931 Cent Issue

	Good	Fine	XF
S2260 10 Cents			
1.10.1931. Green and red. Building on slope at left. Back: Green. Portrait SYS at center.			
a. Red seal centered below denomination. *(S/M #K24-10a).*	40.00	100.	225.
b. Red seal to left, new Chinese signature at right. with old Chinese signature obliterated. *(S/M #24-10b).*	—	—	—

#S2265-2270 *Deleted.* See #S2256a; S2257b; S2258b; S2259b.

1933 Issue

	Good	Fine	XF
S2276 10 Cents			
1.5.1933. Red and yellow. Vertical. SYS at center. Back: Blue. Horizontal. Mausoleum of "72 Martyrs of the Yellow Flower Hill" at right. Printer: ABNC.			
a. Signature Hsu and Ch'en.	—	—	—
b. Signature Huang and Ch'en.	—	—	—
S2277 20 Cents			
1.5.1933. Orange on light blue underprint. Vertical. SYS at center. Back: Black. Horizontal. Modern bridge at left center. Printer: ABNC. *(S/M #K24-41).*	—	—	—

1928 Issue

	Good	Fine	XF
S2278 1 Dollar			
1.5.1933. Light brown on pale green underprint. Monument at center. Vertical. Back: Purple. SYS at center. Horizontal.			
a. Chinese and English signature with red serial #. *(S/M #K24-50a).*	10.00	35.00	100.
b. Chinese signature with red serial #. *(S/M #K24-50c).*	10.00	35.00	100.
c. Chinese signature with dark blue serial #. *(S/M #K24-50b).*	7.50	20.00	50.00
S2279 5 Dollars			
1.5.1933. Green on pale lilac underprint. Large Building at upper center. Vertical. Back: Red-violet. Horizontal.			
a. Chinese and English signature with red serial #. *(S/M #K24-51a).*	10.00	35.00	100.
b. Chinese signature with red serial #. *(S/M #K24-51c).*	10.00	35.00	100.
c. Chinese signature with dark blue serial #. *(S/M #K24-51b).*	7.50	20.00	50.00

1933 Issue

	Good	Fine	XF
S2280 10 Dollars			
1.5.1933. Red on green and yellow underprint. Government building at center. Back: Olive. SYS at center.			
a. Chinese and English signature with red serial #. *(S/M #K24-52a).*	25.00	100.	250.
b. Chinese signature with red serial #. *(S/M #K24-52c).*	25.00	75.00	250.
c. Chinese signature with dark blue serial #. *(S/M #K24-52b).*	25.00	75.00	250.

1928 Issue

	Good	Fine	XF
S2281 50 Dollars			
1933. Blue and black on multicolor underprint. Public building at center. Back: Orange. *(S/M #K24-53).*	175.	550.	—
S2285 50 Dollars			
1935. Violet and multicolor. *(S/M #K24-).* Reported not confirmed.	—	—	—

Kwangsi Official Currency Bureau

號錢銀官西廣

Kuang Hsi Kuan Yin Ch'ien Hao

1909 Issue

	VG	VF	UNC
S2287 1 Tael			
Yr. 1 (1909). *Kweilin. (S/M #K31-1).*	275.	750.	—
S2289 10 Taels			
Yr. 1 (1909). *Kweilin. (S/M #K31-2).*	300.	900.	—
S2290 1 Tael			
Yr. 1 (1909). *Lungchow. (S/M #K31-10).*	275.	750.	—
S2292 10 Taels			
Yr. 1 (1909). *Lungchow. (S/M #K31-11).*	300.	900.	—

Kwangsi Farmers Bank

行銀民農西廣

Kuang Hsi Nung Min Yin Hang

1938 Issue

	VG	VF	UNC
S2295 1 Yüan			
1938. Blue. Mythical man at left, farming at right. Back: Red. *(S/M #K32-1).*	75.00	225.	—

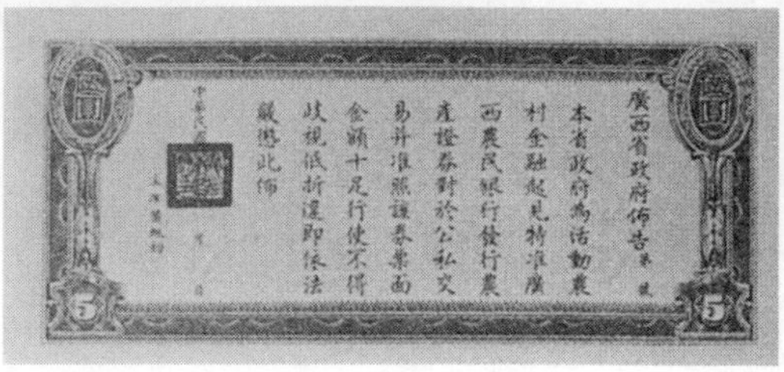

	VG	VF	UNC
S2296 5 Yüan			
1938. Green. Mythical man at left, farming at right. Back: Brown. *(S/M #K32-2).*	25.00	75.00	225.

Kwangsi Provincial Treasury Notes

(券)庫金省西廣

Kuang Hsi Sheng Chin K'u (Ch'üan)

1923 Issue

	Good	Fine	XF
S2301 1 Yüan			
1923. *(S/M #K33-1).* Reported not confirmed.	—	—	—
S2302 5 Yüan			
1923. *(S/M #K33-2).* Reported not confirmed.	—	—	—
S2303 10 Yüan			
1923. Green and brown. Back: Green. *(S/M #K33-3).*	125.	300.	750.

NOTE: #S2301-S2303 are believed by some to be a military issue.

1931 Issue

	Good	Fine	XF
S2303A 1 Yüan			
1931. National star in all 4 corners. Vertical format.			
a. *Kweilin. (S/M #K33-6a).*	—	—	—
b. *Liuchow. (S/M #K33-6b).*	—	—	—
c. *Nanning. (S/M #K33-6c).*	—	—	—
d. *Wuchow. (S/M #K33-6d).*	—	—	—

NOTE: #S2303A is considered by some to be a military issue.

1934 Issue

	Good	Fine	XF
S2304 1 Dollar			
1934. Orange and multicolor. Government buildings at upper center. Vertical format. Back: Olive-green. Building above silver dollar at center. Printer: W&S.			
a. Serial # suffix *N. Nanning. (S/M #K33-10a).*	25.00	75.00	200.
b. Serial # suffix *W. Wuchow. (S/M #K33-10b).*	25.00	75.00	200.

1936 Issue

	Good	Fine	XF
S2309 10 Silver Yüan			
1936. Blue and green. Back: Brown. Overprint: *Kwangsi Bank. (S/M #K33-11).*	125.	375.	—

Kwangsi Provincial Government

券通流幣輔省西廣
Kuang Hsi Sheng Fu Pi Liu T'ung Ch'üan

1949 Issue

	VG	VF	UNC
S2311 10 Cents ND (1949). Green and multicolor. Building at center. Back: Brown. Printer: HKPA. *(S/M #K34-1).*	10.00	30.00	100.

	VG	VF	UNC
S2312 20 Cents ND (1949). Brown and multicolor. Building at right. Back: Red. Printer: HKPA. *(S/M #K342).*	10.00	30.00	100.

	VG	VF	UNC
S2313 50 Cents ND (1949). Brown and multicolor. Building at center. Back: Brown. Printer: HKPA. *(S/M #K34-3).*	7.50	25.00	75.00

	VG	VF	UNC
S2314 100 Cents ND (1949). Green and multicolor. Building at right. Back: Brown. Printer: HKPA. *(S/M #K34-4).*	10.00	30.00	100.
S2315 500 Cents ND (1949). Red and multicolor. Building at center. Back: Red. Printer: HKPA. *(S/M #K34-5).*	25.00	75.00	200.

Provincial Bank of Kwangsi (Kwangse)

行銀省西廣
Kuang Hsi Sheng Yin Hang

1922 Issue

	Good	Fine	XF
S2318 10 Cents 1922. Green on red and light green underprint. Lake scene at center. Back: Brown on light blue underprint. *(S/M #K35-).*	—	—	—
S2319 20 Cents 1922. Blue. Specimen.	—	Unc	500.
S2320 50 Cents 1922. Olive green. Specimen.	—	Unc	500.
S2323 5 Dollars 1922. Green. *(S/M #K35-).*	—	—	—

1926 Issues

#S2325-S2327 with large rectangular overprint refer to Military - Chinese Republic Army, Navy and Air Force Sub. headquarters #S3828-S3830.

	Good	Fine	XF
S2325 1 Dollar Jan. 1926. Green and yellow. Pagoda at left, park at right. Back: Green and red. Coliseum at center.			
a.	20.00	50.00	—
b. *Kweilin. (S/M #K35-1b).*	20.00	50.00	—
c. *Liuchow. (S/M #K35-1c).*	20.00	50.00	—
d. *Lungchow. (S/M #K35-1d).*	20.00	50.00	—
e. *NANNING. (S/M #K35-1e).*	20.00	50.00	—
f. *Watlam. (S/M #K35-1f).*	20.00	50.00	—
g. *WUCHOW. (S/M #K35-1g).*	20.00	50.00	—
r. Remainder without place name. *(S/M #K35-1r).*	—	Unc	100.
S2326 5 Dollars Jan. 1926. Dark blue and black on red underprint. Park at left, shoreline, boats at right. Back: Gray on green underprint. Great Wall at center.			
a.	25.00	75.00	—
b. *Kweilin. (S/M #K35-2b).*	25.00	75.00	—
c. *Liuchow. (S/M #K35-2c).*	25.00	75.00	—
d. *Lungchow. (S/M #K35-2d).*	25.00	75.00	—
e. Green *NANNING* on back. *(S/M #K35-2e).*	25.00	75.00	—
f. *Watlam. (S/M #K35-2f).*	25.00	75.00	—
h. *Pai Sze/WUCHOW. (S/M #K35-2g).*	25.00	75.00	—
i. Black *NANNING* on back. *(S/M #K35-2e).*	25.00	75.00	—
j. *WUCHOW. (S/M #K35-2g).*	25.00	75.00	—
r. Remainder without place name. *(S/M #K35-2r).*	—	Unc	100.

#S2366A *Deleted*. See #S2326j.

	Good	Fine	XF
S2327 10 Dollars Jan. 1926. Brown and black on olive-gray underprint. Park at left, shoreline, boats at right. Back: Blue-gray on light blue underprint. Great Wall at center.			
a.	25.00	75.00	—
b. *Kweilin. (S/M #K35-3b).*	25.00	75.00	—
c. *Liuchow. (S/M #K35-3c).*	25.00	75.00	—
d. *Lungchow. (S/M #K35-3d).*	25.00	75.00	—
e. *NANNING. (S/M #K35-3e).*	25.00	75.00	—
f. *Watlam. (S/M #K35-3f).*	25.00	75.00	—
g. *WUCHOW. (S/M #K35g).*	25.00	75.00	—
r. Remainder without place name. *(S/M #K35-3r).*	—	Unc	100.

#S2328 *Deleted*. See #2327g.

1928 Issue

	Good	Fine	XF
S2331 1 Chiao = 10 Cents 1928. *(S/M #K35-10).* Reported not confirmed.	—	—	—
S2332 2 Chiao = 20 Cents 1928. Blue on brown underprint. House by bridge at top center. Back: Blue-gray. *(S/M #K35-11).*	40.00	100.	—
S2333 5 Chiao = 50 Cents 1928. Houses at top center. Back: Blue. *(S/M #K35-12).*			
a. Green on multicolor underprint.	25.00	75.00	—
b. Black on multicolor underprint.	25.00	75.00	—

1928 Local Currency Issue

	Good	Fine	XF
S2337 25 Dollars 1928. Violet and multicolor. Rural scene at right. *(S/M #K35-20).*			
a. Issued note.	75.00	225.	—
r. Remainder without signature seals.	—	Unc	150.

1929 Issue

	Good	Fine	XF
S2339 1 Dollar 1929. Black and multicolor. River scene at center. Back: Red. Printer: ABNC.			
a.	5.00	15.00	50.00
b. *Kweilin. (S/M #K35-30b).*	5.00	15.00	50.00
c. *Liuchow. (S/M #K35-30c).*	5.00	15.00	50.00
d. *Lungchow. (S/M #K35-30d).*	5.00	15.00	50.00
e. *Nanning. (S/M #K35-30e).*	5.00	15.00	50.00
f. *Watlam. (S/M #K35-30f).*	5.00	15.00	50.00
g. *Wuchow. (S/M #K35-30g).*	5.00	15.00	50.00
h. *Wuchow* with additional overprint: *Pa Pu. (S/M #K35-30h).*	5.00	15.00	50.00
i. *Chengchow. (S/M #K35-30).*	5.00	15.00	50.00
r. Remainder without place name. *(S/M #K35-30r).*	—	Unc	100.
S2340 5 Dollars 1929. Green and multicolor. River scene at center. Back: Purple. Printer: ABNC.			
a.	5.00	15.00	40.00
b. *Kweilin. (S/M #K35-31b).*	5.00	15.00	40.00
c. *Liuchow. (S/M #K35-31c).*	5.00	15.00	40.00
d. *Lungchow. (S/M #K35-31d).*	5.00	15.00	40.00
e. *Nanning. (S/M #K35-31e).*	5.00	15.00	40.00
f. *Watlam. (S/M #K35-31f).*	5.00	15.00	40.00
g. *Wuchow. (S/M #K35-31g).*	5.00	15.00	40.00
h. *Wuchow* with additional overprint: *Pa Pu. (S/M #K35-31h).*	5.00	15.00	40.00
i. *Chengchow. (S/M #K35-31).*	5.00	15.00	40.00
j. *Pimlok. (S/M #K35-31).*	5.00	15.00	40.00
r. Remainder without place name. *(S/M #K35-31r).*	—	Unc	60.00
S2341 10 Dollars 1929. Blue and multicolor. River scene at center. Back: Brown. Printer: ABNC.			
a.	5.00	15.00	50.00
b. *Kweilin. (S/M #K35-32b).*	5.00	15.00	50.00
c. *Liuchow. (S/M #K35-32c).*	5.00	15.00	50.00
d. *Lungchow. (S/M #K35-32d).*	5.00	15.00	50.00
e. *Nanning. (S/M #K35-32e).*	5.00	15.00	50.00
f. *Watlam. (S/M #K35-32f).*	5.00	15.00	50.00
g. *Wuchow. (S/M #K35-32g).*	5.00	15.00	50.00
h. *Wuchow* with additional overprint: *Pa Pu. (S/M #K35-32h).*	5.00	15.00	50.00
i. *Chengchow. (S/M #K35-32i).*	5.00	15.00	40.00
r. Remainder without place name. *(S/M #K35-32r).*	—	Unc	75.00

1932 Issue

	Good	Fine	XF
S2342 10 Cents 1932. Brown and green. Back: Orange. *(S/M #K35-40).*	50.00	150.	—

Kwangsi Bank

行銀西廣
Kuang Hsi Yin Hang

1904 Imperial Tael Issue

		Good	Fine	XF
S2343	**1 Tael** Yr. 30 (1904). *(S/M #K36-).*	—	—	—
S2344	**10 Taels** Yr. 30 (1904). *(S/M #K36-).*	—	—	—

1909 Imperial Issue

		Good	Fine	XF
S2345	**1 Yüan** Yr. 2 (1909). Black. Silver dollar at center. Facing dragons at left and right. *(S/M #K36-).*	—	—	—
S2346	**5 Yüan** Yr. 2 (1909). Black. 5 silver dollars at center. Facing dragons at left and right. Back: Green and black. *(S/M #K36-).*	150.	350.	1000.

1912 Military Hao Issue

		Good	Fine	XF
S2347	**1 Hao** June 1912. *(S/M #K36-).*	125.	300.	900.
S2347A	**2 Hao** June 1912. *(S/M #K36-).*	125.	300.	900.
S2347B	**5 Hao** June 1912. *(S/M #K36-).*	150.	350.	1000.

1912 Military Ch'iao Issue

		Good	Fine	XF
S2348	**10 Cents** Sept. 1912. *(S/M #K36-1).*	100.	275.	800.
S2349	**20 Cents** Sept. 1912. *(S/M #K36-1.5).*	125.	375.	1100.
S2350	**50 Cents** Sept. 1912. *(S/M #K36-2).*	125.	375.	1100.
S2351	**1 Dollar** 1912. Gray-green and purple-violet on yellow underprint. Mountain pass at left, modern building along shoreline at right. Serial # varieties. Various hand stamps in different colored inks. Back: Dark brown on pale blue underprint.			
	a. *KWEILIN. (S/M #K36-10a).*	20.00	50.00	125.
	b. *LIUCHOW. (S/M #K36-10b).*	10.00	25.00	75.00
	c. *LUNGCHOW. (S/M #K36-10c).*	7.50	20.00	50.00
	d. *NANNING.* (2 varieties for *Ning*). *(S/M #K36-10d).*	7.50	20.00	50.00
	e. *WUCHOW.* (or *Wu*). (S/M #K36-10e).	10.00	30.00	100.
	f. *WATLAM. (S/M #K36-10f).*	10.00	30.00	100.
S2352	**5 Dollars** 1912. Dark brown and orange on light blue underprint. Mountain pass at left, modern building along shoreline at right. Serial # varieties. Various hand stamps in different colored inks. Back: Orange on pale green underprint.			
	a. *KWEILIN. (S/M #K36-11a).*	25.00	75.00	200.
	b. *LIUCHOW. (S/M #K36-11b).*	25.00	75.00	200.
	c. *LUNGCHOW. (S/M #K36-11c).*	20.00	40.00	100.
	d. *NANNING. (S/M #K36-11d).*	20.00	40.00	100.
	e. *WUCHOW. (S/M #K36-11e).*	40.00	75.00	150.

		Good	Fine	XF
S2353	**10 Dollars** 1912. Green on yellow underprint. Mountain pass at left, modern building along shoreline at right. Serial # varieties. Various hand stamps in different colored inks. Back: Green.			
	a. *KWEILIN. (S/M #K36-12a).*	45.00	125.	—
	b. *LIUCHOW. (S/M #K36-12b).*	45.00	125.	—
	c. *LUNGCHOW. (S/M #K36-12c).*	45.00	125.	—
	d. *NANNING. (S/M #K36-12d).*	45.00	125.	—
	e. *WUCHOW. (S/M #K36-12e).*	45.00	125.	—

1915 Military Issue

		Good	Fine	XF
S2354	**10 Cents** 1915. Blue and red. Mountain pass at left, modern building along shoreline at right. Serial # varieties. Various hand stamps in different colored inks. Back: Orange and blue. *KWEILIN. (S/M #K36-20).*	45.00	125.	—
S2354A	**50 Cents** 1915. Green on yellow underprint. Mountain pass at left, modern building along shoreline at right. Serial # varieties. Various hand stamps in different colored inks. *(S/M #K36-22).*	50.00	125.	—

1917 Military Issue

		Good	Fine	XF
S2355	**10 Cents** 1917. Gray-green and purple-violet on yellow underprint. Mountain pass at left, modern building along shoreline at right. Serial # varieties. Various hand stamps in different colored inks. Back: Dark brown on pale blue underprint. *(S/M #K36-24).*	20.00	50.00	—

1918 Military Issue

		Good	Fine	XF
S2356	**50 Cents** 1918. *(S/M #K36-28).*	75.00	225.	—

1920 Military Issue

		Good	Fine	XF
S2357	**10 Cents** Oct. 1920. Blue and orange. Mountain pass at left, modern building along shoreline at right. Serial # varieties. Various hand stamps in different colored inks. Back: Orange and blue. *WUCHOW. (S/M #K36-30).*	20.00	75.00	225.

#S2358 *Deleted.* See #S2357.

		Good	Fine	XF
S2359	**20 Cents** 1920. Blue. Mountain pass at left, modern building along shoreline at right. Serial # varieties. Various hand stamps in different colored inks. Back: Blue. *(S/M #K36-31).*	50.00	125.	—
S2361	**50 Cents** 1920. Green on yellow underprint. Mountain pass at left, modern building along shoreline at right. Serial # varieties. Various hand stamps in different colored inks. Back: Violet. *(S/M #K36-32).*	50.00	125.	—

#S2362 *Deleted.* See #S2361.

1921 Military Issues

		Good	Fine	XF
S2363	**10 Cents** 1921. Blue and red. Back: Orange and blue. *KWEILIN. (S/M #K36-40).*	20.00	40.00	100.
S2365	**50 Cents** Feb. Yr. 10 (1921). Deep blue-green on orange underprint. Red octagonal seal: *ISSUED BY KWANGSI BANK-Tenth Year of the Republic of China.* Back: Violet on pale green underprint. Oval hand stamp with similar message as front in Chinese. *WUCHOW. (S/M #K36-41).*	15.00	35.00	—
S2366	**1 Dollar** Yr. 10 (1921 - old date Yr. 1). Red octagonal seal: *ISSUED BY KWANGSI BANK-Tenth Year of the Republic of China.* Back: Oval handstamp with similar message as front in Chinese. Overprint: On #2351e. *WUCHOW. (S/M #K36-42).*	15.00	50.00	—
S2367	**2 Dollars** 1921. *KWEILIN. (S/M #K36-44).*	125.	400.	—
S2368	**5 Dollars** 1921. Brown and orange. Back: Orange and green. *LUNGCHOW. (S/M #K36-50).*	125.	400.	—
S2369	**5 Dollars** 1921. Back: Title: *KWEILIN BANK KWEILIN. (S/M #K36-51).*	125.	400.	—

1922 Military Dollar Issues

		Good	Fine	XF
S2370	**10 Cents** 1922. Gray. *Kweilin. (S/M #K36-55).*	40.00	100.	—
S2372	**50 Cents** 1922. Green and orange. *(S/M #K36-56).*	40.00	100.	—
S2373	**1 Dollar** 1922. Green on yellow underprint. Back: Green on pink u nderprint. *(S/M #K36-57).*	40.00	100.	350.
S2374	**1 Dollar** 1922. Gray. *Kweilin. (S/M #K36-58).*	40.00	100.	350.
S2375	**2 Dollars** 1922. *Kweilin. (S/M #K36-59).* Reported not confirmed.	—	—	—

1923 Military Hao Issue

		Good	Fine	XF
S2376	**1 Hao** 1923. Blue on pink underprint. Back red. *(S/M #K36-).*	40.00	100.	225.

1936 Provincial Issue

		VG	VF	UNC
S2380	**1 Chiao** 1936. Dark blue. Building at left and right. Back: Red. Printer: HHEC. No place name. *(S/M #K36-60).*	10.00	25.00	75.00

1938 Issues

		VG	VF	UNC
S2381	**5 Chiao** 1938. Green. Bridge at left. Back: Orange and multicolor. Printer: CMPA. *(S/M #K36-70).*	15.00	30.00	100.
S2382	**5 Chiao** ND. Violet. Shoreline at right. Back: Green and multicolor. Printer: CMPA. *(S/M #K36-80).*	40.00	100.	225.

Kwangtung Currency Bureau

局錢東廣
Kuang Tung Ch'ien Chü

1904 Issue

		Good	Fine	XF
S2385	**1 Dollar** Yr. 30 (1904). Black on ochre underprint. Back: Pale brown-orange. Black text. Printer: PYOG. *(S/M #K51-1).*	275.	750.	—

1905 Issue

		Good	Fine	XF
S2388	**1 Dollar** Yr. 31 (1905). Black on pale green. Back: Grayish purple. *(S/M #K51-20).*	350.	1000.	—

1907 Issue

		Good	Fine	XF
S2389	**1 Dollar** Yr. 33 (1907). Black. Dragon dollar coins not touching frame at left or right. Solid frame below house at bottom center. Back: Yellow-orange. Rectangular frame, black text and three vertical rectangular hand stamps. Printer: PYOG. *(S/M #K51-).*	275.	750.	—
S2390	**5 Dollars** Yr. 33 (1907). Black. Dragon dollar coins not touching frame at left or right. Solid frame below house at bottom center. Back: Light green. Rectangular frame, black text and three vertical rectangular hand stamps. Printer: PYOG. *(S/M #K51-).*	200.	600.	—
S2391	**10 Dollars** Yr. 33 (1907). Black. Dragon dollar coins not touching frame at left or right. Solid frame below house at bottom center. Back: Red. Rectangular frame, black text and three vertical rectangular hand stamps. Printer: PYOG. *(S/M #K51-).*	500.	1500.	—

TYPE II

	Good	Fine	XF
S2392 1 Dollar			
Yr. 33 (1907). Black. Dragon dollar coins touch frame at left and right with broken frame below house at bottom center. Back: Text between scrollwork and ornate denominations; red seal with black signature at lower right. Printer: JIPB. *(S/M #K51-20a).*	275.	750.	—
S2393 5 Dollars			
Yr. 33 (1907). Black. Dragon dollar coins touch frame at left and right with broken frame below house at bottom center. Back: Text between scrollwork and ornate denominations; red seal with black signature at lower right. Printer: JIPB. *(S/M #K51-).*	300.	900.	—
S2394 10 Dollars			
Yr. 33 (1907). Black. Dragon dollar coins touch frame at left and right with broken frame below house at bottom center. Back: Text between scrollwork and ornate denominations; red seal with black signature at lower right. Printer: JIPB. *(S/M #K51-).*	500.	1500.	—

S#2392 & S2394 with additional large seal overprint are reported as a military reissue ca. 1911.

Provincial Bank of Kwangtung Province

行銀省東廣

Kuang Tung Sheng Yin Hang Tui Huan Ch'üan

1913 Exchange Notes Issue

	Good	Fine	XF
S2395 50 Cents			
1913. Printer: ABNC. *Canton. (S/M #K55-1).*	100.	275.	—
S2396 1 Dollar			
1913. Green and multicolor. Back: Red. Printer: ABNC. *Canton. (S/M #K55-10).*	150.	450.	—
S2397 2 Dollars			
1913. Printer: ABNC. *Canton. (S/M #K55-11)*	175.	500.	—
S2398 5 Dollars			
1.1.1913. Dark green on multicolor underprint. Large Building at center. Printer: ABNC. *Canton. (S/M #K55-12).*			
a. Issued note.	200.	600.	—
b. Punched hole cancelled.	125.	300.	—
p. Proof.	—	Unc	1250.
s. Specimen.	—	Unc	750.
S2399 10 Dollars			
1.1.1913. *Canton. (S/M #K55-13).*			
p. Proof.	—	Unc	1500.
s. Specimen.	—	Unc	1250.

NOTE: For #S2398 and S2399 with additional overprint, see Bank of China #29 and 29A, Vol. 2.

	Good	Fine	XF
S2401 1 Dollar			
1.1.1918. Dark blue on multicolor underprint. Pagoda at center. *CANTON.* Back: Dark green. Printer. ABNC.			
a. 2 red signature seals at left. Large black signature at right. without signature title. *(S/M #K55-20).*	10.00	25.00	75.00
b. 2 red signature seals at left, signature title: *GEN. MANAGER* at right. *(S/M #K55-20d).*	10.00	25.00	75.00
c. English signature 25mm square blue overprint at center. *(S/M #K55-20).*	7.50	20.00	50.00
d. Signature titles: *CASHIER* and *MANAGING DIRECTOR* below English Signature. *(S/M #K55-20a).*	7.50	20.00	50.00
e. *Sheng Li* at top center English signature without titles. *(S/M #K55-20b.).*	2.50	5.00	15.00
f. Large red hexagonal seal at left, black overprint with pagoda at center and with additional 5 digit serial #. *(S/M #K55-20).*	25.00	75.00	175.
g. Like e., but without 5 digit serial #. *(S/M #K55-20c).*	10.00	25.00	75.00
p. Proof.	—	Unc	300.
s. Specimen.	—	Unc	400.

NOTE: For #S2401 with overprint of 6 character new bank name see #469, Vol. 2.

1918 Exchange Notes Issue

	Good	Fine	XF
S2402 5 Dollars			
1.1.1918. Orange on multicolor underprint. Large building at center, *Sheng Li* at top center. *CANTON.* Back: Purple. Printer: ABNC.			
a. Signature titles: *CASHIER* and *MANAGING DIRECTOR* below English Signature. *(S/M #K55-21a).*	7.50	15.00	40.00
b. English signature without titles. *(S/M #K55-21b).*	5.00	10.00	25.00
c. Large red seal at left, Large black overprint with pagoda at center with additional 5 digit serial #. *(S/M #K55-21).*	15.00	40.00	100.
d. Like c, but without 5 digit serial #. *(S/M #K55-21c).*	7.50	15.00	45.00
p. Proof.	—	Unc	300.
s. Specimen.	—	Unc	400.
S2403 10 Dollars			
1.1.1918. Dark green on multicolor underprint. Theatre at center. *Sheng Li* at left and right of bank name. *CANTON.* Back: Orange. Printer: ABNC.			
a. Signature titles: *CASHIER and MANAGING DIRECTOR below English Signature, Large 7 in date. (S/M #K55-22a).*	10.00	20.00	50.00
b. Like a., but with small *7* in date. *(S/M #K55-22a).*	10.00	20.00	50.00
c. English signature without titles,. Large *7* in date. *(S/M #K55-22b).*	5.00	10.00	30.00
d. English signature without titles., small *7* in date. *(S/M #K55-22b).*	5.00	10.00	30.00
e. *Swatow*with *CANTON. (S/M #K55-22).*	40.00	100.	225.
f. Large red seal at left, Large black overprint with pagoda at center, small *7* in date, with additional 5 digit serial #. *(S/M #K55-22).*	40.00	100.	225.
g. Like f., but small *7* in date. *(S/M #K55-22).*	40.00	100.	225.
h. Like f., but without 5 digit serial #. *(S/M #K55-22c).*	20.00	40.00	100.
i. Like g., but without 5 digit serial #. *(S/M #K55-22c).*	20.00	40.00	100.
p. Proof.	—	Unc	300.
s. Specimen.	—	Unc	400.

	Good	Fine	XF
S2404 50 Dollars			
1.1.1918. Dark brown on multicolor underprint. Pavilion, pool at center. *Sheng Li* at top center. *CANTON.* Back: Olive-green. Printer: ABNC.			
a. Signature titles: *CASHIER* and *MANAGING DIRECTOR* below printed black English Signature *(S/M #K55-23a).*	10.00	20.00	60.00
b. Like a., but signature at left handwritten in various colors. *(S/M #K55-23a).*	10.00	20.00	60.00
c. English signature without titles. *(S/M #K55-23b).*	5.00	10.00	25.00
d. Like c., but signature at left handwritten in various colors. *(S/M #K55-).*	20.00	40.00	100.
e. Large red seal at left, Large black overprint with pagoda at center, with additional 5 digit serial #. *(S/M #K55-23).*	40.00	100.	225.
f. Like e., but without 5 digit serial #. *(S/M #K55-23).*	30.00	75.00	200.
s. Specimen.	—	Unc	400.
S2405 100 Dollars			
1.1.1918. Olive-green on multicolor underprint. University at center. *CANTON.* Back: Blue-black. Printer: ABNC.			
a. Signature titles: *CASHIER* and *MANAGING DIRECTOR* below printed black English Signature *(S/M #K55-24a).*	15.00	40.00	100.
b. Like a., but signature at right handwritten in various colors. *(S/M #K55-24a).*	20.00	40.00	100.
c. Printed English signature without titles. *(S/M #K55-24b).*	7.50	20.00	40.00
d. English signature without titles, but signature at right handwritten. *(S/M #K55-24b).*	7.50	40.00	100.
e. Large red seal at left, Large black overprint with pagoda at center, with additional 5 digit serial #. *(S/M #K55-24).*	40.00	100.	225.
f. Like e., but without 5 digit serial #. *(S/M #K55-24).*	25.00	50.00	125.
p. Proof.	—	Unc	300.
s. Specimen.	—	Unc	400.

NOTE: Modern forged signature titles of #S2401-S2405 exist.

1922 Exchange Notes Issue

	Good	Fine	XF
S2407 20 Cents			
1.1.1922. Black. Tunnel at left. Back: Blue and multicolor. Printer: ABNC. *(S/M #K55-30).*			
a. Issued note.	2.50	5.00	15.00
s. Specimen.	—	Unc	400.
S2408 50 Cents			
1.1.1922. Orange. Large building at center. Back: Green. Printer: ABNC. *(S/M #K55-31).*			
a. Issued note.	2.50	5.00	15.00
s. Specimen.	—	Unc	400.

Kwangtung Provincial Bank

行銀省東廣

Kuang Tung Sheng Yin Hang

1931 National Currency Issue

	Good	Fine	XF
S2411 1 Dollar			
1931. Blue-gray on multicolor underprint. SYS at center. Back: Blue. Bank building at center. Printer: ABNC.			
a. Signature A-B. *(S/M #K56-2a).*	25.00	50.00	150.
b. *HAIKOW. (S/M #K56-2b).*	75.00	150.	450.
c. *SWATOW. (S/M #K56-2c).*	75.00	150.	450.
S2414 5 Dollars			
1931. Green on multicolor underprint. SYS at center. Back: Green. Bank building at center. Printer: ABNC.			
a. Signature A-B. *(S/M #K56-11a).*	40.00	100.	300.
b. *SWATOW. (S/M #K56-11b).*	75.00	150.	450.
c. Signature D-E-F. *(S/M #K56-11c).*	40.00	100.	300.
d. *HAIKOW. (S/M #K56-11d).*	100.	200.	600.
S2417 10 Silver Yüan			
1931. Red-brown on multicolor underprint. Signature A-B. SYS at center. Back: Red-brown. Bank building at center. Printer: ABNC. *(S/M #K56-).*	75.00	150.	500.

1931 Local Currency Issue

		VG	VF	UNC
S2421	**1 Dollar**			
	1931. Orange on multicolor underprint. SYS at right. Back: Olive. Bank building at center. Printer: ABNC.			
	a. Signature A-B. *(S/M #K56-1a).*	.50	2.50	7.50
	b. Signature C-B. *(S/M #K56-1b).*	.50	2.50	7.50
	c. Signature D-E. *(S/M #K56-1c).*	.50	2.50	7.50
	d. Signature D-E-F. *(S/M #K56-1d).*	.50	2.50	7.50
	e. *SWATOW.* signature G-B. *(S/M #K56-1e).*	15.00	40.00	100.
	f. *PAK HOI.* signature G-B. *(S/M #K56-1f).*	20.00	50.00	125.
S2422	**5 Dollars**			
	1931. Green on multicolor underprint. SYS at right. Back: Orange. Bank building at center. Printer: ABNC.			
	a. Signature A-B. *(S/M #K56-10a).*	.50	2.50	7.50
	b. Signature C-B. *(S/M #K56-10b).*	.50	2.50	7.50
	c. Signature D-E. *(S/M #K56-10c).* Reported not confirmed.	20.00	50.00	125.
	d. Signature D-E-F. *(S/M #K56-10d).*	.50	2.50	7.50
	e. *SWATOW. (S/M #K56-10e).*	15.00	45.00	100.
	f. *PAK HOI. (S/M #K56-10f).*	20.00	50.00	125.
S2423	**10 Dollars**			
	1931. Red on multicolor underprint. SYS at right. Back: Brown. Bank building at center. Printer: ABNC.			
	a. Signature A-B. *(S/M #K56-14a).*	5.00	10.00	30.00
	b. Signature C-B. *(S/M #K56-14b).*	5.00	10.00	30.00
	c. Signature D-E. *(S/M #K56-14c).* Reported not confirmed.	25.00	50.00	125.
	d. Signature D-E.F. *(S/M #K56-14d).*	5.00	10.00	30.00
	e. *Nan Hsiung. (S/M #K56-14e).*	25.00	100.	225.
	f. *SWATOW. (S/M #K56-14).*	20.00	60.00	100.
	g. *PAK HOI (S/M #K56-14-).*	20.00	60.00	100.
S2424	**100 Dollars**			
	1931. Olive-brown on multicolor underprint. SYS at right. Signature A-B. Back: Blue. Bank building at center. Printer: ABNC. *(S/M #K56-17).*	40.00	75.00	225.

1931 Provisional Issues

#S2425-S2429 overprint: *LOCAL CURRENCY* on National currency issue.

		VG	VF	UNC
S2425	**1 Dollar**			
	1931. Brown and multicolor. Back: Brown. Overprint: *LOCAL CURRENCY.*			
	a. Signature D-E-F. *(S/M #K56-3b).*	2.00	5.00	10.00
	b. Black overprint signature D-E-F. *(S/M #K56-4b).*	2.00	5.00	10.00
	c. Signature A-B. *(S/M #K56-4).*	2.00	5.00	10.00
	d. As c. *Nan Hsiung blocked out at lower left and right. (S/M #K56-6).*	25.00	75.00	225.
S2426	**5 Dollars**			
	1931. Red and multicolor. Signature D-E-F. Back: Red. Overprint: *LOCAL CURRENCY. (S/M #K56-12b).*	2.50	10.00	25.00
S2427	**5 Dollars**			
	1931. Dark blue and multicolor. Signature A-B. Back: Blue. Overprint: *LOCAL CURRENCY. (S/M #K56-13b).*			
	a. Issued note.	2.50	10.00	25.00
	b. *Nan Hsiung* blocked out at lower left and right. *(S/M #K56-13).*	15.00	45.00	125.
S2428	**10 Dollars**			
	1931. Violet and multicolor. Signature A-B. Back: Violet. Overprint: *LOCAL CURRENCY. (S/M #K56-15b).*	7.50	20.00	50.00
S2429	**10 Dollars**			
	1931. Green and multicolor. Signature A-B. Back: Green. Overprint: *LOCAL CURRENCY.*			
	a. Signature D-E-F. *(S/M #K56-16b).*	5.00	15.00	40.00
	b. Black overprint signature D-E-F. *(S/M #K56-16b).*	5.00	10.00	30.00

1932 Issue

		VG	VF	UNC
S2429A	**10 Cents**			
	1932. Brown. SYS at left. Back: Pagoda at center. *Haikow* at left and right in frame. *(S/M #K56-18).*	15.00	45.00	100.
S2430	**20 Cents**			
	1932. Brown. SYS at left. Back: Pagoda at center. *Haikow* at left and right in frame. *(S/M #K56-19).*	20.00	50.00	125.

1934 Issue

		VG	VF	UNC
S2431	**10 Cents**			
	1934. Red. Shoreline, sampan at left. Printer: HHEC.			
	a. Without place name. *(S/M #K56-20a).*	2.50	5.00	10.00
	b. *PAK HOI. (S/M #K56-20b).*	5.00	10.00	30.00
	c. *Swatow. (S/M #K56-20).*	5.00	10.00	30.00
S2432	**50 Cents**			
	1934. Blue. Back: Red-violet. Printer: HHEC. *(S/M #K56-21).*	5.00	10.00	30.00

1935 National/Foreign Currency Issue

		VG	VF	UNC
S2433	**10 Cents**			
	1935. Brown. SYS at left with *Ta Yang* (foreign or Mexican coins) at left and right in frame. Back: Pagoda at center. Printer: HKPA. *(S/M #K56-29).*	50.00	100.	250.
S2434	**20 Cents**			
	1935. Brown and violet. SYS at left with *Ta Yang* (foreign or Mexican coins) at left and right in frame. Back: Brown and green. Pagoda at center. Printer: HKPA. *(S/M #K56-31).*	75.00	150.	350.

1935 Local Currency Issue

		VG	VF	UNC
S2436	**10 Cents**			
	1935. Red on multicolor underprint. SYS at right. Back: Junk (sampan) in harbor at center. Printer: ABNC.			
	a. Without place name. *(S/M #K56-30a).*	2.50	5.00	10.00
	b. *PAK HOI. (S/M #K56-30b).*	5.00	10.00	35.00
	c. *SWATOW. (S/M #K56-30c).*	5.00	10.00	35.00
	p. As a. Proof.	—	Unc	300.
	s1. As a. Specimen.	—	Unc	400.
	s2. As b. Specimen.	—	Unc	400.
	s3. As c. Specimen.	—	Unc	400.
S2437	**20 Cents**			
	1935. Green on multicolor underprint. SYS at right. Back: Green. Junk (sampan) in harbor at center. Printer: ABNC.			
	a. Without place name, black signature *(S/M #K56-32a).*	2.50	5.00	15.00
	b. Green signature *(S/M #K56-32a).*	1.00	2.50	7.50
	c. *PAK HOI. (S/M #K56-32b).*	5.00	10.00	30.00
	d. *SWATOW. (S/M #K56-32).*	5.00	10.00	30.00
	p1. As a. Proof.	—	Unc	300.
	p2. As b. Proof.	—	Unc	300.
	s1. As a. Specimen.	—	Unc	400.
	s2. As b. Specimen.	—	Unc	400.
	s3. As c. Specimen.	—	Unc	400.
	s4. As d. Specimen.	—	Unc	400.
	s5. Brown Chinese character overprint. Specimen.	—	Unc	600.
	s6. Without signature. Specimen.	—	Unc	400.
S2438	**50 Cents**			
	1935. Blue on multicolor underprint. SYS at right. Back: Blue. Junk (sampan) in harbor at center. Printer: ABNC. *(S/M #K56-33).*			
	a. Issued note.	5.00	10.00	30.00
	p. Without signature Proof.	—	Unc	300.
	s. Without signature Specimen.	—	Unc	400.

1936 National Currency Issue

		VG	VF	UNC
S2440	**20 Cents**			
	1936. Blue and multicolor. Memorial building at center. Back: Blue and brown. Printer: CHB.			
	a. Signature A-B. *(S/M #K56-40).*	20.00	50.00	150.
	b. Signature D-E-F. *(S/M #K56-40).*	20.00	50.00	150.

1936 Local Currency Issue

		VG	VF	UNC
S2442	**1 Dollar**			
	ND (1936). Red and green. Shoreline at right. Back: Green. Printer: CHB. *(S/M #K56-50).*	7.50	20.00	50.00

		VG	VF	UNC
S2443	**5 Dollars**			
	ND (1936). Green and tan. Shoreline at center. Back: Green. Printer: CHB. *(S/M #K56-51).*	7.50	20.00	50.00

1939 Hainan Island District Issue

#S2446 and S2447 issued during the Japanese occupation of Hainan Island.

		VG	VF	UNC
S2446	**20 Cents**			
	1939. Blue and multicolor. Back: Red. *(S/M #K56-60).*	75.00	125.	300.
S2447	**1 Dollar**			
	1939. Red. SYS at right, SYS Memorial building in Canton at center. Back: Blue and green. *(S/M #K56-70).*			
	a. Issued note.	75.00	125.	300.
	s. Specimen with signature	—	Unc	400.

1940 Issue

#S2449 and S2450 issued during the Japanese occupation.

	VG	VF	UNC
S2449 1 Dollar 1940. Red. SYS at right, SYS Memorial building in Canton at center. Back: Blue and green. *(S/M #K56-80).*			
a. Signature 1.	50.00	125.	350.
b. Signature 2.	50.00	125.	350.
r. Remainder.	—	Unc	100.
s. Specimen without signature.	—	Unc	400.
S2450 5 Dollars 1940. Orange. SYS at right, Memorial to Canton martyrs at left. Back: Green. *(S/M #K56-81).*			
a. Signature 1.	125.	375.	1000.
b. Signature 2.	125.	375.	1000.

1949 Issue

	VG	VF	UNC
S2452 1 Cent 1949. Red. SYS at left. Uniface. Printer: CHB. *(S/M #K57-1).*	1.00	2.50	7.50
S2453 5 Cents 1949. Violet and green. SYS at left. Uniface. Printer: CHB. *(S/M #K57-2).*	1.00	2.00	5.00
S2454 10 Cents 1949. Violet and brown. SYS at center. Back: Brown. Government building at center. Printer: CHB. *(S/M #K57-3).*	1.00	2.00	5.00
S2455 50 Cents 1949. Brown and blue. SYS at center. Back: Blue. Government building at center. Printer: CHB. *(S/M #K57-4).*	1.00	2.00	5.00
S2456 1 Yüan 1949. Blue and green. SYS at left. Uniface. Back: Blue. Government building at center. Printer: CHB. *(S/M #K57-10).*	1.00	2.50	7.50

	VG	VF	UNC
S2457 5 Yüan 1949. Green. SYS at left. Back: Government building at center. Printer: CHB. *(S/M #K57-11).*	1.00	2.50	7.50

	VG	VF	UNC
S2458 10 Yüan 1949. Violet. SYS at left. Back: Government building at center. Printer: CHB. *(S/M #K57-12).*	1.00	3.00	10.00

	VG	VF	UNC
S2459 100 Yüan 1949. Red. SYS at left. Back: Government building at center. Printer: CHB. *(S/M #K57-13).*	2.50	10.00	40.00

Kweichow Provincial Government General Treasury

貴州省政府總金庫

Kuei Chou Sheng Cheng Fu Tsung Chin K'u

1930 Issue

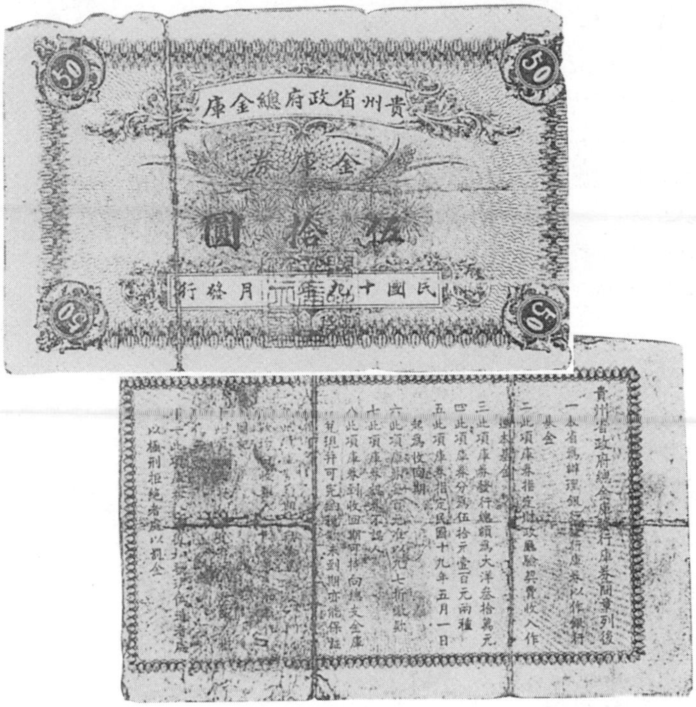

	VG	VF	UNC
S2460 50 Yüan 1930. *(S/M #K70.5-11).*	100.	250.	750.
S2460A 100 Dollars 1930. *(S/M #K70.5-12).*	100.	250.	750.

1932 Issue

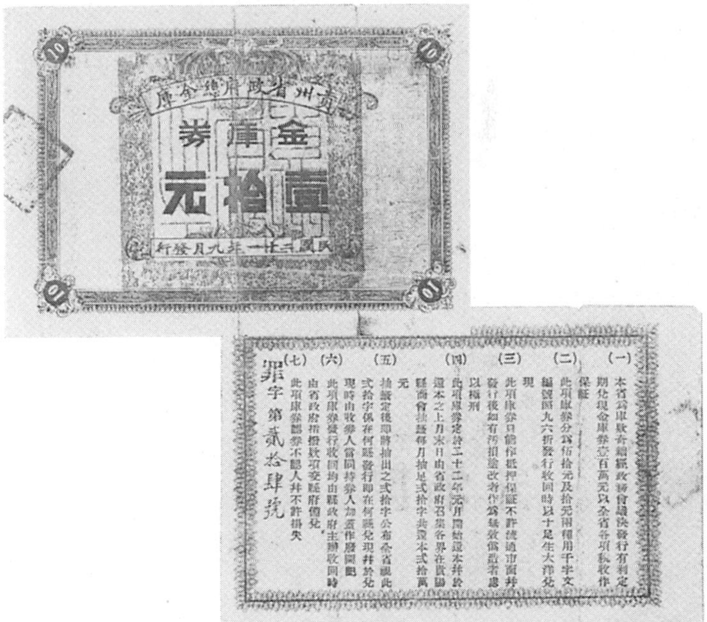

	VG	VF	UNC
S2460B 10 Yüan 1932. *(S/M #K70.5-15).*	100.	250.	750.
S2460C 50 Yüan 1932. *(S/M #K70.5-16).*	100.	250.	750.

Provincial Bank of Kweichow

貴州省銀行
Kuei Chou Sheng Yin Hang

1949 Issue

	VG	VF	UNC
S2461 1 Cent 1949. Orange. Back: Modern building at center. Printer: CPFA. *(S/M #K71-1).*	5.00	10.00	25.00
S2462 5 Cents 1949. Green and multicolor. Back: Green. Modern building at center. Printer: CPFA. *(S/M #K71-2).*	10.00	25.00	50.00

	VG	VF	UNC
S2463 10 Cents 1949. Red and blue. Back: Red. Modern building at center. Printer: CPFA. *(S/M #K71-3).*	10.00	25.00	50.00

Kweichow Bank
Kueichow Bank
Bank of Kweichow

貴州銀行
Kuei Chou Yin Hang

1912 Issue

	Good	Fine	XF
S2465 10 Cents 1912. Green. Birds of Paradise facing at upper left and right. Back: Yellow. Printer: WTBC. *(S/M #K72-1).*	40.00	125.	—
S2466 20 Cents 1912. Green. Bird of Paradise facing at upper left and right. Back: Yellow. Printer: WTBC. *(S/M #K72-2).*	40.00	125.	—
S2467 50 Cents 1912. Green. Birds of Paradise facing at upper left and right. Back: Brown. Printer: WTBC. *(S/M #K72-3).*	50.00	150.	—

	Good	Fine	XF
S2468 1 Yüan 1912. Blue, black and yellow. Birds of Paradise facing at upper left and right.			
a. Serial #. *(S/M #K72-10a).*	20.00	75.00	—
b. Without serial #. *(S/M #K72-10b).*	—	Unc	225.

	Good	Fine	XF
S2469 5 Yüan 1912. Blue and multicolor. Birds of Paradise facing at upper left and right. Back: Orange. Printer: WTBC. *(S/M #K72-11).*	75.00	225.	—
S2470 10 Yüan 1912. Green and multicolor. Birds of Paradise facing at upper left and right. Back: Green. Printer: WTBC. *(S/M #K72-12).*	75.00	225.	—

1918 Issue

	Good	Fine	XF
S2471 10 Cents 1918. Green. *(S/M #K72-20).*	50.00	150.	—
S2472 20 Cents 1918. Blue. *(S/M #K72-21).*	75.00	225.	—
S2473 50 Cents 1918. Brown. Back: Yellow. *(S/M #K72-22).*	50.00	150.	—

1922 Issue

	Good	Fine	XF
S2474 1 Yüan 1.11.1922. Blue and green. Peacocks facing at center. Back: Green. *(S/M #K72-30).*	75.00	225.	—

1925 ND Issue

	Good	Fine	XF
S2477 10 Cents ND (1925). Green. Temple at right. Back: Modern building complex, shoreline. *(S/M #K72-40).*	50.00	150.	—
S2478 20 Cents ND (1925). Blue. *(S/M #K72-41).*	50.00	150.	—
S2479 50 Cents ND (1925). Brown. Temple at right. Back: Modern building complex, shoreline. *(S/M #K72-).*	75.00	225.	—

	Good	Fine	XF
S2480 1 Yüan ND (1925). Blue and multicolor. Buildings at left and right. Back: Blue and red. *(S/M #K72-42).*	75.00	225.	—
S2482 10 Yüan ND (1925). Green. Pavilion, bridge at center. Back: Yellow-green. Rural scenes at left and right. *(S/M #K72-44).*	75.00	225.	—

1930 Issue

	Good	Fine	XF
S2483 50 Cents 1930. Building, trees at left. Back: Building, bridge at center. *(S/M #K72-50).*	75.00	225.	—
S2484 1 Dollar 1930. Green. Back: Blue. *(S/M #K72-60).*	75.00	225.	—

#S2485 *Deleted.* See #S2482.

#S2486 and S2487 *Deleted.* (local issue).

Ninghsia Provincial Bank

行銀省夏寧

Ning Hsia Sheng Yin Hang

1942 Issue

	Good	Fine	XF
S2488 10 Cents 1942. Red. Back: Violet. Printer: BEPP. *(S/M #N16-1).*	50.00	150.	—

	Good	Fine	XF
S2489 20 Cents 1942. Green. Printer: BEPP. *(S/M #N16-2).*	75.00	225.	—

Hunan Pao Hsing Mineral Bank
Hunan Pow Shing Mining Bank

行銀業鑛興寶

(Hunan) Pao Hsing Kuang Yeh Yin Hang

1912 Issue

	Good	Fine	XF
S2489A 50 Coppers 1912. Black on yellow underprint. Back: Blue and brown.	75.00	225.	600.
S2489F 50 Coppers 1.1.1912. Black on pale green and pale yellow-orange underprint. Ornate frame with flowers, fish, urns. Oval city view at center. Back: Floral design. *S/M #P10-0.4).*	150.	400.	—
S2490 100 Coppers 1.1.1912. *(S/M #P10-0.5)*	—	—	—

	Good	Fine	XF
S2490A 1 Dollar 1.1.1912. *(S/M #P10-0.7).* (Not issued).	—	—	—

1912 Tael Issues

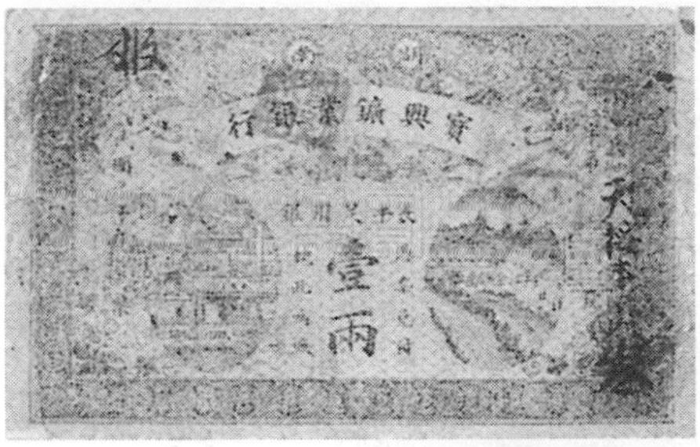

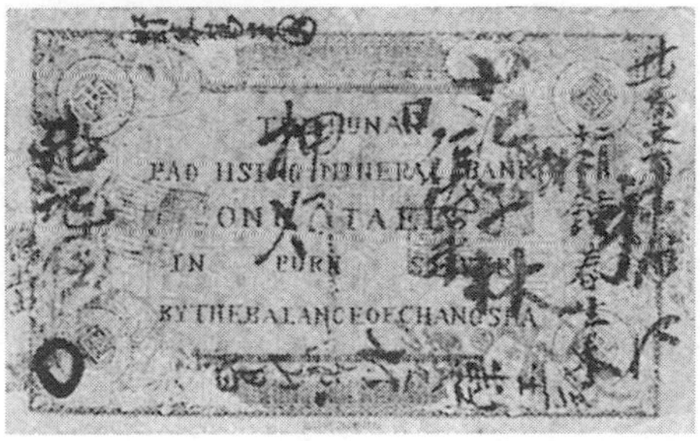

	Good	Fine	XF
S2490B 1 Tael 1912. Black on tan underprint. Buildings at left, rural scene at right. Back: Blue on yellow underprint. *Changsha. (S/M #P10-1).*	200.	600.	—
S2490C 3 Taels 1912. Buildings at left, rural scene at right. *Changsha. (S/M #P10-2).*	200.	600.	—
S2490D 5 Taels 1912. Buildings at left, rural scene at right. *Changsha. (S/M #P10-3).*	400.	1000.	—
S2490E 10 Taels 1912. Black on ochre underprint. Buildings at left, rural scene at right. Back: Blue on red underprint. *Changsha. (S/M #P10-4).*	400.	1000.	—
S2490G 10 Taels 1912. Two flags above hemisphere at center. Back: Buildings at mine at center. *(S/M #P10-15).*	500.	1250.	—

Altai District

阿爾泰通用銀券
O Erh T'ai T'ung Yung Yin Ch'uan

1918 Current Silver Note Issue

		Good	Fine	XF
S2490J 1 Yüan	1918. Gray-violet. Horse drawn wagon with people at center. Back: Green. *(S/M #03-1)*.	100.	225.	—
S2490K 5 Yüan	1918. Olive-green. Horse drawn wagon with people at center. Back: Orange. *(S/M #03-2)*.	150.	400.	—
S2490L 10 Yüan	1918. Orange. Horse drawn wagon with people at center. Back: Blue. *(S/M #03-3)*.	250.	750.	—

Peiping Municipal Bank

北平市銀行
Pei P'ing Shih Yin Hang

1936 Issue

		VG	VF	UNC
S2491 20 Coppers	1936. Brown. Printer: BEPP. Specimen. *(S/M #P27-1)*.	—	—	350.
S2492 25 Coppers	1936. Blue. Back: Pagoda at center. Printer: BEPP. Specimen. *(S/M #P27-2)*.	—	—	350.

		VG	VF	UNC
S2495 20 Cents	1936. Brown. Back: Brown and red. Printer: BEPP. Specimen. *(S/M #P27-10)*.	—	—	350.
S2497 1 Yüan	1936. Green and yellow. Shoreline, tower at center. Back: Green. Printer: BEPP. Specimen. *(S/M #P27-20)*.	—	—	350.
S2498 5 Yüan	1936. Orange. Printer: BEPP. Specimen. *(S/M #P27-21)*.	—	—	350.

1937 Issue

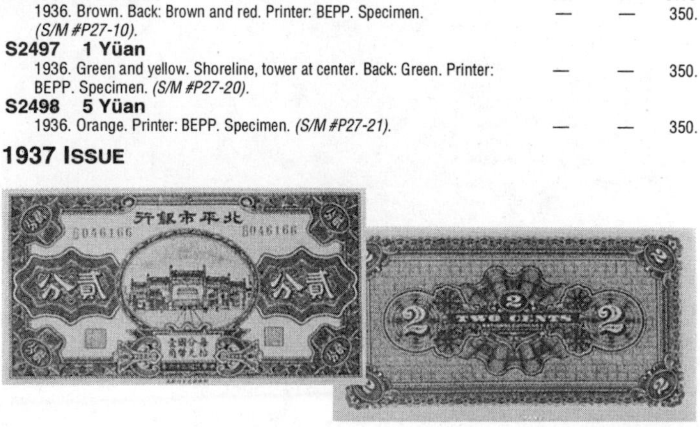

		VG	VF	UNC
S2501 2 Cents	1937. Gateway at center. Printer: BEPP. *(S/M #P27-)*.			
	a. Issued note.	100.	225.	400.
	s. Specimen.	—	—	350.

Pei-Yang Kin-Fu Bank

北洋經武銀號
Pei Yang Ching Wu Yin Hao

1906 Issue

		Good	Fine	XF
S2505 3 Taels	CD 1906. Vertical format. Printer: BWC. Specimen. *(S/M #-)*.	—	Unc	1250.

NOTE: See also #S2521.

Commercial Guarantee Bank of Chihli

北洋保商銀行
Pei Yang Pao Shang Yin Hang

ND Issue

		Good	Fine	XF
S2509 5 Dollars	ND. Black and red. Back: Red and green. Ship at lower left, lighthouse at bottom center, steam train at lower right. Remainder. *(S/M #P33-1)*.	125.	275.	750.

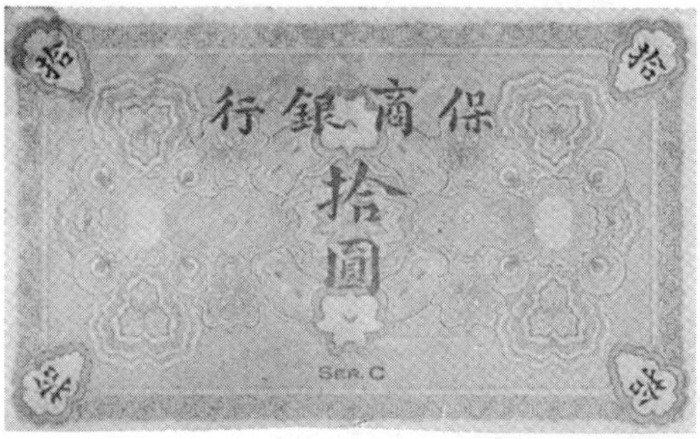

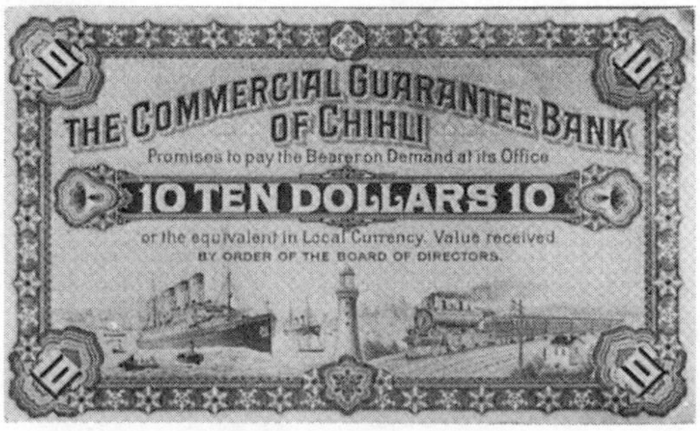

		Good	Fine	XF
S2510 10 Dollars	ND. Black and blue. Ship at lower left, lighthouse at bottom center, steam train at lower right. Back: Blue and red. Remainder. *(S/M #P33-2)*.	200.	450.	1250.

1908-11 Issue

		Good	Fine	XF
S2510A	**1 Dollar** (ca.1908-11). Green. Back: Orange. Remainder. *(S/M #P33-).*	150.	400.	900.

		Good	Fine	XF
S2511	**5 Dollars** (ca.1908-11). Brown and multicolor. Back: Orange and green. Remainder. *(S/M #P33-3).*	150.	400.	900.
S2512	**10 Silver Yüan** (ca.1908-11). Brown. Back: Orange. Remainder. *(S/M #P33-4).*	200.	500.	1500.
S2512A	**50 Dollars** (ca.1908-11). Violet. Back: Green and red. Remainder. *(S/M#P33-).*	225.	600.	1750.

		Good	Fine	XF
S2513	**100 Dollars** (ca.1908-11). Green and multicolor. Back: Green and red. Specimen. *(S/M #P33-5).*	—	Unc	2500.

1912 Issue

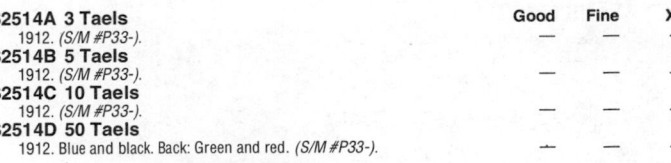

		Good	Fine	XF
S2514	**1 Tael** 1912. *(S/M #P33-).*	—	—	—
S2514A	**3 Taels** 1912. *(S/M #P33-).*	—	—	—
S2514B	**5 Taels** 1912. *(S/M #P33-).*	—	—	—
S2514C	**10 Taels** 1912. *(S/M #P33-).*	—	—	—
S2514D	**50 Taels** 1912. Blue and black. Back: Green and red. *(S/M #P33-).*	—	—	—

		Good	Fine	XF
S2514E	**100 Taels** 1912. Vertical format. *(S/M #P33-).*	—	—	—
S2514F	**500 Taels** 1912. Yellow and multicolor. Back: Brown and green. Specimen. *(S/M #P33-).*	—	—	—

1919 Issue

S2515 1 Dollar — Good / Fine / XF

1.1.1919. Purple on multicolor underprint. Bank building at left without place name. Printer: ABNC.

	Good	Fine	XF
a. *Peiping. (S/M #P33-9a).*	150.	450.	—
b. *Tientsin (S/M #P33-9b).*	150.	450.	—
p. Proof.	—	Unc	350.

S2515A 5 Dollars — Good / Fine / XF

1.1.1919. Violet on multicolor underprint. Bank building at right. Back: Violet. Printer: ABNC.

	Good	Fine	XF
a. *PEIPING. (S/M #P33-10a).*	75.00	225.	—
b. With additional numerical overprint: *3-5; 13. (S/M #P33-10b).*	75.00	225.	—
c. *TIENTSIN.* with additional numerical overprint: *21. (S/M #P33-10c).*	75.00	225.	—

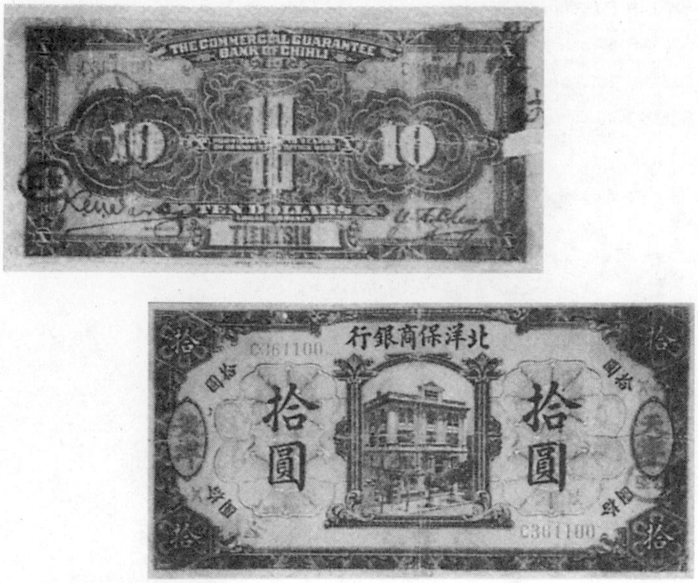

S2516 10 Dollars	Good	Fine	XF
1.1.1919. Green on multicolor underprint. Back: Green. Printer: ABNC.			
a. *PEIPING. (S/M #P33-11a).*	125.	375.	—
b. As a. with additional numerical overprint: *7; 13. (S/M #P33-11b).*	125.	375.	—
c. *TIENTSIN. (S/M #P33-11c).*	125.	375.	—

S2516A 5 Dollars	Good	Fine	XF
1.1.1919. Green on multicolor underprint. Similar to #S2516 but with different guilloche. Back: Green. Printer: ABNC.			
a. Issued note.	100.	300.	—
p. Proof. without place name. *(S/M #P33-11.5).*	—	Unc	350.

S2517A 10 Dollars			
1.1.1919. Similar to #S2516 but with different guilloche. Without place name. Printer: ABNC. Proof. *(S/M #P33-12).*	—	Unc	400.

1933 Issue

S2518 1 Dollar	Good	Fine	XF
1.7.1933. Lilac and multicolor. Great Wall at left and right. Back: Brown. Printer: W&S.			
a. *PEIPING.* Large signature *(S/M #P33-20a).*	30.00	100.	—
b. *PEIPING.* Large signature with additional numerical overprint: *55-88,* etc. *(S/M #P33-20c).*	30.00	100.	—
c. *PEIPING.* Small signature *S/M #P33-20b).*	30.00	100.	—
d. *PEIPING.* Small signature with additional numerical overprint: *55-88,* etc. *(S/M #P33-20d).*	30.00	100.	—
e. *TIENTSIN.* Large signature *(S/M #P33-20e).*	30.00	100.	—
f. *TIENTSIN.* Large signature with additional numerical overprint: *55-88,* etc. *(S/M #P33-20f).*	30.00	100.	—
g. *TIENTSIN.* Small signature *(S/M #P33-20g).*	30.00	100.	—
h. *TIENTSIN.* Small signature with additional numerical overprint: *55-88,* etc. *(S/M #P33-20h).*	30.00	100.	—

Peiyang Tientsin Bank

北洋天津銀行
Pei Yang T'ien Ching Yin Hao

1910 Tael Issue

S2521 1 Tael	VG	VF	UNC
(ca. 1910). Multicolor. Dragons facing above portrait. Li Hung Chan with harbor view at bottom. Back: Blue and orange. Remainder. *(S/M #P35-1).*	75.00	225.	750.

S2522 3 Taels	VG	VF	UNC
(ca. 1910). Dragons facing above portrait. Li Hung Chan with harbor view at bottom. Vertical format. Back: Red and green. Remainder. *(S/M #P35-2).*	—	200.	900.

NOTE: See also #S2505.

S2523 5 Taels			
(ca. 1910). Dragons facing above portrait. Li Hung Chan with harbor view at bottom. Back: Red and green. Remainder. *(S/M #P35-3).*	—	200.	900.
S2524 10 Taels			
(ca. 1910). Dragons facing above portrait. Li Hung Chan with harbor view at bottom. Back: Orange and blue. Remainder. *(S/M #P35-4).*	—	250.	1100.
S2525 100 Taels			
(ca. 1910). Dragons facing above portrait. Li Hung Chan with harbor view at bottom. Remainder. *(S/M #P35-5).*	—	400.	1250.

1910 Dollar Issue

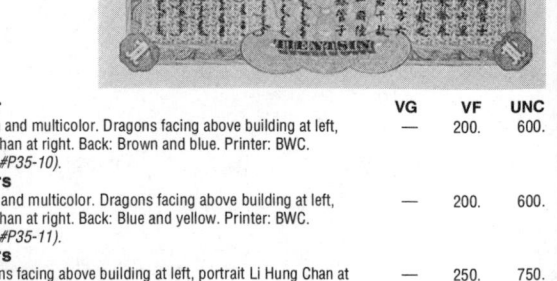

S2526 1 Dollar	VG	VF	UNC
(ca. 1910). Brown and multicolor. Dragons facing above building at left, portrait Li Hung Chan at right. Back: Brown and blue. Printer: BWC. Remainder. *(S/M #P35-10).*	—	200.	600.
S2527 3 Dollars			
(ca. 1910). Green and multicolor. Dragons facing above building at left, portrait Li Hung Chan at right. Back: Blue and yellow. Printer: BWC. Remainder. *(S/M #P35-11).*	—	200.	600.
S2528 5 Dollars			
(ca. 1910). Dragons facing above building at left, portrait Li Hung Chan at right. Printer: BWC. Remainder. *(S/M #P35-12).*	—	250.	750.
S2529 10 Dollars			
(ca. 1910). Dragons facing above building at left, portrait Li Hung Chan at right. Printer: BWC. Remainder. *(S/M #P35-13).*	—	250.	750.
S2529A 50 Dollars			
(ca. 1910). Red and multicolor. Dragons facing above building at left, portrait Li Hung Chan at right. Back: Green and red. Printer: BWC. Remainder. *(S/M #P35-13.5).*	—	300.	1200.

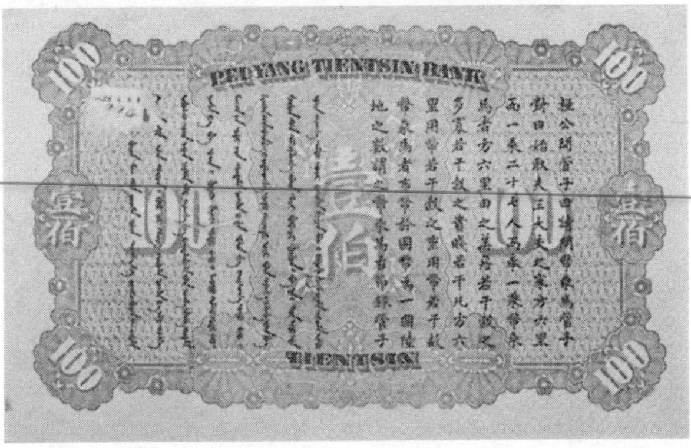

		VG	VF	UNC
S2530	**100 Dollars** (ca. 1910). Red and multicolor. Dragons facing above building at left, portrait Li Hung Chan at right. Back: Green and red. Printer: DWC. Remainder. *(S/M #P35-14).*	—	600.	2000.

NOTE: For #S2526 and S2530 with additional overprint, see Provincial Bank of Chihli #S1257-S1260.

Peiyang Currency Bureau

北洋銀元局
Pei Yang Yin Yüan Chü

1905 Issue

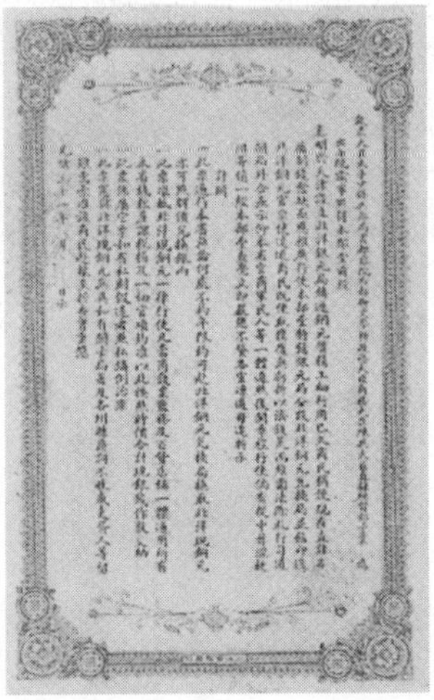

		Good	Fine	XF
S2531	**500 Cash** Yr. 31 (1905). Blue on yellow underprint. Dragons facing at upper left and right. Vertical format. Back: Orange text. *(S/M #P36-1).*	600.	2000.	—

ILLUSTRATIONS

Illustrations of bank notes used throughout this catalog are 42% of the actual size.

Frontier Bank

邊業銀行
Pien Yeh Yin Hang

1919 Issue

		Good	Fine	XF
S2535	**1 Dollar** 1919. Greenish black. Camel caravan at center. Back: Black on greenish black and red underprint. Overprint: Red letter. Printer: BEPP. Калганъ ***(Kalgan). U. (S/M #P42-).***	150.	450.	—

1920 Issue

		Good	Fine	XF
S2538	**10 Cents** 1920. Brown and green. Back: Green and multicolor. Printer: BEPP. *Kalgan. (S/M #P42-1).*	75.00	225.	—
S2539	**20 Cents** 1920. Gray and red. Back: Blue and multicolor. *Kalgan. (S/M #P42-).*	100.	300.	—

1920 Provisional Issues

#S2544-S2546 overprint on Kirin Yung Heng Provincial Bank

		Good	Fine	XF
S2544	**10 Cents** ND (1920 -old date 1918). Overprint: On #S1009. *(S/M #P42-2).*	150.	450.	—
S2545	**10 Cents** ND (1920 -old date 1918). Overprint: On #S1006. *(S/M #P42-3).*	150.	450.	—
S2546	**10 Cents** ND (1920 -old date 1918). Overprint: On #S1007. *(S/M #P42-4).*	125.	375.	—
S2549	**3 Dollars** ND (1920 -old date 1917). Overprint: On #S990. *(S/M #P42-10).*	175.	500.	—

1921 Regular Issue

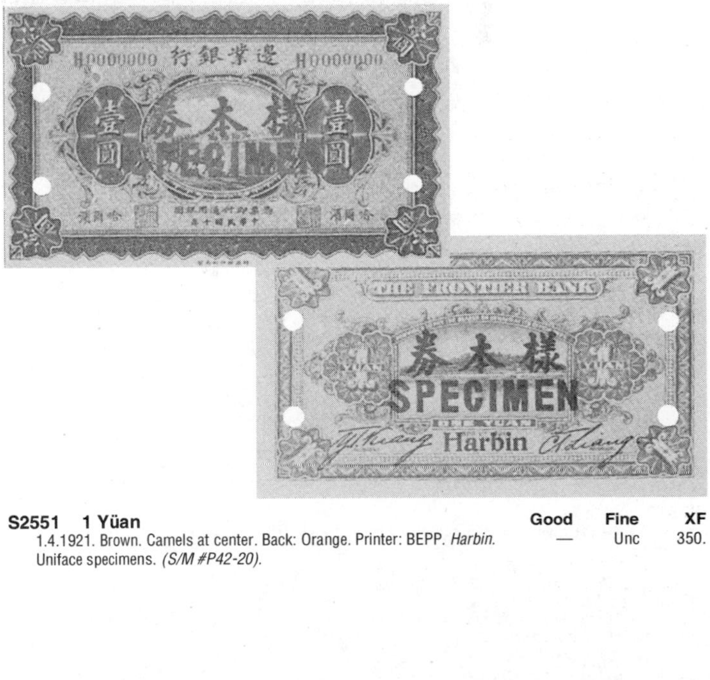

		Good	Fine	XF
S2551	**1 Yüan** 1.4.1921. Brown. Camels at center. Back: Orange. Printer: BEPP. *Harbin.* Uniface specimens. *(S/M #P42-20).*	—	Unc	350.

S2552 5 Yüan	Good	Fine	XF
1.4.1921. Green. Camel caravan, tents at center. Back: Brown. Printer: BEPP.			
a. *Tientsin. (S/M #P42-21a).*	100.	300.	—
s. *Harbin.* Two part uniface specimen. *(S/M #P42-21b).*	—	Unc	500.

S2553 10 Yüan	Good	Fine	XF
1.4.1921. Violet. Camel caravan at center. Back: Orange. Printer: BEPP. *Harbin. (S/M #P42-22).*			
a. Issued note.	125.	375.	—
s. Harbin. Two part uniface specimen. Overprint and punch hole cancelled.	—	Unc	800.

1924 ND Provisional Issue

#S2556-S2561 overprint on Kirin Yung Heng Provisional Bank.

	Good	Fine	XF
S2556 10 Cents			
ND (1924 -old date 1923). Overprint: On #S1045. *(S/M #P42-30).* Reported not confirmed.	—	—	—
S2557 20 Cents			
ND (1924 -old date 1923). Overprint: On #S1046. *(S/M #P42-31).* Reported not confirmed.	—	—	—
S2559 1 Yüan			
ND (1924 -old date 1923). Overprint: On #S1051. *(S/M #P42-40).*	150.	450.	—
S2560 5 Yüan			
ND (1924 -old date 1923). Overprint: On #S1052. *(S/M #P42-41).*	200.	600.	—
S2561 10 Yüan			
ND (1924 -old date 1923). Overprint: On #S1053. *(S/M #P42-42).*	200.	600.	—

1925 Issues

S2563 10 Cents	Good	Fine	XF
1.1.1925. Green. Printer: BEPP.			
a. *TIENTSIN. (S/M #P42-50).*	100.	250.	—
b. *MUKDEN. (S/M #P42-50).*	75.00	175.	—

S2564 10 Cents	Good	Fine	XF
1.1.1925. Orange. Harvesting at center. Printer: BEPP.			
a. *PEKING AND TIENTSIN CURRENCY. (S/M #P42-).*	25.00	75.00	—
b. *MUKDEN. (S/M #P42-).*	25.00	75.00	—

	Good	Fine	XF
S2565 20 Cents			
1.1.1925. Green. Harvesting at center. *PEKING & TIENTSIN CURRENCY.* Printer: BEPP.			
a. *TIENTSIN. (S/M #P42-51).* Orange.	40.00	100.	—
b. *PEKING AND TIENTSIN CURRENCY. (S/M #P42-).* Green.	40.00	100.	—
c. *MUKDEN. (S/M #P42-).* Green.	40.00	100.	—
S2565A 20 Cents			
Orange. Temple complex view. Printer: BEPP. *TIENTSIN.*	150.	450.	
S2566 50 Cents			
1.1.1925. Violet. Back: Violet and red. Printer: BEPP. *MUKDEN. (S/M #P42-52).*	25.00	75.00	—

	VG	VF	UNC
S2568 1 Yüan			
1.7.1925. Green on multicolor underprint. Hut at center. Back: Green. Printer: ABNC.			
a. *HARBIN.* with additional Chinese 4 character overprint *(S/M #P42-60b).*	125.	375.	—
s1. *HARBIN.* Specimen. *(S/M #P42-60a).*	—	—	350.
s2. As a. Specimen. *(S/M #P42-60b).*	—	—	350.
s3. *MUKDEN.* Specimen. *(S/M #P42-60c).*	—	—	350.
S2569 1 Yüan			
1.7.1925. Brown on multicolor underprint. Hut at center. Back: Red-violet. Printer: ABNC.			
a. *MUKEN.*	100.	300.	—
s1. *HARBIN.* Specimen. *(S/M #P42-61a).*	—	—	350.
s2. *HARBIN.* with additional Chinese 4 character official overprint. Specimen. *(S/M #P42-61b).*	—	—	350.
s3. *MUKDEN.* Specimen. *(S/M #P42-61c).*	—	—	350.

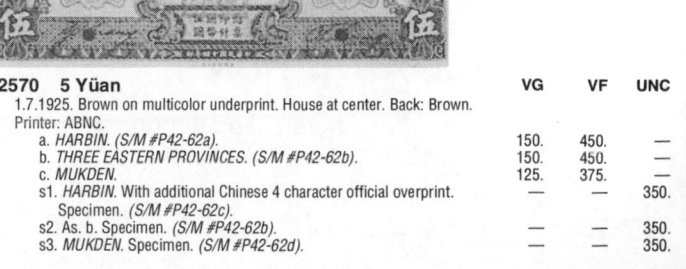

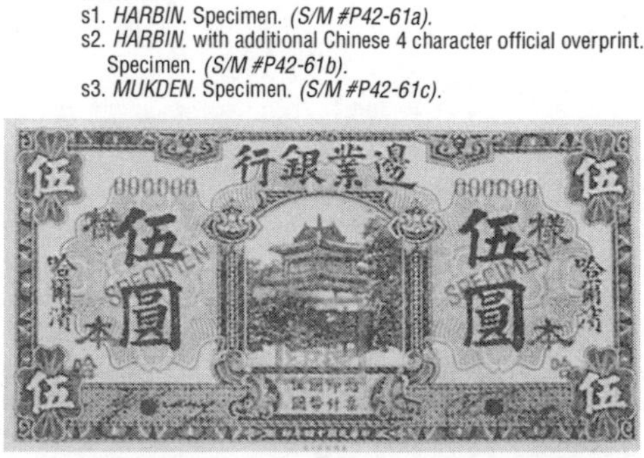

S2570 5 Yüan	VG	VF	UNC
1.7.1925. Brown on multicolor underprint. House at center. Back: Brown. Printer: ABNC.			
a. *HARBIN. (S/M #P42-62a).*	150.	450.	—
b. *THREE EASTERN PROVINCES. (S/M #P42-62b).*	150.	450.	—
c. *MUKDEN.*	125.	375.	—
s1. *HARBIN.* With additional Chinese 4 character official overprint. Specimen. *(S/M #P42-62c).*	—	—	350.
s2. As. b. Specimen. *(S/M #P42-62b).*	—	—	350.
s3. *MUKDEN.* Specimen. *(S/M #P42-62d).*	—	—	350.

S2571 5 Yüan

	VG	VF	UNC
1.7.1925. Orange on multicolor underprint. House at center. Back: Orange. Printer: ABNC. *MUKDEN. (S/M #P42-63).*	150.	400.	—

S2572 10 Yüan

	VG	VF	UNC
1.7.1925. Blue on multicolor underprint. Printer: ABNC.			
a. *HARBIN. (S/M #P42-64a).*	125.	350.	—
b. Like b., With additional overprint: *Harbin* above signature and control character *Hei* at left and right. *HARBIN* over control letters *S.S.* at left and r. on back. *(S/M #P42-64d).*	125.	350.	—
c. *HARBIN.* With additional Chinese 4 character official overprint and Harbin. *(S/M #P42-64c).*	100.	250.	—
d. *THREE EASTERN PROVINCES.*	100.	250.	—
e. *MUKDEN.*	75.00	200.	—
s1. As c. Specimen. *(S/M #P42-64c).*	—	—	350.
s2. *THREE EASTERN PROVINCES.* Specimen. *(S/M #P42-64b).*	—	—	350.

S2573 10 Yüan

	VG	VF	UNC
1.7.1925. Dark green and multicolor. Like #S2572. Back: Green. Printer: ABNC. *MUKDEN. (S/M #P42-65).*	15.00	45.00	125.

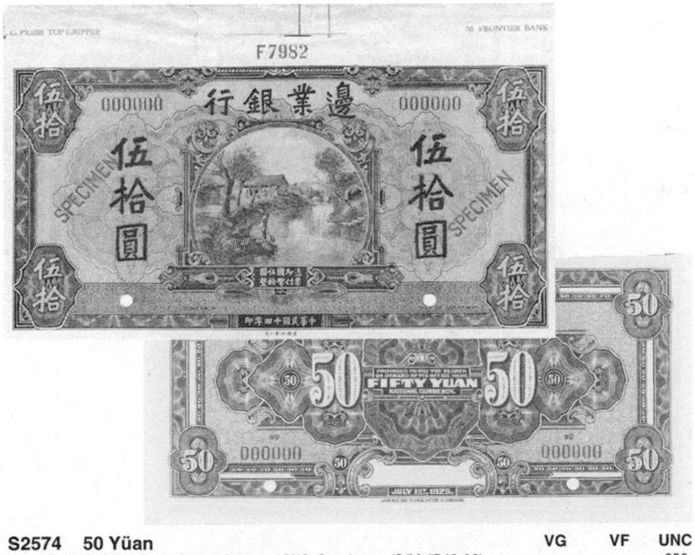

S2574 50 Yüan

	VG	VF	UNC
1.7.1925. Olive. Back: Green. Printer: ABNC. Specimen. *(S/M #P42-66).*	—	—	350.

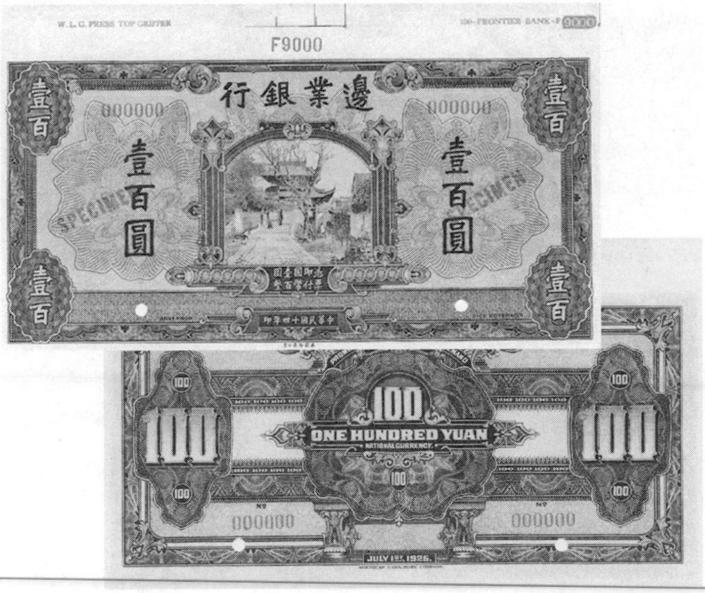

S2575 100 Yüan

	VG	VF	UNC
1.7.1925. Violet on multicolor underprint. Printer: ABNC. Specimen. *(S/M #P42-67).*	—	—	350.

1929 Issues

S2576 10 Cents

	VG	VF	UNC
1.12.1929. Brown and red. *HARBIN.* Back: Brown. Overprint: Chinese four character. *(S/M #P42-70a).*			
a. Issued note.	100.	225.	—
s. Specimen.	—	—	350.

S2577 10 Cents

	VG	VF	UNC
1.12.1929. Orange. Overprint: Chinese four character. *MUKDEN. (S/M #P42-70b).*	125.	300.	—

S2578 20 Cents

	VG	VF	UNC
1.12.1929. Red. Overprint: Four character Chinese. *HARBIN. (S/M #P42-71a).*			
a. Issued note.	125.	300.	—
s. Specimen.	—	—	350.

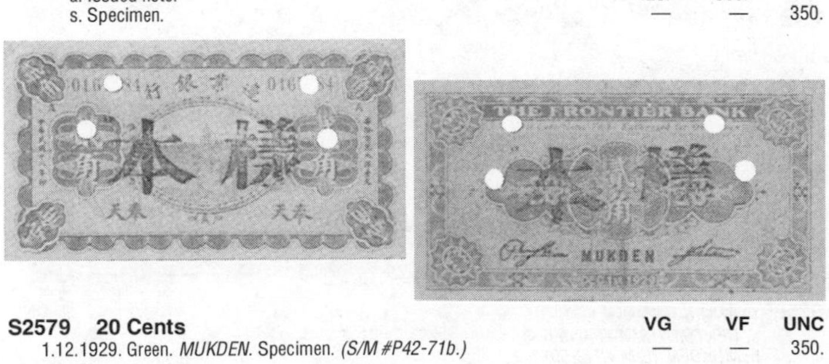

S2579 20 Cents

	VG	VF	UNC
1.12.1929. Green. *MUKDEN.* Specimen. *(S/M #P42-71b.)*	—	—	350.

S2580 50 Cents	VG	VF	UNC
1.12.1929. Orange. Overprint: Chinese four character. *HARBIN. (S/M #P42-72a).*			
a. Issued note.	100.	250.	—
s. Specimen.	—	—	350.

S2581 50 Cents	VG	VF	UNC
1.12.1929. Brown. *MUKDEN. (S/M #P42-72b.)*			
a. Issued note.	125.	300.	—
s. Specimen.	—	—	350.

1932 Issue

S2585 1 Yüan	VG	VF	UNC
1932. Brown on multicolor underprint. Temple of Heaven at center. *TIENTSIN. (S/M #P42-).*	125.	300.	—

Market Stabilization Currency Bureau

局錢官市平
P'ing Shih Kuan Ch'ien Chüan

1924 Copper Coin Issue

S2589 10 Coppers	VG	VF	UNC
13.7.1924. Brown and tan. Gateway at center. Back: Blue. *Kiangsu. (S/M #P50-1).*	125.	350.	—

S2590 100 Coppers	VG	VF	UNC
13.7.1924. Red and tan. Gateway at center. Back: Orange. *Kiangsu. (S/M #P50-2).*	200.	500.	—

Shan Hsi Zing Fun Bank

行銀豐泰西陝
Shan Hsi Ch'in Feng Yin Hang

1912 Liang (Tael) Issue

S2593 1 Liang (Tael)	VG	VF	UNC
1.5.1912. Violet and multicolor. Back: Blue. Printer: CMPA. Remainder. *(S/M #S16-1).*	—	75.00	300.
S2594 5 Liang (Taels)			
1.5.1912. Violet. Printer: CMPA. Specimen. *(S/M #S16 -).*	—	Unc	120.

1913 Liang (Tael) Issue

S2597 5 Liang (Taels)	Good	Fine	XF
1913. Green and orange. Two spheres at center. Uniface. Printer: CMPA. *(S/M #S16-2).*			
r1. Remainder.	—	Unc	160.
r2. Remainder with perforations and cancellation overprint.	—	Unc	140.

S2598 10 Liang (Taels)	VG	VF	UNC
1913. Black and violet. Back: Blue and green. Ship at left, train at right. Printer: CMPA. *(S/M #S16-3).*	40.00	125.	350.

Fu Ching Chien Chü / Shensi
Fu Ching Bank of Shensi
Fu Ching Bank

陝西富泰錢局
Shan Hsi Fu Ch'in Ch'ien Chü

陝西富泰銀行
Shan Hsi Fuy Ch'in Yin Hang

富泰錢局
Fu Ch'in Ch'ien Chü

1919 Tael Issue

S2599 50 Taels — Good 125. | Fine 375. | XF 1000.
1919. Purple. Pagoda, buildings at center. Back: Brown on green underprint. Diagonally cut cancelled at center right. *(S/M #S17-0-8)*.

1922 Yüan Issue

S2600 1 Yüan — Good 25.00 | Fine 75.00 | XF 225.
1922. Green. Fortress at center. Back: Violet and multicolor. Printer: BEPP. *(S/M #S20-1)*.

S2600A 5 Yüan — Good 25.00 | Fine 75.00 | XF 225.
1922. Blue. Fortress at center. Back: Violet and multicolor. Printer: BEPP. *(S/M #S20-2)*.

S2600B 10 Yüan — Good 40.00 | Fine 125. | XF 350.
1922. Orange. Fortress at center. Back: Violet and multicolor. Printer: BEPP. *(S/M #S20-3)*.

NOTE: For #S2600-S2600B with additional overprint, see Military - National Army Combined Headquarters #S3918-S3920.

1923 Cash Issue

#S2601#S2602

S2601 100 Cash — Good 30.00 | Fine 125. | XF 300.
1.3.1923. Violet. Mountain view at top. Vertical format. Back: Green and red. Printer: BEPP. *(S/M #S17-1)*.

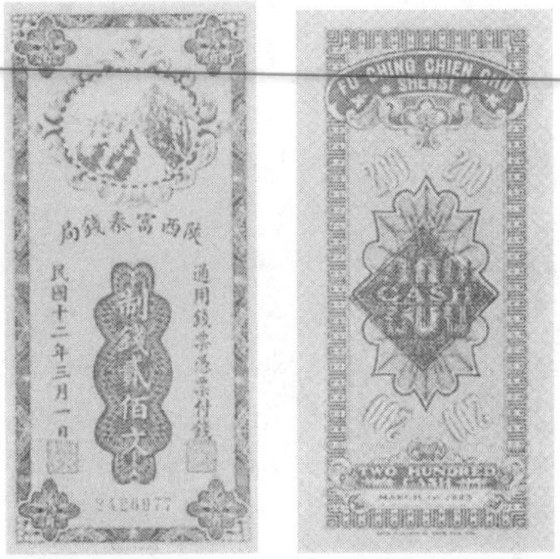

S2602 200 Cash — Good 40.00 | Fine 150. | XF 400.
1.3.1923. Mountain view at center. Printer: BEPP. *(S/M #S17-1.3)*.

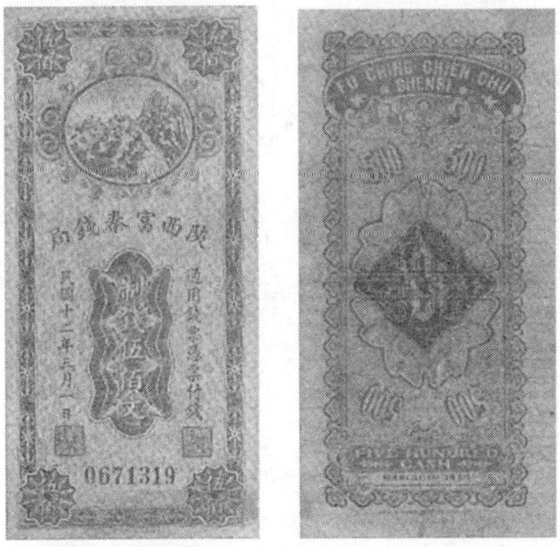

		Good	Fine	XF
S2603	**500 Cash** 1.3.1923. Red-orange. Mountain view at top. Vertical format. Back: Olive on red-orange underprint. Printer: BEPP. *(S/M #S17-1.6)*.	50.00	175.	600.
S2604	**1000 Cash** 1923. Mountain view at top. Printer: BEPP. *(S/M #S17-2)*.	60.00	200.	750.

1926 Ch'uan Issue

		Good	Fine	XF
S2606	**1 Ch'uan** 1926. Blue and yellow. Building at top. Vertical format. Back: Brown. Printer: ILBC. *(S/M #S17-10)*.	60.00	200.	750.

1927 Ch'uan Issue

		Good	Fine	XF
S2607	**1 Ch'uan** 1.2.1927. *(S/M #S17-15)*.	60.00	200.	750.
S2607A	**2 Ch'uan** 1.2.1927. Red. Temple at center. *(S/M #S17-16)*.	100.	250.	800.
S2607B	**2 Ch'uan** 1.2.1927. Dull red. Pagoda, trees at center. *(S/M #S17-17)*.	100.	250.	800.
S2608	**10 Cents** 1927. *(S/M #S17-20)*.	100.	250.	800.
S2609	**30 Cents** 1927. Green and red. Back: Blue. *(S/M #S17-21)*.	125.	400.	1000.
S2610	**50 Cents** 1927. *(S/M #S17-22)*.	125.	400.	1000.

NOTE: For #S2608-S2610 with additional overprint, see Military - National Army #S3907-S3909.

1928 Cash Issue

	Good	Fine	XF
S2613 1000 Cash 1928. Green on tan underprint. Steam train at center. Back: Green.	75.00	200.	400.

	Good	Fine	XF
S2614 2000 Cash Aug. 1928. Purple on light yellow-green underprint. Monument in city at center. *(S/M #S17-29).*	75.00	200.	400.
S2615 2000 Cash 1928. Red and yellow. Back red .*(S/M #S17-30).*	50.00	150.	300.

1931 Copper Coin Issue

	Good	Fine	XF
S2616 50 Coppers 1931. Brown on pale green underprint. Farm buildings at center. Back: Biplane at center. *(S/M #S17-42).*	50.00	150.	300.

1935 Copper Coin Issue

	Good	Fine	XF
S2617 10 Copper Coins 1935. Dark green and black. Great Wall view. Back: Dark green.	50.00	150.	300.

	Good	Fine	XF
S2618 20 Coppers 1935. Specimen. *(S/M #S17-51).*	—	Unc	350.

#S2621-S2623 *Deleted.* See #S2599-S2600B.

Shansi Provincial Railway

山西省鐵兩行聯合辦事處
Shan Hsi Sheng T'ien Liang Hang Lian Ho Pan Shih Ch'u

1940 Issue

	Good	Fine	XF
S2624 25 Cents June 1940. Purple on pink underprint. Building at left. Back: Red. *(S/M #S22.5-6).*	20.00	50.00	150.

Shanse Provincial Bank
Shansi Provincial Bank

山西省銀行
Shan Hsi Sheng Yin Hang

1919 Issue

	Good	Fine	XF
S2625 10 Cents 1919. *(S/M #S23-1).* Reported not confirmed.	—	—	—
S2626 20 Cents 1919. *(S/M #S23-2).* Reported not confirmed.	—	—	—

	Good	Fine	XF
S2627 50 Cents 1919. *(S/M #S23-3).* Reported not confirmed.	—	—	—

	Good	Fine	XF
S2628 1 Dollar 1919. Blue on green and ochre underprint. Rural house at center. Back: Blue. Shoreline at center.			
a. *TAIYUAN.* (3mm). signature Y. C. Yen and P. C. Hao without signature titles. *(S/M #S23-10a).*	10.00	25.00	75.00
b. *TAIYUAN.* (3mm). signature C. Y. Chia and J. C. Hsü with titles *Co-Director* and *Director.*	10.00	25.00	75.00
c. As b. *TAIYUAN.* (4mm). Signature (?). P. Chi and J. C. Hsü with titles.	10.00	25.00	75.00
d. *TIENTSIN. (S/M #S23-10c).*	25.00	75.00	225.
e. *TAIKU.* Signature like c.	—	—	—
f. *HUNGTUNG.* Signature like c.	—	—	—
g. *YANGCHÜAN.* Signature like c.	—	—	—
h. *SHIHKIACHWANG.* Signature like c.	—	—	—
i. *TAIYUAN,* overprint in black over another place name (like *KIAOCHENG* or *YUNGCHENG*). Signature like c.	—	—	—
s. *PEIPING.* Specimen. *S/M #S23-10b).*	—	Unc	350.
S2628A 1 Dollar 1919. Blue on brown and purple underprint. Rural house cat center. Back: Blue. Shoreline at center. *SHANSI. (S/M #S23-10d).*	40.00	125.	300.
S2629 5 Dollars 1919. Blue and brown. Back: Blue. Printer: BEPP. *TAIYUAN. (S/M #S23-11).*	50.00	150.	400.

S2630 10 Dollars	Good	Fine	XF
1919. Black on blue and brown underprint. Shoreline houses at center. Back: Blue. Printer: BEPP.			
a. *TAIYUAN. (S/M #S23-12a).*	50.00	150.	400.
s. *PEIPING.* Specimen. *(S/M #S23-12b).*	—	Unc	350.

S2631 50 Dollars

1919. Printer: BEPP. *TAIYUAN. (S/M #S23-13).* Reported not confirmed.	—	—	—

S2632 100 Dollars

1919. Printer: BEPP. *TAIYUAN. (S/M #S23-14).* Reported not confirmed.	—	—	—

1922 Issue

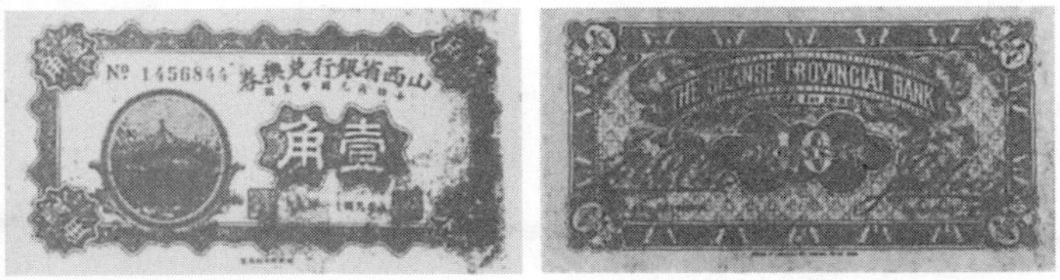

S2632A 10 Cents	Good	Fine	XF
1.3.1922. Brown on red underprint. Pavilion at left. Back: Green and dark brown. Printer: BEPP. *(S/M #S23-15).*	25.00	75.00	225.

1924 Issue

S2633 10 Coppers	Good	Fine	XF
ND (1924). Brown on green underprint. Back: Dark blue on red underprint.			
a. *Fen Yang. (S/M #S23-20a).*	20.00	50.00	150.
b. Black. *P'ing Yao. (S/M #S23-20b).*	15.00	40.00	100.
c. Black. *Tai Yuan. (S/M #S23-20c).*	15.00	40.00	100.
d. Red. *Tai Yuan. (S/M #S23-20d).*	20.00	50.00	150.
e. *Yu Tz'u. (S/M #S23-20e).*	20.00	50.00	150.
f. Black. *Tai Hsien. (S/M #S23-20f).*	20.00	50.00	150.
g. *Sin Hsien.*	40.00	100.	300.

S2634 20 Coppers	Good	Fine	XF
ND (1924). Blue on pink underprint. *(S/M #S23-21).*			
a. *Tái Yuan.* Red or black. *(S/M #S23-21a).*	20.00	50.00	150.
b. *Tái Hsien. (S/M #S23-21b).*	25.00	60.00	175.
c. *Sin Hsien.*	25.00	60.00	175.

S2635 50 Coppers

ND (1924). *(S/M #S23-22).*	60.00	175.	450.

S2636 100 Coppers

ND (1924). Red on gray underprint. two size varieties. *SINHSIEN (S/M #S23-23).*	75.00	200.	500.

1926 Issue

S2637 10 Cents	Good	Fine	XF
1926. Violet. Waterfront scene at right. 2 signature varieties. Printer: BEPP.			
a. *PEIPING. (S/M #S23-30b).*	25.00	75.00	225.
b. *TIENTSIN. (S/M #S23-30a).*	25.00	75.00	225.
c. *TAIYUAN.* Signature C. Y. Chia and J. C. Hsü with titles: *Co-Director* and *Director. (S/M #S23-30c).*	15.00	45.00	125.
d. Signature Y. C. Yen as *Co-Director* at left and right. *(S/M #S23-30d).*	15.00	45.00	125.

S2638 10 Cents

1926. Dark green. Waterfront scene at right. 2 signature varieties. Back: Green. Printer: BEPP. *TAIYUAN. (S/M #S23-).*	40.00	125.	300.

S2639 20 Cents	Good	Fine	XF
1926. Red. Rural house at right. Printer: BEPP.			
a. *TIENTSIN. (S/M #S23-30a).*	20.00	50.00	150.
b. *TAIYUAN.* As #S2637c. 2 signature varieties. *(S/M #S23-30b).*	20.00	50.00	150.
c. *TAIYUAN.* As #S2637d. *(S/M #S23-30c).*	20.00	50.00	150.
d. *TAIYUAN.* Signature Chi and Hsü.	20.00	50.00	150.

S2641 1 Dollar

1926. Printer: BEPP. *(S/M #S23-40).* Reported not confirmed.	—	—	—

1928 Issues

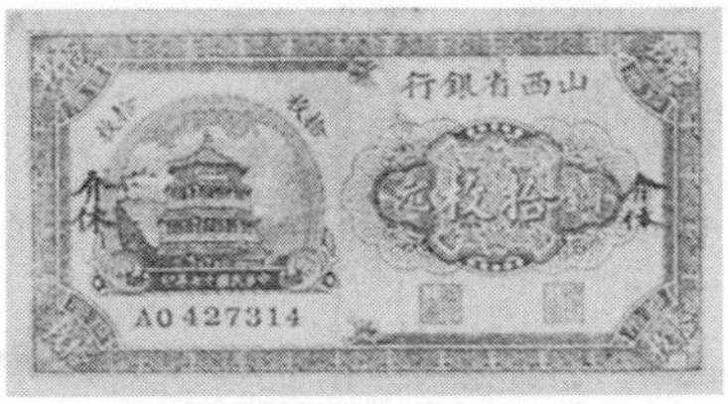

S2644 10 Coppers	Good	Fine	XF
1928. Blue-black on ochre and pale blue underprint. Temple at left. Back: Brown. Printer: BEPP.			
a. *Fen Hsiu. (S/M #S23-45a).*	20.00	40.00	125.
b. *Tai Yuan. (S/M #S23-45b).*	20.00	40.00	125.
c. *Sin Hsien. (S/M #S23-45c).*	40.00	125.	300.

S2645 20 Coppers	Good	Fine	XF
1928. Brown on multicolor. Fortress at left. Printer: BEPP.			
a. *Fen Hsiu. (S/M #S23-46a).*	40.00	125.	300.
b. *Tai Yuan. (S/M #S23-46b).*	40.00	125.	300.

S2647 10 Cents

1928. Blue. Back: Green. Printer: BEPP *(S/M #S23-50).* Reported not confirmed.	—	—	—

S2648 20 Cents	Good	Fine	XF
1928. Purple. Pagoda at left. Back: Dark olive. Printer: BEPP. *TAIYUAN. (S/M #S23-51).*			
a. Place name 4mm high.	20.00	50.00	150.
b. Place name 6mm high.	40.00	125.	300.

Formerly listed #S2649 has been determed to be a color shade variety of #S2648.

S2651 1 Dollar

1928. Brown. Hillside buildings at center. Back: Green. *TAIYUAN. (S/M #S23-53).*	25.00	75.00	225.

S2651A 1 Dollar	Good	Fine	XF
1928. Blue-violet on multicolor underprint. River, city, tower along wall at right. *TAIYUAN. (S/M #S23-54).*	50.00	150.	400.

S2652 5 Dollars

	Good	Fine	XF
1928. Dark blue-gray. Building with clock tower at center. *TAIYUAN. (S/M #S23-55).*	45.00	125.	300.

S2652A 5 Dollars

	Good	Fine	XF
1928. Brown on ochre underprint. Hillside village at right. *TAIYUAN. (S/M #S23-56).*	75.00	225.	600.

S2653 10 Dollars

	Good	Fine	XF
1928. Dark green. Bank building at center. *TAIYUAN. (S/M #S23-57).*	75.00	225.	600.

S2653A 10 Dollars

	Good	Fine	XF
1928. Brown-violet on multicolor and light blue underprint. Houses and trees at right. Back: Brown on yellow underprint. Hillside village at left. *TAIYUAN. (S/M #S23-58).*	100.	250.	750.

1930 Issues

S2654 10 Cents

1930. Brown. Hillside buildings at left. Back: Building with clock tower. Printer: BEPP.

	Good	Fine	XF
a. *TAIYUAN. (S/M #S23-60a).*	25.00	75.00	225.
b. *KIUSIU. (S/M #S23-60b).*	25.00	75.00	225.
c. *PINGYAO. (S/M #S23-60c).*	25.00	75.00	225.
d. *SUIYUAN. (S/M #S23-60d).*	25.00	75.00	225.
e. *TAIHSIEN. (S/M #S23-60e).*	25.00	75.00	225.
f. *Fantsun.*	25.00	75.00	225.
g. *Kiaocheng.*	15.00	45.00	125.
h. *Siaoyi.*	15.00	45.00	125.
i. *Sinhsien.*	15.00	45.00	125.
j. *Taiku.*	15.00	45.00	125.
k. *Yinghsien.*	15.00	45.00	125.
l. *Yutzuhsien.*	15.00	45.00	125.

S2655 20 Cents

1930. Brown. Shoreline, large building in distance at left. Back: Peking fortress gate at center. Printer: BEPP. *TAIYUAN. (S/M #S23-60.5).*

	Good	Fine	XF
e. *SHOHSIEN.*	15.00	45.00	125.
f. *PINGYAO.*	15.00	45.00	125.
g. *SIAOYI.*	15.00	45.00	125.
h. *WENSHUI.*	15.00	45.00	125.

S2655A 20 Cents

1930. Deep olive-green. Shoreline, large building in distance at left. Back: Peking fortress gate at center. Printer: BEPP.

	Good	Fine	XF
a. *SUIYUAN. (S/M #S23-61a).*	20.00	50.00	150.
b. *FANTSAN. (S/M #S23-61b).*	20.00	50.00	150.
c. *TAIKU. (S/M #S23-61c).*	20.00	50.00	150.
d. *TAIYUAN. (S/M #S23-61d).*	20.00	50.00	150.

S2656 50 Cents

	Good	Fine	XF
1930. Red. Back: Violet. Printer: BEPP. *(S/M #S23-62).*	20.00	50.00	150.

S2657 1 Yüan

1.8.1930. Brown on multicolor underprint. Shoreline at center. Back: Brown. Printer: BEPP.

	Good	Fine	XF
a. *CHANGCHIH.* 2 signature varieties. *(S/M #S23-70a).*	25.00	75.00	225.
b. *CH'UWO.* 2 signature varieties. *(S/M #S23-70b).*	25.00	75.00	225.
c. *FENYANG. (S/M #S23-70c).*	25.00	75.00	225.
d. *HUNGTIEN. (S/M #S23-70d).*	25.00	75.00	225.
e. *KIAOCHENG. (S/M #S23-70e).*	25.00	75.00	225.
f. *KIEHSIU. (S/M #S23-70f).*	25.00	75.00	225.
g. *LINFEN. (S/M #S23-70g).*	25.00	75.00	225.
h. *PINGYAO. (S/M #S23-70h).*	25.00	75.00	225.
i. *SHOHSIEN. (S/M #S23-70i).*	25.00	75.00	225.
j. *SIAOYI. (S/M #S23-70j).*	25.00	75.00	225.
k. *SINHSIEN. (S/M #S23-70k).*	25.00	75.00	225.
l. *SUIYUAN. (S/M #S23-70l).*	25.00	75.00	225.
m. *TAIYUAN.* 2 signature varieties. *(S/M #S23-70m).*	20.00	50.00	150.
n. *TATUNG. (S/M #S23-70n).*	25.00	75.00	225.
o. *TSING CHENG. (S/M #S23-70o).*	25.00	75.00	225.
p. *YUTZE. (S/M #S23-70p).*	25.00	75.00	225.
q. *CHIHSIEN. (S/M #S23-70q).*	25.00	75.00	225.
r. *WENSHUI.* 2 signature varieties. *(S/M #S23-70r).*	25.00	75.00	225.
s. *YUNCHENG.* 2 signature varieties. *(S/M #S23-70s).*	25.00	75.00	225.
t. *HUNGTUNG. (S/M #S23-70t).*	35.00	125.	350.
u. *TAIKU.* 2 signature varieties. *(S/M #S23-70u).*	35.00	125.	350.
v. *CHIHSIEN. (S/M #S23-70x).*	35.00	125.	350.
w. *YANGCHÜAN. (S/M #S23-70w).*	35.00	125.	350.
x. *FANTSUN. (S/M #S23-70x).*	35.00	125.	350.
y. *SINKIANG.* 2 signature varieties. *(S/M #S23-70y).*	35.00	125.	350.
z. *YINGHSIEN. (S/M #S23-70z).*	35.00	125.	350.
aa. *TAIHSIEN.*	35.00	125.	350.
ab. *TSINGYUAN.*	35.00	125.	350.

S2657A 1 Yüan

	Good	Fine	XF
Violet with bright multicolor guilloches. Like #S2657 with similar branch office overprints. Printer: BEPP. *(S/M #S23-70).*	50.00	150.	400.

S2657B 1 Yüan

	Good	Fine	XF
Violet with dull multicolor guilloches. Like #S2657A with similar branch office overprints. Printer: BEPP. *(S/M #23-70).*	50.00	150.	400.

NOTE: Confirmation of various branch overprints for #S2657A and S2657B is requested.

S2658 5 Yüan

	Good	Fine	XF
1930. Yellow. Printer: BEPP. *TAIYUAN. (S/M #S23-71).*	50.00	150.	400.

S2659 10 Yüan

	Good	Fine	XF
1930. Green. Printer: BEPP. *TAIYUAN. (S/M #S23-72).*	50.00	150.	400.

#S2660 *Deleted.* See #S2654.

#S2663 *Deleted.* See #S2657A and #S2657B.

1932 Issue

S2666 10 Coppers

1932. Dark brown. Pagodas at left, rural house at right. Back: Red. Printer: BEPP. *TAIYUAN.*

	Good	Fine	XF
a. Issued note. *(S/M #S23-75a).*	15.00	45.00	125.
b. With additional 8 Chinese character overprint at left and right on back. *(S/M #S23-75b).*	15.00	45.00	125.

S2667 20 Coppers	Good	Fine	XF
1932. Black. Pagodas at left, rural house at right. Back: Brown. Printer: BEPP. *TAIYUAN.*			
a. Issued note. *(S/M #S23-76a).*	15.00	45.00	125.
b. With additional 6 Chinese character overprint at left and r. on back. *(S/M #S23-76b).*	15.00	45.00	125.
S2671 1 Yüan			
1932. Red and brown. Back: Brown. Printer: BEPP. *(S/M #S23-80).*	50.00	150.	400.
S2672 5 Yüan			
1932. Yellow. Printer: BEPP. *(S/M #S23-81).*	50.00	150.	400.

S2673 10 Yüan	Good	Fine	XF
1932. Green on multicolor underprint. Railroad, ore cars, factory and workers at center. Back: Green. Printer: BEPP.			
a. *TAIYUAN. (S/M #S23-82a).*	40.00	125.	350.
b. *T'AIKU. (S/M #S23-82b).*	50.00	150.	400.
c. *TATUNG.*	50.00	150.	400.
d. *FENYANG.*	30.00	100.	275.

1933 Issue

S2675 5 Yüan	Good	Fine	XF
1.9.1933. Red on light blue underprint. Watchtower at Peking at center. Back: Red. Factories at center. Printer: BEPP.			
a. *TAIYUAN.* Signature Y. Fu - S. Wang. *(S/M #S23-90a).*	25.00	75.00	225.
b. *TAIYUAN.* Signature Y. Fu - C. L. Lu. *(S/M #S23-90b).*	25.00	75.00	225.
c. *TAIKU.* Signature Y. Fu - S. Wang. *(S/M #S23-90c).*	50.00	150.	400.
d. *HUNGTUNG.* Signature Y. Fu - S. Wang. *(S/M #S23-90d).*	50.00	150.	400.
e. *PINGYAO.* Signature Y. Fu - S. Wang. *(S/M #S23-90e).*	50.00	150.	400.

1936 Issue

S2677 1 Yüan	Good	Fine	XF
July 1936. Varying shades of green on light blue underprint. Pagoda at center. Back: Dark blue. Printer: NWPF. *SHANSI. (S/M #S23-99).*	10.00	25.00	75.00

1937 ND Provisional Issue

S2678 1 Yüan	Good	Fine	XF
ND (1937 -old date July 1936). Olive-green on light blue underprint. Back: Different serial #. Overprint: 2 vertical sets of 4 Chinese characters at left and right on #S2677. *(S/M #S23-100).*	60.00	175.	450.

1937 Regular Issue

S2679 5 Yüan	Good	Fine	XF
1937. Brown on multicolor underprint. Watchtower at Peking at left or right. Back: Orange. Pavillion at center. Printer: NWPF. *SHANSI (S/M #S23-110).*	50.00	150.	400.

S2680 10 Yüan	Good	Fine	XF
1937. Black and multicolor. Watch tower at Peking at left or right. Back: Green. Mountain village. Printer: NWPF. *SHANSI. (S/M #S23-111).*	20.00	60.00	175.

Provincial Bank of Shensi

陝西省銀行

Shan Hsi Sheng Yin Hang

1930 ND Provisional Issue

S2681 1 Dollar	VG	VF	UNC
ND (1930 -old date 1.8.1928). Brown. Overprint: On #S3887D. *SHENSI/SHANTUNG. (S/M #S24-1).*			
a. Issued note.	75.00	225.	—
s. Specimen with 3 Chinese character overprint, punched hole cancelled.	—	—	350.

	Good	Fine	XF
S2682 5 Dollars			
ND (1930 -old date 1.8.1928). Deep green. Overprint: On #S3888C. *SHENSI/SHANTUNG. (S/M #S24-2).*			
a. Issued note.	100.	275.	—
s. Specimen as #S2681s.	—	—	400.
S2683 10 Dollars			
ND (1930 -old date 1.8.1928). Red-brown. Overprint: On #s3889D. *SHENSI/SHANTUNG. (S/M #S24-3).*			
a. Issued note.	125.	350.	—
s. Specimen as #S2681s.	—	—	550.

1931 Issue

	VG	VF	UNC
S2684 1 Dollar			
1931. Brown. Back: Brown. Printer: BEPP. *SHENSI. (S/M #S24-10).*	50.00	150.	400.
S2685 5 Dollars			
1931. Green. Back: Green. Printer: BEPP. *SHENSI. (S/M #S24-11).*	60.00	175.	450.
S2686 10 Dollars			
1931. Blue. Back: Blue. Biplane at center. *SHENSI. (S/M #S24-12).*	100.	275.	650.

1932 Issue

	VG	VF	UNC
S2687 10 Cents			
1.4.1932. Red. Barns with tower at left. Back: Red. Biplane at center. Printer: BEPP. *SHENSI. (S/M #S24-20).*			
a. Issued note.	40.00	125.	350.
s. Specimen.	—	—	450.

	VG	VF	UNC
S2688 20 Cents			
1.4.1932. Green. Barns with tower at left. Back: Green. Monoplane at center. Printer: BEPP. *SHENSI. (S/M #S24-21).*			
a. Issued note.	40.00	125.	350.
s. Specimen.	—	—	500.

1939 ND Provisional Issue

#S2691-S2692A overprint new bank name on unissued notes of Shensi Fu Ching Bank.

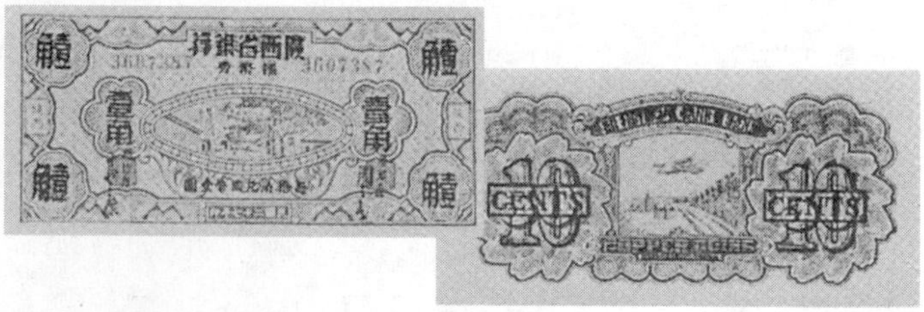

	VG	VF	UNC
S2691 1 Chiao = 10 Cents on 50 Coppers			
ND (1939 -old date Yr. 17). Blue. Rural building at center. Back: Blue. Biplane at center. *(S/M #S24-30).*	40.00	125.	350.
S2692 2 Chiao = 20 Cents			
ND (1939 -old date Yr. 17). Red. Back: Red. *(S/M #S24-31).*	25.00	75.00	225.
S2692A 5 Chiao = 50 Cents			
ND (1938 -old date Yr. 17). Green. Rural building at center. Back: Gray. Biplane at center. *(S/M #S24-32).*	60.00	175.	450.

1949 Issue

	VG	VF	UNC
S2693 20 Cents			
1949. Pagoda at right. *(S/M #S24-42).*	60.00	175.	450.

Bank of Shansi

陝西銀行流通券
Shan Hsi Yin Hang Liu T'ung Ch'üan

ND Issue

	VG	VF	UNC
S2694 1 Yüan			
ND (ca.1912). Blue on yellow underprint. Back: Black. Remainder. *(S/M #S26.5-10).*	100.	275.	650.

Shantung Commercial Bank

山東商業銀行
Shan Tung Shang Yeh Yin Hang

1920 ND Provisional Issue

	Good	Fine	XF
S2695 5 Dollars			
ND (1920). Overprint: On #S2768. *(S/M #S42-0.5).*	60.00	175.	—
S2696 10 Dollars			
ND (1920). Overprint: On #S2769. *(S/M #S42-1).*	100.	300.	—

1926 Regular Issue

	Good	Fine	XF
S2700 10 Dollars			
1926. Green and multicolor. Back: Green. Printer: BEPP. *(S/M #S42-).*	100.	300.	—

Shantung Exchange Bureau

山東平市官錢換局
Shan Tung P'ing Shih Kuan Ch'ien Tsung Chü

1932 Issue

	Good	Fine	XF
S2703 10 Cents			
1932. Red. Printer: HTCN. *Chinan. (S/M #S41.5-11).*	30.00	100.	—

1933 Issue

	Good	Fine	XF
S2708 10 Cents			
1933. Red. Printer: SSPC. *(S/M #S41.5-12).*	40.00	125.	—

S2708A 20 Cents	Good	Fine	XF
1933. Dark blue on blue underprint. Gateway at center. Vertical format. *(S/M #S41.5-13).*	25.00	75.00	—

1936 Copper Coin Issue

S2709 10 Coppers	Good	Fine	XF
Yr. 25 (1936). Dark blue-gray on blue-gray underprint. 3 tower gate at center. Back: Control letters A-A . *(S/M #S41.5-19).*	5.00	10.00	35.00

S2710 20 Coppers	Good	Fine	XF
Yr. 25 (1936). Dark green on green underprint. Waterfront village at left. *(S/M #S41.5-20).*	10.00	25.00	75.00

S2711 50 Coppers	Good	Fine	XF
Yr. 25 (1936). Steam passenger train at center. *(S/M #S41.5-21).*			
a. Control letters *A-A* on back.	15.00	45.00	125.
b. Control letters *B-B* on back.	15.00	45.00	125.

S2712 100 Coppers	Good	Fine	XF
Yr. 25 (1936). Red on yellow-orange underprint. Building with clock tower at center. *(S/M #S41.5-22).*	15.00	45.00	125.

S2713 100 Coppers	Good	Fine	XF
1936. Brown on blue-green underprint. Bank building at center. *(S/M #S41.5-23).*	50.00	150.	400.

Shantung Provincial Treasury

山東省金庫券

Shan Tung Sheng Chin K'u Ch'üan

1926 Issue

	Good	Fine	XF
S2715 10 Cents 1926. House at left, gardening at right. Printer: SOPO. *(S/M #S43-1).* Reported not confirmed.	—	—	—
S2716 20 Cents 1926. House at left, gardening at right. Printer: SOPO. *(S/M #S43-2).* Reported not confirmed.	—	—	—

	Good	Fine	XF
S2718 1 Yüan 1926. Orange and yellow. House at left, gardening at right. Back: Violet. Printer: SOPO. *(S/M #S43-10).*	60.00	175.	500.
S2719 5 Yüan 1926. Blue and green. House at left, gardening at right. Back: Green. Printer: SOPO. *(S/M #S43-11).*	75.00	225.	625.

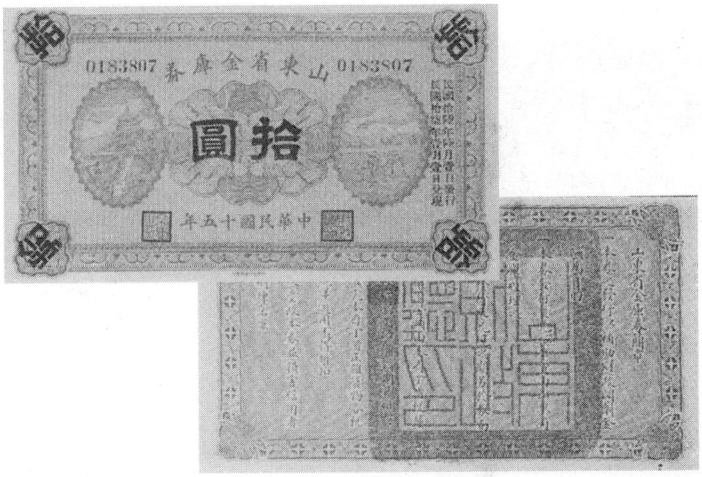

S2720 10 Yüan	Good	Fine	XF
1926. Gray and brown. House at left, gardening at right. Back: Brown. Printer: SOPO. *(S/M #S43-12).*	75.00	225.	625.

Shantung Provincial Treasury

山東省庫券

Shan Tung Sheng K'u Ch'uan

1932 Issue

	Good	Fine	XF
S2723 1 Dollar 1932. Blue.			
a. *Chefoo. (S/M #S43.5-10a).*	60.00	175.	500.
b. *Shantung. (S/M #S43.5-10b).*	60.00	175.	500.
S2724 5 Dollars 1932. *Shantung. (S/M #S45.5-11).*	—	—	—
S2725 10 Dollars 1932. *Shantung. (S/M #S43.5-12).*	—	—	—

Shantung Min Sheng Bank

山東省民生銀行

Shan Tung Sheng Min Sheng Yin Hang

1936 Issue

S2731 10 Cents	Good	Fine	XF
1936. Brown. Sampan at center. Back: Brown. Printer: SSPC. *(S/M #S45-1).*	5.00	15.00	45.00

	Good	Fine	XF
S2732 20 Cents 1936. Dark gray-green. Shoreline at center. Printer: SSPC. *(S/M #S45-3).*	5.00	15.00	45.00
S2733 50 Cents 1936. Orange. Printer: SSPC. *(S/M #S45-5).*	10.00	30.00	100.
S2734 1 Dollar 1936. Printer: SSPC. *(S/M #S45-10).* Reported not confirmed.	—	—	—
S2735 5 Dollars 1936. Printer: SSPC. *(S/M #S45-11).* Reported not confirmed.	—	—	—
S2736 10 Dollars 1936. Printer: SSPC. *(S/M #S45-12).* Reported not confirmed.	—	—	—

1937 Issue

	Good	Fine	XF
S2737 5 Cents 1937. *(S/M #S45-20).* Reported not confirmed.	—	—	—
S2738 10 Cents 1937. *(S/M #S45-21).* Reported not confirmed.	—	—	—
S2739 20 Cents 1937. *(S/M #S45-22).* Reported not confirmed.	—	—	—

1940 Issue

	Good	Fine	XF
S2740 50 Cents 1940. Black. Gateway at center. *(S/M #S45-28).*	5.00	15.00	45.00

	Good	Fine	XF
S2742 5 Yüan 1940. Green on yellow underprint. Peasants cultivating at center. Additional red serial # overprint. Back: Gray. Printer: SSPC. *(S/M #S45-32).*			
a. Issued note.	5.00	15.00	45.00
b. With additional red serial # on back.	7.50	20.00	60.00

1943 Issue

	Good	Fine	XF
S2744 10 Yüan 1943. Red on yellow underprint. Back: Brown. *(S/M #S45-40).*	15.00	45.00	125.

NOTE: For #S2744 with overprint: *Yu Min Yin Hang* on back see #S3785 (Communist).

Provincial Bank of Shantung

山東省銀行
Shan Tung Sheng Yin Hang

1925 ND Provisional Issue

#S2745-S2747 Overprint new bank name on Tsingtao (Regional) City Bank.

	Good	Fine	XF
S2745 1 Yüan ND (1925 -old date 15.4.1924). Overprint: On #S1302U. *SHANTUNG. (S/M #S46-1).*	25.00	75.00	225.
S2746 5 Yüan ND (1925 -old date 15.4.1924). Overprint: On #S1302K. *SHANTUNG. (S/M #S46-2).*	25.00	75.00	225.

	Good	Fine	XF
S2747 10 Yüan ND (1925 -old date 15.4.1924). Overprint: On #S1302L. *SHANTUNG. (S/M #S46-3).*	30.00	100.	275.

1925 Tiao Issue

	Good	Fine	XF
S2748 1 Tiao = 49 Copper Cents Sept. 1925. Brown on blue underprint. Back: Railway city gate at center. Unsigned remainder. *(S/M #S46-7).*	—	Unc	300.

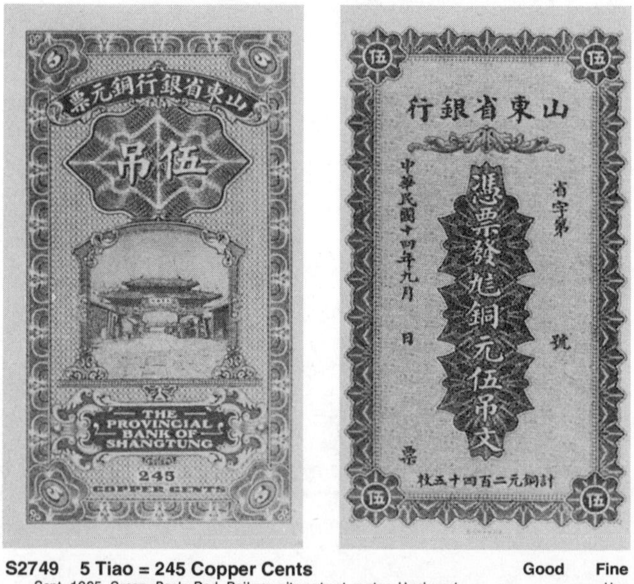

	Good	Fine	XF
S2749 5 Tiao = 245 Copper Cents Sept. 1925. Green. Back: Red. Railway city gate at center. Unsigned remainder. *(S/M #S46-8).*	—	Unc	300.

1925 First Regular Issue

S2751 1 Yüan	Good	Fine	XF
15.8.1925. Green and multicolor. Monument at center. Back: Green. Printer: BEPP.			
a. *SHANTUNG. (S/M #S46-20b).*	20.00	60.00	175.
b. *SHANTUNG/TSINGTAO. (S/M #S46-20c).*	45.00	125.	350.
c. *CHINGTAO/Shantung. (S/M #S46-20d).*	45.00	125.	350.
d. Without place name. *(S/M #S46-20a).*	—	Unc	250.

S2752 5 Yüan	Good	Fine	XF
15.8.1925. Blue and multicolor. Monument at center. Back: Blue. Printer: BEPP.			
a. *SHANTUNG. (S/M #S46-22a).*	25.00	75.00	225.
b. *CHINGTAO/SHANTUNG* with additional serial #. *(S/M #S46-22b).*	50.00	150.	400.

NOTE: For #S2751 and S2752 with additional overprint, see Military - Chihli - Shantung #S3812a nd S3813.

S2753 10 Yüan			
15.8.1925. Monument at center. Printer: BEPP. *(S/M #S46-24).* Reported not confirmed.	—	—	—

1925 Second Regular Issue

S2754 10 Cents	Good	Fine	XF
1.10.1925. Yellow. Back: Blue. Printer: ABNC. *(S/M #S46-10).*	25.00	75.00	225.

S2755 20 Cents	Good	Fine	XF
1.10.1925. Black. Shoreline at center. Back: Blue and red. Printer: ABNC. *(S/M #S46-11).*			
a. *TSINAN.*	75.00	225.	600.
b. *TSINGTAU.*	40.00	125.	350.

S2756 50 Cents			
1.10.1925. Brown. Back: Brown and multicolor. Printer: ABNC. *TSINGTAO. (S/M #S46-).*	100.	300.	750.

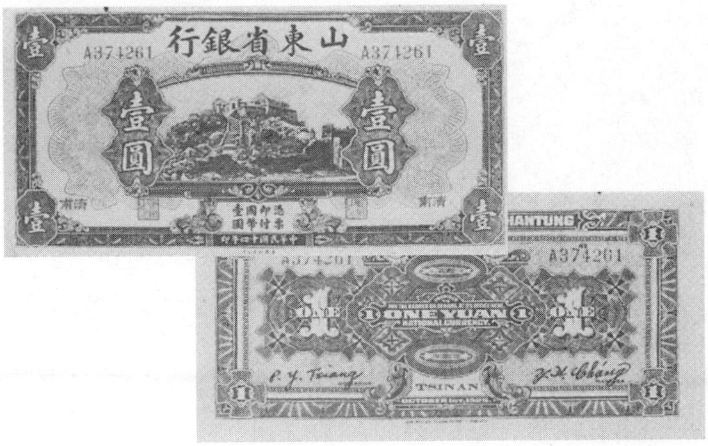

S2757 1 Yüan	Good	Fine	XF
1.10.1925. Blue and multicolor. House on top of hill at center. Back: Blue. Printer: ABNC. *(S/M #S46-21).*			
a. *TSINAN.*	50.00	150.	450.
b. *KIANGSU.*	50.00	150.	450.

S2758 5 Yüan			
1.10.1925. Violet and multicolor. House on top of hill at center. Back: Violet. Printer: ABNC.			
a. *TSINAN. (S/M #S46-23a).*	25.00	75.00	225.
b. *TIENTSIN. (S/M #S46-23b).*	40.00	125.	350.
c. *SHANGHAI. (S/M #S46-23c).*	50.00	150.	450.

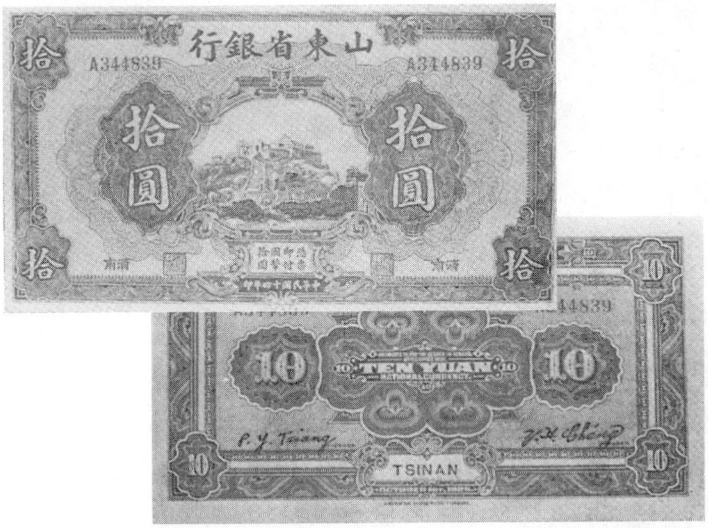

S2759 10 Yüan	Good	Fine	XF
1.10.1925. Red and multicolor. House on top of hill at center. Back: Red. Printer: ABNC. *TSINAN. (S/M #S46-25).*	15.00	45.00	125.

S2760 50 Yüan	Good	Fine	XF
1.10.1925. Black on multicolor underprint. House on top of hill at center. Printer: ABNC. Specimen. *(S/M #S46-26).*	—	Unc	350.

S2761 100 Yüan			
1.10.1925. Brown on multicolor underprint. House on top of hill at center. Printer: ABNC. *(S/M #S46-27).*			
a. Issued note.	—	—	—
s. Specimen.	—	Unc	500.

1926 Issue

		Good	Fine	XF
S2762	**10 Cents** 1.8.1926. Green. Rural house at center. Back: Brown and green. Printer: BEPP.			
	a. *TSINAN. (S/M #S46-30a).*	50.00	150.	450.
	b. *TSINGTAU. (S/M #S46-30b).*	50.00	150.	450.
	c. *TIENTSIN. (S/M #S46-30c).*	50.00	150.	450.
S2763	**20 Cents** 1.8.1926. Blue. Printer: BEPP. *TSINAN. (S/M #S46-31).*	50.00	150.	450.

1926 Tiao Issue

		Good	Fine	XF
S2763B	**2 Tiao = 100 Copper Coins** Oct. 1926. Green. Similar to #S2749. *(S/M #S46-53).*	50.00	150.	450.

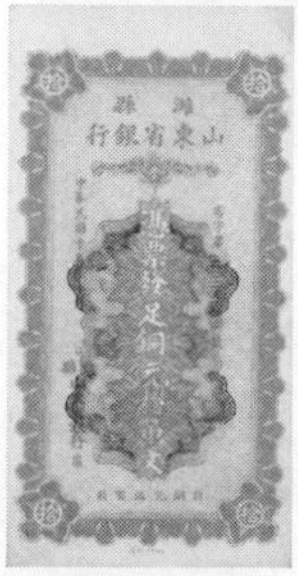

		Good	Fine	XF
S2764	**10 Tiao = 500 Copper Coins** Oct. 1926. Red and blue. Similar to #S2749. Back: Red. *(S/M #S46-55).*	40.00	125.	375.

Shantung Bank
Bank of Shantung

行銀東山
Shan Tung Yin Hang

1912 Issue

		VG	VF	UNC
S2765	**1 Yüan** 1912. Black and multicolor. Back: Black. Printer: CHCP. *Chinan. (S/M #S50-1).*	125.	250.	600.

Note: Previously listed 1 and 3 Ch'uan notes #S2766 and #S2767 dated 1914 are modern fabrications.

ND Dollar Issue

		VG	VF	UNC
S2768	**5 Dollars** ND. Blue and violet. House at left, pavillion at right. Back: Green. *(S/M #S50-9).*	125.	250.	600.
S2769	**10 Silver Yüan** ND. House at left, pavillion at right. *(S/M #S50-10).*	125.	250.	600.

NOTE: For #S2768 and S2769 with additional overprint, see Shantung Commercial Bank #S2695-S2696.

1916 Dollar Issue

		Good	Fine	XF
S2770	**1 Dollar** 1916. *(S/M #S50-20).* Reported not confirmed.	—	—	—

		Good	Fine	XF
S2771	**5 Dollars** 1916. Blue and violet. House at left, pavillion at right. Back: Green. *(S/M #S50-21).*	150.	450.	—

		Good	Fine	XF
S2772	**10 Silver Yüan** 1916. Violet and multicolor. House at left, pavillion at right. Back: Green on pale gold underprint. *SHANTUNG. (S/M #S50-22).*			
	a. Issued note.	125.	375.	900.
	s. Specimen. Perforated 4 Chinese characters.	—	Unc	500.

Suiyuan Provincial Bank

局錢官市平遠綏
Sui Yüan P'ing Shih Kuan Ch'ien Chü

1923 Issue

		Good	Fine	XF
S2773	**10 Coppers** 1923. Brown on green. Bridge at left. Back: Blue. Steam Train at center.	—	—	—
S2774	**20 Coppers** 1923. Violet and green. Back: Brown. Printer: BEPP. Specimen. *(S/M #S91-).*	—	Unc	400.

		Good	Fine	XF
S2775	**30 Coppers** 1923. Red and blue. Shoreline at left. Printer: BEPP. Specimen. *(S/M #S91-1).*	—	Unc	400.
S2778	**10 Cents** 1923. Green. *(S/M #S91-).*	—	—	—
S2779	**20 Cents** 1923. Red. *(S/M #S91-).*	—	—	—

1925 Issue

		Good	Fine	XF
S2780	**10 Coppers** 1925. Brown on green underprint. Two pavillions at left. Back: Blue. Steam passenger train at center. *Paotow. (S/M #S91-).*	—	—	—
S2781	**20 Coppers** 1925. Dark olive-green on light oange underprint. Two pavillions at left. Back: Light red-orange. Steam passenger train at center. *Kuei Sui. (S/M #S91-).*	30.00	100.	—
S2782	**60 Coppers** 1925. *(S/M #S91-).*	—	—	—

S2785 1 Yüan	Good	Fine	XF
1.2.1925. Gateway at center. Printer: BEPP. *Suiyuan*. Specimen. *(S/M #S91-)*.	—	Unc	400.

S2786 5 Yüan	Good	Fine	XF
1.2.1925. House at center. Printer: BEPP. *Suiyuan*. Specimen. *(S/M #S91-)*.	—	Unc	500.

1923 Issue

S2787A 10 Coppers	Good	Fine	XF
1927. Brown on green underprint. Gazebo with trees at left. Back: Brown. Steam Train at center.	—	—	—

S2787B 10 Coppers	Good	Fine	XF
1927. Orange on green underprint. Gazebo with trees at left. Back: Brown. Steam Train.	—	—	—

1927 Issue

S2789 50 Coppers	Good	Fine	XF
1927. Shoreline at left. Back: Steam passenger train at center. *(S/M #S91-)*.			
s1. Chinese overprint Specimen.	—	Unc	400.
s2. English overprint: *SPECIMEN* on back.	—	Unc	400.

1930 Issue

S2791 1 Yüan	Good	Fine	XF
1.7.1930. Green. Bridge to house at center. Printer: BEPP. *Suiyuan*. *(S/M #S91-10)*.			
a. Issued note.	30.00	100.	300.
s. Specimen.	—	Unc	450.
S2792 5 Yüan			
1.7.1930. Blue. Pavilion on dock at center. Printer: BEPP. *Suiyuan*. *(S/M #S91-11)*.	30.00	100.	300.

S2793 10 Yüan	Good	Fine	XF
1.7.1930. Mountain fortress at center. Printer: BEPP. *Suiyuan*. *(S/M #S91-12)*.			
a. Issued note.	40.00	125.	375.
s. Specimen.	—	Unc	500.

1932 Issue

	Good	Fine	XF
S2795 10 Coppers			
1932. Blue. Back: Blue and yellow. Printer: BEPP. *(S/M #S91-21)*.	—	—	—
S2796 20 Coppers			
1932. Green. Back: Green. Printer: BEPP. *(S/M #S91-22)*.	—	—	—
S2798 60 Coppers			
1932. Violet and blue. Back: Violet. Printer: BEPP. *(S/M #S91-24)*.	—	—	—
S2800 1 Chiao = 10 Cents			
1932. Green. Back: Green. Printer: BEPP. *Suiyuan*. *(S/M #S91-26)*.	—	—	—
S2801 2 Chiao = 20 Cents			
1932. Red. Back: Red. Printer: BEPP. *Suiyuan*. *(S/M #S91-28)*.	—	—	—

1935 Issue

		Good	Fine	XF
S2802	**1 Chiao = 10 Cents** 1935. Blue on yellow underprint. Building at center. Back: Blue. *(S/M #S91-31).*	—	—	—
S2802A	**2 Chiao = 20 Cents** 1935. Brown.	—	—	—

Szechuan Provincial Bank

四川官錢局
Szu Ch'uan Kuan Ch'ien Chü

1923 Issue

		Good	Fine	XF
S2804	**1 Dollar** 1923. *(S/M #S96-1).* Reported not confirmed.	—	—	—
S2805	**3 Dollars** 1923. *(S/M #S96-2).* Reported not confirmed.	—	—	—

1924 Cash Issue

		Good	Fine	XF
S2808	**1000 Cash = 100 Coppers** March 1924. Green. Pagoda at left, house at right. Back: Green. Overprint: Red seal. Remainder. *(S/M #S96-10).*	35.00	125.	375.

Szechuan Official Bank

四川官銀號
Szu Ch'uan Kuan Yin

四川官銀局
Szu Ch'uan Kuan Yin Hao

ND Dollar Issue

		Good	Fine	XF
S2809	**1 Dollar** ND. Green and yellow. Back: Blue. Painting of emperor and subjects. *(S/M #S100-1).*	20.00	50.00	150.

1923 Cash Issue

		Good	Fine	XF
S2810	**1000 Cash** 1923. Blue and yellow. Back: Violet. *(S/M #S100-5).*	35.00	125.	375.

1923 Dollar Issue

		Good	Fine	XF
S2811	**1 Dollar** 1923. Blue. Vertical format. Back: Painting of child up tree, 2 women below. *(S/M #S100-10).*	50.00	150.	450.

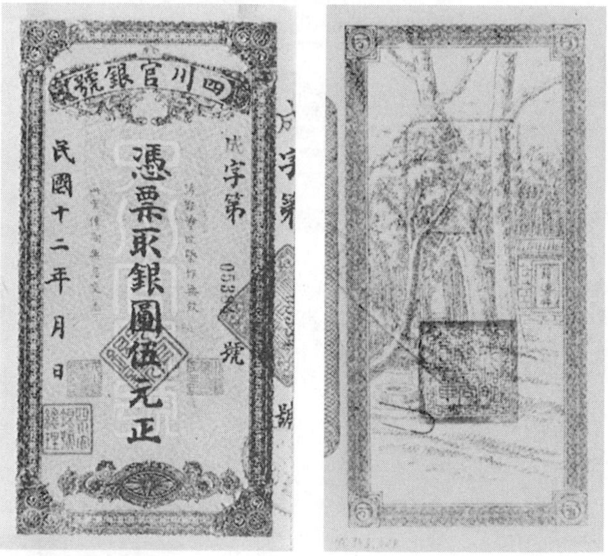

		Good	Fine	XF
S2812	**5 Dollars** 1923. Purple. Vertical format. Back: Painting of trees. *(S/M #S100-11).*	150.	450.	1400.

1924 Cash Issue

		Good	Fine	XF
S2813	**200 Cash** 1924. *(S/M #S100-20).* Reported not confirmed.	—	—	—
S2814	**500 Cash** 1924. *(S/M #S100-21).* Reported not confirmed.	—	—	—
S2815	**1000 Cash** 1924. *(S/M #S100-22).*	60.00	175.	500.

Szechuan Provincial Government

四川省政府建設庫券
Szu Ch'uan Sheng Cheng Fu Chien She K'u Ch'üan

1936 Reconstruction Notes

		Good	Fine	XF
S2816	**50 Dollars** 1936. Blue and green. Buildings at center. Back: Blue. *(S/M #S102-1).*	100.	300.	900.
S2817	**100 Dollars** 1936. Orange and yellow. Buildings at left and right. *(S/M #S102-2).*	125.	375.	1200.

NOTE: For #S2816 and S2817 with additional overprint, see Farmers Bank of China #472 and 473, Vol. 2.

Szechuen Provincial Bank

四川省銀行
Szu Ch'uan Sheng Yin Hang

1935 ND Provisional Issue

S2819 50 Cents	Good	Fine	XF
ND (1935 -old date 1934). Green. Overprint: New bank name on Bank of Chungking. *(S/M #S103-0.5).*	125.	375.	1200.

1936; 1937 Regular Issue

	Good	Fine	XF
S2821 50 Cents			
1.7.1936. Red. Buildings at upper center. Vertical format. Back: Brown and green. *(S/M #S103 1).*	25.00	75.00	225.
S2823 5 Dollars			
1.7.1937. Green and multicolor. Mountains, tower at upper center. Back: Green. *(S/M #S103-10).*	50.00	150.	450.
S2824 10 Silver Yüan			
1.7.1937. Violet and multicolor. Back: Violet. *(S/M #S103-11).*	50.00	150.	450.

NOTE: For #S2823 and S2824 with additional overprint, see Farmers Bank of China #470 and 471, Vol. 2.

1949 Issue

	Good	Fine	XF
S2825 5 Cents			
1949. Green. Hillside village at top. Back: Szechuan Republican coin. *(S/M #S103.1-12).*	30.00	100.	300.
S2825A 10 Cents			
1949. Blue. Hillside village at top. Back: Szechuan Republican coin. *(S/M #S103.1-13).*	30.00	100.	300.

S2826 50 Cents	Good	Fine	XF
1949. Red. Hillside village at top. Vertical format. Back: Szechuan Republican coin. *(S/M #S103.1-16).*	30.00	100.	300.

Szechuen Province

四川兌換券
Szu Ch'uan Tui Huan Ch'üan

1921 Issue

S2827 1 Dollar	Good	Fine	XF
1921. Blue and green. House at left, pagoda at right. Back: Green and red. Shelter in trees at center.			
a. *CHUNGKING. (S/M #S104.5-11a).*	25.00	75.00	225.
b. Without place name. *(S/M #S104.5-11b).*	—	—	150.

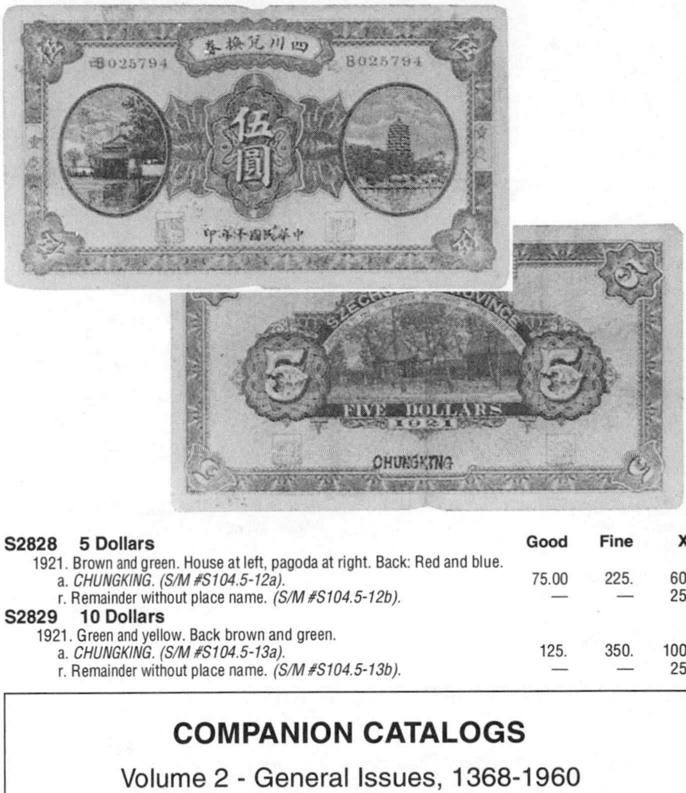

	Good	Fine	XF
S2828 5 Dollars			
1921. Brown and green. House at left, pagoda at right. Back: Red and blue.			
a. *CHUNGKING. (S/M #S104.5-12a).*	75.00	225.	600.
r. Remainder without place name. *(S/M #S104.5-12b).*	—	—	250.
S2829 10 Dollars			
1921. Green and yellow. Back brown and green.			
a. *CHUNGKING. (S/M #S104.5-13a).*	125.	350.	1000.
r. Remainder without place name. *(S/M #S104.5-13b).*	—	—	250.

Szechuan Copper Currency Bureau

局元銅/川四

Szu Ch'uan/T'ung Yüan Chü

1904 Issue

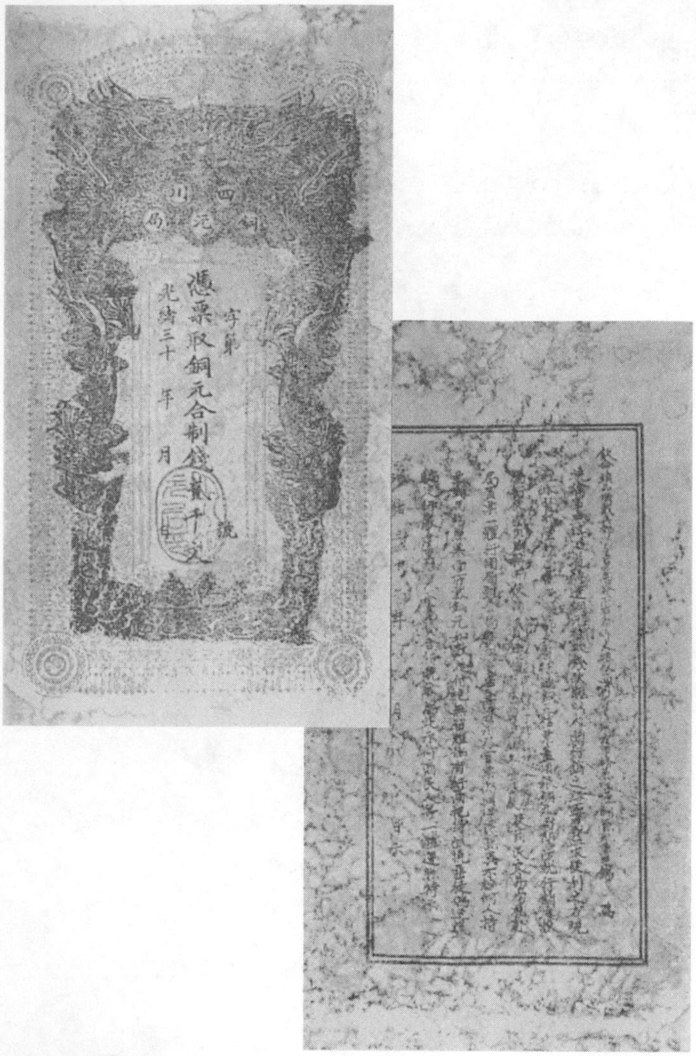

	Good	Fine	XF
S2830 2000 Cash Yr. 30 (1904). Dark blue and red. Facing dragons at upper left and right. Back: Black. *(S/M #S105-0.4).*	250.	600.	—

1908 Issue

	Good	Fine	XF
S2831 1000 Cash ND (ca.1908). Brown and black. *(S/M #S105-0.9).*	200.	600.	—
S2832 2000 Cash ND (ca.1908). Brown and black. Back: Blue. *(S/M #S105-1).*	250.	750.	—

Tihua Official Currency Bureau

局錢官化廸

Ti Hua Kuan Ch'ien Chü

1923 Issue

	Good	Fine	XF
S2833A 40 Cash 1923. Black. Crossed flags with horizontal stripes at top, floral design at left and right. Cloth. *Ili. (S/M #T116-0.2).*	75.00	225.	—

1924 Issue

	Good	Fine	XF
S2833B 40 Cash 1924. Black. Crossed flags with horizontal stripes at top, floral design at left and right. Cloth. *(S/M #T116-0.3).*	75.00	225.	—

1925 Issue

	Good	Fine	XF
S2833C 40 Cash 1925. Black. *(S/M #T116-0.4).*	50.00	150.	400.

1926 Issue

	Good	Fine	XF
S2834 40 Cash 1926. Black and yellow. Uniface. *(S/M #T116-0.5).*	75.00	225.	600.

1927 Issue

	Good	Fine	XF
S2834A 40 Cash 1927. Black. *(S/M #T116-0.7).*	50.00	150.	400.

1928 Issue

	Good	Fine	XF
S2835 40 Cash 1928. *Sinkiang. (S/M #T116-1).*	50.00	150.	400.

1929 Issue

	Good	Fine	XF
S2836 40 Cash 1929. *Sinkiang. (S/M #T116-10).*	50.00	150.	400.

1930 Issue

	Good	Fine	XF
S2837 40 Cash 1930. Black and yellow. *Sinkiang. (S/M #T116-20).*	75.00	225.	600.

1931 Issue

	Good	Fine	XF
S2838 40 Cash 1931. Black and yellow. *Sinkinag. (S/M #T116-30).*	75.00	225.	600.

1932 Issue

	Good	Fine	XF
S2839 40 Cash 1932. Black. Crossed flags with sunburst in canton at top, floral design at left and right, waves at bottom. Cloth. *Sinkiang. (S/M #T116-40).*	75.00	225.	600.
S2841 100 Cash 1932. Sun at top and bottom, leaves at left and right. *Sinkiang. (S/M #T116-41).*	150.	450.	1000.

Tientsin Bank

行銀津天

T'ien Ching Yin Hao

1905 Issue

	Good	Fine	XF
S2843 1 Dollar Yr. 31 (1905). Green and red. Facing dragons at upper left and right. Back: Blue. *(S/M #T170.5-11).*	225.	650.	—

Bureau of Finance Ching Hai (Tsing Hai)

券持維廳政財

(Ch'ing Hai) Ts'ai Cheng T'ing Wei Ch'ih Ch'üan

1930 Maintenance Notes Issue

	Good	Fine	XF
S2845 10 Cents 1930. Blue. Cloth. *Tsinghai. (S/M #T191-).*	300.	800.	2000.
S2846 1 Dollar 1930. Blue. *Tsinghai. (S/M #T191-).*	400.	1000.	2750.
S2847 5 Dollars 1930. Red. *(S/M #T191-).*	550.	1400.	3250.

1935 Maintenance Notes Issue

		Good	Fine	XF
S2848	**1 Yüan** 1935. Chinghai Province. Printer: BEPP. *(S/M #T191-1).* Reported not confirmed.	—	—	—

		Good	Fine	XF
S2849	**5 Yüan** 1935. Red. Buildings on hillside at center. Chinghai Province. Back: Sampans at center. Printer: BEPP. Remainder. *(S/M #T191-2).*	—	Unc	200.
S2850	**10 Yüan** 1935. Chinghai Province. Printer: BEPP. *(S/M #T191-3).* Reported not confirmed.	—	—	—

Fukien South - Eastern Bank

建福/行銀南東
Tung Nan Yin Hang/Fu Chien

1928 Issue

		Good	Fine	XF
S2851	**1 Dollar** 1928. Green. Shelter in park at center. *FUKIEN.* Back: Brown. *(S/M #F30-11).*			
	a. Issued note.	150.	450.	—
	s. Specimen.	—	Unc	500.
S2852	**5 Dollars** Brown on multicolor underprint. Building in center. *FUKIEN.* Back: Red on pale orange underprint.	75.00	225.	650.
S2853	**10 Dollars** 1928. Building at center. *FUKIEN.* Specimen. *(S/M #F30-11).*	—	Unc	600.

Provincial Bank of the Three Eastern Provinces Bank of Manchuria

БАНК МАНЬЧЖУРIИ

Provincial Bank of Manchuria

Eastern Provincial Bank

Toong San Sang Government Bank

行銀省三東
Tung San Sheng Yin Hang

行銀官省三東
Tung San Sheng Kuan Yin Hang

號銀官省三東
Tung San Sheng Kuan Yin Hao

券兌 號銀官省三東
Tung San Sheng Kuan Yin Hui Tui Ch'üan

1908 Issue

		Good	Fine	XF
S2854	**10 Cents** Yr. 1 (1908). Printer: PYOG. *(S/M #F10-20).*	175.	400.	—
S2854A	**20 Cents** Yr. 1 (1908). Printer: PYOG. *(S/M #F10-21).*	175.	400.	—
S2854B	**50 Cents** Yr. 1 (1908). Printer: PYOG. *(S/M #F10-22).*	175.	400.	—
S2854C	**100 Cents** Yr. 1 (1908). Printer: PYOG. *(S/M #F10-23).*	225.	600.	—
S2854D	**1 Dollar** Yr. 1 (1908). Printer: PYOG. *(S/M #F10-24).*	225.	600.	—
S2854E	**5 Dollars** Yr. 1 (1908). Printer: PYOG. *(S/M #F10-25).*	275.	750.	—
S2854F	**10 Dollars** Yr. 1 (1908). Printer: PYOG. *(S/M #F10-26).*	300.	850.	—

1909 Chiao Issue

		Good	Fine	XF
S2855	**1 Chiao = 10 Cents** 1.4.1909. Multicolor. *(S/M #T214-).*	175.	400.	—
S2856	**2 Chiao = 20 Cents** 1.4.1909. *(S/M #T214-).* Reported not confirmed.	—	—	—
S2857	**5 Chiao = 50 Cents** 1.4.1909. *(S/M #T214-).* Reported not confirmed.	—	—	—

		Good	Fine	XF
S2858	**10 Chiao = 100 Cents** 1.4.1909. Gray and orange. Back: Gray and green. *(S/M #T214-).*	225.	600.	—
S2859	**50 Chiao = 500 Cents** 1.4.1909. *(S/M #T214-).* Reported not confirmed.	—	—	—
S2860	**100 Chiao = 1000 Cents** 1.4.1909. *(S/M #T214-).* Reported not confirmed.	—	—	—

1910 Chiao Issue

		Good	Fine	XF
S2861	**1 Chiao = 10 Cents** 1910. Printer: PYOG. *(S/M #T214-1).* Reported not confirmed.	—	—	—
S2862	**2 Chiao = 20 Cents** 1910. Printer: PYOG. *(S/M #T214-2).* Reported not confirmed.	—	—	—
S2863	**5 Chiao = 50 Cents** 1910. Printer: PYOG. *(S/M #T214-3).* Reported not confirmed.	—	—	—
S2864	**10 Chiao = 100 Cents** 1910. Printer: PYOG. *(S/M #T214-4).* Reported not confirmed.	—	—	—
S2865	**50 Chiao = 500 Cents** 1910. Printer: PYOG. *(S/M #T214-5).* Reported not confirmed.	—	—	—
S2866	**100 Chiao = 1000 Cents** 1910. Printer: PYOG. *(S/M #T214-6).* Reported not confirmed.	—	—	—

1912 Chiao Issue

		Good	Fine	XF
S2867	**1 Chiao = 10 Cents** 1912. Gray and green. Back: Blue. Printer: PYPO. *(S/M #T214-).*	150.	450.	—
S2868	**2 Chiao = 20 Cents** 1912. Tan. Back: Bistre. Printer: PYPO. *(S/M #T214-).*	150.	450.	—

1913 Chiao Issue

		Good	Fine	XF
S2873	**1 Chiao = 10 Cents** 1913. *(S/M #T214-10).* Reported not confirmed.	—	—	—
S2874	**2 Chiao = 20 Cents** 1913. *(S/M #T214-11).* Reported not confirmed.	—	—	—
S2875	**5 Chiao = 50 Cents** 1913. *(S/M #T214-12).* Reported not confirmed.	—	—	—
S2876	**10 Chiao = 100 Cents** 1913. *(S/M #T214-13).* Reported not confirmed.	—	—	—
S2877	**50 Chiao = 500 Cents** 1913. *(S/M #T214-14).* Reported not confirmed.	—	—	—

		Good	Fine	XF
S2878	**100 Chiao = 1000 Cents** 1913. *(S/M #T214-15).*	600.	1200.	—

1915 Chiao Issue

		Good	Fine	XF
S2880	**1/2 Chiao = 5 Cents** 1915. Blue and green. Steam passenger train at right. Back: Violet. Woded hills at center. *(S/M #T21420).*	30.00	100.	300.

S2881 1 Chiao = 10 Cents

	Good	Fine	XF
1915. Blue and green. Wooded hills at right. Back: Brown. Fortress gateway at center. *(S/M #T214-21).*	50.00	150.	450.

	Good	Fine	XF
S2882 2 Chiao = 20 Cents			
1915. Blue on yellow underprint. Blue on yellow underprint. Back: Brown. Temple at center. *(S/M #T214-22a).*	25.00	75.00	225.
S2882A 2 Chiao = 20 Cents			
1915. Blue on pink underprint. Wooded hills at right. Back: Gray. *(S/M #T214-22b).*	45.00	125.	375.
S2883 5 Chiao = 50 Cents			
1915. *(S/M #T214-23).* Reported not confirmed.	—	—	—
S2884 10 Chiao = 100 Cents			
1915. *(S/M #T214-24).* Reported not confirmed.	—	—	—
S2885 50 Chiao = 500 Cents			
1915. *(S/M #T214-25).* Reported not confirmed.	—	—	—
S2886 100 Chiao = 1000 Cents			
1915. *(S/M #T214-26).* Reported not confirmed.	—	—	—

1916 Issue

	Good	Fine	XF
S2887 5 Coppers			
1916. *(S/M #T214-30).* Reported not confirmed.	—	—	—
S2888 10 Coppers			
1916. *(S/M #T214-31).* Reported not confirmed.	—	—	—
S2889 20 Coppers			
1916. *(S/M #T214-32).* Reported not confirmed.	—	—	—
S2890 50 Coppers			
1916. *(S/M #T214-33).* Reported not confirmed.	—	—	—
S2891 100 Coppers			
1916. *(S/M #T214-34).* Reported not confirmed.	—	—	—

	Good	Fine	XF
S2892 1 Dollar			
1.5.1916. Yellow. Wooded hillside. *MUKDEN.* Back: Black. Printer: BEPP. *(S/M #T214-40).*	75.00	225.	—
S2893 5 Dollars			
1.5.1916. *MUKDEN.* Printer: BEPP. *(S/M #T214-41).*	100.	300.	—
S2894 10 Dollars			
1.5.1916. *MUKDEN.* Printer: BEPP. *(S/M #T214-42).*	125.	375.	—
S2895 50 Dollars			
1.5.1916. *MUKDEN.* Printer: BEPP. *(S/M #T214-43).*	125.	375.	—

1917 Issue

	Good	Fine	XF
S2897 1 Dollar			
1917. Orange. Back: Green and black. Temple of Heaven at center. Printer: BEPP. *Fengtien. (S/M #T214-50).*	75.00	225.	—
S2898 5 Dollars			
1917. Blue. Back: Green and black. Temple of Heaven at center. Printer: BEPP. *Fengtien. (S/M #T214-51).*	75.00	225.	—

	Good	Fine	XF
S2899 10 Dollars			
1917. Green. Back: Blue and black. Temple of Heaven at center. Printer: BEPP. *Fengtien. (S/M #T214-52).*	100.	300.	—

1918 Issue

	Good	Fine	XF
S2901 10 Cents			
1918. Printer: TCPL. *Fengtien. (S/M #T214-60).* Reported not confirmed.	—	—	—
S2902 20 Cents			
1918. Printer: TCPL. *Fengtien. (S/M #T214-61).* Reported not confirmed.	—	—	—
S2903 50 Cents			
1918. Printer: TCPL. *Fengtien. (S/M #T214-62).* Reported not confirmed.	—	—	—

1919 Issue

	Good	Fine	XF
S2906 50 Cents			
1919. Printer: PYOG. *(S/M #T214-70).* Reported not confirmed.	—	—	—
S2908 1 Tael			
1919. Printer: ABNC. *(S/M #T214-80).* Reported not confirmed.	—	—	—
S2909 5 Taels			
1919. Printer: ABNC. *(S/M #T214-81).* Reported not confirmed.	—	—	—
S2910 10 Taels			
1919. Printer: ABNC. *(S/M #T214-82).* Reported not confirmed.	—	—	—
S2911 50 Taels			
1919. Printer: ABNC. *(S/M #T214-83).* Reported not confirmed.	—	—	—
S2912 100 Taels			
1919. Printer: ABNC. *(S/M #T214-84).* Reported not confirmed.	—	—	—

1920 Issue

	Good	Fine	XF
S2913 10 Cents			
1920. Buildings at center. Printer: PYOG. *(S/M #T214-90).* Reported not confirmed.	—	—	—

	Good	Fine	XF
S2916 1 Dollar			
1920. Green. Back: Blue with black text. Printer: BEPP. *Harbin. (S/M #T214-100).*	75.00	225.	—

	Good	Fine	XF
S2917 5 Dollars			
1920. Brown. Buildings at center. Back: Red. Overprint: *BANK OF MANCHURIA / HARBIN* on back. Printer: BEPP. *Harbin. (S/M #T214-101).*			
a. Issued note.	150.	450.	—
s. Specimen.	—	Unc	500.

	Good	Fine	XF
S2918 10 Dollars			
1920. Blue. Buildings at center. Back: Green. Printer: BEPP. *Harbin. (S/M #T214-102).*			
a. Issued note.	150.	450.	—
s. Specimen.	—	Unc	500.

1921 Issues

	Good	Fine	XF
S2920 5 Cents			
1921. Printer: TCPL. *FENGTIEN. (S/M #T214-110).* Reported not confirmed.	—	—	—
S2920A 10 Cents			
1921. Printer: TCPL. *FENGTIEN. (S/M #T214-111).* Reported not confirmed.	—	—	—
S2920B 20 Cents			
1921. Printer: TCPL. *FENGTIEN. (S/M #T214-113).* Reported not confirmed.	—	—	—
S2920C 50 Cents			
1921. Printer: TCPL. *FENGTIEN. (S/M #T214-116).* Reported not confirmed.	—	—	—

	Good	Fine	XF
S2921 5 Cents			
1.1.1921. Violet and blue. Buildings at left. Back: Blue and multicolor. Printer: BEPP. *HARBIN. (S/M #T214-).*			
a. Issued note.	40.00	125.	350.
b. With otfficial Chinese 4 character overprint.	40.00	125.	350.

	Good	Fine	XF
S2922 10 Cents			
1.1.1921. Blue and yellow. Buildings at left. *HARBIN.* Back: Orange and blue. Printer: BEPP.			
a. Issued note. *(S/M #T214-112a).*	50.00	150.	450.
b. With otfficial Chinese 4 character overprint. *(S/M #T214-112b).*	50.00	150.	450.
S2923 20 Cents			
1.1.1921. Blue and yellow. Buildings at left. Back: Violet and multicolor. Printer: BEPP. *HARBIN. (S/M #T214-114).*	25.00	75.00	—

	Good	Fine	XF
S2925 20 Cents			
1.1.1921. Brown on light blue underprint. Without imprint. Back: Dark green and multicolor.			
a. Issued note. *(S/M #T214-115a).*	20.00	50.00	—
b. With otfficial Chinese 4 character overprint *(S/M #T214-115b).*	20.00	50.00	—
S2926 50 Cents			
1.1.1921. *(S/M #T214-117).* Reported not confirmed.	—	—	—

	Good	Fine	XF
S2927 1 Dollar			
July 1921. Yellow-orange and multicolor. Building at center. *HARBIN.* Back: Yellow-orange. Printer: ABNC.			
a. Issued note. *(S/M #T214-120a).*	50.00	150.	—
b. With otfficial Chinese 4 character overprint *(S/M #T214-120b).*	50.00	150.	—
s. Specimen overprint on #S2927b. *(S/M #T214-120c).*	—	Unc	400.

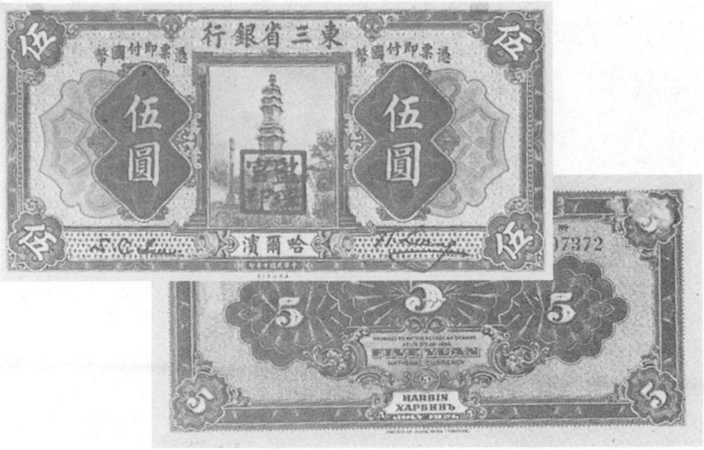

	Good	Fine	XF
S2928 5 Dollars			
July 1921. Olive and multicolor. Tower at center. *HARBIN.* Back: Olive. Printer: ABNC.			
a. Issued note. *(S/M #T214-121a).*	75.00	225.	—
b. With otfficial Chinese 4 Character overprint *(S/M #T214-121b).*	75.00	225.	—
s. Specimen overprint on #S2928b. *(S/M #T214-121c).*	—	Unc	550.

	Good	Fine	XF
S2929 10 Dollars			
July 1921. Purple and multicolor. Tower gates at center. *HARBIN.* Back: Violet. Printer: ABNC.			
a. Issued note. *(S/M #T214-122a).*	75.00	225.	—
b. With otfficial Chinese 4 character overprint at center on face. *(S/M #T214-122b).*	75.00	225.	—
s. Specimen overprint on #S2929b. *(S/M #T214-122c).*	—	Unc	500

1922 Issue

	Good	Fine	XF
S2931 5 Coppers			
1922. Printer: TCPL. *Fengtien. (S/M #T214-130).* Reported not confirmed.	—	—	—
S2932 10 Coppers			
1922. Printer: TCPL. *Fengtien. (S/M #T214-131).* Reported not confirmed.	—	—	—
S2933 20 Coppers			
1922. Printer: TCPL. *Fengtien. (S/M #T214-132).* Reported not confirmed.	—	—	—
S2934 50 Coppers			
1922. Printer: TCPL. *Fengtien. (S/M #T214-133).* Reported not confirmed.	—	—	—
S2935 100 Coppers			
1922. Printer: TCPL. *Fengtien. (S/M #T214-134).* Reported not confirmed.	—	—	—

	Good	Fine	XF
S2936 1 Dollar			
1922. Orange. Back: Green. Temple of heaven at center. *Fengtien. (S/M #T214-140).*	25.00	75.00	225.

S2937 5 Dollars	Good	Fine	XF
1922. Dark blue. Back: Green. Temple of Heaven at center. *Fengtien. (S/M #T214-141).*	125.	375.	—

S2938 10 Dollars	Good	Fine	XF
1922. Green. Back: Blue. Temple of Heaven at center. *Fengtien. (S/M #T214-142).*	75.00	225.	—

S2940 5 Cents	Good	Fine	XF
1.4.1923. Blue and yellow. Buildings at left. Without imprint. *Harbin.* Back: Violet and multicolor.			
a. Issued note. *(S/M #T214-150a).*	20.00	50.00	150.
b. With otfficial Chinese 4 character overprint. *(S/M #T214-150b).*	20.00	50.00	150.
s. Specimen overprint on #S2940b. *(S/M #T214-150c).*	—	Unc	350.

S2941 10 Cents	Good	Fine	XF
1.4.1923. Brown and yellow-green. Buildings at left. *Harbin.* Without imprint. Back: Brown, orange and green.			
a. Issued note. *(S/M #T214-151a).*	25.00	75.00	225.
b. With otfficial Chinese 4 character overprint. *(S/M #T214-151b).*	25.00	75.00	225.
s. Specimen overprint on #S2941b. *(S/M #T214-151c).*	—	Unc	350.
S2942 20 Cents			
1.4.1923. Buildings at left. *Harbin.* Without imprint. *(S/M #T214-152).* Reported not confirmed.	—	—	—
S2943 50 Cents			
1.4.1923. Buildings at left. *Harbin.* Without imprint. *(S/M #T214-153).* Reported not confirmed.	—	—	—
S2944 1 Dollar			
1923. Printer: BEPP.			
a. *Fengtien. (S/M #T214-160a).* Reported not confirmed.	—	—	—
b. *Harbin. (S/M #T214-160b).* Reported not confirmed.	—	—	—
c. *Tientsin. (S/M #T214-160c).* Reported not confirmed.	—	—	—
S2945 5 Dollars			
1923. Printer: BEPP.			
a. *Fengtien. (S/M #T214-161a).* Reported not confirmed.	—	—	—
b. *Harbin. (S/M #T214-161b).* Reported not confirmed.	—	—	—
c. *Tientsin. (S/M #T214-161c).* Reported not confirmed.	—	—	—
S2946 10 Dollars			
1923. Printer: BEPP.			
a. *Fengtien. (S/M #T214-162a).* Reported not confirmed.	—	—	—
b. *Harbin. (S/M #T214-162b).* Reported not confirmed.	—	—	—
c. *Tientsin. (S/M #T214-162c).* Reported not confirmed.	—	—	—

1924 Issue

S2947 1 Dollar	Good	Fine	XF
1924. Printer: TCPL. *Fengtien. (S/M #T214-170).* Reported not confirmed.	—	—	—
S2948 5 Dollars			
1924. Printer: TCPL. *Fengtien. (S/M #T214-172).* Reported not confirmed.	—	—	—
S2949 10 Dollars			
1924. Printer: TCPL. *Fengtien. (S/M #T214-174).* Reported not confirmed.	—	—	—

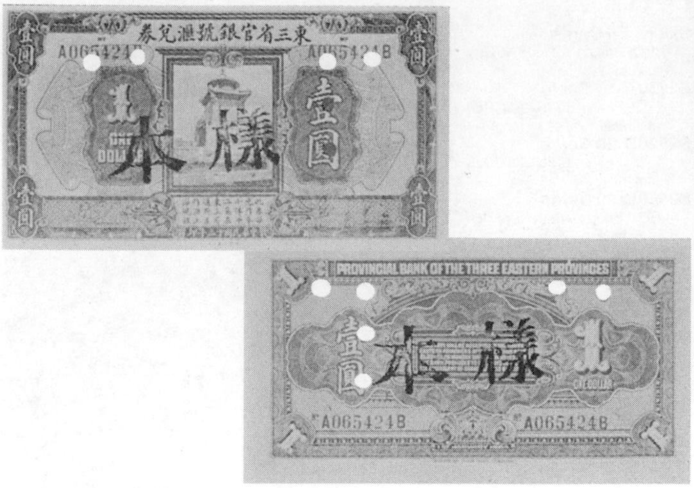

S2951 1 Dollar	VG	VF	UNC
1.1.1924. Blue and multicolor. Tower at center. Back: Green. Printer: ABNC.			
a. Issued note. *(S/M #T214-171a).*	50.00	150.	225.
s. Specimen. *(S/M #T214-171b).*	—	—	400.

S2952 5 Dollars	VG	VF	UNC
1.1.1924. Green and multicolor. Tower at center. Back: Orange. Printer: ABNC.			
a. Issued note. *(S/M #T214-173a).*	50.00	150.	225.
s. Specimen. *(S/M #T214-173b).*	—	—	400.

S2953 10 Dollars	VG	VF	UNC
1.1.1924. Dark brown on pink, green, and multicolor underprint. Tower at center. Back: Red. Printer: ABNC. *(S/M #T214-175).*			
a. 171 x 86mm.	50.00	150.	450.
b. 165 x 84mm.	50.00	150.	450.
S2954 50 Dollars			
1.1.1924. Green and multicolor. Tower at center. Back: Brown. Printer: ABNC. *(S/M #T214-176).*	100.	300.	800.

S2955 100 Dollars	VG	VF	UNC
1.1.1924. Violet and multicolor. Tower at center. Back: Black. Printer: ABNC.	125.	375.	1000.

1929 First Issue

	Good	Fine	XF
S2956 10 Cents			
1929. Printer: TCPL. *Fengtien. (S/M #T214-180).* Reported not confirmed.	—	—	—
S2957 20 Cents			
1929. Printer: TCPL. *Fengtien. (S/M #T214-182).* Reported not confirmed.	—	—	—
S2958 50 Cents			
1929. Printer: TCPL. *Fengtien. (S/M #T214-184).* Reported not confirmed.	—	—	—

1929 Second Issue

	Good	Fine	XF
S2959 10 Cents			
1.12.1929. Green. Large building at center. *MUKDEN.*			
a. Issued note. *(S/M #T214-181a).*	20.00	60.00	175.
b. With additional control # overprint: *2. (S/M #T214-181b).*	20.00	60.00	175.
S2960 20 Cents			
1.12.1929. Brown. Bridge at center. *MUKDEN. (S/M #T214-183).*	20.00	60.00	175.
S2961 50 Cents			
1.12.1929. Blue. *MUKDEN. (S/M #T214-185).*	30.00	100.	300.

S2962 1 Dollar	Good	Fine	XF
Nov. 1929. Black and multicolor. Pavillion by pool at center. Back: Black. Printer: ABNC.			
a. *THREE EASTERN PROVINCES. (S/M #T214-190c).*	35.00	100.	300.
b. *TIENTSIN/THREE EASTERN PROVINCES. (S/M #T214-190b).*	40.00	125.	375.
p1. As a. Proof.	—	Unc	400.
p2. *TIENTSIN.* Proof.	—	Unc	600.
r. Remainder. Without place name. *(S/M #T214-190a).*	—	Unc	200.
s1. As a. Specimen.	—	Unc	600.
s2. *TIENTSIN.* Specimen.	—	Unc	650.

S2963 5 Dollars	Good	Fine	XF
Nov. 1929. Brown and multicolor. Pavillion by pool at center. Back: Brown. Printer: ABNC.			
a. *THREE EASTERN PROVINCES. (S/M #T214-191c).*	75.00	225.	600.
b. *TIENTSIN/THREE EASTERN PROVINCES. (S/M #T214-191b).*	75.00	225.	600.
p1. As a. Proof.	—	Unc	400.
p2. *TIENTSIN.* Proof.	—	Unc	600.
r. Remainder. Without place name. *(S/M #T214-191a).*	—	Unc	200.
s1. As a. Specimen.	—	Unc	600.
s2. *TIENTSIN.* Specimen.	—	Unc	650.

1929 First Issue

S2964 10 Dollars	Good	Fine	XF
Nov. 1929. Green and multicolor. Back: Green.			
a. *THREE EASTERN PROVINCES. (S/M #T214-192c).*	30.00	100.	300.
b. *TIENTSIN/THREE EASTERN PROVINCES. (S/M #T214-192b).*	45.00	125.	375.
p1. As a. Proof.	—	Unc	450.
p2. *TIENTSIN.* Proof.	—	Unc	600.
r. Remainder. Without place name. *(S/M #T214-192a).*	—	Unc	200.
s1. As a. Specimen.	—	Unc	600.
s2. *TIENTSIN.* Specimen.	—	Unc	700.

1929 Second Issue

S2965 100 Dollars	Good	Fine	XF
Nov. 1929. Red and multicolor. Pavillion by pool at center. Printer: ABNC.			
a. *THREE EASTERN PROVINCES. (S/M #T214-193c).*	175.	550.	—
b. *TIENTSIN/THREE EASTERN PROVINCES. (S/M #T214-193b).*	300.	850.	—
p. As a. Proof.	—	Unc	700.
r. Remainder. Without place name. *(S/M #T214-193a).*	—	Unc	300.
s. As a. Specimen.	—	Unc	850.

For #S2962-S2965 with additional overprint, see Chanan Bank #J118-J119 amd Central Bank of Manchukuo #J120-J122, Vol. 2.

Provincial Bank of Honan

局钱银官泉豫
Yü Ch'üan Kuan Yin Ch'ien Chü

1904 Issue

	Good	Fine	XF
S2971 500 Cash			
Yr. 30 (1904). *(S/M #Y20-).* Reported not confirmed.	—	—	—
S2972 1000 Cash			
Yr. 30 (1904). Red and green. Back: Black. *(S/M #Y20-1).*	150.	450.	—
S2973 1000 Cash			
Yr. 30 (1904). Orange and blue. *(S/M #Y20-).* Reported not confirmed.	—	—	—
S2974 2000 Cash			
Yr. 30 (1904). *(S/M #Y20-).* Reported not confirmed.	—	—	—

1918 Issue

	Good	Fine	XF
S2977 10 Coppers 15.7.1918. Dark olive-green on pink underprint. Portrait old man at lower left. Back: Red on yellow underprint. *(S/M #Y20-10).*	30.00	100.	300.

	Good	Fine	XF
S2978 20 Coppers 15.7.1918. Violet on tan underprint. Portrait old man at lower left. Back: Dark blue on olive-green underprint. *(S/M #Y20-11).*	50.00	150.	450.
S2979 50 Coppers 15.7.1918. *(S/M #20-12).* Reported not confirmed.	—	—	—
S2980 100 Coppers 15.7.1918. *(S/M #Y20-13).* Reported not confirmed.	—	—	—

	Good	Fine	XF
S2981 1 Dollar 15.7.1918. Blue. Portrait old man at center. Back: Blue on green and tan underprint. Printer: ABNC. *(S/M #Y20-20).*	70.00	225.	—
S2982 5 Dollars 15.7.1918. Orange. Portrait old man at center. Back: Red on blue and brown underprint. Printer: ABNC. *(S/M #Y20-21).*	90.00	250.	—
S2983 10 Dollars 15.7.1918. Dark red on blue and brown underprint. Portrait old man at center. Back: Green on blue and tan underprint. Printer: ABNC. *(S/M #Y20-22).*	100.	225.	—

1921 Issue

	Good	Fine	XF
S2985 1 Dollar 1921. Green. Back: Red and blue. *(S/M #Y20-30).*	18.50	55.00	—

NOTE: For #S2985 with large square red seal overprint, see Military - Hunan Province Treasury #S3855.

Yu Sien Bank
Yü Hsiang Bank

行銀湘裕
Yü Hsiang Yin Hang

1918 Issue

	Good	Fine	XF
S2988 10 Coppers June 1918. Brown and blue. House at left, roadway to walled city at right. *CHANGSHA*. Back: Orange and blue. Bank building at center. Printer: CMPA. *(S/M #Y24-1).*	25.00	80.00	—
S2989 10 Coppers 1918. Brown and green. House at left, roadway to walled city at right. *CHANGSHA*. Back: Red and blue. Bank building at center. Printer: CMPA. *(S/M #Y24-2).*	25.00	80.00	—
S2990 20 Coppers 1918. Green and brown. House at left, roadway to walled city at right. *CHANGSHA*. Back: Blue and yellow. Bank building at center. Printer: CMPA. *(S/M #Y24-3).*	25.00	80.00	—

	Good	Fine	XF
S2992 100 Coppers June 1918. Green and orange. House at left, roadway to walled city at right. *CHANGSHA*. Back: Brown and blue. Bank building at center. Printer: CMPA. *(S/M #Y24-4).*	20.00	60.00	—

	Good	Fine	XF
S2994 1 Silver Dollar 15.7.1918. Red. House at left, roadway to walled city at right. *HUNAN // CHANGSHA*. Back: Red and multicolor. Printer: ABNC. *(S/M #Y24-10).*			
a. Issued note.	25.00	75.00	225.
p. Without place name. Proof.	—	Unc	300.

	Good	Fine	XF
S2995 5 Silver Dollars 15.7.1918. Dark blue. House at left, roadway to walled city at right. *HUNAN // CHANGSHA*. Back: Dark blue and multicolor. Printer: ABNC. *(S/M #Y24-11).*			
a. Issued note.	75.00	225.	650.
p. Without place name. Proof.	—	Unc	300.
S2995A 10 Silver Dollars 15.7.1918. House at left, roadway to walled city at right. *HUNAN // CHANGSHA*. Without place name. Printer: ABNC. Proof. *(S/M #Y24-12).*	—	—	—

New Fu-T'ien Bank
Yunnan Fu-T'ien Bank

行銀新滇富南雲
Yün Nan Fu T'ien Hsin Yin Hang

1929 Issue

	Good	Fine	XF
S2996 1 Dollar			
1929. Blue and multicolor. Phoenix and horse facing above globes. Back: Blue. Printer: ABNC. *(S/M #Y67-1).*			
a. Issued note.	15.00	45.00	125.
s. Specimen.	—	Unc	500.
S2997 5 Dollars			
1929. Brown and multicolor. Phoenix and horse facing above globes. Back: Brown. Printer: ABNC. *(S/M #Y67-2).*			
a. Issued note.	15.00	45.00	125.
s. Specimen.	—	Unc	450.

	Good	Fine	XF
S2998 10 Dollars			
1929. Violet and multicolor. Phoenix and horse facing above globes. Back: Violet. Printer: ABNC. *(S/M #Y67-3).*			
a. Issued note.	25.00	75.00	225.
s. Specimen.	—	Unc	450.
S2999 50 Dollars			
1929. Green and multicolor. Phoenix and horse facing above globes. Back: Green. Printer: ABNC. *(S/M #Y67-4).*			
a. Issued note.	50.00	150.	450.
s. Specimen.	—	Unc	600.

	Good	Fine	XF
S3000 100 Dollars			
1929. Red and multicolor. Phoenix and horse facing above globes. Back: Red. Printer: ABNC. *(S/M #Y67-5).*			
a. Issued note.	50.00	150.	450.
s. Specimen.	—	Unc	600.

1933 Issue

	Good	Fine	XF
S3001 5 Cents			
1933. Blue and red. Temple at center. Back: Blue. *(S/M #Y67-12).*	60.00	175.	525.
S3002 10 Cents			
1933. Violet. Pagoda on hillside at center. *(S/M #Y67-).*	125.	350.	900.
S3003 20 Cents			
1933. Green on red underprint. *(S/M #Y67-).*	125.	350.	900.
S3004 50 Cents			
1933. Red and blue. *(S/M #Y67-).*	10.00	25.00	75.00

Fu-Tien Bank
Yunnan "Fu-Tien" Bank
Yunnan "Futten" Bank

行銀滇富南雲
Yün Nan Fu T'ien Yin Hang

行銀滇富
Fu Tien Yin Hang

1913 Issue

	Good	Fine	XF
S3009 5 Dollars 1913. Brown, green and red. Crossed flags at top center. Back: Dark green and red. Printer: YOPO. *(S/M #Y70-0.5).*	200.	600.	1400.

	Good	Fine	XF
S3009A 10 Dollars 1913. Blue and multicolor. Crossed flags at top center. Back: Brown and yellow. Printer: YOPO. *(S/M #Y70-1).*	200.	600.	1400.

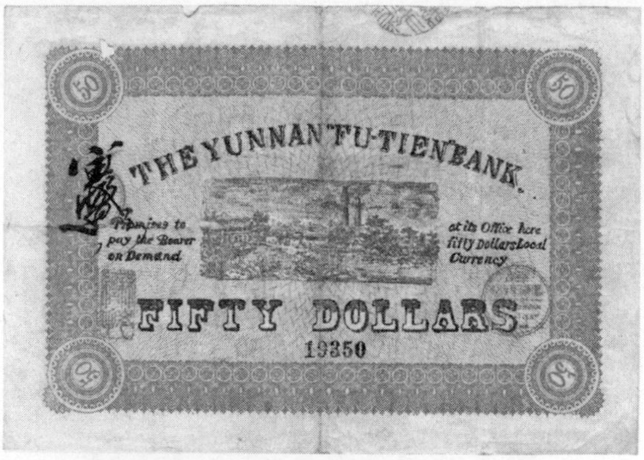

S3009B 50 Dollars

Yr. 16 (1927). Crossed flags at top center. Back: City view at center. Printer: YOPO. *(S/M #Y70-)*.

Good	Fine	XF
400.	1200.	—

S3009C 100 Dollars

Yr. 16 (1927). Crossed flags at top center. Back: Antique steam passenger train at center. Printer: YOPO. *(S/M #Y70-)*.

Good	Fine	XF
400.	1200.	—

NOTE: Confirmation of date of issue for #S3009B and S3009C is requested.

1916 Commemorative Issue

S3009E 1 Yüan

Yr. 5 (1916). Black and olive-brown. Rural scene at left. Portrait general at right. Back: Rural village. In memory of the Chinese Republican Revolution in Yunnan Province. Specimen with perforations. *(S/M #Y70-)*. Rare.

Good	Fine	XF
—	—	—

S3009F 5 Yüan

Yr. 5 (1916). Black and brown on pale blue underprint. Rural scene at left. Portrait general at right. In Memory of the CHinese Republican Revolution in Yunnan Province. Specimen with perforations. *(S/M #Y70-)*. Rare.

Good	Fine	XF
—	—	—

S3009G 10 Yüan

Yr. 5 (1916). Black and blue-black. Gazebo at left. Portrait general at right. Back: Blue-gray. In Memory of the Chinese Republican Revolution in Yunnan Province. Specimen with perforations. *(S/M #Y70-)*. Rare.

Good	Fine	XF
—	—	—

1919 Issue

S3009J 20 Cash

1920. Blue on pink underprint.

Good	Fine	XF
40.00	125.	—

S3010 1 Dollar

1919. Purple on light blue underprint. Back: Red on green underprint. *(S/M #Y70-)*.

Good	Fine	XF
150.	450.	—

1921 ND Issue

S3011 10 Cents

ND (1921). Black. Phoenix and horse facing above globes. Back: Blue and multicolor. Printer: ABNC. *(S/M #Y70-11)*.

Good	Fine	XF
25.00	75.00	—

S3012 20 Cents	Good	Fine	XF
ND (1921). Dark blue. Phoenix and horse facing above globes. Back: Dark blue on multicolor underprint. Printer: ABNC. *(S/M #Y70-12.)*			
a. Issued note.	25.00	75.00	—
b. Punched hole cancelled, hand stamps.	20.00	50.00	—

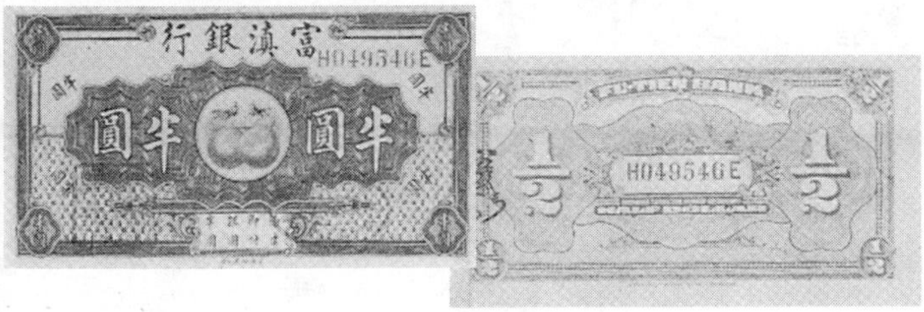

S3013 50 Cents	Good	Fine	XF
ND (1921). Dark green. Phoenix and horse facing above globes. 2 signature varieties. Back: Green and multicolor. Printer: ABNC. *(S/M #Y70-13).*	40.00	125.	—

S3014 1 Dollar	Good	Fine	XF
ND (1921). Olive and multicolor. Phoenix and horse facing above globes. Back: Green. Gateway at center. Printer: ABNC. *(S/M #Y70-20).*	50.00	150.	—

S3015 5 Dollars	Good	Fine	XF
ND (1921). Violet on multicolor underprint. Phoenix and horse facing above globes. Back: Red. Gateway at center. Printer: ABNC. *(S/M #Y70-21).*			
a. Issued note.	75.00	225.	—
s. Specimen.	—	Unc	350.

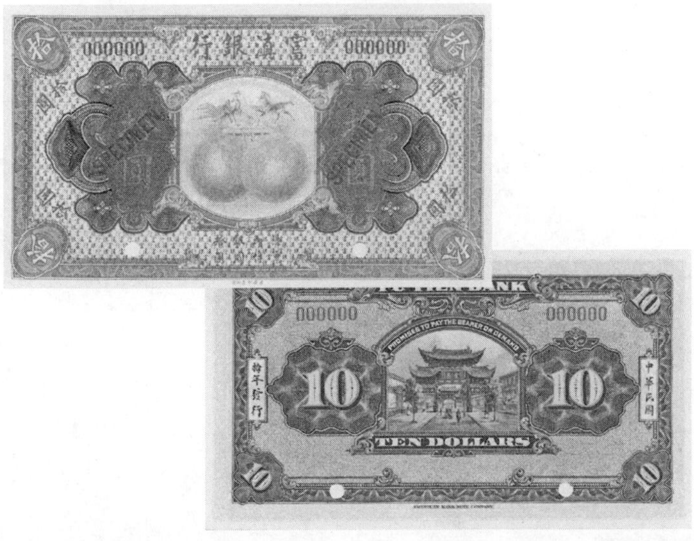

S3016 10 Dollars	Good	Fine	XF
ND (1921). Orange on green underprint. Phoenix and horse facing above globes. Back: Green. Printer: ABNC. *(S/M #Y70-22).*			
a. Issued note.	100.	300.	—
s. Specimen.	—	Unc	450.

S3017 50 Dollars	Good	Fine	XF
ND (1921). Blue on brown underprint. Phoenix and horse facing above globes. Back: Brown. Printer: ABNC. Specimen. *(S/M #Y70-23).*	—	Unc	450.

S3018 100 Dollars	Good	Fine	XF
ND (1921). Brown on blue underprint. Phoenix and horse facing above globes. Back: Green. Printer: ABNC. Specimen. *(S/M #Y70-24).*	—	Unc	600.
S3019 500 Dollars			
ND (1921). Phoenix and horse facing above globes. Printer: ABNC. *(S/M #Y70-25).* Reported not confirmed.	—	—	—
S3020 1000 Dollars			
ND (1921). Phoenix and horse facing above globes. Printer: ABNC. *(S/M #Y70-26).* Reported not confirmed.	—	—	—

1927 Issue

S3021 1 Dollar	Good	Fine	XF
1927. Printer: YOPO. *(S/M #Y70-30).* Reported not confirmed.	—	—	—
S3022 5 Dollars			
1927. Printer: YOPO. *(S/M #Y70-31).* Reported not confirmed.	—	—	—

S3023 10 Dollars	Good	Fine	XF
1927. Blue and green. Crossed flags at upper center. Back: Red and brown. Printer: YOPO. *(S/M #Y70-32).*	125.	375.	—

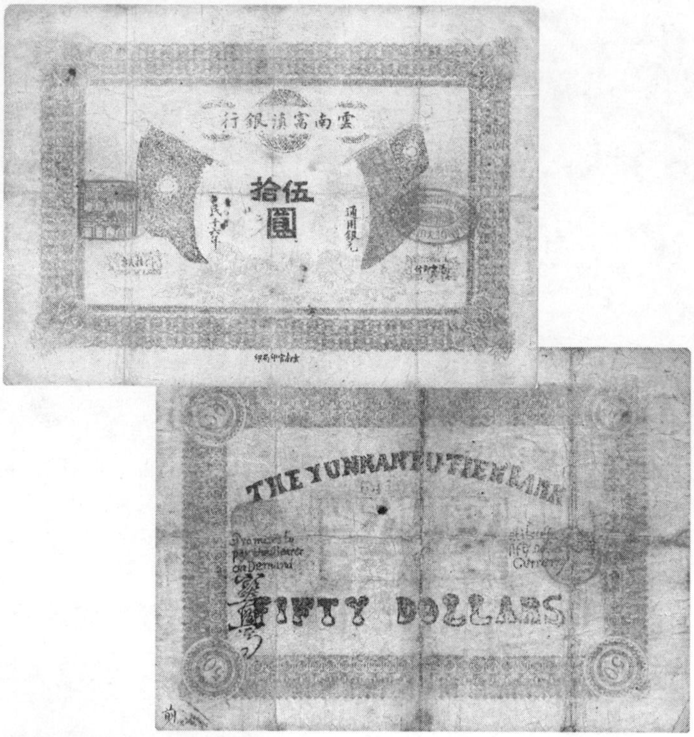

	Good	Fine	XF
S3023A 50 Dollars			
1927. Brown and multicolor. Crossed flags. Printer: YOPO.	375.	1000.	—
S3023B 100 Dollars			
1927. Blue on rose underprint. Crossed flags. Back: Brown and blue. Village scene. Printer: YOPO.	500.	1250.	—

1929 Issue

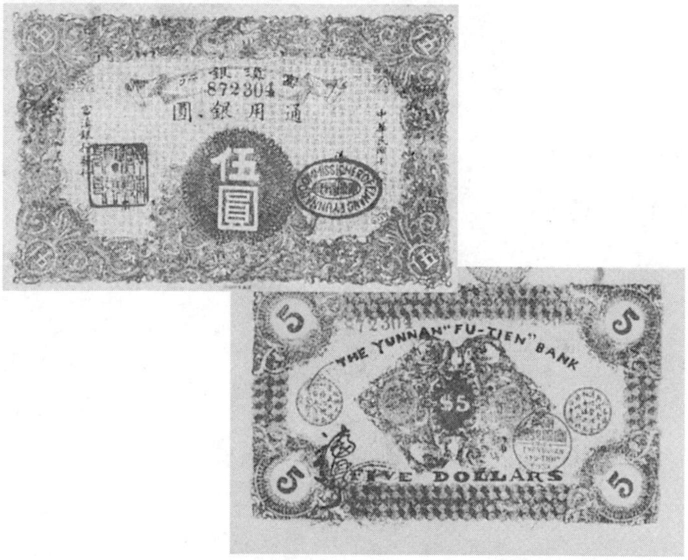

	Good	Fine	XF
S3023D 5 Dollars			
1929. Dark blue on pale orange underprint. Back: Red on pink underprint. Black text. *(S/M #Y70-35)*.	15.00	45.00	125.

Yunnan Official Currency Bureau

局錢官南雲

Yün Nan Kuan Ch'ien Chü

1907 Tael Issue

	Good	Fine	XF
S3023E 3 Taels 6 Mace			
Yr. 33 (1907). Black on orange underprint. Facing dragons at top, waves at bottom. Back: Black text, large red square seal. *(S/M #Y70.5-13)*.	—	—	—

Yunnan Provincial Bank

票本額定圓銀行銀省南雲

Yün Nan Sheng Yin Hang Yin Yüan Ting O Pen P'iao

1949 Silver Yüan Cashier's Checks Issue

	VG	VF	UNC
S3024 1 Silver Yüan			
1949. Red on light blue underprint. Back: Red. City gates at center. Printer: HKPA.			
a. Issued note. *(S/M #Y71-0.4a)*.	5.00	15.00	45.00
b. With additional large red hand stamped signature seal and violet Chinese 4 character overprint: *Ting O Pen P'iao. (S/M #Y71-0.4b)*.	5.00	15.00	45.00

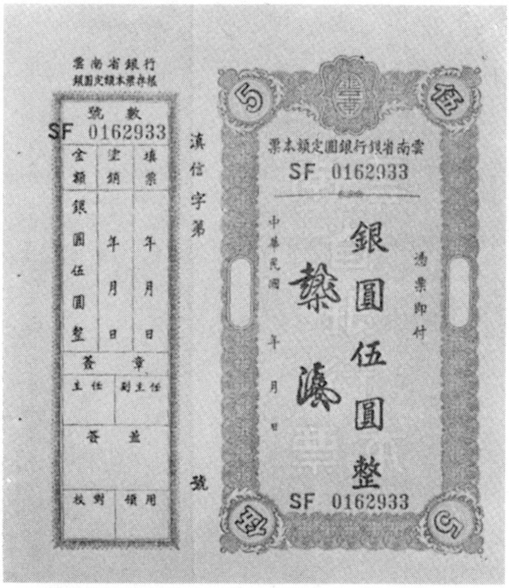

	VG	VF	UNC
S3025 5 Silver Yüan			
1949. Red and blue. Uniface. Vertical format. *(S/M #Y71-)*.			
a. Issued note.	25.00	75.00	225.
r1. Remainder without counterfoil.	—	—	150.
r2. Remainder with counterfoil.	—	—	125.
S3026 10 Silver Yüan			
1949. Blue and yellow. Uniface. *(S/M #Y71-1)*.			
a. Issued note.	30.00	100.	300.
r1. Remainder without counterfoil.	—	—	100.
r2. Remainder with counterfoil.	—	—	100.

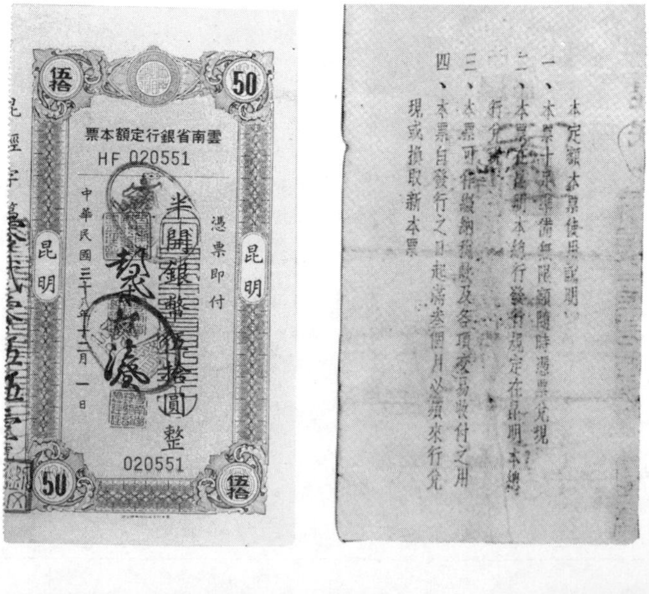

	VG	VF	UNC
S3027 50 Silver Yüan			
4.7.1949; 1.12.1949. *Kumming. (S/M #Y71-3).*			
a. Issued note.	50.00	150.	—
b. Cancelled.	20.00	50.00	—
S3028 100 Silver Yüan			
1.12.1949. *(S/M #Y71-4).*			
a. Issued note.	50.00	150.	—
b. Cancelled.	20.00	50.00	—

1949 Cashier's Checks (O Pen P'iao) Issue

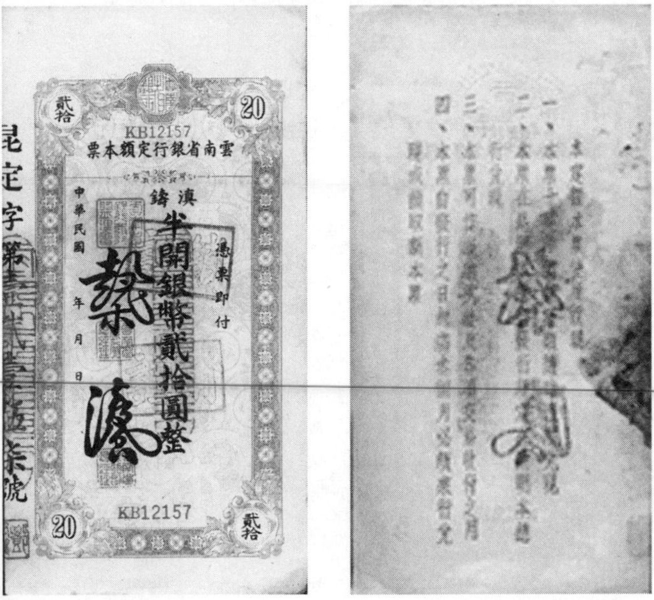

	VG	VF	UNC
S3029 10 Silver Yüan			
(ca.1949). Red with black text. Embossed bank seal at top center with text. Series A. Back: *Payable in Yunnan Provincial silver 1/2 dollars. (S/M #71-11).*			
a. Issued note.	50.00	150.	—
b. Cancelled.	20.00	50.00	—

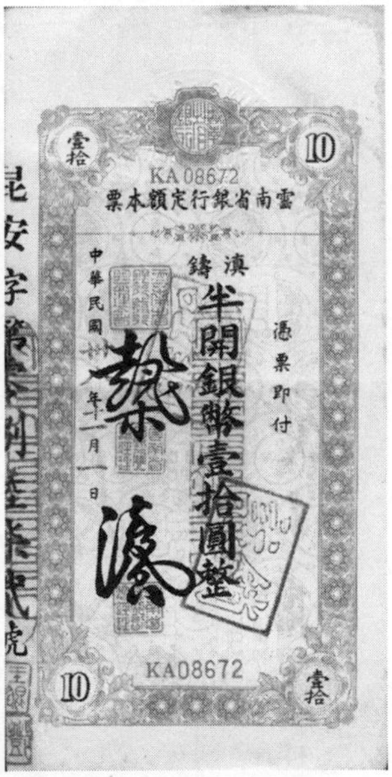

	VG	VF	UNC
S3029A 20 Silver Dollars			
(ca. 1949). Green with black text. Series A. *(S/M #71-12).*	50.00	150.	450.

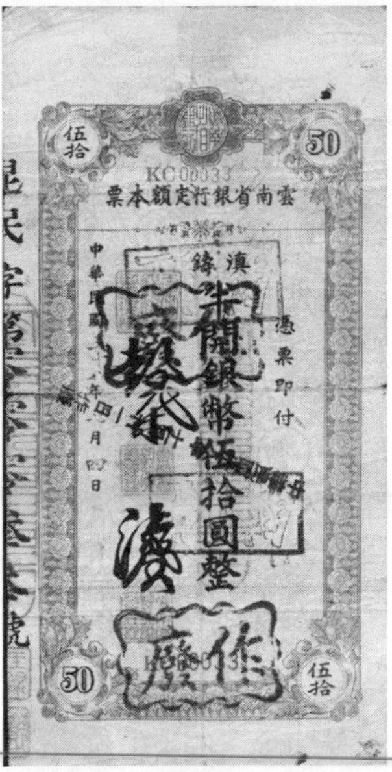

	VG	VF	UNC
S3029B 50 Silver Dollars			
(ca. 1949). Series A. *(S/M #71-13).*	—	—	—

1949 Cashier's Checks (O Pen P'iao) Issue

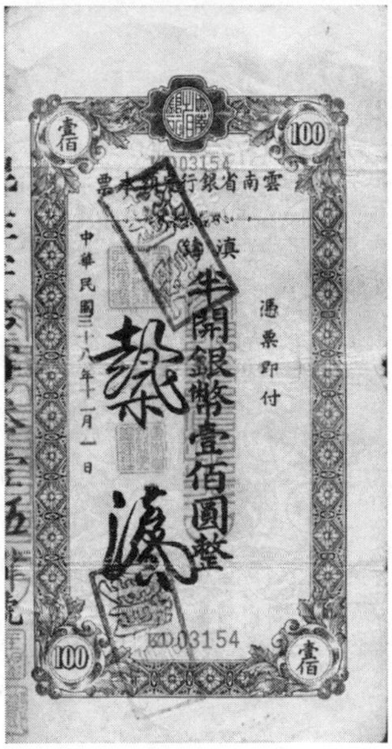

	VG	VF	UNC
S3029C 100 Silver Dollars			
4.7.1949. Series A. *(S/M 71-14).*	100.	300.	—

SENDING SCANNED IMAGES BY E-MAIL

We have been receiving an ever-increasing flow of scanned images from sources world wide. Unfortunately, many of these scans could not be used due to the type of scan, or simple incompatibility with our systems. We appreciate the effort it takes to produce these images and accuracy they add to the catalog listings.

Here are a few simple instructions to follow when producing these scans. We encourage you to continue sending new images or upgrades to those currently illustrated and please do not hesitate to ask questions about this process.

- Scan all images within a resolution of 300 dpi.
- Size setting should be at 100%
- Please include in the e-mail the actual size of the image in millimeters height x width
- Scan in true 4-color
- Save images as jpeg and name in such a way which clearly indentifies the country of the note and catalog number
- Do not compress files
- Please e-mail with a request to confirm receipt of the attachment
- Please send multiple images on a disc if available
- Please send images to: george.cuhaj@fwmedia.com

1949 Kunming Branch Cashier's Checks Issue

		VG	VF	UNC
S3031	**5 Dollars** 1.12.1949. Green with black text. Uniface. Printer: HKPA. *(S/M #Y71-21).*	45.00	125.	375.
S3031A	**10 Dollars** (ca. 1949). Printer: HKPA. *(S/M #Y71-22).*	25.00	75.00	225.
S3031B	**20 Dollars** (ca. 1949). Printer: HKPA. *(S/M #Y71-23).*	—	—	—
S3031C	**50 Dollars** 1.12.1949. Purple. Printer: HKPA. *(S/M #Y71-24).*	—	—	—
S3031D	**100 Dollars** (ca. 1949). Printer: HKPA. *(S/M #Y71-25).*	—	—	—

Bank of Territorial Development of Yunnan

雲南官商合辦殖邊銀行
Yün Nan Kuan Shang Ho Ban Chih Pien Yin Hang

雲南官商合辦殖邊銀行兌換券
Yün Nan Kuan Shang Ho Ban Chih Pien Yin Hang Tui Huan Ch'üan

1927 Issue

		VG	VF	UNC
S3033	**1 Dollar** 1.5.1927. Monument by fortress at center. *YUNNAN.* Back: Hillside village at center. Printer: ABNC. Proof. *(S/M #Y70.7-1).*	150.	450.	—
S3034	**5 Dollars** 1.5.1927. Monument by fortress at center. Back: Hillside village at center. Printer: ABNC. Proof. *(S/M #Y70.7-2).*	150.	450.	—
S3035	**10 Silver Yüan** 1.5.1927. Monument by fortress at center. *YUNNAN.* Back: Hillside village at center. Printer: ABNC. Proof. *(S/M #Y70.7-3).*	150.	450.	—
S3036	**50 Dollars** 1.5.1927. Monument by fortress at center. *YUNNAN.* Back: Hillside village at center. Proof. *(S/M #Y70.7-4).*	150.	450.	—

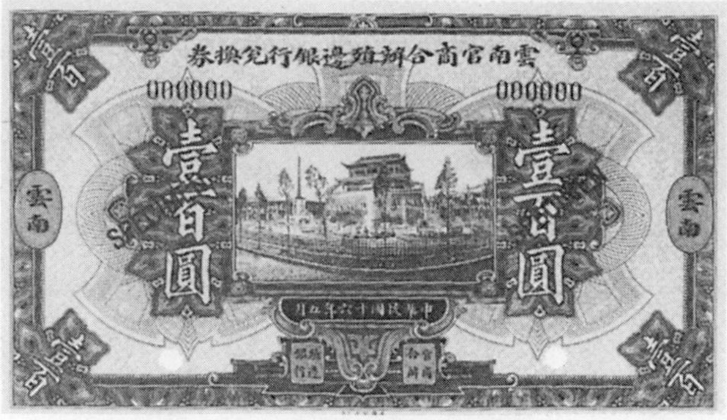

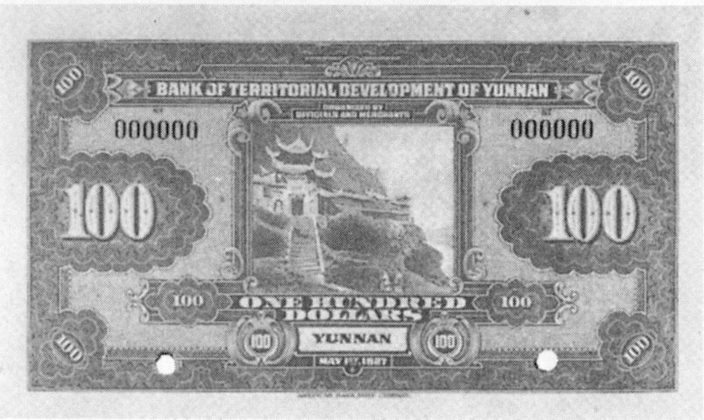

		VG	VF	UNC
S3037	**100 Dollars** 1.5.1927. Monument by fortress at center. *YUNNAN.* Back: Hillside village at center. Printer: ABNC. *(S/M #Y70.7-5).*			
	p. Proof.	—	—	500.
	s. Specimen.	—	—	750.

Islamic Republic of Turkestan
United Islamic Republicof East Turkestan
Revolutionary or Supreme Government, Khotan

1933 Silver Dachin Issue

		VG	VF	UNC
S3039	**100 Silver Dachin** AH1352 (1933). Black with red text. Cloth. Large red-brown handstamped seal. Back: Dark blue-green, black text on red underprint.	30.00	100.	—

1933 Copper Cash Issue

		Good	Fine	XF
S3041	**400 Copper Cash** AH1352 (1933). Blue, black text on red violet. Uniface. Back: Two reddish brown hand stamped seals on back. *(S/M #-)*	45.00	125.	375.

Islamic Republic of East Turkestan

1933 Issue

		Good	Fine	XF
S3045	**5 Miscal = 1/2 Tael** ND (1933). *(S/M #-).*	75.00	225.	650.
S3046	**1 Sar = 1 Tael** AH1352 (1933). Star and crescent at center. *(S/M #-).*			
	a. Cloth.	120.	350.	1000.
	b. Paper.	60.00	175.	550.

Communist Banks

REPUBLIC PERIOD

An increasingly uneasy association between the Kuomintang and the Chinese Communist Party developed and continued until April 12, 1927, when Chiang Kai-shek, Sun Yat-sen's political heir, instituted a bloody purge to stamp out the Communists within the *Kuomintang* and the government and virtually paralyzed their ranks throughout China. Some time after the mid-1927 purges, the Chinese Communist Party turned to armed force to resist Chiang Kai-shek and during the period of 1930-34 acquired control over large parts of Kiangsi (Jiangxi), Fukien (Fujian), Hunan and Hupeh (Hbei). The Nationalist Nanking government responded with a series of campaigns against the soviet power bases and, by October 1934, succeeded in driving the remnants of the Communist army to a refuge in Shensi (Shaanxi) Province. There the Communists reorganized under the leadership of Mao Tse-tung, defeated the Nationalist forces, and on Sept. 21, 1949 established the Peoples Republic of China. Thereafter relations between Russia and Communist China steadily deteriorated until 1958 when China emerged as an independent center of Communist power.

SOVIET PERIOD

Prior to 1949, the Peoples Republic of China did not exist as such, but the Communists did control areas known as "Soviets". Most of the "Soviets" were established on the borders of two or more provinces and were named according to the provinces involved. Thus there were such "Soviets" as the Kiangsi-Hunan Soviet, the Hunan-Hupeh-Kiangsi Soviet, the Hupeh-Honan-Anhwei Soviet and others. In 1931 some of the "Soviets" in the southern Kiangsi area were consolidated into the Chinese Soviet Republic, which lasted until the Long March of 1934.

NOTE: The following listings are incomplete as other issuers exist which will be added when developed for future editions of this volume.

MONETARY SYSTEM:

10 Wen (Cash) = 1 Fen (Cent)
10 Fen (Cents) = 1 Chiao (Hao)
10 Chiao = 1 Yüan (Dollar)

Bank of Chang Chung
#S3050-S3057
行 銀 城 長
Ch'ang Chung Yin Hang

Bank of Eastern Chekiang
#S3058-S3059B
行 銀 東 浙
Che Tung Yin Hang

Bank of Kirin
#S3060-S3063A
行銀省林吉
Chi Lin Sheng Yin Hang

Bank of Chinan
#S3063F-S3105
行 銀 南 冀
Chi Nan Yin Hang

Kiangsi Workers and Farmers Bank
#S3108-S3111
行銀農工西江
Chiang Hsi Kung Nung Yin Hang

Kiang Hwai Bank of China
#S3116-S3134
行 銀 淮 江
Chiang Huai Yin Hang

Bank of Kiangnan (nau)
#S3135A-S3135B
行 銀 南 江
Chiang Nan Yin Hang

7th Administrative District Shansi-Charhar-Hopei Border Area Cooperative Society
#S3135P-S3135T
區政行七第區邊冀察晋
Chin Ch'a Chi Pien Chü Ti Ch'i Hsing Cheng Ch'ü

Bank of Shansi, Chahar and Hopei
#S3136-S3211
行銀區邊冀察晋
Chin Ch'a Chi Pien Chü Yin Hang

Szechuan-Shensi Provincial Soviet Wrokers and Farmers Bank
#S3215-S3224
行銀農工/府政埃維蘇省陝川
Ch'uan Shan Sheng Su Wei Ai Cheng Fu / Kung Nung Yin Hang

Bank of Soviet Szechuan-Shensi Provincial Workers and Farmers
#S3228-S3229
府政埃維蘇陝川
Ch'uan Shan Sheng Su Wei Ai Cheng Fu / Kung Nung Yin Hang

Chung Chou Farmers Bank
Farmers Bank of Chung Chou
#S3232-S3241
行銀民農州中
Chung Chou Nung Min Yin Hang

Chinese Soviet Republic / Szechuan-Shensi Provincial Workers and Farmers Bank
#S3243
國和共埃維蘇華中
Chung Hua Su Wei Ai Kung Ho Kuo / Ch'uan Shan Sheng Kung Nung Yin Hang Ch'ien Hang

Chinese Soviet Republic National Bank
Chinese Soviet Republic Economic Reconstruction Bonds
#S3244-S3247
行銀 家國國和共埃維蘇華中
Chung Hua Su Wei Ai Kung Ho Kuo Kuo Chi Yin Hang

Kuo Chi Yin Hang
Worker and Peasants Bank
#S3249
(行銀)省陝川國和共埃維蘇華中
Chung Hua Su Wei Ai Kung Ho Kuo Ch'uan Shan Sheng (Yin Hang)

Chinese Soviet Republic National Bank
#S3250-S3270
行銀家國國和共埃維蘇華中
Chung Hua Su Wei Ai Kung Ho Kuo Kuo Chia Yin Hang
行 銀 家 國
Kuo Chia Yin Hang

Chinese Soviet Republic National Bank / Hunan-West Hupei Special Branch
#S3273-S3274
行分省贛湘 行銀 家國國和共埃維蘇華中
Chung Hua Su Wei Ai Kung Ho Kuo Kuo Chia Yin Hang

Hsiang O Hsi T'a Chü Fen Hang
行分區特西鄂湘行銀家國
(Short form) *Kuo Chia Yin Hang Hsizng O Hsi T'e Chü Fen Hang*

Chinese Soviet National Bank, Hunan-Kwangsi Province
Cjung Hua Su Wei Ai Kung
#S3274A-S3275
行分區特西鄂湘行銀家國國和共埃維蘇華中
Ho Kuo Kuo Chia Yin Hang Hsiang Kan Sheng Fen Hang

Chinese Soviet Republic Government Bank
#S3276-S3288
行銀 家國國和共埃維蘇華中
Chung Hua Su Wei Ai Kung Ho Kuo Kuo Chia Yin Hang
行 銀 家 國
Kuo Chia Yin Hang

Farmers Bank of Northwest China (Shansi)
Sibei(o) Nung Min Inzang
#S3289-S3325
行銀民農北西晉
Shan Hsi Pei Nung Min Yin Hang

Hunan-Hupei-Kiangsi Workers and Farmers Bank
#S3327-S3345
行銀農工省贛鄂湘
Hsiang O Kan Sheng Kung Nung Yin Hang

Hunan-Hupei Soviet Bank
#S3349
行銀埃維蘇省兩鄂湘
Hsiang O Liang Sheng Su Wei Ai Yin Hang

Provincial Treasury of Hupeh, East Hupeh, Branch
#S3351 and S3353
庫分東鄂庫省北湖
Hu Pei Sheng K'u O T'ung Fen K'u

Bank of Central China
#S3355-S3418
行銀中華
Hua Chung Yin Hang

Huainan Bank
#S3418B-S3419L
行銀南淮
Huai Nan Yin Hang

Northwest Anhwei Special District Soviet Bank
#S3421-S3423D
行銀埃維蘇區特地北西皖
Huan Hsi Pei Ti T'e Chü Su Wei Ai Yin Hang

Bank of Rehher Sheeng
#S3424-S3428
行銀省河熱
Je Ho Sheng Yin Hang

Northeast Kiangsi Soviet Bank
#S3433-S3438
行銀埃維蘇(省)北東贛
Kan Tung Pei (Sheng) Su Wei Ai Yin Hang

Northeast Kiangsi Soviet Bank / North Fukien Branch
#S3440-S3440C
行銀北閩行銀埃維蘇(省)北東贛
Kan Tung Pei Sheng Su Wei Ai Yin Hang / Min Pei Yin Hang

Kiangsi, Hunan, Anhwei Soviet Workers and Farmers Bank
#S3441

行銀農工埃蘇皖豫贛
Kan Yü Huan Su Wei Ai Kung Nung Yin Hang

Bank of Kuantung
#S3445-S3449

行銀東關
Kuan Tung Yin Hang

Bank of West Shantung
#S3450-S3462

行銀西魯
Lu Hsi Yin Hang

Fukien-Chekian-Kiangsi Soviet Bank
#S3465-S3480

行銀埃維蘇省贛浙閩
Min Che Kan Sheng Su Wei Ai Yin Hang

Fukien-Chekiang-Kiangsi Soviet Bank / North Fukien Branch
#S3481-S3481B

行銀北閩/行銀埃維蘇省贛浙閩
Min Che Kan Sheng Su Wei Ai Yin Hang / Min Pei Yin Hang

Fukien-Kwangtung-Kiangsi Border Area Bank
#S3482

行銀區邊贛粵閩
Min Yüeh Kan Pien Chü Yin Hang

Southern Peoples Bank
#S3483-S3489

行銀民人方南
Nan Fang Jen Min Yin Hang

Inner Mongolia Peoples Bank
#S3494-S3506

行銀民人古蒙内
Nei Mung Ku Jen Min Yin Hang

Bank of Inner Mongolia
#S3507-S3507A

行銀蒙内
Nei Mung Yin Hang

Bank of Inner Chiang
#S3507J-S3507R

行銀省江嫩
Nen Chiang Sheng Yin Hang

West Hupeh Peasants Bank
#S3508A-S3508J

行銀民農西鄂
O Hsi Nung Min Yin Hang

North Hupeh Peasants Bank
#S3508P-S3508Q

行銀民農北鄂
O Pei Nung Min Yin Hang

East Hupei Workers and Peasants Bank
#S3509-S3512

O Tung Kung Nung Yin Hang

Southeast Hupei Workers, Peasants and Soldiers Bank
#S3515-S3525

O Tung Nan Kung Nung Ping Yin Hang

Southeast Hupei Workers and Farmers Bank
#S3526-S3529

O Tung Nan Kung Nung Yin Hang

Hupei-Honan-Anhwei Soviet Bank
#S3538

O Yü Huan Sheng Su Wei Ai Yin Hang

Hupei-Honan-Anhwei Province
Soviet Workers and Peasants Bank
#S3539-S3540C

O Yü Huan Sheng Su Wei Ai Kung Neng Yin Hang

Bank of Bai Hai, Bo Xai Inxang, B. X. Inxiang
Pei Hai Bank of China, Pei Hai Bank, Bank of Pei Hei
#S3541-S3623N

Pei Hai Yin Hang

P'ing Chiang Workers and Farmers Bank
#S3624-S3625

行銀農工縣江平
P'ing Chiang Hsien Kung Nung Yin Hang

Maojgungs Liutungkyan
#S3630-S3648

司公易貿/區邊寧甘陝
Shan Kan Ning Pien Ch'u / Mao I Kung Szu

Shaan Gan Ning Bianky Inxan (g)

Shensi-Kansu-Ninghsia Border Area Bank
#S3651-S3670

Shan Kan Ning Pien Ch'ü Yin Hang

Bank of Shantong
#S3671-S3675

Shang Tang Yin Hang

Soviet Bank (Hopei-Honan-Anhwei Soviet Economic Commune)
#S3676-S3677

行銀埃維蘇
Su Wei Ai Yin Hang

Ta Chiang Bank / Dagiang Inxaz(g)
#S3680-S3710

行銀江大
Ta Chiang Yin Hang

Eastern Mongolian Bank
#S3715-S3717

行銀蒙東
Tung Mung Yin Hang

Kwangsi-Kweichow-Yunnan Border District
Dian-Kian-Gui Bianky
#S3719-S3720

局易貿區邊桂黔滇
T'ien Ch'ien Kuei Pien Ch'ü Mao I Chü

Bank of Dung Bai
Bank of Dung Pai
Tung Pei Bank of China
#S3725-S3770

Tung Pei Yin Hang

Guangxua Shangdian
#S3775-S3781

店商華光安延
Yen An Kuang Hua Shang Tien

店商華光
Kuang Hua Shang Tien

NOTE: Colors may vary greatly even with significant changes in many issues due to the shortage of quality materials and access to modern printing facilities.

Bank of Chang Chung

行 銀 城 長
Ch'ang Chung Yin Hang

1948 Issue

		Good	Fine	XF
S3050	**100 Yüan** 1948. Brown and yellow. Great Wall at left. Back: Green. *(S/M #C6-1).*	15.00	45.00	125.

		Good	Fine	XF
S3052	**200 Yüan** 1948. Black on orange underprint. Great Wall at left. Back: Red. *(S/M #C6-2).*	10.00	30.00	100.
S3053	**500 Yüan** 1948. Black on violet underprint. Mao Tse-tung at left. Back: Red. *(S/M #C6-3).*	7.50	25.00	75.00
S3053A	**500 Yüan** 1948. Blue on light blue underprint. Mao Tse-tung at left. Back: Red-brown. *(S/M #C6-).*	10.00	30.00	100.

		Good	Fine	XF
S3054	**500 Yüan** 1948. Blue on orange underprint. Mao Tse-tung at left. Back: Brown. *(S/M #C6-4).*	7.50	25.00	75.00
S3055	**1000 Yüan** 1948. Brown and yellow. Plowing with horses. Red serial #. Back: Violet. *(S/M #C6-5).*	7.50	25.00	75.00
S3056	**1000 Yüan** 1948. Brown and red. Plowing with horses. Blue serial #. Back: Violet. *(S/M #C6-6).*	7.50	25.00	75.00
S3057	**5000 Yüan** 1948. Black on blue underprint. Shanhaikuan city gate. Back: Blue. *(S/M #C6-7).*			
	a. Serial # at upper left, red control letters at upper right, red vertical Chinese characters at left and right *(S/M #C6-7a).*	15.00	45.00	125.
	b. Serial # at upper right, red control letters at upper left, black vertical Chinese characters at left and right *(S/M #C6-7b).*	10.00	30.00	100.

Bank of Eastern Chekiang

浙東銀行
Che Tung Yin Hang

1945 Issue

		Good	Fine	XF
S3058	**2 Chiao** 1945. Vertical format. Uniface. Back: Square seal stamping on back. *(S/M #C27-).*	30.00	100.	300.
S3058A	**5 Chiao = 50 Cents** 1945. Two peasants operating foot-powered water conveyor at right. Uniface. Back: Square seal stamping. *(S/M #C27-).*	15.00	45.00	125.

		Good	Fine	XF
S3058B	**5 Chiao** 1945. Farming scene at center right. *(S/M #C27-).*	10.00	30.00	100.

		Good	Fine	XF
S3058C	**1 Yüan** 1945. Rural street scene at center. *(S/M #C27-).*	20.00	60.00	175.

		Good	Fine	XF
S3058D	**1 Yüan** 1945. Rural scene at center right. *(S/M #C27-).*			
	a. Green back.	25.00	75.00	225.
	b. Brown back.	25.00	75.00	225.

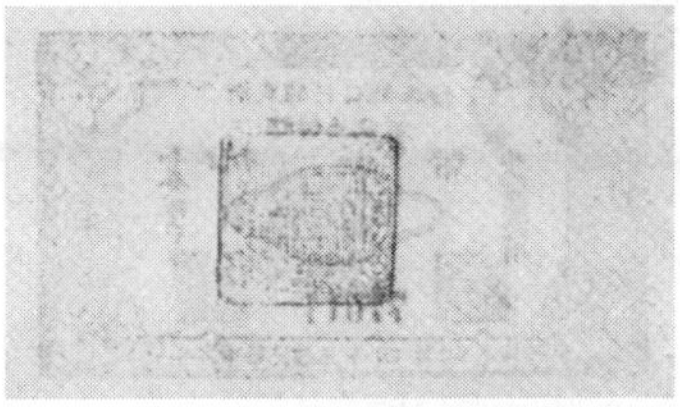

		Good	Fine	XF
S3058E	**1 Yüan** 1945. Uniface. Back: Square seal stamping. *(S/M #C27-).*	40.00	125.	375.

		Good	Fine	XF
S3058F	**1 Yüan** 1945. Peasants operating foot-powered water conveyor at left center. *(S/M #C27-).*	25.00	75.00	225.

		Good	Fine	XF
S3058G	**5 Yüan** 1945. Rural scene at center right. *(S/M #C27-).*	40.00	125.	375.
S3058H	**10 Yüan** 1945. Black on brown underprint. Rural scene at center right. Back: Brown. *(S/M #C27-).*	50.00	150.	450.

1945 Circulating Bearer Checks Emergency Issue

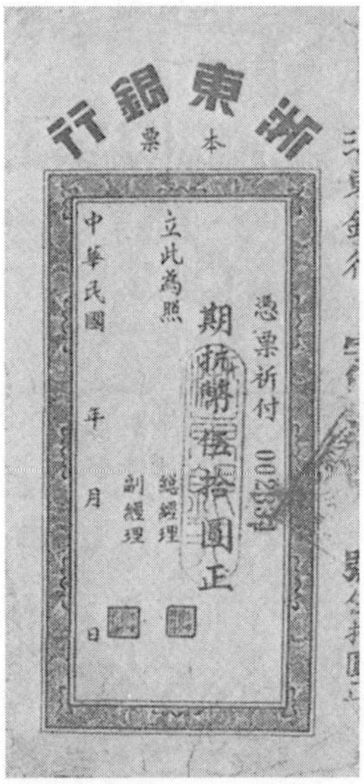

		Good	Fine	XF
S3059	**50 Yüan** 1945. Vertical format. *(S/M #C27-).*	25.00	75.00	225.

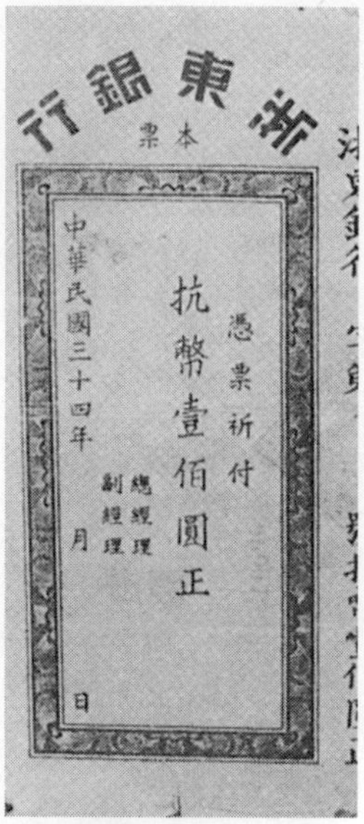

S3059A 50 Yüan

	Good	Fine	XF
1945. Vertical format. *(S/M #C27-).*	50.00	150.	450.

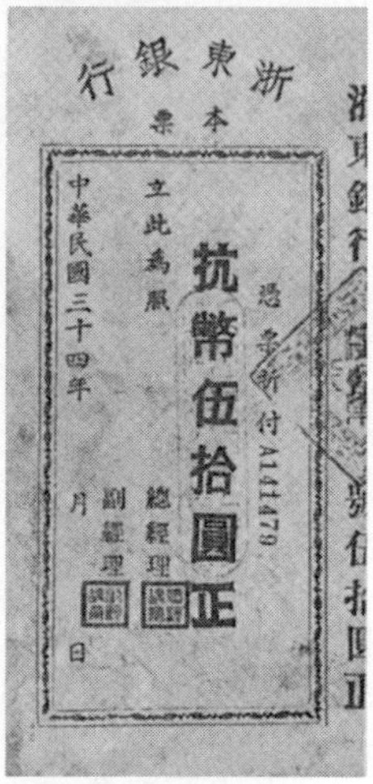

S3059B 100 Yüan

	Good	Fine	XF
1945. Vertical format. *(S/M #C27-).*	50.00	150.	450.

Bank of Kirin

行銀省林吉

Chi Lin Sheng Yin Hang

1946 Issue

S3060 5 Yüan

	Good	Fine	XF
1946. Red. Back: Violet. *(S/M #C73-1).*	25.00	75.00	225.

S3061 10 Yüan

	Good	Fine	XF
1946. Olive. Biplane over city, river, bridges at center. Back: Maroon. *(S/M #C73-1.5).*	20.00	60.00	175.

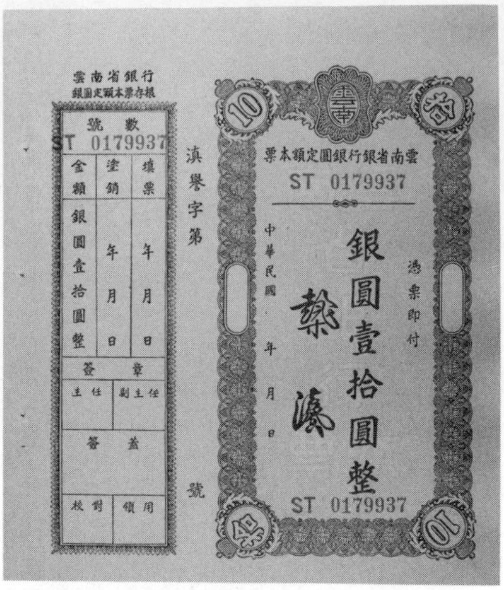

S3062 50 Yüan

	Good	Fine	XF
1946. Green. Back: Red. *(S/M #C73-2).*	25.00	75.00	225.

S3063 100 Yüan

	Good	Fine	XF
1946. Dark blue or blue on red underprint. Back: Red. *(S/M #C73-).*	10.00	25.00	75.00

S3063A 100 Yüan

	Good	Fine	XF
1946. Purple on red underprint. Back: Red. *(S/M #C73-).*	7.50	20.00	60.00

Bank of Chinan

行銀南冀

Chi Nan Yin Hang

1932 Circulating Cashiers Check Issue

S3063F 200 Yüan

	Good	Fine	XF
1932. *(S/M #C81-).*	15.00	45.00	125.

S3063G 500 Yüan

	Good	Fine	XF
1932. *(S/M #C81-).*	15.00	45.00	125.

1939 Regular Issues

S3064 1 Chiao = 10 Cents

	Good	Fine	XF
1939. Greenish black. Steam passenger train crossing bridge with mountains in background at lower left. *(S/M #C81-0.1.*			
a. Brown back.	7.50	20.00	60.00
b. Green back.	7.50	20.00	60.00

S3065 2 Chiao = 20 Cents

	Good	Fine	XF
1939. Blue-gray or green-gray. Village along river at right. *(S/M #C81-0.2).*	7.50	20.00	60.00

S3065A 2 Chiao 5 Fen = 25 Cents

	Good	Fine	XF
1939. Purple. Towered bridge, mountain behind at left. Back: Steam passenger train at center. *(S/M #C81-0.3).*	10.00	30.00	100.

S3066 5 Chiao = 50 Cents

	Good	Fine	XF
1939. Gray-green. City fortress gate at Peking at left. Back: Brown. *(S/M #C81-0.4).*	5.00	15.00	45.00

S3066A 5 Chiao = 50 Cents

	Good	Fine	XF
1939. Steam passenger train at left. *(S/M #C81-0.5).*	25.00	75.00	225.

S3067 1 Yüan

	Good	Fine	XF
1939. Dark green on pink underprint. Building, mountains at left. Back: Ship at center. *(S/M #C81-0.7).*	5.00	15.00	45.00

S3068 2 Yüan

	Good	Fine	XF
1939. Olive-green on pink underprint. Temple at right. Back: Violet-brown. Bank building at center. *(S/M #C81-1).*	5.00	15.00	45.00

S3068A 3 Yüan

	Good	Fine	XF
1939. Green. Gazebo on hill behind houses at left. Back: Red-orange. *(S/M #C81-1.1).*	25.00	75.00	225.

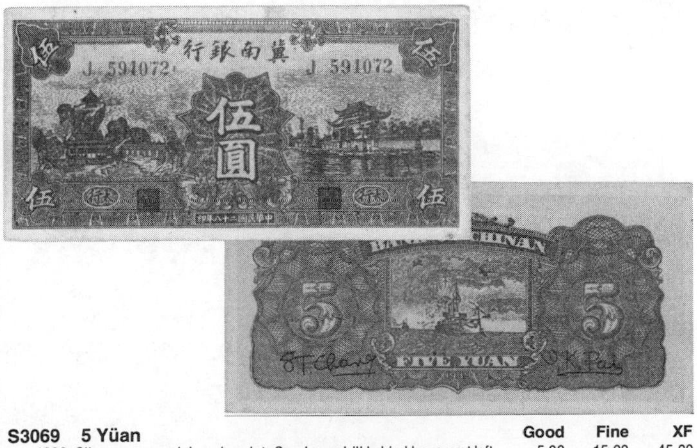

S3069 5 Yüan

	Good	Fine	XF
1939. Olive-green on pink underprint. Gazebo on hill behind houses at left, gateway by shoreline at right. Back: Brown. Warships and planes at center. *(S/M #C81-1.3).*	5.00	15.00	45.00

S3069A 5 Yüan

	Good	Fine	XF
1939. Olive-green on pink underprint. Gazebo on hill hehind houses at left, gateway by shoreline at right. *(S/M #C81-1.4).*			
a. Black overprint: *T'ai Hang* at lower left and r. oval frames.	5.00	15.00	45.00
b. With *T'ai Yüeh* in oval frame.	10.00	30.00	100.
c. Red overprint: *T'ai Yüeh* without frame.	15.00	45.00	100.

#S3069B *Deleted*. See #S3069A.

S3069C 5 Yüan

	Good	Fine	XF
1939. Red and black on light green underprint. Gazebo on hill behind houses at left, gateway by shoreline at right. Back: Green. *(S/M #C81-1.6).*			
a. Without place name.	5.00	15.00	45.00
b. Blue overprint: *T'ai Hang* at lower left and r.	10.00	30.00	100.

S3069D 5 Yüan

	Good	Fine	XF
1939. Steam passenger trains at left. Back: Buildings at center. *(S/M #C81-1.7).*	15.00	45.00	100.

S3069E 10 Yüan

	Good	Fine	XF
1939. Brown-violet on pale blue underprint. Steam passenger train at center. Back: Black. Tea house at center. *(S/M #C81-2).*	5.00	15.00	45.00

S3070 10 Yüan

	Good	Fine	XF
1939. Dark green on pink underprint. Steam passenger train at center. Back: Red. Tea house at center. *(S/M #C81-2.5).*			
a. Without place name. *(S/M #C81-2.5a).*	5.00	15.00	45.00
b. Black *T'ai Yüeh*. *(S/M #C81-2.5b).*	25.00	75.00	225.
c. Red *T'ai Hang* at left and right.	25.00	75.00	225.

S3070A 10 Yüan

	Good	Fine	XF
1939. Orange on yellow underprint. Fortress at left, steam passenger train at right. Back: Violet. *Ping Yüan*. *(S/M #C81-3).*	45.00	125.	375.

S3070B 20 Yüan

	Good	Fine	XF
1939. Purple. Buildings at left. Back: Red. Bridge over river at center. *T'ai Yüeh*. *(S/M #C81-4).*	30.00	100.	300.

S3070C 20 Yüan

	Good	Fine	XF
1939. Building at center. *(S/M #C81-5).*	15.00	45.00	125.

S3070D 50 Yüan

	Good	Fine	XF
1939. Red-orange. Temple of Heaven at right. Back: Green. Temple at center. *(S/M #C81-6).*			
a. Without place name.	25.00	75.00	225.
b. *T'ai Hang*.	25.00	75.00	225.
c. *T'ai Yüeh*.	25.00	75.00	225.

S3070E 50 Yüan

	Good	Fine	XF
1939. Pagoda at right. *(S/M #C81-6.5).*			
a. Without place name.	25.00	75.00	225.
b. *P'ing Yüan*.	25.00	75.00	225.

S3070F 100 Yüan	Good	Fine	XF
1939. Deep blue on red underprint. Buildings at center. Back: Red. Steam passenger train at center. *(S/M #C81-7).*			
a. Without place name.	20.00	60.00	175.
b. *T'ai Hang.*	25.00	75.00	225.

1940 Issue

S3071 20 Cents	Good	Fine	XF
1940. Steam passenger train at lower right. *(S/M #C81-8).*	15.00	45.00	125.

1941 Issue

S3073 10 Coppers	Good	Fine	XF
1941. Red-orange. Seventeen-Arch bridge at Summer Palace at center. *(S/M #C81-9.3).*			
a. Back light green.	15.00	45.00	125.
b. Back dark green.	15.00	45.00	125.

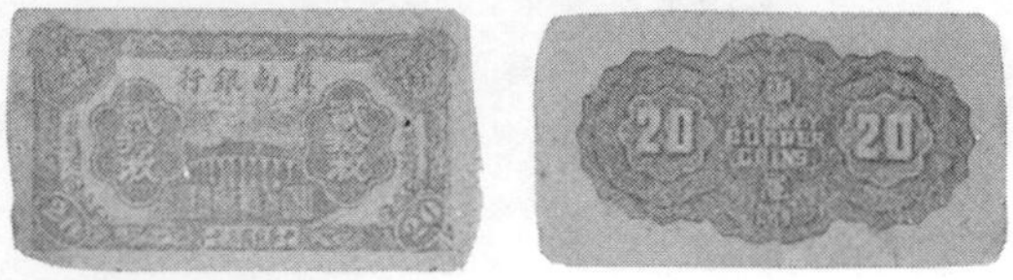

S3073A 20 Coppers	Good	Fine	XF
1941. Gray-green. Colors vary grey to purple. Seventeen-Arch bridge at Summer Palace at center. Back: Brown. *(S/M #C81-9.5).*	10.00	30.00	100.
S3073B 20 Coppers			
1941. Gray. Seventeen-Arch bridge at Summer Palace at center. Back: Dark blue. *(S/M #C81-).*	15.00	45.00	125.
S3073C 20 Coppers			
1941. Purple. Back: Dark blue. *(S/M #C81-).*	15.00	45.00	125.
S3073F 50 Coppers			
1941. *(S/M #C81-9.7).*			
a. Purple.	50.00	150.	—
b. Gray-violet.	50.00	150.	—

1942 Issues

S3074 25 Yüan	Good	Fine	XF
1942. Green. Gazebo at upper center. Vertical format. *(S/M #C81-9.7).*	5.00	15.00	45.00

S3075 50 Yüan	Good	Fine	XF
1942. Brown-violet. Steam passenger train at upper center. Vertical format. Back: Blue-gray. *(S/M #C81-10).*	5.00	15.00	45.00

S3076 100 Yüan	Good	Fine	XF
1942. Brown. Temple at upper center. Vertical format. Back: Blue. *(S/M #C81-11).*	5.00	15.00	45.00

S3077 100 Yüan	Good	Fine	XF
1942. Blue. Planting rice at left. Back: Cultivating with horses at left and right. *(S/M #C81-12).*			
a. Back green.	15.00	45.00	125.
b. Back black.	5.00	15.00	45.00
S3077A 100 Yüan			
1942. Deep brown. Planting rice at left. Back: Cultivating with horses at left and right. *(S/M #C81-12.5).*			
a. Back black.	15.00	45.00	125.
b. Back blue.	7.50	20.00	60.00

S3078 200 Yüan	Good	Fine	XF
1942. Blue. Peasant at left. Back: Brown. Building at center. *(S/M #C81-13).*	5.00	15.00	45.00
S3078A 200 Yüan			
1942. Violet-brown. Peasant at left. Back: Blue-gray. *(S/M #C81-13.5).*	7.50	20.00	60.00
S3079 500 Yüan			
1942. Blue-black. Fortress at left. Back: Brown. *(S/M #C81-14).*	10.00	30.00	100.

S3080 1000 Yüan	Good	Fine	XF
1942. Green on pink underprint. Steam passenger train at center. Back: Red-brown. Gateway along river at center. *(S/M #C81-15).*			
a. 2 serial #.	10.00	30.00	100.
b. Block letters at left, serial # at right.	7.50	20.00	60.00

1943 Emergency Circulating Cashiers Check Issue

S3080F 200 Yüan	Good	Fine	XF
1943. Red. Uniface. *(S/M #C81-).*	50.00	150.	450.

S3080G 500 Yüan	Good	Fine	XF
1943. Blue-violet. Uniface. *(S/M #C81-).*	50.00	150.	450.

1943 Regular Issue

S3081 200 Yüan	Good	Fine	XF
1943. Red on yellow underprint. Pagoda at left. *(S/M #C81-15.2).*	30.00	100.	300.
S3082 1000 Yüan			
1943. Black on lilac underprint. Pagoda at left. *(S/M #C87-15.4).*	45.00	125.	375.

1944 Issue

S3083 20 Yüan	Good	Fine	XF
1944. Brown-violet. Factory buildings at left. *(S/M #C81-15.6).*	15.00	45.00	125.

S3084 50 Yüan	Good	Fine	XF
1944. Red-orange on yellow underprint. Temple of Heaven at right. Back: Deep green. Temple at center.			
a. Without place name. *(S/M #C81-15.8a).*	15.00	45.00	125.
b. *T'ai Hang* in red. *(S/M #C81-15.8b).*	15.00	45.00	125.
c. *T'ai Yüeh* in blue. *(S/M #C81-15.8c).*	15.00	45.00	125.

S3084A 100 Yüan	Good	Fine	XF
1944. Blue. City square, gateway at center. Back: Red. Steam passenger train at center. *(S/M #C81-15.9).*			
a. Without place name.	20.00	60.00	175.
b. *T'ai Hang.*	20.00	60.00	175.

1945 Issues

S3085 5 Yüan	Good	Fine	XF
1945. Green. Building on hillside at right. Back: Red. *(S/M #C81-16).*	30.00	100.	300.
S3086 10 Yüan	**Good**	**Fine**	**XF**
1945. Red brown. Steam passenger train at right. Back: Brown. *(S/M #C81-17).*	10.00	30.00	100.
S3086A 25 Yüan			
1945. Purple. Boat at center, pagoda at right. Back: Black. *(S/M #C81-18).*	50.00	150.	450.
S3086B 50 Yüan			
1945. Blue-black. Steam passenger train at right. Back: Brown. Temple at left center.			
a. Without place name.	7.50	20.00	60.00
b. *T'ai Hang. (S/M #C81-19b).*	15.00	45.00	125.
c. *P'ing Yüan. (S/M #C81-19c).*	10.00	30.00	100.
p. Proof. Face and back.	—	Unc	350.
S3087 100 Yüan			
1945. Blue. Tower at center. Back: Red. City gateway at center. *P'ing Yüan. (S/M #C81-20).*	10.00	30.00	100.
S3088 100 Yüan			
1945. Red. City fortress gate at Peking at center. Back: Green. *(S/M #C81-21).*	15.00	45.00	125.
S3089 100 Yüan			
1945. Brown on yellow underprint. City fortress gate at Peking at center. Back: Blue-gray. *(S/M #C81-21.5).*			
a. White paper.	10.00	30.00	100.
b. Buff paper.	10.00	30.00	100.
S3090 500 Yüan			
1945. Brown and green. Plowing at center. Back: Blue. Warship at center. *(S/M #C81-22).*	7.50	20.00	60.00
S3090A 500 Yüan			
1945. Blue-green on pink underprint. Plowing at center. Back: Brown. *(S/M #C81-22.5).*	7.50	20.00	60.00

S3090B 500 Yüan	Good	Fine	XF
1945. Brown on yellow underprint. Plowing at center. Back: Green.	15.00	45.00	125.
S3090C 500 Yüan			
1945. Dark blue on pink underprint. Back brown. Like #S3090.	15.00	45.00	125.
S3091 500 Yüan			
1945. Green and yellow. Plowing. Back: Brown. *(S/M #C81-23).*			
a. Bold serial #.	7.50	20.00	60.00
b. Regular serial #.	7.50	20.00	60.00

1946 Issue

S3093 100 Yüan	Good	Fine	XF
1946. Blue-green on yellow underprint. Village gateway at center. Back: Brown. Temple of Heaven at center. *(S/M #C81-28).*	15.00	45.00	125.
S3095 500 Yüan			
1946. Gray-green. Building, steam passenger train at center. Back: Black.			
a. Buff paper. *(S/M #C81-30a).*	5.00	15.00	45.00
b. White paper. *(S/M #C81-30b).*	5.00	15.00	45.00
p. Proof. Face and back.	—	Unc	350.

1948 Issues

S3099 500 Yüan	Good	Fine	XF
1948. Red. Harvesting grain at right. Back: Blue. *(S/M #C81-40).*	5.00	15.00	45.00

S3100 500 Yüan	Good	Fine	XF
1948. Red on green and orange underprint. Steam passenger train at center. Back: Pagoda at left. *(S/M #C81-41).*	10.00	30.00	100.

#S3101 *Deleted.* See #S3100.

S3102 500 Yüan	Good	Fine	XF
1948. Brown and green. Horse drawn cart at right. Back: Brown. *(S/M #C81-43).*	10.00	30.00	100.

#S3103 *Deleted.* See #S3102.

S3105 2000 Yüan	Good	Fine	XF
1948. Green and yellow. Steam passenger train at right. Back: Brown. *(S/M #C81-44).*	10.00	30.00	100.

Kiangsi Workers and Farmers Bank

江西工農銀行

Chiang Hsi Kung Nung Yin Hang

ND Issue

S3108 1 Dollar	Good	Fine	XF
ND. Back: V Lenin. Karl Marx. *(S/M #C96-1).*	25.00	75.00	225.

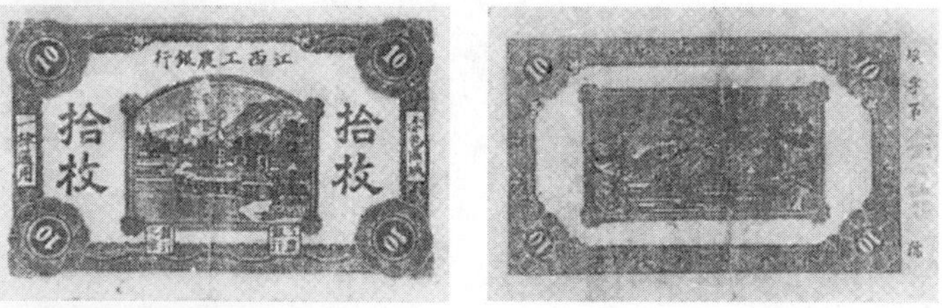

S3109 100 Coppers	Good	Fine	XF
ND. Green. River front village at center. Denomination as: 10 x 10 coppers coin. Back: Red. Mountains and river at center. *(S/M #C96-8).*	100.	300.	900.

S3110 500 Coppers	Good	Fine	XF
ND. Green. Rural house at left, building and tower at right. w/denomination as: 50 x 10 coppers coin. Back: Red. Rural building left and view at right. *(S/M #C96-10).*	125.	375.	1100.

S3111 1000 Coppers	Good	Fine	XF
ND. Buildings at left and right. *(S/M #C96-20).*	150.	450.	1300.

Kiang Hwai Bank of China

江淮銀行

Chiang Huai Yin Hang

1941 Issues

#S3115 *Deleted.*

S3116 5 Chiao = 50 Cents	Good	Fine	XF
1941. Blue-violet and red. Plowing with ox. Back: Green. *(S/M #C104-2).*	30.00	100.	300.

S3117 1 Yüan	Good	Fine	XF
1941. Dark blue. Sawing wood, rice paddy at center. Back: Orange. *Su Chung. (S/M #C104-10a).*	30.00	100.	300.

S3117A 1 Yüan	Good	Fine	XF
1941. Dark blue. Sawing wood, rice paddy at center. Back: Orange. *Yan Fu (S/M #C104-10b).*	50.00	150.	450.

1941 Provisional Issue

S3118 5 Yüan on 1 Yüan	Good	Fine	XF
1941. Dark blue. Back: Orange. Overprint: *Tso 5 Yuan* at left and right on #3117. *Su Chung. (S/M #C104-11).*	25.00	75.00	225.

S3118A 5 Yüan on 1 Yüan	Good	Fine	XF
1941. Dark blue. Back: Orange. Overprint: *Tso 5 Yuan* at left and right on #3117. *Yan Fu. (S/M #C104-11b).*	30.00	100.	300.

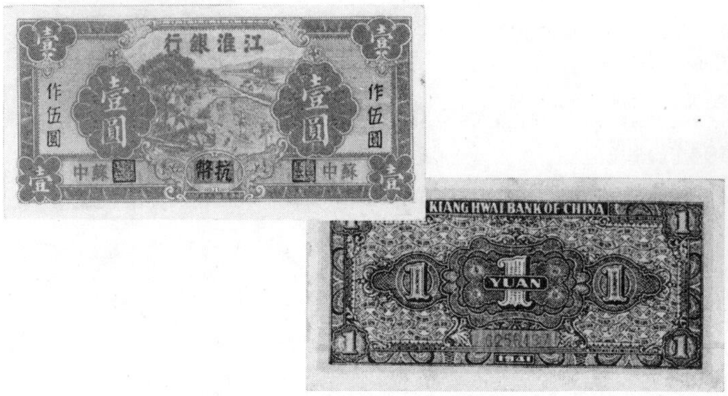

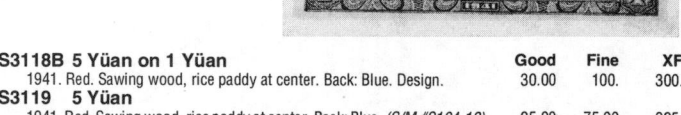

S3118B 5 Yüan on 1 Yüan	Good	Fine	XF
1941. Red. Sawing wood, rice paddy at center. Back: Blue. Design.	30.00	100.	300.

S3119 5 Yüan	Good	Fine	XF
1941. Red. Sawing wood, rice paddy at center. Back: Blue. *(S/M #C104-12).*	25.00	75.00	225.

1943 Issues

S3123 2 Chiao = 20 Cents	Good	Fine	XF
1943. Sampans at center. *(S/M #C104-19).*	15.00	45.00	125.

S3124 5 Chiao = 50 Cents	Good	Fine	XF
1943. Blue. Plowing with ox. Back: Brown. *(S/M #C104-20).*	15.00	45.00	125.

S3125 50 Cents	Good	Fine	XF
1943. Green. Sampans at left center. Back: Red. *(S/M #C104-21).*	20.00	60.00	175.

S3126 1 Yüan	Good	Fine	XF
1943. Red. Factory scene. Back: Blue. *(S/M #C104-30).*	20.00	60.00	175.

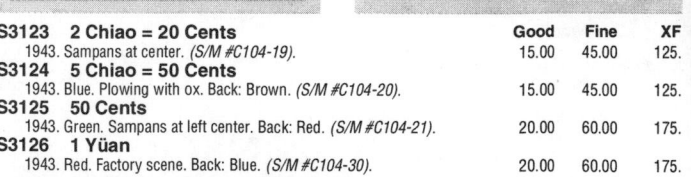

S3127 1 Yüan	Good	Fine	XF
1943. Red. Buildings and factories at center. Back: Blue. *Su Chung.*	20.00	60.00	175.

1944 Issues

	Good	Fine	XF
S3129 1 Yüan			
1944. Black. Farmer and water wheel. Back: Violet. *(S/M #C104-40).*	25.00	75.00	225.
S3130 1 Yüan			
1944. Brown. Planting rice. Back: Green. *(S/M #C104-41).*	25.00	75.00	225.

	Good	Fine	XF
S3131 5 Yüan			
1944. Blue. Portrait Mao Tse-tung at right. Back: Violet. Great Wall at right.			
a. Without place name. *(S/M #C104-42a).*	25.00	75.00	225.
b. *Su Chung. (S/M #C104-42b).*	30.00	100.	300.
S3132 10 Yüan			
1944. Blue. Automobile. Back: Brown. *(S/M #C104-43).*	30.00	100.	300.

	Good	Fine	XF
S3133 20 Yüan			
1944. Green. Portrait Mao Tse-tung at right. Back: Violet on light green underprint. *(S/M #C104-44).*	50.00	150.	450.
S3134 50 Yüan			
1944. Red. Portrait Mao Tse-tung at right. Back: Brown. Printer: KHPF. *(S/M #C104-45).*	50.00	150.	450.

NOTE: For #S3134 with additional Chinese 4 characters overprint. see Bank of Central China #S3356.

Bank of Kiangnan (NAU)

行 銀 南 江

Chiang Nan Yin Hang

1945 Issue

	Good	Fine	XF
S3135A 1 Yüan = 1 Dollar			
1945. Blue-black. Peasants working in rice field at left center. Back: Dark red. *(S/M #C106-14).*	25.00	75.00	225.

	Good	Fine	XF
S3135B 5 Yüan			
1945. Red on pink underprint. Arched bridge to house at left. Back: Dark brown. *(S/M #C106-15).*	25.00	75.00	225.

7th Administrative District Shansi-Chahar-Hopei Border Area Cooperative Society ("Zinchagi Dicixingzhengky")

區政行七第區邊冀察晋

Chin Ch'a Chi Pien Chü Ti Chi'i Hsing Cheng Ch'ü

1941 Issues

	Good	Fine	XF
S3135P 1 Chiao = 10 Cents			
1941. Dark blue. Buildings along river at upper center. Vertical format. *(S/M #C167.5-11).*			
a. Back pale olive-green.	5.00	15.00	45.00
b. Back brown.	7.50	20.00	60.00
S3135Q 1 Chiao = 10 Cents			
1941. Violet. Buildings along river at upper center. Vertical format. Back: Red-orange. *(S/M #C167.5-12).*	5.00	15.00	45.00

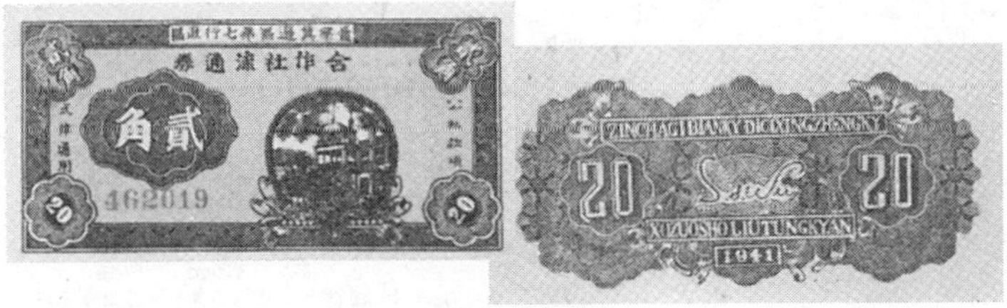

	Good	Fine	XF
S3135R 2 Chiao = 20 Cents			
1941. Dark blue on orange underprint. Building at lower right. Back: Red. *(S/M #C167.5-13).*	15.00	45.00	125.

	Good	Fine	XF
S3135S 5 Chiao = 50 Cents			
1941. Deep purple on yellow-green underprint. Two people in boat near Seventeen-Arch bridge at Summer Palace. Vertical format. Back: Red-violet. *(S/M #C167.5-14).*	5.00	15.00	45.00

1942 Issue

S3135T 5 Chiao

1942. Brown-violet on pink underprint. Buildings with steeples at upper center. Vertical format. Back: Violet. *(S/M #C167.5-16).*

	Good	Fine	XF
a. Blue serial #.	15.00	45.00	125.
b. Red serial #.	15.00	45.00	125.

Bank of Shansi, Chahar and Hopei

行銀區邊冀察晋

Chin Ch'a Chi Pien Ch'ü Yin Hang

1938 Issue

	Good	Fine	XF
S3136 1 Chiao = 10 Cents 1938. Brown. Gazebo at upper center. Vertical format. Back: Olive. *(S/M #C168-1).*	5.00	15.00	45.00
S3137 2 Chiao = 20 Cents 1938. Violet. Pagoda. Vertical format. Back: Green. *(S/M #C168-2).*	60.00	175.	500.

	Good	Fine	XF
S3138 5 Chiao = 50 Cents 1938. Purple. Pagoda at upper center. Vertical format. Back: Brown. *(S/M #C168-3).*	5.00	15.00	45.00
S3139 1 Yüan 1938. Orange and black. Farmer plowing with horse at left. Back: Light brown. *(S/M #C168-).*	25.00	75.00	225.

	Good	Fine	XF
S3140 5 Yüan 1938. Brown. Tower bridge at center. *(S/M #C168-).*	25.00	75.00	225.

1939 Issues

	Good	Fine	XF
S3143 10 Coppers 1939. Green and blue. Summer palace. Back: Brown. *(S/M #C168-10).*	15.00	45.00	125.

	Good	Fine	XF
S3144 20 Coppers 1939. Green. Statue of bull with gazebo in background at upper center. Vertical format. Back: Brown. *(S/M #C168-11).*	7.50	20.00	60.00
S3147 1 Yüan 1939. Olive-green on yellow-orange underprint. Peking Memorial at right. Back: Violet. *(S/M #C168-20).*	5.00	15.00	45.00

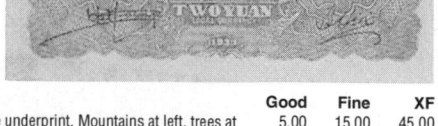

	Good	Fine	XF
S3148 2 Yüan 1939. Red-brown on yellow-orange underprint. Mountains at left, trees at right. Back: Olive. *(S/M #C168-21).*	5.00	15.00	45.00

	Good	Fine	XF
S3149 5 Yüan 1939. Red-orange on green underprint. Great Wall at left and right, sky in background. Series A; B; C; D. Back: Brown and green. Pavillion at center. *(S/M #C168-22).*	10.00	30.00	100.

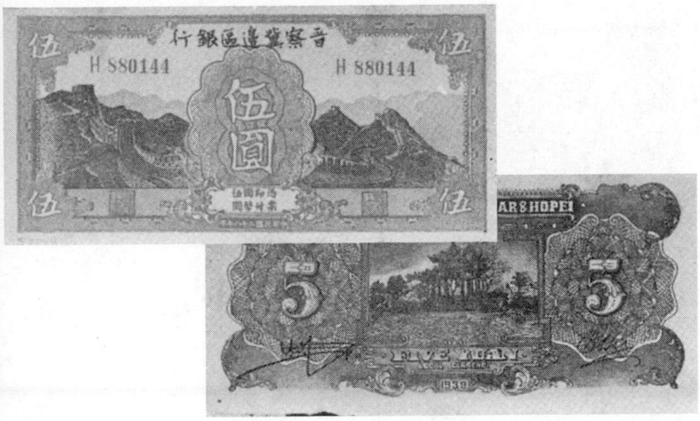

S3149A 5 Yüan	Good	Fine	XF
1939. Red-orange on green underprint. Great Wall at left and right. Series E; F; G; H. *(S/M #C168-23).*	7.50	20.00	60.00
S3150 5 Yüan			
1939. City gate at center. *(S/M #C168-).*	25.00	75.00	225.

1940 Issue

S3151 2 Chiao = 20 Cents	Good	Fine	XF
1940. Violet. Hills in Peking. Vertical format. Back: Orange. *(S/M #C168-30).*	5.00	15.00	45.00

S3152 5 Chiao = 50 Cents	Good	Fine	XF
1940. Red. Woman spinning at left, sheep at right. Back: Dark blue. *(S/M #C168-).*	15.00	45.00	125.

S3156 10 Yüan	Good	Fine	XF
1940. Brown, black and multicolor. Temple of Heaven at center. Back: Olive on light yellow-green. *(S/M #C168-40).*	7.50	20.00	60.00

1941 Issue

S3158 50 Yüan	Good	Fine	XF
1941. Farmer by well at left, bridge over stream at right. Back: Great Wall at center. *(S/M #C168-).*	25.00	75.00	225.

1943 Issue

S3160 10 Yüan	Good	Fine	XF
1943. Red. Shepherd with sheep. 2 signature varieties. Back: Red. *(S/M #C168-50).*	7.50	20.00	60.00
S3161 50 Yüan			
1943. Brown and violet-gray. Rural scene at left, plowing with ox at right. Back: Green. *(S/M #C168-51).*	10.00	30.00	100.

1944 Issue

S3165 50 Yüan	Good	Fine	XF
1944. Brown on light blue underprint. Planting rice at center. *(S/M #C168-60).*	25.00	75.00	225.
S3166 100 Yüan			
1944. Violet. Planting rice. Back: Green. *(S/M #C168-61).*	10.00	30.00	100.
S3167 500 Yüan			
1944. Brown and red-brown. Plowing with ox. Back: Brown. *(S/M #C168-62).*	10.00	30.00	100.
S3168 1000 Yüan			
1944. Red and brown. Planting rice. Back: Brown. *(S/M #C168-63).*	20.00	60.00	175.
S3169 5000 Yüan			
1944. Rural scene at right. Back: Plow horse at center. Specimen. *(S/M #C168-).*	—	Unc	450.

1945 Issues

S3170 5 Yüan	Good	Fine	XF
1945. Sampans at center. *Hopei, Liaoning* and *Jehol.* (S/M #C168-).	25.00	75.00	225.

S3171 5 Yüan	Good	Fine	XF
1945. Olive on yellow underprint. Pagoda at center. Back: Brown. *(S/M #C168-70).*	5.00	15.00	45.00

S3172 10 Yüan	Good	Fine	XF
1945. Brown. Cultivating with horse and an ox. *Hopei, Liaoning* and *Jehol.* Back: Orange. (S/M #C168-71).	25.00	75.00	225.

S3172A 10 Yüan	Good	Fine	XF
1945. Brown. Cultivating with horse and an ox. Clouds in background. *(S/M #C168-71a).*	15.00	45.00	125.

	Good	Fine	XF
S3173 10 Yüan 1945. Red-brown on light blue underprint. Great Wall at center. Back: Purple. *(S/M #C168-72).*	5.00	15.00	45.00
S3174 10 Yüan 1945. Red. Sheep at left. Hopei, Liaoning and Jehol. Back: Violet. *(S/M #C168-73).*	30.00	100.	300.
S3174A 10 Yüan 1945. Brown-violet on ochre underprint. Sheep at left. Hopei, Liaoning and Jehol. Back: Brown. *(S/M #C168-73a).*	30.00	100.	300.
S3174B 10 Yüan 1945. Brown on light yellow underprint. Sheep at left. Back: Brown. Pagoda at center. *(S/M #C168-).*			
a. 2 serial #.	25.00	75.00	225.
b. 2 block #.	25.00	75.00	225.

	Good	Fine	XF
S3174C 10 Yüan 1945. Peasants cultivating at upper center. Series 3; 5. Without serial #. Vertical format. Back: Red-orange. *(S/M #C168-73.5).*	5.00	15.00	45.00
S3175 50 Yüan 1945. Olive-green. Small river boat, shoreline houses. *(S/M #C168-74).*	25.00	75.00	225.
S3176 50 Yüan 1945. Brown. Temple at center. Back: Brown. *(S/M #C168-75).*	10.00	30.00	100.
S3177 50 Yüan 1945. Brown-orange and deep brown. Back: Olive-green. Plowing. *(S/M #C168-76).*	25.00	75.00	225.

#S3178 *Deleted.* See #S3176.

	Good	Fine	XF
S3179 50 Yüan 1945. Violet. Flock of sheep. *Hopei, Liaoning* and *Jehol.* 2 serial # varieties. Back: Olive-green. *(S/M #C168-).*	20.00	60.00	175.
S3179A 50 Yüan 1945. Brown. Flock of sheep. *Hopei, Liaoning* and *Jehol.* 2 serial # varieties. Back: Oive-green. *(S/M #C168-80).*	20.00	60.00	175.

	Good	Fine	XF
S3180 100 Yüan 1945. Green. Plowing with ox at lower right. Back: Brown. *(S/M #C168-81).*	20.00	60.00	175.

	Good	Fine	XF
S3181 100 Yüan 1945. Brown-orange on yellow underprint. Planting rice at lower center right. Back: Brown. *Chi Chung. (S/M #C168-).*	15.00	45.00	125.

	Good	Fine	XF
S3182 100 Yüan 1945. Brown on yellow underprint. Plowing with horse at left, horse drawn cart at right. Back: Green. *(S/M #C168-82).*	7.50	20.00	60.00

	Good	Fine	XF
S3183 100 Yüan 1945. Brown. Great Wall. Back: Green. Hillside pagoda at center. *(S/M #C168-83).*	7.50	20.00	60.00
S3184 100 Yüan 1945. Orange-brown on yellow underprint. Harvesting rice at lower right. Back: Brown or orange-brown. *Hopei. (S/M #C168-84).*	10.00	30.00	100.

	Good	Fine	XF
S3185 200 Yüan 1945. Brown. Plowing with horse at right. Back: Blue. Farmer and sheep at center. *(S/M #C168-85).*	10.00	30.00	100.
S3186 500 Yüan 1945. Red and brown on yellow-green underprint. Bridge. Back: Brown. Junk at center. *(S/M #C168-86).*	7.50	20.00	60.00

1946 Issues

	Good	Fine	XF
S3190 10 Yüan 1946. Violet and red. Steam passenger train at center right. Back: Violet. *Hopei, Liaoning* and *Jehol*. *(S/M #C168-90)*.	25.00	75.00	225.
S3191 50 Yüan 1946. Violet. Back: Red. *(S/M #C168-91)*.	25.00	75.00	225.
S3192 100 Yüan 1946. Red. Tea house at left. Back: Brown. *(S/M #C168-92)*.	7.50	20.00	60.00
S3193 100 Yüan 1946. Green. Farmers at right. Back: Brown. *(S/M #C168-93)*.	15.00	45.00	125.
S3194 200 Yüan 1946. Red-brown and grayish green on light yellow-green underprint. Farmer with irrigation bucket at right. Back: Lilac. Men at center. *(S/M #C168-94)*.	10.00	15.00	45.00
S3194A 200 Yüan 1946. Steam passenger train at left. *Hopei, Liaoning* and *Jehol*. *(S/M #C168-)*.	15.00	45.00	125.
S3195 500 Yüan 1946. Red-brown and black on yellow underprint. Cattle with rancher. Back: Brown. *(S/M #C168-95)*.	10.00	30.00	100.
S3196 500 Yüan 1946. Red and yellow. Harvesting at right. Back: Violet. *(S/M #C168-96)*.	10.00	30.00	100.
S3197 500 Yüan 1946. Brown and black. Rural scenes at left and right. Back: Brown. *Hopei, Liaoning* and *Jehol*. *(S/M #C168-97)*.	10.00	30.00	100.
S3198 500 Yüan 1946. Brown and black. Pack horse at left, plowing with horse at right. Back: Blue and green. *(S/M #C168-100)*.	5.00	15.00	45.00
S3199 500 Yüan 1946. Brown on light green and ochre underprint. Back: Pale brown-orange. *(S/M #C168-101)*.			
a. Issued note.	5.00	15.00	45.00
b. With 2 additional square red hand stamped seals: *Wang Chun Chuan* at left and *Li Run Tian* at right.	10.00	30.00	100.
S3200 1000 Yüan 1946. Brown on yellow-orange and light green underprint. Automobile crossing girder bridge at center. Back: Tan on yellow underprint. *(S/M #C168-102)*.	7.50	20.00	60.00
S3201 1000 Yüan 1946. Black on light blue underprint. Horses grazing. Back: Brown on ochre underprint. *(S/M #C168-103)*.	7.50	20.00	60.00

1947 Issues

	Good	Fine	XF
S3205 1000 Yüan 1947. Brown on light blue and ochre underprint. Gazebo at center. *(S/M #C168-110)*.	7.50	20.00	60.00
S3206 1000 Yüan 1947. Violet. Horse pump at right. Back: Violet. *Hopei, Liaoning* and *Jehol*. *(S/M #C168-111)*.	7.50	20.00	60.00
S3207 2000 Yüan 1947. Green. Steam passenger train at left. Back: Brown. *Hopei, Liaoning* and *Jehol*. *(S/M #C168-112)*.	7.50	20.00	60.00
S3208 5000 Yüan 1947. Violet on green and yellow underprint. Junks at right. Back: Brown. *(S/M #C168-113)*.	7.50	20.00	60.00
S3209 5000 Yüan 1947. Red and green. Plowing. Back: Brown. *(S/M #C168-114)*.	7.50	20.00	60.00
S3210 5000 Yüan 1947. Brown and black. Junks at right. Back: Brown. *(S/M #C168-115)*.	5.00	15.00	45.00
S3211 5000 Yüan 1947. Brown-violet on yellow underprint. Bridge at left. Back: Red-brown. *Hopei, Liaoning* and *Jehol*. *(S/M #C168-116)*.	5.00	15.00	45.00

Szechuan-Shensi Provincial Soviet Workers and Farmers Bank

川陝省蘇維埃政府/工農銀行

Ch'uan Shan Sheng Su Wei Ai Cheng Fu / Kung Nung Yin Hang

1932 Issue

	Good	Fine	XF
S3215 2 Ch'uan 1932. Black.			
a. White cloth. *(S/M #C242-1a)*.	135.	400.	1200.
b. Blue cloth. *(S/M #C242-1b)*.	135.	400.	1200.

Many fake examples are on the market.

1933 Issue

	Good	Fine	XF
S3217 1 Ch'uan 1933. Black. Red oval validation hand stamp. Paper: Gray cloth. *(S/M #C242-5)*. Vertical format.	100.	300.	900.

The 1 Ch'uan note is a fantasy.

	Good	Fine	XF
S3218 2 Ch'uan 1933. Black. Back: Black. Solid *2* in circle at center. Vertical format.			
a. White cloth. *(S/M #C242-10a)*.	50.00	150.	450.
b. Blue cloth. *(S/M #C242-10b)*.	65.00	200.	600.
c. Red oval validation hand stamp. *(S/M #C242-10-)*.	50.00	150.	450.
S3219 3 Ch'uan 1933. Black. Back: Black. Vertical format.			
a. White cloth. *(S/M #C242-11a)*.	60.00	180.	550.
b. Red oval validation handstamp *(S/M #C242-11b)*.	60.00	180.	550.
c. Blue cloth. *(S/M #C242-11c)*.	60.00	180.	550.
d. Green cloth. *(S/M #C242-11d)*.	65.00	200.	600.

NOTE: High quality counterfeits of #S3215, S3217-S3219 printed on gray cloth are often encountered.

1933-35 Issue

	Good	Fine	XF
S3220 1 Ch'uan 1934. Blue. *(S/M #C242-20)*. Vertical format.	100.	300.	—
S3221 3 Ch'uan 1934. Red. *(S/M #C242-21)*. Vertical format.	75.00	225.	—
S3222 5 Ch'uan ND. Cloth. *(S/M #C242-)*. Vertical format.	900.	2750.	—
S3223 10 Ch'uan ND. (1933?). Black on brown underprint. Cloth. *(S/M #C242-)*. Vertical format.	1100.	3500.	—
S3224 300 Cash 1935. *(S/M #C242-30)*. Vertical format. Reported not confirmed.	—	—	—

Bank of Soviet Szechuan-Shensi Provincial Workers and Farmers

川陝蘇維埃政府

Ch'uan Shan Sheng Su Wei Ai Cheng Fu / Kung Nung Yin Hang

1933 Issue

	Good	Fine	XF
S3228 1 Dollar ND (1933). Blue with red star at left and right. Portrait Vladimir I Lenin at center. Back: Green. Clenched fist smashing imperialists. *(S/M #C243-1)*.	175.	525.	1500.
S3229 1 Dollar ND (1933). Portrait Lenin at left, Marx at right. Back: Tractors, factory at center. *(S/M #C243-)*.	375.	1100.	3500.

Chung Chou Farmers Bank
Farmers Bank of Chung Chou

中州農民銀行

Chung Chou Nung Min Yin Hang

1946 Issue

	Good	Fine	XF
S3232 20 Yüan 1946. Red. Rural river view at lower left. Back: Black. Buildings at center. *(S/M #C252-12)*.	15.00	45.00	125.
S3233 50 Yüan 1946. Green on pink underprint. Temple at left. Back: Violet. *(S/M #C252-13)*.	10.00	30.00	100.
S3234 100 Yüan 1946. Dark blue on pink underprint. Steam passenger train at center. Back: Deep blue-green. Hillside shelter at center. *(S/M #C252-14)*.	15.00	45.00	125.

1948 Issues

	Good	Fine	XF
S3235 2 Yüan 1948. Blue. *(S/M #C252-21)*.			
a. Back red-brown.	10.00	30.00	100.
b. Back black.	7.50	20.00	60.00
S3235A 2 Yüan 1948. Blue. Gazebos on bridge at right. Back: Brown-violet. *(S/M #C252-22)*.	25.00	75.00	225.
S3235B 3 Yüan 1948. Orange. Farmers planting rice at left. Back: Blue-green. *(S/M #C252-23)*.	40.00	125.	375.
S3236 5 Yüan 1948. Black on pink underprint. Rural buildings at center. Back: Red-brown. *(S/M #C252-24)*.			
a. Issued note.	25.00	75.00	225.
s. Specimen.	—	Unc	350.
S3236A 5 Yüan 1948. Blue. Farmer plowing at center. Back: Black.	50.00	150.	450.
S3237 10 Yüan 1948. Green. Gazebo at left. *(S/M #C252-25)*.	25.00	75.00	225.

NOTE: Many fake examples are on the market.

	Good	Fine	XF
S3237A 10 Yüan 1948. Grayish black. Gazebo at center. Back: Brown.			
a. Back retrograde (mirror image) *(S/M #C252-26a)*.	5.00	15.00	45.00
b. Back normal. *(S/M #C252-26b)*.	5.00	15.00	45.00
S3237B 10 Yüan 1948. Green. Peasants working in field at center. Back: Red-brown. *(S/M #C252-27)*.	15.00	45.00	125.
S3238 20 Yüan 1948. Gray-green. Boats at left. Back: Dark gray-green. *(S/M #C252-28)*.	15.00	45.00	125.
S3240 100 Yüan 1948. Brown-violet on light yellow-green underprint. Gazebo on bridge at right. Back: Blue-green.			
a. Back blue-green. *(S/M #C252-30a)*.	10.00	15.00	45.00
b. Back blue-gray. *(S/M #C252-30b)*.	15.00	45.00	125.
p. Proof. Face and back.	—	Unc	500.
s. Specimen.	—	Unc	750.
S3241 200 Yüan 1948. Red brown and multicolor. Ships in harbor. Back: Brown. *(S/M #C252-31)*.	30.00	100.	300.

Chinese Soviet Republic

Szechuan-Shensi Provincial Workers and Farmers Bank

中華蘇維埃共和國

Chung Hua Su Wei Ai Kung Ho Kuo / Ch'uan Shan Sheng Kung Nung Yin Hang Ch'ien Hang

1933 Issue

	Good	Fine	XF
S3243 1 Yüan 1933. Green on yellow underprint. Portrait Joseph Stalin at center. Back: Green on light green underprint. Red star between two soldiers at center.			
a. Paper. *(S/M #-)*.	375.	1100.	3250.
b. Cloth. *(S/M #-)*.	450.	1250.	3750.

CHINESE SOVIET REPUBLIC NATIONAL BANK

行銀 家國國和共埃維蘇華中

Chung Hua Su Wei Ai Kung Ho Kuo Kuo Chia Yin Hang Kuo Chia Yin Hang

1936 CHINESE SOVIET REPUBLIC ECONOMIC RECONSTRUCTION BONDS ISSUE

		Good	Fine	XF
S3244	**50 Cents** 1936. Green. Flag and hemisphere. Back: Red. *(S/M #C272-1).*	25.00	75.00	225.
S3246	**2 Dollars** 1936. Green. Flag and hemisphere. Back: Red. *(S/M #C272-10).*	30.00	100.	300.
S3247	**5 Dollars** 1936. Green. Back: Red. *(S/M #C272-).*	50.00	150.	450.

WORKER AND PEASANTS BANK

(行銀)省陝川國和共埃維蘇華中

Chung Hua Su Wei Ai Kung Ho Kuo Ch'uan Shan Sheng (Yin Hang)

1934 ISSUE

		Good	Fine	XF
S3249	**3 Ch'uan** 1934. Black, blue and orange. Star above three horses at center. Vertical format. Back: Hammer and sickle above Lenin. *(S/M #C273-1).*	200.	600.	1800.

CHINESE SOVIET REPUBLIC NATIONAL BANK

行銀家國國和共埃維蘇華中行 銀 家 國

Chung Hua Su Wei Ai Kung Ho Kuo Kuo Chia Yin Hang Kuo Chia Yin Hang

1932 ISSUE

		Good	Fine	XF
S3250	**5 Fen** 1932. Green. Soldiers at center. Back: Violet. Arms at center. *(S/M #C274-1).*	15.00	45.00	125.
S3251	**1 Chiao** 1932. Red. Back: Red. *(S/M #C274-2).*			
	a. Without black letter.	20.00	60.00	175.
	b. Block letter before serial #.	20.00	60.00	175.
	c. Serial # printed on face of note.	20.00	60.00	175.
S3251A	**2 Chiao** 1932. Blue. Portrait Lenin at center. Back: Pale violet. *(S/M #C274-2.5).*			
	a. With *No.* printed on back.	20.00	60.00	175.
	b. With *No. D* printed on back.	20.00	60.00	175.
	c. As a but printed on face.	20.00	60.00	175.

#S3252 *Deleted.*

		Good	Fine	XF
S3253	**1 Yüan** 1932-33. Light brown on light blue underprint. Portrait Vladimir I Lenin at center. Back: Green. *(S/M #C274-10).*	15.00	45.00	125.

1933 ISSUES

		Good	Fine	XF
S3255	**1 Chiao** 1933. *(S/M #C274-20).* Reported not confirmed.	—	—	—
S3257	**5 Chiao** 1933. Violet and green. Back: Red-brown. *(S/M #C274-21).*	7.50	20.00	60.00
S3258	**5 Chiao** 1933. Violet on ochre underprint. Back: Red-brown. *(S/M #C274-22).*	15.00	45.00	125.
S3259	**1 Yüan** 1933. Reddish brown on light blue underprint. Portrait Vladimir I. Lenin at center. Back: Deep green. *(S/M #C274-29).*	25.00	75.00	225.

NOTE: #S3259 believed to be spurious issue by some authorities.

1934 ISSUES

		Good	Fine	XF
S3260	**10 Coppers** 1934. Soldiers with flag above sphere at center. *(S/M #C274-31).*	25.00	75.00	225.
S3262	**2 Chiao** 1934. Blue and black on yellow underprint. Portrait Vladimir I. Lenin at center. Back: Black. Arms at center. *(S/M #C274-41).*	25.00	75.00	225.
S3263	**5 Chiao** 1934. *(S/M #C274-42).* Reported not confirmed.	—	—	—
S3264	**1 Yüan** 1934. N. Lenin. *(S/M #C274-50).*	30.00	100.	300.
S3265	**1 Yüan** 1934. K. Marx. *(S/M #C274-51).*	50.00	150.	450.

#S3268 *Deleted.*

1936 ISSUE

		Good	Fine	XF
S3270	**1 Yüan** 1936. Lenin. *(S/M #C274-70).*	30.00	100.	300.

CHINESE SOVIET REPUBLIC NATIONAL BANK

行分省贛湘 行銀 家國國和共埃維蘇華中

Chung Hua Su Wei Ai Kung Ho Kuo Kuo Chia Yin Hang Hsiang O Hsi T'a Chü Fen Hang

行分區特西鄂湘行銀家國

(Short form) Kuo Chia Yin Hang Hsiang O Hsi T'e Chü Fen Hang

HUNAN - WEST HUPEI SPECIAL BRANCH

1931 ISSUE

		Good	Fine	XF
S3273	**1 Chiao** 1931. Black. Building at center. Back: Blue. Rural hillside buildings at center. *(S/M #C275-1).*	45.00	125.	375.
S3273A	**2 Chiao** 1931. Black. Temple at lower center. Back: Green. Hammer and sickle on a star at center. *(S/M #C275-2).*	60.00	175.	525.
S3273B	**2 Chiao** 1931. Black. Building at lower center. Back: Red. Village at center. *(S/M #C275-3).*	60.00	175.	525.
S3273C	**5 Chiao** 1931. Temple of Heaven at center. *Changsha. (S/M #C275-4).*	100.	300.	900.
S3274	**1 Yüan** 1931. Back: Hillside buildings at center. *Changsha. (S/M #C275-2).*	100.	300.	900.

CHINESE SOVIET REPUBLIC BANK OF HUNAN-KWANGSI PROVINCE

行分省贛湘 行銀 家國國和共埃維蘇華中

Chung Hua Su Wei Ai Kung Ho Kuo Kuo Chia Yin Hang Hsiang Kan Sheng Fen Hang Kuo Chia Yin Hang

1933 ISSUE

		Good	Fine	XF
S3274A	**5 Fen** 1934. Red. Back: Dark blue. *(S/M #C274-).*	15.00	45.00	125.

1934 CHIAO ISSUES

		Good	Fine	XF
S3274B	**1 Chiao** 1933. Red. Hammer and sickle on globe at center. Back: Building at center.			
	a. Back brown. *(S/M #C274-40a).*	7.50	20.00	60.00
	b. Back dark green. *(S/M #C274-40b).*	15.00	45.00	125.
	c. Back deep olive-green. *(S/M #C274-40c).*	25.00	75.00	225.
S3274C	**1 Chiao** 1934. Brown. Back: Green. *(S/M #C274-40).*	25.00	75.00	225.

1934 COPPER COIN ISSUE

		Good	Fine	XF
S3275	**10 Coppers** 1934. Black. Soldiers with flag above globe at center. *(S/M #C274-51).*	10.00	30.00	100.

NOTE: Many counterfeits are on the market.

CANTON

1933 ISSUE

		Good	Fine	XF
S3275A	**2 Chiao** 1933. Dark brown. Youngsters with flag on globe at center. Back: Red. Temple at center. *(S/M #C274-42).*	45.00	125.	375.
S3275B	**1 Yüan** 1933. Vladimir I. Lenin at center. Back: Blue. *(S/M #C274-48).*	100.	300.	900.

CHINESE SOVIET REPUBLIC GOVERNMENT BANK

行銀 家國國和共埃維蘇華中

Chung Hua Su Wei Ai Kung Ho Kuo Kuo Chia Yin Hang

行 銀 家 國

Kuo Chia Yin Hang

NORTHWEST

1935 ISSUE

		Good	Fine	XF
S3276	**5 Fen** 1935. Black. Uniface. *(S/M #C276-1).*	25.00	75.00	225.
S3278	**2 Chiao** 1935. Black. Worker holding up hammer and peasant holding up sickle, flag in background. Uniface. *(S/M #C276-2).*	30.00	100.	300.
S3279	**2 Chiao** 1935. Worker holding up hammer and peasant holding up sickle, flag in background. Vertical format. Cloth. Back: Radiant star on shield behind horseman at center. *(S/M #C276-3).*	50.00	150.	450.
S3281	**1 Yüan** 1935. Vladimir I. Lenin in star at center. Cloth. Back: Farmer, worker and soldier with flag at center. *(S/M #C276-10).*	150.	450.	1200.

1936 ISSUE

		Good	Fine	XF
S3282	**1 Fen** 1936. Man in circular frame at left, denomination in oval frame at center right. *(S/M #C276-3).*	30.00	100.	300.
S3284	**1 Chiao** 1936. Black. J. Stalin at upper center. Vertical format. Uniface.			
	a. Paper. *(S/M #C276-20a).*	60.00	175.	525.
	b. Cloth. *(S/M #C276-20b).*	75.00	225.	650.
S3285	**2 Chiao** 1936. Foot soldiers in trench about to advance behind leader. Uniface. *(S/M #C276-21).*	45.00	125.	375.
S3286	**5 Chiao** ND (1936). Crowd rallying at center. Uniface. *(S/M #C276-22).*	50.00	150.	450.

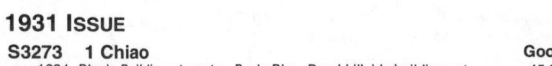

		Good	Fine	XF
S3287	**1 Yüan** 1936. *(S/M #C276-23).*	125.	375.	—

S3288 2 Yüan
ND. *(S/M #C276-).* Reported not confirmed. — — —

Farmers Bank of Northwest China (Shansi)

行銀民農北西晉

Shan Hsi Pei Nung Min Yin Hang

1940 Issues

	Good	Fine	XF
S3289 5 Fen			
1940. Purplish black. Summer house at top center. Vertical format. *(S/M #H76-0.3).*			
a. Issued note.	75.00	225.	650.
s. Specimen.	—	Unc	700.
S3290 1 Chiao = 10 Cents			
1940. Black. Building at right. *(S/M #H76-0.5).*	10.00	30.00	100.
S3290A 2 Chiao = 20 Cents			
1940. Blue. Back: Red.	10.00	30.00	100.
S3290B 5 Chiao = 50 Cents			
1940. Pagoda at lower left. *(S/M #H76-0.7).*	15.00	45.00	125.
S3291 5 Chiao = 50 Cents			
1940. Tan. Gazebo at left. Back: Blue-gray. *(S/M #H76-1).*	30.00	100.	300.
S3292 5 Chiao = 50 Cents			
1940. Dark brown-violet. Four people in boat at lower left. Back: Dark brown-violet. *(S/M #H76-1.5).*			
a. Issued note.	15.00	45.00	125.
b. Violet serial #.	30.00	100.	300.
S3293 1 Yüan			
1940. Black and pale olive-green. Farmers at left, bridge at right. Back: Brown-violet. Two steam ships at center. *(S/M #H76-2).*			
a. Issued note withoutverprint on 1st character of bank name.	25.00	75.00	225.
b. Without overprint on 1st character of bank name.	50.00	150.	450.
S3294 1 Yüan			
1940. Dark green and dark brown. Farmer plowing with horse at left, farmer at right. Back: Purple and red-orange. Building at center. *(S/M #H76-3).*			
a. Issued note.	25.00	75.00	225.
s. Specimen.	—	Unc	350.
S3295 2 Yüan			
1940. Dark brown on pink underprint. Temple at center. Back: Dark brown. Gazebo at left, fortress gate at right. *(S/M #H76-4).*	7.50	20.00	60.00
S3295A 2 Yüan			
1940. Green on yellow underprint. House at center. *(S/M #H76-4.5).*			
a. Back brown-orange.	15.00	45.00	125.
b. Back yellow.	20.00	60.00	175.

1941 Issue

	Good	Fine	XF
S3296 5 Yüan			
1941. Black on ochre underprint. Rural scene at left and right. Back: Purple. Bridge by gazebo at center. *(S/M #H76-5).*			
a. Issued note.	30.00	100.	300.
s. Specimen.	—	Unc	450.

1942 Issue

	Good	Fine	XF
S3297 10 Yüan			
1942. Blue-black. Small shrines in woods near bridge at right. *(S/M #H76-).*	30.00	100.	300.

1943 Issues

	Good	Fine	XF
S3298 50 Yüan			
1943. Blue-black. Three peasants working at left, sheep grazing at right. Back: Green. *(S/M #H76-7).*			
a. Issued note.	40.00	125.	375.
s. Specimen.	—	Unc	450.
S3298A 50 Yüan			
1943. Red-brown on blue underprint. Temple in trees at right. Back: Blue-grey. *(S/M #H76-9).*	30.00	100.	300.
S3298B 50 Yüan			
1943. Dark blue. Temple in trees at right. Back: Blue-grey. *(S/M #H76-).*			
a. Back violet-brown.	25.00	75.00	225.
b. Red italic serial # Back red.	15.00	45.00	125.
S3298C 100 Yüan			
1943. Blue on yellow underprint. Great Wall at center. Back: Green. *(S/M #H76-9.7).*	45.00	125.	375.
S3298D 100 Yüan			
1943. Green. Sheepo at right. *(S/M #H76-10).*			
a. Back green.	30.00	100.	300.
b. Back blue-black.	45.00	125.	375.
S3298E 100 Yüan			
1943. Brown. Sheep at right. Back: Blue. *(S/M #H76-11).*	30.00	100.	300.

1945 Issues

	Good	Fine	XF
S3299A 10 Yüan			
1945. Dark blue. Boat passing under village bridge at upper center. Vertical format. Back: Green. *(S/M #H76-13).*	45.00	125.	375.
S3299B 10 Yüan			
1945. Blue. Boat passing under village bridge at upper center. Vertical format. Back: Green. *(S/M #H76-14).*	45.00	125.	375.
S3299C 100 Yüan			
1945. Great Wall at center. Unissued remainder without serial # or seals. *(S/M #H76-16).*	—	—	450.
S3300 500 Yüan			
1945. Red and black. Yanan headquarters at center. Back: Blue. Building at center. *(S/M #H76-20).*	25.00	75.00	225.
S3301 500 Yüan			
1945. Blue-gray. Seated person at left, sheep at right. Back: Blue. *(S/M #H76-23).*	40.00	125.	375.

#S3301A *Deleted.* See #S3300.

1946 Issues

	Good	Fine	XF
S3304 100 Yüan			
1946. Violet-brown on yellow-orange underprint. Cow, sheep and horse at right. Back: Brown. Three people at center. *(S/M #H76-30).*	30.00	100.	300.
S3305 500 Yüan			
1946. Pagoda at center. Back: Temple. *(S/M #H76-30.5).*	30.00	100.	300.
S3306 500 Yüan			
1946. Blue and brown. Pagoda at left. Back: Green. Gazebo at center. *(S/M #H76-31).*	45.00	125.	375.
S3307 1000 Yüan			
1946. Blue-gray on ochre underprint. Boat passing under village bridge at left. Specimen. *(S/M #H76-33).*	—	—	450.
S3308 1000 Yüan			
1946. Blue. Boat, bridge at left. Back: Red. *(S/M #H76-36).*	25.00	75.00	225.

1947 Issues

	Good	Fine	XF
S3313 1000 Yüan			
1947. Violet. Plowing with ox. Back: Green. *(S/M #H76-42).*	40.00	125.	375.

#S3313A *Deleted.* See #S3314.

	Good	Fine	XF
S3314 2000 Yüan			
1947. Brown-violet on ochre underprint. Farmer plowing with ox at center right. Back: Green. *(S/M #H76-43).*			
a. Issued note.	75.00	225.	675.
b. Brown rays in background.	25.00	75.00	225.
S3315 2000 Yüan			
1947. Blue. Sheep. Back: Red. *(S/M #H76-44).*	45.00	125.	375.
S3316 5000 Yüan			
1947. Light blue-black on pink underprint. Flock of sheep grazing at right. Back: Red. *(S/M #H76-45).*	25.00	75.00	225.
S3317 5000 Yüan			
1947. Violet. Farmer, cows. Back: Green. *(S/M #H76-46).*	45.00	125.	375.
S3318 10,000 Yüan			
1947. Black. Great Wall at left and right. Back: Black. Steer at left, sheep at right. *(S/M #H76-50).*	50.00	150.	450.

#S3320 *Deleted.*

1948 Issues

	Good	Fine	XF
S3321 1000 Yüan			
1948. Black. Farm at left, hillside pagoda at right. Back: Red. Temple at center.			
a. Large serial #. *(S/M #H76-61a).*	30.00	100.	300.
b. Small serial #. *(S/M #H76-61b).*	30.00	100.	300.
S3322 5000 Yüan			
1948. Black. Rural scene at left, pagoda at right. Back: Red. *(S/M #H76-62).*	30.00	100.	300.
S3323 10,000 Yüan			
1948. Blue-black. Irrigation system. Serial # in regular or italic font. Back: Red. *(S/M #H76-63).*			
a. Regular serial #.	10.00	30.00	100.
b. Italic serial #.	50.00	150.	450.
S3324 10,000 Yüan			
1948. Black. Rural scene at left, pagoda at right. Back: Red. *(S/M #H76-64).*	5.00	15.00	45.00

	VG	VF	UNC
S3325 50,000 Yüan			
1948. Purplish black. Camels at left, fortress at right. Specimen. *(S/M #H76-68).*		—	600.

Hunan-Hupei-Kiangsi Workers and Farmers Bank

行銀農工省贛鄂湘

Hsiang O Kan Sheng Kung Nung Yin Hang

ND Issue

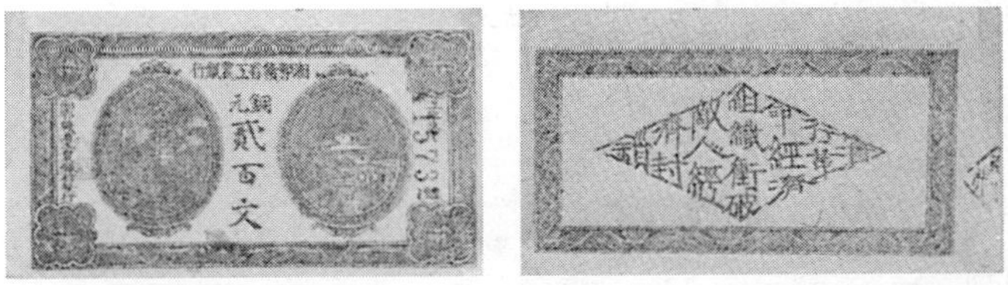

	Good	Fine	XF
S3327 200 Cash			
ND. Black. Pagoda at left, building at right. Back: Red. *(S/M #H101-11).*			
a. Issued note.	20.00	60.00	175.
r. Uniface remainder.	—	Unc	600.

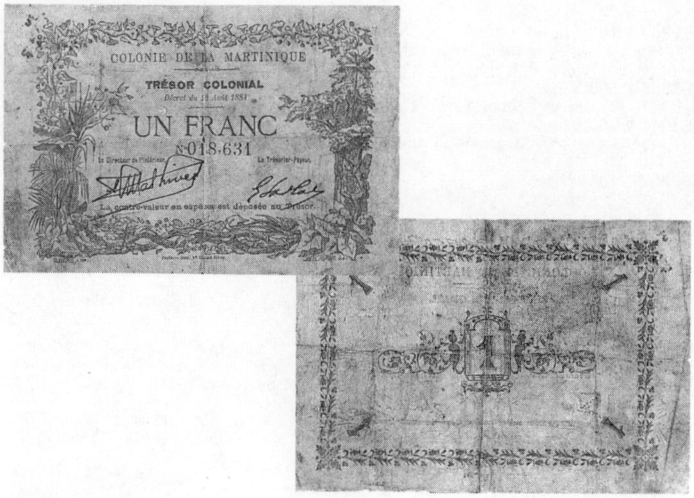

	Good	Fine	XF
S3328 200 Cash ND. Blue-green. Pagoda at left, building at right. Back: Red. *(S/M #H101-2)*.	50.00	150.	450.

1931 Issue

	Good	Fine	XF
S3329 1 Ch'uan 1931. Blue. Printer: PCYC. *(S/M #H101-10)*. Reported not confirmed.	—	—	—

	Good	Fine	XF
S3333 1 Chiao 1931. Black. Rural family scenes at left and right. *(S/M #H101-20)*.			
a. Issued note.	75.00	225.	675.
b. Hand stamped Chinese characters in rectangular frame "Full Cash Paid."	45.00	125.	375.

	Good	Fine	XF
S3333A 1 Chiao 1931. Blue. Rural family scenes at left and right. *(S/M #H101)*.	150.	450.	1250.
S3333B 1 Chiao 1931. Green. Rural family scenes at left and right. *(S/M #H101-)*.	150.	450.	1250.

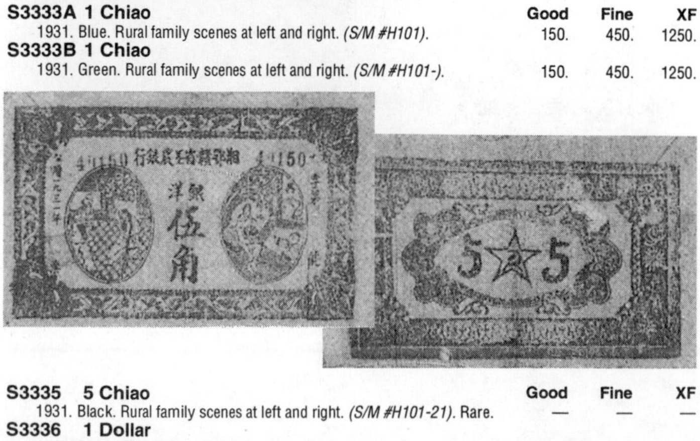

	Good	Fine	XF
S3335 5 Chiao 1931. Black. Rural family scenes at left and right. *(S/M #H101-21)*. Rare.	—	—	—
S3336 1 Dollar 1931. Black. *(S/M #H101-30)*. Rare.	—	—	—

1932 Issue

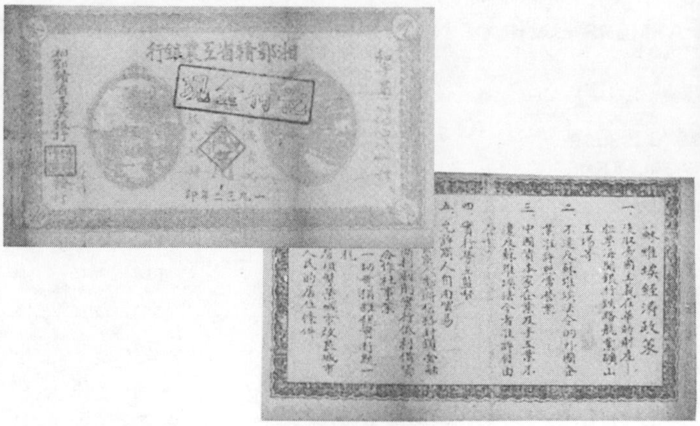

	Good	Fine	XF
S3340 2 Chiao 1932. Red on olive underprint. Back: Black. *(S/M #H101-40)*.			
a. Issued note.	60.00	175.	550.
b. 3 character overprint in rectangle (Paid).	30.00	100.	300.
S3340A 2 Chiao 1932. Red on black underprint. Like #S3340. Back: Black. 18 columns of text. *(S/M #H101-)*.	45.00	125.	375.
S3340B 2 Chiao 1932. Red and black. Like #S3340. Back: Black. 25 columns of text. *(S/M #H101-)*.	175.	550.	1500.
S3341 3 Chiao 1932. Black with red text. Portrait bearded man at left, pagoda at right. Back: Brown-violet. Village at center. *(S/M #H101-41)*.			
a. Issued note.	100.	300.	900.
b. Hand stamped 3 Chinese characters in rectangular frame "Full Cash Paid."	75.00	225.	675.

NOTE: The old man depicted on #S3341 is not Karl Marx but copied from a locally issued note.

1933 Issue

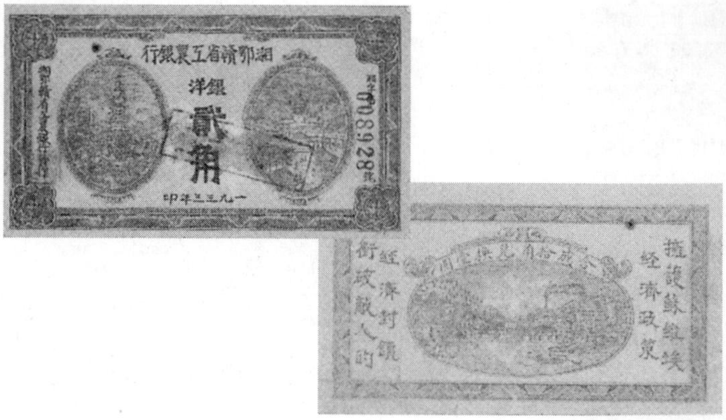

	Good	Fine	XF
S3344 2 Chiao 1933. Dark blue. Pagoda at left, temple at right. Back: Red. Shoreline village, bridge and boats at center.			
a. Issued note. Rare.	—	—	—
b. Violet hand stamp 4 Chinese characters in rectangular frame.	125.	375.	1000.
S3345 3 Chiao 1933. Red. *(S/M #H101-51)*. Rare.	—	—	—

Hunan-Hupei Soviet Bank

行銀埃維蘇省兩鄂湘

Hsiang O Liang Sheng Su Wei Ai Yin Hang

1931 Issue

	Good	Fine	XF
S3349 1 Yüan 1931. *(S/M #H102-1)*.	150.	450.	1250.

Provincial Treasury of Hupeh

庫分東鄂庫省北湖

Hu Pei Sheng K'u O T'ung Fen K'u

East Hupeh

1940-42 Issue

	VG	VF	UNC
S3351 5 Chiao 1940. Blue-black on light blue underprint. Back: Violet. Specimen. *(S/M #H172.5-13)*.	—	—	500.
S3353 1 Yüan 1942. Blue on multicolor underprint. Back: Purple. Specimen. *(S/M #H172.5-24)*.		—	500.

Bank of Central China

華中銀行
Hua Chung Yin Hang

1944 Issue

	Good	Fine	XF
S3355 10 Yüan 1944. Red. Logging at right. Back: Black and yellow. *(S/M #H180-1)*.			
a. 3mm serial #.	15.00	45.00	125.
b. 5mm serial #.	15.00	45.00	125.

1944 Provisional Issue

	Good	Fine	XF
S3356 50 Yüan 1944. Red. Back: Brown. Overprint: On #3134. *(S/M #H180-2)*.	80.00	250.	750.

1945 Regular Issues

	Good	Fine	XF
S3358 5 Chiao = 50 Cents 1945. Villagers working at left and right. *(S/M #H180-)*.	15.00	45.00	125.
S3359 5 Chiao = 50 Cents 1945. Dark blue. Temple with pagoda in background at left center. Back: Red. *(S/M #H180-9)*.	7.50	20.00	60.00

	Good	Fine	XF
S3360 1 Yüan 1945. Blue. Steam passenger train at right. Back: Red. *(S/M #H180-20)*.	10.00	30.00	100.
S3361 1 Yüan 1945. Blue. Junks at left, ships at right. Back: Brown. *(S/M #H180-21)*.	7.50	20.00	60.00
S3361A 1 Yüan 1945. Red. Junks at left, ships at right.	7.50	20.00	60.00
S3362 2 Yüan 1945. Violet. Planting rice. Back: Green. *(S/M #H180-23)*.	10.00	30.00	100.
S3363 2 Yüan 1945. Blue. Planting rice. Back: Brown. *(S/M #H180-24)*.	15.00	45.00	125.
S3364 5 Yüan 1945. Blue. Irrigation system at right. Back: Brown. *(S/M #H180-25)*.	10.00	30.00	100.
S3364A 5 Yüan 1945. Purple. Irrigation system at right. *(S/M #H180-25.5)*.	25.00	75.00	225.

	Good	Fine	XF
S3365 5 Yüan 1945. Violet. Army bugler by Great Wall. Back: Green. *(S/M #H180-26)*.	10.00	30.00	100.
S3366 5 Yüan 1945. Green. Planting rice. Back: Green. *(S/M #H180-27)*.	15.00	45.00	125.
S3367 5 Yüan 1945. Green. Rural scene. Back: Violet. *(S/M #H180-30)*.	15.00	45.00	125.

	Good	Fine	XF
S3368 10 Yüan 1945. Red. Portrait Mao Tse-tung at right. Back: Green. *(S/M #H180-31)*.	30.00	100.	300.
S3369 20 Yüan 1945. Green. Plowing. *(S/M #H180-32)*.	25.00	75.00	225.

	Good	Fine	XF
S3370 20 Yüan 1945. Green. Farm scene at right. Back: Yellow and multicolor. *(S/M #H180-33)*.	25.00	75.00	225.

	Good	Fine	XF
S3371 50 Yüan 1945. Violet. Ship and plane at right. Back: Blue. English. *(S/M #H180-34)*.	15.00	45.00	125.

	Good	Fine	XF
S3372 50 Yüan 1945. Deep purple. Ship and plane at right. Back: Blue-black. Without English. *(S/M #H180-35)*.	15.00	45.00	125.

S3373 50 Yüan	Good	Fine	XF
1945. Dark brown. Ship, turbine and steam passenger train at right. Back: Dark blue, dark brown and green. *(S/M #H180-36).*			
a. One block letter, 3mm high serial #.	20.00	60.00	175.
b. Two block letters, 4mm high serial #.	20.00	60.00	175.
S3374 50 Yüan			
1945. Brown. Ships at dockside. Back: Blue. *(S/M #H180-37).*	15.00	45.00	125.

S3375 100 Yüan	Good	Fine	XF
1945. Green. Great Wall. Back: Brown. Printer: HCBN. *(S/M #H180-40).*	10.00	30.00	100.
S3375A 100 Yüan			
1945. Green. Great Wall. Back: Brown. *(S/M #H180-40.5).*	10.00	30.00	100.

S3376 100 Yüan	Good	Fine	XF
1945. Brown. Portrait Mao Tse-tung at right. *(S/M #H180-41).*	40.00	125.	375.

S3377 100 Yüan	Good	Fine	XF
1945. Green. Bugler by Great Wall. Back: Violet. *(S/M #H180-42).*			
a. Small serial #.	25.00	75.00	225.
b. Large serial #.	25.00	75.00	225.
S3378 100 Yüan			
1945. Green. City wall. Back: Violet. *(S/M #H180-43).*	25.00	75.00	225.

1946 Issues

S3380 5 Yüan	Good	Fine	XF
1946. Red and blue. Burgler by Great Wall. Back: Blue. *(S/M #H180-50).*	25.00	75.00	225.
S3381 5 Yüan			
1946. Blue and green. Burglar by Great Wall. Back: Violet. *(S/M #H180-51).*	25.00	75.00	225.
S3382 5 Yüan			
1946. Violet and green. Burglar by Great Wall. Back: Green. *(S/M #H180-52).*	25.00	75.00	225.
#S3383 *Deleted.*			
S3384 20 Yüan			
1946. Green. Plowing. Back: Green. *(S/M #H180-54).*	25.00	75.00	225.

S3385 20 Yüan	Good	Fine	XF
1946. Blue and green. Temple of Heaven at right. Back: Pagoda at center. *(S/M #H180-54.5).*	10.00	30.00	100.

S3386 50 Yüan	Good	Fine	XF
1946. Brown. Bridge, pavillion with tower in background at center. right. *(S/M #H180-55).*			
a. Back green.	10.00	30.00	100.
b. Back brown.	10.00	30.00	100.

S3387 50 Yüan	Good	Fine	XF
1946. Violet. Pagoda and bridge. *(S/M #H180-56).*	25.00	75.00	225.
S3388 100 Yüan			
1946. Violet. Great Wall. *(S/M #H180-56.5).*	25.00	75.00	225.

S3389 200 Yüan	Good	Fine	XF
1946. Blue. Hillside pagoda at right. Back: Violet. Steam passenger train at center. *(S/M #H180-57).*	25.00	75.00	225.

		Good	Fine	XF
S3390	**200 Yüan** 1946. Blue. Temple of Heaven at center. Back: Violet. *(S/M #H180-60).*	15.00	45.00	125.
S3391	**200 Yüan** 1946. Green. Temple of Heaven at center. Back: Brown. *(S/M #H180-61).*	15.00	45.00	125.
S3392	**200 Yüan** 1946. Blue. Summer Palace. Back: Brown. *(S/M #H180-62).*	25.00	75.00	225.

		Good	Fine	XF
S3393	**200 Yüan** 1946. Blue. Pagoda along river at right. Back: Modern buildings along river at center. *(S/M #H180-62.5).*	10.00	30.00	100.
S3393A	**200 Yüan** 1946. Black. Pagoda along river at right. Back: Dark blue. Modern buildings along river at center. *(S/M #H180-).*			
	a. White paper.	10.00	30.00	100.
	b. Gray paper.	15.00	45.00	125.

		Good	Fine	XF
S3393B	**200 Yüan** 1946. Orange. Peasant plowing with ox at lower right. Back: Yellow-orange. *(S/M #H180-62.7).*	25.00	75.00	225.

		Good	Fine	XF
S3394	**500 Yüan** 1946. Deep red. Steam passenger train, ship at right. *(S/M #H180-63).*			
	a. Back brown. Ship at right.	—	—	—
	b. Back blue, without ship.	—	—	—

		Good	Fine	XF
S3394A	**500 Yüan** 1946. Deep red. Steam passenger train, ship at right. Back: Blue. Value. *(S/M #H180-).*	25.00	75.00	225.
S3395	**500 Yüan** 1946. Brown. Steam passenger train, ship at right. Back: Blue-black. *(S/M #H180-64).*	25.00	75.00	225.

1947 Issue

		Good	Fine	XF
S3397	**1000 Yüan** 1947. Brown. Peasant with cows at center. Back: Blue-gray. *(S/M #H180-70).*			
	a. Regular serial #.	10.00	30.00	100.
	b. Bold serial #.	10.00	30.00	100.

1948 Issues

		Good	Fine	XF
S3399	**50 Yüan** 1948. Violet. Monument. *(S/M #H180-70.3).*	10.00	30.00	100.
S3400	**100 Yüan** 1948. Bugler by Great Wall. *(S/M #H180-70.6).*	10.00	30.00	100.
S3401	**200 Yüan** 1948. Deep brown. Sawing logs at center right. Back: Brown. *(S/M #H180-71)*	7.50	20.00	60.00
S3402	**200 Yüan** 1948. Blue. Wood sawing. *(S/M #H180-71.3).*	10.00	30.00	100.
S3403	**200 Yüan** 1948. Violet. Temple. *(S/M #H180-71.6.*	10.00	30.00	100.
S3405	**500 Yüan** 1948. Blue. Great Wall at right. Back: Brown. *(S/M #H180-72).*	10.00	30.00	100.
S3406	**500 Yüan** 1948. Blue-black. Pagoda at center. Back: Brown. *(S/M #H180-73).*	10.00	30.00	100.

		Good	Fine	XF
S3407	**1000 Yüan** 1948. Pale blue. Steam passenger train at right. Back: Green. Ships dockside at center. *(S/M #H180-74).*	10.00	30.00	100.
S3408	**1000 Yüan** 1948. Brown. Pagoda at left center. Back: Green. *(S/M #H180-75).*	10.00	30.00	100.
S3409	**1000 Yüan** 1948. Red. Windmill at center right. Back: Green. Sampans at center. *(S/M #H180-76).*	10.00	30.00	100.
S3410	**1000 Yüan** 1948. Black. Hillside summer palace, pagoda along shoreline at center right. Back: Brown. *(S/M #H180-77).*	10.00	30.00	100.
S3411	**2000 Yüan** 1948. Brown and yellow. Hillside pagoda along shoreline at left. Back: Green. *(S/M #H180-80).*	7.50	20.00	60.00
S3412	**2000 Yüan** 1948. Blue. Sampan by house and bridge at center. *(S/M #H180-81).*			
	a. 2 Black letters with serial #. Back brown.	7.50	20.00	60.00
	b. 2 Serial #'s on face. Back green and brown.	10.00	30.00	100.
S3413	**2000 Yüan** 1948. Green. Shrine. Back: Blue. *(S/M #H180-82).*			
	a. Issued note.	10.00	30.00	100.
	s. Specimen.	—	Unc	400.
S3414	**2000 Yüan** 1948. Red. Summer palace. Back: Blue. *(S/M #H180-83).*	10.00	30.00	100.
S3415	**2000 Yüan** 1948. Brown on yellow underprint. Army bugler at left, Great Wall at left and right. Back: Dark green. *(S/M #H180-84).*	10.00	30.00	100.

1949 Issues

	Good	Fine	XF
S3416 5000 Yüan 1949. Brown. Minehead at right. Back: Green. Temple at center. *(S/M #H180-90).*	10.00	30.00	100.
S3417 5000 Yüan 1949. Brown on light green underprint. Ship at dockside at lower left. Back: Dark green. Cattle at center. *(S/M #H180-91).*	10.00	30.00	100.
S3418 5000 Yüan 1949. Violet and green. Dump truck. Back: Blue. *(S/M #H180-92).*	25.00	75.00	225.

Huainan Bank

行銀南淮

Huai Nan Yin Hang

1942 Issue

	Good	Fine	XF
S3418B 10 Yüan 1942. House in woods at left. Back: Birds over junk at left. *(S/M #H194-13).*	—	—	—

1943 Issue

	Good	Fine	XF
S3418D 5 Yüan 1943. Military observation post at right. *(S/M #H194-22).*	—	—	—
S3418F 10 Yüan 1943. Crowd rallied before speaker at right. *(S/M #H194-23).*	—	—	—

1944 Issues

	Good	Fine	XF
S3419 1 Chiao = 10 Cents 1944. Ox driven irrigation system at right. *(S/M #H194-31).*	—	—	—
S3419C 5 Chiao = 50 Cents 1944. Worker, soldier, and peasant at center. *(S/M #H194-32).*	—	—	—
S3419E 1 Yüan 1944. School class at left, farming and industrial scenes at right. *(S/M #H194-34).*	—	—	—
S3419G 5 Yüan 1944. Rural home at left. *(S/M #194-34).*	—	—	—
S3419J 10 Yüan 1944. Watermark: Mao Tse-tung at left. *(S/M #H194-35).*	—	—	—
S3419L 10 Yüan July 1944. Planting rice at right. *(S/M #H194-36).*	—	—	—

Northwest Anhwei Special District Soviet Bank

行銀埃維蘇區特地北西皖

Huan Hsi Pei Ti T'e Chü Su Wei Ai Yin Hang

1932 Issue

	Good	Fine	XF
S3421 2 Chiao 1932. Portrait Karl Marx at center. *(S/M #H195-1).*	150.	450.	1250.

#S3422 Deleted.

	Good	Fine	XF
S3423 1 Yüan 1932. Black. Government building at center. Back: Yellow. Hammer and sickle in rays above top of globe at center. Printer: HHPC. *(S/M #H195-3).*	100.	300.	900.
S3423A 1 Yüan 1932. Government building at center. Similiar to #S3423 but reduced size. *(S/M #H195-4).*	50.00	150.	450.
S3423B 1 Yüan 1932. Green and black. Government building at center. Back: Green. Karl Marx at lower left; top of globe at lower right. *(S/M #H195-5).*	50.00	150.	450.
S3423C 1 Yüan 1932. Green and brown. Government building at center. *(S/M #H195-6).*	75.00	225.	675.

1923 Issue

	Good	Fine	XF
S3423D 5 Yüan 1923. Government building at center. Back: Karl Marx at center. *(S/M #H195-7).*	100.	300.	900.

Bank of Rehher Sheeng

行銀省河熱

Je Ho Sheng Yin Hang

1946 Issue

	Good	Fine	XF
S3424 50 Yüan 1946. Black on light green. Cattle at left, farming at right. Back: Light blue-gray. Great Wall at center. *(S/M #J3-).*	45.00	125.	375.
S3424A 100 Yüan 1946. Red on light blue-green underprint. Steam passenger train at center. Back: Brown. Rural scenes at left and center right. *(S/M #J3-).*	50.00	150.	450.

1947 Issues

	Good	Fine	XF
S3425 10 Yüan 1947. Light red-brown. Modern buildings at left. Back: Brown. *(S/M #J3-).*	50.00	150.	450.
S3425A 20 Yüan 1947. Red on light yellow underprint. Rural village at center. Back: Brown. Rural scene at center. *(S/M #J3-).*	50.00	150.	450.
S3425B 20 Yüan 1947. Dark brown-violet on light yellow-green underprint. Pagoda, rural scene at center. Back: Purple. Gazebo at center. *(S/M #J3-).*	30.00	100.	300.
S3426 50 Yüan 1947. Green. Great Wall at left. Back: Brown. *(S/M #J3-).*	25.00	75.00	225.
S3427 100 Yüan 1947. Lilac on yellow underprint. Plowing with oxen at left. Back: Gray. *(S/M #J3-1).*	7.50	20.00	60.00
S3427A 100 Yüan 1947. Brown-violet on yellow-green underprint. Rural village with fortress gate at center right. "18th special district" in Chinese at left and right. Back: Light olive-green. *(S/M #J3-).*	25.00	75.00	225.
S3427B 100 Yüan 1947. Rural village with fortress gate at center right. *(S/M #J3-).*	25.00	75.00	225.
S3428 200 Yüan 1947. Gray on pink underprint. Gateway at left. Back: Red. *(S/M #J3-2).*	25.00	75.00	225.

Northeast Kiangsi Soviet Bank

行銀埃維蘇(省)北東贛

Kan Tung Pei (Sheng) Su Wei Ai Yin Hang

1932 Issue

	Good	Fine	XF
S3433 5 Ch'uan 1932. *(S/M #K13-1).* Reported not confirmed.	—	—	—
S3434 10 Cents 1932. Blue on red underprint. Flag on hemisphere at center. Back: Black on red underprint. *(S/M #K13-).*	50.00	150.	450.
S3435 10 Cents 1932. Blue and red. Flag on hemisphere at center. Back: Red and black. Overprint: On #S3468. *(S/M #K13-10).* Reported not confirmed.	—	—	—
S3437 50 Cents 1932. Red. Star, hammer and sickle. Back: Green. *(S/M #K13-11).*	50.00	150.	450.
S3438 1 Yüan 1932. Overprint: On #3471. *(S/M #K13-20).* Reported not confirmed.	—	—	—

Northeast Kiangsi Soviet Bank

行銀北閩行銀埃維蘇(省)北東贛

Kan Tung Pei Sheng Su Wei Ai Yin Hang / Min Pei Yin Hang

North Fukien Branch

1932 Issue

	Good	Fine	XF
S3440 1 Chiao Jan. 1932. Hammer and sickle on star at center. Back: Text, date and various hand stamps. *(S/M #K13.5-1).*	50.00	150.	450.
S3440A 2 Chiao Jan. 1932. Deep blue-green and red on yellow underprint. Hammer and sickle on star at center. Back: Text, date and various hand stamps. *(S/M #K13.5-2).*			
a. Issued note.	50.00	150.	450.
r. Remainder without serial # filled in lower frame.	—	—	350.
S3440B 5 Chiao Jan. 1932. Hammer and sickle on star at center. Back: Text, date and various hand stamps. *(S/M #K13.5-3).*	50.00	150.	450.

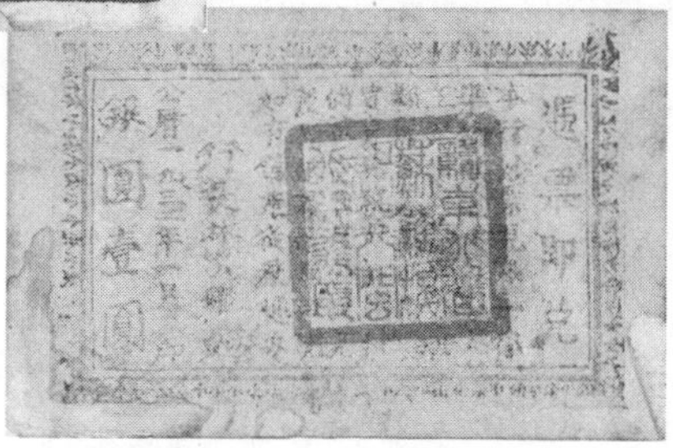

	Good	Fine	XF
S3440C 1 Yüan Jan. 1932. Blue on red and tan underprint. Hammer and sickle on star at center. Back: Large red hand stamped seal. Printer: Text, date and various hand stamps. *(S/M #K13.5-4).*			
a. Issued note.	—	—	—
r. Remainder without serial # in lower frame.	—	—	500.

Kiangsi, Hunan, Anhwei Soviet Workers and Farmers Bank

行銀農工埃蘇皖豫贛

Kan Yü Huan Su Wei Ai Kung Nung Yin Hang

1932 Issue

	Good	Fine	XF
S3441 1 Yüan 1932. *(S/M #K14-1).* Reported not confirmed.	—	—	—

Bank of Kuantung

行銀東關
Kuan Tung Yin Hang

1948 Issue

	Good	Fine	XF
S3445 1 Yüan 1948. Orange. Mountain lake at center. Back: Ocean liner at center. *(S/M #K20-1).*	15.00	45.00	125.
S3446 5 Yüan 1948. Green and gray. Mountain lake at center. Back: Ocean liner at center. *(S/M #K20-2).*	25.00	75.00	225.
S3447 10 Yüan 1948. Red and blue. Mountain lake at center. Back: Red. Ocean liner at center. *(S/M #K20-3).*	30.00	100.	300.
S3448 50 Yüan 1948. Violet and black. Mountain lake at center. Back: Violet. Ocean liner at center. *(S/M #K20-4).*	60.00	175.	525.
S3449 100 Yüan 1948. Black on pale blue and lilac underprint. Mountain lake at left. Back: Black. Ocean liner. *(S/M #K20-5).*	60.00	175.	525.

Bank of West Shantung

行銀西魯
Lu Hsi Yin Hang

1940 Issue

	Good	Fine	XF
S3450 1 Chiao 1940. Gazebo on hill at upper center. *(S/M #L24-0.2).*	60.00	175.	525.
S3451 2 Chiao 1940. Temple of Heaven at right. *(S/M #L24-0.4).*	60.00	175.	525.

	Good	Fine	XF
S3452 5 Chiao 1940. Brown. Farmer at center. Back: Ochre. *(S/M #L24-0.6).*	45.00	125.	375.
S3452A 1 Yüan 1940. Rural scenes at left and right. *(S/M #L24-0.8).*	45.00	125.	375.
S3453 20 Yüan 1940. Blue and red. Buildings, mountains at left. Back: Orange. *(S/M #L24-1).*	45.00	125.	375.
S3453A 50 Yüan 1940. Green on yellow underprint. Large building at right. Back: Violet.	60.00	175.	525.

1941 Issue

	Good	Fine	XF
S3454 4 Fen 1941. Rural scene at left and right. Back: House at center. *(S/M #L24-3).*	50.00	150.	450.
S3454A 5 Fen 1941. Ship at left, truck at right. *(S/M #L24-4).*	60.00	175.	525.
S3454B 20 Cents 1941. Farmer at upper center. *(S/M #L24-5).*	60.00	175.	525.
S3454C 25 Cents 1941. Farmer plowing with horse at left. *(S/M #L24-6).*	75.00	225.	675.
S3454D 2 Yüan 1941. Fortress at left, steam passenger train at right. *(S/M #L24-7).*	100.	300.	900.

1942 Issue

	Good	Fine	XF
S3454E 5 Yüan 1942. Blue. Back: Green. *(S/M #L24-).*	40.00	125.	375.
S3454F 10 Yüan 1942. Purple and black. Back: Blue. *(S/M #L24-).*	60.00	175.	525.
S3455 20 Yüan 1942. Green. Temple of Heaven at left, gazebo at right. Back: Brown. *(S/M #L24-10).*	75.00	225.	675.

1943 Issue

	Good	Fine	XF
S3456 10 Yüan 1943. Tan on yellow underprint. Planting rice at center. *(S/M #L24-12).*			
a. Back blue-green.	75.00	225.	675.
b. Back light brown. *Tai Yun.*	100.	300.	900.
s. Specimen.	—	Unc	750.
S3456A 50 Yüan 1943. Brown. Bridge and lake at left. Back: Dark green. Pagoda at left and right. *(S/M #L24-13).*	125.	375.	1100.
S3456B 100 Yüan 1943. Gateway at right. *(S/M #L24-14).*	75.00	225.	675.
	VG	**VF**	**UNC**
S3456C 200 Yüan 1943. Harvesting at center. Specimen. *(S/M #L24-15).*		—	750.
S3456D 500 Yüan 1943. Plowing with horse at left. Specimen. *(S/M #L24-16).*		—	750.

1944 Issue

	Good	Fine	XF
S3456E 10 Yüan 1944. Dark blue and dark brown. Temple of Heaven at left, tower at right. *(S/M #L24-17).*			
a. Issued note. *HUSI* in oval frames at left and right.	125.	375.	1100.
s. Specimen.	—	Unc	750.
S3457 100 Yüan 1944. Blue and yellow. Steam passenger train at center. Back: Brown. *(S/M #L24-20).*	75.00	225.	675.
S3458 300 Yüan 1944. Temple of Heaven at upper center. Vertical format. Back: Shoreline hillside village at center. *(S/M #L24-22).*	40.00	125.	375.
	VG	**VF**	**UNC**
S3459 500 Yüan 1944. Ship at left, steam passenger train at right. Specimen. *(S/M #L24-25).*	—	—	750.

1945 Issue

	Good	Fine	XF
S3461 10 Yüan 1945. Green. Rural scene at left, building at right. *(S/M #L24-30).*	75.00	225.	675.
S3462 25 Yüan 1945. Hillside temple at right. *(S/M #L24-33).*	60.00	175.	525.

Fukien-Chekiang-Kiangsi Soviet Bank

行銀埃維蘇省贛浙閩
Min Che Kan Sheng Su Wei Ai Yin Hang

ND Issue

	Good	Fine	XF
S3465 1 Chiao ND. Blue. Uniface. Crude hammer, sickle and star at center. *(S/M #M15-1).*			
a. Thick (fat) star. Blue validation seals at right and left borders.	45.00	125.	375.
b. Slim star. Red validation seals at right and left borders.	45.00	125.	375.

1932 Issue

	Good	Fine	XF
S3468 1 Chiao 1932. Blue and red. Flag on hemisphere at center. Back: Red and black. *(S/M #M15-10).*	45.00	125.	375.
S3469 2 Chiao 1932. Green. Back: Brown. *(S/M #M15-20).*	60.00	175.	525.
S3470 5 Chiao 1932. Violet. Back: Green. *(S/M #M15-21).*	60.00	175.	525.

	Good	Fine	XF
S3471 1 Yüan 1932. Dark green and red. Flag and hemisphere. Back: Dark blue and red. *(S/M #M15-30).*	75.00	225.	675.

NOTE: For #S3468 and S3471 with additional overprint, see #S3435 and #S3438.

1933 Issue

	Good	Fine	XF
S3473 1 Chiao 1933. *(S/M #M15-40).*	125.	375.	1100.

	Good	Fine	XF
S3476 1 Yüan 1933. Light green and red. Flag and hemisphere. *(S/M #M15-50).*	150.	450.	1250.
S3478 10 Yüan 1933. *(S/M #M15-51).*	225.	675.	1750.

1934 Issue

	Good	Fine	XF
S3480 1 Yüan 1934. Green and red. Back: Blue and red. *(S/M #M15-60).*	225.	675.	1750.

Fukien-Chekiang-Kiangsi Soviet Bank

行銀北閩 /行銀埃維蘇省贛浙閩

Min Che Kan Sheng Su Wei Ai Yin Hang / Min Pei Yin Hang

North Fukien Branch

1934 Issue

	Good	Fine	XF
S3481 1 Chiao Nov. 1934. Hammer and sickle on star at center. Back: Text. *(S/M #M15.5-1).*	100.	300.	900.
S3481A 2 Chiao Nov. 1934. Hammer and sickle on star at center. Back: Text. *(S/M #M15.5-2).*	100.	300.	900.
S3481B 1 Yüan Nov. 1934. Black and red. Hammer and sickle on star at center. Back: Text. Paper: Brown. *(S/M #M15.5-4).*	75.00	225.	675.

Fukien-Kwangtung-Kiangsi Border Area Bank

行銀區邊贛粵閩

Min Yüeh Kan Pien Chü Yin Hang

ND Provisional Issue

	Good	Fine	XF
S3482 10 Yüan ND (- old date 1949). Overprint: On #S3489. *(S/M #M17-).*	10.00	30.00	100.

NOTE: #S3482 is considered to be spurious by some authorities.

Southern Peoples Bank

行銀民人方南

Nan Fang Jen Min Yin Hang

1949 Issue

	Good	Fine	XF
S3483 1 Chiao 1949. Red and black. Ornamental frame around denomination at center. *(S/M #N5-).*	10.00	30.00	100.
S3483A 1 Chiao 1949. Modern municipal building complex at center.	25.00	75.00	225.
S3483B 2 Chiao 1949. Worker and farmer leaning on shield; modern municipal building at left. *(S/M #N5-0.3).*	25.00	75.00	225.
S3485 5 Chiao 1949. Red. Teahouse in woods at center. Back: Red. Drying rice at center. *(S/M #N5-0.5).*	25.00	75.00	225.
S3486 5 Chiao 1949. Green. Worker and farmer leaning on shield, modern municipal building at left. Back: Green. Cows at center. *(S/M #N5-0.7).*	30.00	100.	300.
S3487 1 Yüan 1949. Blue and green. Pagoda at right. Back: Blue. *(S/M #N5-1).*	25.00	75.00	225.
S3488 5 Yüan 1949. Violet. Gazebo at right. Back: Violet. *(S/M #N5-2).*	25.00	75.00	225.

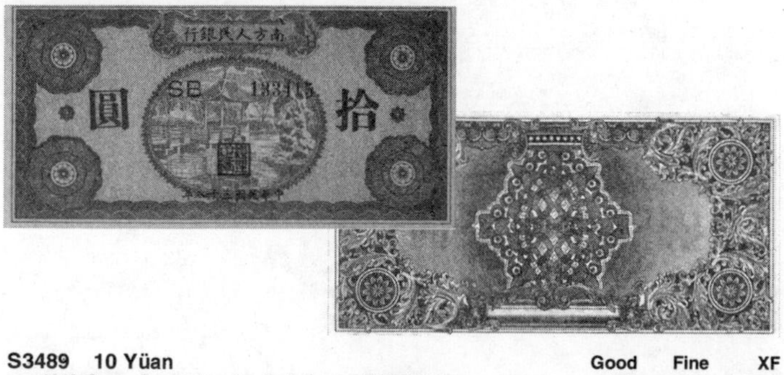

	Good	Fine	XF
S3489 10 Yüan 1949. Green. Gazebo at center. Back: Green. *(S/M #N5-3).*	1.00	3.00	10.00

NOTE: For #S3489 with additional red Chinese characters overprint, see #S3482.

Inner Mongolia Peoples Bank

行銀民人古蒙內

Nei Mung Ku Jen Min Yin Hang

1948 Issue

	Good	Fine	XF
S3494 200 Yüan 1948. Black on blue underprint. Herdsman with horses at center. Back: Purple. Man with ox drawn cart at center. *(S/M #N12-0.5).*	45.00	125.	375.
S3495 500 Yüan 1948. Violet. Back: Green. *(S/M #N12-1).*	45.00	125.	375.
S3498 2000 Yüan 1948. Sheep. *(S/M #N12-).*	60.00	175.	525.

1949 Issue

	Good	Fine	XF
S3501 100 Yüan 1949. Herdsman with horses at center. *(S/M #N12-10).*	45.00	125.	375.
S3502 500 Yüan 1949. *(S/M #N12-11).* Reported not confirmed.	—	—	—
S3503 1000 Yüan 1949. *(S/M #N12-12).* Reported not confirmed.	—	—	—
S3505 5000 Yüan 1949. *(S/M #N12-13).* Reported not confirmed.	—	—	—
S3506 10,000 Yüan 1949. Red. Back: Brown. *(S/M #N12-14).*	60.00	175.	525.

Bank of Inner Mongolia

行銀蒙內

Nei Mung Yin Hang

1947 Issue

	Good	Fine	XF
S3507 200 Yüan 1947. Red on yellow underprint. Bank building at right. Back: Blue-black. *(S/M #N12.5-6).*	100.	300.	900.
S3507A 500 Yüan 1947. Steam passenger train at lower center. Back: Monument at upper center. *(S/M #N12.5-7).*	125.	375.	1100.

Bank of Inner Chiang

行銀省江嫩

Nen Chiang Sheng Yin Hang

1946 Issue

	Good	Fine	XF
S3507J 5 Yüan 1946. Army machine gun crew at center right. *(S/M #N12.7-5).*	25.00	75.00	225.
S3507K 10 Yüan 1946. Peasant and mule by hut at center. *(S/M #N12.7-7).*	25.00	75.00	225.
S3507L 10 Yüan 1946. Steam passenger train, buildings at right. *(S/M #N12.7-9).*	25.00	75.00	225.
S3507M 10 Yüan 1946. Steam passenger train at right. *(S/M #N12.7-9).*	25.00	75.00	225.
S3507P 50 Yüan 1946. Blue-black and yellow on light blue underprint. Soldiers at left. Back: Red-violet. Bank building at center. Printer: Tung Pei Hifan. *(S/M #N12.7-13).*	10.00	30.00	100.
S3507Q 100 Yüan 1946. Two soldiers at left. Back: Bank building at center. 112 x 54mm. *(S/M #N12.7-14).*	25.00	75.00	225.
S3507R 100 Yüan 1946. Deep blue-green on light green underprint. Two soldiers at left. Back: Green and yellow. Bank building at center. 150 x 69mm. *(S/M #N12.7-15).*	175.	525.	1500.

West Hupei Peasants Bank

行銀民農西鄂

O Hsi Nung Min Yin Hang

1930 Issue

	Good	Fine	XF
S3508A 1 Chiao 1930-1931. Red. Hammer and sickle on star at center. Back: Blue. *(S/M #O4-0.2).*	25.00	75.00	225.
S3508D 1 Yüan 1930. Temple of Heaven at center. *(S/M #O4-0.5).*	25.00	75.00	225.

1931 Issues

	Good	Fine	XF
S3508F 2 Chiao 1931. Tea house at center. *(S/M #O4-1).*	25.00	75.00	225.
S3508G 2 Chiao 1931. *(S/M #O4-2).*	25.00	75.00	225.
S3508J 1 Yüan 1931. Temple of Heaven at right. Back: Rural hillside view. *(S/M #O4-5).*	25.00	75.00	225.

North Hupeh Peasants Bank

行銀民農北鄂

O Pei Nung Min Yin Hang

1931 Issue

	Good	Fine	XF
S3508P 5 Chiao 1931. Portrait Vladimir I. Lenin at center. *(S/M #O5.5-11).*	25.00	75.00	225.
S3508Q 1 Yüan 1931. Portrait Vladimir I. Lenin at center. *(S/M #O5.5-12).*	25.00	75.00	225.

East Hupei Workers and Peasants Bank

O Tung Kung Nung Yin Hang

1932 Issue

#	Denomination / Description	Good	Fine	XF
S3509	**1 Ch'uan** 1932. Brown. *(S/M #06-1).*	25.00	75.00	225.
S3510	**2 Ch'uan** 1932. Gray. City fortress gate at left and right. *(S/M #06-2).*	25.00	75.00	225.
S3512	**10 Ch'uan** 1932. Black. Bridge at left, and buildings at right. *(S/M #06-3).*	25.00	75.00	225.

Southeast Hupei Workers, Peasants and Soldiers Bank

O Tung Nan Kung Nung Ping Yin Hang

1931 Issue

#	Denomination / Description	Good	Fine	XF
S3515	**500 Cash** 1931. *(S/M #07-0.3).*	75.00	225.	675.
S3517	**1 Ch'uan** 1931. Black. *(S/M #07-0.5).*	100.	300.	900.
S3518	**2 Ch'uan** 1931. City gate. *(S/M #07-0.6).*	100.	300.	900.
S3519	**5 Ch'uan** 1931. Black. Rural house in woods at center. Back: Green. *(S/M #07-0.7).*	175.	525.	1500.

#S3521, 3522 *Deleted.* See #S3526, S3527.

1932 Issue

#	Denomination / Description	Good	Fine	XF
S3524	**5 Ch'uan** 1932. Blue. *(S/M #07-0.9).*	100.	300.	900.

Southeast Hupei Workers and Peasants Bank

O Tung Nan Kung Nung Yin Hang

1932 Issue

#	Denomination / Description	Good	Fine	XF
S3526	**200 Cash** 1932. Black. Village at center. Back: Text. *(S/M #07-1).*	75.00	225.	675.
S3527	**500 Cash** 1932. Blue and green. *(S/M #07-2).*	75.00	225.	675.
S3529	**5 Ch'uan** 1932. Dark blue. Rural house in woods at center. Back: Text with large red hand stamped seal. *(S/M#07-10).*			
	a. Issued note.	100.	300.	900.
	r. Remainder without serial # or Large hand stamped seal on back.	60.00	175.	525.

Hupei-Hunan Reconstruction Bank

<TRN>O Yü Chien She Yin Hang

#S3531-S3537 *Deleted.*

Hupei-Honan-Anhwei Soviet Bank

O Yü Huan Sheng Su Wei Ai Yin Hang

1931 Issue

#	Denomination / Description	Good	Fine	XF
S3538	**10 Chiao** 1931. *(S/M #011-1).* Reported not confirmed.	—	—	—

Hupei-Honan-Anhwei Province Soviet Workers & Peasants Bank

O Yü Huan Sheng Su Wei Ai Kung Neng Yin Hang

1923 Issue

#	Denomination / Description	Good	Fine	XF
S3539	**2 Chiao** ND. Portrait Karl Marx at center. Back: Upper hemisphere at center. *(S/M #011-2).*	75.00	225.	675.
S3540	**5 Chiao** 1923. Government building at center. Back: Peasant, worker and soldier at center. *(S/M #011-3).*	50.00	150.	450.

1932 Issue

#	Denomination / Description	Good	Fine	XF
S3540A	**5 Chiao** 1932. Dark green on gray underprint. Pagoda at left, temple at right. Back: Red. Peasant, worker and soldier at center. *(S/M #011-4).*	60.00	175.	525.
S3540B	**1 Yüan** 21.1.1932. Dark green on light olive-green underprint. Government building at center. Back: Light yellow-green. Rural scene at center with bank name above in Chinese. *(S/M #011-4).*	60.00	175.	525.
S3540C	**1 Yüan** 1932. Dark green on light olive-green underprint. Government building at center. Back: Light yellow-green. Rural scene at center with bank name in Russian text. *(S/M #011-5).*	75.00	225.	675.

Bank of Bai Hai, Beei Hai Bank, Bo Xai Inxang, B. X. Inxang, Bank of Pei Hai

Pei Hai Bank of China

Pei Hai Yin Hang

1938 ND Issue

#	Denomination / Description	Good	Fine	XF
S3541	**1 Chiao** ND (1938). Blue on pink underprint. Rural building with fence in yard. Back: Red. *Chiaotung. (S/M #P21-0.1).*	7.50	20.00	60.00
S3541A	**10 Cents** ND (1938). Grey-green. Building at right. Back: Dark blue.	20.00	60.00	175.
S3541B	**2 Chiao** ND (1938). Green. Rural building with courtyard at left. Back: Purple.			
	a. *Chiaotung. (S/M #P21-0.2a).*	15.00	45.00	125.
	b. *Yeh Hsien. (S/M #P21-0.2b).*	15.00	45.00	125.
S3542	**5 Chiao** ND (1938). Red. City gate at left. Back: Brown. *Chiaotung. (S/M #P21-0.3).*	20.00	60.00	125.
S3543	**1 Yüan** ND (1938). Red. Rural waterfront village at left. Back: Brown. Overprint: *Fan* at left and right. *(S/M #P21-0.4).*	30.00	100.	300.

1938 Issues

#	Denomination / Description	Good	Fine	XF
S3543A	**5 Chiao** 1938. Blue. Building at left. Back: Purple. *(S/M #P21-).*	25.00	75.00	225.
S3543B	**5 Chiao** 1938. Blue. Building at left. Back: Purple. *Ch'ing-ho. (S/M #P21-).*	25.00	75.00	225.
S3543C	**1 Yüan** 1938. Red. Gateways at left. Back: Brown. *(S/M #P21-).*			
	a. Issued note with serial # on face and back and signature seals.	25.00	75.00	225.
	b. *Nan.* without serial # or signature seals.	25.00	75.00	225.
	c. *Nanhai.* without serial # or signature seals.	25.00	75.00	225.
	d. *Tunghai.*	25.00	75.00	225.
	e. *Yeh Hsien.* with serial # and signature seals.	25.00	75.00	225.
	f. *Enan Pei* at left and right, with serial # and signature seals on face.	25.00	75.00	225.

1940 Issues

#	Denomination / Description	Good	Fine	XF
S3543E	**1 Chiao** 1940. Deep green. Peasant hoeing at right. Back: Yellow. *Ch'ingho. (S/M #P21-).*	15.00	45.00	125.
S3543F	**2 Chiao** 1940. Blue. Back: Brown. *Ch'ingho. (S/M #P21-).*	25.00	75.00	225.
S3543G	**5 Chiao** 1940. Orange. Plowing at right. Back: Orange. *Lu Nan.*	25.00	75.00	225.
S3544	**5 Yüan** 1940. Gateway at left.			
	a. *Sheng* at left and right. *Chiaotung. (S/M #P21-0.6b).*	15.00	45.00	125.
	s. *Jung* at left and right. Specimen. *(S/M #P21-0.6a).*	—	Unc	450.
S3544A	**5 Yüan** 1940. Blue. Back: Purple. *(S/M #P21-).*			
	a. Without place name.	10.00	30.00	100.
	b. *Chiaotung.*	25.00	75.00	225.
	c. *Chi Lu Pian.*	25.00	75.00	225.
S3545	**10 Yüan** 1940. Red. Temple of Heaven at left, fortress gate at right. Back: Shoreline cliffs, house and gazebo at center. *(S/M #P21-0.7).*			
	a. Bright red. Block letters and serial # in italics. Signature Seals at left and right. *Chiaotung.*	25.00	75.00	225.
	b. Wine red. Without block letters. Signature seals both at right. *Nong* or Tsen at left and right.	25.00	75.00	225
	s. Specimen.	—	Unc	450.

1941 Issues

#S3549 *Deleted.* See #S3551B.

#	Denomination / Description	Good	Fine	XF
S3546	**1 Chiao** 1941. Brown. *Chi Lu Pien. (S/M #P21).*	25.00	75.00	225.
S3548	**1 Yüan** 1941. (In center of lower frame.) Red. Rural waterfront village at left. Back: Brown.			
	a. *Fa, Jin* or *Nong* at left and right. *(S/M #P21-0.9a).*	15.00	45.00	125.
	s. *Chan* at left and right. *Giao Dung (Chiaotung).* Specimen. *(S/M #P21-0.9b).*	—	Unc	450.
S3549	**5 Yüan** 1941. Blue on yellow underprint. Temple of Heaven at right. Back: Olive. *Shantung.*	25.00	75.00	225.
S3550	**5 Yüan** 1941. Blue-gray. Junk at left, waterfront house at right. Back: Gazebo at left, modern building at right. *GIAO DUNG (Chiaotung). (S/M #P21-2).*	20.00	60.00	175.
S3550A	**5 Yüan** 1941. Junk at left, waterfront house at right. *Giao Dung (Chioatung).* (twice) at left and right. Back: Gazebo at left, modern building at right. *(S/M #P21-).*	20.00	60.00	175.
S3550B	**10 Yüan** 1941. Red. Pagoda at left, steam passenger train at right. Back: Red. Temple of Heaven at center. *(S/M #P21-3).*			
	a. *Giao Dung (Chiaotung).*	15.00	45.00	125.
	b. As a without overprint *Chien* at left and right. *(S/M #P21-0.9a).*	15.00	45.00	125.
	c. *Cing Xo (Ch'ingho).*	20.00	60.00	175.
	d. *GILU BIAN.*	20.00	60.00	175.
	e. *Gi Lu Bian. (Chi Lu Pian).*	25.00	75.00	225.
	s. Specimen. *(S/M #P21-0.9b).*			

1942 Issues

#	Denomination / Description	Good	Fine	XF
S3551	**2 Chiao** 1942. Green. City gate at left. Back: Olive-green. *Shantung. (S/M #P21-).*	25.00	75.00	225.

	Good	Fine	XF
S3551A 5 Chiao			
1942. Green. Sheep. Back: Blue. *Chi Lu Pien. (S/M #P21-3.3).*	15.00	45.00	125.
S3551B 5 Chiao			
1942. Green. Lakeside park. *(S/M #P21-).*	15.00	45.00	125.
S3551C 5 Chiao			
1942. Dark blue. Peasant hoeing at right. Back: Dark brown. *Ching Ho. (S/M #P21-).*			
a. *Kai* at left in Chinese on face. *Kai* in script English at lower left and right on back.	25.00	75.00	225.
b. *Yüan* at left in Chinese on face. *Yüan in script English at lower left and right on back.*	25.00	75.00	225.
S3551D 5 Chiao			
1942. Dark brown. Fortress gate at right. *Ch'ingho* at left, *Shantung* at right. *(S/M #P21-).*	25.00	75.00	225.
S3551F 1 Yüan			
1942. Brown. Shepherd with sheep. Back: Orange. *Chi Lu Pien. (S/M #P21-3.6).*	7.50	20.00	60.00
S3552 1 Yüan			
1942. Blue-black. Rural waterfront village at left. Back: Brown.			
a. Without place name. Large date. *(S/M #P21-4a).*	5.00	15.00	45.00
b. Without place name. Small date. *(S/M #P21-4d).*	5.00	15.00	45.00
s1. As b. Small date. Specimen. *(S/M #P21-0.4b).*	—	Unc	450.
s2. As b. Small date. *Chiaotung.* Specimen. *(S/M #P21-0.4c).*	—	Unc	450.
S3552A 1 Yüan			
1942. Dark green. Rural waterfront village at left. Back: Dark blue. *Chiaotung. (S/M #P21-5).*	10.00	30.00	100.
S3552B 1 Yüan			
1942. Red. Rural waterfront village at left. Back: Red-brown. *(S/M #P21-).*	10.00	30.00	100.
S3552C 1 Yüan			
1942. Steam passenger train at center. *Shantung. (S/M #P21-).*	15.00	45.00	125.

	Good	Fine	XF
S3552D 2 Yüan			
1942. Blue-green. Farmer plowing at right. Back: Green.	45.00	125.	375.
S3552E 2 Yüan			
1942. Dark green. Plowing at right. Back: Factory at center. *Shantung.*	45.00	125.	375.
S3553 5 Yüan			
1942. Purple on lilac underprint. Modern Ocean liner at center. Bank building at center. *Chiaotung. (S/M #P21-).*	25.00	75.00	225.
S3553A 10 Yüan			
1942. Back: Bank building at center. Modern ocean liner at center. *Chiaotung. (S/M #P21-7).*	15.00	45.00	125.

	Good	Fine	XF
S3553B 10 Yüan			
1942. Grayish green. Hillside view at left, mountain waterfall, stream at right. Back: Blue. Temple at center, steam passenger train crossing bridge over river at right. *Shantung. (S/M #P21-8).*			
a. Issued note.	20.00	60.00	175.
s. Specimen.	—	Unc	450.
S3553C 10 Yüan			
Grayish green. Hillside view at left, mountain waterfall, stream at right. Back: Blue. *Ch'ingho. (S/M #P21-).*	15.00	45.00	125.
S3553F 50 Yüan			
1942. Blue on brown underprint. Riverside village at center. Back: Ocean liner. *Chiaotung. (S/M #P21-).*	15.00	45.00	125.

1943 Issues

	Good	Fine	XF
S3553J 2 Chiao = 20 Cents			
1943. Blue. Sampans (Junks) at center. Back: Brown. *Shantung. (S/M #P21-).*	7.50	20.00	60.00
S3554 5 Chiao = 50 Cents			
1943. Brown. Farmer plowing with ox at right. Back: Green. *Shantung. (S/M #P21-9).*	10.00	30.00	100.

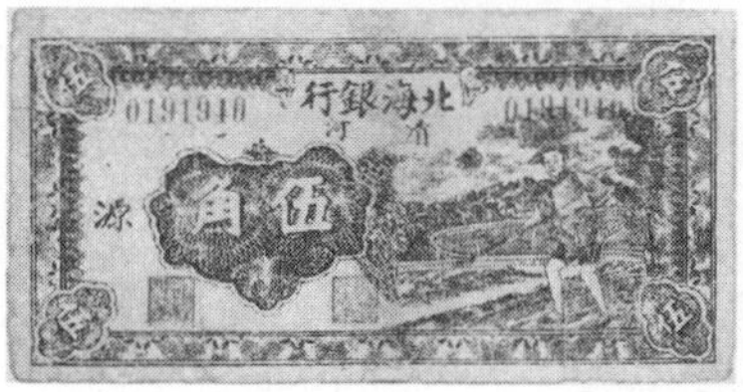

	Good	Fine	XF
S3554A 5 Chiao = 50 Cents			
1943. Blue. Peasant spading. Back: Purple. *Ch'ingho. (S/M #P21-).*			
a. overprint: *Yuan* at left and r.	25.00	75.00	225.
b. overprint: *Kai* at left and r.	25.00	75.00	225.
S3555 1 Yüan			
1943. Brown. Pack mules at center. Back: Yellow. *(S/M #P21-10).*			
a. *Shantung.* Block #.	10.00	30.00	100.
b. *Pohai.* Blue serial #.	10.00	30.00	100.
S3555A 1 Yüan			
1943. Blue. Sampan at center. Back: Farm scene at center. *Pohai. (S/M #P21-10.3).*	30.00	100.	300.
S3555B 1 Yüan			
1943. Rural scene at lower right. *Shantung. (S/M #P21-10.7).*	25.00	75.00	225.

	Good	Fine	XF
S3555C 1 Yüan			
1943. Red-brown. Steam passenger train at lower left, city gate at lower center. Back: Brown. *Luchung. (S/M #P21-).*	25.00	75.00	225.
S3556 5 Yüan			
1943. Violet and brown. Plowing. Back: Violet. *(S/M #P21-11).*	25.00	75.00	225.
S3556A 5 Yüan			
1943. Purple. Peasant beside stream at center. Back: Purple and red. Rural scene at center. *Pohai. (S/M #P21-11.3).*			
a. Issued note.	30.00	100.	300.
s. Specimen.	—	Unc	450.
S3556B 5 Yüan = Guinque (Cinque) Argentens			
1943. Peasants stacking harvest at left, peasant laboring at irrigation system at right. Back: Construction scene at cente. *Pohai. (S/M #P21-11.7).*			
a. Blue. Red serial # and place name. Propaganda words and bank name as signatures on back.	60.00	175.	525.
b. Brown. Black serial # and place name. No words or signatures on back. Back brown.	60.00	175.	525.
s. Specimen.	—	Unc	450.
S3556C 5 Yüan			
1943. Red. Pavilion at center. *Luchung. (S/M #P21-).*	25.00	75.00	225.
S3556D 5 Yüan			
1943. Blue. Pavillion at center. *Luchung. (S/M #P21-).*	25.00	75.00	225.
S3557 10 Yüan			
1943. Purple. Farming scene at left and right. Back: Blue-green. Farm scene at center. *Chiaotung. (S/M #P21-12a).*	25.00	75.00	225.
S3557A 10 Yüan			
1943. Blue-gray. Farming scene at left and right. *Chiaotung. (S/M #P21-12b).*			
a. Back brown.	15.00	45.00	125.
b. Back purple.	10.00	30.00	100.
S3557B 10 Yüan = Decem Argentens			
1943. Multiple arch bridge at left, rural house at right. Back: Peasants cultivating at center. *Pohai. (S/M #P21-12.5b).*			
a. Issued note.	75.00	225.	675.
s. Specimen.	—	Unc	450.
S3557C 10 Yüan			
1943. Brown on blue underprint. Back: Green. *Luchung. (S/M #P21-).*	15.00	45.00	125.

	Good	Fine	XF
S3557D 10 Yüan			
1943. Back: Orange. *Pinhai. (S/M #P21-).*	15.00	45.00	125.
S3557E 10 Yüan			
1943. Red on yellow underprint. Fortress on right. Back: Brown. Rural houses at center. *Shantung. (S/M #P21-).*	25.00	75.00	225.
S3557F 50 Yüan			
1943. Rural mountain scene at right. *Pinhai. (S/M #P21-).*	10.00	30.00	100.
S3557G 50 Yüan			
1943. Harbor scene at right. *Luchung. (S/M #P21-).*	25.00	75.00	225.
S3558 100 Yüan			
1943. Trees along mountainous slopes at right. *New democracy* and *Free China* as signatures. Back: Brown. *Shantung. (S/M #P21-12.5).*			
a. Small (2.5mm) serial #. Dark blue. Back brown.	10.00	30.00	100.
b. Large (4mm) serial #. Black. Back brown. *Pao.*	10.00	30.00	100.
S3559 100 Yüan			
1943. Green. Trees along mountainous slopes at right. *New democracy* and *Free China* as signatures. *(S/M #P21-13).*	10.00	30.00	100.
S3560 100 Yüan			
1943. Red. Truck. Back: Red. *Shantung. (S/M #P21-14).*			
a. Serial # at left and right.	10.00	30.00	100.
b. Block letters at left, serial # at right.	10.00	30.00	100.

1944 Issues

	Good	Fine	XF
S3560B 5 Chiao = 50 Cents			
1944. Green. Farm scene at left. *Pohai. (S/M #P21-17).*	10.00	30.00	100.
S3561 1 Yüan			
1944. Farmer plowing with horse at center. *Pohai. (S/M #P21-19).*	15.00	45.00	125.
S3561A 1 Yüan			
1944. Red. Rural scene at right. Back: Brown. *Shantung.*	15.00	45.00	125.
S3562 1 Yüan			
1944. Red-brown and red. Peasant with cart at center. *Giao Dung (Chiaotung). (S/M #P21-20).*			
a. Back brown-orange.	10.00	30.00	100.
b. Back blue-green.	10.00	30.00	100.
S3562A 5 Yüan			
1944. Orange. Farm scene at left. Back: Ochre. Steam passenger train, control tower at center. *Shantung. (S/M #P21-20.2).*	15.00	45.00	125.
S3562B 5 Yüan			
1944. Blue. Farmer walking in rural area at left. *Pohai.*	15.00	45.00	125.
S3563 5 Yüan			
1944. Blue. Drawing water at right. Back: Brown. *Shantung. (S/M #P21-05).*	10.00	30.00	100.
S3563A 5 Yüan			
1944. Red. Ship at left, steam passenger train at right. Back: Blue. *Nanlu. (S/M #P21-).*	10.00	30.00	100.

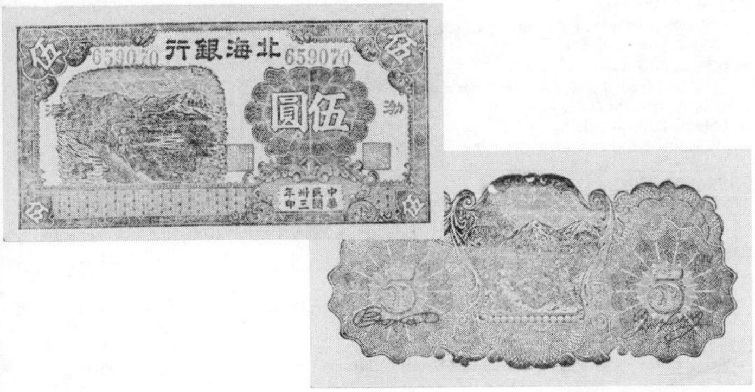

	Good	Fine	XF
S3563B 5 Yüan			
1944. Blue. *Pohai.*	25.00	75.00	225.
S3564 10 Yüan			
1944. Red. Mountains, farm. Back: Red. *Shantung. (S/M #P21-21).*	15.00	45.00	125.

	Good	Fine	XF
S3565 10 Yüan			
1944. Blue. Houses by lake at center. Back: Blue. *Luchung. (S/M #P21-22).*	25.00	75.00	225.
S3565A 10 Yüan			
1944. Red. Houses by lake at center. Back: Brown. *Shantung. (S/M #P21-).*	15.00	45.00	125.
S3565B 10 Yüan			
1944. Blue-black (to gray). Houses bt lake at center. Back: Blue. *Shantung. (S/M #P21-).*			
a. Serial # with prefix letter.	15.00	45.00	125.
b. Serial # without prefix letter.	15.00	45.00	125.
S3565C 10 Yüan			
1944. Blue-green. Houses by lake at center. Back: Blue. *Shantung. (S/M #P21-).*	20.00	60.00	175.
S3565D 10 Yüan			
1944. Red on yellow-orange underprint. Irrigation scene at left, peasant plowing with ox at right. Back: Sampan at center. *Pohai (S/M #P21-).*	15.00	45.00	125.
S3566 10 Yüan			
1944. Red. Forest. Back: Violet. *(S/M #P21-23).*	15.00	45.00	125.
S3566A 10 Yüan			
1944. Green. Sampan at left, peasant plowing with ox at right. Back: Purple. Farm at center. *Ch'ing ho. (S/M #P21-).*	30.00	100.	300.
S3566B 50,000 Cash			
1944. Red. Houses by lake at left. Back: Ox cart and farm scene. *Pin Hoi.*	30.00	100.	300.
S3567 10 Yüan			
1944. Yellow. Rural mountain scene at center. Back: Green. *Shantung. (S/M #P21-24).*	30.00	100.	300.
S3567A 10 Yüan			
1944. Red. Rural mountain scene at center. Back: Red. *Shantung. (S/M #P21-).*	15.00	45.00	125.
S3568 10 Yüan			
1944. Blue and green. Irrigation system. Back: Brown. *Giao Dung. (S/M #P21-24.5).*	15.00	45.00	125.
S3568A 10 Yüan			
1944. Red and yellow. Irrigation system. Back: Brown. *Giao Dung. (S/M #P21-24.6).*			
a. Block letter and serial #.	15.00	45.00	125.
b. Serial # with prefix letter. *Shantung.*	15.00	45.00	125.
S3569 50 Yüan			
1944. Violet. Peasant winnowing rice at right. *Shantung. (S/M #P21-25).*			
a. Back green.	25.00	75.00	225.
b. Back blue.	25.00	75.00	225.
S3569A 50 Yüan			
1944. Rural industries at center *Pohai. (S/M #P21-26).*	25.00	75.00	225.
S3569B 50 Yüan			
1944. Purple and green. Streamlined passenger train at center. Back: Temple of Heaven at center. *Chiaotung. (S/M #P21-28).*			
a. Issued note.	50.00	150.	450.
s. Specimen.	—	Unc	550.
S3569C 50 Yüan			
1944. Red and green. Peasant drawing water at left. Back: Brown. *(S/M #P21-29).*			
a. Dark blue overprint: *Chiaotung.*	30.00	100.	300.
b. Red overprint: *Shantung.*	15.00	45.00	100.
S3570 50 Yüan			
1944. Red and green. Drawing water at left. Back: Brown. *Shantung. (S/M #P21-30a).*			
a. Orange and light green. Back olive.	25.00	75.00	225.
b. Red on light green. Back brown.	25.00	75.00	225.

	Good	Fine	XF
S3570A 50 Yüan			
1944. Orange on pale green. Drawing water at left. Back: Brown. *(S/M #P21-30b).*	25.00	75.00	225.
S3571 50 Yüan			
1944. Blue. Pagodas, hillside village at right. Back: Green. Peasants hauling goods along rural trail at center. *Shantung. (S/M #P21-31).*			
a. Serial #s only on back.	45.00	125.	375.
b. *"New Democracy"* and *"Free China"* on back.	25.00	75.00	225.
S3572 100 Yüan			
1944. Red. Truck at lower center. Back: Red. *Shantung. (S/M #P21-32).*	15.00	45.00	125.
S3572A 100 Yüan			
1944. Rice fields at center. Back: Trees. *Chiaotung. (S/M #P21-).*	15.00	45.00	125.
S3572B 100 Yüan			
1944. Plowing with water buffalo at right. *Pohai. (S/M #P21-).*	15.00	45.00	125.
S3573 200 Yüan			
1944. Red-orange. Peasant hoeing at center. 3 serial # varieties.			
a. Issued note. *(S/M #P21-33a).*	15.00	45.00	125.
b. Black or red overprint: *Shantung. (S/M #P21-33b).*	15.00	45.00	125.
c. Red overprint: *Shantung (S/M #P21-33c).*	15.00	45.00	125.
d. *Pohai. (S/M #P21-33d).*	15.00	45.00	125.
S3574 200 Yüan			
1944. Black. Back: Blue. *Shantung. (S/M #P21-34).*	15.00	45.00	125.

#S3575 *Deleted.* See #S3573C.

	Good	Fine	XF
S3576 200 Yüan			
1944. Blue. Peasant hoeing at center. Back: Green. Overprint: *Shantung. Pohai. (S/M #P21-36).*	15.00	45.00	125.

1945 Issue

	Good	Fine	XF
S3577 5 Chiao = 50 Cents			
1945. Red. Peasants cultivating, mountains in background. Back: Blue. *Giaodung. (S/M #P21-37).*	15.00	45.00	125.
S3577A 1 Yüan			
1945. Red-orange. Truck on rural highway at center. Back: Brown. *Shantung.*			
a. Blue serial #. *(S/M #P21-38a).*	15.00	45.00	125.
b. Block letters. *(S/M #P21-38b).*	7.50	20.00	60.00
S3578 1 Yüan			
1945. Horsedrawn farm equipment at center. *Min* at left and right. *Chiaotung. (S/M #P21-39).*	15.00	45.00	125.
S3578A 2 Yüan			
1945. Red. Shrine at left. Back: Red. *Shantung. (S/M #P21-39.5).*	15.00	45.00	125.
S3579 5 Yüan			
1945. Green. Truck on rural road at center. Back: Green. *Shantung. (S/M #P21-40).*	15.00	45.00	125.
S3579A 5 Yüan			
1945. Blue. Shrine at center. Back: Brown. *Shantung. (S/M #P21-40.5).*	15.00	45.00	125.
S3579B 5 Yüan			
1945. Blue-gray. Drawing water at right. Back: Blue. *Shantung. (S/M #P21-).*	7.50	20.00	60.00
S3580 10 Yüan			
1945. Red-orange. Peasant spearing in paddy at left. Back: Red. *Shantung.*			
a. 2 serial #. 12 different Chinese characters as overprints are known. (S/M #P21-41a).	10.00	30.00	100.
b. Double block letters at left, small serial # at right. *(S/M #P21-41b).*	7.50	20.00	60.00
S3580A 10 Yüan			
1945. Red. Farmer seated with basket of corn cobs at left. Back: Green. *Chiaotung. (S/M #P21-41.3).*	15.00	45.00	125.
S3580B 10 Yüan			
1945. Red. Trees, farm animals, mountain at horizon. Back: Red. *Pohai (S/M #P21-).*	15.00	45.00	125.
S3581 10 Yüan			
1945. Blue and brown. Rural scene. Back: Olive. Sampans at center. *Chiaotung//GIAO DUNG. (S/M #P21-41.6).*	25.00	75.00	225.
S3582 10 Yüan			
1945. Blue. Cars traveling along highway. *Shantung. (S/M #P21-42).*			
a. Back blue. Reported not confirmed.	—	—	—
b. Back green.	10.00	30.00	100.
S3582A 10 Yüan			
1945. Green. Cars traveling along highway. Back: Blue. *Shantung. (S/M #P21-).*	10.00	30.00	100.
S3582B 10 Yüan			
1945. Brown. Cars traveling along highway. Back: Green. *SHANTUNG. (S/M #P21-).*	10.00	30.00	100.
S3582C 10 Yüan			
1945. Red. Winnowing rice at center. *Chiaotung. (S/M #P21).*	25.00	75.00	225.
S3582D 10 Yüan			
1945. Red. Trees by stream at center. *Pohai. (S/M #P21-).*	25.00	75.00	225.
S3583 25 Yüan			
1945. Red. Planting rice at left, blue seals, serial # and block letter. Back: Blue. *Chiaotung//GIAO DUNG. (S/M #P21-42.3).*	25.00	75.00	225.
S3583A 25 Yüan			
1945. Blue on gray underprint. Planting rice at left. Red seals and serial #. Back: Green. *Chiaotung//GIAO DUNG. (S/M #P21-42.6).*	30.00	100.	300.

	Good	Fine	XF
S3584 50 Yüan			
1945. Olive. Plowing with water buffalo. Back: Red. *Shantung. (S/M #P21-43).*	25.00	75.00	225.
S3584A 50 Yüan			
1945. Brown. Plowing with water buffalo. Back: Red. *Shantung. (S/M #P21-).*	25.00	75.00	225.

	Good	Fine	XF
S3585 50 Yüan			
1945. Violet. Terraced hillside at center. *Shantung. (S/M #P21-44).*	15.00	45.00	125.
S3585A 50 Yüan			
1945. Dark blue. Terraced hillside at center. *Shantung. (S/M #P21-).*	15.00	45.00	125.
S3586 50 Yüan			
1945. Blue on tan underprint. Terraced hillside at center. Back: Green. *Shantung//SHAN DUNG. (S/M #P21-50).*	25.00	75.00	225.
S3586A 50 Yüan			
1945. Red. Terraced hillside at center. Back: Brown. *Shantung. (S/M #P21-).*	25.00	75.00	225.
S3586B 50 Yüan			
1945. Green on tan underprint. Terraced hillside at center. Back: Blue with red bar across bank name Shantung//*SHAN DUNG.* (S/M #P21-).	25.00	75.00	225.
S3587 50 Yüan			
1945. *Shantung. (S/M #P21-46).*			
a. Orange. Back red.	15.00	45.00	125.
b. Blue. Back grey-blue.	30.00	100.	300.
c. Grey-blue. Back blue.	30.00	100.	300.
S3587A 50 Yüan			
1945. Violet. Hillside village at left, *YWENTY FIFTY YUAN* (error) below. Back: Violet. Rural houses. *Shantung. (S/M #P21-).*	30.00	100.	300.
S3587B 50 Yüan			
1945. Purple. Hillside village at left, value *YWENTY FIFTY YUAN* below. Back: Violet. Rural houses. *(S/M #P21-).*			
a. Dark blue, 3mm serial #.	30.00	100.	300.
b. light blue, 2mm serial #.	30.00	100.	300.
S3588 50 Yüan			
1945. Violet. Winnowing rice. Back: Blue.			
a. Without place name. *(S/M #P21-51a).*	15.00	45.00	125.
b. *Shantung. (S/M #P21-51b).*	15.00	45.00	125.
S3588A 50 Yüan			
1945. Blue. Winnowing rice at center. Back: Purple. *Chiaotung//GIAO DUNG. (S/M #P21-).*	15.00	45.00	125.
S3588B 50 Yüan			
1945. Red on pale yellow-orange underprint. Winnowing rice at center. Back: Red-brown. *New democracy* and *Free Ching* as signature. *Chiaotung//GIAO DUNG. (S/M #P21-).*	15.00	45.00	125.
S3588C 50 Yüan			
1945. Red. Winnowing rice at center. Back: Brown.	15.00	45.00	125.
S3589 50 Yüan			
1945. Blue. Army bugler and two people at left, farming scene at right. Back: Red. *Shantung. (S/M #P21-52).*			
a. Issued note.	30.00	100.	300.
s. Specimen.	—	Unc	450.
S3589A 50 Yüan			
1945. Red-orange. Army buglar and two people at left, farming scene at right. Back: Brown. *Shantung. (S/M #P52.5).*	25.00	75.00	225.
S3590 50 Yüan			
1945. Red. Farmer and worker. Back: Brown. *Giaodung. (S/M #P21-53).*	25.00	75.00	225.
S3591 100 Yüan			
1945. Violet. Ship, steam passenger train at dockside. Back: Orange. With *New democracy* and *Free Ching. Shantung. (S/M #P21-54).*	30.00	100.	300.
S3591A 100 Yüan			
1945. Blue-black on pink underprint. Trees along mountainous slopes at right. Back: Brown. *Shantung. (S/M #P21-).*	15.00	45.00	125.

S3591B 100 Yüan	Good	Fine	XF
1945. Black. Hillside village at left. Back: Deep olive-green. Rural buildings at center with red *New democracy* and *Free Ching* as signature. *Shantung. (S/M #P21-).*			
a. Issued note.	25.00	75.00	225.
s. Specimen.	—	Unc	450.

S3592 100 Yüan	Good	Fine	XF
1945. Blue. Hillside. Back: Green. *Shantung. (S/M #P21-55).*	25.00	75.00	225.

S3593 100 Yüan	Good	Fine	XF
1945. Red. Ornamental design. Back: Brown. *Shantung. (S/M #P21-60).*	25.00	75.00	225.

S3594 100 Yüan	Good	Fine	XF
1945. Red. Peasant farmer with hoe at right. Back: Red. *Chiaotung//GIAO DUNG. (S/M #P21-61).*	25.00	75.00	225.
S3594A 100 Yüan			
1945. Brown on multicolor underprint. Water buffalo. Back: Brown. *Chiaotung. (S/M #P21-).*	25.00	75.00	225.
S3594B 100 Yüan			
1945. Black and multicolor. Water buffalo. Back: Red-brown. *Chiaotung. (S/M #P21-).*	25.00	75.00	225.
S3594C 100 Yüan			
1945. Purple and multicolor. Cutting trees at left. Back: Red. *Pohai. (S/M #P21-).*	25.00	75.00	225.
S3594D 100 Yüan			
1945. Red. Peasant hoeing at right. *Chiaotung.*	25.00	75.00	225.
S3595 200 Yüan			
1945. Blue. Ornamental design. Back: Brown. *Shantung//SHAN DUNG. (S/M #P21-62).*	25.00	75.00	225.
S3596 200 Yüan			
1945. Brown-violet on pink underprint. Ornamental design. Back: Blue-gray. *Shantung. (S/M #P21-63).*	15.00	45.00	125.
S3596A 200 Yüan			
1945. Purple on pink underprint. Ornamental design. Back: Purple. *Shantung. (S/M #P21-).*	15.00	45.00	125.
S3597 200 Yüan			
1945. Yellow. Mountain scene. Back: Blue. *(S/M #P21-64).*	25.00	75.00	225.

1946 Issues

	Good	Fine	XF
S3599 1 Yüan			
1946. Red. Irrigation system. Back: Green. *(S/M #P21-71).*	10.00	30.00	100.
S3599A 1 Yüan			
1946. Red. Steam passenger train crossing bridge over river at right. Back: Red. *Shantung. (S/M #P21-).*	10.00	30.00	100.
S3599B 1 Yüan			
1946. Red. Mountains at right. Back: Red. *Shantung. (S/M #P21-).*	10.00	30.00	100.
S3602 25 Yüan			
1946. Red. Sheep. Back: Brown. *Shantung. (S/M #P21-71.5).*	10.00	30.00	100.
S3603 100 Yüan			
1946. Brown. Monument at center. Back: Brown. *Shantung. (S/M #P21-72).*	10.00	30.00	100.
S3604 100 Yüan			
1946. Brown. Monument at center. Back: Blue. *Shantung. (S/M #P21-73).*	10.00	30.00	100.
S3605 100 Yüan			
1946. Blue on green underprint. Monument at center. Back: Green. *Shantung. (S/M #P21-74).*	10.00	30.00	100.
S3606 100 Yüan			
1946. Blue. Monument at center. Back: Blue. *Shantung. (S/M #P21-74.5).*	10.00	30.00	100.
S3607 100 Yüan			
1946. Black. Monument at center. Back: Brown. *Shantung. (S/M #P21-75).*	15.00	45.00	125.
S3608 100 Yüan			
1946. Blue on pink underprint. Monument at center. Back: Green. *Shantung. (S/M #P21-80).*	15.00	45.00	125.
S3609 100 Yüan			
1946. Red. Monument at center. Back: Brown. *Shantung. (S/M #P21-81).*	10.00	30.00	100.
S3610 100 Yüan			
1946. Green. Monument at center. Back: Blue. *Shantung. (S/M #P21-82).*	10.00	30.00	100.
S3610A 100 Yüan			
1946. Brown. Monument at center. *Shantung. (S/M #P21-).*	10.00	30.00	100.
S3611 100 Yüan			
1946. Green. Plowing with ox at right. Back: Yellow. *Shantung. (S/M #P21-83).*	15.00	45.00	125.
S3611A 100 Yüan			
1946. Dark blue. Back: Plowing with water buffalo at right; with signature *New democracy* and *Free Ching. Shantung. (S/M #P21-83.5).*			
a. Back brown.	10.00	30.00	100.
b. Back purple.	10.00	30.00	100.
S3612 200 Yüan			
1946. Red. Mountain farm. Back: Red. *TWENTY HUNDRED YUAN* (error). *(S/M #P21-84).*	25.00	75.00	225.
S3613 200 Yüan			
1946. Reddish brown. Threshing at right. Back: Green. *Shantung. (S/M #P21-85).*	25.00	75.00	225.

1947 Issues

	Good	Fine	XF
S3614 1 Yüan			
Red. Steam train in center. Back: Orange. Factory gate.	75.00	225.	675.
S3615 50 Yüan			
1947. Red. Shanghai waterfront. Back: Violet. *Shantung. (S/M #P21-90).*	15.00	45.00	125.
S3618 200 Yüan			
1947. Brown. Threshing. *Shantung.* 2 serial # varieties. Back: Brown. *(S/M #P21-91).*	15.00	45.00	125.
S3620 500 Yüan			
1947. Blue. Truck on highway at center. Back: Brown. *Shantung.*			
a. Serial # at left. Block letters at right. *(S/M #P21-92a).*	15.00	45.00	125.
b. Serial # at left, without block letters at right. *(S/M #P21-92b).*	15.00	45.00	125.
S3620A 500 Yüan			
1947. Blue. Radio station at right. Back: Brown. *Shantung. (S/M #P21-93).*	15.00	45.00	125.

ILLUSTRATIONS

Illustrations of bank notes used throughout this catalog are 42% of the actual size.

	Good	Fine	XF
S3620B 500 Yüan			
1947. Brown and yellow. Gathering straw. Back: Blue. *Shantung. (S/M #P21-94).*	30.00	100.	300.
S3620C 500 Yüan			
1947. Brown. Gathering straw at center. Back: Violet. *(S/M #P21-95).*			
a. *Pohai.*	25.00	75.00	225.
b. *Shantung.*	15.00	45.00	125.
S3620D 500 Yüan			
1947. Brown on yellow underprint. Planting rice at right. Back: Blue. *Shantung. (S/M #P21-100).*	15.00	45.00	125.
S3620E 500 Yüan			
1947. Blue. Lakeside dock at center. Back: Brown. *Shantung. (S/M #P21-101).*	15.00	45.00	125.

#S3620F *Deleted.* See #S3620.

1948 Issues

	Good	Fine	XF
S3621 200 Yüan			
1948. Red-orange. Farm tractor hauling wagons at right. Back: Blue. *Shantung. (S/M #P21-110).*	15.00	45.00	125.
S3622 500 Yüan			
1948. Brown. Cattle grazing at center. Back: Red-brown. *Shantung. (S/M #P21-111).*	5.00	15.00	45.00
S3622A 500 Yüan			
1948. Brown and yellow. Mountain temple at center. Back: Green. *Shantung. (S/M #P21-112).*	7.50	20.00	60.00
S3622B 500 Yüan			
1948. Mountain temple at left. *Shantung. (S/M #P21-113).*			
a. Brown, back violet. One black letter and serial # only at left.	15.00	45.00	125.
b. Olive, back brown. Serial # at left, two block letters at right.	15.00	45.00	125.
S3622D 500 Yüan			
1948. Blue. Mountain temple at left. Back: Reddish-brown. *(S/M #P21-113.6).*	15.00	45.00	125.
S3622E 500 Yüan			
1948. Brown. Factory. Back: Brown. *(S/M #P21-114).*	15.00	45.00	125.
S3623 500 Yüan			
1948. Bugler along Great Wall at right. *Shantung. (S/M #P21-).*	15.00	45.00	125.
S3623A 1000 Yüan			
1948. Blue and green. Monument by modern city buildings at right. Back: Olive-green. Steam passenger train at center. *Shantung. (S/M #P21-120).*	25.00	75.00	225.
S3623B 1000 Yüan			
1948. Violet on multicolor underprint. Portrait Mao Tse-tung. *(S/M #P21-).*	40.00	125.	375.
S3623C 1000 Yüan			
1948. Green and multicolor. Farmer and worker. *(S/M #P21-).*	25.00	75.00	225.
S3623D 1000 Yüan			
1948. Red and black. Pagoda at right. *Shantung. (S/M #P21-).*	25.00	75.00	225.
S3623E 1000 Yüan			
1948. Black and green. Steam train at mine at left. *Shantung. (S/M #P21-).*	25.00	75.00	225.
S3623G 1000 Yüan			
1948. Brown and yellow. Steam train at mine at left. Back: Brown. *(S/M #P21-115).*	25.00	75.00	225.
S3623H 1000 Yüan			
1948. Green on multicolor underprint. Steam train at mine at left. *(S/M #P21-).*	25.00	75.00	225.
S3623I 1000 Yüan			
1948. Black on multicolor underprint. Steam train at mine at left. *(S/M #P21-).*	25.00	75.00	225.
S3623J 1000 Yüan			
1948. Red on multicolor underprint. Steam train at mine at left. *(S/M #P21-).*	25.00	75.00	225.
S3623K 2000 Yüan			
1948. Brown. Summer palace at right. Back: Red. *Shantung. (S/M #P21-121).*	25.00	75.00	225.
S3623L 2000 Yüan			
1948. Blue-black on yellow underprint. Army bugler along Great Wall at left. Back: Gray. *(S/M #P21-122).*	7.50	20.00	60.00
S3623M 2000 Yüan			
1948. Green. Factory. Back: Brown. *(S/M #P21-123).*	15.00	45.00	125.
S3623N 2000 Yüan			
1948. Blue. Ship at dockside at left. Back: Violet. Junks at center. *(S/M #P21-124).*	25.00	75.00	225.
S3623P 100,000 Yüan			
1948.	25.00	75.00	225.

P'ing Chiang Workers and Farmers Bank

行銀農工縣江平

P'ing Chiang Hsien Kung Nung Yin Hang

1931 Issue

	Good	Fine	XF
S3624 1 Chiao			
1931. Blue. *(S/M #P47-1).*	25.00	75.00	225.
S3625 2 Chiao			
1931. Green. *(S/M #P47-2).*	30.00	100.	300.

Maojgungs Liutungkyan

司公易貿/區邊寧甘陝

Shan Kan Ning Pien Ch'ü / Mao I Kung Szu

1944 Issue

	Good	Fine	XF
S3630 50 Yüan			
1944. Blue and green. Vertical format. Back: Black. *(S/M #S31-1).*	25.00	75.00	225.
S3631 100 Yüan			
1944. Violet and green. Back: Blue. *(S/M #S31-2).*	25.00	75.00	225.
S3632 200 Yüan			
1944. Blue. Back: Blue. *(S/M #S31-3).*	25.00	75.00	225.

1945 Issue

	Good	Fine	XF
S3635 5 Yüan			
1945. Green. Vertical format. Back: Black. *(S/M #S31-10).*	15.00	45.00	125.
S3636 10 Yüan			
1945. Red. Vertical format. Back: Black. *(S/M #S31-11).*	15.00	45.00	125.
S3637 20 Yüan			
1945. Black. Vertical format. Back: Black. *(S/M #S31-12).*	15.00	45.00	125.
S3638 50 Yüan			
1945. Brown. Vertical format. Back: Brown. *(S/M #S31-13).*	25.00	75.00	225.
S3639 100 Yüan			
1945. Vertical format. *(S/M #S31-14).* Reported not confirmed.	—	—	—
S3640 250 Yüan			
1945. Brown on light green underprint. Vertical format. Back: Brown. *(S/M #S31-15).*	25.00	75.00	225.
S3640A 500 Yüan			
1945. Orange. Great Wall at upper center. *(S/M #S31-17).*	25.00	75.00	225.

1946 Issues

	Good	Fine	XF
S3641 500 Yüan			
1946. Red. Vertical format. Back: Blue. *(S/M #S31-20).*	20.00	60.00	175.
S3642 1000 Yüan			
1946. Blue. Vertical format. Back: Blue. *(S/M #S31-21).*	20.00	60.00	175.
S3643 1000 Yüan			
1946. Light green. Factory at upper center. Vertical format.			
a. Back grayish tan. *(S/M #S31-21.5a).*	20.00	60.00	175.
b. Back pale violet. *(S/M #S31-21.5b).*	20.00	60.00	175.
S3644 5000 Yüan			
1946. Orange. Vertical format. Back: Blue. *(S/M #S31-22).*	20.00	60.00	175.

1947 Issues

	Good	Fine	XF
S3645 2000 Yüan			
1947. Black. Vertical format. Back. Blue. *(S/M #S31-30).*	20.00	60.00	175.
S3646 5000 Yüan			
1947. Violet. Gateway. Vertical format. Back: Blue. *(S/M #S31-31).*	20.00	60.00	175.
S3647 5000 Yüan			
1947. Red. Gateway. Vertical format. Back: Blue. *(S/M #S31-32).*	20.00	60.00	175.
S3648 5000 Yüan			
1947. Brown. Gateway. Vertical format. Back: Blue. *(S/M #S31-33).*	20.00	60.00	175.

Shaan Gan Ning Bianky Inxan(g) Shensi-Kansu-Ninghsia Border Area Bank

Shan Kan Ning Pien Ch'ü Yin Hang

1941 Issue

	Good	Fine	XF
S3651 1 Chiao = 10 Cents			
1941. Brown. Rural scene with pagoda on hill in distance. Back: Blue. Paper: Pink or buff. *(S/M #S32-1).*	15.00	45.00	125.
S3652 2 Chiao = 20 Cents			
1941. Dark blue. Sheep at center. Back: Brown. Paper: Pink or buff. *(S/M #S32-2).*	15.00	45.00	125.
S3655 5 Yüan			
1941. Blue and yellow. City gate at center right. Back: Violet. *(S/M #S32-11).*	15.00	45.00	125.
S3656 5 Yüan			
1941. Blue and violet. Rural scene. Back: Blue. *(S/M #S32-11.5).*	30.00	100.	300.
S3656A 10 Yüan			
1941. Blue-gray. Rural scene at center. *(S/M #S32-12).*	15.00	45.00	125.
S3657 10 Yüan			
1941. Violet. Government building at center. Back: Black and blue. *(S/M #S32-13).*	30.00	100.	300.

1942 Issue

	Good	Fine	XF
S3658 50 Yüan			
1942. Black. Government building at center. Back: Violet. *(S/M #S32-20).*	30.00	100.	300.
S3659 100 Yüan			
1942. Brown. Assembly hall. Back: Brown-violet. Pagoda on hillside at center. *(S/M #S32-21).*			
a. Issued note.	25.00	75.00	225.
b. Punched hole cancelled.	—	Unc	200.
S3660 100 Yüan			
1942. Violet. Government building at center. Back: Black and blue. *(S/M #S32-).*	25.00	75.00	225.

1943 Issue

	Good	Fine	XF
S3662 50 Yüan			
1943. Blue-gray. Building at center. Back: Brown-violet. Building at center. *(S/M #S32-).*	25.00	75.00	225.
S3663 100 Yüan			
1943. Purple. Camels at center. Back: Building at center. *(S/M #S32-30).*			
a. Back blue. *(S/M #S32-30a).*	25.00	75.00	225.
b. Back brown-violet. *(S/M #S32-30b).*	25.00	75.00	225.

No.	Description	Good	Fine	XF
S3664 200 Yüan	1943. Dark or light blue. Sheep at center. Back: Red-brown. Building at center. *(S/M #S32-31b).*			
	a. Issued note.	25.00	75.00	225.
	b. With additional overprint: *A-D; G*, etc. *(S/M #S32-31a).*	45.00	125.	375.
S3665 500 Yüan	1943. Red. Yenan Headquarters at center. *(S/M #S32-32b).*			
	a. Without letter to left and right of building.	30.00	100.	300.
	b. Additional letter overprint: *A; B; C* etc. *(S/M #S32-32a.)*	30.00	100.	300.
S3666 1000 Yüan	1943. Blue. Yenan Headquarters at center. Back: Hillside pagoda at right. *(S/M #S32-33).*			
	a. Large serial #.	60.00	175.	525.
	b. Small serial # with prefix letters.	60.00	175.	525.
S3667 5000 Yüan	Yenan Headquarters at center. 1943. *(S/M #S32-34).*	75.00	225.	675.

1945 Issue

No.	Description	Good	Fine	XF
S3668 10 Yüan	1945. Great Wall at center. Remainder. *(S/M #S32-41).*	—	100.	300.

1946 Issue

		VG	VF	UNC
S3669 10,000 Yüan	1946. Back: Camels at center. Specimen. *(S/M #S32-51).*	—	—	650.
S3670 50,000 Yüan	1946. Specimen. *(S/M #S32-55).*	—	—	850.

Bank of Shangtong

Shang Tang Yin Hao

1938 Issue

No.	Description	Good	Fine	XF
S3670A 5 Fen	1938. Olive.	30.00	100.	300.
S3671 1 Chiao = 10 Cents	1938. Blue on light green underprint. Rural railway station at left. Back: Purple. Rural building by bridge at center. *(S/M #S56.5-1).*	30.00	100.	300.
S3672 2 Chiao = 20 Cents	1938. Rural scene at left. Back: Bridge at center. *(S/M #S56.5-2).*	30.00	100.	300.

No.	Description	Good	Fine	XF
S3672A 2 Chiao = 20 Cents	1938. Purple. Tall temple on hillside at left. Back: Blue-green. Large value at center.	30.00	100.	300.
S3672B 2 Chiao = 20 Cents	1938. Blue. Hillside pagoda at left. Back: Green.	30.00	100.	300.
S3673 5 Chiao = 50 Cents	1938. Blue-gray. Building at left. Back: Purple. Ship at center. *(S/M #S56.5-3).*	30.00	100.	300.
S3674 1 Dollar	1938. Green. Temple of Heaven at center. Back: Dark green. Bridge at center. *(S/M #S56.5-4).*	45.00	125.	375.
S3675 5 Dollars	1938. Red on pink underprint. Rural scene at center. Back: Red. Rural building by bridge at center. *(S/M #S56-5).*			
	a. Issued note.	75.00	225.	675.
	r. Remainder. without serial #.	—	Unc	250.
S3675A 5 Dollars	1938. Brown and blue. Portrait SYS at right. Back: Blue. Boat at center.	75.00	225.	675.

Soviet Bank (Hopei-Honan-Anhwei Soviet Economic Commune)

行銀埃維蘇

Su Wei Ai Yin Hang

1932 Issue

No.	Description	Good	Fine	XF
S3676 2 Tiao	1932. Brown-violet on blue-green underprint. Buildings at left and right. Back: Blue-green. Horseman with flag at center. *(S/M #S84.5-12).*	75.00	225.	675.
S3677 2 Tiao	1932. Brown-violet on blue-green underprint. Outline of Vladimir I. Lenin at left, municipal building at right. Back: Blue-green. Horseman with flag at center. *(S/M #S84.5-14).*	75.00	225.	675.

Ta Chiang Bank / Dagiang Inxan(g)

行銀江大

Ta Chiang Yin Hang

1942 Issue

No.	Description	Good	Fine	XF
S3680 5 Chiao	1942. Scenes at left and right. *(S/M #T2-5).*	25.00	75.00	225.

1944 Issues

No.	Description	Good	Fine	XF
S3685 1 Chiao	1944. Single arch stone bridge at center. Back: People's Army in march. *(S/M #T2-11).*	25.00	75.00	225.
S3686 1 Chiao	1944. Junks at left, lighthouse at right. Back: People's supply column. *(S/M #T2-12).*	25.00	75.00	225.
S3687 5 Chiao	1944. Teacher, doctor, soldier, peasant, and factory worker at center. Back: Hoe, hammer, rifle, etc. *(S/M #T2-14).*	25.00	75.00	225.
S3689 2 Yüan	1944. Teacher, doctor, soldier, peasant and factory worker at left center. Back: Hammer, rifle, cycle, etc.			
	a. Square signature seals on face. *(S/M #T2-16a).*	25.00	75.00	225.
	b. Square signature seals on back. *(S/M #T2-16b).*	25.00	75.00	225.
S3690 5 Yüan	1944. Single arch stone bridge at right. Back: Peasant woman harvesting grain with sickle at right. *(S/M #T2-18).*	25.00	75.00	225.
S3691 10 Yüan	1944. Teacher, doctor, etc. at left center. *(S/M #T2-19).*	25.00	75.00	225.

1945 Issues

No.	Description	Good	Fine	XF
S3693 5 Chiao	1945. Mountain scene at center. *S/M #T2-20).*	20.00	60.00	175.
S3694 1 Yüan	1945. Single arch stone bridge at center right. *(S/M #T2-21).*	20.00	60.00	175.
S3695 1 Yüan	1945. People's Army in march at center. Vertical format. *(S/M #T2-22).*	20.00	60.00	175.
S3696 1 Yüan	1945. Rural army sentry under tree, mountains in distance at left. *(S/M #T2-23).*	20.00	60.00	175.
S3697 1 Yüan	1945. Rural buildings, mountains in distance at left. *(S/M #T2-24).*	20.00	60.00	175.
S3698 1 Yüan	1945. Teacher, doctor, etc. at left center. Back: Hammer, rifle, sickle, etc. *(S/M #T2-25).*	20.00	60.00	175.
S3699 2 Yüan	1945. Two peasants at center. *(S/M #T2-26).*	20.00	60.00	175.
S3700 2 Yüan	1945. Soldiers raising flag in triumph at center. Vertical format. *(S/M #T2-27).*	20.00	60.00	175.
S3701 2 Yüan	1945. Building, single arch bridge over river at left. *(S/M #T228).*	20.00	60.00	175.
S3702 2 Yüan	1945. Peasants harvesting grain at center. Vertical format. *(S/M #T2-29).*	20.00	60.00	175.
S3703 2 Yüan	1945. People's Army marching from Great Wall at center. Vertical format. *(S/M #T2-30).*	20.00	60.00	175.
S3704 2 Yüan	1945. Rural building, mountains in background at center. Vertical format. *(S/M #T2-31).*	20.00	60.00	175.
S3705 5 Yüan	1945. Lighthouse, junks at left center. *(S/M #T2-41).*	25.00	75.00	225.
S3706 5 Yüan	1945. Rural scene, trees, mountains in background at center right. *(S/M #T2-42).*	25.00	75.00	225.
S3707 5 Yüan	1945. Rural buildings, peasant at center right. *(S/M #T2-43).*	25.00	75.00	225.
S3708 10 Yüan	1945. Single arch stone bridge at center right. *(S/M #T2-46).*	25.00	75.00	225.
S3709 10 Yüan	1945. Peasants plowing with oxen at center. *(S/M #T2-47).*	25.00	75.00	225.
S3710 20 Yüan	1945. Pagoda at center. Vertical format. Back: Planting rice at center. *(S/M #T2-450).*	25.00	75.00	225.

Eastern Mongolian Bank

行銀蒙東

Tung Mung Yin Hang

1946 Issue

No.	Description	Good	Fine	XF
S3715 50 Yüan	1946. Red on green underprint. Lakeside village at left. Back: Green. Ship at center. *(S/M #T212.5-9).*	75.00	225.	675.
S3716 100 Yüan	1946. Blue and yellow. Steam passenger train at center. Back: Red. Modern municipal at center. *(S/M #T212.5-11).*	75.00	225.	675.
S3717 100 Yüan	1946. Brown-violet. Gateway at center. Back: Green. Monument at center. *(S/M #T212.5-14).*	75.00	225.	675.

Kwangsi-Kweichow-Yunnan Border District Dian-Kian-Gui Bianky

局易貿區邊桂黔滇

T'ien Ch'ien Kuei Pien Ch'ü Mao I Chü

1949 Circulating Notes (*Liu T'ung Ch'üan*) Issue

	Good	Fine	XF
S3719 1 Yüan 1949. Orange-brown. Mao Tse-tung at left, row of men at right. Back: Black. Peasants and oxen at left center. *(S/M #T125.5-11).*	45.00	125.	375.
S3720 5 Yüan ND (1949). Mao Tse-tung at right. Back: Harvesting grain at center right. *(S/M #T125.5-12).*	45.00	125.	375.

NOTE: Similar watermarked paper was used for some North Vietnamese issues.

Bank of Dung Bai Bank of Dung Pai Tung Pei Bank of China

Tung Pei Yin Hang

1945 Issues

	Good	Fine	XF
S3725 1 Yüan 1945. Red. Summer palace at left, Temple of Heaven at right. Back: Green. *(S/M #T213-1).*	7.50	20.00	60.00

Many counterfeits have been found in the market.

	Good	Fine	XF
S3726 5 Yüan 1945. Red. Farmer. Back: Green. Village. *(S/M #T213-2).*	7.50	20.00	60.00
S3727 5 Yüan 1945. Red. Sawing logs at left. Back: Small seascape at center. *Liaotung. (S/M #T213-3).*			
a. *Liaotung* at upper center, control letter and # at left and right, serial # at upper left and right. Back black.	10.00	30.00	100.
b. *Liaotung* at left and right, control letter and # at upper left and right. Back green.	7.50	20.00	60.00
S3728 5 Yüan 1945. Red on light blue-green underprint. Horse and irrigation system. Back: Dark olive-green. Buildings at center. *(S/M #T213-).*			
a. With black serial # at upper right.	10.00	30.00	100.
b. With red block # at upper right.	7.50	20.00	60.00
S3729 10 Yüan 1945. Brown on pink underprint. Back: Red. *Liaotung. (S/M #T213-4).*			
a. Black. *Liaotung* . Block letters on sides, 6 digit serial #.	5.00	15.00	45.00
b. Red. *Liaotung* . Block letter at left, 3 digit serial # at right.	5.00	15.00	45.00
S3729A 10 Yüan 1945. Violet. Like #S3729. *Liaotung. (S/M #T213-).*	5.00	15.00	45.00
S3730 10 Yüan 1945. Blue. Plowing. Back: Violet. House at center. *(S/M #T213-5).*	7.50	20.00	60.00
S3731 50 Yüan 1945. Red. Modern steamship at center. Blue serial # and block letters. Back: Brown. *Liaotung. (S/M #T213-10).*			
a. 4mm Serial #.	7.50	20.00	60.00
b. 3mm Serial #.	7.50	20.00	60.00
S3732 50 Yüan 1945. Red-brown. Rural railway station at left. Red block letters and serial #. Back: Red. *Liaotung. (S/M #T213-11).*	7.50	20.00	60.00
S3733 100 Yüan 1945. Yellow. Kitchen. Back: Red. Flags. *(S/M #T213-12).*	15.00	45.00	125.
S3734 100 Yüan 1945. Blue on pink underprint. Government building at left. Back: Red. *(S/M #T213-14).*			
a. Two block letters, 6 sigit serial #.	10.00	30.00	100.
b. Three fraction type block letters, 7 digit serial #.	10.00	30.00	100.

1946 Issues

	Good	Fine	XF
S3735 5 Chiao = 50 Cents 1946. Pale olive-green. Boat dockside at right. Back: Pale blue. *(S/M #T213-16).*	10.00	30.00	100.
S3736 1 Yüan 1946. Red. Farmer plowing with ox at right. Back: Orange. *Liaotung. (S/M #T213-18).*	5.00	15.00	45.00
S3736A 1 Yüan 1946. Red. Boat and tower. *Liaoxi.*	30.00	100.	300.
S3737 5 Yüan 1946. Green. Ship. Back: Green. *Liaotung. (S/M #T213-20).*	7.50	20.00	60.00
S3738 5 Yüan 1946. Red. Plowing. Back: Green. Village. *(S/M #T213-21).*	7.50	20.00	60.00
S3739 10 Yüan 1946. Brown on light green underprint. Peasant operating irrigation system at right. Back: Black. Temple of Heaven at center. *(S/M #T213-21.3).*	10.00	30.00	100.
S3739A 10 Yüan 1946. Light Brown. Peasant operating irrigation system at right. Back: Olive-brown. Large value *10* at center. *(S/M #T213-21.4).*			
a. Issued note.	30.00	100.	300.
b. Issued note with Chinese text for *EXCHANGE.*	30.00	100.	300.
S3740 10 Yüan 1946. Black on green underprint. Municipal building at right (with national flag!). Back: Red-violet. Temple of Heaven at center. *Liaohsi. (S/M #T213-21.5).*	10.00	30.00	100.

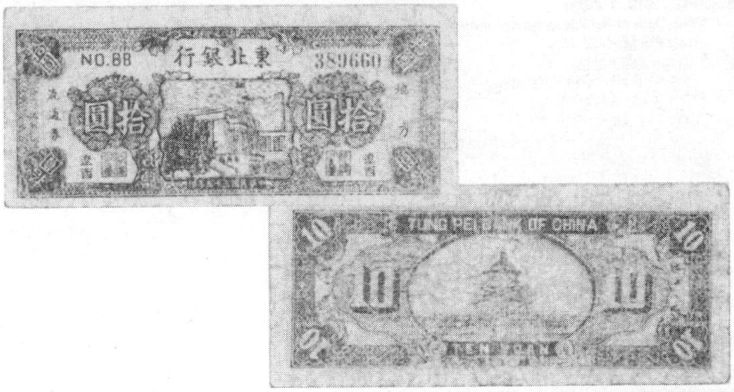

	Good	Fine	XF
S3740A 10 Yüan 1946. Blue. Building at center.	75.00	225.	675.
S3741 50 Yüan 1946. *(S/M #T213-21.7).*	10.00	30.00	100.
S3742 100 Yüan 1946. Green. Building. *Liaoshi. (S/M #T213-22).*	45.00	125.	375.
S3743 100 Yüan 1946. Blue-gray on gray underprint. Steam passenger train at right. Back: Purple. Municipal building at center. *Liaohsi. (S/M #T213-24).*	45.00	125.	375.
S3744 100 Yüan 1946. Red-violet and black. Gazebo and boat at left. Back: Red. *Liaoshi. (S/M #T213-27).*	45.00	125.	375.

1947 Issue

	Good	Fine	XF
S3745 10 Yüan 1947. Back: Violet. Planting rice at right.			
a. Green underprint. *(S/M #T213-30).*	10.00	30.00	100.
b. Gray underprint.	10.00	30.00	100.
S3746 50 Yüan 1947. Violet on light blue-green underprint. Soldier and peasant at left center. Back: Brown. *S/M #T213-31).*	10.00	30.00	100.
S3747 100 Yüan 1947. Red on yellow underprint. Blue serial #. Cultivating with horses. Back: Purple-brown. *(S/M #T213-32).*	10.00	30.00	100.
S3748 100 Yüan 1947. Red on brown-orange underprint. Black serial #. Cultivating with horses. Back: Green. *(S/M #T213-33).*	7.50	20.00	60.00

	Good	Fine	XF
S3749 100 Yüan 1947. Red. Red serial #. Cultivating with horses. Back: Red. *(S/M #T213-34).*	7.50	20.00	60.00
S3750 100 Yüan 1947. Red and yellow. Back: Brown. *(S/M #T213-40).*	7.50	20.00	60.00
S3751 200 Yüan 1947. Red and black on gray underprint. Steam passenger train at right. Back: Dark blue. Temple of Heaven at center. *Liaoshi. (S/M #T213-40.5).*	25.00	75.00	225.
S3751A 200 Yüan	60.00	175.	525.
S3752 500 Yüan 1947. Blue on red underprint. Portrait Mao Tse-tung at right. Back: Red. Building at center. *(S/M #T213-41)*	10.00	30.00	100.
S3753 500 Yüan 1947. Red. Portrait Mao Tse-tung at left. Back: Violet. *(S/M #T213-42).*	10.00	30.00	100.
S3754 500 Yüan 1947. Blue on light orange underprint. Portrait Mao Tse-tung at center. Back: Red. Building at center. *(S/M #T213-43).*	10.00	30.00	100.

1948 Issues

	Good	Fine	XF
S3755 250 Yüan 1948. Violet on red underprint. Soldier and farmer at left center. Back: Red. Bank building at center. *(S/M #T213-50).*	10.00	30.00	100.
S3756 500 Yüan 1948. Green. Farmers and workers. Back: Red. *(S/M #T213-51).*	10.00	30.00	100.
S3757 1000 Yüan 1948. Brown on yellow-green underprint. Farmer and worker at right. Back: Violet. Bank building at center. *(S/M #T213-52).*	10.00	30.00	100.
a. Plain block letters, bold serial #.	10.00	30.00	100.
b. Block letters in parentheses, plain serial #.	10.00	30.00	100.
S3758 1000 Yüan 1948. Brown on ochre underprint. Farmer and worker at right. Back: Brown-violet. Bank building at center. *(S/M #T213-52.5).*	10.00	30.00	100.

	Good	Fine	XF
S3759 5000 Yüan 1948. Black on pale blue underprint. Bank building at right. Back: Purple. *(S/M #T213-53a).*	10.00	30.00	100.
S3759A 5000 Yüan 1948. Brown on pale blue underprint, violet guilloche. Bank building at right. Back: Purple. *(S/M #T213-53b).*	15.00	45.00	125.
S3760 10,000 Yüan 1948. Black and blue. Temple courtyard. Back: Violet. Bank building at center. *(S/M #T213-54).*	15.00	45.00	125.
S3761 10,000 Yüan 1948. Blue-gray on brown-violet underprint. Temple courtyard. Back: Violet. Bank building at center. *(S/M #T213-55).*	15.00	45.00	125.
S3762 10,000 Yüan 1948. Tower. *(S/M #T213-56).*	40.00	125.	375.
S3763 50,000 Yüan 1948. Gray-green on light blue underprint. Steam passenger train at left, ship at right. Back: Brown. Bank building at center. *(S/M #T213-57).*	25.00	75.00	225.

1949 Issue

	Good	Fine	XF
S3764 10,000 Yüan 1949. *(S/M #T213-58).* Reported not confirmed.	—	—	—
S3765 100,000 Yüan 1949. Brown-violet, black and gray. Plowing with horses at left, shoveling ore at right. Back: Fortress gate at center. *(S/M #T213-59).*	50.00	150.	450.
S3765A 10,000 Yüan 1949. Brown. Vertical format. *Liao Ning.*	50.00	150.	450.

1950 Issue

	Good	Fine	XF
S3766 500 Yüan 1950. Dark blue on light blue underprint. Cultivating with tractor at right. Back: Blue-violet. Building at center. *(S/M #T213-60).*	5.00	15.00	45.00

1948 Circulating Cashier's Checks Issue

	Good	Fine	XF
S3770 Various Amounts Dec. 1948. Black text and large red seal hand stamp on ochre underprint. Overprint in blue on Central Bank of Manchukuo cashier's check. *(S/M #T213-).*			
a. 5,500,000 Dollars (18.12.1948).	25.00	75.00	225.
b. 100,000,000 Dollars (28.12.1948).	25.00	75.00	225.

Guangxua Shangdian

店商華光安延
Yen An Kuang Hua Shang Tien

店商華光
Kuang Hua Shang Tien

1938 Issue

	Good	Fine	XF
S3775 2 Fen = 2 Cents 1938. Dark blue on red-orange underprint. Back: Black. *(S/M #Y3-1).*	25.00	75.00	225.
S3776 5 Fen = 5 Cents 1938. Dark blue on red-orange underprint. Back: Black. *(S/M #Y3-2).*	30.00	100.	300.
S3777 1 Chiao = 10 Cents 1938. *(S/M #Y3-4).*	30.00	100.	300.
S3778 2 Chiao = 20 Cents 1938. Rural village with mountains in background. *(S/M #Y3-6).*	30.00	100.	300.
S3779 5 Chiao = 50 Cents 1938. Black on light blue underprint. Gazebo at lower right. *(S/M #Y3-8).*	25.00	75.00	225.

1940 Issue

	Good	Fine	XF
S3780 5 Chiao = 50 Cents 1940. Red. Woman seated at left, sheep at right. Back: Dark blue. *(S/M #Y3-10).*	25.00	75.00	225.
S3781 7 Chiao 5 Fen = 75 Cents 1940. Brown. Rural scene at left with pagoda on hill in distance. Back: Blue. *(S/M #Y3-11).*	30.00	100.	300.

Military, 1912-30

The first military issues were soon released in the first year of the developing Republic as various parts of China were finally put under the control of the new Sun Yat-sen government. It wasn't very long after Yuan-Shi-K'ai became president that his plans to become emperor of China became obvious and that divided China's forces once again.

Throughout the following years military forces under war lords severely taxed the unresting populace in the areas under their control.

These military issues were soon followed by the many communist issues which were first released in the early 1930's and ceased in 1950 when the Chinese mainland became the Peoples Republic.

Certain military issues are also to be found listed under the Provincial section and once determined as strictly military in nature they will be moved to this section.

These listings are not virtually complete as new finds of this material are occasionally encountered.

For further information refer to *A Brief Illustrated History of Chinese Military Notes and Bonds* by S. P. Ting, Taipei, Taiwan (1981).

票鈔用軍
Chün Yung Ch'ao P'iao

票手用軍
Chün Yung Shou P'iao

NOTE: These phrases appear as overprints or in clauses used in principal heading on a number of notes. In most instances they are written horizontally but in some occasions they occur in two vertically written pairs.

Chen Wei, 3rd and 4th Army Corps Treasury Notes (trans)
#S3791-S3796

券庫站兵團軍 面方 四三第 軍 威鎮
Chen Wei Chün Ti San Szu Fang Mien Chün T'uan Ping Chan K'u Ch'üan

Chihli Provincial Military
#S3803-S3807
券通流用軍省隸直
Chih Li Sheng Chün Yung Lin T'ung Ch'üan

Chihli-Shantung Military
#S3809-S3813
券用軍省魯直
Chih Lu Sheng Chün Yung Ch'üan

Republican Fukien Government Bank
#S3813A-S3813E
行銀建福華中
Chung Hua Fu Chien Yin Hang

Chinese National Pacification Army Notes
#S3814-S3816

Chung Hua Min Kuo Ching Kuo Chün Chün Yung Ch'ao Piao

Republican China Military - Shanghai
#S3818-S3820
票鈔用軍/國民華中
Chung Hua Min Kuo / Chün Yung Ch'ao P'iao

Republican China Military - Nanking
#S3822
票鈔用軍 京南/國民華中
Chung Hua Min Kuo / Nan Ching Chün Yung Ch'ao P'iao

Chinese Republic Army, Navy and Air Force Headquarters
#S3824-S3826
部令司總軍空海陸國民華中
Chung Hua Min Kuo Lu Hai K'ung Chün Tsung Szu Ling Pu

Chinese Republic Army, Namvy and Air Force Sub-headquarters
#S3828-S3834
部令司總副軍空海陸國民華中
Chung Hua Min Kuo Lu Hai K'ung Chün Fu Tsung Szu Lin Pu

Kwangtung Republican Military Government
#S3836-S3839
府政軍省粵國民華中
Chung Hua Min Kuo Yüeh Sheng Chün Cheng Fu

Chinese Republican Military Bank-Anhwei
#S3841-S3842
徽安 行 銀 華 中
Chung Hua Yin Hang An Hui

Honan Province Treasury
#S3855
券通庫金省南河
Ho Nan Sheng Chin K'u T'ung Ch'üan

Honan Province
#S3857-S3859
印省南河
Ho Nan Sheng Yin

Bank of the Northwest
#S3861-S3889
行銀北西
Hsi Pei Yin Hang

Hunan Provincial Treasury
#S3892-S3896
券庫金省南湖
Hu Nan Sheng Chin K'u Ch'üan

Kiangse Bank of the Republic
#S3897-S3900B
行銀國民省贛
Kan (Sen) Sheng Min Kuo Yin Hang

Kansu (Military)
#S3900D
號銀官肅甘
Kan Su Kuan Yin Hao

Kwangsi Military
#S3900F
票手用軍西廣
Kuang Hsi Chüan Yung Shou P'iao

Kwangsi, Military (Provisional)
#S3900J-S3900M
票用軍時臨西廣
Kuang Ksi Lin Shih Chü Yung Piao

Kwangtung Provincial Treasury
#S3901-S3903
券庫金省東廣
Kuang Tung Seng Chin K'u Ch'üan

Kweilin Regional Bank
#S3904 and S3906
行銀方地林桂
Kuei Lin Ti Fang Yin Hang

National Army (Circulatinge Notes)
#S3907-S3916
券通流融金軍民國
Kuo Min Chün Chin Jung Liu Tung Ch'üan

National Army Combined Headquarters
#S3818-S3920

國民軍聯軍總司令部軍用票
Kuo Min Chün Lien Chün Tsung Szu Ling Pu Chün Yung P'iao

National Revolutionary Army
#S3923-S3927

國民革命軍總司令部軍需券
Kuo Min Ke Ming Chün Tsung Szu LIng Pu Chün Hsü Ch'ün

Agricultural, Industrial and Commercial Trust Co., Ltd.
#S3928-S3930A

農工商信託有限公司
Nung Kung Shang Hsin Tok Yu Hsien Kung Szu

Provincial Army of Shantung
#S3931-S3941

山東省軍用票
Shan Tung Sheng Chün Yung P'iao

Local Bank of Szechuan (Szechuan Regional Bank)
#S3943-S3947

四川地方銀行
Szu Ch'üan Ti Fang Yin Hang

Ta Han Szechuan Military Government
#S3948

大漢四川軍政府軍用銀票
Ta Han Szu Ch'üan Chün Cheng Fu Chün Yung Ying P'iao

Yunnan-Kwangtung-Kwangsi United Army for Kiangsi Relief
#S3951-S3953

滇粵桂援贛聯軍軍用票
T'ien Yüeh Kuei Yüan Kan Lien Chün Chün Yung P'iao

Property Control Office Third and Fourth Route Army Headquarters
#S3955

財產管理處
Ts'ai Ch'an Kuan Li Chü

Yunnan National Pacification Army
#S3958-S3960

雲南靖國軍軍用銀行兌換券
Yün Nan Ching Kuo Chün Chün Yung Yin Hang Tui Huan Ch'üan

Chen Wei, 3rd and 4th Army Corps Treasury Notes

鎮威 軍 第三四 方面 軍團兵站庫券
Chen Wei Chün Ti San Szu Fang Mien Chün T'uan Ping Chan K'u Ch'üan

1927 Issue

#S3791-S3793 rural scene at ctr. on back. Printer: BEPP.

	Good	Fine	XF
S3791 1927. Brown on multicolor underprint. Houseboat in river at center *(S/M #C42-0.3)*.	75.00	225.	675.
S3792 1927. Olive-green on multicolor underprint. Rural house at center *(S/M #C42-0.6)*.	150.	450.	1200.
S3793 5 Chiao = 50 Cents 1927. Olive-green on multicolor underprint. Pagoda at center. Back: Rural scene at center. Printer: Bepp. *(S/M #C42-1)*.	450.	1250.	—
S3794 1 Yüan 1.5.1927. Blue on multicolor underprint. Ship, boats at center. *(S/M #C42-10)*.	300.	900.	—

	Good	Fine	XF
S3795 5 Yüan 1.5.1927. Red-brown on multicolor underprint. *(S/M #C42-11)*.			
a. Issued note.	375.	1000.	—
p. Proof.	—	Unc	750.
	VG	VF	UNC
S3796 10 Yüan 1.5.1927. Deep orange on multicolor underprint. Proof. *(S/M #C42-12)*.	—	—	750.

Chihli Provincial Military

直隸省軍用流通券
Chih Li Sheng Chün Yung Liu T'ung Ch'üan

1920's ND Provisional Issue

#S3803-S3807 with rectangular Chinese eight character overprint of new issuer's name at center on Provincial Bank of Chihli.

	Good	Fine	XF
S3803 1 Chiao = 10 Cents ND (- old date 1926). Violet on brown and gray-green underprint. Overprint: Rectangular Chinese eight character of new issuer's name at center on Provincial Bnak of Chihli on # *(S/M #C161-1)*.	45.00	125.	375.
S3804 2 Chiao = 20 Cents ND (- old date 1926). Blue-green on brown and violet underprint. Overprint: Rectangular Chinese eight character of new issuer's name at center on Provincial Bank og Chihli on # *(S/M #C161-2)*.	60.00	175.	525.
S3805 1 Yüan ND (- old date 1926). Violet on multicolor underprint. Overprint: Rectangular Chinese eight character of new issuer's name at center on Provincial Bank og Chihli on # *(S/M #C161-10)*.	60.00	175.	525.
S3806 5 Yüan ND (- old date 1926). Blue-gray on multicolor underprint. Overprint: Rectangular Chinese eight character of new issuer's name at center on Provincial Bank og Chihli on # *(S/M #C161-11)*.	75.00	225.	675.
S3807 10 Yüan ND (- old date 1926). Red on multicolor underprint. Overprint: Rectangular Chinese eight character of new issuer's name at center on Provincial Bank og Chihli on # *(S/M #C161-12)*.	100.	300.	900.

Chihli-Shantung Military

直魯省軍用券
Chih Lu Sheng Chün Yung Ch'üan

1920's ND Provisional Issue

#S3809-S3812A with vertical Chinese six character overprint of new issuer's name on Market Stabilization Currency Bureau, Vol. 2.

	Good	Fine	XF
S3809 1 Chiao = 10 Cents ND (- old date 1.6.1923). Blue. Overprint: Vertical Chinese six character of new issuer's name on Market Stabilization Currency Bureau, Vol. 2 *(S/M #C164-1)*.	60.00	175.	525.
S3810 2 Chiao = 20 Cents ND (- old date 1.6.1923). Purple. Overprint: Vertical Chinese six character of new issuer's name on Market Stabilization Currency Bureau, Vol. 2 *(S/M #C164-2)*.	75.00	225.	675.
S3811 5 Chiao = 50 Cents ND (- old date 1.6.1923). Green. Overprint: Vertical Chinese six character of new issuer's name on Market Stabilization Currency Bureau, Vol. 2 *(S/M #C164-3)*.			
a. Issued note.	75.00	225.	675.
b. Punched hole cancelled.	—	—	200.
S3812 1 Yüan ND (- old date 15.8.1925). Green on multicolor underprint. Overprint: Vertical Chinese six character of new issuer's name on Market Stabilization Currency Bureau, Vol. 2 *(S/M #C164-4)*.	100.	300.	900.
S3812A 5 Yüan ND (- old date 15.8.1925). Blue on multicolor underprint. Overprint: Vertical Chinese six character of new issuer's name on Market Stabilization Currency Bureau, Vol. 2 *(S/M #C164-5)*.	150.	450.	1200.

Republican Fukien Government Bank

中華福建銀行
Chung Hua Fu Chien Yin Hang

1912 Issue

	Good	Fine	XF
S3813A 1 Yüan 1.4.1912. Without vignette. *(S/M #C255.5-1)*.	450.	1200.	—
S3813B 2 Yüan 1.4.1912. Red orange on pale blue with black text. Without vignette. Back: Pale green. *(S/M #C255.5-2)*.	450.	1200.	—
S3813C 3 Yüan 1.4.1912. Without vignette. *(S/M #C255.5-3)*.	450.	1200.	—
S3813D 5 Yüan 1.4.1912. Without vignette. *(S/M #C255.5-4)*.	450.	1200.	—
S3813E 10 Yüan 1.4.1912. Without vignette. *(S/M #C255.5-5)*.	450.	1200.	—

Chinese National Pacification Army Notes

中華民國靖國軍軍用鈔票
Chung Hua Min Kuo Ching Kuo Chün Chün Yung Ch'ao P'iao

1912 ND Issue

	Good	Fine	XF
S3814 1 Dollar ND (1912). Green with black text. Multicolor, crossed flags at top center. Back: Green. *(S/M #C263-1)*.	45.00	125.	375.
S3815 5 Dollars ND (1912). Violet with black text on violet underprint. Multicolor, crossed flags at top center. Back: Violet. *(S/M #C263-2)*.	75.00	225.	675.
S3816 10 Dollars ND (1912). Multicolor crossed flags at top center. *(S/M #C263-3)*.	225.	675.	2000.

Republican China Military - Shanghai

票鈔用軍/國民華中

Chung Hua Min Kuo / Chün Yung Ch'ao P'iao

1912 Issue

#S3818-S3820 dated 9th moon 4609 from an archaic Chinese calendar.

NOTE: This issue was redeemed mostly by the Bank of China in Anhwei Province. Final redemption was made by "The Revolutionary Debts Committee" (RDC) in year 25 (1936).

		Good	Fine	XF
S3817	**50 Cents** Black text on blue underprint. Back: Beige, red. *Shanghai.*	300.	900.	2750.
S3818	**1 Dollar** 4609 (1912). Black text on red-brown underprint. Back: Blue. *(S/M #C264-2a).*			
	a. Issued note.	175.	525.	1500.
	b. With violet rectangular RDC redemption hand stamp.	175.	525.	1500.
S3819	**5 Dollars** 4609 (1912). Black text on orange underprint. Back: Green. *(S/M #C264-3a).*			
	a. Issued note.	200.	600.	1800.
	b. With violet rectangular RDC redemption hand stamp.	200.	600.	1800.
S3820	**10 Dollars** 4609 (1912). Black text on green underprint. Back: Brown. *(S/M #C264-4a).*			
	a. Issued note.	275.	900.	2750.
	b. With violet rectangular RDC redemption hand stamp.	275.	900.	2750.

Republican China Military - Nanking

票鈔用軍 京南/國民華中

Chung Hua Min Kuo / Nan Ching Chün Yung Ch'ao P'iao

1912 Issue

		Good	Fine	XF
S3822	**1 Dollar** 1912. Black text on brown underprint. Back: Green with red seal hand stamp. *(S/M #-).*	375.	1100.	3250.

Chinese Republic Army, Navy and Air Force Headquarters

部令司總軍空海陸國民華中

Chung Hua Min Kuo Lu Hai K'ung Chün Tsung Szu Ling Pu

1930 Issue

		Good	Fine	XF
S3824	**1 Chiao** 1930. Red-brown. Rural waterfront at center. Printer: BEPP. *(S/M #C266-1).*	60.00	175.	525.
S3825	**1 Yüan** 1930. Blue-gray. Gazebo at center. Printer: BEPP. *(S/M #C266-10).*	60.00	175.	525.
S3826	**5 Yüan** 1930. Green. Gazebo at center. Printer: BEPP. *(S/M #C266-11).*	75.00	225.	675.

Chinese Republic Army, Navy and Air Force Sub-headquarters

部令司總副軍空海陸國民華中

Chung Hua Min Kuo Lu Hai K'ung Chün Fu Tsung Szu Lin Pu

1920's First ND Provisional Issue

#S3828-S3830 large rectangular black text overprint including new issuer's name on Provincial Bank of Kwangsi.

		Good	Fine	XF
S3828	**1 Yüan** ND (- old date Jan. 1926). Overprint: Large rectangular black text including new issuer's name on Provincial Bank of Kwangsi. *(S/M #C267-1).*			
	a. Overprint on #S2325e. (Nanning).	30.00	100.	300.
	b. Overprint on #S2325g. (Wuchow).	30.00	100.	300.
S3829	**5 Yüan** ND (- old date Jan. 1926). Overprint: Large rectangular black text including new issuer's name on Provincial Bank of Kwangsi. *(S/M #C267-2).*			
	a. Overprint on #S2326e. (Nanning).	30.00	100.	300.
	b. Overprint on #S2326g. (Wuchow).	30.00	100.	300.
S3830	**10 Yüan** ND (- old date Jan. 1926). Overprint: Large rectangular black text including new issuer's name on Provincial Bank of Kwangsi. *(S/M #C267-3).*			
	a. Overprint on #S2327e. (Nanning).	45.00	125.	375.
	b. Overprint on #S2327g. (Wuchow).	45.00	125.	375.

1920's Second ND Provisional Issue

#S3831-S3834 large text overprint on Bank of the Northwest issue.

		Good	Fine	XF
S3831	**2 Chiao = 20 Cents** ND (- old date 1928).			
	a. Overprint on #S3886a. (Honan). *(S/M #C267-10a).*	15.00	45.00	125.
	b. Overprint on #S3886b. (Kaifeng). *(S/M #C267-10b).*	30.00	100.	300.
	c. Overprint on #S3886c. (Taiyuan). *(S/M #C267-10c).*	30.00	100.	300.
	d. Like a, but old date 1927. *Honan.*	50.00	150.	450.
S3832	**1 Yüan** ND (- old date 1.8.1928). Overprint: On #S3887f. (Honan). *(S/M #C267-20).*	45.00	125.	375.
S3833	**5 Yüan** ND (- old date 1.8.1928). Overprint: On #S3888b. (Honan). *(S/M #C267-21).*	25.00	75.00	225.
S3834	**10 Yüan** ND (- old date 1.8.1928). Overprint: On #S3889b. (Honan). *(S/M #C267-22).*	30.00	100.	300.

Kwangtung Republican Military Government

府政軍省粵國民華中

Chung Hua Min Kuo Yüeh Sheng Chün Cheng Fu

1912 Issue

		Good	Fine	XF
S3836	**5 Chiao = 50 Cents** 1912. Black and tan on light blue and orange underprint. Bugles and swords at left, Hu Han Min at right with crossed flags at top center. Back: Blue with black and blue-green text. Printer: CMPA. *(S/M#C270-2).*	45.00	125.	375.
S3837	**1 Dollar** 1912. Red-brown frame. Bugles and swords at left, Hu Han Min at right with crossed flags at top center. Back: Green with black and red text. Printer: CMPA. *(S/M #C270-10).*	45.00	125.	375.
S3838	**2 Dollars** 1912. Brown-violet frame. Bugles and swords at left, Hu Han Min at right with crossed flags at top center. Back: Orange with black and blue text. Printer: CMPA. *(S/M #C270-11).*	100.	300.	900.
S3839	**5 Dollars** 1912. Green frame. Bugles and swords at left, Hu Han Min at right with crossed flags at top center. Back: Red-brown with black and violet text. Printer: CMPA. *(S/M #C270-12).*	75.00	225.	675.

Chinese Republican Military Bank - Anhwei

徽安 行 銀 華 中

Chung Hua Yin Hang An Hui

1912 Issue

#S3841-S3842 Various Chinese character overprints.

		Good	Fine	XF
S3841	**1 Dollar** 1912. Black and green on red underprint. Pagoda, village at center. Back: Red on light blue underprint. Lion holding crossed flags on globe at center. Overprint: Various chinese character. *(S/M #C277-11).*	150.	450.	1250.
S3842	**5 Dollars** 1912. Black and green on red underprint. Pagoda, village at center. Back: Red on light green underprint. Lion holding crossed flags on globe at center. Overprint: Various Chinese character. *(S/M #C277-12).*	225.	675.	1800.

Honan Province Treasury

券通庫金省南河

Ho Nan Sheng Chin K'u T'ung Ch'üan

1920's ND Provisional Issue

#S3855 overprint new issuer's name on Provincial Bank of Honan.

		Good	Fine	XF
S3855	**1 Yüan** ND (- old date 1921). Green. Overprint: Large red square seal on #S2985. *(S/M #H60-1).*	25.00	75.00	225.

Honan Province

印省南河

Ho Nan Sheng Yin

1920's ND Provisional Issue

#S3857-S3859 Large square red seal overprint with new issuer's name on back Provincial Bank of Honan.

		Good	Fine	XF
S3857	**1 Yüan** ND (- old date 1923). Red on multicolor underprint. Rectangular seal stamp at left. Overprint: Large square red seal with new issuer's name on back Provincial Bank of Honan, #S1688a. *(S/M #H61-1).*	45.00	125.	375.
S3858	**5 Yüan** ND (- old date 1923). Green on multicolor underprint. Rectangular seal stamp at left. Overprint: Large square red seal with new issuer's name on back Provincial Bank of Honan, #S1689a. *(S/M #H61-2).*	45.00	125.	375.
S3859	**10 Yüan** ND (- old date 1923). Violet on multicolor underprint. Rectangular seal stamp at left. Overprint: Large square red seal with new issuer's name on back Provincial Bank of Honan, #S1690a. *(S/M #H61-3).*	45.00	125.	375.

Bank of the Northwest

1920's ND Provisional Issue

#S3861-S3863 overprint with new issuer's name on Tsihar Hsing Yeh Bank.

		VG	VF	UNC
S3861	**1 Chiao = 10 Cents** ND (- old date 1924). Brown and blue. *(S/M #H77-1).*			
	a. Overprint on #S835a. (Peking).	30.00	100.	300.
	b. Overprint on #S835c. (Tulunnoerh).	30.00	100.	300.
S3862	**2 Chiao = 20 Cents** ND (- old date 1924). Puprle, brown and orange. *(S/M #H77-2).*			
	a. Overprint on #S836b. (Peking).	30.00	100.	300.
	b. Overprint on #S836c. (Tulunnoerh).	30.00	100.	300.
S3863	**5 Chiao = 50 Cents** ND (- old date 1924). Blue and brown. *(S/M #H77-3).*			
	a. Overprint on #S837b. (Peking).	35.00	125.	375.
	b. Overprint on #S837c. (Tulunnoerh).	35.00	125.	375.

1925 Regular Issues

	VG	VF	UNC
S3864 10 Coppers			
1.3.1925. 1.3.1925. Pagoda at center. Back: Blue. Printer: BEPP.			
a. *Kalgan. (S/M #H77-10a).*	25.00	75.00	225.
b. Red overprint: *Fengchen. (S/M #H77-10b).*	25.00	75.00	225.
c. Black overprint: *FENGCHEN. (S/M #H77-10c).*	25.00	75.00	225.
S3865 20 Coppers			
1.3.1925. Brown on light green underprint. Pagoda at center. Back: Brown. Printer: BEPP.			
a. *KALGAN. (S/M #H77-11a).*	10.00	30.00	100.
b. *FENGCHEN. (S/M #H77-11b).*	10.00	30.00	100.
c. *Fengchen/KALGAN. (S/M #H77-11c).*	10.00	30.00	100.
d. *SUI YUAN. (S/M #H77-11d).*	30.00	100.	300.
e. Like a. Black 5 character overprint.	30.00	100.	300.
S3866 50 Coppers			
1.3.1925. Red on light blue underprint. Pagoda at center. Back: Red. Printer: BEPP.			
a. *KALGAN. (S/M #H77-12a).*	10.00	30.00	100.
b. *Fengchen/KALGAN. (S/M #H77-12b).*	15.00	45.00	125.
S3867 100 Coppers			
1.3.1925. Blue on light orange underprint. Pagoda at center. Printer: BEPP. *KALGAN. (S/M #H77-12a).*	25.00	75.00	225.
S3868 100 Coppers			
1.3.1925. Green on yellow underprint. Pagoda at center. Printer: BEPP. *KALGAN. (S/M #H77-12b).*	30.00	100.	300.
S3869 1 Chiao = 10 Cents			
1.3.1925. Blue on yellow underprint. Railroad track laying at left. Printer: BEPP. *KALGAN. (S/M #H77-20).*	25.00	75.00	225.
S3870 2 Chiao = 20 Cents			
1.3.1925. Violet on light green underprint. Railroad track laying at left. Printer: BEPP.			
a. *KALGAN. (S/M #H77-21a).*	15.00	45.00	125.
b. *Fengchen/KALGAN. (S/M #H77-21b).*	15.00	45.00	125.

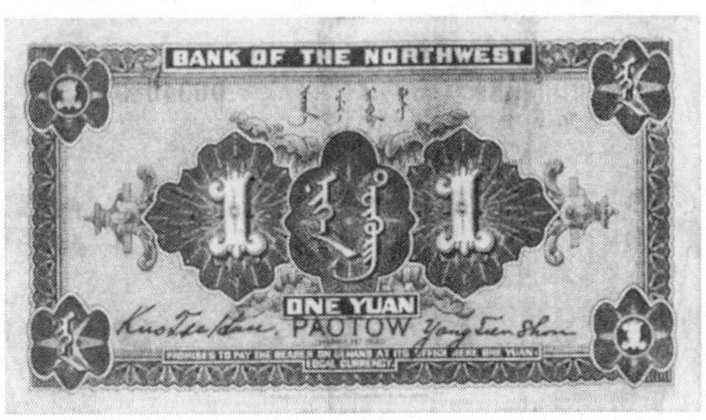

	VG	VF	UNC
S3871 1 Yüan			
1.3.1925. Blue on light blue underprint. Railroad track laying at left. Printer: BEPP.			
a. *FENGCHEN. (S/M #H77-30a).*	10.00	30.00	100.
b. *JEHOL. (S/M #H77-30b).*	10.00	30.00	100.
c. *KALGAN. (S/M #H77-30c).*	7.50	20.00	60.00
d. *Paotow. (S/M #H77-30d).*	30.00	100.	300.
e. *PEKING. (S/M #H77-30e).*	15.00	45.00	125.
f. *SUI YUAN. (S/M #H77-30f).*	25.00	75.00	225.
g. *TIENTSIN. (S/M #H77-30g).*	20.00	60.00	175.
h. *TULUNNOERH. (S/M #H77-30h).*	15.00	45.00	125.
i. *Fengchen/KALGAN. (S/M #H77-30i).*	15.00	45.00	125.

	VG	VF	UNC
S3872 1 Yüan			
1.3.1925. Blue on light blue and multicolor underprint. Railroad track laying at left. Multicolor guilloche.			
a. *JEHOL. (S/M #H77-31a).*	10.00	30.00	100.
b. *KALGAN. (S/M #H77-31b).*	10.00	30.00	100.
c. *PEKING. (S/M #H77-31c).*	15.00	45.00	125.
d. *TIENTSIN. (S/M #H77-31d).*	10.00	30.00	100.
e. *HONAN. (S/M #H77-31e).*	25.00	75.00	225.
r. Remainder.	—	—	350.
S3873 5 Yüan			
1.3.1925. Brown-orange on pale orange underprint. Railroad track laying at left. Printer: BEPP.			
a. *FENGCHEN. (S/M #H77-32a).*	20.00	60.00	175.
b. *JEHOL. (S/M #H77-32b).*	20.00	60.00	175.
c. *KALGAN. (S/M #H77-32c).*	20.00	60.00	175.
d. *PEKING. (S/M #H77-32d).*	25.00	75.00	225.
e. *TIENTSIN. (S/M #H77-32e).*	20.00	60.00	175.
f. *TULUNNOERH. (S/M #H77-32f).*	20.00	60.00	175.
g. *PAOTOW. (S/M #H77-32g).*	30.00	100.	300.
h. *SUI YUAN. (S/M #H77-32h).*	30.00	100.	300.
S3874 5 Yüan			
1.3.1925. Brown-orange on pale orange and multicolor underprint. Railroad track laying at left. Multicolor guilloche. Printer: BEPP.			
a. *JEHOL. (S/M #H77-33a).*	20.00	60.00	175.
b. *KALGAN. (S/M #H77-33b).*	20.00	60.00	175.
c. *PEKING. (S/M #H77-33c).*	20.00	60.00	175.
d. *SHENSI. (S/M #H77-33d).*	25.00	75.00	225.
e. *HONAN. (S/M #H77-33e).*	30.00	100.	300.
f. *NING HSIA. (S/M #H77-33f).*	30.00	100.	300.
S3875 10 Yüan			
1.3.1925. Green on light green underprint. Railroad track laying at left. Printer: BEPP.			
a. *FENGCHEN. (S/M #H77-34a).*	25.00	75.00	225.
b. *KALGAN. (S/M #H77-34b).*	25.00	75.00	225.
c. *PEKING. (S/M #H77-34c).*	25.00	75.00	225.
d. *TIENTSIN. (S/M #H77-34d).*	25.00	75.00	225.
e. *TULUNNOERH. (S/M #H77-34e).*	25.00	75.00	225.
f. *SUI YUAN. (S/M #H77-34f).*	25.00	75.00	225.
S3876 10 Yüan			
1.3.1925. Green on light green and multicolor underprint. Railroad track laying at left. Multicolor guilloche. Printer: BEPP.			
a. *JEHOL. (S/M #H77-35a).*	30.00	100.	300.
b. *KALGAN. (S/M #H77-35b).*	30.00	100.	300.
c. *PEKING. (S/M #H77-35c).*	30.00	100.	300.
d. *SHENSI. (S/M #H77-35c).*	45.00	125.	375.
e. *HONAN. (S/M #H77-35d).*	45.00	125.	375.
f. *KANSU. (S/M #H77-35e).*	45.00	125.	375.

NOTE: #S3876d-f with additional 2 Chinese character city (?) overprint.

1926 Issue

	Good	Fine	XF
S3878 1 Chiao = 10 Cents			
1926. Blue on red underprint. Pagoda on hillside at center. Back: Violet. *KALGAN. (S/M #H77-40).*	45.00	125.	375.
S3878A 10 Cents			
1926. Blue on green and light orange underprint. Railroad station at center. Back: Black on green underprint. *SHENSI.*	45.00	125.	375.
S3879 2 Chiao = 20 Cents			
1926. Red on multicolor underprint. Railroad station at center. Back: Brown. *HONAN. (S/M #H77-41).*	25.00	75.00	225.

1928 Issue

	Good	Fine	XF
S3881 10 Coppers			
1.10.1928. Blue on orange underprint. Troop oath taking at center. Back: Great Wall at center. Printer: BEPP.			
a. *LANCHOW. (S/M #H77-45a).*	45.00	125.	375.
b. *KANSU. (S/M #H77-45b).*	45.00	125.	375.
S3882 20 Coppers			
1.10.1928. Blue on red underprint. Troop oath taking at center. Back: Great Wall at center. Printer: BEPP.			
a. *LANCHOW. (S/M #H77-46a).*	45.00	125.	375.
b. *KANSU. (S/M #H77-46b).*	45.00	125.	375.
c. *SHENSI. (S/M #H77-46c).*	45.00	125.	375.
S3883 50 Coppers			
1.10.1928. Brown on blue underprint. Troop oath taking at center. Back: Great Wall at center. Printer: BEPP.			
a. *LANCHOW. (S/M #H77-47a).*	45.00	125.	375.
b. *KANSU. (S/M #H77-47b).*	45.00	125.	375.
S3884 100 Coppers			
1.10.1928. Red on green underprint. Troop oath taking at center. Back: Great Wall at center. Printer: BEPP.			
a. *LANCHOW. (S/M #H77-48a).*	45.00	125.	375.
b. *KANSU. (S/M #H77-48b).*	45.00	125.	375.

	VG	VF	UNC
S3885			
1928. Blue on multicolor underprint. Back green.			
a. *KALGAN. (S/M #H77-50a).*	45.00	125.	375.
b. *KANSU. (S/M #H77-50b).*	45.00	125.	375.
S3886			
1928. Red on multicolor underprint. Back brown.			
a. *HONAN. (S/M #H77-51a).*	45.00	125.	375.
b. *KAIFENG. (S/M #H77-51b).*	60.00	175.	525.
c. *TAIYUAN. (S/M #H77-51c).*	60.00	175.	525.
d. *LANCHOW. (S/M #H77-51d).*	75.00	225.	675.
e. *KANSU. (S/M #H77-51e).*	75.00	225.	675.

NOTE: For #S3885 and S3886 w/additional overprint. see #S1443-S1444 and #S3831.

	VG	VF	UNC
S3887 1 Yüan			
1.8.1928. Brown. Troop oath taking at center. Back: Great Wall at center.			
a. *SHENSI. (S/M #H77-60a).*	20.00	60.00	175.
b. *Honan/SHENSI. (S/M #H77-60b).*	20.00	60.00	175.
c. *KANSU. (S/M #H77-60c).*	20.00	60.00	175.
d. *SHANTUNG. (S/M #H77-60d).*	30.00	100.	300.
e. *Sian/SHENSI. (S/M #H77-60e).*	45.00	125.	375.
f. *HONAN. (S/M #H77-60f).*	45.00	125.	375.
g. *Kaifeng/HONAN. With circular bank stamp in English at b. (S/M #H77-60f).*	45.00	125.	375.
h. *Sian/SHENSI.*	20.00	60.00	175.

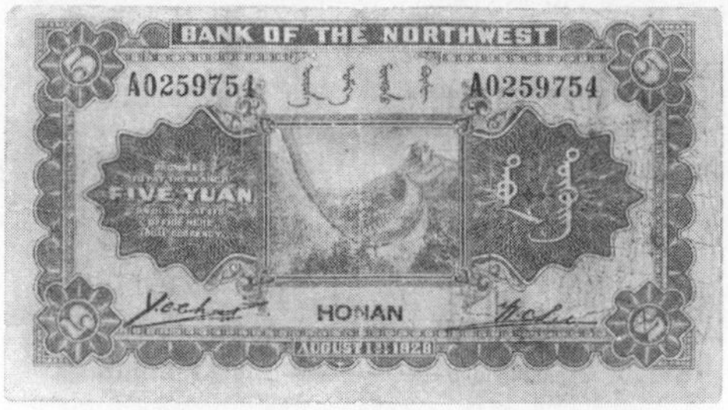

	VG	VF	UNC
S3888 5 Yüan			
1.8.1928. Deep green. Troop oath taking at center. Back: Olive on light green underprint. Great Wall at center. Printer: BEPP.			
a. *Honan/SHENSI. (S/M #H77-61a).*	45.00	125.	375.
b. *HONAN. (S/M #H77-61b).*	45.00	125.	375.
c. *Kaifeng/HONAN.*	45.00	125.	375.
d. *SHANTUNG. (S/M #H77-61c).*	45.00	125.	375.
e. *SHENSI. (S/M #H77-61d).*	100.	300.	900.
S3889 10 Yüan			
1.8.1928. Red-brown. Troop oath taking at center. Back: Great Wall at center.			
a. *Honan/SHENSI. (S/M #H77-62a).*	60.00	175.	525.
b. *HONAN. (S/M #H77-62b).*	60.00	175.	525.
c. *SHENSI. (S/M #H77-62c).*	60.00	175.	525.
d. *SHANTUNG. (S/M #H77-62d).*	60.00	175.	525.
e. *SHANTUNG/TAIAN.*	60.00	175.	525.

NOTE: For #S3887-S3889 with additional overprint. see #S1445-S1447, #S2681-S2683 and #S3832-S3834.

Hunan Provincial Treasury

券庫金省南湖

Hu Nan Sheng Chin K'u Ch'üan

1926 Issue

	VG	VF	UNC
S3892 1 Yüan			
1926. *(S/M #H162-1).*	75.00	225.	675.
S3893 5 Yüan			
1926. *(S/M #H162-2).*	100.	300.	900.
S3894 10 Yüan			
1926. *(S/M #H162-3).*	125.	375.	1100.

1927 Issue

	VG	VF	UNC
S3896 5 Yüan			
1927. Violet on green underprint. *(S/M #H162-10).*	125.	375.	1100.

Kiangse Bank of the Republic

行銀國民省贛

Kan (Sen) Sheng Min Kuo Yin Hang

1912 "Cash" Issue

	Good	Fine	XF
S3897 100 Cash			
4609 (1912). Blue green on yellow underprint. Stylized birds facing at upper left and right with various archaic objects in borders. Vertical format. Back: Green. *(S/M #C97-0.5).*	750.	2250.	—
S3898 1 Ch'uan			
1.1.1912. Blue and red on green underprint. Stylized birds facing at upper left and right with various archaic objects in borders. Vertical format. Back: Green. *(S/M #C97-0.8).*	750.	2250.	—

1912 "Dollar" Issue

	Good	Fine	XF
S3900 1 Dollar			
1.1.1912. Black on blue underprint. Portrait Gen. Ma Yu-Pao at top center. Back: Green. *(S/M #C97-1).*	225.	675.	2000.
S3900A 5 Dollars			
1.1.1912. Portrait Gen. Ma Yu-Pao at top center. *(S/M #C97-2).*	375.	1000.	3000.
S3900B 10 Dollars			
1.1.1912. Green. Portrait Gen. Ma Yu-Pao at top center. Back: Purple and black. *(S/M #C97-3).*	225.	675.	2000.

Kansu (Military)

號銀官肅甘

Kan Su Kuan Yin Hao

1913 Official Note Issue

	Good	Fine	XF
S3900D 1000 Cash			
(ca.1913). Brown and blue on multicolor underprint. Facing phoenix above storks at left and right. Remainder. *(S/M #K6.5-13).*	—	—	400.

Kwangsi Military

票手用軍西廣

Kuang Hsi Chün Yung Shou P'iao

1922 Issue

	Good	Fine	XF
S3900F 1 Yüan			
May 1922. Green on orange underprint. Black text. Uniface. Vertical format. Back: Large square hand stamped seal. *(S/M #K30.5-11).*	50.00	150.	450.

Kwangsi Military (Provisional)

票用軍時臨西廣

Kuang Hsi Lin Shih Chün Yung Piao

1922 Issue

	Good	Fine	XF
S3900J 2 Chiao = 20 Cents			
1922. Antique steam passenger train at center. *(S/M #K31.5-10).*	150.	450.	1250.
S3900K 5 Chiao = 50 Cents			
1922. Antique steam passenger train at left, waterfont village at right. *(S/M #K31.5-11).*	75.00	225.	675.
S3900L 1 Yüan			
1922. Green on yellow underprint. Waterfront village at left, antique steam passenger train at right. Back: Violet. *(S/M #K31.5-12).*	75.00	225.	675.
S3900M 5 Yüan			
1922. Waterfront village at left, antique steam passenger train at right. *(S/M #K31.5-13).*	125.	375.	1000.

Kwangtung Provincial Treasury

券庫金省東廣

Kuang Tung Sheng Chin K'u Ch'üan

1923 Issue

	Good	Fine	XF
S3901 1 Dollar			
1923. Blue-green on lilac underprint. Truck and biplane at center. Without imprint. Back: Red-brown. *(S/M #K52-1).*	100.	300.	900.
S3902 5 Dollars			
1923. Truck and biplane at center. Without imprint. *(S/M #K52-2).*	125.	375.	1000.
S3903 10 Dollars			
1923. Green on tan underprint. Truck and biplane at center. Without imprint. Back: Green. *(S/M #K52-3).*	100.	300.	900.

Kweilin Regional Bank

行銀方地林桂

Kuei Lin Ti Fang Yin Hang

1921-22 Issue

	Good	Fine	XF
S3904 1 Yüan			
1921. Black. Waterfront stone arch at center. *(S/M #K74.5-6.*	100.	300.	900.
S3906 2 Yüan			
1922. Flags at upper center. Back: Boat at left, horseman at right. *(S/M #K74.5-12).*	100.	300.	900.

NOTE: Also see #S2363 and S2368.

National Army

券通流融金軍民國

Kuo Min Chün Chin Jung Liu T'ung Ch'üan

1827 ND Provisional Issue

#S3907-S3909 rectangular ten character overprint of new issuer's name on Fu Chaing Bank of Shensi.

	Good	Fine	XF
S3907			
ND (- old date 1927). Overprint on #S2608. *(S/M #K102-2).*	30.00	100.	300.
S3908 3 Chiao = 30 Cents			
ND (- old date 1927). Overprint: Rectangular ten character of new issuer's name on Fu Chaing Bank of Shensi on #S2609. *(S/M #K102-4).*	45.00	125.	375.
S3909 5 Chiao = 50 Cents			
ND (- old date 1927). Overprint: Rectangular ten character of new issuer's name on Fu Chaing Bank of Shensi on #S2610. *(S/M #K102-5).*	45.00	125.	375.

1927 Issue

	Good	Fine	XF
S3910 1 Chiao = 10 Cents			
1927. Orange on light green underprint. Pagoda at center. Back: Green. Printer: CHCC. *(S/M #K102-1).*	30.00	100.	300.
S3911 2 Chiao = 20 Cents			
1927. Green on red underprint. pagoda at center. Back: Orange. Printer: CHCC. *(S/M #K102-3).*	30.00	100.	300.
S3913 5 Chiao = 50 Cents			
1927. Blue on yellow underprint. Pagoda at center. Printer: CHCC. *(S/M #K102-5).*	45.00	125.	375.
S3914 1 Yüan			
1927. Blue. Pagoda at center. Printer: SASO. *(S/M #K102-10).*	50.00	150.	450.
S3915 2 Yüan			
1927. Violet on orange underprint. Pagoda at center. Back: Light green. *(S/M #K102-11).*	75.00	225.	675.
S3916 5 Yüan			
1927. Red on green underprint. Pagoda at center. Back: Blue. Printer: CHCC. *(S/M #K102-12).*	45.00	125.	375.

National Army Combined Headquarters

票用軍部令司總軍聯軍民國

Kuo Min Chün Lien Chün Tsung Szu Ling Pu Chün Yung P'iao

1920's ND Provisional Issue

#S3918-S3920 with square red nine character and twelve character text overprints on Fu Ching Bank of Shensi.

	Good	Fine	XF
S3918 1 Yüan			
ND (- old date 1922). Green. Overprint: Square red nine character and twelve character text on Fu Ching Bank of Shensi, #S2600. *(S/M #K103-1).*	30.00	100.	300.

		Good	Fine	XF
S3919	**5 Yüan**			
	ND (- old date 1922). Blue. Overprint: Square red nine character and twelve character text on Fu Ching Bank of Shensi, #S2600a. *(S/M #K103-2).*	45.00	125.	375.
S3920	**10 Yüan**			
	ND (- old date 1922). Orange. Overprint: Square red nine character and twelve character text on Fu Ching Bank of Shensi, #S2600b. *(S/M #K103-3).*	60.00	175.	525.

National Revolutionary Army

國民革命軍總司令部軍需券

Kuo Min Ke Ming Chün Tsung Szu Ling Pu Chün Hsü Ch'üan

1926 Issue

		Good	Fine	XF
S3923	**1 Chiao = 10 Cents**			
	Jan. 1926. Black on multicolor underprint. Two peasants, one with axe, the other with hoe at center. Back: Brown. Chinese text. Printer: TIPC. *(S/M #K104-1).*	30.00	100.	300.
S3924	**2 Chiao = 20 Cents**			
	Jan. 1926. Blue on multicolor underprint. Two peasants, one with axe, the other with hoe at center. Back: Violet. Chinese text. Printer: TIPC. *(S/M #K104-2).*	40.00	125.	375.
S3925	**1 Yüan**			
	1926. Black on multicolor underprint. Back: Violet and green. Printer: TIPC. *(S/M #K104-10).*	45.00	125.	375.
S3926	**5 Yüan**			
	1926. Brown on green underprint. Back: Green and red. Printer: TIPC. *(S/M #K104-11).*	50.00	150.	450.
S3927	**10 Yüan**			
	1926. Printer: TIPC. *(S/M #K104-12).* Reported not confirmed.	—	—	—

Agricultural, Industrial and Commercial Trust Co., Ltd.

農工商信託有限公司

Nung Kung Shang Hsin Tok Yu Ksien Kung Szu

1919 Issue

		VG	VF	UNC
S3928	**1 Chiao = 10 Cents**			
	ND (1919). Black and gray-green. SYS at center. Without imprint. Back: Blue-gray and dull purple on light blue underprint. *(S/M #N22.3-1).*	75.00	225.	675.
S3929	**2 Chiao = 20 Cents**			
	ND (1919). SYS at center. Without imprint. *(S/M #N22.3-2).*	100.	300.	900.
S3930	**5 Chiao = 50 Cents**			
	ND (1919). SYS at center. Without imprint. *(S/M #N22.3-3).*	125.	375.	1100.
S3930A	**1 Dollar**			
	ND (1919). Blue-green and brown on red underprint. SYS at center. Without imprint. *(S/M #N22.3-4).*	125.	375.	1100.

Provincial Army of Shantung

山東省軍用票

Shan Tung Sheng Chün Yung P'iao

ND Issue

		Good	Fine	XF
S3931	**1 Chiao = 10 Cents**			
	ND. Red. Gateway over railroad tracks at center. Back: *RPOVINCIAL* (error). Printer: STPO. *(S/M #S44-1).*	20.00	60.00	175.
S3932	**2 Chiao = 20 Cents**			
	ND. Green. Gateway over railroad tracks at center. Back: *RPOVINCIAL* (error). Printer: STPO. *(S/M #S44-2).*	20.00	60.00	175.
S3933	**5 Chiao = 50 Cents**			
	ND. Violet. Gateway over railroad tracks at center. Printer: STPO. *(S/M #S44-3).*	25.00	75.00	225.
S3935	**5 Yüan**			
	ND. Brown on light green underprint. Gateway over railroad tracks at center. Back: Brown. *(S/M #S44-5).*	60.00	175.	525.

1926 Issue

		Good	Fine	XF
S3936	**1 Chiao = 10 Cents**			
	1926. Blue. Fortress on Great Wall at center. Back: Deep blue. Printer: BEPP. *(S/M #S44-10).*	25.00	75.00	225.
S3937	**2 Chiao = 20 Cents**			
	1926. Orange. Fortress on Great Wall at center. Printer: BEPP. *(S/M #S44-11).*	25.00	75.00	225.
S3938	**5 Chiao = 50 Cents**			
	1926. Violet. Fortress on Great Wall at center. Printer: BEPP. *(S/M #S44-12).*	15.00	45.00	125.
S3939	**1 Yüan**			
	1.10.1926. Gray on multicolor underprint. Wooded roadway, gateway at center. Back: Gray. Printer: BEPP. *(S/M #S44-20).*	15.00	45.00	125.
S3940	**5 Yüan**			
	1.10.1926. Red on multicolor underprint. Wooded roadway, gateway at center. Back: Red. Printer: BEPP. *(S/M #S44-21).*	30.00	100.	300.
S3941	**10 Yüan**			
	1.10.1926. Green on multicolor underprint. Wooded roadway, gateway at center. Back: Deep green. Printer: BEPP. *(S/M #S44-22).*	45.00	125.	375.

Local Bank of Szechuan (Szechuan Regional Bank)

四川地方銀行

Szu Ch'uan Ti Fang Yin Hang

1924 Issue

		Good	Fine	XF
S3943	**1 Dollar**			
	1924. *(S/M #S104-1).* Reported not confirmed.	—	—	—
S3944	**5 Dollars**			
	1924. *(S/M #S104-2).* Reported not confirmed.	—	—	—
S3945	**10 Dollars**			
	1924. *(S/M #S104-3).* Reported not confirmed.	—	—	—

1936 Issue

		Good	Fine	XF
S3946	**50 Cents**			
	1.10.1936. Hilltop pagoda above shoreline at upper center. *CHUNGKING. (S/M #S104-13).*	25.00	75.00	225.
S3947	**1 Dollar**			
	1.10.1936. *(S/M #S104-14).*	—	—	—

Ta Han Szechuan Military Government

大漢四川軍政府軍用銀票

Ta Han Szu Chu'an Chün Cheng Fu Chün Yung Yin P'iao

1912 Issue

		Good	Fine	XF
S3948	**1 Yüan**			
	4609 (1912). Brown with black text. Back: Blue. *(S/M #T14-1).*	—	—	—

Note: Illustration of #S3948 is considered a counterfeit by some authorities. Modern replicas exist.

Yunnan-Kwangtung-Kwangsi United Army for Kiangsi Relief

滇粵桂援贛聯軍軍用票

T'ien Yüeh Kuei Yüan Kan Lien Chun Chün Yung P'iao

1916-17 Issue

		Good	Fine	XF
S3951	**1 Dollar**			
	1917. Light blue with black text. Crossed multicolor flags at top center. *(S/M #T174-0.3).*			
	a. Issued note.	200.	600.	—
	r. Unissued remainder without signature.	—	—	400.
S3952	**5 Dollars**			
	1916. Lilac on yellow-orange underprint with black text. Crossed multicolor flags at top center. Unissued remainder without signature. *(S/M #T174-0.6).*	60.00	175.	525.
S3953	**10 Dollars**			
	1916. Brown with black text on yellow-orange underprint. Crossed multicolor flags at top center. *(S/M #T174-1).*			
	a. Issued note.	225.	675.	1800.
	r. Unsigned remainder.	125.	375.	1100.

Third and Fourth Route Army Headquarters Property Control Office

財產管理處

Ts'ai Ch'an Kuan Li Ch'ü

1918 Issue

		Good	Fine	XF
S3955	**5 Ch'uan**			
	1918. Black on yellow underprint. Back: Blue. *(S/M #T180-1).*	75.00	225.	675.

Yunnan National Pacification Army

雲南靖國軍軍用銀行兌換券

Yün Nan Ching Kuo Chün Chün Yung Yin Hang Tui Huan Ch'üan

1917 Issue

		Good	Fine	XF
S3958	**1 Yüan**			
	1917. Brown on green underprint. Back: Blue. Printer: YMSO, Yunnan. *(S/M #Y66-1).*	175.	525.	1500.
S3959	**5 Yüan**			
	1917. Green. Back: Violet. Printer: YMSO, Yunnan. *(S/M #Y66-2).*	125.	375.	1100.
S3960	**10 Yüan**			
	1917. Green. Back: Blue. Printer: YMSO, Yunnan. *(S/M #Y66-3).*	150.	450.	1250.

Japanese Military - WWII

Note: See also Japan #M7-M12.

Japanese Imperial Government

Ta Jih Pen Ti Kuo Cheng Fu

1937 Issue

#M1-M5 Showa yr. 12.

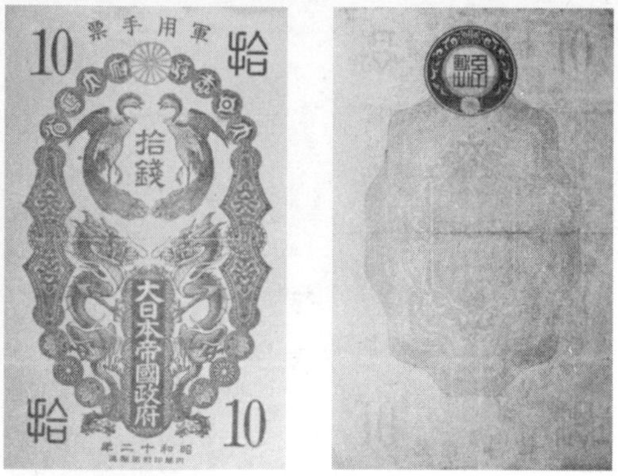

	VG	VF	UNC
M1 10 Sen			
Yr. 12 (1937). Black on blue underprint. Facing Onagadori cockerels at upper center, two facing dragons below. *(S/M #T27-20).*			
a. Issued note.	18.00	90.00	180.
s. Specimen with red overprint: *Mi-hon. Specimen* on back.	—	—	250.
M2 50 Sen			
Yr. 12 (1937). Black on yellow underprint. Facing Onagadori cockerels at upper center, two facing dragons below. *(S/M #T27-22).*			
a. Issued note.	40.00	200.	400.
s. Specimen with red overprint: *Mi-hon. Specimen* on back.	—	—	300.
M3 1 Yen			
Yr. 12 (1937). Black on light lilac underprint. Facing Onagadori cockerels at upper center, two facing dragons below. *(S/M #T27-30).*			
a. Issued note.	50.00	255.	550.
s. Specimen with red overprint: *Mi-hon. Specimen* on back.	—	—	400.
M4 5 Yen			
Yr. 12 (1937). Black on pink underprint. Facing Onagadori cockerels at upper center, two facing dragons below. *(S/M #T27-31).*			
a. Issued note.	400.	750.	2250.
s. Specimen with red overprint: *Mi-hon. Specimen* on back.	—	—	2000.
M5 10 Yen	VG	VF	UNC
Yr. 12 (1937). Black on light green underprint. Facing Onagadori cockerels at upper center, two facing dragons below. *(S/M #T27-32).*			
a. Issued note.	800.	2000.	3500.
s. Specimen with red overprint: *Mi-hon. Specimen* on back.	—	—	2500.

1939-40 ND Issues

TITLES:

A: *Ta Jih Pen Ti Kuo Cheng Fu.*

B: *Ta Jih Pen Ti Kuo Cheng Fu Chung Yung Shou Piao.*

Note: Forgeries exist of #M10. Forgeries exist on #M21 on plain white paper.

Note: For similar notes in different color printings see French Indochina #M1-M7.

	VG	VF	UNC
M6 2 1/2 Rin			
ND (1940). Black on brown underprint. Title A. Vertical note. *(S/M #T30-1).*	200.	550.	1200.

	VG	VF	UNC
M7 1 Sen			
ND (1939). Brown on blue-gray underprint. Dragon at right. Title A. *(S/M #T30-2).*			
a. Issued note.	.50	2.50	7.00
s. Specimen with overprint: *Mi-hon.*	—	—	100.
M8 1 Sen			
ND (1939). Brown on blue-gray underprint. Dragon at right. Title B. *(S/M #T31-1).*	.50	1.75	7.00
M9 5 Sen			
ND (1940). Blue and brown on pink underprint. Dragon at right. Title A. *(S/M #T30-3).*			
a. Issued note.	.25	1.00	4.00
s. Specimen with overprint: *Mi-hon.*	—	—	120.
M10 5 Sen			
ND (1939). Blue and brown on pink overprint. Dragon at right. Title B. *(S/M #T31-2).*	1.00	4.00	12.50

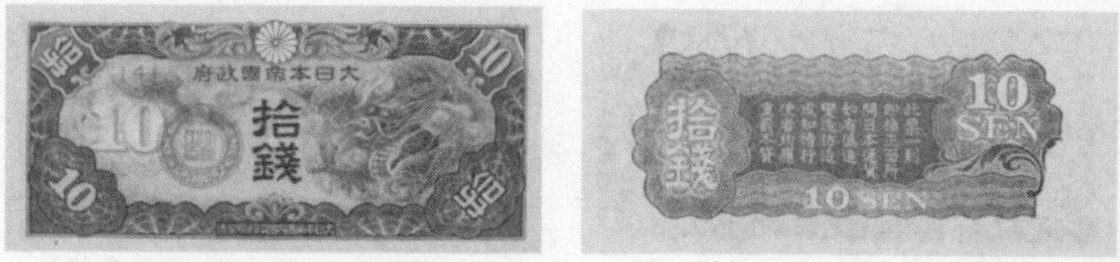

	VG	VF	UNC
M11 10 Sen			
ND (1940). Black on yellow-orange and violet underprint. Dragon at right. Title A. *(S/M #T30-4).*			
a. Issued note.	.50	2.00	8.00
s. Specimen with overprint: *Mi-hon.*	—	—	100.
M12 10 Sen			
ND (1938). Black on yellow-orange and violet underprint. Dragon at right. Title B. *(S/M #T31-3).*	4.50	12.50	40.00
M13 50 Sen			
ND (1940). Black on green and pink underprint. Dragon at left. Title A. *(S/M #T30-5).*	.25	1.50	7.00
M14 50 Sen			
ND (1938). Black on green and pink underprint. Dragon at left. Title B. *(S/M #T31-4).*	.50	1.50	7.00

	VG	VF	UNC
M15 1 Yen			
ND (1940). Black on pink and yellow underprint. Onagadori cock at left. Title A. *(S/M #T30-10).*			
a. Issued note.	2.00	4.00	25.00
s. Specimen with overprint: *Mi-hon.*	—	—	100.
M16 1 Yen			
Black on pink and yellow underprint. Onagadori cock at left. Title B. Back: ND (1939). *(S/M #T31-10).*	10.00	40.00	200.

	VG	VF	UNC
M17 5 Yen			
ND (1940). Black on blue and yellow underprint. Onagadori cock at left and right. Title A. *(S/M #T30-11).*			
a. Issued note.	1.50	3.00	10.00
r. Remainder without serial #, block # or seal.	—	12.50	40.00
s. Specimen with overprint: *Mi-hon.*	—	—	100.

	VG	VF	UNC
M18 5 Yen			
ND (1939). Black on blue and yellow underprint. Onagadori cock at left and right. Title B. *(S?M #T31-11).*			
a. Issued note.	2.00	6.50	20.00
r. Remainder without seal.	—	12.50	40.00

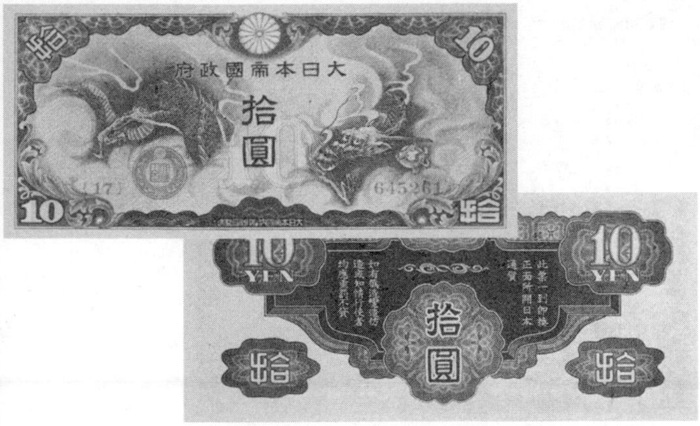

M19 10 Yen

ND (1940). Black on pale blue-green and lilac underprint. Dragon. Title A. *(S/M #T30-13).*

	VG	VF	UNC
a. Issued note.	1.50	3.50	15.00
r. Remainder without serial #, block # or seal.	—	12.50	40.00
s. Specimen with overprint: *Mi-hon.*	—	—	100.

M20 10 Yen

ND (1939). Black on pale blue-green and lilac underprint. Dragon. Title B. *(S/M #T31-12).*

	VG	VF	UNC
a. Issued note.	4.50	12.50	40.00
r. Remainder without serial # or block #.	—	12.50	40.00

1945 ND Issue

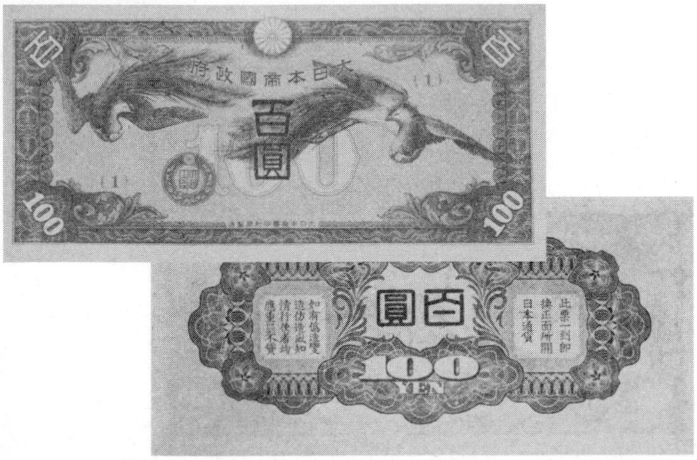

M21 100 Yen

ND (1945). Black on yellow-green underprint. Onagadori cock at left and right. Title A. Back: Green. *(S/M #T30-14).*

	VG	VF	UNC
a. Issued note.	2.50	7.50	20.00
s. Specimen with overprint: *Mi-hon.*	—	—	100.

Military Note

Chun Yung Shou P'iao

1938 ND Issues

M22 1 Yen

ND (1938). Light brown. Overprint: Red. 4 Japanese characters across center, 11 characters below, 8 characters (Bank of Japan) blocked *(S/M #J11-1).*

	VG	VF	UNC
a. Issued note.	7.50	25.00	75.00
b. With handstamp: Type II.	10.00	35.00	—

M23 1 Yen

ND (1938). Light brown. Overprint: 4 Japanese characters across center. *(S/M #T32-1).*

	VG	VF	UNC
a. Issued note.	1.50	4.50	30.00
b. With handstamp: Type II.	4.00	10.00	—
s. Specimen.	—	—	750.

M24 5 Yen

ND (1938). Green and brown underprint. Hooded man at right. Overprint: 4 Japanese characters across center, 11 characters below, 7 characters (Bank of Japan Convertible No *(S/M #J11-2).*

	VG	VF	UNC
a. Issued note.	3.00	15.00	30.00
b. With handstamp: Type II.	10.00	35.00	—

M25 5 Yen

ND (1938; 1944). Green and brown underprint. Overprint: 4 Japanese characters across center.

	VG	VF	UNC
a. Watermark: Plum flowers (1938). *(S/M #T32-2).*	.50	2.00	20.00
b. Watermark: 2 birds (1944). *(S/M #32-3).*	.50	2.00	20.00

M26 10 Yen

ND (1938). Green underprint. Overprint: 4 Japanese characters across center, 11 characters below, 7 characters (Bank of Japan Convertible No *(S/M #J11-3).*

	VG	VF	UNC
a. Issued note.	3.00	12.50	50.00
b. With handstamp: Type II.	10.00	35.00	—

M27 10 Yen

ND (1938). Green underprint. Overprint: 4 Japanese characters across center. *(S/M #T32-4).*

	VG	VF	UNC
a. Issued note.	2.00	7.50	20.00
b. With handstamp: Type II.	2.00	6.00	—
s. Specimen with red overprint: *Mi-hon.*	—	—	100.

1945 ND Hong Kong Issues

		VG	VF	UNC
M28	**100 Yen** ND (1945). Black on light blue and brown underprint. Overprint: 4 Japanese characters across center, 7 characters below, 5 characters at top and 4 vertical characte *(S/M #J11-4).*	2.00	10.00	25.00
M29	**100 Yen** ND (1945). Black on green and violet underprint. Like #M28. Overprint: 4 Japanese characters across center and seal at left. *(S/M #T32-5).*	1.00	7.50	15.00
M30	**100 Yen** ND (1945). Red-brown on green underprint. Similar to #M29. Back: Orange. Overprint: 4 Japanese characters at center. *(S/M #T32-6).*	.50	2.50	10.00

South China Expeditionary Army

1944 Issue

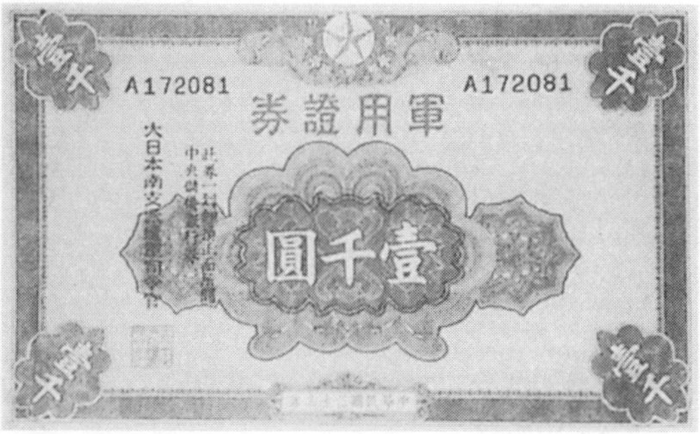

		VG	VF	UNC
M30A	**1000 Yen** Yr. 33 (1944). Red, blue and black on yellow-green underprint. Back: Purple on yellow underprint. *(S/M #T32-7).*	4500.	1000.	—

Russian Military - WWII

Soviet Red Army Headquarters

Su Lien Hung Chun Szu Ling Pu

1945 Issue

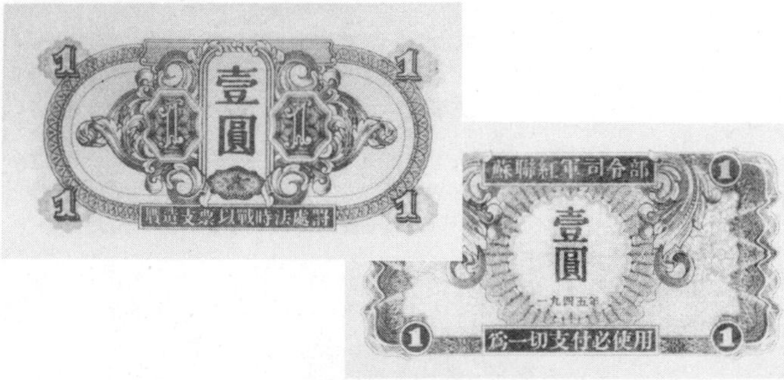

		VG	VF	UNC
M31	**1 Yüan** 1945. Blue on green underprint. *(S/M #S82-1a).*	5.00	20.00	90.00
M32	**5 Yüan** 1945. Brown on green underprint. *(S/M #S82-2a).*	5.00	20.00	90.00

		VG	VF	UNC
M33	**10 Yüan** 1945. Red on lilac underprint. *(S/M #S82-3a).*	2.50	7.50	40.00
M34	**100 Yüan** 1945. Blue on pink underprint. *(S/M #S82-4a).*	5.00	15.00	60.00

1945 ND Revalidated Issue

Note: The 10 Yuan adhesive stamp is also known affixed to Manchukuo 10 Yuan notes. Refer to Manchukuo listings.

		VG	VF	UNC
M35	**10 Yüan** ND (1946 - old date 1945). Red on lilac underprint. Brown revalidation *10 Yuan* adhesive stamp on #M33. *(S/M #S82-3b).*	7.50	20.00	80.00

		VG	VF	UNC
M36	**100 Yüan** ND (1946 - old date 1945). Blue on pink underprint. Green revalidation *100 Yuan* adhesive stamp on #M34. *(S/M #S82-4b).*	5.00	20.00	90.00

Peoples Republic - Military

Military Payment Certificates

Chn Yung Tai Chin Ch'üan

1965 Issue

		VG	VF	UNC
M41	**1 Fen** 1965. Greenish brown. Airplane at left center.	5.00	15.00	60.00
M42	**5 Fen** 1965. Red. Airplane at center.	6.00	30.00	90.00
M43	**1 Chiao** 1965. Purple. Steam passenger train at center right.	15.00	60.00	175.
M45	**1 Yüan** 1965. Green. Truck convoy at left.	15.00	75.00	300.
M46	**5 Yüan** 1965. Truck convoy at left.	25.00	125.	500.

Foreign Exchange Certificates

Bank of China

1979 Issue

		VG	VF	UNC
FX1	**10 Fen** 1979. Brown on multicolor underprint. Waterfall at center.			
	a. Watermark: 1 Large and 4 small stars.	—	—	.50
	b. Watermark: Star and torch.	—	—	1.00
FX2	**50 Fen** 1979. Purple on multicolor underprint. Temple of Heaven at left center. Watermark: Star and torch.	—	—	1.50
FX3	**1 Yüan** 1979. Deep green on multicolor underprint. Pleasure boats in lake with mountains behind at center. Watermark: Star and Torch. .	—	—	1.00

		VG	VF	UNC
FX4	**5 Yüan** 1979. Deep brown on multicolor underprint. Mountain scenery at center. Watermark: Star and Torch.	—	—	2.00

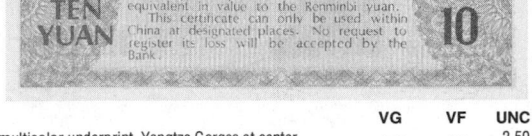

	VG	VF	UNC
FX5 10 Yüan 1979. Deep blue on multicolor underprint. Yangtze Gorges at center.	—	—	2.50
FX6 50 Yüan 1979. Purple and red on multicolor underprint. Mountain lake at Kweilin at center. Watermark: National badge.	—	—	35.00
FX7 100 Yüan 1979. Black and blue on multicolor underprint. Great Wall at center. Watermark: National badge.	—	—	120.

1988 Issue

#FX8-FX9 only uncirculated examples command a premium.

	VG	VF	UNC
FX8 50 Yüan 1988. Black, orange-brown and green on multicolor underprint. Shoreline rock formations at center. Watermark: National badge.	—	—	100.
FX9 100 Yüan 1988. Olive-green on multicolor underprint. Great Wall at center. Watermark: National badge.	—	—	75.00

Off-Shore Island Currency

Bank of Taiwan

T'ai Wan Yin Hang

Kinmen (Quemoy) Branch

1949-51 (1963; 1967) Issue

	VG	VF	UNC
R101 1 Yüan 1949 (1963). Green on multicolor underprint. Portrait SYS at upper center. Printer: CPF. Vertical format.	.25	2.00	10.00

	VG	VF	UNC
R102 1 Yüan 1949 (1952). Green. Portrait SYS at upper center. Printer: FPFT. Vertical format.*(S/M #T74-2)*.	7.50	40.00	150.

	VG	VF	UNC
R102A 1 Yüan 1949. Reddish brown on light orange underprint. Portrait SYS at upper center. Back: Blue. Overprint: Large red outlined character: *Chin Men*. Vertical format. Buff paper. *(S/M #T74-3)*	150.	400.	1000.

	VG	VF	UNC
R102B 5 Yüan 1949. Dark green on light blue and multicolor underprint. Portrait SYS at upper center. Back: Dark green on light green underprint. Overprint: Large red outlined character: *Chin Men*. Vertical format. *(S/M #T74-4)*.	250.	650.	1200.

1950-51 Issues

	VG	VF	UNC
R103 10 Cents 1950 (1952). Blue. Portrait SYS at upper center. Vertical format.			
a. Overprint at bottom of face. *(S/M #T74-10a)*.	7.50	30.00	150.
b. Overprint at middle and bottom of face. *(S/M #T74-10b)*.	6.00	25.00	125.
R104 50 Cents 1950 (1952). Brown. Portrait SYS at upper center. Overprint: *Chin Men* at lower left and right on face. Printer: CPF. Vertical format. *(S/M #T74-11)*.			
a. Overprint: *Chin* at right, *Men* at left on back.	8.00	50.00	175.
b. Overprint: *Chin Men* at left and right on back.	7.50	45.00	160.
R105 10 Yüan 1950 (1952). Blue on multicolor underprint. Portrait SYS at upper center. Printer: FPFT. Vertical format. *(S/M #T74-21)*.	7.50	20.00	75.00
R106 10 Yüan 1950 (1963). Blue. Portrait SYS at upper center. Printer: CPF. Vertical format.	.50	1.50	18.00

	VG	VF	UNC
R107 50 Yüan 1951 (1967). Green. Portrait SYS at upper center. Printer: FPFT. Vertical format.	3.00	20.00	120.

1955-72 Issues

	VG	VF	UNC
R108 5 Yüan 1955 (1956). Violet. Portrait SYS at upper center. Printer: PFBT. Vertical format. *(S/M #T74-40).*	3.00	20.00	150.
R109 5 Yüan 1966. Violet-brown. Portrait SYS at upper center. Printer: CPF. Vertical format.	.75	3.00	20.00

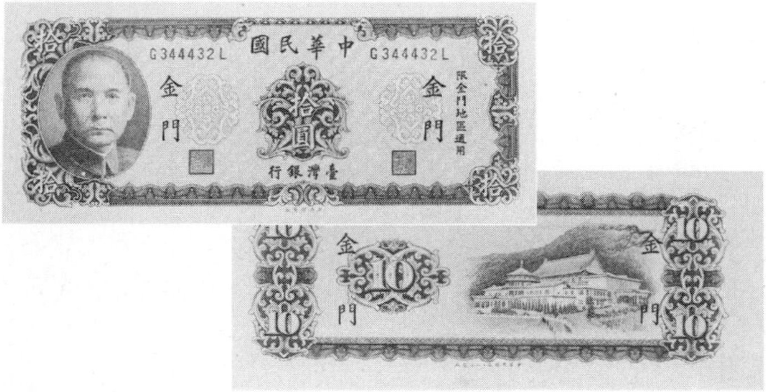

	VG	VF	UNC
R110 10 Yüan 1969 (1975). Red on multicolor underprint. Overprint: Red on #1979a.	1.00	2.00	10.00

	VG	VF	UNC
R111 50 Yüan 1969 (1970). Dark blue on multicolor underprint. SYS at right.	2.00	3.50	25.00

	VG	VF	UNC
R112 100 Yüan 1972 (1975). Overprint: Green on #1983.	4.00	7.50	40.00

1976; 1981 Issue

	VG	VF	UNC
R112A 10 Yüan 1976. Overprint: On #1984.	.25	.75	10.00
R112B 100 Yüan 1981. Overprint: On #1988.	5.00	8.00	30.00
R112C 1000 Yüan 1981. Overprint: On #1988.	35.00	50.00	200.

Matsu Branch

1950-51 Dated (1964; 1967) Issue

	VG	VF	UNC
R113 10 Cents 1950. Specimen. *(S/M #T75-)..* Horizontal format.		—	150.
R114 50 Cents 1950. Green. Specimen. *(S/M #T75-)..* Horizontal format.		—	150.
R115 1 Yüan 1950. Red. Horizontal format.			
a. With imprint. Specimen. *(S/M #T75-).*		—	150.
b. Without imprint. Specimen. *(S/M #T75-).*		—	150.
R116 10 Yüan 1950 (1959). Blue. Printer: FPFT. *(S/M #T75-1).*	7.50	22.50	150.
R117 10 Yüan 1950 (1964). Blue on multicolor underprint. Portrait SYS at upper center. Printer: CPF. Vertical format.	1.00	3.00	25.00

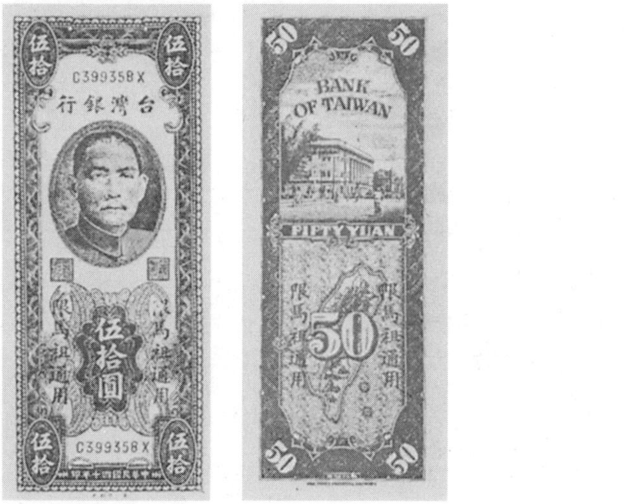

	VG	VF	UNC
R118 50 Yüan 1951 (1967). Green on multicolor underprint. Portrait SYS at upper center. Printer: FPDT. Vertical format.	3.00	8.00	80.00

1969; 1972 Issue

	VG	VF	UNC
R119 1 Yüan 1954 (1959). Brown. Printer: PFBT. *(S/M #T75-20).*	.25	1.00	5.00
R120 1 Yüan 1954. Brown. Printer: CPF. *(S/M #T75-).*	.25	1.00	5.00

ILLUSTRATIONS

Illustrations of bank notes used throughout this catalog are 42% of the actual size.

		VG	VF	UNC
R121	**5 Yüan** 1955 (1959). Dark green. Printer: PFBT. *(S/M #T75-30).*	.75	3.00	15.00

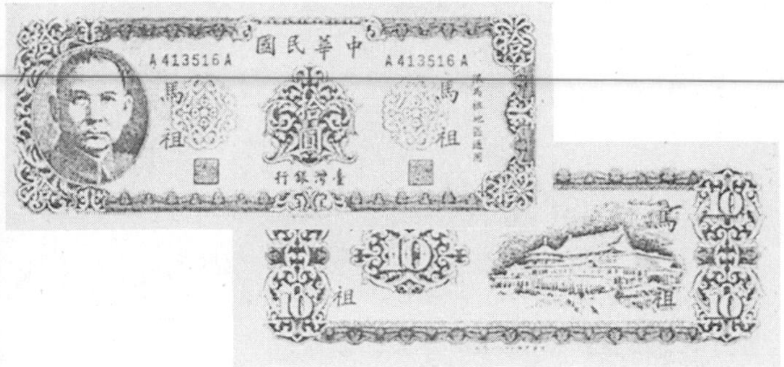

		VG	VF	UNC
R122	**10 Yüan** 1969 (1975). Red on multicolor underprint. Overprint: On #1979a. Printer: CPF.	.50	1.00	10.00

		VG	VF	UNC
R123	**50 Yüan** 1969 (1970). Violet on multicolor underprint. Printer: CPF.	2.00	4.00	30.00
R124	**100 Yüan** 1972 (1975). Dark green, light green and orange on multicolor underprint. Overprint: Green on #1983. Printer: CPF.	4.00	10.00	80.00

1976; 1981 Issue

		VG	VF	UNC
R125	**10 Yüan** 1976. Red on multicolor underprint. Overprint: On #1984.	.40	1.00	8.00
R126	**500 Yüan** 1981. Brown and red-brown on multicolor underprint. Overprint: On #1987.	FV	20.00	80.00
R127	**1000 Yüan** 1981. Blue-black on multicolor underprint. Overprint: On #1988.	FV	37.50	200.

Tachen Branch

1949 Issues

		VG	VF	UNC
R140	**1 Yüan** 1949 (1953). Green. Portrait SYS at upper center. Printer: FPFT. Vertical format. *(S/M #T76-1).*	60.00	160.	500.

1950 Issue

		VG	VF	UNC
R141	**10 Cents** 1950 (1953). Red. Portrait SYS at upper center. Printer: CPF. Vertical format. *(S/M #T76-10).*	110.	325.	750.
R142	**50 Cents** 1950 (1953). Green. Portrait SYS at upper center. Printer: CPF. Vertical format. *(S/M #T76-11).*	110.	325.	750.
R143	**10 Yüan** 1950 (1953). Blue. Portrait SYS at upper center. Printer: FPFT. Vertical format. *(S/M #T76-20).*	90.00	300.	1200.

Japanese Puppet Banks

Central Reserve Bank of China

Chung Yang Ch'u Pei Yin Hang

1940 Issue

		VG	VF	UNC
J1	**1 Fen = 1 Cent** 1940. Red on light brown underprint.			
	a. Imprint and serial #.	1.50	8.00	20.00
	b. Without imprint, With block letters and #.	.50	2.00	5.00
	s1. As a. Specimen with blue overprint: *Yang Pen. Specimen* on back. Uniface pair.	—	—	75.00
	s2. As b. Specimen without overprint: *Yang Pen. Specimen* on back.	—	—	75.00
J2	**5 Fen = 5 Cents** 1940. Green on pale green underprint.			
	a. Imprint and serial #.	1.00	4.00	10.00
	b. Without imprint, With block letters and #.	.25	1.50	4.00
	s1. As a. Specimen with red overprint: *Yang Pen. Specimen* on back. Uniface pair.	—	—	75.00
	s2. As b. Specimen with red overprint: *Yang Pen. Specimen* on back.	—	—	75.00

		VG	VF	UNC
J3	**10 Cents = 1 Chiao** 1940. Green. Back: Multicolor.			
	a. Issued note.	.25	1.50	5.00
	s1. Specimen with red overprint: *Yang Pen. Specimen* on back. Uniface pair.	—	—	75.00
	s2. Specimen with red overprint: *Yang Pen. Specimen* on back.	—	—	75.00

		VG	VF	UNC
J4	**20 Cents = 2 Chiao** 1940. Blue. Back: Multicolor.			
	a. Issued note.	.25	1.25	6.00
	s1. Specimen with red overprint: *Yang Pen. Specimen* on back. Uniface pair.	—	—	60.00
	s2. Specimen with red overprint: *Yang Pen. Specimen* on back.	—	—	60.00

		VG	VF	UNC
J5	**50 Cents = 5 Chiao** 1940. (1941). Red-brown. Back: Multicolor.			
	a. Issued note.	.50	2.50	12.50
	s. Specimen with blue overprint: *Yang Pen.* Red *Specimen* on back.	—	—	75.00

J6	**50 Cents = 5 Chiao**	**VG**	**VF**	**UNC**
	1940. Orange. Back: Multicolor.	1.00	5.00	15.00

J7	**50 Cents = 5 Chiao**	**VG**	**VF**	**UNC**
	1940. Purple. Back: Multicolor.			
	a. Issued note.	.50	3.00	12.50
	s1. Specimen with red overprint: *Yang Pen. Specimen* on back. Uniface pair.	—	—	75.00
	s2. Specimen with red overprint: *Yang Pen. Specimen* on back.	—	—	65.00
J8	**1 Yüan**			
	1940. Green on yellow underprint. Portrait SYS at left, mausoleum of SYS at center. Back: Green with black signature.			
	a. Issued note.	.50	2.50	10.00
	b. Red overprint: *HSING* twice on face and back.	3.00	8.00	20.00
	c. Control overprint: *I (Yi)* twice on face and back.	15.00	40.00	100.
	s. Specimen with red overprint: *Yang Pen. Specimen* on back.	—	—	125.
J9	**1 Yüan**			
	1940. Purple on light blue underprint. Portrait SYS at left, mausoleum of SYS at center. Like #J8. Back: Purple on pink and yellow-green underprint.			
	a. Black signature on back 151 x 79mm. (1.5.1942).	2.00	6.00	18.00
	b. Purple signature Serial # format: LL123456L. 151 x 79mm.	1.00	3.50	12.50
	c. Purple signature Serial # format: L/L 123456L. 146 x 78mm.	1.00	3.50	10.00
	s1. As a. Specimen with red overprint: *Yang Pen. Specimen* on back.	—	—	150.
	s2. As b. Specimen with red overprint: *Yang Pen. Specimen* on back.	—	—	150.

J10	**5 Yüan**	**VG**	**VF**	**UNC**
	1940. Red. Portrait SYS at center. Back: Red. Mausoleum at center.			
	a. Face with yellow and blue-green underprint. Serial # on face and back. Black signature (6.1.1941).	5.00	15.00	45.00
	b. As a. Black control overprint on face and back.	10.00	35.00	100.
	c. Face with pink and blue underprint. Serial # on face only. Black signature (19.12.1941).	1.50	4.00	10.00
	d. As c. Black control overprint on face and back.	3.00	10.00	30.00
	e. As c. Red signature	.25	1.50	4.00
	f. As e. Red overprint: *Wuhan* over seals on face.	3.00	10.00	30.00
	g. As e. Black overprint: *Kwangtung* horizontally on lower corners of face.	3.00	10.00	30.00
	h. Without serial #; black signature	—	—	75.00
	s1. As a. Specimen.	—	—	125.
	s2. As c. Specimen with blue overprint: *Yang Pen. Specimen* on back.	—	—	125.
	s3. As c. Specimen with red overprint: *Mi-hon.*	—	—	125.

Note: Many are of the opinion that overprint: *Wuhan* and *Kwangtung* on #J10 are fantasies.

J11	**5 Yüan**	**Good**	**Fine**	**XF**
	1940. Red with repeated gold Chinese 4 character underprint. Proof.	—	Unc	300.

J12	**10 Yüan**	**VG**	**VF**	**UNC**
	1940. Blue on blue-green and light brown underprint. Portrait SYS at center. Similar to #J10. Back: Blue. Mausoleum at center.			
	a. Bright blue face and back. Serial # on face and back. Black signature (6.1.1941).	12.50	37.50	150.
	b. As a. Red control overprint on face and back.	37.50	150.	—
	c. Dark blue face and back. Serial # on face only, black signature	1.00	4.00	10.00
	d. As c. Red control overprint on face and back.	5.00	20.00	60.00
	e. As c. Black overprint: *Kwangtung* vertically at left and right.	2.50	7.50	25.00
	f. As e. Smaller blue overprint: *Kwangtung.*	2.50	7.50	25.00
	g. As c. Light blue overprint: *Wuhan* over red seals on face.	2.50	7.50	25.00
	h. Color similar to c. Serial # on face only, blue signature (19.12.1941).	.50	1.50	4.00
	i. As h. Overprint: *Wuhan* over signature seals at lower left and right. (as g.).	2.50	7.50	25.00
	j. As h. Overprint: *Wuhan* vertically at sides on face.	2.50	7.50	25.00
	k. As h. Black overprint: *Kwangtung* at left and right. (as e.).	2.50	7.50	25.00
	l. As h. Blue overprint: *Kwangtung* at left and right in different style of type.	2.50	7.50	25.00
	s1. As a. Specimen with red overprint: *Yang Pen. Specimen* on back.	—	—	150.
	s2. As c. Specimen with red overprint: *Yang Pen. Specimen* on back.	—	—	125.
	s3. As c. Specimen with red overprint: *Mi-hon.* Regular serial #.	—	—	100.
	s4. As h. Specimen with red overprint: *Yang Pen. Specimen* on back.	—	—	125.
	s5. As h. Specimen with red overprint: *Mi-hon.* Regular serial #.	—	—	100.

Note: Many are of the opinion that ovpt: *Wuhan* and *Kwangtung* on #J10 are fantasies.

1942 Issue

#J13 *Deleted.* See #J12.

J14	**100 Yüan**	**VG**	**VF**	**UNC**
	1942. Dark green on multicolor underprint. Portrait SYS at center. Back: SYS Mausoleum at center.			
	a. Blue signature	1.50	7.50	20.00
	b. Black signature (17.6.1942).	10.00	32.50	100.
	s. As b. Specimen with red overprint: *Yang Pen. Specimen* on back.	—	—	150.

J15 **500 Yüan**	VG	VF	UNC
1942. Brown on multicolor underprint. Portrait SYS at left. *Kwangtung* at lower left and right. Back: SYS Mausoleum at right on back.			
a. Watermark: *500 Yuan.*	3.00	15.00	50.00
b. Without watermark.	3.00	10.00	30.00
s. Specimen with red overprint: *Yang Pen. Specimen* on back. Without *Kwangtung.*	—	—	150.

1943 Issues

J16 **10 Cents = 1 Chiao**	VG	VF	UNC
1943. Green. SYS Mausoleum at center. Without imprint, with block #.			
a. Issued note.	1.00	5.00	10.00
s. Specimen with red overprint: *Yang Pen.* Uniface pair.	—	—	70.00
J17 **20 Cents = 2 Chiao**			
1943. Blue. SYS Mausoleum at center. Without imprint, with block #.			
a. Issued note.	1.00	5.00	10.00
s. Specimen with red overprint: *Yang Pen.* Uniface pair.	—	—	70.00

J18 **50 Cents = 5 Chiao**	VG	VF	UNC
1943. Red-brown. SYS Mausoleum at center.			
a. Without imprint, With block #.	1.00	4.00	10.00
b. Without imprint, With block letter and #.	1.25	5.00	15.00
s. As a. Specimen with blue overprint: *Yang Pen.* Uniface pair.	—	—	80.00

J19 **1 Yüan**	VG	VF	UNC
1943. Green on light blue underprint. Portrait SYS at center. Back: SYS Mausoleum at center.			
a. Issued note.	1.00	4.00	10.00
s. Specimen with red overprint: *Yang Pen.*	—	—	125.

J20 **10 Yüan**	VG	VF	UNC
1943. Brown on multicolor underprint. Portrait SYS at left. Back: SYS Mausoleum at center.			
a. Issued note.	2.00	8.00	20.00
b. Overprint: *Kwangtung.* vertically at left and right.	3.00	10.00	35.00
s. As a. Specimen with red overprint: *Yang Pen.*	—	—	125.

#J21-J28 portr. SYS at ctr. SYS Mausoleum at ctr. on back.

J21 **100 Yüan**	Good	Fine	XF
1943. Dark olive-green on multicolor underprint. Portrait SYS at center. Back: Light green-dark green. SYS Mausoleum at center. With serial #.			
a. Issued note.	1.00	4.00	10.00
b. Red overprint: *Wuhan.*	3.00	15.00	35.00

#J22 Deleted. See #J21.

J23 **100 Yüan**			
1943 (1944). Blue on multicolor underprint. Portrait SYS at center. Back: Green. SYS Mausoleum at center. With block letters.			
a. Watermark: Clouds.	.50	2.50	8.00
b. Without watermark.	.50	2.50	8.00
s. Specimen overprint: *Yang Pen.*	—	—	125.

J24 **500 Yüan**	VG	VF	UNC
1943 (1944). Brown on multicolor underprint. Portrait SYS at center. Block letters. Back: SYS Mausoleum at center.			
a. Watermark: *500* in Chinese characters.	3.25	10.00	30.00
b. Without watermark.	1.00	4.00	12.50
c. Red overprint: *Kwangtung.*	2.50	7.50	25.00
d. Red overprint: *Wuhan* vertically at left and right.	2.50	7.50	25.00
s1. Specimen with red overprint: *Yang Pen. Specimen* on back.	—	—	125.
s2. Specimen with red overprint: *Mi-hon.*	—	—	125.
s3. As d. Specimen with red overprint: *Yang Pen. Specimen* on back.	—	—	125.
J24A **500 Yüan**			
1943 (1944). Dark brown on multicolor underprint. Portrait SYS at center. Serial #. Back: Dark brown. SYS Mausoleum at center.			
a. Issued note.	5.00	20.00	60.00
s. Specimen with red overprint: *Yang Pen. Specimen* on back.	—	—	125.

J25 500 Yüan

1943 (1944). Deep purple-brownish purple on multicolor underprint. Guilloche in the underprint. Portrait SYS at center. Serial #. Back: Violet, lithographed. SYS Mausoleum at center.

	VG	VF	UNC
a. Watermark: *500* in Chinese characters.	5.00	25.00	55.00
b. Watermark: Cloud forms.	4.00	18.00	40.00
c. Without watermark.	3.00	15.00	30.00
s1. Specimen with red overprint: *Yang Pen. Specimen* on back.	—	—	125.
s2. Specimen with red overprint: *Mi-hon.*	—	—	125.

J26 500 Yüan

1943 (1944). Pale purple on pink underprint. Portrait SYS at center. Like #J25. Back: SYS Mausoleum at center. With plate varieties. Watermark: Cloud form.

	VG	VF	UNC
a. Issued note.	3.50	15.00	35.00
s. Specimen with red overprint: *Yang Pen. Specimen* on back.	—	—	140.

J27 500 Yüan

1943 (1945). Brown on light brown underprint. Brown guilloche. Portrait SYS at center. Block letters. Back: SYS Mausoleum at center.

	VG	VF	UNC
a. Issued note.	2.50	15.00	30.00
s. Specimen with red overprint: *Yang Pen. Specimen* on back.	—	—	125.

J28 500 Yüan

1943. Brown on lilac. Multicolor guilloche. Portrait SYS at center. Block letters. Back: SYS Mausoleum at center.

	VG	VF	UNC
a. Watermark: Cloud forms.	3.00	15.00	30.00
b. Without watermark.	2.50	10.00	25.00
s. Specimen with red overprint: *Yang Pen. Specimen* on back.	—	—	125.

1944 Issues

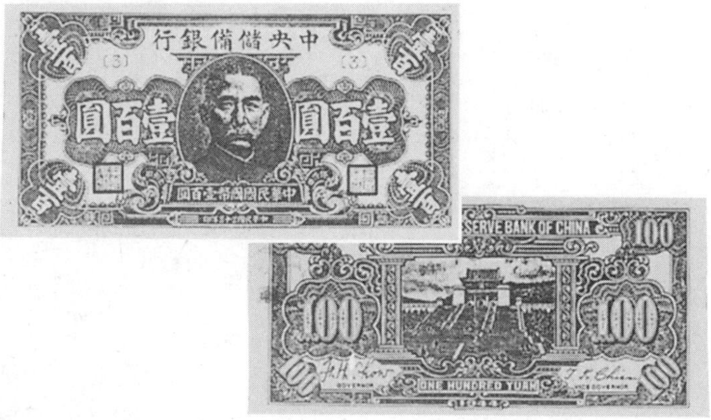

J29 100 Yüan

1944 (1945). Blue on pale green underprint. Portrait SYS at center. Back: Blue. SYS Mausoleum at center. Watermark: Cloud forms.

	VG	VF	UNC
a. Issued note.	3.00	15.00	40.00
s. Specimen with red overprint: *Yang Pen. Specimen* on back.	—	—	125.

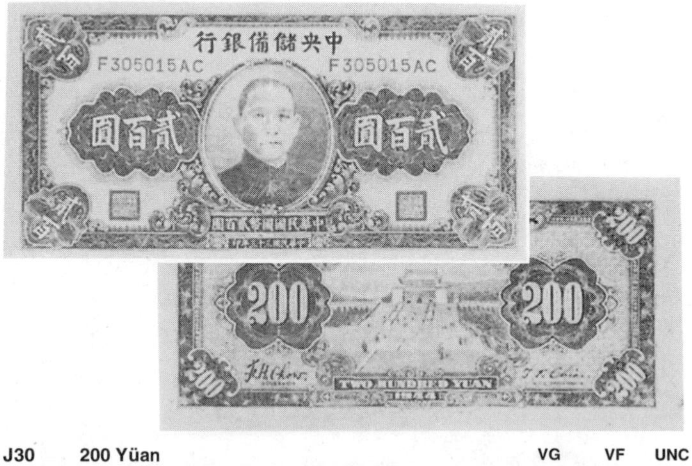

J30 200 Yüan

1944. Red-brown on pink underprint. Portrait SYS at center. Back: Red-brown. SYS Mausoleum at center. Watermark: Cloud forms.

	VG	VF	UNC
a. Issued note.	2.00	10.00	20.00
s. Specimen overprint: *Yang Pen. Specimen* on back.	—	—	125.

Note: #J30 has letters *USAC* hidden in frame design.

J31 1000 Yüan

1944 (1945). Dark blue on multicolor underprint. Portrait SYS at center. Serial #. Back: Deep blue-gray on multicolor underprint. SYS Mausoleum at center. Watermark: Cloud forms.

	VG	VF	UNC
a. Issued note.	5.00	20.00	60.00
s. Specimen with red overprint: *Yang Pen. Specimen* on back.	—	—	125.

J32 1000 Yüan

1944 (1945). Deep gray-blue on multicolor underprint. Portrait SYS at center. Block letters. Back: SYS Mausoleum at center. Watermark: Cloud forms.

	VG	VF	UNC
a. Watermark: Cloud forms.	1.50	7.50	15.00
b. Without watermark.	1.00	5.00	10.00
c. Red overprint: *Wuhan.*	3.00	10.00	35.00
s. Specimen with red overprint: *Yang Pen. Specimen* on back.	—	—	125.

J33 1000 Yüan

1944 (1945). Deep gray-blue on ochre underprint. Portrait SYS at center. Block letters. Back: SYS Mausoleum at center. Watermark: Cloud forms.

	VG	VF	UNC
a. Issued note.	1.50	7.50	15.00
s. Specimen with red overprint: *Yang Pen. Specimen* on back.	—	—	125.

J34 1000 Yüan

1944 (1945). Gray. Portrait SYS at center. Block letters. Back: SYS Mausoleum at center. Watermark: Cloud forms.

	VG	VF	UNC
a. Issued note.	5.00	20.00	80.00
s. Specimen with red overprint: *Yang Pen. Specimen* on back.	—	—	125.

J35 1000 Yüan

1944 (1945). Green on light blue underprint. Portrait SYS at center. Block #. Back: Green. SYS Mausoleum at center. Watermark: Cloud forms.

	VG	VF	UNC
a. Issued note.	15.00	70.00	140.
s1. Specimen with red overprint: *Yang Pen. Specimen* on back.	—	—	125.
s2. As s1. Without *Specimen* on back.	—	—	100.
s3. Specimen with red overprint: *Mi-hon.*	—	—	100.

J36 10,000 Yüan

1944 (1945). Dark brown on pink underprint. Portrait SYS at center. Serial #. Back: SYS Mausoleum at center. Watermark: Cloud forms.

	VG	VF	UNC
a. Watermark: Cloud forms.	20.00	100.	250.
s. Specimen with red overprint: *Yang Pen. Specimen* on back.	—	—	125.

J37 10,000 Yüan

1944 (1945). Dark green on tan or pale yellow-brown underprint. Portrait SYS at center. Serial #. Back: SYS Mausoleum at center. With vignette varieties. Watermark: Cloud forms.

	VG	VF	UNC
a. Back with pink sky in center.	10.00	70.00	150.
b. Back with green sky in center.	15.00	100.	200.
s1. Specimen with red overprint: *Yang Pen. Specimen* on back.	—	—	210.
s2. Specimen with red overprint: *Mi-hon.*	—	—	250.

J38 10,000 Yüan

1944 (1945). Green on pale yellow-brown underprint. Portrait SYS at center. Block letters. Back: SYS Mausoleum at center. Watermark: Cloud forms.

	VG	VF	UNC
a. Issued note.	10.00	70.00	150.
s. Specimen with red overprint: *Yang Pen. Specimen* on back.	—	—	220.

J39 10,000 Yüan

1944 (1945). Green on pale yellow-brown underprint. Portrait SYS at center. Block letters. Back: SYS Mausoleum at center. Watermark: Cloud forms.

	VG	VF	UNC
a. Issued note.	10.00	70.00	150.
s. Specimen with red overprint: *Yang Pen. Specimen* on back.	—	—	250.

1945 Issues

J40 5000 Yüan

1945. Gray-green on pale green underprint. Portrait SYS at center. Serial #. Back: Gray-green. SYS Mausoleum at center.

	VG	VF	UNC
a. Printer: CRBCPW.	7.50	40.00	80.00
b. Without imprint.	10.00	50.00	100.
s. As a. Specimen with red overprint: *Yang Pen. Specimen* on back.	—	—	125.

J41 5000 Yüan

1945. Dark gray-green on pale green underprint. Portrait SYS at center. Block letters. Like #J40. Back: SYS Mausoleum at center.

	VG	VF	UNC
a. Issued note.	7.50	35.00	75.00
s. Specimen with red overprint: *Yang Pen. Specimen* on back.	—	—	125.

J42 5000 Yüan

1945. Black. Portrait SYS at center. Block letters. Back: Dark gray. SYS Mausoleum at center.

	VG	VF	UNC
a. Issued note.	12.50	60.00	120.
s. Specimen with red overprint: *Yang Pen. Specimen* on back.	—	—	140.

J43 100,000 Yüan

1945. Red-violet on pale green underprint. Portrait SYS at center. Serial #. Back: SYS Mausoleum at center.

	VG	VF	UNC
a. Issued note.	100.	500.	1100.
s. Specimen with overprint: *Mi-hon.*	—	—	300.

J44 100,000 Yüan

1945. Purple on yellow-brown underprint. Portrait SYS at center. Back: SYS Mausoleum at center.

	VG	VF	UNC
a. Block letters.	125.	400.	1250.
r. Remainder without block letters or signature seals. Back purple to red-violet.	50.00	150.	450.

Federal Reserve Bank of China

Chung Kuo Lien Ho Chun Pei Yin Hang

1938 First Issue

J45 1/2 Fen

1938. Light blue on yellow underprint. Seventeen arch bridge at summer palace at center. *(S/M #C286-1).*

	VG	VF	UNC
a. Issued note.	3.50	10.00	35.00
s. Specimen with overprint: *Yang Pen. Specimen* on back. Uniface pair.	—	—	60.00

J46 1 Fen

1938. Light brown on pale green underprint. Seventeen arch bridge at summer palace at center. *(S/M #C286-2).*

	VG	VF	UNC
a. Issued note.	1.50	7.00	15.00
s. Specimen with overprint: *Yang Pen. Specimen* on back. Uniface pair.	—	—	75.00

J47 5 Fen

1938; 1939. Red on pink underprint. Seventeen arch bridge at summer palace at center.

	VG	VF	UNC
a. 1938. *(S/M #C286-3).*	1.00	4.00	10.00
b. 1939. *(S/M #C286-30).*	.50	2.00	5.00
s. As a. Specimen with red overprint: *Yang Pen* on face. Blue overprint on back. Uniface pair.	—	—	60.00

J48 10 Fen = 1 Chiao

1938; 1940. Red-brown on pink underprint. Tower of summer palace at right.

	VG	VF	UNC
a. 1938. *(S/M #C286-4).*	.50	2.00	5.00
b. 1940. *(S/M #C286-31).*	1.00	4.00	10.00
s. As a. Specimen with red overprint: *Yang Pen* on face and back. Uniface pair.	—	—	75.00

J49	**20 Fen = 2 Chiao**	**VG**	**VF**	**UNC**
	1938; 1940. Blue on pale blue underprint. Temple of Heaven at right.			
	a. 1938. *(S/M #C286-5).*	.75	2.50	8.00
	b. 1940. *(S/M #C286-32).*	1.00	3.25	10.00
	s. As a. Specimen with red overprint: *Yang Pen* on face and back. Uniface pair.	—	—	70.00

J50	**50 Fen = 5 Chiao**	**VG**	**VF**	**UNC**
	ND (1938). Orange on pale green underprint. Marco Polo bridge at center. *(S/M #C286-60).*			
	a. Issued note.	3.50	10.00	35.00
	s. Specimen with overprint: *Yang Pen. Specimen* on back.	—	—	120.

1938 Second Issue

J51	**10 Cents = 1 Chiao**	**VG**	**VF**	**UNC**
	1938. Brown-violet. Dragon at right. Printer: BEPP. *(S/M #C286-5).*			
	a. Issued note.	15.00	40.00	100.
	s. Specimen with red overprint: *Yang Pen. Specimen* on back. Uniface pair.	—	—	100.

J52	**20 Cents = 2 Chiao**	**VG**	**VF**	**UNC**
	1938. Green. Dragon at right. Printer: BEPP. *(S/M #C286-7).*			
	a. Issued note.	15.00	75.00	150.
	s. Specimen with overprint: *Yang Pen. Specimen* on back. Uniface pair.	—	—	110.

J53	**50 Cents = 5 Chiao**	**VG**	**VF**	**UNC**
	1938. Orange. Dragon at right. Printer: BEPP. *(S/M #C286-8).*			
	a. Issued note.	20.00	100.	200.
	s. Specimen with overprint: *Yang Pen. Specimen* on back. Uniface pair.	—	—	100.

J54	**1 Dollar**	**VG**	**VF**	**UNC**
	1938. Green. Portrait Confucius at left, junks at lower center right, dragon above. *(S/M #C286-10).*			
	a. Issued note.	15.00	70.00	140.
	s. Specimen with overprint: *Yang Pen. Specimen* on back.	—	—	200.

J55	**1 Dollar**	**VG**	**VF**	**UNC**
	1938. Green. Portrait Confucius at left, junks at lower center right, dragon above. Like #J54 but poor printing. *(S/M #C286-11).*	12.50	40.00	120.

Note: Doubtful whether war printing or forgery.

J56	**5 Dollars**	**VG**	**VF**	**UNC**
	1938. Orange. Portrait Yüeh Fei at left, horseback patrol at lower right, dragon above. *(S/M #C286-13).*			
	a. Issued note.	85.00	250.	750.
	s. Specimen with overprint: *Yang Pen. Specimen* on back.	—	—	350.

J57 10 Dollars

	VG	VF	UNC
1938. Blue. Portrait Kuan-yü at left, Great Wall at lower right, dragon above. *(S/M #C286-15).*			
a. Issued note.	85.00	250.	750.
s. Specimen with overprint: *Yang Pen. Specimen* on back.	—	—	350.

J58 100 Dollars

	VG	VF	UNC
1938. Purple. Portrait Huang Ti at left, farm laborer at lower right, dragon above. *(S/M #C286-20).*			
a. Issued note.	200.	700.	2000.
s. Specimen with overprint: *Yang Pen. Specimen* on back.	—	—	800.

J59 100 Yüan

	VG	VF	UNC
1938 (1944). Brown. Great Wall at center, dragon above, portrait Huang Ti at right. Like #J63. Back: Plain pattern. Outer frame has color varieties. *(S/M #C286-22).*	6.50	30.00	90.00

1938 (1939) Issue

#J60 *Deleted.*

J61 1 Yüan

	VG	VF	UNC
1938 (1939). Yellow-green. Boats at center, dragon above, portrait Confucius at right. Back: Pagoda at center. *(S/M #C286-12).*			
a. Issued note.	3.00	15.00	30.00
s. Specimen with red overprint: *Yang Pen. Specimen* on back. Uniface pair.	—	—	125.

J62 5 Yüan

	VG	VF	UNC
1938 (1939). Orange. Horseback patrol at center, dragon above, portrait Yüeh Fei at right. Engraved. *(S/M #C286-14).*			
a. Issued note.	4.00	20.00	40.00
s. Specimen with red overprint: *Yang Pen. Specimen* on back. Uniface pair.	—	—	125.
x. Lithograph counterfeit. Block #4.	—	—	25.00

J63 10 Yüan

	VG	VF	UNC
1938 (1939). Blue. Great Wall at center, dragon above, portrait Huang Ti at right. Paper with many or few fibers. *(S/M #C286-16).*			
a. Issued note.	7.00	30.00	70.00
s. Specimen with red overprint: *Yang Pen. Specimen* on back. Uniface pair.	—	—	125.

J64 100 Yüan

	VG	VF	UNC
1938 (1939). Purple. Ships along shoreline at left, farm laborers at right center, with dragon above, portrait Huang Ti at right. Back: Pagoda at center. *(S/M #C286-21).*			
a. Issued note.	40.00	225.	400.
s. Specimen with red overprint: *Yang Pen. Specimen* on back. Uniface pair.	—	—	150.

#J65 *Deleted.* See #J47.

#J66 *Deleted.* See #J48.

1944 Issue

#J67 *Deleted.* See #J49.

J68 50 Fen = 5 Chiao

	VG	VF	UNC
1944. Violet on ochre and violet underprint. Temple of the clouds at left. *(S/M #C286-40).*			
a. Issued note.	1.00	3.00	10.00
s. Specimen perforated: *Yang Pen.* Uniface pair.	—	—	75.00

J69 1 Yüan

1944. Dark gray on dark olive-green or olive-brown (shades) underprint. Partial view of temple, Confucius at right. *(S/M #C286-50).*

	VG	VF	UNC
a. Issued note.	1.25	4.00	10.00
s. Specimen perforated: *Yang Pen.* Uniface pair.	—	—	75.00

1941 ND Issue

#J70 Deleted. See #J50.

#J71 Deleted. See #J73.

J72 1 Yüan

ND (1941). Gray-green on green and pink overprint. Partial view of temple at left, Confucius at right. *(S/M #C286-70).*

	VG	VF	UNC
a. Issued note.	1.50	5.00	15.00
s. Specimen with red overprint and perforated: *Yang Pen. Specimen* on back.	—	—	100.

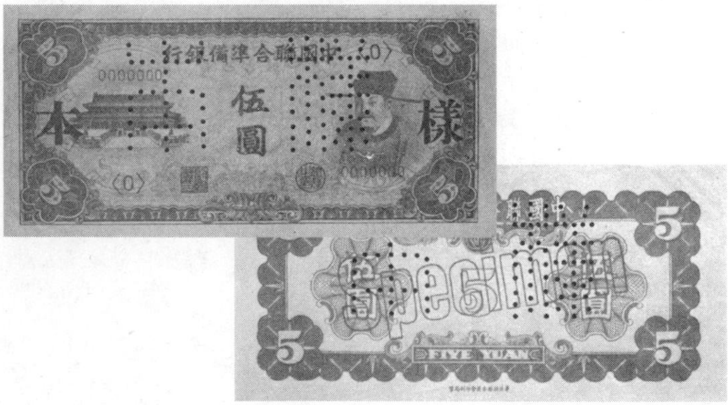

J73 5 Yüan

ND (1941). Orange on multicolor underprint. Temple at left, Yüeh Fei at right. *(S/M #C286-71).*

	VG	VF	UNC
a. Issued note.	3.00	12.50	30.00
s. Specimen with overprint and perforated: *Yang Pen. Specimen* on back. Uniface pair.	—	—	100.

J74 10 Yüan

ND (1941). Blue on multicolor underprint. Wu Ying Hall at left, man with cap at right. *(S/M #C286-74).*

	VG	VF	UNC
a. Issued note.	2.50	10.00	25.00
s. Specimen with red overprint and perforated: *Yang Pen. Specimen* on back.	—	—	120.

J75 100 Yüan

ND (1941). Brown on green and purple underprint. House with stairs at left, Huang Ti at right. Chinese printer. *(S/M #C286-84).*

	VG	VF	UNC
a. Issued note.	8.00	30.00	95.00
s. Specimen with red overprint and perforated: *Yang Pen. Specimen* on back.	—	—	175.

1943 ND Issue

J76 10 Yüan

ND (1943). Dark blue-gray on green and brown underprint. Kuan Yü at left. Jade Peak Pagoda at right. *S/M #C286-73).*

	VG	VF	UNC
a. Issued note.	5.00	20.00	50.00
s. Specimen perforated: *Yang Pen.* Uniface pair.	—	—	140.

J77 100 Yüan

ND (1943). Brown on multicolor underprint. Huang Ti at left. Temple near mountainside at right. *(S/M #C286-83).*

	VG	VF	UNC
a. Issued note.	5.00	20.00	50.00
s. Specimen with overprint and perforated *Yang Pen. Yang Pen on back. Uniface pair.*	—	—	125.

J78 500 Yüan	VG	VF	UNC
ND (1943). Brownish black on pale green and olive underprint. Temple of Heaven at left. Confucius at right. Onagadori cocks underprint at left and at right of vertical denomination at center. Block letters and serial #. Back: *500* once. *(S/M #C286-90).*			
a. Back frame brown. Imprint 26mm.	10.00	35.00	85.00
b. Back frame brown. Imprint 29mm.	5.00	20.00	50.00
s. Back frame red-brown. Imprint 24mm. Specimen perforated: *Yang Pen*. Uniface pair.	—	—	125.

1944 ND Issue

J79 5 Yüan	VG	VF	UNC
ND (1944). Brown on yellow underprint. Small house at left, Yüeh Fei with book at right. *(S/M #C286-72).*			
a. Black on yellow underprint. Seal 8mm high at left. Watermark: Clouds and *FRB* logo.	2.00	7.50	20.00
b. Watermark: *FRB* logo.	2.00	7.50	20.00
c. Dark brown on light brown underprint. Seal 7mm high at left. Without watermark.	3.00	10.00	27.50
s. Specimen perforated: *Yang Pen*. Uniface pair.	—	—	125.

J80 10 Yüan	VG	VF	UNC
ND (1944). Blue on light brown underprint. Kuan-yü at left, wall of house with tree and rock at right. Back: *10 YUAN* at bottom center. *(S/M #C286-75).*			
a. Issued note.	2.00	7.50	20.00
s1. Specimen with red overprint: *Yang Pen*. *Yang Pen* on back. Uniface pair.	—	—	125.
s2. Specimen perforated: *Yang Pen*. Uniface pair.	—	—	125.

J81 10 Yüan	VG	VF	UNC
ND (1944). Purple on multicolor underprint. Man with mustache at right. *(S/M #C286-80).*			
a. Issued note.	3.00	15.00	40.00
s. Specimen with red overprint and perforated: *Yang Pen*.	—	—	125.

J82 10 Yüan	VG	VF	UNC
ND (1944). Blue on multicolor underprint. Man with mustache at right. Similar to #J81. *(S/M #C286-81).*			
a. Issued note.	4.00	15.00	40.00
s1. Specimen with red overprint and perforated: *Yang Pen*.	—	—	125.
s2. Specimen with red overprint: *Mi-hon*.	—	—	100.

J83 100 Yüan	VG	VF	UNC
ND (1944). Dark brown on green-blue and violet. House with stairs at left, Huang Ti at right. Back: Brown and violet. Without imprint. *(S/M #C286-85).*			
a. Issued note.	6.00	20.00	60.00
b. Horizontal quadrille paper.	6.00	20.00	60.00
s1. Specimen with red overprint and perforated: *Yang Pen*.	—	—	150.
s2. Specimen with red overprint: *Mi-hon*.	—	—	150.

J84 500 Yüan	VG	VF	UNC
ND (1944). Dark green on tan and purple underprint. Temple of Heaven at left, Confucius at right. Underprint with Onagadori cock above guilloche at center. Back: Brown on yellow-brown underprint. *500* five times. *(S/M #C286-91).*			
a. Horizontal quadrille paper.	15.00	45.00	140.
b. Non-quadrille paper.	15.00	45.00	140.
s1. Specimen with red overprint and perforated: *Yang Pen*. Uniface pair.	—	—	125.
s2. Specimen with red overprint: *Mi-hon*.	—	—	150.
J84A 500 Yüan			
ND (1944). Blue on light blue-green and yellow-brown underprint. Temple of Heaven at left. Like #J89 but lithographed. Block #1. Back: Brown on yellow underprint. Overprint: Red *Mi-hon*. Specimen.	—	—	200.

1945 ND Issue

J85 1 Yüan	VG	VF	UNC
ND (1945). Dark brown on light orange-brown underprint. Bridge and pavilion at left, numeral at right. (Not issued). *(S/M #C286-65).*			
a. Block #.	—	200.	500.
s. Specimen perforated: *Yang Pen*. Uniface pair.	—	—	500.

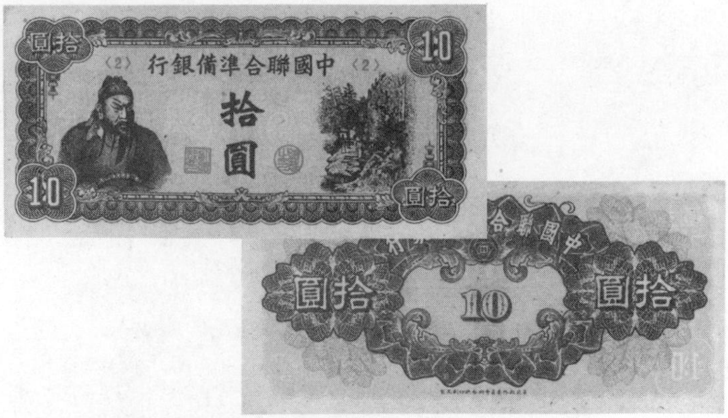

J86 10 Yüan	VG	VF	UNC
ND (1945). Violet on light brown underprint. Kuan-yü at left, wall of house with tree and rock at right. Back: Without *10 YUAN*.			
a. Chinese printer (11 characters). *(S/M #C286-77).*	2.00	7.50	20.00
b. Chinese printer (14 characters). *(S/M #C286-76).*	2.00	7.50	20.00
s. As b. Specimen perforated: *Yang Pen.*	—	—	125.

J87 50 Yüan	VG	VF	UNC
ND (1945). Violet-brown. Man with beard at left. *(S/M #C286-82).*			
a. Watermark. *FRB* logo and clouds. Block #1.	10.00	50.00	110.
b. Without watermark. Block #2.	10.00	25.00	100.
s. As a. Specimen perforated: *Yang Pen.* Uniface pair.	—	—	150.

J88 100 Yüan	VG	VF	UNC
ND (1945). Brown to red-brown. Imperial Resting Quarters near mountainside at at left, Huang Ti at right. Back: Red-brown. *S/M #C286-86).*			
a. Issued note.	2.50	10.00	25.00
s. Specimen perforated: *Yang Pen.* Uniface pair.	—	—	125.

J88A 100 Yüan	VG	VF	UNC
ND (1945). Gray and red-brown. Imperial Resting Quarters near mountainside at at left, Huang Ti at right. Like #J88. Block #16. Back: Brown.	6.00	20.00	60.00

J89 500 Yüan	VG	VF	UNC
ND (1945). Blue on light blue-green and yellow-brown underprint. Temple of Heaven at left. Watermark: *FRB* logo and clouds. *(S/M #C286-92).*			
a. Issued note.	10.00	60.00	150.
s. Specimen perforated: *Yang Pen.* Uniface pair.	—	—	150.

J90 500 Yüan	VG	VF	UNC
ND (1945). Blue-gray on orange-yellow to salmon underprint. Man with beard at left. Like #J87. *(S/M #C286-93).*	5.00	20.00	50.00

J91 1000 Yüan	VG	VF	UNC
ND (1945). Dark green. Great Wall at center right. Back: Ch'ien Men fortress at center. *(S/M #C286-94).*			
a. Engraved, with serial # and block #1-3. Watermark: *1* in oval, ovals horizontal.	10.00	50.00	100.
b. Engraved, with serial # and block #1-3. Watermark: *1* in oval, ovals vertical.	10.00	50.00	100.
c. Watermark: *FRB* logo repeated.	15.00	75.00	150.
r. Remainder, without serial #, block #, or signature seals.	—	—	100.
s. As b. Specimen perforated: *Yang Pen.* Uniface pair.	—	—	150.

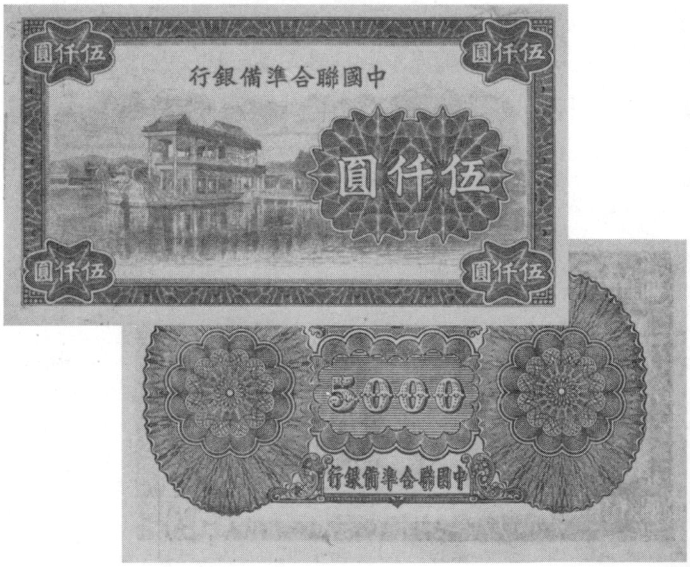

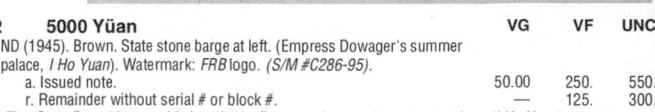

J92 5000 Yüan	VG	VF	UNC
ND (1945). Brown. State stone barge at left. (Empress Dowager's summer palace, *I Ho Yuan*). Watermark: *FRB* logo. *(S/M #C286-95).*			
a. Issued note.	50.00	250.	550.
r. Remainder without serial # or block #.	—	125.	300.

Note: The "State Barge" is a marble boat in the Empress dowager's summer palace *(I Ho Yuan)*, a most unseaworthy craft.

Hua-Hsing Commercial Bank

Hua Hsing Shang Yeh Yin Hang

1938 Issues

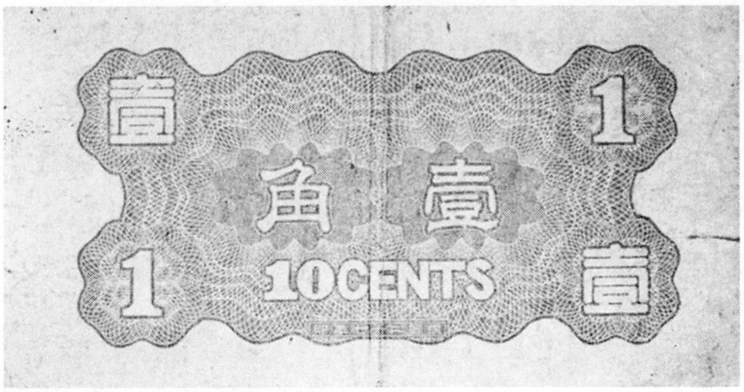

J93 10 Cents = 1 Chiao	VG	VF	UNC
1938. Green on pink and light blue underprint. Junks at left. *S/M #H184-1).*			
a. Issued note.	100.	275.	675.
s. Specimen with overprint: *Yang Pen. Specimen* on back.	—	—	675.

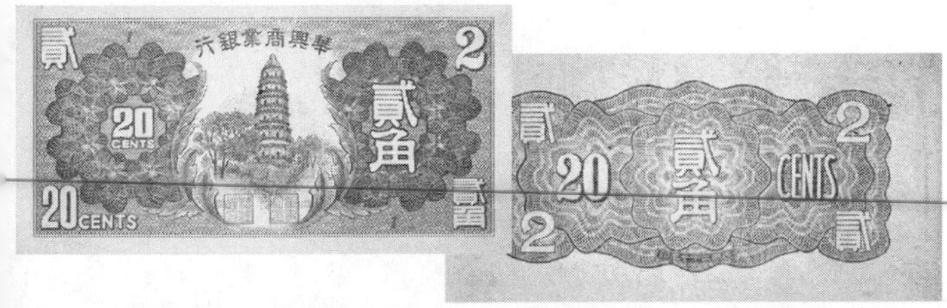

J94 20 Cents = 2 Chiao	VG	VF	UNC
1938. Brown. Pagoda at center. Back: Light blue. *(S/M #H184.2).*			
a. Issued note.	65.00	225.	550.
s. Specimen with overprint: *Yang Pen. Specimen* on back.	—	—	500.

J95 *Deleted.*

J96 1 Yüan	VG	VF	UNC
1938. Green on yellow and gray underprint. Trees along roadway at left center. *(S/M #H184-10).*			
a. Issued note.	180.	500.	1200.
s. Specimen with overprint: *Yang Pen. Specimen* on back.	—	—	600.
J97 5 Yüan			
ND (1938). Blue on multicolor underprint. Liu Ho Pagoda at left, Yüeh Fei at right. *(S/M #184H-11).*			
a. Issued note. Rare.	—	—	—
s. Specimen with overprint: *Yang Pen. Specimen* on back.	—	—	1250.

J98 5 Yüan	VG	VF	UNC
1938. Dark green and black on ochre and gray. House, arch, bridge, and pagoda at center. *(S/M #H184-12).*			
a. Black overprint signature of bank president Ch'en Chin Tao on back.	—	—	550.
s. Specimen with overprint: *Yang Pen* on face and back.	—	—	500.
J99 10 Yüan			
ND (1938). Black on multicolor underprint. Ta Ch'eng Tien building at left. Confucius at right. *(S/M #H184-13).*			
a. Issued note. (Sea salvaged).	1500.	—	—
s. Specimen with overprint: *Yang Pen* on face and back.	—	—	1800.

J100 10 Yüan	VG	VF	UNC
1938. Brown-orange and black on ochre and light green underprint. Temple at center. *(S/M #H184-14).*			
a. Issued note.	180.	425.	725.
r. Remainder without signature	—	—	550.
s. Specimen with overprint: *Yang Pen* on face and back.	—	—	550.

Mengchiang Bank

Meng Chiang Yin Hang

1938-45 ND Issues

J101 5 Fen	VG	VF	UNC
ND (1940). Gray. Herd of sheep at center. Back: Brown-orange. *(S/M #M11-1).*			
a. Issued note.	125.	3.00	12.50
s. Specimen with overprint: *Yang Pen.* on face and back.	—	—	75.00

J101A 1 Chiao	VG	VF	UNC
ND (1940). Brown and black on light blue underprint. Herd of camels at center. Back: Blue-gray. *(S/M #M11-2).*			
a. Issued note.	2.00	6.00	20.00
s. Specimen with red overprint: *Yang Pen* on face and back.	—	—	60.00

J102 5 Chiao	VG	VF	UNC
ND (1944). Black on yellow-brown underprint. Temple courtyard. Back: Green. *(S/M #M11-4).*			
a. Issued note.	40.00	125.	375.
s. Specimen with red-orange overprint: *Mi-hon.*	—	—	200.

J103 5 Chiao = 50 Fen	VG	VF	UNC
ND (1940). Dark purple and black on green and pale blue underprint. Herd of camels at center. Back: Blue-gray. *(S/M #M11-3).*			
a. Issued note.	5.00	20.00	50.00
s. Specimen with red overprint: *Yang Pen* on face and back.	—	—	60.00

J104 1 Yüan	VG	VF	UNC
ND. Dark green on ochre underprint. Great Wall at left center. Back: Blue. *(S/M #M11-10).*	1.50	5.00	15.00

J105 1 Yüan	VG	VF	UNC
ND (1938). Dark green and black on ochre and multicolor underprint. Herd of sheep at center. Back: Blue-gray. *(S/M #M11-11).*			
a. Issued note.	4.00	12.50	50.00
s. Specimen with red overprint: *Yang Pen* on face and back. Toppan Printing Co. imprint. Uniface pair.	—	—	150.

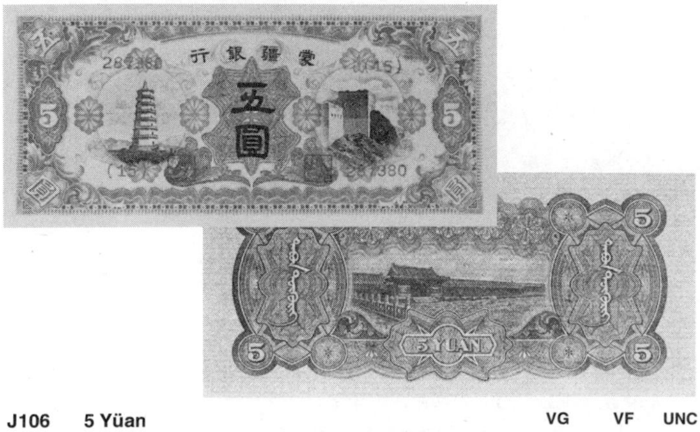

J106 5 Yüan	VG	VF	UNC
ND (1938). Orange-brown and black with violet guilloche. Pagoda at left, fortress at right. Back: Tan. Rural building at center. *(S/M #M11-12).*			
a. Issued note.	3.00	12.50	30.00
s. Specimen with red overprint: *Yang Pen* on face and back. Toppan Printing Co. imprint. Uniface pair.	—	—	150.

J107 5 Yüan	VG	VF	UNC
ND (1944). Purple on pale purple and orange underprint. Lama monastery at left center. Back: Dark blue. Specimen. *(S/M #M11-13).* Rare.	—	—	—

J108 10 Yüan	VG	VF	UNC
ND (1944). Dark blue-gray on yellow underprint. Camel at left, men on horseback, with oxen and horses at center. Back: Light blue. Buddhas at center.			
a. Watermark: Bank logo. Serial # and block #. *(S/M #M11-15).*	15.00	50.00	150.
b. Without watermark. Serial # and block #. *(S/M #M11-).*	5.00	17.50	60.00
c. Block # only. *(S/M #M11-).*	8.00	25.00	75.00

J108A 10 Yüan	VG	VF	UNC
ND (1944). Brown and black on ochre underprint. Camel at left, men on horseback, with oxen and horses at center. Like #J108. Back: Dark red. Buddhas at center. *(S/M #M11-).*			
r. Remainder. Block # only.	8.00	25.00	75.00
s. Specimen with red-orange overprint.	—	—	125.

J109 10 Yüan	VG	VF	UNC
ND (1938). Dark brown. Sheep at center. Back: Blue. *(S/M #M11-14).*			
a. Issued note.	5.00	25.00	75.00
s. Specimen with red overprint: *Yang Pen* on face and back. Toppan Printing Co. imprint. Uniface pair.	—	—	150.

J110 100 Yüan	VG	VF	UNC
ND (1945). Dark green on light brown underprint. Herdsman with goats. *(S/M #M11-22).*			
a. Issued note.	3.00	10.00	30.00
s. Specimen with red-orange overprint: *Mi-hon.*	—	—	125.

J111 100 Yüan	VG	VF	UNC
ND (1945). Black on yellow-green underprint. Lama monastary. *(S/M #M11-21).*	5.00	15.00	40.00

J112 100 Yüan	VG	VF	UNC
ND (1938). Purple and black on olive-geen and multicolor underprint. Pavilion at left, camel at right. *(S/M #M11-21).*			
a. Issued note.	4.00	12.50	55.00
s. Specimen with red overprint: *Yang Pen* on face and back. Toppan Printing Co. imprint. Uniface pair.	—	—	150.

Chi Tung Bank

Chi Tung Yin Hang

1937 Issue

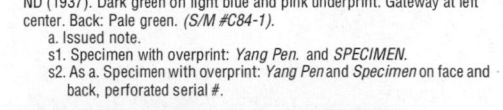

J113 5 Chiao = 50 Fen	VG	VF	UNC
ND (1937). Dark green on light blue and pink underprint. Gateway at left center. Back: Pale green. *(S/M #C84-1).*			
a. Issued note.	275.	700.	1750.
s1. Specimen with overprint: *Yang Pen.* and *SPECIMEN.*	—	—	750.
s2. As a. Specimen with overprint: *Yang Pen* and *Specimen* on face and back, perforated serial #.	—	—	700.

J114 1 Yüan	VG	VF	UNC
ND (1937). Orange on light green and ochre underprint. Great Wall at right. Back: Tan. *(S/M #C284-2).*			
a. Issued note.	275.	700.	1750.
s1. Specimen (English).	—	—	750.
s2. As a. Specimen with overprint: *Yang Pen* and *Specimen* on face and back, perforated serial #.	—	—	700.

J115 5 Yüan	VG	VF	UNC
ND (1937). Purple on multicolor underprint. Tower at Tunghsien at right. *(S/M #C84-3).*			
s1. Specimen (English).	—	—	1500.
s2. Specimen with overprint: *Yang Pen* and *Specimen* on face and back, perforated serial #.	—	—	1400.

J116 10 Yüan	VG	VF	UNC
ND (1937). Black on multicolor underprint. Temple at right. Back: Ochre. *(S/M #C84-4).*			
s1. Specimen (English).	—	—	2500.
s2. Specimen with overprint: *Yang Pen* and *Specimen* on face and back. Perforated serial #.	—	—	2400.

J117 100 Yüan	VG	VF	UNC
ND (1937). Dark blue on multicolor underprint. Building at right. Back: Blue. *(S/M #C84-5).*			
s1. Specimen (English).	—	—	4000.
s2. Specimen with overprint: *Yang Pen* and *Specimen* on face and back. Perforated serial #.	—	—	4000.

Chanan Bank

Ch'a Nan Yin Hang

Provisional Issue

#J118-J119 overprint on notes of the Central Bank of Manchukuo. This is the second overprint w/*Ch'a Nan Yin Hang* in Chinese vertically at l. and r. on face. First overprint is for Central Bank of Manchukuo. Chanan Bank notes have the face overprint for CBM line out, but w/o any new overprint on back leaving the CBM overprint.

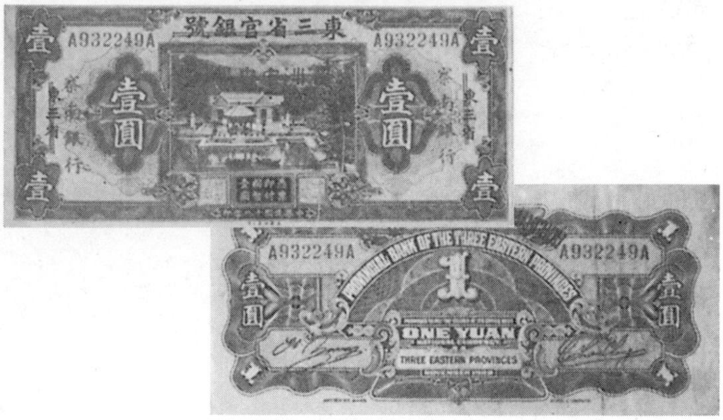

J118 1 Yüan	VG	VF	UNC
ND (1937- old date 1929). Black and multicolor. Overprint: On #J120. *(S/M #C4-1).*			
a. Double line through red overprint below pavilion.	300.	600.	2000.
b. Single line through red overprint below pavilion.	300.	600.	2000.
s. Specimen with red handstamp: *Yang Pen.* Punched hole cancelled.	—	—	600.

J119 10 Yüan	VG	VF	UNC
ND (1937- old date 1929). Green and multicolor. Overprint: On #J122. *(S/M #C4-3).*			
a. Issued note.	1500.	2500.	—
s. Specimen with red handstamp: *Yang Pen.* Punched hole cancelled.	—	—	2500.

Manchukuo

RULERS:

Ta Tung, Years 1-3, 1932-1934
Kang Teh, Years 1-12, 1934-1945

MONETARY SYSTEM:

1 Yuan = 10 Chiao = 100 Fen

Central Bank of Manchukuo

Man Chou Chung Yang Yin Hang

Provisional Issue

#J120-J122 overprint new bank name on notes of the Provincial Bank of the Three Eastern Provinces. Dated first year of Ta Tung (1932).

Note: For #J120 and J122 w/additional vertical Chinese overprint: *Cha Nan Yin Hang,* see Chanan Bank #J118 and #J119.

J120 1 Yüan	VG	VF	UNC
1932 (-old date Nov. 1929). Black and multicolor. Overprint: On #S2962a. *(S/M #M2-1).*			
a. Issued note.	400.	1000.	3000.
s1. Specimen with overprint: *Yang Pen* and *Specimen. Specimen* on back. Uniface pair.	—	—	1000.
s2. As a. Specimen with overprint: *Yang Pen* and *Specimen.* Punched hole cancelled.	—	—	800.

J121 5 Yüan	VG	VF	UNC
1932 (- old date Nov. 1929). Brown and multicolor. Overprint: *Yang Pen* and *Specimen* on back of #S2963a. Specimen. Uniface pair. *(S/M #M2-).*	—	—	1200.

J122 10 Yüan	VG	VF	UNC
1932 (- old date Nov. 1929). Green and multicolor. Overprint: On #S2964a. *(S/M #M2-2).*			
a. Issued note.	1200.	3000.	—
s1. Specimen with overprint: *Yang Pen* and *Specimen* on back. Uniface pair.	—	—	1000.
s2. As a. Specimen with overprint: *Yang Pen.* Punched hole cancelled.	—	—	800.

#J123 *Deleted.*

1932 Issue

J124 5 Chiao = 50 Fen	VG	VF	UNC
ND (1932). Dark blue on ochre underprint. Back: Pale green. *(S/M #M2-10).*			
a. Issued note.	50.00	175.	500.
s. Specimen with overprint: *Yang Pen* and *Specimen* on face and back. Uniface pair.	—	—	450.

1932-33 ND Issue

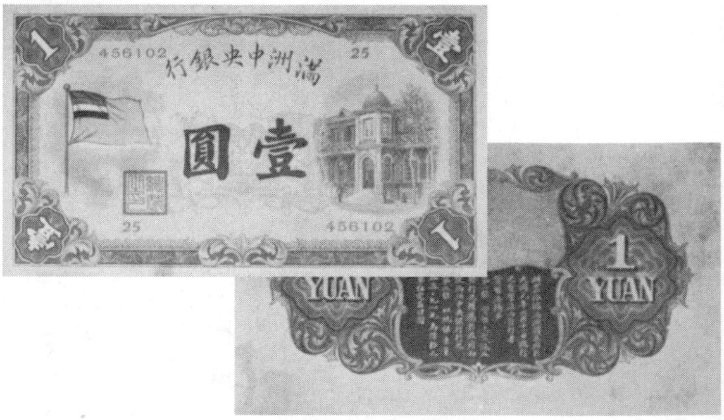

J125 1 Yüan	VG	VF	UNC
ND (1932). Blue on yellow yellow underprint. Multicolor flag at left, building at right. *(S/M #M2-20).*			
a. Issued note.	25.00	125.	280.
s. Specimen with overprint: *Yang Pen* and *Specimen* on face and back. Uniface pair.	—	—	250.

J126 5 Yüan	VG	VF	UNC
ND (1933). Dark brown on tan underprint. Multicolor flag at left, building at right. *(S/M #M2-21).*			
a. Issued note.	100.	300.	650.
s. Specimen with overprint: *Yang Pen* and *Specimen* on face and back. Punched hole cancelled. Uniface pair.	—	—	300.

J127 10 Yüan	VG	VF	UNC
ND (1932). Blue on orange underprint. Multicolor flag at left, building at right. *(S/M #M2-22).*			
a. Issued note.	100.	350.	700.
s. Specimen with overprint: *Yang Pen* and *Specimen* on face and back. Uniface pair.	—	—	350.

J128 100 Yüan	VG	VF	UNC
ND (1933). Blue on yellow-orange underprint. Multicolor flag at left, building at right. *(S/M #M2-23).*			
a. Issued note.	150.	350.	600.
s. Specimen with overprint: *Yang Pen* and *Specimen* on face and back. Uniface pair.	—	—	400.

1935-38 ND Issue

J129 5 Chiao = 50 Fen	VG	VF	UNC
ND (1935). Brown on green and lilac underprint. Ch'ien Lung at right. Back: Brown and olive. *(S/M #M2-30).*			
a. Issued note.	3.00	8.00	40.00
s. Specimen with overprint: *Yang Pen* and *Specimen* on face and back. Uniface pair.	—	—	75.00

J130 1 Yüan	VG	VF	UNC
ND (1937). Black on green and yellow underprint at center. T'ien Ming at right. Back: Green. *(S/M #M2-40).*			
a. 6-digit serial #.	3.00	10.00	30.00
b. 7-digit serial #.	2.00	5.00	12.50
s. Specimen with overprint: *Yang Pen* and *Specimen* on face and back. Uniface pair.	—	—	60.00

J131 5 Yüan	VG	VF	UNC
ND (1938). Black on brown underprint at center. Man with beard wearing feather crown at right. Back: Brown. *(S/M #M2-41).*			
a. 6-digit serial #.	15.00	50.00	150.
b. 7-digit serial #.	8.00	25.00	75.00
s. Specimen with overprint: *Yang Pen* and *Specimen* on face and back. Punched hole cancelled. Uniface pair.	—	—	60.00

J132 10 Yüan	VG	VF	UNC
ND (1937). Black on brown underprint at center. Emperor Ch'ien Lung at right. Back: Purple. *(S/M #M2-42).*			
a. 6-digit serial #.	7.50	20.00	50.00
b. 7-digit serial #.	3.00	8.00	25.00
s. Specimen with overprint: *Yang Pen* and *Specimen* on face and back. Uniface pair.	—	—	60.00

J133 100 Yüan	VG	VF	UNC
ND (1938). Black on green underprint at center. Confucius at right, Ta Ch'eng Tien building at left. Back: Blue. Sheep. *(S/M #M2-43).*			
a. 6-digit serial #.	30.00	100.	200.
b. 7-digit serial #.	6.00	15.00	35.00
s. Specimen with overprint: *Yang Pen* and *Specimen* on face and back. Uniface pair.	—	—	60.00

1944 ND Issue

#J135-J138 w/block # and serial #. New back designs.

J134 5 Chiao = 50 Fen	VG	VF	UNC
ND (1944). Blue-green on pale blue underprint. Ta Ch'eng Tien building at left center. Back: Brown. *(S/M #M2-50).*	10.00	35.00	90.00

J135 1 Yüan	VG	VF	UNC
ND (1944). Black on green and violet underprint at center. T'ien Ming at right. Back: Violet.			
a. Block # and serial #. *(S/M #M2-60).*	1.50	7.50	15.00
b. Block # only. *(S/M #M2-80).*	2.00	7.50	20.00
s1. As a. Specimen with overprint: *Yang Pen. Specimen* on back. Uniface pair.	—	—	60.00
s2. As b. Specimen with overprint: *Yang Pen.*	—	—	75.00

J136 5 Yüan	VG	VF	UNC
ND (1944). Black on orange underprint at center. Man with beard wearing feather crown at right. Back: Green.			
a. Block # and serial #. *(S/M #M2-61).*	2.50	7.50	20.00
s. Block # only. Specimen with overprint: *Yang Pen. (S/M #M2-81).*	—	—	175.

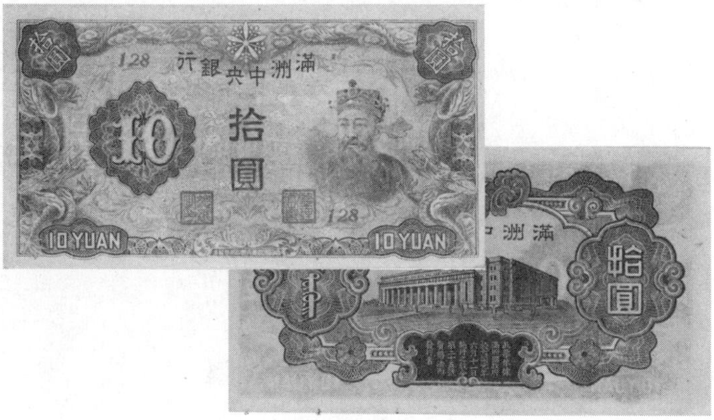

J137 10 Yüan	VG	VF	UNC
ND (1944). Black on green underprint at center. Emperor Ch'ien Lung at right. Back: Blue.			
a. Block # and serial #. Watermark: *MANCHU CENTRAL BANK. (S/M #M2-62).*	2.00	10.00	20.00
b. Revalidation *10 Yuan* adhesive stamp on face. See #M35.	—	—	—
c. Block # only. Watermark. as a. *(S/M #M2-82).*	2.50	12.50	25.00
d. Revalidation *10 Yuan* adhesive stamp on face. See #M35.	—	—	—
e. Block # only. Watermark: Chinese character: *Man* in clouds repeated.	2.50	12.50	30.00
s1. As a. Specimen with overprint: *Yang Pen. Specimen* on back. Uniface pair.	—	—	90.00
s2. As e. Specimen with overprint: *Yang Pen.*	—	—	60.00

J138 100 Yüan	VG	VF	UNC
ND (1944). Black on blue underprint at center. Confucius at right, Ta Ch'eng Tien building at left. Back: Brown. Men and donkey carts by storage silos at center. *(S/M #M2-63).*			
a. Watermark: *MANCHU CENTRAL BANK.*	5.00	15.00	55.00
b. Watermark: Chinese character: *Man* in clouds repeated.	4.00	10.00	35.00
s1. As a. Specimen with overprint: *Yang Pen. Specimen* on back. Block #1. Uniface pair.	—	—	60.00
s2. As b. Specimen with overprint: *Yang Pen.*	—	—	75.00
s3. Specimen. Uniface face and back.	—	—	250.

1941-45 Issue

#J139-J141; J145-J146 w/o serial #, only block letters.

J139 5 Fen	VG	VF	UNC
ND (1945). Blue-green. Back: Orange. Tower at center. *(S/M #M2-70).*	20.00	100.	200.

J140 10 Fen = 1 Chiao	VG	VF	UNC
ND (1944). Yellow-orange underprint. Back: Green. House at center. *(S/M #M2-71).*	1.50	5.00	15.00

J141 5 Chiao = 50 Fen	VG	VF	UNC
ND (1941). Green on pink and orange underprint. Ch'ien Lung at right. Back: Blue. *(S/M #M2-72).*			
a. Issued note.	1.00	3.00	12.00
s. Specimen with overprint: *Yang Pen* and *Specimen.* Uniface pair.	—	—	75.00

#J142-J144 *Deleted.* See #J135b, J136s, J137c.

J145 100 Yüan	VG	VF	UNC
ND (1945). Black on blue underprint at center. Confucius at right, Ta Ch'eng Tien building at left. Like #J138. Back: Brown. Men and donkey carts by storage silos at center. 1 serial #. Local printer. *(S/M #M2-83).*	350.	1000.	—

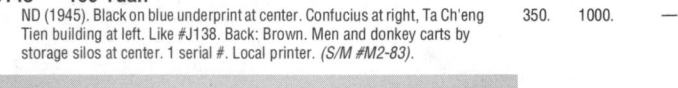

J146 1000 Yüan	VG	VF	UNC
ND (1944). Dark brown and violet. Confucius at right, Ta Ch'eng Tien building at left. Back: Green and brown. Bank building at center. *(S/M #M2-84).*	300.	900.	2700.

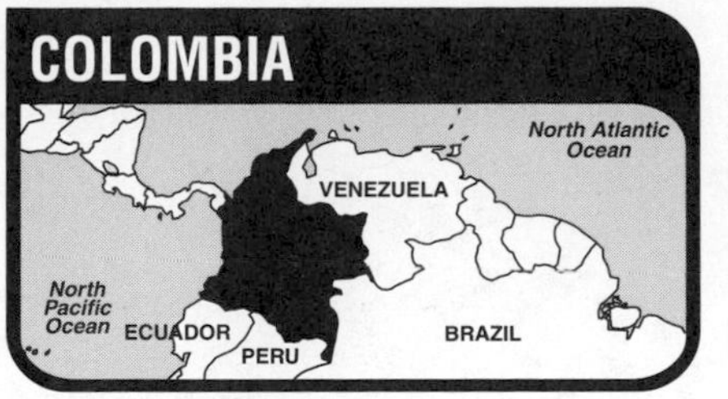

The Republic of Colombia, located in the northwestern corner of South America, has an area of 1.139 million sq. km. and a population of 45.01 million. Capital: Bogotá. The economy is primarily agricultural with a mild, rich coffee the chief crop. Colombia has the world's largest platinum deposits and important reserves of coal, iron ore, petroleum and limestone; precious metals and emeralds are also mined. Coffee, crude oil, bananas, sugar, coal and flowers are exported.

Colombia was one of the three countries that emerged from the collapse of Gran Colombia in 1830 (the others are Ecuador and Venezuela). A 40-year conflict between government forces and anti-government insurgent groups and illegal paramilitary groups - both heavily funded by the drug trade - escalated during the 1990s. The insurgents lack the military or popular support necessary to overthrow the government, and violence has been decreasing since about 2002, but insurgents continue attacks against civilians and large swaths of the countryside are under guerrilla influence. More than 32,000 former paramilitaries had demobilized by the end of 2006 and the United Self Defense Forces of Colombia (AUC) as a formal organization had ceased to function. Still, some renegades continued to engage in criminal activities. The Colombian Government has stepped up efforts to reassert government control throughout the country, and now has a presence in every one of its administrative departments. However, neighboring countries worry about the violence spilling over their borders.

MONETARY SYSTEM:

1 Real = 1 Decimo = 10 Centavos, 1870's
1 Peso = 10 Decimos = 10 Reales, 1880's
1 Peso = 100 Centavos 1993
1 Peso Oro = 100 Centavos to 1993

ARRANGEMENT

Listings for Colombia are divided into four major sections. The first contains regional or state issues issued from 1857 to 1885. The second lists all bank issues for the period 1869 to 1923. The third section consists of various government-sponsored issues from 1880 to 1919 and includes the revolution issue of 1900 under General Urribe. The fourth lists regional or state issues from 1898 to 1919.

The civil war period of 1899-1902 and the years of monetary chaos following are reflected in the many local printings and special overprint issues of the time. It is the plethora of such notes that caused the division of listings into the various sections as outlined above and as detailed below:

Section I, 1857-1885

STATES

BOLÍVAR

Deuda Pública del Distrito de Cartajena, 1878 . . . . . #S80
Deuda Pública del Estado, 1870. . . . . #S90
Estado Soberano de Bolívar, 1877-1885 . . . . . #S101-S130

CAUCA

Estado Soberano del Cauca, 1879-1882 . . . . . #S131-S136
Billete del Estado, 1882 . . . . . #S141-S146

CUNDINAMARCA

Estado de Cundinamarca, 1857 . . . . . #S151
Estado Soberano de Cundinamarca, 1869-1884 . . . . . #S156-S178

PANAMÁ

Estado Soberano de Panamá, 1866-1880 . . . . . #S186-S195
Estado de Panamá, 1861 & 1875. . . . . #S196-S197

SANTANDER

Confederación Granadina. . . . . #S198
Tesorería Jeneral, 1855 . . . . . #S201
Estado de Santander, Billete de Tesorería, 1880 . . . . . #S204-S206

Section II, 1851-1923

BANKS

Banco Americano, 1883 . . . . . #S211-S218
Banco de Antioquía, 187x-1900 . . . . . #S219-S227
Banco de Barranquilla, 1871-1900 . . . . . #S231-S262
Banco de Bogotá, 1873-1919 . . . . . #S271-S299
Banco de Bolívar, 18xx-1884 . . . . . #S301-S303
Banco de Boyacá, 188x-1886. . . . . #S311-S314
Banco de Buga, 187x. . . . . #S316-S320
Banco de Caldas, 19xx-1919 . . . . . #S325-S331
Banco de Cartagena, 1882-1900 . . . . . #S336-S351
Banco de la Provincia de Cartajena, 1851 . . . . . #S351A
Banco del Cauca, 187x-1886 . . . . . #S353-S360
Banco Central, 1887-1907 . . . . . #S366-S372
Banco de Cipaquirá, 1882 . . . . . #S376-S378
Banco de Colombia, 1875-1919 . . . . . #S382-S397
Banco Colombiano (see Guatemala)
Banco del Comercio, 1899 . . . . . #S398-S401
Banco de Credito Hipotecario, 1883. . . . . #S406
Banco de Cundinamarca, 188x-1881 . . . . . #S407-S411
Banco del Departamento de Bolívar, 1885-1888 . . . . . #S421-S424
Banco Dugand, 1919-1922. . . . . #S426-S429
Banco del Estado de Bolívar, 1885. . . . . #S430-S435A
Banco del Estado, 1884-1900. . . . . #S436-S506
Banco Hipotecario, 1881. . . . . #S511-S515
Banco Hipotecario de la Mutualidád, 1919-1921 . . . . . #S516-S518
Banco Hipotecario del Pacífico, 1920-1922 . . . . . #S521-S525
Banco de Honda, 1882. . . . . #S531-S533
Banco del Huila, 1921. . . . . #S541-S542
Banco Industrial, 1883-1923. . . . . #S546-S558
Banco Internacional, 1884 . . . . . #S561-S564
Banco López, 1919-1921 . . . . . #S571-S580
Banco de Marquez, 188x-1883. . . . . #S581-S586
Banco de Medellin, 1895-1899 . . . . . #S591-S608
Banco Mercantil de Medellin, 187x . . . . . #S611
Banco Nacional - Provisional Issues only, 1899 . . . . . #S616-S677
Banco del Norte, 1882. . . . . #S681-S684
Banco del Occidente, 1882 . . . . . #S691-S693
Banco de Oriente, 1884-1900 . . . . . #S696-S701
Banco de Pamplona, 1883-1884. . . . . #S706-S714
Banco de Panamá, 1869. . . . . #S721-S725
Banco de Circulación y Descuento de Perez y Planas, 1865 . . . . . #S726-S730
Banco Popular, 1877-1882 . . . . . #S736-S749
Banco Popular de Bolívar, 1883-1886. . . . . #S756-S762
Banco Popular de Medellin, 1883-1899. . . . . #S766-S778
Banco Popular de Soto, 188x . . . . . #S781-S783
Banco Prendario, 1881-1884. . . . . #S788-S790
Banco Prendario de Soto, 1884. . . . . #S796
Banco del Progreso, 1899 . . . . . #S801-S804
Banco de la República, 188x. . . . . #S807-S810A
Banco Republicano, 1899 . . . . . #S811-S813
Banco de Rio Hacha, 1883-1885. . . . . #S816-S819A
Banco del Ruiz, 1905-1919 . . . . . #S821-S826
Banco de Santander, 1873-1900. . . . . #S831-S835
Banco de Sogamoso, 1882 . . . . . #S841-S844
Banco de Sopetrán, 18xx. . . . . #S845-S846A
Banco de Sucre, 1913-1916 . . . . . #S847-S848
Banco del Sur, 1907-1908. . . . . #S851-S854A
Banco de Tequendama, 1881 . . . . . #S856-S858
Banco del Tolima, 1882. . . . . #S859
Banco de la Union, 1883 . . . . . #S861-S862
Banco Union, 1887-1888. . . . . #S866-S869
Botero Arango e Hijos, 18xx . . . . . #S876
Caja de Propietarios, 188x. . . . . #S881-S886
G. de Caycedo & Ca., 1884. . . . . #S886A
Central American Steam Navigation Co., 1851 . . . . . #S887-S890
Credito Caucano, 1919-1922. . . . . #S891-S892
Exchange Bank of Colón, 1870 . . . . . #S896-S899
La Nueva Compañia Constructora, 188x. . . . . #S900
Señores Fernando Restrepo & Hijos, 1900. . . . . #S900A
Restrepos y Compañia, 1884 . . . . . #S900B
Reyes Gonzales y Hermanos, ND. . . . . #S901-S906
Sociedád de Zancudo, 1882 . . . . . #S908-S909
Uribe e Hijos, 1871 . . . . . #S911-S915
José María Melguizo H. . . . . . #S916-S919
Vicente B. Villa e Hijos, 188x-1889 . . . . . #S921-S923

Note: Issues of the Banco Nacional de los Estados Unidos de Colombia (1881-1885) and Banco Nacional de la República de Colombia (1885-1900) are listed in Vol. 2.

Additionally, all government-sponsored issues formerly listed as Section III in Vol. I have been removed for insertion into Vol. 2. This includes all catalog numbers from #S931 through #S983.

Section III, 1898-1919

REGIONS OR STATES

ANTIOQUIA

Departamento de Antioquia, 1898-1901 . . . . . #S1001-S1024
Casa de Moneda de Medellin, 1919-1920. . . . . #S1026-S1029
Tesoro del Departamento de Antioquia, 1901-1902 . . . . . #S1030-S1044
Gobierno Departamental, 1900-1903 . . . . . #S1051-S1115

BOLÍVAR

Departamento de Bolívar, 1900. . . . . #S1121-S1124

MAGDALENA

Departamento del Magdalena, 1900 . . . . . #S1126-S1130
Gobernación del Magdalena, 1900 . . . . . #S1131-S1143

SANTANDER

Departamento de Santander, 1899-1900 . . . . . #S1151-S1154, #S1157-S1161
La Compañia Empresaria del Camino de Herradura de Bucaramanga á Sabana de Torres, 1887 . . . . . #S1156

TOLIMA

Departamento del Tolima, 1900-1919. . . . . #S1166-S1191

Section IV

REGIONAL FERROCARRIL (RAILROAD) ISSUES, 188x-1912

Ferrocarril de Amaga, 191x. . . . . #S1401
Ferrocarril de Antioquía, 1893-1909 . . . . . #S1501, S1511, S1521
Ferrocarril de Cartagena, 1892 . . . . . #S1531
Ferrocarril del Cauca, 1897-1912 . . . . . #S1541-S1573
Ferrocarril de Cúcuta. . . . . #S1576
Ferrocarril de La Sabana, 1886. . . . . #S1601
Ferrocarril de Santander, 188x-1893. . . . . #S1621-S1651

Note: A great many notes of Colombia are either entirely hand dated or have dates filled in by hand. This accounts for the wide variation of issue dates in any given series.

Section V

Regular Issues, 1819-1900 República de Colombia

1819 Issue . . . . . #1-4
1820s Issue . . . . . #5-7
Tesorería Jeneral de los Estados Unidos de Nueva Granada 1860s Issue . . . . . #59-66
Tesorería Jeneral de los Estados Unidos de Colombia 1860s Issue . . . . . #67
Estados Unidos de Colombia 1863 Treasury Issue. . . . . #71-78
1869 Issue . . . . . #80
1876 Issue. . . . . #81
Billete de Tesoreria . . . . . #91
Banco Nacional de los Estados Unidos de Colombia ND Issue . . . . . #122-123
1881 First Issue . . . . . #134-138
1881 Second Issue . . . . . #141-146
1882 Issue. . . . . #153
1885 Issue. . . . . #161-165; 170-171
Banco Nacional de Colombia 1885 Issue . . . . . #181-182

Section I

State Issues, 1857-1885

Deuda Pública del Distrito de Cartajena

1878 Issue

		Good	Fine	XF
S80	**5 Pesos** 1878. Red. Unsigned remainder.	150.	350.	600.

Deuda Pública del Estado

1870 Issue

		Good	Fine	XF
S90	**5 Pesos** 11.7.1870. Black on red underprint. Arms in border at left. Paper: Light orange.	150.	350.	600.

Estado Soberano de Bolívar

1877 First Issue

		Good	Fine	XF
S101	**10 Centavos = 1 Real** 3.1877. Black. Man at left. Green seal. Back: Green. Large numeral of value and arms at center. Printer: HBNC. Perforated edges.	75.00	150.	350.

		Good	Fine	XF
S102	**10 Centavos = 1 Real** 3.1877. Black. Man at left. Red seal. Straight edges.	75.00	150.	350.

1877 Second Issue

		Good	Fine	XF
S103	**10 Centavos = 1 Real** 3.1877. Man at left. Red seal. Back: Large numeral *10* at left and right. Printer: CCBB.	75.00	150.	350.

		Good	Fine	XF
S106	**1 Peso** 3.1877. Black on red underprint. Large and small ships at upper center. Back: Blue. Printer: CCBB.	150.	350.	600.

		Good	Fine	XF
S107	**5 Pesos** 3.1877. Black. Mining scene at center. Back: Yellow. Printer: CCBB.	200.	400.	750.

1883 First Issue

		Good	Fine	XF
S114	**1 Peso** 15.4.1883. Blue. Farm scenes and steam passenger train at upper center, arms at bottom center. Uniface. Printer: Local.	250.	500.	1000.

1883-85 Issue

S123 50 Centavos	Good	Fine	XF
11.30.1883. Black on orange underprint. Three girls at center. Printer: HBNC.			
a. Back orange. Proof.	—	—	—
b. Back green.	75.00	150.	300.
c. Back brown.	75.00	150.	300.
ct. Color Trials: orange, green, yellow, dark green.	—	Unc	400.

S126 10 Pesos	Good	Fine	XF
9.11.1885. Black on orange underprint. Justice at left, steam passenger train at center. Back: Brown. Hand signature at center. Printer: HBNC.			
a. Issued note.	150.	300.	600.
p. Proof.	—	Unc	1500.
s. Specimen.	—	—	—
S127 10 Pesos			
188x. Black on green underprint. Justice at left, steam passenger train at center. Back: Brown. Hand signature at center. Printer: HBNC. Specimen.	—	—	—

1885 Issues

S128 10 Centavos	Good	Fine	XF
3.1885; 5.1885. Red. Uniface. Back: Oval hand stampings. Printer: Local.	150.	300.	750.
S129 20 Centavos			
3.1885. Blue.	150.	300.	750.
S130 20 Centavos			
5.1885. Black.	150.	300.	750.

Estado Soberano del Cauca

1879 Libranza al Portador Issue

Bill of Exchange to Bearer.

S130A 1 Peso	Good	Fine	XF
14.2.1879. Black. Arms at upper left. "CLASE 1a" at center. Paper: Light gray.			
a. Unsigned remainder.	75.00	150.	300.
b. Cancelled 31.1.1896 with red handwritten text and name vertically in 7 lines on face.	100.	200.	400.

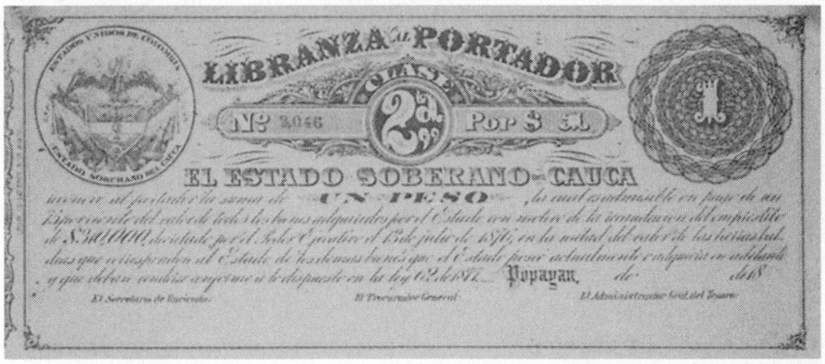

S131 1 Peso	Good	Fine	XF
18xx. Black. Arms at upper left. "*CLASE 2a*" at center. Uniface. Paper: Gray. Printer: Paredes & Ca., Bogotá. Issued under law #62 of 1877.	75.00	150.	300.

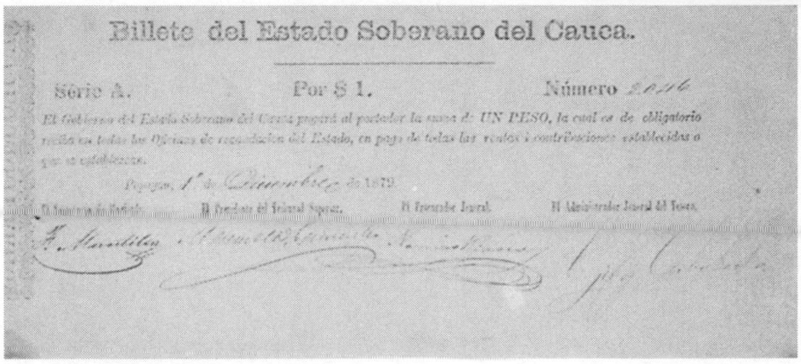

S136 1 Peso	Good	Fine	XF
1.12.1879. Text printed on back of #S131. Series A.	75.00	150.	300.

1878 Billete Flotante Issue

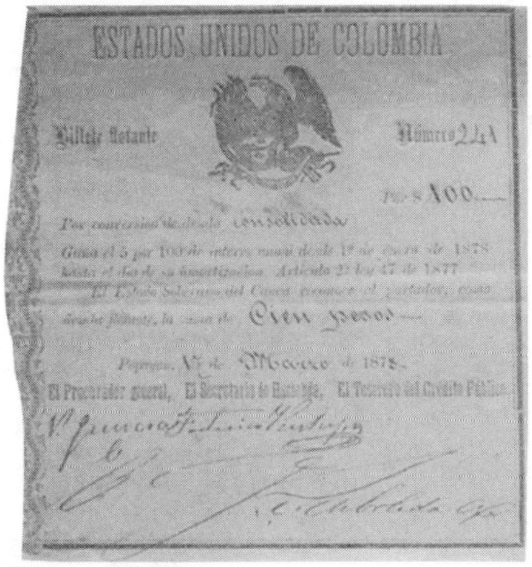

S138 100 Pesos	Good	Fine	XF
17.3.1878. Black. Eagle at upper center. Paper: Brown.	—	—	—

Billete del Estado

1882 Vale al Portador Issue

Promissory Note to Bearer.

Clase 1a or *2a* (1st or 2nd class). Some with word *cinco* handwritten over *diez* in text (5% instead of 10%). Uniface, plain back or with verification (varieties exist).

S141 1 Peso	Good	Fine	XF
1882. Black. Arms at left, 3 hand signatures across bottom. Uniface. Back: Plain or with verification. Printer: D. Paredes, Bogotá.			
a. 1st class. Usual verification on back in 3 straight lines without eagle. 18.2.1882; 15.4.1882.	40.00	100.	200.
b. 2nd class. Lowered to 5%. without verification on back. 15.4.1882.	40.00	100.	200.

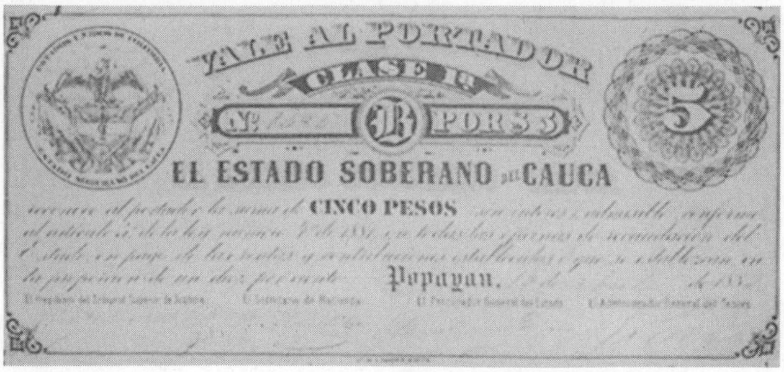

		Good	Fine	XF
S142	**5 Pesos**			
	1882. Black. Arms at upper left, 3 hand signatures across bottom. Uniface. Back: Plain or with verification. Printer: D. Paredes, Bogotá.			
	a. 1st class. Usual verification as #S141a on back. 18.2.1882.	40.00	100.	200.
	b. 2nd class. Lowered to 5%. Usual verification on back. 15.4.1882.	40.00	100.	200.
S143	**10 Pesos**			
	1882. Black. Arms at upper left, 3 hand signatures across bottom. Uniface. Back: Plain or with verification. Printer: D. Paredes, Bogotá.			
	a. 1st class. Usual verification on back. 18.2.1882; 15.4.1882.	40.00	100.	200.
	b. As a, but verification on back with curved lines and eagle at center 15.4.1882.	40.00	100.	200.
	r. Unsigned remainder. 188x.	30.00	75.00	150.

Bono Flotante Issue

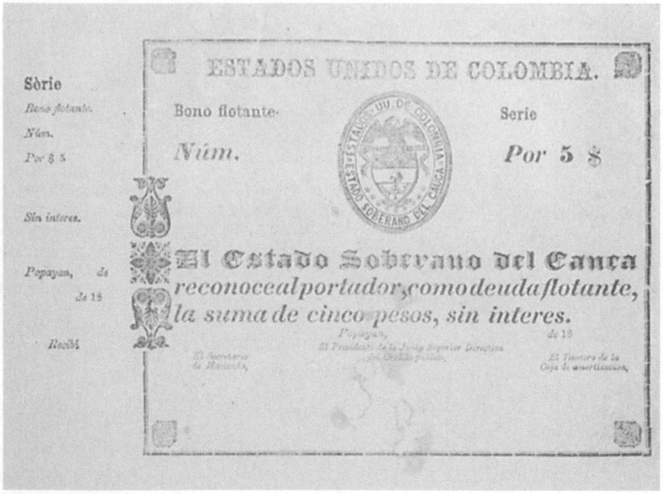

		Good	Fine	XF
S146	**5 Pesos**			
	18xx. Black. Arms at center. Unsigned remainder.	300.	500.	1000.

Estado de Cundinamarca

1857 Vale Flotante de 2a Clase Issue

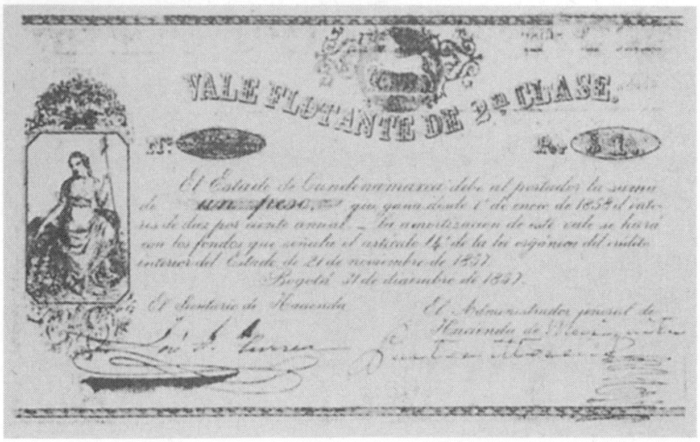

		Good	Fine	XF
S151	**1 Peso**			
	31.12.1857. Black on gray underprint. Seated Liberty at left, horse at top center. Back: Shows interest paid.	150.	300.	600.

Estado Soberano de Cundinamarca

1869-70 Vales de Deuda Flotante Sin Interés Issue

Promissory Note of the Floating Debt Without Interest.

		Good	Fine	XF
S156	**1 Peso**			
	9.11.1869; 19.1.1870; 9.2.1870; 19.2.1870. Black. Arms at center. Uniface. Printer: D. Paredes.	30.00	75.00	150.
S157	**5 Pesos**			
	19.1.1870; 19.5.1870. Black. Arms at center. Uniface. Printer: D. Paredes.	30.00	75.00	150.
S158	**10 Pesos**			
	19.1.1870; 9.2.1870. Black. Arms at center. Uniface. Printer: D. Paredes.	50.00	100.	200.

1871 Bono Flotante al 3% Anual (3% Annual Notes) Issue

		Good	Fine	XF
S161	**1 Peso**			
	27.4.1871; 29.4.1871; 12.5.1871. Black on violet underprint. Eagle, arms, woman and tree at center. Uniface, hole cancelled. Printer: D. Paredes.	50.00	100.	200.
S162	**5 Pesos**			
	1871. Black on blue underprint. Eagle, arms, woman and tree at center. Uniface, hole cancelled. Printer: D. Paredes.	75.00	150.	300.

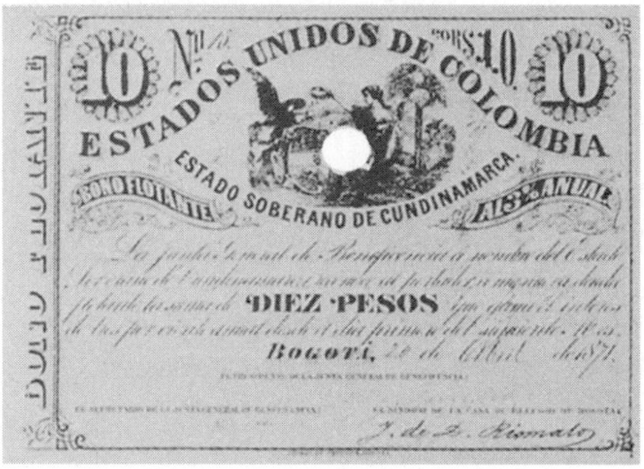

		Good	Fine	XF
S163	**10 Pesos**			
	20.4.1871; 29.4.1871; 12.5.1871. Black on gold underprint. Eagle, arms, woman and tree at center. Uniface, P.O.C. Printer: D. Paredes.	75.00	150.	300.
S165	**50 Pesos**			
	28.4.1871. Black on green underprint. Eagle, arms, woman and tree at center. Uniface, hole cancelled. Printer: D. Paredes.	150.	300.	600.
S166	**100 Pesos**			
	Oct. 1871. Black on red underprint. Eagle, arms, woman and tree at center. Uniface, hole cancelled. Printer: D. Paredes.	300.	400.	750.

NOTE: #S161-S166 Dangerous forgeries exist.

1870 2% Monthly Bill Issue

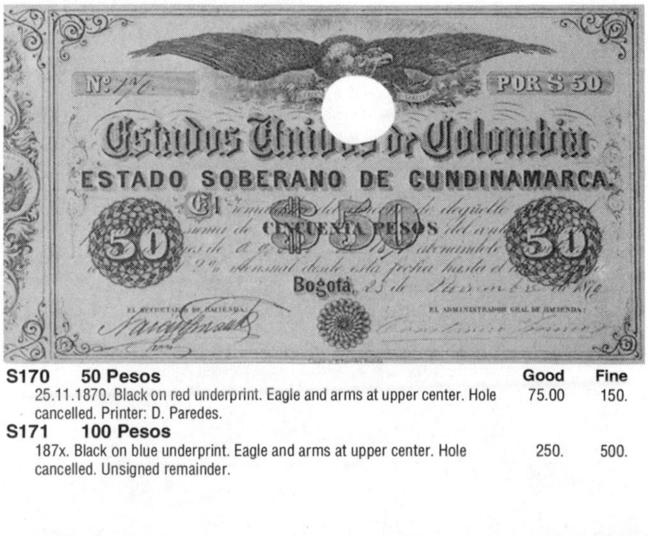

		Good	Fine	XF
S170	**50 Pesos**			
	25.11.1870. Black on red underprint. Eagle and arms at upper center. Hole cancelled. Printer: D. Paredes.	75.00	150.	300.
S171	**100 Pesos**			
	187x. Black on blue underprint. Eagle and arms at upper center. Hole cancelled. Unsigned remainder.	250.	500.	750.

1884 Billetes del Estado Issue

S176 1 Peso	Good	Fine	XF
10.1.1884; 3.3.1884; 30.5.1884. Black on blue underprint. Train station at upper left, arms in underprint. at center. Uniface. Printer: D. Paredes.	100.	200.	400.

S177 5 Pesos	Good	Fine	XF
14.2.1884. Black on orange underprint. Arms at upper left, steam passenger train at upper center.	150.	300.	600.

S178 10 Pesos	Good	Fine	XF
15.4.1884. Black on green underprint. Arms at left, man at right.	150.	350.	750.

Estado Soberano de Panamá

Treasury Bills

Law No. 17 of 1865 - Billetes de Tesoreria Issue

S186 1 Peso	Good	Fine	XF
3.4.1866; 12.10.1869; 20.12.1870. Black on blue underprint. Woman at lower left, boat and mountains in cartouche, standing allegorical woman and plants at center, Gen. T. Herrera at lower right. Uniface. Printer: ABNC.	350.	750.	1500.

S187 2 Pesos	Good	Fine	XF
12.10.1869; 2.5.1872. Black on green underprint. Gen. Herrera at lower left, center design like #S186, standing allegorical woman and cornucopias at lower right. Uniface. Printer: ABNC.	400.	800.	1750.

S188 3 Pesos	Good	Fine	XF
3.4.1866-20.6.1873. Black on brown underprint. Gen. Herrera at lower left, center design like #S186, anchor at lower right. Uniface. Printer: ABNC.	350.	750.	1500.

S189 10 Pesos	Good	Fine	XF
3.4.1866. Black. Gen. Herrera at lower left, center design like #S186, two girls at lower right. Uniface. Printer: ABNC.	500.	1000.	2000.

Law No. 12 of 27.1.1880

S194 50 Centavos	Good	Fine	XF
L.1880. Black.	400.	750.	1500.

S195 1 Peso	Good	Fine	XF
L.1880. Black. Back: Arms at center.	400.	800.	1500.

NOTE: A 2 Pesos denomination requires confirmation.

Estado de Panamá

Law of 28.10.1861

Issue approved by General Buenaventura Correoso.

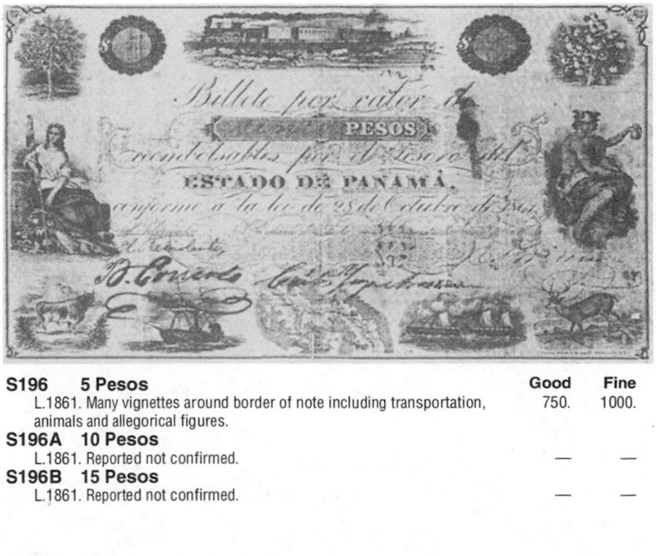

	Good	Fine	XF
S196 5 Pesos L.1861. Many vignettes around border of note including transportation, animals and allegorical figures.	750.	1000.	2000.
S196A 10 Pesos L.1861. Reported not confirmed.	—	—	—
S196B 15 Pesos L.1861. Reported not confirmed.	—	—	—

Decree of 28.10.1875

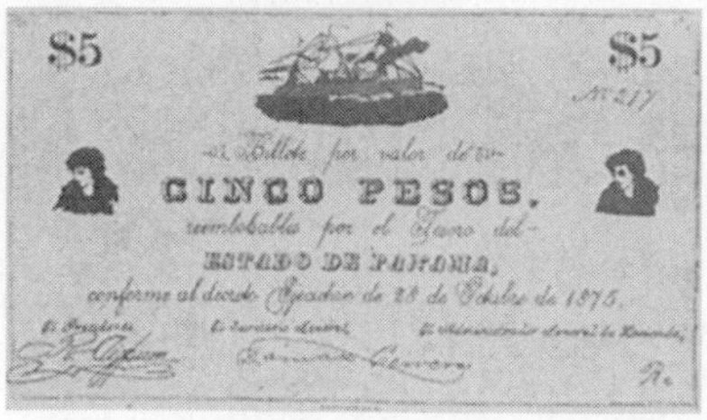

		Good	Fine	XF
S197	**5 Pesos** D.1875. Black on green underprint. Woman at left and right, ship at center.	750.	1250.	2250.
S197A	**20 Pesos**	—	—	—

Confederación Granadina

1859 Issue

		Good	Fine	XF
S198	**10 Pesos** 7.10.1859. Handwritten denomination.	500.	1000.	1500.

Estado de Santander

1855 Tesoreria Jeneral Issue

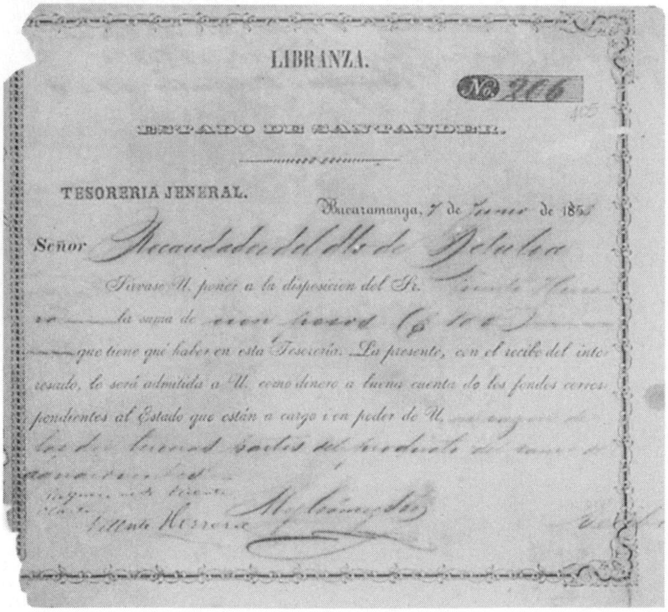

		Good	Fine	XF
S201	**Various Amounts** 7.6.1855. Black. Forms with amounts payable to individuals from the Treasury and usable as money.	200.	300.	600.

Ley 37 of 1879 - Billete de Tesoreria

Issued at Socorro.

		Good	Fine	XF
S204	**1 Peso** 14.4.1880. Black. Allegorical woman seated at lower left. Back: Green.	300.	500.	900.

		Good	Fine	XF
S205	**2 Pesos** 1.5.1880. Black. Eagle at lower left. Back: Green.	400.	750.	1000.

		Good	Fine	XF
S206	**3 Pesos** 3.3.1880. Black. Eagle at lower left. Back: Sepia.	500.	750.	1000.

Section II

Banks, 1851-1923

Banco Americano

1880's Issue

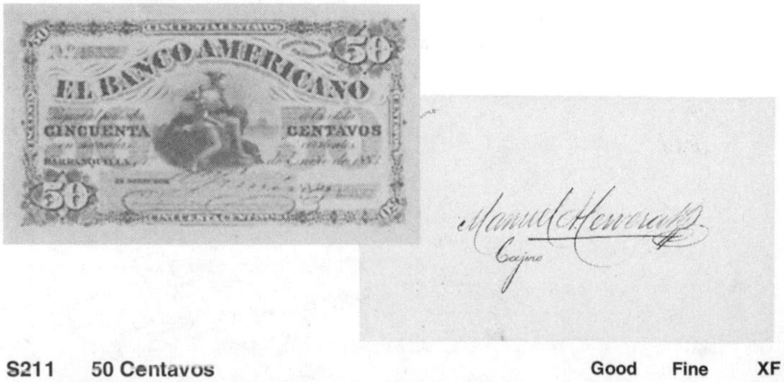

		Good	Fine	XF
S211	**50 Centavos** 1.1.1883; 2.7.1886. Black. Seated Mercury at center. Uniface. Back: Signature. Printer: W&S.	500.	750.	1000.

	Good	Fine	XF
S218 100 Pesos 2.7.1883. Black. Seated Britannia with shield and tree at center. Printer: CS&E.	600.	1000.	1750.

Banco de Antioquia

1870s-1900 Issue

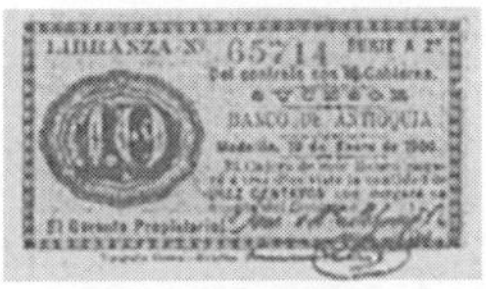

	Good	Fine	XF
S219 10 Centavos 19.1.1900. Dark blue on green underprint. Series A2a or A3a. Printer: Tipografía Central - Medellín.	300.	500.	1000.
S220 1 Peso 1.2.1885. Date finished by hand. Local print.	300.	500.	1000.

	Good	Fine	XF
S221 1 Peso 1.12.1883; 2.7.1886. Green on orange underprint. Sailing ships at upper center. Printer: PBC.	75.00	150.	300.

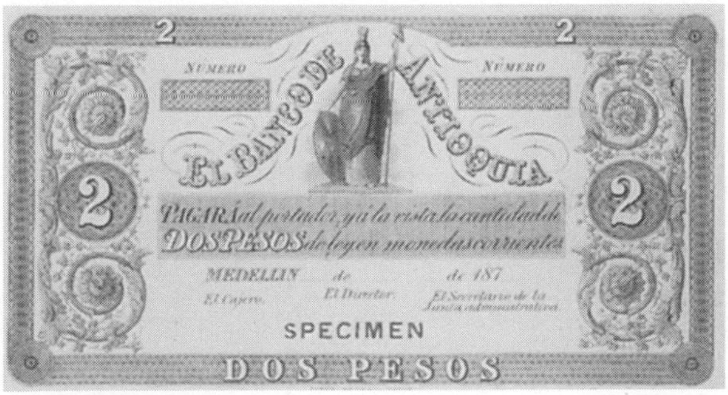

	Good	Fine	XF
S222 2 Pesos 187x. Black on red underprint. Standing Liberty with shield and staff at top center. Printer: PBC.			
p. Proof.	—	Unc	500.
s. Specimen.	—	—	—

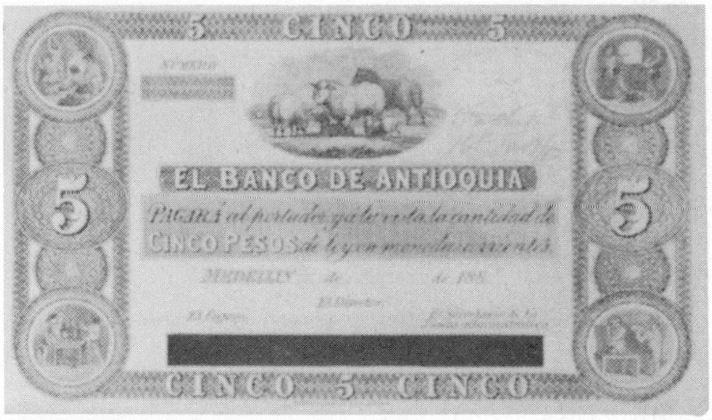

	Good	Fine	XF
S223 5 Pesos 187x; 188x. Black on orange underprint. Sheep at center, small vignettes at each corner. Printer: PBC.			
a. Issued note.	600.	1000.	2000.
b. overprint for José M. Melguizo on back. 19.1.1900.	500.	800.	1600.
p. Proof.	—	Unc	500.

	Good	Fine	XF
S224 10 Pesos 188x. Blue. Justice seated at top center. Printer: PBC. Proof.	—	Unc	500.
S227 100 Pesos 18xx. Proof.	—	Unc	500.

Banco de Barranquilla

1871-86 Issue

	Good	Fine	XF
S231 1 Peso 10.11.1874. Black and tan. Horse and children at lower left, sailor at center, dog and safe at right. Back: Tan. Printer: ABNC.			
a. Issued note.	150.	400.	—
b. Overprint 5 lines of text with date 29.12.1899 on back.	100.	250.	—
c. Like b. but with oval black stamping on face and back: *PAGADERO EN BILLETES DEL BANCO NACIONAL.*	75.00	200.	—
p. Proof.	—	Unc	500.

S232	**2 Pesos**	**Good**	**Fine**	**XF**
	1.3.1871; 1.7.1873; 1.7.1875; 1886. Black and green. Reclining allegorical woman with sheaves and produce at center. Back: Green. Printer: ABNC.			
	a. Issued note.	150.	400.	—
	b. Overprint like #S231b.	100.	250.	—
	p. Proof.	—	Unc	500.
	s. Specimen with serial # but without date or signature	—	—	—

S233	**5 Pesos**	**Good**	**Fine**	**XF**
	12.5.1873; 6.10.1886. Black and orange. Woman with fruit at lower left, large paddle wheel steamer at center, woman at lower right. Back: Orange. Printer: ABNC.			
	a. Issued note.	250.	500.	800.
	b. Overprint like #S231b.	150.	400.	—
	s. Specimen.	—	Unc	750.

S234	**10 Pesos**	**Good**	**Fine**	**XF**
	7.10.1876; 17.3.1877; 6.10.1881. Black on red-orange underprint. Woman with tablet and child at left, Indian woman seated at upper center, woodcarver at lower right. Back: Red-orange. Printer: ABNC.			
	a. Issued note. *DIEZ* in orange letters under numeral at upper left.	300.	600.	1000.
	b. Overprint like #S231b. *CIEN* in orange letters at left. (error).	200.	400.	—
	p. Proof.	—	Unc	500.

S235	**20 Pesos**	**Good**	**Fine**	**XF**
	2.1872; 3.12.1873. Black and brown. Woman with farm tools under tree at lower left, paddle wheel steamer and crocodile at center. Back: Brown. Printer: ABNC.			
	a. Issued note.	300.	600.	1250.
	b. Overprint like #S231b.	150.	400.	1000.
	p. Proof.	—	Unc	500.

S236	**50 Pesos**	**Good**	**Fine**	**XF**
	6.10.1886. Black and blue. Palm vignette at lower left, train at center, vignette of pine tree at lower right. Back: Blue. Printer: ABNC.			
	a. Issued note.	350.	600.	
	b. Overprint like #S231b.	150.	300.	500.
	s. Specimen.	—	Unc	400.

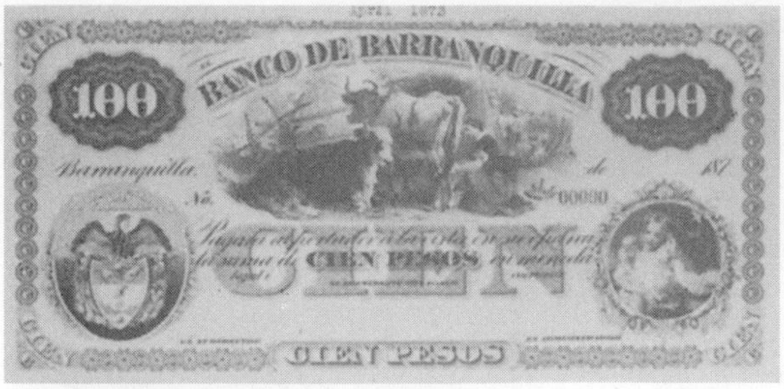

S237	**100 Pesos**	**Good**	**Fine**	**XF**
	1.3.1871. Black on red-brown underprint. Arms at left, woman milking cows at center, two young girls at right. Back: Red-brown. Printer: ABNC. Specimen.	—	Unc	750.

NOTE: Some of #S231-S237 exist with red overprint: *PAGADERO EN MONEDA CORRIENTE* on face and/or back.

1900 Issues

S241	**10 Centavos**	**Good**	**Fine**	**XF**
	3.9.1900. Black on green underprint. Arms at upper left. Series right. Back: Green. Printer: Armenta and Prieto (A&P).	20.00	40.00	100.

S242	**20 Centavos**	**Good**	**Fine**	**XF**
	3.9.1900. Black on orange underprint. Series U. Back: Light orange. Printer: Armenta and Prieto (A&P).	10.00	20.00	40.00

S243	**50 Centavos**	**Good**	**Fine**	**XF**
	7.5.1900. Black. Sailing ship at right. Series left. Printer: Armenta and Prieto (A&P).	25.00	50.00	100.

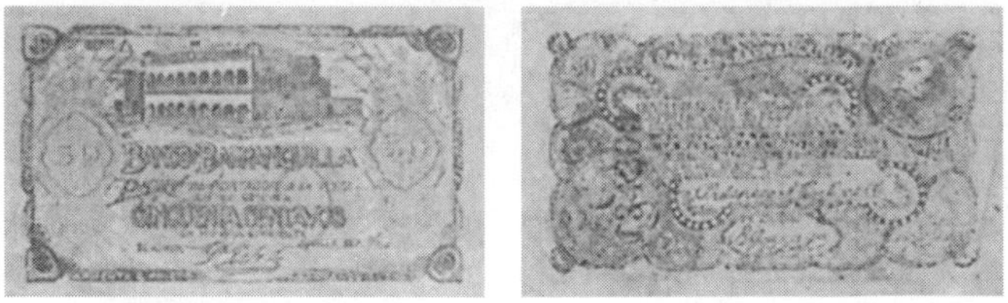

S244	**50 Centavos**	**Good**	**Fine**	**XF**
	3.9.1900. Brown on red underprint. Building "El Cuartel" at top left center. Back: Blue. Bolívar at upper right. Series Δ. Printer: Armenta and Prieto (A&P).	15.00	30.00	75.00
S245	**1 Peso**			
	8.3.1900; 10.3.1900. Printer: A&P.	20.00	40.00	75.00
S246	**1 Peso**			
	1.5.1900. Printer: A&P.	20.00	40.00	75.00

S247	**1 Peso**	**Good**	**Fine**	**XF**
	7.5.1900. Blue on pink underprint. Arms at left, steam train leaving tunnel at right. Series J. Printer: Armenta and Prieto (A&P).	20.00	40.00	75.00

S248 1 Peso	**Good**	**Fine**	**XF**
7.5.1900; 3.9.1900; 19.12.1900. Black on aqua underprint. Arms at left. Series Y. Back: Aqua. Printer: Armenta and Prieto (A&P).	10.00	30.00	75.00
S249 2 Pesos			
1.5.1900. Blue-green. Printer: Armenta and Prieto (A&P).	10.00	30.00	75.00
S250 2 Pesos			
9.6.1900. Printer: A&P.	10.00	30.00	75.00

S251 2 Pesos	**Good**	**Fine**	**XF**
1900. Black on green underprint. Theatre "Emiliano" at top center. Printer: Armenta and Prieto (A&P).			
a. Series K. 7.5.1900.	10.00	30.00	75.00
b. Series W. 3.9.1900.	10.00	30.00	75.00
c. Series Z. 19.12.1900.	10.00	30.00	75.00

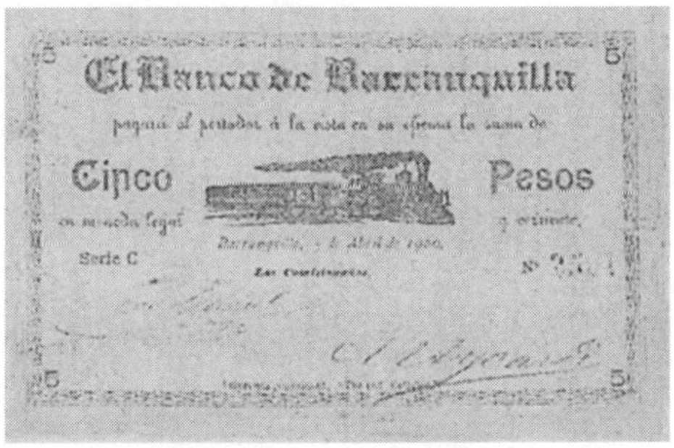

S252 5 Pesos	**Good**	**Fine**	**XF**
3.4.1900. Blue. Train at center. Series C. Paper: Light yellow. Printer: Imprenta Americana.	150.	300.	500.

S253 5 Pesos	**Good**	**Fine**	**XF**
12.6.1900. Brown on tan underprint. Long bridge at lower left, woman with sailing ship in background at right. Series M. Printer: Armenta and Prieto (A&P).	40.00	100.	200.
S254 10 Pesos			
10.3.1900. Printer: Armenta and Prieto (A&P).	200.	350.	500.

S254A 10 Pesos	**Good**	**Fine**	**XF**
5.4.1900. Eagle with wings spread at upper center. Series E. Back: Text and signature. Printer: Armenta and Prieto (A&P).	300.	500.	750.

S255 10 Pesos	**Good**	**Fine**	**XF**
12.6.1900. Black and blue. Paddle wheel steamer at center. Series N. Printer: Armenta and Prieto (A&P).	40.00	75.00	200.
S256 10 Pesos			
1.7.1900; 3.9.1900. Printer: Armenta and Prieto (A&P).	40.00	75.00	200.

S257 20 Pesos	**Good**	**Fine**	**XF**
5.4.1900. Black. Two women standing at left. Series G. Paper: Dark orange. Printer: Armenta and Prieto (A&P).	300.	500.	750.

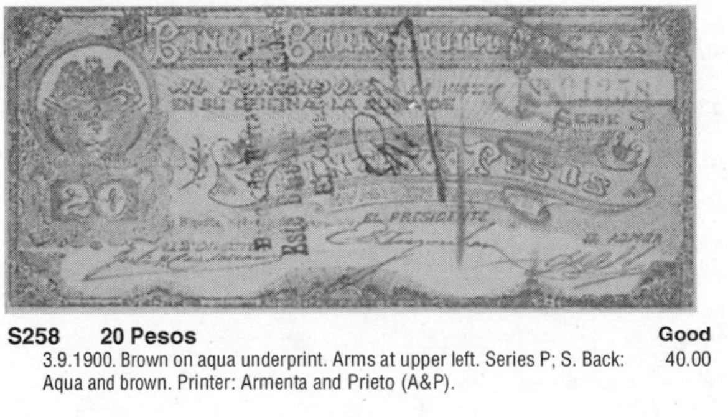

S258 20 Pesos	**Good**	**Fine**	**XF**
3.9.1900. Brown on aqua underprint. Arms at upper left. Series P; S. Back: Aqua and brown. Printer: Armenta and Prieto (A&P).	40.00	150.	300.

No.	Denomination / Description	Good	Fine	XF
S259	**50 Pesos** 15.3.1900. Black on red underprint. Arms at left, paddle wheel steamer at center. Series A. Back: Brown with black text. Printer: Armenta and Prieto (A&P).	40.00	150.	300.

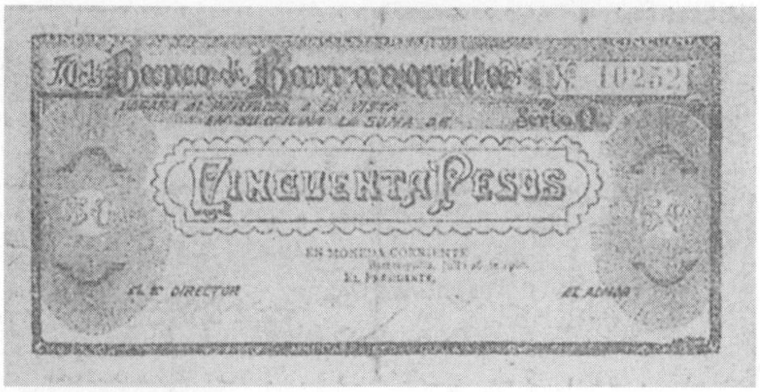

No.	Denomination / Description	Good	Fine	XF
S260	**50 Pesos** 14.7.1900, 22.7.1900, 26.7.1900, 3.9.1900. Black on pink, brown and bluish green underprint. Series Q. Back: Brown and red. Printer: Armenta and Prieto (A&P).	50.00	150.	250.

No.	Denomination / Description	Good	Fine	XF
S261	**100 Pesos** 5.3.1900; 15.3.1900. Black on yellow underprint. Arms at lower left, dog at center. Series A. Back: Green text and red vertical text overprint. Printer: Armenta and Prieto (A&P).	75.00	200.	300.

No.	Denomination / Description	Good	Fine	XF
S262	**100 Pesos** 22.10.1900; 19.12.1900. Brown on green underprint. Government building at center. Series 3. Back: Sailing ship at left, lighthouse at right. Black text overprint with date at center. Printer: Armenta and Prieto (A&P).	100.	300.	500.

Banco de Bogotá

1870's Issue

No.	Denomination / Description	Good	Fine	XF
S271	**1 Peso** 187x. Black. Red numerals. Partially engraved date and space for month and day to be filled in. Without vignettes. Printer: PBC. Rare.	—	—	—
S272	**2 Pesos** 187x. Blue. Orange numerals. Partially engraved date and space for month and day to be filled in. Without vignettes. Printer: PBC. Rare.	—	—	—
S273	**5 Pesos** 187x. Orange. Blue numerals. Partially engraved date and space for month and day to be filled in. Without vignettes. Printer: PBC. Rare.	—	—	—

No.	Denomination / Description	Good	Fine	XF
S274	**10 Pesos** 15.2.1875. Black. Partially engraved date and space for month and day to be filled in. Without vignettes. Back: Signature at center. Printer: PBC. Rare.	—	—	—

NOTE: #S274 as listed is most likely a counterfeit.

No.	Denomination / Description	Good	Fine	XF
S275	**10 Pesos** 187x. Brown. Green numerals. Partially engraved date and space for month and day to be filled in. Without vignettes. Like #S274. Printer: PBC. Rare.	—	—	—
S276	**50 Pesos** 18xx. Black on green underprint. Seated woman at center. Partially engraved date and space for month and day to be filled in. Back: Orange. Printer: PBC. Rare.	—	—	—
S277	**100 Pesos** 187x. Ship. Partially engraved date and space for month and day to be filled in. Printer: PBC. Reported not confirmed.	—	—	—

NOTE: All the above except #S274 are known issued only with red seal overprint: *Banco Nacional* and *30.10.1899* date in overprint on back. For listing see #S616-S620.

1873 Issue

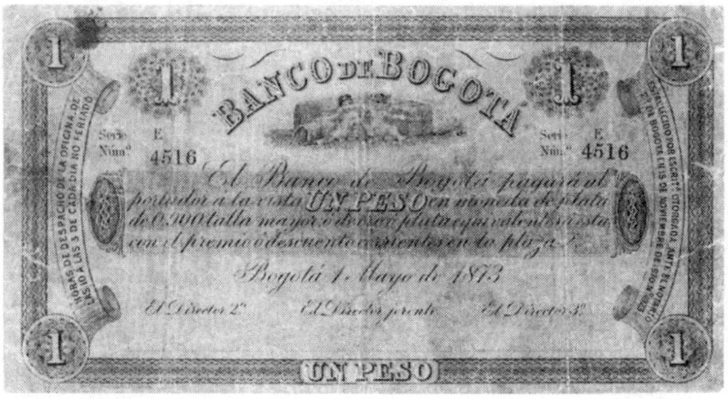

No.	Denomination / Description	Good	Fine	XF
S281	**1 Peso** 1.5.1873. Fully engraved. Black. Two allegorical children with barrel and bale at upper center. Printer: PBC.	—	—	—
S282	**5 Pesos** 1.5.1873. Fully engraved. Blue. Two allegorical children with barrel and bale at upper center. Printer: PBC.	—	—	—
S283	**10 Pesos** 1.5.1873. Fully engraved. Brown. Two allegorical children with barrel and bale at upper center. Printer: PBC.	—	—	—
S284	**50 Pesos** 1.5.1873. Green. Printer: PBC.	—	—	—

NOTE: #S281-S284 are known in issued form only with *Banco Nacional* overprint. and *30.10.1899* date in overprint on back. For listing see #S621-S624.

1876 Issue

No.	Denomination / Description	Good	Fine	XF
S286	**20 Centavos** 7.2.1876. On back. Black. Allegorical woman at center. Back: Green. Printer: D. Paredes, Bogota.	300.	500.	750.

No.	Denomination / Description	Good	Fine	XF
S287	**50 Centavos** 7.2.1876. On back. Black. Portrait Bolívar at left. Back: Blue. Printer: D. Paredes, Bogota.	300.	500.	750.

1880 Issue

		Good	Fine	XF
S291 5 Pesos	1.1.1880. Black. Trees and shoreline with boats at left, Bolívar at right. Series A. Printer: CCBB. Proof.	—	—	—
S292 5 Pesos	27.11.1880. Black on pink underprint. Woman on shore and boats in water at left, Simon Bolívar at right. Series A. Back: Blue-green. Printer: CCBB.	—	—	—
S293 10 Pesos	18xx. Black on blue underprint. Waterfalls at left, Caldas at right. Back: Brown. Printer: CCBB.	—	—	—
S294 50 Pesos	27.11.1880. Black on blue underprint. Officer at left, paddle wheel steamer *Francisco Montoya* at center. Back: Light brown. Printer: CCBB.	—	—	—
S295 100 Pesos	18xx. Black on light red underprint. Pineapple trees and shoreline at center, man at right. Back: Dark blue. Printer: CCBB.	—	—	—

NOTE: #S292-S295 are known issued only with red seal overprint: *Banco Nacional* and *30.10.1899* date in overprint on back. For listing see #S627-S630.

1918 Cedula Hipotecaria Issue

		Good	Fine	XF
S296 10 Pesos	6.4.1918. Added text in red and *a la vista* blocked out on face of #S293.	300.	500.	750.

Ley 7.2.1919 - Cédula Hipotecaria Issue

Mortgage Certificate

		Good	Fine	XF
S297 1 Peso	1.10.1919. Black on light red underprint. Bolívar monument. Condor at left. Series X. Back: Orange. Monument at center. Printer: ABNC.			
	a. Issued note.	100.	200.	400.
	p. Proof.	—	Unc	600.
	s. Specimen.	—	Unc	900.
S298 5 Pesos	19xx. Black on blue underprint. Condor at left. Series Y. Back: Blue. Monument at center. Printer: ABNC.			
	a. Issued note.	200.	500.	1000.
	p. Proof.	—	Unc	750.
	s. Specimen.	—	Unc	1150.
S299 10 Pesos	1.7.1919. Black on grayish brown underprint. Condor at left. Series Z. Back: Grayish brown. Simon Bolivar monument at center. Printer: ABNC.			
	a. Issued note.	250.	600.	1000.
	p. Proof.	—	Unc	600.
	s. Specimen.	—	Unc	1150.

Banco de Bolívar

1884 Issue

		Good	Fine	XF
S301 1 Peso	14.1.1884. Black on orange underprint. Sailing ship at lower left, portrait Simon Bolívar at top center, bridge view at lower right. Back: Orange. Hand signature at center. Printer: A. Macgregor, Liverpool and Manchester.			
	a. Issued note. Rare.	—	—	—
	r. Remainder.	—	—	—

		Good	Fine	XF
S303 10 Pesos	18xx. Black on red underprint. Buildings vignette at left and right, portrait Simon Bolívar at top center. Printer: A. Macgregor, Liverpool and Manchester. Remainder. Rare.	—	—	—

Banco de Boyacá

1886 Issue

		Good	Fine	XF
S311 50 Centavos	2.1886. Brown on pink underprint. Doorway and footbridge at center. Back: Orange.	300.	500.	750.

		Good	Fine	XF
S314 10 Pesos	188x. Black with red denomination and guilloche. Seated woman at top center. Uniface. Printer: Paredes.	400.	800.	1250.

Banco de Buga

1870's Issue

		Good	Fine	XF
S316 1 Peso	187x. Black on red underprint. Arms at upper center. Uniface. Printer: D. Paredes, Bogota. Rare.	—	—	—
S317 5 Pesos	187x. Black on brown underprint. Condor at center. Uniface. Printer: D. Paredes, Bogota. Rare.	—	—	—
S318 10 Pesos	187x. Black on light blue-green underprint. Arms at left, cornucopia at center, two allegorical children at right. Uniface. Printer: D. Paredes, Bogota. Rare.	—	—	—

S319 20 Pesos Good Fine XF

187x. Black on orange underprint. Two allegorical women with eagle and value at center. Uniface. Printer: D. Paredes, Bogota. Rare. — — —

S320 50 Pesos

187x. Black on green underprint. Three allegorical babies and value at center. Uniface. Printer: D. Paredes, Bogota. Rare. — — —

NOTE: #S316-S320 with overprint for Banco del Estado 1900, see #S461-S465.

Banco de Caldas

1910s Issue

	Good	Fine	XF
S325 50 Centavos			
191x. Black on multicolor underprint. Back: Brown. Printer: ABNC.			
p. Proof.	—	Unc	350.
s. Specimen.	—	Unc	750.

	Good	Fine	XF
S326 1 Peso			
17.5.1919; 1.7.1919. Black on green and multicolor underprint. Left signature title: *EL GERENTE*. Back: Green. Printer: ABNC.			
a. 17.5.1919.	150.	300.	600.
b. 1.7.1919.	150.	300.	600.
c. Red oval overprint: *CEDULA HIPOTECARIA* at right on face; red curved overprint: *CEDULA HIPOTECARIA DEL 2% AMORITIZABLE POR SORTEOS ANUALES* in 2 lines on back.	150.	300.	600.
p. Proof, uniface.	—	Unc	500.
s. Specimen. Without overprint.	—	Unc	750.
S327 2 Pesos			
1.7.1919. Black on blue and multicolor underprint. Left signature title: *EL GERENTE*. Back: Blue. Printer: ABNC.			
a. Circular red overprint: *CEDULA HIPOTECARIA...* (as #326c) at right.	150.	300.	600.
p. Proof, uniface.	—	Unc	500.
s. Specimen.	—	Unc	750.

	Good	Fine	XF
S328 5 Pesos			
1.7.1919. Black on orange and multicolor underprint. Left signature title: *EL GERENTE*. Back: Dark orange. Overprint: *CEDULA HIPOTECARIA...* (like #S326c) in red on back. Printer: ABNC.			
a. Issued note.	200.	400.	800.
s. Specimen.	—	Unc	900.
S329 10 Pesos			
191x. Black on multicolor underprint. Portrait Caldas at center. Left signature title: *EL GERENTE*. Back: Orange. Printer: ABNC.			
p. Proof, uniface.	—	Unc	750.
s. Specimen.	—	Unc	1000.

	Good	Fine	XF
S330 20 Pesos			
191x. Black on multicolor underprint. Portrait Caldas at upper right. Left signature title: *EL GERENTE*. Back: Brown. Printer: ABNC.			
p. Proof.	—	Unc	750.
s. Specimen.	—	Unc	1250.
S331 20 Pesos			
19xx (ca.1922). Black. Portrait Caldas at upper right. Left Signature title: *EL PRESIDENTE*. Similar to #S330 but without multicolor guilloche. Archive copy.	—	Unc	1250.

Banco de Cartagena

1882 Issue

	Good	Fine	XF
S336 10 Centavos			
1.1.1882. Green. Dog atop safe at center.	50.00	100.	200.
S337 20 Centavos			
1.1.1882. Blue. Woman.	75.00	150.	300.

	Good	Fine	XF
S338 50 Centavos			
1.1.1882. Blue. Liberty at upper left.	50.00	150.	300.

	Good	Fine	XF
S339 1 Peso			
1.1.1882; 188x. Blue. Woman and wheel at center. Back: Blue-green.	100.	250.	500.

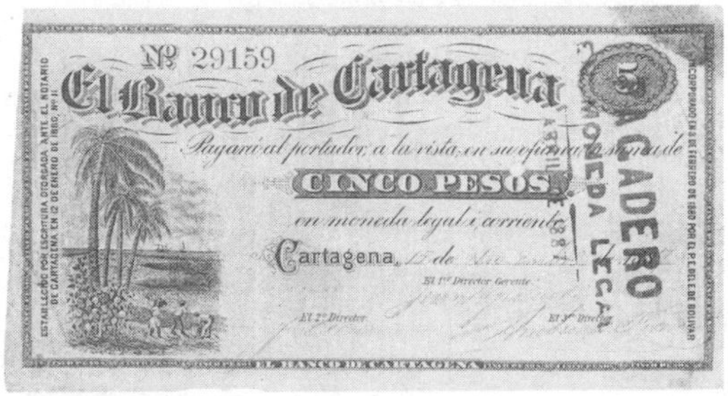

	Good	Fine	XF
S340 5 Pesos			
1.1.1882; 15.2.1887. Green. Palm trees along shoreline at left. Back: Blue.	200.	500.	900.

1900 Issue

	Good	Fine	XF
S344 50 Centavos			
1900. Black. Paper: Pink.	50.00	150.	300.

	Good	Fine	XF
S345 1 Peso			
10.3.1900. Black on red underprint. Back: Blue with black text.			
a. Issued note.	25.00	50.00	150.
b. With additional red overprint vertical text on back. 13.8.1903.	40.00	75.00	200.
S346 2 Pesos			
10.3.1900.	200.	400.	600.

S347 5 Pesos — Good / Fine / XF

10.3.1900. Black. Flowers at left under serial #, building near river at right. Back: Light green. Seated woman and book at center. Overprint: Black vertical text: *Billete de curso forzoso* at left. — 25.00 / 100. / 200.

S348 10 Pesos — Good / Fine / XF

10.3.1900. Black on brown underprint. Seated Indian woman and tree at left in circle. Back: Red. Overprint: Black vertical text: *Billete de curso forzoso* at left.

	Good	Fine	XF
a. Without series.	40.00	150.	300.
b. Series A.	40.00	150.	300.

S349 20 Pesos

10.3.1900. Horseback rider. — 150. / 300. / 600.

S350 50 Pesos — Good / Fine / XF

10.3.1900. Brown on yellow underprint. Monument of Bolívar on horseback in Cartagena at left. Back: Violet. Arms at left, flower at right. Overprint: Black vertical text: *Billete de curso forzoso* at left. — 100. / 200. / 500.

S351 100 Pesos — Good / Fine / XF

10.3.1900. Black on red underprint. Large letters *CIEN* across face. Village view at center, eagle at right. Back: Blue with black overprint text. Two allegorical women at center. — 100. / 200. / 500.

S351A 100 Pesos — Good / Fine / XF

10.3.1900. Village view at center, eagle at right. — 200. / 400. / 800.

Banco de la Provincia de Cartajena

1851 Issue

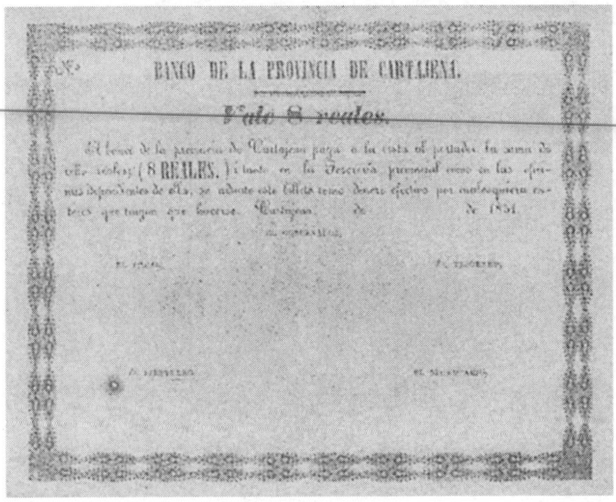

S351B 8 Reales — Good / Fine / XF

1851. Black. Paper: Orange. Unsigned remainder. Rare. — — / — / —

Banco del Cauca

1870-86 Issue

S352 20 Centavos — Good / Fine / XF

1884. Black. Series G. Paper: Peach. — 200. / 400. / 800.

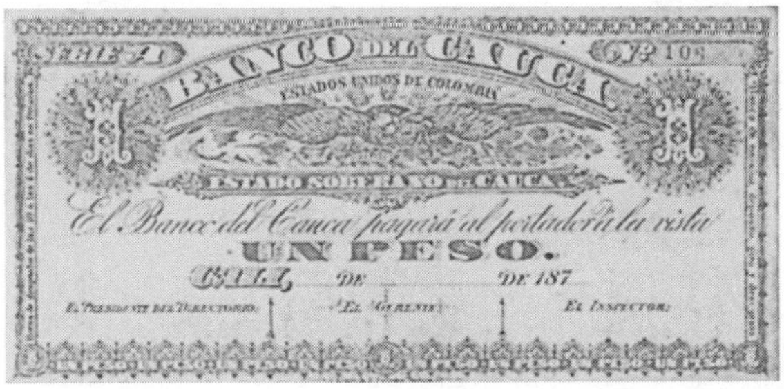

S353 1 Peso — Good / Fine / XF

187x. Black. Eagle at upper center. Uniface. Printer: Lit. D. Paredes. Rare. — — / — / —

S356 20 Centavos — Good / Fine / XF

1.5.1886. Black on red-orange underprint. Simon Bolívar at left. Series G. Back: Brown. Printer: ABNC.

	Good	Fine	XF
a. Issued note.	40.00	100.	200.
p. Proof.	—	Unc	750.

S358 1 Peso

16.5.1881. Black on red-orange underprint. Shepherdess with sheep at left, portrait Caldas at right. Back: Red-orange. Arms at center. Printer: ABNC.

	Good	Fine	XF
a. Issued note.	150.	400.	750.
p. Proof.	—	Unc	750.

S359 5 Pesos

16.5.1881. Black on gold underprint. Allegorical child with fruit plate and sheaf ("Abundance") at upper left, portrait man in uniform at upper center, allegorical woman and two children ("Plenty No. 2") at lower right. Back: Orange. Arms at center. Printer: ABNC.

	Good	Fine	XF
a. Issued note.	200.	500.	1000.
p. Proof.	—	Unc	750.
s. Specimen.	—	Unc	1000.

S360 10 Pesos

16.5.1881. Black on blue underprint. Seated Indian woman ("La Hua de los Incas") at upper left, portrait Simon Bolívar at right. Series C. Back: Blue. Arms at center. Printer: ABNC.

	Good	Fine	XF
a. Issued note.	200.	400.	800.
p. Proof.	—	Unc	750.

NOTE: For #S358-S360 with notes overprint for Banco del Estado 1900, see #S471-S473.

Banco Central

1887-1907 Issue

S366 1 Peso

19.8.1887. Black on red-orange underprint. Standing Justice at left. Portrait Gen. R. Reyes at right or center. Back: Red-orange. Arms at center. Printer: ABNC.

	Good	Fine	XF
a. Issued note.	200.	400.	800.
p. Proof, uniface.	—	Unc	750.
s. Specimen.	—	Unc	950.

S367 1 Peso	Good	Fine	XF
17.7.1907; 15.9.1907. Black on red-orange underprint. Standing Justice at left. Portrait Gen. R. Reyes at right or center. Back: Red-orange. Arms at center. Like #S366 but round date stamping. Printer: ABNC.	200.	400.	800.

S368 5 Pesos

ND (ca. 1900). Black and blue on green underprint. Allegorical woman and child ("History") at left. Portrait Gen. R. Reyes at right or center. Back: Green. Buildings at center. Printer: ABNC.

	Good	Fine	XF
p. Proof, uniface.	—	Unc	750.
r. Unsigned remainder.	—	Unc	400.
s. Specimen.	—	Unc	1000.

S369 10 Pesos

ND (ca.1900). Allegorical woman seated with sheaf and sickle at left. Portrait Gen. R. Reyes at right or center. Back: Brown. Condor on mountain top at center. Printer: ABNC.

	Good	Fine	XF
p. Proof.	—	Unc	750.
s. Specimen.	—	Unc	1000.

NOTE: For #S366-S369 with overprint: *CÉDULA DE TESORERIA* and dated 1919 (formerly #S936-S938) see Vol. 2.

S370 25 Pesos

ND (ca.1900). Black on red-brown underprint. Allegorical woman and children ("Plenty No. 2") at lower left and right. Portrait Gen. R. Reyes at right or center. Back: Red-brown. Lumber barge at center. Printer: ABNC.

	Good	Fine	XF
p. Proof.	—	Unc	750.
s. Specimen.	—	Unc	1000.

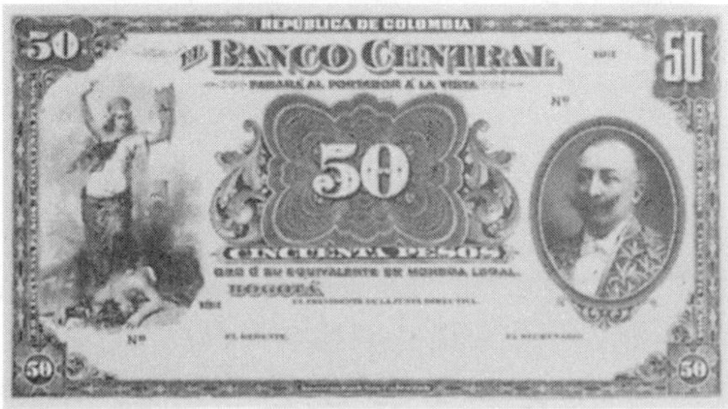

S371 50 Pesos

23.8.1907. Black on light red underprint. Allegorical woman and fallen man at left. Portrait Gen. R. Reyes at right or center. Back: Red. Building at center. Printer: ABNC.

	Good	Fine	XF
a. Issued note. Rare.	—	—	—
p. Proof.	—	Unc	800.
s. Specimen.	—	Unc	1500.

S372 100 Pesos

3.8.1907. Black on purple underprint. Allegorical woman with globe and child ("Civilization") at center right. Portrait Gen. R. Reyes at right or center. Back: Purple. Two women at center. Printer: ABNC.

	Good	Fine	XF
a. Issued note. Rare.	—	—	—
p. Proof.	—	Unc	800.
s. Specimen.	—	Unc	2500.

Banco de Cipaquirá

1882 Issue

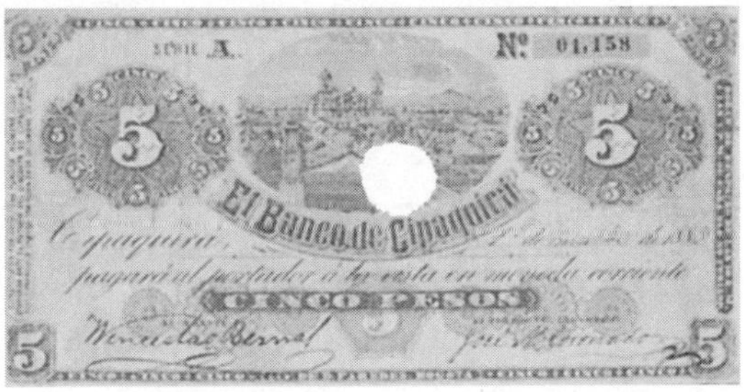

S376 5 Pesos

1.3.1882; 16.8.1882. Black on orange underprint. View of city at center. Series A. Back: Blue. Printer: D. Paredes, Bogota.

	Good	Fine	XF
a. Issued note.	25.00	50.00	100.
b. Oval revalidation stamping with date *Mayo - 86* at left on face only.	25.00	50.00	100.

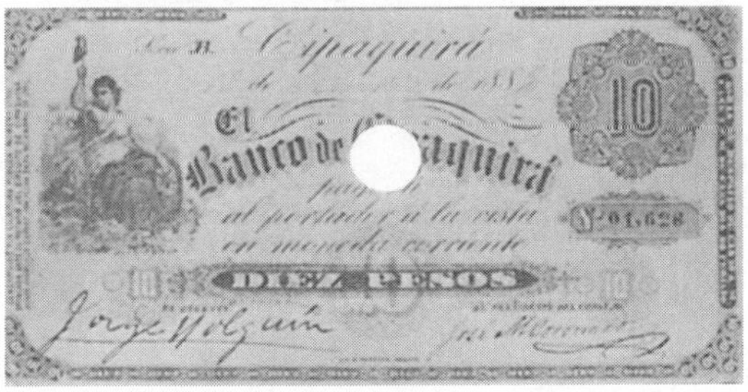

S377 10 Pesos

	Good	Fine	XF
1.2.1882. Black on aqua underprint. Woman seated with staff of Liberty at left. Series B. Back: Red-brown. Printer: D. Paredes, Bogota.	40.00	75.00	150.

S378 50 Pesos

	Good	Fine	XF
29.8.1882. Black on green underprint. Woman with tablet and child at left. Series C. Back: Peach. Printer: D. Paredes, Bogota.	40.00	75.00	150.

NOTE: #S376-S378 are generally found with punched hole cancellation at center.

Banco de Colombia

1875-81 Issue

S382 1 Peso

	Good	Fine	XF
1.4.1875. Black on aqua underprint. Girl with shield and eagle at center right. Uniface. Printer: CCBB. Specimen. Rare.	—	—	—

S384 10 Pesos

20.7.1876. Black on light orange underprint. Two girls with sheaves at center. Back: Light orange. Printer: CCBB.

	Good	Fine	XF
a. Issued note. Rare.	—	—	—
p. Proof.	—	—	—

S385 10 Pesos

	Good	Fine	XF
20.7.1876. Black. Blacksmith shop at upper left. Printer: CCBB. Proof. Rare.	—	—	—

S386 20 Pesos

	Good	Fine	XF
20.7.1876. Black. Ships in harbor at center. Printer: CCBB. Proof. Rare.	—	—	—

S387 50 Pesos

15.12.1881. Black on brown underprint. Man with pack animals at upper center. Back: Brown. Printer: ABNC.

	Good	Fine	XF
a. Issued note. Rare.	—	—	—
p. Proof, uniface.	—	Unc	800.
s. Specimen.	—	Unc	800.

		Good	Fine	XF
S387A	**50 Pesos**			
	15.12.1881. Black on green underprint. Man with pack animals at upper center. Like #S387. Back: Green. Printer: ABNC. Proof.	—	Unc	1100.

		Good	Fine	XF
S388	**100 Pesos**			
	15.12.1881. Black on orange underprint. Columbus landing in New World ("Columbus") at upper center. Back: Orange. Printer: ABNC.			
	p. Proof, uniface.	—	Unc	800.
	s. Specimen.	—	Unc	1100.
S388A	**100 Pesos**			
	15.12.1881. Black on red underprint. Columbus landing in New World ("Columbus") at upper center. Like #S388. Back: Red. Printer: ABNC. Specimen.	—	Unc	800.

1918-19 Cédula Hipotecaria Issue

(Mortgage bill).

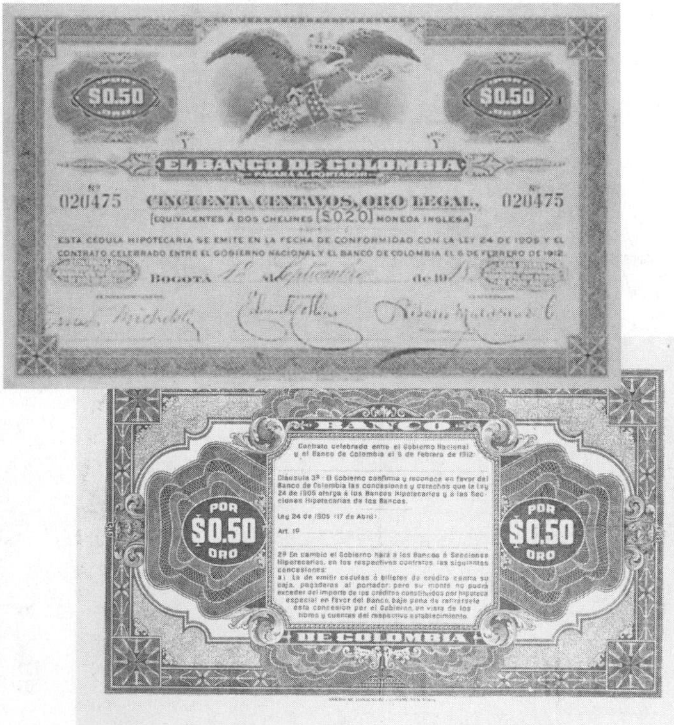

		Good	Fine	XF
S391	**50 Centavos = 2 Shillings**			
	1.7.1918; 1.9.1918. Green and red. Eagle at top center. Back: Green.	50.00	125.	300.

		Good	Fine	XF
S392	**1 Peso = 4 Shillings**			
	1.1.1919. Blue and red. Eagle at top center. Back: Blue.			
	a1. Issued note.	50.00	200.	400.
	s. Specimen.	—	Unc	800.
S397	**500 Pesos = 100 Pounds**			
	(ca.1919). Black, blue and red. Landing of Columbus at upper center, eagle in red at lower center. Back: Blue-gray text. Specimen.	350.	750.	1250.

Banco Colombiano

A Guatemalan bank which had Colombian share capital. Some of its notes may have been in circulation also in Colombia. For a listing of notes from this bank see Guatemala #S121-S126.

Banco del Comercio

1899 Provisional Issue

		Good	Fine	XF
S398	**1 Peso**			
	30.10.1899. Overprint: New bank name on back of Banco Republicano 1 Peso #S811.	350.	800.	1400.

1899 Regular Issue

		Good	Fine	XF
S400	**5 Pesos**			
	8.12.1899. Black on green underprint. Seated woman with hammer at lower left.	400.	900.	1500.

		Good	Fine	XF
S401	**10 Pesos**			
	17.10.1899. Black and red on pink underprint. River scene with church and trees at center. Printer: Tipografia Central Medellin.	400.	900.	1500.

Banco de Credito Hipotecario

1883 Issue

		Good	Fine	XF
S406	**5 Pesos**			
	1.4.1883. Black and brown. Back: Brownish red. Large *X*'s at left and right. Printer: D. Paredes.	400.	900.	1500.

Banco de Cundinamarca

188x-1881 Issue

	Good	Fine	XF
S407 50 Centavos 188x. Black on light brown underprint. Arms at upper right. Series D. Uniface. Unsigned remainder. Rare.	—	—	—
S408 50 Centavos 188x. Arms at center. Uniface. Rare.	—	—	—
S411 5 Pesos 3.1.1881. Eagle. Rare.	—	—	—

Banco del Departamento de Bolívar

1885-88 Issue

	Good	Fine	XF
S421 50 Centavos 1.3.1888. Black on orange underprint. People pouring water from jugs at center. Back: Orange. Printer: HBNC.			
a. Black overprint: *Decreto No. 121 de 1895* and signature at center on back.	100.	200.	400.
p. Proof.	—	Unc	500.

	Good	Fine	XF
S422 1 Peso 1.3.1888. Black on dark orange underprint. Helmeted Athena at left, dog's head at right. Back: Dark orange. Printer: HBNC.			
a. Black overprint: *Decreto...1895* like #S421a, vertically at right on back.	200.	400.	750.
p. Black on green underprint. Proof.	—	Unc	500.

	Good	Fine	XF
S423 5 Pesos 1.3.1888. Black on blue underprint. Campsite with barn and mountains in background at center. Back: Blue. Printer: HBNC.			
a. Black overprint: *Decreto...1895* like #S422a.	200.	400.	750.
p. Proof.	—	Unc	500.
S424 10 Pesos 9.11.1885. Simon Bolívar; steam train. Printer: HBNC. Reported not confirmed.	—	—	—

NOTE: #S421-S423 are known issued only with overprint: *Decreto...1895.*

Banco Dugand

1919-22 Issue

	Good	Fine	XF
S426 1 Peso 20.2.1919. Black on gold underprint. Anchor and sun in circle at top center. Back: Gold. Printer: ABNC.			
a. Issued note.	100.	250.	500.
s. Specimen.	—	Unc	800.
S427 2 Pesos 19xx (ca. 1919). Black on blue underprint. Anchor and sun in circle at top center. Back: Blue. Printer: ABNC. Archive copy.	—	Unc	1000.
S428 5 Pesos ND (ca.1919). Black on red-orange underprint. Anchor and sun in circle at top center. Back: Red-orange. Printer: ABNC. Archive copy.	—	Unc	1000.

	Good	Fine	XF
S429 1 Peso 31.7.1921; 31.1.1922. Black on gold underprint. Anchor and sun in circle at top center. Similar to #S426. Printer: ABNC.			
a. Issued note.	100.	300.	500.
s. Specimen.	—	Unc	1000.

Banco del Estado de Bolívar

1885 Issue

	Good	Fine	XF
S430 20 Centavos 6.1885. Black. Large value numeral at right. Rare.	—	—	—
S431 20 Centavos 6.1885. Black. Without value numeral at right. Rare.	—	—	—
S433 1 Peso 6.1885. Black. Arms at upper center. Rare.	—	—	—
S434 5 Pesos 11.20.1885. Dark red. Arms at center. Rare.	—	—	—
S435 10 Pesos 11.20.1885. Dark blue. Rare.	—	—	—
S435A 100 Pesos 6.1885. Black and red. Arms at center. Rare.	—	—	—

Banco del Estado

1884 Issue

Issues with heading *ESTADO SOBERANO DEL CAUCA.*

		Good	Fine	XF
S436	**20 Centavos** 1.3.1884. Black on blue underprint. Arms with condor at center. Uniface. Series A. Printer: D. Paredes.	75.00	150.	300.
S437	**50 Centavos** 1.3.1884. Black. Arms with condor at center. Uniface. Series B. Printer: D. Paredes.	200.	350.	750.
S438	**1 Peso** 1.3.1884. Black. Arms with condor at center. Uniface. Series C. Printer: D. Paredes.	300.	500.	900.
S439	**5 Pesos** 1.3.1884. Black and brown. Arms with condor at center. Uniface. Series D. Printer: D. Paredes.	150.	400.	750.

		Good	Fine	XF
S440	**10 Pesos** 1.3.1884. Black and red. Arms with condor at center. Uniface. Series E. Printer: D. Paredes.	225.	500.	900.
S441	**25 Pesos** 1.3.1884. Black. Arms with condor at center. Uniface. Series F. Printer: D. Paredes.	300.	600.	1000.
S442	**50 Pesos** 1.3.1884. Black. Arms with condor at center. Uniface. Series G. Printer: D. Paredes.	400.	750.	1250.
S443	**100 Pesos** 1.3.1884. Black. Arms with condor at center. Uniface. Series H. Printer: D. Paredes.	600.	900.	1400.

1886 Issue

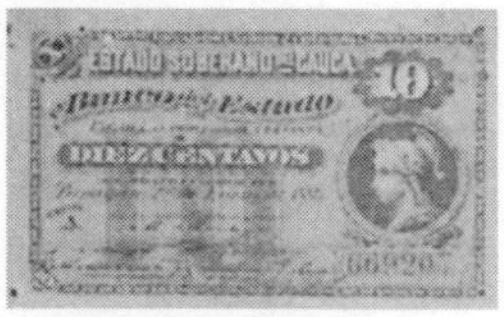

		Good	Fine	XF
S446	**10 Centavos** 2.1.1886. Black on orange underprint. Helmeted woman at right. Series A. Back: Orange. Printer: ABNC.			
	a. Issued note.	50.00	150.	300.
	s. Specimen.	—	Unc	750.

		Good	Fine	XF
S447	**20 Centavos** 2.1.1886. Black on brown underprint. Helmeted Athena at left. Series B. Back: Brown. Printer: ABNC.	100.	200.	350.

		Good	Fine	XF
S448	**50 Centavos** 2.1.1886. Black on green underprint. Man at left. Series C. Back: Green. Printer: ABNC.	75.00	150.	325.

		Good	Fine	XF
S449	**1 Peso** 1.6.1887. Black on green and red-orange underprint. Portrait at left and right, arms at center. Series D. Back: Red-orange. Printer: ABNC.	75.00	150.	325.

		Good	Fine	XF
S450	**5 Pesos** 9.9.1886; 1.6.1887. Black on brown and blue underprint. Arms at left, portrait at right and center. Series E. Back: Brown. Printer: ABNC.	150.	300.	750.

		Good	Fine	XF
S451	**10 Pesos** 21.4.1886. Black on green and red underprint. Portrait Simon Bolívar at left, "Raphael's *Angel*" at center, standing woman ("Caryatides") at right. Series F. Back: Green. Printer: ABNC.			
	a. Issued note.	200.	500.	800.
	p. Proof.	—	Unc	800.

		Good	Fine	XF
S452	**25 Pesos** 5.5.1882; 2.5.1886; 8.5.1886. Black on blue and orange underprint. Arms at left, reclining woman ("La Siesta") at center, portrait at right. Series G. Back: Blue. Printer: ABNC.			
	a. Issued note.	500.	800.	1250.
	p. Proof.	—	Unc	800.

1900 Provisional Issues

		Good	Fine	XF
S460	**1 Peso** 15.2.1900. Overprint: On #S316. Rare.	—	—	—
S461	**1 Peso** 23.2.1900. Overprint: On #S316. Rare.	—	—	—

		Good	Fine	XF
S462	**5 Pesos** 23.2.1900. Back: Brown and black text and new date. Overprint: Brown on face of #S317. Rare.	—	—	—

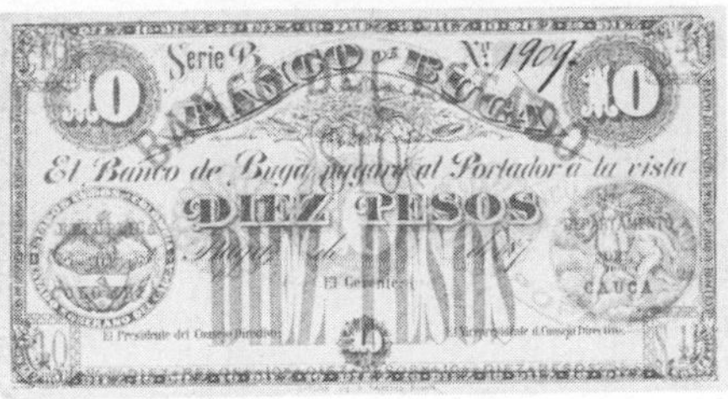

S463 10 Pesos

	Good	Fine	XF
23.2.1900. Back: Red and black text. Overprint: Red on face of #S318. Rare.	—	—	—

S464 20 Pesos

	Good	Fine	XF
23.2.1900. Back: Green and black text. Overprint: Green on face of #S319. Rare.	—	—	—

S465 50 Pesos

	Good	Fine	XF
23.2.1900. Back: Red and black text. Overprint: Red on face of #S320. Rare.	—	—	—

#S471-S473 overprint of new bank name on Banco del Cauca notes (#S358-S360). New bank name overprint on face; several lines of black text and new date overprint on back.

S471 1 Peso

	Good	Fine	XF
23.2.1900. Overprint: Black on face and back of #S358. .	100.	200.	400.

#S471-S473 overprint. new bank name on Banco del Cauca notes (#S358-S360). New bank name overprint. on face; several lines of black text and new date overprint. on back.

S472 5 Pesos

	Good	Fine	XF
23.2.1900. Overprint: On #S359.	200.	400.	800.

S473 10 Pesos

	Good	Fine	XF
23.2.1900. Series C. Overprint: Red on face, black text on back of #S360.	150.	350.	700.

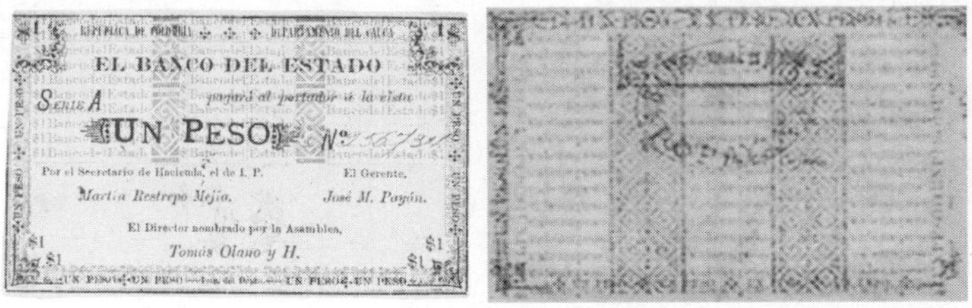

S481 1 Peso

	Good	Fine	XF
23.2.1900. Black on red underprint. Series A. Printer: Imp. del Depto.			
a. Printed names of officials.	75.00	150.	300.
b. Stamped signature of officials.	75.00	150.	300.

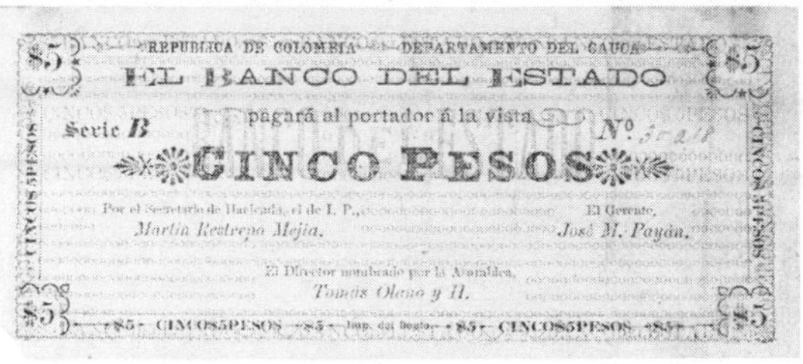

S482 5 Pesos

	Good	Fine	XF
23.2.1900. Black on red underprint. Series B. Printer: Imp. del Depto.	75.00	150.	300.

S483 10 Pesos

	Good	Fine	XF
23.2.1900. Green on red underprint. Series C. Printer: Imp. del Depto.	100.	250.	500.

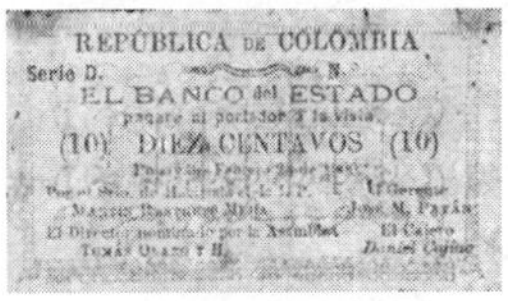

S491 10 Centavos

	Good	Fine	XF
23.2.1900-face. 21.6.1900-back. Black on blue underprint. Series D. Back: Blue.	25.00	75.00	150.

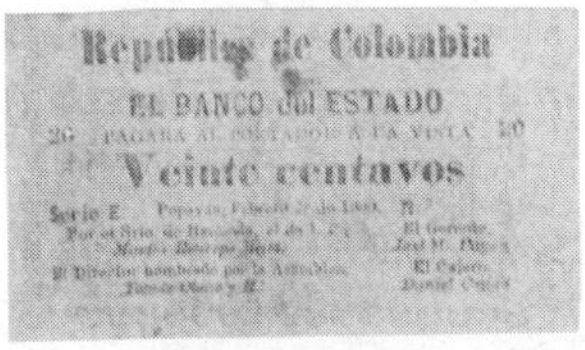

S492 20 Centavos

	Good	Fine	XF
23.2.1900-face. 21.6.1900-back. Black on blue underprint. Series E. Back: Blue.	40.00	100.	200.

S493 50 Centavos

	Good	Fine	XF
23.2.1900-face. 21.6.1900-back. Black on red underprint. Arms at upper left. Series F.	40.00	100.	200.

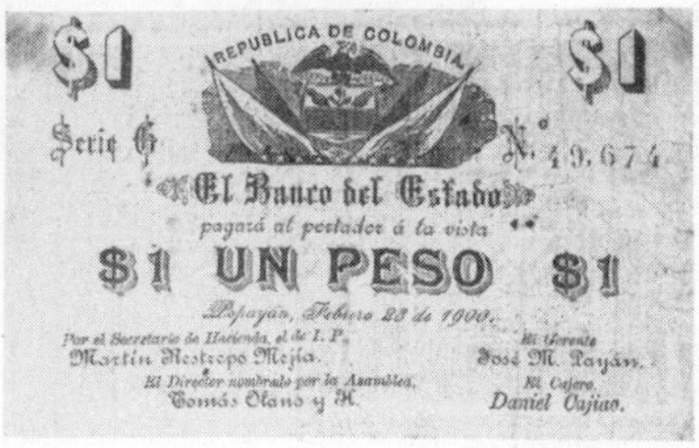

S494 1 Peso — Good / Fine / XF

23.2.1900-face. 21.6.1900-back. Black on yellow underprint. Arms with flags at center. Series G. Back: Yellow. — 40.00 / 100. / 200.

S495 5 Pesos — Good / Fine / XF

23.2.1900-face. 21.6.1900-back. Red on green underprint. Eagle at left, local arms at right. Series I. Back: Red. Printer: Imp. Comercial, Cali. — 25.00 / 75.00 / 150.

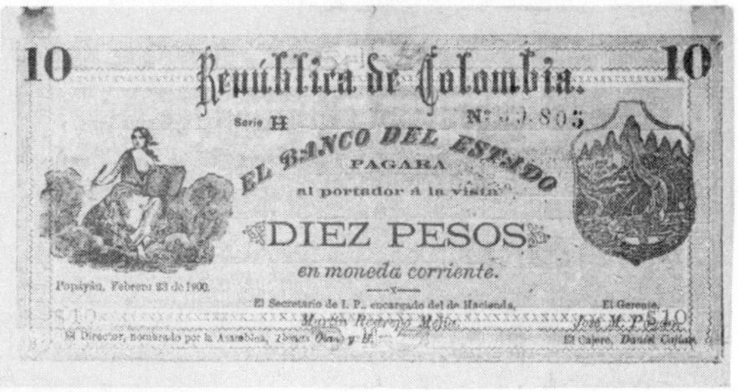

S496 10 Pesos — Good / Fine / XF

23.2.1900-face. 21.6.1900-back. Brown on gray underprint. Woman with tablet at left, local arms at right. Series H. Back: Gray-brown. Printer: Imp. Comercial, Cali. — 75.00 / 150. / 300.

1900 Issue

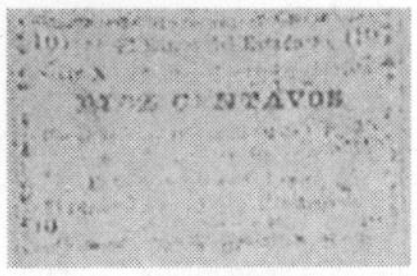

		Good	Fine	XF
S497	**10 Centavos**			
	20.10.1900. Dark red. Series X.	75.00	150.	300.
S499	**50 Centavos**			
	20.10.1900. Light brown. Series V. Paper: Blue.			
	a. Issued note.	75.00	150.	300.
	p. Proof.	—	—	—

1900 Regular Issue

#501-S506 most likely printed in the United States.

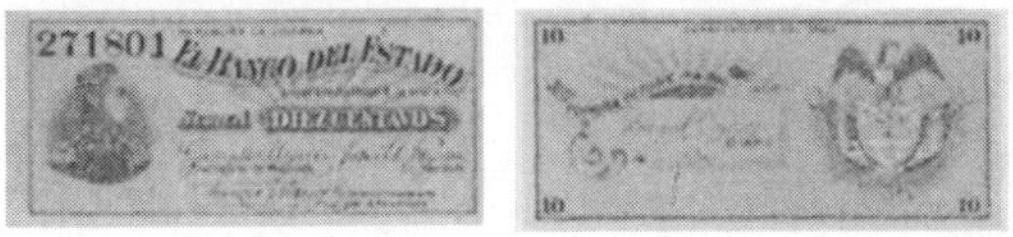

S501 10 Centavos — VG / VF / UNC

1.10.1900. Black on blue underprint. Simon Bolívar at left. Series A. Back: Blue. Signature and date at left, arms at right. — 5.00 / 10.00 / 20.00

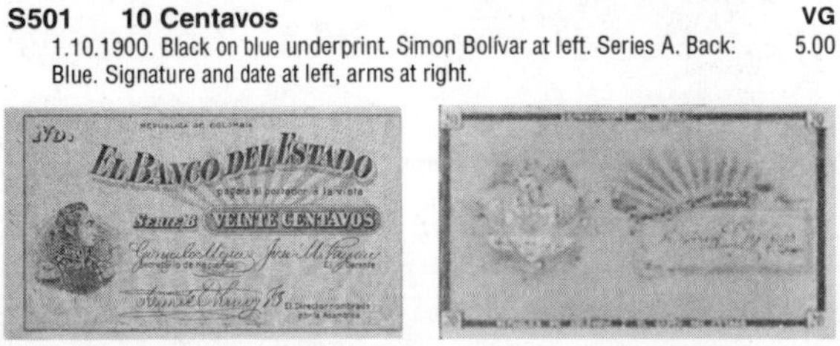

		VG	VF	UNC
S502	**20 Centavos**			
	1.10.1900. Black on brown underprint. Series B. Simon Bolivar at right. Back: Arms at left, date and printed signature at right.			
	a. Issued note.	5.00	10.00	20.00
	b. Uniface with blue bank stamping and handwritten #.	7.50	15.00	30.00

NOTE: Litho plates were found for #S501 and S502 (also others?). Reprints have been made.

S503 50 Centavos — VG / VF / UNC

1.10.1900. Black on orange underprint. A. J. de Sucre at left. Blue or red serial #. Series C. Back: Orange. Arms at left, date and printed signature at right. — 7.50 / 15.00 / 30.00

		VG	VF	UNC
S504	**1 Peso**			
	1.10.1900. Black on green underprint. Justice at left. Series D. Back: Green. Arms at left, date and printed signature at right.			
	a. Printer: *Holden y Motley, Nueva York.*	7.50	15.00	30.00
	b. Printer: *W.L.H. Co., New York.*	10.00	20.00	40.00
	c. Without printer's name, finished note with serial #.	5.00	10.00	25.00
	d. Like c., but without serial #.	2.50	5.00	10.00
	e. Uniface print, face or back.	2.50	5.00	10.00
	f. Like b, but printer: *Hosford & Sons Ptg. Co. N.Y.*	5.00	10.00	25.00
	r. Like b, but without serial #. Remainder.	—	5.00	10.00

S505 5 Pesos — VG / VF / UNC

1.10.1900. Black on orange underprint. Liberty with pole and cap standing at left. Series E. Back: Orange. Arms at left, date and printed signature at right. — 5.00 / 10.00 / 10.00

S506 10 Pesos — VG / VF / UNC

1.10.1900. Black on brown underprint. Arms, flags and seated woman at left. Series F. Back: Brown. Arms at left, date and printed signature at right. — 5.00 / 10.00 / 20.00

NOTE: #S501-S506 may be found as unfinished remainders w/o serial #.

Banco Hipotecario

1881 Issue

S511 5 Pesos	Good	Fine	XF
1.10.1881. Black on brown underprint. Seated woman with sheaf with farm in background ("Mechanics & Agriculture") at left, farmer plowing with horses at right. Series Y. Back: Brown. Printer: ABNC.			
p. Proof.	—	Unc	500.
s. Specimen.	—	Unc	900.

S512 10 Pesos	Good	Fine	XF
1.10.1881. Black on green underprint. Seated woman with sheep at left, three horse heads ("Pharaoh's Horses") in circle at upper right. Series Z. Back: Green. Printer: ABNC.			
p. Proof.	—	Unc	500.
s. Specimen.	—	Unc	900.
S514 50 Pesos			
1.10.1881. Black on orange underprint. Sitting woman with farm produce at left, basket of corn at right. Series W. Back: Orange. Printer: ABNC.			
p. Proof.	—	Unc	500.
s. Specimen.	—	Unc	900.

S515 100 Pesos	Good	Fine	XF
1.10.1881. Black on blue underprint. Griffins at left and right, farm implements and produce in background of portrait, shepherdess with sheep at center. Series V. Back: Blue. Printer: ABNC.			
p. Proof.	—	Unc	500.
s. Specimen.	—	Unc	900.

NOTE: #S511-S515 are known issued only with red seal overprint: *Banco Nacional* and *30.10.1899* date in overprint on back. For listing see #S636-S640.

Banco Hipotecario de la Mutualidád

Ley 24 de 1905

S516 50 Centavos	Good	Fine	XF
1.1.1919. Black on deep blue, red and pale orange underprint. Harvesting coffee beans at upper center. Back: Dark brown on pale green underprint. Arms at center. Printer: Lit. J. L. Arango, Medellin.	200.	400.	800.

#S517 and S518 printer: ABNC.

S517 1 Peso Oro	Good	Fine	XF
ND (ca.1919). Blue on yellow underprint. Harvesting coffee beans at upper center. Similar to #S516. Series A. Back: Blue. Arms at left. Printer: ABNC. 6% interest-bearing note.			
a. Issued note.	200.	400.	800.
s. Specimen.	—	Unc	600.
S518 1 Peso Oro			
ND (ca.1921). Blue. Harvesting coffee beans at upper center. Similar to #S517 but without underprint. Series A. Printer: ABNC. 4% interest-bearing note. Proof.	—	—	—

Banco Hipotecario del Pacífico

1920-22 Bono Bancario Issue

#S521-S523 with solid bar overprint on text below denomination under condor at center. Overprint: *Ley...* on back.

S521 50 Centavos	Good	Fine	XF
8.7.1920. Green on tan underprint. Condor in flight at center. Back: Green. Overprint: Solid bar on text below denomination under condor at center. *Ley...* on back. Printer: ABNC.			
a. Issued note.	75.00	150.	300.
p. Proof without overprint: *Ley...* on back.	—	Unc	500.
s. Specimen.	—	Unc	600.

S522 1 Peso	Good	Fine	XF
1921. Green on lilac underprint. Condor in flight at center. Series A. Back: Green. Overprint: Solid bar on text below denomination under condor at center. *Ley...* on back. Printer: ABNC.			
a. Issued note.	100.	200.	400.
p. Proof without overprint: *Ley...* on back.	—	Unc	500.
s. Specimen.	—	Unc	600.
S523 5 Pesos			
2.1921. Black on red-orange underprint. Condor in flight at center. Back: Red-orange. Overprint: Solid bar on text below denomination under condor at center. *Ley...* on back. Printer: ABNC.			
a. Issued note.	100.	200.	300.
p. Proof without overprint: *Ley...* on back.	—	Unc	600.
s. Specimen.	—	Unc	600.
S524 10 Pesos			
19xx. Blue on olive underprint. Condor in flight at center. Back: Orange. Printer: ABNC.			
p. Proof.	—	Unc	500.
s. Specimen.	—	Unc	600.

S525 20 Pesos	Good	Fine	XF
11.4.1922. Black on light brown and multicolor underprint. Condor in flight at center. Panel of interest markers at right. Back: Brown. Printer: ABNC.			
a. Issued note. Rare.	—	—	—
p. Proof. 19xx.	—	Unc	500.
s. Specimen.	—	Unc	600.

Banco de Honda

1882 Issue

S531 1 Peso	Good	Fine	XF
1882. Blue and black. Steam locomotive. Rare.	—	—	—
S532 5 Pesos			
188x. Rare.	—	—	—
S533 10 Pesos			
188x. Rare.	—	—	—

Banco del Huila

1921 Provisional Bono Boncario Issue

Cat. No. / Description	Good	Fine	XF
S541 50 Centavos			
13.5.1921. Brown on multicolor underprint. Back: Brown. Overprint: On #S821.	100.	200.	400.
S542 20 Pesos			
9.6.1921. Black on multicolor underprint. Back: Olive-green. Overprint: On #S825. Rare.	—	—	—

Banco Industrial

1883-1900 Issue

Issued at Manizales.

Cat. No. / Description	Good	Fine	XF
S546 1 Peso			
20.1.1900. Blue. Two allegorical women at upper center. Back: Orange. Printer: PBC.			
a. Issued note.	200.	400.	800.
p. Proof.	—	Unc	500.
S547 5 Pesos			
188x; 20.1.1890. Orange on orange underprint. Back: Blue. Printer: PBC.	300.	600.	1000.
S548 10 Pesos			
1883. Blue. Woman with flowers. Printer: PBC.	500.	600.	1000.
S549 100 Pesos			
188x. Printer: PBC. Proof.	—	—	—

Ley 24 de 1905; 18 de Mayo de 1918 - Cédula Hipotecaria Issue

Issued at Cartagena.

#S551-S553 interest payable to 1934.

Cat. No. / Description	Good	Fine	XF
S551 1 Peso			
1.5.1919; 30.6.1919. Black and green. Standing woman with globe ("Commerce") at left. Back: Green. Printer: ABNC. Interest payable to 1934.			
a. Issued note.	100.	200.	400.
s. Specimen.	—	Unc	600.
S552 2 Pesos			
1.1.1923. Black and orange. Standing woman with globe ("Commerce") at left. Back: Orange. Printer: ABNC. Interest payable to 1934.			
a. Issued note.	150.	400.	—
p. Proof.	—	Unc	500.
s. Specimen.	—	Unc	600.
S553 5 Pesos			
1.1.1923. Black and blue. Standing woman with globe ("Commerce") at left. Back: Blue. Printer: ABNC. Interest payable to 1934.			
a. Issued note. Rare.	—	—	—
s. Specimen.	—	Unc	600.

1920s Issue

Issued at Cartagena.

#S554-S556 Interest payable to 1932.

Cat. No. / Description	Good	Fine	XF
S554 1 Peso			
ND. Black and green. Standing woman with globe ("Commerce") at left. Back: Green. Printer: ABNC. 156x80mm. Interest payable to 1932.			
p. Proof.	—	Unc	500.
s. Specimen.	—	Unc	600.
S555 2 Pesos			
ND. Black and red-orange. Standing woman with globe ("Commerce") at left. Back: Red-orange. Printer: ABNC. 156x80mm. Interest payable to 1932.			
p. Proof.	—	Unc	500.
s. Specimen.	—	Unc	600.
S556 5 Pesos			
ND. Black and blue. Standing woman with globe ("Commerce") at left. Back: Blue. Printer: ABNC. 156x80mm. Interest payable to 1932.			
p. Proof.	—	Unc	500.
s. Specimen	—	Unc	600.
S558 20 Pesos			
ND (ca.1923). Black on brown underprint. Standing woman with globe ("Commerce") at left. Back: Brown. Interest payable to 1968.			
s. Specimen.	—	Unc	600.

Banco Internacional

1884 Issue

Cat. No. / Description	Good	Fine	XF
S561 1 Peso			
15.12.1884. Black on green underprint. Cart with oxen at center. Back: Green. Printer: ABNC.			
a. Issued note. Rare.	—	—	—
s. Series A. Specimen.	—	Unc	750.
S562 5 Pesos			
15.12.1884. Black on orange underprint. Portrait woman's head at left, allegorical woman with safe, money and scales at center right. Back: Orange. Printer: ABNC.			
p. Proof.	—	Unc	600.
s. Specimen.	—	Unc	750.

Cat. No. / Description	Good	Fine	XF
S563 10 Pesos			
15.12.1884. Black on brown underprint. Justice seated at right. Series C. Back: Brown. Printer: ABNC.			
p. Proof.	—	Unc	600.
s. Specimen.	—	Unc	500.

Cat. No. / Description	Good	Fine	XF
S564 50 Pesos			
15.12.1884. Black on orange underprint. Two seated allegorical women at left, cherubs with globe at center, two girls at right. Series D. Back: Orange. Printer: ABNC.			
p. Proof.	—	Unc	600.

NOTE: #S561-S564 are known issued only with red seal overprint: *Banco Nacional* and *30.10.1899* date in overprint on back. For listing see #S646-S649.

Banco López

1921 Provisional Bono Bancario Issue

#S571 new bank name and other overprint on earlier notes of Banco del Ruiz.

S571 1 Peso	Good	Fine	XF
9.6.1921. Green on multicolor underprint. Back: Green. Overprint: Black and green new bank name on #S822.	75.00	150.	350.

1919 Cédula Hipotecaria Issues

S575 5 Pesos	Good	Fine	XF
1.5.1919. Overprint: Dark green on #S823.			
a. Issued note.	75.00	150.	350.
b. Cancelled with date perforations.	—	—	—

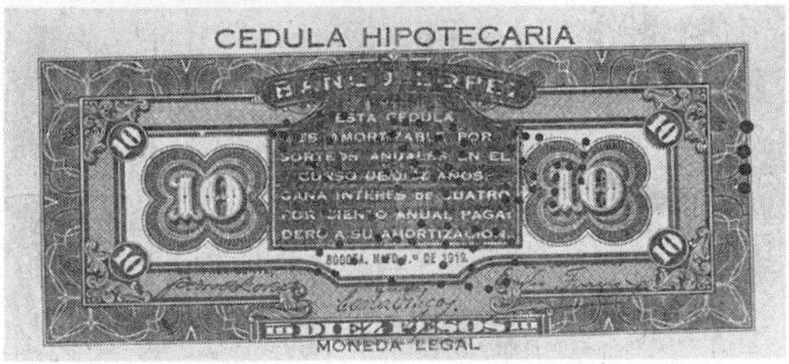

	Good	Fine	XF
S576 10 Pesos			
1.5.1919. Overprint: Black on #S824.	100.	200.	400.
S577 1 Peso			
1.5.1919. Overprint: On #S851.	500.	1000.	1750.
S578 5 Pesos			
1.5.1919. Overprint: On #S852. Rare.	—	—	—
S579 10 Pesos			
1.5.1919. Overprint: On #S853. Rare.	—	—	—
S580 25 Pesos			
1.5.1919. Overprint: On #S854. Rare.	—	—	—

Banco de Marquez

1880s Issue

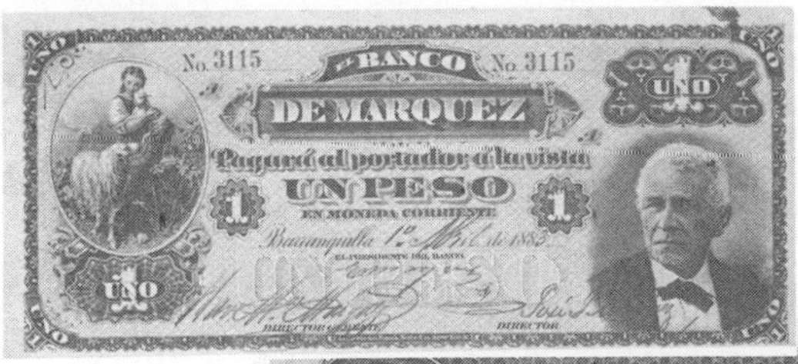

	Good	Fine	XF
S581 1 Peso			
1.4.1883. Black on tan underprint. Shepherdess with sheep at left, man at lower right. Back: Brown. Hand signature at center. Printer: ABNC.			
a. Issued note.	150.	300.	750.
p. Proof.	—	Unc	500.
s. Specimen.	—	Unc	750.
S582 5 Pesos			
188x. Black on green underprint. Man at left, seated woman with flowers at center right. Back: Green. Printer: ABNC.			
p. Proof.	—	Unc	500.
s. Specimen.	—	Unc	750.

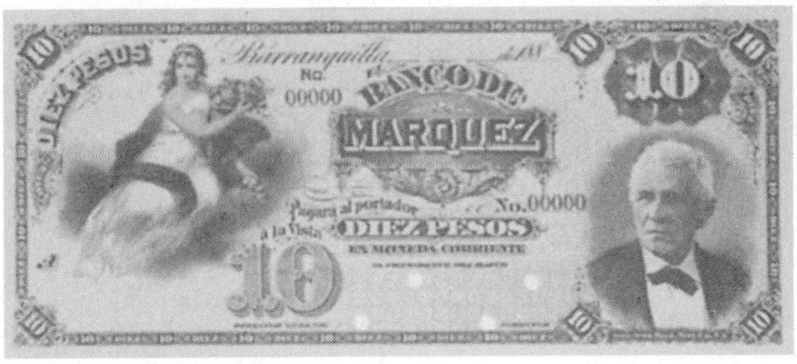

S583 10 Pesos	Good	Fine	XF
188x. Black on orange underprint. Seated woman with fruit ("Vertumna") at left, man at lower right. Back: Orange. Printer: ABNC.			
p. Proof.	—	Unc	500.
s. Specimen.	—	Unc	750.

S585 50 Pesos	Good	Fine	XF
188x. Black on gold underprint. Standing female ("Genius") at left, condor at center, man at lower right. Back: Deep gold. Printer: ABNC.			
p. Proof.	—	Unc	500.
s. Specimen.	—	Unc	750.

S586 100 Pesos — Good / Fine / XF

188x (ca. 1882). Black on blue underprint. Columbus and Indian at left, man at center, "Justice" at right. Back: Blue. Printer: ABNC.

	Good	Fine	XF
p. Proof.	—	Unc	500.
s. Specimen.	—	Unc	750.

NOTE: #S581-S586 are known issued only with red seal overprint: *Banco Nacional* and *30.10.1899* date on back. For listing see #S651-S655.

Banco de Medellin

1895 Issue

		Good	Fine	XF
S591	**50 Centavos** 1.3.1895. Black on gold underprint. Portrait woman with flag at left, beehives at top center, grapes at right. Back: Gold. Printer: BWC.	50.00	150.	300.
S592	**1 Peso** 18xx. Black. Printer: BWC. Specimen. Rare.	—	—	—
S593	**5 Pesos** 18xx. Black. Printer: BWC. Specimen.	—	Unc	750.
S594	**10 Pesos** 18xx. Black. Printer: BWC. Specimen.	—	Unc	750.

		Good	Fine	XF
S597	**100 Pesos** 18xx. Black on orange and green underprint. Portrait woman with flag at left, horses at top center, child with pick at right. Back: Orange and green. Printer: BWC. Specimen.	—	Unc	1250.

1899 Issue

		Good	Fine	XF
S599	**5 Pesos** 17.10.1899. Black. Seated woman with hammer at lower left. Series C. Printer: Tipogfafia Central-Medellin. For similar 5 Pesos see #S777.	75.00	150.	300.

NOTE: For similar 5 Pesos see #S777.

		Good	Fine	XF
S600	**10 Pesos** 17.10.1899; 8.12.1899. Black on red-orange underprint. River scene with church and trees at center. Series A1; A3; A6. Back: Lilac. Printer: Tipografia Central-Medellin.	50.00	100	225.

1899 Provisional Issue

		Good	Fine	XF
S606	**1 Peso** 30.10.1899. Overprint: New bank name and *7.9.1899* date in 7 lines of overprint on back of Banco Republicano #S811.	50.00	100.	225.
S607	**5 Pesos** 30.10.1899. Overprint: New bank name and *7.9.1899* date in 7 lines of overprint on back of Banco Republicano #S812. Rare.	—	—	—

		Good	Fine	XF
S608	**10 Pesos** 1899. Overprint: New bank name and *7.9.1899* date in 7 lines of overprint on back of Banco Republicano #S813. Rare.	—	—	—

Banco Mercantil de Medellin

1870s Issue

		Good	Fine	XF
S610	**5 Pesos** 187x. Black. Uniface. Specimen.	—	—	—
S611	**10 Pesos** 187x. Black. Two seated allegorical women and casks at upper center. Uniface. Paper: White. Proof. Rare.	—	—	—

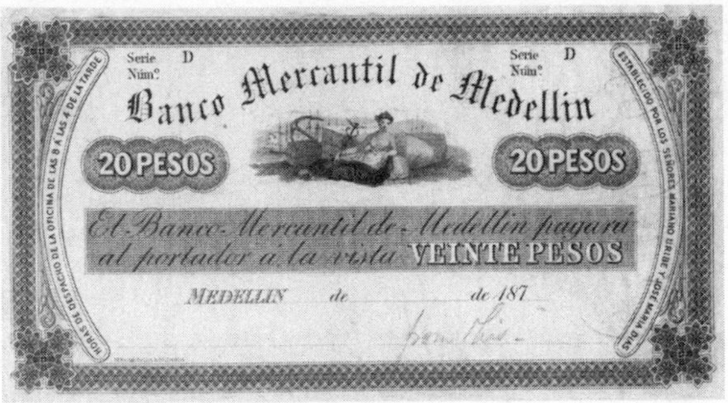

S611A 20 Pesos	Good	Fine	XF
187x. Uniface. Proof.	—	—	—

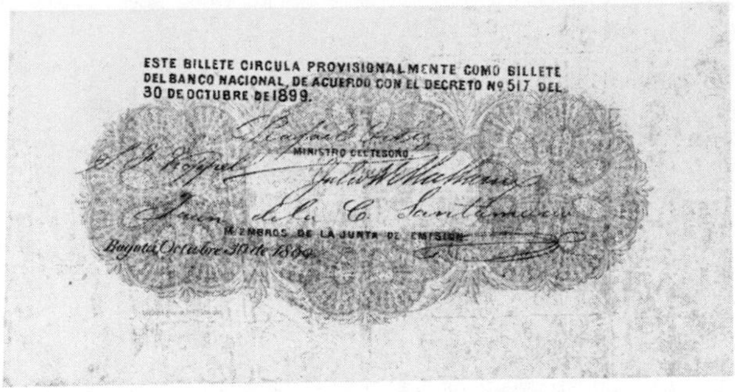

S620 50 Pesos	Good	Fine	XF
30.10.1899. Black on green underprint. Seated woman at center. Back: Orange. Overprint: On #S276. Rare.	—	—	—

S611B 50 Pesos	Good	Fine	XF
187x. Uniface. Proof.	—	—	—

	Good	Fine	XF
S621 1 Peso 30.10.1899. Black. Overprint: On #S281.	150.	350.	750.
S622 5 Pesos 30.10.1899. Blue. Overprint: On #S282.	150.	350.	750.
S623 10 Pesos 30.10.1899. Brown. Overprint: On #S283.	250.	500.	900.
S624 50 Pesos 30.10.1899. Green. Overprint: On #S284. Rare.	—	—	—

Banco Nacional

Provisional Issues Only

1899 Provisional Issues

	Good	Fine	XF
S616 1 Peso 30.10.1899. Black. Red numerals. Overprint: On #S271.	150.	400.	800.
S617 2 Pesos 30.10.1899. Blue. Orange numerals. Overprint: On #S272.	150.	400.	800.

S627 5 Pesos	Good	Fine	XF
30.10.1899. Black on pink underprint. Woman on shore and boats in water at left, Simon Bolívar at right. Back: Blue-green. Overprint: On #S292.	150.	300.	600.

	Good	Fine	XF
S618 5 Pesos 30.10.1899. Orange. Blue numerals. Overprint: On #S273.	150.	400.	800.
S619 10 Pesos 30.10.1899. Brown. Green numerals. Overprint: On #S275.	175.	450.	900.

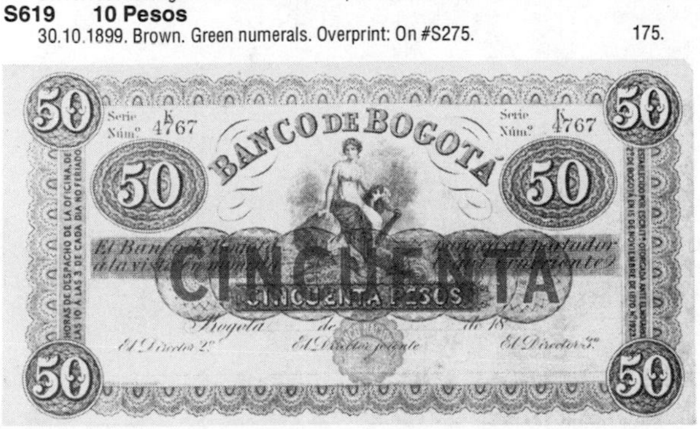

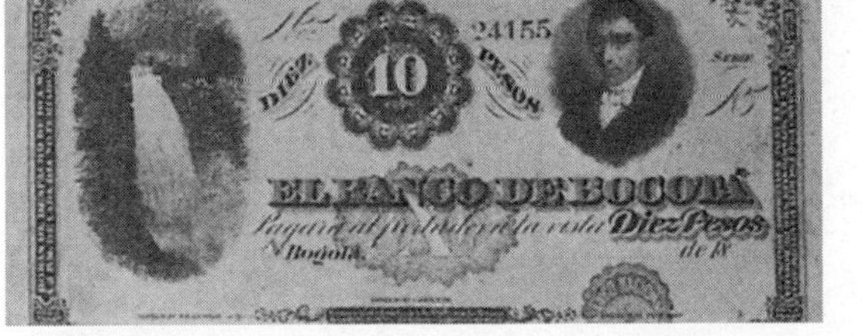

S628 10 Pesos	Good	Fine	XF
30.10.1899. Black on blue underprint. Waterfalls at left, Caldas at right. Back: Brown. Overprint: On #S293.	150.	500.	900.

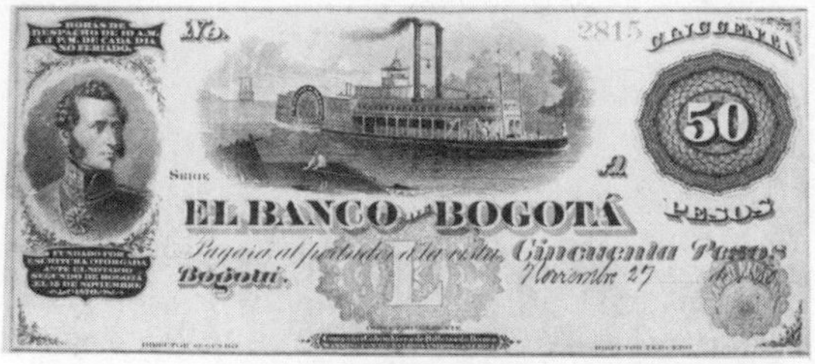

S629 50 Pesos | Good | Fine | XF
30.10.1899. Black on blue underprint. Officer at left, paddle wheel steamer *Francisco Montoya* at center. Back: Light brown. Overprint: On #S294. Rare. | — | — | —

S630 100 Pesos | Good | Fine | XF
30.10.1899. Black on light red underprint. Pineapple trees and shoreline at center, man at right. Back: Dark blue. Overprint: On #S295. Rare. | — | — | —

1899 Overprint on Banco de Hipotecario

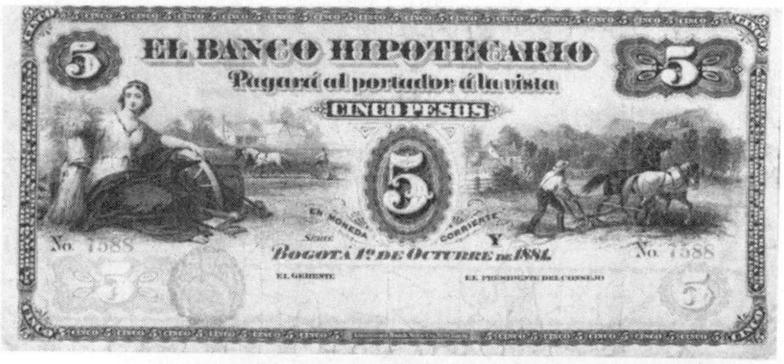

S636 5 Pesos | Good | Fine | XF
30.10.1899. Black on brown underprint. Seated woman with sheaf with farm in background ("Mechanics & Agriculture") at left, farmer plowing with horses at right. Back: Brown. Overprint: On #S511. | 150. | 450. | 800.

S637 10 Pesos | Good | Fine | XF
30.10.1899. Black on green underprint. Seated woman with sheep at left, three horse heads ("Pharaoh's Horses") in circle at upper right. Back: Green. Overprint: On #S512. | 200. | 600. | 1000.

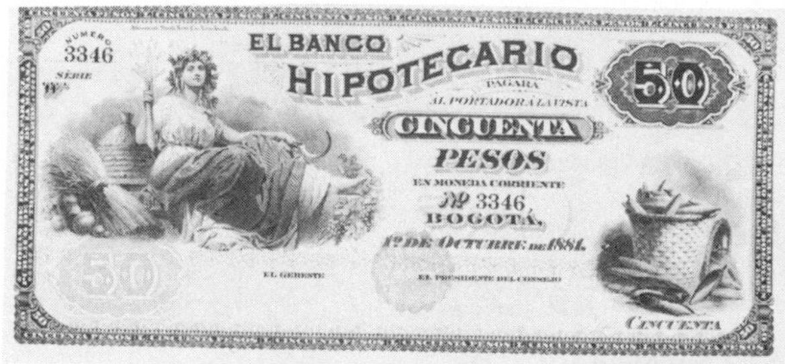

S639 50 Pesos | Good | Fine | XF
30.10.1899. Black on orange underprint. Sitting woman with farm produce at left, basket of corn at right. Back: Orange. Overprint: On #S514. Rare. | — | — | —

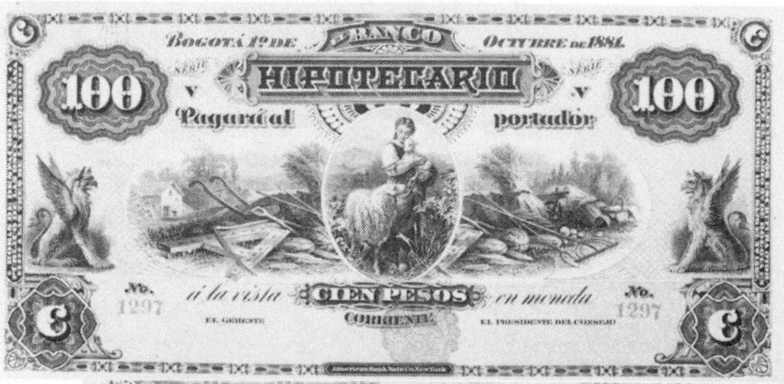

S640 100 Pesos | Good | Fine | XF
30.10.1899. Black on blue underprint. Griffins at left and right, farm implements and produce in background of portrait, shepherdess with sheep at center. Back: Blue. Overprint: On #S515. Rare. | — | — | —

1899 Overprint on Banco Internacional

S646 1 Peso — Good 125. Fine 275. XF 600.
30.10.1899. Black on green underprint. Cart with oxen at center. Back: Green. Overprint: On #S561.

S647 5 Pesos — Good 150. Fine 300. XF 750.
30.10.1899. Black on orange underprint. Portrait woman's head at left, allegorical woman with safe, money and scales at center right. Back: Orange. Overprint: On #S562.

S648 10 Pesos — Good 150. Fine 300. XF 750.
30.10.1899. Black on brown underprint. Justice seated at right. Back: Brown. Overprint: On #S563.

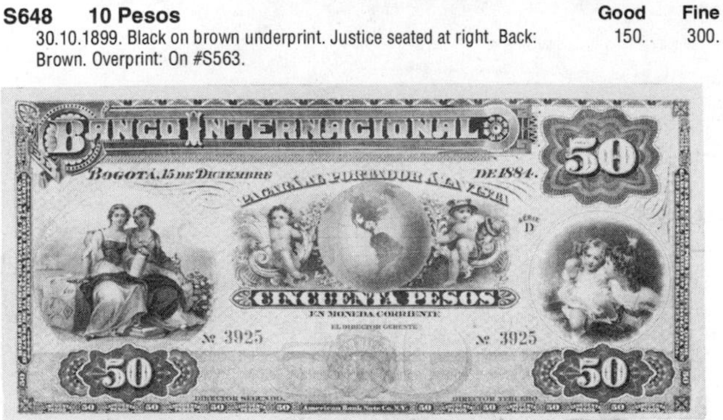

S649 50 Pesos — Good —. Fine —. XF —.
30.10.1899. Black on orange underprint. Two seated allegorical women at left, cherubs with globe at center, two girls at right. Back: Orange. Overprint: On #S564. Rare.

1899 Overprint on Banco de Marquez

S651 1 Peso — Good 125. Fine 275. XF 500.
30.10.1899. Black on tan underprint. Shepherdess with sheep at left, man at lower right. Back: Brown. Hand signature at center. Overprint: On #S581.

S652 5 Pesos — Good 150. Fine 400. XF 800.
30.10.1899. Black on green underprint. Man at left, seated woman with flowers at center right. Back: Green. Overprint: On #S582.

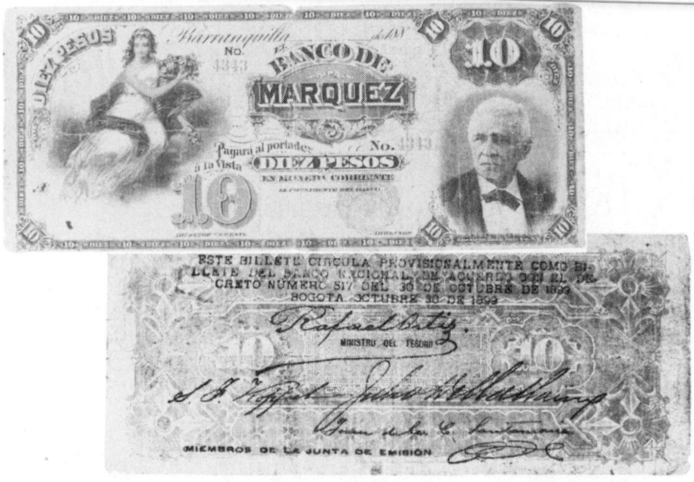

S653 10 Pesos — Good 150. Fine 400. XF 800.
30.10.1899. Black on orange underprint. Seated woman with fruit ("Vertumna") at left, man at lower right. Back: Orange. Overprint: On #S583.

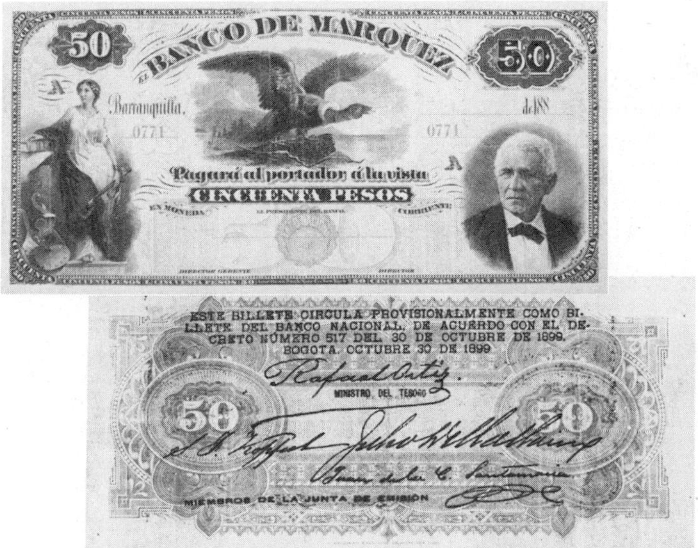

S655 50 Pesos — Good —. Fine —. XF —.
30.10.1899. Black on gold underprint. Standing female ("Genius") at left, condor at center, man at lower right. Back: Deep gold. Overprint: On #S585. Rare.

1899 Overprint on Banco Popular

S655A 100 Pesos — Good —. Fine —. XF —.
Reported not confirmed.

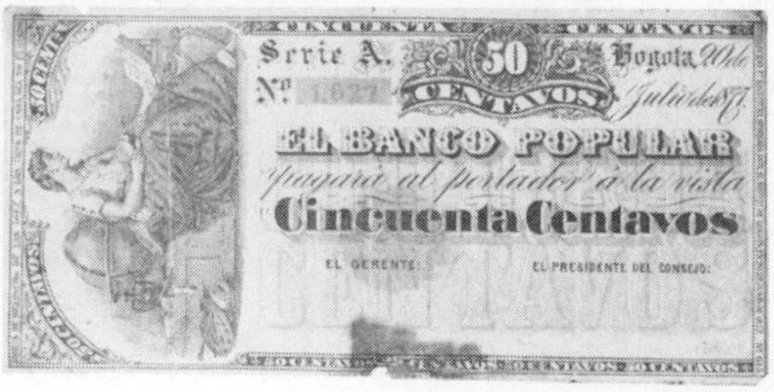

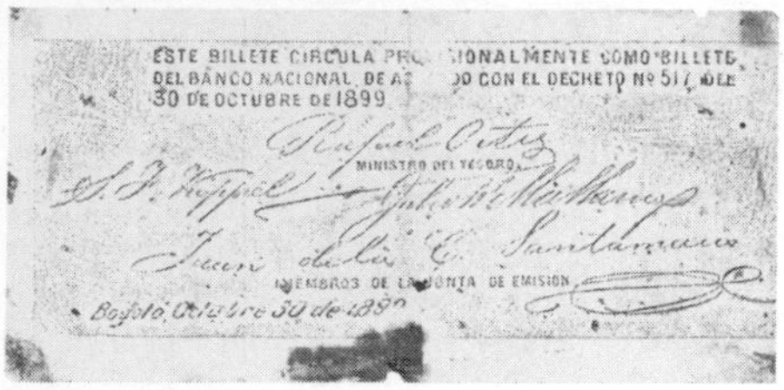

S656 50 Centavos

	Good	Fine	XF
30.10.1899. Black on green underprint. Woman and globe vertically at left. Overprint: On #S736.	150.	300.	750.

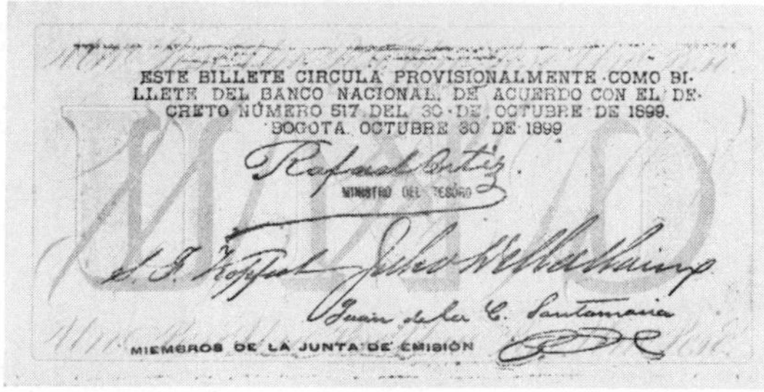

S657 1 Peso

	Good	Fine	XF
30.10.1899. Black on orange underprint. Farmer plowing with oxen at center. Back: Orange. Overprint: On #S737.	150.	300.	750.

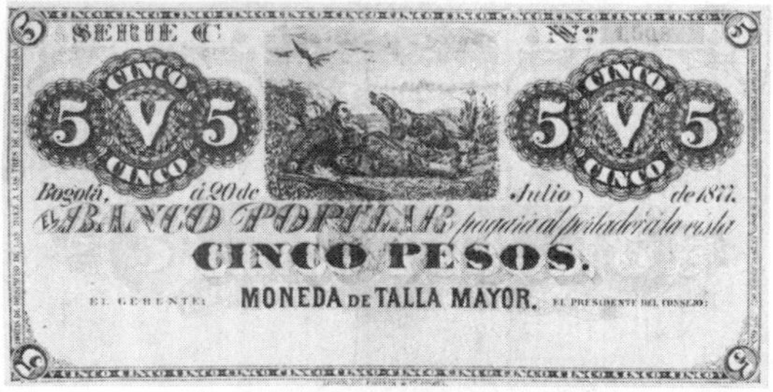

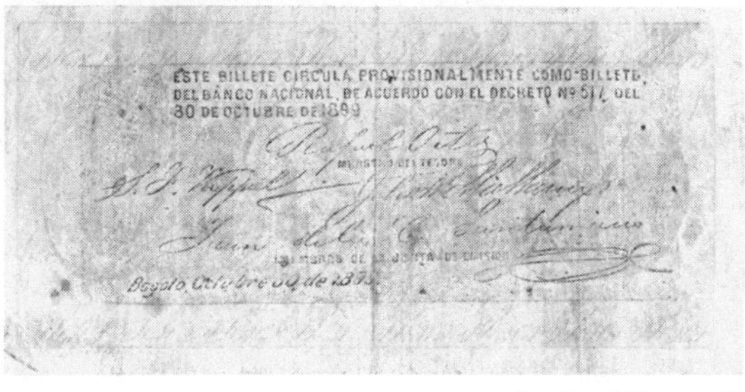

S658 5 Pesos

	Good	Fine	XF
30.10.1899. Black on yellow underprint. Man and dog at center. Text under denomination at center ends in *moneda de talla mayor.* Back: Yellow. Overprint: On #S738.	150.	300.	750.

S659 5 Pesos

	Good	Fine	XF
30.10.1899. Black on blue underprint. Man and dog at center. Text under denomination at center ends in *en moneda corriente.* Back: Blue. Overprint: On #S739.	150.	300.	750.

S660 10 Pesos

	Good	Fine	XF
30.10.1899. Black. Two allegorical women, child and sheep at center. Back: Green. Overprint: On #S740.	150.	300.	750.

S661 25 Pesos

	Good	Fine	XF
30.10.1899. Black on brown underprint. Portrait two girls at left, seated woman with llama at right. Back: Brown. Overprint: On #S747. Rare.	—	—	—

S662 50 Pesos

	Good	Fine	XF
30.10.1899. Black on green underprint. Family on log raft at upper left center, cherub ("Abundance") at lower right. Back: Green. Overprint: On #S748. Rare.	—	—	—

S663 100 Pesos

	Good	Fine	XF
30.10.1899. Black on gold underprint. Reclining allegorical woman with book ("Literature") at left, portrait man at lower right. Back: Orange. Overprint: On #S749. Rare.	—	—	—

1899 Overprint on Banco de La Union

S666 5 Pesos

	Good	Fine	XF
30.10.1899. Black on green underprint. Reclining woman leaning on cask at left, "Raphael's Angel" at center, seated woman with sheaf at right. Back: Green. Overprint: On #S861.	200.	400.	800.

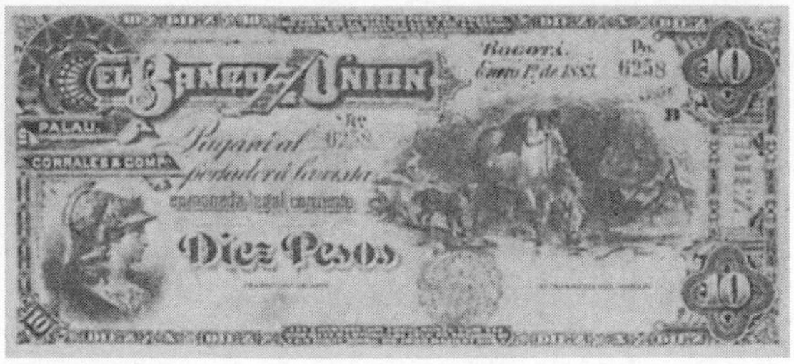

S667 10 Pesos	Good	Fine	XF
30.10.1899. Black on orange underprint. Helmeted female ("Minerva No. 2") at lower left, dog by boy on horseback ("Drinking at the Brook") at center right. Back: Orange. Overprint: On #S862.	225.	450.	900.

#S670 overprint on Banco Union note.

S670 50 Pesos	Good	Fine	XF
30.10.1899. Black on pink underprint. Portrait shepherdess with sheep at left, steam locomotive at center, seated woman at right. Back: Red. Overprint: On #S869. Rare.	—	—	—

1899 Overprint

S672 50 Centavos	Good	Fine	XF
30.10.1899. Light red. Farmers working in field at lower left. Overprint: On #S881.	125.	250.	500.

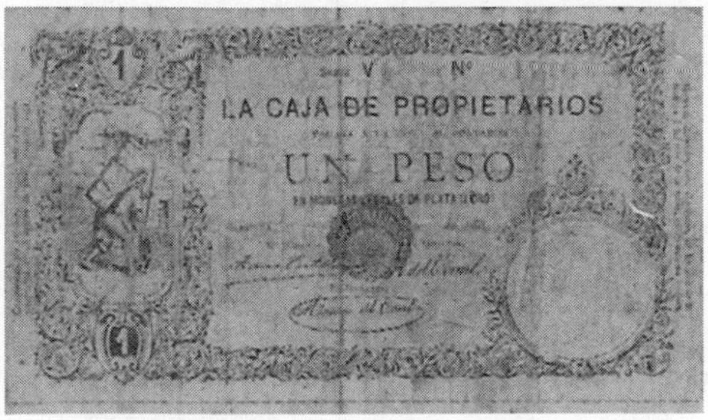

S673 1 Peso	Good	Fine	XF
30.10.1899. Orange. Indian carrying box on back at left. Overprint: On #S882.	125.	250.	500.

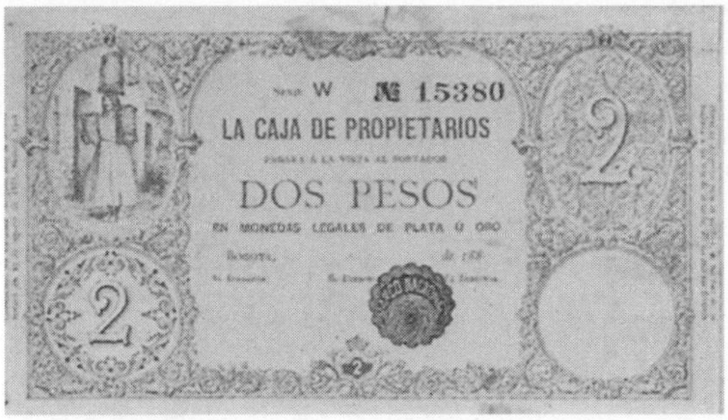

S674 2 Pesos	Good	Fine	XF
30.10.1899. Green. Woman carrying bags at left. Overprint: On #S883.	125.	250.	500.

S675 5 Pesos	Good	Fine	XF
30.10.1899. Violet. Man carrying wide basket at left. Overprint: On #S884.	150.	300.	600.

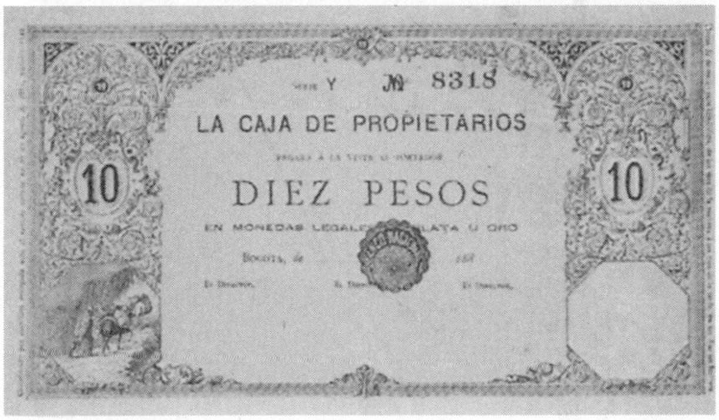

S676 10 Pesos	Good	Fine	XF
30.10.1899. Brown. Man with loaded mules on mountain path at left. Overprint: On #S885.	175.	350.	750.

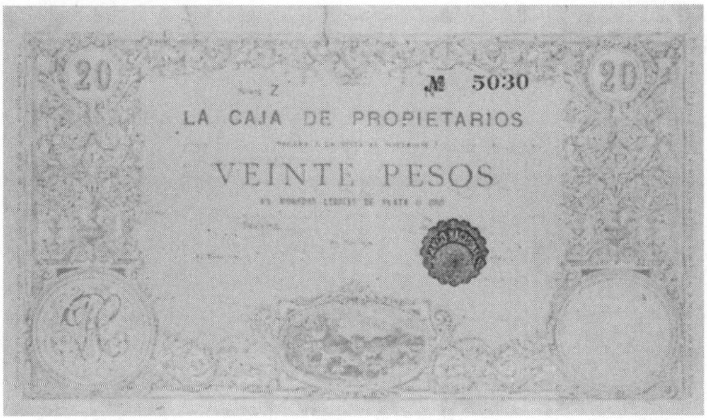

S677 20 Pesos	Good	Fine	XF
30.10.1899. Blue. Monogram at left, cows and horses in oval at lower center. Overprint: On #S886.	250.	600.	1000.

NOTE: All regularly prepared notes issued by the Banco Nacional 1881 to 1900 are listed in Vol. 2.

Banco del Norte

1882 Issue

S681 1 Peso	VG	VF	UNC
1.1.1882. Black on brown underprint. Dog lying down at center. Series A. Back: Brown. Printer: D. Paredes. Unsigned remainder.	20.00	50.00	100.

S682 5 Pesos	VG	VF	UNC
1.1.1882. Black on aqua underprint. Horses at upper left. Series B. Back: Aqua. Printer: D. Paredes. Unsigned remainder.	20.00	50.00	100.

S683 10 Pesos	VG	VF	UNC
1.1.1882. Black on orange underprint. Early steam train by station at upper left. Series C. Back: Deep orange. Printer: D. Paredes. Unsigned remainder.	20.00	50.00	100.

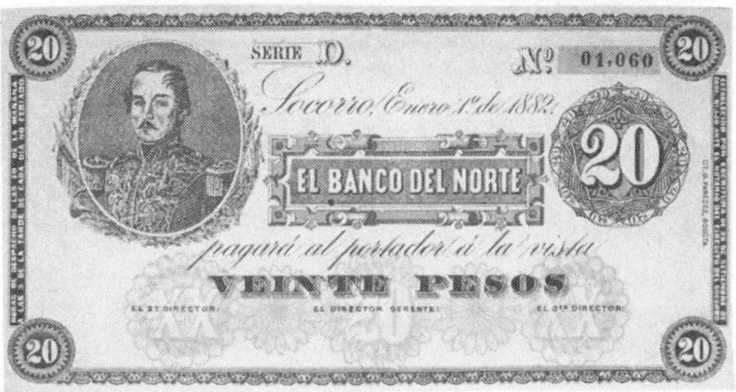

S684 20 Pesos	VG	VF	UNC
1.1.1882. Black on gold underprint. Portrait Gen. Santander at left. Series D. Back: Gold. Printer: D. Paredes. Unsigned remainder.	20.00	50.00	100.

Banco del Occidente

1882 Issue

S691 5 Pesos	Good	Fine	XF
1.5.1882. Steam locomotive. Printer: D. Paredes. Rare.	—	—	—

S692 10 Pesos	Good	Fine	XF
1.5.1882. Black on green underprint. Horses at upper center. Series B. Back: Orange. Printer: D. Paredes. Rare.	—	—	—

Banco del Oriente

1884-1900 Issue

S696 50 Centavos	Good	Fine	XF
2.1.1900. Red-orange. Meadow and mountain scene at upper center. Printer: PBC.	40.00	100.	200.

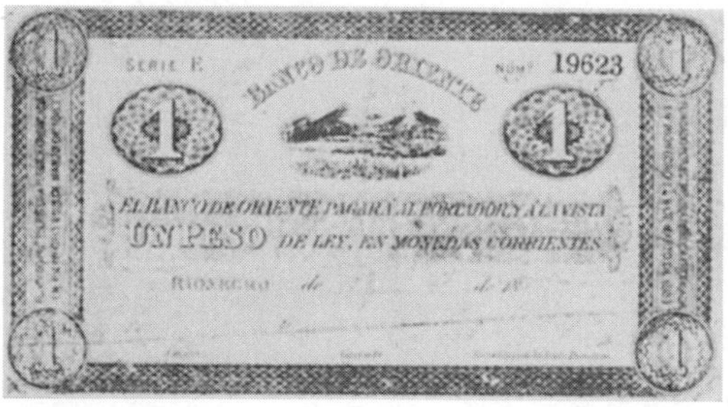

S697 1 Peso	Good	Fine	XF
2.1.1900. Blue. Meadow and mountain scene at upper center. Series E. Printer: PBC.	50.00	125.	250.
S698 5 Pesos			
4.2.1884; 25.2.1887; 5.3.1900. Gold. Meadow and mountain scene at upper center. Series I. Printer: PBC.	75.00	150.	300.
S699 10 Pesos			
22.2.1884; 5.3.1890; 5.3.1900. Green. Meadow and mountain scene at upper center. Series O. Printer: PBC.	75.00	150.	300.

S701 100 Pesos	Good	Fine	XF
5.7.1884; 5.3.1900. Lilac. Meadow and mountain scene at upper center. Series U. Printer: PBC.	100.	200.	400.

NOTE: A large hoard of this series was found in the bank archives and have since been dispersed.

A WORD ON DATE RANGES

Often date ranges or specific dates are listed. These have been observed or reported by our contributors. If a note is outside the published range, it only means that it is a newly reported date, and not necessarily worthy of a premium value.

Banco de Pamplona

1883 Issue

	Good	Fine	XF
S706 5 Pesos 1.1.1883; 2.5.1883; 21.5.1883. Black on red underprint. Woman with tablet and child at left. Series B. Similar to #S378. Back: Red.	125.	250.	500.

1883-84 Issue

	Good	Fine	XF
S711 1 Peso 9.7.1883. Black on gold underprint. Portrait woman at upper center. Series A. Back: Gold. Printer: BWC.			
a. Back without bank stamping.	15.00	40.00	100.
b. Back with bank stamping.	15.00	40.00	100.

	Good	Fine	XF
S712 5 Pesos 4.3.1884. Black on blue underprint. Portrait woman at upper center. Series B. Back: Blue. Printer: BWC.	150.	300.	750.

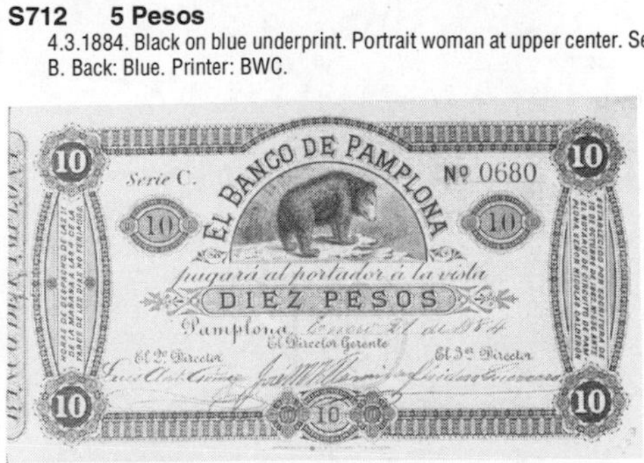

	Good	Fine	XF
S713 10 Pesos 21.1.1884; 4.3.1884; 19.5.1884. Black on green underprint. Bear at upper center. Series C. Back: Green. Printer: BWC.	100.	200.	500.

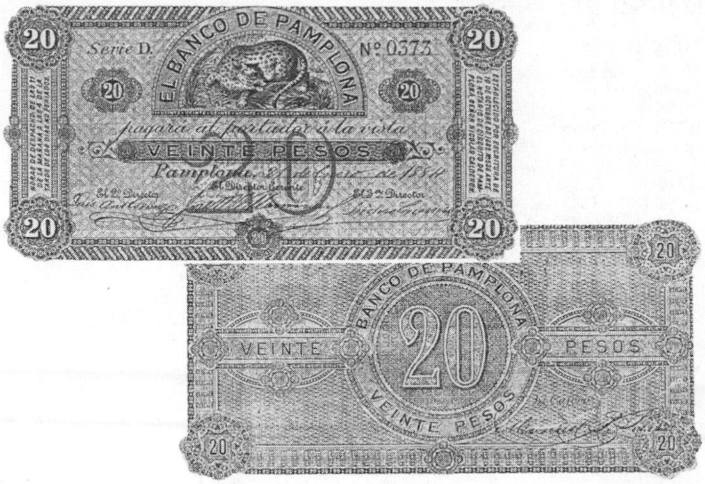

	Good	Fine	XF
S714 20 Pesos 21.1.1884; 4.3.1884. Black on red underprint. Leopard at upper center. Series D. Back: Red. Printer: BWC.	175.	300.	650.

Banco de Panamá

1869 Issue

	Good	Fine	XF
S721 1 Peso ND (ca. 1869). Black on green underprint. A. Planas at upper center. Back: Green. Overprint: Red line on signature at lower right on front, red text vertically at right on back. Printer: ABNC.	250.	500.	1000.
S722 5 Pesos ND (ca. 1869). Black on brown underprint. Portrait A. Planas at left, globe between steamship and steam passenger train at center right. Back: Blue. Overprint: Red text vertically at right on back. Like #S721. Printer: ABNC.	500.	1000.	2000.
S723 10 Pesos ND (ca.1869). Black on brown underprint. Portrait A. Planas at left, globe between steamship and steam passenger train at center right. Similar to #S722. Back: Orange. Printer: ABNC.	600.	1250.	2500.
S724 20 Pesos ND (ca.1869). Black on orange underprint. Globe between steamship and steam passenger train at upper left center, A. Planas at lower right. Back: Brown. Printer: ABNC. Rare.	—	—	—
S725 50 Pesos ND (ca.1869). Black on tan underprint. A. Planas at lower left and right, globe between steamship and steam passenger train at upper center. Back: Orange. Printer: ABNC. Rare.	—	—	—

Banco de Circulación y Descuento de Perez y Planas

1865 Issue

	Good	Fine	XF
S726 1 Peso ND (ca.1865). Black on brown underprint. Portrait A. Planas at left, globe between steamship and steam passenger train at center right. Printer: ABNC. Specimen. Rare.	—	—	—
S727 2 Pesos ND (ca.1865). Black on red and yellow underprint. Portrait A. Planas at left, globe between steamship and steam passenger train at center right. Printer: ABNC. Specimen. Rare.	—	—	—
S728 3 Pesos ND (ca.1865). Black on gold underprint. Portrait A. Planas at left, globe between steamship and steam passenger train at center right. Printer: ABNC. Specimen. Rare.	—	—	—
S729 5 Pesos ND (ca.1865). Black on gold underprint. Portrait A. Planas at left, globe between steamship and steam passenger train at center right. Printer: ABNC. Archive copy. Rare.	—	—	—
S730 10 Pesos ND (ca.1865). Black on brown underprint. Portrait A. Planas at left, globe between steamship and steam passenger train at center right. Printer: ABNC. Specimen. Rare.	—	—	—

Banco Popular

1877 Issue

		Good	Fine	XF
S736	**50 Centavos** 20.7.1877. Black on green underprint. Woman and globe vertically at left. Uniface. Series A. Printer: D. Paredes.	—	—	—
S737	**1 Peso** 20.7.1877. Black on orange underprint. Farmer plowing with oxen at center. Series B. Back: Orange. Printer: D. Paredes.	—	—	—
S738	**5 Pesos** 20.7.1877. Black on yellow underprint. Man and dog at center. Text under denomination at center ends in *moneda de talla mayor*. Series C. Back: Yellow. Printer: D. Paredes.	—	—	—
S739	**5 Pesos** 20.7.1877. Black on blue underprint. Man and dog at center. Like #S738, but text ends in *...en moneda corriente*. Back: Blue. Printer: D. Paredes.	—	—	—
S739A	**5 Pesos** 20.7.1877. Black on blue underprint. Man and dog at center. Like #S739 but text without *En Moneda Corriente*. Series C. Back: Blue.	—	—	—
S740	**10 Pesos** 20.7.1877. Black. Two allegorical women, child and sheep at center. Back: Green. Printer: CCBB.	—	—	—
S743	**100 Pesos** 20.7.1877. Text similar to #S738.	—	—	—

1882 Issue

		Good	Fine	XF
S747	**25 Pesos** 1.1.1882. Black on brown underprint. Portrait two girls at left, seated woman with llama at right. Series D. Back: Brown. Printer: ABNC. Rare.	—	—	—
S748	**50 Pesos** 1.1.1882. Black on green underprint. Family on log raft at upper left center, cherub ("Abundance") at lower right. Series E. Back: Green. Printer: ABNC. Proof.	—	Unc	600.
S749	**100 Pesos** 1.1.1882. Black on gold underprint. Reclining allegorical woman with book ("Literature") at left, portrait man at lower right. Series F. Back: Orange. Printer: ABNC.			
	p. Proof.	—	Unc	600.
	s. Specimen.	—	Unc	900.

NOTE: #S736-S740, S748 and S749 are known in issued form only with red overprint: *Banco Nacional* and *30.10.1899* date in overprint on back. For listing see #S656-S663.

Banco Popular de Bolívar

1883-86 Issue

		Good	Fine	XF
S756	**1 Peso** 20.2.1883. Black on light green and magenta underprint. Back: Gray. Printer: Tip de Antonio Araujo. Rare.	—	—	—
S757	**5 Pesos** 18xx. Black and blue. Horse's head at lower right. Back: Blue. Paper: Pink. Printer: Tip de Antonio Araujo. Rare.	—	—	—
S758	**10 Pesos** 18xx. Black and red. Back: Red. Paper: Pink. Printer: Tip de Antonio Araujo. Rare.	—	—	—
S761	**1 Peso** 11.4.1886. Black on orange underprint. Woman and horse at left, two horses and man leading mule train at right. Back: Orange. Printer: ABNC.			
	a. Issued note. Rare.	—	—	—
	p. Proof.	—	Unc	500.
	s. Specimen.	—	Unc	900.
S762	**5 Pesos** 18xx. Black on blue underprint. Two women at left, man and horses at right. Back: Blue. Printer: ABNC.			
	p. Proof.	—	Unc	500.
	r. Remainder with signature.	—	—	300.
	s. Specimen.	—	Unc	900.

Banco Popular de Medellin

1883-93 Issue

		Good	Fine	XF
S766	**20 Centavos** 12.1893. Black and green on yellow underprint. Uniface. Rare.	—	—	—

		Good	Fine	XF
S770	**50 Centavos** 31.12.1883. Black on light orange underprint. Gauchos roping steers at upper left, girl at upper center right, farmer carrying sheaves at lower right. Series A. Back: Light orange. Printer: ABNC.			
	a. Issued note. Rare.	—	—	—
	p. Proof.	—	Unc	500.
	s. Specimen.	—	Unc	900.
S771	**1 Peso** 3.1885; 1.12.1893. Black on green underprint. Angel at upper left, farm implements and sheaf at upper right center, allegorical woman with torch at right. Series B. Back: Green. Printer: ABNC.			
	p. Proof.	—	Unc	500.
	s. Specimen.	—	Unc	900.
S772	**5 Pesos** 1.5.1883. Black and red-orange. Condor at left, woman with sheaves and sheep at upper right. Series C. Back: Red-orange. Printer: ABNC.			
	a. Issued note.	300.	600.	1200.
	p. Proof.	—	Unc	500.
	s. Specimen.	—	Unc	900.

		Good	Fine	XF
S773	**10 Pesos** 21.12.1883; 1.5.1885. Brown and black. Man watering horses at left, two cherubs and dog on safe at center, standing woman at right. Series D. Back: Brown. Printer: ABNC.			
	a. Issued note.	300.	600.	1200.
	p. Proof.	—	Unc	500.

1899 Provisional Issue

		Good	Fine	XF
S776	**1 Peso** 30.10.1899. Overprint new bank name and *7.9.1899* date in 6 lines of overprint at right on face of Banco Republicano #S811. Back: Two or three hand stamps.	200.	400.	900.
S776A	**5 Pesos** 30.10.1899. Overprint: Overprint new bank name and text in seven lines on back of #S812.	500.	900.	1250.

S777 5 Pesos	Good	Fine	XF
17.10.1899; 8.12.1899. Black on green underprint. Seated woman with hammer at left. Back: Green. Printer: Tipografia Central, Medellin. For similar % Pesos see #S599.	150.	300.	600.

NOTE: For similar 5 Pesos see #S599.

S778 10 Pesos			
17.10.1899. Black and red. Tropical view at center. Similar to #S600. Rare.	—	—	—

Banco Popular de Soto

1880s Issue

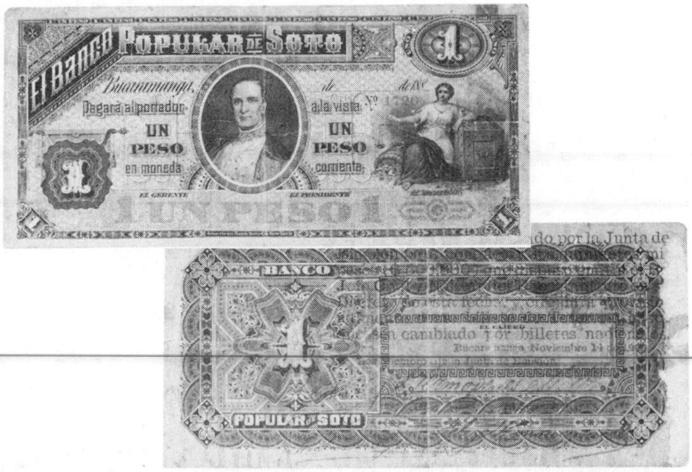

S781 1 Peso	Good	Fine	XF
188x. Black on green underprint. Portrait man at center, seated allegorical woman with money and scales at right. Back: Green. Printer: ABNC.			
a. Overprint: *14.11.1900* date in 9 lines of text and 4 signatures on back.	150.	300.	600.
p. Proof.	—	Unc	500.
S782 5 Pesos			
188x. Black on red-brown underprint. Portrait man at left center, seated Justice at right. Back: Red-brown. Printer: ABNC.			
a. Overprint: *14.11.1900* like #S781a.	150.	300.	600.
p. Proof.	—	Unc	500.
S783 10 Pesos			
188x. Black on red underprint. Bust of Gen. Santander at left, "Raphael's Angel" at center right. Back: Red. Printer: ABNC.			
a. Overprint: *14.11.1900* like #781a.	150.	300.	600.
p. Proof.	—	Unc	500.

Banco Prendario

1881-84 Issue

S788 1 Peso	Good	Fine	XF
1881; 188x. Black on blue underprint. Workers at upper left. Uniface. Printer: D. Paredes.			
a. Issued note. Rare.	—	—	—
r. Unsigned remainder. Series A. Rare.	—	—	—

S790 10 Pesos	Good	Fine	XF
1.6.1884. Black on brown underprint. Eagle at upper left, beehives at upper right. Series C. Uniface. Printer: D. Paredes.			
a. Issued note. Rare.	—	—	—
s. Specimen.	—	—	—

Banco Prendario de Soto

1884 Issue

S796 5 Pesos	Good	Fine	XF
1.1.1884. Black on orange underprint. Allegorical woman with sheaf, beehive and sickle at center. Back: Purple text. Printer: D. Paredes.			
a. Issued note.	25.00	50.00	100.
b. *14.11.1900* date in 9 lines of overprint like #S781a, also red outlined seal of the treasury of the Departamento de Santander at left.	150.	300.	600.

NOTE: A hoard was found of #S796a and has since been absorbed into the marketplace.

Banco del Progreso

1883-99 Issue

S801 50 Centavos	Good	Fine	XF
10.12.1883; 22.11.1899. Black. Seated woman with plants at center. Back: Blue. Printer: PB&Co. Rare.	—	—	—

S802 1 Peso	Good	Fine	XF
22.11.1899. Black on red-brown underprint. Three allegorical women at upper center. Back: Brown. Printer: PB&Co. Rare.	—	—	—

		Good	Fine	XF
S803	**5 Pesos**			
	1.2.1895. Black on green underprint. Allegorical woman and man with wheat and tools at upper center. Back: Green. Printer: PB&Co. Rare.	—	—	—
S804	**10 Pesos**			
	17.10.1899. Scenery. Printer: PB&Co. Rare.	—	—	—
S804A	**100 Pesos**			
	xxxx. Printer: PB&Co. Specimen.	—	—	—

1899 Provisional Issue

		Good	Fine	XF
S805	**1 Peso**			
	1899. Overprint new bank name and date as on #S806 on back of #S811.	100.	200.	400.
S806	**10 Pesos**			
	30.10.1899. Overprint new bank name and *7.9.1899* date in 7 lines of text on back of Banco Republicano #S813.	150.	300.	600.

Banco de la República

188x Issue

		Good	Fine	XF
S807	**1 Peso = 1 Dollar**			
	188x. Black and green. Train crossing bridge at center. Triangular guilloches at upper corners. Printer: HLBNC. Not issued.	—	Unc	400.
S807A	**1 Peso = 1 Dollar**			
	188x. Black and green. Train crossing bridge at center. Similar to #S807, but ornate round guilloches at upper corners. Printer: HLBNC. Cut cancelled. Not issued.	—	Unc	400.
S808	**2 Pesos = 2 Dollars**			
	188x. Black and green. Train emerging from tunnel at lower center. Back: Portrait George Washington at center. Printer: HLBNC. Not issued.	—	Unc	400.
S808A	**2 Pesos = 2 Dollars**			
	188x. Black and green. Minerva reclining with cherub at center. Back: Green. Printer: HLBNC. Not issued.	—	Unc	400.
S809	**5 Pesos = 5 Dollars**			
	188x. Black and green. Portrait George Washington at center. Printer: HLBNC. Not issued.	—	Unc	400.
S809A	**5 Pesos = 5 Dollars**			
	188x. Black and green. Eagle at center. Printer: HLBNC. Punched hole cancelled. Not issued.	—	Unc	400.
S810	**10 Pesos = 10 Dollars**			
	188x. Black and green. Portrait George Washington at lower left, Minerva at lower right. Printer: HLBNC. Not issued.	—	Unc	400.
S810A	**10 Pesos = 10 Dollars**			
	188x. Black and green. Woman standing at left and right. Printer: HLBNC. Not issued.	—	Unc	400.

Banco Republicano

1899 Issue

		Good	Fine	XF
S811	**1 Peso**			
	30.10.1899. Black on red underprint. Flags at left and right, woman at center. Back: Red. Printer: BWC.	150.	300.	600.
S812	**5 Pesos**			
	30.10.1899. Black on red and orange underprint. Flag at left and right, winged Mercury at upper center. Printer: BWC.			
	a. Issued note.	350.	700.	1200.
	s. Specimen.	—	Unc	750.
S813	**10 Pesos**			
	30.10.1899. Black and multicolor on blue underprint. Flags at left and right, cows at center. Back: Blue. Printer: BWC. Rare.	—	—	—

NOTE: Except for #S812, notes of the Banco Republicano are known in issued form only with overprint of other bank names. See #S398, S606, S608, S776 and S806.

Banco de Rio Hacha

1883-85 Issue

		Good	Fine	XF
S816	**20 Centavos**			
	6.12.1885. Black on red-orange underprint. Portrait Simon Bolivár at left, arms at lower right. Series Y. Back: Red-orange. Printer: American Bank Note Co., New York. Litho. Specimen. Rare.	—	—	—
S817	**50 Centavos**			
	1.1.1883. Black on red-orange underprint. Arms at left, seated allegorical woman with sheaf at center, portrait Simon Bolívar at lower right. Series A. Back: Red-orange. Printer: ABNC.			
	a. Issued note. Rare.	—	—	—
	p. Proof.	—	Unc	600.
	s. Specimen.	—	Unc	900.
S818	**1 Peso**			
	1.1.1883. Black on light orange underprint. Portrait Simon Bolívar at lower left, arms and allegorical woman with plants at center, portrait Gen. A. Nariño at lower right. Series B. Back: Light orange. Printer: ABNC.			
	a. Issued note. Rare.	—	—	—
	p. Proof.	—	Unc	600.
	s. Specimen.	—	Unc	900.
S819	**5 Pesos**			
	1.1.1883. Black on brown underprint. Arms at left, Simon Bolívar at center, woman with wheel at right. Series C. Back: Brown. Printer: ABNC.			
	p. Proof.	—	Unc	1000.
	s. Specimen.	—	Unc	1250.
S819A	**10 Pesos**			
	1.1.1883. Black on green underprint. Portrait A. J. de Sucre at lower left, arms and woman with caduceus and eagle at center, portrait Simon Bolívar at lower right. Series D. Back: Green. Printer: ABNC.			
	p. Proof.	—	Unc	1250.
	s. Specimen.	—	Unc	1750.

Banco del Ruiz

1905 Issue

		Good	Fine	XF
S821	**50 Centavos**			
	L.1905. Brown on multicolor underprint. Eagle and mountains in circle at center. Back: Brown. Printer: ABNC.			
	p. Proof.	—	Unc	500.
	s. Specimen.	—	Unc	650.
S822	**1 Peso**			
	L.1905. Green on multicolor underprint. Eagle and mountains in circle at center. Back: Green. Printer: ABNC.			
	p. Proof.	—	Unc	500.
	s. Specimen.	—	Unc	700.
S823	**5 Pesos**			
	L.1905. Red-orange on multicolor underprint. Eagle and mountains in circle at center. Back: Orange. Date 19.8.1919. Printer: ABNC.			
	a. Issued note. 1.8.1919. Rare.	—	—	—
	p. Proof.	—	Unc	500.
	s. Specimen.	—	Unc	750.
S824	**10 Pesos**			
	L.1905. Blue on multicolor underprint. Eagle and mountains in circle at center. Back: Blue. Printer: ABNC.			
	p. Proof.	—	Unc	500.
	s. Specimen.	—	Unc	750.
S825	**20 Pesos**			
	L.1905. Black on multicolor underprint. Eagle and mountains in circle at center. Panel of Interest markers at right. Back: Olive-green. Printer: ABNC.			
	p. Proof.	—	Unc	500.
	s. Specimen.	—	Unc	750.
S826	**50 Pesos**			
	L.1905. Eagle and mountains in circle at center. Back: Date 19.8.1919. Printer: ABNC.	—	Unc	500.

NOTE: Except for #S823, #S821-S825 are known issued only with new bank name overprint. See Banco del Huila and Banco Lopez.

Banco de Santander

1873-1900 Issue

		Good	Fine	XF
S831	**1 Peso**			
	1.6.1873; 18.6.1883. Black. Star at center. Printer: PBC.			
	a. Issued note without overprint. Rare.	—	—	—
	b. 1.6.1873. Overprint: *Pagadero en moneda corriente.*	75.00	150.	300.
	c. Overprint: *Decreto. 6.1.1900* date in 4 lines of overprint text on back. 4 signatures also part of overprint (signature varieties).	25.00	50.00	100.

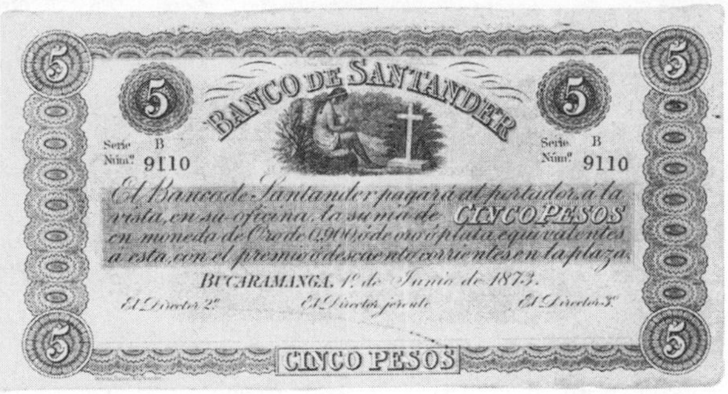

		Good	Fine	XF
S832	**5 Pesos** 1.6.1873; 6.1.1900. Blue. Woman seated near cross at center. Printer: PBC.			
	a. 1.6.1873. Rare.	—	—	—
	b. Overprint: *Decreto. 6.1.1900* like #S831c.	25.00	50.00	100.

		Good	Fine	XF
S833	**10 Pesos** 1.6.1873; 6.1.1900. Brown. Snake at upper center. Printer: PBC.			
	a. 1.6.1873. Rare.	—	—	—
	b. Overprint: *Decreto. 6.1.1900* like #S831c.	25.00	50.00	100.
S834	**20 Pesos** 1.6.1873; 6.1.1900. Green. Mercury with staff at upper center. Printer: PBC.			
	a. 1.6.1873. Rare.	—	—	—
	b. Overprint: *Decreto. 6.1.1900* like #S831c.	200.	400.	800.
S835	**50 Pesos** 1.6.1873; 6.1.1900. Yellow. Printer: PBC.			
	a. 1.6.1873. Rare.	—	—	—
	b. Overprint: *Decreto. 6.1.1900* like #S831c.	50.00	150.	300.

NOTE: Most notes of #S831-S835 are known in issued form only with *1900* date overprint on back.

S836	**100 Pesos** xxxx. Proof.	—	—	—

Banco de Sogamoso

1882 Issue

		Good	Fine	XF
S841	**5 Pesos** 15.8.1882 (hand dated 22.10.1882 or 28.10.1882 at bottom center). Black on green underprint. Horses at center. Series A. Back: Brown. Hand signature at center. Printer: D. Paredes.	50.00	100.	200.

		Good	Fine	XF
S842	**10 Pesos** 15.8.1882 (hand dated 22.11.1882 at bottom center). Black on red-orange underprint. Cows at water at upper center. Series B. Back: Blue-green. Hand signature at center. Printer: D. Paredes.	50.00	100.	200.

		Good	Fine	XF
S843	**50 Pesos** 15.8.1882. Black on blue underprint. Woman with tablet and child at left. Like #S378 and #S706. Text under large numeral at right ends in...*moneda de talla mayor.* Series C. Back: Red-orange. Hand signature at center. Printer: D. Paredes.	50.00	100.	200.

		Good	Fine	XF
S844	**50 Pesos** 15.8.1882. Black on orange underprint. Woman with tablet and child at left. Like #S843 except for text under numeral at right which ends...*moneda corriente.* Series D. Back: Blue. Printer: D. Paredes. Unissued remainder.	50.00	100.	200.

NOTE: All signatures for #S841-S844 are forged.

Banco de Sopetrán

ca.1880s Issue

		Good	Fine	XF
S845	**1 Peso** 18xx. Black. Portrait woman at left, cow head at right. Printer: BWC. Specimen.	—	Unc	1250.
S846	**5 Pesos** 18xx. Black. Portrait woman at left, cow head at right. Similar to #S845. Printer: BWC. Specimen.	—	Unc	2500.
S846A	**10 Pesos** 18xx. Black. Portrait woman at left, cow head at right. Similar to #S845. Printer: BWC. Specimen, perforated B.W & Co/LONDON.	—	Unc	2250.

Banco de Sucre

1913 Issue

		Good	Fine	XF
S847	**50 Centavos** 20.5.1913; 20.5.1916. Black on green underprint. Portrait A. J. de Sucre at left. Series A. Back: Text. Printer: Arango, Medellin.	100.	200.	400.
S848	**1 Peso** 24.9.1913. Black on orange underprint. Allegorical woman at left, portrait A. J. de Sucre at right. Series A. Printer: Arango, Medellin.	200.	350.	700.

Banco del Sur

1907-08 Issue

	Good	Fine	XF
S851 1 Peso 25.8.1908. Black. Portrait Gen. A. Narino at left. Back: Dark green. Printer: ABNC.			
a. Issued note. Rare.	—	—	—
s. Specimen.	—	Unc	1500.
S852 5 Pesos ND (ca.1907). Black. Portrait Gen. A. Narino at left. Back: Dark green. Printer: ABNC.			
a. Issued note. Rare.	—	—	—
p. Proof.	—	Unc	800.
s. Specimen.	—	Unc	1750.
S853 10 Pesos ND (ca.1907). Black. Portrait Gen. A. Narino at center. Back: Dark green. Printer: ABNC.			
p. Proof.	—	Unc	800.
s. Specimen.	—	Unc	1750.
S854 25 Pesos ND (ca.1907). Black. Portrait Gen. A. Narino at right. Back: Dark green. Printer: ABNC. Proof.	—	Unc	600.

NOTE: #S851-S854 are also known with overprint for Banco López. See #S577-S580.

	Good	Fine	XF
S854A 50 Pesos ND (ca.1907). Black. Portrait Gen. A. Narino. Back: Dark green. Printer: ABNC. Proof.	—	Unc	600.

Banco de Tequendama

1881 Issue

	Good	Fine	XF
S856 1 Peso 9.1881. Woman picking from bush at center. Back: Green. Printer: D. Paredes.			
a. Black on orange underprint. Rare.	—	—	—
b. Black text and overprint: *6.8.1900,* also purple stamped signature across center on back. Issued at Ibague. Rare.	—	—	—
S858 10 Pesos 20.9.1881. Black on orange underprint. Buildings and factories at center. Back: Gray. Printer: D. Paredes. Rare.	—	—	—

Banco del Tolima

1882 Issue

	Good	Fine	XF
S859 10 Pesos 1882. Mountain lake with Mt. Tolima in background. Printer: D. Paredes. Neiva. Rare.	—	—	—

Banco de la Union

1883 Issue

	Good	Fine	XF
S861 5 Pesos 1.1.1883. Black on green underprint. Reclining woman leaning on cask at left, "Raphael's Angel" at center, seated woman with sheaf at right. Back: Green. Printer: ABNC. Proof.	—	Unc	600.

	Good	Fine	XF
S862 10 Pesos 1.1.1883. Black on orange underprint. Helmeted female ("Minerva No. 2") at lower left, dog by boy on horseback ("Drinking at the Brook") at center right. Back: Orange. Printer: ABNC. Proof.	—	Unc	600.

NOTE: #S861 and S862 are known in issued form only with red seal overprint: *Banco Nacional* and *30.10.1899* date in overprint on back. For listing see #S666 and S667.

Banco Union

1887-88 Issue

	Good	Fine	XF
S866 1 Peso 15.4.1887; 5.1.1888. Black on light brown underprint. Child at left, sailing ship at center, Liberty at right. Back: Brown. Printer: ABNC.			
a. Issued note.	200.	400.	800.
b. Overprint: *10.2.1900* date in horizontal 7-line text and signature on back. Punched hole cancelled.	100.	250.	500.
p. Proof.	—	Unc	600.

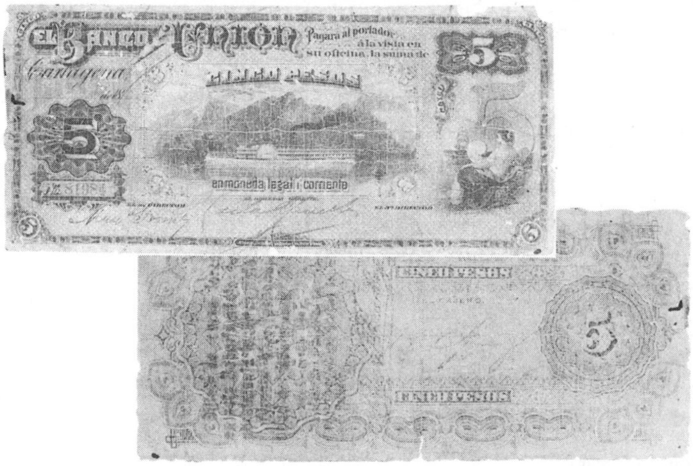

	Good	Fine	XF
S867 5 Pesos 5.1.1888. Black on blue underprint. Paddle wheel steamer at center, seated woman, numeral and sailing ship at right. Back: Purplish gray. Printer: ABNC.			
a. Issued note. Rare.	—	—	—
b. Overprint: *10.2.1900* on back like #S866a.	125.	300.	—
c. Vertical red overprint: *10.2.1900* at left on back.	125.	300.	—
p. Proof.	—	Unc	600.

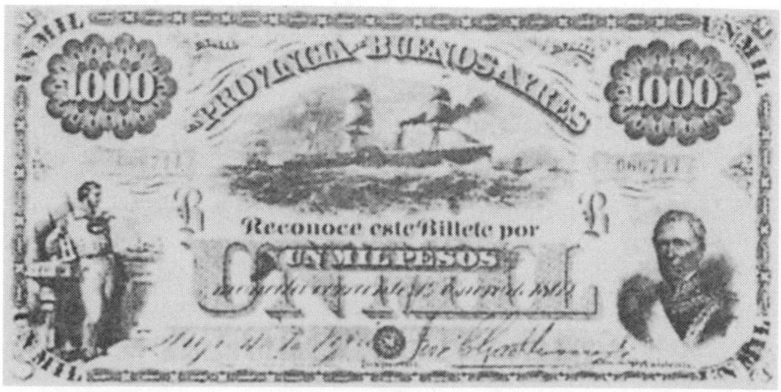

	Good	Fine	XF
S868 10 Pesos 22.2.1887. Black on blue underprint. Seated woman at left, sailing ship at center, seated allegorical woman with vase at right. Back: Blue. Printer: ABNC.			
a. Issued note.	150.	350.	600.
b. Overprint: *10.2.1900* like #S867b but on face at left.	150.	350.	600.
p. Proof.	—	Unc	600.

		Good	Fine	XF
S869	**50 Pesos** 18xx. Black on pink underprint. Portrait shepherdess with sheep at left, steam locomotive at center, seated woman at right. Back: Red. Printer: ABNC. Proof.	—	Unc	600.

NOTE: #S869 is known issued only with red seal overprint: *Banco Nacional* and *30.10.1899* date in overprint on back. For listing see #S670.

Botero Arango e Hijos

18xx Issue

		Good	Fine	XF
S876	**50 Centavos** 18xx. Black. Seated woman with bale at center. Proof. Rare.	—	—	—
S878	**20 Pesos** 1.10.1879. Black on green underprint. Female standing at upper center.	—	—	—

Caja de Propietarios

1880s Issue

		Good	Fine	XF
S881	**50 Centavos** 188x. Light red. Farmers working in field at lower left.	150.	500.	1000.
S882	**1 Peso** 188x. Orange. Indian carrying box on back at left.	150.	500.	1000.
S883	**2 Pesos** 188x. Green. Woman carrying bags at left.	250.	650.	1250.
S884	**5 Pesos** 188x. Violet. Man carrying wide basket at left.	250.	650.	1250.
S885	**10 Pesos** 188x. Brown. Man with loaded mules on mountain path at left.	400.	800.	1250.
S886	**20 Pesos** 188x. Blue. Monogram at left, cows and horses in oval at lower center.	500.	1000.	1750.

NOTE: #S881-S886 are known issued only with red seal overprint: *Banco Nacional* and *30.10.1899* date in overprint on back. For listing see #S672-S677.

G. de Caycedo & Ca.

1884 Issue

		Good	Fine	XF
S886A	**25 Centavos** 1.1.1884. Black on blue underprint. Back: Blue. Printer: Howard y Jones, Grabadores, Londres. Rare.	—	—	—

Central American Steam Navigation Co.

1851 Issue

		Good	Fine	XF
S887	**1/2 Peso = 1/2 Dollar** 1.1.1851. Black. Ship at left, eagle at center, Indian paddling canoe at upper right. Rare.	—	—	—
S888	**1 Peso = 1 Dollar** 1.1.1851. Black. Ship at left, eagle at center, Indian paddling canoe at upper right. Rare.	—	—	—

NOTE: #S888 has error *PESOS* in denomination.

		Good	Fine	XF
S889	**2 Pesos = 2 Dollars** 1.1.1851. Black. Ship at left, eagle at center, Indian paddling canoe at upper right. Rare.	—	—	—
S890	**3 Pesos = 3 Dollars** 1.1.1851. Black. Ship at left, eagle at center, Indian paddling canoe at upper right. Rare.	—	—	—

NOTE: #S888 has error *PESOS* in denomination.

Credito Caucano

1919-22 Cédula Hipotecario Issue

		Good	Fine	XF
S891	**15 Pesos** 14.7.1922. Black on multicolor underprint. Two women ("Reapers No. 3") at left. Back: Brown. Town scene at left. Printer: ABNC.			
	a. Issued note. Rare.	—	—	—
	p. Proof.	—	Unc	750.
	s. Specimen.	—	Unc	1000.
S892	**20 Pesos** ND (ca. 1919). Black on multicolor underprint. Two women ("Reapers No. 3") at left. Back: Green. Printer: ABNC. Proof.	—	Unc	600.

Exchange Bank of Colón

1870 Issue

		Good	Fine	XF
S896	**1 Dollar** ND (ca. 1870). Black. Girl holding produce at left, arms at bottom center, steam locomotive at lower right. Printer: CONB. Unissued remainder. Rare.	—	—	—
S897	**2 Dollars** ND (ca. 1870). Black. Arms at left, loading cotton bales at bottom center, steam train at lower right. Printer: CONB. Unissued remainder. Rare.	—	—	—
S898	**3 Dollars** ND (ca. 1870). Black. Sailor at left, arms at lower right. Printer: CONB. Unissued remainder. Rare.	—	—	—
S899	**5 Dollars** ND (ca. 1870). Black. Arms at upper left, paddle wheel steamboat at center. Printer: CONB. Unissued remainder. Rare.	—	—	—

La Nueva Compañia Constructora

1880s Issue

		Good	Fine	XF
S900	**5 Pesos** 188x. Black and blue. Building at top center. Imprint: Lit. de D. Paredes, Bogotá. Back: Blue.	250.	500.	1000.

Señores Fernando Restrepo & Hijos

1900 Issue

		Good	Fine	XF
S900A	**50 Pesos** 19.5.1900. Black. Paper: Light tan. Rare.	—	—	—

Restrepos y Compañia

1884 Issue

		Good	Fine	XF
S900B	**50 Centavos** xxxx. Specimen.	—	—	—
S900C	**1 Peso** 5.6.1884. Blue. Seated Justice at upper center. Medellin issue. Printer: PBC.			
	a. Issued note. Rare.	—	—	—
	s. Specimen.	—	Unc	900.
S900D	**5 Pesos** xxxx. Specimen.	—	—	—
S900E	**20 Pesos** xxxx. Specimen.	—	—	—
S900F	**80 Pesos** xxxx. Specimen.	—	—	—
S900G	**100 Pesos** xxxx. Specimen.	—	—	—

Reyes Gonzales y Hermanos

1890s Billete Popular Issue

		Good	Fine	XF
S901	**1 Peso** ND. Oval purple stamping: *Tesorería General/ LEGITIMO/Bucaramanga*. Printer: BWC (without imprint).	25.00	75.00	125.
S902	**5 Pesos** ND. Black on blue underprint. Hay in bunches at center. 2 hand signatures. Series B. Back: Blue. Printer: BWC (without imprint).	25.00	75.00	125.
S903	**10 Pesos** ND. Black on yellow underprint. Fishing. Printer: BWC (without imprint).			
	a. Issued note. Rare.	—	—	—
	b. Overprint: *1900*. Reported not confirmed.	—	—	—
S904	**20 Pesos** ND. Black on green underprint. Swans at center. Printer: BWC (without imprint). Rare.	—	—	—
S905	**50 Pesos** ND. Black on light tan underprint. Steam train. Printer: BWC (without imprint). Rare.	—	—	—
S906	**100 Pesos** ND. Black. Printer: BWC (without imprint). Specimen.	—	Unc	600.

Sociedád de Zancudo

1882 Issue

		Good	Fine	XF
S908	**50 Centavos** ND (ca. 1882). Black on brown underprint. Miners at left, portrait Carlos C. Amador at right. Back: Red. Printer: ABNC.			
	a. Issued note.	250.	400.	800.
	p. Proof.	—	Unc	600.
S909	**1 Peso** ND (ca. 1882). Black on green underprint. Four miners at left, portrait Carlos C. Amador at center right. Back: Orange, green, blue and red. Printer: ABNC.			
	a. Issued note.	300.	600.	1200.
	p. Proof.	—	Unc	600.

Uribe e Hijos

1871 Issue

		Good	Fine	XF
S911	**1 Peso** 4.2.1871. Black on green underprint. Four cherubs at left, cows at upper center, seated woman with produce at lower right. Back: Green. Printer: ABNC. Rare.	—	—	—
S913	**5 Pesos** 187x. (ca.1871). Black on blue underprint. Gauchos roping steers at upper left, portrait young girl's head at upper center right, farmer gathering hay at lower right. Back: Blue. Printer: ABNC. Proof. Rare.	—	—	—
S915	**20 Pesos** 5.2.1871. Black on brown underprint. Portrait young girl holding hen with chicks at lower left, Columbus landing in New World ("Columbus") at upper center, portrait girl with dog and puppies at lower right. Back: Orange. Printer: ABNC. Rare.	—	—	—

José María Melguizo H.

1900 Issue

S916 20 Centavos	Good	Fine	XF
19.1.1900. Black on green underprint. Series A2a. Printer: Tipografia Central Medellin.	—	—	—
S918 1 Peso			
19.1.1900. Overprint: Black overprint of new issuer's name and date in six lines on back of unissued #S845.	—	—	—
S919 2 Pesos			
19.1.1900 (- old date 188_). Blue on dark red underprint. Overprint: New date overprint on type of #S222 but with unissued date in 1880s.	—	—	—

Vicente B. Villa e Hijos

1880s Issue

S921 1 Peso	Good	Fine	XF
188x. Black on blue underprint. Man leading horse at left, allegorical woman with sheep at center right. Series A. Back: Blue. Printer: ABNC.			
p. Proof.	—	Unc	600.
r. Unsigned remainder.	—	—	—
s. Specimen.	—	Unc	600.

S922 5 Pesos	Good	Fine	XF
1.2.1885; 1.2.1889. Black on orange underprint. Seated woman ("Study") at left, "Raphael's Angel" at top center right. Series B. Back: Brown. Printer: ABNC.			
a. Issued note.	150.	350.	750.
p. Proof.	—	Unc	600.
s. Specimen.	—	Unc	800.
S923 10 Pesos			
188x. Black on green underprint. Man with scythe ("Farmer") at left, reclinig woman ("L'Orient") at center right. Series C. Back: Green. Printer: ABNC.			
a. Issued note.	150.	350.	750.
p. Proof.	—	Unc	600.
s. Specimen.	—	Unc	800.

#S931 *Deleted.* See Vol. II #242.

#S936-S938 *Deleted.* See Vol. II #313-313B.

#S941 *Deleted.* See Vol. II #90.

#S943 and S946 *Deleted.* See Vol. II #308 and 309.

#S951-S955 *Deleted.* See Vol. II #312-312D.

#S960, S961 and S963 *Deleted.* See Vol. II #314-314B.

#S967 *Deleted.* See Vol. II #243.

#S971-S979 *Deleted.* See Vol. II #283-290.

#S980-S983 *Deleted.* See Vol. II #291-294.

NOTICE

Readers with unlisted dates, signature varieties, etc., are invited to submit photocopies or scans of their notes to:
Standard Catalog of World Paper Money,
700 East State St. Iola, WI 54990-0001,
E-Mail: george.cuhaj@fwmedia.com.

Section III

Regional Issues, 1898-1919

Departamento de Antioquia

1898 Issues

S1001 10 Pesos	Good	Fine	XF
6.10.1898. Black on brown and red underprint. Seated Justice at left, steam locomotive at upper center. Series D. Back: Black on green underprint. Arms with flags and condor at center. Printer: Tip. Central.	150.	350.	750.

Suministros Por Causa De Guerra Issue

S1003 Various Amounts	Good	Fine	XF
30.7.1898. Black. Printer: Tip Del Comercio, Medellin.	—	—	—

1899 Issue

S1005 5 Pesos	Good	Fine	XF
6.1899.	150.	350.	750.

1900 Issues

S1011 10 Centavos	Good	Fine	XF
3.1900. Black on green underprint. Without series or imprint. Like #S1021.			
a. Back brown, without underprint.	20.00	50.00	125.
b. Back red on green underprint.	20.00	50.00	125.
S1012 10 Centavos			
3.1900. Black. Without imprint. Like #S1011.			
a. Series II. Green underprint. on face and back.	20.00	50.00	125.
b. Series III, IV. Blue underprint. on face, brown underprint. on back.	20.00	50.00	125.
S1012A 10 Centavos			
9.1900. Black on pink underprint. Like #S1011. Series VI.	20.00	50.00	100.

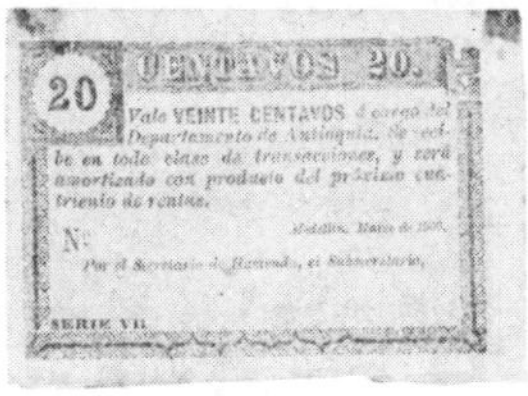

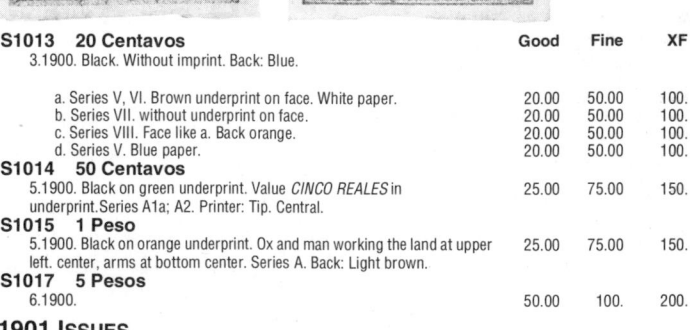

S1013 20 Centavos	Good	Fine	XF
3.1900. Black. Without imprint. Back: Blue.			
a. Series V, VI. Brown underprint on face. White paper.	20.00	50.00	100.
b. Series VII. without underprint on face.	20.00	50.00	100.
c. Series VIII. Face like a. Back orange.	20.00	50.00	100.
d. Series V. Blue paper.	20.00	50.00	100.
S1014 50 Centavos			
5.1900. Black on green underprint. Value *CINCO REALES* in underprint.Series A1a; A2. Printer: Tip. Central.	25.00	75.00	150.
S1015 1 Peso			
5.1900. Black on orange underprint. Ox and man working the land at upper left. center, arms at bottom center. Series A. Back: Light brown.	25.00	75.00	150.
S1017 5 Pesos			
6.1900.	50.00	100.	200.

1901 Issues

S1021 10 Centavos	Good	Fine	XF
1.1901. Black on violet underprint. Without series or imprint. Back: Blue on violet underprint.			
a. Light tan paper. Series VII. Imprint: Imprenta Oficial.	15.00	40.00	100.
b. White paper. Series VII. Imprint like a.	15.00	40.00	100.
c. Light blue paper. Series VIII. Imprint like a.	15.00	40.00	100.
d. Light tan paper. Series VIII but no imprint.	15.00	40.00	100.

	Good	Fine	XF
S1022 20 Centavos			
Jan. 1901. Black. Series IX; X. Printer: Imprenta Oficial.			
a. Brown underprint, light tan paper. Back brown. Series X.	15.00	40.00	100.
b. Violet underprint, blue paper. Back violet. Series X.	15.00	40.00	100.
S1023 50 Centavos			
Feb. 1901. Black on light green underprint. Large numeral at left. Series A1. Printer: Tipografia Central.	40.00	75.00	150.
S1024 1 Peso			
March 1901. Black on yellow underprint. Lion at right. Printer: Tipografia Central.	25.00	50.00	100.

Casa de Moneda de Medellin

1919-20 Gold Certificates of Deposit

	Good	Fine	XF
S1026 2 1/2 Pesos			
15.9.1919; 1.5.1920. Black on green and multicolor underprint. Seated woman with flowers at center. Back: Green. Arms at lower center. Printer: ABNC.			
a. Issued note. 15.9.1919. Rare.	—	—	—
p. Proof, with or without underprint.	—	Unc	700.
s. Specimen.	—	Unc	850.
S1026A 2 1/2 Pesos			
1.5.1920. Black. Seated woman with flowers at center. Back: Arms at lower center. Printer: ABNC. Archive copy. Rare.	—	—	—
S1027 5 Pesos			
15.9.1919. Black on brown and multicolor underprint. Seated woman with flowers at center. Back: Brown. Arms at lower center. Printer: ABNC.			
a. Issued note. Rare.	—	—	—
p. Proof.	—	Unc	700.
s. Specimen.	—	Unc	850.
S1028 10 Pesos			
15.9.1919. Black on orange and multicolor underprint. Seated woman with flowers at center. Back: Orange. Arms at lower center. Printer: ABNC.			
a. Issued note. Rare.	—	—	—
p. Proof.	—	Unc	700.
s. Specimen.	—	Unc	1000.
S1029 20 Pesos			
15.9.1919. Black on blue and multicolor underprint. Seated woman with flowers at center. Back: Blue. Arms at lower center. Printer: ABNC.			
a. Issued note. Rare.	—	—	—
p. Proof.	—	Unc	700.
s. Specimen.	—	Unc	1100.

NOTE: For notes with overprint: *BANCO DE LA REPUBLICA / BILLETE PROVISIONAL*, see Vol. 2, #351-354.

Tesoro del Departamento de Antioquia

1900 Issue

	Good	Fine	XF
S1029A 1 Peso			
5.1900. Black on light red underprint. Ox and man working the land at upper center, arms below. Heading: *TESORO DEPARTAMENTAL*. Paper: Yellow.	50.00	100.	200.

1901 Issues

	Good	Fine	XF
S1030 50 Centavos			
Feb. 1901. Black. Arms at top center. Series F. Printer: Imp. de La Verdad, Medellin.	25.00	50.00	100.

	Good	Fine	XF
S1031 50 Centavos			
Feb. 1901. Black on yellow underprint. Arms at top center. Series G. Printer: Imp. de La Verdad, Medellin.	25.00	50.00	100.
S1032 50 Centavos			
Feb. 1901; Dec. 1901. Black. Open book at upper center. Series G; H. Paper: Pink. Printer: Imp. de La Verdad, Medellin.	25.00	50.00	100.

Decreto 203 del 25 de Mayo de 1900

	Good	Fine	XF
S1033 1 Peso			
March 1901. Black. Steam locomotive at top center Bees at upper left and right on back. Series D.	50.00	100.	200.
S1033C 10 Pesos			
25.5.1900. Black on light blue underprint. Series Z.	—	—	—

1902 Issues

	Good	Fine	XF
S1035 50 Centavos			
6.1902. Black on pink underprint. Series left. Printer: Imp. de La Verdad.	25.00	50.00	150.

	Good	Fine	XF
S1036 1 Peso			
9.1902. Black on blue underprint. Arms at center. Series F. Back: Red. Paper: Pink. Printer: Imp. de La Verdad.	25.00	50.00	150.

	Good	Fine	XF
S1038 5 Pesos			
6.1902. Black on deep pink underprint. Steam locomotive at upper center. Series N. Printer: Imp. de La Verdad.	25.00	75.00	175.
S1040 10 Pesos			
7.1902. Black and red. Smaller sheaf and plow at upper center. Series left. Back: Graygreen. Printer: Imp. de La Verdad.	25.00	75.00	175.
S1041 10 Pesos			
7.1902. Blue and black. Larger sheaf and plow at upper center. Large outlined: *DIEZ PESOS* in underprint. Series Q. Back: Gray-green. Printer: Imp. de La Verdad.	25.00	75.00	175.
S1042 10 Pesos			
9.1902. Black on blue underprint. Larger sheaf and plow at center. Series V. Printer: Imp. de La Verdad.	25.00	75.00	175.
S1042A 10 Pesos			
9.1902. Black on blue underprint. Scale at upper center. Series T. Paper: Pink. Printer: Imp. de La Verdad.	25.00	75.00	175.

	Good	Fine	XF
S1043 10 Pesos			
11.1902. Black. Horse and wagon at upper center, large outlined: *DIEZ PESOS*. Series Y. Back: Blue-black. Paper: Greenish-gray. Printer: Imp. de La Verdad.	25.00	75.00	175.

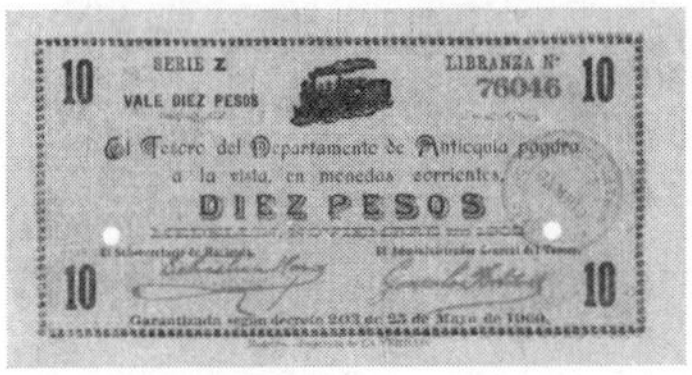

	Good	Fine	XF
S1044 10 Pesos			
11.1902. Black on blue underprint. Train at upper center without large outlined: *DIEZ PESOS* in underprint. Series Z. Back: Blue. Paper: Pink. Printer: Imp. de La Verdad.	25.00	75.00	175.

Gobierno Departamental

1900 Issues

	Good	Fine	XF
S1050 50 Centavos			
5.1900. Black on green underprint. Printer: Tip. del Comercio.	—	—	—
S1051 50 Centavos			
6.1900. Black on tan underprint. Padlock at center. Series A. Printer: Tip. del Comercio.	20.00	40.00	100.

	Good	Fine	XF
S1052 50 Centavos			
9.1900. Black on orange underprint. Padlock at center. Series A; B. Printer: Tip. del Comercio.	20.00	40.00	100.

	Good	Fine	XF
S1053 50 Centavos			
11.1900. Black on orange underprint. Eagle at center. Series C. Without imprint. Back: Black on lilac.	20.00	40.00	100.
S1054 1 Peso			
6.1900. Black. Train at center. Series B.2. Paper: Yellow. Printer: Tip. Central.	20.00	40.00	100.
S1054A 1 Peso			
6.1900. Red on green underprint. Man at right corner, shield at left. corner.	—	—	—
S1055 1 Peso			
6.1900. Black. Bunch of grapes at right. Series A. Back: Deep blue. Paper: Blue.	15.00	35.00	75.00
S1055A 1 Peso			
8.1900. Black on brown underprint. Series B.	—	—	—

	Good	Fine	XF
S1056 1 Peso			
10.1900. Black on green underprint. Grapes at right. Series B. Printer: Tip. del Comercio.	15.00	35.00	75.00

	Good	Fine	XF
S1060 10 Pesos			
6.1900. Black on peach and red underprint. Paddle wheel steamboat at top center. Back: Brown. Printer: Tip. Central. Series D2a.	15.00	50.00	100.

#S1060A-S1062 printer: Tip. del Comercio.

	Good	Fine	XF
S1060A 10 Pesos			
10.1900. Black on red underprint. Arms at upper center. Series left. Printer: Tip. del Comercio.	15.00	50.00	100.
S1061 10 Pesos			
11.1900. Black on green underprint. Arms at upper center. Series F. Printer: Tip. del Comercio.	15.00	50.00	100.
S1062 50 Pesos			
11.1900. Black on green and red underprint. Cow's head at left. Series A. Printer: Tip. del Comercio.	25.00	75.00	150.

1901 Issues

	Good	Fine	XF
S1062A 50 Centavos			
1.1901. Black on red underprint. Eagle at upper center. Series D.	25.00	75.00	150.
S1063 50 Centavos			
2.1901. Series C. Padlock at center. Printer: Tip. del Comercio.	15.00	50.00	100.
S1063A 50 Centavos			
4.1901. Black. Eagle at upper center. Imprint: Tipografía del Foto Club.			
a. Pink underprint. Series A.	15.00	50.00	100.
b. Green underprint. Series C.	15.00	35.00	125.
S1064 50 Centavos			
7.1901; 12.1901. Black on orange underprint. Padlock at top center. Series E. Back: Violet hand stamp: *Departamento de Antioquia/MEDELLIN.* Printer: Tip. del Comercio, Medellin.	25.00	75.00	150.
S1064A 50 Centavos			
12.1901. Black on red-brown underprint. Plow and sheaf at upper center. Series E. Imprint: Tipografía del Foto Club.	15.00	35.00	125.
S1065 1 Peso			
1.1901. Black on red underprint. Train and hill at left, arms at center. Series A.Imprint: Lit. J. L. Arango, Medellin. Back: Green.	25.00	75.00	150.
S1066 1 Peso			
1.1901. Black. Man (B. Franklin?) at upper left. Series B. Back: Red.	25.00	75.00	150.
S1069 1 Peso			
1.1901. Black and red. Grapevine at left. Series E.	25.00	75.00	150.

	Good	Fine	XF
S1070 1 Peso			
1.1901. Black and green. Grapevine at left. Imprint: Imp. del Dpto. Series F. Back: Black on red-brown. Paper: Pink.	25.00	75.00	150.
S1070A 1 Peso			
1.1901. Black and blue. Grapevne at left. Series O. Paper: Pink.	25.00	75.00	150.

	Good	Fine	XF
S1071 1 Peso			
1.1901. Black on red underprint. Arms at left. Imprint: Lit. Oficial. Series H. Back: Black on lilac underprint. Paper: Pink.	25.00	75.00	150.
S1071A 1 Peso			
2.1901. Black. Portrait at upper left. Series B.	25.00	75.00	150.
S1071B 1 Peso			
3.1901. Black. Plow and sheaf at upper center. Imprint: Imp. de La Verdad - Medellin. Series A.	25.00	75.00	150.
S1072 1 Peso			
3.1901. Black. Arms at center. Imprint: Imp. de La Verdad. Series D.	25.00	75.00	150.
S1073 1 Peso			
3.1901. Black on yellow underprint. Horse with Indian runner leading. Series D. Back: Red overprint. Overprint: Red on back.	25.00	75.00	150.
S1074 1 Peso			
3.1901. Steam locomotive at upper center. Series D. Imprint: Imp. de La Verdad.	25.00	75.00	150.

	Good	Fine	XF
S1075 1 Peso			
4.1901. Black on olive underprint. Sheaves and farm tools at upper left. Imprint: Tip. del Foto-Club. Series C. Paper: Pink.	25.00	75.00	150.
S1076 1 Peso			
1901. Black on green underprint. Grapes at right.			
a. Series A. Feb. 1901.	20.00	40.00	100.
b. Series D; E. April 1901.	20.00	40.00	100.
c. Series G. July 1901.	20.00	40.00	100.
S1078 5 Pesos			
6.1901. Black on red underprint. Steam locomotive at upper center. Series C. Back: Red. Printer: Imp. de La Verdad.	25.00	50.00	150.
S1080 5 Pesos			
6.1901. Black on yellow underprint. Sheaf and plow at upper center. Series H. Printer: Imp. de La Verdad.	25.00	50.00	150.
S1082 5 Pesos			
8.1901. Black on pink underprint. Sheaf and plow at upper center. Series N. Imprint: Tip. del Comercio.	25.00	50.00	150.

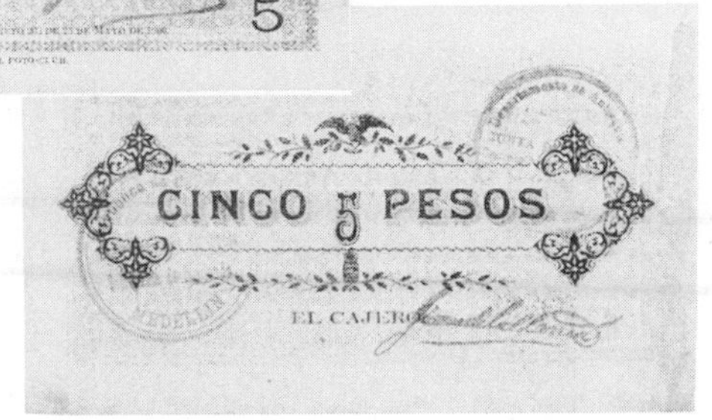

S1085 5 Pesos

	Good	Fine	XF
12.1901. Black on aqua underprint. Horse's head at upper center. Series A; B. Back: Black in inverted position. Paper: Lilac. Printer: Tip. del Foto-Club.	25.00	50.00	150.

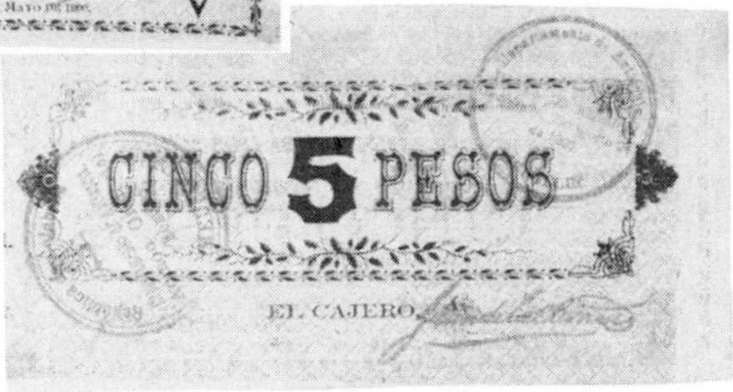

S1086 5 Pesos

	Good	Fine	XF
12.1901. Black on deep pink underprint. Bull's head at upper center. Series B. Printer: Tip. del Foto-Club.	25.00	50.00	150.

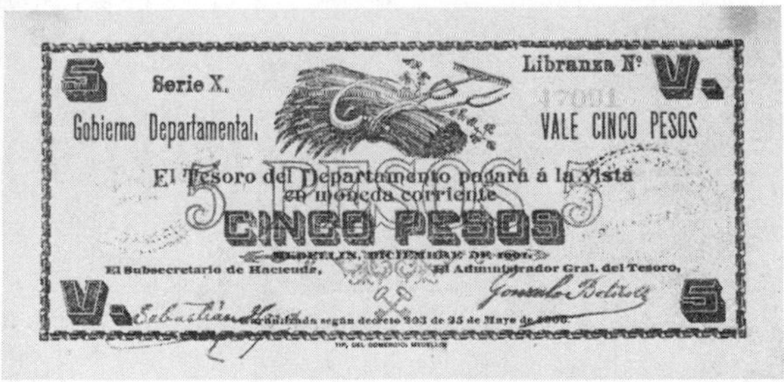

S1088 5 Pesos

	Good	Fine	XF
12.1901. Black. Sheaf and farm tools at upper center. Imprint: Tip. del Comercio.			
a. Blue and red underprint. Back blue. Series V.	25.00	50.00	150.
b. Aqua underprint. Pink paper. Series X.	25.00	50.00	150.

S1092 10 Pesos

2.1901. Black on green and red underprint. Eagle and flag at upper center. Imprint: Imp. de La Verdad. Series D. Back: Blue.	25.00	50.00	150.

S1093 10 Pesos

12.1901. Black on violet underprint. Plow and sheaf at upper center. Series H.	25.00	50.00	150.

1902-03 Issues

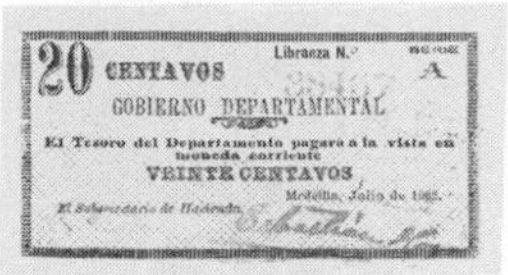

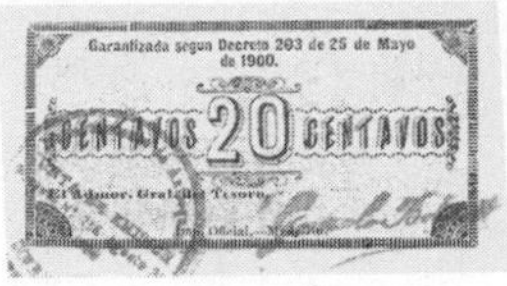

S1097 20 Centavos

	Good	Fine	XF
7.1902. Series A. Printer: Imp. Oficial.	25.00	50.00	150.

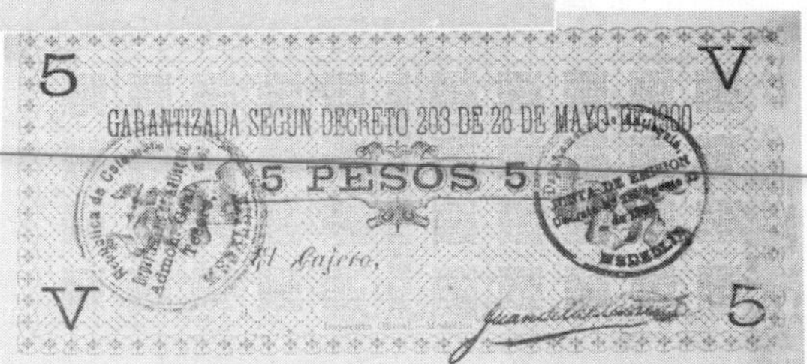

S1103 5 Pesos

	Good	Fine	XF
1.1902. Black and red on tan underprint. Arms at center. Series B. Back: Black on purple underprint. Paper: Pink. Printer: Imp. Oficial.	25.00	50.00	150.

S1106 10 Pesos

	Good	Fine	XF
3.1902. Black on light blue underprint. Arms at left. Series B. Back: Black on red underprint. Local arms at left center. Printer: Imp. Oficial.	25.00	50.00	150.

S1108 20 Pesos

	Good	Fine	XF
7.1902; 11.1902. Black on orange and green underprint. Arms at left. Series A. Back: Black on brown underprint. Printer: Imp. Oficial.	25.00	75.00	200.

S1109 20 Pesos

	Good	Fine	XF
7.1902. Black on orange and green underprint. Woman standing and woman kneeling with sheaf at left. Series B and C. Back: Green on orange underprint. Printer: Imp. del Comercio.	25.00	75.00	200.

		Good	Fine	XF
S1112	**50 Pesos** 7.1902. Black on lilac and green underprint. Eagle and banner at left. Series A. Paper: White or light blue. Printer: Imp. Oficial.	25.00	75.00	200.

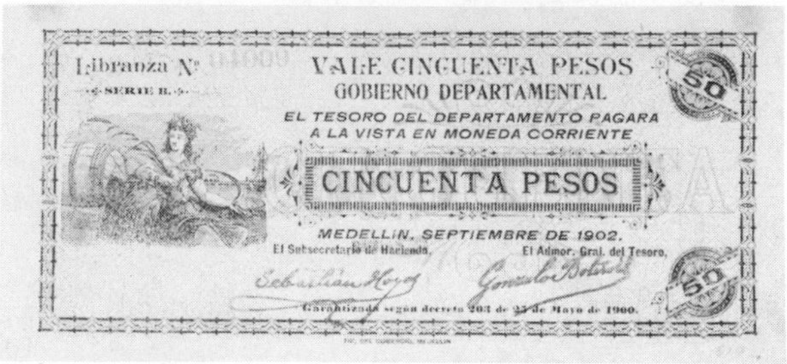

		Good	Fine	XF
S1113	**50 Pesos** 9.1902. Black on light blue and brown underprint. Woman with casks, sheaf and sickle at left. Series B. Back: Blue on green underprint. Paper: Light blue. Printer: Tip. del Comercio.	25.00	75.00	200.
S1115	**50 Pesos** 4.1903. Woman. Printer: Tip. del Comercio.	25.00	75.00	200.

Departamento de Bolívar

Decree 10.7.1900

		Good	Fine	XF
S1120	**10 Centavos** D.1900. Black. Cow at center. Rare.	—	—	—
S1121	**10 Centavos** D. 1900. Arms. Rare.	—	—	—
S1122	**20 Centavos** D. 1900. Ship at center. Rare.	—	—	—
S1123	**50 Centavos** D. 1900. Black on green underprint. Arms at center. Back: Greenish gray. Issued at Lorica. Rare.	—	—	—
S1124	**1 Peso** D.1900. Black on green underprint. Arms at center. Series D. Back: Text at center. Issued at Lorica. Rare.	—	—	—

Departamento del Magdalena

1900 Issue

		Good	Fine	XF
S1126	**20 Centavos** May 1900. Black. Arms at left. Series A. Issued at Riohacha. Rare.	—	—	—
S1128	**1 Peso** 8.1900. Black. Ship at left. Rare.	—	—	—
S1128A	**1 Peso** 8.12.1900. Heading: *EMISION ESPECIAL*. Rare.	—	—	—
S1130	**10 Pesos** 6.1900. Black. Rare.	—	—	—

Gobernación del Magdalena

1900 First Issue

		Good	Fine	XF
S1131	**10 Centavos** 5.4.1900. Black on light green underprint. 2 printed signatures.	50.00	100.	225.

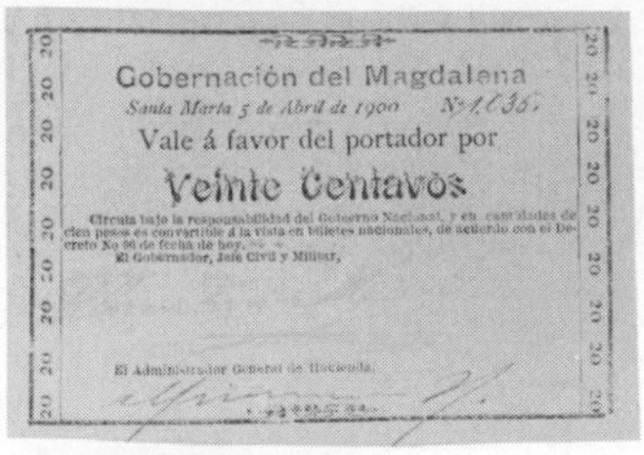

		Good	Fine	XF
S1132	**20 Centavos** 5.4.1900. Black. Uniface, embossed seal at center, 1 stamped and 1 printed signature. No imprint. Paper: White with light blue lines.	50.00	100.	200.
S1133	**50 Centavos** 5.4.1900. Light red. Uniface, embossed seal at center, 1 stamped and 1 printed signature. No imprint. Paper: White with light blue lines.	50.00	100.	200.
S1134	**1 Peso** 5.4.1900. Blue. Uniface, embossed seal at center, 1 stamped and 1 printed signature. No imprint. Paper: White with light blue lines.	50.00	100.	200.

1900 Second Issues

		Good	Fine	XF
S1137	**10 Centavos** 5.4.1900. Maroon-red. Crude print. Printed signature only. Printer: Armenta and Prieto, Barranquilla.	50.00	100.	200.
S1138	**10 Centavos** 5.4.1900. Purple. Crude print. Printed signature only. Printer: Armenta and Prieto, Barranquilla.	50.00	100.	200.

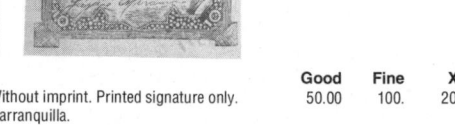

		Good	Fine	XF
S1139	**10 Centavos** 5.4.1900. Blue. Crude print. Without imprint. Printed signature only. Printer: Armenta and Prieto, Barranquilla.	50.00	100.	200.
S1140	**20 Centavos** 5.4.1900. Black. Issued at Riohacha. Printed signature only. Printer: Armenta and Prieto, Barranquilla.	50.00	100.	200.

		Good	Fine	XF
S1141	**50 Centavos** 5.4.1900. Green. Series G. Printed signature only. Printer: Armenta and Prieto, Barranquilla.	50.00	100.	200.

		Good	Fine	XF
S1142	**1 Peso** Black on light pink underprint. Sailing ship at right. Series H. Printed signature only. Printer: Armenta and Prieto, Barranquilla.	50.00	100.	200.
S1143	**1 Peso** 5.4.1900. Blue on light pink underprint. Sailing ship at right. Printed signature only. Printer: Armenta and Prieto, Barranquilla.	50.00	100.	200.

Departamento de Santander

1899 Issue

		Good	Fine	XF
S1151	**20 Centavos** 27.10.1899; 1.11.1899. Black on orange underprint. Horse's head at right. Series AE; AJ. Back: Text. Printer: Tip. Mercantil.	50.00	100.	200.
S1152	**50 Centavos** 1.11.1899. Blue on pink underprint. Palm at left with text: *DEPARTAMENTO NACIONAL DE SANTANDER* in underprint across face. Series A; B; C; F. Back: Blue. Printer: Tip. Mercantil.	50.00	100.	200.
S1153	**1 Peso** 1.11.1899. Black. Legend across face in underprint. Rayed sun at upper left. Printer: Tip. Mercantil.			
	a. Series C; D. Green underprint on face. Back green.	50.00	100.	200.
	b. Series I. Blue underprint on face. Back blue.	50.00	100.	200.
S1154	**5 Pesos** 1.11.1899. Black on pink underprint. Woman carrying branches at center. Series Z. Back: Black. Printer: Tip. Mercantil.	50.00	100.	200.

Provincia de Ocaña

1900 Issue

	Good	Fine	XF
S1155 1 Peso 3.5.1900. Black. Arms at left center. Rare.	—	—	—

La Compañia Empresaria del Camino de Herradura de Bucaramanga a Sabana de Torres

The Managing Company of the Horseshoe Road from Bucaramanga to Sabana de Torres

1887 Issue

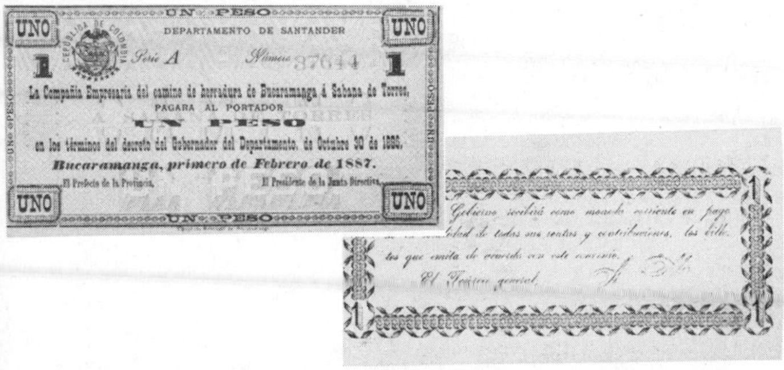

	Good	Fine	XF
S1156 1 Peso 1.2.1887. Black on green underprint. Arms at upper left. Printer: Tipografia Mercantil de Bucaramanga. This note was fully acceptable as money through an agreement wth the government of the department. Rare.	—	—	—

NOTE: #S1156 was fully acceptable as money through an agreement wth the government of the department.

Departamento de Santander

1900 Issues

	Good	Fine	XF
S1157 20 Centavos 1.4.1900. Black on yellow underprint. Small vase at upper left. Series A; D. Printer: Tip. Mercantil.	20.00	50.00	125.
S1158 50 Centavos 1.4.1900. Black on yellow underprint. Small building at upper left. Series C. Back: Small vase at upper left. Printer: Tip. Mercantil.	25.00	75.00	150.
S1158A 50 Centavos 1.4.1900. Portrait of a woman at upper left. Series left. Back: Small vase at upper left. Printer: Tip. Mercantil.	25.00	75.00	150.
S1159 50 Centavos 14.11.1900. Black on brown underprint. Series R; Y. Printer: Tip. Mercantil.	25.00	75.00	150.
S1160 1 Peso 14.11.1900. Black and green. Arms at left. Back: Green. Date line. Printer: Tip. Mercantil.	40.00	100.	300.
S1161 1 Peso 11.1900. Black and green. Eagle on arms at left. Series A. Back: Green. Printer: Tip. Mercantil.	40.00	100.	300.

Departamento del Tolima

1900-19 Issue

	Good	Fine	XF
S1166 10 Centavos 2.7.1900. Rare.	—	—	—
S1167 20 Centavos 2.7.1900; 31.7.1900. Dark blue on green underprint. Back: Green. Rare.	—	—	—
S1168 50 Centavos 2.7.1900. Rare.	—	—	—
S1169 1 Peso 2.7.1900. Rare.	—	—	—

	Good	Fine	XF
S1173 1 Peso 3.7.1900. Black on brown underprint. Series C. Back: Black.	40.00	100.	200.
S1176 20 Pesos 31.7.1900. Rare.	—	—	—
S1177 20 Centavos 15.6.1900; 10.6.1901. Black on brown underprint. Sailing ships at center. Series B. Back: Black.	40.00	100.	200.
S1181 1 Peso 9.1902. Black on red underprint. Series D.	150.	300.	500.
S1191 1 Peso 2.3.1919. Overprint: Overprint on Banco Oriental note. Rare.	—	—	—

Section IV

Regional Ferrocarril (Railroad) Issues

Ferrocarril de Amaga

191x Issue

	Good	Fine	XF
S1401 10 Pesos 191x. Blue. Arms at upper center. Paper: Yellow. Specimen. Rare.	—	—	—

Ferrocarril de Antioquía

1893 Issue

	Good	Fine	XF
S1501 1000 Pesos 1.4.1893. Black and brown on light blue underprint. Standing allegorical figure at left, redemption date of 1902 above. Series J. Printer: Lit. de Villaveces. Printer's specimen. Rare.	—	—	—
S1511 50 Pesos 5.1909. Blue. Train at upper left center. Second series. Unsigned remainder. Rare.	—	—	—

1909 Issue

	Good	Fine	XF
S1521 1 Peso 5.1909. Black on orange and yellow underprint. Trains in mountains at upper left. Printer: Lit. Nacional. Specimen.	—	—	—

Ferrocarril de Cartagena

1892 Issue

	Good	Fine	XF
S1531 100,000 Pesos 20.12.1892. Black.	350.	600.	1000.

Ferrocarril del Cauca

Law of 1896

	Good	Fine	XF
S1541 1000 Pesos 19xx. Black and purple on light blue underprint. Train at upper center. Unsigned remainder.	—	—	—

Laws of 1896; 1897

	Good	Fine	XF
S1551 10 Pesos L.1897. Black on lilac underprint. Woman with bird at upper left. Series B. Tiny arms at upper corners. Printer: Villaveces. Unsigned remainder.	350.	600.	1000.
S1551A 20 Pesos L.1897. Black on orange underprint. Eagle and arms at upper center. Tiny arms at upper corners. Printer: Villaveces. Unsigned remainder.	—	—	—
S1552 50 Pesos L.1897. Black on red-brown underprint. Series C. Tiny arms at upper corners. Printer: Villaveces. Unsigned remainder.	350.	600.	1000.
S1553 100 Pesos L.1897. Black on light green underprint. Girl's head at upper left. Series D. Tiny arms at upper corners. Printer: Villaveces. Unsigned remainder.	350.	600.	1000.
S1555 1000 Pesos L.1897. Black on red underprint. Woman's head at upper left. Series F. Tiny arms at upper corners. Printer: Villaveces. Unsigned remainder.	400.	750.	1250.

1900s Issue

	Good	Fine	XF
S1557 1000 Pesos 190x. Black. Printer: Eugenio Pardo.	—	—	—

1910 Issue

	Good	Fine	XF
S1558 1 Peso 3.1910. Black on yellow underprint. Arms at center in underprint. Specimen.	—	—	—
S1560 10 Pesos 3.1910. Black on brown underprint. Arms at center in underprint. Specimen.	—	—	—
S1561 100 Pesos 3.1910. Black on red underprint. Arms at center in underprint. Specimen.	350.	600.	900.
S1562 500 Pesos 3.1910. Black on light blue underprint. Arms at center in underprint.			
a. Back dark red. Specimen.	—	—	—
b. Back blue. Specimen.	—	—	—

1912 Issue

	Good	Fine	XF
S1573 1000 Pesos 12.1912. Black on light lilac underprint. Specimen.	500.	750.	1250.

ILLUSTRATIONS

Illustrations of bank notes used throughout this catalog are 42% of the actual size.

Ferrocarril de Cucuta

1886 Issue

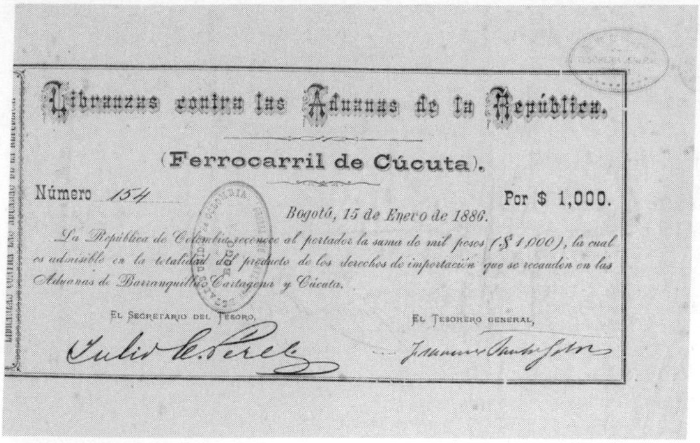

	Good	Fine	XF
S1576 1000 Pesos 15.1.1886. Black.	—	—	—

Ferrocarril de La Sabana

1886 Issue

	Good	Fine	XF
S1601 1 Peso 20.10.1886. Black and blue. Train at center, arms at lower center. Series B. Printer: Lit. de D. Paredes. Rare.	—	—	—

Ferrocarril de Santander

188x Issue

	Good	Fine	XF
S1621 5 Pesos 188x. Blue and black. Steam locomotive at center.	150.	300.	600.
S1625 100 Pesos 188x. Steam locomotive at center.	250.	450.	800.

1893 Issue

	Good	Fine	XF
S1651 1000 Pesos 1.4.1893. Black on red underprint. Eagle at left, arms in underprint at center. Series A. Printer: Villaveces. Rare.	—	—	—

Costa Rica

The Republic of Costa Rica, located in southern Central America between Nicaragua and Panama, has an area of 51,100 sq. km. and a population of 4.19 million. Capital: San Jose. Agriculture predominates; coffee, bananas, beef and sugar contribute heavily to the country's export earnings.

Although explored by the Spanish early in the 16th century, initial attempts at colonizing Costa Rica proved unsuccessful due to a combination of factors, including: disease from mosquito-infested swamps, brutal heat, resistance by natives, and pirate raids. It was not until 1563 that a permanent settlement of Cartago was established in the cooler, fertile central highlands. The area remained a colony for some two and a half centuries. In 1821, Costa Rica became one of several Central American provinces that jointly declared their independence from Spain. Two years later it joined the United Provinces of Central America, but this federation disintegrated in 1838, at which time Costa Rica proclaimed its sovereignty and independence. Since the late 19th century, only two brief periods of violence have marred the country's democratic development. Although it still maintains a large agricultural sector, Costa Rica has expanded its economy to include strong technology and tourism industries. The standard of living is relatively high. Land ownership is widespread.

MONETARY SYSTEM:

1 Peso = 100 Centavos to 1896
1 Colon = 100 Centimos

BANKS:

RAILROAD:

Republic

Banco Anglo-Costarricense

1864 Issue

	Good	Fine	XF
S107 1 Peso 1.1.1864. Printer: BWC. Rare.	—	—	—
S108 10 Pesos 1.1.1864. Ship at left. Portrait Queen Victoria at top center. Watermark: *SAN JOSE DE COSTA RICA* around value in frame. Printer: BWC.			
a. Issued note. Rare.	—	—	—
s. Specimen.	—	Unc	500.
S109 25 Pesos 1.1.1864. Rooster at left. Portrait Queen Victoria at top center. Watermark: *SAN JOSE DE COSTA RICA* around value in frame. Printer: BWC.			
a. Issued note. Rare.	—	—	—
r. Unsigned remainder.	—	—	—
s. Specimen. Rare.	—	—	—
S110 50 Pesos 1.1.1864. Portrai Queen Victoria at top center. Watermark: *SAN JOSE DE COSTA RICA* around value in frame. Printer: BWC. Rare.	—	—	—
S111 100 Pesos 1.1.1864. Black and brown on green underprint. Bull at left. Portrait Queen Victoria at top center. Paper: Orange. Watermark: *SAN JOSE DE COSTA RICA* around value in frame. Printer: BWC.			
a. Issued note. Rare.	—	—	—
p. Proof. Rare.	—	—	—
s. Specimen. Rare.	—	—	—
S111A 100 Pesos 3.12.1902. Black and brown on green underprint. Bull at left. Queen Victora at top center. Back: Text. Paper: Orange. Watermark: *SAN JOSE DE COSTA RICA* around value in frame. Printer: BWC. Rare.	—	—	—

Law of 23.6.1917

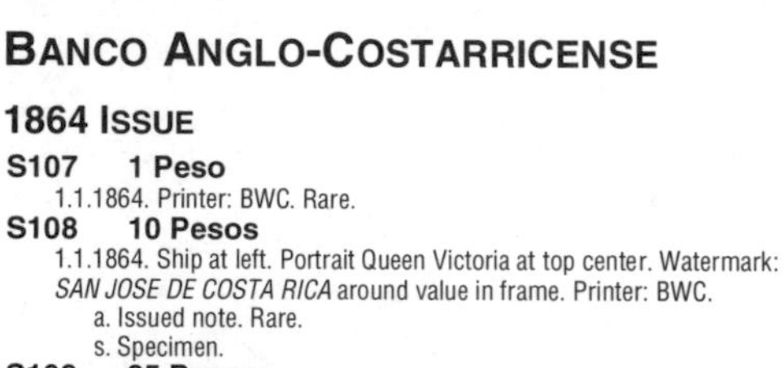

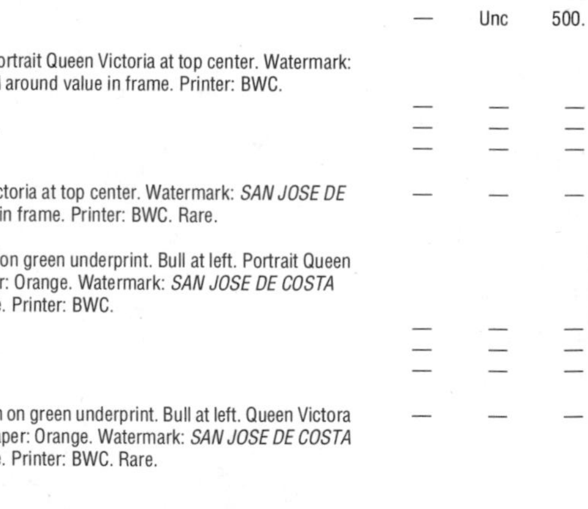

S121 1 Colón

L.1917. Black on multicolor underprint. Portrait man at center. Back: Green. Seated Mercury at center. Printer: ABNC.

	Good	Fine	XF
p. Proof.	—	Unc	1500.
r. Unsigned remainder.	—	Unc	50.00
s1. Specimen with black overprint, with normal serial #. Type A.	—	Unc	750.
s2. Specimen with black overprint, with normal serial #. Type B.	—	Unc	750.
s3. Specimen with red overprint, with normal serial #. Type C.	—	Unc	750.
s4. Specimen.	—	Unc	1650.

NOTE: Remainders with spurious signatures are sometimes seen.

S122 5 Colones

1.1.1903; 1.1.1904; 1.1.1911; 1.1.1917. Black on multicolor underprint. Portrait J. M. Fernandez at upper center. Series A. Back: Brown. Arms at center. Printer: BWC.

	Good	Fine	XF
a. Issued note. Rare.	—	—	—
r. Unsigned remainder.	—	Unc	40.00
s1. Specimen with black overprint, with normal serial #. Type A.	—	Unc	100.
s2. Specimen with black overprint, with normal serial #. Type B.	—	Unc	40.00
s3. Specimen with red overprint, with normal serial #. Type C.	—	Unc	40.00
s4. Archive Specimen.	—	Unc	250.

Specimens are often seen with staple holes.

S123 10 Colones

1.1.1903; 1.1.1904; 1.1.1911; 1.1.1917. Black on multicolor underprint. Portrait B. Carrillo at upper center. Back: Blue. Arms at center. Printer: BWC.

	Good	Fine	XF
a. Issued note. Rare.	—	—	—
r. Unsigned remainder.	—	Unc	50.00
s1. Specimen with black overprint, with normal serial #. Type A.	—	Unc	100.
s2. Specimen with black overprint, with normal serial #. Type B.	—	Unc	40.00
s3. Specimen with red overprint, with normal serial #. Type C.	—	Unc	40.00
s4. Archive Specimen.	—	Unc	250.

Specimens are often seen with staple holes.

S124 20 Colones

1.1.1909; 1.1.1911; 1.1.1917. Black on multicolor underprint. Portrait man at left. Back: Brown and black. Monument at center.

	Good	Fine	XF
a. Issued note. Rare.	—	—	—
r. Unsigned remainder.	—	Unc	75.00
s1. Specimen with black overprint, with normal serial #. Type A.	—	Unc	125.
s2. Specimen with black overprint, with normal serial #. Type B.	—	Unc	50.00
s3. Specimen with red overprint, with normal serial #. Type C.	—	Unc	50.00
s4. Archive Specimen.	—	Unc	250.

Specimens are often seen with staple holes.

S125 50 Colones

1.1.1904; 1.1.1907; 1.1.1909; 1.1.1910; 1.1.1911; 1.1.1912; 1.1.1917. Black on multicolor underprint. Man at left.

	Good	Fine	XF
a. Issued note. Rare.	—	—	—
s. Specimen. Rare.	—	Unc	1250.

S126 100 Colones

1.1.1904; 1.1.1906; 1.1.1907; 1.1.1912. Black on multicolor underprint. Man at left.

	Good	Fine	XF
a. Issued note. Rare.	—	—	—
s. Specimen. Rare.	—	Unc	1250.

Banco Comercial de Costa Rica

1906-11 Issue

S141 5 Colones

1.12.1906. Black on green and red underprint. Rural scene at left, banana plant at right. Series A. Back: Brown. Liberty head at center. Printer: W&S.

	Good	Fine	XF
a. Issued note. Rare.	—	—	—
s. Specimen.	—	Unc	1250.

S142 10 Colones

1906; 1911. Black on orange and pink underprint. Portrait man at left, village scene at center. Back: Red. Liberty head at center. Printer: W&S.

	Good	Fine	XF
a. 1.12.1906. Series A. Rare.	—	—	—
b. 1.9.1911. Series B. Rare.	—	—	—
c. 2.10.1911. Series C. Rare.	—	—	—
d. 2.10.1911. Series D. Rare.	—	—	—
s. Specimen. Rare.	—	Unc	1250.

S144 50 Colones

1906-1911. Black on orange underprint. Man at left, coffee workers at right. Back: Blue. Liberty head at center. Printer: W&S.

	Good	Fine	XF
a. 1.12.1906. Series A. Rare.	—	—	—
b. 1.11.1907. Series B. Rare.	—	—	—
c. 12.8.1910. Series C. Rare.	—	—	—
d. 2.10.1911. Series C. Rare.	—	—	—
s. Specimen.	—	Unc	1250.

S145 100 Colones

1906-1911. Brown and black on green underprint. Man at center. Back: Blue. Shore scenes at left and right. Liberty head at center. Printer: W&S.

	Good	Fine	XF
a. 2.12.1906. Series A. Rare.	—	—	—
b. 1.10.1907. Series B. Rare.	—	—	—
c. 2.10.1911. Series C. Rare.	—	—	—
s. Specimen.	—	Unc	1250.

1914 Issue

S146 5 Colones

2.5.1914. Black on olive and blue underprint. Series B. National Theater at center. Back: Black. Printer: ABNC.

	Good	Fine	XF
a. Issued note.	—	—	—
p. Proof.	—	Unc	900.
s. Specimen.	—	Unc	1250.

S147 10 Colones

2.5.1914. Black on light orange and blue underprint. Series A. National Theater at center. Back: Orange. Liberty at center. Printer: ABNC.

	Good	Fine	XF
a. Issued note. Rare.	—	—	—
p. Proof.	—	Unc	900.
s. Specimen.	—	Unc	1250.

S148 20 Colones

1.11.1913. Black on yellow and orange underprint. Series B. National Theater at center. Back: Blue. Liberty at center. Printer: ABNC.

	Good	Fine	XF
p. Proof.	—	Unc	900.
s. Specimen.	—	Unc	1500.

S149 50 Colones

8.21.1914. Black on red and purple underprint. Series D-E. (E never released). National Theater at center. Back: Blue. Liberty at center. Printer: ABNC.

	Good	Fine	XF
p. Proof.	—	Unc	900.
s. Specimen.	—	Unc	2750.

S150 100 Colones

2.5.1914. Black on purple and brown underprint. Series D.(Series E-H not issued.) National Theater at center. Back: Purple. Liberty at center. Printer: ABNC.

	Good	Fine	XF
p. Proof.	—	Unc	900.
s. Specimen.	—	Unc	1750.

Banco de Costa Rica

1895 Issue

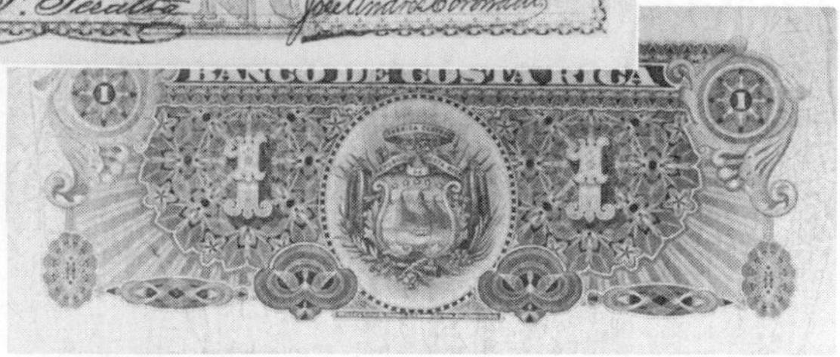

S151 1 Peso	**Good**	**Fine**	**XF**
1.1.1895. Black on blue and orange underprint. Woman with basket and cow at left, portrait woman at center, workers at right. Series A, B. Back: Blue. Arms at center. Printer: W&S.	300.	800.	1500.

S152 2 Pesos	**Good**	**Fine**	**XF**
1.1.1895. Black on yellow underprint. Mythical charioteer at left, seated woman with factory and ships behind at center right. Series A. Back: Green. Arms at center. Printer: W&S.	—	—	—

1891-99 Series

S163 5 Pesos	**Good**	**Fine**	**XF**
1.4.1899. Black on yellow and pale green underprint. Lion at center. Back: Deep olive-brown.			
a. Issued note. Rare.	—	—	—
p. Proof.	—	Unc	500.
r1. Unsigned remainder.	—	Unc	75.00
r2. Unsigned remainder with curved red overprint: *D. AVDO 1899* and Large *5*.	—	Unc	100.
s. Specimen.	—	Unc	500.

S164 10 Pesos	**Good**	**Fine**	**XF**
1.4.1899. Black on red-orange and yellow underprint. American and Canadian Horseshoe Falls at Niagara at center. Back: Red-orange. Woman's head at center. Printer: ABNC.			
a. Issued note. Rare.	—	—	—
p. Proof.	—	Unc	500.
r. Unsigned remainder.	—	Unc	100.
s. Specimen.	—	Unc	2000.

S165 20 Pesos			
1.4.1899. Black on purple and multicolor underprint. Ship at center. Back: Brown on multicolor underprint. Portrait woman with headdress at center. Printer: ABNC.			
a. Issued note. Rare.	—	—	—
p. Proof.	—	Unc	300.
r. Unsigned remainder.	—	Unc	100.
s. Specimen.	—	Unc	1500.

S166 100 Pesos			
1.1.1891; 1.1.1896; 1.3.1897; 1.3.1898. Black on yellow and green underprint. Allegorical women ("Peace") at left, bank at right. Back: Brown. Printer: ABNC.			
p. Proof.	—	Unc	500.
s. Specimen.	—	Unc	2000.

1901 Issue

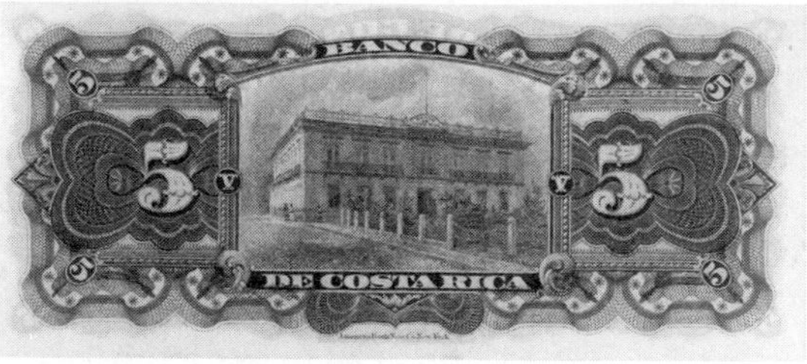

S173 5 Colones	**Good**	**Fine**	**XF**
1901-08. Black on red, brown and green underprint. Seated woman with farm and factory behind at center. Series A-C. Back: Red on violet, red-orange, brown and green underprint. Bank building at center. Printer: ABNC.			
a. 1.1.1901. Series A. With black circular stamp on back *SECRETARIA DE HACIENDA Y COMERCIO*. Rare.	—	—	—
b. 7.1.1905. Series B.	—	—	—
c. 8.1.1908. Series C.	—	—	—
r. Unsigned remainder. Series C.	—	Unc	100.
s. Specimen.	—	Unc	1650.

S174 10 Colones

1901-08. Black on green and multicolor underprint. Steam passenger train at center. Back: Deep olive-green on green and multicolor underprint. Bank building at center. Printer: ABNC.

	Good	Fine	XF
a. 1.1.1901. Series A. With black circular stamp on back: *SECRETARIA DE HACIENDA Y COMERCIO.* Rare.	—	—	—
b. 7.1.1905. Series B. Rare.	—	—	—
c. 8.1.1908. Series C. Rare.	—	—	—
r. Unsigned remainder. Series C.	—	Unc	100.
s. Specimen.	—	Unc	2000.

S175 20 Colones

1.1.1901. Black on brown and multicolor underprint. Miners at center. Back: Dark brown on blue and multicolor underprint. Bank building at center. Printer: ABNC.

	Good	Fine	XF
a. 1.1.1901. Series A. With black circular stamp on back: *SECRETARIA DE HACIENDA Y COMERCIO.* Rare.	—	—	—
b. 7.1.1905. Series B. Rare.	—	—	—
c. 5.1.1914; 10.1.1914. Series D. Rare.	—	—	—
p. Proof. Series A.	—	—	—
r. Unsigned remainder. Series D.	—	Unc	125.
s. Specimen. Series A.	—	Unc	2000.

S176 50 Colones

1901; 1905. Black on blue-green, brown and multicolor underprint. Reclining allegorical woman at left center and center right. Series A-B. Back: Blue-green and multicolor. Bank building at center. Printer: ABNC.

	Good	Fine	XF
a. 1.1.1901. Series A. With black circular stamp on back.	—	—	—
b. 7.1.1905. Series B.	—	—	—

S177 100 Colones

1901; 1905. Black on olive-green and multicolor underprint. Portrait man at left. Series A-B. Back: Olive-green and multicolor. Bank building at center. Printer: ABNC.

	Good	Fine	XF
a. 1.1.1905. Series A. With black circular stamp on back.	—	—	—
b. 7.1.1905. Series B.	—	—	—
p. Proof.	—	—	—
s. Specimen.	—	Unc	1750.

1906 Issue

S179 20 Colones

1.1.1906. Black and red on pink underprint. Soldier's monument at center. Series C. Back: Dark brown. Bank building at center. Printer: W&S.

	Good	Fine	XF
a. Issued note.	—	—	—
r. Unsigned remainder.	—	Unc	100.

Banco Herediano

1885; 1886 Issue

S181 5 Pesos

188x. Black on green underprint. Standing Commerce at left. Winged figure at lower right. Back: Green. Printer: ABNC litho. Issued at Heredia.

	Good	Fine	XF
a. Issued note. Rare.	—	—	—
p. Proof.	—	Unc	500.

S182 10 Pesos

188x. Black on light orange underprint. Standing allegorical woman at left. Winged figure at lower right. Back: Light orange. Printer: ABNC litho. Issued at Heredia.

	Good	Fine	XF
a. Issued note. Rare.	—	—	—
p. Proof.	—	Unc	500.

S183 25 Pesos

188x. Black on light brown underprint. Standing allegorical woman with staff, shield and eagle at left. Winged figure at lower right. Back: Light brown. Printer: ABNC litho. Issued at Heredia.

	Good	Fine	XF
a. Issued note. Rare.	—	—	—
p. Proof.	—	Unc	500.

S184 50 Pesos

188x. Black on red-orange underprint. Two allegorical women with fasces at left. Winged figure at lower right. Back: Red-orange. Printer: ABNC litho. Issued at Heredia.

	Good	Fine	XF
a. Issued note. Rare.	—	—	—
p. Proof.	—	Unc	500.

S185 100 Pesos

188x. Black on blue underprint. Allegorical woman with caduceus at left. Winged figure at lower right. Back: Blue. Printer: ABNC litho. Issued at Heredia.

	Good	Fine	XF
a. Issued note. Rare.	—	—	—
p. Proof.	—	Unc	3000.

Banco Mercantil de Costa Rica

1909-16 Issue

S201 5 Colones	Good	Fine	XF
1.6.1910-1.7.1916. Black on multicolor underprint. Bald eagle at center. Series A. Back: Brown and green underprint. Seated woman with book at center. Printer: ABNC.			
a. Issued note.	300.	750.	—
s. Specimen.	—	Unc	900.

S202 10 Colones	Good	Fine	XF
1.6.1910-1.8.1916. Black on multicolor underprint. Bald eagle at center. Back: Brown on multicolor underprint. Seated woman with shield at center. Printer: ABNC.			
a. Series A. 1.6.1910-1.7.1916. Rare.	—	—	—
b. Series B. 1.8.1916. Rare.	—	—	—
s. Specimen.	—	Unc	1000.

S203 20 Colones	Good	Fine	XF
1.6.1910-1.7.1916. Black on blue and multicolor underprint. Bald eagle at center. Back: Green and multicolor. Woman at center. Printer: ABNC.			
a. Issued note. Rare.	—	—	—
p. Proof.	—	Unc	750.
s. Specimen.	—	Unc	1000.

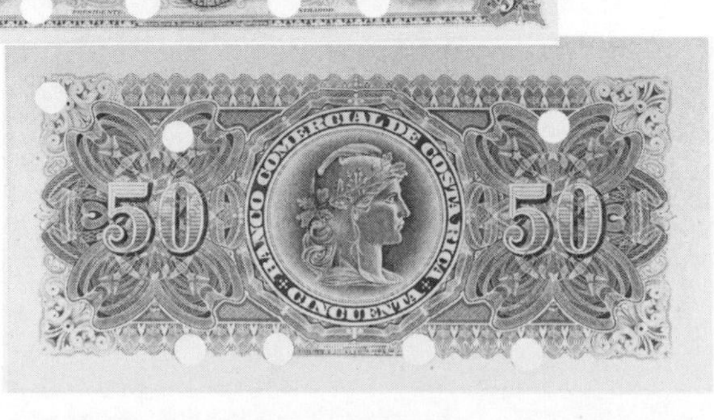

S204 50 Colones	Good	Fine	XF
1910-16. Black on brown and multicolor underprint. Bald eagle at center. Back: Dark blue-gray on blue and brown underprint. Woman at center. Printer: ABNC.			
a. Series A. 1.6.1910-1.7.1916. Rare.	—	—	—
b. Series B. 1.8.1916. Rare.	—	—	—
p. Proof.	—	Unc	750.
s. Specimen.	—	Unc	1250.
S205 100 Colones			
1.6.1910-1.7.1916. Black on orange and multicolor underprint. Bald eagle at center. Back: Olive-green on multicolor underprint. Woman at center. Printer: ABNC.			
a. Issued note. Rare.	—	—	—
p. Proof.	—	—	—
s. Specimen.	—	—	—

Banco Nacional de Costa Rica

1858 Issue

S209 1 Peso	Good	Fine	XF
1858. Portrait Mora at upper left, arms at lower right. Ship at center. Rare.	—	—	—
S210 2 Pesos			
1.6.1858. Red and black. Cherub at upper left, seated woman at center, portrait at left, arms at right. Uniface. Printer: Toppan, Carpenter and Co.	—	—	—
S211 10 Pesos			
18xx. Black. Portrait man at upper left, men with horses plowing field, woman at upper center right, arms at right. Printer: Toppan, Carpenter and Co. Proof.	—	—	—
S212 20 Pesos			
18xx. Black and red. Portrait man at upper left, seated allegorical woman with plow at center, arms at right. Uniface. Series A. Printer: Toppan, Carpenter and Co. Rare.	—	—	—

1878 Issue

S214 10 Pesos	Good	Fine	XF
18xx (ca.1878). Black on orange underprint. Standing woman with fasces by pedestal with arms at left, portrait man at center, sailing ships at lower right. Series A. Back: Orange. Printer: ABNC. Rare.	—	—	—
S215 25 Pesos			
18xx (ca.1878). Black on green underprint. Shrub at left, arms with two seated women at center, man at right. Series A. Back: Green. Printer: ABNC.			
p. Proof.	—	—	—
s. Specimen.	—	—	—
S216 50 Pesos			
18xx (ca.1878). Black on blue underprint. Standing cherub and arms at left, man at center, standing cherub and ship at right. Series A. Back: Blue. Printer: ABNC. Specimen.	—	—	—
S217 100 Pesos			
18xx (ca.1878). Black on brown underprint. Ship, man and train across center, arms at lower right. Series A. Back: Brown. Printer: ABNC.			
p. Proof.	—	—	—
s. Specimen.	—	—	—

NOTE: There was a provisional 1871 issue for the Banco Nacional in Ecuador using overprint notes of this bank. A 2 Peso note is thus listed - see Ecuador #S183. Other values may also exist which require confirmation.

Banco Rural de Credito Hipotecario de Costa-Rica

1873 Bearer Bond Issue

#S218 was issued at 5% interest in a year, thus the S217A could very well have been the interest payment.

S217A 5 Pesos	Good	Fine	XF
1.1.1874. Liberty head.	—	—	—
S218 100 Pesos			
1.10.1873. Black. Issued at 5% interest in a year. #S217A could very well have been the interest payment.	500.	750.	1250.

NOTICE

Readers with unlisted dates, signature varieties, etc., are invited to submit photocopies or scans of their notes to:
Standard Catalog of World Paper Money,
700 East State St. Iola, WI 54990-0001,
E-Mail: george.cuhaj@fwmedia.com.

Banco de la Union

1877 Issue

S219 100 Pesos	Good	Fine	XF
1.11.1877. Black. Christopher Columbus with flags at upper center. Uniface. Paper: Deep yellow. Printer: Eden Fisher & Co., London. Rare.	—	—	—

NOTE: A 25 and 50 Pesos value requires confirmation.

188x; 1887 Issue

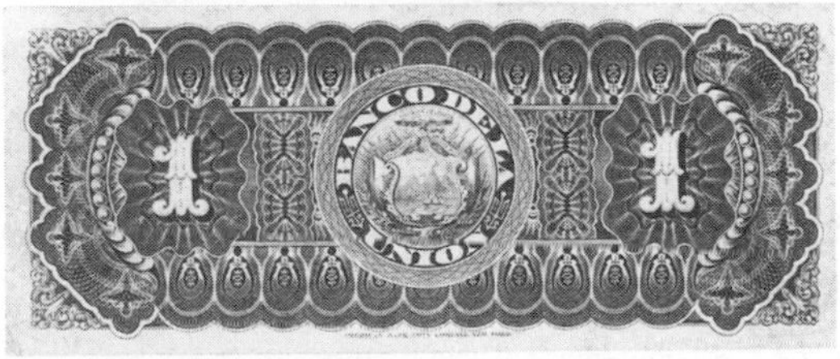

S221 1 Peso	Good	Fine	XF
18xx; 21.10.1886; 1.7.1887; 1.5.1889. Black on blue and red underprint. Raphael's angel at upper center with cherubs at upper corners. Without series; Series A. Back: Blue. Arms at center. Printer: ABNC.			
a. Issued note.	100.	250.	600.
p. Proof.	—	Unc	1500.

S222 2 Pesos	Good	Fine	XF
18xx; 21.10.1886; 1.7.1887; 1.5.1889. Black on pink and green underprint. Eagle at upper center. Without series; Series A. Back: Green. Arms at center. Printer: ABNC.			
a. Issued note. Rare.	—	—	—
p. Proof.	—	Unc	3000.

S223 5 Pesos	Good	Fine	XF
188x; 21.10.1886; 1.7.1887; 1.5.1889. Black on orange and blue underprint. Lion at upper center, griffins at left and right. Without series; Series A. Back: Orange. Arms at center. Printer: ABNC. Specimen.			
a. Issued note.	—	—	—
s. Specimen.	—	Unc	1500.

S224 10 Pesos	Good	Fine	XF
188x; 21.10.1886; 1.7.1887; 1.5.1889. Black on red and green underprint. American and Canadian Horseshoe Falls at Niagara at upper center. Without series; Series A. Back: Red-orange. Arms at center. Printer: ABNC.			
a. Issued note.	—	—	—
s. Specimen	—	Unc	1500.

S225 25 Pesos	Good	Fine	XF
188x; 21.10.1886; 1.7.1887; 1.5.1889. Black on orange and blue underprint. Sailing ship at upper center. Without series; Series A. Back: Blue. Arms at center. Printer: ABNC.			
a. Issued note.	—	—	—
p. Proof.	—	Unc	2750.
s. Specimen.	—	Unc	3000.

S226 50 Pesos	Good	Fine	XF
188x; 21.10.1886; 1.7.1887; 1.5.1889. Black on orange and olive-green underprint. Train crossing bridge at center, facing locomotive at left and right, small train at bottom center. Without series; Series A. Back: Olive-green. Arms at center. Printer: ABNC.			
a. Issued note.	—	—	—
p. Proof.	—	Unc	2500.
s. Specimen.	—	Unc	3000.

S227 100 Pesos	Good	Fine	XF
188x; 21.10.1886; 1.7.1887; 1.5.1889. Black on blue and orange underprint. Allegorical woman at center, allegorical heads at left and right. Without series; Series A. Back: Brown. Arms at center. Printer: ABNC.			
a. Issued note.	—	—	—
p. Proof.	—	Unc	2500.
s. Specimen.	—	Unc	3000.

Railroad

Ferro Carril de Costa Rica

1872 Issue

	Good	Fine	XF
S231 10 Centavos 15.4.1872. Black on brown underprint. Series A-E. Back: Green. Printer: ABNC. Rare.	—	—	—
S232 25 Centavos 15.4.1872. Black on brown underprint. Ship and mountains at center. Series A; B. Back: Green. Printer: ABNC. Rare.	—	—	—

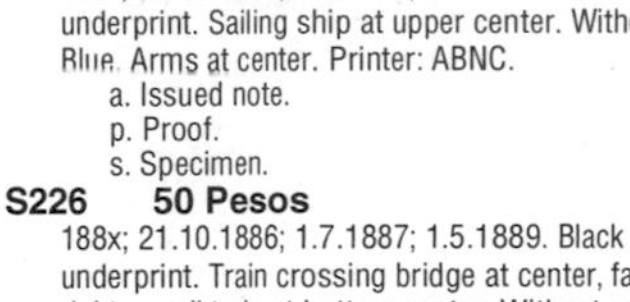

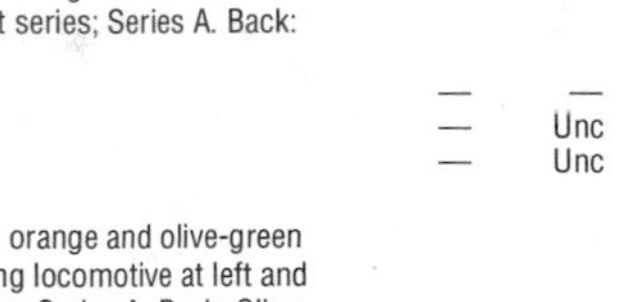

	Good	Fine	XF
S233 50 Centavos 15.4.1872. Black on brown underprint. Ship and mountains at center. Series A; B. Back: Green. Printer: ABNC. Rare.	—	—	—
S234 1 Peso 15.4.1872. Black on brown underprint. Sailing ships at center, arms at lower right. Series A. Back: Green. Printer: ABNC. Rare.	—	—	—
S235 2 Pesos 15.4.1872. Black on brown underprint. Sailing ships and anchor at center. Series A. Back: Green. Printer: ABNC.	—	—	—
S236 5 Pesos 15.4.1872. Black on brown underprint. Steam train at left. center, arms at lower right. Series A. Printer: ABNC.	—	—	—

The Republic of Croatia (Hrvatska), has an area of 56,542 sq. km. and a population of 4.49 million. Capital: Zagreb.

The lands that today comprise Croatia were part of the Austro-Hungarian Empire until the close of World War I. In 1918, the Croats, Serbs, and Slovenes formed a kingdom known after 1929 as Yugoslavia. Following World War II, Yugoslavia became a federal independent Communist state under the strong hand of Marshal Tito. Although Croatia declared its independence from Yugoslavia in 1991, it took four years of sporadic, but often bitter, fighting before occupying Serb armies were mostly cleared from Croatian lands. Under UN supervision, the last Serb-held enclave in eastern Slavonia was returned to Croatia in 1998.

Local Serbian forces supported by the Yugoslav Federal Army had developed a military stronghold and proclaimed an independent "SRPSKE KRAJINA" state in the area around Knin, located in southern Croatia. In August 1995 Croat forces overran this political-military enclave.

RULERS:

Austrian, 1527-1918
Yugoslavian, 1918-1941

MONETARY SYSTEM:

1 Dinar = 100 Para 1918-1941, 1945-
1 Kuna = 100 Banica 1941-1945
1 Kuna = 100 Lipa, 1994-
1 Dinar = 100 Para

PARTISAN - WWII

OBLASNI NAROD. OSLOBOD. ODBOR ZAGREBACKE OBLASTI

ZAGREB GOVERNMENT REGION

1943 ND ISSUE

	Good	Fine	XF
S101 500 Kuna ND (1943). Yellow-green and red. Star in sprays at center within rectangular spray frame. Uniface. Rare.	—	—	—
S102 1000 Kuna ND (1943). Yellow-green and red. Star in sprays at center within rectangular spray frame. Uniface. Rare.	—	—	—
S103 5000 Kuna ND (1943). Yellow-green and red. Star in sprays at center within rectangular spray frame. Uniface. Rare.	—	—	—
S104 10,000 Kuna ND (1943). Yellow-green and red. Star in sprays at center within rectangular spray frame. Uniface. Rare.	—	—	—
S105 50,000 Kuna ND (1943). Yellow-green and red. Star in sprays at center within rectangular spray frame. Uniface. Rare.	—	—	—

ZEMALJSKO ANTIFASISTICKO VIJECE HRVATSKE

CROATIAN ANTI-FASCIST AUTHORITY

1943 ISSUE

	Good	Fine	XF
S106 100 Dinara = 100 Kuna 15.1.1943. Brown, red and blue. Series H-I/V. Rare.	—	—	—
S107 500 Dinara = 500 Kuna 15.1.1943. Brown, red and blue. Series H-I/V. Rare.	—	—	—
S108 1000 Dinara = 1000 Kuna 15.1.1943. Brown, red and blue. Series H-I/V. Rare.	—	—	—
S109 5000 Dinara = 5000 Kuna 15.1.1943. Brown, red and blue. Series H-I/V. Rare.	—	—	—
S110 10,000 Dinara = 10,000 Kuna 15.1.1943. Brown, red and blue. Series H-I/V. Rare.	—	—	—

ZEMALJSKO ANTIFASISTICKO VIJECE NARODNOG

OSLOBODENJA HRVATSKE

CROATIAN ANTI-FASCIST GOVERNMENT AUTHORITY

1943 FIRST ISSUE

	Good	Fine	XF
S111 100 Dinara = 100 Kuna 15.1.1943. Handwritten signature. Without series. Rare.	—	—	—
S112 500 Dinara = 500 Kuna 15.1.1943. Handwritten signature. Without series. Rare.	—	—	—
S113 1000 Dinara = 1000 Kuna 15.1.1943. Handwritten signature. Without series. Rare.	—	—	—
S114 5000 Dinara = 5000 Kuna 15.1.1943. Handwritten signature. Without series. Rare.	—	—	—
S115 10,000 Dinara = 10,000 Kuna 15.1.1943. Handwritten signature. Without series. Rare.	—	—	—

1943 SECOND ISSUE

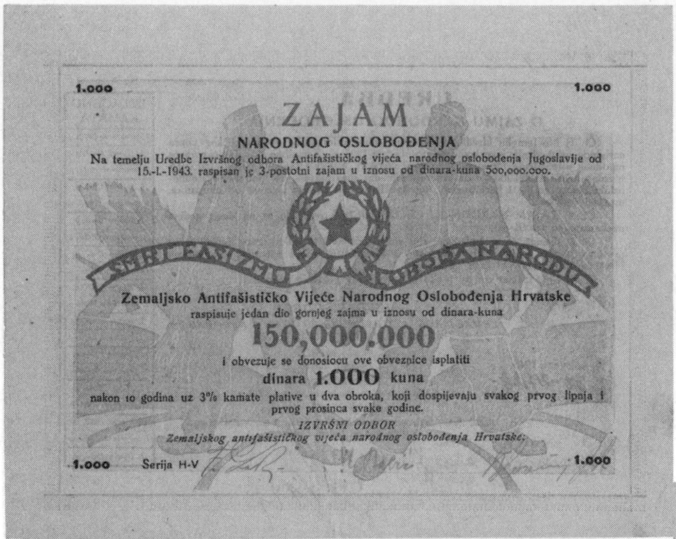

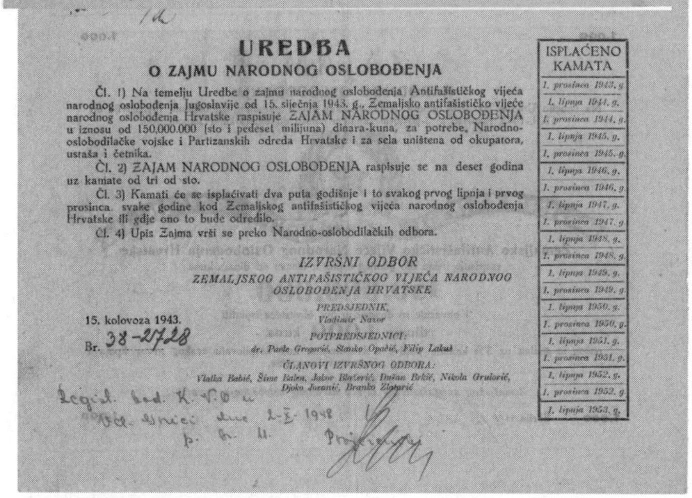

	Good	Fine	XF
S116 100 Dinara = 100 Kuna 15.1.1943. Red and light blue. Handwritten signature. Series H. Rare.	—	—	—
S117 500 Dinara = 500 Kuna 15.1.1943. Red and light blue. Handwritten signature. Series H. Rare.	—	—	—
S118 1000 Dinara = 1000 Kuna 15.1.1943. Red and light blue. Handwritten signature. Series H. Rare.	—	—	—
S119 5000 Dinara = 5000 Kuna 15.1.1943. Red and light blue. Handwritten signature. Series H. Rare.	—	—	—
S120 10,000 Dinara = 10,000 Kuna 15.1.1943. Red and light blue. Handwritten signature. Series H. Rare.	—	—	—
S121 100,000 Dinara = 100,000 Kuna 15.1.1943. Red and light blue. Handwritten signature. Series H. Rare.	—	—	—

1943 THIRD ISSUE

	Good	Fine	XF
S122 100 Dinara = 100 Kuna 15.1.1943. Yellow, red and gray-blue. Printed signature. Without series. Rare.	—	—	—
S123 500 Dinara = 500 Kuna 15.1.1943. Yellow, red and gray-blue. Printed signature. Without series. Rare.	—	—	—
S124 1000 Dinara = 1000 Kuna 15.1.1943. Yellow, red and gray-blue. Printed signature. Without series. Rare.	—	—	—
S125 5000 Dinara = 5000 Kuna 15.1.1943. Yellow, red and gray-blue. Printed signature. Without series. Rare.	—	—	—
S126 10,000 Dinara = 10,000 Kuna 15.1.1943. Yellow, red and gray-blue. Printed signature. Without series. Rare.	—	—	—
S127 100,000 Dinara = 100,000 Kuna 15.1.1943. Yellow, red and gray-blue. Printed signature. Without series. Rare.	—	—	—

1943 FOURTH ISSUE

	Good	Fine	XF
S128 100 Dinara = 100 Kuna 15.1.1943. Brown, blue and red. Without signature. Series I/IV. Rare.	—	—	—
S129 500 Dinara = 500 Kuna 15.1.1943. Brown, blue and red. Without signature. Series I/IV. Rare.	—	—	—
S130 1000 Dinara = 1000 Kuna 15.1.1943. Brown, blue and red. Without signature. Series I/IV. Rare.	—	—	—

1943 FIFTH ISSUE

	Good	Fine	XF
S131 100 Lire 15.1.1943. Red-lilac and violet. Series H and XXII-XXIX.	350.	600.	1000.
S132 500 Lire 15.1.1943. Red-lilac and violet. Series H and XXII-XXIX.	350.	600.	1000.
S133 1000 Lire 15.1.1943. Red-lilac and violet. Series H and XXII-XXIX.	350.	600.	1000.

#S134-S138 *Deleted*. See Bosnia & Herzegovina.

Regional

РЕПУБЛИКА СРПСКА КРАЈИНА

Republika Srpska Krajina

1992 Issue

#R1-R6 Headings in Serbo-Croatian and Cyrillic. Replacement notes: #R1-R34, ZA prefix letters. Note: For notes identical in color and design to #R1-R19 but differing only in text at top, sign. and place of issue Banja Luka, see Bosnia-Herzegovina #133-147.

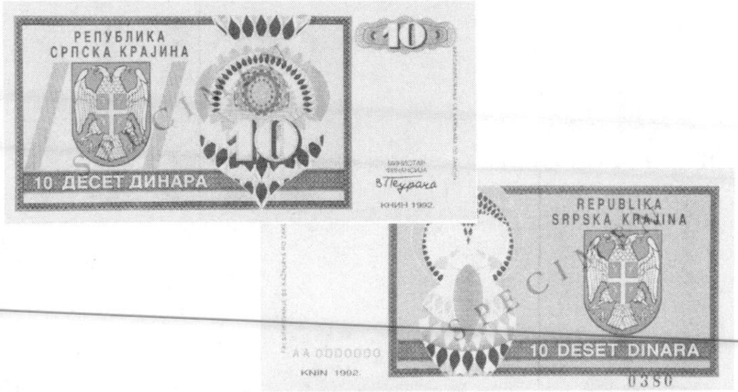

R1 10 Dinara
1992. Deep brown on orange and silver underprint. Arms at left, numerals in heartshaped design below guilloche at center right. Back: Ochre underprint. Curved artistic design at left center, arms at right. Watermark: Young girl.

	VG	VF	UNC
a. Issued note.	.50	1.00	2.50
b. Specimen.	—	—	10.00

R2 50 Dinara
1992. Gray on tan and yellow underprint. Arms at left, numerals in heartshaped design below guilloche at center right. Back: Curved artistic design at left center, arms at right. Watermark: Young girl.

	VG	VF	UNC
a. Issued note.	.50	1.00	2.50
s. Specimen.	—	—	10.00

R3 100 Dinara
1992. Blue-gray on lilac and silver underprint. Arms at left, numerals in heartshaped design below guilloche at center right. Back: Curved artistic design at left center, arms at right. Watermark: Young girl.

	VG	VF	UNC
a. Issued note.	1.00	2.00	4.00
s. Specimen.	—	—	10.00

R4 500 Dinara
1992. Blue-gray on pink and multicolor underprint. Arms at left, numerals in heartshaped design below guilloche at center right. Back: Curved artistic design at left center, arms at right. Watermark: Young boy.

	VG	VF	UNC
a. Issued note.	1.50	4.00	16.00
s. Specimen.	—	—	15.00

R5 1000 Dinara
1992. Deep gray on pink and tan underprint. Arms at left, numerals in heartshaped design below guilloche at center right. Back: Curved artistic design at left center, arms at right.

	VG	VF	UNC
a. Issued note.	1.50	6.00	20.00
s. Specimen.	—	—	15.00

R6 5000 Dinara
1992. Violet on light blue, pink and lilac underprint. Arms at left, numerals in heartshaped design below guilloche at center right. Back: Curved artistic design at left center, arms at right.

	VG	VF	UNC
a. Issued note.	1.50	6.00	20.00
s. Specimen.	—	—	15.00

НАРОДНА БАНКА РЕПУБЛИКЕ СРПСКЕ КРАЈИНЕ

Narodna Banka Republike Srpske Krajine

National Bank of the Serbian Republic - Krajina

1992-93 Issue

#R7-R12 replacement notes: Serial # prefix *ZA*.

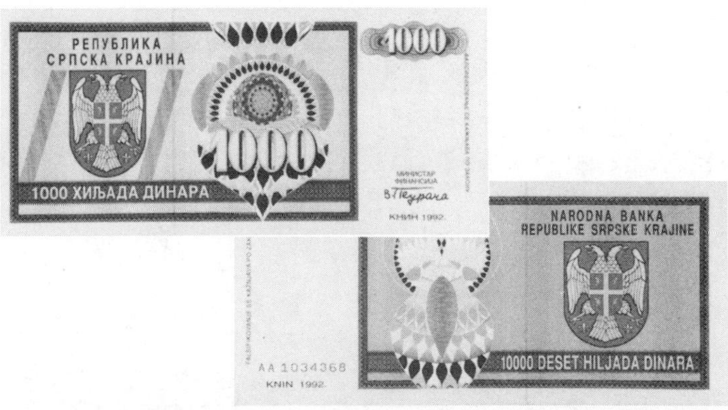

R7 10,000 Dinara
1992. Deep gray-green on light blue and tan underprint. Arms at left, numerals in heartshaped design below guilloche at center right. Back: Curved artistic design at left center, arms at right. Watermark: Young girl.

	VG	VF	UNC
a. Issued note.	1.00	4.00	16.00
s. Specimen.	—	—	15.00

R8 50,000 Dinara

1992. Brown on pale orange and pale olive-green underprint. Arms at left, numerals in heartshaped design below guilloche at center right. Back: Curved artistic design at left center, arms at right. Watermark: Young boy.

	VG	VF	UNC
a. Issued note.	1.50	4.50	20.00
s. Specimen.	—	—	15.00

R9 100,000 Dinara

1993. Dull purple and brown on multicolor underprint. Arms at left, numerals in heartshaped design below guilloche at center right. Back: Curved artistic design at left center, arms at right. Watermark: Young women.

	VG	VF	UNC
a. Issued note.	1.50	6.00	25.00
s. Specimen.	—	—	15.00

R10 1 Million Dinara

1993. Deep purple on multicolor underprint. Arms at left, numerals in heartshaped design below guilloche at center right. Back: Curved artistic design at left center, arms at right. Watermark: Young girl.

	VG	VF	UNC
a. Issued note.	2.00	8.00	30.00
s. Specimen.	—	—	20.00

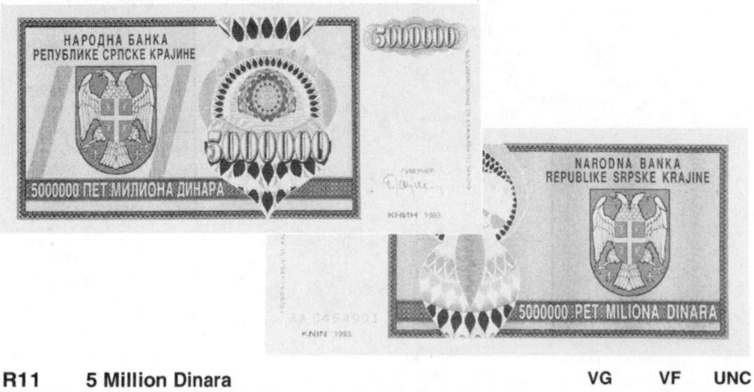

R11 5 Million Dinara

1993. Dark brown on orange and blue-gray underprint. Arms at left, numerals in heartshaped design below guilloche at center right. Back: Curved artistic design at left center, arms at right. Watermark: Young girl.

	VG	VF	UNC
a. Issued note.	1.00	2.50	6.00
s. Specimen.	—	—	10.00

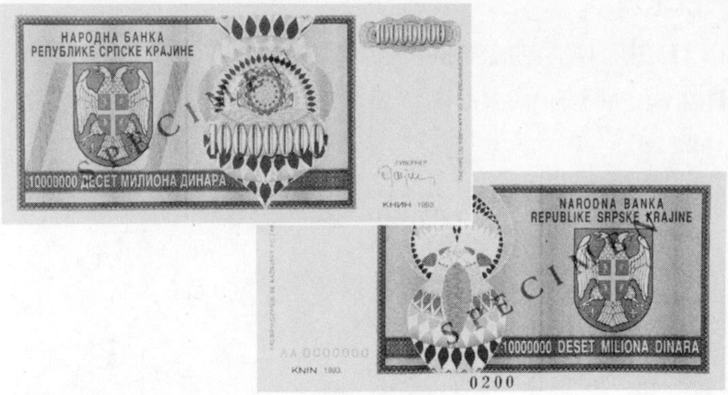

R12 10 Million Dinara

1993. Deep blue on pale olive-green and multicolor underprint. Arms at left, numerals in heartshaped design below guilloche at center right. Back: Curved artistic design at left center, arms at right. Watermark: Young girl.

	VG	VF	UNC
a. Issued note.	1.00	2.50	6.00
s. Specimen.	—	—	10.00

#R13-R19 Replacement notes: Serial # prefix *Z*.

R13 20 Million Dinara

1993. Olive-gray on orange and tan underprint. Arms at left, numerals in heartshaped design below guilloche at center right. Back: Curved artistic design at left center, arms at right. Watermark: Greek design repeated.

	VG	VF	UNC
a. Issued note.	1.50	3.50	8.00
s. Specimen.	—	—	10.00

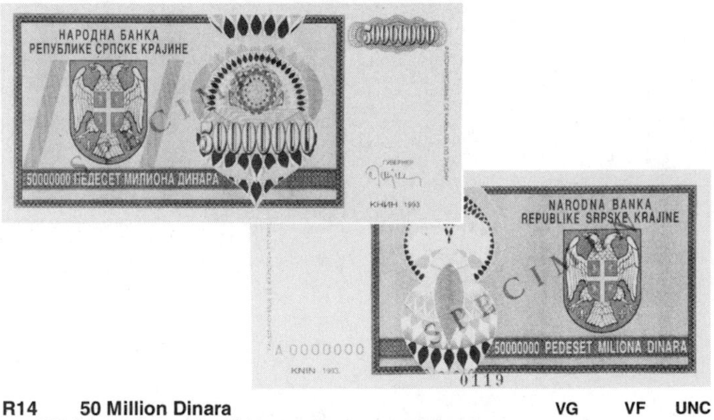

R14 50 Million Dinara

1993. Brown-violet on pink and light gray underprint. Arms at left, numerals in heartshaped design below guilloche at center right. Back: Curved artistic design at left center, arms at right. Watermark: Greek design repeated.

	VG	VF	UNC
a. Issued note.	2.00	4.50	9.00
s. Specimen.	—	—	10.00

R15 100 Million Dinara

1993. Blue-black on light blue and gray underprint. Arms at left, numerals in heartshaped design below guilloche at center right. Back: Curved artistic design at left center, arms at right. Watermark: Greek design repeated.

	VG	VF	UNC
a. Issued note.	1.00	3.00	7.00
s. Specimen.	—	—	10.00

R16 500 Million Dinara

1993. Orange on lilac and yellow underprint. Arms at left, numerals in heartshaped design below guilloche at center right. Back: Curved artistic design at left center, arms at right. Watermark: Greek design repeated.

	VG	VF	UNC
a. Issued note.	1.00	3.00	7.00
s. Specimen.	—	—	10.00

R17 1 Milliard Dinara

1993. Dull brownish orange on pale blue and light orange underprint. Arms at left, numerals in heartshaped design below guilloche at center right. Back: Curved artistic design at left center, arms at right. Watermark: Greek design repeated.

	VG	VF	UNC
a. Issued note.	1.00	3.00	7.00
s. Specimen.	—	—	10.00

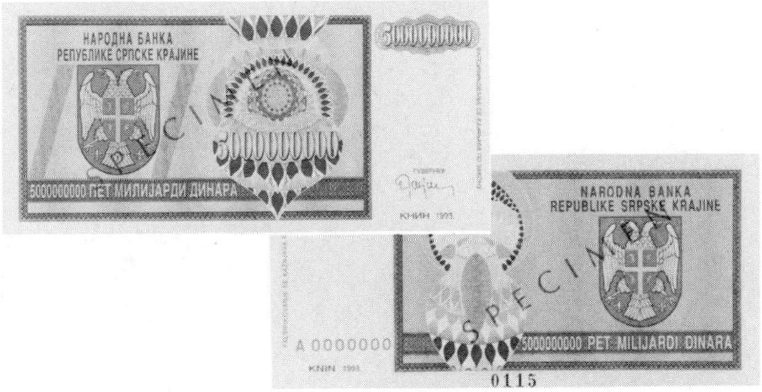

R18 5 Milliard Dinara

1993. Purple on lilac and gray underprint. Arms at left, numerals in heartshaped design below guilloche at center right. Back: Curved artistic design at left center, arms at right. Watermark: Greek design repeated.

	VG	VF	UNC
a. Issued note.	1.50	4.00	10.00
s. Specimen.	—	—	15.00

R19 10 Milliard Dinara

1993. Black on orange and pink underprint. Arms at left, numerals in heartshaped design below guilloche at center right. Back: Curved artistic design at left center, arms at right. Watermark: Greek design repeated.

	VG	VF	UNC
a. Issued note.	2.00	5.00	12.00
s. Specimen.	—	—	15.00

1993 Issue

#R20-R27 Replacement notes: Serial # prefix *Z*.

R20 5000 Dinara

1993. Red-violet and violet on blue-gray underprint. Knin fortress on hill at left center. Back: Serbian arms at center right. Watermark: Greek design repeated.

	VG	VF	UNC
a. Issued note.	.25	1.00	3.00
s. Specimen.	—	—	10.00

R21 50,000 Dinara

1993. Brown, red and red-orange on ochre underprint. Knin fortress on hill at left center. Back: Serbian arms at center right. Watermark: Greek design repeated.

	VG	VF	UNC
a. Issued note.	.25	1.00	3.00
s. Specimen.	—	—	10.00

R22 100,000 Dinara

1993. Violet and blue-gray on pink underprint. Knin fortress on hill at left center. Back: Serbian arms at center right. Watermark: Greek design repeated.

	VG	VF	UNC
a. Issued note.	.25	1.00	3.00
s. Specimen.	—	—	10.00

R23 500,000 Dinara

1993. Brown and gray-green on pale green underprint. Knin fortress on hill at left center. Back: Serbian arms at center right. Watermark: Greek design repeated.

	VG	VF	UNC
a. Issued note.	.25	1.00	3.00
s. Specimen.	—	—	10.00

R24 5 Million Dinara

1993. Orange and gray-green on pale orange underprint. Knin fortress on hill at left center. Back: Serbian arms at center right. Watermark: Greek design repeated.

	VG	VF	UNC
a. Issued note.	.50	1.00	3.50
s. Specimen.	—	—	10.00

R25 100 Million Dinara

1993. Olive-brown and grayish green on light blue underprint. Knin fortress on hill at left center. Back: Serbian arms at center right. Watermark: Greek design repeated.

	VG	VF	UNC
a. Issued note.	.50	1.00	3.50
s. Specimen.	—	—	10.00

R26 500 Million Dinara

1993. Chocolate brown and gray-green on pale olive-green underprint. Knin fortress on hill at left center. Back: Serbian arms at center right. Watermark: Greek design repeated.

	VG	VF	UNC
a. Issued note.	.50	1.50	4.00
s. Specimen.	—	—	10.00

R27 5 Milliard Dinara

1993. Brown-orange and aqua on gray underprint. Knin fortress on hill at left center. Back: Serbian arms at center right. Watermark: Greek design repeated.

	VG	VF	UNC
a. Issued note.	1.00	2.00	6.00
s. Specimen.	—	—	10.00

R28 10 Milliard Dinara

1993. Purple and red on aqua underprint. Knin fortress on hill at left center. Back: Serbian arms at center right. Watermark: Greek design repeated.

	VG	VF	UNC
a. Issued note.	1.00	2.00	7.00
s. Specimen.	—	—	15.00

R29 50 Milliard Dinara

1993. Brown and olive-green on reddish brown underprint. Knin fortress on hill at left center. Back: Serbian arms at center right. Watermark: Greek design repeated.

	VG	VF	UNC
a. Issued note.	1.00	2.00	7.00
s. Specimen.	—	—	15.00

1994 Issue

Replacement notes: Serial # prefix *ZA*.

R30 1000 Dinara

1994. Dark brown and slate-gray on yellow-orange underprint. Knin fortress on hill at left center. Back: Serbian arms at center right. Watermark: Greek design repeated.

	VG	VF	UNC
a. Issued note.	.25	.50	2.00
s. Specimen.	—	—	10.00

R31 10,000 Dinara

1994. Red-brown and dull purple on ochre underprint. Knin fortress on hill at left center. Back: Serbian arms at center right. Watermark: Greek design repeated.

	VG	VF	UNC
a. Issued note.	.25	.50	2.00
s. Specimen.	—	—	10.00

R32 **500,000 Dinara**

1994. Dark brown and blue-gray on grayish green underprint. Knin fortress on hill at left center. Back: Serbian arms at center right. Watermark: Greek design repeated.

	VG	VF	UNC
a. Issued note.	.50	1.00	3.00
s. Specimen.	—	—	10.00

R33 **1 Million Dinara**

1994. Purple and aqua on lilac underprint. Knin fortress on hill at left center. Back: Serbian arms at center right. Watermark: Greek design repeated.

	VG	VF	UNC
a. Issued note.	.50	1.00	3.00
s. Specimen.	—	—	10.00

R34 **10 Million Dinara**

1994. Gray and red-brown on pink underprint. Knin fortress on hill at left center. Back: Serbian arms at center right. Watermark: Greek design repeated.

	VG	VF	UNC
a. Issued note.	.50	1.50	5.00
s. Specimen.	—	—	10.00

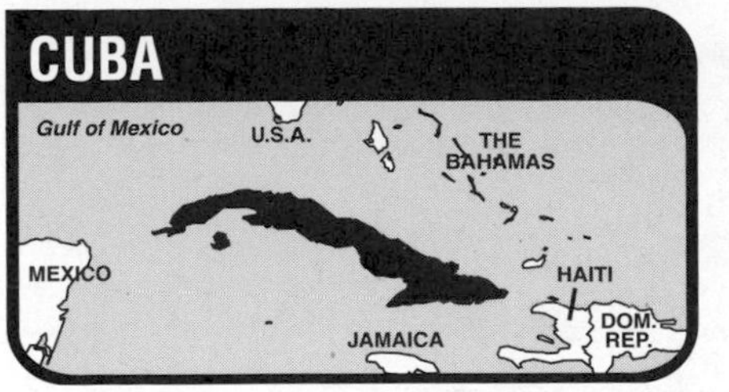

The Republic of Cuba, situated at the northern edge of the Caribbean Sea about 145 km. south of Florida, has an area of 110,860 sq. km. and a population of 11.4 million. Capital: Havana. The Cuban economy is d on the cultivation and refining of sugar, which provides 80 percent of export earnings.

The native Amerindian population of Cuba began to decline after the European discovery of the island by Christopher Columbus in 1492 and following its development as a Spanish colony during the next several centuries. Large numbers of African slaves were imported to work the coffee and sugar plantations, and Havana became the launching point for the annual treasure fleets bound for Spain from Mexico and Peru. Spanish rule, marked initially by neglect, became increasingly repressive, provoking an independence movement and occasional rebellions that were harshly suppressed. It was US intervention during the Spanish-American War in 1898 that finally overthrew Spanish rule. The subsequent Treaty of Paris established Cuban independence, which was granted in 1902 after a three-year transition period. Fidel Castro led a rebel army to victory in 1959; his iron rule held the subsequent regime together for nearly five decades. He stepped down as president in February 2008 in favor of his younger brother Raul Castro. Cuba's Communist revolution, with Soviet support, was exported throughout Latin America and Africa during the 1960s, 1970s, and 1980s. The country is now slowly recovering from a severe economic downturn in 1990, following the withdrawal of former Soviet subsidies. Cuba portrays its difficulties as the result of the US embargo in place since 1961.

RULERS:

Spanish to 1898

MONETARY SYSTEM:

1 Peso = 100 Centavos
1 Peso Convertible = 1 U.S.A. Dollar, 1995-

Spanish Administration

Empresa del Acueducto de Cardenas

1870 Issue

S112 **3 Pesos**

Aug. 1870. Black. Reclining woman at top center, fountains at lower left and lower right.

	Good	Fine	XF
a. Issued note.	2000.	4000.	—
r. Unsigned remainder. 187x.	—	1000.	2500.

NOTE: #S112 exists with falsified signatures added recently.

Foreign Exchange Certificates

The Banco Nacional de Cuba issued four types of peso certificates in series A, B, C and D. The C and D series was issued in two designs and originally required hand issue date and sign. at redemption. Resembling traveler's checks.

Banco Nacional de Cuba

Series A

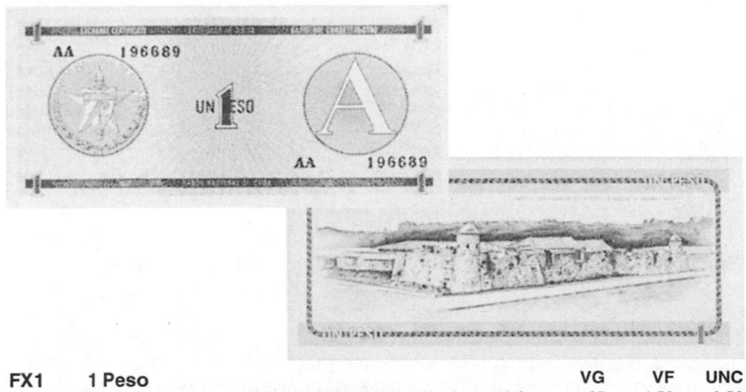

FX1 **1 Peso**

ND (1985). Red -violet on orange and olive-green underprint. Arms at left. Back: Fortress: Castillo San Salvador de la Punta.

VG	VF	UNC
.25	1.50	3.50

No.	Denomination / Description	VG	VF	UNC
FX2	**3 Pesos** ND (1985). Red-violet on orange and pink underprint. Arms at left. Back: Fortress: Castillo San Pedro de la Roca.	.50	3.50	7.00
FX3	**5 Pesos** ND (1985). Red-violet on orange and blue-green underprint. Arms at left. Back: Fortress: Castillo de los Tres Reyes del Morro.	1.00	5.00	10.00
FX4	**10 Pesos** ND (1985). Red-violet on orange and brown underprint. Arms at left. Back: Fortress: Castillo Nuestra Señora de Los Angeles de Jagua.	2.00	9.00	17.50

No.	Denomination / Description	VG	VF	UNC
FX5	**20 Pesos** ND (1985). Red-violet on orange and blue underprint. Arms at left. Back: Fortress: Castillo de la Real Fuerza.	4.00	20.00	40.00

Series B

No.	Denomination / Description	VG	VF	UNC
FX6	**1 Peso** ND (1985). Dark green on light green and olive-brown underprint. Arms at left. Back: Fortress: Castillo San Salvador de la Punta.	.25	1.00	2.50
FX7	**5 Pesos** ND (1985). Dark green on light green and blue-green underprint. Arms at left. Back: Fortress: Castillo de los Tres Reyes del Morro.	1.00	5.00	20.00
FX8	**10 Pesos** ND (1985). Dark green on light green and brown underprint. Arms at left. Back: Fortress: Castillo Nuestra SeÒora de Los Angeles de Jagua.	2.00	10.00	30.00
FX9	**20 Pesos** ND (1985). Dark green on light green and blue underprint. Arms at left. Back: Fortress: Castillo de la Real Fuerza.	4.00	20.00	40.00

No.	Denomination / Description	VG	VF	UNC
FX10	**50 Pesos** ND (1985). Dark green on light green and dull violet underprint. Arms at left. Back: Fortress: Castillo de la Chorrera.	7.50	20.00	70.00

Series C First Issue

No.	Denomination / Description	VG	VF	UNC
FX11	**1 Peso** ND. Pale blue on light blue and light red-brown underprint. Arms at left.	.10	.25	1.50

No.	Denomination / Description	VG	VF	UNC
FX12	**3 Pesos** ND. Pale blue on light blue and violet underprint. Arms at left.	.10	.30	1.75
FX13	**5 Pesos** ND. Pale blue on light blue and light olive underprint. Arms at left.	.10	.50	2.50
FX14	**10 Pesos** ND. Pale blue on light blue and lilac underprint. Arms at left.	.10	.40	2.25
FX15	**20 Pesos** ND. Pale blue on light blue and tan underprint. Arms at left.	.15	.50	3.00
FX16	**50 Pesos** ND. Pale blue on light blue and rose underprint. Arms at left.	.20	.60	3.50
FX17	**100 Pesos** ND. Pale blue on light blue and ochre underprint. Arms at left.	.20	.75	4.00
FX18	**500 Pesos** ND. Pale blue on light blue and tan underprint. Arms at left.	.20	5.00	20.00

Series C Second Issue

No.	Denomination / Description	VG	VF	UNC
FX19	**1 Peso** ND. Blue-violet. Arms at left.	.15	.50	1.25
FX20	**3 Pesos** ND. Blue-violet on light blue and red underprint. Arms at left.	.15	.50	1.25
FX21	**5 Pesos** ND. Blue-violet on light blue and pale olive-green underprint. Arms at left.	.25	1.00	2.00

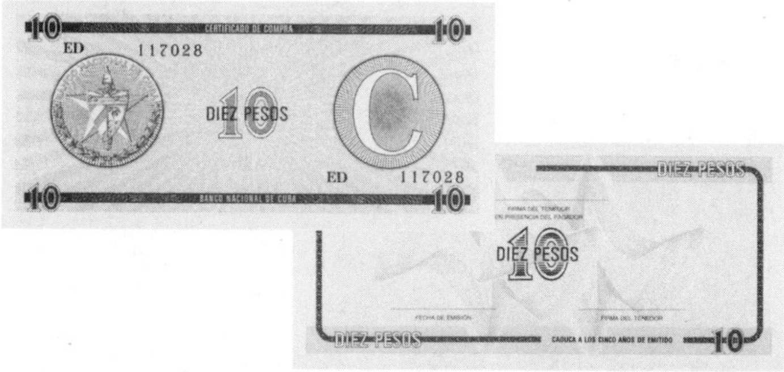

No.	Denomination / Description	VG	VF	UNC
FX22	**10 Pesos** ND. Blue-violet on light blue and brown underprint. Arms at left.	.50	1.50	3.00
FX23	**20 Pesos** ND. Blue-violet on light blue and orange-brown underprint. Arms at left.	.50	2.50	5.00

No.	Denomination / Description	VG	VF	UNC
FX24	**50 Pesos** ND. Blue-violet on light blue and violet underprint. Arms at left.	.50	1.50	5.00
FX25	**100 Pesos** ND. Blue-violet on light blue and gray underprint. Arms at left.	.50	1.50	5.00
FX26	**500 Pesos** ND. Blue-violet. Arms at left.	2.00	5.00	25.00

SENDING SCANNED IMAGES BY E-MAIL

We have been receiving an ever-increasing flow of scanned images from sources world wide. Unfortunately, many of these scans could not be used due to the type of scan, or simple incompatibility with our systems. We appreciate the effort it takes to produce these images and accuracy they add to the catalog listings.

Here are a few simple instructions to follow when producing these scans. We encourage you to continue sending new images or upgrades to those currently illustrated and please do not hesitate to ask questions about this process.

- Scan all images within a resolution of 300 dpi.
- Size setting should be at 100%
- Please include in the e-mail the actual size of the image in millimeters height x width
- Scan in true 4-color
- Save images as jpeg and name in such a way which clearly indentifies the country of the note and catalog number
- Do not compress files
- Please e-mail with a request to confirm receipt of the attachment
- Please send multiple images on a disc if available
- Please send images to: george.cuhaj@fwmedia.com

Series D First Issue

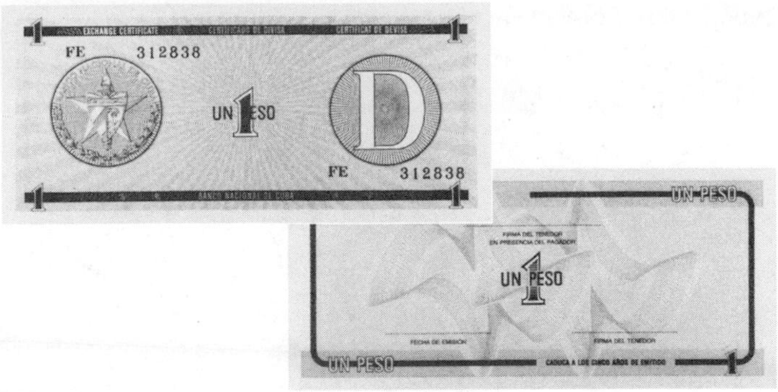

FX27 1 Peso	VG	VF	UNC
ND. Pale red-brown on light orange and orange-brown underprint. Arms at left.	.25	1.50	3.50

FX28 3 Pesos	VG	VF	UNC
ND. Pale red-brown on light orange and pale blue underprint. Arms at left.	.50	3.00	7.00

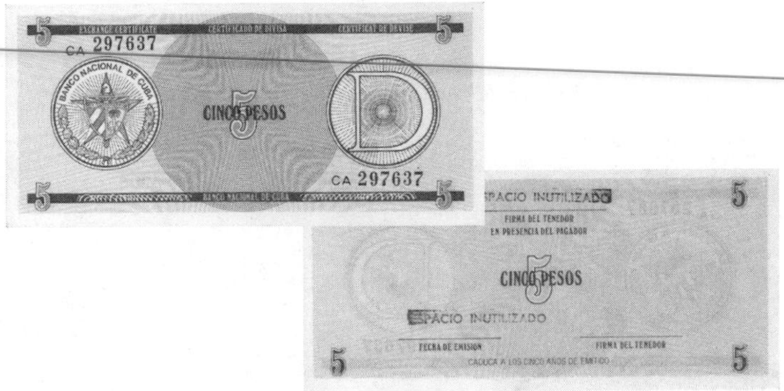

FX29 5 Pesos	VG	VF	UNC
ND. Pale red-brown on light orange and light green underprint. Arms at left.	1.00	5.00	10.00

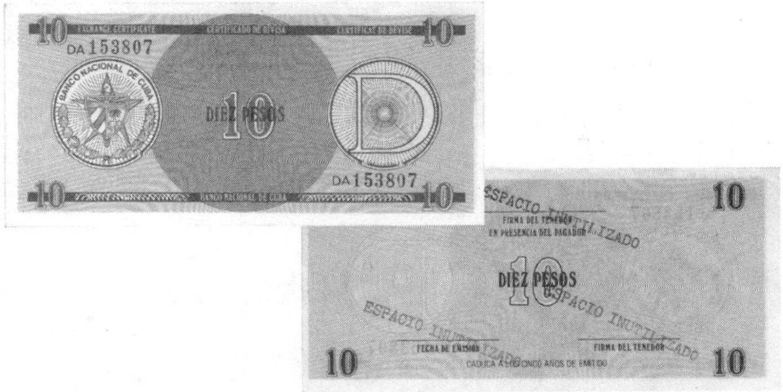

FX30 10 Pesos	VG	VF	UNC
ND. Pale red-brown on light orange and lilac underprint. Arms at left.	2.00	10.00	17.50

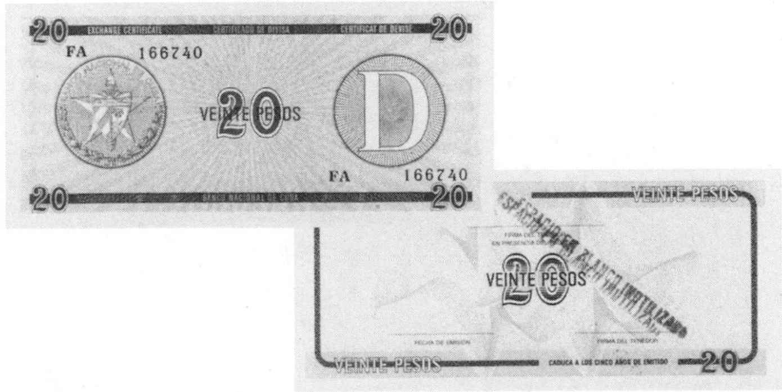

FX31 20 Pesos	VG	VF	UNC
ND. Pale red-brown on light orange and ochre underprint. Arms at left.	4.00	20.00	32.50

Series D Second Issue

FX32 1 Peso	VG	VF	UNC
ND. Dark brown on tan and pale olive-green underprint. Arms at left. With or without various handstamps: *ESPACIO EN BLANCO INUTILIZADO* or *ESPACIO INUTILIZADO* on back.	.10	.30	.60

FX33 3 Pesos	VG	VF	UNC
ND. Dark brown on tan and red underprint. Arms at left. With or without various handstamps: *ESPACIO EN BLANCO INUTILIZADO* or *ESPACIO INUTILIZADO* on back.	.15	.60	1.25

FX34 5 Pesos	VG	VF	UNC
ND. Dark brown on tan and green underprint. Arms at left. With or without various handstamps: *ESPACIO EN BLANCO INUTILIZADO* or *ESPACIO INUTILIZADO* on back.	.25	1.00	2.00

FX35 10 Pesos	VG	VF	UNC
ND. Dark brown on tan and orange underprint. Arms at left. With or without various handstamps: *ESPACIO EN BLANCO INUTILIZADO* or *ESPACIO INUTILIZADO* on back.	.50	2.00	4.00

FX36 20 Pesos	VG	VF	UNC
ND. Dark brown on tan and blue-gray underprint. Arms at left. With or without various handstamps: *ESPACIO EN BLANCO INUTILIZADO* or *ESPACIO INUTILIZADO* on back.	1.00	4.00	8.00

1994 Pesos Convertibles Issue

FX37 1 Peso Convertible	VG	VF	UNC
1994. Orange, brown and olive-green on multicolor underprint. J. Martí monument at right. Back: Arms at center. Watermark: J. Martí.	FV	FV	2.50

FX38 3 Pesos Convertibles	VG	VF	UNC
1994. Dull red, deep blue-green and brown on multicolor underprint. E. "Che" Guevara monument at right. Back: Arms at center. Watermark: J. Martí.	FV	FV	7.00

FX39 5 Pesos Convertibles	VG	VF	UNC
1994. Dark green, orange and blue-black on multicolor underprint. A. Maceo monument at right. Back: Arms at center. Watermark: J. Martí.	FV	FV	10.00

FX40 10 Pesos Convertibles

	VG	VF	UNC
1994. Brown, yellow-green and purple on multicolor underprint. M. Gómez monument at right. Back: Arms at center. Watermark: J. Martí.	FV	FV	17.50

FX41 20 Pesos Convertibles

	VG	VF	UNC
1994. Blue, red and tan on multicolor underprint. C. Cienfuegos monument at right. Back: Arms at center. Watermark: J. Martí.	FV	FV	35.00

FX42 50 Pesos Convertibles

	VG	VF	UNC
1994. Purple, brown and orange on multicolor underprint. C. García monument at right. Back: Arms at center. Watermark: J. Martí.	FV	FV	70.00

FX43 100 Pesos Convertibles

	VG	VF	UNC
1994. Red-violet, brown-orange and purple on multicolor underprint. C. Manuel de Céspedes monument at right. Back: Arms at center. Watermark: J. Martí.	FV	FV	150.

Banco Central de Cuba

2004 Pesos Convertibles Issue

FX44 5 Pesos Convertibles

	VG	VF	UNC
2004; 2005.			
a. 2004. Top left serial # horizontal.	FV	FV	10.00
b. 2005. Top left serial # vertical	FV	FV	10.00

FX45 10 Pesos Convertibles

	VG	VF	UNC
2004.	FV	FV	17.50

2006 Pesos Convertibles

FX46 1 Peso

	VG	VF	UNC
2006. Dark green on yellow and brown underprint.	FV	FV	2.50

FX47 3 Pesos

	VG	VF	UNC
2006. Red on green and red underprint.	FV	FV	5.00

FX48	5 Pesos	VG	VF	UNC
	2006. Green on yellow and red underprint.	FV	FV	10.00

FX49	10 Pesos	VG	VF	UNC
	2006. Multicolor.	FV	FV	17.50
FX50	20 Pesos			
	2006. Blue on light blue and yellow underprint.	FV	FV	35.00
FX51	50 Pesos			
	2006. Purple on red and yellow underprint.	FV	FV	70.00
FX52	100 Pesos			
	2006. Red on yellow and red underprint.	FV	FV	150.

The Republic of Czechoslovakia, located in central Europe, had an area of 49,365 sq. mi. (127,859 sq. km.). Capital: Prague (Praha). Industrial production in the cities and agriculture and livestock in the rural areas were the chief occupations.

The Czech lands to the west were united with the Slovak to form the Czechoslovak Republic on October 28, 1918 upon the dissolution of the Austrian-Hungarian Empire. Tomas G. Masaryk was the first president. In the 1930s Hitlet provoked Czechoslovakia's German minority in the Sudetenland to agitate for autonomy. The territory was broken up for the benefit of Germany, Poland and Hungary by the Munich agreement signed by the United Kingdom, France, Germany and Italy on September 29, 1938. On March 15, 1939, Germany invaded Czechoslovakia and incorporated the Czech lands into the Third Reich as the "Protectorate of Bohemia and Moravia." eastern Slovakia, was constituted as a republic under Nazi infulence. A government-in-exile was set up in London in 1940. The Soviet and American forces liberated the area by May 1945. After World War II the physical integrity and independence of Czechoslovakia was re-established, while bringing it within the Russian sphere of influence. On February 23-25, 1948, the Communists seized control of the government in a *coup d'etat,* and adopted a constitution making the country a "people's republic." A new constitution adopted June 11, 1960, converted the country into a "socialist republic." Communist infulence increased steadily while pressure for liberalization culminated in the overthrow of the Stalinist leader Antonçin Novotny and his associates in January, 1968. The Communist Party then introduced far reaching reforms which received warnings from Moscow, followed by occupation of Warsaw Pact forces on August 21, 1968 resulting in stationing of Soviet troops. Student demonstrations for reform began in Prague on November 17, 1989. The Federal Assembly abolished the Communist Party's sole right to govern. In December, 1989, communism was overthrown. In January, 1990 the Czech and Slovak Federal Republic (CSFR) was formed. The movement for a democratic Slovakia was apparent in the June 1992 elections with the Slovak National Council adopting a declaration of sovereignty. The CSFR was disolved on December 31, 1992, and both new republics came into being on January 1, 1993.

See the Czech Republic and Slovakia sections for additional listings.

MONETARY SYSTEM:

1 Koruna = 100 Haleru

Foreign Exchange Certificates

Podniku Zahranicniho Obchodu Tuzex

1957-58 Issue

FX1	0.50 Koruna	VG	VF	UNC
	1958. Rare.	—	—	—
FX2	1 Koruna			
	1957. Rare.	—	—	—
FX3	5 Korun			
	1957. Rare.	—	—	—
FX4	10 Korun			
	1957. Rare.	—	—	—
FX5	20 Korun			
	1957. Rare.	—	—	—
FX6	50 Korun			
	1957. Rare.	—	—	—
FX7	71.5 Korun			
	1957. Rare.	—	—	—
FX8	100 Korun			
	1957. Rare.	—	—	—

1959 Issue

FX9	0.50 Koruna	VG	VF	UNC
	1959. Rare.	—	—	—
FX10	1 Koruna			
	1959. Rare.	—	—	—
FX11	5 Korun			
	1959. Rare.	—	—	—
FX12	10 Korun			
	1959. Rare.	—	—	—
FX13	20 Korun			
	1959. Rare.	—	—	—
FX14	50 Korun			
	1959. Rare.	—	—	—
FX15	71.5 Korun			
	1959. Rare.	—	—	—
FX16	100 Korun			
	1959. Rare.	—	—	—

1960 Issue

FX17	0.50 Koruna	VG	VF	UNC
	1960.	5.00	15.00	50.00

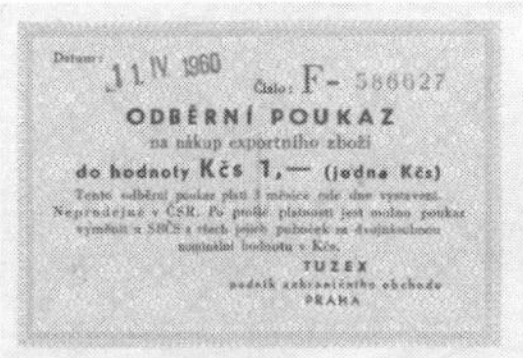

FX18	1 Koruna	VG	VF	UNC
	1960.	7.50	20.00	60.00
FX19	5 Korun			
	1960. Rare.	—	—	—

	VG	VF	UNC
FX20 10 Korun			
1960. Rare.	—	—	—
FX21 20 Korun			
1960. Rare.	—	—	—
FX22 50 Korun			
1960. Rare.	—	—	—
FX23 71.5 Korun			
1960. Rare.	—	—	—
FX24 100 Korun			
1960. Rare.	—	—	—

1961 Issue

	VG	VF	UNC
FX25 0.50 Koruna			
1961.	5.00	12.50	65.00
FX26 1 Koruna			
1961.	5.00	15.00	80.00
FX27 5 Korun			
1961.	10.00	35.00	120.
FX28 10 Korun			
1961. Rare.	—	—	—
FX29 20 Korun			
1961. Rare.	—	—	—
FX30 50 Korun			
1961. Rare.	—	—	—
FX31 71.5 Korun			
1961. Rare.	—	—	—
FX32 100 Korun			
1962. Rare.	—	—	—

1962-69 Issues

Printed date of 1966-69 on FX33-FX39, others w/handstamped date.

	VG	VF	UNC
FX33 0.50 Koruna			
1962-69. Date handstamped or printed (1966-69).			
a. Regular issue.	2.00	5.00	10.00
b. Z (zahranicni) Foreign issue.	2.00	5.00	10.00

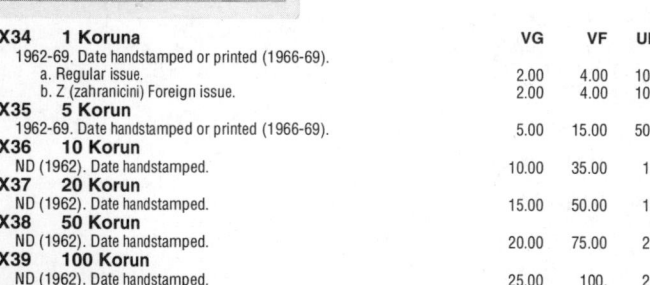

	VG	VF	UNC
FX34 1 Koruna			
1962-69. Date handstamped or printed (1966-69).			
a. Regular issue.	2.00	4.00	10.00
b. Z (zahranicini) Foreign issue.	2.00	4.00	10.00
FX35 5 Korun			
1962-69. Date handstamped or printed (1966-69).	5.00	15.00	50.00
FX36 10 Korun			
ND (1962). Date handstamped.	10.00	35.00	100.
FX37 20 Korun			
ND (1962). Date handstamped.	15.00	50.00	150.
FX38 50 Korun			
ND (1962). Date handstamped.	20.00	75.00	200.
FX39 100 Korun			
ND (1962). Date handstamped.	25.00	100.	250.

1969-73 Issues

Printed date on FX40-FX42, all others w/handstamped date.

	VG	VF	UNC
FX40 0.50 Koruna			
1969-73. Date printed.			
a. Regular issue.	1.25	2.00	5.00
b. Z (zahranicni) Foreign issue.	3.00	7.50	15.00
FX41 1 Koruna			
1969-73. Date printed.			
a. Regular issue.	1.25	2.00	5.00
b. Z (zahranicini) Foreign issue.	3.00	7.50	15.00
FX42 5 Korun			
1969-73. Date printed.			
a. Regular issue.	2.00	4.00	10.00
b. Z (zahranicni) Foreign issue.	5.00	12.50	25.00
FX43 10 Korun	VG	VF	UNC
1969-73. Date handstamped.	5.00	15.00	60.00
FX44 20 Korun			
1969-73. Date handstamped.	10.00	35.00	100.

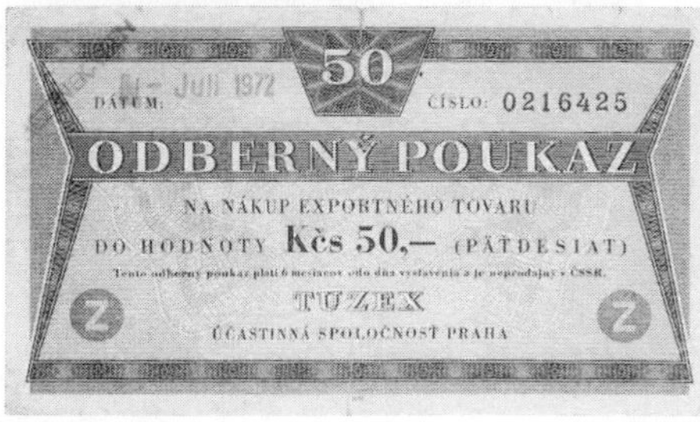

	VG	VF	UNC
FX45 50 Korun			
1969-73. Date handstamped.			
a. Issued note.	15.00	75.00	150.
b. "Z" imprint.	—	—	—
FX46 100 Korun			
1969-73. Date handstamped.	20.00	100.	200.

1973-80 Issues

Printed date on FX47-49, all others w/handstamped date.

	VG	VF	UNC
FX47 0.50 Koruna			
1973-79. Date printed.			
a. Regular issue. 1973-79.	.20	.50	1.00
b. Z (Zahranicni) foreign issue. 1974-78.	.50	1.50	3.00
FX48 1 Koruna			
1973-79. Date printed.			
a. Regular issue. 1973-79.	.20	.50	1.00
b. Z (Zahranicni) foreign issue. 1974-78.	.50	1.50	3.00
FX49 5 Korun			
1973-80. Date printed.			
a. Regular issue. 1973-80.	.50	1.50	3.00
b. Z (Zahranicni) foreign issue. 1974-78.	3.00	7.50	15.00
FX50 10 Korun			
ND (1973). Date handstamped.	4.00	8.00	15.00
FX51 20 Korun			
ND (1973). Date handstamped.	5.00	15.00	30.00
FX52 50 Korun			
ND (1973).	7.50	25.00	75.00
FX53 100 Korun			
ND (1974). Date handstamped.	15.00	90.00	150.
FX54 500 Korun			
ND (1979). Date handstamped.	25.00	150.	350.

1980-88 Issue

#FX55-FX62 white outer edge. *TUZEX* once in text. Date printed for FX55-FX57, others w/handstamped date.

	VG	VF	UNC
FX55 0.50 Koruna			
1980-87. Violet and green. Date printed. Printer: STC-P.	.25	.50	1.00

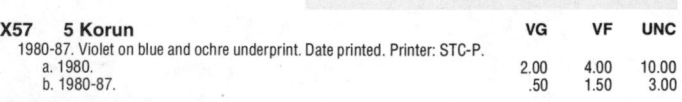

	VG	VF	UNC
FX56 1 Koruna			
1980-87. Green on ochre underprint. Date printed. Printer: STC-P.	.25	.50	1.00

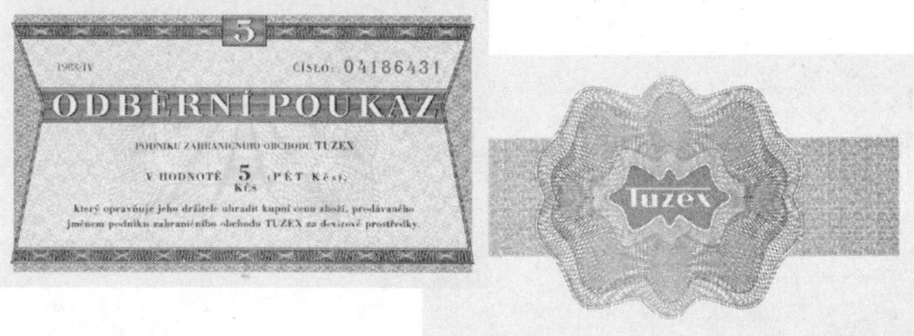

	VG	VF	UNC
FX57 5 Korun			
1980-87. Violet on blue and ochre underprint. Date printed. Printer: STC-P.			
a. 1980.	2.00	4.00	10.00
b. 1980-87.	.50	1.50	3.00

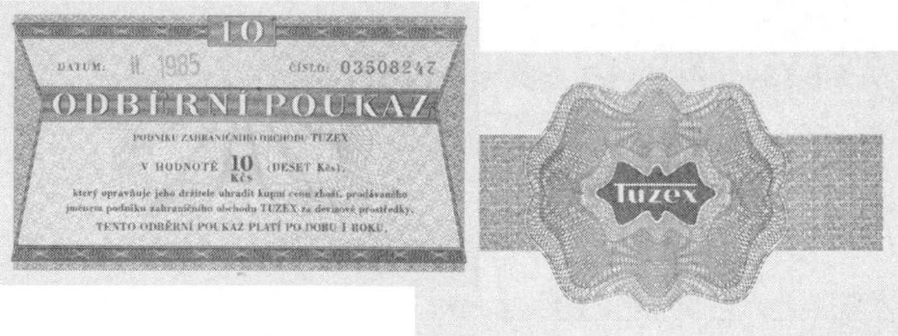

	VG	VF	UNC
FX58 10 Korun			
ND (1980). Dark green on green underprint. Date handstamped. Printer: STC-P.	.75	2.00	5.00
FX59 20 Korun			
ND (1980). Brown on orange and green underprint. Date handstamped. Printer: STC-P.	2.00	5.00	10.00
FX60 50 Korun			
ND (1980). Brown on pink and orange underprint. Date handstamped. Printer: STC-P.	4.00	10.00	20.00

FX61 100 Korun — VG 5.00 | VF 15.00 | UNC 30.00
ND (1980). Violet on green and violet underprint. Date handstamped. Printer: STC-P.

FX62 500 Korun — VG 15.00 | VF 75.00 | UNC 150.
ND (1980). Gray on brown underprint. Date handstamped. Printer: STC-P.

1989-90 Issue

#FX63-FX70 Colors as previous issue but outer edge w/solid color. Date printed for FX63-65, others w/handstamped date.

FX63 0.50 Koruna — VG .25 | VF .50 | UNC 1.00
1989; 1990. Violet edge. Outer edge with solid color. Large globe with *TUZEX* at left and right. Printed date. Printer: STC-P.

	VG	VF	UNC
FX64 1 Koruna 1989; 1990. Yellow-brown edge. Outer edge in solid color. Large globe with *TUZEX* at left and right. Printed date. Printer: STC-P.	.25	.50	1.00
FX65 5 Korun 1989; 1990. Blue and ochre edge. Outer edge with solid color. Large globe with *TUZEX* at left and right. Printed date. Printer: STC-P.	.50	1.50	3.00
FX66 10 Korun ND (1989). Light and dark green edge. Outer edge with solid color. Large globe with *TUZEX* at left and right. Handstamped date. Printer: STC-P.	1.25	2.50	5.00
FX67 20 Korun ND (1989). Yellow-brown and green edge. Outer edge with solid color. Large globe with *TUZEX* at left and right. Handstamped date. Printer: STC-P.	2.00	5.00	10.00
FX68 50 Korun ND (1989). Pink and orange edge. Outer edge with solid color. Large globe with *TUZEX* at left and right. Handstamped date. Printer: STC-P.	4.00	10.00	20.00
FX69 100 Korun ND (1989). Violet and green edge. Outer edge with solid color. Large globe with *TUZEX* at left and right. Handstamped date. Printer: STC-P.	5.00	15.00	30.00
FX70 500 Korun ND (1989). Brown edge. Large globe with *TUZEX* at left and right. Handstamped date. Printer: STC-P.	10.00	65.00	100.

1990-92 Issue

#FX71-FX78 Date printed for FX63-FX65, others w/handstamped date.

FX71 0.50 Koruna — VG .25 | VF .50 | UNC 1.00
1990-92. Globe with *TUZEX*. Printer: VEB Leipzig, Germany.

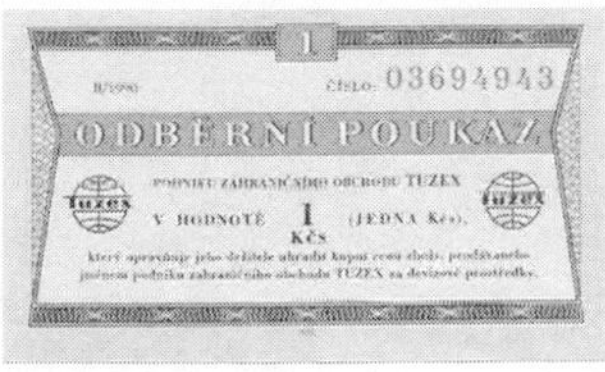

	VG	VF	UNC
FX72 1 Koruna 1990-92. Globe with *TUZEX*. Printer: VEB Leipzig, Germany.	.25	.50	1.00
FX73 5 Korun 1990-92. Globe with *TUZEX*. Printer: VEB Leipzig, Germany.	.50	1.50	3.00
FX74 10 Korun ND (1990). Globe with *TUZEX*. Printer: VEB Leipzig, Germany.	1.00	2.50	5.00
FX75 20 Korun ND (1990). Globe with *TUZEX*. Printer: VEB Leipzig, Germany.	2.00	5.00	10.00
FX76 50 Korun ND (1990). Globe with *TUZEX*. Printer: VEB Leipzig, Germany.	5.00	12.50	20.00
FX77 100 Korun ND (1990). Globe with *TUZEX*. Printer: VEB Leipzig, Germany.	5.00	15.00	30.00
FX78 500 Korun ND (1990). Globe with *TUZEX*. Printer: VEB Leipzig, Germany.	10.00	50.00	100.

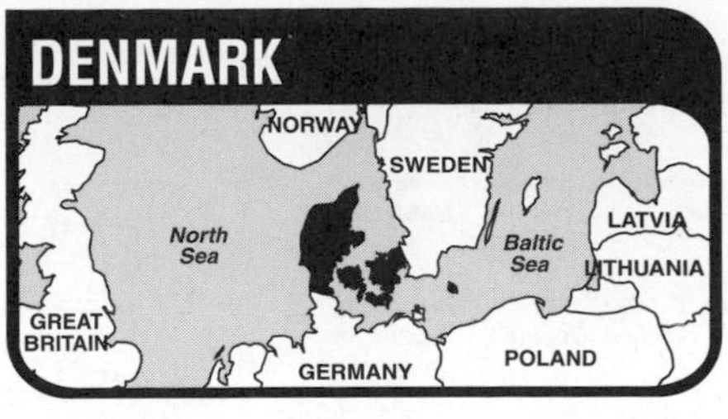

The Kingdom of Denmark, a constitutional monarchy located at the mouth of the Baltic Sea, has an area of 43,094 sq. km. and a population of 5.48 million. Capital: Copenhagen. Most of the country is arable. Agriculture, which used to employ the majority of the people, is now conducted by large farms served by cooperatives. The largest industries are food processing, iron and metal, and shipping. Machinery, meats (chiefly bacon), dairy products and chemicals are exported.

Once the seat of Viking raiders and later a major north European power, Denmark has evolved into a modern, prosperous nation that is participating in the general political and economic integration of Europe. It joined NATO in 1949 and the EEC (now the EU) in 1973. However, the country has opted out of certain elements of the European Union's Maastricht Treaty, including the European Economic and Monetary Union (EMU), European defense cooperation, and issues concerning certain justice and home affairs.

RULERS:

Frederik IV, 1699-1730
Christian VI, 1730-1746
Frederik V, 1746-1766
Christian VII, 1766-1808
Frederik VI, 1808-1839
Christian VIII, 1839-1848
Frederik VII, 1848-1863

MONETARY SYSTEM:

1 Rigsdaler dansk Courant = 96 Skilling Courant = 6 Mark; at the same time,
1 Rigsdaler Species = 120 Skilling Courant, 1713-1813
1 Rigsbankdaler = 96 Rigsbankskilling (= 1/2 Rigsdaler Species), 1813-54
1 Daler Rigsmønt = 96 Skilling Rigsmønt (= 1 Rigsbankdaler), 1854-74
1 Krone = 100 Øre
1 Krone (1/2 Rigsdaler) = 100 Øre 1874-

BANKS:

Kingdom

Aalborg Kreditbank

ND First Issue

	Good	Fine	XF
S101 1 Krone ND. Black text. Uniface. Paper: Yellow-gray.	—	—	—
S102 5 Kroner ND. Black text. Uniface. Paper: Blue. Rare.	—	—	—

ND Second Issue

	Good	Fine	XF
S106 10 Øre ND. Black and gray. Uniface. Vertical format.	—	—	—
S107 25 Øre ND. Black and green. Uniface. Vertical format.	—	—	—
S108 1 Krone ND. Red-brown. Uniface. Vertical format.	—	—	—
S109 5 Kroner ND. Blue. Uniface. Vertical format.	—	—	—
S110 10 Kroner ND. Yellow. Uniface. Vertical format.	—	—	—

ND Third Issue

	Good	Fine	XF
S111 10 Øre ND. Black and gray. Local arms at upper left. Back: Gray.			
a. Issued note.	135.	225.	300.
b. Violet hand stamp: *Serie A* on face at left. (Fourth Issue).	135.	225.	300.
S112 25 Øre ND. Black and green. Local arms at upper left. Back: Black and gray.			
a. Issued note.	125.	250.	400.
b. Violet hand stamp: *Serie A.* (Fourth Issue).	—	—	—
S113 1 Krone ND. Brown. Local arms at upper left. Back: Red-brown.	—	—	—
S114 5 Kroner ND. Light blue. Local arms at upper left. Back: Dark blue.	—	—	—
S115 10 Kroner ND. Yellow-green. Local arms at upper left.	—	—	—

ND Provisional (Fifth) Issue

#S116-S120 overprint 3 lines of text on #S111-S115.

	Good	Fine	XF
S116 10 Øre ND. Black and gray. Local arms at upper left. Handwritten name on 2nd line and printed signature at lower right. Back: Gray. Overprint: Three lines of text on #S111. Rare.	—	—	—

#	Description	Good	Fine	XF
S117	**25 Øre** ND. Black and green. Local arms at upper left. Handwritten name on 2nd line and printed signature at lower right. Back: Black and gray. Overprint: Three lines of text on #S112. Rare.	—	—	—
S118	**1 Krone** ND. Brown. Local arms at upper left. Handwritten name on 2nd line and printed signature at lower right. Back: Red-brown. Overprint: Three lines of text on #S113. Rare.	—	—	—
S119	**5 Kroner** ND. Light blue. Local arms at upper left. Handwritten name on 2nd line and printed signature at lower right. Back: Dark blue. Overprint: Three lines of text on #S114. Rare.	—	—	—
S120	**10 Kroner** ND. Yellow-green. Local arms at upper left. Handwritten name on 2nd line and printed signature at lower right. Overprint: Three lines of text on #S115. Rare.	—	—	—

Aarhus Kreditbank

ND First Issue

#	Description	Good	Fine	XF
S121	**10 Øre** ND. Black and yellow-gray. Town view across top.	65.00	130.	—
S122	**25 Øre** ND. Black and blue-gray. Town view across top.	80.00	150.	—
S123	**1 Krone** ND. Black and red-brown. Town view across top.	100.	175.	—
S124	**2 Kroner** ND. Black and light green. Town view across top.	—	—	—
S125	**5 Kroner** ND. Black and gray-brown. Town view across top.	—	—	—
S126	**10 Kroner** ND. Black and yellow. Town view across top.	—	—	—
S127	**25 Kroner** ND. Black and light brown. Town view across top.	—	—	—

1902 Second Issue

#	Description	Good	Fine	XF
S131	**10 Øre** 1902. Black and gray. Back: Gray-green. Bank at center. Printer: E. Sperling & Co., Aarhus. 120 x 72mm.			
	a. With imprint.	60.00	110.	160.
	b. Without imprint.	50.00	90.00	—
S132	**25 Øre** 1902. Black and gray. Like #S131. Back: Gray-green. Bank at center. Printer: E. Sperling & Co., Aarhus.			
	a. With imprint.	70.00	140.	—
	b. Without imprint.	60.00	125.	—
S132A	**50 Øre** 1902. Light Purple. Back: Gray-green. Bank at center. Printer: E. Sperling & Co., Aarhus. 120 x 72mm. Rare.	—	—	—
S133	**1 Krone** 1902. Black and dark green. Back: Gray-green. Bank at center. Printer: E. Sperling & Co., Aarhus. 120 x 72mm.			
	a. With imprint.	—	—	—
	b. Without imprint.	100.	200.	—

#	Description	Good	Fine	XF
S134	**2 Kroner** 1902. Black and gray-green. Back: Gray-green. Bank at center. Printer: E. Sperling & Co., Aarhus. 120 x 72mm.			
	a. With imprint.	—	—	—
	b. Without imprint.	115.	220.	—
S135	**5 Kroner** 1902. Black and yellow. Back: Gray-green. Bank at center. Printer: E. Sperling & Co., Aarhus. 120 x 72mm.			
	a. With imprint.	—	—	—
	b. Without imprint.	—	—	—
S136	**10 Kroner** 1902. Black and light red. Back: Gray-green. Bank at center. Printer: E. Sperling & Co., Aarhus. 120 x 72mm.			
	a. With imprint.	—	—	—
	b. Without imprint.	—	—	—

Dansk Købmandsbank

1908 Issue

		VG	VF	UNC
S141	**10 Øre** 27.11.1908. Black and gray. Arms of Copenhagen and Frederiksberg at upper and lower left. Litra A.	12.50	25.00	50.00
S142	**25 Øre** 27.11.1908. Black and gray. Arms of Copenhagen and Frederiksberg at upper and lower left. Litra B. Back: Black and red-brown.	20.00	45.00	80.00
S143	**1 Krone** 27.11.1908. Black and gray. Arms of Copenhagen and Frederiksberg at upper and lower left. Litra C. Back: Black and yellow.	60.00	100.	200.
S144	**2 Kroner** 27.11.1908. Arms of Copenhagen and Frederiksberg at upper and lower left. Litra D.	75.00	150.	225.

#	Description	Good	Fine	XF
S145	**5 Kroner** 27.11.1908. Arms of Copenhagen and Frederiksberg at upper and lower left. Litra E.	—	—	—
S146	**10 Kroner** 27.11.1908. Black and gray. Arms of Copenhagen and Frederiksberg at upper and lower left. Litra F. Back: Black and lilac.	—	—	—
S147	**50 Kroner** 27.11.1908. Black and blue-gray. Arms of Copenhagen and Frederiksberg at upper and lower left. Litra F. Back: Black and lilac.	—	—	—

Esbjerg Kreditbank

ND First Issue

#	Description	Good	Fine	XF
S151	**10 Øre** ND. Black and gray. Local arms in small tower at lower left. Back: Lions rampant at left and right of local arms at center.	40.00	80.00	150.
S152	**25 Øre** ND. Black on light blue underprint. Local arms in small tower at lower left. Back: Light blue. Lions rampant at left and right of local arms at center.	40.00	80.00	150.

#	Description	Good	Fine	XF
S153	**1 Krone** ND. Brown and peach. Local arms in small tower at lower left. Back: Light peach. Lions rampant at left and right of local arms at center.	50.00	100.	175.
S154	**5 Kroner** ND. Brown and red-brown. Local arms in small tower at lower left. Back: Light brown. Lions rampant at left and right of local arms at center.	55.00	110.	175.
S155	**10 Kroner** ND. Dark and light brown Local arms in small tower at lower left. Back: Light brown. Lions rampant at left and right of local arms at center.	100.	225.	325.
S156	**25 Kroner** ND. Dark and light green. Local arms in small tower at lower left. Back: Light gray-green. Lions rampant at left and right of local arms at center.	—	—	—

ND First Provisional Issue

#	Description	Good	Fine	XF
S161	**10 Øre** ND. Black and gray. Local arms in small tower at lower left. Back: Lions rampant at left and right of local arms at center. Overprint: 2 lines of text and 2 signatures on face of #S151.	40.00	85.00	150.
S162	**25 Øre** ND. Black on light blue underprint. Local arms in small tower at lower left. Back: Light blue. Lions rampant at left and right of local arms at center. Overprint: 2 lines of text and 2 signatures on face of #S152.	45.00	90.00	160.
S163	**1 Krone** ND. Brown and peach. Local arms in small tower at lower left. Back: Light peach. Lions rampant at left and right of local arms at center. Overprint: 2 lines of text and 2 signatures on face of #S153.	50.00	100.	175.
S164	**5 Kroner** ND. Brown and red-brown. Local arms in small tower at lower left. Back: Light brown. Lions rampant at left and right of local arms at center. Overprint: 2 lines of text and 2 signatures on face of #S154.	65.00	140.	225.
S165	**10 Kroner** ND. Dark and light brown. Local arms in small tower at lower left. Back: Light brown. Lions rampant at left and right of local arms at center. Overprint: 2 lines of text and 2 signatures on face of #S155.	70.00	150.	275.

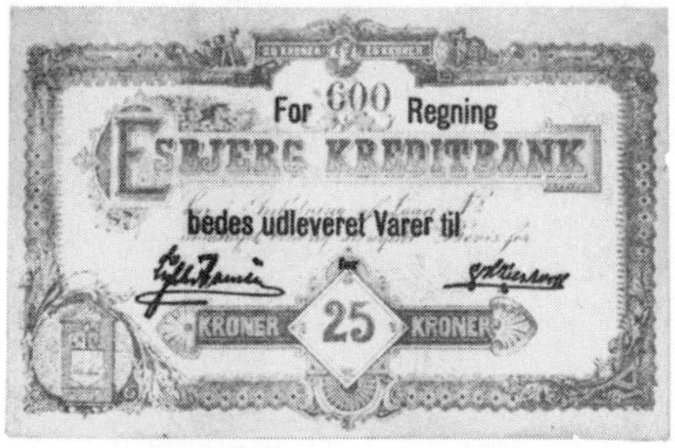

#	Description	Good	Fine	XF
S166	**25 Kroner** ND. Dark and light green. Local arms in small tower at lower left. Back: Light gray-green. Lions rampant at left and right of local arms at center. Overprint: 2 lines of text and 2 signatures on face of #S156.	80.00	175.	375.

ND Second Provisional Issue

#S171-S176 overprint on face like #S161-S166, and *VAREANVISNING* in large letters across back.

#	Description	Good	Fine	XF
S171	**10 Øre** ND. Black and gray. Local arms in small tower at lower left. Back: Lions rampant at left and right of local arms at center. Overprint: 2 lines of text and 2 signatures on face. With *VAREANVISNING* added to back #S161.	50.00	100.	150.
S172	**25 Øre** ND. Black on light blue underprint. Local arms in small tower at lower left. Back: Light blue. Lions rampant at left and right of local arms at center. Overprint: 2 lines of text and 2 signatures on face. With *VAREANVISNING* added to back #S162.	60.00	100.	150.

No.	Description	Good	Fine	XF
S173 1 Krone	ND. Brown and peach. Local arms in small tower at lower left. Back: Light peach. Lions rampant at left and right of local arms at center. Overprint: 2 lines of text and 2 signatures on face. With *VAREANVISNING* added to back #S163.	65.00	110.	160.
S174 5 Kroner	ND. Brown and red-brown. Local arms in small tower at lower left. Back: Light brown. Lions rampant at left and right of local arms at center. Overprint: 2 lines of text and 2 signatures on face. With *VAREANVISNING* added to back #S164.	70.00	125.	200.

No.	Description	Good	Fine	XF
S175 10 Kroner	ND. Dark and light brown. Local arms in small tower at lower left. Back: Light brown. Lions rampant at left and right of local arms at center. Overprint: 2 lines of text and 2 signatures on face. With *VAREANVISNING* added to back #S165.	75.00	150.	250.
S176 25 Kroner	ND. Dark and light green. Local arms in small tower at lower left. Back: Light gray-green. Lions rampant at left and right of local arms at center. Overprint: 2 lines of text and 2 signatures on face. With *VAREANVISNING* added to back #S166.	80.00	150.	275.

ND Fourth Issue

No.	Description	Good	Fine	XF
S181 10 Øre	ND. Black on yellow-green underprint. Small local arms at upper center. SERIES B.	25.00	65.00	125.

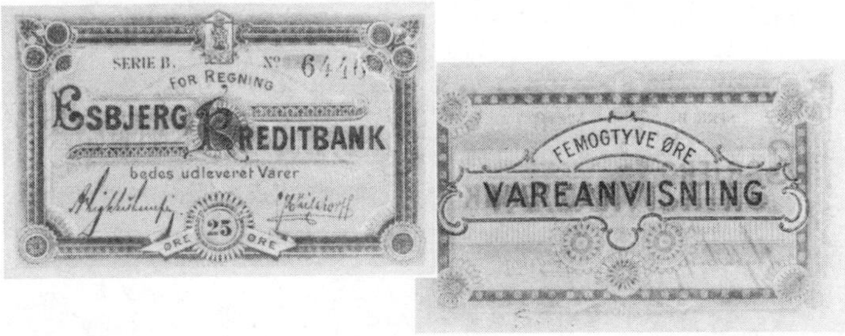

No.	Description	Good	Fine	XF
S182 25 Øre	ND. Brown on blue-gray underprint. Small local arms at upper center. SERIES B.	35.00	75.00	140.
S183 1 Krone	ND. Dark blue on light red underprint. Small local arms at upper center. SERIES B.	40.00	90.00	150.
S184 5 Kroner	ND. Violet on gray underprint. Small local arms at upper center. SERIES B.	45.00	100.	175.

Frederikshavn Kreditbank

ND Issue

No.	Description	Good	Fine	XF
S191 10 Øre	ND. Gray-brown. Standing Mercury with caduceus at left, round building and town at center. Back: Light gray. Remainder with control number.	25.00	70.00	175.
S192 25 Øre	ND. Black and yellow. Standing Mercury with caduceus at left, round building and town at center. Back: Light yellow. Remainder with control number.	25.00	70.00	175.
S193 1 Krone	ND. Brown and red-brown. Standing Mercury with caduceus at left, round building and town at center. Back: Light brown. Remainder with control number.	25.00	70.00	175.
S194 5 Kroner	ND. Blue-gray. Standing Mercury with caduceus at left, round building and town at center. Remainder with control number.	30.00	90.00	200.
S195 10 Kroner	ND. Green. Standing Mercury with caduceus at left, round building and town at center. Remainder with control number.	30.00	90.00	200.

Hjørring Kreditbank

1894 First Issue

No.	Description	Good	Fine	XF
S205 25 Kroner	10.11.1894. Blue-green. Black text. Back: Black text.	200.	450.	—

ND Second Issue

No.	Description	Good	Fine	XF
S211 10 Øre	ND. Gray and black. Standing queen above reclining king on checkerboard at left, school buildings at center.	50.00	150.	225.
S212 25 Øre	ND. Black and gray. Standing queen above reclining king on checkerboard at left, school buildings at center. Back: Light yellow.	60.00	150.	250.
S213 1 Krone	ND. Brown and red-brown. Standing queen above reclining king on checkerboard at left, school buildings at center.	60.00	150.	250.

No.	Description	Good	Fine	XF
S214 5 Kroner	ND. Light green and light blue. Standing queen above reclining king on checkerboard at left, school buildings at center. Back: Light blue.	80.00	175.	275.
S215 10 Kroner	ND. Green. Standing queen above reclining king on checkerboard at left, school buildings at center. Back: Light green.	100.	200.	300.

Odense Kreditbank

ND First Issue

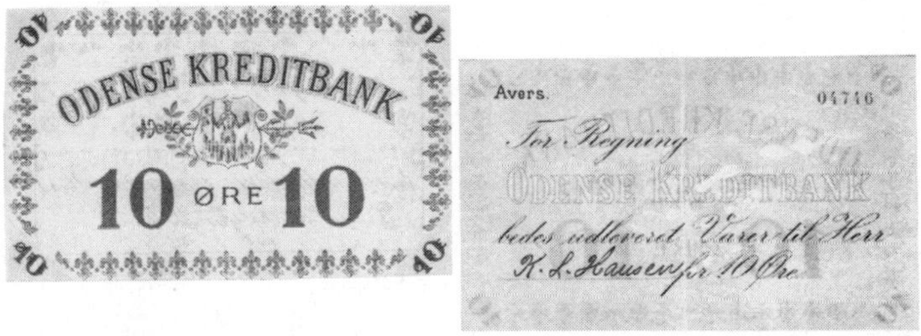

No.	Description	Good	Fine	XF
S221 10 Øre	ND. Black and blue on light orange underprint. Local arms at center. Back: Blue and black. Top line: *Avers* at left and serial # at right.	40.00	70.00	—
S222 25 Øre	ND. Black and blue on orange underprint. Local arms at center. Like #S221. Back: Blue and black. Top line: *Avers* at left and serial # at right.	60.00	90.00	—
S223 1 Krone	ND. Black and orange on light blue underprint. Local arms at center. Back: Orange and black. Top line: *Avers* at left and serial # at right.	30.00	50.00	—
S224 2 Kroner	ND. Black and orange on light blue underprint. Local arms at center. Like #S223. Back: Orange and black. Top line: *Avers* at left and serial # at right.	65.00	90.00	—
S225 5 Kroner	ND. Black and orange on light blue underprint. Local arms at center. Like #S223. Back: Orange and black. Top line: *Avers* at left and serial # at right.	85.00	115.	—
S226 20 Kroner	ND. Black and orange on light blue underprint. Local arms at center. Like #S223. Back: Orange and black. Top line: *Avers* at left and serial # at right.	85.00	115.	—
S227 50 Kroner	ND. Black and orange on light blue underprint. Local arms at center. Like #S223. Back: Orange and black. Top line: *Avers* at left and serial # at right.	200.	275.	—

ND Second Issue

No.	Description	Good	Fine	XF
S233 1 Krone	ND. Black and orange on light blue underprint. Local arms at center. Like #S223. Back: Orange and black. Top line: *Avers* at center and serial # at left and right. Remainder.	125.	250.	—

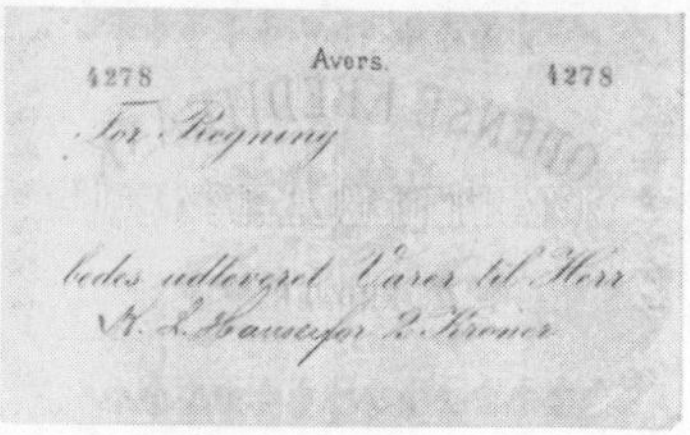

	Good	Fine	XF
S234 2 Kroner			
ND. Black and orange on light blue underprint. Local arms at center. Like #S224. Back: Orange and black. Top line: *Avers* at center and serial # at left and right. Remainder.	—	—	—

Randers Kreditbank

ND First Issue

	Good	Fine	XF
S241 10 Kroner			
ND. Blue-gray. Black text. Back: Black text. (Not redeemable after 31.12.1892.)	—	—	—

ND; 1895 Second Issues

	Good	Fine	XF
S246 10 Øre			
ND. Black and blue. Local arms at upper left, town scene across upper center. Value: *10 ØRE* at lower center.	40.00	70.00	150.
S247 10 Øre			
ND. Black and blue. Local arms at upper left, town scene across upper center. Like #S246 but added line of text: *har i Anl...* across center.	30.00	60.00	100.
S248 25 Øre			
ND. Dark and light blue. Local arms at upper left, town scene across upper center. Value: *25 ØRE* at lower center.	40.00	70.00	185.
S249 25 Øre			
ND. Local arms at upper left, town scene across upper center. Added line of text: *har i Anl...* across center like #S247.	40.00	75.00	185.
S250 1 Krone			
ND. Dark and light red. Local arms at upper left, town scene across upper center. Value: *EN KRONE* at lower center.	40.00	80.00	120.
S251 1 Krone			
ND. Local arms at upper left, town scene across upper center. Added line of text: *har i Anl...* across center like #S247.	40.00	80.00	120.
S252 2 Kroner			
ND. Red. Local arms at upper left, town scene across upper center. Value: *TO KRONER* at lower center.	45.00	90.00	130.
S253 2 Kroner			
ND. Local arms at upper left, town scene across upper center. Added line of text: *har i Anl...* across center like #S247.	40.00	100.	150.
S254 2 Kroner			
ND. Local arms at upper left, town scene across upper center. Back: Added line of text: *har i Anl...* across center. Like #S253.			
a. Issued note.	40.00	100.	150.
b. With Large date overprint: *1895* at upper right. on face.	40.00	100.	150.
S255 5 Kroner			
ND. Brown. Local arms at upper left, town scene across upper center. Value: *FEM KRONER* at lower center. Back: Light brown.	40.00	100.	150.
S256 5 Kroner			
ND. Local arms at upper left, town scene across upper center. Added line of text: *har i Anl...* across center like #S247.	40.00	100.	200.
S257 5 Kroner			
ND. Local arms at upper left, town scene across upper center. Back: Added line of text: *har i Anl...* across center. Like #S256. Overprint: Large date *1895* at upper right on face.	40.00	110.	225.
S258 10 Kroner			
ND. Blue-green. Local arms at upper left, town scene across upper center. Value: *TI KRONER* at lower center. Back: Light blue-green.	40.00	125.	250.
S259 10 Kroner			
ND. Local arms at upper left, town scene across upper center. Added line of text: *har i Anl...* across center like #S247.	40.00	125.	250.
S260 10 Kroner			
Local arms at upper left, town scene across upper center. Back: Added line of text: *har i Anl...* across center. Like #S259.			
a. Issued note.	40.00	125.	250.
b. With Large date overprint: *1895* at upper right. on face.	40.00	125.	250.
S261 20 Kroner			
ND. Violet. Local arms at upper left, town scene across upper center. Value: *20 KRONER* at lower center.	60.00	150.	275.
S262 20 Kroner			
ND. Local arms at upper left, town scene across upper center. Added line of text in red: *har i Anl...* across center like #S247.	60.00	150.	275.
S263 20 Kroner			
ND. Local arms at upper left, town scene across upper center. Back: Added line of text in red: *har i Anl...* across center. Like #S262.			
a. Issued note.	60.00	150.	275.
b. With Large date overprint: *1895* at upper right. on face.	60.00	150.	275.
S264 50 Kroner			
ND. Gray-green. Local arms at upper left, town scene across upper center. Added line of text: *har i Anl...* across center like #S247.	100.	300.	600.

	Good	Fine	XF
S265 50 Kroner			
ND. Gray-green. Local arms at upper left, town scene across upper center. Back: Added line of text: *har i Anl...* across center. Like #S264.			
a. Issued note.	60.00	175.	450.
b. With Large date overprint: *1895* at upper right. on face.	50.00	165.	425.

ND; 1895 Third Issue

	Good	Fine	XF
S271 10 Øre			
ND. Black and grayish blue. Local arms at upper left, town scene across upper center. Similar to #S246 but with value: *ØRE 10 ØRE* at lower center.	30.00	70.00	125.
S272 10 Øre			
ND. Black and grayish blue. Local arms at upper left, town scene across upper center. Value: *ØRE 10 ØRE* at lower center. Like #S271. Back: Printed text.			
a. Issued note.	30.00	70.00	125.
b. With Large date overprint: *1895* at upper right. on face.	30.00	70.00	125.
S273 25 Øre			
ND. Blue and yellow on red underprint. Value: *ØRE 25 ØRE* at lower center. Back: Green.	30.00	80.00	125.
S274 25 Øre			
ND. Blue and yellow on red underprint. Value: *ØRE 25 ØRE* at lower center. Like #S273. Back: Green. Printed text.			
a. Issued note.	35.00	80.00	125.
b. With Large date overprint: *1895* at upper right. on face.	35.00	80.00	175.
S275 1 Krone			
ND. Red and green. Value: *KRONE 1 KRONE* at lower center. Back: Green.	40.00	90.00	175.
S276 1 Krone			
ND. Red and green. Value: *KRONE 1 KRONE* at lower center. Back: Green. Printed text.			
a. Issued note.	40.00	100.	175.
b. With Large date overprint: *1895* at upper right. on face.	40.00	100.	175.

1896-1900 Issue

	Good	Fine	XF
S281 10 Øre			
26.2.1896 (on back). Black, gray-green, and green. Sunburst in underprint. Back: Black text.	30.00	70.00	125.
S282 25 Øre			
1.3.1900. Black, light blue, and red. No rays in underprint. 2 signatures at bottom.	35.00	70.00	125.
S283 1 Krone			
ca.1900. Red, yellow, and green. 2 signatures at bottom.	30.00	75.00	125.
S284 5 Kroner			
1.9.1897 (on back). Gray and brown. Ornately designed with larger and wider town view across upper center and rising sun above.	60.00	125.	200.
S285 10 Kroner			
1.9.1897 (on back). Blue. Ornately designed with larger and wider town view across upper center and rising sun above.	100.	200.	350.
S286 50 Kroner			
1.7.1898 (on back). Red-brown. Ornately designed with larger and wider town view across upper center and rising sun above.	100.	200.	350.

Thisted Kreditbank

ND Issue

	Good	Fine	XF
S291 10 Øre			
ND. Blue-gray with black text. Local arms at center right.	75.00	150.	325.
S292 25 Øre			
ND. Gray with black text. Local arms at center right.	100.	225.	350.
S293 1 Krone			
ND. Light red with black text. Local arms at center right.	125.	315.	—
S294 5 Kroner			
ND. Gray-orange, black text. Local arms at center right.	—	—	—
S295 10 Kroner			
ND. Gray-orange, black text. Local arms at center right. Like #S294.	—	—	—
S296 20 Kroner			
ND. Gray-violet, black text. Local arms at center right.	—	—	—

Varde Kreditbank

ND Provisional Issue

	Good	Fine	XF
S301 10 Øre			
ND. Black and grayish blue. Overprint: New bank name *Kreditbanken Varde* on #S271.	100.	175.	—
S302 25 Øre			
ND. Blue and yellow on red underprint. Back: Green. Overprint: New bank name *Kreditbanken Varde* on #S273.	100.	200.	—
S303 1 Krone			
ND. Red and green. Back: Green. Overprint: New bank name *Kreditbanken Varde* on #S275.	100.	200.	—
S304 2 Kroner			
ND. Overprint: New bank name *Kreditbanken Varde* on #S253.	—	—	—
S305 5 Kroner			
ND. Overprint: New bank name *Kreditbanken Varde* on #S256.	—	—	—
S306 10 Kroner			
ND. Overprint: New bank name *Kreditbanken Varde* on #S259.	—	—	—
S307 20 Kroner			
ND. Overprint: New bank name *Kreditbanken Varde* on #S262.	—	—	—

Vejle Kreditbank

ND Issue

	Good	Fine	XF
S311 10 Øre			
ND. Gray and black. Local arms at upper left. Back: Light gray.	75.00	175.	—
S312 25 Øre			
ND. Light brown. Local arms at upper left.	125.	200.	—
S313 1 Krone			
ND. Green. Local arms at upper left.	—	—	—
S314 5 Kroner			
ND. Local arms at upper left.	—	—	—
S315 10 Kroner			
ND. Blue. Local arms at upper left.	—	—	—
S316 50 Kroner			
ND. Local arms at upper left.	—	—	—

Military

Kgl. Danska Fält-Commisariatet, 1809

Royal Danish Commission

1809 Issue

#M1A-M4A printed w/Danish and Swedish values, printed for planned occupation of south Sweden. (Not issued).

Note: Trial printings exist for 12 Skillingar; 1, 6, 20 and 24 Riksdaler Riksgald.

		Good	Fine	XF
M1A	**8 Skillingar Riksgalds-Mynt** 1809. Printed with Danish and Swedish values. (Not issued.)	—	—	—
M1B	**16 Skillingar Riksgalds-Mynt** 1809. Printed with Danish and Swedish values. (Not issued.)	—	—	—
M1C	**2 Rixdaler Banco Specie** 1809. Printed with Danish and Swedish values. (Not issued.)	—	—	—
M1D	**20 Rixdaler Banco Specie** 1809. Printed with Danish and Swedish values. (Not issued.)	—	—	—

Allierede Overkommando til Brug i Danmark

Allied Command in Denmark, WWII

1945 Issue

		VG	VF	UNC
M1	**25 Øre** ND (1945). Brown on lilac underprint.	10.00	25.00	70.00

		VG	VF	UNC
M2	**1 Krone** ND (1945). Lilac on blue underprint.	3.50	10.00	20.00

		VG	VF	UNC
M3	**5 Kroner** ND (1945). Green.	12.50	35.00	100.
M4	**10 Kroner** ND (1945). Dark brown and blue.	12.50	35.00	100.
M5	**50 Kroner** ND (1945). Violet.	60.00	400.	800.
M6	**100 Kroner** ND (1945). Green-blue.			
	a. Issued note.	—	—	6000.
	s. Specimen.	—	—	5000.

Danske Krigsministerium, Den Danske Brigade

Royal Danish Ministry of War, Post Liberation WWII

1947-58 Issue

#M7-M12 issued for the troops first stationed in Germany, and later in other parts of the world.

		VG	VF	UNC
M7	**5 Øre** ND (1947-58). Blue. Back: Arms at left.	2.50	7.50	20.00
M8	**10 Øre** ND (1947-58). Brown. Back: Arms at left.	2.25	6.00	17.50

		VG	VF	UNC
M9	**25 Øre** ND (1947-58). Blue. Back: Arms at left.	4.00	8.00	22.50
M10	**1 Krone** ND (1947-58). Brown. Back: Arms at left.	5.00	10.00	25.00
M11	**5 Kroner** ND (1947-58). Blue. Back: Arms at left.	35.00	110.	250.

		VG	VF	UNC
M12	**10 Kroner** ND (1947-58). Brown.	75.00	175.	400.

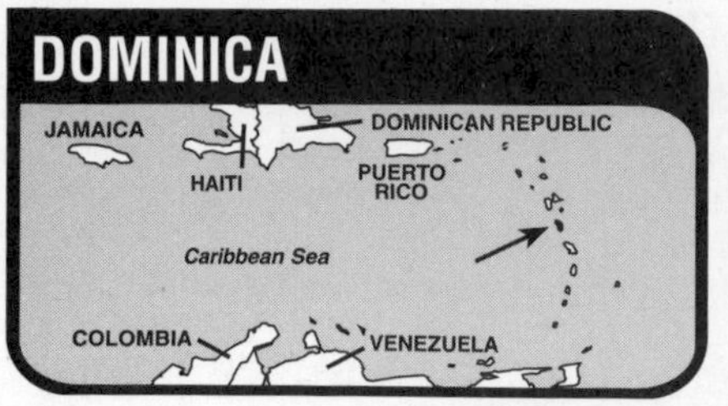

The commonwealth of Dominica, situated in the Lesser Antilles midway between Guadeloupe to the north and Martinique to the south, has an area of 754 sq. km. and a population of 72,500. Capital: Roseau.

Dominica was the last of the Caribbean islands to be colonized by Europeans due chiefly to the fierce resistance of the native Caribs. France ceded possession to Great Britain in 1763, which made the island a colony in 1805. In 1980, two years after independence, Dominica's fortunes improved when a corrupt and tyrannical administration was replaced by that of Mary Eugenia Charles, the first female prime minister in the Caribbean, who remained in office for 15 years. Some 3,000 Carib Indians still living on Dominica are the only pre-Columbian population remaining in the eastern Caribbean.

RULERS:

British

MONETARY SYSTEM:

1 British West Indies Dollar = 4 Shillings 2 Pence
5 British West Indies Dollars = 1 Pound 10 Pence

British Administration

Barclays Bank (Dominion, Colonial and Overseas)

1926 Provisional Issue

	Good	Fine	XF
S101 5 Dollars 1926. Supported royal arms at center. Rare.	—	—	—

1937 Provisional Issue

#S101A and S102 overprint: *ISSUED AT DOMINICA BRANCH* at left and right of center.

S101A 5 Dollars	Good	Fine	XF
1.5.1937; 1.2.1941. Purple on multicolor underprint. Supported royal arms at right. Large black *D* (Dominica) at upper right. Back: Supported royal arms at center. Overprint: *ISSUED AT DOMINICA BRANCH* at left and right of center. Printer: BWC. Issuing office Bridgetown, Barbados.	300.	800.	—

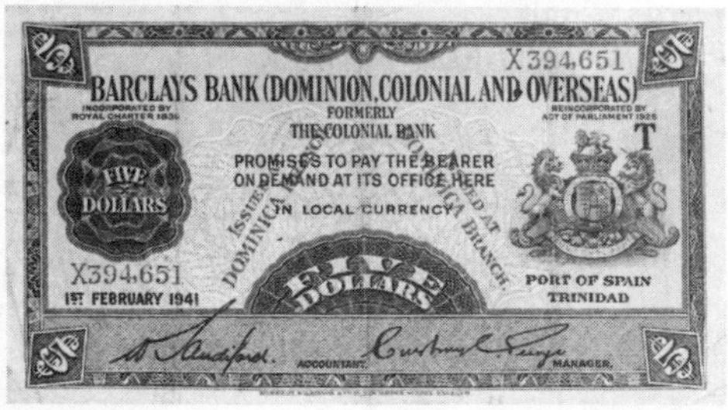

S102 5 Dollars	Good	Fine	XF
1.5.1937; 1.2.1941. Purple on multicolor underprint. Supported royal arms at right. Back: Supported royal arms at center. Overprint: *ISSUED AT DOMINICA BRANCH* at left and right of center on Trinidad #S102. Printer: BWC.	300.	800.	—

Colonial Bank

1900's Issue

S106 5 Dollars	Good	Fine	XF
To 1926. Reported not confirmed.	—	—	—

Royal Bank of Canada

ND Provisional Issue

S111 5 Dollars = 1 Pound 10 Pence	Good	Fine	XF
ND (- old date 2.1.1913). Black on green underprint. Overprint: *DOMINICA* at left and right and *PAYABLE AT ROSEAU/DOMINICA* at center on Canada #1378.			
a. Issued note.	400.	1250.	—
s. Specimen. Rare.	—	—	—

1920 Regular Issue

S112 5 Dollars = 1 Pound 10 Pence	Good	Fine	XF
2.1.1920. Black on green underprint. Steamship at center. With text: *REDEEMABLE ONLY / IN / DOMINICA* at bottom center. Back: Green. Supported royal arms at center.	400.	1250.	—

1938 Issue

S113 5 Dollars = 1 Pound 10 Pence	Good	Fine	XF
3.1.1938. Black on green underprint. Steamship at center. With text: *REDEEMABLE ONLY/IN/DOMINICA* at bottom center. Back: Green. Supported royal arms at center. Printer: CBNC. Similar to #S112 but smaller size.			
a. Issued note.	300.	750.	—
p. Proof.	—	Unc	600.

NOTE: For later issues see British East Caribbean Territories in Vol. 2 and East Caribbean States in Vol. 3.

The Dominican Republic, occupying the eastern two-thirds of the island of Hispañiola, has an area of 48,730 sq. km. and a population of 9.50 million. Capital: Santo Domingo. The agricultural economy produces sugar, coffee, tobacco and cocoa.

Explored and claimed by Christopher Columbus on his first voyage in 1492, the island of Hispaniola became a springboard for Spanish conquest of the Caribbean and the American mainland. In 1697, Spain recognized French dominion over the western third of the island, which in 1804 became Haiti. The remainder of the island, by then known as Santo Domingo, sought to gain its own independence in 1821, but was conquered and ruled by the Haitians for 22 years; it finally attained independence as the Dominican Republic in 1844. In 1861, the Dominicans voluntarily returned to the Spanish Empire, but two years later they launched a war that restored independence in 1865. A legacy of unsettled, mostly non-representative rule followed, capped by the dictatorship of Rafael Leonidas Trujillo from 1930-61. Juan Bosch was elected president in 1962, but was deposed in a military coup in 1963. In 1965, the United States led an intervention in the midst of a civil war sparked by an uprising to restore Bosch. In 1966, Joaquin Balaguer defeated Bosch in an election to become president. Balaguer maintained a tight grip on power for most of the next 30 years when international reaction to flawed elections forced him to curtail his term in 1996. Since then, regular competitive elections have been held in which opposition candidates have won the presidency. Former President (1996-2000) Leonel Fernandez Reyna won election to a second term in 2004 following a constitutional amendment allowing presidents to serve more than one term.

MONETARY SYSTEM:

1 Peso Oro = 100 Centavos Oro

Republic

Banco de la Compañia de Crédito de Puerto Plata

1880's Issue

	Good	Fine	XF
S101 25 Centavos			
18xx. Black on green and brown underprint. Portrait Christopher Columbus at left. Back: Green. Dominican arms. Printer: ABNC.			
r. Unsigned remainder.	10.00	25.00	75.00
s. Specimen.	—	Unc	200.
S102 50 Centavos			
188x. Black on blue and gold underprint. Seated Indian woman ("La Hua de los Incas") at left. Back: Blue. Dominican arms. Printer: ABNC.			
r. Unsigned remainder.	5.00	10.00	25.00
s. Specimen.	—	Unc	200.

	Good	Fine	XF
S103 1 Peso			
188x. Black on red and green underprint. Portrait Christopher Columbus at left, seated woman with jug ("Virgin del Sol") at lower right. Back: Red. Dominican arms. Printer: ABNC.			
r. Unsigned remainder.	7.50	15.00	50.00
s. Specimen.	—	Unc	250.
S104 2 Pesos			
188x. Black on blue and brown underprint. Reclining woman with lamp sitting ("Literature") at left. Back: Blue. Dominican arms. Printer: ABNC.			
r. Unsigned remainder.	15.00	40.00	100.
s. Specimen.	—	Unc	250.

	Good	Fine	XF
S105 5 Pesos			
188x. Black on light red and green underprint. Christopher Columbus seated ("Columbus in His Study") at left, two sailors at lower right. Back: Light brown. Dominican arms. Printer: ABNC.			
r. Unsigned remainder.	15.00	40.00	120.
s. Specimen.	—	Unc	250.

	Good	Fine	XF
S106 10 Pesos			
188x. Black on orange and blue underprint. Christopher Columbus in sight of land ("First Land") at left, "Raphael's Angel No. 2" at center, Mercury at right. Back: Dark brown. Dominican arms. Printer: ABNC.			
r. Unsigned remainder.	—	75.00	200.
s. Specimen.	—	Unc	300.

	Good	Fine	XF
S107 50 Pesos			
188x. Black on green and orange underprint. Sailor with telescope and other marine implements at left, landing of Christopher Columbus at center, women with spool ("Industry") at right. Back: Brown. Dominican arms. Printer: ABNC.			
a. Issued note. Rare.	—	—	—
p. Proof.	—	Unc	300.
s. Specimen.	—	Unc	500.

1899 Provisional Issue

#S111-S112 red overprint of 6 lines of text: *REHABILITADO...* and 2 handwritten signature at bottom. Date *21.7.1899* is included in overprint. Back may have round purple hand stamping: *CONSTITUCIONAL...*

	Good	Fine	XF
S111 25 Centavos			
21.7.1899. Black on green and brown underprint. Portrait Christopher Columbus at left. 2 handwritten signatures at bottom. Back: Green. Dominican arms. Overprint: Red 6 lines of text: *REHABILITADO...* date included on #S101.	40.00	125.	400.
S112 50 Centavos			
21.7.1899. Black on blue and gold underprint. Seated Indian woman ("La Hua de los Incas") at left. 2 handwritten signatures at bottom. Back: Blue. Dominican arms. Overprint: Red 6 lines of text: *REHABILITADO...* date included on #S102.	40.00	125.	400.

NOTE: Higher denominations which have been overprinted require confirmation.

Banco Nacional de Santo Domingo

1869 Issue

	Good	Fine	XF
S119 25 Centavos			
ND (ca.1870). Green on black underprint. Portrait Abraham Lincoln at right. Printer: ABNC. Face proof.	—	Unc	250.
S120 50 Centavos			
ND (ca.1870). Green on black underprint. Portrait George Washington at center. Printer: ABNC. Face proof.	—	Unc	250.

S121 1 Peso	Good	Fine	XF
1.12.1869. Black and dark green on green underprint. Portrait Christopher Columbus at lower left, reclining woman with globe ("Science") at center, anchor at lower right. Back: Green. Text at center. Printer: ABNC.			
a. Issued note. Rare.	—	—	—
p. Proof.	—	Unc	250.
r. Remainder, without serial #, punched hole cancelled.	—	Unc	100.

S122 2 Pesos	Good	Fine	XF
1.12.1869. Black on green underprint. Sailor ("The Hail") at left, woman seated at sugar cane press at right. Back: Green. Text at center. Printer: ABNC.			
a. Issued note. Rare.	—	—	—
p. Proof.	—	Unc	250.
S123 5 Pesos			
1.12.1869. Black on green underprint. Tree with basket and other implements at left, dog on safe ("The Safeguard") at center, woman ("Liberty") at lower right. Back: Green. Text at center. Printer: ABNC. Proof.	—	Unc	250.

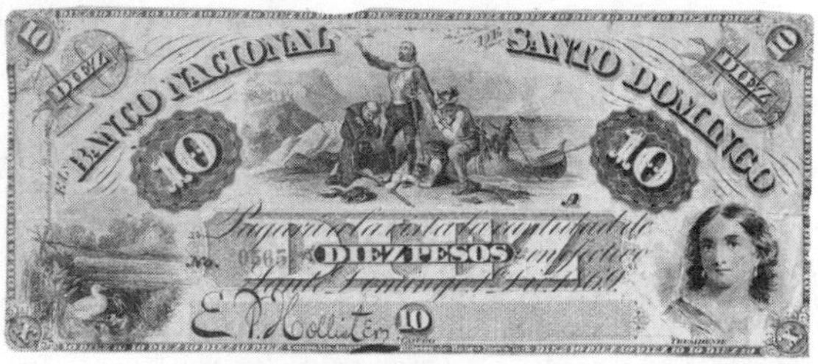

S124 10 Pesos	Good	Fine	XF
1.12.1869. Black on green underprint. Ducks at left, Christopher Columbus landing in new world ("Columbus") at center, girl ("The Bride") at right. Back: Green. Text at center. Printer: ABNC. Rare.	—	Unc	250.
S125 20 Pesos			
1.12.1869. Black on green underprint. Standing woman with basket at left, allegorical woman with staff and bird in foliage scene ("The Tropics") at center, man carrying sheaf at right. Back: Green. Text at center. Printer: ABNC. Proof.			
a. With serial #. (Not issued). Rare.	—	—	—
p. Proof.	—	Unc	250.

NOTE: Beware of remainders with spurious signatures.

1881 Provisional Issue

#S126 and S127 overprint of seven lines of text on back. Date *21.12.1881* is included in the overprint.

S126 1 Peso	Good	Fine	XF
21.12.1881. Black and dark green on green underprint. Portrait Christopher Columbus at lower left, reclining woman with globe ("Science") at center, anchor at lower right. Back: Green. Text at center. Signature and title printed at bottom and vertically at left and right. Overprint: Seven lines of text on back of #S121. Rare.	—	—	—
S127 2 Pesos			
21.12.1881. Black on green underprint. Sailor ("The Hail") at left, woman seated at sugar cane press at right. Back: Green. Text at center. Signature and title printed at bottom and vertically at left and right. Overprint: Seven lines of text on back of #S122. Rare.	—	—	—

NOTE: Higher denominations with this provisional overprint require confirmation.

1889 Issue

S129 25 Centavos	Good	Fine	XF
L.14.8.1889. Black. Helmeted woman at left. Back: Black or orange. Printer: FBNC. Proof.	—	Unc	200.
S130 50 Centavos			
L.14.8.1889. Black. Portrait Christopher Columbus at left. Back: Black or green. Proof.	—	Unc	200.

1889 ND Issue

S131 1 Peso	Good	Fine	XF
ND. Black on green underprint. Portrait Liberty at left, arms at right. Printed signature at right. Series C. Back: Green. Printer: FBNC.			
a. Issued note with hand signature at left, stamping at corner on back.	10.00	40.00	100.
r. Remainder without hand signature at left or stamping on back.	—	Unc	50.00

S132 2 Pesos	Good	Fine	XF
ND. Black on brown underprint. Arms at upper left, portrait Christopher Columbus at lower right. Series D. Back: Brown. Printer: FBNC.			
a. Issued note as #S131a.	15.00	50.00	125.
r. Remainder as #S131b.	—	Unc	75.00

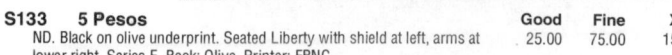

S133 5 Pesos	Good	Fine	XF
ND. Black on olive underprint. Seated Liberty with shield at left, arms at lower right. Series E. Back: Olive. Printer: FBNC.	25.00	75.00	150.

NOTE: #S132a and S133 often have small hole cancellations (3 to 4mm).

Law of 14.8.1889 - 1912 Issue

	Good	Fine	XF
S142 2 Pesos ND. Black on light green underprint. Arms at left with payable text: *PLATA MONEDA MEJICANA* (Silver Mexican Money). Portrait young woman at right. Series A. Back: Green. Printer: CS&E.	125.	350.	—
S143 5 Pesos ND. Black on red and green underprint. Arms at left with payable text: *PLATA MONEDA MEJICANA* (Silver Mexican Money). Portrait Christopher Columbus at upper center. Series B. Back: Red. Printer: CS&E.	125.	350.	—
S145 25 Pesos ND. Arms at left with payable text: *PLATA MONEDA MEJICANA* (Silver Mexican Money). Mercury standing by two seated women at left, arms at upper right. Printer: CS&E. Unsigned remainder.	—	—	—

	Good	Fine	XF
S147 100 Pesos ND. Black on pink and blue underprint. Arms at left with payable text: *PLATA MONEDA MEJICANA* (Silver Mexican Money). Portrait Christopher Columbus at upper right. Series D. Back: Blue. Printer: CS&E. Unsigned remainder.	75.00	150.	400.

1912 Issue

	Good	Fine	XF
S151 1 Peso = 1 Dollar 31.1.1912. Black on blue and brown underprint. Seated allegorical woman at center. Back: Green. Arms at center. Printer: ABNC.			
p. Proof.	—	Unc	1650.
s. Specimen, punched hole cancelled.	—	Unc	1650.
S152 2 Pesos = 2 Dollars 31.1.1912. Black on orange and green underprint. Seated allegorical woman at right. Back: Red-orange. Arms at center. Printer: ABNC. Proof.	—	Unc	1650.

	Good	Fine	XF
S153 5 Pesos = 5 Dollars 31.1.1912. Black on blue and brown underprint. Seated allegorical woman with cherub supporters at center. Back: Blue-gray. Arms at center. Printer: ABNC.			
p. Proof.	—	Unc	1250.
s. Specimen, punched hole cancelled.	—	Unc	2750.
S154 10 Pesos = 10 Dollars 31.1.1912. Black on brown and purple underprint. Allegorical woman seated at center. Back: Brown. Arms at center. Printer: ABNC. Proof.	—	Unc	1750.
S155 25 Pesos = 25 Dollars 31.1.1912. Black on green and orange underprint. Seated allegorical woman with globe at left. Back: Olive-green. Arms at center. Printer: ABNC. Proof.	—	Unc	2500.
S156 50 Pesos = 50 Dollars 31.1.1912. Black on purple and green underprint. Allegorical woman seated at center. Back: Purple. Arms at center. Printer: ABNC. Proof.	—	Unc	3000.
S157 100 Pesos = 100 Dollars 31.1.1912. Black on orange and green underprint. Allegorical woman seated at left and right of denomination numeral at center. Back: Orange. Arms at center. Printer: ABNC.			
p. Proof.	—	Unc	3250.
s. Specimen, punched hole cancelled.	—	Unc	4500.

Government

1875-76 Crédito Público-Deuda Consolidada Issue

Bond of Consolidated Public Debt.

	Good	Fine	XF
S161 5 Pesos 1.6.1875; 4.2.1876. Red. Arms at center. Handwritten date. Uniface.	10.00	25.00	40.00
S162 10 Pesos 1.7.1875. Green. Arms at center. Handwritten date. Uniface. Like #S161.	25.00	50.00	100.

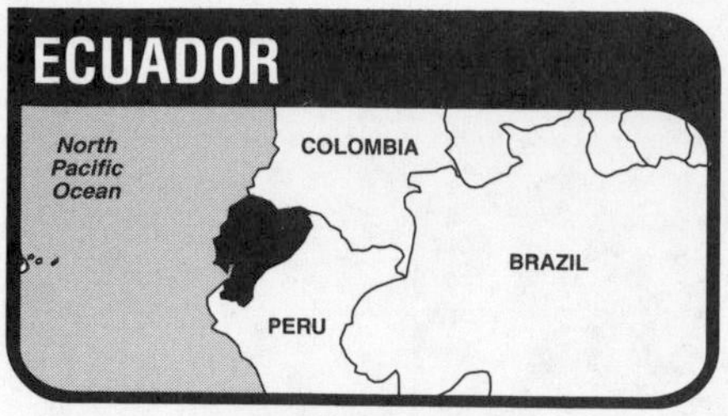

The Republic of Ecuador, located astride the equator on the Pacific coast of South America, has an area of 283,560 sq. km. and a population of 13.93 million. Capital: Quito. Agriculture is the mainstay of the economy but there are appreciable deposits of minerals and petroleum. It is the world's largest exporter of bananas and balsa wood. Coffee, cacao and shrimp are also valuable exports. What is now Ecuador formed part of the northern Inca Empire until the Spanish conquest in 1533. Quito became a seat of Spanish colonial government in 1563 and part of the Viceroyalty of New Granada in 1717. The territories of the Viceroyalty - New Granada (Colombia), Venezuela, and Quito - gained their independence between 1819 and 1822 and formed a federation known as Gran Colombia. When Quito withdrew in 1830, the traditional name was changed in favor of the "Republic of the Equator." Between 1904 and 1942, Ecuador lost territories in a series of conflicts with its neighbors. A border war with Peru that flared in 1995 was resolved in 1999. Although Ecuador marked 25 years of civilian governance in 2004, the period has been marred by political instability. Protests in Quito have contributed to the mid-term ouster of Ecuador's last three democratically elected Presidents. In 2007, a Constituent Assembly was elected to draft a new constitution; Ecuador's twentieth since gaining independence.

MONETARY SYSTEM:

1 Peso = 8 Reales
1 Peso = 100 Centavos
1 Sucre = 10 Decimos = 100 Centavos
1 Condor = 25 Sucres
1 USA Dollar = 25,000 Sucres (March 2001)

BANKS:

GOVERNMENT

BANKS

BANCO ANGLO-ECUATORIANO

MONTECRISTI

1885-86 ISSUE

#S91-S94 Originally printed for issue at Montecristi but actually issued with overprint of: *GUAYAQUIL*.

	Good	Fine	XF
S91 1 Peso			
14.10.1885; 21.10.1885. Black on light brown underprint. Condor on shield with lion and unicorn supporters at center. With text: *En Moneda Fuerte*. Back: Light brown. Mountain scene at center. Overprint: *GUAYAQUIL*. Printer: ABNC.			
p. Proof.	—	Unc	1000.
s. Specimen.	—	Unc	1500.
S92 1 Peso			
4.6.1886. Black on light brown underprint. Condor on shield with lion and unicorn supporters at center. Like #S91 but with text: *En Moneda Corrieute*. Back: Light brown. Mountain scene at center. Overprint: *GUAYAQUIL*. Printer: ABNC. Proof.	—	Unc	1000.
S93 5 Pesos			
ca.1886. Black on orange underprint. Condor on shield with lion and unicorn supporters at center. Woman writing at right. With text: *en Moneda Fuerte*. Back: Mountain scene at center. Overprint: *GUAYAQUIL*. Printer: ABNC.			
p. Back green. Proof.	—	Unc	1750.
s. Back orange. Specimen.	—	Unc	2250.
S94 10 Pesos			
ca.1886. Black on red-orange and green underprint. Condor on shield with lion and unicorn supporters at center. Watering horses at left. With text: *en Moneda Fuerte*. Back: Mountain scene at center. Overprint: *GUAYAQUIL*. Printer: ABNC.			
p. Back blue. Proof.	—	Unc	1750.
s. Back red-orange. Specimen.	—	Unc	2250.

GUAYAQUIL

1885 PROVISONAL ISSUE

	Good	Fine	XF
S95 1 Sucre			
21.10.1885. Black on light brown underprint. Condor on shield with lion and unicorn supporters at center. With text: *En Moneda Fuerte*. Back: Light brown. Mountain scene at center. Overprint: *UN SUCRE* and *GUAYAQUIL* on #S91.	—	—	—

1886 REGULAR ISSUE

	Good	Fine	XF
S96 1 Sucre			
1886. Black on light brown underprint. Condor on shield with lion and unicorn supporters at center. *En Moneda Corriente*. Similar to #S91. Back: Light brown. Mountain scene at center.	—	—	—
S97 5 Sucres			
ca.1886. Black on orange underprint. Condor on shield with lion and unicorn supporters at center. *En Moneda Corriente*. Similar to #S93. Back: Orange. Mountain scene at center. Specimen.	—	Unc	1500.
S98 10 Sucres			
ca.1886. Black on red-orange and green underprint. Condor on shield with lion and unicorn supporters at center. *En Moneda Corriente*. Similar to #S94. Back: Red-orange. Mountain scene at center.			
p. Proof.	—	Unc	900.
s. Specimen.	—	Unc	1500.

BANCO DEL AZUAY

1914-20 ISSUE

	Good	Fine	XF
S101 1 Sucre			
24.4.1914; 1.12.1920; 17.12.1920; 8.7.1921. Black on blue and red underprint. Gil Ramírez Dávalos standing at left. Back: Green. Printer: ABNC.			
a. Issued note.	100.	250.	600.
p. Proof.	—	Unc	700.
S102 2 Sucres			
6.3.1914; 16.3.1914; 16.6.1916; 1.12.1920. Black on orange and green underprint. Two children with bunches of string at center. Back: Dark red. Printer: ABNC.			
a. Issued note.	100.	250.	600.
p. Proof.	—	Unc	750.
S103 5 Sucres			
1.12.1920; 15.11.1924. Black on blue and pink underprint. Old fortress with city behind at left, portrait Alonso de Mercadillo at right. Back: Brown. Printer: ABNC.			
a. Issued note.	150.	400.	—
p. Proof.	—	Unc	850.
S104 10 Sucres			
18.6.1917; 20.2.1920. Black on red and purple underprint. Portrait Diego de Almagro at left, Liberty monument at center, portrait Sebastián de Benalcázar at right. Back: Brown. Ornamental head at center. Printer: ABNC.			
a. Issued note.	100.	200.	450.
p. Proof.	—	Unc	600.

NOTE: Higher values (20, 50, 100, 500 and 1000 Sucres) are reported but not confirmed. Some dates may have capitalization amount overprint. More information is needed.

NOTE: Some notes were issued with overprint: *CAJA CENTRAL DE EMISION Y AMORTIZACION*, see #S282A.

BANCO DE CIRCULACIÓN Y DESCUENTO DE MANUEL ANTONIO DE LUZARRAGA

1860'S ISSUE

	Good	Fine	XF
S111 1 Peso			
1868. Black on orange underprint. Luzarraga at lower left, allegorical woman and plants ("Tropiccs") at upper center, woman at lower right.			
a. 1.10.1868. Rare.	—	—	—
p. Proof. 18xx.	—	Unc	600.

See also #S134 for a provisional issue of the Banco del Ecuador.

	Good	Fine	XF
S112 4 Pesos			
186x. Black on blue underprint. Sailor at lower left, eagle at upper center right. Proof.	—	Unc	600.
S113 4 Pesos			
18xx; 31.12.1862. Black on brown underprint. Eagle at center. Proof.	—	Unc	600.
S113A 5 Pesos			
186x. Black on red-orange underprint. Standing Justice at left, steamship at center right. Proof.	—	Unc	600.
S114 5 Pesos			
18xx. Black on yellow-orange underprint. Portrait girl at upper left, seated woman with tablet and child ("History") at upper center right. Proof.	—	Unc	600.
S115 10 Pesos			
18xx. Black on green underprint. Statue of Freedom at left, seated woman with globe ("Science") at upper center right. Proof.	—	Unc	600.
S116 20 Pesos			
18xx. Black on brown underprint. Allegorical man wearing toga standing under tree at left, arms at right. Proof.	—	Unc	600.

Note: For similar notes dated 1.10.1868 and counterstamped on back see #S137A-S137D.

BANCO DE CIRCULACIÓN Y DESCUENTO DE PLANAS, PÉREZ & OBARRIO

1867 ISSUE

	Good	Fine	XF
S117 4 Reales			
18xx (1867). Black on green underprint. Portrait young girl's head at center. Uniface. Printer: CABB. Proof, punched hole cancelled.	—	Unc	400.
S117A 1 Peso			
18xx (1867). Black on green underprint. Standing woman at left, girl's head at center. Printer: CABB. Archive copy.	—	Unc	400.
S118 5 Pesos			
18xx (1867). Black on orange underprint. Cherub at upper left, seated sailor at center, woman with numeral *V* at right. Printer: CABB. Proof, punched hole cancelled. Rare.	—	—	—
S119 10 Pesos			
18xx (1867). Black on brown underprint. Girl's head at lower left and right, horses at center. Printer: CABB. Rare.	—	—	—
S119A 20 Pesos			
18xx (1867). Black on blue underprint. Tree, basket, sacks and shovel at left, allegorical woman holding sailing ship at upper center Archive copy.	—	Unc	600.

Banco Comercial y Agrícola

1895 Issue

		Good	Fine	XF
S120	**1 Sucre** 1.10.1895; 1.7.1896. Black on green and yellow underprint. Reclining woman with wheel and sheaf at left, portrait man at center. Similar to #S126, but *CAPITAL S/2,000,000* at right border. Back: Green. Printer: ABNC.	125.	300.	—
S121	**5 Sucres** ND (ca.1895). Black on orange and yellow underprint. Cherub with fruit ("Abundance") at left, portraits three men at center right. Similar to #S127, but *CAPITAL S/2,000,000* and minor plate differences. Back: Orange. Printer: ABNC. Archive copy.	—	Unc	1000.
S122	**20 Sucres** ND (ca.1895). Black on blue and yellow underprint. Threshing machine at right. Similar to #S129, but *CAPITAL S/2,000,000.* Back: Blue. Street view in town at right. Printer: ABNC. Specimen or proof.	—	Unc	1250.
S123	**100 Sucres** ND (ca.1895). Black on light brown and yellow underprint. Woman's head at upper left, woman seated ("Naiad") at center right. Similar to #S131, but *CAPITAL S/2,000,000.* Back: Brown. José Joaquín Olmedo monument at left. Printer: ABNC.			
	p. Proof.	—	Unc	900.
	s. Series L. Specimen.	—	Unc	1250.
S124	**1000 Sucres** ND (ca.1895). Black on red, orange and yellow underprint. Woman seated with fruit at left, Liberty at center right. Similar to #S132, but *CAPITAL S/2,000,000.* Series P. Back: Red-orange. Monument with man on horse at left. Printer: ABNC. Specimen.	—	Unc	1250.

1897 Issue

		Good	Fine	XF
S125	**1 Sucre** 1.1.1897 (date only in oval stamping at center on back). Black on green and yellow underprint. Reclining woman with wheel and sheaf at left, portrait man at center. Like #S120. Back: Dark brown. Printer: ABNC.	100.	250.	—

1903-22 Issue

		Good	Fine	XF
S126	**1 Sucre** 1903-25. Black on green and yellow underprint. Reclining woman with wheel and sheaf at left, portrait man at center, *CAPITAL S/5,000,000* at right border. Back: Green. Printer: ABNC.			
	a. 1.1.1903; 1.8.1905; 1.1.1907.	50.00	100.	300.
	b. 1.7.1910; 5.12.1911; 1.10.1913; 5.1.1916; 15.7.1917; 15.9.1917.	50.00	100.	300.
	c. 1.1.1920-17.1.1925.	35.00	75.00	200.
	p. Proof.	—	Unc	550.
S127	**5 Sucres** 1907-25. Black on orange and yellow underprint. Cherub with fruit ("Abundance") at left, portraits three men at center right, *CAPITAL S/5,000,000.* Back: Orange. Printer: ABNC.			
	a. 1.1.1907.	100.	250.	—
	b. 15.1.1915-17.1.1925.	75.00	200.	—
	p. Proof.	—	Unc	1250.
S128	**10 Sucres** 1907-25. Black on light brown underprint. Sailing ship at center, *CAPITAL S/5,000,000.* Back: Brown. Printer: ABNC.			
	a. 1.1.1903; 1.1.1907.	100.	250.	—
	b. 5.1.1916-17.1.1925.	75.00	250.	—
S129	**20 Sucres** 1.1.1907; 15.1.1915; 5.1.1916; 28.2.1923; 17.1.1925. Black on blue and yellow underprint. Threshing machine at right, *CAPITAL S/5,000,000.* Back: Blue. Street view in town at right. Printer: ABNC.	300.	600.	—
S130	**50 Sucres** 5.1.1916; 15.3.1916; 16.3.1918. Black on green underprint. Allegorical woman seated at center, *CAPITAL S/5,000,000.* Back: Dark green. Printer: ABNC.	—	—	—
S131	**100 Sucres** 1.1.1922; 1.10.1922. Black on light brown and yellow underprint. Woman's head at upper left, woman seated ("Naiad") at center right. *CAPITAL S/5,000,000.* Back: Brown. Olmedo monument at left. Rare.	—	—	—
S131A	**500 Sucres** Reported not confirmed.	—	—	—
S132	**1000 Sucres** 15.4.1907; 18.4.1916. Black on red, orange and yellow underprint. Woman seated with fruit at left, Liberty at center right. *CAPITAL S/5,000,000.* Back: Red-orange. Monument with man on horse at left. Rare.	—	—	—

19xx Provisional Issue

		Good	Fine	XF
S132A	**1 Sucre** 19xx. Black bearer check form. Red value numeral and words at center, blue bank stamping at left and right, red bank name and signature title at lower right. Uniface.	—	—	—

Banco de Descuento

1922 Cédula Hipotecaria Issue

		Good	Fine	XF
S132B	**5 Sucres** 26.12.1922. Black. Back: With annual interest table. Paper: Pale green. Printer: W&S (face). Local printer for back. 4% interest-bearing note.	—	—	—

NOTE: #S132B was issued under the law of 6.8.1869.

		Good	Fine	XF
S132C	**5 Sucres** ND. Brown. Like #S132B. Uniface. Specimen.	—	—	—

1923-24 Issue

		Good	Fine	XF
S133	**5 Sucres** 13.11.1923; 13.12.1923; 5.3.1924. Black on blue and red underprint. Seated woman with boy and produce at center. Back: Brown. Printer: W&S.	—	—	—

NOTE: For #S133 dated 1926 and overprint: *CAJA CENTRAL...* see #S283.

		Good	Fine	XF
S136	**50 Sucres** 30.1.1922; 23.10.1923. Green and pink. Three allegorical seated women at center. Printer: W&S.	—	—	—

NOTE: For #S136 overprint: *CAJA CENTRAL...* See #S287. Other denominations reported for this bank include 1, 10, 20, 100 and 1000 Sucres.

Banco del Ecuador

1868 Provisional Issue

#S137A-S137D overprint on notes of Banco de Circulación y Descuento de Manuel Antonio de Luzarraga.

		Good	Fine	XF
S137A	**1 Peso** 1.10.1868. Black on orange underprint. Luzarraga at lower left, allegorical woman and plants ("Tropiccs") at upper center, woman at lower right. Overprint: On #S111.	—	—	—
S137B	**4 Pesos** 1.10.1868. Black on blue underprint. Sailor at lower left, eagle at upper center right. Overprint: On #S112.	—	—	—
S137C	**5 Pesos** 1.10.1868. Black on yellow-orange underprint. Portrait girl at upper left, seated woman with tablet and child ("History") at upper center right. Overprint: On #S114.	—	—	—
S137D	**10 Pesos** 1.10.1868. Black on green underprint. Statue of Freedom at left, seated woman with globe ("Science") at upper center right. Overprint: On #S115.	—	—	—

1870's Issue

		Good	Fine	XF
S138	**2 Reales** 187x. Black on orange underprint. Sailor and anchor at left, woman at right. Printer: ABNC.	—	Unc	500.
S138A	**2 Reales** 187x. Black on green underprint. Sailor and anchor at left, woman at right. Like #S138. Printer: ABNC. Proof.	—	Unc	600.
S139	**4 Reales** 187x. Black on green underprint. Two seated allegorical women at upper center. Back: Green. Printer: ABNC. Proof.	—	Unc	1500.
S141	**1 Peso** 15.12.1870; 21.12.1871; 7.6.1872; 1.10.1872. Brown and blue. Portrait Simón Bolívar at left, seated Minerva at right. Back: Orange, blue and brown. Rare.	—	Unc	750.
S141A	**1 Peso** 1.10.1872. Black and red. Portrait Simón Bolívar at left, seated Minerva at right. Like #S141. Back: Green and violet. Rare.	—	Unc	750.
S141B	**10 Pesos** 18xx. Violet and green. Portrait Simón Bolívar left center, seated Minerva right center. Back: Blue and brown. Proof.	—	Unc	750.
S141C	**10 Pesos** 18xx. Brown and green. Portrait Simón Bolívar left center, seated Minerva right center. Similar to #S141B but for colors. Proof.	—	Unc	900.
S141D	**20 Pesos** 18xx. Green and brown. Portrait Simón Bolívar left center, seated Minerva right center. Similar to #S141B. Back: Brown and blue. Proof.	—	Unc	1000.

1874 Issues

#S142-S164

#S142-S143D originally issued with hand stamps: *BANCO DEL ECUADOR and REPÚBLICA DEL ECUADOR-MINISTERIO DE HACIENDA* on back. Later issued w/only hand stamp: *MINISTERIO.*

		Good	Fine	XF
S142	**1 Peso** 2.1.1874. Black on green and orange underprint. Two sailors at lower left, steam train at center, woman at lower right. Series A. Back: Orange. Printer: ABNC.	100.	300.	—
S142B	**1 Peso** 2.1.1874. Black on salmon and green underprint. Two sailors at lower left, steam train at center, woman at lower right. Series B. Like #S142. Back: Green. Printer: ABNC. Archive copy.	—	Unc	500.
S142C	**1 Peso** 2.1.1874. Black on magenta and brown underprint. Two sailors at lower left, steam train at center, woman at lower right. Series C. Like #S142. Back: Magenta. Printer: ABNC.	—	—	—
S142D	**1 Peso** 2.1.1874. Black on red and green underprint. Two sailors at lower left, steam train at center, woman at lower right. Series D. Like #S142. Back: Purple. Printer: ABNC.			
	a. Issued note.	100.	300.	—
	p. Proof.	—	Unc	1000.
S143	**5 Pesos** 2.1.1874. Black on orange and olive underprint. Tree, shovel, basket and sacks at left, allegorical woman with barrels and crate at center, allegorical woman with cherub and produce at right. Series A. Back: Green. Printer: ABNC. Archive copy.	—	Unc	750.
S143B	**5 Pesos** 2.1.1874. Black on blue and orange underprint. Tree, shovel, basket and sacks at left, allegorical woman with barrels and crate at center, allegorical woman with cherub and produce at right. Series B. Like #S143. Back: Salmon. Printer: ABNC. Archive copy.	—	Unc	750.

S143C 5 Pesos — Good | Fine | XF

2.1.1874. Black on dark green and light orange underprint. Tree, shovel, basket and sacks at left, allegorical woman with barrels and crate at center, allegorical woman with cherub and produce at right. Series C. Like #S143. Back: Purple. Printer: ABNC. Specimen, punched hole cancelled. — | Unc | 600.

S143D 5 Pesos

2.1.1874. Black on orange and blue-gray underprint. Tree, shovel, basket and sacks at left, allegorical woman with barrels and crate at center, allegorical woman with cherub and produce at right. Series D. Like #S143. Back: Red. Printer: ABNC. Archive copy. — | Unc | 750.

1880; 1884 Issue

#S144-S145 issued with hand stamp: *MINISTERIO DE HACIENDA.*

S144 1 Peso — Good | Fine | XF

11.1880-26.5.1886. Black on blue and red underprint. Helmeted female ("Minerva No. 2") at left, woman with cornucopia ("Plenty") at center, "Mercury" at right. With handstamp: *MINISTERIO DE HACIENDA.* Back: Blue. Printer: ABNC. 125. | 400. | —

S145 5 Pesos

1.4.1884; 22.10.1884; 30.5.1887. Black on orange and green underprint. Local arms at left, reclining allegorical woman ("L'Orient") at center. With handstamp: *MINISTERIO DE HACIENDA.* Back: Brown. Printer: ABNC. — | — | —

NOTE: Denominations of 10, 20, 100 and 500 Pesos are reported for one or two full issues.

ND Provisional Issue

#S147 and S148 new currency system values overprint on face in words at left. Each old peso from this bank equalled 80 centavos (80%) of the new sucre.

S147 80 Centavos on 1 Peso — Good | Fine | XF

ND (- old dates 1.2.1886; 22.3.1886; 26.5.1886). Black on blue and red underprint. Helmeted female ("Minerva No. 2") at left, woman with cornucopia ("Plenty") at center, "Mercury" at right. With handstamp: *MINISTERIO DE HACIENDA.* Back: Blue. Overprint: New currency system values on face in words at left on #S144. Printer: ABNC.

a. Issued note. Rare. — | — | —
p. Proof. — | Unc | 2500.

S148 4 Sucres on 5 Pesos — Good | Fine | XF

ND (- old dates 14.8.1885; 30.5.1887). Black on orange and green underprint. Local arms at left, reclining allegorical woman ("L'Orient") at center. With handstamp: *MINISTERIO DE HACIENDA.* Back: Brown. Overprint: New currency system values on face in words at left on #S145. Printer: ABNC. Rare. — | — | —

1887-1926 Regular Issues

S151 1 Sucre — Good | Fine | XF

1887-1901. Black on red and green underprint. Boy with caduceus and fish ("Off Sandy Hook") at center with ship in background. Back: Green. Printer: ABNC.

a. 13.7.1887-9.5.1894 handwritten dates. *CAPITAL S/1,200,000.* 75.00 | 150. | —
b. 1.9.1894. *CAPITAL S/2,000,000.* 75.00 | 200. | —
c. 1.10.1901 printed date. Also *CAPITAL S/2,000,000.* 50.00 | 100. | 350.
p. Proof. — | Unc | 850.

S152 2 Sucres

12.12.1901. Black on blue underprint. Ships at center. Back: Dark blue. Printer: ABNC.

a. *CAPITAL S/2,000,000.* 100. | 300. | —
b. *CAPITAL S/3,000,000.* 100. | 300. | —

S152A 2 Sucres

Black on light orange underprint. Seated woman with bales and caduceus ("Commerce") at center. Series C. Like #S153. Back: Brown. Printer: ABNC. Archive copy. 100. | 300. | —

S153 2 Sucres

1.12.1907. Black on light orange underprint. Seated woman with bales and caduceus ("Commerce") at center. Series E; J. Back: Orange. Printer: ABNC.

a. Issued note. 50.00 | 200. | 600.
p. Proof. — | Unc | 850.

S154 2 Sucres

1.12.1907. Black on light orange underprint. Seated woman with bales and caduceus ("Commerce") at center. Series D. Like #S153. Back: Olive. Printer: ABNC. 50.00 | 200. | 600.

S154A 2 Sucres

Black on light orange underprint. Seated woman with bales and caduceus ("Commerce") at center. Series F. Like #S153. Back: Green. Printer: ABNC. Archive copy. — | — | —

S155 2 Sucres

2.1.1911. Black on light orange underprint. Seated woman with bales and caduceus ("Commerce") at center. Series G. Like #S153. Back: Blue. Printer: Blue.

a. Issued note. 50.00 | 200. | 600.
p. Proof. — | Unc | 750.

S156 2 Sucres

2.1.1911. Black on light orange underprint. Seated woman with bales and caduceus ("Commerce") at center. Series H. Like #S153. Back: Red-orange. Printer: ABNC. 50.00 | 200. | 600.

S156A 2 Sucres — Good | Fine | XF

Black on light orange underprint. Seated woman with bales and caduceus ("Commerce") at center. Series J. Like #S153. Back: Brown. Printer: ABNC. Archive copy. — | — | —

S157 2 Sucres

2.1.1911. Black on light orange underprint. Seated woman with bales and caduceus ("Commerce") at center. Series K. Like #S153. Back: Red-brown. Printer: ABNC.

a. Issued note. 50.00 | 200. | 600.
p. Proof. — | Unc | 950.

S157A 5 Sucres

18xx (ca.1892). Black on orange, yellow and salmon underprint. Sailor at left, portrait woman ("Majesty No. 3") at left center, seated allegorical woman with two children ("Peace") at right. Similar to #S158, but with *CAPITAL S/2,000,000.* Back: Orange. Printer: ABNC. Archive copy. — | — | —

S157B 5 Sucres

18xx. Black on orange, yellow and salmon underprint. Sailor at left, portrait woman ("Majesty No. 3") at left center, seated allegorical woman with two children ("Peace") at right. *CAPITAL S/2,000,000.* Like #S157A. Back: Green. Printer: ABNC. — | — | —

S158 5 Sucres

16.8.1899; 30.7.1919; 15.3.1926. Black on orange underprint. Sailor at left, portrait woman ("Majesty No. 3") at left center, seated allegorical woman with two children ("Peace") at right. *CAPITAL S/3,000,000.* Back: Green. Printer: ABNC.

a. Issued note. 90.00 | 400. | —
p. Proof in black. — | Unc | 750.

S158A 5 Sucres

19xx. Black on orange underprint. Sailor at left, portrait woman ("Majesty No. 3") at left center, seated allegorical woman with two children ("Peace") at right. *CAPITAL S/3,000,000.* Like #S158. Back: Red. Printer: ABNC. — | — | —

S159 10 Sucres

5.5.1902; 6.9.1912; 8.10.1920. Black on orange underprint. Woman with board and child ("Study") at left. Back: Orange. Woman at center. Printer: ABNC.

a. Issued note. — | — | —
p. Proof. — | Unc | 1500.

S160 20 Sucres

3.9.1898; 19xx. Black on green and brown underprint. Sailing ship at lower left, seated man shearing sheep ("South American Sheep Shearing") at center, two standing men at lower right. Back: Brown. Printer: ABNC. — | — | —

S161 50 Sucres

15.3.1926. Black on yellow and brown underprint. Ox-drawn cart at center. Back: Brown. Ornamented head at center. Printer: ABNC.

a. Issued note. — | — | —
p. Proof. — | Unc | 2000.

S161A 100 Sucres

18xx. Black on blue and orange underprint. Allegorical woman reclining ("Literature No. 2") at left, griffins at left and center right, horse's head ("Horse's Head No. 1") at right. Similar to #S162, but with *CAPITAL S/1,200,000.* Back: Orange. Printer: ABNC. Proof. — | — | —

S162 100 Sucres

15.3.1926. Black on blue and red underprint. Allegorical woman reclining ("Literature No. 2") at left, griffins at left and center right, horse's head ("Horse's Head No. 1") at right. *CAPITAL S/3,000,000.* Back: Brown. Printer: ABNC.

a. Issued note. Rare. — | — | —
s. Specimen. — | Unc | 1250.

S163 500 Sucres

18xx; 1911. Black on red and green underprint. Seated allegorical woman seated ("Arts") at upper left, allegorical woman holding ship at right. Back: Green. Printer: ABNC. Specimen. — | Unc | 1750.

S164 1000 Sucres

12.4.1926. Black on orange underprint. Allegorical woman at left. Back: Orange. Liberty at center. Printer: ABNC.

a. Issued note. — | — | —
p. Proof. — | Unc | 2750.

ND Issue

S167 100 Pesos

18xx. Green and red. Simon Bolivar at left, seated figure at right. Remainder. Local printer. — | — | —

Banco Internacional

1886-94 Issue

S171 1 Sucre — Good | Fine | XF

17.5.1887 (stamped); 11.3.1889; 1.3.1891; 1.5.1891 (handwritten). Black on yellow underprint. Portrait Antonio José de Sucre at left, arms at right. Narrow margins. Back: Blue. Printer: W&S.

a. Issued note. 125. | 300. | —
s. Specimen. Red back. — | Unc | 500.

S172 1 Sucre

18xx; also 10.11.1892. Black on green underprint. Portrait Antonio José de Sucre at left, arms at right. Similar to #S171 but with modified portrait details. Wide margins. Series B/A; G/A. Back: Brown. Paper: Pink. Printer: W&S. Unissued remainder. — | Unc | 25.00

S173 1 Sucre

10.11.1892. Black on green underprint. Portrait Antonio José de Sucre at left, arms at right. Like #S172. Back: Brown. Printer: W&S. — | — | —

S174 5 Sucres

1885-93. Black on pink underprint. J. J. Olmedo at left, arms at center. Printer: W&S.

a. Issued note. 14.2.1885; 5.11.1885; 6.6.1893. — | — | —
p. Proof. — | Unc | 300.

S175 10 Sucres

18xx; 6.6.1893. Vicente Rocafuerte at left, arms at right. Printer: W&S. Proof. — | Unc | 300.

S176 20 Sucres

2.8.1894. Arms at left. Printer: W&S. — | — | —

		Good	Fine	XF
S178	**100 Sucres**			
	2.8.1893. Arms at left, Abdón Calderón at center. Printer: W&S.	—	—	—
S179	**500 Sucres**			
	18xx. Blue and yellow. Standing Liberty with pole at center, arms at lower right. Printer: W&S.	—	—	—

		Good	Fine	XF
S179A	**1000 Sucres**			
	18xx. Black on yellow and orange underprint. Standing Simón Bolívar statue at left, arms with cherub supporters at center. Printer: W&S. Proof.	—	Unc	1250.

Banco de Londres y Ecuador

1880's Issue

		Good	Fine	XF
S180	**1 Sucre**			
	18xx (ca. 1887). Black on green underprint. London arms at left, Ecuadorian arms at right. Back: Green. Sucre Theater at center. Printer: ABNC.			
	p. Proof.	—	Unc	1500.
	s. Series B. Specimen.	—	Unc	2000.
S181	**5 Sucres**			
	18xx (ca.1887). Black on blue underprint. London arms at left, Ecuadorian arms at right. Back: Blue. National Palace at center. Printer: ABNC.			
	p. Proof.	—	Unc	1500.
	s. Series A. Specimen.	—	Unc	2000.
S182	**10 Sucres**			
	18xx (ca.1887). Black on orange underprint. London arms at left, Ecuadorian arms at right. "Raphael's Angel" at center. Back: Orange. Road and town scene at center. Printer: ABNC.			
	p. Proof.	—	Unc	1500.
	s. Specimen.	—	Unc	2000.

Banco Nacional

1871 Provisional Issue

		Good	Fine	XF
S183	**2 Pesos**			
	1.3.1871. Overprint: Dark green vertical bank name, city and issue date at left on Banco Nacional de Costa Rica #S210. Rare.	—	—	—

NOTE: Other similarly overprinted values require confirmation.

1871 Regular Issue

		Good	Fine	XF
S186	**2 Reales**			
	187x. Black on brown underprint. Young girl at lower left and cherub at lower right, arms at center. Back: Brown. Printer: ABNC. Proof.	—	Unc	950.
S187	**4 Reales**			
	187x. Liberty at lower left, head of girl at center, arms at lower right. Printer: ABNC.			
	p1. Black on green underprint. Proof.	—	Unc	950.
	p2. Black on blue underprint. Back blue. Proof.	—	—	—
S187A	**4 Reales**			
	187x. Black on blue underprint. Like #S187, but young Indian girl at upper center. Back: Blue. Printer: ABNC. Archive copy.	—	—	—
S191	**1 Peso**			
	9.8.1871. Black on brown underprint. Four cherubs holding denomination numeral at left, reclining allegorical woman at center, arms at lower right. Back: Brown. Printer: ABNC.	—	—	—
S193	**5 Pesos**			
	187x. Black on green underprint. Arms at lower left, five cherubs holding denomination numeral at center, woman at lower right. Back: Green. Printer: ABNC.	—	—	—
S194	**10 Pesos**			
	187x. Black on orange underprint. Arms at left, allegorical woman with coins and marine implements at center, Justice at right. Back: Orange. Printer: ABNC. Archive copy.	—	—	—
S195	**20 Pesos**			
	187x. Black on blue underprint. Boy with staff and sheep ("St. John the Baptist") at lower left, allegorical woman holding staff and bird with foliage behind ("Tropics") at center, arms at right. Back: Blue. Printer: ABNC. Proof.	—	—	—
S195A	**100 Pesos**			
	187x. Black on purple underprint. Condor with wings spread at left, arms at center, portrait woman's head at right. Back: Purple. Printer: ABNC. Specimen.	—	—	—

Banco Particular de Descuento I Circulación de Guayaquil

1862-66 Issues

		Good	Fine	XF
S196	**2 Reales**			
	1.4.1865; 1.4.1866. Black on green underprint. Arms at center. Uniface. Printer: ABNC.			
	a. Issued note.	90.00	—	—
	p. Proof.	—	Unc	750.
S197	**4 Reales**			
	18xx. Black on green underprint. Arms at center. Uniface. Printer: ABNC.			
	p. Proof.	—	Unc	750.
	s. Series A. Specimen.	—	—	—
S198	**1 Peso**			
	1.6.1862. Black. Condor over arms at left, plants at right.	—	—	—
S199	**1 Peso**			
	5.9.1864.	—	—	—

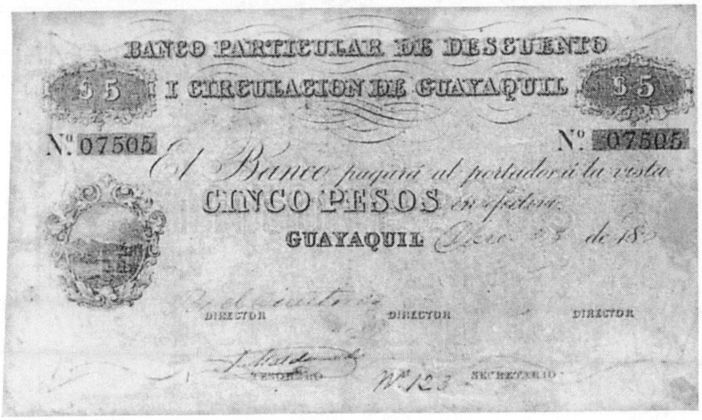

		Good	Fine	XF
S200	**5 Pesos**			
	23.12.1862. Boats along shoreline in ornate frame at left.	600.	—	—

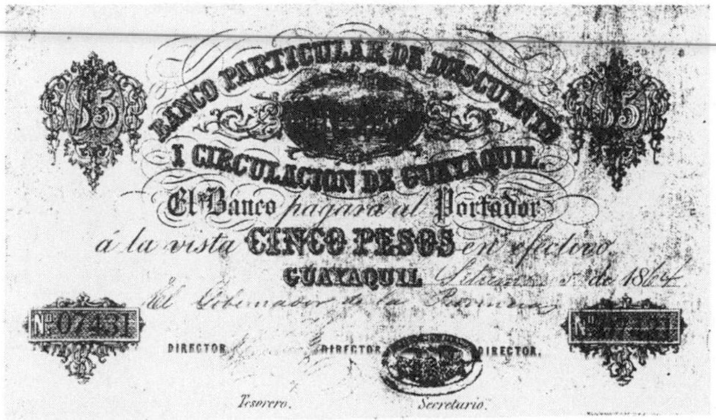

		Good	Fine	XF
S201	**5 Pesos**			
	5.9.1864. Black on brown underprint. Shoreline scene at upper center. Back: Red. Printer: Wm. Brown.	—	—	—

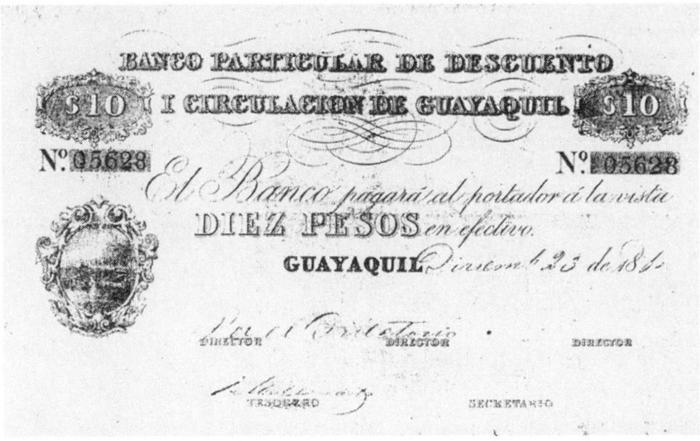

		Good	Fine	XF
S202	**10 Pesos**			
	23.12.1862. Black on brown underprint. Boats along shoreline in ornate frame at left.	—	—	—
S202A	**10 Pesos**			
	5.9.1864.	—	—	—
S203	**20 Pesos**			
	23.12.1862; 5.9.1864. Black on brown underprint. Boats along shoreline in ornate frame at left. Similar to #S202.	—	—	—
S204	**50 Pesos**			
	5.9.1864.	—	—	—
S205	**100 Pesos**			
	5.9.1864.	—	—	—

NOTE: An issue of compulsory acceptance notes using forms of the Banco Particular de Descuento y Circulación de Guayaquil is reported in denominations of 1, 5, 10, 20, 50 and 100 Pesos. Date is 23.12.1862.

Banco del Pichincha

1907-08 Issue

		Good	Fine	XF
S211	**1 Sucre**			
	1907-10. Black and brown. Train at left, helmeted woman at center right. Back: Green. Printer: W&S.			
	a. Overprint: *Compania Anonima Capital S/600,000.* 15.4.1907-8.1.1908.	70.00	225.	—
	b. Overprint: *Capital S/845,000.* 31.1.1910; 18.2.1910; 21.11.1910	70.00	225.	—
	c. ND. Blue and olive green. Back brown. Specimen.	—	—	—

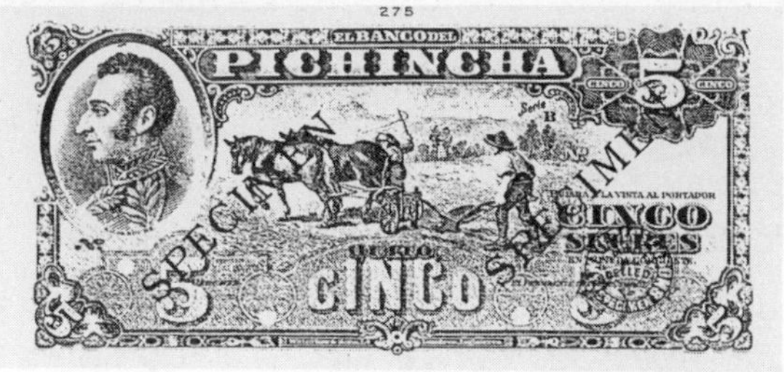

	Good	Fine	XF
S212 5 Sucres 1907; ND. Portrait Antonio José de Sucre at upper left, farmer plowing with horses at center. Printer: W&S.			
a. 29.5.1907.	—	—	—
s. ND. Blue and pink. Back brown. Specimen.	—	—	—
S213 10 Sucres 1908; ND. Seated woman with shield at left. Printer: W&S.			
a. 29.5.1907.	—	—	—
s. ND. Brown and lilac. Back green.	—	—	—
S214 20 Sucres ca.1907. Printer: W&S. Specimen.	—	—	—

NOTE: #S212-S214 with Capital S845,000 require confirmation.

1912-15 Issues

	Good	Fine	XF
S220 1 Sucre ND (ca.1912-14). Black on tan underprint. Portrait man at left. Like #S221. *CAPITAL S/1,000,000.* Back: Olive. Reclining woman playing mandolin at center. Printer: ABNC.			
a. Issued note.	—	—	—
p. Proof.	—	—	—
s. Specimen.	—	Unc	800.
S221 1 Sucre 30.4.1914. Green. Portrait man at left. Back: Olive Reclining woman playing mandolin at center. Printer: ABNC.	—	—	—

NOTE: For #S221 dated 1926 and overprint: *CAJA CENTRAL...* See #S281.

NOTE: Capitalization amount for #S221 needs confirmation.

	Good	Fine	XF
S221A 1 Sucre 20.11.1916; 4.1.1918. Black. Portrait man at left. Like #S221. *CAPITAL S/1,500,000.* Back: Olive. Reclining woman playing mandolin at center. Printer: ABNC.			
p. Proof.	—	—	—
s. Specimen.	—	Unc	650.
S222 1 Sucre 1920-24. Black on brown underprint. Portrait man at left. Like #S221. Back: Olive. Reclining woman playing mandolin at center. Printer: ABNC.			
a. 9.3.1920; 6.8.1920; 6.4.1921; 21.10.1921.	25.00	85.00	150.
b. 2.1.1922; 3.4.1922; 5.4.1922; 18.5.1922; 23.5.1922; 7.11.1922; 17.11.1923; 17.12.1924; 19.12.1924.	20.00	75.00	175.
p. Proof.	—	Unc	1250.
S223 5 Sucres 1912-20. Black on green underprint. Portrait man at center. Back: Green. Woman and globe at center. Printer: ABNC.			
a. 14.10.1912; 14.12.1912.	100.	400.	—
b. 8.1.1917; 9.3.1920; 6.8.1920.	100.	400.	—
p. Proof.	—	Unc	1250.
s. Specimen.	—	Unc	1250.
S224 10 Sucres ND (ca.1912-14) - 1921. Black on orange and yellow underprint. Condor at right. Back: Orange. Allegorical woman holding paddle, cherub at center. Printer: ABNC.			
a. 15.10.1915; 8.1.1917; 7.2.1917.	—	—	—
b. 6.4.1921.	—	—	—
p. ND (ca.1912-14). *CAPITAL S/1,000,000.* Proof.	—	Unc	1250.
s. Specimen.	—	Unc	1250.
S225 20 Sucres ND (ca.1912-14) - 1921. Black on green underprint. Women at left and right of arms at left center. Back: Blue. Men with oxen team at center. Printer: ABNC.			
a. 9.3.1920; 6.8.1920; 19.11.1921.	—	—	—
p. ND (ca.1912-14). *CAPITAL S/1,000,000.* Proof.	—	Unc	1250.
s. Specimen.	—	Unc	1250.
S226 50 Sucres ND (ca.1912-14) - 1921. Black on gold and brown underprint. Allegorical woman seated with globe and lute ("Urania") at left center. Back: Green. Commerce seated with condor and circular scene at center. Printer: ABNC.			
a. 9.3.1920; 6.4.1921.	—	—	—
p. ND (ca.1912-14). *CAPITAL S/1,000,000.* Proof.	—	Unc	1250.
s. Specimen.	—	Unc	1500.
S227 100 Sucres ND (ca.1912-14) - 1922. Black on yellow and green underprint. Woman with produce in sacks and barrels at center right. Back: Brown. Printer: ABNC.			
a. 9.3.1920; 9.11.1921; 19.11.1921; 2.1.1922.	—	—	—
p. ND (ca.1912-14). *CAPITAL S/1,000,000.* Proof.	—	Unc	1250.
s. Specimen.	—	Unc	1750.

NOTE: Issues for 1912-14 have imprint or overprint: *CAPITAL S/1,000,000;* from 1915-17 *CAPITAL S/1,500,000* (some with *CAPITAL S/2,500,000);* from 1920-21 *CAPITAL S/3,000,000;* from 1922-24 *CAPITAL S/4,000,000.*

Banco de Quito

1870s ND Issue

	Good	Fine	XF
S231 2 Reales ND. Black on green underprint. Men with water pitchers at fountain in town at left. Uniface. Back: Two stampings. Printer: NBNC. Proof.	—	—	—

1874-78 Issue

	Good	Fine	XF
S236 1 Peso 1.12.1874; 1.1.1875; 4.3.1875; 1.2.1878; 1.7.1878. Black on orange underprint. Portrait woman in shawl at left, arms at top center, portrait Indian at right. Back: Blue. Printer: CS&E.			
a. Issued note.	—	—	—
s. Specimen (unfinished date).	—	—	—

NOTE: Additional denominations in this series (2, 5, 10, 20, 50 and 100 Pesos) require confirmation.

1880 Issue

	Good	Fine	XF
S241 1 Peso 2.1.1880. Horseman with pack horse at upper left. Printer: ABNC.			
a. Black on tan underprint. Back brown. Issued note.	—	—	—
p1. Black on orange underprint. Back blue. Proof.	—	—	—
p2. Black on pink underprint. Proof.	—	—	—
S242 5 Pesos 2.1.1880. Black on orange underprint. Woman with sheaf and sickle seated at left, woman with wheel ("Fortune") seated at right. Back: Brown. Printer: ABNC.			
p. Proof.	—	—	—
s. Specimen.	—	—	—
S243 10 Pesos 2.1.1880. Black on blue underprint. Female seated with sheaf and sickle ("Agriculture") at left, woman with spool ("Industry") at right. Back: Orange. Printer: ABNC.			
p. Proof.	—	—	—
s. Specimen.	—	—	—
S244 20 Pesos 2.1.1880. Black on green underprint. Seated woman ("Study") at left, reclining woman and globe ("Science") at center right. Back: Red-orange. Printer: ABNC.			
p. Proof.	—	—	—
s. Specimen.	—	—	—
S245 100 Pesos 2.1.1880. Black on brown underprint. Standing Justice at left, arms at left center, Christopher Columbus landing ("Columbus") at right. Back: Deep green. Printer: ABNC.			
p. Proof.	—	—	—
s. Specimen.	—	—	—

1885 Issue

	Good	Fine	XF
S246 1 Sucre 1.1.1885. Black on brown underprint. Portrait Antonio José de Sucre at upper left, Raphael's Angel at upper center right, arms at lower right. Back: Red-orange. Printer: ABNC.			
a. Issued note.	—	—	—
p. Proof.	—	Unc	1250.
s. Specimen.	—	Unc	500.

NOTE: Additional denominations in this series (2, 5, 10, 20, 50 and 100 Sucres) require confirmation.

Banco Sur Americano

1920 Issue

	Good	Fine	XF
S251 1 Sucre 2.1.1920. Black on orange underprint. Condor at left. Back: Brown. Sailing ships at center.			
a. Issued note.	—	—	—
r. Remainder without serial # or signature	—	Unc	1.00
S252 5 Sucres 2.1.1920. Black on yellow underprint. Christopher Columbus on ship deck in sight of land at left. Back: Blue. Standing woman with fasces at center.			
a. Issued note.	—	—	—
r. Remainder without serial # or signature	3.00	6.00	15.00
S252A 10 Sucres 2.1.1920.	—	—	—

	VG	VF	UNC
S253 20 Sucres 2.1.1920. Black. Seated Christopher Columbus with anchor, globe and arms at left. Back: Blue. Men in rowboat heading towards shore at center. Remainder without serial # or signature.			
a. Pink underprint.	.50	1.00	2.00
b. Without underprint.	.75	2.00	3.50
S253A 50 Sucres 2.1.1920.	—	—	—

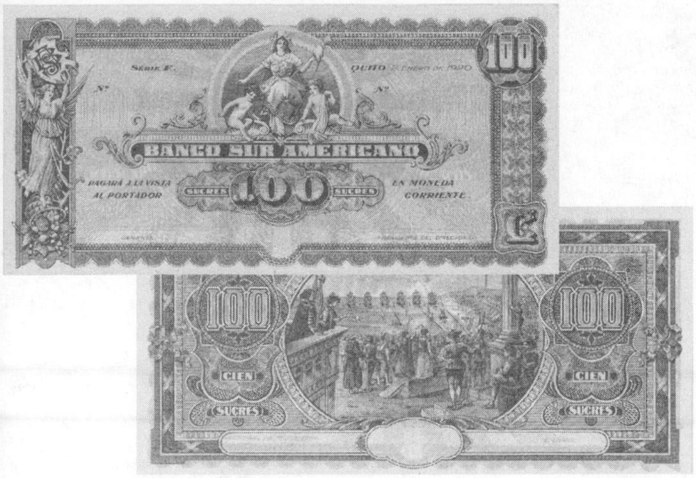

	VG	VF	UNC
S254 100 Sucres 2.1.1920. Black on blue underprint. Woman standing on cornucopia and holding monogram scroll at left, woman and two children at center. Back: Slate-blue. Crowd welcoming returing ships at center. Remainder.	.75	1.50	4.00

Compañia de Crédito Agrícola e Industrial

1921 Issue

NOTE: For #S272 and #S274 dated 1926 with overprint: *CAJA CENTRAL. . .* see #S282 and S284.

	Good	Fine	XF
S272 2 Sucres 2.1.1921; 5.4.1921. Black on multicolor underprint. Reclining allegorical woman with globe (Commerce) at center. Back: Orange. Printer: ABNC.			
a. Issued note.	100.	400.	—
p. Proof.	—	Unc	1000.
s. Specimen.	—	Unc	1000.
S274 10 Sucres 5.4.1921. Black on multicolor underprint. Allegorical man with scythe and sheaf at left, allegorical woman holding ship at right. Back: Brown. Printer: ABNC.			
a. Issued note.	—	—	—
p. Proof.	—	Unc	1000.
s. Specimen.	—	Unc	1250.

Banco de la Unión

1880's Issue

	Good	Fine	XF
S261 1 Peso 2.1.1882. Black on green underprint. Presidential palace at center, "Mercury" at right. Back: Green. Printer: ABNC.			
a. Issued note.	—	—	—
p. Proof.	—	Unc	1000.
S262 5 Pesos 18xx. Black on dark orange underprint. Street scene at left, two cherubs at center right. Back: Dark orange. Printer: ABNC.			
p. Proof.	—	Unc	1100.
s. Specimen.	—	Unc	1250.
S263 10 Pesos 12.10.1887. Black on brown underprint. Cathedral at left, seated allegorical woman with sheaves and sheep at upper center right. Back: Brown. Printer: ABNC.			
p. Proof.	—	—	—
s. Specimen.	—	Unc	11,250.
S264 20 Pesos 18xx. Black on blue underprint. San Francisco Church at center, woman ("May") at right. Back: Blue. Printer: ABNC.			
p. Proof.	—	—	—
s. Specimen.	—	Unc	1750.
S264A 100 Pesos 18xx. Black on orange underprint. Statue of Freedom at left, Jesuit church at center, ram at right. Back: Orange. Printer: ABNC.			
p. Proof.	—	—	—
s. Specimen.	—	Unc	1750.

1887 Provisional Issue

New value overprint on face of older issue.

	Good	Fine	XF
S265 1 Sucre 12.9.1887; 12.10.1887; 14.8.1893. Black on green underprint. Presidential palace at center, "Mercury" at right. Back: Green. Overprint: New value in red at upper center on face of #S261. Printer: ABNC.	—	—	—
S266 5 Sucres (ca.1887.) Black on dark orange underprint. Street scene at left, two cherubs at center right. Back: Dark orange. Overprint: New value on face of #S262. Printer: ABNC.	—	—	—
S267 10 Sucres 12.10.1887. Black on brown underprint. Cathedral at left, seated allegorical woman with sheaves and sheep at upper center right. Back: Brown. Overprint: New value on face of #S263. Printer: ABNC.	—	—	—

1893-94 Regular Issue

	Good	Fine	XF
S268 1 Sucre 12.4.1894; 27.5.1895; 27.12.1895. Black on green underprint. Presidential palace at center, "Mercury" at right. Like #S261. Back: Green. Printer: ABNC.	—	—	—
S269 5 Sucres 14.8.1893; 28.6.1895. Black on dark orange underprint. Street scene at left, two cherubs at center right. Like #S262. Back: Dark orange. Printer: ABNC.	—	—	—
S270 10 Sucres 18xx. Black on brown underprint. Cathedral at left, seated allegorical woman with sheaves and sheep at upper center right. Like #S263. Back: Brown. Printer: ABNC.	—	—	—
S271 20 Sucres 12.1.1893. Black on blue underprint. San Francisco Church at center, woman ("May") at right. Like #S264. Back: Blue. Printer: ABNC.	—	—	—
S271A 100 Sucres 18xx. Black on orange underprint. Statue of Freedom at left, Jesuit church at center, ram at right. Like #S264A. Back: Orange. Printer: ABNC. Proof.	—	—	—

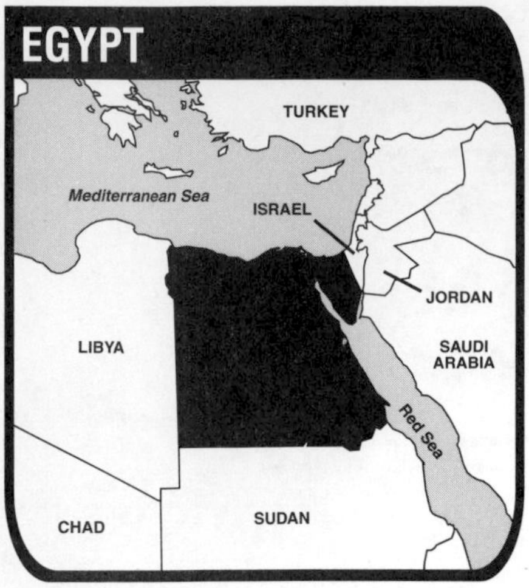

The Arab Republic of Egypt, located on the northeastern corner of Africa, has an area of 1,001,450 sq. km. and a population of 81.71 million. Capital: Cairo. Although Egypt is an almost rainless expanse of desert, its economy is predominantly agricultural. Cotton, rice and petroleum are exported.

The regularity and richness of the annual Nile River flood, coupled with semi-isolation provided by deserts to the east and west, allowed for the development of one of the world's great civilizations. A unified kingdom arose circa 3200 B.C., and a series of dynasties ruled in Egypt for the next three millennia. The last native dynasty fell to the Persians in 341 B.C., who in turn were replaced by the Greeks, Romans, and Byzantines. It was the Arabs who introduced Islam and the Arabic language in the 7th century and who ruled for the next six centuries. A local military caste, the Mamluks took control about 1250 and continued to govern after the conquest of Egypt by the Ottoman Turks in 1517. Following the completion of the Suez Canal in 1869, Egypt became an important world transportation hub, but also fell heavily into debt. Ostensibly to protect its investments, Britain seized control of Egypt's government in 1882, but nominal allegiance to the Ottoman Empire continued until 1914. Partially independent from the UK in 1922, Egypt acquired full sovereignty with the overthrow of the British-backed monarchy in 1952. The completion of the Aswan High Dam in 1971 and the resultant Lake Nasser have altered the time-honored place of the Nile River in the agriculture and ecology of Egypt. A rapidly growing population (the largest in the Arab world), limited arable land, and dependence on the Nile all continue to overtax resources and stress society. The government has struggled to meet the demands of Egypt's growing population through economic reform and massive investment in communications and physical infrastructure.

RULERS:

"OTTOMAN
Abdul Mejid, AH1255-1277, 1839-1861AD
Abdul Aziz, AH1277-1293, 1861-1876AD
Abdul Hamid II, AH1293-1327, 1876-1909AD
"EGYPTIAN
Muhammad V, AH1327-1332, 1909-1914AD
Hussein Kamil, AH1334-1336, 1915-1917AD
Fuad I (Sultan), AH1336-1341, 1917-1922AD
Fuad I (King), AH1341-1355, 1922-1936AD
Farouk I, AH1355-1372, 1936-1952AD

MONETARY SYSTEM:

1 Piastre = 10 Ochr-El-Guerches
1 Pound = 100 Piastres, to 1916
1 Piastre (Guerche) = 10 Milliemes
1 Pound (Junayh) = 100 Piastres, 1916-

Ottoman Administration

Bank of Egypt

1850's Issue

		Good	Fine	XF
S121	**1000 Piastres** 18xx. Pyramid between palm trees behind sphinx and supported arms at top center. Uniface specimen.	—	Unc	2500.

Italian Occupation - WW II

Cassa Mediterranea di Credito per l'Egitto

1942 ND Issue

NOTE: Only one complete specimen set is known. For similar notes w/*PER IL SVDAN* refer to Sudan #M1-M8; for similar notes w/*CASSA MEDITERRANEA...LA GRECIA* refer to Greece #M1-M9.

		VG	VF	UNC
M1	**5 Piastre** ND (1942). Purple on blue. Bust of Apollo at right. Back: Stylized grain at left.			
	a. Issued note. Rare.	—	—	—
	s. Specimen.	—	—	2500.
M2	**10 Piastre** ND (1942). Red-orange. Bust of Apollo at right. Back: Stylized ancient galley prows at left.			
	a. Issued note. Rare.	—	—	—
	s. Specimen.	—	—	2500.

		VG	VF	UNC
M3	**50 Piastre** ND (1942). Red-orange. Portrait Emperor Octavian at left.			
	a. Issued note. Rare.	—	—	—
	s. Specimen.	—	—	2500.
M4	**1 Lira** ND (1942). Dull purple and dark brown on ochre underprint. Portrait Emperor Octavian at left.			
	a. Issued note. Rare.	—	—	—
	s. Specimen.	—	—	2500.

		VG	VF	UNC
M5	**5 Lire** ND (1942). Dark brown and purple on ochre underprint. Portrait Emperor Octavian at left.			
	a. Issued note. Rare.	—	—	—
	s. Specimen.	—	—	2500.
M6	**10 Lire** ND (1942). Violet and purple. Portrait Emperor Octavian at left. Specimen.	—	—	2500.

		VG	VF	UNC
M7	**50 Lire** ND (1942). Dark gray on light gray underprint. Portrait David (by Michelangelo) at left.			
	a. Issued note. Rare.	—	—	—
	s. Specimen.	—	—	2500.
M8	**100 Lire** ND (1942). Portrait David (by Michelangelo) at left.			
	a. Issued note. Rare.	—	—	—
	s. Specimen.	—	—	2500.

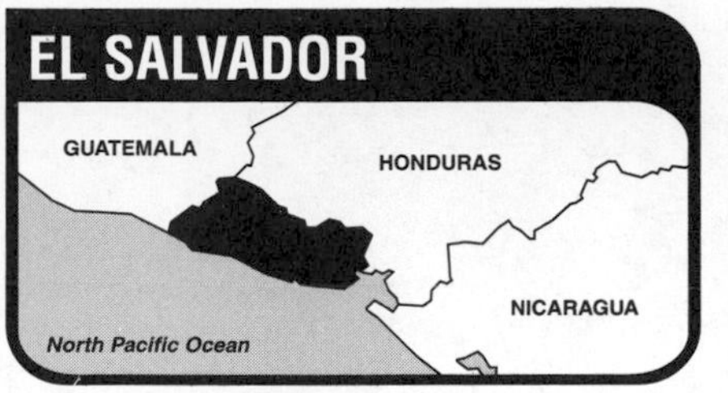

The Republic of El Salvador, a Central American country bordered by Guatemala, Honduras and the Pacific Ocean, has an area of 21,040 sq. km. and a population of 7.07 million. Capital: San Salvador. This most intensely cultivated country of Latin America produces coffee (the major crop), sugar and balsam for export. Gold, silver and other metals are largely unexploited.

El Salvador achieved independence from Spain in 1821 and from the Central American Federation in 1839. A 12-year civil war, which cost about 75,000 lives, was brought to a close in 1992 when the government and leftist rebels signed a treaty that provided for military and political reforms.

On January 1, 2001, a monetary reform established the U.S. dollar as the accounting unit for all financial transactions, and fixed the exchange rate as 8.75 colones per dollar. In addition, the Central Reserve Bank has indicated that it will cease issuing coins and notes.

MONETARY SYSTEM:

1 Peso = 100 Centavos to 1919
1 Colón = 100 Centavos 1919-

COMMERCIAL BANKS:

Banco Agricola Comercial	#S101-S113
Banco de Ahuachapám	#S121-S126
Banco de Centro America y Londres	#S131-S137
Banco Industrial del Salvador	#S141-S145
Banco Internacional del Salvador	#S151-S156
Banco Nacional del Salvador	#S161-S166
Banco Occidental	#S171-S199
Banco Salvadoreño	#S201-S226

NOTE: Some commercial bank issues carry a validation ovpt. on the back, consisting of *TOMOSE RAZON* (or some form thereof), arms, city, date of issue and sign. The bank emissions which did not receive this back ovpt. were Banco Industrial, Banco Internacional and Banco de Centro America y Londres.

DATING SYSTEM:

Dates listed for notes are those found on the face, regardless of the ovpt. issue dates on back which were applied practically on a daily basis as notes were needed for circulation.

REPUBLIC

BANCO AGRICOLA COMERCIAL

1890's ISSUE

	Good	Fine	XF
S101 1 Peso			
189x-1917. Black on green and yellow underprint. Kneeling women at left, seated woman at right, holding shield with denomination at center. Back: Orange. Stylized head of old man at center. Printer: ABNC.			
a. 1.3.1904.	100.	250.	—
b. 25.2.1914-2.3.1917. Serial # varieties.	70.00	200.	—
p. Proof. 189x.	—	Unc	1750.
s. Specimen.	—	Unc	1000.
S102 5 Pesos			
189x-1904. Black on tan and green underprint. Seated woman with sacks, caduceus and tablet ("Commerce") at right. Back: Green. Printer: ABNC.			
a. 1.3.1904.	—	—	—
p. Proof. 189x.	—	Unc	2250.
s. Specimen.	—	Unc	1000.

	Good	Fine	XF
S103 10 Pesos			
189x. Black on red-orange underprint. Seated woman with caduceus at left center, arms at center, seated woman with scales at center right. Back: Blue-black. Printer: ABNC.			
a. Issued note.	—	—	—
p. Proof. 189x.	—	Unc	1750.
s. Specimen. 189x.	—	—	—
S104 25 Pesos			
189x. Black on blue and yellow underprint. Sailing ship at upper left center, allegorical woman with sickle at right. Back: Dark green. Allegorical man at left and right. Printer: ABNC.			
a. Issued note.	—	—	—
p. Proof. 189x.	—	—	—
s. Specimen. 189x.	—	—	—
S105 100 Pesos			
189x. Black on orange, yellow and pink underprint. Seated woman with produce and parrot at center. Back: Red. Arms at center. Printer: ABNC.			
a. Issued note.	—	—	—
p. Proof. 189x.	—	—	—
s. Specimen. 189x.	—	—	—

1915 ISSUE

	Good	Fine	XF
S106 50 Pesos			
1.1.1915. Black on multicolor underprint. Woman seated near globe at center. Back: Olive. Arms at center. Printer: ABNC.			
a. Issued note.	—	—	—
p. Proof. 189x.	—	Unc	2250.
S107 100 Pesos			
19xx. Black on multicolor underprint. Cherub, seated woman and globe at center. Back: Orange. Arms at center. Printer: ABNC.			
a. Issued note.	—	—	—
p. Proof. 189x.	—	Unc	2500.

1922 ISSUES

	Good	Fine	XF
S108 1 Colón			
1.3.1922. Black on multicolor underprint. Side view of bank at center. Series A. Back: Orange. Christopher Columbus at center. Printer: ABNC.			
a. Issued note.	50.00	125.	—
p. Proof. ND.	—	Unc	1000.
s. Specimen. ND.	—	Unc	800.
S109 1 Colón			
1.3.1922. Black on multicolor underprint. Front view of bank at center. Series B. Back: Orange. Christopher Columbus at center. Printer: ABNC.			
a. Issued note.	90.00	250.	—
p. Proof. ND.	—	—	—
s. Specimen.	—	Unc	800.
S110 2 Colones			
1.3.1922. Black on multicolor underprint. Side view of bank at center. Series A. Like #S108. Back: Reddish brown. Christopher Columbus at center. Printer: ABNC.			
a. Issued note.	90.00	275.	—
p. Proof.	—	Unc	1250.
s. Specimen.	—	Unc	1000.
S111 5 Colones			
1.3.1922. Black on multicolor underprint. Side view of bank at center. Series A. Like #S108. Back: Green. Christopher Columbus at center. Printer: ABNC.			
a. Issued note.	—	—	—
s. Specimen.	—	Unc	1750.
S112 10 Colones			
1.3.1922. Black on multicolor underprint. Side view of bank at center. Series A. Like #S108. Back: Brown-black. Christopher Columbus at center. Printer: ABNC.			
a. Issued note.	—	—	—
p. Proof.	—	—	—
s. Specimen.	—	Unc	1750.

	Good	Fine	XF
S113 25 Colones			
1.3.1922. Black on green and multicolor underprint. Front view of bank at center. Series B. Like #S109. Back: Blue. Christopher Columbus at center. Printer: ABNC.			
a. Issued note.	—	—	—
p. Proof.	—	—	—
s. Specimen.	—	Unc	1750.

A WORD ON DATE RANGES

Often date ranges or specific dates are listed. These have been observed or reported by our contributors. If a note is outside the published range, it only means that it is a newly reported date, and not necessarily worthy of a premium value.

Banco de Ahuachapam

1890's Issue

	Good	Fine	XF
S121 1 Peso			
189x. Black on red-orange underprint. Portrait F. Morazan at left, ox-drawn cart at center right. Back: Orange. Arms at center. Printer: ABNC. (Not issued).			
p. Proof.	—	Unc	1000.
r. Unsigned remainder.	—	Unc	350.
s. Specimen.	—	Unc	1000.
S122 2 Pesos			
189x. Black on pink, orange and yellow underprint. Women working at left and right, portrait F. Morazan at center. Back: Red. Arms at center. Printer: ABNC. (Not issued).			
p. Proof.	—	Unc	1000.
s. Specimen.	—	Unc	800.
S123 5 Pesos			
189x. Black on light yellow and brown underprint. Woman kneeling with globe ("Urania") at left center. Back: Purple. Arms at center. Printer: ABNC. (Not issued).			
p. Proof.	—	Unc	1100.
s. Specimen.	—	Unc	800.
S124 10 Pesos			
189x. Black on pink, yellow and brown underprint. Woman seated with children ("Peace") at right. Back: Brown. Allegorical figures at left and right. Arms at center. Printer: ABNC. Proof. (Not issued).	—	Unc	400.
S125 25 Pesos			
189x. Black on green and yellow underprint. People gathered at watering place at left, locomotive at right. Back: Green. Standing allegorical figures at left and right. Arms at center. Printer: ABNC. (Not issued).			
p. Proof.	—	Unc	1250.
s. Specimen.	—	Unc	400.
S126 50 Pesos			
189x. Black on blue and yellow underprint. Cow and calf at upper left, clasped hands at center, landscape at upper right. Back: Blue. Arms at center. Printer: ABNC. (Not issued).			
p. Proof.	—	Unc	450.
s. Specimen.	—	Unc	450.

Banco de Centro America y Londres

1895; 1897 Issue

	Good	Fine	XF
S131 1 Peso			
1895; 8.2.1897; 30.6.1899. Black and brown on green underprint. Portrait Christopher Columbus at left, standing Liberty with flag at right. Back: Bank monogram at center. Printer: W&S.	150.	—	—

	Good	Fine	XF
S132 5 Pesos			
1895. Black on pink underprint. Standing Liberty with flag at left, portrait Christopher Columbus at center right. Back: Green. Bank monogram at center. Printer: W&S.	—	—	—
S133 10 Pesos			
1895. Black on green and pink underprint. Portrait Christopher Columbus at left, Liberty with flag at center. Back: Red. Bank monogram at center. Printer: W&S.	—	—	—
S134 50 Pesos			
26.3.1897. Green and black on orange underprint. Portrait Christopher Columbus at upper left, standing Liberty with flag at center. Back: Blue. Bank monogram at center. Printer: W&S.			
a. Issued note. Rare.	—	—	—
s. Specimen. Rare.	—	—	—
S135 100 Pesos			
1895. Black on red and orange underprint. Portrait Christopher Columbus at upper left, Liberty with flag at center. Back: Bank monogram at center. Printer: W&S.	—	—	—

1905 Provisional Issue

#S136 and S137 overprint: *ORO* on #S131 and S132.

	Good	Fine	XF
S136 1 Peso			
1905. Black and brown on green underprint. Portrait Christopher Columbus at left, standing Liberty with flag at right. Back: Bank monogram at center. Overprint: *ORO* in large letters vertically twice at left and right, on face of #S131. Printer: W&S.	—	—	—

	Good	Fine	XF
S137 5 Pesos			
1905. Black on pink underprint. Standing Liberty with flag at left, portrait Christopher Columbus at center right. Back: Green. Bank monogram at center. Overprint: *ORO* in large letters vertically twice at left and right, on face of #S132. Printer: W&S.	—	—	—

Banco Industrial del Salvador

1890's Issue

	Good	Fine	XF
S141 1 Peso			
189x. Black on orange and yellow underprint. Ox cart loaded with sugar cane at center, refinery in background. Back: Orange. Coin-like design at center. Printer: ABNC.			
a. Issued note.	—	—	—
p. Proof.	—	—	—
s. Specimen.	—	—	—

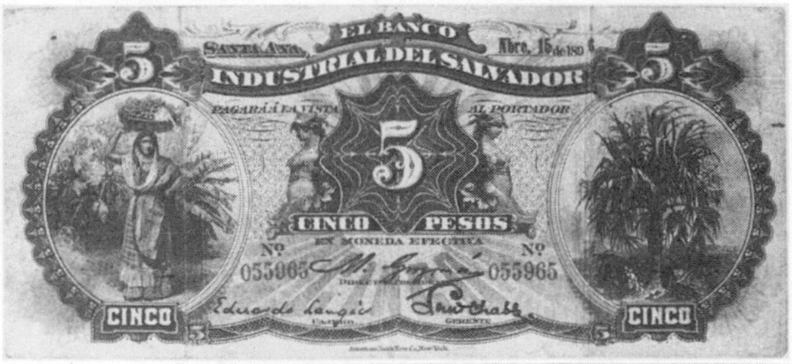

S142 5 Pesos	Good	Fine	XF
1.5.1896-15.1.1897. Black on green and red underprint. Woman with fruit basket on her head at left, tree at right. Back: Green. Obv. and rev. coin-like design similar to Central American Republic coinage of the 1820's and 1830's Printer: ABNC.			
a. Issued note.	100.	325.	—
p. Proof.	—	—	—

S143 10 Pesos	Good	Fine	XF
15.4.1896; 15.8.1896; 15.11.1896; 15.1.1897. Black on blue and brown underprint. Coffee workers at left, building at center, arms at right. Back: Ochre. Coin-like design similar to #S142. Printer: ABNC.			
a. Issued note	175.	—	—
p. Proof.	—	—	—
s. Specimen.	—	—	—

S144 25 Pesos	Good	Fine	XF
1.5.1896. Black on salmon and blue underprint. Church at left, ox cart at center, portrait Liberty at right. Back: Salmon. Coin-like design at left, train at center right. Printer: ABNC.			
a. Issued note.	—	—	—
p. Proof.	—	—	—
s. Specimen.	—	—	—

S145 100 Pesos	Good	Fine	XF
1890; 1896. Black on light blue underprint. Seated allegorical woman at left and right of arms at center. Back: Light blue-gray. Seated woman at left and right of obverse coin design at lower center. Printer: ABNC.			
a. 3.4.1890; 8.4.1896. (Handwritten or hand stamped).	125.	300.	—
s. Specimen. 189x.	—	—	—

Banco Internacional del Salvador

1880-90 Issue

S151 1 Peso	Good	Fine	XF
1.12.1881; 1.6.1882. Black and gray. Seated allegorical woman holding shield with arms at upper left center. Back: Orange. Six flags at center. Printer: Waterlow e Hijos (W&S).	125.	350.	—
S152 5 Pesos			
18xx. Seated allegorical woman holding shield with arms at upper center. Back: Green. Six flags at center. Printer: Waterlow e Hijos (W&S).	—	—	—

S153 10 Pesos	Good	Fine	XF
18xx. Black and gray. Seated allegorical woman holding shield with arms at left. Back: Blue. Six flags at center. Printer: Waterlow e Hijos (W&S).	—	—	—

S154 25 Pesos	Good	Fine	XF
18xx. Black and gray. Seated allegorical woman holding shield with arms at upper left. Printer: Waterlow e Hijos (W&S).	—	—	—

S155 100 Pesos	Good	Fine	XF
1887; 1890; 1895. Black on rose and green underprint. Seated allegorical woman holding shield with arms at upper center. Printer: Waterlow e Hijos (W&S).	—	—	—

S156 500 Pesos	Good	Fine	XF
1890; 1891; 1895. Black on green underprint. Mercury at left, seated allegorical woman holding shield with arms at lower right. Printer: Waterlow e Hijos (W&S).	—	—	—

Banco Nacional del Salvador

1906-08 Issue

S161 1 Peso	Good	Fine	XF
10.4.1908-6.2.1913. Black and red on rose underprint. Large denomination in guilloche at center. Back: Red-orange or brownish red. Large denomination in guilloche at center. Printer: W&S.			
a. 1908. Serie B.	4.00	30.00	100.
b. 1909-13. Serie A.	4.00	30.00	90.00

S162 5 Pesos			
18.9.1906-5.5.1913. Black and green on light red underprint. Large denomination in guilloche at center. Back: Green. Large denomination in guilloche at center. Printer: W&S.			
a. 1906-07. Serie A. Handwritten signature.	3.00	20.00	85.00
b. 1908. Serie A. Printed signature.	3.00	20.00	75.00
c. 1909-13. Serie B. Printed signature.	3.00	20.00	75.00

S163 10 Pesos			
15.2.1907-13.1.1911. Black and purple on brown underprint. Large denomination in guilloche at center. Back: Lilac-brown. Large denomination in guilloche at center. Printer: W&S.			
a. 1907. Serie A. Handwritten signature.	6.00	50.00	125.
b. 1908-11. Serie A. Printed signature. Black overprint on back.	6.00	45.00	110.
c. 6.3.1908. Serie A. Printed signature. Red overprint on back.	6.00	45.00	110.

S164 25 Pesos			
20.4.1907-10.8.1911. Black and tan on light green underprint. Large denomination in guilloche at center. Back: Light brown. Large denomination in guilloche at center. Printer: W&S.	12.00	75.00	225.

S165 50 Pesos	Good	Fine	XF
15.2.1907-6.2.1913. Black and blue on pink underprint. Large denomination in guilloche at center. Back: Blue. Large denomination in guilloche at center. Printer: W&S.	20.00	90.00	275.

S166 100 Pesos			
20.4.1907-9.2.1912. Black and blue on tan underprint. Large denomination in guilloche at center. Back: Blue. Large denomination in guilloche at center. Printer: W&S.			
a. 1907. Serie A. Handwritten signature.	35.00	150.	400.
b. 1908-12. Serie A. Printed signature.	30.00	125.	300.

Banco Occidental

1890-1914 Issues

S171 1 Peso	Good	Fine	XF
30.9.1899. Black on light green and yellow underprint. Cherub holding oval frame with portrait woman at center. Middle signature title: *DIRECTOR.* Back: Dark green. Woman's head at center. Printer: ABNC.			
a. Series H.	50.00	175.	—
p. Proof.	—	Unc	1100.
s. Specimen.	—	Unc	700.

S172 1 Peso	Good	Fine	XF
Dec. 1910; Nov. 1912; Nov. 1914; 31.5.1917. Black on red underprint. Cherub holding oval frame with portrait woman at center. Serial # red or blue. Similar to #S171. Back: Dark green. Woman's head at center. Printer: ABNC.			
a. Back blue. Middle signature title: *PRESIDENTE.*	70.00	200.	—
p. Back green. Middle signature title: *DIRECTOR.* Proof.	—	Unc	1750.
s. As a. Specimen, punched hole cancelled. ND. Series L.	—	Unc	500.

S173 1 Peso			
May 1914. Black on orange underprint. Horseman with mountain and building in background at center. Series L. Back: Blue. Stylized woman's head at center. Printer: NYBNC.	125.	350.	—

S174 2 Pesos

1.6.1913; Oct. 1913; July 1916; 1.6.1918. Black on light blue underprint. Horseman with mountain and building in background at center. Like #S173. Back: Red-brown. Printer: NYBNC.

	Good	Fine	XF
a. Issued note.	200.	—	—
s. July 1916. without Series, punched hole cancelled. Specimen.	—	—	—

S175 5 Pesos

189x. Black on orange and yellow underprint. Standing Justice beside scene of presidential palace at left. Back: Orange. Arms at center. Printer: ABNC. (Not issued).

	Good	Fine	XF
p. Proof.	—	Unc	1100.
r. Unsigned remainder.	—	Unc	750.

S176 5 Pesos

1891-1915. Black on green underprint. Harvesting coffee at left, harbor scene at center. Back: Green. Arms at center. Printer: ABNC.

	Good	Fine	XF
a1. Issued at Santa Ana. Middle signature title: *DIRECTOR.* 10.8.1891; 20.3.1895. Rare.	—	—	—
a2. Series A. 25.5.1905.	—	—	—
b. San Salvador overprint for city of issue. Middle signature title: *PRESIDENTE.* Series A. 31.1.1906.	100.	—	—
c. San Salvador. Series D. Dec. 1914; Jan. 1915.	100.	—	—
p. Proof.	—	Unc	2500.
s. Series G. Specimen. 189x.	—	Unc	1500.

S177 10 Pesos

1893-1917. Black on yellow and brown underprint. Steam locomotive at left, harbor scene at right. Back: Brown. Arms at center. Printer: ABNC.

	Good	Fine	XF
a. Issued at Santa Ana. Middle signature title: *DIRECTOR.* 1.1.1893; 1.7.1893; 25.5.1905.	—	—	—
b. San Salvador overprint for city of issue. Middle signature title: *PRESIDENTE.* 12.1917.	—	—	—
p. Proof.	—	Unc	1000.
s. Specimen. 189x.	—	—	—

S178 25 Pesos

1890; 19xx. Black on orange and yellow underprint. Harbor scene at left center, ship at right. Back: Orange. Arms at center. Printer: ABNC.

	Good	Fine	XF
a. Issued at Santa Ana. Middle signature title: *DIRECTOR.* 1.5.1890.	—	—	—
b. Issued at San Salvador. Middle signature title: *PRESIDENTE.* 19xx.	—	—	—
p. Proof.	—	Unc	1500.
s. Specimen. 189x.	—	—	—

S179 50 Pesos

189x; ND (19xx). Bank at left, harbor scene at right. Back: Arms at center. Printer: ABNC.

	Good	Fine	XF
a. Black on orange and yellow underprint. Back orange. Issued at Santa Ana. Middle signature title: *DIRECTOR.* 189x.	—	—	—
b. Black on purple and yellow underprint. Back purple. Issued at San Salvador. Middle signature title: *PRESIDENTE.* ND (19xx).	—	—	—
p. Santa Ana. Proof. ND.	—	—	—
s. Specimen.	—	Unc	1750.

S180 100 Pesos

189x-1916. Black on olive and yellow underprint. Harbor scene at left, miners at lower right. Back: Olive. Arms at center. Printer: ABNC.

	Good	Fine	XF
a. Issued at Santa Ana. Middle signature title: *DIRECTOR.* 189x.	—	—	—
b. Issued at San Salvador. Middle signature title: *PRESIDENTE.* 19xx; Feb. 1916.	—	—	—
c. Like b., but 19xx not in plate.	—	—	—
p. Santa Ana. Proof. ND.	—	—	—
s. Specimen.	—	Unc	1500.

S181 500 Pesos

189x. Black on blue and yellow underprint. Two seated allegorical women ("Commerce & Agriculture") at left, harbor scene at right. Middle signature title: *DIRECTOR.* Back: Blue. Arms at center. Printer: ABNC. Issued at Santa Ana.

	Good	Fine	XF
p. Proof.	—	—	—
s. Specimen.	—	—	—

1920-29 Issues

S191 1 Colón

1.5.1920. Blue and multicolor in plain white background. Woman ("Kalliope") at center. Series A. Back: Orange. Portrait Christopher Columbus facing right at center. Printer: ABNC.

	Good	Fine	XF
a. 2 printed signatures, 1 hand signature (at right).	35.00	90.00	275.
b. 3 printed signatures.	30.00	85.00	250.
s. Specimen.	—	Unc	400.

S192 1 Colón

1.1.1929. Blue and multicolor in multicolor background. Woman ("Kalliope") at center. Series B. Similar to #S191 but different, larger guilloches and 3 printed signatures. Back: Portrait Christopher Columbus facing right at center. Printer: ABNC.

	Good	Fine	XF
a. Issued note.	20.00	70.00	200.
s. Specimen.	—	Unc	400.

S193 2 Colones

1.5.1920. Blue and multicolor in plain white background. Seated allegorical woman ("Kalliope") at center. Series A. Back: Red-brown. Portrait Christopher Columbus facing right at center. Printer: ABNC.

	Good	Fine	XF
a. Issued note.	80.00	250.	—
p. Proof.	—	—	—
s. Specimen.	—	Unc	700.

S194 2 Colones

1926-29. Blue and multicolor in multicolor background. Seated allegorical woman ("Kalliope") at center. Similar to #S193 but different, larger guilloches. Back: Red-brown. Portrait Christopher Columbus facing right at center. Printer: ABNC.

	Good	Fine	XF
a. Series B. 1.11.1926.	40.00	175.	375.
b. Series C. 1.1.1929.	35.00	150.	300.
s. Specimen.	—	Unc	600.

S194A 5 Colones	Good	Fine	XF
1.5.1920. Blue and multicolor in plain white background. Seated allegorical woman with globe ("Kalliope") at right. Series A in black. Back: Green. Portrait Christopher Columbus facing right at center. Printer: ABNC.			
p. Proof.	—	—	—
s. Specimen.	—	Unc	1250.

S195 5 Colones	Good	Fine	XF
1926-29. Blue and multicolor in multicolor background. Seated allegorical woman with globe ("Kalliope") at right. Similar to #S194A but different, larger guilloches. Back: Green. Portrait Christopher Columbus facing right at center. Printer: ABNC.			
a. Series B. 1.11.1926.	70.00	300.	—
b. Series C. 1.1.1929.	60.00	250.	—
p. Proof.	—	—	—
s. Series B. Specimen. 1.11.1926.	—	Unc	600.
S196 10 Colones			
1.9.1925. Blue on multicolor underprint. Seated allegorical woman with globe ("Kalliope") at center. Series A in red. Back: Dark brown. Portrait Christopher Columbus facing right at center. Printer: ABNC.			
p. Proof.	—	—	—
s. Specimen.	—	Unc	1250.
S197 25 Colones			
1.1.1929. Blue on multicolor underprint. Seated allegorical woman with globe ("Kalliope") at center. Series A. Back: Dark blue. Portrait Christopher Columbus facing right at center. Printer: ABNC.			
a. Issued note.	—	—	—
p. Proof.	—	—	—
s. Specimen.	—	Unc	1500.

S198 100 Colones	Good	Fine	XF
1924-29. Blue on multicolor underprint. Seated allegorical woman with globe ("Kalliope") at left. Back: Olive-green. Portrait Christopher Columbus facing right at center. Printer: ABNC.			
a. Series A in red. 1.9.1924.	—	—	—
b. Series B. 1.1.1929.	—	—	—
p. Proof.	—	—	—
s. Series A. Specimen.	—	Unc	1650.

S199 500 Colones	Good	Fine	XF
1925-29. Blue on multicolor underprint. Seated allegorical woman with globe ("Kalliope") at center. Back: Dark green. Portrait Christopher Columbus facing right at center. Printer: ABNC.			
a. Series A in red. 1.1.1925.	—	—	—
b. Series B. 1.1.1929.	—	—	—
c. As b. Cancelled, perforated *PAGADO.*	—	—	—
p. Proof.	—	Unc	1000.
s. Series A. Specimen.	—	Unc	1500.

Banco Salvadoreño

1899-1913 Issues

S201 1 Peso	Good	Fine	XF
1899-1905. Black on orange and yellow underprint. Two women ("Reapers No. 3") at left, seated allegorical woman with caduceus, arms and eagle at right. Back: Orange. Stylized woman's head at center. Printer: ABNC.			
a. Series A. 14.1.1899; 1.7.1903; 8.1.1904.	75.00	150.	—
b. Series B. 1.10.1905; 1.12.1905.	65.00	150.	325.
p. Proof.	—	—	—
s. Series A. Specimen. 189x.	—	Unc	600.
S202 1 Peso			
1913-19. Black on pink underprint. Two women ("Reapers No. 3") at left, seated allegorical woman with caduceus and arms at right. Like #S201 but reduced size and without eagle at right. Printer: ABNC.			
a. Series C. 1.2.1913.	30.00	90.00	275.
b. Series D. 15.3.1914.	25.00	80.00	250.
c. Series E. 15.11.1914; 1.10.1915; 31.10.1916; 1.7.1918; 1.2.1919.	25.00	80.00	250.
s. Specimen.	—	Unc	600.
S203 5 Pesos			
189x-1916. Black on green underprint. Arms at left, seated woman with quill pen and book near draped flags and cannon at right. Back: Green. Cherub's head at top center. Printer: ABNC.			
a. Series A. 189x.	—	—	—
b. Series B. 15.9.1913.	—	—	—
c. Series C. 31.7.1916.	100.	250.	—
p. Proof.	—	—	—
s. Series A. Specimen. 189x.	—	Unc	800.
S204 10 Pesos			
189x; 15.1.1915; 15.7.1915; 1.7.1918. Black on yellow and purple underprint. Seated woman at left and right of value at upper left, seated woman ("Rose") at upper right. Series A; B. Back: Purple. Printer: ABNC.			
a. Issued note.	—	—	—
b. Cancelled, perforated: *CANCELADO.*	—	—	—
p. Proof.	—	Unc	1500.
s. Specimen.	—	Unc	1650.
S205 25 Pesos			
1893-1915. Black on brown and yellow underprint. Arms at left, seated woman with book by globe ("La Critique") at center. Back: Brown. Printer: ABNC.			
a. Series A. 4.7.1893.	—	—	—
b. Series B. 15.7.1915.	—	—	—
p. Proof.	—	Unc	2000.
s. Specimen.	—	Unc	2150.
S206 100 Pesos			
189x; 15.9.1913. Black on blue and yellow underprint. Reclining woman ("The Siesta") at left, arms at upper center right, seated woman ("Industry") at right. Series A. Back: Blue. Printer: ABNC.			
a. Issued note.	—	—	—
p. Proof.	—	—	—

S207 500 Pesos	Good	Fine	XF
19xx. Black on yellow underprint. Minerva reclining with lion at center. Back: Olive-green. Printer: ABNC.			
a. Issued note.	—	—	—
p. Proof.	—	—	—

1913; 1914 Issue

	Good	Fine	XF
S208 1 Peso 1.2.1913. Black on pink underprint. Two women ("Reapers No. 3") at left, seated allegorical woman with caduceus and arms at right. Series C. Like #S202. Printer: Carlos Parraga, San Salvador C.A. Rare.	—	—	—
S209 5 Pesos 15.9.1913; 15.9.1914. Black on green underprint. Arms at left, seated woman with quill pen and book near draped flags and cannon at right. Series B. Like #S203. Back: Green. Cherub's head at top center. Printer: Carlos Parraga, San Salvador C.A.			
a. Issued note. Rare.	—	—	—
p. Proof.	—	—	—

1920 Issue

	Good	Fine	XF
S211 1 Colón 1.6.1920. Black on multicolor underprint. Seated woman with sheaf and wheel at center. Series A. Back: Orange. Christopher Columbus facing left at center. Printer: ABNC.			
a. Issued note.	30.00	125.	275.
p. Proof.	—	Unc	1500.
s. Specimen.	—	Unc	1000.
S212 2 Colones 1.6.1920. Black on multicolor underprint. Seated woman with sheaf and wheel at left center. Series A. Back: Red-brown. Christopher Columbus facing left at center. Printer: ABNC.			
a. Issued note.	125.	600.	—
p. Proof.	—	Unc	1750.
s. Specimen.	—	Unc	1250.
S213 5 Colones 1.6.1920. Black on multicolor underprint. Seated woman with sheaf and wheel at left center. Series A. Back: Green. Christopher Columbus facing left at center. Printer: ABNC.			
a. Issued note.	50.00	200.	375.
p. Proof.	—	Unc	1500.
s. Specimen.	—	Unc	1250.

	Good	Fine	XF
S214 10 Colones 1.6.1920. Black on multicolor underprint. Seated woman with sheaf and wheel at center. Series A. Back: Dark brown. Christopher Columbus facing left at center. Printer: ABNC.			
a. Issued note.	300.	1100.	—
p. Proof. ND.	—	Unc	2500.
s. Specimen.	—	Unc	1650.
S215 25 Colones 1.6.1920. Black on multicolor underprint. Seated woman with sheaf and wheel at center. Series A. Back: Christopher Columbus facing left at center. Printer: ABNC.	—	—	—

1924 Issue

	Good	Fine	XF
S221 1 Colón 1924-31. Black on red and blue underprint. Seated woman with sheaf and wheel at center. Similar to #S211. Back: Christopher Columbus facing left at center. Printer: W&S.			
a. Series A. 1.11.1924.	25.00	90.00	250.
b. Series B. 1.1.1929.	20.00	80.00	225.
c. Series C. 1.1.1931; 1.10.1931.	20.00	80.00	225.
S222 2 Colones 1.1.1924; 1.1.1929. Black on brown, green and multicolor underprint. Series A. Back: Red-brown. Printer: W&S.			
a. Issued note.	45.00	175.	375.
b. Cancelled with perforations.	—	—	—
S223 5 Colones 1924-31. Black on multicolor underprint. Seated woman with sheaf and wheel at left center. Similar to #S213. Back: Green. Christopher Columbus facing left at center. Printer: W&S.			
a. Series A. 1.11.1924.	50.00	200.	450.
b. Series B. 1.10.1931.	30.00	175.	375.
S224 10 Colones 1924-31. Black on multicolor underprint. Seated woman with sheaf and wheel at center. Similar to #S214. Back: Dark brown. Christopher Columbus facing left at center. Printer: W&S.			
a. Series A. 1.11.1924.	—	—	—
b. Series B. 1.10.1931.	—	—	—

	Good	Fine	XF
S225 25 Colones 1.11.1924. Black on multicolor underprint. Seated woman with sheaf and wheel at center. Series A. Similar to #S215. Back: Christopher Columbus facing left at center. Printer: W&S.	—	—	—
S226 100 Colones 1.11.1924; 1.1.1929. Black on orange and purple underprint. Series A. Back: Green.			
a. Issued note.	—	—	—
b. Cancelled with perforations.	—	—	—

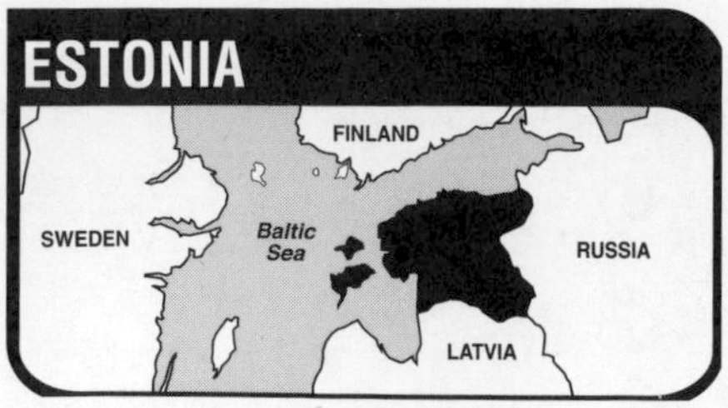

The Republic of Estonia is the northernmost of the three Baltic states in eastern Europe. It has an area of 45,226 sq. km. and a population of 1.31 million. Capital: Tallinn. Agriculture and dairy farming are the principal industries. Butter, eggs, bacon, timber are exported.

After centuries of Danish, Swedish, German, and Russian rule, Estonia attained independence in 1918. Forcibly incorporated into the USSR in 1940 - an action never recognized by the US - it regained its freedom in 1991, with the collapse of the Soviet Union. Since the last Russian troops left in 1994, Estonia has been free to promote economic and political ties with Western Europe. It joined both NATO and the EU in the spring of 2004.

MONETARY SYSTEM

1 Mark = 100 Penni to 1928
1 Kroon = 100 Senti

MILITARY - WW I

FINNISH REGIMENT - SONS OF THE NORTH

1919 ND ISSUES

#M1-M3 overprint: *Pohjan Pojat Rykmentin Rahaston hoitaja.*

		VG	VF	UNC
M1	**50 Penni**			
	ND (1919-old date 1919). Overprint: On #42.	—	—	—
M2	**1 Markka**			
	ND (1919-old date 1916). Overprint: On Finland #19.	—	—	—
M3	**1 Marka**			
	ND (1919-old date 1919). Overprint: On #43.	—	—	—

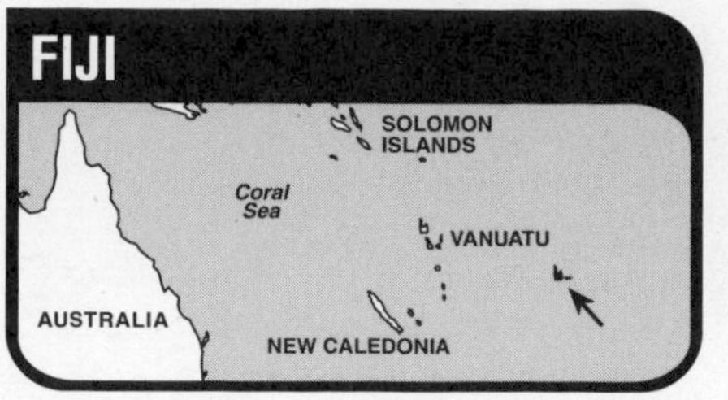

The republic of Fiji is an independent member of the British Commonwealth. It consists of about 320 islands located in the southwestern Pacific 1,770 km. north of New Zealand. The islands have a combined area of 18,270 sq. km. and a population of 931,750. Capital: Suva, on the island of Viti Levu. Fiji's economy is d on agriculture, tourism and mining. Sugar, coconut products, and gold are exported.

Fiji became independent in 1970, after nearly a century as a British colony. Democratic rule was interrupted by two military coups in 1987, caused by concern over a government perceived as dominated by the Indian community (descendants of contract laborers brought to the islands by the British in the 19th century). The coups and a 1990 constitution that cemented native Melanesian control of Fiji, led to heavy Indian emigration; the population loss resulted in economic difficulties, but ensured that Melanesians became the majority. A new constitution enacted in 1997 was more equitable. Free and peaceful elections in 1999 resulted in a government led by an Indo-Fijian, but a civilian-led coup in May 2000 ushered in a prolonged period of political turmoil. Parliamentary elections held in August 2001 provided Fiji with a democratically elected government led by Prime Minister Laisenia Qarase. Re-elected in May 2006, Qarase was ousted in a December 2006 military coup led by Commodore Voreqe Bainimarama, who initially appointed himself acting president. In January 2007, Bainimarama was appointed interim prime minister.

RULERS:

Thakombau (Cakobau), until 1874
British, 1874-1970.

MONETARY SYSTEM:

1 Shilling = 12 Pence
1 Pound = 20 Shillings to 1969
1 Dollar = 100 Cents, 1969-

REGIONAL

KINGDOM OF BAU, CAKOBAU REX

ND TREASURY NOTES

		Good	Fine	XF
S201	**1 Dollar**			
	ND (1867). Black on buff.			
	a. Issued note.	—	—	—
	r. Unissued remainder.	—	—	—

BRITISH ADMINISTRATION

FIJI BANKING AND COMMERCIAL COMPANY

1873 ISSUE

#S211-S215A issued ca. 1873-76.

		Good	Fine	XF
S211	**1 Dollar**			
	(ca.1873). Black on green underprint. Vignette at center. Back: Denomination value in Fijian.			
	a. Issued note.	—	—	—
	r. Unissued remainder.	—	—	—

		Good	Fine	XF
S212	**5 Shillings**			
	(ca.1874-76). Black on green underprint. Back: Denomination value in Fijian.			
	a. Issued note.	—	—	—
	r. Unissued remainder.	—	—	—
S213	**10 Shillings**			
	(ca.1874-76). Black on green underprint. Back: Denomination value in Fijian.			
	a. Issued note.	—	—	—
	r. Unissued remainder.	—	—	—

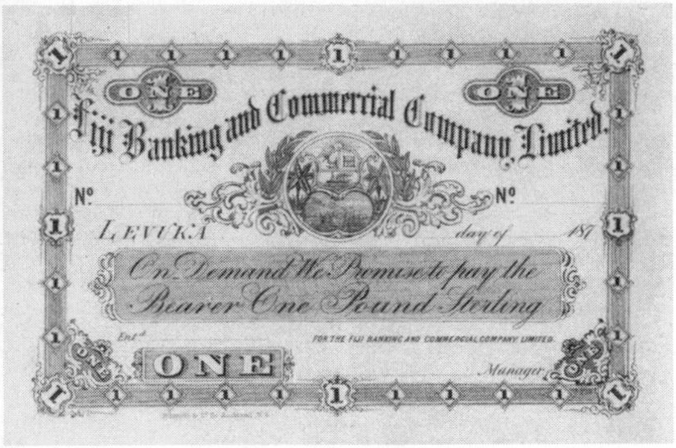

S214 1 Pound	Good	Fine	XF
(ca.1873-76). Black on green underprint. Back: Denomination value in Fijian.			
a. Issued note.	—	—	—
r. Unissued remainder.	—	—	—

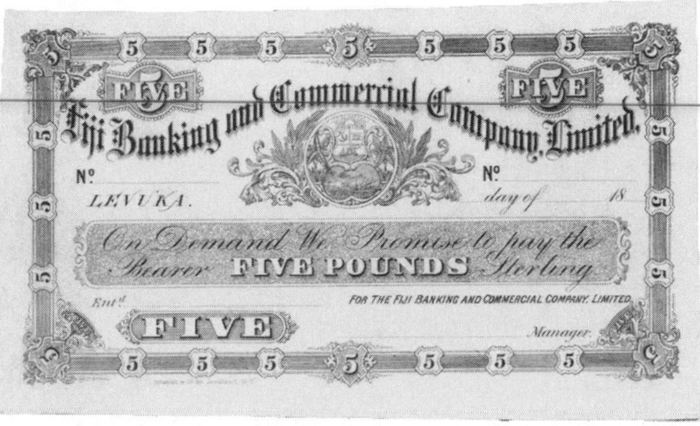

S215 5 Pounds	Good	Fine	XF
(ca.1873-76). Black on blue underprint. Back: Denomination value in Fijian.			
a. Issued note.	—	—	—
r. Unissued remainder.	—	—	—
S215A 10 Pounds			
(ca.1874-76). Black on maroon underprint. Back: Denomination value in Fijian.			
a. Issued note.	—	—	—
r. Unissued remainder.	—	—	—

Bank of New Zealand

1876 First Provisional Issue

#S216-S219 Design is third issue of Bank of New Zealand (listed under New Zealand).

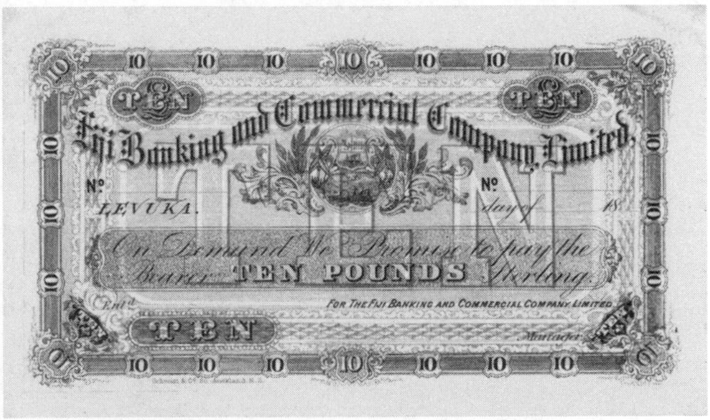

S216 1 Pound	Good	Fine	XF
18xx (1876). Black on green underprint. Maoris at upper left, Kiwis at lower left. Red handwritten: *LEVUKA* substituted for *BLENHEIM* or *NEW PLYMOUTH.* Hand stamped: *PAYABLE IN LEVUKA ONLY* at upper right. Printer: BWC.			
a. *BLENHEIM.*	—	—	—
b. *NEW PLYMOUTH.*	—	—	—
S217 5 Pounds			
18xx (ca. 1876). Black on brown underprint. Maoris at upper left, Kiwis at lower left. Red handwritten: *LEVUKA* substituted for *BLENHEIM* or *NEW PLYMOUTH.* Hand stamped: *PAYABLE IN LEVUKA ONLY* at upper right. Printer: BWC.			
a. *BLENHEIM.*	—	—	—
b. *NEW PLYMOUTH.*	—	—	—

S218 10 Pounds	Good	Fine	XF
18xx (ca. 1876). Black on brown underprint. Maoris at upper left, Kiwis at lower left. Red handwritten: *LEVUKA* substituted for *BLENHEIM* or *NEW PLYMOUTH.* Hand stamped: *PAYABLE IN LEVUKA ONLY* at upper right. Printer: BWC.			
a. *BLENHEIM.*	—	—	—
b. *NEW PLYMOUTH.*	—	—	—
S219 20 Pounds			
18xx (ca. 1876). Black on blue underprint. Maoris at upper left, Kiwis at lower left. Red handwritten: *LEVUKA* substituted for *BLENHEIM* or *NEW PLYMOUTH.* Hand stamped: *PAYABLE IN LEVUKA ONLY* at upper right. Printer: BWC.			
a. *BLENHEIM.*	—	—	—
b. *NEW PLYMOUTH.*	—	—	—

1876 Second Provisional Issue

#S220-S223 Design on third issue of Bank of New Zealand (New Zealand #S191-S194) w/ovpt: *SUVA* on *BLENHEIM* or *NEW PLYMOUTH.*

S220 1 Pound	Good	Fine	XF
18xx (ca. 1876); 1.7.1909. Back on green underprint. Maoris at upper left, Kiwis at lower left. Hand stamped: *PAYABLE IN FIJI ONLY.* Overprint: *SUVA.* Printer: BWC.			
a. *BLENHEIM.*	—	—	—
b. *NEW PLYMOUTH.*	—	—	—
S221 5 Pounds			
18xx (ca. 1876). Black on brown underprint. Maoris at upper left, Kiwis at lower left. Hand stamped: *PAYABLE IN FIJI ONLY.* Overprint: *SUVA.* Printer: BWC.			
a. *BLENHEIM.*	—	—	—
b. *NEW PLYMOUTH.*	—	—	—
S222 10 Pounds			
18xx (ca. 1876). Black on brown underprint. Maoris at upper left, Kiwis at lower left. Hand stamped: *PAYABLE IN FIJI ONLY.* Overprint: *SUVA.* Printer: BWC.			
a. *BLENHEIM.*	—	—	—
b. *NEW PLYMOUTH.*	—	—	—
S223 20 Pounds			
18xx (ca. 1876). Black on blue underprint. Maoris at upper left, Kiwis at lower left. Hand stamped: *PAYABLE IN FIJI ONLY.* Overprint: *SUVA.* Printer: BWC.			
a. *BLENHEIM.*	—	—	—
b. *NEW PLYMOUTH.*	—	—	—

1876 Third Provisional Issue

#S224 has *SUVA* overprint on third issue Bank of New Zealand note #S194.

S224 20 Pounds	Good	Fine	XF
18xx (1876). Black on blue underprint. *PAYABLE IN FIJI ONLY.* Overprint: *SUVA.* Printer: BWC.	—	—	—

1918 Provisional Issue

Overprint on Bank of New Zealand #216.

S225 10 Shillings	Good	Fine	XF
19xx (1918). Red. Paper: Pink. Printer: Whitcombe & Tombs.			
a. Overprint: SUVA.	—	—	—
b. Overprint: LEVUKA.	—	—	—

Bank of New South Wales

1901 Provisional Issue

#S231-S234 overprint: *SUVA* on 1890-1910 issue with vignette at upper center.

S231 1 Pound	Good	Fine	XF
19xx (1901). Black. Printer: CS&E.	—	—	—
S232 5 Dollars			
19xx (1901). Black. Printer: CS&E.	—	—	—
S233 10 Pounds			
19xx (1901). Black. Printer: CS&E.	—	—	—
S234 20 Pounds			
19xx (1901). Black. Printer: CS&E.	—	—	—

The Republic of Finland, the second most northerly state of the European continent, has an area of 338,145 sq. km. and a population of 5.24 million. Capital: Helsinki. Electrical, optical equipment, shipbuilding, metal and woodworking are the leading industries. Paper, wood pulp, plywood and telecommunication equipment are exported.

Finland was a province and then a grand duchy under Sweden from the 12th to the 19th centuries, and an autonomous grand duchy of Russia after 1809. It won its complete independence in 1917. During World War II, it was able to successfully defend its freedom and resist invasions by the Soviet Union - albeit with some loss of territory. In the subsequent half century, the Finns made a remarkable transformation from a farm/forest economy to a diversified modern industrial economy; per capita income is now among the highest in Western Europe. A member of the European Union since 1995, Finland was the only Nordic state to join the euro system at its initiation in January 1999.

RULERS:

Gustaf III, 1771-1792, of Sweden
Gustaf IV Adolph, 1792-1809
Alexander I, 1809-1825, of Russia
Nicholas I, 1825-1855
Alexander II, 1855-1881
Alexander III, 1881-1894
Nicholas II, 1894-1917

MONETARY SYSTEM:

(With Sweden to 1809)
1 Riksdaler Specie = 48 Skilling Specie
(With Russia 1809-1917)
1 Ruble = 100 Kopeks, 1809-1860
1 Markka = 100 Penniä, 1860-1963
1 Markka = 100 "Old" Markkaa, 1963-2001
1 Euro = 100 Cents, 2002-

REGIONAL

FÖRENINGSBANKEN I FINLAND, SUOMEN YHDYSPANKKI

UNION BANK OF FINLAND

1866 ISSUE

	Good	Fine	XF
S101 15 Markkaa 1866. Light brown. Back: Clasped hands in oval at center.	1250.	2500.	—
S102 25 Markkaa 1866. Green. Back: Beehive in oval at upper left.	1500.	3000.	—
S103 100 Markkaa 1866. Black. Back: Mercury running at left.	5000.	15,000.	—

1882 ND ISSUE

	Good	Fine	XF
S104 25 Markkaa ND (1882). Green. Portrait man wearing wolf's head fur skin on his head with wolf at left. Printer: BWC.	450.	900.	—
S105 100 Markkaa ND (1882). Green and pink. Woman standing before starry sky at left. Printer: BWC.			
a. Issued note.	2500.	7500.	—
s. Specimen.	—	—	—

VAASAN OSAKE PANKKI / WASA AKTIE BANK

1918 ACCOUNT CHECKS ISSUE

#S111-S113 This and other banks in 1918 issued numerous emergency "notgeld" notes and checks in various denominations.

	VG	VF	UNC
S111 25 Markkaa 1918. Light brown. Arms at lower center. Serial # prefix letters A; B or C.	25.00	100.	275.

	VG	VF	UNC
S112 100 Markkaa 1918. Brown and tan. Arms at lower center.	50.00	200.	500.
S113 500 Markkaa 1918. Arms at lower center.	1000.	2500.	5000.

FIUME

Fiume (Rijeka) is a major port and industrial center of Croatia, located on the Kvarner Gulf of the Adriatic Sea. The port was a primary for the Yugoslav Navy.

By the 10th century, a recognizable settlement had developed at the present site of Fiume. It was incorporated into Austria in 1471, was made a free port in 1717, was united to Croatia in 1776, and was declared an autonomous city of the Austrian crown in 1770. The French occupied the city during 1809-14, after which it alternated under Austrian, Hungarian and Croatian rule until after World War I when set up as a free city. On September 1919, the Italian military commander D'Annunzio occupied Fiume with his troops, and he proclaimed the "Reggenza Italiana del Carnaro" and the Fiume free State, waiting for the annexation to Italy. Mussolini, who up to the time, had liked enterprise of Fiume, he was obliged by European diplomacy to change direction and, on January 1921 he sent regularly Italian troops to expell D'Annunzio from Fiume. Notes of Austro-Hungarian bank with Fiume overprint circulated since April 1919 up to February 1921. On January 1924, Mussolini proclaimed the Fiume's annexation to Italy. Occupied by the Germans during World War II, Fiume was liberated by the Yugoslavs in May, 1945 and transferred to Yugoslavia by the Italian Peace Treaty of 1947.

MONETARY SYSTEM:

1 Krone = 100 Heller

FREE STATE

CITTA DI FIUME

1919/21 ISSUES

	Good	Fine	XF
S101 1 Krone ND (1919/21- old date 1.12.1916). Overprint: Red on Austria #20.			
a. Overprint Type I.	6.00	15.00	30.00
b. Overprint Type II.	3.50	7.50	15.00
c. Overprint Type III.	90.00	150.	325.

	Good	Fine	XF
S102 1 Krone ND (1919/21- old date 1.12.1916). Overprint: Red on Hungary #10. Serial # above 7000.			
a. Overprint Type I.	11.00	25.00	50.00
b. Overprint Type II.	6.00	12.50	25.00
c. Overprint Type III.	120.	200.	425.

S103 2 Kronen
ND (1919/21- old date 5.8.1914). Overprint: Blue on Austria #17.

	Good	Fine	XF
a. Overprint Type I.	12.50	25.00	50.00
b. Overprint Type II.	6.00	12.50	25.00
c. Overprint Type III.	120.	200.	400.

S104 2 Kronen
ND (1919/21- old date 1.3.1917). Red on gray underprint. Overprint: On Austria #21.

	Good	Fine	XF
a. Overprint Type I.	6.00	12.50	25.00
b. Overprint Type II.	3.50	7.50	15.00
c. Overprint Type III.	120.	200.	400.

1920 ND Issues

S105 2 Kronen
ND (1920- old date 1.3.1917). Red on gray underprint. Overprint: On Hungary #11. Serial # above 7000.

	Good	Fine	XF
a. Overprint Type I.	11.00	22.50	45.00
b. Overprint Type II.	6.00	12.50	25.00
c. Overprint Type III	140.	250.	550.

#S106 *Deleted.* (fabrication).

S107 10 Kronen
ND (1920- old date 2.1.1904). Blue-violet on red and green underprint. Overprint: On Austria #9.

	Good	Fine	XF
a. Overprint Type I.	25.00	50.00	100.
b. Overprint Type II.	11.00	22.50	45.00
c. Overprint Type III.	180.	350.	750.
d. Overprint Type IV.	100.	225.	450.

S108 10 Kronen
ND (1920- old date 2.1.1915). Blue and green. Overprint: On Austria #19.

	Good	Fine	XF
a. Overprint Type I.	11.00	22.50	45.00
b. Overprint Type II.	5.00	10.00	20.00
c. Overprint Type III.	150.	300.	650.
d. Overprint Type IV.	80.00	160.	375.

S109 20 Kronen
ND (1920- old date 2.1.1907). Blue on red-brown and green underprint. Overprint: On Austria #10.

	Good	Fine	XF
a. Overprint Type I.	50.00	100.	200.
b. Overprint Type II.	25.00	50.00	100.
c. Overprint Type III. Rare.	—	—	—
d. Overprint Type IV.	200.	425.	850.

S110 20 Kronen
ND (1920- old date 2.1.1913). Blue on green and red underprint. Overprint: On Austria #13.

	Good	Fine	XF
a. Overprint Type I.	12.50	35.00	70.00
b. Overprint Type II.	5.00	10.00	20.00
c. Overprint Type III.	250.	500.	1000.
d. Overprint Type IV.	75.00	150.	325.

S111 20 Kronen
ND (1920- old date 2.1.1913). Blue on green and red underprint. Overprint: On Austria #14. (II AUFLAGE).

	Good	Fine	XF
a. Overprint Type I.	11.00	25.00	50.00
b. Overprint Type II.	5.00	15.00	30.00
c. Overprint Type III.	250.	525.	1050.
d. Overprint Type IV.	75.00	150.	300.

S112 50 Kronen
ND (1920- old date 2.1.1902). Blue on rose underprint. Overprint: On Austria #6.

	Good	Fine	XF
a. Overprint Type I.	80.00	160.	350.
b. Overprint Type II.	50.00	100.	200.
c. Overprint Type III. Rare.	—	—	—
d. Overprint Type IV.	180.	350.	725.

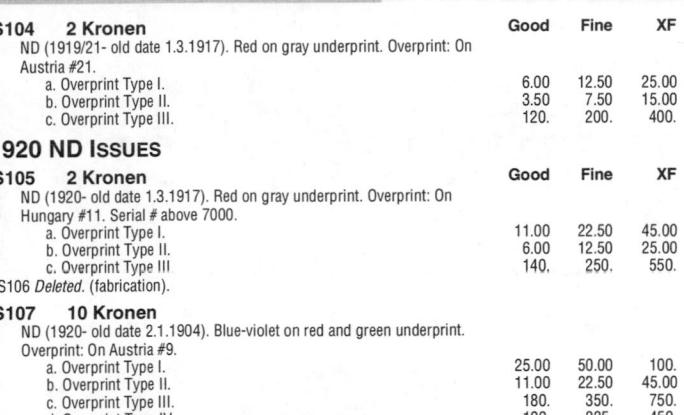

S113 50 Kronen
ND (1920- old date 2.1.1914). Blue and green. Overprint: On Austria #15.

	Good	Fine	XF
a. Overprint Type I.	15.00	30.00	60.00
b. Overprint Type II.	5.00	10.00	20.00
c. Overprint Type III.	300.	600.	1200.
d. Overprint Type IV.	80.00	160.	325.

S114 100 Kronen
ND (1920- old date 2.1.1910). Blue. Overprint: On Austria #11.

	Good	Fine	XF
a. Overprint Type I.	200.	400.	800.
b. Overprint Type II.	200.	400.	800.
c. Overprint Type III. Rare.	—	—	—
d. Overprint Type IV.	350.	725.	1450.

S115 100 Kronen
ND (1920- old date 2.1.1912). Green on red and blue underprint. Overprint: On Austria #12.

	Good	Fine	XF
a. Overprint Type I.	15.00	40.00	80.00
b. Overprint Type II.	5.00	15.00	30.00
c. Overprint Type III. Rare.	—	—	—
d. Overprint Type IV.	80.00	160.	320.

S116 1000 Kronen
ND (1920- old date 2.1.1902). Blue. Overprint: On Austria #8.

	Good	Fine	XF
a. Overprint Type I.	18.00	40.00	80.00
b. Overprint Type II.	7.50	20.00	40.00
c. Overprint Type IV.	120.	250.	525.

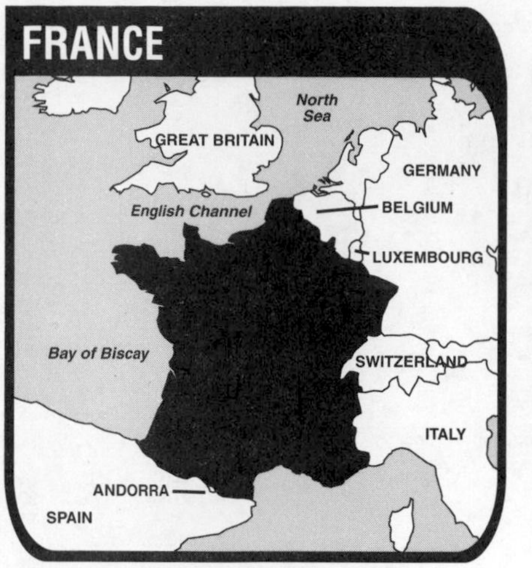

The French Republic, largest of the West European nations, has an area of 547,026 sq. km. and a population of 64.05 million. Capital: Paris. Agriculture, manufacturing and tourism are the most important elements of France's diversified economy. Textiles and clothing, iron and steel products, machinery and transportation equipment, agricultural products and wine are exported.

Although ultimately a victor in World Wars I and II, France suffered extensive losses in its empire, wealth, manpower, and rank as a dominant nation-state. Nevertheless, France today is one of the most modern countries in the world and is a leader among European nations. Since 1958, it has constructed a hybrid presidential-parliamentary governing system resistant to the instabilities experienced in earlier more purely parliamentary administrations. In recent years, its reconciliation and cooperation with Germany have proved central to the economic integration of Europe, including the introduction of a common exchange currency, the euro, in January 1999. At present, France is at the forefront of efforts to develop the EU's military capabilities to supplement progress toward an EU foreign policy.

MONETARY SYSTEM:

1 Livre = 20 Sols (Sous)
1 Ecu = 6 Livres
1 Louis D'or = 4 Ecus to 1794
1 Franc = 10 Decimes = 100 Centimes, 1794-1960
1 Nouveau Franc = 100 "old" Francs, 1960-1962
1 Franc = 100 Centimes, 1962-2002
1 Euro = 100 Cents, 2002-

FRENCH DENOMINATIONS

1 Un	13 Treize	125 Cent Vingt-Cinq
2 Deux	14 Quatorze	200 Deux Cents
3 Trois	15 Quinze	250 Deux Cent Cinquante
4 Quatre	16 Seize	300 Trois Cents
5 Cinq	20 Vingt	400 Quatre Cents
6 Six	25 Vingt-Cinq	500 Cinq Cents
7 Sept	30 Trente	750 Sept Cent cinquante
8 Huit	40 Quarante	1,000 Mille
9 Neuf	10 Cinquante	2,000 Deux Mille
10 Dix	80 Quatre-Vingts	5,000 Cinq Mille
11 Onze	90 Quatre-Vingt-Dix	10,000 Quatre-Vingt-Dix
12 Douze	100 Cent	

COMMERCIAL BANKS

SIEGE

COMMERCIAL BANKS

ACHILLE ADAM, BANQUIER

1800'S ISSUE

		Good	Fine	XF
S101	**20 Francs** 18xx. View of ships in harbor at upper center.	—	750.	1500.
S102	**100 Francs** 18xx. View of ships in harbor at upper center. Like #S101.	—	1000.	2250.

BANQUE DE BORDEAUX

1818-48 ISSUE

		Good	Fine	XF
S103	**100 Francs** 18.3.1848. Black. Two allegorical figures at left with flag, at right with trident; two women reclining at bottom, bank at center. Paper: Light yellow. Rare.	—	—	—
S104	**200 Francs** 18.3.1848. Black. Two allegorical figures at left with flag, at right with trident; two women reclining at bottom, bank at center. Like #S103. Paper: Light green. Rare.	—	—	—
S105	**500 Francs** ND. Allegorical figures at left and right, arms of Bordeaux at bottom. Rare.	—	—	—
S106	**500 Francs** 20.10.1825. Black. Two allegorical figures at left with flag, at right with trident; two women reclining at bottom, bank at center. Like #S103. Paper: Ruby similar to parchment. Rare.	—	—	—
S107	**500 Francs** 10.8.1836; 9.5.1838; 20.6.1844. Black. Two allegorical figures at left with flag, at right with trident; two women reclining at bottom, bank at center. Like #S106. Paper: Pink. Rare.	—	—	—

		Good	Fine	XF
S108	**1000 Francs** 1.7.1819-20.11.1846. Black. Allegorical figures at left and right, arms of Bordeaux at bottom. Like #S105. Rare.	—	—	—
S109	**1000 Francs** ND. Black. Two allegorical figures at left with flag, at right with trident; two women reclining at bottom, bank at center. Like #S106. Rare.	—	—	—

Banque Commerciale du Havre

1800's Issue

		Good	Fine	XF
S110	**100 Francs** 18xx. Unsigned remainder.	—	—	—

Banque de Dijon

1839 Issue

		Good	Fine	XF
S111	**250 Francs** ND. Proof.	—	—	—
S112	**500 Francs** ND. Proof.	—	—	—
S113	**1000 Francs** ND. Proof.	—	—	—

NOTE: No examples of #S111-S113 are presently known.

Banque du Havre

1837-48 Issue

		Good	Fine	XF
S121	**50 Francs** ND. Seated allegorical figure at left and right within frame, ships at bottom left, center and right. Proof. Rare.	—	—	—
S122	**100 Francs** ND. Seated allegorical figure at left and right within frame, ships at bottom left, center and right. Like #S121. Reported not confirmed.	—	—	—
S123	**250 Francs** 15.2.1840. Black. Seated allegorical figure at left and right within frame, ships at bottom left, center and right. Like #S121. Paper: Ruby. Rare.	—	—	—
S124	**250 Francs** 5.1.1840; 15.2.1840. Black. Rare.	—	—	—
S125	**500 Francs** ND (ca.1836). Man's head at left and right within frame, ships at bottom center. Rare.	—	—	—
S126	**500 Francs** 15.2.1840. Black. Seated allegorical figure at left and right within frame, ships at bottom left, center and right. Like #S121. Paper: Gray-blue. Rare.	—	—	—
S127	**1000 Francs** 24.12.1836. Black. Man's head at left and right within frame, ships at bottom center. Like #S125. Proof. Rare.	—	—	—

Banque de Lille

1836-48 Issue

		Good	Fine	XF
S131	**100 Francs** 27.3.1848. Black. Bull's head at upper left, horse's head at upper right. Paper: Green. Rare.	—	—	—
S132	**250 Francs** 1.2.1837. Black. Imprint at bottom: *Normand Fils Del.-Belhatte Sc.* Proof. Rare.	—	—	—
S133	**250 Francs** 23.2.1837. Black. Like #S132. Imprint at bottom: *Normand Fils Del.-Saunier Direcxit-Belhatte Sc.* Proof. Rare.	—	—	—
S134	**500 Francs** ND. Bull's head at upper left, horse's head at upper right. Like #S131. Reported not confirmed. Rare.	—	—	—
S135	**1000 Francs** 13.12.1838. Black. Bull's head at upper left, horse's head at upper right. Like #S131. Proof. Rare.	—	—	—

ILLUSTRATIONS

Illustrations of bank notes used throughout this catalog are 42% of the actual size.

Banque de Limoges, 1848

It is reported that the Banque de Limoges had proofs of notes printed in April of 1848. Denominations at first were from 20 to 1000 Francs, later including 5 and 10 Francs. No examples are presently confirmed.

Banque de Lyon

1835-48 Issue

		Good	Fine	XF
S141	**25 Francs** 20.3.1848. Black. Arms with rampant lion at top center. Back: Blue. Rare.	—	—	—
S142	**100 Francs** 25.3.1848. Black. Arms with rampant lion at top center. Like #S141. Back: Blue. Reported not confirmed.	—	—	—
S143	**250 Francs** 1836. Provisional issue Barre/Porret. Proof.	—	Unc	7500.

		Good	Fine	XF
S144	**250 Francs** 25.1.1839; 12.9.1839. Standing allegorical figures at left and right, cherubs at bottom left and right, arms at top center.	—	Unc	10,000.
S145	**500 Francs** ND. Standing allegorical figures at left and right, cherubs at bottom left and right, arms at top center. Like #S144. Reported not confirmed.	—	—	—
S146	**1000 Francs** 11.7.1844. 3 signatures. Rare.	—	—	—

		Good	Fine	XF
S147	**1000 Francs** 1848. Standing allegorical figures at left and right, cherubs at bottom left and right, arms at top center. Like #S144. Imprint: *Louis Perrin impr.* at left, 2 signatures. Rare.	—	—	—

Banque de Marseille

1836-48 Issue

	Good	Fine	XF
S151 50 Francs 22.3.1848. Black on green underprint. Seated allegorical figure at lower left and right, old view of town at bottom center. Paper texture like vellum. Rare.	—	—	—
S152 100 Francs 25.3.1848. Seated allegorical figure at lower left and right, old view of town at bottom center. Like #S151. Rare.	—	—	—
S153 250 Francs 24.9.1836. Black. Proof. Rare.	—	—	—
S154 250 Francs 28.11.1838. Black. Seated allegorical figure at lower left and right, old view of town at bottom center. Like #S151. Paper: Ruby. Rare.	—	—	—

	Good	Fine	XF
S155 500 Francs 21.8.1839. Seated allegorical figure at lower left and right, old view of town at bottom center. Like #S151. Inscription at upper left and right in two circles. Paper texture like vellum. Rare.	—	—	—
S156 500 Francs 1848. Seated allegorical figure at lower left and right, old view of town at bottom center. Like #S151 but text at center in circle. Reported not confirmed.	—	—	—

	Good	Fine	XF
S157 1000 Francs 24.9.1836. Horse's head at bottom lower left center and bull's head at lower center right. Proof. Rare.	—	—	—
S158 1000 Francs 1848. Seated allegorical figure at lower left and right, old view of town at bottom center. Like #S151. Reported not confirmed.	—	—	—

Banque de Nantes

1818-48 Issue

	Good	Fine	XF
S161 250 Francs Printer: *Cornouailles Fecit*. Proof. Rare.	—	—	—
S162 500 Francs Imprint: *Cornouailles Fecit*. Printer: *Cornouailles Fecit*. Proof. Rare.	—	—	—
S163 1000 Francs Imprint: *Cornouailles Fecit*. Printer: *Cornouailles Fecit*. Proof. Rare.	—	—	—

NOTE: Only 3 proof examples are known for this bank.

Banque d'Orléans

1838-48 Issue

	Good	Fine	XF
S171 25 Francs 1848. Rare.	—	—	—
S172 100 Francs 1848. Rare.	—	—	—
S173 250 Francs 1.1.1839. Steam locomotives at bottom left, arms at top center, ship at bottom right. Rare.	—	—	—
S174 500 Francs 1.1.1839 (?). Rare.	—	—	—
S175 1000 Francs 1.1.1839 (?). Rare.	—	—	—

Banque de Rouen

1807-48 Issue

	Good	Fine	XF
S176 50 Francs 18.3.1848. Green. Ornate left and right border with anchor, fruit, caduceus, cherubs, etc.			
a. Issued note. Rare.	—	—	—
p. Proof.	—	Unc	4000.
S177 100 Francs 1.4.1807. Black. Rare.	—	—	—

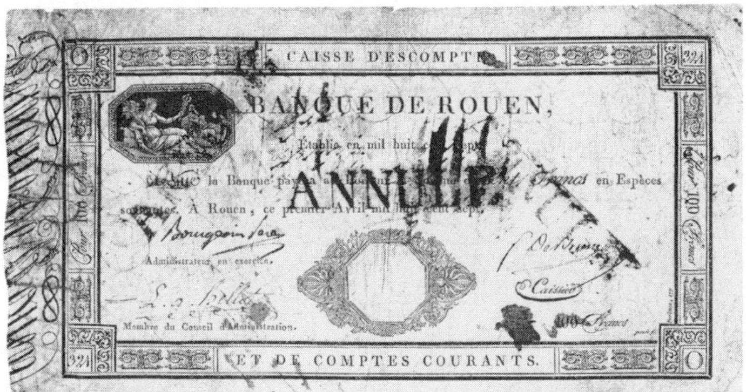

	Good	Fine	XF
S178 100 Francs 18.3.1848.	—	—	—
S179 250 Francs 22.8.1826; 2.9.1826. Text: *La loi punit de mort le contrefacteur*. Rare.	—	—	—

	Good	Fine	XF
S180 250 Francs 26.9.1826. Text: *Le contrefacteur est puni des travaux forces a perpetuite*. Rare.	—	—	—

	Good	Fine	XF
S181 500 Francs 1.4.1807. Red.	5000.	10,000.	—
S182 500 Francs ND (ca.1826). Text: *La loi punit de mort le contrefacteur.* Like #S179. Rare.	—	—	—
S183 500 Francs Red. Text: *Le contrefacteur est puni des travaux forces a perpetuite.* Like #S180. Rare.	—	—	—
S184 1000 Francs ND (ca.1826). Text: *La loi punit de mort le contrefacteur.* Like #S179. Rare.	—	—	—
S185 1000 Francs Text: *Le contrefacteur est puni des travaux forces a perpetuite.* Like #S180. Rare.	—	—	—

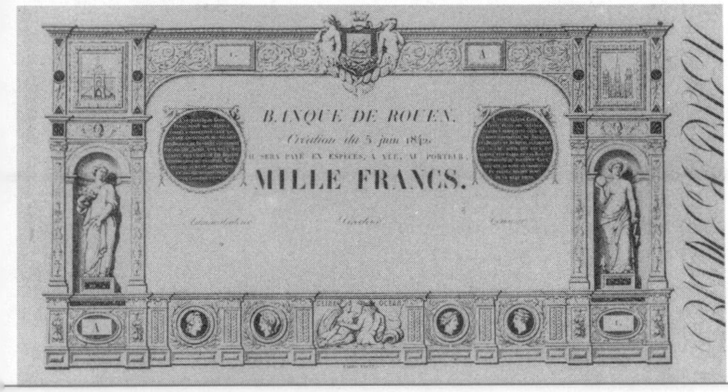

	Good	Fine	XF
S186 1000 Francs 5.6.1842. Standing allegorical woman at left and right, two figures representing Seine and Ocean at bottom center. Designer: Barre. Proof.	—	Unc	7500.

Banque Rouennaise

1871 Issue

	Good	Fine	XF
S188 5 Francs 1871. Cut cancelled, hand stamped: *ANNULE.*	—	750.	1750.

	Good	Fine	XF
S189 10 Francs 1871. Like #S208. Cut cancelled, hand stamped: *ANNULE.*	—	750.	1750.

Banque de Savoie

1851; 1859 Issue

For previously listed #S191-S197, see Italian States #S160-S166.

Banque Territoriale, Paris

1799-1803 Issues

	Good	Fine	XF
S201 50 Francs Black. Paper: Yellow.	—	—	—
S202 100 Francs Black. Paper: Green.	—	—	—
S203 250 Francs Black. Paper: Blue.	—	—	—
S204 500 Francs Black. Paper: Pink.	—	—	6500.
S205 1000 Francs Black. Paper: White.	—	—	5000.

Banque de Toulouse

1838-48 Issue

	Good	Fine	XF
S209 100 Francs 20.3.1848. Red. Five allegorical figures at bottom. Rare.	—	—	—
S210 200 Francs 20.3.1848. Blue. Like #S201. Rare.	—	—	—
S211 250 Francs 1.2.1839. Black. Allegorical figures in border. Proof. Rare.	—	—	—
S212 250 Francs ND. Black. Like #S201. Rare.	—	—	—
S213 500 Francs ND. Like #S201. Reported not confirmed.	—	—	—
S214 500 Francs ND. Like #S203. Rare.	—	—	—
S215 1000 Francs ND. Like #S201. Reported not confirmed.	—	—	—

Caisse de Commerce, Paris

1792 Issue

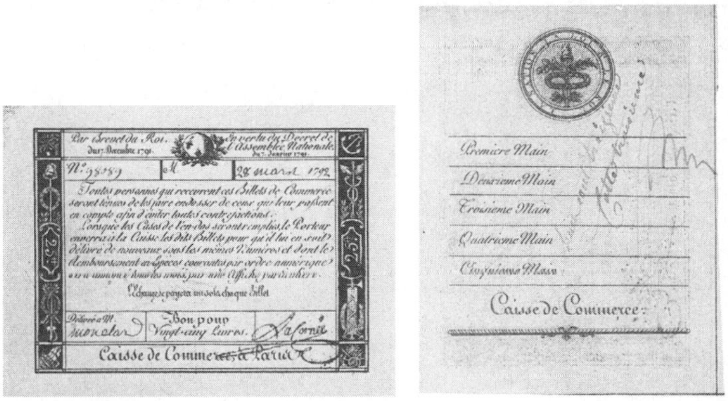

	Good	Fine	XF
S218 25 Livres 25.1.1792-28.3.1792. Black. Handwritten dates with handwritten signature. Back: Handwritten dates with handwritten signature. Paper: Yellow.	40.00	125.	375.

Caisse de Comptes Courants

1795 Issue

	Good	Fine	XF
S221 500 Francs AN4-AN8.	—	—	—
S222 1000 Francs AN4-AN8.	—	—	—

Caisse d'Echange, Caen

1800 Issue

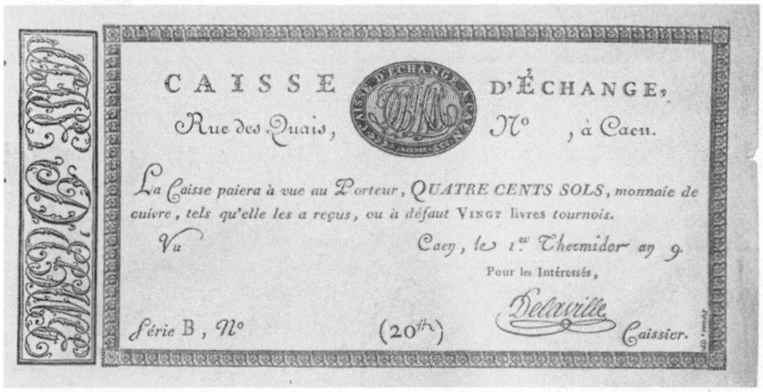

	Good	Fine	XF
S226 400 Sols AN9. Black. (Not issued).	—	225.	675.

Caisse d'Echange, Orléans

1801 Issue

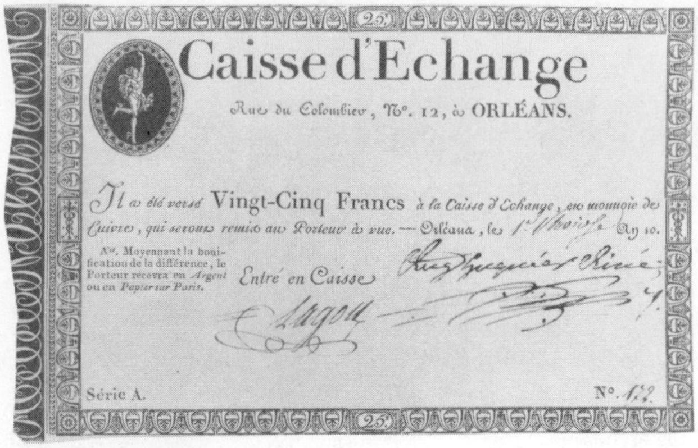

		Good	Fine	XF
S231	**25 Francs** AN10.			
	a. Issued note.	75.00	225.	675.
	r. Unissued remainder.	—	Unc	200.
S232	**50 Francs** AN10.	100.	300.	900.
S233	**100 Francs** AN10.	200.	600.	1750.

Caisse d'Echange des Monnaies, Paris

1798-1804 Issue

		Good	Fine	XF
S236	**12.50 Francs**	75.00	225.	675.
S237	**25 Francs**	75.00	225.	675.

Caisse d'Echange des Monnaies, Rouen

1797-1803 Issue

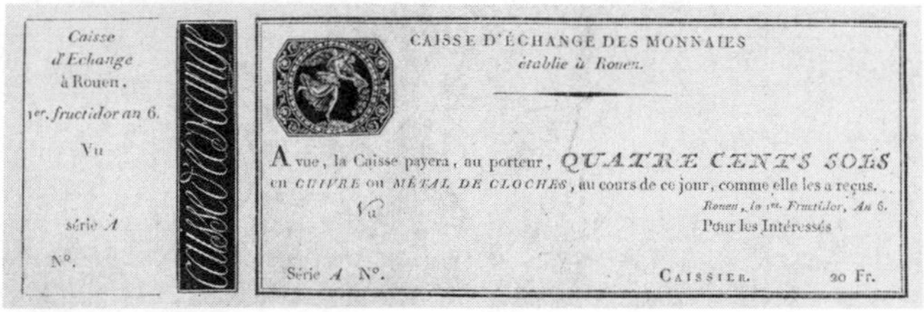

		Good	Fine	XF
S241	**400 Sols** 1 er Fructidor AN6. Angel at upper left spilling cornucopia. (Not issued).	—	275.	800.

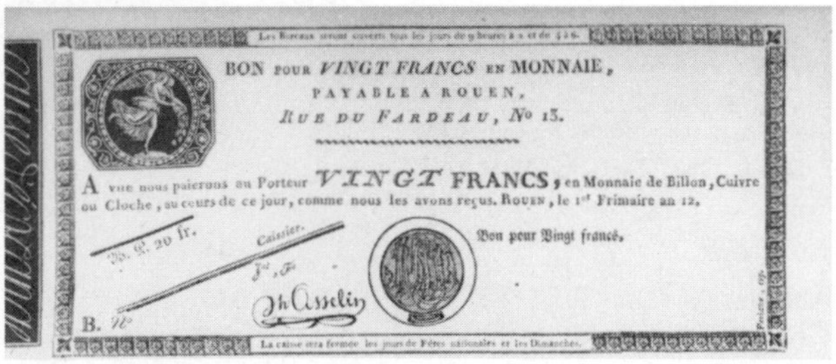

		Good	Fine	XF
S245	**20 Francs** AN10, 12. Angel at upper left spilling cornucopia.			
	a. Date: *1 er Frimaire AN 10.*	25.00	75.00	225.
	b. Date: *1 er Frimaire AN 12.*	25.00	75.00	225.

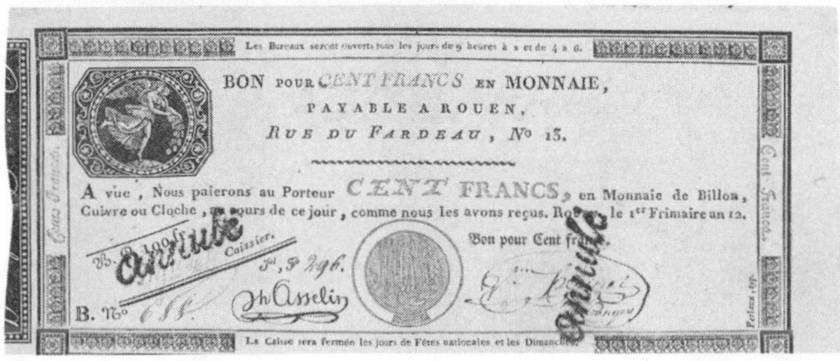

		Good	Fine	XF
S246	**100 Francs** AN12. Angel at upper left spilling cornucopia.			
	a. Issued note.	40.00	125.	375.
	b. Cancelled, overprint: *Annulé.*	20.00	60.00	175.

Caisse d'Escompte du Commerce, Paris

1797-1803 Issue

		Good	Fine	XF
S253	**500 Francs** 24.11.1797-26.8.1803. Vignettes in corners, Mercury at bottom left center, Ceres at bottom center right.	—	4000.	10,000.

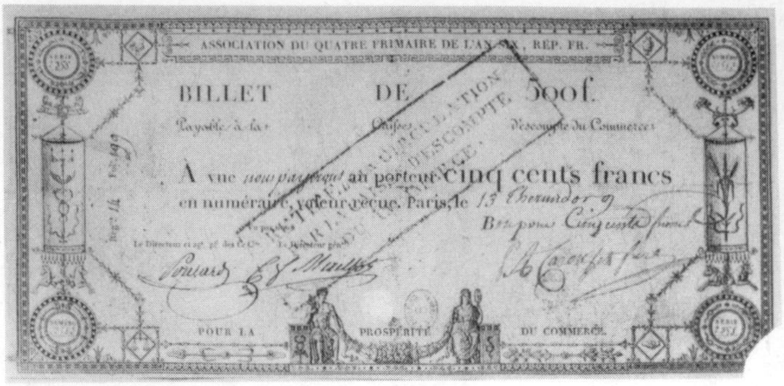

		Good	Fine	XF
S254	**500 Francs** AN6 and other dates. Two allegorical figures sitting with partial wreath at bottom center.	—	4000.	10,000.

Comptoir Commercial, Paris

1800-03 Issue

		Good	Fine	XF
S261	**200 Francs** 1800-03.	—	—	—
S262	**250 Francs** 1800-03.	—	—	—
S263	**300 Francs** 1800-03.	—	—	—
S264	**500 Francs** 1800-03.	—	—	—
S265	**1000 Francs** 1800-03.	—	—	—

Factorerie du Commerce, Parris

Notes are reported ca. 1802, but denominations are unknown.

Societé Générale du Commerce, Rouen

Notes are reported, but denominations are unknown.

Siege

Siege of Lyon

1793 ND Issue

		Good	Fine	XF
S301	**25 Sous** ND (1793). Black. Fleur-de-lis at corners, diamonds in border. With 1 signature at left, embossed arms at right. Uniface.	20.00	60.00	175.

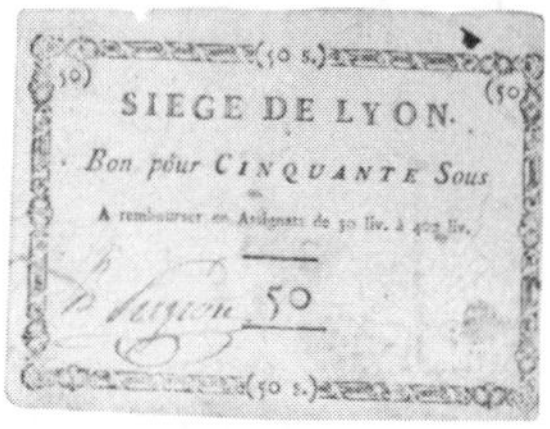

		Good	Fine	XF
S302	**50 Sous** ND (1793). Black. Ornamented border. With 1 signature at left, embossed arms at right. Uniface. Paper: Off-white.	25.00	75.00	225.
S303	**5 Livres** ND (1793). Black. Plain border. With 1 signature at left, embossed arms at right. Uniface. Paper: White.	40.00	125.	375.

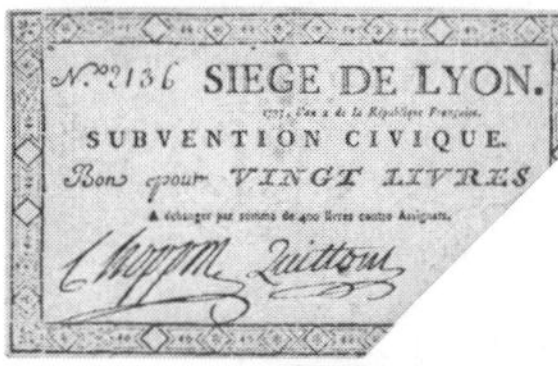

S#303

S#304

		Good	Fine	XF
S304	**20 Livres** ND (1793). Black. Border similar to #S301. With 2 signatures and 2 embossed arms. Cut cancelled.			
	a. Watermark: *Caise.*	40.00	125.	375.
	b. Watermark: *Patriotique.*	40.00	125.	375.
	c. Watermark: *De Lyon.*	40.00	125.	375.

NOTE: #S304 only one uncut example known.

Military

Trésorerie aux Armées

Army Treasury

1917 ND Issue

#M1-M3 French text on back: *up to the end of the second year after the armistice.*

		VG	VF	UNC
M1	**50 Centimes**			
	ND (1917). Blue. Woman with child at left, soldier with dog at right. Back: *RF* monogram in shield at center.	1.50	7.50	40.00
M2	**1 Franc**			
	ND (1917). Light brown. Woman with child at left, soldier with dog at right. Back: *RF* monogram in shield at center.	1.75	8.50	45.00
M3	**2 Francs**			
	ND (1917). Lilac. Woman with child at left, soldier with dog at right. Back: *RF* monogram in shield at center.	5.00	40.00	160.

1919 ND Issue

#M4-M5 French text on back: *up to the end of the fourth year after the armistice.*

		VG	VF	UNC
M4	**50 Centimes**			
	ND (1919). Blue. Woman with child at left. Soldier with dog at right. Back: *RF* monogram in shield at center.	2.00	10.00	50.00
M5	**1 Franc**			
	ND (1919). Light brown. Woman with child at left, soldier with dog at right. Back: *RF* monogram in shield at center.	3.00	15.00	80.00

Tresor Français

1947 ND Issue

#M6-M10 *TRESOR FRANÇAIS.*

		VG	VF	UNC
M6	**5 Francs**			
	ND (1947). Brown, red and multicolor. Woman at center. Back: Wheat harvesting.			
	a. Issued note.	2.50	20.00	95.00
	s. Specimen.	—	—	400.

		VG	VF	UNC
M7	**10 Francs**			
	ND (1947). Light blue and multicolor. Woman at center. Back: Wheat harvesting.			
	a. Issued note.	4.50	27.50	100.
	s. Specimen.	—	—	400.
M8	**50 Francs**			
	ND (1947). Blue and Multicolor. Mercury at center. Back: Reclining woman.	7.50	60.00	225.

		VG	VF	UNC
M9	**100 Francs**			
	ND (1947). Brown and Multicolor. Mercury at center. Back: Reclining woman.	7.50	55.00	200.
M10	**1000 Francs**			
	ND (1947). Blue-green and multicolor. Mercury at center. Back: Reclining woman.	100.	275.	1000.

1955 ND Issue

#M11-M15 *TRESOR PUBLIC.*

		VG	VF	UNC
M11	**100 Francs**			
	ND (1955). Mercury at center. Back: Reclining woman.			
	a. Issued note.	10.00	70.00	300.
	s. Specimen.	—	—	700.
M12	**1000 Francs**			
	ND (1955). Multicolor. Mercury at left center.			
	a. Issued note.	100.	400.	—
	s. Specimen.	—	—	1200.

		VG	VF	UNC
M13	**5000 Francs**			
	ND (1955). Multicolor. Young farm couple at center.			
	a. Issued note.	275.	500.	—
	s. Specimen.	—	—	1500.

1960 ND Issue

		VG	VF	UNC
M14	**5 Nouveaux Francs on 500 Francs**			
	ND (1960). Multicolor. Mercury facing.	60.00	300.	1400.
M14A	**10 Nouveaux Francs on 1000 Francs**			
	ND (1960). Multicolor. Mercury at left center. Overprint: On #M12.	175.	1100.	—
M15	**50 Nouveaux Francs on 5000 Francs**			
	ND (1960). Multicolor. Overprint: On #M13.	200.	1400.	—

Suez Crisis, 1956

Forces Françaises en Mediterranee Orientale

1956 ND Issue

		VG	VF	UNC
M16	**50 Francs**			
	ND (1956). Multicolor. Overprint: On #M8. *FORCES FRANCAISES EN MEDITERRANEE ORIENTALE.*	125.	700.	—
M17	**100 Francs**			
	ND (1956). Overprint: On #M9. *FORCES FRANCAISES EN MEDITERRANEE ORIENTALE.*	100.	600.	—
M18	**1000 Francs**			
	ND (1956). Overprint: On #M10.*FORCES FRANCAISES EN MEDITERRANEE ORIENTALE.*	300.	1800.	—

Regional

Régie des Chemins de Fer des Territoires Occupés

Franco-Belgian Railways Administration in Occupied German Territory

1923 ND Issue

#R1-10 steam locomotive at top ctr. Rhine landscape in unpt. at ctr. Neptune at r. on back.

		VG	VF	UNC
R1	**.05 Franc**			
	ND (1923). Dark blue on orange underprint, red border.	.50	2.00	8.00
R2	**.10 Franc**			
	ND (1923). Dark brown on light blue underprint, green border.	.50	2.00	8.00
R3	**.25 Franc**			
	ND (1923). Violet on lilac underprint, gold border.	.75	2.50	10.00
R4	**.50 Franc**			
	ND (1923). Dark green on olive underprint, gold border.	1.00	3.00	12.00
R5	**1 Franc**			
	ND (1923). Dark blue on gray-green underprint, gold border.	1.50	5.00	20.00

		VG	VF	UNC
R6	**5 Francs**			
	ND (1923). Dark blue on gray underprint, red border.	3.00	7.50	25.00
R7	**10 Francs**			
	ND (1923). Black on gray-blue underprint.	5.00	25.00	75.00
R8	**20 Francs**			
	ND (1923). Violet underprint.	10.00	35.00	125.
R9	**50 Francs**			
	ND (1923). Pink underprint.			
	a. Issued note.	35.00	125.	300.
	b. Series B21. (Not issued).	25.00	100.	225.
R10	**100 Francs**			
	ND (1923). Black on pink underprint, gold border.	50.00	175.	350.

FRENCH INDO-CHINA

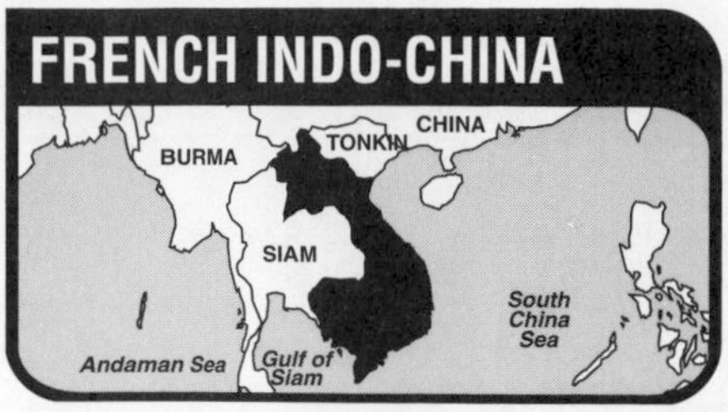

French Indo-China (l'Indo-Chine) was located on the Indo-Chinese peninsula of Southeast Asia. It was a French colonial possession from the later 19th century until 1954. A French Governor-General headed a federal-type central government and colonial administration, but reported directly to France which retained exclusive authority over foreign affairs, defense, customs, finance and public works. The colony covered 286,194 sq. mi. (741,242 sq. km.) and had a population of 24 million. It consisted of 5 protectorates: Tonkin (northern Vietnam), Annam (central Vietnam), Cochin-China (southern Vietnam), Laos and Cambodia. Principal cities were: Saigon, Hanoi, Haiphong, Pnom-Penh and Vientiane. From 1875 to 1951, the exclusive right to issue banknotes within the colony was held by the Bank of Indochina (Banque de l'Indochine). On December 31, 1951 this privilege was transferred to the Issuing Authority of the States of Cambodia, Laos and Vietnam (Institut d'Emission des Etats du Cambodge, du Laos et du Vietnam).

From the moment of their conquest, the Indochinese people resisted French rule. The degree of resistance varied, being strongest in central and northern Vietnam, but was evident throughout Indochina. There were unsuccessful attempts by Vietnamese nationals, headed by Nguyen Ai Quoc (later known as Ho Chi Minh), to gain recognition/independence at the Versailles Peace Conference following World War I.

Japan occupied French Indochina at the start of World War II, but allowed the local French (Vichy) government to remain in power until March 1945. Meanwhile, many nationalists (communist and non-communist alike) followed Ho Chi Minh's leadership in the formation of the League for Independence of Vietnam (Viet-Minh) which took an active anti-Japanese part during the war. France reoccupied the area after the Japanese surrender, and established the Associated States of Indochina, with each of the five political subdivisions having limited independence within the French Union. Disagreement over the degree of independence and the reunification of the three Vietnamese subdivisions led to armed conflict with the Viet-Minh and a protracted war (The First Indochina War). In 1949/1950, in an attempt to retain her holdings, France recognized Laos, Cambodia and Vietnam as semi-independent self governing States within the French Union, but retained financial and economic control. Fighting continued and culminated with the French military disaster at Dien Bien Phu in May 1954. The subsequent Geneva Agreement brought full independence to Laos, Cambodia and Vietnam (*temporarily* divided at the 17th parallel of latitude), and with it, an end to French rule in Indochina.

See also Vietnam, South Vietnam, Laos and Cambodia.

RULERS:

French to 1954

MONETARY SYSTEM:

1 Piastre = 1 (Mexican Silver) Dollar = 100 Cents,1875-1903
1 Piastre = 100 Cents, 1903-1951

JAPANESE OCCUPATION, WW II

JAPANESE IMPERIAL GOVERNMENT

TA JIH PEN TI KUO CHENG FU

1938-40 ND ISSUE

		VG	VF	UNC
M1	**50 Sen** ND (1940). Blue on yellow-green and light purple underprint. Dragon at left. Back: Blue.	50.00	125.	250.
M2	**1 Yen** ND (1940). Purple on yellow-green and brown underprint. Onagadori cockerel at left. Back: Purple.	150.	250.	500.
M3	**5 Yen** ND (1940). Gray-green on gray-blue and light purple underprint. Onagadori cockerel at left and right. Back: Dark green.	600.	1000.	2000.
M4	**10 Yen** ND (1940). Brown on light blue and pink underprint. Onagadori cockerel at left and right. Block # and serial #. Back: Brown.	600.	1000.	2000.
M5	**100 Yen** ND (1938). Blue-green on light lilac underprint. Onagadori cockerel at left and right. Specimen.	—	—	500.

Note: For 100 Yen of same design but different color printing, see China #M21.

1942 ND ISSUE

		VG	VF	UNC
M6	**1 Yen** ND (ca.1942). Purple on yellow-green underprint, lithograph. Onagadori cockerel at left. Only 2 block #. Without *Ro* prefix. Back: Purple. Specimen.	—	—	500.

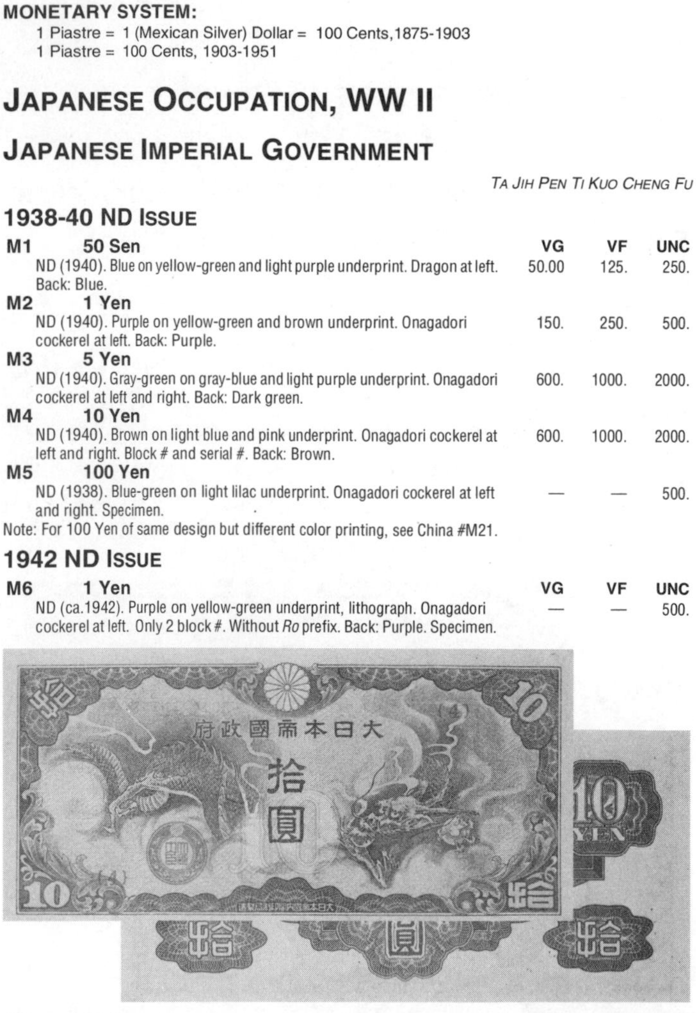

		VG	VF	UNC
M7	**10 Yen** ND (ca.1942). Brown on light blue underprint., lithograph. Onagadori cockerel at left and right. Only 2 block #. Without *Ro* prefix. Back: Brown.	.50	2.50	10.00

GERMAN STATES

Although the origin of the German Empire can be traced to the Treaty of Verdun, 843, that ceded Charlemagne's lands east of the Rhine to German Prince Louis, it was for centuries little more than a geographic expression, consisting of hundreds of effectively autonomous big and little states. Nominally the states owed their allegiance to the Holy Roman Emperor, who was also a German king, but as the emperors exhibited less and less concern for Germany the actual power devolved on the lords of the individual states. The fragmentation of the empire climaxed with the tragic denouement of the Thirty Years War, 1618-48, which devastated much of Germany, destroyed its agriculture and medieval commercial eminence and ended the attempt of the Hapsburgs to unify Germany. Deprived of administrative capacity by a lack of resources, the imperial authority became utterly powerless. At this time Germany contained an estimated 1,800 individual states, some with a population of as little as 300. The German Empire of recent history (the creation of Bismarck) was formed on April 14, 1871, when the King of Prussia became Emperor Wilhelm I of Germany. The new empire comprised four kingdoms, five grand duchies, 13 duchies and principalities, three free cities and the nonautonomous province of Alsace-Lorraine. Prior to the German unification in 1871 the various German States enjoyed varying degrees of political independence including the right to coin and issue money. Most of the paper currency issues of the German States from the middle of the 18th century until the unification are valued in thalers and gulden denominations with the gulden usually worth about half the thaler. There are a few exceptions such as the "Franken" valued notes of the Napoleonic Kingdom of Westphalia and the early "Pfund Banco" notes of the Prussian "Giro und Lehnbank."

After the unification many of these banks issued currency under the new mark system. These notes are listed in the Regional Bank listing which follows this section.

Bank notes of the German States prior to the unification in 1871, official government issues and local bank issues are listed together under the various states.

MONETARY SYSTEM:

Until 1871 the Mark (Marck) was a measure of weight.

North German States until 1837

2 Gulden = 1 Reichsthaler
1 Speciesthaler (before 1753)
1 Convention Thaler (after 1753)

North German States after 1837

30 Groschen = 1 Thaler
1 Vereinsthaler (after 1857)

South German States until 1837

120 Convention Kreuzer = 2 Convention Gulden = 1 Convention Thaler

ANHALT, DUCHY OF

HERZOGLICH ANHALTISCHE STAATSSCHUL DENVERWALTUNG

ANHALT STATE INDEBTEDNESS ADMINISTRATION

1861-67 STATE TREASURY NOTES ISSUE

Issued for statewide circulation.

		Good	Fine	XF
S101	**1 Thaler** 20.5.1861. Light green. Signature Funcke; Siebigk; Holzmann; Medicus. Back: Light brown. Watermark: II EIN THLER II. Printer: Gebr. Katz, Dessau.	450.	900.	1750.
S102	**1 Thaler** 1.8.1866. Green. Back: Light brown.			
	a. With imprint and watermark.	450.	900.	1750.
	b. Without imprint and without watermark.	450.	900.	1750.
S103	**1 Thaler** 31.10.1867. Green. Back: Light brown.	—	—	—

ANHALT-BERNBURG, DUCHY OF

The line died out in 1863, whereupon its territories were united with Anhalt-Dessau.

HERZOGLICH ANHALTISCHES STAATSMINISTERIUM

ANHALT STATE MINISTRY

1850 TREASURY BILLS ISSUE

	Good	Fine	XF
S107 1 Thaler 18.3.1850. Yellow brown. Signature Hempel; Krosigk; Ahlfeld. Back: Pink. Watermark: A.I.B. Printer: Theodor Boesche, Berlin.	450.	900.	1750.
S108 5 Thaler 18.3.1850. Pink. Signature Hempel; Krosigk; Ahlfeld. Back: Green. Watermark: A.5.B. Printer: Theodor Boesche, Berlin.	525.	1050.	2100.

1852-56 TREASURY BILLS ISSUE

	Good	Fine	XF
S109 1 Thaler 5.2.1852.	—	—	—
S110 25 Thaler 26.6.1856. Flesh colored. Signature Schaetzell. Back: Light brown. Watermark: HERZOGLICH ANH . BERNBURG KASSENANWEISUNG.	850.	1750.	3500.

1859 ISSUE

	Good	Fine	XF
S111 1 Thaler 25.7.1859. Black on green underprint. Monogram HAB as underprint. Signature Schaetzell. Watermark: HERZ ANH BERNB KASSENSCHEIN I THALER I. Printer: Theodor Boesche, Berlin.	375.	750.	1500.

ANHALT-CÖTHEN, DUCHY OF

Anhalt-Cöthen was raised from a principality to a duchy when it entered the Confederation of the Rhine in 1807. In 1828 the main Anhalt-Cöthen line died out, whereupon the princes of Anhalt-Cöthen-Pless became the dukes of Anhalt-Cöthen. This line died out in 1847, whereupon its territories were jointly administered by Anhalt-Bernburg and Anhalt-Dessau. In 1863, after the Anhalt-Bernburg line died out, the three Anhalt duchies were united into one.

HERZOGL. ANHALT-CÖTHENSCHE KASSENSCHEIN

ANHALT-CÖTHEN TREASURY

1829 STATE TREASURY NOTES ISSUE

	Good	Fine	XF
S116 1 Thaler Courant 1.1.1829. Light green.	850.	1750.	3500.
S117 5 Thaler Courant 1.1.1829.	—	—	—
S118 10 Thaler Courant 1.1.1829.	—	—	—

HERZOGL. ANHALT-CÖTHENSCHE STAATSSCHULDEN-COMMISSION

ANHALT-CÖTHEN STATE INDEBT EDNESS COMMISSION

1848 TREASURY NOTES ISSUE

Emergency issue during the Revolution of 1848.

	Good	Fine	XF
S121 5 Thaler 1.5.1848. Black. Uniface.	525.	1050.	2100.
S122 1 Thaler 1.6.1848. Green.			
a. With imprint.	375.	750.	1500.
b. Without imprint.	450.	900.	1750.
S123 5 Thaler 1.6.1848. Black on green underprint. Back: Printed.	450.	900.	1750.

ANHALT-CÖTHEN-BERNBURGER EISENBAHN-GESELLSCHAFT

ANHALT-CÖTHEN-BERNBURG RAI LROAD COMPANY

1846 TREASURY NOTES ISSUE

	Good	Fine	XF
S126 1 Thaler 2.3.1846. Light green. Signature Böttger; Friedheim; Hess; Jannasch; Steinthal. Back: Signature Kersten; Braun. Printer: Eduard Haenel, Berlin.	525.	1050.	2100.

1850-56 TREASURY NOTES ISSUE

	Good	Fine	XF
S127 1 Thaler 20.2.1850. Black on green underprint.			
a. With watermark.	375.	750.	1500.
b. Without watermark. (forgery?).	—	—	—

	Good	Fine	XF
S128 5 Thaler 20.2.1850. Light green.	450.	900.	1750.
S129 25 Thaler 1.7.1856. Green on light green. Watermark: 25 CBEG 25. Printer: Albert Falckenberg, Magdeburg.	650.	1300.	2600.

ANHALT-DESSAU, DUCHY OF

The duchy absorbed Anhalt-Cöthen in 1847 and Anhalt-Bernberg in 1863. After uniting the three Anhalt lines, it called itself simply the "Duchy of Anhalt."

HERZOGLICH ANHALT-DESSAUISCHE REGIERUNG

1849 STATE TREASURY NOTES ISSUE

	Good	Fine	XF
S131 1 Thaler 1.8.1849. Gray. Signature Ploetz; Basedow.	375.	750.	1500.
S132 5 Thaler 1.8.1849. Coffee brown. Signature Ploetz; Basedow.	525.	1050.	2100.

1855 STATE TREASURY NOTES ISSUE

	Good	Fine	XF
S133 10 Thaler 1.10.1855. Light green. Signature Basedowith Braunbehrens. Back: Green numbers.	800.	1600.	3250.

ANHALT-DESSAUISCHE LANDESBANK

1847 ISSUE

	Good	Fine	XF
S134 1 Thaler 2.1.1847.	450.	900.	1750.

	Good	Fine	XF
S135 5 Thaler 2.1.1847.	650.	1300.	2600.

1855 ISSUE

	Good	Fine	XF
S136 10 Thaler 1.6.1855.	800.	1600.	3250.
S137 50 Thaler 1.6.1855.	—	—	—

1864 ISSUE

	Good	Fine	XF
S138 1 Thaler 2.1.1864. Green and light brown.	450.	900.	1750.

S139 5 Thaler	Good	Fine	XF
2.1.1864.	650.	1300.	2600.

1874 Issue

S140 100 Mark	Good	Fine	XF
1.7.1874. Printer: G&D.	750.	1500.	3000.

Baden, Grand Duchy of

Grossh. Badische General-Staats-Casse

1849; 1854 Issue

S141 2 Gulden	Good	Fine	XF
1.7.1849. Father Rhine at left, Danube at right, Badenia above. Signature Fruttiger; Friderici. Printer: Hasper in Karlsruhe using plates by C. Naumann.	150.	300.	600.

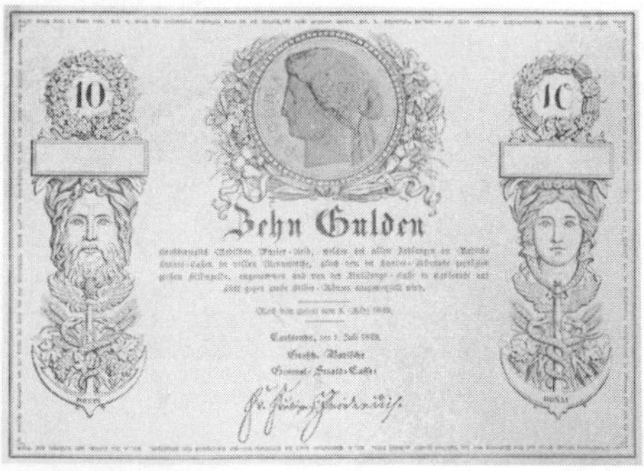

	Good	Fine	XF
S142 10 Gulden 1.7.1849. Father Rhine at left, Danube at right, Badenia above. Signature Fruttiger; Friderici. Printer: Hasper in Karlsruhe using plates by C. Naumann.	525.	1050.	2100.
S143 35 Gulden 1.7.1849. Father Rhine at left, Danube at right, Badenia above. Signature Fruttiger; Friderici. Printer: Hasper in Karlsruhe using plates by C. Naumann.	800.	1600.	3250.
S144 10 Gulden 1.7.1854. Printer: C. Naumann.	800.	1600.	3250.
S145 50 Gulden 1.7.1854. Printer: C. Naumann.	1100.	2200.	4500.

Allgemeine Versorgungsanstalt

1870 State Loan Bank Treasury Notes

An emergency issue of loan notes (Darlehenskassenscheinen) during the monetary stringency caused by the outbreak of the Franco-Prussian War.

	Good	Fine	XF
S148 5 Gulden 30.7.1870.	800.	1600.	3250.
S149 10 Gulden 30.7.1870.	1100.	2200.	4500.

A WORD ON DATE RANGES

Often date ranges or specific dates are listed. These have been observed or reported by our contributors. If a note is outside the published range, it only means that it is a newly reported date, and not necessarily worthy of a premium value.

Badische Bank

Refer to Regional Banks #S901-S915.

Bavaria, Kingdom of

Kgl. Bayer. Staats-Schuldentilgungs-Commission

1866 Issue

Issued to help pay for the costs of the Six Weeks War of 1866, and for the construction of state railroads. In July 1870 another 6 million gulden was issued to pay for the expenses of the Franco-Prussian War; this group is identical in all respects, including date to the 1866 issue.

S151 2 Gulden	Good	Fine	XF
5.9.1866. Signature Sutner; Bayer; Hegnenberg-Dux. Printer: Dondorf & Naumann, Frankfurt/Main.	125.	250.	500.

S152 5 Gulden	Good	Fine	XF
5.9.1866. Blue and black. Father Rhine at right. Signature Sutner; Bayer; Hegnenberg-Dux. Back: Blue and brown. Bavaria at center. Printer: Dondorf & Naumann, Frankfurt/Main.	125.	250.	500.

S153 50 Gulden	Good	Fine	XF
5.9.1866. Signature Sutner; Bayer; Hegnenberg-Dux. Printer: Dondorf & Naumann, Frankfurt/Main.	800.	1600.	3250.

Bayerische Hypotheken-und Wechsel-Bank München

1836-39 Issue

	Good	Fine	XF
S156 10 Gulden 1.6.1836.	1100.	2200.	4500.
S157 100 Gulden 1.6.1839.	800.	1600.	3250.

1841 Issue

	Good	Fine	XF
S158 10 Gulden 1.5.1841.	650.	1300.	2600.

1849 Issue

	Good	Fine	XF
S159 10 Gulden 1.7.1849. Proof.	—	—	—

1850 Issue

	Good	Fine	XF
S160 10 Gulden 1.7.1850. Red and black. With blind embossing.	525.	1050.	2100.
S161 100 Gulden 16.9.1850.	800.	1600.	3200.

1857 Issue

	Good	Fine	XF
S162 35 Gulden 6.1.1857. Essay only.	—	—	—
S163 10 Gulden 1.8.1857.	650.	1300.	2600.

1865 Issue

	Good	Fine	XF
S164 10 Gulden 1.7.1865. Woman and child at left and right. Printer: G&D.	525.	1050.	2100.

1870 Issue

	Good	Fine	XF
S165 100 Gulden 1.10.1870. Printer: G&D.	1100.	2200.	4500.

1874 Issue

	Good	Fine	XF
S166 100 Mark 1.7.1874. Printer: G&D.	—	—	—

Bayerische Notenbank

Refer to Regional Banks, #S921-S943.

Brunswick, Duchy of

Herzogl. Braunschweig-Lüneburgische Leihhaus-Kommission

1813 Deposit Notes Issue

Three-quarters of the issue was in 100-thaler notes.

	Good	Fine	XF
S171 10 Thaler 1813. Deposit note.	—	—	—
S172 20 Thaler 1813. Deposit note.	—	—	—
S173 50 Thaler 1813. Deposit note.	—	—	—
S174 100 Thaler 1813. Deposit note.	—	—	—

1842 Deposit Notes Issue

	Good	Fine	XF
S175 1 Thaler 7.3.1842. Without embossed stamp. Signature Lastroy; Kybitz; Zimmerman. Printer: Gebr. Meyer, Braunschweig.	650.	1300.	2600.
S176 5 Thaler 7.3.1842. Without embossed stamp. Signature Lastroy; Kybitz; Zimmerman. Printer: Gebr. Meyer, Braunschweig.	800.	1600.	3200.
S177 20 Thaler 7.3.1842. Without embossed stamp. Signature Lastroy; Kybitz; Zimmerman. Printer: Gebr. Meyer, Braunschweig.	800.	1600.	3200.

1851 Deposit Notes Issue

	Good	Fine	XF
S178 1 Thaler 7.3.1842 (1851/52). Embossed stamp in upper right corner with horse, crown and initials *L.C.* Signature Lastroy; Kybitz; Zimmerman.	800.	1600.	3200.
S179 5 Thaler 7.3.1842 (1851-52). Embossed stamp in upper right corner with horse, crown and initials *L.C.* Signature Lastroy; Kybitz; Zimmerman.	—	—	—
S180 20 Thaler 7.3.1842 (1851/52). Embossed stamp in upper right corner with horse, crown and initials *L.C.* Signature Lastroy; Kybitz; Zimmerman.	—	—	—

Herzogl. Braunschw.-Lüneburg. Finanz-Collegium

1858 Issue

	Good	Fine	XF
S181 1 Thaler 1.5.1858. Crowned arms at upper left. Signature Thielau; Hantelmann; Kybitz; Zimmerman. Back: Stallion at center.	450.	900.	1800.
S182 10 Thaler 1.5.1858. Signature Thielau; Hantelmann; Kybitz; Zimmermann.	450.	900.	1800.

Darlehns-Bank, Braunschweig

Brunswick

1848 Issue

An emergency issue of the Darlehnsbankscheinen, similar to the Prussian ones, during the Revolution of 1848. #S185 and S186 notes of the BRAUNSCHW.-LUNEBURG. LEIHHAUS-KOMMISSION w/red ovpt: *DARLEHNS-BANKSCHEIN, GESETZ V. 4.5.1848.*

	Good	Fine	XF
S185 1 Thaler 4.5.1848. Signature Lastroy; Kybitz; Zimmerman. Overprint: Red *DARLEHNS-BANKSCHEIN, GESETZ V. 4.5.1848.* on #S175. Printer: Gebr. Meyer, Braunschweig.	800.	1600.	3200.
S186 5 Thaler 4.5.1848. Signature Lastroy; Kybitz; Zimmerman. Overprint: Red *DARLEHNS-BANKSCHEIN, GESETZ V. 4.5.1848.* on #S176. Printer: Gebr. Meyer, Braunschweig.	—	—	—

Braunschweigische Bank

1854 Issue

	Good	Fine	XF
S189 10 Thaler 1.5.1854. Black. Printer: Vieweg, Braunschweig.	800.	1600.	3200.

1856 Issue

	Good	Fine	XF
S190 10 Thaler 1.6.1856. Black. Printer: Vieweg, Braunschweig.	1100.	2200.	4500.

1869 Issue

	Good	Fine	XF
S191 10 Thaler 1.1.1869. Black on brown. Bank at center, lion wearing mural crown and holding sword above jars of money; agriculture at left, commerce at right. Printer: G&D.	450.	900.	1800.

1874 Issue

	Good	Fine	XF
S192 100 Mark 1.7.1874. Printer: G&D.	—	—	—

Bremen, Free and Hanseatic City of

Bremer Bank

1856 Issue

		Good	Fine	XF
S196	**5 Thaler Gold** 1.10.1856. Signature Meier; Renken.	800.	1600.	3200.
S197	**10 Thaler Gold** 1.10.1856. Arms of Bremen at top center. Signature Meier; Renken. Back: Tyche holding key and mappa.	800.	1600.	3200.
S198	**25 Thaler Gold** 1.10.1856. Mercury (commerce) and mermaid (navigation) flanking arms of Bremen. Signature Meier; Renken.	—	—	—
S199	**100 Thaler Gold** 1.10.1856.	—	—	—

1863 Issue

		Good	Fine	XF
S200	**10 Thaler Gold** 1.7.1863.	—	—	—
S201	**20 Thaler Gold** 1.7.1863.	—	—	—
S202	**50 Thaler Gold** 1.7.1863.	—	—	—
S203	**100 Thaler Gold** 1.12.1863.	—	—	—

1870 Issue

		Good	Fine	XF
S204	**5 Thaler Courant** 14.2.1870. Signature Meier; Renken. Printer: G. Hunckel, Bremen.	800.	1600.	3200.
S205	**10 Thaler Courant** 14.2.1870. Arms of Bremen at top center. Denomination printed in orange. Signature Meier; Renken. Back: Tyche holding key and mappa. Printer: G. Hunckel, Bremen.	800.	1600.	3200.

1872 Issue

		Good	Fine	XF
S208	**20 Mark** 1.7.1872. Signature Meier; Renken. Back: Mercury (commerce) and mermaid (navigation) flank denomination in circle and wreath.	600.	1200.	2400.

		Good	Fine	XF
S209	**100 Mark** 1.7.1872. Signature Meier; Renken. Back: Mercury (commerce) and mermaid (navigation) flank arms of Bremen.	900.	1800.	3600.

Frankfurt/Main, Free City of

Rechnei-und Rentenamt

1826-54 Issue

		Good	Fine	XF
S211	**500 Gulden** Black.			
	a. 1826-40. Printer: Andreas'sche Buchdruckerei.	—	—	—
	b. 1841-4.1848. Printer: Benjamin Krebs.	—	—	—
	c. 11.1848-1854. Printer: C. Krebs-Schmitt.	—	—	—

Frankfurter Bank

1855; 1870 Issue

		Good	Fine	XF
S214	**5 Gulden** 1.1.1855. Brown and blue. Woman at left and right (Francofordia). Cancelled.	450.	900.	1800.

		Good	Fine	XF
S215	**10 Gulden** 1.1.1855.	450.	900.	1800.
S216	**35 Gulden** 1.1.1855. Brown and blue. Full-faced portrait of Francofordia at center, in profile above at left and right. Back: Geometric pattern.	800.	1600.	3200.

		Good	Fine	XF
S217	**50 Gulden** 1.1.1855. Like #S215.			
	a. Issued note.	800.	1600.	3200.
	b. Punched hole cancelled.	600.	1200.	2400.
S218	**100 Gulden** 1.1.1855. Like #S215.	1100.	2200.	4500.
S219	**500 Gulden** 1.1.1855. Like #S215.			
	a. Issued note.	1100.	2200.	4500.
	b. Punched hole cancelled.	750.	1500.	3000.
S220	**500 Gulden** 25.7.1870. Deposit certificate.	1100.	2200.	4500.

1874 Issue

		Good	Fine	XF
S223	**100 Mark** 1.1.1874.			
	a. Issued note.	900.	1800.	3600.
	b. Punched hole cancelled.	650.	1300.	2600.
S224	**500 Mark** 1.1.1874.			
	a. Issued note.	950.	1900.	3800.
	b. Punched hole cancelled.	675.	1300.	2600.
S225	**1000 Mark** 1.1.1874.			
	a. Issued note.	1200.	2400.	5000.
	b. Punched hole cancelled.	800.	1600.	3250.

1890 Issue

S226 100 Mark	Good	Fine	XF
1.8.1890.			
a. Issued note.	1200.	2400.	5000.
b. Punched hole cancelled.	800.	1600.	3250.

S227 1000 Mark	Good	Fine	XF
1.8.1890.			
a. Issued note.	1200.	2400.	5000.
b. Punched hole cancelled.	800.	1600.	3250.

Hamburg, Free and Hanseatic City of

Norddeutsche Bank

1857 Bills of Exchange Issue

Circulated as bank notes.

	Good	Fine	XF
S231 10 Thaler			
1857 (1865).	—	—	—
S232 25 Thaler			
1857 (1865).	—	—	—

Hannover, Kingdom of

Magistrat der Königl. Residenzstadt

1846 Treasury Notes Issue

S235 1 Thaler	Good	Fine	XF
7.12.1846.			
a. Brown on yellowish paper.	450.	900.	1800.
b. Black on yellowish paper.	450.	900.	1800.

S236 5 Thaler	Good	Fine	XF
7.12.1846.			
a. Brown on reddish paper.	800.	1600.	3200.
b. Black on reddish paper.	800.	1600.	3200.

1874 Treasury Notes Issue

S239 100 Mark	Good	Fine	XF
ND (1874).			
a. Blue.	1200.	2400.	5000.
b. Green. Proof.	—	—	—

Hannoversche Bank

1857 Issue

S241 10 Thaler	Good	Fine	XF
1.3.1857. Printer: G&D.	450.	900.	1800.

	Good	Fine	XF
S242 20 Thaler			
1.3.1857. Commerce and industry at left, agriculture at right. Back: Arms at center, red *20* printed three times. Printer: G&D.	450.	900.	1800.
S243 50 Thaler			
1.3.1857. Printer: G&D.	800.	1600.	3200.

		Good	Fine	XF
S244	**100 Thaler** 1.3.1857. Printer: G&D.	800.	1600.	3200.

1871 Issue

		Good	Fine	XF
S245	**10 Thaler** 1.7.1871. Printer: G&D.	800.	1600.	3200.

1874 Issue

		Good	Fine	XF
S248	**100 Mark** 1.1.1874. Printer: G&D.	800.	1600.	3200.

Hesse-Darmstadt, Grand Duchy of

Grossherzogl. Hessische Staatsschulden-Tilgungskasse

1848 Issue

		Good	Fine	XF
S251	**1 Gulden** 1.9.1848. Signature Schenck; Hombergk. Printer: C. Naumann and R.L. Venator.	450.	900.	1800.
S252	**5 Gulden** 1.9.1848. Signature Schenck; Hombergk. Printer: C. Naumann and R.L. Venator.	800.	1600.	3200.
S253	**10 Gulden** 1.9.1848. Signature Schenck; Hombergk. Printer: C. Naumann and R.L. Venator.	—	—	—
S254	**35 Gulden** 1.9.1848. Signature Schenck; Hombergk. Printer: C. Naumann and R.L. Venator.	—	—	—
S255	**70 Gulden** 1.9.1848. Signature Schenck; Hombergk. Printer: C. Naumann and R.L. Venator.	—	—	—

1852 Issue

		Good	Fine	XF
S256	**1 Gulden** 28.2.1852. Signature Eckhardt; Rabenau. Printer: C. Naumann and R.L. Venator.	650.	1300.	2600.
S257	**5 Gulden** 28.2.1852. Signature Eckhardt; Rabenau. Printer: C. Naumann and R.L. Venator.	800.	1600.	3200.
S258	**10 Gulden** 28.2.1852. Signature Eckhardt; Rabenau. Printer: C. Naumann and R.L. Venator.	800.	1600.	3200.
S259	**35 Gulden** 28.2.1852. Signature Eckhardt; Rabenau. Printer: C. Naumann and R.L. Venator.	—	—	—

1854 Issue

		Good	Fine	XF
S260	**1 Gulden** 11.11.1854. Signature Eckhardt; Breidenbach. Printer: C. Naumann and R.L. Venator.	450.	900.	1800.
S261	**5 Gulden** 11.11.1854. Signature Eckhardt; Breidenbach. Printer: C. Naumann and R.L. Venator.	—	—	—
S262	**10 Gulden** 11.11.1854. Signature Eckhardt; Breidenbach. Printer: C. Naumann and R.L. Venator.	800.	1600.	3200.

1855 Issue

		Good	Fine	XF
S263	**1 Gulden** 1.11.1855. Signature Eckhardt; Breidenbach. Printer: C. Naumann and R.L. Venator.	650.	1300.	2600.
S264	**5 Gulden** 1.11.1855. Signature Eckhardt; Breidenbach. Printer: C. Naumann and R.L. Venator.	800.	1600.	3200.
S265	**10 Gulden** 1.11.1855. Signature Eckhardt; Breidenbach. Printer: C. Naumann and R.L. Venator.	800.	1600.	3200.
S266	**35 Gulden** 1.11.1855. Signature Eckhardt; Breidenbach. Printer: C. Naumann and R.L. Venator.	—	—	—

1865 Issue

		Good	Fine	XF
S267	**1 Gulden** 1.7.1865. Blue and black. Two medallions, Hassia at left, commerce, agriculture and industry at right. Signature Eckhardt; Hesse. Back: Orange underprint.	350.	700.	1400.
S268	**5 Gulden** 1.7.1865. Signature Eckhardt; Hesse.	450.	900.	1800.
S269	**10 Gulden** 1.7.1865. Signature Eckhardt; Hesse.	800.	1600.	3200.
S270	**50 Gulden** 1.7.1865. Signature Eckhardt; Hesse.	1100.	2200.	4500.

Bank für Süddeutschland

1856 Issue

		Good	Fine	XF
S276	**10 Gulden** 1.7.1856. Printer: C. Naumann, Frankfurt/Main.	800.	1600.	3200.
S277	**10 Thaler** 1.7.1856. Printer: C. Naumann, Frankfurt/Main.	800.	1600.	3200.
S278	**25 Gulden** 1.12.1856. Printer: Maximilian Frommann, Darmstadt.	1100.	2200.	4500.
S279	**50 Gulden** 1.12.1856. Printer: Maximilian Frommann, Darmstadt.	1100.	2200.	4500.
S280	**100 Gulden** 1.12.1856. Printer: Maximilian Frommann, Darmstadt.	1100.	2200.	4500.
S281	**25 Thaler** 1.12.1856. Printer: Maximilian Frommann, Darmstadt.	1100.	2200.	4500.
S282	**50 Thaler** 1.12.1856. Printer: Maximilian Frommann, Darmstadt.	1100.	2200.	4500.
S283	**100 Thaler** 1.12.1856. Printer: Maximilian Frommann, Darmstadt.	1100.	2200.	4500.

1857 Issue

		Good	Fine	XF
S284	**10 Thaler** 21.3.1857. Printer: C. Naumann, Frankfurt/Main.	650.	1300.	2600.

1870 Issue

		Good	Fine	XF
S285	**10 Gulden** 2.1.1870. Putti at lower left and lower right. Back: Tyche at center. Printer: G&D.	650.	1300.	2600.
S286	**25 Gulden** 2.1.1870. Printer: G&D.	800.	1600.	3200.

1874 Issue

		Good	Fine	XF
S287	**100 Mark** 1.1.1874. Printer: G&D.	900.	1800.	3600.

Hesse-Homburg, Landgraviate of

Landgräflich Hessische Concessionirte Landesbank

1855 Issue

		Good	Fine	XF
S291	**5 Gulden** 1.1.1855. Female profiles at left and right. Back: Mirror image of front. Printer: C. Naumann, Frankfurt/Main.	450.	900.	1750.
S292	**10 Gulden** 1.1.1855. Printer: C. Naumann, Frankfurt/Main.	650.	1300.	2600.

Hesse-Cassel, Electorate of

Kurfürstlich Hessische Direktion der Haupt-Staats-Kasse

1848 Issue

		Good	Fine	XF
S295	**1 Thaler** 26.8.1848. Printer: Dondorf, and Theodor Fischer.	450.	900.	1750.
S296	**5 Thaler** 26.8.1848. Printer: Dondorf, and Theodor Fischer.	650.	1300.	2600.
S297	**20 Thaler** 26.8.1848. Printer: Dondorf, and Theodor Fischer.	—	—	—

1849 Issue

		Good	Fine	XF
S298	**1 Thaler** 24.3.1849. Signature Schotten; Stern; Schmerfeld. Printer: Dondorf, and Theodor Fischer.	450.	900.	1750.
S299	**5 Thaler** 24.3.1849. Signature Schotten; Stern; Schmerfeld. Printer: Dondorf, and Theodor Fischer.	—	—	—
S300	**20 Thaler** 24.3.1849. Signature Schotten; Stern; Schmerfeld. Printer: Dondorf, and Theodor Fischer.	—	—	—

In 1866 a new issue was was being printed in 1866 at Giesecke & Devrient in Leipzig when the Prussian troops occupied the city. After the end of the war, when Hesse-Cassel was annexed by Prussia, the notes were entirely destroyed by Giesecke & Devrient.

Kurhessische Leih- und Commerzbank, Kassel

1850 Issue

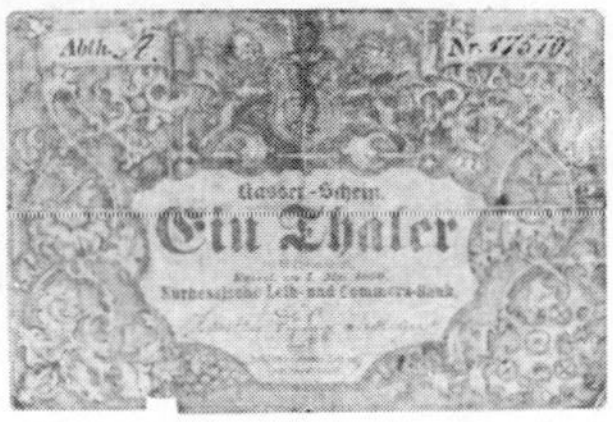

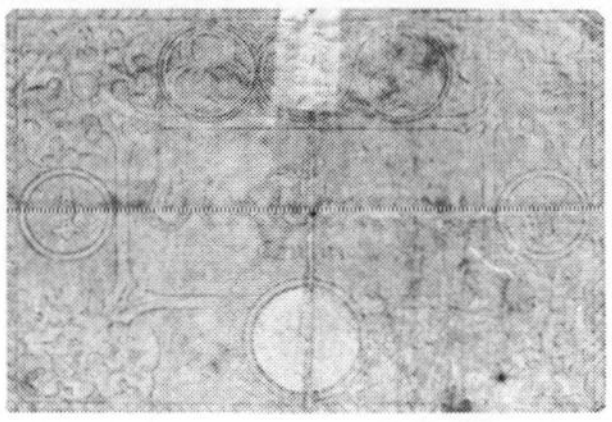

		Good	Fine	XF
S306	1 Thaler 1.5.1850.	375.	750.	1500.

1855 Issue

		Good	Fine	XF
S307	10 Thaler 1.5.1855. Putti representing commerce and industry at left and right. Back: Male portrait at left, Johann Gutenberg at right. Printer: Theodor Fischer, Cassel.	225.	450.	900.

Lübeck, Free and Hanseatic City of

Commerz-Bank in Lübeck

Commerce Bank in Lübeck

1865 Issue

		Good	Fine	XF
S311	10 Thaler 1.7.1865 (1866). Black on green underprint. Commerce and industry at left and right. Signature Rehder; Crome; Possehl; Wolpmann; Borries. Back: Brown. Bank name and denomination.	125.	250.	500.

		Good	Fine	XF
S312	20 Thaler 1.7.1865 (1866). Signature Rehder; Crome; Possehl; Wolpmann; Borries. Back: Blue. Bank name and denomination.	175.	350.	700.
S313	100 Thaler 1.7.1865 (1866). Signature Rehder; Crome; Possehl; Wolpmann; Borries.	350.	700.	1400.

NOTE: An issue of 1871, printed by H. G. Rahtgens in Lübeck, requires confirmation.

1875 Issue

		Good	Fine	XF
S314	100 Mark 1.1.1875. Printer: G&D.	—	—	—

Credit-und Versicherungsbank, Lübeck

Credit and Insurance Bank

1858 Issue

		Good	Fine	XF
S316	20 Thaler 2.1.1858. Printer: G&D. (Not issued).	850.	1700.	3400.
S317	50 Thaler 2.1.1858. Printer: G&D. (Not issued).	850.	1700.	3400.
S318	100 Thaler 2.1.1858. Printer: G&D. (Not issued).	850.	1700.	3400.

Lübecker Privatbank

Lübeck Private Bank

1856-57 Issue

		Good	Fine	XF
S321	10 Thaler 2.1.1856.	—	—	—
S322	20 Thaler 2.1.1856.	—	—	—
S323	100 Thaler 2.1.1856.	—	—	—
S324	200 Thaler 2.1.1857.	—	—	—

1875 Issue

		Good	Fine	XF
S325	100 Mark 1.1.1875. Printer: G&D. (Not issued).	—	—	—

Privat-Disconto-und Darlehen-Kasse zu Lübeck

1819 Issue

		Good	Fine	XF
S328	100-1000 Mark Courant (From 1819.)	—	—	—

Mecklenburg-Schwerin, Grand Duchy of

Renterei-Kassenscheine

1868-69 Issue

2% interest-bearing revenue office bills.

		Good	Fine	XF
S331	25 Thaler 1868-69.	—	—	—
S332	50 Thaler 1868-69.	—	—	—
S333	100 Thaler 1868-69.	—	—	—

1870 Issue

		Good	Fine	XF
S334	**10 Thaler** 1.6.1870. Signature Müller.	850.	1700.	3400.
S335	**25 Thaler** 1.6.1870. Signature Müller.	850.	1700.	3400.
S336	**50 Thaler** 1.6.1870. Signature Müller.	850.	1700.	3400.

Rostocker Bank

Bank of Rostock

1850 Issue

		Good	Fine	XF
S337	**10 Thaler** 1.7.1850.	—	—	—
S338	**20 Thaler** 1.7.1850.	—	—	—
S339	**50 Thaler** 1.7.1850.	—	—	—
S340	**100 Thaler** 1.7.1850.	—	—	—

1862 Issue

		Good	Fine	XF
S341	**10 Thaler** 1.3.1862. Printer: G&D.	850.	1700.	3400.
S342	**20 Thaler** 1.3.1862. Printer: G&D.	850.	1700.	3400.
S343	**50 Thaler** 1.3.1862. Printer: G&D.	850.	1700.	3400.
S344	**100 Thaler** 1.3.1862. Printer: G&D.	850.	1700.	3400.

1866 Issue

		Good	Fine	XF
S345	**10 Thaler** 28.7.1866. Printer: G&D.	—	—	—
S346	**20 Thaler** 28.7.1866. Printer: G&D.	—	—	—
S347	**50 Thaler** 28.7.1866. Printer: G&D.	—	—	—
S348	**100 Thaler** 28.7.1866. Printer: G&D.	—	—	—

1874 Issue

		Good	Fine	XF
S349	**100 Mark** 1.1.1874. Printer: G&D.	600.	1200.	2400.

Mecklenburg-Strelitz, Grand Duchy of

Rentei-Cassenscheine

1866 Issue

		Good	Fine	XF
S351	**5 Thaler** 1.6.1866. Signature Voss; Engel.	1100.	2250.	4500.
S352	**10 Thaler** 1.6.1866. Signature Voss; Engel.	—	—	—
S353	**25 Thaler** 1.6.1866. Signature Voss; Engel.	—	—	—

1869 Issue

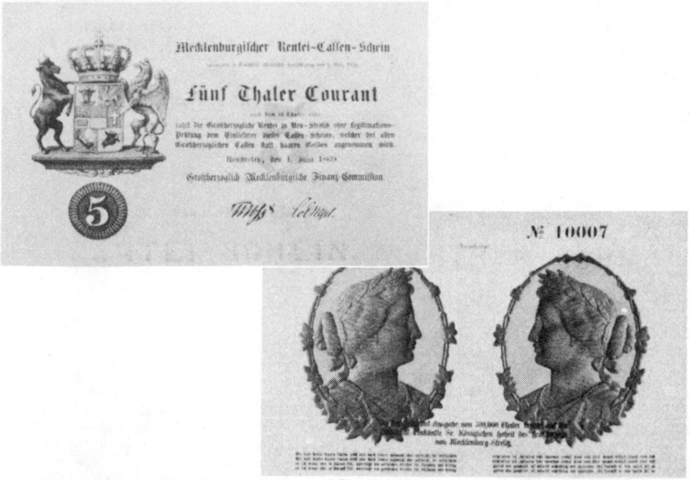

		Good	Fine	XF
S354	**5 Thaler** 1.6.1869. Signature Voss; Engel.	—	—	2250.
S355	**10 Thaler** 1.6.1869. Signature Voss; Engel.	—	—	2250.
S356	**25 Thaler** 1.6.1869. Signature Voss; Engel.	—	—	—

Nassau, Duchy of

Nassauische Landes-Credit-Kasse

Nassau Regional Credit Office, Wiesbaden

1840 Issue

		Good	Fine	XF
S361	**1 Gulden** 3.12.1840 (7.1841). Printer: C. Naumann, Frankfurt/Main.	750.	1500.	3000.

		Good	Fine	XF
S362	**5 Gulden** 3.12.1840 (7.1841). Printer: C. Naumann, Frankfurt/Main.	750.	1500.	3000.

1841 Issue

		Good	Fine	XF
S363	**1 Gulden** 15.6.1841. Printer: C. Naumann, Frankfurt/Main.	750.	1500.	3000.
S364	**5 Gulden** 15.6.1841. Printer: C. Naumann, Frankfurt/Main.	—	—	—
S365	**25 Gulden** 15.6.1841. Printer: C. Naumann, Frankfurt/Main.	—	—	—

1847 Issue

		Good	Fine	XF
S366	**1 Gulden** 12.8.1847. Printer: C. Naumann, Frankfurt/Main.	450.	900.	1750.
S367	**5 Gulden** 12.8.1847. Printer: C. Naumann, Frankfurt/Main.	650.	1300.	2600.
S368	**25 Gulden** 12.8.1847. Printer: C. Naumann, Frankfurt/Main.	750.	1500.	3000.

1848 Issue

No.	Description	Good	Fine	XF
S369	**1 Gulden** 26.2.1848. Printer: C. Naumann, Frankfurt/Main.	—	—	—
S370	**5 Gulden** 26.2.1848. Printer: C. Naumann, Frankfurt/Main.	—	—	—
S370A	**25 Gulden** 26.2.1848. Printer: C. Naumann, Frankfurt/Main.	—	—	—

Nassauische Landesbank, Wiesbaden

Nassau Regional Bank, Wiesbaden

1856-59 Issue

No.	Description	Good	Fine	XF
S371	**5 Gulden** 12.8.1856. Signature Reuter; Brück; Rössler. Back: Signature Weimar.	375.	750.	1500.
S372	**25 Gulden** 12.8.1856. Signature Reuter; Brück; Rössler. Back: Signature Weimar.	750.	1500.	3000.
S373	**10 Gulden** 1.1.1859. Black. Signature Reuter; Brück; Geisse. Back: Brown and blue. Printer: C. Naumann, Frankfurt/Main.	650.	1300.	2600.

1865 Issue

No.	Description	Good	Fine	XF
S374	**5 Gulden** 24.7.1865. Signature Hergenhahn; Langen; Wirth.	650.	1300.	2600.
S375	**50 Gulden** 24.7.1865. Signature Hergenhahn; Langen; Wirth.	1100.	2200.	4500.

Oldenburg, Grand Duchy of

Grossherzogl. Oldenburg. Staatsministerium

Grand Duchy Oldenburg State Ministry

1869 Issue

No.	Description	Good	Fine	XF
S377	**5 Thaler** 1.1.1869. Black on orange underprint. Themis holding mappa, fasces and shield at left, Commerce at right. Signature Zedelius; Tebbenjohanns.	450.	900.	1800.
S378	**10 Thaler** 1.1.1869. Signature Zedelius; Tebbenjohanns.	450.	900.	1800.

Oldenburgische Landesbank

Oldenburg State Bank

1875 Issue

No.	Description	Good	Fine	XF
S381	**100 Mark** 1.4.1875. Printer: Reichsdruckerei.	750.	1500.	3000.

Deutsche Volksbank, Eutin

German Peoples Bank, Eutin

1870 Deposit Notes Issue

No.	Description	Good	Fine	XF
S386	**10 Thaler** 20.5.1870.	175.	350.	700.
S387	**25 Thaler** 20.5.1870.	150.	300.	600.
S388	**50 Thaler** 20.5.1870.	—	—	—
S389	**100 Thaler** 20.5.1870.	—	—	—

Prussia, Kingdom of

Tresorscheine

1806 Treasury Notes Issue

No.	Description	Good	Fine	XF
S391	**5 Thaler** ND (1806). Signature Schulenburg; Stein.	225.	450.	900.
S392	**50 Thaler** ND (1806). Signature Schulenburg; Stein.	—	—	—
S393	**100 Thaler** ND (1806). Signature Schulenburg; Stein.	—	—	—
S394	**250 Thaler** ND (1806). Signature Schulenburg; Stein.	—	—	—

1809 Treasury Notes Issue

No.	Description	Good	Fine	XF
S395	**1 Thaler** ND (1809). Signature Altenstein.			
	a. Overprint: *REALISATIONS-COMPTOIR ZU BERLIN.*	150.	300.	600.
	b. Overprint: *REALISATIONS-COMPTOIR ZU BRESLAU.*	150.	300.	600.
	c. Overprint: *REALISATIONS-COMPTOIR ZU KÖNIGSBERG.*	350.	700.	1400.

Hauptverwaltung der Staats-Schulden

Main Administration of Government Debts

1824 Issue

No.	Description	Good	Fine	XF
S396	**1 Thaler** 6.5.1824.	150.	300.	600.

No.	Description	Good	Fine	XF
S397	**5 Thaler** 6.5.1824.	175.	350.	700.
S398	**50 Thaler** 6.5.1824.	—	—	—

1834 Issue

No.	Description	Good	Fine	XF
S398A	**1 Thaler Courant** 1.1.1834. Black. Crowned and mantled arms with wildman supporters at upper center.	—	—	—

1835 Issue

No.	Description	Good	Fine	XF
S399	**1 Thaler** 2.1.1835.	150.	300.	600.

S400 5 Thaler — Good / Fine / XF
2.1.1835. — 350. / 700. / 1400.

S401 50 Thaler
2.1.1835. — — / — / —

S402 100 Thaler
2.1.1835. — — / — / —

S403 500 Thaler — Good / Fine / XF
2.1.1835. Proof. — — / — / —

1851 Issue

S404 1 Thaler — Good / Fine / XF
2.11.1851. Signature Natan; Köhler; Rolcke; Gamet. Printer: Preussische Staatsdruckerei. — 150. / 300. / 600.

S405 5 Thaler
2.11.1851. Crowned and mantled arms with wildman supporters. Oak and laurel branches at left and right. Signature Natan; Köhler; Rolcke; Gamet. Back: Two putti flanking eagle. Printer: Preussische Staatsdruckerei. — 350. / 700. / 1400.

S406 10 Thaler
2.11.1851. Crowned shield in order collar flanked by two angels. Two seated angels flanking crowned monogram, denomination and order collar. Signature Natan; Köhler; Rolcke; Gamet. Printer: Preussische Staatsdruckerei. — — / — / —

S407 50 Thaler
2.11.1851. Eagle at left standing on Roman helmet, all within oak wreath. Signature Natan; Köhler; Rolcke; Gamet. Back: Female seated on throne flanked by two youth standardbearers. Printer: Preussische Staatsdruckerei. — — / — / —

S408 100 Thaler
2.11.1851. Crowned and mantled shield at left with wildman supporters. Signature Natan; Köhler; Rolcke; Gamet. Back: Two females seated on throne, two putti flanking. Printer: Preussische Staatsdruckerei. — — / — / —

1856 Issue

S409 1 Thaler — Good / Fine / XF
15.12.1856. Black on blue, red, yellow, green and brown underprint. Underprint is a warning of the penalties for counterfeiting. Signature Natan; Gamet, Nobiling; Günther. Back: Putti representing agriculture at left and commerce at right. Printer: Preussische Staatsdruckerei. — 100. / 200. / 400.

S410 5 Thaler — Good / Fine / XF
15.12.1856. Signature Natan; Gamet; Nobiling; Günther. Printer: Preussische Staatsdruckerei. — 125. / 250. / 500.

1861 Issue

S411 1 Thaler — Good / Fine / XF
13.2.1861. Signature Gamet; Günther; Löwe. Printer: Preussische Staatsdruckerei. — 100. / 200. / 400.

Hauptverwaltung der Darlehnskassen

Main Administration of State Loan Banks

1848 Issue

S416 1 Thaler — Good / Fine / XF
15.4.1848. Black on yellow-brown underprint. Signature Lamprecht; Rabe; Meyen; Woywod. — 175. / 350. / 700.

S417 5 Thaler — Good / Fine / XF
15.4.1848. Black on gray underprint. Signature Lamprecht; Rabe; Meyen; Woywod. — 450. / 900. / 1800.

1866 Issue

Issued after the Prussian Landtag had been suspended. The ostensible reason was the mobilization of the Prussian Army and the Overend, Gurney crisis in Britain. It seemed more probable that this was one of Bismarck's methods of raising money when he was denied it during the Prussian Constitutional Conflict; hocking shares of the Cologne-Minden Railroad Company was another. When it re-assembled, the Landtag declared the issue illegal. The issue was legalized after the government asked the Landtag for an indemnity and the Landtag granted it.

	Good	Fine	XF
S418 1 Thaler 18/19.5.1866. Signature Dechend; Scheller; Mendelssohn-Bartholdy; Böse. Control Commission: Costenoble; Conrad; Dehnicke. Printer: Preussische, Staatsdruckerei, C. Ringer, and C. Sc	175.	350.	700.
S419 5 Thaler 18/19.5.1866. Signature Dechend; Scheller; Mendelssohn-Bartholdy; Böse. Control Commission: Costenoble; Conrad; Dehnicke. Printer: Preussische, Staatsdruckerei, C. Ringer, and C. Sc	450.	900.	1800.

	Good	Fine	XF
S420 10 Thaler 18/19.5.1866. Signature Dechend; Scheller; Mendelssohn-Bartholdy; Böse. Control Commission: Costenoble; Conrad; Dehnicke. Printer: Preussische, Staatsdruckerei, C. Ringer, and C. Sc	650.	1300.	2600.
S421 5 Thaler 2.1.1868. Signature Wedell; Löwe; Meinecke.	650.	1300.	2600.

1870 Issue

Issued at the outbreak of the Franco-Prussian War by Prussia on behalf of the North German Confederation. The arms of the North German Confederation are at upper left: a shield divided into three bars of sable, argent and gules. The North German Confederation became the German Empire on January 18, 1871 after Bavaria, Württemberg, Baden, and the southern portion of Hesse-Darmstadt agreed to join.

	Good	Fine	XF
S422 5 Thaler 1.8.1870. Signature Wedell; Löwe; Meinecke; Eck. Printer: Preussische Staatsdruckerei.	350.	700.	1400.

	Good	Fine	XF
S423 10 Thaler 1.8.1870. Signature Wedell; Löwe; Meinecke; Eck. Printer: Preussische Staatsdruckerei.	450.	900.	1800.
S424 25 Thaler 1.8.1870. Signature Wedell; Löwe; Meinecke; Eck. Printer: Preussische Staatsdruckerei.	650.	1300.	2600.

Königliche Giro-und Lehnbank

Royal Endorsement and Loan Bank

1766-69 Issue

	Good	Fine	XF
S426 10 Pfund Banco 29.10.1766.	—	—	—
S427 20 Pfund Banco 29.10.1766.	—	—	—
S428 100 Pfund Banco 29.10.1766.	—	—	—
S429 500 Pfund Banco 29.10.1766.	—	—	—
S430 1000 Pfund Banco 29.10.1766.	—	—	—
S431 4 Pfund Banco 29.10.1766-69.	—	—	—
S432 8 Pfund Banco 29.10.1766-69.	—	—	—

1774 Issue

	Good	Fine	XF
S433 4 Pfund Banco 1774 (1793).	—	—	—
S433A 8 Pfund Banco 1774 (1793).	—	—	—
S433B 10 Pfund Banco 1774 (1793).	—	—	—
S433C 20 Pfund Banco 1774 (1793).	—	—	—
S433D 100 Pfund Banco 1774 (1793).	—	—	—
S433E 500 Pfund Banco 1774 (1793).	—	—	—
S433F 1000 Pfund Banco 1774 (1793).	—	—	—

Bankkassenscheine

Bank Treasury Notes

1798-1836 Issue

	Good	Fine	XF
S435 100 Thaler 1798-1836.	—	—	—
S436 200 Thaler 1798-1836.	—	—	—
S437 300 Thaler 1798-1836.	—	—	—
S438 500 Thaler 1798-1836	—	—	—

Preussische Haupt-Bank

Prussian Main Bank

1846 Issue

	Good	Fine	XF
S441 25 Thaler 31.7.1846.	1100.	2200.	4500.
S442 50 Thaler 31.7.1846.	1100.	2200.	4500.
S443 100 Thaler 31.7.1846.	1100.	2200.	4500.
S444 500 Thaler 31.7.1846.	—	—	—

1856-64 Issue

	Good	Fine	XF
S445 10 Thaler 15.5.1856. Back: Without three-color.	—	—	—
S446 10 Thaler 15.5.1856. Back: Three-color.	850.	1700.	3400.
S447 25 Thaler 26.5.1857.	850.	1700.	3400.
S448 25 Thaler 26.11.1857. Proof.	850.	1700.	3400.
S449 50 Thaler 9.6.1860. Pink and brown. Images of Mercury in profile.	850.	1700.	3400.
S450 100 Thaler 19.12.1864.	850.	1700.	3400.

1867-68 Issue

	Good	Fine	XF
S451 10 Thaler 18.6.1867.	850.	1700.	3400.
S452 500 Thaler 5.12.1867.	1250.	2500.	5000.
S453 25 Thaler 21.9.1868.	850.	1700.	3400.

1874 Issue

	Good	Fine	XF
S454 100 Mark 1.5.1874. Printer: Reichsdruckerei.	850.	1700.	3400.
S455 500 Mark 1.5.1874. Printer: Reichsdruckerei.	1000.	2000.	4000.
S456 1000 Mark 1.5.1874. Printer: Reichsdruckerei.	1100.	2200.	4400.

Kgl. Seehandlungsinstitut Berlin

Royal Institute of Maritime Commerce

1820 ND Issue

	Good	Fine	XF
S461 100 Thaler ND (ca. 1820).	—	—	—
S462 500 Thaler ND (ca. 1820).	—	—	—

Städtische Bank, Breslau Silesia

State Bank, Breslau, Silesia

1848 Issue

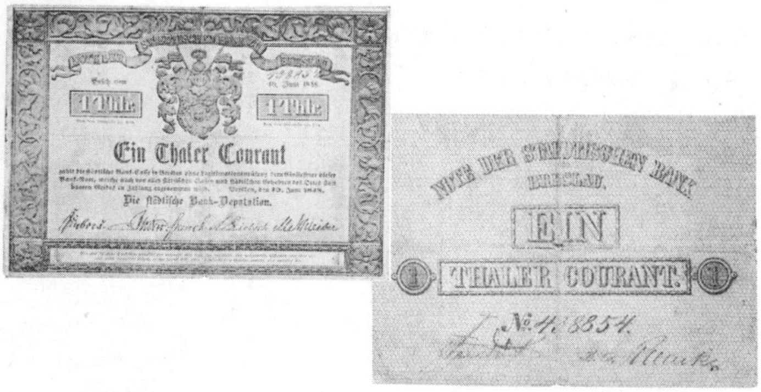

	Good	Fine	XF
S466 1 Thaler 10.6.1848.	350.	700.	1400.
S467 5 Thaler 10.6.1848.	550.	1100.	2200.
S468 25 Thaler 10.6.1848.	800.	1600.	3250.
S469 50 Thaler 10.6.1848.	—	—	—

1863 Issue

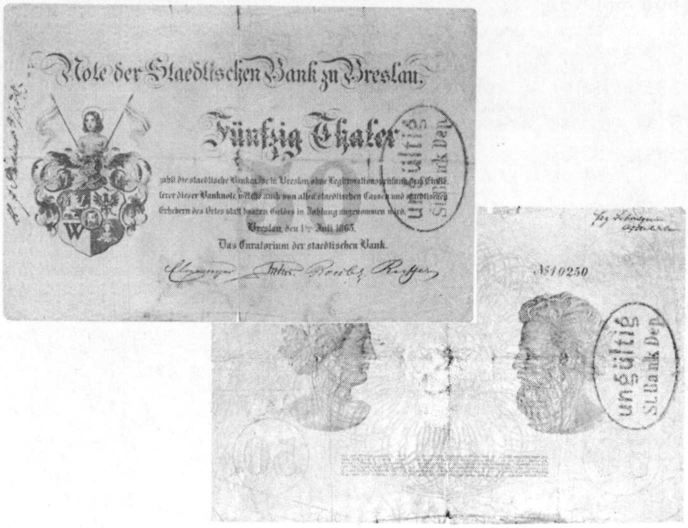

	Good	Fine	XF
S470 10 Thaler 1.7.1863.	550.	1100.	2200.
S471 20 Thaler 1.7.1863.	650.	1300.	2600.
S472 50 Thaler 1.7.1863. a. Issued note.	850.	1700.	3400.
b. Cancelled.	—	—	—
S473 100 Thaler 1.7.1863.	1100.	2200.	4500.

1874 Issue

	Good	Fine	XF
S474 100 Mark 1.7.1874. a. Issued note.	800.	1600.	3250.
b. Cancelled.	—	—	—
S475 1000 Mark 1.7.1874.	1100.	2200.	4400.

Kassen-Verein, Berlin

Treasury Association, Berlin

1825-33 Issue

	Good	Fine	XF
S481 1000 Reichsthaler Preuss. Cour. ND (ca. 1825).	—	—	—
S482 100 Thaler ND (ca. 1825).	—	—	—
S483 200 Thaler ND (1826-33).	—	—	—
S484 300 Thaler ND (1826-33).	—	—	—
S485 500 Thaler ND (1826-33).	—	—	—
S486 1000 Thaler ND (1826-33).	—	—	—

1835 Issue

#S287-S488 BILLS PAYABLE AT SIGHT WHICH CIRCULATED LIKE BANK NOTES.

	Good	Fine	XF
S487 100 Thaler ca. 1835.	—	—	—
S488 200 Thaler ca. 1835. Black on red underprint. Back: Black on pink underprint.	—	—	—

Bank des Berliner Kassen-Vereins

Bank of the Berlin Treasury Association

1850 First Issue

	Good	Fine	XF
S491 10 Thaler 1.10.1850.	—	—	—
S492 20 Thaler 1.10.1850.	—	—	—
S493 50 Thaler 1.10.1850.	—	—	—

		Good	Fine	XF
S494	**100 Thaler** 1.10.1850.	—	—	—
S495	**200 Thaler** 1.10.1850.	—	—	—

1850 (1866) Second Issue

		Good	Fine	XF
S496	**10 Thaler** 1.10.1850.	1100.	2200.	4500.
S497	**20 Thaler** 1.10.1850. Stork in medallion at left, Mercury at right. Signature Riess; Leo; Schmidt. Back: Brown. Large *20*.	1100.	2200.	4500.
S498	**50 Thaler** 1.10.1850.	—	—	—
S499	**100 Thaler** 1.10.1850.	—	—	—
S500	**200 Thaler** 1.10.1850.	—	—	—

Kölnische Privatbank Rheinland

Cologne Private Bank

1856 First Issue

		Good	Fine	XF
S506	**10 Thaler** 1.5.1856. No underprint.	850.	1700.	3400.
S507	**20 Thaler** 1.5.1856. No underprint.	850.	1700.	3400.
S508	**50 Thaler** 1.5.1856. No underprint.	850.	1700.	3400.
S509	**100 Thaler** 1.5.1856. No underprint.	850.	1700.	3400.

1856 (1863) Second Issue

		Good	Fine	XF
S510	**10 Thaler** 1.5.1856. Yellow-brown underprint.			
	a. Issued note.	450.	900.	1800.
	p. Face proof.	—	Unc	2000.

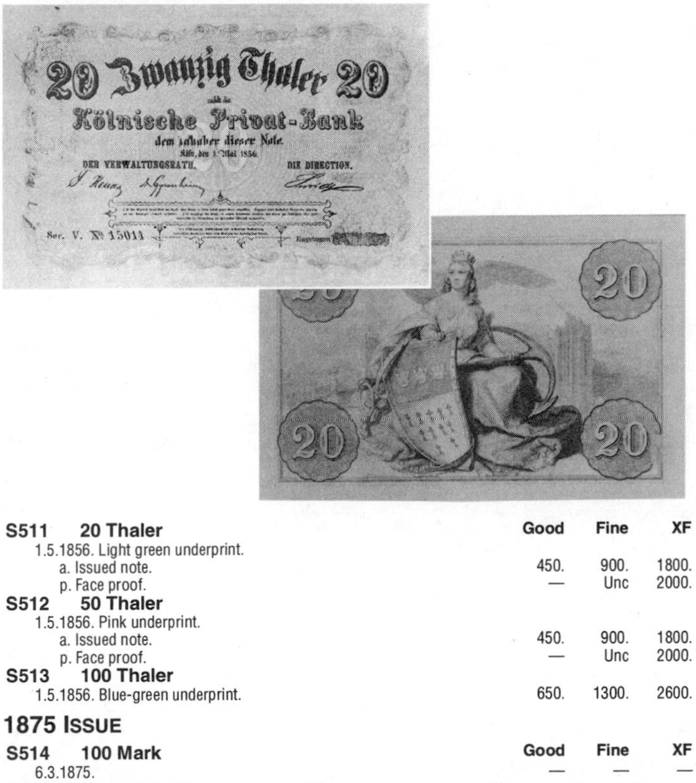

		Good	Fine	XF
S511	**20 Thaler** 1.5.1856. Light green underprint.			
	a. Issued note.	450.	900.	1800.
	p. Face proof.	—	Unc	2000.
S512	**50 Thaler** 1.5.1856. Pink underprint.			
	a. Issued note.	450.	900.	1800.
	p. Face proof.	—	Unc	2000.
S513	**100 Thaler** 1.5.1856. Blue-green underprint.	650.	1300.	2600.

1875 Issue

		Good	Fine	XF
S514	**100 Mark** 6.3.1875.	—	—	—

Communalständische Bank fur die Preussische Oberlausitz Görlitz

Communal Peoples Bank for Prussian Oberlausitz, Silesia

1866 Issue

		Good	Fine	XF
S516	**10 Thaler** 1.5.1866.	850.	1700.	3400.
S517	**20 Thaler** 1.5.1866.	850.	1700.	3400.
S518	**50 Thaler** 1.5.1866.	850.	1700.	3400.
S519	**100 Thaler** 1.5.1866.	850.	1700.	3400.
S520	**200 Thaler** 1.5.1866.	—	—	—

1874 Issue

		Good	Fine	XF
S521	**100 Mark** 31.3.1874.	—	—	—

West Preussen

West Prussia

Danziger Privat-Actien-Bank

1857 Issue

		Good	Fine	XF
S522	**10 Thaler** 1.7.1857. Arms at center. Signature Normann; Frantzius; Schottler. Back: Four allegorical figures, representing from left to right the Vistula, Danzig, Mercury (Commerce) an Printer: G&D.	750.	1500.	3000.
S523	**20 Thaler** 1.7.1857. Printer: G&D.	—	—	—
S524	**50 Thaler** 1.7.1857. Printer: G&D.	—	—	—
S525	**100 Thaler** 1.7.1857. Printer: G&D.	1350.	2750.	5500.

1862-73 Issues

		Good	Fine	XF
S526	**10 Thaler** 1.9.1862. Arms at center. Signature Normann; Frantzius; Schottler. Back: Four allegorical figures, representing from left to right: Visttula, Danzig, Mercury (Commerce) and Printer: G&D.	750.	1500.	3000.
S527	**20 Thaler** 2.1.1865. Printer: G&D.	900.	1800.	3750.
S528	**50 Thaler** 2.1.1865. Printer: G&D.	900.	1800.	3750.
S529	**100 Thaler** 1.7.1867. Arms at left. Back: Like #S526. Printer: G&D.	1350.	2750.	5500.
S530	**100 Thaler** 1.5.1871. Printer: G&D.	—	—	—
S531	**100 Thaler** 1.3.1873. Printer: G&D.	1350.	2750.	5500.

1875 Issue

		Good	Fine	XF
S532	**100 Mark** 1.6.1875. Rare.	—	—	—

1882 Issue

		Good	Fine	XF
S533	**100 Mark** 1.6.1882. Printer: Reichsdruckerei. Rare.	—	—	—

1887 Issue

		Good	Fine	XF
S534	**100 Mark** 1.6.1887. Arms with lions at lower center. Signature Mix; Damme; Langerfeldt; Steimmig; Rodenacker. Back: Like #S522 but under arch. Printer: Reichsdruckerei. Rare.	—	—	—

Ostpreussen

East Prussia

Königsberger Privatbank

Königsberg Private Bank

1857 Issue

		Good	Fine	XF
S535	**10 Thaler** 1.4.1857.	—	—	—
S536	**20 Thaler** 1.4.1857.	2300.	4600.	9250.
S537	**50 Thaler** 1.4.1857.	—	—	—
S538	**100 Thaler** 1.4.1857.	—	—	—

1866 Issue

		Good	Fine	XF
S539	**10 Thaler** 13.10.1866. Arms at upper center. Back: Head of man, either Neptune or River god Pregel, trident, anchor, rudder and seahorse below.	850.	1700.	3400.
S540	**20 Thaler** 13.10.1866.	2300.	4600.	9250.
		Good	Fine	XF
S541	**50 Thaler** 13.10.1866.	850.	1700.	3400.
S542	**100 Thaler** 13.10.1866.	1100.	2200.	4500.

Kurmärkische Privat-Bank, Berlin

Private Bank of the Electoralmark, Berlin

1860's Issue

		Good	Fine	XF
S543	**5 Thaler** 186x. Handwritten day, month and year.	1100.	2200.	4500.

Magdeburger Privatbank

Prussian Province of Saxony

Private Bank of Magdeburg

1856 Issue

		Good	Fine	XF
S544	**10 Thaler** 30.6.1856.	—	—	—
S545	**20 Thaler** 30.6.1856.	—	—	—
S546	**50 Thaler** 30.6.1856.	—	—	—
S547	**100 Thaler** 30.6.1856.	—	—	—

1866 Issue

		Good	Fine	XF
S548	**10 Thaler** 1.7.1866.	1100.	2200.	4500.
S549	**20 Thaler** 1.7.1866.	1100.	2200.	4500.
S550	**50 Thaler** 1.7.1866.	1100.	2200.	4500.
S551	**100 Thaler** 1.7.1866.	1100.	2200.	4500.

1874 Issue

		Good	Fine	XF
S552	**100 Mark** 1.1.1874.	—	—	—

Owinsker General-Kasse, Owinsk b. Posen

General Treasury of Owinsk

1801 Issue

		Good	Fine	XF
S553	**20 Thaler** 1801.	—	—	—

Ritterschaftliche Privatbank in Pommern, Stettin

Private Bank of Knighthood in Pommerania, Stettin

1824-25 Issue

		Good	Fine	XF
S556	**1 Thaler** ND (1824-25). Back: View of Stettin. Signature Bülow; Kleist; Bonin.	250.	375.	750.
S557	**5 Thaler** ND (1824-25).	350.	700.	1400.

1849 Issue

		Good	Fine	XF
S558	**10 Thaler** 24.8.1849.	—	—	—
S559	**20 Thaler** 24.8.1849.	—	—	—
S560	**50 Thaler** 24.8.1849.	—	—	—
S561	**100 Thaler** 24.8.1849.	—	—	—

1860 Issue

		Good	Fine	XF
S562	**10 Thaler** 20.7.1860.	850.	1700.	3500.
S563	**20 Thaler** 20.7.1860.	—	—	—
S564	**50 Thaler** 20.7.1860.	—	—	—
S565	**100 Thaler** 20.7.1860.	—	—	—

1869 Issue

		Good	Fine	XF
S566	**10 Thaler** 20.9.1869.	850.	1700.	3500.
S567	**20 Thaler** 20.9.1869.	1100.	2200.	4500.
S568	**50 Thaler** 20.9.1869.	—	—	—
S569	**100 Thaler** 20.9.1869.	—	—	—

1874 Issue

		Good	Fine	XF
S570	**100 Mark** 6.8.1874.			
	a. Issued note.	700.	1400.	2800.
	p. Proof.	—	Unc	2500.

Provinzial-Actien Bank des Grossherzogthums Posen

Provincial Stock Bank of the Grand Duchy of Posen

1857 Issue

		Good	Fine	XF
S571	**10 Thaler** 1.12.1857. Printer: G&D.	700.	1400.	2800.
S572	**20 Thaler** 1.12.1857. Blue and black. Peace and commerce at left, agriculture at right. Printer: G&D.	850.	1700.	3500.
S573	**50 Thaler** 1.12.1857. Printer: G&D.	1100.	2200.	4500.
S574	**100 Thaler** 1.12.1857. Printer: G&D.	1100.	2200.	4500.
S575	**200 Thaler** 1.12.1857. Printer: G&D.	1100.	2200.	4500.

1867 Issue

		Good	Fine	XF
S576	**10 Thaler** 18.3.1867. Printer: G&D.	850.	1700.	3400.
S577	**20 Thaler** 18.3.1867. Printer: G&D.	1100.	2200.	4500.
S578	**50 Thaler** 18.3.1867. Printer: G&D.	1100.	2200.	4500.
S579	**100 Thaler** 18.3.1867. Printer: G&D.	1100.	2200.	4500.

1874 Issue

		Good	Fine	XF
S580	**100 Mark** 17.3.1874.	—	—	—
S581	**200 Mark** 17.3.1874.	—	—	—
S582	**500 Mark** 17.3.1874.	—	—	—

1883 Issue

		Good	Fine	XF
S583	**100 Mark** 17.3.1883.	—	—	—
S584	**200 Mark** 17.3.1883.	—	—	—
S585	**500 Mark** 17.3.1883.	—	—	—

Reuss Schleiz, Principality of Jüngere Linie

Kommission für die Verwaltung der Staatsschulden

Commission for the Administration of State Debts

1849 Issue

		Good	Fine	XF
S588	**1 Thaler** 27.3.1849. Signature Semmel; Mayer; Hirt.	450.	900.	1800.

1860 Issue

		Good	Fine	XF
S589	**1 Thaler** 7.1.1860. Signature Beulewitz; Glass.	350.	700.	1400.

1870 Issue

		Good	Fine	XF
S590	**1 Thaler** 4.7.1870. Black on green underprint. Arms at upper center. Back: Arms at center. Printer: G&D.	350.	700.	1400.

Geraer Bank

1856 Issue

		Good	Fine	XF
S594	**10 Thaler** 15.1.1856. Black and blue. Arms at center. Back: Monument of angel crowning industry and agriculture. Printer: G&D.	450.	900.	1800.
S595	**50 Thaler** 15.1.1856. Printer: G&D.	700.	1400.	2500.
S596	**100 Thaler** 15.1.1856. Printer: G&D.	—	—	—

1874 Issue

		Good	Fine	XF
S597	**100 Mark** 1.1.1874. Printer: G&D.	750.	1500.	3000.

Reuss Greiz, Principality of

Ältere Linie

Kassenscheine

1858 Treasury Notes Issue

		Good	Fine	XF
S601	**1 Thaler** 15.5.1858. Signature Fritz; Raab; Bergner. Printer: Henning, Greiz.	450.	900.	1800.

1863 Treasury Notes Issue

		Good	Fine	XF
S602	**1 Thaler** 22.4.1863. Black and green. Signature Geldern-Crispendorf; Kommerstädt; Bergner. Printer: Henning, Greiz.	350.	700.	1400.

Saxony, Electorate of

Churfürstl. Sächs. Cassen-Billets

Royal Electoral Saxon Treasury Bills

1772 Issue

		Good	Fine	XF
S606	**1 Reichsthaler** 6.5.1772.	350.	700.	1400.
S607	**2 Reichsthaler** 6.5.1772.	450.	900.	1800.
S608	**5 Reichsthaler** 6.5.1772.	750.	1500.	3000.

		Good	Fine	XF
S609	**10 Reichsthaler** 6.5.1772.	—	—	—
S610	**50 Reichsthaler** 6.5.1772.	—	—	—
S611	**100 Reichsthaler** 6.5.1772.	—	—	—

1804 Issue

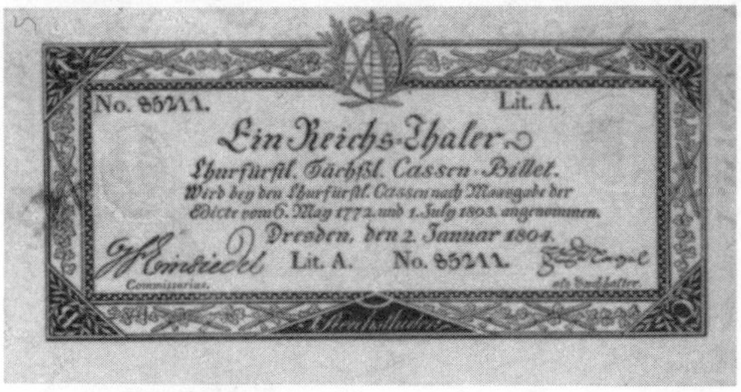

		Good	Fine	XF
S612	**1 Reichsthaler** 2.1.1804.			
	a. Signature Einsiedel; Nagel.	175.	350.	700.
	b. Signature Einsiedel; Winkler.	175.	350.	700.
	c. Signature Leipziger; Nagel.	175.	350.	700.
	d. Signature Leipziger; Winkler.	175.	350.	700.
	e. Signature Richter; Nagel.	175.	350.	700.
	f. Signature Schönberg; Nagel.	175.	350.	700.
	g. Signature Watzdorf; Winkler.	175.	350.	700.
S613	**2 Reichsthaler** 2.1.1804.			
	a. Signature Carlowitz; Winkler.	300.	600.	1200.
	b. Signature Einsiedel; Winkler.	300.	600.	1200.
	c. Signature Leipziger; Winkler.	300.	600.	1200.
	d. Signature Richter; Nagel.	300.	600.	1200.
	e. Signature Watzdorf; Einsiedel.	300.	600.	1200.
	f. Signature Watzdorf; Nagel.	300.	600.	1200.
S614	**5 Reichsthaler** 2.1.1804.	450.	900.	1800.
S615	**1, 2, 5 Reichsthaler** Blank forms.	125.	250.	500.

Saxony, Kingdom of

Königlich Sächsische Interims-Cassen-Scheine

Royal Saxon Treasury Notes

1815 Issue

		Good	Fine	XF
S616	**1 Reichsthaler** 18.12.1815.			
	a. Signature Ferber; Rachel.	225.	450.	900.
	b. Signature Bünau; Rachel.	225.	450.	900.
	c. Signature Carlowitz; Rachel.	225.	450.	900.
	d. Signature Sahr; Rachel.	225.	450.	900.

Königlich Sächsische Cassen Billets

Royal Saxon Treasury Bills

1818 Issue

		Good	Fine	XF
S617	**1 Reichsthaler** 1.10.1818. Without red surcharge.			
	a. Signature Bünau; Rachel.	175.	350.	700.
	b. Signature Carlowitz; Rachel.	175.	350.	700.
	c. Signature Ferber; Rachel.	175.	350.	700.
S618	**2 Reichsthaler** 1.10.1818. Without red surcharge.			
	a. Signature Bünau; Rachel.	225.	450.	900.
	b. Signature Carlowitz; Rachel.	225.	450.	900.
	c. Signature Ferber; Rachel.	225.	450.	900.
	d. Signature Sahr; Rachel.	225.	450.	900.

1818 (1834) Issue

		Good	Fine	XF
S619	**1 Thaler Courant** 1.10.1818 (30.7.1834). Black. One red surcharge: *1 Thlr. Cour.* Paper: Blue, may appear as gray, gray-violet or violet.			
	a. Signature Carlowitz; Rachel.	250.	500.	1000.
	b. Signature Ferber; Rachel.	250.	500.	1000.
	c. Signature Sahr; Rachel.	250.	500.	1000.

1818 Issue

S620 2 Thaler Courant	Good	Fine	XF
1.10.1818 (30.7.1834). One red surcharge: *2 Thlr. Cour.* Paper: Blue, may appear as gray, gray-violet or violet.			
a. Signature Bünau; Rachel.	300.	600.	1200.
b. Signature Carlowitz; Rachel.	300.	600.	1200.
c. Signature Sahr; Rachel.	300.	600.	1200.

1818 (1841) Issue

S620A 1 Thaler Courant	Good	Fine	XF
1.10.1818 (1841). Two red surcharges: *1 Thlr. Cour.* Paper: White.			
a. Signature Bünau; Rachel.	—	—	—
b. Signature Carlowitz; Rachel.	—	—	—

S620B 2 Thaler Courant	Good	Fine	XF
1.10.1818 (1841). Two red surcharges: *2 Thlr. Cour.* Paper: White.			
a. Signature Bünau; Rachel.	—	—	—
b. Signature Carlowitz; Rachel.	—	—	—
c. Signature Ferber; Rachel.	—	—	—

1840 Issue

The first printing was done in Dresden; most of Hirshfeld's personnel transferred there to perform it. Later printings were done in Leipzig.

		Good	Fine	XF
S621	**1 Thaler**			
	16.4.1840 (1.11.1842). Signature Weissenbach; Hübler; Schmidt. Printer: J.B. Hirschfeld, Leipzig.	150.	300.	600.
S622	**5 Thaler**			
	16.4.1840 (1.11.1842). Signature Weissenbach; Hübler; Schmidt. Printer: J.B. Hirschfeld, Leipzig.	250.	500.	1000.
S623	**10 Thaler**			
	16.4.1840 (1.11.1842). Signature Weissenbach; Hübler; Schmidt. Printer: J.B. Hirschfeld, Leipzig.	650.	1300.	2600.

1855 Issue

1855 is the date of the law which authorized this issue; however, the 1 thaler note depicts a coin type which was not issued until 1857.

#S624-S627 values are for cancelled notes.

S624 1 Thaler	Good	Fine	XF
6.9.1855 (1857). Black. Both sides of imaginary thaler at left and right. (based on thaler, KM 1192). Signature Weissenbach; Opelt; Pfotenhauer. Back: Seated allegorical woman (Saxonia) at center, locomotive at right. Paper: Light brown.	125.	250.	500.

		Good	Fine	XF
S625	**5 Thaler**			
	6.9.1855 (1857). Both sides of imaginary 5 thaler coin (based on thaler, KM 1192) at left and right. Signature Weissenbach; Opelt; Pfotenhauer. Back: Seated allegorical woman (Saxonia) at center, locomotive at right.	150.	300.	600.
S626	**10 Thaler**			
	6.9.1855 (1857). Signature Weissenbach; Opelt; Pfotenhauer.	450.	900.	1800.
S627	**20 Thaler**			
	6.9.1855 (1857). Signature Weissenbach; Opelt; Pfotenhauer.	1100.	2200.	4500.
S628	**50 Thaler**			
	6.9.1855 (1857). Signature Weissenbach; Opelt; Pfotenhauer.	—	—	—

1867 Issue

		Good	Fine	XF
S629	**1 Thaler**			
	2.3.1867. Signature Weissenbach; Roch; Pfotenhauer. Printer: G&D.	150.	300.	600.
S630	**5 Thaler**			
	2.3.1867. Signature Weissenbach; Roch; Pfotenhauer. Printer: G&D.	150.	300.	600.
S631	**10 Thaler**			
	2.3.1867. Signature Weissenbach; Roch; Pfotenhauer. Printer: G&D.	450.	900.	1800.

Chemnitzer Stadtbank

Chemnitz City Bank

1848 Credit Note Issue

		Good	Fine	XF
S636	**1 Thaler, 14-thaler-fuss**			
	19.8.1848.	350.	700.	1400.
S637	**1 Thaler, 30-thaler-fuss**			
	19.8.1848.	350.	700.	1400.

1867 Issue

S638 1 Thaler	Good	Fine	XF
10.8.1867.	250.	500.	1000.

1874 Issue

S639 100 Mark	Good	Fine	XF
1.5.1874. Printer: G&D.	1100.	2200.	4500.

Landständische Hypothekenbank für das Königl.

Sächs. Markgrafenthum Oberlausitz, Bautzen

Peoples Mortgage Bank of the Royal Saxon Margraviate Oberlausitz, Bautzen

1850 Issue

		Good	Fine	XF
S641	**1 Thaler**			
	15.11.1850.	—	—	—
S642	**5 Thaler**			
	15.11.1850.	—	—	—

Landständische Bank des Kön. Sächs.

Markgrafthums Oberlausitz

Peoples Bank of the Royal Saxon Margraviate Oberlausitz

1860's Issue

	Good	Fine	XF
S646 5 Thaler 1860.	—	—	—
S647 10 Thaler 1861.	850.	1700.	3500.

	Good	Fine	XF
S648 10 Thaler 10.10.1868.	850.	1700.	3500.

1875 Issue

	Good	Fine	XF
S649 100 Mark 1.1.1875. Printer: G&D.	1100.	2200.	4500.

Leipziger Bank

Bank of Leipzig

1839 Issue

	Good	Fine	XF
S651 100 Thaler 11.3.1839.	—	—	—
S652 200 Thaler 11.3.1839.	—	—	—
S653 500 Thaler 11.3.1839.	—	—	—
S654 20 Thaler Konventionsfuss (1839).	—	—	—
S655 100 Thaler Konventionsfuss (1839).	—	—	—
S656 200 Thaler Konventionsfuss (1839).	—	—	—
S657 500 Thaler Konventionsfuss (1839).	—	—	—
S658 1000 Thaler Konventionsfuss (1839).	—	—	—
S659 100 Thaler 14-thaler-fuss (1839).	—	—	—
S660 500 Thaler 14-thaler-fuss (1839).	—	—	—

1843 Issue

	Good	Fine	XF
S661 50 Thaler 8.10.1843.	—	—	—

1845 Issue

	Good	Fine	XF
S662 20 Thaler 15.7.1845.	—	—	—

1855 Issue

	Good	Fine	XF
S663 20 Thaler 1.3.1855. Printer: G&D.	1100.	2200.	4500.

1860 Issue

	Good	Fine	XF
S664 50 Thaler 1.6.1860. Printer: G&D.	1100.	2200.	4500.
S665 100 Thaler 1.6.1860. Printer: G&D.	1100.	2200.	4500.

1864 Issue

	Good	Fine	XF
S666 10 Thaler 20.6.1864. Printer: G&D.	1100.	2200.	4500.

1866 Issue

	Good	Fine	XF
S667 10 Thaler 18.4.1866. Printer: G&D.	1100.	2200.	4500.

1874 Issue

	Good	Fine	XF
S668 100 Mark 1.1.1874. Printer: G&D.	1100.	2200.	4500.

Leipziger Diskonto-Kasse

Leipzig Discount Bank

1824 Currency Exchange Issue

	Good	Fine	XF
S671 100 Reichsthaler 1824.	—	—	—
S672 200 Reichsthaler 1824.	—	—	—
S673 500 Reichsthaler 1824.	—	—	—
S674 1000 Reichsthaler 1824.	—	—	—

Leipziger Kassenverein

Leipzig Treasury Association

1867 Issue

	Good	Fine	XF
S676 100 Thaler 1.5.1867.	—	—	—

1875 Issue

	Good	Fine	XF
S677 500 Mark 31.3.1875. Printer: G&D.	—	—	—

Leipzig-Dresdner Eisenbahn-Compagnie Eisenbahn-Cassa-Scheine

Leipzig-Dresden Railway Company Railway Treasury Notes

1838-39 Issue

	Good	Fine	XF
S681 1 Thaler, 14-thaler-fuss ND (1838). Black. 2 signatures, Gustav Harkort at right. Back: Brown. Paper: Green.	225.	450.	900.

1855 Issue

	Good	Fine	XF
S682 1 Thaler, 14-thaler-fuss ND (1855). Back: *UMDRUCK VON 1855.*	225.	450.	900.

1857 Issue

	Good	Fine	XF
S683 1 Thaler, 30-thaler-fuss ND (1857).	225.	450.	900.

1870 Issue

	Good	Fine	XF
S684 1 Thaler, 30-thaler-fuss ND (1870). Overprint: *UMDRUCK VON 1870.*	225.	450.	900.

Sächsische Bank zu Dresden

Refer to Regional Banks #S946-S971.

Saxe-Altenburg, Duchy of

Herrschaftl. Floss-Kassen-Billet Fürstl. Kammer-Hauptkasse

Governmental Floating Treasury Bill Royal Government Treasury

1785 Issue

	Good	Fine	XF
S686 5 Thaler 15.12.1785. Hand dated.	1300.	2600.	5250.

Kassenscheine

Treasury Notes

1848 Issue

	Good	Fine	XF
S688 1 Thaler 16.7.1848 (1849). Signature Bryogner; Meissner; Hempel; Reuter. Printer: J. B. Hirschfeld, Leipzig.	450.	900.	1800.

1858 Issue

		Good	Fine	XF
S689	**10 Thaler** 11.11.1858. Signature Geulebrück; Meissner; Gabelentz; Lingke. Printer: G&D.	650.	1300.	2600.

Saxe-Coburg, Duchy of

Grossherzogl. Sachische Kassen-Anweisungen

Ducal Treasury Vouchers

1849 Issue

		Good	Fine	XF
S691	**1 Thaler** 22.1.1849. Signature Hofmann; Braun; Scherzer. Printer: Dietz'sche Hofbuchdruckerei, plates by C. Naumann.	650.	1300.	2600.
S692	**5 Thaler** 22.1.1849. Signature Hofmann; Braun; Scherzer. Printer: Dietz'sche Hofbuchdruckerei, plates by C. Naumann. Reported not confirmed.	—	—	—

1870 Issue

		Good	Fine	XF
S693	**1 Thaler** 30.6.1870. Signature Egidy; Westhäusser; Goebel. Printer: G&D.	450.	900.	1800.
S694	**5 Thaler** 30.6.1870. Signature Egidy; Westhäusser; Goebel. Printer: G&D. Reported not confirmed.	—	—	—

Saxe-Coburg and Gotha, Duchy of

Although unified under one duke in 1826, Coburg and Gotha remained independent of each other in many respects. Coburg and Gotha each had their own Diet. In economic terms Gotha was in the orbit of Frankfurt/Main, Coburg in that of Nuremberg. This explains the separate issues of treasury vouchers for Coburg and Gotha.

Privatbank zu Gotha

Private Bank of Gotha

1857 Issue

		Good	Fine	XF
S701	**10 Thaler** 2.1.1857.	—	—	—
S702	**20 Thaler** 2.1.1857.	850.	1700.	3500.
S703	**100 Thaler** 2.1.1857.	—	—	—

1874 Issue

		Good	Fine	XF
S704	**100 Mark** 1.7.1874. Seated allegorical woman at left.	1100.	2200.	4500.

NOTE: Printer's proofs of higher denominations are valued at *XF $400.00.*

Saxe-Gotha, Duchy of

Herzogl. Kassen Anweisungen in Saxe-Gotha

Ducal Treasury Vouchers

1847 Issue

		Good	Fine	XF
S706	**1 Thaler** 30.9.1847. Printer: Haenels Hofbuchdruckerei, Magdeburg.	650.	1300.	2600.
S707	**5 Thaler** 30.9.1847. Printer: Haenels Hofbuchdruckerei, Magdeburg.	850.	1700.	3500.

1860 Issue

		Good	Fine	XF
S708	**1 Thaler** 12.7.1860. Signature Hess; Grüzmüller; Thauget. Printer: G&D.	450.	900.	1800.
S709	**5 Thaler** 12.7.1860. Signature Hess; Grüzmüller; Thauget. Printer: G&D.	850.	1700.	3500.

Saxe-Meiningen, Duchy of

Kassenanweisungen

Treasury Vouchers

1849 Issue

		Good	Fine	XF
S711	**1 Thaler** 24.5.1849. Brown. Signature Blomeyer; Trinks; Butler; Habersang. Printer: Haenel, Magdeburg.	175.	350.	700.
S712	**10 Thaler** 31.3.1856. Signature Blomeyer; Trinks; Butler; Schaller.	550.	1100.	2200.

Mitteldeutsche Creditbank in Meiningen

Middle German Credit Bank

1856 Issue

		Good	Fine	XF
S714	**10 Thaler** 26.8.1856 (4.1857). Blue on brown underprint. Female portrait in medallion flanking seated knight holding shield and sword at center. Printer: B. Dondorf and C. Naumann's Druckerei.	650.	1300.	2600.

1875 Issue

S715 100 Mark	Good	Fine	XF
2.1.1875. Printer: C. Naumann, Frankfurt/Main. Not placed in circulation.	1100.	2200.	4500.

Saxe-Weimar-Eisenach, Grand Duchy of

Grossherzogl. Sächsische Cassen Anweisung

Grand Ducal Treasury Voucher

1847 Issue

S716 1 Thaler	Good	Fine	XF
27.8.1847. Signature Meyer; Kühne; Horn. Printer: Haenels Hofbuchdruckerei, Magdeburg.	450.	900.	1800.
S717 5 Thaler			
27.8.1847. Signature Meyer; Kühne; Horn. Printer: Haenels Hofbuchdruckerei, Magdeburg.	650.	1300.	2600.

1859 Issue

S718 1 Thaler	Good	Fine	XF
20.4.1859. Signature Hoffmann; Schwendler; Horn. Printer: G&D.	350.	700.	1400.
S719 5 Thaler			
20.4.1859. Signature Hoffmann; Schwendler; Horn. Printer: G&D.	—	—	—

1870 Issue

S720 1 Thaler	Good	Fine	XF
22.6.1870. Boys symbolizing commerce and agriculture at left and right. Young man holding hawk, lion below. Signature Thon; Frier; Horn. Printer: G&D.	250.	500.	1000.
S721 1 Thaler			
Printer: G&D. Proofs in various colors.	150.	300.	600.
S722 5 Thaler			
22.6.1870. Signature Thon; Fries; Horn. Printer: G&D.	550.	1100.	2200.
S723 5 Thaler			
Printer: G&D. Proofs in various colors.	150.	300.	600.

Weimarische Bank

Weimar Bank

1854 Issue

S726 10 Thaler	Good	Fine	XF
4.2.1854. Arms at top center. Back: Tyche of Saxe-Weimar-Eisenach, wearing as a crown the Wartburg plus and rampant lion.	550.	1100.	2200.
S727 10 Thaler			
4.2.1854. Arms at top left, right and center.	1100.	2200.	4500.
S728 20 Thaler			
4.2.1854.	1100.	2200.	4500.
S729 50 Thaler			
4.2.1854.	1100.	2200.	4500.
S730 100 Thaler			
4.2.1854.	—	—	—

1874 Issue

S731 100 Mark	Good	Fine	XF
1.1.1874. Printer: G&D.	550.	1100.	2200.

NOTE: Printer's Proofs of higher denominations are valued at *XF $550.00.*

Schaumburg-Lippe, Principality of

Controll-Commission der Fürstl. Schaumburg-Lippischen Kassen-Anweisungen

Control Commission of the Schaumburg-Lippe Treasury Vouchers

1857 Issue

S733 10 Thaler	Good	Fine	XF
2.1.1857. Black on yellow underprint. Angels at left and right. Signature Campe; Iffland. Back: Black and blue.			
a. Issued note.	350.	700.	1400.
p. Proof.	—	Unc	1500.

Niedersächsische Bank, Bückeburg

Lower Saxony Bank, Bückeburg

1856 Issue

S736 10 Thaler	Good	Fine	XF
12.9.1856. Angels holding shields with emblems of manual and intellectual labor at left and right. Back: Arms at center.	850.	1700.	3400.

1865 Issue

S737 10 Thaler	Good	Fine	XF
28.6.1865. Printer: C. Naumann.	—	—	—

1874 Issue

S738 100 Mark — Good / Fine / XF
1.1.1874. Printer: C. Naumann. — 850. / 1700. / 3400.

Schleswig-Holstein, Duchies of

Danish until 1864. An uprising against Danish rule occured 1848-1850; after a short period of Austro-Prussian military government in 1851, the duchies were restored to Denmark. After Austria and Prussia defeated Denmark in 1864, the duchies were under the military government of Austria and Prussia. Both duchies were annexed by Prussia in 1866.

Oberste Zivilbehörde für Holstein, Kiel

Supreme Civil Authority for Holstein, Kiel

1851 Issue

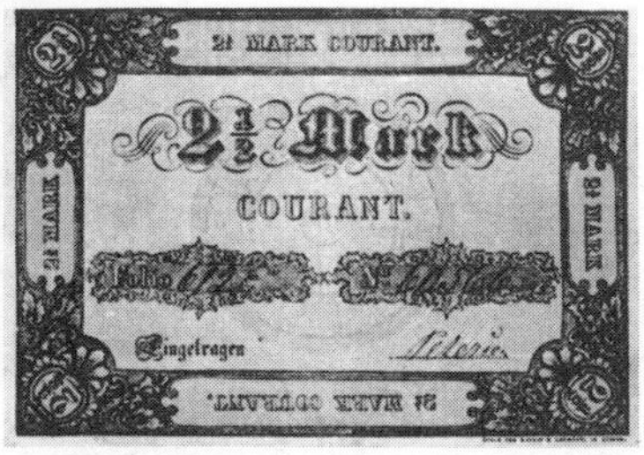

		Good	Fine	XF
S741	**2 1/2 Mark** 17.7.1851. Printer: Kobner & Lehmkul, Altona.	225.	450.	900.
S742	**10 Mark** 17.7.1851. Printer: Kobner & Lehmkul, Altona.	550.	1100.	2200.
S743	**25 Mark** 17.7.1851. Printer: Kobner & Lehmkul, Altona.	1100.	2200.	4400.

Sr. Königl. Majestät Ministerium für die Herzogtümer Holstein und Lauenburg, Kopenhagen

His Royal Majesty's Ministry for the Duchies Holstein and Lauenburg, Kopenhagen

1854 Issue

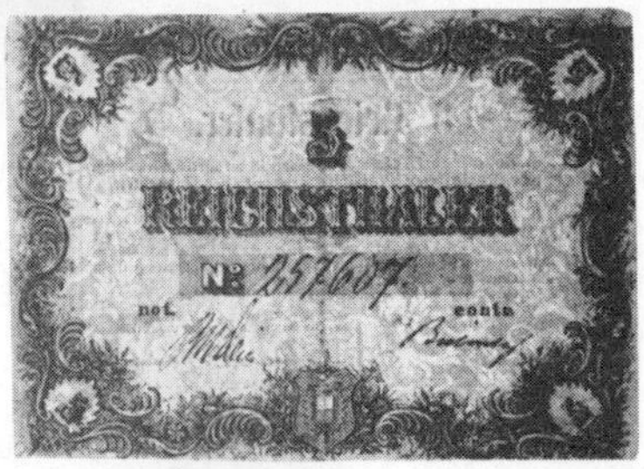

		Good	Fine	XF
S746	**5 Reichsthaler** 1.9.1854.	850.	1700.	3400.
S747	**20 Reichsthaler** 1.9.1854.	—	—	—

Königliches Finanz-Kollegium

Royal Financial Registry

1807 Issue

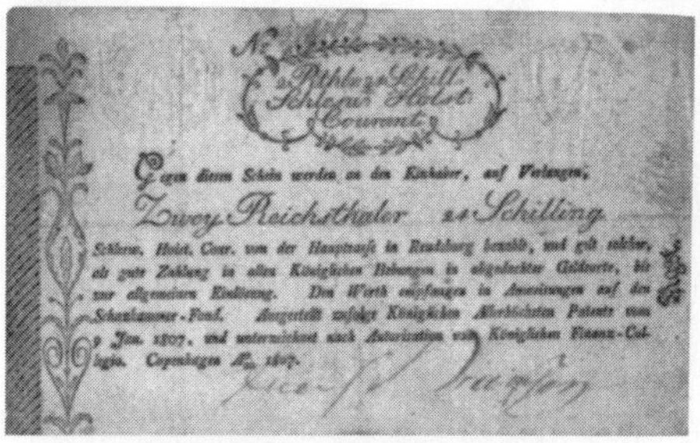

		Good	Fine	XF
S751	**2 Reichsthaler 24 Schilling** 9.1.1807. Kopenhagen, *Anweisung auf den Schatzkammer-Fond.*	450.	900.	1800.
S752	**20 Reichsthaler** 9.1.1807. Kopenhagen, *Anweisung auf die Einnahmen des Schatzkammer-Abtragsfonds.*	—	—	—

1808-15 Issue

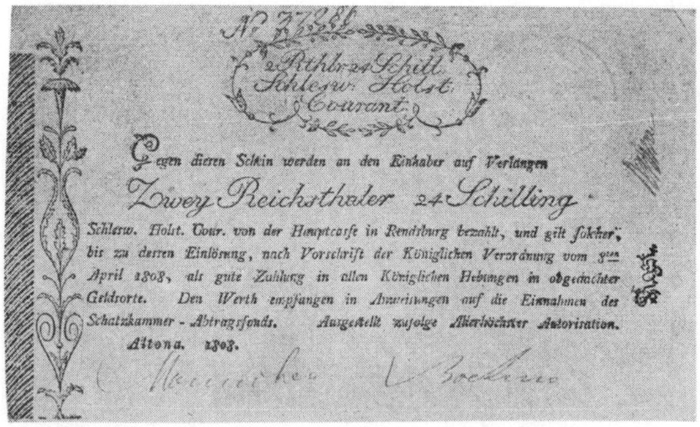

		Good	Fine	XF
S753	**2 Reichsthaler 24 Schilling** 8.4.1808. Altona, *Anweisung auf die Einnahmen des Schatzkammer-Abtragsfonds.*			
	a. Round embossed stamp.	175.	350.	700.
	b. Octagonal embossed stamp.	350.	700.	1400.
S754	**20 Reichsthaler** 8.4.1808. Altona.	850.	1700.	3500.
S755	**5 Reichsthaler** 6.12.1815. Kopenhagen.	1100.	2200.	4500.

Schleswig-Holsteinische Species Bank in Altona

Schleswig-Holstein Specie Bank in Altona

1787-1813 Issue

	Good	Fine	XF
S756 8 Thaler Species = 10 Thaler Courant 1787-1813.	850.	1700.	3500.
S757 20 Thaler Species = 25 Thaler Courant 1787-1813.	850.	1700.	3500.
S758 40 Thaler Species = 50 Thaler Courant 1787-1813.	1100.	2200.	4500.
S759 80 Thaler Species = 100 Thaler Courant 1787-1813.	1100.	2200.	4500.

Schleswig-Holsteinisches Leihe-Institut, Altona, Kopenhagen

Schleswig-Holstein Loan Institute, Altona, Kopenhagen

1801 Issue

	Good	Fine	XF
S761 5 Reichsthaler Schlesw.-Holst. Courant 1801. Serial letter A, B, C and D (redeemable in different years).	850.	1700.	3400.

1802 Issue

	Good	Fine	XF
S762 5 Reichsthaler Schlesw.-Holst. Courant 1802. Serial letter A, B, C and D (redeemable in different years).	850.	1700.	3400.

1803 Issue

	Good	Fine	XF
S763 5 Reichsthaler Schlesw.-Holst. Courant 1803. Serial letter A, B, C and D (redeemable in different years).	—	—	—

1810 Issue

	Good	Fine	XF
S764 25 Reichsthaler 1810. Serial letter A, B, C and D (redeemable in different years).	—	—	—
S765 50 Reichsthaler 1810. Serial letter A, B, C and D (redeemable in different years).	—	—	—
S766 75 Reichsthaler 1810. Serial letter A, B, C and D (redeemable in different years).	—	—	—
S767 100 Reichsthaler 1810. Serial letter A, B, C and D (redeemable in different years).	—	—	—

Schlesw. Holst. Kassen-Scheine

Provisional Government

1848 Issue

	Good	Fine	XF
S771 1 Thaler = 2 1/2 Mark Courant 31.7.1848. Signature J. C. Ravit; H. W. Baudissin; M. Moltke; P. Lüders; Matthiessen; Tiedemann.	225.	450.	900.
S772 4 Thaler = 10 Mark Courant 31.7.1848. Signature J. C. Ravit; H. W. Baudissin; M. Moltke; P. Lüders; Matthiessen; Tiedemann.	350.	700.	1400.
S773 10 Thaler = 25 Mark Courant 31.7.1848. Signature J. C. Ravit; H. W. Baudissin; M. Moltke; P. Lüders; Matthiessen; Tiedemann.	650.	1300.	2600.

Schleswig-Holstein, Statthalterschaft der Herzogtümer

Schleswig-Holstein, Governorship of the Duchies

1850, different values, are obligations.

Freiwillige Anleihe des Schleswig-Holst. Finanz-Departements

Voluntary Loan of the Schleswig-Holstein Finance Department

1863, 5 and 10 Thalers, are promissory notes.

Schwarzburg-Rudolstadt, Principality of Kassenbillets

1848 Issue

	Good	Fine	XF
S776 1 Thaler 4.12.1848. Signature Schwartz; Bamberg.			
a. Edge light blue.	350.	700.	1400.
b. Edge white.	350.	700.	1400.

1851-55 Issue

	Good	Fine	XF
S777 1 Thaler 30.5.1851. Count Albert VII at top, castles of Schwarzburg and Rudolstadt at left and right. Signature Schwartz; Bamberg. Back: Pink underprint. Watermark: SIR. Printer: Theodor Boesche, Berlin.	225.	450.	900.
S778 10 Thaler 1.12.1855 (1.1856). Signature Ketelhodt; Hercher; Bergmann.	650.	1300.	2600.

Schwarzburg-Sondershausen, Principality of

Verwaltung des Kammerschulden-Tilgungsfonds

Administration of the Governmental Debt Redemption Treasury Assignments

1854-55 Issue

	Good	Fine	XF
S781 1 Thaler 11.3.1854. Themis holding scales and sword at left, arms at right. Signature Cannabich; Gottschalck; Liebers. Back: Numeral I.	450.	900.	1800.
S782 5 Thaler 11.3.1854. Signature Cannabich; Gottschalck; Liebers.	—	—	—
S783 10 Thaler 20.12.1855. Signature Cannabich; Gottschalck; Liebers.	—	—	—

1859 Issue

	Good	Fine	XF
S784 1 Thaler 25.10.1859. Signature Cannabich; Huschke; Linke.	350.	700.	1400.

1866 Issue

		Good	Fine	XF
S785	**1 Thaler** 25.2.1866. Signature Cannabich; Möller; Linke.	225.	450.	900.

Thüringische Bank

Thuringian Bank

1856 Issue

		Good	Fine	XF
S788	**20 Thaler** 1.3.1856.	850.	1700.	3500.

1870 Issue

		Good	Fine	XF
S789	**20 Thaler** 29.3.1870.	850.	1700.	3500.

Waldeck, Principality of

Fürstl. Waldecksche Staatsschulden-Verwaltung

Royal Waldeck State Indebtedness Administration

1854 Issue

		Good	Fine	XF
S791	**1 Thaler** 13.11.1854. Signature Schumacher; Steineck. Printer: Dondorf & Naumann, Frankfurt/Main.	650.	1300.	2600.
S792	**10 Thaler** 13.11.1854. Printer: Dondorf & Naumann, Frankfurt/Main.	850.	1700.	3500.

Westphalia, Kingdom of

Obligationen der Reichsschulden-Amortisations-Casse

Obligations of the Imperial Debt Amortizations Treasury

Decree of October 19, 1808

		Good	Fine	XF
S796	**25 Franken** 19.10.1808. Black.	125.	250.	500.
S797	**50 Franken** 19.10.1808. Black.	125.	250.	500.
S798	**100 Franken** 19.10.1808. Black.	125.	250.	500.
S799	**200 Franken** 19.10.1808. Black.	125.	250.	500.

Obligationen der Reichsschulden-Amortisations-Casse

Quarterly Interest Coupons to the Obligations of the Imperial Debt Amortizations Treasury

1812-20 Issue

		Good	Fine	XF
S801	**2 Franken** 1812-20. Black. Without red stamp *F.W.*	30.00	60.00	125.
S802	**3 Franken** 1812-20. Black. Without red stamp *F.W.*	30.00	60.00	125.
S803	**4 Franken** 1812-20. Black. Without red stamp *F.W.*	30.00	60.00	125.
S804	**5 Franken** 1812-20. Black. Without red stamp *F.W.*	30.00	60.00	125.

		Good	Fine	XF
S805	**6 Franken** 1812-20. Black. Without red stamp *F.W.*	30.00	60.00	125.
S806	**10 Franken** 1812-20. Black. Without red stamp *F.W.*	30.00	60.00	125.
S807	**2 Franken** 1812-20. Black. Red stamp *F.W.*	40.00	80.00	160.
S808	**3 Franken** 1812-20. Black. Red stamp *F.W.*	40.00	80.00	160.
S809	**4 Franken** 1812-20. Black. Red stamp *F.W.*	40.00	80.00	160.
S810	**5 Franken** 1812-20. Black. Red stamp *F.W.*	40.00	80.00	160.
S811	**6 Franken** 1812-20. Black. Red stamp *F.W.*	40.00	80.00	160.
S811A	**10 Franken** 1812-20. Black. Red stamp *F.W.*	40.00	80.00	160.

1812 Treasury Notes Issue

		Good	Fine	XF
S812	**20 Franken** 12.6.1812. Values handwritten.	150.	300.	600.
S813	**50 Franken** 12.6.1812. Values handwritten.	150.	300.	600.
S814	**100 Franken** 12.6.1812. Values handwritten.	150.	300.	600.
S815	**250 Franken** 12.6.1812. Values handwritten.	150.	300.	600.
S816	**20 Franken** 8.7.1812. Values printed.	175.	350.	700.
S817	**50 Franken** 8.7.1812. Values printed.	175.	350.	700.

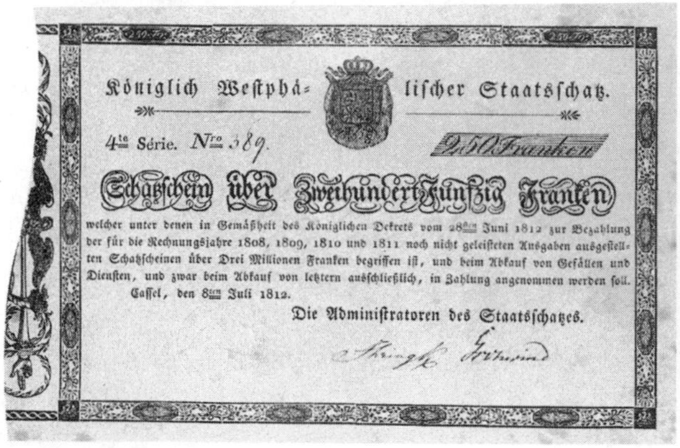

		Good	Fine	XF
S818	**250 Franken** 8.7.1812. Values printed.	175.	350.	700.

Issues of Westphalia were not intended to be legal tender for circulation and therefore cannot be considered paper money.

Württemberg, Kingdom of

Königl. Staats-Haupt-Kasse

Royal State Treasury

1849 Issue

		Good	Fine	XF
S841	**2 Gulden** 1.8.1849. Minerva at top; putti symbolizing agriculture and commerce at bottom. Signature Herdegen; Schickhardt. Printer: C. Naumann, Frankfurt/Main.	450.	900.	1800.
S842	**10 Gulden** 1.8.1849. Signature Herdegen; Schickhardt. Printer: C. Naumann, Frankfurt/Main.	750.	1500.	3000.
S843	**35 Gulden** 1.8.1849. Signature Herdegen; Schickhardt. Printer: C. Naumann, Frankfurt/Main.	750.	1500.	3000.

1858 Issue

		Good	Fine	XF
S844	**10 Gulden** 1.1.1858. Signature Vogel; Schickhardt. Printer: C. Naumann, Frankfurt/Main.	750.	1500.	3000.

1871 Issue

		Good	Fine	XF
S845	**10 Gulden** 1.12.1871. Signature Neuschler; Heider. Printer: C. Naumann, Frankfurt/Main.	750.	1500.	3000.

Württembergischer Cassen-Verein von G. Müller und Genossen

Württemberg Treasury Association of G. Müller and Associates

1870 Issue

		Good	Fine	XF
S846	**5 Gulden** 1.8.1870. Punched.	125.	250.	500.

Note: Interest bearing notes in higher denomination were also issued.

Württembergische Notenbank

See Regional Bank Issues #S975-S999.

Principalities

Fürstlich Anhalt-Cöthen-Plessner Rent-Kammer-Scheine

Princely Anhalt-Cöthen-Pless Governmental Interest Bearing Notes

1807-21 Issue

	Good	Fine	XF
S851 5 Silbergroschen 1807-21.	—	—	—
S852 10 Silbergroschen 1807-21.	450.	900.	1800.
S853 15 Silbergroschen 1807-21.	—	—	—
S854 1 Reichsthaler 1807-21.	—	—	—
S855 5 Reichsthaler 1807-21.	—	—	—
S856 10 Reichsthaler 1807-21.	—	—	—

Anhalt-Dessau, Herzogl. Anhalt-Dessauisches Steueramt

Anhalt-Dessau, Ducal Tax Bureau

1863 ND Issue

Dated by the use of the suffix "Dessau," which was not used after the absorption of Anhalt-Bernburg in 1863. Used during a period of shortage of copper money.

	Good	Fine	XF
S857 3 Pfennig ND (pre 1863). Red stamp: HERZ. ANH. DESSAU STEURAMT, DESSAU. Back: Handwritten: 3 PFENNIG. Cardboard.	—	—	—

Fürstl. Carolath-Beuthen'sche Kammer, Kassenanweisungen der Rent-Kasse

Princely Carolath-Beuthen Government Treasury Vouchers of the Revenue Fund

1830 Issue

	Good	Fine	XF
S858 1 Thaler Preuss. Courant 1.7.1830.			
a. Issued note.	450.	900.	1800.
p. Proof.	—	Unc	1250.

Fürst Pückler-Muskau in Muskau O.L., Schlesien

Treasury Vouchers

1826 ND Issue

	Good	Fine	XF
S859 1 Thaler ND (1826).	1100.	2200.	4500.
S860 5 Thaler ND (1826).	1500.	3000.	6000.

Solms-Hohensolms-Lich, Oberhessen, Fürst

1814 Issue

	Good	Fine	XF
S861 5 Thaler 1814.	—	—	—

Solms-Laubach, Oberhessen, Gräfl. Solms-Laubachische Kassenanweisungen

1847 Issue

	Good	Fine	XF
S862 1 Gulden 1847. Printer: C. Naumann, Frankfurt/Main.	1500.	3000.	6000.
S863 5 Gulden 1847. Printer: C. Naumann, Frankfurt/Main.	1500.	3000.	6000.

Stolberg-Rossla, Prov. Sachsen, Grafen

1706 Issue

An emergency issue when Electoral Saxon troops occupied the previously independent earldom in a *coup de main.*

	Good	Fine	XF
S864 3 Pfennig 1706.	—	—	—
S865 6 Pfennig 1706.	—	—	—
S866 1 Silbergroschen 1706.	—	—	—
S867 2 Silbergroschen 1706.	—	—	—

	Good	Fine	XF
S868 6 Silbergroschen 1706.	—	—	—
S869 12 Silbergroschen 1706.	—	—	—

1813 Issue

Issued after the earldoms were liberated by Prussia; the small denominations were issued under a common law of the three Stolberg lines. Redeemed 1817.

	Good	Fine	XF
S870 3 Pfennig 11.1813.	—	—	—
S871 6 Pfennig 11.1813.	—	—	—
S872 1 Silbergroschen 11.1813.	—	—	—
S873 2 Silbergroschen 11.1813.	—	—	—
S874 6 Silbergroschen 11.1813.	—	—	—
S875 12 Silbergroschen 11.1813.	—	—	—

Stolberg-Stolberg, Prov. Sachsen, Grafen

1706 Issue

An emergency issue when Electroal Saxon troops occupied the previously independent earldom in a *coup de main.*

	Good	Fine	XF
S876 3 Pfennig 1706.	—	—	—
S877 6 Pfennig 1706.	—	—	—
S878 1 Silbergroschen 1706.	—	—	—
S879 2 Silbergroschen 1706.	—	—	—
S880 6 Silbergroschen 1706.	—	—	—
S881 12 Silbergroschen 1706.	—	—	—

1813 Issue

Issued after the earldoms were liberated by Prussia; the small denominations were issued under a common law of the three Stolberg lines. Redeemed 1817.

	Good	Fine	XF
S882 3 Pfennig 11.1813.	—	—	—
S883 6 Pfennig 11.1813.	—	—	—
S884 1 Silbergroschen 11.1813.	—	—	—
S885 2 Silbergroschen 11.1813.	—	—	—
S886 6 Silbergroschen 11.1813.	—	—	—
S887 12 Silbergroschen 11.1813.	—	—	—

Stolberg-Wernigerode, Prov. Sachsen, Grafen

1813 Issue

	Good	Fine	XF
S888 3 Pfennig 11.1813.	—	—	—
S889 6 Pfennig 11.1813.	—	—	—
S890 1 Silbergroschen 11.1813.	—	—	—
S891 2 Silbergroschen 11.1813.	—	—	—
S892 6 Silbergroschen 11.1813.	—	—	—
S893 12 Silbergroschen 11.1813.	—	—	—
S894 1 Thaler 11.1813.	—	—	—
S895 2 Thaler 11.1813.	—	—	—
S896 3 Thaler 11.1813.	—	—	—
S897 5 Thaler 11.1813.	—	—	—
S898 10 Thaler 11.1813.	—	—	—
S899 20 Thaler 11.1813.	—	—	—

Ysenburg-Büdingen, Oberhessen, Fürst

1814 Issue

	Good	Fine	XF
S900 5 Thaler 1814.	—	—	—

Regional Banks

Notes issued by many banks during 1914-18 as well as those made during the inflation period by numerous states and banks are not included in this section. Only those from regional banks having had a history of issues over a number of years are included: Badische Bank, Bayerische Notenbank, Sächsische Bank and Württembergische Notenbank.

Badische Bank

Bank of Baden

1870-74 Issue

	Good	Fine	XF
S901 10 Gulden 1.12.1870. Black on gray and green underprint. Allegorical woman with two small angels at lower left and right. Back: River god of the Rhine at left and goddess of the river Neckar at right. Printer: Naumann.	900.	1800.	3600.

	Good	Fine	XF
S902 50 Gulden 1.7.1871. Black and blue on yellow-brown underprint. Allegorical woman with two small angels at lower left and right. Back: River god of the Rhine at left and goddess of the river Neckar at right. Printer: Naumann.	1300.	2600.	5250.
S903 100 Mark 1.1.1874. Black and blue on yellow-brown underprint. Allegorical woman with two small angels at lower left and right. Back: River god of the Rhine at left and goddess of the river Neckar at right. Printer: Naumann.	450.	900.	1800.

1890 Issue

	Good	Fine	XF
S904 100 Mark 1.1.1890. Black and blue on light blue underprint. Allegorical woman with two small angels at lower left and right. Back: River god of the Rhine at left and goddess of the river Neckar at right. Printer: Naumann.	1350.	2700.	3400.

1902 Issue

	Good	Fine	XF
S905 100 Mark 1.10.1902. Black and blue on light blue underprint. Allegorical woman with two small angels at lower left and right. Back: River god of the Rhine at left and goddess of the river Neckar at right. Printer: Naumann.	15.00	30.00	60.00

1907 Issue

	Good	Fine	XF
S906 100 Mark 1.1.1907. Black and blue on light blue underprint. Allegorical woman with two small angels at lower left and right. Back: Gray on light blue underprint. River god of the Rhine at left and goddess of the river Neckar at right. Printer: Naumann.			
a. Printer: C. Naumann's Druckerel.	10.00	15.00	30.00
b. Without imprint.	5.00	10.00	20.00

1918-22 Issues

	VG	VF	UNC
S907 100 Mark 15.12.1918. Black on blue and blue-green underprint. Back: Black on blue underprint.	2.00	5.00	25.00
S908 500 Mark 1.8.1922. Black-green on brown and gray underprint. Griffins and arms at center. Back: Factory and field work.	2.00	5.00	25.00

	VG	VF	UNC
S909 5000 Mark 1.12.1922. Brown on violet and gold underprint. Two large stylized griffins at center. Back: Small scenes at corners, Large allegorical scene at center.	2.00	7.50	30.00

1923 Issue

	VG	VF	UNC
S910 10,000 Mark 1.4.1923. Light brown on blue and green underprint. Two stylized griffins and arms at center. Back: 2-faced head with one facing left and one facing right at center.	1.50	4.00	15.00

		VG	VF	UNC
S911	**500,000 Mark** 1.8.1923. Dark brown on gray-brown and violet underprint. Back: Man with torch and hammer.	1.50	3.00	7.50
S912	**1 Million Mark** 7.8.1923. Black on violet underprint. Uniface.	1.50	3.00	7.50

		VG	VF	UNC
S913	**2 Milliarden Mark** 25.9.1923. Dark brown on gray-green underprint. Overprint: Red new denomination across 20 Millionen Mark on face and back.	1.50	3.00	7.50
S914	**100 Milliarden Mark** 30.10.1923. Dark brown on brown-violet and light blue underprint.	2.00	7.50	30.00

1924 Issue

		VG	VF	UNC
S915	**50 Reichsmark** 11.10.1924. Dark blue on brown and green underprint. Johann Peter Hebel at right.			
	a. Issued note.	450.	900.	1800.
	b. Cancelled, stamped: *Ungültig*.	60.00	125.	250.

Bayerische Notenbank

Bavarian Note Issuing Bank

1875 Issue

		VG	VF	UNC
S921	**100 Mark** 3.11.1875. Black on blue underprint. Two seated allegorical figures with child at left and right, arms at bottom center. Printer: G&D. Made from the same plate as #S166.	500.	1000.	2000.

1900 Issue

		VG	VF	UNC
S922	**100 Mark** 1.1.1900. Black on blue and multicolor underprint. Two seated allegorical figures with child at left and right, arms at bottom center. Like #S921. Printer: G&D.	3.00	6.00	12.00

1922 Issue

		VG	VF	UNC
S923	**100 Mark** 1.1.1922. Black on multicolor underprint. Back: Arms at right.	.75	1.50	4.50

		VG	VF	UNC
S924	**1000 Mark** 1.10.1922. Blue-black on blue and brown underprint. Back: Brown on light blue underprint.	1.00	3.00	10.00
S925	**5000 Mark** 1.12.1922. Multicolor.	1.00	3.00	10.00

1923 First Issue

		VG	VF	UNC
S926	**20,000 Mark** 1.3.1923. Dark blue on blue and orange underprint. Back: Arms at center.	1.00	3.00	12.50

		VG	VF	UNC
S927	**50,000 Mark** 15.3.1923. Black on gray and multicolor underprint. Back: Blue on green and light brown underprint.	1.00	3.00	12.50

		VG	VF	UNC
S928	**100,000 Mark** 15.6.1923. Black on green and red underprint. Back: Blue on light olive. Griffins with arms at left and right, Bavaria Monument at Munich.	1.00	3.00	12.50

		VG	VF	UNC
S929	**1 Million Mark** 15.8.1923. Black and blue on tan and orange underprint. Two stylized figures at center. Back: Blue and red. Arms at center.	1.00	3.00	12.50

1923 Second Issue

		VG	VF	UNC
S930	**500,000 Mark** 18.8.1923. Dark blue on violet and lilac underprint. Back: Arms in underprint.	1.00	3.00	12.50
S931	**1 Million Mark** 20.8.1923. Dark brown on yellow and blue-green underprint. Back: Blue-green.	1.00	3.00	12.50
S932	**5 Millionen Mark** 20.8.1923. Dark brown on green and red-brown underprint. Back: Brown and red Arms at center.	1.50	4.00	15.00
S933	**25 Millionen Mark** 20.8.1923. Blue and brown.	1.50	4.00	15.00
S934	**50 Millionen Mark** 20.8.1923. Black on light olive and red-brown underprint. Fruit baskets at left and right. Back: Arms.	1.50	4.00	15.00
S935	**10 Millionen Mark** 1.9.1923. Blue and brown.	1.25	3.00	12.50

		VG	VF	UNC
S936	**1 Milliarde Mark** 1.10.1923. Dark brown on violet underprint. Back: Violet.	1.50	4.00	15.00
S937	**5 Milliarden Mark** 18.10.1923. Black on red, pink and gray-blue underprint. Uniface.	1.50	4.50	20.00
S938	**50 Milliarden Mark** 24.10.1923. Dark green.	2.00	7.50	30.00
S939	**500 Milliarden Mark** ND (-old date 1.8.1923). Multicolor. Overprint: Red-brown New denomination on 100 Millionen Mark.	45.00	90.00	175.

1924 Issue

		VG	VF	UNC
S940	**50 Reichsmark** 30.8.1924. Brown-violet. Venetian woman by Albrecht Dürer. Like Federal Republic of Germany #18. Proof. (Not issued).	—	—	1500.
S941	**50 Reichsmark** 11.10.1924. Green. Arms at upper right.	450.	900.	1800.
S942	**100 Reichsmark** 11.10.1924. Blue. Back: Arms.	375.	750.	1500.

1925 Issue

		VG	VF	UNC
S943	**50 Reichsmark** 1.9.1925. Brown and green. Hieronymus Holzschuher (by Albrecht Dürer) at right.	375.	750.	1500.

Sächsische Bank

Bank of Saxony

1866 Issue

		Good	Fine	XF
S946	**10 Thaler** 15.1.1866. Portrait woman at left, Mercury at right. Printer: G&D.	1200.	2400.	4800.
S947	**20 Thaler** 15.1.1866. Portrait woman at left, Mercury at right. Printer: G&D.	1500.	3000.	6000.
S948	**50 Thaler** 15.1.1866. Portrait woman at left, Mercury at right. Printer: G&D.	—	—	—
S949	**100 Thaler** 15.1.1866. Portrait woman at left, Mercury at right. Printer: G&D.	—	—	—

1874 Issue

		VG	VF	UNC
S950	**100 Mark** 1.1.1874. Black on green and brown underprint. Portrait woman at left, Mercury at right. Back: Brown and gray on green underprint. Printer: G&D.	60.00	125.	250.
S951	**500 Mark** 1.1.1874. Black and brown on pink underprint. Portrait woman at left, Mercury at right. Printer: G&D. Reported not confirmed.	—	—	—

1890; 1911 Issue

		VG	VF	UNC
S952	**100 Mark** 1890; 1911. Black on blue and brown underprint. Portrait woman at left, Mercury at right. Printer: G&D.			
	a. 15.6.1890.	8.00	30.00	75.00
	b. 2.1.1911.	3.00	10.00	25.00
S953	**500 Mark** 1890; 1911. Black on red-brown and blue underprint. Portrait woman at left, Mercury at right. Printer: G&D.			
	a. 15.6.1890.	30.00	80.00	175.
	b. 2.1.1911.	7.00	20.00	75.00

1922 Issue

	VG	VF	UNC
S954 500 Mark			
1.7.1922. Blue-black on blue, red and multicolor underprint. Portrait woman at left, Mercury at right. Back: Dark green and brown. Printer: G&D. Lithographed.			
a. Back with folio # at lower left, signature at lower right.	1.00	3.00	15.00
b. Without folio # or signature on back.	1.00	3.00	15.00
S955 500 Mark			
12.9.1922. Blue on yellow underprint.	1.00	7.50	50.00
S956 1000 Mark			
12.9.1922. Dark olive on light olive underprint.	1.00	7.50	50.00

1923 Issue

	VG	VF	UNC
S957 5000 Mark			
12.3.1923. Black on blue-green and green underprint.	1.00	3.00	10.00
S958 10,000 Mark			
1.3.1923. Green and pink.	1.00	2.50	12.50

	VG	VF	UNC
S959 50,000 Mark			
25.7.1923. Blue-black on green and brown underprint. Back: Green on brown underprint.	1.00	3.00	10.00
S960 100,000 Mark			
2.7.1923. Black on green and pink underprint. Back: Brown and green. Printer: G&D.	1.00	3.00	10.00

	VG	VF	UNC
S961 500,000 Mark			
15.8.1923. Black on green, violet and blue underprint. Back: Black on green underprint.	.75	2.00	7.50
S962 1 Million Mark			
18.8.1923. Brown and light blue.	.75	2.00	7.50
S963 2 Millionen Mark			
1.9.1923. Black on brown-olive underprint. Bridge at left. Back: Blue and lilac. Printer: Rommler & Jonas.	.75	2.00	7.50
S964 5 Millionen Mark			
12.8.1923. Dark brown on peach and gray-green underprint. Printer: Stengel.	1.00	3.50	10.00
S965 100 Millionen Mark			
1.10.1923. Blue-black on multicolor underprint. Back: Red on blue underprint.	1.50	4.00	12.50
S966 20 Milliarden Mark			
20.10.1923. Brown-violet and green.	4.00	10.00	50.00
S967 100 Milliarden Mark			
20.10.1923. Brown-violet and light brown.	10.00	30.00	120.
S968 1 Billion Mark			
15.11.1923. Green and olive.	30.00	100.	200.
S969 10 Billionen Mark			
15.11.1923. Lilac and blue.	40.00	120.	250.

1924 Issue

	VG	VF	UNC
S970 50 Reichsmark			
11.10.1924. Brown. Portrait Ludwig Richter (painter) at left.	400.	800.	1600.
S971 100 Reichsmark			
11.10.1924. Dark blue and brown. Portrait Gotthold Ephraim Lessing (writer) at left.	450.	900.	1800.

Württembergische Notenbank

Württemberg Note Issuing Bank

1871 Issue

	Good	Fine	XF
S975 10 Gulden			
15.11.1871. Three small cherubs at left and right, arms at upper center. Printer: C. Naumann.	1200.	2400.	4800.

	Good	Fine	XF
S976 35 Gulden			
15.11.1871. Three small cherubs at left and right, arms at upper center. Back: Like #S975. Printer: C. Naumann.	1300.	2600.	5250.

1874-75 Issue

	Good	Fine	XF
S977 100 Mark			
1874-75. Dark brown on light brown and blue underprint. Three small cherubs at left and right, arms at upper center. Bank name in 2 lines. Printer: C. Naumann.			
a. 1.1.1874.	750.	1500.	3000.
b. 1.1.1875.	1000.	2000.	4000.

1890 Issue

		Good	Fine	XF
S978	**100 Mark** 1.1.1890. Three small cherubs at left and right, arms at upper center. Similar to #S977 but smaller size. Printer: Dondorf & Naumann. Punched hole cancelled.	550.	1100.	2200.

1902; 1911 Issue

		VG	VF	UNC
S979	**100 Mark** 1902; 1911. Black on blue and light brown underprint. Three small cherubs at left and right, arms at upper center. Back: Supported royal arms at center. Printer: G&D.			
	a. 1.1.1902.	120.	240.	475.
	b. 1.1.1911. Signature Koerper; Steinhäuser.	4.50	8.00	20.00
	c. 1.1.1911. Signature Koerper; Lotter.	4.50	8.00	20.00

1918 Issue

		VG	VF	UNC
S980	**100 Mark** 15.12.1918. Dark green on olive-brown underprint. Overprint: *Müsterdruck.* Undertype for #S991, without new value overprint. Known only as Specimen.	—	400.	900.

1922 Issue

		VG	VF	UNC
S981	**1000 Mark** 1.9.1922. Blue on gray-violet underprint.	3.00	8.00	30.00

1923 First Issue

		VG	VF	UNC
S982	**10,000 Mark** 20.2.1923. Blue-black on yellow-brown underprint. Back: Brown and blue.	1.00	3.00	12.50
S983	**20,000 Mark** 15.6.1923. Dark green and red on light brown underprint. Ludwig Uhland at left. Back: Green on light brown underprint. Arms at top center.	.75	2.00	10.00

		VG	VF	UNC
S984	**50,000 Mark** 10.6.1923. Green and red-brown on lilac underprint. Back: Two deer and arms in underprint.	.75	2.00	10.00
S985	**100,000 Mark** 15.6.1923. Dark green and blue on brown underprint. Back: Two deer and arms in underprint. Similar to #S984.	.75	2.00	10.00
S986	**1 Million Mark** 15.6.1923. Blue-black and red-brown on brown underprint. Back: Two deer and arms in underprint. Similar to #S984.	.75	2.00	10.00

		VG	VF	UNC
S987	**1 Million Mark** 1.8.1923. Black and red on orange underprint. Portrait Friedrich Schiller at upper center. Back: Brown and green. Rising sun over hills at center.	.75	2.00	10.00
S988	**5 Millionen Mark** 1.8.1923. Black on red underprint. Back: Brown arms in underprint at center.	1.00	3.00	12.50

		VG	VF	UNC
S989	**100 Millionen Mark** 1.8.1923. Black on dark blue underprint. Back: Similar to #S988; green arms.	1.50	4.00	15.00
S990	**10 Milliarden Mark** 15.10.1923.			
	a. Good until 30.11.1923.	2.50	7.50	25.00
	b. Good until 31.12.1923.	2.50	7.50	25.00
S991	**50 Milliarden Mark** ND (1923-old date 15.12.1918). Overprint: On 100 Mark, #S980.	10.00	25.00	60.00
S992	**500 Milliarden Mark** 20.11.1923. Black-brown on olive-brown and purple underprint. Back: Brown with black text. Arms across center.	30.00	100.	250.

1923 Second Issue

		VG	VF	UNC
S993	**4.20 Goldmark = 1 Dollar** 5.12.1923. (Not issued).	—	—	—
S994	**21 Goldmark = 5 Dollars** 5.12.1923. (Not issued).	—	—	—
S995	**105 Goldmark = 25 Dollars** 5.12.1923. (Not issued).	—	—	—

1924 Issue

		VG	VF	UNC
S996	**50 Reichsmark** 11.10.1924. Brown. Portrait Johannes Kepler at left.	300.	600.	1200.
S997	**100 Reichsmark** 11.10.1924. Dark blue. Portrait Jörg Syrlin der Ältere (wood carver) at right.	375.	750.	1500.

1925 Issue

		VG	VF	UNC
S998	**50 Reichsmark** 1.8.1925. Dark brown and green. Portrait Christian Friedrich Daniel Schubart (port) at left.	350.	700.	1400.

1930 Issue

		VG	VF	UNC
S999	**50 Reichsmark** 1.10.1930. Dark brown and dark green. Portrait Friedrich List (economist) at left. (Not issued).	—	—	1500.

Germany, a nation of north-central Europe which from 1871 to 1945 was, successively, an empire, a republic and a totalitarian state, attained its territorial peak as an empire when it comprised a 208,780 sq. mi. (540,740 sq. km.) homeland and an overseas colonial empire.

As the power of the Roman Empire waned, several warlike tribes residing in northern Germany moved south and west, invading France, Belgium, England, Italy and Spain. In 800 AD the Frankish King Charlemagne, who ruled most of present-day France and Germany, was crowned Emperor of the Holy Roman Empire. Under his successors, this empire was divided into France in the West and Germany (including the Emperor's title) in the East. Over the centuries the German part developed into a loose federation of an estimated 1,800 German States that lasted until 1806. Modern Germany was formed from the eastern part of Charlemagne's empire.

In 1815, the German States were reduced to a federation of 32, of which Prussia was the strongest. In 1871, Prussian Chancellor Otto Von Bismarck united the German States into an empire ruled by Wilhelm I, the Prussian king. The empire initiated a colonial endeavor and became one of the world's greatest powers. Germany disintegrated as a result of World War I, and was reestablished as the Weimar Republic. The humiliation of defeat, economic depression, poverty and discontent gave rise to Adolf Hitler in 1933, who reconstituted Germany as the Third Reich and after initial diplomatic and military triumphs, led it to disaster in World War II. During the postwar era, the western provinces were occupied by the Allied forces while the eastern provinces were occupied and administered by the Soviet Union. East Germany and West Germany were established in 1949.

The post-WWII division of Germany ended on Oct. 3, 1990, when the German Democratic Republic (East Germany) ceased to exist and its five constituent provinces were formally admitted to the Federal Republic of Germany. An election held on Dec. 2, 1990 chose representatives to the united federal parliament (Bundestag), which then conducted its opening session in Berlin in the old Reichstag building. The Capital remained in Bonn until 1999.

For subsequent history, see German Federal Republic and German Democratic Republic.

RULERS:

Wilhelm I, 1871-1888
Friedrich III, 1888
Wilhelm II, 1888-1918

MONETARY SYSTEM:

1 Mark = 100 Pfennig
1 Mark = 100 Pfennig to 1923
1000 Milliarden Mark = 1 Billion Mark = 1 Rentenmark = 100 Rentenpfennig, 1923-1924
1 Rentenmark = 1 Reichsmark = 100 Reichspfennig, 1924-1948
1 AMC Mark = 100 AMC Pfennig, 1945-1948
1 Million = 1,000,000
10 Millionen = 10,000,000
1 Milliarde = 1,000,000,000 (English 1 Billion)
10 Milliarden = 10,000,000,000
1 Billion = 1,000,000,000,000 (English 1 Trillion)
10 Billionen = 10,000,000,000,000

French Zone of Occupation, 1947

Baden

1947 Fractional Currency Issue

	VG	VF	UNC
S1001 5 Pfennig			
1947. Brown and green. Value at center. Back: Arms at center.			
a. *No.* with series A; B; C.	1.00	7.50	25.00
b. *Nr.* with series A.	2.00	10.00	30.00
S1002 10 Pfennig			
1947. Blue and gray. Value at center, arms at left and right. Back: Arms at center.			
a. *No.* with series A; B; C; D.	1.00	7.50	25.00
b. *Nr.* with series C; D.	2.00	15.00	30.00
S1003 50 Pfennig			
1947. Red and yellow on orange underprint. Value at center. Series A. Back: Arms at center.	15.00	75.00	200.

Rheinland-Pfalz

1947 Fractional Currency Issue

	VG	VF	UNC
S1004 5 Pfennig			
15.10.1947. Brown and violet-brown. Wheat ears at center. Series A, B, C. Back: Castle "*Stolzenfels*" and Rhine River.	1.00	7.50	25.00
S1005 10 Pfennig			
15.10.1947. Blue and blue-green. Wheat ears at center. Series A-F. Back: Castle "*Stolzenfels*" and Rhine River.	1.00	7.50	25.00
S1006 50 Pfennig			
15.10.1947. Lilac and red on olive-gray underprint. Wheat ears at center. Series A. Back: Castle "*Stolzenfels*" and Rhine River.	10.00	65.00	150.

Württemberg-Hohenzollern

1947 Fractional Currency Issue

	VG	VF	UNC
S1007 5 Pfennig			
10.1947. Dark and light brown. Back: Castle Lichtenstein at center.			
a. Series A, B, C, D.	1.00	5.00	20.00
b. Series C, D with asterisk.	1.00	5.00	20.00
S1008 10 Pfennig			
10.1947. Dark and light blue. Back: Castle at Sigmaringen.			
a. Series A, B, C, D.	1.00	5.00	20.00
b. Series C, D with asterisk.	1.00	5.00	20.00

Note: The 10 and 50 Pfennig notes of the above issues circulated under the 1948 monetary reform with one-tenth of their former face value until 31.5.1949.

	VG	VF	UNC
S1009 50 Pfennig			
10.1947. Red and pink. Back: Gateway to Castle Hohentübingen.			
a. Series A with *No.*	10.00	50.00	125.
b. Series A with asterisk.	10.00	50.00	125.

Note: The 10 and 50 Pfennig notes of the above issues circulated under the 1948 monetary reform with one-tenth of their former face value until 31.5.1949.

Railroads - Post WWI

Deutsche Reichsbahn Berlin (German Railroad)

Reichsverkehrsministerium Ministry of Transport

1923 Issue

	VG	VF	UNC
S1011 1 Million Mark			
12.8.1923. Brown on orange underprint. Winged wheel at upper center. Uniface.	.20	.50	2.00

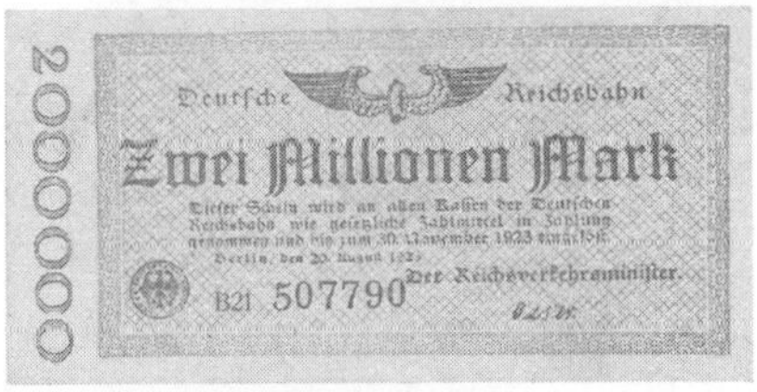

	VG	VF	UNC
S1012 2 Millionen Mark			
20.8.1923. Brown on green and lilac-brown underprint. Winged wheel at upper center. Uniface.			
a. Watermark: Interlaced squares.	.20	.50	2.00
b. Watermark: Cups.	.25	.50	2.00
c. Watermark: H-S-H.	.50	1.00	4.00
S1013 5 Millionen Mark			
22.8.1923. Dark brown on lilac and light green. Winged wheel at upper center. Uniface. Similar to #S1011.			
a. Watermark: Stars and hexagons.	.20	.50	2.00
b. Watermark: Interlaced squares.	.20	.50	2.00
c. Watermark: Waves.	.20	.50	2.00
d. Watermark: H-S-H.	.50	1.00	4.00
S1014 10 Millionen Mark			
2.9.1923. Black on lilac and light brown underprint. Winged wheel in underprint. Uniface. Paper: Light green.	.20	.50	2.00

	VG	VF	UNC
S1015 20 Millionen Mark			
18.9.1923. Green on lilac-brown and olive underprint. Steam locomotive in underprint. Uniface. Paper: Light green.	.20	.50	2.00
S1016 50 Millionen Mark			
18.9.1923. Brown on green underprint. Steam locomotive in underprint. Uniface. Paper: Light green.	.25	.50	3.00

	VG	VF	UNC
S1017 100 Millionen Mark 25.9.1923. Black on brown and light violet underprint. Uniface. Paper: Light green.			
a. Without black star near serial #.	.50	1.00	5.00
b. Black star near serial #.	1.00	2.00	7.50

	VG	VF	UNC
S1018 200 Millionen Mark 10.10.1923. Black on lilac and light brown underprint. Winged wheel in underprint. Uniface. Similar to #S1014. Paper: Light green.	.50	1.00	5.00
S1019 500 Millionen Mark 10.10.1923. Black on gray-green and olive underprint. Winged wheel in underprint. Uniface. Like #S1018.	.75	1.25	5.00
S1020 1 Milliarde Mark 18.10.1923. Black text on green and blue underprint. Steam locomotive in underprint. Back: Olive. City views of Cologne, Mainz at top; Steel works in Rheinhausen, Castle of Hambach at bottom; Pfalz Paper: Light green.	.75	1.25	5.00

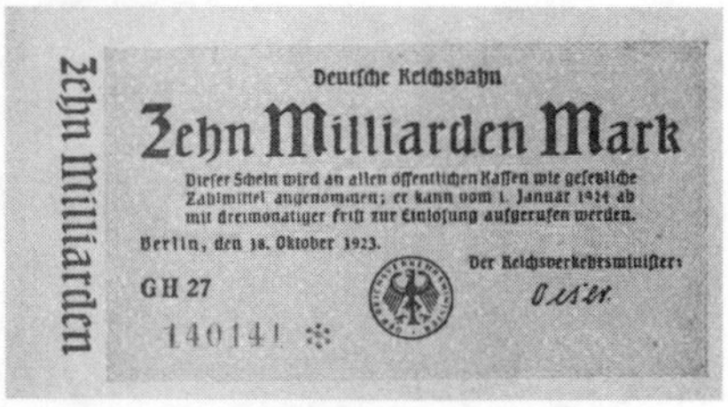

	VG	VF	UNC
S1021 10 Milliarden Mark 18.10.1923. Black text on violet underprint. Steam locomotive in underprint. Paper: Pink.	1.00	2.00	7.50
S1022 20 Milliarden Mark 18.10.1923. Black text on dull brown-violet and dark brown underprint. Steam locomotive in underprint. Similar to #S1020. With or without serial #. Back: Dull brown-violet. Paper: Light green.	.50	1.00	5.00
S1023 50 Milliarden Mark 18.10.1923. Black text on brown underprint. Steam locomotive in underprint. Like #S1020. Uniface. Paper: Yellow.	1.50	3.00	10.00
S1024 100 Milliarden Mark 27.10.1923. Black on green underprint. Uniface. Paper: Yellow.	1.00	2.00	7.50
S1025 200 Milliarden Mark 5.11.1923. Black on gray underprint. Winged wheel in underprint. Uniface. Paper: Pink.	1.50	7.50	25.00
S1026 500 Milliarden Mark 3.11.1923. Brown on lilac underprint. Serial # at left below or right above. Paper: Light green.	1.50	3.00	10.00
S1027 1 Billion Mark 27.10.1923. Black on brown and blue strips. Back: Five church views: Wittenberg, Ulm at top; Freiburg/Br., Danzig at bottom, Munich at center.	1.50	3.00	10.00
S1028 2 Billionen Mark 6.11.1923. Brown on light brown underprint. Uniface. Paper: Yellow.	1.50	3.00	10.00
S1029 5 Billionen Mark 27.10.1923. Black on blue underprint and strips. Uniface.	1.75	3.00	10.00
S1030 10 Billionen Mark 27.10.1923. Brown and pink and blue strips. Back: Deep orange. Views of: Porta Nigra in Trier, fortress Ehrenbreitstein at top; Imperial palace in Goslar, castle in Nürnberg at bottom; War Memorial near Detmold (victory over the Romans) at center on back.	2.00	3.50	12.50
S1031 20 Billionen Mark 5.11.1923. Black on olive underprint. Uniface. Paper: Pink.	2.00	4.00	15.00

Wertbeständige Anteilscheine

1923 Issue

	VG	VF	UNC
S1032 0.42 Mark Gold = 1/10 Dollar 23.10.1923. Black on brown underprint. Uniface. Paper: Yellow.	3.00	7.50	20.00
S1033 1.05 Mark Gold = 1/4 Dollar 23.10.1923. Black on green underprint. Uniface. Paper: Yellow.	4.00	12.00	35.00
S1034 2.10 Mark Gold = 1/2 Dollar 23.10.1923. Black on brown underprint. Uniface. Paper: Yellow.	6.00	30.00	75.00

Wertbeständige Geldscheine

1923 Issue

	VG	VF	UNC
S1035 0.42 Mark Gold = 1/10 Dollar 7.11.1923. Black on olive-brown underprint. Large value: *1/10* in underprint. Uniface.	1.00	4.00	20.00
S1036 1.05 Mark Gold = 1/4 Dollar 7.11.1923. Brown on light lilac underprint. Large value: *1/4 in underprint. Uniface.*	2.00	8.00	35.00
S1037 2.10 Mark Gold = 1/2 Dollar 7.11.1923. Brown on light brown underprint. Large value *1/2* in underprint. Uniface.	3.00	12.00	45.00
S1038 4.20 Mark Gold = 1 Dollar 7.11.1923. Red-brown on brown and olive underprint. Large value: *1* in underprint. Uniface.	5.00	30.00	75.00
S1039 8.40 Mark Gold = 2 Dollars 7.11.1923. Black on blue-gray underprint. Uniface. Paper: Pink.	10.00	60.00	125.
S1040 21 Mark Gold = 5 Dollars 7.11.1923. Black on lilac-gray underprint. Uniface. Paper: Pink.	15.00	75.00	175.

Regional Railroads - Post WWI

NOTE: For railroad notes w/*Deutsche Reichsbahn, Berlin* see #S1011-S1040.

Reichsverkehrsministerium Zweigstelle Bayern

Ministry of Transport, Bavarian Branch

1923 Issue

	VG	VF	UNC
S1101 1 Million Mark 15.8.1923. Black on blue underprint. Two cherubs at left and right of container with letters at center. 2 signature varieties. Back: Arms with steam train at center.	.50	1.00	5.00
S1102 5 Millionen Mark 15.8.1923. Dark and light brown. Two cherubs at left and right of container with letters at center. 2 signature varieties. Like #S1101. Back: Arms with steam train at center.	.50	1.00	5.00
S1103 10 Millionen Mark 15.8.1923. Dark and light green. Two cherubs at left and right of container with letters at center. 2 signature varieties. Like #S1101. Back: Arms with steam train at center.	.50	1.00	5.00
S1104 20 Millionen Mark 15.8.1923. Blue-violet and lilac. Two cherubs at left and right of container with letters at center. 2 signature varieties. Like #S1101. Back: Arms with steam train at center.	1.00	3.00	10.00

	VG	VF	UNC
S1105 10 Milliarden Mark 26.10.1923. Deep purple on light tan underprint. Two cherubs at left and right of container with letters at center. 2 signature varieties. Like #S1101. Back: Arms with steam train at center.	1.00	3.00	12.50

	VG	VF	UNC
S1106 50 Milliarden Mark 26.10.1923. Black on light brown and light green underprint. Color strip at left.	5.00	20.00	100.
S1107 50 Milliarden Mark 26.10.1923. Black on light tan and light green underprint. Color strip at right. Uniface.			
a. Color strip light brown at top.	5.00	12.50	25.00
b. Color strip light green at top.	5.00	12.50	25.00
S1107A 100 Milliarden Mark 26.10.1923. Black on pink and gray.	5.00	12.50	35.00
S1108 100 Milliarden Mark 26.10.1923. Green on gray-brown and olive green underprint.			
a. *Münhen* instead of *München* in dateline. Without imprint.	5.00	15.00	40.00
b. Correct spelling *München* with imprint. 2 watermark varieties.	5.00	15.00	40.00
c. Correct spelling but without imprint.	5.00	12.50	35.00
d. Error like a., imprint *A. MEINDL, MÜNCHEN-PASING.*	5.00	15.00	45.00
S1109 500 Milliarden Mark 26.10.1923. Black.			
a. Rose and lilac underprint.	12.50	30.00	100.
b. Additional gray-blue underprint.	10.00	25.00	80.00
S1110 1 Billion Mark 26.10.1923. Black on brown and blue underprint.			
a. Brown underprint at left, blue underprint at right.	10.00	25.00	100.
b. Blue underprint at left, brown underprint at right.	10.00	25.00	80.00

Reichsbahndirektion Altona

Regional Railroad Office Altona

1923 Issue

	VG	VF	UNC
S1111 500,000 Mark 8.8.1923. Dark brown on gray underprint. Winged wheel in underprint at upper center. Watermark: 3 varieties.	.25	1.00	5.00
S1112 1 Million Mark 8.8.1923. Green on gray underprint. Winged wheel in underprint at upper center. Watermark: 2 varieties.	.25	1.00	5.00

No.	Denomination / Description	VG	VF	UNC
S1113	**2 Millionen Mark** 8.8.1923. Blue on gray underprint. Winged wheel in underprint at upper center. Watermark: 3 varieties.	.50	1.50	7.50
S1114	**5 Millionen Mark** 8.8.1923. Purple on gray underprint. Winged wheel in underprint at upper center.	.25	1.00	5.00
S1115	**100 Millionen Mark** 1.10.1923. Black on lilac underprint. Winged wheel in underprint at upper center. Color strip at left.	.25	1.00	5.00
S1116	**200 Millionen Mark** 1.10.1923. Purple on lilac underprint. Winged wheel in underprint at upper center.	.25	1.00	5.00
S1117	**500 Millionen Mark** 1.10.1923. Green on lilac underprint. Winged wheel in underprint at upper center.	.50	1.25	5.00
S1118	**1 Milliarde Mark** 23.10.1923. Black on gray underprint.	.50	1.25	5.00
S1119	**5 Milliarden Mark** 23.10.1923. Brown on gray underprint.	.50	1.25	5.00
S1120	**10 Milliarden Mark** 23.10.1923. Blue on gray underprint.	.50	1.50	7.50
S1121	**20 Milliarden Mark** 23.10.1923. Brown on gray underprint.			
	a. With watermark.	.50	1.50	7.50
	b. Without watermark.	1.50	4.00	20.00
S1122	**50 Milliarden Mark** 23.10.1923. Red on gray underprint.			
	a. Printer's monogram.	1.50	4.00	12.50
	b. Printer's name.	1.00	2.00	7.50
S1123	**100 Milliarden Mark** 23.10.1923. Green on gray underprint. Watermark: 2 varieties.	1.00	2.00	7.50
S1124	**500 Milliarden Mark** 5.11.1923. Blue on gray underprint. Watermark: 2 varieties.	1.00	2.00	7.50
S1125	**1 Billion Mark** 14.11.1923. Purple on gray underprint.	1.50	4.00	35.00

Reichsbahndirektion Breslau

Regional Railroad Office Breslau

1923 Issues

No.	Denomination / Description	VG	VF	UNC
S1131	**500,000 Mark** 15.8.1923. Black on blue underprint. Winged wheel at upper left.	1.00	5.00	20.00
S1132	**1 Million Mark** 15.8.1923. Black on green underprint. Winged wheel at upper left.	1.00	3.00	20.00
S1133	**2 Millionen Mark** 15.8.1923. Black on red underprint. Winged wheel at upper left.	1.00	3.00	20.00
S1134	**5 Millionen Mark** 15.8.1923. Black on brown-orange underprint. Winged wheel at upper left.	1.00	4.00	20.00
S1135	**5 Millionen Mark** 23.8.1923. Black on brown-orange underprint. Winged wheel at upper left. Series A. Like #S1134.	1.00	4.00	30.00

#S1136 and S1137 winged wheel at ctr. on face. Lg. winged wheel at ctr. on back.

No.	Denomination / Description	VG	VF	UNC
S1136	**50 Millionen Mark** 27.9.1923. Black on gray underprint. Winged wheel at center. Back: Large winged wheel at center.	1.00	3.00	15.00
S1137	**100 Millionen Mark** 27.9.1923. Black on purple underprint. Winged wheel at center. Back: Large winged wheel at center.	1.00	2.50	7.50
S1138	**50 Milliarden Mark** ND (- old date 23.8.1923). Overprint: Red value on unissued 2 Millionen Mark.	6.00	12.00	35.00

#S1139-S1141 winged wheel at upper ctr. Uniface.

No.	Denomination / Description	VG	VF	UNC
S1139	**50 Milliarden Mark** 25.10.1923. Black on light brown and lilac underprint. Winged wheel at upper center. Uniface. Watermark: Two varieties.	1.00	2.00	7.50
S1140	**100 Milliarden Mark** 25.10.1923. Black on gray-blue underprint. Winged wheel at upper center. Uniface.	1.00	2.00	7.50
S1141	**500 Milliarden Mark** 7.11.1923. Black on green and light brown underprint. Winged wheel at upper center. Uniface. Watermark: 2 varieties.	1.50	5.00	20.00

Reichsbahndirektion Cassel

Regional Railroad Office Cassel

1923 First Issue

No.	Denomination / Description	VG	VF	UNC
S1146	**1 Million Mark** 10.8.1923. Black on green underprint. Winged wheel in underprint at left. Text at bottom: *...Eisenbahnkassen in Cassel...* with C serial # prefix.	1.50	5.00	20.00
S1147	**2 Millionen Mark** 10.8.1923. Black on green underprint. Winged wheel in underprint at left. Text at bottom: *...Eisenbahnkassen in Cassel...* with C serial # prefix.	2.00	6.00	25.00
S1148	**5 Millionen Mark** 10.8.1923. Black on light brown underprint. Winged wheel in underprint at left. Text at bottom: *...Eisenbahnkassen in Cassel...* with C serial # prefix.	6.00	12.00	40.00

1923 Second Issue

No.	Denomination / Description	VG	VF	UNC
S1149	**1 Million Mark** 10.8.1923. Black on green underprint. Winged wheel in underprint at left. Text at bottom: *. . .Eisenbahnkassen in Göttingen. . .* with *G* serial # prefix. Like #S1146.	2.50	7.00	25.00
S1150	**2 Millionen Mark** 10.8.1923. Black on green underprint. Winged wheel in underprint at left. Text at bottom: *. . .Eisenbahnkassen in Göttingen. . .* with *G* serial # prefix. Like #S1147.	4.00	10.00	35.00
S1151	**5 Millionen Mark** 10.8.1923. Black on light brown underprint. Winged wheel in underprint at left. Text at bottom: *. . .Eisenbahnkassen in Göttingen. . .* with *G* serial # prefix. Like #S1148. Reported not confirmed.	—	—	—

1923 Third Issue

No.	Denomination / Description	VG	VF	UNC
S1152	**1 Million Mark** 10.8.1923. Black on green underprint. Winged wheel in underprint at left. Text at bottom: *...Eisenbahnkassen in Nordhausen und Sangerhausen...* with *N* serial # prefix. Like #S1146.	12.50	27.50	65.00
S1153	**2 Millionen Mark** 10.8.1923. Black on green underprint. Winged wheel in underprint at left. Text at bottom: *...Eisenbahnkassen in Nordhausen und Sangerhausen...* with *N* serial # prefix. Like #S1147.	12.50	27.50	65.00
S1154	**5 Millionen Mark** 10.8.1923. Black on light brown underprint. Winged wheel in underprint at left. Text at bottom: *...Eisenbahnkassen in Nordhausen und Sangerhausen...* with *N* serial # prefix. Like #S1148. Reported not confirmed.	—	—	—

1923 Fourth Issue

No.	Denomination / Description	VG	VF	UNC
S1155	**1 Million Mark** 10.8.1923. Black on green underprint. Winged wheel in underprint at left. Text at bottom: *...Eisenbahnkassen in Paderborn...* with *P* serial # prefix. Like #S1146.	1.50	20.00	90.00
S1156	**2 Millionen Mark** 10.8.1923. Black on green underprint. Winged wheel in underprint at left. Text at bottom: *...Eisenbahnkassen in Paderborn...* with *P* serial # prefix. Like #S1147.	2.50	27.50	100.
S1157	**5 Millionen Mark** 10.8.1923. Black on light brown underprint. Winged wheel in underprint at left. Text at bottom: *...Eisenbahnkassen in Paderborn...* with *P* serial # prefix. Like #S1148.	17.50	120.	250.

1923 Fifth Issue

No.	Denomination / Description	VG	VF	UNC
S1158	**500,000 Mark** 10.8.1923. Black on light blue underprint. Text at bottom: *...Eisenbahnkassen des Reichsbahndirektionsbezirks Cassel...* with *U:* serial # prefix.	.75	2.00	7.50
S1159	**1 Million Mark** 10.8.1923. Black on green underprint. Winged wheel in underprint at left. Text at bottom: *...Eisenbahnkassen des Reichsbahndirektionsbezirks Cassel...* with *U:* serial # prefix. Like #S1146.	.75	2.00	7.50
S1160	**2 Millionen Mark** 10.8.1923. Black on green underprint. Winged wheel in underprint at left. Text at bottom: *...Eisenbahnkassen des Reichsbahndirektionsbezirks Cassel...* with >I>U: serial # prefix. Like #S1147.	.50	1.50	7.50
S1161	**5 Millionen Mark** 10.8.1923. Black on light brown underprint. Winged wheel in underprint at left. Text at bottom: *...Eisenbahnkassen des Reichsbahndirektionsbezirks Cassel...* with *U:* serial # prefix. Like #S1148.	.50	1.50	7.50
S1162	**10 Millionen Mark** 10.8.1923. Black on purple underprint. Text at bottom: *...Eisenbahnkassen des Reichsbahndirektionsbezirks Cassel...* with *U:* serial # prefix.	.75	2.00	7.50

1923 Sixth Issue

No.	Denomination / Description	VG	VF	UNC
S1163	**10 Milliarden Mark** 24.10.1923. Green. Long text at center. Winged wheel in underprint at left.	1.00	2.50	10.00
S1164	**20 Milliarden Mark** 24.10.1923. Brown. Long text at center. Winged wheel in underprint at left.	1.00	2.50	10.00
S1165	**50 Milliarden Mark** 24.10.1923. Blue. Long text at center. Winged wheel in underprint at left.	1.00	3.00	12.50
S1166	**100 Milliarden Mark** 24.10.1923. Black on yellow underprint. Long text at center. Winged wheel in underprint at left.	1.00	3.50	12.50
S1167	**500 Milliarden Mark** 24.10.1923. Black on green underprint. Long text at center. Winged wheel in underprint at left.	1.00	3.00	12.50
S1168	**1 Billion Mark** 24.10.1923. Blue on brown-orange underprint. Long text at center. Winged wheel in underprint at left.	1.50	4.00	12.50
S1169	**5 Billionen Mark** 24.10.1923. Black on red underprint. Long text at center. Winged wheel in underprint at left.	1.50	5.00	20.00

Reichsbahndirektion Dresden

Regional Railroad Office Dresden

1923 Issue

No.	Denomination / Description	VG	VF	UNC
S1171	**500,000 Mark** 11.8.1923. Dark brown on olive underprint. Watermark: 2 varieties.	.40	1.00	5.00
S1172	**1 Million Mark** 11.8.1923. Red on gray underprint. Back: Red. Eagle at center.	.40	1.00	5.00
S1173	**2 Millionen Mark** 13.8.1923. Black and blue-gray. Back: Red-orange. Paper: Red-orange.	1.00	2.50	10.00
S1174	**3 Millionen Mark** 16.8.1923. Black and green. Back: Green. Paper: Blue-gray.	1.00	2.50	10.00
S1175	**3 Millionen Mark** 20.8.1923. Black and orange. Back: Orange. Paper: Green.	1.00	2.50	10.00

No.	Denomination / Description	VG	VF	UNC
S1176	**5 Millionen Mark** 21.8.1923. Black on blue-gray and orange underprint.	.40	1.00	5.00

		VG	VF	UNC
S1177	**100 Millionen Mark** 25.9.1923. Black on light green and lilac underprint.	1.00	2.50	10.00

		VG	VF	UNC
S1178	**50 Milliarden Mark** 26.10.1923. Black and red on blue-green underprint. Paper: Dark yellow.	1.00	3.00	12.50

		VG	VF	UNC
S1179	**100 Milliarden Mark** 26.10.1923. Black on light blue, green and light orange underprint.	1.50	4.00	15.00
S1180	**500 Milliarden Mark** 26.10.1923. Black on blue-gray, olive and red underprint. Similar to #S1179.	2.00	7.00	20.00
S1181	**10 Billionen Mark** 22.11.1923. Green on light brown underprint. Rare.	—	—	—

NOTE: #S1181 ONLY 1 EXAMPLE KNOWN.

Reichsbahndirektion Elberfeld

Regional Railroad Office Elberfeld

1923 Issues

		VG	VF	UNC
S1186	**1 Million Mark** 11.8.1923. Black. Handwritten style.	1.50	5.00	17.50
S1187	**1 Million Mark** 11.8.1923. Red to red-brown. Handwritten style.	1.00	3.50	12.50
S1188	**2 Millionen Mark** 16.8.1923. Green.	1.00	3.00	10.00
S1189	**2 Millionen Mark** 16.8.1923. Blue.	1.00	3.50	12.50
S1190	**5 Millionen Mark** 17.8.1923. Blue on gray-green underprint. Winged wheel at upper center, building at center in underprint.	1.00	3.00	10.00
S1191	**10 Millionen Mark** 18.8.1923. Black on lilac and gray-green underprint. Eagle at left and right in underprint. Expiration date in text 30.9.1923.	1.00	3.00	10.00
S1192	**10 Millionen Mark** 18.8.1923. Black on lilac and gray-green underprint. Eagle at left and right in underprint. Like #S1191 but without expiration date text.	1.00	3.00	10.00
S1193	**50 Milliarden Mark** 26.10.1923. Black on blue-green and blue-violet underprint.	1.50	4.00	12.50
S1194	**100 Milliarden Mark** 2.11.1923. Green on light blue and pale yellow underprint.	2.50	7.00	20.00
S1195	**1 Billion Mark** 14.11.1923. Lilac-brown on brown and olive underprint.	7.00	85.00	175.

Reichsbahndirektion Erfurt

Regional Railroad Office Erfurt

1923 Issue

		VG	VF	UNC
S1201	**1 Million Mark** 12.8.1923. Black on green underprint. Winged wheel at each corner in underprint.	.75	2.00	7.50
S1202	**3 Millionen Mark** 12.8.1923. Black on lilac-rose underprint. Two winged wheels.	1.00	3.00	10.00
S1203	**5 Millionen Mark** 12.8.1923. Black on lilac-blue underprint.	1.00	3.00	10.00
S1204	**10 Millionen Mark** 12.8.1923. Black on greenish blue underprint.	.75	2.00	7.50
S1205	**100 Millionen Mark** 22.9.1923. Black on lilac-blue underprint. Winged wheel in underprint at center.	1.00	3.00	10.00
S1206	**500 Millionen Mark** 22.9.1923. Black on green underprint.	1.00	3.50	12.50
S1207	**10 Milliarden Mark** 20.10.1923. Blue on gray underprint. Winged wheel in underprint at center.	1.50	4.00	12.50
S1208	**50 Milliarden Mark** 20.10.1923. Black-green on gray-green underprint. Winged wheel in underprint at center. Similar to #S1207.	1.50	4.00	12.50
S1209	**100 Milliarden Mark** 26.10.1923. Black on orange underprint. Three winged wheels in underprint at center.	1.50	4.50	15.00
S1210	**500 Milliarden Mark** 3.11.1923. Black on blue underprint.	2.50	7.00	20.00
S1211	**1 Billion Mark** 3.11.1923. Black on green underprint.	8.50	25.00	65.00
S1212	**5 Billionen Mark** 3.11.1923. Red on yellow underprint.	15.00	37.50	125.
S1213	**10 Billionen Mark** 3.11.1923. Black on green underprint.	22.50	50.00	140.

Reichsbahndirektion Frankfurt am Main

Regional Railroad Office Frankfurt am Main

1923 Issue

		VG	VF	UNC
S1216	**500,000 Mark** 10.8.1923. Gray and black. Gray ornament at left.	.50	1.50	7.50
S1217	**1 Million Mark** 10.8.1923. Gray and black. Gray ornament at left.	.50	1.50	7.50
S1218	**5 Millionen Mark** 10.8.1923. Gray and black. Gray ornament at left.	.50	1.50	7.50
S1219	**10 Millionen Mark** 1.9.1923. Dark green on light green underprint. Eagle at corners in underprint.	.50	1.50	7.50
S1220	**20 Millionen Mark** 1.9.1923. Dark brown on yellow underprint. Eagle at corners in underprint. Like #S1219.	.50	1.50	7.50
S1221	**200 Millionen Mark** 26.9.1923. Dark brown on orange underprint. Eagle at corners in underprint. Like #S1219.	.50	1.75	7.50

#S1222-S1227 TWO WMK. VARIETIES.

#S1222-S1224 WINGED WHEEL IN UNPT. AT CTR.

		VG	VF	UNC
S1222	**20 Milliarden Mark** 22.10.1923. Black on green underprint. Winged wheel in underprint at center. Watermark: Two varieties.	.75	2.00	7.50
S1223	**50 Milliarden Mark** 22.10.1923. Dark brown on purple underprint. Winged wheel in underprint at center. Watermark: Two varieties.	.75	2.00	7.50
S1224	**100 Milliarden Mark** 22.10.1923. Dark green on lilac-red underprint. Winged wheel in underprint at center. Watermark: Two varieties.	1.00	3.00	10.00

		VG	VF	UNC
S1225	**500 Milliarden Mark** 22.10.1923. Dark brown on gray-violet underprint. Winged wheel at lower center. Watermark: Two varieties.	1.50	4.00	12.50
S1226	**1 Billion Mark** 2.11.1923. Black on orange underprint. Winged wheel at left and right. Watermark: Four varieties.	1.50	4.00	12.50

No.	Denomination / Description	VG	VF	UNC
S1227	**5 Billionen Mark** 6.11.1923. Black on rose underprint. Winged wheel at upper center. Watermark: Two varieties.	1.50	4.00	12.50
S1228	**10 Billionen Mark** 6.11.1923. Dark brown on brown underprint. Winged wheel at left and right.	1.50	4.50	15.00

Reichsbahndirektion Osten in Frankfurt a.d. Oder

Regional Railroad Office in the East at Frankfurt a.d. Oder

1923 Issue

No.	Denomination / Description	VG	VF	UNC
S1231	**10 Milliarden Mark** 27.10.1923. Dark red on green underprint.	3.00	8.00	25.00
S1232	**20 Milliarden Mark** 27.10.1923. Dark green on green underprint.	2.50	7.00	20.00
S1233	**50 Milliarden Mark** 27.10.1923. Purple on green underprint.	2.00	6.00	20.00
S1234	**100 Milliarden Mark** 3.11.1923. Blue on gray underprint.	6.00	12.50	50.00
S1235	**200 Milliarden Mark** 3.11.1923. Brown on gray underprint.	7.00	15.00	50.00
S1236	**500 Milliarden Mark** 14.11.1923. Black on yellow-brown underprint.	8.00	40.00	125.
S1237	**1 Billion Mark** 14.11.1923. Black on lilac underprint.	35.00	90.00	200.

Reichsbahndirektion Halle (S.)

Regional Railroad Office Halle (S.)

1923 Issue

No.	Denomination / Description	VG	VF	UNC
S1241	**500,000 Mark** ND (- good until 1.10.1923). Dark green on light green underprint.	1.00	2.50	10.00
S1242	**1 Million Mark** ND. Brown on rose underprint. Like #S1241.	1.00	2.50	10.00
S1243	**100 Millionen Mark** 26.9.1923. Black on brown underprint.	1.00	2.50	10.00
S1244	**500 Millionen Mark** 26.9.1923. Black on light blue underprint.	1.00	3.00	20.00
S1245	**10 Milliarden Mark** 24.10.1923. Black on purple underprint.	1.00	3.50	20.00
S1246	**20 Milliarden Mark** 24.10.1923. Black on gray underprint.	1.50	4.00	25.00
S1247	**50 Milliarden Mark** 24.10.1923. Black on light green underprint.	1.50	4.50	25.00
S1248	**100 Milliarden Mark** 2.11.1923. Purple on gray-violet underprint.	2.00	6.00	30.00
S1249	**500 Milliarden Mark** 2.11.1923. Dark brown on gray-blue underprint. Watermark: 2 varieties.	2.00	6.00	30.00
S1250	**1 Billion Mark** 2.11.1923. Dark brown on orange underprint.	4.00	10.00	35.00

Reichsbahndirektion Hannover

Regional Railroad Office Hannover

1923 Issue

No.	Denomination / Description	VG	VF	UNC
S1251	**100,000 Mark** 2.8.1923. Red on gray underprint. Winged wheel.	1.00	3.50	12.50
S1252	**200,000 Mark** 29.7.1923. Gray on orange underprint.	2.50	7.00	20.00
S1253	**300,000 Mark** 2.8.1923. Purple on gray underprint.	1.50	4.50	15.00
S1254	**500,000 Mark** 2.8.1923. Blue on gray underprint. Winged wheel in underprint at center.			
	a. *Good until 11.8.1923.* Rare.	—	—	—
	b. *Good until 31.8.1923.*	.75	2.00	7.50
S1255	**1 Million Mark** 2.8.1923. Green on gray underprint.	1.00	2.00	7.50
S1256	**20 Milliarden Mark** 24.10.1923. Olive.			
	a. Gray underprint.	1.00	3.50	12.50
	b. Light blue underprint.	1.00	3.50	12.50
S1257	**50 Milliarden Mark** 24.10.1923. Lilac-brown.			
	a. Gray underprint.	1.50	4.50	15.00
	b. Light blue underprint.	2.00	6.00	17.50
S1258	**100 Milliarden Mark** 24.10.1923. Green on gray underprint.	1.50	4.50	15.00
S1259	**200 Milliarden Mark** 24.10.1923. Lilac-brown on gray underprint.	1.50	5.00	17.50
S1260	**1 Billion Mark** 24.10.1923.			
	a. Blue on gray and green underprint. Rare.	—	—	—
	b. Purple on gray and green underprint.	5.00	12.00	40.00
S1261	**2 Billionen Mark** 24.10.1923. Blue on gray and green underprint.	7.00	70.00	150.

Reichsbahndirektion Karlsruhe

Regional Railroad Office Karlsruhe

1923 Issues

No.	Denomination / Description	VG	VF	UNC
S1266	**1 Million Mark** 10.8.1923. Dark green on green underprint. Back: Winged wheel at lower center.	1.00	1.50	7.50
S1267	**2 Millionen Mark** 10.8.1923. Dark brown on orange underprint. Back: Winged wheel at lower center.	1.00	1.50	7.50

No.	Denomination / Description	VG	VF	UNC
S1268	**5 Millionen Mark** 10.8.1923. Dark purple on lilac underprint. Back: Winged wheel at lower center.	1.00	1.50	7.50
S1269	**10 Millionen Mark** 20.8.1923. Dark gray on gray underprint. Women and children at center.	1.00	1.75	7.50
S1270	**20 Millionen Mark** 20.8.1923. Red-violet on peach underprint. Women and children at center. Like #S1269.	1.00	1.75	7.50
S1271	**1 Milliard Mark** 20.8.1923. Dark brown on brown underprint.	1.00	2.00	10.00
S1272	**100 Milliarden Mark** 15.10.1923. Black on grayish blue underprint. Value: *Hundert*. Railroad bridge at Murg-Valley with steam passenger train at center. Back: Winged wheel at center.	2.50	7.00	20.00
S1273	**100 Milliarden Mark** 15.10.1923. Black on grayish blue underprint. Railroad bridge at Murg-Valley with steam passenger train at center. Like #S1272 but with value: *Einhundert* in heading. Back: Winged wheel at center. Watermark: 2 varieties.	1.00	3.00	10.00
S1274	**200 Milliarden Mark** 15.10.1923. Dark brown on light brown underprint. Railroad bridge at Murg-Valley with steam passenger train at center. Like #S1273. First line *Gutschein,* second line *Deutsche Reichsbahn.* Back: Winged wheel at center.	1.50	4.00	12.50
S1275	**200 Milliarden Mark** 15.10.1923. Dark brown on light brown underprint. Railroad bridge at Murg-Valley with steam passenger train at center. Like #S1274 but first line *Deutsche Reichsbahn* and second line *Gutschein.* Back: Winged wheel at center.	2.00	6.00	20.00
S1276	**500 Milliarden Mark** 15.10.1923. Dark green on light green underprint. Railroad bridge at Murg-Valley with steam passenger train at center. First line *Deutsche Reichsbahn* and second line *Gutschein.* Like #S1275. Back: Winged wheel at center.	1.00	3.50	12.50
S1277	**1 Billion Mark** 15.10.1923. Blue on green underprint. Steam locomotive at center. Back: Light green. Winged wheel center. Watermark: 2 varieties.	1.50	4.00	12.50

No.	Denomination / Description	VG	VF	UNC
S1278	**10 Billionen Mark** 15.10.1923. Dark blue on blue-green underprint. Steam locomotive at center. Like #S1277. Back: Winged wheel center.	2.00	6.00	20.00
S1279	**5 Billionen Mark** 15.11.1923. Black on gray-brown and blue underprint. Steam passenger trains at upper left and right.	1.50	5.00	17.50

Reichsbahndirektion Köln

Regional Railroad Office Cologne

1923 First Issue

Most notes have winged wheel at upper l. or r. on face, and at ctr. on back.

		VG	VF	UNC
S1280	**500,000 Mark** 11.8.1923. Used as undertype for #S1290. (Not issued).	—	—	—
S1281	**1 Million Mark** 11.8.1923. Black on light brown underprint.	1.50	4.00	12.50
S1282	**2 Millionen Mark** 11.8.1923. Black on blue underprint.	1.50	4.00	12.50
S1283	**3 Millionen Mark** 11.8.1923. Black on red underprint.	1.50	4.00	12.50
S1284	**10 Millionen Mark** 11.8.1923. Black on green underprint. Watermark: 3 varieties.	1.00	2.50	10.00
S1285	**20 Millionen Mark** 11.8.1923. Black on purple underprint.	1.00	3.00	10.00

1923 Second Issue

		VG	VF	UNC
S1286	**10 Millionen Mark** 2.9.1923. Black on green underprint.	1.00	3.00	10.00
S1287	**20 Millionen Mark** 2.9.1923. Brown-black on purple underprint.	1.00	3.00	10.00
S1288	**100 Millionen Mark** 25.9.1923. Black on gray and red-orange underprint.	1.00	3.50	12.50
S1289	**500 Millionen Mark** 10.10.1923. Black on blue-green and lilac underprint. Watermark: Two varieties.	1.00	3.50	12.50
S1290	**1 Milliard Mark** ND (- old date 11.8.1923). Black on gray-green underprint. New denomination in words printed across face and back in carmine on unissued 500,000 Mark note #S1280. Back: Locomotive.	1.00	3.00	10.00
S1291	**10 Milliarden Mark** 18.10.1923. Black on orange and green underprint.	1.50	4.00	12.50
S1292	**100 Milliarden Mark** 18.10.1923. Black on light brown and red underprint. Watermark: Three varieties.	5.00	12.00	40.00
S1293	**500 Milliarden Mark** 18.10.1923. Black on green underprint. Watermark: Two varieties.	10.00	25.00	75.00
S1294	**1 Billion Mark** 18.11.1923. Rare.	—	—	—
S1295	**5 Billionen Mark** 18.11.1923. Blue on gray underprint. Rare.	—	—	—
S1296	**10 Billionen Mark** 18.11.1923. Rare.	—	—	—

Reichsbahndirektion Königsberg/Pr.

Regional Railroad Office Königsberg/Prussia

1923 First Issue

		VG	VF	UNC
S1301	**1 Million Mark** 10.8.1923. Dark blue.	2.50	7.00	20.00

1923 Second Issue

		VG	VF	UNC
S1302	**100,000 Mark** 18.8.1923. Brownish red.	3.00	8.00	25.00
S1303	**5 Millionen Mark** 18.8.1923. Green.	4.00	10.00	30.00
S1304	**20 Milliarden Mark** ND (- old date 18.8.1923). Green. Overprint: Red new denomination in text across face of #S1303.	12.00	30.00	90.00

Note: Counterfeits of #S1304 without watermarks exist.

		VG	VF	UNC
S1305	**50 Milliarden Mark** 26.10.1923. Brown.	5.00	12.00	40.00
S1306	**100 Milliarden Mark** 26.10.1923. Purple.	12.00	35.00	100.
S1307	**1 Billion Mark** 5.11.1923. Dark green on gray-green underprint. Steam locomotive at center in underprint. Watermark: Two varieties.	25.00	55.00	165.
S1308	**5 Billionen Mark** 5.11.1923. Watermark: Two varieties. Rare.	—	—	—

Reichsbahndirektion Magdeburg

Regional Railroad Office Magdeburg

1923 Issue

		VG	VF	UNC
S1311	**500,000 Mark** 9.8.1923. Black and blue on green underprint.	1.50	3.00	10.00
S1312	**2 Millionen Mark** 9.8.1923. Black and red on light brown underprint. Watermark: 2 varieties.	1.00	2.00	7.50
S1313	**5 Millionen Mark** 9.8.1923. Black and green on gray-blue underprint.	1.00	3.00	10.00

#S1314-S1317 winged wheel at ctr.

		VG	VF	UNC
S1314	**200 Milliarden Mark** 29.10.1923. Black on light brown underprint. Winged wheel at center.	2.00	6.00	60.00
S1315	**500 Milliarden Mark** 14.11.1923. Black on purple underprint. Winged wheel at center.	10.00	50.00	140.
S1316	**1 Billion Mark** 20.11.1923. Black on rose underprint. Winged wheel at center.	10.00	50.00	140.
S1317	**5 Billionen Mark** 22.11.1923. Black on green underprint. Winged wheel at center.	15.00	60.00	175.

Reichsbahndirektion Münster/Westf.

Regional Railroad Office Münster/Westf.

1923 First Issue

		VG	VF	UNC
S1321	**1 Million Mark** 15.8.1923. Red on gray underprint. Winged wheel in underprint at center.	1.50	4.00	12.50
S1322	**3 Millionen Mark** 15.8.1923. Blue on gray underprint. Winged wheel in underprint at center.	1.50	4.00	12.50
S1323	**5 Millionen Mark** 15.8.1923. Purple on gray underprint. Winged wheel in underprint at center.	1.50	4.00	12.50

1923 Second Issue

		VG	VF	UNC
S1323A	**1 Million Mark** 20.8.1923.	1.00	3.00	10.00
S1323B	**3 Millionen Mark** 20.8.1923.	1.00	3.00	10.00
S1323C	**5 Millionen Mark** 20.8.1923.	1.00	3.00	10.00
S1324	**1 Milliarde Mark** 25.10.1923. Winged wheel in underprint at center.	15.00	45.00	100.

#S1325-S1327 two wmk. varieties.

		VG	VF	UNC
S1325	**5 Milliarden Mark** 25.10.1923. Brown-red on green underprint. Winged wheel in underprint at center. Watermark: Two varieties.	2.50	7.00	20.00
S1326	**10 Milliarden Mark** 25.10.1923. Dark green on green underprint. Winged wheel in underprint at center. Watermark: Two varieties.	1.50	5.00	17.50
S1327	**20 Milliarden Mark** 25.10.1923. Dark green on green underprint. Winged wheel in underprint at center. Watermark: Two varieties.	2.50	7.00	20.00

		VG	VF	UNC
S1328	**50 Milliarden Mark** 25.10.1923. Dark brown on green underprint. Winged wheel in underprint at center. Watermark: Three varieties.	7.50	15.00	50.00
S1329	**100 Milliarden Mark** 25.10.1923. Grayish purple on green underprint. Winged wheel in underprint at center. Watermark: Two varieties.	2.50	7.00	20.00
S1330	**200 Milliarden Mark** 25.10.1923. Lilac on green underprint. Winged wheel in underprint at center.	4.00	10.00	30.00
S1331	**500 Milliarden Mark** 25.10.1923. Winged wheel in underprint at center. Rare.	—	—	—
S1332	**1 Billion Mark** 25.10.1923. Blue on green underprint. Winged wheel in underprint at center.	15.00	40.00	120.
S1333	**2 Billionen Mark** 25.10.1923. Winged wheel in underprint at center. Rare.	—	—	—
S1334	**5 Billionen Mark** 25.10.1923. Winged wheel in underprint at center. Rare.	—	—	—
S1335	**10 Billionen Mark** 25.10.1923. Winged wheel in underprint at center. Rare.	—	—	—

Reichsbahndirektion Oppeln, Oberschlesische Eisenbahnen

Regional Railroad Office Oppeln, Upper Silesian Railroads

1923 Issue

	VG	VF	UNC
S1341 50,000 Mark 16.8.1923. Brown. Eagle at left, winged wheel in underprint at center.	2.50	7.00	20.00
S1342 100,000 Mark 16.8.1923. Green. Eagle at left, winged wheel in underprint at center. Like #S1341.	4.00	10.00	35.00
S1343 500,000 Mark 16.8.1923. Rose. Eagle at left, winged wheel in underprint at center. Like #S1341.	1.50	5.00	20.00
S1344 1 Million Mark 16.8.1923. Dark blue.	1.50	4.00	12.50
S1345 500 Millionen Mark 27.9.1923. Olive green. Eagle at left, winged wheel in underprint at center. Similar to #S1341.	2.50	7.00	20.00
S1346 20 Millionen Mark 28.9.1923. Orange.	1.50	5.00	17.50
S1347 50 Millionen Mark 28.9.1923. Blue.	2.50	7.00	20.00
S1348 100 Millionen Mark 28.9.1923. Purple.	3.00	10.00	25.00
S1349 10 Milliarden Mark 25.10.1923. Rose. Eagle at left, winged wheel in underprint at center. Similar to #S1341.	2.50	10.00	20.00
S1350 20 Milliarden Mark 25.10.1923. Gray-blue. Eagle at left, winged wheel in underprint at center. Like #S1341.	3.00	10.00	25.00
S1351 100 Milliarden Mark 25.10.1923. Blue.	4.00	12.50	30.00
S1352 500 Milliarden Mark 25.10.1923. Light brown.	17.50	45.00	125.
S1353 1 Billion Mark 6.11.1923. Lilac. Eagle at left, winged wheel in underprint at center. Similar to #S1341.	40.00	100.	275.
S1354 5 Billionen Mark 13.11.1923. Orange. Eagle at left, winged wheel in underprint at center. Similar to #S1341. Rare.	—	—	—

Reichsbahndirektion Stettin

Regional Railroad Office Stettin

1923 First Issue

	VG	VF	UNC
S1356 500,000 Mark 11.8.1923. Black. Handwritten style.	17.50	45.00	125.
S1357 1 Million Mark 11.8.1923. Black. Handwritten style.	17.50	45.00	125.
S1358 3 Millionen Mark 11.8.1923. Black. Handwritten style.	17.50	45.00	125.

1923 Second Issue

#S1359-S1370 most notes have winged wheel at ctr. on face.

	VG	VF	UNC
S1359 500,000 Mark 20.8.1923. Black on green underprint.	1.50	5.00	17.50

	VG	VF	UNC
S1360 1 Million Mark 20.8.1923. Black on peach underprint. Watermark: With and without.	3.00	8.00	25.00
S1361 5 Millionen Mark 20.8.1923. Black on brown underprint.	2.50	7.00	20.00
S1362 1 Milliarde Mark 26.10.1923. Black on blue underprint.	3.00	8.00	25.00
S1363 5 Milliarden Mark 26.10.1923. Black on lilac underprint.	4.00	10.00	35.00

#S1364-S1366 two wmk. varieties.

	VG	VF	UNC
S1364 10 Milliarden Mark 26.10.1923. Black on green underprint. Watermark: Two varieties.	4.00	10.00	35.00
S1365 20 Milliarden Mark 26.10.1923. Black on brown underprint. Watermark: Two varieties.	4.00	10.00	35.00
S1366 50 Milliarden Mark 26.10.1923. Black on red-brown underprint. Watermark: Two varieties.	4.00	10.00	40.00
S1367 100 Milliarden Mark 26.10.1923. Black on green-gray underprint.	4.00	10.00	40.00
S1368 200 Milliarden Mark 5.11.1923. Dark brown on light blue underprint.			
a. White paper.	4.00	10.00	40.00
b. Rose paper.	7.00	15.00	50.00
S1369 500 Milliarden Mark 5.11.1923. Black on dark brown underprint.			
a. White paper.	10.00	40.00	90.00
b. Rose paper.	15.00	45.00	100.
S1370 1 Billion Mark 5.11.1923. Black and red on light green underprint.	20.00	50.00	125.

Reichsbahndirektion Stuttgart

Regional Railroad Office Stuttgart

1923 Issue

	VG	VF	UNC
S1371 1 Million Mark 13.8.1923. Brown on light brown underprint. Winged wheel. Railroad Headquarter building at Stuttgart.	2.00	5.00	17.50
S1371A 1 Million Mark 21.8.1923. Brown on light brown underprint. Winged wheel. Railroad Headquarter building at Stuttgart. Similar to #S1371.	3.00	6.00	17.50
S1372 5 Millionen Mark 18.8.1923. Brown on light tan underprint. Winged wheel. Back: Eagle.			
a. Red-brown.	2.00	5.00	17.50
b. Brownish black.	2.00	5.00	17.50

	VG	VF	UNC
S1373 50 Millionen Mark 26.9.1923. Black on blue-green underprint. Winged wheel. Back: Green. Steam locomotive at center.	.75	3.00	10.00
S1374 1 Milliarde Mark 26.9.1923. Dark brown on olive-brown underprint. Winged wheel. Back: Multiple arched railroad viaduct over the Neckar at Cannstadt.	1.00	3.00	10.00

	VG	VF	UNC
S1375 20 Milliarden Mark 19.10.1923. Black on blue-gray underprint. Winged wheel. Back: Stuttgart railroad terminal.	1.00	3.00	10.00
S1376 50 Milliarden Mark 23.10.1923. Black on brown underprint. Winged wheel. Back: Interior of Stuttgart railroad terminal.	1.00	3.00	10.00
S1377 100 Milliarden Mark 23.10.1923. Black on gray underprint. Winged wheel. Back: Viaduct.	1.50	4.00	15.00
S1378 500 Milliarden Mark 30.10.1923. Dark brown on pale rose underprint. Winged wheel. Back: Steamship.	1.50	5.00	17.50

		VG	VF	UNC
S1379	**1 Billion Mark** 5.11.1923. Dark purple on dull orange underprint. Winged wheel. Back: Interior of Stuttgart railroad terminal.	1.50	5.00	17.50

		VG	VF	UNC
S1380	**5 Billionen Mark** 9.11.1923. Dark green on light green underprint. Winged wheel. Back: Steel railroad bridge.	2.00	6.00	20.00

SIEGE

COLBERG

1807 FIRST *KOMMISSIONS-KUPON* ISSUE

#S1451-S1453 WERE AUTHORIZED BY A COINAGE COMMISSION, THEREFORE THE NAME. THESE NOTES ARE ON CARDBOARD.

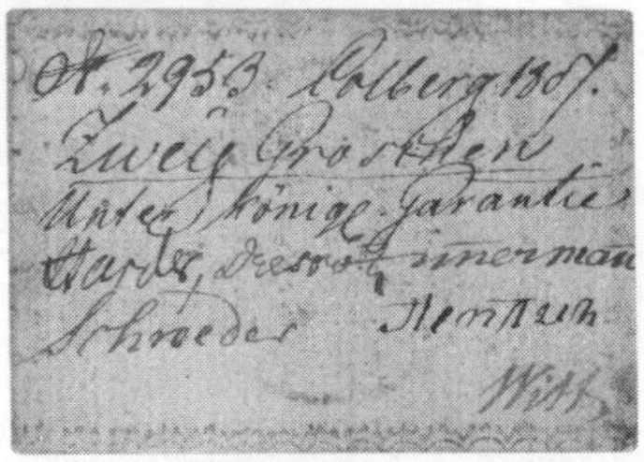

		Good	Fine	XF
S1451	**2 Groschen** 1807. Black ink. Handwritten with 6 signatures. Back: Hand stamped: *Kon. Preuss. Gouvernement zu Colberg.*	90.00	180.	360.

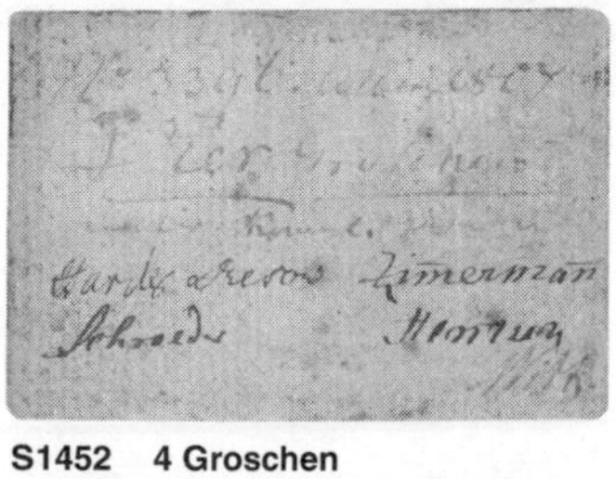

		Good	Fine	XF
S1452	**4 Groschen** 1807. Blue ink. Handwritten with 6 signatures. Back: Hand stamped: *Kon. Preuss. Gouvernement zu Colberg.*	90.00	180.	360.
S1453	**8 Groschen** 1807. Red ink. Handwritten with 6 signatures. Back: Hand stamped: *Kon. Preuss. Gouvernement zu Colberg.*	125.	250.	500.

1807 SECOND *MEINECKE-KUPONS* ISSUE

#S1454-S1456 are named after the Counselor for War and Crown Lands.

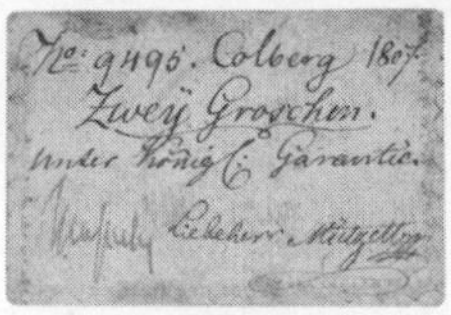

		Good	Fine	XF
S1454	**2 Groschen** 1807. Black ink. Handwritten with 3 signatures. Like #S1451. Back: Hand stamped: *Kon. Preuss. Gouvernement zu Colberg.*	125.	250.	500.
S1455	**4 Groschen** 1807. Blue ink. Handwritten with 3 signatures. Like #S1452. Back: Hand stamped: *Kon. Preuss. Gouvernement zu Colberg.*	125.	250.	500.

		Good	Fine	XF
S1456	**8 Groschen** 1807. Red ink. Handwritten with 3 signatures. Like #S1453. Back: Hand stamped: *Kon. Preuss. Gouvernement zu Colberg.*	140.	280.	550.

ERFURT

1813 ISSUE

		Good	Fine	XF
S1461	**2 Groschen** 1.11.1813. Black. Flowered border, Arms of Erfurt (wheel design) at upper center and in embossed seal at right. Uniface. Printer: Johann Immanuel Uckermann.			
	a. Without imprint.	—	—	—
	b. With imprint.	—	—	—
S1462	**3 Groschen** 1.11.1813. Black. Arms of Erfurt (wheel design) at upper center and in embossed seal at right. Similar to #S1461 but border has oval and diamond design. Uniface. Printer: Johann Immanuel Uckermann.			
	a. Without imprint.	—	—	—
	b. With imprint.	—	—	—
S1463	**4 Groschen** 1.11.1813. Black. Border at upper left and right has various symbolic designs, lower left and right have scenes of sunrise over city views. Uniface. Printer: Johann Immanuel Uckermann.			
	a. Without imprint.	—	—	—
	b. With imprint.	—	—	—

		Good	Fine	XF
S1464	**8 Groschen** 1.11.1813. Black. Arms of Erfurt (wheel design) at upper center and in embossed seal at right. Similar to #S1461 but border has design of leaves and branches. Uniface. Printer: Johann Immanuel Uckermann.			
	a. Without imprint.	—	—	—
	b. With imprint.	—	—	—

		Good	Fine	XF
S1465	**12 Groschen** 1.11.1813. Black. Arms at upper center, ornamental border at top and bottom, wheel design at right. Uniface. Printer: Johann Immanuel Uckermann.			
	a. Without imprint.	—	—	—
	b. With imprint.	—	—	—

	Good	Fine	XF
S1466 1 Thaler			
1.11.1813. Black. Wheel design at upper center, anchors in lower border. Uniface. Printer: Johann Immanuel Uckermann.			
a. Without imprint.	—	—	—
b. With imprint.	—	—	—
S1467 2 Thaler			
1.11.1813. Black. Arms at upper center, zigzag design in border. Uniface. Printer: Johann Immanuel Uckermann.			
a. Without imprint.	—	—	—
b. With imprint.	—	—	—
S1468 5 Thaler			
1.11.1813. Black. Wheel design and branches at upper center, wheel design at right. Uniface. Printer: Johann Immanuel Uckermann.			
a. Without imprint.	—	—	—
b. With imprint	—	—	—

Mainz

Mayence

1793 First Issue

	Good	Fine	XF
S1471 20 Sous			
5.1793 (- old date 4.1.1792.) Back: Handwritten value, signature with handstamping: *SIEGE DE MATENCE* on back of 10 Sous #A53.	300.	600.	1200.

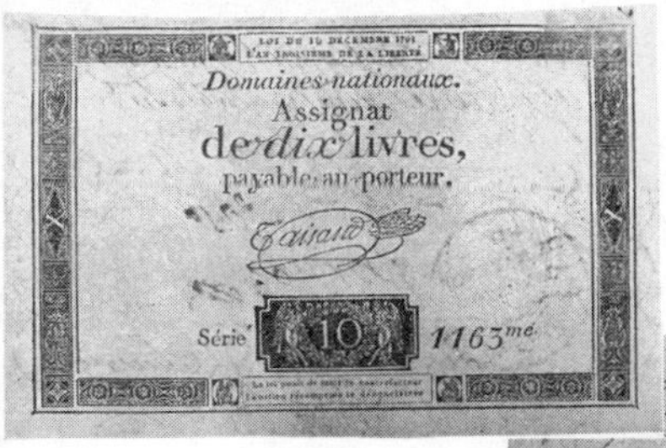

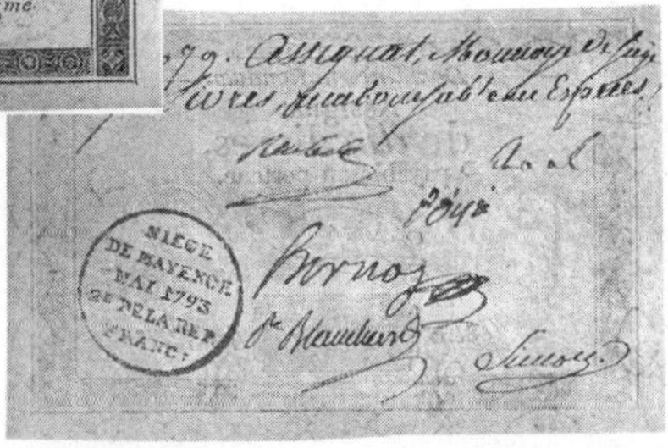

	Good	Fine	XF
S1472 20 Livres			
5.1793. (- old date 16.12.1791.) Back: Handwritten value, signature with handstamping: *SIEGE DE MATENCE* on back of 10 Livres #A51.	225.	450.	900.
S1473 20 Livres			
5.1793. (- old date 24.10.1792.) Back: Handwritten value, signature with handstamping: *SIEGE DE MATENCE* on back of 10 Livres #A66.	—	—	—
S1474 50 Livres			
5.1793. (- old date 24.10.1792.) Back: Handwritten value, signature with handstamping: *SIEGE DE MATENCE* on back of 25 Livres #A67.	300.	600.	1200.

1793 Second Issue

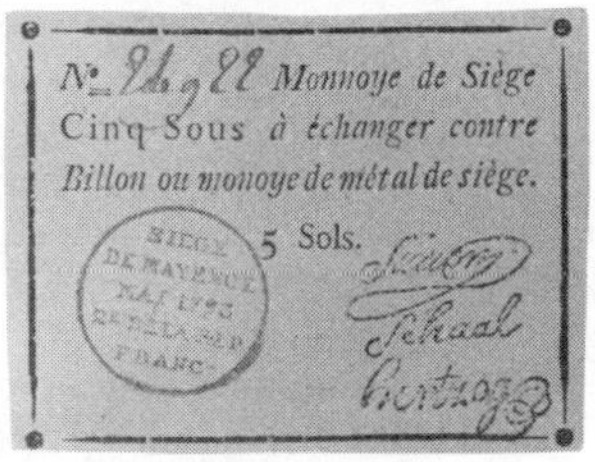

	Good	Fine	XF
S1475 5 Sous			
May 1793. Black. Red stamping in circle at left. 3 signatures. Without series letter. Uniface.			
a. Hand signatures.	150.	300.	600.
b. Printed signatures.	75.00	150.	300.
x. Error *écharger* instead of *échanger*.	350.	700.	1400.
S1476 10 Sous			
May 1793. Black. Red hand stamp in circle at left. 3 signatures. Without series letter. Uniface. Like #S1475.			
a. Hand signatures.	150.	300.	600.
b. Printed signatures.	75.00	150.	300.
x. Error like #S1475x.	350.	700.	1400.

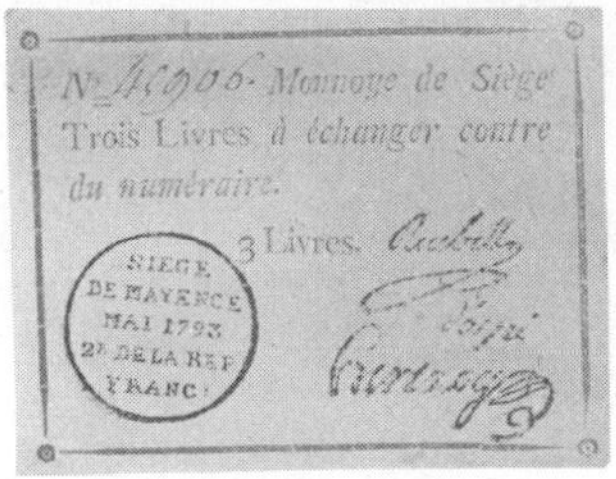

	Good	Fine	XF
S1477 3 Livres			
May 1793. Red. Black stamping at left. 3 signatures. Without series letter. Uniface.			
a. Hand signatures.	175.	350.	700.
b. Printed signatures.	100.	200.	400.
x. Error like #S1475x.	350.	700.	1400.

#S1478-S1481 w/series letter, otherwise like previous issue.

	Good	Fine	XF
S1478 5 Sous			
May 1793. Black. Red stamping in circle at left. 3 signatures. Series A. Uniface. Like #S1475.			
a. Issued note.	125.	250.	500.
x. Error like #S1475x.	350.	700.	1400.
S1479 10 Sous			
May 1793. Black. Red stamping in circle at left. 3 signatures. Series A. Uniface. Like #S1476.			
a. Issued note.	125.	250.	500.
x. Error like #S1475x.	350.	700.	1400.
S1480 3 Livres			
May 1793. Red. Black hand stamp at left. 3 signatures. Series A. Uniface. Like #S1477.			
a. Issued note.	125.	250.	500.
x. Error like #S1475x.	350.	700.	1400.
S1481 3 Livres			
May 1793. Red. Black hand stamp at left. 3 signatures. Series B. Uniface. Like #S1477.			
a. Issued note.	125.	250.	500.
x. Error like #S1475x.	600.	1200.	2400.

Military Payment Certificates

Etappen - Inspektion

Base Inspectorate I, 1st Army

1915 Issue

	VG	VF	UNC
M1 50 Centimes			
1915. Issued in occupuied French territory.	40.00	70.00	120.
M2 1 Franc			
1915. Issued in occupuied French territory.	40.00	70.00	120.

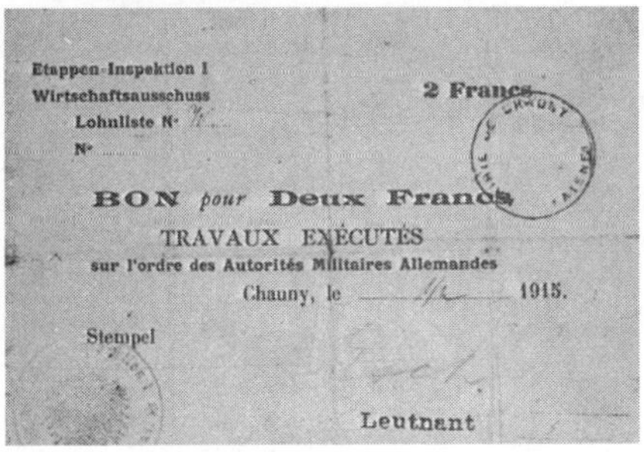

	VG	VF	UNC
M3 2 Francs			
1915. Issued in occupuied French territory.	30.00	50.00	100.
M4 5 Francs			
1915. Issued in occupuied French territory.	30.00	50.00	100.

Etappen - Kommandantur

Base Local Headquarters

1915 Issue

	VG	VF	UNC
M5 50 Centimes			
1915. Issued in occupied French territory.	40.00	70.00	120.
M6 1 Franc			
1915. Issued in occupied French territory.	30.00	50.00	100.
M7 2 Francs			
1915. Issued in occupied French territory.	30.00	50.00	100.

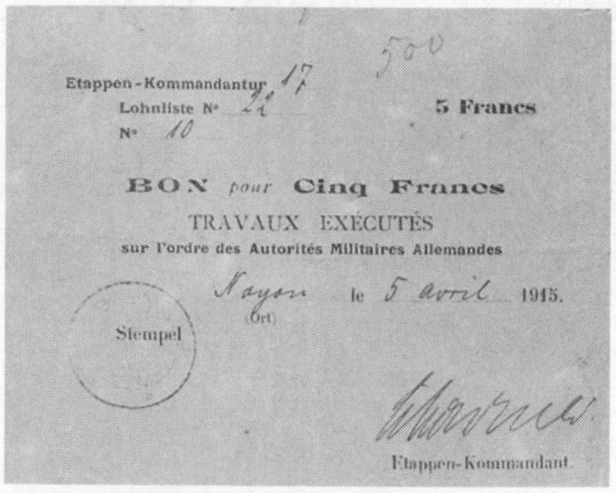

		VG	VF	UNC
M8	**5 Francs** 1915. Issued in occupied French territory.	30.00	50.00	100.

Etappen - Inspektion

Base Inspectorate, 2nd Army

1914-15 Issue

		VG	VF	UNC
M9	**5 Francs** 1914-15. Issued in occupied French territory, so called "Deichmann-Bons", with different handstamps of various French municipalities.	40.00	125.	250.
M10	**10 Francs** 1914-15. Issued in occupied French territory, so called "Deichmann-Bons", with different handstamps of various French municipalities.	40.00	150.	300.
M11	**20 Francs** 1914-15. Issued in occupied French territory, so called "Deichmann-Bons", with different handstamps of various French municipalities.	40.00	150.	300.

		VG	VF	UNC
M12	**50 Francs** 1914-15. Issued in occupied French territory, so called "Deichmann-Bons", with different handstamps of various French municipalities.	40.00	200.	400.
M13	**100 Francs** 1914-15. Issued in occupied French territory, so called "Deichmann-Bons", with different handstamps of various French municipalities.	40.00	200.	400.

#M14-M18 Deleted, see #M9-M13.

Etappen - Inspektion

Base Inspectorate, 3rd Army

1915 Issue

		VG	VF	UNC
M19	**1 Franc** 1915. Issued in occupied French territory.	40.00	125.	250.
M20	**2 Francs** 1915. Issued in occupied French territory.	40.00	125.	250.
M21	**3 Francs** 1915. Issued in occupied French territory.	40.00	125.	250.
M22	**5 Francs** 1915. Issued in occupied French territory.	40.00	125.	250.
M23	**10 Francs** 1915. Issued in occupied French territory.	40.00	125.	250.
M24	**25 Francs** 1915. Issued in occupied French territory.	40.00	125.	250.
M25	**100 Francs** 1915. Issued in occupied French territory.	40.00	150.	300.
M26	**100 Francs** 1915. Issued in occupied French territory.	40.00	150.	300.

Reichsmarine des Ostseebereiches

Reich's Navy of the Baltic Sea Zone

Kiel

1923 Issue

		VG	VF	UNC
M27	**1 Milliarde Mark** 27.10.1923.	10.00	20.00	40.00

		VG	VF	UNC
M28	**5 Milliarden Mark**	7.00	15.00	40.00
M29	**20 Milliarden Mark**	7.00	15.00	40.00
M30	**50 Milliarden Mark**	7.00	15.00	40.00

Behelfszahlungsmittel für die Deutsche Wehrmacht

Auxiliary Payment Certificates, German Armed Forces

1940 ND Issue

Intended as legal tender within the services during World War II. Worth 10 times the face value if spent in military channels.

		VG	VF	UNC
M31	**1 Reichspfennig** ND (1940). Lilac-brown. Swastika at center in underprint. Intended as legal tender within the services during World War II. Worth 10 times the face value if spent in military channels.	25.00	100.	250.

1942 ND Issue

		VG	VF	UNC
M32	**1 Reichspfennig** ND (1942). Blue. Eagle with small swastika in underprint at center.	2.00	4.00	10.00
M33	**5 Reichspfennig** ND (1942). Red. Eagle with small swastika in underprint at center.	2.00	4.00	10.00

		VG	VF	UNC
M34	**10 Reichspfennig** ND (1942). Green. Eagle with small swastika in underprint at center.	1.00	3.00	15.00
M35	**50 Reichspfennig** ND (1942). Red-orange. Eagle with small swastika in underprint at center.	2.00	10.00	35.00

		VG	VF	UNC
M36	**1 Reichsmark** ND (1942). Brown on orange underprint. Eagle with small swastika in underprint at center.	5.00	15.00	75.00

		VG	VF	UNC
M37	**2 Reichsmark** ND (1942). Dark blue on lilac underprint. Eagle with small swastika in underprint at center.	15.00	75.00	250.

Note: Also see Greece #M19-M22.

Verrechnungsscheine für die Deutsche Wehrmacht

Clearing Notes for German Armed Forces

1944 Issue

M38 1 Reichsmark	VG	VF	UNC
15.9.1944. Green.	.50	1.00	5.00

M39 5 Reichsmark	VG	VF	UNC
15.9.1944. Blue. .	.75	2.50	10.00

M40 10 Reichsmark	VG	VF	UNC
15.9.1944. Red.	.50	1.50	7.50

M41 50 Reichsmark	VG	VF	UNC
15.9.1944. Lilac-brown.	5.00	12.50	40.00

Regional - Occupation of Lithuania - WWI

Ostbank für Handel und Gewerbe, Darlehnskassenscheine

State Loan Bank Currency Notes, Eastern Bank of Commerce and Industry, Posen (Poznan)

1916 Issue

R120 20 Kopeken	VG	VF	UNC
17.4.1916. Blue-green. Circulated in Lithuania until 1922.	20.00	40.00	80.00

R121 50 Kopeken	VG	VF	UNC
17.4.1916. Black on red-brown and blue-green underprint. Circulated in Lithuania until 1922.			
a. *ASTUN GADEEM* last 2 words at bottom right on back. Capital letters of bottom text 1.8mm tall. *AISDEWU KASES SIME* at right. With *S* in form of *f*.	15.00	35.00	80.00
b. As above but capital letters only. 1.2-1.4mm tall.	25.00	80.00	150.
c. *ASTONI GADEEM* last 2 words at bottom right on back. Capital letter of bottom text 1.8mm tall. *AISDEWU KASES SIHME* at right.	15.00	35.00	70.00
d. As above but capital letters only 1.2-1.4mm tall. Text poorly printed.	15.00	35.00	70.00

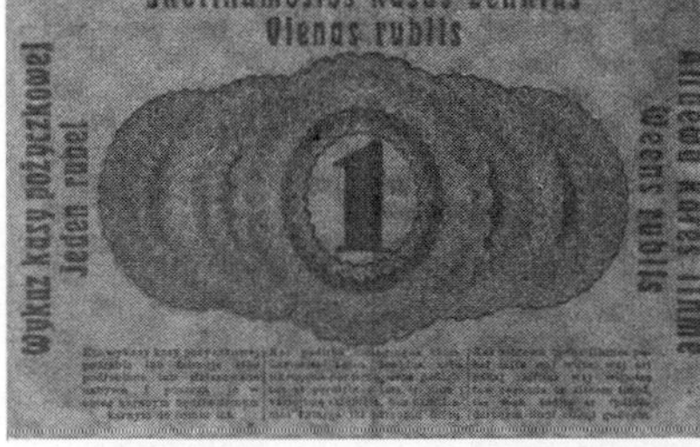

R122 1 Rubel	VG	VF	UNC
17.4.1916. Black on blue and brown underprint. Circulated in Lithuania until 1922.			
a. Like #R121a.	15.00	35.00	70.00
b. Like #R121b.	20.00	80.00	150.
c. Like #R121c.	15.00	35.00	70.00
d. Like #R121d.	15.00	35.00	70.00

R123 3 Rubel	VG	VF	UNC
17.4.1916. Dark brown on green and lilac underprint. Circulated in Lithuania until 1922.			
a. *AIFDEWU* with crossed *F* (Gothic *F*).	60.00	100.	400.
b. *AIFDEWU* with uncrossed *F* (Gothic *S*).	20.00	50.00	150.

R124 10 Rubel	VG	VF	UNC
17.4.1916. Red-brown on red and green underprint. Circulated in Lithuania until 1922.	100.	150.	250.

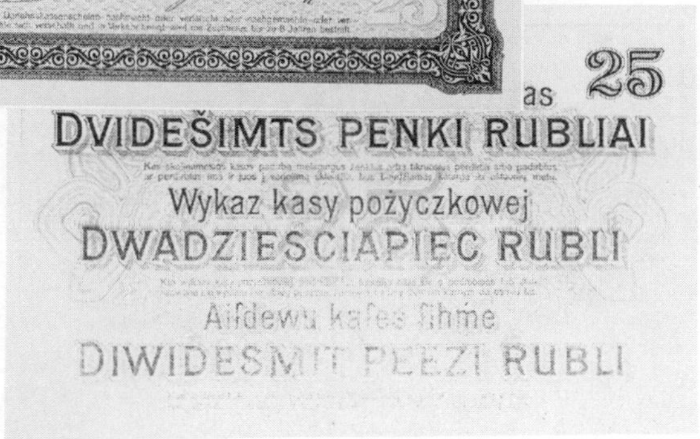

R125 25 Rubel

	VG	VF	UNC
17.4.1916. Dark blue on lilac underprint. Circulated in Lithuania until 1922.	110.	250.	450.

R126 100 Rubel

	VG	VF	UNC
17.4.1916. Blue. Woman at left, man wearing helmet at right. Circulated in Lithuania until 1922.	150.	300.	500.

Darlehnskasse Ost

State Loan Bank East

Kowno (Kaunas)

1918 Issue

R127 1/2 Mark

	VG	VF	UNC
4.4.1918. Black on lilac and light brown underprint. Circulated in Lithuania until 1922.	20.00	30.00	50.00

R128 1 Mark

	VG	VF	UNC
4.4.1918. Dark brown on green underprint. Circulated in Lithuania until 1922.	15.00	25.00	40.00

R129 2 Mark

	VG	VF	UNC
4.4.1918. Red-brown on lilac underprint. Circulated in Lithuania until 1922.	50.00	100.	300.

R130 5 Mark

	VG	VF	UNC
4.4.1918. Brown and blue. Circulated in Lithuania until 1922.	15.00	25.00	60.00

R131 20 Mark

	VG	VF	UNC
4.4.1918. Red-brown on green and pink underprint. Circulated in Lithuania until 1922.	30.00	60.00	100.

R132 50 Mark

	VG	VF	UNC
4.4.1918. Dark blue on gray-violet underprint. Circulated in Lithuania until 1922.	35.00	60.00	120.

R133 100 Mark

	VG	VF	UNC
4.4.1918. Brown. Woman at left, man wearing helmet at right. Similar to #R126. Circulated in Lithuania until 1922.	40.00	70.00	150.

R134 1000 Mark	VG	VF	UNC
4.4.1918. Green. Mercury and youth in armor at right. Circulated in Lithuania until 1922.			
a. 6 digit serial #, black signatures.	80.00	200.	400.
b. 7 digit serial #, green signatures.	70.00	150.	350.
c. 6 digit serial #, green signatures. Rare.	—	—	—
d. 7 digit serial #, black signatures. Rare.	—	—	—

GERMAN OCCUPIED TERRITORIES - WWII

REICHSKREDITKASSEN

REICH'S CREDIT TREASURY NOTES

1940 ISSUE

#R135-R140 legal tender alongside the currency of the country in numerous occupied countries and territories during WW II.

R135 50 Reichspfennig	VG	VF	UNC
ND (1940-45). Green on tan underprint.	5.00	15.00	30.00

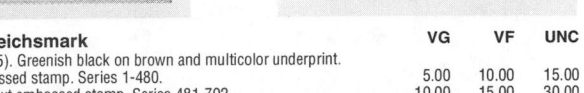

R136 1 Reichsmark	VG	VF	UNC
ND (1940-45). Greenish black on brown and multicolor underprint.			
a. Embossed stamp. Series 1-480.	5.00	10.00	15.00
b. Without embossed stamp. Series 481-702.	10.00	15.00	30.00

COMPANION CATALOGS

Volume 2 - General Issues, 1368-1960
Volume 3 - Modern Issues, 1961- present
The Companion Catalogs in the Standard Catalog of World Paper Money series include: The General Issues volume which lists national notes dated and used, before 1960. It is updated periodically, now in it's 12th edition. The Modern Issues Book includes national notes issued since 1961, and is updated annually.
Inquiries about the availability of both these volumes are invited to contact F+W Publications, 700 East State Street, Iola, WI 54990-0001. You may visit our website at: shopnumismaster.com

R137 2 Reichsmark	VG	VF	UNC
ND (1940-45). Grayish brown on green and tan underprint.			
a. Embossed stamp. 7 digit serial #.	3.00	7.00	15.00
b. Without embossed stamp. 8 digit serial #.	10.00	15.00	30.00

R138 5 Reichsmark	VG	VF	UNC
ND (1940-45). Blue-black on brown and gray underprint. Portrait farmer at left, factory worker at right. Back: Berlin War Memorial at center.			
a. Embossed stamp. 7 digit serial #.	7.00	15.00	30.00
b. Without embossed stamp, 8 digit serial #.	10.00	17.00	25.00

R139 20 Reichsmark	VG	VF	UNC
ND (1940-45). Dark brown on red-brown and pale olive underprint. "The Architect" by A. Durer at right. Back: Brandenburg Gate at center.	10.00	15.00	30.00

R140 50 Reichsmark	VG	VF	UNC
ND (1940-45). Blue-black on dull violet underprint. Portrait woman at right. Back: Marienburg castle at center.	12.00	18.00	35.00

Note: Immediately after the end of the war, Reichs Credit Treasury Notes were authorized in the British zone of occupation in the denominations of 5, 20 and 50 Reichsmark, provided they had been given a stamp of a Reichsbank office located in the British zone of occupation. All such notes with different stamps are scarce ($75.00 each).

The German Democratic Republic (East Germany), located on the great north European plain, ceased to exist in 1990. During the closing days of World War II in Europe, Soviet troops advancing into Germany from the east occupied the German provinces of Mecklen-burg, Brandenburg, Saxony- Anhalt, Saxony and Thuringia. These five provinces comprised the occupation zone administered by the Soviet Union after the cessation of hostilities. The other three zones were administered by the United States, Great Britain and France. Under the Potsdam agreement, questions affecting Germany as a whole were to be settled by the commanders in chief of the occupation zones acting jointly and by unanimous decision. When Soviet intransigence rendered the quadripartite commission inoperable, the three western zones were united to form the Federal Republic of Germany, May 23, 1949. Thereupon the Soviet Union dissolved its occupation zone and established it as the Democratic Republic of Germany, Oct. 7, 1949. East and West Germany became reunited as one country on Oct. 3, 1990.

MONETARY SYSTEM:

1 Mark = 100 Pfennig

Foreign Exchange Certificates

Forum-Aussenhandelsgesellschaft m.b.H.

1979 Issue

Certificates issued by state-owned export-import company. These were in the form of checks for specified amounts for purchase of special (mostly imported) goods.

1 Mark = 1 DM (West German Mark)

#FX1-FX7 replacement notes: Serial # prefix *ZA, ZB.*

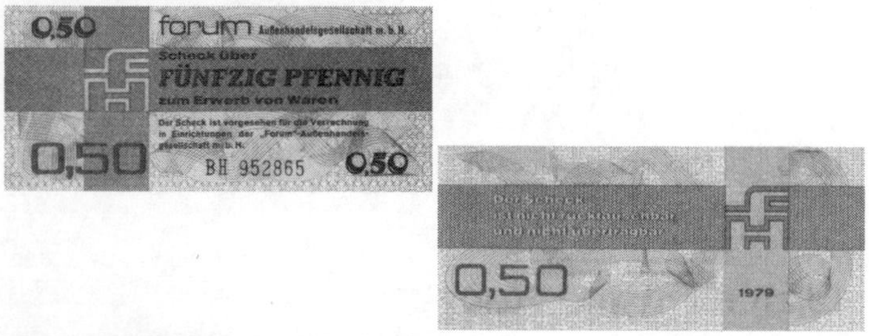

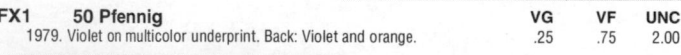

FX1	**50 Pfennig**	**VG**	**VF**	**UNC**
	1979. Violet on multicolor underprint. Back: Violet and orange.	.25	.75	2.00

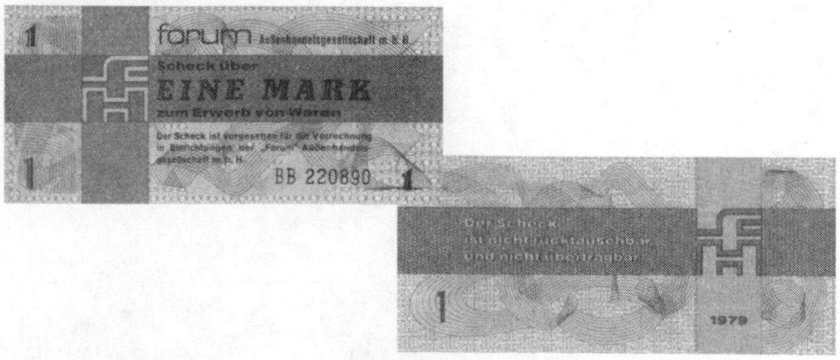

FX2	**1 Mark**	**VG**	**VF**	**UNC**
	1979. Brown and rose.	.25	.75	3.00

FX3	**5 Mark**	**VG**	**VF**	**UNC**
	1979. Green and peach.	.50	1.50	5.00

FX4	**10 Mark**	**VG**	**VF**	**UNC**
	1979. Blue and light green.	.50	1.50	5.00

FX5	**50 Mark**	**VG**	**VF**	**UNC**
	1979. Light red and orange.	.50	1.50	5.00

FX6	**100 Mark**	**VG**	**VF**	**UNC**
	1979. Olive and green. Back: Olive and yellow.	1.00	3.00	7.50

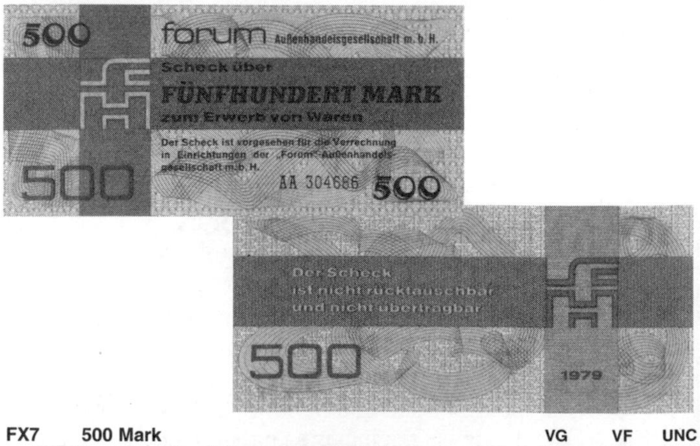

FX7	**500 Mark**	**VG**	**VF**	**UNC**
	1979. Gray-brown and purple. Back: Gray-brown and blue.	2.50	5.00	10.00

A set of specimens of FX1-FX7 are available in two varieties: w/overprint: *MUSTER* and w/o serial #s, or perforation *SPECIMEN* and serial # AA000000. Value at $700.

GREAT BRITAIN

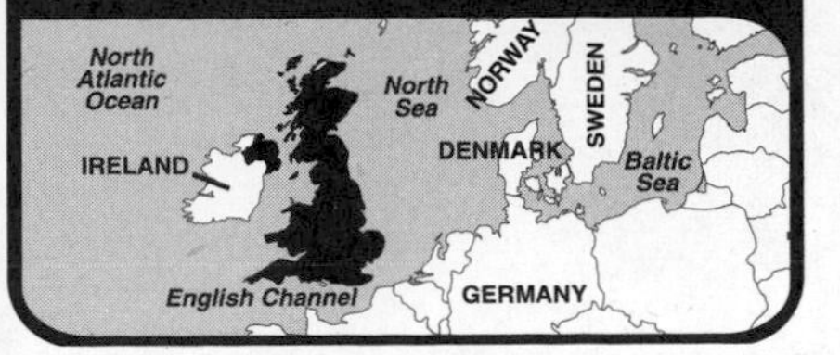

The United Kingdom of Great Britain and Northern Ireland, (including England, Scotland, Wales and Norhtern Ireland) is located off the northwest coast of the European continent, has an area of 94,227 sq. mi. (244,046 sq. km.), and a population of 59.45 million. Capital: London.

The economy is d on industrial activity, trading and financial services. Machinery, motor vehicles, chemicals and textile yarns and fabrics are exported.

After the departure of the Romans, who brought Britain into an active relationship with Europe, Britain fell prey to invaders from Scandinavia and the Low Countries who drove the original Britons into Scotland and Wales, and established a profusion of kingdoms that finally united in the 11th century under the Danish King Canute. Norman rule, following the conquest of 1066, stimulated the development of those institutions which have since distinguished British life. Henry VIII (1509-47) turned Britain from continental adventuring and faced it to the sea - a decision that made Britain a world power during the reign of Elizabeth I (1558-1603). Strengthened by the Industrial Revolution and the defeat of Napoleon, 19th century Britain turned to the remote parts of the world and established a colonial empire of such extent and prosperity that the world has never seen its like. World Wars I and II sealed the fate of the Empire and relegated Britain to a lesser role in world affairs by draining her resources and inaugurating a worldwide movement toward national self-determination in her former colonies.

By the mid-20th century, most of the former British Empire had gained independence and had evolved into the Commonwealth of Nations. This association of equal and and autonomous states, set out to agree views and special relationships with one another (appointing High Commissioners rather than Ambassadors) for mutual benefit, trade interests, etc. The Commonwealth is presently (1999) composed of 54 member nations, including the United Kingdom. All recognize the monarch as Head of the Commonwealth; 16 continue to recognize Queen Elizabeth II as Head of State. In addition to the United Kingdom, they are: Antigua & Barbuda, Australia, The Bahamas, Barbados Belize, Canada, Grenada, Paupa New Guinea, St. Christopher & Nevis, St. Lucia, St. Vincent & the Grenadines, Solomon Islands.

RULERS:

William III, 1694-1702
Anne, 1702-1714
George I, 1714-1727
George II, 1727-1760
George III, 1760-1820
George IV, 1820-1830
William IV, 1830-1837
Victoria, 1837-1901
Edward VII, 1901-1910
George V, 1910-1936
Edward VIII, 1936
George VI, 1936-1952
Elizabeth II, 1952-

MONETARY SYSTEM:

1 Shilling = 12 Pence
1 Pound = 20 Shillings to 1971
1 Pound = 100 (New) Pence, 1971-

PRIVATE AND COMMERCIAL JOINT STOCK BANKS

This series of note issues is very extensive, starting in the mid-18th century and extending into the earlier years of the 20th century. The history of these issues and their impact on the economic life of Great Britain is totally interwoven with the history of the country itself, and is a very complex story. There were literally hundreds of different banks, with the greatest concentration of note issues taking place during the first part of the 19th century. As centralization became stronger the need and influence of private note issues became less, until it finally ceased altogether.

In accordance with the Bank Charter Act of 1844, the number of issuing banks in England and Wales decreased considerably. In 1900 notes of the following banks were still in circulation.

Bank NameLast Date of Issue

Ashford Bank, Pomfret, Burra & Co.	1902
Aylesbury Old Bank, Cobb Bartlett & Co.	1902
Banbury Bank, Gillet & Co.	1918
Banbury Old Bank, T.R. Cobb & Sons	1902
Bank of Whitehaven Ltd.	1916
Bedford Bank, Thomas Barnard & Co.	1915
Bicester & Oxfordshire Bank - Tibb & Co.	1920
Bradford Banking Co. Ltd.	1910
Bradford Commercial Banking Co. Ltd.	1904
Buckingham Bank - Bartlett & Co.	1902
Cambridge & Cambridgeshire Bank Ltd. - Fosters	1904
Canterbury Bank, Hammand, Pumptre, Hilton, McMaster & Furley	1903
Carlisle & Cumberland Banking Co. Ltd.	1911
City Bank, Exeter - Milford, Snow & Co.	1901
Cumberland Union Banking Co. Ltd.	1901
Derby Bank, Samuel Smith & Co.	1902
East Riding Bank, Beckett & Co., York	1920
Exeter Bank - Sanders & Co.	1901
Faversham Bank, Hilton, Rigden & Rigden	1902
Halifax Commercial Banking Co., Ltd.	1919
Halifax & Huddersfield Union Bank Ltd.	1910
Hull & Kingston-upon-Hull, Samuel Smith	1902
Ipswich Bank, Bacon Cobbold & Co.	1904
Kington & Radnorshire Bank Ltd. - Davies, Banks & Co.	1910
Knaresborough & Claro Banking Co. Ltd.	1903
Lancaster Banking Co. Ltd.	1907
Leeds Bank, Beckett & Co. Leeds	1920
Leeds Union Bank, William Williams, Brown & Co.	1900
Leicestershire Banking Co., Ltd.	1900
Lincoln Bank, Smith, Ellison & Co.	1902
Lincoln & Lindsey Banking Co. Ltd.	1913
Llandovery & Llandilo Bank - David Jones & Co.	1909
Moore & Robinson, Notts Banking Co. Ltd.	1901
Naval Bank, Plymouth, Harris, Bulteel & Co.	1914
Newark Bank, Samuel Smith & Co.	1902
Newark & Sleaford Bank, Peacock, Wilson & Co.	1912
Newcastle upon Tyne Joint Stock Banking Co.	1908
Newmarket Bank, Hammand & Co.	1905
North & South Wales Bank Ltd.	1908
Nottingham Bank, Samuel Smith & Co.	1902
Nottingham & Nottingham Banking Co. Ltd.	1919
Oxford Old Bank, Parsons Thomson & Co.	1900
Oxfordshire Witney Bank, Gillett & Co.	1918
Pares' Leicestershire Banking Co. Ltd.	1902
Reading Bank, Simonds & Co.	1913
Richmond Bank, Yorkshire, Roper & Priestman	1902
Sheffield Banking Co. Ltd.	1905
Sheffield & Hallamshire Bank Ltd.	1913
Sheffield & Rotherham Joint Stock Banking Co. Ltd.	1907
Stamford, Spalding & Boston Banking Co. Ltd.	1907
Stuckeys Banking Co. Ltd.	1909
Tring Bank & Chesham Bank, Thomos Butcher & Sons	1900
Uxbridge Old Bank - Woodbridge, Lacy, Hartland, Hibbert & Co.	1900
Wakefield & Barnsley Union Bank Ltd.	1906
Wallingford Bank, Hedges Wells & Co.	1905
Wellington, Somerset Bank, Fox, Fowler & Co.	1921
West Riding Bank, Leathern Tew & Co.	1906
West Riding Union Banking Co. Ltd.	1902
West Yorkshire Banking Co. Ltd.	1919
Whitehaven Joint Stock Banking Co. Ltd.	1908
Witts & Dorset Banking Co. Ltd.	1914
Worcester Old Bank, Berwick Lechmere & Co.	1905
Yarmouth, Norfolk & Suffolk Bank Ltd. - Lancons, Youell & Kemp	1901
York City & County Banking Co. Ltd.	1909
Yorkshire Banking Co. Ltd.	1901
York Union Banking Co. Ltd.	1902

MILITARY

BRITISH MILITARY AUTHORITY

1943 ND ISSUE

Originally issued in 1943 for use by British troops in North Africa. One Pound notes w/ovpt: *BULGARIA, FRANCE* and *GREECE* were prepared but not issued. The remaining stock was later sent to Cyprus in 1956.

		VG	VF	UNC
M1	**6 Pence** ND (1943). Red-brown on green and peach underprint. Lion on crown device. Back: Red, green, blue and purple.	6.00	20.00	70.00

		VG	VF	UNC
M2	**1 Shilling** ND (1943). Black on gray and violet underprint. Lion on crown device. Back: Purple on brown, green and blue underprint.	3.00	12.00	35.00

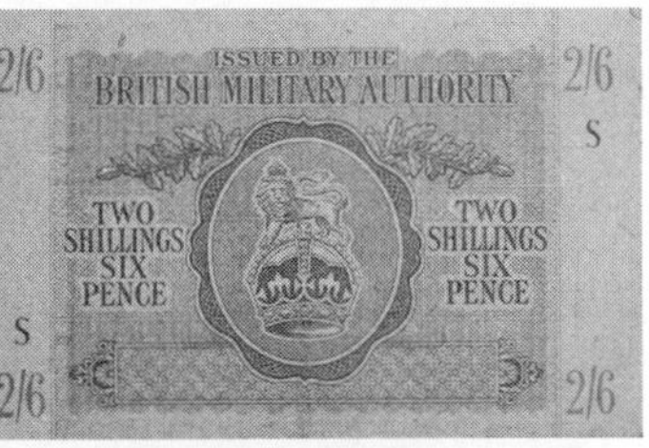

		VG	VF	UNC
M3	**2 Shillings - 6 Pence** ND (1943). Green on pink underprint. Lion on crown device. Back: Olive green and brown on lilac and olive underprint.	4.00	17.50	40.00

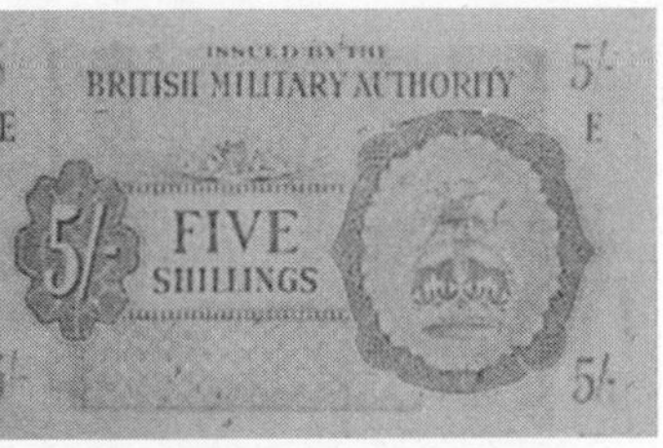

		VG	VF	UNC
M4	**5 Shillings** ND (1943). Brown on blue and green underprint. Lion with crown device. Back: Violet on green and blue underprint.	5.00	20.00	50.00

M5 10 Shillings	VG	VF	UNC
ND (1943). Blue on olive and lilac underprint. Lion on crown device. Back: Olive brown on gray and brown underprint.	8.00	35.00	80.00

M6 1 Pound	VG	VF	UNC
ND (1943-45). Purple on orange and green underprint. Lion on crown face. Back: Orange, green and black.			
a. Issued note without overprint.	15.00	45.00	100.
b. Overprint: *BULGARIA*. 25 prepared.	—	—	1500.
c. Overprint: *FRANCE*. 50 prepared.	—	—	1000.
d. Overprint: *GREECE*. 25 prepared.	—	—	1500.

British Armed Forces

1946 ND Token Issue

M7 1/2 Penny	VG	VF	UNC
ND (1946). Black on dark brown. Round printed disk of laminated paper. Printer: TDLR (without imprint).	4.00	10.00	25.00

M8 1 Penny	VG	VF	UNC
ND (1946). Black on dark brown. Round printed disk of laminated paper. Printer: TDLR (without imprint).	4.00	10.00	25.00

British Armed Forces, Special Vouchers

1946 ND First Series

Originally issued on Aug. 1, 1946 for use by British forces in occupied Germany and Austria. They were later released to British forces in occupied Japan on May 6, 1947. Some notes of the First Series are found w/ovpt: *ISSUED IN H.M. SHIPS AFLOAT FOR USE IN NAAFI CANTEENS ONLY*, which were used by Force T marines also assigned to Japan. They were part of the B.C.O.F.

	VG	VF	UNC
M9 3 Pence			
ND (1946). Lilac on orange and green underprint. Printer: TDLR.			
a. Issued note.	3.00	35.00	80.00
b. Overprint: ...*NAAFI CANTEENS ONLY*.	40.00	150.	300.
M10 6 Pence			
ND (1946). Brown on lilac and blue underprint. Printer: TDLR.			
a. Issued note.	3.00	20.00	60.00
b. overprint: ...*NAAFI CANTEENS ONLY*.	40.00	150.	300.
M11 1 Shilling			
ND (1946). Gray-blue on olive green and orange underprint. Printer: TDLR.			
a. Issued note.	6.00	35.00	90.00
b. Overprint: ...*NAAFI CANTEENS ONLY*.	40.00	150.	300.

	VG	VF	UNC
M12 2 Shillings - 6 Pence			
ND (1946). Pale red on green and violet underprint. Back: Pale red and violet. Printer: TDLR.			
a. Issued note.	10.00	45.00	120.
b. Overprint: ...*NAAFI CANTEENS ONLY*.	40.00	150.	300.
M13 5 Shillings			
ND (1946). Green on violet and orange underprint. Back: Green and pale red. Printer: TDLR.			
a. Issued note.	15.00	50.00	130.
b. Overprint: ...*NAAFI CANTEENS ONLY*.	40.00	150.	300.
M14 10 Shillings			
ND (1946). Purple on orange and red-brown underprint. Printer: TDLR.			
a. Issued note.	12.00	50.00	130.
b. Overprint: ...*NAAFI CANTEENS ONLY*.	40.00	150.	300.

M15 1 Pound	VG	VF	UNC
ND (1946). Blue on red and green underprint. Printer: TDLR.			
a. Issued note.	20.00	55.00	150.
b. Overprint: ...*NAAFI CANTEENS ONLY*.	100.	250.	—

1948 ND Second Series

Note: This series was retired in 1971.

M16 3 Pence	VG	VF	UNC
ND (1948). Brown on light red and green underprint. Printer: TDLR.			
a. Paper with metal strip. (1948).	1.00	4.00	17.50
b. Watermark paper. (1961).	.50	2.50	10.00

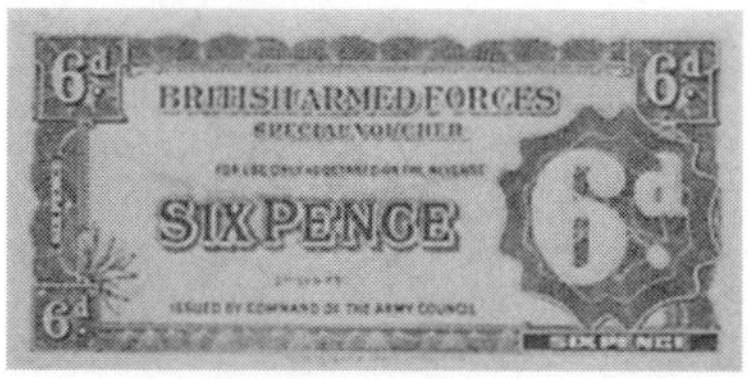

M17 6 Pence	VG	VF	UNC
ND (1948). Greenish blue on green and orange underprint. Printer: TDLR.			
a. Paper with metal security strip.	1.00	4.00	20.00
b. Watermark paper. (1961).	.50	2.50	12.00

	VG	VF	UNC
M18 1 Shilling			
ND (1948). Red-orange on purple and green underprint. Printer: TDLR.			
a. Paper with metal security strip. (1948).	1.00	4.50	30.00
b. Watermark paper. (1961).	.50	2.50	15.00
M19 2 Shillings - 6 Pence			
ND (1948). Lilac on light green and orange underprint. Printer: TDLR.			
a. Paper with metal security strip.	1.25	4.50	20.00
b. Watermark paper. (1961).	1.00	3.00	15.00

		VG	VF	UNC
M20	**5 Shillings**			
	ND (1948). Blue on orange and light red underprint. Printer: TDLR.			
	a. Paper with metal security strip. (1948).	6.00	15.00	30.00
	b. Watermark paper, black serial #. (1961).	4.00	10.00	25.00
	c. Watermark paper, red serial #.	4.00	10.00	25.00
	d. Cancelled remainder with normal serial # and 2 punched holes.	—	Unc	4.00
M21	**10 Shillings**			
	ND (1948). Green. Printer: TDLR.			
	a. Paper with metal security strip. (1948).	2.00	5.00	25.00
	b. Watermark paper. (1961).	2.00	5.00	25.00

		VG	VF	UNC
M22	**1 Pound**			
	ND (1948). Lilac on red and blue underprint. Printer: TDLR.			
	a. Paper with metal strip. (1948).	.50	1.50	3.00
	b. Watermark paper.	—	—	—

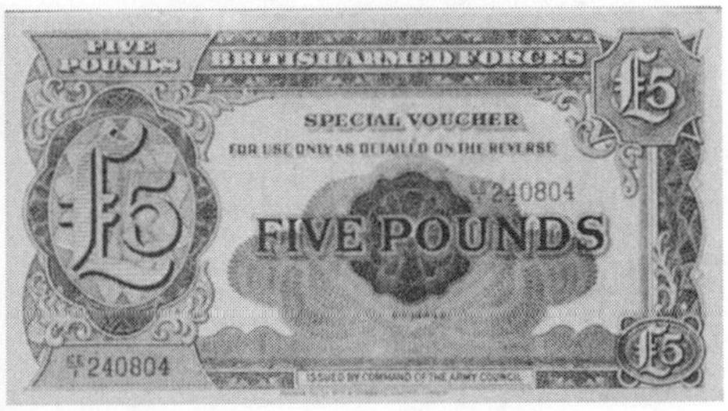

		VG	VF	UNC
M23	**5 Pounds**			
	ND (1958). Dark blue on olive and brown underprint. Printer: TDLR. Watermark paper.	.50	1.50	4.00

1956 ND Third Series

Printed in 1948, they were not issued until 1956 for use during the Suez Canal crisis. This situation was quickly resolved, lasting only 2 months.

		VG	VF	UNC
M24	**3 Pence**			
	ND (1956). Green, orange and pink. Imprint: TDLR. Back: Green. Printer: J. Waddington Ltd.	60.00	150.	250.

		VG	VF	UNC
M25	**6 Pence**			
	ND (1956). Lilac and green. Imprint: TDLR. Printer: J. Waddington Ltd.	20.00	60.00	120.

		VG	VF	UNC
M26	**1 Shilling**			
	ND (1956). Blue and pink. Imprint: TDLR. Printer: J. Waddington Ltd.			
	a. Without punch cancel holes.	10.00	35.00	100.
	b. Cancelled remainder with 2 punched holes.	—	—	4.00
	s. Specimen with 1 punched hole.	—	—	35.00

		VG	VF	UNC
M26A	**2 Shillings - 6 Pence**			
	ND. Imprint: TDLR. Printer: J. Waddington Ltd. Specimen.	—	—	300.
M27	**5 Shillings**			
	ND (1956). Orange and green. Imprint: TDLR. Printer: J. Waddington Ltd.	60.00	150.	250.

		VG	VF	UNC
M28	**10 Shillings**			
	ND (1956). Red, green and orange. Imprint: TDLR. Printer: J. Waddington Ltd.			
	a. Without punch cancel holes.	4.00	20.00	80.00
	b. Cancelled remainder with normal serial # and 2 punched holes.	—	Unc	4.00

		VG	VF	UNC
M29	**1 Pound**			
	ND (1956). Brown, pink and purple. Imprint: TDLR. Printer: J. Waddington Ltd.	—	—	3.00

1962 ND Fourth Series

#M30-M36 Not issued.

		VG	VF	UNC
M30	**3 Pence**			
	ND (1962). Slate on violet and light green underprint. Specimen. Without imprint. Rare.	—	—	—

		VG	VF	UNC
M31	**6 Pence**			
	ND (1962). Blue on violet and light green underprint. Specimen. Without imprint. Rare.	—	—	—
M32	**1 Shilling**			
	ND. Dark brown on olive and orange underprint. Without imprint.			
	a. Normal serial #, but without punch cancellations.	6.00	25.00	150.
	b. Cancelled remainder with 2 punched holes.	—	—	3.50
	c. Specimen with 1 punched hole. Rare.	—	—	—
M33	**2 Shillings - 6 Pence**			
	ND (1962). Red-orange on violet and light green underprint. Specimen. Without imprint. Rare.	—	—	—

M34 5 Shillings	VG	VF	UNC
ND. Green on light brown underprint. Specimen only. Without imprint. Rare.	—	—	—

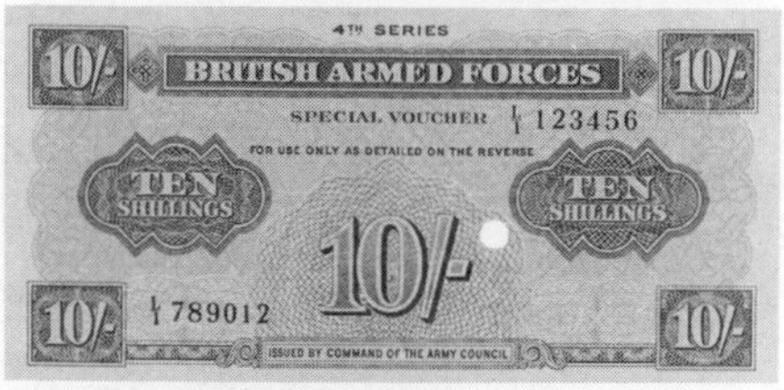

M35 10 Shillings	VG	VF	UNC
ND. Violet on blue and green underprint. Without imprint.			
a. Normal serial # but without punch cancellations.	5.00	25.00	150.
b. Cancelled remainder with normal serial # and 2 punched holes.	—	—	5.00
c. Specimen with special serial # and 1 punched hole. Rare.	—	—	—

M36 1 Pound	VG	VF	UNC
ND. Violet on pale green and lilac underprint. Without imprint.			
a. Normal serial #, without punch cancellations.	—	—	1.00
b. Specimen with special serial # and 1 punched hole. Rare.	—	—	—

1960s Fifth Series

#M37-M43 are not know in issued form, only as specimens and a few proof examples.

	VG	VF	UNC
M37 3 Pence			
ND. Red-brown, purple and green. Specimen. Rare.	—	—	—
M38 6 Pence			
ND. Green, turquoise and light brown. Specimen. Rare.	—	—	—
M39 1 Shilling			
ND. Lilac and green. Specimen. Rare.	—	—	—
M40 2 Shillings - 6 Pence			
ND. Purple, turquoise and light brown. Specimen. Rare.	—	—	—
M41 5 Shillings			
ND. Blue, red and turquoise. Specimen. Rare.	—	—	—
M42 10 Shillings			
ND. Orange, green and slate. Specimen. Rare.	—	—	—
M43 1 Pound			
ND. Olive and red-brown. Specimen. Rare.	—	—	—

1972 Sixth Series

M44 5 New Pence	VG	VF	UNC
ND (1972). Orange-brown and green. Printer: TDLR.			
a. Issued note.	—	—	2.00
s. Specimen.	—	—	450.

M45 10 New Pence	VG	VF	UNC
ND (1972). Violet, green and olive. Printer: TDLR.			
a. Issued note.	—	—	3.00
s. Specimen.	—	—	450.

M46 50 New Pence	VG	VF	UNC
ND (1972). Green on pink underprint. Printer: TDLR.			
a. Issued note.	—	—	4.00
s. Specimen.	—	—	450.

1972 Sixth Series Second Issue

	VG	VF	UNC
M47 5 New Pence			
ND (1972). Orange-brown and green. Printer: BWC.	—	—	1.00
M48 10 New Pence			
ND (1972). Violet, green and olive. Printer: BWC.	—	—	1.00
M49 50 New Pence			
ND (1972). Green on pink underprint. Printer: BWC.	—	—	1.00

The Hellenic Republic of Greece is situated in southeastern Europe on the southern tip of the Balkan Peninsula. The republic includes many islands, the most important of which are Crete and the Ionian Islands. Greece (including islands) has an area of 131,940 sq. km. and a population of 10.72 million. Capital: Athens. Greece is still largely agricultural. Tobacco, cotton, fruit and wool are exported. Greece achieved independence from the Ottoman Empire in 1829. During the second half of the 19th century and the first half of the 20th century, it gradually added neighboring islands and territories, most with Greek-speaking populations. In World War II, Greece was first invaded by Italy (1940) and subsequently occupied by Germany (1941-44); fighting endured in a protracted civil war between supporters of the king and Communist rebels. Following the latter's defeat in 1949, Greece joined NATO in 1952. A military dictatorship, which in 1967 suspended many political liberties and forced the king to flee the country, lasted seven years. The 1974 democratic elections and a referendum created a parliamentary republic and abolished the monarchy. In 1981, Greece joined the EC (now the EU); it became the 12th member of the European Economic and Monetary Union in 2001.

RULERS:

John Capodistrias, 1827-1831
Othon (Otto of Bavaria) 1832-1862
George I, 1863-1913
Constantine I, 1913-1923
George II, 1922-1923, 1935-1947
Paul I, 1947-1964
Constantine II, 1964-1973

MONETARY SYSTEM:

1 Phoenix = 100 Lepta, 1828-31
1 Drachma = 100 Lepta, 1841-2001
1 Euro = 100 Cents, 2002-

REGIONAL

ΠΡΟΗΟΜΙΟΥΧΟΣ ΤΡΑΠΕΖΑ ΗΠΕΙΡΟΘΕΣΣΑΛΙΑΣ

PRIVILEGED BANK OF EPIRUS AND THESSALY

1882 ISSUE

	Good	Fine	XF
S101 10 Drachmai 31.3.1882. Blue and brown. Woman holding torch, angel below at left, arms at right. Back: Head at left and right. Printer: G. Richard, Paris.	750.	1500.	—
S102 25 Drachmai 31.3.1882. Blue and brown. Two cherubs supporting arms at left, reclining woman with lion at lower right. Back: Three allegorical figures at center. Printer: G. Richard, Paris. Rare.	—	—	—
S103 100 Drachmai 31.3.1882. Lilac and brown. Arms and allegorical figure at left. Back: Allegory of Justice and Law. Printer: G. Richard, Paris. Rare.	—	—	—

1885 ISSUE

	Good	Fine	XF
S104 1 Drachma 21.12.1885. Brown on gray underprint. Portrait Alexander of Macedon at left. Back: Green. Arms at center. Printer: BWC.	100.	200.	400.
S105 2 Drachmai 21.12.1885. Brown on blue and tan underprint. Portrait Alexander of Macedon at left, portrait helmeted Athena at right. Back: Green. Arms at center. Printer: BWC.	100.	200.	400.
S106 1 Drachma 21.12.1885 (issued 1897). Black on blue and brown underprint. Portrait helmeted Athena at left. Back: Green. Arms at center. Printer: BWC.	100.	200.	400.
S107 2 Drachmai 21.12.1885 (issued 1897). Black on blue and brown underprint. Hermes at right. Back: Green. Arms at center. Printer: BWC.	100.	200.	400.

NOTE: For notes similar to #S104-S107 but with brown backs see #S145-S148; with blue backs see Vol. II, #35-38.

1887-88 ISSUE

	Good	Fine	XF
S108 25 Drachmai 1.3.1887. Brown, green and blue. Arms at left, allegorical figures at right. Printer: G. Richard, Paris. Rare.	—	—	—
S109 100 Drachmai 2.1.1888. Blue, brown and black. Supported arms at upper left, seated allegorical woman at lower right. Back: Two reclining figures at center. Printer: G. Richard, Paris. Rare.	—	—	—

ΙΟΝΙΚΗ ΤΡΑΠΕΖΑ

IONIAN BANK

ΚΕΦΑΛΛΗΝΙΑ CEPHALONIA BRANCH

1840'S ISSUE

	Good	Fine	XF
S110 10 Shillings 184x. Ionian Bank arms with English and Greek flags at top center. Printer: PB&P. Specimen. Rare.	—	—	—
S111 1 Pound 184x. Ionian Bank arms with English and Greek flags at top center. Printer: PB&P. Specimen. Rare.	—	—	—
S112 2 Pounds 184x. Ionian Bank arms with English and Greek flags at top center. Printer: PB&P. Specimen. Rare.	—	—	—
S113 5 Pounds 184x. Ionian Bank arms with English and Greek flags at top center. Printer: PB&P. Specimen. Rare.	—	—	—

1843-44 ISSUE

	Good	Fine	XF
S114 2 Colonata 1843-69. Ionian Bank arms with English and Greek flags at top center. Printer: PBC. Rare.	—	—	—
S115 5 Colonata 1844-69. Ionian Bank arms with English and Greek flags at top center. Back: Blue. Printer: PBC. Rare.	—	—	—
S119 100 Colonata 1844-69. Ionian Bank arms with English and Greek flags at top center. Printer: PBC. Rare.	—	—	—

NOTE: Additional denominations require confirmation.

KERKYRA (CORFU) BRANCH

1840'S ISSUE

	Good	Fine	XF
S120 10 Shillings 184x. Ionian Bank arms with English and Greek flags at top center. Printer: PB&P. Specimen. Rare.	—	—	—
S121 1 Pound 184x. Ionian Bank arms with English and Greek flags at top center. Printer: PB&P. Specimen. Rare.	—	—	—
S122 2 Pounds 184x. Ionian Bank arms with English and Greek flags at top center. Printer: PB&P. Specimen. Rare.	—	—	—
S123 5 Pounds 184x. Ionian Bank arms with English and Greek flags at top center. Printer: PB&P. Specimen. Rare.	—	—	—

1843-44 ISSUE

	Good	Fine	XF
S124 2 Colonata 1843-69. Ionian Bank arms with English and Greek flags at top center. Printer: PBC. Rare.	—	—	—
S125 5 Colonata 1844-69. Ionian Bank arms with English and Greek flags at top center. Printer: PBC. Rare.	—	—	—
S129 100 Colonata 1844-69. Ionian Bank arms with English and Greek flags at top center. Printer: PBC. Rare.	—	—	—

NOTE: Additional denominations require confirmation.

ZANTE BRANCH

1840'S ISSUE

	Good	Fine	XF
S130 10 Shillings 184x. Ionian Bank arms with English and Greek flags at top center. Printer: PB&P. Specimen. Rare.	—	—	—
S131 1 Pound 184x. Ionian Bank arms with English and Greek flags at top center. Printer: PB&P. Specimen. Rare.	—	—	—
S132 2 Pounds 184x. Ionian Bank arms with English and Greek flags at top center. Printer: PB&P. Specimen. Rare.	—	—	—
S133 5 Pounds 184x. Ionian Bank arms with English and Greek flags at top center. Printer: PB&P. Specimen. Rare.	—	—	—

1843-44 ISSUE

	Good	Fine	XF
S134 2 Colonata 1843-69. Ionian Bank arms with English and Greek flags at top center. Printer: PBC. Rare.	—	—	—
S135 5 Colonata 1844-69. Ionian Bank arms with English and Greek flags at top center. Printer: PBC. Rare.	—	—	—
S139 100 Colonata 1844-69. Ionian Bank arms with English and Greek flags at top center. Printer: PBC. Rare.	—	—	—

NOTE: Additional denominations require confirmation.

W/OUT BRANCH NAME

1876 ISSUE

	Good	Fine	XF
S140 10 New Drachmai 1876-83. Black. Arms of King George at upper left, Ionian Bank arms with English and Greek flags at upper center. Back: Brown and red. Bank name in French. Printer: PBC. Rare.	—	—	—
S141 25 New Drachmai 1876-83. Black on green underprint. Arms of King George at upper left, Ionian Bank arms with English and Greek flags at upper center. Back: Blue. Bank name in French. Printer: PBC. Rare.	—	—	—
S142 100 New Drachmai 1876-83. Black on blue underprint. Arms of King George at upper left, Ionian Bank arms with English and Greek flags at upper center. Back: Green. Bank name in French. Printer: PBC. Rare.	—	—	—

ΙΟΝΙΚΗ ΤΡΑΠΕΖΑ LIMITED

IONIAN BANK LIMITED

1883-1907 ISSUE

		Good	Fine	XF
S143	**10 New Drachmai** 1884-1907. Black. Arms of King George at upper left, Ionian Bank arms with English and Greek flags at upper center. Similar to #S140 except for addition of *LIMITED* and [Greek] BAS. *EPITROPOS* (King's Comm Back: Brown and red. Bank name in French.			
	a. Issue A. 27.12.1884. Printer: PBC. Rare.	—	—	—
	b. Issue B. 3.9.1895-10.9.1907. Printer: W&S. Rare.	—	—	—
S144	**25 New Drachmai** 1883. Black on green underprint. Arms of King George at upper left, Ionian Bank arms with English and Greek flags at upper center. Similar to #S141 except for addition of *LIMITED* and [Greek] BAS. *EPITROPOS* (King's Comm Back: Blue. Bank name in French. Rare.	—	—	—

1885 ISSUE

		Good	Fine	XF
S145	**1 Drachma** 21.12.1885. Black on blue and tan underprint. Portrait Alexander of Macedon at left. Back: Brown. Arms at center. Printer: BWC.	45.00	100.	225.

		Good	Fine	XF
S146	**2 Drachmai** 21.12.1885. Black on blue and tan underprint. Portrait Alexander of Macedon at left, portrait helmeted Athena at right. Back: Brown. Arms at center. Printer: BWC.	45.00	125.	250.

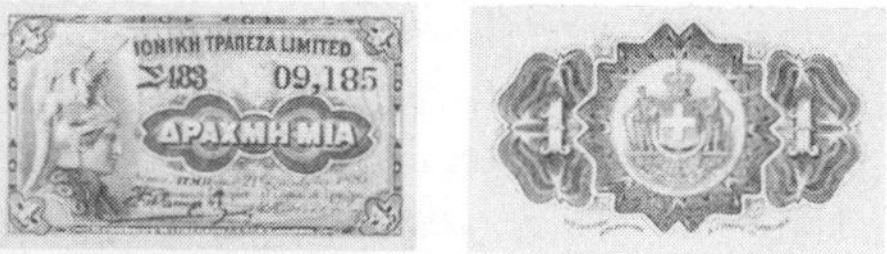

		Good	Fine	XF
S147	**1 Drachma** 21.12.1885 (issued 1887). Black on blue and brown underprint. Portrait helmeted Athena at left. Back: Brown. Arms at center. Printer: BWC.	25.00	75.00	150.

		Good	Fine	XF
S148	**2 Drachmai** 21.12.1885 (issued 1887). Black on blue and brown underprint. Hermes at right. Back: Brown. Arms at center. Printer: BWC.	30.00	100.	200.

NOTE: For notes similar to #S145-S148 but with green backs see #S104-S107; with blue backs see Vol. II, #34 and 35, #40 and 41, and also #301 and 302.

1888 ISSUE

		Good	Fine	XF
S149	**25 Drachmai** 23.3.1889; 22.10.1894; 30.11.1898. Gray on yellow underprint. Arms of King George at upper left, bank arms with flags at upper center. Athena at upper right. Back: Green. Printer: W&S.	650.	1300.	2600.
S150	**100 Drachmai** 1888-99. Black on blue-green underprint. Arms of King George at upper left, bank arms with flags at upper center. Back: Green. Printer: PBC.	800.	1600.	3200.

1900 ISSUE

		Good	Fine	XF
S151	**25 Drachmai** 1900-20. Blue-black on light orange underprint. Arms of King George at upper left, bank arms with flags at upper center. Athena at upper right. Like #S149. Back: Green. Printer: W&S.	350.	700.	1400.

		Good	Fine	XF
S152	**100 Drachmai** 18.1.1903-1.3.1919. Black on blue underprint. Arms of King George at upper left, bank arms with flags at upper center. Like #S150. Back: Green. Printer: PBC.	450.	900.	180.

ΤΡΑΠΕΖΑ ΚΡΗΤΗΣ

BANK OF CRETE

1900-26 ISSUE

		Good	Fine	XF
S153	**25 Drachmai** 2.1.1909-26.9.1915. Black on orange and green underprint. Arms at upper center, portrait King George at upper right. Sitting figure from ancient coin at left. Back: Green. Printer: BWC.	60.00	125.	250.

		Good	Fine	XF
S154	**100 Drachmai**			
	1900-17. Black on orange and green underprint. Arms at upper center, portrait King George at upper right. Head from ancient coin at left. Back: Blue. Printer: BWC.			
	a. 2.1.1900; 25.1.1901.	175.	350.	700.
	b. 26.4.1914; 26.3.1915; 9.9.1916; 3.3.1917.	45.00	100.	200.

Partisan - WWII

ΠΟΛΙΤΙΚΗ ΕΠΙΤΡΟΠΗ ΕΘΝΙΚΗΣ ΑΠΕΛΕΥΘΕΡΩΣΗΣ

Civilian Committee of National Liberation

1944 Issue

		VG	VF	UNC
S161	**5 Oka**			
	5.6.1944. Black on green and yellow underprint. Burning houses at left, standing soldier with rifle at center, and farmers at right. Back: Aqua and black. Hand stamp (if any).			
	a. Handwritten serial #.	30.00	60.00	100.
	b. Stamped serial #.	30.00	50.00	100.
	r. Remainder without serial #.	—	Unc	125.
S162	**25 Oka**			
	5.6.1944. Black on green and yellow underprint. Burning houses at left, standing soldier with rifle at center, and farmers at right. Back: Aqua and black. Hand stamp (if any).			
	a. Handwritten serial #.	35.00	75.00	150.
	b. Stamped serial #.	35.00	75.00	150.
S163	**100 Oka**			
	5.6.1944. Black on green and yellow underprint. Burning houses at left, standing soldier with rifle at center, and farmers at right. Back: Aqua and black. Hand stamp (if any).			
	a. Handwritten serial #.	150.	300.	600.
	b. Stamped serial #.	150.	300.	600.
S164	**500 Oka**			
	5.6.1944. Black on green and yellow underprint. Burning houses at left, standing soldier with rifle at center, and farmers at right. Back: Aqua and black. Hand stamp (if any). (Not issued).			
	a. Handwritten serial #. Rare.	—	—	—
	x. Overprint: *ΑΝΑΜΝΗ Σ ΤΙΚΟΝ. (Souvenir Commemorative.)*	—	—	25.00

Italian Occupation - WWII

Cassa Mediterranea di Credito per la Grecia

1941 Issue

		VG	VF	UNC
M1	**5 Drachmai**			
	ND (1941). Green. Wheat at left. Back: Hermes at right.	2.00	12.50	40.00

		VG	VF	UNC
M2	**10 Drachmai**			
	ND (1941). Red-orange. Prow of ancient ship at left. Back: Hermes at right.	2.00	15.00	50.00
M3	**50 Drachmai**			
	ND (1941). Blue. Wheat at left. Back: Hermes at right.	2.00	15.00	65.00
M4	**100 Drachmai**			
	ND (1941). Brown on orange underprint. Prow of ship at left. Back: Hermes at right.	2.50	17.50	70.00

		VG	VF	UNC
M5	**500 Drachmai**			
	ND (1941). Dark green. Michaelangelo's *David* at left.	5.00	30.00	175.
M6	**1000 Drachmai**			
	ND (1941). Light brown. Michaelangelo's *David* at left.	7.00	20.00	100.
M7	**5000 Drachmai**			
	ND (1941). Lilac. Michaelangelo's *David* at left.	10.00	50.00	250.

		VG	VF	UNC
M8	**10,000 Drachmai**			
	ND (1941). Gray. Michaelangelo's *David* at left.	25.00	75.00	350.
M9	**20,000 Drachmai**			
	ND (1941). Blue. Michaelangelo's *David* at left.	25.00	125.	450.

Ionian Islands

Biglietto a Corso Legale per le Isole Jonie

1941 ND Issue

#M11-M18 issued for the Ionian Islands.

		VG	VF	UNC
M11	**1 Drachma**			
	ND (1941). Dark green. Back: Tan underprint.	1.50	10.00	40.00

		VG	VF	UNC
M12	**5 Drachmai**			
	ND (1941). Red. Alexander at left. Back: Ancient picture at center.	5.00	15.00	60.00
M13	**10 Drachmai**			
	ND (1941). Green. Alexander at left. Back: Ancient picture at center.	7.50	15.00	70.00
M14	**50 Drachmai**			
	ND (1941). Brown. Old man at left.	7.50	15.00	75.00

		VG	VF	UNC
M15	**100 Drachmai**			
	ND (1941). Blue. Old man at left.	7.50	15.00	75.00
M16	**500 Drachmai**			
	ND (1941). Lilac on blue underprint. Caesar head at left. Back: Ancient frieze of two horsemen.			
	a. Issued note.	15.00	50.00	150.
	b. Blue Imperial handstamp. Signature at left.	100.	500.	1000.
M17	**1000 Drachmai**			
	ND (1941). Brown. Caesar head at left. Back: Ancient frieze of two horsemen.			
	a. Issued note.	2.50	10.00	45.00
	b. Blue Imperial handstamp. Signature at left.	100.	500.	1000.

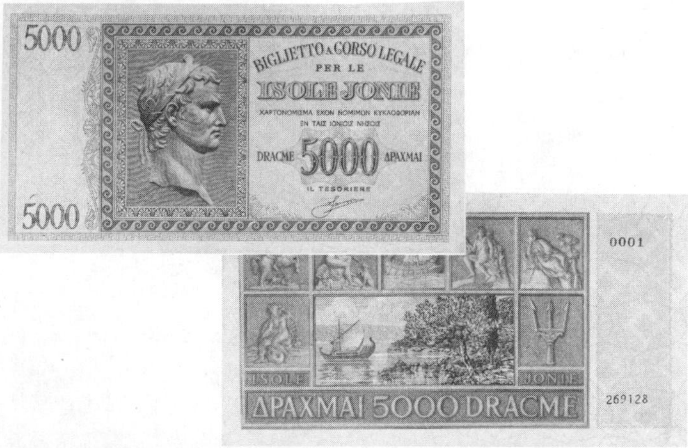

		VG	VF	UNC
M18	**5000 Drachmai**			
	ND (1941). Blue on gray underprint. Caesar head at left. Back: Ionian emblems and landscape at center.			
	a. Issued note.	15.00	75.00	250.
	b. Blue Imperial handstamp. Signature at left.	100.	500.	1000.

German Occupation - WWII

German Armed Forces

Auxiliary Payment Certificates

#M19-M22 issued for the German Armed Forces.

German Nazi (3 varieties), Salonika-Aegean and Greek handstamps on back of Germany #M32-M35.

		VG	VF	UNC
M19	**1 Pfennig**			
	ND. Blue. Stamped on Germany #M32.	4.00	20.00	50.00

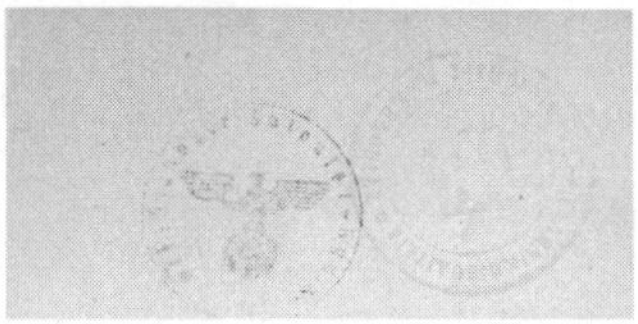

		VG	VF	UNC
M20	**5 Pfennig**			
	ND. Red. Stamped on Germany #M33.	4.00	20.00	50.00
M21	**10 Pfennig**			
	ND. Green. Stamped on Germany #M34.	4.00	20.00	50.00
M22	**50 Pfennig**			
	ND. Orange. Stamped on Germany #M35.	125.	450.	900.

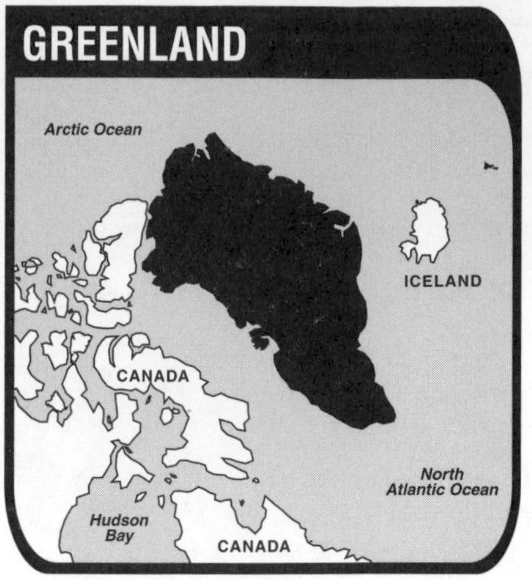

Greenland, an integral part of the Danish realm, is a huge island situated between the North Atlantic Ocean and the Polar Sea, almost entirely within the Artic Circle. It has an area of 2.166 million sq. km. and a population of 57,564. Capital: Nuuk (Godthab). Greenland is the world's only source of natural cryolite, a fluoride of sodium and aluminum important in making aluminum. Fish products and minerals are exported.

Greenland, the world's largest island, is about 81% ice-capped. Vikings reached the island in the 10th century from Iceland; Danish colonization began in the 18th century, and Greenland was made an integral part of Denmark in 1953. It joined the European Community (now the EU) with Denmark in 1973, but withdrew in 1985 over a dispute centered on stringent fishing quotas. Greenland was granted self-government in 1979 by the Danish parliament; the law went into effect the following year. Denmark continues to exercise control of Greenland's foreign affairs in consultation with Greenland's Home Rule Government.

RULERS:
Danish

MONETARY SYSTEM:
1 Rigsbankdaler = 96 Skilling to 1874
1 Krone = 48 Skilling
1 Krone = 100 Óre, 1874-

Military

Grønlands Administration

1940's Trade Certificates

#M1-M4 are perforated, narrow cardboard tokens with denomination and *Grl. Adm.* Issued for American troops stationed in Greenland during World War II.

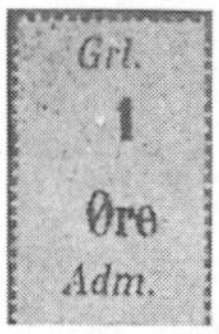

		VG	VF	UNC
M1	**1 Øre**			
	ND. Brown cardboard.	25.00	55.00	140.
M2	**2 Øre**			
	ND. Yellow cardboard.	25.00	55.00	140.
M3	**5 Øre**			
	ND. Violet cardboard.	50.00	150.	500.
M4	**10 Øre**			
	ND. White cardboard.	60.00	170.	400.

1941 ND Trade Certificates

		VG	VF	UNC
M5	**1 Skilling**			
	ND (1941). Red. Embossed circular seal with crown over *GRONLANDS ADMINISTRATION* at left. Like #M6.	250.	500.	850.

		VG	VF	UNC
M6	**5 Skilling**			
	ND (1941). Blue. Embossed circular seal with crown over *GRONLANDS ADMINISTRATION* at left.	275.	550.	1100.
M7	**20 Skilling**			
	ND (1941). Green. Embossed circular seal with crown over *GRONLANDS ADMINISTRATION* at left. Like #M6.			
	a. Issued note.	25.00	65.00	200.
	s. Specimen.	—	—	200.

Note: A quantity of #M7 was made available during 1981-83, and it has since been absorbed into the marketplace.

1942 ND Trade Certificates

		VG	VF	UNC
M8	**1 Skilling** ND (1942). Red. Black oval handstamp: *GRONLANDS ADMINISTRATION* around crown at left. Like #M10.	—	—	20.00
M9	**5 Skilling** ND (1942). Blue. Black oval handstamp: *GRONLANDS ADMINISTRATION* around crown at left. Like #M10.	—	—	20.00

		VG	VF	UNC
M10	**20 Skilling** ND (1942). Green. Black oval handstamp: *GRONLANDS ADMINISTRATION* around crown at left.			
	a. Issued note.	—	—	20.00
	s. Specimen.	—	—	500.

Note: A quantity of #M8-M10 was made available in 1981-83, and they have since been absorbed into the marketplace.

WWII Emergency Issue

		VG	VF	UNC
M11	**50 Kroner** July 1944. Egedesmunde.	5000.	14,000.	—

GRENADA

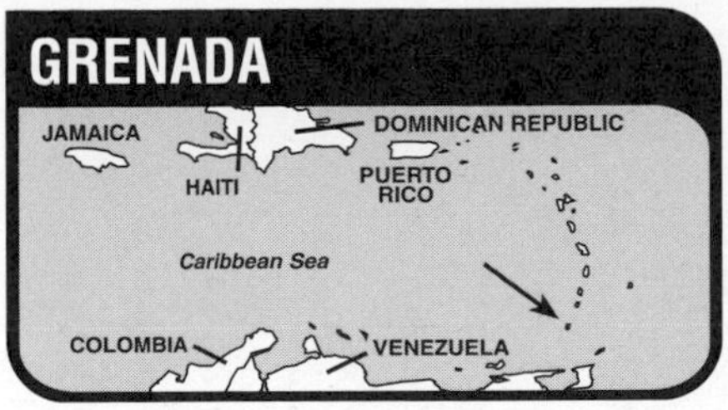

Grenada, located in the Windward islands of the Caribbean Sea 145 km. north of Trinidad, has (with Carriacou and Petit Martinique) an area of 344 sq. km. and a population of 90,343. Capital: St. George's. Carib Indians inhabited Grenada when COLUMBUS discovered the island in 1498, but it remained uncolonized for more than a century. The French settled Grenada in the 17th century, established sugar estates, and imported large numbers of African slaves. Britain took the island in 1762 and vigorously expanded sugar production. In the 19th century, cacao eventually surpassed sugar as the main export crop; in the 20th century, nutmeg became the leading export. In 1967, Britain gave Grenada autonomy over its internal affairs. Full independence was attained in 1974, making Grenada one of the smallest independent countries in the Western Hemisphere. Grenada was seized by a Marxist military council on 19 October 1983. Six days later the island was invaded by US forces and those of six other Caribbean nations, which quickly captured the ringleaders and their hundreds of Cuban advisers. Free elections were reinstituted the following year and have continued since that time. Hurricane Ivan struck Grenada in September of 2004 causing severe damage.

RULERS:

British

MONETARY SYSTEM:

1 Shilling = 12 Pence
1 Pound = 20 Shillings to 1970
1 Dollar = 100 Cents
1 British West Indies Dollar = 4 Shillings-2 Pence

Banks

Barclays Bank (Dominion, Colonial and Overseas)

1926 Provisional Issue

		Good	Fine	XF
S106	**5 Dollars** 1.9.1926. Black on pink and blue-green underprint. Overprint: *ISSUED AT GRENADA BRANCH* twice on face on Barbados #S101. Printer: BWC. Rare.	—	—	—

1937 Provisional Issue

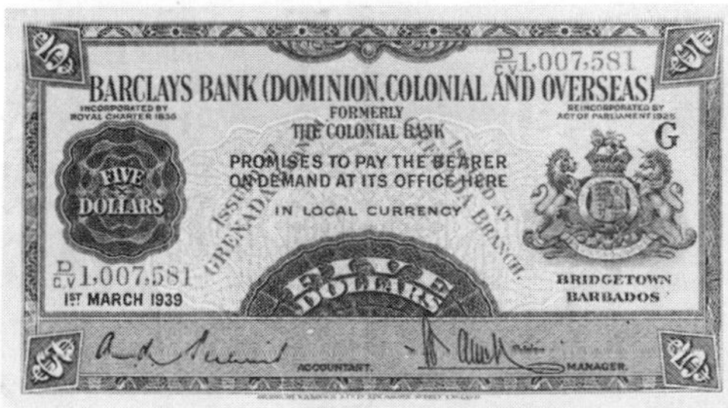

		Good	Fine	XF
S107	**5 Dollars** 1937-40. Purple on multicolor underprint. Royal arms at right. Overprint: *ISSUED AT GRENADA BRANCH* twice on face on Barbados #S111. Printer: BWC.			
	a. 1.5.1937.	375.	750.	1500.
	b. 1.3.1939.	350.	700.	1400.
	c. 1.3.1940.	225.	600.	1250.

1941 Provisional Issue

		Good	Fine	XF
S108	**5 Dollars** 1.2.1941. Purple on multicolor underprint. Supported royal arms at right. Overprint: On Trinidad #S102b.	225.	600.	1250.

Colonial Bank

1880s Provisional Issue

S111 5 Dollars	Good	Fine	XF
ND (ca. 1882-1912). Brown. Supported royal arms at upper center. Overprint: *ISSUED AT GRENADA BRANCH* (twice) on Barbados #S141. Specimen.	—	Unc	5500.

1925 Provisional Issue

S113 5 Dollars	Good	Fine	XF
1.1.1925. Black on pink underprint. Supported royal arms at upper center. Overprint: *ISSUED AT GRENADA BRANCH* (twice) and Large *G* at upper right on Barbados #S151.			
a. Issued note. Rare.	—	—	—
s. Specimen.	—	Unc	2250.

Royal Bank of Canada

1909 Provisional Issue

S116 5 Dollars = 1 Pound 10 Pence	Good	Fine	XF
2.1.1909. Black on green and yellow underprint. Overprint: Blue *GRENADA* twice vertically, vertical *PAYABLE AT ST. GEORGE'S GRENADA* at center. Overprint on Canada #S1371. Specimen.	—	Unc	2250.

1920 Issue

S117 5 Dollars = 1 Pound 10 Pence	Good	Fine	XF
2.1.1920. Black on green underprint. Steamship at center. Back: Green. Printer: ABNC. Large size. Specimen.			
p. Proof.	—	Unc	750.
s. Specimen.	—	Unc	2000.

1938 Issue

S118 5 Dollars = 1 Pound 10 Pence	Good	Fine	XF
3.1.1938. Black on green underprint. Steamship at center. Similar to #S117 but reduced size. Back: Green. Printer: CBNC.			
a. Issued note.	250.	700.	1400.
p. Proof.	—	Unc	750.

NOTE: For later issues see East Caribbean states Vol. II and III.

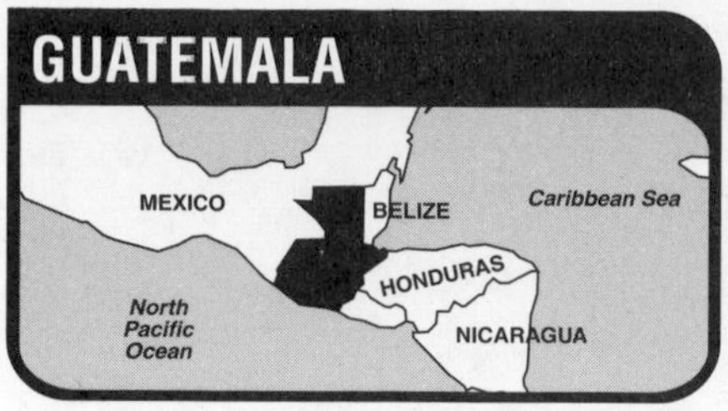

The Republic of Guatemala, the northernmost of the five Central American republics, has an area of 108,890 sq. km. and a population of 13 million. Capital: Guatemala City. The economy of Guatemala is heavily dependent on resources which are being developed. Coffee, cotton and bananas are exported.

The Mayan civilization flourished in Guatemala and surrounding regions during the first millennium A.D. After almost three centuries as a Spanish colony, Guatemala won its independence in 1821. During the second half of the 20th century, it experienced a variety of military and civilian governments, as well as a 36-year guerrilla war. In 1996, the government signed a peace agreement formally ending the conflict, which had left more than 100,000 people dead and had created, by some estimates, some 1 million refugees.

MONETARY SYSTEM:

1 Peso = 100 Centavos to 1924
1 Quetzal = 100 Centavos, 1924-

Availability of Early Bank Issues

A rising inflation from about 1900 to 1924 created a need for more and more bank notes to be listed. Their value decreased, higher denominations were introduced, and by the time of the 1924 currency reform it took 60 old pesos to equal 1 new quetzal. The Caja Reguladora reissued notes of 20 Pesos or more into the new system but all lower peso values ceased to circulate. Many notes of these earlier banks are still readily available today.

BANKS:

GOVERNMENT

Banks

Banco Agricola Hipotecario

1895-1926 Issue

S101 1 Peso	Good	Fine	XF
1895-1920. Black on pink and blue underprint. Seated woman with caduceus at left, woman in winged chariot drawn by lions at center, girls with sheep and cow at right. Back: Red. Woman at center. Printer: W&S.			
a. 14.4.1895-26.3.1900.	30.00	90.00	225.
b. 26.3.1920; 30.6.1920.	15.00	40.00	100.
c1. Black overprint: *PAGADERO EN QUEZALTENANGO* in box on back. Date partially printed and filled in by hand. __de__de 189x.	—	—	—
c2. Like c1, but with printed date. 30.4.1895.	60.00	300.	650.
d1. *QUEZALTENANGO* lined out and overprint: *GUATEMALA* on bottom of overprint in box on back. Date partially overprint: *30... ABRIL... 5.*	—	—	—
d2. Date entirely printed 6.4.1895; 30.4.1895.	—	—	—

S102 5 Pesos	Good	Fine	XF
1895-1920. Black on red-orange and violet underprint. Woman with winged cap at left, woman in winged chariot drawn by lions at center, man with staff and seated woman at right. Back: Red. Woman at center. Printer: W&S.			
a. Date partially overprint: *5... ABRIL... 5.*	—	—	—
b. Printed date. 5.4.1895; 2.7.1895.	50.00	150.	600.
c. 1.8.1914; 1.6.1917; 30.6.1920.	20.00	60.00	250.
d. Overprint in box like #S101c. 5.4.1895.	—	—	—
e. Altered overprint like #S101d. 2.7.1895.	25.00	80.00	350.

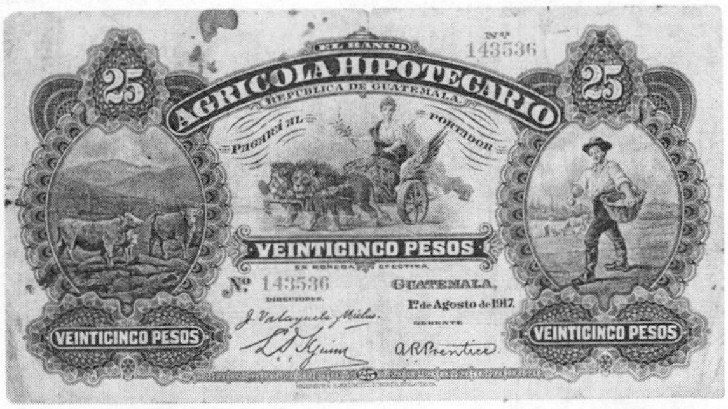

S103 25 Pesos

1.8.1917; 11.1.1923. Black on red and violet underprint. Cattle at left, woman in winged chariot drawn by lions at center, farmer sowing at right. Back: Red. Woman at center. Printer: W&S.

	Good	Fine	XF
	30.00	60.00	300.

S104 50 Pesos

1917-26. Black on red, blue and olive underprint. Woman feeding bird ("Paloma") at center. Back: Orange. Liberty at center. Printer: ABNC.

	Good	Fine	XF
a. 1.8.1917.	50.00	175.	300.
b. Caja Reguladora reissue, 2 sets of serial # (red and blue). 11.2.1924; 4.2.1926.	100.	250.	650.
p. Proof.	—	Unc	350.

S105 100 Pesos

1892-1926. Black on pink and blue underprint. Woman standing with pedestal, anchor and beehive at left, woman in winged chariot drawn by lions at center, farmer plowing at right. Back: Red. Woman at center. Printer: W&S.

	Good	Fine	XF
a. Handwritten signature. 8.5.1892-31.8.1915.	125.	350.	800.
b. Printed signature. 1.6.1917; 11.2.1924.	100.	275.	650.
c. Overprint in box like #S101c.	—	—	—
d. Date partially filled in by hand. *5... Marzo... 96.*	—	—	—
e. Caja Reguladora reissue, 2 sets of serial #. 15.2.1926.	100.	300.	750.

S106 500 Pesos

1.6.1917. Black on multicolor underprint. Man with trident in chariot drawn by three horses at left. Woman in winged chariot drawn by lions at lower right. Back: Red. Woman at center. Printer: W&S.

	Good	Fine	XF
a. Issued note. Rare.	300.	600.	900.
s. Specimen.	—	Unc	1200.

Banco Americano de Guatemala

1895-1926 Issues

S111 1 Peso

1895-1920. Black on gray underprint. Two seated women with symbols of Agriculture and Commerce, and arms af Guatemala at left, arms of the United States at right. Series A. Back: Red-orange. Scene of three mountains overlooking village and train at center. Printer: ABNC.

	Good	Fine	XF
a. 29.8.1895-30.4.1902.	30.00	60.00	100.
b. 2.11.1914-15.6.1920.	15.00	30.00	60.00
p. Proof.	—	Unc	125.
s. Specimen.	—	Unc	125.

S112 5 Pesos

1897-1920. Black on gray underprint. Two seated women with symbols of Agriculture and Commerce, and arms af Guatemala at left, arms of the United States at right. Series B. Back: Brown. Scene of three mountains overlooking village and train at center. Printer: ABNC.

	Good	Fine	XF
a. 23.1.1897; 5.3.1897; 30.4.1902.	50.00	100.	200.
b. 2.11.1914-15.6.1920.	30.00	60.00	120.
s. Specimen.	—	Unc	125.

S113 25 Pesos

2.11.1914-25.6.1918. Black on blue underprint. Two seated women with symbols of Agriculture and Commerce, and arms af Guatemala at left, arms of the United States at right. Series C. Back: Blue. Scene of three mountains overlooking village and train at center. Printer: ABNC.

	Good	Fine	XF
	40.00	125.	200.

S114 100 Pesos

1913-25. Black on gray and orange underprint. Two seated women with symbols of Agriculture and Commerce, and arms af Guatemala at left, arms of the United States at right. Series D. Back: Brown. Scene of three mountains overlooking village and train at center. Printer: ABNC.

	Good	Fine	XF
a. 19.3.1913; 2.11.1914; 4.8.1915; 28.3.1922; 26.1.1923; 29.10.1924.	175.	250.	425.
b. Caja Reguladora reissue, 2 sets of red serial #. 14.1.1925	200.	350.	600.
p. Proof.	—	Unc	350.
s. Specimen.	—	Unc	200.

S115 500 Pesos

1895-1925. Black on orange underprint. Two seated women with symbols of Agriculture and Commerce, and arms af Guatemala at left, arms of the United States at right. Series E. Back: Orange. Scene of three mountains overlooking village and train at center. Printer: ABNC.

	Good	Fine	XF
a. 11.10.1895. Handwritten date at right.	225.	350.	650.
b. Date at right. 22.10.1917; 27.3.1920; 28.3.1922; 11.8.1922.	125.	275.	500.
c. Date at center. 26.1.1923; 14.1.1925.	125.	275.	500.
d. Caja Reguladora reissue, 2 sets of red serial #. ND.	200.	425.	650.
p. Proof.	—	Unc	350.
s. Specimen.	—	Unc	500.

S116 1 Peso

26.1.1923. Black on gray underprint. Two seated women with symbols of Agriculture and Commerce, and arms af Guatemala at left, arms of the United States at right. Series C. Similar to #S111. Back: Red-orange. Scene of three mountains overlooking village and train at center. Printer: W&S.

	Good	Fine	XF
a. Issued note.	20.00	35.00	75.00
s. Specimen.	—	Unc	250.

S117 5 Pesos

22.5.1919; 15.5.1923. Black on gray underprint. Two seated women with symbols of Agriculture and Commerce, and arms af Guatemala at left, arms of the United States at right. Series B; C. Similar to #S112. Back: Brown. Scene of three mountains overlooking village and train at center. Printer: W&S.

	Good	Fine	XF
a. Issued note.	30.00	75.00	125.
s. Specimen.	—	Unc	250.

S118 25 Pesos

25.6.1918; 22.5.1919; 15.5.1923. Black on blue underprint. Two seated women with symbols of Agriculture and Commerce, and arms af Guatemala at left, arms of the United States at right. Series B; C. Similar to #S113. Back: Blue. Scene of three mountains overlooking village and train at center. Printer: W&S.

	Good	Fine	XF
a. Issued note.	40.00	80.00	200.
s. Specimen.	—	Unc	300.

S119 100 Pesos

22.5.1919-14.1.1925. Black on light brown underprint. Two seated women with symbols of Agriculture and Commerce, and arms af Guatemala at left, arms of the United States at right. Series B; C. Similar to #S114. Back: Brown. Scene of three mountains overlooking village and train at center. Printer: W&S.

	Good	Fine	XF
a. Issued note.	75.00	200.	325.
s. Specimen.	—	Unc	350.

S120 500 Pesos

4.2.1926; 15.2.1926. Black on orange underprint. Two seated women with symbols of Agriculture and Commerce, and arms af Guatemala at left, arms of the United States at right. Series C. Similar to #S115. Back: Orange. Scene of three mountains overlooking village and train at center. Printer: W&S. Caja Reguladora reissue, 2 sets of serial # (red and black).

	Good	Fine	XF
a. Issued note.	225.	450.	800.
s. Specimen.	—	Unc	600.

BANCO COLOMBIANO

1879-1901 ISSUE

S121 1 Peso

1879-1900. Black on green underprint. Standing soldier in armor with shield and spear with Liberty cap at left, small arms of Guatemala at center left and of Colombia at center right. Ox-drawn cart at top center. Back: Green. Printer: BWC.

	Good	Fine	XF
a. 17.10.1879. Small black serial #.	—	—	—
b. 5.4.1900; 17.4.1900. Large black serial #.	40.00	75.00	250.

S122 5 Pesos

1884-1901. Black on reddish brown underprint. Standing soldier in armor with shield and spear with Liberty cap at left, small arms of Guatemala at center left and of Colombia at center right. Cactus plants at top center. Back: Red-brown. Printer: BWC.

	Good	Fine	XF
a. Black serial #. 16.5.1884; 16.3.1887.	—	—	—
b. Red serial #. 19.9.1901; 21.9.1901; 23.9.1901.	75.00	275.	450.

S123 10 Pesos

1887; 1901. Black on blue underprint. Standing soldier in armor with shield and spear with Liberty cap at left, small arms of Guatemala at center left and of Colombia at center right. Boat loading at top center. Back: Blue. Printer: BWC.

	Good	Fine	XF
a. 23.4.1887; 30.4.1887. Handsigned. Black serial #.	—	—	—
b. 24.9.1901. Printed signature. Red serial #.	95.00	275.	600.

S124 20 Pesos

1890; 1901. Black on gold underprint. Standing soldier in armor with shield and spear with Liberty cap at left, small arms of Guatemala at center left and of Colombia at center right. Farm work scene at top center. Back: Gold. Printer: BWC.

	Good	Fine	XF
a. 12.7.1890. Handsigned. Black serial #.	—	—	—
b. 25.9.1901. Printed signature. Black serial #.	225.	650.	950.

S125 50 Pesos

1885-1901. Black on lilac underprint. Standing soldier in armor with shield and spear with Liberty cap at left, small arms of Guatemala at center left and of Colombia at center right. Harvest scene at top center. Back: Lilac. Printer: BWC.

	Good	Fine	XF
a. Red serial #. 4.3.1885; 14.3.1885.	400.	1050.	1850.
b. Black serial #. 25.4.1889; 16.6.1890.	325.	800.	1500.
c. Blue serial #. 25.9.1901.	250.	550.	1000.

S126 100 Pesos

	Good	Fine	XF
28.2.1889. Black on red underprint. Standing soldier in armor with shield and spear with Liberty cap at left, small arms of Guatemala at center left and of Colombia at center right. Cows at top center. Black serial #. Back: Red. Printer: BWC. Rare.	—	—	—

Banco Comercial de Guatemala

1890's Issue

S131 1 Peso

1892-94. Black on blue underprint. Woman with sheaf of wheat at left. Back: Brown and blue. Printer: IBNC.

	Good	Fine	XF
a. 1.11.1892; 15.11.1892; 15.2.1893. Hand dated.	—	—	—
b. 31.3.1894. Printed date.	—	—	—
p. Proof.	—	—	—

S132 5 Pesos

31.12.1892; 31.3.1894. Black on green underprint. Woman with sheaf of wheat at left. Back: Light brown and orange. Printer: IBNC.

	Good	Fine	XF
a. Issued note, hand dated.	—	—	—
p. Proof.	—	—	—

S133 25 Pesos

189x. Black on green underprint. Woman with sheaf of wheat at left. Similar to #S132 but larger size. Back: Light brown and orange. Printer: IBNC.

	Good	Fine	XF
p. Proof.	—	—	—
s. Specimen.	—	—	—

S134 100 Pesos

	Good	Fine	XF
189x. Black on green underprint. Woman with sheaf of wheat at left. Similar to #S132 but larger size. Back: Light brown and orange. Printer: IBNC. Proof.	—	—	—

S135 500 Pesos

	Good	Fine	XF
189x. Black on green underprint. Woman with sheaf of wheat at left. Similar to #S132 but larger size. Back: Light brown and orange. Printer: IBNC. Proof.	—	—	—

Banco de Guatemala

1895-1926 Issue

S141 1 Peso

1895-1915. Black on blue underprint. Woman's head at lower left and right corners; arms between steam passenger trains at upper center. Back: Brown. Printer: IBNC.

	Good	Fine	XF
a. Small red serial #. 15.7.1895-25.6.1900. Blue underprint in center, tan at sides.	40.00	100.	225.
b. Large red serial #. 27.5.1914; 1.8.1914; 1.3.1915. Blue and tan underprint in center, blue at left, tan at right.	25.00	75.00	225.

#S142 *Deleted.* See #S149.

S143 5 Pesos

1895-1915. Black on blue underprint. Woman's head at lower left and right corners; arms between steam passenger trains at upper center. Back: Red-orange. Printer: IBNC.

	Good	Fine	XF
a. 15.7.1895.	150.	275.	525.
b. Small red serial # 15.6.1899-1.2.1905.	100.	225.	425.
c. Large red serial # 17.4.1914; 4.2.1915; 4.4.1915.	75.00	175.	350.

#S144 *Deleted.* See #S149A.

S145 5 Pesos

	Good	Fine	XF
30.9.1922. Black on blue underprint. Train at left, ship at right of arms at center. Woman's head at lower corners. Back: Red-orange. Printer: W&S.	50.00	125.	300.

S146 25 Pesos

1905-25. Black on blue underprint. Woman's head at lower left and right corners; arms between steam passenger trains at upper center. Back: Olive. Printer: IBNC.

	Good	Fine	XF
a. 29.8.1905-1919. Blue underprint ends at red serial # which is in block type.	75.00	200.	325.
b. 1920-14.2.1926. Blue underprint very near *NO.* above regular ABNCo serial #.	75.00	200.	325.
c. Caja Reguladora reissue, 2 sets of red serial #. 14.1.1925.	90.00	225.	525.

S147 100 Pesos

1895-1926. Black on blue underprint. Woman's head at lower left and right corners; arms between steam passenger trains at upper center. Back: Brown. Printer: IBNC.

	Good	Fine	XF
a. Handwritten date. 30.8.1895.	150.	325.	—
b. 27.9.1895.	150.	325.	—
c. 21.6.1907-1919. Block serial #.	100.	250.	500.
d. 1920-14.2.1926. Standard ABNCo. serial #.	75.00	225.	475.
e. Caja Reguladora reissue, 2 sets of red serial #. 14.1.1925; 15.2.1926.	90.00	250.	475.

S148 500 Pesos

1915-26. Black on blue underprint. Woman's head at lower left and right corners; arms between steam passenger trains at upper center. Back: Green. Printer: IBNC.

	Good	Fine	XF
a. 5.8.1915-4.2.1926.	180.	350.	700.
b. Caja Reguladora reissue, red and black serial #. 4.2.1926.	225.	400.	750.
c. Caja Reguladora reissue, black serial #. 15.2.1926.	225.	400.	750.

QUEZALTENANGO

1895-1926 ISSUE

S149 1 Peso	Good	Fine	XF
1.9.1896-2.12.1897. Black on red-orange underprint. Woman's head at lower left and right corners; arms between steam passenger trains at upper center. Like #S141. With added text: *SUCURSAL QUEZALTENANGO* at top. Back: Red-orange. With added text: *SUCURSAL QUEZALTENANGO* at top.	200.	425.	800.

S149A 5 Pesos	Good	Fine	XF
10.9.1896; 17.9.1896; 29.9.1896. Black on red underprint. Woman's head at lower left and right corners; arms between steam passenger trains at upper center. Like #S143. With added text: *SUCURSAL QUEZALTENANGO* at top. Back: Brown. With added text: *SUCURSAL QUEZALTENANGO* at top.	350.	750.	1125.

S149B 25 Pesos			
17.9.1896. Black on blue underprint. Woman's head at lower left and right corners; arms between steam passenger trains at upper center. Like #S146. With added text: *SUCURSAL QUEZALTENANGO* at top. Back: Olive. With added text: *SUCURSAL QUEZALTENANGO* at top.	600.	1250.	1600.

S149C 100 Pesos			
29.9.1896. Black on blue underprint. Woman's head at lower left and right corners; arms between steam passenger trains at upper center. Like #S147. With added text: *SUCURSAL QUEZALTENANGO* at top. Back: Brown. With added text: *SUCURSAL QUEZALTENANGO* at top.	1100.	1750.	2500.

BANCO INTERNACIONAL DE GUATEMALA

1878-1926 ISSUE

S150 1 Peso	Good	Fine	XF
(ca.1878). Back: Green. Printer: PBC. Proof.	—	—	—

S150A 1 Peso			
(ca.1878). Back: Red. Printer: PBC. Proof.	—	—	—

S151 1 Peso			
1879-99. Black on gray underprint. Hand holding eight flags. Signature title: *JERENTE* below date. Back: Orange. Printer: NBNC.			
a. Handwritten date. 7.1.1879; 25.4.1879.	200.	400.	550.
b. Stamped date. 30.6.1879.	100.	200.	400.
c. Partially printed date. 5.7.1893-20.12.1899. Also with ABNC monogram.	25.00	40.00	75.00
p. Proof.	—	Unc	150.

S152 1 Peso			
1900-16. Black. Hand holding eight flags. Similar to #S151. Signature title: GERENTE below date. Series 2. Printer: W&S.			
a. 4 signatures. 30.6.1900.	30.00	55.00	125.
b. 3 signatures across. 2.10.1916/1914.	25.00	40.00	100.
s. Specimen.	—	Unc	150.

S153 1 Peso	Good	Fine	XF
1917-23. Black. Hand holding eight flags. Like #S151. Signature title: *JERENTE* below date. Series 2A. Printer: NBNC.			
a. 3 signatures across. 23.10.1917; 5.4.1920 (2 var.).	20.00	45.00	80.00
b. 3 signatures, 2 at left and 1 at right. 18.5.1923.	20.00	45.00	80.00

S154 5 Pesos	Good	Fine	XF
1885-1900. Black on gray underprint. Hand holding eight flags. Counterfoil at left margin. Uniface. Printer: NBNC.			
a. Without ABNC monogram. 6.4.1885.	125.	350.	650.
b. ABNC monogram added. 8.1.1900.	100.	300.	550.

S155 5 Pesos	Good	Fine	XF
1900-16. Black on gray underprint. Hand holding eight flags. Similar to #S154. Printed without counterfoil at left. Series 2. Back: Blue. Bank at center. Printer: W&S.			
a. 30.6.1900.	75.00	200.	550.
b. 14.3.1913; 2.10.1916/1914.	50.00	150.	450.

S156 5 Pesos			
1917-23. Black on gray underprint. Hand holding eight flags. Similar to #S155. Series 2A. Back: Blue. Steam passenger train at center. Printer: ABNC.			
a. Handwritten signature. 23.10.1917.	60.00	125.	200.
b. Printed signature. 5.4.1920; 18.5.1923.	50.00	100.	175.
s. Specimen.	—	Unc	250.

S156A 25 Pesos			
5.4.1895; 6.4.1895. Black on brown underprint. Hand holding eight flags. Counterfoil at left margin. Uniface. Printer: NBNC.	—	Unc	300.

S157 25 Pesos			
1900-16. Black on brown underprint. Hand holding eight flags. Series 2. Back: Brown. Bank at center. Printer: W&S.			
a. 30.9.1907/1900; 14.3.1913; 2.10.1916/1914.	75.00	150.	350.
p. Face and back proof. 30.9.1900.	—	Unc	150.

S158 25 Pesos			
1917-25. Black on brown underprint. Hand holding eight flags. Similar to #S157. Series 2A. Back: Brown. Steam passenger train at center. Printer: ABNC.			
a. Handwritten signature. 23.10.1917; 5.4.1920.	75.00	150.	350.
b. Printed signature. 28.1.1925.	60.00	125.	325.
s. Specimen.	—	Unc	300.

S159 100 Pesos			
18xx; 1909-14. Black on blue underprint. Hand holding eight flags. Back: Black, brown and blue. Printer: face, NBNC; back, ABNC.			
a. 1.9.1909; 2.10.1914.	75.00	200.	500.
p. Face and back proof. 18xx.	—	Unc	150.

S160 100 Pesos	Good	Fine	XF
1917-25. Black on blue underprint. Hand holding eight flags. Similar to #S159 but smaller size. Series 2A. Back: Black, brown and blue. Printer: ABNC.			
a. 23.10.1917-20.11.1922.	90.00	150.	425.
b. Caja Reguladora reissue, 2 sets of serial #, red and black. 14.1.1925.	75.00	125.	400.
p. Proof.	—	Unc	150.
s. Specimen.	—	Unc	300.

S160A 500 Pesos	Good	Fine	XF
18xx (ca.1890). Black on green underprint. Hand holding eight flags. Counterfoil at left margin. Back: Green. Steam passenger train at center. Printer: ABNC. Face and back proof.	—	Unc	200.

S161 500 Pesos			
1917-26. Black on green underprint. Hand holding eight flags. Similar to #S160A. Back: Green. Steam passenger train at center. Printer: ABNC.			
a. 23.10.1917; 5.4.1920; 25.10.1920.	250.	400.	750.
b. Caja Reguladora reissue, black and red serial #. 4.2.1926.	200.	400.	750.
c. Caja Reguladora reissue. 15.2.1926.	200.	—	—
s. Specimen.	—	Unc	450.

Banco Nacional de Guatemala

1874 ND Issue

		Good	Fine	XF
S166	**1 Real** ND. Red. Back: Green arms and black printed signature. Local printing. Rare.	—	—	—

		Good	Fine	XF
S167	**1 Peso** ND. Black on red underprint. Seated allegorical woman at lower left and at lower right, portrait Pres. J. Rufino Barrios at left, J. M. Samayoa at right. Back: Green. Printer: CCBB.	850.	1750.	3000.
S168	**5 Pesos** ND. Black. Portraits Pres. J. R. Barrios at left, J. M. Samayoa at right, allegorical women with sheaves at center.	—	—	—
S169	**10 Pesos** ND. Black. Portraits Pres. J. R. Barrios at top left, J. M. Samayoa at bottom left, standing allegorical woman with tablet inscribed: *30 DE JUNIO DE 1871* at center.	—	—	—
S170	**20 Pesos** ND. Black. Portraits Pres. J. R. Barrios and J. M. Samayoa at left and right center, allegorical woman at center.	—	—	—
S170A	**50 Pesos** ND. Black. Portraits Pres. J. R. Barrios and J. M. Samayoa at left and right center, Indians at lower left, seated allegorical woman at lower right.	—	—	—
S170B	**100 Pesos** ND. Black. Portraits Pres. J. R. Barrios at left, J. M. Samayoa at right, man with horse at center.	—	—	—

Banco de Occidente en Quezaltenango

1881-1926 Issue

		Good	Fine	XF
S171	**25 Centavos** 20.8.1881. Seated woman at left. Rare.	—	—	—
S172	**50 Centavos** 15.8.1900; 20.12.1916. Black on pink underprint. Woman at left, green quetzal bird at center, standing woman with basket on head with other women harvesting at right. Back: Green. Arms at center. Printer: W&S.	25.00	45.00	100.
S173	**1 Peso** 188x-1914. Black on green, red, blue, brown and orange underprint. Arms at left, seated woman with bales and caduceus ("Commerce") at center, quetzal at right. Back: Green. Printer: ABNC.			
	a. 188x; 1890/8x. Hand signature at left and right.	55.00	125.	300.
	b. Stamped date on printed line. 14.6.1899; 15.7.1899; 4.12.1899.	30.00	60.00	175.
	c. Printed date. 1.7.1909; 1.8.1914.	20.00	45.00	95.00
	p. Proof. 188x.	—	Unc	100.
	s. Specimen.	—	Unc	150.

#S174 *Deleted*. See #S184.

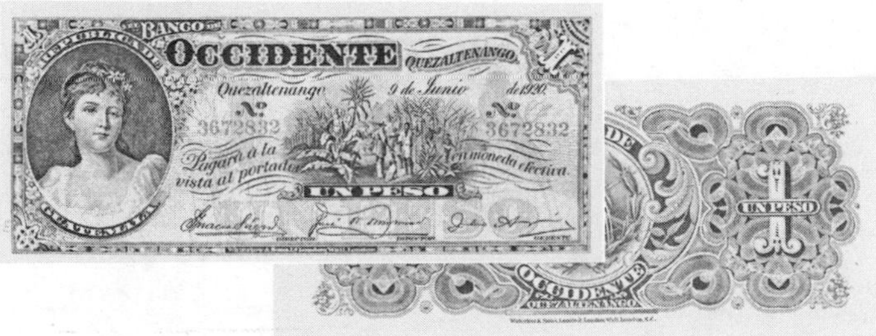

		Good	Fine	XF
S175	**1 Peso** 1900-21. Black. Portrait woman at left, sugar plantation at center. Back: Brown. Arms at center. Printer: W&S.			
	a. Green and lilac underprint. 15.8.1900.	40.00	95.00	250.
	b. Blue and green underprint. 20.12.1916; 9.6.1920; 2.11.1921.	25.00	55.00	150.

		Good	Fine	XF
S176	**5 Pesos** 1890-1919. Black on multicolor underprint. Arms at left, woman with cogwheel and bales at center, quetzal at right. Back: Green. Printer: ABNC.			
	a. Handwritten date. 5.3.1890/188x; 24.10.1890; 1.6.1898.	75.00	200.	350.
	b. Printed date. 14.2.1903-2.6.1919.	50.00	125.	300.
	s. Specimen.	—	Unc	250.

		Good	Fine	XF
S177	**5 Pesos** 15.1.1918; 19.6.1920. Black on gray and orange underprint. Woman at left, Mercury at center. Back: Orange. Arms at center. Printer: W&S.	30.00	100.	250.
S178	**5 Pesos** 2.11.1921. Black on gray and orange underprint. Woman at left, Mercury at center. Like #S177. Back: Green. Arms at center. Printer: W&S. Smaller size.	25.00	90.00	225.

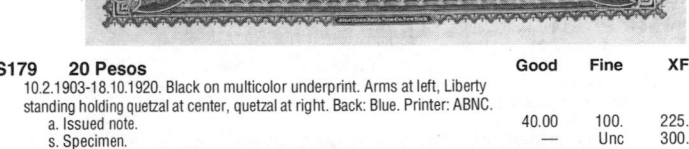

		Good	Fine	XF
S179	**20 Pesos** 10.2.1903-18.10.1920. Black on multicolor underprint. Arms at left, Liberty standing holding quetzal at center, quetzal at right. Back: Blue. Printer: ABNC.			
	a. Issued note.	40.00	100.	225.
	s. Specimen.	—	Unc	300.

		Good	Fine	XF
S180	**20 Pesos** 15.1.1918. Black on multicolor underprint. Arms at left, seated woman with caduceus at center. Back: Red. Arms at center. Printer: W&S.	75.00	250.	450.
S181	**20 Pesos** 1921-25. Black on multicolor underprint. Arms at left, seated woman with caduceus at center. Similar to #S180 but smaller size. Back: Blue. Arms at center. Printer: W&S.			
	a. 2.11.1921.	45.00	80.00	200.
	b. Caja Reguladora reissue, 2 sets of serial #. 14.1.1925 (old date lined out).	60.00	150.	325.

S182 100 Pesos	Good	Fine	XF
1890-1920. Black on multicolor underprint. Arms at left, coffee harvesting scene ("Coffee Plantation") at center, quetzal at right. Back: Red-orange. Printer: ABNC.			
a. Handwritten date and signature. 29.4.1890; 25.5.1893; 15.8.1900; 22.5.1902.	100.	300.	650.
b. Printed date and signature. 20.10.1902-18.10.1920.	75.00	225.	525.
s. Specimen.	—	Unc	450.

S183 100 Pesos			
1921-26. Black on multicolor underprint. Arms at left, coffee harvesting scene ("Coffee Plantation") at center, quetzal at right. Similar to #S182 but much smaller size. Printer: W&S.			
a. Printed date, red serial #. 2.11.1921.	40.00	125.	350.
b. Overprint date, black serial #. 10.10.1925; 18.1.1926.	30.00	90.00	300.
c. Caja Reguladora reissue, 2 sets of serial #. 15.2.1926.	75.00	150.	400.

Guatemala City

1800's Issue

S184 1 Peso	Good	Fine	XF
16.7.1894. Black on orange, blue, green and brown multicolor underprint. Arms at left, seated woman with bales and caduceus ("Commerce") at center, quetzal at right. Like #S173 but with branch name added at top. Back: Blue. Overprint: Red vertical *PAGADERO UNICAMENTE EN GUATEMALA* in box at center. Rare.	—	—	—
S185 5 Pesos			
18xx. Black on multicolor underprint. Arms at left, woman with cogwheel and bales at center, quetzal at right. Like #S176 but with branch name added at top. Back: Green. Specimen.	—	—	—
S186 20 Pesos			
18xx. Black on multicolor underprint. Arms at left, Liberty standing holding quetzal at center, quetzal at right. Like #S179 but with branch name added at top. Back: Orange. Proof.	—	—	—
S187 100 Pesos			
18xx. Black on multicolor underprint. Arms at left, coffee harvesting scene ("Coffee Plantation") at center, quetzal at right. Like #S182 but with branch name added at top. Back: Red-orange.			
p. Proof.	—	—	—
s. Specimen.	—	—	—

Comite Bancario de Guatemala

1899 Issue

S191 1 Peso	Good	Fine	XF
15.4.1899-3.8.1899. Black on gray underprint. Steamship at lower left, arms between seated Liberty and Justice at upper center, steam passenger train at lower right. Back: Orange-brown. Printer: HBNC (without imprint).	50.00	150.	450.
S192 5 Pesos			
2.6.1899-13.7.1899. Black on gray underprint. Steamship at lower left, arms between seated Liberty and Justice at upper center, steam passenger train at lower right. Back: Blue. Printer: HBNC (without imprint).	100.	350.	600.
S193 25 Pesos			
2.6.1899; 15.6.1899; 22.6.1899; 3.7.1899; 6.7.1899; 13.7.1899. Black on gray underprint. Steamship at lower left, arms between seated Liberty and Justice at upper center, steam passenger train at lower right. Back: Brown. Printer: HBNC (without imprint).	225.	600.	1000.

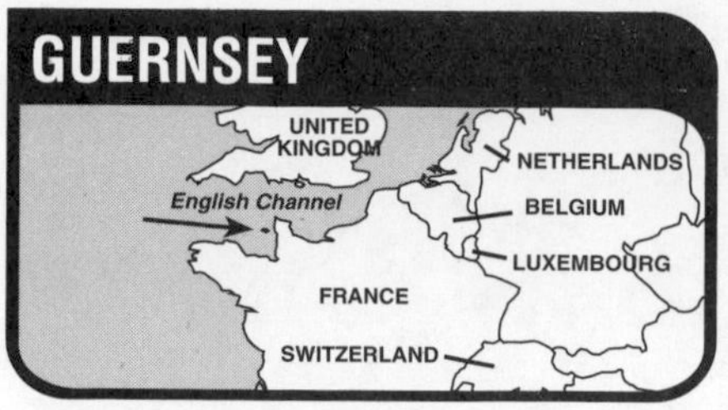

The Bailiwick of Guernsey, a British crown dependency located in the English Channel 48 km. west of Normandy, France, has an area of 78 sq. km., including the Isles of Alderney, Jethou, Herm, Brechou and Sark, and a population of 58,681. Capital: St. Peter Port. Agriculture and cattle breeding are the main occupations.

Guernsey and the other Channel Islands represent the last remnants of the medieval Dukedom of Normandy, which held sway in both France and England. The islands were the only British soil occupied by German troops in World War II. Guernsey is a British crown dependency, but is not part of the UK. However, the UK Government is constitutionally responsible for its defense and international representation.

United Kingdom bank notes and coinage circulate concurrently with Guernsey money as legal tender.

RULERS:

British to 1940, 1944-
German Occupation, June 1940-June 1944

MONETARY SYSTEM:

1 Penny = 8 Doubles
1 Shilling = 12 Pence
5 Shillings = 6 Francs
1 Pound = 20 Shillings to 1971
1 Pound = 100 New Pence 1971-

British Administration

Guernsey Banking Co. Ltd.

1861-1906 Issue

S151 1 Pound	Good	Fine	XF
1861-87. Arms at upper left, ship at center, woman with bales at upper right with title: *GUERNSEY BANKING COMPANY*. Printer: PBC.			
a. Signature titles: *MANAGER* and *CHAIRMAN*. 1.8.1887.	—	—	—
s. Signature title: *MANAGER*. Specimen. 22.8.1861.	—	—	—
S153 1 Pound			
1.7.1906. Arms at upper left, ship at center, woman with bales at upper right. Similar to #S151, but with title: *GUERNSEY BANKING COMPANY LIMITED*. Signature titles: *MANAGER* and *CHAIRMAN*. Printer: PBC.	—	—	—

Guernsey Commercial Banking Co. Ltd.

1886-1916 Issue

S171 1 Pound	Good	Fine	XF
6.12.1886; 2.1.1906. Commerce seated at upper center with sailing ships in background with title: *GUERNSEY COMMERCIAL BANKING COMPANY*. 3 signatures. Printer: PB&P. Rare.	—	—	—

NOTE: Issue dates of 2.12.1868 and 6.9.1869 are not confirmed.

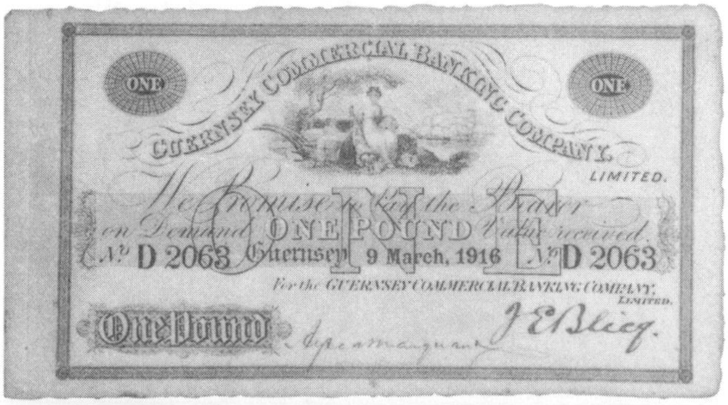

S173 1 Pound	Good	Fine	XF
9.3.1916. Commerce seated at upper center with sailing ships in background. Similar to #S171, but with title: *GUERNSEY COMMERIAL BANKING COMPANY LIMITED*. 2 signatures.			
a. Issued note. Rare.	—	—	—
p. Proof. (ca.1913).	—	—	—

Southern District Banking Company

Guernsey

1838 Issue

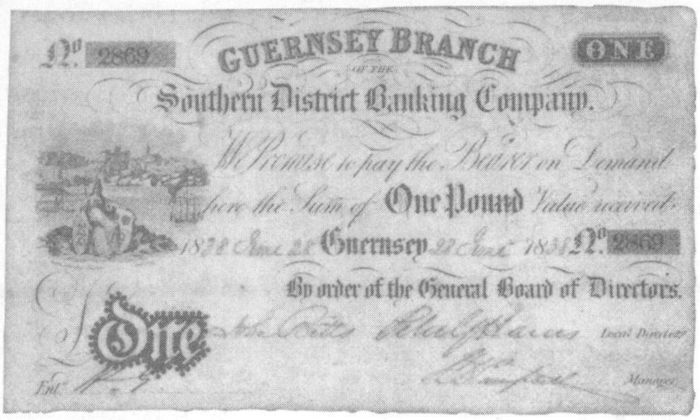

	Good	Fine	XF
S177 1 Pound 28.6.1838. Landscape at left.	—	4000.	—

Regional

Alderney Commercial Bank

1810 Issue

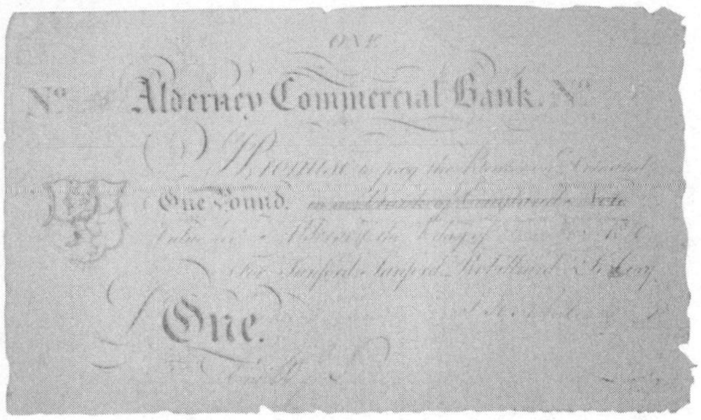

	Good	Fine	XF
S181 1 Pound 26.12.1810. Black. Arms at left.	—	—	4250.

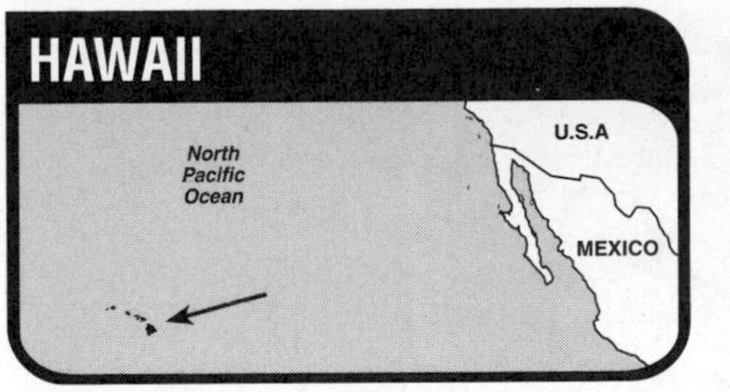

Hawaii consists of eight main islands and numerous smaller islands of coral and volcanic origin situated in the central Pacific Ocean 2,400 miles (3,862 km.) from San Francisco. The archipelago has an area of 6,471 sq. mi. (16,641 sq. km.) and a population of 1.1 million. Capital: Honolulu. The principal industries are tourism and agriculture. Cane sugar and pineapples are exported.

The islands, originally populated by Polynesians who traveled from the Society Islands, were discovered by British navigator Capt. James Cook in 1778. He named them the Sandwich Islands. King Kamehameha the Great united the islands under one kingdom (1795-1810) which endured until 1893 when Queen Liliuokalani, the gifted composer of "Aloha Oe" and other songs, was deposed and a provisional government established. This was followed by a republic which governed Hawaii until 1898 when it ceded itself to the United States. Hawaii was organized as a territory in 1900 and became the 50th state of the United States on Aug. 21, 1959.

RULERS

King Kalakaua, 1874-1891
Queen Liliuokalani, 1891-1893
Provisional Govt., 1893-1894
Republic, 1894-1898
Annexed to U.S., 1898-1900
Territory, 1900-1959

MONETARY SYSTEM

1 Dollar = 100 Cents

Kingdom

Bank of Claus Spreckels & Co.

1886-87 Silver Certificate of Deposit Issue

	Good	Fine	XF
S101 10 Dollars 24.9.1887. Purple. Seated figure in rowboat at left. Hand cancelled by tearing off the signature at lower right. Back: Yellow. Rare.	—	—	—
S102 20 Dollars 15.1.1887. Blue. Seated figure in rowboat at left. Hand cancelled by tearing off the signature at lower right. Back: Red. Rare.	—	—	—
S103 50 Dollars 1.10.1886. Red. Seated figure in rowboat at left. Hand cancelled by tearing off the signature at lower right. Back: Green. Rare.	—	—	—
S104 100 Dollars 1.10.1886. Green. Seated figure in rowboat at left. Hand cancelled by tearing off the signature at lower right. Back: Blue. Rare.	—	—	—

NOTE: A single set of #S101-S104 was presented as a new discovery and sold at auction by Lyn F. Knight, Inc. at the 1997 Memphis Paper Money Show.

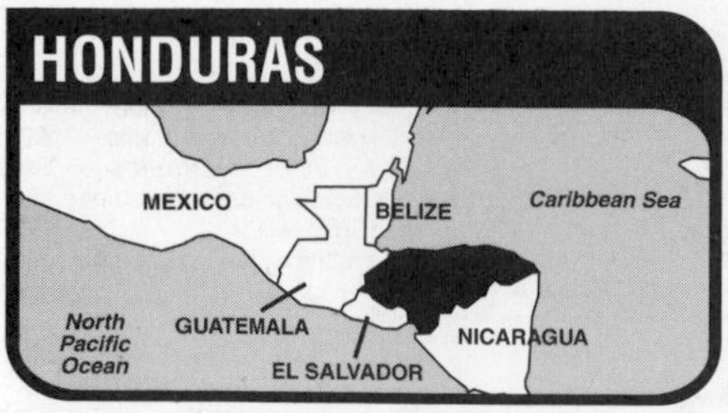

The Republic of Honduras, situated in Central America between El Salvador, Nicaragua and Guatemala, has an area of 43,277 sq. mi. (112,088 sq. km.) and a population of 6.48 million. Capital: Tegucigalpa. Tourism, agriculture, mining (gold and silver), and logging are the chief industries. Bananas, timber and coffee are exported.

Once part of Spain's vast empire in the New World, Honduras became an independent nation in 1821. After two and a half decades of mostly military rule, a freely elected civilian government came to power in 1982. During the 1980s, Honduras proved a haven for anti-Sandinista contras fighting the Marxist Nicaraguan Government and an ally to Salvadoran Government forces fighting leftist guerrillas. The country was devastated by Hurricane Mitch in 1998.

MONETARY SYSTEM:

I Peso = 100 Centavos, 1871-1926
1 Lempira = 100 Centavos, 1926-

BANKS:

REVOLUTION

REPUBLIC

Note: Certain listings encompassing issues circulated by provincial, state and commercial banking authorities are contained in Volume 1.

BANKS

AGUAN NAVIGATION AND IMPROVEMENT COMPANY

1886 ISSUE

	Good	Fine	XF
S101 50 Centavos 25.6.1886. Black on red underprint. Portrait woman at left, portrait Pres. Bográn at center. Back: Green. Printer: HLBNC.	30.00	75.00	200.
S103 2 Pesos ND (1886). Black on yellow underprint. Sailing ship and steam passenger train at left, portrait Pres. Bográn at center, ship loading at right. Back: Green. Medallion of helmeted Minerva at upper center. Printer: HLBNC. Rare.	—	—	—
S104 5 Pesos 25.6.1886. Black on gold underprint. Portrait Pres. Bográn at left, ship at right. Back: Green. Printer: HLBNC.			
a. Issued note.	175.	450.	950.
s. Proof.	—	Unc	300.
S105 10 Pesos 25.6.1886. Black on red underprint. Portrait Pres. Bográn at upper left, ship at lower right. Back: Green. Printer: HLBNC.	275.	750.	1250.
S107 50 Pesos 25.6.1886. Black on green underprint. Portrait Pres. Bográn at lower left, Justice seated between two children at center, paddle wheel steamer at lower right. Back: Green. Printer: HLBNC.	1000.	2500.	—

BANCO ATLANTIDA

1913-19 ISSUE

	Good	Fine	XF
S111 1 Peso 1.4.1913-14.1.1919. Black on green and brown underprint. Female seated by seashore at center. Back: Green. Arms at center. Printer: ABNC.			
a. Hand signature. 1.4.1913.	60.00	250.	450.
b. Printed signature. 1.4.1913.	60.00	250.	450.
c. Overprint: *Decree No. 11 of 14.1.1919* date in 5 lines of red text (in Spanish) on face.	175.	350.	600.
p. Proof.	—	Unc	500.
s. Specimen.	—	Unc	800.
S113 5 Pesos 1.4.1913-14.1.1919. Black on blue underprint. Female seated by seashore at center. Like #S111. Back: Blue. Arms at center. Printer: ABNC.			
a. Issued note. Rare.	—	—	—
b. Overprint: *Decree No. 11 of 14.1.1919* date like #S111c. Rare.	—	—	—
p. Proof.	—	Unc	700.
s. Specimen.	—	Unc	1000.

	Good	Fine	XF
S115 20 Pesos 1.4.1913. Black on orange and yellow underprint. Female seated by seashore at center. Like #S111. Back: Orange. Arms at center. Printer: ABNC.			
p. Proof.	—	Unc	1500.
s. Specimen.	—	Unc	2150.

NOTE: Additional denominations require confirmation.

1932 ISSUE

	Good	Fine	XF
S121 1 Lempira 1932. Black on green and multicolor underprint. Female seated by seashore at center. Similar to #S111. Back: Olive-brown. Arms at center. Printer: ABNC.			
a. Series A. Left hand signature title: *PRESIDENTE*. 1.3.1932.	55.00	100.	250.
b. Series A. Left hand signature title: *VICE-PRESIDENTE*. 1.3.1932.	55.00	100.	250.
c. Series B. 1.7.1932.	55.00	100.	250.
p. Proof	—	Unc	300.
s. Specimen.	—	Unc	400.
S122 2 Lempiras 1932. Black on blue, orange and multicolor underprint. Helmeted woman protecting child at center. Back: Red. Bank at center. Printer: ABNC.			
a. Series A. 1.3.1932.	60.00	150.	275.
b. Series B. 1.7.1932.	60.00	150.	275.
s. Specimen.	—	Unc	300.
S123 5 Lempiras 1932-43. Black on pink, orange and multicolor underprint. Female seated by seashore at center. Similar to #S121. Back: Blue. Arms at center. Printer: ABNC.			
a. Series A. 1.3.1932.	65.00	175.	300.
b. Series B. Left hand signature title: *PRESIDENTE*. 1.7.1932.	65.00	175.	300.
c. Series B. Left hand signature title: *VICE-PRESIDENTE*. 1.7.1932.	65.00	175.	300.
d. Series C. Left hand signature title: *VICE-PRESIDENTE*. 1.2.1943.	65.00	175.	300.
e. Series C. Left hand signature title: *PRESIDENTE*. 1.2.1943.	65.00	175.	300.
p. Proof.	—	Unc	250.
s. Specimen.	—	Unc	500.
S124 10 Lempiras 1932-43. Black on multicolor underprint. Seated woman and child at left and right. Back: Brown. Bank at center. Printer: ABNC.			
a. Series A. 1.3.1932.	100.	225.	450.
b. Series B. 1.7.1932.	100.	225.	450.
c. Series C. Left hand signature title: *PRESIDENTE*. 1.2.1943.	100.	225.	450.
d. Series C. Left hand signature title: *VICE-PRESIDENTE*. 1.2.1943.	100.	225.	450.
p. Proof.	—	Unc	500.
s. Specimen.	—	Unc	600.
S125 20 Lempiras 1932-45. Black on green and multicolor underprint. Woman reclining at center. Back: Green. Arms at center. Printer: ABNC.			
a. Series A. 1.3.1932.	150.	250.	700.
b. Series B. 1.7.1932.	150.	250.	700.
c. Series C. 17.5.1945.	150.	250.	700.
p. Proof.	—	Unc	600.
s. Specimen.	—	Unc	1000.

BANCO CENTRO-AMERICANO

1888 ISSUE

	Good	Fine	XF
S131 1 Peso 30.11.1888. Black on brown and yellow underprint. Arms at left, woman ("Spanish Girl") at center right. Back: Brown. Griffins at left and right. Printer: ABNC.			
a. Issued note. Rare.	500.	1750.	—
p. Proof.	—	Unc	700.
s. Specimen.	—	Unc	800.
S132 2 Pesos 30.11.1888. Black on green and yellow underprint. Ship at upper left and center, steam train at upper center right, arms at right. Back: Green. Figures at left and right. Printer: ABNC.			
p. Proof.	—	Unc	750.
s. Specimen.	—	Unc	1000.
S133 5 Pesos 30.11.1888. Black on orange and yellow underprint. Goats at left, arms at center, woman pouring water from pitcher ("Rebecca") at right. Back: Orange. Printer: ABNC. Specimen.			
p. Proof.	—	Unc	800.
s. Specimen.	—	Unc	1200.
S134 10 Pesos 30.11.1888. Black on blue and yellow underprint. Standing woman with ship's wheel ("Fortuna") at left, ships at left center, arms at right. Back: Blue. Printer: ABNC.			
p. Proof.	—	Unc	800.
s. Specimen.	—	Unc	1200.
S135 20 Pesos 30.11.1888. Black on green and yellow underprint. Woman with sheaf at upper left, arms at center, miners working at right. Back: Olive-green. Printer: ABNC.			
p. Proof.	—	Unc	900.
s. Specimen.	—	Unc	2000.
S136 50 Pesos 30.11.1888. Black on brown and yellow underprint. Woman with three children ("Education") above arms at left, seated Indian ("Alerta") at right. Back: Red-brown. Printer: ABNC. Specimen.	—	Unc	2500.

		Good	Fine	XF
S137	**100 Pesos** 30.11.1888. Black on orange and yellow underprint. Seated woman ("Study") at left, steer's head at center, arms at right. Back: Orange. Printer: ABNC. Specimen.	—	Unc	4000.

1888 Emergency Issue

		Good	Fine	XF
S139	**1 Peso** 30.11.1888. Black. Arms handstamped at center. Back: Black. Paper: Light brown. Tegucigalpa local printing.	—	—	—

Banco de Comercio

1915 Issue

		Good	Fine	XF
S141	**1 Peso** 16.2.1915. Black on multicolor underprint. Equestrian statue at left. Back: Green. Arms at center. Printer: ABNC.			
	a. Issued note. Rare.	750.	—	—
	s. Specimen.	—	Unc	500.
S143	**5 Pesos** 16.2.1915. Black on multicolor underprint. Equestrian statue at right. Series A. Back: Purple. Arms at center. Printer: ABNC.			
	a. Issued note. Rare.	—	—	—
	s. Specimen.	—	Unc	750.
S144	**10 Pesos** 16.2.1915. Black on multicolor underprint. Equestrian statue at left. Similar to #S141. Back: Blue. Arms at center. Printer: ABNC.			
	a. Issued note. Rare.	—	—	—
	p. Proof.	—	Unc	750.
	s. Specimen.	—	Unc	1250.
S145	**20 Pesos** 16.2.1915. Black on multicolor underprint. Equestrian statue at left. Similar to #S143. Back: Brown. Arms at center. Printer: ABNC.			
	p. Proof.	—	Unc	1450.
	s. Specimen.	—	Unc	2000.

Banco Nacional de Honduras

1908 Issue

		Good	Fine	XF
S148	**5 Pesos** ND (ca. 1908). Black on green, orange and brown underprint. Two standing allegorical woman ("North & South") at right. Back: Green. Arms at center. Printer: ABNC.			
	p. Proof.	—	Unc	1000.
	s. Specimen.	—	Unc	2600.

Banco Nacional Hondureño

1889 Issue

		Good	Fine	XF
S151	**10 Centavos** 1889. Black on yellow underprint. Helmeted female head ("Minerva No. 3") at right. Back: Brown. Printer: ABNC.			
	a. Issued note.	175.	550.	850.
	p. Proof.	—	Unc	250.
	s. Specimen.	—	Unc	400.
S152	**25 Centavos** 1889. Black on green underprint. Miners at left. Back: Green. Printer: ABNC.			
	a. Issued note.	175.	550.	850.
	p. Proof.	—	Unc	300.
	s. Specimen.	—	Unc	400.

		Good	Fine	XF
S153	**50 Centavos** 1889. Black on orange underprint. Locomotive at left. Back: Orange. Printer: ABNC.			
	a. Issued note.	350.	900.	1250.
	p. Proof.	—	Unc	500.
	s. Specimen.	—	Unc	750.
S154	**1 Peso** 1889. Black on brown underprint. Woman seated at left, portrait Pres. General Luis Bográn at lower right. Back: Brown. Printer: ABNC.			
	a. Issued note.	650.	1550.	—
	p. Proof.	—	Unc	750.
	s. Specimen.	—	Unc	1000.
S155	**2 Pesos** 1889. Black on orange underprint. Standing sailor at left, supported portrait Pres. General Luis Bográn at center. Back: Orange. Printer: ABNC.			
	a. Issued note.	1200.	2500.	—
	p. Proof.	—	Unc	900.
	s. Specimen.	—	Unc	1400.

NOTE: #S154 and S155 sometimes with hand stamp on back showing issue at San Pedro Sula branch.

		Good	Fine	XF
S156	**5 Pesos** 1889. Black on blue underprint. Seated allegorical woman at left, arms at center right, portrait Pres. General Luis Bográn at right. Back: Blue. Printer: ABNC.			
	a. Issued note. Rare.	—	—	—
	p. Proof.	—	Unc	1200.
	s. Specimen.	—	Unc	1800.
S157	**10 Pesos** 1889. Black on green underprint. Man at left, seated allegorical woman at upper center. With portrait Pres. General Luis Bográn. Back: Green. Printer: ABNC.			
	p. Proof.	—	Unc	1200.
	s. Specimen.	—	Unc	2000.
S158	**50 Pesos** 1889. Black on orange underprint. Portrait Pres. General Luis Bográn left, reclining woman with pitcher and lute ("Naiad") at left center. Back: Orange. Printer: ABNC.			
	p. Proof.	—	Unc	1800.
	s. Specimen.	—	Unc	2600.
S159	**100 Pesos** 1889. Black on red underprint. Seated allegorical woman ("Tropics No. 3") at left and a different one at right, portrait Pres. General Luis Bográn at upper center. Back: Red. Printer: ABNC.			
	p. Proof.	—	Unc	2200.
	s. Specimen.	—	Unc	5000.

1935 Revolution

Banco Territorial de Honduras

1935 Issue

		Good	Fine	XF
S161	**1 Lempira** ND (ca.1935). Liberty at center. Back: Arms at left, hill and town at center. Revolution overprint at left.	—	—	—
S161A	**10 Lempiras** ND. Liberty at center. Back: Arms at left, hill and town at center. Like #S161, but without revolution overprint.	—	—	—

República de Honduras

Billete Aduanero

Customs Notes

Decree of 5.10.1927

		Good	Fine	XF
S162	**1 Peso** 1928. Blue on light tan underprint. Arms at left. Back: Blue. Ornamental design. Printer: ABNC. Specimen or proof.	—	Unc	1500.
S163	**2 Pesos** 1928. Brown on light tan underprint. Arms at left. Back: Brown. Ornamental design. Printer: ABNC. Proof.	—	Unc	1500.
S164	**5 Pesos** 1928. Black on lilac underprint. Arms at left. Back: Olive-brown. Ornamental design. Printer: ABNC. Proof.	—	Unc	2250.
S165	**10 Pesos** 1928. Red on pink underprint. Arms at left. Back: Red. Ornamental design. Printer: ABNC. Proof.	—	Unc	2250.
S165A	**50 Pesos** 1928. Dark green on light tan underprint. Arms at left. Back: Dark green. Ornamental design. Printer: ABNC. Proof.	—	Unc	2000.
S165B	**100 Pesos** 1928. Orange on light tan underprint. Arms at left. Back: Orange. Ornamental design. Printer: ABNC. Proof.	—	Unc	2000.

Decreto Legislativo No. 72 de Marzo de 1937

		Good	Fine	XF
S166	**1 Lempira** 1937. Light blue on gray underprint. Arms at left. Series L. Back: Light blue. Ornamental design. Printer: ABNC.			
	a. Issued note.	25.00	50.00	100.
	p. Proof.	—	Unc	200.
	s. Specimen.	—	Unc	300.

	Good	Fine	XF
S167 2 Lempiras			
1937. Dark brown on gray underprint. Arms at left. Series K. Back: Dark brown. Ornamental design. Printer: ABNC.			
a. Issued note.	25.00	50.00	100.
p. Proof.	—	Unc	200.
s. Specimen.	—	Unc	300.
S168 5 Lempiras			
1937. Olive-green on light blue underprint. Arms at left. Series J. Back: Olive-green. Ornamental design. Printer: ABNC.			
a. Issued note.	30.00	75.00	125.
b. Issued note. Punched hole cancelled.	15.00	40.00	80.00
p. Proof.	—	Unc	200.
s. Specimen.	—	Unc	300.
S169 10 Lempiras			
1937. Red on gray underprint. Arms at left. Series I. Back: Red. Ornamental design. Printer: ABNC.			
a. Issued note.	50.00	125.	200.
p. Proof.	—	Unc	200.
s. Specimen.	—	Unc	300.
S170 50 Lempiras			
1937. Green on gray underprint. Arms at left. Series H. Back: Green. Ornamental design. Printer: ABNC.			
a. Issued note.	65.00	140.	225.
b. Issued note. Punched hole cancelled.	25.00	60.00	125.
p. Proof.	—	Unc	250.
s. Specimen.	—	Unc	350.
S171 100 Lempiras			
1937. Gold on peach underprint. Arms at left. Back: Gold. Ornamental design. Printer: ABNC.			
p. Proof.	—	Unc	250.
s. Specimen.	—	Unc	350.

The Hungarian Republic, located in central Europe, has an area of 93,030 sq. km. and a population of 9.93 million. Capital: Budapest. The economy is d on agriculture and a rapidly expanding industrial sector. Machinery, chemicals, iron and steel, and fruits and vegetables are exported.

Hungary became a Christian kingdom in A.D. 1000 and for many centuries served as a bulwark against Ottoman Turkish expansion in Europe. The kingdom eventually became part of the polyglot Austro-Hungarian Empire, which collapsed during World War I. The country fell under Communist rule following World War II. In 1956, a revolt and an announced withdrawal from the Warsaw Pact were met with a massive military intervention by Moscow. Under the leadership of Janos Kadar in 1968, Hungary began liberalizing its economy, introducing so-called "Goulash Communism." Hungary held its first multiparty elections in 1990 and initiated a free market economy. It joined NATO in 1999 and the EU in 2004.

RULERS:

Austrian to 1918

MONETARY SYSTEM:

1 Korona = 100 Fillér to 1926
1 Pengö = 100 Fillér to 1946
1 Milpengö = 1 Million Pengö
1 B(illió) Pengö = 1 Billion Pengö
1 Adopengö = 1 Tax Pengö
1 Forint = 100 Fillér 1946- 1 Forint (Florin) = 60 Krajczar

Austrian Administration

Iparmütári Alapitvány Jegy

1847 Issue

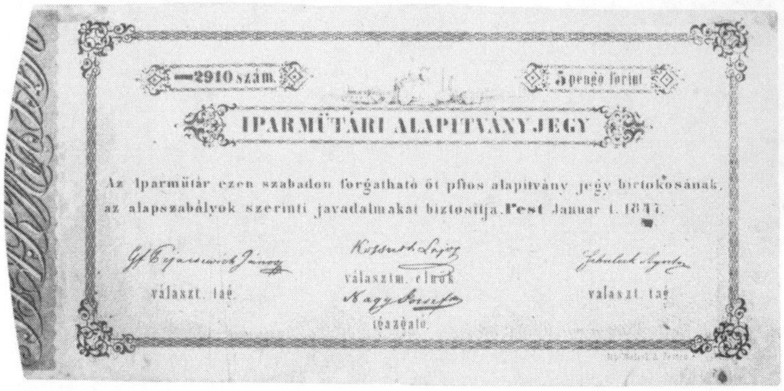

	Good	Fine	XF
S91 5 Pengö Forint 1.1.1847. Black. Kossuth signature. Uniface.	—	—	—

Kamatos Utalvány

Interest-Paying Legal Tender Treasury Bills

1848 First Issue

#S101-S103 Issued for a 6-month loan. Interest tables on backs.

	Good	Fine	XF
S101 50 Forint 1848. Black on light blue underprint. Different handwritten dates. Back: Interest tables. 232x130mm. Rare.	—	—	—
S102 100 Forint 1848. Black on light brown underprint. Different handwritten dates. Back: Interest tables. 232x130mm. Rare.	—	—	—
S103 500 Forint 1848. Black on light gray underprint. Different handwritten dates. Back: Interest tables. 232x130mm. Rare.	—	—	—

1848 Second Issue

#S104-S106 Notes issued for 12-month loan and have coupons 47 x 130mm which were to be removed after six months. Interest tables on backs.

	Good	Fine	XF
S104 50 Forint 1848. Black on yellow underprint. Different handwritten dates. Back: Interest tables. 185x130mm. Rare.	—	—	—
S105 100 Forint 1848. Black on pink underprint. Different handwritten dates. Back: Interest tables. 185x130mm. Rare.	—	—	—
S106 500 Forint 1848. Black on light gray underprint. Different handwritten dates. Back: Interest tables. 185x130mm. Rare.	—	—	—

NOTE: Coupons were for values of 1 Fr 15 Kr (50 Forint), 2 Fr 30 Kr (100 Forint) and 12 Fr 30 Kr (500 Forint).

1848 Third Issue

#S107-S109 like previous issue but notes w/o coupons.

		Good	Fine	XF
S107	**50 Forint** 1848. Black on yellow underprint. Different handwritten dates. Like #S104. Back: Interest tables. 138x130mm. Rare.	—	—	—
S108	**100 Forint** 1848. Black on pink underprint. Different handwritten dates. Like #S105. Back: Interest tables. 138x130mm. Rare.	—	—	—

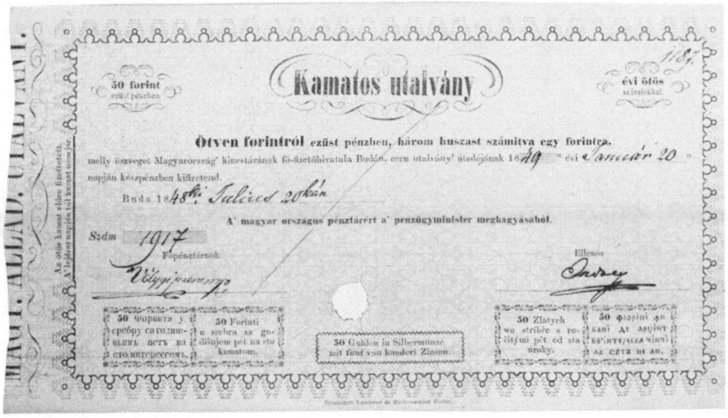

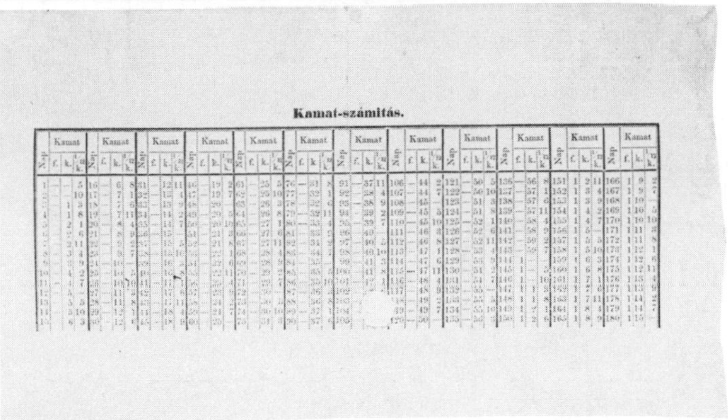

		Good	Fine	XF
S109	**500 Forint** 1848. Black on light gray underprint. Different handwritten dates. Like #S106. Back: Interest tables. 138x130mm. Rare.	—	—	—

Magyar Kereskedelmi Bank

Hungarian Commercial Bank

1848 Issue

		Good	Fine	XF
S111	**1 Forint** ND (1848). Black on brown underprint. Arms in underprint at bottom center. Printed signature of Kossuth as Finance Minister, Ferenc Volgyi as Chief of State Treasury, and Janos Rogler as Bank Cashier.	3.00	10.00	35.00

		Good	Fine	XF
S112	**2 Forint** ND (1848). Black on light red underprint. Arms at bottom center. Printed signature of Kossuth as Finance Minister, Ferenc Volgyi as Chief of State Treasury, and Janos Rogler as Bank Cashier. Back: Green underprint.	2.00	6.00	35.00

Pénzjegy

State Notes, Finance Ministry

1848 Issue

		Good	Fine	XF
S116	**5 Forint** 1.9.1848. Gray underprint. Printed signature of Kossuth as Minister of Finance. Penzjegy is in first line of small text under written out denomination. Back: Dark pink underprint. Green text.			
	a. Red-brown face color.	2.00	6.00	35.00
	b. Brown face color.	2.00	6.00	35.00

		Good	Fine	XF
S117	**10 Forint** 1.9.1848. Black on gray underprint. Arms at bottom center. Printed signature of Kossuth as Minister of Finance. Penzjegy is in first line of small text under written out denomination. Back: Dull olive underprint. Black text.	3.00	10.00	60.00

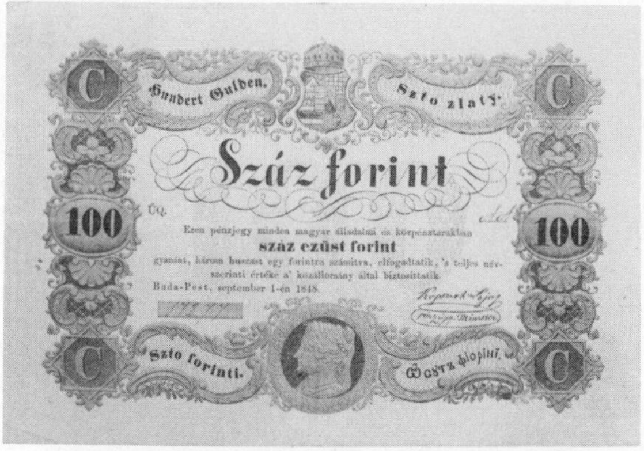

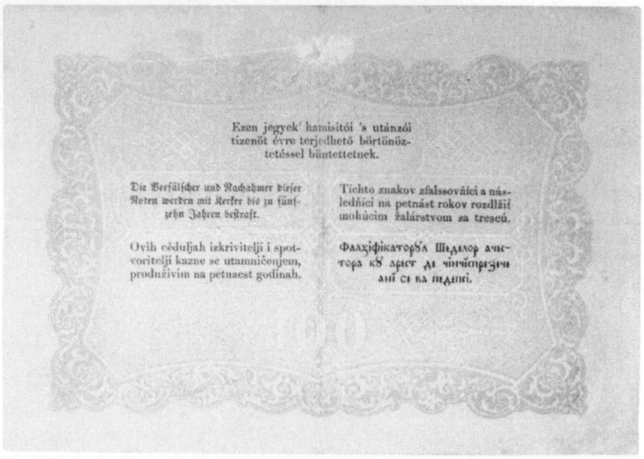

S118 100 Forint

	Good	Fine	XF
1.9.1848. Black on gray underprint. Arms at top and woman at bottom center. Printed signature of Kossuth as Minister of Finance. Penzjegy is in first line of small text under written out denomination. Back: Gray underprint. Black text.	30.00	85.00	250.

Kincstári Utalvány, Országos Honvédelmi Bizottmány

State Treasury Notes, National Army Defense Committee

1849 Issue

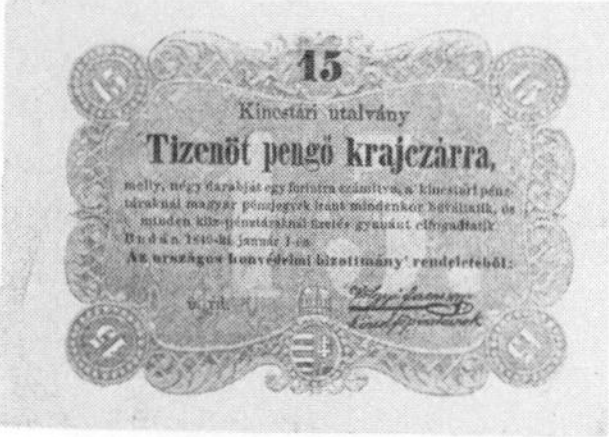

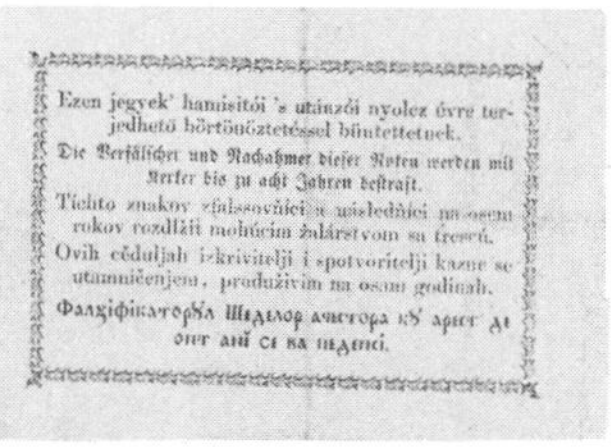

S121 15 Pengö Krajczár

	Good	Fine	XF
1.1.1849. Black on red-brown or brown underprint. Arms at bottom center and printed signature of Ferenc Volgyi as Chief of State Treasury. Back: Black text.	1.50	6.00	35.00

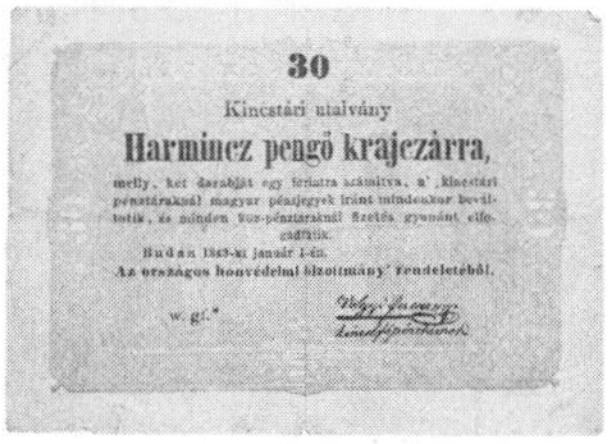

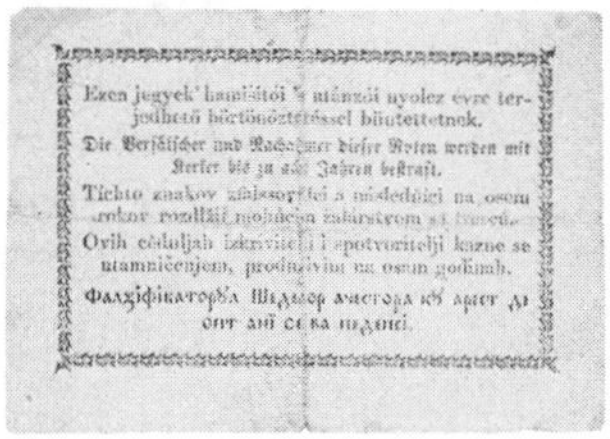

S122 30 Pengö Krajczár

	Good	Fine	XF
1.1.1849. Black on gray underprint. Arms at bottom center and printed signature of Ferenc Volgyi as Chief of State Treasury. Back: Black text.	1.50	6.00	35.00

Kincstári Utalvány

State Treasury Note, Finance Ministry

1849 Issue

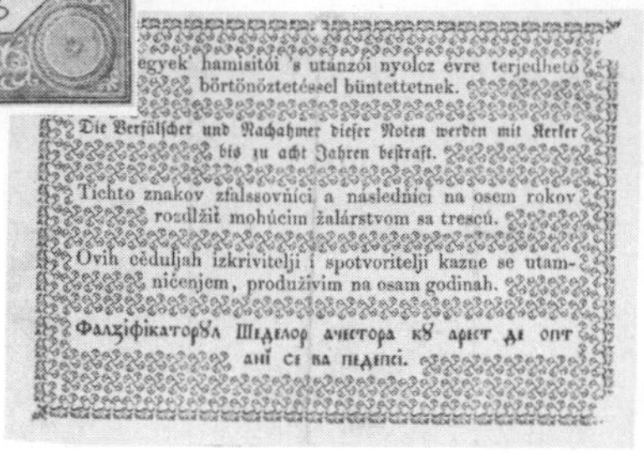

S126 2 Pengö Forint

	Good	Fine	XF
1.7.1849. Black. Arms without crown at bottom center.			
a. Signature Kossuth and Ferenc Duschek as Governor of Hungary and Minister of Finance, respectively.	10.00	30.00	90.00
b. Signature Kossuth and Bertalan Szemere, Prime Minister. Rare.	—	—	—

S127 10 Pengö Forint

1.7.1849. Black. Signature Kossuth and Szemere. Rare.	—	—	—

Non-Hungarian Issues

Nyugtatvány Receipt

1851 Issue

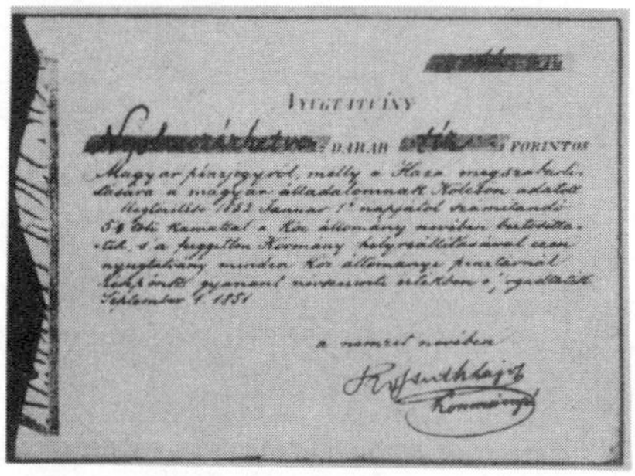

S131 Various amounts

	Good	Fine	XF
1.9.1851. Black. Counterfoil at left margin.	—	—	—

Hungarian Fund, New York

1852 Issue

S136 1 Dollar

	VG	VF	UNC
2.2.1852. Black. L. Kossuth at lower left, Hungaria with sword over fallen crowned figure at center, Liberty at lower right. Arms at upper corners. Large *ONE* protector. Printed date. English text. Letters A-C. Paper: Thin white. Printer: Danforth, Bald and Co.			
a. Issued note (with serial #).	—	7.50	25.00
b. Sheet of 3 subjects.	—	—	50.00
r. Unissued remainder (without serial #).	—	—	10.00

S137 5 Dollars — VG | VF | UNC

2.2.1852. Black. L. Kossuth at lower left, arms at center, standing Liberty with Hungarian shield at lower right. Handwritten date. Letter A. English text. Uniface. Printed signature L. Kossuth. Printer: Danforth, Bald and Co. — 5.00 | 15.00 | 75.00

S137A 5 Dollars

2.2.1852. Black. Like #S137 but with large *FIVE* protector. Printed date. Letter B. English text. Uniface. Printed signature L. Kossuth. Printer: Danforth, Bald and Co. — 5.00 | 15.00 | 75.00

S138 10 Dollars — VG | VF | UNC

1.1.1852. Black. L. Kossuth at lower left, seated Liberty with shield and two women at upper center, woman with globe at right. Handwritten date. Letter A. English text. Uniface. Printed signature L. Kossuth. Printer: Danforth, Bald and Co. — 25.00 | 55.00 | 125.

S138A 10 Dollars

1.1.1852. Black. Like #S138 but with large *TEN* protector. Printed date. Letter A. English text. Uniface. Printed signature L. Kossuth. Printer: Danforth, Bald and Co. — 25.00 | 55.00 | 125.

S139 50 Dollars

2.2.1852; 1.7.1852. Black. Standing Liberty with Hungarian shield and pole at lower left, portrait L. Kossuth at upper center, seated woman with United States shield at right. Large *FIFTY* protector. Letters A; B. Handwri Printer: Danforth, Bald and Co. — 150. | 300. | —

S140 100 Dollars — VG | VF | UNC

1.1.1852; 1.7.1852. Black. Woman in flowing robe at left and right of portrait of left. Kossuth at upper center. Large *100* protector. Letter A. Handwritten signature. Printer: Danforth, Bald and Co. — 175. | 325. | —

PÉNZJEGY, PHILADELPHIA

FINANCE MINISTRY

1852 ND ISSUE

S141 1 Forint — VG | VF | UNC

ND (1852). Black. Three standing women at left, Hungaria over fallen crowned figure with flags and cannon at center, woman with pedestal at lower right. Printed signature L. Kossuth. Hungarian text. Uniface. Letters A- Printer: Toppan, Carpenter, Casilear and Co.

- r1. Unissued remainder. — — | 3.00 | 12.50
- r2. Sheet of 4 subjects. — — | — | 50.00

S142 2 Forint

ND (1852). Black. Seated Justice with scale at left, Liberty with Hungarian shield and fasces at center, standing Athena at right. Letters A-H. Printed signature L. Kossuth. Hungarian text. Uniface. Printer: Toppan, Carpenter, Casilear and Co.

- r1. Unissued remainder. — — | 3.00 | 12.50
- r2. Sheet of 4 subjects. — — | — | 50.00

S143 5 Forint — VG | VF | UNC

ND (1852). Black. Seated woman with sickle at upper left, arm and hammer at center, beehive below, seated woman with bales at upper right. Arms at lower corners. Printed signature L. Kossuth. Hungarian text. Uniface. L Printer: Toppan, Carpenter, Casilear and Co.

- r1. Unissued remainder. — — | 3.00 | 12.50
- r2. Sheet of 3 subjects. — — | — | 50.00

PÉNZJEGY, LONDON

FINANCE MINISTRY

1860-61 ND ISSUE

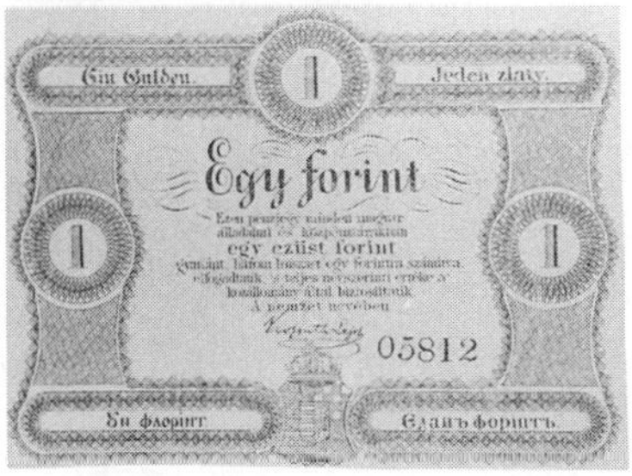

S146 1 Forint — Good | Fine | XF

ND (1860-61). Black. Arms with crown at bottom center. Printed signature of L. Kossuth "in the name of the nation." No large heading at top or center. Uniface. Watermark: Arms, value and *RESURGO* (revolt against). Printer: Day and Son. Rare. — — | — | —

S147 2 Forint

ND (1860-61). Red. Printed signature of L. Kossuth "in the name of the nation." No large heading at top or center. Uniface. Watermark: Arms, value and *RESURGO* (revolt against). Printer: Day and Son. Rare. — — | — | —

S148 5 Forint

ND (1860 61). Green. Printed signature of L. Kossuth "in the name of the nation." No large heading at top or center. Uniface. Watermark: Arms, value and *RESURGO* (revolt against). Printer: Day and Son. Rare.

NOTE: At the request of Austrian Emperor Franz Josef, #S146-S148 were confiscated by the British government, taken to the Bank of England, and burned. Only a very few were saved.

KINCSTÁR UTALVÁNY/KINCSTÁR JEGY, TORINO

STATE TREASURY NOTES

1866 ISSUE

Plates for #S151-S153 were prepared by the sons of Lajos Kossuth and notes were printed in Torino, Italy in 1866. Denominations were in *garas* (= groats).

S151 2 Valto Garas — VG | VF | UNC

1.7.1866.

- a. Issued note. — — | — | —
- b. Reprint from the original plate. — — | — | —

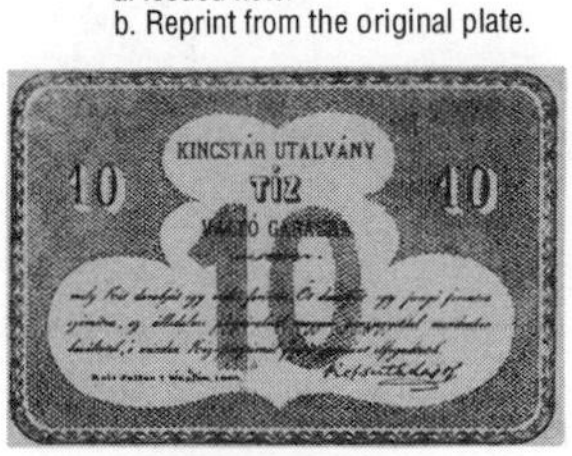

S152 10 Valto Garas — VG | VF | UNC

1.7.1866.

- a. Issued note. — — | — | —
- b. Reprint from the original plate. — — | — | —

S153 1 Forint — VG | VF | UNC

1.7.1866.

- a. Issued note. — — | — | —
- b. Reprint from the original plate. — — | — | —

Siege

Arad

1848-49 ND Issues

		Good	Fine	XF
S161	**1 Kreuzer** ND. With K.K./F.z.A. Round.	—	—	—
S162	**3 Kreuzer** ND. With K.K./F.z.A. Round.	—	—	—

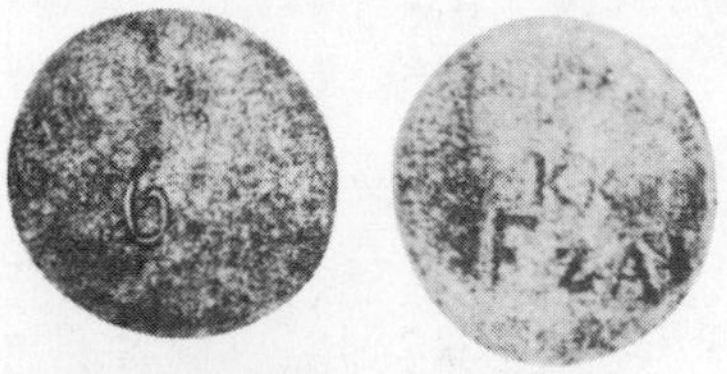

		Good	Fine	XF
S163	**6 Kreuzer** ND. With K.K./F.z.A. Round.	—	—	—
S164	**6 Kreuzer** ND. Square.	—	—	—

		Good	Fine	XF
S165	**6 Kreuzer** ND. Square.	—	—	—
S166	**10 Kreuzer Conv. Münz** ND. Handwritten; signature Saffran and Müller.	125.	250.	—
S167	**10 Kreuzer** ND. Handwritten and seal, signature Saffran and Müller.	125.	250.	—
S168	**10 Kreuzer** ND. Printed.	—	—	—
S169	**18 Kreuzer C. M.** ND.	—	—	—
S170	**20 Kreuzer** ND. Signature Alois.	—	—	—
S171	**20 Kreuzer Convenzs. Münze** ND. Signature Saffran and Müller.	125.	250.	—
S172	**1 Gulden** ND. Signature Joh. Dietrich v. Hermannsthal.	—	—	—

		Good	Fine	XF
S173	**1 Gulden Covmüz** ND. Signature Saffran and Müller with seal.	125.	250.	—
S174	**5 Gulden Co. Müz** ND. Signature Saffran and Müller, with seal. Value in Roman numeral.	125.	250.	—
S175	**10 Gulden Co. Müz** ND. Signature Saffran and Müller, with seal. Value in Arabic numerals.	125.	250.	—

1849 Issue

		Good	Fine	XF
S176	**5 Gulden Conv. Fuss** 20.4.1849. Value in Roman numeral.	125.	250.	—
S177	**10 Gulden** 20.4.1849. Value in Roman numeral.	125.	250.	—

Komárom

1849 First Issue

		Good	Fine	XF
S179	**1 Kraiczár** ND (1849).	—	—	—

		Good	Fine	XF
S180	**2 Kraiczár** ND (1849). Like #S179.	—	—	—

		Good	Fine	XF
S181	**8 Pengö Krajczár** 6.4.1849.	20.00	40.00	—

1849 Second Issue

#S182 and S183 different design variants. Forgeries exist.

		Good	Fine	XF
S182	**5 Pengö Krajczár** 13.7.1849. 3 varieties.	20.00	40.00	—
S183	**10 Pengö Krajczár** 13.7.1849. 3 varieties.	20.00	40.00	—

Temesvár

1849 Issue

		Good	Fine	XF
S191	**1 Kreuzer W.W.** ND. Small cardboard.	—	—	—
S192	**3 Kreuzer W.W.** ND.	—	—	—
S193	**6 Krajcár C.M.** 19.3.1849.	—	—	—
S194	**8 Krajcár C.M.** 19.3.1849.	—	—	—
S197	**5 Gulden C.M.** 1.5.1849.			
	a. Issued note.	—	—	—
	b. Punched hole cancelled.	—	—	—
S198	**10 Gulden C.M.** 1.5.1849. Like #S197.			
	a. Issued note.	—	—	—
	b. Punched hole cancelled.	—	—	—

Russian Army Occupation - WWII

A Vöröshadsereg Parancsnoksága

1944 Issue

		VG	VF	UNC
M1	**1 Pengö** 1944. Blue on light brown underprint. Without serial #. Printing size on date side. 106 x 49mm.			
	a. Underprint horizontal wavy lines.	.50	1.50	6.00
	b. Underprint vertical wavy lines.	.50	1.50	6.00

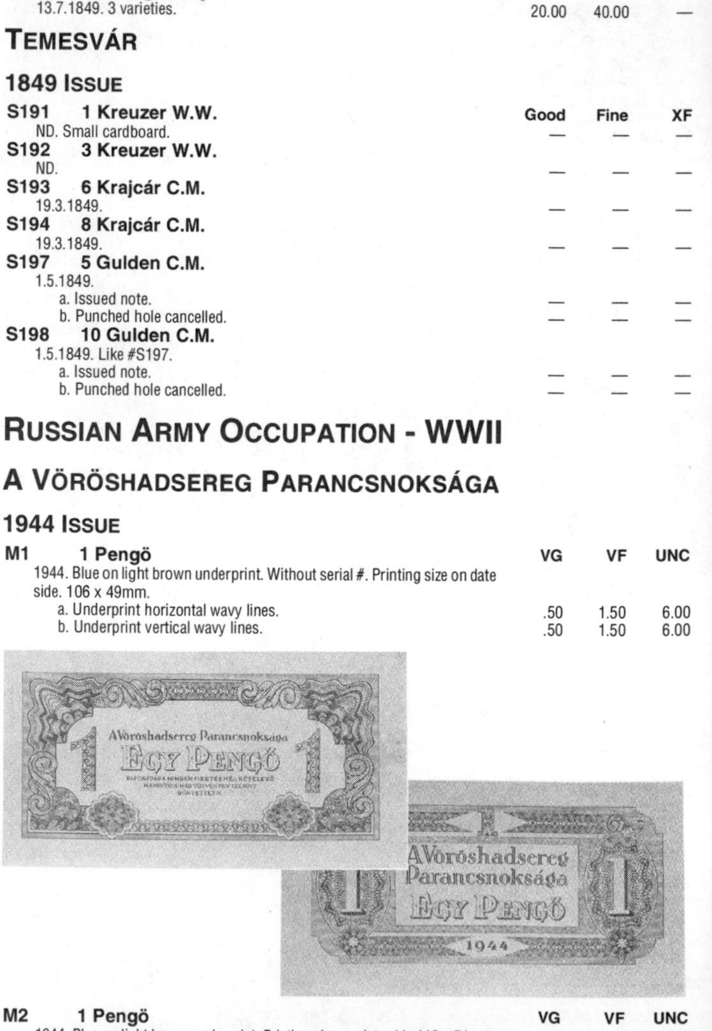

		VG	VF	UNC
M2	**1 Pengö** 1944. Blue on light brown underprint. Printing size on date side 118 x 54mm.			
	a. Without serial #. With horizontal wavy lines.	.25	.50	3.00
	b. Without serial #. With vertical wavy lines.	.25	.50	3.00
	c. With serial #.	8.00	20.00	50.00

M3 2 Pengö	VG	VF	UNC
1944. Blue on green underprint.	.25	.50	3.00

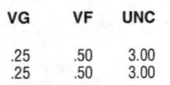

M4 5 Pengö	VG	VF	UNC
1944. Lilac on light blue underprint.			
a. With horizontal wavy lines.	.25	.50	3.00
b. With vertical wavy lines.	.25	.50	3.00

M5 10 Pengö	VG	VF	UNC
1944. Dark green on lilac and green underprint.	.50	2.00	8.00

M6 20 Pengö	VG	VF	UNC
1944. Gray on dull olive underprint.			
a. Without serial #.	10.00	25.00	60.00
b. With serial #. 2 serial # varieties.	.50	2.00	8.00

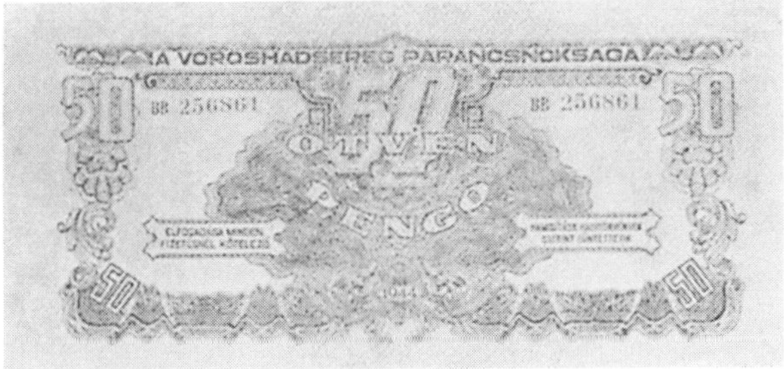

	VG	VF	UNC
M7 50 Pengö 1944. Olive on light brown and blue underprint. 2 serial # varieties.	.50	1.50	10.00
M8 100 Pengö 1944. Dark brown on dull orange underprint. 2 serial # varieties.	.50	1.50	10.00

M9 1000 Pengö	VG	VF	UNC
1944. Red on light blue underprint.	3.50	8.00	30.00

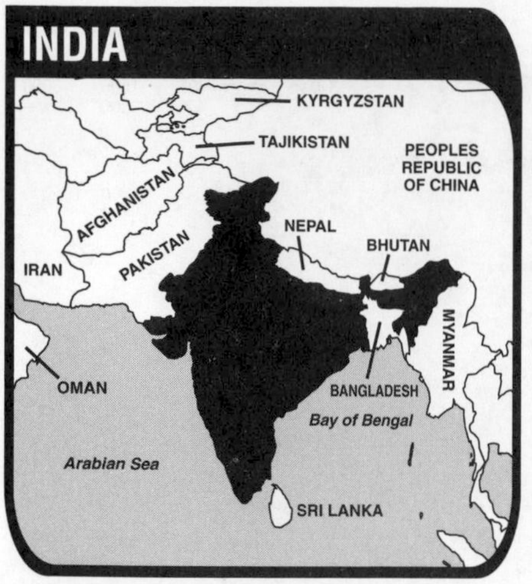

The Republic of India, a subcontinent jutting southward from the mainland of Asia, has an area of 3,287,590 sq. km. and a population of 1,147.9 million, second only to that of the Peoples Republic of China. Capital: New Delhi. India's economy is d on agriculture and industrial activity. Engineering goods, cotton apparel and fabrics, handicrafts, tea, iron and steel are exported.

Aryan tribes from the northwest infiltrated onto the Indian subcontinent about 1500 B.C.; their merger with the earlier Dravidian inhabitants created the classical Indian culture. The Maurya Empire of the 4th and 3rd centuries B.C. - which reached its zenith under Ashoka - united much of South Asia. The Golden Age ushered in by the Gupta dynasty (4th to 6th centuries A.D.) saw a flowering of Indian science, art, and culture. Arab incursions starting in the 8th century and Turkic in the 12th were followed by those of European traders, beginning in the late 15th century. By the 19th century, Britain had assumed political control of virtually all Indian lands. Indian armed forces in the British army played a vital role in both World Wars. Nonviolent resistance to British colonialism led by Mohandas Gandhi and Jawaharlal Nehru brought independence in 1947. The subcontinent was divided into the secular state of India and the smaller Muslim state of Pakistan. A third war between the two countries in 1971 resulted in East Pakistan becoming the separate nation of Bangladesh. India's nuclear weapons testing in 1998 caused Pakistan to conduct its own tests that same year. The dispute between the countries over the state of Kashmir is ongoing, but discussions and confidence-building measures have led to decreased tensions since 2002. Despite impressive gains in economic investment and output, India faces pressing problems such as significant overpopulation, environmental degradation, extensive poverty, and ethnic and religious strife.

RULERS:

British to 1947

Note: Staple holes and condition:

Perfect uncirculated notes are rarely encountered without having at least two tiny holes made by staples, stick pins or stitching having been done during age old accounting practices before and after a note is released to circulation. Staples were officially discontinued in 1998.

Note: Certain listings encompassing issues circulated by various commercial bank and regional authorities are contained in Volume 1.

Persian Gulf

Known as "Gulf Rupees." Intended for circulation in areas of Oman, Bahrain, Qatar and Trucial States during 1950's and early 1960's. "Z" prefix in serial #.

Government of India

ND Issue

		VG	VF	UNC
R1	**1 Rupee** ND. Red. Redesigned coin with Asoka column at right. Signature A. K. Roy; left K. Jha or H. V. R. lengar.	25.00	50.00	200.

Reserve Bank of India

ND Issue

		VG	VF	UNC
R2	**5 Rupees** ND. Orange. Redesigned panels at left and right. Signature H. V. R. lengar.	100.	200.	500.

		VG	VF	UNC
R3	**10 Rupees** ND. Red. Hindi corrected. Letter A. Signature H. V. R. lengar.	25.00	125.	350.

		VG	VF	UNC
R4	**100 Rupees** ND. Green. Hindi corrected. Signature H. V. R. lengar.	65.00	350.	1350.

Haj Pilgrim

Intended for use by Moslem pilgrims in Mecca, Saudi Arabia.

Reserve Bank of India

(ND) Issue

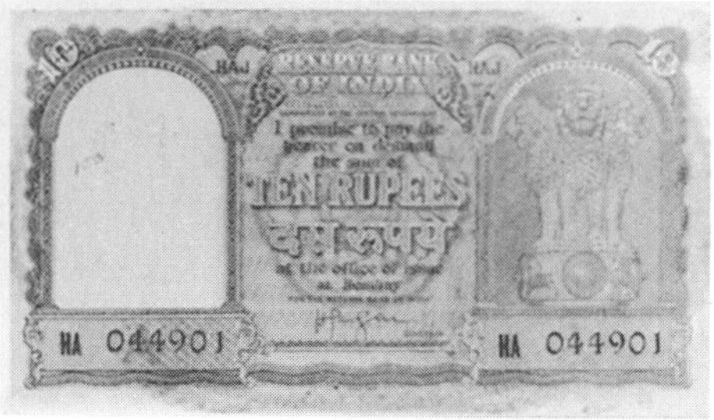

		VG	VF	UNC
R5	**10 Rupees** ND. Blue. Asoka column at right. Letters *HA* near serial number, and *HAJ* at left and right of bank title at top. Like # 39c.	250.	500.	1000.
R6	**100 Rupees** ND. Red. Asoka column at right. Letters *HA* near serial number, and *HAJ* at left and right of bank title at top. Signature H. V. R. lengar.	500.	1000.	—

INDIA - BRITISH

The civilization of India, which began about 2500 B.C., flourished under a succession of empires - notably those of Chandragupta, Asoka and the Mughals - until undermined in the 18th and 19th centuries by European colonial powers.

The Portuguese were the first to arrive, off Calicut in May 1498. It was not until 1612, after the Portuguese and Spanish power had begun to wane, that the British East India Company established its initial settlement at Surat. Britain could not have chosen a more propitious time. The northern Mogul Empire, the central girdle of petty states, and the southern Vijayanagar Empire were crumbling and ripe for foreign exploitation. By the end of the century, English traders were firmly established in Bombay, Madras, Calcutta and lesser places elsewhere, and Britain was implementing its announced policy to create such civil and military institutions as may be the foundation of secure English domination for all time. By 1757, following the successful conclusion of a war of colonial rivalry with France during which the military victories of Robert Clive, a young officer with the British East India Company, made him the most powerful man in India, the British were firmly settled in India as not only traders but as conquerors. During the next 60 years, the British East India Company acquired dominion over most of India by bribery and force, and governed it directly or through puppet princelings.

Because of the Sepoy Mutiny of 1857-58, a large scale mutiny among Indian soldiers of the Bengal army, control of the government of India was transferred from the East India Company to the British Crown in 1858. At this point in world history, India was the brightest jewel in the imperial diadem of the British lords of the earth, but even then a movement for greater Indian representation in government presaged the Indian Empire's twilight hour less than a century hence - it would pass into history on August 15, 1947.

All private bank issues ceased by 1862.

MONETARY SYSTEM:

1 Rupee = 16 Annas
1 Anna = 4 Pice
1 Pice = (Paisa) = 3 Pies

BANKS:

Asiatic Bank .... #S5-S8
Bank of Bengal .... #20-S95
Bank of Bombay .... #S100-S117
Bank of Hindostan .... #S120-S137
Bank of Madras .... #S140-S153
Bank of Western India .... #S154
Calcutta Bank .... #S155-S160
Commercial Bank .... #S166-S171
Commercial Bank of India .... #S175
Hindostan Bank .... #S180
Madras Government Bank .... #S185-S186
Oriental Bank .... #S190-S193
Union Bank .... #S195-S198

BRITISH ADMINISTRATION

ASIATIC BANK

1800S ISSUE

	Good	Fine	XF
S5 5 Star Pagodas, 17.5 Arcot Rupees 18xx. Black. India holding snake and mace seated with tiger, mountains in background at upper left. Unsigned remainder.	600.	3000.	6000.
S6 10 Star Pagodas, 35 Arcot Rupees 18xx. Black. India holding snake and mace seated with tiger, mountains in background at upper left. Unsigned remainder.	600.	3000.	6000.
S7 100 Star Pagodas, 350 Arcot Rupees 1.2.1820. Black. India holding snake and mace seated with tiger, mountains in background at upper left.	600.	3000.	6000.
S8 500 Star Pagodas, 1750 Arcot Rupees 18xx. Black. India holding snake and mace seated with tiger, mountains in background at upper left. Unsigned remainder.	600.	3000.	6000.

BANK OF BENGAL

1812 ISSUE

	Good	Fine	XF
S20 20 Sicca Rupees 13.9.1812-29.5.1819. Black. Serial # at lower right.			
a. Issued note.	600.	1500.	3000.
b. Issued note with cut signature.	400.	800.	—

1815-16 ISSUE

	Good	Fine	XF
S24 16 Sicca Rupees / 1 Gold Mohur 7.9.1816-16.12.1820. Black. Serial # at upper left and lower right.			
a. Issued note.	600.	1500.	3000.
b. Issued note with cut signature.	400.	800.	—
S25 500 Sicca Rupees 13.7.1815-27.11.1820. Black. Serial # at upper left and lower right.			
a. Issued note.	600.	1500.	3000.
b. Issued note with cut signature.	400.	800.	—

1824-26 ISSUE

	Good	Fine	XF
S30 10 Sicca Rupees 8.12.1824-11.7.1826. Black. Commerce seated at top center, value in Bengali, Persian and Kaithi above. Back: Bank name in scroll.			
a. Issued note.	600.	1500.	3000.
b. Issued note with cut signature.	400.	800.	—
S31 16 Sicca Rupees / 1 Gold Mohur 6.4.1825. Black. Commerce seated at top center, value in Bengali, Persian and Kaithi above. Back: Bank name in scroll.			
a. Issued note.	600.	1500.	3000.
b. Issued note with cut signature.	400.	800.	—
S32 50 Sicca Rupees 4.12.1824-5.1.1828. Black. Commerce seated at top center, value in Bengali, Persian and Kaithi above. Back: Bank name in scroll.			
a. Issued note.	600.	1500.	3000.
b. Issued note with cut signature.	400.	800.	—
S33 100 Sicca Rupees 27.10.1824-18.6.1829. Black. Commerce seated at top center, value in Bengali, Persian and Kaithi above. Back: Bank name in scroll.			
a. Issued note.	600.	1500.	3000.
b. Issued note with cut signature.	400.	800.	—
S34 250 Sicca Rupees 18xx. Commerce seated at top center, value in Bengali, Persian and Kaithi above. Uniface. Back: Bank name in scroll. Overprint: *SPECIMEN*. Proof.			
a. Issued note.	—	Unc	3000.
b. Issued note with cut signature.	—	—	—
S35 500 Sicca Rupees 16.8.1824-31.12.1827. Black. Commerce seated at top center, value in Bengali, Persian and Kaithi above. Back: Bank name in scroll.			
a. Issued note.	600.	1500.	3000.
b. Issued note with cut signature.	400.	800.	—
S36 1000 Sicca Rupees 16.1.1826; 2.2.1826. Black. Commerce seated at top center, value in Bengali, Persian and Kaithi above. Back: Bank name in scroll.			
a. Issued note.	600.	1500.	3000.
b. Issued note with cut signature.	400.	800.	—
p. Proof with overprint: *SPECIMEN*.	—	Unc	3000.
r. Remainder without signature	—	Unc	1250.

1827-29 ISSUE

	Good	Fine	XF
S40 10 Sicca Rupees 15.5.1828-28.10.1836. Black. Commerce seated at top center, value in Bengali, Persian and Kaithi above. Value under right serial #. Back: Bank name in scroll. Printer: P&H.			
a. Issued note.	600.	1500.	3000.
b. Issued note with cut signature.	400.	800.	—
S41 50 Sicca Rupees 3.1.1828-27.2.1829. Black. Commerce seated at top center, value in Bengali, Persian and Kaithi above. Value under right serial #. Back: Bank name in scroll. Printer: P&H.			
a. Issued note.	600.	1500.	3000.
b. Issued note with cut signature.	400.	800.	—
S42 100 Sicca Rupees 8.7.1829-18.1.1837. Black. Commerce seated at top center, value in Bengali, Persian and Kaithi above. Value under right serial #. Back: Bank name in scroll. Printer: P&H.			
a. Issued note.	600.	1500.	3000.
b. Issued note with cut signature.	400.	800.	—
S43 1000 Sicca Rupees 21.3.1827; 1.4.1827. Black. Commerce seated at top center, value in Bengali, Persian and Kaithi above. Value under right serial #. Back: Bank name in scroll. Printer: P&H.			
a. Issued note.	600.	1500.	3000.
b. Issued note with cut signature.	400.	800.	—

1828-33 ISSUE

	Good	Fine	XF
S45 20 Sicca Rupees 30.12.1828. Black. Commerce seated at top center, top border with Persian script, bottom with Kaithi. Back: Bank name in center scroll. Printer: P&H.			
a. Issued note.	600.	1500.	3000.
b. Issued note with cut signature.	400.	800.	—
S46 25 Sicca Rupees 20.1.1833. Black. Commerce seated at top center, top border with Persian script, bottom with Kaithi. Back: Bank name in center scroll. Printer: P&H.			
a. Issued note.	600.	1500.	3000.
b. Issued note with cut signature.	400.	800.	—

1828-34 THIRD ISSUE

	Good	Fine	XF
S50 10 Sicca Rupees 31.10.1828-2.11.1835. Black. Commerce seated at upper center. Back: Value in languages. Printer: P&B.			
a. Issued note.	600.	1500.	3000.
b. Issued note with cut signature.	400.	800.	—
S51 16 Sicca Rupees / 1 Gold Mohur 20.3.1833-28.8.1834. Black. Commerce seated at upper center. Back: Value in languages. Printer: P&B.			
a. Issued note.	600.	1500.	3000.
b. Issued note with cut signature.	400.	800.	—
S52 20 Sicca Rupees 18.12.1833-2.1.1836. Black. Commerce seated at upper center. Back: Value in languages. Printer: P&B.			
a. Issued note.	600.	1500.	3000.
b. Issued note with cut signature.	400.	800.	—
S53 25 Sicca Rupees 17.12.1833-2.1.1836. Black. Commerce seated at upper center. Back: Value in languages. Printer: P&B.			
a. Issued note.	600.	1500.	3000.
b. Issued note with cut signature.	400.	800.	—
S54 50 Sicca Rupees 26.11.1829-26.1.1836. Black. Commerce seated at upper center. Back: Value in languages. Printer: P&B.			
a. Issued note.	600.	1500.	3000.
b. Issued note with cut signature.	400.	800.	—
S55 100 Sicca Rupees 13.9.1832-23.10.1835. Black. Commerce seated at upper center. Back: Value in languages. Printer: P&B.	600.	1500.	3000.
S56 250 Sicca Rupees 18.1.1834-12.11.1835. Black. Commerce seated at upper center. Back: Value in languages. Printer: P&B.			
a. Issued note.	600.	1500.	3000.
b. Issued note with cut signature.	400.	800.	—

No.	Description	Good	Fine	XF
S57	**500 Sicca Rupees** 25.2.1832-14.3.1834. Black. Commerce seated at upper center. Back: Value in languages. Printer: P&B.			
	a. Issued note.	600.	1500.	3000.
	b. Issued note with cut signature.	400.	800.	—
S58	**1000 Sicca Rupees** 12.5.1832-10.4.1835. Black. Commerce seated at upper center. Back: Value in languages. Printer: P&B.			
	a. Issued note.	600.	1500.	3000.
	b. Issued note with cut signature.	400.	800.	—

1837-47 Issue

No.	Description	Good	Fine	XF
S60	**10 Company Rupees** 28.2.1842; 28.3.1842. Black. Commerce seated at top center. Serial # handwritten. Printer: P&B.			
	a. Issued note.	600.	1500.	3000.
	b. Issued note with cut signature.	400.	800.	—
S61	**15 Company Rupees** 28.2.1842-8.7.1845. Black. Commerce seated at top center. Serial # handwritten. Printer: P&B.			
	a. Issued note.	600.	1500.	3000.
	b. Issued note with cut signature.	400.	800.	—
S62	**20 Company Rupees** 22.9.1837; 25.1.1841. Black. Commerce seated at top center. Serial # handwritten. Printer: P&B.			
	a. Issued note.	600.	1500.	3000.
	b. Issued note with cut signature.	400.	800.	—
S63	**25 Company Rupees** 25.1.1841. Black. Commerce seated at top center. Serial # handwritten. Printer: P&B.			
	a. Issued note.	600.	1500.	3000.
	b. Issued note with cut signature.	400.	800.	—
S64	**50 Company Rupees** 8.11.1842; 20.12.1843. Black. Commerce seated at top center. Serial # handwritten. Printer: P&B.			
	a. Issued note.	600.	1500.	3000.
	b. Issued note with cut signature.	400.	800.	—
S65	**100 Company Rupees** 23.1.1841; 10.1.1842. Black. Commerce seated at top center. Serial # handwritten. Printer: P&B.			
	a. Issued note.	600.	1500.	3000.
	b. Issued note with cut signature.	400.	800.	—
S66	**500 Company Rupees** 3.12.1847. Black. Commerce seated at top center. Serial # handwritten. Printer: P&B.			
	a. Issued note.	600.	1500.	3000.
	b. Issued note with cut signature.	400.	800.	—

1840-53 Issue

No.	Description	Good	Fine	XF
S70	**10 Company Rupees** 27.5.1852. Black. Commerce seated at top center. Serial # typescript. Printer: PBC.			
	a. Issued note.	600.	1500.	3000.
	b. Issued note with cut signature.	400.	800.	—
S71	**15 Company Rupees** 3.5.1852-26.2.1857. Black. Commerce seated at top center. Serial # typescript. Printer: PBC.			
	a. Issued note.	600.	1500.	3000.
	b. Issued note with cut signature.	400.	800.	—
S72	**20 Company Rupees** 17.2.1840-9.10.1852. Black. Commerce seated at top center. Serial # typescript. Printer: PBC.			
	a. Issued note.	600.	1500.	3000.
	b. Issued note with cut signature.	400.	800.	—
S73	**25 Company Rupees** 17.12.1842-20.3.1854. Black. Commerce seated at top center. Serial # typescript. Printer: PBC.			
	a. Issued note.	600.	1500.	3000.
	b. Issued note with cut signature.	400.	800.	—
S74	**50 Company Rupees** 28.9.1852-18.11.1853. Black. Commerce seated at top center. Serial # typescript. Printer: PBC.			
	a. Issued note.	600.	1500.	3000.
	b. Issued note with cut signature.	400.	800.	—
S75	**100 Company Rupees** 16.1.1852-10.11.1852. Black. Commerce seated at top center. Serial # typescript. Printer: PBC.			
	a. Issued note.	600.	1500.	3000.
	b. Issued note with cut signature.	400.	800.	—
S76	**250 Company Rupees** 25.7.1845-10.5.1847. Black. Commerce seated at top center. Serial # typescript. Printer: PBC.			
	a. Issued note.	600.	1500.	3000.
	b. Issued note with cut signature.	400.	800.	—
S77	**1000 Company Rupees** 15.4.1853. Black. Commerce seated at top center. Serial # typescript. Printer: PBC.			
	a. Issued note.	600.	1500.	3000.
	b. Issued note with cut signature.	400.	800.	—

1853 Issue

No.	Description	Good	Fine	XF
S80	**10 Company Rupees** 15.4.1853-15.8.1855. Black. Commerce seated at top center. Without native scripts. Printer: PBC.			
	a. Issued note.	600.	1500.	3000.
	b. Issued note with cut signature.	400.	800.	—
S81	**15 Company Rupees** 15.4.1853-1.9.1855. Black. Commerce seated at top center. Without native scripts. Printer: PBC.			
	a. Issued note.	600.	1500.	3000.
	b. Issued note with cut signature.	400.	800.	—
S82	**20 Company Rupees** 15.4.1853. Black. Commerce seated at top center. Without native scripts. Printer: PBC.			
	a. Issued note.	600.	1500.	3000.
	b. Issued note with cut signature.	400.	800.	—
S83	**25 Company Rupees** 15.4.1853. Black. Commerce seated at top center. Without native scripts. Printer: PBC.			
	a. Issued note.	600.	1500.	3000.
	b. Issued note with cut signature.	400.	800.	—
S84	**50 Company Rupees** 15.4.1853. Black. Commerce seated at top center. Without native scripts. Printer: PBC.			
	a. Issued note.	600.	1500.	3000.
	b. Issued note with cut signature.	400.	800.	—
S85	**100 Company Rupees** 15.4.1853. Black. Commerce seated at top center. Without native scripts. Printer: PBC.			
	a. Issued note.	600.	1500.	3000.
	b. Issued note with cut signature.	400.	800.	—
S86	**250 Company Rupees** 15.4.1853. Black. Commerce seated at top center. Without native scripts. Printer: PBC.			
	a. Issued note.	600.	1500.	3000.
	b. Issued note with cut signature.	400.	800.	—
S87	**500 Company Rupees** 15.4.1853. Black. Commerce seated at top center. Without native scripts. Printer: PBC.			
	a. Issued note.	600.	1500.	3000.
	b. Issued note with cut signature.	400.	800.	—
S88	**1000 Company Rupees** 15.4.1853. Black. Commerce seated at top center. Without native scripts. Printer: PBC.			
	a. Issued note.	600.	1500.	3000.
	b. Issued note with cut signature.	400.	800.	—

1857 Issue

No.	Description	Good	Fine	XF
S90	**10 Rupees** 31.8.1857; 12.4.1859. Black on purple underprint. Justice and Commerce seated with Britannia and lion at upper center. Back: Black and blue. Large value in scroll.			
	a. Issued note.	600.	1500.	3000.
	p. Proof overprint: *SPECIMEN.*	—	Unc	3000.
S91	**25 Rupees** 2.9.1857; 3.9.1857. Black on blue underprint. Justice and Commerce seated with Britannia and lion at upper center. Back: Black and blue. Large value in scroll.			
	a. Issued note.	600.	1500.	3000.
	p. Proof overprint: *SPECIMEN.*	—	Unc	3000.
S92	**50 Rupees** 19.10.1857. Black on red underprint. Justice and Commerce seated with Britannia and lion at upper center. Back: Black and blue. Large value in scroll.			
	a. Issued note.	600.	1500.	3000.
	p. Proof overprint: *SPECIMEN.*	—	Unc	3000.
S93	**100 Rupees** 17.11.1857. Black on green underprint. Justice and Commerce seated with Britannia and lion at upper center. Back: Black and blue. Large value in scroll.			
	a. Issued note.	600.	1500.	3000.
	p. Proof overprint: *SPECIMEN.*	—	Unc	3000.
S94	**500 Rupees** 18.12.1857. Black on orange underprint. Justice and Commerce seated with Britannia and lion at upper center. Back: Black and blue. Large value in scroll.			
	a. Issued note.	600.	1500.	3000.
	p. Proof overprint: *SPECIMEN.*	—	Unc	3000.
S95	**1000 Rupees** 27.1.1858. Black on red underprint. Justice and Commerce seated with Britannia and lion at upper center. Back: Black and blue. Large value in scroll.			
	a. Issued note.	600.	1500.	3000.
	p. Proof overprint: *SPECIMEN.*	—	Unc	3000.

Bank of Bombay

1846-54 Issue

No.	Description	Good	Fine	XF
S100	**10 Rupees** 5.1.1854-10.10.1856. Black. Statues of standing Mountstuart Elphinstone at left, John Malcolm at right, starbursts at top and bottom center. Native legends in four border quadrants.	600.	1500.	3000.
S101	**15 Rupees** 2.7.1849. Black. Statues of standing Mountstuart Elphinstone at left, John Malcolm at right, starbursts at top and bottom center. Native legends in four border quadrants.	600.	1500.	3000.
S102	**25 Rupees** 18xx. Black. Statues of standing Mountstuart Elphinstone at left, John Malcolm at right, starbursts at top and bottom center. Native legends in four border quadrants.	600.	1500.	3000.
S103	**50 Rupees** 15.4.1846. Black. Statues of standing Mountstuart Elphinstone at left, John Malcolm at right, starbursts at top and bottom center. Native legends in four border quadrants.	600.	1500.	3000.
S104	**100 Rupees** 2.9.1853. Statues of standing Mountstuart Elphinstone at left, John Malcolm at right, starbursts at top and bottom center. Native legends in four border quadrants.	600.	1500.	3000.
S105	**10000 Rupees** 18xx. Black. Statues of standing Mountstuart Elphinstone at left, John Malcolm at right, starbursts at top and bottom center. Native legends in four border quadrants. Overprint: *SPECIMEN.* Proof.	—	Unc	3000.

1853-55 Issue

	Good	Fine	XF
S110 10 Rupees 22.3.1853-1.11.1860. Black on brown or maroon underprint. Native legends in two border quadrants.			
a. Issued note.	600.	1500.	3000.
p. Proof overprint: *SPECIMEN.*	—	Unc	3000.
S111 25 Rupees 6.8.1855-18.11.1866. Black on pink underprint. Native legends in two border quadrants.			
a. Issued note.	600.	1500.	3000.
p. Proof overprint: *SPECIMEN.*	—	Unc	3000.
S112 100 Rupees 1.1.1855; 10.8.1855. Black on brown underprint. Native legends in two border quadrants.			
a. Issued note.	600.	1500.	3000.
p. Proof overprint: *SPECIMEN.*	—	Unc	3000.
S113 1000 Rupees 18xx. Black. Native legends in two border quadrants. Overprint: *SPECIMEN*. Proof.	—	Unc	3000.

1859-60 Issue

	Good	Fine	XF
S115 10 Rupees 1.11.1860. Black on brown underprint. Bombay town hall at upper center, statues of standing Elphinstone at left, Malcolm at right, starburst at top center. Bombay arms at bottom center. Native text in four border quadrants.			
a. Issued note.	600.	1500.	3000.
p. Proof overprint: *SPECIMEN.*	—	Unc	3000.
S116 25 Rupees 29.9.1859. Black on rose underprint. Bombay town hall at upper center, statues of standing Elphinstone at left, Malcolm at right, starburst at top center. Bombay arms at bottom center. Native text in four border quadrants.	600.	1500.	3000.
S117 100 Rupees 29.9.1859. Black on green underprint. Bombay town hall at upper center, statues of standing Elphinstone at left, Malcolm at right, starburst at top center. Bombay arms at bottom center. Native text in four border quadrants.	600.	1500.	3000.

Bank of Hindostan

1823-27 Issue

	Good	Fine	XF
S120 4 Sicca Rupees 28.11.1823. Black on blue underprint.	600.	2250.	4500.
S121 16 Sicca Rupees 5.1.1827. Black on blue underprint.	750.	3000.	6000.
S122 20 Sicca Rupees 8.12.1823. Black on blue underprint.	750.	3000.	6000.

1820s First Issue

	Good	Fine	XF
S125 50 Sicca Rupees 18xx. Black. Tiger lying down at lower center. Printer: P&B. Unsigned remainder.	750.	3000.	6000.
S126 100 Sicca Rupees 18xx. Black. Tiger lying down at lower center. Printer: P&B. Unsigned remainder.	750.	3000.	6000.
S127 250 Sicca Rupees 18xx. Black. Tiger lying down at lower center. Printer: P&B. Unsigned remainder.	750.	3000.	6000.
S128 500 Sicca Rupees 18xx. Black. Tiger lying down at lower center. Printer: P&B. Unsigned remainder.	750.	3000.	6000.
S129 1000 Sicca Rupees 18xx. Black. Tiger lying down at lower center. Printer: P&B. Unsigned remainder.	750.	3000.	6000.

1820s Second Issue

	Good	Fine	XF
S130 4 Sicca Rupees 18xx. Black on red underprint.	750.	3000.	6000.
S131 20 Sicca Rupees 18xx. Black on red underprint.	750.	3000.	6000.

1830s Issue

	Good	Fine	XF
S135 4 Sicca Rupees 183x. Black.	225.	1100.	3000.
S136 10 Sicca Rupees 183x. Black.	600.	2250.	6000.
S137 16 Sicca Rupees 183x. Black.	225.	1100.	3000.

Bank of Madras

1845-49 Issue

	Good	Fine	XF
S140 10 Rupees 1.5.1845. Black.	600.	3000.	6000.
S141 20 Rupees 24.7.1849. Black.	600.	3000.	6000.
S142 25 Rupees 27.4.1849. Black.	600.	3000.	6000.
S143 50 Rupees 10.4.1849. Black.	600.	3000.	6000.
S144 100 Rupees 184x. Black.	600.	3000.	6000.
S145 500 Rupees 1.4.1845. Black.	600.	3000.	6000.
S146 1000 Rupees 2.1.1845. Black.	600.	3000.	6000.
S147 3000 Rupees 184x. Black.	600.	3000.	6000.

1849-61 Issue

	Good	Fine	XF
S149 10 Rupees 25.7.1861. Black.	600.	3000.	6000.
S150 15 Rupees 1.4.1856; 4.4.1856. Black.	600.	3000.	6000.
S151 25 Rupees 20.8.1849. Black.	600.	3000.	6000.
S152 50 Rupees 20.7.1859. Black.	600.	3000.	6000.
S153 100 Rupees 6.1.1860. Black.	600.	3000.	6000.

Bank of Western India

1844 Issue

	Good	Fine	XF
S154 5 Rupees 1.5.1844. Black.	600.	3000.	6000.

Calcutta Bank

1824-25 Issue

	Good	Fine	XF
S155 5 Sicca Rupees 11.1.1824. Black. Allegorical figure of Agriculture seated at upper center. Back: Bank name in scroll.	450.	1500.	3000.
S156 10 Sicca Rupees 5.1.1825. Black. Allegorical figure of Agriculture seated at upper center. Back: Bank name in scroll.	450.	1500.	3000.
S157 20 Sicca Rupees 18xx. Black. Allegorical figure of Agriculture seated at upper center. Back: Bank name in scroll.	450.	1500.	3000.
S158 500 Sicca Rupees 18xx. Black. Allegorical figure of Agriculture seated at upper center. Back: Bank name in scroll.	450.	1500.	3000.
S159 1000 Sicca Rupees 18xx. Black. Allegorical figure of Agriculture seated at upper center. Back: Bank name in scroll.	450.	1500.	3000.
S160 5000 Sicca Rupees 18xx. Black. Allegorical figure of Agriculture seated at upper center. Back: Bank name in scroll.	450.	1500.	3000.

Commercial Bank

1820s First Issue

	Good	Fine	XF
S166 8 Sicca Rupees 18xx. Black. Britannia seated at upper left, Commerce and Mercury at upper center right, Ganga statue at upper right. Persian script flanking central design. Proof.	—	Unc	3000.
S167 10 Sicca Rupees 18xx. Black. Britannia seated at upper left, Commerce and Mercury at upper center right, Ganga statue at upper right. Persian script flanking central design. Proof.	—	Unc	3000.
S168 20 Sicca Rupees 18xx. Black. Britannia seated at upper left, Commerce and Mercury at upper center right, Ganga statue at upper right. Persian script flanking central design. Proof.	—	Unc	3000.
S168A 500 Sicca Rupees 18xx. Black. Proof.	—	Unc	16,000.

1820s Second Issue

	Good	Fine	XF
S170 5 Sicca Rupees 18xx. Black. Britannia seated at upper left, Commerce and Mercury at upper center right, Ganga statue at upper right. Proof.	—	Unc	3000.
S171 16 Sicca Rupees 18xx. Black. Britannia seated at upper left, Commerce and Mercury at upper center right, Ganga statue at upper right. Proof.	—	Unc	3000.

Commercial Bank of India

1845 Issue

	Good	Fine	XF
S175 10 Rupees 18xx. Black. Unsigned remainder.	—	3000.	6000.

Hindostan Bank

1800s Issue

	Good	Fine	XF
S180 5 Sicca Rupees 18xx. Dark brown on red underprint. Unissued remainder.	—	Unc	3750.

Madras Government Bank

1816-22 Issue

	Good	Fine	XF
S185 2 Star Pagodas, 7 Rupees 9.10.1816. Black.	—	3000.	6000.
S186 5 Rupees 24.5.1822. Black.	—	3000.	6000.

Oriental Bank

1848 Issue

	Good	Fine	XF
S190 5 Rupees 184x. Unsigned remainder.	—	3000.	6000.
S191 50 Rupees 10.11.1845. Black.	—	3000.	6000.
S191A 100 Rupees 184x. Brown. Unsigned remainder.	—	—	10,000.
S192 500 Rupees 184x. Black. Unsigned remainder.	—	3000.	6000.
S193 1000 Rupees 184x. Black. Unsigned remainder.	—	3000.	6000.

Union Bank

1840s Issue

	Good	Fine	XF
S195 5 Rupees 25.5.1847. Black. Elephant at left and right border.	—	3000.	6000.
S196 10 Company Rupees 18xx. Black. Elephant at left, tiger at right border. Unissued remainder.	—	3000.	6000.
S197 20 Company Rupees 30.3.1841. Black. Snake at left and right border. Unsigned remainder.	—	3000.	6000.
S198 250 Company Rupees 18xx. Black. Ganga standing at left, tiger at right border.	—	3000.	6000.

India - Princely States

Only four Native States ever prepared bank notes for issue - Jammu and Kashmir in 1876, Dhrangadhra and Hyderabad in 1918, and Kutch in 1946. Kutch never released its notes, while those of Jammu and Kashmir were recalled shortly afterward. Dhrangadhra's notes may have been used briefly. Only Hyderabad's issues enjoyed a lengthy circulation until their withdrawal about 1953.

As World War II progressed, the British Indian colonial coinage became in short supply, especially after the Japanese had invaded Burma and then the Imphal-Kohima-Manipur region of India in 1943-1944. A number of the Native States devised CASH COUPONS to meet the shortage - small ticket-like cardboards, some were prepared from postage or revenue stamp plates, others created with coin pictures, etc. Most were tightly controlled, as attested by their series letters and control numbers - and apparently very few were saved by the populace.

Except for small hoards of Bikaner, Bundi, Indergadh and Junagadh, few specimens have survived since their period of issue. India had few paper money collectors during World War II.

Other Indian state notes may exist.

For purposes of visual clarity, bank notes are shown in this section at 42% of actual size; cash coupons are shown at 65 to 70% of actual size; and stamp money at 100%.

PRINCELY STATES OF INDIA

Ambliara	Indergadh	Navanagar
Bajana	Jaipur	Nawalgarh
Balwan	Jaisalmir	Palitana
Bikaner	Jammu and Kashmir	Rajkot
Bundi	Jasdan	Ramgarh Raj
Chuda	Junagadh	Sailana
Dhar	Kutch	Sayala
Dhrangadhra	Mangrol	Sitamau
Dinajpur	Mengani	Tonk
Gondal	Muli	Vithalgadh
Hyderabad	Mysore	

MONETARY SYSTEM:

1 Paise (Pice) = 3 Pies
1 Anna = 4 Paisa
1 Rupee = 16 Annas

Ambliara

A small princely state located in the Sabar Kantha Agency of Western India with an area of 80 sq. mi. (207 sq. km.).

Government

ND Issue

	Good	Fine	XF
S201 1 Paisa (Pice) ND. Black text. Paper: Brown pressboard. Unique.	—	—	—

Bajana

An estate located in the Western India States Agency between the Ranu of Kutch and Ahmadabad with an area of 183 sq. mi. (474 sq. km.).

Government

ND WWII Cash Coupon Stamp Money Issue

	Good	Fine	XF
S202 1 Anna ND. Red. Purple signature. Paper: White pressboard.	7.50	30.00	60.00

Balwan

An estate located at the extreme northerly border of Kotah State wholly within the boundaries of the Indargarh *kotri.*

Government

ND WWII Emergency Cash Coupons Issue

	Good	Fine	XF
S206 1/4 Anna ND. Black. Paper: Tan pressboard.	5.00	15.00	30.00
S207 1 Anna ND. Dark green. Paper: Tan pressboard.	5.00	15.00	30.00
S209 4 Annas ND. Red-brown. Paper: Tan pressboard.	7.50	17.50	35.00

Bikaner

A state in the Rajputana Agency, with an area of 23,317 sq. mi. (60,407 sq. km.). Also called Bikanir.

Government

ND WWII Emergency Cash Coupons Issue

		VG	VF	UNC
S211	**1 Pice** ND. Back: Oval handstamp: *SADAR TREASURY-BIKANER.* Paper: Square pressboard.	3.00	10.00	17.50

		VG	VF	UNC
S212	**1 Anna** ND. Back: Oval handstamp: *SADAR TREASURY-BIKANER.* Paper: Square pressboard.	4.00	10.00	27.50
S213	**2 Annas** ND. Back: Oval handstamp: *SADAR TREASURY-BIKANER.* Paper: Square pressboard.	4.00	10.00	25.00
S214	**4 Annas** ND. Back: Oval handstamp: *SADAR TREASURY-BIKANER.* Paper: Square pressboard.	5.00	15.00	30.00

Bundi

A state located in the Western Rajputana States Agency with an area of 21,200 sq. mi. (54,922 sq. km.).

Government

ND WWII Emergency Cash Coupon Stamp Money Issue

#S221-S224 similar to postage or revenue stamps. Ovpt: *CASH COUPON* on face, control # on back.

		VG	VF	UNC
S221	**3 Pies = 1 Paisa (Pice)** ND. Violet. Maharaja between brahma bulls at center. English and Hindi denomination. Overprint: *CASH COUPON BUNDI STATE* on face, control # on back. Paper: Pressboard.	5.00	10.00	25.00

		VG	VF	UNC
S222	**1 Anna** ND. Red. Maharaja between brahma bulls at center. English and Hindi denomination. Similar to #S221. Overprint: *CASH COUPON BUNDI STATE* on face, control # on back. Paper: Pressboard.	7.50	15.00	35.00
S224	**4 Annas** ND. Green. Court Fee stamp design. Overprint: *CASH COUPON BUNDI STATE* on face, control # on back. Paper: Pressboard.	7.50	17.50	40.00

Chuda

A small state located in the Western India States Agency between Ahmadabad and Rajkot with an area of 78 sq. mi. (202 sq. km.).

Government

ND WWII Emergency Cash Coupon Stamp Money Issue

		VG	VF	UNC
S226	**1 Paisa** ND. Portrait of *thakor*. Rare.	—	—	—
S227	**2 Paisa** ND. Portrait of *thakor*.			
	a. Blue pressboard.	30.00	75.00	—
	b. Cream to light yellow pressboard.	45.00	125.	—

Dhar

A state in the Southern States and Malwa Agency in Central India with an area of 1,800 sq. mi.

Dhar State Bank

ND WWII Emergency Cash Coupons Issue

		VG	VF	UNC
S231	**1 Pice** ND. Seal of Dhar State Bank at left. Pressboard.	12.50	30.00	55.00
S232	**1 Anna** ND. Seal of Dhar State Bank at left. Like #S231. Small letters: *ONE ANNA.*	15.00	35.00	60.00

		VG	VF	UNC
S233	**1 Anna** ND. Seal of Dhar State Bank at left. Like #S231. Large letters: *ONE ANNA* in English and Hindi.	12.50	30.00	55.00

Dhrangadhra

A small feudatory state located in Gujarat State with an area of 1,167 sq. mi. (3,023 sq. km.).

Jhalawad Bank

ND Circulating Checks Issue

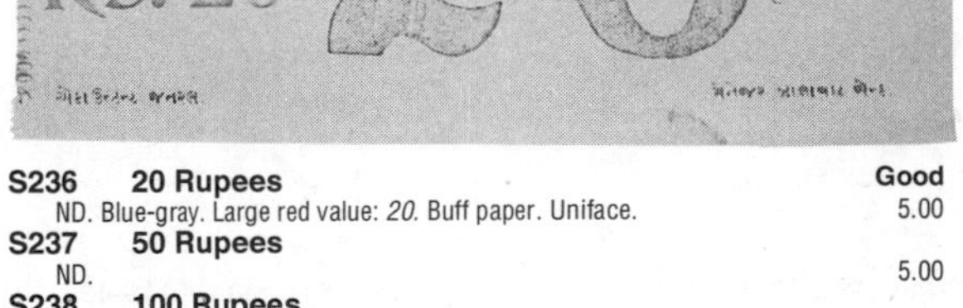

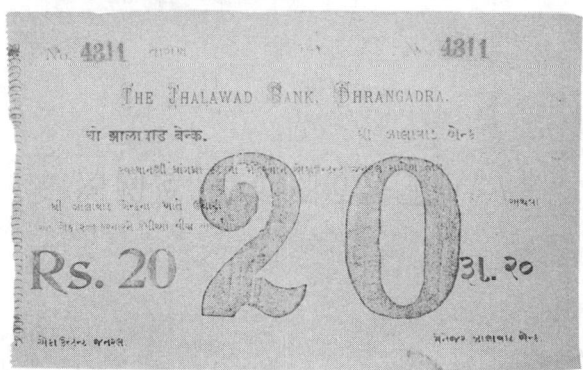

		Good	Fine	XF
S236	**20 Rupees** ND. Blue-gray. Large red value: *20.* Buff paper. Uniface.	5.00	12.50	30.00
S237	**50 Rupees** ND.	5.00	12.50	30.00
S238	**100 Rupees** ND.	5.00	12.50	30.00

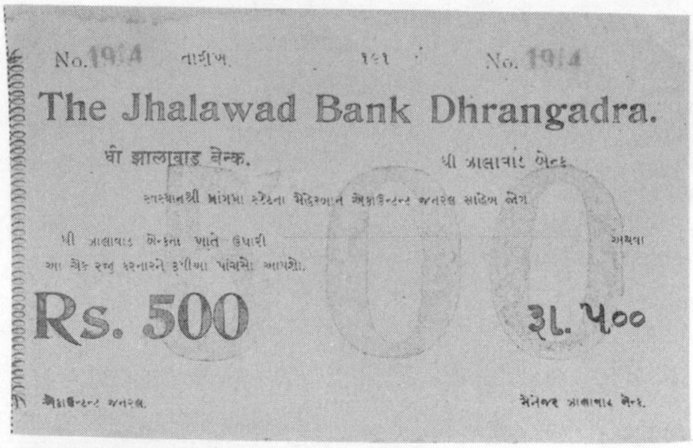

		Good	Fine	XF
S239	**500 Rupees** ND. Blue-gray. Large red value: *20*. Like #S236. Buff paper. Uniface.	5.00	15.00	45.00

1918 Treasury Notes Issue

		Good	Fine	XF
S241	**5 Rupees** 1.5.1918. Black and red-brown. Numerals and text in Hindi with 3 handwritten signatures. Paper: Native laid paper. Uniface.	10.00	20.00	35.00
S244	**50 Rupees** 1.5.1918. Black and red-brown. Numerals and text in Hindi with 3 handwritten signatures. Paper: Native laid paper. Uniface.	10.00	20.00	35.00

Dinajpur

Previously listed 1 Pice and 1 Anna cash coupons have been determined to be fantasies.

Gondal

A state in Kathiawar in the Western India States Agency with an area of 1,024 sq. mi. (2,653 sq. km.). These cash coupons also circulated in the neighboring states of Rajkot, Virpur and Jetpur.

Government

ND WWII Cash Coupons Issue

		VG	VF	UNC
S251	**1 Paiso (Pice)** ND. Gujarati text: *Gondal State Stamp 1 Paiso.* Series T. Paper: Light brown pressboard.	12.50	30.00	55.00

Hyderabad

Largest of the Princely States located in south central India with an area of 82,313 sq. mi. Ruled by Muslim Nizams until invaded and annexed by India in 1948. Issued notes 1948-53 under British Indian rule.

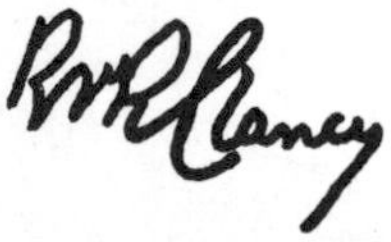

A. Sir Reginald R. Clancy, 1918-19

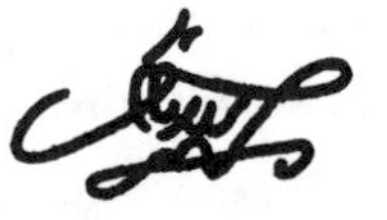

B. Fakhr-ud-Din Ahmad, 1919-20

C. Hyder Nawaz Jung, 1921-36

D. Fakhr-Yar Jung, 1936-38, 1940-41

E. Mehdi Yar Jung, 1939

F. Ghulam Muhammad, 1941-45

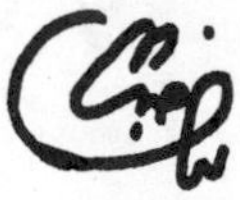

G. Liaquat Jung, 1945, 1946-47

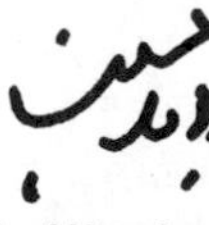

H. Zahed Husain, 1945-46

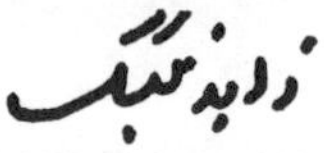

I. Zahed Jung, 1946

J. Moin Nawaz Jung, 1947-48

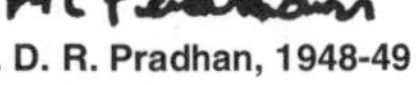

K. D. R. Pradhan, 1948-49

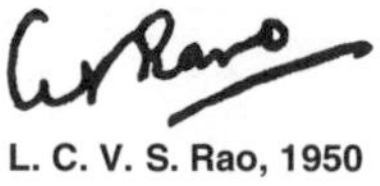

L. C. V. S. Rao, 1950

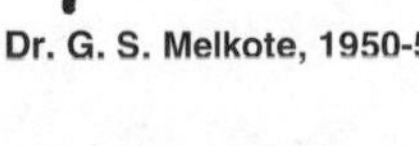

M. Dr. G. S. Melkote, 1950-53

Government

1915-36 Issue

		Good	Fine	XF
S261	**1 Rupee** ND (1919). Black on peach underprint. Obverse of coin at upper left, reverse at upper right. Back: Light brown. Printer: W&S. Rare.	—	—	—
S262	**1 Rupee** ND (1919). Bicolored. Printer: W&S.	—	—	—

		Good	Fine	XF
S263	**5 Rupees** FE 1331-47 (1920-36). Green. Back: Five-1 Rupee coins. Printer: W&S.			
	a. Series IQ. Without signature. Sea salvage note (most with stamping), unissued. FE 1331 (1920).	60.00	125.	—
	b. Series LX. Signature C. FE 1337 (1926).	40.00	100.	200.
	c. Series MC. Signature C. FE 1346 (1935).	30.00	75.00	175.
	d. Series MD-ME. Signature D. FE 1347 (1936).	30.00	75.00	175.
S264	**10 Rupees** FE 1327 (1916). Yellow-brown and black on lilac underprint. Series AB. Signature A. Printer: W&S.	125.	225.	450.
S265	**10 Rupees** FE 1331-47 (1920-36). Yellow-brown and black on lilac underprint. Like #S264 but rectangular panel added for date on lower left center frame. Printer: W&S.			
	a. Series AI. Without signature. Sea salvage note (most with stamping), unissued. FE 1331 (1920).	60.00	125.	—
	b. Series AN. Signature C. FE 1333 (1922).	60.00	125.	300.
	c. Series ?. Signature C. FE 1338 (1927).	55.00	100.	300.
	d. Series BK. Signature C. FE 1339 (1928).	55.00	100.	300.
	e. Series BW. Signature C. FE 1342 (1931).	55.00	100.	300.
	f. Series ?. Signature C. FE 1344 (1933).	55.00	100.	300.
	g. Series CH. Signature C. FE 1346 (1935).	55.00	100.	300.
	h. Series CZ. Signature D. FE 1347 (1936).	60.00	120.	325.

S266 100 Rupees	Good	Fine	XF
FE 1331-39 (1920-28). Blue and black on tan underprint. Printer: W&S.			
a. Series PS. Without signature. Sea salvage note (most with stamping), unissued. FE 1331 (1920).	75.00	150.	—
b. Series PY-PZ. Signature C. FE 1339 (1928).	75.00	175.	375.
c. Series QA. Signature C.	75.00	175.	375.
d. Series PT. Signature C. FE 1334 (1923).	100.	200.	425.

S267 1000 Rupees	Good	Fine	XF
FE 1340 (1929); 1341 (1930). Red and black on light green underprint. Series AA. Signature C. Printer: W&S.	150.	300.	900.

1939-53 Issue

S271 1 Rupee	VG	VF	UNC
ND (1939-46). Brown and multicolor. Wording in 4 lines at center. Back: Obverse and reverse of 1 Rupee coin at center. Printer: Security Press, Nasik (without imprint).			
a. Series A. Signature E. ND (1939).	4.00	10.00	25.00
b. Series B-M. Signature D. ND (1940-41).	4.00	10.00	25.00
c. Series B-X. Signature F, G. ND (1941-45).	4.00	10.00	25.00
d. Series S-W. Signature H. ND (1945-46).	4.00	10.00	25.00
e. Series X-Y. Signature I. ND (1946).	4.00	10.00	25.00

S272 1 Rupee	VG	VF	UNC
ND (1945-53). Brown and multicolor. Similar to #S271 except that wording is in 2 lines at center. Series W-Z, AB-AQ. Back: Obverse and reverse of 1 Rupee coin at center. Printer: Security Press, Nasik (without imprint).			
a. Series Z, AB. Signature G. ND (1946-47).	2.00	5.00	15.00
b. Signature H. ND (1945-46).	2.00	5.00	15.00
c. Signature I. ND (1946).	2.00	5.00	15.00
d. Signature J. ND (1947-48).	3.00	10.00	30.00
e. Signature K. ND (1948-49).	3.00	10.00	30.00
f. Signature L. ND (1950).	2.00	5.00	15.00
g. Signature M. ND (1950-53).	2.00	5.00	15.00

NOTE: #S271 and S272 issued from 1939-48 under Muslim rulers, 1948-53 under Indian occupation.

S273 5 Rupees	VG	VF	UNC
ND (1938-47). Green and multicolor. Series MH-PX. Back: Five 1 Rupee coins dated FE 1347. Printer: Security Press, Nasik (without imprint).			
a. Signature D. ND (1938; 1940-41).	6.00	17.50	60.00
b. Signature E. ND (1939).	6.00	17.50	60.00
c. Signature F. ND (1941-45).	6.00	17.50	60.00
d. Signature H. ND (1945-46).	6.00	17.50	60.00
e. Signature G. ND (1946-47).	6.00	17.50	60.00

S274 10 Rupees	VG	VF	UNC
ND (1938-47). Light brown and multicolor. Series CP-JI. Printer: Security Press, Nasik (without imprint).			
a. Signature D. ND (1938; 1940-41).	6.00	17.50	60.00
b. Signature E. ND (1939).	6.00	25.00	75.00
c. Signature F. ND (1941-45).	6.00	25.00	75.00
d. Signature H. ND (1945-46).	6.00	25.00	75.00
e. Signature G. ND (1946-47).	6.00	25.00	75.00
S275 100 Rupees			
ND (1939-45). Blue and multicolor. Printer: Security Press, Nasik (without imprint).			
a. Series QC. Signature D. ND (1938; 1940-41).	30.00	100.	275.
b. Series QF; QH; QI; QJ. Signature E. ND (1939).	30.00	100.	275.
c. Series QN; QP. Signature F. ND (1941-45).	30.00	100.	275.
d. Series QS. Signature G. ND (1945; 1946-47).	30.00	100.	275.
e. Series QY. Signature H. ND (1945-46).	30.00	100.	275.

Indergadh

A state located in the northern tip of Kotah State now merged into Rajasthan with an area of 400 sq. mi. (109 sq. km.).

Government

1933-42 WWII Emergency Cash Coupons Issue

S282 1 Anna	VG	VF	UNC
1933 (1942). Reverse of 1 Anna coin of George V at center, control # at top.	5.00	10.00	25.00
S283 2 Annas			
1939 (1942). Reverse of 2 Anna coin of George VI at center. Pressboard.	6.00	15.00	30.00

Jaipur

Formerly listed #S291 is a 1935 dated 4 Annas dual portr. donation receipt from "Their Majesties' Silver Jubilee Fund."

Jaisalmir

A state located in the Western Raiputana States Residency with an area of 16,062 sq. mi. (41,611 sq. km.).

Government

ND WWII Cash Coupons Issue

S301 1/4 Anna	Good	Fine	XF
ND. Hindi text and Western control #. Paper: Thick pressboard. Rare.	—	—	—

		Good	Fine	XF
S302	**1/2 Anna** ND. Hindi text and Western control #. Paper: Thick pressboard. Rare.	—	—	—
S303	**3/4 Anna** ND. Hindi text and Western control #. Paper: Thick pressboard. Rare.	—	—	—
S304	**1 3/4 Annas** ND. Different Hindi text and Western control #. Rare.	—	—	—
S305	**2 Annas** ND. Different Hindi text and Western control #. Overprint: On #S304. Rare.	—	—	—

JAMMU AND KASHMIR

A large state in the extreme north of India with an area of 85,885 sq. mi. (222,500 sq. km.). India and Pakistan are in continual dispute over control of the area. The two states had the same sovereign.

GOVERNMENT

1934 SRI KAR TEMPLE TOKENS ISSUE

		Good	Fine	XF
S311	**1 Rupee** VS 1934 (1876). Brown-orange. Hindi and Urdu script, radiant sunface at top center, Persian stamped seal of Jammu at lower center. Rare.	—	—	—
S312	**2 Rupees** VS 1934 (1876). Hindi and Urdu script, radiant sunface at top center, Persian stamped seal of Jammu at lower center. Rare.	—	—	—
S313	**5 Rupees** VS 1934 (1876). Hindi and Urdu script, radiant sunface at top center, Persian stamped seal of Jammu at lower center. Rare.	—	—	—
S314	**10 Rupees** VS 1934 (1876). Hindi and Urdu script, radiant sunface at top center, Persian stamped seal of Jammu at lower center. Rare.	—	—	—
S315	**20 Rupees** VS 1934 (1876). Hindi and Urdu script, radiant sunface at top center, Persian stamped seal of Jammu at lower center. Rare.	—	—	—
S316	**50 Rupees** VS 1934 (1876). Hindi and Urdu script, radiant sunface at top center, Persian stamped seal of Jammu at lower center. Rare.	—	—	—

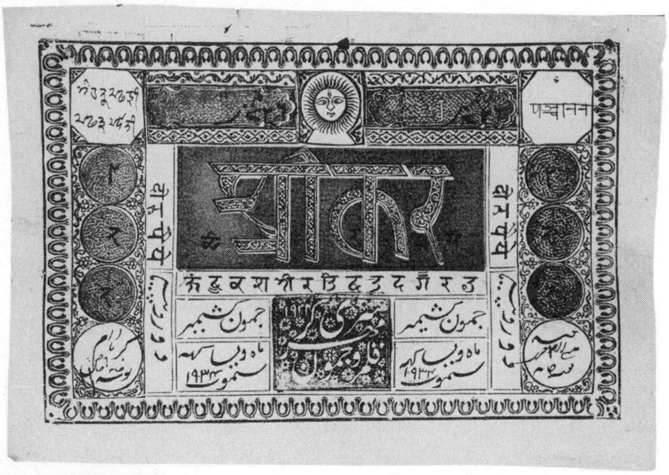

		Good	Fine	XF
S317	**100 Rupees** VS 1934 (1876). Hindi and Urdu script, radiant sunface at top center, Persian stamped seal of Jammu at lower center. Rare.	—	—	—

JASDAN

A state located in Western India States Agency with an area of 296 sq. mi. (767 sq. km.).

GOVERNMENT

1942 WWII EMERGENCY CASH COUPONS ISSUE

		VG	VF	UNC
S321	**1 Pice** ND (1942). Large Gujarati numeral *1* and *LOT NO.* With series letter at right, control # at right margin. Lot No. G. Gujarati legends. Pressboard.	10.00	30.00	60.00

		VG	VF	UNC
S322	**1 Anna** 1933 (1942). 1 Anna coin of King George V at right. Lot No. B. Gujarati legends. Pressboard.	12.50	30.00	75.00

JUNAGADH

A state located in Kathiawar in the Western India States Agency with an area of 3,337 sq. mi. (8,645 sq. km.). It was also known as Soruth or Saurashtra. It gave its name to the Saurashtra Union in 1948 when India took control.

GOVERNMENT

1943 ND WWII CASH COUPONS ISSUE

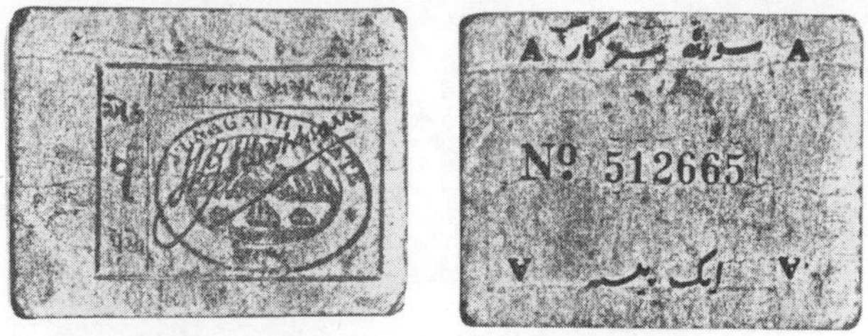

		VG	VF	UNC
S332	**1 Paisa** ND (1943). Green. Oval seal stamp: *JUNAGADH STATE.*	4.00	10.00	25.00

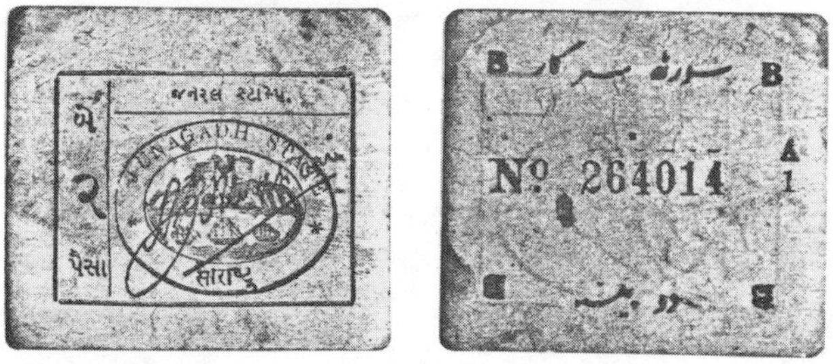

		VG	VF	UNC
S333	**2 Paisa** ND (1943). Red. Oval seal stamp: *JUNAGADH STATE.*	4.00	10.00	25.00
S334	**1 Anna** ND (1943). Violet. Oval seal stamp: *JUNAGADH STATE.*	4.00	12.50	30.00

KUTCH

GOVERNMENT

1946 ND ISSUE

		Good	Fine	XF
S341	**25 Koris** ND (1946). Maharajah Vijaya Rajji at right. Printer: W&S. Specimen. Rare.	—	—	—
S342	**50 Koris** ND (1946). Maharajah Vijaya Rajji at right. Printer: W&S. Specimen. Rare.	—	—	—
S343	**100 Koris** ND (1946). Maharajah Vijaya Rajji at right. Printer: W&S. Specimen. Rare.	—	—	—
S344	**500 Koris** ND (1946). Maharajah Vijaya Rajji at right. Printer: W&S. Specimen. Rare.	—	—	—

NOTE: Only a specimen set is known at this time.

MANGROL

A tiny state located in Kathiawar on the Arabian Sea coast, midway between Porbandar and Portuguese Diu with an area of 227 sq. mi. (588 sq. km.).

GOVERNMENT

ND WWII EMERGENCY CASH COUPON STAMP MONEY ISSUE

		VG	VF	UNC
S352	**1 Paisa (Pice)** ND. Value in Gujarati and English. 5-digit control # and signature. Paper: Pink pressboard. 50x50mm.	7.50	17.50	40.00
S353	**2 Paisa (Pice)** ND. Value in Gujarati and English. 5-digit control # and signature. Paper: White pressboard. 50x50mm.	12.50	30.00	60.00
S354	**1 Anna** ND. Value in Gujarati and English. 5-digit control # and signature. Paper: Gray-green pressboard.	7.50	17.50	40.00

MENGANI

A small state located in Kathiawar in Bombay Presidency, 15 miles south of Rajkot city with an area of 34 sq. mi. (88 sq. km.). The Talukdar paid an annual tribute to the British government and his affairs were looked after by a Kathiawar manager.

GOVERNMENT

ND WWII CASH COUPON STAMP MONEY ISSUE

		VG	VF	UNC
S361	**1 Paiso** ND. Scroll below, cow at center with *MANGNI TALUKA* in English, and *STATE MENGNI TALUKA REVENUE STAMP, ONE PAISO* in Gujarati. Paper: Pressboard.	6.00	15.00	30.00

MULI

A small state located in the Western India States Agency with an area of 133 sq. mi. (344 sq. km.).

RULERS:
Harish Chandra Sinhji

GOVERNMENT

1943-45 WWII CASH COUPON STAMP MONEY ISSUE

		VG	VF	UNC
S371	**1 Paisa (Pice)** ca. 1943-45. Sinhji at center. Paper: Black pressboard.	3.00	7.50	15.00
S372	**2 Paisa (Pice)** ca. 1943-45. Sinhji at center. Paper: Light blue pressboard.	3.00	7.50	15.00
S373	**4 Annas** ca. 1943-45. Sinhji at center. Paper: Light brown pressboard.	4.00	10.00	25.00

Mysore

Formerly listed #S381-S383 with portrait of Maharaja at center are donation receipts of the Imperial Indian Relief Fund.

NAVANAGAR

"Swasthan Nawanagar" (Navangar State) in Western India States Agency with an area of 3,791 sq. mi. (9,821 sq. km.).

GOVERNMENT

1943-44 WWII CASH COUPON STAMP MONEY ISSUE

		VG	VF	UNC
S391	**2 Pice** 1943-44. Revenue stamps with portrait C. Maharaja Digvijaysingh at center. Gujarati control # at top. Paper: Pressboard. Perforated: *NS* (Navanagar State).	12.50	30.00	60.00
S392	**1 Anna** 1943-44. Revenue stamps with portrait C. Maharaja Digvijaysingh at center. Gujarati control # at top. Paper: Pressboard. Perforated: *NS* (Navanagar State).	12.50	30.00	60.00
S393	**2 Annas** 1943-44. Revenue stamps with portrait C. Maharaja Digvijaysingh at center. Gujarati control # at top. Paper: Pressboard. Perforated: *NS* (Navanagar State).	12.50	30.00	60.00
S394	**4 Annas** 1943-44. Revenue stamps with portrait C. Maharaja Digvijaysingh at center. Gujarati control # at top. Paper: Pressboard. Perforated: *NS* (Navanagar State).	12.50	30.00	60.00

NAWALGARH

A small city state located in Rajasthan.

GOVERNMENT

ND WWII EMERGENCY CASH COUPONS ISSUE

		VG	VF	UNC
S401	**1 Paisa (Pice)** ND. Embossed Indian numeral value. Devnagri text. Back: Hand stamped oval seal: *THIKANA OFFICE NAWALGARH.* Paper: Dull brown pressboard.	5.00	15.00	40.00
S402	**1 Anna** ND. Embossed Indian numeral value. Devnagri text. Back: Hand stamped oval seal: *THIKANA OFFICE NAWALGARH.* Paper: Cream pressboard.	5.00	15.00	40.00
S403	**2 Annas** ND. Embossed Indian numeral value. Devnagri text. Back: Hand stamped oval seal: *THIKANA OFFICE NAWALGARH.* Paper: Dull green pressboard.	5.00	15.00	40.00
S404	**4 Annas** ND. Embossed Indian numeral value. Devnagri text. Back: Hand stamped oval seal: *THIKANA OFFICE NAWALGARH.* Paper: Pink pressboard.	5.00	15.00	40.00
S405	**8 Annas** ND. Embossed Indian numeral value. Devnagri text. Back: Hand stamped oval seal: *THIKANA OFFICE NAWALGARH.* Paper: Light green pressboard. Uniface.	12.50	30.00	75.00

PALITANA

A small state in Kathiawar, Western India States Agency with an area of 300 sq. mi. (777 sq. km.). Joined Saurashtra Union in 1948.

GOVERNMENT

1943 WWII CASH COUPONS ISSUE

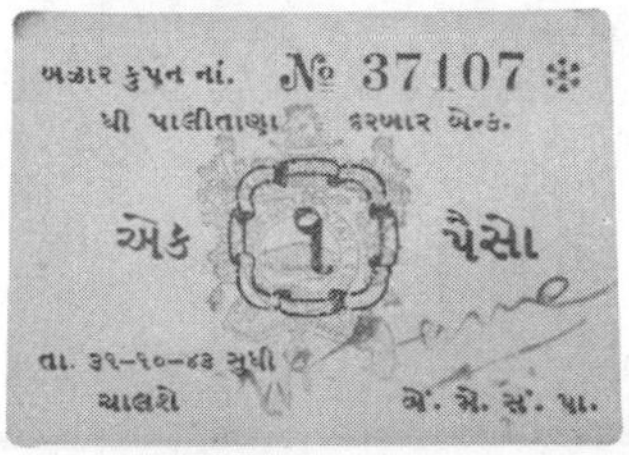

		VG	VF	UNC
S411	**1 Paisa** 31.10.1943. Gujarati numeral of value within scroll printed over Palitana State arms. Western control # and hand signature.	15.00	40.00	75.00
S412	**1/2 Anna** 31.10.1943. Gujarati numeral of value within scroll printed over Palitana State arms. Western control # and hand signature.	15.00	40.00	75.00
S413	**1 Anna** 31.10.1943. Gujarati numeral of value within scroll printed over Palitana State arms. Western control # and hand signature.	25.00	55.00	100.

ND WWII CASH COUPON STAMP MONEY ISSUE

		Good	Fine	XF
S415	**1 Paise** ND. Printed revenue stamps. Paper: Pressboard.			
S416	**2 Paisa** ND. Printed revenue stamps. Paper: Pressboard.			
S417	**1 Anna** ND. Printed revenue stamps. Paper: Pressboard.			
S418	**2 Annas** ND. Printed revenue stamps. Paper: Pressboard.			
S419	**4 Annas** ND. Printed revenue stamps. Paper: Pressboard.			
S420	**8 Annas** ND. Printed revenue stamps. Paper: Pressboard.			

RAJKOT

A state in Kathiawar, Western India States Agency with an area of 344 sq. mi. (891 sq. km.). Joined Saurashtra Union in 1948.

GOVERNMENT

ND WWII EMERGENCY CASH COUPON STAMP MONEY ISSUE

		VG	VF	UNC
S421	**1 Pice** ND. Gray. Printed revenue stamps. Pressboard.	6.00	15.00	40.00
S422	**2 Pice** ND. Green. Printed revenue stamps. Pressboard.	6.00	15.00	40.00
S423	**1 Anna** ND. Red. Portrait ruler of Rajkot. Printed revenue stamps. Pressboard. Reported not confirmed.	—	—	—

Ramgarh Raj

Previously listed #S481 1 Anna is a fantasy (printed on post-WWII era postcards). A 1/2 Anna fantasy printed on different paper stock has recently been reported.

SAILANA

A small state located in Southern States and Malwa Agency with an area of 297 sq. mi. (769 sq. km.).

GOVERNMENT

ND WWII EMERGENCY CASH COUPON STAMP MONEY ISSUE

		Good	Fine	XF
S430	**1 Paisa (Pice)** ND. Black. Portrait Dileep Singh, Rajah. Paper: Rose pressboard. Rare.	—	—	—
		VG	**VF**	**UNC**
S431	**1 Anna** ND. Black and red. Portrait Dileep Singh, Rajah. Maharaja at center.			
	a. Overprint: *1 ANNA.*	5.00	15.00	30.00
	b. Overprint: *ANNA.* (error).	45.00	125.	225.

NOTE: #S431b appears once in a full sheet of 16 examples.

#S432 Deleted.

SAYALA

A small state located in the Western India State Agency near Chuda with an area of 225 sq. mi. (583 sq. km.).

GOVERNMENT

ND WWII CASH COUPONS ISSUE

		VG	VF	UNC
S435	**1 Paisa (Pice)** ND. Black. Arms at left. Series D-F. Uniface.	5.00	10.00	25.00

SITAMAU

A small state located in Central India residency, in Mandsor district, with an area of 191 sq. mi. (495 sq. km.). Founded 1660. Merged w/India 1947.

GOVERNMENT

1942-43 WWII CASH COUPONS ISSUE

		Good	Fine	XF
S441	**1 Anna** 1942-43. State seal. Back: Control #, date, value and signature. Rare.	—	—	—
S442	**2 Annas** 1942-43. State seal. Back: Control #, date, value and signature. Rare.	—	—	—
S443	**4 Annas** 1942-43. State seal. Back: Control #, date, value and signature. Rare.	—	—	—

TONK

The only Muslim-ruled state in Rajputana, Jaipur Residency with an area of 2,553 sq. mi. (6,614 sq. km.).

GOVERNMENT

1943 ND WWII CASH COUPONS ISSUE

		Good	Fine	XF
S451	**1 Pice** ND (1943). Denomination in English, Hindi and Perso-Arabic. Pressboard.	17.50	45.00	—
S453	**4 Annas** ND (1943).			
	a. *ANNAS 4.* Large letters: Control # on back.	40.00	100.	175.
	b. *ANNAS 4.* Small letters.	40.00	100.	175.
S454	**1 Pice** ND (1943). Tower at left. Paper: Black pressboard.	40.00	85.00	—
S455	**1 Anna** ND (1943). Minaret at left, airplanes at upper right. Paper: Blue pressboard.	40.00	85.00	—

1943 WAR PURPOSES FUND ISSUE

		VG	VF	UNC
S456	**4 Annas** ND (1943). Blue with red text.	75.00	175.	—

VITHALGADH

A small state in the Western India States Agency with an area of 56 sq. mi. (145 sq. km.).

GOVERNMENT

ND WWII CASH COUPON STAMP MONEY ISSUE

		VG	VF	UNC
S461	**1 Anna** ND. Gujarati script: *VITHALGADH* at center and denomination across bottom, portrait Maharaja at center.	12.50	25.00	55.00
S462	**2 Annas** ND. Gujarati script: *VITHALGADH* at center and denomination across bottom, portrait Maharaja at center.	12.50	25.00	55.00

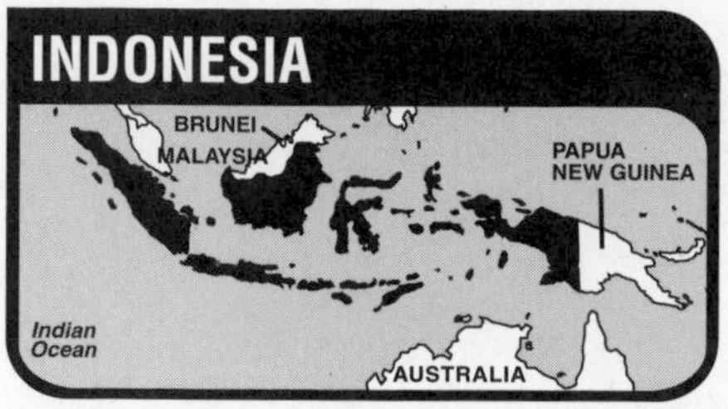

The Republic of Indonesia, the world's largest archipelago, extends for more than 4,827 km. along the equator from the mainland of southeast Asia to Australia. The 13,667 islands comprising the archipelago have a combined area of 1,919,440 sq. km. and a population of 237.5 million, including East Timor. Capital: Jakarta. Petroleum, timber, rubber and coffee are exported.

The Dutch began to colonize Indonesia in the early 17th century; the islands were occupied by Japan from 1942 to 1945. Indonesia declared its independence after Japan's surrender, but it required four years of intermittent negotiations, recurring hostilities, and UN mediation before the Netherlands agreed to relinquish its colony. Indonesia is the world's largest archipelagic state and home to the world's largest Muslim population. Current issues include: alleviating poverty, preventing terrorism, consolidating democracy after four decades of authoritarianism, implementing financial sector reforms, stemming corruption, holding the military and police accountable for human rights violations, and controlling avian influenza. In 2005, Indonesia reached a historic peace agreement with armed separatists in Aceh, which led to democratic elections in December 2006. Indonesia continues to face a low intensity separatist movement in Papua.

MONETARY SYSTEM:

1 Gulden = 100 Cents to 1948
1 Rupiah = 100 Sen, 1945-

GENERAL INTRODUCTION

A. VARIATIONS

This listing does *not* include the wide range of variations in the emergency paper money, e.g.

COLOR: In most cases only the main colors are listed; green may vary from blue-green to yellow-green, red from dark stone red to red-orange, etc.

PAPER: White, brown, thin (rice paper), thick, with or w/o wmk., and even notebook paper are used for the notes.

UNDERPRINT (unpt.): Is sometimes clear, but mostly vague or almost absent.

NUMBERING: There is a wide range of combinations, 1 to 5 letters, 5 or 6 digits, square or round digits, differences in style of the letters (sans serif or not).

STAMPS or POSTMARKS: In most cases not listed as it is easy to produce hand stamped notes, and falsifications do exist.

B. COMMON WORDS FOUND ON INDONESIAN BANKNOTES

Tanda pembajaran jang sah	legal currency
Uang (or oeang *)	money
Uang kertas	paper money
Coupon penukaran	exchange coupon
Mandat pertahanan	defense mandate
Bon	coupon
Beredar	circulate
Berlaku	valid
Palsu	false
Tidak berlaku	not valid
Darurat	emergency
Istimewa	special
Ketetapan	decree
Gubernur	governor
Propinsi	Province
Sub-propinsi	Sub-province
Bupati	regent
Kabupaten	regency
Daerah	district, region
Kepala daerah	head of district/region
Kas negara	state treasury
Menteri keuangan	minister of finance
Djabatan keuangan	finance office
Residen	resident
Keresidenan	residency
Kewedanaan	district

NOTE: In January 1947 Indonesia changed the spelling "oe" to "u" because of the Dutch origin of the spelling "oe". On notes the spelling is sometimes "oe" and sometimes "u", e.g. Boepati/Bupati, Keoeangan/Keuangan, Poeloeh/Puluh.

C. NUMBERS

1/2	setengah	40	empat puluh
1	satu	50	lima puluh
2 1/2	dua setengah	100	seratus
5	lima	250	dua ratus lima puluh
10	sepuluh	400	empat ratus
20	dua puluh	500	lima ratus
25	dua puluh lima	1000	seribu

D. ABBREVIATIONS

N.R.I.	Negara Republik Indonesia (*negara* means state)
T.N.I.	Tentara Negara Indonesia (*tentara* means army)

I. REGIONAL ISSUES REPUBLIC OF INDONESIA

A. JAVA

A1. Bodjonegoro .... #S61-S63
1. Djokjakarta (Jogjakarta) .... #S107-S111
1A. Kediri .... #S112-S113B
1B. Madiun .... #S113C-S114
2. Magelang .... #S116
2A. Patjitan .... #S118
3. Serang .... #S121-S125
4. Surakarta .... #S130-S134

B. SUMATRA

1. Asahan .... #S141-S154

1A. Barus .... #S157
2. Bengkoeloe (Bengkulu) .... #S161-S168
3. Bukit Barisan .... #S171
4. Bukittinggi (B. Tinggi) .... #S181-S195
4A. Issue for the Province of Sumatra .... #S181-S195
4B. Issue for the sub-province of South Sumatra .... #S201-S203
4C. Issue for East Sumatra .... #S211-S213
4D. Issue for West Sumatra .... #S221
4E. Issue for Aceh .... #S231-S232
4F. Issue for Djambi .... #S236
4G. Issue for Riau .... #S241
4H. Issue for Tapanuli .... #S251-S253
5. Djambi .... #S261-S269
6. Koealoeh Leidong (Kualuh Leidong) .... #S271-S279
7. Koetaradja (Kutaradja) .... #S281-S286
8. Kutatjane .... #S291-S293
9. Labuhan Batu .... #S301-S303
10. Labuhan Bilik .... #S308-S314
11. Langsa .... #S316-S317
11A. Lima Poeloeh .... #S318-S318A
11B. Membang Moeda .... #S319-S320B
12. Nias .... #S321-S325
12A. Pagar Alam .... #S327-S330
13. Palembang .... #S330A-S339
14. Panai .... #S341
14A. Pekanbaru .... #S340
15. Pematang Siantar .... #S351-S354
15A. Pendopo .... #S354A-S355
16. Rantau Prapat .... #S361-S374
17. Tandjungkarang .... #S380-S388
18. Tapanoeli (Tapanuli) .... #S390-S398
19. Tigabinanga .... #S401-S403
20. Tjurup .... #S406
21. No place of issue; issue for the special military district of South Sumatra ... #S410-S412
22. No place of issue shown; issue in North Lampung for town of Kotabumi .... #S419-S421

REBELLIOUS MOVEMENTS AGAINST THE REPUBLIC OF INDONESIA

Movement/Region

JAVA
Pemerintah Negara Islam Indonesia .... #S431-S432

SUMATRA
Pemerintah Revolusioner Republik Indonesia (P.R.R.I.) .... #S461-S481

NORTH CELEBES
Piagan Perdjuangarn Semesta (Permesta) .... #S491-S501

SOUTH CELEBES
Republik Islam Indonesia .... #S510-S530

MOLUCCAS
Republik Maluku Selatan (R.M.S.) .... #S531

REPUBLIC REGIONALS

BLITA

1948 ISSUE

	Good	Fine	XF
S50 1 Rupiah 8.8.1948. Dark blue.	—	—	—
S51 5 Rupiah 8.8.1948. Red.	—	—	—

BODJONEGORO

1948 ISSUE

#S61-S63 redeemable after 14.1.1949.

	Good	Fine	XF
S60 1/2 Rupiah 15.11.1948. Stamped signature. Uniface. Paper: Brown packing.	—	—	—
S61 1 Rupiah 15.11.1948. Black and red. Stamped signature. Uniface. Paper: Brown packing.	—	—	—
S62 5 Rupiah 15.11.1948. Black and red. Stamped signature. Uniface. Paper: Brown packing.	—	—	—

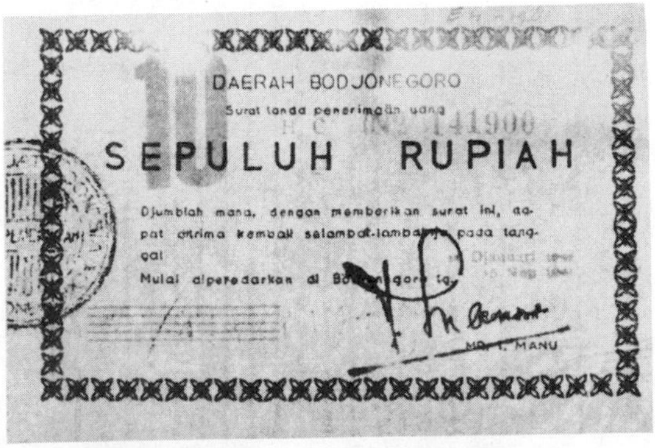

	Good	Fine	XF
S63 10 Rupiah 15.11.1948. Black and red. Stamped signature. Uniface. Paper: Brown packing. Rare.	—	—	—

NOTE: Modern fakes have begun appearing on the market.

DJOKJAKARTA

JOGJAKARTA

1948 ISSUE

#S107-S109 signed by the Sultan of Jogjakarta, Hamengkubuwono IX. Central text: Daerah Istimewa Jogjakarta (Special region of Jogjakarta). Redeemable after 10.1.1949

	Good	Fine	XF
S107 2 1/2 Rupiah 10.11.1948. Black on green underprint. Signed by the Sultan of Jogjakarta, Hamengkubuwono IX. Central text: Daerah Istimewa Jogjakarta (Special region of Jogjakarta). Denomination underprint. Uniface.			
a. Stub at left. Rare.	—	—	—
b. No stub at left. Rare.	—	—	—

	Good	Fine	XF
S108 5 Rupiah 10.11.1948. Black on green underprint. Signed by the Sultan of Jogjakarta, Hamengkubuwono IX. Central text: Daerah Istimewa Jogjakarta (Special region of Jogjakarta). Denomination underprint. Uniface.			
a. Stub at left. Rare.	—	—	—
b. No stub at left. Rare.	—	—	—
S109 10 Rupiah 10.11.1948. Black on green underprint. Signed by the Sultan of Jogjakarta, Hamengkubuwono IX. Central text: Daerah Istimewa Jogjakarta (Special region of Jogjakarta). Denomination underprint. Uniface. Rare.	—	—	—

#S110 and S111 *Deleted.*

KEDIRI

1948 TOWN ISSUE

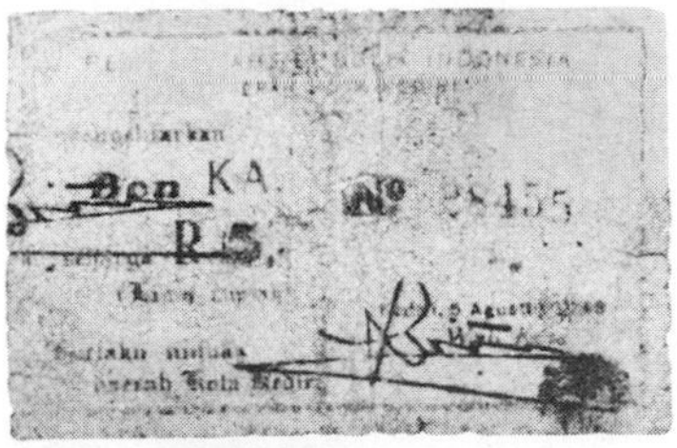

	Good	Fine	XF
S112 5 Rupiah 5.8.1948. Red. Kediri. Uniface.	—	—	—

1948 RESIDENCE'S ISSUE

	Good	Fine	XF
S113 2 1/2 Rupiah 16.10.1948. Red. Kediri Residency. Uniface.	—	—	—
S113A 5 Rupiah 16.10.1948. Red. Kediri Residency. Uniface.	—	—	—
S113B 10 Rupiah 16.10.1948.	—	—	—

MADIUN

1948 CITY ISSUE

	Good	Fine	XF
S113C 1/2 Rupiah 1.9.1948. Uniface.	—	—	—
S113D 1 Rupiah 1.9.1948. Black. 1 red stripe.	—	—	—
S113E 2 1/2 Rupiah 1.9.1948. Black. 2 red stripes.	—	—	—
S113F 5 Rupiah 1.9.1948. Black. 3 red stripes. Uniface.	—	—	—

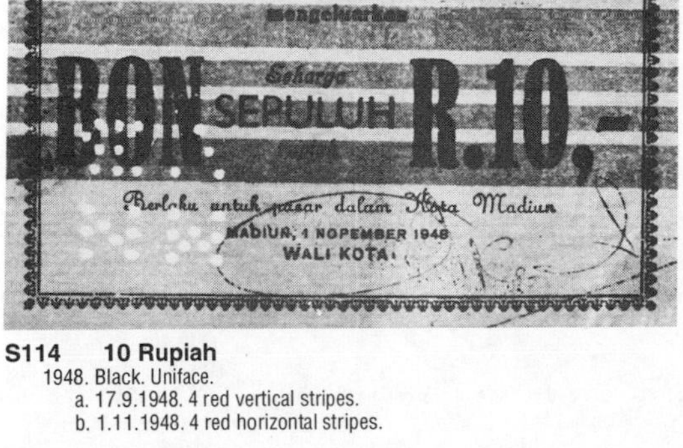

	Good	Fine	XF
S114 10 Rupiah 1948. Black. Uniface.			
a. 17.9.1948. 4 red vertical stripes.	—	—	—
b. 1.11.1948. 4 red horizontal stripes.	—	—	—

1949 Military Territory Issue

	Good	Fine	XF
S115 25 Rupiah 5.10.1949. Black. Uniface.	—	—	—

Magelang

1948 Residency Issue

	Good	Fine	XF
S116 2 1/2 Rupiah 25.10.1948. Black and green. Landscape.	—	—	—
S117 5 Rupiah 25.10.1948.	—	—	—

1949 Defense Issue

	Good	Fine	XF
S117A 2 1/2 Rupiah 1.8.1948. Black.	—	—	—
S117B 5 Rupiah 1.8.1948. Black.	—	—	—

Magetan

1948 Issue

	Good	Fine	XF
S117D 1 Rupiah 17.9.1948. 1 vertical stripe.	—	—	—
S117E 2 1/2 Rupiah 17.9.1948. 2 vertical stripes.	—	—	—
S117F 5 Rupiah 17.9.1948. 3 vertical stripes.	—	—	—
S117G 10 Rupiah 17.9.1948. 4 vertical stripes.	—	—	—

Patjitan

1947 ND Issue

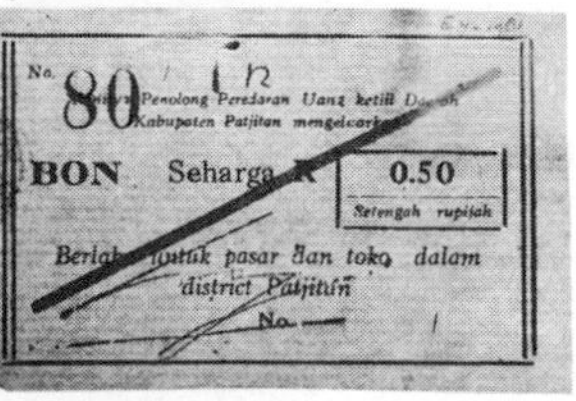

	Good	Fine	XF
S118 1/2 Rupiah ND (ca.1948). Uniface.	—	—	—
S118A 1 Rupiah ND(1948). Rare.	—	—	—
S118B 5 Rupiah ND(1948). Rare.	—	—	—
S118C 10 Rupiah ND(1948). Rare.	—	—	—

Semarang

1949 Issue

	Good	Fine	XF
S119 25 Rupiah 1.11.1949. Coconut tree at left.	—	—	—

Serang

1947-48 Issue

#S121-S125 modern fakes exist of #S121-S125; made by the original printer's son.

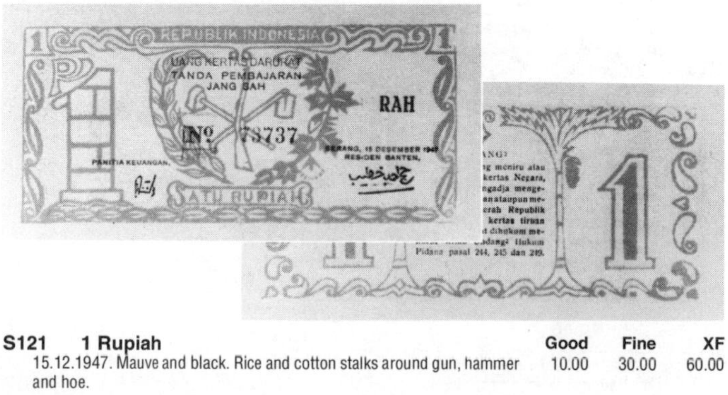

	Good	Fine	XF
S121 1 Rupiah 15.12.1947. Mauve and black. Rice and cotton stalks around gun, hammer and hoe.	10.00	30.00	60.00

	Good	Fine	XF
S122 5 Rupiah 15.12.1947. Green and black. Ancient gate at center.	6.00	12.00	25.00

	Good	Fine	XF
S123 10 Rupiah 15.12.1947. Green and black on light green underprint. Minaret at center.	15.00	30.00	65.00

	Good	Fine	XF
S124 25 Rupiah 15.12.1947. Red to red-brown. Tower at left, gate at right.			
a. Hand stamped: *palsu* (false) in black or blue.	2.00	5.00	10.00

NOTE: Contemporary fakes exist of #S124.

	Good	Fine	XF
S125 50 Rupiah 11.8.1948. Purple to red-violet and black. Tower at left, gate at right.	2.50	5.00	10.00

NOTE: Contemporary fakes exist of #S125.

SURAKARTA

1948-49 CITY ISSUES

	Good	Fine	XF
S130 1 Rupiah 1.11.1948. Black, red value. Torch at lower center. Uniface.	—	—	—
S131 2 1/2 Rupiah 1.11.1948. Black, red value. Lamp at lower center. Rare.	—	—	—

	Good	Fine	XF
S132 5 Rupiah 1.11.1948. Black, red value. Lamp at lower center. Large value: *5* at right. Uniface. Like #S131.	—	—	—
S132A 5 Rupiah 1.11.1949. Black, red value. Ember at lower center.	—	—	—
S133 10 Rupiah 1.11.1949. Fighting lion and buffalo at lower center.			
a. Black, red value. Rare.	—	—	—
b. Yellow, red value. Rare.	—	—	—
S134 25 Rupiah 1.11.1949. Temple at lower center.			
a. Black, red value.	—	—	—
b. Blue, red value.	—	—	—

NOTE: Modern fakes exist of #S130, S132, S132A.

TJEPU

1948 ISSUE

	Good	Fine	XF
S135 1 Rupee 17.8.1948. Legendary figure and serpent at left.	—	—	—
S135A 5 Rupee 17.8.1948. Legendary figure at upper left, dove in center.	—	—	—

ASAHAN

1947 ISSUES

	Good	Fine	XF
S141 10 Sen 21.8.1947. Value in circle.			
a. Purple.	—	—	—
b. Black.	—	—	—
c. Sepia.	—	—	—
S142 50 Sen 21.8.1947. Value in circles.			
a. Red-brown.	—	—	—
b. Green.	300.	—	—

	Good	Fine	XF
S143 1 Rupiah 21.8.1947. Black. Value in circles.			
a. Black.	300.	—	—
b. Sepia.	—	—	—
S144 2 1/2 Rupiah 21.8.1947. Purple. Value in circles.			
a. Purple.	—	—	—
b. Green.	—	—	—
c. Black.	—	—	—

	Good	Fine	XF
S145 5 Rupiah 21.8.1947.			
a. Black.	30.00	60.00	150.
b. Red-brown.	30.00	60.00	150.
c. Grey-purple.	—	—	—
d. Green.	—	—	—
S146 10 Rupiah 21.8.1947. Banana tree at right.			
a. Purple.	—	—	—
b. Red.	—	—	—
c. Black.	—	—	—
S147 25 Rupiah 21.8.1947. Coconut trees at right.			
a. Black.	—	—	—
b. Brown.	15.00	30.00	60.00
c. Green.	20.00	40.00	80.00
S148 50 Rupiah 21.8.1947. Coconut trees at left and right.			
a. Brown.	10.00	25.00	50.00
b. Red.	10.00	25.00	50.00
c. Black.	10.00	25.00	50.00
S149 100 Rupiah 21.8.1947. Landscape at left, flowers at right.			
a. Green.	25.00	50.00	100.
b. Black.	—	—	—
S150 2500 Rupiah 21.8.1947. Brown-red. Landscape at left, flowers at right.	—	—	—

1948 ISSUES

#S150A-S150D HAND STAMPS ON BACK.

	Good	Fine	XF
S150A 1000 Rupiah 12.2.1948. Black.	—	—	—
S150B 2500 Rupiah 27.2.1948.			
a. Red.	—	—	—
b. Black.	—	—	—
c. Purple, blue, green.	—	—	—
S150C 5000 Rupiah 1948.			
a. Red.	—	—	—
b. Blue.	—	—	—
S150D 20,000 Rupiah 3.3.1948.			
a. Black.	—	—	—
b. Blue.	—	—	—

1947 ISSUES

	Good	Fine	XF
S151 100,000 Rupiah 21.8.1947. Green. Back: Hand stamps.	30.00	60.00	110.

	Good	Fine	XF
S152 100,000 Rupiah 7.2.1948. Back: Hand stamps.			
a. Purple.	—	—	—
b. Green.	—	—	—
c. Black.	—	—	—
S153 100,000 Rupiah 7.2.1948. Green. Back: Hand stamps.	—	—	—

S154 250,000 Rupiah	Good	Fine	XF
7.2.1948. Flower at lower center. Back: Hand stamps.			
a. Green (Test).	—	—	—
b. Blush.	—	—	—
c. Blue-green.	—	—	—

Barus

1948 Issue

S157 500 Rupiah	Good	Fine	XF
26.12.1948.	—	—	—

Bengkoeloe

Bengkulu

1947 Issue

#S161-S165 seal and printed sign., handwritten initials. *MANDAT P(anitia) M(akanan) R(akjat) Kas Negara di Bengkoeloe* (Mandate Committee for people's food - state treasury Bengkulu).

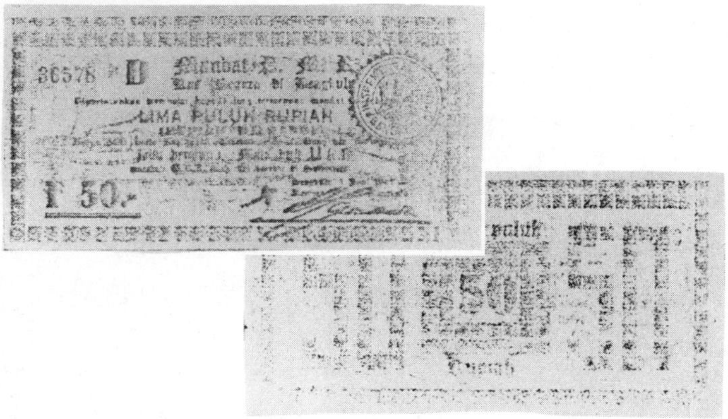

S161 50 Rupiah	Good	Fine	XF
1.6.1947. Red on purple underprint. Seal and printed signature, handwritten initials.	20.00	30.00	75.00

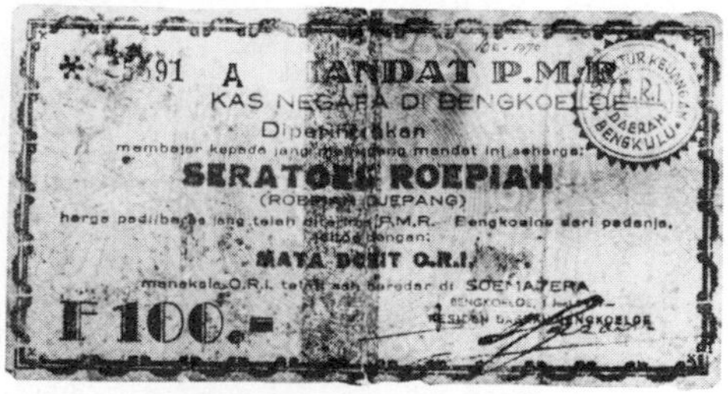

S162 100 Rupiah	Good	Fine	XF
1.6.1947. Green on yellow underprint. Seal and printed signature, handwritten initials.	15.00	25.00	60.00

S163 250 Rupiah	Good	Fine	XF
1.6.1947. Red on yellow underprint. Seal and printed signature, handwritten initials.	10.00	25.00	50.00

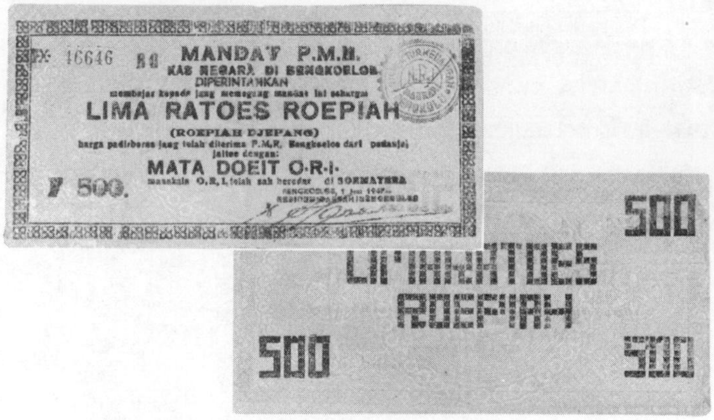

S164 500 Rupiah	Good	Fine	XF
1.6.1947. Black on pink underprint. Seal and printed signature, handwritten initials.			
a. Denomination with thin type *ROEPIAH DJEPANG* 41 1/2mm long.	8.50	12.50	31.00
b. Denomination with thick serif type: *ROEPIAH DJEPANG* 48mm long.	8.00	12.00	35.00

S165 1000 Rupiah	Good	Fine	XF
1.6.1947. Dark brown to violet on green underprint. With or without underprint. Seal and printed signature, handwritten initials.			
a. Blue seal, signature and serial #.	6.00	12.00	25.00
b. Red seal, signature and serial #.	5.00	10.00	20.00
c. Black seal, signature and serial #.	6.00	12.00	25.00

1947 Sub-Province Issue

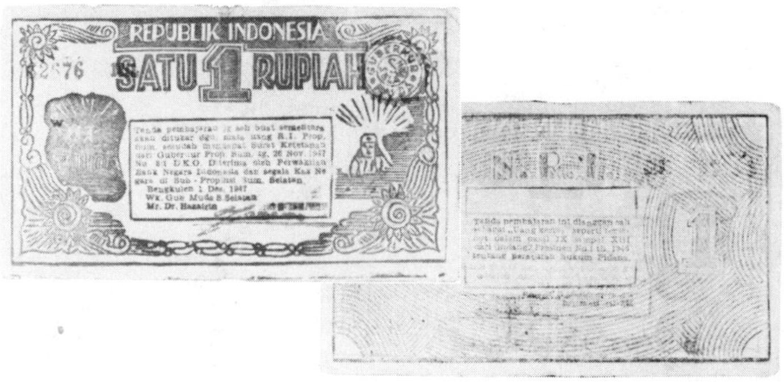

S166 1 Rupiah	Good	Fine	XF
1.12.1947. Green. Nurse at right. Red seal and printed signature without initials.	6.00	12.50	25.00

S167 5 Rupiah	Good	Fine	XF
1.12.1947. Brown-violet. Coast scene at upper center. Red seal and printed signature without initials.	10.00	20.00	45.00

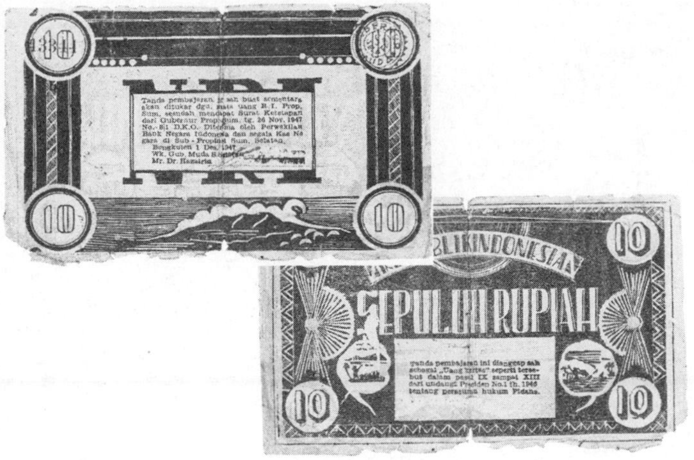

S168 10 Rupiah
1.12.1947. Blue. Country scene at left and center. Red seal and printed signature without initials.

	Good	Fine	XF
S168	5.00	15.00	30.00

Bukit Barisan

1949 Issue

S171 20 Rupiah
1.5.1949. Mounted lancer at left, buffalo at center.

	Good	Fine	XF
a. Dark green.	15.00	30.00	50.00
b. Red-brown.	12.00	20.00	40.00

Bukittinggi

B. Tinggi

Propinsi Sumatera

Province of Sumatera

1947 First Issue

S181 1/2 Rupiah
17.8.1947. Dark red-brown. Religious houses. Central text: *Propinsi Sumatera* (Province of Sumatra).

	Good	Fine	XF
S181	6.00	12.00	25.00

S182 1 Rupiah
17.8.1947. Red-brown. Sukarno at left. Central text: *Propinsi Sumatera* (Province of Sumatra).

	Good	Fine	XF
S182	3.00	9.00	18.00

S183 2 1/2 Rupiah
17.8.1947. Red-brown on tan underprint. Portrait Sukarno at left. Central text: *Propinsi Sumatera* (Province of Sumatra).

	Good	Fine	XF
S183	10.00	25.00	60.00

S184 5 Rupiah
17.8.1947. Blue on light blue to green underprint. Sukarno at left, Borobudur temple at right. Central text: *Propinsi Sumatera* (Province of Sumatra).

	Good	Fine	XF
S184	3.00	8.00	15.00

S185 10 Rupiah
17.8.1947. Mountain scenery at left, falls at right. Central text: *Propinsi Sumatera* (Province of Sumatra).

	Good	Fine	XF
S185	3.00	8.00	15.00

S186 25 Rupiah
17.8.1947. Green. Sukarno at center. Central text: *Propinsi Sumatera* (Province of Sumatra).

	Good	Fine	XF
S186	20.00	40.00	60.00

1947 Second Issue

S187 2 1/2 Rupiah	Good	Fine	XF
17.12.1947. Mauve on yellow-green underprint. Woman at right.			
a. With serial #.	3.00	6.00	15.00
b. With block letters only.	3.00	6.00	15.00

1948 First Issue

S188 1 Rupiah	Good	Fine	XF
1.1.1948. Brown.			
a. Blue underprint. With 2 serial #.	4.00	7.00	17.50
b. Without underprint. With 1 serial #.	—	—	—

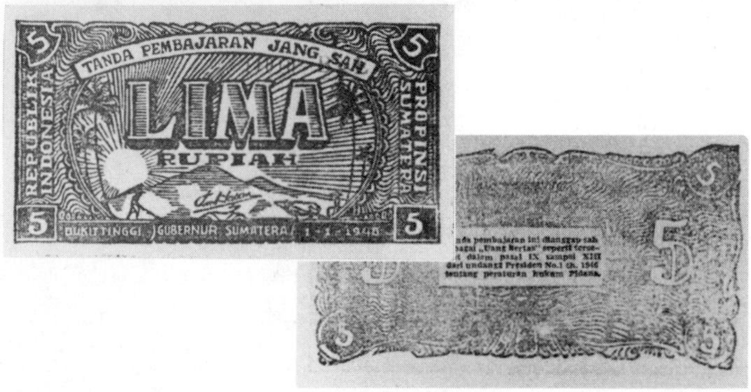

S189 5 Rupiah	Good	Fine	XF
1.1.1948. Green. Rising sun behind mountains at left.			
a. 2 serial #.	1.50	4.00	12.00
b. 1 serial #.	1.50	4.00	12.00

S190 10 Rupiah	Good	Fine	XF
1.1.1948. Rice stalks at left, coconut at right.			
a. Purple on yellow underprint.	1.50	4.00	12.00
b. Blue on green underprint.	1.50	4.00	12.00
c. Blue, without underprint.	1.50	4.00	12.00

S191 25 Rupiah	Good	Fine	XF
17.1.1948. Transports at left.			
a. Red (color variations from orange to brown-violet).	2.00	5.00	10.00
b. Green.	3.00	6.00	15.00
c. Blue, without underprint. Black serial #.	6.00	11.00	20.00
d. Black, without underprint. Red serial #.	4.00	8.00	15.00
e. As a. Printed on tissue paper.	5.00	10.00	20.00

NOTE: For #S191a, d, 184, 189, 192 with *Segel-Inflasi R5* (inflation stamp) see #S410a-b.

1948 Second Issue

S192 5 Rupiah	Good	Fine	XF
1.4.1948. Rising sun behind mountains. Like #S189.			
a. Green, red serial #.	2.00	5.00	11.00
b. Brown on yellow underprint. Black serial #.	1.50	4.00	10.00
c. Brown, red serial #. Without underprint.	1.50	4.00	10.00

S193 10 Rupiah	Good	Fine	XF
1.4.1948. Rice stalks at left, coconut at right. Like #S190.			
a. Dark green on yellow underprint.	1.50	3.00	8.00
b. Light green.	1.50	3.00	8.00

S194 50 Rupiah	Good	Fine	XF
1.4.1948. Factory at left; refinery at right.			
a. Dark brown on yellow underprint.	3.00	8.00	15.00
b. Light brown to red-brown, without underprint.	3.00	8.00	15.00
c. Green on yellow underprint.	8.00	12.00	25.00

NOTE: For #S194 with text overprint. (1949) see #S412.

		Good	Fine	XF
S195	**100 Rupiah** 17.4.1948.			
	a. Green on pink underprint.	17.50	30.00	55.00
	b. Brown-red, without underprint.	10.00	25.00	45.00
	c. Black, without underprint, handwritten serial #. (Printed in Djambi).	17.50	30.00	55.00

Sumatera Selatan

South Sumatera

1948 Issue

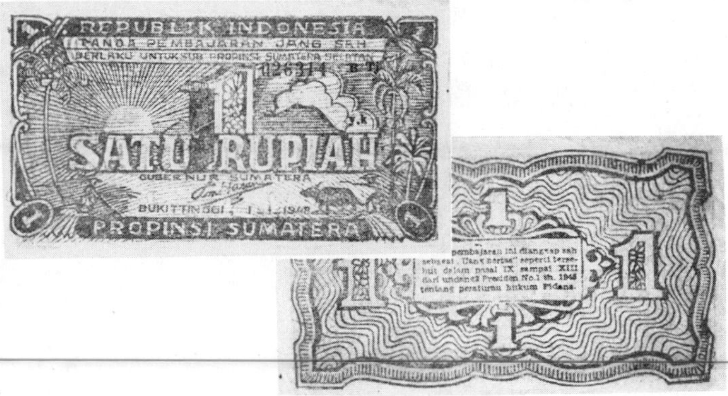

		Good	Fine	XF
S201	**1 Rupiah** 1.1.1948. Green. Central text: *Berlaku untuk sub propinsi Sumatera Selatan* (Valid in the sub-province of South Sumatera). Signed by Governor of Sumatra, Teuku A. M. Hassan.	3.00	6.00	12.00

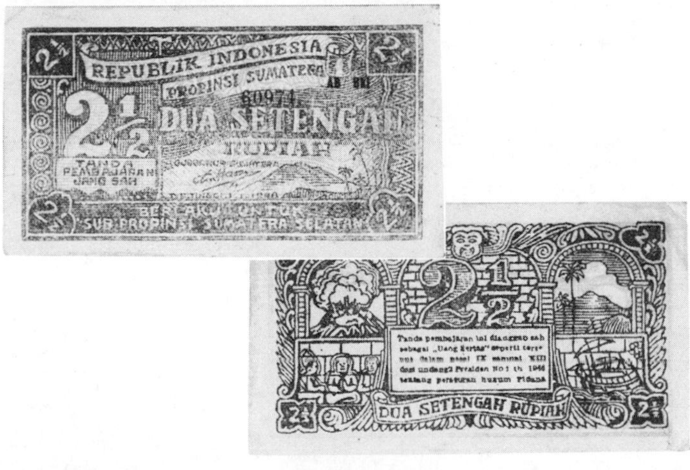

		Good	Fine	XF
S202	**2 1/2 Rupiah** 1.1.1948. Red on yellow underprint. Central text: *Berlaku untuk sub propinsi Sumatera Selatan* (Valid in the sub-province of South Sumatera). Signed by Governor of Sumatra, Teuku A. M. Hassan.	2.00	4.00	8.00

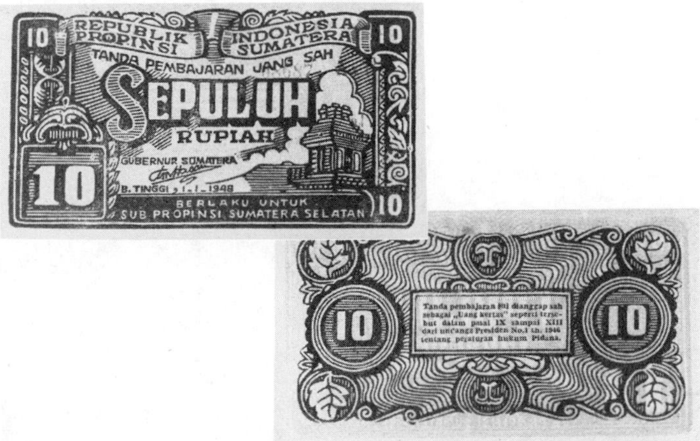

		Good	Fine	XF
S203	**10 Rupiah** 1.1.1948. Light blue to dark blue. Temple at right. Central text: *Berlaku untuk sub propinsi Sumatera Selatan* (Valid in the sub-province of South Sumatera). Signed by Governor of Sumatra, Teuku A. M. Hassan.	2.50	6.00	11.00

NOTE: All notes are signed by the Governor of Sumatra, Teuku A. M. Hassan.

Sumatera Timur

East Sumatera

1948 Issue

		Good	Fine	XF
S211	**10 Sen** 1.1.1948. Lilac on gray underprint. Central text: *Sumatera Timur* (East Sumatera). Signed by Governor of Sumatra, Teuku A. M. Hassan.	—	—	—
S212	**1/2 Rupiah** 1.1.1948. Purple on gray underprint. Central text: *Sumatera Timur* (East Sumatera). Signed by Governor of Sumatra, Teuku A. M. Hassan.	—	—	—

		Good	Fine	XF
S213	**5 Rupiah** 1.1.1948. Blue on gray underprint. Lake at center. Central text: *Sumatera Timur* (East Sumatera). Signed by Governor of Sumatra, Teuku A. M. Hassan.	10.00	25.00	45.00

NOTE: All notes are signed by the Governor of Sumatra, Teuku A. M. Hassan.

Sumatera Barat

West Sumatera

1948 Issue

#S221 central text: *Berlaku untuk daerah S. Barat* (Valid for the of West Sumatra region).

		Good	Fine	XF
S221	**10 Rupiah** 17.1.1948. Blue. Central text: *Berlaku untuk daerah S. Barat* (Valid for the West Sumatra region). Imam Bonjol at left, traditional houses at right. Signed by Governor of Sumatra, Teuku A. M. Hassan.	10.00	25.00	45.00

NOTE: All notes are signed by the Governor of Sumatra, Teuku A. M. Hassan.

Atjeh

Atcheh

1948 Issue

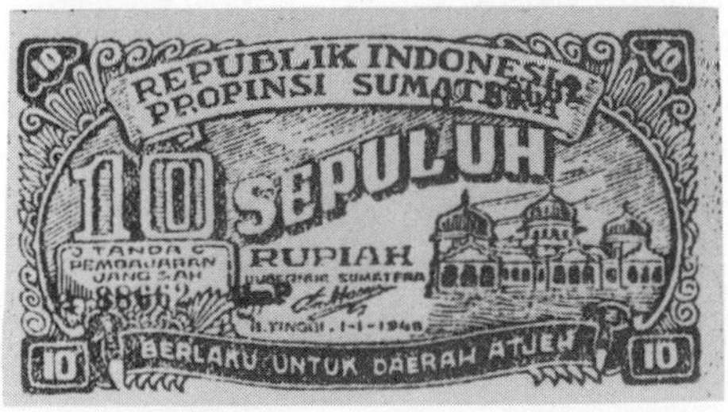

		Good	Fine	XF
S231	**10 Rupiah** 1.1.1948. Blue. Great Mosque at right. Central text: *Berlaku untuk daerah Atjeh* (Valid for the Atcheh region). Signed by Governor of Sumatra, Teuku A. M. Hassan.	10.00	25.00	45.00

S232 25 Rupiah	**Good**	**Fine**	**XF**
1.1.1948. Terraced rice field at left. Central text: *Berlaku untuk daerah Atjeh* (Valid for the Atcheh region). Signed by Governor of Sumatra, Teuku A. M. Hassan.			
a. Green on yellow underprint.	20.00	40.00	60.00
b. Blue on yellow underprint.	25.00	45.00	65.00
c. Brown.	20.00	40.00	60.00

NOTE: All notes are signed by the Governor of Sumatra, Teuku A. M. Hassan.

Djambi

1947 Issue

#S236 central text: *Berlaku untuk daerah Djambi* (Valid for the Djambi region).

S236 10 Rupiah	**Good**	**Fine**	**XF**
17.12.1947. Blue on green underprint. Ships at left. Central text: *Berlaku untuk daerah Djambi* (Valid for the Djambi region). Signed by Governor of Sumatra, Teuku A. M. Hassan.	10.00	25.00	45.00

NOTE: All notes are signed by the Governor of Sumatra, Teuku A. M. Hassan.

Riau

1947 Issue

S241 5 Rupiah	**Good**	**Fine**	**XF**
17.12.1947. Female dancer at left. Central text: *Berlaku untuk daerah Riau* (Valid in the Riau region).Signed by Governor of Sumatra, Teuku A. M. Hassan.			
a. Dark brown, dark brown-green underprint.	10.00	25.00	45.00
b. Green.	20.00	40.00	65.00

NOTE: All notes are signed by the Governor of Sumatra, Teuku A. M. Hassan.

Tapanoeli

Tapanuli

1948 Issue

S251 5 Rupiah	**Good**	**Fine**	**XF**
1.1.1948. Dark Blue. Toba lake at center. Central text: *Berlaku buat daerah Tapanuli* (Valid for the Tapanuli region).Signed by Governor of Sumatra, Teuku A. M. Hassan.	10.00	25.00	45.00

#S252 and S253 *Deleted.*

Djambi

1947 Issues

S261 1/2 Rupiah	**Good**	**Fine**	**XF**
1947. Red. Handwritten # and hand stamped signature.			
a. 24.10.1947.	17.50	32.50	50.00
b. 28.11.1947.	17.50	32.50	50.00
S262 1 Rupiah			
17.9.1947. Black. Handwritten # and hand stamped signature.			
a. Left hand signature title: *a/n Ketua Muda D.P.R.*	15.00	30.00	50.00
b. Left hand signature title: *Ketua Muda D.P.R.*	15.00	30.00	50.00
c. Left hand signature title: *Komisi Keuangan.*	15.00	30.00	50.00

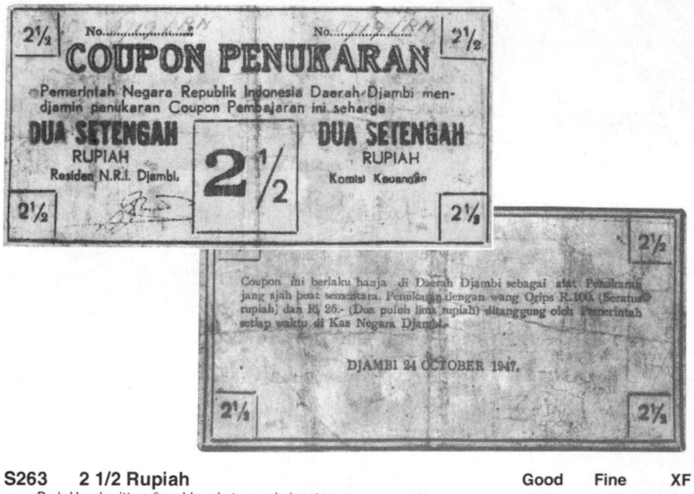

S263 2 1/2 Rupiah	**Good**	**Fine**	**XF**
Red. Handwritten # and hand stamped signature.			
a. 24.10.1947.	15.00	25.00	45.00
b. 28.11.1947.	15.00	25.00	45.00
S263A 5 Rupiah			
17.11.1947. Black. Handwritten # and hand stamped signature.	—	—	—

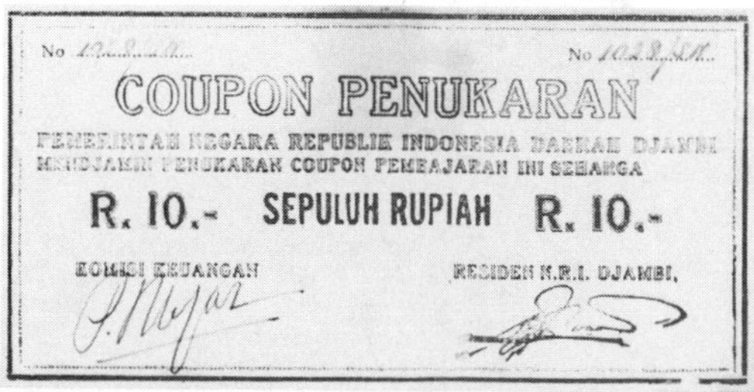

S263B 10 Rupiah	**Good**	**Fine**	**XF**
17.11.1947. Black. Handwritten # and hand stamped signature.	—	—	—

1947; 1948 Issue

S263C 1 Rupiah	**Good**	**Fine**	**XF**
Blue on light green underprint. Printed # and signature. Stamped letters.			
a. 31.3.1948.	17.50	30.00	50.00
b. 1.4.1948.	17.50	30.00	50.00
S264 2 1/2 Rupiah			
1947. Printed # and signature. Stamped letters. Similar to #S267.			
a. 27.12.1917. Red on yellow underprint.	7.50	15.00	30.00
b. 20.15.1947.	3.00	8.00	15.00

S265 5 Rupiah	Good	Fine	XF
1947; 1948. Red on yellow underprint. Printed # and signature. Stamped letters.			
a. 27.12.1947.	10.00	17.50	27.50
b. 31.3.1948.	7.50	12.00	25.00

S266 10 Rupiah	Good	Fine	XF
1947; 1948. Red on pale red underprint. Printed # and signature. Stamped letters.			
a. 27.12.1947.	12.50	25.00	40.00
b. 31.3.1948.	12.50	25.00	40.00

1948 Issue

S268 5 Rupiah	Good	Fine	XF
20.5.1948. Light green on yellow underprint. Printed # and signature. Stamped letters.	6.00	15.00	30.00

S269 25 Rupiah	Good	Fine	XF
20.5.1948. Brown-red on blue-green underprint. Printed # and signature. Stamped letters.	17.00	27.00	42.00

NOTE: #S270-S279, formerly listed here, see #S319-S319L.

Koetaradja

Kutaradja

1947-48 Issue

S281 1/2 Rupiah	Good	Fine	XF
15.9.1947. Black on yellow. Great Mosque at center. *Keresidenan Atjeh* (Atcheh residency).	10.00	20.00	40.00

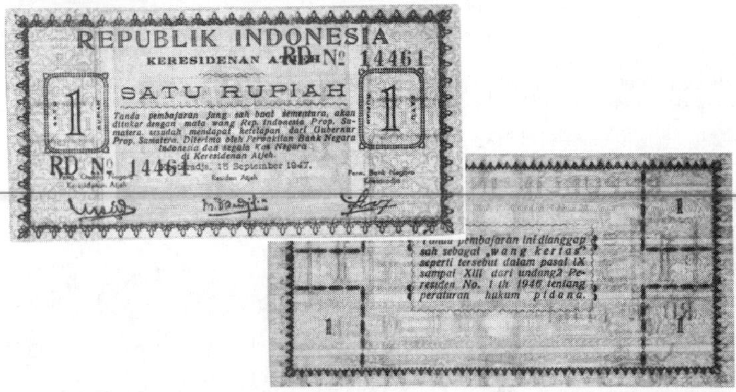

S282 1 Rupiah	Good	Fine	XF
15.9.1947. Black on pink. *Keresidenan Atjeh* (Atcheh residency).	7.50	15.00	30.00

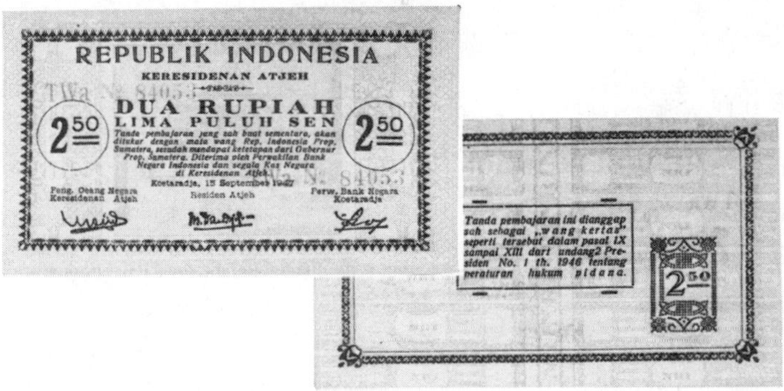

S283 2 1/2 Rupiah	Good	Fine	XF
15.9.1947. Black on green. *Keresidenan Atjeh* (Atcheh residency).	7.50	18.00	35.00
S283A 2 1/2 Rupiah 1.12.1947. Brown. Scenery in center. *Keresidenan Atjeh* (Atcheh residency).	—	—	—
S283B 5 Rupiah 1.12.1947. Dark blue. *5* in circles. *Keresidenan Atjeh* (Atcheh residency).	—	—	—

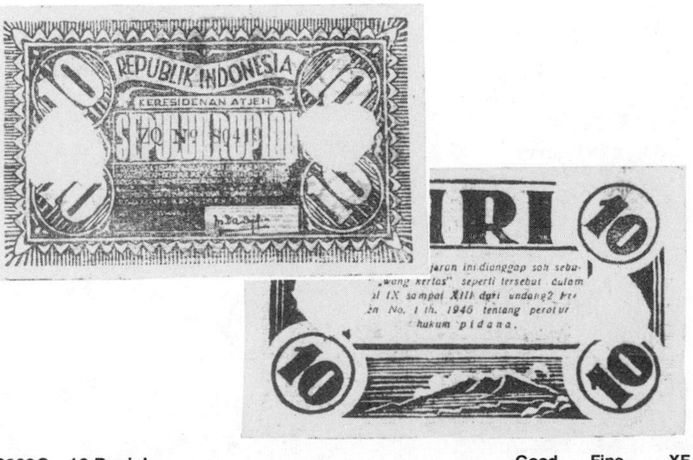

S283C 10 Rupiah	Good	Fine	XF
1.12.1947. Black. *10* in circles. *Keresidenan Atjeh* (Atcheh residency). Rare.	—	—	—
S284 5 Rupiah 15.1.1948. Black on green. Sukarno at left. *Keresidenan Atjeh* (Atcheh residency). Rare.	—	—	—

1949 Issues

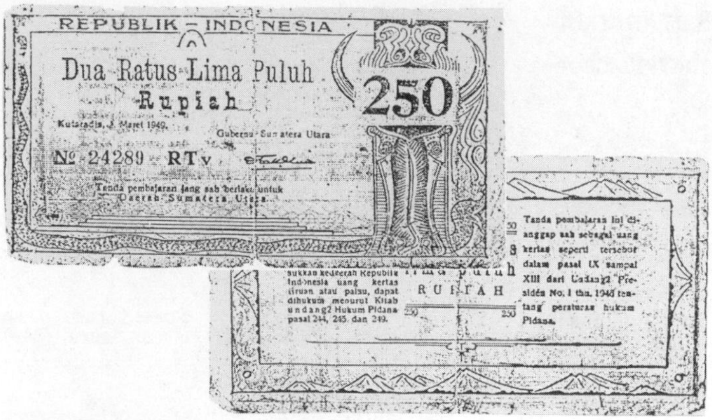

		Good	Fine	XF
S285	**250 Rupiah**			
	1.3.1949. Blue on yellow underprint. Atchenese dagger at right. Central text: *Daerah Sumatera Utara* (District of North Sumatra).	7.50	25.00	50.00

		Good	Fine	XF
S286	**250 Rupiah**			
	1.3.1949. Black on purple underprint. Atchenese dagger. Central text: *Daerah Sumatera Utara* (District of North Sumatra).	6.00	12.50	30.00

Kutatjane

1948 Issue

#S291-S293 are of Res(imen) I Div(ision) X of the Tentara Negara Indonesia (National Army of Indonesia), Southeast Atcheh.

		Good	Fine	XF
S291	**1 Rupiah**			
	1948. Black on yellow underprint. Guns.	—	—	—
S292	**5 Rupiah**			
	1948. Black. Soldiers.	—	—	—
S293	**10 Rupiah**			
	1948. Black on red underprint. Landscape.	—	—	—

NOTE: Former #S301-S303 are the same as #S361, S362 and S370.

Laboehan Bilore

1948 Issue

		Good	Fine	XF
S306	**5 Rupiah**			
	23.12.1947.	—	—	—
S307	**10 Rupiah**			
	23.12.1947.	—	—	—

Labuhan Bilik

1948 Issues

		Good	Fine	XF
S308	**25 Rupiah**			
	23.12.1948. Black.	—	—	—

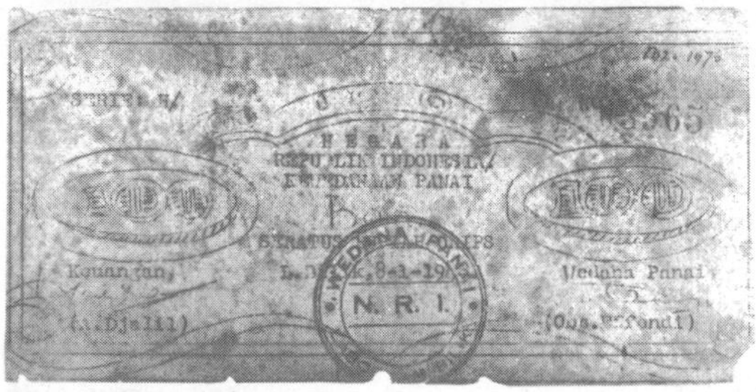

		Good	Fine	XF
S309	**100 Rupiah**			
	19.1.1948. *100* in block left and right.			
	a. Black.	—	—	—
	b. Green.	—	—	—
S310	**100 Rupiah**			
	5.2.1948. *100* in block left and right. Like #S309.			
	a. Blue.	—	—	—
	b. Red-brown.	—	—	—
S311	**100 Rupiah**			
	14.2.1948. Coastal scenery at left and right.	—	—	—
S311A	**10,000 Rupiah**			
	24.2.1948. Red.	—	—	—

		Good	Fine	XF
S311B	**50,000 Rupiah**			
	6.3.1948.	—	—	—
S312	**100,000 Rupiah**			
	24.2.1948. Red.	—	—	—
S312A	**250,000 Rupiah**			
	25.3.1948. Orange.	—	—	—
S313	**500,000 Rupiah**			
	9.4.1948. Black.	—	—	—

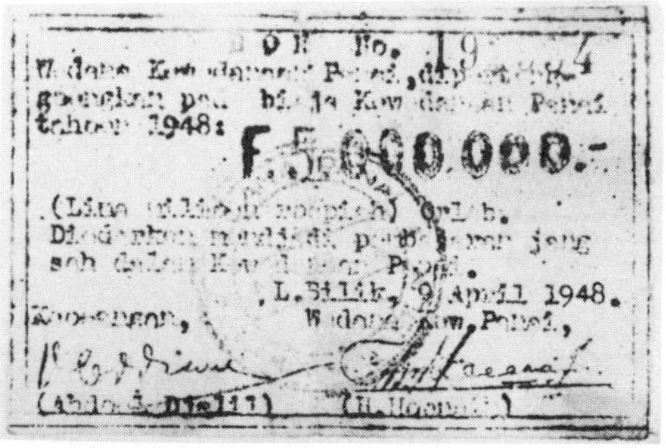

		Good	Fine	XF
S313A	**5,000,000 Rupiah**			
	9.4.1948.	—	—	—
S313B	**25,000,000 Rupiah**			
	7.5.1948. Similar to #S313A.	—	—	—
S314	**25,000,000 Rupiah**			
	7.5.1948. Black.	—	—	—

Langsa

1949 Issue

		Good	Fine	XF
S316	**100 Rupiah**			
	2.1.1949. Red.			
	a. Without signature.	—	—	—
	b. With signatures.	—	—	—

NOTE: Modern fakes of #S316 on coarse paper exist.

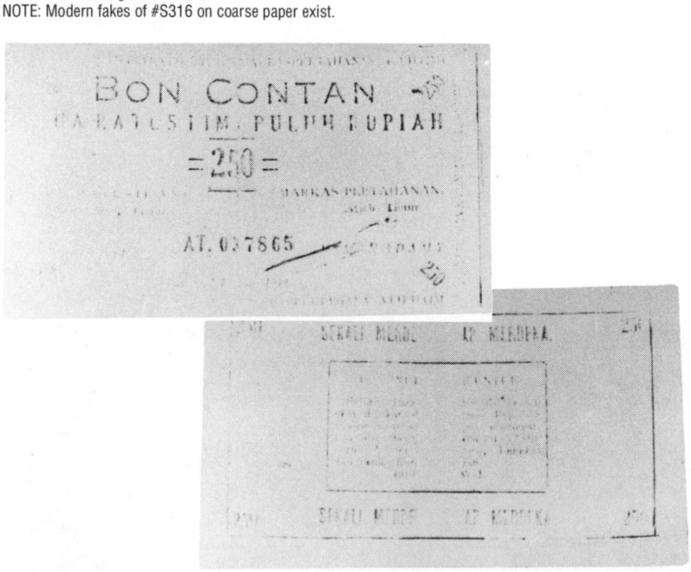

		Good	Fine	XF
S317	**250 Rupiah**			
	2.1.1949.			
	a. Black.	35.00	105.	175.
	b. Green.	35.00	105.	175.

NOTE: Modern fakes of #S317 on coarse paper exist.

Lima Poeloeh

1947 Issue

	Good	Fine	XF
S318 50 Rupiah 1.9.1947. Red. Value in heart-shaped guilloche at left and right. Back: Blue hand stamp. Rare.	—	—	—

	Good	Fine	XF
S318A 100 Rupiah 1.9.1947; 10.9.1947. Red. Value in diamond design at center. Rare.	—	—	—

Membang Moeda (M. Muda)

1947-48 Issues

	Good	Fine	XF
S319A 50 Rupiah 1.9.1947. Black.	—	—	—

	Good	Fine	XF
S319B 100 Rupiah 1.9.1947. Red.	—	—	—
S319C 250 Rupiah 10.1947. Green. Two lines of trees at left or right.	—	—	—

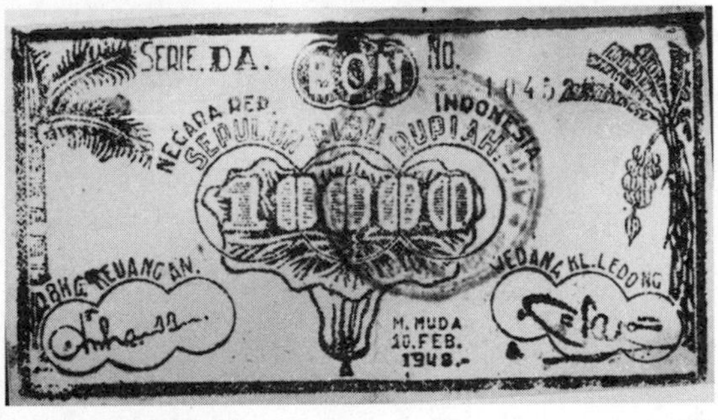

	Good	Fine	XF
S319D 1000 Rupiah 10.12.1947. Red-brown. Coconut tree at left and right.	—	—	—
S319E 2500 Rupiah 1.1.1948. Dark brown. Thunderbolt at left and right.	—	—	—
S319F 5000 Rupiah 15.1.1948. Brown. Mountain scene at left and right.	—	—	—
S319G 10,000 Rupiah 20.1.1948. Brown. Lighthouse at left and right. Palms at left and right.	—	—	—
S319H 10,000 Rupiah 10.2.1948. Brown. Tree at left and right.	—	—	—
S319I 25,000 Rupiah 22.2.1948. Brown. Trees at left and right.	—	—	—
S319J 50,000 Rupiah 3.3.1948. Green. Floral design.	—	—	—

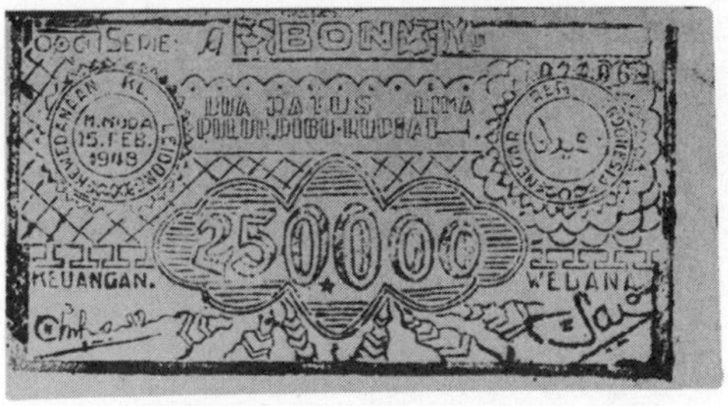

	Good	Fine	XF
S319K 250,000 Rupiah 15.2.1948. Green. Value in floral design.	—	—	—

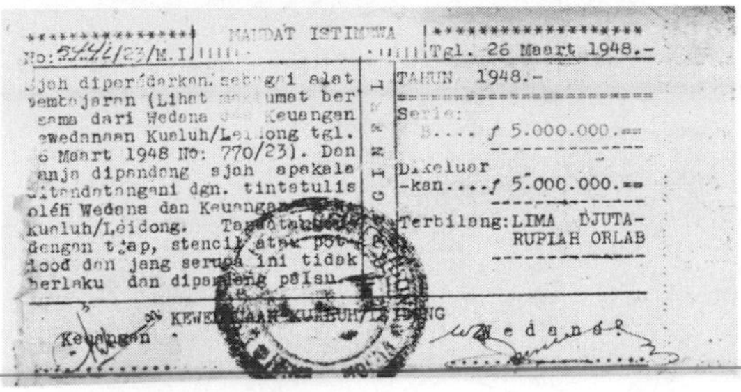

MANDAT ISTIMEWA
Tgl. 26 Maart 1948.-
TAHUN 1948.-
Serie: B.... f 5.000.000.-
Dikeluar-kan.... f 5.000.000.-
Terbilang: LIMA DJUTA-RUPIAH ORLAB

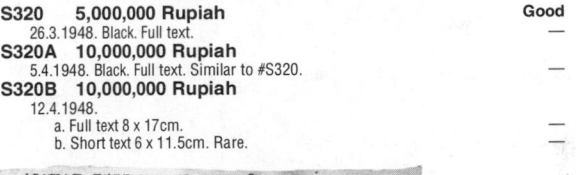

	Good	Fine	XF
S320 5,000,000 Rupiah 26.3.1948. Black. Full text.	—	—	—
S320A 10,000,000 Rupiah 5.4.1948. Black. Full text. Similar to #S320.	—	—	—
S320B 10,000,000 Rupiah 12.4.1948.			
a. Full text 8 x 17cm.	—	—	—
b. Short text 6 x 11.5cm. Rare.	—	—	—

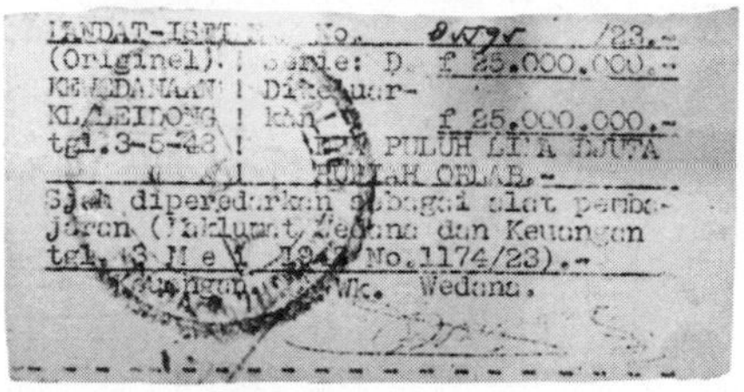

MANDAT-ISTI... No. /23.-
(Originel). Serie: D. f 25.000.000.-
f 25.000.000.-
DUA PULUH LIMA DJUTA RUPIAH ORLAB.-

	Good	Fine	XF
S320C 25,000,000 Rupiah 3.5.1948. Black.	—	—	—

Nias

1947-49 Issues

	Good	Fine	XF
S321 1 Rupiah 25.9.1947. Black on yellow underprint. Central text: *Alat pembajar berlaku dalam Kabupaten Nias* (Legal tender valid in the Nias regency).	—	—	—
S321A 100 Rupiah 20.12.1948. Black. Central text: *Alat pembajar berlaku dalam Kabupaten Nias* (Legal tender valid in the Nias regency).	—	—	—
S321B 200 Rupiah 20.12.1948. Black on yellow. Leaves all around. Central text: *Alat pembajar berlaku dalam Kabupaten Nias* (Legal tender valid in the Nias regency).	—	—	—

#S322 *Deleted.*

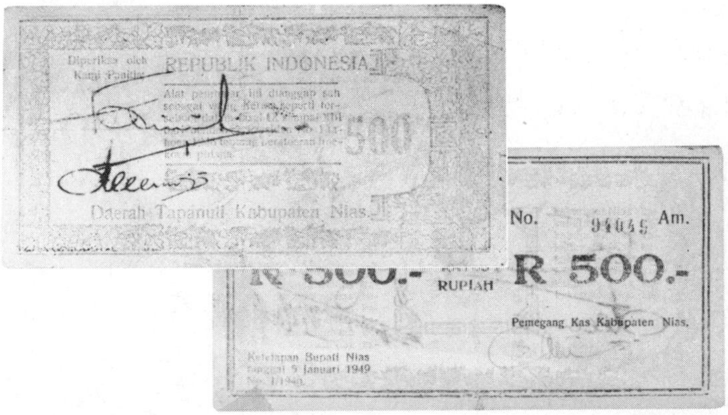

	Good	Fine	XF
S323 500 Rupiah 5.1.1949. Leaves all around. Central text: *Alat pembajar berlaku dalam Kabupaten Nias* (Legal tender valid in the Nias regency).			
a. Black on green.	10.00	30.00	60.00
b. Black on orange underprint.	20.00	40.00	60.00
c. Black on light blue.	10.00	20.00	40.00
S324 500 Rupiah 7.1.1949. Green. Central text: *Alat pembajar berlaku dalam Kabupaten Nias* (Legal tender valid in the Nias regency).	7.50	25.00	50.00

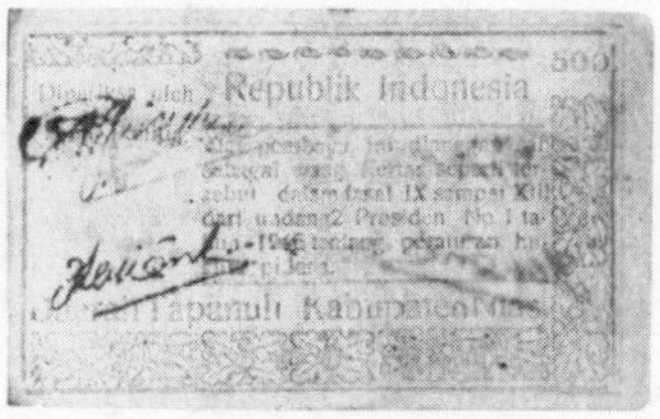

S325 500 Rupiah	Good	Fine	XF
12.11.1949. Black on light blue underprint.	—	—	—

P. Alam

Pagar Alam

1947 Issue

S326 10 Rupiah	Good	Fine	XF
12.17.1947. Black. Eagle on mountain at left.	—	—	—

S327 50 Rupiah	Good	Fine	XF
17.12.1947. Eagle on mountain at lower center. Uniface.			
a. Red.	—	—	—
b. Blue.	—	—	—
S328 100 Rupiah			
17.12.1947. Blue. Eagle on mountain at center.	—	—	—

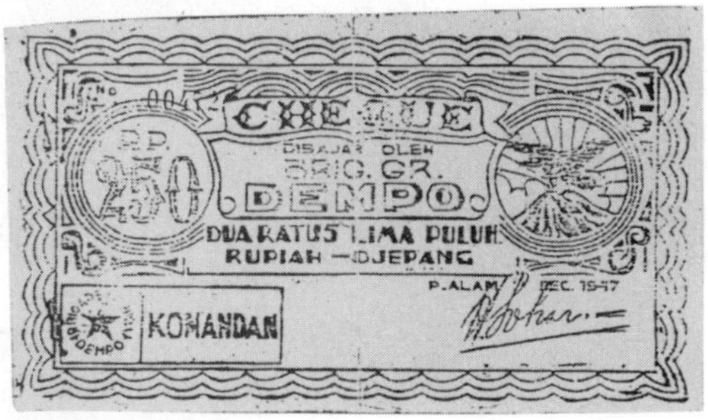

S329 250 Rupiah	Good	Fine	XF
17.12.1947. Black. Eagle on mountain at right.	—	—	—
S330 1000 Rupiah			
17.12.1947. Red. Eagle and mountain at left center.	—	—	—

Palembang

1947 Issues

S331 50 Rupiah	Good	Fine	XF
1.8.1947. Flag in circle at left and right. Central text: *Mandat D(ewan) P(ertahanan) D(aerah) P(alembang)* (Mandate Board of Defense District of Palembang).			
a. Blue.	—	—	—
b. Green.	—	—	—

S332 250 Rupiah	Good	Fine	XF
1.8.1947. Red. Central text: *Mandat D(ewan) P(ertahanan) D(aerah) P(alembang)* (Mandate Board of Defense District of Palembang).	7.50	25.00	50.00

S333 500 Rupiah	Good	Fine	XF
1.8.1947. Green on brown. Central text: *Mandat D(ewan) P(ertahanan) D(aerah) P(alembang)* (Mandate Board of Defense District of Palembang).	—	—	—

S334 1000 Rupiah	Good	Fine	XF
1.8.1947. Blue. *1000* in 4 corners. Value at left, blue seal. Central text: *Mandat D(ewan) P(ertahanan) D(aerah) P(alembang)* (Mandate Board of Defense District of Palembang).	3.00	8.00	20.00

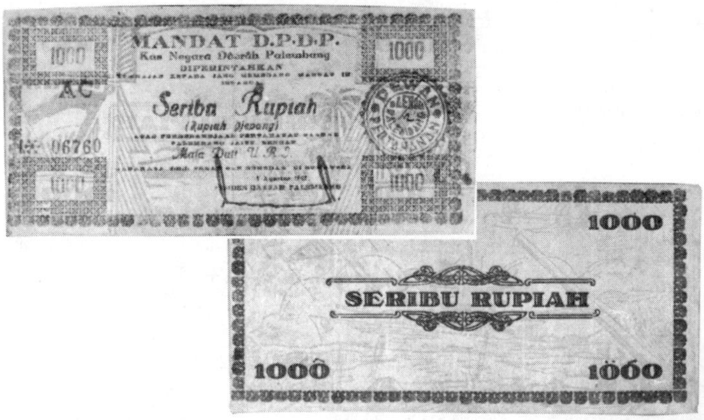

S335 1000 Rupiah	Good	Fine	XF
1.8.1947. Blue to blue-green on light green underprint. Value at left, blue seal. Central text: *Mandat D(ewan) P(ertahanan) D(aerah) P(alembang)* (Mandate Board of Defense District of Palembang).			
a. Blue.	5.00	8.00	20.00
b. Blue. Uniface.	6.00	9.00	20.00
c. Green.	8.00	12.00	25.00
d. Green. Uniface.	8.00	12.00	25.00

1949 First Issue

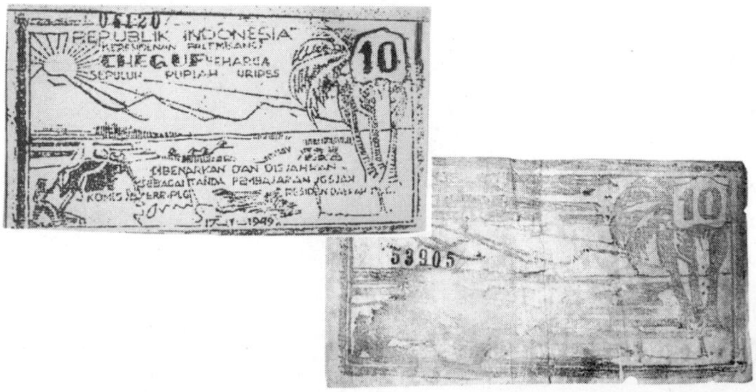

S336 10 Rupiah	Good	Fine	XF
17.4.1949. Gray. Rice field. Text: *Cheque Keresidenan Palembang.* Uniface.	7.50	25.00	50.00

S337 50 Rupiah	Good	Fine	XF
17.4.1949. Coconut tree at left. Text: *Cheque Keresidenan Palembang*. Uniface.			
a. Black.	7.50	25.00	50.00
b. Green.	6.00	17.50	45.00

1949 Second Issue

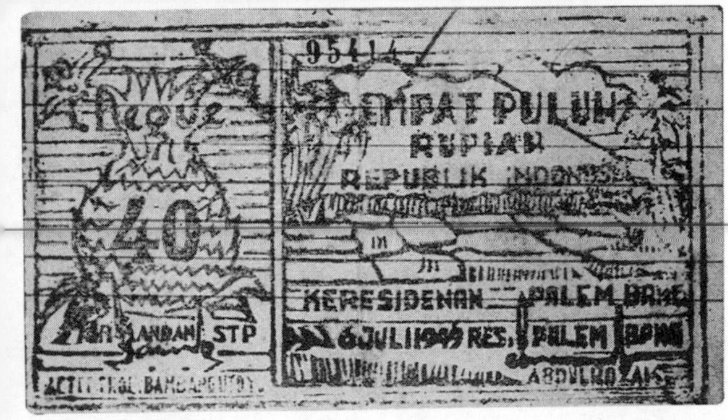

S338 40 Rupiah	Good	Fine	XF
6.7.1949. Pineapple at left. Text: *Cheque Keresidenan Palembang*. Uniface.			
a. Red.	7.50	25.00	50.00
b. Green.	12.00	25.00	50.00
c. Orange.	8.00	20.00	40.00
d. Dark brown.	10.00	25.00	50.00
S339 50 Rupiah			
18.11.1949. Leaves and candle.			
a. Blue.	—	—	—
b. Black.	—	—	—

Pekanbaru

1940 Exchange Coupon Issue

S342 1 Rupiah	Good	Fine	XF
1.7.1940. Green.	—	—	—

Pematang Siantar

1947 Issue

S351 1 Rupiah	Good	Fine	XF
31.3.1947. Dark red on blue underprint. Portrait Sukarno at left, volcano at right. Central text: *Propinsi Soematera* (Province of Sumatra).	5.00	9.00	20.00

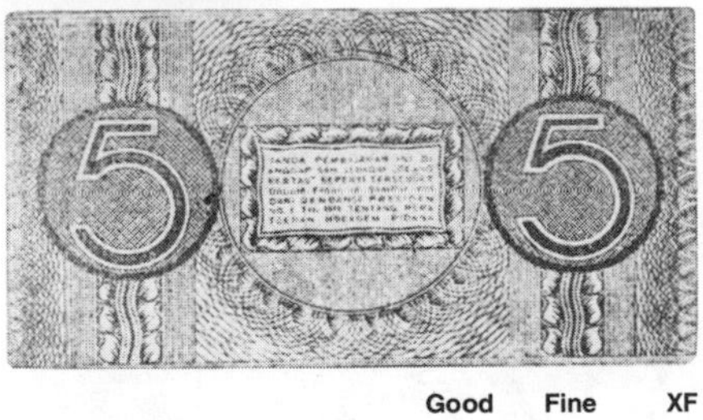

S352 5 Rupiah	Good	Fine	XF
31.3.1947. Sukarno at left. Central text: *Propinsi Soematera* (Province of Sumatra).			
a. Green on yellow underprint.	4.00	8.00	17.50
b. Blue on red underprint.	6.00	12.50	25.00

S353 10 Rupiah	Good	Fine	XF
31.3.1947. Sukarno at left. Central text: *Propinsi Soematera* (Province of Sumatra).			
a. Deep purple on pink underprint.	3.00	6.00	20.00
b. Green on light green underprint.	4.00	8.00	22.50
x. Blue-violet on lilac underprint. (Counterfeit).	—	—	—

S354 100 Rupiah	Good	Fine	XF
31.3.1947. Sukarno at left. Central text: *Propinsi Soematera* (Province of Sumatra).			
a. Lilac on yellow and light blue underprint.	10.00	25.00	60.00
b. Violet on yellow and light blue underprint.	10.00	25.00	60.00

NOTE: Modern fakes of #S345 exists (prefix CN).

Pendopo

1949 Issue

S354A 10 Rupiah	Good	Fine	XF
17.1.1949. Black. Uniface.	—	—	—

S355 25 Rupiah	Good	Fine	XF
17.1.1949. Uniface.			
a. Red.	—	—	—
b. Black.	—	—	—

NOTE: For #S355 with inflation strip, see #S411C.

Rantau Prapat

1947-48 Issues

#S361-S374 Mimeographed.

S361 2 1/2 Rupiah	Good	Fine	XF
ND(1947). Value in center. Central text: *Kaboepaten Laboean Batoe, Rantau Prapat* (Labuan Batu regency, Rantauprapat).	—	—	—
S361A 5 Rupiah			
ND(1947). Black. Value in center. Central text: *Kaboepaten Laboean Batoe, Rantau Prapat* (Labuan Batu regency, Rantauprapat).	—	—	—
S362 10 Rupiah			
ND(1947). Value in center. Central text: *Kaboepaten Laboean Batoe, Rantau Prapat* (Labuan Batu regency, Rantauprapat).	—	—	—
S363 50 Rupiah			
ND(1947). Black. Value in center. Central text: *Kaboepaten Laboean Batoe, Rantau Prapat* (Labuan Batu regency, Rantauprapat).	—	—	—

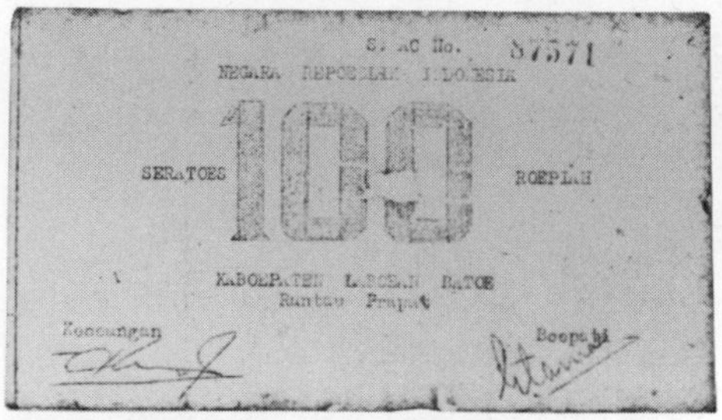

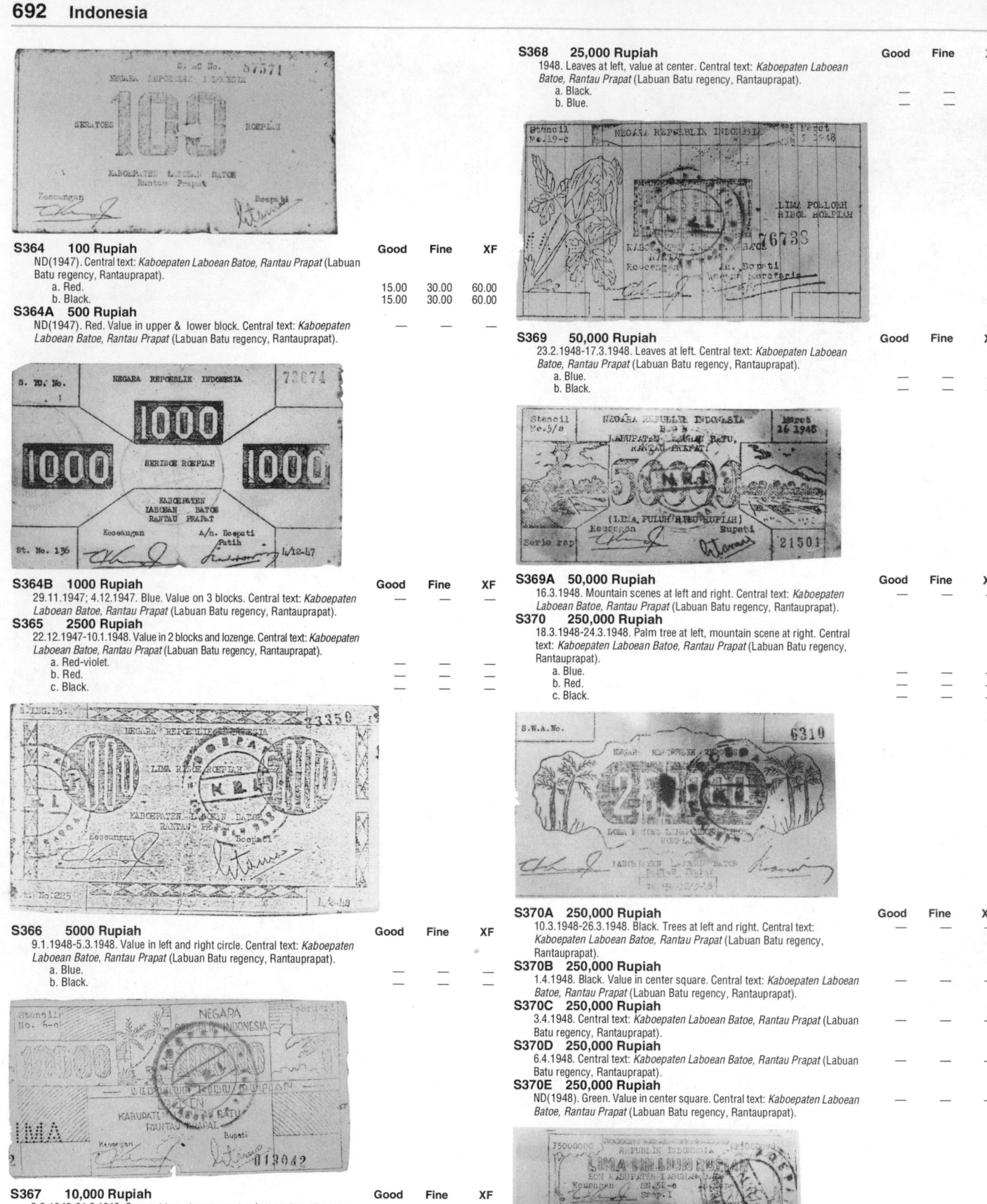

S364 100 Rupiah	Good	Fine	XF
ND(1947). Central text: *Kaboepaten Laboean Batoe, Rantau Prapat* (Labuan Batu regency, Rantauprapat).			
a. Red.	15.00	30.00	60.00
b. Black.	15.00	30.00	60.00
S364A 500 Rupiah			
ND(1947). Red. Value in upper & lower block. Central text: *Kaboepaten Laboean Batoe, Rantau Prapat* (Labuan Batu regency, Rantauprapat).	—	—	—

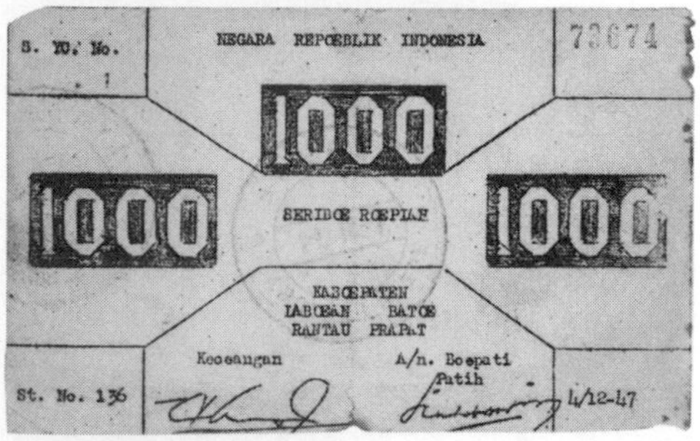

S364B 1000 Rupiah	Good	Fine	XF
29.11.1947; 4.12.1947. Blue. Value on 3 blocks. Central text: *Kaboepaten Laboean Batoe, Rantau Prapat* (Labuan Batu regency, Rantauprapat).	—	—	—
S365 2500 Rupiah			
22.12.1947-10.1.1948. Value in 2 blocks and lozenge. Central text: *Kaboepaten Laboean Batoe, Rantau Prapat* (Labuan Batu regency, Rantauprapat).			
a. Red-violet.	—	—	—
b. Red.	—	—	—
c. Black.	—	—	—

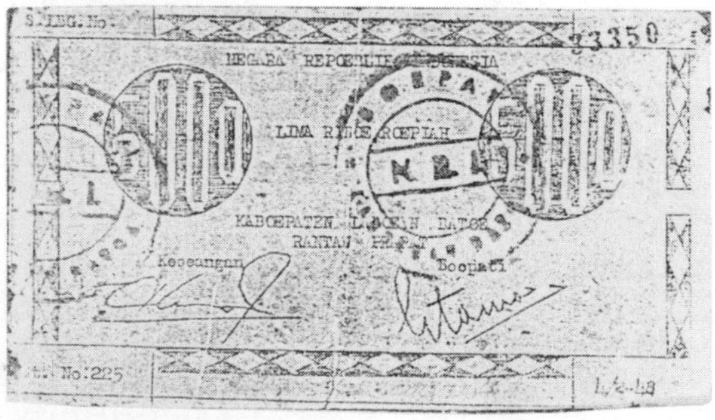

S366 5000 Rupiah	Good	Fine	XF
9.1.1948-5.3.1948. Value in left and right circle. Central text: *Kaboepaten Laboean Batoe, Rantau Prapat* (Labuan Batu regency, Rantauprapat).			
a. Blue.	—	—	—
b. Black.	—	—	—

S367 10,000 Rupiah	Good	Fine	XF
3.2.1948-21.2.1948. Coconut tree at upper center, banana tree at upper right. Central text: *Kaboepaten Laboean Batoe, Rantau Prapat* (Labuan Batu regency, Rantauprapat).			
a. Blue.	—	—	—
b. Black.	—	—	—
S367A 10,000 Rupiah			
6.2.1948-21.2.1948. Value within three conjoined circles. Central text: *Kaboepaten Laboean Batoe, Rantau Prapat* (Labuan Batu regency, Rantauprapat).			
a. Blue.	—	—	—
b. Black.	—	—	—

S368 25,000 Rupiah	Good	Fine	XF
1948. Leaves at left, value at center. Central text: *Kaboepaten Laboean Batoe, Rantau Prapat* (Labuan Batu regency, Rantauprapat).			
a. Black.	—	—	—
b. Blue.	—	—	—

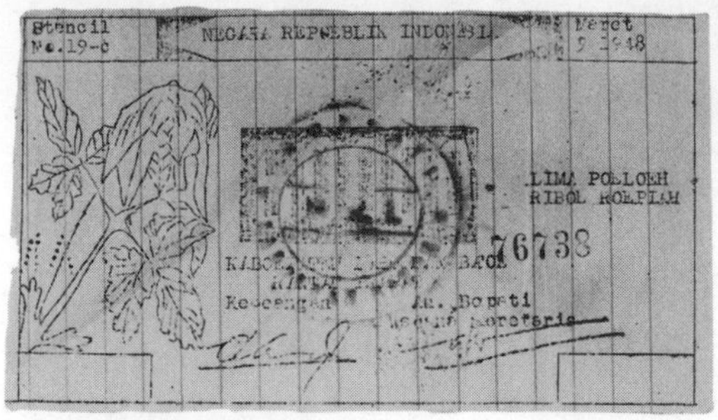

S369 50,000 Rupiah	Good	Fine	XF
23.2.1948-17.3.1948. Leaves at left. Central text: *Kaboepaten Laboean Batoe, Rantau Prapat* (Labuan Batu regency, Rantauprapat).			
a. Blue.	—	—	—
b. Black.	—	—	—

S369A 50,000 Rupiah	Good	Fine	XF
16.3.1948. Mountain scenes at left and right. Central text: *Kaboepaten Laboean Batoe, Rantau Prapat* (Labuan Batu regency, Rantauprapat).	—	—	—
S370 250,000 Rupiah			
18.3.1948-24.3.1948. Palm tree at left, mountain scene at right. Central text: *Kaboepaten Laboean Batoe, Rantau Prapat* (Labuan Batu regency, Rantauprapat).			
a. Blue.	—	—	—
b. Red.	—	—	—
c. Black.	—	—	—

S370A 250,000 Rupiah	Good	Fine	XF
10.3.1948-26.3.1948. Black. Trees at left and right. Central text: *Kaboepaten Laboean Batoe, Rantau Prapat* (Labuan Batu regency, Rantauprapat).	—	—	—
S370B 250,000 Rupiah			
1.4.1948. Black. Value in center square. Central text: *Kaboepaten Laboean Batoe, Rantau Prapat* (Labuan Batu regency, Rantauprapat).	—	—	—
S370C 250,000 Rupiah			
3.4.1948. Central text: *Kaboepaten Laboean Batoe, Rantau Prapat* (Labuan Batu regency, Rantauprapat).	—	—	—
S370D 250,000 Rupiah			
6.4.1948. Central text: *Kaboepaten Laboean Batoe, Rantau Prapat* (Labuan Batu regency, Rantauprapat).	—	—	—
S370E 250,000 Rupiah			
ND(1948). Green. Value in center square. Central text: *Kaboepaten Laboean Batoe, Rantau Prapat* (Labuan Batu regency, Rantauprapat).	—	—	—

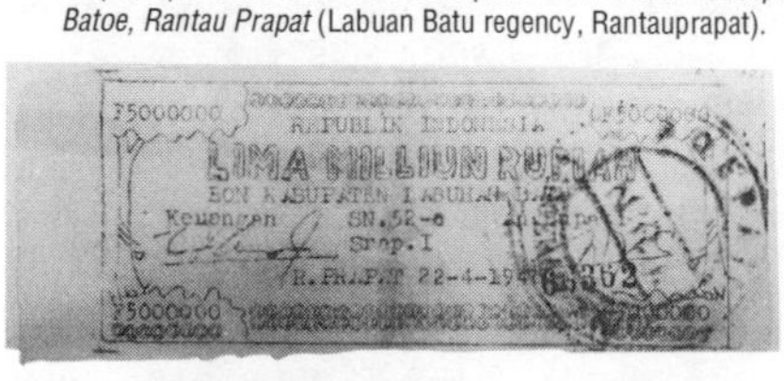

S371 5,000,000 Rupiah	Good	Fine	XF
9.21.1948-24.4.1948. Black. Trees at center. Central text: *Kaboepaten Laboean Batoe, Rantau Prapat* (Labuan Batu regency, Rantauprapat).			
a. Black.	—	—	—
S371 5,000,000 Rupiah			
b. Blue.	—	—	—
c. Orange.	—	—	—

S371A 5,000,000 Rupiah

14.4.1948. Black. Value in center block. Central text: *Kaboepaten Laboean Batoe, Rantau Prapat* (Labuan Batu regency, Rantauprapat).

	Good	Fine	XF
	—	—	—

S372 25,000,000 Rupiah

9.4.1948-8.5.1948. Mountains at lower center. Central text: *Kaboepaten Laboean Batoe, Rantau Prapat* (Labuan Batu regency, Rantauprapat).

	Good	Fine	XF
a. Red.	—	—	—
b. Brown.	—	—	—
c. Black.	—	—	—
d. Green.	—	—	—

S374 25,000,000 Rupiah

12.5.1948. Black. Central text: *Kaboepaten Laboean Batoe, Rantau Prapat* (Labuan Batu regency, Rantauprapat).

	Good	Fine	XF
	—	—	—

TANDJUNGKARANG

1947 ISSUES

S380 25 Rupiah

15.11.1947. Black. Red seal, 1 red and 1 black signature. Central text: *Mandat Pertahanan Daerah Lampung* (Defense Mandate of Lampung Region).

	Good	Fine	XF
	15.00	30.00	60.00

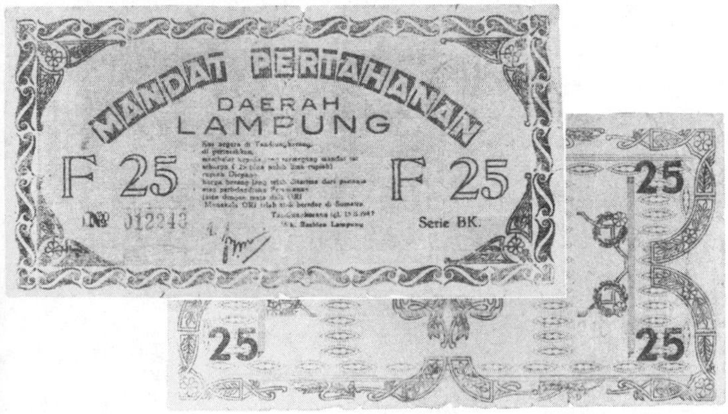

S381 25 Rupiah

15.11.1947. Orange and black. Like #S380 but with floral underprint. Violet seal, 1 blue and 1 black signature. Central text: *Mandat Pertahanan Daerah Lampung* (Defense Mandate of Lampung Region).

	Good	Fine	XF
	18.00	35.00	75.00

1948 FIRST ISSUE

S382 50 Rupiah

15.1.1948. Black. Dagger at left. One handwritten initial. Central text: *Mandat Pertahanan Keresidenan Lampung* (Defense Mandate Lampung Residency).

	Good	Fine	XF
a. Red seal.	10.00	20.00	50.00
b. Black seal.	10.00	20.00	50.00
c. Blue seal.	15.00	25.00	60.00

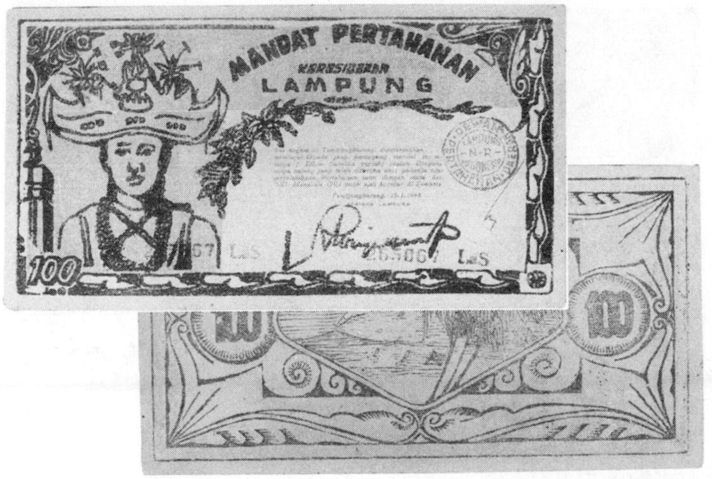

S383 100 Rupiah

15.1.1948. Black. Female at left. One handwritten initial. Central text: *Mandat Pertahanan Keresidenan Lampung* (Defense Mandate Lampung Residency).

	Good	Fine	XF
a. Red seal.	15.00	30.00	60.00
b. Black seal.	15.00	30.00	60.00
c. Blue seal.	20.00	35.00	65.00

1948 SECOND ISSUE

S384 1/2 Rupiah

1.6.1948. Gray-green. Central text: *Republik Indonesia, Propinsi Sumatera, Keresidenan Lampung* (Republic of Indonesia, Province of Sumatera, Lampung Residency). Uniface.

	Good	Fine	XF
a. Red seal, red serial #.	3.00	8.00	20.00
b. Black seal, black serial #.	3.00	8.00	20.00

S385 1 Rupiah

1.6.1948. Dark purple. Central text: *Republik Indonesia, Propinsi Sumatera, Keresidenan Lampung* (Republic of Indonesia, Province of Sumatera, Lampung Residency). Uniface.

	Good	Fine	XF
a. Blue seal.	3.00	9.00	20.00
b. Black seal.	2.50	5.00	12.50
c. Red seal.	2.00	4.00	10.00

S386 2 1/2 Rupiah

1.6.1948. Central text: *Republik Indonesia, Propinsi Sumatera, Keresidenan Lampung* (Republic of Indonesia, Province of Sumatera, Lampung Residency).

	Good	Fine	XF
a. Red.	2.00	5.00	10.00
b. Pink.	2.50	6.00	10.00

S387 5 Rupiah

1.6.1948. Black. Industry at left, trees at right. Central text: *Republik Indonesia, Propinsi Sumatera, Keresidenan Lampung* (Republic of Indonesia, Province of Sumatera, Lampung Residency).

	Good	Fine	XF
a. Red seal, red serial #.	3.00	8.00	15.00
b. Black seal, black serial #.	3.00	8.00	15.00

S388 10 Rupiah

1.6.1948. Black. Dagger at left and right. Central text: *Republik Indonesia, Propinsi Sumatera, Keresidenan Lampung* (Republic of Indonesia, Province of Sumatera, Lampung Residency).

	Good	Fine	XF
a. Red seal, red serial #.	3.00	8.00	17.00
b. Black seal, black serial #.	3.00	8.00	17.00

TAPANOELI

TAPANULI DISTRICT

1947-48 ISSUES

S390 5 Rupiah — Good 12.50 · Fine 25.00 · XF 55.00

8.8.1947. Black on red. Central text: *Harga R 5* and *Alat pembajar berlakoe dalam daerah Tapanoeli* (Legal tender valid in the district Tapanuli).

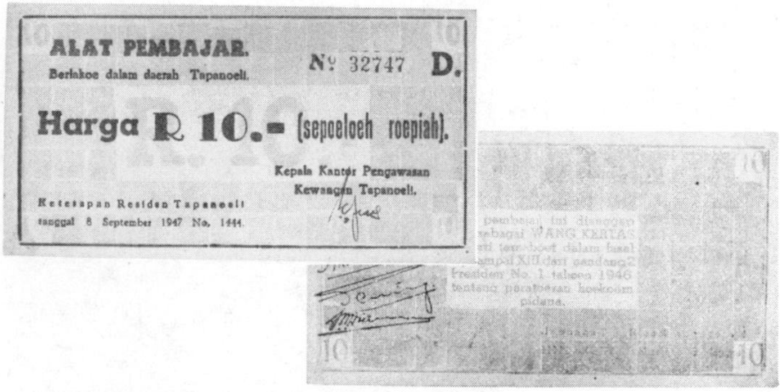

S391 10 Rupiah — Good 20.00 · Fine 40.00 · XF 85.00

8.9.1947. Black on pink underprint. Central text: *Harga R 10* and *Alat pembajar berlakoe dalam daerah Tapanoeli* (Legal tender valid in the district Tapanuli).

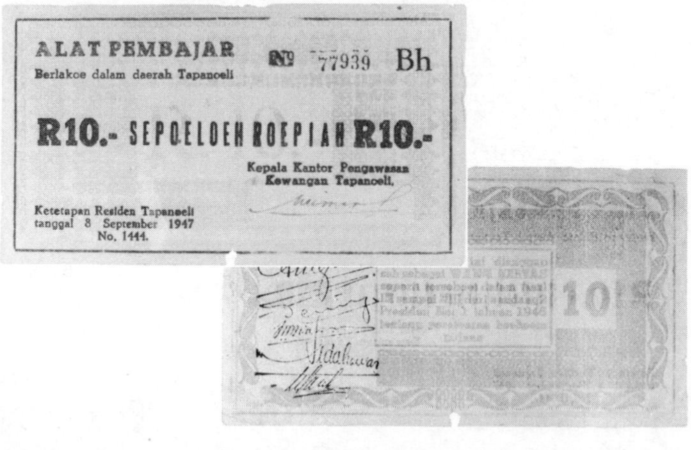

S392 10 Rupiah — Good 20.00 · Fine 30.00 · XF 60.00

8.9.1947. Black on red underprint. Central text: *R 10* and *Alat pembajar berlakoe dalam daerah Tapanoeli* (Legal tender valid in the district Tapanuli).

#S393 *Deleted.*

S394 25 Rupiah — Good 15.00 · Fine 35.00 · XF 75.00

18.11.1947. Black on pink. Central text: *Harga R 25* and *Alat pembajar berlakoe dalam daerah Tapanoeli* (Legal tender valid in the district Tapanuli).

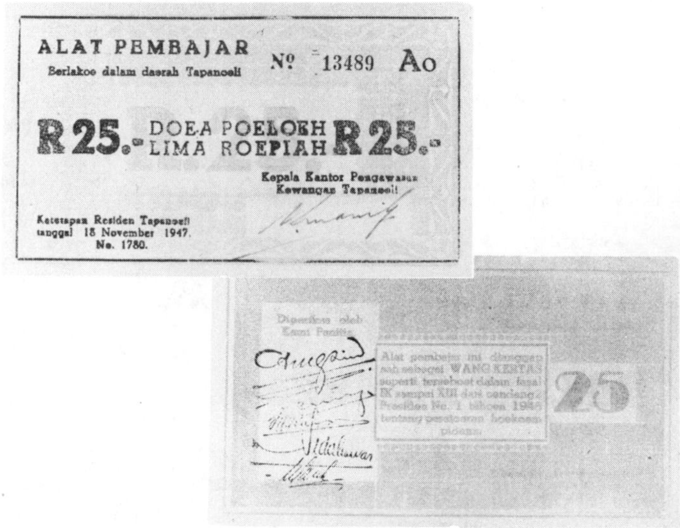

S395 25 Rupiah — Good 7.50 · Fine 20.00 · XF 50.00

18.11.1947. Central text: *R 25* and *Alat pembajar berlakoe dalam daerah Tapanoeli* (Legal tender valid in the district Tapanuli).

S396 50 Rupiah

28.4.1948. Black on pink. Central text: *Alat pembajar berlakoe dalam daerah Tapanoeli* (Legal tender valid in the district Tapanuli).

	Good	Fine	XF
a. Number of decree *464* (lower left corner).	12.50	27.50	60.00
b. Number of decree *646* (lower left corner).	10.00	25.00	55.00

S397 100 Rupiah

11.10.1948. Central text: *Alat pembajar berlakoe dalam daerah Tapanoeli* (Legal tender valid in the district Tapanuli).

	Good	Fine	XF
a. Black on light red.	12.50	30.00	65.00
b. Black on green.	15.00	35.00	70.00
c. Black on yellow-green.	12.50	30.00	65.00

S398 200 Rupiah

23.11.1948. Black on green. Central text: *Alat pembajar berlakoe dalam daerah Tapanoeli* (Legal tender valid in the district Tapanuli).

	Good	Fine	XF
a. Green underprint.	20.00	45.00	90.00
b. Yellow underprint.	15.00	40.00	85.00

TIGABINANGA

1947-49 ISSUE

	Good	Fine	XF
S399 50 Rupiah 17.9.1947. Black. Typewritten.	—	—	—
S400 100 Rupiah 3.11.1947. Black. Typewritten.	—	—	—

S401 250 Rupiah

	Good	Fine	XF
17.9.1947; 17.10.1947; 20.11.1947. Black. Typewritten.	—	—	—

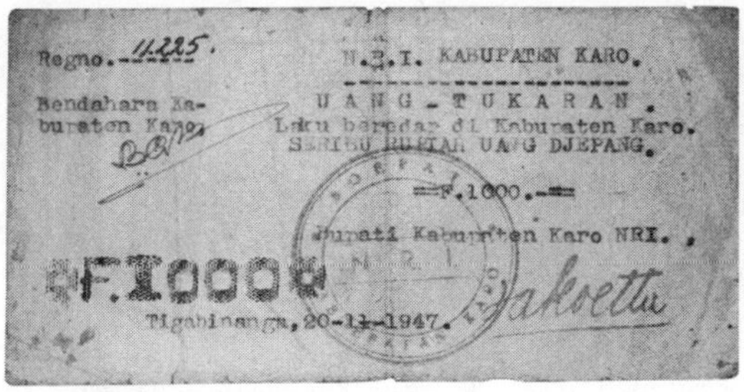

S402 1000 Rupiah

20.11.1947.

	Good	Fine	XF
a. Red.	—	—	—
b. Blue.	—	—	—
c. Black.	—	—	—

NOTE: Modern fakes of #S401-S402 exist.

TJURUP

CURUP

1949 ISSUE

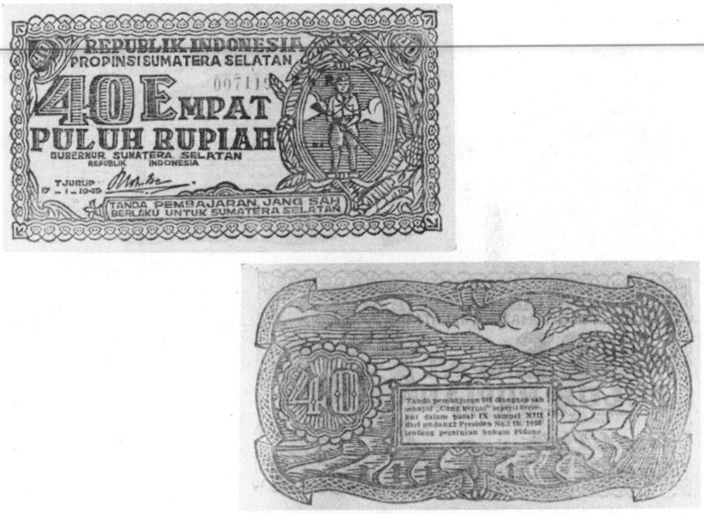

S406 40 Rupiah

	Good	Fine	XF
17.1.1949. Purple on yellow underprint. Soldier with rifle at right.	3.00	10.00	25.00

DAERAH MILITER ISTIMEWA SUMATERA SELATAN

SPECIAL MILITARY REGION OF SOUTH SUMATRA

1949 ND PROVISIONAL ISSUE

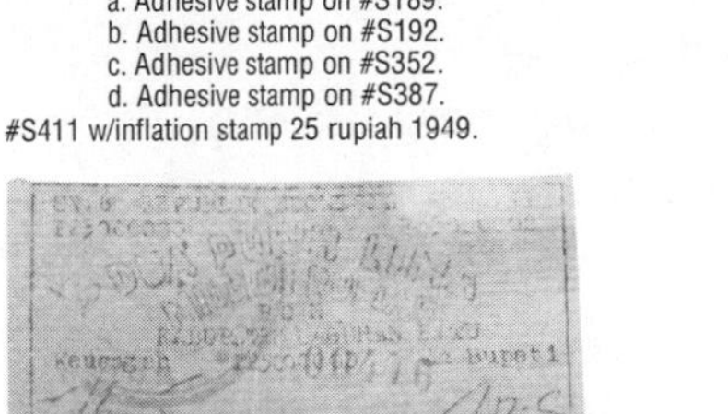

S410 5 Rupiah

ND (1949). Yellow.

	Good	Fine	XF
a. Adhesive stamp on #S189.	5.00	10.00	20.00
b. Adhesive stamp on #S192.	5.00	10.00	20.00
c. Adhesive stamp on #S352.	5.00	10.00	20.00
d. Adhesive stamp on #S387.	—	—	—

#S411 w/inflation stamp 25 rupiah 1949.

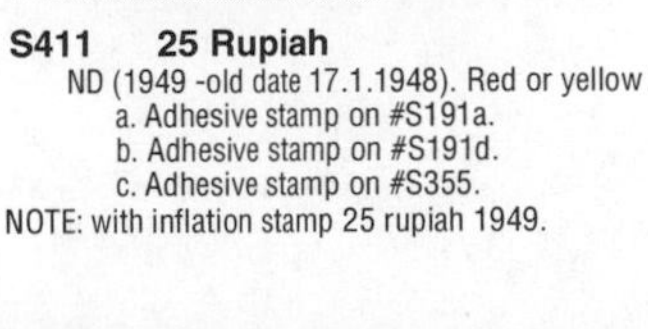

S411 25 Rupiah

ND (1949 -old date 17.1.1948). Red or yellow underprint.

	Good	Fine	XF
a. Adhesive stamp on #S191a.	2.00	8.00	15.00
b. Adhesive stamp on #S191d.	2.00	8.00	15.00
c. Adhesive stamp on #S355.	—	—	—

NOTE: with inflation stamp 25 rupiah 1949.

		Good	Fine	XF
S412	**50 Rupiah** ND (1949 -old date 1.4.1948). Factory at left; refinery at right. Overprint: Red text with ornamental border and serial # on back of #S1949.	4.00	10.00	25.00

NOTE: The military governor of South Sumatra called in all notes of 5 and 25 rupiah and for every two notes one was returned with stamp in an attempt to control inflation.

Kotabumi

1949 Issue

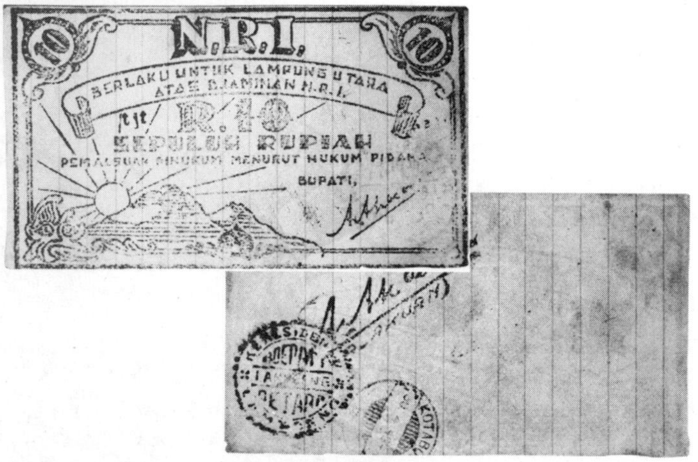

		Good	Fine	XF
S419	**10 Rupiah** 1949. Green. Rising sun at left. With title: *LAMPUNG UTARA* (North Lampung) with postmark of issuing place.	—	—	—

		Good	Fine	XF
S421	**50 Rupiah** 1949. With title: *LAMPUNG UTARA* (North Lampung) with postmark of issuing place.			
	a. Purple. (ca.1949).	5.00	12.00	25.00
	b. Black. 4.5.1949.	2.00	8.00	15.00
	c. Blue. 15.4.1949.	5.00	12.00	25.00

NOTE: Modern counterfeits exist of #S421b.

Rebellious Movements

Pemerintah Negara Islam Indonesia (PNII)

Government of the Islamic State of Indonesia

Tjirebon, West Java

1949 Issue

#S431 place of issue Karesidenan Tjirebon (Tjirebon residency).

		Good	Fine	XF
S431	**5 Rupiah** 10.10.1949.	—	—	—

ND Issue

#S432 place of issue Daerah Tjirebon (Tjirebon district).

		Good	Fine	XF
S432	**5 Rupiah** ND. Similar to #S431.	—	—	—

Pemerintah Revolusioner Republik Indonesia (PRRI)

Revolutionary Government of the Republic Indonesia

1959 Local Issue

#S461-S464 locally printed notes, w/engraved wooden blocks.

		Good	Fine	XF
S461	**1 Rupiah** 9.1959. Green. Native houses at lower left. No serial #. (Not issued).	—	—	—
S462	**5 Rupiah** 9.1959. Dark blue on yellow underprint. Batek house at left, Atchente dagger at right.	1.50	4.00	10.00
S463	**25 Rupiah** 9.1959. Red on yellow underprint. Torpgan house at lower left, boat at right.	1.50	4.00	10.00

		Good	Fine	XF
S464	**100 Rupiah** 9.1959. Brown on light brown underprint. Minangkabau house of lower left, Mt. Merapi at right.	3.00	7.50	25.00

1959 Belgian Issue

#S470-S475 reportedly to have been printed in Belgium. Not issued for use by the Free Atcheh Movement.

		Good	Fine	XF
S470	**1 Rupiah** ND (ca.1959).	—	—	—
S471	**5 Rupiah** ND (ca.1959). Purple.	—	—	—
S472	**10 Rupiah** ND (ca.1959). Green.	—	—	—
S473	**50 Rupiah** ND (ca.1959). Dark brown.	—	—	—
S474	**100 Rupiah** ND (ca.1959). Red-brown.	—	—	—
S475	**1000 Rupiah** ND (ca.1959). Blue-green.	—	—	—

1960 Issue

#S481 local PRRI issue of Bonabulu.

		Good	Fine	XF
S481	**100 Rupiah** 1.1.1960. Red. Tin of rice. Uniface.	—	—	—

Piagam Perdjuangan Semesta (Permesta)

Total Revolutionary Charter

1958 Issue

		Good	Fine	XF
S491	**5 Rupiah** 1958. Black on blue.	25.00	50.00	100.
S492	**10 Rupiah** 1958. Red on black.	22.00	45.00	85.00

	Good	Fine	XF
S493 25 Rupiah 1958. Black on red.	10.00	25.00	45.00

	Good	Fine	XF
S494 50 Rupiah 1958. Gray-green on yellow.	15.00	30.00	60.00
S495 100 Rupiah 1958. Red on yellow.	7.50	20.00	40.00
S495A 500 Rupiah 1958. Blue on pink.	10.00	20.00	40.00
S496 1000 Rupiah 1958. Red and green on yellow.	20.00	50.00	100.

1959 Issue

	Good	Fine	XF
S497 100 Rupiah 1959. Red.	12.00	30.00	60.00
S498 250 Rupiah 1959. Reported not confirmed.	—	—	—
S499 500 Rupiah 1959. Black and green on purple.	15.00	30.00	60.00
S500 1000 Rupiah 1959. Black and yellow on green.	20.00	40.00	80.00

	Good	Fine	XF
S501 5000 Rupiah 1959. Black on green.	17.50	40.00	80.00

1953-65 Rebellion

At the beginning of 1952 Lt. Col. Kahar Muzakkar, in charge of government operations against the rebellious Republic of the South Moluccas (RMS), placed himself under the orders of the Imam S. M. Kartosuwiryo as commander in South Sulawesi (Celebes). On August 7, 1953 he proclaimed Sulawesi and adjacent territories to be part of the Islamic State. See also PNII.

Republik Islam Indonesia (RII)

Islamic Republic of Indonesia

1953-65 Provisional ND Gulden Issue

#S510-S516 genuine overprints on notes:

	Good	Fine	XF
S510 1/2 Gulden ND. 1 signature. Overprint: On N.I. #122.	2.50	5.00	10.00
S511 1 Gulden ND. 1 signature. Overprint: Purple, black, green, red, red-orange, pink, red-purple on back, face or both back and face on N.I	2.00	4.00	8.00
S512 5 Gulden ND. 2 signature. Overprint: Purple, black, red, orange on N.I. #124c.	3.00	6.00	12.00

	Good	Fine	XF
S513 10 Gulden ND. 2 signature. Overprint: Purple, black, green, red, blue, orange on back or face on N.I. #125c.	2.50	5.00	10.00

1953-65 Genuine Ovpt. Provisional ND Roepiah Issue

	Good	Fine	XF
S514 10 Roepiah ND. 2 signature. Overprint: Purple, black, red, blue, grey on N.I. #131.	2.00	4.00	8.00
S515 10 Roepiah ND. 2 signature. Overprint: Purple, black on falsification of N.I.#131 (not known without overprint.).	3.00	6.00	12.00

1953-65 Genuine Ovpt. Provisional ND Dollar Issue

	Good	Fine	XF
S516 10 Dollars ND. Overprint: Black, blue, gray on Malaya #M7c.	4.00	8.00	15.00

1953-65 Modern False Ovpt. Provisional ND Gulden Issue

#S521-S530 modern false overprints on notes:

	Good	Fine	XF
S521 1/2 Gulden ND. Overprint: On N.I. #122b.	—	—	—
S522 1 Gulden ND. Overprint: On N.I. #123c.	—	—	—
S523 5 Gulden ND. Overprint: On N.I. #124c.	—	—	—
S524 10 Gulden ND. Overprint: On N.I. #125c.	—	—	—

1953-65 False Ovpt. Provisional ND Roepiah Issue

	Good	Fine	XF
S525 1/2 Roepiah ND. Overprint: On N.I. #128.	—	—	—
S526 1 Roepiah ND. Overprint: On N.I. #129.	—	—	—
S527 5 Roepiah ND. Overprint: On N.I. #130.	—	—	—
S528 10 Roepiah ND. Overprint: On N.I. #131.	—	—	—
S529 100 Roepiah ND. Overprint: On N.I. #132.	—	—	—

1953-65 False Ovpt. Provisional ND Dollar Issue

	Good	Fine	XF
S530 10 Dollars ND. Overprint: On Malaya #M7c.			
a. Black overprint.	—	—	—
b. Red overprint.	—	—	—
c. Lilac overprint.	—	—	—

NOTE: The above exist w/either black, red or lilac ovpt.

1950-66 Rebellion

In July 1950 the RMS government ordered an ovpt. on notes of the Dutch East Indies in circulation at that time. The oval ovpt. bears the sign. of Mr. G. G. H. Apituley, Secretary of the Ministry of Finance of the RMS.

Republik Maluku Selatan (RMS)

Republic of the South Moluccas

1950-66 Dutch Ovpt. Issue

Bar-type ovpt. (see example illus.) as well as oval ovpt. from the island of Saparua are not recognized as genuine by the RMS government-in-exile.

NOTE: No market valuations are quoted for the RMS notes as it is easy to falsify this type of overstamp.

	Good	Fine	XF
S531 Various Denominations Overprint: Mainly red and blue on back, often upside down.	—	—	—

NOTE: Dangerous falsifications exist.

Regional - Irian Barat

Republik Indonesia

1963 ND Provisional Issue

R1 1 Rupiah

	VG	VF	UNC
ND (1963 - old date 1961). Orange. President Sukarno at left with overprint at lower right. Overprint: *IRIAN BARAT.*	4.00	10.00	30.00

R2 2 1/2 Rupiah

	VG	VF	UNC
ND (1963 - old date 1961). Violet. President Sukarno at left with overprint at lower right. Overprint: *IRIAN BARAT.*	5.00	12.00	35.00

Bank Indonesia

1963 ND Provisional Issue

R3 5 Rupiah

	VG	VF	UNC
ND (1963 - old date 1960). Gray-olive. President Sukarno at left with overprint. Overprint: *IRIAN BARAT.*	7.50	20.00	60.00

R4 10 Rupiah

	VG	VF	UNC
ND (1963 - old date 1960). Red. President Sukarno at left with overprint. Overprint: *IRIAN BARAT.*	6.00	17.50	50.00

R5 100 Rupiah

	VG	VF	UNC
ND (1963 - old date 1960). Green. President Sukarno at left with overprint. Overprint: *IRIAN BARAT.*	50.00	100.	300.

Regional - Riau

Republik Indonesia

1963 ND Provisional Issue

R6 1 Rupiah

	VG	VF	UNC
ND (1963 - old date 1961). Orange. President Sukarno at left with overprint at lower right. Overprint: *RIAU.*	7.50	20.00	50.00

R7 2 1/2 Rupiah

	VG	VF	UNC
ND (1963 - old date 1961). Blue. President Sukarno at left with overprint at lower right. Overprint: *RIAU.*	7.50	20.00	60.00

Contemporary counterfeits on fragile paper with artificial blue fibers exist.

Bank Indonesia

1963 ND Provisional Issue

R8 5 Rupiah

	VG	VF	UNC
ND (1963 - old date 1960). Violet. President Sukarno at left with overprint on #82a. Prefix *X* in serial number. Back: Female dancer at right. Overprint: *RIAU.* Watermark: Sukarno	7.50	22.50	55.00

Modern counterfeits on #82b but without prefix X on serial number exist.

R9 10 Rupiah

ND (1963 - old date 1960). Red. President Sukarno at left with overprint. Overprint: *RIAU.*

	VG	VF	UNC
R9	6.00	17.50	45.00

R10 100 Rupiah

ND (1963 - old date 1960). Green. President Sukarno at left with overprint. Overprint: *RIAU.*

	VG	VF	UNC
R10	25.00	100.	400.

The Islamic Republic of Iran, located between the Caspian Sea and the Persian Gulf in southwestern Asia, has an area of 1,648,000 sq. km. and a population of 65.87 million. Capital: Tehran. Although predominantly an agricultural state, Iran depends heavily on oil for foreign exchange. Crude oil, carpets and agricultural products are exported.

Known as Persia until 1935, Iran became an Islamic republic in 1979 after the ruling monarchy was overthrown and the shah was forced into exile. Conservative clerical forces established a theocratic system of government with ultimate political authority vested in a learned religious scholar referred to commonly as the Supreme Leader who, according to the constitution, is accountable only to the Assembly of Experts. US-Iranian relations have been strained since a group of Iranian students seized the US Embassy in Tehran on 4 November 1979 and held it until 20 January 1981. During 1980-88, Iran fought a bloody, indecisive war with Iraq that eventually expanded into the Persian Gulf and led to clashes between US Navy and Iranian military forces between 1987 and 1988. Iran has been designated a state sponsor of terrorism for its activities in Lebanon and elsewhere in the world and remains subject to US and UN economic sanctions and export controls because of its continued involvement in terrorism and conventional weapons proliferation. Following the election of reformer Hojjat ol-Eslam Mohammad Khatami as president in 1997 and similarly a reformer Majles (parliament) in 2000, a campaign to foster political reform in response to popular dissatisfaction was initiated. The movement floundered as conservative politicians, through the control of unelected institutions, prevented reform measures from being enacted and increased repressive measures. Starting with nationwide municipal elections in 2003 and continuing through Majles elections in 2004, conservatives reestablished control over Iran's elected government institutions, which culminated with the August 2005 inauguration of hardliner Mahmud Ahmadi-Nejad as president.

RULERS: Qajar Dynasty

Sultan Ahmad Shah, AH1327-44/1909-25AD Pahlavi Dynasty
Reza Shah, SH1304-20/1925-41AD
Mohammad Reza Pahlavi, SH1320-58/1941-79AD

PRESIDENTS:

Islamic Republic of Iran
Abolhassan Bani Sadr, SH1358-60 (AD1979-Jun 81)
Mohammad Ali Rajai, SH1360 (AD-1981 Jun-Oct)
Hojjatoleslam Ali Khamene'i, SH1360-(AD1981-)

MONETARY SYSTEM:

1 Shahi = 50 Dinars
1 Kran (Qiran) = 20 Shahis
1 Toman = 10 Krans AH1241-1344, SH1304-09 (1825-1931)
1 Shahi = 5 Dinars
1 Rial 100 Dinars = 20 Shahis
1 Toman = 10 Rials SH1310- (1932-)

Military

German Treasury - WWI

1916-17 Issue

M1 12 Kran 10 Shahi on 5 Mark

ND (1916-17 - old date 3.10.1904). Overprint: Red; denomination in Persian on both sides of Germany #8.

	Good	Fine	XF
M1	1500.	3000.	5000.

M2 25 Kran on 10 Mark

ND (1916-17 - old date 6.10.1906). Overprint: Red; denomination in Persian on both sides of Germany # 9.

	Good	Fine	XF
M2	1000.	2000.	3000.

M3 **5 Tomans on 20 Mark**

	Good	Fine	XF
ND (1916-17 - old date 19.2.1914). Overprint: Red; on Germany #40.	625.	1250.	2500.

M4 **25 Tomans on 100 Mark**

	Good	Fine	XF
ND (1916-17 - old date 21.4.1910). Overprint: Red; on Germany #42.			
a. Issued note. Rare.	—	—	—
s. Specimen perforated: *DRUCKPROBE.*	—	—	—

M5 **250 Tomans on 1000 Mark**

	Good	Fine	XF
ND (1916-17 - old date 21.4.1910). Overprint: Red; on Germany #44.			
a. Issued note. Rare.	—	—	—
s. Specimen perforated: *DRUCKPROBE.*	—	—	—

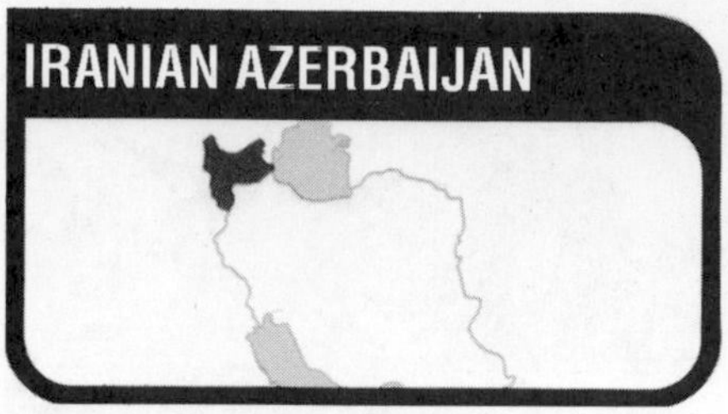

Former province of northwestern Iran. In 1938 it was divided into Eastern and Western Azerbaijan. In November of 1945 a Communist-led revolt broke out against the central government of Iran. On December 15 an autonomous republic was proclaimed. It lasted until December 11, 1946 when troops of the Iranian central government reoccupied the territory.

MONETARY SYSTEM:
1 Toman = 10 Krans

Iranian Azerbaijan

Autonomous Government

1946 Issue

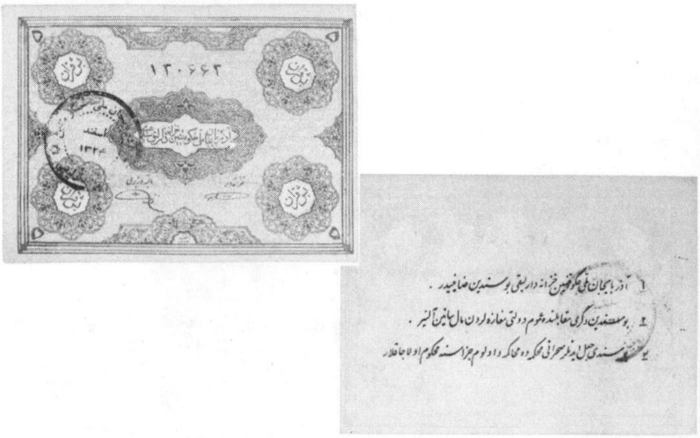

S101 **5 Krans**

	VG	VF	UNC
AH1324 (1946). Red on olive underprint. Hand stamp. Back: Persian text.	7.50	20.00	45.00

S102 **1 Toman**

	VG	VF	UNC
AH1324 (1946). Violet on gray underprint. Ornate guilloches. Back: Persian text with perforated denomination numerals at upper center.			
a. With hand stamp on face. Small or large signature.	7.50	20.00	45.00
b. Without hand stamp.	7.50	20.00	45.00

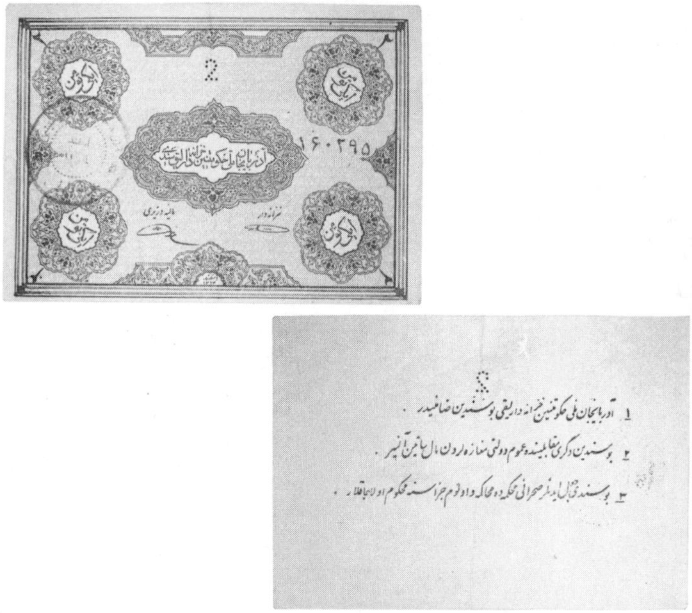

S103 **2 Tomans**

	VG	VF	UNC
AH1324 (1946). Blue on gray underprint. Ornate guilloches. Back: Persian text with perforated denomination numerals at upper center.			
a. With hand stamp on face.	10.00	30.00	60.00
b. Without hand stamp.	10.00	30.00	60.00

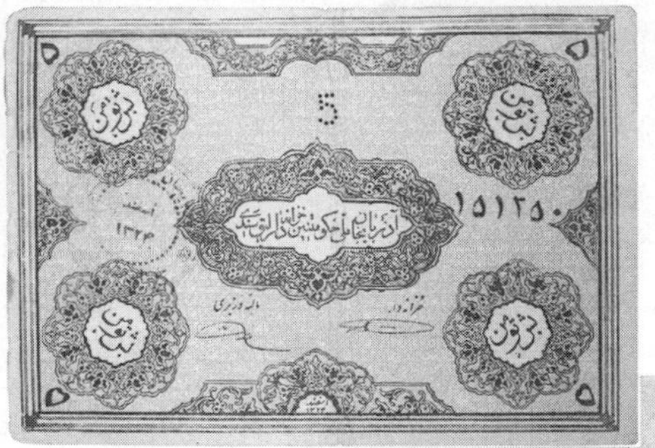

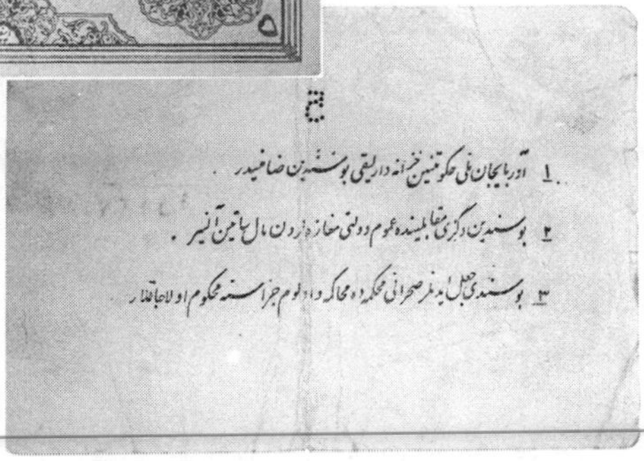

S104 5 Tomans
AH1324 (1946). Green on gray underprint. Ornate guilloches. Back: Persian text with perforated denomination numerals at upper center.

	VG	VF	UNC
a. With hand stamp on face.	20.00	45.00	75.00
b. Without hand stamp.	15.00	35.00	70.00

S105 10 Tomans
AH1324 (1946). Red on gray underprint. Ornate guilloches. Back: Persian text with perforated denomination numerals at upper center.

	VG	VF	UNC
a. With hand stamp on face.	15.00	35.00	70.00
b. Without hand stamp.	20.00	45.00	75.00

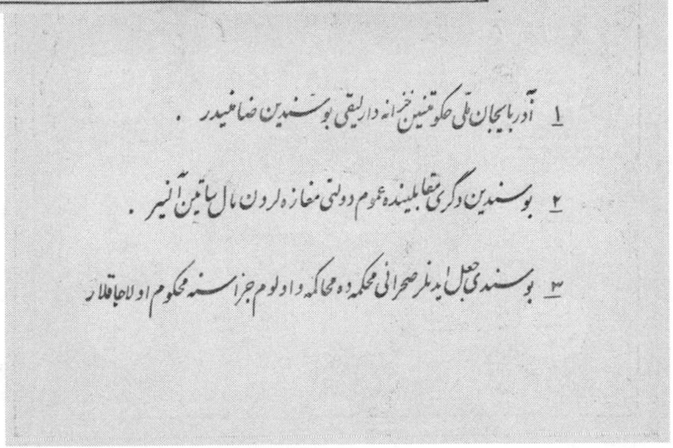

S106 50 Tomans
AH1324 (1946). Blue on gray underprint. Ornate guilloches. Back: Persian text with perforated denomination numerals at upper center.

	VG	VF	UNC
a. With hand stamp, handwritten signature.	20.00	45.00	90.00
b. With hand stamp, stamped signature.	15.00	45.00	80.00
r. Without hand stamp or perforated denomination numeral. Remainder.	7.50	15.00	35.00

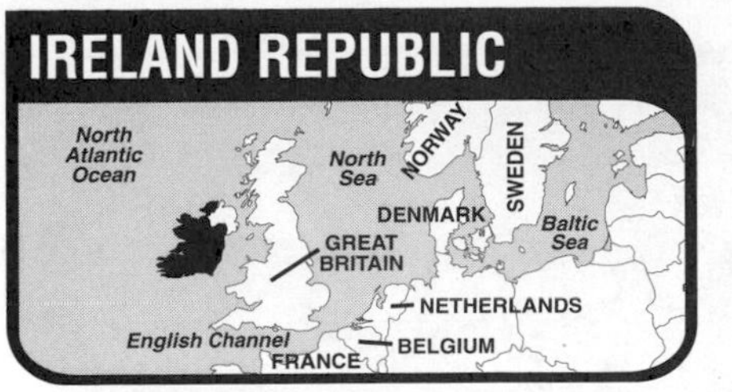

The Republic of Ireland, occupying five-sixths of the island of Ireland located in the Atlantic Ocean west of Great Britain, has an area of 70,280 sq. km. and a population of 4.16 million. Capital: Dublin.

Celtic tribes arrived on the island between 600-150 B.C. Invasions by Norsemen that began in the late 8th century were finally ended when King Brian Boru defeated the Danes in 1014. English invasions began in the 12th century and set off more than seven centuries of Anglo-Irish struggle marked by fierce rebellions and harsh repressions. A failed 1916 Easter Monday Rebellion touched off several years of guerrilla warfare that in 1921 resulted in independence from the UK for 26 southern counties; six northern (Ulster) counties remained part of the UK. In 1949, Ireland withdrew from the British Commonwealth; it joined the European Community in 1973.

RULERS:
British to 1921

MONETARY SYSTEM:
1 Shilling = 12 Pence
1 Pound = 20 Shillings to 1971
1 Pound = 100 Pence, 1971-2001
1 Euro = 100 Cent, 2002-

IRELAND (EIRE)

IRISH REPUBLIC

1866-67 NATIONAL PROMISSORY BONDS ISSUE

National promissory bonds or notes in various denominations were printed in several series during 1866-67. Only those pieces most resembling paper currency are included in this listing. There are a number of other bond issues but they are outside the scope of this catalog.

#S101-S104 fully or partially printed dates. Printer: CONB.

S101 5 Dollars
17.3.1866. Black. Standing allegorical woman at left, portrait of man at lower right. Uniface. Printer: CONB.

	Good	Fine	XF
	50.00	150.	450.

REPUBLIC OF IRELAND

1866-67 ISSUE

S102 10 Dollars — Good | Fine | XF

1866-1919. Black on green underprint. Portrait of men at lower left and right. Two *10* protectors in underprint at lower left center and lower center right. Eagle perched on sword and flag on mountain peak at upper center. Back: Green. Printer: CONB.

	Good	Fine	XF
a. Original issue 1866-67.	40.00	125.	375.
b. Reissue Jan. 1919.	150.	450.	—

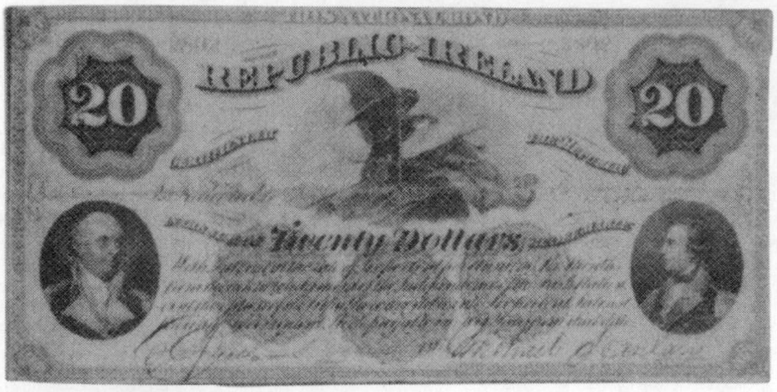

S103 20 Dollars

	Good	Fine	XF
1866-67. Black on green underprint. Similar to #S102 but different portrait at lower left and right. Eagle perched on sword and flag on mountain peak at upper center. Back: Green. Printer: CONB.	75.00	225.	675.

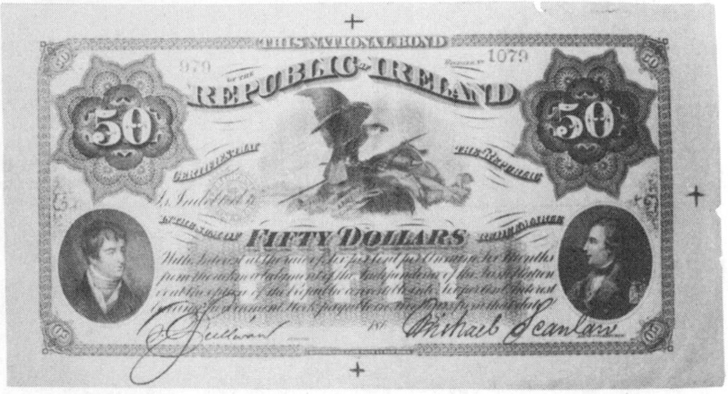

S104 50 Dollars

	Good	Fine	XF
1866-67. Black on green underprint. Similar to #S103 but different portrait at lower left and right. Large *FIFTY* protector in underprint at lower center. Eagle perched on sword and flag on mountain peak at upper center. Back: Green. Printer: CONB.	75.00	225.	675.

S105 100 Dollars

	Good	Fine	XF
1866-67. Reported not confirmed.	—	—	—

S106 500 Dollars

	Good	Fine	XF
1866-67. Reported not confirmed.	—	—	—

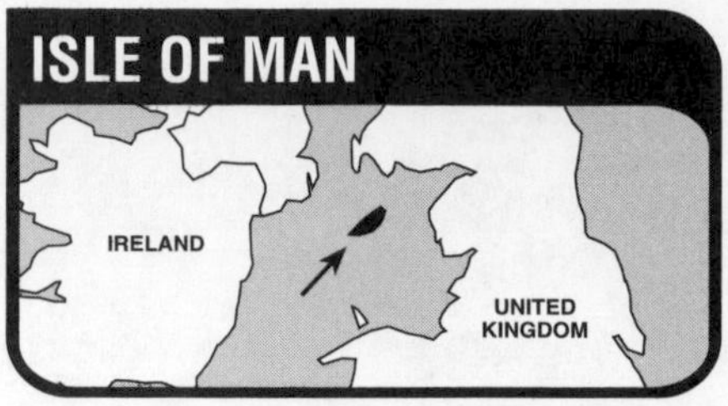

The Isle of Man, a dependency of the British Crown located in the Irish Sea equidistant from Ireland, Scotland and England, has an area of 572 sq. km. and a population of 76,220. Capital: Douglas. Agriculture, dairy farming, fishing and tourism are the chief industries.

Part of the Norwegian Kingdom of the Hebrides until the 13th century when it was ceded to Scotland, the isle came under the British crown in 1765. Current concerns include reviving the almost extinct Manx Gaelic language. Isle of Man is a British crown dependency but is not part of the UK. However, the UK Government remains constitutionally responsible for its defense and international representation. The Sovereign of the United Kingdom (currently Queen Elizabeth II) holds the title Lord of Man. The Isle of Man is ruled by its own legislative council and the House of Keys, one of the oldest legislative assemblies in the world. Acts of Parliament passed in London do not affect the island unless it is specifically mentioned.

United Kingdom bank notes and coinage circulate concurrently with Isle of Man money as legal tender.

RULERS:

British

MONETARY SYSTEM:

1 Pound = 20 Shillings to 1971
1 Pound = 100 Pence, 1971-

BANKS:

Castle Rushen	#S111
Douglas & Isle of Man Bank (Dumbell's)	#S121-S122
Douglas & Isle of Man Bank (Holmes')	#S121-S122
Dumbell's Banking Co. Ltd.	#S141-S143

Private Banks

Castle Rushen

1790s Issue

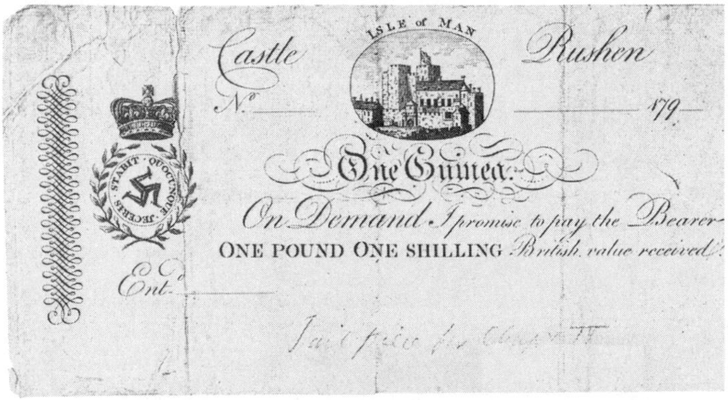

S111 1 Guinea = 1 Pound 1 Shilling

	Good	Fine	XF
179x. Black. Crowned arms at left, castle at upper center. Uniface. Unsigned remainder.	150.	300.	—

Douglas & Isle of Man Bank (Dumbell's)

1854-65 Issue

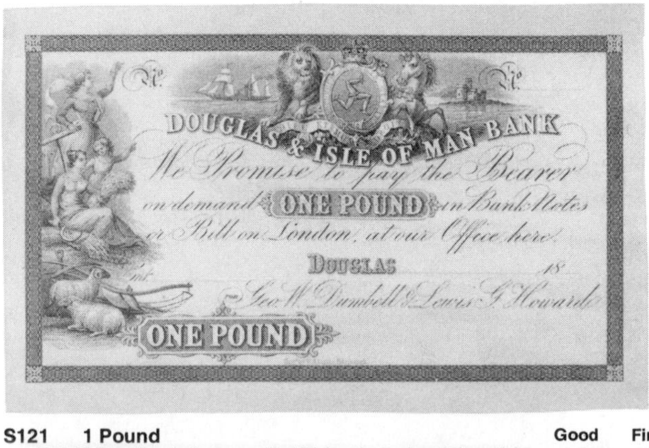

S121 1 Pound

1854-65. Two allegorical women with child, farm tools, sheep below at left, crowned shield with triskeles with lion and unicorn as supports at top center. 2 signatures at lower right.

	Good	Fine	XF
a. Issued note.	1100.	2250.	—
r. Unsigned remainder.	—	Unc	1000.

1865-74 Issue

S122 1 Pound	Good	Fine	XF
1865-74. Two allegorical women with child, farm tools, sheep below at left, crowned shield with triskeles with lion and unicorn as supports at top center. Like #S121a but 3 signatures at lower right.	175.	350.	700.

Douglas & Isle of Man Bank (Holmes')

1844 Issue

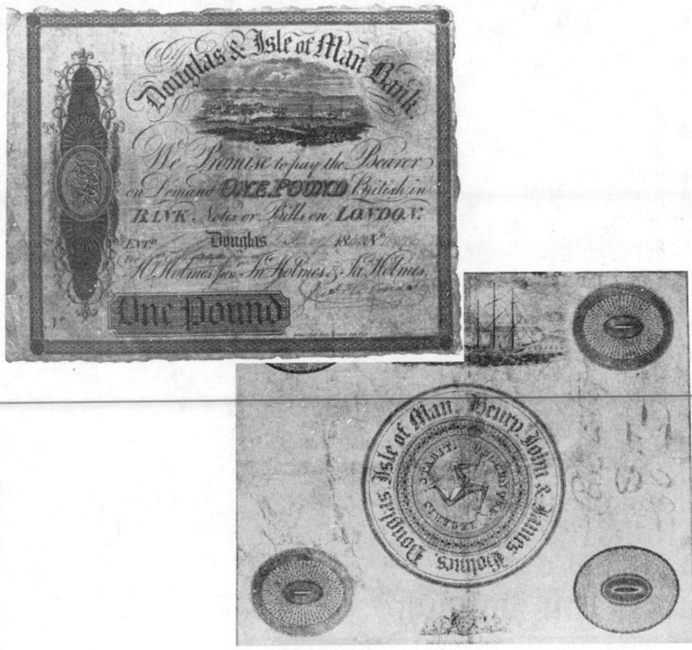

S131 1 Pound	Good	Fine	XF
1.1.1844. Black. Harbor scene at upper center right. Back: Ships and Isle arms.	50.00	100.	—

NOTE: Although the two banks listed above bear the same title, they were actually run by different individuals.

Dumbell's Banking Co. Ltd.

1874-75 Provisional Issue

S141 1 Pound	Good	Fine	XF
1874-75. Two allegorical women with child, farm tools, sheep below at left, crowned shield with triskeles with lion and unicorn as supports at top center. Overprint: New bank name on #S122.	300.	600.	—

1875-99 Issue

S142 1 Pound	Good	Fine	XF
1875-78. Lion, triskeles and unicorn above bank name at top center.	375.	750.	—

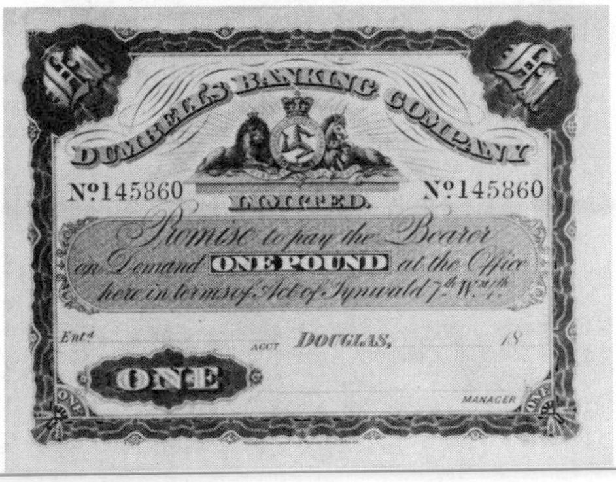

S143 1 Pound	Good	Fine	XF
21.12.1891; 7.8.1885; 21.5.1897; 4.11.1899. Lion and unicorn supporting crowned shield with triskeles below bank name at upper center.			
a. Issued note.	450.	900.	—
r. Remainder without date.	350.	700.	1400.

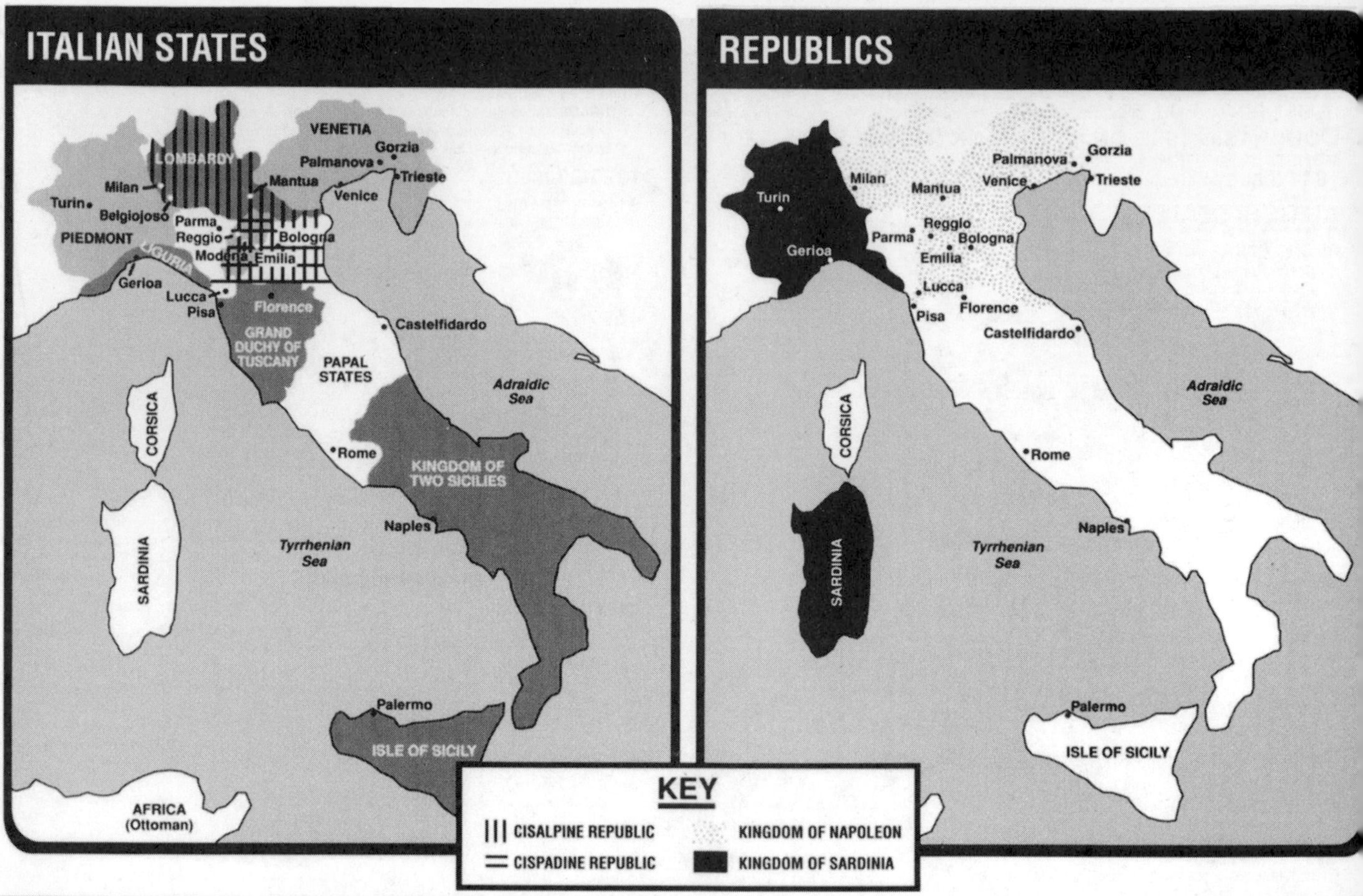
ITALIAN STATES
VENETIA
LOMBARDY
Gorzia
Palmanova
Trieste
Milan
Mantua
Venice
Turin
Belgiojoso
Parma
Reggio
Bologna
PIEDMONT
Modena
Emilia
LIGURIA
Gerioa
Lucca
Pisa
Florence
GRAND DUCHY OF TUSCANY
Castelfidardo
PAPAL STATES
Adraidic Sea
CORSICA
Rome
KINGDOM OF TWO SICILIES
Naples
Tyrrhenian Sea
SARDINIA
Palermo
ISLE OF SICILY
AFRICA (Ottoman)
REPUBLICS
Palmanova
Gorzia
Trieste
Milan
Mantua
Venice
Turin
Reggio
Parma
Bologna
Emilia
Gerioa
Lucca
Pisa
Florence
Castelfidardo
Adraidic Sea
CORSICA
Rome
Naples
Tyrrhenian Sea
SARDINIA
Palermo
ISLE OF SICILY
KEY
CISALPINE REPUBLIC
CISPADINE REPUBLIC
KINGDOM OF NAPOLEON
KINGDOM OF SARDINIA

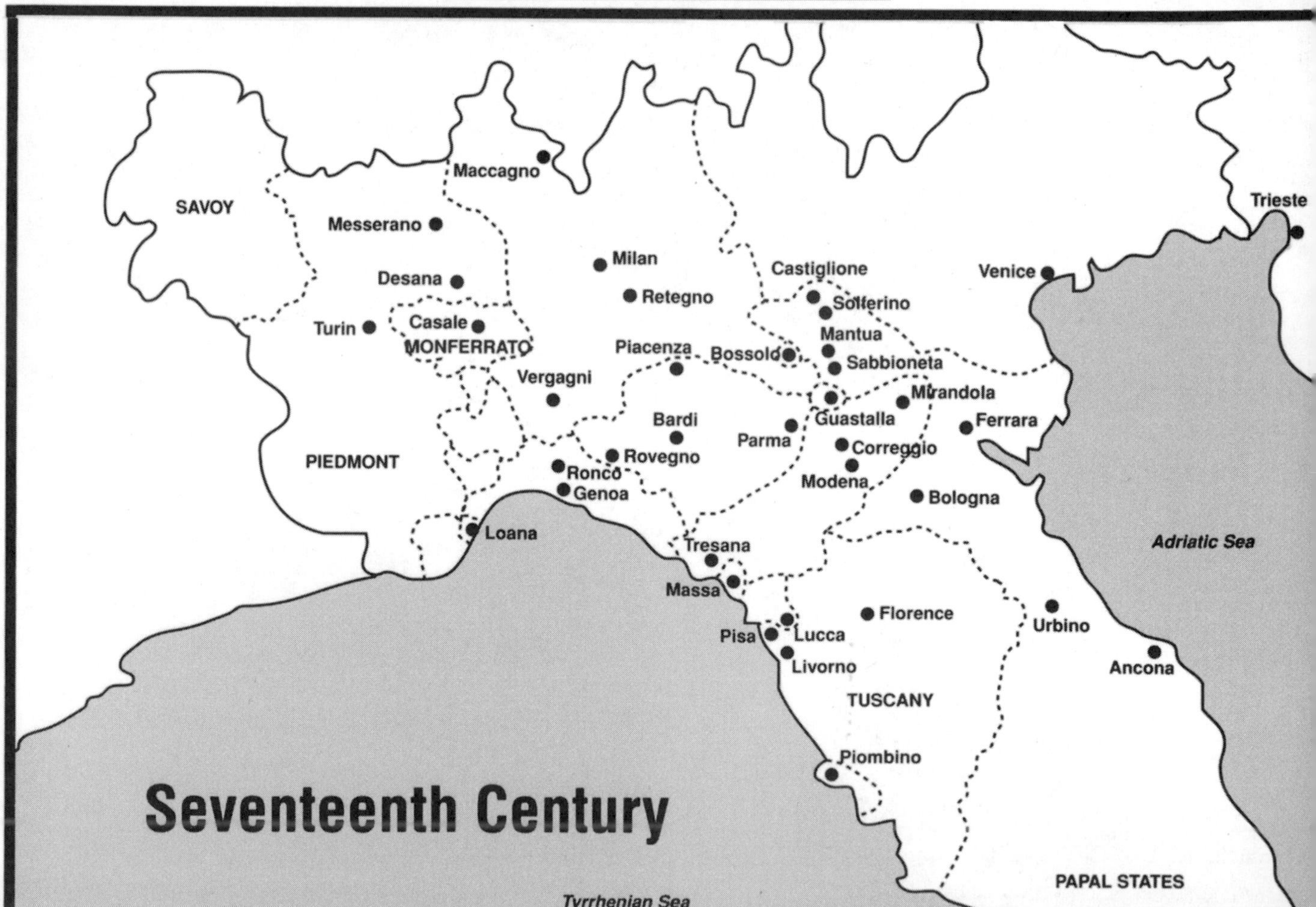
Maccagno
SAVOY
Messerano
Milan
Desana
Retegno
Castiglione
Solferino
Venice
Trieste
Turin
Casale
MONFERRATO
Mantua
Piacenza
Bossolo
Sabbioneta
Vergagni
Mirandola
Guastalla
Ferrara
Bardi
Parma
Correggio
PIEDMONT
Rovegno
Ronco
Modena
Genoa
Bologna
Loana
Tresana
Adriatic Sea
Massa
Florence
Urbino
Pisa
Lucca
Livorno
Ancona
TUSCANY
Piombino
Seventeenth Century
PAPAL STATES
Tyrrhenian Sea

From the fall of Rome until modern times, "Italy," a 700 mile-long peninsula, was little more than a geographical expression. Although nominally included in the Empire of Charlemagne and the Holy Roman Empire, it was in reality divided into a number of independent states and kingdoms presided over by wealthy families, soldiers of fortune or hereditary rulers. The 19th century unification movement fostered by Mazzini, Garibaldi and Cavour attained fruition in 1860-70 with the creation of the Kingdom of Italy and the installation of Victor Emanuele, House of Savoy, as King.

MONETARY SYSTEM:
1 Lira = 100 Centesimi

ANTICHI STATI ITALIANI - OLD ITALIAN STATES

REGNO DI SARDEGNA - Kingdom of Sardinia
- Regie Finanze-Torino, 1746-99 .... #S101-S133
- Special Issues for Sardinia, 1780-81 .... #S134-S135
- Monte di San Secondo, 1794-99 .... #S140-S141
- Repubblica Cisalpina-Nazione Piemontese, 1800 .... #S145-S148
- Banca di Genova, 1848-49 .... #S150-S153
- Banca di Torino, 1849 .... #S155-S157
- Banca di Savoia, 1851-59 .... #S160-S166
- Banca Nazionale negli Stati Sardi, 1851-72 .... #S170-S175

LOMBARDO-VENETO
- Banco Giro di Venezia, 1798 .... #S181-S184
- Venetian Republic-Moneta patriottica, 1848 .... #S185-S190
- Venetian Republic-Moneta del Comune, 1848-49 .... #S191-S196
- Regno Lombardo-Veneto-Viglietto del Tesoro, 1849 .... #S197-S205
- Citta' di Fiume, 1848-50 .... #S206-S210
- Monte Lombardo Veneto, 1859 .... #S211-S215
- I. R. Monte Veneto, 1866 .... #S216-S218

SIEGE
- Mantova, 1796 .... #S221-S229
- Zara, 1813 .... #S231-S232
- Palmanova, 1814 .... #S233-S236
- Osoppo, 1848 .... #S237-S243
- Palmanova, 1848 .... #S244-S249

PRINCIPATO DI LUCCA E PIOMBINO - Princedom of Lucca and Piombino
- Banca di Lucca, 1813 .... #S261-S263

GRANDUCATO DI TOSCANA - Grand Duchy of Tuscany
- Banca D. P. Adami e C., 1859 .... #S291-S292

STATO PONTIFICIO-PAPAL STATES
- S. Monte Della Pieta' Di Roma, 1785-97 .... #S301-S376
- Banco Di S. Spirito Di Roma, 1786-96 .... #S377-S519

Prima Repubblica Romana (1798-99)
- Banco Di S. Spirito, 1798 .... #S521-S525
- Monte Di Pieta', 1798 .... #S526-S530
- Assegnati, 1798-99 .... #S531-S540
- Banca Romana, 1834-50 .... #S551-S555
- Buoni del Tesoro, 1848 .... #S556-S562
- Legazione di Bologna-Boni Provinciali, 1848-49 .... #S563-S568

Seconda Repubblica Romana (1849)
- Boni Centrali, 1849 .... #S571-S583
- Boni Provinciali, 1849 .... #S584-S623
- Boni Comunali, 1849 .... #S631-S648
- Commissariato Pontificio per le 4 Legazioni-Bologna, 1849 .... #S651
- Boni del Tesoro in Sostituzione, 1849 .... #S652-S657
- Boni del Tesoro in Surrogazione, 1851 .... #S658-S663
- Banco di Santo Spirito, 1855 .... #S665
- Banca Pontificia per le 4 Legazioni, 1855 .... #S671-S674
- Banca Dello Stato Pontificio-Provisional Issue, 1851 .... #S681-S685
- Banca Dello Stato Pontificio-Regular Issue, 1853-67 .... #S686-S696
- Banca Dello Stato Pontificio, 1867-70 .... #S701-S708

REGNO DELLE DUE SICILIE
- Governo Provvisorio di Sicilia, 1849 .... #S711

REGNO D'ITALIA - KINGDOM OF ITALY

GOVERNMENT BANKS
- Banca Nazionale nel Regno d'Italia, Provisional Issue, 1866 .... #S721-S723
- Banca Nazionale nel Regno d'Italia, Regular Issue, 1866-96 .... #S731-S747
- Banca Nazionale Toscana, 1866-83 .... #S751-S770
- Banca Toscana di Credito, 1864-80 .... #S771-S782
- Banca Romana, 1870-90 .... #S791-S802
- Banco di Napoli, 1866-1922 .... #S811-S859
- Banco di Sicilia, 1866-1921 .... #S861-S899

CREDITO AGRARIO - Agrarian Credit Banks and Associations
- Cassa di Risparmio di Bologna, 1871-87 .... #S901-S904
- Banca Agricola Nazionale, 1870 .... #S905-S911
- Monte dei Paschi di Siena, 1870-98 .... #S912-S917
- Banca Generale di Roma, 1880-92 .... #S918-S919
- Banca Agraria Commerciale di Foggia, 1882 .... #S920
- Banca Agricola Sarda, 1871-80 .... #S921-S924
- Credito Agricolo Industriale Sardo, 1874-84 .... #S925-S928

COMMERCIAL BANKS - ABUSIVE ISSUES
- Banca del Popolo, 1867-71 .... #S941-S945
- Monte dei Paschi di Siena, 1866-71 .... #S951-S955
- Banca di Valdinievole in Pescia, 1871 .... #S961-S963
- Banca Italo-Germanica, 1871-72 .... #S971-S978

REGNO DI SARDEGNA

KINGDOM OF SARDINIA

Victor Amadeus II, duke of Savoy, after acquiring Sardinia by means of the Treaty of the Hague, in 1720 transformed into a kingdom the state that Berthold had made a county in 999 starting from the region of Moriana in Savoy; at the beginning of 1400, Victor Amadeus VIII had transformed this county into a dukedom. From then on the House of Savoy directed its expansionist interests towards the Italian regions to the point of becoming the interpreter and guide the movements of the Risorgimento det

Vittorio Amadeo II, 1720-1730
Carlo Emanuele III, 1730-1773
Vittorio Amadeo III, 1773-1796
Carlo Emanuele IV, 1796-1802
Vittorio Emanuele I, 1802-1821
Carlo Felice, 1821-1831
Carlo Alberto, 1831-1849
Vittorio Emanuele II, 1849-1861 later King of Italy

REGIE FINANZE-TORINO

1746 ISSUE

	Good	Fine	XF
S101 100 Lire 1.1.1746. Paper: White-cream. Watermark: Design.			
a. Issued note.	1250.	3000.	6000.
r. Remainder.	—	—	350.
S102 200 Lire 1.1.1746. Paper: White-cream. Watermark: Design.			
a. Issued note.	1250.	3000.	6000.
r. Remainder.	—	—	350.
S103 500 Lire 1.1.1746. Paper: White-cream. Watermark: Design. Rare.	—	—	—
S104 1000 Lire 1.1.1746. Paper: White-cream. Watermark: Design.	—	6000.	12,000.
S105 3000 Lire 1.1.1746. Paper: White-cream. Watermark: Design.	—	12,500.	17,500.

1750 ISSUE

	Good	Fine	XF
S106 100 Lire 1.1.1750. Black. Paper: White-creme. Rare.	—	—	—
S107 200 Lire 1.1.1750. Black. Paper: White-creme. Rare.	—	—	—

1756 ISSUE

	Good	Fine	XF
S108 50 Lire 1.8.1756. Black. Paper: White-creme. Watermark: Design. Rare.	—	—	—
S109 100 Lire 1.8.1756. Black. Paper: White-creme. Watermark: Design. Rare.	—	—	—

1760 ISSUE

	Good	Fine	XF
S110 50 Lire 1.4.1760. Black. Paper: White-creme. Watermark: Design. Unknown.	—	—	—
S111 100 Lire 1.4.1760. Black. Paper: White-creme. Watermark: Design. Unknown.	—	—	—

1765 ISSUE

	Good	Fine	XF
S112 50 Lire 1.1.1765. Black. Paper: White-creme. Watermark: Design.			
a. Issued note. Rare.	—	—	—
r. Remainder.	—	—	350.
S113 100 Lire 1.1.1765. Black. Paper: White-creme. Watermark: Design.			
a. Issued note. Rare.	—	—	—
r. Remainder.	—	—	300.

1774 ISSUE

	Good	Fine	XF
S114 50 Lire 25.2.1774. Black. Overprint: New date on #S112. Paper: White-creme. Rare.	—	—	—
S115 50 Lire 1.4.1774. Black. Like #S112. Paper: White-creme. Watermark: Design. Rare.	—	—	—
S116 100 Lire 25.2.1774. Black. Overprint: New date on #S113. Paper: White-creme. Watermark: Design. Rare.	—	—	—
S117 100 Lire 1.4.1774; 1.10.1776. Black. Like #S113. Paper: White-creme. Watermark: Design. Rare.	—	—	—

1781; 1794 ISSUE

		Good	Fine	XF
S118	**50 Lire**			
	1.6.1781; 1.7.1786; 1.10.1792; 1.6.1794; 1.10.1794. Paper: Tinted.			
	a. Issued note.	50.00	100.	200.
	r. Remainder, 1794.	—	—	300.
S119	**100 Lire**			
	1.6.1781. Paper: Tinted. Rare.	—	—	—

1785 Issue

		Good	Fine	XF
S120	**100 Lire**			
	1.7.1785. Black. Paper: White-creme.	450.	900.	1750.
S121	**200 Lire**			
	1.7.1785. Black. Paper: White-creme.	300.	600.	1250.

1786 Issue

		Good	Fine	XF
S122	**100 Lire**			
	1.7.1786; 1.10.1792; 15.5.1794; remainder, 1794. Black. Paper: White-creme.			
	a. Issued note.	125.	300.	600.
	r. Remainder. 1794.	—	—	300.
S123	**200 Lire**			
	1.7.1786; 1.10.1792. Black. Paper: White-creme.	450.	900.	1800.

1792; 1794 Issue

		Good	Fine	XF
S124	**10 Lire**			
	1.4.1793; 1.6.1794; 1.10.1794. Black. Paper: Blue.	300.	750.	1500.
S125	**15 Lire**			
	1.4.1793; 1.6.1794; 1.10.1794. Black. Paper: Amaranth. Rare.	—	—	—
S126	**25 Lire**			
	1.10.1792; 1.6.1794; 1.10.1794. Black. Paper: White-creme.			
	a. Issued note.	45.00	100.	250.
	r. Remainder. 1792-94.	—	—	150.
S127	**300 Lire**			
	1.4.1793. Black. Paper: White-creme.	300.	750.	1500.
S128	**600 Lire**			
	1.4.1793. Black. Paper: White-creme.	450.	1000.	2800.

1796 Issue

		Good	Fine	XF
S129	**25 Lire**			
	1.4.1796. Black. Paper: White-creme. Watermark: Design.	45.00	100.	250.

		Good	Fine	XF
S130	**50 Lire**			
	1.4.1796. Black. Paper: White-creme. Watermark: Design.			
	a. Issued note.	60.00	125.	250.
	r. Remainder.	—	—	250.

1799 Issue

		Good	Fine	XF
S131	**50 Lire**			
	1.9.1799. Black. Seated allegorical woman holding portrait man at left. Paper: White-creme. Watermark: Design.	40.00	75.00	225.

		Good	Fine	XF
S132	**100 Lire**			
	1.9.1799. Black. Seated allegorical woman at left, angel at right. Paper: White-creme.	50.00	150.	450.

		Good	Fine	XF
S133	**200 Lire**			
	1.9.1799. Black. Bust on pedestal at left, standing Mercury at right. Paper: White-creme.	75.00	225.	675.

Special Issues for Sardinia

1780 Issue

		Good	Fine	XF
S134	**50 Lire**			
	1.7.1780. Black. Crowned arms at left.			
	a. Issued note without counterfoil. Rare.	—	—	—
	r. Remainder with counterfoil.	—	—	350.

1781 Issue

		Good	Fine	XF
S135	**5 Scudi**			
	1.7.1781. Black. Vertical format.			
	a. Issued note. Rare.	—	—	—
	r. Remainder with counterfoil.	—	—	30,000.

Monte di San Secondo

1794; 1800 Issues

Issue to replace the Regie Finanze notes.

		Good	Fine	XF
S140	**500 Lire**			
	1794-1800. Bull in crowned oval. Rare.	—	—	—
S141	**1000 Lire**			
	1794-1800. Bull in crowned oval. Rare.	—	—	—

Repubblica Cisalpina - Nazione Piemontese

1800 Issue

This issue was withdrawn from circulation after three months.

		Good	Fine	XF
S145	**50 Lire**			
	11.9.1800. Rare.	—	—	—
S146	**250 Lire**			
	11.9.1800.	—	—	—
S147	**500 Lire**			
	11.9.1800.	—	—	—
S148	**1000 Lire**			
	11.9.1800.	—	—	—

Banca di Genova

1848; 1849 Issue

		Good	Fine	XF
S150	**100 Lire**			
	13.9.1848; 26.10.1849. Red. Genoa arms at top, Janus at bottom, value across center. Uniface. Rare.	—	—	—
S151	**250 Lire**			
	22.12.1848. Green. Columbus in medallion with Industry and Abundance allegories at left, Janus in medallion with Commerce and Science allegories at right, Genoa arms at top center. Uniface. Rare.	—	—	—
S152	**500 Lire**			
	13.9.1848. Yellow. Columbus in medallion with Industry and Abundance allegories at left, Janus in medallion with Commerce and Science allegories at right, Genoa arms at top center. Uniface. Rare.	—	—	—
S153	**1000 Lire**			
	7.9.1848. Black. Columbus in medallion with Industry and Abundance allegories at left, Janus in medallion with Commerce and Science allegories at right, Genoa arms at top center. Uniface. Rare.	—	—	—

Banca di Torino

1849 Issue

	Good	Fine	XF
S155 200 Lire 15.9.1849. Blue. Standing figures at left and right, arms of Turin at top center. Uniface. Rare.	—	—	—
S156 500 Lire 15.9.1849. Black. Standing figures at left and right, arms of Turin at top center. Uniface. Paper: Cream. Rare.	—	—	—
S157 1000 Lire 15.9.1849. Black. Standing figures at left and right, arms of Turin at top center. Uniface. Rare.	—	—	—

Banca di Savoia

1851 Issue

	Good	Fine	XF
S160 50 Livres 1.12.1851. Black on gray underprint. Man at left and right. Rare.	—	—	—
S161 100 Livres 1.12.1851. Black.			
a. Pink underprint. Rare.	—	—	—
b. Without underprint. Rare.	—	—	—
S162 250 Livres 1.12.1851. Black.			
a. Green underprint. Rare.	—	—	—
b. Without underprint. Rare.	—	—	—
S163 500 Livres 1.12.1851. Black.			
a. Orange underprint. Rare.	—	—	—
b. Without underprint. Rare.	—	—	—
S164 1000 Livres 1.12.1851. Black. Rare.	—	—	—

1859 Issue

	Good	Fine	XF
S165 20 Livres 1.7.1859. Black. Arms at top center. Paper: Yellow.	3000.	5000.	—
S166 50 Livres 1.7.1859. Black. Value: *50* at left and right. Rare.	—	—	—

Banca Nazionale negli Stati Sardi

1851; 1857 Issue

	Good	Fine	XF
S170 20 Lire 8.1.1857-30.10.1867. Black. Crowned arms of Genoa and Turin between reclining gods at top center, portrait Christopher Columbus in medallion at bottom center, ornamental border. Uniface. Paper: Yellow.	250.	800.	2000.
S171 50 Lire 8.1.1857-23.1.1867. Black. Crowned arms of Genoa and Turin between reclining gods at top center, portrait Christopher Columbus in medallion at bottom center, ornamental border. Uniface. Paper: White.	300.	1000.	2500.
S172 100 Lire 1.7.1851-17.1.1872. Black. Crowned arms of Genoa and Turin between reclining gods at top center, portrait Christopher Columbus in medallion at bottom center, ornamental border. Uniface. Paper: Red.	150.	400.	1250.
S173 250 Lire 1.7.1851-19.7.1871. Black. Crowned arms of Genoa and Turin between reclining gods at top center, portrait Christopher Columbus in medallion at bottom center, ornamental border. Uniface. Paper: Green.	300.	1000.	2500.
S174 500 Lire 1.7.1851-17.1.1872. Black. Crowned arms of Genoa and Turin between reclining gods at top center, portrait Christopher Columbus in medallion at bottom center, ornamental border. Uniface. Paper: Cream.	500.	2500.	6000.
S175 1000 Lire 1.7.1851-19.7.1871. Black. Crowned arms of Genoa and Turin between reclining gods at top center, portrait Christopher Columbus in medallion at bottom center, ornamental border. Uniface. Paper: White. Rare.	—	—	—

Lombardo - Veneto

Comprised of the northern Italy duchies of Milan and Mantua and the Venetian Republic, which were absorbed by the Kingdom of Napoleon in 1805. After Napoleon fell in 1815, they were awarded by Austria and incorporated as Kingdom of Lombardy-Venice. This kingdom ceased after the conquest of Lombardy in 1859, and the conquest of Venetian territory in 1866, by the King of Italy, Vittorio Emanuele II.

Banco Giro di Venezia

1798 Issue

	VG	VF	UNC
S181 10 Ducati 1.10.1798. Black. Crowned double-headed Austro-Hungarian imperial eagle at top center. Winged lion with gospel (Venice symbol) at bottom center. Uniface. Watermark: Design.	15.00	30.00	100.
S182 50 Ducati 1.10.1798. Black. Crowned double-headed Austro-Hungarian imperial eagle at top center. Winged lion with gospel (Venice symbol) at bottom center. Uniface. Watermark: Design.	15.00	50.00	200.
S183 100 Ducati 1.10.1798. Black. Crowned double-headed Austro-Hungarian imperial eagle at top center. Winged lion wtih gospel (Venice symbol) at bottom center. Uniface. Watermark: Design.	15.00	30.00	100.
S184 500 Ducati 1.10.1798. Black. Crowned double-headed Austro-Hungarian imperial eagle at top center. Winged lion with gospel (Venice symbol) at bottom center. Uniface. Watermark: Design. Reported not confirmed.	—	—	—

Venetian Republic - Moneta Patriottica

1848 Issue

	VG	VF	UNC
S185 1 Lira 1848. Black. Ornamental border with winged horses, flowers. Without bank name indicated, with or without watermark. Back: Orange seal of Venice, with or without handwritten signature.	2.50	7.50	25.00
S186 2 Lire 1848. Black. Seated Neptune at left, Justice at right. Without bank name indicated, with or without watermark. Back: Orange seal of Venice, with or without handwritten signature.	5.00	25.00	50.00
S187 3 Lire 1848. Black. Two cherubs at center, coat-of-arms of Venice and Milan at upper left and right. Without bank name indicated, with or without watermark. Back: Orange seal of Venice, with or without handwritten signature.	2.50	7.50	25.00
S188 5 Lire 1848. Black. Coat-of-arms of Venice and Milan at upper left and right. Without bank name indicated, with or without watermark. Back: Orange seal of Venice, with or without handwritten signature.	2.50	7.50	25.00
S189 50 Lire 1848. Black on pink underprint. Allegorical figures, coat-of-arms of Venice at lower left, Milan at top right. Bank name around *S. Marco* Lion in embossed seal.	20.00	75.00	350.
S190 100 Lire 1848. Black on pink underprint. Coat-of-arms of Venice at top center, Milan at bottom center. Bank name around *S. Marco* Lion in embossed seal.	7.50	40.00	125.

Venetian Republic - Moneta del Comune

1848; 1849 Issue

	Good	Fine	XF
S191 50 Centesimi 1849. Black and gray. Banco Nazionale di Venezia name around *S. Marco* Lion in embossed seal. Orange seal of Venice.			
a. Issued note (=1 Lira).	450.	1250.	3500.
b. Cut left or right half (= 50 centesimi).	45.00	125.	375.

NOTE: #S191 was printed w/the possibility to be cut in half and used as fifty centesimi, while whole it was worth 1 lira.

	Good	Fine	XF
S192 1 Lira 1848. Black and gray. Coat-of-arms of Venice and Milan at bottom left and right. Banco Nazionale di Venezia name around *S. Marco* Lion in embossed seal. Back: Orange seal of Venice.	35.00	100.	350.

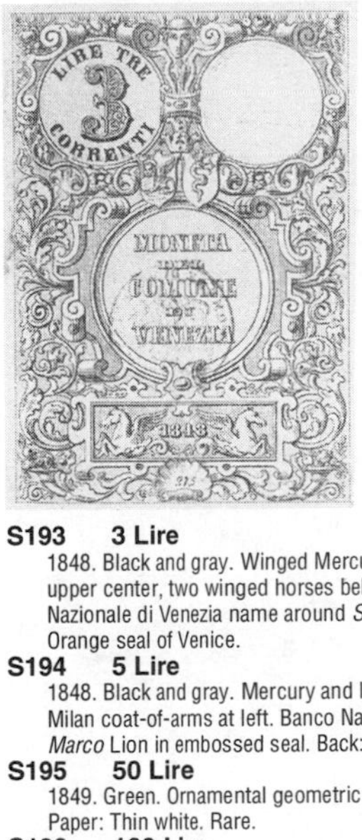

	Good	Fine	XF
S193 3 Lire 1848. Black and gray. Winged Mercury head at top center, two arms at upper center, two winged horses below, ornamental border. Banco Nazionale di Venezia name around *S. Marco* Lion in embossed seal. Back: Orange seal of Venice.	75.00	225.	675.
S194 5 Lire 1848. Black and gray. Mercury and Industry at lower center, Venetian and Milan coat-of-arms at left. Banco Nazionale di Venezia name around *S. Marco* Lion in embossed seal. Back: Orange seal of Venice.	175.	550.	1700.
S195 50 Lire 1849. Green. Ornamental geometric border. Back: Orange seal of Venice. Paper: Thin white. Rare.	—	—	—
S196 100 Lire 1849. Red. Standing allegorical *Italia* at left. With white lance and shield representing Venice, Milan coat-of-arms in left hand. Back: Orange seal of Venice. Rare.	—	—	—

Regno Lombardo-Veneto - Viglietto del Tesoro

1849 Issue

#	Description	Good	Fine	XF
S197	**5 Lire** 1.4.1849. Black on light cream underprint. Two embossed seals of the Milan Administration with crowned double-headed Austro-Hungarian imperial eagle. Uniface. Watermark: Design.	150.	450.	1350.
S198	**10 Lire** 1.4.1849. Black on rose underprint. Two embossed seals of the Milan Administration with crowned double-headed Austro-Hungarian imperial eagle. Uniface. Watermark: Design.	300.	900.	2750.
S199	**15 Lire** 1.4.1849. Black on light green underprint. Two embossed seals of the Milan Administration with crowned double-headed Austro-Hungarian imperial eagle. Uniface. Watermark: Design.	375.	1250.	3750.
S200	**30 Lire** 1.4.1849. Grey on light green underprint. Back: Prospectus of interest.			
	a. Issued note. Unknown.	—	—	—
	b. Green formulare.	750.	2250.	—
S201	**60 Lire** 1.4.1849. Blue on light azure underprint. Back: Prospectus of interest.			
	a. Issued note - unknown. Rare.	—	—	—
	b. Green formulare.	—	—	—
S202	**120 Lire** 1.4.1849. Back: Prospectus of interest.			
	a. Issued note - unknown. Rare.	—	—	—
	b. Green formulare.	—	—	—
S203	**600 Lire** 1.4.1849. Back: Prospectus of interest.			
	a. Issued note - unknown.	—	—	—
	b. Green formulare.	—	—	—
S204	**1200 Lire** 1.4.1849. Back: Prospectus of interest.			
	a. Issued note - unknown.	—	—	—
	b. Green formulare.	—	—	—
S205	**2400 Lire** 1.4.1849.			
	a. Issued note - unknown.	—	—	—
	b. Green formulare.	—	—	—

Citta' di Fiume

1848-50 Issue

#S206-S210 1 Austrian Florin = 60 Carantani

#	Description	Good	Fine	XF
S206	**3 Carantani** 8.5.1849. Red. Uniface.	225.	450.	1250.
S207	**3 Carantani** 1.5.1850. Black. Uniface.	275.	750.	2250.
S208	**5 Carantani** 17.10.1848. Red. Uniface.	225.	675.	2000.
S209	**5 Carantani** 1.5.1850. Blue-green. Uniface.	225.	675.	2000.
S210	**10 Carantani** 17.10.1848. Red. Uniface.	275.	750.	2250.

Monte Lombardo-Veneto - Vaglia

1859 Issue

#	Description	Good	Fine	XF
S211	**1 Fiorino** 15.6.1859. Black. Female allegories at bottom center, crowned Austro-Hungarian imperial eagle at top center. Watermark: *KKCK*. Uniface.	150.	450.	1400.
S212	**5 Fiorini** 15.6.1859. Black. Two allegories at left and right, crowned Austro-Hungarian imperial eagle at bottom center. Watermark: *KKCK*. Uniface.	375.	1200.	3600.
S213	**10 Fiorini** 15.6.1859. Black. Two allegories at left and right, crowned Austro-Hungarian imperial eagle at bottom center. Watermark: *KKCK*. Uniface.	750.	2250.	6000.
S214	**100 Fiorini** 15.6.1859. Black. Two allegories at left and right, crowned Austro-Hungarian imperial eagle at bottom center. Watermark: *KKCK*. Uniface. Rare.	—	—	—
S215	**1000 Fiorini** 15.6.1859. Many allegories in the borders, crowned Austro-Hungarian eagle at bottom center. Rare.	—	—	—

I. R. Monte Veneto

1866 Issue

#S216-S218 issued in Treviso, Udine and Verona.

#	Description	Good	Fine	XF
S216	**1 Fiorino** 1.9.1866. Country woman at left, workman at right, crowned Austro-Hungarian imperial eagle at top center. Rare.	—	—	—

#	Description	Good	Fine	XF
S217	**10 Fiorini** 1.9.1866. Farmer at left and country woman at right, crowned Austro-Hungarian imperial eagle at bottom center. Rare.	—	—	—
S218	**100 Fiorini** 1.9.1866. Two angels standing at left and right, two angels flying at top center, crowned Austro-Hungarian imperial eagle at bottom center.	—	—	—

Sieges

Mantova

1796 Issue

#	Description	Good	Fine	XF
S221	**10 Soldi** 6.10.1796. Black. Two red seals with crowned Austro-Hungarian imperial eagle. Uniface. Rare.	—	—	—
S222	**1 Lira** 6.10.1796. Black. Two red seals with crowned Austro-Hungarian imperial eagle. Uniface. Rare.	—	—	—
S223	**3 Lire** 6.10.1796. Black. Two red seals with crowned Austro-Hungarian imperial eagle. Uniface.	125.	375.	1100.
S224	**6 Lire** 6.10.1796. Black. Two red seals with crowned Austro-Hungarian imperial eagle. Uniface.	150.	450.	1350.
S225	**9 Lire** 6.10.1796. Black. Two red seals with crowned Austro-Hungarian imperial eagle. Uniface.	300.	900.	2750.
S226	**12 Lire** 6.10.1796. Black. Two red seals with crowned Austro-Hungarian imperial eagle. Uniface.	750.	2250.	6500.
S227	**18 Lire** 6.10.1796. Black. Two red seals with crowned Austro-Hungarian imperial eagle. Uniface.	1100.	3300.	10,000.
S228	**45 Lire** 6.10.1796. Black. Two red seals with crowned Austro-Hungarian imperial eagle. Uniface.	—	—	—
S229	**135 Lire** 6.10.1796. Black. Two red seals with crowned Austro-Hungarian imperial eagle. Uniface.	—	—	—

Zara

1813 ND Issue

#	Description	Good	Fine	XF
S231	**1 Franc** ND (1813). Black. Brown-red seal. Unique.	—	—	—
S232	**2 Francs** ND (1813). Black. Brown-red seal. Rare.	—	—	—

Palmanova, 1814

1814 Issue

#	Description	Good	Fine	XF
S233	**2 Lire** 1814. Black seal. Blue seal with French imperial eagle and serial #. Paper: Laid. Uniface. Unique.	—	—	—
S234	**5 Lire** 1814. Remainder.	—	2000.	6000.
S235	**10 Lire** 1814. Unknown.	—	—	—
S236	**25 Lire** 1814. Black seal. Blue seal with French imperial eagle and serial #. Paper: Laid. Uniface.	—	—	—

Osoppo

1848 ND Issue

#	Description	Good	Fine	XF
S237	**50 Centesimi** ND (1848). Handwritten with three rectangular black seals and partial circular black seal in upper left corner. Rare.	—	—	—
S238	**1 Lira** ND (1848). Handwritten with three rectangular black seals and partial circular black seal in upper left corner.	750.	2250.	6500.
S239	**2 Lire** ND (1848). Handwritten with three rectangular black seals and partial circular black seal in upper left corner.	800.	2400.	7250.
S240	**3 Lire** ND (1848). Handwritten with three rectangular black seals and partial circular black seal in upper left corner.	900.	2750.	8250.
S241	**6 Lire** ND (1848). Handwritten with three rectangular black seals and partial circular black seal in upper left corner.	1200.	3600.	11,000.
S242	**50 Lire** ND (1848). Handwritten with three rectangular black seals and partial circular black seal in upper left corner. Rare.	—	—	—
S243	**100 Lire** ND (1848). Handwritten with three rectangular black seals and partial circular black seal in upper left corner. Rare.	—	—	—

Palmanova, 1848

1848 Issue

#	Description	Good	Fine	XF
S244	**25 Centesimi** 1848. Black. Hand signature. Watermark: Design.	150.	450.	1350.
S245	**50 Centesimi** 1848. Black. Hand signature.	75.00	225.	675.

		Good	Fine	XF
S246	**1 Lira** 1848. Black text, value in red, date in green with 4 hand signatures. Watermark: Design.			
	a. Value word printed.	45.00	125.	375.
	b. Value word handwritten.	—	—	—
S247	**2 Lire** 1848. Black text, value in red, date in green with 4 hand signatures. Watermark: Design.	45.00	125.	375.
S248	**3 Lire** 1848. Black text, value in red, date in green with 4 hand signatures. Watermark: Design.	45.00	125.	375.
S249	**6 Lire** 1848. Black text, value in red, date in green with 4 hand signatures. Watermark: Design.	100.	300.	900.

PRINCIPATO DI LUCCA E PIOMBINO

PRINCEDOM OF LUCCA AND PIOMBINO

The Grand Duchy of Lucca and the Princedom of Piombino had during the centuries independent histories. The former was a republic from the 15th century and remained as such until the Napoleonic conquest. The latter was variously ruled or occupied by the Appiani first and then by the Buoncompagni from whom Napoleon took it away. On March 18, 1805 Napoleon united the two small states and granted them to his sister Elisa Bonaparte Baciocchi as a French principality. This new small state had a short

BANCA DI LUCCA

1813 ND ISSUE

		Good	Fine	XF
S261	**50 Soldi** ND (ca.1813). Black. Paper: Brown, thin. Reported not confirmed.	—	—	—
S262	**5 Lire** ND (ca.1813). Black. Paper: Brown, thin. Reported not confirmed.	—	—	—
S263	**30 Lire** ND (ca.1813). Black. Paper: Brown, thin. Rare.	—	—	—

GRANDUCATO DI TOSCANA

GRAND DUCHY OF TUSCANY

The Medici family ruled the State from 1421 to 1737, when, as a consequence of the Spanish succession war, Tuscany fell under the Austrian influence with the Lorena House. This influence lasted until 1860, when the Grand Duchy joined the Kingdom of Italy. After the accession of Napoleon, from 1809 to 1814, the Grand Duchy was united to France and, after Napoleon's fall, underwent the indirect rule of Austria before joining the Kingdom of Italy.

The last Granduchi:

Ferdinando III, 1790-1801
and for a second period, 1814-1824
Leopoldo II, 1824-1859
Ferdinando II, 1859-1860
From 1817 up until 1856, the following Granducal Banks issued paper money:
Cassa di Sconto de Firenze
Banca di Sconto di Firenze
Banca di Sconto di Livorno
Banca di Siena
Banca di Arezzo
Banca di Pisa
Banca di Lucca

In 1857, all these banks merged to form Banca Nazionale Toscana and in 1859, this institute issued bank notes in the amount of nearly 10 million Lire. Until today, not one of the many different notes issued during the Granducal period is known to exist

BANCA D. P. ADAMI & C.

1859 ISSUE

		VG	VF	UNC
S291	**100 Lire** 1.3.1859. Black. Embossed seal. Back: Two circular black seals. Paper: Heavy grease-proof paper.	300.	900.	2750.
S292	**500 Lire** 1.3.1859. Black. Embossed seal. Back: Two circular black seals. Paper: Heavy grease-proof paper.	150.	450.	1350.

STATO PONTIFICIO

PAPAL STATES

During many centuries prior to the formation of the unified Kingdom of Italy, Italy was divided into numerous independent papal and ducal states. The Popes held temporal sovereignty over an area in central Italy comprising some 17,000 sq. mi. (44,030 sq. km.) including the city of Rome. At the time of the general unification of Italy under the Kingdom of Sardinia, 1861, the papal dominions beyond Rome were acquired by that kingdom, diminishing the Pope's sovereignty to Rome and its environs. In

PONTIFFS:

Clement XIII, 1758-1769
Sede Vacante, Feb. 2 - May 19, 1769
Clement XIV, 1769-1774
Sede Vacante, Sept. 22, 1774 - Feb. 15, 1775
Pius VI (Sextus), 1775-1799
Pius VII, 1800-1823
Sede Vacante, Aug. 20 - Sept. 28, 1823
Leo XII, 1823-1829
Sede Vacante, Feb. 10 - Mar. 31, 1829
Pius VIII, 1829-1830
Sede Vacante, Nov. 30, 1830 - Feb. 2, 1831
Gregory XVI, 1831-1846
Sede Vacante, June 1-16, 1846
Pius IX, 1846-1878

MONETARY SYSTEM:

100 Bajocchi = 1 Scudo
30 Paoli = 1 Doppia

S. MONTE DELLA PIETA' DI ROMA

1785-95 ISSUE

		Good	Fine	XF
S301	**3 Scudi** 14.9.1795. 135x100mm.	25.00	75.00	225.
S302	**4 Scudi** 14.9.1795. 135x100mm.	25.00	75.00	225.
S303	**5 Scudi** 1785-97. Black. Watermark: Design. 200x145mm.	12.50	40.00	125.
S304	**6 Scudi** 1785-97. Black. Watermark: Design. 200x145mm.	12.50	40.00	125.
S305	**7 Scudi** 1785-97. Black.	15.00	45.00	135.
S306	**8 Scudi** 1785-97. Black. Watermark: Design. 200x145mm.	15.00	45.00	135.
S307	**9 Scudi** 1785-97. Black. Watermark: Design. 200x145mm.	15.00	45.00	135.
S308	**10 Scudi** 1785-97. Black. Watermark: Design. 200x145mm.	15.00	45.00	135.
S309	**11 Scudi** 1785 97. Black. Watermark: Design. 200x145mm.	15.00	45.00	135.
S310	**12 Scudi** 1785-97. Black. Watermark: Design. 200x145mm.	15.00	45.00	135.
S311	**13 Scudi** 1785-97. Black. Watermark: Design. 200x145mm.	15.00	45.00	135.
S312	**14 Scudi** 1785-92. Black. Watermark: Design. 200x145mm.	15.00	45.00	135.
S313	**15 Scudi** 1785-97. Black. Watermark: Design. 200x145mm.	15.00	45.00	135.
S314	**16 Scudi** 1785-92. Black. Watermark: Design. 200x145mm.	20.00	60.00	175.
S315	**17 Scudi** 1785-92. Black. Watermark: Design. 200x145mm.	20.00	60.00	175.
S316	**18 Scudi** 1785-95. Black. Watermark: Design. 200x145mm.	20.00	60.00	175.
S317	**19 Scudi** 1786-97. Black. Watermark: Design. 200x145mm.	20.00	60.00	175.
S318	**20 Scudi** 1786-97. Black. Watermark: Design. 200x145mm.	20.00	60.00	175.
S319	**21 Scudi** 1786-97. Black. Watermark: Design. 200x145mm.	20.00	60.00	175.
S320	**22 Scudi** 1786-97. Black. Watermark: Design. 200x145mm.	20.00	60.00	175.
S321	**23 Scudi** 1786-97. Black. Watermark: Design. 200x145mm.	20.00	60.00	175.
S322	**24 Scudi** 1786-97. Black. Watermark: Design. 200x145mm.	20.00	60.00	175.
S323	**25 Scudi** 1786-97. Black. Watermark: Design. 200x145mm.	20.00	60.00	175.
S324	**26 Scudi** 1786-97. Black. Watermark: Design. 200x145mm.	20.00	60.00	175.
S325	**27 Scudi** 1786-97. Black. Watermark: Design. 200x145mm.	20.00	60.00	175.
S326	**28 Scudi** 1786-97. Black. Watermark: Design. 200x145mm.	20.00	60.00	175.
S327	**29 Scudi** 1786-97. Black. Watermark: Design. 200x145mm.	20.00	60.00	175.

		Good	Fine	XF
S328	**30 Scudi** 1786-97. Black. Watermark: Design. 200x145mm.	20.00	60.00	175.
S329	**31 Scudi** 1786-97. Black. Watermark: Design. 200x145mm.	25.00	75.00	225.
S330	**32 Scudi** 1786-97. Black. Watermark: Design. 200x145mm.	25.00	75.00	225.
S331	**33 Scudi** 1786-97. Black. Watermark: Design. 200x145mm.	25.00	75.00	225.
S332	**34 Scudi** 1786-97. Black. Watermark: Design. 200x145mm.	25.00	75.00	225.
S333	**35 Scudi** 1786-97. Black. Watermark: Design. 200x145mm.	25.00	75.00	225.
S334	**36 Scudi** 1786-97. Black. Watermark: Design. 200x145mm.	25.00	75.00	225.
S335	**37 Scudi** 1786-97. Black. Watermark: Design. 200x145mm.	25.00	75.00	225.
S336	**38 Scudi** 1786-97. Black. Watermark: Design. 200x145mm.	25.00	75.00	225.
S337	**39 Scudi** 1786-97. Black. Watermark: Design. 200x145mm.	25.00	75.00	225.
S338	**40 Scudi** 1786-97. Black. Watermark: Design. 200x145mm.	25.00	75.00	225.
S339	**41 Scudi** 1786-97. Black. Watermark: Design. 200x145mm.	25.00	75.00	225.
S340	**42 Scudi** 1786-97. Black. Watermark: Design. 200x145mm.	25.00	75.00	225.
S341	**43 Scudi** 1786-97. Black. Watermark: Design. 200x145mm.	25.00	75.00	225.
S342	**44 Scudi** 1786-97. Black. Watermark: Design. 200x145mm.	25.00	75.00	225.
S343	**45 Scudi** 1786-97. Black. Watermark: Design. 200x145mm.	25.00	75.00	225.
S344	**46 Scudi** 1786-97. Black. Watermark: Design. 200x145mm.	25.00	75.00	225.
S345	**47 Scudi** 1786-97. Black. Watermark: Design. 200x145mm.	25.00	75.00	225.
S346	**48 Scudi** 1786-97. Black. Watermark: Design. 200x145mm.	25.00	75.00	225.
S347	**49 Scudi** 1786-97. Black. Watermark: Design. 200x145mm.	25.00	75.00	225.
S348	**50 Scudi** 1786-97. Black. Watermark: Design. 200x145mm.	25.00	75.00	225.
S349	**55 Scudi** 1786-97. Black. Watermark: Design. 200x145mm.	30.00	100.	300.
S350	**60 Scudi** 1786-97. Black. Watermark: Design. 200x145mm.	30.00	100.	300.
S351	**65 Scudi** 1786-97. Black. Watermark: Design. 200x145mm.	30.00	100.	300.
S352	**70 Scudi** 1786-97. Black. Watermark: Design. 200x145mm.	30.00	100.	300.
S353	**75 Scudi** 1786-97. Black. Watermark: Design. 200x145mm.	30.00	100.	300.
S354	**80 Scudi** 1786-97. Black. Watermark: Design. 200x145mm.	30.00	100.	300.
S355	**85 Scudi** 1786-97. Black. Watermark: Design. 200x145mm.	30.00	100.	300.
S356	**90 Scudi** 1786-97. Black. Watermark: Design. 200x145mm.	30.00	100.	300.
S357	**95 Scudi** 1786-97. Black. Watermark: Design. 200x145mm.	30.00	100.	300.
S358	**100 Scudi** 1786-97. Black. Watermark: Design. 200x145mm.	60.00	175.	525.
S359	**110 Scudi** 1788-95. Black. Watermark: Design. 200x145mm.	225.	675.	2000.
S360	**120 Scudi** 1788-95. Black. Watermark: Design. 200x145mm.	225.	675.	2000.
S361	**130 Scudi** 1788. Black. Watermark: Design. 200x145mm.	225.	675.	2000.
S362	**140 Scudi** 1788. Black. Watermark: Design. 200x145mm.	225.	675.	2000.
S363	**150 Scudi** 1788-92. Black. Watermark: Design. 200x145mm.	225.	675.	2000.
S364	**200 Scudi** 1788-92. Black. Watermark: Design. 200x145mm.	225.	675.	2000.
S365	**250 Scudi** 1788-92. Black. Watermark: Design. 200x145mm.	225.	675.	2000.
S366	**300 Scudi** 1788-92. Black. Watermark: Design. 200x145mm.	225.	675.	2000.
S367	**350 Scudi** 1788. Black. Watermark: Design. 200x145mm.	225.	675.	2000.
S368	**400 Scudi** 1788. Black. Watermark: Design. 200x145mm.	225.	675.	2000.
S369	**450 Scudi** 1788. Black. Watermark: Design. 200x145mm. Rare.	—	—	—
S370	**500 Scudi** 1788. Black. Watermark: Design. 200x145mm.	225.	675.	2000.
S371	**600 Scudi** 1788. Black. Watermark: Design. 200x145mm. Rare.	—	—	—
S372	**700 Scudi** 1788. Black. Watermark: Design. 200x145mm. Rare.	—	—	—
S373	**800 Scudi** 1788. Black. Watermark: Design. 200x145mm.	375.	1150.	3400.
S374	**900 Scudi** 1788. Black. Watermark: Design. 200x145mm.	300.	900.	2750.
S375	**1000 Scudi** 1788-97. Black. Watermark: Design. 200x145mm.	375.	1150.	3400.
S376	**1500 Scudi** 1788. Black. Watermark: Design. 200x145mm.	525.	1750.	5000.

NOTE: During First Roman Republic, some S. Monte Della Pietà notes were overprint by the Republican Municipal Administration with the seal of about 20 different towns, to ratify the validity of circulation. All the Republican validated notes are rare, and in comparison with the normal notes, a price increase up to double the value for common seals and up to five times for rarer seals.

Banco di S. Spirito di Roma

1786; 1795 Issue

#S377 and S378 White wmk. paper.

		Good	Fine	XF
S377	**3 Scudi** 15.9.1795. Black. 135x100mm.	30.00	100.	300.
S378	**4 Scudi** 15.9.1795. Black. 135x100mm.	30.00	100.	300.
S379	**5 Scudi** 1786-96. Black. Watermark: Design. 200x145mm.	20.00	60.00	175.
S380	**6 Scudi** 1786-96. Black. Watermark: Design. 200x145mm.	20.00	60.00	175.
S381	**7 Scudi** 1786-96. Black. Watermark: Design. 200x145mm.	20.00	60.00	175.
S382	**8 Scudi** 1786-96. Black. Watermark: Design. 200x145mm.	20.00	60.00	175.
S383	**9 Scudi** 1786-96. Black. Watermark: Design. 200x145mm.	20.00	60.00	175.
S384	**10 Scudi** 1786-96. Black. Watermark: Design. 200x145mm.	20.00	60.00	175.
S385	**11 Scudi** 1786-96. Black. Watermark: Design. 200x145mm.	20.00	60.00	175.
S386	**12 Scudi** 1786-96. Black. Watermark: Design. 200x145mm.	20.00	60.00	175.
S387	**13 Scudi** 1786-96. Black. Watermark: Design. 200x145mm.	20.00	60.00	175.
S388	**14 Scudi** 1786-96. Black. Watermark: Design. 200x145mm.	20.00	60.00	175.
S389	**15 Scudi** 1786-96. Black. Watermark: Design. 200x145mm.	20.00	60.00	175.
S390	**16 Scudi** 1786-96. Black. Watermark: Design. 200x145mm.	20.00	60.00	175.
S391	**17 Scudi** 1786-96. Black. Watermark: Design. 200x145mm.	25.00	75.00	225.
S392	**18 Scudi** 1786-96. Black. Watermark: Design. 200x145mm.	25.00	75.00	225.
S393	**19 Scudi** 1786-96. Black. Watermark: Design. 200x145mm.	25.00	75.00	225.
S394	**20 Scudi** 1786-96. Black. Watermark: Design. 200x145mm.	25.00	75.00	225.
S395	**21 Scudi** 1786-96. Black. Watermark: Design. 200x145mm.	25.00	75.00	225.
S396	**22 Scudi** 1786-96. Black. Watermark: Design. 200x145mm.	25.00	75.00	225.
S397	**23 Scudi** 1786-96. Black. Watermark: Design. 200x145mm.	30.00	100.	300.
S398	**24 Scudi** 1786-96. Black. Watermark: Design. 200x145mm.	30.00	100.	300.
S399	**25 Scudi** 1786-96. Black. Watermark: Design. 200x145mm.	30.00	100.	300.
S400	**26 Scudi** 1786-96. Black. Watermark: Design. 200x145mm.	30.00	100.	300.
S401	**27 Scudi** 1786-96. Black. Watermark: Design. 200x145mm.	30.00	100.	300.
S402	**28 Scudi** 1786-96. Black. Watermark: Design. 200x145mm.	30.00	100.	300.
S403	**29 Scudi** 1786-96. Black. Watermark: Design. 200x145mm.	30.00	100.	300.
S404	**30 Scudi** 1786-96. Black. Watermark: Design. 200x145mm.	30.00	100.	300.
S405	**31 Scudi** 1786-96. Black. Watermark: Design. 200x145mm.	30.00	100.	300.
S406	**32 Scudi** 1786-96. Black. Watermark: Design. 200x145mm.	30.00	100.	300.
S407	**33 Scudi** 1786-96. Black. Watermark: Design. 200x145mm.	30.00	100.	300.
S408	**34 Scudi** 1786-96. Black. Watermark: Design. 200x145mm.	30.00	100.	300.
S409	**35 Scudi** 1786-96. Black. Watermark: Design. 200x145mm.	30.00	100.	300.
S410	**36 Scudi** 1786-96. Black. Watermark: Design. 200x145mm.	40.00	125.	375.
S411	**37 Scudi** 1786-96. Black. Watermark: Design. 200x145mm.	40.00	125.	375.
S412	**38 Scudi** 1786-96. Black. Watermark: Design. 200x145mm.	40.00	125.	375.
S413	**39 Scudi** 1786-96. Black. Watermark: Design. 200x145mm.	40.00	125.	375.
S414	**40 Scudi** 1786-96. Black. Watermark: Design. 200x145mm.	40.00	125.	375.
S415	**41 Scudi** 1786-96. Black. Watermark: Design. 200x145mm.	40.00	125.	375.
S416	**42 Scudi** 1786-96. Black. Watermark: Design. 200x145mm.	75.00	225.	675.
S417	**43 Scudi** 1786-96. Black. Watermark: Design. 200x145mm.	45.00	135.	400.
S418	**44 Scudi** 1786-96. Black. Watermark: Design. 200x145mm.	45.00	135.	450.
S419	**45 Scudi** 1786-96. Black. Watermark: Design. 200x145mm.	45.00	135.	450.
S420	**46 Scudi** 1786-96. Black. Watermark: Design. 200x145mm.	45.00	135.	450.
S421	**47 Scudi** 1786-96. Black. Watermark: Design. 200x145mm.	45.00	135.	450.

		Good	Fine	XF
S422	**48 Scudi** 1786-96. Black. Watermark: Design. 200x145mm.	45.00	135.	450.
S423	**49 Scudi** 1786-96. Black. Watermark: Design. 200x145mm.	45.00	135.	450.
S424	**50 Scudi** 1786-96. Black. Watermark: Design. 200x145mm.	45.00	135.	450.
S425	**51 Scudi** 1786-96. Black. Watermark: Design. 200x145mm.	60.00	200.	600.
S426	**52 Scudi** 1786-96. Black. Watermark: Design. 200x145mm.	75.00	225.	675.
S427	**53 Scudi** 1786-96. Black. Watermark: Design. 200x145mm.	75.00	225.	675.
S428	**54 Scudi** 1786-96. Black. Watermark: Design. 200x145mm.	75.00	225.	675.
S429	**55 Scudi** 1786-96. Black. Watermark: Design. 200x145mm.	75.00	225.	675.
S430	**56 Scudi** 1786-96. Black. Watermark: Design. 200x145mm.	75.00	225.	675.
S431	**57 Scudi** 1786-96. Black. Watermark: Design. 200x145mm.	75.00	225.	675.
S432	**58 Scudi** 1786-96. Black. Watermark: Design. 200x145mm.	75.00	225.	675.
S433	**59 Scudi** 1786-96. Black. Watermark: Design. 200x145mm.	75.00	225.	675.
S434	**60 Scudi** 1786-96. Black. Watermark: Design. 200x145mm.	75.00	225.	675.
S435	**61 Scudi** 1786-96. Black. Watermark: Design. 200x145mm.	80.00	250.	750.
S436	**62 Scudi** 1786-96. Black. Watermark: Design. 200x145mm.	80.00	250.	750.
S437	**63 Scudi** 1786-96. Black. Watermark: Design. 200x145mm.	80.00	250.	750.
S438	**64 Scudi** 1786-96. Black. Watermark: Design. 200x145mm.	80.00	250.	750.
S439	**65 Scudi** 1786-96. Black. Watermark: Design.	80.00	250.	750.
S440	**66 Scudi** 1786-96. Black. Watermark: Design. 200x145mm.	80.00	250.	750.
S441	**67 Scudi** 1786-96. Black. Watermark: Design. 200x145mm.	80.00	250.	750.
S442	**68 Scudi** 1786-96. Black. Watermark: Design. 200x145mm.	80.00	250.	750.
S443	**69 Scudi** 1786-96. Black. Watermark: Design. 200x145mm.	80.00	250.	750.
S444	**70 Scudi** 1786-96. Black. Watermark: Design. 200x145mm.	80.00	250.	750.
S445	**71 Scudi** 1786-96. Black. Watermark: Design. 200x145mm.	125.	375.	1200.
S446	**72 Scudi** 1786-96. Black. Watermark: Design. 200x145mm.	125.	375.	1200.
S447	**73 Scudi** 1786-96. Black. Watermark: Design. 200x145mm.	125.	375.	1200.
S448	**74 Scudi** 1786-96. Black. Watermark: Design. 200x145mm.	125.	375.	1200.
S449	**75 Scudi** 1786-96. Black. Watermark: Design. 200x145mm.	125.	375.	1200.
S450	**76 Scudi** 1786-96. Black. Watermark: Design. 200x145mm.	125.	375.	1200.
S451	**77 Scudi** 1786-96. Black. Watermark: Design. 200x145mm.	125.	375.	1200.
S452	**78 Scudi** 1786-96. Black. Watermark: Design. 200x145mm.	125.	375.	1200.
S453	**79 Scudi** 1786-96. Black. Watermark: Design. 200x145mm.	125.	375.	1200.
S454	**80 Scudi** 1786-96. Black. Watermark: Design. 200x145mm.	125.	375.	1200.
S455	**81 Scudi** 1786-96. Black. Watermark: Design. 200x145mm.	125.	375.	1200.
S456	**82 Scudi** 1786-96. Black. Watermark: Design. 200x145mm.	125.	375.	1200.
S457	**83 Scudi** 1786-96. Black. Watermark: Design. 200x145mm.	125.	375.	1200.
S458	**84 Scudi** 1786-96. Black. Watermark: Design. 200x145mm.	125.	375.	1200.
S459	**85 Scudi** 1786-96. Black. Watermark: Design. 200x145mm.	125.	375.	1200.
S460	**86 Scudi** 1786-96. Black. Watermark: Design. 200x145mm.	125.	375.	1200.
S461	**87 Scudi** 1786-96. Black. Watermark: Design. 200x145mm.	125.	375.	1200.
S462	**88 Scudi** 1786-96. Black. Watermark: Design. 200x145mm.	125.	375.	1200.
S463	**89 Scudi** 1786-96. Black. Watermark: Design. 200x145mm.	80.00	250.	750.
S464	**90 Scudi** 1786-96. Black. Watermark: Design. 200x145mm.	80.00	250.	750.
S465	**91 Scudi** 1786-96. Black. Watermark: Design. 200x145mm.	80.00	250.	750.
S466	**92 Scudi** 1786-96. Black. Watermark: Design. 200x145mm.	125.	375.	1200.
S467	**93 Scudi** 1786-96. Black. Watermark: Design. 200x145mm.	125.	375.	1200.
S468	**94 Scudi** 1786-96. Black. Watermark: Design. 200x145mm.	125.	375.	1200.
S469	**95 Scudi** 1786-96. Black. Watermark: Design. 200x145mm.	125.	375.	1200.
S470	**96 Scudi** 1786-96. Black. Watermark: Design. 200x145mm.	125.	375.	1200.
S471	**97 Scudi** 1786-96. Black. Watermark: Design. 200x145mm.	125.	375.	1200.
S472	**98 Scudi** 1786-96. Black. Watermark: Design. 200x145mm.	125.	375.	1200.
S473	**99 Scudi** 1786-96. Black. Watermark: Design. 200x145mm.	80.00	250.	750.
S474	**100 Scudi** 1786-96. Black. Watermark: Design. 200x145mm.	75.00	225.	675.
S475	**105 Scudi** 1786-96. Black. Watermark: Design. 200x145mm.	135.	400.	1200.
S476	**110 Scudi** 1786-96. Black. Watermark: Design. 200x145mm.	135.	400.	1200.
S477	**115 Scudi** 1786-96. Black. Watermark: Design. 200x145mm.	135.	400.	1200.
S478	**120 Scudi** 1786-96. Black. Watermark: Design. 200x145mm.	135.	400.	1200.
S479	**125 Scudi** 1786-96. Black. Watermark: Design. 200x145mm.	135.	400.	1200.
S480	**130 Scudi** 1786-96. Black. Watermark: Design. 200x145mm.	135.	400.	1200.
S481	**135 Scudi** 1786-96. Black. Watermark: Design. 200x145mm.	135.	400.	1200.
S482	**140 Scudi** 1786-96. Black. Watermark: Design. 200x145mm.	135.	400.	1200.
S483	**145 Scudi** 1786-96. Black. Watermark: Design. 200x145mm.	135.	400.	1200.
S484	**150 Scudi** 1786-96. Black. Watermark: Design. 200x145mm.	135.	400.	1200.
S485	**155 Scudi** 1786-96. Black. Watermark: Design. 200x145mm.	135.	400.	1200.
S486	**160 Scudi** 1786-96. Black. Watermark: Design. 200x145mm.	135.	400.	1200.
S487	**165 Scudi** 1786-96. Black. Watermark: Design. 200x145mm.	135.	400.	1200.
S488	**170 Scudi** 1786-96. Black. Watermark: Design. 200x145mm.	135.	400.	1200.
S489	**175 Scudi** 1786-96. Black. Watermark: Design. 200x145mm.	135.	400.	1200.
S490	**180 Scudi** 1786-96. Black. Watermark: Design. 200x145mm.	135.	400.	1200.
S491	**185 Scudi** 1786-96. Black. Watermark: Design. 200x145mm.	135.	400.	1200.
S492	**190 Scudi** 1786-96. Black. Watermark: Design. 200x145mm.	135.	400.	1200.
S493	**195 Scudi** 1786-96. Black. Watermark: Design. 200x145mm.	135.	400.	1200.
S494	**200 Scudi** 1786-96. Black. Watermark: Design. 200x145mm.	135.	400.	1200.
S495	**210 Scudi** 1786-96. Black. Watermark: Design. 200x145mm.	150.	500.	1500.
S496	**220 Scudi** 1786-96. Black. Watermark: Design. 200x145mm.	150.	500.	1500.
S497	**230 Scudi** 1786-96. Black. Watermark: Design. 200x145mm.	150.	500.	1500.
S498	**240 Scudi** 1786-96. Black. Watermark: Design. 200x145mm.	150.	500.	1500.
S499	**250 Scudi** 1786-96. Black. Watermark: Design. 200x145mm.	150.	500.	1500.
S500	**260 Scudi** 1786-96. Black. Watermark: Design. 200x145mm.	150.	500.	1500.
S501	**270 Scudi** 1786-96. Black. Watermark: Design. 200x145mm.	150.	500.	1500.
S502	**280 Scudi** 1786-96. Black. Watermark: Design. 200x145mm.	150.	500.	1500.
S503	**290 Scudi** 1786-96. Black. Watermark: Design. 200x145mm.	150.	500.	1500.
S504	**300 Scudi** 1786-96. Black. Watermark: Design. 200x145mm.	150.	500.	1500.
S505	**320 Scudi** 1786-96. Black. Watermark: Design. 200x145mm.	175.	600.	1800.
S506	**340 Scudi** 1786-96. Black. Watermark: Design. 200x145mm.	175.	600.	1800.
S507	**360 Scudi** 1786-96. Black. Watermark: Design. 200x145mm.	175.	600.	1800.
S508	**380 Scudi** 1786-96. Black. Watermark: Design. 200x145mm.	175.	600.	1800.
S509	**400 Scudi** 1786-96. Black. Watermark: Design. 200x145mm.	175.	600.	1800.
S510	**450 Scudi** 1786-96. Black. Watermark: Design. 200x145mm.	225.	700.	2500.
S511	**500 Scudi** 1786-96. Black. Watermark: Design. 200x145mm.	225.	700.	2500.
S512	**600 Scudi** 1786-96. Black. Watermark: Design. 200x145mm. Rare.	—	—	—
S513	**700 Scudi** 1786-96. Black. Watermark: Design. 200x145mm. Rare.	—	—	—
S514	**800 Scudi** 1786-96. Black. Watermark: Design. 200x145mm. Rare.	—	—	—
S515	**900 Scudi** 1786-96. Black. Watermark: Design. 200x145mm. Rare.	—	—	—
S516	**1000 Scudi** 1786-96. Black. Watermark: Design. 200x145mm. Rare.	—	—	—
S517	**1500 Scudi** 1786-96. Black. Watermark: Design. 200x145mm. Rare.	—	—	—
S518	**2000 Scudi** 1786-96. Black. Watermark: Design. 200x145mm. Unknown.	—	—	—
S519	**3000 Scudi** 1786-96. Black. Watermark: Design. 200x145mm. Unknown.	—	—	—

NOTE: During First Roman Republic, some Banco Di S. Spirito notes were overprint by the Republican Municipal Administration with the seal of about 15 different towns, to ratify the validity of circulation. All the Republican validated notes are rare and, in comparison with the normal notes, prices increase up to double the value for common seals and up to five times for rarer seals.

PRIMA REPUBBLICA ROMANA

BANCO DI S. SPIRITO

1798 ISSUE

		VG	VF	UNC
S521	**25 Bajocchi** 8.6.1798-5.8.1798. Black. Republican seal at top left and right. Various handwritten dates. Watermark: Design.			
	a. Value in words.	25.00	75.00	225.
	b. Value in numerals.	45.00	100.	300.
S522	**40 Bajocchi** 5.8.1798-27.8.1798. Black. Republican seal at top left and right. Various handwritten dates. Watermark: Design.	25.00	75.00	225.
S523	**50 Bajocchi** 23.6.1798-4.9.1798. Black. Republican seal at top left and right. Various handwritten dates. Watermark: Design.			
	a. Value in words.	20.00	60.00	175.
	b. Value in numerals.	30.00	100.	300.
S524	**60 Bajocchi** 3.7.1798-4.8.1798. Black. Republican seal at top left and right. Various handwritten dates. Watermark: Design.	30.00	100.	300.
S525	**10 Paoli = 100 Bajocchi** 3.7.1798-4.9.1798. Black. Republican seal at top left and right. Various handwritten dates. Watermark: Design.	15.00	45.00	125.

MONTE DI PIETA'

1798 ISSUE

		VG	VF	UNC
S526	**25 Bajocchi** 11.6.1798-30.10.1798. Black. Republican seal at top left and right. Various handwritten dates. Watermark: Design.			
	a. Value in words.	25.00	75.00	225.
	b. Value in numerals.	30.00	100.	300.
S527	**40 Bajocchi** 11.8.1798-4.9.1798. Black. Republican seal at top left and right. Various handwritten dates. Watermark: Design.	25.00	75.00	225.
S528	**50 Bajocchi** 3.7.1798-4.9.1798. Black. Republican seal at top left and right. Various handwritten dates. Watermark: Design.			
	a. Value in words.	15.00	45.00	125.
	b. Value in numerals.	25.00	75.00	225.
S529	**60 Bajocchi** 6.8.1798-4.9.1798. Black. Republican seal at top left and right. Various handwritten dates. Watermark: Design.	25.00	75.00	225.
S530	**10 Paoli = 100 Bajocchi** 6.7.1798-4.9.1798. Black. Republican seal at top left and right. Various handwritten dates. Watermark: Design.	15.00	45.00	125.

ASSEGNATI - ASSIGNATS

1798 ISSUE

		VG	VF	UNC
S531	**3 Bajocchi** ANNO 7 (1798). Black. Value printed. Back: Black seal. Watermark: Design.	40.00	125.	375.
S532	**5 Bajocchi** ANNO 7 (1798). Black. Value printed. Back: Black seal. Watermark: Design.	225.	675.	2250.
S533	**10 Bajocchi = 1 Paolo** ANNO 7 (1798). Black. Value printed. Back: Black seal. Watermark: Design.	175.	525.	1600.
S534	**1 1/2 Paoli** ANNO 7 (1798). Black. Value printed. Back: Black seal. Watermark: Design.	25.00	75.00	225.
S535	**2 Paoli** ANNO 7 (1798). Black. Value printed. Back: Black seal. Watermark: Design.	40.00	125.	375.
S536	**2 1/2 Paoli** ANNO 7 (1798). Black. Value printed. Back: Black seal. Watermark: Design.	40.00	125.	375.
S537	**7 Paoli** ANNO 7 (1798). Black. Value printed. Back: Black seal. Watermark: Design.	15.00	45.00	125.
S538	**8 Paoli** ANNO 7 (1798). Black. Value printed. Back: Black seal. Watermark: Design.	15.00	45.00	125.

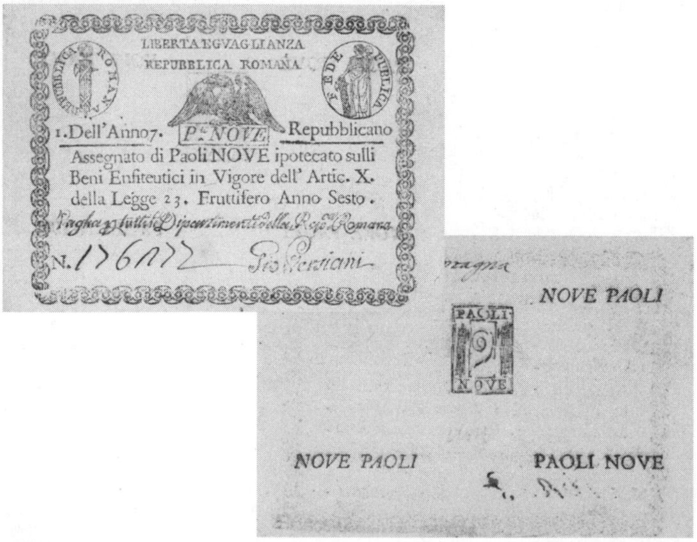

		VG	VF	UNC
S539	**9 Paoli** ANNO 7 (1798). Black. Value printed. Back: Black seal. Watermark: Design.	15.00	45.00	125.

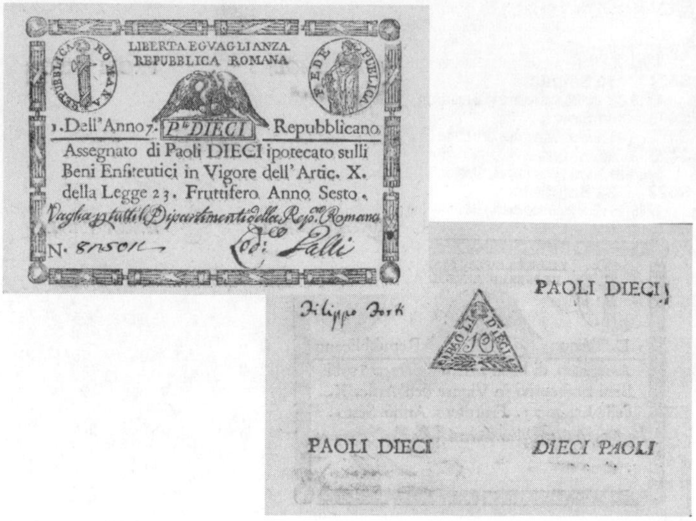

		VG	VF	UNC
S540	**10 Paoli** ANNO 7 (1798). Black. Value printed. Back: Black seal. Watermark: Design.			
	a. Value in triangle on back.	7.50	20.00	60.00
	b. Value in circle on back.	7.50	20.00	60.00
	c. Value in square on back.	7.50	20.00	60.00
	d. Value in rhombus on back.	7.50	20.00	60.00

BANCA ROMANA

1834; 1849 ISSUE

		Good	Fine	XF
S551	**5 Scudi** 1835-49. Light gray. Fortune at left and right. Back: Seal with *Banca Romana* and value. Watermark: Design.	1500.	4500.	12,500.
S552	**10 Scudi** 1835-49. Light brick red. Tevere allegory at top left and right. Back: Seal with *Banca Romana* and value. Watermark: Design. Rare.	—	—	—
S553	**20 Scudi** 1834-49. Orange. Allegorical figure all around in oval. Back: Seal with *Banca Romana* and value. Watermark: Design. Rare.	—	—	—
S554	**50 Scudi** 1834-49. Blue on azure underprint. Allegory all around in oval. Back: Seal with *Banca Romana* and value. Watermark: Design. Rare.	—	—	—
S555	**100 Scudi** 1834-49. Gray on white. Allegorical figure all around. Back: Seal with *Banca Romana* and value. Watermark: Design. Rare.	—	—	—

BUONI DEL TESORO

1848 ISSUE

		Good	Fine	XF
S556	**1 Scudo** 1848. Brown, rose on creme underprint. Embossed seal and 2-1/2 seals. Back: Red seal. Watermark: Design. Rare.	—	—	—
S557	**2 Scudi** 1848. Deep gray on yellow underprint. Embossed seal and 2-1/2 seals. Back: Red seal. Watermark: Design.	225.	675.	2000.
S558	**5 Scudi** 1848. Gray-olive. Embossed seal and 2-1/2 seals. Back: Red seal. Paper: White. Watermark: Design.	375.	1100.	3250.
S559	**10 Scudi** 1848. Gray-green. Embossed seal and 2-1/2 seals. Back: Red seal. Paper: Green. Watermark: Design.	750.	2250.	6750.
S560	**20 Scudi** 1848. Embossed seal and 2-1/2 seals. Back: Red seal. Watermark: Design. Reported not confirmed.	—	—	—
S561	**50 Scudi** 1848. Embossed seal and 2-1/2 seals. Back: Red seal. Watermark: Design. Reported not confirmed.	—	—	—
S562	**100 Scudi** 1848. Red on rose underprint. Embossed seal and 2-1/2 seals. Back: Red seal. Watermark: Design. Rare.	—	—	—

LEGAZIONE DI BOLOGNA - BONI PROVINCIALI

1848; 1849 PROVISIONAL ISSUE

		Good	Fine	XF
S563	**5 Scudi** 14.8.1848; 3.1.1849. Deep blue. Paper: Light blue. Watermark: Design. Rare.	—	—	—
S564	**10 Scudi** 14.8.1848; 3.1.1849. Black on blue. Paper: Light blue. Watermark: Design. Rare.	—	—	—
S565	**20 Scudi** 14.8.1848; 3.1.1849. Deep blue. Paper: Light blue. Watermark: Design. Rare.	—	—	—
S566	**30 Scudi** 3.1.1849. Deep blue. Paper: Light blue. Watermark: Design. Rare.	—	—	—
S567	**50 Scudi** 14.8.1848; 3.1.1849. Deep blue. Paper: Light blue. Watermark: Design. Rare.	—	—	—
S568	**100 Scudi** 14.8.1848. Deep blue. Paper: Light blue. Watermark: Design. Rare.	—	—	—

<LOC>SECONDA REPUBBLICA ROMANA

Boni Centrali

1849 Issue

No.	Denomination / Description	Good	Fine	XF
S571	**10 Bajocchi** 1849. Black. Republican eagle at top center, embossed seal with Republican eagle.	40.00	125.	375.
S572	**16 Bajocchi** 1849. Black on gray underprint. Republican eagle at top center, embossed seal with Republican eagle.	40.00	125.	375.
S573	**24 Bajocchi** 1849. Black. Republican eagle at top center, embossed seal with Republican eagle. Paper: Yellow.	40.00	125.	375.
S574	**24 Bajocchi** 1849. Black. Republican eagle at top center, embossed seal with Republican eagle. Paper: Yellow. New typology. Rare.	—	—	—
S575	**32 Bajocchi** 1849. Blue on azure underprint. Republican eagle at top center, embossed seal with Republican eagle.	150.	450.	1350.
S576	**40 Bajocchi** 1849. Black on green underprint. Republican eagle at top center, embossed seal with Republican eagle.	150.	450.	1350.
S577	**1 Scudo** 1849. Slate on gray underprint. Republican eagle at top center, embossed seal with Republican eagle.	125.	375.	1100.
S578	**2 Scudi** 1849. Slate on gray underprint. Republican eagle at top center, embossed seal with Republican eagle.	150.	450.	1350.
S579	**5 Scudi** 1849. Slate. Republican eagle at top center, embossed seal with Republican eagle.	300.	900.	2750.
S580	**10 Scudi** 1849. Olive on green underprint. Republican eagle at top center, embossed seal with Republican eagle. Rare.	—	—	—
S581	**20 Scudi** 1849. Slate. Republican eagle at top center, embossed seal with Republican eagle. Rare.	—	—	—
S582	**50 Scudi** 1849. Slate on light azure-green underprint. Republican eagle at top center, embossed seal with Republican eagle. Rare.	—	—	—
S583	**100 Scudi** 1849. Republican eagle at top center, embossed seal with Republican eagle. Reported not confirmed.	—	—	—

Boni Provinciali

Ancona

1849 Issue

No.	Denomination / Description	Good	Fine	XF
S584	**5 Bajocchi** 10.6.1849. Black. Back: Several stampings.	375.	1100.	3250.
S585	**5+5 Bajocchi** 1849. Black. Back: Several stampings.			
	a. Issued note (= 10 Bajocchi).	300.	900.	2750.
	b. Cut left or right half (= 5 Bajocchi).	125.	375.	1100.
S586	**10 Bajocchi** 1849. Black. Back: Several stampings.	450.	1250.	3750.
S587	**20 Bajocchi** 1849. Black. Back: Several stampings. Rare.	—	—	—
S588	**25 Bajocchi** 1849. Black. Back: Several stampings. Rare.	—	—	—
S589	**30 Bajocchi** 1849. Black. Back: Several stampings. Rare.	—	—	—
S590	**40 Bajocchi** 1849. Black. Back: Several stampings.	450.	1350.	4250.
S591	**50 Bajocchi** 1849. Black. Back: Several stampings. Rare.	—	—	—

Ascoli

ND Issue

No.	Denomination / Description	Good	Fine	XF
S592	**1 1/2 Bajocchi** ND. Paper: Green. Reported not confirmed.	—	—	—
S593	**3 Bajocchi** ND. Paper: Blue. Reported not confirmed.	—	—	—
S594	**5 Bajocchi** ND. Paper: Creme. Reported not confirmed.	—	—	—
S595	**10 Bajocchi** ND. Paper: White. Reported not confirmed.	—	—	—
S596	**20 Bajocchi** ND. Paper: Yellow. Reported not confirmed.	—	—	—
S597	**30 Bajocchi** ND. Paper: Rose. Reported not confirmed.	—	—	—
S598	**50 Bajocchi** ND. Paper: White. Reported not confirmed.	—	—	—

Bologna

Ordinance of March 7, 1849

No.	Denomination / Description	Good	Fine	XF
S599	**5 Bajocchi** L. 1849. Black. Embossed seal. Back: Blue seal. Paper: Blue.	75.00	225.	675.
S600	**10 Bajocchi** L. 1849. Black. Embossed seal. Back: Blue seal. Paper: White.	75.00	225.	675.
S601	**20 Bajocchi** L. 1849. Black. Embossed seal. Back: Blue seal. Paper: Orange.	100.	300.	900.
S602	**1/2 Scudo** L. 1849. Black on creme underprint. Embossed seal. Back: Blue seal.	175.	525.	1575.
S603	**1 Scudo** L. 1849. Black on rose underprint. Embossed seal. Back: Blue seal. Paper: White.	300.	900.	2750.
S604	**2 1/2 Scudi** L. 1849. Black. Embossed seal. Back: Blue seal. Paper: White. Rare.	—	—	—

Civitavecchia

1849 Issue

No.	Denomination / Description	Good	Fine	XF
S605	**10 Bajocchi** 14.5.1849. Reported not confirmed.	—	—	—
S606	**20 Bajocchi** 14.5.1849. Black. Paper: Red. Rare.	—	—	—
S607	**30 Bajocchi** 14.5.1849. Reported not confirmed.	—	—	—
S608	**50 Bajocchi** 14.5.1849. Black. Paper: Yellow. Rare.	—	—	—
S609	**1 Scudo** 14.5.1849. Black. Paper: Green. Rare.	—	—	—

Forli

1849 Issue

No.	Denomination / Description	Good	Fine	XF
S611	**5 Bajocchi** 14.4.1849. Black. Embossed seal. Paper: White. Rare.	—	—	—
S612	**20 Bajocchi** 14.4.1849. Black. Embossed seal. Paper: Rose. Rare.	—	—	—
S613	**1 Scudo** 14.4.1849. Black. Embossed seal. Paper: White. Rare.	—	—	—

Frosinone

ND Issue

No.	Denomination / Description	Good	Fine	XF
S614	**5 Bajocchi** ND. Blue. Blue seal. Back: Red seal. Paper: White. Rare.	—	—	—

Perugia

ND Issue

No.	Denomination / Description	Good	Fine	XF
S620	**5 Bajocchi** ND. Slate. Paper: Creme. Rare.	—	—	—

Rieti

ND Issue

No.	Denomination / Description	Good	Fine	XF
S621	**6 Bajocchi** ND. Black. Red seal. Paper: White. Rare.	—	—	—
S622	**14 Bajocchi** ND. Black. Red and black seals. Paper: White. Rare.	—	—	—
S623	**35 Bajocchi** ND. Black. Red and black seals. Paper: Creme. Rare.	—	—	—

Boni Comunali

Albano

ND Issue

No.	Denomination / Description	Good	Fine	XF
S631	**5 Bajocchi** ND. Black. Paper: White. Rare.	—	—	—
S632	**7 1/2 Bajocchi** ND. Black. Paper: Creme. Watermark: Design. Rare.	—	—	—
S633	**12 1/2 Bajocchi** ND. Black. Paper: Yellow. Watermark: Design. Rare.	—	—	—

Arsoli

ND Issue

No.	Denomination / Description	Good	Fine	XF
S634	**3 Bajocchi** ND. Black. Paper: Light green. Rare.	—	—	—
S635	**5 Bajocchi** ND. Black. Paper: Light azure. Rare.	—	—	—
S636	**10 Bajocchi** ND. Black. Paper: Light green. Rare.	—	—	—

Monsanvito

ND Issue

No.	Denomination / Description	Good	Fine	XF
S641	**2 1/2 Bajocchi** ND. Black. Paper: White. Unique.	—	—	—

Pesaro

ND Issue

No.	Denomination / Description	Good	Fine	XF
S642	**5 Bajocchi** ND. Blue and black. Rare.	—	—	—
S643	**10 Bajocchi** ND. Blue. Red seal. Back: Blue. Rare.	—	—	—
S644	**20 Bajocchi** ND. Blue. Red seal. Back: Blue. Rare.	—	—	—
S645	**50 Bajocchi** ND. Blue. Red seal. Back: Blue. Rare.	—	—	—
S646	**1 Scudo** ND. Red. Black seal. Back: Two seals. Rare.	—	—	—
S647	**2 Scudi** ND. Red. Black seal. Back: Two seals. Rare.	—	—	—
S648	**5 Scudi** ND. Orange. Seal. Back: Two seals. Rare.	—	—	—

Commissariato Pontificio per le 4 Legazioni-Bologna

1849 Issue

	Good	Fine	XF
S651 20 Bajocchi 1.6.1849. Black. Embossed seal. Back: Two seals. Paper: White.	100.	300.	900.

Boni del Tesoro in Sostituzione

1849 Issue

	Good	Fine	XF
S652 1 Scudo 3.8.1849. Slate. Full seal with two partial circular seals at upper and lower left. Back: Red seal. Paper: Gray-azure. Watermark: Design.	175.	525.	1575.
S653 2 Scudo 3.8.1849. Slate. Full seal with two partial circular seals at upper and lower left. Back: Red seal. Paper: Yellow. Rare.	—	—	—
S654 5 Scudi 3.8.1849. Slate. Full seal with two partial circular seals at upper and lower left. Back: Red seal. Paper: Creme. Watermark: Design.	300.	900.	2750.
S655 10 Scudi 3.8.1849. Slate. Full seal with two partial circular seals at upper and lower left. Back: Red seal. Paper: Green-yellow. Watermark: Design. Rare.	—	—	—
S656 20 Scudi 3.8.1849. Olive on light green underprint. Full seal with two partial circular seals at upper and lower left. Back: Red seal. Watermark: Design. Rare.	—	—	—
S657 50 Scudi 3.8.1849. Slate on deep green underprint. Full seal with two partial circular seals at upper and lower left. Back: Red seal. Watermark: Design.	175.	525.	1575.

Boni del Tesoro in Surrogazione

1851 Issue

	Good	Fine	XF
S658 1 Scudo 10.6.1851. Red on rose underprint. Blue seal. Back: Red seal. Watermark: Design.	300.	900.	2750.
S659 5 Scudi 10.6.1851. Red on azure underprint. Blue seal. Back: Red seal. Watermark: Design.	600.	1800.	5400.
S660 10 Scudi 10.6.1851. Blue-green on azure underprint. Blue seal. Back: Red seal. Watermark: Design. Rare.	—	—	—
S661 20 Scudi 10.6.1851. Blue seal. Back: Red seal. Watermark: Design. Rare.	—	—	—
S662 50 Scudi 10.6.1851. Blue seal. Back: Red seal. Watermark: Design.	150.	450.	1350.
S663 100 Scudi 10.6.1851. Blue seal. Back: Red seal. Watermark: Design. Reported not confirmed.	—	—	—

Banco di Santo Spirito

1855; 1858 Issue

	Good	Fine	XF
S665 20 Scudi 1855-58. Black on blue underprint. Black seal at lower center. Rare.	—	—	—

Banca Pontificia per le 4 Legazioni

1855 ND Provisional Issue

	Good	Fine	XF
S671 10 Scudi ND (1855- old date 1853). Female head at left and at right, allegorical figure around. Overprint: *BIGLIETTO PROVVISORIO/DELLA BANCA DI BOLOGNA PER LE 4 LEGAZIONI/PAGABILE IN BOLOGNA* on #S692.			
a. Issued note. Rare.	—	—	—
r. Remainder.	—	—	300.
S672 20 Scudi ND (1855- old date 1853). Green. Allegorical figures all around in oval. Overprint: *BIGLIETTO PROVVISORIO/DELLA BANCA DI BOLOGNA PER LE 4 LEGAZIONI/PAGABILE IN BOLOGNA* on #S694.			
a. Issued note. Rare.	—	—	—
r. Remainder.	—	—	500.
S673 50 Scudi ND (1855- old date 1853). Yellow. Allegorical figures all around in oval. Overprint: *BIGLIETTO PROVVISORIO/DELLA BANCA DI BOLOGNA PER LE 4 LEGAZIONI/PAGABILE IN BOLOGNA* on #S695. Reported not confirmed.	—	—	—
S674 100 Scudi ND (1855- old date 1853). Red. Allegorical figures all around in oval. Overprint: *BIGLIETTO PROVVISORIO/DELLA BANCA DI BOLOGNA PER LE 4 LEGAZIONI/PAGABILE IN BOLOGNA* on #S696. Reported not confirmed.	—	—	—

Banca dello Stato Pontificio

1851-52 ND Provisional Issue

	Good	Fine	XF
S681 5 Scudi ND (1851-52- old dates 1835-49). Light gray. Fortune at left and right. Back: Seal with *Banca Romana* and value. Overprint: *Biglietto Provvisorio della Banca della Stato Pontificio* on back of #S551. Rare.	—	—	—
S682 10 Scudi ND (1851-52- old dates 1835-49). Light brick red. Tevere allegory at top left and right. Back: Seal with *Banca Romana* and value. Overprint: *Biglietto Provvisorio della Banca della Stato Pontificio* on back of #S552. Rare.	—	—	—
S683 20 Scudi ND (1851-52- old dates 1834-49). Orange. Allegorical figure all around in oval. Back: Seal with *Banca Romana* and value. Overprint: *Biglietto Provvisorio della Banca della Stato Pontificio* on back of #S553. Rare.	—	—	—
S684 50 Scudi ND (1851-52- old dates 1834-49). Blue on azure underprint. Allegory all around in oval. Back: Seal with *Banca Romana* and value. Overprint: *Biglietto Provvisorio della Banca della Stato Pontificio* on back of #S554. Rare.	—	—	—
S685 100 Scudi ND (1851-52- old dates 1834-49). Gray on white. Allegorical figure all around. Back: Seal with *Banca Romana* and value. Overprint: *Biglietto Provvisorio della Banca della Stato Pontificio* on back of #S555. Rare.	—	—	—

Banca dello Stato Pontificio - Regular Issue

1853-61 ND Issue

	Good	Fine	XF
S686 1 Scudo ND (1853). Black. Paper: White.	300.	900.	2750.
S687 1 Scudo 1866; 1867. Blue. Back: Italian lire denomination. Paper: White.	250.	750.	2250.
S688 2 Scudi ND (1856). Blue. Paper: White. Reported not confirmed.	—	—	—
S689 5 Scudi ND (1853). Azure. Paper: White.	350.	1150.	3450.
S690 5 Scudi ND (1861). Female head at left and at right, allegorical figure around. Rare.	—	—	—
S691 5 Scudi 1866; 1867. Red. Allegorical figure all around in oval. Rare.	—	—	—
S692 10 Scudi ND (1853). Female head at left and at right, allegorical figure around. Rare.	—	—	—
S693 10 Scudi ND (1859). Reported not confirmed.	—	—	—
S694 20 Scudi (1853). Green. Allegorical figures all around in oval. Rare.	—	—	—
S695 50 Scudi (1853). Yellow. Allegorical figures all around in oval. Reported not confirmed.	—	—	—
S696 100 Scudi (1853). Red. Allegorical figures all around in oval. Reported not confirmed.	—	—	—

Banca dello Stato Pontificio

1867 Italian Lire Issue

	Good	Fine	XF
S701 5 Lire 1867-70. Black and blue. Back: Woman's head. Watermark: Design. Rare.	—	—	—
S702 10 Lire 1867-70. Blue. Woman with headpiece at left. Watermark: Design. Rare.	—	—	—
S703 20 Lire 1867-70. Allegorical women at left and at right. Watermark: Design. Rare.	—	—	—
S704 50 Lire 1867-70. Agriculture at left and Industry at right. Watermark: Design. Rare.	—	—	—
S705 100 Lire 1867-70. Allegorical women standing at left and at right. Watermark: Design. Rare.	—	—	—
S706 200 Lire 1867-70. Two columns at left and at right with allegorical figures. Watermark: Design, Rare.	—	—	—
S707 500 Lire 1867-70. Seated allegorical figures at left and at right, allegories below. Watermark: Design. Rare.	—	—	—
S708 1000 Lire 1867-70. Six allegories including Industry and Agriculture. Watermark: Design. Rare.	—	—	—

Regno delle Due Sicilie

Kingdom of the Two Sicilies

The Kingdom was formally created in 1816 from the ashes of the Napoleonic empire; but the history of the two regions continually crosses starting from the 12th century with Roger II, followed by the Angevin occupation in 1266, the Aragonese one in 1442, the very short French one during the first years of 1500. In 1905 the two areas became provinces of the Spanish monarchy ruled by a viceroy. After a short Austrian occupation subsequent to the Treaty of Utrecht (1713), the two provinces retu

Ferdinando I, 1816-1825
Francesco I, 1825-1830
Ferdinando II, 1830-1859
Francesco II, 1859-1861

Governo Provvisorio di Sicilia

1849 Issue

	Good	Fine	XF
S711 4 Oncia 23.4.1849. Gray and hazel.	325.	975.	2800.

REGNO D'ITALIA

From the fall of the Roman empire until last century, Italy was divided into many independent states and kingdoms, and some of them were sometimes occupied by other European States. The *Risorgimento* unification movement, fostered by Cavour, Garibaldi and Mazzini, with the help of England and France, attained fruition in 1860-70 with the creation of the Kingdom of Italy (March 1861) and the installation of Victor Emanuele II, King of Sardinia, as King of Italy.

Government Banks

Banca Nazionale nel Regno d'Italia

1866 ND Provisional Marca da Bollo Stamp Issue

#S721-S723 portr. Kg. Victor Emanuele II, w/bar ovpt. across *DA BOLLA*.

		Good	Fine	XF
S721	**5 Lire** ND (1866). Portrait King Victor Emanuele II. Overprint: Bar across *DA BOLLA*.	150.	450.	1350.
S722	**10 Lire** ND (1866). Portrait King Victor Emanuele II. Overprint: Bar across *DA BOLLA*.	300.	1000.	3000.
S723	**15 Lire** ND (1866). Portrait King Victor Emanuele II. Overprint: Bar across *DA BOLLA*. Rare.	—	—	—

1866-96 Regular Issues

		Good	Fine	XF
S731	**1 Lira** 20.1.1869; 17.7.1872; 15.1.1873. Black on green underprint. Head at lower left and right, date in circles at lower center. Back: Portraits of Cavour and Manin at upper and lower left, Columbus and Dante at upper and lower right.	7.50	25.00	100.

		Good	Fine	XF
S732	**2 Lire** 25.7.1866; 22.1.1868. Black. Count Cavour at center. Back: Green. Date at top.	15.00	45.00	140.
S733	**5 Lire** 29.8.1866. Black. Head of Italia at upper left. Paper: White.	100.	400.	1500.
S734	**5 Lire** 30.10.1867; 15.1.1873. Black on blue underprint. Portraits of Cavour at upper left, Columbus at upper right, heads at lower left and right. Back: Black on olive underprint.	15.00	45.00	140.
S735	**10 Lire** 19.5.1866. Dark blue. Victor Emanuele II at upper center.	300.	1500.	3500.

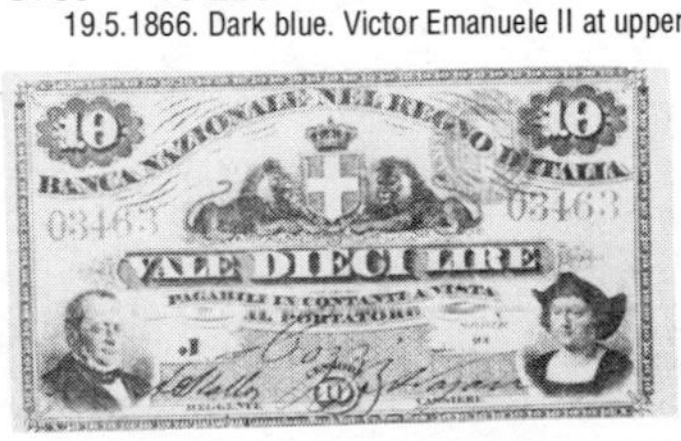

		Good	Fine	XF
S736	**10 Lire** 16.5.1866-28.9.1870. Black. Count Cavour at lower left, supported royal arms at upper center, Columbus at lower right. Back: Blue. Date at top, text at center.	15.00	45.00	200.

		Good	Fine	XF
S737	**10 Lire** 17.7.1872. Black on peach and green underprint. Two allegories at left and right, crowned Austro-Hungarian imperial eagle at bottom center. Similar to #S212. Back: Blue and black. Portrait Italia at center.	15.00	45.00	200.
S738	**25 Lire** 25.7.1866; 30.10.1867; 22.7.1868. Black. Paper: Red.	125.	375.	1600.
S739	**25 Lire** 24.1.1883-20.7.1892. Dark blue on orange underprint. Three cherubs at lower center, seated woman with fasces and cornucopia at right, arms at top center. Back: Blue. Bust of Italia at center, head at each corner.	100.	300.	1300.
S740	**40 Lire** 25.7.1866. Black. Paper: Olive. Rare.	—	—	—

		Good	Fine	XF
S741	**50 Lire** 1874-24.6.1895. Blue. Arms at upper center, portrait Italia at left, seated Justice at bottom center. Back: Anchor between two medallion portraits at center. Paper: Ivory.	60.00	250.	800.
S742	**100 Lire** 15.1.1873-18.5.1896. Black. Paper: Rose.	60.00	250.	800.
S743	**250 Lire** 15.1.1873. Black. Paper: Light green.	750.	2250.	6750.
S744	**500 Lire** 17.7.1872-24.6.1895. Black. Paper: Yellow.	300.	1000.	3000.
S745	**1000 Lire** 17.7.1872; 15.1.1873. Black. Paper: White. Rare.	—	—	—
S746	**1000 Lire** 16.1.1878-18.5.1896. Yellow-brown. Cherubs at sides, allegorical figures of Industry and Agriculture seated at bottom center, arms at top center. Back: Bust of Italia. Paper: Light blue.	750.	2250.	6750.

Banca Nazionale Toscana

1859-73 Issues

		Good	Fine	XF
S751	**50 Centesimi** 1873. Black on orange underprint. Back: Orange. Facing heads of Italia at center.	7.50	25.00	80.00
S752	**1 Lira** 1873. Black. Back: Green. Head of Italia at center.	12.50	30.00	100.
S753	**2 Lire** 1873. Black on red underprint. Portrait Dante at left. Back: Red. Similar to #S262.	45.00	100.	400.
S754	**5 Lire** 1873. Black on purple underprint. Similar to #S263. Back: Purple. Four heads of Italia.	125.	400.	1500.
S755	**10 Lire** 1873. Black on red underprint. Similar to #S753. Back: Red. Two facing heads of Italia at center.	175.	1000.	3000.
S756	**20 Lire** 19.5.1866; 17.7.1866. Black. Paper: Green.	150.	500.	2000.
S757	**20 Lire** 3.9.1872. Black on peach underprint. Back: Red-orange and green. Italia at center.	375.	1200.	3500.
S758	**25 Lire** 1883. Red and green on red-orange underprint.	175.	525.	1600.
S759	**50 Lire** 19.5.1866; 4.7.1866; 17.7.1866. Black. Like #S246. Paper: Pink.	225.	675.	2250.
S760	**50 Lire** 1872. Black on rose underprint. Italia at left, Daente at right. Back: Red-orange and brown.	300.	900.	2750.
S761	**50 Lire** 23.12.1883. Blue-green on gray.	175.	600.	1800.
S762	**100 Lire** 19.5.1866; 17.7.1866. Rare.	—	—	—
S763	**100 Lire** 2.1.1865. Rare.	—	—	—

		Good	Fine	XF
S764	**100 Lire** 9.9.1869-23.12.1883. Black on violet underprint. Back: Violet. Paper: Tan.	175.	600.	1800.
S765	**200 Lire** 2.1.1865. Reported not confirmed.	—	—	—
S766	**200 Lire** 9.9.1869; 18.8.1870. Black on green underprint. Back: Green. Paper: Light blue.	525.	2000.	6000.
S767	**500 Lire** 2.1.1865. Reported not confirmed.	—	—	—
S768	**500 Lire** 9.9.1869; 18.8.1870. Black on orange underprint. Back: Orange. Paper: Yellow. Rare.	—	—	—
S769	**1000 Lire** 2.1.1865. Rare.	—	—	—
S770	**1000 Lire** 9.9.1869; 18.8.1870. Black on blue and light tan underprint. Back: Orange. Rare.	—	—	—

Banca Toscana di Credito

1864-80 Issue

		Good	Fine	XF
S771	**20 Lire** 30.6.1866. Black. Uniface. Paper: Yellow.	225.	600.	2000.
S772	**20 Lire** 1.1.1873; 17.9.1876. Black. Italia head in oval at left. Back: Peach. Paper: Yellow and white. Printer: BWC. Rare.	—	—	—
S773	**50 Lire** 2.1.1864; 1.7.1874. Italia head in oval at left. Similar to 20 Lire, #S772. Printer: BWC. Rare.	—	—	—
S774	**50 Lire** 2.1.1880. Italia head in oval at left. Similar to #S773 but larger size. Printer: BWC. Rare.	—	—	—
S775	**100 Lire** 2.1.1864; 1.7.1874. Italia head in oval at left. Similar to 20 Lire, #S772. Printer: BWC. Rare.	—	—	—
S776	**100 Lire** 2.1.1880. Italia head in oval at left. Similar to #S775 but larger size. Printer: BWC.	1500.	4500.	13,500.
S777	**200 Lire** 2.1.1864. Italia head in oval at left. Similar to 20 Lire, #S772. Printer: BWC. Rare.	—	—	—
S778	**200 Lire** 2.1.1880. Italia head in oval at left. Similar to #S777 but larger size. Printer: BWC. Rare.	—	—	—
S779	**500 Lire** 2.1.1868; 1.7.1874. Black. Back: Arms. Paper: Peach. Printer: BWC. Rare.	—	—	—
S780	**500 Lire** 2.1.1880. Black. Similar to #S779 but larger size. Back: Arms. Paper: Peach. Printer: BWC. Rare.	—	—	—
S781	**1000 Lire** 2.1.1864. Printer: BWC. Proof. Unique.	—	—	—
S782	**5000 Lire** 2.1.1864. Printer: BWC. (2 known.) Rare.	—	—	—

Banca Romana

1872; 1890 Issue

		VG	VF	UNC
S791	**50 Centesimi** 1872. Black on violet underprint. Italia at right. Back: One head at left. Printer: BWC.	20.00	60.00	175.
S792	**1 Lira** 1872. Black on brown underprint. Italia at left. Back: One head at center. Printer: BWC.	25.00	75.00	225.

		Good	Fine	XF
S793	**2 Lire** ND. Cameo portrait woman at upper center. Printer: A.B.C. Proof.	—	—	—
S794	**5 Lire** 1872. Black on orange underprint. Italia at lower left, wolf with twins at bottom center, arms at right. Back: Green. No heads. Printer: A.B.C.	150.	500.	1500.
S795	**10 Lire** 1872. Black on green underprint. Similar to #S273. Back: Brown. No heads. Printer: A.B.C.	125.	450.	1500.
S796	**20 Lire** 1872. Brown on orange underprint. Italia at left, Roma at right. Back: Green. Three heads. Rare.	—	—	—
S797	**25 Lire** 1883. Black on orange underprint. Like #S281. Back: Red.	60.00	180.	550.
S798	**50 Lire** 1872; 1890. Black on green underprint. Portrait Italia and arms at upper left, wolf with twins at center, portrait Roma and arms at upper right. Back: Brown. Six heads. Paper: Yellow.	45.00	140.	450.
S799	**100 Lire** 1872-90. Blue on green underprint. Portrait Italia at left, arms at upper center, wolf with twins at lower center, portrait Roma at right. Back: Green. Six heads. Paper: Yellow.	275.	750.	2250.
S800	**200 Lire** 1872-90. Blue on orange underprint. Portrait Italia at left, arms at upper center, wolf with twins at lower center, portrait Roma at right. Back: Red. Six heads. Paper: Light green.	450.	1500.	4500.
S801	**500 Lire** 1872-90. Blue on orange underprint. Portrait Italia at left, arms at upper center, wolf with twins at lower center, portrait Roma at right. Back: Green. Seven heads, eight arms. Paper: Cream.	600.	2500.	—
S802	**1000 Lire** 1872-90. Blue on brown underprint. Portrait Italia at left, arms at upper center, wolf with twins at lower center, portrait Roma at right. Back: Red. Ten heads, eight arms. Paper: Cream.	1500.	—	—

Banco di Napoli

1866 Fedi di Credito - Provisional Cash Receipt Issue

		Good	Fine	XF
S811	**1 Lira** 1866; 1867. Red. Embossed seal. Uniface. Watermark: Design.	120.	350.	1150.
S812	**2 Lire** 1867. Green. Embossed seal. Uniface. Watermark: Design.	120.	350.	1150.
S813	**5 Lire** 1866-67. Blue. Embossed seal. Uniface. Watermark: Design.	150.	450.	1350.
S814	**10 Lire** 1866. Black. Embossed seal. Uniface. Watermark: Design.	150.	450.	1350.

1867-70 Fedi di Credito - Regular Cash Receipt Issues

		Good	Fine	XF
S815	**50 Centesimi** 1868; 1873. Black. Paper: White thin.	15.00	45.00	125.
S816	**1 Lira** 3.9.1868. Black. Paper: Red thin.	150.	450.	1500.
S817	**1 Lira** 1.1.1867; 1.6.1867. Black on light blue underprint. 3 signatures. Back: Light blue.	120.	350.	1150.
S818	**1 Lira** 1.7.1867-1.12.1867. Like #S997 but with 2 signatures.	120.	350.	1150.
S819	**1 Lira** 1.5.1869. Black on blue underprint.	150.	450.	1500.
S820	**1 Lira** 1.10.1870; 1.5.1874. Black on blue underprint.	30.00	100.	300.
S821	**2 Lire** ND (1867). Black on green underprint. Paper: White.	225.	675.	2000.
S822	**5 Lire** ND (1867). Black on red-rose underprint.	300.	900.	2750.
S823	**5 Lire** 1868. Black on rose underprint.	300.	900.	2750.
S824	**5 Lire** 1.5.1869. Black on light rose underprint. Back: Maroon.	300.	900.	2750.
S825	**5 Lire** 1870-73. Black on brown underprint. Back: Brown.	75.00	350.	1150.
S826	**10 Lire** ND (1867). Black on green underprint. Horse at left and right. 3 signatures. Rare.	—	—	—
S827	**10 Lire** 1868-69. Black on light green underprint. Horse at left and right.	300.	1500.	4500.
S828	**10 Lire** 1870-72. Brown and blue. Horse at left and right. Rare.	—	—	—
S829	**20 Lire** ND (1867). Black on light red underprint. Horse at left and right. Rare.	—	—	—
S830	**20 Lire** 1868. Black on red underprint. Horse at left and right. Rare.	—	—	—
S831	**20 Lire** 1869-72. Black on rose underprint. Horse at left and right. Rare.	—	—	—
S832	**50 Lire** ND (1867). Black on rose underprint. Horse at left and right. Rare.	—	—	—
S833	**50 Lire** 1868. Black on light rose underprint. Horse at left and right. Rare.	—	—	—
S834	**50 Lire** 1869-76. Black on red underprint. Horse at left and right. Rare.	—	—	—
S835	**100 Lire** ND (1867). Green and rose. Horse at left and right. Rare.	—	—	—
S836	**100 Lire** 1868. Light green and rose. Rare.	—	—	—
S837	**100 Lire** 1869; 1872. Black, green and blue on peach underprint. Two female heads at left and reverse image at right. Back: Green. Rare.	—	—	—
S838	**250 Lire** 1.7.1867. Black on green, yellow and red-brown underprint. Portrait Italia at left and reverse image at right. Back: Gray-green. Paper: Yellow. Unique.	—	—	—
S839	**250 Lire** 1.11.1869. Black on yellow and blue underprint. Portrait Leonardo da Vinci at left, portrait Art at right. Rare.	—	—	—
S840	**500 Lire** 1.7.1867. Black on light green and rose-brown underprint. Italia at left and right. Rare.	—	—	—
S841	**500 Lire** 1.11.1869-1.11.1870. Black on green and red-brown underprint. Italia at left and at right. Rare.	—	—	—

Number	Description	Good	Fine	XF
S842 1000 Lire	1.11.1869-1.11.1870. Green and brown. Portrait Galileo at left, portrait Flavo Gioia at right. Horse at each corner of center design. Back: Red. Proof. Rare.	—	—	—

1877-1905 Regular Bank Notes Issues

Number	Description	Good	Fine	XF
S843 25 Lire	1.8.1883. Black and brown. Portrait Cavour at left. Back: Brown. Two Mercury heads.	275.	825.	2450.
S844 50 Lire	29.1.1877-1.6.1879. Black on red underprint. Horse at left and right. Back: Red and green. Printer: BWC.	325.	1000.	3500.
S845 50 Lire	6.9.1881. Brown and black. Portraits of Galileo at left, G. Manna at right. Back: Brown.	90.00	275.	1000.
S846 50 Lire	1896; 1903. Green. Industry with caduceus and book at right. Back: Violet and green. Mercury at left and right.	75.00	225.	675.
S847 100 Lire	29.1.1877; 18.8.1880. Brown on blue-cream underprint. Portrait woman at left, mirror image at right. Back: Purple and green. Printer: BWC.	375.	1500.	4500.
S848 100 Lire	6.9.1881. Green and black. Portraits of Leonardo Da Vinci at left, King Vittorio Emanuele II at right. Back: Green.	150.	450.	1500.
S849 100 Lire	30.6.1896; 22.10.1903. Black on red-brown underprint. Agriculture with sickle and corn at right. Back: Brown and red. Woman at left and right.	135.	400.	1200.
S850 200 Lire	1877; 1883. Black on red rose underprint. Portrait Leonardo da Vinci at left, woman at right. Back: Dark green. Paper: Red. Printer: BWC. Rare.	—	—	—
S851 500 Lire	1877; 1885. Black on blue underprint. Portrait Italia at left and reverse image at right. Back: Green and blue-violet.	600.	1800.	5000.
S852 500 Lire	1896; 1905. Black on rose and yellow underprint. Portrait Leonardo da Vinci at left. Back: Green-violet.	900.	3000.	—
S853 1000 Lire	1877; 1885. Black on rose and creme underprint. Portrait Galileo at left, F. Gioia at right. Back: Green and red.	1200.	4500.	—
S854 1000 Lire	2.3.1896; 22.10.1903. Black on violet-brown underprint. Portrait Galileo at left, horse at each corner of center design. Rare.	—	—	—

1908-21 Issues

		VG	VF	UNC
S855 25 Lire	17.8.1918; 4.6.1919. Black on gray and blue underprint. Arms at left. Back: Green-gray.	150.	450.	1350.
S856 50 Lire	1909-21. Black on blue-gray underprint. Portrait S. Rosa at lower left. Back: Dark blue. Portrait Minerva at lower right.	100.	300.	900.
S857 100 Lire	1908-21. Black on blue underprint. Portrait T. Tasso at left. Back: Red-brown. Classic head of Platone/Dionysius at right.	125.	375.	1150.
S858 500 Lire	1909-21. Black on green-gray underprint. Portrait G. Filangieri at left. Back: Brown. Medusa at right.	125.	375.	1200.
S859 1000 Lire	1909; 1921. Black on lilac and gray underprint. Portrait G. Vico at left. Back: Dark green. Head of Heraclea at right.	150.	450.	1350.

Banco di Sicilia

Banco Regio

1866 Polizzini di Cassa Provisional Issue

Number	Description	Good	Fine	XF
S861 2 Lire	1866. Red and black. Embossed seal. Uniface. Watermark: Design.			
	a. White paper.	450.	1500.	—
	b. Blue paper.	450.	2000.	—
S862 3 Lire	1866. Embossed seal. Uniface. Watermark: Design.			
	a. White paper.	600.	1800.	—
	b. Light blue paper. Rare.	—	—	—
S863 5 Lire	1866. Embossed seal. Uniface. Watermark: Design.			
	a. White paper.	450.	2000.	—
	b. Light blue paper. Rare.	—	—	—
S864 6 Lire	1866. Embossed seal. Uniface. Watermark: Design.			
	a. White paper. Rare.	—	—	—
	b. Light blue paper. Rare.	—	—	—
S865 7 Lire	1866. Black. Embossed seal. Uniface. Watermark: Design.			
	a. White paper. Rare.	—	—	—
	b. Light blue paper. Rare.	—	—	—
S866 8 Lire	1866. Embossed seal. Uniface. Watermark: Design.			
	a. White paper. Rare.	—	—	—
	b. Light blue paper. Rare.	—	—	—
S867 9 Lire	1866. Black. Embossed seal. Uniface. Watermark: Design.			
	a. White paper. Rare.	—	—	—
	b. Light blue paper. Rare.	—	—	—
S868 10 Lire	1866. Embossed seal. Uniface. Watermark: Design.			
	a. White paper.	750.	2250.	—
	b. Light blue paper. Rare.	—	—	—

1866 Tesoreria Provinciale di Palermo Provisional Issue

Number	Description	Good	Fine	XF
S869 2 Lire	1866. Green and black. Black seal *Cassa di Palermo Ore e Argento.* Watermark: Design.			
	a. White paper.	450.	1500.	—
	b. Light blue paper. Rare.	—	—	—
S870 5 Lire	1866. Green and black. Black seal *Cassa di Palermo Ore e Argento.* Watermark: Design.			
	a. White paper.	550.	1750.	—
	b. Light blue paper. Rare.	—	—	—
S871 10 Lire	1866. Black seal *Cassa di Palermo Ore e Argento.* Watermark: Design.			
	a. White paper.	375.	1150.	3450.
	b. Light blue paper. Rare.	—	—	—

1866 Fedi di Credito Provisional Issue

Number	Description	Good	Fine	XF
S872 2 Lire	1866; 1867. Black. Printed seal *Cassa oro e argento di Palermo* and embossed seal. Watermark: Design.	550.	1500.	—
S873 3 Lire	1866; 1867. Black. Printed seal *Cassa oro e argento di Palermo* and embossed seal. Watermark: Design.	600.	1800.	—
S874 5 Lire	1866; 1867. Black. Printed seal *Cassa oro e argento di Palermo* and embossed seal. Watermark: Design.	425.	1275.	—

1867; 1868 Polizzini di Cassa Provisional Issue

Number	Description	Good	Fine	XF
S875 2 Lire	1867. Blue-green. Embossed seal. Watermark: Design.			
	a. Palermo branch.	550.	1650.	—
	b. Messina branch. Rare.	—	—	—
S876 3 Lire	1867-69. Blue-green. Embossed seal. Watermark: Design. Rare.	—	—	—
S877 5 Lire	1868. Blue-green. Embossed seal. Watermark: Design. Rare.	—	—	—

1868 Fedi di Credito Issue

Number	Description	Good	Fine	XF
S878 1 Lira	3.9.1868. Black on blue underprint. Ceres Agriculture at left, portrait Italia at lower right. Back: Blue. Arms of Savoy at center.	375.	1100.	3300.

1870; 1876 Fedi di Credito Issue

Number	Description	Good	Fine	XF
S879 1 Lira	27.4.1870. Black on blue underprint. Red seal with bank arms at top center. Back: Blue. Printer: BWC (without imprint).	75.00	225.	675.
S880 2 Lire	24.7.1870. Dark blue on orange underprint. Red seal with bank arms at top center. Back: Orange. Printer: BWC (without imprint).	125.	375.	1150.
S881 5 Lire	24.7.1870. Black on blue underprint. Red seal with bank arms at top center. Back: Blue. Printer: BWC (without imprint).	300.	900.	2750.
S882 10 Lire	24.7.1870. Black on tan underprint. Red seal with bank arms at top center. Back: Tan. Bank arms at top center, three-leg design (triquetra) at left and right. Printer: BWC (without imprint).	300.	900.	2750.
S883 20 Lire	27.4.1870. Dark blue on orange and green underprint. Red seal with bank arms at top center. Back: Green. Bank arms at top center, three-leg design (triquetra) at left and right. Printer: BWC (without imprint). Rare.			
S884 50 Lire	24.7.1870; 2.1.1875. Black on green and rose underprint. State arms at upper center. Red seal with bank arms at top center. Back: Red. Bank arms at top center, three-leg design (triquetra) at left and right. Printer: BWC (without imprint).	150.	450.	1350.
S885 100 Lire	27.4.1870; 2.1.1875. Black on tan underprint. State arms at upper center. Red seal with bank arms at top center. Back: Tan. Bank arms at top center, three-leg design (triquetra) at left and right. Printer: BWC (without imprint).	225.	675.	2000.
S886 200 Lire	1870; 1876. Black on azure and peach underprint. State arms at upper center. Red seal with bank arms at top center. Back: Blue-green. Bank arms at top center, three-leg design (triquetra) at left and right. Printer: BWC (without imprint).	425.	1275.	3750.
S887 500 Lire	1870; 1876. Black on brown underprint. Neptune at left, Italia at right. Red seal with bank arms at top center. Back: Brown. Printer: BWC (without imprint).	750.	2250.	6750.
S888 1000 Lire	1870; 1876. Brown on azure and creme underprint. Red seal with bank arms at top center. Back: Brown on azure underprint. Printer: BWC (without imprint). Rare.	—	—	—

1879; 1892 Bank Notes Issues

Number	Description	Good	Fine	XF
S889 25 Lire	17.5.1883; 25.2.1891. Black and blue on tan underprint. Neptune at left. Back: Tan. Italia head at center. Printer: BWC.	350.	1150.	3450.
S890 50 Lire	11.4.1879; 5.7.1892. Black and green on rose underprint. Red seal with bank arms at top center. Back: Red and green. Printer: BWC (without imprint).	400.	1200.	3600.
S891 100 Lire	11.4.1879; 5.7.1892. Black and red on creme underprint. Red seal with bank arms at top center. Back: Tan. Printer: BWC (without imprint).	250.	750.	2250.
S892 200 Lire	23.9.1879. Black and azure on creme underprint. Red seal with bank arms at top center. Back: Orange and green. Printer: BWC (without imprint). Rare.	—	—	—

	Good	Fine	XF
S893 500 Lire 1879; 1892. Black and brown on blue underprint. Neptune at left, portrait Italia at right. Red seal with bank arms at top center. Back: Brown and blue. Printer: BWC (without imprint). Rare.	—	—	—
S894 1000 Lire 1879; 1892. Black and green on red underprint. Neptune at left, portrait Italia at right. Red seal with bank arms at top center. Back: Green and red. Printer: BWC (without imprint). Rare.	—	—	—

1896; 1920 Issues

	Good	Fine	XF
S895 25 Lire 21.2.1918; 6.8.1918. Black and olive on lilac underprint. Red medallic head of Italia seal at bottom center. Neptune statue at left. Back: Red-brown. Seven classic heads in circle at center. Printer: *STADERINI* (vertical imprint at left).	75.00	225.	675.
S896 50 Lire 1897; 1915. Black and brown on creme underprint. Red medallic head of Italia seal at bottom center. Neptune statue at left. Back: Gray and rose. Seven classic heads in circle at center and triquetra at right. Printer: *STADERINI* (vertical imprint at left).	25.00	75.00	225.
S897 100 Lire 1896; 1915. Black and gray-blue on light gray underprint. Red medallic head of Italia seal at bottom center. Neptune statue at left. Back: Blue and gray. Seven classic heads in circle at center and triquetra at right. Printer: *STADERINI* (vertical imprint at left).	30.00	120.	400.
S898 500 Lire 1897; 1919. Black and blue on brown underprint. Red medallic head of Italia seal at bottom center. Neptune statue at left. Back: Brown. Seven classic heads in circle at center and triquetra at right. Printer: *STADERINI* (vertical imprint at left).	135.	400.	1200.
S899 1000 Lire 1897; 1920. Black and brown on gray underprint. Red medallic head of Italia seal at bottom center. Neptune statue at left. Back: Azure. Seven classic heads in circle at center and triquetra at right. Printer: *STADERINI* (vertical imprint at left).	200.	600.	1800.

Credito Agrario

Agrarian Credit Banks and Associations

Cassa di Risparmio di Bologna

1871; 1887 Issue

	Good	Fine	XF
S901 30 Lire 5.3.1871. Black on creme underprint. Re head at left. Back: Multicolor. Watermark: Design. Printer: BWC.			
a. Issued note. Reported not confirmed.	—	—	—
s. Specimen.	—	Unc	2000.
S902 40 Lire 5.3.1871. Black on red underprint. Back: Multicolor. Watermark: Design. Printer: BWC.			
a. Issued note. Reported not confirmed.	—	—	—
s. Specimen.	—	Unc	2000.
S903 50 Lire 5.3.1871. Black on rose underprint. Head of L. Malvasia at left. Back: Multicolor. Watermark: Design. Printer: BWC.			
a. Issued note. Reported not confirmed.	—	—	—
s. Specimen.	—	Unc	2000.
S904 100 Lire 1874; 1887. Black on red underprint. Head of P. Crescenzio at left. Back: Multicolor. Watermark: Design. Printer: BWC.			
a. Issued note. Rare.	—	—	—
s. Specimen.	—	Unc	2000.

Banca Agricola Nazionale

1870 Issue

	Good	Fine	XF
S905 30 Lire 1.6.1870. Black and rose. Bust of Italia at upper center, two women reclining with crowned shield below. Printer: BWC.			
a. Issued note. Reported not confirmed.	—	—	—
s. Specimen.	—	Unc	2000.
S906 40 Lire 1.6.1870. Black on green underprint. Bust of Italia at upper center, two women reclining with crowned shield below. Printer: BWC.			
a. Issued note. Reported not confirmed.	—	—	—
s. Specimen.	—	Unc	2000.
S907 50 Lire 1.6.1870. Black and brown. Bust of Italia at upper center, two women reclining with crowned shield below. Printer: BWC.			
a. Issued note. Reported not confirmed.	—	—	—
s. Specimen.	—	Unc	2000.
S908 100 Lire 1.6.1870. Black and red. Bust of Italia at upper center, two women reclining with crowned shield below. Printer: BWC.			
a. Issued note. Reported not confirmed.	—	—	—
s. Specimen.	—	Unc	2000.
S909 250 Lire 1.6.1870. Black on brown underprint. Bust of Italia at upper center, two women reclining with crowned shield below. Printer: BWC.			
a. Issued note. Reported not confirmed.	—	—	—
s. Specimen.	—	Unc	2000.
S910 500 Lire 1.6.1870. Black and azure on rose underprint. Bust of Italia at upper center, two women reclining with crowned shield below. Printer: BWC.			
a. Issued note. Reported not confirmed.	—	—	—
s. Specimen.	—	Unc	2500.
S911 1000 Lire 1.6.1870. Black and light amaranth.			
a. Issued note. Reported not confirmed.	—	—	—
s. Specimen. Rare.	—	Unc	2500.

Monte dei Paschi di Siena

1870; 1898 Issue

	Good	Fine	XF
S912 30 Lire 1870; 1898. Black and yellow on creme underprint. Portrait Abate at left, allegorical cherub at right. Back: Green. Printer: BWC. Rare.	—	—	—
S913 40 Lire 1870; 1876. Black and violet. Portrait Abate at left, allegorical cherub at right. Back: Brown. Printer: BWC.			
a. Issued note. Reported not confirmed.	—	—	—
s. Specimen.	—	Unc	2500.

	Good	Fine	XF
S914 50 Lire 1870; 1898. Black on rose underprint. Portrait Abate at left, allegorical cherub at right. Back: Red. Printer: BWC.			
a. Issued note. Rare.	—	—	—
s. Specimen.	—	Unc	2500.
S915 100 Lire 1870; 1898. Black and amaranth on yellow. Portrait Abate at left, allegorical cherub at right. Back: Brown. Printer: BWC.			
a. Issued note. Rare.	—	—	—
s. Specimen.	—	Unc	2500.
S916 200 Lire 1870; 1898. Black on red and blue underprint. Portrait Abate at left, allegorical cherub at right. Back: Red. Printer: BWC. Rare.	—	—	—
S917 500 Lire 1870; 1898. Reported not confirmed.	—	—	—

Biglietti Consorziale For previously listed #S491-S499, refer to Vol. II.

Biglietti Gia' Consorziale For previously listed #S501-S508, refer to Vol. II.

Banca Generale di Roma

1880; 1892 Issue

	Good	Fine	XF
S918 30 Lire 1880; 1892. Black. Two children with bunch of grapes at left, Italia head at right, she-wolf with twins at lower center. Back: Blue. Printer: BWC.	300.	900.	2750.
S919 50 Lire 1880; 1892. Black. Two children with bunch of grapes at left, Italia head at right, she-wolf with twins at lower center. Back: Blue. Printer: BWC. Rare.	—	—	—

Banca Agraria Commerciale di Foggia

1882 Issue

	Good	Fine	XF
S920 30 Lire 2.6.1882. Black on azure and rose underprint. Allegorical child with plow at left, agricultural wagon at left. Printer: BWC. Rare.	—	—	—

Banca Agricola Sarda

1871; 1880 Issue

	Good	Fine	XF
S921 30 Lire 1871-80. Black. Portrait E. d'Arborea at left, portrait Priore at right. Back: Profile head of Italia at left and mirror image at right. Paper: Lilac. Printer: BWC.			
a. Florence. 10.2.1871.	30.00	100.	300.
b. Rome. 1.9.1875.	30.00	100.	300.
c. Oristano. 1870; 1.1.1878; 1880.	15.00	45.00	125.

	Good	Fine	XF
S922 50 Lire 10.12.1871. Black and green. Portrait E. d'Arborea at left, portrait Priore at right. Back: Green. Profile head of Italia at left and mirror image at right. Paper: White. Printer: BWC.	150.	450.	1350.

	Good	Fine	XF
S923 100 Lire 15.1.1872. Dark blue and green. Portrait E. d'Arborea at left, portrait Priore at right. Back: Green. Profile head of Italia at left and mirror image at right. Paper: White. Printer: BWC. Rare.	—	—	—
S924 250 Lire 1.11.1872. Black. Portrait E. d'Arborea at lower center. Back: Green. Paper: Green.			
a. Issued note. Reported not confirmed.	—	—	—
b. Specimen.	—	—	—

Credito Agricolo Industriale Sardo

1874; 1884 Issue

	Good	Fine	XF
S925 30 Lire 1.3.1874. Black and brown. Portrait helmeted Roman warrior at left, agriculture allegory at right. Red seal. Back: Brown. Printer: BWC.	7.50	25.00	80.00
S926 30 Lire 1.1.1884. Black and green on green underprint. Portrait helmeted Roman warrior at left, agriculture allegory at right. Red seal. Back: Green. Printer: BWC.	300.	900.	2750.
S927 50 Lire 1.1.1874. Black and brown. Portrait helmeted Roman warrior at left, agriculture allegory at right. Blue *50*protector at center, with red seal. Back: Brown. Printer: BWC.	15.00	45.00	150.

	Good	Fine	XF
S928 100 Lire 1.1.1874. Black on brown underprint. Portrait helmeted Roman warrior at left, agriculture allegory at right. Red seal. Printer: BWC.	50.00	150.	450.

Commercial Banks - Abusive Issues

Banca del Popolo

1866; 1871 Issue

	Good	Fine	XF
S941 10 Lire 23.11.1867. Black, brown and red. Two reclining allegories flanking crowned shield at top center, coat-of-arms at left and right, bust of Italia at bottom center. Paper: White. Rare.	—	—	—
S942 20 Lire 2.9.1867. Black. Two reclining allegories flanking crowned shield at top center, coat-of-arms at left and right, bust of Italia at bottom center. Paper: White. Rare.	—	—	—
S943 30 Lire 1866; 1871. Black on brown underprint. Two reclining allegories flanking crowned shield at top center, coat-of-arms at left and right, bust of Italia at bottom center. Rare.	—	—	—
S944 50 Lire 1866; 1871. Black on yellow-green underprint. Two reclining allegories flanking crowned shield at top center, coat-of-arms at left and right, bust of Italia at bottom center. Similar to #S943. Rare.	—	—	—
S945 100 Lire 1866; 1871. Black on light green underprint. Two reclining allegories flanking crowned shield at top center, coat-of-arms at left and right, bust of Italia at bottom center. Similar to #S943. Rare.	—	—	—

Monte dei Paschi di Siena

1866; 1871 Issue

	Good	Fine	XF
S951 10 Lire 1866; 1869. Black. Paper: Blue-violet.			
a. Issued note. Rare.	—	—	—
r. Remainder.	—	Unc	750.
S952 25 Lire 1866; 1869. Reported not confirmed.	—	—	—
S953 50 Lire 1866; 1871. Black. Paper: Rose.			
a. Issued note. Rare.	—	—	—
b. Punched hole cancelled.	—	—	600.
S954 100 Lire 1866; 1871. Reported not confirmed.	—	—	—
S955 200 Lire 1866; 1871. Rare.	—	—	—

Banca di Valdinievole in Pescia

1871 ND Issue

	Good	Fine	XF
S961 20 Lire ND (ca.1871). Black and green on brown underprint. Back: Brown.			
a. Issued note. Rare.	—	—	—
r. Remainder.	—	Unc	750.

	Good	Fine	XF
S962 50 Lire			
ND. Reported not confirmed.	—	—	—
S963 100 Lire			
ND. Reported not confirmed.	—	—	—

Banca Italo - Germanica

1871; 1872 Issue

	Good	Fine	XF
S971 5 Lire			
1871; 1872. Black. Heads of Italia and Germania at right. Back: Red and green. Heads of Italia and Germania at right. Printer: BWC.			
a. Issued note. Rare.	—	—	—
r. Remainder.	—	Unc	1250.
S972 10 Lire			
1871; 1872. Black. Tevere bridge at left, Main bridge at right. Back: Green, red and blue. Printer: BWC.			
a. Issued note. Rare.	—	—	—
r. Remainder.	—	Unc	1200.
S973 20 Lire			
1871; 1872. Black. Hadrian's tomb at left, castle at right. Back: Blue and violet. Printer: BWC.			
a. Issued note. Rare.	—	—	—
r. Remainder.	—	Unc	1350.
S974 50 Lire			
1871; 1872. Black. Castle at left, Ducal palace of Venice at right. Back: Prospectus of interest. Printer: BWC.			
a. Issued note. Rare.	—	—	—
r. Remainder.	—	Unc	1250.
S975 100 Lire			
1871; 1872. Black. Standing Italia with shield and baton at left. Back: Prospectus of interest. Printer: BWC.			
a. Issued note. Rare.	—	—	—
r. Remainder.	—	Unc	1350.

	Good	Fine	XF
S976 250 Lire			
1871; 1872. Black. Standing Italia with books and shield at left. Back: Prospectus of interest. Printer: BWC.			
a. Issued note. Rare.	—	—	—
r. Remainder.	—	Unc	1000.
s. Specimen.	—	Unc	1500.
S977 500 Lire			
1871; 1872. Black. Germania with shield and spear at left. Back: Prospectus of interest. Printer: BWC.			
a. Issued note. Rare.	—	—	—
r. Remainder.	—	Unc	1500.

	Good	Fine	XF
S978 1000 Lire			
1871; 1872. Black. Germania and Italia with four cherubs at left. Back: Prospectus of interest. Printer: BWC.			
a. Issued note. Rare.	—	—	—
r. Remainder.	—	Unc	1500.
s. Specimen.	—	Unc	1500.

The Italian Republic, a 700-mile-long peninsula extending into the heart of the Mediterranean Sea, has an area of 301,230 sq. km. and a population of 58.14 million. Captal: Rome. The economy centers about agriculture, manufacturing, forestry and fishing. Machinery, textiles, clothing and motor vehicles are exported.

Italy became a nation-state in 1861 when the regional states of the peninsula, along with Sardinia and Sicily, were united under King Victor Emmanuel II. An era of parliamentary government came to a close in the early 1920s when Benito Mussolini established a Fascist dictatorship. His alliance with Nazi Germany led to Italy's defeat in World War II. A democratic republic replaced the monarchy in 1946 and economic revival followed. Italy was a charter member of NATO and the European Economic Community (EEC). It has been at the forefront of European economic and political unification, joining the Economic and Monetary Union in 1999. Persistent problems include illegal immigration, organized crime, corruption, high unemployment, sluggish economic growth, and the low incomes and technical standards of southern Italy compared with the prosperous north.

RULERS:

Umberto I, 1878-1900
Vittorio Emanuele III, 1900-1946

MONETARY SYSTEM:

1 Lira = 100 Centesimi, to 2001
1 Euro = 100 Cents, 2001-

DECREES:

There are many different dates found on the following notes of the Banca d'Italia. These include ART. DELLA LEGGE (law date) and the more important DECRETO MINISTERIALE (D. M. date). The earliest D.M. date is usually found on the back of the note while later D.M. dates are found grouped together. The actual latest date (of issue) is referred to in the following listings.

PRINTERS:

Further differentiations are made in respect to the printers w/the place name *Roma* or *L'Aquila* (1942-44).

Note: Certain listings encompassing issues circulated by various bank and regional authorities are contained in Volume 1.

Military

REPLACEMENT NOTES:

#M10-M23, asterisk in front of serial number.

Cassa Veneta dei Prestiti

Currency Notes

Buoni di Cassa

	VG	VF	UNC
M1 5 Centesimi			
2.1.19118. Black on blue underprint. Serial # with or without *No.*	.50	1.00	3.00

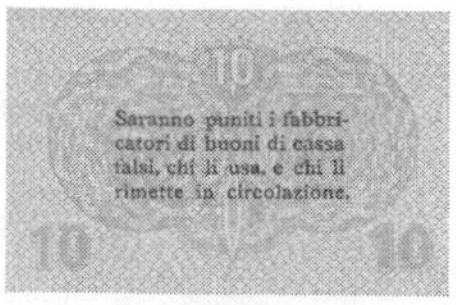

	VG	VF	UNC
M2 10 Centesimi			
2.1.1918. Black on light brown underprint.	.50	1.00	3.00

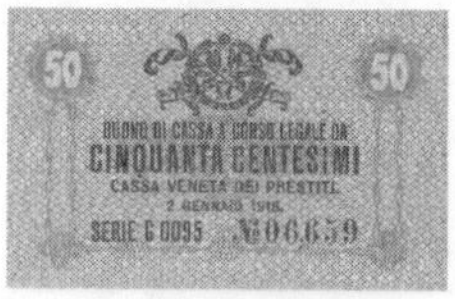

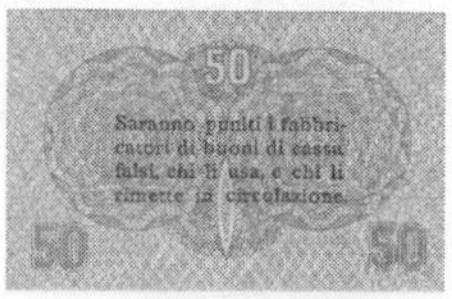

	VG	VF	UNC
M3 50 Centesimi			
2.1.1918. Black on red underprint.	.50	1.00	3.00

		VG	VF	UNC
M4	**1 Lira**			
	2.1.1918. Lilac. *Italia* at left. 2 serial # varieties.	1.00	2.00	4.00
M5	**2 Lire**			
	2.1.1918. Green. *Italia* at left. 3 serial # varieties.	1.00	2.50	5.00

		VG	VF	UNC
M6	**10 Lire**			
	2.1.1918. Blue. *Italia* at left. 2 serial # varieties.	1.50	5.00	10.00

		VG	VF	UNC
M7	**20 Lire**			
	2.1.1918. Red-violet. *Italia* at left. 2 serial # varieties.	3.00	10.00	20.00
M8	**100 Lire**			
	2.1.1918. Brown and green. *Italia* at left.	15.00	50.00	100.
M9	**1000 Lire**			
	2.1.1918. Brown. *Italia* at left.	65.00	175.	650.

Allied Military Currency

Series 1943

REPLACEMENT NOTES:
#M10-M23, asterisk in front of serial number.

		VG	VF	UNC
M10	**1 Lira**			
	1943. Blue and brown.			
	a. *F.*	.20	1.00	5.00
	b. Without *F.*	.20	1.00	5.00
M11	**2 Lire**			
	1943. Violet and brown.			
	a. *F.*	.20	1.00	6.00
	b. Without *F.*	.20	1.00	6.00
M12	**5 Lire**			
	1943. Green and brown.			
	a. *F.*	.30	1.25	12.50
	b. Without *F.*	.30	2.00	15.00

		VG	VF	UNC
M13	**10 Lire**			
	1943. Black and brown.			
	a. *F.*	1.00	7.00	50.00
	b. Without *F.*	1.00	8.00	55.00
M14	**50 Lire**			
	1943. Blue.			
	a. *F.*	2.00	7.50	75.00
	b. Without *F.*	3.00	10.00	85.00
M15	**100 Lire**			
	1943. Violet and blue.			
	a. *F.*	4.00	10.00	100.
	b. Without *F.*	4.00	12.50	125.
M16	**500 Lire**			
	1943. Green and blue.			
	a. *F.*	35.00	150.	600.
	b. Without *F.*	40.00	175.	700.

		VG	VF	UNC
M17	**1000 Lire**			
	1943. Black and blue.			
	a. *F.*	80.00	225.	900.
	b. Without *F.*	75.00	200.	850.

Series of 1943 A

		VG	VF	UNC
M18	**5 Lire**			
	1943. A. Green and brown. Printer: Forbes.			
	a. Serial # prefix/suffix A-A.	.50	1.50	7.50
	b. Serial # prefix/suffix A-B.	.50	1.50	7.50
	s. Specimen perforated: *SPECIMEN.*	—	—	140.
M19	**10 Lire**			
	1943.A. Black and brown. Printer: Forbes.			
	a. Serial # prefix/suffix A-A.	.50	2.00	12.50
	b. Serial # prefix/suffix A-B.	.50	2.00	12.50
	s. Specimen perforated: *SPECIMEN.*	—	—	140.
M20	**50 Lire**			
	1943. A. Blue.			
	a. Serial # prefix/suffix A-A.	2.00	7.00	50.00
	b. Serial # prefix/suffix A-B.	2.00	7.00	50.00
	s. Specimen perforated: *SPECIMEN.*	—	—	175.

M21 100 Lire	VG	VF	UNC
19843. A. Violet and blue.			
a. Serial # prefix/suffix A-A.	2.00	7.00	50.00
b. Serial # prefix/suffix A-B.	2.00	7.00	50.00
c. Serial # prefix/suffix A-C.	2.00	7.00	50.00
s. Specimen perforated: *SPECIMEN.*	—	—	150.
M22 500 Lire			
1943. A. Green and blue.			
a. Issued note.	25.00	75.00	500.
s. Specimen perforated: *SPECIMEN.*	—	—	850.
M23 1000 Lire			
1943. A. Black and blue.			
a. Issued note.	20.00	70.00	450.
s. Specimen perforated: *SPECIMEN.*	—	—	850.

Governo delle Isole Italiane dell'Egeo

Dodecanese

Government of Italian Islands in the Aegean

1944 Issue

M24 50 Lire	Good	Fine	XF
15.4.1944-21.4.1944. Green and brown on yellow underprint. Wolf with Romulus and Remus at center, island fortress in background.	1000.	3500.	5500.

M25 100 Lire	Good	Fine	XF
15.4.1944-21.4.1944. Blue and brown on yellow underprint. Stag at left.	400.	1300.	3000.

CAUTION: Forgeries have appeared on the Italian market. They may be recognized by the bad quality printing, especially the signature and the missing yellow unpt.

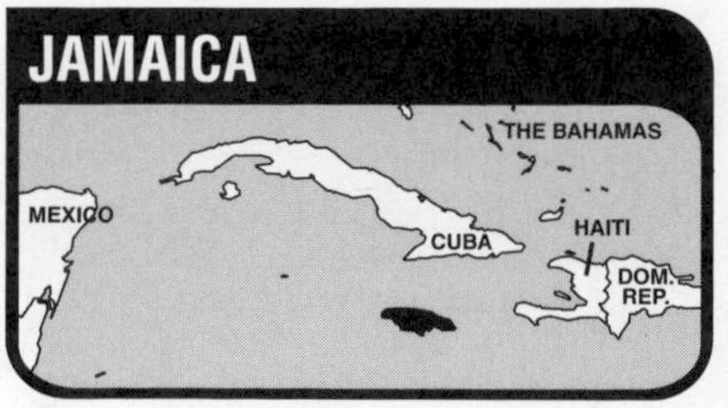

Jamaica, a member of the British Commonwealth situated in the Caribbean Sea 90 miles south of Cuba, has an area of 10,991 sq. km. and a population of 2.8 million. Capital: Kingston. The economy is founded chiefly on mining, tourism and agriculture. Alumina, bauxite, sugar, rum and molasses are exported.

The island - discovered by Christopher Columbus in 1494 - was settled by the Spanish early in the 16th century. The native Taino Indians, who had inhabited Jamaica for centuries, were gradually exterminated and replaced by African slaves. England seized the island in 1655 and established a plantation economy d on sugar, cocoa, and coffee. The abolition of slavery in 1834 freed a quarter million slaves, many of whom became small farmers. Jamaica gradually obtained increasing independence from Britain, and in 1958 it joined other British Caribbean colonies in forming the Federation of the West Indies. Jamaica gained full independence when it withdrew from the Federation in 1962. Deteriorating economic conditions during the 1970s led to recurrent violence as rival gangs affiliated with the major political parties evolved into powerful organized crime networks involved in international drug smuggling and money laundering. Violent crime, drug trafficking, and poverty pose significant challenges to the government today. Nonetheless, many rural and resort areas remain relatively safe and contribute substantially to the economy.

Jamaica is a member of the Commonwealth of Nations. Elizabeth II is the Head of State, as Queen of Jamaica.

A decimal standard currency system was adopted on Sept. 8, 1969.

RULERS:

British

MONETARY SYSTEM:

1 Shilling = 12 Pence
1 Pound = 20 Shillings to 1969
1 Dollar = 100 Cents, 1969-

Note: Certain listings encompassing issues circulated by various bank and regional authorities are contained in Volume 1.

British Administration

Island Treasury

1822 Issue

	Good	Fine	XF
S101 5 Pounds			
12.1822.	—	—	—
S102 10 Pounds			
12.1822.	—	—	—
S103 20 Pounds			
12.1822.	—	—	—
S104 50 Pounds			
12.1822.	—	—	—
S105 100 Pounds			
12.1822. Proof.	—	—	—

1840's Issue

S106 1 Pound	Good	Fine	XF
184x. Proof.	—	—	—

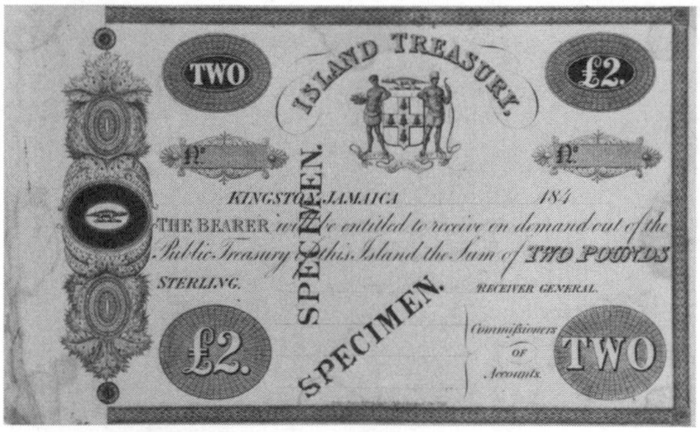

	Good	Fine	XF
S107 2 Pounds			
184x. Arms at upper center. Proof. Handstamped: *SPECIMEN.*	—	—	—
S108 3 Pounds			
184x. Proof.	—	—	—
S109 4 Pounds			
184x. Proof.	—	—	—
S110 10 Pounds			
184x. Proof.	—	—	—
S111 50 Pounds			
184x. Proof.	—	—	—
S112 100 Pounds			
184x. Proof.	—	—	—

Bank of Jamaica

1830's Issue

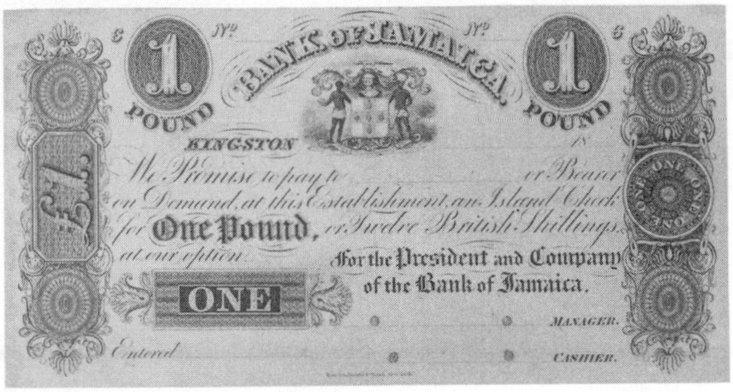

		Good	Fine	XF
S121	**1 Pound**			
	18xx. Arms at upper center. Proof, punched hole cancelled.	—	Unc	5000.
S122	**2 Pounds**			
	18xx. Arms at upper center. Proof, punch hole cancelled.	—	—	—
S123	**4 Pounds**			
	18xx. Proof.	—	—	—
S124	**10 Pounds**			
	18xx. Proof.	—	—	—

NOTE: Additional denominations require confirmation.

Bank of Nova Scotia

1900; 1919-20 Issue

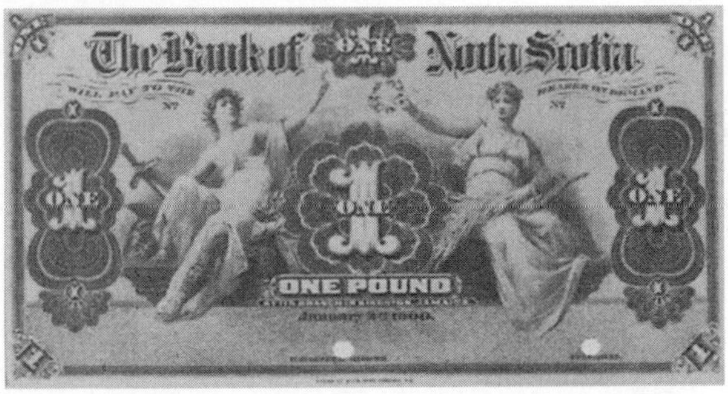

		Good	Fine	XF
S131	**1 Pound**			
	1900; 1919-20. Black on green and pale yellow underprint. Value between woman with helmet and sword at left; woman with palm branch and wreath at right. Back: Green. Printer: ABNC.			
	a. Signature. J. Y. Payzant. 2.1.1919. Rare.	—	—	—
	p. Proof.	—	Unc	2500.
	s. Specimen.	—	Unc	3000.

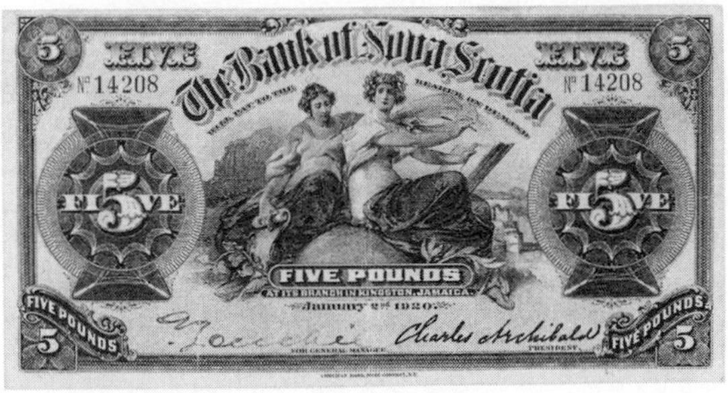

		Good	Fine	XF
S132	**5 Pounds**			
	1900; 1920. Black on orange and pale yellow underprint. Two women with scroll and book at center. Back: Brown. Printer: ABNC.			
	a. Signature. J. Y. Payzant. 2.1.1900. Rare.	—	—	—
	b. Signature. C. Archibald. 2.1.1920.	450.	900.	—
	p. Proof.	—	Unc	2500.

1930 Issue

		Good	Fine	XF
S139	**1 Pound**			
	2.1.1930. Black on green, yellow, and blue underprint. Woman seated among produce at center. 2 signature varieties. Back: Green. Printer: CBNC.	200.	600.	—

Barclays Bank (Dominion, Colonial and Overseas)

1926-35 Issue

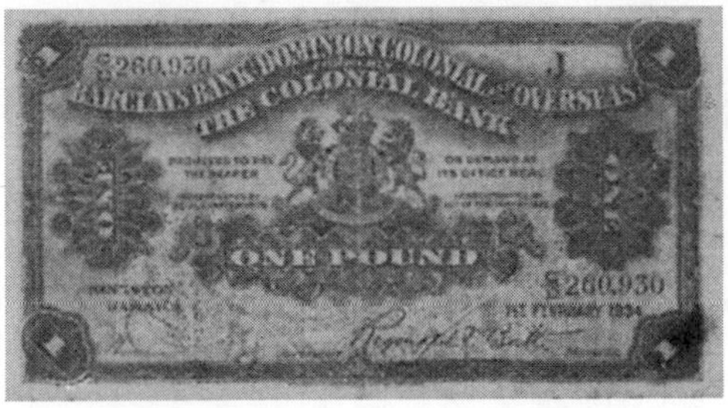

		Good	Fine	XF
S141	**1 Pound**			
	1926-35. Black on orange underprint. Arms at center. Serial # prefix C. Hand signed. Printer: BWC.			
	a. 1.9.1926; 15.12.1927; 1.6.1929.	525.	1050.	—
	b. 1.4.1932; 1.2.1934; 1.1.1935.	450.	900.	—
	s. Specimen.	—	Unc	3000.
S142	**5 Pounds**			
	1.9.1926. Black on yellow underprint. Arms at center. Serial # prefix C. Hand signed. Printer: BWC. Rare.	—	—	—
S143	**10 Pounds**			
	1.9.1926. Black on green underprint. Arms at center. Serial # prefix C. Hand signed. Printer: BWC. Rare.	—	—	—

1937; 1940 Issue

		Good	Fine	XF
S146	**1 Pound**			
	1937-41. Black on red underprint. Arms at right. Serial # prefix D. Printer: BWC.			
	a. 1.1.1937.	375.	1125.	—
	b. 1.5.1937.	325.	975.	—
	c. 1.2.1938.	300.	900.	—
	d. 1.3.1939.	—	—	—
	e. 1.2.1941.	275.	825.	—
S147	**5 Pounds**			
	1.3.1940. Black on orange underprint. Arms at right. Serial # prefix D. Printer: BWC.	1100.	3300.	—

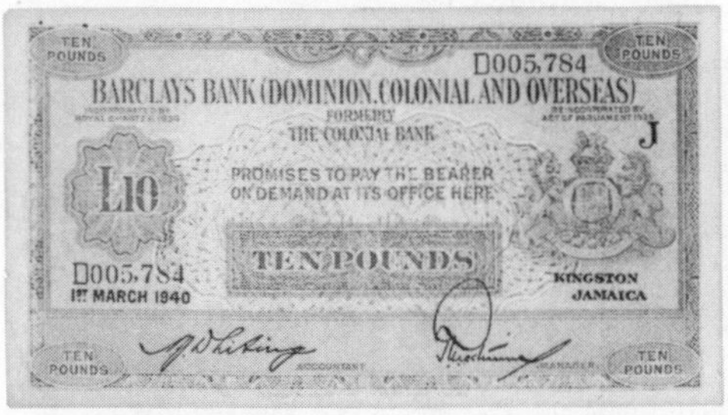

S148 **10 Pounds**	Good	Fine	XF
1937-40. Black on blue and mauve underprint. Arms at right. Serial # prefix D. Printer: BWC.			
a. 1.1.1937.	750.	2250.	—
b. 1.5.1937.	600.	1800.	—
c. 1.3.1940.	150.	300.	900.

Canadian Bank of Commerce

1921 Issue

S151 **1 Pound**	Good	Fine	XF
1.3.1921. Black on orange underprint. Three allegorical figures at center. No letter designation. Back: Brown. Mercury at center with allegorical women at left and right of bank arms at center. Printer: ABNC.			
a. Issued note.	—	—	—
p. Proof.	—	Unc	2500.
S151A **1 Pound**			
1.3.1921. Black on orange underprint. Three allegorical figures at center. Like #S151, but letter designation *B*. Back: Brown. Mercury at center with allegorical women at left and right of bank arms at center. Printer: CBN.	—	—	—

S152 **5 Pounds**	Good	Fine	XF
1.3.1921. Black on green and red underprint. Woman sitting at center. Back: Green. Mercury at center with allegorical women at left and right of bank arms at center. Printer: ABNC Ottawa.			
a. Issued note.	—	—	—
p. Proof.	—	—	—

1938 Issue

S156 **1 Pound**	Good	Fine	XF
1.6.1938. Black on orange underprint. Three allegorical figures at center. Similar to #S151A. Back: Brown. Mercury and allegorical woman at left and right of bank arms at center. Printer: CBN.	—	—	—

S157 **5 Pounds**	Good	Fine	XF
1.6.1938. Black. Woman sitting at center. Like #S152. Back: Mercury and allegorical woman at left and right of bank arms at center. Specimen.	—	Unc	2500.

NOTE: #S157 was prepared for issue, but all were withheld from circulation and destroyed.

Colonial Bank

1840's Issue

S161 **1 Pound 5 Shillings Sterling = 6 Dollars or 2 Pounds 1 Shilling 8 Pence**	Good	Fine	XF
10.3.1840. (ca.1838-83). Arms at upper center. Rare.	—	—	—

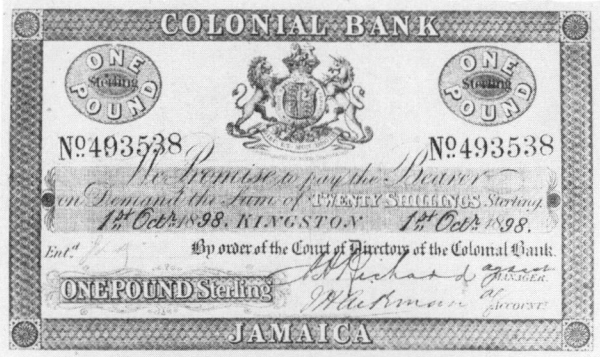

S162 **5 Pounds Sterling = 24 Dollars or 8 Pounds 6 Shillings 8Pence**	Good	Fine	XF
ca.1838-1.1.1883. Arms at upper center. Rare.	—	—	—

1885 Issue

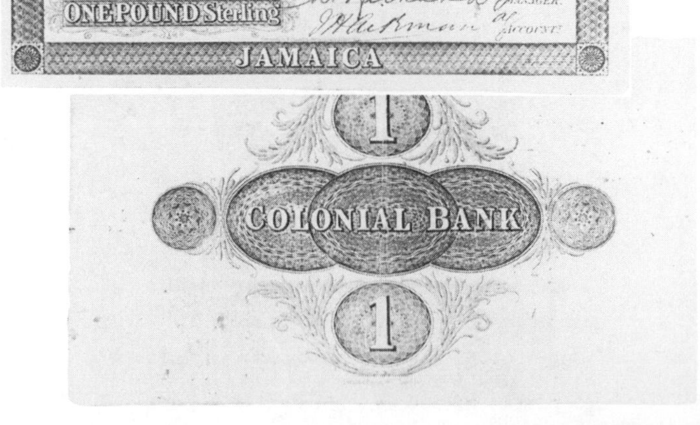

		Good	Fine	XF
S171	**1 Pound** 1.1.1885; 1.1.1896; 1.10.1898; 1.10.1902. Black. Supported royal arms at upper center. Printer: PBC.	1350.	4000.	—

1907 Issue

Issued after 1900. Notes have serial # prefix A.

		Good	Fine	XF
S181	**1 Pound** 1.1.1907; 1.5.1912. Black on orange underprint. Supported royal arms at upper center with large curved *COLONIAL BANK* in ornate underprint. Rare.	—	—	—
S182	**5 Pounds** 1907. Black on yellow underprint. Supported royal arms at upper center with large curved *COLONIAL BANK* in ornate underprint. Rare.	—	—	—

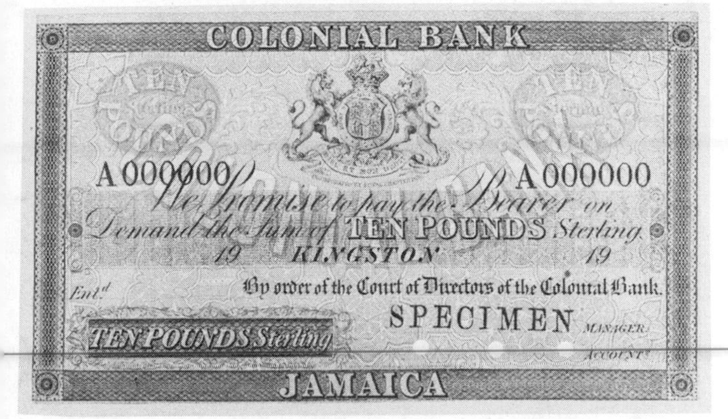

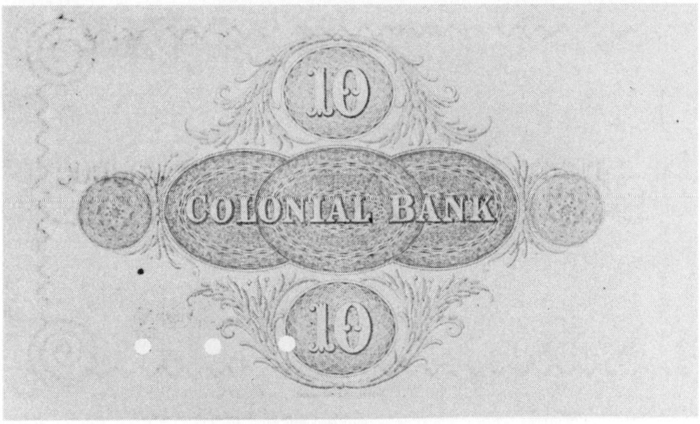

		Good	Fine	XF
S183	**10 Pounds** 1907. Black on green and orange underprint. Supported royal arms at upper center with large curved *COLONIAL BANK* in ornate underprint. Rare.	—	—	—

1917-20 Issue

		Good	Fine	XF
S191	**1 Pound** 1.11.1917; 1.4.1925. Supported royal arms at upper center, with serial # prefix B and large *J* (Jamaica) at upper right.			
	a. Issued note.	1100.	3300.	—
	s. Specimen.	—	Unc	3500.
S192	**5 Pounds** 1.11.1920. Supported royal arms at upper center, with serial # prefix B and large *J* (Jamaica) at upper right.			
	a. Issued note.	—	—	—
	s. Specimen.	—	Unc	3500.
S193	**10 Pounds** 1.6.1919; 1.4.1925. Supported royal arms at upper center, with serial # prefix B and large *J* (Jamaica) at upper right. Rare.	—	—	—

London and Colonial Bank Limited

1800's Issue

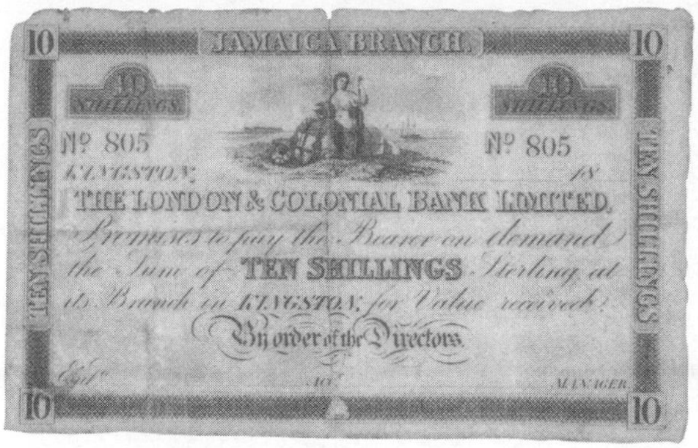

		Good	Fine	XF
S201	**10 Shillings** 18xx. Seated allegory of Commerce at upper center. Printer: Batho. Remainder.	—	—	—

Planters Bank

1839 Issue

		Good	Fine	XF
S206	**1 Pound** 1.11.1839. Blue. Rare.	—	—	—

1844 Issue

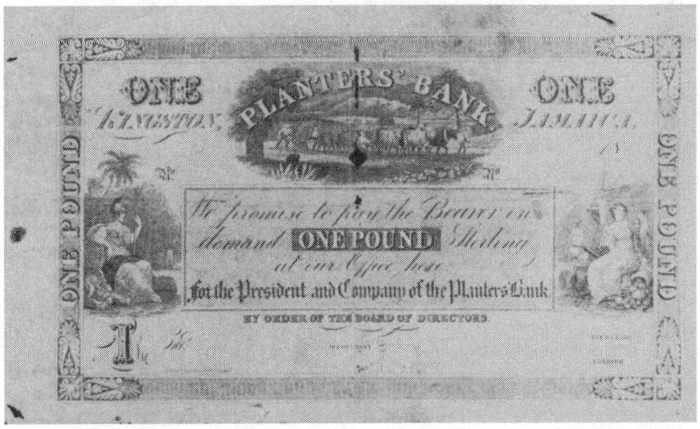

		Good	Fine	XF
S211	**1 Pound** 1.9.1844. Black. Seated Britannia with lion, sailing ships in background at left, farmers with cows at upper center, seated woman with produce, sailing ship in background at right. Printer: John Scott, Glasgow.			
	a. Issued note. Rare.	—	—	—
	r. Unsigned remainder.	—	—	2000.

S212 **3 Pounds**	Good	Fine	XF
(ca.1844). Black. Seated Britannia with lion and sailing ships in ornate border at left, two allegorical figures with ship at upper center. Printer: John Scott, Glasgow.			
a. Issued note. Rare.	—	—	—
r. Unsigned remainder. Rare.	—	—	—

S213 **5 Pounds**	Good	Fine	XF
(ca.1844). Black. Two allegorical figures at upper center with sailing ship at left, plantation at right. Printer: John Scott, Glasgow.			
a. Issued note. Rare.	—	—	—
r. Unsigned remainder.	—	—	2000.

S214 **10 Pounds**	Good	Fine	XF
18xx. Black. Horseman, dockyard at left, seated Britannia with shield and lion at upper center, trader checking goods at right. Printer: John Scott, Glasgow.	—	—	—
S215 **50 Pounds**			
Black. Printer: John Scott, Glasgow. Proof. Rare.	—	—	—
S216 **100 Pounds**			
Printer: John Scott, Glasgow. Proof. Rare.	—	—	—

NOTICE

Readers with unlisted dates, signature varieties, etc., are invited to submit photocopies or scans of their notes to:
Standard Catalog of World Paper Money,
700 East State St. Iola, WI 54990-0001,
E-Mail: george.cuhaj@fwmedia.com.

Royal Bank of Canada

1911 Issue

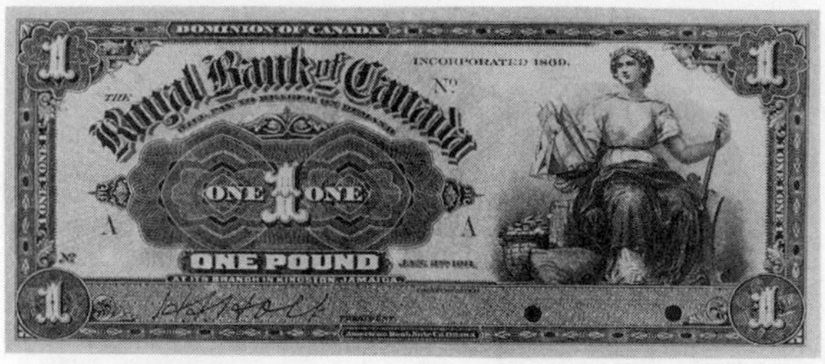

S221 **1 Pound**	Good	Fine	XF
2.1.1911. Black on green and pale yellow underprint. Woman seated with lyre and model ship at right. Back: Green. Arms at center. Printer: ABNC.			
a. Issued note.	600.	1200.	—
p. Proof without plate letter A or signature	—	Unc	2000.
r. Proof with plate letter A and signature H. S. Holight	—	Unc	1000.

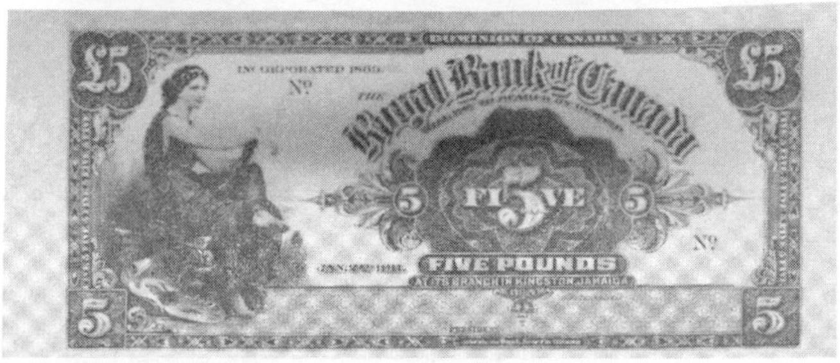

S222 **5 Pounds**	Good	Fine	XF
2.1.1911. Black on red-orange and light green underprint. Seated woman ("Study") at left. Back: Brown. Arms at center. Printer: ABNC. Proof.	—	Unc	2000.

1938 Issue

S226 **1 Pound**	Good	Fine	XF
3.1.1938. Black on green and pale yellow underprint. Woman seated with lyre and model ship at right. Similar to #S221. Back: Green. Arms at center. Printer: CBNC.			
a. Issued note.	750.	—	—
p. Proof.	—	Unc	2000.

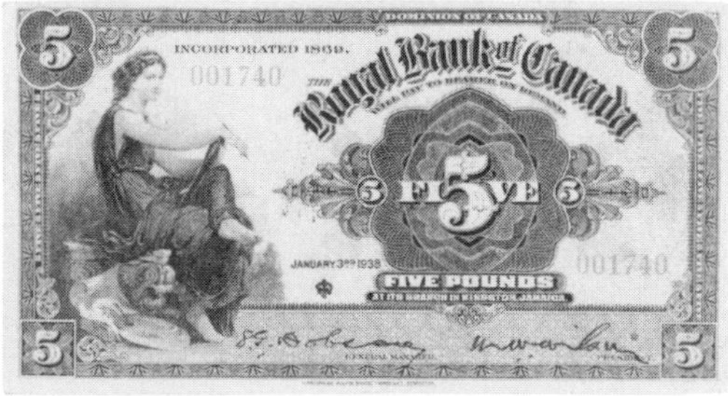

S227 **5 Pounds**	Good	Fine	XF
3.1.1938. Black on red-orange and light green underprint. Seated woman ("Study") at left. Similar to #S222. Back: Brown. Arms at center. Printer: CBNC.			
a. Issued note. Rare.	—	—	—
p. Proof.	—	Unc	2500.

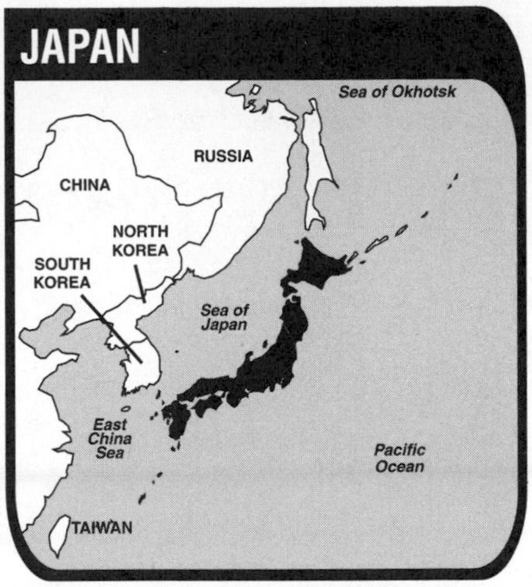

Japan, a constitutional monarchy situated off the east coast of Asia, has an area of 377,835 sq. km. and a population of 127.29 million. Capital: Tokyo. Japan, one of the three major industrial nations of the free world, exports machinery, motor vehicles, textiles and chemicals.

In 1603, a Tokugawa shogunate (military dictatorship) ushered in a long period of isolation from foreign influence in order to secure its power. For more than two centuries this policy enabled Japan to enjoy stability and a flowering of its indigenous culture. Following the Treaty of Kanagawa with the US in 1854, Japan opened its ports and began to intensively modernize and industrialize. During the late 19th and early 20th centuries, Japan became a regional power that was able to defeat the forces of both China and Russia. It occupied Korea, Formosa (Taiwan), and southern Sakhalin Island. In 1931-32 Japan occupied Manchuria, and in 1937 it launched a full-scale invasion of China. Japan attacked US forces in 1941 - triggering America's entry into World War II - and soon occupied much of East and Southeast Asia. After its defeat in World War II, Japan recovered to become an economic power and a staunch ally of the US. While the emperor retains his throne as a symbol of national unity, elected politicians - with heavy input from bureaucrats and business executives - wield actual decisionmaking power. The economy experienced a major slowdown starting in the 1990s following three decades of unprecedented growth, but Japan still remains a major economic power, both in Asia and globally.

See also Burma, China (Japanese military issues, Central Reserve Bank, Federal Reserve Bank, Hua Hsing Commercial Bank, Mengchiang Bank, Chanan Bank, Chi Tung Bank and Manchukuo), Hong Kong, Indochina, Malaya, Netherlands Indies, Oceania, the Philippines, Korea and Taiwan.

RULERS:

Mutsuhito (Meiji), Years 1-45, (1868-1912) 明治
Mutsuhito (Meiji), 1868-1912
Yoshihito (Taisho), 1912-1926
Hirohito (Showa), 1926-1989
Akihito (Heisei), 1989-

MONETARY SYSTEM:

1 Sen = 10 Rin
1 Yen = 100 Sen
1 Shu = 1000-1750 Mon (copper or iron "cash" coins)
1 Bu (fun) = 4 Shu
1 Ryo = 4 Bu to 1870
1 Sen = 10 Rin
1 Yen = 100 Sen, 1870-

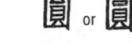

両 Ryo　匁 Monme　朱 Shu　分 Bu　文 Mon

圓 or 圓 or 円 Yen　銭 Sen　厘 Rin

METALS

金 Gold (Kin)　銀 Silver (Gin)　銅 Copper (Zeni)

REVALIDATION SEAL OVERPRINT:

3
Rin
Finance
Ministry

NUMERICAL

A - CONVENTIONAL

B - FORMAL

NUMBER	CONVENTIONAL	FORMAL
1	一	壹 or 弌
2	二	弐 or 貳
3	三	叄 弎
4	四	肆
5	五	伍
6	六	陸
7	七	柒
8	八	捌
9	九	玖
10	十	拾
20	十 二 or 廿	拾貳
25	五 十 二 or 五廿	伍拾貳
30	十 三 or 卅	拾叄
100	百 一	佰壹
1,000	千 一	仟壹
10,000	萬 一 or 万	萬壹
100,000	萬 十 or 万十	萬拾
1,000,000	萬百一	萬佰壹

Note: This table has been adapted from *Chinese Bank Notes* by Wars Smith and Brian Matravers.

GOVERNMENT

NOTE: The market valuations for Oin-satsu are for the more common varieties of the basic Han-satsu.

OIN-SATSU

1872 ND PROVISIONAL ISSUE

NOTE: The market valuations for Oin-satsu are for the more common varieties of the basic Han-satsu.

		Good	Fine	XF
S101	**1 Rin** ND (1872).	4.00	10.00	20.00
S102	**2 Rin** ND (1872).	4.00	10.00	20.00
S103	**3 Rin** ND (1872).	4.00	10.00	20.00
S104	**4 Rin** ND (1872).	4.00	10.00	20.00
S105	**5 Rin** ND (1872).	4.00	10.00	20.00
S106	**6 Rin** ND (1872).	5.00	12.00	24.00
S107	**7 Rin** ND (1872).	5.00	12.00	24.00
S108	**8 Rin** ND (1872).	5.00	12.00	24.00
S109	**9 Rin** ND (1872).	5.00	12.00	24.00
S110	**1 Sen** ND (1872).	5.00	12.00	24.00
S112	**1 Sen 2 Rin** ND (1872).	6.00	15.00	30.00
S113	**1 Sen 3 Rin** ND (1872).	6.00	15.00	30.00
S114	**1 Sen 4 Rin** ND (1872).	6.00	15.00	30.00
S115	**1 Sen 5 Rin** ND (1872).	6.00	15.00	30.00
		Good	**Fine**	**XF**
S116	**1 Sen 6 Rin** ND (1872).	6.00	15.00	30.00
S117	**1 Sen 7 Rin** ND (1872).	6.00	15.00	30.00
S118	**1 Sen 8 Rin** ND (1872).	6.00	15.00	30.00

		Good	Fine
S119 1 Sen 9 Rin ND (1872).	6.00	15.00	30.00
S120 2 Sen ND (1872).	6.00	15.00	32.00
S121 2 Sen 1 Rin ND (1872).	7.00	17.50	35.00
S124 2 Sen 4 Rin ND (1872).	7.00	17.50	35.00
S125 2 Sen 5 Rin ND (1872).	7.00	17.50	35.00
S126 2 Sen 6 Rin ND (1872).	7.00	17.50	35.00
S127 2 Sen 7 Rin ND (1872).	7.00	17.50	35.00
S129 2 Sen 9 Rin ND (1872).	7.00	17.50	35.00
S130 3 Sen ND (1872).	7.00	17.50	35.00
S131 3 Sen 1 Rin ND (1872).	8.00	20.00	40.00
S132 3 Sen 2 Rin ND (1872).	8.00	20.00	40.00
S133 3 Sen 3 Rin ND (1872).	8.00	20.00	40.00
S135 3 Sen 5 Rin ND (1872).	8.00	20.00	40.00
S138 3 Sen 8 Rin ND (1872).	8.00	20.00	40.00
S139 3 Sen 9 Rin ND (1872).	8.00	20.00	40.00
S140 4 Sen ND (1872).	10.00	25.00	50.00
S142 4 Sen 2 Rin ND (1872).	12.50	30.00	60.00
S145 4 Sen 5 Rin ND (1872).	12.50	30.00	60.00
S148 4 Sen 8 Rin ND (1872).	12.50	30.00	60.00

NOTE: The market valuations for Oin-satsu are for the more common varieties of the basic Han-satsu.

GOVERNMENT

EDO - YOKOHAMA BAKAFU (SHOGUNATE)

TOKYO

1867 GOLD NOTE ISSUE

	Good	Fine	XF
S150 1 Ryo Yr. 3 Keio (1867).	600.	1250.	1500.
S151 5 Ryo Yr. 3 Keio (1867).	750.	1500.	2000.
S152 10 Ryo Yr. 3 Keio (1867).	750.	1500.	2000.

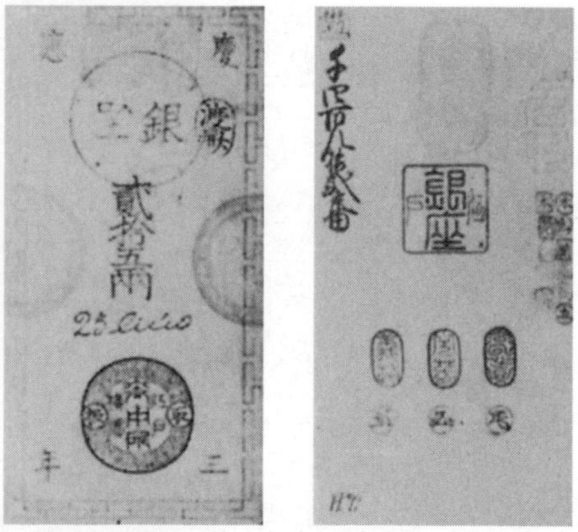

	Good	Fine	XF
S153 25 Ryo Yr. 3 Keio (1867).	1250.	2000.	2500.

EDO & EIGHT PROVINCES OF THE KANTO

1867 GOLD NOTE ISSUE

	Good	Fine	XF
S154 1 Ryo Yr. 3 Keio (1867).	600.	1250.	1500.
S155 25 Ryo Yr. 3 Keio (1867).	750.	1500.	2000.
S156 50 Ryo Yr. 3 Keio (1867).	1000.	1750.	2250.

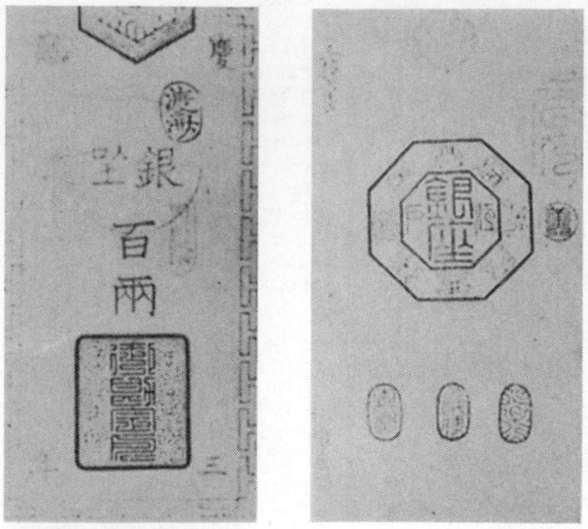

	Good	Fine	XF
S157 100 Ryo Yr. 3 Keio (1867).	1250.	2000.	2500.
S158 200 Ryo Yr. 3 Keio (1867).	1500.	2500.	3000.

HYOGO PORT-DEVELOPMENT

KOBE

1867 ISSUE

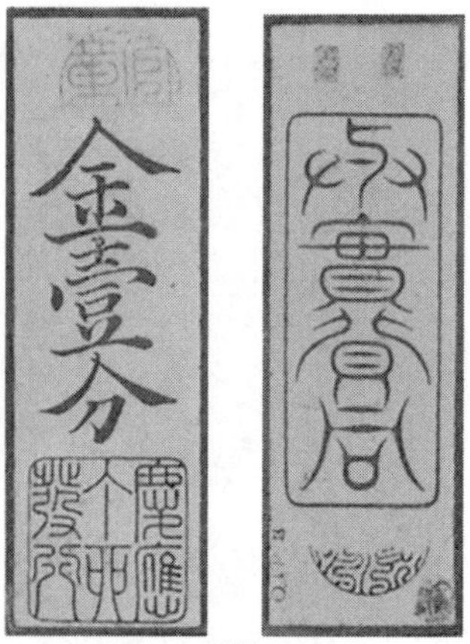

S159

S160

S161

	Good	Fine	XF
S159 1 Fun Yr. 3 Keio (1867). Black.	20.00	35.00	75.00
S160 2 Fun Yr. 3 Keio (1867). Black.	20.00	55.00	75.00
S161 1 Ryo Yr. 3 Keio (1867). Black.	35.00	55.00	90.00

DAJOKAN-SATSU

CABINET

1868 GOLD NOTE ISSUE

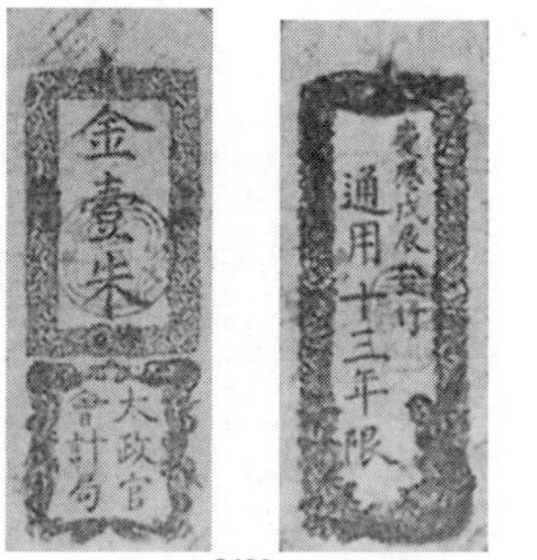

S162

S163

	Good	Fine	XF
S162 1 Shu Yr. 4 Keio (1868).	20.00	35.00	50.00
S163 1 Bu Yr. 4 Keio (1868).	15.00	35.00	50.00

S164

S165

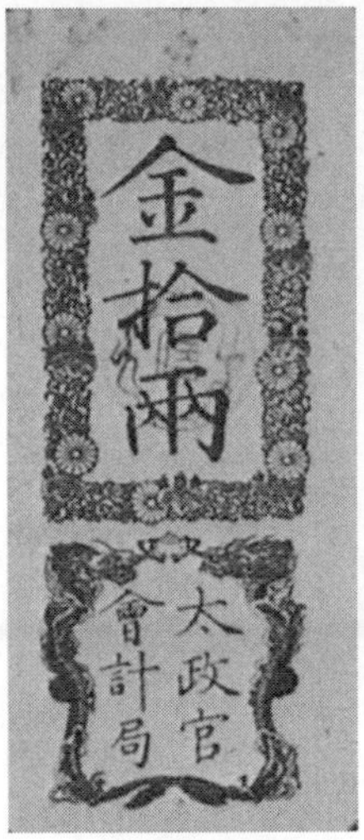

S166

		Good	Fine	XF
S164	**1 Ryo** Yr. 4 Keio (1868).	40.00	70.00	100.
S165	**5 Ryo** Yr. 4 Keio (1868).	75.00	175.	300.
S166	**10 Ryo** Yr. 4 Keio (1868).	100.	220.	310.

Minbusho-Satsu

Civil Department

1869 Gold Note Issue

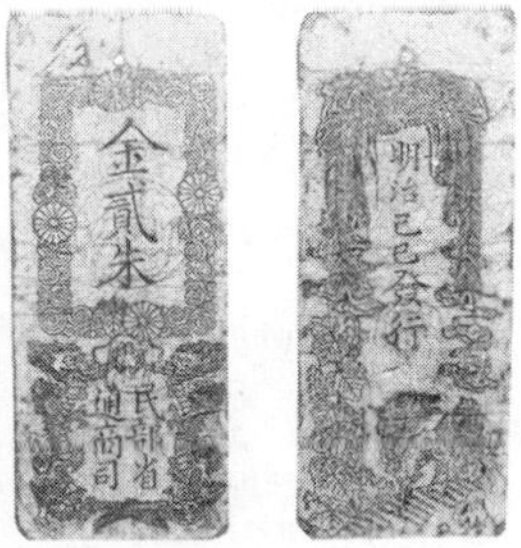

S167

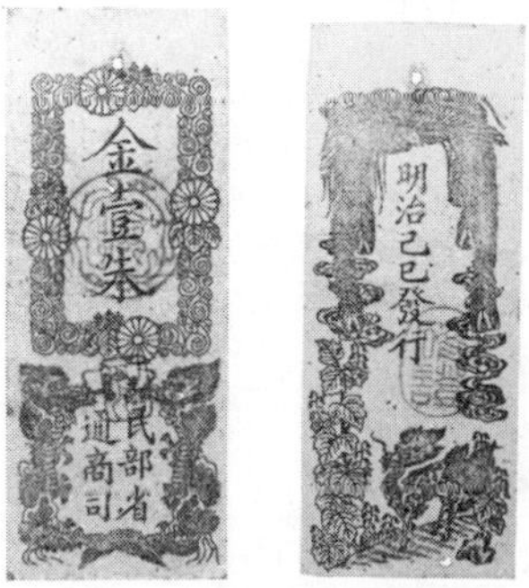

S168

		Good	Fine	XF
S167	**1 Shu** Yr. 2 Meiji (1869). Black. Two facing dragons at bottom. Back: Dragon at bottom.	20.00	50.00	75.00
S168	**2 Shu** Yr. 2 Meiji (1869). Black. Two facing dragons at bottom. Back: Dragon at bottom.	20.00	50.00	75.00

S169

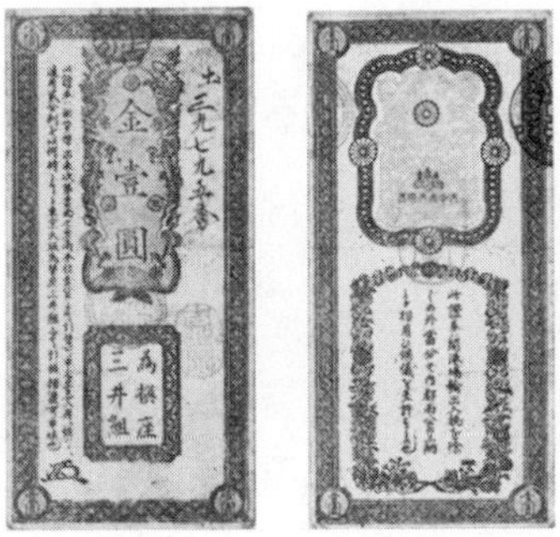

S170

		Good	Fine	XF
S169	**1 Bu** Yr. 2 Meiji (1869). Black. Two facing dragons at bottom. Back: Dragon at bottom.	25.00	55.00	80.00
S170	**2 Bu** Yr. 2 Meiji (1869). Black. Two facing dragons at bottom. Back: Dragon at bottom.	25.00	55.00	90.00

Okurasho Dakan Shoken

Finance Ministry

1871 Convertible Gold Note Issue

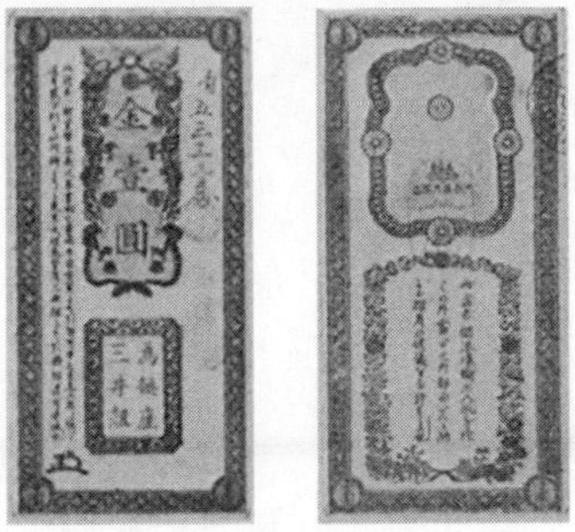

S171

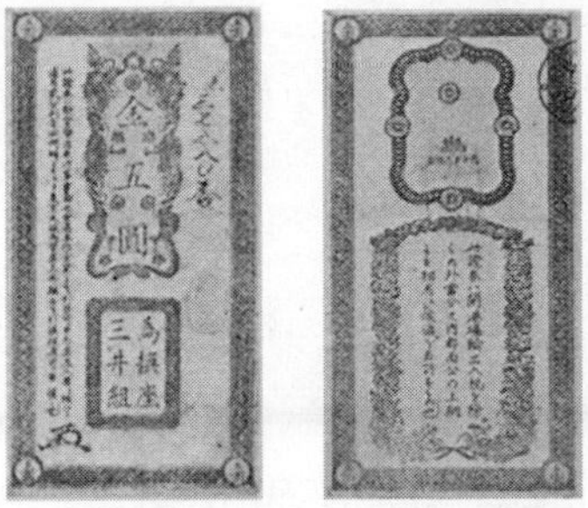

S172

		Good	Fine	XF
S171	**1 Yen** ND (1871). Back: Blue-gray adhesive stamp with impressed oval vermillion seal.	125.	250.	400.
S172	**5 Yen** ND (1871). Back: Blue-gray adhesive stamp with impressed oval vermillion seal.	450.	1000.	1750.
S173	**10 Yen** ND (1871). Back: Blue-gray adhesive stamp with impressed oval vermillion seal.	900.	1500.	2000.

Kaitakushi Dakan Shoken

Development Office

1872 Convertible Note Issue

#S174-S179 Higher denominations may also have a black overprint of the denomination.

S174

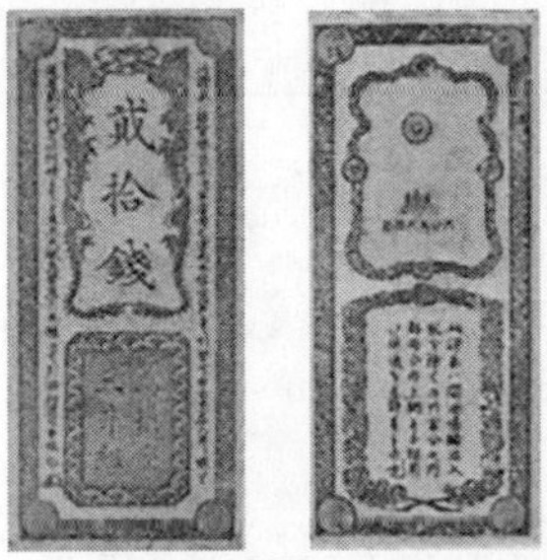

S175

		Good	Fine	XF
S174	**10 Sen** ND (1872). Black. Circular red seal of the development office. Back: Blue-gray adhesive stamp with impressed oval vermillion seal.	25.00	50.00	90.00
S175	**20 Sen** ND (1872). Black. Circular red seal of the development office. Back: Blue-gray adhesive stamp with impressed oval vermillion seal.	30.00	75.00	125.

S176

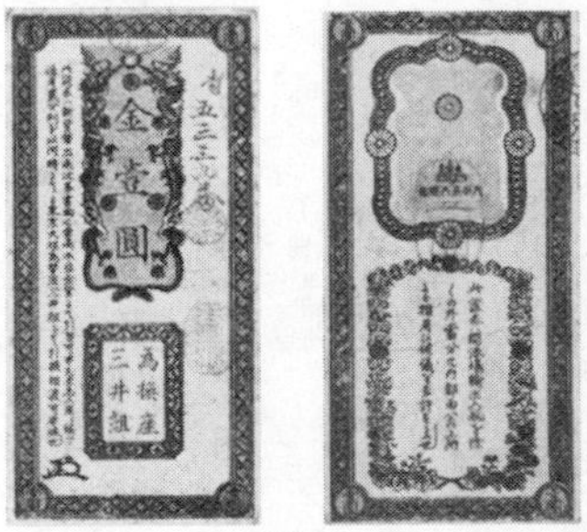

S177

		Good	Fine	XF
S176	**50 Sen** ND (1872). Black. Circular red seal of the development office. Back: Blue-gray adhesive stamp with impressed oval vermillion seal.	60.00	120.	175.
S177	**1 Yen** ND (1872). Black. Circular red seal of the development office. Back: Blue-gray adhesive stamp with impressed oval vermillion seal.	200.	500.	750.

		Good	Fine	XF
S178	**5 Yen** ND (1872). Black. Circular red seal of the development office. Back: Blue-gray adhesive stamp with impressed oval vermillion seal. Rare.	—	—	—
S179	**10 Yen** ND (1872). Black. Circular red seal of the development office. Back: Blue-gray adhesive stamp with impressed oval vermillion seal. Rare.	—	—	—

Exchange Banks

Tokyo Kawase Kaisha

Tokyo

1869 Silver Note Issue

		Good	Fine	XF
S180	**3 Momme 7 Fun 5 Rin** ND (1869). Black.	15.00	25.00	45.00

1869 Multi-Office Gold Note Issue

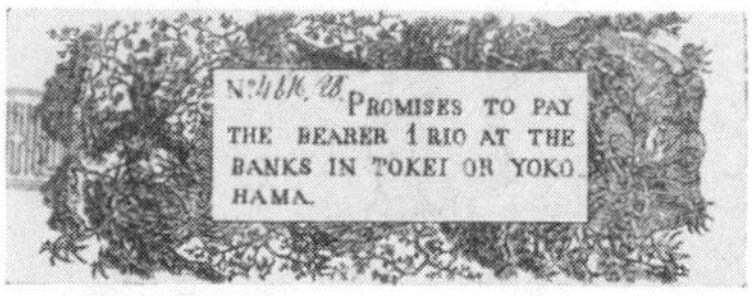

		Good	Fine	XF
S181	**1 Ryo** ND (1869). Black. Crane superimposed over rising sun at top, sailboat at bottom. Back: Turtle at bottom.			
	a. Red 2 character oval overprint: *Tokyo.*	85.00	175.	250.
	b. Red 2 character rectangular overprint: *Yokohama.*	165.	350.	500.
	c. Red 2 character square overprint: *Niigata.* Rare.	—	—	—

NOTICE

Readers with unlisted dates, signature varieties, etc., are invited to submit photocopies or scans of their notes to:
Standard Catalog of World Paper Money,
700 East State St. Iola, WI 54990-0001,
E-Mail: george.cuhaj@fwmedia.com.

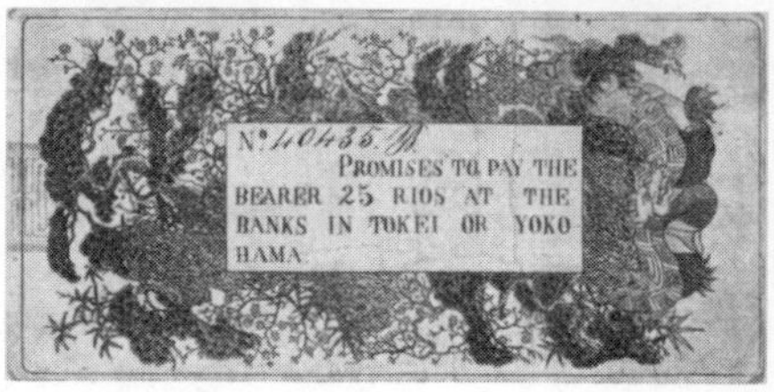

		Good	Fine	XF
S182	**25 Ryo** ND (1869). Black. Crane superimposed over rising sun at top, sailboat at bottom. Back: Turtle at bottom.			
	a. Red 2 character oval overprint: *Tokyo.*	350.	800.	1250.
	b. Red 2 character rectangular overprint: *Yokohama.* Rare.	—	—	—
	c. Red 2 character square overprint: *Niigata.* Rare.	—	—	—
	d. Violet 2 character oval overprint: *Kobe.* Rare.	—	—	—

Kyoto

1869 Copper Note Issue

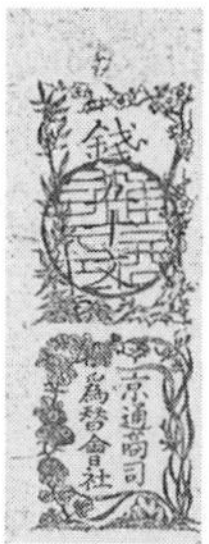

S183

S184

		Good	Fine	XF
S183	**50 Mon** ND (1869). Black.	15.00	25.00	50.00
S184	**100 Mon** ND (1869). Black.	15.00	25.00	55.00

S185

S186

		Good	Fine	XF
S185	**200 Mon** ND (1869). Black.	20.00	35.00	50.00
S186	**500 Mon** ND (1869). Black.	30.00	60.00	80.00

Osaka

1869 Copper Note Issue

S187

S188

S189

	Good	Fine	XF
S187 100 Mon Yr. 2 Meiji (1869). Black.	17.50	25.00	40.00
S188 200 Mon Yr. 2 Meiji (1869). Black.	20.00	30.00	45.00
S189 500 Mon Yr. 2 Meiji (1869). Black.	30.00	40.00	60.00

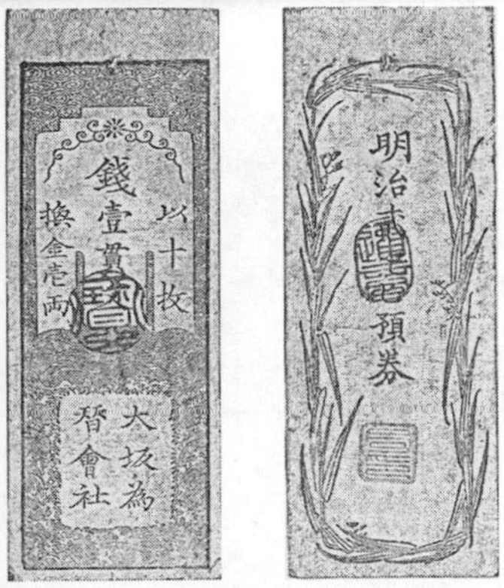

	Good	Fine	XF
S190 1 Kan Mon = 1000 Mon Yr. 2 Meiji (1869). Black.	125.	250.	400.

1869 Multi-Office Gold Note Issue

	Good	Fine	XF
S191 1 Ryo ND (1869). Black.			
a. Red 1 character circular overprint: *Kyoto.*	55.00	110.	150.
b. Red 2 character oval overprint: *Otsu.*	125.	200.	300.
c. Red 2 character fundo overprint: *Tsuruga.*	175.	300.	500.

	Good	Fine	XF
S192 1 Ryo ND (1869). Black. Saikyo *(Kyoto).*	125.	225.	300.

Hikone

1870 Issue

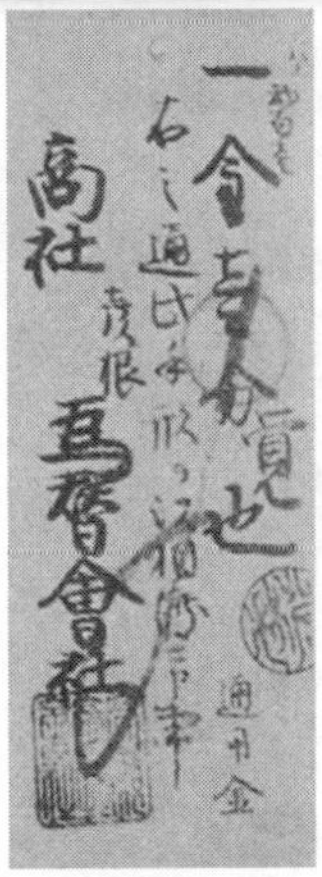

S193

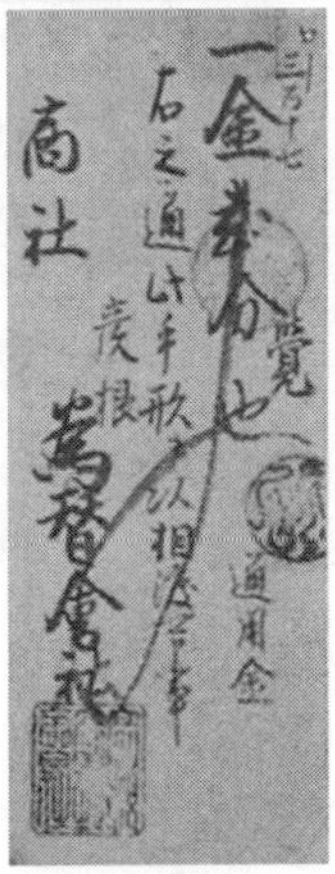

S194

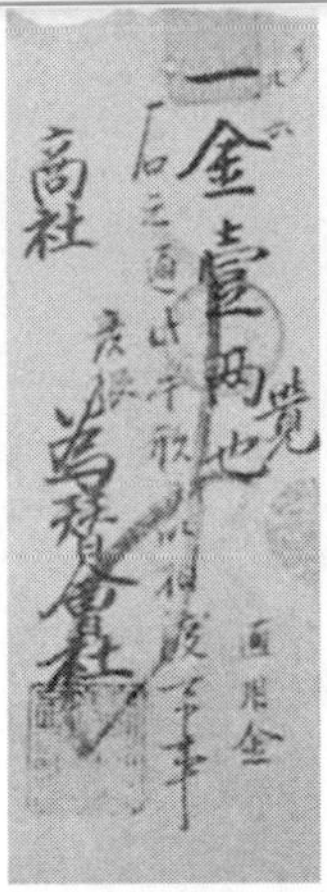

S195

	Good	Fine	XF
S193 1 Bu Yr. 3 Meiji (1870). Black.	175.	350.	500.
S194 2 Bu Yr. 3 Meiji (1870). Black.	175.	350.	500.
S195 1 Ryo Yr. 3 Meiji (1870). Black.	175.	350.	500.

Matsuzaka

1870 Issue

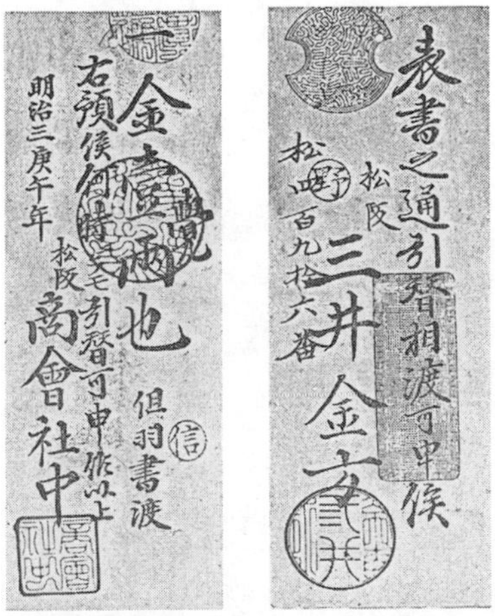

	Good	Fine	XF
S195A 1 Ryo Yr. 3 Meiji (1870). Black. Rare.	—	—	—

OSAKA

1870 FOREIGN SILVER NOTE ISSUE

	Good	Fine	XF
S196 25 Mexican Dollars Yr. 3 Meiji (1870). Photographic print of Osaka Exchange Office glued with impressed oval seal at bottom. Rare.	—	—	—
S197 50 Mexican Dollars Yr. 3 Meiji (1870). Photographic print of Osaka Exchange Office glued with impressed oval seal at bottom. Rare.	—	—	—

1869 GOLD NOTE ISSUE

	Good	Fine	XF
S198 1 Ryo Yr. 2 Meiji (1869). Black. Photographic print of Osaka Exchange Office glued with impressed oval seal at bottom.	125.	200.	400.
S199 5 Ryo Yr. 2 Meiji (1869). Black. Photographic print of Osaka Exchange Office glued with impressed oval seal at bottom.	400.	800.	1500.
S200 10 Ryo Yr. 2 Meiji (1869). Black. Photographic print of Osaka Exchange Office glued with impressed oval seal at bottom. Rare.	—	—	—

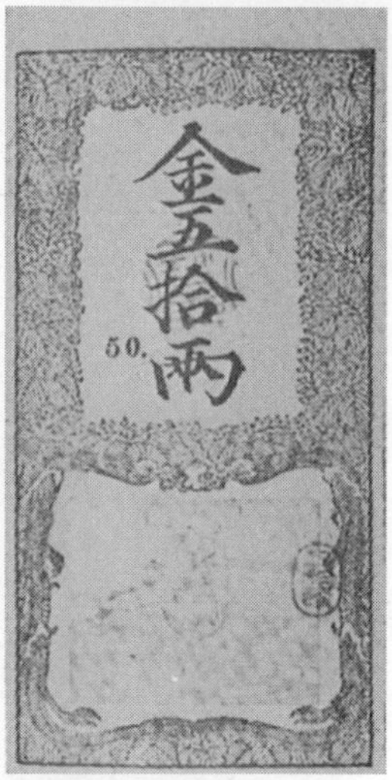

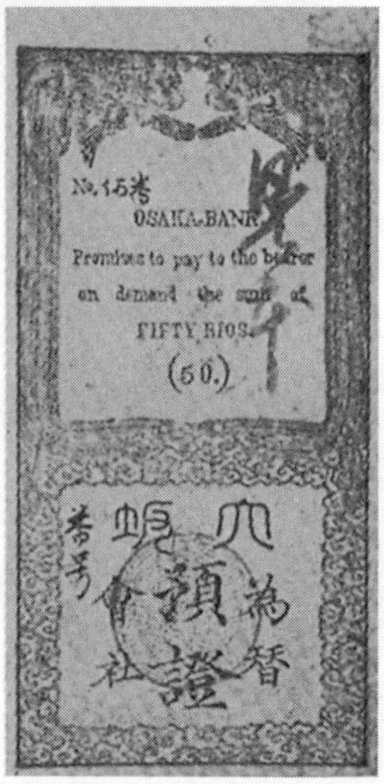

	Good	Fine	XF
S201 50 Ryo Yr. 2 Meiji (1869). Black. Photographic print of Osaka Exchange Office glued with impressed oval seal at bottom. Rare.	—	—	—

	Good	Fine	XF
S202 100 Ryo Yr. 2 Meiji (1869). Black. Photographic print of Osaka Exchange Office glued with impressed oval seal at bottom. Rare.	—	—	—

YOKOHAMA

1870 FOREIGN SILVER NOTE ISSUE

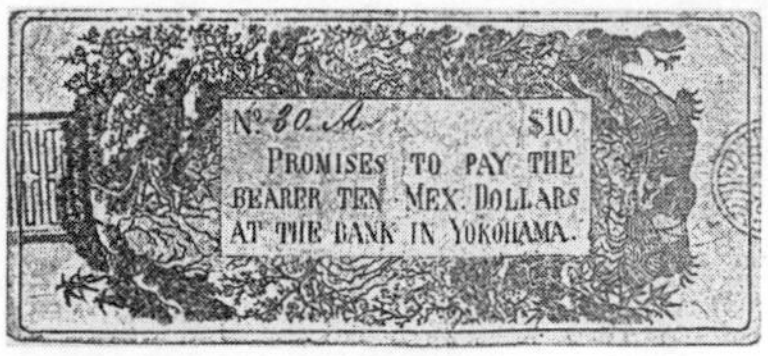

	Good	Fine	XF
S203 10 Mex(ican) Dollars ND (1870). Black. Rare.	—	—	—
S204 100 Mex(ican) Dollars ND (1870). Black. Rare.	—	—	—

1872 LOCAL CURRENCY - FOREIGN SILVER NOTE ISSUE

	Good	Fine	XF
S205 5 Dollars Yr. 5 Meiji (1872). Black. Mt. Fuji in frame of two facing dragons at top center. Back: Two dragon frame. Printer: PBC. Rare.	—	—	—

	Good	Fine	XF
S206 10 Dollars Yr. 5 Meiji (1872). Blue. Mt. Fuji in frame of two facing dragons at top center. Back: Two dragon frame. Printer: PBC.			
a. Issued note. Rare.	—	—	—
b. Proof in black.	—	—	—
S207 20 Dollars Yr. 5 Meiji (1872). Maroon. Mt. Fuji in frame of two facing dragons at top center. Back: Two dragon frame. Printer: PBC.			
a. Issued note. Rare.	—	—	—
b. Proof in black.	—	—	—
S208 50 Dollars Yr. 5 Meiji (1872). Green. Mt. Fuji in frame of two facing dragons at top center. Back: Two dragon frame. Printer: PBC.			
a. Issued note. Rare.	—	—	—
b. Proof in black.	—	—	—
S209 100 Dollars Yr. 5 Meiji (1872). Blue. Mt. Fuji in frame of two facing dragons at top center. Back: Black. Two dragon frame. Printer: PBC.			
a. Issued note. Rare.	—	—	—
b. Proof in black.	—	—	—
S210 500 Dollars Yr. 5 Meiji (1872). Blue. Mt. Fuji in frame of two facing dragons at top center. Back: Two dragon frame. Printer: PBC.			
a. Issued note. Rare.	—	—	—
b. Proof in black.	—	—	—
S211 1000 Dollars Yr. 5 Meiji (1872). Green. Mt. Fuji in frame of two facing dragons at top center. Back: Black. Two dragon frame. Printer: PBC.			
a. Issued note. Rare.	—	—	—
b. Proof in black.	—	—	—

Foreign Banks

Central Bank of Western India

1866 Issue

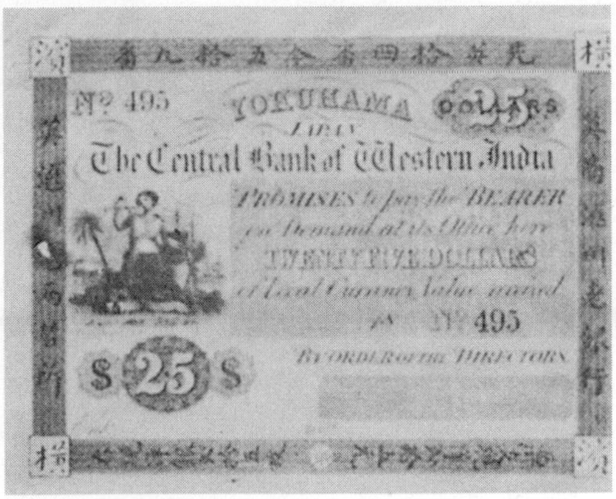

S224 25 Dollars	Good	Fine	XF
9.2.1866. Seated Justice with scale at left, ship and palm trees in background. Printer: Batho Sprague & Co.			
a. Issued note, hand cancelled. Rare.	—	—	—
r. Remainder. Rare.	—	—	—

NOTE: Additional denominations require confirmation.

Chartered Mercantile Bank of India, London & China

1860's Issue

	Good	Fine	XF
S228 5 Dollars May 1866. Black on blue underprint. Back: Black. Printer: PBC. Specimen. Rare.	—	—	—
S229 10 Dollars 18xx. Printer: PBC. Specimen. Rare.	—	—	—
S230 50 Dollars 18xx. Printer: PBC. Specimen. Rare.	—	—	—
S231 100 Dollars 18xx. Printer: PBC. Specimen. Rare.	—	—	—

NOTE: #S228-S231 exist as specimens in the collection of HK & SBC Ltd.

Commercial Bank Corporation of India & the East

1866 Issue

	Good	Fine	XF
S235 10 Dollars 3.2.1866.	—	—	—

NOTE: One issued note is known.

Hong Kong & Shanghai Banking Corporation

Hiogo

1870's Issue

	Good	Fine	XF
S240 5 Dollars 18xx. Green on brown underprint. Printer: BLF. Specimen. Rare.	—	—	—
S241 10 Dollars 18xx. Blue on brown underprint. Printer: BLF. Specimen. Rare.	—	—	—

#S242 Deleted.

	Good	Fine	XF
S243 50 Dollars 18xx. Violet on brown underprint. Printer: BLF. Specimen. Rare.	—	—	—

NOTE: Color trials with modified underprint exist for #S243.

	Good	Fine	XF
S244 100 Dollars 18xx. Printer: BLF. Rare.	—	—	—

Yokohama

1866 Provisional Issue

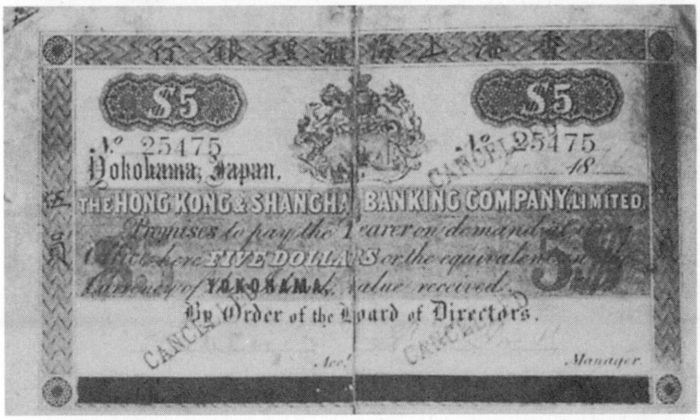

	Good	Fine	XF
S246 5 Dollars 2.7.1866. Black on blue underprint. Back: Green. Overprint: *YOKOHAMA, JAPAN* and *YOKOHAMA* on Hong Kong notes. Printer: Ashby & Co. Rare.	—	—	—
S247 10 Dollars 18xx. Overprint: *YOKOHAMA, JAPAN* and *YOKOHAMA* on Hong Kong notes. Printer: Ashby & Co. Reported not confirmed.	—	—	—

	Good	Fine	XF
S248 25 Dollars 2.7.1866. Gray. Back: Orange. Overprint: *YOKOHAMA, JAPAN* and *YOKOHAMA* on Hong Kong notes. Printer: Ashby & Co. Rare.	—	—	—
S249 50 Dollars 18xx. Overprint: *YOKOHAMA, JAPAN* and *YOKOHAMA* on Hong Kong notes. Printer: Ashby & Co. Reported not confirmed.	—	—	—
S250 100 Dollars 18xx. Overprint: *YOKOHAMA, JAPAN* and *YOKOHAMA* on Hong Kong notes. Printer: Ashby & Co. Reported not confirmed.	—	—	—

1870's Issue

	Good	Fine	XF
S252 5 Dollars 18xx. Black on red underprint. Bank arms at top center with *YOKOHAMA* in frame. Printer: Ashby & Co. Specimen. Rare.	—	—	—
S253 10 Dollars 18xx. Black on red underprint. Bank arms at top center with *YOKOHAMA* in frame. Printer: Ashby & Co. Specimen. Rare.	—	—	—
S254 25 Dollars 18xx. Black on red underprint. Bank arms at top center with *YOKOHAMA* in frame. Printer: Ashby & Co. Specimen. Rare.	—	—	—
S255 50 Dollars 18xx. Black on red underprint. Bank arms at top center with *YOKOHAMA* in frame. Printer: Ashby & Co.			
a. Issued note. Rare.	—	—	—
s. Specimen. Rare.	—	—	—
S256 100 Dollars 18xx. Black on red underprint. Bank arms at top center with *YOKOHAMA* in frame. Printer: Ashby & Co. Specimen. Rare.	—	—	—

A WORD ON DATE RANGES

Often date ranges or specific dates are listed. These have been observed or reported by our contributors. If a note is outside the published range, it only means that it is a newly reported date, and not necessarily worthy of a premium value.

		Good	Fine	XF
S257	**500 Dollars** 18xx. Back: Green. Specimen. Rare.	—	—	—

New Oriental Bank Corporation Ltd.

1886 Issue

		Good	Fine	XF
S260	**1 Dollar** 1.1.1886; 1.3.1886. Black on pink underprint. Mexican eagle at left, portrait Minerva at right. Back: Octagonal *tri-grams* at center.			
	a. Issued note.	750.	2250.	—
	s. Specimen.	—	Unc	4000.

Japanese Military Currency

See also China, Hong Kong and occupation issues for Burma, French Indochina, Malaya, Netherlands Indies, Oceania and the Philippines.

Great Japanese Government - Ministry of Finance

Dai Nip-pon Sei-fu O-kura-sho

1904 Russo-Japanese War Issue

Issued in Korea, North China and Sakhalin in Eastern Siberia. Meiji yr. 37.

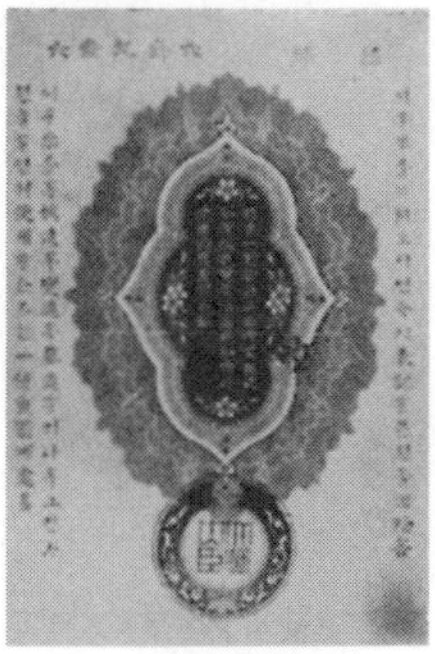

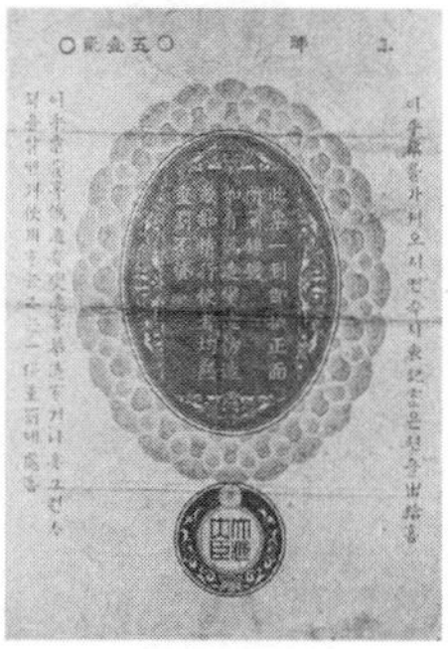

		Good	Fine	XF
M1	**10 Sen** 1904. Meiji year 37. Black on light red-brown underprint. Back: Red-brown.			
	a. With serial # at top on back.	20.00	40.00	75.00
	b. Without serial # on back.	10.00	20.00	40.00
M2	**20 Sen** 1904. Meiji year 37. Black on green underprint. Back: Green.			
	a. With serial # at top on back.	75.00	150.	300.
	b. Without serial # on back.	40.00	75.00	150.
M3	**50 Sen** 1904. Meiji year 37. Black on light gray-violet underprint. Back: Light gray-violet.			
	a. With serial # at top on back.	75.00	150.	300.
	b. Without serial # on back.	40.00	75.00	150.

Note: For issues with design like #M1-M3 but having a 10-pointed star above cockerels' heads, see Korea #7-9.

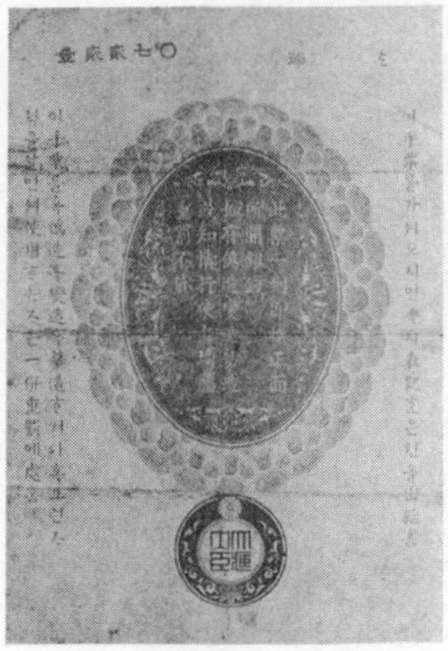

		Good	Fine	XF
M4	**1 Yen** 1904. Meiji year 37. Black on ochre underprint. Back: Yellow-brown.			
	a. With serial # at top on back.	125.	250.	500.
	b. Without serial # on back.	80.00	200.	400.
M5	**5 Yen** 1904. Meiji year 37. Black on light blue-gray underprint. Back: Blue-gray.			
	a. With serial # at top of rack.	750.	1500.	3000.
	b. Without serial # on back.	500.	1250.	2500.
M6	**10 Yen** 1904. Meiji year 37. Black on light brown-violet underprint. Back: Brown-violet.			
	a. With serial # at top on back.	1000.	2000.	—
	b. Without serial # on back.	700.	1750.	—

1914 Occupation of Tsingtao Provisional Issue

#M7-M12 English legends - in silver at l. and r. and at top on back. Taisho yr. 3.

		Good	Fine	XF
M6A	**10 Sen** ND. Pica type overprint on face only of #M1.	375.	750.	1250.
M6B	**50 Sen** ND. Pica type overprint on face only of #M3.	650.	1250.	2500.

1914 Occupation of Tsingtao Issue

#M7-M12 English legends - *in silver* at left, and rright and at top on back. Taisho yr. 3 (except #M7a and M9a, Meiji Yr. 37).

		Good	Fine	XF
M7	**10 Sen** 1914. Taisho year 3. Black on red-brown. English legends-*in silver* at left and right. Back: Red-brown. English legends-*in silver* at top.			
	a. Like #M1 but overprint: *10 SEN IN SILVER* in pica type letters. Meiji year 37.	300.	500.	1000.
	b. Overprint in itallic scrpit.	750.	1000.	2500.
M8	**20 Sen** 1914. Taisho year 3. Black on light green underprint. English legends-*in silver* at left and right. Back: Light green. English legends-*in silver* at top.	375.	950.	1250.
M9	**50 Sen** 1914. Taisho year 3. Black on light purple underprint. English legends-*in silver* at left and right. Back: Light purple. English legends-*in silver* at top.			
	a. Like #M3 but overprint: *50 SEN IN SILVER* in pica type. Meiji year 37.	375.	950.	1500.
	b. Overprint in italic script.	1200.	2000.	4000.
M10	**1 Yen** 1914. Taisho year 3. Black on yellow underprint. English legends-*in silver* at left and right. Back: Orange. English legends-*in silver* at top.	1000.	1750.	3500.

		Good	Fine	XF
M11	**5 Yen** 1914. Taisho year 3. Black on light blue underprint. English legends-*in silver* at left and right. Back: Blue-gray. English legends-*in silver* at top. Rare.	—	—	—
M12	**10 Yen** 1914. Taisho year 3. Black on light red-brown underprint. English legends-*in silver* at left and right. Back: Red-brown. English legends-*in silver* at top. Rare.	—	—	—

1918 Occupation Of Siberia Issue

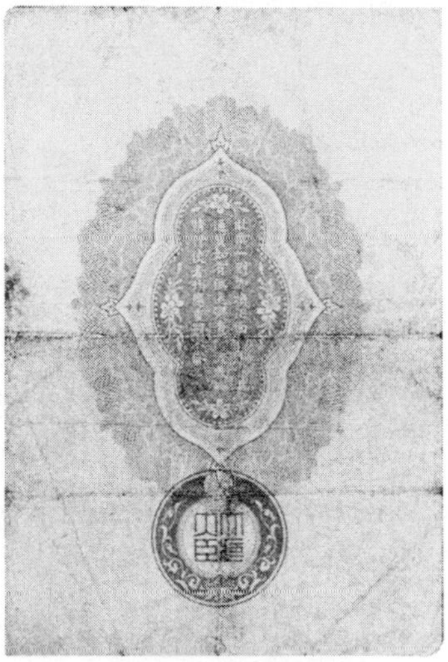

		Good	Fine	XF
M13	**10 Sen** 1918. Taisho year 7. Black on ochre underprint. Russian legends at left and right. Back: Yellow-brown.	50.00	100.	200.
M14	**20 Sen** 1918. Taisho year 7. Black on light green underprint. Russian legends at left and right. Back: Light green.	60.00	125.	250.
M15	**50 Sen** 1918. Taisho year 7. Black on tan underprint. Russian legends at left and right. Back: Brown.	75.00	350.	500.

		Good	Fine	XF
M16	**1 Yen** 1918. Taisho year 7. Black on light blue underprint. Russian legends at left and right. Back: Dark blue.	250.	500.	1000.
M17	**5 Yen** 1918. Taisho year 7. Black on light brown-violet underprint. Russian legends at left and right. Back: Brown -violet.	1100.	2250.	4500.
M18	**10 Yen** 1918. Taisho year 7. Black. Russian legends at left and right.			
	a. Light purple underprint. Back blue-violet.	1250.	2500.	5500.
	s. Light violet underprint. Back violet. Specimen. Rare.	—	—	—

Note: For similar notes dated Showa year 12 (1937), see China #M1-M5.

1940's ND Occupation of Russian Territory Issue

		Good	Fine	XF
M19	**10 Kopeks** ND. Gray-green on blue underprint. Russian text and block #. Not issued. Rare.	—	—	—
M20	**50 Kopeks** ND. Red-brown on pink underprint. Russian text and block #. Similar to Malaya 50 cents, #M4. Not issued. Rare.	—	—	—
M21	**1 Ruble** ND. Brown on tan underprint. Russian text and block #. Similar to Malaya 1 Dollar, #M5. Not issued. Rare.	—	—	—
M22	**5 Rubles** ND. Blue on pale blue underprint. Russian text and block #. Similar to Malaya 5 Dollars, #M6. Not issued. Rare.	—	—	—
M23	**1 Chervonetz** ND. Dark blue on pale blue. Russian text and block #. Two peasant women at right. Similar to Oceania 1£, #4. Not issued. Rare.	—	—	—

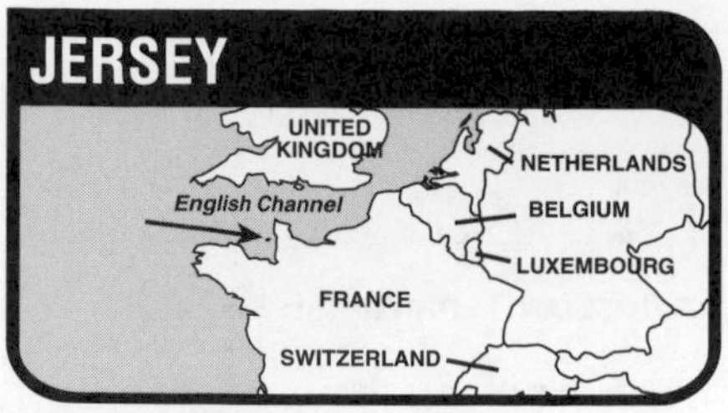

The Bailiwick of Jersey, a British Crown dependency located in the English Channel 12 miles (19 km.) west of Normandy, France, has an area of 45 sq. mi. (117 sq. km.) and a population of 90,000. Capital: St. Helier. The economy is d on agriculture and cattle breeding - the importation of cattle is prohibited to protect the purity of the island's world-famous strain of milk cows.

Jersey and the other Channel Islands represent the last remnants of the medieval Dukedom of Normandy that held sway in both France and England. These islands were the only British soil occupied by German troops in World War II. Jersey is a British crown dependency but is not part of the UK. However, the UK Government is constitutionally responsible for its defense and international representation.

RULERS:

British

MONETARY SYSTEM:

1 Shilling = 12 Pence
1 Pound = 20 Shillings to 1971
1 Pound = 100 Pence, 1971-

BANKS AND CHURCHES

PARISHES

From 1816 to 1941, only two notes circulated as government issues: a 5 Pound 1840 Bearer Bond (see #A1 in Volume 2) and a 1 Pound 1874 Harbour Committee note. Some States politicians were bankers who apparently wanted fiscal control to remain with their banks. Eventually, over 100 banks, parishes and individuals became note issuers. Notes were often issued for road-building and other public works. Bank and parish issues sometimes became intertwined with those of private companies. The notes catalogued here are church, parish or bank issues which seemed to serve the general public in some capacity.

Banks and Churches

Bible Christian Church

1872 ND Issue

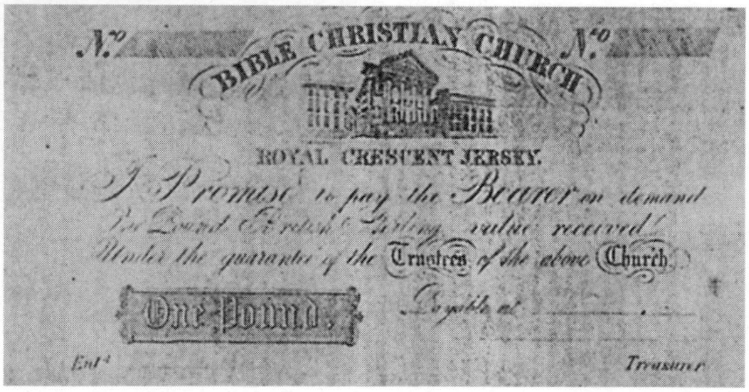

S121	1 Pound	Good	Fine	XF
	ND (ca.1872-84). Green. Building with marble-columned façade at top center. Uniface. Remainder.	—	—	125.

Bible Christian Society

ND Issue

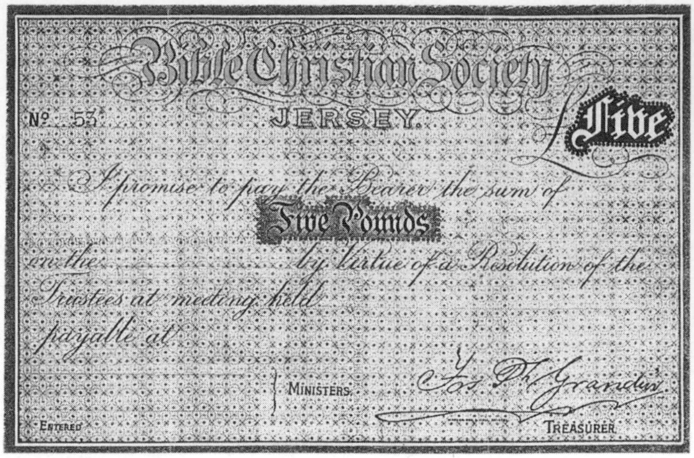

S126	5 Pounds	Good	Fine	XF
	ND. Black text. Paper: Tan. Remainder.	—	—	—

Esplanade

1858 Issue

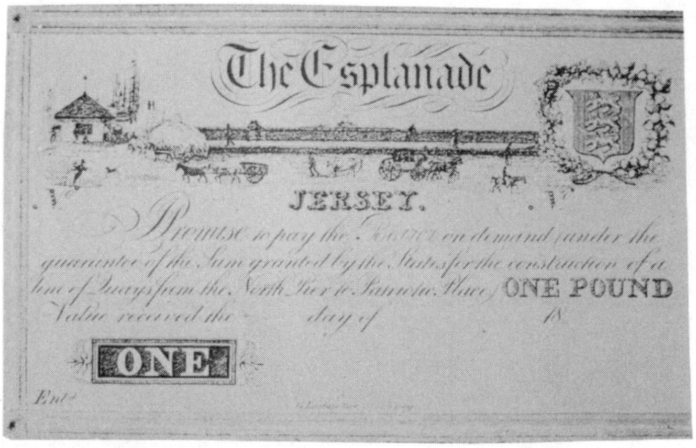

S136	1 Pound	Good	Fine	XF
	1858. Farm at upper left, street scene at upper center, arms at upper right.	—	1250.	—

International Bank

1865 Issue

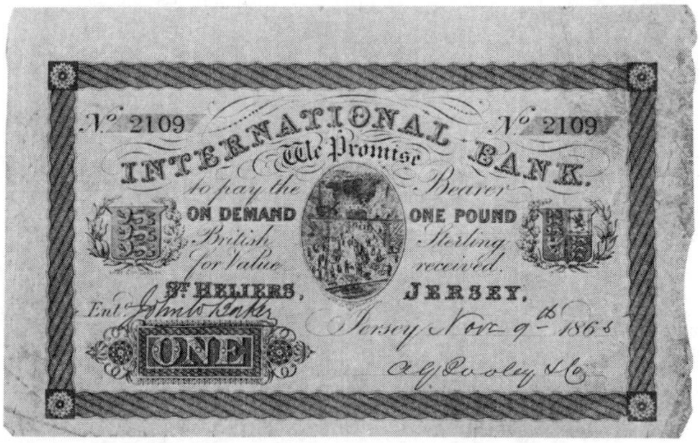

S161	1 Pound	Good	Fine	XF
	9.11.1865. Black. Arms at left and right, construction scene at center. Uniface. Printer: Rowe Co., London.	75.00	225.	675.

Jersey Agricultural Association, Trinity Bank

1835 Issue

S166 1 Pound — Good: — Fine: — XF: —
20.10.1835. Farm tools at upper center. Rare.

Jersey Mercantile Union Bank

1850's Issue

S208 1 Pound — Good: — Fine: — XF: —
18xx. Black. Harbor scene at upper left, arms at upper center, three allegorical figures at upper right, *BRITISH STERLING* in bottom frame. Back: Blue-gray. Printer: CS&E. Specimen.

1860's Issue

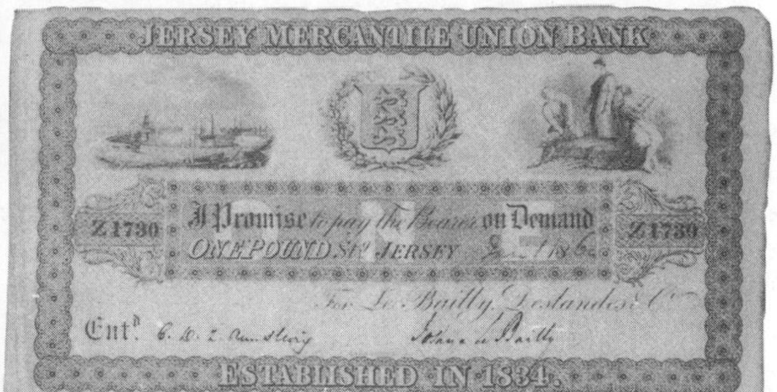

S213 1 Pound — Good: 1000. Fine: 3000. XF: —
1.1.1864. Black. Harbor scene at upper left, arms at upper center, three allegorical figures at upper right. Similar to #S208 but date within central panel, *ESTABLISHED IN 1834* in bottom frame.

NOTE: A similar issue exists drawn on this bank by Le Bailly, Deslandes & Co.

Masonic Temple Company, Limited

1866 Issue

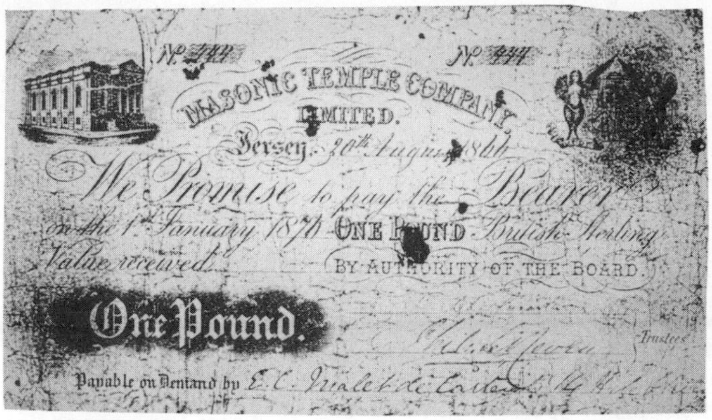

S226 1 Pound — Good: — Fine: — XF: —
1.1.1866. Building at upper left, arms at upper right. Rare.

NOTE: Poor quality reprints of an 1844 date exist.

Town Vingtaine of St. Helier

1830's Issue

S236 1 Pound — Good: — Fine: — XF: —
10.5.1834. Shield and shore scene at left.

S238 1 Pound — Good: — Fine: — XF: —
18xx. Gray and orange. Harbor and town at upper center. Like #S241 but uniface.

1850's Issue

S241 1 Pound — Good: — Fine: — XF: 125.
18xx. Gray and orange. Harbor and town at upper center. Printer: PBC. Remainder.

Vingtaine du Mont au Pretre

1838 Issue

S292 1 Pound — Good: — Fine: — XF: —
7.12.1838.

Wesleyan Methodist Country Chapels Bank

1835-50 Issue

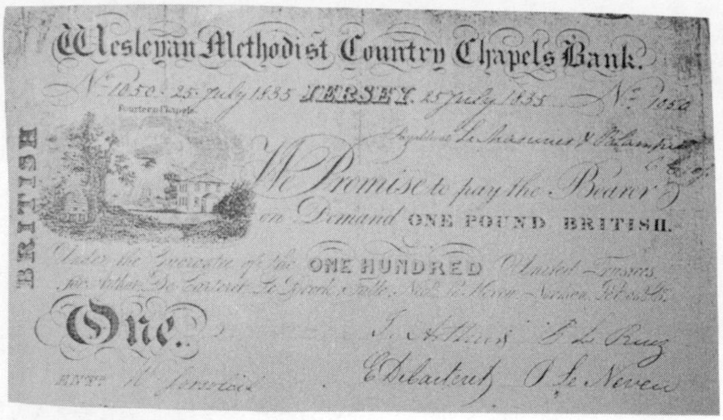

S301 1 Pound — Good — Fine — XF
25.7.1835; 1850. Beehive and chapels at left. Rare. — — —

NOTE: Blue printings appearing as proofs without dates may be reprints.

Parishes

Parish of St. Brelade

1859; 1886 Issue

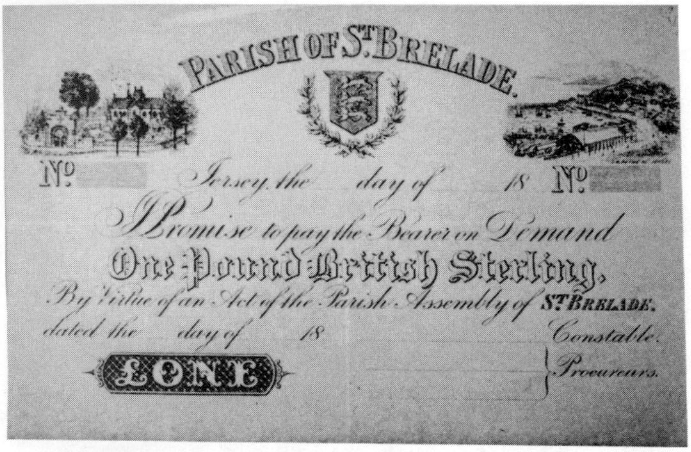

S306 1 Pound	Good	Fine	XF
7.10.1859; 12.2.1886. Church and grounds at upper left, seacoast road with hill at upper right.	75.00	225.	475.

St. Clement's Parish Bank

1800's Issue

S308 1 Pound	Good	Fine	XF
18xx. Black. Arms at upper left, church building at upper right. Remainder.	—	—	—

Parish of St. Helier

1835 Issue

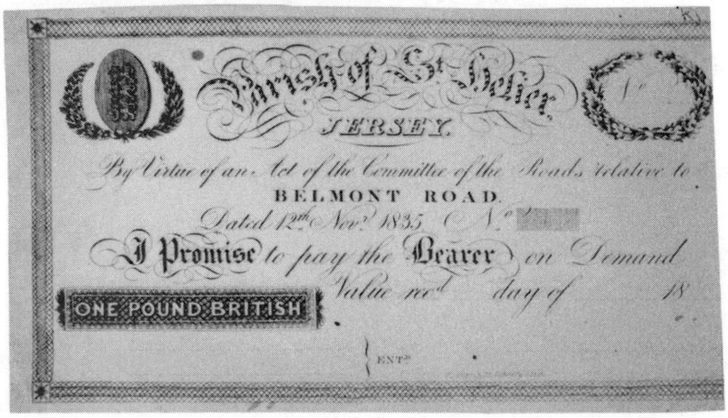

·S311 1 Pound	Good	Fine	XF
L.12.11.1835. Arms at upper left. Belmont road issue. Rare.	—	—	—

Town and Parish of St. Helier

1858 Issue

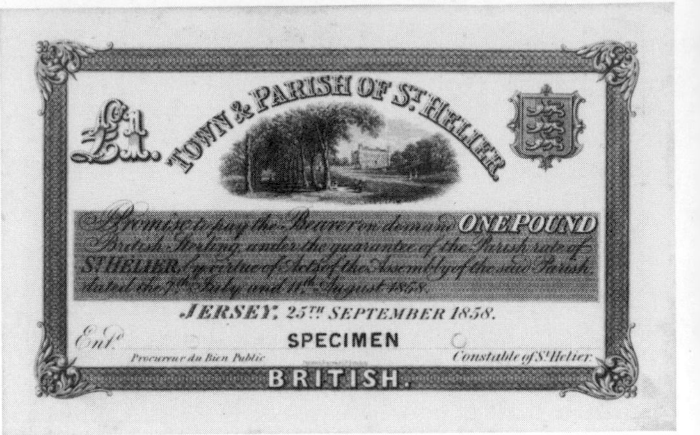

S316 1 Pound	Good	Fine	XF
25.9.1858. Trees and building at upper center, arms at right. Printer: PBC. Proof. Rare.	—	—	—

NOTE: Several other Parish of St. Helier issues are reported in association with various public works.

St. John's Bank

1800's Issue

S318 1 Pound	Good	Fine	XF
18xx. Black. Church building at left, old town view at top center. Remainder.			

NOTE: A collectors reprint (250) was produced dated 1982.

St. Martin's Parish Bank

1897 Issue

S320 1 Pound	Good	Fine	XF
18xx. Arms at upper left, castle on hill at right. Similar to #S321, but without frame border. Uniface.	—	—	

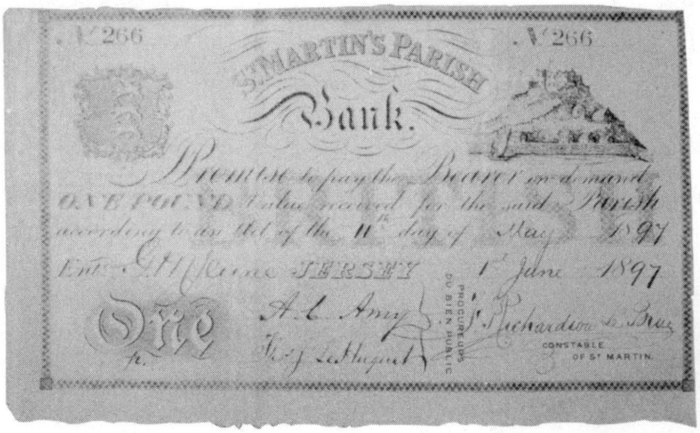

S321 1 Pound	Good	Fine	XF
1.6.1897. Arms at upper left, castle on hill at right. Rare.	—	—	—

NOTE: The date 1831 is reported for a St. Martin's Parish Bank note. It requires confirmation.

St. Mary's Parochial Bank

1850's Issue

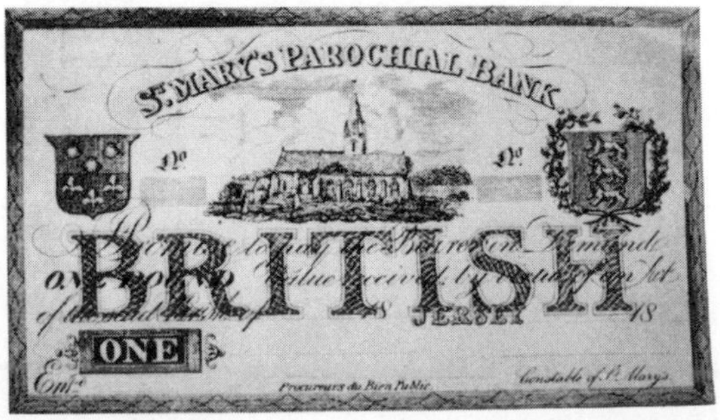

S326 1 Pound	Good	Fine	XF
18xx. Arms at left and right, church at center. Paper: Plain blue.	—	—	150.

S327 1 Pound | Good — | Fine — | XF 200.
18xx. Brown-black. Arms at left and right, church at center. Like #S326. Paper: Plain white. Proof.

S328 1 Pound | Good — | Fine — | XF 200.
18xx. Black. Arms at left and right, church at center. Like #S326. Paper: White. Watermark: *Island of Jersey* and Jersey shield of arms. Proof.

NOTE: Additional varieties require confirmation.

St. Peter's Parochial Bank

1830's Issue

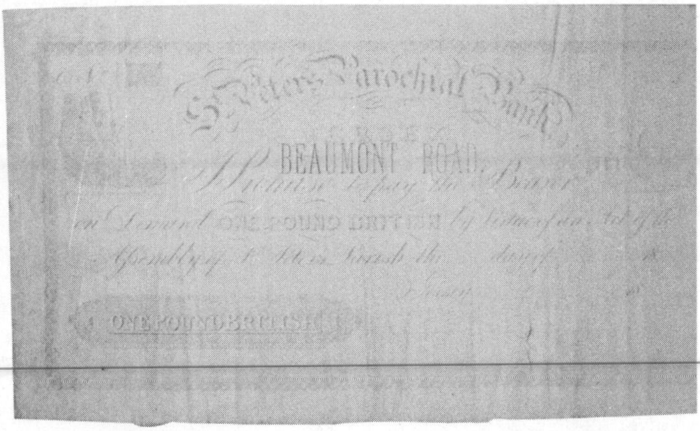

S331 1 Pound	Good	Fine	XF
18xx. House with trees at upper left, church at upper right.			
a. Overprint: *BEAUMONT ROAD* upper center. Rare.	—	—	—
r. Unsigned remainder. Rare.	—	—	—

NOTE: Reported colors for #S331 are black or orange. A variety dated 1827 with inscription: *bon pour un louis* requires confirmation.

St. Peter's Valley Road

1828 Issue

S336 1 Pound	Good	Fine	XF
1.1.1828. House and horses at left. Rare.	—	—	—

Parish of St. Peter

1890's Issue

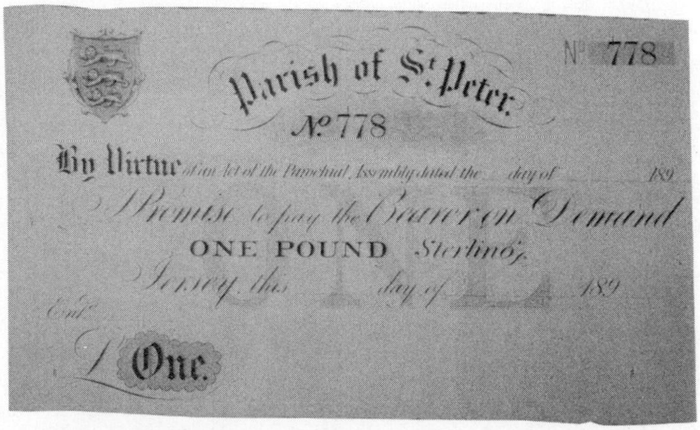

S341 1 Pound	Good	Fine	XF
189x. Arms at upper left.			
a. Blue underprint and back. Rare.	—	—	—
b. Brown underprint. Rare.	—	—	—

Parish of St. Saviour

St. Saviour's Bank

1832 Issue

S346 1 Pound	Good	Fine	XF
12.5.1832. Church at upper left, arms and lion at upper right.	75.00	225.	675.

Parish of Trinity

1836 Issue

S350 1 Pound	Good	Fine	XF
1836. Proof.	—	—	—

Note: Issued for paving of the Rozel Road and for other public works.

KEELING COCOS

Keeling Cocos Islands are a group of 27 small coral islands located in the Indian Ocean. Discovered by Captain Keeling of the East India Company in 1609, they became a British protectorate in 1857. The islands were successfully administered from Ceylon from 1878, the Straits Settlements from 1886, and the Crown Colony of Singapore from 1903. However, the real administration was vested in the hands of the Clunies-Ross family, who established themselves in the islands in about 1827. In 1955 the administration of the islands was transferred from the United Kingdom to Australia on the understanding that the Clunies-Ross family would retain their ownership of their property although the islanders have been given the opportunity to acquire Australian citizenship. In July 1978 the Australian Government announced that it had arranged to buy the islands from Mr. John Clunies-Ross, thus ending the grant of territory in perpetuity by Queen Victoria.

RULERS:
British since 1857

MONETARY SYSTEM:
1 Rupee = 100 Cents

BRITISH ADMINISTRATION

COCOS

1887-88 ISSUE

	Good	Fine	XF
S101 1/4 Rupee 1887-88. Title: *COCOS* at top. Hand dated and signed by J. C. Ross. Embossed seal at center. Uniface. Sheepskin.	—	—	—

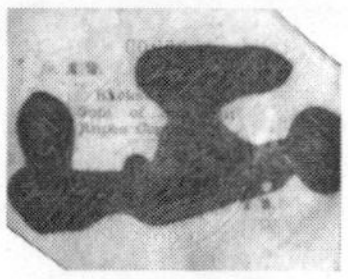

	Good	Fine	XF
S102 1/2 Rupee 24.7.1888. Title: *COCOS* at top. Hand dated and signed by J. C. Ross. Embossed seal at center. Uniface. Sheepskin. Rare.	—	—	—

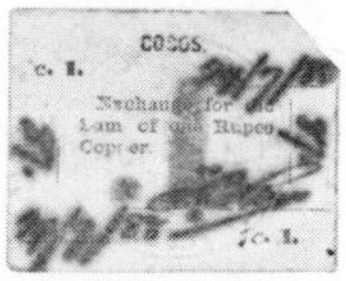

	Good	Fine	XF
S103 1 Rupee 1888. Title: *COCOS* at top. Hand dated and signed by J. C. Ross. Embossed seal at center. Uniface. Sheepskin. Rare.	—	—	—

	Good	Fine	XF
S104 2 Rupees 1888. Title: *COCOS* at top. Hand dated and signed by J. C. Ross. Embossed seal at center. Uniface. Sheepskin. Rare.	—	—	—

KEELING COCOS ISLANDS

1888 ISSUE

	Good	Fine	XF
S111 1/4 Rupee 1888. Title: *KEELING COCOS ISLANDS* by arms at top center. Embossed seal at center. Hand signed by J. C. Ross, hand dated. Uniface. Sheepskin.	900.	2700.	—

	Good	Fine	XF
S112 1/2 Rupee 1888. Title: *KEELING COCOS ISLANDS* by arms at top center. Embossed seal at center. Hand signed by J. C. Ross, hand dated. Uniface. Sheepskin.	450.	1350.	—
S113 1 Rupee 1888. Title: *KEELING COCOS ISLANDS* by arms at top center. Embossed seal at center. Hand signed by J. C. Ross, hand dated. Uniface. Sheepskin.	450.	1350.	—

	Good	Fine	XF
S114 2 Rupees 1888. Title: *KEELING COCOS ISLANDS* by arms at top center. Embossed seal at center. Hand signed by J. C. Ross, hand dated. Uniface. Sheepskin.	450.	1350.	—

	Good	Fine	XF
S115 3 Rupees 1888. Title: *KEELING COCOS ISLANDS* by arms at top center. Embossed seal at center. Hand signed by J. C. Ross, hand dated. Uniface. Sheepskin.	450.	1350.	—

	Good	Fine	XF
S116 5 Rupees 1888. Title: *KEELING COCOS ISLANDS* by arms at top center. Embossed seal at center. Hand signed by J. C. Ross, hand dated. Uniface. Sheepskin.	450.	1350.	—

1897 ISSUE

	Good	Fine	XF
S117 1/4 Rupee 1897. Black. Arms at top center. Hand written serial # and signature of G. Clunies Ross. Uniface.	175.	525.	1575.

	Good	Fine	XF
S118 1/2 Rupee 1897. Black. Arms at top center. Hand written serial # and signature of G. Clunies Ross. Uniface.	175.	525.	1575.

	Good	Fine	XF
S119 1 Rupee 1897. Black. Arms at top center. Hand written serial # and signature of G. Clunies Ross. Uniface.	175.	525.	1575.
S120 2 Rupees 1897. Black. Arms at top center. Hand written serial # and signature of G. Clunies Ross. Uniface.	175.	525.	1575.
S121 3 Rupees 1897. Black. Arms at top center. Hand written serial # and signature of G. Clunies Ross. Uniface.	175.	525.	1575.
S122 5 Rupees 1897. Black. Arms at top center. Hand written serial # and signature of G. Clunies Ross. Uniface.	175.	525.	1575.

1902 Issue

S123 1/10 Rupee	Good	Fine	XF
1902. Black. Arms at top center. Printed signature of G. Clunies Ross. Uniface.	—	Unc	100.

S124 1/4 Rupee	Good	Fine	XF
1902. Black. Arms at top center. Printed signature of G. Clunies Ross. Uniface.	—	Unc	100.

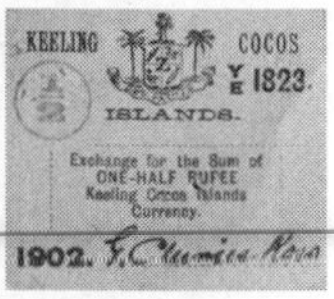

S125 1/2 Rupee	Good	Fine	XF
1902. Black. Arms at top center. Printed signature of G. Clunies Ross. Uniface.	—	Unc	150.

S126 1 Rupee	Good	Fine	XF
1902. Black. Arms at top center. Printed signature of G. Clunies Ross. Uniface.	—	Unc	300.

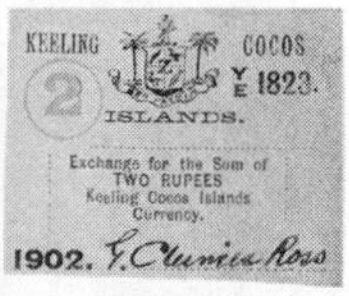

S127 2 Rupees	Good	Fine	XF
1902. Black. Arms at top center. Printed signature of G. Clunies Ross. Uniface.	—	Unc	300.

S128 5 Rupees	Good	Fine	XF
1902. Black. Arms at top center. Printed signature of G. Clunies Ross. Uniface.	—	Unc	350.

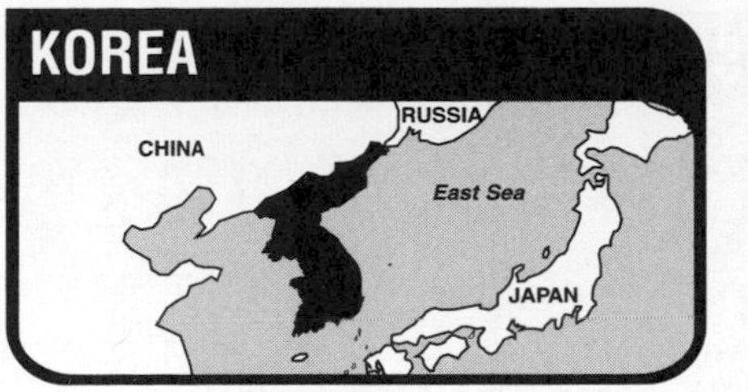

Korea,"Land of the Morning Calm", occupies a mountainous peninsula in northeast Asia bounded by Manchuria, the Yellow Sea and the Sea of Japan. According to legend, the first Korean dynasty, that of the House of Tangun, ruled from 2333 BC to 1122 BC. It was followed by the dynasty of Kija, a Chinese scholar, which continued until 193 BC and brought a high civilization to Korea. The first recorded period in the history of Korea, the Period of the Three Kingdoms, lasted from 57 BC to 935 AD and achieved the first political unification on the peninsula. The Kingdom of Koryo, from which Korea derived its name, was founded in 935 and continued until 1392, when it was superseded by the Yi dynasty of King Yi, Sung Kye which was to last until the Japanese annexation in 1910.

At the end of the 16th century Korea was invaded and occupied for 7 years by Japan, and from 1627 until the late 19th century it was a semi-independent tributary of China. Japan replaced China as the predominant foreign influence at the end of the Sino-Japanese War (1894-95), only to find its position threatened by Russian influence from 1896 to 1904. The Russian threat was eliminated by the Russo-Japanese War (1904-05) and in 1905 Japan established a direct protectorate over Korea. On Aug. 22, 1910, the last Korean ruler signed the treaty that annexed Korea to Japan as a government general in the Japanese Empire. Japanese suzerainty was maintained until the end of World War II.

The Potsdam conference (1945) set the 38th parallel as the line dividing the occupation forces of the United States in the South and the Soviet Union in the north.

A contingent of the United States Army landed at Inchon to begin the acceptance of the surrender of Japanese forces in the South on Sept. 8, 1945. Unissued Japanese printed stock was released during the U.S. Army's administration for circulation in the southern sector.

NOTE: For later issues see Korea/North and Korea/South.

* * * This section has been partially renumbered. * * *

The Potsdam conference in 1945 set the 38th parallel as the line dividing the occupation forces of the United States in the south and the Soviet Union in the north.

A contingent of the United States Army landed at Inchon to begin the acceptance of the surrender of Japanese forces in the south on Sept. 8, 1945. Unissued Japanese printed stock was released during the U.S. Army's administration for circulation in the southern sector.

RULERS:

Japanese, 1910-1945
Yi Hyong (Kojong), 1864-1897
as Kwangmu, 1897-1907
Yung Hi, 1907-1910

MONETARY SYSTEM:

1 Yang = 100 Fun
1 Whan = 5 Yang to 1902
1 Won = 100 Chon 1902-
1 Yen = 100 Sen

MONETARY UNITS:

Fun
Mun
Yang, Niang
Chon
Won
Hwan

MONETARY UNITS:

Mun .... Yang

Kingdom

Keijo-Pusan Railway Company

1900 Issue

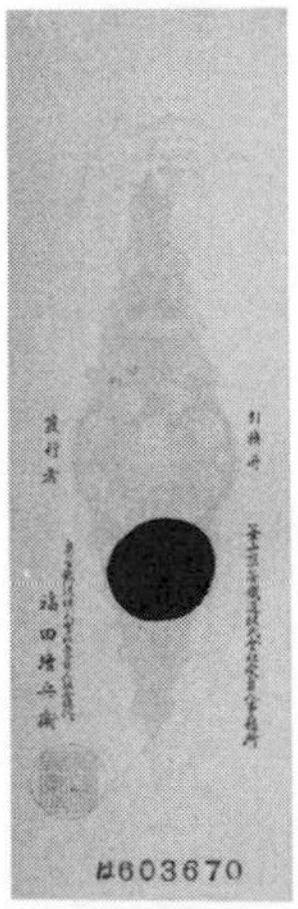

S101 50 Mun	Good	Fine	XF
1900. Blue on light blue underprint. Steam train at upper center. Back: Orange. Vertical format.			
a. Issued note.	—	—	—
b. Punched hole cancelled.	75.00	225.	675.

		Good	Fine	XF
S102	**100 Mun**			
	1900. Brown on light tan underprint. Steam train at upper center. Back: Orange. Vertical format.			
	a. Issued note. Rare.	—	—	—
	b. Punched hole cancelled.	75.00	225.	675.
S103	**300 Mun**			
	1900. Steam train at upper center. Back: Orange. Vertical format. Reported not confirmed.	—	—	—
S104	**500 Mun**			
	1900. Orange on light tan underprint. Steam train at upper center. Back: Orange. Vertical format.			
	a. Issued note. Rare.	—	—	—
	b. Punched hole cancelled.	80.00	240.	725.

Seoul Exchange Office

ND Issue

		Good	Fine	XF
S115	**100 Corean Dollars**			
	ND. Brown with black text on green underprint. Back: Black and ochre with blue, green and black text.	—	—	—

Kuang Tong Company

ND Issue

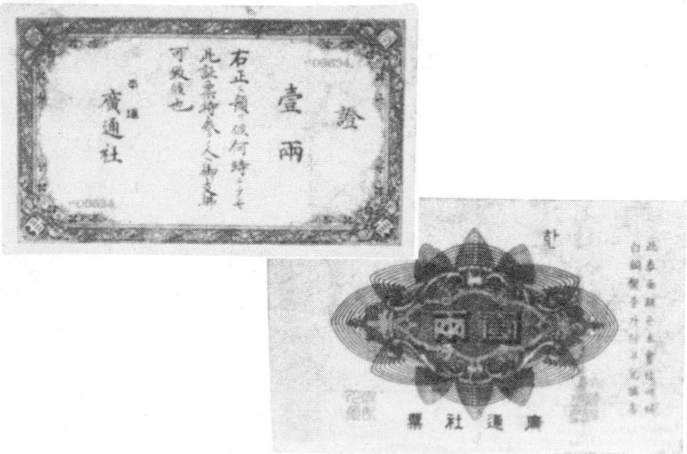

		Good	Fine	XF
S121	**1 Yang**			
	ND. Black on pale blue-green underprint. Back: Dark blue.	—	—	—

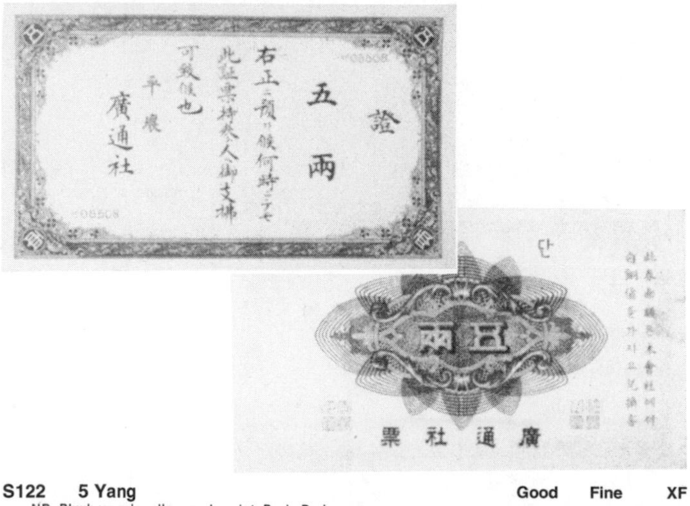

		Good	Fine	XF
S122	**5 Yang**			
	ND. Black on pale yellow underprint. Back. Dark green.	—	—	—

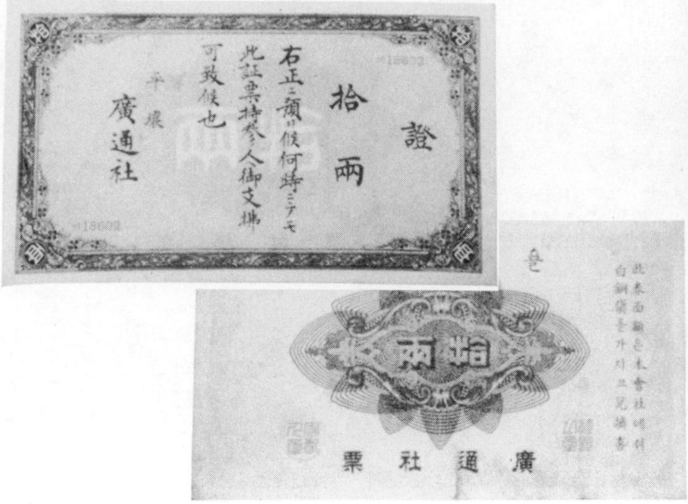

		Good	Fine	XF
S123	**10 Yang**			
	ND. Black on pale blue underprint. Back: Red-brown.	—	—	—

Kuang Tung Chon Hiang

Kuang Tung Cash Bank

ND Issue

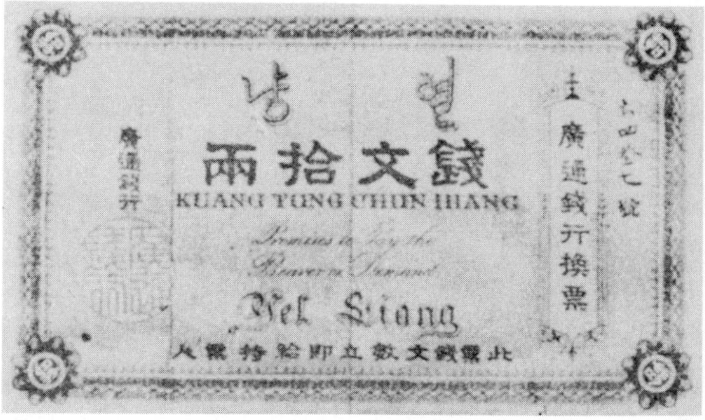

		Good	Fine	XF
S133	**10 Yang**			
	ND.	—	—	—

Tong Sun Tai Hoa

ND Issue

#S141-S145 denominations given in Yang Yopchon.

		Good	Fine	XF
S141	**25 Yang**			
	ND.	—	—	—

		Good	Fine	XF
S142	**50 Yang** ND. Black and orange on blue underprint. Back: Pale blue.	—	—	—
S143	**100 Yang** ND.	—	—	—
S144	**500 Yang** ND.	—	—	—

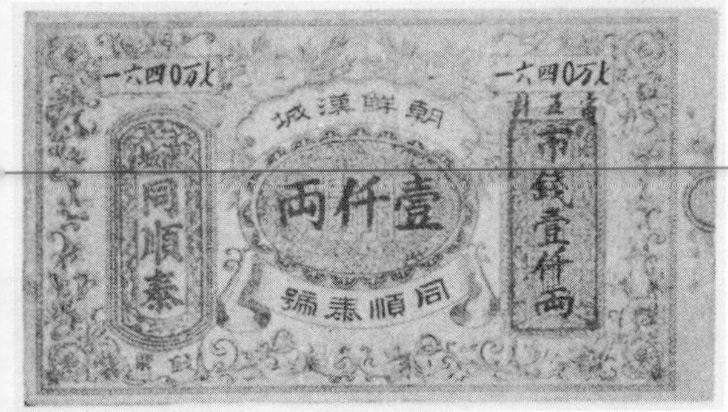

		Good	Fine	XF
S145	**1000 Yang**	—	—	—
S151	**10,000 Mun**	—	—	—

CHINDO BANK

SHOTOKU CHOSEN GINKO

ND ISSUE

#S171-S177 denominations given in Yang Yopchon. No relation to the Vol. 2 book.

		Good	Fine	XF
S171	**1 Yang** ND.	—	—	—

		Good	Fine	XF
S173	**10 Yang** ND. Black on plae green underprint. Back: Brown.	—	—	—

		Good	Fine	XF
S174	**50 Yang** ND. Black on ochre underprint. Back: Ochre.	—	—	—

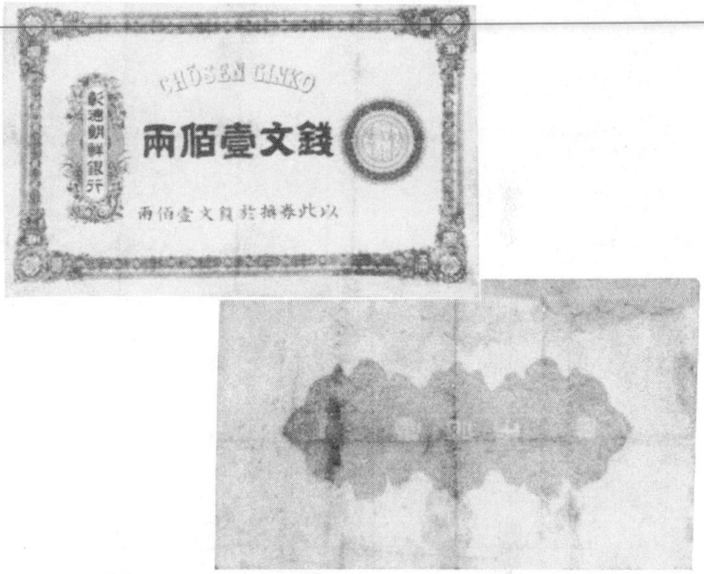

		Good	Fine	XF
S175	**100 Yang** ND. Black on pale purple underprint. Back: Pale green.	—	—	—

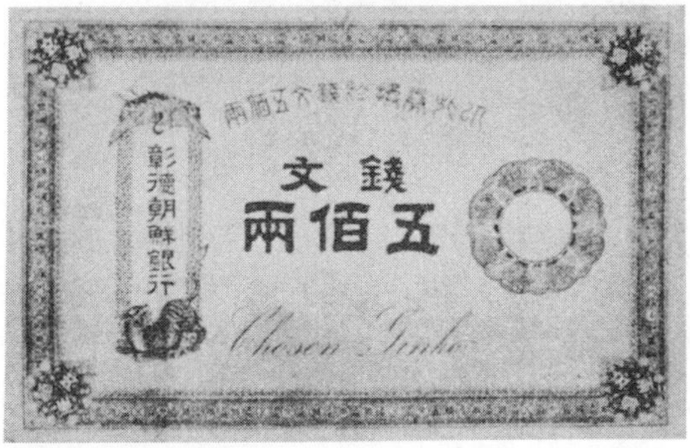

		Good	Fine	XF
S176	**500 Yang** ND.	—	—	—
S177	**1000 Yang** ND.	—	—	—

NOTE: No relation to Chosen Ginko listed in Vol. 2.

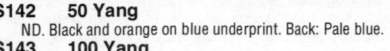

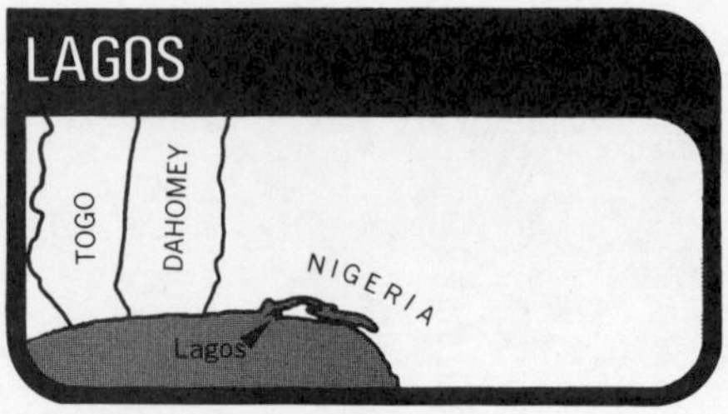

After centuries of self-determination, followed by various colonial occupations, Lagos (so named by the Portuguese because of its many lakes and lagoons) fell under British rule in 1861. The British administered Lagos at first from Sierra Leone, then as part of the Gold Coast. Lagos became a separate colony from 1886 to 1906; it was then conjoined with southern Nigeria. Lagos became the capital of Nigeria in 1960 and is located in the southwestern part of the country.

British Administration

African Banking Corporation Ltd.

1891 Issue

		Good	Fine	XF
S101	**1 Pound** 1.10.1891. Black and green. Portrait woman at left. Back: Green. Printer: BWC.			
	a. Issued note.	—	—	—
	s. Specimen. Perforated: *SPECIMEN B.W. & CO/LONDON.*	—	Unc	2500.
S102	**5 Pounds** 1.10.1891. Black and brown. Portrait woman supported by two cherubs at left. Back: Brown. Printer: BWC.			
	a. Issued note.	—	—	—
	s. Specimen. Perforated: *SPECIMEN B.W. & CO/LONDON.*	—	Unc	2500.

Bank of British West Africa Limited

1890s Issue

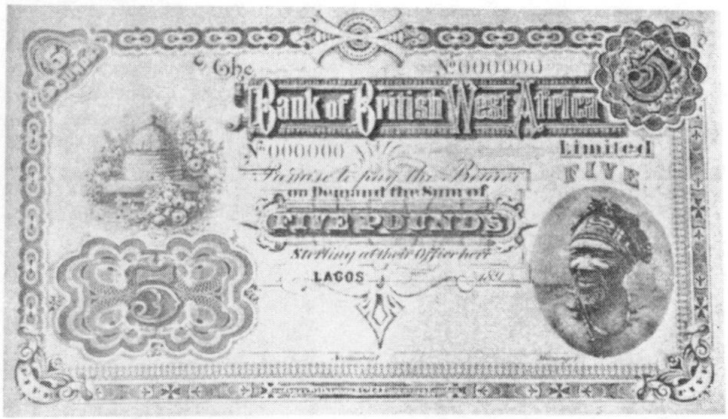

		Good	Fine	XF
S111	**5 Pounds** 189x. Beehive at upper left, man in headdress at lower right. Printer: BWC. Proof.	—	—	—

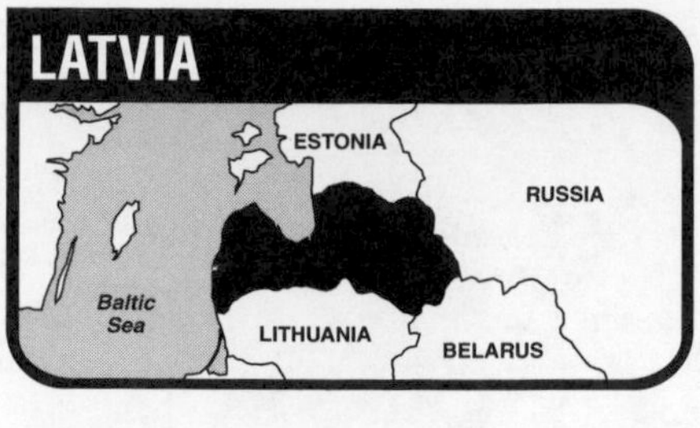

The Republic of Latvia, the central Baltic state in east Europe, has an area of 24,595 sq. mi. (43,601 sq. km.) and a population of 2.4 million. Capital: Riga. Livestock raising and manufacturing are the chief industries. Butter, bacon, fertilizers and telephone equipment are exported.

The name "Latvia" originates from the ancient Latgalians, one of four eastern Baltic tribes that formed the ethnic core of the Latvian people (ca. 8th-12th centuries A.D.). The region subsequently came under the control of Germans, Poles, Swedes, and finally, Russians. A Latvian republic emerged following World War I, but it was annexed by the USSR in 1940 - an action never recognized by the US and many other countries. Latvia reestablished its independence in 1991 following the breakup of the Soviet Union. Although the last Russian troops left in 1994, the status of the Russian minority (some 30% of the population) remains of concern to Moscow. Latvia joined both NATO and the EU in the spring of 2004.

MONETARY SYSTEM:

1 Rublis = 100 Kapeikas, 1919-22
1 Lats = 100 Santimu, 1923-40; 1992
1 Lats = 200 Rublu, 1993
1 Rublis = 1 Russian Ruble, 1992

Regional

Rigas Stradneeku Deputatu Padomes

Riga's Workers Deputies' Soviet

1919 Issue

Note: #R1-R4 also exist as unfinished notes. Unfinished sheets of #R3 and R4 with printing on only 1 side were used in producing some Latvian postage stamps.

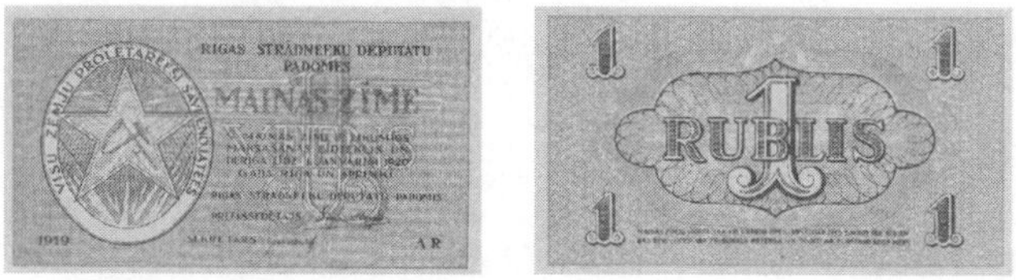

		VG	VF	UNC
R1	**1 Rublis** 1919. Red and brown. Star with hammer and sickle. Watermark: Design. Circulated in all parts of Latvia.	2.00	5.00	10.00

		VG	VF	UNC
R2	**3 Rubli** 1919. Red, olive green and black. Star, with hammer and sickle. Watermark: Design. Circulated in all parts of Latvia.			
	a. Issued note.	3.00	6.00	12.00
	x. Back inverted. Rare.	—	—	—

		VG	VF	UNC
R3	**5 Rubli** 1919. Red and blue. Star, with hammer and sickle. Watermark: Design. Circulated in all parts of Latvia.			
	a. Issued note.	4.00	8.00	15.00
	x. Back inverted. Rare.	—	—	—
R4	**10 Rubli** 1919. Red, green and lilac. Star, with hammer and sickle. Watermark: Design. Circulated in all parts of Latvia.	5.00	10.00	20.00

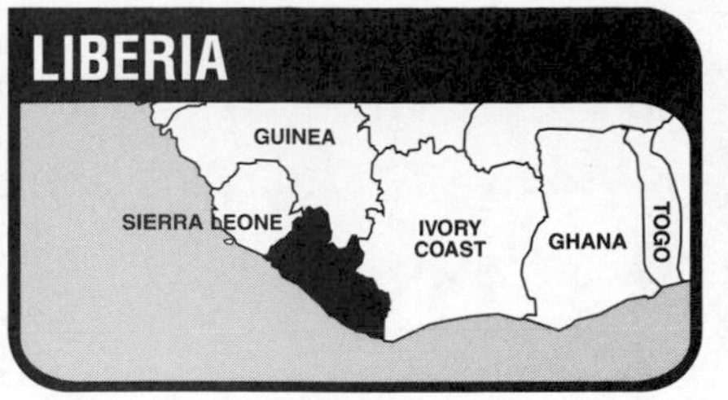

The Republic of Liberia, located on the southern side of the west African bulge between Sierra Leone and the Ivory Coast, has an area of 38,250 sq. mi. (111,369 sq. km.) and a population of 3.26 million. Capital: Monrovia. The major industries are agriculture, mining and lumbering. Iron ore, diamonds, rubber, coffee and cocoa are exported.

Settlement of freed slaves from the US in what is today Liberia began in 1822; by 1847, the Americo-Liberians were able to establish a republic. William Tubman, president from 1944-71, did much to promote foreign investment and to bridge the economic, social, and political gaps between the descendents of the original settlers and the inhabitants of the interior. In 1980, a military coup led by Samuel Doe ushered in a decade of authoritarian rule. In December 1989, Charles Taylor launched a rebellion against Doe's regime that led to a prolonged civil war in which Doe himself was killed. A period of relative peace in 1997 allowed for elections that brought Taylor to power, but major fighting resumed in 2000. An August 2003 peace agreement ended the war and prompted the resignation of former president Charles Taylor, who faces war crimes charges in The Hague related to his involvement in Sierra Leone's civil war. After two years of rule by a transitional government, democratic elections in late 2005 brought President Ellen Johnson Sirleaf to power. The UN Mission in Liberia (UNMIL) maintains a strong presence throughout the country, but the security situation is still fragile and the process of rebuilding the social and economic structure of this war-torn country will take many years.

MONETARY SYSTEM:

1 Dollar = 100 Cents

United States Administration

American Colonization Society

1840's Issue

S101 50 Cents	Good	Fine	XF
18xx. Black. Portrait Benjamin Franklin at upper left, two cherubs with barrel and bale at upper center, portrait George Washington at upper right. Printer: UBS&H/DU. Proof.	—	Unc	500.

S102 1 Dollar	Good	Fine	XF
1840. Black. Two seated allegorical children writing and reading at top center. Printer: UBS&H/DU.	—	Unc	500.

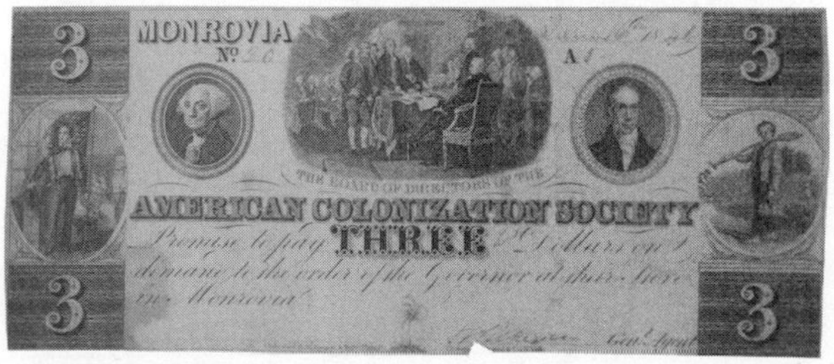

S103 3 Dollars	Good	Fine	XF
16.6.1846. Black. Boy with flag at far left, portrait George Washington at upper left, signing of Declaration of Independence at center, portrait man at upper right, boy with shovel at far right. Printer: UBS&H/DU.	—	—	—

Colonial Agent, Monrovia

1834 Issue

S106 5 Cents	Good	Fine	XF
4.7.1834. Wild pig at center with text: *The Colonial Agent promises to pay to the bearer, on demand, five cents.*	—	—	—
S107 10 Cents			
4.7.1834. Sheep at center with text: *The Colonial Agent. . . ten cents.*	175.	525.	1575.

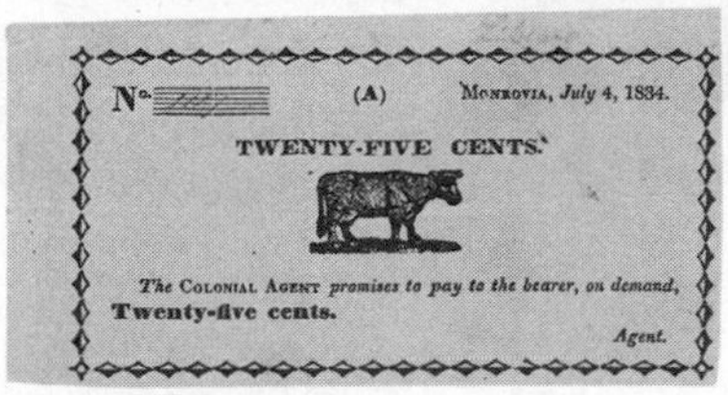

S108 25 Cents	Good	Fine	XF
4.7.1834. Cow at center with text: *The Colonial Agent . . . twenty-five cents.*	175.	525.	1575.

Maryland State Colonization Society

1837 Issue

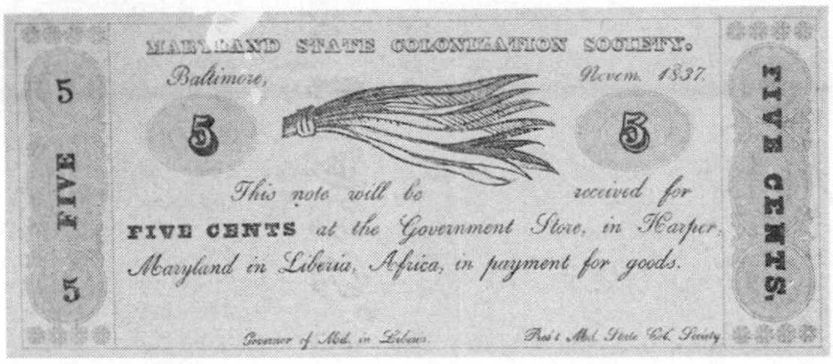

S111 5 Cents	Good	Fine	XF
Novem. 1837. Black and golden brown. Tobacco leaves at upper center with text: *This. . . will be received for five cents at the government store, in Harper, Maryland in Liberia, Africa, in payment for goods.* Paper: Pink.			
a. Issued note.	—	—	—
rp. Reprint with watermark: 1883....	—	Unc	400.

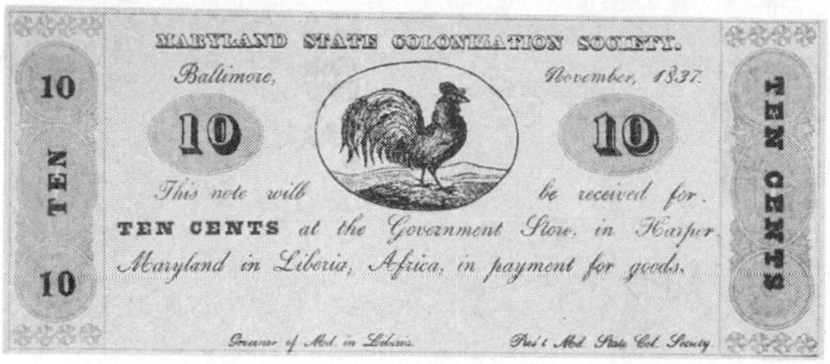

S112 10 Cents	Good	Fine	XF
November 1837. Black and golden brown. Rooster at upper center with text: *This. . . will be received for ten cents at the government store, in Harper, Maryland in Liberia, Africa, in payment for goods.* Paper: Pink.			
a. Issued note.	—	—	—
rp. Reprint with watermark: 1883....	—	Unc	400.
S113 25 Cents			
November 1837. Black and golden brown. Duck at upper center with text: *This. . . will be received for twenty-five cents at the government store, in Harper, Maryland in Liberia, Africa, in payment for goods.* Paper: Pink.			
a. Issued note.	—	—	—
rp. Reprint with watermark: 1883....	—	Unc	400.

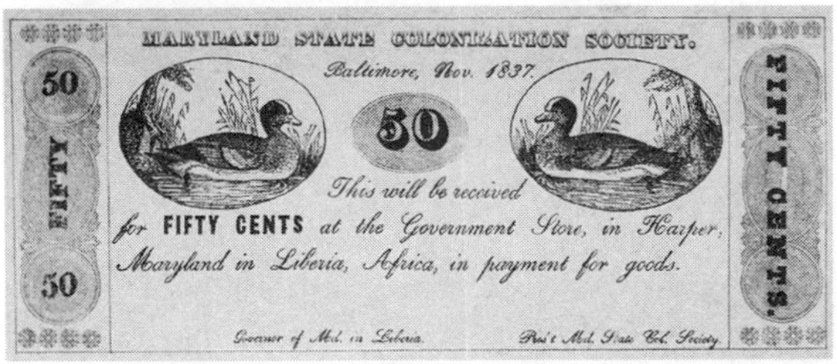

S114 50 Cents	Good	Fine	XF
Nov. 1837. Black and golden brown. Facing ducks at upper left and right with text: *This. . . will be received for fifty cents at the government store, in Harper, Maryland in Liberia, Africa, in payment for goods.* Paper: Pink.			
a. Issued note.	—	—	—
rp. Reprint with watermark: 1883....	—	Unc	400.

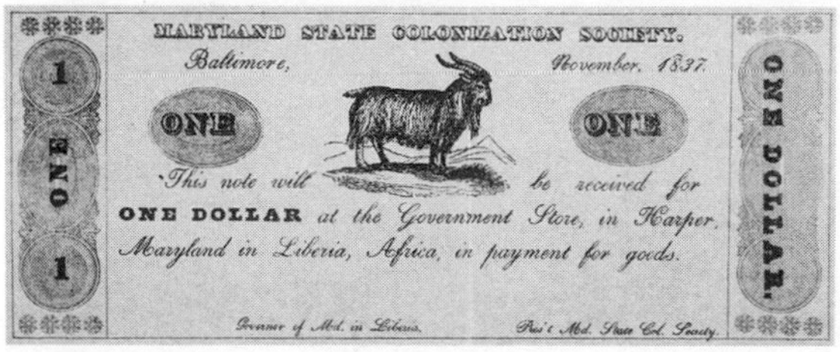

S115 1 Dollar	Good	Fine	XF
November, 1837. Black and golden brown. Goat at top center with text: *This. . . will be received for one dollar at the government store, in Harper, Maryland in Liberia, Africa, in payment for goods.* Paper: Pink.			
a. Issued note.	—	—	—
rp. Reprint with watermark: 1883....	—	Unc	400.

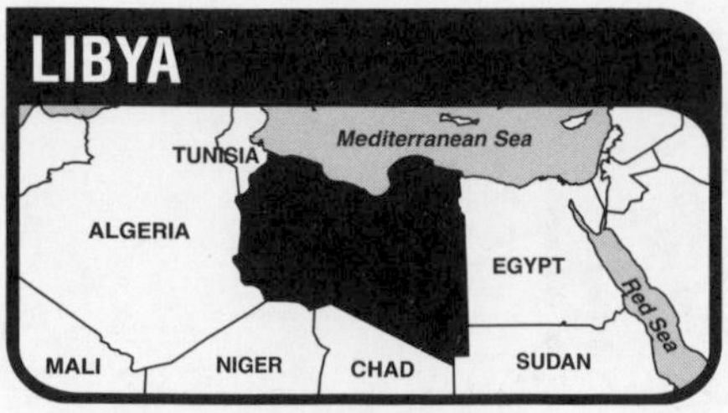

The Socialist People's Libyan Arab Jamahiriya, located on the north central coast of Africa between Tunisia and Egypt, has an area of 679,359 sq. mi. (1,759,540 sq. km.) and a population of 6.39 million. Capital: Tripoli. Crude oil, which accounts for 90 percent of the export earnings, is the mainstay of the economy.

The Italians supplanted the Ottoman Turks in the area around Tripoli in 1911 and did not relinquish their hold until 1943 when defeated in World War II. Libya then passed to UN administration and achieved independence in 1951. Following a 1969 military coup, Col. Muammar Abu Minyar al-Qadhafi began to espouse his own political system, the Third Universal Theory. The system is a combination of socialism and Islam derived in part from tribal practices and is supposed to be implemented by the Libyan people themselves in a unique form of "direct democracy." Qadhafi has always seen himself as a revolutionary and visionary leader. He used oil funds during the 1970s and 1980s to promote his ideology outside Libya, supporting subversives and terrorists abroad to hasten the end of Marxism and capitalism. In addition, beginning in 1973, he engaged in military operations in northern Chad's Aozou Strip - to gain access to minerals and to use as a of influence in Chadian politics - but was forced to retreat in 1987. UN sanctions in 1992 isolated Qadhafi politically following the downing of Pan AM Flight 103 over Lockerbie, Scotland. During the 1990s, Qadhafi began to rebuild his relationships with Europe. UN sanctions were suspended in April 1999 and finally lifted in September 2003 after Libya accepted responsibility for the Lockerbie bombing. In December 2003, Libya announced that it had agreed to reveal and end its programs to develop weapons of mass destruction and to renounce terrorism. Qadhafi has made significant strides in normalizing relations with Western nations since then. He has received various Western European leaders as well as many working-level and commercial delegations, and made his first trip to Western Europe in 15 years when he traveled to Brussels in April 2004. The US rescinded Libya's designation as a state sponsor of terrorism in June 2006. In January 2008, Libya assumed a nonpermanent seat on the United Nations Security Council for the 2008/09 term. In August 2008, the US and Libya signed a bilateral comprehensive claims settlement agreement to compensate claimants in both countries who allege injury or death at the hands of the other country, including the Lockerbie bombing, the LaBelle disco bombing, and the UTA 772 bombing. In October 2008, the US Government received $1.5 billion pursuant to the agreement to distribute to US national claimants, and as a result effectively normalized its bilateral relationship with Libya. The two countries then exchanged ambassadors for the first time since 1973 in January 2009.

RULERS:

Idris I, 1951-1969

MONETARY SYSTEM:

1 Piastre = 10 Milliemes
1 Pound = 100 Piastres = 1000 Milliemes, 1951-1971
1 Dinar = 1000 Dirhams, 1971-

British Occupation - WW II

Military Authority in Tripolitania

1943 ND Issue

		VG	VF	UNC
M1	**1 Lira**			
	ND (1943). Green. Lion on crown at center or at right.			
	a. Issued note.	1.00	8.00	40.00
	s. Specimen.	—	—	200.
M2	**2 Lire**			
	ND (1943). Blue on green underprint. Lion on crown at center or at right.			
	a. Issued note.	5.00	40.00	120.
	s. Specimen.	—	—	200.

Note: #M2 is scarce as there was a coin of equivalent value in circulation at the time of issue.

		VG	VF	UNC
M3	**5 Lire**			
	ND (1943). Green on red-brown underprint. Lion on crown at center or at right.			
	a. Issued note.	1.00	7.50	40.00
	s. Specimen.	—	—	350.
M4	**10 Lire**			
	ND (1943). Lilac on green underprint. Lion on crown at center or at right.			
	a. Issued note.	4.00	15.00	65.00
	s. Specimen.	—	—	400.

		VG	VF	UNC
M5	**50 Lire**			
	ND (1943). Brown. Lion on crown at center or at right.			
	a. Issued note.	10.00	50.00	135.
	s. Specimen.	—	—	500.
M6	**100 Lire**			
	ND (1943). Red-orange on blue underprint. Lion on crown at center or at right.			
	a. Issued note.	15.00	60.00	185.
	s. Specimen.	—	—	600.

		VG	VF	UNC
M7	**500 Lire**			
	ND (1943). Green on blue underprint. Lion on crown at center or at right.			
	a. Issued note.	80.00	400.	1150.
	s. Specimen.	—	—	1000.
M8	**1000 Lire**			
	ND (1943). Blue on brown underprint. Lion on crown at center or at right.			
	a. Issued note.	300.	1250.	2500.
	s. Specimen.	—	—	2000.

French Occupation of the Fezzan - WW II

Republique Francaise

1936-38 ND Issue

#M9-M11 black handstamp: *R-F/FEZZAN* (in rectangle); letters in stamp 12 and 14mm high on Banque de l'Afrique Occidentale notes. Forgeries, created for collectors, exist (with letters in stamp taller and different dates after 1940).

Note: There is a possibility that all Fezzan overprint notes except some of #M9 are spurious.

		VG	VF	UNC
M9	**5 Francs**			
	ND (-old date 10.3.1938). Multicolor. Overprint: On French West Africa #21.	150.	275.	—

		VG	VF	UNC
M10	**25 Francs**			
	ND (-old date 10.3.1938). Overprint: On French West Africa #24.	—	—	—

		VG	VF	UNC
M11	**100 Francs**			
	ND (-old date 17.11.1936). Overprint: On French West Africa #26.	—	—	—

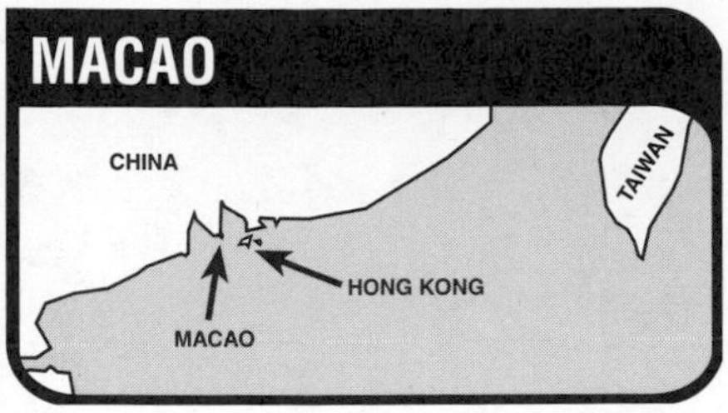

The Macau R.A.E.M., a former Portuguese overseas province located in the South China Sea 35 miles (56 km.) southwest of Hong Kong, consists of the peninsula and the islands of Taipa and Coloane. It has an area of 14 sq. mi. (21.45 sq. km.) and a population of 415,850. Capital: Macau. The economy is d on tourism, gambling, commerce and gold trading - Macau is one of the few entirely free markets for gold in the world. Cement, textiles, vegetable oils and metal products are exported.

Established by the Portuguese in 1557, Macau is the oldest European settlement in the Far East. Pursuant to an agreement signed by China and Portugal on 13 April 1987, Macau became the Macau Special Administrative Region (SAR) of the People's Republic of China on 20 December 1999. In this agreement, China promised that, under its "one country, two systems" formula, China's socialist economic system would not be practiced in Macau, and that Macau would enjoy a high degree of autonomy in all matters except foreign and defense affairs for the next 50 years.

RULERS:

Portuguese from 1849-1999

MONETARY SYSTEM:

1 Dollar = 100 Cents
1 Pataca = 100 Avos

DATING

Most notes were issued in the year of the Chinese Republic but occasionally the old Chinese lunar calendar was used. These dates are listed as "CD". Refer to China-Introduction for Cyclical Date Chart.

DATE CHART

	庚	辛	壬	癸	甲	乙	丙	丁	戊	己
戌	1850 1910		1862 1922		1874 1934		1886 1946		1838 1898	
亥		1851 1911		1863 1923		1875 1935		1887 1947		1839 1899
子	1840 1900		1852 1912		1864 1924		1876 1936		1888 1948	
丑		1841 1901		1853 1913		1865 1925		1877 1937		1889 1949
寅	1830 1890		1842 1902		1854 1914		1866 1926		1878 1938	
卯		1831 1891		1843 1903		1855 1915		1867 1927		1879 1939
辰	1880 1940		1832 1892		1844 1904		1856 1916		1868 1928	
巳		1881 1941		1833 1893		1845 1905		1857 1917		1869 1929
午	1870 1930		1882 1942		1834 1894		1846 1906		1858 1918	
未		1871 1931		1883 1943		1835 1895		1847 1907		1859 1919
申	1860 1920		1872 1932		1884 1944		1836 1896		1848 1908	
酉		1861 1921		1873 1933		1885 1945		1837 1897		1849 1909

PRIVATE BANKS

During the 1920's and early 1930's the private banks of Macao issued various circulating checks in dollars to facilitate trade with Chinese firms. These apparently circulated freely along with the Pataca issues of the Banco Nacional Ultramarino which quite obviously were in short supply. Most examples known have appropriate colonial revenue adhesive stamps affixed as found on bills of exchange and private checks. The additional large brush strokes or marks obliterating the denomination indicates the sum has been paid. A similar circulating check was issued in 1944 by the Tai Fong Cambista.

Portuguese Administration

Chan Tung Cheng Bank

1934 Issue

		Good	Fine	XF
S92	**10 Dollars** 1934. Black on pink underprint. Back: Red. Government building at center. Printer: HKPP.	150.	450.	1350.

Chee Cheong Bank

1934 Interest Bearing Notes Issue

		Good	Fine	XF
S101	**100 Dollars** 1934.	75.00	225.	675.
S102	**200 Dollars** 1934.	75.00	225.	675.
S103	**800 Dollars** 1934.	100.	300.	900.

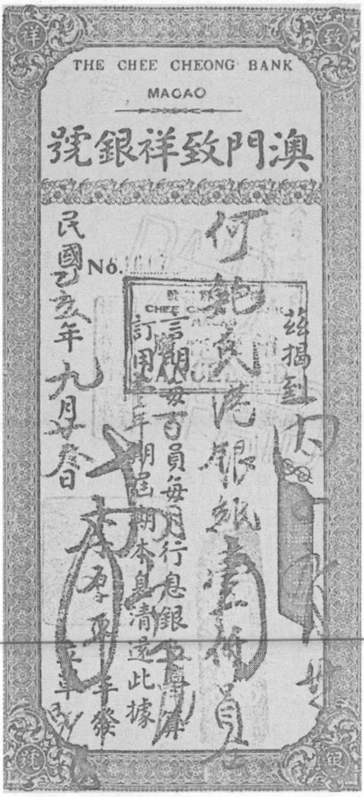

		Good	Fine	XF
S104	**1000 Dollars** 23.7.1934. Maroon on yellow underprint. Back: Red text. Vertical format.	125.	375.	1150.

Foo Hang Bank

1937 Issue

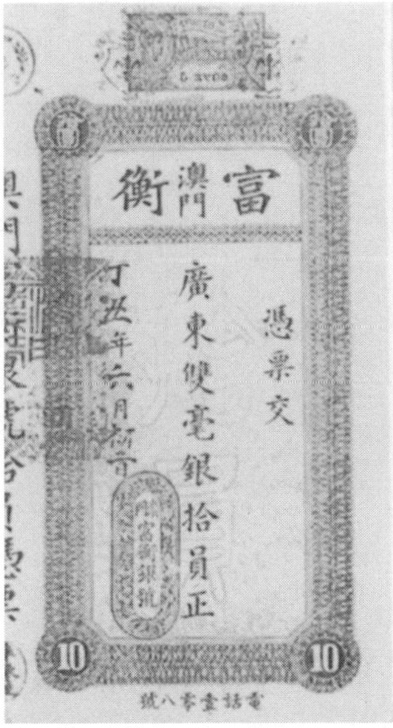

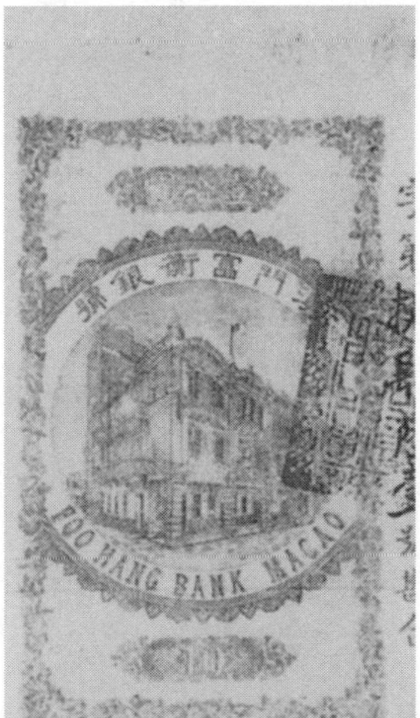

		Good	Fine	XF
S105	**10 Dollars** 1937. Blue on pale green underprint. Back: Red. Government building at center.	30.00	100.	300.

Fu Quei Cambista

1933 Cashier's Checks Issue

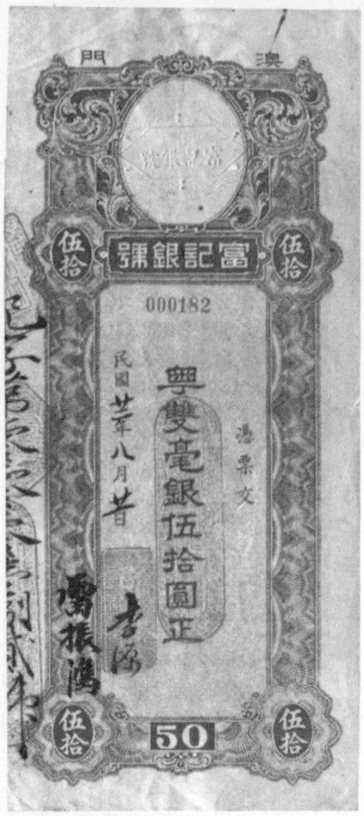

S106	**50 Dollars**	**Good**	**Fine**	**XF**
	1933. Green on light ochre underprint. Back: Red. Pagoda at center. Vertical face//horizontal back.	200.	600.	1800.

Hang Hing Bank

1931 Issue

S107	**50 Dollars**	**Good**	**Fine**	**XF**
	23.1.1931. Green on yellow-green underprint. Two cherubs holding shield at top. Back: Red-brown.	150.	450.	1350.

Kwong Yuen Bank

1924; 1925 Cashier's Checks Issue

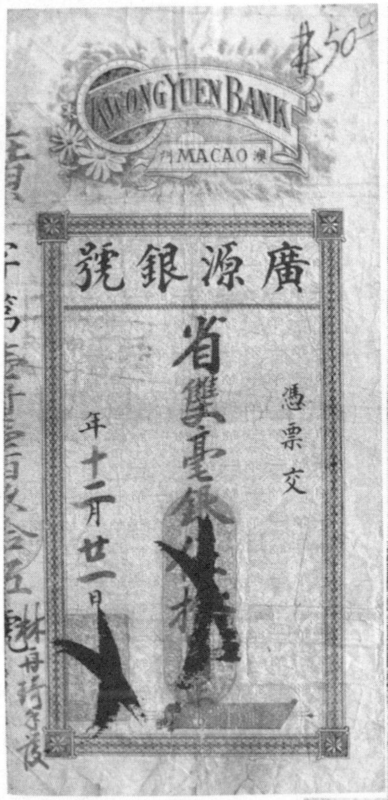

S108	**50 Dollars**	**Good**	**Fine**	**XF**
	27.11.1924; 21.12.1924. Green on yellow underprint. Uniface. Vertical format.	60.00	180.	550.

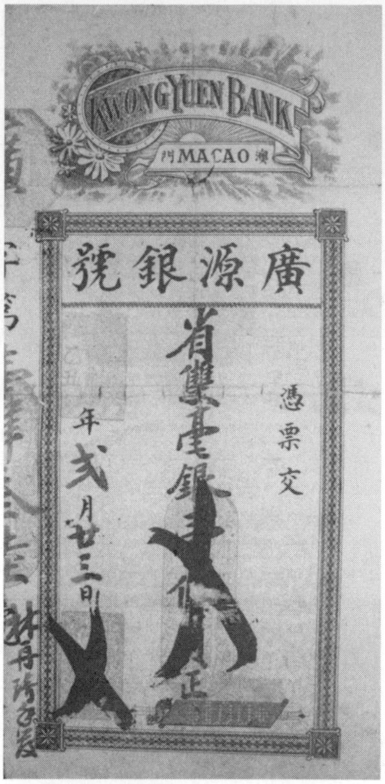

S109	**100 Dollars**	**Good**	**Fine**	**XF**
	23.2.1925; 1.10.1930. Uniface. Vertical format.	60.00	180.	550.

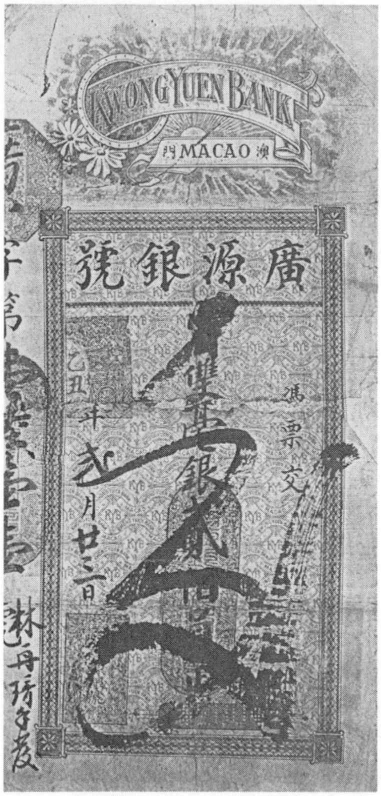

S110	**200 Dollars**	**Good**	**Fine**	**XF**
	17.10.1924; 23.2.1925. Uniface. Vertical format.	60.00	180.	550.

1932 Cashier's Checks Issue

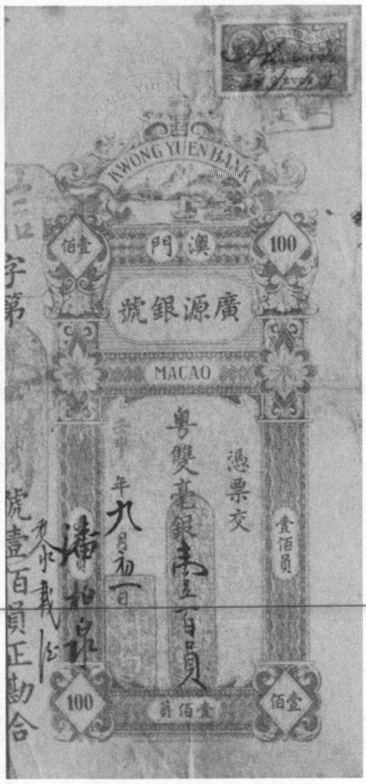

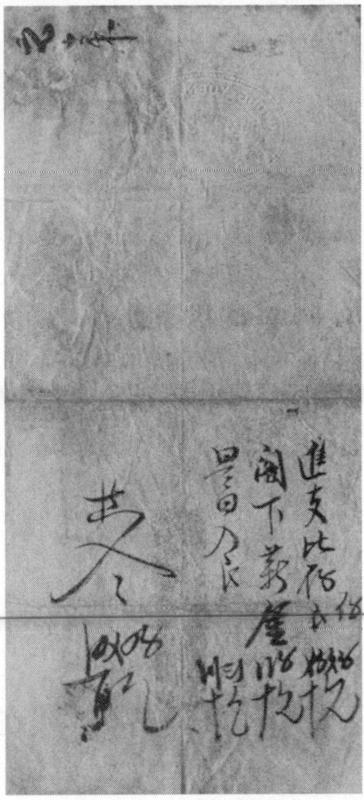

		Good	Fine	XF
S111	**50 Dollars** 1.9.1932; 1.10.1932. Brown-violet on light green underprint. Shoreline view at upper center. Uniface. Vertical format.	125.	375.	1150.
S112	**100 Dollars** CD 1.9.1932. Red. Uniface. Vertical format.	125.	375.	1150.

Lee Yuen

1931 Cashier's Checks Issue

		Good	Fine	XF
S116	**10 Dollars** 1.4.1931. Vertical format.	225.	675.	1350.

Pao Shin Bank

1927 Cashier's Checks Issue

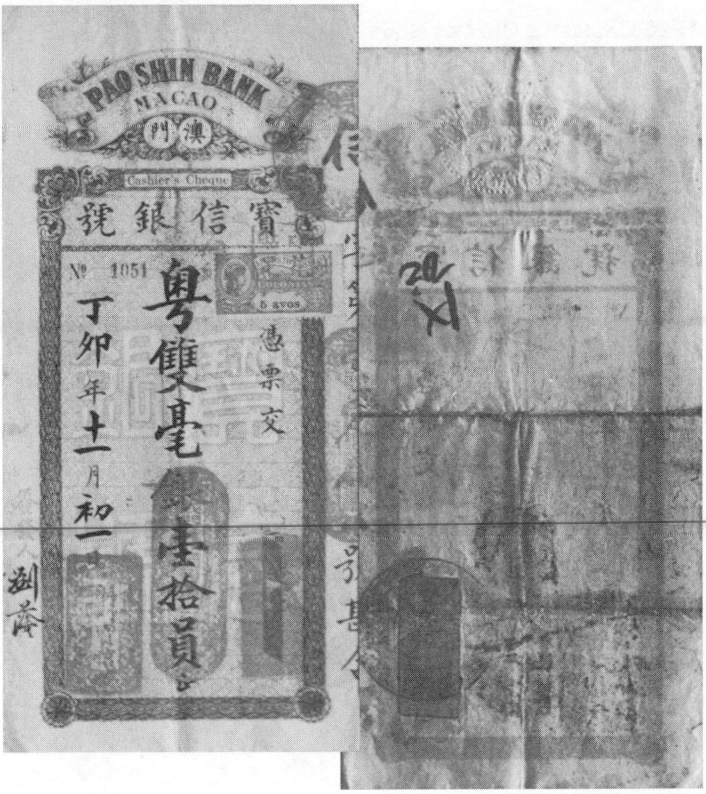

		Good	Fine	XF
S121	**10 Dollars** CD 1.11.1927. Brown-violet on olive-green underprint. Uniface. Vertical format.	225.	675.	1350.

Po Wing Bank, Macao

1928 Cashier's Checks Issue

		Good	Fine	XF
S126	**1 Dollar** Reported not confirmed.	—	—	—
S127	**5 Dollars** Reported not confirmed.	—	—	—

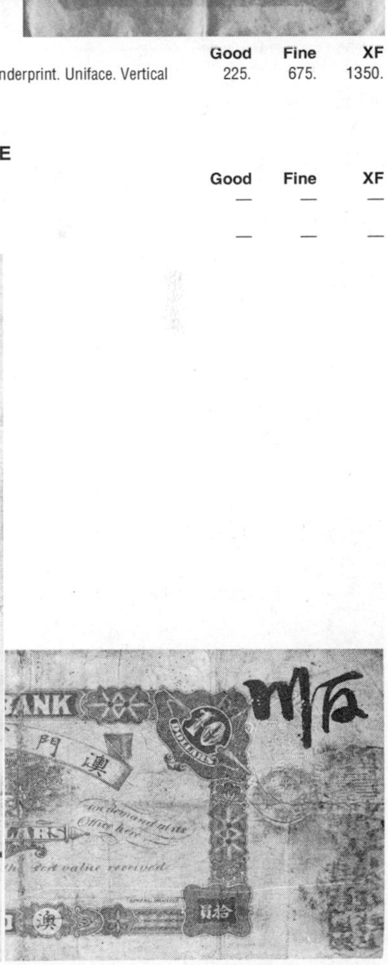

		Good	Fine	XF
S128	**10 Dollars** 1.7.1928. Purple on dull green. Vertical. Back: Purple on ochre. Boats along shoreline at center. Horizontal.			
	a. With *CASHIER'S CHEQUE* on face at top.	150.	450.	1350.
	b. Without *CASHIER'S CHEQUE* on face.	150.	450.	1350.

Banco Pou-Seng

Pou-Seng Bank

1926 Cashier's Checks Issue

		Good	Fine	XF
S131	**100 Dollars** 3.1.1926. Black on ochre and light blue underprint. Back: Dull brown. Arch at center. Vertical format.	225.	675.	2250.
S132	**100 Dollars** 17.3.1926. Dark green on yellow underprint. Back: Purple on yellow underprint. Bank at center.	225.	675.	2250.

Shing Shun Bank, Macao

1931 Cashier's Checks Issue

		Good	Fine	XF
S136	**1 Dollar** ND (1931). Printer: YPFC.	150.	450.	1350.
S137	**5 Dollars** ND (1931). Printer: YPFC.	150.	450.	1350.

		Good	Fine	XF
S138	**10 Dollars** 26.2.1931. Brown and light brown. Vertical. Back: Red. Sampan at center. Horizontal. Printer: YPFC.	150.	450.	1350.

		Good	Fine	XF
S139	**50 Dollars** 6.2.1931. Green. Vertical. Back: Brown. Sampan at center. Horizontal. Printer: YPFC.	175.	525.	1575.

Shun Woo Bank

ND Cashier's Checks Issue

		Good	Fine	XF
S141	**10 Dollars** ND. Violet and green.	225.	675.	2250.

Sum Yick Bank

1944 Cashier's Checks Issue

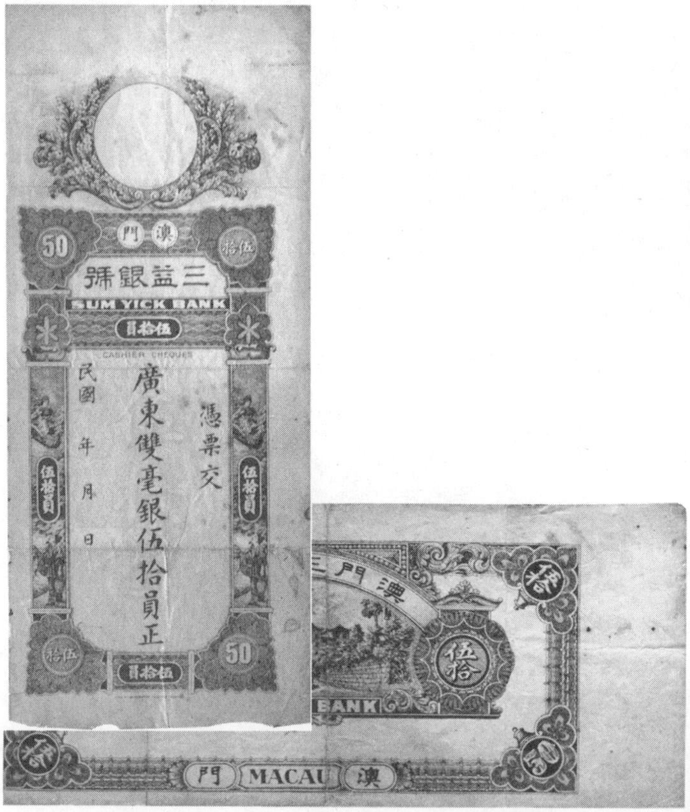

		Good	Fine	XF
S146	**50 Dollars** ND. Blue. Vertical. Back: Purple. Building at center. Horizontal.	225.	675.	2250.

Tai Fong Cambista

ND Issue

		Good	Fine	XF
S148	50 Dollars ND. Red and orange, with blue center guilloche, on peach underprint.	125.	375.	1150.

1944 Cashier's Checks Issue

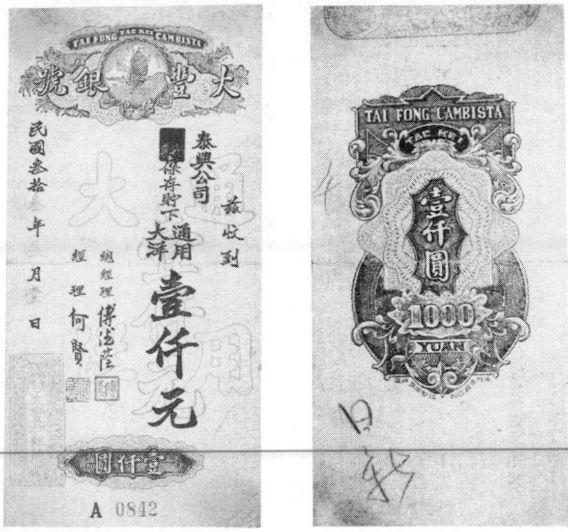

		VG	VF	UNC
S151	1000 Yuan 1.5.1944. Brown and lilac on yellow underprint. Sampan at top center. Back: Black and lilac. Vertical format.	75.00	225.	675.

Tai Seng Bank

1930 Cashier's Checks Issue

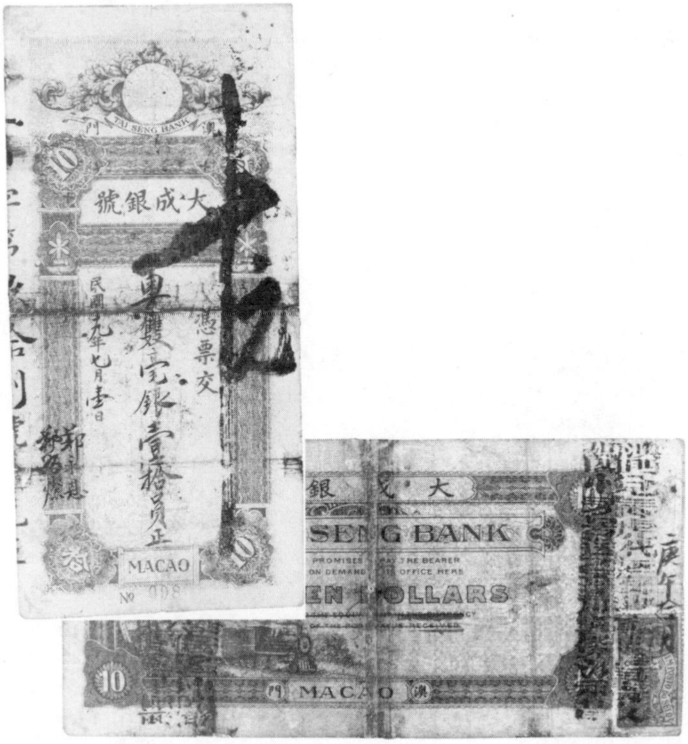

		Good	Fine	XF
S156	10 Dollars 1.7.1930. Violet on ochre underprint. Vertical. Back: Blue-gray on tan underprint. Steam locomotive at lower left. Horizontal.	225.	675.	2000.

Tong Tak Iün Kel Cambista

1944 Cashier's Checks Issue

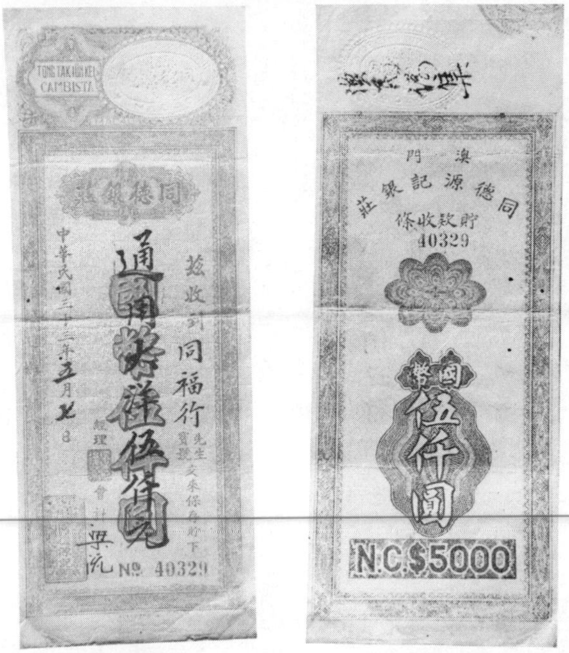

		Good	Fine	XF
S161	5000 Yuan 7.5.1944. Brown on green and gold underprint. Back: Brown on yellow underprint. Vertical format.	150.	450.	1350.

Banco Vui Hang

1923 Cashier's Checks Issue

		Good	Fine	XF
S171	10 Patacas 1923. Gray. Vertical. Back: Dull green. Steamship at center. Horizontal.	225.	675.	2000.

Yick Kee Bank

1927 Cashier's Checks Issue

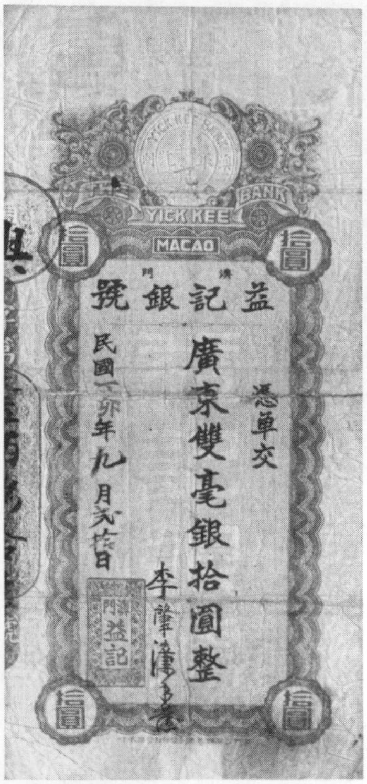

S176	10 Dollars	Good	Fine	XF
	20.9.1927. Olive-green on orange underprint. Vertical. Back: Red-brown. Horizontal.	150.	450.	1350.

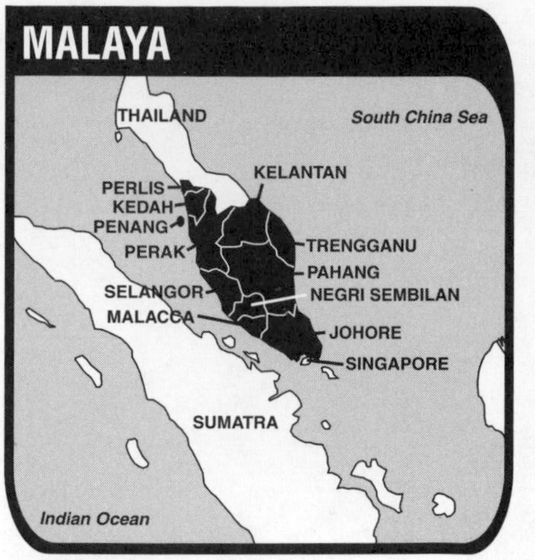

Malaya, a former member of the British Commonwealth located in the southern part of the Malay Peninsula, consisted of 11 states: the unfederated Malay states of Johore, Kedah, Kelantan, Perlis and Trengganu; the federated Malay states of Negri Sembilan, Pahang, Perak and Selangor; and former members of the Straits Settlements, Malacca and Penang. The federation had an area of about 60,000 sq. mi. (155,400 sq. km.). Capital: Kuala Lumpur. It was occupied by Japan from 1941-1945. Malaya was organized February 1, 1948, was granted full independence on August 31, 1957, and became part of the Federation of Malaysia on September 16, 1963.

See also Straits Settlements and Malaysia.

RULERS:
British

MONETARY SYSTEM:
1 Dollar = 100 Cents

Japanese Occupation - WW II

Japanese Government

1942-45 Issue

#M1-M10 block letters commencing with M.

Note: Many modern *'replicas'* from paste-up plates in strange colors have entered the market from sources in Southeast Asia.

M1	1 Cent	VG	VF	UNC
	ND (1942). Dark blue on light green underprint.			
	a. 2 block letters, format: MA.	.10	2.00	4.00
	b. Fractional block letters, format: M/AA.	.05	.50	1.00
	s. As a. Specimen with red overprint: *Mi-hon. SPECIMEN* on back.	—	—	120.

M2	5 Cents	VG	VF	UNC
	ND (1942). Brown-violet and gray.			
	a. 2 block letters.	.10	1.00	6.00
	b. Fractional block letters.	.10	.60	1.00
	s. As a. Specimen with red overprint: *Mi-hon. SPECIMEN* on back.	—	—	150.

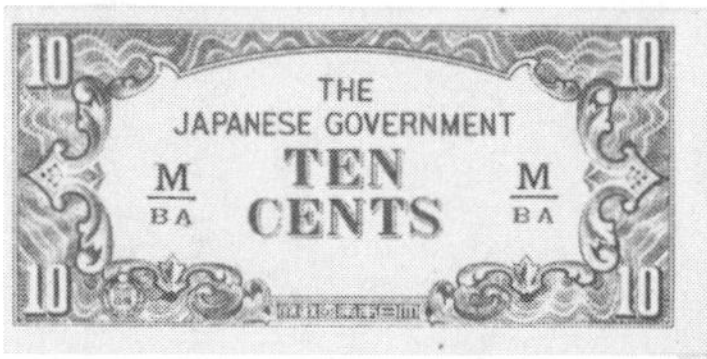

M3	10 Cents	VG	VF	UNC
	ND (1942). Green and light blue.			
	a. 2 block letters.	.50	2.00	8.00
	b. Fractional block letters.	.10	.50	1.00
	s. As a. Specimen with red overprint: *Mi-hon. SPECIMEN* on back.	—	—	120.

M4 50 Cents	VG	VF	UNC
ND (1942). Brown. Fan-like tree at right.			
a. Without watermark. Block letters: MA; MB.	1.00	5.00	17.50
b. With watermark. Block letters: MC-MT.	.10	.50	2.00
s. As a. Specimen with red overprint: *Mi-hon. SPECIMEN* on back.	—	—	150.

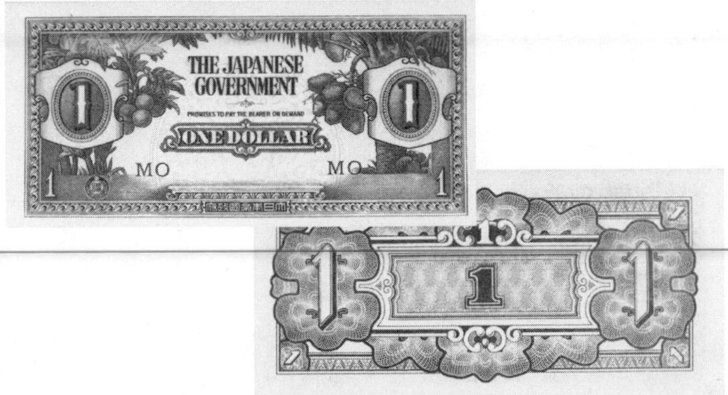

M5 1 Dollar	VG	VF	UNC
ND (1942). Dark blue on pink underprint. Breadfruit tree at left, coconut palm at right.			
a. Without watermark. Block letters: MA With serial #.	12.50	60.00	160.
b. With watermark. Block letters: MB-MH; MJ-MN; MR.	.25	1.00	4.00
c. With watermark. Block letters: MI; MO; MS.	.20	.40	1.00
s. Block letters: MB. Specimen with red overprint: *Mi-hon. SPECIMEN* on back.	—	—	150.

M6 5 Dollars	VG	VF	UNC
ND (1942). Lilac on orange underprint. Coconut palm at left, paw-paw tree at right.			
a. Block letters: MA with serial #.	5.00	20.00	90.00
b. Block letters MB-MJ; MO; MP.	1.00	3.00	9.00
c. Block letters MK; MR.	.20	.50	1.00
d. Woven paper.	.30	1.25	4.00
s. As b. Specimen with red overprint: *Mi-hon. SPECIMEN* on back.	—	—	150.

M7 10 Dollars	VG	VF	UNC
ND (1942-44). Blue-green on light yellow underprint. Trees and fruits. Back: Green to bluish green or light blue. Ship on horizon.			
a. Block letters with serial #.	5.00	20.00	90.00
b. Block letters: MB-MP. M with vertical upstroke and downstroke. With watermark.	.25	.50	2.50
c. Block letters without serial #. *M* with sloping upstroke and downstroke. Paper with silk threads, without watermark. MP. (1944).	.10	.25	1.00
s. As b. Specimen with red overprint: *Mi-hon. SPECIMEN* on back.	—	—	150.

M8 100 Dollars	VG	VF	UNC
ND (1944). Brown. Hut and trees on the water. Back: Man with buffalos in river.			
a. M with vertical upstroke and downstroke. Watermark. paper.	.25	2.00	6.00
b. *M* with sloping upstroke and downstroke. Paper with silk threads, without watermark.	.15	.50	3.00
c. Block letters only. Watermark. woven paper.	.50	3.00	6.00
s. As a. Specimen with red overprint: *Mi-hon. SPECIMEN* on back.	—	—	150.
x. Purple face (probable error). Block letters MT.	2.50	10.00	35.00

M9 100 Dollars	VG	VF	UNC
ND (1945). Brown. Workers on a rubber estate at right. Back: Green. Houses and seashore at center.	5.00	10.00	25.00

M10 1000 Dollars	VG	VF	UNC
ND (1945). Greenish black on green underprint. Ox cart at center. Back: Green. Man with buffalos in river.			
a. Black block letters. M with vertical upstroke and downstroke. With watermark.	60.00	300.	750.
b. Red block letters. *M* with sloping upstroke and dowstroke. Paper with silk threads, without watermark.	2.00	7.00	25.00
s. As a. Specimen with red overprint: *Mi-hon.*	—	—	900.

Note: Many new "replicas" from paste-up plates in strange colors are entering the market from Southeast Asian sources.

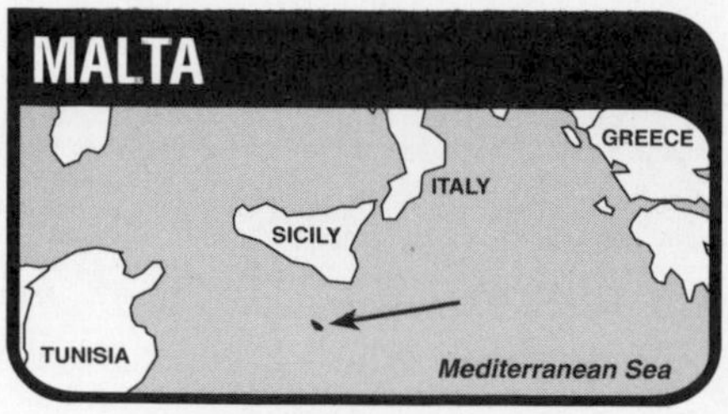

The Republic of Malta, an independent parliamentary democracy within the British Commonwealth, is situated in the Mediterranean Sea between Sicily and North Africa. With the islands of Gozo and Comino, Malta has an area of 122 sq. mi. (316 sq. km.) and a population of 379,000. Capital: Valletta. With the islands of Gozo (Ghawdex), Comino, Cominetto and Filfla, Malta has no proven mineral resources, an agriculture insufficient to its needs and a small but expanding, manufacturing facility. Clothing, textile yarns and fabrics, and knitted wear are exported.

Great Britain formally acquired possession of Malta in 1814. The island staunchly supported the UK through both World Wars and remained in the Commonwealth when it became independent in 1964. A decade later Malta became a republic. Since about the mid-1980s, the island has transformed itself into a freight transshipment point, a financial center, and a tourist destination. Malta became an EU member in May 2004 and began to use the euro as currency in 2008.

RULERS:

British to 1974

MONETARY SYSTEM:

1 Shilling = 12 Pence
1 Pound = 20 Shillings to 1971
1 Lira = 100 Centesimi, 1972-2007
1 Euro = 100 Cents, 2008-

British Administration

Anglo-Egyptian Banking Company, Ltd.

1866 Issue

	Good	Fine	XF
S101 10 Shillings 1.10.1866. Black. Portrait Grand Master La Valette at left, arms below. Paper: Pink. Printer: BWC. Rare.	—	—	—
S102 1 Pound 1.10.1866. Black. Portrait Grand Master La Valette at left, arms below. Paper: Pink. Printer: BWC. Rare.	—	—	—
S103 5 Pounds 1.10.1866. Black. Portrait Grand Master La Valette at left, arms below. Paper: Pink. Printer: BWC. Rare.	—	—	—
S104 10 Pounds 1.10.1866. Black. Portrait Grand Master La Valette at left, arms below. Paper: Pink. Printer: BWC. Rare.	—	—	—

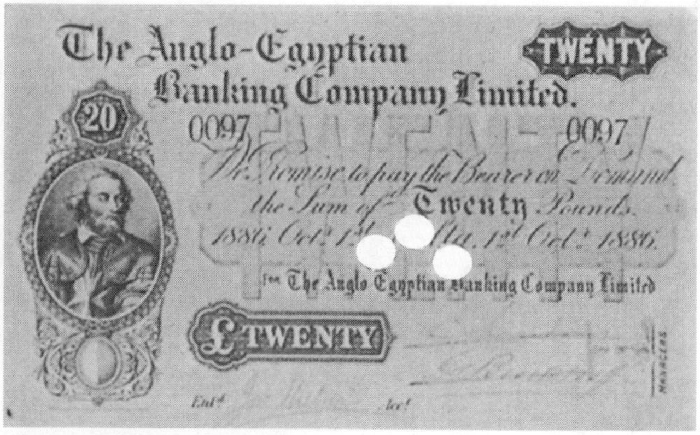

	Good	Fine	XF
S105 20 Pounds 1.10.1866. Black. Portrait Grand Master La Valette at left, arms below. Paper: Pink. Printer: BWC. Rare.	—	—	—

Banco Anglo Maltese

1880s Issue

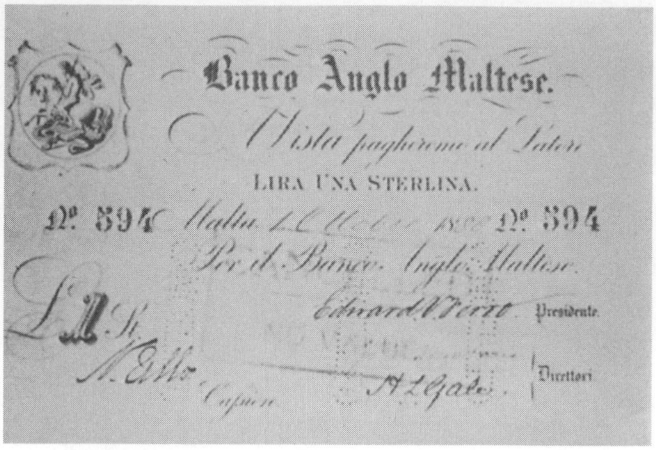

	Good	Fine	XF
S111 1 Pound 1.10.1888. Black. St. George slaying dragon at upper left. Rare.	—	—	—
S112 5 Pounds 18xx. Black. St. George slaying dragon at upper left. Rare.	—	—	—
S113 10 Pounds 18xx. Black. St. George slaying dragon at upper left. Rare.	—	—	—
S114 20 Pounds 18xx. Black. St. George slaying dragon at upper left. Rare.	—	—	—
S115 30 Pounds 18xx. Black. St. George slaying dragon at upper left. Rare.	—	—	—

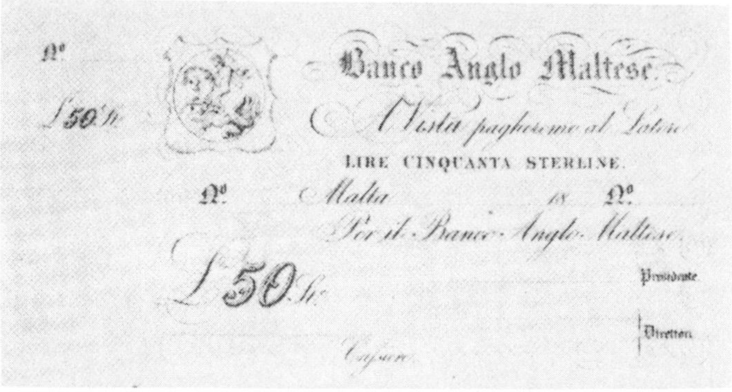

	Good	Fine	XF
S116 50 Pounds 18xx. Black. St. George slaying dragon at upper left. Rare.	—	—	—

Banco di Malta

1812 Issue

	Good	Fine	XF
S121 5 Scudi 1812. Black. St. Paul in oval frame at upper left. Printer: A. Oaby, London. Rare.	—	—	—

	Good	Fine	XF
S122 10 Scudi 1812. Black. St. Paul in oval frame at upper left. Printer: A. Oaby, London. Rare.	—	—	—
S123 20 Scudi 1812. Black. St. Paul in oval frame at upper left. Printer: A. Oaby, London. Rare.	—	—	—
S124 30 Scudi 1812. Black. St. Paul in oval frame at upper left. Printer: A. Oaby, London. Rare.	—	—	—

		Good	Fine	XF
S125	**40 Scudi** 1812. Black. St. Paul in oval frame at upper left. Printer: A. Oaby, London. Rare.	—	—	—
S126	**100 Scudi** 1812. Black. St. Paul in oval frame at upper left. Printer: A. Oaby, London. Rare.	—	—	—
S127	**100 Scudi** 1812. Black. St. Paul in oval frame at upper left. Printer: A. Oaby, London. Rare.	—	—	—
S128	**150 Scudi** 1812. Black. St. Paul in oval frame at upper left. Printer: A. Oaby, London. Rare.	—	—	—
S129	**200 Scudi** 1812. Black. St. Paul in oval frame at upper left. Printer: A. Oaby, London. Rare.	—	—	—
S130	**250 Scudi** 1812. Black. St. Paul in oval frame at upper left. Printer: A. Oaby, London. Rare.	—	—	—
S131	**300 Scudi** 1812. Black. St. Paul in oval frame at upper left. Printer: A. Oaby, London. Rare.	—	—	—
S132	**500 Scudi** 1812. Black. St. Paul in oval frame at upper left. Printer: A. Oaby, London. Rare.	—	—	—
S133	**1000 Scudi** 1812. Black. St. Paul in oval frame at upper left. Printer: A. Oaby, London. Rare.	—	—	—

ND First Issue

		Good	Fine	XF
S141	**5 Scudi** 18xx. Black. Without vignette. Rare.	—	—	—
S142	**10 Scudi** 18xx. Black. Without vignette. Rare.	—	—	—
S143	**20 Scudi** 18xx. Black. Without vignette. Rare.	—	—	—
S144	**30 Scudi** 18xx. Black. Without vignette. Rare.	—	—	—
S145	**40 Scudi** 18xx. Black. Without vignette. Rare.	—	—	—

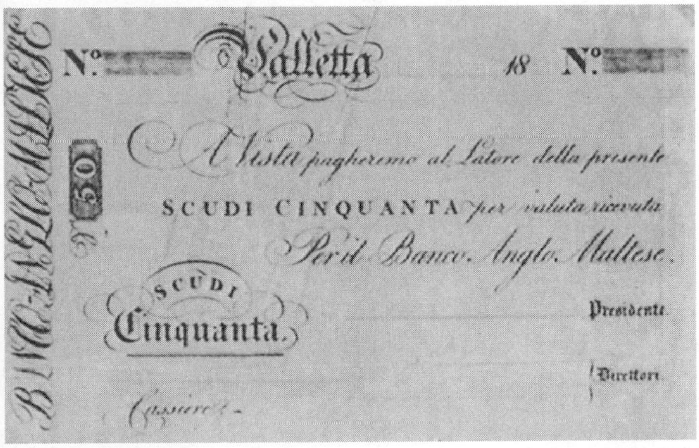

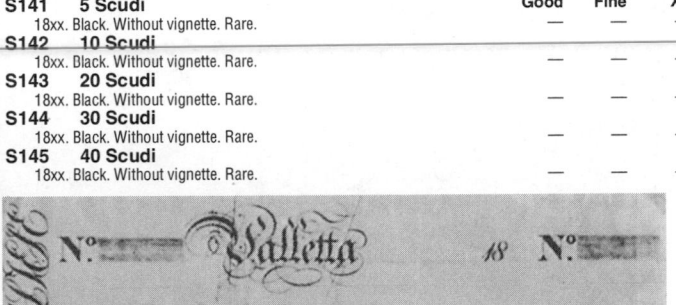

		Good	Fine	XF
S146	**50 Scudi** 18xx. Black. Without vignette. Rare.	—	—	—
S147	**100 Scudi** 18xx. Black. Without vignette. Rare.	—	—	—
S148	**150 Scudi** 18xx. Black. Without vignette. Rare.	—	—	—
S149	**200 Scudi** 18xx. Black. Without vignette. Rare.	—	—	—
S150	**250 Scudi** 18xx. Black. Without vignette. Rare.	—	—	—
S151	**300 Scudi** 18xx. Black. Without vignette. Rare.	—	—	—
S152	**500 Scudi** 18xx. Black. Without vignette. Rare.	—	—	—
S153	**1000 Scudi** 18xx. Black. Without vignette. Rare.	—	—	—

ND Second Issue

#S161-S165 Denominations in sterling lire.

		Good	Fine	XF
S161	**5 Lire** 18xx. Black. St. Paul in oval frame at upper left. Printer: Batho & Co., London. Unsigned remainder.	—	—	150.

		Good	Fine	XF
S162	**10 Lire** 18xx. Black. St. Paul in oval frame at upper left. Printer: Batho & Co., London. Unsigned remainder.	—	—	150.
S163	**20 Lire** 18xx. Black. St. Paul in oval frame at upper left. Printer: Batho & Co., London. Unsigned remainder.	—	—	200.
S164	**50 Lire** 18xx. Black. St. Paul in oval frame at upper left. Printer: Batho & Co., London. Unsigned remainder.	—	—	200.
S165	**100 Lire** 18xx. Black. St. Paul in oval frame at upper left. Printer: Batho & Co., London. Unsigned remainder.	—	—	250.

NOTE: #S161-S165 are encountered in sets of remainders.

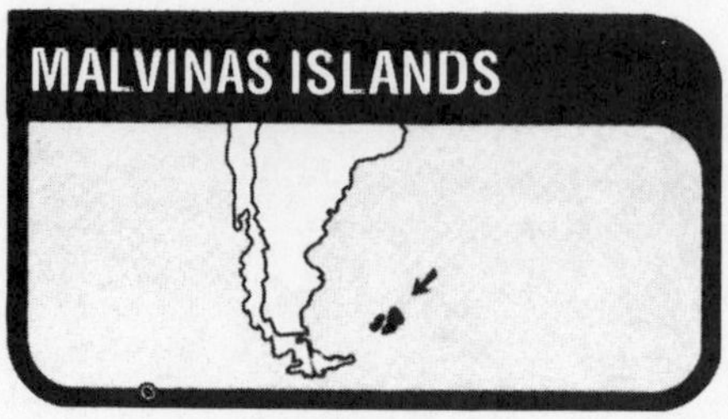

Malvinas Islands, generally known as the Colony of the Falkland Islands and Dependencies, a British colony located in the South Atlantic about 500 miles northeast of Cape Horn, has an area of 4,700 sq. mi. (12,173 sq. km.). East Falkland and West Falkland, South Georgia, and South Sandwich are the dependencies and are the largest of the 200 islands. Capital: Port Stanley.

The Malvinas were discovered by British navigator John Davis (Davys) in 1592. French navigator Louis de Bougainville established the first settlement, at Port Louis, in 1764. The following year Capt. John Byron claimed the islands for Britain and left a small party at Saunders Islands. Spain later forced the French and British to abandon their settlements but did not implement its claim to the islands. In 1829 the Republic of Buenos Aires, which claimed to have inherited the Spanish rights, sent Louis Vernet to develop a colony on the island. In 1831 he seized three American sailing vessels, whereupon the men of the corvette, *U.S.S. Lexington,* destroyed his settlement and proclaimed the Malvinas to be *free of all governance.* Britain, which had never renounced its claim, then re-established its settlement in 1833. Argentine military forces invaded the Falkland Islands on April 2, 1982 which resulted in a confrontation of war; these occupation forces surrendered to the British between June 14-15, 1982. In April 1990 the Argentine Congress declared the Falkland and other British-held South Atlantic islands all part of the new Argentine province of Tierra del Fuego.

RULERS:
British

Republic of Buenos Aires Regional

Isla de Malvinas

1924 Issue

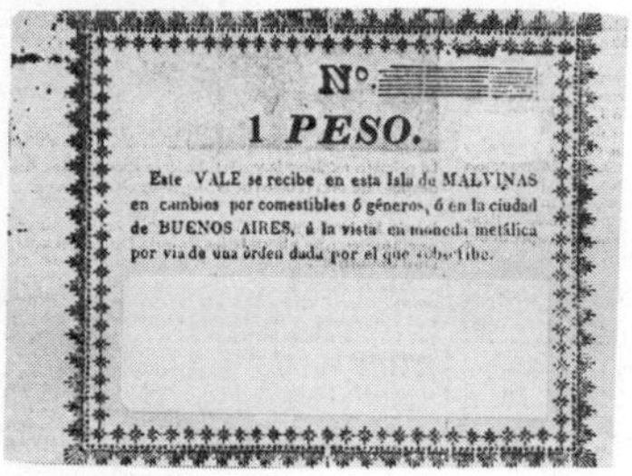

		Good	Fine	XF
S101	**1 Peso** ND. (ca.1824-29). Black. Uniface. Unsigned remainder.	—	—	—

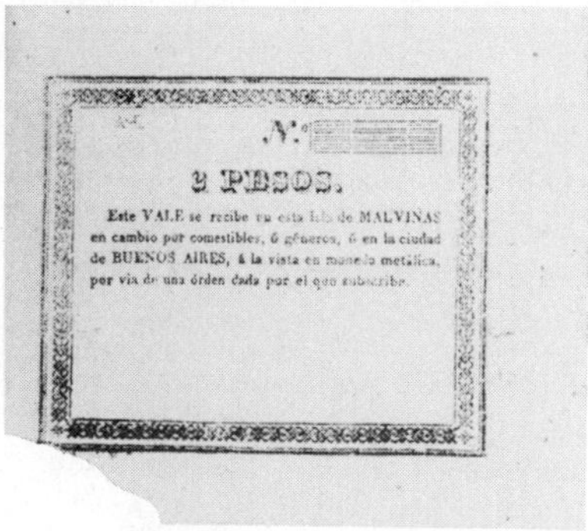

		Good	Fine	XF
S102	**2 Pesos** ND. (ca.1824-29). Black. Uniface. Unsigned remainder. Rare.	—	—	—
S103	**5 Pesos** ND. (ca.1824-29). Black. Uniface. Unsigned remainder. Rare.	—	—	—

		Good	Fine	XF
S104	**10 Pesos** ND. (ca.1824-29). Black. Farmer with plow at top center. Uniface. Rare.	—	—	—

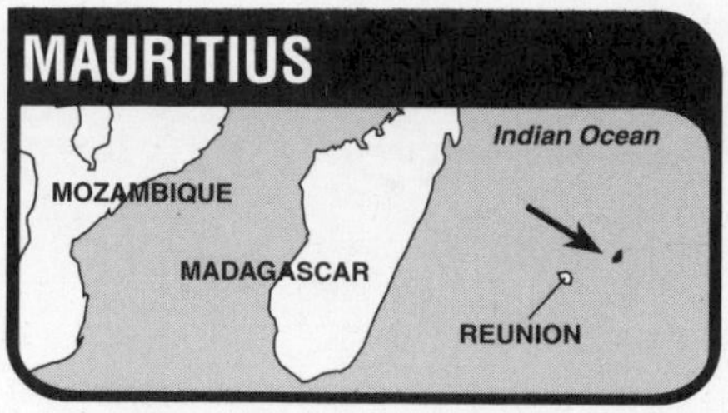

The island of Mauritius, a member of the British Commonwealth located in the Indian Ocean 500 miles (805 km.) east of Madagascar, has an area of 790 sq. mi. (2,045 sq. km.) and a population of 1.18 million. Capital: Port Louis. Sugar provides 90 percent of the export revenue.

Although known to Arab and Malay sailors as early as the 10th century, Mauritius was first explored by the Portuguese in the 16th century and subsequently settled by the Dutch - who named it in honor of Prince Maurits van Nassau - in the 17th century. The French assumed control in 1715, developing the island into an important naval overseeing Indian Ocean trade, and establishing a plantation economy of sugar cane. The British captured the island in 1810, during the Napoleonic Wars. Mauritius remained a strategically important British naval , and later an air station, playing an important role during World War II for anti-submarine and convoy operations, as well as the collection of signals intelligence. Independence from the UK was attained in 1968. A stable democracy with regular free elections and a positive human rights record, the country has attracted considerable foreign investment and has earned one of Africa's highest per capita incomes. Recent poor weather, declining sugar prices, and declining textile and apparel production, have slowed economic growth, leading to some protests over standards of living in the Creole community.

NOTE: Certain listings encompassing issues circulated by various bank and regional authorities are contained in Volume 1.

British Administration

Colonial Bank of Mauritius Bourbon & Dependencies

1810s Issue

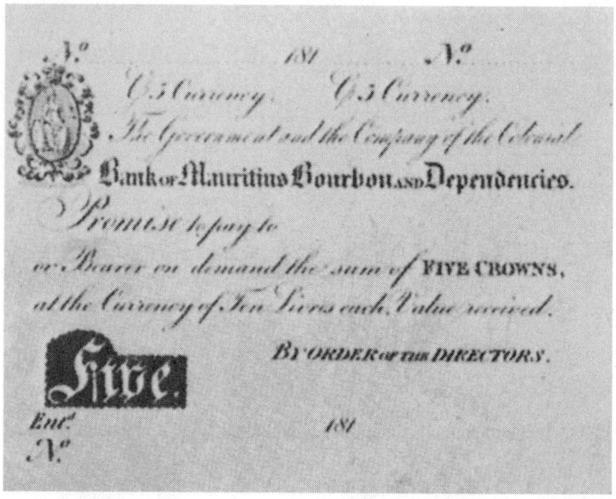

		Good	Fine	XF
S103	**5 Crowns** 181x. Black. Britannia seated in ornate frame at upper left. Unsigned remainder.	—	—	1750.

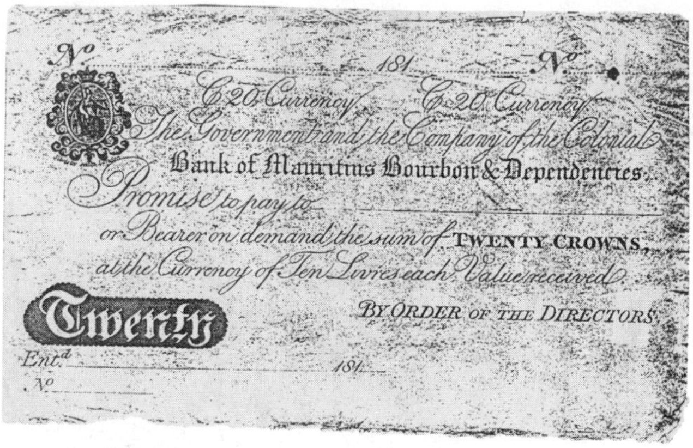

		Good	Fine	XF
S105	**20 Crowns** 181x. Black. Britannia seated in ornate frame at upper left. Uniface. Unsigned remainder.	—	—	2400.

Mauritius Bank

1830-35 Issue

		Good	Fine	XF
S111	**10 Dollars** 1830-35.	—	—	—
S112	**15 Dollars** 1830-35.	—	—	—

	Good	Fine	XF
S113 20 Dollars			
1830-35.	—	—	—
S114 100 Dollars			
1830-35.	—	—	—
S115 200 Dollars			
1830-35.	—	—	—

Mauritius Commercial Bank

1838-40 Issues

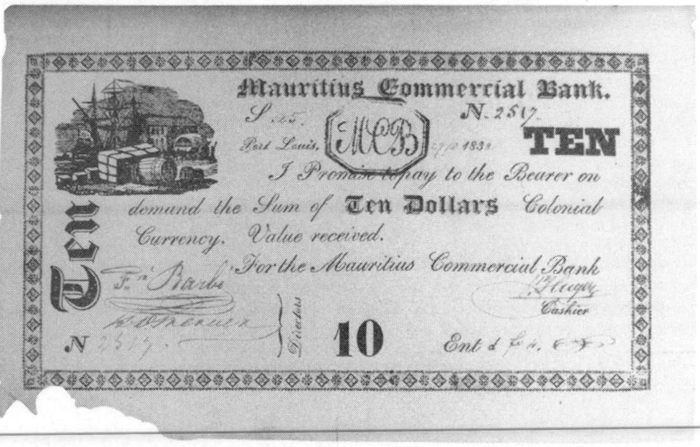

	Good	Fine	XF
S121 10 Dollars			
27.8.1838. Blue-black. Sailing ship, barrel and bales dockside at upper left. Signature varieties.	900.	2750.	8250.

	Good	Fine	XF
S122 10 Dollars			
16.4.1839; 2.3.1843. Black. Waterfront scene at center. Signature varieties. Back: Orange.			
a. Issued note.	30.00	100.	300.
r. Remainder without signature. 2.3.1843.	—	Unc	200.
S123 15 Dollars			
27.8.1838. Blue-black. Signature varieties.	50.00	150.	450.

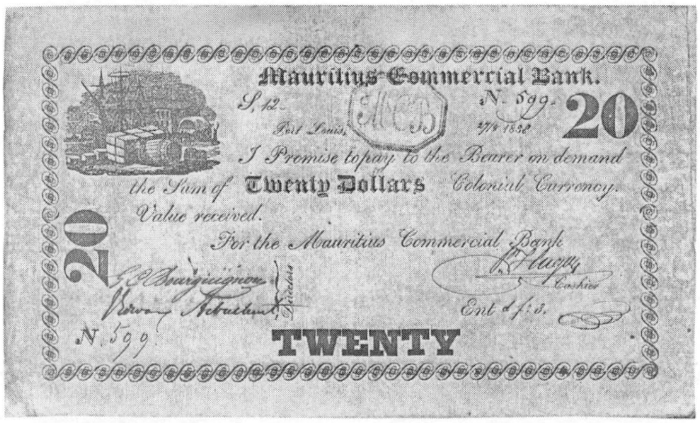

	Good	Fine	XF
S124 20 Dollars			
27.8.1838. Black. Sailing ship, barrel and bales dockside at upper left. Signature varieties.	625.	1875.	5500.

	Good	Fine	XF
S125 20 Dollars			
8.2.1839-18.10.1839. Black. Waterfront scene at center. Signature varieties. Similar to #S122. Uniface.	50.00	150.	450.

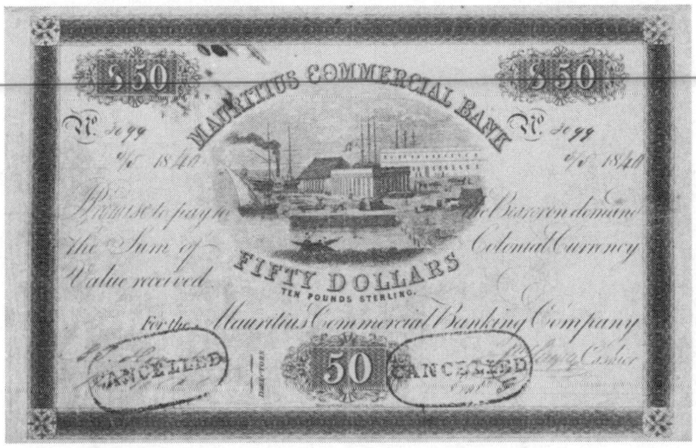

	Good	Fine	XF
S126 50 Dollars			
16.1.1840; 5.5.1840. Black. Waterfront scene at center. Signature varieties. Like #S125.	50.00	150.	450.

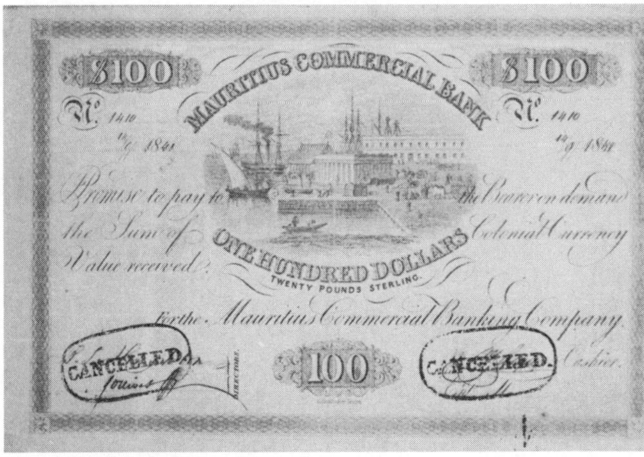

	Good	Fine	XF
S127 100 Dollars			
4.4.1839; 5.4.1839; 8.4.1839; 9.4.1839; 14.9.1841. Black. Waterfront scene at center. Signature varieties. Like #S125.			
a. Issued note.	100.	300.	900.
r. Overprint: *CANCELLED*.	—	Unc	200.
S128 200 Dollars			
2.4.1839; 3.4.1839; 7.4.1839; 9.4.1839. Signature varieties.	150.	450.	1350.
S129 500 Dollars			
28.6.1839; 25.7.1839. Signature varieties.	225.	675.	2000.
S130 1000 Dollars			
7.8.1839; 7.11.1839. Signature varieties.	450.	1350.	4250.

ND Issue

	Good	Fine	XF
S136 50 Rupees			
(Not issued).	—	Unc	1500.

Oriental Bank Corporation

1858 Issue

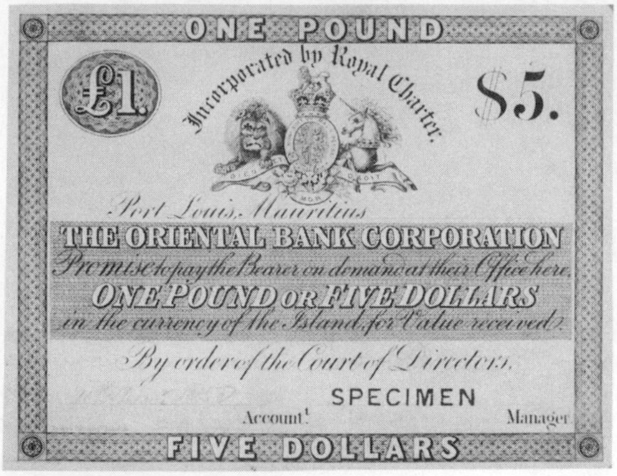

S141 1 Pound = 5 Dollars | **Good** | **Fine** | **XF**
11.12.1858. Supported royal arms, ornate border. Printer: PBC. Specimen. — Unc 4000.

S142 5 Pounds = 25 Pounds | **Good** | **Fine** | **XF**
Supported royal arms, ornate border. Similar to #S141. Printer: PBC. Specimen. — Unc 4000.

The United States of Mexico, located immediately south of the United States, has an area of 1,222,612 sq. mi. (1,967,183 sq. km.) and a population of 98.88 million. Capital: Mexico City. The economy is based on agriculture, manufacturing and mining. Cotton, sugar, coffee and shrimp are exported.

Mexico was the site of highly advanced Indian civilizations 1,500 years before conquistador Hernando Cortes conquered the wealthy Aztec empire of Montezuma, 1519-1521, and founded a Spanish colony which lasted for nearly 300 years. During the Spanish period, Mexico, then called New Spain, stretched from Guatemala to the present states of Wyoming and California, its present northern boundary having been established by the secession of Texas (1836) and the war of 1846-1848 with the United States.

Independence from Spain was declared by Father Miguel Hidalgo on Sept. 16, 1810, Mexican Independence Day, and was achieved by General Agustin de Iturbide in 1821. Iturbide became emperor in 1822 but was deposed when a republic was established a year later. For more than half a century following the birth of the republic, the political scene of Mexico was characterized by turmoil which saw two emperors (including the unfortunate Maximilian), several dictators and an average of one new government every nine months passing swiftly from obscurity to oblivion. The land, social, economic and labor reforms promulgated by the Reform Constitution of Feb. 5, 1917 established the basis for a sustained economic development and participative democracy that have made Mexico one of the most politically stable countries of modern Latin America.

MONETARY SYSTEM

1 Escudo = 16 Reales to 1897 1 Peso = 100 Centavos, 1863-

BANKS

Banco Comercial de Chihuahua (Chihuahua) .... #S124-S131B
Banco de Aguascalientes (Aguascalientes) .... #S101-S107
Banco de Campeche (Campeche) .... #S108-S112
Banco de Chiapas (Chiapas) .... #S113-S115
Banco de Chihuahua (Chihuahua) .... #S115A-S123
Banco de Coahuila (Coahuila) .... #S195-S204
Banco de Durango (Durango) .... #S272-S281
Banco de Empleados (Distrito Federal) .... #S204A-S204F
Banco de Guanajuato (Guanajuato) .... #S287-S297
Banco de Guerrero (Guerrero) .... #S298-S303
Banco de Hidalgo (Hidalgo) .... #S304-S310
Banco de Hidalgo, Parral (Chihuahua) .... #S138-S142
Banco de Jalisco (Jalisco) .... #S312-S328
Banco de Londres y México (Distrito Federal) .... #S232-S241
Banco de Londres Mexico y Sud America (Distrito Federal) .... #S216-S230
Banco de Michoacán (Michoacán) .... #S338-S344
Banco de Morelos (Morelos) .... #S345-S351
Banco de Nuevo Leon (Nuevo Leon) .... #S358-S365
Banco de Oaxaca (Oaxaca) .... #S371-S375
Banco de Patricio Milmo (Nuevo Leon) .... #S366-S370
Banco de Querétaro (Querétaro) .... #S390-S398
Banco de San Ignacio (Sinaloa) .... #S415-S418
Banco de San Luis Potosí (San Luis Potosí) .... #S399-S407
Banco de Santa Eulalia (Chihuahua) .... #S187-S193
Banco de Sonora (Sonora) .... #S419-S423
Banco de Tabasco (Tabasco) .... #S424-S428
Banco de Tamaulipas (Tamaulipas) .... #S429-S436
Banco de Veracruz (Veracruz) .... #S436A
Banco de Zacatecas (Zacatecas) .... #S474-S481
Banco del Estado de Chihuahua (Chihuahua) .... #S131C-S137
Banco del Estado de Durango (Durango) .... #S284-S286
Banco del Estado de Mexico (México) .... #S329-S337
Banco Industrial de México, Sociedad Anónima (Distrito Federal) .... #S205-S206
Banco Internacional e Hipotecario de México (Distrito Federal) .... #S207-S215A
Banco Mejicano (Chihuahua) .... #S143-S149A
Banco Mercantil de Monterrey (Nuevo Leon) .... #S352-S357
Banco Mercantil de Veracruz (Veracruz) .... #S437-S444
Banco Mercantil de Yucatán (Yucatán) .... #S445-S457
Banco Mercantil Mexicano (Distrito Federal) .... #S242-S248
Banco Mexicano (Chihuahua) .... #S150-S159
Banco Minero (Chihuahua) .... #S160-S171
Banco Minero Chihuahuense (Chihuahua) .... #S172-S182
Banco Minero de Chihuahua (Chihuahua) .... #S183-S186
Banco Nacional de Mexico (Distrito Federal) .... #S254-S263
Banco Nacional Mexicano (Distrito Federal) .... #S249-S253B
Banco Occidental de Mexico (Sinaloa) .... #S408-S414
Banco Oriental de Mexico (Puebla) .... #S376-S389
Banco Peninsular Mexicano (Yucaán) .... #S458-S465
Banco Yucateco (Yucatán) .... #S466-S473

GOVERNMENT

Ejército Nacional (Jalisco) .... #S311

PAWN SHOP

Nacional Monte de Piedad (Distrito Federal) .... #S264-S271

NOTE: Catalog numbers in ( ) are cross references to The Complete Encyclopedia of Mexican Paper Money by Duane Douglas, Claudio Verrey & Alberto Hidalgo c1982 Krause Publications.

Aguascalientes

Banco de Aguascalientes

1902-10 Issue

S101 5 Pesos	Good	Fine	XF
Black on green underprint. Portrait P.J.G. Rojas at left, Church of San Marcos at right. Back: Green. Gypsy woman. Printer: ABNC.			
a. Series A. 1.10.1902. *(BK-AGU-1).*	50.00	150.	—
b. Series B. 19.11.1906. *(BK-AGU-2).*	45.00	125.	—
c. Series C. 1.7.1910. *(BK-AGU-3).*	45.00	125.	—
d. Overprint: *GUADALAJARA.* 15.4.1903/1.10.1902. *(BK-AGU-4).*	125.	375.	—
p. Proof. Without series. ND.	—	Unc	500.
s1. Specimen. Series B. 19xx.	—	Unc	750.
s2. Specimen. Series C. 1.7.1910.	—	Unc	750.

S102 10 Pesos	Good	Fine	XF
1902-10. Black on yellow and brown underprint. Church of San Marcos at left, man with ox-cart at right. Back: Brown. Gypsy woman. Printer: ABNC.			
a. Series A. 1.10.1902; 3.4.1903; 14.10.1903; *(BK-AGU-7).*	50.00	150.	—
b. Series B. 19.11.1906; 1.5.1907. *(BK-AGU-8).*	50.00	150.	450.
c. Series C. 1.7.1910. *(BK-AGU-9).*	45.00	125.	375.
d. Overprint: *GUADALAJARA.* 30.11.1904/14.10.1903; 25.5.1903/3.4.1905. *(BK-AGU-10).*	75.00	225.	—
p. Proof.	—	Unc	500.
s. Specimen. Series B. 1.7.1910.	—	Unc	750.

S103 20 Pesos	Good	Fine	XF
1902-07. Black on orange underprint. Church of San Marcos at left, seated female at right. Back: Orange. Gypsy woman. Printer: ABNC.			
a. Series A. 1.10.1902. *(BK-AGU-12).*	125.	375.	—
b. Series B. 19.11.1906; 1.5.1907. *(BK-AGU-13).*	150.	450.	1350.
c. Red overprint: *GUADALAJARA.* 1.10.1903/1.10.1902; 15.5.1905/1.10.1902. *(BK-AGU-14).*	125.	375.	—
d. Black overprint: *GUADALAJARA.* 15.4.1903/1.10.1902. *(BK-AGU-15).*	125.	375.	—
e. Overprint: *SUCURSAL EN GUADALAJARA.* 19.11.1906. *(BK-AGU-16).*	125.	375.	—
s. Specimen. Series B. ND.	—	Unc	750.

S104 50 Pesos	Good	Fine	XF
1902-07. Black on blue and yellow underprint. Chruch of San Marcos at center, horsedrawn plow at left, men gathering wood at right. Back: Blue. Gypsy woman. Printer: ABNC.			
a. Series A. 1.10.1902-14.10.1903. *(BK-AGU-18).*	600.	1800.	—
b. Series B. 1.5.1907. *(BK-AGU-19).*	450.	1350.	—
c. Overprint: *GUADALAJARA.* 3.4.1903/25.5.1903; 14.10.1903/1.9.1905. *(BK-AGU-20).*	600.	1800.	—

S105 100 Pesos	Good	Fine	XF
1902-07. Black on yellow and pink underprint. Chruch of San Marcos at left, portrait female head at right. Back: Red. Gypsy woman. Printer: ABNC.			
a. Series A. 14.10.1902; 3.4.1903; 14.10.1903. *(BK-AGU-22).*	600.	1800.	—
b. Series B. 1.5.1907. *(BK-AGU-23).*	600.	1800.	5400.
c. Overprint: *GUADALAJARA.* 15.8.1904/14.10.1903. *(BK-AGU-24).*	600.	1800.	—

S106 500 Pesos	Good	Fine	XF
1.10.1902. Black on yellow and olive-green underprint. Church of San Marcos at left, farmer plowing with oxen at right. Series A. Back: Olive-green. Gypsy woman. Printer: ABNC.			
a. Issued note.	6500.	15,000.	—
r. Unsigned remainder.	—	Unc	250.

S107 1000 Pesos	Good	Fine	XF
19xx (ca.1902). Black on orange underprint. Church of San Marcos at left, portrait P.J.G. Rojas at right. Series A. Back: Orange. Gypsy woman. Printer: ABNC.			
p. Proof.	—	Unc	1000.
s. Specimen.	—	Unc	1500.

CAMPECHE

BANCO DE CAMPECHE

1903-09 ISSUE

S108 5 Pesos	Good	Fine	XF
1.7.1903-09. Black on green underprint. State arms at left center, two standing females at right. Series A. Back: Green. Scene of village landscape. Printer: ABNC. *(BK-CAM-1).*			
a. Issued note.	2250.	6750.	—
p. Proof.	—	Unc	1000.
s. Specimen.	—	Unc	1500.

S109 10 Pesos	Good	Fine	XF
1.7.1903-ca.1906. Black on orange and yellow underprint. Justice at left, State arms at center. Series B. Back: Red. Scene of village landscape. Printer: ABNC. *(BK-CAM-3).*			
a. Issued note.	3750.	11,000.	—
p. Proof.	—	Unc	1250.
s. Specimen.	—	Unc	1500.

S110 20 Pesos	Good	Fine	XF
1.7.1903; 1.7.1909. Black on blue and yellow underprint. State arms at left, ship at right. Series C. Back: Blue-gray. Scene of village landscape. Printer: ABNC. *(BK-CAM-4).*			
a. Issued note.	3750.	11,000.	—
b. Overprint: *SURCUSAL EN MÉRIDA.* 2.7.1906/1.7.1903. *(BK-CAM-5).*	3750.	11,000.	—
p. Proof.	—	Unc	1750.
s. Specimen.	—	Unc	2000.

S111 50 Pesos	Good	Fine	XF
19xx (ca.1903-06). Black on brown and yellow underprint. State arms at left, lion at center. Series D. Back: Brown. Scene of village landscape. Printer: ABNC. *(BK-CAM-7).*			
p. Proof.	—	Unc	2000.
s. Specimen.	—	Unc	2500.

S112 100 Pesos	Good	Fine	XF
19xx (ca.1903-06). Black on olive-green and yellow underprint. State arms at left, standing allegorical woman with sword and shield at right. Back: Olive-green. Scene of village landscape. Printer: ABNC. *(BK-CAM-8).*			
p. Proof.	—	Unc	2500.
s. Specimen.	—	Unc	3000.

CHIAPAS

BANCO DE CHIAPAS

1901-06 ISSUE

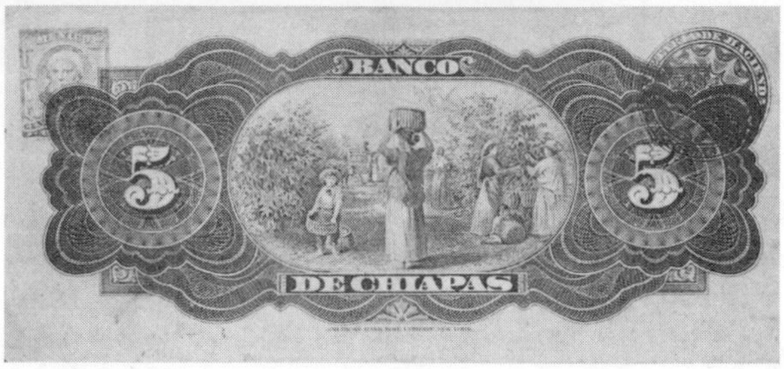

S113 5 Pesos	Good	Fine	XF
12.2.1902. Black on green and yellow underprint. Portrait man at left. Series A. Back: Green. Crop workers at center. Printer: ABNC. *(BK-CHIP-1).*			
a. Issued note.	2250.	6750.	15,000.
p. Proof.	—	Unc	1200.
s. Specimen.	—	Unc	1500.

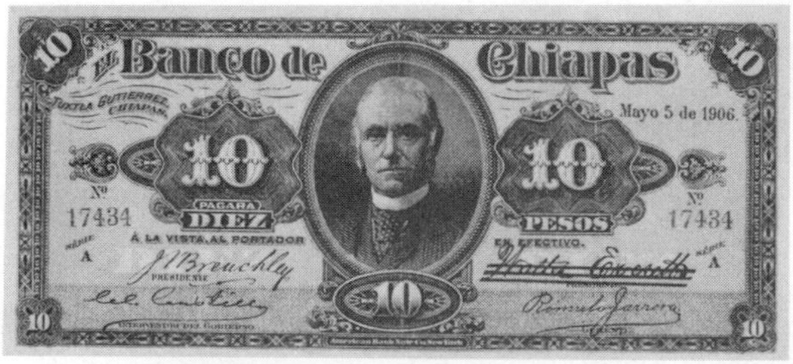

S114 10 Pesos	Good	Fine	XF
12.2.1902; 5.5.1906; 4.4.1909. Black on orange underprint. Portrait man at center. Series A. Back: Orange. Man with ox-cart at center. Printer: ABNC. *(BK-CHIP-3).*			
a. Issued note.	2250.	6750.	15,000.
p. Proof.	—	Unc	1500.
s. Specimen.	—	Unc	1750.

S115 20 Pesos	Good	Fine	XF
ND (ca.1901-06). Black on blue and yellow underprint. Three Indians at left. Back: Blue-gray. Men leading oxen team at center. Printer: ABNC. *(BK-CHIP-5).*			
p. Proof.	—	Unc	1500.
s. Specimen.	—	Unc	1750.

Chihuahua

Banco de Chihuahua

1874-89 Issue

S115A 25 Centavos	Good	Fine	XF
1876. Black. Allegorical woman with sheaves and beehive at center. Series C. Back: Brown. Two beehives at center. Printer: NBNC. Proof.	—	—	—

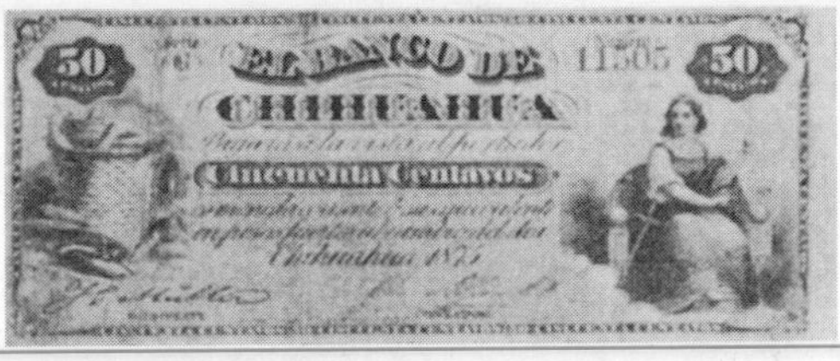

S116 50 Centavos	Good	Fine	XF
1875. Black. Basket of corn at left, seated female holding scales ("Justice") at right. Series B. Back: Blue. Printer: NBNC. *(BK-CHI-1)*.	600.	1800.	5400.

S117 1 Peso	Good	Fine	XF
1874. Black. Harvest at lower left, horsemen at center, woman with flowers ("May") at lower right. Series A. Back: Green. Printer: NBNC. *(BK-CHI-2)*.	900.	2750.	7500.

#S118-S123 printer: ABNC.

S118 25 Centavos	Good	Fine	XF
1889. Black on yellow underprint. Woman with children at right. Series A. Back: Green. Printer: ABNC. *(BK-CHI-3)*.			
a. Issued note.	125.	375.	1150.
p. Proof.	—	Unc	1000.
s. Specimen.	—	Unc	1250.

S119 50 Centavos	Good	Fine	XF
1889. Black on yellow-green underprint. Woman with fruit at left. Series A. Back: Blue. Printer: ABNC. *(BK-CHI-6)*.			
a. Issued note.	175.	525.	1600.
p. Proof.	—	Unc	1000.
s. Specimen.	—	Unc	1250.

S120 1 Peso	Good	Fine	XF
1889. Black on yellow and brown underprint. Woman at left, man with child at right. Back: Brown. Dog on safe at center. Printer: ABNC.			
a. Issued note. *(BK-CHI-8)*.	700.	2100.	6250.
b. Overprint: *BANCO MINERO DE CHIHUAHUA* and *Creel Hernan*. *(BK-CHI-9)*.	750.	2250.	6750.
p. Proof.	—	Unc	1000.
s. Specimen.	—	Unc	1250.

S121 5 Pesos	Good	Fine	XF
1889. Black on orange and yellow underprint. Woman with flowers ("Rose") at left, helmeted female head ("Minerva No. 3") at center right. Series A. Back: Green. Cattle at pond in center. Printer: ABNC. *(BK-CHI-9a)*.			
p. Proof.	—	Unc	1000.
s. Specimen.	—	Unc	1250.

S122 10 Pesos	Good	Fine	XF
1889. Black on green and yellow underprint. Seated allegorical woman with shield and plant at left, steam passenger train at right. Series A. Back: Brown. Steam train exiting overpass at center. Printer: ABNC. *(BK-CHI-10)*.			
a. Issued note.	—	—	—
p. Proof.	—	Unc	1000.
s. Specimen.	—	Unc	1250.

S123 20 Pesos	Good	Fine	XF
1889. Black on blue and yellow underprint. Reclining allegorical woman ("The Siesta") at left, seated female with child ("Cupid Disarmed") at right. Series A. Back: Blue. Ships at center. Printer: ABNC. *(BK-CHI-11)*.			
p. Proof.	—	Unc	1000.
s. Specimen.	—	Unc	1250.

Banco Comercial de Chihuahua

1889-99 Issue

S124 25 Centavos

1889. Black on orange underprint. Portrait Hidalgo at center. Series A. Back: Blue. Raphael's Angel at center. Printer: ABNC. *(BK-CHI-135).*

	Good	Fine	XF
a. Issued note.	100.	300.	900.
p. Proof.	—	Unc	1000.
s. Specimen.	—	Unc	1250.

S125 50 Centavos

1889. Black on yellow underprint. Hidalgo at left, steam locomotive at right. Series A. Back: Green. Miner at left. Printer: ABNC. *(BK-CHI-137).*

	Good	Fine	XF
a. Issued note.	125.	375.	1100.
p. Proof.	—	Unc	1000.
s. Specimen.	—	Unc	1250.

S126 1 Peso

1889. Black on orange and yellow underprint. Hidalgo at left, cow with calf at right. Series A. Back: Red. Men and horses at center. Printer: ABNC. *(BK-CHI-138).*

	Good	Fine	XF
a. Issued note.	550.	1650.	4750.
p. Proof.	—	Unc	1000.
s. Specimen.	—	Unc	1250.

S127 5 Pesos

1889. Black on brown and yellow underprint. Portrait Hidalgo at left, young Mercury with caduceus and fish ("Off Sandy Hook") at right. Series A. Back: Seated Mercury. Printer: ABNC. Text: *EN MONEDA DE PLATA DEL CUÑO MEXICANO* at lower left. Middle signature title: *DIRECTOR. (BK-CHI-139).*

	Good	Fine	XF
a. Issued note.	450.	1350.	4000.
p. Proof.	—	Unc	1250.
s. Specimen.	—	Unc	1500.

S127A 5 Pesos

1898. Black on brown and yellow underprint. Portrait Hidalgo at left, young Mercury with caduceus and fish ("Off Sandy Hook") at right. Back: Brown. Seated Mercury. Printer: ABNC. Like #S127, but with text: *A LA PAR, EN EFECTIVO* at lower left. Middle signature title: *GERENTE.*

	Good	Fine	XF
a. Issued note. 5.2.1898. Series B.	450.	1350.	4000.
b. Overprint: *GÓMEZ PALACIO.* 20.5.1898-15.6.1898. *(BK-CHI-140).*	450.	1350.	4000.
p. Proof. 1898. Series D.	—	Unc	1500.
s. Specimen. 1898. Series D.	—	Unc	1750.

S128 10 Pesos

1889. Black on blue and yellow underprint. Portrait Hidalgo at center left, workers at right. Series A. Back: Blue. Seated Mercury. Printer: ABNC. Text: *EN MONEDA DE PLATA DEL CUÑO MEXICANO* at lower left center. Middle signature title: *DIRECTOR. (BK-CHI-142).*

	Good	Fine	XF
a. Issued note.	450.	1350.	4000.
b. Overprint: *GÓMEZ PALACIO.* 20.10.1898. *(BK-CHI-140).*	450.	1350.	4000.
p. Proof.	—	Unc	1500.
s. Specimen.	—	Unc	1750.

S128A 10 Pesos

1898-99. Black on blue and yellow underprint. Portrait Hidalgo at center left, workers at right. Series A. Back: Blue. Seated Mercury. Printer: ABNC. Like #S128, but with text: *A LA PAR, EN EFECTIVO* at lower left center. Middle signature title: *GERENTE.*

	Good	Fine	XF
a. Issued note.	450.	1350.	4000.
p. Proof.	—	Unc	1500.
s. Specimen.	—	Unc	1750.

S129 20 Pesos

1889. Black on orange and yellow underprint. Portrait Hidalgo at left, sheep at center, woman with bow and arrows at right. Series A. Back: Orange. Seated Mercury. Printer: ABNC. Text: *EN MONEDA DE PLATA DEL CUÑO MEXICANO* at lower center. Middle signature title: *DIRECTOR.*

	Good	Fine	XF
p. Proof.	—	Unc	1750.
s. Specimen.	—	Unc	2000.

S129A 20 Pesos

1898-99. Black on orange and yellow underprint. Portrait Hidalgo at left, sheep at center, woman with bow and arrows at right. Series B. Hand signed & issued. Back: Orange. Seated Mercury. Printer: ABNC. Like #S129, but with text: *A LA PAR, EN EFECTIVO* at lower center. Middle signature title: *GERENTE.*

	Good	Fine	XF
a. Overprint: *GÓMEZ PALACIO.* 19.8.1899/1898; 19.19.1899. *(BK-CHI-144).*	600.	1800.	5400.
p. Proof.	—	Unc	1500.
s. Specimen.	—	Unc	2000.

S130 50 Pesos	Good	Fine	XF
1889. Black on green and yellow underprint. Hidalgo at center, Christopher Columbus with Indian maiden at right. Series A. Back: Green. Seated Mercury. Printer: ABNC. Text: *EN MONEDA DE PLATA DEL CUÑO MEXICANO* at lower left. Middle signature title: *DIRECTOR. (BK-CHI-145).*			
p. Proof.	—	Unc	1750.
s. Specimen.	—	Unc	2000.

S130A 50 Pesos	Good	Fine	XF
1898-99. Black on green and yellow underprint. Hidalgo at center, Christopher Columbus with Indian maiden at right. Back: Green. Seated Mercury. Printer: ABNC. Like #S130, but with text: *A LA PAR, EN EFECTIVO* at lower left. Middle signature title: *GERENTE.*			
a. Overprint: *GÓMEZ PALACIO.* 1.5.1898; 20.10.1898. Series B. *(BK-CHI-146).*	450.	1350.	4000.
s. Specimen. 1898. Series B; 1899. Series C.	—	Unc	2000.

S131 100 Pesos	Good	Fine	XF
1899. Black on orange and yellow underprint. Steam passenger train through mountain pass at left, portrait Hidalgo at center, miner at right. Series A. Back: Red-orange. Seated Mercury. Printer: ABNC. Text: *EN MONEDA DE PLATA DEL CUÑO MEXICANO* at lower center. Signature title: *DIRECTOR* at right.			
p. Proof.	—	Unc	1750.
s. Specimen.	—	Unc	2000.

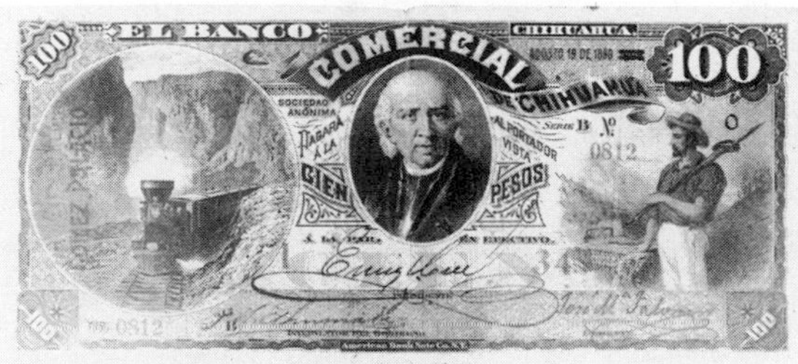

S131A 100 Pesos	Good	Fine	XF
1898-99. Black on orange and yellow underprint. Steam passenger train through mountain pass at left, portrait Hidalgo at center, miner at right. Back: Red-orange. Seated Mercury. Printer: ABNC. Similar to #S131, but with text: *A LA PAR, EN EFECTIVO* at lower center. Signature title: *GERENTE* at right.			
a. Overprint: *GÓMEZ PALACIO.* 20.10.1898. 19.8.1899/1898. Series B. *(BK-CHI-147).*	1500.	4500.	—
s. Specimen. 1898. Series B; 1899. Series C.	—	Unc	2000.

S131B 500 Pesos	Good	Fine	XF
1889. Black on brown and yellow underprint. Standing Liberty at left, allegorical woman holding cherub ("Spring") at center, portrait Hidalgo at right. Series A. Back: Brown and black. Seated Mercury. Printer: ABNC. Text: *EN MONEDA DE PLATA DEL CUÑO MEXICANO* at lower center. Middle signature title: *DIRECTOR.*			
p. Proof.	—	Unc	1750.
s. Specimen.	—	Unc	2000.

Banco del Estado de Chihuahua

Decree of 12.12.1913

S131C 1 Peso	Good	Fine	XF
D.1913 (ca.1915). Black on multicolor underprint. Loggers at center. Series A. Back: Orange. National arms at center. Printer: ABNC. Not issued.			
p. Proof.	—	Unc	1750.
s. Specimen.	—	Unc	2000.

S132 5 Pesos	VG	VF	UNC
D.1913. Black on multicolor underprint. Miner with drill at center. Series A. Back: Orange. National arms at center. Printer: ABNC. *(BK-CHI-148).*			
a. Issued note with 1 signature.	2.25	7.50	20.00
b. Uncut sheet of four. *(BK-CHI-148A).*		—	500.
p. Proof.	—	Unc	350.
s. Specimen.	—	Unc	500.

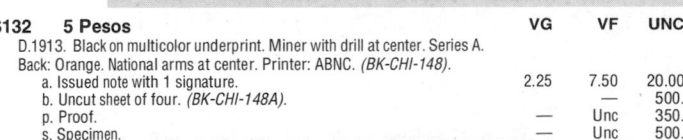

S133 10 Pesos

D.1913. Black on multicolor underprint. Cowboy herding cattle at center. Series A. Back: Orange. National arms at center. Printer: ABNC. *(BK-CHI-149).*

	VG	VF	UNC
a. Issued note with 1 signature.	2.25	7.50	20.00
b. Uncut sheet of four. *(BK-CHI-149A).*	—	Unc	500.
p. Proof.	—	Unc	500.
s. Specimen.	—	Unc	750.

S134 20 Pesos

D.1913. Black on multicolor underprint. Harvesting scene at center. Series A. Back: Orange. National arms at center. Printer: ABNC. *(BK-CHI-150).*

	VG	VF	UNC
a. Issued note with 1 signature.	2.50	7.50	20.00
p. Proof.	—	Unc	500.
s. Specimen.	—	Unc	750.

S135 50 Pesos

D.1913. Black on multicolor underprint. Steam passenger train by station at center. Series A. Back: Orange. National arms at center. Printer: ABNC. *(BK-CHI-151).*

	VG	VF	UNC
a. Issued note with 1 signature.	7.50	20.00	85.00
b. Uncut sheet of 4. *(BK-CHI-151A).*	—	Unc	500.
p. Proof.	—	Unc	500.
s. Specimen.	—	Unc	750.

S136 100 Pesos

D.1913. Black on multicolor underprint. Ceres (Goddess of Agriculture), Goddess Juno, and Industry at center. Series A. Back: Orange. National arms at center. Printer: ABNC. *(BK-CHI-153).*

	VG	VF	UNC
a. Issued note with 1 signature.	17.50	45.00	125.
p. Proof.	—	Unc	500.
s. Specimen.	—	Unc	750.

S137 500 Pesos

D.1913. Black on multicolor underprint. Women with young boys representing "Work" & "Knowledge" at center. Series A. Back: Orange. National arms at center. Printer: ABNC. *(BK-CHI-154).*

	VG	VF	UNC
a. Issued note with 1 signature.	30.00	100.	300.
p. Proof.	—	Unc	500.
s. Specimen.	—	Unc	750.

El Banco de Hidalgo, Parral

1883 Issue

S138 25 Centavos

1883. Black on blue underprint. Portrait Hidalgo at left. Series A. Back: Brown. Printer: HLBNC. *(BK-CHI-125).*

	Good	Fine	XF
a. Issued note.	600.	1800.	5400.
p. Proof.	—	Unc	500.

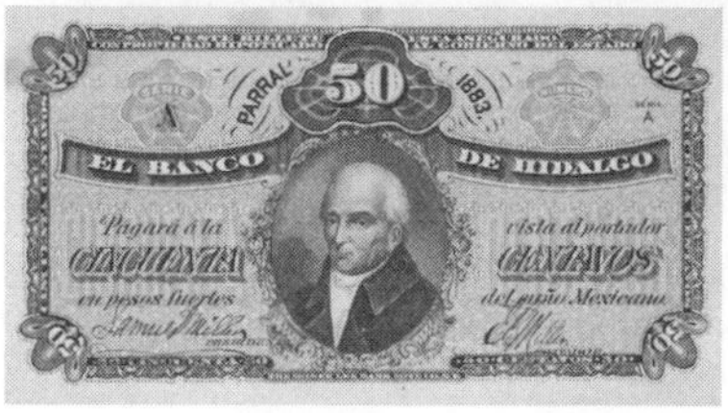

S139 50 Centavos

1883. Portrait Hidalgo at lower center. Series A. Printer: HLBNC.

	Good	Fine	XF
a. Black on red-orange underprint. *(BK-CHI-126).*	600.	1800.	—
p. Proof. Black on green underprint. Back green. *(BK-CHI-127).*	—	Unc	500.

S140 1 Peso

1883. Black on brown underprint. Portrait Hidalgo at center, cherubs at left and right in underprint. Series A. Back: Green. Printer: HLBNC.

	Good	Fine	XF
a. Black on brown underprint. *(BK-CHI-128).*	1200.	3600.	—
p. Proof. Black on green underprint. Back green. *(BK-CHI-129).*	—	Unc	500.
s. Specimen. *(BK-CHI-130).*	—	Unc	750.

S141 5 Pesos

1883. Black on green underprint. Portrait Hidalgo at upper left, steam passenger train at lower right. Series A. Back: Green. Printer: HLBNC.

	Good	Fine	XF
p. Proof.	—	Unc	3250.
s. Specimen. *(BK-CHI-131).*	—	Unc	3500.

S142 10 Pesos

1883. Black on green underprint. Mining scenes at lower left, portrait Hidalgo at upper right. Series A. Back: Green. Printer: HLBNC.

	Good	Fine	XF
p. Proof. *(BK-CHI-134).*	—	Unc	3250.
s. Specimen. *(BK-CHI-133).*	—	Unc	3500.

Banco Mejicano

1878 Issue

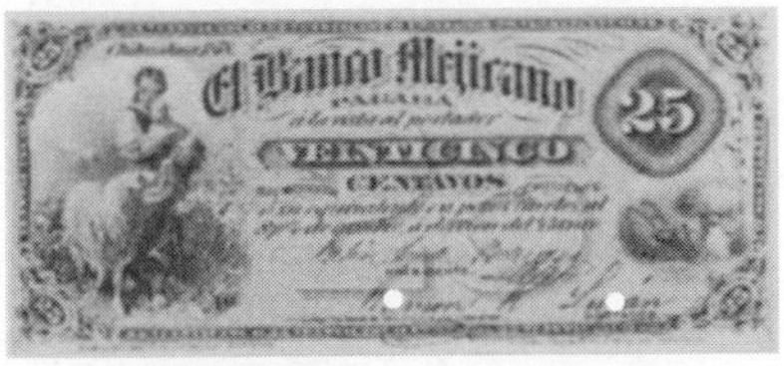

S143 25 Centavos

1878. Black on blue underprint. Shepherdess holding lamb with sheep at left, plow and sheaf at right. Back: Dark orange. Plow and sheaf at center. Printer: NBNC.

	Good	Fine	XF
a. Issued note. *(BK-CHI-22).*	10.00	30.00	100.
p. Proof.	—	Unc	300.
r. Remainder without serial #. *(BK-CHI-23).*	—	Unc	50.00
s. Specimen.	—	Unc	500.

S144 50 Centavos

1878. Black on white with pale orange underprint. Man plowing at left, seated female ("Plenty") at right. Back: Blue. Printer: NBNC.

	Good	Fine	XF
a. Issued note. *(BK-CHI-25).*	125.	375.	1100.
b. Large red overprint: *BATOPILAS.*	150.	450.	1250.
p. Proof.	—	Unc	500.
s. Specimen.	—	Unc	750.

S145 1 Peso

	Good	Fine	XF
1878. Black on green-orange underprint. Agriculture work at center. Series A-E. Back: Brown. National arms at center. Printer: NBNC. *(BK-CHI-27).*	225.	675.	2000.

1883 Issue

S146 1 Peso

1883. Black on tan underprint. Steam train by station ("Anthracite Burner") at center. Series A. Back: Tan. Printer: ABNC. *(BK-CHI-28)*

	Good	Fine	XF
a. Issued note.	525.	1600.	5400.
p. Proof.	—	Unc	1500.
s. Specimen.	—	Unc	1750.

S147 2 Pesos

1883. Black on green underprint. Helmeted Athena at left, two prospectors at right. Series B. Back: Green. Printer: ABNC.

	Good	Fine	XF
p. Proof.	—	Unc	1000.
s. Specimen.	—	Unc	1250.

S148 5 Pesos

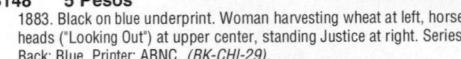

	Good	Fine	XF
1883. Black on blue underprint. Woman harvesting wheat at left, horses heads ("Looking Out") at upper center, standing Justice at right. Series C. Back: Blue. Printer: ABNC. *(BK-CHI-29).*	2250.	6750.	—

S149 10 Pesos

	Good	Fine	XF
1883. Black on orange underprint. Town square scene at left, Ceres (Goddess of Agriculture) at center, market scene at right. Series D. Back: Orange. Printer: ABNC. Punched hole cancelled. *(BK-CHI-30).*	2250.	6750.	—

S149A 20 Pesos

1883. Black on brown underprint. Man plowing field with palm trees in background at left, village scene with people, water fountain, and buildings at right. Series E. Back: Brown. Printer: ABNC.

	Good	Fine	XF
p. Proof.	—	Unc	1000.
s. Specimen.	—	Unc	1250.

Banco Mexicano

1888 Issue

S150 25 Semillas (seeds)

	Good	Fine	XF
1888. Black. Eagle in underprint. *(BK-CHI-31).*	200.	600.	1800.

S151 25 Centavos

1888. Black on yellow underprint. Farmer with sheaf at left. Series A. Back: Brown. Indian ("Chola") at center. Printer: ABNC. *(BK-CHI-32).*

	Good	Fine	XF
a. Issued note.	20.00	60.00	200.
p. Proof.	—	Unc	1000.
s. Specimen. Serie A.	—	Unc	1250.

S152 50 Centavos

1888. Black on yellow underprint. Two goats at right. Series A. Back: Orange. Steam locomotive at center. Printer: ABNC. *(BK-CHI-35).*

	Good	Fine	XF
a. Issued note.	150.	450.	750.
p. Proof.	—	Unc	500.
s. Specimen.	—	Unc	500.

S153 1 Peso

1888. Black on yellow and orange underprint. Woman with chickens at left, female at right. Series A. Back: Brown. Cow's head at center. Printer: ABNC. *(BK-CHI-37).*

	Good	Fine	XF
a. Issued note.	100.	375.	650.
p. Proof.	—	Unc	500.
s. Specimen.	—	Unc	500.

S154 2 Pesos

1888. Black on brown and yellow underprint. Christopher Columbus in sight of land ("First Land") at left, Indian with feather headdress at lower right. Series A. Back: Dark red. Girl and horse at center. Printer: ABNC.

	Good	Fine	XF
a. Issued note. *(BK-CHI-39).*	1500.	2500.	—
p. Proof.	—	Unc	500.
s. Specimen.	—	Unc	500.

S155 5 Pesos

1888. Black on green underprint. Seated female ("La Critique") at center. Series A. Back: Olive-green. Woman's head at center. Printer: ABNC.

	Good	Fine	XF
a. Issued note. *(BK-CHI-41).*	2500.	7500.	—
b. Back proof. *(BK-CHI-41A).*	—	Unc	500.
p. Proof.	—	Unc	1000.
s. Specimen.	—	Unc	1250.

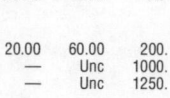

S156 10 Pesos

1888. Black on olive-brown underprint. Cherub representing "Electricity" at left, standing woman ("Fortuna") at right. Series A. Back: Green. Church at center. Printer: ABNC.

	Good	Fine	XF
p. Proof.	—	Unc	1000.
s. Specimen.	—	Unc	1250.

S157 20 Pesos

1888. Black on brown underprint. Woman symbolizing "Commerce" at center, "Study" at right. Series A. Back: Dark brown. Church at center. Printer: ABNC.

	Good	Fine	XF
a. Issued note. *(BK-CHI-43).*	2250.	6750.	—
p. Proof.	—	Unc	1000.
s. Specimen.	—	Unc	1250.

S158 50 Pesos

1886; 1888. Black on orange and yellow underprint. Dog ("Dog and Treasury") at lower left with building in background, cherub ("Bacchus") at right. Series A. Back: Red-brown. Church at center. Printer: ABNC.

	Good	Fine	XF
a. Issued note. *(BK-CHI-45).*	3000.	9000.	—
p. Proof.	—	Unc	1000.
s. Specimen.	—	Unc	1250.

S159 100 Pesos

1888. Black on yellow-green underprint. Farmer plowing at left center, man shearing sheep at right. Series A. Back: Blue. Church at center. Printer: ABNC.

	Good	Fine	XF
a. Issued note. *(BK-CHI-47).*	2250.	6750.	—
p. Proof.	—	Unc	1000.
s. Specimen.	—	Unc	1250.

Banco Minero

1888-1914 Issue

S160 25 Centavos

1888. Black on brown underprint. Seated woman with quill and book ("Industry") at right. Text: *EN MONEDA DE PLATA DEL CUÑO MEXICANO.* Back: Orange. Seated woman with sheep at center. Printer: ABNC. *(BK-CHI-67).*

	Good	Fine	XF
a. Issued note. Series A-C.	75.00	225.	675.
p. Proof. Series A.	—	Unc	1000.
s. Specimen. Series A.	—	Unc	1250.

S161 50 Centavos

1888. Black on pink underprint. Women with shawl ("Spanish Girl") at left, Minerva at right. Series A. Text: *EN MONEDA DE PLATA DEL CUÑO MEXICANO.* Back: Brown. Seated female at center. Printer: ABNC. *(BK-CHI-70).*

	Good	Fine	XF
a. Issued note.	60.00	175.	525.
p. Proof.	—	Unc	1000.
s. Specimen.	—	Unc	1250.

S162 1 Peso

1888-1914. Black on green underprint. Seated Indian ("La Hua de los Incas") at left, seated woman at right. Text: *EN MONEDA DE PLATA DEL CUÑO MEXICANO.* Back: Green. Banco Minero at center. Printer: ABNC.

	Good	Fine	XF
a. Series A. 1888. *(BK-CHI-72).*	50.00	150.	450.
b. Series B. 1888. *(BK-CHI-73).*	40.00	125.	375.
c. Series C. 1895. *(BK-CHI-74).*	30.00	100.	300.
d. Series A-D. Reissued 23.4.1914; 24.4.1914. *(BK-CHI-75).*	3.00	10.00	30.00
e. Series E. 7.7.1914.	3.00	10.00	30.00
f. Series F1-F10. 22.6.1914; 7.7.1914. *(BK-CHI-75).*	3.00	10.00	30.00
g. Series G1-G10. 22.6.1914; 7.7.1914. *(BK-CHI-75).*	3.00	10.00	30.00
p. Proof. Series A. 1888.	—	Unc	1000.
s1. Specimen. Series B. ca.1888.	—	Unc	1250.
s2. Specimen. Series C. 1895.	—	Unc	1250.
s3. Specimen. Series E; F1; F2.	—	Unc	1250.
s4. Specimen. Without series. ND.	—	Unc	1250.

NOTE: Reports of specific dates from 1888-1914 are requested.

S163 5 Pesos

1888-97. Black on orange and yellow underprint. Seated female ("Justice") at left, seated female ("Tropics No. 3") at right. Text: *EN MONEDA DE PLATA DEL CUÑO MEXICANO.* Back: Blue. Allegorical woman with safe and coins at left, miners at center. Printer: ABNC.

	Good	Fine	XF
a. Series A. 1888. *(BK-CHI-77).*	75.00	225.	675.
b. Series B. 1895. *(BK-CHI-78).*	30.00	100.	300.
c. Series A. 1896. *(BK-CHI-79).*	30.00	100.	300.
d. Series B. 1897. *(BK-CHI-80).*	15.00	45.00	100.
p. Proof. Series A. 1888.	—	Unc	1000.
s1. Specimen. Series A. 1888.	—	Unc	1250.
s2. Specimen. Series A52.	—	Unc	1250.
s3. Specimen. Series B.	—	Unc	1250.

NOTE: Reports of specific dates from 1888-1914 are requested.

S163A 5 Pesos

1898-1914. Black on orange and yellow underprint. Seated female ("Justice") at left, seated female ("Tropics No. 3") at right. Like #S163 but with text: *A LA PAR EN EFECTIVO.* Back: Blue. Allegorical woman with safe and coins at left, miners at center. Printer: ABNC.

	Good	Fine	XF
a. Seriec C. 1898-1899. *(BK-CHI-81).*	7.50	20.00	60.00
f. Series D. 3.5.1900/1899. *(BK-CHI-82).*	7.50	20.00	60.00
g. 12.11.1901; 20.1.1902-1909. *(BK-CHI-83).*	6.00	17.50	50.00
h. 16.3.1910-1.8.1914. *(BK-CHI-84).*	3.00	10.00	30.00
i. Overprint: *CHIHUAHUA.* 11.9.1903/1903-31.5.1911/1911. *(BK-CHI-85).*	6.00	20.00	60.00
j. Overprint: *GÓMEZ PALACIO.* 16.7.1900/1899; 1901. *(BK-CHI-86).*	30.00	90.00	100.
k. Overprint: *HERMOSILLO.* 3.3.1903; 24.8.1903; 25.8.1903. *(BK-CHI-87).*	25.00	75.00	225.
l. Overprint: *HERMOSILLO/CHIHUAHUA.* 3.4.1903/1904; 3.3.1905/1903/1904. *(BK-CHI-88).*	25.00	75.00	225.
s1. Specimen. Series C; E.	—	Unc	1250.
s2. Specimen. Series D; F1; F2.	—	Unc	1250.
s3. Specimen. Series H4; J3; O3; R3; U50; U51; Y32.	—	Unc	1250.
s4. Specimen. Series H. 1902; L. 1903; P. 1904.	—	Unc	1250.
s5. Specimen. Without series. 1903; 1906-07.	—	Unc	1250.
s6. Specimen. Without series. ND.	—	Unc	1250.

NOTE: Reports of specific dates from 1888-1914 are requested.

S164 10 Pesos

1888. Black on orange and yellow underprint. Female head with helmet at left, Banco Minero at center. Text: *en moneda de plata del cuño mexicano.* Back: Brown. Cattle and sheep ("Cattle on the Road") at center. Printer: ABNC.

	Good	Fine	XF
p. Proof. Series A. 1888.	—	Unc	1000.
s. Specimen. Series A. 1888.	—	Unc	1250.

NOTE: Reports of specific dates from 1888-1914 are requested.

S164A 10 Pesos

1897-1914. Black on orange and yellow underprint. Female head with helmet at left, Banco Minero at center. Like #S164 but with text: *a la par en efectivo*. Back: Brown. Cattle and sheep ("Cattle on the Road") at center. Printer: ABNC.

	Good	Fine	XF
a. Series B. 1897. *(BK-CHI-91).*	30.00	100.	300.
b. 1898. *(BK-CHI-92).*	20.00	60.00	175.
c. 20.3.1900-1.8.1914. *(BK-CHI-93).*	6.00	20.00	60.00
d. Overprint: *CHIHUAHUA*. 13.4.1903/1903-21.11.1912/ 1912. *(BK-CHI-94).*	10.00	30.00	100.
e. Overprint: *GÓMEZ PALACIO*. 20.3.1900.	45.00	125.	375.
f. Overprint: *HERMOSILLO/CHIHUAHUA*. 21.8.1903/1903. *(BK-CHI-96).*	30.00	100.	300.
p1. Proof. Series B; C.	—	Unc	1000.
p2. Proof. Without series. ND.	—	Unc	1000.
s1. Specimen. Series B.	—	Unc	1250.
s2. Specimen. Series A26-A28; E4; J3; L3; L4; O; U25.	—	Unc	1250.
s3. Specimen. Series F; Without series. 1903; 1906.	—	Unc	1250.
s4. Specimen. Without series. ND.	—	Unc	1250.

NOTE: Reports of specific dates from 1888-1914 are requested.

S165 20 Pesos

1888. Black on orange and yellow underprint. Seated female with child at left, public water well scene at right. Text: *EN MONEDA DE PLATA DEL CUÑO MEXICANO*. Back: Red. Steam locomotive at center. Printer: ABNC.

	Good	Fine	XF
a. Issued note. *(BK-CHI-99).*	125.	375.	1000.
p. Proof. Series A.	—	Unc	1000.
s. Specimen. Series A.	—	Unc	1250.

NOTE: Reports of specific dates from 1888-1914 are needed.

S165A 20 Pesos

1898-1908. Black on orange and yellow underprint. Seated female with child at left, public water well scene at right. Like #S165 but with text: *a la par en efectivo* and curved *CHIHUAHUA 1903*. Back: Red. Steam locomotive at center. Printer: ABNC.

	Good	Fine	XF
a. 20.3.1900-25.7.1914. *(BK-CHI-100).*	20.00	60.00	175.
b. Overprint: *CHIHUAHUA*. 9.7.1906/1906/1903. Series C. 24.12.1908/1908/1903. Series E. 4.12.1908/1908/1903. *(BK-CHI-101).*	25.00	75.00	225.
c. Overprint: *GÓMEZ PALACIO/CHIHUAHUA*. 9.7.1906/1903. *(BK-CHI-102).*	75.00	225.	675.
p. Proof. Without series. ND.	—	Unc	1000.
s1. Specimen. Series C. 1903.	—	Unc	1250.

NOTE: Reports of specific dates from 1888-1914 are needed.

S165B 20 Pesos

1910-14. Black on orange and yellow underprint. Seated female with child at left, public water well scene at right. Text: *a la par en efectivo*. Like #S165A but *CHIHUAHUA* in straight line. Back: Red. Steam locomotive at center. Printer: ABNC.

	Good	Fine	XF
a. Series F; H. 27.1.1910.	15.00	45.00	125.
b. Series R. 30.12.1912.	15.00	45.00	125.
c. Series W. 24.3.1913.	15.00	45.00	125.
d. Series J.10. 21.4.1914; 3.7.1914.	15.00	45.00	125.
e. Series N.11. 7.7.1914.	15.00	45.00	125.
s1. Specimen. Series A10; D12; E11; S-V.	—	Unc	1000.
s2. Specimen. Without series. ND.	—	Unc	1250.

NOTE: Reports of specific dates from 1888-1914 are requested.

S166 50 Pesos

1888-97. Black on yellow and blue underprint. Banco Minero at center, Urania (Muse of Astrology) at right. Text: *EN MONEDA DE PLATA DEL CUÑO MEXICANO*. Back: Blue. Seated Indian with hatchet at center. Printer: ABNC.

	Good	Fine	XF
p. Proof. Series A. 1888.	—	Unc	1000.
s. Specimen. Series A. 1888.	—	Unc	1250.

NOTE: Reports of specific dates from 1888-1914 are requested.

S166A 50 Pesos

1900-14. Black on yellow and blue underprint. Banco Minero at center, Urania (Muse of Astrology) at right. Like #S166 but with text: *A LA PAR EN EFECTIVO*. Back: Blue. Seated Indian with hatchet at center. Printer: ABNC.

	Good	Fine	XF
a. 1898-17.7.1914. *(BK-CHI-106).*	125.	375.	1100.
b. Overprint: *GÓMEZ PALACIO*. 26.6.1900/1899-20.2.1907/1903. *(BK-CHI-109).*	225.	675.	2000.
c. Overprint: *CHIHUAHUA*. 6.2.1902/1901-30.12.1912/ 1913. *(BK-CHI-108).*	125.	375.	1100.
p1. Proof. Series A. ND; 1903.	—	Unc	1000.
p2. Proof. Without series. ND.	—	Unc	1000.
s1. Specimen. Series A. ND; 1903.	—	Unc	1250.
s2. Specimen. 3.1901. Series B-D; F; N; O; T7.	—	Unc	1250.
s3. Specimen. Series A8.	—	Unc	1250.
s4. Specimen. Without series. ND.	—	Unc	1250.

NOTE: Reports of specific dates from 1888-1914 are requested.

S167 100 Pesos

1888; 1897; 5.5.1899. Black on yellow and olive underprint. Cherubs at lower left, woman in canoe ("La Verdulera") at center, cow with calf at lower right. Text: *EN MONEDA DE PLATA DEL CUÑO MEXICANO*. Back: Olive-green. Three children ("The Young Students") at left. Printer: ABNC.

	Good	Fine	XF
a. Series B. 1888. *(BK-CHI-111).*	225.	675.	2000.
p. Proof. Series A. 1888.	—	Unc	1000.
s1. Specimen. Series A. 1888.	—	Unc	1250.
s2. Specimen. Series E.	—	Unc	1250.

NOTE: Reports of specific dates from 1888-1914 are requested.

S168 100 Pesos

1899-1914. Black on yellow and olive underprint. Cherubs at lower left, woman in canoe ("La Verdulera") at center, cow with calf at lower right. Like #S167 but with text: *A LA PAR EN EFECTIVO*. Back: Olive-green. Three children ("The Young Students") at left. Printer: ABNC.

	Good	Fine	XF
a. 5.5.1899-21.4.1914. *(BK-CHI-112-113).*	125.	375.	1100.
b. Overprint: *CHIHUAHUA*. 31.4.1903/1899-1912/5.12.1911. Series P. *(BK-CHI-114).*	125.	375.	1100.
c. Overprint: *SUC. DEL BANCO MINERO*. 16.7.1908; 26.8.1907/1907/1903. *(BK-CHI-115).*	150.	450.	1350.
d. Overprint: *GÓMEZ PALACIO*. 16.6.1900; 23.4.1908-28.4.1908/ 11.11.1898. *(BK-CHI-116).*	375.	1100.	3300.
e. Overprint: *HERMOSILLO/CHIHUAHUA*.; 3.3.1903/8.4.1908/1903; 3.3.1903/16.3.19-/1903. *(BK-CHI-117).*	175.	525.	1575.
p1. Proof. Series A.	—	Unc	1000.
p2. Proof. Without series. ND.	—	Unc	1000.
s1. Specimen. Series A5; A6; A7; C. ca.1898.	—	Unc	1250.
s2. Specimen. Series E; F. 1902; O; P; R; X.	—	Unc	1250.
s3. Specimen. Without series. ND; 1902; 1903.	—	Unc	1250.

NOTE: Reports of specific dates from 1888-1914 are requested.

S169 1000 Pesos	Good	Fine	XF
1888-1914. Black on multicolor underprint. Reclining woman at left center. Back: Black on multicolor underprint. Woman at center. Printer: ABNC.			
a. Overprint: *CHIHUAHUA.* 10.7.1908/1908/1904. *(BK-CHI-119).*	5000.	15,000.	—
b. 1909. Archive copy.	—	—	—
s1. Specimen. 1902.	—	Unc	1250.
s2. Specimen. Series J.2; N.1. ND (1914).	—	Unc	1250.

NOTE: Reports of specific dates from 1888-1914 are requested.

S169A 1000 Pesos			
ND (ca.1908). Black on green underprint. Allegorical woman holding book and boy at left, allegorical woman holding scythe and fruit with boy at right. Back: Green. Printer: ABNC. Proof. (Not issued).	—	—	—

1910 Commemorative Issue

#S170-S171 100th Anniversary of Independence ovpt. on face.

S170 5 Pesos	Good	Fine	XF
1910. Black on brown and yellow underprint. Seated female ("Justice") at left, seated female ("Tropics No. 3") at right. Series T3. Back: Red, white and green (National colors). Text around coin design at center. Overprint: *1810-CENTENARIO-1910* on face of #S163. Printer: ABNC. *(BK-CHI-90).*			
a. Issued note.	175.	525.	1575.
p. Proof.	—	Unc	1000.
s. Specimen.	—	Unc	1250.
S171 10 Pesos			
1910. Black on orange underprint. Female head with helmet at left, Banco Minero at center. Back: Red, white and green (National colors). Commemorative text around coin design at center. Overprint: *1810-CENTENARIO-1910* on face on #S164. Printer: ABNC. *(BK-CHI-98).*			
a. Issued note.	125.	375.	1100.
p. Proof.	—	Unc	1250.
s. Specimen. Series U3; V3.	—	Unc	1250.

Banco Minero Chihuahuense

1880-87 Issue

S172 25 Centavos	Good	Fine	XF
1880. Black on salmon underprint. Miners working at left. Series A. Back: Deep blue. Printer: ABNC.			
a. *(BK-CHI-52).* 1880.	45.00	125.	375.
b. Overprint: 1882. *(BK-CHI-52a).*	100.	300.	900.
c. Overprint: 1883. *(BK-CHI-52a).*	—	—	—
d. Overprint: *BATOPILAS.* (4 different varieties known). 1880. *(BK-CHI-53).*	125.	375.	1150.
e. Overprint: *ADMOR. GRAL. DE RENTAS, 1880* with additional signature	175.	525.	1550.
p. 1880. Proof.	—	Unc	1000.
s. 1880. Specimen.	—	Unc	1250.

S173 50 Centavos	Good	Fine	XF
1880-ca.1887. Black on orange underprint. Helmeted female head ("Minerva No. 2") at center. Back: Brown. Printer: ABNC.			
a. Series A. 1880. *(BK-CHI-57).*	125.	375.	1150.
b. Overprint: 1882.	—	—	—
p1. Proof. Series A. 1880.	—	Unc	1000.
p2. Proof. Series B. 1880 (ca.1887).	—	Unc	1000.
s1. Specimen. Series A. 1880.	—	Unc	1250.
s2. Specimen. Series B. 1880.	—	Unc	1250.

S174 1 Peso	Good	Fine	XF
1880. Black on green underprint. Standing female with child ("Charity & Commerce") at center. Series A. Back: Green. Printer: ABNC.			
a. Handwritten signature 1880. *(BK-CHI-60).*	125.	375.	1100.
b. Red overprint: *1882/1880.* Printed signature *(BK-CHI-61).*	125.	375.	1100.
c. Red vertical overprint: *VALE POR PESOS FUERTES A LA PAR* twice on face. *(BK-CHI-).*	175.	525.	1575.
d. Red vertical overprint similar to c. Large text: *VALE PESOS FUERTES A LA PAR* added across face. *(BK-CHI-63.)*	175.	525.	1575.
p. Proof.	—	Unc	1000.
r. Unsigned remainder. *(BK-CHI-62).*	—	Unc	250.
s. Specimen.	—	Unc	1250.

S175 1 Peso	Good	Fine	XF
1880; 1882. Black on tan underprint. Standing female with child ("Charity & Commerce") at center. Series A, B. Like #S174. Back: Brown. Overprint: Red: *VALE POR PESOS FUERTES A LA PAR* across face. Printer: ABNC. *(BK-CHI-64).*			
a. 1880.	175.	525.	1575.
b. 1882/1880.	—	—	—
p. Proof. 1880.	—	Unc	1000.
s. Specimen. Series A; B. 1880.	—	Unc	1250.
S176 1 Peso			
1880. Black on pink underprint. Standing female with child ("Charity & Commerce") at center. Series B. Like #S174. Back: Red-orange. Printer: ABNC. *(BK-CHI-65).*			
a. Issued note.	300.	900.	2750.
p. Proof.	—	Unc	1000.
s. Specimen.	—	Unc	1250.

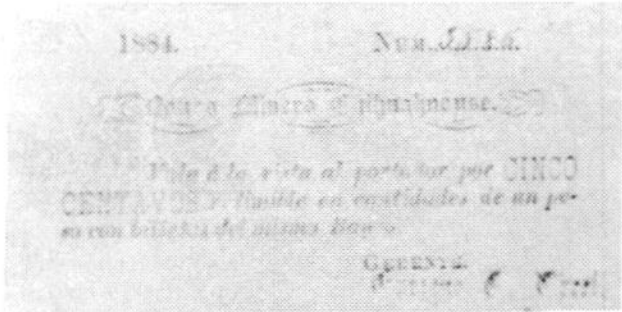

S180 5 Centavos	Good	Fine	XF
1884. Black. *APRIL 16, 1884* in inked seal. *(BK-CHI-49).*	75.00	225.	675.
S181 10 Centavos			
1884. *April 15, 1884* in inked seal. Value: *DIEZ CENTAVOS* in thin letters. *(BK-CHI-50).*	90.00	275.	825.

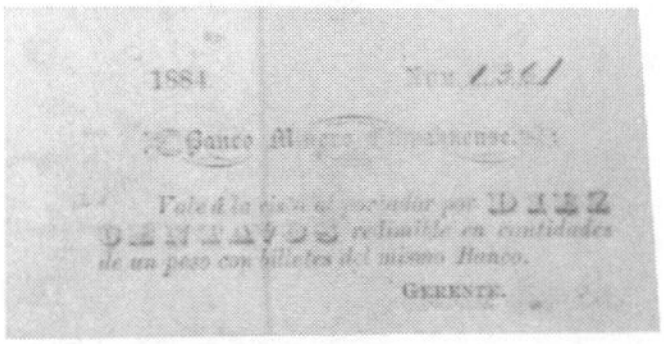

S182 10 Centavos	Good	Fine	XF
1884. *April 15, 1884* in inked seal. *DIEZ CENTAVOS* in thick letters. *(BK-CHI-51).*	100.	300.	900.

Banco Minero de Chihuahua

1914 Issue

	Good	Fine	XF
S183 50 Centavos 1914. Black on green-yellow underprint. Without pictorial design. Back: Brown. Printer: Eduardo I. Aguilar. *(BK-CHI-121).*	225.	675.	200.

	Good	Fine	XF
S184 2 Pesos 7.2.1914-5.9.1914. Black on pink underprint. Mining scene at center. Back: Red. Minero Bank at center. Printer: AB&PC. *(BK-CHI-122).*	5.00	15.00	45.00

	Good	Fine	XF
S185 5 Pesos 19.5.1914-9.6.1914. Black on tan underprint. Euthenia (Goddess of Plenty) by beehive at left, portrait young woman at top center right. Back: Brown. National arms at center. Printer: B&S. *(BK-CHI-123).*	5.00	15.00	45.00

	Good	Fine	XF
S186 10 Pesos 9.5.1914-24.6.1914. Black on green underprint. Standing female at right. Back: Green. National arms at center. Printer: B&S. *(BK-CHI-124).*	5.00	15.00	45.00

Banco de Santa Eulalia

1875-84 Issue

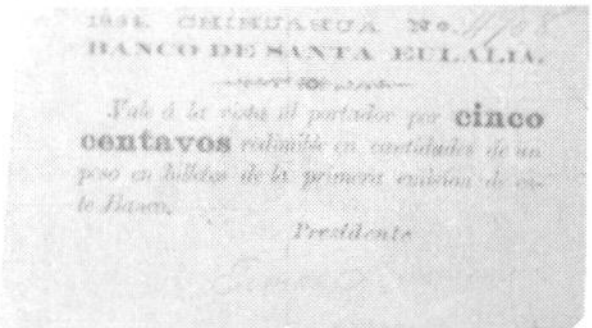

	Good	Fine	XF
S187 5 Centavos 1884. *(BK-CHI-12).*	75.00	225.	675.

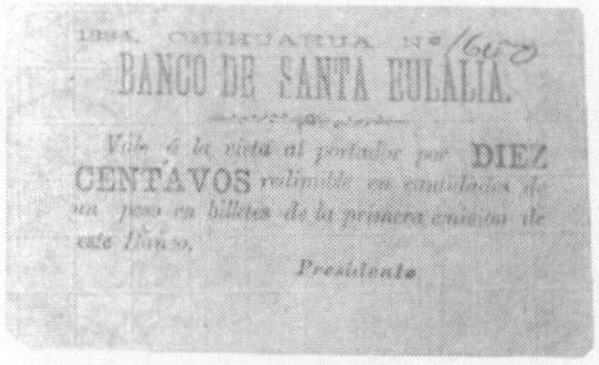

	Good	Fine	XF
S188 10 Centavos 1884. *(BK-CHI-13).*	125.	375.	1100.

	Good	Fine	XF
S189 25 Centavos 1875 (ca.1875-82). Black on pale-orange underprint. Woman's head at lower left and right, steam locomotive at center. Back: Brown. Printer: ABNC.			
a. Series A; B. *(BK-CHI-14).*	100.	300.	900.
p. Proof. Series A.	—	Unc	1000.
s. Specimen. Series A.	—	Unc	1250.

NOTE: on Series A the signature on the right is handsigned; for Series B, the signature on the right is printed.

	Good	Fine	XF
S190 50 Centavos 1875 (ca.1881). Black on orange underprint. Man with wool pack at left, miners at right. Back: Orange. Printer: ABNC.			
a. Series A; B. *(BK-CHI-16).*	100.	300.	900.
p. Proof. Series A.	—	Unc	1000.
s. Specimen. Series A.	—	Unc	1250.

NOTE: on Series A the signature on the right is handsigned; for Series B, the signature on the right is printed.

	Good	Fine	XF
S191 1 Peso 1875 (ca.1875-82). Black on tan and green underprint. Herdsman at left, train at right. Back: Tan. Printer: ABNC.			
a. Series A; B. *(BK-CHI-18).*	225.	675.	2000.
p. Proof. Series A.	—	Unc	1000.
s. Specimen. Series A.	—	Unc	1250.
S192 5 Pesos 1882. Black on orange underprint. Helmeted allegorical man representing "Electricity" and allegorical woman with wings at center. Series C. Back: Green. Five 8 reales coins at center. Printer: ABNC.			
p. Proof. Series A.	—	Unc	1000.
s. Specimen. Series A.	—	Unc	1250.

S193 10 Pesos

1882-83. Black on pink underprint. Seated female ("Tropics No. 2") at left, "Raphael's Angel No. 2" at right. Back: Blue. Ten 8 reales coins, 5 at left, 5 at right. Printer: ABNC.

	Good	Fine	XF
a. Series C. *(BK-CHI-20).*	2250.	6750.	—
p. Proof. Series C.	—	Unc	1000.

NOTE: The following text was prepared as an overprint on #S189-S193 ca.1884-86: *BANCO DE SANTA EULALIA PAGARÁ A LA VISTA EL VALOR DE ESTE BILLETE EN PLATA A LA PAR. 1884*. This overprint was made in two styles: the first in black, the second in blue. No examples are known.

Coahuila

Banco de Coahuila

1898-1914 Issue

S195 5 Pesos

1898-1914. Black on light green underprint. Seated female ("Agriculture") at left. Portrait Arizpe at left, portrait Cepeda at right. Back: Green. Reclining female ("National Emblems") at center. Printer: ABNC.

	Good	Fine	XF
a. Series E. 15.1.1898; 16.5.1898.	30.00	100.	300.
b. Series E. 5.3.1900-5.5.1912.	15.00	45.00	125.
c. Series E. 15.2.1914. *(BK-COA-5).*	10.00	30.00	100.
p. Proof. Without series. ND.	—	Unc	1000.
s. Specimen. Without series. ND.	—	Unc	1250.

NOTE: Reports of specific dates from 1898-1914 are requested.

S196 10 Pesos

1898-1914. Black on tan underprint. Seated female ("Commerce") at right. Portrait Arizpe at left, portrait Cepeda at right. Back: Brown. Cowboy herding cattle at center. Printer: ABNC.

	Good	Fine	XF
a. Series S. 3.3.1898; 16.5.1898; 5.5.1902. *(BK-COA-8).*	30.00	100.	300.
b. Series S. 5.3.1900; 15.11.1900; 15.9.1909. *(BK-COA-9).*	25.00	75.00	225.
c. Series S. 15.2.1914. *(BK-COA-10).*	15.00	45.00	125.
d. Overprint: *Torreon.* Series S. 3.3.1898.	45.00	100.	300.
p. Proof. Without series. ND.	—	Unc	1000.
s. Specimen. Without series. ND.	—	Unc	1250.

NOTE: Reports of specific dates from 1898-1914 are requested.

S197 20 Pesos

1898-1914. Black on orange underprint. Woman at left, sheep at right. Portrait Arizpe at left, portrait Cepeda at right. Back: Orange. Sheep and country landscape at center, train by station at center. Printer: ABNC.

	Good	Fine	XF
a. Series C. 3.3.1898; 16.5.1898. *(BK-COA-15).*	75.00	225.	675.
b. Series C. 5.3.1900; 15.11.900. *(BK-COA-17).*	50.00	150.	450.
c. Series C. 15.9.1909; 7.6.1910; 5.2.1914. *(BK-COA-17).*	40.00	125.	375.
d. Overprint: *Torreon.* Series C. 3.3.1898. *(BK-COA-18).*	100.	300.	900.
p. Proof. Without series. ND.	—	Unc	1000.
s. Specimen. Without series. ND.	—	Unc	1250.

NOTE: Reports of specific dates from 1898-1914 are requested.

S198 50 Pesos

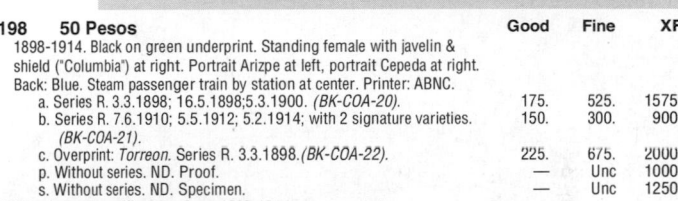

1898-1914. Black on green underprint. Standing female with javelin & shield ("Columbia") at right. Portrait Arizpe at left, portrait Cepeda at right. Back: Blue. Steam passenger train by station at center. Printer: ABNC.

	Good	Fine	XF
a. Series R. 3.3.1898; 16.5.1898;5.3.1900. *(BK-COA-20).*	175.	525.	1575.
b. Series R. 7.6.1910; 5.5.1912; 5.2.1914; with 2 signature varieties. *(BK-COA-21).*	150.	300.	900.
c. Overprint: *Torreon.* Series R. 3.3.1898.*(BK-COA-22).*	225.	675.	2000.
p. Without series. ND. Proof.	—	Unc	1000.
s. Without series. ND. Specimen.	—	Unc	1250.

NOTE: Reports of specific dates from 1898-1914 are requested.

S199 100 Pesos

1898-1914. Black on orange and yellow underprint. Female at right. Portrait Arizpe at left, portrait Cepeda at right. Back: Orange. Woman at center. Printer: ABNC.

	Good	Fine	XF
a. Series I. 3.2.1898. *(BK-COA-24).*	525.	1575.	5000.
b. Series I. 5.3.1900; 15.9.1909. *(BK-COA-25).*	450.	1350.	4000.
c. Series I. 7.6.1910; 5.5.1912. *(BK-COA-26).*	450.	1350.	4000.
p. Proof. Without series. ND.	—	Unc	1000.
s. Specimen. Without series. ND.	—	Unc	1250.

NOTE: Reports of specific dates from 1898-1914 are requested.

S200 500 Pesos	Good	Fine	XF
1897-98. Black on olive-green and yellow underprint. Woman with basket on head at left, palm tree at right. Portrait Arizpe at left, portrait Cepeda at right. Back: Olive-green. Minerva (Goddess of Science, Art and War) at left, woman at right. Printer: ABNC.			
a. Series T-1. 16.5.1898. *(BK-COA-28).*	3000.	9000.	—
b. Overprint: *Torreon.* Series T. 3.2.1898. *(BK-COA-29).*	3000.	9000.	—
p. Proof. Without series. ND.	—	Unc	1000.
s. Specimen. Without series. ND.	—	Unc	1250.

S201 1000 Pesos	Good	Fine	XF
1897-98. Black on purple and yellow underprint. Art and Literature at right. Portrait Arizpe at left, portrait Cepeda at right. Back: Purple. Sheep and cattle. Printer: ABNC. *(BK-COA-31).*			
p. Proof. Without series. ND.	—	Unc	1000.
s. Specimen. Without series. ND.	—	Unc	1250.

S202 1 Peso	Good	Fine	XF
2.4.1914; 15.7.1914. Black on green underprint. Portrait Arizpe at left, portrait Cepeda at right. Series U. Back: Green. Coahuila Bank at center. Printer: AB&PC. *(BK-COA-1).*	12.50	35.00	125.

S203 2 Pesos	Good	Fine	XF
2.4.1914; 14.7.1914. Black on orange underprint. Portrait Arizpe at left, portrait Cepeda at right. Series N. Back: Red. Coahuila Bank at center. Printer: AB&PC. *(BK-COA-2).*	7.50	25.00	75.00

S204 10 Pesos	Good	Fine	XF
15.2.1914; 1.5.1914. Black on light green underprint. Standing female at right. Series S. Back: Olive-green. National arms at center. Printer: B&S. *(BK-COA-13).*	6.00	20.00	60.00

Distrito Federal - México City

Banco de Empleados

1800s Issue

S204A 5 Pesos Fuertes	Good	Fine	XF
18xx. Portrait woman at left, national arms at right. Vignette at left and right. Printer: BWC. Specimen.	—	Unc	750.
S204B 10 Pesos Fuertes			
18xx. National arms at left, woman at right. Vignette at left and right. Printer: BWC. Specimen.	—	Unc	750.

S204C 20 Pesos Fuertes	Good	Fine	XF
18xx. Portrait woman at left and right, national arms at upper center. Vignette at left and right. Printer: BWC. Specimen.	—	Unc	750.
S204D 50 Pesos Fuertes			
18xx. Boy kneeling at bookcase at left, national arms at right. Vignette at left and right. Printer: BWC. Specimen.	—	Unc	750.

S204E 100 Pesos Fuertes

	Good	Fine	XF
18xx. Palace at left, portrait woman at right, national arms at upper center. Vignette at left and right. Printer: BWC. Specimen.	—	Unc	750.

S204F 500 Pesos Fuertes

	Good	Fine	XF
18xx. Boy kneeling at bookcase at left, palace at right, national arms at upper center. Vignette at left and right. Printer: BWC. Specimen.	—	Unc	750.

Banco Industrial de México, Sociedad Anónima

1898 Issue

S205 50 Centavos

	Good	Fine	XF
6.3.1898. Maritime Progress and Industry at left. *(BK-DF-379).*	375.	1100.	3300.

S206 100 Centavos

	Good	Fine	XF
6.3.1898. Maritime Progress and Industry at left. *(BK-DF-380).*	—	Unc	1250.

Banco Internacional e Hipotecario de México

1800s Issue

S207 1 Peso

	Good	Fine	XF
18xx (ca.1889). Black on blue and yellow underprint. Standing allegorical woman with flags at left center, portrait M. Lerdo de Tejada at right. Back: Blue. Indian at center. Printer: ABNC. *(BK-DF-360).* (Not issued).			
p. Proof.	—	Unc	1000.
s. Specimen.	—	Unc	1250.

S208 2 Pesos

	Good	Fine	XF
18xx (ca.1889). Black on green and yellow underprint. Portrait two women at left, two children seated ("The Turo Republics") at right. Back: Brown. Indian at center. Printer: ABNC. *(BK-DF-362).* (Not issued).			
p. Proof.	—	Unc	1000.
s. Specimen.	—	Unc	1250.

S209 5 Pesos

	Good	Fine	XF
18xx (ca.1889). Black on olive and yellow underprint. Standing woman ("Fortuna") at left, steam passenger train at center. Back: Olive. Aztec calendar superimposed on five 8 reales coins at center. Printer: ABNC. *(BK-DF-364).* (Not issued).			
p. Proof.	—	Unc	1000.
s. Specimen.	—	Unc	1250.

S210 10 Pesos

	Good	Fine	XF
18xx (ca.1889). Black on brown and yellow underprint. Crop worker at left, portrait woman ("Columbia") with cherub supporters at right. Back: Green. Steam passenger train at center. Printer: ABNC. *(BK-DF-366).* (Not issued).			
p. Proof.	—	Unc	1000.
s. Specimen.	—	Unc	1250.

S211 20 Pesos

	Good	Fine	XF
18xx (ca.1889). Black on orange and yellow underprint. Child supporting shield with value flanked by allegorical women at left and right at center. Back: Orange. Woman with sheep at center. Printer: ABNC. *(BK-DF-368).* (Not issued).			
p. Proof.	—	Unc	1000.
s. Specimen.	—	Unc	1250.

S212 50 Pesos

	Good	Fine	XF
18xx (ca.1889). Black on brown and yellow underprint. Seated Indian with bow and arrow ("Alerta") at left, rural vista at center right. Back: Brown. Steer's head at center. Printer: ABNC. *(BK-DF-370).* (Not issued).			
p. Proof.	—	Unc	1000.
s. Specimen.	—	Unc	1250.

NOTICE

Readers with unlisted dates, signature varieties, etc., are invited to submit photocopies or scans of their notes to:
Standard Catalog of World Paper Money,
700 East State St. Iola, WI 54990-0001,
E-Mail: george.cuhaj@fwmedia.com.

S213 100 Pesos | Good | Fine | XF

18xx (ca.1889). Black on blue and yellow underprint. Man seated playing guitar on mule ("El Guitarrista") at left, two children ("The Two Republics") seated at right. Back: Blue-black. Cattle wading at center. Printer: ABNC. *(BK-DF-372).* (Not issued).

	Good	Fine	XF
p. Proof.	—	Unc	1000.
s. Specimen.	—	Unc	1250.

S214 500 Pesos | Good | Fine | XF

18xx (ca.1889). Black on orange and yellow underprint. Fleet of ships at left, boy with large hat ("Craig Colgate") at right. Back: Black and orange. Woman at left. Printer: ABNC. *(BK-DF-374).* (Not issued).

	Good	Fine	XF
p. Proof.	—	Unc	1000.
s. Specimen.	—	Unc	1250.

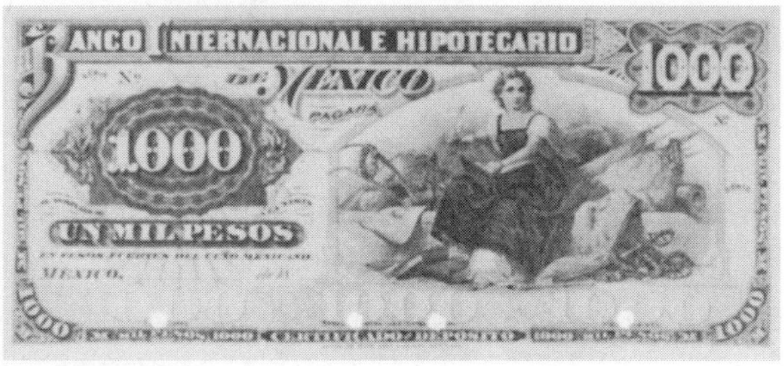

S215 1000 Pesos | Good | Fine | XF

18xx (ca.1889). Black on green and yellow underprint. Seated female at center right. Back: Black and green. Allegorical woman with globe and child at center. Printer: ABNC. *(BK-DF-375).* (Not issued).

	Good	Fine	XF
p. Proof. 18xx.	—	Unc	1000.
s. Specimen. 18xx.	—	Unc	1250.

1914 Gold Certificate of Deposit Issue

S215A 1000 Grams	Good	Fine	XF
ND (ca.1914). Black on green and yellow underprint. National arms and seated Justice wearing crown and holding key at left. Series A. Back: Orange. Building at upper center. Printer: ABNC. Specimen. *(BK-DF-378).*	—	Unc	1250.

Banco de Londres México y Sud America

1867-78 Issue

S216 5 Pesos	Good	Fine	XF
15.11.1867. Pale orange underprint. Man on horseback at left, British crowned supported arms at upper center, Cathedral of Mexico at right. Uniface. *(BK-DF-1).*	250.	750.	2250.

S217 10 Pesos	Good	Fine	XF
2.9.1878. Portrait Montezuma at left, donkey with cart at right. Printer: BWC. *(BK-DF-2).*	7500.	—	—

1800s Text Varieties Issues

Type I: No branch name engraved.

Type II: Payable at Distrito Federal.

S220 2 Pesos	Good	Fine	XF
6.11.1883. Black on green and orange underprint. Young girl at lower left, portrait Queen Victoria at upper center, woman with child at lower right. Series A-F. Text Type II. Back: Blue. Printer: ABNC. *(BK-DF-3).*	2700.	7500.	—

S221 20 Pesos | Good | Fine | XF

18xx (ca.1868-81). Reclining female ("Science") at upper left, "Mule Train" at center, men with telescope ("Looking Out") at lower right. Text Type II. Printer: ABNC. *(BK-DF-5).*

	Good	Fine	XF
p1. Proof. 18xx (ca.1868). Black on blue underprint. Series A.	—	Unc	2500.
p2. Proof. 18xx (ca.1874-81). Black on blue and brown underprint. Back blue. Series B.	—	Unc	2500.
s. Specimen. Series B.	—	Unc	3000.

S222 50 Pesos | Good | Fine | XF

18xx (ca.1868-81). Young sailor at lower left, "Mule Train" at center, woman kneeling ("Rebecca") at lower right. Type II. Series A. Printer: ABNC. *(BK-DF-6).*

	Good	Fine	XF
p1. Proof. 18xx (ca.1868). Black on brown underprint.	—	Unc	3000.
p2. Proof. 18xx (ca.1874-81). Black on brown and blue underprint. Back blue.	—	Unc	3000.
s. Specimen.	—	Unc	3500.

S223 100 Pesos	Good	Fine	XF
18xx (ca.1866-81). Girl with dog ("The Pets") at lower left, "Mule Train" at center, seated allegorical woman with cherub at lower right. Series A. Back: Blue. Printer: ABNC. *(BK-DF-7).*			
p1. Proof. 18xx (ca.1866). Black on green underprint. Text Type I.	—	Unc	3000.
p2. Proof. 18xx (ca.1868-81). Black on green and orange underprint. Text Type II.	—	Unc	3000.
s. Specimen.	—	Unc	3500.

S223A 500 Pesos	Good	Fine	XF
18xx (ca.1866-79). Anchor at lower left, "Mule Train" at center, chickens at lower right. Series A. Back: Blue. Printer: ABNC.			
p1. Proof. 18xx (ca.1866). Black on green underprint. Text Type I.	—	Unc	4000.
p2. Proof. 18xx (ca.1868-79). Black on green and orange underprint. Text Type II.	—	Unc	4000.
s. Specimen.	—	Unc	4500.

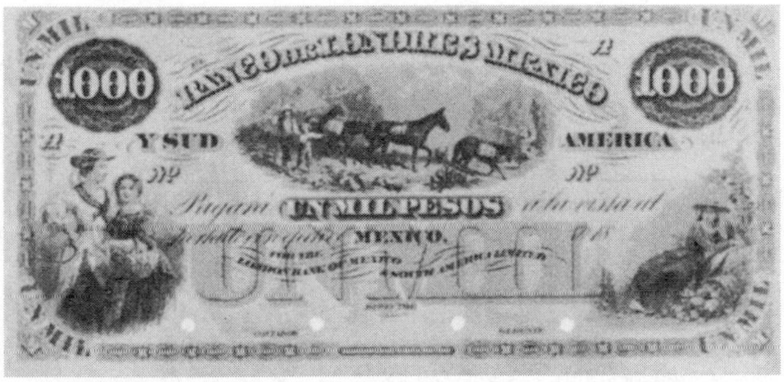

S223B 1000 Pesos	Good	Fine	XF
18xx (ca.1866-75). Two women ("The Sisters") at left, woman with fruit at right. Series A. Back: Blue. Printer: ABNC.			
p1. Proof. 18xx (ca.1866). Black on green underprint. Text Type I.	—	Unc	4500.
p2. Proof. 18xx (ca.1868-75). Black on green and orange underprint. Text Type II.	—	Unc	4500.

S224 5 Pesos	Good	Fine	XF
1887-89. Black on green underprint. Portrait Pablo Benito Juárez at left, national arms at upper center. Bull's head at lower right. Back: Green. Building and landscape at center. Printer: BWC.			
a. Series F. 1.9.1887. *(BK-DF-9).*	4500.	12,500.	—
b. Overprint: *Puebla.* Series F. 1.2.1889. *(BK-DF-10).*	4500.	12,500.	—
c. Overprint: *Veracruz.* Series F. 1.9.1887. *(BK-DF-11).*	4500.	12,500.	—

S225 10 Pesos	Good	Fine	XF
1.5.1889. Portrait Pablo Benito Juárez at left, national arms at upper center. Horse at right. Series E. Overprint: *GUANAJUATO*. Printer: BWC. *(BK-DF-13).*	2500.	7500.	—

S226 10 Pesos	Good	Fine	XF
18xx. Portrait Pablo Benito Juárez at left, national arms at upper center. Woman with bunch of grapes at lower right. Series E. Printer: BWC. Proof. *(BK-DF-14).*	—	Unc	1250.

S227 20 Pesos	Good	Fine	XF
1887. Black on pale blue underprint. Portrait Pablo Benito Juárez at left, national arms at upper center. Dog's head at lower right. Back: Blue. Building and landscape at center. Printer: BWC.			
a. Series D. 1.9.1887. *(BK-DF-15).*	5000.	15,000.	—
b. Overprint: *Puebla.* Series D. 1.9.1887. *(BK-DF-16).*	5000.	15,000.	—

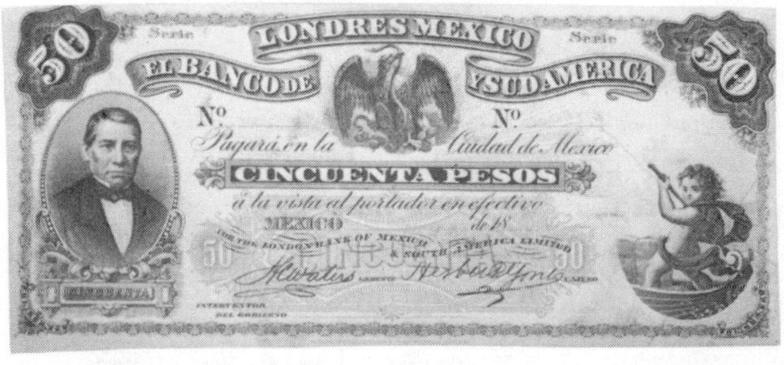

S228 50 Pesos	Good	Fine	XF
18xx. Portrait Pablo Benito Juárez at left, national arms at upper center. Young boy in boat at right. Series C. Printer: BWC. Proof. *(BK-DF-17).*	—	Unc	2000.

S229 100 Pesos	Good	Fine	XF
18xx. Portrait Pablo Benito Juárez at left, national arms at upper center. Three children at right. Series B. Printer: BWC. Proof. *(BK-DF-18).*	—	Unc	2000.

S230 500 Pesos	Good	Fine	XF
18xx. Portrait Pablo Benito Juárez at left, national arms at upper center. Mercury seated at right. Series A. Back: Dark green. Palace and landscape at center. Printer: BWC. *(BK-DF-19).*			
p1. Face proof.	—	Unc	2250.
p2. Back proof overprint: *SPECIMEN.*	—	Unc	2250.

Banco de Londres y México

1889-1914 Issue

S232 1 Peso	Good	Fine	XF
ND. Without pictorial design. Proof.	—	Unc	2500.

S233 5 Pesos	Good	Fine	XF
1889-1913. Black on green and yellow underprint. Portrait Pablo Benito Juárez at left, seated female with two children ("Peace") at right. Back: Green. National arms. Printer: ABNC.			
a. Center signature title: *Cajero*. Series A. 9.1.1891; 15.5.1893. *(BK-DF-25)*.	22.50	65.00	185.
b. Center signature title: *Consejero* Series B. 2.1.1894-2.7.1897. *(BK-DF-26)*.	7.50	20.00	60.00
c. Series C. 1.1.1902; D. 1.5.1906; E. 1.7.1909. *(BK-DF-27)*.	4.00	12.50	35.00
d. Series E. 1.7.1910; F. 2.1.1912; G. 2.1.1913; H. 1.10.1913; I. 1.10.1913. *(BK-DF-28)*.	4.00	12.50	35.00
e. Overprint: *AGUASCALIENTES*. 1.5.1906; 1.7.1910. *(BK-DF-31)*.	10.00	30.00	100.
f. Overprint: *DURANGO*. 1.1.1902; 1.5.1906; 1.7.1910. *(DK-DF-32)*.	15.00	45.00	125.
g. Overprint: *GUADALAJARA*. 1.5.1906; 2.1.1912; 2.1.1913. *(BK-DF-33)*.	10.00	30.00	100.
h. Overprint: *GUADALAJARA* and *COCULA*. 1.5.1906. *(BK-DF-34)*.	25.00	75.00	225.
i. Overprint: *GUANAJUATO*. 1.7.1897; 1.7.1909; 1.7.1910. *(BK-DF-35)*.	12.50	35.00	100.
j. Overprint: *LERDO*. 1.7.1897. *(BK-DF-36)*.	15.00	45.00	125.
k. Overprint: *MAZATLÁN*. 1.7.1897; 1.5.1906. *(BK-DF-37)*.	15.00	45.00	125.
l. Overprint: *MONTERREY*. 1.7.1897; 1.5.1906; 2.1.1912. *(BK-DF-38)*.	12.50	35.00	100.
m. Overprint: *MORELIA*. 1.7.1897; 1.7.1909; 1.7.1910. *(BK-DF-39)*.	10.00	30.00	100.
n. Overprint: *PUEBLA*. 1.7.1889 (printed date). (BK-DF-40).	45.00	125.	375.
o. Overprint: *PUEBLA*. 1.7.1897. *(BK-DF-41)*.	10.00	30.00	100.
p. Overprint: *QUERÉTARO*. 15.5.1893-2.1.1913. *(BK-DF-42)*.	10.00	30.00	100.
p. Overprint: *QUERÉTARO*. 15.5.1893-2.1.1913. *(BK-DF-42)*.	10.00	30.00	100.
q. Overprint: *SAN LUIS POTOSÍ*. 1.9.1894-2.1.1913. *(BK-DF-43)*.	10.00	30.00	100.
r. Overprint: *TORREÓN*. 1.1.1902-1.7.1910. *(BK-DF-44)*.	12.50	35.00	100.
s. Overprint: *VERACRUZ*. 16.6.189x-2.1.1913. *(BK-DF-45)*.	10.00	30.00	100.
s. Overprint: *VERACRUZ*. 16.6.189x-2.1.1913. *(BK-DF-45)*.	10.00	30.00	100.

S234 10 Pesos	Good	Fine	XF
1889-1913. Black on brown and yellow underprint. Portrait Pablo Benito Juárez at left, miners at center and at right. Back: Dark brown. National arms. Printer: ABNC.			
a. Center signature title: *Cajero*. Series A. 1.7.1889. (printed date). *(BK-DF-46)*.	45.00	125.	375.
b. Series A. 1.9.1891-22.2.1897. *(BK-DF-47)*.	15.00	45.00	125.
c. Center signature title: *Consejero*. Series B. 1.7.1897. *(BK-DF-48)*.	5.00	15.00	45.00
d. Series C. 1.1.1902; D. 1.5.1906; E. 1.7.1909; 1.7.1910; F. 2.1.1912. *(BK-DF-49)*.	4.00	12.50	35.00
e. Series G. 2.1.1913; H. 1.10.1913; I. 1.10.1913. *(BK-DF-50)*.	4.00	12.50	35.00
f. Overprint: *AGUASCALIENTES*. 1.1.1902; 1.5.1906; 1.7.1910. *(BK-DF-52)*.	10.00	30.00	100.
g. Overprint: *DURANGO*. 1.1.1902; 1.5.1906; 1.7.1910. *(BK-DF-53)*.	10.00	30.00	100.
h. Overprint: *GUADALAJARA*. 1.7.1889.	30.00	100.	300.
i. Overprint: *GUADALAJARA*. 1.1.1902; 2.1.1912; 2.1.1913. *(BK-DF-55)*.	12.50	35.00	100.
j. Overprint: *GUANAJUATO*. 1.7.1897-1.7.1910. *(BK-DF-56)*.	12.50	35.00	100.
k. Overprint: *LERDO*. 1.7.1897. *(BK-DF-57)*.	15.00	45.00	125.
l. Overprint: *MAZATLÁN*. 1.7.1897. *(BK-DF-58)*.	15.00	45.00	125.
m. Overprint: *MONTERREY*. 1.7.1897; 1.1.1902; 2.1.1912. *(BK-DF-59)*.	12.50	35.00	100.
n. Overprint: *MORELIA*. 1.7.1897; 1.7.1909; 1.7.1910. *(BK-DF-60)*.	10.00	30.00	100.
o. Overprint: *PUEBLA*. 1.7.1889. *(BK-DF-61)*.	45.00	125.	375.
p. Proof. Series A. 189x.	10.00	30.00	100.
p. Proof. Series A. 189x.	—	Unc	500.
q. Overprint: *QUERÉTARO*. 1.7.1897-1.7.1910. *(BK-DF-63)*.	10.00	30.00	100.
r. Overprint: *SAN LUIS POTOSÍ*. *1.9.1897; 1.9.1891; 1.1.1902; 2.1.1912; 2.1.1913. (BK-DF-64)*.	10.00	30.00	100.
s. Overprint: *TORREÓN*. 1.7.1897; 1.9.1891; 1.1.1902; 1.7.1909; 1.7.1910. *(BK-DF-65)*.	12.50	35.00	100.

	Good	Fine	XF
s. Overprint: *TORREÓN*. 1.7.1897; 1.9.1891; 1.1.1902; 1.7.1909; 1.7.1910. *(BK-DF-65)*.	—	Unc	750.
t. Overprint: *VERACRUZ*. 1.7.1889. *(BK-DF-66.)*	45.00	125.	375.
u. Overprint: *VERACRUZ*. 1.1.1902; 2.1.1912; 2.1.1913. *(BK-DF-67)*.	20.00	60.00	175.

S235 20 Pesos	Good	Fine	XF
1889-1913. Black on orange-brown and yellow underprint. Portrait Pablo Benito Juárez left, Friar Bartolome de las Casas at center. Back: Brown. National arms. Printer: ABNC.			
a. Center signature title: *Cajero*. Series A. 1.7.1889 (printed date); 1.9.1891; 2.1.1894. *(BK-DF-68)*.	25.00	75.00	225.
b. Series A. 1.9.1891-22.2.1897. *(BK-DF-69)*.	15.00	45.00	125.
c. Center signature title: *Consejero*. Series B. 1.7.1897; C. 1.1.1902. *(BK-DF-70)*.	7.50	20.00	60.00
d. Series D. 1.7.1910; E. 2.1.1913; F. 2.1.1913; G. 1.10.1913; H. 1.10.1913. *(BK-DF-71)*.	7.50	20.00	60.00
e. Overprint: *AGUASCALIENTES*. 1.1.1902. *(BK-DF-73)*.	30.00	100.	300.
f. Overprint: *COCULA*. 1.1.1902. *(BK-DF-74)*.	30.00	100.	300.
g. Overprint: *DURANGO*. 1.1.1902; 1.7.1910. *(BK-DF-75)*.	30.00	100.	300.
h. Overprint: *GUADALAJARA*. 1.7..1897; 2.1.1912; 2.1.1913. *(BK-DF-76)*.	25.00	75.00	225.
i. Overprint: *GUANAJUATO*. 1.7.1889; 1.7.1897; 1.7.1910. *(BK-DF-77)*.	30.00	100.	300.
j. Overprint: *LERDO*. 1.7.1897. *(BK-DF-78)*.	30.00	100.	300.
k. Overprint: *MAZATLAN*. 1.7.1897. *(BK-DF-79)*.	30.00	100.	300.
l. Overprint: *MONTERREY*. 1.7.1897; 2.1.1912. *(BK-DF-80)*.	30.00	100.	300.
m. Overprint: *MORELIA*. 1.7.1897; 1.7.1910. *(BK-DF-81)*.	30.00	100.	300.
n. Overprint: *PUEBLA*. 1.7.1897; 1.7.1889. *(BK-DF-82)*.	25.00	75.00	225.
o. Overprint: *QUERÉTARO*. 1.7.1897; 1.7.1910. *(BK-DF-83)*.	30.00	100.	300.
p. Overprint: *SAN LUIS POTOSÍ*. 1.7.1897; 1.9.1891; x.1.1893 - handwritten date; 1.7.1910; 2.1.1912. *(BK-DF-84)*.	25.00	75.00	225.
p. Proof. Series A. 189x.	—	Unc	500.
q. Overprint: *TORREÓN*. 1.1.1902; 1.7.1910. *(BK-DF-85)*.	30.00	100.	300.
r. Overprint: *VERACRUZ*. 9.1.1891. *(BK-DF-86)*.	30.00	100.	300.
s. Specimen. Series A. 1.7.1889.	—	Unc	750.

S236 50 Pesos	Good	Fine	XF
1889-1913. Black on blue and yellow underprint. Portrait Pablo Benito Juárez at left, cowboy with longhorns at right. Back: Blue. National arms. Printer: ABNC.			
a. Center signature title: *Cajero*. Series A. 1.7.1889 (printed date). *(BK-DF-87)*.	125.	375.	1100.
b. Series A. 1.9.1891-22.2.1897. *(BK-DF-88)*.	45.00	125.	375.
c. Center signature title: *Consejero*. Series B. 1.7.1897. *(BK-DF-89)*.	45.00	125.	375.
d. Series C. 1.1.1902. *(BK-DF-90)*.	45.00	125.	375.
e. Series D. 1.7.1910; E. 2.1.1912. *(BK-DF-91)*.	45.00	125.	375.
f. Series F. 2.1.1913; G. 1.10.1913.	30.00	100.	300.
g. Series H. 1.10.1913. *(BK-DF-93)*.	30.00	100.	300.
h. Overprint: *AGUASCALIENTES*. 1.1.1902. *(BK-DF-95)*.	60.00	175.	525.
i. Overprint: *DURANGO*. 1.1.1902. *(BK-DF-96)*.	45.00	125.	375.
j. Overprint: *GUADALAJARA*. 1.9.1891; 1.7.1897; 2.1.1912. *(BK-DF-97)*.	60.00	175.	525.
k. Overprint: *GUANAJUATO*. 1.7.1889; 1.7.1897. *(BK-DF-98)*.	60.00	175.	525.
l. Overprint: *LERDO*. 1.7.1897. *(BK-DF-99)*.	75.00	225.	675.
m. Overprint: *MONTERREY*. 1.7.1897. *(BK-DF-100)*.	60.00	175.	525.
n. Overprint: *MORELIA*. 1.7.1897. *(BK-DF-101)*.	60.00	225.	675.
o. Overprint: *PUEBLA*. 1.7.1889; 1.7.1897; 2.7.1897. *(BK-DF-102)*.	45.00	125.	375.

	Good	Fine	XF
p. Proof. Series A. 189x.	60.00	225.	525.
p. Proof. Series A. 189x.	—	Unc	500.
q. Overprint: *SAN LUIS POTOSÍ.* 9.1.1891-2.1.1912. *(BK-DF-104).*	45.00	125.	375.
r. Overprint: *TORREÓN.* 1.1.1902; 1.7.1910. *(BK-DF-105).*	60.00	225.	525.
s. Overprint: *MAZATLAN.* 3.8.1897.	60.00	175.	525.
s. Overprint: *MAZATLAN.* 3.8.1897.	—	Unc	750.

S237 100 Pesos

1889-1913. Black on orange and yellow underprint. Cattle at left, portrait Pablo Benito Juárez at center, men with horses at right. Back: Orange and black. National arms. Printer: ABNC.

	Good	Fine	XF
a. Center signature title: *Cajero.* Series A. 1.7.1889 (printed date). *(BK-DF-106).*	125.	375.	1100.
b. Series A. 1.9.1891; 19.9.1891; 1.8.1896. *(BK-DF-107).*	60.00	175.	525.
c. Center signature title: *Consejero.* Series B. 1.7.1897. *(BK-DF-108).*	45.00	125.	375.
d. Series C. 1.1.1902; D. 1.7.1910; E. 2.1.1912. *(BK-DF-109).*	45.00	125.	375.
e. Series F. 2.1.1913; G. 1.10.1913; H. 1.10.1913. *(BK-DF-110).*	45.00	125.	375.
f. Overprint: *AGUASCALIENTES.* 1.1.1902. *(BK-DF-112).*	125.	375.	1100.
g. Overprint: *DURANGO.* 1.1.1902.	75.00	225.	675.
h. Overprint: *GUANAJUATO.* 1.7.1897. *(BK-DF-114).*	125.	375.	1100.
i. Overprint and needle punched: *MAZATLAN.* 1.7.1897. *(BK-DF-115).*	125.	375.	1100.
j. Overprint: *MONTERREY.* 1.7.1897.	75.00	225.	675.
k. Overprint: *QUERÉTARO.* 1.7.1897.	75.00	225.	675.
l. Overprint: *SAN LUIS POTOSÍ.* 1.7.1897; 1.7.1910. *(BK-DF-118).*	75.00	225.	675.
m. Overprint: *TORREON.* Series C. 1.1.1902.	75.00	225.	675.
p. Proof. Series A. 189x.	—	Unc	500.
s. Specimen. Series A. 1.7.1889.	—	Unc	750.

S238 500 Pesos

1889-1913. Black on yellow and olive underprint. Pride of lions ("Lion at Home") at center, portrait Pablo Benito Juárez at right. Back: Olive-green. Men walking horses ("Horse Breaking") at center. Printer: ABNC.

	Good	Fine	XF
a. Center signature title: *Consejero.* Series B. 1.7.1897; C. 10.1.1903; E. 1.7.1909; 1.10.1910; F. 1.5.1911; G. 1.10.1913; H. 19.10.1913. *(BK-DF-119).*	750.	2250.	6750.
b. Overprint: *DURANGO.* 10.1.1903. *(BK-DF-121).*	750.	2250.	6750.
p. Proof. Center signature title: *Cajero.* Series A. 189x.	—	Unc	750.
s. Specimen. Series A. 1.7.1889.	—	Unc	1000.

S239 1000 Pesos

1889-1913. Black on orange and yellow underprint. Seated female ("Arts") at left center, portrait B. Juárez at right. Back: Black and orange. Train at center. Printer: ABNC.

	Good	Fine	XF
a. Center signature title: *Consejero.* Series B. 1.7.1897; E. 1.7.1909; F. 1.5.1911; G. 1.10.1913. *(BK-DF-122).*	1000.	3000.	9000.
p. Proof. Center signature title: *Cajero.* Series A. 189x.	—	Unc	1500.
s. Specimen. Series A. 1.7.1889.	—	Unc	1750.

S240 1 Peso

	Good	Fine	XF
14.2.1914. Black on orange underprint. Seated Justice and Peace at right. Back: Brown. Printer: B&S. *(BK-DF-20).*	5.00	15.00	45.00

S241 2 Pesos

	Good	Fine	XF
14.2.1914. Black on orange underprint. Seated Faith and Happiness at left. Back: Green. Printer: B&S. *(BK-DF-22).*	5.00	15.00	45.00

NOTE: For #S233-S239, reports of specific dates from 1889-1913 are requested.

Banco Mercantil Méxicano

1882 Text Varieties Issue

Type I: Payable at *CIUDAD DE MÉXICO.*

Type II: Payable at various branches w/*Ciudad de. . .* engraved.

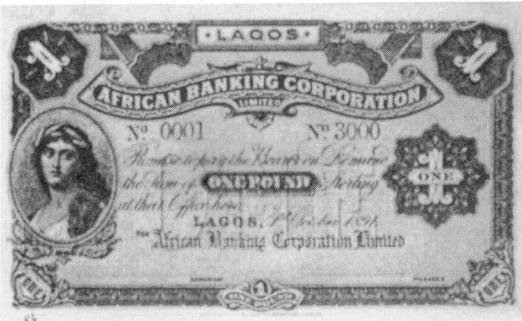

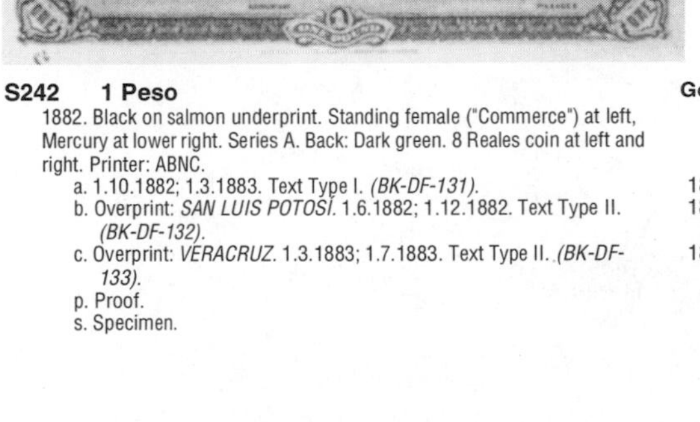

S242 1 Peso

1882. Black on salmon underprint. Standing female ("Commerce") at left, Mercury at lower right. Series A. Back: Dark green. 8 Reales coin at left and right. Printer: ABNC.

	Good	Fine	XF
a. 1.10.1882; 1.3.1883. Text Type I. *(BK-DF-131).*	1800.	5400.	—
b. Overprint: *SAN LUIS POTOSÍ.* 1.6.1882; 1.12.1882. Text Type II. *(BK-DF-132).*	1800.	5400.	—
c. Overprint: *VERACRUZ.* 1.3.1883; 1.7.1883. Text Type II. *(BK-DF-133).*	1800.	5400.	—
p. Proof.	—	Unc	1500.
s. Specimen.	—	Unc	1750.

S243 5 Pesos	Good	Fine	XF
1882. Black on orange underprint. Sailing ships at left, Raphael's Angel at center, woman with spool ("Industry") at right. Series A. Back: Dark green. Monument to Christopher Columbus. Printer: ABNC. *(BK-DF-134).*			
a. Overprint: *QUERÉTARO.* 1.6.1882. Text Type II.	3750.	7500.	—
p. Proof.	—	Unc	1750.
s. Specimen.	—	Unc	2000.

S244 10 Pesos	Good	Fine	XF
1882. Black on green underprint. Anchor at left, allegorical woman with sheaf and tools at right. Series A. Back: Red. Monument to Christopher Columbus. Printer: ABNC. *(BK-DF-136).*			
a. 1.6.1882. Text Type I.	3750.	—	—
p. Proof.	—	Unc	2000.
s. Specimen.	—	Unc	2250.

S245 20 Pesos	Good	Fine	XF
1882. Black on blue underprint. Portrait shepherdess with sheep at left, allegorical woman with marine implements at lower right. Series A. Back: Brown. Monument to Christopher Columbus. Printer: ABNC. *(BK-DF-137).*			
a. Overprint: *GUANAJUATO.* 1.6.1882. Text Type II.	3750.	—	—
p. Proof.	—	Unc	2000.
s. Specimen.	—	Unc	2250.

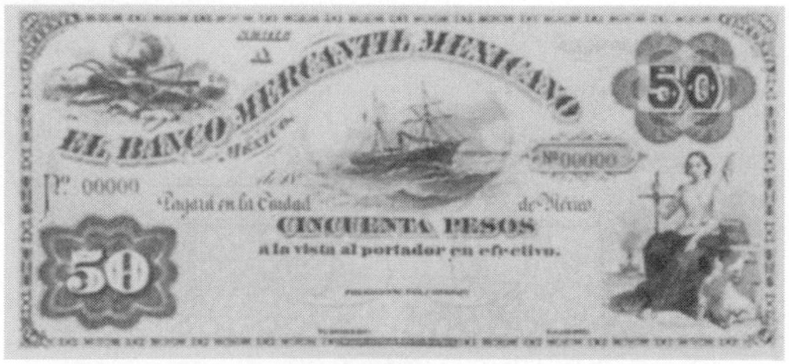

S246 50 Pesos	Good	Fine	XF
18xx. Black on orange underprint. Farm implements at upper left, sailing ship at center, seated Justice with sword and flag at right. Series A. Back: Blue. Monument to Christopher Columbus. Printer: ABNC.			
p. Proof. Series A.	—	Unc	2500.
s. Specimen.	—	Unc	2750.

S247 100 Pesos	Good	Fine	XF
18xx. Black on brown underprint. Reclining allegorical woman ("L'Orient") at left center, woman writing ("Trade") at right. Series A. Back: Green. Monument to Christopher Columbus. Printer: ABNC.			
p. Proof. Series A.	—	Unc	2500.
s. Specimen.	—	Unc	2750.

S247A 500 Pesos	Good	Fine	XF
18xx. Black on olive underprint. Indian woman holding plant ("La Hua de los Incas") at left, allegorical woman leaning on crate ("Manufacturers") at right. Series A. Back: Red-brown. Monument to Christopher Columbus. Printer: ABNC.			
p. Proof.	—	Unc	3000.
s. Specimen.	—	Unc	3500.

S248 1000 Pesos	Good	Fine	XF
18xx. Black on brown underprint. Steam train at left, woman holding pitcher ("Virgin del sol") at center, ships at right. Series A. Back: Orange. Monument to Christopher Columbus. Printer: ABNC. *(BK-DF-138).*			
p. Proof.	—	Unc	3000.
s. Specimen.	—	Unc	3500.

Banco Nacional Méxicano

1882 Issue

S249 1 Peso	Good	Fine	XF
1882. Black on green underprint. National arms at center. Back: Blue. Reverse design of 8 reales coin. Printer: ABNC.			
a. 1.7.1882; 10.7.1882; 31.10.1882. *(BK-DF-124).*	2750.	8250.	—
b. Overprint and pin hole punched: *SAN LUIS POTOSÍ.* 10.7.1882.	2750.	8250.	—
c. Overprint and pin hole punched: *VERA CRUZ.* 31.10.1882. *(BK-DF-125).*	2750.	8250.	—
p. Proof.	—	Unc	3000.
s. Specimen.	—	Unc	3500.

S250 2 Pesos

1882. Black on light green underprint. National arms at center. Back: Red-brown. Reverse design of 8 reales coin. Printer: ABNC.

	Good	Fine	XF
a. 1882. *(BK-DF-126).*	3000.	9000.	—
b. Overprint and pin hole punched: *VERA CRUZ*. 1882. *(BK-DF-126).*	3000.	9000.	—
p. Proof.	—	Unc	2500.
s. Specimen.	—	Unc	3000.

S251 5 Pesos

18xx. Black on light green underprint. National arms at center. Back: Orange. Reverse design of 8 reales coin. Printer: ABNC.

	Good	Fine	XF
p. Proof.	—	Unc	2000.
s. Specimen.	—	Unc	2250.

S252 10 Pesos

10.2.1882. Black on light brown underprint. National arms at left. Back: Green. Printer: ABNC. *(BK-DF-128).*

	Good	Fine	XF
a. Issued note.	4250.	8500.	—
p. Proof.	—	Unc	2000.
s. Specimen.	—	Unc	2250.

S252A 20 Pesos

18xx. Black on light brown underprint. National arms at left. Back: Dark brown. Printer: ABNC.

	Good	Fine	XF
p. Proof.	—	Unc	2000.
s. Specimen.	—	Unc	2250.

S252B 50 Pesos

18xx. Black on light brown underprint. National arms at left. Back: Orange. Printer: ABNC.

	Good	Fine	XF
p. Proof.	—	Unc	2000.
s. Specimen.	—	Unc	2250.

S253 100 Pesos

23.2.1882. Black on gray underprint. National arms at left. Back: Brown. Reverse design of 8 reales coin. Printer: ABNC.

	Good	Fine	XF
a. Issued note.	5250.	11,000.	—
p. Proof.	—	Unc	2000.
s. Specimen.	—	Unc	2250.

S253A 500 Peso

18xx. Black on gray underprint. National arms at left. Back: Red. Reverse design of 8 reales coin. Printer: ABNC.

	Good	Fine	XF
p. Proof.	—	Unc	2000.
s. Specimen.	—	Unc	2250.

S253B 1000 Pesos

18xx. Black on olive-brown underprint. National arms at left. Back: Blue. Reverse design of 8 reales coin. Printer: ABNC.

	Good	Fine	XF
p. Proof.	—	Unc	2000.
s. Specimen.	—	Unc	2250.

Banco Nacional de México

1885-1913 Issue

#S254-S263 Many city overprint are usually encountered with the same city name pin-hole punched also.

S254 50 Centavos

ND (ca.1914). Black on green underprint. Christopher Columbus in sight of land ("First Land") at left. Back: Brown. 50 centavos coin at left and center right. Printer: ABNC. (Not issued). *(BK-DF-139).*

	Good	Fine	XF
p. Proof.	—	Unc	2000.
s. Specimen.	—	Unc	2250.

S255 1 Peso

1885-1913. Black on green and yellow underprint. Portrait M. García Teruel at left, steam locomotive ("Anthracite Burner") at center. Back: Green. 8 reales coin at left and center right. Printer: ABNC.

	Good	Fine	XF
a. 1.1.1885. *(BK-DF-141).*	100.	300.	900.
b. 6.12.1913. *(BK-DF-142).*	4.00	12.50	35.00
c. Overprint: *CHIHUAHUA*. 1.1.1885; 1.1.1888; 1.1.1889; 1.5.1889. *(BK-DF-144).*	45.00	125.	375.
d. Overprint: *CHIHUAHUA*. Overprint on back: *Pagadero en Mexicoo y en todas las Sucursales sin descuento*. 1.5.1889. *(BK-DF-145).*	20.00	60.00	175.
e. Overprint: *DURANGO*. 1.12.1890. *(BK-DF-146)*	100.	300.	900.
f. Overprint: *GUADALAJARA*. 1.1.1885. *(BK-DF-147).*	60.00	175.	525.
g. Overprint: *MONTERREY*. 1.12.1889; 1.8.1890. *(BK-DF-148).*	100.	300.	900.
h. Overprint: *OAXACA*. 1.1.1888; 1.8.1890. *(BK-DF-149).*	100.	300.	900.
i. Overprint: *SAN LUIS POTOSÍ*. 1.1.1885. *(BK-DF-150).*	50.00	150.	450.
j. Overprint: *VERACRUZ*. 1.1.1885; 1.1.1887. *(BK-DF-151).*	30.00	100.	300.
k. Overprint: *PAGADERO EN PUEBLA*, perforated: *PUEBLA*. 1.1.1885.	200.	600.	1800.
p1. Proof. 188x.	—	Unc	1500.
p2. Proof. ND.	—	Unc	1750.
s1. Specimen. 188x.	—	Unc	1500.
s2. Specimen. ND.	—	Unc	1750.

S256 2 Pesos

1885-1913. Black on yellow and orange underprint. Portrait M. García Teruel at left, prospectors at right. Back: Orange. National arms at center. Printer: ABNC.

	Good	Fine	XF
a. 6.12.1913. *(BK-DF-152).*	5.00	15.00	45.00
b. Overprint: *CHIHUAHUA*. 1.1.1885. *(BK-DF-154).*	60.00	175.	525.
c. Overprint: *CHIHUAHUA* and needle punched: *E. CHIHUAHUA*. 1.1.1885. *(BK-DF-155).*	75.00	225.	675.
d. Overprint: *GUADALAJARA*. 1.1.1885. *(BK-DF-156).*	125.	375.	1125.
e. Overprint: *GUANAJUATO*. 1.1.1885. *(BK-DF-157).*	125.	375.	1125.
f. Overprint: *SAN LUIS POTOSÍ*. 1.1.1885. *(BK-DF-158).*	125.	375.	1125.
g. Overprint: *VERACRUZ*. 1.1.1885. *(BK-DF-159).*	75.00	225.	675.
p1. Proof. 188x.	—	Unc	1500.
p2. Proof. ND.	—	Unc	1500.
s1. Specimen. 188x.	—	Unc	2000.
s2. Specimen. ND.	—	Unc	2000.

S257 5 Pesos

1885-1913. Black on yellow and brown underprint. Seated female ("Literature") at left, portrait M. García Teruel at right. Back: Brown. Christopher Columbus discovering America at center. Printer: ABNC.

	Good	Fine	XF
a. 1.1.1885; 1.1.1888; 1.10.1889; 1.12.1890. *(BK-DF-160).*	30.00	100.	300.
b. 1.8.1895; 8.8.1896; 26.7.1897. *(BK-DF-161).*	10.00	30.00	100.
c. 1.7.1901-6.12.1913. *(BK-DF-162).*	4.00	12.50	35.00
d. Overprint: *ACAPULCO.* 1.10.1906. *(BK-DF-166).*	25.00	75.00	225.
e. Overprint: *AGUASCALIENTES.* 1.12.1902. *(BK-DF-167).*	15.00	45.00	125.
f. Overprint: *AUTLÁN, JAL.* 1.8.1905. *(BK-DF-168).*	15.00	45.00	125.
g. Overprint: *BRAVOS, Chilpancingo.* 1.12.1902. *(BK-DF-169).*	15.00	45.00	125.
h. Overprint: *CAMPECHE.* 1.10.1906. *(BK-DF-170).*	12.50	35.00	100.
i. Overprint: *CHIHUAHUA.* 1.4.1902. *(BK-DF-172).*	25.00	75.00	225.
j. Overprint: *C. GUZMÁN, JAL.* 1.8.1905. *(BK-DF-171).*	15.00	45.00	125.
k. Overprint: *C. JUÁREZ.* 1.8.1905. *(BK-DF-174).*	15.00	45.00	125.
l. Overprint: *CIUDAD VICTORIA.* 1.8.1905. *(BK-DF-173).*	12.50	35.00	100.
m. Overprint: *COLIMA.* 1.42.1902; 1.12.1902. *(BK-DF-175).*	20.00	60.00	175.
n. Overprint: *CÓRDOBA.* 1.3.1910. *(BK-DF-176).*	10.00	30.00	100.
o. Overprint: *CUERNAVACA.* 1.8.1905. *(BK-DF-17).*	20.00	60.00	175.
p. Overprint: *DURANGO.* 1.4.1902. *(BK-DF-178).*	20.00	60.00	175.
p1. Proof. 188x.	—	Unc	1500.
p2. Proof. ND.	—	Unc	1750.
q. Overprint: *GUADALAJARA.* 1.4.1902. *(BK-DF-179).*	25.00	75.00	225.
r. Overprint: *GUAYMAS.* 1.12.1902. *(BK-DF-180).*	15.00	45.00	125.
r. Overprint: *GUAYMAS.* 1.12.1902. *(BK-DF-180).*	15.00	45.00	125.
s. Overprint: *HERMOSILLO, SON.* 1.10.1906. *(BK-DF-181).*	20.00	60.00	175.
s1. Specimen. 188x; 189x.	—	Unc	1500.
s2. Specimen. ND.	—	Unc	1750.
t. Overprint: *IRAPUATO.* 1.10.1906. *(BK-DF-182).*	15.00	45.00	125.
u. Overprint: *LAGOS.* 1.7.1905; 1.8.1905. *(BK-DF-183).*	15.00	45.00	125.
v. Overprint: *LA PIEDAD.* 1.8.1905. *(BK-DF-184).*	25.00	75.00	225.
w. Overprint: *LERMA/PACHUCA.* ND. *(BK-DF-185).*	25.00	75.00	225.
x. Overprint: *MATEHUALA.* 1.4.1902. *(BK-DF-186).*	20.00	60.00	175.
y. Overprint: *MAZATLÁN.* 1.4.1902. *(BK-DF-187).*	20.00	60.00	175.
z. Overprint: *MÉRIDA.* 1.4.1902. *(BK-DF-188).*	20.00	60.00	175.
aa. Overprint: *MONCLOVA.* 1.8.1905.*(BK-DF-189).*	20.00	60.00	175.
ab. Overprint: *MONTERREY.* and needle punched: 1.12.1890. *(BK-DF-190).*	20.00	60.00	175.
ac. Overprint: *MONTERREY.* 1.4.1902. *(BK-DF-191).*	20.00	60.00	175.
ad. Overprint: *MORELIA.* 1.12.1902. *(BK-DF-192).*	25.00	75.00	225.
ae. Overprint: *PACHUCA..* 1.8.1905. *(BK-DF-1193).*	10.00	30.00	100.
af. Overprint: *PUEBLA.* 1.4.1902. *(BK-DF-194).*	25.00	75.00	225.
ag. Overprint: *PURUANDIRO.* 1.8.1905. *(BK-DF-195).*	15.00	45.00	125.
ah. Overprint: *QUERÉTARO.* 1.7.1905; 1.8.1905; 1.10.1906. *(BK-DF-196).*	15.00	45.00	125.
ai. Overprint: *RIOVERDE.* 1.8.1905. *(BK-DF-197).*	20.00	60.00	175.
aj. Overprint: *S. ANDRÉS TUSTLA.* 1.8.1905. *(BK-DF-198).*	20.00	60.00	175.
ak. Overprint: *SAN LUIS POTOSÍ.* 1.4.1902. *(BK-DF-199).*	15.00	45.00	125.
al. Overprint: *SOMBRERETE.* 1.3.1910. *(BK-DF-200).*	20.00	60.00	175.
am. Overprint: *TANTOYUCA.* 1.12.1902; 1.8.1905. *(BK-DF-201).*	20.00	60.00	175.
an. Overprint: *TAPACHULA.* 1.1.1908. *(BK-DF-202).*	15.00	45.00	125.
ao. Overprint: *TEHUACÁN.* 1.9.1909. *(BK-DF-203).*	25.00	75.00	225.
ap. Overprint: *TEPIC.* 1.8.1905. *(BK-DF-204).*	25.00	75.00	225.
aq. Overprint: *TEZIUTLÁN.* 1.12.1902; 1.7.1901. *(BK-DF-205).*	25.00	75.00	225.
ar. Overprint: *TLALTENANGO.* 1.10.1906. *(BK-DF-206).*	20.00	60.00	175.
as. Overprint: *TOLUCA.* 1.12.1902. *(BK-DF-207).*	12.50	35.00	100.
at. Overprint: *TORREON.* 1.12.1902. *(BK-DF-208).*	25.00	75.00	225.
au. Overprint: *TULANCINGO.* 1.10.1906. *(BK-DF-209).*	25.00	75.00	225.
av. Overprint: *TUXLA GUTIÉRREZ.* 1.8.1905. *(BK-DF-210).*	15.00	45.00	125.
aw. Overprint: *URUAPÁN MICH.* 1.8.1905. *(BK-DF-211).*	25.00	75.00	225.
ax. Overprint: *VERACRUZ.* 1.4.1902. *(BK-DF-212).*	20.00	60.00	175.
ay. Overprint: *XALAPA.* 1.8.1905. *(BK-DF-213).*	20.00	60.00	175.
az. Overprint: *PAGADERO EN ZACATECAS.* 1.12.1890; 1.4.1902. *(BK-DF-214).*	15.00	45.00	125.
ba. Overprint: *PAGADERO IN TAMPICO.* 1.4.1902.	25.00	75.00	225.

S258 10 Pesos

1885-1913. Black on yellow and blue underprint. Portrait M. García Teruel at left. Seated female ("Tropics No. 2") at center right. Back: Blue. National Bank of Mexico at center. Printer: ABNC.

	Good	Fine	XF
a. 1.1.1885. *(BK-DF-215).*	50.00	150.	450.
b. 1.12.1886; 1.1.1887; 1.1.1888. *(BK-DF-216).*	25.00	75.00	225.
c. 1.10.1889-26.7.1897. *BK-DF-217).*	7.50	20.00	60.00
d. 1.7.1901-1.1.1908. *(BK-DF-218).*	4.00	12.50	35.00
e. 1.9.1909-6.12.1913. *(BK-DF-219).*	4.00	12.50	35.00
f. Overprint: *ACAPULCO.* 1.10.1906. *(BK-DF-222).*	25.00	75.00	225.
g. Overprint: *AGUASCALIENTES.* 1.12.1902. *(BK-DF-223).*	30.00	100.	300.
h. Overprint: *AUTLÁN, JAL.* 1.8.1905. *(BK-DF-224).*	25.00	75.00	225.
i. Overprint: *BRAVOS CHILPANCINGO.* 1.12.1902. *(BK-DF-225).*	15.00	45.00	125.
j. Overprint: *CAMPECHE.* 1.10.1906. *(BK-DF-226).*	10.00	30.00	100.
k. Overprint: *CHIHUAHUA.* 1.4.1902. *(BK-DF-228).*	25.00	75.00	225.
l. Overprint: *C. GUZMÁN, JAL.* 1.8.1905. *(BK-DF-227).*	15.00	45.00	125.
m. Overprint: *C. JUÁREZ.* 1.8.1905. *(BK-DF-230).*	15.00	45.00	125.
n. Overprint: *CIUDAD VICTORIA.* 1.8.1905. *(BK-DF-229).*	25.00	75.00	225.
o. Overprint: *COLIMA.* 1.12.1902. *(BK-DF-231).*	15.00	45.00	125.
p. Overprint: *CÓRDOBA.* 1.3.1911. *(BK-DF-232).*	10.00	30.00	100.
p1. Proof. 188x.	—	Unc	750.
p2. Proof. ND.	—	Unc	750.
q. Overprint: *CUERNAVACA.* 1.8.1905. *(BK-DF-233).*	15.00	45.00	125.
r. Overprint: *DURANGO.* 1.4.1902. *(BK-DF-234).*	30.00	100.	300.
s. Overprint: *GUADALAJARA.* 1.5.1889. *(BK-DF-235).*	45.00	125.	375.
s1. Specimen. 188x.	—	Unc	750.
s2. Specimen. ND.	—	Unc	750.
t. Overprint: *GUANAJUATO.* 1.5.1889. *(BK-DF-236).*	45.00	125.	375.
u. Overprint: *GUAYMAS.* 1.12.1902. *(BK-DF-237).*	25.00	75.00	225.
v. Overprint: *HERMOSILLO, SON.* 1.10.1906; 1.4.1902. *(BK-DF-238).*	25.00	75.00	225.
w. Overprint: *HUAUCHINANGO, PUE.* 1.3.1911. *(BK-DF-239).*	45.00	125.	375.
x. Overprint: *RAPUATO.* 1.10.1906. *(BK-DF-240).*	45.00	125.	375.
y. Overprint: *LAGOS.* 1.12.1902. *(BK-DF-241).*	15.00	45.00	125.
z. Overprint: *LA PIEDAD.* 1.8.1905. *(BK-DF-242).*	15.00	45.00	125.
aa. Overprint: *MATEHUALA* (Agencia en). 26.7.1897. *(BK-DF-243).*	50.00	150.	450.
ab. Overprint: *MAZATLÁN.* 1.5.1889. *(BK-DF-244).*	45.00	125.	375.
ac. Overprint: *MÉRIDA.* 4.6.1889. *(BK-DF-245).*	45.00	125.	375.
ad. Overprint: *MONCLOVA, COAH.* 1.8.1905; 1.7.1901. *(BK-DF-246).*	45.00	125.	375.
ae. Overprint: *MONTERREY.* 1.4.1902. *(BK-DF-247).*	45.00	125.	375.
af. Overprint and needle punched: *MONTERREY.* 1.12.1890. *(BK-DF-248).*	45.00	125.	375.
ag. Overprint: *OAXACA.* 1.10.1889; 1.8.1890; 1.4.1902. *(BK-DF-249).*	45.00	125.	375.
ah. Overprint: *PACHUCA.* 1.12.1902. *(BK-DF-250).*	10.00	30.00	100.
ai. Overprint: *PUEBLA.* 1.4.1902. *(BK-DF-251).*	25.00	75.00	225.
aj. Overprint: *QUERÉTARO.* 1.8.1905; 1.1.1902. *(BK-DF-252).*	15.00	45.00	125.
ak. Overprint: *RIO VERDE.* 1.8.1905. *(BK-DF-253).*	25.00	75.00	225.
al. Overprint: *S. ANDRÉS TUXTLA.* 1.8.1905. *(BK-DF-254).*	10.00	15.00	45.00
am. Overprint: *SOMBRERETE.* 1.3.1910. *(BK-DF-255).*	25.00	75.00	225.
an. Overprint: *TABASCO.* 1.4.1902. *(BK-DF-256).*	25.00	75.00	225.
ao. Overprint: *TAMPICO.* 1.4.1902. *(BK-DF-257).*	25.00	75.00	225.
ap. Overprint: *TANTOYUCA.* 1.10.1906. *(BK-DF-258).*	25.00	75.00	225.
aq. Overprint: *TEHUACÁN.* 1.3.1910. *(BK-DF-259).*	25.00	75.00	225.
ar. Overprint: *TEPIC.* 1.8.1905. *(BK-DF-260).*	25.00	75.00	225.
as. Overprint: *TEZIUTLÁN.* 26.7.1897; 1.7.1901. *(BK-DF-261).*	25.00	75.00	225.
at. Overprint: *TLALTENANGO.* 1.10.1906. *(BK-DF-262).*	25.00	75.00	225.
au. Overprint: *TOLUCA.* 1.12.1902. *(BK-DF-263).*	15.00	45.00	125.
av. Overprint: *TORREON.* 1.12.1902. *(BK-DF-264).*	15.00	45.00	125.
aw. Overprint: *TULANCINGO.* 1.10.1906. *(BK-DF-265).*	25.00	75.00	225.
ax. ND. Remainder with overprint: *BILLETE SIN VALOR.* 1.8.1905. *(BK-DF-220).*	—	Unc	25.00

S259 20 Pesos

1885-1913. Black on green and ochre underprint. Portrait M. García Teruel at left, cowboys rounding up cattle at right. Back: Green. Monument at center. Printer: ABNC.

	Good	Fine	XF
a. 1.1.1887. *(BK-DF-271).*	30.00	100.	300.
b. 1.12.1890; 26.7.1897. *(BK-DF-272).*	20.00	60.00	175.
c. 1.7.1901-1.1.1908. *(BK-DF-273).*	7.50	20.00	60.00
d. 1.9.1909-15.9.1913. *(BK-DF-274).*	5.00	15.00	45.00
e. Overprint: *ACAPULCO.* 1.10.1906. *(BK-DF-277).*	45.00	125.	375.
f. Overprint: *AUTLÁN, JAL.* 1.8.1905. *(BK-DF-278).*	25.00	75.00	225.
g. Overprint: *CHIHUAHUA.* 1.4.1902. *(BK-DF-280).*	45.00	125.	375.
h. Overprint: *C. GUZMÁN JAL.* 1.8.1905. *(BK-DF-279).*	45.00	125.	375.
i. Overprint: *CIUDAD VICTORIA.* 1.8.1905. *(BK-DF-281).*	45.00	125.	375.
j. Overprint: *COLIMA.* 1.4.1902; 1.12.1902. *(BK-DF-282).*	45.00	125.	375.
k. Overprint: *CÓRDOBA.* 1.3.1911. *(BK-DF-283).*	25.00	75.00	225.
l. Overprint: *CUERNAVACA.* 1.8.1905. *(BK-DF-284).*	45.00	125.	375.
m. Overprint: *DURANGO.* 15.10.1890/188x. *(BK-DF-285).*	50.00	150.	450.
n. Overprint: *GUANAJUATO.* 1.5.1889. *(BK-DF-286).*	45.00	125.	375.
o. Overprint: *GUAYMAS.* 1.12.1902. *(BK-DF-287).*	45.00	125.	375.
p. Overprint: *HERMOSILLO SON.* 1.10.1906. *(BK-DF-288).*	45.00	125.	375.
p1. Proof. 188x.	—	Unc	750.
p2. Proof. ND.	—	Unc	750.
q. Overprint: *IRAPUATO.* 1.10.1906.	45.00	125.	375.
r. ND. Remainder with overprint: *BILLETE SIN VALOR.* *(BK-DF-275).*	45.00	125.	375.
r. ND. Remainder with overprint: *BILLETE SIN VALOR.* *(BK-DF-275).*	—	Unc	500.
s. Overprint: *MAZATLÁN.* 1.5.1889. *(BK-DF-291).*	45.00	125.	375.
s1. Specimen. 188x.	—	Unc	1000.
s2. Specimen. ND.	—	Unc	1000.
t. Overprint and needle punched: *MÉRIDA.* 4.6.1889. *(BK-DF-292).*	45.00	125.	375.
u. Overprint: *MÉRIDA.* 1.4.1902. *(BK-DF-293).*	25.00	75.00	225.
v. Overprint: *MONCLOVA, COAH.* 1.8.1905. *(BK-DF-294).*	45.00	125.	375.
w. Overprint: *MONTERREY.* 1.4.1902. *(BK-DF-295).*	45.00	125.	375.

	Good	Fine	XF
x. Overprint: *NUEVO LAREDO.* 26.7.1897; 1.7.1901. *(BK-DF-296).*	45.00	125.	375.
y. Overprint: *PUEBLA.* 1.1.1887. *(BK-DF-297).*	45.00	125.	375.
z. Overprint: *PUEBLA.* 1.4.1902. *(BK-DF-298).*	45.00	125.	375.
aa. Overprint: *PURUANDIRO.* 1.8.1905. *(BK-DF-299).*	45.00	125.	375.
ab. Overprint: *RIO VERDE.* 1.8.1905. *(BK-DF-30).*	25.00	75.00	225.
ac. Overprint: *SALTILLO.* 1.4.1902. *(BK-DF-301).*	45.00	125.	375.
ad. Overprint: *TABASCO.* 1.4.1902. *(BK-DF-302).*	45.00	125.	375.
ae. Overprint: *TAMPICO.* 1.4.1902. *(BK-DF-303).*	45.00	125.	375.
af. Overprint: *TEHUACÁN.* 1.3.1910. *(BK-DF-304).*	45.00	125.	375.
ag. Overprint: *TEPIC.* 1.8.1905. *(BK-DF-305).*	45.00	125.	375.
ah. Overprint: *TLALTENANGO.* 1.10.1906.. *(BK-DF-306).*	45.00	125.	375.
ai. Overprint: *TORREON.* 1.12.1902. *(BK-DF-307).*	45.00	125.	375.
aj. Overprint: *TULANCINGO.* 1.10.1906. *(BK-DF-308).*	45.00	125.	375.
ak. Overprint: *TUXTLA GUTIÉRREZ.* 1.8.1905. *(BK-DF-309).*	45.00	125.	375.
al. Overprint: *URUAPAN, MICH.* 1.8.1905. *(BK-DF-310).*	45.00	125.	375.
am. Overprint: *VERACRUZ.* 1.4.1902. *(BK-DF-311).*	45.00	125.	375.
an. Overprint and needle punched: *ZACATECAS.* 1.12.1890. 188x. *(BK-DF-312).*	50.00	150.	450.
ao. Overprint: *ZACATECAS..* 1.4.1902. *(BK-DF-313).*	45.00	125.	375.
ap. Overprint: *AGUASCALIENTES.* 1.7.1901. *(BK-DF-277A).*	45.00	125.	375.
aq. Overprint: *BRAVOS.* 1.12.1902. *(BK-DF-278A).*	45.00	125.	375.
ar. Overprint: *CIUDAD JUAREZ.* 1.8.1905. *(BK-DF-280A).*	45.00	125.	375.
as. Overprint and needle punched: *PAGADERO EN.* *(BK-DF-297A).*	45.00	125.	375.
at. Branch overprint: *QUERETARO.* 1.8.1905. *(BK-DF-299A).*	45.00	125.	375.
au. Overprint: *SAN ANDRES TUXTLA.* 1.8.1905. *(BK-DF-301A).*	45.00	125.	375.
av. Overprint: *TANTOYUCA.* 1.6.1906. *(BK-DF-303A).*	45.00	125.	375.
aw. Branch overprint: *VERACRUZ.* 1.1.1885.	200.	600.	1750.

S260 50 Pesos

1885-1913. Black on yellow and and brown underprint. Reclining female ("La Siesta") at left, portrait M. García Tereul at right. Back: Brown. Church and street scene at center. Printer: ABNC.

	Good	Fine	XF
a. 1.1.1885. *(BK-DF-314).*	100.	300.	900.
b. 1.12.1890; 26.7.1897. *(BK-DF-315).*	30.00	100.	300.
c. 1.7.1901-1.1.1908. *(BK-DF-316).*	25.00	75.00	225.
d. 1.9.1909-5.11.1913. *(BK-DF-317).*	15.00	45.00	125.
e. Overprint: *CUERNAVACA.* 1.12.1902; 1.8.1905. *(BK-DF-320).*	75.00	225.	675.
f. Overprint: *GUAYMAS.* 1.12.1902. *(BK-DF-321).*	75.00	225.	675.
g. Overprint: *MAZATLÁN.* 1.7.1901. *(BK-DF-322).*	75.00	225.	675.
h. Overprint and needle punched: *MERIDA.* 1.5.1889. *(BK-DF-323).*	100.	300.	900.
i. Overprint and needle punched: *MERIDA.* 1.4.1902. *(BK-DF-324).*	75.00	225.	675.
j. Overprint: *MONTERREY.* 1.8.1890. *(BK-DF-325).*	100.	300.	900.
k. Overprint: *PURUANDIRO.* 1.8.1905. *(BK-DF-326).*	75.00	225.	675.
l. Overprint: *S. ANDRÉS TUXTLA.* 1.12.1902. *(BK-DF-327).*	75.00	225.	675.
m. Overprint: *SOMBRERETE.* 1.3.1910. *(BK-DF-328).*	75.00	225.	675.
n. Overprint: *TABASCO.* 1.7.1901. *(BK-DF-320).*	75.00	225.	675.
o. Overprint and needle punched: *ZACATECAS.* 1.12.1890. *(BK-DF-330).*	100.	300.	900.
p. Overprint: *PAGADERO EN VERACRUZ.* 1.4.1902.	150.	450.	1250.
p1. Proof. 188x.	—	Unc	500.
p2. Proof. ND.	—	Unc	500.
q. Overprint: *PUEBLA.* 1.12.1890.	100.	300.	900.
r. ND. Remainder with overprint: *BILLETE SIN VALOR.* *(BK-DF-318).*	—	Unc	250.
s. Overprint: *TUXTLA GUTIÉRREZ.* 1.8.1905. *(BK-DF-229A).*	100.	300.	900.
s1. Specimen. 188x.	—	Unc	750.
s2. Specimen. ND.	—	Unc	750.
t. Overprint: *VERACRUZ.* 1.4.1902. *(BK-DF-329b).*	100.	300.	900.

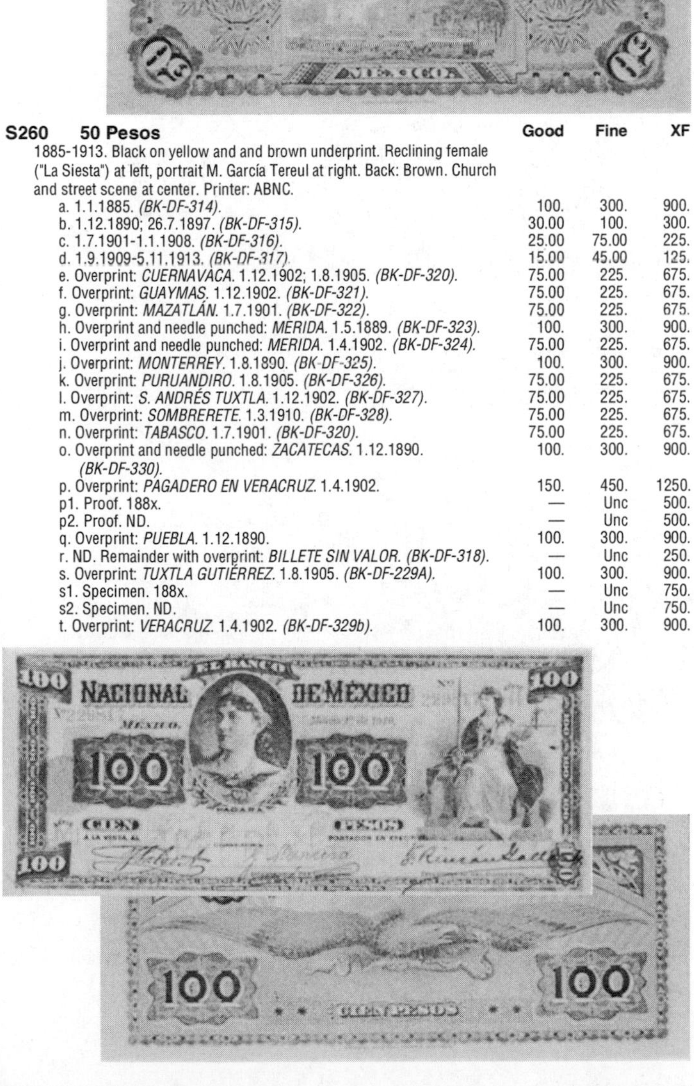

S261 100 Pesos

1885-1911. Black on yellow and brown underprint. Portrait M. García Teruel at left center, "Justice" at right. Back: Blue-gray. Eagle with wings spread eye to eye with snake at center. Printer: ABNC.

	Good	Fine	XF
a. 1.1.1885; 1.6.1886. *(BK-DF-331).*	125.	375.	1100.
b. 1.1.1888. *(BK-DF-332).*	125.	375.	1100.
c. 1.12.1890/1888-1.12.1902. *(BK-DF-334).*	75.00	225.	675.
d. 1.1.1908-1.3.1911. *(BK-DF-334).*	45.00	125.	375.
e. Overprint: *CAMPECHE.* 1.10.1906. *(BK-DF-338).*	100.	300.	900.
f. Overprint and needle punched: *GUANAJUATO.* 1.1.1885. *(BK-DF-339).*	125.	375.	1100.
g. Overprint: *MATEHUALA.* 5.11.1901. *(BK-DF-340).*	100.	300.	900.
h. Overprint and needle punched: *MERIDA.* 1.1.1888. *(BK-DF-341).*	125.	375.	1100.
i. Overprint: *MORELIA.* 1.12.1902. *(BK-DF-342).*	100.	300.	900.
j. Overprint: *QUERETARO.* 1.12.1902. *(BK-DF-343).*	100.	300.	900.
k. Overprint: *SAN ANDRÉS TUXTLA.* 1.1.1902. *(BK-DF-344).*	100.	300.	900.
l. Overprint: *TUXTLA GUTIÉRREZ.* 1.12.1902. *(BK-DF-345).*	100.	300.	900.
m. Overprint: *VERACRUZ.* 1.1.1885; 1.1.1888. *(BK-DF-346).*	125.	375.	1100.
n. Overprint: *VERACRUZ. VERACRUZ.* 1.3.188x. *(BK-DF-346).*	125.	375.	1100.
o. Overprint and needle punched: *ZACATECAS.* 1.12.1890. *(BK-DF-348).*	125.	375.	1100.
p. Overprint: *CUERNAVACA.* 1.12.1902. *(BK-DF-338A).*	100.	300.	900.
p1. Proof. 188x.	—	Unc	500.
p2. Proof. ND.	—	Unc	500.
q. Overprint: *TABASCO.* 5.11.1901. *(BK-DF-344A).*	100.	300.	900.
r. ND. Remainder with overprint: *BILLETE SIN VALOR.* *(BK-DF-335).*	—	Unc	300.
s1. Specimen. 188x.	—	Unc	750.
s2. Specimen. ND.	—	Unc	750.

S261A 100 Pesos

	Good	Fine	XF
19xx (ca.1913). Black on blue, green and brown underprint. Arms at right. Back: Green. Building at center. Printer: ABNC. Proof.	—	Unc	750.

S262 500 Pesos

1885-1913. Black on yellow and orange underprint. Seated female ("History") at left, portrait M. García Teruel at center, seated female with globe & jug ("Allegory") at right. Back: Orange and black. Herdsmen and wild horses ("Lassoing") at center. Printer: ABNC.

	Good	Fine	XF
a. Series A. 1.1.1885. *(BK-DF-349).*	600.	1800.	5400.
b. 26.7.1897-11.12.1913. *(BK-DF-350).*	450.	1350.	4000.
c. Overprint: *MONTERREY.* 12.8.188x. *(BK-DF-351).*	500.	1500.	4500.
p1. Proof 188x.	—	Unc	750.
p2. Proof. ND.	—	Unc	750.
r. ND. Remainder with overprint: *BILLETE SIN VALOR* on face or back. *(BK-DF-352).*	—	Unc	250.
s1. Specimen. 188x.	—	Unc	1000.
s2. Specimen. 189x.	—	Unc	1000.
s3. Specimen. ND.	—	Unc	1000.

S263 1000 Pesos

1885-1913. Black on multicolor underprint. Portrait M. García Teruel at left, reclining female ("L'Orient") at right. Back: Red-orange and black. Reclining woman with water jug ("Naiad") at center. Printer: ABNC.

	Good	Fine	XF
a. 25.10.1888-1.4.1913. *(BK-DF-355).*	750.	2250.	6750.
p1. Proof. 188x.	—	Unc	750.

	Good	Fine	XF
p2. Proof. ND.	—	Unc	750.
r. ND. Remainder with overprint: *BILLETE SIN VALOR* on face or back. *(BK-DF-356).*	—	Unc	350.
s1. Specimen. 188x.	—	Unc	1000.
s2. Specimen. 189x.	—	Unc	1000.
s3. Specimen. ND.	—	Unc	1000.

NOTE: For #S258-S263, reports of specific dates from 1885-1913 are requested.

National Pawn Shop

Nacional Monte de Piedad

1880-81 Certificates Issue

S264 1 Peso

12.7.1880-15.10.1881. Black on green underprint. Portrait P. Romero de Terreros at left, seated female with wheat and lamb ("Agriculture") at right. Series A. Back: Brown. Monte de Piedad building at center. Printer: ABNC. *(PR-DF-22).*

	Good	Fine	XF
a. Issued certificate.	175.	525.	1575.
p. Proof.	—	Unc	750.
r1. Remainder without counterfoil.	—	Unc	250.
r2. Remainder with counterfoil. *(PR-DF-24).*	—	Unc	250.
s. Specimen.	—	Unc	1000.

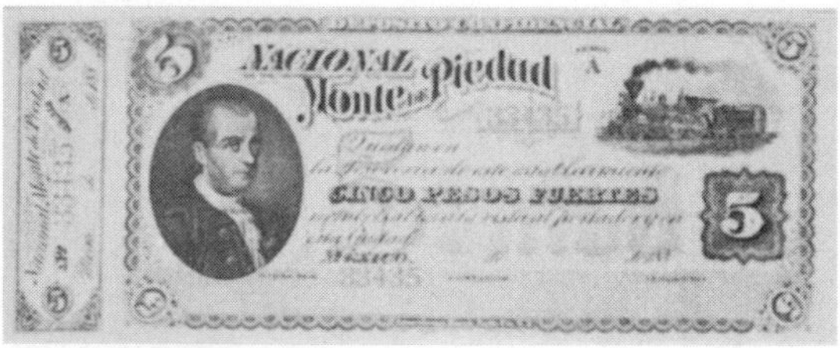

S265 5 Pesos

12.7.1880; 17.1.1881. Black on green underprint. Portrait P. Romero de Terreros at left, locomotive at upper right. Series A. Back: Brown. Monte de Piedad building at center. Printer: ABNC. *(PR-DF-27).*

	Good	Fine	XF
a. Issued certificate.	300.	900.	2750.
p. Proof.	—	Unc	750.
r1. Remainder without counterfoil. Series A. *(PR-DF-28).*	—	Unc	250.
r2. Remainder with counterfoil. *(PR-DF-29).*	—	Unc	250.
s. Specimen.	—	Unc	1000.

S266 10 Pesos

188x. Black on brown underprint. Deer ("Deer Drinking") at upper left center, portrait P. Romero de Terreros at lower right. Series A. Back: Blue. Monte de Piedad building at center. Printer: ABNC.

	Good	Fine	XF
p. Proof.	—	Unc	750.
r1. Remainder without counterfoil. *(PR-DF-32).*	—	Unc	250.
r2. Remainder with counterfoil. *(PR-DF-33).*	—	Unc	250.
s. Specimen.	—	Unc	1000.

S267 20 Pesos

188x. Black on brown underprint. Portrait P. Romero de Terreros at left center, farm produce at lower right. Back: Blue. Monte de Piedad building at center. Printer: ABNC.

	Good	Fine	XF
p. Proof.	—	Unc	750.
r1. Remainder without counterfoil. *(PR-DF-36).*	—	Unc	250.
r2. Remainder with counterfoil. *(PR-DF-37).*	—	Unc	250.
s. Specimen.	—	Unc	750.

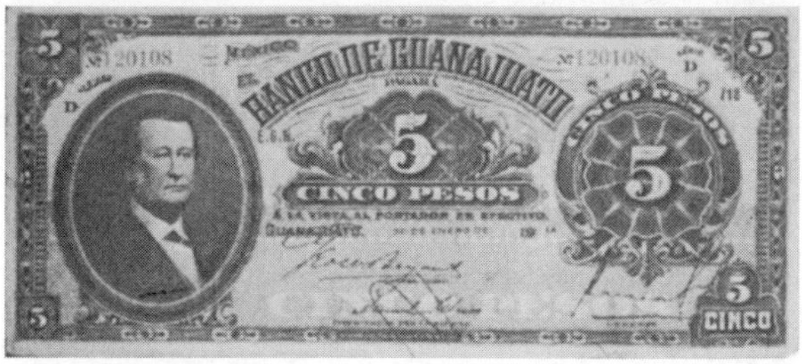

S268 50 Pesos

188x. Black on brown underprint. Portrait P. Romero de Terreros at upper left, cherub holding sheaf of grain ("Abundance") at right. Back: Blue. Monte de Piedad building at center. Printer: ABNC.

	Good	Fine	XF
p. Proof.	—	Unc	500.
r1. Remainder without counterfoil. *(PR-DF-40).*	—	Unc	250.
r2. Remainder with counterfoil. *(PR-DF-41).*	—	Unc	250.
s. Specimen.	—	Unc	750.

S269 100 Pesos

188x. Black on orange underprint. Seated female ("The Reaper") at left, portrait P. Romero de Terreros at center, horse's head at right. Back: Green. Monte de Piedad building at center. Printer: ABNC.

	Good	Fine	XF
p. Proof.	—	Unc	500.
r1. Remainder without counterfoil. *(PR-DF-44).*	—	Unc	250.
r2. Remainder with counterfoil. *(PR-DF-45).*	—	Unc	250.
s. Specimen.	—	Unc	750.

S270 500 Pesos

188x. Black on orange underprint. Sailing ship at left center, portrait P. Romero de Terreros at center, steam locomotive at center right. Back: Green. Monte de Piedad building at center. Printer: ABNC.

	Good	Fine	XF
p. Proof.	—	Unc	500.
r1. Remainder without counterfoil. *(PR-DF-48).*	—	Unc	250.
r2. Remainder with counterfoil. *(PR-DF-49).*	—	Unc	250.
s. Specimen.	—	Unc	750.

S271 1000 Pesos	Good	Fine	XF
188x. Black on orange underprint. Market scene at lower left, portrait P. Romero de Terreros at center, Female at lower right. Back: Green. Monte de Piedad building at center. Printer: ABNC.			
p. Proof.	—	Unc	500.
r1. Remainder without counterfoil. *(PR-DF-52).*	—	Unc	250.
r2. Remainder with counterfoil. *(PR-DF-53).*	—	Unc	250.
s. Specimen.	—	Unc	750.

Durango

Banco de Durango

1891 Issue

S272 1 Peso	Good	Fine	XF
1891-1901. Black on blue and yellow underprint. Allegorical figures flanking shield at left center. Back: Blue. Allegorical woman's head at center. Printer: ABNC.			
a. Series A. 15.6.1891; 1.9.1892. *(BK-DUR-5).*	150.	450.	1300.
b. Series B. 30.6.1893. *(BK-DUR-5).*	150.	450.	1300.
c. Without bank seals; 3.3.1901. *(BK-DUR-6).*	125.	375.	1150.
p. Proof. Series A.	—	Unc	750.
r. Remainder. ND. Series C. *(BK-DUR-7).*	7.50	20.00	60.00
s1. Specimen. Series A-C.	—	Unc	750.
s2. Specimen. Series G. 1914.	—	Unc	750.

S273 5 Pesos	Good	Fine	XF
1891-1913. Black on red-orange and yellow underprint. Miners at center, seated Irene (Goddess of Peace) at right. Text: *PAGARÁ A LA VISTA* at upper left. Serial # at right only. Back: Red-orange. Printer: ABNC.			
a. Series D. 1.1.1900. *(BK-DUR-11).*	25.00	75.00	225.
b. Series E. 11.5.1903. *(BK-DUR-12).*	20.00	60.00	175.
c. Series F. 5.9.1906; 10.5.1907; 1.1.1910. *(BK-DUR-12).*	20.00	60.00	175.
d. Series G. 18.6.1913. *(BK-DUR-13).*	15.00	45.00	125.
e. Overprint: *PAGADERO EN GÓMEZ PALACIO.* Series E. 11.5.1903.	45.00	125.	375.
f. Series B. 30.6.1893. *(BK-DUR-10A).*	60.00	175.	525.
p1. Proof. Series A.	—	Unc	750.
p2. Proof. Without series.	—	Unc	750.
s1. Specimen. Series A.	—	Unc	1000.
s2. Specimen. Series B.	—	Unc	1000.
s3. Specimen. Without series; series D; G.	—	Unc	1000.
s4. Specimen. Series E.	—	Unc	1000.

S273A 5 Pesos			
ND (ca.1914). Black on red-orange and yellow underprint. Miners at center, seated Irene (Goddess of Peace) at right. Similar to #S273, but with text: *PAGARÁ A LA VISTA...* at lower center. Serial # at left and right. Series J. Back: Red-orange. Printer: ABNC.			
p. Proof.	—	Unc	750.
s. Specimen.	—	Unc	1000.

S274 10 Pesos	Good	Fine	XF
1891-1914. Black on orange and yellow underprint. Cathedral of Durango at left, farmer mowing at right. Back: Orange. Printer: ABNC.			
a. Series B. 15.6.1891; 30.6.1893; 1.8.1896. *(BK-DUR-18).*	45.00	125.	375.
b. Series D. 1.1.1900. *(BK-DUR-19).*	25.00	75.00	225.
c. Series E. 11.5.1903; F. 5.9.1906; 10.5.1907; 1.1.1910. *(BK-DUR-20).*	20.00	60.00	175.
d. Series G. 18.6.1913; J. March 1914. *(BK-DUR-21).*	20.00	60.00	175.
e. Overprint: *PAGADERO EN GÓMEZ PALACIO.* Series E. 11.5.1903. *(BK-DUR-22).*	50.00	150.	450.
p1. Proof. Series A.	—	Unc	750.
p2. Proof. Without series.	—	Unc	750.
s1. Specimen. Series A.	—	Unc	1000.
s2. Specimen. Series B; D; E; G; J.	—	Unc	1000.
s3. Specimen. Series C.	—	Unc	1000.
s4. Specimen. Without series.	—	Unc	1000.

S275 20 Pesos	Good	Fine	XF
1891-1914. Black on brown and yellow underprint. Steam passenger train traveling through prairie with mountain in distance at left center, Harvest at right. Back: Sepia. Printer: ABNC.			
a. Series C. 1.8.1896. *(BK-DUR-25).*	60.00	175.	525.
b. Series D. 1.1.1900; E. 11.5.1903; F. 11.11.1903; 10.5.1907; 1.11.1910. *(BK-DUR-26).*	45.00	125.	375.
c. Series H. 1.3.1914; J, March 1914. *(BK-DUR-27).*	30.00	100.	300.
d. Overprint: *PAGADERO EN GÓMEZ PALACIO.* 11.5.1903. *(BK-DUR-28).*	75.00	225.	675.
p1. Proof. Series A.	—	Unc	750.
p2. Proof. Without series.	—	Unc	750.
s1. Specimen. Series A.	—	Unc	1000.
s2. Specimen. Without series; series C-E; H; J.	—	Unc	1000.

S276 50 Pesos	Good	Fine	XF
1891-1907. Black on green and yellow underprint. Child reclining on fish ("Off Sandy Hook") at left, seated Liberty with eagle and child ("Constitution") at right. Back: Green. 50 printed 3 times, allegorical figure at left and center right. Printer: ABNC.			
a. Series A. 1.6.1891. *(BK-DUR-30).*	225.	675.	2000.
b. Series C. 1.8.1896; D. 1.1.1900; E. 11.5.1903; F. 10.5.1907; 30.6.1907. *(BK-DUR-31).*	175.	525.	1500.
p. Proof. Series A.	—	Unc	750.

S276A 50 Pesos	Good	Fine	XF
1913-14. Black on green and yellow underprint. Child reclining on fish ("Off Sandy Hook") at left, seated Liberty with eagle and child ("Constitution") at right. Similar to #S276. Back: Green. 50 printed 5 times, allegorical figure at left and center right. Printer: ABNC.			
a. Series G. 18.6.1913; J. Feb. 1914; H. 1.3.1914. *(BK-DUR-32).*	135.	400.	1200.
p. Proof. Without series.	—	Unc	750.
s1. Specimen. Series G.	—	Unc	1000.
s2. Specimen. Series H; J.	—	Unc	1000.

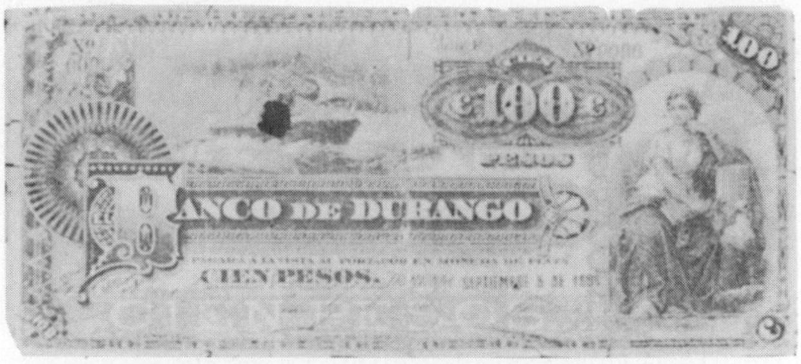

S277 100 Pesos	Good	Fine	XF
1888-1907. Black on brown and yellow underprint. Ship at upper left center, seated Justice at right. Back: Brown. Printer: ABNC.			
a. Series D. 1.1.1900; F. 5.9.1906; 30.6.1907. *(BK-DUR-34).*	600.	1800.	5400.
s. Specimen. Series A. ca.1888; B. ND.	—	Unc	1000.

S277A 100 Pesos	Good	Fine	XF
1913-14. Black on brown and yellow underprint. Ship at upper left center, seated Justice at right. Similar to #S277, but different denomination guilloches. Back: Brown. Printer: ABNC.			
a. Series H. 18.6.1913; J. Feb. 1914. *(BK-DUR-35).*	225.	675.	2000.
p. Proof. Without series. ND.	—	Unc	750.
s. Specimen. Without series; series J. ND.	—	Unc	1000.
S278 500 Pesos			
ND (ca.1914). Black on yellow and green underprint. Bank of Durango at center. Series A. Back: Blue-gray. Printer: ABNC. *(BK-DUR-36).* (Not issued).			
a. Issued note.	15.00	45.00	125.
s. Specimen.	—	Unc	1000.

NOTE: For #S272-S277A, reports of specific dates from 1891-1914 are requested.

1914 Issue

S280 5 Pesos	Good	Fine	XF
23.5.1914. Black on tan underprint. Ceres at left. Series E.S.P. Back: Brown. Printer: B&S. *(BK-DUR-16).*	5.00	15.00	45.00

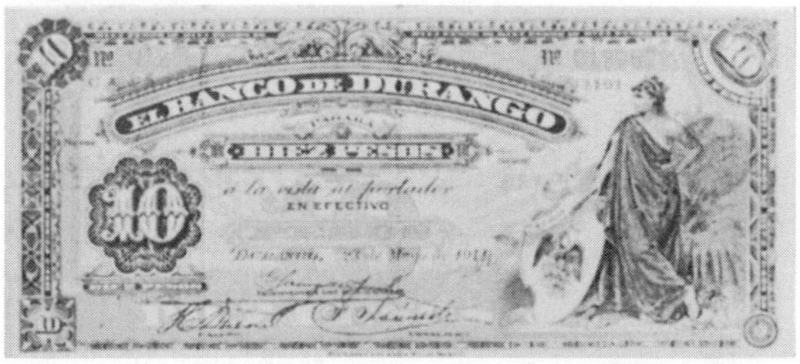

S281 10 Pesos	Good	Fine	XF
23.5.1914. Green and black. Polyhymnia (Muse of Lyrical Poetry) at right. Series E.S.P. Back: Green. Printer: B&S. *(BK-DUR-24).*	5.00	15.00	45.00

Banco del Estado de Durango

1882 Issue

S284 25 Centavos	Good	Fine	XF
5.1.1882. Portrait M. Hidalgo at left. Printer: H. S. Crocker & Co., S.F.			
a. Issued note. *(BK-DUR-1).*	150.	450.	1350.
r. Remainder. *(BK-DUR-2).*	—	Unc	500.

S285 50 Centavos	Good	Fine	XF
5.1.1882. Black on white. Portrait M. Hidalgo at left. Printer: H. S. Crocker & Co., S.F. *(BK-DUR-3).*	300.	900.	2700.

S286 1 Peso	Good	Fine	XF
5.1.1882. Black on white. Portrait M. Hidalgo at left. Steam passenger train at right. Back: Green. Printer: H. S. Crocker & Co., S.F. Remainder. *(BK-DUR-4).*	225.	675.	2000.

Guanajuato

Banco de Guanajuato

1913 Issue

S287 1 Peso	Good	Fine	XF
1913-14. Black on yellow underprint. Seated female with mirror at center. Back: Olive-green. State arms at center. Printer: ABNC.			
a. Series A. 3.12.1913; B. 3.12.1913. *(BK-GUA-1).*	7.50	20.00	60.00
b. Series C. 26.6.1914; 10.7.1914; 20.7.1914.	7.50	20.00	60.00
p. Proof. Without series. ND.	—	Unc	500.
s. Specimen. Series B; C. 19xx. *(BK-GUA-2s).*	—	Unc	750.

S288 2 Pesos	Good	Fine	XF
1913-14. Black on blue and brown underprint. Seated female holding branch at right. Back: Blue. State arms at center. Printer: ABNC.			
a. Series A and B. 3.12.1913; B and C. 1.6.1914. *(BK-GUA-3).*	7.50	20.00	60.00
p. Proof. Without series. ND.	—	Unc	500.
r. Unsigned remainder. ND. *(BK-GUA-4).*	12.50	35.00	100.
s. Specimen. Series B; C. 19xx. *(BK-GUA-5s).*	—	Unc	750.

S289 5 Pesos	Good	Fine	XF
1900-14. Black on green underprint. Portrait M. Doblado at left. Back: Green. Printer: ABNC.			
a. Series A. 15.10.1900; 30.10.1900; 29.10.1901. *(BK-GUA-6).*	15.00	45.00	125.

	Good	Fine	XF
b. Series B. 14.10.1902; 9.12.1902.	10.00	30.00	100.
c. Series C. 1.3.1903-6.7.1910. *(BK-GUA-7).*	15.00	45.00	125.
d. Series D. 30.1.1914; E. 20.7.1914. *(BK-GUA-8).*	25.00	75.00	225.
e. Overprint: *IRAPUATO.* Series A, 30.11.1900. *(BK-GUA-9).*	30.00	120.	375.
p. Proof. Without series. ND.	—	Unc	500.
s. Specimen. Series D; E. 19xx. *(BK-GUA-10s).*	—	Unc	750.

NOTE: For #S289, reports of specific dates from 1903-10 are requested.

S290 10 Pesos	Good	Fine	XF
1900-14. Black on red-orange and pale yellow-green underprint. State arms at left, cherub at center right. Back: Red-orange. Printer: ABNC.			
a. Series A. 15.10.1900; 29.10.1901. *(BK-GUA-11).*	20.00	60.00	200.
b. Series B. 8.9.1902; 9.12.1902; C. 19.9.1907; 3.8.1909; 6.7.1910. *(BK-GIA-12).*	30.00	45.00	125.
c. Series D. 12.4.1911; 30.1.1914; E. 26.6.1914; 10.7.1914; 20.7.1914. *(BK-GUA-13).*	10.00	15.00	45.00
d. Overprint: *IRAPUATO.* Series A. 15.10.1900; B. 14.10.1902. *(BK-GUA-14).*	30.00	45.00	125.
p. Proof. Without series. ND.	—	Unc	500.
s. Specimen. Series A; B; C; E; F. 19xx. *(BK-GUA-15s).*	—	Unc	750.

S291 20 Pesos	Good	Fine	XF
1900-14. Black on blue and yellow underprint. Woman's head at left, woman holding flowers ("Juanita") at right. Back: Blue-gray. State arms at center. Printer: ABNC.			
a. Series A. 15.10.1900. *(BK-GUA-16).*	45.00	125.	375.
b. Series A. 20.3.1902; 8.9.1902; 14.10.1902; B. 1.3.1903; 3.8.1909. *(BK-GUA-17).*	30.00	100.	300.
c. Series B. 3.5.1912. *(BK-GUA-18).*	30.00	100.	300.
d. Overprint: *IRAPUATO. Series A. 15.10.1900. (BK-GUA-19).*	75.00	225.	675.
e. Series C. 30.1.1914; E; F. 20.7.1914.	30.00	100.	300.
p. Proof. Without series. ND.	—	Unc	500.
s. Specimen. Series D; E. 19xx. *(BK-GUA-20s).*	—	Unc	750.

S292 50 Pesos	Good	Fine	XF
1901-14. Black on olive-green and yellow underprint. State arms at right. Back: Dark green. Printer: ABNC.			
a. Series A. 30.11.1900; 1.8.1901; 29.10.1901; 14.10.1902. *(BK-GUA-21).*	225.	675.	2100.
b. Series B. 3.8.1909; B; C. 3.5.1912; B; D. 30.1.1914; E. 1.6.1914. *(BK-GUA-22).*	175.	525.	1575.
p. Proof. Without series. ND.	—	Unc	500.
r. Remainder. Series F. ND. *(BK-GUA-23).*	—	Unc	200.
s. Specimen. Series B. 19xx.	—	Unc	750.

S293 100 Pesos	Good	Fine	XF
1900-14. Black on red and yellow underprint. Miner holding pick and lamp ("Miner No. 1") at center. Back: Red. State arms at center. Printer: ABNC.			
a. Series A. 15.10.1900; 1.8.1901; B. 1.3.1903. *(BK-GUA-25).*	375.	1150.	3450.
b. Series B. 1.12.1909; 30.1.1912; C. 1.3.1913; B; D. 30.1.1914; B; D; E. 1.6.1914; 20.7.1914. *(BK-GUA-26).*	550.	1650.	5000.
p. Proof. Without series. ND.	—	Unc	750.
s. Specimen. Series A; B. 19xx.	—	Unc	1000.

S294 500 Pesos	Good	Fine	XF
(ca.1900-14). Black on brown and yellow underprint. State arms at left, portrait M. Doblado at right. Back: Brown. Minerva (Goddess of Science, Art and War) at center. Printer: ABNC.			
a. Series C. 1.12.1909; 1.4.1914; 20.7.1914. *(BK-GUA-28).*	1800.	5250.	—
p1. Proof. Series A. 19xx (ca.1900).	—	Unc	1500.
p2. Proof. Without series. ND.	—	Unc	1500.

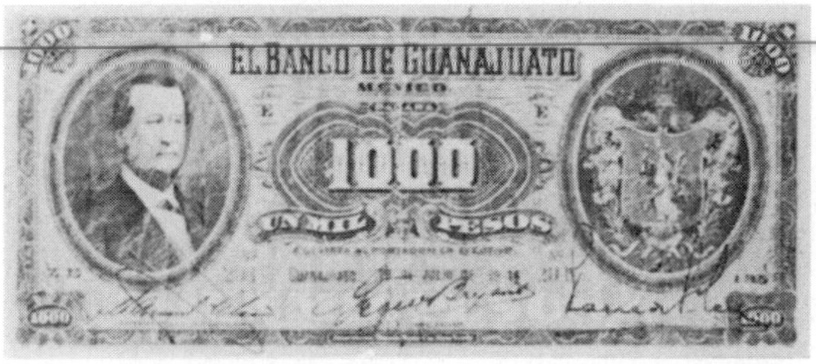

S295 1000 Pesos	Good	Fine	XF
(ca.1900-14). Black on purple and yellow underprint. Portrait M. Doblado at left, State arms at right. Back: Purple. Printer: ABNC.			
a. Series E. 20.7.1914. *(BK-GUA-32).*	2000.	6000.	—
p. Proof. Series A. 19xx (ca.1900).	—	Unc	750.

NOTE: For #S294 and S295, reports of specific dates are requested.

1914 Issue

S296 5 Pesos	Good	Fine	XF
1.6.1914. Brown and black. Euthenia (Goddess of Plenty) at left. Series G. Back: Brown. National arms at center. Printer: B&S. *(BK-GUA-34).*	5.00	15.00	50.00

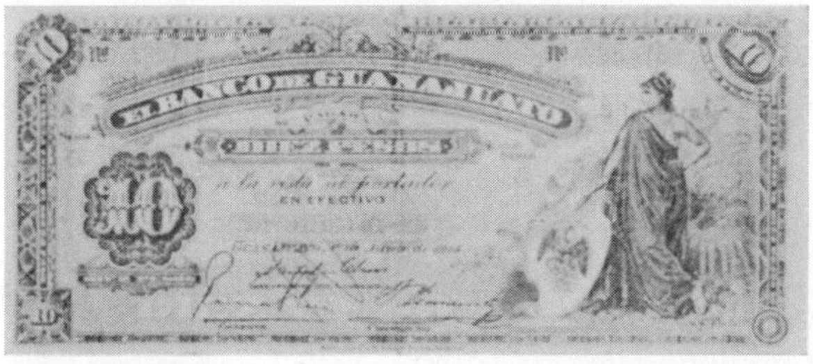

S297 10 Pesos	Good	Fine	XF
1.6.1914. Green, yellow and black. Standing female at right. Series G. Back: National arms at center. Printer: B&S. *(BK-GUA-35).*	5.00	15.00	50.00

Guerrero

Banco de Guerrero

1906-14 Issue

S298 5 Pesos	Good	Fine	XF
1906-14. Black on green underprint. Young girl with fruit basket at center. Back: Green. Portrait of Acapulco. Printer: ABNC.			
a. Series A. 5.5.1906. *(BK-GUE-1).*	100.	300.	900.
b. Series A. 6.2.1914. *(BK-GUE-2).*	75.00	225.	675.
c. Series B. 19xx (ca.1914). Perforated: *AMORTIZADO. (BK-GUE-3).*	—	Unc	25.00
p. Proof. Without series. 190x.	—	Unc	500.
s1. Specimen. Series A. 190x.	—	Unc	750.
s2. Specimen. Series B. 19xx.	—	Unc	750.
s3. Specimen. Without series. ND.	—	Unc	750.

S299 10 Pesos	Good	Fine	XF
(ca.1906-14). Black on brown and green underprint. Portrait V. G. Saldana at center. Back: Blue. Portrait of Acapulco. Printer: ABNC.			
a. Series A. 5.5.1906. *(BK-GUE-6).*	125.	375.	1150.
b. Series B. 19xx (ca.1914). Perforated: *AMORTIZADO. (BK-GUE-7).*	—	Unc	25.00
p. Proof. Without series. 190x.	—	Unc	500.
s1. Specimen. Series A. 190x.	—	Unc	750.
s2. Specimen. Series B. 19xx.	—	Unc	750.
s3. Specimen. Without series. ND.	—	Unc	750.

S300 20 Pesos	Good	Fine	XF
(ca.1906-14). Black on green underprint. Miners working at center. Back: Blue-gray. Portrait of Acapulco. Printer: ABNC.			
a. Series A. 5.5.1906. *(BK-GUE-9).*	150.	450.	1250.
b. Series B. 19xx (ca.1914). Perforated: *AMORTIZADO. (BK-GUE-10).*	—	Unc	25.00
p. Proof. Without series. 190x.	—	Unc	500.
s1. Specimen. Series A. 190x.	—	Unc	750.
s2. Specimen. Series B. 19xx.	—	Unc	750.
s3. Specimen. Without series. ND.	—	Unc	750.

NOTE: For #S299 and S300, confirmation is requested for the 1914 date as issued notes.

S301 50 Pesos	Good	Fine	XF
1906-14. Black on green underprint. Portrait V. G. Saldana at left. Back: Dark red. Portrait of Acapulco. Printer: ABNC.			
a. Series A. 5.5.1906. *(BK-GUE-12).*	150.	450.	1250.
b. Series A. Jan. 1914; 15.1.1914. *(BK-GUE-13).*	100.	300.	900.
c. Series B. 21.4.1914. *(BK-GUE-13).*	100.	300.	900.
d. Series B. 19xx (ca.1914). Perforated: *AMORTIZADO. (BK-GUE-14).*	—	Unc	50.00
p. Proof. Without series. 190x.	—	Unc	500.
s1. Specimen. Series A. 190x.	—	Unc	750.
s2. Specimen. Series B. 19xx.	—	Unc	750.
s3. Specimen. Without series. ND.	—	Unc	750.

S302 100 Pesos	Good	Fine	XF
1906-14. Black on brown underprint. Cathedral of Taxco at center right. Back: Brown. Portrait of Acapulco. Printer: ABNC.			
a. Series A. 5.5.1906. *(BK-GUE-16).*	900.	2750.	7500.
b. Series A. 15.1.1914. *(BK-GUE-17).*	900.	2750.	7500.
c. Series B. 28.5.1908. Perforated: *AMORTIZADO. (BK-GUE-18).*	—	Unc	50.00
p. Proof. Without series. 190x.	—	Unc	750.
s1. Specimen. Series A. 190x.	—	Unc	1000.
s2. Specimen. Series B. 19xx.	—	Unc	1000.

S303 500 Pesos	Good	Fine	XF
190x (ca.1904). Black on orange and yellow underprint. Ships at left center. Series A. Back: Orange. Portrait of Acapulco. Printer: ABNC. *(BK-GUE-20).*			
p. Proof.	—	Unc	750.
s. Specimen.	—	Unc	1000.

Hidalgo

Banco de Hidalgo

1902-14 Issue

S304 1 Peso	Good	Fine	XF
1914. Black on blue and yellow underprint. Mining scene at center. Back: Blue-gray. Hidalgo at center. Printer: ABNC.			
a. Series A. 5.5.1914. *(BK-HID-1).*	7.50	20.00	60.00
b. Series A. 19xx. Perforated: *AMORTIZADO. (BK-HID-2).*	—	Unc	20.00
p. Proof. Without series. ND.	—	Unc	750.
s. Specimen. Series A. ND.	—	Unc	1000.

S305 5 Pesos

1902-14. Black on orange and pale green underprint. Monument to Miguel Hidalgo at left, miners at right. Back: Orange. City view of Pachuca at center. Printer: ABNC.

	Good	Fine	XF
a. Series A. 23.9.1902. *(BK-HID-4).*	12.50	35.00	100.
b. Series B. 1.12.1913. *(BK-HID-5).*	7.50	20.00	60.00
c. Series C. 21.4.1914. *(BK-HID-6).*	7.50	20.00	60.00
d. Series C. 19xx. Perforated: *AMORTIZADO. (BK-HID-7).*	—	Unc	25.00
p1. Face proof. Without series. 190x.	—	Unc	500.
p2. Back proof.	—	Unc	500.
s. Specimen. Series B.	—	Unc	750.

S306 10 Pesos

1902-14. Black on green and yellow underprint. Miners at left and right, portrait Juan C. Doria at center. Back: Green. City view of Pachuca at center. Printer: ABNC.

	Good	Fine	XF
a. Series A. 23.9.1902; 1.11.1902; 6.6.1906. *(BK-HID-10).*	45.00	125.	375.
b. Series A. 1.9.1910: B. 21.4.1914. *(BK-HID-11).*	30.00	100.	300.
c. Series B. 19xx. Perforated: *AMORTIZADO. (BK-HID-12).*	—	Unc	25.00
d. Overprint: *TULANCINGO* on back; Series A. 1.11.1902; 23.9.1902. *(BK-HID-13).*	60.00	175.	525.
p. Proof. Without series. 190x.	—	Unc	500.
s. Specimen. Series A. 190x; Series B. 19xx.	—	Unc	750.

S307 20 Pesos

1902-10. Black on brown and yellow underprint. Monument to Miguel Hidalgo at left, factory at center right. Back: Brown. City view of Pachuca at center. Printer: ABNC.

	Good	Fine	XF
a. Series A. 23.9.1902; 1.11.1902; 6.6.1903. *(BK-HID-15).*	45.00	125.	375.
b. Series A. 1.9.1910; 23.11.1910; B. 21.4.1914. *(BK-HID-16).*	30.00	100.	300.
c. Series A. 1.9.1910. Perforated: *AMORTIZADO.* with 3 signatures *(BK-HID-17).*	25.00	75.00	225.
d. Series A. 1.9.1910. Perforated: *AMORTIZADO.* with 2 signatures *(BK-HID-18).*	—	Unc	100.
e. Overprint: *TULANCINGO* on back. Series A. 6.6.1903. *(BK-HID-21).*	60.00	175.	525.
p. Proof. Without series. 190x.	—	Unc	500.
r1. Unsigned remainder with back seals. Series A. 1.9.1910. Perforated: *AMORTIZADO. (BK-HID-19).*	—	Unc	50.00
r2. Unsigned remainder. Series B. 19xx. Perforated: *AMORTIZADO. (BK-HID-20).*	—	Unc	50.00
s1. Specimen. Series A. 190x.	—	Unc	750.
s2. Specimen. Series B. 19xx.	—	Unc	750.

S308 50 Pesos

1902-14. Black on blue and ochre underprint. Portrait P. Romero de Terreros at left, mining scene at right. Back: Dark blue on blue underprint. City view of Pachuca at center. Printer: ABNC.

	Good	Fine	XF
a. Series A. 23.9.1902-1.9.1910. *(BK-HID-23).*	150.	450.	1350.
p. Proof. Without series. 190x.	—	Unc	750.
r. Unsigned remainder. Series B. 19xx. Perforated: *AMORTIZADO. (BK-HID-24).*	—	Unc	100.
s. Specimen. Without series. 19xx; Series B. 19xx.	—	Unc	1000.

NOTE: For #S308, confirmation is erquested for the 1914 date as an issued note.

S309 100 Pesos

1904-14. Black on yellow and olive-green underprint. Monument to Miguel Hidalgo at left, portrait Juan C. Doria at right. Series A-C. Back: Olive-green. City view of Pachuca at center. Printer: ABNC.

	Good	Fine	XF
a. 16.7.1904; 1.1.1914; 21.4.1914. *(BK-HID-26).*	—	—	—
b. Series A. 2.4.1903.	900.	2700.	—
p. Proof. Without series. 190x.	—	Unc	1000.
s. Specimen. Series A. 190x; Series B. 19xx.	—	Unc	1250.

NOTE: For #S309, a note dated ca.1910 is reported in archive records. No examples are known.

S310 500 Pesos

ca.1906; 1914. Black on red amd yellow underprint. Portrait Miguel Hidalgo at left, miners working at center right. Back: Red. Bank at center. Printer: ABNC.

	Good	Fine	XF
a. Series B. 22.1.1914.	—	—	—
p. Proof. 190x (ca.1906).	—	Unc	750.
s. Specimen. 190x (ca.1906).	—	Unc	1000.

JALISCO

EJÉRCITO NACIONAL

1864 BONO ISSUE

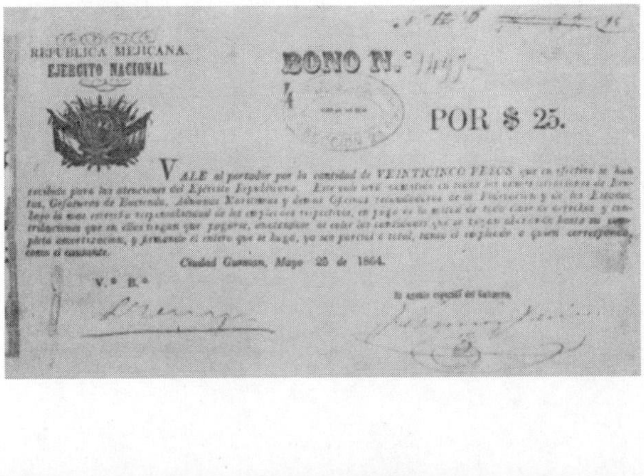

REPUBLICA MEJICANA.
EJERCITO NACIONAL.
BONO N.° 1497
POR $ 25.
VALE al portador por la cantidad de VEINTICINCO PESOS ...
Ciudad Guzman, Mayo 23 de 1864.

S311 25 Pesos	Good	Fine	XF
25.5.1864. Arms at upper left. Black text. Paper: Blue-gray. *(PR-JAL-11).*	225.	675.	2000.

S311A 50 Pesos	Good	Fine	XF
25.5.1864. Arms at upper left. Black text. Paper: Blue-gray. *(PR-JAL-12).*	225.	675.	2000.

Banco de Jalisco

1900-14 First Issue

S312 50 Centavos

1914. Pink and black. Woman's head at left, horses's head at right. With or without date. Back: Orange and pink. City view of Guadalajara at center. Printer: BWC.

	Good	Fine	XF
a. 1.5.1914. *(BK-JAL-1).*	15.00	45.00	120.
r. Remainder. 1.5.1914. *(BK-JAL-3).*	—	Unc	250.
s. Specimen.	—	Unc	750.

S313 1 Peso

20.1.1914/18xx. Black and blue. Dog's head at left, Ceres (Goddess of Agriculture) at center, ram at right. Back: Green and blue. City view of Guadalajara at center. Printer: BWC. *(BK-JAL-4).*

	Good	Fine	XF
a. Issued note.	15.00	45.00	120.
s. Specimen.	—	Unc	750.

S314 5 Pesos

5.9.1900. Portrait Eleutheria (Goddess of Liberty) at left, portrait Mercury (God of Commerce) at right. Series A. Back: City view of Guadalajara at center. Printer: BWC. *(BK-JAL-6).*

	Good	Fine	XF
a. Issued note.	1500.	4500.	—
b. Overprint: *COLIMA. (BK-JAL-7).*	1550.	4600.	—
c. Overprint: *TEPIC/COLIMA. (BK-JAL-8).*	1550.	4600.	—
s. Specimen.	—	Unc	750.

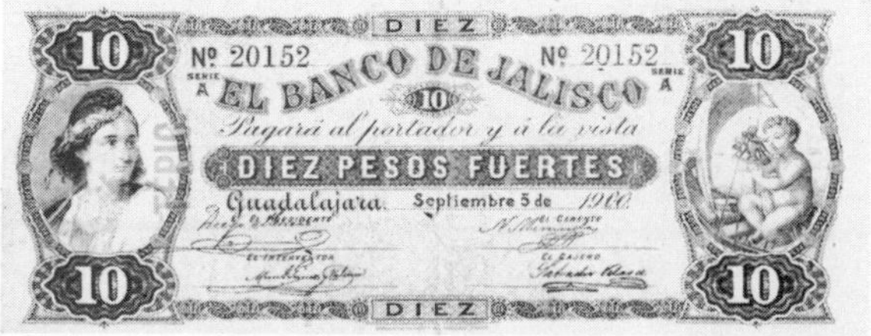

S315 10 Pesos

1898-1900. Yellow and green underprint. Portrait Eleutheria (Goddess of Liberty) at left, child on sailboat at right. Series A. Back: Green and yellow. City view of Guadalajara at center. Printer: BWC.

	Good	Fine	XF
a. 28.11.1898; 5.9.1900. *(BK-JAL-9).*	750.	2250.	—
b. Overprint: *TEPIC.* 5.9.1900. *(BK-JAL-10).*	750.	2250.	—
c. Overprint: *TEPIC/COLIMA.* 5.9.1900. *(BK-JAL-11).*	750.	2250.	—
s. Specimen.	—	Unc	750.

S316 20 Pesos

20.5.1900. Portrait Polyhymnia (Muse of Lyrical Poetry) at left, herd of cattle at right. Series A. Back: City view of Guadalajara at center. Printer: BWC. *(BK-JAL-12).*

	Good	Fine	XF
a. Issued note.	3000.	9000.	—
s. Specimen.	—	Unc	750.

S317 50 Pesos

28.11.1898; 3.12.1900. Portrait Chloris (Goddess of Flowers) at left, allegory of Spring at right. Series A. Back: City view of Guadalajara at center. Printer: BWC. *(BK-JAL-13).*

	Good	Fine	XF
a. Issued note.	3000.	9000.	—
s. Specimen.	—	Unc	750.

S318 100 Pesos

1.3.1900. Portrait Minerva (Goddess of Science, Art and War) at left, oxen drawing hay wagon at right. Series A. Back: City view of Guadalajara at center. Printer: BWC. *(BK-JAL-14).*

	Good	Fine	XF
a. Issued note.	3000.	9000.	—
s. Specimen.	—	Unc	750.

S319 500 Pesos

18xx. Red, green and black. Boy at left, steam locomotive at right. Back: City view of Guadalajara at center. Printer: BWC.

	Good	Fine	XF
p. Proof.	—	Unc	1000.
s. Specimen.	—	Unc	1250.

S319A 1000 Pesos

18xx

	Good	Fine	XF
s. Specimen.	—	Unc	1250.

1900-14 Second Issue

S320 5 Pesos

1902-14. Black on green and yellow underprint. State arms at left. Back: Green. City view of Guadalajara at center. Printer: ABNC.

	Good	Fine	XF
a. Series A. 1.8.1902; B. 1.2.1903; 5.5.1903. *(BK-JAL-16).*	15.00	45.00	125.
b. Series C. 15.10.1908; 15.12.1908; D. 1.2.1910. *(BK-JAL-17).*	15.00	45.00	125.
c. Series E. 5.1.1911; F. 26.3.1914. *(BK-JAL-18).*	15.00	45.00	125.
d. Overprint: *TEPIC.* Series B. 1.2.1903; 5.5.1903. *(BK-JAL-19).*	25.00	75.00	225.
e. Overprint: *ZAMORA.* Series A. 1.8.1902; Series B. 1.2.1903. *(BK-JAL-20).*	25.00	75.00	225.
f. Overprint: *ZAPOTLÁN.* Series A. 10.9.1902. *(BK-JAL-21).*	25.00	75.00	225.
p. 19xx. Proof.	—	Unc	500.
s. Specimen.	—	Unc	750.

S321 10 Pesos

1902-14. Black on orange underprint. State arms at left, woman and child at lower right. Back: Orange. City view of Guadalajara at center. Printer: ABNC.

	Good	Fine	XF
a. Series A. 1.2.1903. *(BK-JAL-25).*	25.00	75.00	225.
b. Series B. 25.3.1908; D. 1.2.1910. *(BK-JAL-26).*	25.00	75.00	225.
c. Series E. 5.1.1911; 1.2.1911; F. 26.3.1914. *(BK-JAL-27).*	25.00	75.00	225.
d. Overprint: *TEPIC.* Series A. 1.2.1903. *(BK-JAL-28).*	30.00	100.	300.
e. Overprint: *ZAMORA.* Series A. 10.9.1902; 1.2.1903. *(BK-JAL-29).*	30.00	100.	300.
p. Proof. 19xx.	—	Unc	500.
s. Specimen.	—	Unc	750.

S322 20 Pesos

1902-14. Black on blue underprint. State arms at left, standing female with fasces & wreath at right. Back: Blue. City view of Guadalajara at center. Printer: ABNC.

	Good	Fine	XF
a. Series A. 10.9.1902; 5.5.1902. *(BK-JAL-31).*	60.00	175.	525.
b. Series B. 12.3.1907; D. 1.2.1910. *(BK-JAL-32).*	60.00	175.	525.
c. Series E; F. 26.3.1914. *(BK-JAL-33).*	60.00	175.	525.
p1. Face proof. Green and black, mounted on card. *(BK-JAL-33A).*	—	Unc	500.
p2. Proof. 19xx.	—	Unc	500.
s. Specimen.	—	Unc	750.

S323 50 Pesos

(ca.1902-14). Black on olive-green and yellow underprint. State arms at left, ceramic workers and their wares at right. Back: Olive-green. City view of Guadalajara at center. Printer: ABNC.

	Good	Fine	XF
a. 25.3.1908. *(BK-JAL-35).*	375.	1100.	3300.
b. Series A. 16.7.1909; B. 16.7.1909; E. 1.1.1911; F. 26.3.1914. *(BK-JAL-36).*	300.	900.	2700.
p. Proof. 19xx. (ca.1902).	—	Unc	500.
s. Specimen.	—	Unc	750.

S324 100 Pesos

(ca.1902-09). Black on brown and yellow underprint. State arms at left center, men and burros at right. Back: Brown. City view of Guadalajara at center. Printer: ABNC.

	Good	Fine	XF
a. Series B. 16.7.1909. *(BK-JAL-38).*	2250.	6750.	—
p. Proof. 19xx (ca.1902).	—	Unc	500.
s. Specimen.	—	Unc	750.

S325 100 Pesos

1.2.1910; 5.1.1911. Black on green and purple underprint. Female liberty head at left, State arms at right. Series D; E. Back: Purple. City view of Guadalajara at center. Printer: ABNC.

	Good	Fine	XF
a. Issued note. *(BK-JAL-39).*	450.	1300.	4000.
p. Proof.	—	Unc	500.
s. Specimen. *(BK-JAL-39s).*	—	Unc	750.

S326 500 Pesos

1.2.1910; 5.1.1911. Black on pink, green and brown underprint. Reclining woman at left. State arms at center right. Series D; E. Back: Blue-gray. City view of Guadalajara at center. Printer: ABNC.

	Good	Fine	XF
a. Issued note. *(BK-JAL-41).*	2250.	6750.	—
p. Proof.	—	Unc	1000.
s. Specimen. *(BK-JAL-42s).*	—	Unc	1250.

NOTE: For #S325 and S326, a note dated ca.1914 is listed in archive records. No examples are known.

S327 1000 Pesos

19xx (ca.1909-14). Black on brown, purple and blue underprint. Seated allegorical woman holding globe at left, state arms at right. Back: Red. City view of Guadalajara at center. Printer: ABNC.

	Good	Fine	XF
p. Proof.	—	Unc	1000.
s. Specimen. *(BK-JAL-43s).*	—	Unc	1250.

1914 ND Issue

S328 5 Pesos

	Good	Fine	XF
ND. Green. State arms at left. Series B. Printer: NBNC. Unsigned remainder. *(BK-JAL-44).*	500.	1500.	4500.

México (Estado de)

Banco del Estado de México

1897-1914 Issue

S329 5 Pesos

1897-1912. Black on yellow and brown underprint. Nike (Victory) at left, national arms at left center, seated female with globe at right. Back: Brown. Steam passenger train traveling through mountain pass at center. Printer: ABNC.

	Good	Fine	XF
a. Series A. 5.11.1897; 18.7.1898; 2.4.1899. Series A. Signature title: *DIRECTOR GERENTE* at right. *(BK-MEX-3).*	30.00	100.	300.
b. Series B. 26.8.1901; 29.10.1902. Series A & B. Signature title: *CAJERO* at right. *(BK-MEX-4).*	25.00	75.00	225.
c. Series B. 19.11.1907-22.10.1912. *(BK-MEX-5).*	25.00	75.00	225.
d. Overprint: *MORELIA.* 21.10.1908; 22.10.1912. *(BK-MEX-6).*	25.00	75.00	225.
p1. Proof. Without series. 189x.	—	Unc	500.
p2. Proof. Series A. ND.	—	Unc	500.
s1. Specimen. Without series. 189x.	—	Unc	750.
s2. Specimen. Without series. ND.	—	Unc	750.
s3. Specimen. Series B. ND.	—	Unc	750.

S330 10 Pesos

1898-1912. Black on green and yellow underprint. Woman at left. National arms at right. Back: Green. Allegorical man at left and right. Steam passenger train traveling through mountain pass at center. Printer: ABNC.

	Good	Fine	XF
a. Series A. 1.1.1898; 18.7.1898; 2.4.1899. Signature title: *DIRECTOR GERENTE* at right. *(BK-MEX-9).*	30.00	100.	300.
b. Series B. 26.8.1901-5.11.1909. Signature title: *CAJERO* at right. *(BK-MEX-10).*	25.00	75.00	225.
c. Series B. 16.7.1910; 1.7.1911; 22.10.1912. *(BK-MEX-11).*	25.00	75.00	225.
d. Overprint: *MORELIA.* 19.11.1907; 2.10.1908; x.11.1910. *(BK-MEX-12).*	30.00	100.	300.
p. Proof. Without series. 189x.	—	Unc	500.
s. Specimen. Without series. 189x.	—	Unc	750.

S331 20 Pesos

1898-1912. Black on orange and yellow underprint. Flying female with light ("Electricity") at center. National arms at right. Back: Orange. Steam passenger train traveling through mountain pass at center. Printer: ABNC.

	Good	Fine	XF
a. Series A. 1.1.1898; 18.7.1898; 22.9.1899; 5.2.1900. Signature title: *DIRECTOR GERENTE* at right. *(BK-MEX-14).*	75.00	225.	675.
b. Series B. 26.8.1901-25.11.1905. Signature title: *CAJERO* at right. *(BK-MEX-15).*	60.00	175.	525.
c. Series B. 2.4.1909-22.10.1912. *(BK-MEX-16).*	60.00	175.	525.
d. Overprint: *MORELIA.* 26.8.1901; 25.11.1905; 22.10.1912. *(BK-MEX-17).*	100.	300.	900.
p. Proof. Without series. 189x.	—	Unc	500.
s. Specimen. Without series. ND.	—	Unc	750.

S332 50 Pesos

1898-1912. Black on yellow and olive underprint. Seated female with globe & lyre ("Urania") at left. National arms at right. Back: Brown. Steam passenger train traveling through mountain pass at center. Printer: ABNC.

	Good	Fine	XF
a. Series A. 1.1.1898; 18.7.1898; 5.2.1900. Signature title: *DIRECTOR GERENTE* at right. *(BK-MEX-19).*	300.	900.	2700.
b. Series B. 26.8.1901; 25.11.1905. Signature title: *CAJERO* at right. *(BK-MEX-20).*	225.	675.	2000.
c. Series B. 1.7.1911; 22.10.1912. *(BK-MEX-21).*	175.	525.	1575.
d. Overprint: *MORELIA.* 1.7.1911. *(BK-MEX-22).*	300.	900.	2750.
p. Proof. Without series. 189x.	—	Unc	1000.
s. Specimen. Without series. 189x.	—	Unc	1250.

S333 100 Pesos

1898-1911. Black on blue and yellow underprint. Ship at left, seated female at right. National arms at center. Back: Blue. Steam passenger train traveling through mountain pass at center. Printer: ABNC.

	Good	Fine	XF
a. Series A. 1.1.1898; 18.7.1898; 5.2.1900. Signature title: *DIRECTOR GERENTE* at right. *(BK-MEX-24).*	600.	1800.	5400.
b. Series B. 25.8.1901/189x; 25.11.1905. Signature title: *CAJERO* at right. *(BK-MEX-25).*	525.	1550.	4600.
c. Series B. 1.7.1911; 22.10.1912. *(BK-MEX-26).*	525.	1550.	4600.
p. Proof. Without series. 189x.	—	Unc	1000.
s. Specimen. Without series. 189x.	—	Unc	1250.

S334 500 Pesos	Good	Fine	XF
(ca.1897-1911). Black on red-orange and yellow underprint. Two supporting figures around Mexican seal. National arms at center. Signature title: *DIRECTOR GERENTE* at right. Back: Red. Steam passenger train traveling through mountain pass at center. Printer: ABNC. *(BK-MEX-28).*			
a. Series B. 1.7.1911.	3000.	9000.	—
p. Proof. Without series. 189x (ca.1897).	—	Unc	1000.
s. Specimen. Without series. 189x (ca.1897).	—	Unc	1250.

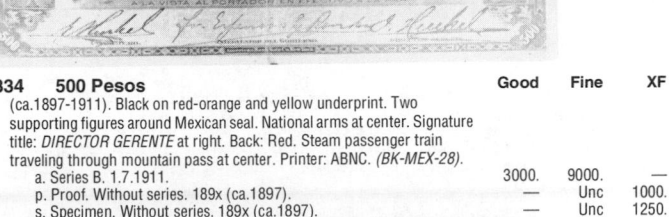

S335 1000 Pesos	Good	Fine	XF
(ca. 1897-1900). Black on blue and yellow underprint. Liberty head at left center. National arms at right. Signature title: *DIRECTOR GERENTE* at right. Back: Dark blue. Steam passenger train traveling through mountain pass at center. Printer: ABNC. *(BK-MEX-30).*			
a. Series A. 6.2.1900.	5500.	11,000.	—
p. Proof. Without series. 189x (ca.1897).	—	Unc	1000.
s. Specimen. Without series. 189x (ca.1897).	—	Unc	1250.

1914 Issue

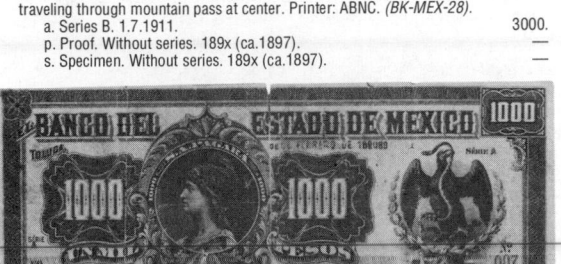

S336 1 Peso	Good	Fine	XF
9.2.1914. Black on green underprint. Portrait Miguel Hidalgo at center. Series C.D., E.F. Back: Green. Steam passenger train traveling through mountain pass at center. Printer: AB&PC. *(BK-MEX-1).*	7.50	20.00	60.00

S337 2 Pesos	Good	Fine	XF
9.2.1914. Orange and black. Portrait Miguel Hidalgo at center. Series NO, PQ. Back: Red. Steam passenger train traveling through mountain pass at center. Printer: AB&PC. *(BK-MEX-2).*	5.00	15.00	45.00

Michoacán

Banco de Michoacán

1903 Issue

S338 5 Pesos	Good	Fine	XF
5.1.1903; 6.8.1903. Black on green and yellow underprint. Portrait José M. Morelos Pavón at left, lion at center, winged cherub at right. Series A. Back: Green. Cathedral at center. Printer: ABNC. *(BK-MIC-1).*			
a. Issued note.	1350.	4250.	12,500.
b. Overprint: *MOROLEÓN.* 6.8.1903. *(BK-MIC-2).*	1350.	4250.	12,500.
c. Overprint: *PURUANDIRO.* 5.1.1903. *(BK-MIC-3).*	1350.	4250.	12,500.
d. Overprint: *ALAMBARO.* ND. *(BK-MIC-4).*	1350.	5000.	15,000.
p. Proof.	—	Unc	1250.
s. Specimen.	—	Unc	1500.

S339 10 Pesos	Good	Fine	XF
5.1.1903; 6.8.1903. Black on orange and yellow underprint. Man carrying water jug at left. Series A. Back: Orange. Cathedral at center. Printer: ABNC. *(BK-MIC-7).*			
a. Issued note.	1500.	4500.	13,500.
b. Overprint: *COTIJA.* 6.8.1903. *(BK-MIC-8).*	1500.	4500.	13,500.
c. Overprint: *MOROLEÓN.* 5.1.1903. *(BK-MIC-9).*	1500.	4500.	13,500.
d. Overprint: *PURUANDIRO.* 5.1.1903. *(BK-MIC-10).*	1500.	4500.	13,500.
p. Proof.	—	Unc	2000.
s. Specimen.	—	Unc	2500.

S340 20 Pesos	Good	Fine	XF
5.1.1903. Black on blue and yellow underprint. Portrait José Michelena at center. Series A. Back: Blue-gray. Cathedral at center. Printer: ABNC. *(BK-MIC-12).*			
a. Issued note.	2250.	6750.	20,000.
p. Proof.	—	Unc	2250.
s. Specimen.	—	Unc	2500.

S341 50 Pesos	Good	Fine	XF
6.2.1903. Black on brown and yellow underprint. Women kneeling preparing food at left. Series A. Back: Brown. Cathedral at center. Printer: ABNC. *(BK-MIC-14).*			
a. Issued note.	5500.	17,500.	—
p. Proof.	—	Unc	2250.
s. Specimen.	—	Unc	2500.

S342 100 Pesos	Good	Fine	XF
16.2.1903. Black on olive-green and yellow underprint. Portrait Vasco de Quiroga at center. Series A. Back: Olive-green. Cathedral at center. Printer: ABNC. *(BK-MIC-16).*			
a. Issued note.	5500.	11,000.	—
p. Proof.	—	Unc	2250.
s. Specimen.	—	Unc	2500.

S343 500 Pesos	Good	Fine	XF
19xx (ca.1906). Black on red and yellow underprint. Man with farm tool at left. Back: Brown. Cathedral at center. Printer: ABNC.			
p. Proof.	—	Unc	2250.
s. Specimen.	—	Unc	2500.

S344 1000 Pesos	Good	Fine	XF
19xx (ca. 1906). Black on purple and yellow underprint. Farmer beside wagon at center. Back: Purple. Cathedral at center. Printer: ABNC.			
p. Proof.	—	Unc	2250.
s. Specimen.	—	Unc	2500.

Morelos

Banco de Morelos

1903 Issue

S345 5 Pesos	Good	Fine	XF
1903-10. Black on green underprint. Horse at left, standing female ("Paloma") at right. Back: Green. Printer: ABNC.			
a. 25.3.1903-20.12.1904. *(BK-MOR-2)*.	40.00	125.	375.
b. Series C. 11.2.1910. *(BK-MOR-3)*.	30.00	100.	300.
c. Overprint: *ACAPULCO*. 14.8.1903. *(BK-MOR-4)*.	45.00	125.	375.
p. Proof. Without series. ND.	—	Unc	750.
s. Specimen. Series C. ND.	—	Unc	1000.

S346 10 Pesos	Good	Fine	XF
1903-10. Black on brown underprint. Two seated women at left, standing female at right. Back: Brown. Allegorical woman's head at center. Printer: ABNC.			
a. Series A; E. 25.3.1903-20.12.1904. *(BK-MOR-7)*.	45.00	125.	375.
b. Series A: E. 11.2.1910. *(BK-MOR-8)*.	30.00	100.	300.
c. Overprint: *ACAPULCO*. 14.8.1903. *(BK-MOR-9)*.	45.00	125.	375.
p. Proof. Without series. ND.	—	Unc	750.
s. Specimen. Series E. ND.	—	Unc	1000.

S347 20 Pesos	Good	Fine	XF
1903-10. Black on blue underprint. Two females ("The Reapers") at left, seated woman holding national arms next to lion at right. Back: Blue-black. Printer: ABNC.			
a. Series A; D. 3.6.1903; 14.8.1903; 29.10.1903; 20.12.1904. *(BK-MOR-011)*.	60.00	175.	525.
b. Series D. 11.2.1910. *(BK-MOR-12)*.	60.00	175.	525.
c. Overprint: *ACAPULCO*. 14.8.1903. *(BK-MOR-13)*.	75.00	225.	675.
p. Proof. Without series. ND.	—	Unc	750.
s. Specimen. Without series. ND.	—	Unc	1000.

S348 50 Pesos	Good	Fine	XF
1903-10. Black on blue underprint. Seated female with children at center. Back: Blue. Printer: ABNC.			
a. 3.6.1903; 14.8.1903; 29.10.1903. *(BK-MOR-15)*.	125.	375.	1100.
b. Series A; F. 11.2.1910. *(BK-MOR-16)*.	125.	375.	1100.
p. Proof. Without series. ND.	—	Unc	750.
s. Specimen.	—	Unc	1000.

S349 100 Pesos	Good	Fine	XF
1903-10. Black on red underprint. Standing female with scales and child ("Equity") at left, portrait Jose M. Morelos at center right. Back: Red. Allegorical woman's head at center. Printer: ABNC.			
a. Series A; G. 3.6.1903-20.12.1904. *(BK-MOR-18)*.	600.	1800.	5400.
b. Series A. ND (ca.1903). Specimen or proof.	—	Unc	1000.
p. Proof. Without series. ND.	—	Unc	1000.
s. Specimen. Series A.	—	Unc	1250.

S350 500 Pesos	Good	Fine	XF
ND (ca.1902). Black on olive-green underprint. Lion facing left at center. Series B. Back: Olive-green. Lion's head at center. Printer: ABNC. Specimen or proof. *(BK-MOR-20)*.	—	Unc	1250.

1914 Issue

S351 1 Peso	Good	Fine	XF
31.7.1914. Portrait Jose M. Morelos y Pavón at left, woman (Abundance) at right. Printer: E.I.A. *(BK-MOR-1)*.	600.	1800.	5400.

Nuevo León

Banco Mercantil de Monterrey

1900-11 Issue

S352 5 Pesos	Good	Fine	XF
1900. Black on green and yellow underprint. Portrait M. Escobedo at left, ore loading platform at center. Text: *EN MONEDA DE PLATA.* Middle signature title: *PRESIDENTE.* Back: Green. City of Monterrey at center. Printer: ABNC. *(BK-NUE-39).*			
a. Series E. 2.4.1900; 15.8.1900.	150.	450.	1300.

S352A 5 Pesos	Good	Fine	XF
1906; 1911. Black on green and yellow underprint. Portrait M. Escobedo at left, ore loading platform at center. Like #S352 but text: *EN MONEDA CORRIENTE.* Middle signature title: *CONSEJERO.* Back: Green. City of Monterrey at center. Printer: ABNC. (BK-NUE-40).			
a. 23.10.1906.	75.00	225.	675.
b. Series L; N. 27.7.1911. *(BK-NUE-41).*	60.00	175.	525.
p. Proof. Series A. 19xx.	—	Unc	1000.
s. Specimen. Series A. 19xx; without series, ND.	—	Unc	1250.

S353 10 Pesos	Good	Fine	XF
1900. Black on brown and yellow underprint. Railroad depot at left, portrait M. Escobedo at center right. Text; *EN MONEDA DE PLATA.* Middle signature title: *PRESIDENTE.* Back: Brown. City of Monterrey at center. Printer: ABNC. *(BK-NUE-44).*			
a. Series K; M. 2.4.1900; 15.8.1900.	125.	375.	1100.
b. Overprint: *LINARES.* Series M. 2.4.1900; 15.8.1900. *(BK-NUE-47).*	175.	525.	1575.
p. Proof. Series H. 19xx.	—	Unc	1000.
s. Specimen. Series H. 19xx.	—	Unc	1250.

S353A 10 Pesos	Good	Fine	XF
1906; 1911. Black on brown and yellow underprint. Railroad depot at left, portrait M. Escobedo at center right. Like #S353 but text:*EN MONEDA CORRIENTE.* Middle signature title:*CONSEJERO.* Back: Brown. City of Monterrey at center. Printer: ABNC. (BK-NUE-45).			
a. 23.10.1906.	125.	375.	1100.
b. Series R. 27.7.1911.	100.	300.	1000.
s. Specimen. Series T, ND.	—	Unc	1250.

S354 20 Pesos	Good	Fine	XF
1900. Black on olive-green underprint. Portrait M. Escobedo at left, cathedral at right. Text: *EN MONEDA DE PLATA.* Middle signature title: *PRESIDENTE.* Back: Olive-green. City of Monterrey at center. Printer: ABNC. *(BK-NUE-49).*			
a. Series P. 15.8.1900.	300.	900.	2700.
p. Proof. Series R. 19xx.	—	Unc	1000.
s. Specimen. Series R. 19xx.	—	Unc	1250.

S354A 20 Pesos	Good	Fine	XF
6.3.1907. Black on olive-green underprint. Portrait M. Escobedo at left, cathedral at right. Like #S354 but text: *EN MONEDA CORRIENTE.* Middle signature title: *CONSEJERO.* Series S. Back: Olive-green. City of Monterrey at center. Printer: ABNC. *(BK-NUE-50).*	350.	1100.	3300.

S355 50 Pesos	Good	Fine	XF
1900. Black on red-orange underprint. Portrait M. Escobedo at left, theater building at right. Text: *EN MONEDA DE PLATA.* Middle signature title: *PRESIDENTE.* Back: Orange. City of Monterrey at center. Printer: ABNC. *(BK-NUE-52).*			
a. Series S. 2.4.1900; 6.3.1902.	600.	1800.	5400.
b. Series T; U; V. 15.8.1900.	525.	1100.	3300.
S355A 50 Pesos			
(ca.1906).ND. Black on red-orange underprint. Portrait M. Escobedo at left, theater building at right. Like #S355 but with text: *EN MONEDA CORRIENTE.* Middle signature title: *CONSEJERO.* Back: Orange. City of Monterrey at center. Printer: ABNC. Specimen.	—	Unc	1250.
S356 100 Pesos			
2.4.1900-6.3.1907. Black on blue and yellow underprint. Portrait M. Escobedo at left, building at center. Text: *EN MONEDA DE PLATA* Middle signature title: *PRESIDENTE.* Series W. Back: Blue-black. City of Monterrey at center. Printer: ABNC. *(BK-NUE-54).*	1500.	4500.	13,000.

S356A 100 Pesos			
6.3.1907. Black on blue and yellow underprint. Portrait M. Escobedo at left, building at center. Like #S356 but with text: *EN MONEDA CORRIENTE;* middle signature title: *CONSEJERO.* Series Z. Back: Blue-black. City of Monterrey at center. Printer: ABNC.			
p. Proof.	—	Unc	1000.
s. Specimen.	—	Unc	1250.

S357 500 Pesos	Good	Fine	XF
19xx. Black on red and yellow underprint. Portrait M. Escobedo at left, large building at center right. Text: *EN MONEDA DE PLATA.* Middle signature title: *PRESIDENTE.* Series Z. Back: Red. City of Monterrey at center. Printer: ABNC. *(BK-NUE-55s).*	525.	1100.	3300.

S357A 500 Pesos			
(ca.1907). Black on red and yellow underprint. Portrait M. Escobedo at left, large building at center right. Like #S357 but with text: *EN MONEDA CORRIENTE;* middle signature title: *CONSEJERO.* Back: Red. City of Monterrey at center. Printer: ABNC.			
p. Proof.	—	Unc	1000.
s. Specimen.	—	Unc	1250.

Banco de Nuevo León

1893-1914 Issue

S358 50 Centavos	Good	Fine	XF
ND. I. Zaragoza at right. Without signature. Essay. *(BK-NUE-6).*	—	Unc	1500.

S359 1 Peso	Good	Fine	XF
1892-1914. Black on yellow and brown underprint. Portrait I. Zaragoza at left, helmeted female head ("Minera No. 3") at center, beehives at right. Back: Brown. State seal at center. Printer: ABNC. *(BK-NUE-7).*			
a. 12.1.1892; 15.1.1893; 5.2.1893; 5.5.1893; 1893- ca.1913. Righthand signature title: *EL CAJERO.*	150.	450.	1300.
b. Perforated: *CANCELADO.* 5.2.1914. *(BK-NUE-8).*	—	—	250.
c. Issues with needle punched cancel: *CANCELADO.* 1.1.1913. *(BK-NUE-7A).*	125.	375.	1100.
s. Specimen. (ca.1913-14). Righthand signature title: *EL GERENTE.*	—	Unc	1250.

S360 5 Pesos	Good	Fine	XF
1892-1912. Black on green and yellow underprint. Jaguar at left center, portrait I. Zaragoza at right. Back: Green. State seal at center. Printer: ABNC.			
a. Series G. 1.12.1892; 15.5.1895; 4.7.1897. Righthand signature title: *EL CAJERO. (BK-NUE-11).*	100.	300.	900.
b. 25.9.1900/18xx-5.2.1903/19xx. Righthand signature title: *EL GERENTE. (BK-NUE-12).*	35.00	100.	300.
c. Series G. 20.2.1907; 1.1.1910-15.5.1912. *(BK-NUE-13).*	30.00	100.	300.
d. Perforated: *CANCELADO.* ND. *(BK-NUE-14).*	—	—	250.
e. Overprint: *ALLENDE.* 25.9.1900/18xx.	100.	300.	900.
f. 1.1.1913. *(BK-NUE-14A).*	—	—	250.

S361 10 Pesos	Good	Fine	XF
1895-1913. Black on orange and yellow underprint. Seated allegorical females flanking portrait I. Zaragoza at center. Back: Orange. State seal at center. Printer: ABNC.			
a. 1.1.1895; 15.7.1896/2.2.1896; 4.7.1897; 2.4.1900. Righthand signature title: *EL CAJERO. (BK-NUE-17).*	100.	300.	900.
b. 14.7.1900-16.10.1909. Righthand signature title: *EL GERENTE. (BK-NUE-18).*	75.00	225.	675.
c. Series L. 16.9.1910-1.1.1913. *(BK-NUE-19).*	75.00	225.	675.
d. Perforated: *CANCELADO.* 1.1.1913. With or without date. *(BK-NUE-21).*	—	—	250.
e. Overprint: *TORREÓN, COAH.* 14.7.1900. *(BK-NUE-20).*	125.	375.	1150.

S362 20 Pesos	Good	Fine	XF
1894-1912. Black on blue and yellow underprint. Progress at left center, portrait I. Zaragoza at right. Back: Blue. State seal at center. Printer: ABNC.			
a. 5.5.1893; 5.2.1894; 2.4.1896; 4.7.1897; 18.10.1897; 25.9.1900; 25.3.1904. Righthand signature title: *EL CAJERO. (BK-NUE-23).*	250.	750.	2250.
b. 27.11.1906; 21.11.1908. Righthand signature title: *EL GERENTE. (BK-NUE-24).*	225.	675.	2000.
c. Series A. 1.1.1910-15.5.1912. *(BK-NUE-25).*	175.	525.	1575.
d. Perforated: *CANCELADO.* ND. *(BK-NUE-26).*	—	—	300.
e. 1.1.1913. *(BK-NUE-26A).*	175.	525.	1575.

S363 50 Pesos	Good	Fine	XF
1893-1913. Black on yellow and olive-green underprint. Woman standing at left, portrait I. Zaragoza at top left center, woman kneeling with eagle at right. Back: Olive-green. State seal at center. Printer: ABNC.			
a. 5.5.1893; 18.10.1897. Righthand signature title: *EL CAJERO. (BK-NUE-28).*	400.	1200.	3600.
b. 5.5.1893; 14.7.1900. Righthand signature title: *EL GERENTE. (BK-NUE-28).*	400.	1200.	3600.
c. 19.9.1907; 1.1.1911; 5.2.1912; 15.5.1912. *(BK-NUE-29).*	375.	1450.	3300.
d. Perforated: *CANCELADO.* 1.1.1913. *(BK-NUE-30).*	125.	375.	1100.
s. Specimen. 18xx (ca.1899). Righthand signature title: *EL GERENTE.*	—	Unc	1000.

S364 100 Pesos	Good	Fine	XF
1893-1913. Black on orange, yellow and pink underprint. Standing female ("Commerce") at left, river scene with mountain in background at center, portrait I. Zaragoza at right. Back: Red. State seal at center. Printer: ABNC.			
a. 5.2.1893. Righthand signature title: *EL CAJERO. (BK-NUE-33).*	600.	1800.	5400.
b. 25.9.1900/18xx; 15.9.1904. Righthand signature title: *EL GERENTE. (BK-NUE-33).*	600.	1800.	5400.
c. Series I. 5.5.1910; 16.9.1910; 1.1.1911; 5.2.1912; 15.5.1912. *(BK-NUE-34).*	525.	1575.	4600.
d. Perforated: *CANCELADO.* 1.1.1913. *(BK-NUE-35).*	—	—	400.

S365 500 Pesos	Good	Fine	XF
(ca.1893-1.1.1913). Black on yellow and brown underprint. Portrait I. Zaragoza at left, city view at center right, griffin at right. Back: Dark brown. State seal at center. Printer: ABNC.			
a. Perforated: *CANCELADO.* 1.1.1913. *(BK-NUE-37).*	—	—	400.
s1. Specimen. 18xx. Righthand signature title: *EL CAJERO.*	—	Unc	1000.
s2. Specimen. 18xx. Righthand signature title: *EL GERENTE.*	—	Unc	1000.
s3. Specimen. 19xx.	—	Unc	1250.

NOTE: For #S360-S365, reports of specific dates from 1893-1913 are requested.

Banco de Patricio Milmo

1800s Issue

		Good	Fine	XF
S366	**5 Pesos** 18xx. Vaquero on horseback at center. Printer: KBNC. Unsigned remainder. *(BK-NUE-1).*	—	Unc	1500.
S367	**10 Pesos** 18xx. Vaquero on horseback at center. Printer: KBNC. Unsigned remainder. *(BK-NUE-2).*	—	Unc	1500.
S368	**20 Pesos** 18xx. Vaquero on horseback at center. Printer: KBNC. Unsigned remainder. *(BK-NUE-3).*	—	Unc	1800.
S369	**50 Pesos** 18xx. Vaquero on horseback at center. Printer: KBNC. Unsigned remainder. *(BK-NUE-4).*	—	Unc	1800.

		Good	Fine	XF
S370	**100 Pesos** 18xx. Vaquero on horseback at center. Printer: KBNC. Unsigned remainder. *(BK-NUE-5).*	—	Unc	1800.

Oaxaca

Banco de Oaxaca

1903-07 Issue

S371 5 Pesos — Good — Fine — XF

1903-07. Black on green and yellow underprint. Monument to Pablo Benito Juarez at lower left, seated female with child ("Plenty No. 2") at center. Back: Green. Tehuana at center. Printer: ABNC. *(BK-OAX-1).*

	Good	Fine	XF
a. Series B; C. 10.3.1903-1.7.1907.	375.	750.	2250.
p. Proof. Without series. ND.	—	Unc	1250.
s. Specimen. Series D or without series. ND.	—	Unc	1500.

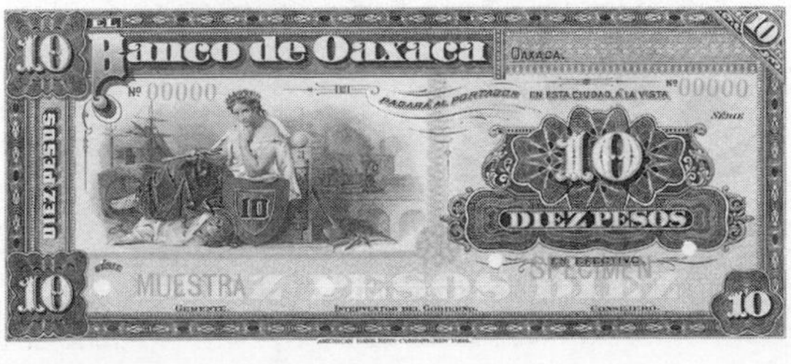

S372 10 Pesos

10.3.1903-21.3.1907. Black on orange and yellow underprint. Seated female representing Commerce at left. Back: Orange. Tehuana at center. Printer: ABNC.

	Good	Fine	XF
a. Series E; J. *(BK-OAX-3).*	1000.	3000.	9000.
p. Proof. Without series. ND.	—	Unc	1500.
s. Specimen.	—	Unc	1750.

S373 20 Pesos

1903-05. Black on red and yellow underprint. Two female heads at center. Series F. Back: Red. Tehuana at center. Printer: ABNC.

	Good	Fine	XF
a. 23.5.1903; 2.4.1905. *(BK-OAX-5).*	1800.	5400.	15,000.
b. Overprint: *ISTMO.* 2.4.1905. *(BK-OAX-6).*	1800.	5400.	15,000.
p. Proof. Without series. ND.	—	Unc	2000.
s. Specimen.	—	Unc	1750.

S374 50 Pesos

10.3.1903. Black on olive-green underprint. Monument to Pablo Benito Juarez at left. Back: Olive-green. Tehuana at center. Printer: ABNC.

	Good	Fine	XF
a. Series G. *(BK-OAX-9).*	3000.	9000.	25,000.
p. Proof.	—	Unc	1500.
s. Specimen.	—	Unc	1750.

S375 100 Pesos

ND (ca.1903). Black on yellow and brown underprint. Monument to Pablo Benito Juarez at center. Back: Brown. Tehuana at center. Printer: ABNC.

	Good	Fine	XF
p. Proof. Without series. ND.	—	Unc	1500.
s. Specimen. Series H.	—	Unc	1750.

Puebla

Banco Oriental de México

1913 ND Issue

S376 5 Pesos

ND (1913). Banco Oriental de Mexico at center. Back: State arms at center. Printer: AB&PC.

	Good	Fine	XF
a. With printed signature. Face proof. *(BK-PUE-23).*	1000.	3000.	—
x. Inverted 10 Peso guilloche. Face proof. *(BK-PUE-24).*	—	—	1500.

S377 10 Pesos	Good	Fine	XF
ND (1914). Banco Oriental de Mexico at center. Back: State arms at center. Printer: AB&PC. Proof. *(BK-PUE-33).*	375.	1100.	3300.

1914 ND Issue

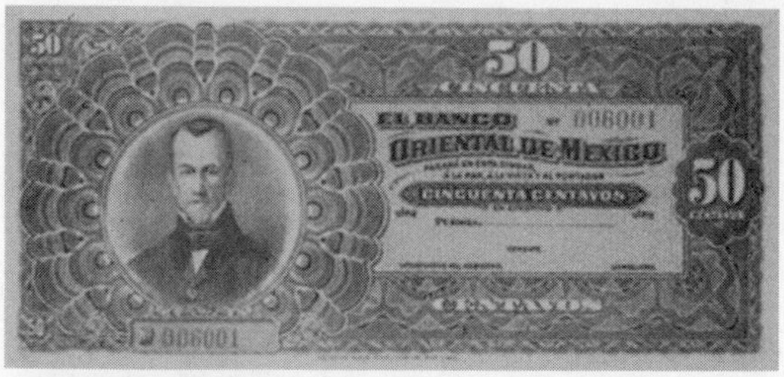

S378 50 Centavos	Good	Fine	XF
ND (ca.1914). Black on bright green underprint. Portrait Estebán de Antunano at left. Back: Green. Aztec calendar at center. Printer: ABNC. *(BK-PUE-1).*			
p. Proof.	—	Unc	1000.
s. Specimen.	—	Unc	1250.

S379 1 Peso	Good	Fine	XF
ND (ca.1914). Black on purple, orange and blue underprint. Bank building at left. Back: Orange. Indian woman at center. Printer: ABNC. *(BK-PUE-4).*			
p. Proof.	—	Unc	1000.
s. Specimen.	—	Unc	1250.

S380 2 Pesos	Good	Fine	XF
ND (ca.1914). Black on red, orange, and multicolor underprint. Bank building at center. Back: Red. Indian woman at center. Printer: ABNC. *(BK-PUE-7).*			
p. Proof.	—	Unc	1000.
s. Specimen.	—	Unc	1250.

1900-10 Issue

S381 5 Pesos	Good	Fine	XF
1900-14. Black on orange and yellow underprint. Portrait Estebán de Antunano at left, Cathedral of Puebla at right. Back: Orange. State arms at center. Printer: ABNC.			
a. 1.3.1900; 12.3.1900; 15.3.1900. *(BK-PUE-8).*	7.50	20.00	60.00
b. 1.5.1901; 30.6.1901; 1.9.1909. *(BK-PUE-9).*	5.00	15.00	45.00
c. 3.2.1910-24.4.1914. *(BK-PUE-10).*	3.00	10.00	30.00
d. ND. *(BK-PUE-11).*	7.50	20.00	60.00
e. Overprint: *ATLIXCO.* 15.3.1900. *(BK-PUE-14).*	25.00	75.00	225.
f. Overprint: *HUAJUAPAM.* 3.2.1910. *(BK-PUE-15).*	15.00	45.00	125.
g. Overprint: *JUCHITAN.* 3.2.1910. *(BK-PUE-16).*	15.00	45.00	125.
h. Overprint: *OAXACA.* 1.5.1901. *(BK-PUE-17).*	25.00	75.00	225.
i. Overprint: *SANTA ANA.* 3.2.1910. *(BK-PUE-18).*	20.00	60.00	100.
j. Overprint: *TEHUAÇÁN.* 15.3.1900; 30.6.1901. *(BK-PUE-19).*	20.00	60.00	100.
k. Overprint: *TEHUÁNTEPEC.* 3.2.1910. *(BK-PUE-20).*	15.00	45.00	125.
l. Overprint: *TEZIUTLÁN.* 15.3.1900. *(BK-PUE-21).*	20.00	60.00	100.
m. Overprint: *TLAXCALA.* 3.2.1910. *(BK-PUE-22).*	15.00	45.00	125.
p. Proof. Without series. ND.	—	Unc	1000.
s. Specimen. Without series. ND.	—	Unc	1250.

S382 10 Pesos	Good	Fine	XF
1900-14. Black on olive-green underprint. Portrait Estebán de Antunano at left, city of Puebla at right. Back: Dark green. State arms at center. Printer: ABNC.			
a. 23.5.1900; 1.5.1900; 30.6.1901. *(BK-PUE-25).*	7.50	20.00	60.00
b. 1.5.1901 - 1.9.1909. *(BK-PUE-26).*	5.00	15.00	45.00
c. 3.2.1910 - 22.4.1914. *(BK-PUE-27).*	3.00	10.00	30.00
d. Overprint: *ATLIXCO.* 13.5.1900. *(BK-PUE-29).*	30.00	100.	300.
e. Overprint: *OAXACA.* 1.5.1901. *(BK-PUE-30).*	30.00	100.	300.
f. Overprint: *TEHUACÁN.* 30.6.1901. *(BK-PUE-31).*	25.00	75.00	225.
g. Overprint: *TEZIUTLÁN.* 23.5.1900; 1.6.1901; 30.6.1901. *(BK-PUE-32).*	25.00	75.00	225.
p. Proof. Without series.	—	Unc	1000.
s. Specimen. Without series.	—	Unc	1250.

S383 20 Pesos	Good	Fine	XF
1900-14. Black on brown underprint. Monument of Liberty at left, portrait Estebán de Antunáno at right. Back: Brown. State arms at center. Printer: ABNC.			
a. 30.6.2900. *(BK-PUE-35).*	12.50	35.00	100.
b. 1.5.1901; 12.6.1901; 1.9.1909. *(BK-PUE-36).*	12.50	35.00	100.
c. 1.9.1909-1.4.1914. *(BK-PUE-37).*	7.50	20.00	60.00
d. Overprint: *OAXACA.* 1.5.1901. *(BK-PUE-39).*	30.00	100.	300.
e. Overprint: *TEHUACÁN.* 12/1.6.1901; 30.6.1901. *(BK-PUE-40).*	30.00	100.	300.
f. Overprint: *TEZIUTLÁN.* 12/1.6.1901; 30.6.1901. *(BK-PUE-41).*	30.00	100.	300.
p. Proof. Without series. ND.	—	Unc	1000.
s. Specimen. Without series. ND.	—	Unc	1250.

S384 50 Pesos	Good	Fine	XF
1900-14. Black on green underprint. Portrait Estebán de Antunano at left, standing female with horn & cherub at right. Back: Green. State arms at center. Printer: ABNC.			
a. 30.6.1900. *(BK-PUE-42).*	15.00	45.00	125.
b. 1.5.1901-1.9.1909. *(BK-PUE-43).*	15.00	45.00	125.
c. 3.1.1914; 12.1.1914; 14.3.1914; 1.4.1914. *(BK-PUE-44).*	7.50	20.00	60.00
d. Overprint: *OAXACA.* 1.5.1901; 12/1.6.1901. *(BK-PUE-45).*	30.00	100.	300.
e. Overprint: *TEHUACAN.* 2.3.1903. *(BK-PUE-45A).*	30.00	100.	300.
p. Proof. Without series. ND.	—	Unc	1000.
s. Specimen. Without series. ND.	—	Unc	1250.

S385 100 Pesos	Good	Fine	XF
1901-14. Black on red underprint. Portrait Estebá de Antunano at left, Government Palace at center. Back: Red. State arms at center. Printer: ABNC.			
a. 11.6.1900; 12.6.1901; 30.6.1901. *(BK-PUE-47).*	30.00	100.	300.
b. 1.9.1909. *(BK-PUE-48).*	30.00	100.	300.
c. 3.2.1910; 3.1.1914; 10.3.1914. *(BK-PUE-49).*	25.00	75.00	225.
d. ND. Without signature of *Gerente. (BK-PUE-50).*	25.00	75.00	225.
e. Overprint: *ATLIXCO.* ND. *(BK-PUE-52).*	50.00	150.	450.
f. Overprint: *TEZIUTLÁN.* 30.6.1901. *(BK-PUE-53).*	50.00	150.	450.
g. Overprint: *TEHUACAN.* 11.6.1901. *(BK-PUE-52a).*	75.00	225.	675.
p. Proof. Without series. ND.	—	Unc	1000.
s. Specimen. Without series. ND.	—	Unc	1250.

S386 500 Pesos	Good	Fine	XF
1901-14. Black on blue and yellow underprint. Two seated female ("War & Peace") at left, portrait Estebán de Antunano at right. Back: Dark blue. State arms at center. Printer: ABNC.			
a. 30.6.1901. *(BK-PUE-54).*	500.	1500.	4500.
b. 1.4.1914; 3.1.1914; 14.2.1914. *(BK-PUE-55).*	300.	900.	2750.
p1. Face proof. *(BK-PUE-55a).*	—	Unc	1000.
p2. Proof. Without series. ND.	—	Unc	1250.
s. Specimen. Without series. 19xx.	—	Unc	1250.

S387 1000 Pesos	Good	Fine	XF
1901-14. Black on orange and yellow underprint. Sailor at left, portrait Estebán de Antunano at center, standing female with scythe & wheat at right. Back: Orange. State arms at center. Printer: ABNC.			
a. 30.6.1901. *(BK-PUE-57).*	600.	1800.	5400.
b. 17.6.1913-1.4.1914. *(BK-PUE-58).*	750.	2250.	6750.
p. Proof. Without series. ND.	—	Unc	1500.
s. Specimen. Without series. 19xx.	—	Unc	1750.

NOTE: For #S383-S387, reports of specific dates from 1900-14 are requested.

1914 Issue

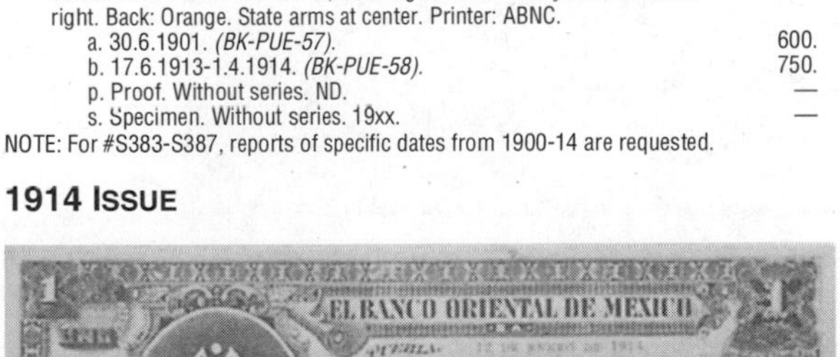

S388 1 Peso	Good	Fine	XF
1914. Black, green and yellow. Monogram at left, Fort Loreto at center right. Back: Olive-green. State arms at center. Printer: AB&PC.			
a. Circular seals on face. 12.1.1914-28.4.1914. *(BK-PUE-2).*	2.00	5.00	15.00
b. Square seals on face. 1.4.1914; 22.4.1914. *(BK-PUE-3).*	2.00	5.00	15.00

S389 2 Pesos	Good	Fine	XF
1914. Black, lilac and yellow. Monogram at left, Fort Loreto at center right. Back: Lilac. State arms at center. Printer: AB&PC.			
a. Circular seals on face. 12.1.1914-26.2.1914. *(BK-PUE-5).*	2.00	5.00	15.00
b. Square seals on face. 22.4.1914. *(BK-PUE-6).*	5.00	15.00	45.00

Querétaro

Banco de Querétaro S.A.

1903-14 Issue

S390 5 Pesos	Good	Fine	XF
1903-14. Black on green underprint. Ox-cart at left, state arms at center right. Series A. Back: Green. Steam passenger train traveling below aquaduct at center. Printer: ABNC.			
a. 30.7.1903; 4.1.1905; 1.11.1905; 15.1.1906. *(BK-QUE-3).*	40.00	125.	375.
b. New signature overprint at left and at center. 10.4.1914. *(BK-QUE-4).*	25.00	75.00	225.
c. Overprint: *IRAPUATO.* 30.7.1903; 15.1.1906. *(BK-QUE-6).*	40.00	125.	375.
p. Proof. Without series. ND.	—	Unc	1500.
s. Specimen. Series A. ND.	—	Unc	1750.

S391 10 Pesos	Good	Fine	XF
1903-14. Black on brown underprint. Portrait Guadalupe Obregón (as a child) at left, state arms at right. Series A. Back: Dark brown. Steam passenger train traveling below aquaduct at center. Printer: ABNC.			
a. 1.11.1895; 15.1.1906. *(BK-QUE-7).*	40.00	125.	375.
b. New signature overprint at left and at center. 10.4.1914. *(BK-QUE-8).*	25.00	75.00	225.
c. Overprint: *IRAPUATO.* 30.7.1903; 15.1.1906. *(BK-QUE-10).*	40.00	125.	375.
p. Proof. Without series; Series A. ND.	—	Unc	1250.
s. Specimen. Series A. ND.	—	Unc	1500.

S392 20 Pesos	Good	Fine	XF
1903-14. Black on orange underprint. Man carrying water jugs at left, portrait J. A. U. Arana at right. Series A. Back: Brown. Steam passenger train traveling below aquaduct at center. Printer: ABNC.			
a. 30.7.1903; 1.11.1905. *(BK-QUE-11).*	175.	525.	1575.
b. 15.4.1914. *(BK-QUE-12).*	175.	525.	1575.
c. Overprint: *IRAPUATO.* 30.7.1903. *(BK-QUE-14).*	1750.	525.	1575.
p. Proof. Without series. ND.	—	Unc	1250.
s. Specimen. Series A. ND.	—	Unc	750.

S393 50 Pesos	Good	Fine	XF
1903-14. Black on blue and yellow underprint. Portrait J. O. Domínguez at left, state arms at right. Series A. Back: Blue. Steam passenger train traveling below aquaduct at center. Printer: ABNC.			
a. 30.7.1903; 1.11.1905; 15.1.1906. *(BK-QUE-15).*	400.	1200.	3600.
b. 15.4.1914. *(BK-QUE-16).*	300.	900.	2700.
c. Overprint: *IRAPUATO.* 30.7.1903. *(BK-QUE-18).*	450.	1350.	4000.
p. Proof. Without series. ND.	—	Unc	1000.
s. Specimen. Series A. ND.	—	Unc	1250.

S394 100 Pesos	Good	Fine	XF
1903-10. Black on red underprint. Standing female ("Liberty") at left, state arms at right. Series A; B. Back: Dark red. Steam passenger train traveling below aquaduct at center. Printer: ABNC.			
a. 30.7.1903; 1.9.1910. *(BK-QUE-19).*	600.	1800.	5400.
b. Overprint: *IRAPUATO.* 30.7.1903; 15.1.1906. *(BK-QUE-21).*	750.	2250.	6750.
s. Specimen. Series B. ND.	—	Unc	1250.

S395 500 Pesos	Good	Fine	XF
1903-10. Black on olive-green underprint. Portrait J. A. U. Arana at left, Minerva (Goddess of Science, Art and War) at right. Series A. Back: Dark green. Steam passenger train traveling below aquaduct at center. Printer: ABNC.			
a. 30.7.1903; 1.9.1910. *(BK-QUE-22).*	1500.	4500.	13,500.
b. Overprint: *IRAPUATO.* 30.7.1903. *(BK-QUE-23).*	1800.	5400.	15,000.
s. Specimen.	—	Unc	2250.

S396 1000 Pesos			
ND (ca.1903-09). Black on red underprint. J. O. Domínguez at left, state arms at right. Series A. Back: Orange. Steam passenger train traveling below aquaduct at center. Printer: ABNC. *(BK-QUE-25).*			
p. Proof.	—	Unc	1000.
s. Specimen.	—	Unc	1250.

1914 Issue

S397 1 Peso	Good	Fine	XF
1914. Blue and black. State arms at left, man with pack mule at right. National arms at center. Back: Blue. Printer: AB&PC.			
a. Series A. 1.1.1914. *(BK-QUE-1).*	12.50	35.00	100.
b. Series B. 15.2.1914. *(BK-QUE-1).*	12.50	35.00	100.
c. Series C. 15.4.1914. *(BK-QUE-1).*	12.50	35.00	100.

S398 2 Pesos	Good	Fine	XF
1914. Orange and yellow underprint. State arms at left, seated Indian at center right, ox-cart at right. National arms at center. Back: Red-orange. Printer: AB&PC.			
a. Series A. 1.1.1914. *(BK-QUE-2).*	15.00	45.00	125.
b. Series B. 15.2.1914. *(BK-QUE-2).*	15.00	45.00	125.

San Luis Potosí

Banco de San Luis Potosí

1897-98 Issue

S399 5 Pesos	Good	Fine	XF
1898-1913. Black on green and yellow underprint. Portrait Mariano Arista at left. State arms. Back: Green. National arms at center. Printer: ABNC.			
a. Series A. 20.7.1898. *(BK-SAN-3).*	50.00	150.	450.
b. Series A. 6.8.1900; 18.2.1901; 10.3.1903. *(BK-SAN-4).*	45.00	125.	375.
c. Series B. 10.3.1903; 8.11.1911; C. 15.10.1913. *(BK-SAN-5).*	40.00	125.	375.
d. Overprint: *CELAYA.* 1.9.1898. *(BK-SAN-7).*	60.00	175.	525.
e. Overprint: *LEÓN.* 28.2.1898. *(BK-SAN-8).*	60.00	175.	525.
p. Proof. Series A. ND.	—	Unc	500.
s. Specimen. Series. A; B; C. ND.	—	Unc	750.

S400 10 Pesos	Good	Fine	XF
1897-1913. Black on brown underprint. Female at left, seated female ("Agriculture") at right. State arms. Back: Brown. National arms at center. Printer: ABNC.			
a. Series A. 4.11.1897; 9.11.1897; 20.11.1897; 11.12.1897; 28.2.1898; 12.8.1898. *(BK-SAN-9).*	75.00	225.	675.
b. Series A; B. 18.2.1901; B. 10.3.1903. *(BK-SAN-10).*	45.00	125.	375.
c. Series C. 15.10.1913. *(BK-SAN-11).*	50.00	150.	450.
d. Overprint: *CELAYA.* 10.2.1900; 1.4.1900. *(BK-SAN-13).*	60.00	175.	525.
e. Overprint: *LEÓN.* 12.8.1898; 28.2.1898. *(BK-SAN-14).*	60.00	175.	525.
p. Proof. Series A. ND.	—	Unc	500.
s. Specimen. Series A; B. ND.	—	Unc	750.

S401 20 Pesos

1897-1913. Black on orange and yellow underprint. Two seated females ("Commerce & Agriculture") at right. State arms. Back: Orange. National arms at center. Printer: ABNC.

	Good	Fine	XF
a. Series A. 20.12.1897; 10.6.1898; 26.11.1899. *(BK-SAN-15).*	60.00	175.	525.
b. Series A. 18.1.1898; 28.2.1898; B. 26.11.1899; 18.12.1899; 28.12.1899; 18.2.1901. *(BK-SAN-16).*	50.00	150.	450.
c. Series B. 18.2.1911; 8.11.1911; C. 15.10.1913. *(BK-SAN-17).*	40.00	125.	375.
d. Overprint: *CELAYA.* 1.9.1899; 18.2.1901. *(BK-SAN-19).*	60.00	175.	525.
e. Overprint: *LEÓN.* 28.2.1898-18.2.1901. *(BK-SAN-20).*	50.00	150.	450.
p. Proof. Series A. ND.	—	Unc	500.
s. Specimen. Series A. ND.	—	Unc	750.

S402 50 Pesos

1898-1913. Black on blue underprint. Seated female with child at center. State arms. Back: Blue. National arms at center. Printer: ABNC.

	Good	Fine	XF
a. Series A. 18.5.1898; 1.2.1899; B. 18.2.1901. *(BK-SAN-21).*	225.	675.	2000.
b. Series B. 8.11.1911; C. 15.10.1913. *(BK-SAN-22).*	200.	600.	1800.
c. Overprint: *CELAYA.* 18.2.1901. *(BK-SAN-24).*	225.	675.	2000.
d. Overprint: *LEÓN.* 26.5.1898. *(BK-SAN-25).*	225.	675.	2000.
p. Proof. Series A. ND.	—	Unc	1000.
s. Speciman. Series A. ND.	—	Unc	1250.

S403 100 Pesos

(ca.1897-1913). Black on yellow, orange and red underprint. Seated female ("Commerce") at right. State arms. Back: Red. National arms at center. Printer: ABNC.

	Good	Fine	XF
a. Series A. 1.6.1899. *(BK-SAN-26).*	450.	1350.	4000.
b. Series B. 18.2.1901; 6.12.1909. *(BK-SAN-27).*	400.	1200.	3600.
c. Overprint: *LEÓN.* 8.12.1898. *(BK-SAN-29).*	525.	1575.	4600.
p. Proof. Series A. ND.	—	Unc	1250.
s1. Specimen. Series A. ND.	—	Unc	1500.
s2. Specimen. Series C. ND.	—	Unc	1500.

S404 500 Pesos

1897-1913. Black on olive-green underprint. Mining scene at right. State arms. Back: Olive-green. National arms at left. Printer: ABNC.

	Good	Fine	XF
a. Series A. 21.6.1900. *(BK-SAN-30).*	1500.	4500.	13,000.
b. Series B. 18.2.1901. *(BK-SAN-30).*	1500.	4500.	13,000.
p. Proof. Series A. ND.	—	Unc	2250.
s1. Specimen. Series A. ND.	—	Unc	2500.
s2. Specimen. Series C. ND.	—	Unc	2500.

S405 1000 Pesos

ND (ca.1897-1913). Black on orange and yellow underprint. Portrait Mariano Arista at center. State arms. Back: Orange. National arms at center. Printer: ABNC. *(BK-SAN-32s).*

	Good	Fine	XF
p. Proof. Series A. ND.	—	Unc	2250.
s1. Specimen. Series A. ND.	—	Unc	2500.
s2. Specimen. Series B. ND.	—	Unc	2500.
s3. Specimen. Series C. ND.	—	Unc	2500.

1914 Issue

S406 1 Peso

	Good	Fine	XF
15.2.1914. Orange and black. State arms at center right, bank building at left. Series D. Back: Red. National arms at center. Printer: AB&PC. *(BK-SAN-1).*	7.50	20.00	60.00

S407 2 Pesos

	Good	Fine	XF
15.2.1914. Green and black. State arms at center right, bank building at left. Series D. Back: Green. National arms at center. Printer: AB&PC. *(BK-SAN-2).*	7.50	20.00	60.00

Sinaloa

Banco Occidental de México

1898-1913 Issue

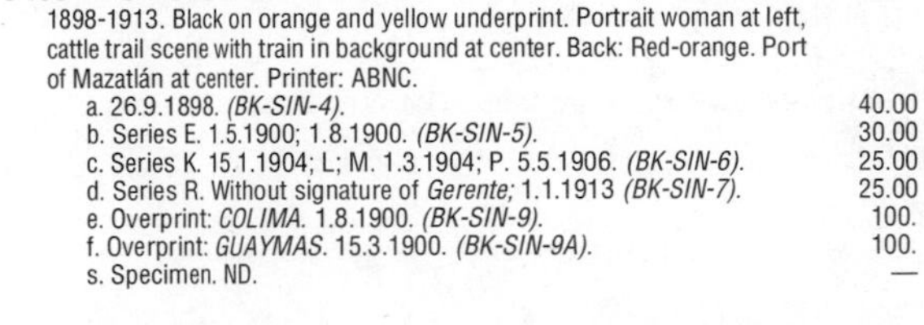

S408 5 Pesos

1898-1913. Black on orange and yellow underprint. Portrait woman at left, cattle trail scene with train in background at center. Back: Red-orange. Port of Mazatlán at center. Printer: ABNC.

	Good	Fine	XF
a. 26.9.1898. *(BK-SIN-4).*	40.00	120.	360.
b. Series E. 1.5.1900; 1.8.1900. *(BK-SIN-5).*	30.00	100.	300.
c. Series K. 15.1.1904; L; M. 1.3.1904; P. 5.5.1906. *(BK-SIN-6).*	25.00	75.00	225.
d. Series R. Without signature of *Gerente;* 1.1.1913 *(BK-SIN-7).*	25.00	75.00	225.
e. Overprint: *COLIMA.* 1.8.1900. *(BK-SIN-9).*	100.	300.	900.
f. Overprint: *GUAYMAS.* 15.3.1900. *(BK-SIN-9A).*	100.	300.	900.
s. Specimen. ND.	—	Unc	750.

S409 10 Pesos

1900-13. Black on green underprint. Portrait woman at left, train at center. Back: Green. Port of Mazatlán at center. Printer: ABNC.

	Good	Fine	XF
a. Series M; R. 1.4.1900-1.3.1904. *(BK-SIN-10).*	30.00	100.	300.
b. Series R. 16.10.1909. *(BK-SIN-11).*	25.00	75.00	225.
c. 1.1.1913. *(BK-SIN-12).*	30.00	100.	300.
d. Overprint: *COLIMA.* Series F. 1.8.1900. *(BK-SIN-14).*	40.00	120.	360.
e. Overprint: *GUAYMAS.* 15.3.1900. *(BK-SIN-15).*	45.00	125.	375.
s. Specimen. ND.	—	Unc	1000.

S410 20 Pesos

1900-13. Black on brown underprint. Sailor standing at left and right, portrait woman at center. Back: Brown. Port of Mazatlán at center. Printer: ABNC.

	Good	Fine	XF
a. Series D. 15.3.1900; 1.4.1900; E. 1.5.1900; G. 1.9.1900; 15.10.1900; N. 1.3.1904. *(BK-SIN-16).*	300.	900.	2750.
b. 1.1.1913. *(BK-SIN-17).*	350.	1000.	3000.
c. Overprint: *PAGADERO EN COLIMA.* Series G. 1.8.1900; 15.10.1900. *(BK-SIN-19).*	300.	900.	2700.
d. Overprint: *PAGADERO EN GUAYMAS.* 1.12.1900. *(BK-SIN-20).*	300.	900.	2700.
s. Specimen.	—	Unc	1250.

S411 50 Pesos

1898-1904. Black on blue and yellow underprint. Standing Themis (Justice) at left, portrait woman at center, seated winged male at right. Back: Blue. Port of Mazatlán at center. Printer: ABNC.

	Good	Fine	XF
a. Series B. 1.1.1900; G. 1.9.1900; N. 1.3.1904. *(BK-SIN-1).*	900.	2700.	7500.
b. Overprint: *PAGADERO EN CULIACÁN.* 25.10.1898. *(BK-SIN-24).*	900.	2700.	7500.
c. Overprint: *PAGADERO EN GUAYMAS.* Series C. 15.3.1900. *(BK-SIN-25).*	800.	2400.	7250.
d. Overprint: *COLIMA.* Series H. 15.10.1900. *(BK-SIN-26).*	800.	2400.	7250.
s. Specimen.	—	Unc	1250.

S412 100 Pesos

1900. Black on red and yellow underprint. Cherubs at left and right. Supporting portrait of woman at left center. Back: Red. Port of Mazatlán at center. Printer: ABNC.

	Good	Fine	XF
a. Series C. 1.1.1900; D. 1.4.1900; G. 1.9.1900; H. 15.10.1900; I. 1.12.1900. *(BK-SIN-27).*	600.	1800.	5400.
b. Overprint: *PAGADERO EN GUAYMAS.* Series C. 15.3.1900. *(BK-SIN-29).*	625.	1850.	5500.
c. Overprint: *PAGADERO EN COLIMA.* ND; 15.10.1900; *(BK-SIN-30).*	625.	1850.	5500.

NOTE: For #S409-S412, notes dated ca.1898 are reported in archive records. No issued examples are known.

S413 500 Pesos

ND (ca. 1900). Black on olive-green underprint. Woman at left, Aztec calendar at right center. Back: Olive-green. Port of Mazatlán at center. Printer: ABNC.

	Good	Fine	XF
p. Proof.	—	Unc	1000.
s. Specimen. *(BK-SIN-31s).*	—	Unc	1250.

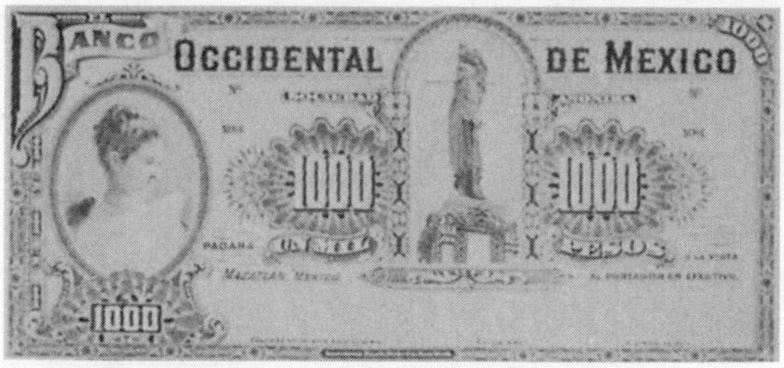

S414 1000 Pesos

ND (ca.1900). Black on brown underprint. Portrait woman at left, monument to Cuauhtémoc at center. Back: Dark brown. Portrait of Mazatlan at center. Printer: ABNC.

	Good	Fine	XF
p. Proof. *(BK-SIN-32).*	—	Unc	1000.
s. Specimen. *(BK-SIN-33s).*	—	Unc	1250.

Banco de San Ignacio (Ignatio)

1878 Issue

S415 Dos (2) Reales

	Good	Fine	XF
1878. Black. Woman at center. Back: Green. Man at center. Printer: S. C. Toof & Co. Lith., Memphis, TN. *(BK-SIN-1).*	20.00	60.00	175.

S416 Quatro (4) Reales

	Good	Fine	XF
1878. Printer: S. C. Toof & Co. Lith., Memphis, TN. Reported not confirmed.	—	—	—

S417 1 Peso

	Good	Fine	XF
1878. Black. Woman hugging child at upper left. Series A. Back: Green. Dog's head at center. Printer: S. C. Toof & Co. Lith., Memphis, TN. *(BK-SIN-2).*	100.	300.	900.

S418 5 Pesos

	Good	Fine	XF
1878. Farm family with horse and wagon at left. Series A. Back: Steam train by station at center. Printer: S. C. Toof & Co. Lith., Memphis, TN. *(BK-SIN-3).*	300.	900.	2700.

Sonora

Banco de Sonora

1897-1911 Issue

S419 5 Pesos	Good	Fine	XF
1897-1911. Black on brown and yellow underprint. Portrait Hortensia C. Vélez at left, cherub at left center, female ("Strength") at right. Back: Brown. Printer: ABNC.			
a. Series B. 4.4.1898; 1.8.1899. *(BK-SON-1).*	60.00	175.	525.
b. 1.7.1901-24.11.1909. *(BK-SON-2).*	15.00	45.00	125.
c. Series CK. 2.1.1911. *(BK-SON-3).*	12.50	35.00	100.
d. Overprint: *CHIHUAHUA.* 1.7.1903/1902. *(BK-SON-4).*	60.00	175.	525.
p. Proof. Series E. 1.7.1902. Back dark brown with brown underprint.	—	Unc	1000.
r. Unissued remainder. Series DI; DN; DU; DZ. (ND). *(BK-SON-5).*	—	—	25.00
s. Specimen.	—	Unc	1250.

NOTE: Reports of specific dates from 1897-1911 are requested.

S420 10 Pesos	Good	Fine	XF
1897-1911. Black on green and yellow underprint. Portrait Hortensia C. Vélez at left, cowboys and cattle scene at right. Back: Green. Printer: ABNC.			
NOTE: reports of specific dates from 1897-1911 are needed			
a. 1.9.1899; 1.11.1899. *(BK-SON-7).*	60.00	175.	525.
b. Grill underprint on back with printed signature. 1.7.1902-14.8.1906/1.1.1906; 24.11.1909. *(BK-SON-8).*	30.00	100.	300.
c. Series DD; DJ. 2.1.1911. *(BK-SON-9).*	4.00	12.50	35.00
d. Overprint: *CHIHUAHUA.* 1.7.1903/2. *(BK-SON-10).*	60.00	175.	525.
p. Proof. Series B. 1.7.1902. Back dark green with green underprint.	—	Unc	750.
r. Unissued remainder. Series DL; DM; DO; DT; DQ; DU. (ND). *(BK-SON-11).*	—	—	30.00
s. Specimen. Series B. 1.7.1902.	—	Unc	1000.

NOTE: Backs for #S419 and S420 *EL* in bank title (ca.1897-99). Later dates with out *EL* on back.

S421 20 Pesos	Good	Fine	XF
1897-1911. Black on orange and yellow underprint. Reclining female ("River Source") at left, portrait Hortensia C. Vélez at right. Back: Orange. Printer: ABNC.			
a. 1.6.1899. *(BK-SON-12).*	75.00	225.	675.
b. 1.7.1901-24.11.1909. *(BK-SON-13).*	60.00	175.	525.
c. Series DL; DP; DR; DS. 2.1.1911. *(BK-SON-14).*	45.00	125.	375.
p. Proof. Series B. 1.7.1902. Back dark orange with orange underprint.	—	Unc	750.
r. Unissued remainder. Series DT; DU; DV. ND. *(BK-SON-15).*	—	—	30.00
s. Specimen. Series B. 1.7.1902.	—	Unc	1000.

NOTE: Reports of specific dates from 1897-1911 are requested.

S422 50 Pesos	Good	Fine	XF
1899-1911. Black on green and yellow underprint. Men working at left, portrait Hortensia C. Vélez at right. Back: Blue-gray. Head of allegorical woman at center. Printer: ABNC.			
a. Series CF. 1.12.1899. *(BK-SON-16).*	125.	375.	1100.
b. Printed signature. Grill underprint on back. 1.7.1901-24.11.1909. *(BK-SON-17).*	100.	300.	900.
c. Series CF. 2.1.1911. *(BK-SON-18).*	100.	300.	900.
p. Proof. Series M. 1.7.1902. Back blue-black with blue-gray underprint.	—	Unc	750.
r. Remainder. Series DP-DT; DW; DX. (ND). *(BK-SON-19).*	—	—	50.00
s. Specimen. Series M. 1.7.1902.	—	Unc	1000.

NOTE: Reports of specific dates from 1897-1911 are requested.

S423 100 Pesos	Good	Fine	XF
1898-1911. Black on olive-brown and yellow underprint. Portrait Hortensia C. Vélez at left, sailing ships at center. Back: Olive-brown. Printer: ABNC.			
a. Series CP. 1.11.1898. *(BK-SON-20).*	450.	1350.	4000.
b. Grill underprint on back. 1.7.1903/1902-1.1.1906. *(BK-SON-21).*	375.	1100.	3300.
c. Series CL; CP. 2.1.1911. *(BK-SON-22).*	375.	1100.	3300.
p. Proof. Series D. 1.7.1902. Back olive-green with light olive underprint.	—	Unc	750.
r. Remainder. Series DR; DT; DV; DW; DX; DZ. (ND). *(BK-SON-23).*	—	—	50.00
s. Specimen. Series D. 1.7.1902.	—	Unc	1000.

NOTE: Reports of specific dates from 1897-1911 are requested.

Tabasco

Banco de Tabasco

1901-03 Issue

S424 5 Pesos	Good	Fine	XF
1901-03. Black on green and yellow underprint. State arms at left, Marina "La Malinche" at right. Back: Green. Villahermosa on the Grijalva River at center. Printer: ABNC.			
a. 1.1.1901; 15.10.1901; 19.9.1903. *(BK-TAB-1).*	30.00	100.	300.
b. Needle punched: *LAGUNA.* 19.9.1903. *(BK-TAB-2).*	150.	450.	1250.
c. Overprint: *PICHUCALCO.* 19.9.1903. *(BK-TAB-3).*	40.00	125.	375.

S425 10 Pesos — Good | Fine | XF

1901-03. Black on orange and yellow underprint. Government Palace at right. Back: Orange. Villahermosa on the Grijalva River at center. Printer: ABNC.

	Good	Fine	XF
a. 1.1.1901; 15.10.1901; 19.9.1903. *(BK-TAB-5).*	75.00	225.	675.
b. Overprint: *PICHUCALCO.* 19.9.1903. *(BK-TAB-6).*	100.	300.	900.
c. Needle punched: *LAGUNA.* 19.3.1903. *(BK-TAB-7).*	150.	450.	1300.
s. Specimen. 1903.	—	Unc	1000.

S426 20 Pesos — Good 1200. | Fine 3600. | XF 11,000.

1.1.1901. Black on blue and yellow underprint. Lumberjacks cutting trees at left. Series A. Back: Blue. Villahermosa on the Grijalva River at center. Printer: ABNC. *(BK-TAB-9).*

S427 50 Pesos — Good 600. | Fine 1800. | XF 5400.

1.1.1901. Black on olive-green underprint. Vaquero herding cattle at left, workers picking fruits at right. Series A. Back: Greenish brown. Villahermosa on the Grijalva River at center. Printer: ABNC. *(BK-TAB-11).*

S428 100 Pesos — Good 1500. | Fine 4500. | XF 13,000.

1.1.1901. Black on red and yellow underprint. Palm tree at left, harvesting of sugar cane at center right. Series A. Back: Red. Villahermosa on the Grijalva River at center. Printer: ABNC. *(BK-TAB-13).*

Tamaulipas

Crédito del Estado de Tamaulipas

1876 Emergency Issue

S428A 12 1/2 Centavos = Un Real — Good 25.00 | Fine 75.00 | XF 225.

1876. Violet. Oval black seals: *gobierno del estado* above eagle and *SECRETARIO DEL GOBIERNO DE TAMAULIPAS.*

S428B 25 Centavos = 4 Reales — Good 12.50 | Fine 35.00 | XF 100.

1876. Violet. Oval black seals: *gobierno del estado* above eagle and *SECRETARIO DEL GOBIERNO DE TAMAULIPAS.*

S428C 50 Centavos — Good 12.50 | Fine 35.00 | XF 100.

1876. Gray. Oval black seals: *gobierno del estado* above eagle and *SECRETARIO DEL GOBIERNO DE TAMAULIPAS.* Paper: Pale lilac.

S428D 1 Peso — Good 12.50 | Fine 35.00 | XF 100.

1876. Pale brown. Oval black seals: *gobierno del estado* above eagle and *SECRETARIO DEL GOBIERNO DE TAMAULIPAS.*

S428E 5 Pesos — Good 25.00 | Fine 75.00 | XF 225.

1876. Gray-blue. Oval black seals: *gobierno del estado* above eagle and *SECRETARIO DEL GOBIERNO DE TAMAULIPAS.*

S428F 10 Pesos — Good 25.00 | Fine 75.00 | XF 225.

1876. Pale brown. Oval black seals: *gobierno del estado* above eagle and *SECRETARIO DEL GOBIERNO DE TAMAULIPAS.*

S428G 25 Pesos — Good 25.00 | Fine 75.00 | XF 225.

1876. Pale brown. Oval black seals: *gobierno del estado* above eagle and *SECRETARIO DEL GOBIERNO DE TAMAULIPAS.*

Banco de Tamaulipas

1902 Issue

S429 5 Pesos

1902-14. Black on green underprint. Portrait Guadalupe Obregón (as a child) at center. Back: Green. Dogs at shoreline, man in canoe at center. Printer: ABNC.

	Good	Fine	XF
a. Series A. 15.10.1902; B. 15.11.1902; C. 15.7.1903; 12.12.1910. *(BK-TAM-3).*	12.50	35.00	100.
b. Series D. 25.10.1911; E. 25.10.1911; F. 21.1.1913; 31.8.1913. *(BK-TAM-4).*	7.50	20.00	60.00
c. Series G. 31.3.1914; H. 21.4.1914. *(BK-TAM-5).*	5.00	15.00	45.00
d. Series H. (ND). *(BK-TAM-7)*	2.50	7.50	20.00
p. Proof.	—	Unc	500.
r. Unsigned remainder. Series G; H. 31.3.1914. *(BK-TAM-6).*	—	—	25.00
s. Specimen. Series H.	—	Unc	750.

S430 10 Pesos

1902-14. Black on orange and light green underprint. Cattle at center. Back: Orange. Dogs at shoreline, man in canoe at center. Printer: ABNC.

	Good	Fine	XF
a. Series A. 15.10.1902; C. 15.7.1903. *(BK-TAM-10).*	30.00	100.	300.
b. Series D. 12.12.1910; E. 25.10.1911; F. 31.8.1913; 10.1.1914. *(BK-TAM-11).*	25.00	75.00	225.
c. Series H. (ND). *(BK-TAM-12).*	5.00	15.00	45.00
p. Proof.	—	Unc	500.
s1. Specimen. Series B. 190x.	—	Unc	750.
s2. Specimen. Series D. 190x.	—	Unc	750.
s3. Specimen. Series G. 31.3.1914.	—	Unc	750.

S431 20 Pesos

1902-14. Black on blue and light green underprint. Train at center. Back: Blue. Dogs at shoreline, man in canoe at center. Printer: ABNC.

	Good	Fine	XF
a. Series A. 15.10.1902; C. 15.7.1903. *(BK-TAM-14).*	100.	300.	900.
b. Series D. 12.12.1910; F. 31.8.1913. *(BK-TAM-15).*	75.00	225.	675.
c. Series H. 21.4.1914. *(BK-TAM-15).*	75.00	225.	675.
d. Series H. (ND). *(BK-TAM-17).*	7.50	20.00	60.00
p. Proof.	—	Unc	500.
r. Unsigned remainder. Series G. 31.3.1914. *(BK-TAM-16).*	—	—	50.00
s. Specimen. Series D; H. 190x.	—	Unc	750.

S432 50 Pesos

1902-14. Black on brown and yellow underprint. Two females representing Commerce at center. Back: Brown. Dogs at shoreline, man in canoe at center. Printer: ABNC.

	Good	Fine	XF
a. Series A. 15.10.1902; C. 15.7.1903. *(BK-TAM-18).*	375.	1100.	3300.
b. Series D. 12.12.1910; F. 10.1.1914. *(BK-TAM-19).*	300.	900.	2700.
c. Series H. 21.4.1914. *(BK-TAM-19).*	300.	900.	2700.
d. Series H. (ND). *(BK-TAM-21).*	30.00	100.	300.
p. Proof.	—	Unc	500.
r. Unsigned remainder. Series G. 31.3.1914. *(BK-TAM-20).*	40.00	125.	375.
s. Specimen. Series H.	—	Unc	750.

S433 100 Pesos

1902-14. Black on olive-green underprint. Sailing ships at center. Back: Dark green. Dogs at shoreline, man in canoe at center. Printer: ABNC.

	Good	Fine	XF
a. Series B. 15.10.1902; C. 15.7.1903. *(BK-TAM-23).*	450.	1350.	4000.
b. Series D. 12.12.1910. *(BK-TAM-24).*	300.	900.	2700.
c. Series F. 10.1.1914. *(BK-TAM-24).*	375.	1100.	3300.
p. Proof. Series A. 190x (ca.1902).	—	Unc	500.
r1. Remainder. Series G. 31.3.1914. *(BK-TAM-26).*	—	—	375.
r2. Remainder. Series H. (ND). *(BK-TAM-27).*	—	—	225.
s1. Specimen. Series A. 190x.	—	Unc	750.
s2. Specimen. Series D. 190x (ca.1903).	—	Unc	750.
s3. Specimen. Series H. ND.	—	Unc	750.

S434 500 Pesos

(ca.1902-14). Black on red and yellow underprint. Workers at docks at left, portrait Juan de la Garza at center. Back: Red. Dogs at shoreline, man in canoe at center. Printer: ABNC.

	Good	Fine	XF
a. Series H. 21.4.1914. *(BK-TAM-29).*	1000.	3000.	9000.
p. Proof. Series A. 190x (ca.1902).	—	Unc	1250.
r. Unsigned remainder. Series G. 31.3.1914. *(BK-TAM-30).*	—	—	1000.
s1. Specimen. Series A. 190x (ca.1903).	—	Unc	1500.
s2. Specimen. Series C. 190x (ca.1903).	—	Unc	1500.
s3. Specimen. Without series. ND.	—	Unc	1500.

S435 1000 Pesos	Good	Fine	XF
(ca.1902-14). Black on olive-brown underprint. Two seated females with a child between them at center right. Back: Brown. Dogs at shoreline, man in canoe at center. Printer: ABNC.			
a. Series B. 15.10.1902. *(BK-TAM-32).*	3000.	9000.	27,000.
p. Proof. Series A. 190x (ca.1902).	—	Unc	1250.
r. Unsigned remainder. Series G. 31.3.1914. *(BK-TAM-33).*	—	—	1000.
s1. Specimen. Series A. 190x.	—	Unc	1500.
s2. Specimen. Series D. 190x (ca.1903).	—	Unc	1500.
s3. Specimen. Without series. ND.	—	Unc	1500.

1914 Issue

S436 1 Peso	Good	Fine	XF
15.2.1914. Black on orange underprint. Oil rigs, storage tanks, steam freight train and tanker ship at upper center. Series 1A:1J; 1A:1P. 2 signature varieties. Back: Red. Standing Mercury on dock, sailing ship and fortress in background at center. Printer: AB&PC. *(BK-TAM-1).*	7.50	20.00	60.00

Veracruz

El Banco de Veracruz

1890 Issue

S436A 1 Peso Fuerte	Good	Fine	XF
1.9.1890. Portrait Prosperity at lower left, national arms at right. Series A. Printer: BWC.	25.00	75.00	225.

A WORD ON DATE RANGES

Often date ranges or specific dates are listed. These have been observed or reported by our contributors. If a note is outside the published range, it only means that it is a newly reported date, and not necessarily worthy of a premium value.

Banco Mercantil de Veracruz

1898-1910 Issue

S437 5 Pesos	Good	Fine	XF
1898-1910. Black on green and yellow underprint. Seated female at center. Back: Green. Harbor of Veracruz. Blue stamp and red seal. Printer: ABNC.			
a. 15.3.1898. *(BK-VER-1).*	15.00	45.00	125.
b. 20.2.1902-8.11.1905. *(BK-VER-2).*	15.00	45.00	125.
c. 13.4.1910. *(BK-VER-3).*	12.50	35.00	110.
d. Overprint: *ORIZABA.* 14.4.1904. *(BK-VER-5).*	25.00	75.00	225.
e. Overprint: *ANDRÉS TUXTLA* 15.7.1905. *(BK-VER-6).*	25.00	75.00	225.
f. Overprint: *XALAPA.* 14.4.1904. *(BK-VER-7).*	25.00	75.00	225.
p. Proof. Without series. ND.	—	Unc	500.
s. Specimen. Without series. ND.	—	Unc	750.

S438 10 Pesos	Good	Fine	XF
15.3.1898. Black on brown and yellow underprint. Steam passenger train at left, sugar cane harvest at center, pine tree at right. Back: Brown. Harbor of Veracruz. Printer: ABNC. *(BK-VER-8).*			
a. Issued note.	2250.	6750.	19,500.
p. Proof. Without series. ND.	—	Unc	2250.
s. Specimen. Without series. ND.	—	Unc	2500.

S439 10 Pesos	Good	Fine	XF
1900-14. Black on brown and yellow underprint. Portrait Miguel Lerdo de Tejada at left. Back: Blue. Harbor of Veracruz. Printer: ABNC.			
a. 2.4.1900. *(BK-VER-9).*	60.00	100.	300.
b. 31.8.1903-8.11.1905. *(BK-VER-10).*	25.00	75.00	225.
c. 13.4.1910; 20.4.1914. *(BK-VER-11).*	15.00	45.00	125.
d. Overprint: *ORIZABA.* 14.4.1904. *(BK-VER-13).*	25.00	75.00	225.
e. Overprint: *XALAPA.* 14.4.1904. *(BK-VER-15).*	25.00	75.00	225.
f. Overprint: *S. ANDRÉS TUXTLA. 15.7.1905. (BK-VER-14).*	25.00	75.00	225.
p. Proof. Without series. ND.	—	Unc	500.
s. Specimen. Without series. ND.	—	Unc	750.

S440 20 Pesos

1898-1905. Black on olive-green and yellow underprint. Seated woman with fruit at center. Back: Olive-green. Harbor of Veracruz. Orange stamp and blue seal. Printer: ABNC.

	Good	Fine	XF
a. 15.3.1898. *(BK-VER-16).*	75.00	225.	675.
b. 20.2.1902-8.2.1905. *(BK-VER-17).*	75.00	225.	675.
c. Overprint: *ORIZABA.* 14.4.1904. *(BK-VER-19).*	75.00	225.	675.
d. Overprint: *XALAPA.* 14.4.1904. *(BK-VER-20).*	75.00	225.	675.
p. Proof. Without series. ND.	—	Unc	500.
s. Specimen. Without series. ND.	—	Unc	750.

S441 50 Pesos

1898-1905. Black on orange and yellow underprint. Sailing ships at center. Back: Orange. Harbor of Veracruz. Printer: ABNC.

	Good	Fine	XF
a. 15.3.1898. *(BK-VER-21).*	150.	450.	1300.
b. 31.8.1903; 8.11.1905. *(BK-VER-22).*	150.	450.	1300.
c. Overprint: *S. ANDRÉS TUXTLA.* 15.7.1905. *(BK-VER-24).*	200.	600.	1800.
d. Overprint: *ORIZABA.* 14.4.1904.	150.	450.	1350.
p. Proof. Without series. ND.	—	Unc	750.
s. Specimen. Without series. ND.	—	Unc	1000.

S442 100 Pesos

(ca.1898-1914). Black on blue and yellow underprint. Horsemen and steam passenger train at center. Back: Blue-gray. Harbor of Veracruz. Green stamp and blue seal. Printer: ABNC.

	Good	Fine	XF
a. 15.3.1898. *(BK-VER-25).*	425.	1300.	3900.
b. 20.2.1902-15.7.1905; 8.11.1905. *(BK-VER-26).*	375.	1150.	3450.
d. Overprint: *ORIZABA.* 14.4.1904. *(BK-VER-29).*	375.	1150.	3450.
e. Overprint: *XALAPA.* 14.4.1904. *(BK-VER-30).*	425.	1300.	3900.
p. Proof. Without series. ND.	—	Unc	1250.
r. Unissued remainder. Perforated: *PAGADO;* ND. *(BK-VER-27).*	200	600	1800
s. Specimen. Without series. ND.	—	Unc	1250.

S443 500 Pesos

15.3.1898. Black on orange and yellow underprint. Sailing ships at center, steam train at upper right. Back: Red. Harbor of Veracruz. Printer: ABNC. *(BK-VER-31).*

	Good	Fine	XF
a. Issued note.	1100.	3300.	10,000.
p. Proof. Without series. ND.	—	Unc	1750.
s. Specimen. Without series. ND.	—	Unc	2000.

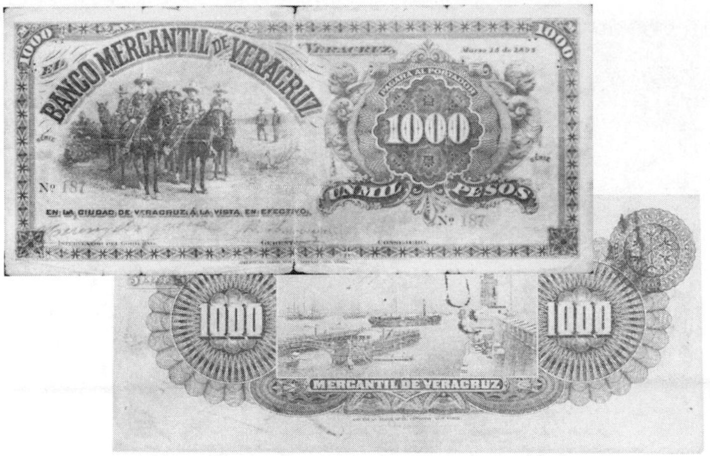

S444 1000 Pesos

(ca.1898-1914). Black on yellow and purple underprint. Group of horsemen at left. Back: Purple. Harbor of Veracruz. Printer: ABNC. *(BK-VER-33).*

	Good	Fine	XF
a. 15.3.1898.	2000.	6000.	18,000.
p. Proof. Without series. ND.	—	Unc	1750.
s. Specimen. Without series. ND.	—	Unc	2250.

NOTE: For #S437-S444, reports of specific dates from 1898-1914 are requested.

Yucatán

Banco Mercantil de Yucatán

1890-92 Issue

S445 1 Peso

1.2.1892. Green on orange underprint. Locomotive at left, seated female ("Mechanics") at right. Back: Green. Printer: HLBNC. *(BK-YUC-31).*

	Good	Fine	XF
	450.	1350.	4000.

S446 5 Pesos

1890. Black on blue and brown underprint. Female head with Liberty cap at left, ship dockside at center right. Back: Blue. Helmeted man's head at center. Printer: HLBNC. Proof. *(BK-YUC-34).*

	Good	Fine	XF
	—	Unc	1250.

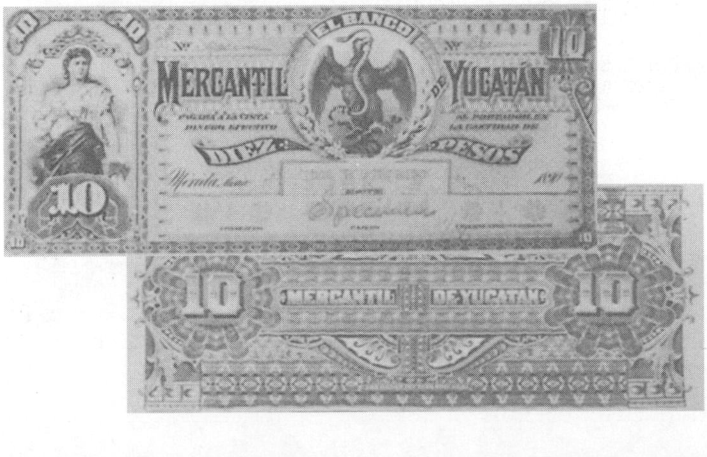

S447 10 Pesos	Good	Fine	XF
1890. Black on blue and orange underprint. Woman at left, national arms at center right. Back: Blue. Printer: HLBNC. Proof. *(BK-YUC-39).*	—	Unc	1250.

S448 20 Pesos	Good	Fine	XF
1890. Black on brown and blue underprint. Indian warrior at left, female at right. Back: Brown. Printer: HLBNC. Proof. *(BK-YUC-43).*	—	Unc	1250.

S449 50 Pesos	Good	Fine	XF
9.4.1890. Dog's head at left, reclining female ("Science") at right. Back: Brown. Steam locomotive at center. Printer: HLBNC. *(BK-YUC-46).*			
a. Issued note.	2250.	6750.	19,500.
p. Proof. 189x.	—	Unc	1250.

S450 100 Pesos	Good	Fine	XF
30.6.1893. Seated female ("Reverie") at left, portrait Miguel Hidalgo at right. Back: Green. Printer: HLBNC.	—	Unc	1250.

S451 500 Pesos	Good	Fine	XF
189x. Seated woman with anchor, sailing ships in background at left, dog's head at right. Back: Orange. National arms at left. Printer: HLBNC. Proof. *(BK-YUC-58).*	—	Unc	1250.

S452 1000 Pesos	Good	Fine	XF
1890. Steam train crossing viaduct bridge with merchants below at left, two females ("Prosperity") overlooking the harvest at right. Back: Blue. Helmeted man at lower left and right center, national arms at center. Printer: HLBNC. Proof. *(BK-YUC-61).*	—	Unc	1250.

NOTE: For #S446-S452, an issue with the printed date *189x* was reportedly made. Only #S449 and S451 have been confirmed with this style so far.

1897-1900 Issue

S452A 5 Pesos	Good	Fine	XF
30.8.1897. Black on green and yellow underprint. Allegorical woman reading, reclining on sacks and barrels at center. Series B. Back: Green. Printer: ABNC. *(BK-YUC-36).*	2250.	6750.	19,500.

NOTE: Reports of specific dates from 1897-1904 are requested.

S453 5 Pesos	Good	Fine	XF
1898-ca.1903. Black on green and yellow underprint. Allegorical woman reading, reclining on sacks and barrels at center. Similar to #S452A, but with text: *A LA PAR* added at left. Back: Green. Printer: ABNC.			
p. Proof. Series C. 1898.	—	Unc	1750.
s1. Specimen. Series D. 1899.	—	Unc	2000.
s2. Specimen. Series G. Dec.190x.	—	Unc	2000.
s3. Specimen. Series H. 190x (ca.1903).	—	Unc	2000.
s4. Specimen. Series C. 1898.	—	Unc	2000.

NOTE: Reports of specific dates from 1897-1904 are requested.

S454 10 Pesos	Good	Fine	XF
1900-04. Black on blue and yellow underprint. Seated female and boy ("Industries") at left. Back: Blue-gray. Printer: ABNC.			
a. Series H. Perforated: *CANCELADO;* 28.5.1904. *(BK-YUC-41).*	15.00	45.00	125.
p. Proof. Without series. ND.	—	Unc	500.
s. Specimen. Series G. Dec.190x.	—	Unc	750.

NOTE: Reports of specific dates from 1897-1904 are requested.

S455 50 Pesos

1897. Black on orange, yellow and brown underprint. Gypsy woman ("Haidee") at left, female head with Liberty cap ("Liberty") at right. Similar to #S456, but *PORTADOR EN DINERO* at upper center right. Printer: ABNC.

	Good	Fine	XF
p1. Proof. Without series. ND.	—	Unc	1000.
p2. Proof. Series B. 1897.	—	Unc	1000.
s. Specimen. Series G. Dec.190x.	—	Unc	1250.

NOTE: Reports of specific dates from 1897-1904 are requested.

S456 50 Pesos

1898-1904. Black on orange, yellow and brown underprint. Gypsy woman ("Haidee") at left, female head with Liberty cap ("Liberty") at right. *PORTADOR* above denomination numeral at upper center, *A LA PAR* added at upper center right. Back: Brown. Printer: ABNC.

	Good	Fine	XF
a. Series C. 28.6.1898; 18.11.1899; 1.5.1900. *(BK-YUC-49).*	225.	675.	2000.
p1. Proof. Without series. ND.	—	Unc	1000.
p2. Proof. Series B. 1897.	—	Unc	1000.
s1. Specimen. Series C. 1898.	—	Unc	1250.
s2. Specimen. Series D. 1899.	—	Unc	1250.
s3. Specimen. Series E. 1900.	—	Unc	1250.
s4. Specimen. Series G. Dec.190x.	—	Unc	1250.
s5. Specimen. Series H. 190x (ca.1903).	—	Unc	1250.

NOTE: Reports of specific dates from 1897-1904 are requested.

S457 100 Pesos

1900-04. Black on olive-brown underprint. Columbus and his men sighting land at left, two standing females ("North and South") at right. Back: Olive-brown. Printer: ABNC.

	Good	Fine	XF
a. Series G. 1900. *(BK-YUC-55).*	1200.	3600.	11,000.
b. Series B. 10.11.1900; 10.12.1900; 28.3.1904.	525.	1575.	5000.
p1. Proof. Without series. ND.	—	Unc	1250.
p2. Proof. Series G. Dec.190x.	—	Unc	1250.
s. Specimen. Series G. 1900.	—	Unc	1500.

NOTE: Reports of specific dates from 1897-1904 are requested.

S457A 500 Pesos

(ca.1900-04). Black on yellow and purple underprint. Seated woman and child with books ("Study") at left. Back: Purple. Women's head at center. Printer: ABNC.

	Good	Fine	XF
p1. Proof. Without series. ND.	—	Unc	1250.
p2. Proof. Series G. Dec.190x.	—	Unc	1250.
s1. Specimen. Series F. 1900.	—	Unc	1500.
s2. Specimen. Series H. 190x.	—	Unc	1500.

NOTE: Reports of specific dates from 1897-1904 are requested.

Banco Peninsular Mexicano

1893-1901 Provisional Issues

#S458-S460 overprint new bank name on notes of the Banco Yucateco.

S458 5 Pesos

29.6.1901; 1.10.1903. Black on red-orange and yellow underprint. Steam locomotive at left, men working dockside at right. Back: Red-orange. Allegorical figures at left and center right. Overprint: On #S467.

	Good	Fine	XF
a. 29.6.1901; 1.10.1903. *(BK-YUC-7).*	20.00	60.00	175.
b. Overprint: *SUCURSAL DE CÁRMEN* and perforated: *CAMPECHE;* 1.10.1903. *(BK-YUC-9).*	25.00	75.00	225.
c. Purple handstamp: *SUCURSAL EN CÁRMEN* and perforated: *LAGUNA, CAMPECHE.* ND *(BK-YUC-9).*	60.00	175.	525.
r. Remainder. Without series. 2 signatures handwritten.	—	—	100.

S459 10 Pesos

1897-1904. Black on green and yellow underprint. Helmeted female head ("Minerva No. 3") and seated female ("National Emblems") at left, man feeding horse at right. Back: Dark green. Overprint: On #S468. *(BK-YUC-14).*

	Good	Fine	XF
a. Perforated: *CAMPECHE.* 1.11.1897; 6.10.1898. *(BK-YUC-15).*	25.00	75.00	225.
b. Overprint: *Sucursal de Campeche* and perforated: *CAMPECHE.* 9.8.1898; 6.10.1898. *(BK-YUC-16).*	30.00	100.	300.
c. Overprint: *Sucursal en Cármen, Campeche* and perforated: *LAGUNA.* ND. *(BK-YUC-17).*	60.00	175.	525.
d. Without branch overprint. Handwritten date. 1.8.1897; 7.1.1899; 29.6.1901.	60.00	175.	525.
e. Without branch overprint. Engraved date. 1.10.1903.	30.00	100.	300.

S460 20 Pesos

1895-1902. Black on blue and yellow underprint. Two female ("Union") at left center, seated woman with sheaf and water jug at right. Back: Blue. Overprint: On #S469.

	Good	Fine	XF
a. 11.9.1895-11.11.1902. *(BK-YUC-21).*	25.00	75.00	225.
b. Overprint: *Sucursal en Campeche* and perforated: *CAMPECHE.* 1.11.1897; 10.5.1898; 7.6.1898. *(BK-YUC-22).*	45.00	125.	375.

S461 50 Pesos

19.6.1898-16.4.1904. Black on orange, yellow and brown underprint. Gypsy woman ("Haidee") at left, female head with Liberty cap ("Liberty") at right. Back: Brown. Overprint: New bank name on #S456. *(BK-YUC-51).*

	Good	Fine	XF
	150.	450.	1350.

S462 100 Pesos

30.6.1893. Seated female ("Reverie") at left, portrait Miguel Hidalgo at right. Back: Green. Overprint: New bank name on #S450. *(BK-YUC-52).*

	Good	Fine	XF
	2250.	6750.	20,000.

S463 100 Pesos

10.11.1900; 17.11.1900; 10.12.1900; 28.3.1904. Black on olive-brown underprint. Columbus and his men sighting land at left, two standing females ("North and South") at right. Back: Olive-brown. Overprint: New bank name on #S457. *(BK-YUC-57).*

	Good	Fine	XF
	525.	1575.	5000.

1913-14 Issues

S464 1 Peso

30.11.1913. Black on yellow and orange underprint. Indian woman at left, sailing ship at right. Series A. Back: Green. Printer: AB&PC.

	Good	Fine	XF
a. Handwritten signature at left. *(BK-YUC-63).*	10.00	30.00	100.
b. Printed signature at left. *(BK-YUC-64).*	3.00	10.00	30.00
p. Proof.	—	Unc	750.
s. Specimen.	—	Unc	1000.

S464A 1 Peso

1913. Black on yellow and orange underprint. Indian woman at left, sailing ship at right. Series A. Similar to #S464. Back: Green. Printer: ABNC. Proof.

	Good	Fine	XF
	—	Unc	750.

S465 5 Pesos

1.4.1914. Black on yellow and orange underprint. Steam locomotive at left, dock workers at right. Series A. Back: Orange. Allegorical figures at left and center right. Printer: ABNC.

	Good	Fine	XF
a. Issued note.	2.00	5.00	15.00
p. Proof. Without series. 189x.	—	Unc	750.
s1. Specimen. Without series. 189x.	—	Unc	750.
s2. Specimen. Series A. 19xx.	—	Unc	750.

Banco Yucateco

1889-1903 Issue

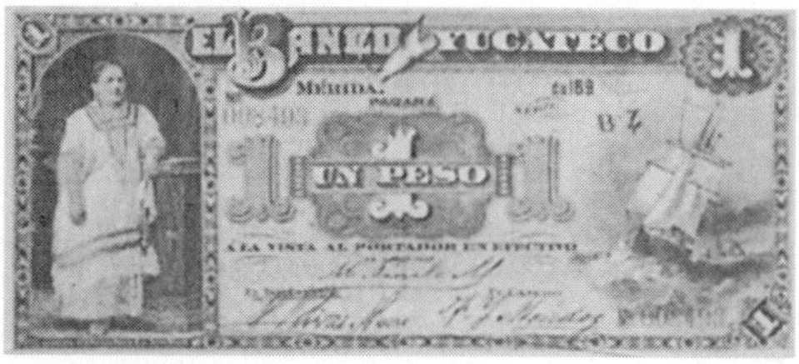

S466 1 Peso

1.11.1891; 1.1.1892. Black on brown-yellow underprint. Indian woman at left, sailing ship at right. Series BZ. Back: Olive-green. Printer: ABNC. *(BK-YUC-1).*

	Good	Fine	XF
a. Issued note.	200.	600.	1800.
p. Proof. Without series. 189x.	—	Unc	750.
s. Specimen.	—	Unc	1000.

S467 5 Pesos

(ca.1890-1903). Black on red-orange and yellow underprint. Steam locomotive at left, men working dockside at right. Back: Red-orange. Allegorical figures at left and center right. Printer: ABNC.

	Good	Fine	XF
a. 5.1.1899. *(BK-YUC-4).*	75.00	225.	675.
b. Series TA. 29.6.1901. *(BK-YUC-4).*	75.00	225.	675.
c. Series HC. 1.10.1903. *(BK-YUC-4).*	75.00	225.	675.
d. Overprint: *Sucursal de Campeche* and perforated: *CAMPECHE.* 9.8.1897; 2.12.1901; 1.10.1903. *(BK-YUC-6).*	45.00	125.	375.
p. Proof. Without series. 189x (ca.1890).	—	Unc	500.
s1. Specimen. Without series. 189x.	—	Unc	750.
s2. Specimen. Series TM. 189x (ca.1898).	—	Unc	750.
s3. Specimen. Series OO. 1xxx (ca.1899).	—	Unc	750.
s4. Specimen. Series MGT. 19xx (ca.1903).	—	Unc	750.
s5. Specimen. Series TA. 1xxx.	—	Unc	750.
s6. Specimen. Series HC. 19xx.	—	Unc	750.

S468 10 Pesos

ca.1890-1903. Black on green and yellow underprint. Helmeted female head ("Minerva No. 3") and seated female ("National Emblems") at left, man feeding horse at right. Back: Dark green. Printer: ABNC.

	Good	Fine	XF
a. 13.10.1900; 1.11.1900; 29.6.1901; 28.9.1901. *(BK-YUC-10).*	30.00	100.	300.
b. Perforated: *CAMPECHE.* 189x; 6.10.1898. *(BK-YUC-12).*	45.00	125.	375.
c. Overprint: *Sucursal de Campeche* and perforated: *CAMPECHE.* 6.8.1898; 9.8.1898; 23.9.1899. *(BK-YUC-13).*	50.00	150.	450.
p. Proof. 189x (ca.1890).	—	Unc	500.
s1. Specimen. Without series. 189x.	—	Unc	750.
s2. Specimen. Series LA. 189x (ca.1898).	—	Unc	750.
s3. Specimen. Series EC. 1xxx (ca.1899).	—	Unc	750.
s4. Specimen. Series CA. 1xxx (ca.1900).	—	Unc	750.
s5. Specimen. Series MH. 1xxx (ca.1903).	—	Unc	750.

S469 20 Pesos

ca.1890-1903. Black on blue and yellow underprint. Two female ("Union") at left center, seated woman with sheaf and water jug at right. Back: Blue. Printer: ABNC. *(BK-YUC-18).*

	Good	Fine	XF
a. 1897-1902.	45.00	125.	375.
b. Overprint: *Sucursal en Campeche* and perforated: *CAMPECHE.* 1.11.1897; 7.6.1898. *(BK-YUC-20).*	60.00	175.	525.
p1. Proof. Without series. 189x (ca.1890).	—	Unc	500.
p2. Proof. Without series. 190x.	—	Unc	500.
p3. Proof. Series YU. 190x (ca.1900).	—	Unc	500.
s1. Specimen. Without series. 189x.	—	Unc	750.
s2. Specimen. Series OM. 189x (ca.1898).	—	Unc	750.
s3. Specimen. Series AT. 1xxx (ca.1898).	—	Unc	750.
s4. Specimen. Series YU. 190x (ca.1900).	—	Unc	750.
s5. Specimen. Series MGG. 190x (ca.1903).	—	Unc	750.

S470 50 Pesos

(ca.1890-1903). Black on red-brown and yellow underprint. Sailing ship at left, reclining woman ("Navigation") at right. Back: Brown. Printer: ABNC. *(DK-YUC-23).*

	Good	Fine	XF
a. 24.5.1898; 24.7.1899.	1500.	4500.	13,500.
p. Proof. Without series. 189x (ca.1890).	—	Unc	1000.
s1. Specimen. Without series. 189x.	—	Unc	1250.
s2. Specimen. Series RC. 189x (ca.1898).	—	Unc	1250.
s3. Specimen. Series UC. 1xxx (ca.1899).	—	Unc	1250.
s4. Specimen. Series DE. 1xxx (ca.1900).	—	Unc	1250.
s5. Specimen. Series JDC. 1xxx (ca.1903).	—	Unc	1250.

S471 100 Pesos

(ca.1890-1903). Black on orange and yellow underprint. Helmsman at wheel ("At the Helm") at left, Indian woman in canoe ("La Verdulera") at center right. Back: Orange. Printer: ABNC. *(BK-YUC-25).*

	Good	Fine	XF
a. Series MGT. 29.5.1902; 16.3.1903.	2250.	6750.	20,000.
p. Proof. Without series. 189x (ca.1890).	—	Unc	1250.
s1. Specimen. Without series. 189x.	—	Unc	1500.
s2. Specimen. Series AR. 189x (ca.1898).	—	Unc	1250.
s3. Specimen. Series OY. 1xxx (ca.1899).	—	Unc	1250.
s4. Specimen. Series DA. 1xxx (ca.1900).	—	Unc	1250.
s5. Specimen. Series JDC. 1xxx (ca.1903).	—	Unc	1250.
s6. Specimen. Without series. 1xxx.	—	Unc	1250.

S472 500 Pesos

(ca.1890-1903). Black on brown and gold underprint. Electricity at left center, ships at right. Back: Black and brown. Allegorical animals at left and center right, profile of Minerva (Goddess of Science, Art and War) a Printer: ABNC. *(BK-YUC-27).*

	Good	Fine	XF
a. 1.5.1889; 7.10.1897.	2500.	7500.	22,500.
p. Proof. Without series. 189x (ca.1890).	—	Unc	2000.
s1. Specimen. Without series. 189x.	—	Unc	2250.
s2. Specimen. Series NC. 1xxx (ca.1899).	—	Unc	2250.
s3. Specimen. Series RI. 1xxx (ca.1900).	—	Unc	2250.
s4. Specimen. Series CC. 1xxx (ca.1902).	—	Unc	2250.
s5. Specimen. Series JIL. 1xxx (ca.1903).	—	Unc	2250.

S473 1000 Pesos

(ca.1890-1903). Black on olive-green, red and orange underprint. Seated female with children ("Peace") at left, seated woman with shield and plant ("Contemplation") at right. Back: Black and red. Allegorical woman ("Arts") at center. Printer: ABNC. *(BK-YUC-29).*

	Good	Fine	XF
a. Series BA, ca.1891.	2000.	6000.	18,000.
p. Proof. Without series. 189x (ca.1890).	—	Unc	2250.
s1. Specimen. Without series. 189x.	—	Unc	2500.
s2. Specimen. Series ME. 1xxx (ca.1900).	—	Unc	2000.
s3. Specimen. Series NEP. 1xxx (ca.1902).	—	Unc	2000.
s4. Specimen. Series PD. 1xxx (ca.1903).	—	Unc	2000.

NOTE: For #S467-S473, reports of specific dates from 1889-1903 are requested.

Zacatecas

Banco de Zacatecas

1891 Issue

S474 1 Peso

8.12.1891. Black on orange and yellow underprint. Young girl ("Helen") at left, portrait F. G. Salinas at right. Series A. Back: Orange. Village landscape. Printer: ABNC. *(BK-ZAC-1).*

	Good	Fine	XF
a. Issued note.	900.	2700.	7500.
p. Proof.	—	Unc	1250.
s. Specimen.	—	Unc	1500.

S475 5 Pesos	Good	Fine	XF
1891-1914. Black on green and yellow underprint. Farmer plowing at left, portrait F. G. Salinas at right. Back: Green. Village landscape. Printer: ABNC.			
a. Series A. 8.12.1891. *(BK-ZAC-4).*	30.00	100.	300.
b. Series H. 20.6.1896; 15.8.1900. *(BK-ZAC-5).*	15.00	45.00	125.
c. Series K. 2.3.1906: L. 18.11.1908; M. 22.9.1909. *(BK-ZAC-6).*	10.00	30.00	100.
d. Series N. 1.11.1912; 1.11.913; Ñ. 15.2.1914: O. 15.5.1914. *(BK-ZAC-11).*	7.50	20.00	60.00
e. *AGUASCALIENTES.* 2.3.1906. *(BK-ZAC-11).*	45.00	125.	375.
f. Overprint: *LAGOS.* 2.3.1906. *(BK-ZAC-11).*	45.00	125.	375.
p. Proof.	—	Unc	1250.
r. Remainder. Without signature or series. ND.	—	—	30.00
s. Specimen. Without series. 1xxx.	—	Unc	1500.

S476 10 Pesos	Good	Fine	XF
1891-1914. Black on brown and yellow underprint. Panoramic view of factory at left, portrait F. G. Salinas at center. Back: Brown. Village landscape. Printer: ABNC.			
a. Series A. 8.12.1891. *(BK-ZAC-13).*	45.00	125.	375.
b. 15.8.1900. Series K. 2.3.1906; 8.11.1908; Series M. 22.9.1909. *(BK-ZAC-14).*	30.00	100.	300.
c. Series N. 1.11.1912; 15.2.1914. *(BK-ZAC-15).*	45.00	125.	375.
d. Overprint: *AGUASCALIENTES.* 1.3.1906. *(BK-ZAC-18).*	60.00	180.	550.
e. Overprint: *LAGOS.* 2.3.1906. *(BK-ZAC-19).*	60.00	180.	550.
p. Proof.	—	Unc	750.
r. Remainder. Without signature or series. ND. *(BK-ZAC-16).*	—	—	45.00
s. Specimen.	—	Unc	1000.

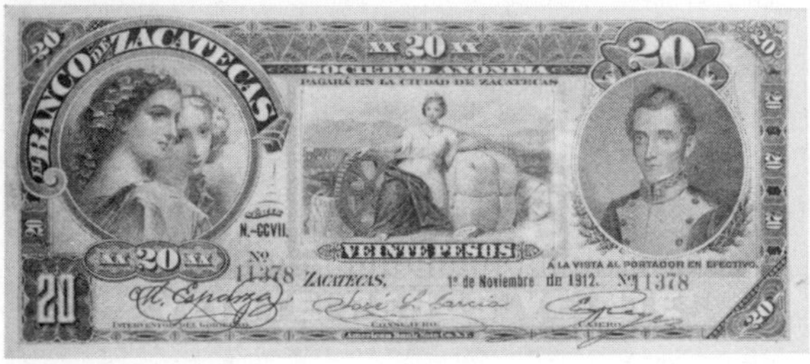

S477 20 Pesos	Good	Fine	XF
1891-1914. Black on orange and yellow underprint. Two women at left, seated female ("Advance") at center, portrait F. G. Salinas at right. Back: Orange. Street scene. Printer: ABNC.			
a. Series B. 20.12.1891; 15.5.1895; 8.7.1897; 1.7.1899. *(BK-ZAC-20).*	375.	1150.	3500.
b. 15.8.1900; 18.11.1908. *(BK-ZAC-21).*	375.	1150.	3500.
c. Series N. 1.11.1912; Ñ 15.2.1914. *(BK-ZAC-22).*	300.	900.	2700.
p. Proof.	—	Unc	1000.
s. Specimen.	—	Unc	1250.

S478 50 Pesos	Good	Fine	XF
(ca.1891-1912). Black on blue and green underprint. Farmer with scythe at left, young girl feeding cow at center, portrait F. G. Salinas at right. Back: Blue. Street scene. Printer: ABNC.			
a. 7.8.1897; 1.11.1898; 1.7.1899. *(BK-ZAC-24).*	375.	1150.	3450.
b. Series H. 15.8.1900. *(BK-ZAC-25).*	350.	1100.	3300.
c. Series K. 2.3.1906.	350.	1100.	3300.
d. Series N. 1.11.1912. *(BK-ZAC-26).*	300.	900.	2700.
e. Overprint: *LAGOS.* 2.3.1906. *(BK-ZAC-30).*	400.	1200.	3600.
p. Proof. 1xxx (ca.1891).	—	Unc	1000.
r. Remainder. *(BK-ZAC-27).*	—	—	125.
s. Specimen.	—	Unc	1250.

S479 100 Pesos	Good	Fine	XF
1891-1912. Black on red, orange and yellow underprint. Cherub with harp at left, portrait F. G. Salinas at center, young girl ("The Brunette") at right. Back: Red. Miners at center. Printer: ABNC.			
a. Series B. 20.12.1891. *(BK-ZAC-31).*	900.	2700.	8000.
b. Series E. 7.8.1897; F. 15.11.1898. *(BK-ZAC-31).*	900.	2700.	8000.
c. Series H. 15.8.1900; I, 5.5.1903. *(BK-ZAC-32).*	800.	2400.	7250.
d. Series N. 1.11.1912. *(BK-ZAC-32).*	800.	2400.	7250.
p. Proof.	—	Unc	1000.
r. Remainder. ND. *(BK-ZAC-33).*	—	—	125.
s. Specimen.	—	Unc	1250.

S480 500 Pesos	Good	Fine	XF
(ca.1891-1906). Black on brown and yellow underprint. Seated female ("Mechanics No. 2") at left, portrait F. G. Salinas at right. Back: Brown and black. Allegorical woman with eagle at center right, head of allegorical woman at right. Printer: ABNC.			
a. Series G. 1.7.1899. *(BK-ZAC-35).*	3000.	9000.	—
b. 2.3.1906. *(BK-ZAC-35).*	3000.	9000.	—
p. Proof. 1xxx (ca.1891).	—	Unc	2500.
r. Remainder. ND. *(BK-ZAC-36).*	—	—	750.
s. Specimen. 1xxx.	—	Unc	3000.

NOTE: For #S475-S480, reports of specific dates from 1891-1914 are needed to augment these listings.

1914 Issue

S481 1 Peso	Good	Fine	XF
1914. Red and yellow or gray. Monument at center. Printer: E.I.A. Back proof. *(BK-ZAC-3).*	—	Unc	750.

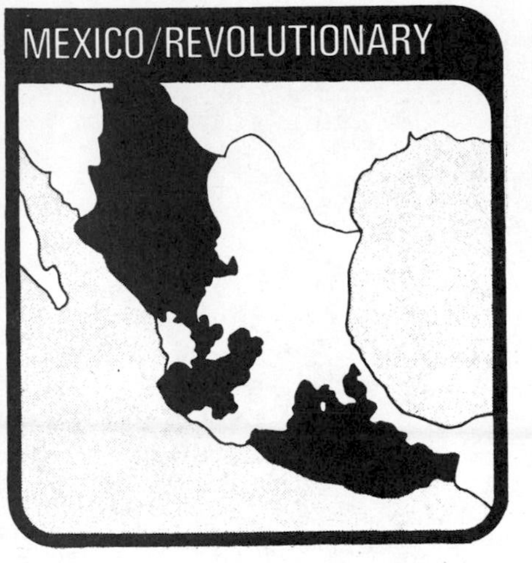

The Mexican independence movement is of interest and concern to collectors because of the warfare-induced activity of local and state mints, which began with the Sept. 15, 1810 march on the capital led by Father Miguel Hidalgo, a well-intentioned man of imagination and courage who proved to be an inept organizer and leader. Hidalgo was captured and executed within 10 months. His revolution, led by such as Morelos, Guerrero and Iturbide, continued and culminated in Mexican independence in 1821. Turbulent years followed. From 1821 to 1867 there were two emperors, several dictators, and enough presidents to provide a change of government on the average of once every nine months. Porfirio Diaz, who had the longest tenure of any dictator in Latin American history, seized power in 1876 and did not relinquish it until 1911.

The final phase of Mexico's lengthy revolutionary period began in 1910 and lasted through the adoption of a liberal constitution and the election of a new congress in 1917. The 1910-17 revolution was agrarian in character and intended to destroy the regime of Díaz and to make Mexico economically and diplomatically independent. The republic experienced a state of upheaval that saw most of the leading figures of the revolution (Villa, Carranza, Obregón, Zapata, Calles) fighting each other at one time or another. Carranza eventually emerged as the most powerful figure of the early revolution. As de facto president in 1916, he convened a constitutional convention which produced a constitution in which the aims of the revolution were formalized.

MONETARY SYSTEM

1 Peso = 100 Centavos

REVOLUTION

1910-17

Issues of state, regional, municipal and military authorities

Administración General de Rentas del Estado (Guanajuato) . . . . #S772-S773
Administración General de Rentas del Estado (Querétaro) . . . . #S985A
Ayuntamiento de 1915, Iguala (Guerrero) . . . . #S790-S808
Banco de Coahuila/Banco de la Laguna (Coahuila) . . . . #S563-S569
Banco de Coahuila/Banco Nacional de México (Coahuila) . . . . #S570-S572
Banco Español Refaccionario S.A./Banco Oriental de México (Puebla) . . . . #S964-S967
Banco de la Laguna/Banco de Coahuila (Coahuila) . . . . #S579-S591
Banco de la Laguna/Banco de Londres y México (Coahuila) . . . . #S592-S596A
Banco de la Laguna/Banco Minero (Coahuila) . . . . #S597-S602
Banco de Londres y México/Deutsch-Sudamerikanische Bank (Berlin) (Coahuila) . . . . #S603-S606
Banco de Londres y México/Banco de la Laguna (Coahuila) . . . . #S607-S608
Banco de Londres y México/Banco Nacional de México (Coahuila) . . . . #S609-S612
Banco Minero/Banco de la Laguna, Gómez Palacio (Durango) . . . . #S762-S766
Banco Nacional de México/Banco de Coahuila (Coahuila) . . . . #S613-S614
Banco Nacional de México/Deutsch-Sudamerikanische Bank (Berlin) (Coahuila) . . . . #S615-S617
Banco Nacional de México/Banco de Londres y México . . . . #S618-S621
Banco Revolucionario de Guerrero . . . . #S785-S789
Bonos al Portador, Durango . . . . #S717-S723
Brigada Azuara (Hidalgo) . . . . #S828-S830
Brigada Serdan . . . . S#984B-C
La Caja de Ahorros de la R.M., S.A. (Chihuahua) . . . . #S542-S544
La Caja de la Brigada CABALLERO, Tampico (Tamaulipas) . . . . #S1083-S1084
Circulación Forzosa en el Estado de Morelos, Cuernavaca . . . . #S899-S902
La Comisión Reguladora del Comercio de Zacatecas . . . . #S1139-S1142
Comisión Reguladora del Mercado de Henequén y la Tesorería General del Estado (Yucatan) . . . . #S1120-S1127
Compañiá Real del Monte y Pachuca/Bank of Montreal (Hidalgo) . . . . #S831-S839
Cuartel General del Ejército Constitucionalista de la Sierra Norte de Puebla . . . . #S985
Cuerpo de Ejército del Noreste (Nuevo Leon) . . . . #S940-S941
Cuerpo de EJ>E?>rcito del Noroeste, Tepic (Nayarit) . . . . #S916-S917B
Deutsch-Sudamerikanische Bank (Berlin)/Banco de Londres y México (Coahuila) . . . . #S573-S575
Deutsch-Sudamerikanische Bank (Berlin)/Banco Nacional de México (Coahuila) . . . . #S576-S578
Dirección General de Rentas del Estado, Cuernavaca (Morelos) . . . . #S903-S905
La Dirección General de Rentas del Estado, Guadalajara (Jalisco) . . . . #S844-S856
Distrito de Matamoros (Puebla) . . . . #S972-S984A
Distrito de Morelos (Tlaxcala) . . . . #S1085-S1087
División Almazán, Huajuapán (Oaxaca) . . . . #S942
División del Bravo, Monterrey (Nuevo Leon) . . . . #S935-S939
Ejército Constitucionalista (San Luis Potosí) . . . . #S986-S989
Ejército Constitucionalista Uruapán (Michoacán) . . . . #S898
Ejército Constitucionalista, Cuerpo de Ejército del Noroeste, Culiacán (Sinaloa) . . . . #S990-S999
Ejército Constitucionalista, División del Norte, Torreón (Coahuila) . . . . #S652-S654
Ejército Constitucionalista, División de Occidente, Guadalajara (Jalisco) . . . . #S860-S862
Ejército Constitucionalista de México (Chihuahua) . . . . #S523-S526
Ejército Constitucionalista de México, Tampico (Tamaulipas) . . . . #S1082
Ejército Constitucionalista, Parras (Coahuila) . . . . #S638-S641
Ejército Constitucionalista del Sur (Guerrero) . . . . #S809-S812
Ejército Libertador de Guerrero, Chilpancingo . . . . #S812A
Ejército Revolucionario de Guerrero . . . . #S813-S816
Estado de Aguascalientes - Tesorería Municipal (Aguascalientes) . . . . #S501-S503
El Estado de Chihuahua (Chihuahua) . . . . #S527-S538
El Estado de Coahuila . . . . #S655-S659
El Estado de Durango . . . . #S724-S753
El Estado de Durango, San José de la Boca . . . . #S768
El Estado de Durango, Topia . . . . #S769-S770
El Estado de Jalisco . . . . #S873-S875
El Estado Libre y Soberano de Colima . . . . #S662-S663
Estado Libre y Soberano de México . . . . #S877-S882
El Estado Libre y Soberano de Sinaloa . . . . #S1041-S1048
El Estado de Michoacán de Ocampo . . . . #S883
Estado de Sinaloa, Culiacán . . . . #S1000-S1004
Estado de Sinaloa, Mazatlán . . . . #S1005-S1008
El Estado de Sinaloa, San Blas . . . . #S1026-S1040
El Estado de Sonora, Hermosillo . . . . #S1062-S1078
Gobierno Constitucionalista, Brigada Morales y Molina (Guerrero) . . . . #S817-S824
Gobierno Constitucionalista del Estado de Durango . . . . #S754-S758
Gobierno Constitucionalista del Estado Libre y Soberano del Veracruz, Llave . . . . #S1091-S1096
Gobierno Constitucionalista de Mexico, La Paz (Baja, California) . . . . #S504-S508
Gobierno Constitucionalista de Mexico, Monclova (Coahuila) . . . . #S625-S635
Gobierno Constitucionalista de México, República (Distrito Federal) . . . . #S681-S684
Gobierno Constitucionalista Provisional de Chihuahua (Chihuahua) . . . . #S539-S540
Gobierno Constitucionalista, República Méxicana (Distrito Federal) . . . . #S685-S689
Gobierno Constitucionalista Territorio de la Baja, Cfa., La Paz la Jefatura Politica (Baja, California) . . . . #S509-S522
El Gobierno Constitucionalista del Territorio de Tepic y del Estado de Sinaloa, Rosario . . . . #S1009-S1014
Gobierno Constitucionalista de Yucatán, Tesorería General . . . . #S1128-S1133
Gobierno Convencionista, Cuernavaca (Morelos) . . . . #S906-S908
Gobierno Convencionista de México (Morelos) . . . . #S909-S912
Gobierno Convencionista de Mexico (Toluca) . . . . #S882
Gobierno del Estado de Colima . . . . #S660-S661
Gobierno del Estado de Durango . . . . #S759-S761
Gobierno Federal de la República Mexicana (Distrito Federal) . . . . #S690-S696
Gobierno de Nuevo León, Monterrey . . . . #S934
Gobierno Preconstitucional del Estado de Oaxaca . . . . #S950-S951
Gobierno Provisional de México, (Distrito Federal) México . . . . #S701-S712
Gobierno Provisional de México, República (Distrito Federal) . . . . #S697-S700
Gobierno Provisional de México, Veracruz . . . . #S1097-S1115
Gobierno Provisional de Michoacán . . . . #S884-S887
Gobierno Provisional de Zacatecas . . . . #S1143-S1145
Jefatura de Armas - M.S. González, Muzquiz (Coahuila) . . . . #S637
Jefatura de Armas, Morelia (Michoacán) . . . . #S888-S893
Jefatura de Armas, Yautepec (Morelos) . . . . #S913-S915
Jefatura de Hacienda en el Estado (Chihuahua) . . . . #S541
Jefatura de Hacienda en el Estado Jalisco . . . . #S875A
La Jefatura de Hacienda, Guaymas (Sonora) . . . . #S1055-S1057
La Jefatura Municipal, Guanaceví (Durango) . . . . #S767
Jefe de la Columna Territorio do Tepic (Nayarit) . . . . #S920-S928
Jefe de la División de Occidente (Jalisco) . . . . #S876
Jefe Político del Territorio (Nayarit) . . . . #S918-S919
Junta Comercial, Chalchicomula (Puebla) . . . . #S968-S969
Municipio de San Pedro (Coahuila) . . . . #S648-S651
Obligación Provisional del Erario Federal (Distrito Federal) . . . . #S713-S716
La Pagaduría del Cuerpo de Ejército del Noroeste (Jalisco) . . . . #S863-S867
La Pagaduría General de la Brigada Avila, Jérez (Zacatecas) . . . . #S1146-S1147
Pagaduría General de la Brigada de Sinaloa, San Blas . . . . #S1049-S1054
La Pagaduría Gral. del Cuerpo de Ejército del Noroeste (Jalisco) . . . . #S868-S872
La Pagaduría Gral. de la Brigada de Sinaloa . . . . #S1015-S1021
La Tesorería de la Federación, Guaymas (Sonora) . . . . #S1058-S1061
La Tesorería de la Federacion, Saltillo (Coahuila) . . . . #S642-S647
Tesorería General del Estado (Chihuahua) . . . . #S548-S561
La Tesorería General del Estado de Colima . . . . #S664-S680
Tesorería General del Estado - Transitorio (Chihuahua) . . . . #S545-S547
Tesorería General del Estado (Guanajuato) . . . . #S774-S784
La Tesorería General del Estado de Oaxaca . . . . #S948-S949
La Tesorería General del Estado de Oaxaca, Oaxaca de Juárez . . . . #S952-S960
La Tesorería General del Estado de Sinaloa . . . . #S1022-S1025
La Tesorería General del Estado de Tabasco, San Juan Batista . . . . #S1079-S1081
Tesorería General Territorio de Tepic (Nayarit) . . . . #S929-S933
La Tesorería General, Tliaxiaco (Oaxaca) . . . . #S963
Tesorería General del Estado de Veracruz Llave . . . . #S1116-S1119
Tesorería de la Junta Comercial de Chalchicomula (Puebla) . . . . #S970-S971
La Tesorería Municipal de C. Jiménez (Chihuahua) . . . . #S562
Tesorería Municipal, Municipio de Matamoros (Coahuila) . . . . #S622-S624
Tesorería Municipal, Monclova (Coahuila) . . . . #S636
La Tesorería Municipal, Pátcuaro (Michoacán) . . . . #S894-S895
Tesorería Municipal, Puruandiro (Michoacán) . . . . #S896-S897
La Tesorería Municipal de esta Ciudad Tliaxcala . . . . #S1088-S1090
La Tesorería Provisional del Comercio, Huajuapán (Oaxaca) . . . . #S943-S947
Tesorería Provisional, Tamazola (Oaxaca) . . . . #S961-S962

AGUASCALIENTES

TESORERÍA MUNICIPALESTADO DE AGUASCALIENTES TESORERÍA MUNICIPAL

ND ISSUE

		Good	Fine	XF
S501	**5 Centavos** ND. Black. Eagle at center. Paper: Brown/green pasteboard. *(SI-AGU-1).*	10.00	30.00	90.00

S502 10 Centavos	**Good**	**Fine**	**XF**
ND. Black. Eagle at center. Paper: Violet/green pasteboard. *(SI-AGU-2).*	10.00	30.00	90.00

S503 20 Centavos	**Good**	**Fine**	**XF**
ND. Black. Eagle at center. Paper: Red/green pasteboard. *(SI-AGU-3).*	12.50	35.00	125.

Baja California

Gobierno Constitucionalista de México, La Paz

ND Issue

S504 5 Centavos	**Good**	**Fine**	**XF**
ND. Black. Eagle at center. Paper: Pale green pasteboard. *(MI-BAJ-1).*	25.00	75.00	225.

S505 10 Centavos	**Good**	**Fine**	**XF**
ND. Black. Eagle at center. Paper: Pasteboard. *(MI-BAJ-2).*	25.00	75.00	225.

S506 20 Centavos	**Good**	**Fine**	**XF**
ND. Black. Eagle at center. Paper: Gray pasteboard. *(MI-BAJ-3).*	25.00	75.00	225.

S507 50 Centavos	**Good**	**Fine**	**XF**
ND. Black. Eagle at center. Paper: Red, pink pasteboard. *(MI-BAJ-4).*	25.00	75.00	225.
S508 50 Centavos			
ND. Black. *(MI-BAJ-5).*			
a. Red pasteboard.	25.00	75.00	225.
b. Gray pasteboard.	25.00	75.00	225.
c. Salmon pasteboard.	25.00	75.00	225.

Gobierno Constitucionalista Territorio de la Baja Cfa, LaPaz, La Jefatura Politica

1914 Issue

S509 5 Pesos	**Good**	**Fine**	**XF**
21.8.1914. Black. Paper: Gray pasteboard. Violet circular seal *JEFATURA POLITICA DEL DISTRITO DE LA DAJA CALIFORNIA * LA PAZ ** on face or back. *(MI-BAJ-6).*	22.50	65.00	200.

S510 5 Pesos	**Good**	**Fine**	**XF**
21.8.1914. Black. Paper: Green pasteboard. Violet circular seal *JEFATURA POLITICA DEL DISTRITO DE LA DAJA CALIFORNIA * LA PAZ ** on face or back.			
a. Issued note. *(MI-BAJ-7).*	30.00	90.00	270.
b. Overprint: *DISTRITO DE MAZATLAN. RETIRADO DE LA CIRCULACION* (withdrawn from circulation). *(MI-BAJ-8).*	50.00	150.	450.

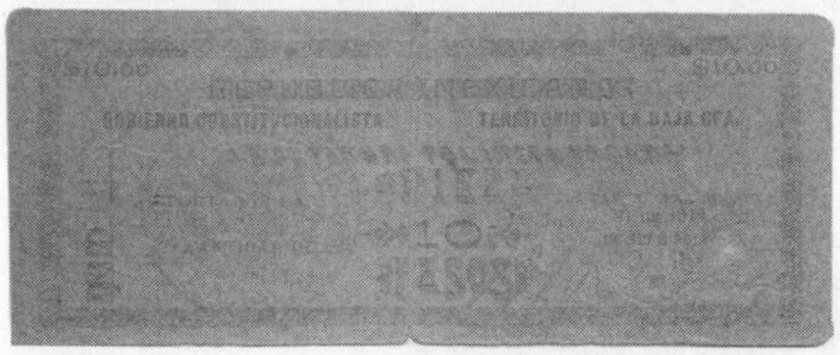

S511 10 Pesos	**Good**	**Fine**	**XF**
21.8.1914. Black. Paper: Maroon pasteboard. Violet circular seal *JEFATURA POLITICA DEL DISTRITO DE LA DAJA CALIFORNIA * LA PAZ ** on face or back. *(MI-BAJ-9).*	30.00	90.00	270.

S512 20 Pesos	**Good**	**Fine**	**XF**
21.8.1914. Black. Paper: Light pink thin paper. Watermark: *REGIST...* Violet circular seal *JEFATURA POLITICA DEL DISTRITO DE LA DAJA CALIFORNIA * LA PAZ ** on face or back. *(MI-BAJ-10).*	30.00	90.00	270.

Chiapas

Gobierno Preconstitucional - Caja de Cambio

1914 Issue

S513 5 Centavos	**Good**	**Fine**	**XF**
28.12.1914. Black. National arms at left. Series A. Paper: Tan pasteboard. *(SI-CHIP-1).*	12.50	35.00	110.
S514 10 Centavos			
28.12.1914. Black. National arms at left. Series B. Paper: Blue pasteboard. *(SI-CHIP-3).*	12.50	35.00	110.
S515 20 Centavos			
28.12.1914. Blue. National arms at left. Series C. Paper: White pasteboard. *(SI-CHIP-5).*	25.00	75.00	225.
S516 50 Centavos			
28.12.1914. Orange. National arms at left. Series D. Paper: Cream pasteboard. *(SI-CHIP-7).*	25.00	75.00	225.

1915 Issue

S517 5 Centavos	**Good**	**Fine**	**XF**
12.5.1915. Black. National arms at left. Series A. Paper: Blue pasteboard. *(SI-CHIP-2).*	10.00	30.00	90.00
S518 10 Centavos			
12.5.1915. Black. National arms at left. Series B. Paper: Orange pasteboard. *(SI-CHIP-4).*	20.00	60.00	180.
S519 20 Centavos			
12.5.1915. Black. National arms at left. Series C. Paper: Cream pasteboard. *(SI-CHIP-6).*	20.00	60.00	180.
S520 50 Centavos			
12.5.1915. Black. National arms at left. Series D. Paper: Brown pasteboard. *(SI-CHIP-8).*			
a. Issued note.	10.00	30.00	90.00
b. Without serial # and back seal. 12.5.1915.	30.00	90.00	270.

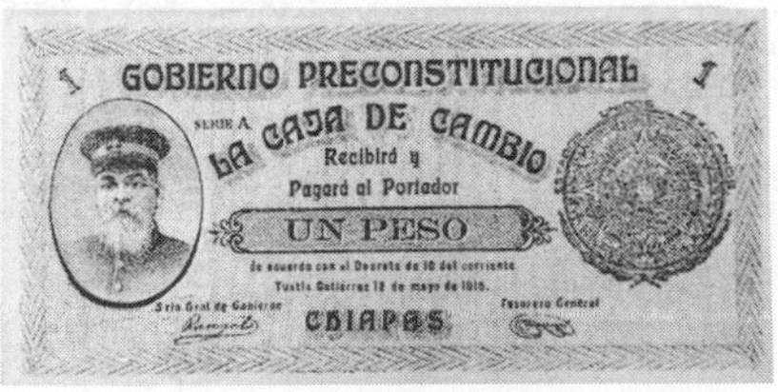

S521	**1 Peso**	**Good**	**Fine**	**XF**
	ND. Portrait J. Carranza at left, Aztec calendar stone at right. Series A. *(SI-CHIP-9).*	60.00	180.	540.

S522	**2 Pesos**	**Good**	**Fine**	**XF**
	ND. Portrait B. Dominguez at left, Aztec calendar stone at right. Series A. *(SI-CHIP-10).*	50.00	150.	450.

CHIHUAHUA

DE MÉXICOEJÉRCITO CONSTITUCIONALISTA DE MÉXICO

DECREE OF FEBRUARY 12, 1914

S523	**1 Peso**	**Good**	**Fine**	**XF**
	30.3.1914. Black on pink underprint. National coat-of-arms at center. Series A. Back: Liberty cap and rays at center.			
	a. Issued note. *(MI-CHI-68).*	2.00	6.00	18.00
	b. Overprint: *MICHOACÁN DE OCAMPO. TESORERÍA GENERAL, RETIRADO* in purple, red, green or black. *(MI-CHI-69).*	15.00	45.00	135.
	c. Overprint: *HACIENDA DE SAN JOAQUIN, 1916. (MI-CHI-70).*	18.00	55.00	165.
	d. As b. With *VILA HIDALGO.*	15.00	45.00	135.

S524	**5 Pesos**	**Good**	**Fine**	**XF**
	30.3.1914. Black on green underprint. National coat-of-arms at center. Series B. Back: Liberty cap and rays at center. *(MI-CHI-71).*	2.00	6.00	18.00

S525	**10 Pesos**	**Good**	**Fine**	**XF**
	30.3.1914. Black on lilac underprint. National coat-of-arms at center. Series C. Back: Liberty cap and rays at center. *(MI-CHI-72).*			
	a. Black seal.	3.00	9.00	27.00
	b. Brown seal.	3.00	9.00	27.00
	s. Specimen. Perforated: *SPECIMEN.*	—	Unc	250.

S526	**20 Pesos**	**Good**	**Fine**	**XF**
	30.3.1914. Black on orange underprint. National coat-of-arms at center. Series D. Back: Liberty cap and rays at center. *(MI-CHI-73).*	3.00	9.00	27.00

EL ESTADO DE CHIHUAHUA

DECRETO 10.2.1914

S527	**50 Centavos**	**VG**	**VF**	**UNC**
	Various dates in 1915. Blue. Back: Green. National arms at center. *(MI-CHI-37).*			
	a. Issued note.	2.00	6.00	18.00
	b. Inverted Treasury seal on back.	6.00	18.00	55.00

S528 50 Centavos

D. 1914. Various dates in 1915. Green and black. Series U. Back: Green. National arms at center.

	VG	VF	UNC
a. Circular black treasury and scalloped red state seals; Large signature at left and right. *(MI-CHI-38).*	2.00	6.00	18.00
b. Scalloped red seal; small signature at left and right. Circular black treasury seal on back. *(MI-CHI-39).*	2.00	6.00	18.00
c. Small signature at left and right. Circular red treasury seal and horizontal control letters on back. *(MI-CHI-40).*	2.00	6.00	18.00
d. Small signature at left and right. Vertical scalloped red treasury seal and control letters on back. *(MI-CHI-41).*	2.00	6.00	18.00
e. Like c, but with date below control letters on back. 20.4.1915; 1.6.1915.	2.00	6.00	18.00
f. Violet overprint: *FALSO* on c.	4.00	12.00	35.00
g. Small signature at left and right. Back without seal or control letters. *(MI-CHI-43).*	2.00	6.00	18.00
h. Without serial # or seals. *(MI-CHI-).*	5.00	15.00	45.00

S529 1 Peso

D. 1914. Blue and black. Portrait Francisco I. Madero at left, portrait Gov. A. González at right. Series A. Back: Blue. Capitol building at center.

	VG	VF	UNC
a. Large printed signature. Red scalloped state seal. Black or blue-black circular treasury seal on back. *(MI-CHI-44).*	4.00	12.00	35.00
b. Small printed signature. Red scalloped treasury seal on back. *(MI-CHI-46).*	2.00	6.00	18.00
c. Like a, but with date at center on back. 5.10.1915; 10.7.1915.	2.00	6.00	18.00
d. Without serial # or signature at left and right. *(MI-CHI-45).*	7.50	27.50	85.00
e. Scalloped red seal on face, circular black or blue-black seal on back.	2.50	7.50	25.00
f. Red circular treasury seal on back.	2.50	7.50	25.00
g. Red scalloped treasury seal and control letters on back.	2.00	6.00	18.00
x. Error: overprint inverted.	—	—	—

S530 1 Peso

June 1915. Blue and black. Portrait Francisco I. Madero at left, portrait Gov. A. González at right. Like #S529 but with small printed signature. Series I. Back: Blue. Capitol building at center.

	VG	VF	UNC
a. Circular red treasury seal on back. *(MI-CHI-47).*	2.00	6.00	18.00
b. Scalloped red treasury seal on back.	2.00	6.00	18.00
c. Red seal on blank back. *MI-CHI-48).*	10.00	30.00	90.00
d. Like a, but with date at center on back. 11.1.1915.	2.00	6.00	18.00
e. Like b, but with date at center on back. 20.6.1915-10.11.1915.	2.00	6.00	18.00

S531 5 Pesos

D. 1914. Black on pink underprint. Portrait Francisco I. Madero at left, portrait Gov. A. González at right. Back: Red. Capitol building at center.

	VG	VF	UNC
a. Large signature at left and right. Blue scalloped state seal. Black circular treasury seal on back. *(MI-CHI-49).*	4.00	12.50	35.00
b. Without blue scalloped state seal on face.	4.00	12.50	35.00
c. Small signature *(MI-CHI-50).*	4.00	12.50	35.00
d. Black scalloped treasury seal on back.	4.00	12.50	35.00
e. Without treasury seal, signature, date or serial #. *(MI-CHI-51).*	15.00	45.00	125.
f. Black circular seal on back.	3.00	9.00	27.50
g. With large printed signature and rubber stamp seal on back. *(MI-CHI-51a).*	3.00	9.00	27.50

S532 5 Pesos

Jan. 1915. Black on pink underprint. Portrait Francisco I. Madero at left, portrait Gov. A. González at right. Like #S531. Series H. Back: Red. Capitol building at center.

	VG	VF	UNC
a. Black scalloped treasury seal on back. *(MI-CHI-52).*	3.00	9.00	27.50
b. Black scalloped seal on blank back. *(MI-CHI-53).*	17.50	55.00	85.00
c. Blue scalloped treasury seal on back. *(MI-CHI-54).*	2.00	6.00	18.00
d. Blue scalloped treasury seal on blank back. *(MI-CHI-55).*	17.50	55.00	85.00
e. Like #S532b with date at center on back. 1.6.1915; 10.6.1915.	1.25	4.00	12.50

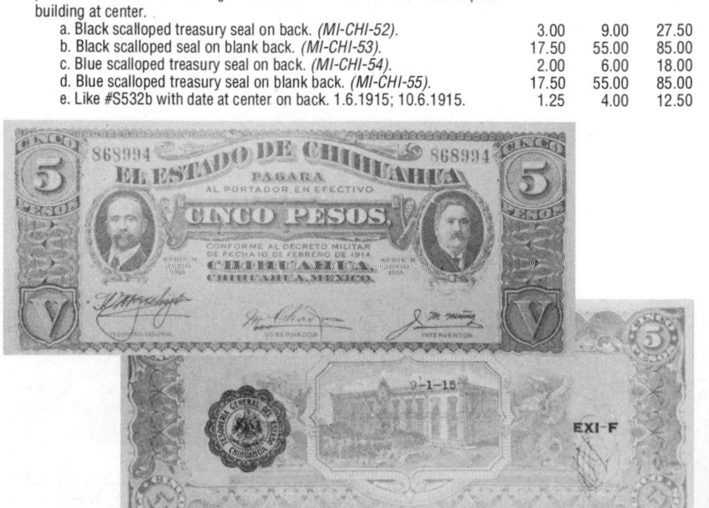

S532A 5 Pesos

June 1915. Black on pink underprint. Portrait Francisco I. Madero at left, portrait Gov. A. González at right. Like #S532. Series M. Back: Red. Capitol building at center.Date at center. 1.6.1915-11.1.1915.

	VG	VF	UNC
	1.25	4.00	12.50

S533 10 Pesos

D. 1914. Black on yellow-orange underprint. Portrait Francisco I. Madero at left, portrait Gov. A. González at right. Series D. Back: Green. Capitol building at center.

	VG	VF	UNC
a. 2 handwritten signatures at left and right. Black circular treasury seal on back. *(MI-CHI-56).*	12.50	35.00	110.
b. Dark blue circular treasury seal and 2 dark blue small printed signatures at left and right. *(MI-CHI-57).*	6.00	18.00	54.00
c. Small black printed signature at left and right. Red circular treasury seal on back. *(MI-CHI-58).*	3.00	9.00	27.50
d. Red circular treasury seal on blank back. *(MI-CHI-58a).*	17.50	55.00	85.00
e. Black scalloped treasury seal on back. *(MI-CHI-58b).*	3.00	9.00	27.50
f. Overprint: *FALSO* on d.	5.00	15.00	45.00
g. Red scalloped treasury seal on back. *(MI-CHI-59).*	2.00	6.00	17.50
h. Without signature. With seal on back.	17.50	55.00	150.
i. Without signature. Without seal on back. (Counterfeit).	6.00	17.50	55.00
s. Specimen. As c. Perforated: *SPECIMEN.*	—	—	300.
x1. Error: overprint inverted.	—	—	—
x2. Error: overprint on face.	—	—	—

S534 10 Pesos

Jan. 1915. Black on yellow-orange underprint. Portrait Francisco I. Madero at left, portrait Gov. A. González at right. Like #S533. Series J. Back: Green. Capitol building at center.

	VG	VF	UNC
a. Red circular treasury seal on back.	1.50	5.00	15.00
b. Red scalloped treasury seal on back. *(MI-CHI-59).*	1.50	5.00	15.00
c. Red scalloped treasury seal on blank back. *(MI-CHI-60).*	15.00	45.00	125.

S535 10 Pesos

June 1915. Black on yellow-orange underprint. Portrait Francisco I. Madero at left, portrait Gov. A. González at right. Like #S534. Series N. Back: Green. Capitol building at center. *(MI-CHI-61).*

	VG	VF	UNC
a. Without date at center on back.	1.50	5.00	15.00
b. With date at center on back. 20.8.1915; 9.10.1915.	1.50	5.00	15.00
c. Red scalloped treasury seal on blank back. *(MI-CHI-62).*	15.00	45.00	125.

S536 20 Pesos

D. 1914. Brown and black. Portrait Francisco I. Madero at left, portrait Gov. A. González at right. Two handwritten signatures. Series E. Back: Brown. Capitol building at center.

	VG	VF	UNC
a. Black circular treasury seal and red scalloped state seal on back. *(MI-CHI-63).*	10.00	30.00	90.00
b. Small black printed signature. Circular black treasury seal on back.	1.50	5.00	15.00
c. Circular red seal on back.	2.00	6.00	18.00

S537 20 Pesos

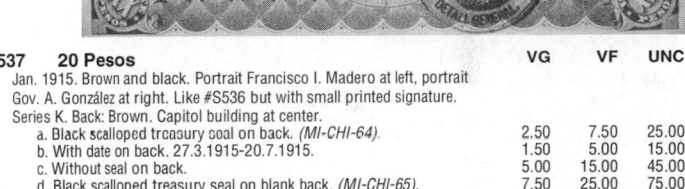

Jan. 1915. Brown and black. Portrait Francisco I. Madero at left, portrait Gov. A. González at right. Like #S536 but with small printed signature. Series K. Back: Brown. Capitol building at center.

	VG	VF	UNC
a. Black scalloped treasury seal on back. *(MI-CHI-64).*	2.50	7.50	25.00
b. With date on back. 27.3.1915-20.7.1915.	1.50	5.00	15.00
c. Without seal on back.	5.00	15.00	45.00
d. Black scalloped treasury seal on blank back. *(MI-CHI-65).*	7.50	25.00	75.00
e. Black circular treasury seal on back.	3.00	9.00	27.50
f. Inverted black scalloped treasury seal, date and block letters on back.	15.00	45.00	135.

S538 50 Pesos

D. 1914. Green and black. Portrait Francisco I. Madero at left, portrait Gov. A. González at right. Two handwritten signatures. Series F. Back: Yellow to orange. Capitol building at center. *(MI-CHI-66).*

	VG	VF	UNC
a. Violet circular treasury seal on back.	2.50	7.50	27.50
b. Violet scalloped treasury seal on back.	4.00	12.50	35.00
c. Red scalloped treasury seal on back.	4.00	12.50	35.00
d. Red scalloped state and black circular treasury seal on back.	4.00	12.50	35.00
e. Black circular treasury seal on back.	4.00	12.50	35.00
f. Violet scalloped treasury seal on blank back.	7.50	25.00	75.00
r. Remainder without serial #, left and right signature or seal on back. *(MI-CHI-67).*	7.50	25.00	75.00

Gobierno Constitucionalista Provisional de Chihuahua

1916 Issue

S539 10 Centavos

1916. National arms at upper center. Paper: Green pasteboard. *(MI-CHI-1).*

	Good	Fine	XF
	3.00	9.00	27.50

S540 20 Centavos

1916. Brown to yellow-black on green underprint. National arms at upper center. *(MI-CHI-2).*

	Good	Fine	XF
	3.00	9.00	27.50

Jefatura de Hacienda en el Estado de Chihuahua

1913 Issue

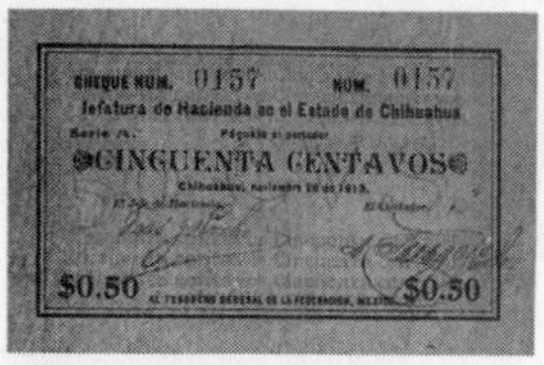

	Good	Fine	XF
S541 50 Centavos 20.11.1913. Black on pink underprint. *(SI-CHI-4).*	70.00	200.	625.

La Caja de Ahorros de la R.M., S.A.

1913 Issue

	Good	Fine	XF
S542 20 Centavos 25.10.1913. Black on yellow underprint. *(PI-CHI-1).*	17.50	55.00	165.
S543 50 Centavos 25.10.1913. Black on green underprint. Like #S542. *(PI-CHI-2).*	17.50	55.00	165.
S544 1 Peso 25.10.1913. Black on orange underprint. Like #S542. *(PI-CHI-3).*	17.50	55.00	165.

Tesorería General del Estado - Transitorio

ND Issue

#S545-S547 circular hand stamp: *TESORERÍA GENERAL DEL ESTADO CHIHUAHUA.*

	Good	Fine	XF
S545 5 Centavos ND. Green. Circular hand stamp: *TESORERIA GENERAL DEL ESTADO CHIHUAHUA.* Series A; B. Paper: Maroon pasteboard. *(SI-CHI-1).*	5.00	15.00	45.00
S546 5 Centavos ND. Green. Circular hand stamp: *TESORERIA GENERAL DEL ESTADO CHIHUAHUA.* Series A. Paper: Orange pasteboard. *(SI-CHI-2).*	5.00	15.00	45.00
S546A 5 Centavos ND. Green. Circular hand stamp: *TESORERIA GENERAL DEL ESTADO CHIHUAHUA.* Series B. Paper: White pasteboard. *(SI-CHI-3).*	4.00	12.50	35.00
S546B 5 Centavos ND. Green. Circular hand stamp: *TESORERIA GENERAL DEL ESTADO CHIHUAHUA.* Series B. Paper: Red pasteboard. *(SI-CHI-3A).*	4.00	12.50	35.00
S546C 5 Centavos ND. Green. Circular hand stamp: *TESORERIA GENERAL DEL ESTADO CHIHUAHUA.* Without *D* before and after *5.* Paper: White pasteboard. *(SI-CHI-).*	6.00	17.50	55.00
S547 5 Centavos ND. Black on red-violet. Circular hand stamp: *TESORERIA GENERAL DEL ESTADO CHIHUAHUA. (SI-CHI-3B).*	5.00	15.00	45.00

Tesorería General del Estado

General State Treasury

1913 Issue

	Good	Fine	XF
S548 5 Centavos 10.12.1913. Black and yellow. Series A. *(MI-CHI-3).*	175.	525.	1575.
S549 10 Centavos 10.12.1913. Black and pink. Straight text: *TESORERÍA. . .*Series A. *(MI-CHI-4).*	270.	850.	2550.
S550 10 Centavos 10.12.1913. Curved text: *TESORERÍA. . . (MI-CHI-5).*	1.50	5.00	15.00
S551 25 Centavos 10.12.1913. Black on pink underprint. Large or small signature. Series C. *(MI-CHI-6).*			
a. Large seal on back. Imp. A.	22.50	65.00	185.
b. Imp. B. *(MI-CHI-7).*	3.00	9.00	27.50
c. Small black treasury seal on back. Series H.	3.00	9.00	27.50
d. Large black seal on back. Imp. C. *(MI-CHI-8).*	1.50	5.00	15.00
e. Small black seal on back. Imp. C. Series N; BB. *(MI-CHI-9).*	1.50	5.00	15.00
f. Overprint: *Revalidado por Decreto del 17 de Diciembre de 1914. (MI-CHI-10).*	7.50	22.50	65.00
g. Small red seal on back. *(MI-CHI-11).*	1.50	5.00	15.00
h. Small blue seal on back. *(MI-CHI-12).*	1.50	5.00	15.00
i. Small green seal on back. *(MI-CHI-13).*	2.00	6.00	18.00
j. Red circular treasury seal type B, red vertical date at upper left, without NUM at upper right. Series CC; DD. 7.12.(19)15; 7.21.(19)15. *(MI-CHI-14).*	1.50	5.00	15.00
S552 50 Centavos 10.12.1913. Black. *(MI-CHI-15).*			
a. Imp. B.	40.00	120.	360.
b. Imp. C. Series D; G. *(MI-CHI-16).*	27.50	80.00	240.
c. Blue on light brown underprint. Imp. A. *(MI-CHI-16A).*	22.50	65.00	185.
d. Imp. C. Overprint: *Revalidado por Decreto de 17 de Diciembre de 1914 .*	25.00	75.00	225.

	Good	Fine	XF
S553 1 Peso 10.12.1913. Black on green underprint. *(MI-CHI-17).*			
a. Series A; C-F.	9.00	27.50	85.00
b. Imp. C. Series B; D; G-J; L; P; Q; T; U. *(MI-CHI-18).*	5.00	15.00	45.00
c. Imp. A. Series A; C. *(MI-CHI-18A).*	15.00	45.00	135.
d. Imp C. Overprint: *Revalidado por Decreto de 17 de Diciembre de 1914. (MI-CHI-19).*	9.00	27.50	85.00
e. Imp. C. Hand stamped: *FALSO.*	9.00	27.50	85.00
f. Imp C. Watermark: *Oldham...* Series O.	9.00	27.50	85.00
S553A 5 Pesos 10.12.1913. Black on brown underprint. 2 handwritten signatures. Uniface. Without imprint. Series A.	15.00	45.00	135.

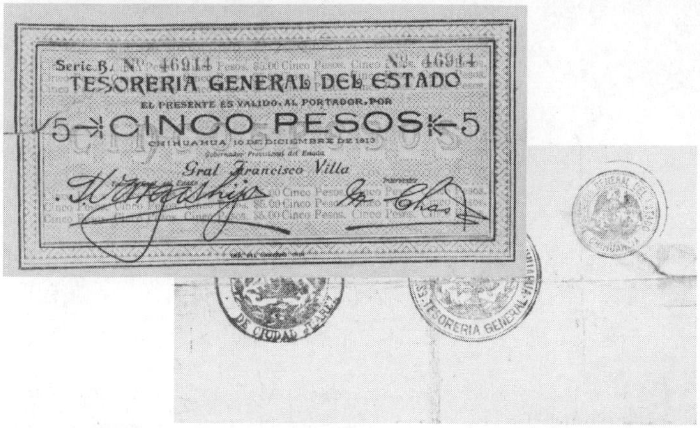

	Good	Fine	XF
S554 5 Pesos 10.12.1913. Black on brown underprint. Imp. B. Series A-D.			
a. Handwritten signature. *(MI-CHI-20a).*	30.00	90.00	270.
b. Printed signature. *(MI-CHI-20).*	3.00	9.00	27.50
c. Overprint: *Revalidado por Decreto de 17 de Diciembre de 1914. (MI-CHI-21).*	5.00	15.00	45.00
d. Violet hand stamped.	4.00	12.50	35.00
e. *Goberñado* (error) for *Gobernador. (MI-CHI-21a).*	4.00	12.50	35.00

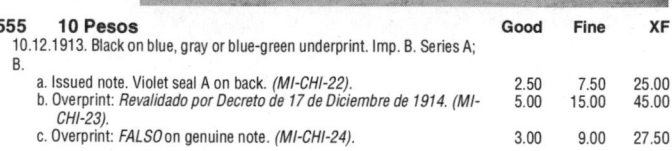

	Good	Fine	XF
S555 10 Pesos 10.12.1913. Black on blue, gray or blue-green underprint. Imp. B. Series A; B.			
a. Issued note. Violet seal A on back. *(MI-CHI-22).*	2.50	7.50	25.00
b. Overprint: *Revalidado por Decreto de 17 de Diciembre de 1914. (MI-CHI-23).*	5.00	15.00	45.00
c. Overprint: *FALSO* on genuine note. *(MI-CHI-24).*	3.00	9.00	27.50

		Good	Fine	XF
S556	**20 Pesos** 10.12.1913. Black on pale green underprint. Imp. B. Series A. Back: Seal A. *(MI-CHI-25).*			
	a. Issued note.	4.00	12.50	35.00
	b. Overprint: *Revalidado por Decreto de 17 de Diciembre de 1914. (MI-CHI-27).*	6.00	17.50	55.00
	c. Overprint: *FALSO* on genuine note. *(MI-CHI-26).*	5.00	15.00	45.00
	x. Error: *VIENTE* instead of *VEINTE. (MI-CHI-28).*	250.	750.	2250.

		Good	Fine	XF
S557	**50 Pesos** 10.12.1913. Black on green underprint. Imp. B. Series A.			
	a. 2 handwritten signatures. *(MI-CHI-30).*	30.00	90.00	270.
	b. 2 printed signatures. *(MI-CHI-29).*	30.00	90.00	270.
	c. Overprint: *Revalidado por Decreto de 17 de Diciembre de 1914. (MI-CHI-31).*	30.00	90.00	270.

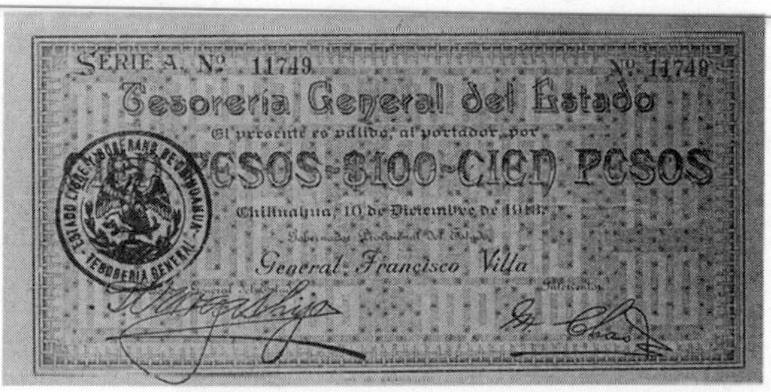

		Good	Fine	XF
S558	**100 Pesos** 10.12.1913. Black on red underprint. Imp. B. Series A.			
	a. 2 handwritten signatures. *(MI-CHI-33).*	50.00	150.	450.
	b. 2 printed signatures. *(MI-CHI-32).*	45.00	135.	400.
	c. Overprint: *Revalidado por Decreto de 17 de Diciembre de 1914.*	45.00	135.	400.

#S559-S561 overprint: *República Mexicana-Ejército Libertador-Comandancia; Estado Libre y Soberano de Chihuahua-Tesorería General; República Mexicana-Ejército Libertador-Brigada Pacheco-Detall* on back.

		Good	Fine	XF
S559	**1 Peso** 10.12.1913. Black on blue underprint. *(MI-CHI-34).*	175.	525.	1600.

		Good	Fine	XF
S560	**2 Pesos** 10.12.1913. Black on blue underprint. Without imprint. Series B.			
	a. Issued note. *(MI-CHI-35).*	200.	600.	1800.
	b. Additional overprint: *Brigada Malpica* on back.	225.	675.	1950.
S561	**10 Pesos** 10.12.1913. Black on blue underprint. Without imprint. Series B. *(MI-CHI-36).*	125.	375.	1100.

La Tesorería Municipal de C. Jiménez

1915 Issue

		Good	Fine	XF
S562	**25 Centavos** 24.12.1915. Black. *(SI-CHI-5).*	20.00	60.00	175.

Coahuila

Bank on Bank Checks

These checks were issued by the banks of Torreón, Coahuila, payable to the bearer in Mexico City once the railroad was reopened. They were cleverly devised by the local bank executives when under pressure by General Francisco Villa who demanded cash to pay his troops. Thus, these bank on bank checks became legal tender and the bank executives met a dire commitment.

Banco de la Leguna (RefaccionaBanco de Coahuila / Banco de la Laguna (Refaccionario)

1913 Issue

		Good	Fine	XF
S563	**1 Peso** 7.10.1913. Black on green underprint. Series A. Printer: Tip. C. Mountauriol. *(MI-COA-20).*	25.00	75.00	225.

		Good	Fine	XF
S564	**5 Pesos** 7.10.1913. Black. Series A. Printer: Tip. C. Mountauriol. *(MI-COA-21).*	20.00	60.00	180.
S565	**10 Pesos** 7.10.1913. Green. Series A. Printer: Tip. C. Mountauriol. *(MI-COA-22).*	25.00	75.00	225.
S566	**20 Pesos** 7.10.1913. Red. Series A. Printer: Tip. C. Mountauriol.			
	a. Issued note. *(MI-COA-23).*	25.00	75.00	225.
	b. Overprint: *San Luis Potosí. (MI-COA-24).*	45.00	135.	400.

1914 Issue

		Good	Fine	XF
S567	**5 Pesos** 5.2.1914. Black. Series B. Printer: Tip. Valdez. *(MI-COA-25).*	25.00	75.00	225.
S568	**10 Pesos** 5.2.1914. Green. Series B. Printer: Tip. Valdez. *(MI-COA-26).*	25.00	75.00	225.
S569	**20 Pesos** 5.2.1914. Red. Series B. Printer: Tip. Valdez.			
	a. Issued note. *(MI-COA-27).*	50.00	150.	450.
	b. Overprint: *Guadalajara. (MI-COA-28).*	50.00	150.	450.

Banco de Coahuila/Banco Nacional de México

1913 Issue

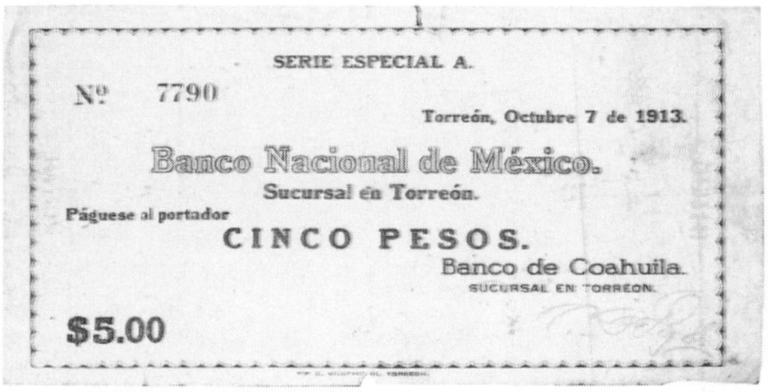

		Good	Fine	XF
S570	**5 Pesos** 7.10.1913. Black. Series A. Printer: Tip. C. Mountauriol. *(MI-COA-29).*	25.00	75.00	225.
S571	**10 Pesos** 7.10.1913. Green. Series A. Printer: Tip. C. Mountauriol. *(MI-COA-30).*	25.00	75.00	225.
S572	**20 Pesos** 7.10.1913. Red. Series A. Printer: Tip. C. Mountauriol. *(MI-COA-31).*	25.00	75.00	225.

Deutsch-Sudamerikanische Bank (Berlin) / Banco de Londres y México

1913 Issue

	Good	Fine	XF
S573 5 Pesos			
7.10.1913. Black. Series A. Printer: Tip. C. Mountauriol.			
a. Issued note. *(MI-COA-32).*	50.00	150.	450.
b. Cancellation: *Banco Germanico (Sucursal Mexico) Pagado. (MI-COA-33).*	100.	300.	900.
S574 10 Pesos			
7.10.1913. Green. Series A. Printer: Tip. C. Mountauriol.			
a. Issued note. *(MI-COA-34).*	75.00	225.	675.
b. Perforated: *CANCELADO. (MI-COA-35).*	125.	375.	1100.
S575 20 Pesos			
7.10.1913. Red. Series A. Printer: Tip. C. Mountauriol.			
a. Issued note. *(MI-COA-36).*	90.00	270.	800.
b. Perforated: *CANCELADO. (MI-COA-37).*	135.	400.	1200.

Deutsch-Sudamerikanische Bank (Berlin) / Banco Nacional de México

1913 Issue

#S576-S578 w/o imprint.

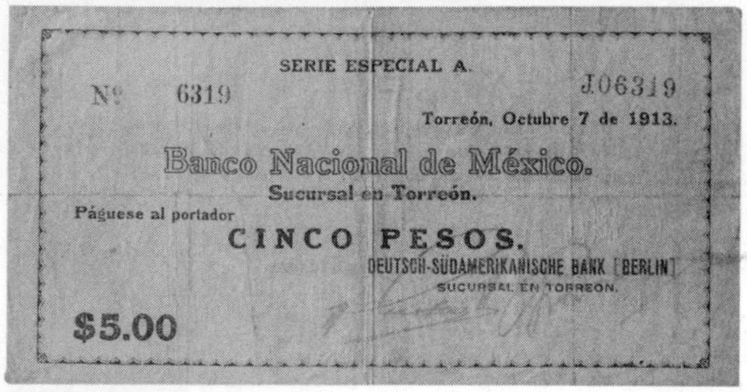

	Good	Fine	XF
S576 5 Pesos			
7.10.1913. Black. Series A.			
a. Issued note. *(MI-COA-38).*	55.00	165.	550.
b. Perforated: *CANCELADO. (MI-COA-39).*	100.	300.	900.
S577 10 Pesos			
7.10.1913. Green. Series A.			
a. Issued note. *(MI-COA-40).*	75.00	225.	675.
b. Perforated: *CANCELADO. (MI-COA-41).*	120.	360.	1050.
S578 20 Pesos			
7.10.1913. Red. Series A.			
a. Issued note. *(MI-COA-42).*	10.00	300.	900.
b. Perforated: *CANCELADO. (MI-COA-43).*	150.	450.	1350.

Banco de la Laguna (Refaccionario) / Banco de Coahuila

1913 Issues

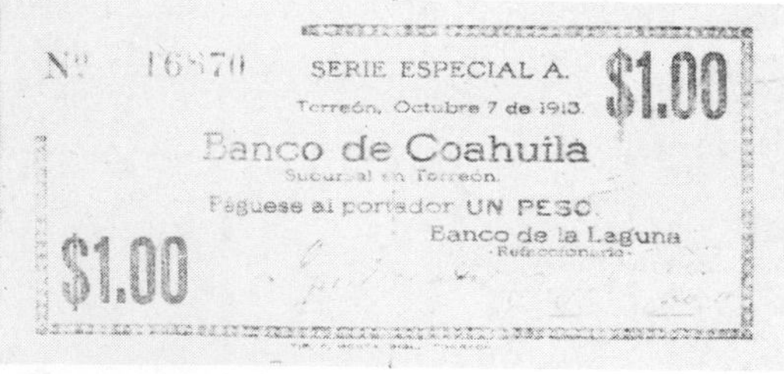

	Good	Fine	XF
S579 1 Peso			
7.10.1913. Black on green underprint. Series A. Printer: Tip. C. Mountauriol. *(MI-COA-44).*	25.00	75.00	225.
S580 5 Pesos			
7.10.1913. Black. Series A. Printer: Tip. C. Mountauriol. *(MI-COA-45).*	20.00	60.00	180.
S581 10 Pesos			
7.10.1913. Green. Series A. Printer: Tip. C. Mountauriol.			
a. Issued note. *(MI-COA-46).*	25.00	75.00	225.
b. Hand stamped: *FALSO (MI-COA-47).*	15.00	45.00	135.
S582 20 Pesos			
7.10.1913. Red. Series A. Printer: Tip. C. Mountauriol.			
a. Issued note. *(MI-COA-48).*	20.00	60.00	180.
b. Hand stamped: *FALSO. (MI-COA-49).*	15.00	45.00	135.
S583 50 Pesos			
18.12.1913. Series A. Paper: Thick blue. Printer: Tip. C. Mountauriol.			
a. Issued note. *(MI-COA-50).*	45.00	135.	400.
b. Hand stamped: *FALSO. (MI-COA-50a).*	45.00	135.	400.
S584 50 Pesos			
18.12.1913. Series A. Paper: Thin blue. Printer: Tip. C. Mountauriol. *(MI-COA-51).*	55.00	165.	500.

1914 Issues

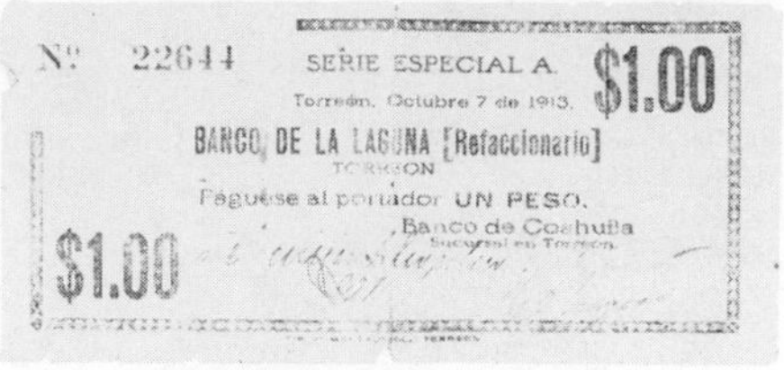

	Good	Fine	XF
S585 1 Peso			
5.1.1914. Black on blue-green underprint. Hand stamped signature. Series B. Printer: Tip. C. Mountauriol, Torreon. *(MI-COA-52).*	12.50	35.00	100.
S586 2 Pesos			
5.1.1914. Black on green underprint. Hand stamped signature. Series B. Printer: Tip. C. Mountauriol, Torreon. *(MI-COA-53).*	12.50	35.00	100.
S587 5 Pesos			
5.1.1914. Black. Like #S580. Series B. Printer: Tip. C. Mountauriol, Torreon.			
a. Issued note. *(MI-COA-55).*	35.00	100.	300.
b. Overprint: *GUADALAJARA. (MI-CA-56).*	35.00	100.	300.
S588 5 Pesos			
5.1.1914. Black. Series B. Printer: Tip. S. de la Peña. *(MI-COA-54).*	25.00	75.00	225.

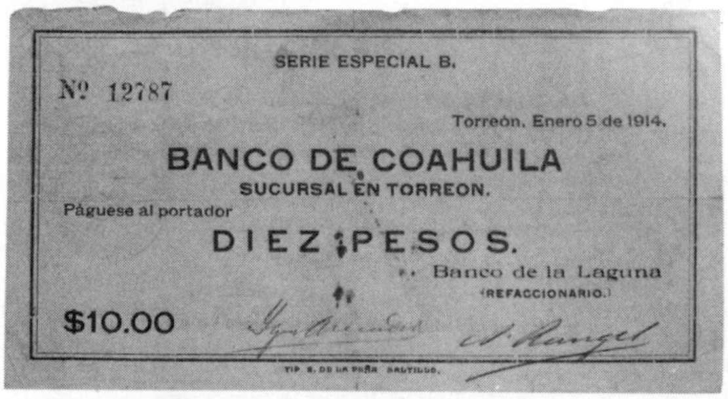

	Good	Fine	XF
S589 10 Pesos			
5.1.1914. Blue. Series B. Printer: Tip. S. de la Peña. *(MI-COA-57).*	25.00	75.00	225.
S590 20 Pesos			
5.1.1914. Sepia. Series B. Printer: Tip. S. de la Peña. *(MI-COA-58).*	25.00	75.00	225.
S591 50 Pesos			
5.1.1914. Series B. Printer: Tip. S. de la Peña. *(MI-COA-59).*	65.00	200.	600.

Banco de la Laguna (Refaccionario) / Banco de Londres y México

1913 Issue

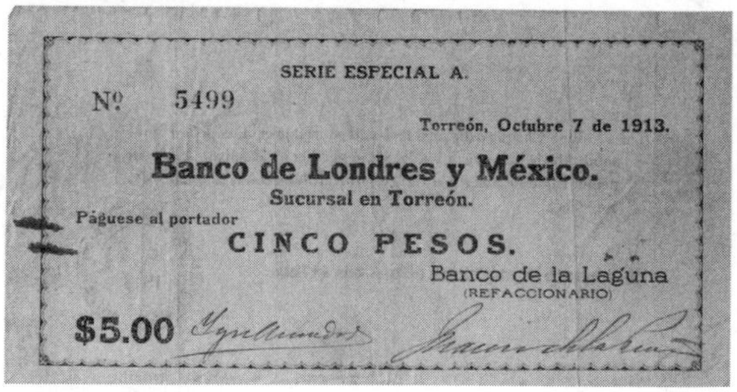

	Good	Fine	XF
S592 5 Pesos			
7.10.1913. Black. Series A.			
a. Issued note. *(MI-COA-60).*	25.00	75.00	225.
b. Hand stamped: *FALSO. (MI-COA-61).*	15.00	45.00	135.

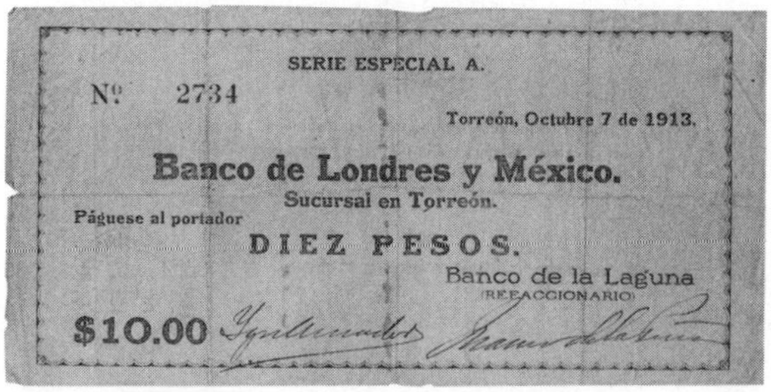

	Good	Fine	XF
S593 10 Pesos			
7.10.1913. Green. Series A.			
a. Issued note. *(MI-COA-62).*	25.00	75.00	225.
b. Hand stamped: *FALSO. (MI-COA-63).*	15.00	45.00	135.
c. Hand stamped: *CANCELADO. (MI-COA-63A).*	25.00	75.00	225.
S594 5 Pesos	**Good**	**Fine**	**XF**
7.10.1913. Watermark: *OLD HAMPSHIRE BOND.* Printer: Tip. C. Mountauriol, Torreón. Reported not confirmed.	—	—	—

		Good	Fine	XF
S595	**10 Pesos**			
	7.10.1913. Green. Watermark: *OLD HAMPSHIRE BOND.* Printer: Tip. C. Mountauriol, Torreón.			
	a. Issued note.	25.00	75.00	225.
	b. Large violet hand stamp: *CANCELADO.*	25.00	75.00	225.
	c. Large black hand stamp: *CANCELADO.*	25.00	75.00	225.
	d. Blue rectangular outlined hand stamp: *CANCELADO/MEXICO.*	25.00	75.00	225.
	e. Perforated: *AMORTIZADO.*	25.00	75.00	225.
	f. Small violet hand stamp: *CANCELADO.*	25.00	75.00	225.

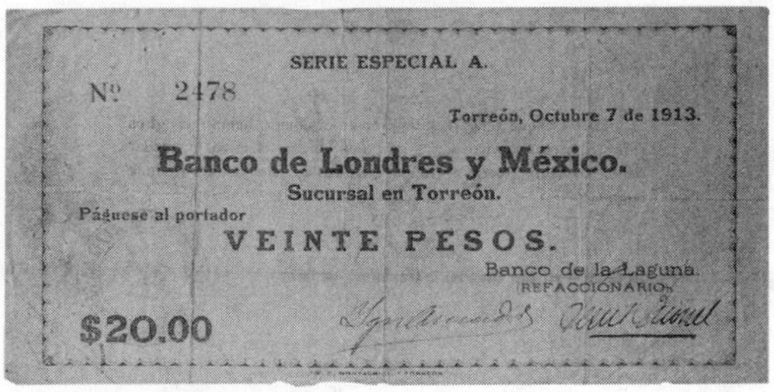

		Good	Fine	XF
S596	**20 Pesos**			
	7.10.1913. Red. Series A. Watermark: *OLD HAMPSHIRE BOND.* Printer: Tip. C. Mountauriol, Torreón.			
	a. Issued note. *(MI-COA-64).*	35.00	100.	300.
	b. Hand stamped: *FALSO. (MI-COA-65).*	35.00	100.	300.
S596A	**50 Pesos**			
	7.10.1913. Watermark: *OLD HAMPSHIRE BOND.* Printer: Tip. C. Mountauriol, Torreón. Reported not confirmed.	—	—	—

Banco de la Laguna (Refaccionario) / Banco Minero

1913 Issue

		Good	Fine	XF
S597	**5 Pesos**			
	7.10.1913. Black. Small text: *SUCURSAL...*Series A. Printer: Tip. C. Mountauriol. *(MI-COA-66).*	25.00	75.00	225.

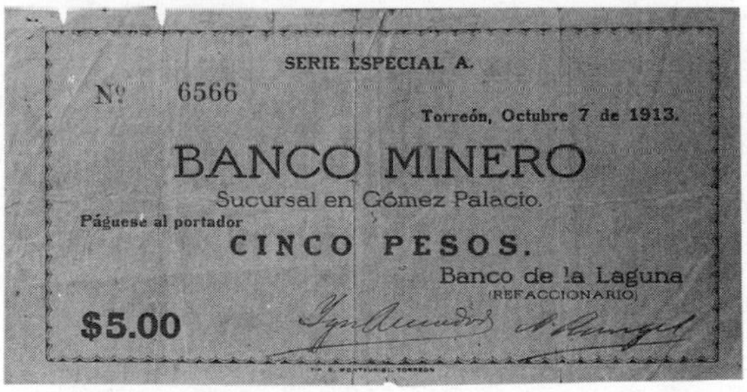

		Good	Fine	XF
S598	**5 Pesos**			
	7.10.1913. Large text: *SUCURSAL...*Series A. Printer: Tip. C. Mountauriol. *(MI-COA-67).*	25.00	75.00	225.
S599	**10 Pesos**			
	7.10.1913. Green. Series A. Printer: Tip. C. Mountauriol.			
	a. Issued note. *(MI-COA-68).*	12.50	35.00	110.
	b. Hand stamped: *FALSO. (MI-COA-69).*	15.00	45.00	135.
S600	**20 Pesos**			
	7.10.1913. Red. Small text: *SUCURSAL...*Series A. Printer: Tip. C. Mountauriol. *(MI-COA-70).*	15.00	45.00	135.
S601	**20 Pesos**			
	7.10.1913. Red. Large text: *SUCURSAL...*Series A. Printer: Tip. C. Mountauriol.			
	a. Issued note. *(MI-COA-71).*	15.00	45.00	135.
	b. Hand stamped: *FALSO. (MI-COA-72).*	20.00	60.00	180.
S602	**50 Pesos**			
	18.12.1913. Blue. Series A. Printer: Tip. C. Mountauriol.			
	a. Issued note. *(MI-COA-73).*	65.00	200.	600.
	b. Hand stamped: *CANCELADO.*	45.00	135.	400.

Banco de Londres y México / Deutsch-Sudamerikanische Bank (Berlin)

1913 Issue

#S603-S605 w/o imprint.

		Good	Fine	XF
S603	**5 Pesos**			
	7.10.1913. Black. Series A. *(MI-COA-74).*	50.00	150.	450.
S603A	**5 Pesos**			
	7.10.1913. Black. Similar to #S603 but with *Torreón* and date centered.	50.00	150.	450.
S604	**10 Pesos**			
	7.10.1913. Green. Series A. *(MI-COA-75).*	75.00	225.	675.
S605	**20 Pesos**			
	7.10.1913. Red. Series A. *(MI-COA-76).*	90.00	270.	800.
S606	**20 Pesos**	**Good**	**Fine**	**XF**
	7.10.1913. Red. Torreón and date at center. Both serial # printed. Series A. Printer: Mountauriol, Torreón. *(MI-COA-77)*	125.	375.	1100.

Banco de Londres y México / Banco de la Laguna (Refaccionario)

1913 Issue

#S607 and S608 printer: Tip. C. Mountauriol.

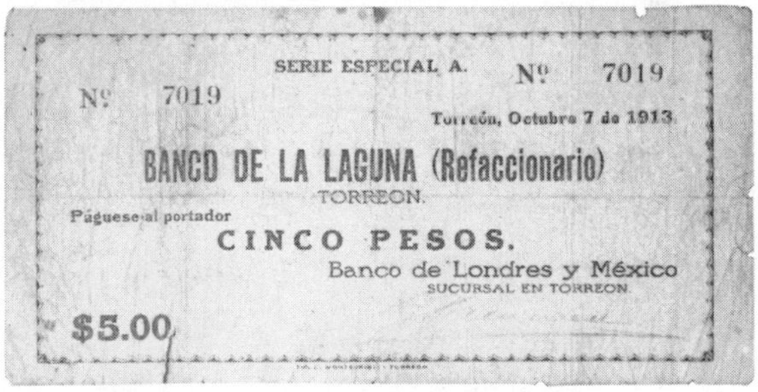

		Good	Fine	XF
S607	**5 Pesos**			
	7.10.1913. Series A. Printer: Tip. C. Mountauriol. *(MI-COA-78).*	50.00	150.	450.
S608	**10 Pesos**			
	7.10.1913. Green. Series A. Printer: Tip. C. Mountauriol.			
	a. Issued note. *(MI-COA-79).*	65.00	200.	600.
	b. Hand stamped: *CANCELADO. (MI-COA-80).*	65.00	200.	600.

Banco de Londres y México / Banco Nacional de México

1913 Issue

		Good	Fine	XF
S609	**1 Peso**			
	7.10.1913. Black on green underprint. Series A. Printer: Tip. C. Mountauriol. *(MI-COA-81).*	35.00	110.	225.

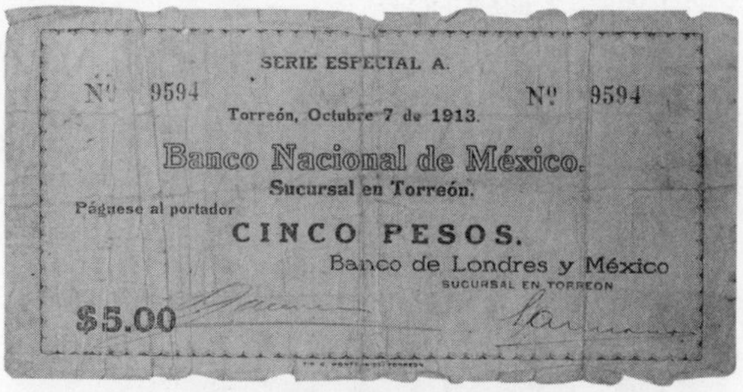

S610 5 Pesos	Good	Fine	XF
7.10.1913. Black. Series A. Printer: Tip. C. Mountauriol. *(MI-COA-82).*	35.00	110.	225.

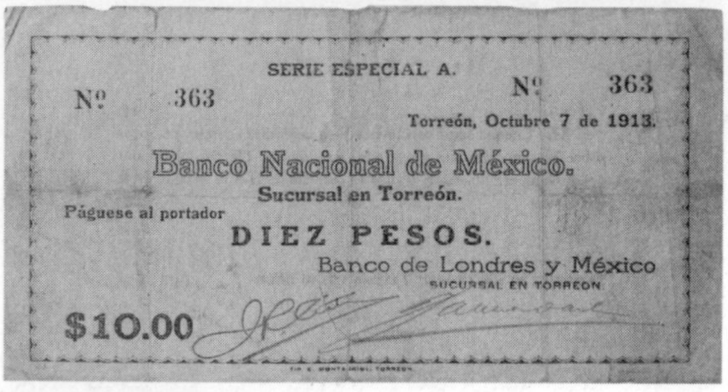

S611 10 Pesos	Good	Fine	XF
7.10.1913. Series A. Printer: Tip. C. Mountauriol. *(MI-COA-83).*	45.00	135.	400.
S612 20 Pesos			
7.10.1913. Series A. Printer: Tip. C. Mountauriol. *(MI-COA-84).*	45.00	135.	400.

Banco Nacional de México / Banco de Coahuila

1913 Issue

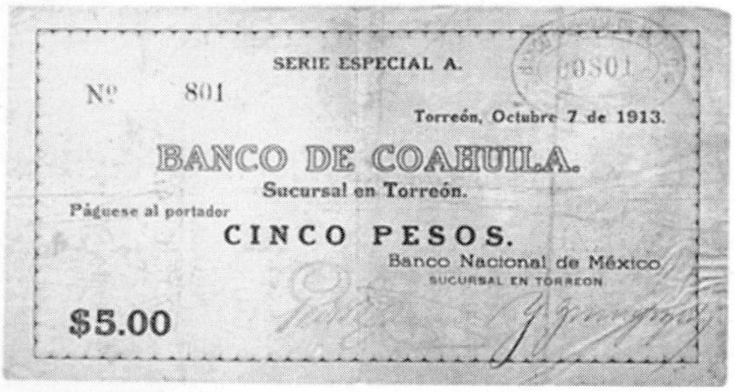

S613 5 Pesos	Good	Fine	XF
7.10.1913. Black. Series A. *(MI-COA-85).*	35.00	110.	330.
S614 10 Pesos			
7.10.1913. Green. Series A. *(MI-COA-86).*	20.00	60.00	180.

Banco Nacional de México / Deutsch-Sudamerikanische Bank (Berlin)

1913 Issue

S615 5 Pesos	Good	Fine	XF
7.10.1913. Black. Series A. Printer: Tip. C. Mountauriol. *(MI-COA-87).*	50.00	150.	450.
S616 10 Pesos			
7.10.1913. Series A. Printer: Tip. C. Mountauriol. *(MI-COA-88).*	75.00	225.	675.
S617 20 Pesos			
7.10.1913. Series A. Printer: Tip. C. Mountauriol. *(MI-COA-89).*	90.00	270.	800.

Banco Nacional de México / Banco de Londres y México

1913 Issue

S618 1 Peso	Good	Fine	XF
7.10.1913. Series A. Printer: Tip. C. Mountauriol. *(MI-COA-90).*	30.00	90.00	270.

S619 5 Pesos	Good	Fine	XF
7.10.1913. Series A. Printer: Tip. C. Mountauriol. *(MI-COA-91).*	30.00	90.00	270.

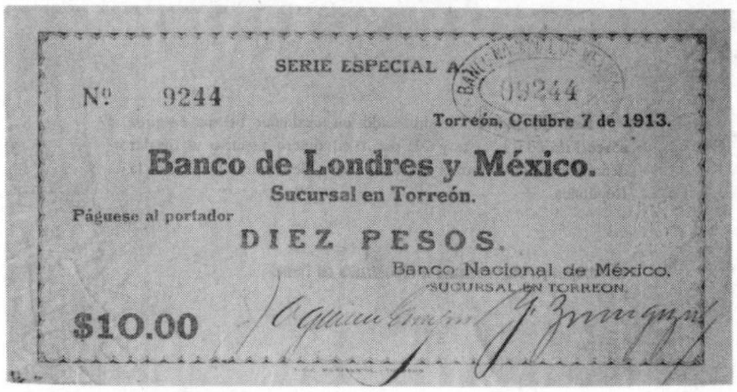

S620 10 Pesos	Good	Fine	XF
7.10.1913. Green. Series A. Printer: Tip. C. Mountauriol.			
a. Issued note. *(MI-COA-92).*	20.00	60.00	180.
b. Overprint: *EL CHEQUE LÉJITIMO DEL CONTENIDO DE ESTE FUE PAGADO. (MI-COA-93).*	20.00	60.00	180.
c. Hand stamped: *CANCELADO.*	15.00	45.00	135.

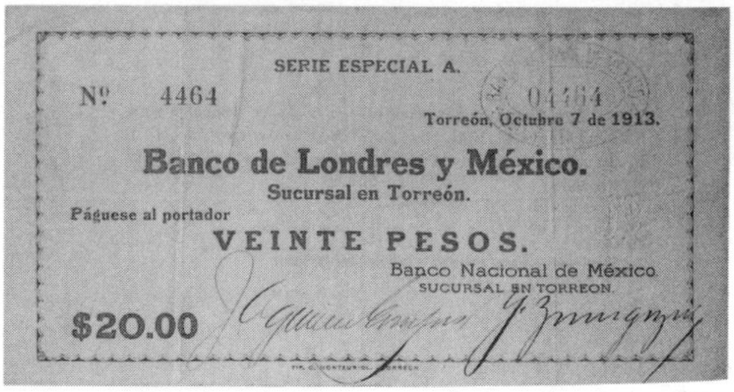

S621 20 Pesos	Good	Fine	XF
7.10.1913. Red. Series A. Printer: Tip. C. Mountauriol.			
a. Issued note. *(MI-COA-94).*	20.00	60.00	180.
b. Overprint: *EL CHEQUE LÉJITIMO DEL CONTENIDO DE ESTE FUE PAGADO. (MI-COA-95).*	20.00	60.00	180.

Tesorería Municipal, Municipio de Matamoros

ND Issue

S622 5 Centavos	Good	Fine	XF
ND. Black. Paper: Cream pasteboard. *(SI-COA-1).*	7.50	20.00	60.00
S623 10 Centavos			
ND. Red. Series A. Paper: Cream pasteboard. *(SI-COA-2).*	7.50	20.00	60.00

S624 20 Centavos	Good	Fine	XF
ND. Blue. Series A. Paper: Cream pasteboard. *(SI-COA-3).*	7.50	20.00	60.00

Gobierno Constitucionalista de México, Monclova

Decree of April 26, 1913

This was the first issue of paper money emitted by revolutionary forces and consequently, the first military issue of the revolution. These notes were issued by General Venustiano Carranza's forces when they were fighting against those of President Victoriano Huerta.

VALIDATION HAND STAMPS:

1. REVALIDADO POR DECRETO DE 17 DE DICIEMBRE DE 1914.
2. DIVISION DEL NORTE, EJERCITO CONSTITUCIONALISTA, JEFATURA DE ARMAS.
3. PREFECTURA DEL DISTRITO DE NAZAS - ESTADO DE COAHUILA, MEXICO.
4. TESORERIA GENERAL DEL ESTADO DE SONORA, HERMOSILLO.
5. RENTA DEL TIMBRE, PRINCIPAL DE NUEVO LEON.
6. JEFATURA POLITICAL DEL DISTRITO NORTE, ENSENADA.
7. PRESIDENCIA MUNICIPAL DE CANANEA, SONORA, MEX.
8. LA PAZ, B.C. (eagle above)
9. RECAUDACION DE RENTAS DEL DISTRITO DE MAZATLAN. RETIRADO DE LA CIRCULACION.
10. BRIGADA CARRASCO, 3A, DIVISION.

S625 1 Peso	Good	Fine	XF
28.5.1913. Black. Series A. Back: Green. Circular red seal.			
a. Small signature at right.	6.00	17.50	55.00
b. As a. with overprint: *REVALIDADO/POR DECRETO DE 17 DE DICEMBRE DE 1914.*	10.00	30.00	90.00
c. Large printed signature at right.	1.50	5.00	15.00
d. As c. with overprint: *REVALIDADO/POR DECRETO DE 17 DE DICIEMBRE DE 1914.*	2.00	6.00	17.50

S626 1 Peso	Good	Fine	XF
20.5.1913. Black. Like #S626 but with different guilloches around numerals. Series A. Back: Green. Circular red seal. *(MI-COA-1).*	1.50	5.00	15.00
S627 5 Pesos			
28.5.1913. Black. Narrow *5's* in corners. Series B. Back: Green. Narrow *5's* at left and right. *(MI-COA-2).*	7.50	20.00	60.00
S628 5 Pesos			
28.5.1913. Black. Large *5's* in lower corners, small *5's* in upper corners. Series B. Back: Green.			
a. Small signature at right.	1.50	5.00	15.00
b. As a. with overprint: *REVALIDADO/POR DECRETO DE 17 DE DICIEMBRE DE 1914.*	1.50	5.00	15.00
c. Large signature at right. *(MI-COA-3).*	1.50	5.00	15.00
S629 10 Pesos			
28.5.1913. Black. Series C. Back: Green. Large: *DIEZ* at upper left and right. Poor quality printing. *(MI-COA-4).*	5.00	15.00	45.00
S630 10 Pesos			
28.5.1913. Black. Series C. Like #S629 but with narrow 0's in 10's. Back: Green. Small *DIEZ* at upper left and right.	5.00	15.00	45.00
S631 10 Pesos			
28.5.1913. Black Back: Green. Large: *DIEZ* at upper left and right. Like #S629 but better quality printing. *(MI-COA-5).*	3.00	10.00	30.00
S632 20 Pesos			
28.5.1913. Black. *VIENTE* (error) in upper and lower borders. Series D.			
a. Small signature at right. *(MI-COA-6).*	5.00	15.00	45.00
b. As a. with overprint: *REVALIDADO/POR DECRETO DE 17 DE DICIEMBRE DE 1914* on a.	5.00	15.00	45.00
c. Large signature at right.	5.00	15.00	45.00
d. As c. with overprint: *REVALIDADO/POR DECRETO DE 17 DE DICIEMBRE DE 1914* on c.	5.00	15.00	45.00
S633 20 Pesos			
28.5.1913. Black. Like #S629 but with retouched 20's at lower left and right and *VEINTE* corrected in borders. Series D. Back: Green. *(MI-COA-7).*	—	—	—

NOTE: Serial #'s have been recorded for #S632 both above and below #S633. The crude appearance of the *20's* at lower left and right similar to the *10's* on #S630 may prove the claims of earlier catalogers of a spurious issue.

S634 50 Pesos	Good	Fine	XF
28.5.1913. Black. Series E. Back: Orange.			
a. 1 handwritten and 1 printed signature. *(MI-COA-8).*	15.00	45.00	135.
b. 2 printed signatures. *(MI-COA-9).*	30.00	90.00	270.
S635 100 Pesos			
28.5.1913. Black. Series F. Back: Orange.			
a. 2 handwritten signatures. *(MI-COA-10).*	25.00	75.00	225.
b. 1 handwritten and 1 printed signature. *(MI-COA-11).*	30.00	90.00	270.
c. Without signature.	40.00	120.	360.

Tesorería Municipal, Monclova

1914 ND Issue

S636 5 Centavos	Good	Fine	XF
ND. Paper: Green pasteboard. *(SI-COA-4).*	45.00	135.	400.

Jefatura de Armas - M.S. González, Muzquiz

1914 Issue

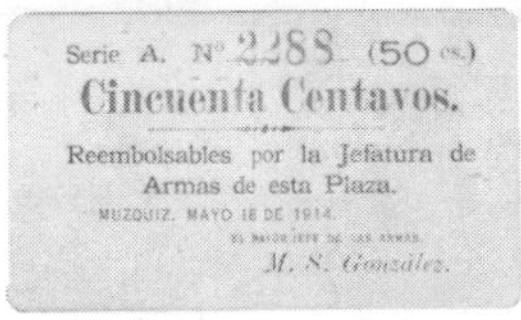

S637 50 Centavos	Good	Fine	XF
18.5.1914. *(MI-COA-12).*	40.00	120.	360.

Ejército Constitucionalista, Parras

1914 Issue

S638 25 Centavos	Good	Fine	XF
30.4.1914. Black on yellow underprint. Hand stamped signature of Roberto Rivas.			
a. Issued note. *(MI-COA-13).*	50.00	150.	450.
b. Hand stamped: *AMORTIZADO.*	45.00	135.	400.
S639 50 Centavos			
30.4.1914. Green on yellow underprint. Hand stamped signature of Roberto Rivas. *(MI-COA-14).*	50.00	150.	450.

S640 1 Peso	Good	Fine	XF
30.4.1914. Orange on gray underprint. Hand stamped signature of Roberto Rivas.			
a. Issued note. *(MI-COA-15).*	50.00	150.	450.
b. Hand stamped: *AMORTIZADO.*	45.00	135.	400.

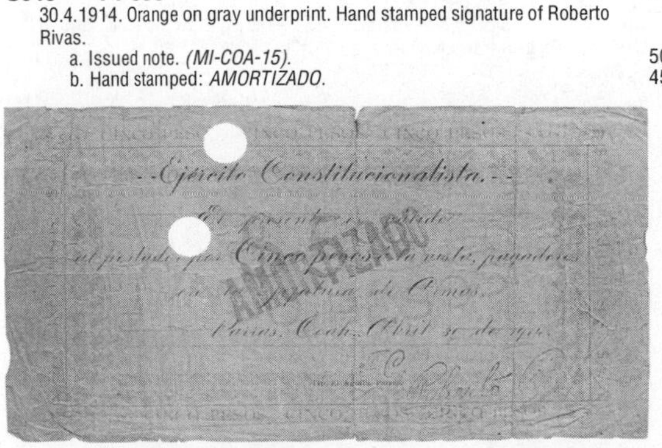

S641 5 Pesos	Good	Fine	XF
30.4.1914. Black on yellow and pink underprint. Hand stamped signature of Roberto Rivas. Paper: Thin.			
a. Issued note. *(MI-COA-16).*	65.00	200.	600.
b. Hand stamped: *AMORTIZADO.*	50.00	150.	450.

La Tesorería de la Federación, Saltillo

1914 Issue

		Good	Fine	XF
S642	**10 Centavos** 27.1.1914. Black on pale pink underprint. National arms at center. Series F. Back: Red. Mining town at center. *(SI-COA-5).*	1.50	5.00	15.00
S643	**25 Centavos** 27.1.1914. Black on yellow underprint. National arms at center. Series E. Back: Brown. Mining town at center. *(SI-COA-6).*	15.00	45.00	135.
S644	**50 Centavos** 27.1.1914. Black on dull purple underprint. National arms at center. Series D-B; D-E; D-G. Back: Dull purple. Mining town at center. *(SI-COA-7).*	1.50	5.00	15.00
S645	**1 Peso** 27.1.1914. Black on pale blue underprint. National arms at center. Series B; C. Back: Mining town at center. *(SI-COA-8).*	1.50	5.00	15.00
S646	**2 Pesos** 27.1.1914. Black on pale green underprint. National arms at center. Series C. Back: Mining town at center. *(SI-COA-9).*	1.50	5.00	15.00
S647	**5 Pesos** 27.1.1914. Black on pink underprint. National arms at center. Series A. Back: Red. Mining town at center. *(SI-COA-10).*	2.00	6.00	18.00

Municipio de San Pedro

1916 Issue

		Good	Fine	XF
S648	**5 Centavos** 1916. Series A. Paper: Gray pasteboard. *(SI-COA-11).*	7.50	20.00	60.00
S649	**10 Centavos** 1916. Like #S648. Series D. Paper: Green pasteboard. *(SI-COA-12).*	7.50	20.00	60.00
S650	**25 Centavos** 1916. Like #S648. Paper: Pasteboard. *(SI-COA-13).*	10.00	30.00	90.00
S651	**50 Centavos** 1916. Like #S648. Paper: Orange pasteboard. *(SI-COA-14).*	10.00	30.00	90.00

Ejército Constitucionalista - División del Norte, Torreón

General Francisco"Pancho" Villa

1913 Issue

		Good	Fine	XF
S652	**5 Centavos** 20.11.1913. National arms at center. *(MI-COA-17).*	40.00	120.	360.
S653	**50 Centavos** 20.11.1913. National arms at center. *(MI-COA-18).*	40.00	120.	360.

		Good	Fine	XF
S654	**1 Peso** 20.11.1913. Blue. National arms at center. *(MI-COA-19).*	40.00	120.	360.

El Estado de Coahuila

Decree of September 1, 1914

Translation of back text: "This Emission is Authorized by the First Chief of the Constitutionalist Army, in Charge of the Executive Power of the Nation."

		Good	Fine	XF
S655	**50 Centavos** D.1914. Series A. *(MI-COA-96).*	175.	525.	1575.
S656	**1 Peso** D.1914. Seated Justice at left. Series B. *(MMI-COA-97).*	175.	525.	1575.

		Good	Fine	XF
S657	**5 Pesos** D.1914. Black on brown underprint. Standing Justice at left. Series C. *(MI-COA-98).*	150.	450.	1350.

		Good	Fine	XF
S658	**10 Pesos** D.1914. Black on green underprint. Seated Justice at left. Series D. *(MI-COA-97).*	150.	450.	1350.
S659	**20 Pesos** D.1914. Black on brown underprint. Standing Justice at left. Like #S657. Series E. *(MI-COA-100).*	175.	525.	1575.

Colima

Gobierno del Estado de Colima

ND Issue

		Good	Fine	XF
S660	**5 Centavos** ND. Black. Back: Palm tree at left center, national arms at center. Paper: Gray pasteboard. *(SI-COL-20).*	20.00	60.00	180.
S661	**10 Centavos** ND. Red. Back: Palm tree at left center, national arms at center. Paper: Gray pasteboard. *(SI-COL-21).*	20.00	60.00	180.

El Estado Libre y Soberano de Colima

ND Issue

		Good	Fine	XF
S662	**50 Centavos** ND. Arms at left, national arms at center. Printer: Imprenta Franco Mexicana, S.A. Remainder. (Not issued). *(SI-COL-16).*	135.	400.	1200.

		Good	Fine	XF
S663	**1 Peso** ND. Black on green underprint. Arms at left, national arms at center. Printer: Imprenta Franco Mexicana, S.A. *(SI-COL-17).*			
	a. Issued note. *(SI-COL-17A).*	150.	450.	1350.
	r. Remainder.	125.	375.	1100.

La Tesorería General del Estado de Colima

ND Issue

		Good	Fine	XF
S664	**5 Centavos** ND. National arms at center. Paper: Blue pasteboard. *(SI-COL-18).*	20.00	60.00	180.
S665	**10 Centavos** ND. National arms at center. Like #S664. Paper: Brown pasteboard. *(SI-COL-19).*	20.00	60.00	180.

Decree No. 117 of April 22, 1914

		Good	Fine	XF
S666	**10 Centavos** June 1914. Orange on cream. Series A. *(SI-COL-1).*	45.00	135.	400.

		Good	Fine	XF
S667	**50 Centavos** June 1914. Green on orange underprint. National arms at upper center. *(SI-COL-2).*	45.00	135.	400.

	Good	Fine	XF
S668 1 Peso June 1914. Blue on brown underprint. *(SI-COL-3).*	35.00	110.	330.

Decree of July 22, 1914

	Good	Fine	XF
S669 10 Centavos 22.7.1914. *(SI-COL-4).*	50.00	150.	450.

	Good	Fine	XF
S670 20 Centavos 22.7.1914. Black on orange underprint. Volcanoes, palm trees at right. Series B. *(SI-COL-5).*	50.00	150.	450.

	Good	Fine	XF
S671 50 Centavos 22.7.1914. Black on blue underprint. Volcanoes, palm trees at right. Series B. *(SI-COL-6).*	30.00	90.00	270.

Decree of January 18, 1915

	Good	Fine	XF
S672 5 Centavos 18.1.1915. Blue. *(SI-COL-7).*	65.00	200.	600.
S673 10 Centavos 18.1.1915. *(SI-COL-8).*	90.00	270.	800.
S674 20 Centavos 18.1.1915. Series A. *(SI-COL-9).*	50.00	150.	450.

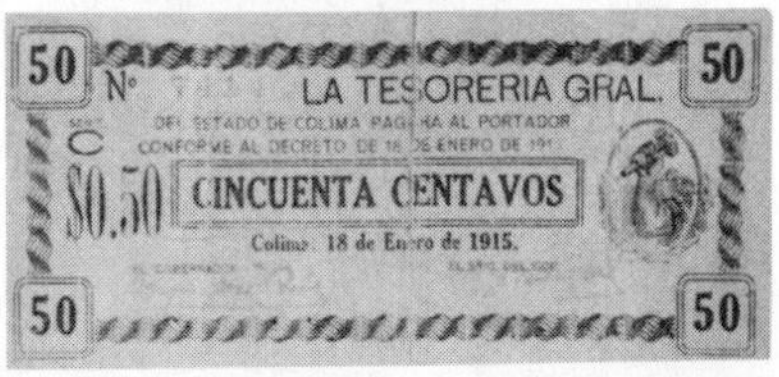

	Good	Fine	XF
S675 50 Centavos 18.1.1915. Arm and hammer at right. Series C. *(SI-COL-10).*	50.00	150.	450.

	Good	Fine	XF
S676 1 Peso 18.1.1915. Blue on pink underprint. National arms at center. Series A.			
a. Issued note. *(SI-COL-11).*	65.00	200.	600.
b. Overprint: *AMORTIZADO.*	65.00	200.	600.

Decree of June 4, 1915

	Good	Fine	XF
S677 20 Centavos 15.6.1915. Black. Series A. Printer: Lit. de J. M. Iguiniz Guada. *(SI-COL-12).*	20.00	60.00	180.
S678 50 Centavos 15.6.1915. Black on light green underprint. Series B. Printer: Lit. de J. M. Iguiniz Guada. *(SI-COL-13).*	20.00	60.00	180.
S679 1 Peso 15.6.1915. Black on brown underprint. Government building at center. Series C. Printer: Lit. de J. M. Iguiniz Guada. *(SI-COL-14).*	20.00	60.00	180.

	Good	Fine	XF
S680 5 Pesos 15.6.1915. Black on brown underprint. Government building at center. Series C. Like #S679. Printer: Lit. de J. M. Iguiniz Guada. *(SI-COL-15).*	75.00	225.	675.

Distrito Federal

Gobierno Constitucionalista de México, República

ND Transitorio Issue

	Good	Fine	XF
S681 5 Centavos ND. Standing Justice at center. Eagle's head to left. Handstamped *GMC* monogram. Back: National arms at center. Paper: Orange pasteboard. *(MI-DF-67).*	1.00	3.00	10.00
S682 5 Centavos ND. Standing Justice at center. Eagle's head to right. Handstamped *GMC* monogram. Back: National arms at center. Paper: Pink pasteboard.			
a. Issued note. *(MI-DF-68).*	1.50	5.00	15.00
b. Overprint: *C. I. JUAREZ. (MI-DF-69).*	1.50	5.00	15.00
c. Overprint: *Durango. (MI-DF-70).*	1.50	5.00	15.00
d. Overprint *PARRAL. (MI-DF-71).*	1.50	5.00	15.00
e. Overprint: *NOGALES.*	2.00	6.00	18.00
S683 10 Centavos ND. Standing Justice at center. Eagle's head to left. Handstamped *GMC* monogram. Like #S681. Back: National arms at center. Paper: Dark blue pasteboard.			
a. Issued note. *(MI-DF-72).*	1.50	5.00	15.00
b. Overprint: *NOGALES.*	1.50	5.00	15.00
S684 10 Centavos ND. Standing Justice at center. Eagle's head to right. Handstamped *GMC* monogram. Like #S682. Back: National arms at center. Paper: Light blue pasteboard.			
a. Issued note. *(MI-DF-73).*	1.00	3.00	9.00
b. Overprint: *C. JUAREZ (MI-DF-74).*	1.00	3.00	9.00
c. Overprint: *Durango.*	1.00	3.00	9.00
d. Overprint: *MATAMOROS.*	1.50	5.00	15.00

Gobierno Constitucionalista, República Mexicana

Decree of July 21, 1915 - "Infalsificables" Issue

	Good	Fine	XF
S685 5 Pesos D.1915. Black, green, and multicolor. Monument to Cuauhtémoc at left. Series C. Back: Green. Printer: ABNC.			
a. Issued note. *(SI-DF-5).*	1.50	5.00	15.00
p. Proof.	—	Unc	250.
s. Specimen.	—	Unc	300.

S686 10 Pesos	Good	Fine	XF
D.1915. Black, blue, and multicolor. Portrait Jose M. Morelos y Pavón at center. Series I. Back: Blue. Printer: ABNC.			
a. Issued note.*(SI-DF-6)*.	1.00	3.00	9.00
p. Proof.	—	Unc	250.
s. Specimen.	—	Unc	300.

S687 20 Pesos	Good	Fine	XF
D.1915. Black, pale orange and multicolor. Monument to Juárez at left. Series X. Back: Orange. Printer: ABNC.			
a. Issued note. *(SI-DF-7)*.	2.00	6.00	18.00
p. Proof.	—	Unc	250.
s. Specimen.	—	Unc	300.

S688 50 Pesos	Good	Fine	XF
D.1915. Black, tan, and multicolor. Courtyard at center. Series E. Back: Brown. Printer: ABNC.			
a. Issued note. *(SI-DF-8)*.	12.50	35.00	110.
p. Proof.	—	Unc	250.
s. Specimen. Series E. ND.	—	Unc	350.
S689 100 Pesos			
D.1915. Black, pale green, and multicolor. Indigenous ruins at center. Series M. Back: Olive-green. Printer: ABNC.			
a. Issued note. *(SI-DP-9)*.	9.00	27.50	80.00
p. Proof.	—	Unc	250.
s. Specimen.	—	Unc	350.

Gobierno Federal de la República Mexicana

1915 Issue

S690 1 Peso	Good	Fine	XF
1.8.1915. Black on green underprint. National arms at center. Printer: ABNC. Proof. *(SI-DF-18)*.	—	Unc	350.
S691 2 Pesos			
1.8.1915. Black on orange underprint. National arms at center. Printer: ABNC. Proof. *(SI-DF-19)*.	—	Unc	350.

S692 5 Pesos	Good	Fine	XF
1.8.1915. Black on green underprint. National arms at center. Printer: ABNC. Proof. *(SI-DF-20)*.	—	Unc	350.
S693 10 Pesos			
1.8.1915. Black on tan underprint. National arms at center. Printer: ABNC. Proof. *(SI-DF-21)*.	—	Unc	450.
S694 20 Pesos			
1.8.1915. Black on olive-green underprint. National arms at center. Printer: ABNC. Proof. *(SI-DF-22)*.	—	Unc	450.
S695 50 Pesos			
1.8.1915. Black on tan underprint. National arms at center. Printer: ABNC. Proof. *(SI-DF-23)*.	—	Unc	450.

S696 100 Pesos	Good	Fine	XF
1.8.1915. Black on tan underprint. National arms at center. Printer: ABNC. Proof. *(SI-DF-24)*.	—	Unc	500.

Gobierno Provisional de México, República

1914 ND Issue

S697 5 Centavos	VG	VF	UNC
ND. Seated Justice at center. Back: National arms at left. Overprint: Brown or red: *V*. Paper: Deep orange or yellow-orange pasteboard. *(MI-DF-1)*.	1.00	3.00	9.00
S698 10 Centavos	**VG**	**VF**	**UNC**
ND. Standing Justice at left. Back: National arms at center. Overprint: *X*. Paper: Gray or blue pasteboard. *(MI-DF-2)*.	1.00	3.00	9.00
S699 20 Centavos	**VG**	**VF**	**UNC**
ND. Liberty at left. Back: Aztec calendar stone at center. Paper: Gray pasteboard. *(MI-DF-3)*.	1.00	3.00	9.00

1914 Issue

S700 20 Centavos	VG	VF	UNC
1914. Justice at center. Series U; Y. Back: National arms at center. Paper: Light brown pasteboard. *(MI-DF-4)*.	1.00	3.00	9.00

Gobierno Provisional de México, Mexico City

Decreto 19.9.1914; 1914 Issue

S701 1 Peso	Good	Fine	XF
20.10.1914. Black on tan underprint. Seated Liberty at left, national arms with Popocatepetl and Ixtaccihuatl (volcanoes) in background at center. Series A. Back: Brown.			
a. Issued note. *(MI-DF-5)*.	2.00	6.00	18.00
b. Overprint: *REVALIDADO/por decreto 17....* with serial # on face. *(MI-DF-6)*.	1.00	3.00	9.00
c. Without serial # or seals on back. *(MI-DF-7)*.	7.50	20.00	60.00
d. Back blank. *(MI-DF-8)*.	25.00	75.00	225.
e. Overprint: *ATOYAC, AGENCIA DEL TIMBRE. (MI-DF-10)*.	6.00	18.00	55.00
f. Overprint: *ADMON. PRINCIPAL DEL TIMBRE, GUADALAJARA. (MI-DF-11>*.	3.00	9.00	27.50
g. Overprint: *ADMON. PRINCIPAL DEL TIMBRE, REVALIDADO, SAN LUIS POTOSI. (MI-DF-12)*.	3.00	9.00	27.50
h. Overprint: *ADMINISTRACION SUBALTERNA DEL TIMBRE, CIUDAD GUZMAN. (MI-DF-13)*.	3.00	9.00	27.50
i. Overprint: *ADMINISTRACION SUBALTERNA DEL TIMBRE, COCULA. (MI-DF-14)*.	6.00	18.00	55.00
j. Overprint: *AGENCIA DEL TIMBRE, SAN GABRIEL. (MI-DF-15)*.	6.00	18.00	55.00
k. Overprint: *AGENCIA DEL TIMBRE, SAYULA. (MI-DF-16)*.	6.00	18.00	55.00
l. Overprint: *AGENCIA DEL TIMBRE, ZACOALCO. (MI-DF-17)*.	6.00	18.00	55.00
m. Overprint: *DEPARTAMENTO DE HACIENDA, MARZO 15, 1915, ZAMORA. (MI-DF-18)*.	5.00	15.00	45.00
n. Overprint: *REPUBLICA MEXICANA, SECRETARIA DE HACIENDA, REVALIDADO. (MI-DF-19)*.	6.00	18.00	55.00
o. Overprint: *REVALIDADO POR ORDEN DEL DEPARTAMENTO DE HACIENDA, CELAYA, MARZO DE 1915. (MI-DF-20)*.	5.00	15.00	45.00
p. Overprint: *REVALIDADO/POR DECRETO, SAN MIGUEL DE ALLENDE. (MI-DF-21)*.	6.00	18.00	55.00
q. Overprint: *REVALIDADO CONFORME A LA CIRCULAR DE HACIENDA DE 17 DE FEBRERO DE 1915, SAN MARCOS. (MI-DF-22)*.	7.50	20.00	60.00
r. Overprint: *TEOCUITATLAN. (MI-DF-23)*.	6.00	18.00	55.00
s. Overprint: *TAMAZULA, AGENCIA DEL TIMBRE. (MI-DF-24)*.	5.00	15.00	45.00
t. Overprint: *PAGADURIA GENERAL DE LA OFICINA DE OPERACIONES 15 MARZO DE 1915, MICHOACAN. (MI-DF-25)*.	7.50	20.00	60.00
u. Overprint: *ADMON. SUBALTERNA DEL TIMBRE, TAPALPA. (MI-DF-26)*.	6.00	18.00	55.00
v. Overprint: *AGENCIA DEL TIMBRE, 9o CANTON, TUXPAN. (MI-DF-27)*.	6.00	18.00	55.00
w. Overprint: *REVALIDADO POR ACUERDO DEL DEPARTAMENTO DE HACIENDA, QUERETARO. (MI-DF-28)*.	5.00	15.00	45.00
x. Overprint: *SECRETARIA DE HACIENDA, VERACRUZ.*	5.00	15.00	45.00
y. Face proof. *(MI-DF-9)*.	—	Unc	250.
S702 5 Pesos	**Good**	**Fine**	**XF**
20.10.1914. Black on light green underprint. Seated Liberty at left, national arms with Popocatepetl and Ixtaccihuatl (volcanoes) in background at center. Series B. Back: Green.			

a. Issued note. *(MI-DF-29).*	2.00	6.00	18.00
b. Overprint: *REVALIDADO/por decreto 17.... (MI-DF-30).*	1.50	5.00	15.00
c. Back blank. *(MI-DF-32).*	18.00	55.00	165.
d. Overprint: *ADMINISTRACION PRINCIPAL DEL TIMBRE, REVALIDADO, SAN LUIS POTOSI. (MI-DF-33).*	6.00	18.00	55.00
e. Overprint: *REVALIDADO POR ACUERDO DEL DEPARTAMENTO DE HACIENDA. AGUASCALIENTES, ENERO 1915. (MI-DF-34).*	6.00	18.00	55.00
f. Overprint: *REVALIDADO ACUERDO DEL DEPARTAMENTO DE HACIENDA, CHIHUAHUA. (MI-DF-35).*	9.00	27.50	85.00
g. Overprint: *REVALIDADO POR ACUERDO DEL DEPARTAMENTO DE HACIENDA, SAN LUIS POTOSI. (MI-DF-36).*	6.00	18.00	55.00
h. Overprint:*REVALIDADO POR ACUERDO DEL DEPARTAMENTO DE HACIENDA, CELAYA. (MI-DF-37).*	6.00	18.00	55.00
i. Overprint: *ADMINISTRACION PRAL. DEL TIMBRE LEON, GTO. (MI-DF-38).*	6.00	18.00	55.00
j. Overprint: *QUERETARO REVALIDADO POR ACUERDO DEL DEPARTAMENTO DE HACIENDA. (MI-DF-39).*	9.00	27.50	85.00
k. Overprint: *ADMON. PRINCIPAL DEL TIMBRE, CHIHUAHUA. (MI-DF-40).*	9.00	27.50	85.00
l. Overprint: *AGENCIA DEL TIMBRE, ZACOALCO. (MI-DF-41).*	9.00	27.50	85.00

S703 5 Pesos

20.10.1914. Black on light green underprint. Seated Liberty at left, national arms with Popocatepetl and Ixtaccihuatl (volcanoes) in background at center. Series B. Back: Green. Thin paper. *(MI-DF-31).*	2.00	6.00	18.00

S704 10 Pesos

20.10.1914. Black on brown underprint. Seated Liberty at left, national arms with Popocatepetl and Ixtaccihuatl (volcanoes) in background at center. Series C. Overprint: *REVALIDADO/por decreto 17.... (MI-DF-42).*	1.50	5.00	15.00

S705 20 Pesos

20.10.1914. Black on brown underprint. Seated Liberty at left, national arms with Popocatepetl and Ixtaccihuatl (volcanoes) in background at center. Series D. Lower text at right: *EL S. S. encargado de la Sria, de Hacienda.* Overprint: *REVALIDADO/por decreto 17.... (MI-DF-45).*	1.50	5.00	15.00

S706 20 Pesos

	Good	Fine	XF
20.10.1914. Black on brown underprint. Seated Liberty at left, national arms with Popocatepetl and Ixtaccihuatl (volcanoes) in background at center. Series D. Like #S705 but lower text at right: *El OM encarga de la Sria, de Hacienda.<NI* Overprint: *REVALIDADO por decreto 17.... (MI-DF-46).*	3.00	9.00	27.50

S707 50 Pesos

	Good	Fine	XF
20.10.1914. Black on light blue underprint. Seated Liberty at left, national arms with Popocatepetl and Ixtaccihuatl (volcanoes) in background at center. Series E.			
a. Issued note. *(MI-DF-47).*	5.00	15.00	45.00
b. Without date, signature, serial #, series letters or seals on back. *(MI-DF-48).*	15.00	45.00	135.
c. Without date, signature or serial #; With seals on back. *(MI-DF-49).*	15.00	45.00	135.
d. Back blank. *(MI-DF-50).*	30.00	90.00	270.
e. Overprint: *REVALIDADO/por decreto 17...(MI-DF-51).*	1.50	5.00	15.00
f. Overprint: *REVALIDADO/por decreto 17...,* without signature or date; with seals on back. *(MI-DF-52).*	30.00	90.00	270.
g. Overprint: *PAGADURIA GENERAL, TORREÓN, COAH. (MI-DF-53).*	6.00	18.00	55.00
h. Overprint: Needle punch perforation: *TAMPICO. (MI-DF-54).*	5.00	15.00	45.00
i. Overprint: *ADM. PRINCIPAL DEL TIMBRE GUADALAJARA* around eagle. *(MI-DF-55).*	6.00	18.00	55.00
j. Overprint: *ADM. PRAL. DEL TIMBRE, GUADALAJARA. (MI-DF-56).*	2.50	7.50	20.00
k. Overprint: *REVALIDADO. Reynosa* signature at right. 20.10.1914. *(MI-DF-51A).*	9.00	27.50	85.00
l. Overprint: *ADMINISTRACIÓN de ARENTAS, URUAPAN, MICH. (MI-DF-56A).* 20.10.1914.	9.00	27.50	85.00

S708 100 Pesos

	Good	Fine	XF
28.9.1914. Black on red-brown to pink underprint. Seated Liberty at left, national arms with Popocatepetl and Ixtaccihuatl (volcanoes) in background at center. Series F.			
a. Issued note. *(MI-DF-57).*	1.50	5.00	15.00
b. Overprint: *REVALIDADO/por decreto 17...(MI-DF-58).*	1.50	5.00	15.00
c. Overprint: *REVALIDADO/por decreto 17...*without signature or date, with seals on back. *(MI-DF-60).*	30.00	80.00	270.
d. Overprint: *ESTADO DE MICHOACAN, REVALIDADO CONFORME AL DECRETO DE ENERO DE 1915. (MI-DF-62).*	9.00	27.50	85.00
e. Overprint: *REPUBLICA MEXICANA, BUENAVISTA, GUERRERO. (MI-DF-63).*	10.00	30.00	90.00
f. Overprint: *ADM. PRINCIPAL DEL TIMBRE, GUADALAJARA,* around eagle. *(MI-DF-64).*	6.00	18.00	55.00
g. Overprint: *TESORERIA MUNICIPAL, PARRAL, CHIHUAHUA. (MI-DF-65).*	10.00	30.00	90.00
h. Overprint: *ADM. PRAL. DEL TIMBRE, GUADALAJARA. (MI-DF-66).*	1.50	5.00	15.00
x. Error: *SEPT. 1914,* lacking day of month in date. *(MI-DF-61).*	9.00	27.50	85.00

NOTE: Also see #S875A and S876 under Jalisco for more overprint varieties.

Decree of April 3, 1916

S709 1 Peso

	VG	VF	UNC
1.5.1916. Black and green. Statue of Christopher Columbus at left, national arms with Popocatepetl and Ixtaccihuatl (volcanoes) in background at left center, Toltec stone head at lower right. Series A-U. Back: Blue. Printer: Oficina de Gobierno Mexico. *(SI-DF-10).*	1.50	5.00	15.00

S710 1 Peso

	VG	VF	UNC
5.1.1916. Black. Statue of Christopher Columbus at left, Aztec throne at left center, Toltec stone head at lower right. Series J. Back: Brown. Printer: Oficina de Gobierno Mexico.			
a. Issued note. *(SI-DF-15).*	1.50	5.00	15.00
p1. Face proof. *(SI-DF-13).*	—	—	250.
p2. Back proof. *(SI-DF-14).*	—	—	250.

S711 2 Pesos

	VG	VF	UNC
5.1.1916. Black. Statue of Christopher Columbus at left, Aztec throne at left center, Toltec stone head at lower right. Like #S710. Vertical text at right: *Circulación Provisional.* Back: Brown. Printer: Oficina de Gobierno Mexico.			
a. Series A; B. *(SI-DF-12).*	1.50	5.00	15.00
b. Series B with inverted B at upper left.	—	—	—

S712 2 Pesos

5.1.1916. Black. Statue of Christopher Columbus at left, Aztec throne at left center, Toltec stone head at lower right. Like #S711 but without vertical legend at right. Series Z. Back: Brown. Printer: Oficina de Gobierno Mexico.			
a. Issued note. *(SI-DF-16).*	1.50	5.00	15.00
p1. Gray proof. *(SI-DF-17).*	—	—	350.
p2. Sepia proof.	—	—	350.
p3. Green proof.	—	—	350.

Obligación Provisional del Erario Federal

1914 Federal Treasury Bonds Issue

		VG	VF	UNC
S713	**1 Peso**			
	25.7.1914. Black on pale green underprint. National arms at left. Series A. Back: Green. Printer: Oficina Impresora de Estampillas. *(SI-DF-1).*	1.50	5.00	15.00
S713A	**5 Pesos**			
	25.7.1914. Dark green-black on light blue underprint. National arms at left. Series B. Back: Blue. Printer: Oficina Impresora de Estampillas. *(SI-DF-2).*	1.50	5.00	15.00
S714	**5 Pesos**			
	25.7.1914. Black on pale blue underprint. National arms at left. Series B. Back: Blue. Printer: Oficina Impresora de Estampillas.	1.50	5.00	15.00
S715	**25 Pesos**			
	25.7.1914. Black on pink underprint. National arms at left. Series C. Back: Violet. Printer: Oficina Impresora de Estampillas. *(SI-DF-3).*	3.00	9.00	27.50
S716	**50 Pesos**			
	25.7.1914. Black on pale orange underprint. National arms at left. Series D. Back: Orange. Printer: Oficina Impresora de Estampillas. *(SI-DF-4).*	1.50	5.00	15.00

Durango

Bonos al Portador, Durango

1913 First Issue

		Good	Fine	XF
S717	**20 Centavos**			
	Aug. 1913. Black on brown underprint. *(SI-DUR-1).*	30.00	90.00	270.
S718	**50 Centavos**			
	Aug. 1913. Black on green underprint. Like #S717. *(SI-DUR-2).*	9.00	27.50	85.00
S719	**1 Peso**			
	Aug. 1913. Black on yellow underprint. Like #S717. *(SI-DUR-3).*	6.00	18.00	55.00
S720	**5 Pesos**			
	Aug. 1913. Black on red underprint. Like #S717. *(SI-DUR-4).*	9.00	27.50	85.00

1913 Second Issue

		Good	Fine	XF
S721	**20 Centavos**			
	3.10.1913. Black on brown underprint. Like #S717. *(SI-DUR-5).*	9.00	27.50	85.00
S722	**50 Centavos**			
	3.10.1913. Black on green underprint. Like #S717. *(SI-DUR-6).*	9.00	27.50	85.00
S723	**1 Peso**			
	3.10.1913. Black on yellow underprint. Like #S717. *(SI-DUR-7).*	6.00	18.00	55.00

Estado de Durango

1913 Issues

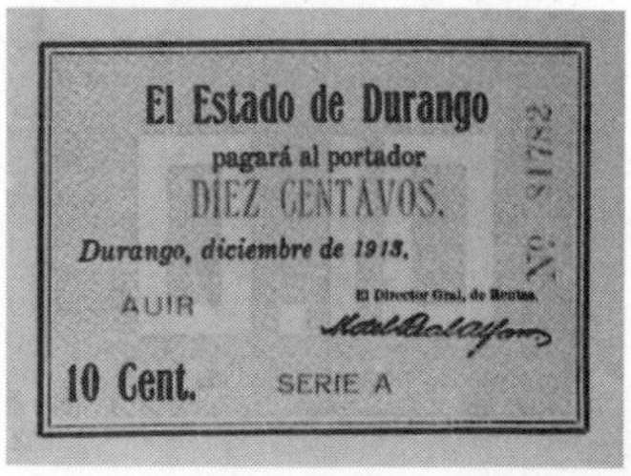

		Good	Fine	XF
S724	**10 Centavos**			
	Dec. 1913. Red and black on light blue underprint. Series A. *(SI-DUR-8).*	15.00	45.00	135.

		Good	Fine	XF
S725	**50 Centavos**			
	Dec. 1913. Black and red on green underprint. Series A.			
	a. Issued note. *(SI-DUR-9).*	15.00	45.00	135.
	b. Overprint: *AMORTIZADO. (SI-DUR-10).*	9.00	27.50	55.00

		Good	Fine	XF
S726	**1 Peso**			
	Dec. 1913. Black and red on yellow underprint. Series A; B.			
	a. Issued note. *(SI-DUR-11).*	15.00	45.00	135.
	b. Overprint: *AMORTIZADO. (SI-DUR-12).*	9.00	27.50	55.00

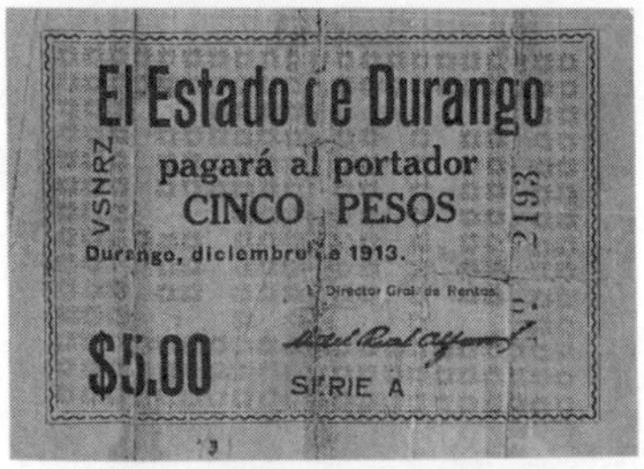

		Good	Fine	XF
S727	**5 Pesos**			
	Dec. 1913. Black on orange underprint. Series A. *(SI-DUR-13).*	9.00	27.50	55.00

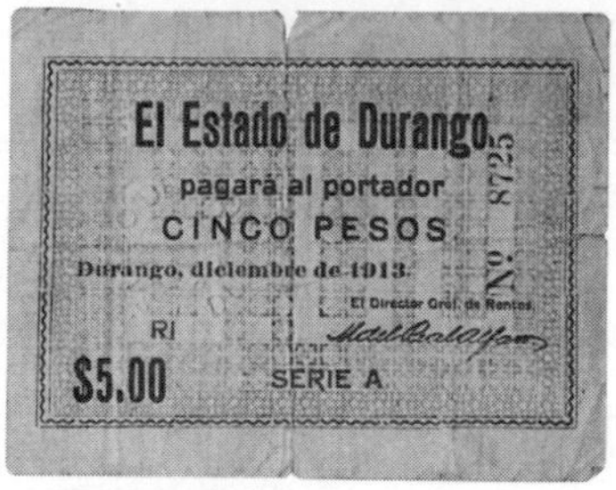

		Good	Fine	XF
S728	**5 Pesos**			
	Dec. 1913. Black on brown underprint. Series A. *(SI-DUR-14).*	15.00	45.00	135.

1914 Issues

		Good	Fine	XF
S729	**50 Centavos**			
	Jan. 1914. Black. Standing Liberty with flag at left. Without Series, Series A;B. Back: Red.			
	a. Issued note. *(SI-DUR-15).*	1.50	5.00	15.00
	b. Overprint: *Revalidado por Decreto...(SI-DUR-16).*	5.00	15.00	45.00
S730	**1 Peso**			
	Jan. 1914. Black on brown-orange underprint. Standing Liberty with flag at left. Denomination: *UN PESO* upside down in upper and lower borders. Back: Green.			
	a. Issued note. *(SI-DUR-17).*	2.50	7.50	20.00
	b. Overprint: *Revalidado por Decreto...(SI-DUR-18).*	5.00	15.00	45.00

		Good	Fine	XF
S731	**1 Peso**			
	Jan. 1914. Black on brown-orange underprint. Standing Liberty with flag at left. Like #S729 but *UN PESO* normal in upper and lower borders. Series F-J. Back: Green.			
	a. Issued note. *(SI-DUR-19).*	1.50	5.00	15.00
	b. Overprint: *Revalidado por Decreto...(SI-DUR-20).*	4.00	12.50	35.00
	c. Overprint: *Jefatura de Hacienda en el Estados de Jalisco. (SI-DUR-19a).*	4.00	12.50	35.00

S732 5 Pesos	Good	Fine	XF
Jan. 1914. Black on red underprint. Standing Liberty with flag at left. 3 signature Series B-D. Back: Blue-gray.			
a. Issued note. *(SI-DUR-21).*	1.50	5.00	15.00
b. Circular overprint: *Distrito De Culiacán Comandancia Militar. (SI-DUR-21A).*	4.00	12.50	35.00
c. Overprint: *Revalidado por Decreto...(SI-DUR-21).*	1.00	3.00	9.00
S733 5 Pesos			
Jan. 1914. Black. Standing Liberty with flag at left. Like #S729 but 1 signature. Back: Red.			
a. Issued note. *(SI-DUR-23).*	6.00	18.00	55.00
b. Overprint: *Revalidado por Decreto...(SI-DUR-25).*	5.00	15.00	45.00
c. Overprint: *Jefatura Politica del Distrito Norte, Ensenada. (SI-DUR-22).*	6.00	18.00	55.00
d. Overprint: *Jefatura en el Estado-Jalisco. (SI-DUR-24).*	6.00	18.00	55.00
S734 10 Centavos			
March 1914. Black and red-orange on pale blue-gray underprint. Series B. Printer: TIP.DORADOR.DGO. *(SI-DUR-26).*			
a. Issued note.	7.50	20.00	60.00
b. Violet handstamp seal with *BONOS/eagle/SERIE A.*	—	—	—

S735 50 Centavos	Good	Fine	XF
March 1914. Black and orange on pale green underprint. Series C. Printer: TIP.DORADOR.DGO. *(SI-DUR-27).*	7.50	20.00	60.00
S736 5 Pesos			
Aug. 1914. Black on pink underprint. Like #S732. Series E; F.			
a. Issued note. *(SI-DUR-28).*	2.50	7.50	20.00
b. Overprint: *Revalidado por Decreto...(SI-DUR-29).*	5.00	15.00	45.00
c. Overprint: *Leon, Gto. (SI-DUR-30).*	9.00	27.50	85.00
d. Overprint: *AMORTIZADO. (SI-DUR-31).*	5.00	15.00	45.00
e. Overprint: two black seals on back.	5.00	15.00	45.00
S737 50 Pesos			
Aug. 1914. Black on brown underprint. Like #S732. Series A. *(SI-DUR-32).*	7.50	20.00	60.00

Decree of December 12, 1913

S738 1 Peso	Good	Fine	XF
Oct. 1914. Black on light orange underprint. National arms at center right. Series L; M. *(SI-DUR-33).*	2.50	7.50	20.00
S739 50 Centavos			
Dec. 1914. Black on pale blue underprint. Series C; D; E. Back: Blue and green. *(SI-DUR-34).*	2.00	6.00	18.00

S740 50 Centavos	Good	Fine	XF
31.12.1914. Black. Standing Liberty with flag at left. Series F. Back: Brown. *(SI-DUR-35).*	7.50	20.00	60.00
S741 1 Peso			
31.12.1914. Black on pale brown underprint. Standing Liberty with flag at left. Series F. Back: Maroon. *(SI-DUR-36).*	3.00	9.00	27.50

S742 5 Pesos	Good	Fine	XF
31.12.1914. Black. Standing Liberty with flag at left. Series F. Paper: Blue. *(SI-DUR-37).*	5.00	15.00	45.00
S743 10 Pesos			
31.12.1914. Black on blue. Standing Liberty with flag at left. Series F. Back: Green. *(SI-DUR-38).*	25.00	75.00	225.

Decree of December 12, 1913; 1915 Issue

S744 1 Peso	Good	Fine	XF
Jan. 1915. Black on light orange underprint. National arms at center right. Like #S738. Series N. *(SI-DUR-39).*	2.50	7.50	20.00

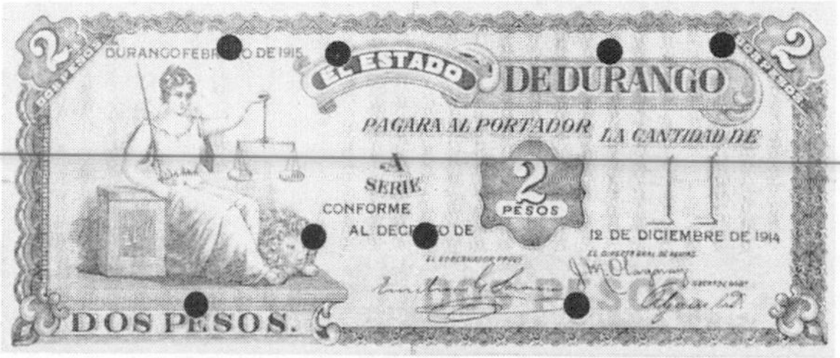

S745 2 Pesos	Good	Fine	XF
Feb. 1915. Seated Justice at left. Series A. Punched hole cancelled. *(SI-DUR-40).*	5.00	15.00	45.00

S746 5 Pesos	Good	Fine	XF
Aug. 1915. Black. Seated Justice at left. Series A. Like #S745. Back: Blue.			
a. Issued note. *(SI-DUR-42).*	25.00	75.00	225.
b. Overprint: *Revalidado, Octubre, 1915...* on back. *(SI-DUR-43).*	3.00	9.00	27.50

S747 25 Centavos	Good	Fine	XF
ND. Black. National arms at center without series; Series A. Back: Pink. *(SI-DUR-44).*	1.50	5.00	15.00
S748 25 Centavos			
ND. Back: Portrait Gen. J. E. Garciá at center. Back proof. *(SI-DUR-45).*	—	Unc	350.

S749 50 Centavos	Good	Fine	XF
Sept. 1915. Black on pale blue underprint. Series F. Back: Blue. Like #S747. *(SI-DUR-46).*	1.50	5.00	15.00

		Good	Fine	XF
S750	**2 Pesos** Sept. 1915. Black. National arms at center right. Series A. *(SI-DUR-47).*	3.00	9.00	27.50
S751	**5 Pesos** Sept. 1915. Black. National arms at center right. Without seals, with black serial #. Back: Blue. *(SI-DUR-48).*	5.00	15.00	45.00
S752	**5 Pesos** Sept. 1915. Black. National arms at center right. Red seals, red serial #. Like #S751. Back: Blue. *(SI-DUR-49).*	2.50	7.50	20.00

		Good	Fine	XF
S753	**10 Pesos** Oct. 1915. Pale orange. Seated Justice at left. Series A. Back: Brown. *(SI-DUR-50).*	5.00	15.00	45.00

Gobierno Constitucionalista del Estado de Durango

1914 Issue

		VG	VF	UNC
S754	**5 Pesos** Dec. 1914. Black on cream. Back: Hand stamped seal, hand signed. *(SI-DUR-51).*	40.00	120.	360.
S755	**10 Pesos** Dec. 1914. Black on cream. Printed signature. *(SI-DUR-52).*	40.00	120.	360.

1915 Issue

		VG	VF	UNC
S756	**5 Pesos** March 1915. Black on cream. Back: Hand stamped seal. *(SI-DUR-53).*			
	a. Denomination in upper border.	30.00	90.00	270.
	b. Denomination in upper and lower border.	30.00	90.00	270.

		VG	VF	UNC
S757	**10 Pesos** March 1915. Black on cream. Without denomination in border. *(SI-DUR-54).*	45.00	135.	400.

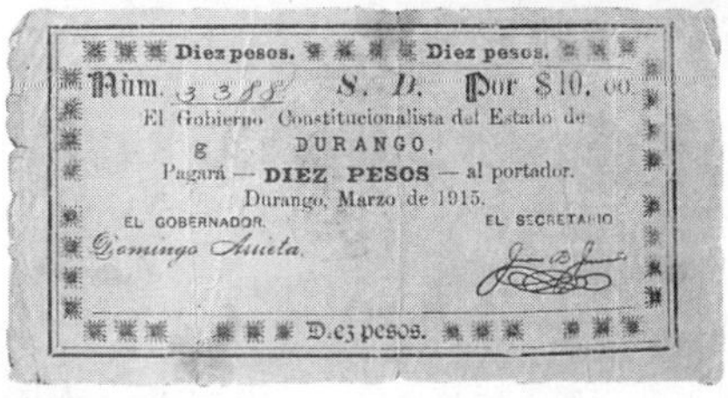

		VG	VF	UNC
S758	**10 Pesos** March 1915. Denomination in border three times. *(SI-DUR-55).*	45.00	135.	400.

Gobierno del Estado de Durango

ND Issue

		Good	Fine	XF
S759	**5 Centavos** ND. Indian head at center. Series A. Back: Farmer plowing with oxen. Paper: Orange pasteboard. *(SI-DUR-56).*	3.00	9.00	27.50
S760	**10 Centavos** ND. Indian head at center. Series A. Back: Farmer plowing with oxen. Paper: Gray pasteboard. *(SI-DUR-57).*	3.00	9.00	27.50
S761	**20 Centavos** ND. Indian head at center. Series A. Back: Farmer plowing with oxen. Paper: Brown pasteboard. *(SI-DUR-58).*	5.00	15.00	45.00

Banco Minero / Banco de la Laguna, Gómez Palacio

1913 Issue

		Good	Fine	XF
S762	**5 Pesos** 7.10.1913. Red. Series A. *(MI-DUR-4).*	45.00	135.	400.
S763	**5 Pesos** 7.10.1913. Black. Series A. *(MI-DUR-5).*	45.00	135.	400.
S764	**10 Pesos** 7.10.1913. Black. Series A. *(MI-DUR-6).*	50.00	150.	450.
S765	**20 Pesos** 7.10.1913. Red. Series A. *(MI-DUR-7).*	90.00	270.	800.
S766	**50 Pesos** 7.10.1913. Series A. *(MI-DUR-8).*	135.	400.	1200.

La Jefatura Municipal, Guanaceví

1913 Issue

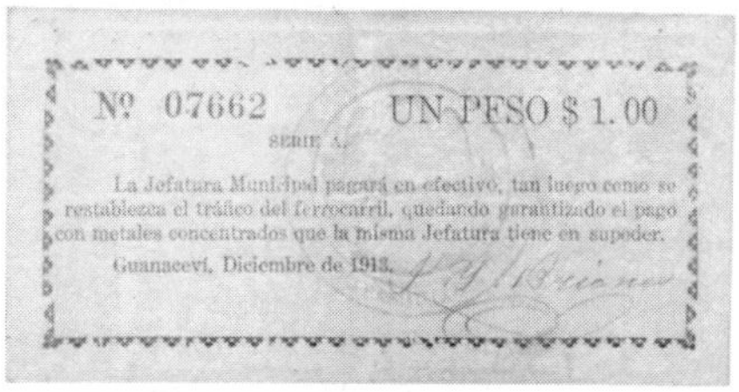

		Good	Fine	XF
S767	**1 Peso** Dec. 1913. Series A. *(SI-DUR-59).*	70.00	210.	625.

El Estado de Durango, San José de la Boca

1914 Issue

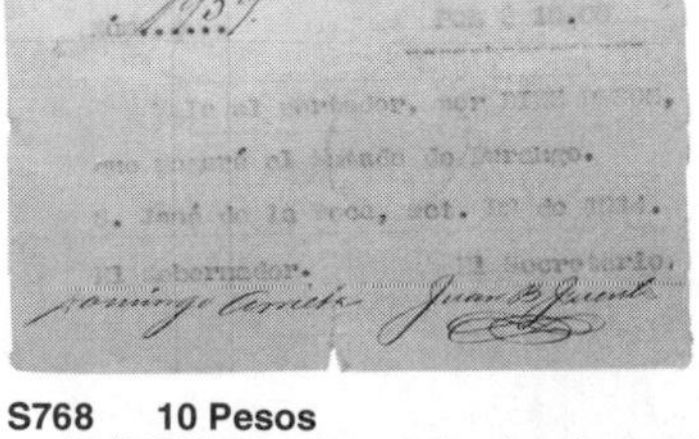

		Good	Fine	XF
S768	**10 Pesos** 22.10.1914. Typewritten voucher signed by Gov. D. Arrieta. *(SI-DUR-62).*	50.00	150.	450.

El Estado de Durango, Topia

1914 Issue

		Good	Fine	XF
S769	**1 Peso** Dec. 1914. Black on white. *(SI-DUR-63).*	70.00	210.	625.

1915 Issue

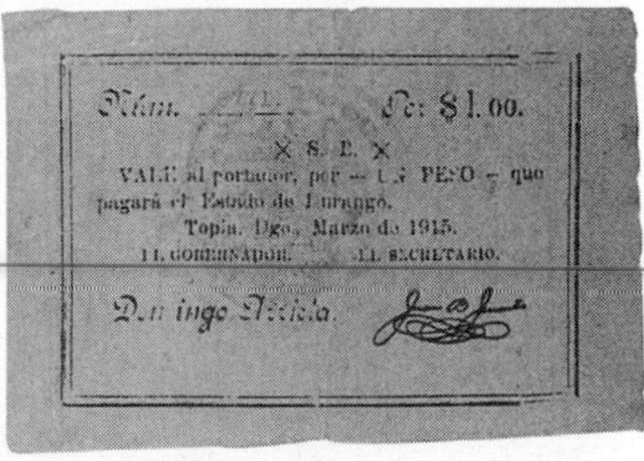

		Good	Fine	XF
S770	**1 Peso** March 1915. Black. *(SI-DUR-64).*	50.00	150.	450.

Guanajuato

Administración General de Rentas del Estado

ND Issue

		Good	Fine	XF
S771	**10 Centavos** ND. Red on tan. Back: State of arms at center. Vertical format on back. *(SI-GUA-58).*	7.50	20.00	60.00
S772	**50 Centavos** ND. Black. Statue of man at left. Series A. Back: State arms at center. *(SI-GUA-59).*	6.00	18.00	55.00
S773	**50 Centavos** ND. Violet. Statue of man at left. Series G. Back: State arms at center. *(SI-GUA-60).*	6.00	18.00	55.00

Tesorería General del Estado

ND Bonos de Circulación Obligatoria Issue

#S774-S779 Name of original issuer is blocked out and *Tesorería General del Estado* is printed below. Originally printed for Guanajuato in 1883.

		Good	Fine	XF
S774	**5 Centavos** ND. Orange. Mining scene at upper center. Printer: Kendall Bank Note Co., New York. *(SI-GUA-52).*	7.50	20.00	60.00
S775	**10 Centavos** ND. Green. Mining scene at upper center. Printer: Kendall Bank Note Co., New York. *(SI-GUA-53).*	7.50	20.00	60.00
S776	**20 Centavos** ND. Blue. Mining scene at upper center. Printer: Kendall Bank Note Co., New York. *(SI-GUA-54).*	7.50	20.00	60.00
S777	**30 Centavos** ND. Brown. Mining scene at upper center. Printer: Kendall Bank Note Co., New York. *(SI-GUA-55).*	9.00	27.50	85.00
S778	**40 Centavos** ND. Sepia. Mining scene at upper center. Printer: Kendall Bank Note Co., New York. *(SI-GUA-56).*	10.00	30.00	90.00
S779	**50 Centavos** ND. Black. Mining scene at upper center. Printer: Kendall Bank Note Co., New York. *(SI-GUA-57).*	9.00	27.50	85.00

1914 First Bonos Issue

		Good	Fine	XF
S780	**50 Centavos** 6.1.1914. Black on blue underprint. State arms at left. *(SI-GUA-47).*	40.00	120.	360.
S781	**1 Peso** 6.1.1914. Black on blue underprint. State arms at left. Like #S780. *(SI-GUA-48).*	70.00	210.	625.

1914 Second Bonos Issue

		Good	Fine	XF
S782	**25 Centavos** 16.4.1914. State arms at left. *(SI-GUA-49).*	90.00	270.	800.
S783	**50 Centavos** 16.4.1914. Green. State arms at left. *(SI-GUA-50).*	90.00	270.	800.
S784	**1 Peso** 16.4.1914. State arms at left. *(SI-GUA-51).*	40.00	120.	360.

Guerrero

Banco Revolucionario de Guerrero

Decree of October 6, 1914

		Good	Fine	XF
S785	**1 Peso** 1.1.1914. Black on light blue underprint. Series B. Back: Sunburst State seal at center.			
	a. Issued note. *(SI-GUE-6).*	50.00	150.	450.
	b. Perforated cancellation. *(SI-GUE-7).*	40.00	120.	360.

		Good	Fine	XF
S786	**2 Pesos** 1.12.1914. Red. Steam passenger train at center. Series A.			
	a. Issued note. 65 x 38mm. *(SI-GUE-8).*	135.	400.	1200.
	r. Remainder without serial # and seal. *(SI-GUE-9).*	180.	550.	1650.
S787	**5 Pesos** 6.10.1914. Blue. Series A. Back: Boys at center.			
	a. Black printed signature *(SI-GUE-10).*	120.	360.	1100.
	b. Red printed signature *(SI-GUE-11).*	150.	450.	1350.

		Good	Fine	XF
S788	**10 Pesos** 20.10.1914. Black. Miguel Hidalgo y Costilla at upper left center. Series A. *(SI-GUE-12).*	500.	1500.	4500.
S789	**20 Pesos** 20.10.1914. Black. Series A. *(SI-GUE-13).*	225.	675.	2100.

Ayuntamiento de 1915, Iguala

1915 Issue

		Good	Fine	XF
S790	**2 Centavos** 1915. Brown. Straight line border. Back: National arms. *(SI-GUE-34).*	7.50	20.00	60.00
S790A	**2 Centavos** 1915. Without border. Back: National arms. *(SI-GUE-34A).*	7.50	20.00	60.00
S790B	**2 Centavos** 1915. Pink ornate border. Back: National arms. *(SI-GUE-34B).*	7.50	20.00	60.00
S791	**3 Centavos** 1915. Brown. Straight line border. Back: National arms. *(SI-GUE-35).*	7.50	20.00	60.00
S792	**3 Centavos** 1915. Ornate border. Back: National arms. Paper: Brown pasteboard. *(SI-GUE-36).*	7.50	20.00	60.00
S793	**4 Centavos** 1915. Brown. Straight line border. Back: National arms. *(SI-GUE-37).*	7.50	20.00	60.00

	Good	Fine	XF
S794 4 Centavos			
1915. Brown. Without border. Back: National arms. *(SI-GUE-38).*	7.50	20.00	60.00
S795 4 Centavos			
1915. Ornate border. Back: National arms. *(SI-GUE-39).*	7.50	20.00	60.00
S796 5 Centavos			
1915. Brown. Straight line border. Back: National arms. *(SI-GUE-40).*	7.50	20.00	60.00
S797 5 Centavos			
1915. Brown. Without border. Back: National arms. *(SI-GUE-41).*	7.50	20.00	60.00
S798 10 Centavos			
1915. Brown. Straight line border. Back: National arms. *(SI-GUE-42).*	5.00	15.00	45.00
S799 10 Centavos			
1915. Brown. Without border. Back: National arms. *(SI-GUE-43).*	7.50	20.00	60.00
S800 10 Centavos			
1915. Ornate border. Back: National arms. Paper: White pasteboard. *(SI-GUE-44).*	6.00	18.00	55.00
S801 20 Centavos			
1915. Straight line border. Back: National arms. Paper: Red-brown pasteboard. *(SI-GUE-45).*	7.50	20.00	60.00
S802 20 Centavos			
1915. Without border. Back: National arms. Paper: Red-brown pasteboard. *(SI-GUE-46).*	7.50	20.00	60.00
S803 20 Centavos			
1915. Black. Ornate border. Back: National arms.			
a. Pink/white pasteboard. *(SI-GUE-47).*	7.50	20.00	60.00
b. Blue pasteboard.	7.50	20.00	60.00
c. White pasteboard.	7.50	20.00	60.00
S804 25 Centavos			
1915. Black. Straight line border. Back: National arms.			
a. White-salmon pasteboard. *(SI-GUE-48).*	12.50	35.00	110.
b. Orange pasteboard.	12.50	35.00	110.
c. Violet pasteboard.	12.50	35.00	110.
d. Brown pasteboard.	12.50	35.00	110.
S805 25 Centavos			
1915. Black. Red, ornate border. Back: National arms. Paper: White-salmon pasteboard. *(SI-GUE-49).*	4.00	12.50	35.00
S806 50 Centavos			
1915. Black. Straight line border. Back: National arms. Paper: White pasteboard. *(SI-GUE-50).*	5.00	15.00	45.00
S807 50 Centavos			
1915. Black. Ornate border. Back: National arms.			
a. White pasteboard. *(SI-GUE-51).*	4.00	12.50	35.00
b. Green pasteboard.	4.00	12.50	35.00
c. Brown pasteboard.	4.00	12.50	35.00
d. Red pasteboard.	4.00	12.50	35.00
e. Pink paper.	4.00	12.50	35.00
f. Orange pasteboard.	4.00	12.50	35.00
g. Gray pasteboard.	4.00	12.50	35.00
h. Lilac pasteboard.	4.00	12.50	35.00
S808 1 Peso			
1915. Black. Ornate border. Back: National arms.			
a. Blue pasteboard. *(SI-GUE-53).*	2.50	7.50	20.00
b. Brown pasteboard.	2.50	7.50	20.00
c. Gray paper.	2.50	7.50	20.00
d. Buff pasteboard. with green hand stamp *MUNICIPAL IGUALA* on face. Serial # on back.	2.50	7.50	20.00

Ejército Constitucionalista del Sur

ND Issue

	Good	Fine	XF
S809 5 Centavos			
ND. Black. National arms at center. Paper: Pasteboard. *(MI-GUE-14).*	40.00	120.	360.

	Good	Fine	XF
S810 10 Centavos			
ND. Black. National arms at center. Paper: Pasteboard. *(MI-GUE-15).*	40.00	120.	360.
S811 50 Centavos			
ND. Black. National arms at center. Paper: Cream pasteboard. *(MI-GUE-16).*	25.00	75.00	225.
S812 1 Peso			
ND. National arms at center.			
a. Orange pasteboard. *(MI-GUE-17).*	25.00	75.00	225.
b. Yellow pasteboard.	25.00	75.00	225.
c. Blue pasteboard.	25.00	75.00	225.
d. Violet pasteboard.	25.00	75.00	225.
e. Overprint: *AMORTIZADO. (MI-GUE-18).*	25.00	75.00	225.
f. Cream pasteboard.	25.00	75.00	225.

Ejército Libertador de Guerrero, Chilpancingo

Decree of October 6, 1914

	Good	Fine	XF
S812A 1 Peso			
D.6.10.1914. Black. Arms at center. Series A. *(MI-GUE-5).*	600.	1800.	5400.

Ejército Revolucionario de Guerrero

ND Issue

	Good	Fine	XF
S813 10 Centavos			
ND. Black. Paper: White pasteboard. *(MI-GUE-29).*	25.00	75.00	225.

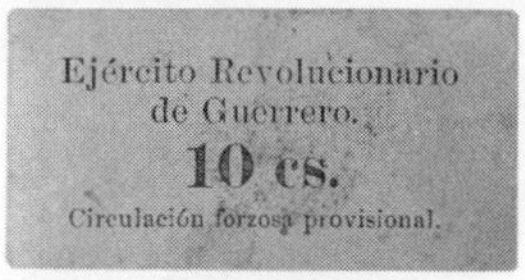

	Good	Fine	XF
S814 10 Centavos			
ND. Black. Paper: Gray pasteboard. *(MI-GUE-30).*	15.00	45.00	135.
S815 20 Centavos			
ND. Black. Paper: Pink or white pasteboard. *(MI-GUE-31).*	20.00	60.00	180.
S816 50 Centavos			
ND. Black. Paper: Tan pasteboard. *(MI-GUE-32).*	20.00	60.00	180.

Gobierno Constitucionalista, Brigada Morales y Molina

ND Issue

	Good	Fine	XF
S817 10 Centavos			
ND. Black. Paper: Red pasteboard. *(MI-GUE-33).*	15.00	45.00	135.

	Good	Fine	XF
S818 20 Centavos			
ND. Black. Paper: Orange pasteboard.			
a. Issued note. *(MI-GUE-34).*	15.00	45.00	135.
b. Overprint: *AMORTIZADO.*	15.00	45.00	135.
S819 50 Centavos			
ND. Black.			
a. Cream pasteboard. *(MI-GUE-35).*	5.00	15.00	45.00
b. Pink pasteboard.	5.00	15.00	45.00
c. Red pasteboard.	5.00	15.00	45.00
d. Green pasteboard.	5.00	15.00	45.00
e. White pasteboard.	5.00	15.00	45.00
S820 1 Peso			
ND. Black. National arms at center.			
a. White pasteboard. *(MI-GUE-36).*	5.00	15.00	45.00
b. Blue pasteboard.	5.00	15.00	45.00

	Good	Fine	XF
S821 1 Peso			
ND. Black. Back: Signature: *Morales y Molina* handwritten. Paper: Tan pasteboard.			
a. Issued note. *(MI-GUE-37).*	6.00	18.00	55.00
b. Overprint: *AMORTIZADO.*	6.00	18.00	55.00
S822 1 Peso			
ND. Black on tan underprint. National arms at center. *(MI-GUE-38).*	5.00	15.00	45.00
S823 5 Pesos			
ND. Black. National arms at center.			
a. Deep pink underprint. *(MI-GUE-39).*	9.00	27.50	55.00
b. Pale salmon underprint.	9.00	27.50	55.00
S824 10 Pesos			
ND. Gray. National arms at center.			
a. Issued note. *(MI-GUE-40).*	20.00	60.00	180.
b. Overprint: *AMORTIZADO.*	20.00	60.00	180.

Hidalgo

Brigada Azuara

1915 Issue

		Good	Fine	XF
S825	**50 Centavos** 12.1.1915. Black. *(MI-HID-1).*	40.00	120.	360.
S826	**1 Peso** 12.1.1915. Black. *(MI-HID-2).*	40.00	120.	360.

		Good	Fine	XF
S827	**1 Peso** 20.1.1915. Black on brown. Series A. *(MI-HID-3).*	45.00	135.	400.

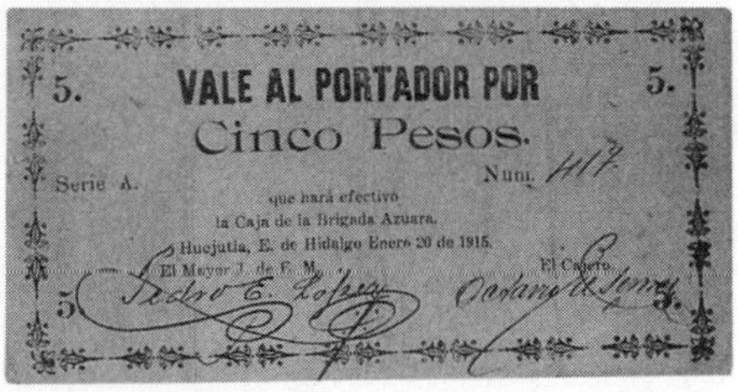

		Good	Fine	XF
S828	**5 Pesos** 20.1.1915. Black. Series A. *(MI-HID-4).*	45.00	135.	400.

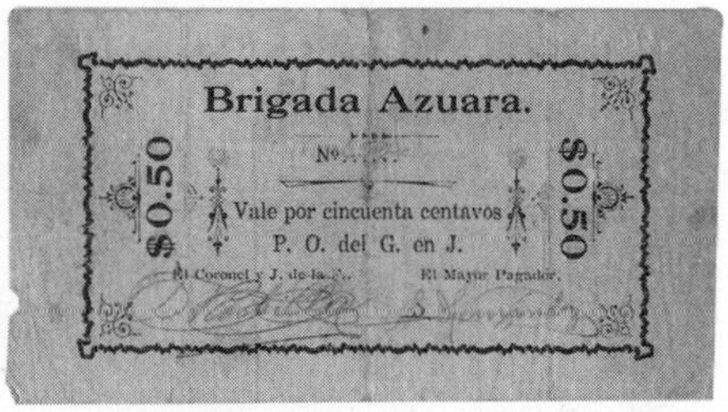

		Good	Fine	XF
S829	**50 Centavos** ND. Blue on white underprint. *(MI-HID-5).*	125.	375.	1100.
S830	**1 Peso** ND. *(MI-HID-6).*	125.	375.	1100.

Compañiá Real del Monte y Pachuca / Bank of Montreal

1915 First Issue

		Good	Fine	XF
S831	**5 Pesos** 28.5.1915. Black on pale tan underprint. Hand signed adhesive fiscal stamp. Series I. Back: Hand stamped seal. *(PI-HID-58).*	425.	1275.	3750.
S832	**10 Pesos** 28.5.1915. Black on pale green underprint. Hand signed adhesive fiscal stamp. Series N. Back: Hand stamped seal. *(PI-HID-59).*	425.	1275.	3750.
S833	**20 Pesos** 28.5.1915. Black. Hand signed adhesive fiscal stamp. Series M. Back: Hand stamped seal. *(PI-HID-60).*	425.	1275.	3750.

1915 Second Issue

		Good	Fine	XF
S834	**1 Peso** 1915. Green. Hand signed adhesive fiscal stamp. Back: Hand signed seal. *(PI-HID-61).*			
	a. Various dates. Series A.	25.00	75.00	225.
	b. ND. Series A.	15.00	45.00	135.
S835	**2 1/2 Pesos** 1915. Yellow. Hand signed adhesive fiscal stamp. Series E. Back: Hand signed seal. *(PI-HID-62).*	150.	450.	1350.
S836	**5 Pesos** 1915. Green. Hand signed adhesive fiscal stamp. Series B. Back: Hand signed seal. *(PI-HID-63).*	70.00	210.	625.
S837	**5 Pesos** 1915. Blue. Hand signed adhesive fiscal stamp. Series B. Back: Hand signed seal. *(PI-HID-64).*	30.00	90.00	270.
S838	**10 Pesos** 1915. Cream. Hand signed adhesive fiscal stamp. Series C. Back: Hand signed seal. *(PI-HID-66).*	50.00	150.	450.
S839	**20 Pesos** 1915. Pink. Hand signed adhesive fiscal stamp. Series D. Back: Hand signed seal. *(SI-HID-67).*	75.00	225.	675.

Estado Libre y Soberano de Hidalgo

1915 Issue

		Good	Fine	XF
S840	**10 Centavos** 1.5.1915. Black. Series E. Paper: Pink pasteboard. *(SI-HID-2).*	3.00	9.00	27.50
S841	**20 Centavos** 1.5.1915. Paper: Pasteboard. *(SI-HID-3).*	25.00	75.00	225.
S842	**25 Centavos** 1.5.1915. Black on pale green underprint. Series C. Paper: Pasteboard. *(SI-HID-4).*	6.00	18.00	55.00
S843	**50 Centavos** 1.5.1915. Black on pale green underprint. Series B; G. Paper: Pasteboard. *(SI-HID-5).*	3.00	9.00	27.50

Jalisco

La Dirección General de Rentas del Estado, Guadalajara

Decree No. 2 of June 18, 1914

		Good	Fine	XF
S844	**5 Centavos** 19.7.1914. Black on pale orange underprint. Series A. Back: National arms at center.			
	a. Issued note. *(SI-JAL-12).*	7.50	22.50	65.00
	b. Without serial #; perforated: *PAGADO. (SI-JAL-13).*	—	—	65.00
S845	**10 Centavos** 19.7.1914. Black on pale blue underprint. Series A. Back: National arms at center.			
	a. Issued note. *(SI-JAL-14).*	7.50	22.50	65.00
	b. Without serial #; perforated: *PAGADO. (SI-JAL-15).*	—	—	65.00

		Good	Fine	XF
S846	**20 Centavos** 19.7.1914. Black on pink underprint. Series A.			
	a. Issued note. *(SI-JAL-16).*	10.00	30.00	90.00
	b. Without serial #; perforated: *PAGADO. (SI-JAL-17).*	—	—	90.00
S847	**50 Centavos** 19.7.1914. Black on light blue underprint. Men at left. Series B.			
	a. Issued note. *(SI-JAL-18).*	10.00	30.00	90.00
	b. Without serial #; perforated: *PAGADO. (SI-JAL-19).*	—	—	90.00

Decree No. 12 of August 11, 1914

		Good	Fine	XF
S848	**5 Centavos** 15.8.1914. Sepia and green. State arms at center in underprint. Series B.			
	a. Issued note. *(SI-JAL-20).*	3.00	9.00	27.50
	b. Without serial #; perforated: *PAGADO. (SI-JAL-21).*	—	—	27.50
S849	**10 Centavos** 15.8.1914. Black and brown. Series B. Back: National arms at center.			
	a. Issued note. *(SI-JAL-22).*	15.00	45.00	135.
	b. Without serial #; perforated: *PAGADO. (SI-JAL-23).*	—	—	135.
S850	**20 Centavos** 15.8.1914. Black on pink. Series B. Back: State arms at center.			
	a. Issued note. *(SI-JAL-24).*	5.00	15.00	45.00
	b. Without serial #; perforated: *PAGADO. (SI-JAL-25).*	—	—	45.00
S851	**50 Centavos** 15.8.1914. Black on sepia. Series C.			
	a. Issued note. *(SI-JAL-26).*	4.00	12.50	35.00
	b. Without serial #; perforated: *PAGADO. (SI-JAL-27).*	—	—	35.00
S852	**5 Centavos** 30.10.1914. Black and green. State arms at center in underprint. Series C. *(SI-JAL-28).*	5.00	15.00	45.00
S853	**10 Centavos** 30.10.1914. Black and brown. State arms at center in underprint. Series C. *(SI-JAL-29).*	18.00	55.00	165.
S854	**20 Centavos** 30.10.1914. Black on pink underprint. Series C. Back: State arms at center. *(SI-JAL-30).*	6.00	18.00	55.00
S855	**50 Centavos** 30.10.1914. Black on sepia. Series D. *(SI-JAL-31).*	2.50	7.50	20.00

Decree No. 59 of February 1, 1915

		Good	Fine	XF
S856	**50 Centavos**			
	1.2.1915. Black on sepia. Series E. Back: Green. *(SI-JAL-32).*	4.00	12.50	35.00

Decree No. 65 of May 29, 1915

		Good	Fine	XF
S857	**5 Centavos**			
	8.6.1915. Brown and green. State arms at center in underprint. Series E.			
	a. Issued note. *(SI-JAL-33).*	2.50	7.50	20.00
	b. Decree No. 64 (error). *(SI-JAL-34).*	9.00	27.50	80.00
S858	**20 Centavos**			
	8.6.1915. Black on pink underprint. Series F. Back: State arms at center. *(SI-JAL-35).*	2.50	7.50	20.00

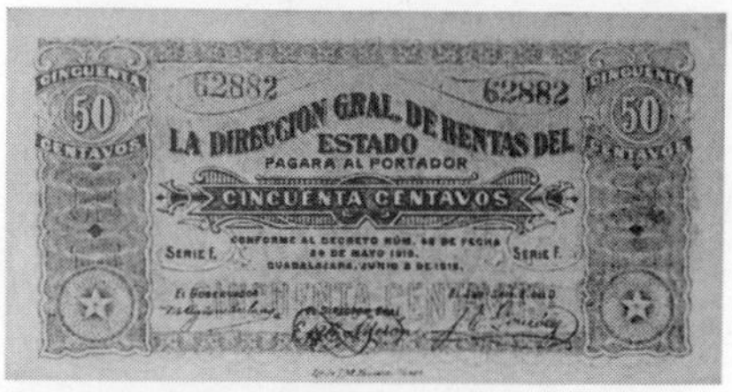

		Good	Fine	XF
S859	**50 Centavos**			
	8.6.1915. Black on dull red-brown underprint. Series F. Back: Green. *(SI-JAL-36).*	2.50	7.50	20.00

Ejército Constitucionalista, División de Occidente, Guadalajara

1915 Issue

		VG	VF	UNC
S860	**1 Peso**			
	20.1.1915. Black on pink underprint. Portrait Ramon Corona at left, Government building at right. Series A. *(MI-JAL-22).*	2.50	7.50	20.00
S861	**5 Pesos**			
	20.1.1915. Brown on blue underprint. Portrait Ramon Corona at left, Government building at right. Series A. Back: Green. *(MI-JAL-23).*	3.00	9.00	27.50
S862	**10 Pesos**			
	20.1.1915. Brown on pale green underprint. Portrait Ramon Corona at left, Government building at right. Series A. *(MI-JAL-24).*	7.50	20.00	60.00

La Pagaduríá del Cuerpode Ejército del Noroeste

1914 Issue

		Good	Fine	XF
S863	**50 Centavos**			
	1.8.1914. Black on orange underprint. Series C. *(MI-JAL-10).*	25.00	75.00	225.

		Good	Fine	XF
S864	**1 Peso**			
	1.8.1914. Black on green underprint. Series C. *(MI-JAL-11).*	40.00	120.	360.

		Good	Fine	XF
S865	**5 Pesos**			
	1914; 1915. Black on rose underprint. Francisco I. Madero at left, Liberty at right. Back: Deep blue. Field artillery troops with cannon at center, arms at left and right.			
	a. Issued note. Series C. 1.8.1914. *(MI-JAL-12).*	25.00	75.00	225.
	r. Remainder without serial #. Series D. 1.5.1915. *(MI-JAL-13).*	45.00	135.	400.
S866	**10 Pesos**			
	1.8.1914. Black on orange underprint. Francisco I. Madero at left, Liberty at right. Series C. *(MI-JAL-14).*	30.00	90.00	270.
S867	**20 Pesos**			
	1.8.1914. Black on green underprint. Francisco I. Madero at left, Liberty at right. Series C. *(MI-JAL-15).*	45.00	135.	400.

La Pagaduríá Gral. del Cuerpo de Ejército del Noroeste

1915 Issue

		Good	Fine	XF
S868	**50 Centavos**			
	1.5.1915. Black on pale orange underprint. Series D; E. Signature General Serrano. *(MI-JAL-16).*	4.00	12.50	35.00
S869	**1 Peso**			
	1.5.1915. Black on green underprint. Series D. Signature General Serrano. *(MI-JAL-17).*	7.50	20.00	60.00

		Good	Fine	XF
S870	**5 Pesos**			
	1.5.1915. Black on pink underprint. Francisco I. Madero at left, Liberty at right. Series D. Signature General Serrano. Back: Soldiers and cannon at center. Paper and cardboard.			
	a. Issued note. *(MI-JAL-18).*	4.00	12.50	36.00
	b. Without serial #. *(MI-JAL-19).*	4.00	12.50	36.00
S871	**10 Pesos**			
	1.5.1915. Black on yellow and green underprint. Francisco I. Madero at left, Liberty at right. Series D. Signature General Serrano. Back: Red. Arms at left, soldiers with cannon at center. *(MI-JAL-20).*			
	a. Issued note.	10.00	30.00	90.00
	r. Remainder without serial #.	10.00	30.00	90.00
S872	**20 Pesos**			
	1.5.1915. Black on olive green underprint. Francisco I. Madero at left, Liberty at right. Series D. Signature General Serrano. *(MI-JAL-21).*	25.00	75.00	225.

Estado de Jalisco

ND Issue

		Good	Fine	XF
S873	**5 Centavos**			
	ND. Back: National arms at center. Paper: Blue pasteboard. *(SI-JAL-9).*	2.50	7.50	20.00
S874	**10 Centavos**			
	ND. Series F. Back: National arms at center. Paper: Purple pasteboard. *(SI-JAL-10).*	2.50	7.50	20.00
S875	**20 Centavos**			
	ND. Red. Back: National arms at center.			
	a. Blue pasteboard. *(SI-JAL-11).*	2.50	7.50	20.00
	b. Green pasteboard.	2.50	7.50	20.00

Jefatura de Hacienda en el Estado Jalisco

1915 Issue

		Good	Fine	XF
S875A	**50 Pesos** 22.2.1915. Like #S876, similar overprint. Back: Overprint text in circle, also 5 lines of text and date. Issued at Guadalajara.	17.50	55.00	165.

Jefe de la División de Occidente

1915 Issue

These are #S707 notes lacking date, signatures and serial letters and bearing a lg. red face ovpt: *Circulá-Forzosamente este Billete con la sola Firma del Subscrito, por carecer de las ordinarias. Guadalajara, Enero 28, 1915. El Gral. Jefe de la Division de Occidente.* (May this Bill be of compulsory circulation with the lone signature appearing below, because the ordinary ones are unavailable. Guadalajara, January 28, 1915. Commander General of the Western Division). Signed by M. M. Diéguez.

		Good	Fine	XF
S876	**50 Pesos** 28.1.1915. Seated Liberty at left, national arms at center.			
	a. Overprint: *RETIRADO* on face and back. *(MI-JAL-25).*	17.50	55.00	165.
	b. With seal on back: *Jefatura de Hacienda en el Estado. Jalisco. Autorizado...Febrero 22 de 1915.* Overprint: *RETIRADO* on face and back.	45.00	135.	400.
	c. Like a. but without *RETIRADO* on face or back.	—	—	—

México (Estado de)

Estado Libre y Soberano de México, Toluca

Decree No. 4 of March 1, 1915

		Good	Fine	XF
S877	**5 Centavos** 1.3.1915. Stamped coin-like. Paper: Gray pasteboard.			
	a. Without dot after: *TOLUCA.*	25.00	75.00	225.
	b. With dot after: *TOLUCA.*	25.00	75.00	225.

		VG	VF	UNC
S878	**20 Centavos** 1.3.1915. Brown on blue underprint. Eagle on pedestal at left. Series A. *(SI-MEX-9).*	1.50	5.00	15.00
S879	**50 Centavos** 1.3.1915. Blue. Eagle on pedestal at left. Series A; B; C; D; F. Paper: Pale orange pasteboard or paper. *(SI-MEX-10).*	3.00	9.00	27.50

		VG	VF	UNC
S880	**1 Peso** 1.3.1915. Black on green and tan underprint. Christopher Columbus monument at center. Series A. Back: Blue. *(SI-MEX-11).*	6.00	18.00	54.00
S881	**1 Peso** 1.3.1915. Blue. Christopher Columbus monument at center. Series B-F. *(SI-MEX-12).*	1.50	5.00	15.00

Gobierno Convencionista de México, Toluca

1915 Issue

		VG	VF	UNC
S882	**50 Centavos** 16.8.1915. Black on yellow underprint. Justice at left. Series A. Back: Purple. Coin at center. *(SI-MEX-7).*	1.50	5.00	15.00

Michoacán

El Estado de Michoacán de Ocampo, Morelia

Military Decree of February 5, 1915

		VG	VF	UNC
S883	**10 Pesos** 5.2.1915. Brown-violet on pink underprint. Printed signature. Black or blue serial #. Back: Blue-green. Arms at upper center, red circular Treasury seal. Watermark: Titanic Bond.			
	a. Issued note. *(MI-MIC-8).*	2.00	6.00	18.00
	b. Without serial #. *(MI-MIC-9).*	2.00	6.00	18.00
	c. Overprint: *Comandancia Militar, La Union, Gro. (MI-MIC-10).*	2.00	6.00	18.00
	d. Without underprint.	2.00	6.00	18.00
	e. With serial # and Without underprint.	2.00	6.00	18.00

Gobierno Provisional de Michoacán

1915 ND Transitorio Issue

		Good	Fine	XF
S884	**5 Centavos** ND (1915). Black. Melchor Ocampo at center. Signature varieties. Series O. Back: National arms at center. Paper: Pink pasteboard. *(SI-MIC-9).*	5.00	15.00	45.00
S885	**10 Centavos** ND (1915). Green. Melchor Ocampo at center. Signature varieties. Series N. Back: National arms at center. Paper: Brown pasteboard. *(SI-MIC-10).*	4.00	12.50	36.00
S886	**20 Centavos** ND (1915). Violet. Melchor Ocampo at center. Signature varieties. Series E. Back: National arms at center. Paper: Brown pasteboard. *(SI-MIC-11).*	4.00	12.50	36.00
S887	**50 Centavos** ND (1915). Red-orange. Melchor Ocampo at center. Signature varieties. Back: National arms at center. Paper: White pasteboard.			
	a. Issued note. Series A; D; E. *(SI-MIC-12).*	2.00	6.00	18.00
	b. Circular overprint: *Cuerpo de Ejercito del Norte* and various dates ca.1915.	5.00	15.00	45.00
	c. Oval overprint: *Angangueo.* Series B. *(SI-MIC-14).*	12.50	35.00	110.

Jefatura de Armas, Morelia

1915 Issue

		Good	Fine	XF
S888	**1 Centavo** July 1915. *(MI-MIC-2).*	12.50	35.00	110.
S889	**5 Centavos** July 1915. *(MI-MIC-3).*	7.50	20.00	60.00
S890	**5 Centavos** July 1915. *(MI-MIC-4).*	7.50	20.00	60.00
S891	**10 Centavos** July 1915. *(MI-MIC-5).*			
	a. Paper.	7.50	20.00	60.00
	b. Pasteboard.	7.50	20.00	60.00
S892	**20 Centavos** July 1915. *(MI-MIC-6).*	12.50	35.00	110.
S893	**50 Centavos** July 1915. *(MI-MIC-7).*	12.50	35.00	110.

La Tesorería Municipal, Pátzcuaro

1915 Issue

		Good	Fine	XF
S894	**10 Centavos** 1.6.1915. Black and red. Paper: Yellow pasteboard. *(SI-MIC-15).*	10.00	30.00	90.00
S895	**20 Centavos** 1.6.1915. Brown and red. Paper: White pasteboard. *(SI-MIC-16).*	12.50	35.00	110.

Tesorería Municipal, Puruandiro

1915 Issue

		Good	Fine	XF
S896	**5 Centavos** (ca.1915). Various dates. Series A. Paper: Brown. *(SI-MIC-17).*	15.00	45.00	135.
S897	**10 Centavos** (ca.1915). Various dates. Series A. Paper: Brown. *(SI-MIC-18).*	15.00	45.00	135.

Ejército Constitucionalista, Uruapán

1914 Issue

		Good	Fine	XF
S898	**5 Pesos** 20.12.1914. Black on green underprint. Series B. *(SI-MIC-20).*	10.00	30.00	90.00

Morelos

Circulación Forzosa en el Estado de Morelos, Cuernavaca

ND Issue

		Good	Fine	XF
S899	**10 Centavos** ND. Paper: Pasteboard. *(SI-MOR-23).*	15.00	45.00	135.
S900	**20 Centavos** ND. Paper: Brown pasteboard. *(SI-MOR-24).*	5.00	15.00	45.00
S901	**1 Peso** ND. Paper: Gray pasteboard. *(SI-MOR-25).*	10.00	30.00	90.00
S902	**1 Peso** ND. Black. *(SI-MOR-26).*			
	a. Gray paper.	1.00	3.00	9.00
	b. Brown paper.	1.00	3.00	9.00
	c. Pink paper.	1.00	3.00	9.00
	d. Orange paper.	1.00	3.00	9.00
	e. Maroon paper.	1.00	3.00	9.00
	f. White paper.	1.00	3.00	9.00

Dirección General de Rentas del Estado, Cuernavaca

1914 Issue

		Good	Fine	XF
S903	**10 Centavos** June 1914. Green. *(SI-MOR-7).*	15.00	45.00	135.
S904	**20 Centavos** June 1914. Red. *(SI-MOR-8).*	15.00	45.00	135.

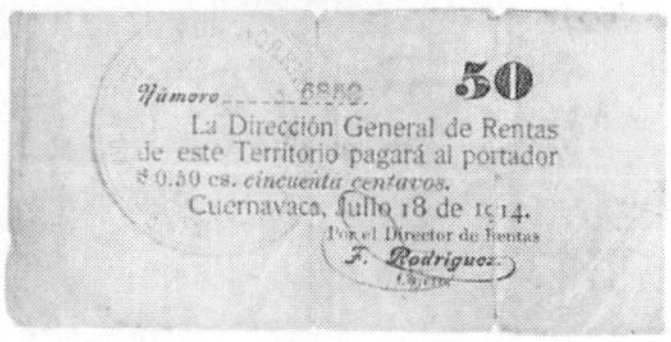

		Good	Fine	XF
S905	**50 Centavos** 28.7.1914. Black. *(SI-MOR-9).*	15.00	45.00	135.

Gobierno Convencionista, Cuernavaca

1915 Transitorio Issue

		Good	Fine	XF
S906	**5 Centavos** 1915. Paper: Pink pasteboard. *(SI-MOR-10).*	10.00	30.00	90.00
S907	**10 Centavos** 1915. Series B. Back: Sunface at center. Paper: Yellow pasteboard. *(SI-MOR-11).*	10.00	30.00	90.00
S908	**20 Centavos** 1915. Series A. Back: Sunface at center. Like #S907. Paper: Red pasteboard. *(SI-MOR-12).*	4.00	12.50	35.00

Gobierno Convencionista de México

Decree of October 1, 1915

		Good	Fine	XF
S909	**5 Pesos** 12.10.1915. Black on tan underprint. Justice at left.			
	a. Issued note, printed top to top. *(SI-MOR-16).*	2.00	6.00	18.00
	b. Inverted back.	30.00	90.00	270.

Decree of December 27, 1915

		Good	Fine	XF
S910	**50 Centavos** ND. Yellow. Farmer and laborer at center. Back: Red seal. *(SI-MOR-13).*	18.00	54.00	155.
S911	**50 Centavos** ND. Red. *(SI-MOR-14).*	15.00	45.00	135.

Decree of January 10, 1916

		Good	Fine	XF
S912	**2 Pesos** D.1916. Black on green underprint. Woman at right. *(SI-MOR-15).*	1.00	3.00	9.00

Jefatura de Armas, Yautepec

1915 Issue

		Good	Fine	XF
S913	**5 Centavos** Jan. 1915. Paper: White pasteboard. *(MI-MOR-4).*	9.00	27.00	80.00
S914	**10 Centavos** Jan. 1915. Series R. Paper: Green pasteboard. *(MI-MOR-5).*	9.00	27.00	80.00
S915	**20 Centavos** Jan. 1915. Series C. Paper: Violet pasteboard. *(MI-MOR-6).*	9.00	27.00	80.00

Nayarit

Cuerpo de Ejército del Noroeste, Tepic

Army of the Northwest

1914 Issue

		Good	Fine	XF
S916	**50 Centavos** 10.6.1914. Blue. National arms at upper left. Series D. Back: Denomination and monogram. *(MI-NAY-3).*	9.00	27.00	80.00

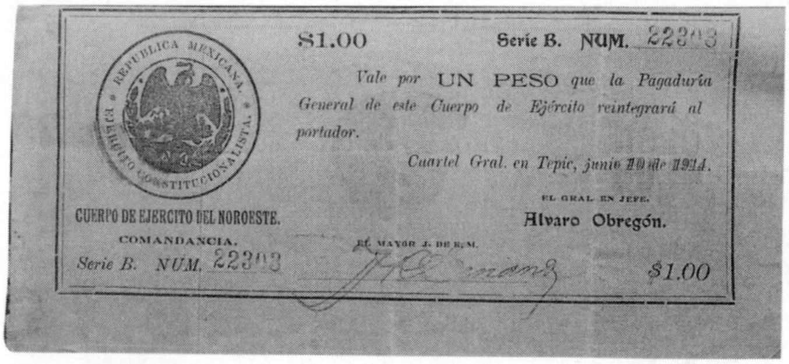

		Good	Fine	XF
S917	**1 Peso** 10.6.1914. National arms at upper left. Series B. Back: Denomination and monogram. *(MI-NAY-4).*	60.00	180.	550.
S917B	**10 Pesos** 10.6.1914. Red. National arms at upper left. Similar to #S917. Series B. Back: Denomination and monogram. *(MI-NAY-4).*	80.00	240.	750.

Gobierno Constitucionalista, Territorio de Tepic

1913 Issue

		Good	Fine	XF
S917F	**10 Pesos** Nov. 1913. *(MI-NAY-4A).*	—	—	—

Jefe Político del Territorio

ND Issue

		Good	Fine	XF
S918	**5 Centavos** ND. Overprint: *Gral Juan Carrasco. (SI-NAY-29).*			
	a. Red pasteboard.	25.00	75.00	225.
	b. Pink pasteboard.	25.00	75.00	225.
	c. Green pasteboard.	25.00	75.00	225.

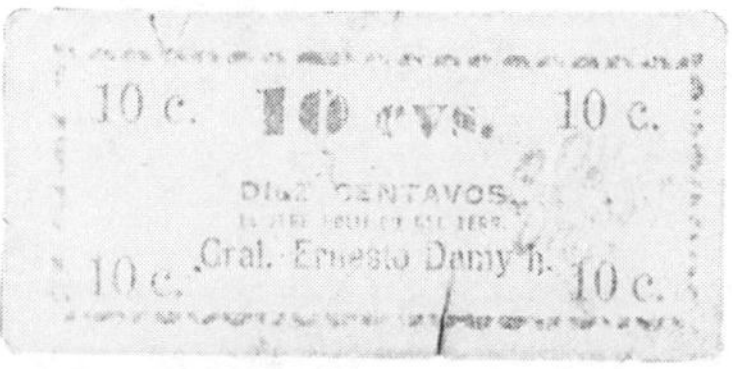

		Good	Fine	XF
S919	**10 Centavos** ND. Overprint: *Gral Juan Carrasco. (SI-NAY-30).*			
	a. Lilac pasteboard.	25.00	75.00	225.

	Good	Fine	XF
b. Gray pasteboard.	25.00	75.00	225.
c. Blue pasteboard.	25.00	75.00	225.
d. Pink pasteboard.	25.00	75.00	225.

JEFE DE LA COLUMNA, TERRITORIO DE TEPIC

1915 ISSUE

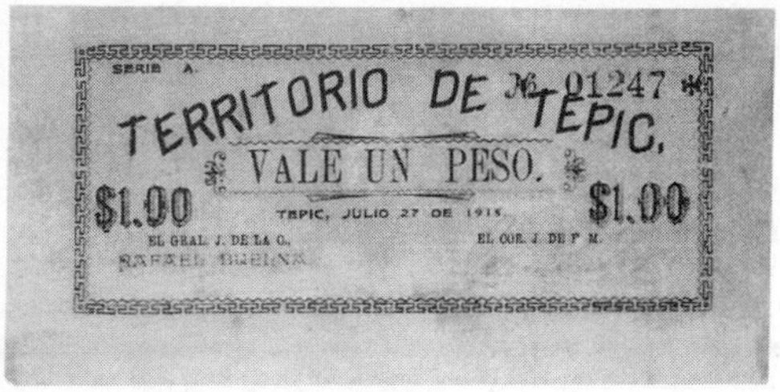

	Good	Fine	XF
S920 1 Peso 27.7.1915. Black on pink underprint. Series A. *(SI-NAY-5).*	45.00	135.	400.

ND ISSUES

	Good	Fine	XF
S921 5 Centavos ND. Green. *(SI-NAY-20).*	15.00	45.00	135.
S922 10 Centavos ND. Yellow. *(SI-NAY-21).*	6.00	18.00	55.00
S923 20 Centavos ND. Paper: Gray pasteboard. *(SI-MAY-23).*	6.00	18.00	55.00

	Good	Fine	XF
S924 50 Centavos ND. Black. *(SI-NAY-24).*	18.00	55.00	165.

	Good	Fine	XF
S925 50 Centavos ND. *(SI-NAY-25).*	18.00	55.00	165.
S926 50 Centavos ND. *(SI-NAY-26).*	18.00	55.00	165.
S927 50 Centavos ND. Brown. *(SI-NAY-27).*	5.00	15.00	45.00
S928 50 Centavos ND. Overprint: With diagonal *STAL MEXI. (SI-NAY-28).*	5.00	15.00	45.00
S928A 50 Centavos ND. Ornamental border. Back: Ornamental border.	5.00	15.00	45.00

TESORERÍA GENERAL, TERRITORIO DE TEPIC

ND ISSUE

	Good	Fine	XF
S929 5 Centavos ND. Pale blue. *(SI-NAY-15).*	25.00	75.00	225.
S930 10 Centavos ND. Pale blue. *(SI-NAY-16).*	25.00	75.00	225.
S931 20 Centavos ND. Pale blue. *(SI-NAY-17).*	25.00	75.00	225.
S932 50 Centavos ND. Pale blue. *(SI-NAY-18).*	25.00	75.00	225.

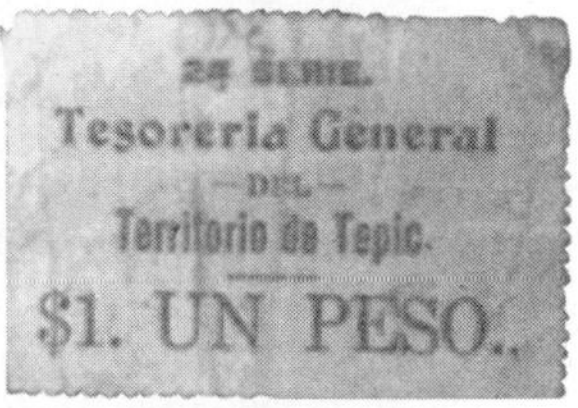

	Good	Fine	XF
S933 1 Peso ND. Pale blue. *(SI-NAY-19).*	25.00	75.00	225.

NUEVO LEÓN

GOBIERNO DE NUEVO LEÓN, MONTERREY

1914 ISSUE

	Good	Fine	XF
S934 1 Centavo 1914. Black on light green underprint. Violet monogram stamping. Paper: Pasteboard. *(SI-NUE-3).*	2.00	6.00	18.00

DIVISIÓN DEL BRAVO, MONTERREY

1914 ISSUE

#S935-S939 The symmetrical back design is usually the same color w/some shade varieties as the unpt. of the face. The 1, 2 and 5 peso denominations bear 3 circular printed seals on back. The 10 and 50 centavos are w/o seals.

VALIDATION HAND STAMPS:

1. .... JEFATURA DE HACIENDA, MONTERREY, N.I.
2. .... EJERCITO NACIONAL, DIVISION DEL BRAVO.
3. .... GOBIERNO DE ESTADO LIBRE Y SOBERANO DE NUEVO LEON.

	Good	Fine	XF
S935 10 Centavos 8.1.1914. Black on blue or green underprint. National arms at center. Series E; F. Back: Symmetrical design. *(MI-NUE-1).*	4.00	12.50	36.00
S936 50 Centavos 8.1.1914. Black on blue underprint. National arms at center. Back: Symmetrical design.			
a. Large signature at center. Series D. *(MI-NUE-2).*	2.00	6.00	18.00
b. Hand stamped: *DIVISION DEL BRAVO / JEFATURA DE ARMAS DE N. LAREDO*CUARTEL GENERAL* around eagle overprint (MI-NUE-3).*	5.00	15.00	45.00
c. Small signature at center. Series D-A; D-B; D-C; D-D; D-E; E-B.	2.00	6.00	18.00
S937 1 Peso 8.1.1914. Black on pink underprint. National arms at center. Series C; C.A-C.D. Back: Symmetrical design. Three circular printed seals. *(MI-NUE-4)).*	2.00	6.00	18.00
S938 2 Pesos 8.1.1914. Black on gray underprint. National arms at center. Series B; C.A.; C.B. Back: Symmetrical design. Three circular printed seals. *(MI-NUE-5).*	2.00	6.00	18.00
S939 5 Pesos 8.1.1914. Black on brown underprint. National arms at center. Series A. Back: Symmetrical design. Three circular printed seals. *(MI-NUE-6).*	4.00	12.50	36.00

UNDETERMINED ORIGIN

CUERPO DE EJÉRCITO DEL NOROESTE

ND ISSUE

	Good	Fine	XF
S940 1 Peso ND. Green. Constitutionalist Army seal, handwritten signature. Series B.			
a. Regular paper. *(MI-NUE-10).*	30.00	90.00	270.
b. Tan ledger paper.	30.00	90.00	270.

	Good	Fine	XF
S941 5 Pesos ND. Green. Constitutionalist Army seal, handwritten signature. Series A.			
a. Issued note. *(MI-NUE-11).*	45.00	135.	400.
b. Overprint: *AMORTIZADO.*	45.00	135.	400.
r. Remainder, without Army seal. Printed signature. Series B. *(MI-NUE-12).*	40.00	120.	360.

OAXACA

DIVISIÓN ALMAZÁN, HUAJUAPÁN

1916 ISSUE

		Good	Fine	XF
S942	**1 Peso** 1.4.1916. Black. Seated woman at left, national arms at center. Series A. *(MI-OAX-1).*	75.00	225.	675.

La Tesorería Provisional del Comercio, Huajuapán

1915 Issue

		Good	Fine	XF
S943	**5 Centavos** 19.10.1915. Black. *(PI-OAX-12).*	6.00	18.00	55.00
S944	**10 Centavos** ND. Black. *(PI-OAX-13).*	7.50	20.00	60.00
S945	**20 Centavos** ND. Black. *(PI-OAX-14).*	7.50	20.00	60.00

		Good	Fine	XF
S946	**50 Centavos** 18.9.1915; 10.5.1915. Black. *(PI-OAX-15).*	6.00	18.00	55.00
S947	**1 Peso** 18.9.1915. Black. *(PI-OAX-16).*	7.50	20.00	60.00

La Tesorería General del Estado de Oaxaca, Nochixtlán

1916 Issue

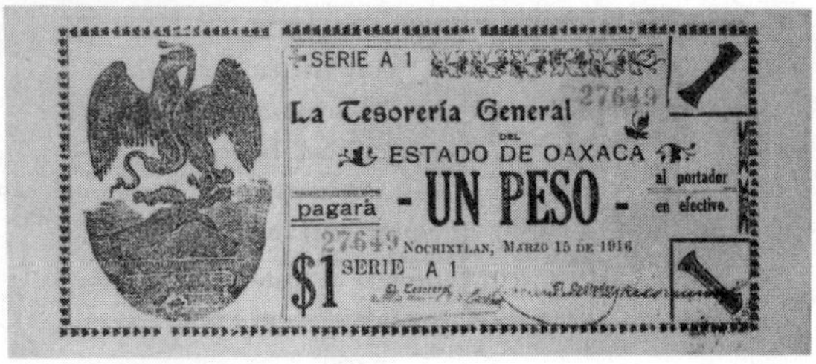

		Good	Fine	XF
S948	**1 Peso** 15.3.1916. Black. National arms at left. Series A1. Back: Miguel Hidalgo at left. *(SI-OAX-4).*			
	a. Without signature.	15.00	45.00	135.
	b. Stamped signature at left, without signature at right.	2.00	6.00	18.00
S949	**5 Pesos** 15.3.1916. Black. National arms at left. Series O. Back: Miguel Hidalgo at left.			
	a. Stamped violet signature at left, handwritten signature at right. *(SI-OAX-5).*	6.00	18.00	55.00
	b. 2 stamped violet or blue signatures. *(SI-OAX-6).*	1.50	5.00	15.00
	r. Remainder. *(SI-OAX-6a).*	2.50	7.50	20.00

Gobierno Preconstitucional del Estado de Oaxaca

Decree of April 1, 1916

		Good	Fine	XF
S950	**50 Centavos** 1.4.1916. Blue. Paper: White pasteboard. *(SI-OAX-26).*	6.00	18.00	55.00

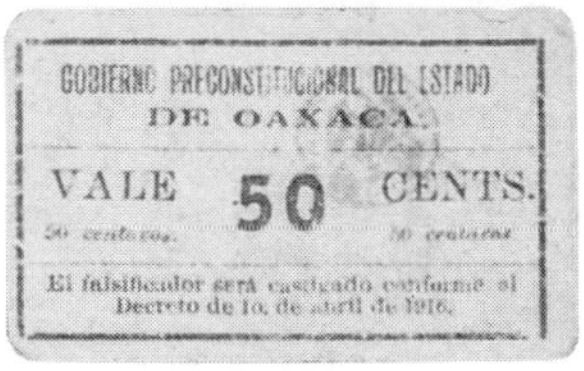

		Good	Fine	XF
S951	**50 Centavos** 1.4.1916. Blue. Paper: Maroon pasteboard. *(SI-OAX-27).*	6.00	18.00	55.00

La Tesorería General del Estado de Oaxaca, Oaxaca de Juárez

1914 Issue

		Good	Fine	XF
S952	**5 Centavos** 8.4.1914; May 1914. Black on pink underprint. *(SI-OAX-7).*	45.00	135.	400.

Decrees of 19.2.1915; 10.7.1915; 8.11.1915; 12.1.1916; 18.1.1916

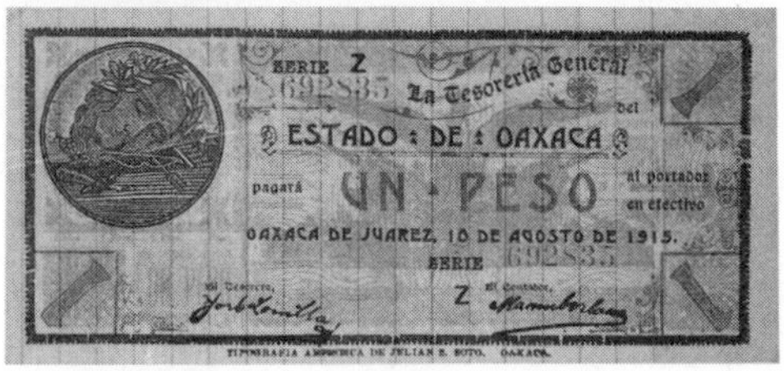

		Good	Fine	XF
S953	**1 Peso** Various dates ca.1915. Green and red on yellow to ochre and yellow-green to olive-green underprint. Wreathed head of woman at upper left. Back: Large Portrait Pablo Benito Juárez at left.			
	a. Series A; D; E; J; P; R; U; Z. *(SI-OAX-8).*	1.00	3.00	9.00
	b. Small bust of Juarez.	2.00	6.00	12.50
	c. Blue paper. Series I. 15.11.1915. *(SI-OAX-10).*	2.00	6.00	12.50
	d. Ledger paper. Series A. 3.9.1915.	15.00	45.00	135.
	e. As d. Series P. 10.8.1915.	15.00	45.00	135.
	x. Error: *NU PESO* instead of *UN PESO*. Series P. 24.9.1915. *(SI-OAX-9).*	150.	450.	1350.

		Good	Fine	XF
S954	**5 Pesos** Various dates ca.1915-16. Blue and green on orange and yellow underprint. Wreathed head of woman at upper left. Series A; D; E; I; J; R; U; Y; Z. Back: Large Portrait Pablo Benito Juárez at left. *(SI-OAX-11).*	1.50	5.00	15.00
S955	**5 Pesos** Various dates ca.1915. Blue and green on orange and yellow underprint. Wreathed head of woman at upper left. Like #S954 but upper serial # above series letter. Series J; Z. Back: Small Portrait Pablo Benito Juárez at left. *(SI-OAX-12).*	4.00	12.50	35.00
S956	**5 Pesos** ND (ca.1915). Back: Miguel Hildago at center. Back proof. *(SI-OAX-13).*	125.	375.	1150.
S957	**10 Pesos** Various dates ca.1915-16. Blue, maroon, brown, gray, gold on pink underprint. Wreathed head of woman at left. Back: Portrait Pablo Benito Juárez at right.			
	a. Issued note. Series A; D; W; X. *(SI-OAX-14).*	5.00	15.00	45.00
	b. Blue paper. Series A; I. 15.11.1915. *(SI-OAX-15).*	5.00	15.00	45.00
S958	**10 Pesos** Various dates ca.1915. Purple. Wreathed head of woman at left. Back: Portrait Pablo Benito Juárez at right.			
	a. Issued note. *(SI-OAX-16).*	2.00	6.00	18.00
	x. Error: without underprint on back. *(SI-OAX-17).*	7.50	20.00	60.00
S959	**20 Pesos** Various dates ca.1915. Green and brown. Wreathed head of woman at left. Back: Portrait Pablo Benito Juárez at right.			
	a. Oil cloth. Series D. *(SI-OAX-19).*	5.00	15.00	45.00
	b. Paper on cloth. Series D; P. *(SI-OAX-20).*	5.00	15.00	45.00
	c. Paper. Series Z. *(SI-OAX-21).*	25.00	75.00	225.
	d. Paper on cloth. Series Z. *(SI-OAX-21a).*	35.00	115.	345.

		Good	Fine	XF
S960	**50 Pesos** 10.11.1915. Red, orange and blue. Wreathed head of woman at left. Series LA; LI. Back: Portrait Pablo Benito Juárez at left. *(SI-OAX-22)*.	12.50	35.00	135.

Tesorería Provisional, Tamazola

1915 Issue

		Good	Fine	XF
S961	**20 Centavos** 20.7.1915. Like #S962. Paper: Pasteboard. *(SI-OAX-28)*.	18.00	55.00	165.
S962	**25 Centavos** 20.7.1915. Paper: Pasteboard. *(SI-OAX-29)*.	18.00	55.00	165.

La Tesorería General, Tlaxiaco

Decree of June 24, 1916

		Good	Fine	XF
S963	**50 Centavos** 26.6.1916. Series F. Paper: Light brown thin pasteboard. *(SI-OAX-30)*.			
	a. Issued note.	2.00	6.00	12.50
	r. Remainder without handstamped seal on back.	—	—	40.00

Puebla

Banco Español Refaccionario S.A.

Banco Oriental de México

1914 Issue

#S964-S967 checks payable to bearer w/printed denominations.

		Good	Fine	XF
S964	**5 Centavos** 1.7.1914. Blue and brown. *(PI-PUE-10)*.	18.00	55.00	165.
S965	**10 Centavos** 1.7.1914. Brown. *(PI-PUE-11)*.	18.00	55.00	165.
S966	**20 Centavos** 1.7.1914. Brown. *(PI-PUE-12)*.	18.00	55.00	42.50
S967	**50 Centavos** 1.7.1914. Black and red. Back: Red. Paper: Pink. *(PI-PUE-13)*.	25.00	75.00	225.

Junta Comercial, Chalchicomula

ND Issue

		Good	Fine	XF
S968	**10 Centavos** ND. Green. Coin at left. Paper: Cream pasteboard. *(PI-PUE-6)*.	7.50	20.00	60.00
S969	**20 Centavos** ND. Blue. Coin at left. Paper: Cream pasteboard. *(PI-PUE-7)*.	7.50	20.00	60.00

Tesorería de la Junta Comercial de Chalchicomula

ND Issue

		Good	Fine	XF
S970	**50 Centavos** ND. Green and black. Paper: Cream. *(PI-PUE-2)*.	45.00	135.	400.
S971	**1 Peso** ND. Brown and black. Paper: Cream.			
	a. Issued note. *(PI-PUE-3)*.	60.00	180.	550.
	b. Overprint: *Revalidado Cincuenta Centavos Papel Infalsificable*. *(PI-PUE-5)*.	45.00	135.	400.

Distrito de Matamoros

ND Issue

		Good	Fine	XF
S972	**2 Centavos** ND. Ornate borders. Series C. Back: Ornate borders. Paper: Violet pasteboard. *(SI-PUE-13)*.	6.00	18.00	55.00
S973	**5 Centavos** ND. Ornate borders. Back: Ornate borders. Paper: Orange pasteboard. *(SI-PUE-14)*.	6.00	18.00	55.00

		Good	Fine	XF
S974	**10 Centavos** ND. Ornate borders. Series B. Back: Ornate borders. Paper: Pasteboard. *(SI-PUE-15)*.	6.00	18.00	55.00
S975	**20 Centavos** ND. Green. Ornate borders. Series B; C. Back: Ornate borders. Paper: Yellow pasteboard. *(SI-PUE-16)*.	6.00	18.00	55.00
S976	**25 Centavos** ND. Ornate borders. Series A-C. Back: Ornate borders. Paper: Purple pasteboard. *(SI-PUE-17)*.	6.00	18.00	55.00
S977	**50 Centavos** ND. Ornate borders. Series B. Back: Ornate borders. Paper: Green pasteboard. *(SI-PUE-18)*.	6.00	18.00	55.00

#S978 *Deleted*. See #S984A.

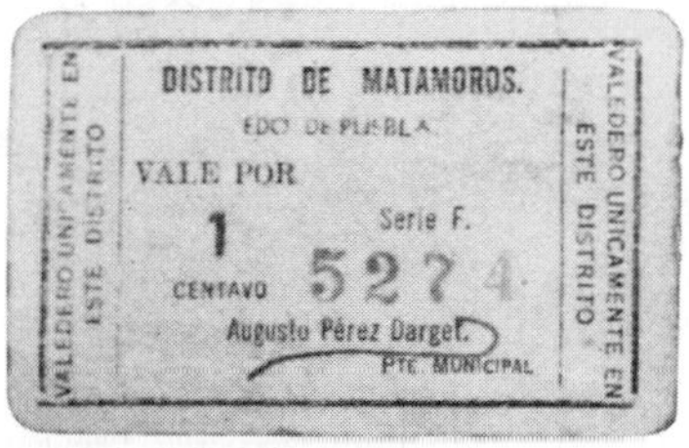

		Good	Fine	XF
S979	**1 Centavo** ND. Straight line borders. Series F. Back: Straight line borders. Paper: Dull yellow pasteboard. *(SI-PUE-20)*.	6.00	18.00	55.00
S980	**2 Centavos** ND. Straight line borders. Series E. Back: Straight line borders. Paper: Gold, tan pasteboard. *(SI-PUE-21)*.	6.00	18.00	55.00

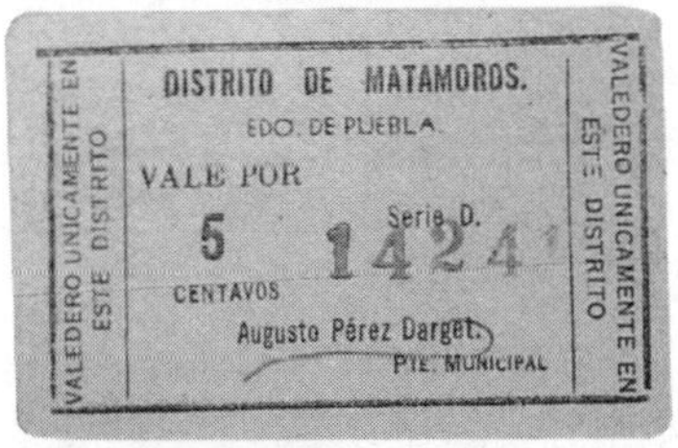

		Good	Fine	XF
S981	**5 Centavos** ND. Straight line borders. Series D. Back: Straight line borders. Paper: Salmon pasteboard. *(SI-PUE-22)*.	6.00	18.00	55.00

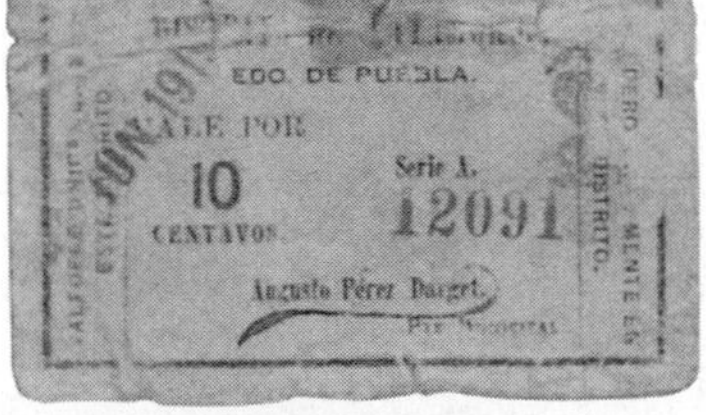

		Good	Fine	XF
S982	**10 Centavos** ND. Straight line borders. Series A. Back: Straight line borders. Paper: Pink pasteboard. *(SI-PUE-23)*.	6.00	18.00	55.00
S983	**20 Centavos** ND. Straight line borders. Series A. Back: Straight line borders. Paper: Yellow pasteboard. *(SI-PUE-24)*.	6.00	18.00	55.00
S984	**50 Centavos** ND. Straight line borders. Series A. Back: Straight line borders. *(SI-PUE-25)*.			
	a. Light green pasteboard.	6.00	18.00	55.00
	b. ND. Gray-type variety pasteboard.	6.00	18.00	55.00
S984A	**1 Peso** ND. Straight line borders. Series B; C. Back: Straight line borders. Paper: White pasteboard. *(SI-PUE-19)*.	7.50	20.00	60.00

Brigada Serdan

1914-15 Issue

Number	Description	Good	Fine	XF
S984B	**50 Centavos** 5.12.1914. Black on light gold underprint. Arms at center. Series A. Back: Aqua.	—	—	—
S984C	**50 Centavos** 14.3.1915. Black on green underprint. Arms at center.	—	—	—

Cuartel General del Ejército Constitucionalista de la Sierra Norte de Puebla

ND Issue

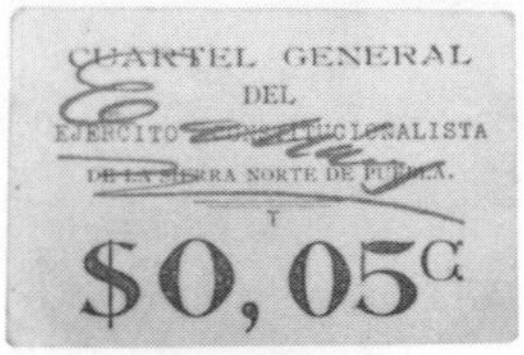

Number	Description	Good	Fine	XF
S985	**5 Centavos** ND. *(SI-PUE-20).*	25.00	75.00	225.

Queretaro

La Administracion General de Rentas del Estado

1924 Issue

Number	Description	Good	Fine	XF
S985A	**2 Pesos** 1924. Black. Back: Arms in red at center. Paper: Blue security.	30.00	90.00	270.

San Luis Potosí

Ejército Constitucionalista

ND Issue

Number	Description	Good	Fine	XF
S986	**5 Centavos** ND. Orange. Liberty with flags at center. Paper: Red pasteboard. *(MI-SAN-4).*	6.00	18.00	55.00
S987	**10 Centavos** ND. Blue. Liberty with flags at center. Paper: White pasteboard. *(MI-SAN-5).*	6.00	18.00	55.00
S988	**20 Centavos** ND. Blue. Liberty with flags at center. Paper: Gray pasteboard. *(MI-SAN-6).*	6.00	18.00	55.00
S989	**50 Centavos** ND. Yellow. Liberty with flags at center. Paper: Orange pasteboard. *(MI-SAN-7).*	2.50	7.50	20.00

Sinaloa

Ejército Constitucionalista, Cuerpo de Ejército del Noroeste, Culiacán

Constitutionalist Army of the Northwest

1914 Issue

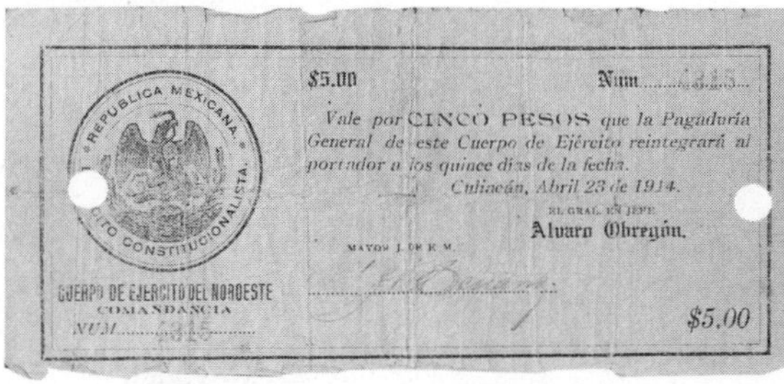

Number	Description	Good	Fine	XF
S990	**5 Pesos** 23.4.1914. Black. National arms at left. Printed signature of Alvaro Obregon and handwritten signature of Francisco Serano. *(MI-SIN-1).*	25.00	75.00	225.
S991	**10 Pesos** 23.4.1914. Black. National arms at left. Printed signature of Alvaro Obregon and handwritten signature of Francisco Serano. *(MI-SIN-2).*	30.00	90.00	270.
S992	**20 Pesos** 23.4.1914. Black. National arms at left. Printed signature of Alvaro Obregon and handwritten signature of Francisco Serano. *(MI-SIN-3).*	30.00	90.00	270.
S993	**50 Pesos** 23.4.1914. Black. National arms at left. Printed signature of Alvaro Obregon and handwritten signature of Francisco Serano. *(MI-SIN-4).*	30.00	90.00	270.

1914 Comandancia Issue

Number	Description	Good	Fine	XF
S994	**50 Centavos** 1.5.1914. National arms at left. Back: Seal. *(MI-SIN-5).*	40.00	120.	360.
S995	**1 Peso** 1.5.1914. Brown. National arms at left. Back: Seal.			
	a. Issued note. *(MI-SIN-6).*	30.00	90.00	270.
	b. Overprint: *AMORTIZADO. (MI-SIN-7).*	30.00	90.00	270.

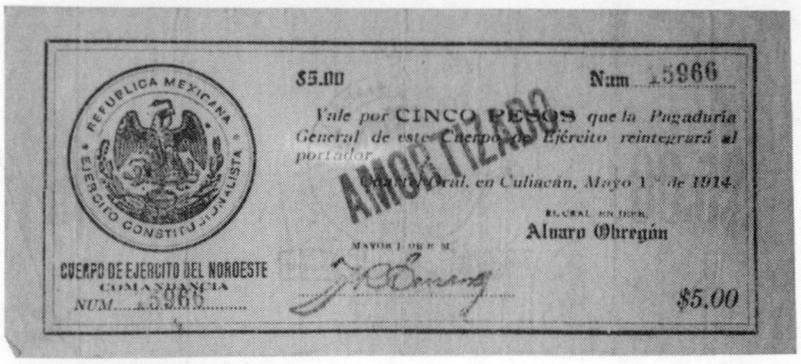

Number	Description	Good	Fine	XF
S996	**5 Pesos** 1.5.1914. Black. National arms at left. Back: Seal.			
	a. Issued note. *(MI-SIN-8).*	15.00	45.00	135.
	b. Overprint: *AMORTIZADO. (MI-SIN-9).*	15.00	45.00	135.
S997	**10 Pesos** 1.5.1914. Orange. National arms at left. Back: Seal. *(MI-SIN-10).*	15.00	45.00	135.
S998	**20 Pesos** 1.5.1914. Dark pink. National arms at left. Back: Seal. *(MI-SIN-11).*	18.00	55.00	165.

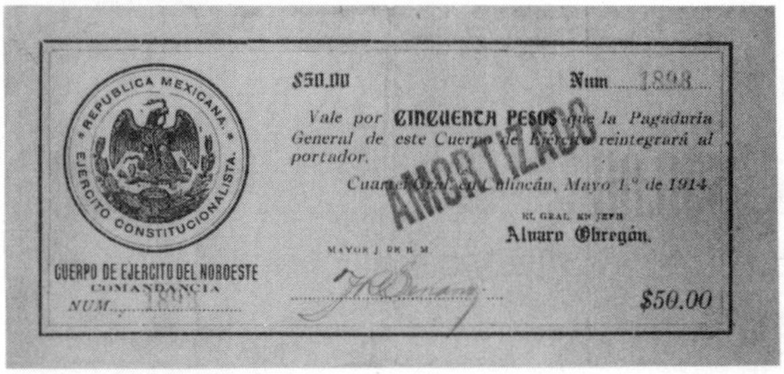

Number	Description	Good	Fine	XF
S999	**50 Pesos** 1.5.1914. Blue. National arms at left. Back: Seal.			
	a. Issued note. *(MI-SIN-12).*	18.00	55.00	165.
	b. Overprint: *AMORTIZADO. (MI-SIN-13).*	18.00	55.00	165.

Estado de Sinaloa, Culiacán

Decree No. 17 of December 13, 1913

Number	Description	Good	Fine	XF
S1000	**1 Peso** 13.12.1913. Orange. National arms at left. Printed signature of Felipe Riveros and Jose G. Heredia. Series C. Overprint: *AMORTIZADO. (SI-SIN-1).*	7.50	20.00	60.00

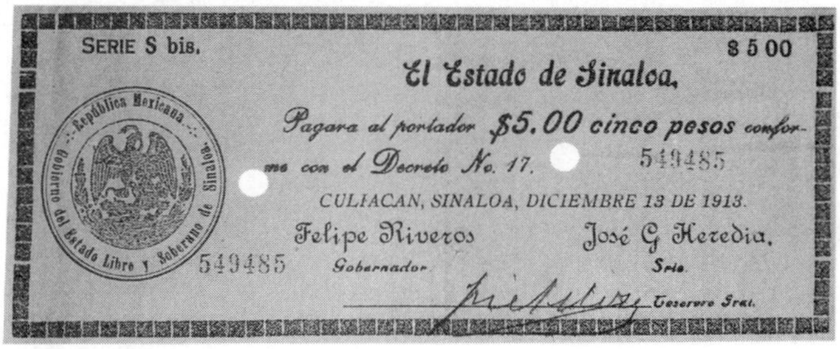

Number	Description	Good	Fine	XF
S1001	**5 Pesos** 13.12.1913. Blue. National arms at left. Printed signature of Felipe Riveros and Jose G. Heredia. Series G; P; S; W; Y. *(SI-SIN-2).*	6.00	18.00	55.00
S1002	**10 Pesos** 13.12.1913. Black. National arms at left. Printed signature of Felipe Riveros and Jose G. Heredia. Series L; T; U. *(SI-SIN-3).*	7.50	20.00	60.00

Decree No. 2 of April 15, 1915

Number	Description	Good	Fine	XF
S1003	**5 Centavos** 15.4.1915. National arms at center. Paper: Brown pasteboard. *(SI-SIN-4).*	6.00	18.00	55.00
S1004	**10 Centavos** 15.4.1915. National arms at center. Series A. Paper: Green pasteboard. *(SI-SIN-5).*	6.00	18.00	55.00

Estado de Sinaloa, Mazatlán

1916 First Issue

Number	Description	Good	Fine	XF
S1005	**1 Peso** 1.7.1916. Dark blue and gray. Seated Mercury with globe at center. Series A. Back: Green underprint. Red text. *(SI-SIN-10).*	30.00	90.00	270.
S1006	**2 Pesos** 1.7.1916. Brown and gray. Seated Mercury with globe at center. Series B. Back: Green underprint. Blue text. *(SI-SIN-12).*	30.00	90.00	270.

1916 Second Issue

	Good	Fine	XF
S1007 1 Peso 15.8.1916. Purple and gray. Seated Mercury with globe at center. *(SI-SIN-11).*	30.00	90.00	270.
S1008 2 Pesos 15.8.1916. Purple and gray on white. Seated Mercury with globe at center. *(SI-SIN-13).*	55.00	165.	550.

El Gobierno Constitucionalista del Territorio de Tepic ydel Estado de Sinaloa, Rosario

1913 Issue

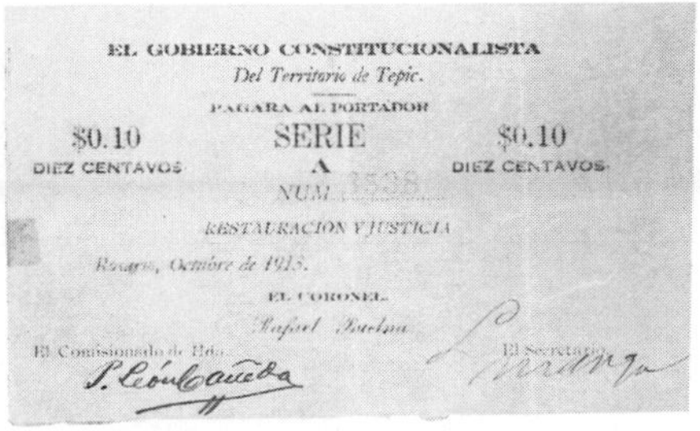

	Good	Fine	XF
S1009 10 Centavos Oct. 1913. Black on brown underprint. Handwritten signature. Series A. *(MI-SIN-23).*	90.00	270.	800.
S1010 20 Centavos Oct. 1913. Handwritten signature. Series A. *(MI-SAN-24).*	90.00	270.	800.
S1011 50 Centavos Oct. 1913. Handwritten signature. Series C. *(MI-SIN-25).*	90.00	270.	800.

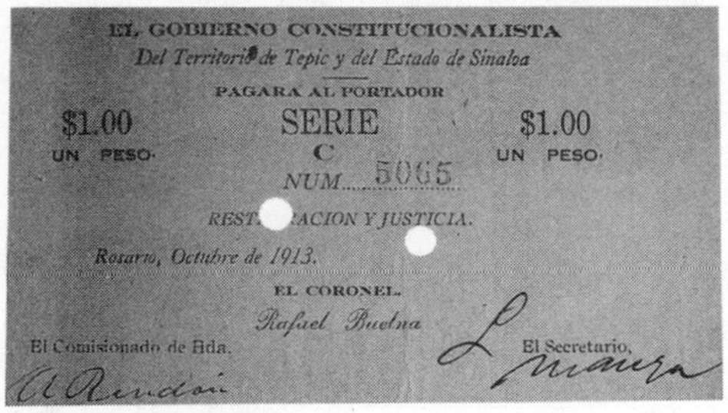

	Good	Fine	XF
S1012 1 Peso Oct. 1913. Black on brown. Handwritten signature. Series C. *(MI-SIN-26).*	60.00	180.	550.
S1013 5 Pesos Oct. 1913. Handwritten signature. Series C. *(MI-SIN-27).*	90.00	270.	800.
S1014 20 Pesos Oct. 1913. Handwritten signature. Series C. *(MI-SIN-28).*	90.00	270.	800.

La Pagaduría Gral. de la Brigada de Sinaloa

Law of 19 August 1914

	Good	Fine	XF
S1015 25 Centavos 21.8.1914. Black. National arms at upper center. Series A. Printer: Imprenta Moderna-Mazatlan. *(MI-SIN-15).*	25.00	75.00	225.

	Good	Fine	XF
S1016 50 Centavos 21.8.1914. Black. National arms at upper center. Series A. Printer: Imprenta Moderna-Mazatlan.			
a. Issued note. *(MI-SIN-16).*	25.00	75.00	225.
b. Overprint: *AMORTIZADO. (MI-SIN-17).*	25.00	75.00	225.
S1017 1 Peso 21.8.1914. Black on pink underprint. National arms at upper center. Series A-C. Printer: Imprenta Moderna-Mazatlan.			
a. Issued note. *(MI-SIN-18).*	2.50	7.50	20.00
b. Overprint for Mazatlan and *Retirado de la Circulacion.*	2.50	7.50	20.00
c. Overprint: *JEFATURA DE HACIENDA MAZATLAN.*	2.50	7.50	20.00
S1018 5 Pesos 21.8.1914. Blue on orange underprint. National arms at upper center. Series A-C. Printer: Imprenta Moderna-Mazatlan. *(MI-SIN-19).*	3.00	9.00	27.50
S1019 10 Pesos 21.8.1914. Red on pale blue underprint. National arms at upper center. Series A; C. Printer: Imprenta Moderna-Mazatlan. *(MI-SIN-20).*	5.00	15.00	45.00
S1020 20 Pesos 21.8.1914. Blue. National arms at upper center. Series A; B. Printer: Imprenta Moderna-Mazatlan. *(MI-SIN-21).*	15.00	45.00	135.
S1021 50 Pesos 21.8.1914. Orange and black on light green underprint. National arms at upper center. Series A. Printer: Imprenta Moderna-Mazatlan. *(MI-SIN-22).*	15.00	45.00	135.

La Tesorería General del Estado de Sinaloa

1914 Issue

	Good	Fine	XF
S1022 10 Centavos 25.2.1914. Green. Series C. Back: National arms. *(SI-SIN-6).*	5.00	15.00	45.00
S1023 20 Centavos 25.2.1914. Blue-green. Series B. Back: National arms. *(SI-SIN-7).*	5.00	15.00	45.00
S1024 50 Centavos 25.2.1914. Black on pale orange underprint. Series A. Back: National arms. *(SI-SIN-8).*	3.00	9.00	27.50
S1025 50 Centavos 10.4.1914. Black on pale orange underprint. Series B. Back: National arms. *(SI-SIN-9).*	2.50	7.50	20.00

Estado de Sinaloa, San Blas

Decree No. 3 of July 13, 1913

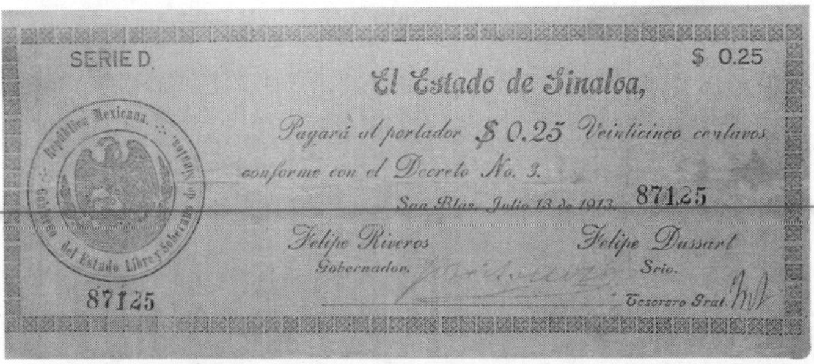

	Good	Fine	XF
S1026 25 Centavos 13.7.1913. Black. National arms at left. Printed signatures of Felipe Riveros and Felipe Dassart and two handwritten signatures. Series O. *(SI-SIN-14).*	40.00	120.	360.
S1027 50 Centavos 13.7.1913. Black. National arms at left. Printed signatures of Felipe Riveros and Felipe Dassart and two handwritten signatures. Series D.			
a. Issued note. *(SI-SIN-15).*	30.00	90.00	270.
b. Overprint: *AMORTIZADO. (SI-SIN-16).*	25.00	75.00	225.

	Good	Fine	XF
S1028 1 Peso 13.7.1913. Orange on cream. National arms at left. Printed signatures of Felipe Riveros and Felipe Dassart and two handwritten signatures. Series R. *(SI-SIN-17).*	40.00	120.	360.
S1029 5 Pesos 13.7.1913. Blue on cream. National arms at left. Printed signatures of Felipe Riveros and Felipe Dassart and two handwritten signatures. Series C. *(SI-SIN-18).*	30.00	90.00	270.
S1030 10 Pesos 13.7.1913. National arms at left. Printed signatures of Felipe Riveros and Felipe Dassart and two handwritten signatures. Series C. *(SI-SIN-19).*	30.00	90.00	270.

Decree No. 11 of September 15, 1913

	Good	Fine	XF
S1031 25 Centavos 15.9.1913. Black. National arms at left. Printed signatures of Felipe Riveros and Fidencio E. Schmidt and two handwritten signatures. Series F. *(SI-SIN-20).*	25.00	75.00	225.

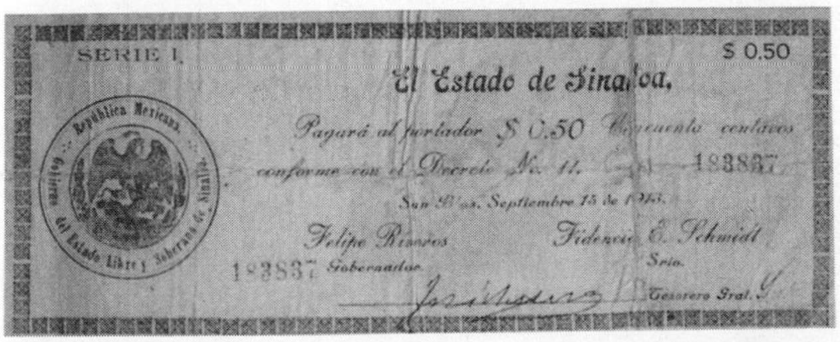

	Good	Fine	XF
S1032 50 Centavos 15.9.1913. National arms at left. Printed signatures of Felipe Riveros and Fidencio E. Schmidt and two handwritten signatures. Series I. *(SI-SIN-21).*	25.00	75.00	225.

S1033 1 Peso — Good | Fine | XF

15.9.1913. National arms at left. Printed signatures of Felipe Riveros and Fidencio E. Schmidt and two handwritten signatures. *(SI-SIN-22).* — 25.00 | 75.00 | 225.

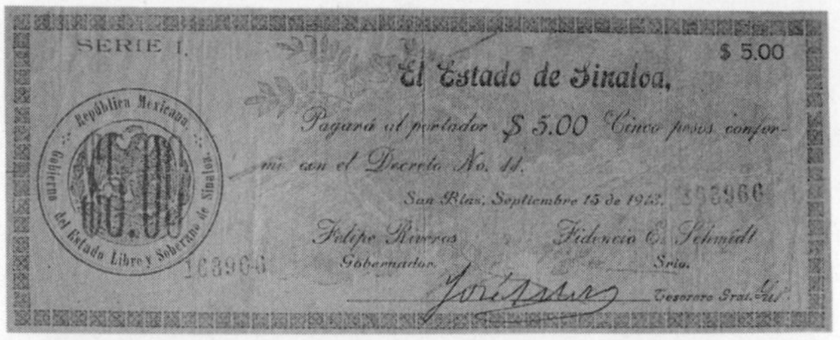

S1034 5 Pesos — Good | Fine | XF

15.9.1913. Blue on pale orange underprint. National arms at left. Printed signatures of Felipe Riveros and Fidencio E. Schmidt and two handwritten signatures. Series I. *(SI-SIN-23).* — 25.00 | 75.00 | 225.

S1035 10 Pesos

15.9.1913. National arms at left. Printed signatures of Felipe Riveros and Fidencio E. Schmidt and two handwritten signatures. Series G. *(SI-SIN-24).* — 25.00 | 75.00 | 225.

Decree No. 14 of October 23, 1913

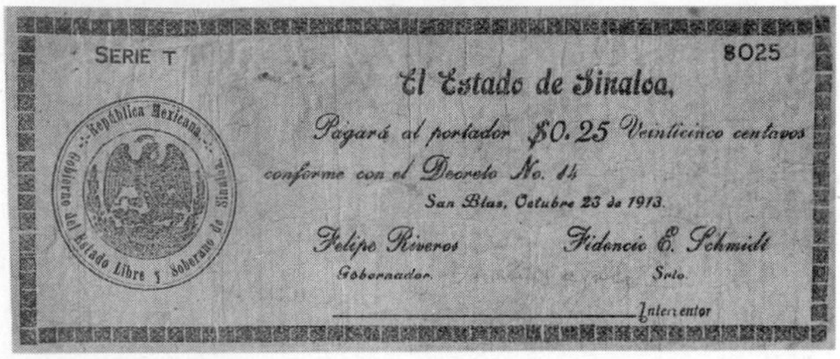

S1036 25 Centavos — Good | Fine | XF

23.10.1913. Black. National arms at left. Printed signatures of Felipe Riveros and Fidencio E. Schmidt and one or two handwritten signatures.
- a. Signature title: *Interventor.* Series T. *(SI-SIN-25).* — 18.00 | 55.00 | 165.
- b. Signature title: *Tesoreria Gral.* Series N. *(SI-SIN-26).* — 18.00 | 55.00 | 165.

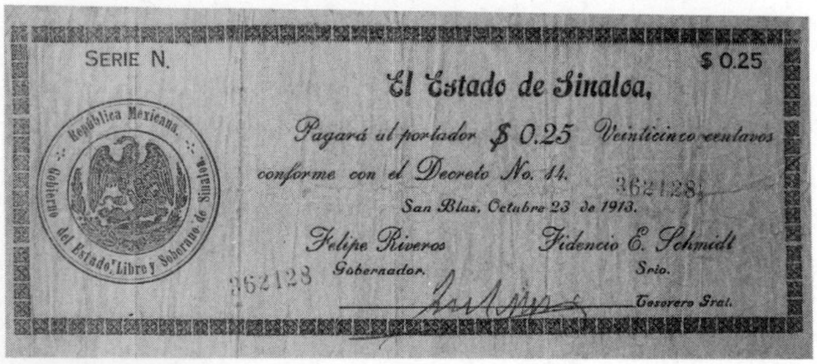

S1037 50 Centavos — Good | Fine | XF

23.10.1913. Black. National arms at left. Printed signatures of Felipe Riveros and Fidencio E. Schmidt and one or two handwritten signatures.
- a. Signature title: *Interventor. (SI-SIN-27).* — 40.00 | 120. | 360.
- b. Signature title: *Tesoreria Gral.* Series Y. *(SI-SIN-28).* — 18.00 | 55.00 | 165.

S1038 1 Peso

23.10.1913. Orange on cream. National arms at left. Printed signatures of Felipe Riveros and Fidencio E. Schmidt and one or two handwritten signatures. Signature title: *Tesoreria Gral.* Series Z. *(SI-SIN-29).* — 18.00 | 55.00 | 165.

S1039 5 Pesos

23.10.1913. Blue and brown on red underprint. National arms at left. Printed signatures of Felipe Riveros and Fidencio E. Schmidt and one or two handwritten signatures. Signature title: *Tessoreria Gral.* Series V. *(SI-SIN-30).* — 18.00 | 55.00 | 165.

S1040 10 Pesos

23.10.1913. Black on green underprint. Series U. *(SI-SIN-31).* — 18.00 | 55.00 | 165.

El Estado Libre y Soberano de Sinaloa

Decree of February 22, 1915

S1041 25 Centavos — VG | VF | UNC

D.1915. Black on tan underprint. Portrait Pablo Benito Juárez at left, portrait Francisco I. Madero at right. Series A; C; D; F; H; I. Back: Light green. Circular violet treasury handstamp. Printer: Britton & Rey, San Francisco, California. *(SI-SIN-32).* — 2.00 | 6.00 | 18.00

S1042 50 Centavos — VG | VF | UNC

D.1915. Black on light blue underprint. Portrait Pablo Benito Juárez at left, portrait Francisco I. Madero at right. Series A; C-J. Back: Orange. Circular violet treasury handstamp. Printer: Britton & Rey, San Francisco, California. *(SI-SIN-33).* — 2.00 | 6.00 | 18.00

S1043 1 Peso

D.1915. Black on pale purple underprint. Portrait Pablo Benito Juárez at left, portrait Francisco I. Madero at right. Series A-J. Back: Tan. Circular violet treasury handstamp. Printer: Britton & Rey, San Francisco, California.
- a. With blue circular treasury seal of Sinaloa on back. Series A; B; C. *(SI-SIN-34).* — 2.00 | 6.00 | 18.00
- b. Typewritten overprint on back: *Esta Emisión se cangeará en su oportunidad por emisión constitucionalista. P. O. del Gral. J.D.E.M.* and handwritten signature of R. Dominguez. *(SI-SIN-35).* — 15.00 | 45.00 | 135.
- c. Without blue circular treasury seal of *SINALOA* on back. Series B; D; E; F; G; H; I; J. — 2.00 | 6.00 | 18.00

S1044 5 Pesos

D.1915. Black on pale yellow-orange underprint. Portrait Pablo Benito Juárez at left, portrait Francisco I. Madero at right. Back: Dull red. Circular violet treasury handstamp. Printer: Britton & Rey, San Francisco, California.
- a. 2 printed signatures. Series A; C; D; E; G; H; J. *(SI-SIN-36).* — 2.00 | 6.00 | 18.00
- b. 2 printed signatures, and 2 handwritten signatures. Treasury overprint: *SINALOA* at right on back. Series A; C; D; E; G; J. *(SI-SIN-37).* — 9.00 | 27.00 | 80.00
- c. Handwriting on back: *Este billete ... P.O. del Gral. J.D.E.M.* and handwritten signature of R. Dominguez. Series H. *(SI-SIN-38).* — 15.00 | 45.00 | 135.
- r. Unsigned remainder. Series F. — 5.00 | 15.00 | 45.00

NOTE: #S1044a Series H exists with printed narrow serial # and handstamped wide serial #.

S1045 10 Pesos — UNC

D.1915. Black on pale green underprint. Portrait Pablo Benito Juárez at left, portrait Francisco I. Madero at right. Back: Deep blue. Circular violet treasury handstamp. Printer: Britton & Rey, San Francisco, California.
- a. 2 printed signatures. *(SI-SIN-39).* — 2.00 | 6.00 | 18.00
- b. 2 printed signatures, and 2 handwritten signatures. Treasury overprint: *SINALOA* at right on back. Series A; C; D; E. *(SI-SIN-40).* — 9.00 | 27.00 | 80.00
- c. Typewritten overprint: *Esta emisión se cangerá en su oportunidad por emisión constitucionalista. P. O. del Gral. J.D.E.M.* and handwritten signature of R. Dominguez on back. *(SI-SIN-41).* — 15.00 | 45.00 | 135.
- r. Unsigned remainder. Series F. Punch hole cancelled. — 5.00 | 15.00 | 45.00

#S1046-S1048 With 2 additional blue control # sideways.

S1046 20 Pesos

D.1915. Black on yellow underprint. Portrait Pablo Benito Juárez at left, portrait Francisco I. Madero at right. 4 signatures. Series E; F; G; J. Back: Deep olive-green. Circular violet treasury handstamp. Printer: Britton & Rey, San Francisco, California. *(SI-SIN-42).* — 10.00 | 30.00 | 90.00

S1047 50 Pesos

D.1915. Black on brown and yellow underprint. Portrait Pablo Benito Juárez at left, portrait Francisco I. Madero at right. Series D; E; I. Back: Dull purple. Circular violet treasury handstamp. Printer: Britton & Rey, San Francisco, California. *(SI-SIN-43).*
- a. Issued note. — 10.00 | 30.00 | 90.00
- r. Remainder, without serial #. Punch hole cancelled. — 6.00 | 18.00 | 55.00

S1048 100 Pesos

D.1915. Black on pink underprint. Portrait Pablo Benito Juárez at left, portrait Francisco I. Madero at right. Series O. Back: Light brown. Circular violet treasury handstamp. Printer: Britton & Rey, San Francisco, California. *(SI-SIN-44).* — 50.00 | 150. | 450.

Pagaduría General de la Brigada de Sinaloa, San Blas

Decree of September 15, 1913

		Good	Fine	XF
S1049 25 Centavos	1913. *(MI-SIN-29).*	40.00	120.	360.
S1050 50 Centavos	1913. *(MI-SIN-30).*	40.00	120.	360.
S1051 1 Peso	1913. *(MI-SIN-31).*	40.00	120.	360.
S1052 5 Pesos	1913. *(MI-SIN-32).*	40.00	120.	360.

Decree of October 15, 1913

		Good	Fine	XF
S1053 50 Centavos	ND. *(MI-SIN-33).*	40.00	120.	360.
S1054 1 Peso	ND. *(MI-SIN-34).*	40.00	120.	360.

México (Estado de)

La Jefatura de Hacienda, Guaymas

1914 Issue

S1055 10 Centavos — Good | Fine | XF

1.4.1914. Black on orange underprint. Uniface. Series G. *(SI-SON-8).* — 15.00 | 45.00 | 135.

Sonora

La Jefatura de Hacienda, Guaymas

S1056 50 Centavos — Good | Fine | XF

1.4.1914. Black on green underprint. Uniface.
- a. Issued note. *(SI-SON-9a).* — 2.50 | 7.50 | 20.00
- b. "A" before *PROVISIONAL* in underprint. *(SI-SON-9A).* — 5.00 | 15.00 | 45.00

S1057 1 Peso

1.4.1914. Black on brown underprint.
- a. Issued note. *(SI-SON-10).* — 2.00 | 6.00 | 18.00
- b. "A" before *PROVISIONAL* in underprint. *(SI-SON-10A).* — 5.00 | 15.00 | 45.00
- c. Handstamped seal *Division del Yaqui, General en Jefe. (SI-SON-10B).* — 5.00 | 15.00 | 45.00

La Tesorería de la Federación, Guaymas

Law of September 6, 1913

#S1058-S1061 With or without stamped sign. or revalidation hand stamps on back.

	VG	VF	UNC
S1058 10 Centavos			
16.3.1914. Black on red and yellow underprint. National arms at upper right. Series D. Back: Harbor scene at center. *(SI-SON-4)*.	1.00	3.00	9.00
S1059 50 Centavos			
16.3.1914. Black on red and yellow underprint. National arms at upper right. Series C. Back: Harbor scene at center. *(SI-SON-5)*.			
a. Issued note.	1.00	3.00	9.00
b. Revalidation hand stamp:..SALINA CRUZ...DE POLICIA...? on back.	2.00	6.00	18.00
S1060 1 Peso			
16.3.1914. Black on red and yellow underprint. National arms at upper right. Series B. Back: Harbor scene at center. *(SI-SON-6)*.	1.00	3.00	9.00
S1061 2 Pesos			
16.3.1914. Black on red and yellow underprint. National arms at upper right. Series A. Back: Harbor scene at center. *(SI-SON-7)*.	1.00	3.00	9.00

El Estado de Sonora, Hermosillo

Decrees No. 13 of August 27, 1913 and No. 40 of February 12, 1914

VALIDATION HAND STAMPS:

Different series, w/ or w/o seals. The 5 and 10 peso notes are hand signed. This series bears resellos on the 5 and 10 peso denominations as follows:

1. ....DISTRITO DE GUAYMAS, RIO YAQUI, SONORA.
2. ....FUERZAS DEL ESTADO DE SONORA, DETALL, GENERAL.
3. ....ADUANA MARITIMA DE GUAYMAS, ADMINISTRACION.
4. ....EJÉRCITO CONSTITUCIONALISTA - COMANDANCIA
5. ....ADUANA FRONTERIZA DE NOGALES, SON. IADMINISTRACIONI FEB 14 1915. MILITAR, LA PAZ, B. CFA.

	VG	VF	UNC
S1062 5 Centavos			
L.1913-14. Black on pale green underprint. *(SI-SON-11)*.	9.00	27.00	75.00
S1063 10 Centavos			
L.1913-14. Black on red underprint. Similar to #S1062. *(SI-SON-12)*.	25.00	75.00	225.

Decree No. 13 of August 27, 1913

A.................W/o series. W/sign. *Augustín Lewels* w/title: *EL. CONT. E. DE LA TRIA. GRAL.*
B.........................Series 1-4. W/sign. *Carlos E. Randall* w/title: *EL TESORERO GENERAL.*

	Good	Fine	XF
S1064 25 Centavos			
L.1913. Black on brown underprint. State seal at upper left. Back: Brown and green. Printer: Imp. del Estado.			
a. Face plate 117 x 50mm. Without series. Signature A. Back plate 118 x 50mm. With 35mm government seal. *(SI-SON-)*.	25.00	75.00	225.
b. Without series. *(SI-SON-13)*.	25.00	75.00	225.
c. Series 2.	25.00	75.00	225.
d. Series 3.	25.00	75.00	225.
e. Face plate 122 x 53mm. Series 4. Signature B. Back plate 121 x 53mm. With 39mm government seal. *(SI-SON-13)*.	25.00	75.00	225.
r. Remainder. Series 4. Without oval seal or serial #. *(SI-SON-16)*.	7.50	20.00	60.00
S1065 50 Centavos			
L.1913. Black on green underprint. State seal at upper left. Back: Green. Printer: Imp. del Estado.			
a. Without series. Signature A. *(SI-SON-)*.	25.00	75.00	225.
b. Series 2-4. Signature B. *(SI-SON-15)*.	25.00	75.00	225.
r. Remainder. Series 4. Without oval seal or serial #. *(SI-SON-16)*.	7.50	20.00	60.00
S1066 1 Peso			
L.1913. Black on pale yellow-orange underprint. Blue-gray oval seal. Printer: Imp. del Estado.			
a. Without series. Handwritten signature. *(SI-SON-17)*.	7.50	20.00	60.00
b. Series 2. With 38mm government seal.	—	—	—
c. Series 3. Signature B. With 35mm or 38mm government seal. *(SI-SON-17)*.	3.00	9.00	27.50
d. Series 4. Signature B. With 38mm government seal. *(SI-SON-17)*.	3.00	9.00	27.50
r. Remainder. Series 4. Without oval seal or serial #. *(SI-SON-18)*.	7.50	20.00	60.00
S1067 5 Pesos			
L.1913. Black on pale blue underprint. Printer: Imp. del Estado.			
a. Without series. Signature A. *(SI-SON-19)*.	7.50	20.00	60.00
b. Series 2. Signature B. With 35mm government seal. *(SI-SON-19)*.	7.50	20.00	60.00
c. Series 3 or 4. With 35mm government seal. Red 4th signature title: *INTERVENTOR* at lower left. *(SI-SON-19)*.	7.50	20.00	60.00
d. Series 4. With 38mm seal. Red 4th signature title: *INTERVENTOR* at lower left. *(SI-SON-19)*.	7.50	20.00	60.00
S1068 10 Pesos			
L.1913. Black on pink underprint. Handwritten signature. Printer: Imp. del Estado.			
a. Without series, signature A. *(SI-SON-)*.	15.00	45.00	135.
b. Series 1. *(SI-SON-20)*.	12.50	35.00	110.
c. Series 2. Signature B. With 35mm government seal. *(SI-SON-20)*.	12.50	35.00	110.
d. Series 2; 3. Signature B. With 38mm government seal. *(SI-SON-20)*.	6.00	18.00	55.00
e. Series 4. With 35mm government seal. 4th signature title: *INTERVENTOR* at right. *(SI-SON-20)*.	6.00	18.00	55.00
f. Series 4. With 38mm government seal. 4th signature title: *INTERVENTOR* at right. *(SI-SON-20)*.	12.50	35.00	110.

NOTE: #S1068d Series 2 also exists with *PROVSIONAL* or *PROVIISIONAL* (errors) at left.

Decree No. 13 of August 27, 1913

	VG	VF	UNC
S1069 25 Centavos			
1.1.1915. Black. Portrait Francesco I. Madero at left, portrait J.M. Pino Suarez at right. Series A-J. Printed signature. Back: Green. Printer: ABNC. *(SI-SON-21)*.	1.00	3.00	9.00

	VG	VF	UNC
S1070 50 Centavos			
1.1.1915. Black. Portrait Francesco I. Madero at left, portrait J.M. Pino Suarez at right. Printed signature. Series A-J. Printer: ABNC. *(SI-SON-22)*.	1.00	3.00	9.00
S1071 1 Peso			
1.1.1915. Black on pale yellow underprint. Portrait Francesco I. Madero at left, portrait J.M. Pino Suarez at right. Printed signature. Series B-I. Printer: ABNC. *(SI-SON-23)*.	1.00	3.00	9.00

	VG	VF	UNC
S1072 5 Pesos			
1.1.1915. Black on pale blue underprint. Portrait Francesco I. Madero at left, portrait J.M. Pino Suarez at right. Printed signature. Series A; C-L. Printer: ABNC. *(SI-SON-24)*.	1.00	3.00	9.00
S1073 10 Pesos			
1.1.1915. Black on pink underprint. Portrait Francesco I. Madero at left, portrait J.M. Pino Suarez at right. Printed signature. Series A-J. Printer: ABNC. *(SI-SON-25)*.	2.00	6.00	18.00

	VG	VF	UNC
S1074 20 Pesos			
1.3.1915. Black on pale green underprint. Portrait Francesco I. Madero at left, portrait J.M. Pino Suarez at right. Printer: ABNC.			
a. 2 printed and 2 handwritten signatures.	7.50	20.00	60.00
r. Remainder with 2 printed signatures. Series L; M; N. *(SI-SON-26)*.	6.00	18.00	55.00
s. Specimen, perforated hole cancelled. Series N. 1915.	—	—	350.

S1075 50 Pesos	VG	VF	UNC
1.3.1915. Black on lilac underprint. Portrait Francesco I. Madero at left, portrait J.M. Pino Suarez at right. Printer: ABNC.			
a. 2 printed and 2 handwritten signatures.	50.00	150.	450.
r. Remainder with 2 printed signatures. Series L; N. *(SI-SON-27).*	45.00	135.	400.
s. Specimen. Series L.	—	—	600.

S1076 100 Pesos	VG	VF	UNC
1.3.1915. Black on pale pink and blue underprint. Portrait Francesco I. Madero at left, portrait J.M. Pino Suarez at right. Printer: ABNC.			
a. 2 printed and 2 handwritten signatures.	45.00	135.	400.
r. Remainder with 2 printed signatures. Series L-N. *(SI-SON-28).*	40.00	120.	360.
s. Specimen. Series M.	—	—	600.

Decree No. 70 of April 16, 1915

S1077 5 Centavos	VG	VF	UNC
D.1915. Black on pink underprint. Back: Red.			
a. Issued note. *(SI-SON-29).*	5.00	15.00	45.00
b. Without seal or serial #. *(SI-SON-30).*	2.00	6.00	18.00
S1078 10 Centavos			
D.1915. Black on blue underprint.			
a. Issued note. *(SI-SON-31).*	2.00	6.00	18.00
a. Without seal or serial #. *(SI-SON-32).*	2.00	6.00	18.00

Tabasco

La Tesorería General del Estado de Tabasco, San Juan Bautista

1914 Issue

S1078A 20 Centavos	Good	Fine	XF
22.5.1914. Series J; S. *(SI-TAB-4).*	120.	360.	1100.
S1078B 50 Centavos			
22.5.1914. *(SI-TAB-5).*	120.	360.	1100.

Decree of March 22, 1915

S1079 20 Centavos	Good	Fine	XF
Mar. 1915. Black on pink or blue underprint. Series D. *(SI-TAB-6).*	25.00	75.00	225.

S1080 50 Centavos	Good	Fine	XF
Mar. 1915. Black on gray. *50* at center. Series F. *(SI-TAB-7).*	35.00	110.	330.

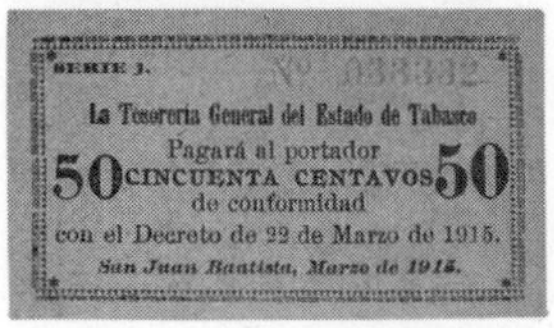

S1081 50 Centavos	Good	Fine	XF
Mar. 1915. Black. *50* at each side. Series J. *(SI-TAB-8).*	30.00	90.00	270.

ILLUSTRATIONS

Illustrations of bank notes used throughout this catalog are 42% of the actual size.

Tamaulipas

Ejército Constitucionalista de México, Tampico

1914 Issue

S1082 20 Pesos	Good	Fine	XF
6.7.1914. Black on pink underprint. National arms at left. Series B.			
a. Issued note. *(MI-TAM-6).*	75.00	225.	675.
b. Overprint: *AMORTIZADO. (MI-TAM-7).*	60.00	180.	540.

La Caja de la Brigada Caballero, Tampico

1914 Issue

S1083 50 Centavos	Good	Fine	XF
6.6.1914. Black on green underprint. Series A. Back: Dark blue. Eagle at center.			
a. Issued note. *(MI-TAM-3).*	125.	375.	1100.
b. Overprint: *AMORTIZADO. (MI-TAM-4).*	90.00	270.	800.
S1084 1 Peso			
6.6.1914. Green underprint. Series A. Back: Blue. Small eagle in oval at center. *(MI-TAM-5).*	90.00	270.	800.

Tlaxcala

Distrito de Morelos

ND Issue

S1085 5 Centavos	Good	Fine	XF
ND. Red and black on dark blue underprint. Ceres (Goddess of Agriculture) seated with plow at left center. Series A. *(SI-TLA-1).*	—	—	1000.
S1086 20 Centavos			
ND. Green and blue on cream. Girl with cattle at left center. Series A. *(SI-TLA-2).*	—	—	1000.

S1087 50 Centavos	Good	Fine	XF
ND. Locomotive at center. Series A. Paper: Dark brown pasteboard. *(SI-TLA-3).*	—	—	1000.

La Tesorería Municipal de Ciudad Tlaxcala

1914 Issue

	Good	Fine	XF
S1088 5 Centavos 1.10.1914. *(SI-TLA-4).*	125.	375.	1100.

	Good	Fine	XF
S1089 10 Centavos 25.8.1914. *(SI-TLA-5).*	125.	375.	1100.
S1090 20 Centavos 1.10.1914. *(SI-TLA-6).*	125.	375.	1100.

Veracruz

Gobierno Constitucionalista del Estado Libre y Soberano de Veracruz-Llave

ND First Issue

	VG	VF	UNC
S1091 5 Centavos ND. Portrait Francisco Madero at center. Series B; F. Back: Arms at center. Paper: Pink pasteboard. *(MI-VER-8).*	3.00	9.00	27.50
S1092 10 Centavos ND. Portrait Pablo Benito Juárez at center. Series K. Back: Arms at center. Paper: Blue pasteboard. *(MI-VER-9).*	3.00	9.00	27.50
S1093 20 Centavos ND. Portrait Miguel Hidalgo at center. Series S. Back: Arms at center. Paper: Yellow pasteboard. *(MI-VER-10).*	3.00	9.00	27.50

ND Second Issue

	VG	VF	UNC
S1094 5 Centavos ND. Portrait Francisco Madero at center. Back: Arms at center. Paper: Pink pasteboard. *(MI-VER-11).*	2.00	6.00	18.00
S1095 10 Centavos ND. Portrait Pedro Benito Juárez at right. Back: Arms at center. Paper: Blue pasteboard. *(MI-VER-12).*	2.00	6.00	18.00
S1096 20 Centavos ND. Portrait Miguel Hidalgo at center. Back: Arms at center. Paper: Yellow pasteboard. *(MI-VER-13).*	2.00	6.00	18.00

Gobierno Provisional de México, Veracruz

Decree of 19.9.1914

	Good	Fine	XF
S1097 1 Peso 1.12.1914. Brown on pale green underprint. Seated Liberty at left, national arms with Popocatepetl and Ixtaccihuatl (volcanoes) in background at center. Small number *1's* in corners. Series A. Back: Peso coins at center. *(MI-VER-14).*	40.00	120.	360.
S1098 1 Peso 1.12.1914. Black on light brown underprint. Seated Liberty at left, national arms with Popocatepetl and Ixtaccihuatl (volcanoes) in background at center. Flat base *1's* with rhombus in corners. Series A. Back: Peso coins at center.			
a. Issued note. *(MI-VER-15).*	2.00	6.00	18.00
b. Overprint: *Michoacán de Ocampo, Retirado.*	2.50	7.50	20.00
S1099 1 Peso 1.12.1914. Black on light brown underprint. Seated Liberty at left, national arms with Popocatepetl and Ixtaccihuatl (volcanoes) in background at center. Flat base *1's*. Series A. Back: Peso coins at center. Flat base *1's*. *(MI-VER-16).*	2.00	6.00	18.00
S1100 1 Peso 1.12.1914. Black on light brown underprint. Seated Liberty at left, national arms with Popocatepetl and Ixtaccihuatl (volcanoes) in background at center. Flat base *1's*. Series A. Back: Peso coins at center. Curved *1's*. *(MI-VER-17).*	2.00	6.00	18.00

	Good	Fine	XF
S1101 1 Peso 5.2.1915. Black on ochre underprint. Seated Liberty at left, national arms with Popocatepetl and Ixtaccihuatl (volcanoes) in background at center. Curved based *1's* in corners. Series A. Back: Peso coins at center.			
a. Issued note. *(MI-VER-18).*	1.00	3.00	9.00
b. Overprint: *Michoacán de Ocampo, Tesorería General/Retirado (MI-VER-23).*	2.00	6.00	18.00
c. Blank back with seal. *(MI-VER-21).*	6.00	18.00	55.00
d. Overprint: *Administración de Rentas de Jalapa/Retirado de la Circulación. (MI-VER-).*	3.00	9.00	27.50
e. Overprint: *Retirado de la Circulación. (MI-VER-18).*	2.00	6.00	18.00
f. Vertical overprint: *VERACRUZ* at left and right.	—	—	—

	Good	Fine	XF
S1102 2 Pesos 5.2.1915. Brown. Seated Liberty at left, national arms with Popocatepetl and Ixtaccihuatl (volcanoes) in background at center. Straight based *2's* in denomination. Series G. Back: Peso coins at center.			
a. Tan underprint. *(MI-VER-24).*	4.00	12.00	36.00
b. Yellow-brown underprint. *(MI-VER-25).*	18.00	55.00	165.
c. Straight based *2's* in denomination. Green underprint. *(MI-VER-26).*	40.00	120.	360.
d. Overprint: *Ret. de la Circulación. (MI-VER-29).*	2.00	6.00	18.00
e. Overprint: *Michoacán de Ocampo Tesorería General Retirado. (MI-VER-30).*	3.00	9.00	27.50
S1103 2 Pesos 5.2.1915. Black on yellow underprint. Seated Liberty at left, national arms with Popocatepetl and Ixtaccihuatl (volcanoes) in background at center. Curved based *2's* in denomination. Series G. Back: Light blue-green. Peso coins at center.			
a. Issued note. *(MI-VER-27).*	1.00	3.00	9.00
b. Back blank with seal. *(MI-VER-28).*	18.00	55.00	165.

	Good	Fine	XF
S1104 5 Pesos 1.12.1914. Dark green underprint. Seated Liberty at left, national arms with Popocatepetl and Ixtaccihuatl (volcanoes) in background at center. Series B. Back: Peso coins at center. Large *5's* in denomination.			
a. Issued note. *(MI-VER-31).*	1.00	3.00	9.00
b. Overprint: *Yucatán, GOBIERNO Constitucionalista. (MI-VER-33).*	15.00	45.00	135.
c. Overprint: *Jefatura de Hacienda Queretaro. (MI-VER-34).*	2.50	7.50	20.00
d. Overprint: *Ga. Jefatura de Hda. Guadalajara. (MI-VER-35).*	2.50	7.50	20.00
S1105 5 Pesos 1.12.1914. Seated Liberty at left, national arms with Popocatepetl and Ixtaccihuatl (volcanoes) in background at center. Series B. Back: Peso coins at center. Small *5's* in denomination.			
a. Issued note. *(MI-VER-32).*	2.00	6.00	18.00
b. Overprint: *Yucatán, GOBIERNO Constitucionalista. (MI-VER-33).*	15.00	45.00	135.
c. Overprint: *Jefatura de Hacienda Querétaro. (MI-VER-34).*	2.50	7.50	20.00
d. Overprint: *Ga. Jefatura de Hda Guadalajara. (MI-VER-35).*	2.50	7.50	20.00

S1106 10 Pesos — Good | Fine | XF

1.12.1914. Black on brown and yellow underprint. Seated Liberty at left, national arms with Popocatepetl and Ixtaccihuatl (volcanoes) in background at center. Small *10* at right. Series C. Back: Peso coins at center. *(MI-VER-36).* — 45.00 | 135. | 400.

S1107 10 Pesos

1.12.1914. Seated Liberty at left, national arms with Popocatepetl and Ixtaccihuatl (volcanoes) in background at center. Series C. Back: Brown. Peso coins at center. Large *10* at right.

	Good	Fine	XF
a. *C* or *D* serial # suffix. *(MI-VER-37).*	1.00	3.00	9.00
b. 4 punched hole cancellation and purple hand stamp: *CANCELADO* on a.	1.00	3.00	9.00

S1108 10 Pesos

1.12.1914. Seated Liberty at left, national arms with Popocatepetl and Ixtaccihuatl (volcanoes) in background at center. Series C. Back: Purple. Peso coins at center.

	Good	Fine	XF
a. Issued note. *(MI-VER-38).*	1.00	3.00	9.00
b. Overprint: *Gto. Jefatura Superior de Hacienda - Estado de Guanajuato. (MI-VER-39).*	2.50	7.50	20.00
c. Overprint: *Yucatán, GOBIERNO Constitucionalista. (MI-VER-40).*	1.50	5.00	15.00
d. Overprint: *Toluca. (MI-VER-41).*	3.00	9.00	27.00
e. Overprint: *Jefatura de Hacienda, Querétaro. (MI-VER-42).*	2.50	7.50	20.00
f. Overprint: *Ga Jefatura de Hda Guadalajara. (MI-VER-43).*	1.50	5.00	15.00
g. Overprint: *Tabasco, Jefatura de Hacienda - Resellado. (MI-VER-44).*	3.00	9.00	27.00
h. Overprint: *Mich. de Ocampo, Jefatura de Hacienda - Resellado. (MI-VER-45).*	3.00	9.00	27.00
i. Overprint: *Mich. de Ocampo Tesorería General Retirado.*	3.00	9.00	27.00

S1109 20 Pesos — Good | Fine | XF

1.12.1914. Seated Liberty at left, national arms with Popocatepetl and Ixtaccihuatl (volcanoes) in background at center. Straight based *2's* in corners. Series D. Back: Peso coins at center. *(MI-VER-46).* — 45.00 | 135. | 400.

S1110 20 Pesos

1.12.1914. Deep gray on dull olive-brown underprint with *VEINTE PESOS* repeated. Seated Liberty at left, national arms with Popocatepetl and Ixtaccihuatl (volcanoes) in background at center. Curved based *2's* in corners. Series D. Back: Blue-gray. Peso coins at center. Printer: México Oficina del Gobierno.

	Good	Fine	XF
a. Olive underprint. *(MI-VER-47).*	1.00	3.00	9.00
b. Brown underprint in pattern without wording.	2.50	7.50	20.00
c. Overprint: *Ebano, S.L.P.* (series) *C//Rgto. de Cab. Gral. José Cavazos.*	4.00	12.00	36.00

S1111 20 Pesos

1.12.1914. Black on brown and yellow underprint. Seated Liberty at left, national arms with Popocatepetl and Ixtaccihuatl (volcanoes) in background at center. Semi-straight based *2's* in corners. Series D. Back: Blue. Peso coins at center. Printer: Oficina del Gobierno.

	Good	Fine	XF
a. Issued note. *(MI-VER-48).*	1.00	3.00	9.00
b. Overprint: *Yucatán, GOBIERNO Constitucionalista. (MI-VER-51).*	2.50	7.50	20.00
c. Overprint: *Campeche, Eduardo Morales. (MI-VER-52).*	2.50	7.50	20.00
d. Overprint: *Jefatura Superior de Hacienda. Estado de Guanajuato. (MI-VER-53).*	2.50	7.50	20.00
e. Overprint: *Jfra. de Hda. Guadlajara. (MI-VER-54).*	4.00	12.00	36.00
f. Overprint: *Michoacán de Ocampo, Tesorería General Retirado. (MI-VER-55).*	4.00	12.00	36.00
g. Overprint: *Michoacán de Ocampo, Amortizado. (MI-VER-56).*	18.00	55.00	165.
h. Overprint: *Jefatura de Hacienda, Querétaro. (MI-VER-57).*	4.00	12.00	36.00

S1112 20 Pesos

1.12.1914. Green underprint. Seated Liberty at left, national arms with Popocatepetl and Ixtaccihuatl (volcanoes) in background at center. Semi-straight based *2's* in corners. Series D. Back: Blue. Peso coins at center.

	Good	Fine	XF
a. Issued note. *(MI-VER-49).*	2.50	7.50	20.00
b. Overprint: *Yucatán, GOBIERNO Constitucionalista. (MI-VER-51).*	2.50	7.50	20.00
c. Overprint: *Campeche, Eduardo Morales. (MI-VER-52).*	2.50	7.50	20.00
d. Overprint: *Jefatura Superior de Hacienda. Estado de Guanajuato. (MI-VER-53).*	2.50	7.50	20.00
e. Overprint: *Jfra. de Hda. Guadalajara. (MI-VER-54).*	5.00	15.00	45.00
f. Overprint: *Michoacán de Ocampo, Retirado. (MI-VER-55).*	5.00	15.00	45.00
g. Overprint: *Michoacán de Ocampo, Amortizado. (MI-VER-56).*	18.00	55.00	165.
h. Overprint: *Jefatura de Hacienda, Querétaro. (MI-VER-57).*	3.00	9.00	27.00

S1113 20 Pesos

1.12.1914. Seated Liberty at left, national arms with Popocatepetl and Ixtaccihuatl (volcanoes) in background at center. Semi-straight *2's*. Series D. Back: Pink. Peso coins at center.

	Good	Fine	XF
a. Issued note. *(MI-VER-50).*	3.00	9.00	27.00
b. Overprint: *Yucatán, GOBIERNO Constitucionalista. (MI-VER-51).*	2.50	7.50	20.00
c. Overprint: *Campeche, Eduardo Morales. (MI-VER-52).*	2.50	7.50	20.00
d. Overprint: *Jefatura Superior de Hacienda. Estado de Guanajuato. (MI-VER-53).*	2.50	7.50	20.00
e. Overprint: *Jfra. de Hda. Guadalajara. (MI-VER-54).*	5.00	15.00	45.00
f. Overprint: *Michoacán de Ocampo, Retirado. (MI-VER-55).*	5.00	15.00	45.00
g. Overprint: *Michoacán de Ocampo, Amortizado. (MI-VER-56).*	18.00	55.00	165.
h. Overprint: *Jefatura de Hacienda, Querétaro. (MI-VER-57).*	3.00	9.00	27.00

S1114 50 Pesos

1.12.1914. Seated Liberty at left, national arms with Popocatepetl and Ixtaccihuatl (volcanoes) in background at center. Series E. Back: Peso coins at center.

	Good	Fine	XF
a. Issued note. *(MI-VER-58).*	2.00	6.00	18.00
b. Overprint: *Yucatán. Gobierno Constitucionalista. (MI-VER-61).*	5.00	15.00	45.00
c. Overprint: *Jefatura de Hda. Guadalajara. (MI-VER-62).*	18.00	55.00	165.
r. Without date, signature or series. *(MI-VER-59).*	40.00	120.	360.

S1115 100 Pesos

1.12.1914. Seated Liberty at left, national arms with Popocatepetl and Ixtaccihuatl (volcanoes) in background at center. Series E: F. Back: Peso coins at center.

	Good	Fine	XF
a. Series E. *(MI-VER-63).*	1.00	3.00	9.00
b. Overprint: *Yucatán, GOBIERNO Constitucionalista. (MI-VER-66).*	2.00	6.00	18.00
c. Series F. *(MI-VER-65).*	2.50	7.50	20.00
d. As c. Overprint: *Yucatán. (MI-VER-67).*	12.50	35.00	110.
e. Without date, signature and series. Back without seals. *(MI-VER-64).*	25.00	75.00	225.
f. As c. Overprint: *TEZIUTLAN.*	7.50	20.00	60.00

Tesorería General del Estado de Veracruz Llave

Decree of June 1, 1915

	Good	Fine	XF
S1116 1 Peso ND. National arms at lower center. Series A. *(SI-VER-9).*	75.00	225.	675.
S1117 5 Pesos ND. National arms at lower center. Series A. *(SI-VER-10).*	75.00	225.	675.
S1118 10 Pesos ND. National arms at lower center. Series A. *(SI-VER-11).*	75.00	225.	675.
S1119 20 Pesos ND. National arms at lower center. Series A. Paper: Pasteboard. *(SI-VER-12).*	100.	300.	900.

Yucatán

Comisión Reguladora del Mercado de Henequén y la Tesorería General del Estado

1914 First Issue

S1120 20 Centavos

27.7.1914. Brown. Crowned state arms at left, sisal harvesting at right. Back: Blue. National arms at center. *(PI-YUC-5).*

	Good	Fine	XF
a. Needle punched *CAMPECHE.* Series A.	4.00	12.00	36.00
b. Series A; B; e; F; G; H; I; J.	4.00	12.00	36.00

S1121 50 Centavos

27.7.1914. Black on orange, pink and yellow underprint. Crowned state arms at left, sisal harvesting at right.Series A; C; F; G; H; I; J; K; M; N; O; P. Back: Pink. National arms at center.

	Good	Fine	XF
a. Issued note. *(PI-YUC-6).*	2.00	6.00	18.00
b. Black overprint: *ORO NACIONAL* on back. *(PI-YUC-7).*	25.00	75.00	225.
c. As b. With red-violet hand stamp: *JEFATURA DE HACIENDA MERIDA RESELLADO.*	45.00	135.	400.

1914 Second Issue

S1122 1 Peso

20.11.1914. Black, green and pink. Yucatan woman at left, worker at right. Series A. Back: Brown. Coin at center.

	Good	Fine	XF
a. Needle punched *CAMPECHE* vertically at right. *(PI-YUC-8A). (PI-YUC-8).*	4.00	12.00	36.00
b. Without needle punched *CAMPECHE. (PI-YUC-8).*	50.00	150.	450.

S1123 5 Pesos

20.11.1914. Black and green. National arms at left center. Series A. Back: Green. Overprint: Circular: *COMISION REGULADORA* around 1/2.

	Good	Fine	XF
a. Issued note. *(PI-YUC-10).*	4.00	12.00	36.00
b. Red overprint: *ORO NACIONAL* on back. *(PI-YUC-11).*	50.00	150.	450.

S1124 20 Pesos

20.11.1914. Black on yellow and brown. Government building at left, sisal harvesting at right. Series B; C; D. Back: Blue.

	Good	Fine	XF
a. Issued note. *(PI-YUC-12).*	2.00	6.00	18.00
b. Overprint: *ORO NACIONAL* on back. *(PI-YUC-13).*	100.	300.	900.
c. Red overprint: *Resellado por la Comisión Reguladora del Mercado de Henequén. Mérida, April 25, 1915* on back. *(PI-YUC-14).*	5.00	15.00	45.00

1915 Issue

	Good	Fine	XF
S1125 100 Pesos 1.3.1915. Black on orange and yellow underprint. Portrait Miguel Hidalgo at left. Series A; B; G. Back: Brown-violet. Gateway at center. *(PI-YUC-15).*	3.00	9.00	27.00

Bono de Caja, Mérida

1916 Issue

	Good	Fine	XF
S1126 20 Pesos 9.5.1916. Green underprint. Building at center. Series F. Back: Gold.			
a. Issued note. *(PI-YUC-17).*	350.	1100.	3300.
r. Remainder without seal. *(PI-YUC-17A).*	180.	550.	1650.

Decree No. 536 of May 9, 1916

	Good	Fine	XF
S1127 100 Pesos 9.5.1916. Brown on tan underprint. Portrait Pedro Benito Juárez above national arms at center. Series G. Back: National arms at center. *(PI-YUC-19).*	225.	675.	2000.

Gobierno Constitucionalista de Yucatán,

Tesorería General

ND Issue

	Good	Fine	XF
S1128 1 Centavo ND. Back: State arms at center. Paper: Gray or pink pasteboard. *(SI-YUC-10).*	4.00	12.00	36.00
S1129 5 Centavos ND. Back: State arms at center. Paper: Red or pink pasteboard. *(SI-YUC-11).*	2.50	7.50	20.00
S1130 10 Centavos ND. Back: State arms at center. Paper: Cream pasteboard. *(SI-YUC-12).*	2.50	7.50	20.00

ND Transitorio Issue

	Good	Fine	XF
S1131 5 Centavos ND. Back: National arms at center. Paper: Red pasteboard. *(SI-YUC-13).*	1.50	5.00	15.00
S1132 10 Centavos ND. Back: National arms at center. Paper: Gray pasteboard. *(SI-YUC-14).*	1.50	5.00	15.00
S1133 20 Centavos ND. Back: National arms at center. Paper: Light brown pasteboard. *(SI-YUC-15).*	1.50	5.00	15.00

Tesorería General del Estado

Decree No. 550 of May 23, 1916

	Good	Fine	XF
S1134 50 Centavos 26.5.1916. Brown on orange underprint. Palm tree and hut at center. Back: Pale gold. Figures at center. *(SI-YUC-1).*	5.00	15.00	45.00
S1135 1 Peso 23.5.1916. Dark brown. Building at center. Series A. Back: Green. Maya ruins at center. *(SI-YUC-2).*	3.00	9.00	27.00
S1136 2 Pesos 23.5.1916. Dark brown on green underprint. Portrait Maya Indian at center. Series B. Back: Blue. *(SI-YUC-4).*	2.00	6.00	18.00

Decree No. 559 of May 22, 1916

	Good	Fine	XF
S1137 5 Pesos 22.5.1916. Seated Euthenia (Goddess of Plenty) at left. *(SI-YUC-5).*	30.00	90.00	270.
S1138 10 Pesos 22.5.1916. Portrait Francisco Madero at center. Series D. Back: National arms at center. *(SI-YUC-7).*	6.00	18.00	55.00

Zacatecas

La Comisión Reguladora del Comercio de Zacatecas

ND Issue

	Good	Fine	XF
S1139 10 Centavos ND. Overprint: *INFALSIFICABLE.* Paper: Brown pasteboard.	4.00	12.00	36.00

	Good	Fine	XF
S1140 20 Centavos ND. Paper: Pasteboard.	7.50	20.00	60.00

	Good	Fine	XF
S1141 50 Centavos ND. Paper: Pasteboard.	7.50	20.00	60.00
S1142 1 Peso ND. Overprint: *INFALSIFICABLE.* Paper: Gray pasteboard.	7.50	20.00	60.00

Gobierno Provisional de Zacatecas

ND Issue

	VG	VF	UNC
S1143 5 Centavos ND. Black. Arms at center. Paper: Pink pasteboard.	2.00	6.00	18.00
S1144 10 Centavos ND. Black. Paper: Gray pasteboard.	1.00	3.00	9.00
S1145 20 Centavos ND. Black. Paper: Light brown pasteboard.	3.00	9.00	27.00

La Pagaduría General de la Brigada Avila, Jérez

1915 Issue

	Good	Fine	XF
S1146 25 Centavos 15.8.1915. Series R. Paper: Ledger. *(MI-ZAC-1).*	50.00	150.	450.

	Good	Fine	XF
S1147 50 Centavos 15.8.1915. Series R. Paper: Ledger. *(MI-ZAC-2).*	50.00	150.	450.

The former independent kingdom of Montenegro, now one of the nominally autonomous federated units of Yugoslavia, was located in southeastern Europe north of Albania. As a kingdom, it had an area of 5,333 sq. mi. (13,812 sq. km.) and a population of about 250,000. The predominantly pastoral kingdom had few industries.

The use of the name Montenegro began in the 15th century when the Crnojevic dynasty began to rule the Serbian principality of Zeta; over subsequent centuries Montenegro was able to maintain its independence from the Ottoman Empire. From the 16th to 19th centuries, Montenegro became a theocracy ruled by a series of bishop princes; in 1852, it was transformed into a secular principality. After World War I, Montenegro was absorbed by the Kingdom of Serbs, Croats, and Slovenes, which became the Kingdom of Yugoslavia in 1929; at the conclusion of World War II, it became a constituent republic of the Socialist Federal Republic of Yugoslavia. When the latter dissolved in 1992, Montenegro federated with Serbia, first as the Federal Republic of Yugoslavia and, after 2003, in a looser union of Serbia and Montenegro. In May 2006, Montenegro invoked its right under the Constitutional Charter of Serbia and Montenegro to hold a referendum on independence from the state union. The vote for severing ties with Serbia exceeded 55% - the threshold set by the EU - allowing Montenegro to formally declare its independence on 3 June 2006.

RULERS:

Nicholas I, 1910-1918

MONETARY SYSTEM:

1 Perper = 100 Para = 1 Austrian Crown

AUSTRIAN OCCUPATION - WW I

K.U.K. MILITAR GENERALGOUVERNEMENT KREISKOMMANDO, 1916-18

MILITARY GOVERNMENT DISTRICT COMMAND

CETINJE ISSUE

1916 ND FIRST PROVISIONAL ISSUE

		Good	Fine	XF
M1	**5 Perpera** ND (1916-old date 25.7.1914). Overprint: On #9. Width of *CETINJE* is 11mm.	2.00	8.00	20.00

		Good	Fine	XF
M2	**10 Perpera** ND (1916-old date 25.7.1914). Overprint: On #10. Width of *CETINJE* is 11mm.	3.00	10.00	25.00
M3	**20 Perpera** ND (1916-old date 25.7.1914). Overprint: On #11. Width of *CETINJE* is 11mm.	3.00	10.00	25.00
M4	**50 Perpera** ND (1916-old date 25.7.1914). Overprint: On #12. Width of *CETINJE* is 11mm.	3.00	10.00	25.00
M5	**100 Perpera** ND (1916-old date 25.7.1914). Overprint: On #13. Width of *CETINJE* is 11mm.	6.00	20.00	50.00

1916 ND SECOND PROVISIONAL ISSUE

#M6-M12 WIDTH OF *CETINJE* IN OVERPRINT 11MM.

		Good	Fine	XF
M6	**1 Perper** ND (1916-old date 25.7.1914). Overprint: On #15. Width of *CETINJE* is 11mm.	2.00	5.00	10.00

		Good	Fine	XF
M7	**2 Perpera** ND (1916-old date 25.7.1914). Overprint: On #16. Width of *CETINJE* is 11mm.	2.00	5.00	10.00
M8	**5 Perpera** ND (1916-old date 25.7.1914). Overprint: On #17. Width of *CETINJE* is 11mm.	2.00	5.00	10.00
M9	**10 Perpera** ND (1916-old date 25.7.1914). Overprint: On #18. Width of *CETINJE* is 11mm.	3.00	9.00	18.00

		Good	Fine	XF
M10	**20 Perpera** ND (1916-old date 25.7.1914). Overprint: On #19. Width of *CETINJE* is 11mm.	3.50	10.00	20.00
M11	**50 Perpera** ND (1916-old date 25.7.1914). Overprint: On #20. Width of *CETINJE* is 11mm.	5.00	15.00	30.00
M12	**100 Perpera** ND (1916-old date 25.7.1914). Overprint: On #21. Width of *CETINJE* is 11mm.	7.00	20.00	40.00

1916 ND THIRD PROVISIONAL ISSUE

#M13-M17 WIDTH OF *CETINJE* IN OVERPRINT 16MM.

		Good	Fine	XF
M13	**5 Perpera** ND (1916-old date 25.7.1914). Overprint: On #9. Width of *CETINJE* is 16mm.	3.50	10.00	20.00

		Good	Fine	XF
M14	**10 Perpera** ND (1916-old date 25.7.1914). Overprint: On #10. Width of *CETINJE* is 16mm.	3.50	10.00	20.00
M15	**20 Perpera** ND (1916-old date 25.7.1914). Overprint: On #11. Width of *CETINJE* is 16mm.	4.00	12.00	25.00

		Good	Fine	XF
M16	**50 Perpera** ND (1916-old date 25.7.1914). Overprint: On #12. Width of *CETINJE* is 16mm.	5.00	15.00	30.00
M17	**100 Perpera** ND (1916-old date 25.7.1914). Overprint: On #13. Width of *CETINJE* is 16mm.	7.00	20.00	40.00

1916 ND Fourth Provisional Issue

#M18-M24 width of *CETINJE* in overprint 16mm.

		Good	Fine	XF
M18	**1 Perper** ND (1916-old date 25.7.1914). Overprint: On #15. Width of *CETINJE* is 16mm.	2.00	5.00	10.00
M19	**2 Perpera** ND (1916-old date 25.7.1914). Overprint: On #16. Width of *CETINJE* is 16mm.	2.00	6.00	12.00
M20	**5 Perpera** ND (1916-old date 25.7.1914). Overprint: On #17. Width of *CETINJE* is 16mm.	3.00	9.00	18.00
M21	**10 Perpera** ND (1916-old date 25.7.1914) Overprint: On #18. Width of *CETINJE* is 16mm.	3.50	10.00	20.00
M22	**20 Perpera** ND (1916-old date 25.7.1914). Overprint: On #19. Width of *CETINJE* is 16mm.	4.00	12.00	25.00
M23	**50 Perpera** ND (1916-old date 25.7.1914). Overprint: On #20. Width of *CETINJE* is 16mm.	5.00	15.00	30.00
M24	**100 Perpera** ND (1916-old date 25.7.1914). Overprint: On #21. Width of *CETINJE* is 16mm.	7.00	20.00	40.00

NOTE: EXAMPLES OF OVERPRINT. NOTES HAVE BEEN OBSERVED WITH A NARROW STAMP OF THE PLACE NAME ON ONE SIDE, A WIDE STAMP OF THE PLACE NAME ON THE OTHER SIDE.

Ipek Issue

1916 ND First Provisional Issue

		Good	Fine	XF
M25	**5 Perpera** ND (1916-old date 25.7.1914). Overprint: On #9.	3.50	10.00	20.00
M26	**10 Perpera** ND (1916-old date 25.7.1914). Overprint: On #10.	5.00	15.00	30.00

		Good	Fine	XF
M27	**20 Perpera** ND (1916-old date 25.7.1914). Overprint: On #11.	7.00	20.00	40.00
M28	**50 Perpera** ND (1916-old date 25.7.1914). Overprint: On #12.	10.00	30.00	60.00
M29	**100 Perpera** ND (1916-old date 25.7.1914). Overprint: On #13.	12.00	35.00	70.00

1916 ND Second Provisional Issue

		Good	Fine	XF
M30	**1 Perper** ND (1916-old date 25.7.1914). Overprint: On #15.	2.00	6.00	12.00
M31	**2 Perpera** ND (1916-old date 25.7.1914). Overprint: On #16.	3.50	10.00	20.00
M32	**5 Perpera** ND (1916-old date 25.7.1914). Overprint: On #17.	5.00	15.00	30.00
M33	**10 Perpera** ND (1916-old date 25.7.1914). Overprint: On #18.	7.00	20.00	40.00
M34	**20 Perpera** ND (1916-old date 25.7.1914). Overprint: On #19.	10.00	25.00	50.00

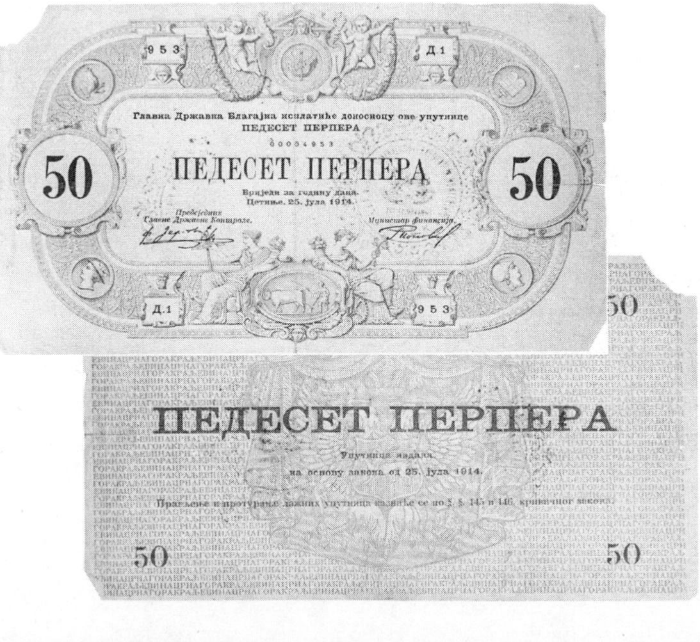

		Good	Fine	XF
M35	**50 Perpera** ND (1916-old date 25.7.1914). Overprint: On #20.	12.00	30.00	60.00
M36	**100 Perpera** ND (1916-old date 25.7.1914). Overprint: On #21.	12.50	35.00	70.00

Kolasin Issue

1916 ND First Provisional Issue

		Good	Fine	XF
M37	**5 Perpera** ND (1916-old date 25.7.1914). Overprint: On #9.	4.00	12.00	25.00
M38	**10 Perpera** ND (1916-old date 25.7.1914). Overprint: On #10.	5.00	15.00	30.00
M39	**20 Perpera** ND (1916-old date 25.7.1914). Overprint: On #11.	10.00	25.00	50.00
M40	**50 Perpera** ND (1916-old date 25.7.1914). Overprint: On #12.	12.00	30.00	60.00
M41	**100 Perpera** ND (1916-old date 25.7.1914). Overprint: On #13.	25.00	75.00	150.

1916 ND Second Provisional Issue

		Good	Fine	XF
M42	**1 Perper** ND (1916-old date 25.7.1914). Overprint: On #15.	2.50	7.50	15.00
M43	**2 Perpera** ND (1916-old date 25.7.1914). Overprint: On #16.	4.00	12.00	25.00
M44	**5 Perpera** ND (1916-old date 25.7.1914). Overprint: On #17.	5.00	15.00	30.00
M45	**10 Perpera** ND (1916-old date 25.7.1914). Overprint: On #18.	6.00	17.50	35.00
M46	**20 Perpera** ND (1916-old date 25.7.1914). Overprint: On #19.	8.00	25.00	50.00
M47	**50 Perpera** ND (1916-old date 25.7.1914). Overprint: On #20.	12.00	35.00	70.00
M48	**100 Perpera** ND (1916-old date 25.7.1914). Overprint: On #21.	20.00	60.00	120.

Niksic Issue

1916 ND First Provisional Issue

#M49-M53 width of *NIKSIC* in overprint 11mm.

		Good	Fine	XF
M49	**5 Perpera** ND (1916-old date 25.7.1914). Overprint: On #9. Width of *NIKSIC* is 11mm.	6.00	17.50	35.00
M50	**10 Perpera** ND (1916-old date 25.7.1914). Overprint: On #10. Width of *NIKSIC* is 11mm.	12.00	35.00	70.00
M51	**20 Perpera** ND (1916-old date 25.7.1914). Overprint: On #11. Width of *NIKSIC* is 11mm.	15.00	50.00	100.
M52	**50 Perpera** ND (1916-old date 25.7.1914). Overprint: On #12. Width of *NIKSIC* is 11mm.	20.00	60.00	120.
M53	**100 Perpera** ND (1916-old date 25.7.1914). Overprint: On #13. Width of *NIKSIC* is 11mm.	35.00	100.	200.

1916 ND Second Provisional Issue

#M54-M60 width of *NIKSIC* in overprint 11mm.

		Good	Fine	XF
M54	**1 Perper** ND (1916-old date 25.7.1914). Overprint: On #15. Width of *NIKSIC* is 11mm.	3.50	10.00	20.00
M55	**2 Perpera** ND (1916-old date 25.7.1914). Overprint: On #16. Width of *NIKSIC* is 11mm.	6.00	17.50	35.00
M56	**5 Perpera** ND (1916-old date 25.7.1914). Overprint: On #17. Width of *NIKSIC* is 11mm.	6.00	17.50	35.00
M57	**10 Perpera** ND (1916-old date 25.7.1914). Overprint: On #18. Width of *NIKSIC* is 11mm.	7.50	22.50	45.00
M58	**20 Perpera** ND (1916-old date 25.7.1914. Overprint: On #19. Width of *NIKSIC* is 11mm.	10.00	30.00	60.00

		Good	Fine	XF
M59	**50 Perpera** ND (1916-old date 25.7.1914). Overprint: On #20. Width of *NIKSIC* is 11mm.	12.50	37.50	75.00

		Good	Fine	XF
M60	**100 Perpera** ND (1916-old date 25.7.1914). Overprint: On #21. Width of *NIKSIC* is 11mm.	25.00	75.00	150.

1916 ND Third Provisional Issue

#M61-M65 width of *NIKSIC* in ovpt. 14mm.

		Good	Fine	XF
M61	**5 Perpera** ND (1916-old date 25.7.1914). Overprint: On #9. Width of *NIKSIC* is 14mm.	5.00	15.00	30.00
M62	**10 Perpera** ND (1916-old date 25.7.1914). Overprint: On #10. Width of *NIKSIC* is 14mm.	7.50	22.50	45.00
M63	**20 Perpera** ND (1916-old date 25.7.1914). Overprint: On #11. Width of *NIKSIC* is 14mm.	10.00	30.00	60.00
M64	**50 Perpera** ND (1916-old date 25.7.1914). Overprint: On #12. Width of *NIKSIC* is 14mm.	12.50	37.50	75.00
M65	**100 Perpera** ND (1916-old date 25.7.1914). Overprint: On #13. Width of *NIKSIC* is 14mm.	25.00	75.00	150.

1916 ND Fourth Provisional Issue

#M66-M72 width of *NIKSIC* in overprint 14mm.

		Good	Fine	XF
M66	**1 Perper** ND (1916-old date 25.7.1914). Overprint: On #15. Width of *NIKSIC* is14mm.	4.00	12.00	25.00
M67	**2 Perpera** ND (1916-old date 25.7.1914). Overprint: On #16. Width of *NIKSIC* is14mm.	5.00	16.00	32.00
M68	**5 Perpera** ND (1916-old date 25.7.1914). Overprint: On #17. Width of *NIKSIC* is14mm.	5.00	16.00	32.00
M69	**10 Perpera** ND (1916-old date 25.7.1914). Overprint: On #18. Width of *NIKSIC* is14mm.	7.00	20.00	40.00
M70	**20 Perpera** ND (1916-old date 25.7.1914). Overprint: On #19. Width of *NIKSIC* is14mm.	8.00	22.50	45.00
M71	**50 Perpera** ND (1916-old date 25.7.1914). Overprint: On #20. Width of *NIKSIC* is14mm.	10.00	30.00	60.00
M72	**100 Perpera** ND (1916-old date 25.7.1914). Overprint: On #21. Width of *NIKSIC* is14mm.	15.00	50.00	100.

Plevlie Issue

1916 ND First Provisional Issue

		Good	Fine	XF
M73	**5 Perpera** ND (1916-old date 25.7.1914). Overprint: On #9.	5.00	15.00	32.00
M74	**10 Perpera** ND (1916-old date 25.7.1914). Overprint: On #10.	7.50	22.50	45.00
M75	**20 Perpera** ND (1916-old date 25.7.1914). Overprint: On #11.	10.00	30.00	60.00

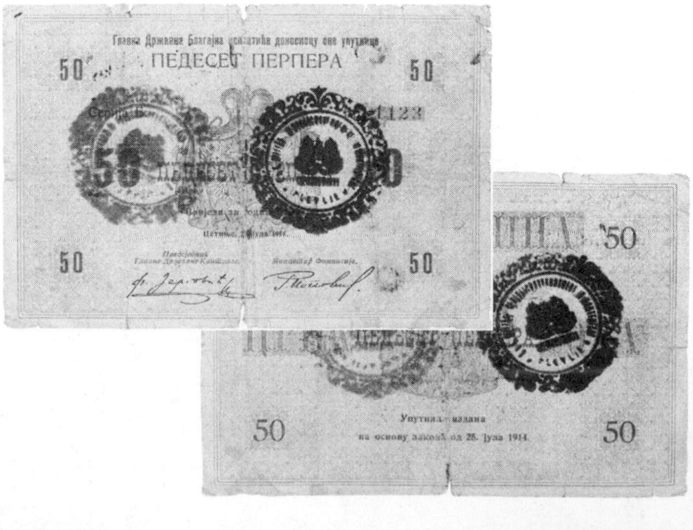

		Good	Fine	XF
M76	**50 Perpera** ND (1916-old date 25.7.1914). Overprint: On #12.	12.50	37.50	75.00
M77	**100 Perpera** ND (1916-old date 25.7.1914). Overprint: On #13.	30.00	100.	200.

1916 ND Second Provisional Issue

		Good	Fine	XF
M78	**1 Perper** ND (1916-old date 25.7.1914). Overprint: On #15.	5.00	15.00	30.00
M79	**2 Perpera** ND (1916-old date 25.7.1914). Overprint: On #16.	5.00	15.00	30.00
M80	**5 Perpera** ND (1916-old date 25.7.1914). Overprint: On #17.	5.00	15.00	30.00
M81	**10 Perpera** ND (1916-old date 25.7.1914). Overprint: On #18.	6.00	17.50	35.00
M82	**20 Perpera** ND (1916-old date 25.7.1914). Overprint: On #19.	7.50	22.50	45.00
M83	**50 Perpera** ND (1916-old date 25.7.1914). Overprint: On #20.	9.00	27.50	55.00
M84	**100 Perpera** ND (1916-old date 25.7.1914). Overprint: On #21.	12.50	37.50	75.00

Podgorica Issue

1916 ND First Provisional Issue

#M85-M89 width of *Podgorica* in overprint 13mm.

		Good	Fine	XF
M85	**5 Perpera** ND (1916-old date 25.7.1914). Overprint: On #9. Width of *PODGORICA* is 13mm.	7.50	22.50	45.00
M86	**10 Perpera** ND (1916-old date 25.7.1914). Overprint: On #10. Width of *PODGORICA* is 13mm.	10.00	30.00	60.00
M87	**20 Perpera** ND (1916-old date 25.7.1914). Overprint: On #11. Width of *PODGORICA* is 13mm.	12.50	37.50	75.00
M88	**50 Perpera** ND (1916-old date 25.7.1914). Overprint: On #12. Width of *PODGORICA* is 13mm.	15.00	50.00	100.
M89	**100 Perpera** ND (1916-old date 25.7.1914). Overprint: On #13. Width of *PODGORICA* is 13mm.	30.00	100.	200.

1916 ND Second Provisional Issue

#M90-M96 width of *Podgorica* in overprint 13mm.

		Good	Fine	XF
M90	**1 Perper** ND (1916-old date 25.7.1914). Overprint: On #15. Width of *Podgorica* is 13mm.	4.00	12.50	25.00
M91	**2 Perpera** ND (1916-old date 25.7.1914). Overprint: On #16. Width of *Podgorica* is 13mm.	5.00	15.00	30.00
M92	**5 Perpera** ND (1916-old date 25.7.1914). Overprint: On #17. Width of *Podgorica* is 13mm.	7.50	22.50	45.00
M93	**10 Perpera** ND (1916-old date 25.7.1914). Overprint: On #18. Width of *Podgorica* is 13mm.	7.50	22.50	45.00
M94	**20 Perpera** ND (1916-old date 25.7.1914). Overprint: On #19. Width of *Podgorica* is 13mm.	10.00	30.00	60.00
M95	**50 Perpera** ND (1916-old date 25.7.1914). Overprint: On #20. Width of *Podgorica* is 13mm.	12.50	37.50	75.00
M96	**100 Perpera** ND (1916-old date 25.7.1914). Overprint: On #21. Width of *Podgorica* is 13mm.	15.00	50.00	100.

1916 ND Third Provisional Issue

#M97-M101 width of *Podgorica* in overprint 13mm.

		Good	Fine	XF
M97	**5 Perpera** ND (1916-old date 25.7.1914). Overprint: On #9. Width of *PODGORICA* is 13mm.	7.50	22.50	45.00
M98	**10 Perpera** ND (1916-old date 25.7.1914). Overprint: On #10. Width of *PODGORICA* is 13mm.	7.50	22.50	45.00
M99	**20 Perpera** ND (1916-old date 25.7.1914). Overprint: On #11. Width of *PODGORICA* is 13mm.	12.50	37.50	75.00
M100	**50 Perpera** ND (1916-old date 25.7.1914). Overprint: On #12. Width of *PODGORICA* is 13mm.	15.00	50.00	100.
M101	**100 Perpera** ND (1916-old date 25.7.1914). Overprint: On #13. Width of *PODGORICA* is 13mm.	30.00	100.	200.

1916 ND Fourth Provisional Issue

#M102-M108 width of *Podgorica* in overprint 13mm.

		Good	Fine	XF
M102	**1 Perper** ND (1916-old date 25.7.1914). Overprint: On #15. Width of *PODGORICA* is 13mm.	7.50	22.50	45.00
M103	**2 Perpera** ND (1916-old date 25.7.1914). Overprint: On #16. Width of *PODGORICA* is 13mm.	9.00	27.50	55.00

		Good	Fine	XF
M104	**5 Perpera** ND (1916-old date 25.7.1914). Overprint: On #17. Width of *PODGORICA* is 13mm.	12.50	37.50	75.00
M105	**10 Perpera** ND (1916-old date 25.7.1914). Overprint: On #18. Width of *PODGORICA* is 13mm.	15.00	50.00	100.
M106	**20 Perpera** ND (1916-old date 25.7.1914). Overprint: On #19. Width of *PODGORICA* is 13mm.	25.00	75.00	150.
M107	**50 Perpera** ND (1916-old date 25.7.1914). Overprint: On #20. Width of *PODGORICA* is 13mm.	30.00	100.	200.
M108	**100 Perpera** ND (1916-old date 25.7.1914). Overprint: On #21. Width of *PODGORICA* is 13mm.	35.00	125.	250.

1916 ND Fifth Provisional Issue

#M109-M113 width of *PODGORICA* in overprint 17mm.

		Good	Fine	XF
M109	**5 Perpera** ND (1916-old date 25.7.1914). Overprint on #9.	6.00	17.50	35.00
M110	**10 Perpera** ND (1916-old date 25.7.1914). Overprint on #10.	7.50	22.50	45.00
M111	**20 Perpera** ND (1916-old date 25.7.1914). Overprint on #11.	10.00	30.00	60.00

		Good	Fine	XF
M112	**50 Perpera** ND (1916-old date 25.7.1914). Overprint on #12.	7.50	22.50	45.00
M113	**100 Perpera** ND (1916-old date 25.7.1914). Overprint on #13.	12.50	37.50	75.00

1916 ND Sixth Provisional Issue

#M114-M120 width of *PODGORICA* in overprint 17mm.

		Good	Fine	XF
M114	**1 Perper** ND (1916-old date 25.7.1914). Overprint: On #15. Width of *PODGORICA* is 17mm.	7.50	22.50	45.00
M115	**2 Perpera** ND (1916-old date 25.7.1914). Overprint: On #16. Width of *PODGORICA* is 17mm.	7.50	22.50	45.00
M116	**5 Perpera** ND (1916-old date 25.7.1914). Overprint: On #17. Width of *PODGORICA* is 17mm.	7.50	22.50	45.00
M117	**10 Perpera** ND (1916-old date 25.7.1914). Overprint: On #18. Width of *PODGORICA* is 17mm.	12.50	37.50	75.00
M118	**20 Perpera** ND (1916-old date 25.7.1914). Overprint: On #19. Width of *PODGORICA* is 17mm.	15.00	50.00	100.
M119	**50 Perpera** ND (1916-old date 25.7.1914). Overprint: On #20. Width of *PODGORICA* is 17mm.	20.00	60.00	125.
M120	**100 Perpera** ND (1916-old date 25.7.1914). Overprint: On #21. Width of *PODGORICA* is 17mm.	25.00	75.00	150.

Stari Bar Issue

1916 ND First Provisional Issue

#M121-125 width of *STARI BAR* in overprint 11mm.

		Good	Fine	XF
M121	**5 Perpera** ND (1916-old date 25.7.1914). Overprint: On #9. Width of *STARI BAR* is 11mm.	12.50	37.50	80.00
M122	**10 Perpera** ND (1916-old date 25.7.1914). Overprint: On #10. Width of *STARI BAR* is 11mm.	20.00	60.00	130.
M123	**20 Perpera** ND (1916-old date 25.7.1914). Overprint: On #11. Width of *STARI BAR* is 11mm.	20.00	60.00	130.
M124	**50 Perpera** ND (1916-old date 25.7.1914). Overprint: On #12. Width of *STARI BAR* is 11mm.	25.00	75.00	175.
M125	**100 Perpera** ND (1916-old date 25.7.1914). Overprint: On # 13. Width of *STARI BAR* is 11mm.	30.00	100.	200.

1916 ND Second Provisional Issue

#M126-M132 width of *STARI BAR* in overprint 11mm.

		Good	Fine	XF
M126	**1 Perper** ND (1916-old date 25.7.1914). Overprint: On #15. Width of *STARI BAR* is 11mm.	15.00	50.00	120.
M127	**2 Perpera** ND (1916-old date 25.7.1914). Overprint: On #16. Width of *STARI BAR* is 11mm.	20.00	50.00	140.
M128	**5 Perpera** ND (1916-old date 25.7.1914). Overprint: On #17. Width of *STARI BAR* is 11mm.	25.00	75.00	160.
M129	**10 Perpera** ND (1916-old date 25.7.1914). Overprint: On #18. Width of *STARI BAR* is 11mm.	30.00	100.	200.
M130	**20 Perpera** ND (1916-old date 25.7.1914). Overprint: On #19. Width of *STARI BAR* is 11mm.	30.00	100.	200.
M131	**50 Perpera** ND (1916-old date 25.7.1914). Overprint: On #20. Width of *STARI BAR* is 11mm.	40.00	125.	275.
M132	**100 Perpera** ND (1916-old date 25.7.1914). Overprint: On #21. Width of *STARI BAR* is 11mm.	50.00	150.	350.

1916 ND Third Provisional Issue

#M133-M137 width of *STARI BAR* in overprint 16mm.

		Good	Fine	XF
M133	**5 Perpera** ND (1916-old date 25.7.1914). Overprint: On #9. Width of *STARI BAR* is 16mm.	12.50	37.50	85.00
M134	**10 Perpera** ND (1916-old date 25.7.1914). Overprint: On #10. Width of *STARI BAR* is 16mm.	25.00	75.00	170.
M135	**20 Perpera** ND (1916-old date 25.7.1914). Overprint: On #11. Width of *STARI BAR* is 16mm.	25.00	75.00	170.
M136	**50 Perpera** ND (1916-old date 25.7.1914). Overprint: On #12. Width of *STARI BAR* is 16mm.	40.00	125.	250.
M137	**100 Perpera** ND (1916-old date 25.7.1914). Overprint: On #13. Width of *STARI BAR* is 16mm.	50.00	150.	350.

1916 ND Fourth Provisional Issue

#M138-M144 width of *STARI BAR* in overprint 16mm.

		Good	Fine	XF
M138	**1 Perper** ND (1916-old date 25.7.1914). Overprint: On #15. Width of *STARI BAR* is 16mm.	7.50	22.50	50.00
M139	**2 Perpera** ND (1916-old date 25.7.1914). Overprint: On #16. Width of *STARI BAR* is 16mm.	7.50	22.50	50.00
M140	**5 Perpera** ND (1916-old date 25.7.1914). Overprint: On #17. Width of *STARI BAR* is 16mm.	7.50	22.50	50.00
M141	**10 Perpera** ND (1916-old date 25.7.1914). Overprint: On #18. Width of *STARI BAR* is 16mm.	12.50	37.50	80.00
M142	**20 Perpera** ND (1916-old date 25.7.1914). Overprint: On # 19. Width of *STARI BAR* is 16mm.	15.00	50.00	120.
M143	**50 Perpera** ND (1916-old date 25.7.1914). Overprint: On #20. Width of *STARI BAR* is 16mm.	20.00	60.00	125.
M144	**100 Perpera** ND (1916-old date 25.7.1914). Overprint: On #21. Width of *STARI BAR* is 16mm.	25.00	75.00	150.

Belgrad Issue

1916 ND Provisional Issue

		Good	Fine	XF
M145	**1 Perper** ND (1916-old date 25.7.1914). Overprint: On #15.	150.	450.	1000.
M146	**10 Perpera** ND (1916-old date 25.7.1914). Overprint: On #18.	150.	450.	1000.

Steuer-u. Zollamt Kolasin Issue

1916 ND Provisional Issue

		Good	Fine	XF
M147	**1 Perper** ND (1916-old date 25.7.1914). Overprint: On #1.	150.	450.	1000.

K.u.K. Kreiskommando Unterabteilung

District Command Subdivision

1916 ND Provisional Issue

		Good	Fine	XF
M147A	**1 Perper** ND (1916-old date 25.7.1914). Overprint: Without place name on #15.	150.	450.	1000.

K.u.K. Stationskommando

1916 Issue

		Good	Fine	XF
M147B	**5 Perpera** ND (1616-old date 25.7.1914). Overprint: Without place name on #17.	—	—	—

K.u.K. Militarverwaltung

Army Administration, 1917-18

1917 Convertable Voucher Issue

		VG	VF	UNC
M148	**1 Perper = 50 Münzperper = 50 Heller** 5.7.1917. Blue-green on orange underprint. Back: Orange with black text on light green underprint.	7.00	20.00	55.00

		VG	VF	UNC
M149	**2 Perper = 1 Münzperper = 1 Krone** 5.7.1917. Violet on green underprint. Back: Olive-green with black text on lilac underprint.	7.00	25.00	70.00
M150	**5 Perper = 2 Münzperper 50 Para = 2 Kronen 50 Heller** 5.7.1917. Purple on green underprint. Back: Green with black text on pink underprint.	10.00	30.00	80.00
M151	**10 Perper = 5 Münzperper = 5 Kronen** 1.6.1917. Blue on brown underprint. Back: Red-brown with black text on green underprint.	7.00	25.00	70.00

		VG	VF	UNC
M152	**20 Perper = 10 Münzperper = 10 Kronen** 20.11.1917. Red-brown on green underprint. Back: Back Green with black text on light red-orange underprint.	15.00	40.00	100.

		VG	VF	UNC
M153	**50 Perper = 25 Münzperper = 25 Kronen** 20.11.1917. Red-brown on green underprint. Back: Brown with black text on red-brown underprint.	25.00	50.00	150.
M154	**100 Perper = 50 Münzperper = 50 Kronen** 20.11.1917. Blue on olive underprint. Back: Brown with black text on blue underprint.	30.00	60.00	200.

NOTE: DURING WORLD WAR II ITALIAN OVERPRINTED NOTES OF YUGOSLAVIA WITH *VERIFICATO* WERE CIRCULATED IN MONTENEGRO. THERE WAS ALSO AN ISSUE OF *SOCIALNIKI DINARA* IN 1945 (STAMP MONEY). FOR DETAILS OF THE *VERIFICATO* NOTES SEE YUGOSLAVIA.

MOROCCO

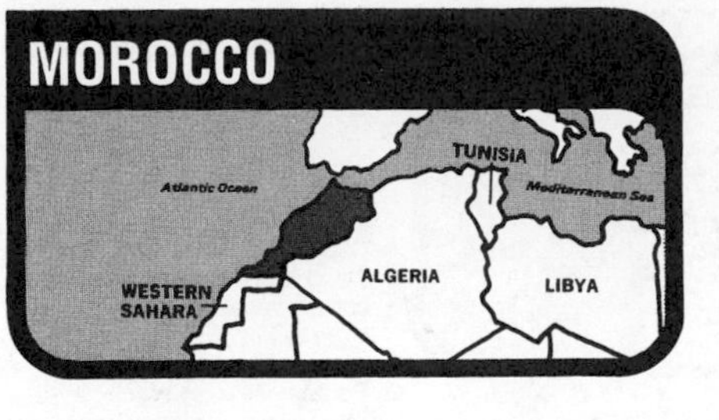

The Kingdom of Morocco, situated on the northwest corner of Africa south of Spain, has an area of 172,413 sq. mi. (712,550 sq. km.) and a population of 28.98 million. Capital: Rabat. The economy is essentially agricultural. Phosphates, fresh and preserved vegetables, canned fish and raw material are exported.

In 788, about a century after the Arab conquest of North Africa, successive Moorish dynasties began to rule in Morocco. In the 16th century, the Sa'adi monarchy, particularly under Ahmad Al-Mansur (1578-1603), repelled foreign invaders and inaugurated a golden age. In 1860, Spain occupied northern Morocco and ushered in a half century of trade rivalry among European powers that saw Morocco's sovereignty steadily erode; in 1912, the French imposed a protectorate over the country. A protracted independence struggle with France ended successfully in 1956. The internationalized city of Tangier and most Spanish possessions were turned over to the new country that same year. Morocco virtually annexed Western Sahara during the late 1970s, but final resolution on the status of the territory remains unresolved. Gradual political reforms in the 1990s resulted in the establishment of a bicameral legislature, which first met in 1997. The country has made improvements in human rights under King Mohammed VI and its press is moderately free. Despite the continuing reforms, ultimate authority remains in the hands of the monarch.

RULERS:

Abd Al-Aziz, AH1311-1325/1894-1908AD
Hafiz, AH1325-1330/1908-1912AD
Yusuf, AH1330-1346/1912-1927AD
Muhammad V, AH1346-1380/1927-1961AD
Hassan II, AH1380-1420 /1961-1999AD
Muhammad VI, AH1420- /1999- AD

MONETARY SYSTEM:

1 Dirham = 50 Mazunas
1 Rial = 10 Dirhams to 1921
1 Franc = 100 Centimes
1 Dirham = 100 Francs, 1921-1974
1 Dirham = 100 Centimes = 100 Santimat, 1974-
1 Riffan = 1 French Gold Franc = 10 British Pence

REGIONAL

STATE BANK OF THE RIFF

1923 ISSUE

ISSUED DURING THE BERBER UPRISING UNDER ABD EL-KRIM, 1921-26.

		VG	VF	UNC
R1	**1 Riffan = 10 Pence** 10.10.1923. Red-orange. Horseman at left and right. Uniface.	—	60.00	90.00
R2	**5 Riffans = 50 Pence** 10.10.1923. Light green. Horseman at left and right.	—	75.00	120.

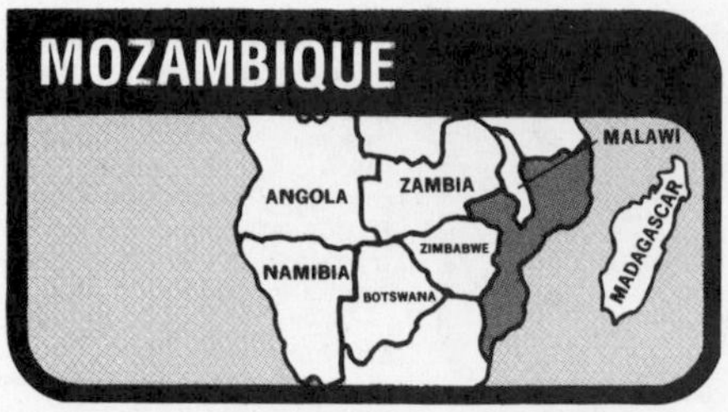

The People's Republic of Mozambique, a former overseas province of Portugal stretching for 1,430 miles (2,301 km.) along the southeast coast of Africa, has an area of 309,494 sq. mi. (783,030 sq. km.) and a population of 19.56 million. Capital: Maputo. Agriculture is the chief industry. Cashew nuts, cotton, sugar, copra and tea are exported.

Almost five centuries as a Portuguese colony came to a close with independence in 1975. Large-scale emigration by whites, economic dependence on South Africa, a severe drought, and a prolonged civil war hindered the country's development until the mid 1990's. The ruling Front for the Liberation of Mozambique (FRELIMO) party formally abandoned Marxism in 1989, and a new constitution the following year provided for multiparty elections and a free market economy. A UN-negotiated peace agreement between FRELIMO and rebel Mozambique National Resistance (RENAMO) forces ended the fighting in 1992. In December 2004, Mozambique underwent a delicate transition as Joaquim Chissano stepped down after 18 years in office. His elected successor, Armando Emilio Guebuza, promised to continue the sound economic policies that have encouraged foreign investment. Mozambique has seen very strong economic growth since the end of the civil war largely due to post-conflict reconstruction.

RULERS:

Portuguese to 1975

MONETARY SYSTEM:

Pound Sterling = Libra Esterlina (pound sterling)
1 Mil Reis = 1000 Reis to 1910
1 Escudo = 100 Centavos, 1911-1975
1 Escudo = 1 Metica = 100 Centimos, 1975-

REGIONAL

BANCO DA BEIRA

1919 LIBRA ISSUES

#R1-R33 values are primarily for cancelled notes. Most of those except for #R2-R4 without cancellations are worth at least double the valuations shown. Cancellations: *CANCELADO* in large letters or *PAGO 30.*(or other day) *11.1942* in small letters and #.

		Good	Fine	XF
R1	**10 Centavos**			
	15.9.1919. Green and yellow. Back: Dark brown. Printer: BWC.			
	a. Issued note.	2.00	6.00	15.00
	b. Cancelled.	2.00	6.00	15.00
R2	**20 Centavos**			
	15.9.1919. Green. Back: Black. Printer: BWC.			
	a. Issued note.	2.00	6.00	15.00
	b. Cancelled.	2.00	6.00	15.00

		Good	Fine	XF
R3	**50 Centavos**			
	15.9.1919. Black on orange-brown and multicolor underprint. Back: Blue. Printer: BWC.			
	a. Large hand signature at left.	3.00	8.00	17.50
	b. Small printed signature at left.	2.00	6.00	15.00
	c. Cancelled.	3.00	8.00	17.50

		Good	Fine	XF
R4	**50 Centavos**			
	15.9.1919. Brown. *PRATA* deep blue in frame at top center. Printer: BWC.			
	a. Issued note.	2.00	6.00	15.00
	b. Cancelled.	2.00	6.00	15.00
R5	**1/2 Libra**			
	15.9.1919. Red on multicolor underprint. Printer: BWC.	2.00	6.00	15.00

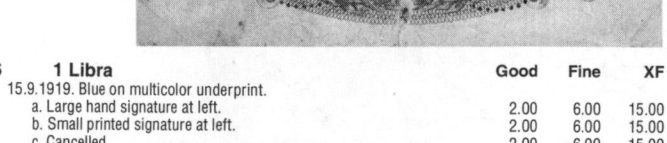

		Good	Fine	XF
R6	**1 Libra**			
	15.9.1919. Blue on multicolor underprint.			
	a. Large hand signature at left.	2.00	6.00	15.00
	b. Small printed signature at left.	2.00	6.00	15.00
	c. Cancelled.	2.00	6.00	15.00

		Good	Fine	XF
R7	**1 Libra**			
	15.9.1919. Blue on multicolor underprint. *OURO* in frame at bottom center. Printer: BWC.			
	a. Issued note.	2.00	6.00	15.00
	b. Cancelled.	2.00	6.00	15.00

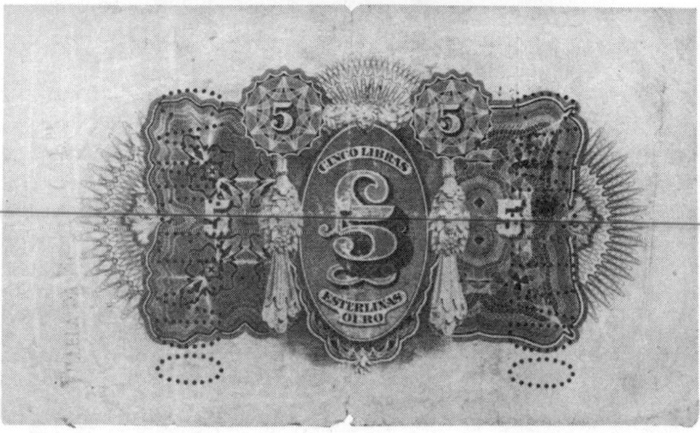

		Good	Fine	XF
R8	**5 Libras**			
	15.9.1919. Blue on multicolor underprint. Printer: BWC.			
	a. Large hand signature at left.	4.00	12.00	30.00
	b. Small printed signature at left.	4.00	12.00	30.00
R9	**5 Libras**			
	15.9.1919. Blue. *OURO* in frame at bottom center. Printer: BWC.	5.00	12.00	30.00
R10	**10 Libras**			
	15.9.1919.	15.00	50.00	175.
R11	**20 Libras**			
	15.9.1919.	25.00	75.00	200.

1919 Escudo Issue

		Good	Fine	XF
R11A	**1 Escudo**			
	15.9.1919. Brown. Back: Greenish gray. Printer: BWC.	5.00	12.00	30.00

1921 Issue

		Good	Fine	XF
R12	**10 Libras**			
	1.2.1921.	25.00	100.	225.
R13	**20 Libras**			
	1.2.1921.	25.00	100.	225.

Companhia de Moçambique, Beira

ND Provisional Libra Issue

#R14-R23 overprint new issuer name in rectangular frame.

		Good	Fine	XF
R14	**10 Centavos**			
	ND (-old date 15.9.1919). Overprint: On #R1. Printer: BWC.	2.00	6.00	20.00
R15	**20 Centavos**			
	ND (-old date 15.9.1919). Overprint: On #R2. Printer: BWC.	2.00	6.00	20.00
R16	**50 Centavos**			
	ND (-old date 15.9.1919). Overprint: On #R3. Printer: BWC.	2.00	6.00	20.00

		Good	Fine	XF
R17	**50 Centavos**			
	ND (-old date 15.9.1919). Overprint: On #R4. Printer: BWC.	2.00	6.00	20.00
R18	**1/2 Libra**			
	ND (-old date 15.9.1919). Overprint: On #R5. Printer: BWC.	2.00	6.00	20.00
R19	**1 Libra**			
	ND (-old date 15.9.1919). Overprint: On #R6. Printer: BWC.			
	a. Large hand signature at left.	2.00	6.00	20.00
	b. Small printed signature at left.	2.00	6.00	20.00

		Good	Fine	XF
R20	**1 Libra**			
	ND (-old date 15.9.1919). Overprint: On R#7. Printer: BWC.	3.00	8.00	20.00
R21	**5 Libras**			
	ND (-old date 15.9.1919). Overprint: On #R8. Printer: BWC.	4.00	15.00	40.00
R21A	**5 Libras**			
	ND (-old date 15.9.1919). Overprint on #R9.	4.00	15.00	40.00
R22	**10 Libras**			
	ND (-old date 1.2.1921). Overprint: On #R12. Printer: BWC.	25.00	100.	200.
R23	**20 Libras**			
	ND (-old date 1.2.1921). Overprint: On #R13. Printer: BWC.	25.00	100.	200.

ND Provisional Escudo Issue

		Good	Fine	XF
R23A	**1 Escudo**			
	ND (-old date 15.9.1919). Overprint: On #R11A.	4.00	15.00	40.00

1930 Regular Issue

		Good	Fine	XF
R24	**1 Libra**			
	1.11.1930. Blue on multicolor underprint. Printer: BWC.			
	a. Issued note.	2.00	6.00	15.00
	b. Cancelled.	2.00	6.00	15.00

1931 Issue

		Good	Fine	XF
R25	**10 Centavos**			
	1.10.1931. Green.	2.00	6.00	15.00

		Good	Fine	XF
R26	**50 Centavos** 1.10.1931. Sepia. Printer: BWC.	2.00	6.00	15.00
R27	**1/2 Libra** 1.9.1931.	2.00	6.00	15.00

1933 Issue

		Good	Fine	XF
R28	**10 Centavos** 20.10.1933. Green. Printer: BWC.	2.00	6.00	15.00

		Good	Fine	XF
R29	**20 Centavos** 25.11.1933. Blue. Printer: BWC.	2.00	6.00	12.00

1934 Issue

		VG	VF	UNC
R30	**1/2 Libra** 15.3.1934. Red on multicolor underprint. Back: Blue-green.			
	a. Issued note.	2.00	6.00	15.00
	s. Specimen.	—	—	35.00

		Good	Fine	XF
R31	**1 Libra** 15.3.1934. Blue. Printer: BWC.	2.00	6.00	15.00
R32	**5 Libras** 15.1.1934. Blue. Printer: BWC.	3.00	15.00	30.00

1937 Issue

		Good	Fine	XF
R33	**1 Escudo** 12.5.1937. Violet. Printer: BWC.	2.00	6.00	15.00

MYANMAR

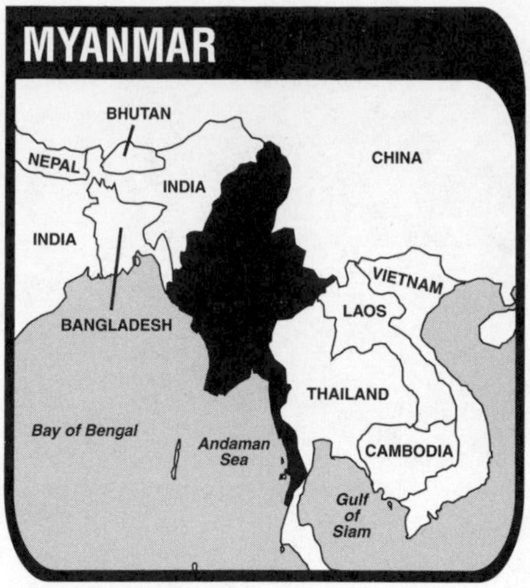

The Socialist Republic of the Union of Myanmar (formally called Burma), a country of Southeast Asia fronting on the Bay of Bengal and the Andaman Sea, has an area of 261,789 sq. mi. (676,552 sq. km.) and a population of 49.34 million. Capital: Rangoon. Myanmar is an agricultural country heavily dependent on its leading product (rice) which embodies two-thirds of the cultivated area and accounts for 40 percent of the value of exports. Petroleum, lead, tin, silver, zinc, nickel, cobalt and precious stones are exported.

Britain conquered Burma over a period of 62 years (1824-1886) and incorporated it into its Indian Empire. Burma was administered as a province of India until 1937 when it became a separate, self-governing colony; independence from the Commonwealth was attained in 1948. Gen. Ne Win dominated the government from 1962 to 1988, first as military ruler, then as self-appointed president, and later as political kingpin. In September 1988, the military deposed Ne Win and established a new ruling junta. Despite multiparty legislative elections in 1990 that resulted in the main opposition party - the National League for Democracy (NLD) - winning a landslide victory, the junta refused to hand over power. NLD leader and Nobel Peace Prize recipient Aung San Suu Kyi, who was under house arrest from 1989 to 1995 and 2000 to 2002, was imprisoned in May 2003 and subsequently transferred to house arrest. After the ruling junta in August 2007 unexpectedly increased fuel prices, tens of thousands of Burmese marched in protest, led by prodemocracy activists and Buddhist monks. In late September 2007, the government brutally suppressed the protests, killing at least 13 people and arresting thousands for participating in the demonstrations. Since then, the regime has continued to raid homes and monasteries and arrest persons suspected of participating in the pro-democracy protests. The junta appointed Labor Minister Aung Kyi in October 2007 as liaison to Aung San Suu Kyi, who remains under house arrest and virtually incommunicado with her party and supporters. Burma in early May 2008 was struck by Cyclone Nargis which official estimates claimed left over 80,000 dead and 50,000 injured. Despite this tragedy, the junta proceeded with its May constitutional referendum, the first vote in Burma since 1990, setting the stage for the 2010 parliamentary elections.The country name in English was changed to Union of Myanmar in 1989.

RULERS:

British to 1948
Japanese, 1942-1945

MONETARY SYSTEM:

1 Rupee (Kyat) = 10 Mu = 16 Annas (Pe) to 1942, 1945-1952
1 Rupee = 100 Cents, 1942-1943
1 Kyat = 100 Pyas, 1943-1945, 1952-

Foreign Exchange Certificates

Central Bank of Myanmar

1993 ND Issue

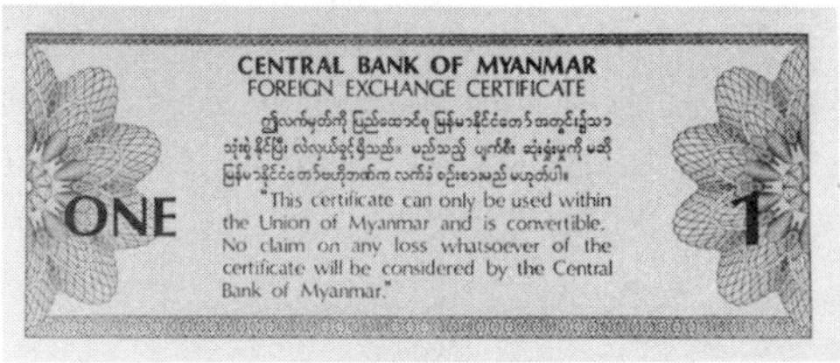

		VG	VF	UNC
FX1	**1 Dollar (USA)** ND (1993). Blue, brown, yellow and green.	—	—	4.00

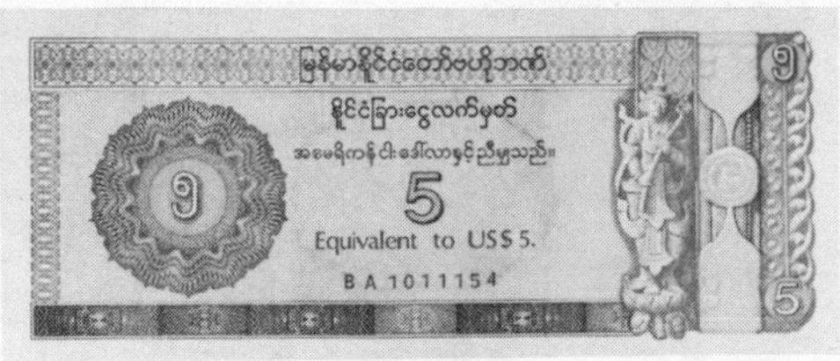

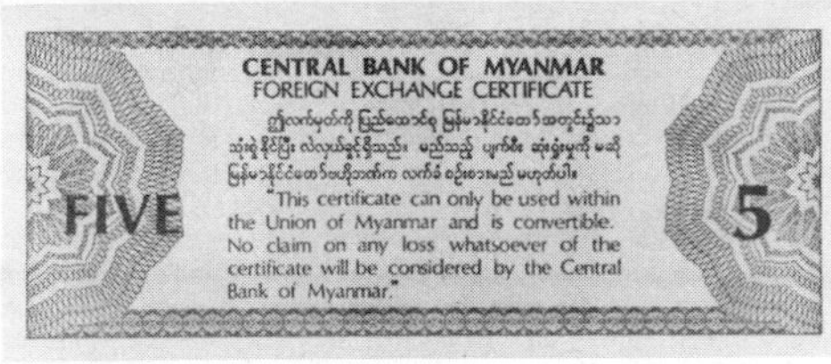

		VG	VF	UNC
FX2	**5 Dollars (USA)** ND (1993). Maroon, yellow and blue.	—	—	12.50

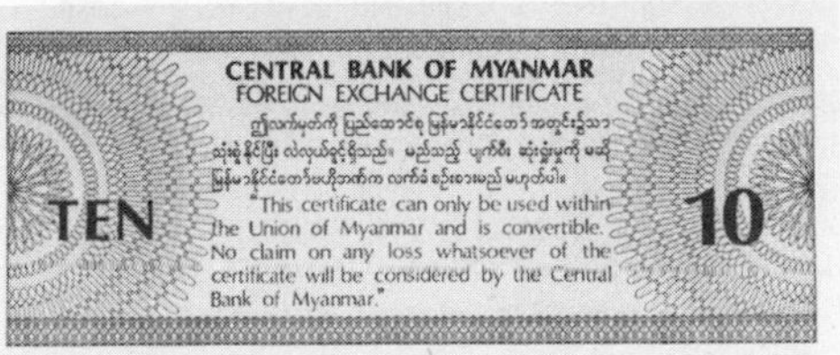

		VG	VF	UNC
FX3	**10 Dollars (USA)** ND (1993). Blue, green and gray.	—	—	27.50
FX4	**20 Dollars (USA)** ND (1997). Maroon, yellow and brown.	—	—	35.00

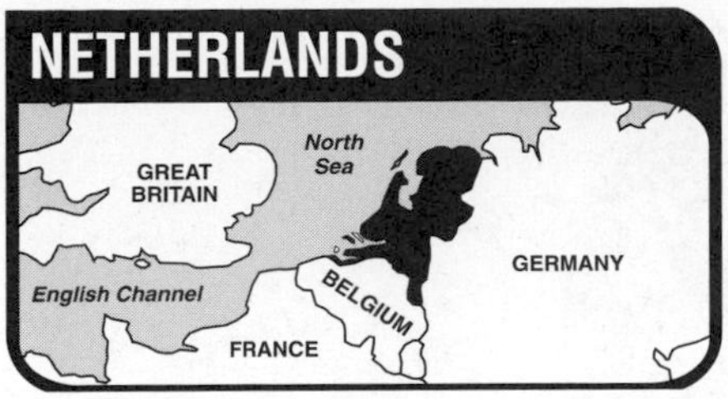

The Kingdom of the Netherlands, a country of western Europe fronting on the North Sea and bordered by Belgium and Germany, has an area of 15,770 sq. mi. (40,844 sq. km.) and a population of 15.87 million. Capital: Amsterdam, but the seat of government is at The Hague. The economy is d on dairy farming and a variety of industrial activities. Chemicals, yarns and fabrics, and meat products are exported.

The Dutch United Provinces declared their independence from Spain in 1579; during the 17th century, they became a leading seafaring and commercial power, with settlements and colonies around the world. After a 20-year French occupation, a Kingdom of the Netherlands was formed in 1815. In 1830 Belgium seceded and formed a separate kingdom. The Netherlands remained neutral in World War I, but suffered invasion and occupation by Germany in World War II. A modern, industrialized nation, the Netherlands is also a large exporter of agricultural products. The country was a founding member of NATO and the EEC (now the EU), and participated in the introduction of the euro in 1999.

Siege

Leyden

1574 Issue

		Good	Fine	XF
S101	**5 Stuiver** 1574. Crowned lion with shield and sword. Legend: *PUGNO PRO PATRIA* (I fight for my country). Back: Legend: *LUGDUNUM BATAVORUM.* 30mm.			
	a. Without countermark.	—	300.	900.
	b. With countermark.	—	350.	1150.
S102	**14 Stuiver** 1574.	—	—	—
S103	**16 Stuiver** 1574.	—	—	—
S104	**18 Stuiver** 1574.	—	—	—
S105	**20 Stuiver** 1574. Crowned lion with Liberty hat on lance. Legend: *HAEC LIBERTATIS ERGO* (This is sustained in behalf of Liberty). Back: Legend: *GODT BEHOEDE LEYDEN.* (May God Protect Leyden). 37mm.	—	—	—

		Good	Fine	XF
S106	**20 Stuiver** 1574. Crowned lion with standard. Back: Legend: *GOD BEHOEDE LEYDEN* (May God protect Leyden) around city arms.			
	a. Without countermark.	—	—	—
	b. With countermark.	—	—	—

		Good	Fine	XF
S107	**28 Stuiver** 1574. Lion with shield and sword. Back: Legend: *GOTT BEHOEDE LEYDEN* within wreath border.	—	—	—

S108	30 Stuiver	Good	Fine	XF
	1574. Lion with sword and shield, crown above. Legend: *HAEC LIBERTATIS ERG.* Back: Legend: *GOTT BEHOEDE LEYDEN* above city arms.			
	a. Without countermark.	—	—	—
	b. With countermark.	—	—	—

Occupation of Germany, Post - WWII

Ministerie van Oorlog

ND Issues

		VG	VF	UNC
M1	**1 Gulden** ND. Brown. Like #M3.	75.00	150.	300.
M2	**5 Gulden** ND. Green. Like #M3.	100.	200.	400.

		VG	VF	UNC
M3	**25 Gulden** ND. Violet.	125.	275.	500.

Netherlands Indies (now Indonesia) comprised Sumatra and adjacent islands, Java with Madura, Borneo (except for Sabah, Sarawak and Brunei), Celebes with Sangir and Talaud Islands, and the Moluccas and Lesser Sunda Islands east of Java (excepting the Portuguese half of Timor and the Portuguese enclave of Oe-Cusse). Netherlands New Guinea (now Irian Jaya) was ceded to Indonesia in 1962. The Dutch colonial holdings formed an archipelago of more than 13,667 islands spread across 3,000 miles (4,824 km.) in southeast Asia. The area is rich in oil, rubber, timber and tin.

Portuguese traders established posts in the East Indies in the 16th century, but they were soon outnumbered by the Dutch VOC (United East India Company) who arrived in 1602 and gradually established themselves as the dominant colonial power. Dutch dominance, interrupted by British incursions during the Napoleonic Wars, established the Netherlands Indies as one of the richest colonial possessions in the world.

One day after the Japanese attack on Pearl Harbor the Netherlands declared war against Japan and therefore a state of war existed between Japan and the Dutch East Indies. The main islands of the archipelago were taken by the Japanese during the first three months of 1942; on March 8, 1942 the Royal Netherlands Indies Army surrendered in Kalidjati (between Jakarta and Bandung on Java island). The Japanese placed Sumatra and former British Malaya (including Singapore) under the administration of the 25th army, Java and Madura under the 16th army and the rest of Indonesia, including Borneo and Sulawesi (Celebes), under the administration of the Japanese navy. The 1942 series was placed in circulation immediately after the conquest of Borneo. Initially the notes were printed in Japan, later they were printed locally.

From September 1944 the 1942 series was replaced by a set in the Indonesian (and Japanese) language instead of Dutch as the Japanese wanted to support the growing nationalist movement in Indonesia in this way as well.

The 100 and 1000 rupiah which are similar to Malayan notes issued in 1942 (#M8-9 and 10) are believed to have been issued in Sumatra only; the 1000 rupiah never reached normal circulation at all (see #126 and 127).

The Japanese surrendered on August 15, 1945 (effective for Java and Sumatra on September 12) and the Republic of Indonesia was proclaimed on August 17, 1945. During 1946-1949 (the first Dutch troops returned to Java March 6, 1946) the struggle for independence by the Indonesian nationalists against the Dutch caused monetary chaos (see also the Indonesia section in Volume One of this catalog) and the Japanese invasion money remained valid in both the Dutch and Indonesian nationalist-controlled areas as late as 1948 and 1949 at different rates to the Netherlands Indies gulden and the Indonesian rupiah.

RULERS:

United East India Company, 1602-1799
Batavian Republic, 1799-1806
Louis Napoleon, King of Holland, 1806-1811
British Administration, 1811-1816
Kingdom of the Netherlands, 1816-1942
Dutch to 1949

MONETARY SYSTEM:

1 Gulden = 100 Cent
1 Roepiah (1943-45) = 100 Sen
Dutch:
1 Rijksdaalder = 48 Stuivers = 0.60 Ducatoon
1 Gulden = 120 Duits = 100 Cents 1854-
British:
1 Spanish Dollar = 66 Stuivers
1 Java Rupee = 30 Stuivers

Dutch Administration

Verenigde Oostindische Compagnie

United East India Company

1703 Credit Letter Issues

		VG	VF	UNC
S50	**5 Rijksdaalders** 15.10.1783. Rare.	—	—	—
S51	**10 Rijksdaalders** 15.10.1783. Rare.	—	—	—
S52	**15 Rijksdaalders** 15.10.1783. Rare.	—	—	—
S53	**20 Rijksdaalders** 15.10.1783. Rare.	—	—	—
S54	**50 Rijksdaalders** 15.10.1783. Rare.	—	—	—

1704 Credit Letter Issues

		VG	VF	UNC
S55	**15 Rijksdaalders** 1784. Paper: Blue. Rare.	—	—	—

1795 Credit Letter Issues

		VG	VF	UNC
S56	**1 Rijksdaalder** 26.4.1796. Rare.	—	—	—
S57	**5 Rijksdaalders** 29.12.1795. Rare.	—	—	—
S58	**10 Rijksdaalders** 29.12.1795. Rare.	—	—	—
S59	**15 Rijksdaalders** 29.12.1795. Rare.	—	—	—

1796 Credit Letter Issues

		VG	VF	UNC
S60	**1 Rijksdaalder** 2.4.1799. Rare.	—	—	—
S61	**5 Rijksdaalders** 2.4.1799. Rare.	—	—	—
S62	**15 Rijksdaalders** 2.4.1799. Rare.	—	—	—

1782 Batavia Issue

	VG	VF	UNC
S101 25 Rijksdaalders 27.12.1782. Dutch and Malay-Arabic text. Paper: Brown ribbed. Rare.	—	—	—
S102 50 Rijksdaalders 27.12.1782. Dutch and Malay-Arabic text. Paper: Brown ribbed. Rare.	—	—	—
S103 100 Rijksdaalders 27.12.1782. Dutch and Malay-Arabic text. Paper: Brown ribbed. Rare.	—	—	—
S104 200 Rijksdaalders 27.12.1782. Dutch and Malay-Arabic text. Paper: Brown ribbed. Rare.	—	—	—
S105 300 Rijksdaalders 27.12.1782. Dutch and Malay-Arabic text. Paper: Brown ribbed. Rare.	—	—	—
S106 400 Rijksdaalders 27.12.1782. Dutch and Malay-Arabic text. Paper: Brown ribbed. Rare.	—	—	—
S107 500 Rijksdaalders 27.12.1782. Dutch and Malay-Arabic text. Paper: Brown ribbed. Rare.	—	—	—
S108 1000 Rijksdaalders 27.12.1782. Dutch and Malay-Arabic text. Paper: Brown ribbed. Rare.	—	—	—

Former #S111-S120 have been re-listed as S126-S135.

1805 Amboina Issue

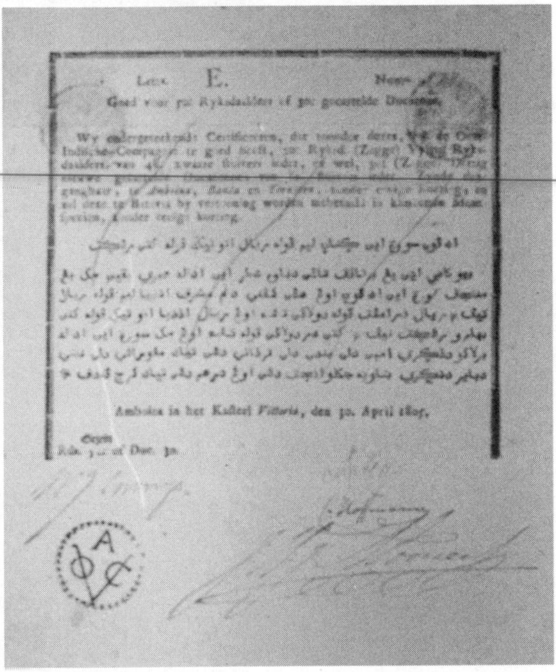

	VG	VF	UNC
S120 50 Rijksdaalders 30.4.1805. Rare.	—	—	—

	VG	VF	UNC
S121 100 Rijksdaalders 30.4.1805. Rare.	—	—	—
S122 100 Rijksdaalders Handwritten text and value. Rare.	—	—	—
S123 200 Rijksdaalders 30.4.1805. Rare.	—	—	—
S124 500 Rijksdaalders 30.4.1805. Rare.	—	—	—
S125 1000 Rijksdaalders 30.4.1805. Rare.	—	—	—

1809 Amboina Issue

	VG	VF	UNC
S126 5 Rijksdaalders 29.3.1809 (- old date 27.7.1808). Rare.	—	—	—
S127 10 Rijksdaalders 29.3.1809 (- old date 27.7.1808). Rare.	—	—	—

1805 Amboina Issue

	VG	VF	UNC
S128 20 Rijksdaalders 29.3.1809 (- old date 27.7.1808). Rare.	—	—	—

Gouvernement General

1807-09 Issue

	Good	Fine	XF
S129 2 Rijksdaalders 13.3.1809.	175.	525.	1575.
S130 5 Rijksdaalders 27.3.1807. Rare.	—	—	—

1811 Lentemmand Issue

	VG	VF	UNC
S131 2 Rijksdaalders 1811. Hand stamp: *V.E.I.C.* in bale mark. Rare.	—	—	—
S132 3 Rijksdaalders 1811. Hand stamp: *V.E.I.C.* in bale mark. Rare.	—	—	—
S133 5 Rijksdaalders 1811. Hand stamp: *V.E.I.C.* in bale mark. Rare.	—	—	—
S134 10 Rijksdaalders 1811. Rare.	—	—	—
S135 15 Rijksdaalders 1811. Rare.	—	—	—

Batavian Republic

Bataviaasch Bank Van Leening

Batavian Bank of Loan

1803 Mortgage Letters Issue

	VG	VF	UNC
S139 15 Rijksdaalders 1803. Java issue.	—	—	—

#S136-S140 are deleted, as they have been determined to be the same as #S121-S125.

Kingdom of Holland and French Empire

Government

1807-11 Provisional Issue

#S140A-S143 w/various dates: Batavian, 1807-11; Amboina, 1808-09; Banda, 1808; Ternaten, 1808-09. Circular hand stamp: *LN* monogram.

	VG	VF	UNC
S140A 1/2 Rijksdaalder 1807-11. Circular hand stamp: *LN* monogram. Rare.	—	—	—
S141 1 Rijksdaalder 1807-11. Circular hand stamp: *LN* monogram. Rare.	—	—	—
S142 2 Rijksdaalders 1807-11. Circular hand stamp: *LN* monogram. Rare.	—	—	—
S143 3 Rijksdaalders 1807-11. Circular hand stamp: *LN* monogram. Rare.	—	—	—

British Administration

Government

1812 Issue

	VG	VF	UNC
S146 1 Spanish Dollar 1.5.1812.	—	—	—
S147 2 Spanish Dollars 1.5.1812.	—	—	—
S148 3 Spanish Dollars 1.5.1812.	—	—	—

1814 Issue

	VG	VF	UNC
S149 5 Java Rupees Oct. 1814. Lombard Bank.	—	—	—
S150 15 Java Rupees 7.4.1814.	—	—	—

Note: For previously listed #S151-S166 refer to Volume II.

Regional - French Influence

Government

1810 Issue

#S171-S176 Circular hand stamp: *LN* monogram *1810* on face and back. Uniface.

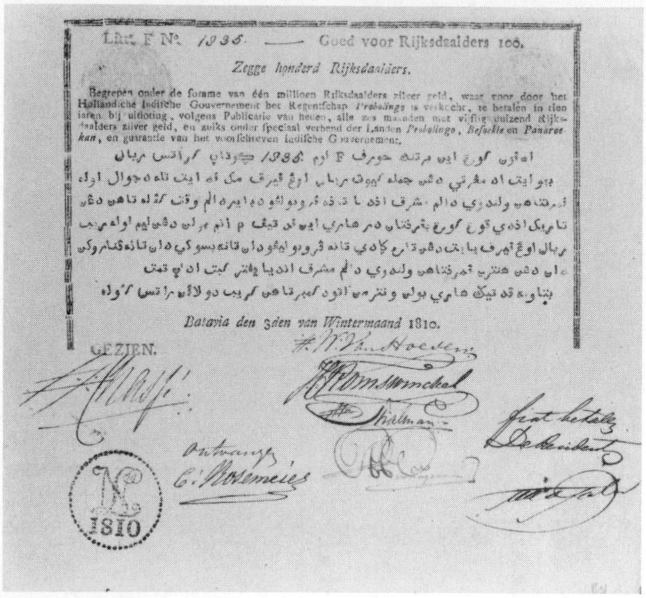

	VG	VF	UNC
S171 100 Rijksdaalders 1810. Dutch text on upper part, Malay-Arabic text on lower part. Circular hand stamp: *LN* monogram *1810*. Back: Circular hand stamp: *LN* monogram *1810*. Rare.	—	—	—
S172 200 Rijksdaalders 1810. Dutch text on upper part, Malay-Arabic text on lower part. Circular hand stamp: *LN* monogram *1810*. Back: Circular hand stamp: *LN* monogram *1810*. Rare.	—	—	—
S173 300 Rijksdaalders 1810. Dutch text on upper part, Malay-Arabic text on lower part. Circular hand stamp: *LN* monogram *1810*. Back: Circular hand stamp: *LN* monogram *1810*. Rare.	—	—	—
S174 400 Rijksdaalders 1810. Dutch text on upper part, Malay-Arabic text on lower part. Circular hand stamp: *LN* monogram *1810*. Back: Circular hand stamp: *LN* monogram *1810*. Rare.	—	—	—
S175 500 Rijksdaalders 1810. Dutch text on upper part, Malay-Arabic text on lower part. Circular hand stamp: *LN* monogram *1810*. Back: Circular hand stamp: *LN* monogram *1810*. Rare.	—	—	—

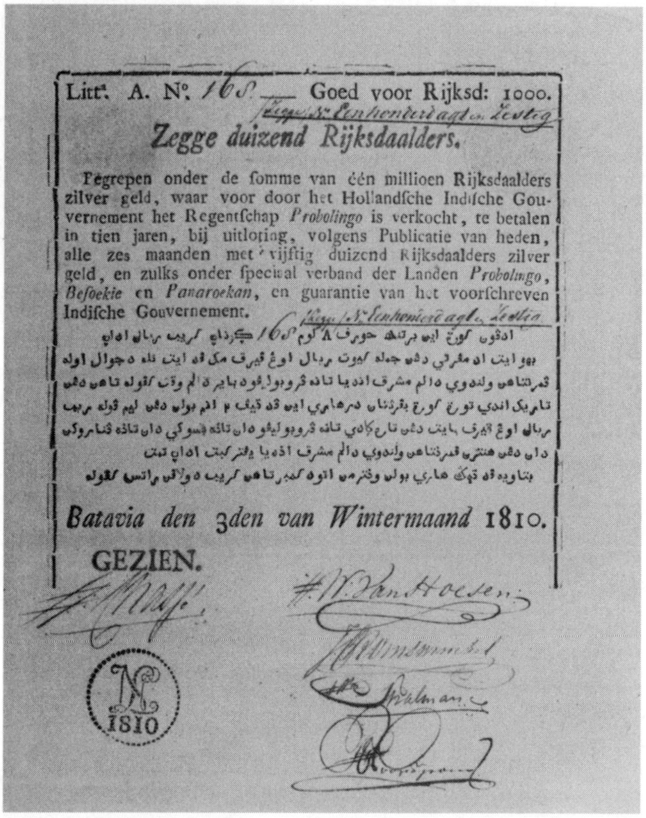

	VG	VF	UNC
S176 1000 Rijksdaalders 1810. Dutch text on upper part, Malay-Arabic text on lower part. Circular hand stamp: *LN* monogram *1810*. Back: Circular hand stamp: *LN* monogram *1810*. Rare.	—	—	—

NEWFOUNDLAND

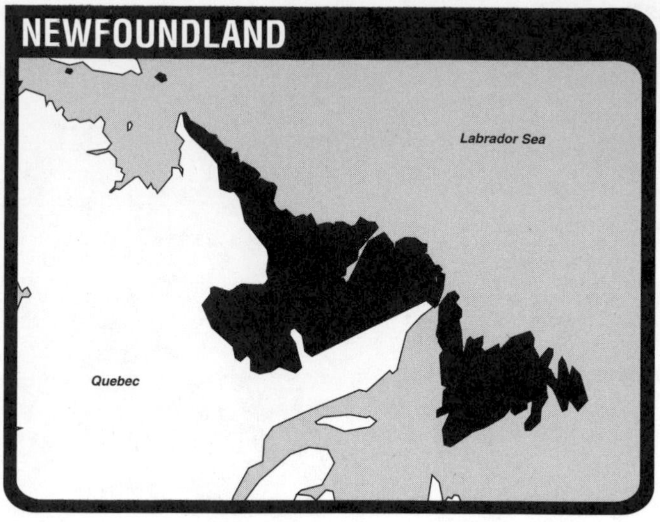

John Cabot, who visited Newfoundland in 1497, is given the title of discoverer although it is likely that Vikings visited its shore on their various trips to the west. Early settlement efforts were made by the British involving such men as Sir Humphrey Gilbert, John Guy and Sir George Calvert. There was much dispute between the French and the British for the island and its fishing rights. Awarded to England by the Treaty of Utrecht of 1713. Granted first governor in 1728. Adequate local government did not develop until the mid 1800s. Made a British colony in 1934 and became a province of Canada (along with Labrador) in 1949.

RULERS:

British

MONETARY SYSTEM:

1 Pound = 4 Dollars = 20 Shillings
1 Dollar = 100 Cents

Chartered Banks

Commercial Bank of Newfoundland

1857-58 Issue

	Good	Fine	XF
S101 1 Pound 25.8.1857; 20.10.1858. Black. Seated Commerce at center. Uniface. Printer: PBC.			
a. Issued note.	1500.	4500.	—
p. Proof. 18xx.	—	Unc	1000.
S102 5 Pounds 18xx. Black. Seated Commerce at center. Uniface. Printer: PBC. Proof.	—	Unc	1000.
S103 10 Pounds 18xx. Black. Seated Commerce at center. Uniface. Printer: PBC. Proof.	—	Unc	1000.
S104 20 Pounds 18xx. Black. Seated Commerce at center. Uniface. Printer: PBC. Proof.	—	Unc	1000.

1865-67 Issue

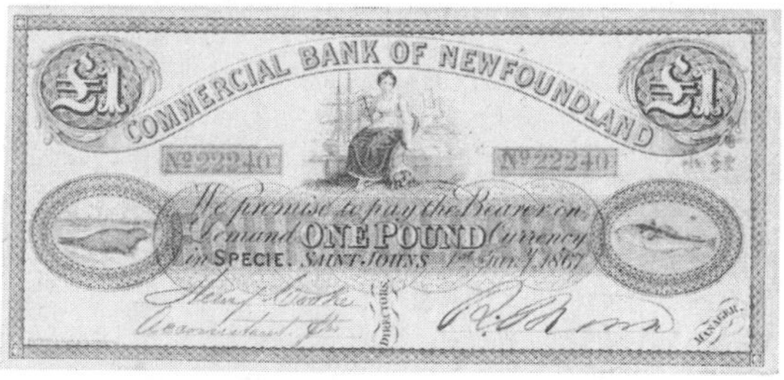

	Good	Fine	XF
S106 1 Pound/4 Dollars 1.1.1867. Black on blue underprint. Seal in oval at left, seated Commerce at center, codfish in oval at right. 2 signature spaces at left. Printer: PBC.	750.	2250.	—
S107 5 Pounds/20 Dollars 1.1.1867. Black on red-brown underprint. Seal in oval at left, seated Commerce at center, codfish in oval at right. 2 signature spaces at left. Printer: PBC.	750.	2250.	—

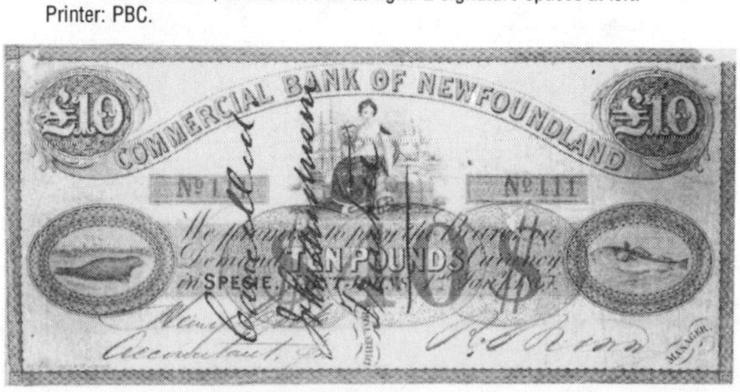

	Good	Fine	XF
S108 10 Pounds/40 Dollars 1865; 1.1.1867. Black on green underprint. Seal in oval at left, seated Commerce at center, codfish in oval at right. 2 signature spaces at left. Printer: PBC.	1200.	3600.	—

1874 Issue

S109 1 Pound/4 Dollars	Good	Fine	XF
1874-84. Black on blue underprint. Seal in oval at left, seated Commerce at center, codfish in oval at right. 1 signature space at left. Like #S106.			
a. 1.1.1874; 1.3.1882.	750.	2250.	—
b. 1.7.1884.	675.	2000.	—

S110 5 Pounds/20 Dollars			
1874; 1885. Black on red-brown underprint. Seal in oval at left, seated Commerce at center, codfish in oval at right. 1 signature space at left. Like #S107, but different guilloche at center.			
a. 1.1.1874.	675.	2000.	—
p. Proof. 1.7.1885.	—	Unc	1000.

1881 Issue

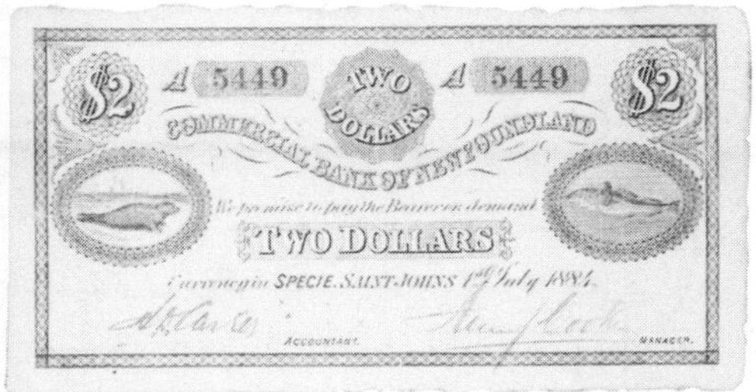

S111 2 Dollars	Good	Fine	XF
1881-84. Black. Seal at left, codfish at right. Back: Blue. Printer: PBC.			
a. 1.1.1881; 1882.	600.	1800.	—
b. 1.7.1884.	525.	1575.	—

1888 Issue

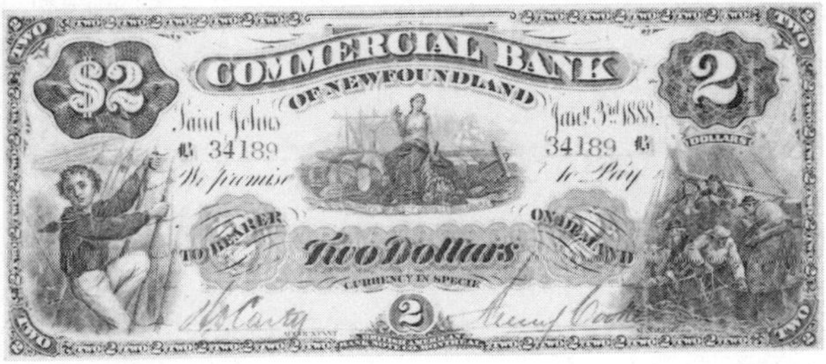

S112 2 Dollars	VG	VF	UNC
3.1.1888. Black on orange underprint. Seated Commerce at top center. Sailor at lower left, fisherman at lower right. Back: Green. Printer: BABNC.	175.	525.	—

S113 2 Dollars			
3.1.1888. Black on green underprint. Seated Commerce at top center. Sailor at lower left, fisherman at lower right. Like #S112. Back: Green. Printer: BABNC.	375.	1250.	—

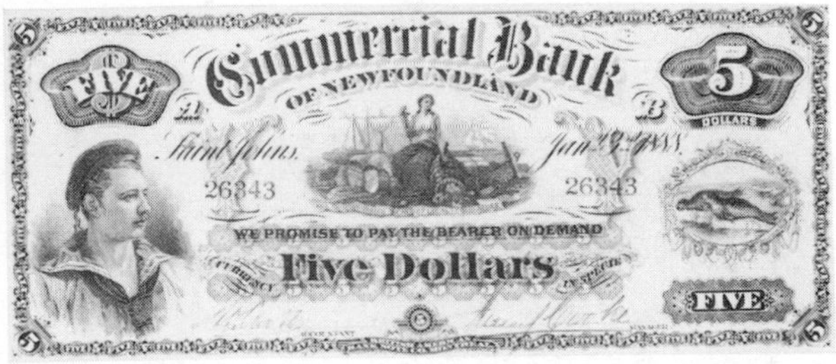

S114 5 Dollars	VG	VF	UNC
3.1.1888. Black on green underprint. Seated Commerce at top center. Sailor at lower left, seals at right. Back: Green. Printer: BABNC.	175.	525.	—

S115 10 Dollars	VG	VF	UNC
3.1.1888. Black on green underprint. Seated Commerce at top center. Portrait Queen Victoria at lower left, sailor at lower right. Back: Green. Printer: BABNC.			
a. Issued note.	525.	1575.	—
b. Redemption overprint: *2 DOLLARS.*	—	—	—

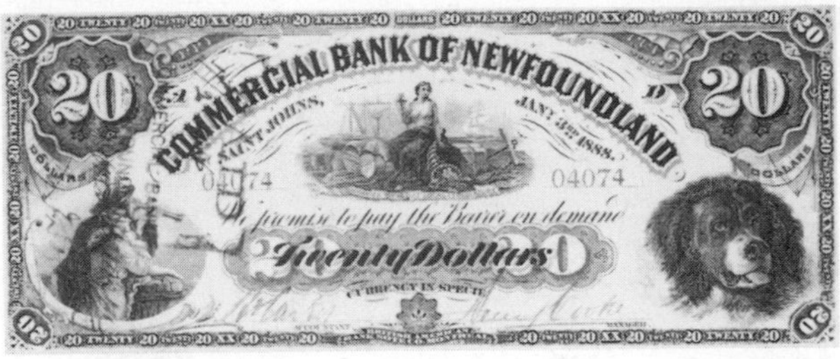

S116 20 Dollars	VG	VF	UNC
3.1.1888. Black on green underprint. Seated Commerce at top center. Man, woman and telescope at lower left, dog's head at lower right. Back: Green. Printer: BABNC.	900.	2700.	—

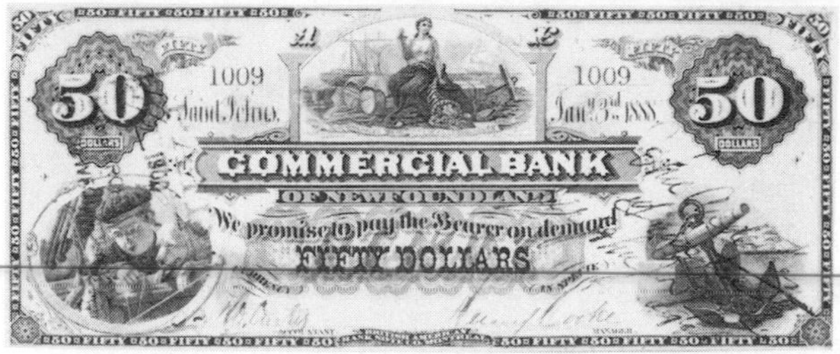

S117 50 Dollars	Good	Fine	XF
3.1.1888. Black on green underprint. Seated Commerce at top center. Boy and dog at lower left, anchor at lower right. Back: Green. Printer: BABNC. Rare.	—	—	—

Union Bank of Newfoundland

1854 Issue

S118 1 Pound	Good	Fine	XF
1854-55. Black. Sailing ship at upper center. Printer: PBC.			
a. Red word protector. Back red. 18.5.1854.	1750.	5250.	—
b. Green word protector. Back green. 1.3.1855.	1750.	5250.	—

S118A 2 Pounds			
18xx. Black. Sailing ship at upper center. Printer: PBC. Proof.	—	Unc	750.

S119 5 Pounds	VG	VF	UNC
18xx. Black. Sailing ship at upper center. Overprint: *SPECIMEN.* Printer: PBC. Proof.	—	Unc	750.

S120 10 Pounds			
18xx. Black. Sailing ship at upper center. Overprint: *SPECIMEN.* Printer: PBC. Proof.	—	Unc	750.

1865 Issue

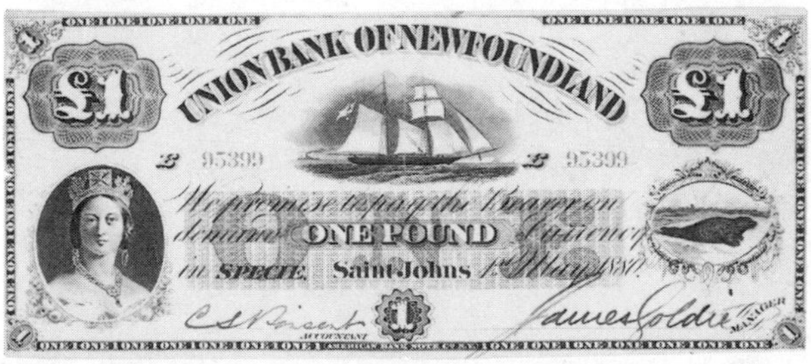

S121 1 Pound	VG	VF	UNC
1865-80. Black on green underprint. Portrait Queen Victoria at lower left, sailing ship "*Fishing Smack*" at upper center. Seal at right. Uniface. Printer: ABNC.			
a. Partially engraved date. 1.5.1865.	900.	2700.	—
b. Fully engraved date. 1.3.1867; 1.9.1877.	750.	2250.	—
c. 1.5.1880.	525.	1550.	4500.

	VG	VF	UNC
S122 5 Pounds 1865-83. Brown on blue underprint. Portrait Queen Victoria at lower left, sailing ship "*Fishing Smack*" at upper center. Similar to #S121, but codfish at right. Uniface. Printer: ABNC.			
a. Partially engraved date. 2.10.1865; 3.4.1876; 1.10.1881.	1350.	3000.	—
b. Fully engraved date. 1.8.1883.	1100.	3300.	—

NOTE: #S122 is sometimes encountered with handstamped guarantee of $16.

S123 10 Pounds 2.10.1865; 3.4.1876; 1.10.1881. Blue on red underprint. Portrait Queen Victoria at lower left, sailing ship "*Fishing Smack*" at upper center. Codfish at right. Similar to #S122. Uniface. Partially engraved date. Printer: ABNC. Rare.	—	—	—

NOTE: #S123 is sometimes encountered with handstamped guarantee of $32.

1882; 1889 Issue

	VG	VF	UNC
S124 2 Dollars 1.5.1882. Black on green underprint. Codfish at lower left, portrait J. Smith at center, dog and safe at lower right. Back: Green. Printer: ABNC.	400.	1200.	3600.

	VG	VF	UNC
S125 5 Dollars 1.5.1889. Black on green and yellow underprint. Sailing ship at left, steamship at center right. Back: Green. Cattle in pond at center. Printer: ABNC.	650.	2000.	6000.

	VG	VF	UNC
S126 10 Dollars 1.5.1889. Black on orange and yellow underprint. Dog's head at lower left, sailing ship *Sealing* at center, sailors at right. Back: Orange. Woman and safe at center. Printer: ABNC.	600.	1800.	5400.

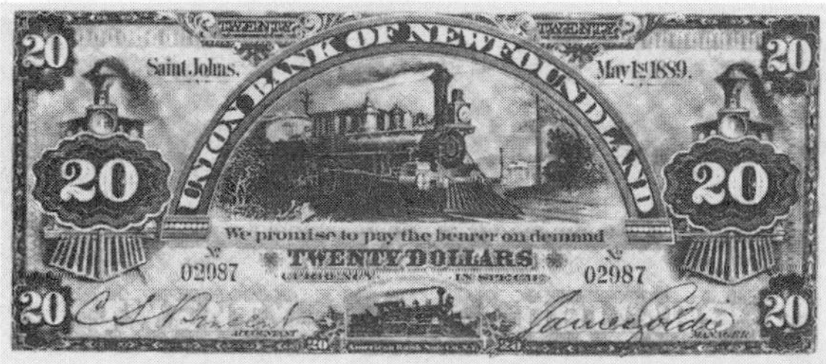

	VG	VF	UNC
S127 20 Dollars 1.5.1889. Black on blue and yellow underprint. Steam locomotive at left and right with value superimposed, steam locomotive at center. Back: Blue. Steam locomotive at center. Printer: ABNC.	650.	2000.	6000.
S128 50 Dollars 1.5.1889. Black on brown and yellow underprint. Allegorical woman at left and right, bank at center. Back: Brown. Dog by safe at center. Printer: ABNC. Rare.	—	—	—

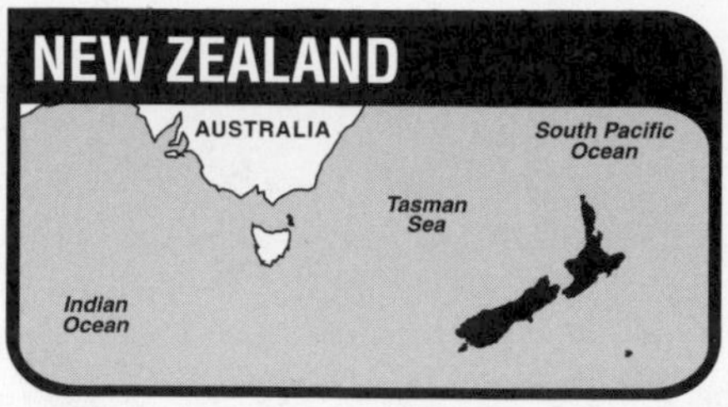

New Zealand, a parliamentary state located in the southwestern Pacific 1,250 miles (2,011 km.) east of Australia, has an area of 103,736 sq. mi. (269,056 sq. km.) and a population of 3.8 million. Capital: Wellington. Wool, meat, dairy products and some manufactured items are exported.

The Polynesian Maori reached New Zealand in about A.D. 800. In 1840, their chieftains entered into a compact with Britain, the Treaty of Waitangi, in which they ceded sovereignty to Queen Victoria while retaining territorial rights. In that same year, the British began the first organized colonial settlement. A series of land wars between 1843 and 1872 ended with the defeat of the native peoples. The British colony of New Zealand became an independent dominion in 1907 and supported the UK militarily in both World Wars. New Zealand's full participation in a number of defense alliances lapsed by the 1980s. In recent years, the government has sought to address longstanding Maori grievances.

RULERS:

British

MONETARY SYSTEM:

1 Shilling = 12 Pence
1 Pound = 20 Shillings (also 2 Dollars) to 1967
1 Dollar = 100 Cents, 1967-

BANKS:

Bank of Aotearoa, ca.1880 .... #S101
Bank of Auckland, 1864-67 .... #S106-S108
Bank of Australasia, 1863-1934 .... #S111-S136
Bank of New South Wales, 1861-1934 .... #S139-S165
Bank of New Zealand, 1861-1934 .... #S171-S240
Bank of Otago Ltd., 1863-74 .... #S241-S243
Colonial Bank of Issue, 1850-56 .... #S246-S247
Colonial Bank of New Zealand, 1874-95 .... #S251-S270
Commercial Bank of Australia, 1912-34 .... #S270A-S286
Commercial Bank of New Zealand Limited, 1865-66 .... #S288-S290
National Bank of New Zealand, 1873-1934 .... #S291-S321
New Zealand Banking Company, 1840-45 .... #S326-S327
New Zealand Banking Corporation, Ltd., 1863-66 .... #S331
Oriental Bank Corporation, 1857-61 .... #S333-S335A
Otago Banking Company, 1851 .... #S336-S338
Union Bank of Australia, 1840-1934 .... #S341-S376
Union Bank of Australia Limited, 1905-23 .... #S361-S376

OFFICES OF ISSUE:

(a) - not named .... (i) - Nelson
(b) - Auckland, Auckland & Wellington .... (j) - Picton
(c) - Christchurch .... (k) - Sydney
(e) - Dunedin .... (l) - Wanganui
(f) - Invercargill .... (m) - Wellington
(g) - Lyttelton .... (y) - Auckland, Wanganui & Dunedin
(h) - Napier, Napier or Wellington .... (z) - Unknown

British Administration

Bank of Aotearoa

1894 Issue

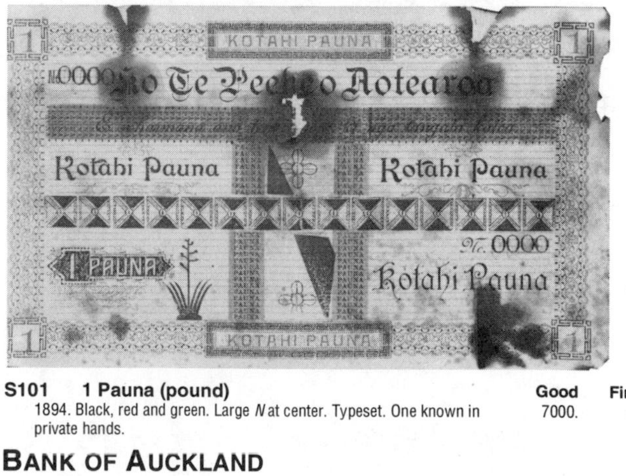

	Good	Fine	XF
S101 1 Pauna (pound) 1894. Black, red and green. Large *N* at center. Typeset. One known in private hands.	7000.	—	—

Bank of Auckland

1864 Issue

	Good	Fine	XF
S104 1 Pound 1.3.1865. Black. Bank name at top. Rare.	—	—	—

1865 Issue

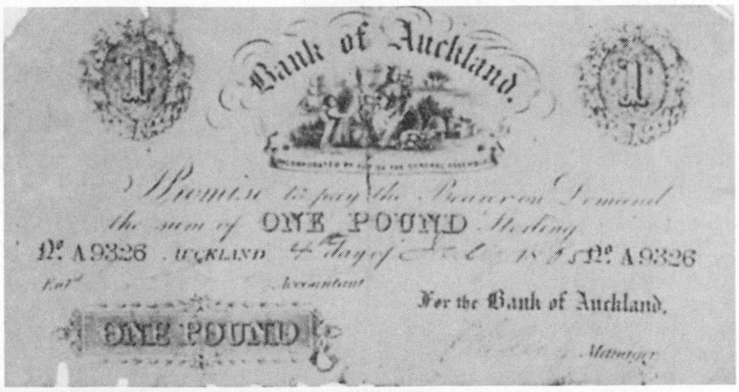

	Good	Fine	XF
S106 1 Pound 4.7.1865; 17.8.1866. Black. Seated woman with symbols of commerce at upper center, ships in background. Printer: CS&E. Rare.	10,000.	—	—

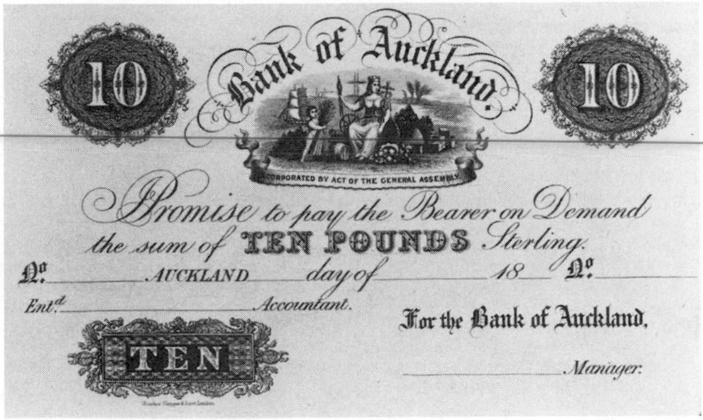

	Good	Fine	XF
S108 10 Pounds ND. Black. Seated woman with symbols of commerce at upper center, ships in background. Similar to #S106.			
p1. Back orange. Proof.	—	Unc	1250.
p2. Back black. Proof.	—	Unc	1250.

Bank of Australasia

1863-79 Issue

#S111-S115 Promissory text varies according to office of issue.

	Good	Fine	XF
S111 1 Pound (ca.1863-86). Black on green center. Two seated women at upper center, arms at upper left. Value numeral in inner guilloche at upper right. Designs in all corner guilloches. Uniface. Printer: PBC.			
b. Auckland. 14.7.1863.	—	—	—
c. Christchurch. 13.10.1868; 13.12.1873; 13.7.1875.	—	—	—
e. Dunedin. 11.10.18xx (ca.1867).	—	—	—
m. Wellington. 13.4.1874.	—	—	—
S112 5 Pounds (ca.1864-86). Black on green center. Two seated women at upper center, arms at upper left. Value numeral in inner guilloche at upper right. Designs in all corner guilloches. Uniface. Printer: PBC.			
c. Christchurch. 13.6.1870; 13.12.1870.	—	—	—
e. Dunedin. 11.10.1864.	—	—	—
S113 10 Pounds (ca.1863-86). Black on green center. Two seated women at upper center, arms at upper left. Value numeral in inner guilloche at upper right. Designs in all corner guilloches. Uniface. Printer: PBC.			
b. Auckland. ND (ca.1867).	—	—	—
c. Christchurch. ND (ca.1863).	—	—	—
e. Dunedin. ND (ca.1867).	—	—	—
h. Napier or Wellington. 6.1875.	—	—	—

	Good	Fine	XF
S114 20 Pounds (ca.1863-76). Black on green center. Two seated women at upper center, arms at upper left. Value numeral in inner guilloche at upper right. Designs in all corner guilloches. Uniface. Printer: PBC.			
c. Christchurch. ND.	—	—	—
h. Napier. ND.	—	—	—
S115 50 Pounds (ca.1863-76). Black on green center. Two seated women at upper center, arms at upper left. Value numeral in inner guilloche at upper right. Designs in all corner guilloches. Uniface. Printer: PBC.	—	—	—

1874 Issue

	Good	Fine	XF
S115A 1 Pound 1.6.1874. Black. Arms at center. Uniface.	—	—	—

1885-1923 Issue

	Good	Fine	XF
S116 10 Shillings 1.6.1918-2.6.1923. Orange on blue underprint. Wellington.	—	—	—

#S117-S121 similar to above, but value spelled out in inner guilloche at upper right. Value numeral in each corner guilloche. Uniface.

	Good	Fine	XF
S117 1 Pound 1885-1923. Black on purple and green underprint. Arms in upper left guilloche. Value spelled out in inner guilloche at upper right. Value numeral in each corner guilloche. Uniface.			
m. Wellington. 2.1.1911-1923.	—	—	—
z. Office of issue unknown. 1907; 1.7.1915.	—	—	—

	Good	Fine	XF
S118 5 Pounds 1907-21. Black on blue and orange underprint. Value spelled out in inner guilloche at upper right. Value numeral in each corner guilloche. Uniface.			
m. Wellington. 5.2.1917-5.8.1921.	—	—	—
z. Office of issue unknown. 1907.	—	—	—

		Good	Fine	XF
S119	**10 Pounds** 1902-21. Black on brown and blue underprint. Value spelled out in inner guilloche at upper right. Value numeral in each corner guilloche. Uniface.			
	c. Christchurch. 13.9.1902.	—	—	—
	m. Wellington. 13.9.1912-14.3.1921.	—	—	—
	z. Office of issue unknown. 1906.	—	—	—
S120	**20 Pounds** (ca.1877-1923). Value spelled out in inner guilloche at upper right. Value numeral in each corner guilloche. Uniface.	—	—	—
S121	**50 Pounds** 1888-1921. Black on red and brown underprint. Value spelled out in inner guilloche at upper right. Value numeral in each corner guilloche. Uniface.			
	c. Christchurch. 17.10.1890; 18.4.1898; 18.4.1904. Rare.	—	—	—
	e. Dunedin. 17.4.1906. Rare.	—	—	—
	m. Wellington. 17.10.1888; 17.4.1913; 18.10.1921. Rare.	—	—	—
	z. Office of issue unknown. 1903.	—	—	—

1923-32 Issues

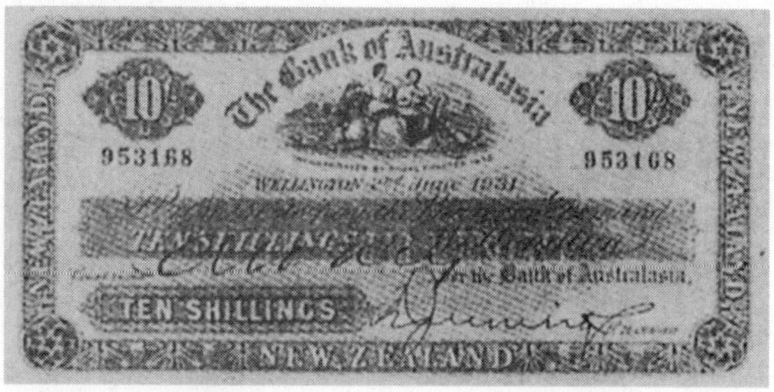

		Good	Fine	XF
S131	**10 Shillings** 1924-2.6.1931. Orange on blue underprint. Printer: PBC.	250.	750.	2250.

		Good	Fine	XF
S132	**1 Pound** 1.7.1923-1.7.1931. Black on purple and green underprint. Value spelled out in inner guilloche at upper right. Value numeral in each corner guilloche. Serial # varieties. Printer: PBC.	250.	750.	2250.
S133	**1 Pound** 19.7.1932. Black on purple and green underprint. Value spelled out in inner guilloche at upper right. Value numeral in each corner guilloche. Similar to #S132. Printer: TDLR.	250.	750.	2250.

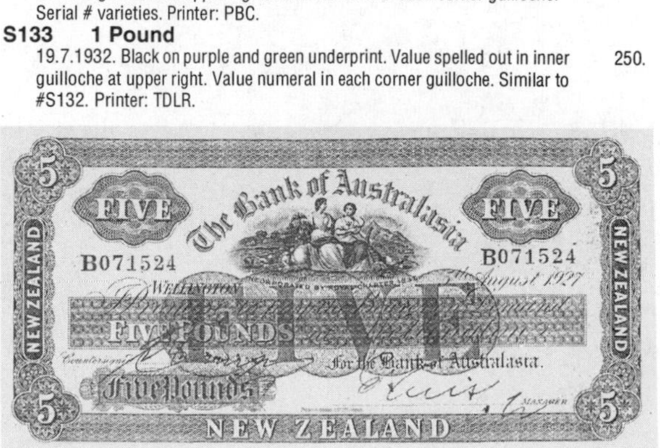

		Good	Fine	XF
S134	**5 Pounds** 5.2.1925-1931. Black on blue and orange underprint. Value spelled out in inner guilloche at upper right. Value numeral in each corner guilloche. Printer: PBC.	300.	900.	2700.
S135	**10 Pounds** 12.3.1927; 10.9.1927. Black on brown and blue underprint. Value spelled out in inner guilloche at upper right. Value numeral in each corner guilloche. Printer: PBC.	375.	1100.	3300.
S136	**50 Pounds** (ca.1923-24). Black on red and green underprint. Value spelled out in inner guilloche at upper right. Value numeral in each corner guilloche. Printer: PBC.	600.	1800.	—

Bank of New South Wales

1840s Issue

		Good	Fine	XF
S139	**1 Pound** 24.10.1844. Black. Seated figure at center.	—	—	—

1861; 1862 Issue

		Good	Fine	XF
S141	**1 Pound** 30.7.1861; 1.6.1866; 15.5.1867. Gray and black. Profile of Queen Victoria at upper left, seated Commerce at upper center, ships in background. Printer: CS&E.	—	—	—
S142	**5 Pounds** 30.7.1861. Blue. Profile of Queen Victoria at upper left, seated Commerce at upper center, ships in background. Printer: CS&E.	—	—	—
S143	**10 Pounds** 30.7.1861. Brown. Profile of Queen Victoria at upper left, seated Commerce at upper center, ships in background. Printer: CS&E.	—	—	—
S144	**20 Pounds** 1.10.1862. Light green. Profile of Queen Victoria at upper left, seated Commerce at upper center, ships in background. Printer: CS&E.	—	—	—

1870 Issue

		Good	Fine	XF
S146	**1 Pound** (ca.1870-90). Black. Seated Commerce at upper center, ships in background. *NEW ZEALAND* at upper and lower borders. Back: Red.			
	b. Auckland. 18xx.	—	—	—
	c. Christchurch. 18xx.	—	—	—
	e. Dunedin. 18xx.	—	—	—
	i. Nelson. 18xx.	—	—	—
	l. Wanganui. 18xx.	—	—	—
	m. Wellington. 18xx.	—	—	—

		Good	Fine	XF
S147	**5 Pounds** (ca.1870-90). Blue. Seated Commerce at upper center, ships in background. *NEW ZEALAND* at upper and lower borders.			
	a. Office of issue not named. ND. Specimen.	—	—	—
	b. Auckland. 18xx.	—	—	—
	c. Christchurch. 18xx. Specimen.	—	—	—
	e. Dunedin. 18xx.	—	—	—
	l. Wanganui. 18xx.	—	—	—
	m. Wellington. 18xx. Specimen.	—	—	—
	y. Auckland, Wanganui and Dunedin. 18xx.	—	—	—
S148	**10 Pounds** (ca.1870-90). Brown. Seated Commerce at upper center, ships in background. *NEW ZEALAND* at upper and lower borders. Back: Red.	—	—	—
S149	**20 Pounds** (ca.1870-90). Light green. Seated Commerce at upper center, ships in background. *NEW ZEALAND* at upper and lower borders. Back: Red.			
	e. Dunedin. 18xx. Specimen.	—	Unc	1000.

1890-1922 Issues

	Good	Fine	XF
S150 5 Shillings 19xx. Seated Commerce at upper center. Bank name at top separated by vignette. Specimen.	—	—	—
S151 10 Shillings 1918. Orange and brown. Vignette of seated Commerce at upper center. *BANK OF NEW SOUTH WALES* in top and bottom margin. Value: *10/-* over *SHILLINGS* at upper left and right.	—	—	—
S152 10 Shillings 1.9.1919; 1921. Orange and brown. Vignette of seated Commerce at upper center. *BANK OF NEW SOUTH WALES* in top and bottom margin. Like #S151 but value: *TEN SHILLINGS* at upper left and right. Back: Circular designs in corners.	—	—	—

	Good	Fine	XF
S153 10 Shillings 1922. Orange and brown. Vignette of seated Commerce at upper center. *BANK OF NEW SOUTH WALES* in top and bottom margin. Similar to #S152, but bank name at top separated by vignette. Back: Oval designs in corners. Smaller size.	—	—	—

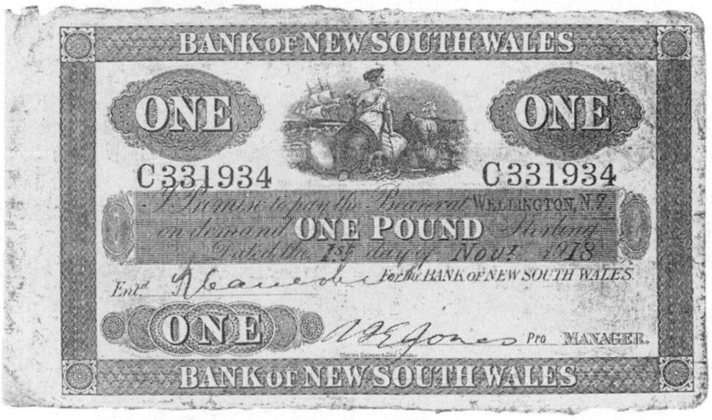

	Good	Fine	XF
S154 1 Pound (ca.1890-1923). Black. Vignette of seated Commerce at upper center. *BANK OF NEW SOUTH WALES* in top and bottom margin. Back: Red.			
a. Office of issue not named. 1.7.1915. Specimen.	—	—	—
e. Dunedin. Specimen.	—	—	—
m. Wellington. 1.5.1914; 1.2.1917; 1.11.1918.	—	—	—
z. Office of issue unknown. 1.1.1891; 1.7.1892; 1.10.1908-14.	—	—	—

NOTE: A specimen of #S154 has been reported with date 1.10.1914, and subsequent hand dates of 1.2.1915 and 1.4.1918. Office of issue unknown.

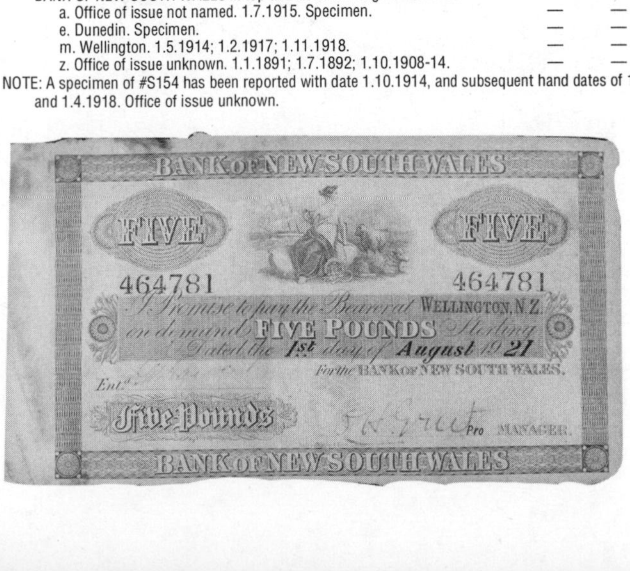

	Good	Fine	XF
S155 5 Pounds (ca.1890-1923). Black and green. Vignette of seated Commerce at upper center. *BANK OF NEW SOUTH WALES* in top and bottom margin.			
m. Wellington. 1.8.1914; 1.8.1921.	—	—	—
z. Office of issue unknown. 5.2.1921.	—	—	—

	Good	Fine	XF
S156 10 Pounds ND (ca.1890-1923). Brown. Vignette of seated Commerce at upper center. *BANK OF NEW SOUTH WALES* in top and bottom margin. Back: Red.			
a. Office of issue not named. 19xx.	—	—	—
m. Wellington. 1.4.1922.	—	—	—
z. Office of issue unknown. 1.3.1918.	—	—	—
S157 20 Pounds (ca.1890-1923). Light green. Vignette of seated Commerce at upper center. *BANK OF NEW SOUTH WALES* in top and bottom margin.			
a. Office of issue not named. 19xx. Specimen.	—	—	—
z. Office of issue unknown. 1890-1923.	—	—	—
S158 50 Pounds (ca.1914-23). Vermilion. Vignette of seated Commerce at upper center. *BANK OF NEW SOUTH WALES* in top and bottom margin.			
a. Office of issue not named. 19xx.	—	—	—
z. Office of issue unknown. 1.4.1914.	—	—	—
S159 100 Pounds (ca.1914-23). Black. Vignette of seated Commerce at upper center. *BANK OF NEW SOUTH WALES* in top and bottom margin.			
a. Office of issue not named. 19xx.	—	—	—
z. Office of issue unknown. 1.11.1914.	—	—	—

1923; 1924 Issue

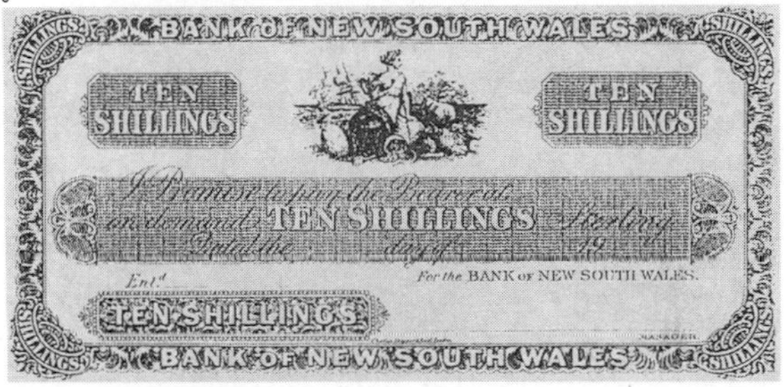

	Good	Fine	XF
S161 10 Shillings 1.1.1924-1.18.1933. Orange and brown. Bank title in full in ornate borders at top and bottom. Printer: CS&E.	—	—	—

NOTE: It is believed that the office of issue is Wellington only.

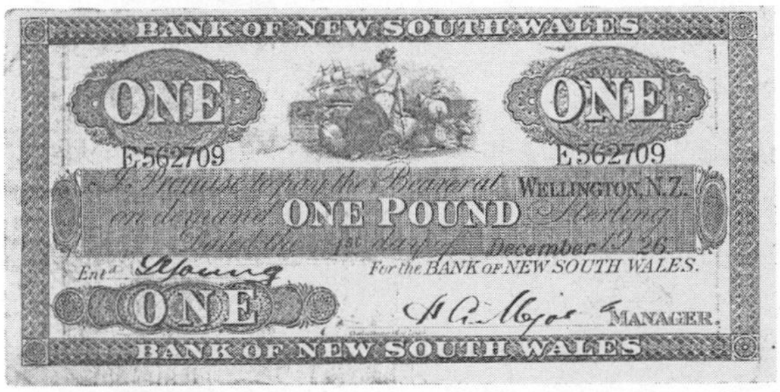

	Good	Fine	XF
S162 1 Pound 1.1.1924; 1.12.1926; 1.9.1931; 1.2.1932. Purple-brown. Bank title in full in ornate borders at top and bottom. Printer: CS&E.	—	—	—

NOTE: It is believed that the office of issue is Wellington only.

S163 5 Pounds	Good	Fine	XF
1.8.1924; 1.3.1926; 1929; 1.19.1931; 1.12.1932. Blue. Bank title in full in ornate borders at top and bottom. Back: Green. Printer: CS&E.	—	—	—

NOTE: It is believed that the office of issue is Wellington only.

S164 10 Pounds			
(ca.1923-34). Brown. Bank title in full in ornate borders at top and bottom. Printer: CS&E. Specimen.	—	—	—

NOTE: It is believed that the office of issue is Wellington only.

S165 20 Pounds			
(ca.1923-34). Light green. Bank title in full in ornate borders at top and bottom. Printer: CS&E. Specimen.	—	—	—

NOTE: It is believed that the office of issue is Wellington only.

Bank of New Zealand

1861 Emergency Issue

S171 1 Pound	Good	Fine	XF
1861. Printer: B.N.Z. Lithograph on plain paper. Dunedin office only.	—	—	—

NOTE: No examples of #S171 are presently known.

1861 Issue

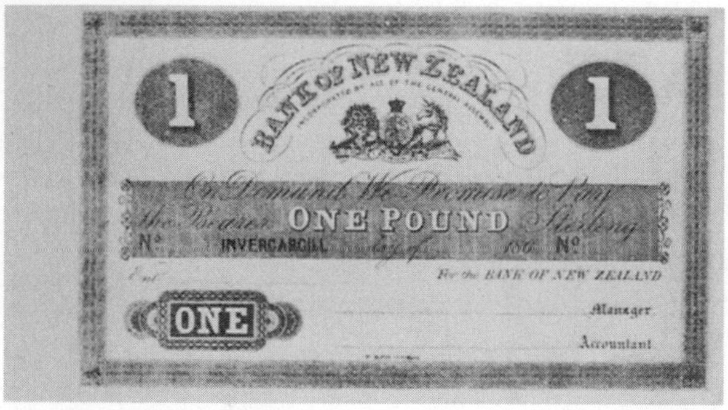

S176 1 Pound	Good	Fine	XF
186x; 1862. Black. Royal arms at top center. Uniface. Printer: W. Moffit & Co., Sydney.			
b. Auckland and Nelson.	—	—	—
f. Invercargill.	—	—	—

S177 5 Pounds	Good	Fine	XF
1861; 1862. Blue. Royal arms at top center. Uniface. Printer: W. Moffit & Co., Sydney.			
b. Auckland, Invercargill and Nelson.	—	—	—

1862 Issue

#S181-S184 Proofs exists from at least 13 domiciles: Auckland, Blenheim, Christchurch, Dundelin, Invercargill, Lyttelton, Napier, Nelson, New Plymouth, Picton, Riverton, Timaru, Wellington and Wangamui.

S181 1 Pound	Good	Fine	XF
(ca.1862-70). Brown. Printer: PBC.			
b. Auckland. 18xx. Specimen.	—	—	—
i. Nelson.	—	—	—

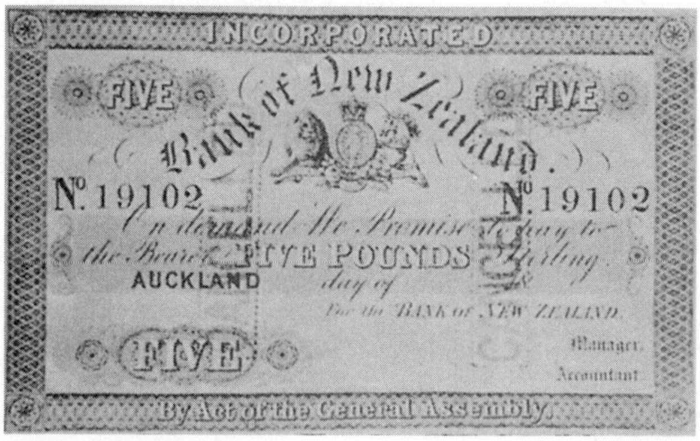

S182 5 Pounds	Good	Fine	XF
(ca.1862). Blue. Printer: PBC.			
b. Auckland. 18xx. Specimen.	—	—	—
f. Invercargill. 18xx. Specimen.	—	—	—
j. Picton. 18xx. Specimen.	—	—	—

S183 10 Pounds	Good	Fine	XF
(ca.1862). Green. Printer: PBC.	—	—	—

S184 20 Pounds			
(ca.1862). Orange. Printer: PBC.			
g. Lyttelton.	—	—	—

1870; 1873 Issue

S191 1 Pound	Good	Fine	XF
1.12.1870; 1.1.1881; 1.4.1884-90. Gray and green. Two Maoris at top left, two kiwis in rural scene at bottom left. Printer: BWC.	—	—	—

S192 5 Pounds	Good	Fine	XF
1903-15. Gray and brown. Two Maoris at top left, two kiwis in rural scene at bottom left. Printer: BWC.			
m. Wellington. 1.1.1913; 19xx.	—	—	—

S193 10 Pounds	Good	Fine	XF
1895-1908. Dark gray and dark brown. Two Maoris at top left, two kiwis in rural scene at bottom left. Printer: BWC.			
m. Wellington. 1.12.1908; 19xx. Two known.	—	12,500.	—

S194 20 Pounds	Good	Fine	XF
1907-26. Gray and blue-green. Two Maoris at top left, two kiwis in rural scene at bottom left. Printer: BWC.			
m. Wellington. 1.8.1924.	300.	900.	—

S195 50 Pounds	Good	Fine	XF
1914-27. Green and mauve. Two Maoris at top left, two kiwis in rural scene at bottom left.			
e. Dunedin. 18xx. Specimen.	—	—	—

S196 100 Pounds	Good	Fine	XF
1928-29. Brown and red. Two Maoris at top left, two kiwis in rural scene at bottom left.			
b. Auckland. 18xx. Specimen.	—	—	—
k. Sydney. 18xx. Specimen.	—	—	—
m. Wellington. 19xx. Specimen.	—	—	—

NOTE: It is reported that #S194-S196 were issued in 1929. Confirmation is needed.

1880's Issue

S201 1 Pound	Good	Fine	XF
18xx. Portrait man at left and right; animals at top left and right. Printer: BWC. Proof.			
a. Red and green underprint.	—	Unc	600.
b. Blue and yellow underprint.	—	Unc	600.

1889 Issue

S202 1 Pound	Good	Fine	XF
18xx. 1888; 1.10.1889; 1.12.1890; 1.12.1891; 1896; 1.3.1898; 1.6.1898. Black and green. Portrait woman at left, two Maoris at right, animals at top left and right, rural scenes at bottom. Back: Brown. Lake scene at center. Printer: BWC.	1750.	5250.	—

1898 Issue

S206 1 Pound	Good	Fine	XF
7.11.1898; 7.12.1899; 1.4.1900; 1.12.1900; 1.4.1901; 1.10.1901; 1.5.1902; 1.5.1903. Black and gray. Woman with cherub, sheep and kiwi at left, arms at upper center. Back: Lake with palms at left, seal and motto of the Colony of New Zealand at center, Maori standing and k	525.	1600.	—

1901 Issue

S212 1 Pound

1.10.1901; 1.12.1912-1918. Black and pink. Two Maoris at top left, two kiwis in rural scene at bottom left. Like #S191, but with continuous underprint. Printer: BWC.

	Good	Fine	XF
a. Without serial # prefix (1902-04).	—	—	—
b. With serial # prefix (1905-16).	—	—	—

S213 1000 Pounds

	Good	Fine	XF
Bank transactions only.	—	—	—

There were also £5000, £10,000, £20,000, £50,000 and £100,000 notes but none have survived.

1916; 1920 Provisional Issue

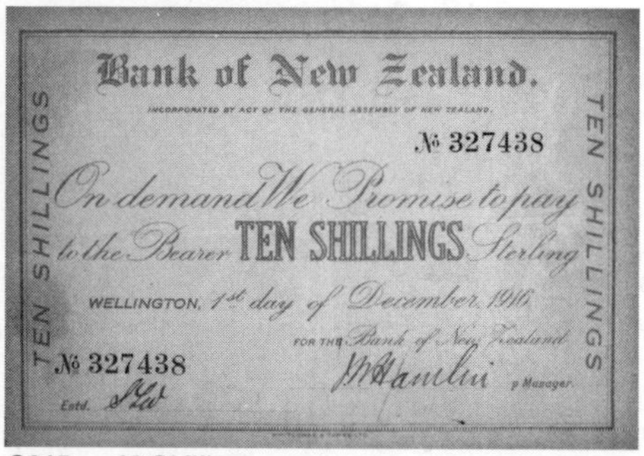

S215 10 Shillings

1916-18. Red. Uniface. Paper: Pink. Printer: Whitcombe & Tombs. Issued at Wellington.

	Good	Fine	XF
a. Without printer's name, date handwritten. 1.8.1916. Rare.	—	—	—
b. Without printer's name, date printed. 1.8.1916. Rare.	—	—	—
c. With printer's name. 1.12.1916; 1.3.1917; 1.9.1917; 1.10.1917; 1.3.1918. Rare.	—	—	—

1916-21 Regular Issues

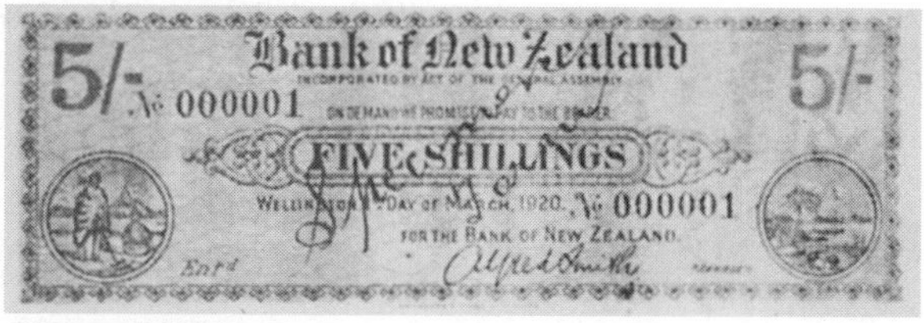

S221 5 Shillings

	Good	Fine	XF
1.3.1920. Black on red underprint. Men at lower left, two kiwis in rural scene at lower right. 5/- in blue. Printer: Whitcombe & Tombs. (Not issued.)	—	—	—

S222 10 Shillings

1.4.1917. Blue and pink. Two Maoris at left, two kiwis in rural scene at right. Back: Brown. Printer: BWC.

	Good	Fine	XF
a. Date handwritten.	1100.	3300.	—
b. Date printed.	1100.	3300.	—

S223 10 Shillings

1.10.1917; 1.10.1918; Blue and pink. Two Maoris at left, two kiwis in rural scene at right. Similar to #S222. *10 SHILLINGS* deleted from top left and right corners. (Applies to #500,001 and above.) Printer: BWC.

	Good	Fine	XF
a. Without serial # prefix.	1000.	3000.	—
b. Serial prefix *A*.	1350.	4000.	—

NOTE: Other full dates of #S223 should be reported.

S224 10 Shillings

	Good	Fine	XF
1.4.1920. Blue and pink. Serial # prefix *B*. Back: Text and figures removed. Printer: BWC.	1500.	4500.	—

S225 1 Pound

	Good	Fine	XF
1.11.1916; 1.12.1916; 1.2.1917; 1.5.1917; 1.6.1917; 1.9.1917; 1.10.1917; 1.4.1918; 1.10.1919; 1.4.19 Multicolor. Two Maoris at left, two kiwis in rural scene at right. Similar to #S222. Printer: BWC.	450.	1350.	4000.

S226 1 Pound

	Good	Fine	XF
1.4.1921; 1.10.1921; 1.12.1922; 1.4.1923; 1.10.1923; 1.4.1924. Multicolor. Two Maoris at left, two kiwis in rural scene at right. Similar to #S222. Back: All text and figures removed. Printer: BWC.	500.	1500.	—

S227 5 Pounds

	Good	Fine	XF
1916-20. Blue on pink and green underprint. Two kiwis in rural scene at lower left, two Maoris at lower right. Back: Brown on gray underprint. Printer: BWC.			
a. Left edge perforated. 1.12.1916; 1.4.1917.	1200.	3600.	—
b. Left edge straight. 1.10.1917; 1.10.1918; 1.4.1920.	1100.	3300.	—

NOTE: Additional dates for #S227 require confirmation.

S228 5 Pounds

	Good	Fine	XF
1.10.1921; 1.10.1922; 1.4.1923; 1.4.1924. Multicolor. Two kiwis in rural scene at lower left, two Maoris at lower right. Similar to #S227. Back: All text and figures removed. Printer: BWC.	1100.	3300.	—

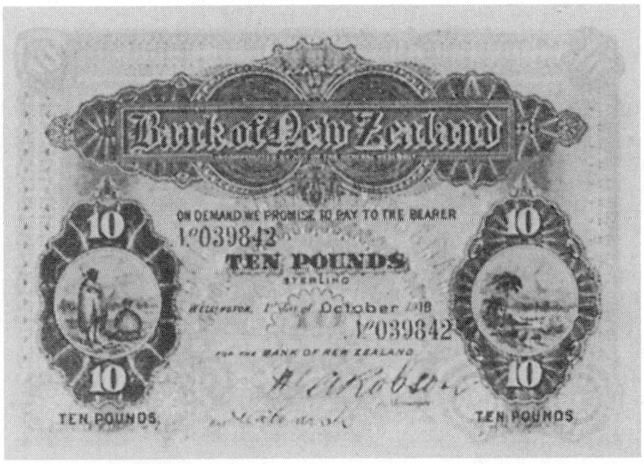

S229 10 Pounds

	Good	Fine	XF
1.10.1916; 1.10.1917; 1.10.1919. Multicolor. Two kiwis in rural scene at lower left, two Maoris at lower right. Similar to #S227. Printer: BWC.	1500.	4500.	—

S230 10 Pounds

	Good	Fine	XF
1.10.1919; 1.10.1920; 1.10.1921; (ca.1921-23). Multicolor. Two kiwis in rural scene at lower left, two Maoris at lower right. Similar to #S227. Back: All text and figures removed.	1500.	4500.	—

1924-29 Issues

S231 10 Shillings

	Good	Fine	XF
1.10.1924; 1.10.1925. Yellow and multicolor. Portrait Maori King Tawhiao at right. Printer: BWC.	750.	2250.	—

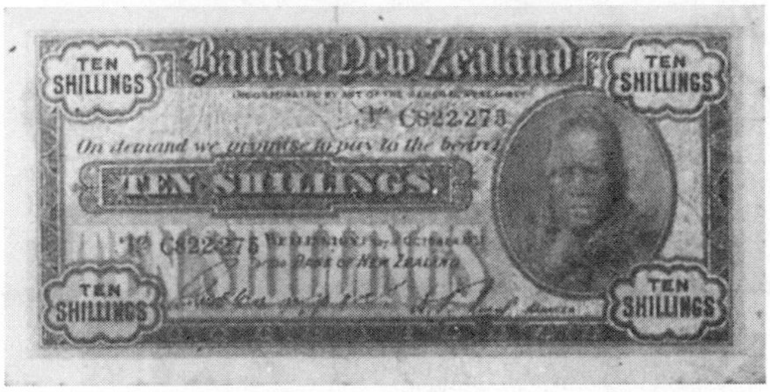

S232 10 Shillings

	Good	Fine	XF
1.10.1926; 1.10.1928; 1.10.1929; 1.10.1931; 1.10.1932. Yellow and multicolor. Portrait Maori King Tawhiao at right. Like #S231 but £1/2 deleted from corners. (Applies to #A500,001 and above.) Printer: BWC.			
a. Signature D. F. Reid.	675.	2000.	—
b. Signature B. A. Moore.	675.	2000.	—

S233 1 Pound

	Good	Fine	XF
1.10.1924; 1.10.1925. Violet and multicolor. Portrait King Tawhiao at center. Bank name arched. Signature A. Hempton. Black serial #. Printer: BWC.	150.	450.	2000.

S234 1 Pound

	Good	Fine	XF
1.10.1926; 1.10.1927; 1.10.1928; 1.10.1929; 1.10.1930; 1.10.1931; 1.10.1932. Violet and multicolor. Portrait King Tawhiao at center. Like #S233 but bank name in straight line. Red serial #. Printer: BWC.			
a. Signature D. F. Reid.	150.	450.	2000.
b. Signature B. A. Moore.	150.	450.	2000.

S235 5 Pounds

	Good	Fine	XF
1.10.1924; 1.10.1925; 1.10.1926; 1.10.1927; 1.10.1928. Blue and multicolor. Portrait King Tawhiao at left. Bank name arched. Printer: BWC.	175.	525.	—

		Good	Fine	XF
S237	**10 Pounds** 1.10.1924; 1.10.1926; 1.10.1927; 1.10.1928. Brown. Portrait King Tawhiao at center. Bank name arched. Like #S233. Printer: BWC.	400.	1200.	—
S238	**20 Pounds** 1.10.1926; (ca.1926-34). Green. Portrait King Tawhiao at right. Printer: BWC.	—	—	—

		Good	Fine	XF
S239	**50 Pounds** 1.10.1929; (ca.1929-34). Pink. Portrait King Tawhiao at right.	—	—	—
S240	**100 Pounds** 24.5.1929; 1.10.1929; (ca.1929-34). Olive. Portrait King Tawhiao at right.	—	—	—

NOTE: For #S231-S240, more full dates are needed for confirmation. Various color shades may exist.

Bank of Otago Ltd.

1864-68 Issue

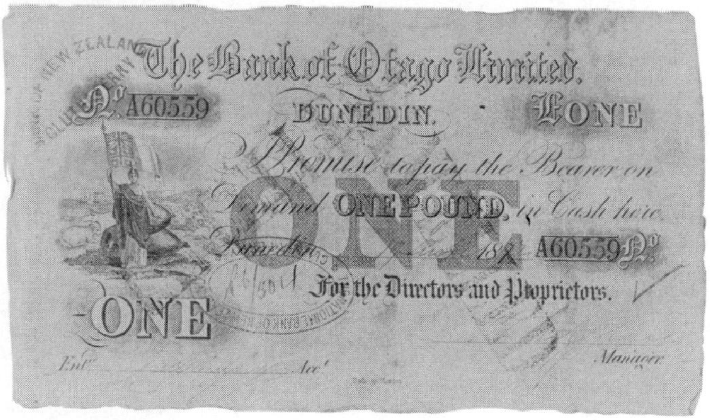

		Good	Fine	XF
S241	**1 Pound** 1.1.1864; 17.4.1867; 21.1.1872; 19.1.1878. Black and blue. Britannia with flag at left. With or without prefix letter in serial #. Back: Bank name in oval guilloche. Printer: Batho & Co.	—	—	—
S242	**5 Pounds** 3.1.1866; 2.5.1868. Black. Britannia with flag at left. With or without prefix letter in serial #. Back: Bank name in oval guilloche. Printer: Batho & Co. Rare.	—	—	—
S243	**10 Pounds** 10.3.1868. Britannia with flag at left. With or without prefix letter in serial #. Back: Bank name in oval guilloche. Printer: Batho & Co. Rare.	—	—	—
S244	**20 Pounds** (ca.1863-73). Reported not confirmed.	—	—	—

Colonial Bank of Issue

1850's Issue

		Good	Fine	XF
S246	**1 Pound** (ca.1850-56). Black. Royal arms at top center. Three different value statements in three corners. Uniface.			
	b. Auckland. Specimen.	—	—	—
	m. Wellington. Specimen.	—	—	—
S247	**5 Pounds** (ca.1850-56). Orange. Royal arms at top center. Three different value statements in three corners. Uniface. Like #S246.			
	e. Dunedin.	—	—	—
	m. Wellington. Specimen.	—	—	—

Colonial Bank of New Zealand

1874 First Issue

		Good	Fine	XF
S251	**1 Pound** 1874. Brown. Woman at upper center. Uniface. Printer: Fergusson & Mitchell. Rare.	—	—	—

1875 Issue

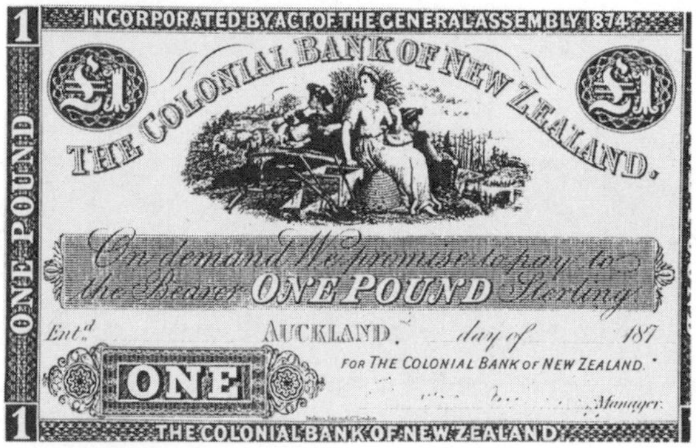

		Good	Fine	XF
S262	**1 Pound** 187x; 188x. Blue and yellow. Allegorical woman flanked by sailors with implements and beehive at upper center. Serial # varieties. Printer: PBC.			
	b. Auckland. 187x.	—	—	—
	c. Christchurch. 187x.	—	—	—
	e. Dunedin. 1.1.1890.	—	—	—
	h. Napier. Proof.	—	—	—
	m. Wellington. Proof.	—	—	—

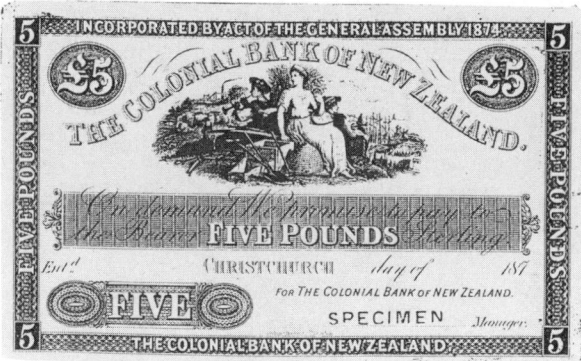

		Good	Fine	XF
S263	**5 Pounds** 187x; 188x. Allegorical woman flanked by sailors with implements and beehive at upper center. Serial # varieties. Printer: PBC.			
	b. Auckland. 187x.	—	—	—
	c. Christchurch. 187x. Specimen.	—	—	—
	e. Dunedin.	—	—	—
	h. Napier. Proof.	—	—	—
S264	**10 Pounds** 187x; 188x. Allegorical woman flanked by sailors with implements and beehive at upper center. Serial # varieties. Printer: PBC.			
	b. Auckland. 187x.	—	—	—
	e. Dunedin.	—	—	—
	h. Napier. Proof.	—	—	—

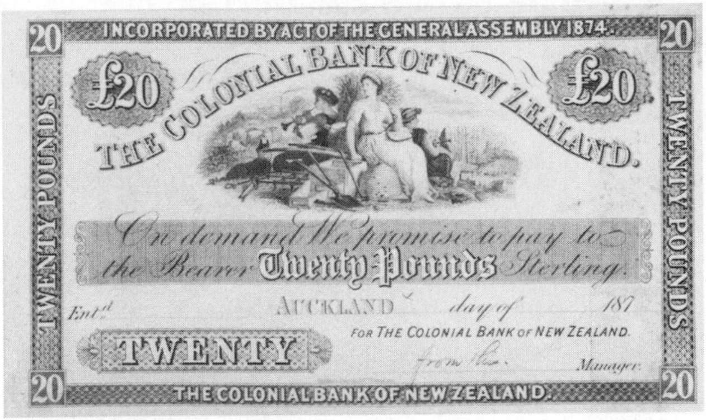

	Good	Fine	XF
S265 20 Pounds 187x; 188x. Allegorical woman flanked by sailors with implements and beehive at upper center. Serial # varieties. Printer: PBC.			
a. Auckland. 187x.	—	—	—
c. Christchurch. 187x.	—	—	—
e. Dunedin. Proof.	—	—	—
h. Napier. Proof.	—	—	—
S266 50 Pounds 187x; 188x. Allegorical woman flanked by sailors with implements and beehive at upper center. Serial # varieties. Printer: PBC.			
h. Napier. Proof.	—	—	—

1880's Issue

	Good	Fine	XF
S267 1 Pound 1.3.1889-95. Blue and yellow. Shield with bank monogram flanked by two women at upper center, ships in background. Back: Green, red and brown. Portraits left and right, building at center. Printer: BWC.			
e. Dunedin.	—	—	—
S268 5 Pounds (ca.1889-95). Grey and yellow. Shield with bank monogram flanked by two women at upper center, ships in background. Back: Brown, grey and pink. Portraits left and right, building at center. Printer: BWC. Proof.	—	—	—
S269 10 Pounds 1.5.18xx (ca.1889-95). Light brown and yellow. Shield with bank monogram flanked by two women at upper center, ships in background. Allegorical head at left and right. Back: Red, green and brown. Portraits left and right, tower building at center. Printer: BWC.			
e. Dunedin. 1.5.18xx. Specimen.	—	—	—
p. Proof.	—	—	—

	Good	Fine	XF
S269A 20 Pounds 1.6.18xx. Light brown and yellow. Shield with bank monogram flanked by two women at upper center, ships in background. Back: Grey, brown, blue and green. Portraits left and right, building at center. Printer: BWC.			
e. Dunedin. 1.6.18xx. Specimen.	—	—	—
p. Proof.	—	—	—
S270 50 Pounds 1.7.18xx. Green. Shield with bank monogram flanked by two women at upper center, ships in background. Back: Green, brown and grey. Portraits left and right, building at center. Printer: BWC.			
e. Dunedin. 1.7.18xx. Unsigned remainder.	—	—	—

NOTE: Wellington office issue may exist for #S267-S270.

Commercial Bank of Australia

1914-19 Issue

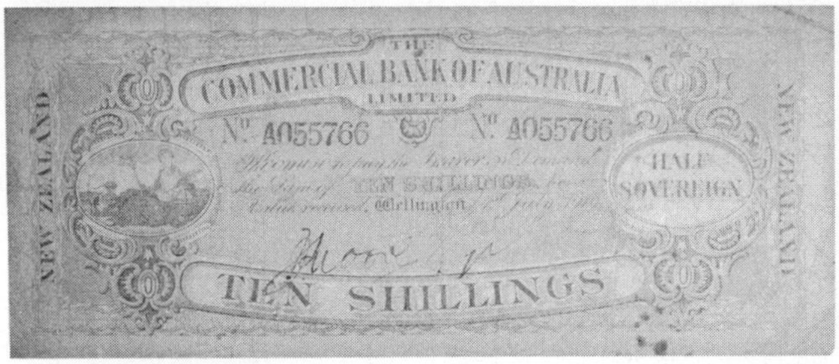

	Good	Fine	XF
S270A 10 Shillings 14.4.1917; 1.7.1919. Yellow and green. Seated woman with globe and caduceus at left. Printer: Sands (without imprint).			
a. Date handwritten.	—	—	—
b. Date printed.	1800.	5400.	—

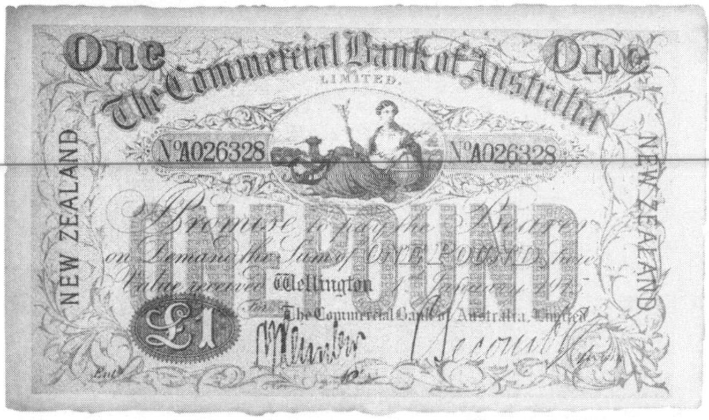

	Good	Fine	XF
S271 1 Pound 1914; 1.1.1915; 1.1.1917; 1.1.1919. Purple. Seated woman with globe and caduceus at center. Back: Facing female head at left and right. Printer: Sands (without imprint).	1800.	5400.	—

	Good	Fine	XF
S272 5 Pounds 18.8.1914; 1916. Blue. Seated woman with globe and caduceus at center. Printer: Sands (without imprint).	—	—	—

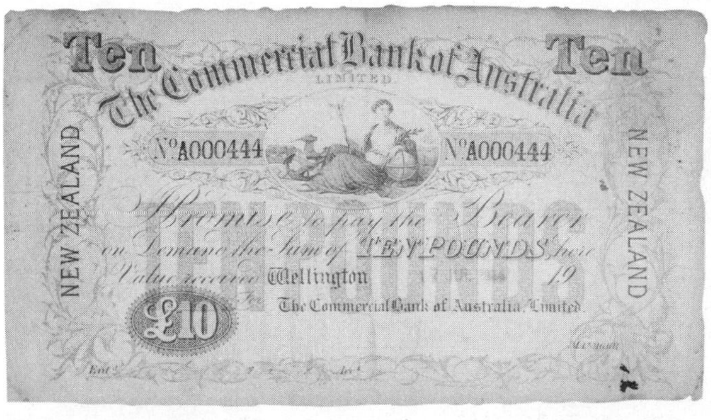

	Good	Fine	XF
S273 10 Pounds 12.7.1914; 1915. Brown. Seated woman with globe and caduceus at center. Printer: Sands (without imprint).	—	—	—

		Good	Fine	XF
S275	**100 Pounds** (ca.1914-19). Green. Seated woman with globe and caduceus at center. Printer: Sands (without imprint).	—	—	—
S276	**1000 Pounds** (ca.1914-19). Bank transactions only.	—	—	—

1917-19 Issue

		Good	Fine	XF
S277	**10 Shillings** 1919; 1.1.1923. Yellow. Reclining Industry at left. Printer: W&S.	—	—	—
S278	**1 Pound** 1.1.1919; (ca.1919-24). Purple. Reclining Industry at left. Printer: W&S.	—	—	—
S279	**5 Pounds** 1917; (ca.1919-24). Blue. Reclining Industry at left. Printer: W&S.	—	—	—
S280	**10 Pounds** (ca.1919-24). Brown. Reclining Industry at left. Printer: W&S.	—	—	—
S280A	**50 Pounds** (ca.1919-24). Red. Reclining Industry at left. Printer: W&S. Reported not confirmed.	—	—	—
S280B	**100 Pounds** (ca.1919-24). Green. Reclining Industry at left. Printer: W&S. Reported not confirmed.	—	—	—

1926 Issue

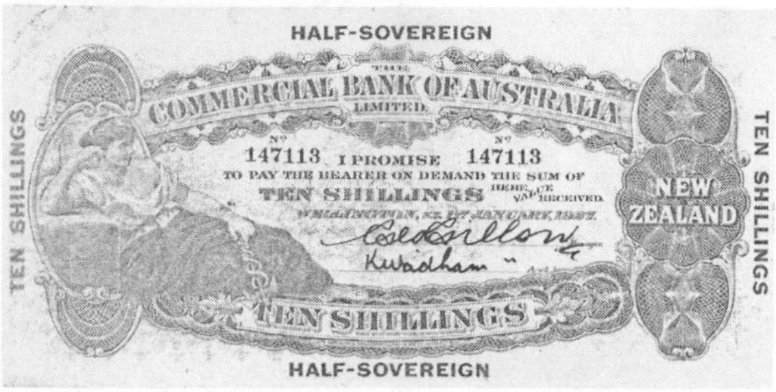

		Good	Fine	XF
S281	**10 Shillings** 1.1.1923; 1.1.1927; 1.6.1929. Yellow and orange. Reclining Industry at left. Printer: W&S.	900.	2700.	—

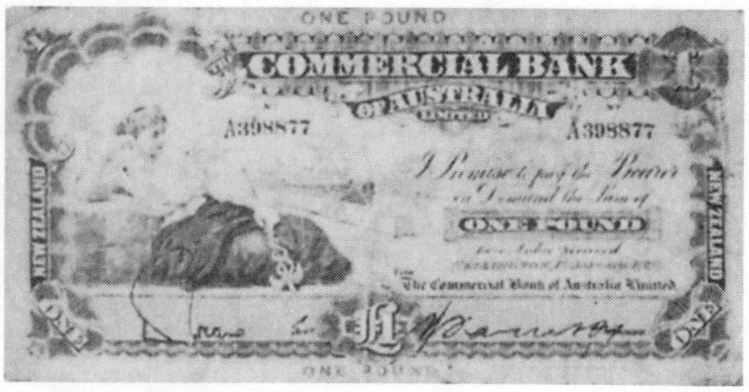

		Good	Fine	XF
S282	**1 Pound** 1.1.1926; 1.1.1927; 1.1.1928; 1930. Purple and green. Reclining Industry at left. Back: Purple. Printer: W&S.	600.	1800.	—
S283	**5 Pounds** 1.1.1926. Blue and green. Reclining Industry at left. Back: Blue. Printer: W&S.	—	—	—
S284	**10 Pounds** 1926. Brown. Reclining Industry at left. Printer: W&S.	—	—	—
S285	**50 Pounds** 1926. Red and green. Reclining Industry at left. Back: Red. Printer: W&S.	—	—	—
S286	**100 Pounds** 19xx. (ca.1924-34). Green. Reclining Industry at left. Printer: W&S.	—	—	—

A WORD ON DATE RANGES

Often date ranges or specific dates are listed. These have been observed or reported by our contributors. If a note is outside the published range, it only means that it is a newly reported date, and not necessarily worthy of a premium value.

Commercial Bank of New Zealand Limited

1865 Issue

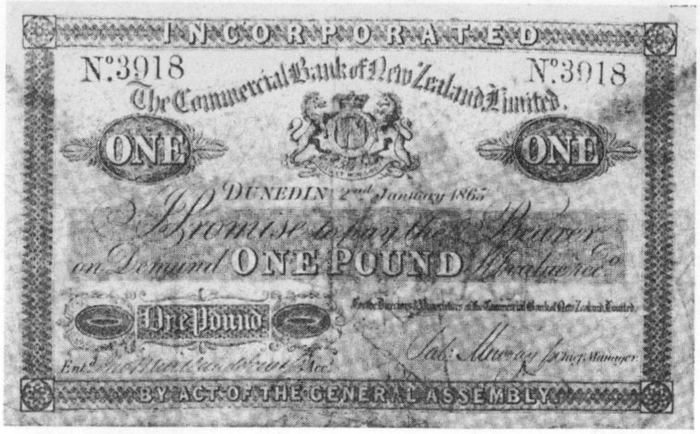

		Good	Fine	XF
S288	**1 Pound** 2.1.1865. Arms at top center. Printer: PBC. Dunedin.	—	—	—
S289	**5 Pounds** (ca.1865-66). Printer: PBC. Specimen.	—	—	—
S289A	**10 Pounds** (ca.1865-66). Printer: PBC. Specimen.	—	—	—
S289B	**20 Pounds** (ca.1865-66). Printer: PBC. Specimen.	—	—	—

		Good	Fine	XF
S289C	**50 Pounds** 2.1.1865. Arms at top center. Dunedin. Specimen.	—	—	—
S290	**100 Pounds** (ca.1865-66). Specimen.	—	—	—

Note: A second issue was prepared in 1866 but was probably never issued. It differs from the first issue only by the addition of the words *here or at Dundin* after *value received.*

National Bank of New Zealand

1873 Issue

		Good	Fine	XF
S291	**1 Pound** ND (ca.1873-77). Gray. Arms with crowned lion and unicorn facing right. No incorporation clause below bank name. Uniface. Printer: PBC.			
	a. Office of issue not named. Specimen.	—	—	—
	b. Auckland. Specimen.	—	—	—
	e. Dunedin. Specimen.	—	—	—
S292	**5 Pounds** ND (ca.1873-77). Blue. Arms with crowned lion and unicorn facing right. No incorporation clause below bank name. Uniface. Printer: PBC.			
	a. Office of issue not named. Specimen.	—	—	—
	b. Auckland.	—	—	—
S293	**10 Pounds** ND (ca.1873-77). Brown. Arms with crowned lion and unicorn facing right. No incorporation clause below bank name. Uniface. Printer: PBC.			
	a. Office of issue not named. Specimen.	—	—	—
	b. Auckland.	—	—	—
S294	**20 Pounds** ND (ca.1873-77). Green. Arms with crowned lion and unicorn facing right. No incorporation clause below bank name. Uniface. Printer: PBC.			
	a. Office of issue not named. Specimen.	—	—	—
	c. Christchurch.	—	—	—

S295 50 Pounds	Good	Fine	XF
ND (ca.1873-77). Orange. Arms with crowned lion and unicorn facing right. No incorporation clause below bank name. Uniface. Printer: PBC.			
b. Auckland.	—	—	—

1877 Issue

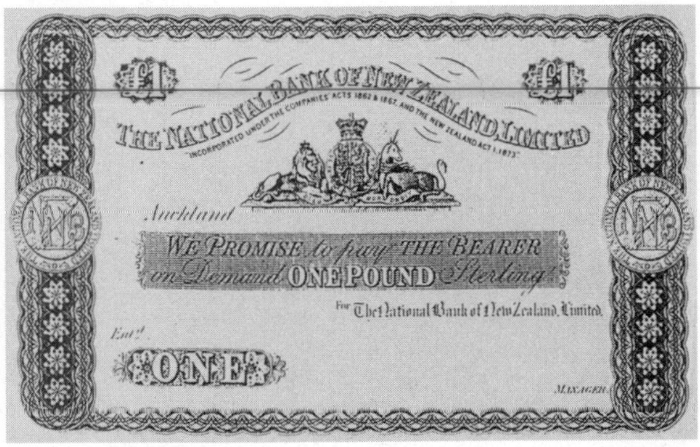

S296 1 Pound	Good	Fine	XF
ND (ca.1877-1894). Gray and green. Arms with crowned lion and unicorn facing right. With incorporation text line below bank title. Printer: PBC. 190 x 115mm.			
b. Auckland.	—	—	—
c. Christchurch. 18xx.	—	—	—
e. Dunedin. 18xx.	—	—	—
m. Wellington. 18xx.	—	—	—
S297 5 Pounds			
ND (ca.1877-1894). Blue and dark brown. Arms with crowned lion and unicorn facing right. With incorporation text line below bank title. Printer: PBC.			
b. Auckland. 18xx.	—	—	—
c. Christchurch. 18xx.	—	—	—
e. Dunedin. 18xx.	—	—	—
m. Wellington. 18xx.	—	—	—
S298 10 Pounds			
ND (ca.1877-1894). Brown and green. Arms with crowned lion and unicorn facing right. With incorporation text line below bank title. Printer: PBC.			
b. Auckland. 19xx.	—	—	—
c. Christchurch. 19xx.	—	—	—
e. Dunedin. 18xx.	—	—	—
m. Wellington. 19xx.	—	—	—
S299 20 Pounds			
ND (ca.1877-1894). Green and orange. Arms with crowned lion and unicorn facing right. With incorporation text line below bank title. Printer: PBC.			
b. Auckland. 18xx.	—	—	—
c. Christchurch. 19xx.	—	—	—
e. Dunedin. 18xx.	—	—	—
m. Wellington. 19xx; 1.1.1912.	—	—	—
S300 50 Pounds			
ND (ca.1877-1894). Pink and dark blue. Arms with crowned lion and unicorn facing right. With incorporation text line below bank title. Printer: PBC.			
b. Auckland. 18xx.	—	—	—
c. Christchurch. 18xx.	—	—	—
e. Dunedin. 18xx.	—	—	—
m. Wellington. 18xx; 19xx.	—	—	—

Formerly listed S301-S305 have been incorporated into S296-S300.

ILLUSTRATIONS

Illustrations of bank notes used throughout this catalog are 42% of the actual size.

1910-22 Issue

#S306-S311 Wellington Office (other offices need confirmation).

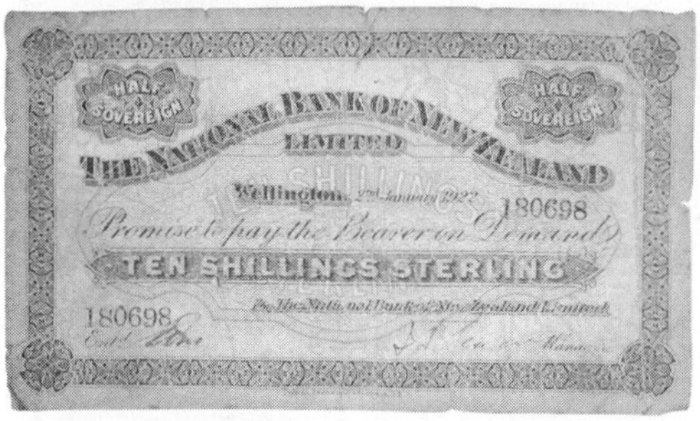

S306 10 Shillings	Good	Fine	XF
1.10.1920; 2.1.1922; 1.1.1923. Gray and green. Larger arms.	1800.	5400.	—

#S307-S311 denomination unpt. at ctr.

S307 1 Pound	Good	Fine	XF
1.1.1910-1.1.1917; 1.1.1921; 1.1.1923. Gray and green. Larger arms. Denomination underprint at center.	900.	2700.	—

S308 5 Pounds	Good	Fine	XF
1.1.1916; 1.1.1919; 1.1.1923. Blue and chocolate brown. Larger arms. Denomination underprint at center.	1500.	4500.	—

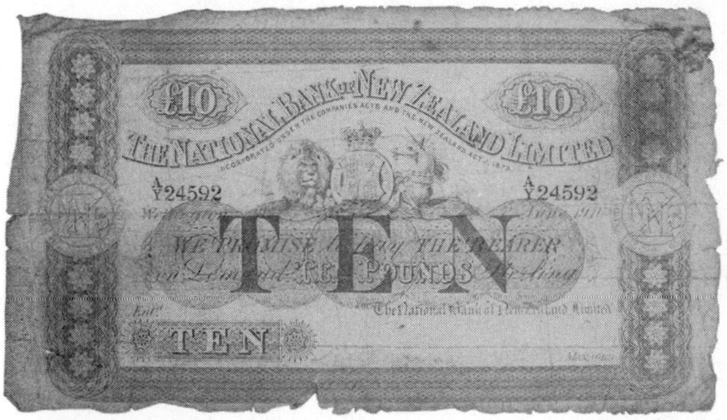

S309 10 Pounds	Good	Fine	XF
1.6.1910; 1.1.1912; 1.1.1916; 1921. Brown and green. Larger arms. Denomination underprint at center.	—	—	—

	Good	Fine	XF
S310 20 Pounds 1.1.1912; 1.6.1916. Green and orange. Larger arms. Denomination underprint at center.	—	—	—
S311 50 Pounds 1916; 1921. Pink and blue. Larger arms. Denomination underprint at center.	—	—	—

NOTE: For #S307-S311, notes may be dated from ca.1910-24. Additional dates other than those listed require confirmation.

1925; 1926 Issue

	Good	Fine	XF
S316 10 Shillings 1.1.1925-1.7.1933. Orange and purple. Bank name in double lined capital letters. Uniface.	900.	2700.	7500.

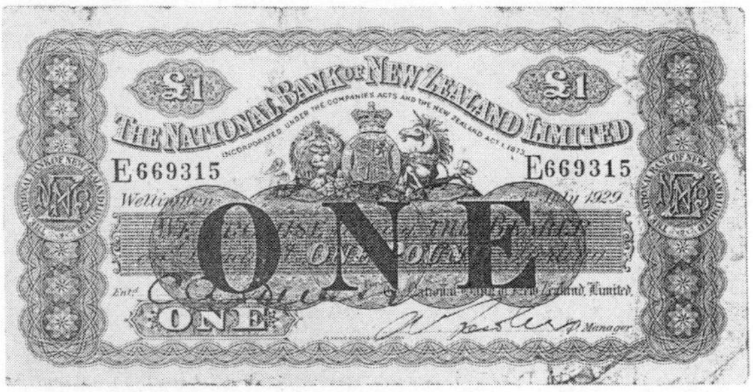

	Good	Fine	XF
S317 1 Pound 1.1.1925-1.8.1930. Purple and dark brown. Bank name in double lined capital letters. Uniface.	375.	1100.	3300.

	Good	Fine	XF
S318 5 Pounds 1.1.1924-1930. Blue and dark brown. Bank name in double lined capital letters. Back: Blue.	750.	2250.	—

	Good	Fine	XF
S319 10 Pounds 1.6.1924; 1.6.1925; 1.6.1926. Brown and dark green. Bank name in double lined capital letters. Back: Brown.	—	—	—
S320 20 Pounds 1926. Green and orange. Bank name in double lined capital letters. Back: Green.	—	—	—
S321 50 Pounds 1925. Pink and dark blue. Bank name in double lined capital letters. Back: Pink.	—	—	—

NOTE: For #S316-S321, notes may be dated from ca.1924-34. Additional dates other than those listed require confirmation.

New Zealand Banking Company

1840 Issue

	Good	Fine	XF
S326 1 Pound (ca.1840-45). Black. Britannia at upper left.	—	—	—
S327 5 Pounds (ca.1840-45). Black. Britannia at upper left. Like #S326.	—	—	—

New Zealand Banking Corporation, Ltd.

1885 Issue

	Good	Fine	XF
S331 1 Pound 2.1.1865. Black frame. Uniface. (Not issued.)	—	—	—

Oriental Bank Corporation

1857 Issue

	Good	Fine	XF
S333 1 Pound (ca.1857-61). Black. Arms at upper center. Printer: PBC.			
a. Issued note. Wellington. 1.1.1857. Rare.	—	—	—
s. Specimen. Auckland.	—	—	—

	Good	Fine	XF
S334 5 Pounds (ca.1857-61). Light brown. Arms at upper center. Printer: PBC. Auckland. Specimen.	—	—	—

		Good	Fine	XF
S335	**10 Dollars** (ca.1857-61). Arms at upper center. Printer: PBC. Reported not confirmed.	—	—	—
S335A	**20 Pounds** (ca. 1857-61). Arms at upper center. Printer: PBC. Auckland. Specimen.	—	—	—

Otago Banking Company

1851 Issue

#S336-S338 Notes are inscribed *BANK OF OTAGO* do not confuse with those of the Bank of Otago Ltd.

		Good	Fine	XF
S336	**10 Shillings** (ca.1851). Blue. Scottish arms at top center. (Not issued.)	—	—	—

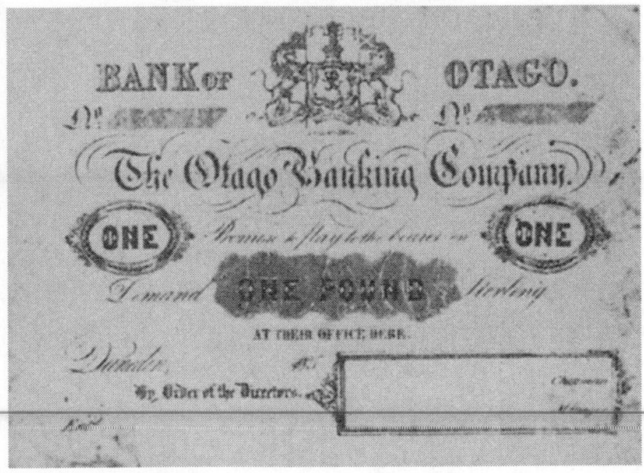

		Good	Fine	XF
S337	**1 Pound** (ca.1851). Black. Scottish arms at top center. (Not issued.)	450.	—	—
S338	**5 Pounds** (ca.1851). Black and blue. Scottish arms at top center. (Not issued.)	525.	—	—

Union Bank of Australia

1840 Issue

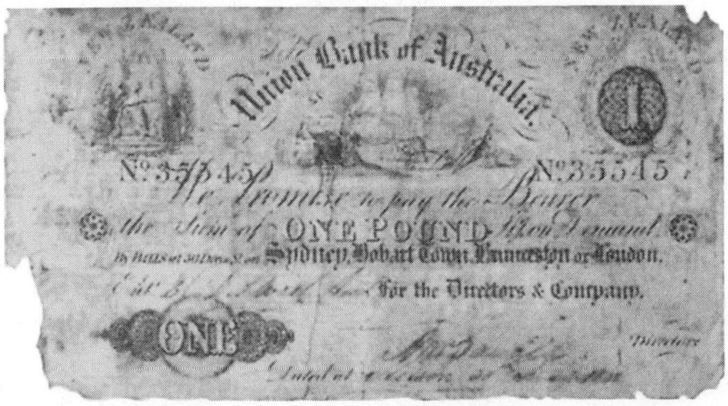

		Good	Fine	XF
S341	**1 Pound** 24.3.1840; 30.5.1842. Black. Enthroned Queen Victoria at upper left, Britannia and ships at top center. Uniface. Printer: PBC. Rare.	—	—	—

NOTE: Additional values of 2, 5, 10 and 20 Pound require confirmation.

1856 Issue

		Good	Fine	XF
S346	**1 Pound** 1.3.1859; 1.4.186x. Greenish black. Queen Victoria at upper left, ship at center. Date handwritten. Uniface. Printer: PBC. Christchurch.	—	—	—
S347	**5 Pounds** (ca.1852-60). Black. Queen Victoria at upper left, ship at center. Date handwritten. Uniface. Printer: PBC.	—	—	—
S348	**10 Pounds** (ca.1852-60). Black. Queen Victoria at upper left, ship at center. Date handwritten. Uniface. Printer: PBC.	—	—	—
S349	**20 Pounds** (ca.1852-60.). Queen Victoria at upper left, ship at center. Date handwritten. Uniface. Printer: PBC. Specimen.	—	—	—

1861 Issue

		Good	Fine	XF
S351	**1 Pound** 1866. Greenish black. Partial date printed. Uniface.	—	—	—
S352	**5 Pounds** (ca.1861-78). Black. Partial date printed. Uniface.	—	—	—

		Good	Fine	XF
S353	**10 Pounds** (ca.1861-78). Black. Partial date printed. Uniface.			
	m. Wellington. 1.3.186x.	—	—	—
	s. Napier. Specimen. 18xx.	—	—	—

1878 Issue

#S356-S359 back design initiated. Printer: PBC.

There are 6 varieties of each:

name as *UNION BANK OF AUSTRALIA*

name as *UNION BANK OF AUSTRALIA LIMITED.*

name as *THE UNION BANK OF AUSTRALIA LIMITED.*

£ symbol in circle before figure of value

Printer's imprint shortened to *Perkins, Bacon & Co. Ld.*

Printer's imprint omitted.

		Good	Fine	XF
S356	**1 Pound** (ca.1878-1904). Black. Britannia seated with symbols of commerce, lion and kangaroo at top center. Overprint: Green. Printer: PBC.	—	—	—
S357	**5 Pounds** (ca.1878-1904). Black. Printer: PBC.	—	—	—
S358	**10 Pounds** (ca.1878-1904). Black. Printer: PBC.	—	—	—
S359	**20 Pounds** (ca.1878-1904). Gray. Back: Brown. Printer: PBC.	—	—	—

1905 Issue

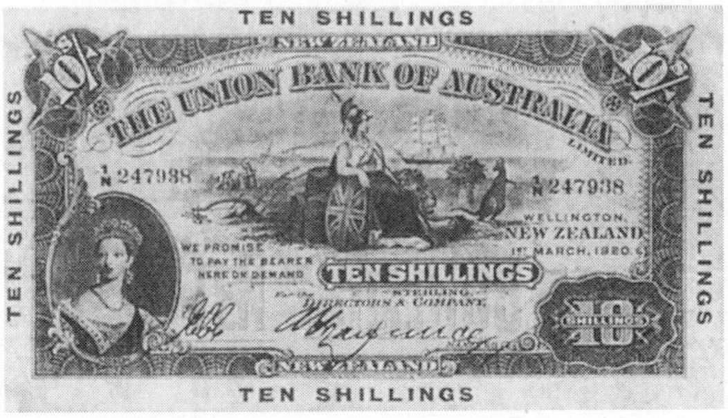

		Good	Fine	XF
S361	**10 Shillings** 1.3.1920. Blue on red underprint. Portrait Queen Victoria at lower left, Britannia seated with symbols of commerce, lion and kangaroo at center. Printer: W&S.	1800.	5400.	—

NOTICE

Readers with unlisted dates, signature varieties, etc., are invited to submit photocopies or scans of their notes to:
Standard Catalog of World Paper Money,
700 East State St. Iola, WI 54990-0001,
E-Mail: george.cuhaj@fwmedia.com.

S362 1 Pound	Good	Fine	XF
1.3.1905. Black, dark green and red. Portrait Queen Victoria at left, Britannia and symbols of commerce at top center. Back: Green. Printer: W&S.			
a. Plain margins.	—	—	—
b. *NEW ZEALAND* added in upper and lower margins.	600.	1800.	—

S363 5 Pounds	Good	Fine	XF
1.3.1905. Black on green underprint. Portrait Queen Victoria at top center, Britannia and symbols of commerce at lower right. Back: Red. Printer: W&S.			
a. Plain margins.	—	—	—
b. *NEW ZEALAND* added in margins.	1550.	4650.	—
S364 10 Pounds			
1.3.1905. Black and orange. Back: Blue. Printer: W&S.			
a. Plain margin.	—	—	—
b. *NEW ZEALAND* in margins.	—	—	—
S365 20 Pounds			
1.3.1905. Black on light blue underprint. Queen Victoria at lower right. Back: Mustard. Printer: W&S.			
a. Plain margins.	—	—	—
b. *NEW ZEALAND* added in margins and *20* in sunburst at upper corners.	—	—	—
c. As b but without sunbursts.	—	—	—

S366 50 Pounds	Good	Fine	XF
1.3.1905. Black on pink underprint. Queen Victoria at upper left, Britannia seated with symbols of commerce at center. Back: Brown. Printer: W&S.			
a. Plain margins.	—	—	—
b. *NEW ZEALAND* added in margins.	—	—	—
p. Proof.			

1923 Issue

#S371-S376 Wellington office.

S371 10 Shillings	Good	Fine	XF
1.10.1923. Orange on green underprint. Portrait Queen Victoria at lower left, Britannia and symbols of commerce at center. Back: Orange. Printer: W&S.			
a. Text: with *STERLING.*	750.	2250.	6750.
b. Without *STERLING.*	750.	2250.	6750.

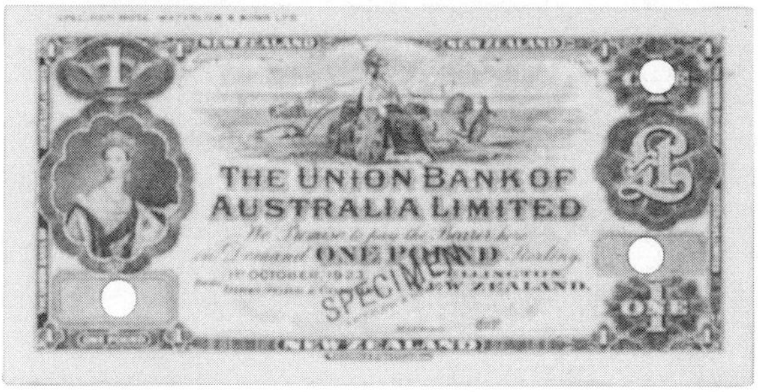

S372 1 Pound	Good	Fine	XF
1.10.1923. Mauve and green. Portrait Queen Victoria at left, Britannia and symbols of commerce at top center. Back: Mauve. Printer: W&S.			
a. Issued note.	450.	1750.	—
s. Specimen.	—	Unc	1750.
S373 5 Pounds			
1.10.1923. Blue and pink. Portrait Queen Victoria at top center, Britannia and symbols of commerce at lower right. Back: Brown. Printer: W&S.	1500.	4500.	—
S374 10 Pounds			
1.10.1923. Brown and green. Queen Victoria at right. Back: Brown. Printer: W&S.	—	—	—
S375 20 Pounds			
1.10.1923. Green and purple. Queen Victoria at lower right. Back: Green. Printer: W&S.	—	—	—
S376 50 Pounds			
1.10.1923. Red. Queen Victoria. Printer: W&S.	—	—	—

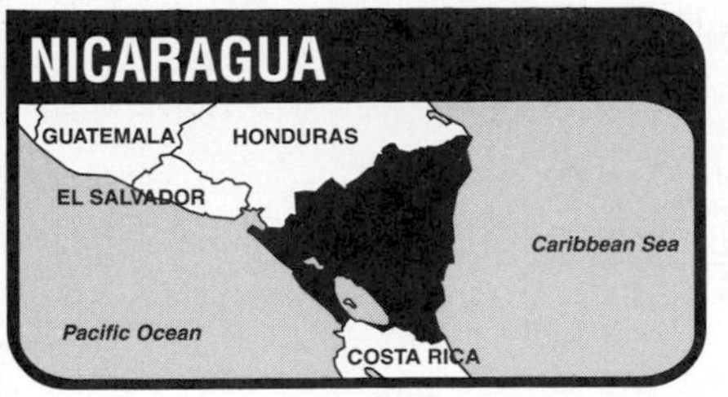

The Republic of Nicaragua, situated in Central America between Honduras and Costa Rica, has an area of 50,193 sq. mi (130,000 sq. km.) and a population of 4.69 million. Capital: Managua. Agriculture, mining (gold and silver) and hardwood logging are the principal industries. Cotton, meat, coffee, tobacco and sugar are exported.

The Pacific coast of Nicaragua was settled as a Spanish colony from Panama in the early 16th century. Independence from Spain was declared in 1821 and the country became an independent republic in 1838. Britain occupied the Caribbean Coast in the first half of the 19th century, but gradually ceded control of the region in subsequent decades. Violent opposition to governmental manipulation and corruption spread to all classes by 1978 and resulted in a short-lived civil war that brought the Marxist Sandinista guerrillas to power in 1979. Nicaraguan aid to leftist rebels in El Salvador caused the US to sponsor anti-Sandinista contra guerrillas through much of the 1980s. Free elections in 1990, 1996, and 2001, saw the Sandinistas defeated, but voting in 2006 announced the return of former Sandinista President Daniel Ortega Saavedra. Nicaragua's infrastructure and economy - hard hit by the earlier civil war and by Hurricane Mitch in 1998 - are slowly being rebuilt.

MONETARY SYSTEM:

1 Peso = 100 Centavos to 1912
1 Córdoba = 100 Centavos, 1912-1987
1 New Córdoba = 1000 Old Córdobas, 1988-90
1 Córdoba Oro = 100 Centavos, 1990-

BANKS

#S101 and S102 *Deleted*. See #S131-S132.

BANCO AGRICOLA-MERCANTIL

1888 ISSUE

S106 50 Centavos	Good	Fine	XF
6.11.1888. Black. Animals feeding at left. Printer: ABNC. Lithograph.			
a. Issued note.	—	—	—
s. Specimen.	—	Unc	1250.

S107 1 Peso	Good	Fine	XF
6.11.1888. Black on orange underprint. Sitting child with lyre at left, woman and sheep at top center, cow's head at right. Back: Red. Printer: ABNC.			
a. Issued note.	—	—	—
p. Proof.	—	Unc	1250.
r. Unsigned remainder.	—	Unc	300.
s. Specimen.	—	Unc	1500.

NOTE: For #S107 and S108 with overprint: *TESORERIA GENERAL* see #A14 and A15 in Volume 2.

S108 5 Pesos	Good	Fine	XF
6.11.1888. Black on yellow-green and brown underprint. Seated woman ("Industry") at left, farm scene at center. Back: Brown. Printer: ABNC.			
a. Issued note.	—	—	—
p. Proof.	—	Unc	1250.
s. Specimen.	—	Unc	1250.

#S109 *Deleted*.

NOTE: For #S107 and S108 with overprint: *TESORERIA GENERAL* see #A14 and A15 in Volume 2.

S110 25 Pesos	Good	Fine	XF
6.11.1888. Black on green and blue underprint. Seated woman at left, woman with farm produce ("The Tropics No. 2") at center, farm animals at lower right. Back: Blue. Printer: ABNC. Specimen.	—	Unc	1250.

S111 50 Pesos	Good	Fine	XF
6.11.1888. Black on blue, yellow and green underprint. Sailor at left, reclining woman ("Agriculture") at center. Back: Green. Printer: ABNC.			
a. Issued note.	—	—	—
r. Unsigned remainder with serial #.	—	Unc	300.
s. Specimen.	—	Unc	1250.

S112 100 Pesos

6.11.1888. Black on yellow and tan underprint. Cow's head at left center. Seated Mercury at right with ship in background. Back: Brown. Printer: ABNC.

	Good	Fine	XF
a. Issued note.	—	—	—
r. Unsigned remainder with serial #.	—	Unc	300.
s. Specimen.	—	Unc	1250.

Banco de Centro America y Londres

1889 Issue

S115 1 Peso

	Good	Fine	XF
18xx. Christopher Columbus at left, standing Liberty with flag at right. Back: Bank monogram at center. Rare.	—	—	—

S119 100 Pesos

	Good	Fine	XF
18xx. Specimen. Rare.	—	—	—

Banco de Nicaragua

1889; 1890 Issue

S121 50 Centavos

	Good	Fine	XF
17.9.1890; 22.12.1893. Brown on yellow underprint. Standing Liberty with flag at left, arms at center right. Back: Blue. Printer: W&S.	120.	360.	1150.

S122 1 Peso

	Good	Fine	XF
8.11.1889; 27.4.1891; 24.8.1891; 27.8.1891; 22.12.1893. Brown and black on gold underprint. Portrait Medina at left, standing Liberty with flag at right. Back: Dull red. Printer: W&S.	225.	675.	2000.

S123 5 Pesos

18xx. Standing Liberty with flag at left, portrait E. Carazo at center. Printer: W&S.

	Good	Fine	XF
a. Issued note.	—	—	—
s. Specimen.	—	Unc	1250.

S124 10 Pesos

18xx. Black on brown and gold underprint. Portrait Pres. A. Cardenas at left, standing Liberty with flag at center. Back: Green. Arms. Printer: W&S.

	Good	Fine	XF
a. Issued note.	—	—	—
s. Specimen.	—	Unc	1250.

S125 50 Pesos

	Good	Fine	XF
18xx. Portrait J. Zavala at center. Printer: W&S.	—	—	—

S126 100 Pesos

	Good	Fine	XF
18xx. Printer: W&S. Reported not confirmed.	—	—	—

MILITARY

WILLIAM WALKER MILITARY SCRIPT

A notaphilic oddity of Nicaragua, which might rank with the Papel Moneda of El Salvador, is the "Military Script" of William Walker, one time President of Nicaragua. Walker, a United States citizen, achieved a degree of fame in 1855 when he and a group of followers captured the city of Granada on behalf of a Nicaraguan political interest group. Walker, however, soon established himself as the real power in Nicaraguan politics and made peace with certain opposition groups. Though in control of the country, his domination was short-lived as a result of Commodore Cornelius Vanderbilt's sponsorship of Walker's overthrow in respoinse to restriction placed on transit of the Isthmus. Vanderbilt was part owner of a company which had previouisly had the right of transit. Walker made several attempts to invade Central America again, only to be apprehended by the British who turned him over to authorities in HOnduras in 1860 where he was promply executed.

While President of Nicaragua, Walker issued "Military Script" to his followers as payment for services rendered. While not technically money because the issues were not declared to be legal tender for all debts public and private, the notes did serve as a form of near money. All specimens are believed to be quite scarce and of considerable historical significance.

SIGNATURE VARIETIES

1. F. (emin) Ferrer
2. M. (anual) Carrascosa
3. Wm. K. Rogers

1856 ISSUE

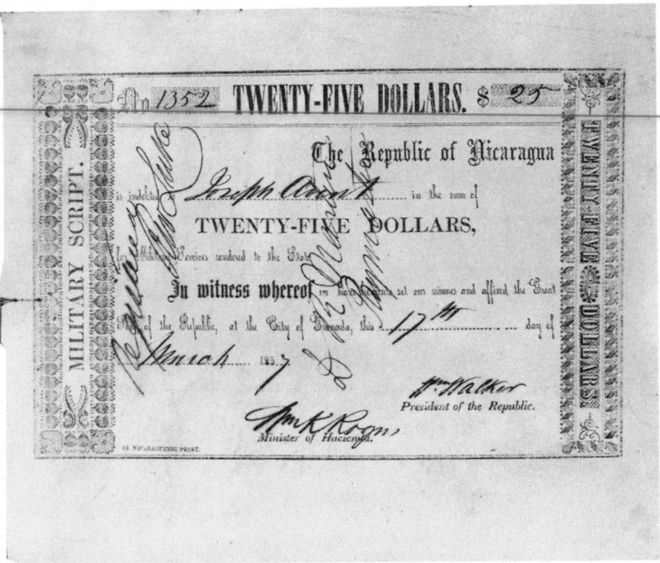

		Good	Fine	XF
S131	**25 Dollars** 29.7.1856; 20.2.1857; 17.3.1857. Dry seal of the Republic at lower left center. Soft paper.	1200.	3600.	11,000.

NOTE: #S131 with signature 3 in XF sold at Smythe auction 6/98 for $8,250.

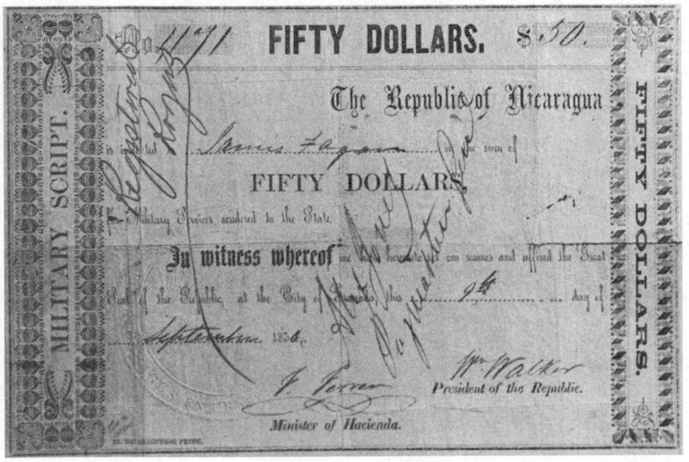

		Good	Fine	XF
S132	**50 Dollars** 31.10.1856. Dry seal of the Republic at lower left center. Soft paper.	2250.	6750.	19,500.

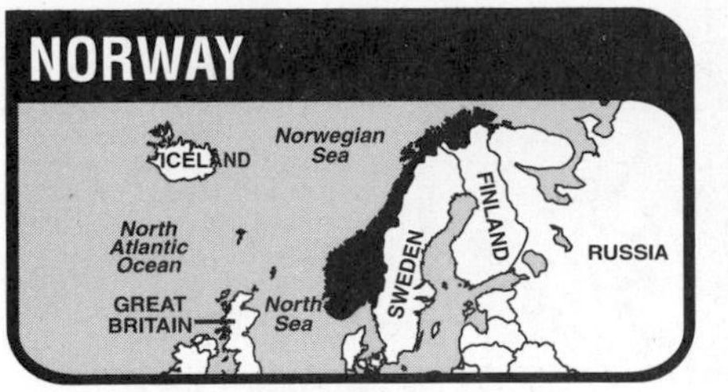

The Kingdom of Norway, a constitutional monarchy located in northwestern Europe, has an area of 150,000 sq. mi. (388,500 sq. km.) including the island territories of Spitzbergen (Svalbard) and Jan Mayen, and a population of 4.46 million. Capital: Oslo. The diversified economic of Norway includes shipping, fishing, forestry, agriculture and manufacturing. Nonferrous metals, paper and paperboard, paper pulp, iron, steel and oil are exported.

Two centuries of Viking raids into Europe tapered off following the adoption of Christianity by King Olav Tryggvason in 994. Conversion of the Norwegian kingdom occurred over the next several decades. In 1397, Norway was absorbed into a union with Denmark that lasted more than four centuries. In 1814, Norwegians resisted the cession of their country to Sweden and adopted a new constitution. Sweden then invaded Norway but agreed to let Norway keep its constitution in return for accepting the union under a Swedish king. Rising nationalism throughout the 19th century led to a 1905 referendum granting Norway independence. Although Norway remained neutral in World War I, it suffered heavy losses to its shipping. Norway proclaimed its neutrality at the outset of World War II, but was nonetheless occupied for five years by Nazi Germany (1940-45). In 1949, neutrality was abandoned and Norway became a member of NATO. Discovery of oil and gas in adjacent waters in the late 1960s boosted Norway's economic fortunes. The current focus is on containing spending on the extensive welfare system and planning for the time when petroleum reserves are depleted. In referenda held in 1972 and 1994, Norway rejected joining the EU.

RULERS:

Christian V, 1670-1699
Frederik IV, 1699-1730
Christian VI, 1730-1746
Frederik V, 1746-1766
Christian VII, 1766-1808
Frederik VI, 1808-1814
Carl XIII, 1814-1818
Carl XIV Johan, 1818-1844
Oscar I, 1844-1859
Carl XV, 1859-1872
Oscar II, 1872-1905
Haakon VII, 1905-1957
Olav V, 1957-1991
Harald V, 1991-

MONETARY SYSTEM:

1 Speciedaler = 96 Skilling to 1816
1 Speciedaler = 120 Skilling, 1816-1873
1 Krone = 100 Øre, 1873-

MILITARY - WW II

IHENDEHAVARGJELDSBREV

ARMY HIGH COMMAND

1940 ISSUE

Issued by Maj. Gen. W. Steffens in Voss with the approval of the branch of the Norges Bank.

		VG	VF	UNC
M1	**5 Kroner** 14.4.1940. Black. Ornamental border at left. Uniface.	300.	550.	700.

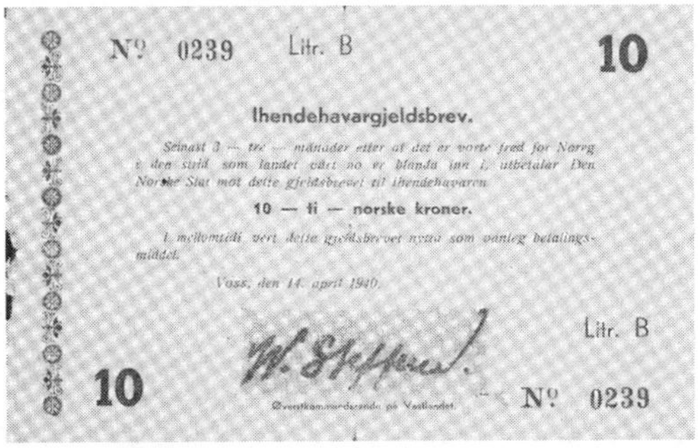

		VG	VF	UNC
M2	**10 Kroner** 14.4.1940. Black. Ornamental border at left. Uniface.	225.	400.	600.
M3	**100 Kroner** 14.4.1940. Black. Ornamental border at left. Uniface.	—	—	—

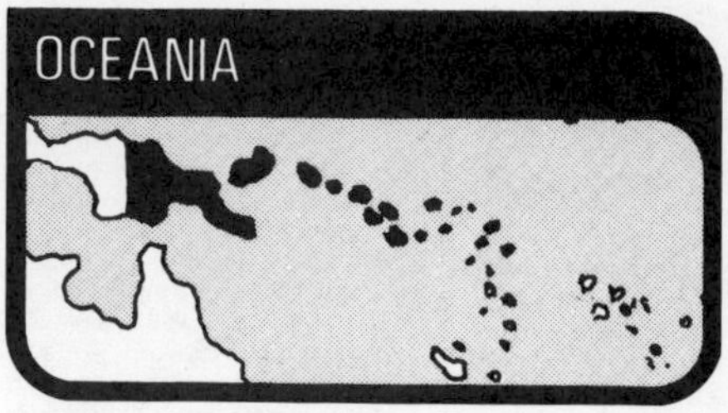

In general usage, Oceania is the collective name for the islands scattered throughout most of the Pacific Ocean. It has traditionally been divided into four parts: Australasia (Australia and New Zealand), Melenesia, Micronesia and Polynesia.

Numismatically, Oceania is the name applied to the Gilbert and Solomon Islands, New Britain, and Papua New Guinea, hence the British denominations. See also French Oceania.

MONETARY SYSTEM:

1 Pound = 20 Shillings

Japanese Occupation - WW II

Australian "Replicas"

1943 ND Issue

Note: Reprints of #1, 2 and 4 were reportedly made in Australia in 1943 (poor printing paper with a weak watermark), mostly with overprint: *REPLICA* on back.

More recent copies also exist.

		VG	VF	UNC
R1	**1/2 Shilling** ND (1943). Purple on yellow-brown underprint. Palm trees along the beach at right with red overprint: *REPLICA*. Block letters: OC.	12.50	35.00	100.
R2	**1 Shilling** ND (1943). Bright blue on green underprint. Breadfruit tree at left, palm trees along the beach at right. Red overprint: *REPLICA*. Block letters: OC.	12.50	35.00	100.
R3	**1 Shilling** ND (1943). Dark blue-gray. Without guilloche or overprint: *REPLICA*. Block letters : OC.	12.50	35.00	100.
R4	**1 Pound** ND (1943). Green with modified blue guilloche. Red overprint: *REPLICA* on back. Block letters : OA.	15.00	50.00	125.
R5	**1 Pound** ND (1943). Back: Without overprint: *REPLICA*.			
	a. Green with modified pale blue guilloche.	12.50	35.00	100.
	b. Dark olive-green.	15.00	50.00	—
	c. Bright green.	15.00	50.00	—

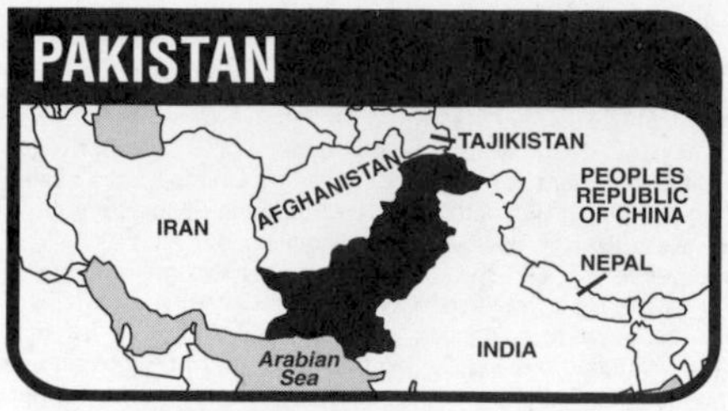

The Islamic Republic of Pakistan, located on the Indian subcontinent between India and Afghanistan, has an area of 310,404 sq. mi. (803,943 sq. m.) and a population of 156 million. Capital: Islamabad. Pakistan is mainly an agricultural land. Yarn, cotton, rice and leather are exported.

The Indus Valley civilization, one of the oldest in the world and dating back at least 5,000 years, spread over much of what is presently Pakistan. During the second millennium B.C., remnants of this culture fused with the migrating Indo-Aryan peoples. The area underwent successive invasions in subsequent centuries from the Persians, Greeks, Scythians, Arabs (who brought Islam), Afghans, and Turks. The Mughal Empire flourished in the 16th and 17th centuries; the British came to dominate the region in the 18th century. The separation in 1947 of British India into the Muslim state of Pakistan (with West and East sections) and largely Hindu India was never satisfactorily resolved, and India and Pakistan fought two wars - in 1947-48 and 1965 - over the disputed Kashmir territory. A third war between these countries in 1971 - in which India capitalized on Islamabad's marginalization of Bengalis in Pakistani politics - resulted in East Pakistan becoming the separate nation of Bangladesh. In response to Indian nuclear weapons testing, Pakistan conducted its own tests in 1998. The dispute over the state of Kashmir is ongoing, but discussions and confidence-building measures have led to decreased tensions since 2002. Mounting public dissatisfaction with President Musharraf, coupled with the assassination of the prominent and popular political leader, Benazir Bhutto, in late 2007, and Musharraf's resignation in August 2008, led to the September presidential election of Asif Zardari, Bhutto's widower. Pakistani government and military leaders are struggling to control Islamist militants, many of whom are located in the tribal areas adjacent to the border with Afghanistan. The November 2008 Mumbai attacks again inflamed Indo-Pakistan relations. The Pakistani Government is also faced with a deteriorating economy as foreign exchange reserves decline, the currency depreciates, and the current account deficit widens.

MONETARY SYSTEM:

1 Rupee = 16 Annas to 1961

1 Rupee = 100 Paisa (Pice), 1961-

REPLACEMENT NOTES:

#24, 24A, 24B, 1/X or 2/X prefix. #25-33, X as first of double prefix letters.

Regional

Government of Pakistan

1950 ND Pilgrim Issue

		VG	VF	UNC
R1	**100 Rupees** ND (1950). Red. Crescent moon and star at right. Like #7 but with overprint: *FOR PILGRIMS FROM PAKISTAN FOR USE IN SAUDI ARABIA AND IRAQ.*	—	—	—

State Bank of Pakistan

1950 ND Haj Pilgrim Issue

		VG	VF	UNC
R2	**10 Rupees** ND (1950). Green. Shalimar Gardens in Lahore. Like #13 but with overprint: *FOR HAJ PILGRIMS FROM PAKISTAN FOR USE IN SAUDI ARABIA ONLY.* 3 signature varieties. Back: Tombs near Thatta.	25.00	100.	275.
R3	**10 Rupees** ND. Green on multicolor underprint. Portrait of Mohammed Ali Jinnah at left. Two signature varieties. Back: Shalimar Gardens. Watermark: Portrait of Mohammed Ali Jinnah. Like #16 but with overprint.	15.00	40.00	75.00

R4	10 Rupees	VG	VF	UNC
	ND. Purple on multicolor underprint. Portrait of Mohammed Ali Jinnah at left. Back: Shalimar Gardens. Like #16 and #21 but with overprint.	5.00	7.00	10.00

R5	100 Rupees	VG	VF	UNC
	ND. Brown on multicolor underprint. Mohammed Ali Jinnah at left. Back: Badshahi Mosque, Lahore. Like #23; black overprint.	50.00	100.	225.

1970 ND Haj Pilgrim Issue

Haj Pilgrim notes were discontinued in 1994 and notes on hand were destroyed.

R6	10 Rupees	VG	VF	UNC
	ND (1978). Blue-black on multicolor underprint. Portrait of Mohammed Ali Jinnah at right. Back: View of Moenjodaro. Urdu text line A beneath upper title. Watermark: Portrait of Mohammed Ali Jinnah. Like #34; black overprint.	4.00	7.00	10.00

R7	100 Rupees	VG	VF	UNC
	ND (1975-78). Gold on multicolor underprint. Portrait of Mohammed Ali Jinnah at right. Two signature varieties. Back: Islamic College, Peshawar. No Urdu text line beneath upper title. Like #31; dark brown overprint.	5.00	10.00	20.00

PAPUA NEW GUINEA

Papua New Guinea, an independent member of the British Commonwealth, occupies the eastern half of the island of New Guinea. It lies north of Australia near the equator and borders on West Irian. The country, which includes nearby Bismarck Archipelago, Buka and Bougainville, has an area of 462,820 sq. km. and a population of 5.93 million. Capital: Port Moresby. The economy is agricultural, and exports include copra, rubber, cocoa, coffee, tea, gold and copper.

The eastern half of the island of New Guinea - second largest in the world - was divided between Germany (north) and the UK (south) in 1885. The latter area was transferred to Australia in 1902, which occupied the northern portion during World War I and continued to administer the combined areas until independence in 1975. A nine-year secessionist revolt on the island of Bougainville ended in 1997 after claiming some 20,000 lives.

RULERS:
British

MONETARY SYSTEM:
1 Kina = 100 Toea, 1975-
1 Shilling = 12 Pence
1 Crown = 5 Shillings
1 Pound = 4 Crowns

Territory of Papua

Bank of New South Wales

Port Moresby

1910 Issue

		Good	Fine	XF
S111	**1 Pound** 1.5.1910; 1.6.1910. Black. Seated allegorical woman holding caduceus by sheep with sailing ship in background at top center. Printer: CS&E.	—	—	—
S112	**5 Pounds** (ca.1910). Reported not confirmed.	—	—	—
S113	**10 Pounds** (ca.1910). Reported not confirmed.	—	—	—

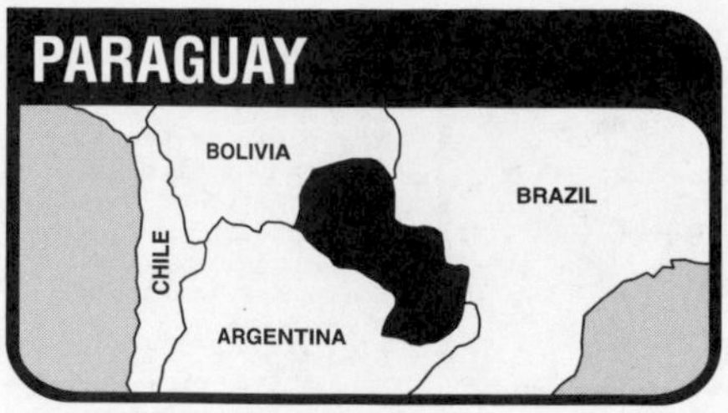

The Republic of Paraguay, a landlocked country in the heart of South America surrounded by Argentina, Bolivia and Brazil, has an area of 157,042 sq. mi. (406,752 sq. km.) and a population of 5.5 million, 95 percent of whom are of mixed Spanish and Indian descent. Capital: Asunción. The country is predominantly agrarian, with no important mineral deposits or oil reserves. Meat, timber, oilseeds, tobacco and cotton account for 70 percent of Paraguay's export revenue.

In the disastrous War of the Triple Alliance (1865-70) - between Paraguay and Argentina, Brazil, and Uruguay - Paraguay lost two-thirds of all adult males and much of its territory. It stagnated economically for the next half century. In the Chaco War of 1932-35, Paraguay won large, economically important areas from Bolivia. The 35-year military dictatorship of Alfredo Stroessner ended in 1989, and, despite a marked increase in political infighting in recent years, Paraguay has held relatively free and regular presidential elections since then.

MONETARY SYSTEM:

1 Peso = 100 Centavos to 1870
1 Peso = 8 Reales to 1872
1 Peso = 100 Centésimos to 1870
1 Peso = 100 Centavos (Centésimos) to 1944
1 Guaraní = 100 Céntimos, 1944-

Banks

Banco de Comercio

1886 Issues

	Good	Fine	XF
S102 1 1/2 Pesos 6.3.1866. Steam locomotive at left. Series A. Printer: Stiller y Laass, Buenos Aires. Rare.	—	—	—

	Good	Fine	XF
S103 2 Pesos 6.3.1886. Black on brown underprint. Railroad depot at center right. Series B. Back: Brown. Arms at center. Printer: Stiller y Laass, Buenos Aires. Rare.	—	—	—
S104 5 Pesos 6.3.1886. Black on orange underprint. Building with tower at left. Printer: Stiller y Laass, Buenos Aires. Rare.	—	—	—

NOTE: Additional denominations require confirmation.

	Good	Fine	XF
S104A 10 Pesos Rare.	—	—	—
S105 1 1/2 Pesos 6.3.1886. Brown on light blue underprint. Passenger train at center. Printer: G&D. Face proof.	—	Unc	1250.
S106 2 Pesos 6.3.1886. Black and red on light green underprint. Government building at upper left. Printer: G&D. Face proof.	—	Unc	1250.
S107 5 Pesos 6.3.1886. Black and brown on light green underprint. Government building at upper right. Back: Brown on blue underprint. Printer: G&D. Proof.	—	Unc	1400.
S108 10 Pesos 6.3.1886. Black on blue and orange underprint. Portrait man at left, plantation scene at center right. Back: Brown and violet. Arms at center. Printer: G&D. Proof.	—	Unc	1600.
S109 20 Pesos 6.3.1886. Black on light orange and blue underprint. Portrait man at upper right, workers building native huts at lower center. Printer: G&D. Face proof.	—	Unc	1250.
S110 50 Pesos 6.3.1886. Black on red and purple underprint. River scene at center, portrait man at right. Printer: G&D. Proof.	—	Unc	1250.

Banco del Paraguay

1879-82 Issue

	Good	Fine	XF
S111 5 Centavos 1879; 1882. Black. Deer running at center. Uniface. Printer: Litografía Nacional, Buenos Aires.			
a. 1.1.1879.	—	—	—
b. 1.1.1882.	—	—	—

	Good	Fine	XF
S112 10 Centavos 1879; 1882. Black. Cows at center. Uniface. Printer: Litografía Nacional, Buenos Aires.			
a. 1.1.1879.	—	—	—
b. 1.1.1882.	—	—	—

	Good	Fine	XF
S113 20 Centavos 1879; 1882. Black. Fox at center. Uniface. Printer: Litografía Nacional, Buenos Aires.			
a. 1.1.1879.	—	—	—
b. 1.1.1882.	—	—	—

	Good	Fine	XF
S114 50 Centavos 1879; 1882. Black. Green numeral *50* at center. Lion under tree at right. Uniface. Printer: Litografía Nacional, Buenos Aires.			
a. 1.1.1879.	—	—	—
b. 1.1.1882.	—	—	—
S119 20 Pesos 1.1.1882. Dog's head at lower left, horses at upper center. Printer: Litografía Nacional, Buenos Aires.	—	—	—

1882 Issue

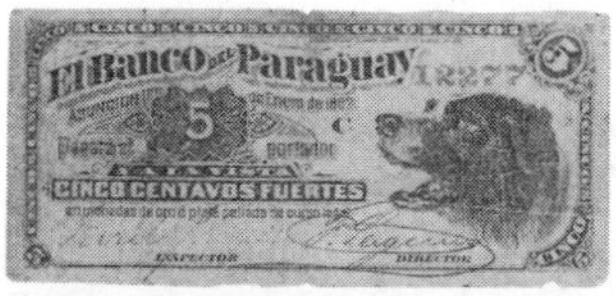

	Good	Fine	XF
S121 5 Centavos 1.1.1882. Black on blue underprint. Dog's head at right. Uniface. Printer: ABNC.			
a. Issued note.	40.00	120.	360.
p. Proof.	—	Unc	750.

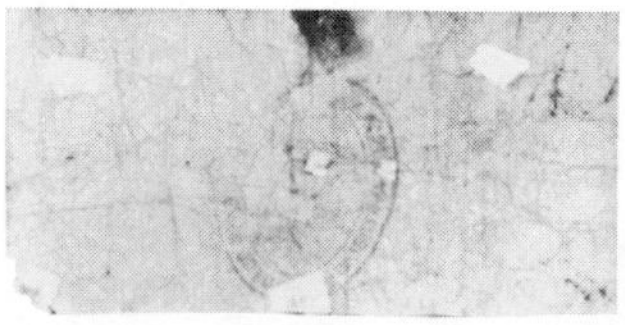

	Good	Fine	XF
S122 10 Centavos 1.1.1882. Black on gold underprint. Bull at left. Uniface. Printer: ABNC.			
a. Issued note.	45.00	135.	300.
p. Proof.	—	Unc	750.

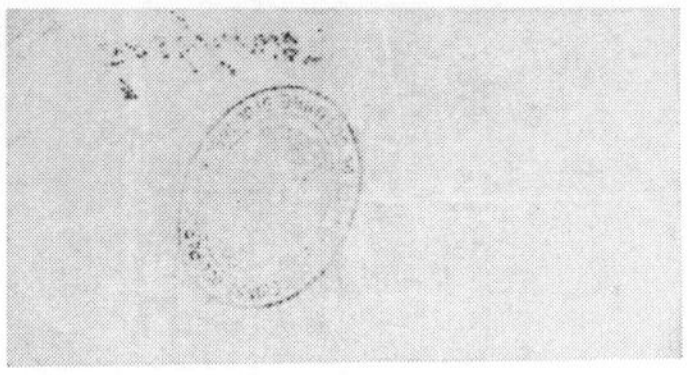

S123 20 Centavos

1.1.1882. Black on brown underprint. Jaguar at center. Uniface. Printer: ABNC.

	Good	Fine	XF
a. Issued note.	60.00	180.	540.
p. Proof.	—	Unc	750.

S124 50 Centavos

1.1.1882. Black on red underprint. Horse at left under tree, value between griffens at center right. Uniface. Printer: ABNC.

	Good	Fine	XF
a. Issued note.	75.00	225.	675.
p. Proof.	—	Unc	750.

S125 1 Peso

1.1.1882. Black on brown underprint. Steam locomotive at upper left, young woman at lower right. Back: Brown. Printer: ABNC.

	Good	Fine	XF
p. Proof.	—	Unc	1000.
s. Specimen.	—	Unc	1250.

S126 2 Pesos

1.1.1882. Black on green underprint. Steam passenger train at center. Back: Green. Printer: ABNC.

	Good	Fine	XF
a. Issued note.	—	—	—
p. Proof.	—	Unc	1000.

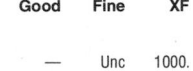

S127 5 Pesos

1.1.1882. Black on red underprint. Arms at left, crowned woman at right. Back: Orange. Printer: ABNC.

	Good	Fine	XF
p. Proof.	—	Unc	1000.
s. Specimen.	—	Unc	1250.

S128 10 Pesos

1.1.1882. Black on olive-green underprint. Sailing ship at center right. Back: Olive-green. Printer: ABNC.

	Good	Fine	XF
p. Proof.	—	Unc	1000.
s. Specimen.	—	Unc	1250.

S129 20 Pesos

1.1.1882. Black on lilac underprint. Ships at left center, woman at right. Back: Purple. Printer: ABNC.

	Good	Fine	XF
p. Proof.	—	Unc	1000.
s. Specimen.	—	Unc	1250.

Banco Nacional del Paraguay

1886 Issue

#S141-S152 Law of 31.10.1883 but later issue date.

S141 5 Centavos

1.1.1886. Black on blue underprint. Dog's head at right. Similar to #S121. Uniface. Printer: ABNC.

	Good	Fine	XF
a. Issued note.	5.00	15.00	50.00
p. Proof.	—	Unc	750.

S142 10 Centavos

1.1.1886. Black on gold underprint. Bull at left. Similar to #S122. Uniface. Printer: ABNC.

	Good	Fine	XF
a. Issued note.	7.50	25.00	75.00
p. Proof.	—	Unc	750.

S143 20 Centavos

1.1.1886. Black on pink underprint. Jaguar at center. Similar to #S123. Uniface. Printer: ABNC.

	Good	Fine	XF
a. Issued note.	12.50	35.00	135.
p. Proof.	—	Unc	750.

S144 50 Centavos

1.1.1886. Black on brown underprint. Horse at left under tree, value between griffens at center right. Similar to #S124. Uniface. Printer: ABNC.

	Good	Fine	XF
a. Issued note.	15.00	45.00	150.
p. Proof.	—	Unc	750.

		Good	Fine	XF
S145	**1 Peso**			
	1.1.1886. Black on brown underprint. Steam locomotive at upper left, young woman at lower right. Similar to #S125. Back: Brown. Printer: ABNC.			
	a. Issued note.	30.00	100.	300.
	p. Proof.	—	Unc	750.

		Good	Fine	XF
S146	**2 Pesos**			
	1.1.1886. Black on green underprint. Steam passenger train at center. Similar to #S126. Back: Green. Printer: ABNC.	—	—	—
S147	**5 Pesos**			
	1.1.1886. Printer: ABNC. Reported not confirmed.	—	—	—
S148	**10 Pesos**			
	1.1.1886. Printer: ABNC. Reported not confirmed.	—	—	—
S149	**20 Pesos**			
	1.1.1886. Black on lilac underprint. Ships at left center, woman at right. Series B. Similar to #S129. Back: Purple. Printer: ABNC. Proof.	—	—	—
S150	**50 Pesos**			
	1.1.1886. Black on green and red underprint. Man at left, arms at center, allegorical woman with globe and pitcher at right. Series A. Back: Orange. Woman with spool at center. Printer: ABNC. Proof.	—	—	—

		Good	Fine	XF
S151	**100 Pesos**			
	1.1.1886. Black on orange and blue underprint. Liberty standing at left, arms at center, portrait Gen. Bernardino Caballero at right. Series A. Back: Blue. Woman writing ("Trade") at center. Printer: ABNC. Proof.			
	a. Issued note. Rare.	—	—	—
	p. Proof.	—	Unc	750.
S152	**200 Pesos**			
	1.1.1886. Black on green and red underprint. Portrait Gen. Escobar at left, horses at upper center, arms at right. Series A. Back: Brown. Steam passenger trains in terminal ("The New Depot"). Printer: ABNC. Proof.	—	Unc	750.

Banco del Paraguay y Rio de la Plata

1889 Issue

		Good	Fine	XF
S161	**1 Peso - 25 Centavos**			
	26.12.1889. Black on green underprint. Seated woman with safe at left, arms at right. Back: Green. Printer: ABNC.			
	a. Issued note.	45.00	135.	400.
	p. Proof.	—	Unc	1250.

		Good	Fine	XF
S162	**2 Pesos**			
	26.12.1889. Black on blue and yellow underprint. Portrait H. Ponzini at left, arms at right. Back: Blue. Printer: ABNC.			
	a. Issued note.	75.00	225.	675.
	p. Proof.	—	Unc	1250.

		Good	Fine	XF
S163	**5 Pesos**			
	26.12.1889. Black on brown underprint. Portrait A. Schmied at left, seated woman at left center, arms at right. Back: Brown. Printer: ABNC.			
	a. Issued note.	—	—	—
	p. Proof.	—	Unc	1000.

		Good	Fine	XF
S164	**10 Pesos**			
	26.12.1889. Black on brown underprint. Hope at the Seashore at left, arms at center, portrait Higinio Uriarte at right. Back: Brown. Figures at left and center right. Printer: ABNC. Proof.			
	a. Issued note.	—	—	—
	p. Proof.	—	Unc	1250.

		Good	Fine	XF
S165	**20 Pesos**			
	26.12.1889. Black on orange and yellow underprint. Arms at left, allegorical woman and child ("Cupid Disarmed") at center, portrait J. A. Meza at right. Back: Orange. Printer: ABNC.			
	a. Purple overprint.	175.	525.	1575.
	b. Without overprint.	175.	525.	1575.
	p. Proof.	—	Unc	1400.

		Good	Fine	XF
S166	**50 Pesos**			
	26.12.1889. Black on yellow and brown underprint. Portrait Gen. Bernardino Caballero at left, seated female ("Tropics") at upper center, arms at right. Back: Dark brown. Indian woman paddling at center. Printer: ABNC. Proof.	—	Unc	2250.

S167 100 Pesos — Good | Fine | XF

26.12.1889. Black on green and yellow underprint. Portrait T. Dugan at left, allegorical child and fish ("Off Sandy Hook") at center, arms at lower right. Back: Green. Viaduct at left center, steam train at center right. Printer: ABNC. Proof. — — | Unc | 1750.

S168 200 Pesos — Good | Fine | XF

26.12.1889. Black on orange and gold underprint. Portrait Gen. Escobar at left, woman and child ("Peace") at center, arms at right. Back: Orange. Two women at center. Printer: ABNC. Proof. Rare. — — | — | —

#S171 and S172 printer: CSABB.

S171 1 Peso - 25 Centavos

20.12.1889. Portrait Higinio Uriarte at left, arms at right. Printer: CSABB. Rare. — — | — | —

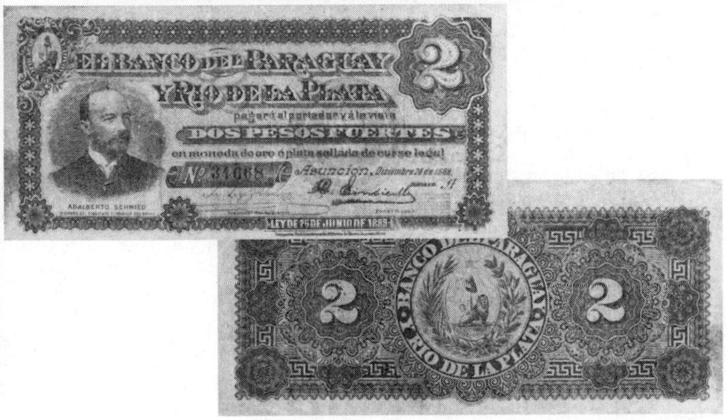

S172 2 Pesos — Good | Fine | XF

20.12.1889. Black on brown underprint. Portrait A. Schmied at left. Back: Green. Arms at center. Printer: CSABB. Rare. — — | — | —

Argentine Occupation

Issued by Argentine military authority for occupation of Paraguay 1870. Uniface. Printer: Lit. San Martin, Buenos Aires.

Lezica y Lanús

Army Supplies

1870's Issue

S181 50 Centimos — Good | Fine | XF

187x. Black. Arms at left, dog on strongbox at center. Paper: Dark blue. — — | Unc | 300.

S182 1 Peso

1.3.1870. Arms at upper center. Rare. — — | — | —

S184 5 Pesos — Good | Fine | XF

1.3.1870. Blue and black. Arms at upper left, two women seated at upper center. Blue hand stamp: *PROVEEDURA / DEL / EJERCITO* over arms. — 600. | 1800. | 5400.

S185 10 Pesos — Good | Fine | XF

1.3.1870. Black and blue-green. Woman at left, arms at upper center. Blue hand stamp: *PROVEEDURA / DEL / EJERCITO* over arms. Paper: Dark pink. — 600. | 1800. | 5400.

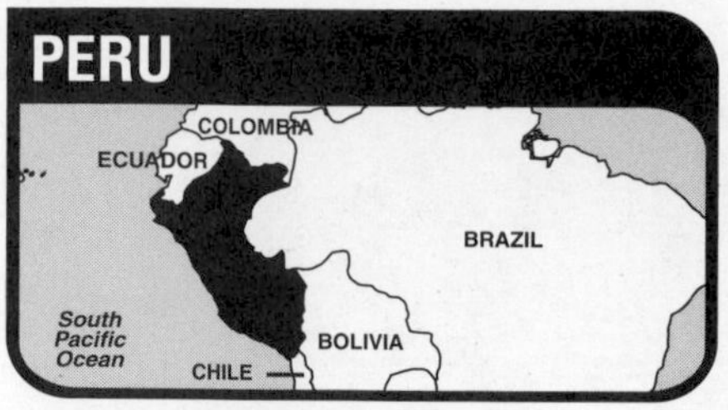

The Republic of Perú, located on the Pacific coast of South America, has an area of 496,222 sq. mi. (1,285,216 sq. km.) and a population of 25.66 million. Capital: Lima. The diversified economy includes mining, fishing and agriculture. Fish meal, copper, sugar, zinc and iron ore are exported.

Ancient Peru was the seat of several prominent Andean civilizations, most notably that of the Incas whose empire was captured by the Spanish conquistadors in 1533. Peruvian independence was declared in 1821, and remaining Spanish forces defeated in 1824. After a dozen years of military rule, Peru returned to democratic leadership in 1980, but experienced economic problems and the growth of a violent insurgency. President Alberto Fujimori's election in 1990 ushered in a decade that saw a dramatic turnaround in the economy and significant progress in curtailing guerrilla activity. Nevertheless, the president's increasing reliance on authoritarian measures and an economic slump in the late 1990s generated mounting dissatisfaction with his regime, which led to his ouster in 2000. A caretaker government oversaw new elections in the spring of 2001, which ushered in Alejandro Toledo Manrique as the new head of government - Peru's first democratically elected president of Native American ethnicity. The presidential election of 2006 saw the return of Alan Garcia Perez who, after a disappointing presidential term from 1985 to 1990, returned to the presidency with promises to improve social conditions and maintain fiscal responsibility.

MONETARY SYSTEM:

1 Sol = 1 Sol de Oro = 100 Centavos, 1879-1985
1 Libra = 10 Soles
1 Inti = 1000 Soles de Oro, 1986-1991
1 Nuevo Sol = 100 Centimes = 1 Million Intis, 1991-
1 Sol = 100 Centavos (10 Dineros)

BANKS:

Banco Anglo-Peruano .... #S101-S108
Banco de Arequipa .... #S111-S124
Banco de la Compañia General del Perú .... #S131-S134
Banco de la Emancipación .... #S141-S143
Banco de Emisión del Cerro .... #S151-S153
Banco Garantizador .... #S161-S168
Banco La Providencia .... #S191-S236
Banco de Lima .... #S241-S246
Banco de Londres y Sud America .... #S251-S257
Banco de Londres Mexico y Sud America .... #S261-S298

Banco Nacional del Perú

Regular Issues .... #S301-S328
Tacna Branch Issue .... #S331-S335
Yquique Branch Issue .... #S341-S345
Banco del Perú .... #S351-S368
Banco de Piura .... #S371-S374
Banco de Tacna .... #S381-S387
Issues under Chilean Occupation .... #S391-S394
Banco de Trujillo .... #S401-S414
Banco del Valle de Chicama .... #S421-S425
Compañia de Obras Públicas y Fomento del Perú .... #S441-S449

PAWN SHOPS

Monte de Piedad de Callao .... #S552-S555
Monte de Piedad de Lima .... #S564

REVOLUTION

Iquitos Revolution .... #S601-S607

BANKS

BANCO ANGLO-PERUANO

1875 FIRST ISSUE

S101 20 Centavos
1.7.1875. Black. Back: English and Peruvian arms at center. Printer: CNBB/NBNC.

	Good	Fine	XF
a. Back green.	50.00	150.	450.
b. Back orange.	75.00	225.	675.

S101A 40 Centavos
1.7.1875. Black on brown underprint. Back: Brown. English and Peruvian arms at center. Printer: CNBB/NBNC.

	Good	Fine	XF
a. Issued note.	50.00	150.	450.
p. Proof.	—	Unc	350.

S101B 50 Centavos
1.7.1875. Black on blue underprint. Back: Blue. English and Peruvian arms at center. Printer: CNBB/NBNC.

Good	Fine	XF
100.	300.	900.

1875 SECOND ISSUE

S102 40 Centavos
1.7.1875. Black on yellow-orange underprint. Signature R. J. Jameson at right. Back: Brown-orange. English and Peruvian arms at center. Printer: CNBB/NBNC. Proof.

Good	Fine	XF
—	Unc	350.

S103 50 Centavos
1.7.1875. Black on dark brown underprint. Signature R. J. Jameson at right. Back: Dark brown. English and Peruvian arms at center. Printer: CNBB/NBNC. Proof.

Good	Fine	XF
—	Unc	350.

S103A 1 Sol
ca. 1875. Brown. Bank monogram at center. Back: English and Peruvian arms at center. Printer: CNBB/NBNC. Back proof.

Good	Fine	XF
—	Unc	200.

1874-75 ISSUE

	Good	Fine	XF
S104 1 Sol 1.9.1874. Green. Mercury on globe at right. Printer: Dondorf & Naumann, Frankfurt a/M. Rare.	—	—	—
S105 5 Soles 17.3.1875. Brown. Mercury on globe at right. Similar to #S104. Printer: Dondorf & Naumann, Frankfurt a/M. Rare.	—	—	—

S106 10 Soles
1.9.1874. Blue. Cherubs at bottom center. Printer: Dondorf & Naumann, Frankfurt a/M. Rare.

Good	Fine	XF
—	—	—

	Good	Fine	XF
S107 20 Soles 1.9.1874; 17.3.1875. Brown. Woman and cherubs at left. Printer: Dondorf & Naumann, Frankfurt a/M. Rare.	—	—	—
S108 100 Soles 187x. Green. Woman and cherubs at left. Similar to #S107. Printer: Dondorf & Naumann, Frankfurt a/M. Rare.	—	—	—

Banco de Arequipa

1870's Issue

	Good	Fine	XF
S111 20 Centavos ND. Black and red. Man and llama with city view in back at center. Printer: Abele y Ca., Lima.	25.00	75.00	225.

	Good	Fine	XF
S112 40 Centavos ND. Blue. Man and llama with city view in back at center. Similar to #S111. Printer: Abele y Ca., Lima.	25.00	75.00	225.

	VG	VF	UNC
S116 40 Centavos 1.10.1874. Black on green underprint. Seated woman with safe and shield at center; city, train and mountain in background. Back: Green. Printer: CNBB.	7.50	22.50	65.00

	VG	VF	UNC
S117 1 Sol 18xx. Black on green underprint. Seated woman with safe and shield at center; city, train and mountain in background. Similar to #S116. Back: Green. Printer: CNBB.	7.50	22.50	65.00
S118 2 Soles 18xx. Black on orange underprint. Seated woman with safe and shield at center; city, train and mountain in background. Similar to #S116. Back: Orange. Printer: CNBB.	12.50	35.00	110.

	VG	VF	UNC
S119 5 Soles 187x. Black on brown underprint. Similar to #S116 but cow at left, wheat at right. Back: Brown. Printer: CNBB.	30.00	90.00	270.

	VG	VF	UNC
S120 10 Soles 187x. Black on brown underprint. Similar to #S116 but man ("Farmer") at left, roosters at right. Back: Brown. Printer: CNBB.	50.00	150.	450.

	VG	VF	UNC
S121 20 Soles 187x. Black on brown underprint. Similar to #S116 but ducks at left, train at right. Printer: CNBB.	—	—	300.

	VG	VF	UNC
S122 50 Soles 187x. Black on brown underprint. Similar to #S116 but basket of corn at left, sheep at right. Printer: CNBB.	—	—	300.

	VG	VF	UNC
S123 100 Soles 187x. Black on red underprint. Similar to #S116 but man at left, anchor at right. Printer: CNBB.	—	—	300.

	VG	VF	UNC
S124 500 Soles 1.8.1872. Black on yellow underprint. Similar to #S116 but sailing ship ("Outward Bound") at left, scroll at right. Printer: CNBB.	—	—	400.

Banco de la Compañia General del Perú

1873 Issue

#S131-S134 colors and printers: face, black and green, NBNC; back, green, ABNC. Proofs, punched hole cancelled.

		VG	VF	UNC
S131	**1 Sol** 1873. Portrait J. Galvez between sailing ship and steam train at upper left, steam train at lower center. Back: Steam train.			
	p. Proof.	—	—	500.
	r. Unissued remainder.	—	—	150.
S132	**5 Soles** 1873. Man with horses and mule train at upper center, train below. Laureated J. Galvez at right. Back: Man with llamas at left, steam train at right.	—	—	300.

		VG	VF	UNC
S133	**20 Soles** 1873. Portrait J. Galvez at left, woman seated at center, train below. Back: Steam train at center.	—	—	350.
S134	**100 Soles** 1873. Woman in feather headdress with sword and lion ("Libertad") at left, laureated portrait J. Galvez at left center, train below. Back: Steam train at left, man with llamas at right.	—	—	400.

NOTE: For #S131, S132 and S134 overprint in Incas as issued in 1881, see Volume II, #11-13.

Banco de la Emancipación

Paper-Money Auxiliary Bank

1822 Issue

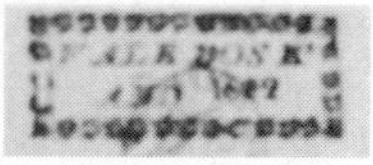

		Good	Fine	XF
S141	**2 Reales** 1822. Black. Rare.	—	—	—

		Good	Fine	XF
S142	**4 Reales** 1822. Black. Rare.	—	—	—

		Good	Fine	XF
S143	**1 Peso = 8 Reales** 5.1822. Black. Rare.	—	—	—

Banco del Emisión del Cerro

1870's Issue

		Good	Fine	XF
S151	**1 Dinero = 1/10 Sol** Reported not confirmed.	—	—	—
S153	**1/2 Sol** Reported not confirmed.	—	—	—

Banco Garantizador

1876 Issue

		Good	Fine	XF
S161	**10 Centavos** 1.9.1876. Black on green underprint. Helmeted Minerva at left. Back: Green. Printer: NBNC.	150.	450.	1350.

		Good	Fine	XF
S162	**20 Centavos** 1.9.1876. Black on brown underprint. Woman and fruit at upper center. Back: Brown. Printer: NBNC.	150.	450.	1350.

		Good	Fine	XF
S163	**40 Centavos** 1.9.1876. Black on red-orange underprint. Eagle at center. Back: Orange. Printer: NBNC.	180.	540.	1600.

		Good	Fine	XF
S164	**1 Sol** 1.9.1876. Black and blue. Farm family at center. Fully printed, or partially printed and stamped date. Back: Blue. Two men at center. Printer: NBNC.	180.	540.	1600.

		Good	Fine	XF
S165	**2 Soles** 1.9.1876. Black and orange. Woman sitting with bale ("Manufactures") at center. Fully printed, or partially printed and stamped date. Back: Orange. Printer: NBNC.	135.	400.	1200.

		Good	Fine	XF
S166	**5 Soles** 1.9.1876. Black and brown. Large ornaments at left and right, portrait girl ("La Perla de Lima") at upper center. Fully printed, or partially printed and stamped date. Back: Brown. Printer: NBNC.	150.	450.	1350.

	Good	Fine	XF
S167 10 Soles 1.9.1876. Black and green. Portrait three girls ("The Young Students") at upper center. Fully printed, or partially printed and stamped date. Printer: NBNC.	180.	540.	1600.

	Good	Fine	XF
S168 50 Soles 1.9.1876. Black and green. Cherub with fruit ("Abundance") at lower left, three allegorical women ("Exchange") at upper center, cotton at lower right. Fully printed, or partially printed and stamped date. Back: Street scene of bank facade. Printer: NBNC.			
a. Issued note. Rare.	—	—	—
s. Specimen.	—	Unc	750.

Banco La Providencia

1863 First Issue

	Good	Fine	XF
S191 5 Pesos 18xx-(7.1863). Black. Woman and child at upper left, cornucopias and caduceus at lower right. Uniface. Rare.	—	—	—
S192 25 Pesos 31.12.1863. Black. Woman and child at upper left, cornucopias and caduceus at lower right. Uniface. Rare.	—	—	—
S193 50 Pesos 31.12.1863. Black. Woman and child at upper left, cornucopias and caduceus at lower right. Uniface. Rare.	—	—	—
S194 100 Pesos 31.12.1863. Black. Woman and child at upper left, cornucopias and caduceus at lower right. Uniface. Rare.	—	—	—
S195 500 Pesos 31.12.1863. Black. Woman and child at upper left, cornucopias and caduceus at lower right. Uniface. Rare.	—	—	—

1863 Second Issue

	Good	Fine	XF
S201 25 Pesos 31.12.1863. Black. Woman and child at upper left, cornucopias and caduceus at lower right. Large denomination word in red at center in underprint. Rare.	—	—	—

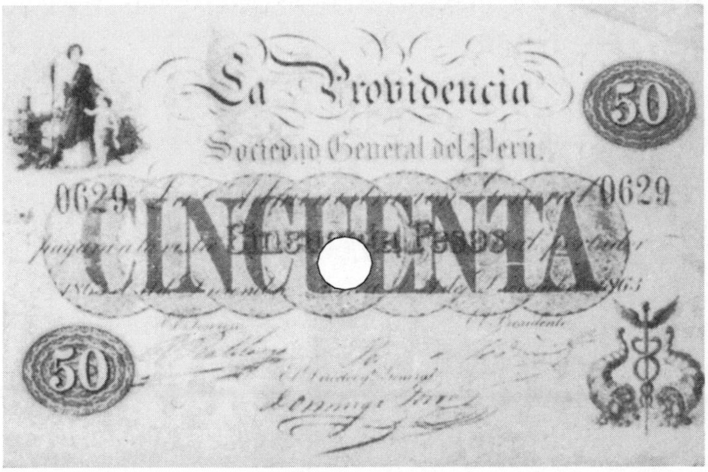

	Good	Fine	XF
S202 50 Pesos 31.12.1863. Black. Woman and child at upper left, cornucopias and caduceus at lower right. Large denomination word in blue at center in underprint. Rare.	—	—	—
S203 100 Pesos 31.12.1863. Black. Woman and child at upper left, cornucopias and caduceus at lower right. Large denomination word in yellow at center in underprint. Rare.	—	—	—
S204 500 Pesos 31.12.1863. Black. Woman and child at upper left, cornucopias and caduceus at lower right. Large denomination word in green at center in underprint. Rare.	—	—	—

1864 Issue

#S209-S214 similar to #S191-S195 but center design guilloche is more ornate and has word plus numerals at either side. They also express value in soles as well as pesos in special text near lower ctr.

	Good	Fine	XF
S209 5 Soles 30.6.1864. Black. Woman and child at upper left, cornucopias and caduceus at lower right. Ornate center guilloche with word plus numerals on each side. Special text with value in soles and pesos near lower center. Rare.	—	—	—
S211 20 Soles = 25 Pesos 30.6.1864. Black. Yellow protector. Woman and child at upper left, cornucopias and caduceus at lower right. Ornate center guilloche with word plus numerals on each side. Special text with value in soles and pesos near lower center. Rare.	—	—	—

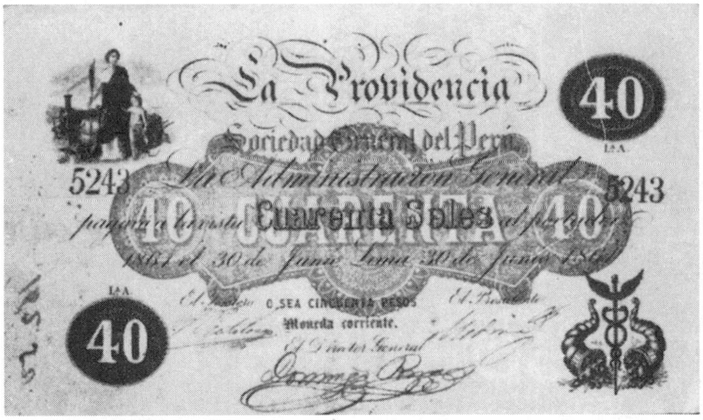

	Good	Fine	XF
S212 40 Soles = 50 Pesos 30.6.1864. Black. Red protector. Woman and child at upper left, cornucopias and caduceus at lower right. Ornate center guilloche with word plus numerals on each side. Special text with value in soles and pesos near lower center. Rare.	—	—	—
S213 80 Soles = 100 Pesos 30.6.1864. Black. Green protector. Woman and child at upper left, cornucopias and caduceus at lower right. Ornate center guilloche with word plus numerals on each side. Special text with value in soles and pesos near lower center. Rare.	—	—	—
S214 200 Soles = 250 Pesos 30.6.1864. Black. Yellow protector. Woman and child at upper left, cornucopias and caduceus at lower right. Ornate center guilloche with word plus numerals on each side. Special text with value in soles and pesos near lower center. Rare.	—	—	—

#S221 and S222 printer: NBNC.

S221 4 Soles

	Good	Fine	XF
1869. Black and red. Woman standing ("Commerce") at left, rayed head at center, anchor at right. Printer: NBNC. Rare.	—	—	—

S222 8 Soles

	Good	Fine	XF
1869. Black and red. Two men at left, sailing ship at center, cotton at right. Printer: NBNC. Rare.	—	—	—

1867-77 Issue

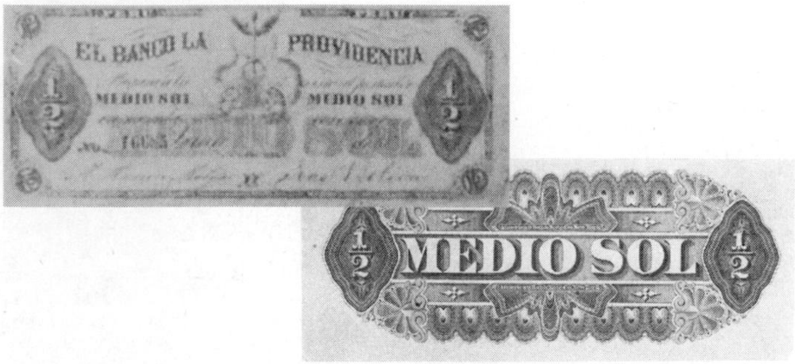

S226 1/2 Sol

	Good	Fine	XF
18xx. Black on green underprint. Cornucopias and caduceus at center. Back: Green. Printer: ABNC.			
a. Issued note.	135.	400.	1200.
p. Proof.	—	Unc	1500.

S227 1 Sol

	Good	Fine	XF
5.4.1867; 10.11.1872. Black on green underprint. Woman and child ("Charity & Commerce") at left, two cornucopias and caduceus at right. Back: Green. Llamas. Printer: ABNC.	150.	450.	1350.

S228 2 Soles

	Good	Fine	XF
2.8.1867; 17.4.1868; 1.1.1875. Black on green underprint. Woman and child ("Charity & Commerce") at left, two cornucopias and caduceus at right. Similar to #S227. Back: Brown. Llamas. Printer: ABNC. Rare.	—	—	—

NOTE: According to archive records, two back color varieties exist for #S227 and S228.

S229 4 Soles

	Good	Fine	XF
1.1.1875. Black on green underprint. Woman and child ("Charity & Commerce") at left, two cornucopias and caduceus at right. Similar to #S227. Back: Llamas. Overprint: Large star at upper center right. Printer: ABNC.	135.	400.	1200.

S230 5 Soles

	Good	Fine	XF
1877. Black on green underprint. Woman and child ("Charity & Commerce") at left, two cornucopias and caduceus at right. Similar to #S229. Back: Llamas. Overprint: Large star at upper center right. Printer: ABNC. Rare.	—	—	—

S231 10 Soles

	Good	Fine	XF
1877. Black on green underprint. Woman and child ("Charity & Commerce") at left, two cornucopias and caduceus at right. Similar to #S229. Back: Llamas. Overprint: Large star at upper center right. Printer: ABNC. Rare.	—	—	—

S232 20 Soles

	Good	Fine	XF
20.7.1877. Black on green underprint. Woman and child ("Charity & Commerce") at left, two cornucopias and caduceus at right. Similar to #S229 but man with llamas added at center. Overprint: Large star at upper center right. Printer: ABNC. Rare.	—	—	—

S233 50 Soles

	Good	Fine	XF
20.7.1877. Black on green underprint. Woman and child ("Charity & Commerce") at left, two cornucopias and caduceus at right, man with llamas added at center. Similar to #S232. Overprint: Large star at upper center right. Printer: ABNC. Rare.	—	—	—

S234 100 Soles

	Good	Fine	XF
20.7.1877. Black on green underprint. Woman and child ("Charity & Commerce") at left, two cornucopias and caduceus at right, man with llamas added at center. Similar to #S232. Overprint: Large star at upper center right. Printer: ABNC. Rare.	—	—	—

S235 500 Soles

	Good	Fine	XF
18xx. Black on green underprint. Woman and child ("Charity & Commerce") at left, two cornucopias and caduceus at right, man with llamas added at center. Similar to #S232. Overprint: Large star at upper center right. Printer: ABNC. Rare.	—	—	—

S236 1000 Soles

	Good	Fine	XF
20.7.1877. Black on green underprint. Woman and child ("Charity & Commerce") at left, two cornucopias and caduceus at right, man with llamas added at center. Similar to #S232. Overprint: Large star at upper center right. Printer: ABNC. Rare.	—	—	—

Banco de Lima

1870-76 Issue

#S241-S246 printer: CNBB.

S241 1 Sol — Good — Fine — XF
1.7.1870; 1.11.1875. Black on orange underprint. Indian woman with sword and flag standing at left, mountain view at center, llamas at right. Back: Deep orange. Printer: CNBB. — — —

S242 4 Soles
1.1.1870 (hand stamped or handwritten dates). Black on green underprint. Girls ("Summer") at lower left, two women and shield at upper left, train and shield at right. Back: Blue-green. Printer: CNBB.

	Good	Fine	XF
a. Issued note.	225.	675.	2000.
p. Proof.	—	Unc	1250.

S243 8 Soles — Good — Fine — XF
1.1.1870; 1.2.1876. Black on blue underprint. Three girls ("The Young Students") at lower left, two women and sunface at lower right. Back: Blue. Printer: CNBB. Rare. — — —

S244 20 Soles — Good — Fine — XF
1.11.1875. Black on blue underprint. Sailing ship at left, seated woman with produce and shield at upper center, Mercury at lower right. Back: Light blue. Printer: CNBB. Rare. — — —

S245 80 Soles — Good — Fine — XF
1.1.1871. Black on brown underprint. Liberty with constitution at left, steamship at right. Back: Brown. Printer: CNBB. Rare. — — —

S246 400 Soles — Good — Fine — XF
1.9.1875. Black on yellow underprint. Sitting woman at lower left, harbor scene at center, angel and scroll at lower right. Printer: CNBB. Rare. — — —

Banco de Londres y Sud America

1800's Issue

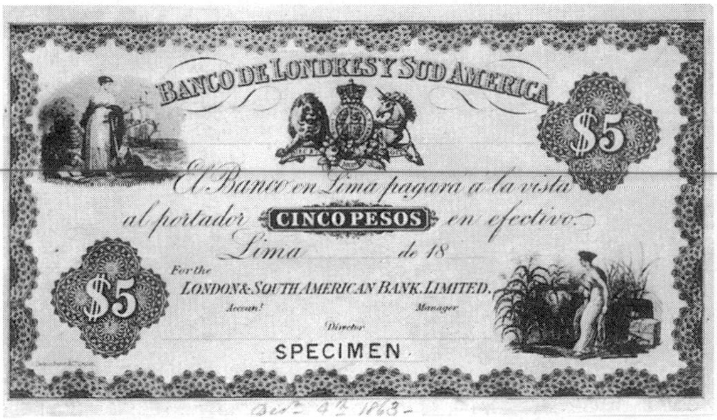

		Good	Fine	XF
S251	**5 Pesos** 18xx. Black. Standing woman by beehive with sailing ship in background at upper left, crowned royal arms at upper center, standing woman in cornfield at lower right. Printer: PBC. Rare.	—	—	—
S253	**25 Pesos** 18xx. Black. Standing woman by beehive with sailing ship in background at upper left, crowned royal arms at upper center, standing woman in cornfield at lower right. Printer: PBC. Rare.	—	—	—
S255	**100 Pesos** 18xx. Black. Standing woman by beehive with sailing ship in background at upper left, crowned royal arms at upper center, standing woman in cornfield at lower right. Printer: PBC. Rare.	—	—	—
S257	**1000 Pesos** 18xx. Black. Standing woman by beehive with sailing ship in background at upper left, crowned royal arms at upper center, standing woman in cornfield at lower right. Printer: PBC. Rare.	—	—	—

Banco de Londres Mexico y Sud America

1860's Issue

		Good	Fine	XF
S261	**5 Pesos** 18xx. Black. Standing woman by beehive with sailing ship in background at upper left, crowned royal arms at upper center, standing woman in cornfield at lower right. Rare.	—	—	—
S263	**25 Pesos** 18xx. Black. Standing woman by beehive with sailing ship in background at upper left, crowned royal arms at upper center, standing woman in cornfield at lower right. Rare.	—	—	—
S265	**100 Pesos** 18xx. Black. Standing woman by beehive with sailing ship in background at upper left, crowned royal arms at upper center, standing woman in cornfield at lower right. Rare.	—	—	—

		Good	Fine	XF
S267	**1000 Pesos** 18xx. Black. Standing woman by beehive with sailing ship in background at upper left, crowned royal arms at upper center, standing woman in cornfield at lower right. Rare.	—	—	—

1866-72 Issues

		Good	Fine	XF
S271	**2 Soles** 1.1.1866. Black on orange underprint. Girl at lower left, portrait Queen Victoria at center, woman with child at lower right. Date filled in by hand. Back: Blue. Printer: ABNC. Rare.	—	—	—
S272	**5 Soles** 1866; 1.3.1870. Black on green underprint. Two girls at lower left, two seated women and English shield at center, woman at right. Date filled in by hand. Back: Blue. Printer: ABNC. Rare.	—	—	—
S273	**5 Soles** 1.3.1870. Black on red underprint. Two girls at lower left, two seated women and English shield at center, woman at right. Date filled in by hand. Like #S272. Back: Blue. Printer: ABNC. Rare.	—	—	—

		Good	Fine	XF
S274	**10 Soles** 1.1.1866. Black on red underprint. Woman holding rabbit at lower left, boys and mule train at top center, shield with flags with portrait Queen Victoria at lower right. Date filled in by hand. Back: Blue. Printer: ABNC. Rare.	—	—	—

		Good	Fine	XF
S275	**25 Soles** 1.10.1871. Black on red underprint. Boys and mule train at upper left, girl holding dog at lower right. Date filled in by hand. Back: Blue. Printer: ABNC. Rare.	—	—	—

		Good	Fine	XF
S276	**100 Soles** 1.6.1872; 1.1.1875. Black on green underprint. Sailors at lower left, two women and Peruvian shield at upper center, two horses at lower right. Date filled in by hand. Back: Blue. Printer: ABNC. Rare.	—	—	—

		Good	Fine	XF
S277	**500 Soles** 18xx. Black on green underprint. Two girls at lower left, lion and reclining woman with portrait Queen Victoria at upper center, helmeted figure at right. Date filled in by hand. Back: Blue. Printer: ABNC. Rare.	—	—	—

		Good	Fine	XF
S278	**1000 Soles** 18xx. Black on green underprint. Two girls with sheaves at lower left, two women seated at upper center, shield with flags with portrait Queen Victoria at lower right. Date filled in by hand. Back: Blue. Printer: ABNC. Rare.	—	—	—

1871 Issue

		Good	Fine	XF
S281	**1 Sol** 20.9.1871. Blue. Woman's head at left. Printer: TDLR. Rare.	—	—	—

		Good	Fine	XF
S282	**2 Soles** 20.9.1871. Purple. Woman's head at lower center. Printer: TDLR. Rare.	—	—	—

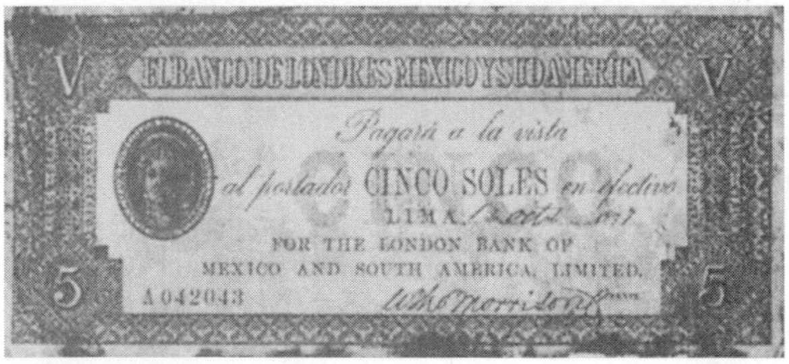

		Good	Fine	XF
S283	**5 Soles** 1.10.1871. Green. Woman's head at left. Printer: TDLR. Rare.	—	—	—

		Good	Fine	XF
S284	**10 Soles** 1.10.1871. Yellow. Woman's head at upper center. Printer: TDLR. Rare.	—	—	—

1873-74 Issue

		Good	Fine	XF
S291	**1 Sol** 1.1.1873. Blue. People with horse at lower left, arms at upper center, laureated woman at lower right. Printer: ABNC.			
	a. Issued note. Rare.	—	—	—
	p. Proof.	—	Unc	3500.

		Good	Fine	XF
S292	**2 Soles** 1.1.1873. Blue. Girl at lower left, portrait Queen Victoria at center, woman with child at lower right. Printed date. Like #S271. Printer: ABNC. Rare.	—	—	—
S293	**5 Soles** 1.1.1873. Black on brown and green underprint. Two girls at lower left, two seated women and English shield at center, woman at right. Printed date. Like #S272. Printer: ABNC.			
	a. Issued note. Rare.	—	—	—
	s. Specimen.	—	Unc	1250.
S294	**5 Soles** 1.1.1873. Brown and blue. Two girls at lower left, two seated women and English shield at center, woman at right. Printed date. Like #S293. Printer: ABNC. Rare.	—	—	—
S295	**10 Soles** 1.1.1873. Light brown on gray underprint. Woman holding rabbit at lower left, boys and mule train at top center, shield with flags with portrait Queen Victoria at lower right. Printed date. Like #S274. Back: Blue. Printer: ABNC. Rare.	—	—	—
S295A	**10 Soles** 18xx (ca.1872). Black on brown and green underprint. Woman holding rabbit at lower left, boys and mule train at top center, shield with flags with portrait Queen Victoria at lower right. Printed date. Like #S295. Printer: ABNC. Archive copy.	—	Unc	1250.
S296	**25 Soles** 18xx (ca.1874). Brown on blue underprint. Boys and mule train at upper left, girl holding dog at lower right. Printed date. Like #S275. Printer: ABNC. Archive copy.	—	Unc	1250.
S297	**100 Soles** 18xx (ca.1874). Green on brown underprint. Sailors at lower left, two women and Peruvian shield at upper center, two horses at lower right. Printed date. Like #S276. Printer: ABNC. Archive copy.	—	Unc	1250.
S298	**500 Soles** 18xx (ca.1874). Printer: ABNC. Reported in archive records, not confirmed.	—	Unc	1250.

Banco Nacional del Perú

1873 First Fractional Issue

		Good	Fine	XF
S301	**20 Centavos** 1.1.1873. Black on blue underprint. Woman at center. Signature titles: *DIRECTOR* and *GERENTE*. Back: Blue. Printer: ABNC.	22.50	66.00	200.

		Good	Fine	XF
S302	**40 Centavos** 1.1.1873. Black on green underprint. Girl with necklace at center. Signature titles: *DIRECTOR* and *GERENTE*. Back: Green. Printer: ABNC.	30.00	90.00	270.

1873 Second Fractional Issue

		Good	Fine	XF
S303	**10 Centavos** 1.1.1873. Black on green underprint. Girl at center. Signature titles: *GERENTE* and *GERENTE*. Back: Green. Printer: ABNC.	15.00	45.00	135.
S303A	**20 Centavos** 1.1.1873. Black on blue underprint. Woman at center. Signature titles: *GERENTE* and *GERENTE*. Like #S301. Printer: ABNC.			
	a. Issued note.	60.00	180.	540.
	p. Proof.	—	Unc	1250.

		Good	Fine	XF
S304	**20 Centavos** 1.1.1873. Black on orange underprint. Woman at center. Signature titles: *GERENTE* and *GERENTE*. Series A. Like #S301. Back: Orange. Printer: ABNC.	30.00	90.00	270.
S305	**40 Centavos** 1.1.1873. Black on peach underprint. Girl with necklace at center. Signature titles combined read: *LOS GERENTES*. Series A. Like #S302. Back: Peach.	45.00	135.	400.

1871-73 Issue

#S311-S318 engraved partial date 18xx.

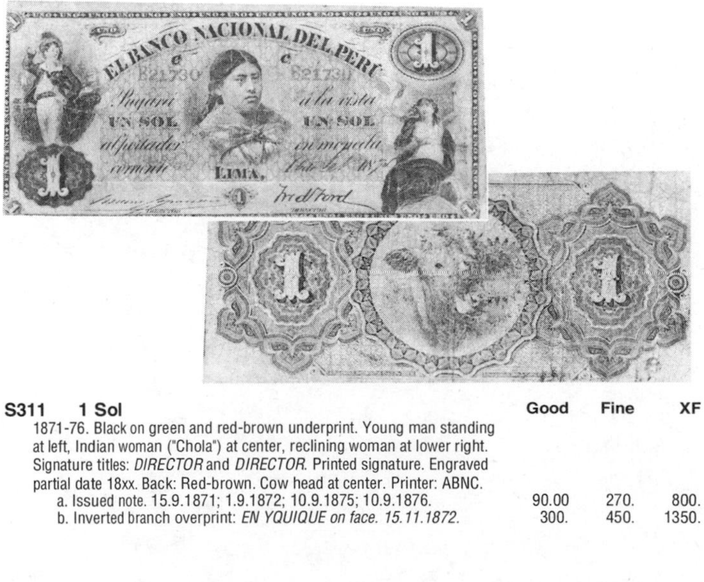

		Good	Fine	XF
S311	**1 Sol** 1871-76. Black on green and red-brown underprint. Young man standing at left, Indian woman ("Chola") at center, reclining woman at lower right. Signature titles: *DIRECTOR* and *DIRECTOR*. Printed signature. Engraved partial date 18xx. Back: Red-brown. Cow head at center. Printer: ABNC.			
	a. Issued note. 15.9.1871; 1.9.1872; 10.9.1875; 10.9.1876.	90.00	270.	800.
	b. Inverted branch overprint: *EN YQUIQUE on face. 15.11.1872.*	300.	450.	1350.

S312 2 Soles	Good	Fine	XF
1.9.1872; 10.9.1875; 5.5.1876. Black on red and green underprint. Boy with sheep ("St. John the Baptist") at left, Indian woman with child at center, cows at right. Signature titles: *DIRECTOR* and *DIRECTOR*. Printed signature. Engraved partial date 18xx. Back: Green. Goat head at left and right. Printer: ABNC.	90.00	270.	800.

S313 5 Soles	Good	Fine	XF
187x. Black on gold and blue underprint. Cherub at upper left, man on mule at center, girl at right. Signature titles: *DIRECTOR* and *DIRECTOR*. Hand signed. Engraved partial date 18xx. Back: Blue. Two women, cherubs and denomination numeral at center. Printer: ABNC.	225.	675.	2000.

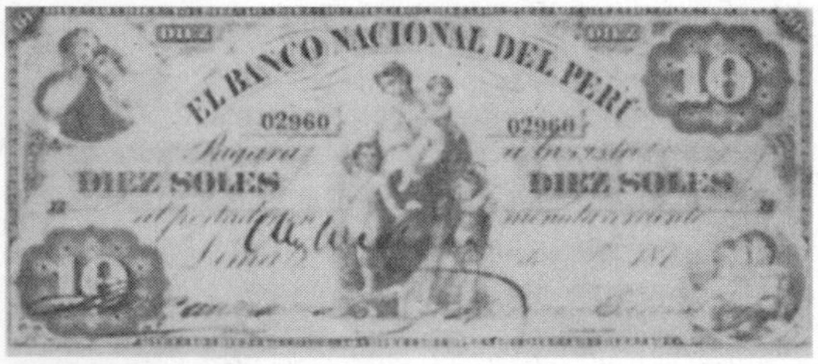

S314 10 Soles	Good	Fine	XF
1.9.1872; 1.1.1874. Black on orange underprint. Two women at upper left, woman and three cherubs ("Charity No. 2") at center, two girls at lower right. Signature titles: *GERENTE* and *GERENTE*. Engraved partial date 18xx. Back: Green. Dog head at center. Printer: ABNC.			
a. Issued note.	—	—	—
p. Proof.	—	Unc	1750.

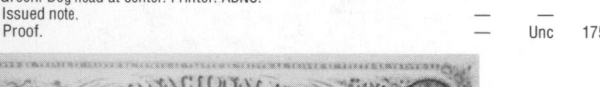

S315 20 Soles	Good	Fine	XF
187x. Black on blue underprint. Man at upper left, men loading llamas at center, dog and safe at lower right. Signature titles: *GERENTE, DIRECTOR, GERENTE*. Engraved partial date 18xx. Back: Red. Men and horses at center. Printer: ABNC. Specimen.	—	Unc	1500.

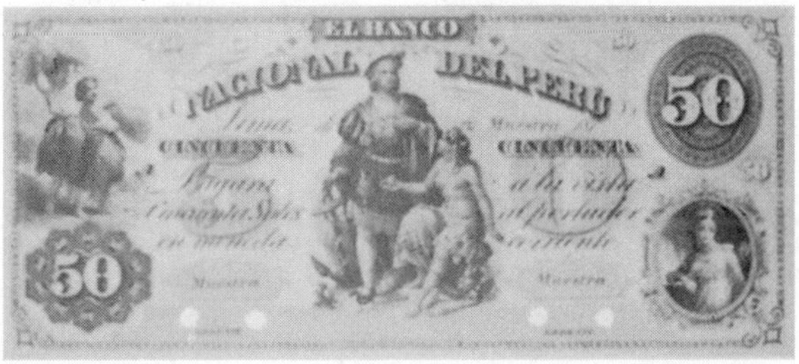

S316 50 Soles	Good	Fine	XF
187x. Black on green underprint. Two girls with sheaves at upper left, Spanish man and Indian woman ("Columbus") at center, portrait woman at lower right. Signature titles: *GERENTE, DIRECTOR, GERENTE*. Engraved partial date 18xx Back: Brown. Men leading horses at center. Printer: ABNC.			
p. Proof.	—	Unc	1250.
s. Specimen.	—	Unc	1500.

S317 100 Soles	Good	Fine	XF
10.9.1873; 10.9.1875; 10.11.1875. Black on orange and gray underprint. Dog at upper left, man roping steer at center, girl at right. Signature titles: *GERENTE, DIRECTOR, GERENTE*. Engraved partial date 18xx. Back: Brown. Funeral of Atahualpa scene at center. Like #S327. Printer: ABNC.	—	—	—

NOTE: #S314-S317 back colors come from archive copies and may not be those used for issued notes.

S318 500 Soles	Good	Fine	XF
15.6.1874. Black on orange underprint. Woman at upper left, standing female with sword and fasces ("America") at center, Indian man at right. Signature titles: *GERENTE, DIRECTOR, GERENTE*. Engraved partial date 18xx. Back: Funeral of Atahualpa scene at center. Like #S327. Printer: ABNC.			
a. Issued note.	—	—	—
p. Proof.	—	Unc	1250.

1877 Provisional Issue

#S321-S328 face designs like previous issue. All have black oval ovpt: *EMISION PAGADERA POR EL GOBIERNO 1877* (payable by the government) on back for #S321-S325 and on face for #S327-328. All notes have printed date and sign.

S321 1 Sol	Good	Fine	XF
10.9.1877. Black on green and red underprint. Young man standing at left, Indian woman ("Chola") at center, reclining woman at lower right. Signature titles: *GERENTE* and *GERENTE*. Printed date and signature. Like #S311. Back: Brown. 1 Sol coin at center. Overprint: Black oval: *EMISION PAGADERA POR EL GOBIERNO 1877* on back.	7.50	22.00	70.00

S322 2 Soles	Good	Fine	XF
10.9.1877. Black on red and green underprint. Boy with sheep ("St. John the Baptist") at left, Indian woman with child at center, cows at right. Signature titles: *GERENTE* and *GERENTE*. Printed date and signature. Like #S312. Back: Green. 1 Sol coin at left and right. Overprint: Black oval: *EMISION PAGADERA POR EL GOBIERNO 1877* on back.			
a. Issued note.	12.50	36.00	115.
b. Black with overprint: *COMISION DE SUBSIDIOS AREQUIPA 1881* in circle at left and right on back.	60.00	180.	540.
p. Proof.	—	Unc	1250.

S323 5 Soles — Good 7.50 · Fine 22.00 · XF 70.00
10.9.1877. Black on gold and blue underprint. Cherub at upper left, man on mule at center, girl at right. Signature titles: *GERENTE* and *GERENTE*. Printed date and signature. Like #S313. Back: Blue. Dog and safe at center. Overprint: Black oval: *EMISION PAGADERA POR EL GOBIERNO 1877* on back.

S324 10 Soles — Good — · Fine — · XF —
10.9.1877. Overprint: Black oval: *EMISION PAGADERA POR EL GOBIERNO 1877* on back. Reported not confirmed.

S325 20 Soles — Good — · Fine — · XF —
10.9.1877. Black on blue underprint. Man at upper left, men loading llamas at center, dog and safe at lower right. Signature titles: *GERENTE, GERENTE* and *DIRECTOR*. Printed date and signature. Like #S315. Back: Orange. Farm scene. Overprint: Black oval: *EMISION PAGADERA POR EL GOBIERNO 1877* on back. Printer: ABNC.

S326 50 Soles — Good — · Fine — · XF —
10.9.1877. Printer: ABNC. Reported not confirmed.

S327 100 Soles — Good — · Fine — · XF —
10.9.1877. Black on orange and gray underprint. Dog at upper left, man roping steer at center, girl at right. Signature titles: *GERENTE, GERENTE* and *DIRECTOR*. Printed date and signature. Like #S317. Back: Black and brown. Funeral of Atahualpa scene at center. Overprint: Black oval: *EMISION PAGADERA POR EL GOBIERNO 1877* on face. Printer: ABNC. Rare.

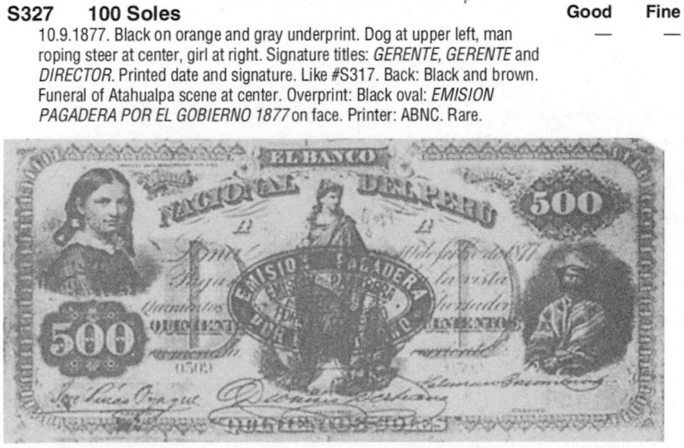

S328 500 Soles — Good — · Fine — · XF —
10.9.1877. Black on orange underprint. Woman at upper left, standing female with sword and fasces ("America") at center, Indian man at right. Signature titles: *GERENTE, GERENTE and DIRECTOR.*. Printed date and signature. Like #S318. Back: Funeral of Atahualpa scene at center. Overprint: Black oval: *EMISION PAGADERA POR EL GOBIERNO 1877* on face. Printer: ABNC. Rare.

Tacna

1870s Issue

S331 1 Sol — Good — · Fine Unc · XF 500.
187x. Green and orange. Indian woman and child at center. Printer: ABNC. Proof.

S332 2 Soles — Good — · Fine Unc · XF 500.
187x. Green and orange. Men loading llamas at lower left, Indian man at lower right. Printer: ABNC. Proof.

S333 5 Soles — Good — · Fine Unc · XF 550.
187x. Yellow and blue. Indian woman ("Chola") at lower left, men loading llamas at center, young girl at right. Printer: ABNC. Proof.

S334 20 Soles — Good — · Fine Unc · XF 550.
187x. Green. Indian woman and child at lower left, field workers harvesting at center, young girl at lower right. Printer: ABNC. Proof.

S335 100 Soles — Good — · Fine Unc · XF 600.
187x. Brown. Woman with three cherubs ("Charity No. 2") at left, cattle at center, Indian woman ("Chola") at lower right. Back: Blue. Printer: ABNC. Archive copy.

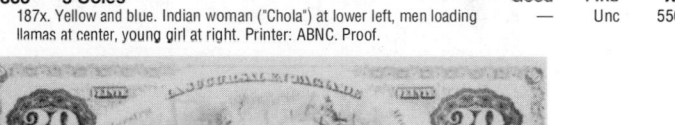

Yquique
1870s Issue

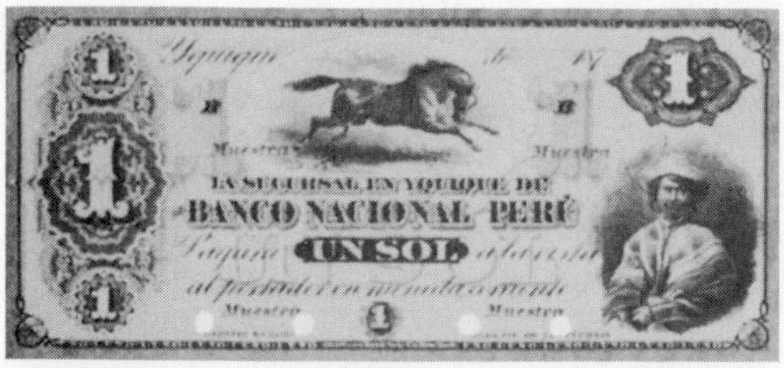

S341 1 Sol	Good	Fine	XF
187x. Orange and red. Running horse at upper center, Indian man at lower right. Back: Brown. 1 Sol coin at center. Like #S321. Printer: ABNC. Proof.	—	Unc	500.

S342 2 Soles	Good	Fine	XF
187x. Green and red. Indian woman ("Chola") at left, reclining woman with produce at upper center. Back: Green. 1 Sol coin at left and right. Like #S322. Printer: ABNC. Proof.	—	Unc	500.

S343 5 Soles	Good	Fine	XF
187x. Red and orange. Man, woman and child near boat and anchor at center. Back: Blue. Dog and safe at center. Like #S323. Printer: ABNC. Proof.	—	Unc	550.

S344 20 Soles	Good	Fine	XF
187x. Black and red. Arms at center, with scenes of boats, mountains and llamas in background. Back: Woman milking cows in farm scene. Printer: ABNC. Proof.	—	Unc	550.
S345 100 Soles 187x. Black on pinkish red underprint. Sailor and marine implements at center. Back: Green. Funeral of Atahualpa scene at center. Like #S327. Printer: ABNC. Archive copy.	—	Unc	600.

Banco del Perú
1864-69 Issues

S351 5 Pesos	Good	Fine	XF
15.6.1864. Black on green underprint. Large denomination numeral at left, seated woman and shield at upper left center, worker at right. Radiant sunface at right. Back: Green. Printer: Face, CNBB; back, CABB.	—	—	—

S352 10 Pesos	Good	Fine	XF
15.6.1869. Black on red and green underprint. Liberty seated at left, woman and shield at upper center. Radiant sunface at right. Printer: Face, CABB; back, CNBB.	—	—	—

S353 100 Pesos	Good	Fine	XF
15.12.1864; 5.1.1867. Black on green and brown underprint. Woman seated at left, woman and shield at upper center. Radiant sunface at right. Similar to #S352 but different woman at left. Printer: Face, CABB; back, CNBB.			
a. Issued note.	—	—	—
p. Proof.	—	Unc	500.
s. Specimen.	—	Unc	750.

S354 500 Pesos	Good	Fine	XF
1.7.1867. Black on green and brown underprint. Liberty seated at left, woman and shield at upper center. Radiant sunface at right. Similar to #S352 but woman and ornate shield at left. Printer: Face, CABB; back, CNBB. Rare.	—	—	—

S355 1000 Pesos	Good	Fine	XF
18xx. Black on green and red underprint. Woman and shield at left, Indian and sailor at upper center. Radiant sunface at right. Uniface. Printer: Face, CABB; back, CNBB. Proof. Rare.	—	Unc	600.

1864-77 Issue

S361 1 Sol	Good	Fine	XF
2.11.1864. Black on green underprint. Radiant sunface at center. Back: Green. Pillar with names at center. Printer: Face, ABNC; back, CNBB.			
a. Issued note. Series J.	50.00	150.	450.
p. Proof.	—	Unc	600.

S362 2 Soles	Good	Fine	XF
1.5.1869; 1.5.1871; 1.12.1873. Black on green underprint. Woman's head at upper left, small radiant woman's head at center. Back: Green. Radiant woman's head at lower left. Printer: Face, CNBB; back, CONB.	60.00	180.	540.

NOTE: All examples seen of #S362 exist with varieties of black text: *a la vista y en moneda corriente hoy* (at sight in current money today) overprint in curved line near center.

S363 4 Soles	Good	Fine	XF
1871-73. Black on green underprint. Radiant woman's head at left, woman at right. Back: Green. Liberty at left. Printer: Face, CNBB; back, CONB.			
a. 1.5.1871. Without round black stamping at left on face.	60.00	180.	540.
b. 1.12.1873. Round black stamping: *CIRCULACION AUTORIZADA POR EL GOBIERNO* (arms center) at left on face.	100.	300.	900.

NOTE: All examples seen of #S363 varieties of black text overprint similar to that on #S362 except that the word hoy (today) is deleted at the end.

S364 4 Soles	Good	Fine	XF
1.1.1874. Black on green underprint. Bank monogram at left. Back: Green. Bank monogram at center. Printer: NBNC.			
a. Round black stamping like #S363b, at left on face and at right on back.	30.00	100.	300.
b. No round black stamping but oval overprint: *EMISION PAGADERA...* like #S321-S325 at center on back.	30.00	100.	300.

S365 10 Soles	Good	Fine	XF
1.1.1874. Black on orange underprint. Bank monogram at left. Similar to #S364. Back: Brown. Overprint: Black like #S364b at center on back.	250.	750.	—

S366 20 Soles	Good	Fine	XF
186x. Black and brown on gold underprint. Two reclining women with wreath on pillar at center, small faces around border. Back: Brown on gold underprint. Radiant sunface at center. Printer: NBNC. Rare.	—	—	—

Note: Trial prints of #S366 are known in about six different colors.

S367 20 Soles	Good	Fine	XF
1.12.1877. Black on green underprint. Woman wearing plumes at left, radiant woman's head at center. Back: Black on orange underprint. Woman at center. Overprint: Black like #S364b at center on back. Printer: Face, CNBB; back, CONB.	525.	1550.	—

S368 100 Soles	Good	Fine	XF
1.12.1877; 1.5.1878. Black on green underprint. Radiant woman's head at left, woman at center with men and ship in background. Printer: Face, CNBB; back, CONB. Rare.	—	—	—

Banco de Piura

1873-78 Issue

S371 1 Sol	Good	Fine	XF
1.12.1873. Black on green underprint. Boy and woman at lower left, worker gathering cotton at lower right. Printer: G&D. Rare.	—	—	—

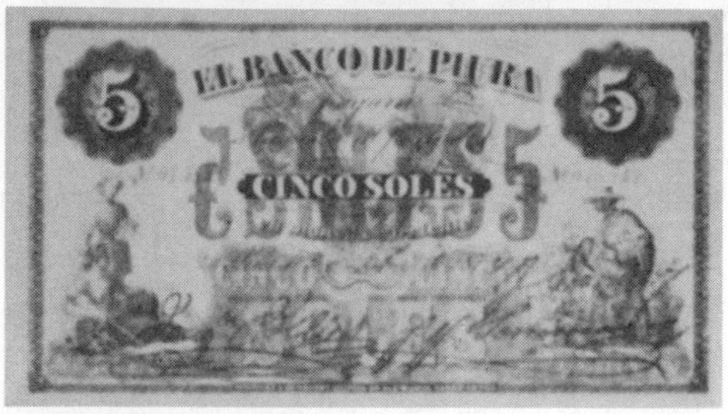

S372 5 Soles	Good	Fine	XF
20.10.1878. Black on red underprint. Boy and woman at lower left, worker gathering cotton at lower right. Printer: G&D. Rare.	—	—	—

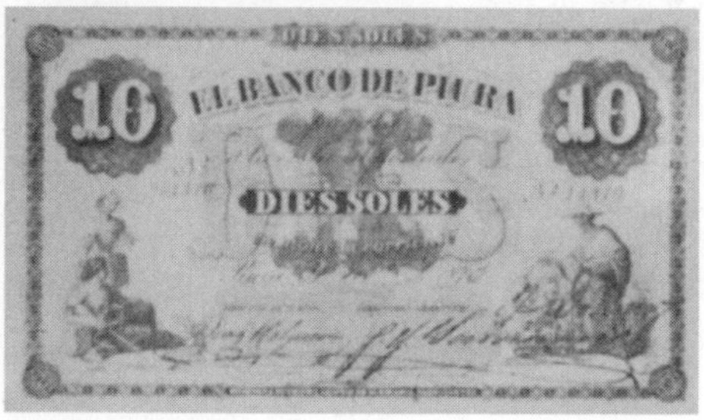

S373 10 Soles	Good	Fine	XF
31.1.1875. Black on blue underprint. Boy and woman at lower left, worker gathering cotton at lower right. Printer: G&D. Rare.	—	—	—

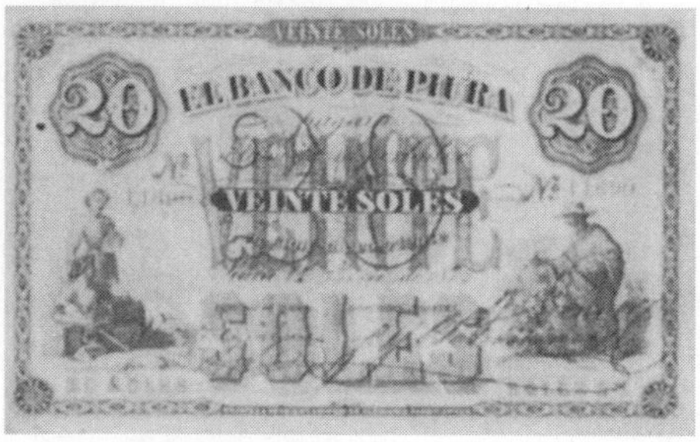

S374 20 Soles	Good	Fine	XF
30.12.1874; 1.1.1875. Black on brown underprint. Boy and woman at lower left, worker gathering cotton at lower right. Printer: G&D. Rare.	—	—	—

Banco de Tacna

1870's Issue

S381 1/2 Sol	Good	Fine	XF
(18xx). Black. Farm animals at upper left. Back: Black and green. Cow head at center. Printer: CNBB/NBNC.			
a. Issued note. Rare.	—	—	—
r. Unsigned remainder.	—	Unc	150.

S382 1 Sol	Good	Fine	XF
(18xx). Black on brown underprint. Girl's head at upper left ("Nina") and lower right ("Lola"), steam train on rural bridge at center. Back: Brown. Printer: CNBB/NBNC.			
a. Issued note. Rare.	—	—	—
r. Unsigned remainder.	—	Unc	175.

S383 2 Soles	Good	Fine	XF
(18xx). Black and brown. Steam passenger train at upper left center, woman with child at lower right. Printer: CNBB/NBNC.	225.	675.	—

S384 5 Soles	Good	Fine	XF
(18xx). Black and green. Standing woman at left, llamas with men at center. Back: Green. Printer: CNBB/NBNC.			
a. Issued note. Rare.	—	—	—
r. Unsigned remainder.	—	Unc	150.

S385 10 Soles	Good	Fine	XF
(18xx). Black and blue. Fruit and basket at lower left, miners at lower center, woman and cornucopia at lower right ("Plenty"). Back: Blue. Printer: CNBB/NBNC.			
a. Issued note.	—	—	—
r. Unsigned remainder.	—	Unc	125.

S386 50 Soles	Good	Fine	XF
(18xx). Black and yellow. Woman seated with gear and tools ("Mechanics") at left. Printer: CNBB/NBNC. Unsigned remainder. Rare.	—	—	—

S387 100 Soles — Good / Fine / XF
(18xx). Black. Woman holding small pitcher at center ("Virgin del Sol"). Printer: CNBB/NBNC. Proof. Rare. — — —

1886 ND Chilean Occupation Issue

After the war between Peru and Chile, the area including Tacna was occupied by Chilean forces. The Banco de Tacna was reorganized under the laws of Chile in 1884, and notes were authorized to be issued.

Three notes w/provisional ovpt. are known from the Chilean epoch.

S391 1 Sol — Good / Fine / XF
ND. Black on brown underprint. Girl's head at upper left ("Nina") and lower right ("Lola"), steam train on rural bridge at center. Back: Brown. Overprint: *EN QUINTOS DE BOLIVIANO A LA PAR* in 2 lines across face of #S382. Rare. — — —

S392 1 Peso on 1 Sol — Good / Fine / XF
1.4.1886. Overprint: *TACNA* (date) *CINCO QUINTOS BOLIVIANOS POR PESO O SU EQUIVALENTE EN MONEDA CORRIENTE*. Rare. — — —

S394 10 Soles — Good / Fine / XF
1.4.1886. Black and blue. Chilean Casa de Moneda round stamping at right, word *SOLES* cut out at upper center. Back: Blue. Overprint: Vertical: *CINCO QUINTOS BOLIVIANOS POR PESO O SU EQUIVALENTE EN MONEDA CORRIENTE* on #S385. Rare. — — —

Note: For reported 1 Peso of the Banco de Tacna under Chilean occupation, see Chile #S441.

Banco de Trujillo

1872-74 Issue

S401 50 Centavos

	Good	Fine	XF
1.8.1872. Black on orange underprint. Dog at center. Curved signature title: *GERENTE*, 1 signature. Hand dated. Back: Orange. Printer: ABNC.			
a. Issued note.	125.	250.	—
p. Proof.	—	Unc	750.
r. Unsigned remainder.	—	Unc	125.

NOTE: For 1876 issue of #S401, see #S413.

S402 1 Sol — Good / Fine / XF
1.5.1872. Black on blue and green underprint. Sitting woman with sheaf and sickle at lower left, arms at top center, young boy ("Oscar") at lower right. Hand dated. Printer: ABNC. Rare. — — —

NOTE: For 1876 issue of #S402, see #S414.

S403 5 Soles

	Good	Fine	XF
1.6.1874. Black on green underprint. Dog at lower left, man and woman watering horses at upper center, woman at lower right. Hand dated. Printer: ABNC.			
a. Issued note. Rare.	—	—	—
p. Proof.	—	Unc	750.

S404 10 Soles — Good / Fine / XF
1.1.1872. Black on red underprint. Seated woman with scale at left, winged woman blowing trumpet with globe and eagle at center, woman at right. Hand dated. Printer: ABNC. Rare. — — —

S405 50 Soles
18xx (ca.1871). Black on orange underprint. Justice at left, explorer landing at center, farmer with sheep at right. Back: Orange. Printer: ABNC. Archive copy. — Unc 750.

S406 100 Soles
18xx (ca.1871). Black on blue underprint. Liberty with shield and flag at left, mythical bird holding bank arms at upper center, reclining allegorical figure with globe at right. Back: Brown. Printer: ABNC. Archive copy. — Unc 750.

1876 Issue

S411 10 Centavos

	Good	Fine	XF
1.5.1876. Black on blue underprint. Woman at center. Printed date. Back: Blue. Printer: ABNC.			
a. Issued note.	75.00	225.	675.
p. Proof.	—	Unc	1250.

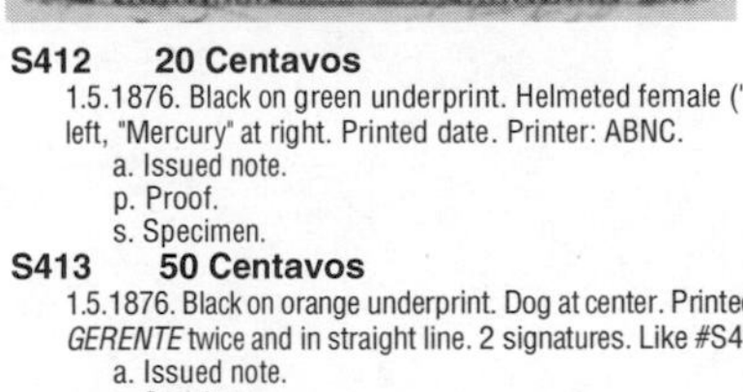

S412 20 Centavos

	Good	Fine	XF
1.5.1876. Black on green underprint. Helmeted female ("Minerva No. 2") at left, "Mercury" at right. Printed date. Printer: ABNC.			
a. Issued note.	75.00	225.	675.
p. Proof.	—	Unc	1000.
s. Specimen.	—	Unc	1250.

S413 50 Centavos

	Good	Fine	XF
1.5.1876. Black on orange underprint. Dog at center. Printed date. Signature title: *GERENTE* twice and in straight line. 2 signatures. Like #S401. Printer: ABNC.			
a. Issued note.	75.00	225.	675.
s. Specimen.	—	Unc	1250.

S414	**1 Sol**			
	1.5.1876. Black on blue and green underprint. Sitting woman with sheaf and sickle at lower left, arms at top center, young boy ("Oscar") at lower right. Printed date. Like #S402. Printer: ABNC. Proof.	—	Unc	1000.

Banco del Valle de Chicama

1800's Issue

		Good	Fine	XF
S421	**20 Centavos = 1/5 Sol**			
	18xx. Black. Farmer with sheaf and plow at upper center. Back: Brown. Printer: ABNC.	30.00	90.00	275.

		Good	Fine	XF
S422	**50 Centavos = 1/2 Sol**			
	18xx. Black. Dog at center. Back: Brown. Printer: ABNC.	40.00	120.	360.

		Good	Fine	XF
S423	**1 Sol**			
	18xx. Black on orange underprint. Portrait young woman's head at lower left and right, standing woman with tablet and column at center. Back: Orange. Printer: ABNC.			
	p. Proof.	—	Unc	1000.
	r. Unsigned remainder.	60.00	180.	540.

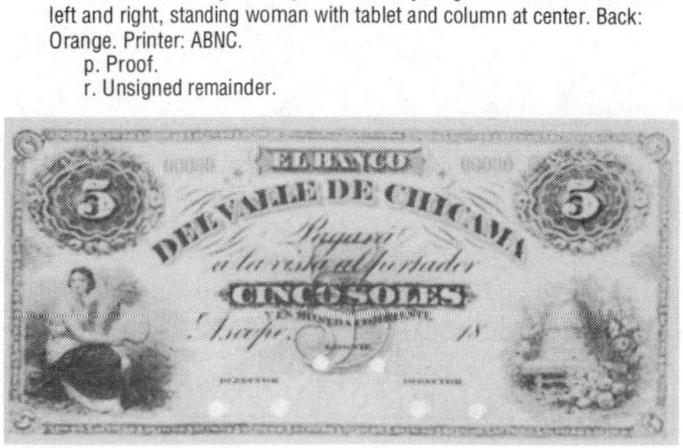

		Good	Fine	XF
S424	**5 Soles**			
	18xx. Black on green underprint. Sitting woman with sheaf and sickle at lower left, beehive at lower right. Printer: ABNC.			
	p. Proof.	—	Unc	1000.
	r. Unsigned remainder.	90.00	270.	800.

		Good	Fine	XF
S425	**50 Soles**			
	18xx. Black on blue underprint. Plow, farming tools at lower left, two horses at upper center, steam locomotive at lower right. Printer: ABNC.			
	p. Proof.	—	Unc	1000.
	r. Unsigned remainder.	125.	375.	1100.

Compañia de Obras Públicas y Fomento del Perú

1876 Issue

		Good	Fine	XF
S441	**10 Centavos**			
	4.7.1876. Black on blue underprint. Seated woman with shield at left. Back: Blue. Printer: CNBB/NBNC.	15.00	45.00	125.

		Good	Fine	XF
S442	**20 Centavos**			
	4.7.1876. Black on green underprint. Steam train on high trestle at left. Back: Green. Printer: CNBB/NBNC.	20.00	60.00	180.

		Good	Fine	XF
S443	**40 Centavos**			
	4.7.1876. Black on brown underprint. Street scene with steam passenger train on viaduct at left. Back: Brown. Printer: CNBB/NBNC.			
	a. Issued note.	40.00	120.	360.
	p. Proof.	—	Unc	1000.

		Good	Fine	XF
S444	**1 Sol**			
	4.7.1876. Black on green underprint. Steam train at center. Back: Green. Printer: CNBB/NBNC.			
	a. Issued note.	40.00	120.	360.
	b. Oval black overprint: *EMISION PAGADERA . . .* like #S321-S325 on back.	30.00	90.00	270.

S445 5 Soles	Good	Fine	XF
4.7.1876. Black on brown underprint. Steam train on rural bridge at center. Back: Brown. Printer: CNBB/NBNC.			
a. Issued note.	40.00	120.	360.
b. Oval black overprint like #S444b on back.	30.00	90.00	270.

S446 10 Soles	Good	Fine	XF
4.7.1876. Black on orange underprint. Worker viewing train emerging from tunnel at center. Back: Orange. Printer: CNBB/NBNC.			
a. Issued note.	40.00	120.	360.
b. Oval black overprint like #S444b on back.	40.00	120.	360.
p. Proof.	—	Unc	750.

S447 20 Soles	Good	Fine	XF
4.7.1876. Black on gold underprint. Reclining woman pouring water from jug and holding rudder ("Naiad") at left. Back: Gold. Printer: CNBB/NBNC.			
a. Oval black overprint like #S444b on back.	75.00	225.	675.
p. Proof.	—	Unc	750.

S448 50 Soles	Good	Fine	XF
4.7.1876. Black on blue underprint. Seated woman ("Study") at left, steam train under archway at right. Back: Blue. Printer: CNBB/NBNC.			
a. Issued note. Rare.	—	—	—
b. Oval black overprint like #S444b on back. Rare.	—	—	—
p. Proof.	—	Unc	750.

S449 100 Soles	Good	Fine	XF
4.7.1876. Black on brown underprint. Steam locomotive at upper left. Series A. Back: Brown. Printer: CNBB/NBNC.			
a. Oval black overprint like #S444b on back.	300.	900.	—
p. Proof.	—	Unc	1000.

NOTE: Though dated 4.7.1876 the above issue was not released until February 1877.

Pawn Shops

Monte de Piedad de Callao

1800's Issue

	Good	Fine	XF
S552 1 Sol 18xx. Black on green underprint. Allegorical woman at left, man, woman and child near shoreline at center, sailor at right. Back: Red. Printer: ABNC. Archive copy.	—	Unc	750.
S553 2 Soles 18xx. Black on green underprint. Woman and marine implements at left, man and boy in marine scene at right. Back: Brown. Printer: ABNC. Archive copy.	—	Unc	750.

	Good	Fine	XF
S554 5 Soles 18xx. Black on green underprint. Woman sitting with scale at left, girl at center, man seated and man with spyglass ("Looking Out") at right. Printer: ABNC. Uniface specimen.	—	Unc	1000.

NOTE: Blue back for #S554 is known only from archive copy.

	Good	Fine	XF
S555 5 Soles 18xx. Black on brown underprint. Woman sitting with scale at left, girl at center, man seated and man with spyglass ("Looking Out") at right. Similar to #S554 except that girl at center is different.	—	Unc	1000.

Monte de Piedad de Lima

1870's Issue

	Good	Fine	XF
S564 4 Soles 187x. Black on green underprint. Mother with child at left, Abundance reclining with cornucopia at upper center, arms at lower right. Back: Green. Printer: ABNC.	225.	675.	—

Revolution

Iquitos Revolution

Guillermo Cervantes

1921 Cheque Provisional Issue

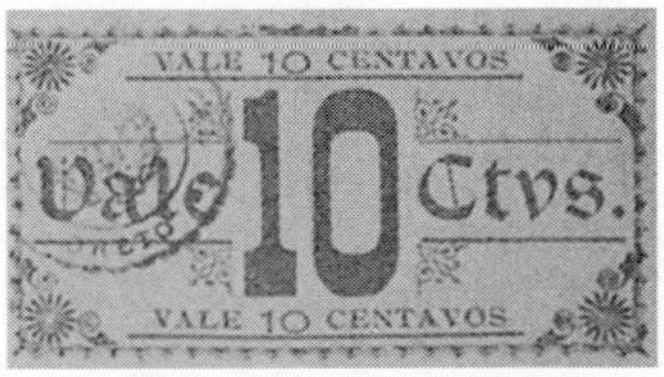

	Good	Fine	XF
S601 10 Centavos on 1 Sol 1.10.1921. Black with brown overprint. Indian facing left at center. Back: Black. Printer: El Oriente.	2.50	7.50	22.50

		Good	Fine	XF
S602	**20 Centavos on 1 Sol** 1.10.1921. Black with dark red overprint. Indian facing left at center. Back: Black. Printer: El Oriente.	2.50	7.50	22.50
S603	**50 Centavos on 1 Sol** 1.10.1921. Black with green overprint. Indian facing left at center. Back: Black. Printer: El Oriente.	4.00	12.50	36.00

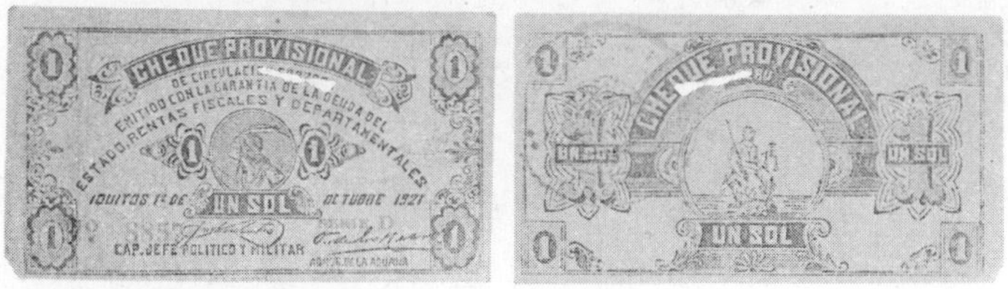

		Good	Fine	XF
S604	**1 Sol** 1.10.1921. Black. Indian facing left at center. Back: Black. Seated woman with staff and scale. Paper: Red-brown. Printer: El Oriente.	2.50	7.50	22.50

		Good	Fine	XF
S605	**1/2 Libra** 1.10.1921. Black on blue underprint. Indian facing right at center. Back: Blue. Arms at center. Printer: El Oriente.	3.00	9.00	27.50

		Good	Fine	XF
S606	**1 Libra** 1.10.1921. Black on red underprint. Angel with wreath and branch at left. Back: Red. Arms at center. Printer: El Oriente.			
	a. Without series or embossed seal.	5.00	15.00	45.00
	b. Embossed seal at left. Series B.	6.00	17.50	50.00

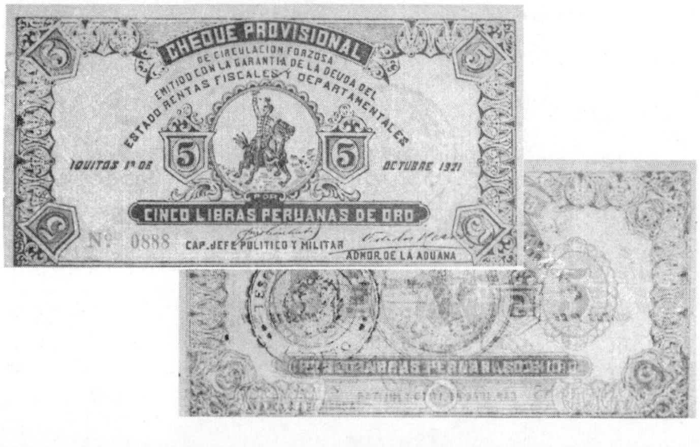

		Good	Fine	XF
S607	**5 Libras** 1.10.1921. Dark blue on yellow underprint. Rider in uniform on horseback at center. Back: Yellow. Soldiers at center. Printer: El Oriente.	12.50	36.00	100.

Republic

Banco de Credito del Perú / Banco Central de Reserva del Perú

1985 Emergency Check Issue

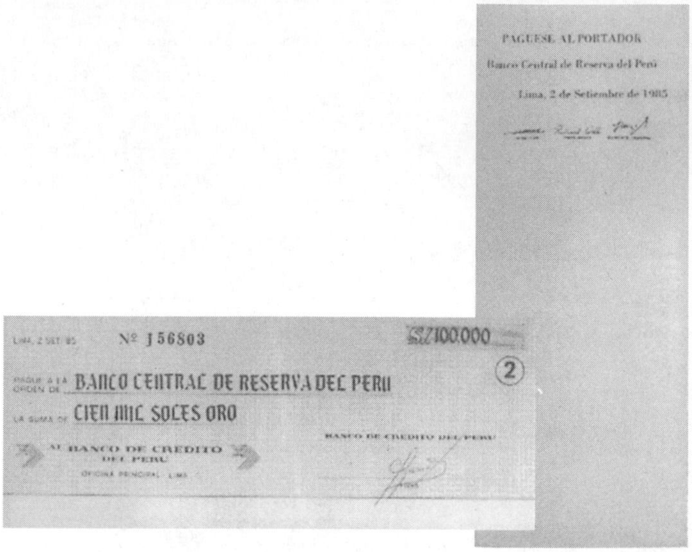

		VG	VF	UNC
R2	**100,000 Soles** 2.9.1985. Black text on light blue text underprint. Two signature varieties.	35.00	150.	—

Banco de la Nación / Banco Central de Reserva del Perú

1985 Cheques Circulares de Gerencia Issue

#R6-R8 bank monogram at upper l.

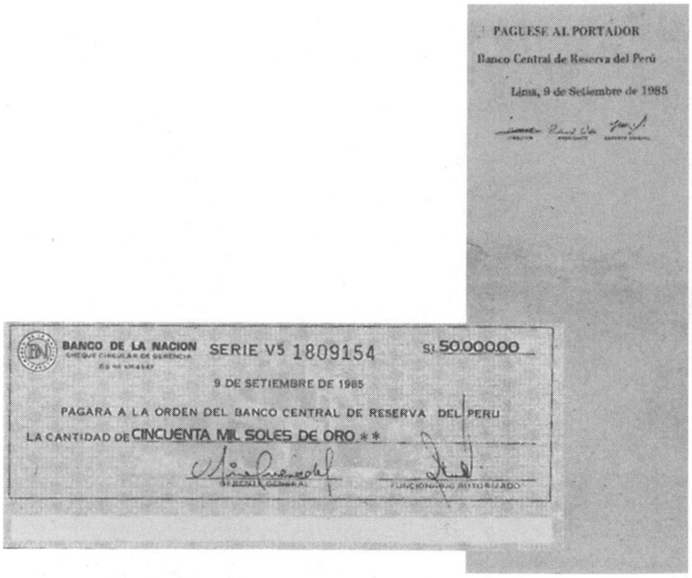

		VG	VF	UNC
R6	**50,000 Soles** 9.9.1985; 16.9.1985. Black text on tan underprint. Bank at center, bank monogram at upper left.	35.00	125.	—
R7	**100,000 Soles** 2.9.1985. Black text on light blue underprint. Bank at center, bank monogram at upper left.	35.00	125.	—
R8	**200,000 Soles** 2.9.1985. Black text on pink underprint. Bank at center, bank monogram at upper left.	35.00	125.	—

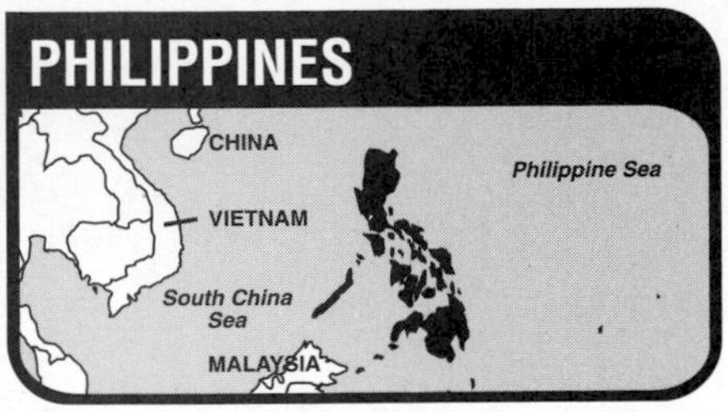

The Republic of the Philippines, an archipelago in the western Pacific 500 miles (805 km.) from the southeast coast of Asia, has an area of 115,830 sq. mi. (300,000 sq. km.) and a population of 75.04 million. Capital: Manila. The economy of the 7,000-island group is d on agriculture, forestry and fishing. Timber, coconut products, sugar and hemp are exported.

The Philippine Islands became a Spanish colony during the 16th century; they were ceded to the US in 1898 following the Spanish-American War. In 1935 the Philippines became a self-governing commonwealth. Manuel Quezon was elected president and was tasked with preparing the country for independence after a 10-year transition. In 1942 the islands fell under Japanese occupation during World War II, and US forces and Filipinos fought together during 1944-45 to regain control. On 4 July 1946 the Republic of the Philippines attained its independence. The 20-year rule of Ferdinand Marcos ended in 1986, when a "people power" movement in Manila ("EDSA 1") forced him into exile and installed Corazon Aquino as president. Her presidency was hampered by several coup attempts, which prevented a return to full political stability and economic development. Fidel Ramos was elected president in 1992 and his administration was marked by greater stability and progress on economic reforms. In 1992, the US closed its last military s on the islands. Joseph Estrada was elected president in 1998, but was succeeded by his vice-president, Gloria Macapagal-Arroyo, in January 2001 after Estrada's stormy impeachment trial on corruption charges broke down and another "people power" movement ("EDSA 2") demanded his resignation. Macapagal-Arroyo was elected to a six-year term as president in May 2004. The Philippine Government faces threats from three terrorist groups on the US Government's Foreign Terrorist Organization list, but in 2006 and 2007 scored some major successes in capturing or killing key wanted terrorists. Decades of Muslim insurgency in the southern Philippines have led to a peace accord with one group and on-again/off-again peace talks with another.

RULERS:

Spanish to 1898
United States, 1898-1946

MONETARY SYSTEM:

1 Peso = 100 Centavos to 1967
1 Piso = 100 Sentimos, 1967-

PROVINCES

Abra	Capiz	Marinduque	Rizal
Agusan	Cavite	Masbate	Romblon
Albay	Cebu	Mindoro	Samar
Antique	Cotabato	Misamis Occidental	Sorsogon
Bataan	Davao	Misamis Oriental	Sulu
Batanes	Ilocos Norte	Mountain Province	Surigao
Batangas	Ilocos Sur	Negros Occidental	Tarlac
Bohol	Iloilo	Negros Oriental	Tayabas
Bukidnon	Isabela	Nueva Ecija	Zambales
Bulacan	La Union	Nueva Vizcaya	Zamboanga
Cagayan	Laguna	Palawan	
Camarines Norte	Lanao	Pampanga	
Camarines Sur	Leyte	Pangasinan	

Each *Province* was governed by a *Provincial Board* consisting of the *Governor* and two elected *Board Members*. The Provincial Treasurer, Provincial Auditor and <i>Provincial Fiscal (equivalent of an Attorney General) were appointed by the national government. They could be, and often were, transferred from one province to another.

CHARTERED CITIES

Manila	Davao (1936)
Baguio	Iloilo (1936)
Bacolod (1938)	Quezon (1939)
Cavite (1940)	San Pablo (1940)
Cebu (1936)	Tagatay (1938)
Dansalan (1940)	Zamboanga (1936)

WWII EMERGENCY & GUERRILLA CURRENCY

APAYAO LEGAL TENDER NOTES

1942 ND ISSUE

#S109-S117 Border styles #S109-S111: TYPE I: coarse lines in shading. TYPE II: fine lines in shading. Top and bottom border areas show these differences.

	Good	Fine	XF
S101 5 Centavos ND. Green (shades). Eagle with wings outstreched at center. Serial # for #S101 and S102: 00,011 to 08,110. Back: Eagle with wings outstreched at center.	1.50	3.00	10.00
S102 5 Centavos ND. Slate blue (shades). Eagle with wings outstreched at center. Back: Eagle with wings outstreched at center.	1.50	3.00	10.00
S103 10 Centavos ND. Lavender. Eagle with wings outstreched at center. Serial # for #S103 and S104: 00,011 to 08,210. Back: Eagle with wings outstreched at center.	1.50	3.00	10.00
S104 10 Centavos ND. Light brown. Eagle with wings outstreched at center. Back: Eagle with wings outstreched at center.	1.50	3.00	10.00
S105 20 Centavos ND. Olive-green (shades). Eagle with wings outstreched at center. Serial #: 00,011 to 07,110. Back: Eagle with wings outstreched at center.	1.50	3.00	10.00

#S106 *Deleted*. See #S105.

	Good	Fine	XF
S107 50 Centavos ND. Brown (shades). Eagle with wings outstreched at center. Serial #00,011 to 07,510. Back: Eagle with wings outstreched at center.			
a. Issued note.	1.00	2.00	6.00
x. Counterfeit. Crude serial #.	—	—	—

#S109-S115 arms in orange, and black text on back.

#S109-S117 Philippine arms at ctr. on face.

Border styles #S109-S111:

TYPE I: coarse lines in shading.

TYPE II: fine lines in shading.

Top and bottom border areas show these differences.

	Good	Fine	XF
S109 1 Peso ND. Purple. Philippine arms at center. TYPE I borders: coarse lines in shading. Serial #00,011 to 00,408 plus some mixed with #S110. Back: Arms in orange, and black text. Tree at left.			
a. White paper.	6.00	12.00	35.00
b. Manila paper.	6.00	12.00	35.00
S110 1 Peso ND. Buff. Philippine arms at center. TYPE I borders: coarse lines in shading. Serial #00,426 to 03,248. Back: Arms in orange, and black text.			
a. White paper.	1.50	3.00	10.00
b. Manila paper.	3.00	10.00	30.00
S111 1 Peso ND. Buff. Philippine arms at center. TYPE II borders: fine lines in shading. Serial #03,324 to 08,710. Back: Arms in orange, and black text.			
a. White paper.	3.00	10.00	30.00
b. Manila paper.	1.50	3.00	10.00

Lettering styles #S112-S113: TYPE: *TWO PESOS* at center and bottom in thick letters. TYPE II: *TWO PESOS* at center and bottom in thin letters.

	Good	Fine	XF
S112 2 Pesos ND. Green. Philippine arms at center. TYPE I denomination word: *TWO PESOS* at center and bottom in thick letters. Serial #00,011 to 03,005. Back: Arms in orange, and black text. Paper: White.	1.50	3.00	10.00
S113 2 Pesos ND. Green. Philippine arms at center. TYPE II denomination words: *TWO PESOS* at center and bottom in thin letters. Serial #04,812 to 08,410. Back: Arms in orange, and black text. Paper: Manila.	1.50	3.00	10.00

NOTE: Serial # 03,006 to 04,811 are Types I and II lettering mixed.

	Good	Fine	XF
S114 5 Pesos ND. Maroon. Philippine arms at center. Serial # for #S114 and S115: 00,011 to 06,110. Back: Arms in orange, and black text. Statue at left.			
a. White paper.	4.00	8.00	25.00
b. Manila paper.	3.00	10.00	30.00
S115 5 Pesos ND. Light brown (shades). Philippine arms at center. Back: Arms in orange, and black text.			
a. White paper.	2.50	5.00	15.00
b. Manila paper.	2.50	5.00	15.00
S116 10 Pesos ND. Dark red-brown. Philippine arms in green at center. Serial # for #S116 and S117: 00,011 to 04,110. Back: Green text. Sunrise over terraced hill at left.	6.00	12.00	35.00
S117 10 Pesos ND. Light brown (shades). Philippine arms at center.	4.00	8.00	25.00

EMERGENCY SCRIPT OF THE PHILIPPINES

1943 ND ISSUE

#S121-S127 all Series A. Serial # are estimates. Mimeographed in sheets of ten and/or twelve on a different color paper for each denomination. More than one stencil was prepared for some denominations, resulting in numerous minor varieties due to typing mistakes in spacing, alignment and spelling.

	Good	Fine	XF
S121 10 Centavos ND. Serial #1 to 8,853. Paper: Yellow.	1.50	3.00	10.00
S122 20 Centavos ND. Serial #1 to 10,813. Paper: Dull rose.	1.50	3.00	10.00
S123 50 Centavos ND. Serial #1 to 8,955. Paper: White.	1.50	3.00	10.00
S124 1 Peso ND. Serial #1 to 8,912. Paper: Pale buff.	1.50	3.00	10.00
S125 2 Pesos ND. Serial #1 to 5,446. Paper: Green (shades).	1.50	3.00	10.00
S126 5 Pesos ND. Serial #1 to 9,671. Paper: Salmon.	2.50	5.00	15.00
S127 10 Pesos ND. Serial #1 to 2,330. Paper: Gray-blue.	3.00	6.00	20.00

NOTE: #S121-S127 have no indication of origin except for signature which carry over from the previous issue.

NOTE: Many Apayao notes were printed on paper which had previously been stamped in purple:

FOR OFFICIAL USE ONLY

MOUNTAIN PROVINCE

COMMONWEALTH OF THE PHILIPPINES

1942 SERIES - OFFICIAL ISSUE

	Good	Fine	XF
S131 10 Centavos 1942. Black. Commonwealth arms at lower right. Serial #1 to 203,258. Back: Countersigned.			

	Good	Fine	XF
a. Back: pen signature of Treas., initials of Aud. and Fiscal (serial #1 to 1100).	6.00	12.00	35.00
b. Back: facsimile signature of all 3 Members (serial #1101 to 4300).	3.00	6.00	20.00
c. Back: pen signature of Treas. and Aud., facsimile signature of Fiscal (serial #4301 to 5300).	3.00	6.00	20.00
d. Back: pen initial of one Member, facsimile signature of 2 Members (serial #5301 to 203,258).	.50	1.00	2.00

S132 25 Centavos

1942. Black. Commonwealth arms at lower right. No engraver's initials at lower left corner. Serial #1 to 206,200. Back: Countersigned.

	Good	Fine	XF
a. Back: pen signature of Aud., initials of Treas. and Fiscal (serial #1 to 1100).	6.00	12.00	35.00
b. Back: pen initial of Treas., facsimile signature of Aud. and Fiscal (serial #1101 to 3500; 4501 to 21,700; 22,701 to 27,700; 28,601 to 37,700).	1.50	3.00	10.00
c. Back: pen initial of Treas., without facsimile signature (Serial #3601 to 4400).	3.00	6.00	20.00
d. Back: facsimile signature of Aud. and Fiscal, without pen signature (serial #28,201 to 28,300).	—	—	—
e. Back: pen initial of Treas., facsimile signature of Aud. and Fiscal (serial #38,301 to 47,500).	1.50	3.00	10.00
f. Back: like "e" except pen initial of Clerk (serial #47,701 to 206,200).	.50	1.00	3.00

S133 25 Centavos

	Good	Fine	XF
1942. Black. Commonwealth arms at lower right. Engraver's initials *F. D.* at lower left corner. Serial #206,301 to 397,687. Back: Countersigned. Like #S132f.	.50	1.00	3.00

S134 50 Centavos

1942. Black. Commonwealth arms at lower right. Serial #1 to 401,388. Back: Countersigned.

	Good	Fine	XF
a. Back: pen signature or initials of each Member (serial #1 to 1100).	4.00	10.00	—
b. Back: facsimile signature of each Member (serial #1101 to 4300).	2.00	5.00	8.50
c. Back: pen initials of Treas. and Aud., facsimile signature of Fiscal (serial #4301 to 4700).	2.00	5.00	8.50
d. Back: pen initial of one Member, small facsimile signature of Treas. and Fiscal.	.25	.50	1.00
e. Back: like "d" except Large facsimile signature (serial # for #S134d and e, 4801 to 401,388).	.25	.50	1.00
x. Counterfeit.	—	—	—

#S135-S137 black. Lg. Commonwealth arms at r.

S135 1 Peso

1942. Black. Large Commonwealth arms at right. Serial #1 to 80,553. Back: Countersigned.

	Good	Fine	XF
a. Back: pen signature of all 3 Members (serial #1 to 400; 701 to 900; 1101 to 4300).	4.00	10.00	—
b. Back: facsimile signature of all 3 Members (serial #501 to 600; 901 to 1000).	—	—	—
c. Back: pen signature of Treas. and Aud., facsimile signature of Fiscal (serial #1001 to 1100).	3.00	6.00	20.00
d. Back: pen signature of Fiscal, facsimile signature of Treas. and Aud. (serial #401 to 500; 601 to 700).	—	—	—
e. Back: pen signature of Aud., facsmile signature of Treas. and Fiscal (serial #4301 to 80,553).	.50	1.00	3.00
x. Counterfeit.	—	—	—

S136 5 Pesos

1942. Black. Large Commonwealth arms at right. Serial #1 to 195,574 and 203,572 to 208,764. Back: Countersigned.

	Good	Fine	XF
a. Back: pen signature of Treas., small facsimile signature of Aud. and Fiscal (serial #1 to 22,000).	1.00	2.00	6.00
b. Back: like "a" but without pen signature (serial # included in "a".	—	—	—
c. Back: pen signature of Treas., facsimile signature of Treas. and Aud. (serial #106,701 to 107,700).	—	—	—
d. Back: pen signature of Treas., large facsimile signature of Aud. and Fiscal (serial # groups 22,001 to 96,700; 98,901 to 106,700; 108,201 to 122,900; 125,001 to 127,000; 128,901 to 131,000; 133,301 to 133,700; 135,401 to 144,500; 146,301 to 147,400; 149,601 to 167,100; 172,901 to 185,800; 187,751 to 195,574; 203,572 to 205,300).	.50	1.00	3.00
e. Back: pen signature of Aud., facsimile signature of Aud. and Fiscal (serial #96,701 to 98,900).	1.50	3.00	10.00
f. Back: pen signature of Fiscal, facsimile signature of Aud. and Fiscal (serial # groups 122,901 to 125,000; 127,001 to 128,900; 131,101 to 133,300; 133,901 to 135,400; 144,501 to 146,300; 147,401 to 149,400; 167,101 to 172,900; 185,801 to 187,750).	.50	1.00	3.00
g. Back: facsimile signature of Aud. and Fiscal, without pen signature (serial #205,301 to 208,764).	1.00	2.00	6.00
h. White paper. Countersignature and serial # in with "d".	2.50	5.00	15.00
i. White paper. Countersignature and serial # in with "f".	3.00	6.00	20.00
x. Counterfeit. Numerous varieties.	9.00	20.00	60.00

S137 10 Pesos

1942. Black. Large Commonwealth arms at right. Serial #1 to 185,462 and 192,555 to 208,741. Back: Countersigned.

	Good	Fine	XF
a. Back: pen signature of all 3 Members (serial #1 to 62,700).	1.50	3.00	10.00
b. Back: pen signature of Aud. and Fiscal only (serial # included in "a").	—	—	—
c. Back: pen signature of Treas. and Fiscal, facsimile signature of Aud. (serial #62,701 to 98,800).	1.50	3.00	10.00
d. Back: pen signature of Treas. and Fiscal only (serial # included in "c").	—	—	—
e. Back: pen signature of 1 Member, facsimile signature of Aud. (serial #98,901 to 158,000).	1.00	2.00	6.00
f. Back: pen signature Treas. only (serial # included in "e").	—	—	—
g. Back: pen signature of Treas. on 1 end, facsimile signature of Treas. and Fiscal together at opposite end (serial #158,001 to 159,000 and 161,000 to 185,462).	1.00	2.00	6.00
h. White paper. Countersignature and serial # in with "g".	3.00	6.00	20.00
i. Back: without countersignature (serial # 192,555 to 195,500).	1.50	3.00	10.00
j. Back: facsimile signature of Aud. and Fiscal (serial #195,501 to 208,741).	1.50	3.00	10.00
x. Counterfeit. Numerous varieties.	9.00	20.00	60.00

1943 Series - Official Issue

S138 1 Peso

	Good	Fine	XF
1943. Black. No engraver's initials on seal at lower right. Serial #1 to 87,900 (approx.). Back: Pen initial of Aud., facsimile signature of Treas. and Fiscal.	1.00	2.00	6.00

S139 1 Peso

1943. Engraver's initials F. D. on seal at lower right. Serial # (approx.) 88,001 to 279,485. Back: Countersigned.

	Good	Fine	XF
a. Back: pen initial of Aud., facsimile signature of Treas. and Fiscal (serial # groups 88,001 to 97,500; 125,601 to 126,600; 127,901 to 128,600).	.50	1.00	3.00
b. Back: pen signature of Clerk, facsimile signature of Treas. and Fiscal (serial # groups 98,401 to 125,300; 127,001 to 127,800; 129,001 to 279,485).	.50	1.00	3.00

1942 Series - Illegal Issue

S141 25 Centavos

	Good	Fine	XF
1942. Black. Commonwealth arms at lower right. Engraver's initials *F. D.* at lower left corner. Like #S133. Serial #397,688 upwards. Back: Countersigned.	—	—	—

S142 50 Centavos

	Good	Fine	XF
1942. Black. Commonwealth arms at lower right. Like #S134. Serial #401,389 upwards. Back: Countersigned.	—	—	—

	Good	Fine	XF
S143 5 Pesos 1942. Black. Large Commonwealth arms at right. Like #S136. Serial #195,575 to 203,571 and 208,765 upwards. Back: Countersigned.			
a. Back: pen signature of Fiscal, fascimile signature of Aud. and Fiscal (serial #195,575 to 198,500).	—	—	—
b. Back: pen signature of Treas., facsimile signature of Aud. and Fiscal (serial #200,701 to 203,571).	—	—	—
c. Back: facsimile signature of Aud. and Fiscal. Without pen signature but may have a forged signature (serial #198,501 to 200,600 and 208,765 upwards).	—	—	—
S144 10 Pesos 1942. Black. Large Commonwealth arms at right. Like #S137. Serial #185,463 to 192,554 and 208,742 upwards. Back: Countersigned.			
a. Back: pen signature of Treas., facsimile signature of Aud. and Fiscal (serial #185,463 to 190,800).	7.50	15.00	45.00
b. White paper. Countersignature and serial # in with "a".	7.50	15.00	45.00
c. Back: facsimile signature of Aud. and Fiscal. Without pen signature but may have a forged signature (serial #191,801 to 192,554 and 208,742 to approx. 212,000).	7.50	15.00	45.00
d. Face: without serial #, but has false serial # applied with captured numbering machine, Serial # always very faint, and ranges from around 220,000 up to 800,000. Back like "c".	—	—	—

1943 Series - Illegal Issue

	Good	Fine	XF
S145 1 Peso 1943. Engraver's initials F. D. on seal at lower right. Like #S139. Serial #279,486 upwards.			
a. Back: pen signature of Clerk, facsimile signature of Treas. and Fiscal.	5.00	10.00	30.00
b. Back: facsimile signature of Aud. and Fiscal only. Without pen signature but may have a forged signature of a Board Member.			

BUKIDNON

(Grinstead Issue, 109th Div. USFIP)

Refer to Mindanao Military Issues.

Currency Board

1942 ND Second Issue

	Good	Fine	XF
S161 10 Centavos ND (1942). Paper: Cream.			
a. Yellow-green stamp. Serial #18,001 to 19,569.	35.00	70.00	225.
x. Error; correct stamp, and *0.10* stamped on back, on 20 Centavos form.	—	—	—
S162 20 Centavos ND (1942). Orange-yellow stamp. Serial #16,001 to 17,299. Paper: Light brown.	40.00	80.00	240.
S163 50 Centavos ND (1942).			
a. Cream paper. Greenish gold stamp. Serial # 14,001 to 15,256.	45.00	90.00	270.
x. Error; correct stamp, and *0.50* stamped on back, on 20 Centavos form.	—	—	—
S164 1 Peso 1942. Light brown stamp. Paper: White.			
a. Serial #10,001 to 11,465.	45.00	90.00	270.
s. Handwritten: *Sample.*	—	—	—
S165 2 Pesos 1942. Red stamp. Paper: White.			
a. Serial #20,001 to 21, 474.	45.00	90.00	270.
s. Handwritten: *Sample.*	—	—	—
S166 2.50 Pesos 1942. Salmon stamp. Serial #12,001 to 12,514. Paper: Gold.	60.00	120.	350.
S167 4 Pesos 1942. Dark blue stamp. Paper: Blue.			
a. Serial #13,001 to 13,891.	45.00	90.00	270.
s. Handwritten: *Sample.*	—	—	—
x. Counterfeit.	—	—	—
S168 5 Pesos 1942. Dark blue stamp. Paper: Buff.			
a. Serial #80,001 to (approx.) 82,995.	40.00	80.00	240.
s. Handwritten: *Sample.*	—	—	—
x. Counterfeit.	—	—	—

	Good	Fine	XF
S169 10 Pesos 1942. Green stamp. Paper: Dull rose.			
a. Serial #10,001 to 10,852.	40.00	80.00	240.
s. Handwritten: *Sample.*	—	—	—
x. Counterfeit.	—	—	—
S170 20 Pesos 1942. Orange-yellow stamp. Paper: Dark green.			
a. Serial #90,001 to 90,669.	50.00	100.	300.
s. Handwritten: *Sample.*	—	—	—
x. Counterfeit.	—	—	—
S171 50 Pesos 1942. Orange stamp. Paper: Pale green.			
a. Serial #40,001 to 40,337.	60.00	120.	350.
b. Handwritten: *Sample.*	—	—	—
S172 200 Pesos 1942. Dark brown stamp. Serial # 11,001 to 11,046. Paper: Salmon.	1500.	3000.	—

NOTE: #S161-S163 state redemption in gold coin and are not dated. There is no 100 Pesos denomination in this issue because no revenue stamps of that value were on hand.

1942 ND Third Issue

	Good	Fine	XF
S173 50 Centavos ND. Purple. Facsimile *WAR BILL* stamp imprinted at left. Serial #15,257 to 15,680. Paper: Cream.	125.	250.	—

424 notes printed.

1942 ND Fourth Issue

	Good	Fine	XF
S174 10 Centavos ND. Purple. Serial #0001 to 4265.			
a. Black text and names.	5.00	10.00	30.00
b. Green text and names.	5.00	10.00	30.00
S175 20 Centavos ND. Green. Serial #0001 to 7790.	7.50	15.00	45.00

	Good	Fine	XF
S176 50 Centavos ND. Brown. Green or black text. Serial # 0101 to 14,279; 23,030 to 24,588.			
a. Without watermark.	4.00	8.00	20.00
b. Commercially watermark paper.	7.50	15.00	45.00
x. Counterfeit.	—	—	—

#S177-S185 similar to #S174-S176. Small size, 77 x 43mm.

	Good	Fine	XF
S177 1 Centavo ND. Brown. Serial #0001 to 2600.	—	—	—
S178 5 Centavos ND. Green. Serial #0001 to 36,300.			
a. Black text.	.50	1.00	2.00
b. Red text.	1.50	3.00	10.00
S179 10 Centavos ND. Purple. Back: Serial #4307 to 9393.			
a. Issued note.	1.50	3.00	10.00
x. Counterfeit.	—	—	—

	Good	Fine	XF
S180 10 Centavos ND. Purple. Serial #9419 to 64,600.			
a. Issued note.	.50	1.00	2.00
x1. Counterfeit.	—	—	—
S180A 10 Centavos ND. Purple. Back: Brown.	—	—	—
S181 10 Centavos ND. Brown. Serial # mixed with #S180.	6.00	12.00	35.00
S182 20 Centavos ND. Green. Back: Serial #7816 to 11,896.	1.50	3.00	10.00

	Good	Fine	XF
S183 20 Centavos ND. Green. Serial #11,981 to 65,000.			
a. Black text.	1.00	2.00	6.00
b. Red text.	1.00	2.00	6.00
x. Counterfeit.	—	—	—
S184 50 Centavos ND. Brown. Back: Serial #14,303 to 15,299.	1.50	3.00	10.00

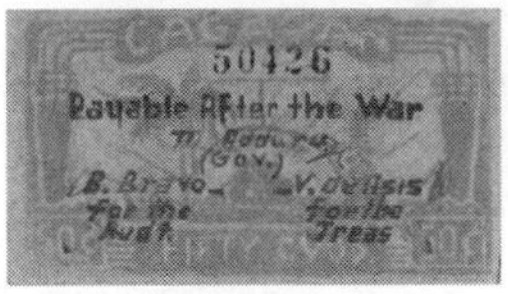

	Good	Fine	XF
S185 50 Centavos ND. Brown. Serial #15,471 to 22,963; 24,706 to 63,700.			
a. Issued note.	.50	1.00	3.00
x. Counterfeit.	—	—	—

ND Emergency Peso Certificate Issue

	Good	Fine	XF
S186 1 Peso ND. Purple. Eagle at center. Serial #0101 to 21,000. Back: No upper corner numerals or words *ONE PESO* at bottom. Paper: White laid.			
a. Black text face and back.	2.50	5.00	15.00
b. Green text face and back.	2.50	5.00	15.00

S187 1 Peso	Good	Fine	XF
ND. Purple. Eagle at center. Serial #26,000 to 65,700. Back: New plate; 1 at upper corners, *ONE PESO* at bottom. Paper: Manila.	1.00	2.00	6.00

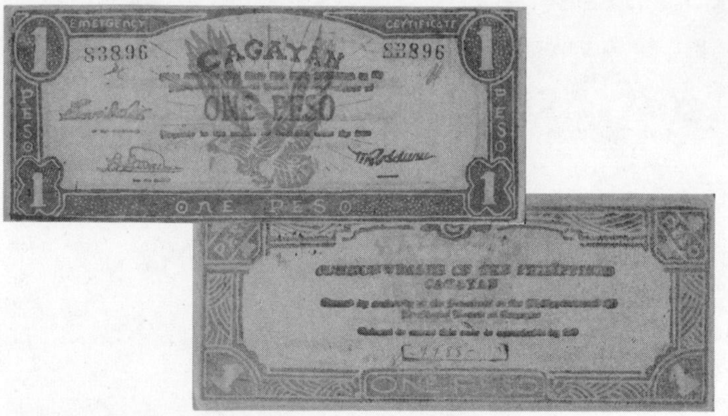

S188 1 Peso	Good	Fine	XF
ND. Green. Eagle in brown at center. Like #S187. Serial #65,800 to 92,300. Back: New plate; 1 at upper corners, *ONE PESO* at bottom. Paper: Manila.	.50	1.00	3.00

	Good	Fine	XF
S189 2 Pesos ND. Green. Eagle in brown at center. Large dashes under top border. Serial #0201 to 23,290. Back: Farmer plowing at center. Paper: Manila.	1.50	3.00	10.00
S190 2 Pesos ND. Green. Eagle in brown at center. Similar to #S189 but small dashes under top border. Serial #23,330 to #64,800. Back: Farmer plowing at center. Paper: Manila.	1.50	3.00	10.00

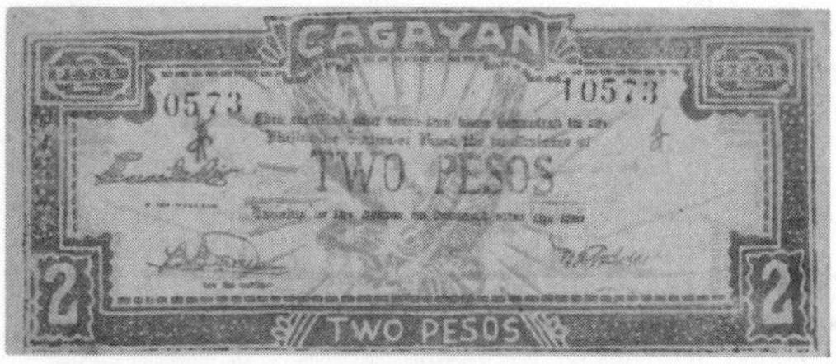

S190A 2 Pesos	Good	Fine	XF
ND. Green. Eagle in brown at center. Small dashes under top border. Like #S190 but with *TWO PESO* (error) at center. Serial # in with #S190. Back: Farmer plowing at center. Paper: Manila.	12.00	25.00	75.00

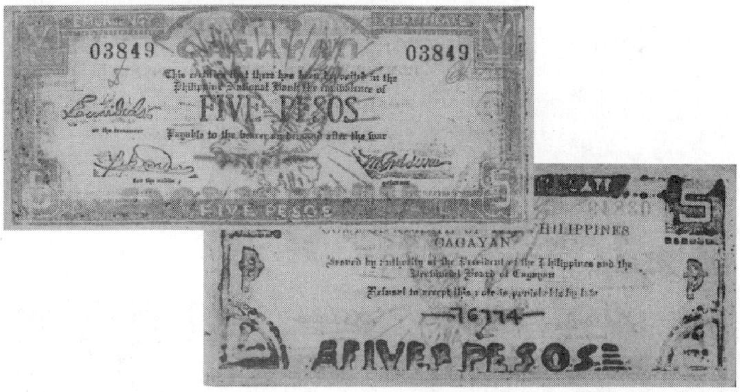

S191 5 Pesos	Good	Fine	XF
ND. Brown (shades). Eagle at center. Back: Numeral *5* at upper corners, without vignette under text at center.			
a. White laid paper. Black or green text. Serial #00501 to 28,400.	1.50	3.00	10.00
b. Manila paper. Black or green text. Serial #31,000 to 42,700.	1.50	3.00	10.00
x. Counterfeit.	—	—	—

S192 5 Pesos	Good	Fine	XF
ND. Brown with green text. Eagle at center. Like #S191. Serial #43,200 to 58,700. Back: *V* at upper corners. Hills, plants, buildings and Statue of Liberty under text across center. Paper: Manila.	1.50	3.00	10.00

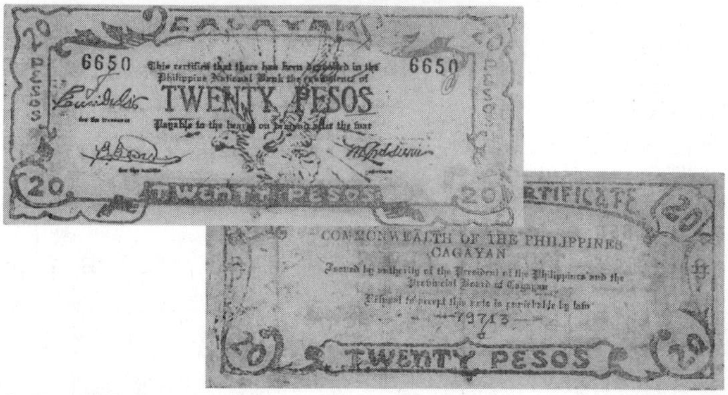

S193 20 Pesos	Good	Fine	XF
ND. Green with black text. Eagle at center. *TWENTY PESOS* at bottom. Serial #2001 to 7300. Back: No vignette across center. Paper: White laid.			
a. Issued note.	9.00	20.00	60.00
x. Counterfeit.	—	—	—

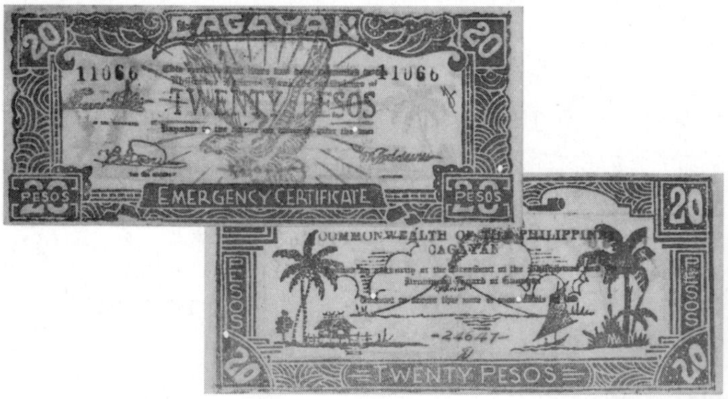

S194 20 Pesos	Good	Fine	XF
ND. Green with black text. Eagle in red-brown at center. *EMERGENCY CERTIFICATE* at bottom. Serial #7400 to 11,698. Back: Mt. Mayon and native scenes across center.			
a. White paper without watermark.	6.00	12.00	35.00
b. Commercially watermark paper.	9.00	20.00	60.00

NOTE: The Second and Fourth Cagayan Issues are known with 3-line rubber stamping *Registered/Countersigned/Prov. Troas. (Troas, not Treas.)* with dates from August through October, 1945. The Fourth Issue may also be found overprint in purple with ¢ and $ symbols.

Currency Committee

Emergency Loose Change of 1943 Provincial Issue

	Good	Fine	XF
S201 50 Centavos 1943. Paper: Manila.			
a. Issued note.	30.00	60.00	180.
x1. Counterfeit.	—	—	—
S201A 50 Centavos 1943. Back: Like #S201 but with *COMMITEE* (error). Paper: Manila.	30.00	60.00	180.
S202 1 Peso 1943. Paper: White.			
a. Issued note.	30.00	60.00	180.
x1. Counterfeit.	—	—	—
S202A 1 Peso 1943. Back: Like #S202 but with *COMMITEE* (error). Paper: White.	25.00	50.00	150.

Aklan Military

1942 Emergency Bills Issue

		Good	Fine	XF
S204	**5 Centavos** 1942. Paper: Thick manila. *First Issue, 8 Dec. 42.* 100,000 notes.	90.00	270.	—
S205	**10 Centavos** 3.12.1942. 100,000 notes.			
	a. Denomination 15mm long.	125.	250.	—
	b. Denomination 30mm long.	125.	250.	—
	c. Denomination in italics.	125.	250.	—
S206	**20 Centavos** 50,000 notes.			
	a. Value *20* in italics.	125.	250.	—
	b. Value *20* regular type.	125.	250.	—
	c. Value *20* at left larger than at right.	125.	250.	—
S207	**50 Centavos** 50,000 notes.	125.	250.	—
S208	**1 Peso** 2.2.1943. Blue. Paper: Coarse white. 25,000 notes.	125.	250.	—
S209	**2 Pesos** 12,500 notes. Rare.	—	—	—

Philippine National Bank - Cebu

1941 Official Emergency Circulating Note Issue

		Good	Fine	XF
S211	**5 Centavos** 1941. Green. Bank arms at center. Like #S301. Serial #1 to 100,000. Paper: Yellow.	1.50	3.00	10.00
S212	**10 Centavos** 1941. Blue. Bank arms at center. Like #S302. Serial #1 to 50,000. Paper: Yellow.	1.50	3.00	10.00
S213	**20 Centavos** 1941. Red. Bank arms at center. Like #S303. Serial #1 to 100,000. Paper: Yellow.	1.50	3.00	10.00
S214	**50 Centavos** 1941. Yellow. Bank arms at center. Like #S304. Serial #1 to 50,000. Paper: Yellow.	1.50	3.00	10.00
S215	**1 Peso** 1941. Blue. Serial #1 to 1,000,000. Back: Light orange. Paper: White bond.	.25	.50	1.50
S216	**5 Pesos** 1941. Black on green underprint. Serial #1 to 180,000. Watermark: Vertical bars.	1.50	3.00	10.00
S217	**10 Pesos** 1941. Black on yellow underprint. Serial #1 to 300,000.			
	a. Without watermark. Serial #1 to approx. 75,000.	1.00	2.00	6.00
	b. Bais paper. watermark: Vertical bars. Serial # approx. 75,001 upwards.	1.00	2.00	6.00
	x1. Printed counterfeit. Two varieties known.	—	—	—
	x2. Hand-drawn counterfeit, quality from crude to excellent.	—	—	—
S218	**20 Pesos** 1941. Black on orange underprint. Serial #1 to 302,500. Paper: Bais. Watermark: Vertical bars.			
	a. Issued note.	1.00	2.00	6.00
	x1. Printed counterfeit.	—	—	—
	x2. Hand-drawn counterfeit.	—	—	—

1941 Cebu Guerrilla Issue

		Good	Fine	XF
S219	**5 Pesos** 1941. Black on green underprint. Like #S216. Serial #180,001 to 200,000. Watermark: Vertical bars.	12.00	25.00	75.00
S220	**20 Pesos** 1941. Black on orange underprint. Like #S218. Serial #302,501 to 325,000. Paper: Bais. Watermark: Vertical bars.	6.00	20.00	60.00

Cebu Emergency Currency Board

Treasury Emergency Currency Certificates

1942 Series - Official Issue

		Good	Fine	XF
S221	**5 Pesos** 1942. Black on brown underprint. Serial #1 to 500. Back: Without countersignature.	—	—	—
S222	**10 Pesos** 1942. Black on green or aqua underprint. Quezon at upper left. Serial #1 to 500. Back: Without countersignature.	—	—	—

#S223-S224 three countersign on back. Like #S222.

		Good	Fine	XF
S223	**10 Pesos** 1942. Black on green or aqua underprint. Quezon at upper left. Serial #501 to 6000 and 30,601 to 30,800. Like #S222. Back: Three countersignatures on back.	20.00	40.00	120.
S224	**20 Pesos** 1942. Black on orange underprint. Quezon at upper left. Serial #1 to 41,000. Like #S222. Back: Three countersignatures on back.			
	a. Pen countersignature of all 3 Board Members.	12.00	25.00	75.00
	b. Pen countersignature of del Bando and Macrohon, facsmiile signature of Elizalde.	30.00	60.00	180.
	c. Facsimile signature of all 3 Board Members.	3.00	6.00	20.00

1942 Illegal Issue

		Good	Fine	XF
S226	**5 Pesos** 1942. Black on brown underprint. Like #S221. Serial #501 upwards. Back: Without countersignature.	—	—	—
S227	**10 Pesos** 1942. Black on green or aqua underprint. Quezon at upper left. Serial #6001 to 30,600 and 30,801 upwards.			
	a. With countersignature. Like #S223.	30.00	60.00	180.
	b. Without countersignature. Like #S222.	—	—	—
S228	**20 Pesos** 1942. Black on orange underprint. Serial #41,000 upwards.			
	a. With countersignature. Like #S224.	6.00	12.00	25.00
	b. Without countersignature.	—	—	—

NOTE: As all legally issued 20 pesos had countersignature, many of the looted notes which were without them had forged signatures applied in India ink.

Culion Leper Colony

1942 First Issue

		Good	Fine	XF
S241	**1 Centavo** 1942. Serial #1 to 20,800. Back: Without typed Presidential Authority.	45.00	90.00	270.
S242	**5 Centavos** 1942. Serial #1 to 18,400. Back: Without typed Presidential Authority.	50.00	100.	300.
S243	**20 Centavos** 1942. Serial #1 to 16,800. Back: Without typed Presidential Authority.	60.00	120.	360.
S244	**50 Centavos** 1942. Serial #1 to 16,000. Back: Without typed Presidential Authority.			
	a. Issued note.	60.00	120.	360.
	x. Error; *FIFTY CENTAVOS* typed over *TWENTY CENTAVOS.*	110.	225.	675.
S245	**1 Peso** 1942. Serial #1 to 16,999; 23,000 to 23,999; 34,000 to 34,999; 45,000 to 46,000. Back: Without typed Presidential Authority.	60.00	180.	540.
S246	**5 Pesos** 1942. Serial #1 to 14,400. Back: Without typed Presidential Authority.	75.00	150.	450.
S247	**20 Pesos** 1942. Serial #1 to 2000. Back: Without typed Presidential Authority.	—	—	—

1942 Second Issue

#S251-S253 After the telegram from President Quezon was received, an additional clause citing Presidential authority was typewritten on the back. The following denominations are known, but there may be others. Serial #'s are included in the previous listing.

		Good	Fine	XF
S251	**1 Centavo** 1942. Like #S241. Back: With typed Presidential Authority.	60.00	120.	360.
S252	**5 Centavos** 1942. Like #S242. Back: With typed Presidential Authority.	75.00	150.	450.
S253	**20 Centavos** 1942. Like #S243. Back: With typed Presidential Authority.	75.00	150.	450.

NOTE: 10,000 pesos in Culion scrip was loaned to, and issued by, the Municipality of Coron on Palawan. It is possible that such notes were stamped for identification. At any rate, Culion notes without the typewritten Presidential authority are known with the following facsimile signature stamped on the back:

Province of Ilocos Norte

1942 First Emergency Treasury Certificates Issue

#S261-S269 dated March 1942. No Series.

		Good	Fine	XF
S261	**5 Centavos** 1942. Handsigned. Typewritten serial #1 to 720. Overprint: Large. Paper: White.	25.00	50.00	150.
S262	**10 Centavos** 1942. Handsigned. Typewritten serial #1 to 655. Overprint: Large. Paper: White.	25.00	50.00	150.
S263	**50 Centavos** 1942. Handsigned. Typewritten serial #1 to 910. Overprint: Small. Paper: White.	25.00	50.00	150.

		Good	Fine	XF
S264	**1 Peso** 1942. Handsigned. Typewritten serial #1 to 537. Overprint: Large. Paper: White.	25.00	50.00	150.
S265	**2 Pesos** 1942. Handsigned. Typewritten serial #1 to 540. Overprint: Large. Paper: White.	25.00	50.00	150.
S266	**5 Pesos** 1942. Handsigned. Typewritten serial #1 to 627. Overprint: Large. Paper: White.	25.00	50.00	150.
S267	**10 Pesos** 1942. Handsigned. Typewritten serial #1 to 620. Overprint: Large. Paper: White.	25.00	50.00	150.
S268	**20 Pesos** 1942. Handsigned. Typewritten serial #1 to 900. Overprint: Small. Paper: White.	25.00	50.00	150.
S269	**50 Pesos** 1942. Handsigned. Typewritten serial #1 to 465. Overprint: Small. Paper: White.	—	—	—

1942 Second Emergency Treasury Certificates Issue

#S270-S276 dated April 1, 1942. Second Series.

		Good	Fine	XF
S270	**1 Peso** 1.4.1942. Printed signature. Typewritten serial #538 to 2753. 2 text varieties, 5 or 6 lines of text. Overprint: Small. Paper: White.	25.00	50.00	150.
S271	**2 Pesos** 1.4.1942. Printed signature. Typewritten serial #541 to 5331. Back: 3 text varieties of last line: *punishable by law, able by law, ble by law.* Overprint: Small. Paper: White.	25.00	50.00	150.
S272	**5 Pesos** 1.4.1942. Printed signature. Typewritten serial #628 to 2682. Overprint: Small. Paper: White.	25.00	50.00	150.
S273	**10 Pesos** 1.4.1942. Printed signature. Typewritten serial #621 to 2540. Overprint: Small. Paper: White.	25.00	50.00	150.
S274	**20 Pesos** 1.4.1942. Printed signature. Typewritten serial #901 to 2327. Overprint: Small. Paper: White.	25.00	50.00	150.
S275	**50 Pesos** 1.4.1942. Printed signature. Typewritten serial #466 to 956. Overprint: Small. Paper: White.			
	a. Issued note.	45.00	90.00	270.
	x. Counterfeit. Dated *March 1942* but inscribed *SECOND SERIES.*	—	—	—

S276 100 Pesos — Good / Fine / XF

1.4.1942. Printed signature. Typewritten serial #1 to 477. Overprint: Small. Paper: White.

- a. Issued note. — — —
- x1. Counterfeit. Dated *March 3, 1942,* inscribed *FIRST SERIES.* — — —
- x2. Counterfeit. Dated *March 1942,* inscribed *SECOND SERIES.* — — —
- x3. Counterfeit. Dated *April 15, 1942,* inscribed *THIRD SERIES.* — — —

1942 Third Emergency Treasury Certificates Issue

#S277-S281 April 15, 1942. Third Series.

S277 1 Peso — Good / Fine / XF

15.4.1942. Typewritten serial #2754 to 8124. Two text varieties, title at right *Provincial Governor* or *Provincial Board* (typing error). Overprint: Small. Paper: White. 22.50 45.00 140.

S278E 2 Pesos

15.4.1942. Typewritten serial #957 to 2212. Overprint: Small purple error; *P2.00* on 50 Pesos #S281 mimeographed form. Paper: White. — — —

S279 10 Pesos

15.4.1942. Typewritten serial #2541 to 4384 in black or red. Two text varieties, 5 or 6 lines of text. Overprint: Small. Paper: White.

- a. Issued note. 25.00 50.00 150.
- x. Counterfeit. Correctly dated but inscribed *FOURTH SERIES.* — — —

S280 20 Pesos

15.4.1942. Typewritten serial #2328 to 3457. Overprint: Small. Paper: White. 25.00 50.00 150.

S281 50 Pesos

15.4.1942. Typewritten serial #957 to 2212. Back: Two text varieties of last line *punishable by law* or *nisable by law.* Overprint: Small. Paper: White.

- a. Issued note. 30.00 60.00 180.
- x. Counterfeit. Dated *April, 1942* (no day), inscribed *THIRD SERIES.* — — —

1942 Fourth Emergency Treasury Certificates Issue

#S282-S283 May 4, 1942. Fourth Series.

S282 5 Pesos — Good / Fine / XF

4.5.1942. Typewritten serial #1328 to 5333. Two text varieties of last line: *after the war* or *ter the war.* Overprint: Small. Paper: White. 25.00 50.00 150.

Note: Serial #1328 to #2682 for #S282 mistakenly duplicated those of April 1st printing.

S283 10 Pesos

4.5.1942. Serial #4385 to 12,772. Back: Two text varieties of last line: *able by law* or *law.* Overprint: Small.

- a. Typewritten serial #4385 to 9400. 25.00 50.00 150.
- b. Printed serial #9401 to 9971 in purple. 25.00 50.00 150.
- c. Printed serial #9972 to 12,772 in black. 25.00 50.00 150.

#S284 May 12, 1942. Fourth Series.

S284 1 Peso

12.5.1942. Serial #8125 to 18,144 (est.). Back: Two text varieties of last line: 6 words or 1 word. Overprint: Small.

- a. White paper. Typewritten serial #8125 to 12,633. 25.00 50.00 150.
- b. Manila paper. Printed serial #12,634 to 13,400. 25.00 50.00 150.
- c. White paper. Printed serial #13,401 to 18,144 (est.). 25.00 50.00 150.

#S285-S288 two text varieties of last line on back: *nisable by law* or *law.*

#S285 and S286 May 15, 1942. Second Series.

S285 50 Centavos

15.5.1942. Typewritten serial #911 to 3679. Back: Two text varieties of last line: *nisable by law* or *law.* Overprint: Small *P.50.* 25.00 50.00 150.

S286 50 Centavos — Good / Fine / XF

15.5.1942. Printed serial #3680 to 11,414 (est.). Back: Two text varieties of last line: *nisable by law* or *law.* Overprint: Small *P0.50*.

- a. Manila paper. Serial #3680 to 7748 and 10,341 to 11,414. 25.00 50.00 150.
- b. White paper. Serial #7749 to 10,340. 25.00 50.00 150.

1942 Various Series Emergency Treasury Certificates Issue

S287 5 Centavos — Good / Fine / XF

20.5.1942. Second Series. Serial # 721 to 4100. Back: Two text varieties of last line: *nisable by law* or *law.* Overprint: Small *P.05.* Paper: Manila.

- a. Typewritten serial # 721 to 1900. 25.00 50.00 150.
- b. Printed serial # 1901 to 4100. 25.00 50.00 150.

S288 5 Centavos

20.5.1942. Second Series. Serial #4101 to 6457. Back: Two text varieties of last line: *nisable by law* or *law.* Overprint: Large *P.05.* Paper: Manila. 25.00 50.00 150.

#S289-S293 two text varieties of last line on face: *deemable after the war* or *after the war.*

S289 10 Centavos

20.5.1942. Second Series. Serial #656 to 2000. Two text varieties of last line: *deemable after the war* or *after the war.* Overprint: Small *P.10.* Paper: Manila. 25.00 50.00 150.

S290 10 Centavos

20.5.1942. Second Series. Serial #2001 to 2100 and 2616 to 3542 (approx.). Two text varieties of last line: *deemable after the war* or *after the war.* Overprint: Small *P0.10.* Paper: Manila. 25.00 50.00 150.

S291 10 Centavos

20.5.1942. Second Series. Serial #3575 (approx.) to 6667. Two text varieties of last line: *deemable after the war* or *after the war.* Overprint: Large *P0.10*.

- a. Manila paper. Serial #3575 to 4823. 25.00 50.00 150.
- b. White paper. Serial #4824 to 6667. 25.00 50.00 150.

NOTE: Serial #2101-2600 are #S290 and S291 intermixed.

S292 20 Centavos

20.5.1942. First Series. Typewritten serial #1 to 2950. Two varieties: with or without value in box at upper right corner. Two text varieties of last line: *deemable after the war* or *after the war.* Overprint: Small *P.20*. Paper: Manila. 25.00 50.00 150.

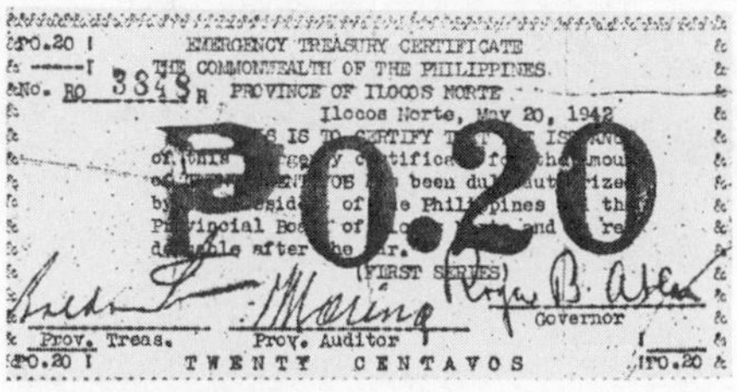

S293 20 Centavos — Good / Fine / XF

20.5.1942. First Series. Printed serial #2951 to 8760. Two varieties: with or without value in box at upper right corner. Two text varieties of last line: *deemable after the war* or *after the war.* Overprint: Large *P0.20.* Paper: White. 25.00 50.00 150.

S294 5 Pesos

20.5.1942. Fifth Series. Printed serial # in purple or black 5334 to 8400. Two text varieties. Overprint: Small. Paper: Manila. 25.00 50.00 150.

June 6, 1942 Issue

S295 5 Pesos — Good / Fine / XF

6.6.1942. Light manila. Sixth Series. Serial #9755 to 15,600 (approx.). Two text varieties.

- a. With 2 zeroes after decimal point. 25.00 50.00 150.
- b. Without 2 zeroes after decimal point. — — —

June 15, 1942 Issue

S296 1 Peso — Good / Fine / XF

15.6.1942. Fifth Series. Serial #18,164 (approx.) to 29,397. Back: Two text varieties of first line: *President* or *Presedint* (error). 25.00 50.00 150.

S297 5 Pesos

15.6.1942. Seventh Series. Serial # 15,601 (approx.) to 23,347. Back: Two text varieties of last line: 8 or 4 words. 25.00 50.00 150.

Philippine National Bank - Iloilo

1941 Emergency Circulating Note Issue

Pre-Surrender Issue.

S301 5 Centavos — Good / Fine / XF

1941. Green. Bank arms at center. Ornamental border. Like #S211. Serial #1 to 297,000. 1.50 3.00 10.00

S302 10 Centavos — Good / Fine / XF

1941. Blue. Bank arms at center. Ornamental border. Like #S212. Serial #1 to 259,000. 1.50 3.00 10.00

S303 20 Centavos

1941. Red. Bank arms at center. Ornamental border. Like #S213. Serial #: official, 1 to 281,000; estimated, 1 to 285,000. 1.50 3.00 10.00

S304 50 Centavos

1941. Yellow. Bank arms at center. Ornamental border. Like #S214. Serial #1 to 181,000. 2.50 5.00 15.00

NOTE: Orange to brown colored 50 Centavos notes are color changelings, a result of oxidation.

S305 1 Peso

1941. Black on green underprint. Eagle in large *V* at center. Eagle facing right. Serial #1 to 240,000. 3.00 6.00 20.00

S306 2 Pesos

1941. Black on blue underprint. Eagle in large *V* at center. Eagle's wings spread. Serial #1 to 942,000.

- a. Issued note. 1.50 3.00 10.00
- x. Counterfeit. — — —

S307 5 Pesos

1941. Black on red underprint. Eagle in large *V* at center. Eagle's wings spread like #S306. *THE* in bank title. 1.50 3.00 10.00

S307A 5 Pesos

1941. Black on red underprint. Eagle in large *V* at center. Eagle's wings spread. Like #S307 but without *THE* in bank title. 4.50 9.00 30.00

NOTE: Serial #1 - 220,000 are #S307. Serial #220,001-268,000 are #S307 and #S307A intermixed.

S308 10 Pesos

1941. Black on brown underprint. Eagle in large *V* at center. Handsigned. Eagle facing right like #S305. Serial #1 to 10,000. 22.50 45.00 135.

		Good	Fine	XF
S309	**10 Pesos**			
	1941. Black on brown underprint. Eagle in large *V* at center. Like #S308 but printed signature. Serial #10,001 to 290,000.			
	a. Issued note.	1.50	3.00	10.00
	x1. Counterfeit. Corner numerals thicker than genuine.	15.00	30.00	90.00
	x2. Counterfeit. Corner numerals thinner than genuine.	15.00	30.00	90.00

POST-SURRENDER ISSUES

1942 Emergency Circulating Note Issue

First Dialosa Printing

		Good	Fine	XF
S311	**50 Centavos**			
	1942. Yellow with green text. Serial #1 to 6466.	15.00	30.00	90.00
S312	**2 Pesos**			
	1942. Dark blue with brown text. Filipino *tao* at left. Serial #1 to 5000.	25.00	50.00	150.
S313	**5 Pesos**			
	1942. Dark red with black text. MacArthur at left, eagle at center. Serial #1 to 24,800.			
	a. Issued note.	5.00	10.00	30.00
	x1. Counterfeit. Portrait better than genuine.	—	—	—
	x2. Counterfeit. Very crude portrait	—	—	—
S314	**10 Pesos**			
	1942. Brown with black text. Quezon at left. Serial #1 to 1850.	7.50	15.00	45.00
S315	**20 Pesos**			
	1942. Green with black text. Roosevelt at left. Serial #1 to 55,200.			
	a. Issued note.	2.50	5.00	15.00
	x1. Counterfeit. Portrait better than genuine.	—	—	—
	x2. Counterfeit. Crude portrait	—	—	—

Second Dialosa Printing

		Good	Fine	XF
S316	**5 Pesos**			
	1942. Dull salmon-red with black text. MacArthur at left, eagle at center. Like #S313. Serial #24,801 to 294,000.	1.50	3.00	10.00
S317	**10 Pesos**			
	1942. Brown with black text. Quezon at left. Like #S314. Serial #1851 to 421,000.			
	a. Dark brown, serial # to 296,000.	1.50	3.00	10.00
	b. Light brown, very high serial # (for example 395,222).	1.50	3.00	10.00
S318	**20 Pesos**			
	1942. Green with black text. Roosevelt at left. Like #S315. Serial #55,201 to 998,000. Back: Standing woman with hammer and Mt. Mayon design (as on Philippine silver coins) at center. 4 plates used.			
	a. Issued note.	1.00	2.00	6.00
	x. Counterfeit. Misspelling *ROOSAVELT* (with *A*) under portrait.	6.00	12.00	35.00
S322	**100 Pesos**			
	1942. Yellow-orange with black text. Mt. Mayon at left. Ribbon directly above drapes *over* bar. Serial #1 to 23,000 and 229,001 to 300,000.			
	a. Issued note.	4.00	8.00	25.00
	x1. Counterfeit. Ribbon above Mt. Mayon is pierced by bar. 5-digit serial #.	3.00	6.00	20.00
	x2. Counterfeit. Different type. 6-digit serial #.	—	—	—

Villalon Printing

#S324 and S325 eagle and *V* design of some 1941 notes.

		Good	Fine	XF
S324	**1 Peso**			
	1942. Black on green underprint. Eagle in large *V* at center. Similar to #S305 but eagle with wings spread. Serial #1 to 75,000.	7.50	15.00	45.00
S325	**5 Pesos**			
	1942. Black on red underprint. Eagle in large *V* at center. Eagle's wings spread. Similar to #S307. Serial #1 to 30,000.	6.00	12.00	35.00

1943 Emergency Circulating Note Issue

Villalon Printing

		Good	Fine	XF
S326	**50 Centavos**			
	1943. Black. Red arms at center. Serial #1 to 200,000.	6.00	12.00	35.00
S327	**2 Pesos**			
	1943. Black on blue underprint. Eagle in large *V* at center. Eagle's wings spread. Similar to #S306. Serial #1 to 37,400.	4.00	8.00	25.00
S328	**5 Pesos**			
	1943. Black on red to violet underprint. Eagle in large *V* at center. Eagle's wings spread. Like #S325. Serial #1 to 455,000.			
	a. White paper.	3.00	6.00	20.00
	b. Yellow paper.	4.50	9.00	30.00
	x. Counterfeit.	—	—	—

NOTE: 5 Pesos notes with serial #363,001 to 367,000 and 367,501 to 368,000 were reported stolen and officially prohibited from circulating.

		Good	Fine	XF
S329	**10 Pesos**			
	1943. Black on brown underprint. Eagle in large *V* at center. Eagle's wings spread. Like #S328. Serial #1 to 200,000.			
	a. White paper.	1.50	3.00	9.00
	b. Yellow paper.	3.00	6.00	20.00
S330	**20 Pesos**			
	1943. Black on green underprint. Eagle in large *V* at center. Eagle's wings spread. Like #S328. Serial #1 to 5000.	40.00	80.00	240.
S331	**50 Pesos**			
	1943. Black on mauve underprint. Eagle in large *V* at center. Eagle's wings spread. Like #S328. Serial #1 to 20,000.	12.00	25.00	75.00

1944 Treasury Certificate Issue

		Good	Fine	XF
S332	**20 Centavos**			
	1944. Serial #000,001 to 020,000. Rare.	—	—	—
S334	**50 Centavos**			
	1944. Initials *smc*, *pav* and *mvb* in upper left, upper right, and lower right corners respectively. Serial #00,001 to (approx.) 160,000.	7.50	15.00	45.00
S335	**50 Centavos**			
	1944. Like #S334 but no initials at corners. Serial # (approx.) 165,001 to 539,980.	7.50	15.00	45.00
S337	**50 Centavos**			
	1944. Back: *SPECIAL MUNICIPALITY OF SIBUYAN ROMBLON PHILS* stamped.	30.00	60.00	180.

1944 Emergency Circulating Note Issue

Dialosa Printing

		Good	Fine	XF
S338	**50 Centavos**			
	1944. Black. Red arms at center. Serial #1 to 150,000.			
	a. Plain paper.	1.00	2.00	6.00
	b. Watermark paper.	—	—	—
S339	**1 Peso**			
	1944. Black. Red arms at center. Serial #1 to 500,000.	1.00	2.00	6.00
S340	**2 Pesos**			
	1944. Black. Red arms at center. Serial #1 to 494,000.			
	a. Issued note.	1.00	2.00	6.00
	x. Counterfeit.	—	—	—
S341	**5 Pesos**			
	1944. Dull salmon-red with black text. MacArthur at left, eagle at center. Like #S316. Serial #1 to 206,000.	1.00	2.00	6.00

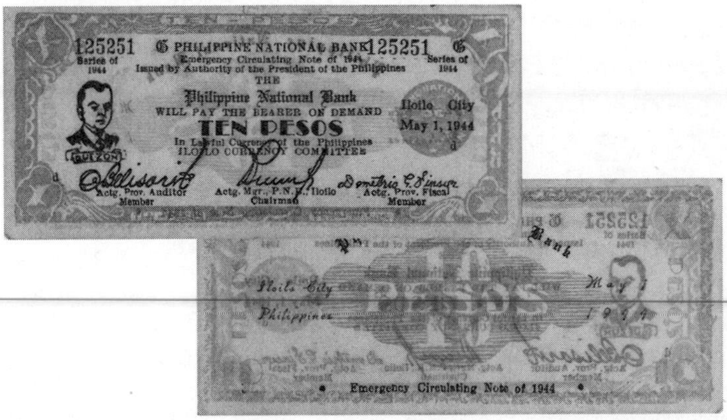

		Good	Fine	XF
S342	**10 Pesos**			
	1944. Brown with black text. Quezon at left. Like #S317. Serial #1 to 263,000.	1.00	2.00	6.00

Province of Isabela

1942 ND First Emergency Legal Tender Issue

		Good	Fine	XF
S351	**1 Peso**			
	ND (1942). Without numerals of value.			
	a. Without denomination stamped on back.	30.00	60.00	180.
	b. Denomination stamped on back.	30.00	60.00	180.
S352	**5 Pesos**			
	ND (1942). Without numerals of value.			
	a. Without denomination stamped on back.	30.00	60.00	180.
	b. Denomination stamped on back.	30.00	60.00	180.
S353	**10 Pesos**			
	ND (1942). Without numerals of value.			
	a. Without denomination stamped on back.	30.00	60.00	180.
	b. Denomination stamped on back.	30.00	60.00	180.
S354	**20 Pesos**			
	ND (1942). Without numerals of value.			
	a. Without denomination stamped on back.	30.00	60.00	180.
	b. Denomination stamped on back.	30.00	60.00	180.

1942 ND Second Emergency Legal Tender Issue

		Good	Fine	XF
S361	**10 Centavos**			
	ND (1942). Numerals of value.	—	—	—
S362	**20 Centavos**			
	ND (1942). Numerals of value.	—	—	—
S364	**1 Peso**			
	ND (1942). Numerals of value.	—	—	—
S365	**2 Pesos**			
	ND (1942). Numerals of value.	—	—	—
S366	**5 Pesos**			
	ND (1942). Numerals of value.	—	—	—
S367	**10 Pesos**			
	ND (1942). Numerals of value.	—	—	—

KKKK

Refer to Masbate #S461-S462.

Philippine National Bank - Lanao

1942 Emergency Circulating Notes Issue

There are two types of Lanao currency:

TYPE I: With *titles* of Committee Members.

TYPE II: With *names* of Committee Members.

		Good	Fine	XF
S372	**20 Centavos**			
	1942. Type I: with *titles* of Committee Members. Facsimile signature stamped in blue. Paper: Manila.	40.00	80.00	240.
S374	**50 Centavos**			
	1942. Type I: with *titles* of Committee Members. Handsigned. Paper: Yellow.	30.00	60.00	180.
S376	**50 Centavos**			
	1942. Type I: with *titles* of Committee Members. Printed signature. Paper: Yellow.	30.00	60.00	180.
S377	**1 Peso**			
	1942. Type I: with *titles* of Committee Members. Handsigned. Paper: White.	30.00	60.00	180.

		Good	Fine	XF
S378	**1 Peso**			
	1942. Type II: with *names* of Committee Members. Handsigned. Paper: White.			
	a. Issued note.	40.00	80.00	240.
	x1. Counterfeit. Typewritten.	—	—	—
	x2. Counterfeit. Crudely printed.	—	—	—
S380	**2 Pesos**			
	1942. Green. Type I: with *titles* of Committee Members. Printed signature. Back: Blue. Moro stringed musical instrument called a *kotivapi* in red across center. Paper: White.	40.00	80.00	240.

1942 Spurious Issue

		Good	Fine	XF
S380X	**10 Pesos**			
	1.20.1942. Spurious note.	—	—	—

NOTE: A 10 Pesos note dated "Enero 20, 1942" is completely spurious. It is mentioned here not only to acquaint collectors with its true status but also as an example of the confusion brought about by the numerous types and varieties of currency being issued which resulted in an entirely bogus issue being placed in circulation.

Free Lanao Provisional Government

1942 Ovpt. Issue

		Good	Fine	XF
S381	**Type I ovpt. on:**			
	c. 10 Pesos Mindanao 1942, #S473.	—	—	—
	e. 1 Peso Cebu 1941, #S215.	—	—	—
	f. 5 Pesos Cebu 1941, #S216.	—	—	—
	h. 20 Pesos Cebu 1941, #S218.	—	—	—
S382	**Type II ovpt. on:**			
	a. 2 Pesos Mindanao 1942, #S471.	—	—	—
	c. 10 Pesos Mindanao 1942, #S473.	—	—	—
	d. 20 Pesos Mindanao 1942, #S474.	—	—	—
	e. 1 Peso Cebu 1941, #S215.	—	—	—
	f. 5 Pesos Cebu 1941, #S216.	—	—	—
	h. 20 Pesos Cebu 1941, #S218.	—	—	—
S383	**Type III A ovpt. on:**			
	h. 20 Pesos Cebu 1941, #S218.	—	—	—
S383A	**Type III B ovpt. on:**			
	c. 10 Pesos Mindanao, 1942, #S473.	—	—	—
	h. 20 Pesos Cebu 1941, #S218.	—	—	—
S384	**Type IV ovpt. on:**			
	b. 5 Pesos Mindanao 1942, #S472.	—	—	—
	h. 20 Pesos Cebu 1941, #S218.	—	—	—

Leyte Emergency Currency Board

1942 Treasury Emergency Certificate Issue

		Good	Fine	XF
S391	**5 Centavos**			
	1942. Black. Back: Red arms at center. Paper: Light blue. 34,932 notes.			
	a. Type I underprint in yellow.	15.00	30.00	90.00
	b. Type II underprint in yellow.	15.00	30.00	90.00
S392	**10 Centavos**			
	1942. Green. Type I underprint. Red arms at center. 9,750 notes.	75.00	150.	450.
S393	**20 Centavos**			
	1942. Blue. Type I underprint in yellow. Red arms at center. 8,100 notes.	30.00	60.00	180.
S394	**1 Peso**			
	April 1942. Green. Orange arms at center. Filipino plowing with carabao at left. Series A. 50,500 notes.	7.50	15.00	45.00

1942 Treasury Emergency Currency Certificate Issue

		Good	Fine	XF
S395	**10 Pesos**			
	1942. Black. Palm and Rizal Monument at left, seal and palm at right. 44,054 notes.			
	a. Type I underprint in yellow on face only.	12.00	25.00	75.00
	b. Type I underprint in yellow on face and back.	12.00	25.00	75.00
	c. Type II underprint in yellow on face only.	15.00	30.00	90.00
S396	**20 Pesos**			
	1942. Blue. Underprint in yellow. Filipinos cultivating rice at left, arms at right. 6,300 notes.			
	a. Type I underprint on face only.	40.00	80.00	240.
	b. Type I underprint on face and back.	40.00	80.00	240.

SERIES 1943

1943 Series First Issue

#S403-S410 printed from wood plates. All are *Plate A.*

		Good	Fine	XF
S403	**20 Centavos**			
	1943. Serial #00,101 to 99,100. Back: Arms and signature in red, purple or brown.			
	a. Issued note.	7.50	15.00	45.00
	x. *ERROR:* Inverted back.	—	—	—
S404	**50 Centavos**			
	1943. Serial #00,101 to 159,100. Back: Arms and signature in red or purple.			
	a. Issued note.	6.00	12.00	35.00
	x. Counterfeit.	—	—	—
S405	**1 Peso**			
	1943. Black. Serial #00,101 to 120,700. Back: Arms and signature in red, purple or brown.	7.50	15.00	45.00
S406	**2 Pesos**			
	1943. Black. Carabao head at left, red arms at right. Serial #00,101 to 41,000.			
	a. Issued note.	7.50	15.00	45.00
	x. Counterfeit (the carabao is smiling!).	—	—	—
S407	**2 Pesos**			
	1943. Blue. Carabao head at left. Red or purple seal at right. Like #S406. Back: Smaller size serial #. Serial #42,001 to 50,000.	30.00	60.00	180.
S408	**5 Pesos**			
	Brown. Native village at left, seal in plate at right. Serial #0101 to 88,000. Back: Green.			
	a. Thin to medium thick white paper.	15.00	30.00	90.00
	b. Ruled ledger paper.	15.00	30.00	90.00
	c. Dark brown paper.	15.00	30.00	90.00
S409	**10 Pesos**			
	1943. Black. Rice terraces at left, red seal at right. Serial #101 to 24,300. Back: Red.			
	a. White paper.	25.00	50.00	150.
	b. Ruled ledger paper.	—	—	—
	x. Counterfeit.	—	—	—
S410	**20 Pesos**			
	1943. Black on yellow underprint. Red or maroon serial # and seal. Mt. Mayon at left. Serial #101 to 16,000. Back: Light blue-green.	30.00	60.00	180.

NOTE: Serial # of 20 Pesos notes destroyed by orders of Col. Kangleon are as follows: 1401 to 4400; 4601 to 6600; 7501 to 8600; 13,201 to 14,600; also 3 individual notes (12,903, 12,912, 12,913).

1943 Series Second Issue

#S411-S415 printed from rubber plates.

		Good	Fine	XF
S411	**20 Centavos**			
	1943. Olive-green. Banana tree at left, seal in plate at right. Plate B. Serial #99,101 to 121,900.			
	a. Issued note.	25.00	50.00	150.
	r. Remainder without serial #.	—	—	—
S412	**50 Centavos**			
	1943. Rust-brown. Palm tree at left, seal in plate at right. Plate B. Serial #159,101 to 199,500.			
	a. Issued note.	25.00	50.00	150.
	r. Remainder without serial #.	—	—	—
S413	**1 Peso**			
	1943. Purple. Antelope head at left, seal in plate at right. Plate B. Serial #121,001 to 180,300. Paper: Pink.	25.00	50.00	150.
S414	**2 Pesos**			
	1943. Blue. Carabao head at left, purple printed seal at right. Plate A2 (face only). Serial #51,001 to 101,600. Back: Smaller size serial #. Like #S407.	25.00	50.00	150.

NOTE: #S414 face is from rubber plate; back is from wood plate.

		Good	Fine	XF
S415	**5 Pesos**			
	1943. Plate B. Serial #88,001 to 96,400.	—	—	—

NOTE: No examples of #S415 are known at this time.

1943 Military Issue

Luzon USAFFE Guerrilla Army Force

1942 Issue

		Good	Fine	XF
S421	**100 Pesos**			
	22.2.1942. Black. Portrait President Roosevelt at left, "Keep 'Em Flying" symbol of the Army Air Force at right. Embossed seal at center. Facsimile signature of Maj. Walter M. Cushing and Capt. W. H. Stephens. Paper: Pink.	25.00	50.00	150.
S422	**500 Pesos**			
	22.2.1942. Black. Portrait President Roosevelt at left, "Keep 'Em Flying" symbol of the Army Air Force at right. Embossed seal at center. Facsimile signature of Maj. Walter M. Cushing and Capt. W. H. Stephens. Paper: Pink.	60.00	120.	360.

Marking's Guerrillas

ND First Issue

Mimeographed in October 1942.

		Good	Fine	XF
S427	**5 Pesos**			
	ND.	—	—	—
S428	**10 Pesos**			
	ND.	—	—	—

Second Issue

Printed in blue. *Advised by Col. Hugh Straughn.* No examples known.

ND Third Issue

Printed in blue. *Advised by Gen. W. W. Fertig.*

		Good	Fine	XF
S438	**10 Pesos**			
	ND. Without inked thumbprints. Remainder.	—	—	—

ND Fourth Issue

Exchange notes.

		Good	Fine	XF
S443	**1000 Pesos**			
	ND. Light blue. *Col. Hugh Straughn* x'd out and *Gen. W. W. Fertig* typed in. Tree and mountain at left, U.S. and Philippine flags at center, huts and trees at right. Back: Large *V* at center. Rare.	—	—	—

President Quezon's Own Guerrillas (PQOG)

ND Emergency Certificate Issue

		Good	Fine	XF
S448	**100 Pesos**			
	ND. Black. Guerrilla fighter on hill at center. PQOG and eagle with Philippine arms in underprint. Facsimile signature of light Col. Benedicto S. Valenzona. Back: PQOG and eagle with Philippine arms. Paper: Pink. Mimeographed.	—	—	—

Masbate Consolidated Mining Co.

1941 ND Token Notes Issue

		Good	Fine	XF
S451	**50 Centavos**			
	ND (1941). Green. Series A. Rare.	—	—	—
S452	**1 Peso**			
	ND (1941). Green. Series A. Rare.	—	—	—
S453	**5 Pesos**			
	ND (1941). Green. Series A. Rare.	—	—	—

Province of Masbate

1942 Emergency Treasury Certificates Issue

Serial numbers are estimates.

	Good	Fine	XF
S456 50 Centavos 15.1.1942. Serial #1 to 4000. Paper: White.	—	—	—
S457 1 Peso 15.1.1942. Serial #1 to 4000. Paper: White.	30.00	60.00	180.
S458 2 Pesos 15.1.1942. Serial #1 to 4000. Paper: White.	—	—	—
S459 5 Pesos 15.1.1942. Serial #1 to 2600. Paper: Cream to yellow.	—	—	—
S460 10 Pesos 15.1.1942. Serial #1 to 1300. Paper: Cream to yellow.	—	—	—

POST-SURRENDER ISSUES

KKKK Katipunan Sa Kaluwasan Sang Ka-anakan Sang Kapupud-an

ND Loose Change Issue

	Good	Fine	XF
S461 50 Centavos ND. Slate black on orange underprint. Red KKKK seal at left, two guerrilla fighters with flag at right. Back: Brown. Crossed rifle, knife and gear at center. Overprint: Black: *FIFTY CENTAVOS* on back. Paper: Ruled ledger.	120.	240.	675.

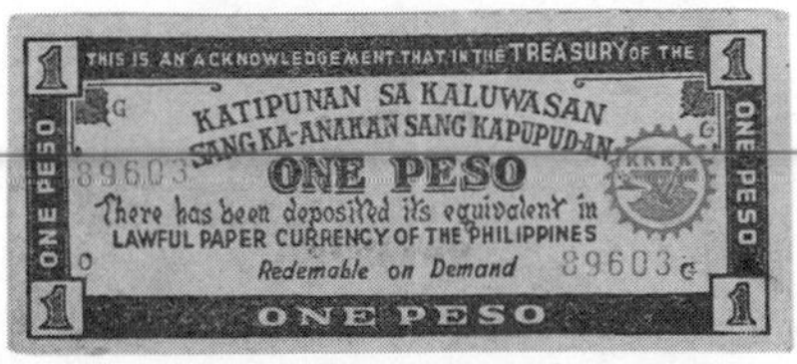

	Good	Fine	XF
S462 1 Peso ND. Black. Red KKKK seal at right. Back: Orange. Crossed rifle, knife and gear at center. Like #S461. Paper: Thin light manila.	120.	240.	675.

FREE MASBATE

Mindanao Emergency Currency Board

1942 Emergency Currency Certificate Issue

	Good	Fine	XF
S471 2 Pesos 1942. Black on blue underprint. Serial #0001 to 90,000.	1.50	3.00	10.00

	Good	Fine	XF
S472 5 Pesos 1942. Blue on green underprint. Serial #0001 to 76,338. Back: Tan underprint.	3.00	6.00	20.00

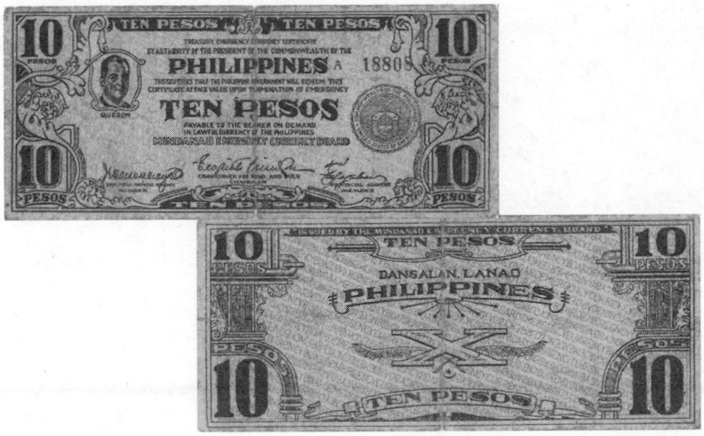

	Good	Fine	XF
S473 10 Pesos 1942. Black on reddish brown underprint. Quezon at left. Serial #0001 to 29,000.	3.00	6.00	20.00

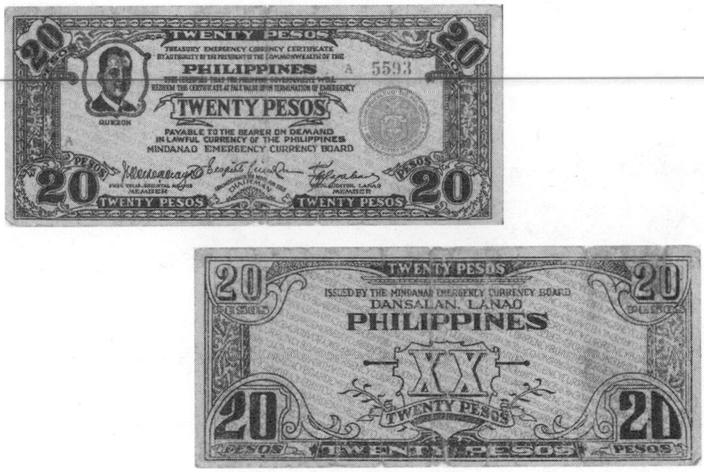

	Good	Fine	XF
S474 20 Pesos 1942. Black on green underprint. Quezon at left. Serial #0001 to 52,900. Similar to #S473.	3.00	6.00	20.00

Second Mindanao Emergency Currency Board

1943 First Treasury Emergency Currency Certificate Issue

(Matugas, Misamis Occ., April 5 to June 25, 1943)

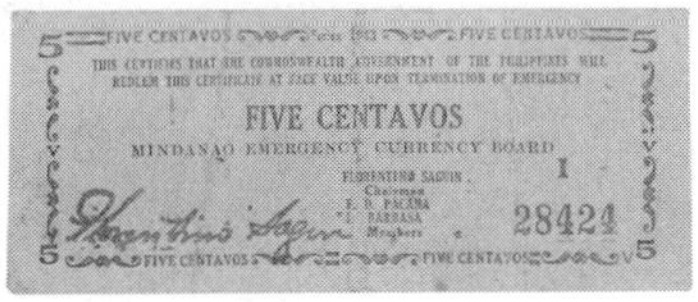

	Good	Fine	XF
S481 5 Centavos 1943. Series *I*. Serial #00,001 to 62,400.			
a. Initials. Serial #00,001 to 08,000.	—	—	—
b. Without initials. Serial #08,001 to 62,400.	6.00	12.00	35.00
S482 10 Centavos 1943. Series *H*. Serial #00,001 to 68,000.			
a. Initials. Serial #00,001 to 08,000.	—	—	—
b. Without initials. Serial #08,001 to 68,000.	6.00	12.00	35.00
S483 20 Centavos 1943. Series *G*. Serial #00,001 to 68,000.			
a. Initials. Serial #00,001 to 08,000.	—	—	—
b. Without initials. Serial #08,001 to 68,000.	6.00	12.00	35.00
S484 50 Centavos 1943. Series *F*. Serial #00,001 to 60,000. *SERIES OF 1943.*	7.50	15.00	45.00
S485 1 Peso 1943. Series *E*. Serial #00,001 to 60,000.			
a. Countersignature Crispin Pangalinan.	—	—	—
b. Countersignature Armando Ala.	—	—	—
c. Countersignature Pedro G. Perez.	—	—	—
d. Countersignature Pedro Dagandan.	—	—	—
e. Countersignature Vicente D. Roa.	—	—	—
f. Without countersignature.	4.50	9.00	30.00
S486 2 Pesos 1943. Series *D*. Serial #0,001 to 84,000.			
a. Countersignature F. D. Pacana.	—	—	—
b. Countersignature I. Barbasa, without stamped title.	—	—	—
c. Countersignature L. J. Oteyza.	—	—	—
d. Countersignature Gabriel Cuerpo.	5.00	10.00	30.00
e. Countersignature Armando Ala.	3.00	6.00	20.00
f. Countersignature Pedro G. Perez.	3.00	6.00	20.00

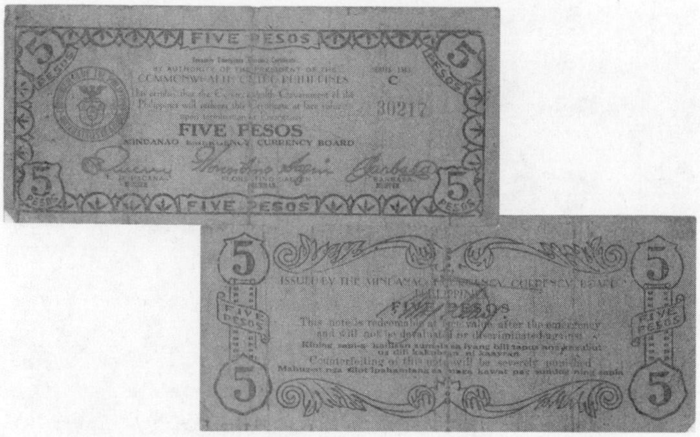

S487 5 Pesos

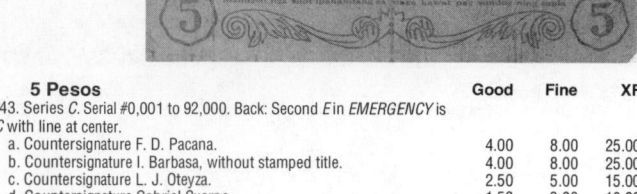

	Good	Fine	XF
1943. Series *C*. Serial #0,001 to 92,000. Back: Second *E* in *EMERGENCY* is a *C* with line at center.			
a. Countersignature F. D. Pacana.	4.00	8.00	25.00
b. Countersignature I. Barbasa, without stamped title.	4.00	8.00	25.00
c. Countersignature L. J. Oteyza.	2.50	5.00	15.00
d. Countersignature Gabriel Cuerpo.	1.50	3.00	10.00
e. Countersignature Leoncio Mendoza. Serial #89,001 to 90,000.	—	—	—
f. Countersignature Pedro Dagandan. Serial #90,001 to 92,000.	—	—	—
g. Without countersignature. Serial #69,001 to 73,000.	—	—	—

S488 10 Pesos

	Good	Fine	XF
1943. Series *B*. Serial #0,001 to 82,000.			
a. Countersignature F. D. Pacana.	2.50	5.00	15.00
b. Countersignature I. Barbasa, with stamped title.	4.00	8.00	25.00
c. Countersignature I. Barbasa, without stamped title.	5.00	10.00	30.00
d. Countersignature L. J. Oteyza.	2.50	5.00	15.00
e. Countersignature Gabriel Cuerpo.	4.00	8.00	25.00
x1. Counterfeit. Misspelling *Chariman* in title. Forged countersignature I. Barbasa on back.	4.50	9.00	30.00
x2. Counterfeit. Top ornaments connected; without countersignature.	.50	1.00	3.00

NOTE: #S488x1 was produced in Bohol. Few if any reached Mindanao.

NOTE: #S488x2 was produced in the Manila area for the *black market* when Japanese military notes had depreciated to the point that any other currency was preferable.

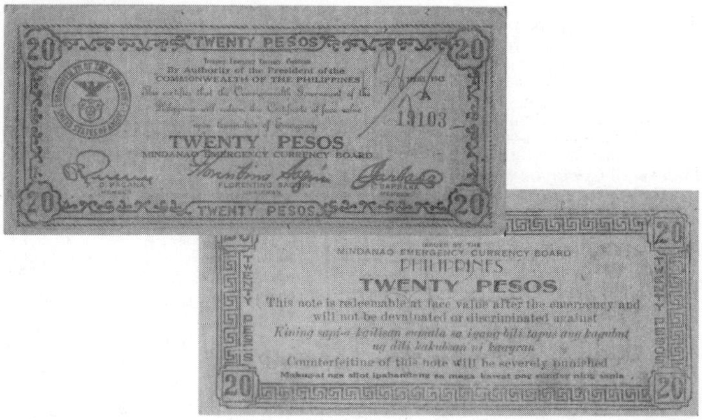

S489 20 Pesos

	Good	Fine	XF
1943. Series *A*. Serial #00,001 to 58,000.			
a. Countersignature F. D. Pacana.	1.50	3.00	10.00
b. Countersignature I. Barbasa, without stamped title.	3.00	6.00	20.00
c. Countersignature L. J. Oteyza.	3.00	6.00	20.00
d. Countersignature Gabriel Cuerpo.	4.00	8.00	25.00
x. Counterfeit. Crude printing.	—	—	—

NOTE: #S489 w/serial # 45,001 to 47,000 were officially reported lost *due to enemy action*.

1943 Second Treasury Emergency Currency Certificate Issue

(Liangan, Lanao, September 6 to November 1, 1943)

#S491-S495 were printed on manila paper.

#S496-S499 were printed on white bond paper (delivered by submarine), some of which has commercial wmks. Linen Bond or PREMIER BOND. Border cuts for #S497 had somehow been misplaced, so new cuts were made which differ slightly from the previous ones. To avoid duplication of serial numbers the Series letters were doubled. Countersigning was dispensed with.

	Good	Fine	XF
S491 5 Centavos			
1943. Series *II*. Serial #00,001 to 84,000. Paper: Manila.	3.00	6.00	20.00
S492 10 Centavos			
1943. Series *HH*. Serial # 00,001 to 84,000. Paper: Manila.	3.00	6.00	20.00
S493 20 Centavos			
1943. Series *GG*. Serial # 00,001 to 84,000. Paper: Manila.	3.00	6.00	20.00
S494 50 Centavos			
1943. Series *FF*. Serial #00,001 to 84,000. *SERIES OF 1943*. Paper: Manila.	3.00	6.00	20.00
S495 1 Peso			
1943. Series *EE*. Serial #00,001 to 84,000. Paper: Manila.	3.00	6.00	20.00

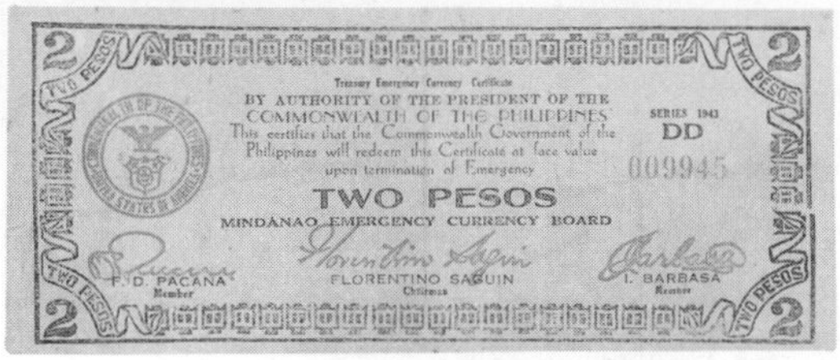

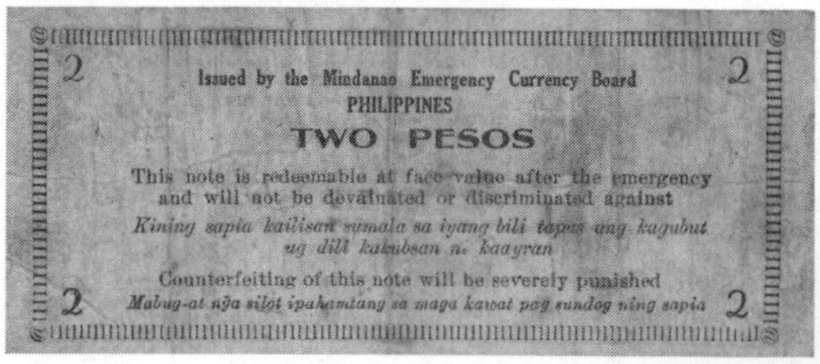

	Good	Fine	XF
S496 2 Pesos			
1943. Series *DD*. Serial #000,001 to 010,100; 10,101 to 68,000. Paper: White bond.	1.00	2.00	6.00
S497 5 Pesos			
1943. Series *CC*. Serial #000,001 to 010,100; 10,101 to 68,000. Back: Second *E* in *EMERGENCY* like #S487. Paper: White bond.	1.50	3.00	10.00
S498 10 Pesos			
1943. Series *BB*. Serial #000,001 to 010,100; 10,101 to 68,000. Paper: White bond.	1.00	2.00	6.00
S499 20 Pesos			
1943. Series *AA*. Serial #00,001 to 69,000. Paper: White bond.			
a. Issued note.	3.00	6.00	20.00
x. Counterfeit.	—	—	—

NOTE: #S496-S499 all started with 6-digit serial # but later went to 5 digits to conserve ink.

1943 Third Treasury Emergency Currency Certificate Issue

(Esperanza, Agusan, Dec. 13, 1943 to Jan. 23, 1944)

#S502-S508 printed from metal plates brought in by USS NARWHAL, #S501 and S509 from previous type and wood border cuts. All notes printed on white paper delivered with the plates. Paper ranged from ordinary book to bond paper. Some of the bond paper has commercial PREMIER BOND wmk. Serial numbers continued from where the Second printing left off.

	Good	Fine	XF
S501 5 Centavos			
1943. Series *II*. Serial #84,001 to 117,200. Paper: White.	4.00	8.00	25.00
S502 10 Centavos			
1943. Series *HH*. Serial #84,001 to 323,100. Paper: White.	1.50	3.00	10.00

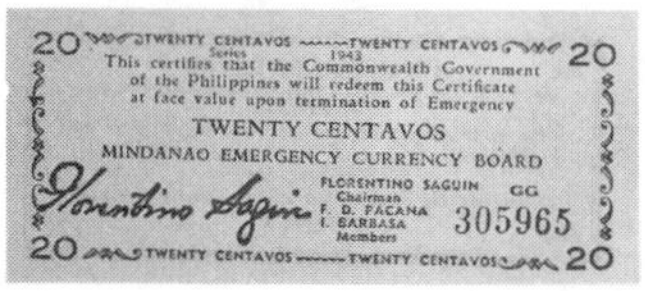

	Good	Fine	XF
S503 20 Centavos			
1943. Series *GG*. Serial #84,001 to 340,800. Paper: White.	1.50	3.00	10.00
S504 50 Centavos			
1943. Series *FF*. Serial #84,001 to 286,900. Paper: White.	1.50	3.00	10.00
S505 1 Peso			
1943. Series *EE*. Serial #84,001 to 421,300. Paper: White.	1.50	3.00	10.00

ILLUSTRATIONS

Illustrations of bank notes used throughout this catalog are 42% of the actual size.

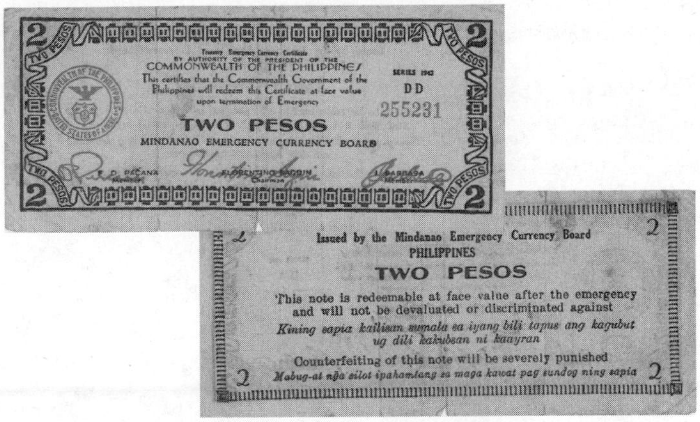

S506 2 Pesos	Good	Fine	XF
1943. Series *DD*. Serial #68,001 to 275,100. Paper: White.	1.50	3.00	10.00
S507 5 Pesos			
1943. Series *CC*. Serial #68,001 to 299,400. Back: Second *E* in *EMERGENCY* is a *C*. Paper: White.	1.50	3.00	10.00

S508 10 Pesos	Good	Fine	XF
1943. Series *BB*. Serial #68,001 to 296,400. Paper: White.			
a. Series *BB* wide.	1.50	3.00	10.00
b. Series *BB* narrow.	4.00	8.00	25.00

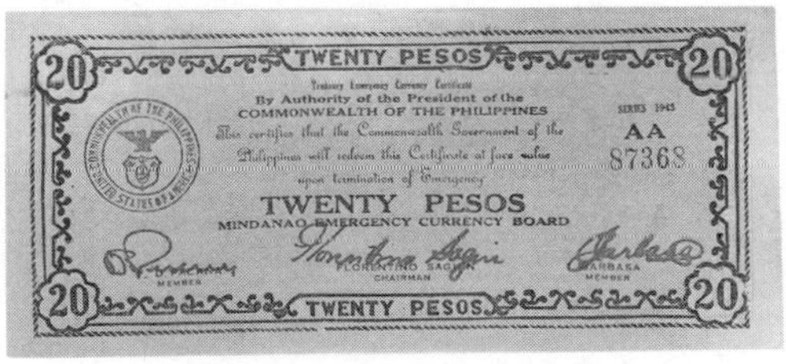

S509 20 Pesos	Good	Fine	XF
1943. Series *AA*. Serial #69,001 to 98,400. Paper: White.	1.50	3.00	10.00

1943 Illegal Issues

S510 10 Pesos	Good	Fine	XF
1943. Series *BB*. Like #S508. Paper: White. Serial numbers: 172,701 to 173,400; 174,801 to 176,200; 176,901 to 183,900; 184,601 to 186,000; 186,701 to 189,500; 191,601 to 195,100; 195,801 to 196,500; 197,901 to 198,600; 201,401 to 202,100; 222,401 to 223,100; 225,901 to 226,600.	—	—	—

1943 Fourth Treasury Emergency Currency Certificate Issue

(Loreto, Agusan, March 18 to July 5, 1944 and November 4 to 15, 1944)

Printed from the same paper stock as the Third printing, so some may also be found with commercial wmk. *PREMIER BOND*. As this printing showed the change in date from 1943 to 1944, serial numbers started over again and with single series letters.

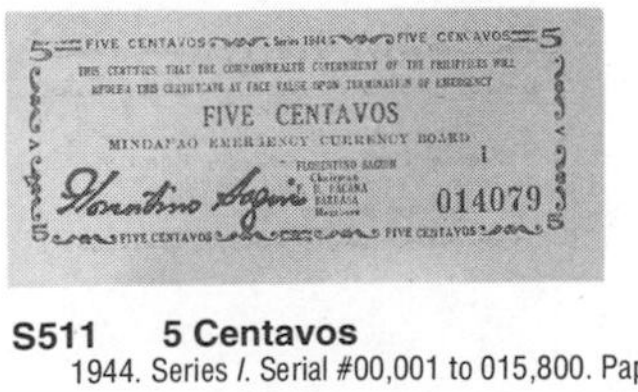

S511 5 Centavos	Good	Fine	XF
1944. Series *I*. Serial #00,001 to 015,800. Paper: White.	6.00	12.00	35.00

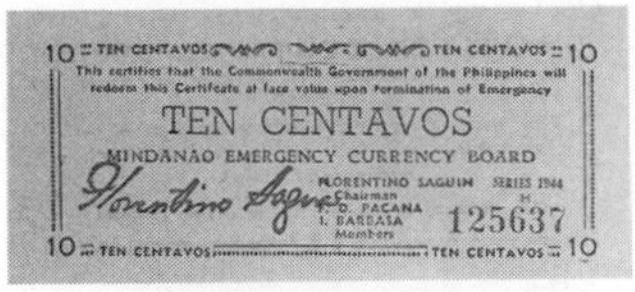

S512 10 Centavos	Good	Fine	XF
1944. Series *H*. Serial #0,001 to 140,000. Paper: White.			
a. *Series 1944* (upper and lower case).	3.00	9.00	30.00
b. *SERIES 1944* (all upper case).	4.00	8.00	25.00

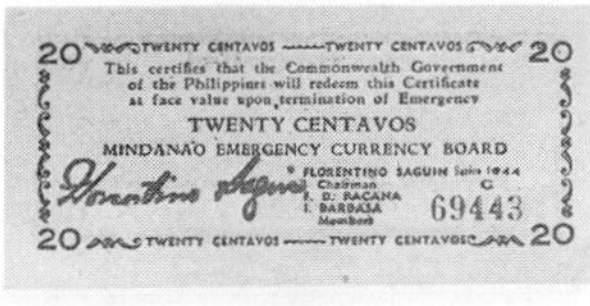

S513 20 Centavos	Good	Fine	XF
1944. Series *G*. Serial #00,001 to 117,600. Date at right. Paper: White.			
a. *Series 1944.*	2.50	5.00	15.00
b. *SERIES 1944.*	—	—	—

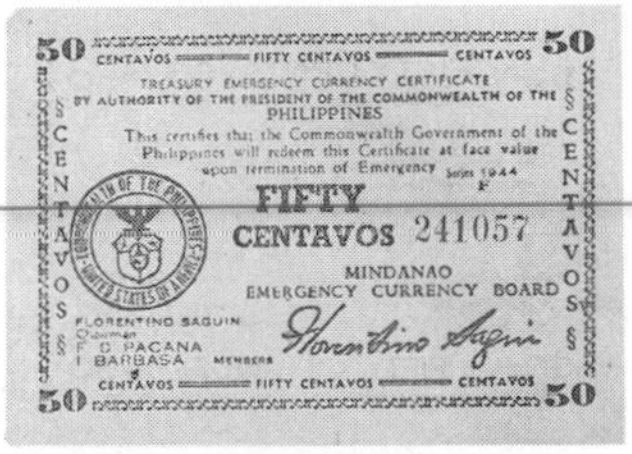

S514 50 Centavos	Good	Fine	XF
1944. Series *F*. Serial #00,001 to 285,700. Paper: White.			
a. *Series 1944* is 10mm. long (narrow date).	1.00	2.00	6.00
b. *Series 1944* is 12mm. long (wide date).	1.50	3.00	10.00

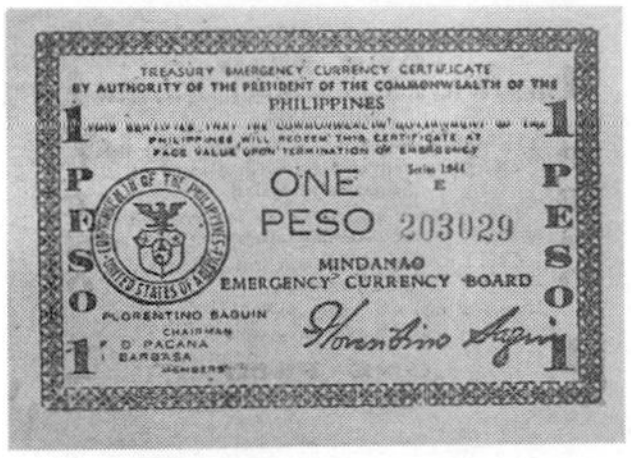

S515 1 Peso	Good	Fine	XF
1944. Series *E*. Serial #00,001 to 273,300. Paper: White.	1.00	2.00	6.00

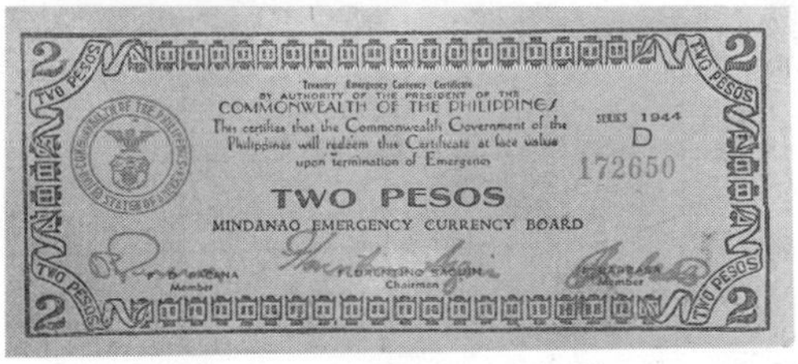

S516 2 Pesos	Good	Fine	XF
1944. Series *D*. Serial #00,001 to 263,200. Paper: White.			
a. *SERIES 1944* is 11 1/2mm. long (narrow date).	1.00	2.00	6.00
b. *SERIES 1944* is 17mm. long (wide date).	1.50	3.00	10.00

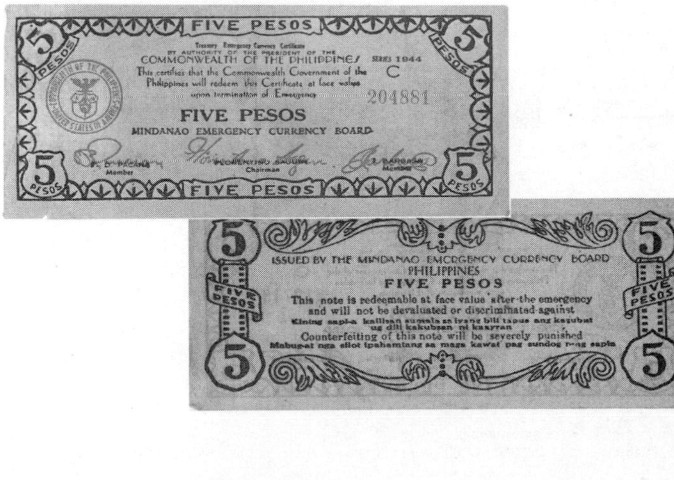

S517 5 Pesos

1944. Series *C*. Serial #00,001 to 259,200. Back: *EMERGENCY* like #S507. Paper: White.

	Good	Fine	XF
a. *SERIES 1944* is 11 1/2mm. long (narrow date).	1.00	2.00	6.00
b. *SERIES 1944* is 15mm. long (wide date).	1.00	2.00	6.00

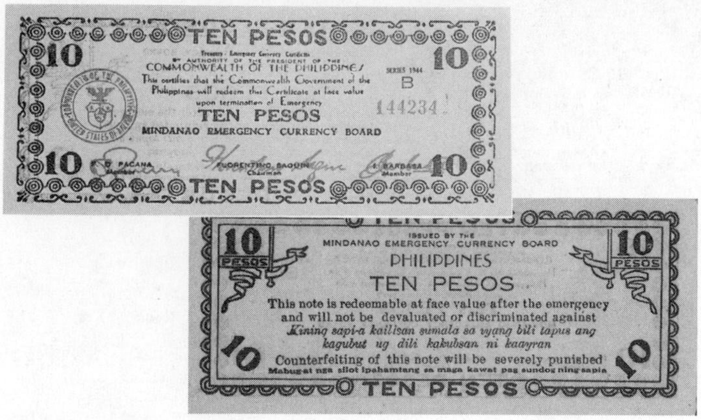

S518 10 Pesos

1944. Series *B*. Serial #00,001 to 170,700. Paper: White.

	Good	Fine	XF
a. *SERIES 1944* is 11mm. long (narrow date).	1.00	2.00	6.00
b. *SERIES 1944* is 15mm. long (wide date).	1.50	3.00	10.00

1944 Treasury Emergency Currency Certificate Issue

S521 20 Centavos

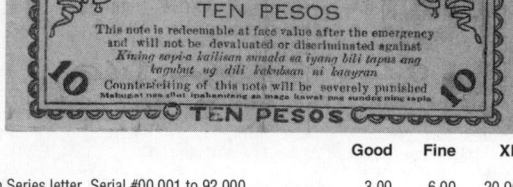

	Good	Fine	XF
1944. No Series letter. Date at top. Serial # 00,001 to 15,000. Paper: White.	7.50	15.00	45.00

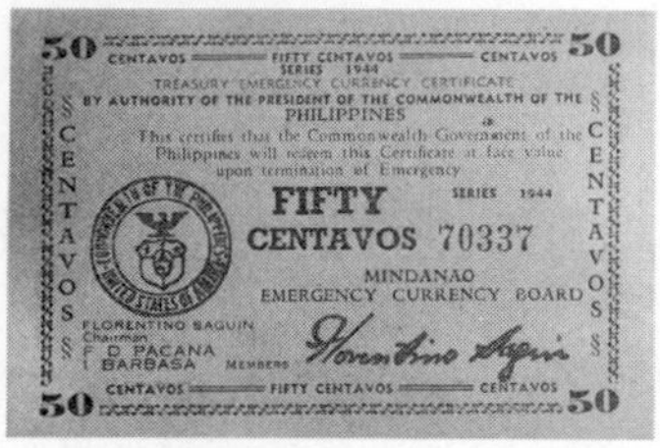

S522 50 Centavos

1944. Date at top and at center right. Paper: White.

	Good	Fine	XF
a. No Series letter. Serial #00,001 to 44,900.	3.00	6.00	20.00
b. *Series 5*. Serial #44,901 to 71,800.	3.00	6.00	20.00

S523 1 Peso

1944. Paper: White.

	Good	Fine	XF
a. No Series letter. *Series 1944*. Serial # (for "a" and "b"): 00,001 to 99,000.	3.00	6.00	20.00
b. No Series letter. *SERIES 1944*.	1.50	3.00	10.00
c. Series *V*. Serial #00,001 to 19,300.	4.00	8.00	25.00
d. Series *V5*. Serial #19,301 to 57,700.	1.50	3.00	10.00

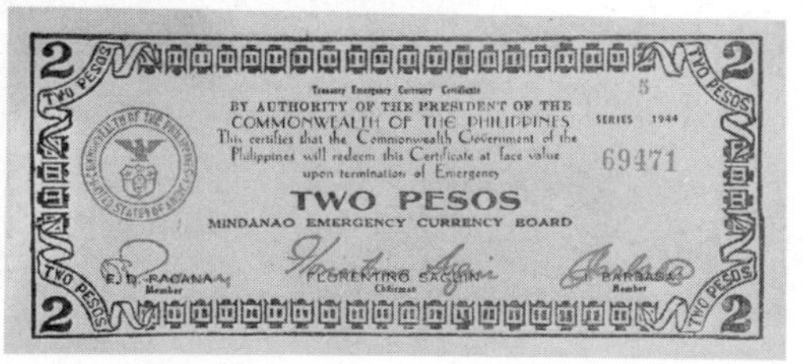

S524 2 Pesos

1944. Paper: White.

	Good	Fine	XF
a. No Series letter. Serial #00,001 to 32,200.	2.50	5.00	15.00
b. Series *5*. Serial #32,201 to 88,600.	2.50	5.00	15.00

S525 5 Pesos

1944. Type I. Wide date. Paper: White.

	Good	Fine	XF
a. No Series letter. Type I and Type II mixed in serial #00,001 to 69,000.	1.00	2.00	6.00
b. Series *5*. Type I and Type II mixed in serial #69,001 to 99,000.	1.50	3.00	10.00
c. Series *T*. Serial #00,001 to 07,100.	7.50	15.00	45.00

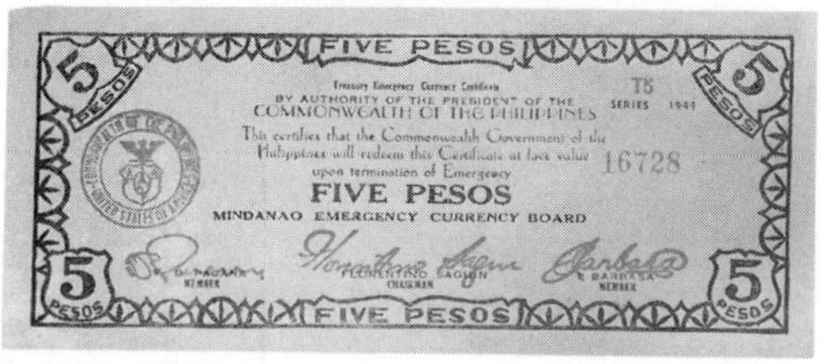

S526 5 Pesos

1944. Type II. Paper: White.

	Good	Fine	XF
a. No Series letter. Type I and Type II mixed in serial #00,001 to 69,000.	1.00	2.00	6.00
b. Series *5*. Type I and Type II mixed in serial #69,001 to 99,000.	1.50	3.00	10.00
c. Series *T5*. Serial #07,101 to 39,600.	2.50	5.00	15.00

NOTE: For #S525-S526, Type I has a 2 1/2 circular ornaments in r. border and was printed from a metal plate made in Australia. Type II has 3 circular ornaments in r. border and was printed from the wooden plate previously used at Liangan.

S527 10 Pesos

1944. Paper: White.

	Good	Fine	XF
a. *Series 1944*. No Series letter. Serial #00,001 to 92,000.	3.00	6.00	20.00
b. *SERIES 1944*. No Series letter. Serial # included in "a".	1.50	3.00	10.00
c. Series *5*. Serial #92,001 to 99,000.	3.00	6.00	20.00
d. Series *S*. Serial #00,001 to 16,600.	1.50	3.00	10.00
e. Series *S5*. Serial #16,601 to 99,000.	1.00	2.00	6.00
f. Series *SA5*. Serial #00,001 to 04,200.	7.50	15.00	45.00

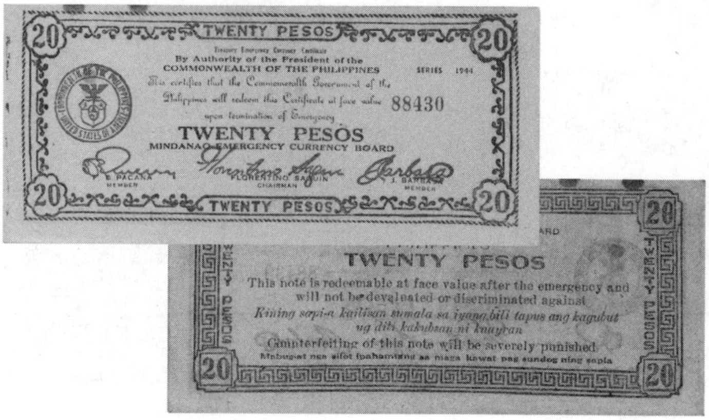

S528 20 Pesos

1944. Paper: White.

	Good	Fine	XF
a. No Series letter. Serial #00,001 to 99,000.	1.50	3.00	10.00
b. Series *R*. Serial #00,001 to 25,700.	1.50	3.00	10.00
c. Series *R5*. Serial #25,701 to 99,000.	1.00	2.00	6.00
d. Series *RA5*. Serial #00,001 to 70,300.	1.00	2.00	6.00
x. Counterfeit. Series *RA5*. Companion piece to #S488x2.	.50	1.00	2.00

NOTE: For #S528 the *R* of *RA5* is slightly wider on serial # 00,001 to 36,300 than the others.

1945 Treasury Emergency Currency Certificate Issue

(Loreto, Agusan, January 2 to 5, 1945)

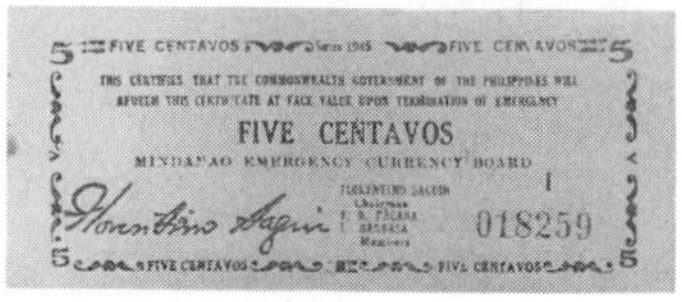

S531 5 Centavos

	Good	Fine	XF
1945. Series *I*. Serial #000,001 to 024,900.	7.50	15.00	45.00

S532 10 Centavos

1945. Series *H*. Serial #000,001 to 041,900.

	Good	Fine	XF
a. *Series 1945*.	6.00	12.00	35.00
b. *SERIES 1945*.	7.50	15.00	45.00

S533 20 Centavos

	Good	Fine	XF
1945. Series *G*. Serial #000,001 to 044,900.	6.00	12.00	35.00

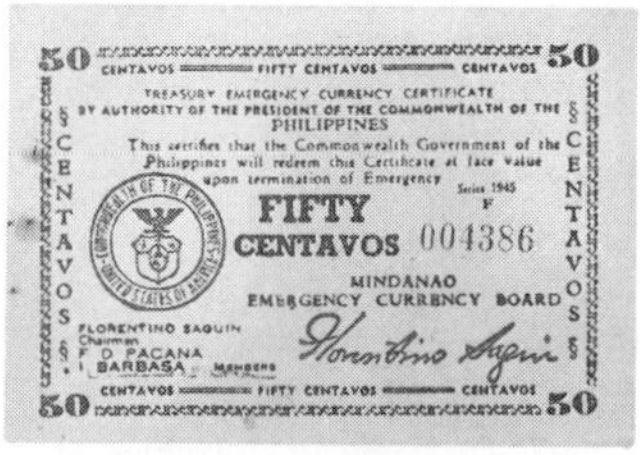

S534 50 Centavos

	Good	Fine	XF
1945. Series *F*. Serial #000,001 to 056,200.	1.50	3.00	10.00

S535 1 Peso

	Good	Fine	XF
1945. Series *E*. Serial #000,001 to 028,200.	1.50	3.00	10.00

		Good	Fine	XF
S536	**2 Pesos**			
	1945. Series *D*. Serial #000,001 to 056,000.	1.00	2.00	6.00
S537	**5 Pesos**			
	1945. Series *C*. Serial #000,001 to 046,100. Back: *EMERGENCY* like #S507.	1.00	2.00	6.00

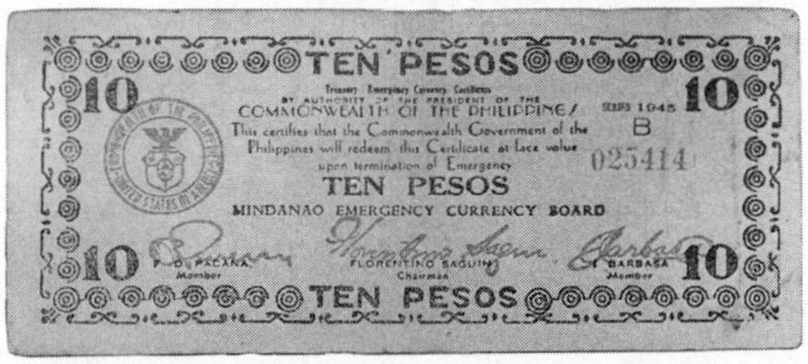

		Good	Fine	XF
S538	**10 Pesos**			
	1945. Series *B*. Serial #000,001 to 038,100.	1.00	2.00	6.00

109th Division USFIP, Series 1944

1944 Negotiable Receipt

		Good	Fine	XF
S546	**5 Pesos**			
	1944. Rare.	—	—	—

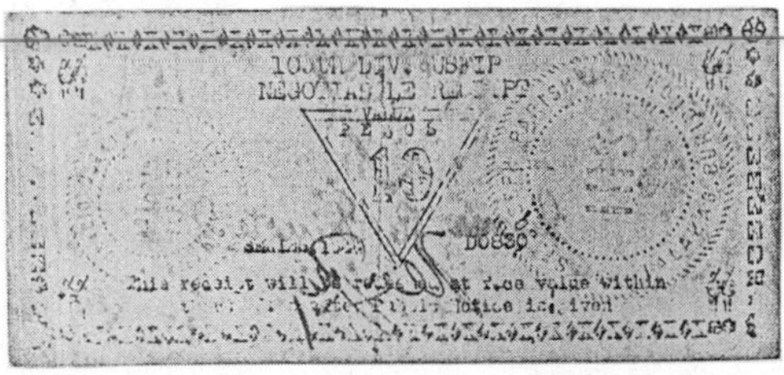

		Good	Fine	XF
S547	**10 Pesos**			
	1944. Rare.	—	—	—
S548	**20 Pesos**			
	1944. Rare.	—	—	—

116th Infantry Regiment USFIP, 1943-44

1943-44 Issue

		Good	Fine	XF
S551	**5 Centavos**			
	Serial # E1 to E535.	—	—	—
S552	**10 Centavos**			
	Serial # D1 to D3339.	—	—	—

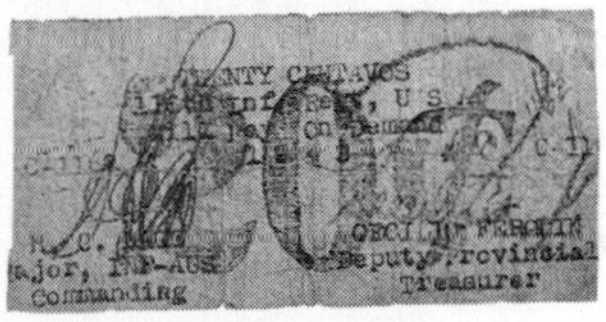

		Good	Fine	XF
S553	**20 Centavos**			
	Serial # C1 to C2564.	—	—	—
S554	**50 Centavos**	Good	Fine	XF
	Serial # B1 to B2029.	—	—	—
S555	**1 Peso**			
	Serial # A1 to A17,526.	—	—	—
S556	**2 Pesos**			
	Serial # AA1 to AA13,778.	—	—	—
S557	**5 Pesos**			
	Serial # AAA1 to AAA865 and V866 to V15,143.	—	—	—
S558	**10 Pesos**			
	Serial # X1 to X885.	—	—	—

Philippine National Bank - Misamis Occidental

1942 First Emergency Circulating Note Issue

		Good	Fine	XF
S571	**50 Centavos**			
	1942. Orange. Handsigned. Serial #00,001 to 30,000. Paper: White.	12.00	25.00	75.00
S572	**1 Peso**			
	1942. Black. Handsigned. Serial #00,001 to 60,000. Back: Inverted. Paper: White.			
	a. Issued note.	12.00	25.00	75.00
	x. Counterfeit.	—	—	—

1942 Second Emergency Circulating Note Issue

		Good	Fine	XF
S573	**10 Centavos**			
	1942. Serial #0001 to 100,000. Back: Inverted. Paper: Black print on manila paper.	15.00	30.00	90.00

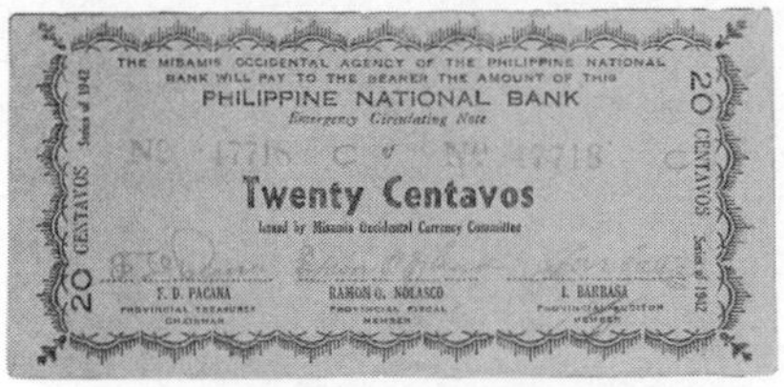

		Good	Fine	XF
S574	**20 Centavos**			
	1942. Serial #0001 to 100,000. Paper: Black print on manila paper.	12.00	25.00	75.00

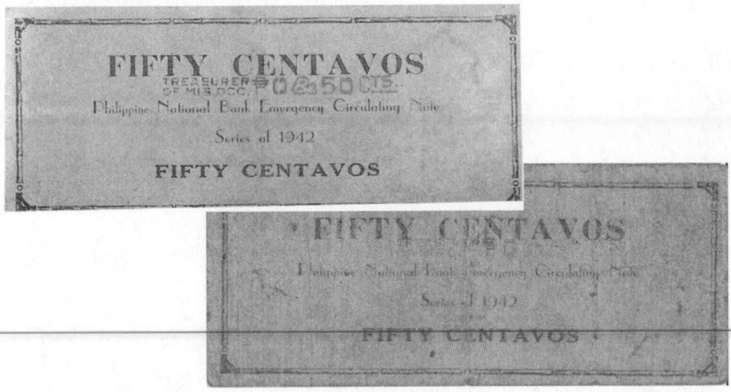

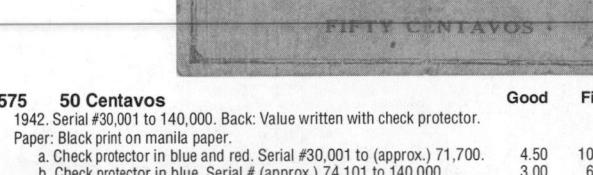

		Good	Fine	XF
S575	**50 Centavos**			
	1942. Serial #30,001 to 140,000. Back: Value written with check protector. Paper: Black print on manila paper.			
	a. Check protector in blue and red. Serial #30,001 to (approx.) 71,700.	4.50	10.00	30.00
	b. Check protector in blue. Serial # (approx.) 74,101 to 140,000.	3.00	6.00	20.00

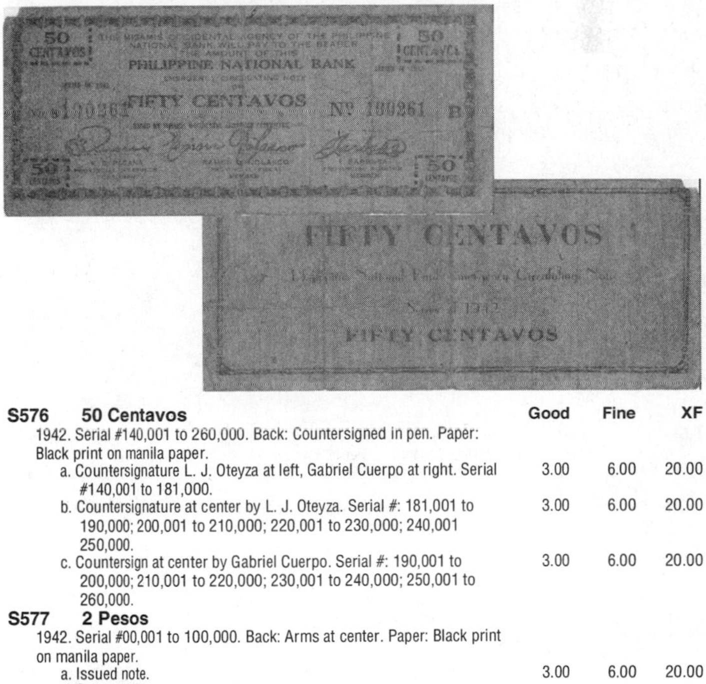

		Good	Fine	XF
S576	**50 Centavos**			
	1942. Serial #140,001 to 260,000. Back: Countersigned in pen. Paper: Black print on manila paper.			
	a. Countersignature L. J. Oteyza at left, Gabriel Cuerpo at right. Serial #140,001 to 181,000.	3.00	6.00	20.00
	b. Countersignature at center by L. J. Oteyza. Serial #: 181,001 to 190,000; 200,001 to 210,000; 220,001 to 230,000; 240,001 250,000.	3.00	6.00	20.00
	c. Countersign at center by Gabriel Cuerpo. Serial #: 190,001 to 200,000; 210,001 to 220,000; 230,001 to 240,000; 250,001 to 260,000.	3.00	6.00	20.00
S577	**2 Pesos**			
	1942. Serial #00,001 to 100,000. Back: Arms at center. Paper: Black print on manila paper.			
	a. Issued note.	3.00	6.00	20.00
	x. Counterfeit.	—	—	—
S578	**5 Pesos**	Good	Fine	XF
	1942. Quezon at left, seal in red at right. Serial #00,001 to 120,000. Back: Arms at center. Countersigned in pen. Paper: Black print on manila paper.			
	a. Countersignature I. Barbasa at left, F. D. Pacana at right. Serial #00,001 to 60,000.	3.00	6.00	20.00
	b. Countersignature at center by I. Barbasa. Serial # 60,001 to 70,000; 80,001 to 90,000; 100,001 to 110,000.	3.00	6.00	20.00
	c. Countersignature at center by F. D. Pacana. Serial #70,001 to 80,000; 90,001 to 100,000; 110,001 to to 120,000.	3.00	6.00	20.00
	x. Counterfeit.	—	—	—

Oriental Misamis Agency - Philippine National Bank

1941 Emergency Circulating Note - Series A Issue

		Good	Fine	XF
S581	**10 Centavos**			
	1941. Black print. Serial #0001 to 20,000.	—	—	—
S582	**20 Centavos**			
	1941. Black print. Serial #0001 to 10,000.	—	—	—
S583	**50 Centavos**			
	1941. Black print. Serial #0001 to 6,000.	—	—	—
S584	**1 Peso**			
	1941. Black print. Serial #0001 to 3,000.	—	—	—

1942 Emergency Circulating Note - Series B Issue

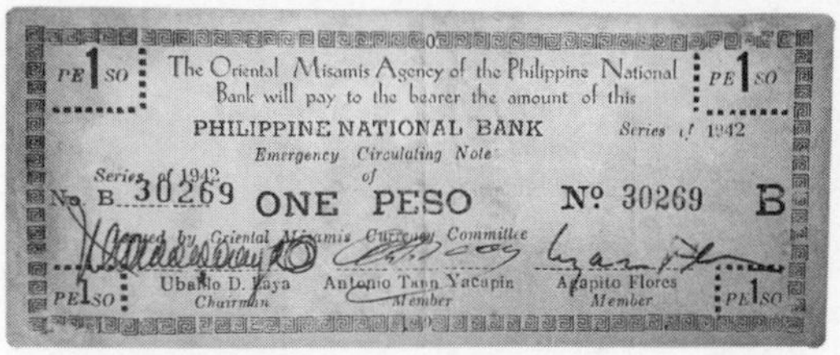

S585 1 Peso | Good 45.00 | Fine 90.00 | XF 270.
1942. Black. Serial #0001 to 34,000.

Mountain Province Emergency Board

Resolution No. 5, Series 1942 First Issue

#S591-S594 black on thin white paper, facsimile stamped sign. All serial # data is approximate.

	Good	Fine	XF
S591 5 Centavos 1942. Black. Serial #0,001 to 22,353 (approx.). Paper: Thin white.	1.00	2.00	6.00

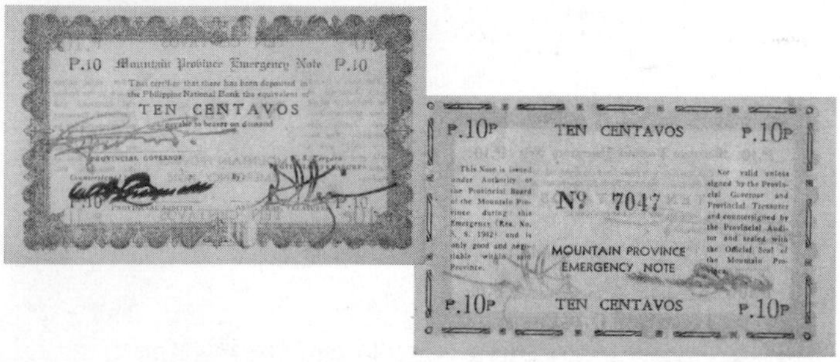

	Good	Fine	XF
S592 10 Centavos 1942. Black. Serial #0,001 to 39,163 (approx.). Paper: Thin white.	1.00	2.00	6.00
S593 20 Centavos 1942. Black. Serial #0,001 to 9,587 (approx.). Paper: Thin white.	1.00	2.00	6.00

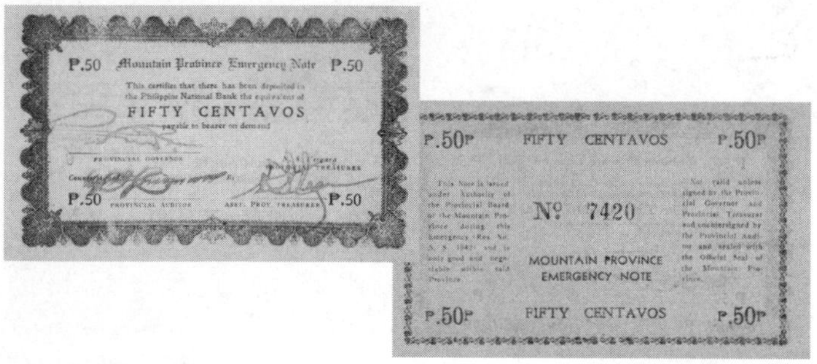

	Good	Fine	XF
S594 50 Centavos 1942. Black. Serial #0,001 to 39,262 (approx.). Paper: Thin white.			
a. First 2 lines of text equal in length.	1.00	2.00	6.00
b. First line longer than second.	1.50	3.00	10.00

#S595-S598 black on white bond paper, handsigned. Some have commercial wmk: *HAMMERMILL BOND.* Redemption clause payable to bearer on demand.

#S595-S597 lg. size heading.

	Good	Fine	XF
S595 1 Peso 1942. Black. Handsigned. Redemption clause payable to bearer on demand. Large size heading. Serial #0,001 to 40,508 (approx.). Back: Red to brownish red. Paper: White bond. Watermark: Some have commercial: *HAMMERMILL BOND.*			
a. First 2 lines of text equal in length.	1.00	2.00	6.00
b. First line longer than second.	1.50	3.00	10.00
S596 2 Pesos 1942. Black. Handsigned. Redemption clause payable to bearer on demand. Large size heading. Serial #0,001 to 9,956 (approx.). Back: Blue. Paper: White bond. Watermark: Some have commercial: *HAMMERMILL BOND.*			
a. First 2 lines of text equal in length.	2.50	5.00	15.00
b. First line longer than second.	2.50	5.00	15.00
S597 5 Pesos 1942. Black. Handsigned. Redemption clause payable to bearer on demand. Large size heading. Serial #0,001 to 1,387 (approx.). Back: Yellow. Paper: White bond. Watermark: Some have commercial: *HAMMERMILL BOND.*	6.00	12.00	35.00

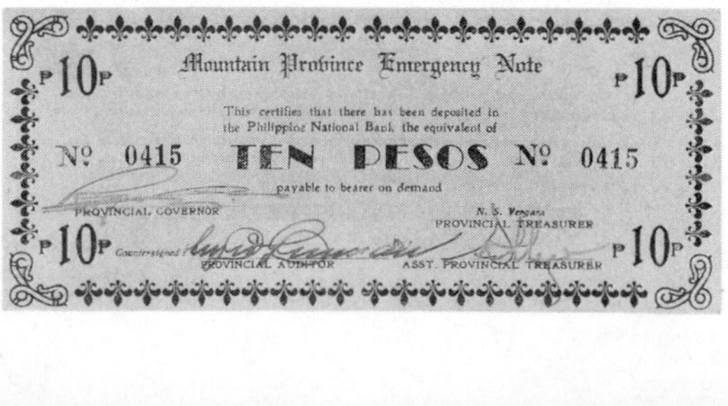

	Good	Fine	XF
S598 10 Pesos 1942. Black. Handsigned. Redemption clause payable to bearer on demand. Smaller size heading like Second Issue. Serial #0,001 to 0,999 (approx.). Back: Brown. Paper: White bond. Watermark: Some have commercial: *HAMMERMILL BOND.*	6.00	12.00	35.00

Resolution No. 5, ND Second Issue

#S601-S604 w/o Resolution date on back. Smaller size heading (like #S598). Series A. Black on manila paper. Stamped facsimile sign. Longer redemption clause, *Redeemable in the Currency of the Philippine Commonwealth after this Emergency.* All serial # data is approximate.

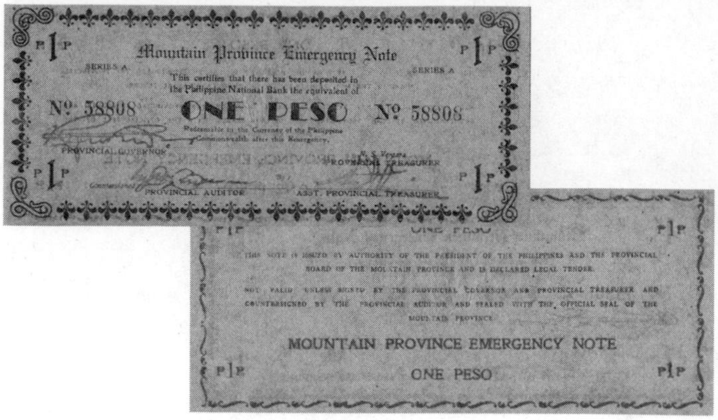

	Good	Fine	XF
S601 1 Peso ND. Black. *Redeemable in the Currency of the Philippine Commonwealth after this Emergency.* Series A. Smaller size heading. Serial #41,065 to 60,952 (approx.). Back: Red to brownish red. Without Resolution date. Paper: Manila.	1.00	2.00	6.00

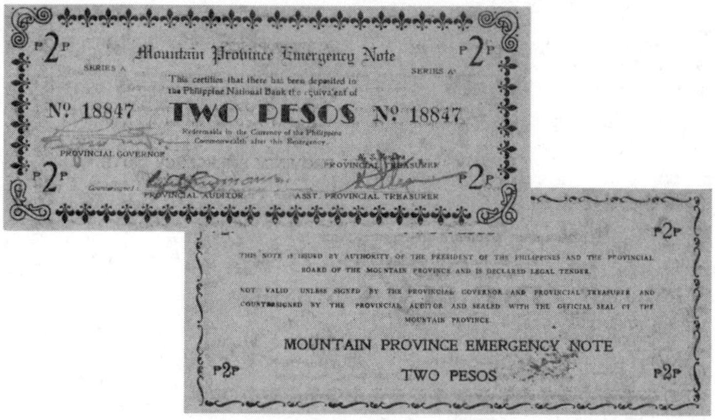

	Good	Fine	XF
S602 2 Pesos ND. Black. *Redeemable in the Currency of the Philippine Commonwealth after this Emergency.* Series A. Smaller size heading. Serial #10,945 to 24,857 (approx.). Back: Blue. Without Resolution date. Paper: Manila.	1.00	2.00	6.00

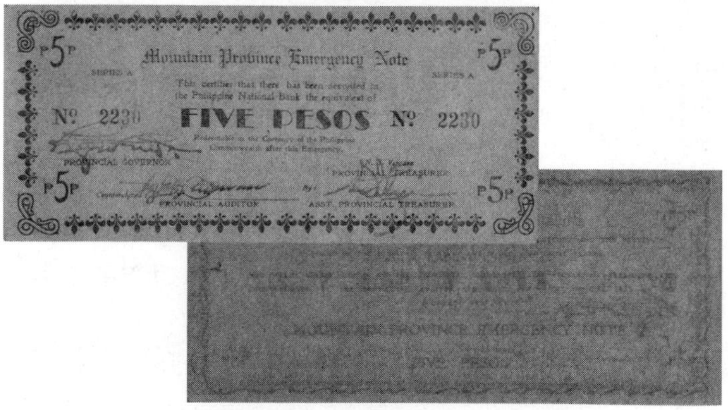

	Good	Fine	XF
S603 5 Pesos ND. Black. *Redeemable in the Currency of the Philippine Commonwealth after this Emergency.* Series A. Smaller size heading. Serial #2,122 to 16,944 (approx.). Back: Yellow. Without Resolution date. Paper: Manila.	1.50	3.00	10.00
S604 10 Pesos ND. Black. *Redeemable in the Currency of the Philippine Commonwealth after this Emergency.* Series A. Smaller size heading. Serial #1,094 to 8,409 (approx.). Back: Brown. Without Resolution date. Paper: Manila.			
a. Issued note.	3.00	6.00	20.00
x. Error; inverted back.	—	—	—

NOTE: Many Mountain Province notes may be found with various countersigning applied when notes were presented for redemption during the Japanese occupation. Those also marked *PAID* are from 3,000 such pesos looted from the Treasury during the bombing attack in 1945.

Negros Occidental Currency Committee - Philippine National Bank

1941 First Emergency Circulating Note Issue

	Good	Fine	XF
S611 1 Peso			
1941. Black on green underprint. Large numeral at left, arms at right. Handsigned. Serial #1 to 30,000. Paper: White bond. Printer: Filma Press.			
a. Handsigned Buenaventura.	12.00	25.00	75.00
b. Handsigned Ramos	15.00	30.00	90.00
c. Handsigned Arellano.	12.00	25.00	75.00

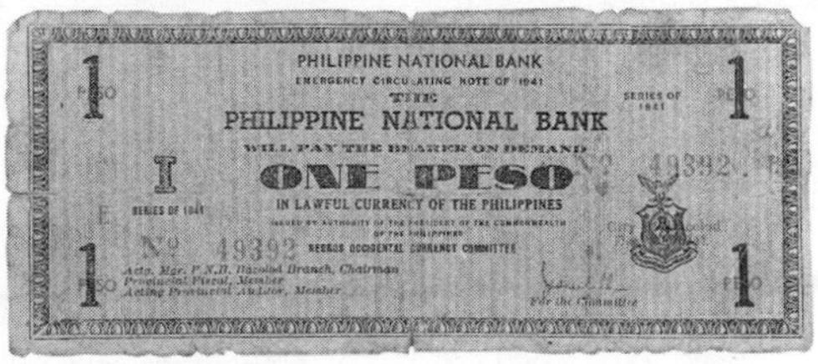

	Good	Fine	XF
S612 1 Peso			
1941. Black on green underprint. Large numeral at left, arms at right. Like #S611 but printed signature. Serial #30,001 to 100,000. Paper: White bond. Printer: Filma Press.			
a. Signature Buenaventura.	4.00	8.00	25.00
b. Signature Ramos.	5.00	10.00	30.00
c. Signature Arellano.	5.00	10.00	30.00

#S613-S617 plate differences:

TYPE I - face, solid *5* in top corners. Back text: *December 29 and 30, 1941.*

Type II - face, shaded *5* in top corners. Back w/o date.

Type III - face, shaded *5* like Type II. Back text like Type I w/dates.

	Good	Fine	XF
S613 5 Pesos			
1941. Black on orange underprint. Solid *5* in top corners. Handsigned. Serial #1 to 5,000. Type I. Back: Text: *December 29 and 30, 1941.* Paper: White bond. Printer: Filma Press.	12.00	25.00	75.00
S614 5 Pesos			
1941. Shaded *5* in top corners. Handsigned. Serial #5,001 to 10,000 and 15,001 to 20,000. Type II. Back: Without date. Paper: White bond. Printer: Filma Press.	7.50	15.00	45.00
S615 5 Pesos			
1941. Shaded *5* in top corners. Handsigned. Serial #10,001 to 15,000. Type III. Back: Text: *December 29 and 30, 1941.* Paper: White bond. Printer: Filma Press.	12.00	25.00	75.00

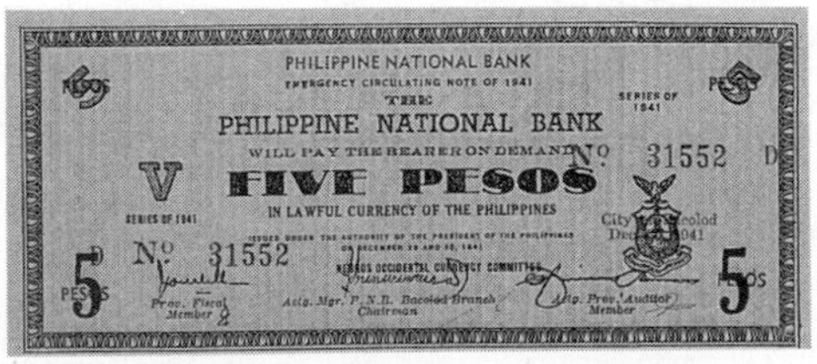

	Good	Fine	XF
S616 5 Pesos			
1941. Shaded *5* in top corners. Printed signature. Serial #25,001 to 30,000. Type II. Back: Without date. Paper: White bond. Printer: Filma Press.	12.00	25.00	75.00
S617 5 Pesos			
1941. Shaded *5* in top corners. Printed signature. Serial #20,001 to 25,000 and 30,001 to 35,000. Type III. Back: Text: *December 29 and 30, 1941.* Paper: White bond. Printer: Filma Press.	7.50	15.00	45.00

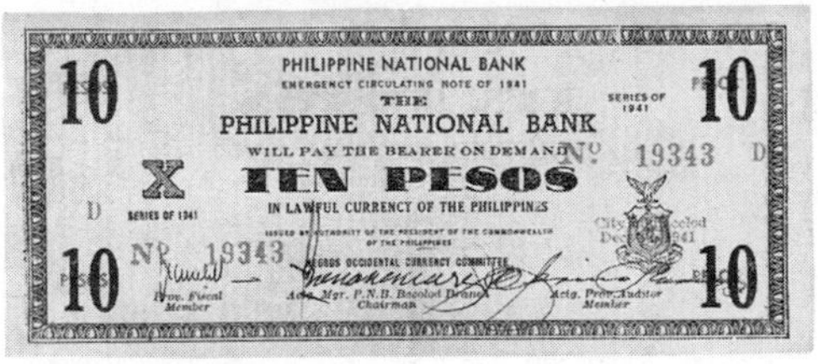

	Good	Fine	XF
S618 10 Pesos			
1941. Black on light yellow underprint. Handsigned. Serial # for this and #S619: 1 to 20,000. Back: Numeral *X* is 6mm high. Paper: White bond. Printer: Filma Press.	4.50	9.00	30.00
S619 10 Pesos			
1941. Handsigned. Serial # mixed with those for #S618. Back: Numeral *X* is 7-1/2mm high. Paper: White bond. Printer: Filma Press.	4.50	9.00	30.00

1941 Second Emergency Circulating Note Issue

#S621-S627 printed by Filma Press. Centavo notes on colored paper, 1 and 2 Pesos and most 10 Pesos on Bais paper, the 5 Pesos and part of the 10 Pesos on white bond paper (some commercial wmk: *(LANCASTER BOND)*.

	Good	Fine	XF
S621 10 Centavos			
1941. Serial #1 to 37,500. Back: Arms at center. Printer: Filma Press.			
a. Pink paper.	22.50	45.00	135.
b. White paper.	—	—	—
x. Error: *Philipipne* in heading.	35.00	70.00	200.
S622 20 Centavos			
1941. Serial #1 to 37,500. Back: Arms at center. Printer: Filma Press.			
a. Blue paper.	22.50	45.00	135.
b. White paper.	30.00	60.00	180.
x. Error: *Philipipne* in heading.	22.50	45.00	135.

	Good	Fine	XF
S623 50 Centavos			
1941. Serial #1 to 25,000. Back: Arms at center. Paper: Yellow. Printer: Filma Press.			
a. Issued note.	22.50	45.00	135.
x. Error: *Philipipne* in heading.	30.00	60.00	180.
S624 1 Peso			
1941. Black on green underprint. Serial #100,001 to 195,000. Paper: Bais. Printer: Filma Press.			
a. *PESO* (in red) at lower left is 7mm long. Serial #100,001 to (approx.) 148,826.	3.00	6.00	20.00
b. *PESO* at lower left is 10mm long. Serial # (approx.) 151,586 to 195,000.	3.00	6.00	20.00
S625 2 Pesos			
1941. Black on blue underprint. Serial #1 to 65,000. Paper: Bais. Printer: Filma Press.			
a. Issued note.	4.50	9.00	30.00
x. Counterfeit.	—	—	—
S626 5 Pesos			
1941. Black on orange underprint. Serial #40,001 to 106,000. Paper: White bond. Printer: Filma Press.			
a. Issued note.	2.50	5.00	15.00
x. Counterfeit.	—	—	—

	Good	Fine	XF
S627 10 Pesos			
1941. Black on yellow underprint. Serial #20,001 to 104,500. Printer: Filma Press.			
a. Bond paper. Serial #20,001 to 50,000.	4.00	8.00	25.00
b. Bais paper. Serial #50,001 to 104,500.	2.50	5.00	15.00
x. Counterfeit.	—	—	—

Commonwealth of the Philippines

January 13, 1942 Couponized Check Issue

	Good	Fine	XF
S629 10 Centavos			
13.1.1942. Green underprint. Serial # for this and #S631: 1 to 150,000.	15.00	30.00	90.00
S630 20 Centavos			
13.1.1942. Dark yellow underprint. Serial # for this and #S632: 1 to 75,000. Back: Lower numerals are 6mm high.	30.00	60.00	180.
S630A 20 Centavos			
13.1.1942. Dark yellow underprint. Back: Like #S630, but lower numerals are 7-1/2mm high.	25.00	50.00	150.

#S631-S633 reduced size.

	Good	Fine	XF
S631 10 Centavos			
13.1.1942. Dark yellow underprint. Serial # included with #S629.	12.00	25.00	75.00
S632 20 Centavos			
13.1.1942. Dark yellow underprint. Serial # included with #S630.	15.00	45.00	135.
S633 50 Centavos			
13.1.1942. Dark yellow underprint. Serial # 1 to 40,000.	15.00	30.00	90.00

#S634-S639 larger size (same as #S629-S630).

	Good	Fine	XF
S634 1 Peso			
13.1.1942. Brown underprint. Serial #1 to 50,000.	12.00	25.00	75.00

	Good	Fine	XF
S635 2 Pesos			
13.1.1942. Dark yellow underprint. Serial # for this and #S636: 1 to 50,000. Back: Lower numerals are 6mm high.	4.50	9.00	30.00

S636 2 Pesos
13.1.1942. Serial # included with #S635. Back: Lower numerals are 7-1/2mm high. — 5.00 / 10.00 / 30.00

	Good	Fine	XF
S637 5 Pesos 13.1.1942. Dark yellow underprint. Serial #1 to 10,000. Back: Lower numerals are 6mm high. Like #S635.	5.00	10.00	30.00
S638 5 Pesos 13.1.1942. Serial #10,001 to 20,000. Back: Lower numerals are 7-1/2mm high. Like #S636.	5.00	10.00	30.00
S639 10 Pesos 13.1.1942. Orange underprint. Serial #1 to 20,000.	10.00	20.00	60.00

Negros Occidental Provincial Currency Committee

1942 Emergency Circulating Note Issue

	Good	Fine	XF
S640 5 Centavos 1942. Bluish or purple. Small red Commonwealth arms at right. Signature Encarnacion. Serial # for this and #S641: 1 to 600,000.			
a. Bond paper.	1.50	3.00	10.00
b. Bais paper.	1.50	3.00	10.00
S641 5 Centavos 1942. Small red Commonwealth arms at right. Signature Ramos. Serial # included in #S640.	1.50	3.00	10.00
S642 10 Centavos 1942. Brown. Small red Commonwealth arms at right. Signature Encarnacion. Serial # for this and #S643: 1 to 100,500. Back: Black.	4.50	10.00	30.00
S643 10 Centavos 1942. Small red Commonwealth arms at right. Signature Ramos. Serial # included in #S642.			
a. Bond paper.	4.50	10.00	30.00
b. Bais paper.	4.50	10.00	30.00

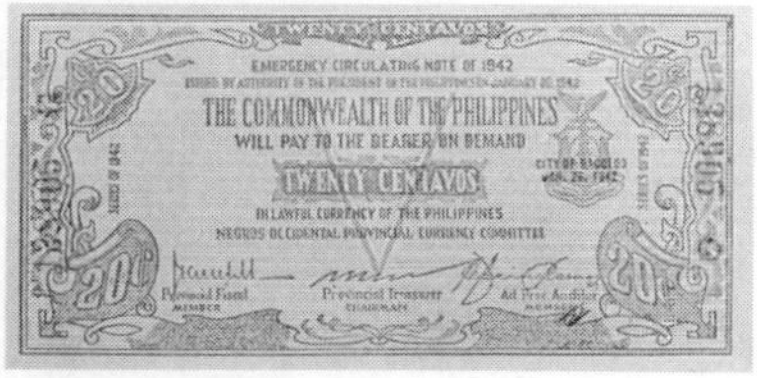

	Good	Fine	XF
S644 20 Centavos 1942. Green. Small red Commonwealth arms at right. Large *V* at center. Serial #1 to 501,500. Back: Black. Paper: Bond.	5.00	10.00	30.00
S645 50 Centavos 1942. Black on green underprint. Small red Commonwealth arms at right. Similar to #S644. Serial #1 to 20,500. Back: Green.	7.50	15.00	45.00

#S646-S650 Quezon at l., red or pale red-orange Commonwealth seal at r. Lg. *V* at ctr. on back.

	Good	Fine	XF
S646 1 Peso 1942. Black on orange underprint. Quezon at left, red or pale red-orange Commonwealth seal at right. Serial #1 to 402,000. Back: Red. Large *V* at center. Paper: Bond.			
a. *PESOS* at left and right on back facing in.	1.00	2.00	6.00
b. *PESOS* at left and right on back facing out.	1.00	2.00	6.00
S647A 2 Pesos 1942. Blue on blue underprint. Quezon at left, red or pale red-orange Commonwealth seal at right. Serial #1 to (approx.) 250,000. Back: Large *V* at center. Paper: Bond.	1.00	2.00	6.00

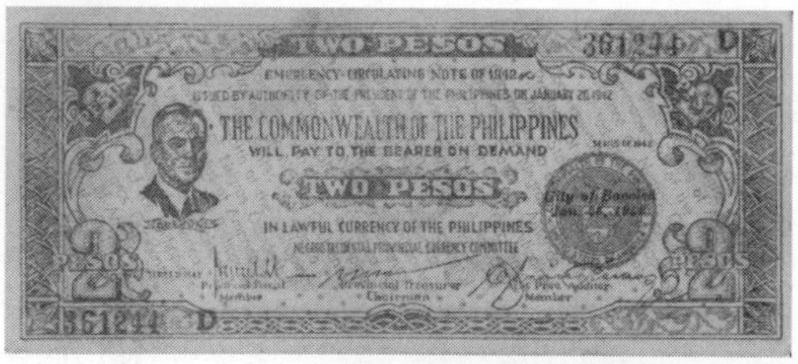

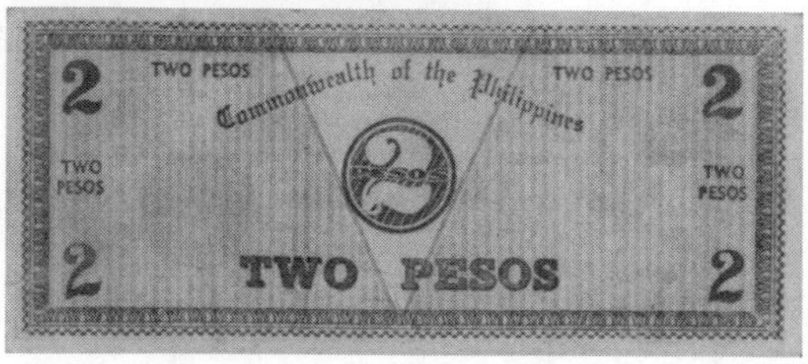

	Good	Fine	XF
S647B 2 Pesos 1942. Purple on purple underprint. Quezon at left, red or pale red-orange Commonwealth seal at right. Serial # (approx.) 275,001 to 678,000. Back: Large *V* at center. Paper: Bais.	1.00	2.00	6.00
S648 5 Pesos 1942. Black on yellow underprint. Quezon at left, red or pale red-orange Commonwealth seal at right. Serial #1 to 341,850. Back: Yellow. Large *V* at center.			
a. Bond paper. Serial #1 to (approx.) 240,000.	1.00	2.00	6.00
b. Bais paper. Serial # (approx.) 244,001 to 341,850.	1.00	2.00	6.00

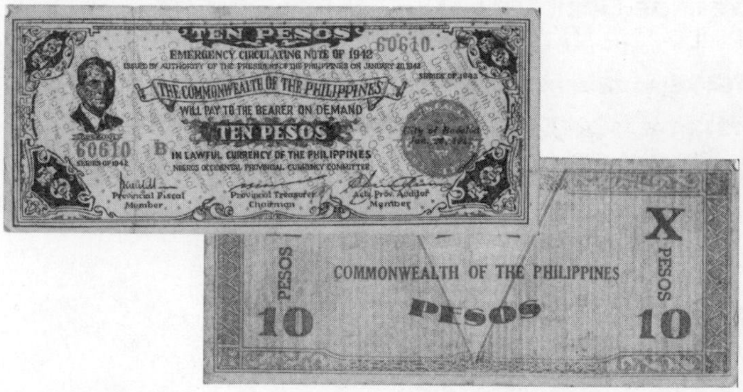

	Good	Fine	XF
S649 10 Pesos 1942. Black on brown underprint. Quezon at left, red or pale red-orange Commonwealth seal at right. Serial #1 to 120,750. Back: Brown. Large *V* at center.			
a. Bond paper. *PESOS* at left and right on back facing in. Serial #1 to (approx.) 58,000.	1.00	2.00	6.00
b. Bond paper. *PESOS* at left and right on back facing out. Serial # included in "a".	1.00	2.00	6.00
c. Bais paper. *PESOS* at left and right on back facing in. Serial # (approx.) 60,001 to 120,000.	1.00	2.00	6.00
d. Bais paper. *PESOS* at left and right on back facing out. Serial # included in "c".	1.00	2.00	6.00

#S650 unofficially issued.

S650 5 Pesos
1942. Black on yellow underprint. Quezon at left, red or pale red-orange Commonwealth seal at right. Serial #341,851 to 359,100. Like #S648. Back: Yellow. Large *V* at center. — — — —

#S650 unofficially issued.

Commonwealth of the Philippines

1942 Couponized Check Issue

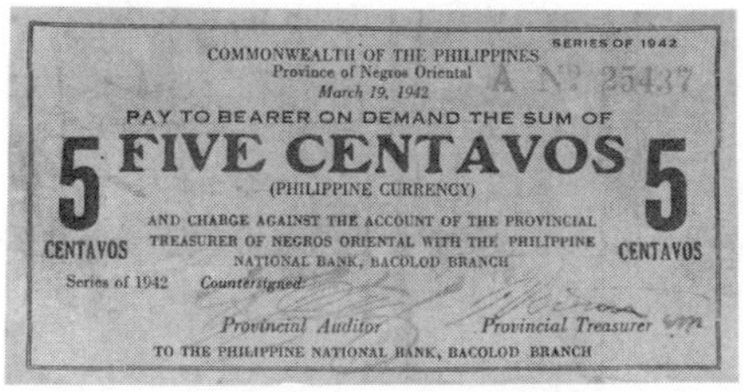

	Good	Fine	XF
S651 5 Centavos 19.3.1942. Dark brown. Serial #1 to 34,000. Back: Green.			
a. Manila paper.	15.00	30.00	90.00
b. Bais paper.	25.00	50.00	150.
S652 10 Centavos 19.3.1942. Dark brown. Serial #1 to 34,000. Back: Green. Paper: Manila.	15.00	30.00	90.00
S653 20 Centavos 19.3.1942. Dark brown. Serial #1 to 34,000. Back: Green. Paper: Manila.	25.00	50.00	150.

#S654-S655 blue on white Bais paper; orange backs.

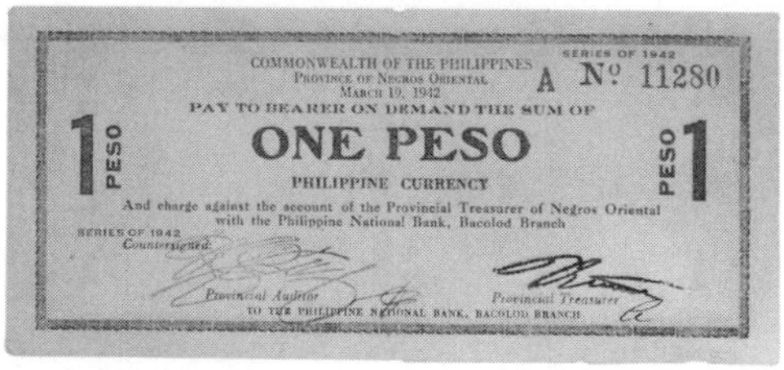

	VG	VF	UNC
S654 1 Peso 19.3.1942. Blue. Serial #1 to 13,000. Back: Orange. Paper: White Bais.			
a. Blue ink.	12.00	25.00	75.00
b. Gray ink.	12.00	25.00	75.00
S655 2 Pesos 19.3.1942. Blue. Serial #1 to 13,000. Back: Orange. Paper: White Bais.			
a. Blue ink.	12.00	25.00	75.00
b. Gray ink.	12.00	25.00	75.00

March 12, 1942 Spurious Issue

	Good	Fine	XF
S656x 20 Pesos 12.3.1942. (Spurious note.)	—	—	—

Negros Oriental Currency Committee Issue

1942 Emergency Circulating Note Issue

	Good	Fine	XF
S658 5 Pesos 1942. Black. Serial #D00501 to D02900; E02901 to E03900; F03901 to F05100; H01300 to H05100. Paper: White.			
a. Regular paper.	12.00	25.00	75.00
b. Bais paper.	15.00	30.00	90.00

Number	Denomination	Good	Fine	XF
S659	**5 Pesos**			
	1942. Black. Without serial #. Paper: White.			
	x. Error. Printed on face only. No serial #.	—	—	—

Negros Emergency Currency Board

1943 Treasury Emergency Currency Certificate Issue

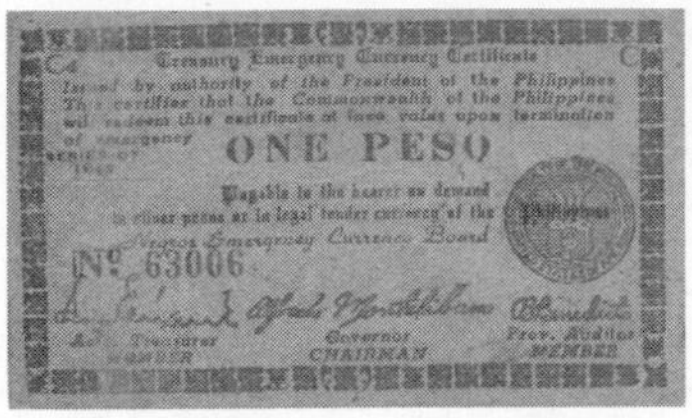

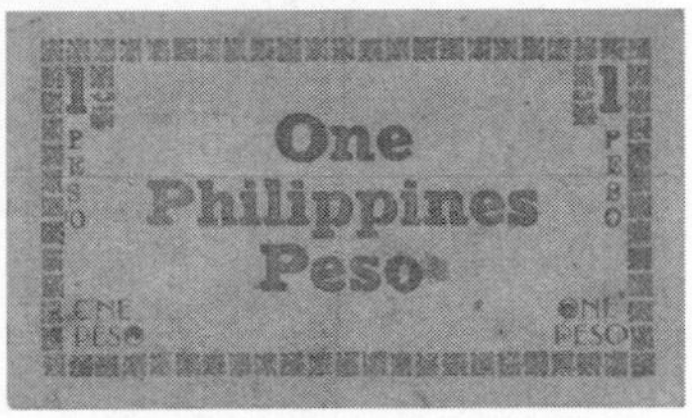

Number	Denomination	Good	Fine	XF
S661	**1 Peso**			
	1943. Red. Green Commonwealth seal at right. Serial #1 to 403,600 A1-A3; B1 1,001 to 21,700; 1751 to 280,000 C1-C4. Back: Green.			
	a. Yellow paper. Normal or small 3 in date.	1.00	2.00	6.00
	b. Manila paper. Normal or small 3 in date.	1.00	2.00	6.00
	c. Gray paper.	1.50	3.00	10.00

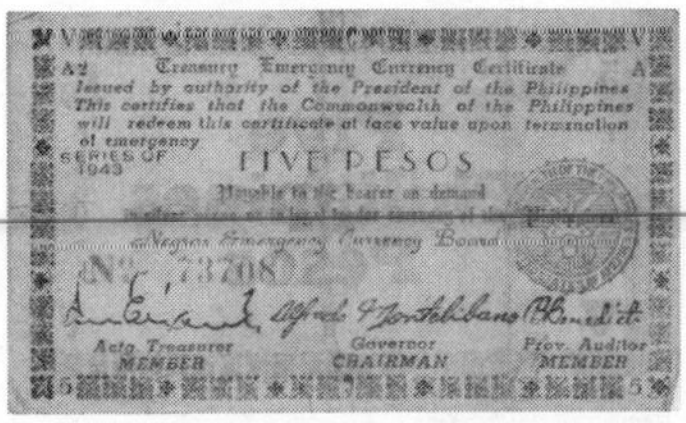

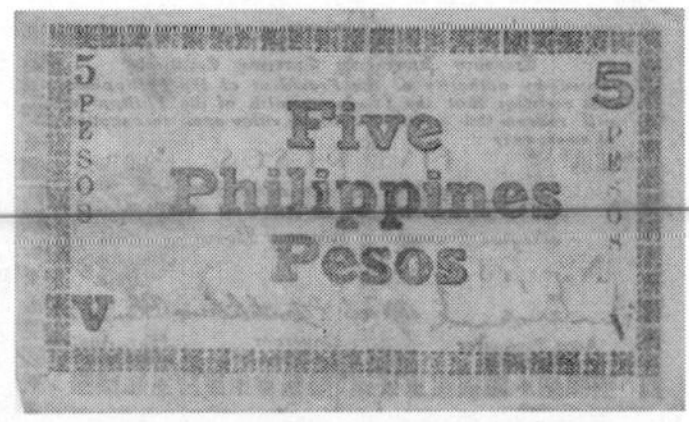

Number	Denomination	Good	Fine	XF
S662	**5 Pesos**			
	1943. Black. Green Commonwealth seal at right. Serial #1 to 150,000 A1-A4; 1,001 to 88,370 B1-B4. Normal or small 3 in date. Back: Green. Paper: White.	1.50	3.00	10.00

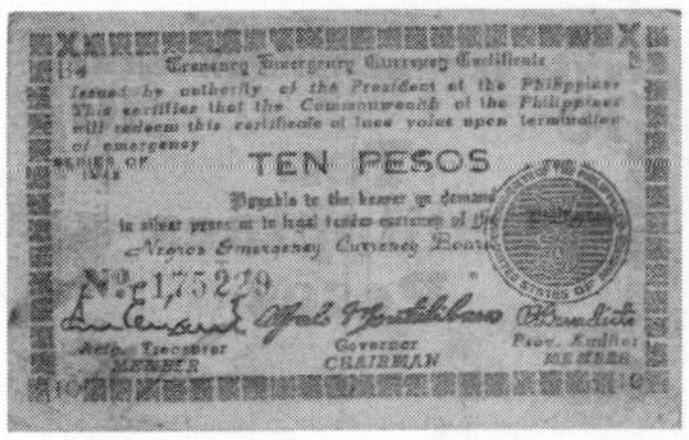

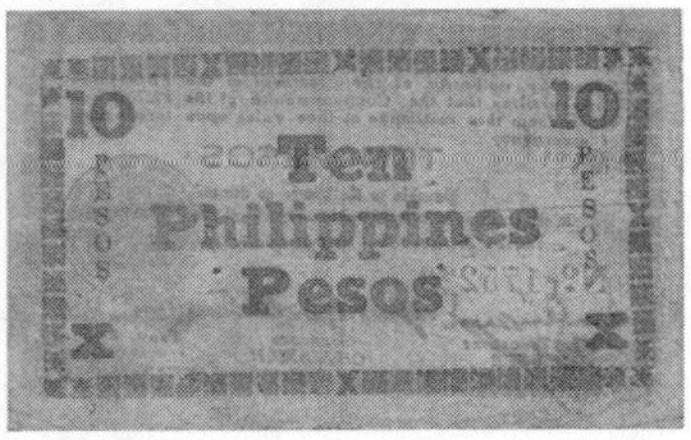

Number	Denomination	Good	Fine	XF
S663	**10 Pesos**			
	1943. Black. Green Commonwealth seal at right.			
	a. White paper. Serial # 1 to 138,280 A1-A4: 1,001 to 239,000 B1-B4. Normal or small 3 in date.	1.00	2.00	6.00
	x. Counterfeit, brown paper.	—	—	—

Number	Denomination	Good	Fine	XF
S664	**20 Pesos**			
	1943. Black. Green Commonwealth seal at right. Serial #1 to 60,000 A1-A3. Paper: White.	1.50	3.00	10.00
S665	**50 Pesos**			
	1943. Black. Orange seal at right. Serial #A1-A2 1 to 40,000. Back: Orange. Countersigned by Treasurer and Auditor. Paper: White.	12.00	25.00	75.00

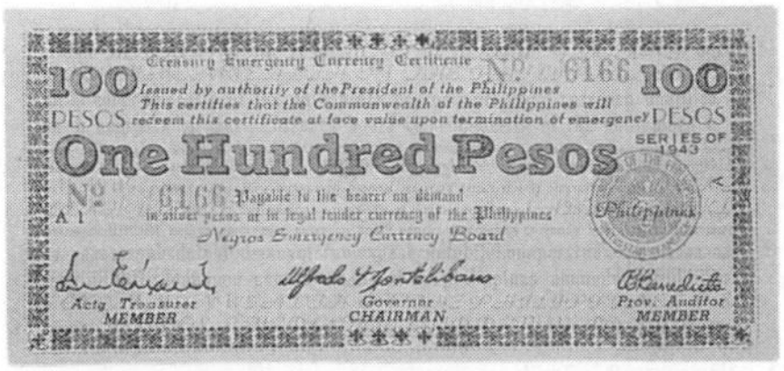

Number	Denomination	Good	Fine	XF
S666	**100 Pesos**			
	1943. Black. Orange seal at right. Serial #1 to 15,100 A1-A2 (#15,100 to 20,965 not issued). Like #S665. Back: Countersigned by Gov. Montelibano.	20.00	40.00	120.
S667	**500 Pesos**			
	1943. Blue on yellow underprint. Red seal at right. Green numerals at corners, also large words across center. Serial #A1 1 to 1,700 (#1,701 to 4,240 not issued). Back: Blue on yellow underprint. Countersigned by all 3 Members. Paper: White.			
	a. Montelibano signature at bottom.	75.00	150.	450.
	b. Montelibano signature at top.	45.00	90.00	270.
	c. Watermaked paper.	75.00	150.	450.

1944 Treasury Emergency Currency Certificate Issue

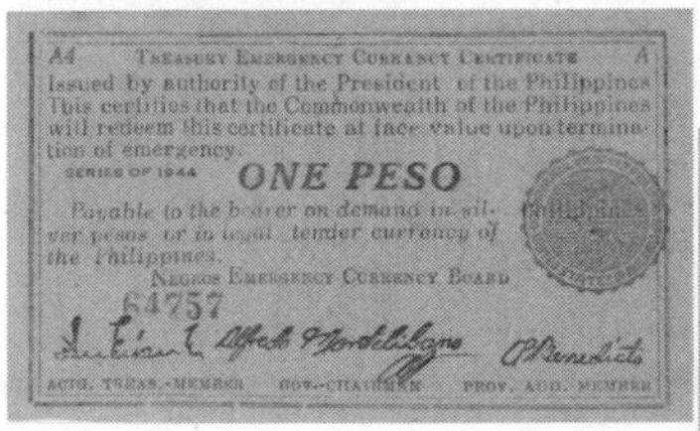

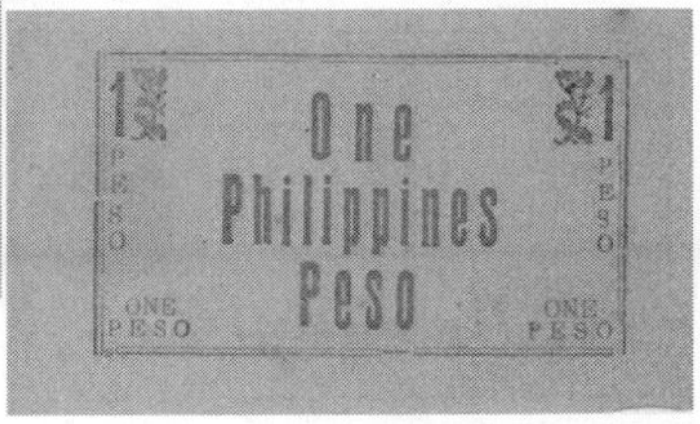

Number	Denomination	Good	Fine	XF
S668	**1 Peso**			
	1944. Blue text, red-orange seal and serial #. Back: Red-brown. Paper: White.			
	a. Normal serial #; A1-A4 0,001 to 80,000.	1.00	2.00	6.00
	b. Serial # with crude narrow *A* suffix. Serial #A1-A4 0,001A to 120,000A.	1.00	2.00	6.00
S669	**1 Peso**			
	1944. Blue text, black seal and serial #. Serial # included in #S668. Back: Slate black. Paper: White.	—	—	—
S670	**1 Peso**			
	1944. Black text, blue seal and serial #. Serial #B1-B4 0,001 to 100,000. Back: Blue. Paper: White.	1.00	2.00	6.00
S671	**1 Peso**			
	1944. Black text, seal and serial #. Serial # included in #S670. Back: Slate black. Paper: White.	—	—	—

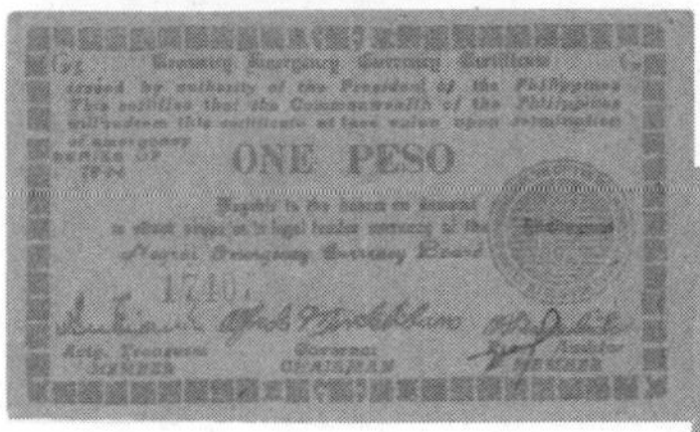

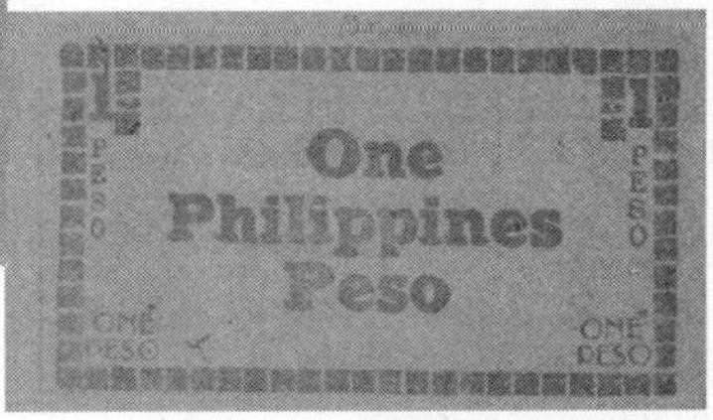

Number	Denomination	Good	Fine	XF
S672	**1 Peso**			
	1944. Red text, green seal and serial #. Serial #D1-D4 0,001 to 100,000; E1-E3 0,001 to 60,000; F1-F4 0,001 to 60,000; G1-G3 0,001 to 60,000. Back: Dark green. Paper: Brown (varieties).	1.00	2.00	6.00
S673	**1 Peso**			
	1944. Like #S672 but different border ornaments at top left and right. Serial #H1-H4 0,001 to 200,000.	3.00	6.00	20.00
S674	**5 Pesos**			
	1944. Black. Green seal and serial #. Serial #C1-C4 0,001 to 200,000. Back: Dark green. Paper: Brown (varieties).	1.50	3.00	10.00
S675	**5 Pesos**			
	1944. Green. Red seal and serial #. Serial #D1-D4 0,001 to 200,000. Back: Red. Paper: Brown (varieties).	1.50	3.00	10.00

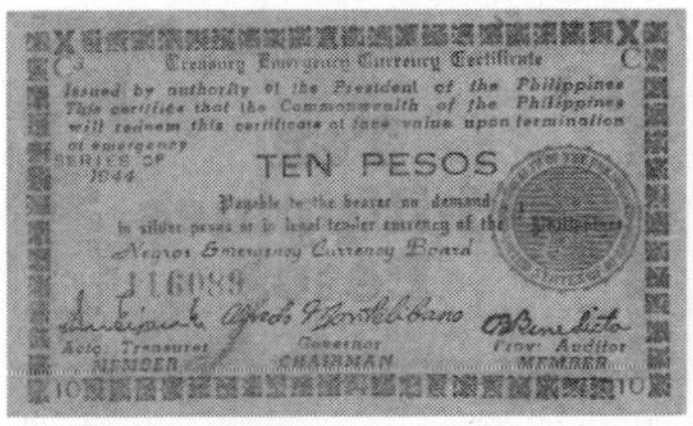

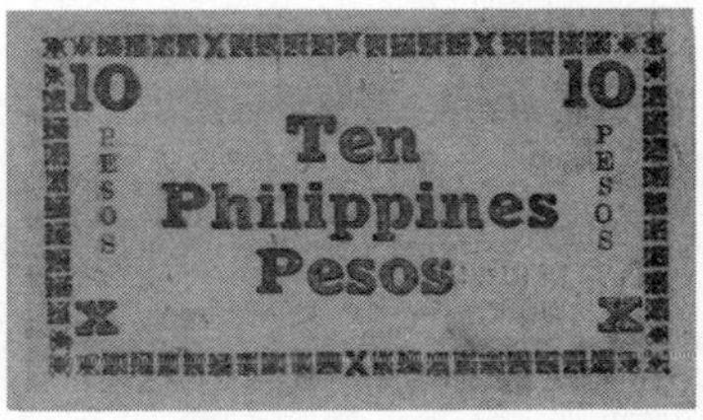

Number	Denomination	Good	Fine	XF
S676	**10 Pesos**			
	1944. Black. Green seal and serial #. Smaller words *TEN PESOS* at center, letters 4mm tall. Serial #C1-C4 0,001 to 200,000; D1-D4 0,001 to 100,000; E1-E4 0,001 to 100,000; F1-F4 0,001 to 100,000. Paper: Brown (varieties).			
	a. Issued note.	1.00	2.00	6.00
	x1. Counterfeit, ornate serial # 4mm high.	—	—	—
	x2. Counterfeit, like x1 but plain serial # 5mm high.	—	—	—

	Good	Fine	XF
S677 10 Pesos 1944. Black. Like #S676 except that words *TEN PESOS* at center are larger, 5mm tall. Serial #G1-G4 0,001 to 100,000; H1-H4 0,001 to 100,000; I1-I4 0,001 to 100,000.			
a. Issued note.	1.00	2.00	6.00
x. Counterfeit, Large *TEN PESOS* but series *D2* which occurs only on genuine notes with small *TEN PESOS*, #S676.	—	—	—
S678 20 Pesos 1944. Black. Green seal and serial #. Serial #B1-B3 1 to 57,000. Paper: White.	1.50	3.00	10.00
S679 20 Pesos 1944. Black. Green seal and serial #. Serial #1 to 24,600 C1-C3. Like #S678. Paper: Pink.	2.50	5.00	15.00

	Good	Fine	XF
S680 20 Pesos 1944. Black. Green seal and serial #. Serial #0,001 to 249,300 D1-D3. Like #S678. Paper: Brown (varieties).			
a. Issued note.	1.00	2.00	6.00
x. Counterfeit, brown paper but series *B1* which occurs only on genuine notes of white paper, #S678.	—	—	—

1945 Treasury Emergency Currency Certificate Issue

	Good	Fine	XF
S681 1 Peso 1945. Red. Green seal and serial #. Serial # I1-I4 0,001 to 100,000; J1-J4 0,001 to 100,000. Back: Dark green. Paper: Brown.	1.50	3.00	10.00
S683 10 Pesos 1945. Black. Green seal and serial #. Serial # J1-J4 0,001 to 199,000 (#199,001 to 200,000 not issued). Paper: Brown.	4.00	8.00	25.00

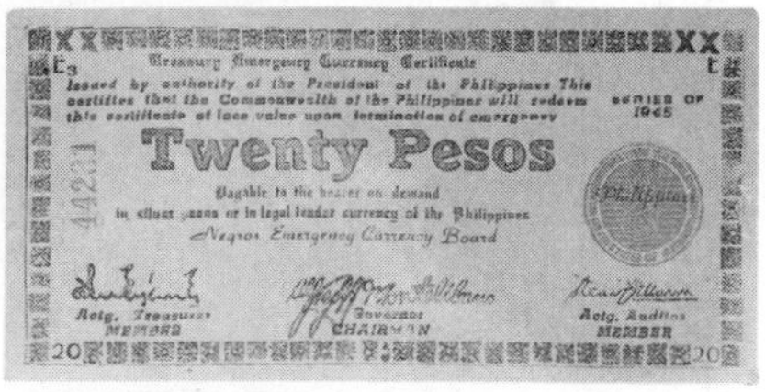

	Good	Fine	XF
S684 20 Pesos 1945. Dark green. Red seal and serial #. Serial #E1-E3 0,001 to 46,000 (#46,001 to 51,000 not issued). Paper: Brown.	6.00	12.00	35.00
S685 20 Pesos 1945. Dark green. Red seal and serial #. Serial #G1 1,001 to 3,000 (#G1-G3 3,001 to 75,000 not issued). Serial #I1 0,001 to 4,000 (#I1-I3 4,001 to 75,000 not issued). Serial #J1 0,001 to 1,000 (#J1-J3 1,001 to 75,000 not issued). Paper: White.	7.50	15.00	45.00

NOTE: 20 Pesos notes serial # F1-F3 0,001 to 75,000 not issued. 20 Pesos notes serial # H1-H3 0,001 to 75,000 not issued. In addition, some 140,000 1 Peso notes printed at the Tolong press were not issued.

Free Negros Military Currency Committee

ND Issue

	Good	Fine	XF
S691 10 Pesos (30).	—	—	—
S692 20 Pesos (74).	—	—	—
S693 30 Pesos (25).	—	—	—
S694 40 Pesos (5).	—	—	—
S695 50 Pesos (70).	—	—	—
S696 100 Pesos (152).	—	—	—
S697 150 Pesos (1).	—	—	—
S698 200 Pesos (114).	—	—	—
S699 300 Pesos (1).	—	—	—
S700 500 Pesos (78).	—	—	—
S701 1,000 Pesos (35).	—	—	—
S702 2,000 Pesos (45).	—	—	—
S703 2,500 Pesos (1).	—	—	—
S704 3,000 Pesos (10).	—	—	—
S705 4,000 Pesos (1).	—	—	—
S706 5,000 Pesos (23).	—	—	—

NOTE: Elizalde's support of the Negros guerrilla movements, from the very beginning, was recognized by Governor Montelibano who appointed him Acting Provincial Treasurer of the *Free Negros* government and a Member of the Negros Emergency Currency Board. Elizalde personally supervised printing of Free Negros emergency currency printed by this Board.

IV Philippine Corps

1943 Military Script Issue

Army of the United States of America

	Good	Fine	XF
S711 2 Pesos 1943. Black. Serial #10,001 to 50,796. Back: Frame is 133 x 53mm, top of *TWO* is 7mm below top frame line. Paper: Brown.	12.00	25.00	75.00
S711A 2 Pesos 1943. Black. Like #S711. Back: Frame is 126 x 52mm. Top of *TWO* is 4mm below top frame line. Paper: Brown.	12.00	25.00	75.00

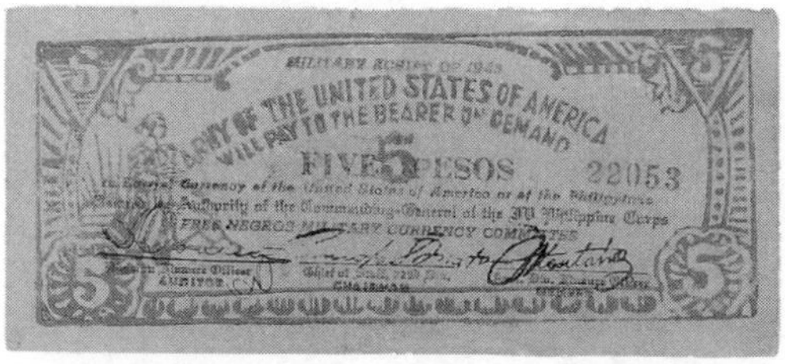

	Good	Fine	XF
S712 5 Pesos 1943. Brown with black text. Woman standing at left looking towards a smoking volcano, sun behind. Serial #10,001 to 29,213. Back: Light orange.	20.00	40.00	120.

	Good	Fine	XF
S713 10 Pesos 1943. Pale brown with black text. Cannon with man behind at left, eagle at center. Serial #1,001 to 21,835.	20.00	40.00	120.
S714 20 Pesos 1943. Green with black text. Armed guerrillas at left. Serial #1,001 to 6,064. Back: Brown. Standing woman holding hammer on anvil at center.	20.00	40.00	120.

1943 7th Military District Issue

	Good	Fine	XF
S715 1 Peso 1943. Black. Serial #1,001 to 41,756. Back: Greenish slate.	7.50	15.00	45.00

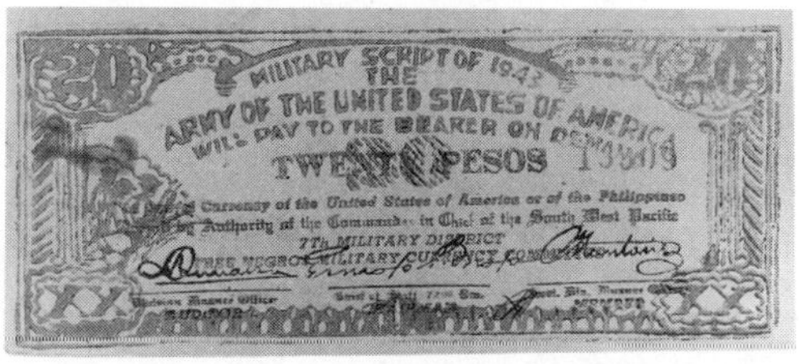

	Good	Fine	XF
S716 20 Pesos 1943. Green with black text. Armed guerrillas a left. Like #S714 except for changes in authorization text. Serial #6,065 to 19,805. Back: Brown. Standing woman holding hammer on anvil at center.			
a. Issued note.	20.00	40.00	120.
x. Counterfeit.	—	—	—

U.S. Forces in the Philippines - Local Military

7th Military District

1944 Issue

	Good	Fine	XF
S724 50 Centavos 1944. Black. (1/100 of a 50-Peso Montelibano note.)	—	—	—

Central Negros Sector

1944 Emergency Chit Issue

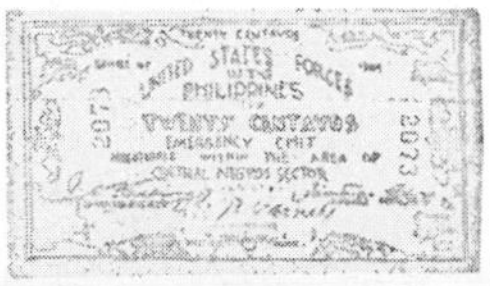

	Good	Fine	XF
S743 20 Centavos 1944. Signature of Sector Commander Maj. Abenir D. Bornales. Paper: Brown. Rare.	—	—	—

	Good	Fine	XF
S744 50 Centavos 1944. Signature of Sector Commander Maj. Abenir D. Bornales. Paper: Brown. Rare.	—	—	—

SPDHQT (Special District Headquarters Troops)

1944 Certificate Issue

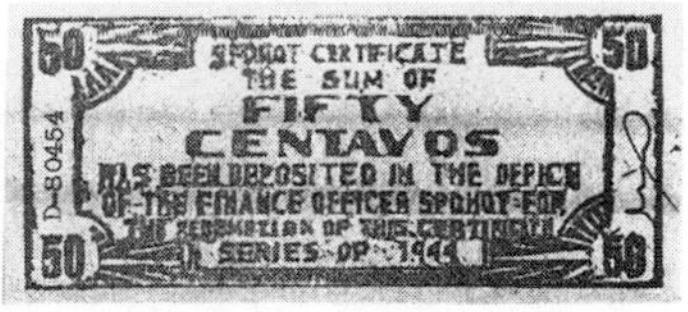

	Good	Fine	XF
S759 50 Centavos 1944. Black. Embossed seal of Notary Public Juez de Paz, of Manjuyod. Uniface. Paper: Pink. Rare.	—	—	—

CPW Area (Command Post W - Sector not known)

ND Circulating Chit Issue

	Good	Fine	XF
S784 50 Centavos ND. Back: Inked fingerprint. Paper: Pink. Mimeographed. Rare.	—	—	—
S785 1 Peso ND. Like #S784. Back: Inked fingerprint. Paper: Pink. Rare.	—	—	—

Provincial Government of Nueva Vizcaya

ND Issue

	Good	Fine	XF
S791 20 Centavos ND. Paper: White laid.			
a. Without embossed seal. Serial #0001 to (approx.) 3,200.	45.00	90.00	270.
b. Embossed seal of Justice of the Peace. Serial # (approx.) 3,201 to (approx.) 4,900.	45.00	90.00	270.
S792 20 Centavos ND. Seal of Justice of the Peace. Serial # (approx.) 10,100 to 16,121. Paper: White laid. Mimeo.	30.00	60.00	180.

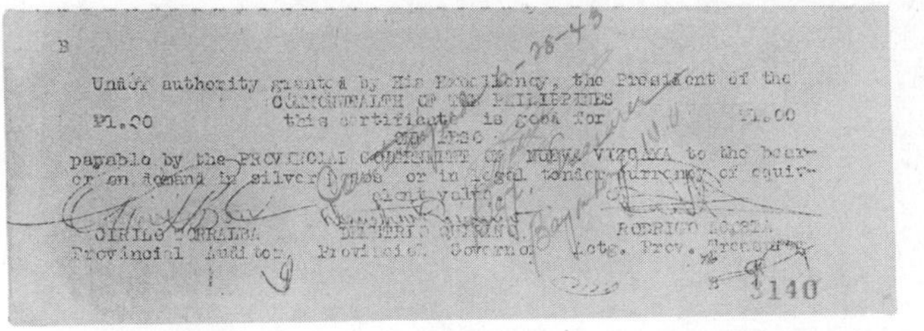

	Good	Fine	XF
S793 1 Peso ND. Paper: Yellow.			
a. Embossed seal of Provincial Auditor. Serial #1 to (approx.) 5,100.	30.00	60.00	180.
b. Without embossed seal. Serial # (approx.) 5,200 to (approx.) 11,500.	30.00	60.00	180.
c. Embossed seal of Justice of the Peace. Serial # (approx.) 13,400 to (approx.) 14,000.	30.00	60.00	180.

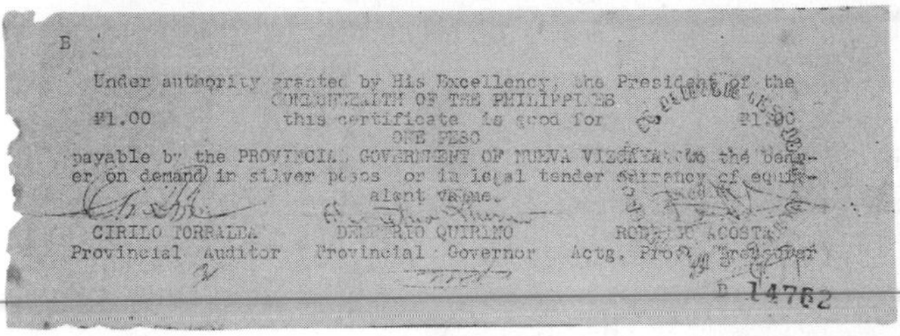

	Good	Fine	XF
S794 1 Peso ND. Seal of Justice of the Peace. Serial # (approx.) 14,762 to 25,134. Paper: Yellow. Mimeo.	30.00	60.00	180.
S795 5 Pesos ND. Serial #0001 to 3,348. Paper: White bond.			
a. Embossed seal of Provincial Auditor. Serial #0001 to (approx.) 1,400.	45.00	90.00	270.
b. Embossed seal of Justice of the Peace. Serial # (approx.) 2,000 to 3,348.	45.00	90.00	270.

NOTE: In July 1943 the puppet Philippine Executive Commission authorized redemption of pre-surrender emergency notes, but specifically excluded any notes printed by mimeograph. Even though this excluded the notes of Nueva Vizcaya, Governor Quirino ordered them accepted for registration in the vain hope they would be included. Thus, many of these notes may be found countersigned in red pen on the face, or with a circular *RECEIVED* date stamp in purple on the back. Catalog values are for notes as originally issued. Countersigned notes are worth only about half as much.

Province Issues under Provincial Authority

1942 Circulating Paper Bill Issue

Resolution No. 53, Series 1942 December 10, 1942

	Good	Fine	XF
S801 10 Centavos 10.12.1942. Typewritten in pica or elite type. Serial #1 to 400. Uniface. Paper: White.	—	—	—
S802 50 Centavos 10.12.1942. Typewritten in pica or elite type. Serial #1 to 200. Uniface. Paper: White.	—	—	—
S803 1 Peso 10.12.1942. Typewritten in pica or elite type. Serial #1 to 500. Uniface. Paper: White.	—	—	—
S804 2 Pesos 10.12.1942. Typewritten in pica or elite type. Serial #1 to 2,000. Uniface. Paper: White.	—	—	—

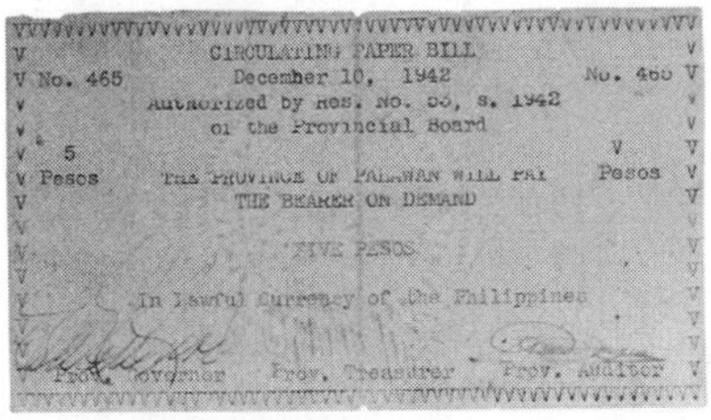

	Good	Fine	XF
S805 5 Pesos 10.12.1942. Typewritten in pica or elite type. Serial #1 to 1,900. Uniface. Paper: White.	—	—	—

1943 First Circulating Paper Bill Issue

Resolution No. 5, Series 1943. January 23, 1943

	Good	Fine	XF
S806 5 Pesos 23.1.1943. Typewritten. Serial #1,901 to 2,500. Uniface. Paper: White.	—	—	—

1943 Second Circulating Paper Bill Issue

Resolution No. 20, Series 1943. February 25, 1943

	Good	Fine	XF
S807 5 Pesos 25.2.1943. Typewritten. Serial #2,501 to 2,900. Uniface. Paper: White.	—	—	—

1943 Third Circulating Paper Bill Issue

Resolution No. 22, Series 1943. March 15, 1943

	Good	Fine	XF
S808 5 Pesos 15.3.1943. Typewritten. Serial #2,901 to 3,000. Uniface. Paper: White.	—	—	—

1943 Fourth Circulating Paper Bill Issue
Resolution No. 24, Series 1943. March 15, 1943

	Good	Fine	XF
S809 2 Pesos 15.3.1943. Mimeographed. Serial #1A to 3,000A. Back: Numeral *2* is 47mm high. Paper: White.	—	—	—
S810 5 Pesos 15.3.1943. Mimeographed. Serial #1-A to 2,000-A. Back: Numeral *5* is 47mm high. Paper: White.	—	—	—
S811 10 Pesos 15.3.1943. Mimeographed. Serial #1-A to 2,000-A. Back: *P10* is 19-1/2mm high. Paper: White.	—	—	—
S812 20 Pesos 15.3.1943. Mimeographed. Serial #1-A to 500-A. Back: *P20* is 19-1/2mm high. Paper: White.	—	—	—

1943 Fifth Circulating Paper Bill Issue
Resolution No. 56, Series 1943. April 30, 1943

	Good	Fine	XF
S813 10 Pesos 30.4.1943. Mimeographed. Serial # (for #S813 and S815): 1-B to 1,500-B. Back: *P10* is 19-1/2mm high.	—	—	—
S814 20 Pesos 30.4.1943. Mimeographed. Serial # (for #S814 and S816): 1-B to 1,000-B. Back: *P20* is 19-1/2mm high.	—	—	—

1943 Sixth Circulating Paper Bill Issue
Resolution No. 56, Series 1943. May 3, 1943

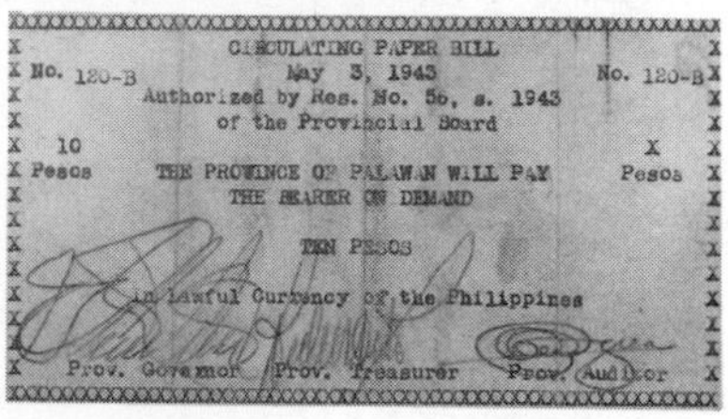

	Good	Fine	XF
S815 10 Pesos 3.5.1943. Mimeographed. Serial # mixed with #S813. Back: *P10* is 19 1/2mm high.			
a. Graph paper.	—	—	—
b. White paper.	—	—	—
x. Counterfeit. Typewritten. Graph or white paper. Back: *P10* is 23mm high.	—	—	—
S816 20 Pesos 3.5.1943. Mimeographed. Serial # mixed with #S814. Back: *P20* is 19-1/2mm high.			
a. Issued note.	—	—	—
x. Counterfeit. Typewritten. Back: *P20* is 23mm high.	—	—	—

1943 Seventh Circulating Paper Bill Issue
Resolution No. 56, Series 1943 *as amended*

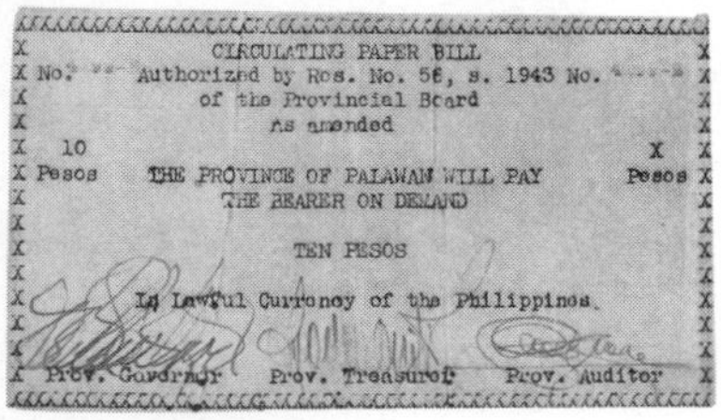

	Good	Fine	XF
S817 10 Pesos 1943. Mimeographed. Signature of Provincial Auditor Paguia. Serial # (for #S817, S819, S820): 1,501-B to 7,126-B. Back: *P10* is 19-1/2mm high.			
a. White paper.	—	—	—
b. Manila paper.	—	—	—
c. Blue paper.	—	—	—
d. Ledger or document paper.	—	—	—
S818 20 Pesos 1943. Mimeographed. Signature of Provincial Auditor Paguia. Serial # (for #S818, S821, S822): 1,001-B to 8,716-B. Back: *P20* is 19-1/2mm high.			
a. White paper.	—	—	—

1943 Eighth Circulating Paper Bill Issue
Resolution No. 56, Series 1943 *as amended*

	Good	Fine	XF
S819 10 Pesos 1943. Mimeographed. Signature of Provincial Auditor Reynosa. Serial # mixed with #S817 and S820. Uniface.			
a. White paper.	—	—	—
b. Brown paper.	—	—	—
S820 10 Pesos 1943. Mimeographed. Signature of Provincial Auditor Reynosa. Serial # mixed with S817 and S819. Like #S819. Back: *P10* is 19-1/2mm high.			
b. Brown paper.	—	—	—
S821 20 Pesos 1943. Mimeographed. Signature of Provincial Auditor Reynosa. Serial # mixed with S818 and S822. Back: *P20* is 19-1/2mm high.			
a. White paper.	—	—	—
b. Brown paper.	—	—	—
c. Ledger or document paper.	—	—	—
S822 20 Pesos 1943. Mimeographed. Signature of Provincial Auditor Reynosa. Serial # mixed with S818 and S821. Uniface. Like #S821. Back: *P20* is 19-1/2mm high.			
a. White paper.	—	—	—

NOTE: 20 Pesos notes serial # 8,717-B to 10,288-B were not issued.

Municipal Issues Under Provincial Authority

Agutaya

May 13, 1943 Circulating Paper Bill Issue

	Good	Fine	XF
S830 10 Centavos 13.5.1943. Typewritten, with carbon copies. Handsigned. Paper: Rose.	—	—	—
S833 1 Peso 13.5.1943. Typewritten, with carbon copies. Handsigned. Back: *P1*. Paper: Rose.	—	—	—
S834 1 Peso 13.5.1943. Typewritten, with carbon copies. Handsigned. Back: *ONE 1 PESO*. Paper: Rose.	—	—	—
S835 2 Pesos 13.5.1943. Typewritten, with carbon copies. Handsigned. Back: *P2*. Paper: Rose.			
a. Typewritten serial #.	—	—	—
b. Printed serial #.	—	—	—
S837 5 Pesos 13.5.1943. Typewritten, with carbon copies. Handsigned. Back: *P5*. Paper: Rose.	—	—	—

#S840-S843 hectograph printing in purple. Rose paper. Printed sign. Stamped denomination on back.

	Good	Fine	XF
S840 20 Centavos 13.5.1943. Hectograph printing in purple. Printed signature. Back: Stamped denomination. Paper: Rose.	—	—	—
S842 1 Peso 13.5.1943. Hectograph printing in purple. Printed signature. Back: Stamped denomination. Paper: Rose.	—	—	—
S843 2 Pesos 13.5.1943. Hectograph printing in purple. Printed signature. Back: Stamped denomination. Paper: Rose.	—	—	—

#S846 and S849 hectograph printing in purple. Green paper. Printed sign. Stamped denomination on back.

	Good	Fine	XF
S846 20 Centavos 13.5.1943. Hectograph printing in purple. Printed signature. Back: Stamped denomination. Paper: Green.	—	—	—
S849 2 Pesos 13.5.1943. Hectograph printing in purple. Printed signature. Back: Stamped denomination. Paper: Green.	—	—	—

June 2, 1943 First Circulating Paper Bill Issue

	Good	Fine	XF
S852 20 Centavos 2.6.1943. Typewritten with carbon copies. Handsigned. Back: Stamped denomination. Paper: Manila.	—	—	—
S854 1 Peso 2.6.1943. Typewritten with carbon copies. Handsigned. Back: Stamped denomination. Paper: Manila.	—	—	—

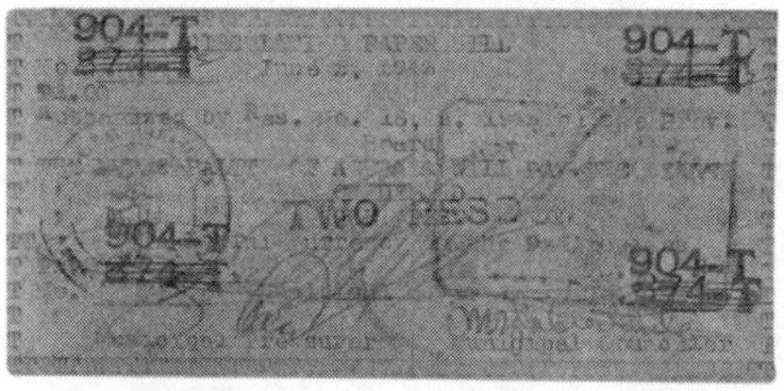

	Good	Fine	XF
S855 2 Pesos 2.6.1943. Typewritten with carbon copies. Handsigned. Back: Stamped denomination. Paper: Manila.	—	—	—
S856 5 Pesos 2.6.1943. Typewritten with carbon copies. Handsigned. Back: Stamped denomination. Paper: Manila.	—	—	—

June 2, 1943 Second Circulating Paper Bill Issue

#S858-S864 new Municipal Mayor: Segundo Raguin.

	Good	Fine	XF
S858 10 Centavos 2.6.1943. Typewritten with carbon copies. Handsigned. Back: Stamped denomination.			
a. Manila paper.	—	—	—
b. White document paper.	—	—	—
S859 20 Centavos 2.6.1943. Typewritten with carbon copies. Handsigned. Back: Stamped denomination.			
a. Manila paper.	—	—	—
S861 1 Peso 2.6.1943. Typewritten with carbon copies. Handsigned. Back: Stamped denomination.			
a. Manila paper.	—	—	—
b. White document paper.	—	—	—
S862 2 Pesos 2.6.1943. Typewritten with carbon copies. Handsigned. Back: Stamped denomination.			
a. Manila paper.	—	—	—
b. White document paper.	—	—	—
S863 5 Pesos 2.6.1943. Typewritten with carbon copies. Handsigned. Back: Stamped denomination.			
a. Manila paper.	—	—	—
b. White document paper.	—	—	—

S864 10 Pesos Good Fine XF
2.6.1943. Typewritten with carbon copies. Handsigned. Back: Stamped denomination.
b. White document paper. — — —

July 2, 1943 Circulating Paper Bill Issue

S867 5 Pesos Good Fine XF
2.7.1943. Typewritten with carbon copies. Handsigned. Back: Stamped denomination. Paper: Manila. — — —

August 4, 1943 Circulating Paper Bill Issue

S870 2 Pesos Good Fine XF
4.8.1943. Typewritten, with carbon copies. Handsigned. Back: Stamped denomination. Paper: Manila. — — —

September 30, 1943 Circulating Paper Bill Issue

S873 1 Centavo Good Fine XF
30.9.1943. Typewritten, with carbon copies. Handsigned. Back: *ONE 01 CENTAVO*. Paper: Manila. — — —

S874 1 Centavo
30.9.1943. Typewritten, with carbon copies. Handsigned. Back: *ONE 1 CENTAVO*. Paper: Manila. — — —

S876 5 Centavos
30.9.1943. Typewritten, with carbon copies. Handsigned. Back: *FIVE 5 CENTAVOS*.
a. Manila paper. — — —
b. White document paper. — — —

S877 10 Centavos
30.9.1943. Back: Stamped denomination.
a. Manila paper. — — —
b. White document paper. — — —

S878 20 Centavos
30.9.1943. Back: Stamped denomination.
a. Manila paper. — — —
x. Error. Border composed of repeated *V* instead of *H*. — — —

S879 50 Centavos
30.9.1943. Back: Stamped denomination.
a. Manila paper. — — —

S880 1 Peso
30.9.1943. Back: Stamped denomination.
a. Manila paper. — — —
b. White document paper. — — —

S881 2 Pesos
30.9.1943. Back: Stamped denomination.
a. Manila paper. — — —
b. White document paper. — — —

S883 5 Pesos
30.9.1943. Back: Stamped denomination.
a. Manila paper. — — —
b. White document paper. — — —

S884 10 Pesos
30.9.1943. Back: Stamped denomination.
b. White document paper. — — —

ND Circulating Paper Bill Issue

S887 10 Pesos Good Fine XF
ND. Typewritten, with carbon copies. Handsigned. Back: Stamped denomination. Paper: White document. — — —

Bacuit

Circulating Paper Bill

Resolution No. 20, Series of 1944, of the Provincial Board

S893 5 Pesos Good Fine XF
9.8.1944. Typewritten. Handsigned. Back: Municipal stamping and denomination. Paper: White bond. — — —

Balabac

Resolutions No. 18 and 19, Series 1943 of the Provincial Board. February 25, 1943

S900 50 Centavos Good Fine XF
25.2.1943. Typewritten. Handsigned. Embossed seal of Justice of the Peace. Paper: White bond. — — —

S901 1 Peso
25.2.1943. Typewritten. Handsigned. Embossed seal of Justice of the Peace. Initial for first names of Members. Paper: White bond.
a. Top 2 lines in lower case letters. — — —

S902 1 Peso
25.2.1943. Typewritten. Handsigned. Embossed seal of Justice of the Peace. First names of Members spelled out. Paper: White bond.
b. Top 2 lines in upper case letters. — — —

S904 2 Pesos
25.2.1943. Typewritten. Handsigned. Embossed seal of Justice of the Peace. First names of Members spelled out. Paper: White bond.
a. Top 2 lines in lower case letters. — — —
b. Top 2 lines in upper case letters. — — —

Brooke's Point

Circulating Paper Bills

Resolution No. 18, Series 1943 of the Provincial Board

Notes Dated September 24, 1943

S913 50 Centavos Good Fine XF
19.4.1943. Typewritten with (a) original copy, (b) black carbon copy. Signed by Justice of the Peace. Paper: Manila. — — —

S914 1 Peso Good Fine XF
19.4.1943. Typewritten with (a) original copy, (b) black carbon copy. Signed by Mayor. Paper: White bond. — — —

S915 2 Pesos
19.4.1943. Typewritten with (a) original copy, (b) black carbon copy. Signed by Mayor. Paper: White bond. — — —

S916 5 Pesos
19.4.1943. Typewritten with (a) original copy, (b) black carbon copy. Signed by Mayor. Paper: Grayish cloth. — — —

S917 10 Pesos
19.4.1943. Typewritten with (a) original copy, (b) black carbon copy. Signed by Mayor. Paper: Grayish cloth. — — —

Resolution No. 33, Series 1943 of the Provincial Board

Notes Dated September 24, 1943

S920 20 Centavos Good Fine XF
24.9.1943. Typewritten with (a) original, (b) black carbon, and (c) blue carbon copy. Paper: White. — — —

S921 50 Centavos
24.9.1943. Typewritten with (a) original, (b) black carbon, and (c) blue carbon copy. Paper: White. — — —

S922 1 Peso
24.9.1943. Typewritten with (a) original, (b) black carbon, and (c) blue carbon copy. Numeral *1* is 25mm high.
a. White paper. — — —
b. Bluish green paper. — — —

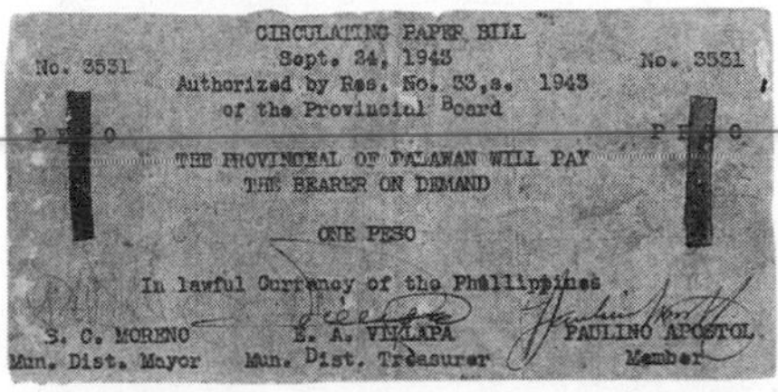

S923 1 Peso Good Fine XF
24.9.1943. Typewritten with (a) original, (b) black carbon, and (c) blue carbon copy. Numeral *1* is 33mm high.
b. Bluish green paper. — — —

S924 1 Peso
24.9.1943. Typewritten with (a) original, (b) black carbon, and (c) blue carbon copy. Paper: White. — — —

S925 2 Pesos
24.9.1943. Typewritten with (a) original, (b) black carbon, and (c) blue carbon copy. Paper: White. — — —

S926 2 Pesos
24.9.1943. Typewritten with (a) original, (b) black carbon, and (c) blue carbon copy. Paper: White document. — — —

S928 5 Pesos
24.9.1943. Typewritten with (a) original, (b) black carbon, and (c) blue carbon copy. Paper: Brown. — — —

Authorized Letter P.T. (Prov. Treas.) of Nov. 6, 1943.

Notes Dated May 27, 1944

S931 1 Peso Good Fine XF
27.5.1944. Typewritten with (a) original, (b) black carbon, and (c) blue carbon copies. Paper: Manila. — — —

S932 2 Pesos
27.5.1944. Typewritten with (a) original, (b) black carbon, and (c) blue carbon copies. Paper: Manila. — — —

S933 5 Pesos
27.5.1944. Typewritten with (a) original, (b) black carbon, and (c) blue carbon copies. Paper: Manila. — — —

Authorized Letter P.T. (Prov. Treas.) of May 9, 1944.

Notes Dated May 29, 1944

S935 20 Centavos Good Fine XF
29.5.1944. Typewritten with (a) original, (b) black carbon, and (c) blue carbon copies. — — —

S936 1 Peso
29.5.1944. Typewritten with (a) original, (b) black carbon, and (c) blue carbon copies. Paper: Manila. — — —

S937 2 Pesos
29.5.1944. Typewritten with (a) original, (b) black carbon, and (c) blue carbon copies. Paper: Manila. — — —

S938 5 Pesos
29.5.1944. Typewritten with (a) original, (b) black carbon, and (c) blue carbon copies. Paper: Manila. — — —

S940 20 Pesos
29.5.1944. Typewritten with (a) original, (b) black carbon, and (c) blue carbon copies. — — —

September 22, 1944 Issue

S945 20 Pesos Good Fine XF
22.9.1944. Paper: Manila. — — —

Authorized Letter P.T. (Prov. Treas.) of October 23, 1944

S948 2 Pesos Good Fine XF
May 27, 1944. Typewritten with black carbon copies. Paper: Brown. Unsigned remainder. — — —

S949 2 Pesos
Jan. 2, 1945. Typewritten with black carbon copies. Paper: Brown. Unsigned remainder. — — —

		Good	Fine	XF
S950	**5 Pesos** May 27, 1944. Typewritten with black carbon copies. Paper: Brown.	—	—	—
S952	**10 Pesos** May 27, 1944. Typewritten with black carbon copies. Paper: Brown.	—	—	—
S955	**20 Pesos** Jan. 2, 1945. Typewritten with black carbon copies. Paper: Manila or brown.	—	—	—

Resolution No. 5, Series 1944 of the Provincial Board

Notes Dated 1945

		Good	Fine	XF
S956	**5 Pesos** 1.3.1945. Typewritten with black carbon copies. Paper: Brown. Unsigned remainder.	—	—	—
S957	**5 Pesos** 1.4.1945. Typewritten with black carbon copies. Paper: Brown. Unsigned remainder.	—	—	—
S958	**10 Pesos** 1.3.1945. Typewritten with black carbon copies. Paper: Brown. Unsigned remainder.	—	—	—

Cagayancillo

A total of 17,627.50 pesos was issued, but none are presently known which cite provincial authority.

Coron

A total of 11,260 pesos was issued, but none are presently known which cite provincial authority.

Cuyo

Circulating Paper Bills

Resolution No. 18, Series 1943 of the Provincial Board

Authorization 7,600 Pesos for Public Works

		Good	Fine	XF
S971	**1 Peso** 1943. Mimeographed signature, printed serial #. Serial #1 to 950.	—	—	—
S972	**2 Pesos** 1943. Mimeographed signature, printed serial #. Serial #1 to 950.	—	—	—
S973	**5 Pesos** 1943. Mimeographed signature, printed serial #. Serial #1 to 950.	—	—	—

Resolution No. 18, Series 1943 of the Provincial Board

Authorization 5,000 Pesos for Teacher's Salaries

		Good	Fine	XF
S974	**1 Peso** 1943. Handsigned. Typewritten serial #. Serial #951-A to 1,575-A.	—	—	—
S975	**2 Pesos** 1943. Handsigned. Typewritten serial #. Serial # 951-A to 1,575-A.	—	—	—

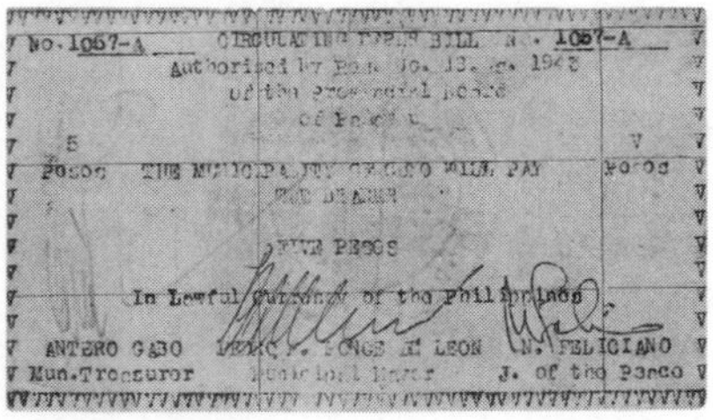

		Good	Fine	XF
S976	**5 Pesos** 1943. Handsigned. Typewritten serial #. Serial #951-A to 1,575-A.	—	—	—

Resolution No. 42, Series 1943 of the Provincial Board

Authorization 3,000 Pesos for Civilian Relief

		Good	Fine	XF
S977	**1 Peso** 1943. Handsigned. Typewritten serial #. Serial #1 to 375.	—	—	—
S978	**2 Pesos** 1943. Handsigned. Typewritten serial #. Serial #1 to 375.	—	—	—
S979	**5 Pesos** 1943. Handsigned. Typewritten serial #. Serial #1 to 375.	—	—	—

Resolution No. 43, Series 1943 of the Provincial Board

Authorization 3,000 Pesos Additional for Civilian Relief

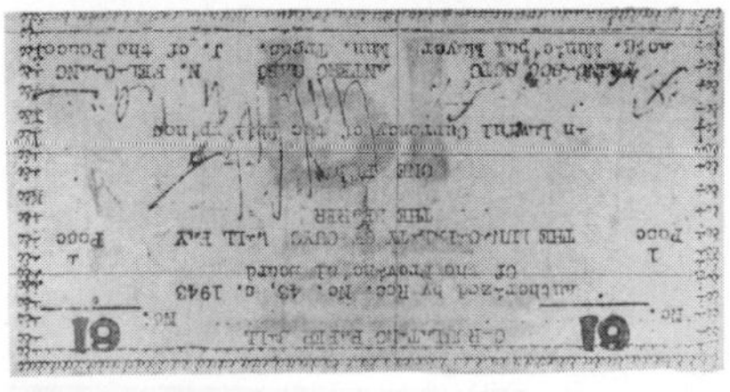

		Good	Fine	XF
S980	**1 Peso** 1943. Mimeographed signature. Printed serial #. Serial #1 to 375.	—	—	—
S981	**2 Pesos** 1943. Mimeographed signature. Printed serial #. Serial #1 to 375.	—	—	—
S982	**5 Pesos** 1943. Mimeographed signature. Printed serial #. Serial #1 to 375.	—	—	—

Resolution No. 5, Series 1944 of the Provincial Board

Authorization 3,000 Pesos for Fiscal Year 1944-45

		Good	Fine	XF
S983	**1 Peso** 1944. Mimeographed signature. Printed serial #. Serial #1 to 375.	—	—	—
S984	**2 Pesos** 1944. Mimeographed signature. Printed serial #. Serial #1 to 375.	—	—	—
S985	**5 Pesos** 1944. Mimeographed signature. Printed serial #. Serial #1 to 375.	—	—	—

Resolution No. 16, Series 1944 of the Provincial Board

Authorization 6,000 Pesos forSalaries of Teachers

		Good	Fine	XF
S986	**1 Peso** 1944. Mimeographed signature. Printed serial #. Serial #1 to 750.	—	—	—
S987	**2 Pesos** 1944. Mimeographed signature. Printed serial #. Serial #1 to 750.	—	—	—

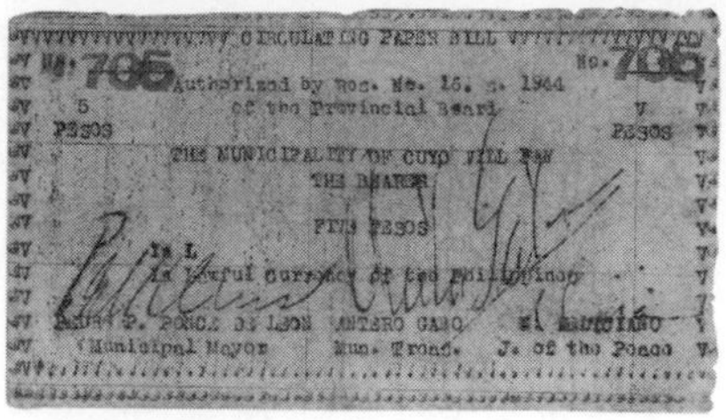

		Good	Fine	XF
S988	**5 Pesos** 1944. Mimeographed signature. Printed serial #. Serial #1 to 750.	—	—	—

Resolution No. 29, Series 1944 of the Provincial Board

Authorization 5,000 Pesos for Use by the Province

		Good	Fine	XF
S989	**1 Peso** 1944. Mimeographed signature. Printed serial #. Serial #1 to 625.	—	—	—
S990	**2 Pesos** 1944. Mimeographed signature. Printed serial #. Serial #1 to 625.	—	—	—
S991	**5 Pesos** 1944. Mimeographed signature. Printed serial #. Serial #1 to 625.	—	—	—

Dumaran

Circulating Paper Bills

Authorized by the Governor of Palawan

Dated November 9, 1943

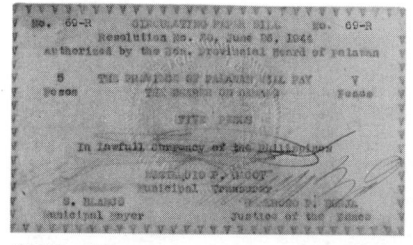

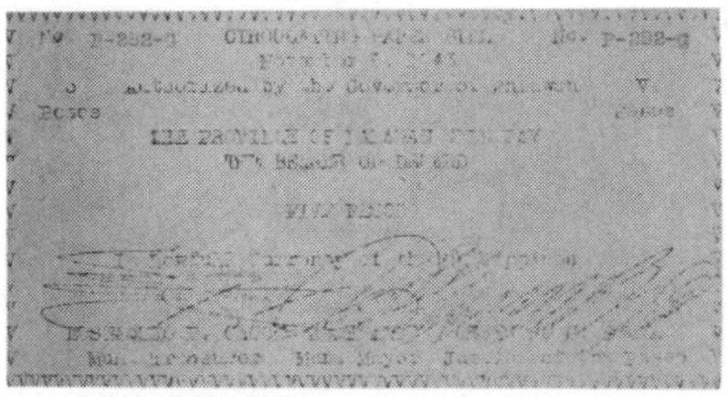

		Good	Fine	XF
S998	**5 Pesos** 9.11.1943. Mimeographed. Embossed seal of Justice of the Peace. Typewritten serial #. Back: *P5*.			
	a. White bond paper.	—	—	—
	b. Manila paper.	—	—	—

Resolution No. 20, Series 1944 of the Provincial Board

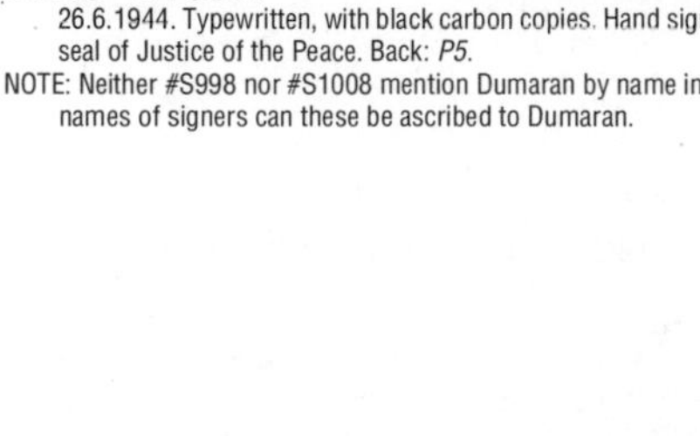

		Good	Fine	XF
S1008	**5 Pesos** 26.6.1944. Typewritten, with black carbon copies. Hand signed. Embossed seal of Justice of the Peace. Back: *P5*.	—	—	—

NOTE: Neither #S998 nor #S1008 mention Dumaran by name in the text. Only through embossed seals and names of signers can these be ascribed to Dumaran.

Puerto Princesa

Circulating Paper Bills

Resolution No. 5, Series 1944 of the Provincial Board

Dated August 24, 1944

	Good	Fine	XF
S1012 10 Pesos 24.8.1944. Typewritten. Handsigned. Uniface. Paper: Manila.	—	—	—

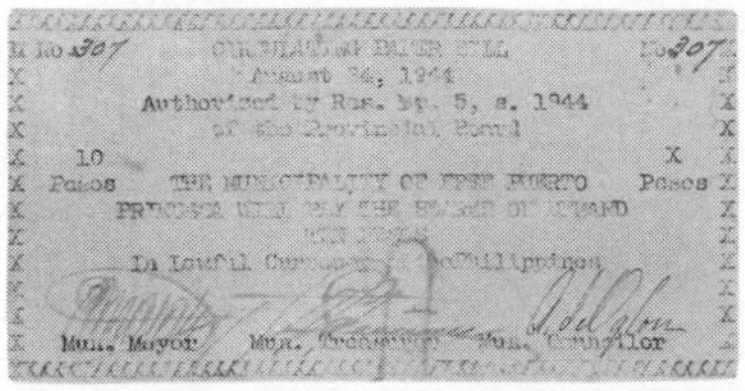

	Good	Fine	XF
S1014 10 Pesos 24.8.1944. Mimeograhped. Handsigned. Pen serial #. Uniface. Paper: Manila.	—	—	—

Taytay

Small Circulating Paper Bills

Resolution No. 18, Series 1943 of the Provincial Board

Dated April 10, 1943

	Good	Fine	XF
S1022 2 Pesos 10.14.1943. Typewritten (pica type) with carbon copies. Back: *P2*. Paper: White.	—	—	—

Large Circulating Paper Bills

Resolution No. 18, Series 1943 of the Provincial Board

Dated April 10, 1943

	Good	Fine	XF
S1026 1 Peso 10.4.1943. Typewritten (elite type) with carbon copies. Back: *P1*. Paper: White.	—	—	—

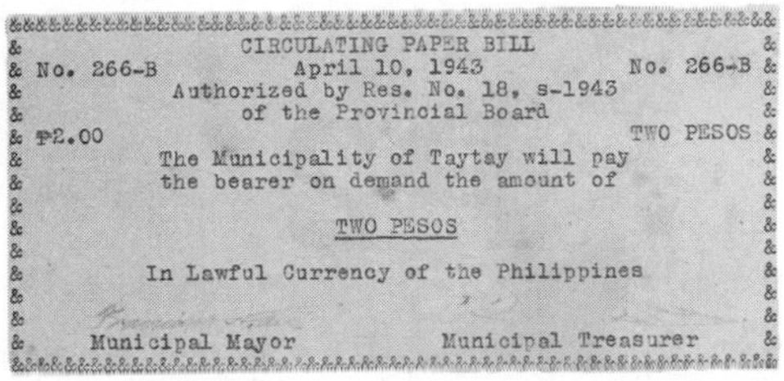

	Good	Fine	XF
S1027 2 Pesos 10.4.1943. Typewritten (elite type) with carbon copies. Back: *P2*. Paper: White.	—	—	—
S1028 5 Pesos 10.4.1943. Typewritten (elite type) with carbon copies. Back: *P5*. Paper: White.	—	—	—
S1030 20 Pesos 10.4.1943. Typewritten (elite type) with carbon copies. Back: *P20*. Paper: White.	—	—	—

Circulating Paper Bills

Resolution No. 20, Series 1944 of the Provincial Board

Dated September 20, 1944

Municipal Mayor: .... Francisco H. Alli
Municipal Treasurer: .... Julio Arzaga
Municipal Councilor: .... Alejandro Sarabia

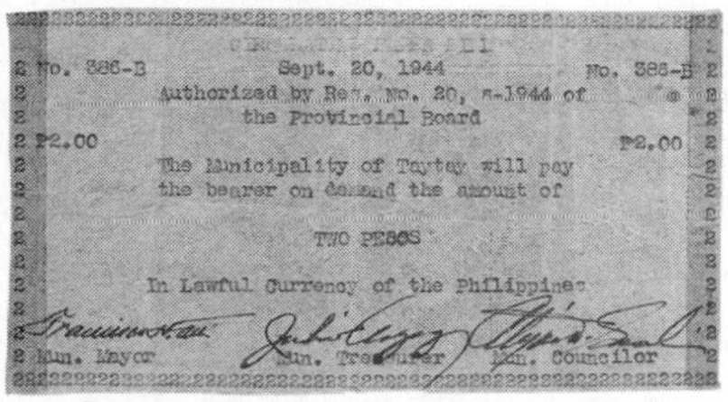

	Good	Fine	XF
S1042 2 Pesos 20.9.1944. Typewritten (pica type) with carbon copies. Back: *P2*. Paper: Manila.	—	—	—
S1044 10 Pesos 20.9.1944. Typewritten (pica type) with carbon copies. Back: *P10*. Paper: Manila.	—	—	—
S1045 20 Pesos 20.9.1944. Typewritten (pica type) with carbon copies. Back: *P20*. Paper: Manila.	—	—	—

Romblon

ND First Issue

#S1061-S1065 mimeographed on manila paper. Each denomination has a crudely drawn head of an animal on the face. Serial # is on back, along with different combinations of stamped facsimile sign. Quantity issued is not known, but serial # indicate an amount in excess of 25,000 pesos.

	Good	Fine	XF
S1061 1 Centavo ND. Pig head at center, palm tree at either side of head. Mimeographed. Back: Serial # and stamped facsimile signatures. Paper: Manila.	—	—	—
S1062 5 Centavos ND. Ox head at center, palm trees like #S1061. Mimeographed. Back: Serial # and stamped facsimile signatures. Paper: Manila.	—	—	—

	Good	Fine	XF
S1063 10 Centavos ND. Carabao head at center, palm trees like #S1061. Mimeographed. Back: Serial # and stamped facsimile signatures. Paper: Manila.	—	—	—

	Good	Fine	XF
S1064 20 Centavos ND. Horse head at center facing left, Large leaf at left and right. Mimeographed. Back: Serial # and stamped facsimile signatures. Paper: Manila.	—	—	—

	Good	Fine	XF
S1065 50 Centavos ND. Dog head at center facing right, decorative border. Mimeographed. Back: Serial # and stamped facsimile signatures. Paper: Manila.	—	—	—

ND Second Issue

	Good	Fine	XF
S1075 50 Centavos ND. Purple. Ornamental design. Printed signature. Back: Serial #. Paper: White.	—	—	—
S1076 1 Peso ND. Purple. Ornamental design. Printed signature. Back: Serial #. Paper: White.	—	—	—

WWII Emergency & Guerrilla Currency

USAFFE Currency Board

ND First Issue

#S1081-S1084 mimeographed on Postal Money Order forms.

	Good	Fine	XF
S1081 1 Peso ND. Mimeographed. Back: *ONE PESO*. Paper: Pink Postal money order form.	—	—	—
S1082 1 Peso ND. Mimeographed. Back: *ONE PESO*. Paper: Yellow Postal money order form.	—	—	—
S1083 2 Pesos ND. Mimeographed. Back: *TWO PESOS*. Paper: Pink Postal money order form.	—	—	—
S1084 2 Pesos ND. Mimeographed. Back: *TWO PESOS*. Paper: Yellow Postal money order form.	—	—	—

ND Second Issue

	Good	Fine	XF
S1085 1 Peso ND. Mimeographed. Serial #00001 to 01,100. Back: *ONE PESO*. Paper: Manila.	—	—	—
S1086 2 Pesos ND. Mimeographed. Serial #00001 to 01,100. Back: *TWO PESOS*. Paper: Manila.	—	—	—

Free Samar Currency Committee

1943 Treasury Emergency Currency Certificate Issue

AUSA Free Samar 1943

	Good	Fine	XF
S1090 20 Centavos			
1943. Serial #A0001 to A50,000. Back: Facsimile signature stamped in purple.			
a. White document paper.	12.00	25.00	75.00
b. Off-white document or ledger paper.	12.00	25.00	75.00
c. Manila document paper.	15.00	30.00	90.00
S1091 50 Centavos			
1943. *SERIES OF 1943* in 2 lines at top. Serial #A0001 to A20,000. Back: Stamped signature in black.			
a. White paper.	25.00	50.00	150.
b. Brown paper.	25.00	50.00	150.
S1092 50 Centavos			
1943. *Series of 1943* in 1 line at top. Serial # B0001 to B20,000. Back: Stamped signature in black. Paper: Manila or brown.	20.00	40.00	120.
S1093 50 Centavos			
1943. *Series of 1943* in 1 line. Inverted border. Serial #C0001 to C20,000. Back: Stamped signature in purple. Paper: Manila or brown.	25.00	50.00	150.

	Good	Fine	XF
S1094 1 Peso			
1943. Neat *FREE SAMAR* 3mm high. Serial #A0001 to A10,000. Back: Large facsimile signature stamped in black. Paper: Manila or brown.	12.00	25.00	75.00
S1095 1 Peso			
1943. Crude *FREE SAMAR* 2mm high. Serial #B0001 to B10,000; C0001 to C10,000; D0001 to D10,000; E0001 to E10,000. Back: Small facsimile signature stamped in purple. Paper: Manila or brown.	12.00	25.00	75.00
S1096 2 Pesos			
1943. *FREE SAMAR* 2mm high. Serial #A0001 to (approx.) A5,200. Paper: Manila or brown.			
a. Large facsimile signature on back. Serial #0001 to (approx.) 4,900.	20.00	40.00	120.
b. Small facsimile signature on back. Serial # (approx.) 5,000 to 5,200.	—	—	—

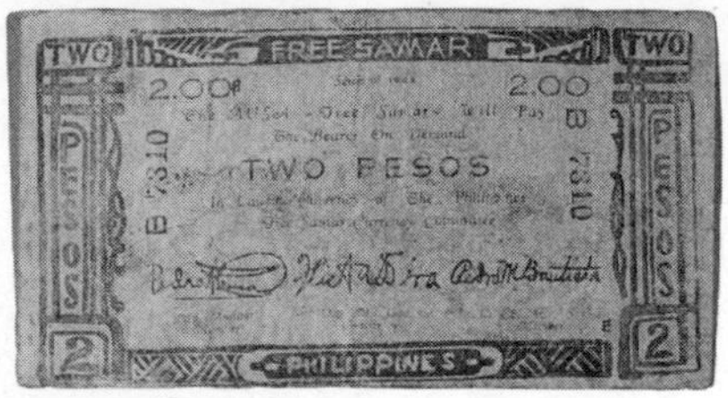

	Good	Fine	XF
S1097 2 Pesos			
1943. *FREE SAMAR* 3 1/2mm high. Serial # (approx.) A5,201 to A10,000; B0001 to B10,000. Back: Small purple facsimile signature. Paper: Thin to thick brown.	15.00	30.00	90.00
S1098 5 Pesos			
1943. *FREE SAMAR* 4mm high. Serial #A0001 to (approx.) A1,000. Back: Large facsimile signature in black. Paper: White.	—	—	—
S1099 5 Pesos			
1943. *FREE SAMAR* 2mm high. Serial # (approx.) A2,300 to A10,000; B0001 to B10,000; C0001 to (approx.) C4,000. Back: Large signature as #S1098. Paper: Manila or brown.	12.00	25.00	75.00
S1100 5 Pesos			
1943. Crude *FREE SAMAR* 3mm high. Serial # (approx.) C4,300 to C10,000. Back: Small purple facsimile signature. Paper: Manila or brown.	15.00	30.00	90.00

NOTE: Some denominations may be found with serial # either 3-1/2 or 4mm high.

Free Samar Currency Board

1943 Treasury Emergency Currency Certificate Issue

	Good	Fine	XF
S1101 10 Centavos			
1943. Serial # for S1101 and S1102: A 0,001 to 60,000. Back: Denomination in black.			
a. White document paper.	15.00	30.00	90.00
b. Off-white document paper.	15.00	30.00	90.00
c. Manila paper.	15.00	30.00	90.00
S1102 10 Centavos			
1943. Serial # mixed with #S1101. Back: Denomination in purple. Paper: Off-white.	—	—	—
S1103 20 Centavos			
1943. Serial #A 0,001 to 50,000. Back: Denomination in black.			
a. White document paper.	10.00	20.00	60.00
b. Manila paper.	10.00	20.00	60.00
x. Error; denomination omitted from back.	—	—	—
S1105 50 Centavos			
1943. Serial #A 0,001 to 20,000; B 0,001 to 20,000; C 0,001 to 20,000. Paper: Manila.	10.00	20.00	60.00
S1106 1 Peso			
1943. Serial #A 0,001 to 10,000; B 0,001 to 10,000; C 0,001 to 10,000; D 0,001 to 10,000; E 0,001 to 10,000. Paper: Manila or brown.	10.00	20.00	60.00
S1107 2 Pesos			
1943. Neat border plate. Serial #A 0,001 to 10,000; B 0,001 to 10,000; C 0,001 to (approx.) 8,000. Paper: Manila.	10.00	20.00	60.00
S1108 2 Pesos			
1943. Worn border plate, blurred printing. Serial #C (approx.) 8,001 to 10,000; D 0,001 to 10,000. Paper: Manila.	10.00	20.00	60.00
S1109 2 Pesos			
1943. New, neat border plate. Serial #E 0,001 to 10,000. Paper: Manila.	7.50	15.00	45.00

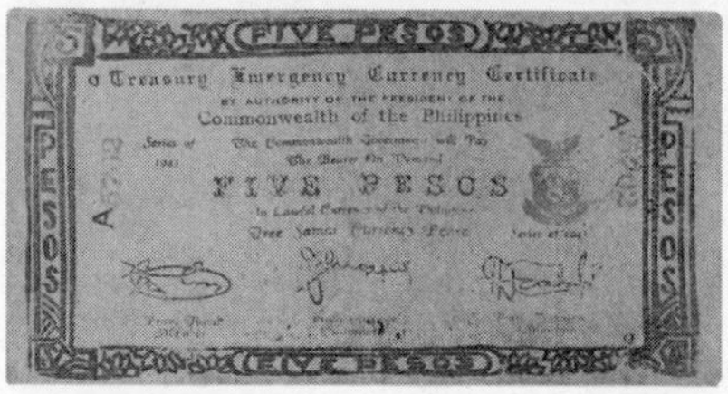

	Good	Fine	XF
S1110 5 Pesos			
1943. *FIVE PESOS* at top 3mm high. Serial # (series A, low numbers). Paper: Manila.	—	—	—

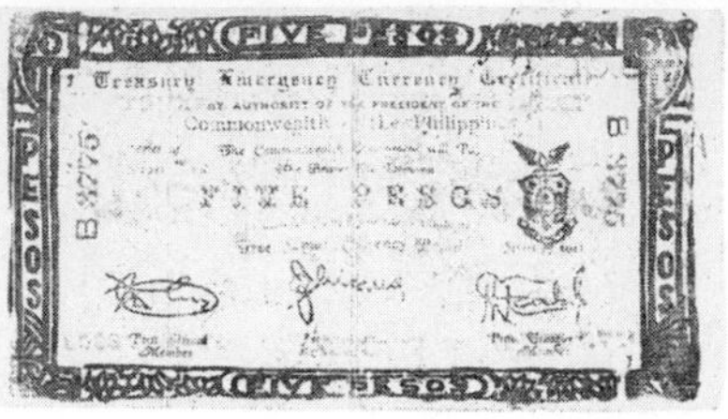

	Good	Fine	XF
S1111 5 Pesos			
1943. Worn plate, blurred printing. Border line above *PESOS* at top slopes downward. Serial # (series A, high numbers; series B, low numbers). Paper: Manila or brown.	12.00	25.00	75.00
S1112 5 Pesos			
1943. Badly worn plate, blurred printing. Line above *PESOS* at top is horizontal. Serial # (series B, high numbers). Paper: Manila or brown.	—	—	—

NOTE: On #S1110-S1112 serial # A 0,001 to 10,000; B 0,001 to 10,000.

	Good	Fine	XF
S1113 5 Pesos			
1943. New, neat border plate. *FIVE PESOS* at top is 3 3/4mm high. Serial #C 0,001 to 10,000; D 0,001 to 10,000; E 0,001 to 10,000.			
a. White paper.	12.00	25.00	75.00
b. Manila paper.	12.00	25.00	75.00
S1114 10 Pesos			
1943. Serial #A 0,001 to 10,000; B 0,001 to 10,000; C 0,001 to 10,000; D 0,001 to 10,000; E 0,001 to 10,000. Back: Winged *X* at center. Paper: Brown.	10.00	20.00	60.00

NOTE: Serial # on all denominations may be either 3-1/2 or 4mm high. They are not listed as sub-varieties because those printed in red are often faded to the point of illegibility.

1944 Issue

	Good	Fine	XF
S1116 1 Peso			
1944. Serial #F 0,001 to 10,000. Back: New design. Paper: Manila or brown.	12.00	25.00	75.00
S1117 2 Pesos			
1944. Serial #F 0,001 to 10,000; G 0,001 to 10,000; H 0,001 to 10,000; I 0,001 to 10,000; J 0,001 to 10,000. Back: New design. Paper: Manila or brown.	12.00	25.00	75.00
S1118 5 Pesos			
1944. Serial #F 0,001 to 10,000. Paper: White.	12.00	25.00	75.00
S1119 10 Pesos			
1944. Serial #F 0,001 to 6,000. Paper: Brown.	15.00	30.00	90.00
S1120 20 Pesos			
1944. Serial #A 0,001 to 10,000; B 0,001 to 2,500. Back: Denominational guilloche in red. Paper: White.	12.00	25.00	75.00

Free Sulu Provincial Government

1943 Tubig-Indangan Issue

	Good	Fine	XF
S1132 2 Centavos			
26.4.1943. Mimeographed. Dated Tubig-Indangan, Sulu April 26, 1943. Both mimeographed and pen signature of Harun Alibasa, Treasurer. Back: *2¢*. Paper: White. Rare.	—	—	—

125th Infantry Regiment

1943 Emergency Money Issue

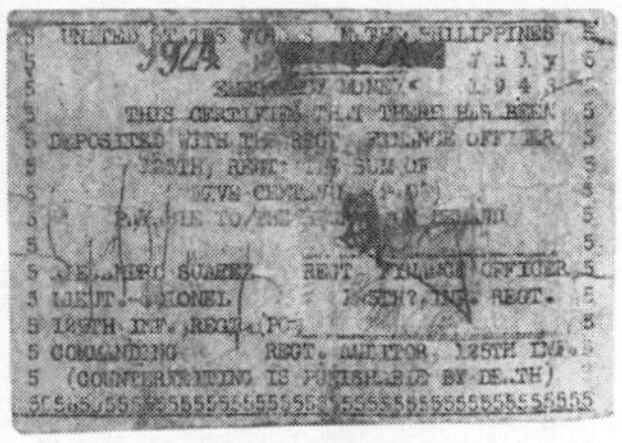

	Good	Fine	XF
S1141 5 Centavos July 1943. Mimeographed. Stamped with crude cut of an eagle. Mimeographed signature of Col. Suarez, pen signature of Regimental Finance Officer and Auditor. Back: *5*. Paper: White. Rare.	—	—	—
S1143 20 Centavos July 1943. Mimeographed. Stamped with crude cut of an eagle. Mimeographed signature of Col. Suarez, pen signature of Regimental Finance Officer and Auditor. Back: *20*. Paper: White. Rare.	—	—	—
S1144 50 Centavos Dec. 1943. Mimeographed. Stamped with crude cut of an eagle. Mimeographed signature of Col. Suarez, pen signature of Regimental Finance Officer and Auditor. Back: *50*. Paper: White. Rare.	—	—	—
S1145 1 Peso Dec. 1943. Mimeographed. Stamped with crude cut of an eagle. Mimeographed signature of Col. Suarez, pen signature of Regimental Finance Officer and Auditor. Back: *P1.00*. Paper: White. Rare.	—	—	—

Zamboanga City Issues

1942 Series A Issue

	Good	Fine	XF
S1161 50 Centavos 1942. Green. Signed by Cashier Rafael Peredes, Sr. for Manager, and by Accountant Mateo Paulino, of Philippine National Bank.	—	—	—
S1162 1 Peso 1942. Red. Signed by Cashier Rafael Peredes, Sr. for Manager, and by Accountant Mateo Paulino, of Philippine National Bank.	—	—	—
S1163 2 Pesos 1942. Blue. Signed by Cashier Rafael Peredes, Sr. for Manager, and by Accountant Mateo Paulino, of Philippine National Bank.	—	—	—
S1164 5 Pesos 1942. Black. Signed by Cashier Rafael Peredes, Sr. for Manager, and by Accountant Mateo Paulino, of Philippine National Bank.	—	—	—
S1165 10 Pesos 1942. Black. Signed by Cashier Rafael Peredes, Sr. for Manager, and by Accountant Mateo Paulino, of Philippine National Bank.	—	—	—

1942 Series B Issue

	Good	Fine	XF
S1166 50 Centavos 1942. Green. Signed by Assistant City Treasurer L. R. Barinaca and City Auditor Jose G. Concepcion.	—	—	—
S1167 1 Peso 1942. Red. Signed by Assistant City Treasurer L. R. Barinaca and City Auditor Jose G. Concepcion.	—	—	—
S1168 2 Pesos 1942. Blue. Signed by Assistant City Treasurer L. R. Barinaca and City Auditor Jose G. Concepcion.	—	—	—
S1169 5 Pesos 1942. Black. Signed by Assistant City Treasurer L. R. Barinaca and City Auditor Jose G. Concepcion.	—	—	—
S1170 10 Pesos 1942. Black. Signed by Assistant City Treasurer L. R. Barinaca and City Auditor Jose G. Concepcion. Reported not confirmed.	—	—	—

1942 Series C Issue

	Good	Fine	XF
S1171 50 Centavos 1942. Green.			
a. Signed by Cashier and Agent.	40.00	80.00	240.
b. Signed by Cashier and *for* Agent.	40.00	80.00	240.

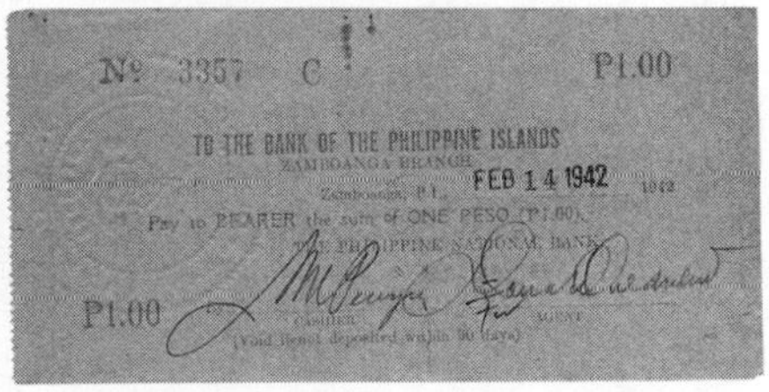

	Good	Fine	XF
S1172 1 Peso 1942. Red.			
b. Signed by Cashier and *for* Agent.	—	—	—
S1173 2 Pesos 1942. Blue.			
b. Signed by Cashier and *for* Agent.	—	—	—
S1174 5 Pesos 1942. Black.			
a. Signed by Cashier and Agent.	—	—	—
b. Signed by Cashier and *for* Agent.	—	—	—
S1175 10 Pesos 1942. Black. Reported not confirmed.	—	—	—

1942 Series D Issue

#S1176-S1180 two different date stamps used, 3-1/2mm high and 5mm high.

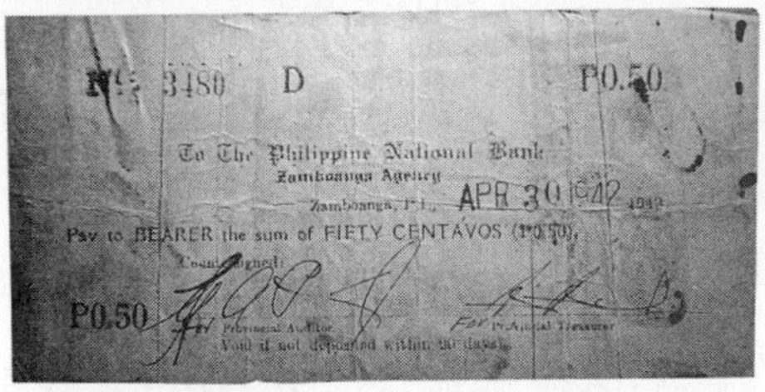

	Good	Fine	XF
S1176 50 Centavos 1942. Green.			
a. Signed by Provincial Treasurer Lazaro J. Agapito, and *for* Provincial Auditor. Serial #0,001 to (approx.) 0.812.	—	—	—
b. Signed *for* Provincial Treasurer stamped facsimile signature in violet of Provincial Auditor. (Only #1001 seen).	—	—	—
c. Signed *for* Provincial Treasurer, and *for* Provincial Auditor. Serial # (approx.) 1,398 upward.	—	—	—
S1177 1 Peso 1942. Red.			
c. Signed *for* Prov. Treasurer, and *for* Prov. Auditor.	—	—	—
S1178 2 Pesos 1942. Blue.			
c. Signed *for* Prov. Treasurer, and *for* Prov. Auditor.	—	—	—
S1179 5 Pesos 1942. Black.			
c. Signed *for* Prov. Treasurer, and *for* Prov. Auditor.	—	—	—
S1180 10 Pesos 1942. Black. Reported not confirmed.	—	—	—

Zamboanga Province Issue

Philippine National Bank - Zamboanga

1942 Emergency Circulating Note Issue

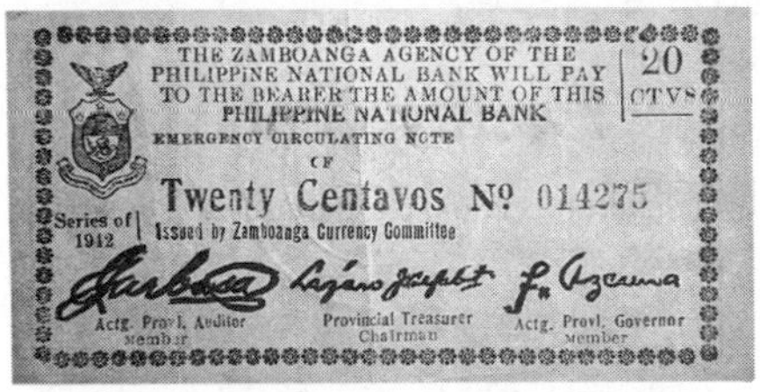

	Good	Fine	XF
S1181 20 Centavos 1942. Serial #000,001 to 020,000. Paper: Manila.	—	—	—
S1182 50 Centavos 1942. Serial #000,001 to 020,000. Paper: Manila.	60.00	120.	360.
S1183 1 Peso 1942. Serial #000,001 to 030,000. Paper: White.			
a. *"Porvl."* Governor (misspelling). Highest Serial # seen - 000457.	—	—	—
b. Corrected spelling. Lowest Serial # seen - 001257.	60.00	120.	360.
x. Counterfeit.	—	—	—

The Republic of Poland, formerly the Polish Peoples Republic, located in central Europe, has an area of 120,725 sq. mi. (312,677 sq. km.) and a population of 38.73 million. Capital: Warsaw. The economy is essentially agricultural, but industrial activity provides the products for foreign trade. Machinery, coal, coke, iron, steel and transport equipment are exported.

Poland is an ancient nation that was conceived near the middle of the 10th century. Its golden age occurred in the 16th century. During the following century, the strengthening of the gentry and internal disorders weakened the nation. In a series of agreements between 1772 and 1795, Russia, Prussia, and Austria partitioned Poland amongst themselves. Poland regained its independence in 1918 only to be overrun by Germany and the Soviet Union in World War II. It became a Soviet satellite state following the war, but its government was comparatively tolerant and progressive. Labor turmoil in 1980 led to the formation of the independent trade union "Solidarity" that over time became a political force and by 1990 had swept parliamentary elections and the presidency. A "shock therapy" program during the early 1990s enabled the country to transform its economy into one of the most robust in Central Europe, but Poland still faces the lingering challenges of high unemployment, underdeveloped and dilapidated infrastructure, and a poor rural underclass. Solidarity suffered a major defeat in the 2001 parliamentary elections when it failed to elect a single deputy to the lower house of Parliament, and the new leaders of the Solidarity Trade Union subsequently pledged to reduce the Trade Union's political role. Poland joined NATO in 1999 and the European Union in 2004. With its transformation to a democratic, market-oriented country largely completed, Poland is an increasingly active member of Euro-Atlantic organizations.

RULERS:

Stanislaw Augustus, 1764-1795
Fryderyk August I, King of Saxony, as Grand Duke, 1807-1814
Alexander I, Czar of Russia, as King, 1815-1825
Nikolaj (Mikolay) I, Czar of Russia, as King, 1825-1855

MONETARY SYSTEM:

1 Marka = 100 Fenigow to 1919
1 Zloty = 100 Groszy, 1919-

FOREIGN EXCHANGE CERTIFICATES

PEKAO TRADING CO. (P.K.O.) / BANK POLSKA

BON TOWAROWY (TRADE VOUCHER)

1960 FIRST SERIES

#FX1-FX10 serial # prefix A; B.

		VG	VF	UNC
FX1	**1 Cent** 1960. Pale blue and lilac. Serial # prefix A; B.	1.50	4.50	7.50
FX2	**5 Cents** 1960. Serial # prefix A; B.	10.00	17.50	30.00
FX3	**10 Cents** 1960. Serial # prefix A; B.	5.00	12.00	20.00
FX4	**50 Cents** 1960. Serial # prefix A; B.	8.00	20.00	35.00
FX5	**1 Dollar** 1960. Serial # prefix A; B.	—	—	—
FX6	**5 Dollars** 1960. Serial # prefix A; B.	—	—	—
FX7	**10 Dollars** 1960. Serial # prefix A; B.	—	—	—
FX8	**20 Dollars** 1960. Serial # prefix A; B.	50.00	—	—
FX9	**50 Dollars** 1960. Serial # prefix A; B.	—	—	—
FX10	**100 Dollars** 1960. Serial # prefix A; B.	—	—	—

1960 SECOND SERIES

#FX11-FX20 similar to #FX1-FX10 but with text on modified backs. Serial # prefix C; D.

		VG	VF	UNC
FX11	**1 Cent** 1960. Serial # prefix C; D.	2.50	6.00	10.00
FX12	**5 Cents** 1960. Serial # prefix C; D.	7.50	18.00	30.00
FX13	**10 Cents** 1960. Serial # prefix C; D.	5.00	12.00	20.00
FX14	**50 Cents** 1960. Serial # prefix C; D.	8.00	20.00	35.00
FX15	**1 Dollar** 1960. Serial # prefix C; D.	7.50	18.00	30.00
FX16	**5 Dollars** 1960. Serial # prefix C; D.	12.00	30.00	—
FX17	**10 Dollars** 1960. Serial # prefix C; D.	15.00	40.00	—
FX18	**20 Dollars** 1960. Serial # prefix C; D.	20.00	50.00	—
FX19	**50 Dollars** 1960. Serial # prefix C; D.	40.00	100.	—
FX20	**100 Dollars** 1960. Serial # prefix C; D.	80.00	200.	—

1969 SERIES

#FX21-FX33 serial # prefix E; F; G.

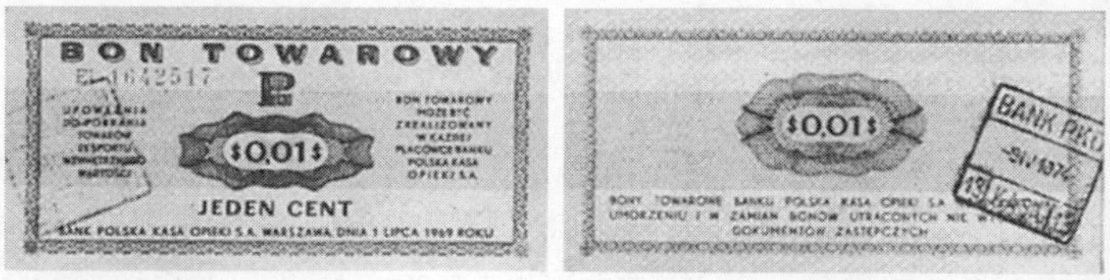

		VG	VF	UNC
FX21	**1 Cent** 1969. Black and blue on pale blue underprint. Back: Brown on pale blue underprint.	1.25	3.00	5.00

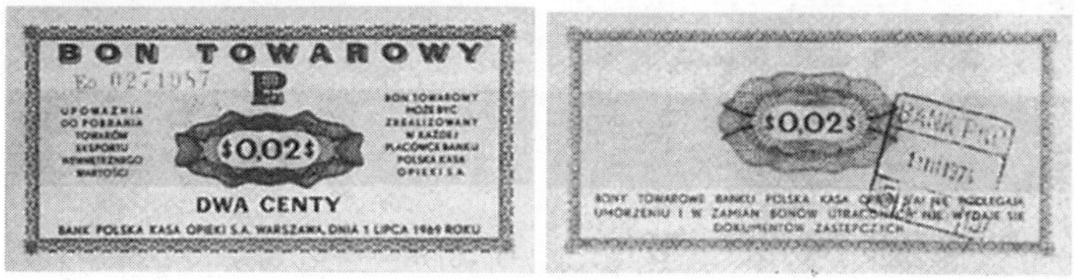

		VG	VF	UNC
FX22	**2 Cents** 1969. Black and green on orange and pink underprint. Back: Red on pink underprint.	1.25	3.00	5.00

		VG	VF	UNC
FX23	**5 Cents** 1969. Black on orange underprint. Back: Brown on orange underprint.	1.50	4.50	7.50

		VG	VF	UNC
FX24	**10 Cents** 1969. Blue and black on orange and yellow underprint. Back: Olive on yellow underprint.	2.50	6.00	10.00
FX25	**20 Cents** 1969.	3.50	10.00	15.00
FX26	**50 Cents** 1969.	3.50	10.00	17.50
FX27	**1 Dollar** 1969. Brown and green on lilac and violet underprint.	5.00	12.50	20.00
FX28	**2 Dollars** 1969.	10.00	15.00	25.00
FX29	**5 Dollars** 1969.	10.00	25.00	—
FX30	**10 Dollars** 1969.	12.50	35.00	—
FX31	**20 Dollars** 1969.	17.50	45.00	—
FX32	**50 Dollars** 1969.	35.00	85.00	—
FX33	**100 Dollars** 1969.	100.	175.	—

1979 SERIES

#FX34-FX46 serial # prefix H; I.

		VG	VF	UNC
FX34	**1 Cent** 1979. Serial number prefix H; I.	.50	1.50	2.50

		VG	VF	UNC
FX35	**2 Cents** 1979. Brown on pink and tan underprint.	.75	1.75	3.00

		VG	VF	UNC
FX36	**5 Cents** 1979. Brown-violet on pale green and yellow underprint. Serial number prefix H; I. Back: Lilac on light green underprint.	1.00	2.50	4.00

		VG	VF	UNC
FX37	**10 Cents** 1979. Deep green on pink and lilac underprint.	1.00	2.75	4.50

		VG	VF	UNC
FX38	**20 Cents** 1979. Serial number prefix H; I.	1.25	3.00	5.00

		VG	VF	UNC
FX39	**50 Cents** 1979. Brown on orange and yellow underprint. Serial number prefix H; I. Back: red-brown on yellow underprint.	1.75	4.50	7.50
FX40	**1 Dollar** 1979. Olive-green on light blue and lilac underprint. Serial number prefix H; I.	3.00	7.50	12.50
FX41	**2 Dollars** 1979. Serial number prefix H; I.	5.00	12.00	20.00
FX42	**5 Dollars** 1979. Serial number prefix H; I.	5.00	15.00	35.00
FX43	**10 Dollars** 1979. Serial number prefix H; I.	12.00	30.00	50.00
FX44	**20 Dollars** 1979. Serial number prefix H; I.	17.50	45.00	80.00
FX45	**50 Dollars** 1979. Serial number prefix H; I.	30.00	75.00	125.
FX46	**100 Dollars** 1979. Serial number prefix H; I.	50.00	125.	200.

Marynarski Bon Towarowy

Seamen's Trade Vouchers

1973 Series

#FX47-FX52 winged anchor w/knot at l.

		VG	VF	UNC
FX47	**1 Cent** 1.7.1973. Winged anchor with knot at left.	4.00	10.00	—
FX48	**2 Cents** 1.7.1973. Winged anchor with knot at left.	5.00	12.50	—
FX49	**5 Cents** 1.7.1973. Winged anchor with knot at left.	6.00	15.00	—
FX50	**10 Cents** 1.7.1973. Winged anchor with knot at left.	7.00	17.50	—
		VG	VF	UNC
FX51	**20 Cents** 1.7.1973. Winged anchor with knot at left.	8.00	17.50	—
FX52	**50 Cents** 1.7.1973. Blue and green on green underprint. Winged anchor with knot at left. Back: Black on green underprint.	10.00	20.00	—
FX53	**1 Dollar** 1.7.1973.	15.00	25.00	—
FX54	**2 Dollars** 1.7.1973.	20.00	30.00	—
FX55	**5 Dollars** 1.7.1973.	25.00	40.00	—
FX56	**10 Dollars** 1.7.1973.	35.00	50.00	—

Note: Higher denominations may have been issued.

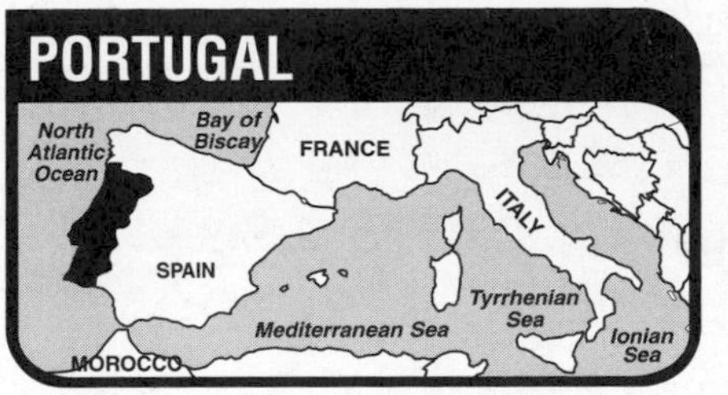

The Portuguese Republic, located in the western part of the Iberian Peninsula in southwestern Europe, has an area of 35,553 sq. mi. (91,905 sq. km.) and a population of 9.79 million. Capital: Lisbon. Portugal's economy is d on agriculture and a small but expanding industrial sector. Textiles, machinery, chemicals, wine and cork are exported.

Following its heyday as a global maritime power during the 15th and 16th centuries, Portugal lost much of its wealth and status with the destruction of Lisbon in a 1755 earthquake, occupation during the Napoleonic Wars, and the independence of its wealthiest colony of Brazil in 1822. A 1910 revolution deposed the monarchy; for most of the next six decades, repressive governments ran the country. In 1974, a left-wing military coup installed broad democratic reforms. The following year, Portugal granted independence to all of its African colonies. Portugal is a founding member of NATO and entered the EC (now the EU) in 1986.

RULERS:

Spanish, 1580-1640
Luis I, 1861-1889
Carlos I, 1889-1908
Manuel II, 1908-1910
Republic, 1910-

MONETARY SYSTEM:

1 Mil Reis = 1000 Reis to 1910
1 Escudo = 100 Centavos, 1910-2001
Note: Prata = Silver, Ouro = Gold.

BANKS

Banco Alliança . . . #S141-S145
Banco Commercial de Braga . . . #S151
Banco Commercial do Porto . . . #S161-S166
Banco de Guimarães . . . #S171-S174
Banco Industrial do Porto . . . #S181-S182
Banco de Lisboa . . . #S191-S248
Banco Mercantil Portuense . . . #S251-S258
Banco de Minho . . . #S261-S265
Banco Uniáo do Porto . . . #S271-S275

TREASURY FOR COMMODITIES

Contracto do Sabão . . . #S281
Contracto do Tabaco . . . #S291-S293

PUBLIC UTILITIES

A Empreza de Estrada de Lisboa Ao Porto . . . #S301
Nova Companhia de Utilidade Publica . . . #S311-S315

The later struggle for the Portuguese throne necessitated a reissue of the old imperial issues dated 1798, 1799, 1805 and 1807 w/red revalidation ovpt. of each of the warring brothers.

Banks

Banco Alliança

1870's Issue

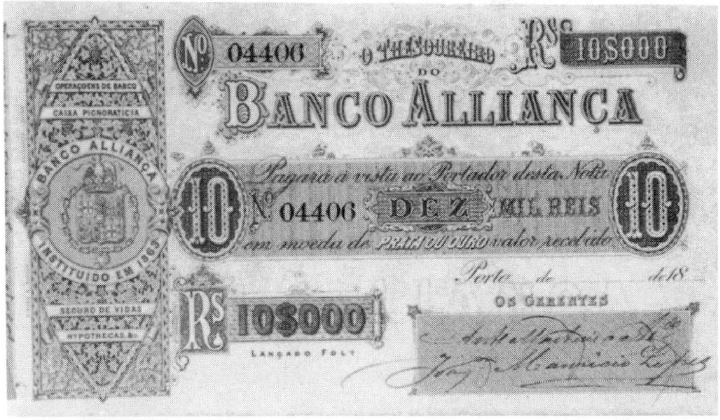

		Good	Fine	XF
S141	**10,000 Reis** 18xx (ca.1870). Red-brown. Arms at left. Printer: Nissen and Parker, London.	—	—	—
S142	**20,000 Reis** 18xx (ca.1870). Light red-brown. Arms at left. Printer: Nissen and Parker, London. Unissued remainder.	—	—	—
S143	**20,000 Reis** 18xx. Blue. Arms at left. Like #S142. Printer: Nissen and Parker, London.	—	—	—
S144	**50,000 Reis** 2.1.1873. Blue. Arms at left. Printer: Nissen and Parker, London.	—	—	—
S145	**100,000 Reis** 18xx (ca.1870). Orange. Arms at left. Printer: Nissen and Parker, London. Unissued remainder.	—	—	—

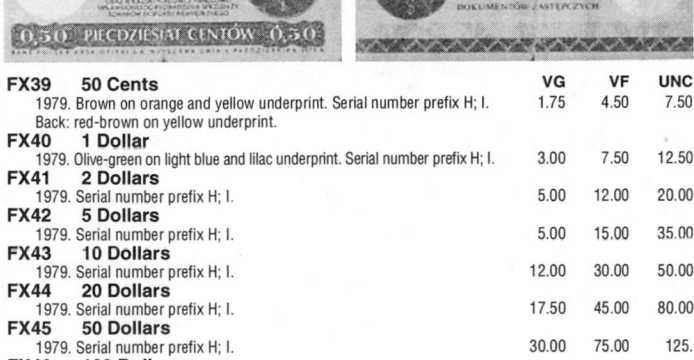

Banco Commercial de Braga

1870's Issue

		Good	Fine	XF
S151	**20,000 Reis** 18xx. Black and orange. Four cartouches and statue in counterfoil area at left.	—	—	—

Banco Commercial do Porto

1830's Issue

		Good	Fine	XF
S161	**10,000 Reis** 18xx. Black. Diamond-shaped inner border.	—	—	—
S162	**20,000 Reis** 18xx. Neptune at center.	—	—	—

		Good	Fine	XF
S163	**50,000 Reis** 4.4.1837. Blue. Ornate octagonal-shaped inner border, large leaves at upper corners.			
	a. Issued note.	—	—	—
	b. Handwritten cancellation.	—	—	—
S164	**100,000 Reis** 18xx. Mercury at center.	—	—	—

1859 Issue

		Good	Fine	XF
S165	**10,000 Reis** 31.12.1859. Helmeted Greek warrior with shield in counterfoil area at left, building at center.	—	—	—
S166	**50,000 Reis** 31.12.1859. Helmeted Greek warrior with shield in counterfoil area at left, large building at center. Printer: BWC.	—	—	—

Banco de Guimarães

1873; 1891 Issue

		Good	Fine	XF
S171	**5000 Reis** 1.6.1891. Black. Arms in counterfoil area at left. Paper: Blue-green.	—	—	—

NOTICE

Readers with unlisted dates, signature varieties, etc., are invited to submit photocopies or scans of their notes to:
Standard Catalog of World Paper Money,
700 East State St. Iola, WI 54990-0001,
E-Mail: george.cuhaj@fwmedia.com.

		Good	Fine	XF
S172	**10,000 Reis** 1.6.1891. Black. Arms in counterfoil area at left.	—	—	—
S173	**20,000 Reis** 4.11.1873. Black. Arms in counterfoil area at left. Paper: Yellow.	—	—	—
S174	**50,000 Reis** 4.11.1873. Green. Arms in counterfoil area at left.	—	—	—

Banco Industrial do Porto

1800's Issue

		Good	Fine	XF
S181	**10,000 Reis** 18xx. Green and orange. Building at upper center. Unissued remainder.	—	—	—
S182	**20,000 Reis** 18xx. Brown and purple. Sailing ships at upper center.	—	—	—

Banco de Lisboa

Bank of Lisbon

1820-46 Issues

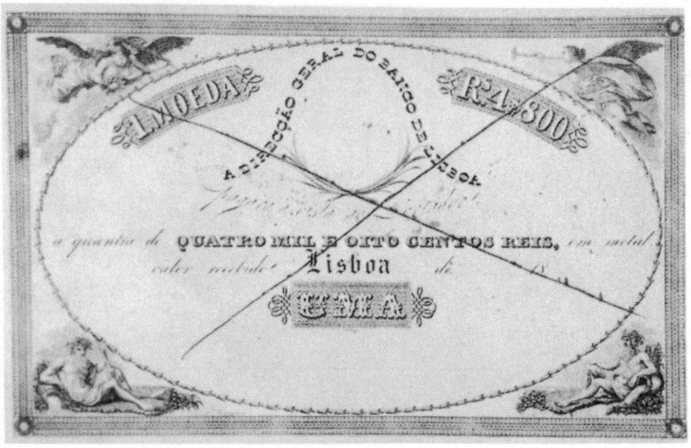

		Good	Fine	XF
S191	**1 Moeda = 4800 Reis** 18xx. Black. Allegorical vignette at each corner. Oval inner borders.	—	—	—
S192	**1 Moeda = 4800 Reis** 6.9.1839. Black. Allegorical vignette at each corner, and more embellishments in text over center. Oval inner borders.	—	—	—

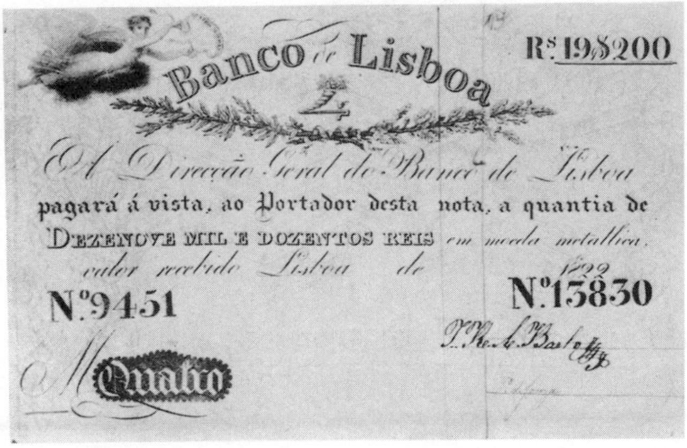

S193 1 Moeda = 4800 Reis

18xx. Black. Similar style to #S192, but 4 different vignettes at corners. Oval inner borders.

S194 1 Moeda = 4800 Reis

19.5.1843. Black. Elongated octagonal inner border, 4 different vignettes at corners.

S195 1 Moeda = 4800 Reis

1.5.1846. Black. Elongated octagonal inner border with thin eagle at upper center, standing allegorical woman at each corner.

S196 4 Moedas = 19,200 Reis

1822. Black. Justice standing at lower center.

	Good	Fine	XF
S193	—	—	—
S194	—	—	—
S195	—	—	—
S196	—	—	—

S197 4 Moedas = 19,200 Reis

1822. Black. Woman with barrel at upper left.

	Good	Fine	XF
S197	—	—	—

S198 4 Moedas = 19,200 Reis

1822. Allegorical winged woman with ribbon at upper left.

S199 4 Moedas = 19,200 Reis

1824. Black. Cherub with long ribbon of flowers across top.

	Good	Fine	XF
S198	—	—	—
S199	—	—	—

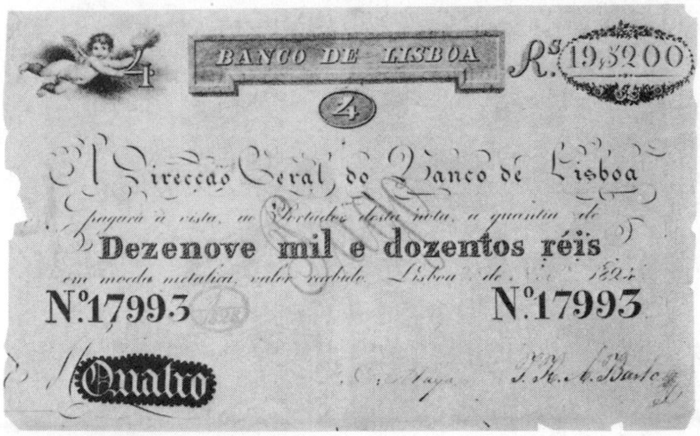

S200 4 Moedas = 19,200 Reis

20.11.1824. Black. Winged cherub at upper left.

S201 4 Moedas = 19,200 Reis

16.11.1825. Winged Mercury at upper left.

	Good	Fine	XF
S200	—	—	—
S201	—	—	—

S202 4 Moedas = 19,200 Reis

12.8.1836. Allegorical figure with torch at upper left, cherub with cornucopia at lower center.

S203 4 Moedas = 19,200 Reis

18xx. Black. Chapel at upper left.

	Good	Fine	XF
S202	—	—	—
S203	—	—	—

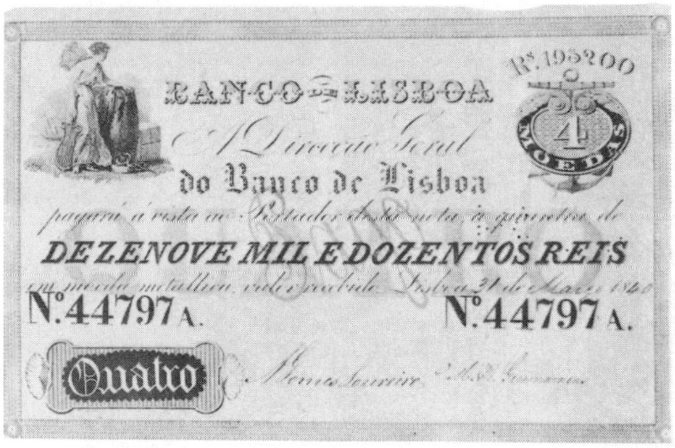

S204 4 Moedas = 19,200 Reis

31.3.1840. Allegorical figure with barrel and bale at upper left.

	Good	Fine	XF
S204	—	—	—

S205 4 Moedas = 19,200 Reis

26.3.1841. Black. Helmeted woman with trident at upper left.

	Good	Fine	XF
S205	—	—	—

	Good	Fine	XF
S206 4 Moedas = 19,200 Reis 18xx. Black. Woman in circle at upper left.	—	—	—
S207 10 Moedas = 48,000 Reis 4.8.1822. Bird at upper left.	—	—	—

	Good	Fine	XF
S208 10 Moedas = 48,000 Reis 1822. Value in wreath at upper left.	—	—	—
S209 10 Moedas = 48,000 Reis 1824. Seated allegorical woman with shield at upper center.	—	—	—
S210 10 Moedas = 48,000 Reis 17.11.1825. Two allegorical figures with cherub above at upper center.	—	—	—

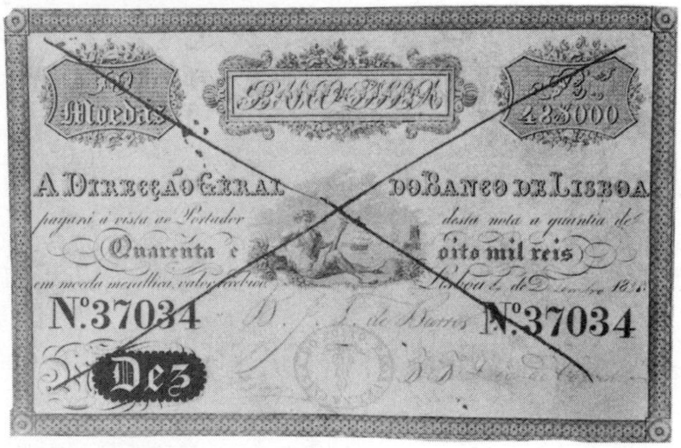

	Good	Fine	XF
S211 10 Moedas = 48,000 Reis 4.12.1838. Seated Neptune at center.	—	—	—
S212 10 Moedas = 48,000 Reis 21.4.1839. Three allegorical figures and cherub at center.	—	—	—

	Good	Fine	XF
S213 10 Moedas = 48,000 Reis 18xx. Neptune with other figures and sea horses at center, value in curved lines with cornucopias at upper left and right.	—	—	—

	Good	Fine	XF
S214 10 Moedas = 48,000 Reis 18xx. Neptune with other figures and sea horses at center, with cornucopias at upper left and right. Similar to #S213, but value in straight line at upper corners.	—	—	—
S215 10 Moedas = 48,000 Reis 21.1.1845. Scarred trees with church behind *(Invicta Serra Do Pilar)* at center.	—	—	—
S216 10 Moedas = 48,000 Reis 18xx. Large building with people at center.	—	—	—

	Good	Fine	XF
S217 20 Moedas = 96,000 Reis 182x. Allegorical woman with crown and caduceus at lower left center.	—	—	—

	Good	Fine	XF
S218 20 Moedas = 96,000 Reis 1822. Angel with cherubs at upper left.	—	—	—
S219 20 Moedas = 96,000 Reis 1825. Two allegorical figures at upper center.	—	—	—
S220 20 Moedas = 96,000 Reis 16.3.1833. Three cherubs with barrels and bales at upper center.	—	—	—

S221 50 Moedas = 240,000 Reis
1825. Cherubs with barrels and bales at center.

Good	Fine	XF
—	—	—

S222 100 Moedas = 480,000 Reis
1825. Neptune seated at center.

Good	Fine	XF
—	—	—

1840's Low Denomination Issues

S223 1200 Reis
18xx. Allegorical women with crowned shield at upper center.

Good	Fine	XF
—	—	—

S224 1200 Reis
10.12.1846; 12.12.1846; 1.10.1847. Black. Cherub at upper left and right, helmeted soldier at lower left, old man at lower right.

Good	Fine	XF
600.	1800.	—

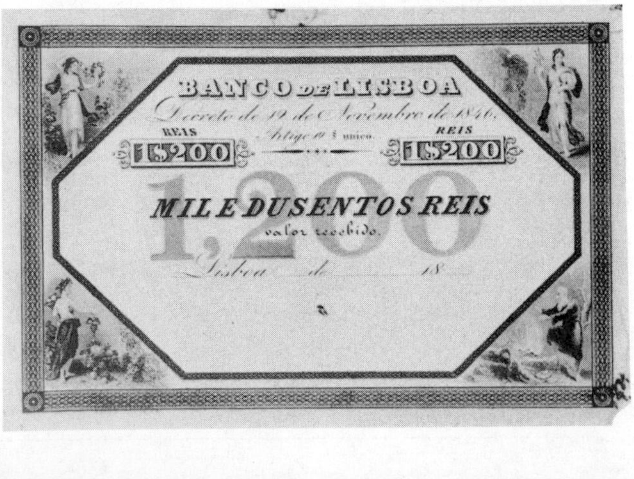

S225 1200 Reis
18xx. Standing figure in each corner.

Good	Fine	XF
—	—	—

1830's Cobre ou Bronze Issues

S226 4 Moedas = 19,200 Reis
183x. Red. Allegorical figure with box and cornucopia at upper left.

Good	Fine	XF
—	—	—

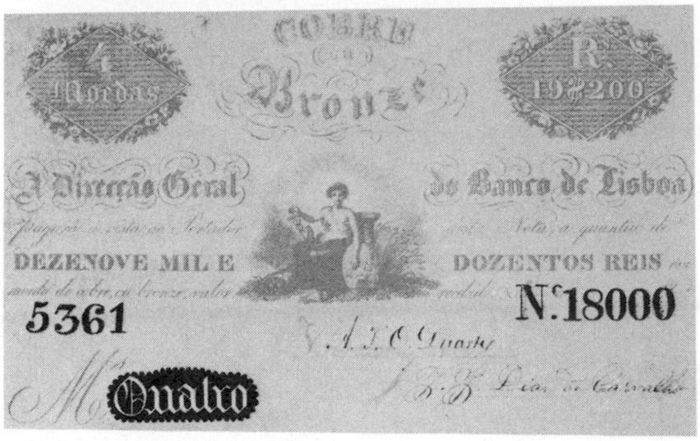

S227 4 Moedas = 19,200 Reis
18xx. Red. Seated figure with shield at center.

S228 4 Moedas = 19,200 Reis
18xx. Red. Two winged cherubs at center.

	Good	Fine	XF
S227	—	—	—
S228	—	—	—

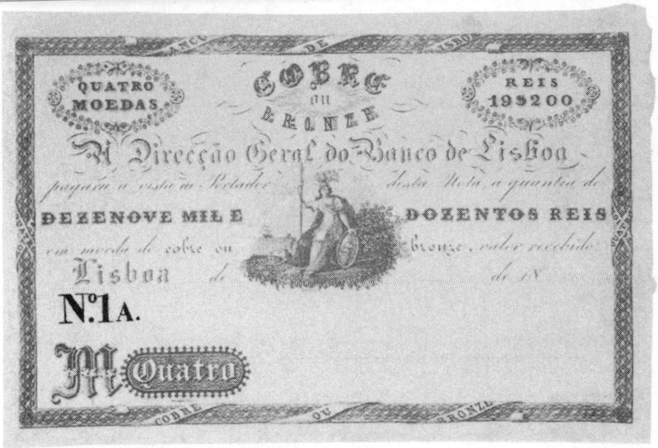

S229 4 Moedas = 19,200 Reis
18xx. Red. Helmeted woman with spear and shield at center.

S230 4 Moedas = 19,200 Reis
4.10.1845. Blue. Three allegorical women at center.

	Good	Fine	XF
S229	—	—	—
S230	—	—	—

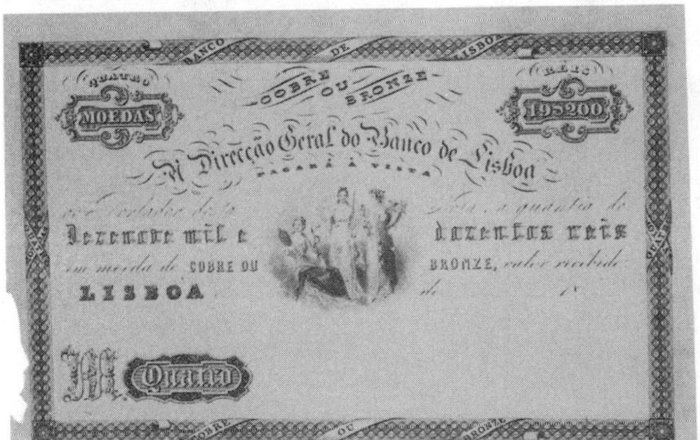

S231 4 Moedas = 19,200 Reis
18xx. Red. Three allegorical women at center. Like #S230.

S232 4 Moedas = 19,200 Reis
18xx. Black. Three allegorical women at center. Like #S230.

	Good	Fine	XF
S231	—	—	—
S232	—	—	—

		Good	Fine	XF
S233	**10 Moedas = 48,000 Reis** 183x. Blue. Two allegorical figures with small monument and bank name at center.	—	—	—
S234	**10 Moedas = 48,000 Reis** 183x. Black. Two cherubs with coin cornucopia at upper right.	—	—	—

		Good	Fine	XF
S235	**2400 Reis** D.19.11.1846. Crowned arms with barrel, plants and anchor at upper center.	—	—	—
S236	**1 Moeda = 4800 Reis** 5.12.1837. Blue. Value at lower left and upper right.	—	—	—
S237	**1 Moeda = 4800 Reis** 16.2.1841. Blue. Value at lower left and upper right. Similar to #S236, but many stylistic changes.	—	—	—
S238	**1 Moeda = 4800 Reis** 18.3.1842. Blue. Reclining women vertically at left, two cherubs with bales at upper center.	—	—	—

		Good	Fine	XF
S239	**1 Moeda = 4800 Reis** 30.9.1845. Blue. Seated Justice at left, two allegorical women with beehive, barrels and bales at upper center.	—	—	—
S240	**1 Moeda = 4800 Reis** 18xx. Blue. Winged allegorical woman at left, three allegorical women at upper center.	—	—	—

1833 ND Circulating Bearer Checks Issue

		Good	Fine	XF
S246	**9600 Reis** ND. *COBRE AU BRONZE - PAYABLE TO BEARER.*	—	—	—
S247	**14,400 Reis** 2.3.1833. *COBRE AU BRONZE - PAYABLE TO BEARER.*	—	—	—
S248	**10 Moedas = 48,000 Reis** ND. Cherub at left. *COBRE AU BRONZE - PAYABLE TO BEARER.*	—	—	—

Banco Mercantil Portuense

1830's Issue

		Good	Fine	XF
S251	**9000 Reis** 18xx. Green.	—	—	—
S252	**18,000 Reis** 18xx. Black.	—	—	—

1859-85 Issue

		Good	Fine	XF
S253	**50,000 Reis** 15.11.1859. Red and black. Arms in medallion at left.	—	—	—
S254	**100,000 Reis** 20.8.1863. Green. Arms in medallion at left.	—	—	—
S255	**10,000 Reis** 31.1.1885. Black. Arms in medallion at left. Back: Red-brown. Paper: Green.	—	—	—
S256	**20,000 Reis** 31.1.1885. Black. Arms in medallion at left. Back: Red-brown. Paper: Pink.	—	—	—
S257	**50,000 Reis** 7.2.1885. Blue. Arms in medallion at left. Back: Red-brown.	—	—	—

		Good	Fine	XF
S258	**100,000 Reis** 2.3.1885. Black. Arms in medallion at left. Back: Green.	—	—	—

Banco do Minho

1874; 1887 Issue

		Good	Fine	XF
S261	**2500 Reis** 1.4.1887. Black and green. Various scenes in five ornate cartouches in counterfoil area at left. Back: Brown. Paper: Yellowish.	—	—	—
S262	**5000 Reis** 1.7.1874. Black and blue. Various scenes in five ornate cartouches in counterfoil area at left. Back: Blue. Paper: Pink.	—	—	—
S263	**10,000 Reis** 1.4.1887. Black and red. Various scenes in five ornate cartouches in counterfoil area at left. Back: Black. Paper: Dark blue.	—	—	—
S264	**20,000 Reis** 1.4.1887. Black and blue. Various scenes in five ornate cartouches in counterfoil area at left. Back: Black.	—	—	—
S265	**50,000 Reis** 1.4.1887. Blue and orange. Various scenes in five ornate cartouches in counterfoil area at left. Back: Orange.	—	—	—

Banco Uniáo do Porto

1886-88 Issue

		Good	Fine	XF
S271	**10,000 Reis** 18xx. Blue. Hands clasping at top center.	—	—	—

#S272-S275 arms in counterfoil area at l.

		Good	Fine	XF
S272	**10,000 Reis** 2.5.1888. Black. Arms in counterfoil area at left. Paper: Yellow.	—	—	—
S273	**20,000 Reis** 2.5.1888. Black and blue. Arms in counterfoil area at left.	—	—	—
S274	**50,000 Reis** 18xx. Green. Arms in counterfoil area at left.	—	—	—
S275	**100,000 Reis** 7.6.1886. Red. Arms in counterfoil area at left.	—	—	—

Treasury For Commodities

Contracto do Sabão

Contract for Soap

1840's Issue

		Good	Fine	XF
S281	**1 Moeda = 4800 Reis** 18xx. Two cherubs at upper center.	—	—	—

Contracto do Tabaco

Contract for Tobacco

1840's Issue

		Good	Fine	XF
S291	**1 Moeda = 4800 Reis** 18xx. Allegorical woman with barrels blowing trumpet at upper center.	—	—	—
S292	**1 Moeda = 4800 Reis** 18xx. Two cherubs at center.	—	—	—

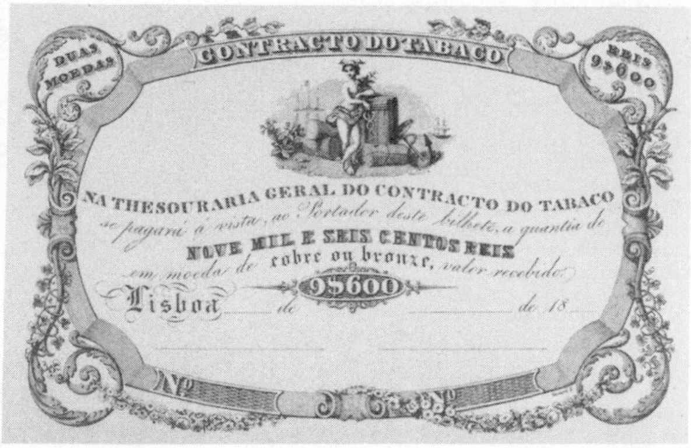

		Good	Fine	XF
S293	**9600 Reis** 18xx. Mercury with barrel at upper center.	—	—	—

Public Utilities

A Empreza de Estrada de Lisboa Ao Porto

Road Construction Lisbon to Porto

1840's Issue

		Good	Fine	XF
S301	**1 Moeda = 4800 Reis** 184x. Woman with plant, boxes and ships at upper center.	—	—	—

Nova Companhia Utilidade Pública

New Public Utilities Company

1877-89 Issue

		Good	Fine	XF
S311	**5000 Reis** 15.1.1877. Red. Boat and animals in river at upper center.	—	—	—
S312	**10,000 Reis** 20.4.1889. Black and blue. Factory row in vertical silhouette at left. Boat and animals in river at upper center. Back: Blue.	—	—	—
S313	**20,000 Reis** 1.5.1888. Black and green. Lumberyard vertically at left. Boat and animals in river at upper center. Back: Green.	—	—	—
S314	**50,000 Reis** 15.1.1877. Black. Boat and animals in river at upper center. Back: Purple.	—	—	—
S315	**100,000 Reis** 15.1.1877. Black and red. Boat and animals in river at upper center. Back: Red.	—	—	—

Sending Scanned Images by e-mail

We have been receiving an ever-increasing flow of scanned images from sources world wide. Unfortunately, many of these scans could not be used due to the type of scan, or simple incompatibility with our systems. We appreciate the effort it takes to produce these images and accuracy they add to the catalog listings.

Here are a few simple instructions to follow when producing these scans. We encourage you to continue sending new images or upgrades to those currently illustrated and please do not hesitate to ask questions about this process.

- Scan all images within a resolution of 300 dpi.
- Size setting should be at 100%
- Please include in the e-mail the actual size of the image in millimeters height x width
- Scan in true 4-color
- Save images as jpeg and name in such a way which clearly indentifies the country of the note and catalog number
- Do not compress files
- Please e-mail with a request to confirm receipt of the attachment
- Please send multiple images on a disc if available
- Please send images to: george.cuhaj@fwmedia.com

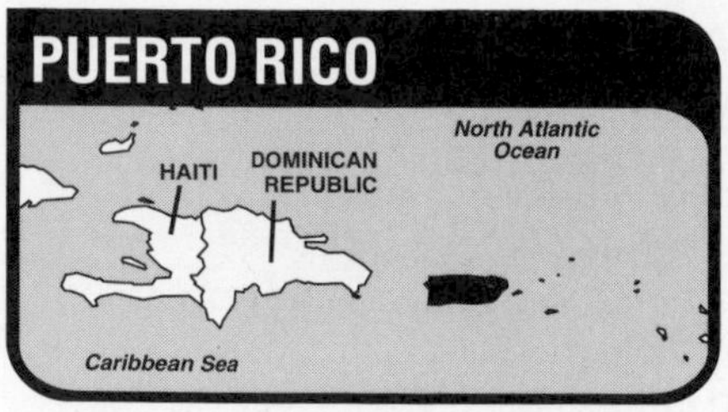

The Commonwealth of Puerto Rico, the easternmost island of the Greater Antilles in the West Indies, has an area of 3,435 sq. mi. (9,104 sq. km.) and a population of 3.3 million. Capital: San Juan. The commonwealth has its own constitution and elects its own governor. Its people are citizens of the United States, liable to the draft - but not to federal taxation. The chief industries of Puerto Rico are manufacturing, agriculture, and tourism. Manufactured goods, cement, dairy and livestock products, sugar, rum, and coffee are exported, mainly to the United States.

Puerto Rico ("Rich Port") was discovered by Columbus who landed on the island and took possession for Spain on Oct. 19, 1493 - the only time Columbus set foot on the soil of what is now a possession of the United States. The first settlement, Caparra, was established by Ponce de Leon in 1508. The early years of the colony were not promising. Considerable gold was found, but the supply was soon exhausted. Efforts to enslave the Indians caused violent reprisals. Hurricanes destroyed crops and homes. French, Dutch, and English freebooters burned the towns. Puerto Rico remained a Spanish possession until 1898, when it was ceded to the United States following the Spanish-American War. Puerto Ricans were granted a measure of self-government and U.S. citizenship in 1917. Effective July 25, 1952, a Congressional resolution elevated Puerto Rico to the status of a free commonwealth associated with the United States.

Vieque (or Crab Island), located to the east of Puerto Rico, is the largest of the Commonwealth's major offshore islands. The others are Culebra, a naval station to the east, and Mona to the west.

RULERS:

Spanish, 1493-1898 United States of America, 1898-present

MONETARY SYSTEM:

1 Peso = 5 Pesetas = 100 Centavos to 1898
1 Dollar = 100 Cents, 1898-

SPANISH ADMINISTRATION

COMPAÑIA DE LOS FERRO-CARRILES DE PUERTO RICO

PUERTO RICO RAILROAD COMPANY

1880 ND ISSUE

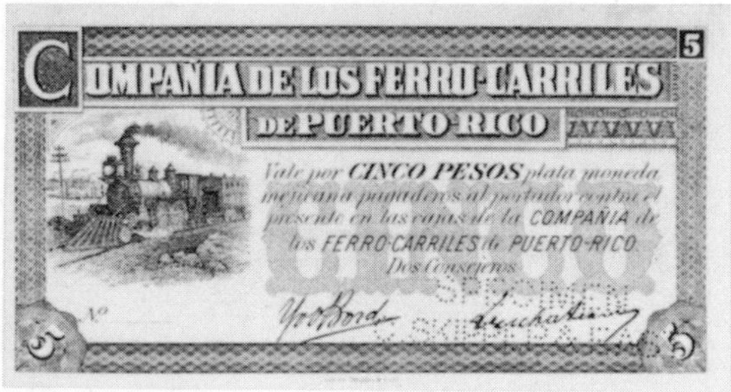

		VG	VF	UNC
S101	**5 Pesos**			
	ND (ca.1880). Black on orange underprint. Steam passenger train at left. Back: Blue. Printer: CS&E.			
	a. Issued note.	750.	2250.	—
	s1. Specimen.	—	—	2250.
	s2. Specimen. Without pinholes.	—	—	2500.

Note: Color proofs are known, but more information is needed.

LA CAJA DE AHORROS DE PONCE

SAVINGS BANK OF PONCE

ND ISSUE

		Good	Fine	XF
S107	**3 Pesos**			
	ND. Black on blue underprint. Minerva seated at top center. Similar to #S110. Rare.	—	—	—

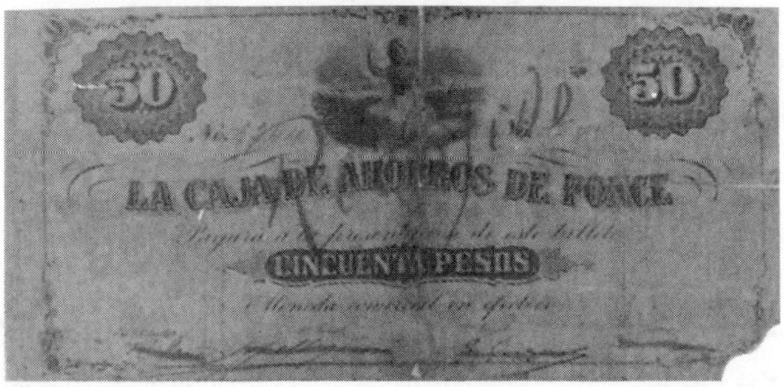

		Good	Fine	XF
S110	**50 Pesos**			
	ND. Black on red underprint. Minerva seated at top center. Rare.	—	—	—

U.S.A. NATIONAL BANKS

FIRST NATIONAL BANK OF PORTO RICO AT SAN JUAN

CHARTER #6484 - THIRD CHARTER PERIOD 1902-22

		Good	Fine	XF
S121	**10 Dollars**			
	1902. Black. Portrait William McKinley at left. Red seal at lower right. Back: Green. Without dates *1902-1908*. Rare.	—	—	—
S122	**20 Dollars**			
	1902. Black. H. McCulloch at left. Red seal at lower right. Back: Green. Without dates *1902-1908*. Rare.	—	—	—
S123	**50 Dollars**			
	1902. Black. Portrait J. Sherman at left. Red seal at lower right. Back: Green. Without dates *1902-1908*. Rare.	—	—	—

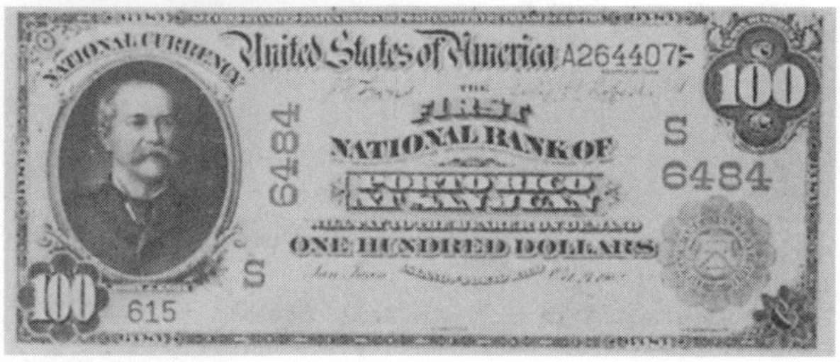

		Good	Fine	XF
S124	**100 Dollars**			
	27.10.1902. Black. Portrait J. J. Knox at left. Red seal at lower right. Back: Green. Without date. Rare.	—	—	—

1902-08 ISSUE

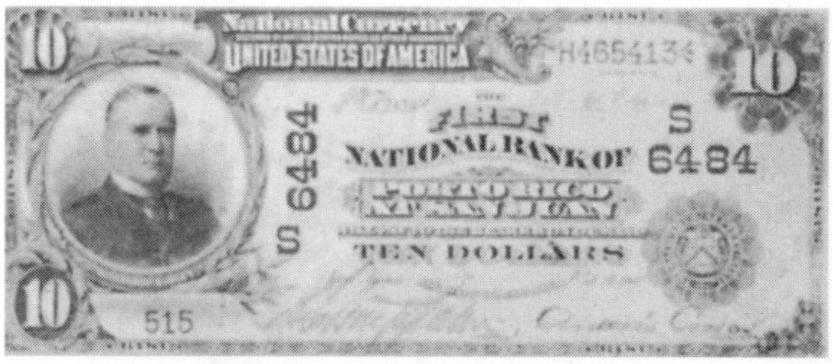

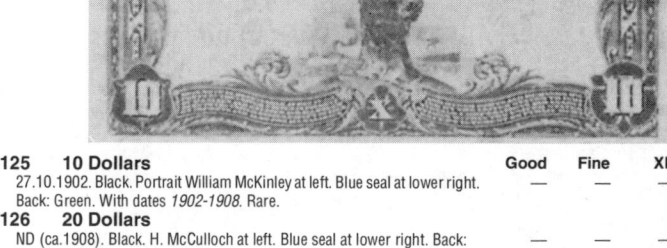

		Good	Fine	XF
S125	**10 Dollars**			
	27.10.1902. Black. Portrait William McKinley at left. Blue seal at lower right. Back: Green. With dates *1902-1908*. Rare.	—	—	—
S126	**20 Dollars**			
	ND (ca.1908). Black. H. McCulloch at left. Blue seal at lower right. Back: Green. With dates *1902-1908*. Rare.	—	—	—
S127	**50 Dollars**			
	ND (ca.1908). Black. Portrait J. Sherman at left. Blue seal at lower right. Back: Green. With dates *1902-1908*. Rare.	—	—	—
S128	**100 Dollars**			
	ND (ca.1908). Black. Portrait J. J. Knox at left. Blue seal at lower right. Back: Green. With dates *1902-1908*. Rare.	—	—	—

RHODESIA

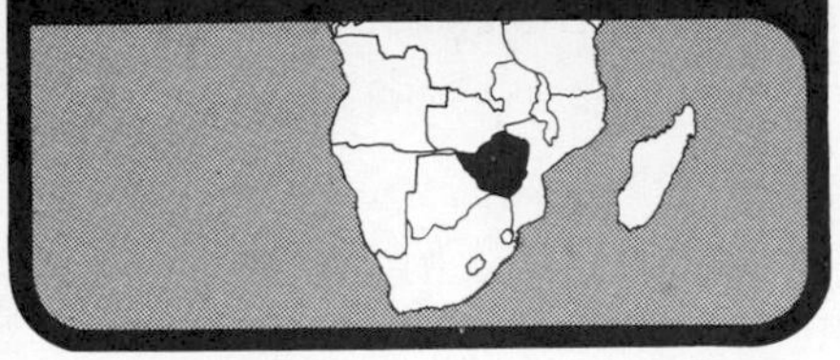

The "Republic of" Rhodesia (never recognized by the British government and was referred to as Southern Rhodesia, now Zimbabwe) located in the east-central part of southern Africa, has an area of 150,804 sq. mi. (390,580 sq. km.) and a population of 9.9 million. Capital: Harare. The economy is d on agriculture and mining. Tobacco, sugar, asbestos, copper and chrome ore and coal are exported.

The Rhodesian area, the habitat of paleolithic man, contains extensive evidence of earlier civilizations, notably the world-famous ruins of Zimbabwe, a gold-trading center that flourished about the 14th or 15th century AD. The Portuguese of the 16th century were the first Europeans to attempt to develop south-central Africa, but it remained for Cecil Rhodes and the British South Africa Co. to open the hinterlands. Rhodes obtained a concession for mineral rights from local chiefs in 1888 and administered his African empire (named Southern Rhodesia in 1895) through the British South Africa Co. until 1923, when the British government annexed the area after the white settlers voted for existence as a separate entity, rather than for incorporation into the Union of South Africa.

From Sept. of 1953 through 1963 Southern Rhodesia was joined with the British protectorates of Northern Rhodesia and Nyasaland into a multiracial federation. When the federation was dissolved at the end of 1963, Northern Rhodesia and Nyasaland became the independent states of Zambia and Malawi.

Britain was prepared to grant independence to Southern Rhodesia but declined to do so when the politically dominant white Rhodesians refused to give assurances of representative government. In November 1965, the white minority government of Southern Rhodesia unilaterally declared Southern Rhodesia an independent dominion. The United Nations and the British Parliament both proclaimed this unilateral declaration of independence null and void. Following a conference in London in December 1979, the opposition government conceded and it was agreed that the British government should resume control. In 1970, the government proclaimed a republic, but this too received no recognition. In 1979, the government purported to change the name of the Colony to Zimbabwe Rhodesia, but again this was never recognized. A British governor soon returned to Southern Rhodesia. One of his first acts was to affirm the nullification of the purported declaration of independence. On April 18, 1980, pursuant to an act of the British Parliament, the colony of Southern Rhodesia became independent within the commonwealth as the Republic of Zimbabwe.

RULERS:

British to 1970 (1980)

MONETARY SYSTEM:

1 Shilling = 12 Pence
1 Pound = 20 Shillings to 1970

BRITISH ADMINISTRATION

AFRICAN BANKING CORPORATION

BULAWAYO

1896 ISSUE

		Good	Fine	XF
S101	**10 Shillings** ND. Proof.	—	—	—

		Good	Fine	XF
S102	**1 Pound** ND (ca.1896). Allegorical woman's portrait at left. Back: Map of Africa at center. Printer: BWC. Payable at Cape Town. Specimen.	—	—	—
S103	**5 Pounds** ND (ca.1896). Cherubs holding allegorical woman's portrait at left. Back: Map of Africa at center. Printer: BWC. Payable at Cape Town. Specimen.	—	—	—
S104	**10 Pounds** ND (ca.1896). Prince standing at left. Back: Map of Africa at center. Printer: BWC. Payable at Cape Town. Specimen.	—	—	—

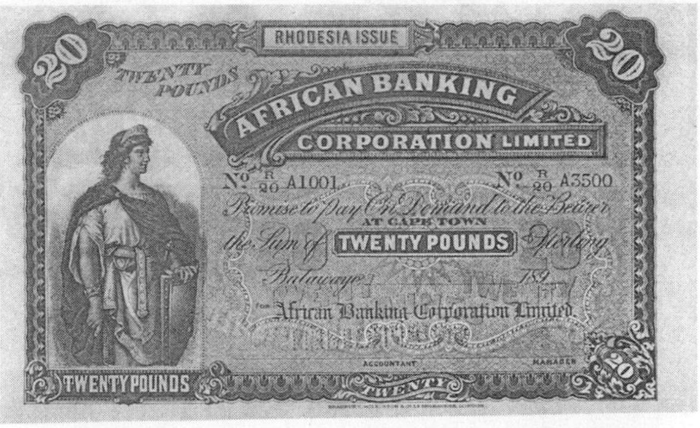

		Good	Fine	XF
S105	**20 Pounds** ND (ca.1896). *Africa* with shield at left. Back: Map of Africa at center. Printer: BWC. Payable at Cape Town. Specimen.	—	—	—

		Good	Fine	XF
S105A	**100 Pounds** ND (ca.1896). Allegorical woman with shield of Africa and lion at left. Back: Map of Africa at center. Printer: BWC. Payable at Cape Town. Specimen.	—	—	—

1920 ISSUE

		Good	Fine	XF
S105B	**1 Pound** ND (ca.1920). Springbok at upper center. Specimen.	—	—	—

BANK OF AFRICA LIMITED

1901 ISSUE

#S106 ovpt: *RHODESIA ISSUE* on Durban note.

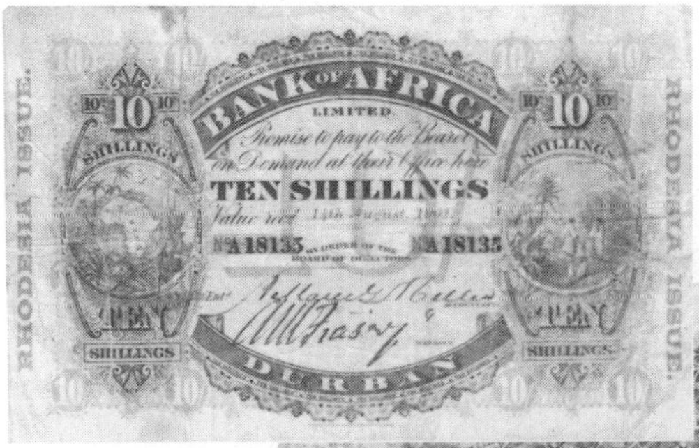

	Good	Fine	XF
S106 10 Shillings 1901. Black on olive underprint. Map of Africa in cartouche at left, field workers in cartouche at right. Back: Purple. Overprint: Red *RHODESIA ISSUE*. Printer: W&S.			
a. Large letters overprint: *RHODESIA ISSUE* at sides. 10.8.1901. Rare.	—	—	—
b. Small letters overprint at sides. 14.8.1901. Rare.	—	—	—

Barclays Bank (Dominion, Colonial and Overseas)

Salisbury

1926 Issue

#S111-S113 Ovpt. *RHODESIAN ISSUE* at upper margin.

	Good	Fine	XF
S111 10 Shillings 1.9.1926; 2.1.1928; 1.10.1931; 1.1.1936; 1.12.1936; 1.8.1938. Red and multicolor. Seated woman with sheep at left, Victoria Falls at right. Signature varieties. Back: Lion resting at bottom center. Overprint: *RHODESIAN ISSUE* at upper margin. Printer: W&S.			
a. Issued note.	225.	675.	2000.
s. Punched hole specimen.	—	Unc	1250.

	Good	Fine	XF
S112 1 Pound 1.9.1926; 1.12.1930; 1.6.1936; 1.9.1937. Blue and multicolor. Seated woman with sheep at left, Victoria Falls at right. Signature varieties. Back: Lion resting at bottom center. Overprint: *RHODESIAN ISSUE* at upper margin. Printer: W&S.			
a. Issued note.	250.	750.	2250.
s. Punched hole specimen.	—	Unc	1250.
S113 5 Pounds 1.9.1926. Green and multicolor. Seated woman with sheep at left, Victoria Falls at right. Signature varieties. Back: Lion resting at bottom center. Overprint: *RHODESIAN ISSUE* at upper margin. Printer: W&S.			
a. Issued note.	—	—	—
s. Punched hole specimen.	—	Unc	1250.

National Bank of South Africa Limited

1921 Provisional Issue

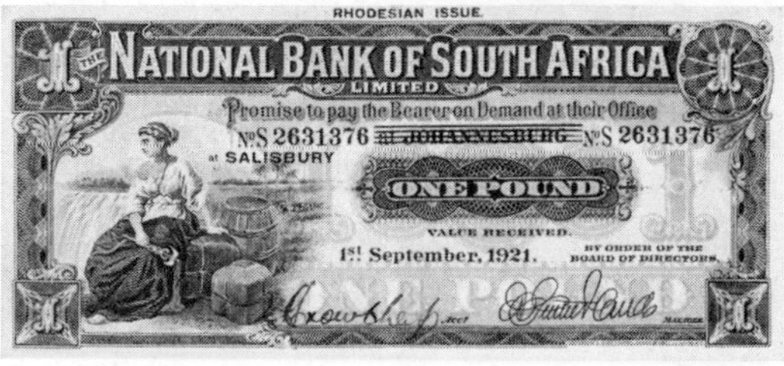

	Good	Fine	XF
S119 1 Pound ND (- old date 1.9.1921). Overprint: *RHODESIAN ISSUE* in upper margin on South Africa #S572. Printer: W&S.	450.	1350.	4000.

1922 Regular Issue

	Good	Fine	XF
S121 10 Shillings 1.7.1922. Green on red-orange underprint. Child with cornucopia at left. Back: Blue-gray. Head at center. Overprint: *RHODESIAN ISSUE* in upper margin. Printer: W&S.			
a. Issued note.	450.	1350.	4000.
s. Punched hole specimen.	—	Unc	1250.
S122 1 Pound 1.7.1922. Black and yellow. Seated woman at left, with Victoria Falls in background. Overprint: *RHODESIAN ISSUE* in upper margin. Printer: W&S.			
a. Issued note.	450.	1350.	4000.
s. Specimen. Punch hole cancelled.	—	Unc	1250.

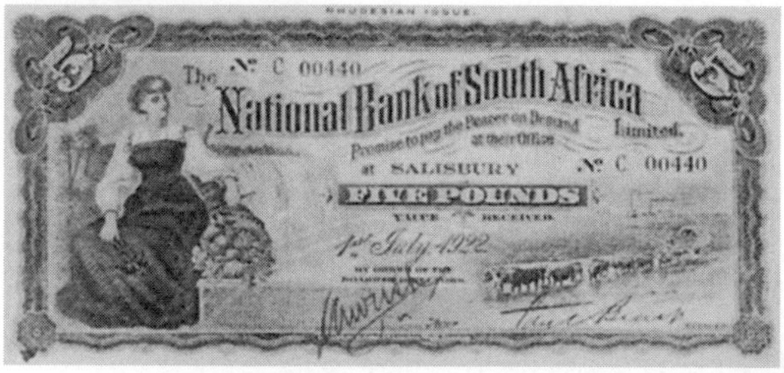

	Good	Fine	XF
S123 5 Pounds 1.7.1922. Blue, yellow and orange. Seated woman with cornucopia at left, Victoria Falls in background at left, cattle and wagon crossing stream at lower right. Back: Portrait woman at center. Overprint: *RHODESIAN ISSUE* in upper margin. Printer: W&S.			
a. Issued note.	—	—	—
s. Specimen. Punch hole cancelled.	—	Unc	1500.

Standard Bank of South Africa

1896 Provisional Issue

	Good	Fine	XF
S132 1 Pound 27.8.1896. Overprint: On Durban Branch Issues, South Africa. Rare.	—	—	—
S133 5 Pounds 27.8.1896. Overprint: On Durban Branch Issues, South Africa. Rare.	—	—	—
S134 10 Pounds 27.8.1896. Overprint: On Durban Branch Issues, South Africa. (Not issued.) Rare.	—	—	—

A WORD ON DATE RANGES

Often date ranges or specific dates are listed. These have been observed or reported by our contributors. If a note is outside the published range, it only means that it is a newly reported date, and not necessarily worthy of a premium value.

1911 Issue

S138 5 Pounds — Good / Fine / XF
1.8.1911; 13.12.1911; 8.7.1912; 1.5.1913. Black on yellow underprint. Standing Britannia with flag and shield at left. Various date and signature varieties. Overprint: *RHODESIAN ISSUE* at upper margin. Printer: W&S. Rare. — — —

1916 Issue

S139 5 Pounds — Good / Fine / XF
1916-17. Red. Statue of Jan Van Riebeeck at left, standing Britannia with flag and shield at right. Various date and signature varieties. Overprint: *RHODESIAN ISSUE* at upper margin. Printer: W&S.

	Good	Fine	XF
a. Issued note. 1.1.1917.	450.	1350.	4000.
s. Specimen. 1.12.1916.	—	Unc	1250.

1917-33 Issue

S146 10 Shillings — Good / Fine / XF
1917-38. Black, green and orange. Statue of Jan Van Riebeeck at left, *R* script letter at center, standing Britannia with flag at right. Various date and signature varieties. Back: Green. Overprint: *RHODESIAN ISSUE* at upper margin. Printer: W&S.

	Good	Fine	XF
a. 1.7.1917; 1.3.1920; 22.6.1925; 2.1.1928; 31.1.1930.	300.	900.	2700.
b. 3.12.1932; 17.11.1933; 4.4.1936; 5.4.1938.	175.	525.	1575.

1925; 1933 Issue

S147 1 Pound — Good 150. / Fine 450. / XF 1350.
30.6.1925; 30.6.1925; 30.9.1927; 30.6.1928-3.12.1937; 1938. Brown, green and multicolor. Standing Britannia with flag and shield at left. Various date and signature varieties. Back: Brown and black. Overprint: *RHODESIAN ISSUE* at upper margin. Printer: W&S.

S148 5 Pounds — Good — / Fine — / XF —
17.11.1933. Blue, black and multicolor. View of Johannesburg and bank. Various date and signature varieties. Overprint: *RHODESIAN ISSUE* at upper margin. Printer: W&S.

Romania, located in southeast Europe, has an area of 91,699 sq. mi. (237,500 sq. km.) and a population of 22.5 million. Capital: Bucharest. Machinery, foodstuffs, raw minerals and petroleum products are exported.

The principalities of Wallachia and Moldavia - for centuries under the suzerainty of the Turkish Ottoman Empire - secured their autonomy in 1856; they united in 1859 and a few years later adopted the new name of Romania. The country gained recognition of its independence in 1878. It joined the Allied Powers in World War I and acquired new territories - most notably Transylvania - following the conflict. In 1940, Romania allied with the Axis powers and participated in the 1941 German invasion of the USSR. Three years later, overrun by the Soviets, Romania signed an armistice. The post-war Soviet occupation led to the formation of a Communist "people's republic" in 1947 and the abdication of the king. The decades-long rule of dictator Nicolae Ceausescu, who took power in 1965, and his Securitate police state became increasingly oppressive and draconian through the 1980s. Ceausescu was overthrown and executed in late 1989. Former Communists dominated the government until 1996 when they were swept from power. Romania joined NATO in 2004 and the EU in 2007.

RULERS:

Carol I (as Prince), 1866-81 (as King) 1881-1914
Ferdinand I, 1914-1927
Mihai I, 1927-1930
Carol II, 1930-1940
Mihai I, 1940-1947

MONETARY SYSTEM:

1 Leu = 100 Bani

German Occupation - WW I

Banca Generala Romana

1917 Issue

#M1-M8 often found w/numerous different handstamps of military units and Romanian authorities. Such notes are generally well worn.

M1 25 Bani — VG .50 / VF 2.00 / UNC 8.00
ND (1917). Olive-brown. Mercury at right. Printer: German.

M2 50 Bani — VG .50 / VF 2.50 / UNC 12.50
ND (1917). Pale blue-gray. Woman at upper left. Printer: German.

M3 1 Leu — VG .50 / VF 3.00 / UNC 15.00
ND (1917). Black text on green underprint. Mercury at left, laureate woman's head at right. Printer: German.

		VG	VF	UNC
M4	**2 Lei** ND (1917). Black text on pale red underprint. Woman at left, Mercury at right. Printer: German.	.50	4.00	18.00

		VG	VF	UNC
M5	**5 Lei** ND (1917). Black text on lilac underprint. Woman at left and at right. Back: Blue-gray. Printer: German.	1.00	6.00	24.00
M6	**20 Lei** ND (1917). Black text on brown underprint. Back: Woman at left, Mercury at right. Printer: German.	2.00	8.50	40.00
M7	**100 Lei** ND (1917). Black text on olive and blue underprint. Back: Mercury at left, woman at right. Printer: German.	6.00	20.00	85.00
M8	**1000 Lei** ND (1917). Brown and multicolor. Like #M7. Back: Mercury at left, woman at right. Printer: German.	12.00	32.50	95.00

#M9 not assigned.

Russian Occupation - WW II

Comandamentul Armatei Rossii

1944 Issue

#M9 Deleted.

		VG	VF	UNC
M10	**5 Lei** 1944. Blue.	15.00	30.00	100.

		VG	VF	UNC
M11	**10 Lei** 1944. Brown.	15.00	40.00	120.
M12	**20 Lei** 1944. Blue.	25.00	60.00	150.
M13	**100 Lei** 1944. Brown-olive.	50.00	100.	225.

		VG	VF	UNC
M14	**500 Lei** 1944. Brown on blue underprint.	60.00	125.	275.
M15	**1000 Lei** 1944.	75.00	150.	350.

		VG	VF	UNC
M16	**5000 Lei** 1944. Rare.	—	—	—

Romanian Occupation of U.S.S.R. - WW II, Transnistria Region

Institutul de Finantare Externa (INFINEX)

1941-44 Bon de Credit Issue

Note: This issue bears unusual denominations because of the exchange rate set by Germany, as follows:

6 Lei = 10 Reichspfennig or 1 Ruble/Karbowanez (Ukrainian German Issue).
1200 Lei = 20 Reichsmark or 200 Rubles/Karbowanez.

		Good	Fine	XF
M17	**1 Leu** ND (1941-44). Gray.	100.	300.	700.
M18	**6 Lei** ND (1941-44). Gray-blue.	100.	300.	700.

		Good	Fine	XF
M19	**24 Lei** ND (1941-44). Brown.	100.	300.	750.

		Good	Fine	XF
M20	**120 Lei** ND (1941-44). Blue. Sunflower at right.	125.	375.	800.

A WORD ON DATE RANGES

Often date ranges or specific dates are listed. These have been observed or reported by our contributors. If a note is outside the published range, it only means that it is a newly reported date, and not necessarily worthy of a premium value.

		Good	Fine	XF
M21	**600 Lei** ND (1941-44). Gray on brown-violet underprint. Cross at center.	125.	375.	850.

		Good	Fine	XF
M22	**1200 Lei** ND (1941-44). Gray on tan underprint. Grapes at center. Back: Boat on river at center.	100.	350.	700.

Regional

Treasury

1919 First Provisional Issue

Romania Timbru Special handstamp on the Austrian (for Bukovina) or Hungarian (for Siebenbérgen and Banat) side of Austro-Hungarian bank notes. All issued in 1919.

#R1-R11 handstamp on Austrian side (Bukovina). Also frequently encountered w/additional Hungarian or Yugoslav handstamps (usually of military units).

		Good	Fine	XF
R1	**10 Kronen** ND (1919 - old date 2.1.1904). Handstamp on Austria #9.	6.00	15.00	30.00
R2	**10 Kronen** ND (1919 - old date 2.1.1915). Handstamp on Austria #19.	4.00	10.00	20.00
R3	**20 Kronen** ND (1919 - old date 2.1.1907). Handstamp on Austria #10.	60.00	150.	300.
R4	**20 Kronen** ND (1919 - old date 2.1.1913). Handstamp on Austria #13.	6.00	15.00	30.00
R5	**20 Kronen** ND (1919 - old date 2.1.1913). Handstamp on Austria #14.	2.00	5.00	10.00
R6	**50 Kronen** ND (1919 - old date 2.1.1902). Handstamp on Austria #6.	60.00	150.	300.

		Good	Fine	XF
R7	**50 Kronen** ND (1919 - old date 2.1.1914). Handstamp on Austria #15.	4.00	10.00	20.00
R8	**100 Kronen** ND (1919 - old date 2.1.1910). Handstamp on Austria #11.	60.00	150.	300.

		Good	Fine	XF
R9	**100 Kronen** ND (1919 - old date 2.1.1912). Handstamp on Austria #12.	2.00	5.00	10.00
R10	**1000 Kronen** ND (1919 - old date 2.1.1902). Handstamp on Austria #8.	4.00	10.00	20.00
R11	**10,000 Kronen** ND (1919 - old date 2.11.1918). Handstamp on Austria #25.	10.00	25.00	50.00

1919 Second Provisional Issue

#R12-R22 handstamp on Hungarian side (Siebenbérgen and Banat). Also frequently encountered w/additional Hungarian or Yugoslav handstamps (usually of military units).

		Good	Fine	XF
R12	**10 Korona** ND (1919 - old date 2.1.1904). Back: Handstamp on Austria #9.	6.00	15.00	30.00
R13	**10 Korona** ND (1919 - old date 2.1.1915). Back: Handstamp on Austria #19.	4.00	10.00	20.00
R14	**20 Korona** ND (1919 - old date 2.1.1907). Back: Handstamp on Austria #10.	60.00	150.	300.

		Good	Fine	XF
R15	**20 Korona** ND (1919 - old date 2.1.1913). Back: Handstamp on Austria #13.	6.00	15.00	30.00
R16	**20 Korona** ND (1919 - old date 2.1.1913). Back: Handstamp on Austria #14.	2.00	5.00	10.00

		Good	Fine	XF
R17	**50 Korona** ND (1919 - old date 2.1.1902). Back: Handstamp on Austria #6.	60.00	150.	300.
R18	**50 Korona** ND (1919 - old date 2.1.1914). Back: Handstamp on Austria #15.	4.00	10.00	20.00
		Good	Fine	XF
R19	**100 Korona** ND (1919 - old date 2.1.1910). Back: Handstamp on Austria #11.	60.00	150.	300.
R20	**100 Korona** ND (1919 - old date 2.1.1912). Back: Handstamp on Austria #12.	2.00	5.00	10.00
R21	**1000 Korona** ND (1919 - old date 2.1.1902). Back: Handstamp on Austria #8.	4.00	10.00	20.00
R22	**10,000 Korona** ND (1919 - old date 2.11.1918). Back: Handstamp on Austria #25.	10.00	25.00	50.00

RUSSIA

Russia, (formerly the central power of the Union of Soviet Socialist Republics and now of the Commonwealth of Independent States) occupying the northern part of Asia and the far eastern part of Europe, has an area of 17,075,200 sq. km. and a population of 140.7 million. Capital: Moscow. Exports include machinery, iron and steel, oil, timber and nonferrous metals.

Founded in the 12th century, the Principality of Muscovy, was able to emerge from over 200 years of Mongol domination (13th-15th centuries) and to gradually conquer and absorb surrounding principalities. In the early 17th century, a new Romanov Dynasty continued this policy of expansion across Siberia to the Pacific. Under Peter I (ruled 1682-1725), hegemony was extended to the Baltic Sea and the country was renamed the Russian Empire. During the 19th century, more territorial acquisitions were made in Europe and Asia. Defeat in the Russo-Japanese War of 1904-05 contributed to the Revolution of 1905, which resulted in the formation of a parliament and other reforms. Repeated devastating defeats of the Russian army in World War I led to widespread rioting in the major cities of the Russian Empire and to the overthrow in 1917 of the imperial household. The Communists under Vladimir Lenin seized power soon after and formed the USSR. The brutal rule of Iosif STALIN (1928-53) strengthened Communist rule and Russian dominance of the Soviet Union at a cost of tens of millions of lives. The Soviet economy and society stagnated in the following decades until General Secretary Mikhail Gorbachev (1985-91) introduced glasnost (openness) and perestroika (restructuring) in an attempt to modernize Communism, but his initiatives inadvertently released forces that by December 1991 splintered the USSR into Russia and 14 other independent republics. Since then, Russia has shifted its post-Soviet democratic ambitions in favor of a centralized semi-authoritarian state whose legitimacy is buttressed, in part, by carefully managed national elections, former President Putin's genuine popularity, and the prudent management of Russia's windfall energy wealth. Russia has severely disabled a Chechen rebel movement, although violence still occurs throughout the North Caucasus.

RULERS:

Catherine II (the Great), 1762-1796
Paul I, 1796-1801
Alexander I, 1801-1825
Nicholas I, 1825-1855
Alexander II, 1855-1881
Alexander III, 1881-1894
Nicholas II, 1894-1917

MONETARY SYSTEM:

1 Ruble = 100 Kopeks, until 1997

MONETARY UNITS

KOPEK	КОП., КОПѢИКА, КОПЕЙКА
KOPEKS	КОПЬЕКЪ., КОП., КОПЕЕК
RUBLE	РУБЛЬ
RUBLES	РУБЛЕИ
CHERVONETS	ЧЕРВОНЕЦ
CHERVONTSA (plural)	ЧЕРВОНЦА
KARBOVANETS	КАРБОВАНЕЦ(RUS), КАРБОВАНЕЦЬ(UKR)
KARBOVANTSIV (pl.)	КАРБОВАНЦІВ
HRYVEN	ГРИВЕНЬ
SHAGIV	ШАГІВ

NOTICE

Readers with unlisted dates, signature varieties, etc.,
are invited to submit photocopies or scans of their notes to:
Standard Catalog of World Paper Money,
700 East State St. Iola, WI 54990-0001,
E-Mail: george.cuhaj@fwmedia.com.

CYRILLIC ALPHABET

А	а	А	а	A	С	с	С	с	S
Б	б	Б	б	B	Т	т	Т	т	T
В	в	В	в	V	У	у	У	у	U
Г	г	Г	г	G	Ф	ф	Ф	ф	F
Д	д	Д	д. g	D	Х	х	Х	х	Kh
Е	е	Е	е	ye	Ц	ц	Ц	ц	C
Ё	ё	Ё	ё	yo	Ч	ч	Ч	ч	ch
Ж	ж	Ж	ж	zh	Ш	ш	Ш	ш	sh
З	з	З	з	Z	Щ	щ	Щ	щ	shch
И	и	И	и	I	Ъ*)	ъ*)	—	ъ	'
Й	й	Й	й	J	Ы	ы	—	ы	
К	к	К	k. к	K	Ь**)	ь**)	—	ь	'
Л		Л	л	L	Э		Э		E
М		М	м	M	Ю	ю	Ю	ю	yu
Н		Н	н	N	Я	я	Я	я	ya
О		О	о	O	І	і	І	і	I
П		П	п	P	Ѣ	ѣ	Ѣ	ѣ	ye
Р		Р	р	R					

*) "hard", and **) "soft" signs; both soundless. I and Ѣ were dropped in 1918.

DENOMINATIONS

1	ОДИН, ОДИНЪ or ОДНА
2	ДВА or ДВЕ
3	ТРИ
5	ПЯТЬ
10	ДЕСЯТЬ
20	ДВАДЦАТЬ
25	ДВАДЦАТЬ ПЯТЬ
30	ТРИДЦАТЬ
40	СОРОК or СОРОКЪ
50	ПЯТЬДЕСЯТ or ПЯТЬДЕСЯТЪ
60	ШЕСТЬДЕСЯТ or ШЕСТЬДЕСЯТЬ
100	СТО
250	ДВЬСТИ ПЯТЪДЕСЯТЪ or ДВЕСТИ ПЯТЪДЕСЯТ
500	ПЯТЬСОТ or ПЯТЬСОТЪ
1,000	ТЫСЯЧА
5,000	ПЯТЬ ТЫСЯЧ or ТЫСЯЧЪ
10,000	ДЕСЯТЬ ТЫСЯЧ or ТЫСЯЧЪ
15,000	ПЯТНАДЦАТЬ ТЫСЯЧ or ТЫСЯЧЬ
25,000	ДВАДЦАТЬ ПЯТЬ ТЫСЯЧ
50,000	ПЯТЬ ДЕСЯТ ТЫСЯЧ or ПЯТЬСОТ
100,000	СТО ТЫСЯЧ or ТЫСЯЧЪ
250,000	ДВЬСТИ ПЯТЬДЕСЯТ ТЫСЯЧ
500,000	ПЯТЬ СОТЪ ТЫСЯЧ or ПЯТЬСОТ
1,000,000	ОДИН МИЛЛИОН or МИЛЛИОНЪ
5,000,000	ПЯТЬ МИЛЛИОНОВ

REGIONAL ISSUES

SECTION BREAKDOWN AND IDENTIFICATION LIST

Regional issues of Russia in this catalog are arranged on a geographic basis from north to south, west to east. A number of major locally circulating issues are included as well.

Shown with the breakdown of each section are some of the Russian headings to assist in locating listed issues. In so far as possible these headings are given exactly as they appear on the notes, regardless of grammatical construction.

NORTH RUSSIA

ГОСУДАРСТВЕННЬИ БАНКЪ АРХАНГЕЛЬСКОЕ ОТДѢЛЕНІЕМЪ
Archangel Government (Red and White Regimes)....#S101-S108
МУРМАНСК НА ФИНАНСОВЫЙ ОТДѢЛ.
Murmansk Soviet (Red and White Regimes)....#S111-S118
5% КРАТКОСРОЧНОЕ ОБЯЗАТЕЛЬСТВО ВЕРХОВНАГО
УПРАВЛЕНІЯ СѢВЕРНОЙ ОБЛАСТИ....#S121-S125
5% КРАТКОСРОЧНОЕ ОБЯЗАТЕЛЬСТВО ВРЕМЕННАГО
ПРАВИТЕЛЬСТВА СѢВЕРНОЙ ОБЛАСТИ
Government of the North Region....#S126-S129
СѢВЕРНАЯ РОССІЯ
North Russia....#S131-S186
ОЛОНЕЦКОЙ ГУБЕРНІЙ
Olonets Government....#S191-S195

NORTHWEST RUSSIA

ПОЛЕВОЕ КАЗНА.ЕИЧТВО СѢВЕРОЗАПАДНАГО ФРОНТА
Field Treasury, Northwest Front (Gen. Yudenich)....#S201-S210
КРЕДИТНЫЙ БИЛЕТЪ ПСКОВСКАГО ОБЛАСТНОГО КАЗНА.ЕЙСТВА
Pskov Regional Government (Gen. Vandamm)....#S211-S213
ОТДѢЛЬНЫИ КОРПУСЪ СѢВЕРНОЙ АРМІИ. ГЕН. РОДЗЯНКО
Special Corps of the North Army (Gen. Rodzianko)....#S216-S222
ЗАПАДНАЯ ДОБРОВОЛЬУЕСКАЯ АРМІЯ , ПОЛК АВАЛОВ - БЕРМОНДТЪ
Independent West Army (Col. Avalov-Bermondt)....#S226-S230
ПАРТИ ЗАНСКИЙ ОТРЯД ПОЛК БУЛАК - БАЛАХОВИЧА
Partisan Detachment of Lt. Col. Bulak-Balakhovich....#S231

КРОНШТАДТСКАЯ РЕСПУБЛИКА
Kronstadt Republic (naval mutineers) .... #S232-S235
МОГИЛЕВЧКАЯ ГУБЕРІЯ
Mogilev Region .... #S236-S240A

WHITE RUSSIA

СЛУЦКОЕ УѢЗДНОЕ ЗЕМСТВО.
Slutsk Zemstvo Issue .... #S241-S244

UKRAINE

УКРАЙНСКАЯ СОЦ (ИАЛИСТИУЕСКАЯ) СОВЕТ. РЕСПУБЛ. (МКА)
Ukrainian Socialist Soviet Republic .... #S293-S304
ЕЛИСАБЕТГРАДСК (СКОЕ) ОТДѢЛЕНІЯ ГОСУДАРСТВЕННАГО БАНКА
Elizabetgrad Branch Government Bank .... #S323-S323B
ЕЛИСАБЕТГРАДСКАГО ОТДѢЛЕНІЯ НАРОДНАГО БАНКА
Elizabetgrad Branch Peoples Bank .... #S324-S325
ВСЕУКРАЇНЬСКИЙ КООПЕРАТИВНИЙ БАНК
Ukrainian Cooperative Bank, Kiev .... #S326-S328
УКРАЙНЬСКА ПОВСТАНСКА АРМІЯ (УКРАІНСЬКА ПОВСТАНСЬКА АРМІЯ)
Ukrainian Revolutionary Army (Post-WW II) .... #S330
РАЗМѢННАИ МАРКА Г. ОДЕССЫ РАЗМѢННЫИ БИЛЕТЪ Г. ОДЕССЫ
Odessa .... #S331-S338
ЖИТОМИР
Zhitomir .... #S341-S363
РОЗМІННИЙ БІЛЕТ МІСТА ЖИТОМИРА
Municipal Receipts .... #S341-S343
РАЗМЕНЫЙ БИЛЕТ НАРОДНОГО БАНКА
National Bank .... #S344-S346
АЗОВСКО-ДОНСКОЙ КОММЕРУЕСКІЙ БАНКЪ ЖИТОМИРСКОЕ ОТДѢЛЕНІЕ
Azov-Don Commercial Bank, Zhitomir Branch .... #S351-S356
ЖИТОМИРСКОЕ ОТДѢЛЕНІЕ ГОСУДАРСТВЕНН. БАНКА
Zhitomir Branch, Government Bank .... #S361-S363
СОЕДИНЕННЫЙ БАНКЪ ЖИТОМИРСКОЕ ОТДѢЛЕНІЕ
Zhitomir Branch Soednenni Bank .... #S364-S364D
КРЫМСКОЕ КРАЕВОЕ ПРАВИТЕЛЬСТВО
ОБЯЗАТЕЛСТВО КРЫМСКАГО КРАЕВОГО КАЗНАЧЕЙСТВА
Crimea Territorial Government (Gen. Sulkevich) .... #S366-S372
Provisional Government of Workers and Peasants .... #S375
УПРАВЛЕНІЕ УПОЛНОМОЧ. ПО ПРОД. ХЕСР. ГУБ. ВРЕМЕННАЯ КВИТАНЧІЯ
Kherson Government Plenipotentiary for Food .... #S376-S380

SOUTH RUSSIA

5% КРАТКОСРО.НОЕ ОЬЯЗАТЕЛЬСТВО ВСЕВЕЛИКАГО ВОЙСКА ДОНСКОГО
Don Cossack Government .... #S381-S404
ГЛАВНОЕКОМАНДОВАНІЕ ВООРУЖЕННЫМИ
СИЛАМИ НА ЮГѢ РОССІЙ
South Russia, High Command of the Armed Forces (Generals Denikin and Wrangel)
ВЫПУЩЕНЪ (or A) РОСТОВСКОЙ (УД) ГОСУДАРСТВЕННАГО БАНКА
Rostov Branch Government Bank .... #S406-S419
ВИЛЕТЪ ГОСУДАРСТВЕННАГО КАЗНАЧЕЙСТВА
Government Treasury Notes .... #S420-S434
ГОСУДАРСТВО РОССІЙСКОЕ
Russian Government .... #S435-S440
АСТРАХАНСКАГО КАЗНА.ЕЙСТВА
Astrakhan Region .... #S441-S446

NORTH CAUCASUS

СЕВЕРО КАВКАЗСКАЯ СОЦИАЛИСТИ.ЕСКАЯ COVHTSKAW РЕСПУЬЛИКА
КРАЕВОГО ИСПОЛНИТ. КОМИТЕТА СОВЕТОВ
North Caucasian Soviet Socialist Republic .... #S447-S448
ВРЕМЭН.-ЕНТР. УПРАВЛ. ОТДВЛЕНІЙ НАРОДНАГО БАНКА
Provisional Central Administration of the Branch of the National Bank .... #S451-S453
СЕВ. КАВКАЗА
Area Executive Committee of the N. Caucasian Soviet Republic .... #S456-S460
СЕВЕРО-КАВКАЗСКИЙ ЭМИРАТ
North Caucasian Emirate .... #S461-S478
АРМАВИРСКАГО ОТДѢЛЕНІЯ ГОСУДАРСТВЕННАГО БАНКА
Armavir Branch Government Bank .... #S479A-S479K
КУБАНСКАГО КРАЕВОГО ПРАВИТЕЛЬСТВА
Kuban Territorial Government .... #S481-S488
КУБАНСКАЯ РЕСПУБЛИКА
Kuban Soviet Republic .... #S491-S494
ЕКАТЕРИНОДАРСКОГО ОТДЕЛЕНИЯ ГОСУДАРСТВЕННАГО БАНКА
Ekaterinodar Branch Government Bank .... #S494A-S497
ГОСУДАРСТВЕННАГО БАНКА ЕКАТЕРИНОДАРСКОЕ ОТДѢЛЕНІЕ
ГАРАНТИРОВАННЫЙ ЧЕКЪ
Guaranteed Check, Government Bank Ekaterinodar Branch .... #S498A-S498E
МИНЕРАЛЬНЫЕ ВОДЫ
Mineralnyie Vodyi District .... #S501-S520
ГОСУДАРЧТВЕННЫЙ БАНКЪ СТАВРОПОЛСКОЕ ОТДѢЛЕНІЕ
Stavropol Branch Government Bank .... #S520A-S520H
ТЕРСКО-ДАГЕСТАНСКАЯ ОБЛАСТЬ
Terek-Daghestan Territory .... #S521-S528
ТЕРСКОЙ РЕСПУБЛИКИЙ (ТЕРСК РЕСП.)
Terek Republic .... #S529-S538
ВРЕМЕНН. РАЗМѢННЫЙ ЗНАКЪ
Black Sea Peasant Militia (Voronovich) .... #S539-S544
(ПИАТИГОРСК-) БАТАЛПАЩИНСК КАЗНАЧ.
Piatigorsk-Batalpashchinsk Company of the Independent Army
(Col. A. Shkuro) .... #S551-S565
ТЕРСКОЕ КАЗНАЧЬЕ ВОЙСКО
Terek Cossack Command (Col. Bicherakov) .... #S566-S568
КОМАНДОВАНІЕ КРАСНОЙ АРМИИ. ТЕРСКОЙ ОБЛАСТИ
Terek District Command of the Red Army .... #S569-S570
ВОЛЖСКО-КАМСКІЙ КОММЕР.ЕСКІЙ БАНКЪ
Volga-Kama Commercial Bank-Grozny .... #S571-S573
РУССКО-АЗІАТСКИЙ БАНКЪ
Russo-Asiatic Bank .... #S576-S579
АЗОВЧКО-ДОНЧКОЙ КОММЕР.ЕЧКИИ БАНКЪ
Azov-Don Commercial Bank .... #S581-S584
ВОНЫ СОЧИНСКАГО ГОРОДСКОГО УПРАВЛЕНИЯ
Sochi (City) .... #S585-S585H
ЧЕРНОМОРСКАЯ ЖЕЛЕЗНАЯ ДОРОГА
Black Sea Railroad .... #S586-S591
ОБЩЕСТВА ВЛАДИКАВКАЗСКОЙ ЖЕЛЛЗНОЙ ДОРОГИ
Vladikavkaz Railroad Company .... #S593-S599
ВЛАДИКАВКАЗСКОЕ ОТДѢЛЕНІЕ ГОСУДАРСТВЕННАГО БАНКА
Vladikavkaz Branch Government Bank .... #S600A-S600D

TRANSCAUCASIA

ЗАКАВКАЗСКАГО КОМИССАРІАТА
Transcaucasian Commissariat .... #S601-S607
ФЕДЕРАЦИЯ СОВ. СОЦ. РЕСПУБЛИК
ЗАКАВКАЗЬЯ С.Ф.С.Р.
Federation of Soviet Socialist Republics of Transcaucasia .... #S611-S631
Transcaucasian Socialist Federal Soviet Republic .... #S632-S639
УПРАВЛЕИЕ ЖЕЛЕЗНЫХ ДОРОГ, С.С.Р. ЗАКАВКАЗЬЯ.
Transcaucasian S.S.R. Railroad .... #S641-S645
СОЦИАЛИСТИЧЕСКАЯ СОВЕТСКАЯ РЕСПУБЛИКА АРМЕНИИ (or АРМЕНИР)
Armenian Socialist Soviet Republic .... #S678-S687
АЛЕКСАНДРОПОЛСКІЙ ГОРОДСК ОБЩЕСТВЕНН БАНК$
Alexandropol Bank Issues .... #S691-S692
Shirak Government Corporation Bank $S693-S698
АЗЕРБАЙДЖАНСКАЯ СОЦ. СОВОТ. РЕСПУБЛИКА
Azerbaijan Socialist Soviet Republic .... #S709-S720
БАКИНСКЛЯ ГОРОДСКАЯ УПРАВА СОВѢТЪ БАКИНСКАГО
ГОРОДСКОГО ХОЗЯИСТВА
Baku City Administration .... #S731-S733
БАТУМСКАГО КАЗНА.ЕЙСТВА
Batum Treasury .... #S736-S745
ГРУЗИНСКАЯ СОЦ . СОВЕТСКАЯ РЕСПУБЛИКА
ОБЯЗАТЕЛЬСТВО НАРОДНАГО БАНКА S.C.P. ГРУЗИН.
Georgia Socialist Soviet Republic .... #S761-S769

SIBERIA AND URALS

САМАРСКАЯ ДИРЕКТОРИЯ
Samara Directory (Komuch) .... #S771-S812
СИБИРСКАГО ВРЕМЕННАГО ПРАВИТЕЛЬСТВА
5% КРАТКОСОРО.НОЕ ОБЯЗАТЕЛЬСТВО
ГОСУДАРСТВЕННАГО КАЗНА.ЕЙСТВА СИБИРИ
Siberian Provisional Government .... #S816-S825
СИБИРСКАГО ВРЕМЕННАГО ПРАВИТЕЛЬСТВА
5% КРАТКОСРО.НОЕ ОБЯЗАТЕЛЬСТВО ГОСУДАРСТВЕННАГО КАЗНАЧЕЙСТВА
ГОСУДАРСТВЕННЫЙ КРЕДИТНЫЙ БИЛЕТЪ
БИЛЕТЪ ГОСУДАРСТВЕННЫЙ ВНУТРЕННІИ 4-1/2% ВЫЙГРЫЩНЫЙ
ЗАЕМЪ 1917 ГОДА
Provisional Siberian Government (Kolchak) .... #S826-S878
ИРК. ОТД. ГОС.Б
Irkutsk Branch, Government Bank .... #S881-S892
УПОЛНОМО.ЕННЫЙ МИНИСТРА СНАБЖЕНІЯ И ПРОДОВОЛЬСТВІЯ ПО
ХАБАРОВСКОМУ РАЙОНУ
Minister Representative Plenipotentiary for Provisions for Khabarovsk District .... #S896-S898
РОССИЙСКОЙ СОЦИАЛИСТИЧЕСКОЙ ФЕДЕРАТИВНАЯ СОВЕТСКАЯ РЕСПУБЛИКА
БИЛЕТЪ ГОСУДАРСТВЕННЫИ ВНУТРЕННІЙ 4-1/2% ВЫЙГРЫЩНЫЙ ЗАЕМЪ
Siberian Revolution Committee .... #S899-S904
ЧРЕЗВЫЧАЙНО-УПОЛНОМОЧЕННЫЙ ПРИКАМСКАГО РАЙОНА
Urals and Kama Region .... #S906-S919
РАБОЧЕЕ И КРЕСТЬЯНСКОЕ ПРАВИТЕЛЬСТВО ЕКАТЕРИНБУРГСКОЕ ОТДЕЛЕНИЕ
ГОСУДАРСТВЕННАГО БАНКА
Soviet of the Urals Region, Ekaterinburg Branch Government Bank .... #S921-S923
УРАЛСКАГО КАЗА.ЬЯГО БОЙСКА
Urals Cossack Region .... #S926-S953
УРАЛЬСКОЕ ОТД. Г. Б.
Uralsk Branch, State Bank .... #S956-S958
ПРАВИТЕЛЬСТВО ЦЕНТРОСИБИРИ СИБИРСКИЙ
Government of Central Siberia .... #S961
АКМОЛИНСКОЙ ОБЛАСТИ
Akmolinsk Region Revolutionary Committee .... #S962-S964
КРАСНОЯРСК. ЕНИС. Г. О-БО
Krasnoyarsk .... #S966-S971
ОРЕНБУРГСКАГО ОТДѢЛИНІЯ ГОСУДАРСТВЕННАГО БАНКА
Orenburg Branch Government Bank .... #S976-S983
ПЕРМСКАГО ГОРОДСКОГО ОБЩЕСТВА
Perm City Association .... #S986-S993

RUSSIAN CENTRAL ASIA

Bukhara, Soviet Peoples Republic .... #S1026-S1054
Khwarezm Peoples Soviet Republic .... #S1076-S1114
СЕМИРЕЧЕНСКАЯ ОБЛАСТЬ ДЕНЕЖНЫИ ЗНАКЪ ВРЕМЕНН.
РАЗМѢНН. ЗНАКЪ
Semireche Region .... #S1116-S1133
ЗАКАСПІЙСКАГО ВРЕМЕННАГО ПРАВИТЕЛЬСТВА
Transcaspian Provisional Administration
АСХАБАДСКАГО ОТДѢЛЕНІЯ ГОСУДАРСТВЕННАГО БАНКА
Government Bank, Askhabod Branch .... #S1136
ЗАКАСПІЙСКАГО НАРОДНАГО БАНКА
Transcaspian National Bank .... #S1139
АСХАБАДСКАГО ОТДѢЛЕНІЯ НАРОДНАГО БАНКА
National Bank, Askhabad Branch .... #S1141-S1146
ОБЯЗАТЕЛЬСТВО ВЕЛИКОБРИТАНСКОЙ ВОЕННОЙ МИССИИ
Great Britain Government Military Mission (British Maj. Gen. Malleson) .... #S1148
ТУРКЕСТАНСКІЙ КРАЙ ТАШКЕТСКАГО ОТДѢЛЕНІЯ ГОСУДАРСТВЕННАГО
БАНКА
Turkestan District Tashkent Branch Government Bank .... #S1151-S1175

EAST SIBERIA

ДАЛЬНЕВОСТО.НЫЙ СОВЕТ. НАРОДНЫХ КОМИССАРОВ
Baikalia - Far Eastern Soviet of Peoples Commissars .... #S1181-S1183
ПРАВИТЕЛЬСТВО РОССІЙСКОЙ ВОСТО.НОЙ ОКРАЙНЫ
ГОСУДАРСТВЕННЫЙ БАНКЪ .ИТИНСКОЕ ОТДѢЛЕНІЕ
Government of the Russian Eastern Border Regions .... #S1186-S1188
СИБИРСКАГО ВРЕМЕННАГО ПРАВИТЕЛЬСТВА
Siberian Provisional Administration .... #S1189-S1194
ВРЕМЕННАЯ ЗЕМСКАЯ ВЛАСТЬ ПРИБАЙКАЛЬЯ
Provisional Power of the Pribaikal Region .... #S1196-S1197
ДАЛЬНЕ-ВОСТО.НОЙ РЕСПУБЛИКИ

KEY RUSSIAN WORDS & PHRASES

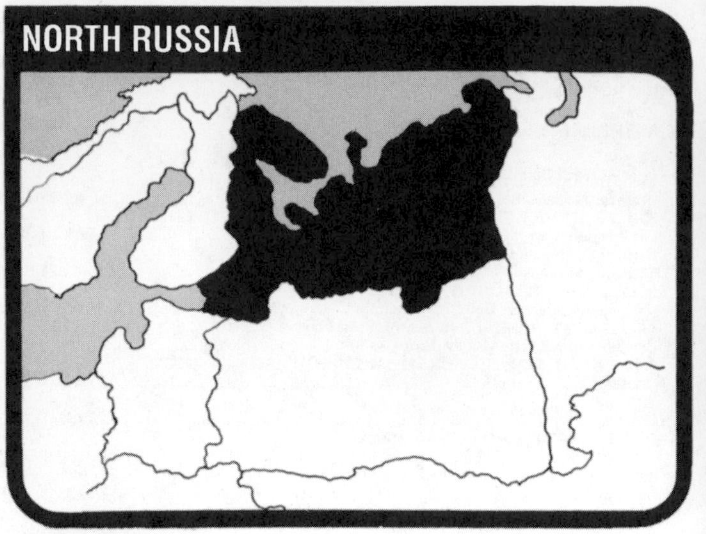

GOVERNMENTS

Archangel Government (Red and White Regimes)
Murmansk Soviet (Red and White Regimes)
Government of the North Region (North Russia)
Olonets Government

ГОСУДАРСТВЕННЫЙ БАНКЪ

GOVERNMENT BANK - RED REGIME

АРХАНГЕЛЬСКОЕ ОТДѢЛЕ НІЕМЪ

ARCHANGEL

1918 ND ISSUE

	VG	VF	UNC
S101 3 Rubles			
ND (1918). Green and black. Fasces at left and right of large *3* at upper center.			
a. Issued note.	7.50	22.50	75.00
x. Misprint: face without black text printing.	15.00	45.00	135.
S102 5 Rubles			
ND (1918). Gray-blue and black.	7.50	22.50	75.00
S103 10 Rubles			
ND (1918). Red-brown and black.			
a. Issued note.	12.50	27.50	80.00
x. Misprint: face without black text printing.	15.00	45.00	135.

		VG	VF	UNC
S104	**25 Rubles** ND (1918). Black on blue-gray underprint. Polar bear at lower left, walrus at lower right.	15.00	45.00	135.

ГОСУДАРСТВЕННЫЙ БАНКЪ

Government Bank - White Regime

1918 Provisional Issue

#S106-S108 issues of the Red regime w/validation ovpt. on back by the White regime. Ovpt. sign. of A. Faddeyev.

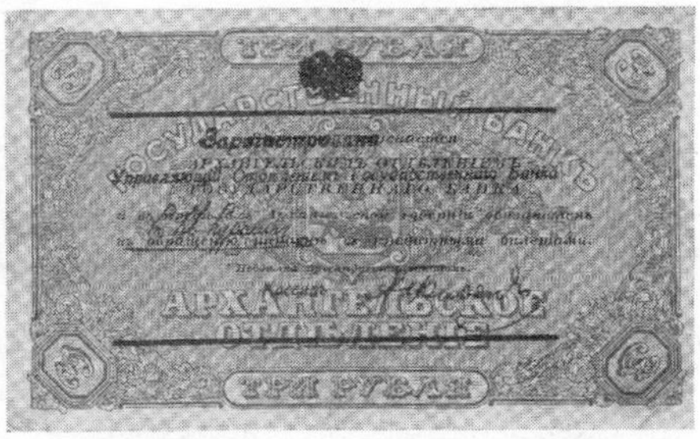

		Good	Fine	XF
S106	**3 Rubles** ND (1918). Green. Fasces at left and right of large *3* at upper center. Overprint: Validation in red on back #S101. Signature of A. Faddeyev.	15.00	45.00	135.
S107	**10 Rubles** ND (1918). Red-brown. Overprint: Validation in black on back #S103. Signature of A. Faddeyev.	20.00	60.00	180.

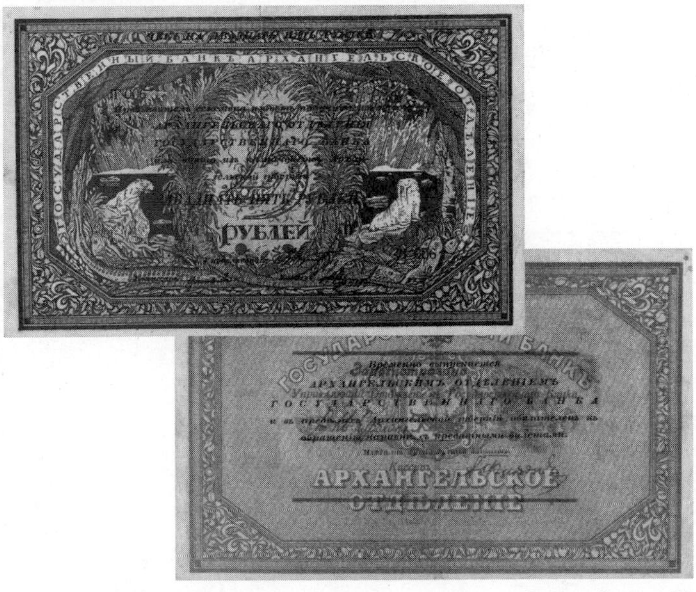

		Good	Fine	XF
S108	**25 Rubles** ND (1918). Gray-blue. Overprint: Validation in red on back #S104. Signature of A. Faddeyev.	20.00	60.00	180.

State Bank - Red Regime

Archangel

1918 Check Issue

		Good	Fine	XF
S111	**3 Rubles** ND (1918).	100.	300.	900.
S112	**10 Rubles** ND (1918).	70.00	210.	625.
S113	**25 Rubles** ND (1918).	70.00	210.	625.

State Bank - White Regime

1918 ND Issue

		Good	Fine	XF
S116	**3 Rubles** ND (1918).	50.00	150.	300.
S117	**10 Rubles** ND (1918).	50.00	150.	300.
S118	**25 Rubles** ND (1918).	50.00	150.	300.

Socialist-Bourgeois government 1918-1920 under Chairman Nikolai Chaikovskii and later under General Eugene Miller. It was supported throughout much of its life by British, American and French troops. The area fell to the Reds in Feb. 1920, after Allied troops had withdrawn.

ВЕРХОВНАГО УПРАВЛЕНІЯ СѢВЕРНОЙ ОБЛАСТИ

1918 5% КРАТКОСРОЧНОЕ ОБЯЗАТЕЛЬСТВО

Debenture Bonds Issue

		Good	Fine	XF
S121	**100 Rubles** 15.8.1918. Yellow. Signed by N. V. Chaikovskii, K. Kurakin and A. Faddeyev with fourth signature.	17.50	50.00	150.

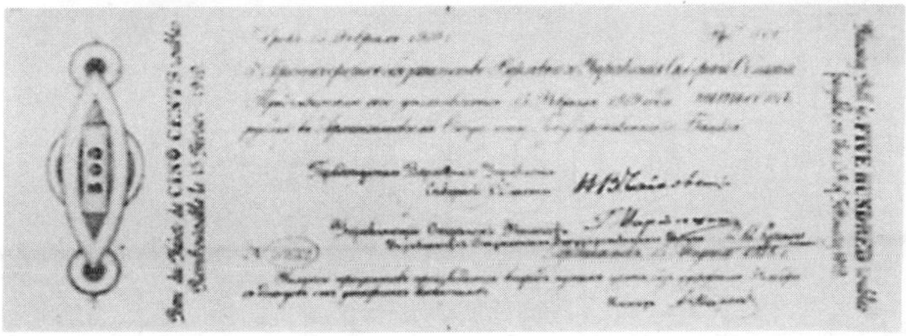

		Good	Fine	XF
S122	**500 Rubles** 15.8.1918. Blue. Signed by N. V. Chaikovskii, K. Kurakin and A. Faddeyev with fourth signature.	30.00	90.00	180.
S123	**1000 Rubles** 15.8.1918. Red. Signed by N. V. Chaikovskii, K. Kurakin and A. Faddeyev with fourth signature.	40.00	120.	360.
S124	**5000 Rubles** 15.8.1918. Signed by N. V. Chaikovskii, K. Kurakin and A. Faddeyev with fourth signature.	60.00	180.	540.
S125	**10,000 Rubles** 15.8.1918. Signed by N. V. Chaikovskii, K. Kurakin and A. Faddeyev.	80.00	240.	725.

ВРЕМЕННАГО ПРАВИТЕЛЬСТВА СѢВЕРНОЙ ОБЛАСТИ

1918 5% КРАТКОСРОЧНОЕ ОБЯЗАТЕЛЬСТВО

Debenture Bonds Issue

Notes exist both w/ or w/o letter И after ФИНАНСОВЪ. This type appeared in Oct. 1918.

		Good	Fine	XF
S126	**50 Rubles** 15.8.1918. Green. Signed by N. V. Chaikovskii, K. Kurakin and A. Faddeyev.	10.00	30.00	90.00
S127	**100 Rubles** 15.8.1918. Signed by N. V. Chaikovskii, K. Kurakin and A. Faddeyev.			
	a. With И.	10.00	30.00	90.00
	b. Without И.	20.00	60.00	180.

		Good	Fine	XF
S128	**500 Rubles** 15.8.1918. Blue. Signed by N. V. Chaikovskii, K. Kurakin and A. Faddeyev.			
	a. With green or black serial #. With И.	20.00	60.00	180.
	b. Without И.	30.00	90.00	270.
S129	**1000 Rubles** 15.8.1918. Red. Signed by N. V. Chaikovskii, K. Kurakin and A. Faddeyev.			
	a. With И.	20.00	60.00	180.
	b. Without I.	30.00	90.00	270.

Chaikovskii Government

1919 ND Small Change Notes Issue

#S131-S134 like Czarist notes #28, #30 and #31 (in Vol. 2) but w/title: СѢВЕРНАЯ РОССІЯ.

		VG	VF	UNC
S131	**10 Kopeks** ND (1919). Green on peach underprint.	10.00	30.00	90.00
S132	**20 Kopeks** ND (1919). Brown on green underprint.	15.00	45.00	135.

		VG	VF	UNC
S133	**50 Kopeks** ND (1919). Blue on yellow underprint. Eagle with crown at upper center.	10.00	30.00	90.00
S134	**50 Kopeks** ND (1919). Eagle without crown.	30.00	90.00	270.

1918 First Issue

#S135-S138 like Czarist issues but w/title: СЪВЕРНАЯ РОССIЯ. Eagle w/crown. W/sign. title: ЧЛЕНЪ ГОСУДАРСТВЕННОЙ ЭМИССIОННОЙ КАССЫ on back.

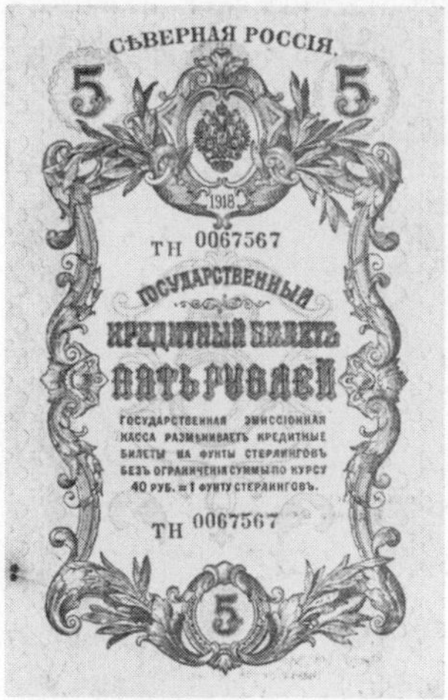

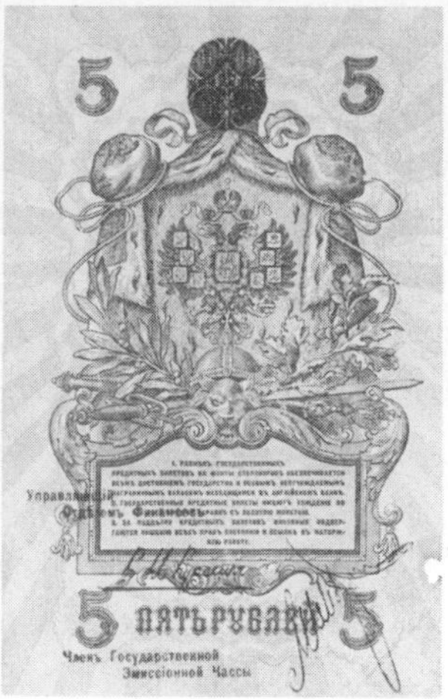

		VG	VF	UNC
S135	**5 Rubles**			
	1918. Blue-green. Eagle with crown. Also known without stamp on back.	10.00	30.00	90.00
S136	**10 Rubles**			
	1918. Red and green. Eagle with crown.	20.00	60.00	180.
S137	**25 Rubles**			
	1918. Pink and green. Eagle with crown.	25.00	75.00	225.

		VG	VF	UNC
S138	**100 Rubles**			
	1918. Brown, red and green. Eagle with crown.	70.00	210.	625.

1918 Second Issue

		VG	VF	UNC
S139	**5 Rubles**			
	1918. Blue-green. Eagle with crown. Back: Signature title: ЧЛЕНЪ ГОРОДСКОЙ ЭМИСIОННОЙ КАССЫ	20.00	60.00	180.

		VG	VF	UNC
S140	**10 Rubles**			
	1918. Black on light red and green underprint. Eagle with crown. Back: Signature title: ЧЛЕНЪ ГОРОДСКОЙ ЭМИСIОННОЙ КАССЫ	25.00	75.00	225.
S141	**25 Rubles**			
	1918. Pink and green. Eagle with crown. Back: Signature title: ЧЛЕНЪ ГОРОДСКОЙ ЭМИСIОННОЙ КАССЫ			
	a. Eagle overprint.	30.00	90.00	180.
	b. Eagle without overprint.	30.00	90.00	180.

		VG	VF	UNC
S142	**100 Rubles**			
	1918. Brown, red and green. Eagle with crown. Back: Black. Signature title: ЧЛЕНЪ ГОРОДСКОЙ ЭМИСIОННОЙ КАССЫ	80.00	240.	725.
S143	**500 Rubles**			
	1918. Eagle with crown. Back: Signature title: ЧЛЕНЪ ГОРОДСКОЙ ЭМИСIОННОЙ КАССЫ	175.	525.	1550.

1919 Issue

#S144-S150 like #1 and #9-14 (in Vol. 2) but text reads: СЪВЕРНАЯ РОССIЯ.

		VG	VF	UNC
S144	**1 Ruble**			
	1919. Blue on red-brown underprint. Eagle without crown. Back: Red-brown.	20.00	60.00	180.

		VG	VF	UNC
S145	**3 Rubles** 1919. Black on green and multicolor underprint. Eagle without crown.	20.00	60.00	180.

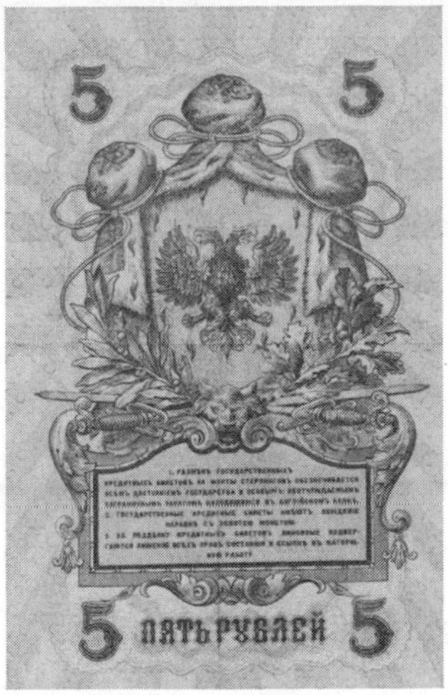

		VG	VF	UNC
S146	**5 Rubles** 1919. Black on blue and light orange underprint. Eagle without crown.	30.00	90.00	270.
S147	**10 Rubles** 1919. Black on light red and green underprint. Eagle without crown. Similar to #S140.	35.00	110.	325.

		VG	VF	UNC
S148	**25 Rubles** 1919. Rose and green. Eagle without crown.	60.00	180.	550.
S149	**100 Rubles** 1919. Brown, red and green. Eagle without crown.	100.	300.	900.
S150	**500 Rubles** 1919. Eagle without crown.	150.	450.	1350.

1919 ГВСО Revalidated Notes Issue

Notes of the Czarist and the Provisional Governments w/perforation: ГВСО. The perforation is frequently forged. Issued from April 14, 1919. Reference # in listings are to notes in Vol. 2.

No.	Denomination / Description	Good	Fine	XF
S151	**50 Kopeks** ND (1919). Blue on yellow underprint. Perforation on #31.	3.00	9.00	27.50
S152	**1 Ruble** ND (1919 -old date 1898). Blue on red-brown underprint. Perforation on #1.	4.00	12.50	37.50

No.	Denomination / Description	Good	Fine	XF
S153	**1 Ruble** ND (1919 -old date 1898). Blue on brown underprint. Perforation on #15.	2.00	6.00	18.00

No.	Denomination / Description	Good	Fine	XF
S154	**3 Rubles** ND (1919 -old date 1905). Black on green and multicolor underprint. Perforation on #9.	3.00	9.00	27.50
S155	**5 Rubles** ND (1919 -old date 1898). Blue on multicolor underprint. Perforation on #3.	20.00	60.00	180.
S156	**5 Rubles** ND (1919 -old date 1909). Blue-black on multicolor underprint. Perforation on #10.	2.00	6.00	18.00
S157	**5 Rubles** ND (1919 -old date 1909). Blue-black on multicolor underprint. Perforation on #35.	3.00	9.00	27.50
S158	**10 Rubles** ND (1919 - old date 1898). Red on multicolor underprint. Perforation on #4.	30.00	90.00	270.
S159	**10 Rubles** ND (1919 -old date 1909). Deep olive-green on green and red underprint. Perforation on #11.	2.00	6.00	18.00
S160	**20 Rubles** ND (1919). Brown on red-brown underprint. Perforation on #38.	2.00	6.00	18.00
S161	**20 Rubles** ND (1919 -old date 1917). Black on yellow underprint. Perforation on #37A.	5.00	15.00	45.00
S162	**25 Rubles** ND (1919 -old date 1909). Red and blue on multicolor underprint. Perforation on #12.	3.00	9.00	18.00

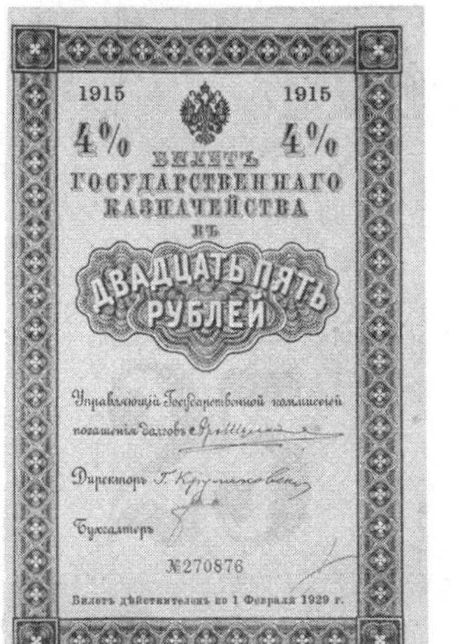

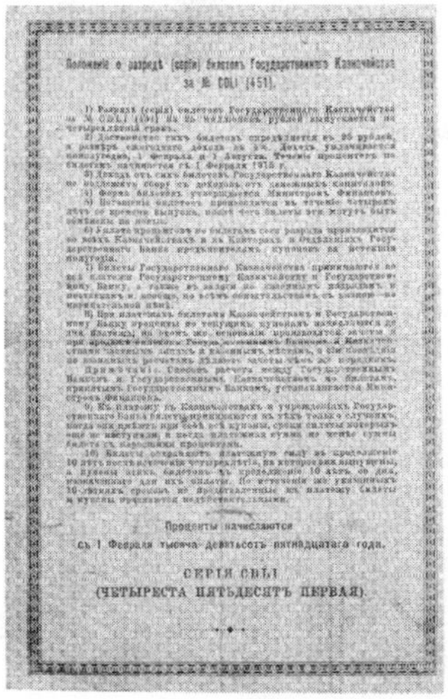

No.	Denomination / Description	Good	Fine	XF
S163	**25 Rubles** ND (1919 -old date 1915). Green on violet underprint. Perforation on #48.	5.00	15.00	45.00
S164	**40 Rubles** ND (1919). Red on green underprint. Perforation on #39.	2.00	6.00	18.00
S165	**40 Rubles** ND (1919 -old date 1917). Black. Perforation on #37B.	10.00	30.00	90.00
S166	**50 Rubles** ND (1919 -old date 1899). Black on multicolor underprint. Perforation on #8.	10.00	30.00	90.00
S167	**50 Rubles** ND (1919 -old date 1909). Brown on green underprint. Perforation on #49.	10.00	30.00	90.00
S168	**50 Rubles** ND (1919 -old date 1914). Brown on green underprint. Perforation on #52.	10.00	30.00	90.00
S169	**50 Rubles** ND (1919 -old date 1915). Brown on green underprint. Perforation on #53.	10.00	30.00	90.00

		Good	Fine	XF
S170	**50 Rubles** ND (1919 -old date 1917). Black on green underprint. Perforation on #37C.	10.00	30.00	90.00
S171	**100 Rubles** ND (1919 -old date 1898). Black on tan and multicolor underprint. Perforation on #5.	30.00	90.00	270.
S172	**100 Rubles** ND (1919 -old date 1910). Light brown. Perforation on #13.	4.00	12.00	36.00
S173	**100 Rubles** ND (1919 -old date 1913). Black on pink underprint. Perforation on #56.	8.00	24.00	75.00
S174	**100 Rubles** ND (1919 -old date 1914). Black on pink underprint. Perforation on #57.	8.00	24.00	75.00
S175	**100 Rubles** ND (1919 -old date 1915). Black on pink underprint. Perforation on #58.	8.00	24.00	75.00
S176	**100 Rubles** ND (1919 -old date 1917). Black on brown underprint. Perforation on #37D.	5.00	15.00	45.00
S177	**250 Rubles** ND (1919 -old date 1917). Black on lilac underprint. Perforation on #36.	3.00	9.00	27.50
S178	**500 Rubles** ND (1919 -old date 1898). Black on multicolor underprint. Perforation on #6.	50.00	150.	450.
S179	**500 Rubles** ND (1919 -old date 1912). Green on multicolor underprint. Perforation on #14.	8.00	24.00	75.00
S180	**500 Rubles** ND (1919 -old date 1915). Black on blue underprint. Perforation on #59.	8.00	24.00	75.00
S181	**500 Rubles** ND (1919 -old date 1916). Black on blue underprint. Perforation on #60.	8.00	24.00	75.00
S182	**1000 Rubles** ND (1919 -old dates 1916; 1917). Lilac-brown. Perforation on #31F-31H.	10.00	30.00	90.00
S183	**1000 Rubles** ND (1919 -old date 1917). Dark brown on green underprint. Perforation on #37.	3.00	9.00	27.50

		Good	Fine	XF
S184	**5000 Rubles** ND (1919 -old dates 1916; 1917). Orange. Perforation on #31I-31J.	8.00	24.00	75.00
S185	**10,000 Rubles** ND (1919 -old dates 1916; 1917). Red. Perforation on #31K-31H.	10.00	30.00	90.00
S186	**100,000 Rubles** ND (1919 -old dates 1916; 1917). Perforation on #31T-31U.	30.00	90.00	270.

ОЛОНЕЦКОЙ ГУБЕРНІЙ

1918 КРЕДИТНЫЙ БИЛЕТЬ Credit Note Issue

		VG	VF	UNC
S191	**1 Ruble** 1918. Yellow. Arms at upper center. Proof. Rare.	—	—	—
S192	**5 Rubles** 1918. Blue. Arms at upper center. Proof. Rare.	—	—	—
S193	**10 Rubles** 1918. Rose. Arms at upper center. Proof. Rare.	—	—	—
S194	**25 Rubles** 1918. Olive-gray. Arms at upper center. Proof. Rare.	—	—	—
S195	**100 Rubles** 1918. Brown. Arms at upper center. Proof. Rare.	—	—	—

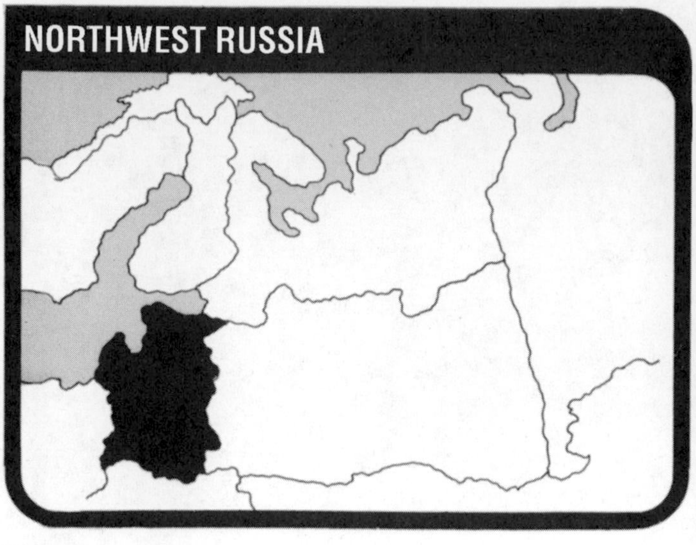

MILITARY

Northwest Front (Gen. N. N. Yudenich)
Pskov Regional Government (Maj. Gen. Vandamm)
Special Corps of the North Army (Gen. Rodzianko)
Independent West Army (Col. Avalov-Bermondt)
Partisan Company of Lt. Col. Bulak-Balakhovich
Kronstadt Republic (Naval Mutineers)
Mogilev Region
Slutsk (White)

ПОЛЕВОЕ КАЗНАЧЕЙСТВО

СѢВЕРОЗАПАДНАГО ФРОНТА

Field Treasury, Northwest Front

1919 ДЕНЕЖНЫЙ ЗНАКЪ Currency Tokens Issue

In May and October, 1919, Yudenich's White army made two unsuccessful attempts to penetrate from Estonia into Petrograd. His elegant notes come in three series - w/o prefix letter and w/A or Б before the serial #. The back of each note shows an uncrowned double eagle and the Peter the Great Monument.

Each note bears two signatures: Yudenich, commander in chief, general of infantry, and St. Lianozov, manager of finance department. Notes were offset printed in Stockholm, Sweden by Centraltryckeriet. Yudenich disbanded his army on Jan. 22, 1920.

		VG	VF	UNC
S201	**25 Kopeks** 1919. Black on light green underprint. Signatures of Yudenich and St. Lianozov. Back: Uncrowned double eagle and Peter the Great monument. Printer: Centraltryckeriet, Stockholm, Sweden.	5.00	15.00	45.00

		VG	VF	UNC
S202	**50 Kopeks** 1919. Black on gray underprint. Signatures of Yudenich and St. Lianozov. Back: Uncrowned double eagle and Peter the Great monument. Printer: Centraltryckeriet, Stockholm, Sweden.	7.00	20.00	60.00

		VG	VF	UNC
S203	**1 Ruble** 1919. Dark green on light green underprint. Signatures of Yudenich and St. Lianozov. Back: Uncrowned double eagle and Peter the Great monument. Printer: Centraltryckeriet, Stockholm, Sweden.	8.00	24.00	75.00
S204	**3 Rubles** 1919. Green on rose underprint. Signatures of Yudenich and St. Lianozov. Back: Uncrowned double eagle and Peter the Great monument. Printer: Centraltryckeriet, Stockholm, Sweden.			
	a. Serial # without letters (first issue).	10.00	30.00	90.00
	b. Serial # prefix: A **(second issue).**	10.00	30.00	90.00

S205 5 Rubles

1919. Black on blue underprint. Signatures of Yudenich and St. Lianozov. Back: Uncrowned double eagle and Peter the Great monument. Printer: Centraltryckeriet, Stockholm, Sweden.

	VG	VF	UNC
a. Like #S204a.	12.00	35.00	110
b. Like #S204b.	12.00	35.00	110.

S206 10 Rubles

1919. Brown on light green underprint. Signatures of Yudenich and St. Lianozov. Back: Uncrowned double eagle and Peter the Great monument. Printer: Centraltryckeriet, Stockholm, Sweden.

	VG	VF	UNC
a. Like #S204a. (first issue)	15.00	45.00	135.
b. Like #S204b. (second issue).	15.00	45.00	135.
c. Serial # prefix: Б **(third issue).**	20.00	60.00	180.

S207 25 Rubles

1919. Black on violet underprint. Double eagle at upper left. Signatures of Yudenich and St. Lianozov. Back: Uncrowned double eagle and Peter the Great monument. Printer: Centraltryckeriet, Stockholm, Sweden.

	VG	VF	UNC
a. Like #S204a.	20.00	60.00	180.
b. Like #S204b.	20.00	60.00	180.
c. Like #S206c.	25.00	75.00	225.

S208 100 Rubles

	VG	VF	UNC
1919. Dark green on light brown underprint. Double eagle at upper left. Signatures of Yudenich and St. Lianozov. Similar to #S207. Back: Uncrowned double eagle and Peter the Great monument. Printer: Centraltryckeriet, Stockholm, Sweden.	25.00	75.00	225.

S209 500 Rubles

	VG	VF	UNC
1919. Blue-black on blue underprint. Signatures of Yudenich and St. Lianozov. Back: Brown on blue-gray underprint. Uncrowned double eagle and Peter the Great monument. Printer: Centraltryckeriet, Stockholm, Sweden.	50.00	150.	450.

S210 1000 Rubles

	VG	VF	UNC
1919. Black-green on light brown underprint. Flags and shields around value at left, double eagle at right. Signatures of Yudenich and St. Lianozov. Back: Brown on lilac underprint. Uncrowned double eagle and Peter the Great monument. Printer: Centraltryckeriet, Stockholm, Sweden.	70.00	200.	600.

ПСКОВСКАГО ОБЛАСТНОГО КАЗНАЧЕЙСТВА

Pskov Regional Government Treasury

1918 КРЕДИТНЫЙ БИЛЕТЪ Treasury Credit Notes Issue

S211 50 Rubles

	VG	VF	UNC
2.11.1918. Dull green and red. Autograph signature of Major General Vandamm, commander of the North Army, and a financial officer and treasurer. Back: Blue and red on green underprint.	35.00	110.	325.

ILLUSTRATIONS

Illustrations of bank notes used throughout this catalog are 42% of the actual size.

1918 Pskov Bank Small Change Notes Issue

Three sign. In 1918 there were also Pskov bonds pressed into use as currency. Not connected with Gen. Vandamm's army, as that organization was not activated until Oct. 12, 1918.

	VG	VF	UNC
S212 1 Ruble 15.3.1918. Orange.	20.00	60.00	180.
S213 5 Rubles 15.3.1918. Blue and brown.	25.00	75.00	225.

ОТДѢЛЬНЫЙ КОРПУСЪ СѢВЕРНОИ АРМIИ, ГЕН. РОДЗЯНКО

Special Corps of Northern Army under Gen. Rodzianko

1919 Stamp Money Issue

	VG	VF	UNC
S216 50 Kopeks ND (1919). Light green. Pastage stamp. Printed. Back: Printed.	50.00	150.	450.

Original size

	VG	VF	UNC
S217 50 Kopeks ND (1919). Light green.			
a. Face only of #S216.	10.00	30.00	90.00
b. Back only of #S216.	10.00	30.00	90.00
S218 50 Kopeks ND (1919). Dark green.			
a. Face only of #S216.	15.00	45.00	135.
b. Back only of #S216.	15.00	45.00	135.

1919 Notes Issue

	VG	VF	UNC
S219 1 Ruble 1919. Brown on yellow.	5.00	15.00	45.00
S220 3 Rubles 1919. Green.	7.00	20.00	60.00
S221 5 Rubles 1919. Blue.	15.00	45.00	135.

	VG	VF	UNC
S222 10 Rubles 1919. Red.	15.00	45.00	135.

ЗАПАДНАЯ ДОБРОВОЛЬЧЕСКАЯ АРМIЯ, ПОЛК АВАЛОВ-БЕРМОНДТЪ

Independent West Army under Colonel Avalov-Bermondt

1919 Kassenscheine (Treasury Notes) Issue

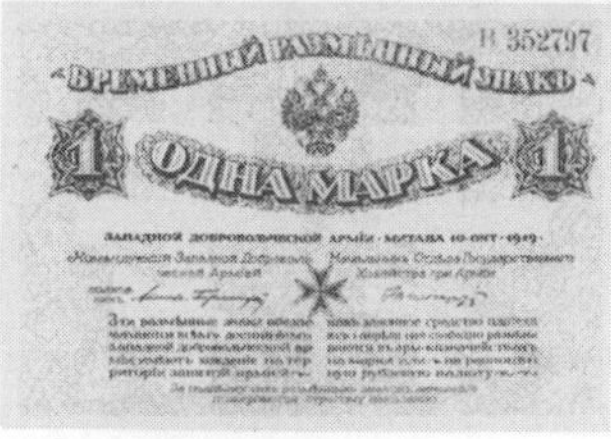

	VG	VF	UNC
S226 1 Mark 10.10.1919. Black on pale blue, red, and gray lines in underprint. Arms at upper center. Text in Russian. Back: Dark blue on light blue. Text in German.			
a. Embossed seal at lower left.	5.00	15.00	45.00
b. No embossed seal.	5.00	15.00	45.00

	VG	VF	UNC
S227 5 Mark 10.10.1919. Black on pale blue, red, and gray lines in underprint. Arms at upper center. Text in Russian. Back: Red on pink underprint. Text in German.			
a. Embossed seal at lower left.	10.00	30.00	90.00
b. No embossed seal.	10.00	30.00	90.00

	VG	VF	UNC
S228 10 Mark 10.10.1919. Black. Arms at upper center. Text in Russian. Back: Brown on pale blue underprint. Text in German. Paper: Green.			
a. Face on green paper with fine lines horizontally in underprint. With embossed seal at lower left.	30.00	90.00	270.
b. Face on white paper without underprint. Seal as above.	15.00	45.00	135.
c. Without embossed seal, Underprint as a.	50.00	150.	450.
d. Without embossed seal Underprint as b.	20.00	60.00	180.

NOTE: Unfinished sheets of #S228 (printed on one side only) were used to print Latvian postage stamps in 1920.

#S229 *Deleted.* See #S228.

	VG	VF	UNC
S230 50 Mark			
10.10.1919. Black. Arms at left. Back: Gray-green on brown underprint.			
a. Stamped imprint.	50.00	150.	450.
b. Without stamped imprint.	50.00	150.	450.

ПАРТИЗАНСКИЙ ОТРЯД ПОЛК БУЛАК-БАЛАХОВИЧА

Partisan Detachment of Lt.Col. Bulak-Balakhovich

1919 ND Issue

	VG	VF	UNC
S231 40 Rubles			
ND (1919). Rare.	—	—	—

КРОНШТАДТСКАЯ РЕСПУБЛИКА

Kronstadt Republic

1917 ND ВРЕМЕННЫЙ БОН

Provisional *Bons* or Notes Issue

#S234 and S235 were apparently intended for issue by the short-lived Kronstadt Republic, a Bolshevik state declared by naval mutineers at the Kronstadt naval fortress outside Petrograd in 1917, which collapsed along with the Bolshevik coup against the Provisional government July 16-18, 1917.

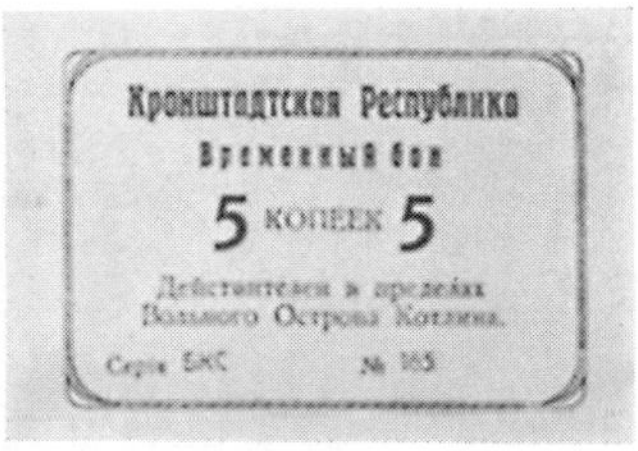

	VG	VF	UNC
S234 5 Kopek			
ND (1917). Black text on bright red underprint. Seriya BKS.	—	—	200.
S235 10 Kopek			
ND (1917). Black text on bright red underprint. Like #S234 but Seriya VTR.	—	—	200.

NOTE: Some authorities question the authenticity of #S234 and S235.

	VG	VF	UNC
S235A 10 Kopek			
ND (1917). Black text on bright red underprint. Seriya VTR. **Like #S235 but reduced in size.** Paper: Off-white.	—	—	300.

МОГИЛЕВСКОЙ ГУБЕРНІИ

Mogilev Region

1918 РАЗМѢННЫЙ БИЛЕТЪ Exchange Notes Issue

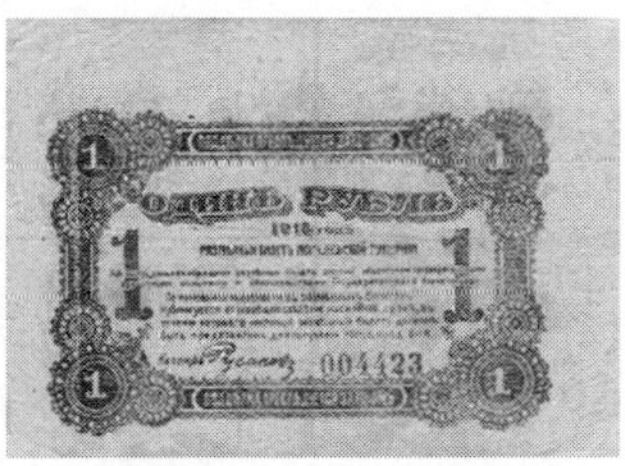

	VG	VF	UNC
S236 1 Ruble			
1918. Blue. Eagle with outstretched wings holding scroll with arms at lower left, three volcanos with center erupting at lower right. Back: Russian text.			
a. Issued note with serial # on lower back.	15.00	45.00	135.
r. Remainder without serial #.	10.00	30.00	90.00

	VG	VF	UNC
S237 3 Rublei			
Black. Eagle with outstretched wings holding scroll with arms at lower left, three volcanos with center erupting at lower right. Back: Polish text. Paper: Blue.			
a. Issued note with serial # on back.	20.00	60.00	180.
r. Remainder without serial # on back.	8.00	24.00	75.00
x. Error with inverted back.	30.00	90.00	270.
S238 5 Rublei			
1918. Black. Eagle with outstretched wings holding scroll with arms at lower left, three volcanos with center erupting at lower right. Back: Russian text. Paper: Blue.			
a. Issued note with serial # on back.	20.00	60.00	180.
r. Remainder without serial #.	8.00	24.00	75.00
S239 10 Rublei			
1918. Eagle with outstretched wings holding scroll with arms at lower left, three volcanos with center erupting at lower right. Back: Russian text.			
a. Issued note with serial # on back.	20.00	60.00	180.
r. Remainder without serial #.	10.00	30.00	90.00
S240 25 Rublei			
1918. Black. Eagle with outstretched wings holding scroll with arms at lower left, three volcanos with center erupting at lower right. Back: Russian text. Paper: Blue.			
a. Issued note with serial # on back.	25.00	75.00	225.
r. Remainder without serial #.	20.00	60.00	180.
S240A 100 Rublei			
1918. Eagle with outstretched wings holding scroll with arms at lower left, three volcanos with center erupting at lower right. Back: Russian text. (Not issued.)	30.00	90.00	270.

СЛУЦКОЕ УѢЗДНОЕ ЗЕМСТВО

Slutsk (White Russia) Zemstvo

1918 КРАТКОСРОЧНАЯ БОНА

Debenture *Bons* or Notes Issue

	Good	Fine	XF
S241 1 Ruble			
1918. Black on red-brown underprint. Handstamp at left. 4 signatures.	20.00	60.00	180.
S242 3 Rubles			
1918. Black on green underprint. Handstamp at left.			
a. Normal underprint.	30.00	90.00	270.
x. Error with reversed underprint.	30.00	90.00	270.

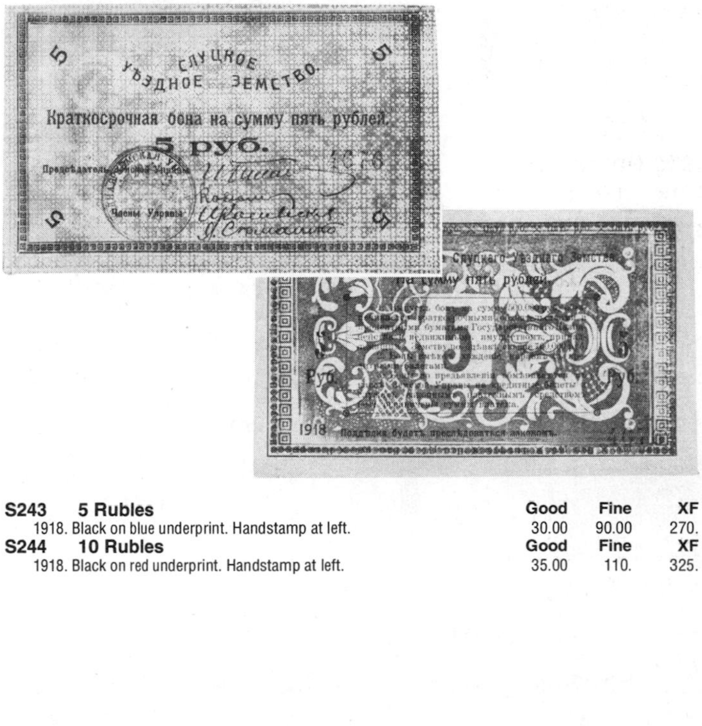

	Good	Fine	XF
S243 5 Rubles			
1918. Black on blue underprint. Handstamp at left.	30.00	90.00	270.
S244 10 Rubles	Good	Fine	XF
1918. Black on red underprint. Handstamp at left.	35.00	110.	325.

UKRAINE & CRIMEA

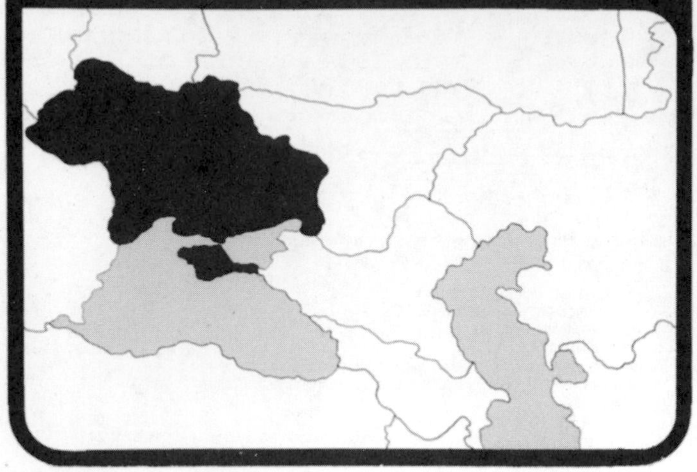

ISSUES OF:

- Ukrainian Socialist Soviet Republic
- Administration of Economic Enterprises
- Elizabetgrad Branch, Government Bank
- Elizabetgrad Branch, Peoples Bank
- Revolutionary Army of Insurgent Ukraine (Makhno)
- Ukrainian Cooperative Bank, Kiev (Kyiv)
- Ukrainian Revolutionary Army (Post-WW II)
- Odessa City
- Zhitomir City
- Zhitomir Branch, Soednenni Bank
- Crimea Territorial Government (Gen. Sulkevich)
- Provisional Govt. of Workers and Peasants
- Kherson Governm

УКРАИНСКОЙ СОЦ. СОВЕТ. РЕСПУБЛ.

1920 ND ЗНАК ДЕРЖАВНОЙ СКАРБНИЦІ ISSUE

		VG	VF	UNC
S293	**10 Karbovanets** ND (1919). Red-brown. With block #. Paper: White. Watermark: Honeycomb.	10.00	30.00	90.00

1919 (1920) ДЕНЕЖНЫЙ ЗНАК CURRENCY TOKEN ISSUE

		VG	VF	UNC
S294	**50 Karbovanets** 1919 (1920). Workers with hammer at left, factory in background. Proofs only.			
	a. Green. Rare.	—	—	—
	b. Light blue. Rare.	—	—	—
	c. Violet. Rare.	—	—	—
	d. Brown. Rare.	—	—	—

УПРАВЛЕНИЕ ХОЗЯЙСТВЕН.

ПРЕДПРЕЯТИЯМИ ВУЦИК.

ADMINISTRATION OF ECONOMIC ENTERPRISES

1923 ISSUE

		VG	VF	UNC
S295	**5 Kopeks** 1923. Green and blue. Handwritten numerator in serial #. Back: Lilac mark of denomination.	15.00	45.00	125.

		VG	VF	UNC
S296	**10 Kopeks** 1923. Green and blue. Handwritten numerator in serial #. Back: Lilac mark of denomination.	15.00	45.00	125.

		VG	VF	UNC
S297	**25 Kopeks** 1923. Green and blue. Handwritten numerator in serial #. Back: Lilac mark of denomination.	20.00	60.00	180.
S298	**50 Kopeks** 1923. Green and blue. Handwritten numerator in serial #. Back: Lilac mark of denomination.	20.00	60.00	180.
S299	**1 Ruble** 1923. Green and blue. Handwritten numerator in serial #. Back: Lilac mark of denomination.	25.00	75.00	225.
S300	**3 Rubles** 1923.	25.00	75.00	225.
S301	**5 Rubles** 1923.	30.00	90.00	270.
S302	**10 Rubles** 1923.	30.00	90.00	270.
S303	**25 Rubles** 1923.	60.00	180.	550.
S304	**50 Rubles** 1923.	75.00	225.	675.

German Occupation - WWII NOTE: For previously listed #S305-S320, see Vol. 2, Ukraine #42-57.

ГОСУДАРСТВЕННАГО БАНКА

GOVERNMENT BANK

ЕЛИСАВЕТГРАСКОЕ ОТДЂ Л

ELIZABETGRAD

1918 РАЗМѢННЫЙ БИЛЕТЪ EXCHANGE NOTES ISSUE

		VG	VF	UNC
S323	**1 Ruble** 1918. Black on brown underprint. Double-headed eagle at left, arms at right. Back: Dull orange. Double-headed eagle at center.	7.50	22.50	65.00
S323A	**3 Rublei** 1918. Black-green. Eagle with outstretched wings and holding scroll with arms at lower left, laureated woman's head at lower right.	7.50	22.50	65.00

		VG	VF	UNC
S323B	**10 Rublei** 1918. Black-green on salmon underprint. Eagle with outstretched wings and holding scroll with arms at lower left, laureated woman's head at lower right. Like #S323A.			
	a. Issued note with serial # at right.	10.00	30.00	90.00
	r. Remainder without serial #.	7.50	22.50	65.00

НАРОДНАГО БАНКА

National Bank

ЕЛИСАБЕТГРАДСКАГО ОТ ДѢЛЕНІЯ

Elizabetgrad

1919 РАЗМѢННІЙ БИЛЕТЪ Exchange Notes Issue

S324 5 Rublei	VG	VF	UNC
1919. Dark blue on light blue underprint. Ornate border. Back: Dark blue on light green underprint. Vertical format.	10.00	30.00	90.00

S324A 25 Rublei	VG	VF	UNC
1919. Black on red and green underprint. Back: Green.			
a. Without series.	5.00	15.00	45.00
b. With series.	8.00	24.00	75.00

1920 РАЗМѢННІЙ БИЛЕТЪ Exchange Notes Issue

S325 50 Rublei	VG	VF	UNC
1920. Black on light brown and light green underprint. Back: Black on brown underprint.			
a. Without series.	10.00	30.00	90.00

S325A 50 Rublei	VG	VF	UNC
1920. Black on brown and green underprint. Back: Black on green underprint.	—	—	—
a. With series.	—	—	—

1st Revolutionary Army of Insurgent Ukraine

Partisan overprints supposedly made on notes of the Denikin Armies by partisan leader N. Makhno at Gulyai-Pole in Ekaterinoslav Guberniya. It is also possible that Makhno could have made some overprint. for propaganda reasons while he was in exile in Paris. However, all examples on the market are bogus and in Unc. or nearly new condition. These began to appear in January 1980.

ВСЕУКРАЇНСЬКИЙ КООПЕРАТИВНИЙ БАНК

Ukrainian Cooperative Bank, Kiev Ukrainbank

1924 ЧЕК Circulating Checks Issue

S326 1 Karbovanets	VG	VF	UNC
1924. Brown.	15.00	45.00	135.

S327 3 Karbovantsi	VG	VF	UNC
1924. Green.	15.00	45.00	135.

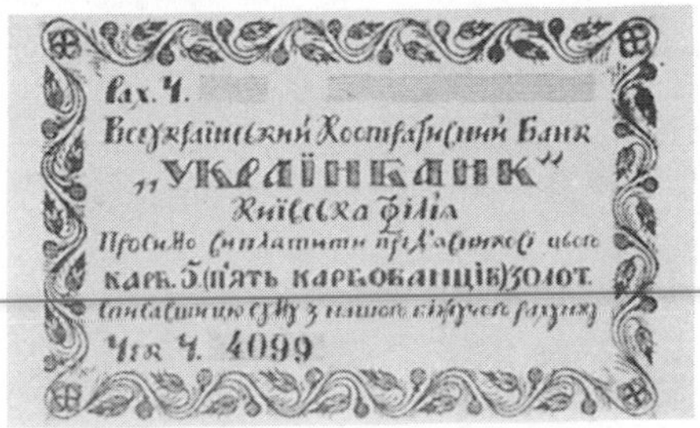

S328 5 Karbovantsiv	VG	VF	UNC
1924. Blue.	20.00	60.00	180.

POST WWII

УКРАИНЬСКА ПОВСТАНСКА АРМІЯ УПА-UPA (УКРАЇНСЬКА ПОВСТАНСЬКА АРМІЯ)

Ukrainian Revolutionary Army

1946 ND Issue

S330 5 Karbovanets	VG	VF	UNC
ND (1946). Brown, violet and multicolor. Soldier at machine gun and soldier with hand grenade. Rare.	—	—	—

ОДЕССА Odessa City

1917 РАЗМѢННАЯ МАРКА Postage Stamp Money Issue

S331 15 Kopeks	VG	VF	UNC
ND (1917). Brown.	5.00	15.00	45.00

S332 20 Kopeks	VG	VF	UNC
ND (1917). Green.	5.00	15.00	45.00

S333 50 Kopeks	VG	VF	UNC
ND (1917). Black and dark blue on brown underprint. Arms at upper center. Back: Wreath.	5.00	15.00	45.00

1917; 1918 РАЗМѢННЫЙИЙ БИЛЕТЬ Г. ОДЕССЫ

EXCHANGE NOTES OF ODESSA AREA ISSUE

Many varieties of color, paper and serial #.

		VG	VF	UNC
S334	**3 Rubles**			
	1917. Dark green. Double eagle with arms at left, Mercury at lower right. Back: Building in underprint.	3.00	9.00	27.50

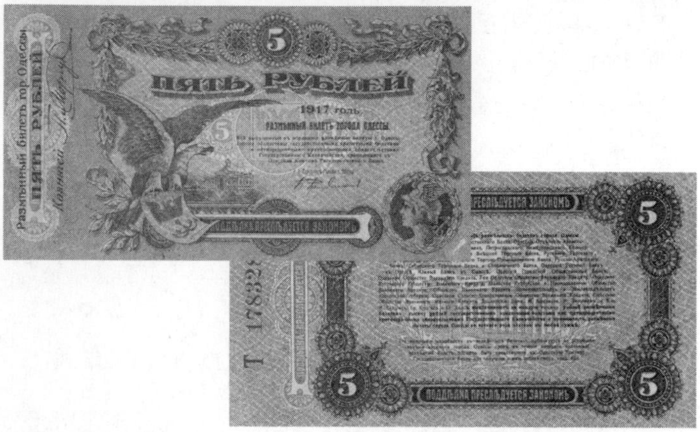

		VG	VF	UNC
S335	**5 Rubles**			
	1917. Blue. Double eagle with arms at left, Mercury at lower right. Similar to #S334. Back: Building in underprint.	3.00	9.00	27.50

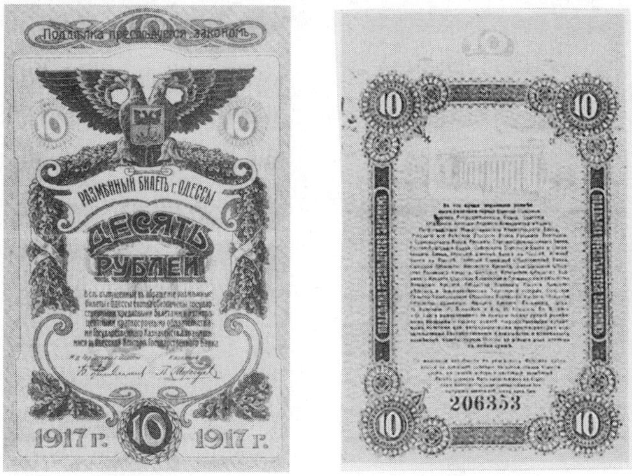

		VG	VF	UNC
S336	**10 Rubles**			
	1917. Dark green on pale green and light red underprint. Double eagle with arms at upper center. Back: Dark brown on pale orange-brown underprint. Building façade at upper center.	5.00	15.00	45.00

		VG	VF	UNC
S337	**25 Rubles**			
	1917. Black on dull green and pink underprint. Double eagle at upper left and right, arms at upper center. Back: Black and deep green on tan underprint. Building at left and at right, arms at upper center.			
	a. Watermark: Waves.	10.00	30.00	90.00
	b. Without watermark. Building underprint, columns at left.	5.00	15.00	45.00
	c. Building underprint, columns at right.	5.00	15.00	45.00
S338	**50 Rubles**			
	1918. Green and blue. Double eagle at upper left and right, arms at upper center. Similar to #S337. Back: Building at left and at right, arms at upper center.	25.00	75.00	225.

NOTE: #S331-S338 were circulating from 1917-20 in southwestern Ukraine.

ЖИТОМИР ZHYTOMYR CITY

1918 РОЗМІННИЙ БІЛЕТ МІСТА ЖИТОМИРА

MUNICIPAL RECEIPTS ISSUE

		VG	VF	UNC
S341	**1 Karbovanets**			
	1918. Black on tan underprint.	8.00	24.00	75.00
S342	**3 Karbovantsi**			
	1918. Green underprint. Like #S343.	10.00	30.00	90.00

		VG	VF	UNC
S343	**5 Karbovantsiv**			
	1918. Blue.			
	a. Black serial #.	10.00	30.00	90.00
	b. Red serial #.	10.00	30.00	90.00

НАРОДНОГО БАНКА NATIONAL BANK

1919-20 РАЗМЕННЫЙ БИЛЕТ TREASURY NOTES ISSUE

		VG	VF	UNC
S344	**50 Rubles**			
	1919. Black on light brown underprint.	7.50	22.50	65.00
S345	**75 Rubles**			
	1919. Black on blue-green underprint.	7.50	22.50	65.00
S346	**100 Rubles**			
	1919. Black on reddish brown underprint.	7.50	22.50	65.00

		VG	VF	UNC
S347	**250 Rubles** 1920. Blue on green underprint.	7.50	22.50	65.00

АЗОВСКО-ДОНСКОЙ КОММЕРЧЕСКІЙ БАНКЪ

Azov-Don Commercial Bank

ЖИТОМИРСКОЕ ОТДЂЛЕНІ Е

Zhytomyr

1918 Circulating Bearer Checks Issue

		VG	VF	UNC
S351	**25 Rubles** 8.4.1918-4.5.1918.	10.00	30.00	90.00
S352	**50 Rubles** 27.1.1918-4.5.1918. (4 types).	10.00	30.00	90.00
S353	**60 Rubles** 27.1.1918-6.3.1918. Rare.	—	—	—
S354	**100 Rubles** 27.1.1918-12.12.1919.	10.00	30.00	90.00
S355	**200 Rubles** 27.1.1918-18.4.1918. (4 types).	10.00	30.00	90.00
S356	**250 Rubles** 20.4.1918-12.12.1919.	10.00	30.00	90.00

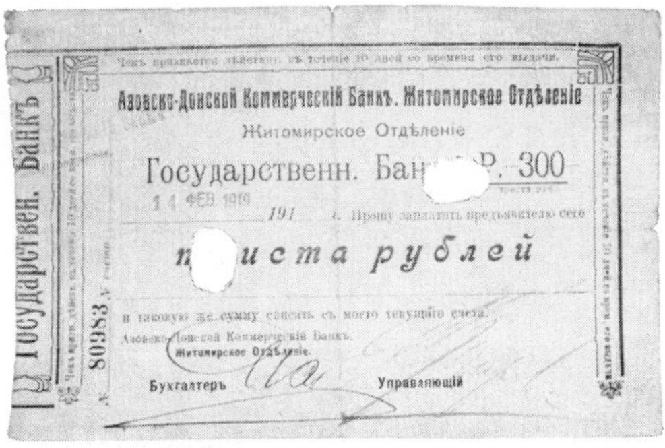

		VG	VF	UNC
S357	**300 Rubles** 14.3.1918-12.12.1919. (4 types).	15.00	45.00	135.
S358	**500 Rubles** 27.1.1918-12.12.1919. (6 types).	15.00	45.00	135.
S359	**1000 Rubles** 14.3.1918-10.5.1920. (9 types).	15.00	45.00	135.

A WORD ON DATE RANGES

Often date ranges or specific dates are listed. These have been observed or reported by our contributors. If a note is outside the published range, it only means that it is a newly reported date, and not necessarily worthy of a premium value.

ГОСУДАРСТВЕНН.БАНКА

Government Bank

ЖИТОМИРСКОЕ ОТДЂАЕНІ Е

Zhytomyr

1918-1919 Circulating Bearer Checks Issue

		Good	Fine	XF
S361	**25 Rubles** 26.3.1918-5.4.1919. (3 Types).	10.00	30.00	90.00
S362	**50 Rubles** 13.2.1918-5.4.1919. (7 Types).	7.50	22.50	65.00

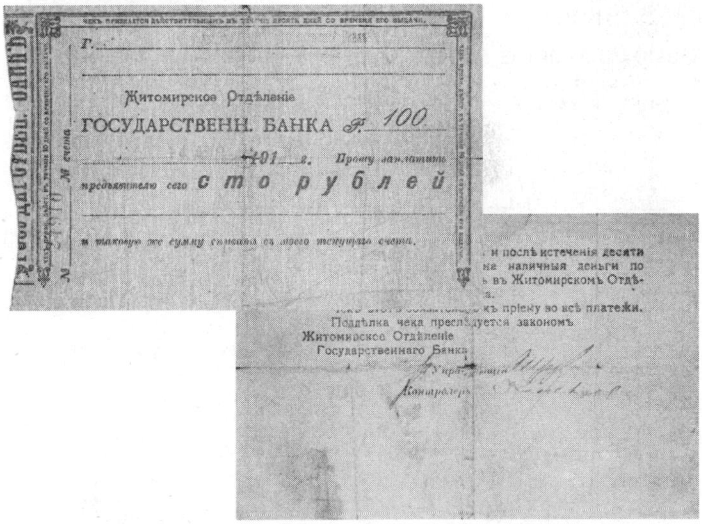

		Good	Fine	XF
S363	**100 Rubles** 13.2.1918-29.4.1918. (4 Types).	15.00	45.00	135.

NOTE: Circulating checks also were issued at Zhitomir by the Union Bank, Vzaimnago Credit Company and a cooperative. Details not available.

СОЕДИНЕННЫЙ БАНКЪ

Soednenni Bank

ЖИТОМИРСКОЕ ОТДЂАЕНІ Е

Zhytomyr

1918 Issue

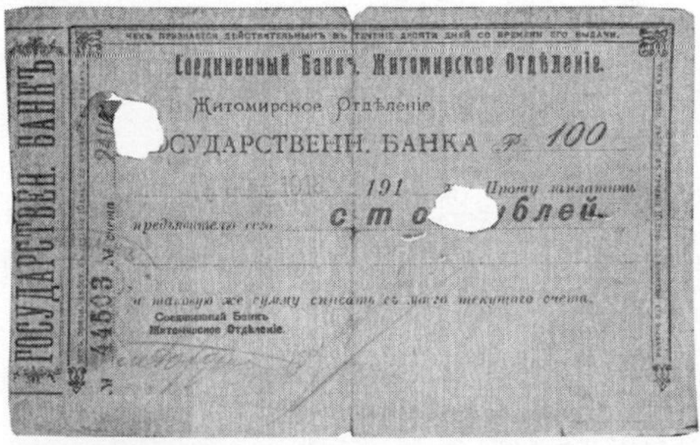

		Good	Fine	XF
S364	**40 Rublei** 26.3.1918. Rare.	—	—	—
S364A	**50 Rublei** 26.3.1918.	40.00	120.	360.

		Good	Fine	XF
S364B	**100 Rublei** 15.6.1918. Black on green underprint. Back: Black text. Punched hole cancelled with 2 holes.	15.00	45.00	135.
S364C	**200 Rublei** 1918-19.	15.00	45.00	135.
S364D	**500 Rublei** 11.4.1918.	45.00	135.	500.

КРЫМСКОЕ КРАЕВОЕ ПРАВИТЕЛЬСТВО

CRIMEA TERRITORIAL GOVERNMENT

1918 ОБЯЗАТЕЛЬСТВО КРЫМСКАГО КРАЕВОГО КАЗНАЧЕЙСТВА

OBLIGATION OFTHE CRIMEA AREA TREASURY ISSUE

		VG	VF	UNC
S366	**500 Rubles** 1.9.1918. Black on green underprint. Double eagle at upper left. Uniface.	15.00	45.00	135.

		VG	VF	UNC
S367	**1000 Rubles** 1.9.1918. Black on green underprint. Double eagle at upper left. Uniface.	15.00	45.00	135.
S368	**5000 Rubles** 1.9.1918. Black on green underprint. Double eagle at upper left. Uniface.			
	a. Issued note.	90.00	270.	800.
	b. Without serial #.	—	—	150.

1918 МАРКА POSTAGE STAMP MONEY ISSUE

		VG	VF	UNC
S369	**50 Kopeks** ND (1918). Brown. Double eagle at center. Back: Double eagle at upper center. Vertical format.	7.50	22.50	65.00

1918 ДЕНЕЖНЫЙ ЗНАКЪ CURRENCY TOKENS ISSUE

		Good	Fine	XF
S370	**5 Rubles** 1918. Blue and brown. Serial # numerator varies from 3 to 6mm. Back: Map of the Crimea	10.00	30.00	90.00
S371	**10 Rubles** 1918. Red and brown. Back: Map of the Crimea.	15.00	45.00	135.

		Good	Fine	XF
S372	**25 Rubles** 1918. Green and lilac. Back: Map of the Crimea.			
	a. Serial # 3.5-6mm high.	15.00	45.00	135.
	b. Serial # 3mm high. (Soviet issue of 1919).	15.00	45.00	135.

PROVISIONAL GOVERNMENT OF WORKERS AND PEASANTS

1919 ISSUE

		Good	Fine	XF
S375	**250 Rubles** 1919. Back: Blank. (Not issued).	—	—	—

УПРАВЛЕНІЕ УПОЛНОМОЧ. ПО ПРОД. ХЕРС. ГУБ.

PLENIPOTENTIARY FOR FOOD OF THE GOVERNMENT TERRITORY OF KHERSON

1919 ОДЕССА ВРЕМЕННАЯ КВИТАНЦІЯ

ODESSA PROVISIONAL RECEIPTS ISSUE

		Good	Fine	XF
S376	**25 Rubles** 10.10.1919. Blue and red. Paper: Brown.	20.00	60.00	180.
S377	**50 Rubles** 10.10.1919. Blue and red. Paper: Green.	20.00	60.00	180.

		Good	Fine	XF
S378	**100 Rubles** 10.10.1919. Blue and red. Paper: Brown.	20.00	60.00	180.
S379	**250 Rubles** 10.10.1919. Blue and red. Paper: Green.	20.00	60.00	180.
S380	**500 Rubles** 10.10.1919. Blue and red. Paper: Brown.	20.00	60.00	180.

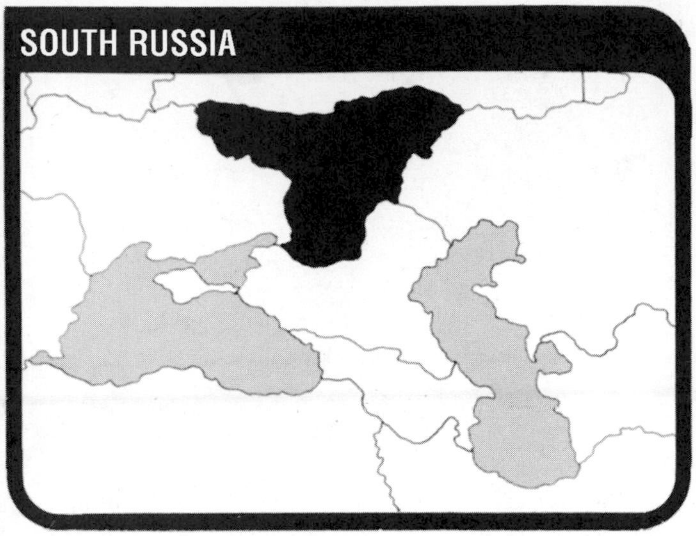

GOVERNMENT
Don Cossack Government

MILITARY
High Command of the Armed Forces in South Russia (Generals Denikin and Wrangel)

ВСЕВЕЛИКАГО ВОЙСКА ДОНСКОГО

Don Cossack Military Government

Astrakhan

1 ЯНВАРЯ 1919 Issue

	Good	Fine	XF
S381 500 Rubles			
1.1.1919. Novocherkassk.	20.00	60.00	180.
S382 1000 Rubles			
1.1.1919. Novocherkassk.	20.00	60.00	180.
S383 5000 Rubles			
1.1.1919. Novocherkassk.	20.00	60.00	180.

	Good	Fine	XF
S384 10,000 Rubles			
1.1.1919. Novocherkassk.	50.00	150.	450.
S385 25,000 Rubles			
1.1.1919. Novocherkassk.	80.00	240.	825.
S386 50,000 Rubles			
1.1.1919. Novocherkassk.	150.	450.	1350.

1 АПРѢЛЯ 1919 Issue

	Good	Fine	XF
S387 500 Rubles			
1.4.1919.			
a. Novocherkassk.	25.00	75.00	225.
b. Taganrog.	25.00	75.00	225.
S388 1000 Rubles			
1.4.1919.			
a. Novocherkassk.	25.00	75.00	225.
b. Taganrog.	35.00	110.	325.
c. Rostov.	—	—	—
S389 5000 Rubles			
1.4.1919.			
a. Novocherkassk.	25.00	75.00	225.
b. Taganrog.	45.00	135.	400.
c. Rostov.	—	—	—
S390 10,000 Rubles			
1.4.1919.			
a. Novocherkassk.	100.	300.	900.
b. Taganrog.	125.	375.	1150.
S391 25,000 Rubles			
1.4.1919.			
a. Novocherkassk.	75.00	225.	675.
b. Rostov.	—	—	—
S392 50,000 Rubles			
1.4.1919. Novocherkassk.	150.	450.	1350.

1 ІЮЛЯ 1919 Issue

	Good	Fine	XF
S393 500 Rubles			
1.7.1919.			
a. Novocherkassk.	15.00	45.00	135.
b. Taganrog.	12.50	35.00	110.
S394 1000 Rubles			
1.7.1919.			
a. Novocherkassk.	15.00	45.00	135.
b. Taganrog.	15.00	45.00	135.
S395 5000 Rubles			
1.7.1919.			
a. Novocherkassk.	15.00	45.00	135.
b. Taganrog.	15.00	45.00	135.
S396 10,000 Rubles			
1.7.1919.			
a. Novocherkassk.	25.00	75.00	225.
b. Taganrog.	40.00	120.	360.
S397 25,000 Rubles			
1.7.1919.			
a. Novocherkassk.	45.00	135.	400.
b. Taganrog.	100.	300.	900.
S398 50,000 Rubles			
1.7.1919.			
a. Novocherkassk.	150.	450.	1350.
b. Taganrog.	—	—	—

1 ОКТЯБРЯ 1919 Issue

	Good	Fine	XF
S399 500 Rubles			
1.10.1919.			
a. Novocherkassk.	15.00	45.00	135.
b. Taganrog.	20.00	60.00	180.
S400 1000 Rubles			
1.10.1919.			
a. Novocherkassk.	15.00	45.00	135.
b. Taganrog.	15.00	45.00	135.
S401 5000 Rubles			
1.10.1919.			
a. Novocherkassk.	25.00	75.00	225.
b. Taganrog.	15.00	45.00	135.
S402 10,000 Rubles			
1.10.1919.			
a. Novocherkassk.	25.00	75.00	225.
b. Taganrog.	20.00	60.00	180.

	Good	Fine	XF
S403 25,000 Rubles			
1.10.1919. Taganrog.	75.00	225.	675.
S404 50,000 Rubles			
1.10.1919. Swastika in the underprint. Taganrog. Misprint; back inverted.	150.	450.	1350.

ГОСУДАРСТВЕННЫЙ БАН К

Government Bank

ВЫМУЩЕН (or А) РОСТОВСК ОЙ НА.ДОНУ КОНТ ОРОЙ

Rostov

General Anton I. Denikin, 1918-20.
General Baron Peter Wrangel, 1920.

#S408-S427 the initial letter of the control # identifies the place of issue. For example, a note numbered Я-060 was issued at Simferopol; one numbered Б-022 was issues at Rostov, etc.

А = Rostov, except:
А = Feodosiya on 3R. Pick #S409.
А = Novorossisk on 1000R. Pick #S424.
А = Feodosiya on all 1920 issues.
А = Ekaterinodar on 50R. Pick #S416.
Б = Rostov
У = Feodosiya
В = Novorossisk
Я = Simferopol
К = Novorossisk
О = Odessa
Л = Kiev

1918 ND РАЗМѢННАЯ МАРКА Postage Stamp Money Issue

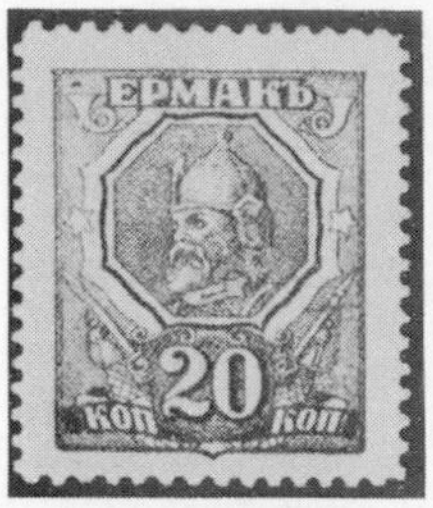

S406 20 Kopeks	VG	VF	UNC
ND (1918). Green. Ermak at center. Back: Printed text and eagle in black. Paper: Thin cardboard.	7.50	22.50	65.00

1918 ND Small Change Notes Issue

S407 50 Kopeks	VG	VF	UNC
ND (1918). Black and gray on light brown underprint. Back: Gen. Platov.	5.00	15.00	45.00

1918 ДЕНЕЖНЫЙ ЗНАКЪ Currency Tokens Issue

Many color shades and print varieties.

S408 1 Ruble	VG	VF	UNC
1918. Black and blue on brown underprint. Double eagle at upper center. Back: Brown on tan underprint.			
a. White, thin paper - Б.	3.00	9.00	27.50
b. Yellow, thick paper - А.	3.00	9.00	27.50

S409 3 Rubles	VG	VF	UNC
1918. Black and green on orange underprint. Double eagle at upper center. Back: Green on yellow underprint.			
a. White, thin paper without watermark. - А; К.	3.00	9.00	27.50
b. Gray, thin paper without watermark. - Л.	3.00	9.00	27.50
c. Yellow, thick paper without watermark. - А.	3.00	9.00	27.50
d. Watermark: Monogram - А.	4.00	12.50	35.00

S410 5 Rubles	VG	VF	UNC
1918. Black and blue on peach underprint. Double eagle at upper center.			
a. Without watermark: - А.	5.00	15.00	45.00
b. Watermark: Monogram - А.	5.00	15.00	45.00
c. Without watermark. Printed on art paper (chalk netting).	5.00	15.00	45.00

S411 10 Rubles	VG	VF	UNC
1918. Red-brown on light green underprint. Double eagle at upper center.			
a. Without watermark: - А.	5.00	15.00	45.00
b. Watermark: Monogram - А.	5.00	15.00	45.00
c. Watermark: Horizontal lines - А.	5.00	15.00	45.00

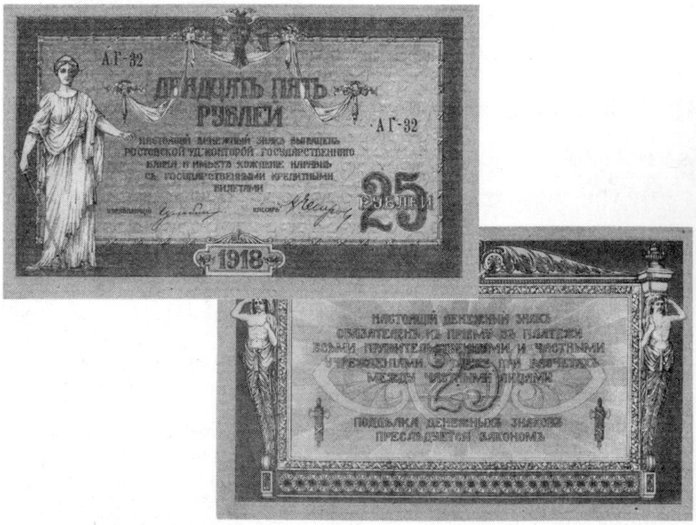

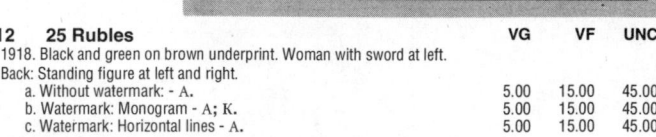

S412 25 Rubles	VG	VF	UNC
1918. Black and green on brown underprint. Woman with sword at left. Back: Standing figure at left and right.			
a. Without watermark: - А.	5.00	15.00	45.00
b. Watermark: Monogram - А; К.	5.00	15.00	45.00
c. Watermark: Horizontal lines - А.	5.00	15.00	45.00

S413 100 Rubles	VG	VF	UNC
1918. Dark brown and gray-blue. Portrait helmeted Ermak supported by seated woman. - А.	5.00	15.00	45.00

S414 250 Rubles	VG	VF	UNC
1918. Black and green on red-brown underprint. Women seated at left and right, Cossack Gen. Platov in uniform at left center. Back: Black on green and light red underprint. Eagle at upper center.			
a. White paper without watermark. - А.	5.00	15.00	45.00
b. Yellowish paper without watermark. - А.	5.00	15.00	45.00
c. Watermark: Monogram - А.	5.00	15.00	45.00

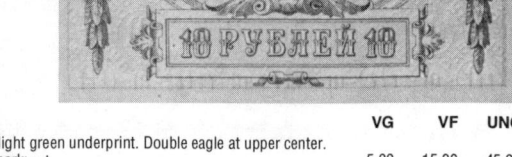

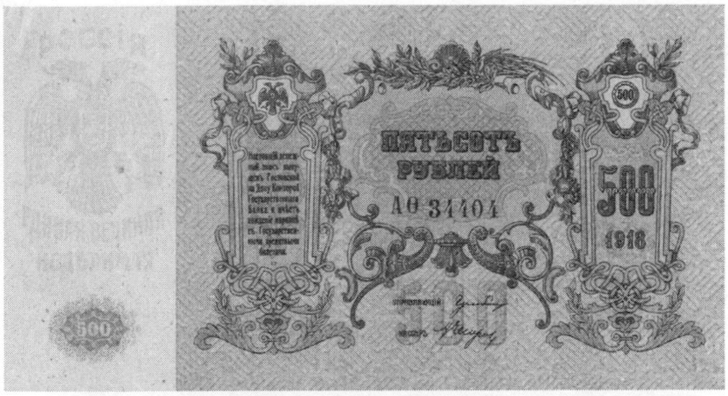

S415 500 Rubles	VG	VF	UNC
1918. Black on green and tan underprint. Small double eagle at upper left. Back: Allegory of Russia seated at left.			
a. White paper without watermark. - A.	5.00	15.00	45.00
b. Yellowish paper without watermark. - A. Serial # or control # (like BA-91).	5.00	15.00	45.00
c. Watermark: Monogram - A; Б; B.	8.00	24.00	75.00
d. Laid paper - AM.	8.00	24.00	75.00

1919 ДЕНЕЖНЫЙ ЗНАКЪ Currency Tokens Issue

S416 50 Rubles	VG	VF	UNC
1919. Brown and blue on gray underprint. Back: Woman with flag. With or without watermark.			
a. Watermark: Monogram *A* - A.	4.00	12.50	35.00
b. Without watermark: - Б.	4.00	12.50	35.00

S417 100 Rubles	VG	VF	UNC
1919. Black on brown and multicolor underprint. Double eagle at upper left. Back: Black on brown underprint. Warrior in armor with standard at right, monument with two warriors behind.			
a. Without watermark. - У.	3.00	9.00	27.50
b. Watermark: Monogram - A.	3.00	9.00	27.50

S418 1000 Rubles	VG	VF	UNC
1919. Black on blue, light green and pink underprint. Double eagle at upper center. Back: Dark blue on gray underprint. Allegory of Russia at center, buildings with spires at lower left and right.			
a. Without watermark. - *Y*.	3.00	9.00	27.50
b. Watermark: Monogram - A; Б; B; Я.	3.00	9.00	27.50
c. Watermark: Mosaic - Я.	3.00	9.00	27.50

S419 5000 Rubles	VG	VF	UNC
1919. Dark brown on orange, green and light brown underprint. Double eagle at upper left, head of Mercury at upper center. Back: Green on brown and orange underprint. St. George with shield, flag and snake at left, eagle at upper center.			
a. Without watermark. Serial # prefix У.	3.00	9.00	27.50
b. Gray paper without watermark. Serial # prefix У.	3.00	9.00	27.50
c. Watermark: Monogram. Serial # prefix A.	3.00	9.00	27.50
d. Watermark: Mosaic. Serial # prefix Я.	3.00	9.00	27.50

1919 БИЛЕТЪ ГОСУДАРСТВЕННАГО КАЗНАЧЕЙСТВА
GOVERNMENT TREASURY NOTES ISSUE

Issued by General Wrangel.

S420 3 Rubles	VG	VF	UNC
1919. Green. Back: Monument with cross honoring the millenium of Russia.			
a. Without watermark. - А.	20.00	60.00	180.
b. Watermark: Mosaic - А.	7.50	22.50	65.00

S421 10 Rubles	VG	VF	UNC
1919. Black on red-brown underprint. Double eagle at upper center. Back: Monument with cross honoring the millenium of Russia and two warriors.			
a. Without watermark. - У.	5.00	15.00	45.00
b. Watermark: Wavy lines - У.	5.00	15.00	45.00

S422 50 Rubles	VG	VF	UNC
1919. Black on olive-brown underprint. Woman with two children at left. Back: Black on light blue and olive-brown underprint. Monument with cross honoring the millenium of Russia.			
a. Watermark: Lines - К; О.	5.00	15.00	45.00
b. Watermark: Spades - О; У.	5.00	15.00	45.00
c. Without watermark. - К.	5.00	15.00	45.00
x. Error with back only. Watermark: Lines.	—	—	60.00

S423 200 Rubles	VG	VF	UNC
1919. Black on brown and gray-violet underprint. Double eagle at upper center. Back: Brown on tan underprint. Monument honoring millenium of Russia. Equestrian statue and soldiers standing in front at center. Watermark: Mosiac. - А; Я.	10.00	30.00	60.00

S424 1000 Rubles	VG	VF	UNC
1919. Multicolor. Bell at left, St. George and dragon at right. Back: Monument with cross honoring the millenium of Russia. Color variations of underprint and top ribbon from light yellow to wine-red.			
a. Without watermark. 3 serial # varieties - А; Б; В; О.	15.00	45.00	135.
b. Watermark: Mosaic - Б II В - **023**; Я.	15.00	45.00	135.

S425 10,000 Rubles	VG	VF	UNC
1919. Brown on green and dull orange underprint. Double eagle at upper center. Back: Monument with cross. Woman seated with lance at left, woman seated with sword at right. Color shade variants. Various series.			
a. Watermark: Mosaic - А; Я.	5.00	15.00	45.00
b. Without watermark. - Я.	5.00	15.00	45.00

1920 БИЛЕТЪ ГОСУДАРСТВЕННАГО КАЗНАЧЕЙСТВА
GOVERNMENT TREASURY NOTES ISSUE

Issued by General Wrangel.

S426 5 Rubles	VG	VF	UNC
1920. Blue-green. Double eagle at upper center. Back: Monument with cross honoring the millenium of Russia.			
a. Printed on both sides. - А. **Rare.**	—	—	—
b. Printed on back only.	25.00	75.00	225.
c. Printed on face only.	25.00	75.00	225.

S427 25,000 Rubles	VG	VF	UNC
1920. Gray-blue and brown. Double eagle at upper center. Back: Monument with cross honoring the millenium of Russia. (Unfinished printing). - А.	25.00	75.00	225.

1920 6% КРАТК. ОБЯЗАТЕЛЬСТВО ГОСУД. КАЗНАЧЕЙСТВА
DEBENTURE BONDS ISSUE

S431 100,000 Rubles	VG	VF	UNC
1.1.1920. Brown on red-brown.			
a. Date Line (СРОК) **1. IV. Rare.**	—	—	—
b. Date Line (СРОК) **15. VIII. Rare.**	—	—	—
c. Date Line (СРОК) **15. XI.**	—	125.	375.

1920 БИЛЕТЪ ГОСУДАРСТВЕННАГО КАЗНАЧЕЙСТВА

Government Treasury Notes Issue

Issued by General Wrangel.

		VG	VF	UNC
S432	**100 Rubles**			
	1920. Red-brown. Double eagle at upper center. Back: Monument with cross honoring the millenium of Russia.			
	a. Watermark: Stars.	5.00	15.00	45.00
	b. Watermark: Wavy lines.	3.00	9.00	27.50
	c. Watermark: Mosaic.	2.00	6.00	17.50
S433	**250 Rubles**			
	1920. Lilac-brown. Double eagle at upper center. Back: Monument with cross honoring the millenium of Russia.			
	a. Brown paper, watermark: Spades.	5.00	15.00	45.00
	b. White paper, watermark: Mosaic.	3.00	9.00	27.50

		VG	VF	UNC
S434	**500 Rubles**			
	1920. Blue or greenish color. Double eagle at upper center. Back: Monument with cross honoring the millenium of Russia.	3.00	9.00	27.50

NOTE: These notes were also overprint for use by Russian Forces trapped in a section of the Ottoman Empire in the early 1920's. More information is needed.

ГОСУДАРСТВО РОССІЙСКОЕ

Russian Government

1920 КАЗНАЧЕИСКІЙ ЗНАКЪ Treasury Tokens Issue

#S435-S438 Never issued due to the Nov. 1920 evacuation of Sevastopol.

		VG	VF	UNC
S435	**1 Ruble**			
	1920. Printer: W&S.	—	—	—
S436	**3 Rubles**			
	1920. Printer: W&S.	—	—	—
S437	**5 Rubles**			
	1920. Blue. Printer: W&S.	—	—	—

		VG	VF	UNC
S438	**50 Rubles**			
	ND (1920). Blue on yellow. Helmeted woman's head at upper left. Back: Eagle. Printer: W&S.	10.00	30.00	90.00

1919 КАЗНАЧЕИСКІЙ ЗНАКЪ Treasury Tokens Issue

#S439 and S440 Never issued due to the Nov. 1920 evacuation of Sevastopol.

		VG	VF	UNC
S439	**100 Rubles**			
	1919. Brown on green. Serial letters in the plate or printed with serial #. Back: Helmeted woman's head at left. Printer: W&S.			
	a. Black serial #.	10.00	30.00	90.00
	b. Brown serial #.	10.00	30.00	90.00

		VG	VF	UNC
S440	**500 Rubles**			
	1919. Green on orange underprint. St. George on horseback at lower left center, lion head at upper center. Back: Helmeted woman's head at center. Printer: W&S.			
	a. Black serial #.	15.00	45.00	135.
	b. Green serial #.	15.00	45.00	135.

АСТРАХАНСКАТО КАЗНАЧЕЙСТВА

Astrakhan Region

1918 ВРЕМЕННЫЙ КРЕДИТНЫЙ БИЛЕТЪ

Provisional Credit Notes Issue

		Good	Fine	XF
S441	**1 Ruble**			
	1918. Dark blue on brown underprint. Double-headed eagle at center. Back: Brown.	20.00	60.00	180.

		Good	Fine	XF
S442	**3 Rublei**			
	1918. Black on light olive green underprint. Back: Double-headed eagle at upper center.	25.00	75.00	225.
S443	**5 Rublei**			
	1918. Dark blue on salmon underprint. Double-headed eagle at center. Similar to #S441.	30.00	90.00	270.
S444	**10 Rublei**			
	1918. Brown on red-brown underprint. Double-headed eagle at center. Like #S443. Back: Green on red and green underprint.	35.00	135.	400.

		Good	Fine	XF
S445	**25 Rublei**			
	1918. Dark blue on green and pink underprint. Back: Brown on green underprint. Double-headed eagle at upper center.	50.00	150.	450.
S445A	**100 Rublei**			
	1918. Brown on yellow underprint. Back: Brown and yellow. Double-headed eagle at upper center. Star of David.	100.	300.	900.

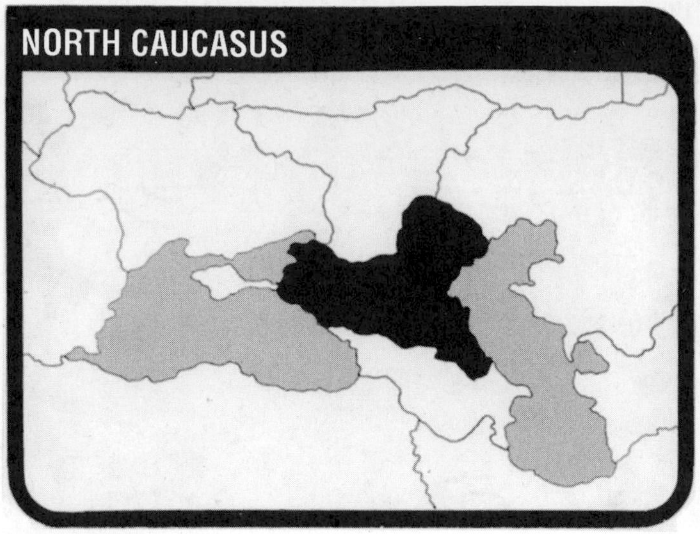

GOVERNMENTS

- North Caucasian Socialist Soviet Republic
- North Caucasian Emirate (Imam Usun-Khadzhi)
- Armavir Branch
- Kuban Territorial Government
- Kuban Soviet Republic
- Ekaterinodar Branch
- Mineralnyie Vodyi District
- Stavropol Branch
- Terek-Daghestan Territory (Imam Gozinskii)
- Terek Republic

MILITARY

- Black Sea Peasant Militia (Chief of Staff Voronovich)
- North Caucasus Volunteer Revolutionary Army
- Piatigorsk-Batalpashchinsk Company of the Independen

СЕВЕРО КАВКАЗСКАЯ СОЦИАЛИСТИЧЕСКАЯ СОВЕТСКАЯ РЕСПУБЛИКА

North Caucasian Socialist Soviet Republic

1918 Issue

		Good	Fine	XF
S447	**10 Rubles**			
	1918. Black on red and yellow underprint. Sickles and corn.			
	a. Text on face: ОВЩЕГОСУДАР ...ОГО.	35.00	100.	300.
	b. Text on face: ОБЩЕГООУДАР ...АГО.	35.00	100.	300.
S448	**25 Rubles**			
	1918. Black on lilac and yellow underprint. Sickles and corn.			
	a. Text on face: ОВЩЕГОСУДАР ...ОГО.	40.00	120.	360.
	b. Text on face: ОБЩЕГООУДАР<FHV ...АГО.	40.00	120.	360.

ВРЕМЕН. ЦЕНТРААЬНАГО УПРАВЛ. ОТДЕАЕНИЯМИ НАРОД. БАНКА

Provisional Central Administration of the Branch of the National Bank

1918 Issue

#S451-S453 printed on bills of exchange paper.

		Good	Fine	XF
S451	**25 Rubles** 1918. Black on blue-green underprint. Back: Purple text.	30.00	90.00	270.
S452	**50 Rubles** 1918. Black on yellow-brown underprint. Back: Purple text.	30.00	90.00	270.
S453	**100 Rubles** 1918. Black on green underprint. Back: Purple text.	30.00	90.00	270.

#S454-S455 *Deleted*, see #S447a and S448.

КРАЕВОГО ИСПОЛНИТ. КОМИТЕТА СОВЕТОВ СЕВ. КАВКАЗА

Area Executive Committee of the North Caucasian Soviet Republic

1918 ДЕНЕЖНЫЙ ЗНАК Currency Tokens Issue

		Good	Fine	XF
S456	**5 Rubles** 1918. Blue and pink.	40.00	120.	360.

		Good	Fine	XF
S457	**50 Rubles** 1918. Green.	50.00	150.	450.

		Good	Fine	XF
S458	**100 Rubles** 1918. Brown and yellow.	50.00	150.	450.
S459	**250 Rubles** 1918. Black on light green and brown underprint.	60.00	180.	550.

		Good	Fine	XF
S460	**500 Rubles** 1918. Multicolor.	70.00	210.	625.

СЕВЕРО-КАВКАЗСКИЙ ЭМИРАТ

North Caucasian Emirate

1919 ND РАЗМѢННЫЙ ЗНАКЪ Exchange Tokens Issue

		Good	Fine	XF
S461	**50 Rubles** ND (1919). Black on orange and tan underprint. Sunburst at center. Like #S534b with circular stamp of Vizier. Back: Brown on green underprint.	90.00	180.	550.
S462	**50 Rubles** ND (1919). Black on orange and tan underprint. Sunburst at center. Like #S534a with circular stamp of Vizier. Back: Brown on green underprint.	30.00	90.00	270.
S463	**100 Rubles** ND (1919). Like #S535 with oval imprint of ring of Imam.	90.00	270.	800.
S464	**100 Rubles** ND (1919). Like #S535 with oval imprint of ring of the Imam and circular stamp of Vizier.	50.00	150.	450.

		Good	Fine	XF
S465	**100 Rubles** ND (1919). Like #S535 with round stamp of Vizier. Handwritten date and text.	90.00	270.	800.
S466	**100 Rubles** ND (1919). Like #S535 with round stamp of Vizier. Without handwritten date and text.	50.00	150.	450.

		Good	Fine	XF
S467	**100 Rubles** ND (1919). Brown and yellow. Like #S458 with round stamp of Vizier. Handwritten date and text.	100.	300.	900.
S468	**100 Rubles** ND (1919). Brown and yellow. Like #S458 with round stamp of Vizier. Without handwritten date and text.	140.	425.	1275.
S469	**500 Rubles** ND (1919). Multicolor. Like #S460 with round stamp of Vizier. Handwritten date and text.	180.	550.	1650.

AH1338/1919 КРЕДИТНЫЙ БИЛЕТЪ

Credit Notes/Billet de Credit Issue

		Good	Fine	XF
S471	**5 Rubles** AH1338/1919. Blue-green. Mountain with flags.			
	a. Printed top to top.	40.00	120.	360.
	b. Back inverted. Rare.	—	—	—
S472	**25 Rubles** AH1338/1919.			
	a. Printed top to top.	100.	300.	900.
	b. Back inverted. Rare.	—	—	—

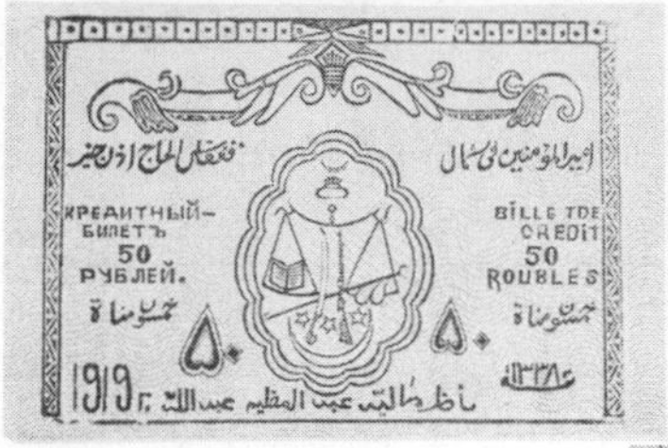

		Good	Fine	XF
S473	**50 Rubles** 1919. Scales at center. Back: Flag on mountain at left.			
	a. Printed top to top.	100.	300.	900.
	b. Back inverted. Rare.	—	—	—

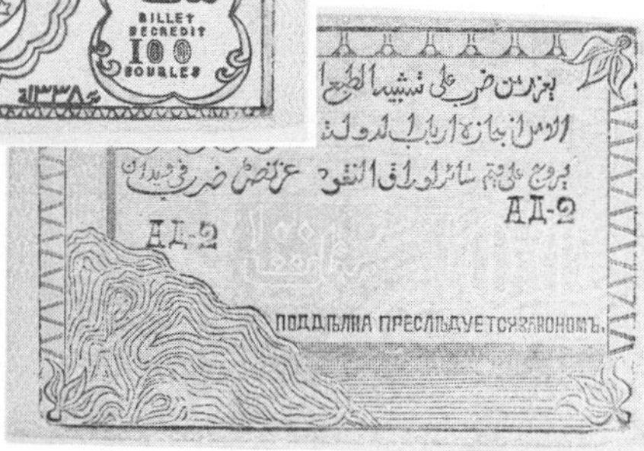

		Good	Fine	XF
S474	**100 Rubles** AH1338/1919. Black on light green and light brown underprint. Scales at center. Similar to #S473. Back: Mountain and flag.			
	a. No text below Arabic numeral of value in underprint on back.	50.00	150.	450.
	b. Like "a" but with Arabic text.	20.00	60.00	180.
	c. Like "a" but back inverted. Rare.	—	—	—

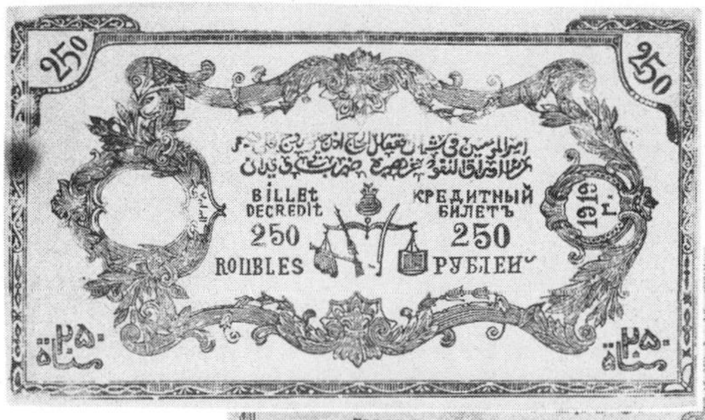

		Good	Fine	XF
S475	**250 Rubles** AH1338/1919. Black on green underprint. Large arms.			
	a. Printed top to top.	50.00	150.	450.
	b. Back inverted. Rare.	—	—	—
S476	**250 Rubles** AH1338/1919. Light blue. Small arms.			
	a. Printed top to top.	50.00	150.	450.
	b. Back inverted. Rare.	—	—	—

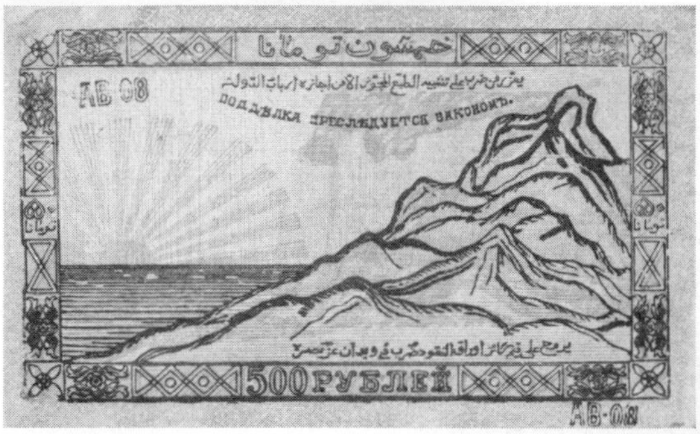

		Good	Fine	XF
S477	**500 Rubles** AH1338/1919. Black on blue and light brown underprint. Back: Mountains and sea with setting sun.			
	a. Printed top to top.	50.00	150.	450.
	b. Back inverted. Rare.	—	—	—

#S478 *Deleted.*

ГОСУДАРСТВЕННАГО БАНКА

Government Bank

АРМАВИРСКАГО ОТДѢЛЕН IЯ

Armavir

1918 Issue

		Good	Fine	XF
S479A	**3 Rublya** 18.6.1918; 1.12.1918. Black on green underprint. Bank stamping across bottom. Back: Black text, red circular stamping at lower left.	30.00	90.00	270.
S479B	**5 Rublei** 18.6.1918; 1.12.1918. Black on blue underprint. Bank stamping across bottom. Back: Black text, red circular stamping at lower left.	30.00	90.00	270.

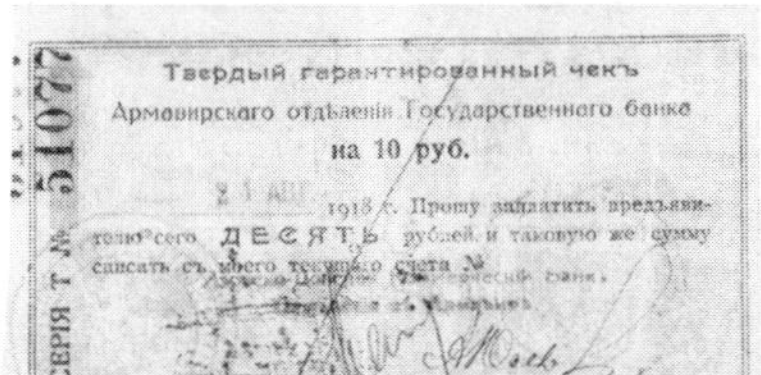

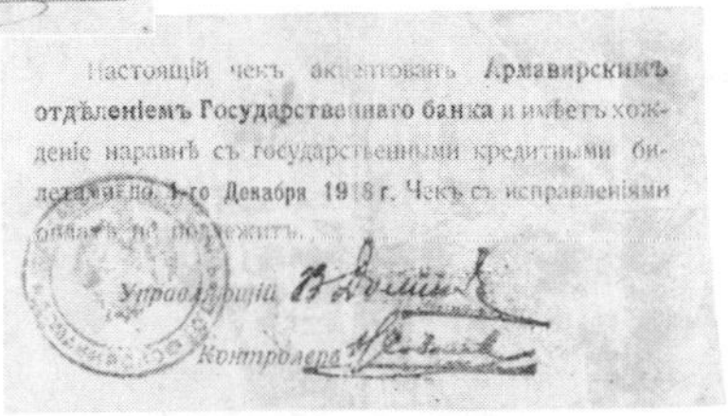

		Good	Fine	XF
S479C	**10 Rublei** 1.7.1918; 21.8.1918; 1.12.1918. Black on red underprint. Bank stamping across bottom. Back: Black text, red circular stamping at lower left.	30.00	90.00	270.
S479D	**25 Rublei** 8.6.1918; 1.7.1918; 1.12.1918. Black on olive green underprint. Bank stamping across bottom. Back: Black text, red circular stamping at lower left.	30.00	90.00	270.

		Good	Fine	XF
S479E	**40 Rublei**			
	1.7.1918; 1.12.1918. Bank stamping across bottom. Back: Black text, red circular stamping at lower left.	30.00	90.00	270.
S479F	**50 Rublei**			
	1.7.1918. Bank stamping across bottom. Back: Black text, red circular stamping at lower left.	50.00	150.	450.
S479G	**100 Rublei**			
	1.7.1918. Bank stamping across bottom. Back: Black text, red circular stamping at lower left.	70.00	210.	625.

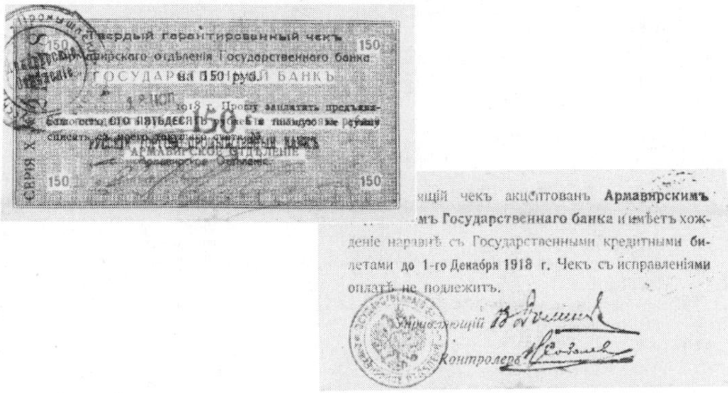

		Good	Fine	XF
S479H	**150 Rublei**			
	18.6.1918; 1.7.1918; 1.12.1918. Black on brown underprint. Bank stamping across bottom. Back: Black text, red circular stamping at lower left.	80.00	240.	725.
S479I	**200 Rublei**			
	1.7.1918. Bank stamping across bottom. Back: Black text, red circular stamping at lower left.	80.00	240.	725.
S479J	**300 Rublei**			
	1.7.1918; 1.12.1918. Bank stamping across bottom. Back: Black text, red circular stamping at lower left.			
	a. Date with correct numerals.	40.00	120.	360.
	x. Error with issue of 1.7. but date 1928.	30.00	90.00	270.
S479K	**500 Rublei**			
	1.7.1918. Bank stamping across bottom. Back: Black text, red circular stamping at lower left.	—	—	—

КУБАНСКАГО КРАЕВОГО ПРАВИТЕЛЬСТВА

Kuban Territorial Government

1918 Bank Issue

		VG	VF	UNC
S481	**50 Kopeks**			
	Ekaterinodar Branch.	30.00	90.00	270.

1918; 1920 Territorial Issue

		VG	VF	UNC
S482	**5 Rubles**			
	15.3.1918.	—	—	—
S483	**3 Rubles**			
	25.3.1918.	—	—	—
S484	**5 Rubles**			
	25.3.1918.	—	—	—
S485	**10 Rubles**			
	25.3.1918.	—	—	—
S486	**20 Rubles**			
	25.3.1918.	—	—	—
S487	**100 Rubles**			
	25.3.1918.	—	—	—

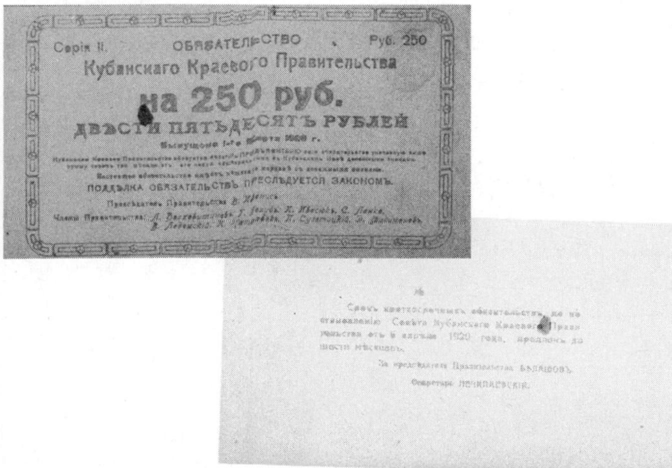

		VG	VF	UNC
S488	**250 Rubles**			
	1.3.1920. Green.			
	a. Text on back: АПРЬЛЯ	20.00	60.00	180.
	b. Text on back: АЛРЬЛЯ	20.00	60.00	180.

КУБАНСКАЯ РЕСПУБЛИКА

Kuban Soviet Republic

1918 ND State Loan Notes Issue

#S491-S494 Russian notes #37A-37D(in Vol. 2) w/square stamp.

		VG	VF	UNC
S491	**20 Rubles**			
	ND (1918). Square stamp on #37A(in Vol. 2).	20.00	60.00	180.
S492	**40 Rubles**			
	ND (1918). Square stamp on #37B(in Vol. 2).	20.00	60.00	180.
S493	**50 Rubles**			
	ND (1918). Square stamp on #37C(in Vol. 2).	20.00	60.00	180.
S494	**100 Rubles**			
	ND (1918). Square stamp on #37D(in Vol. 2).	30.00	90.00	270.

ГОСУДАРСТВЕННОГО БАНКА

Government Bank

ЕКАТЕРИНОДАРСКОГО ОТ ДЕЛЕНИЯ

Ekaterinodar

1918 ND Issue

		VG	VF	UNC
S494A	**50 Kopeks**			
	ND (ca.1918). Blue on tan underprint. Large denomination numeral at center. Back: Large denomination numeral at center.	5.00	15.00	45.00

1918 State Bank Vouchers Issue

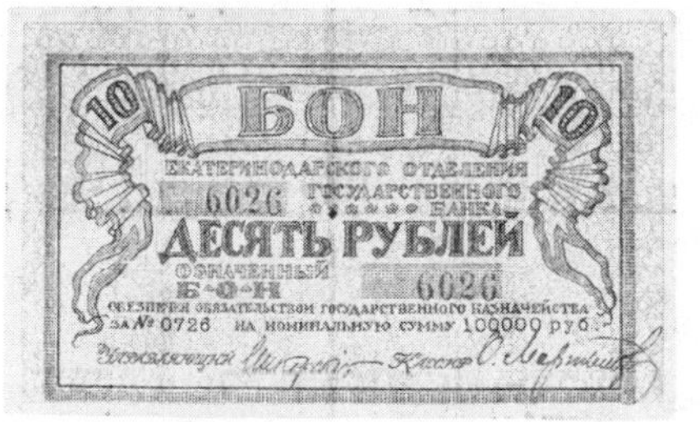

		VG	VF	UNC
S495	**10 Rubles**			
	1918. Blue on brown.			
	a. Retention money 25,000 Rubles.	30.00	90.00	270.
	b. Retention money 50,000 Rubles.	30.00	90.00	270.
	c. Retention money 100,000 Rubles.	30.00	90.00	270.

#S496-S497 are printed on Bill of Exchange paper bearing a wmk. and m/c printed imperial revenue stamp at l.

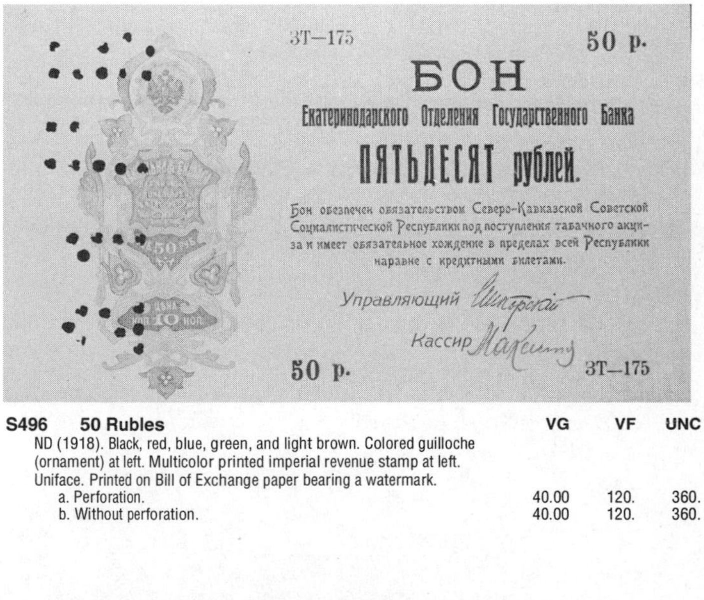

		VG	VF	UNC
S496	**50 Rubles**			
	ND (1918). Black, red, blue, green, and light brown. Colored guilloche (ornament) at left. Multicolor printed imperial revenue stamp at left. Uniface. Printed on Bill of Exchange paper bearing a watermark.			
	a. Perforation.	40.00	120.	360.
	b. Without perforation.	40.00	120.	360.

		VG	VF	UNC
S497	**100 Rubles** ND (1918). Black, red, blue, green, and light brown. Colored guilloche (ornament) at left. Multicolor printed imperial revenue stamp at left. Uniface. Like #S496a. Printed on Bill of Exchange paper bearing a watermark.	15.00	45.00	135.

NOTE: #S496 and S497 state they are issued by the Ekaterinodar Branch of the State Bank for the North Caucasus Soviet Socialist Republic. See #S451-S460.

1918 ГАРАНТИРОВАННЫЙ ЧЕКБ Guaranteed Checks Issue

		Good	Fine	XF
S498A	**50 Rublei** 1918. Black and brown on blue underprint. With or without stamping of various banks. Handwritten date. Uniface.			
	a. Issued note.	30.00	90.00	270.
	b. Punched hole cancelled.	30.00	90.00	270.
S498B	**100 Rublei** 1918. Black and brown on gold underprint. With or without stamping of various banks. Handwritten date. Uniface.			
	a. Issued note.	40.00	120.	360.
	b. Punched hole cancelled.	40.00	120.	360.
S498C	**200 Rublei** 1918. Black and brown on tan underprint. With or without stamping of various banks. Handwritten date. Uniface.			
	a. Issued note.	30.00	90.00	270.
	b. Punched hole cancelled.	30.00	90.00	270.
S498D	**300 Rublei** 1918. Black and brown on light green underprint. With or without stamping of various banks. Handwritten date. Uniface. Punched hole canceled.	40.00	120.	360.
S498E	**500 Rublei** 1918. Black and brown on olive-green and yellow underprint. With or without stamping of various banks. Handwritten date. Uniface. Punched hole canceled.	50.00	150.	450.

МИНЕРАЛЬНЫЕ ВОДЫ

Mineralnyie Vodyi District

1917 First РАЗМѢННЫЙ ЗНАКЪ Exchange Tokens Issue, Letter А, 1917

		Good	Fine	XF
S501	**1 Ruble** 1917.	30.00	90.00	270.
S502	**3 Rubles** 1917.	30.00	90.00	270.
S503	**5 Rubles** 1917.	40.00	120.	360.
S504	**10 Rubles** 1917.	35.00	110.	325.

		Good	Fine	XF
S505	**25 Rubles** 1917.	35.00	110.	325.
S506	**100 Rubles** 1917. Brown, rose and green.	70.00	210.	625.

1918 Second РАЗМѢННЫЙ ЗНАКЪ Exchange Tokens Issue, Letter Б, 1918

		Good	Fine	XF
S507	**1 Ruble** 1918. Black on orange underprint. Arms at left. Back: Orange.	20.00	60.00	180.
S508	**3 Rubles** 1918. Black on green and maroon underprint. Back: Green.	30.00	90.00	270.
S509	**5 Rubles** 1918. Black on blue underprint. Back: Blue.	30.00	90.00	270.

		Good	Fine	XF
S510	**10 Rubles** 1918. Black on red underprint. Back: Brown on red underprint.	20.00	60.00	180.
S511	**25 Rubles** 1918. Black on olive-green underprint.	40.00	120.	360.
S512	**25 Rubles** 1918. Light violet.	30.00	90.00	270.

		Good	Fine	XF
S512G	**50 Rubles** 1918.	25.00	75.00	225.

1919 Third РАЗМѢННЫЙ ЗНАКЪ Exchange Tokens Issue, Letter В, 1919

		Good	Fine	XF
S513	**50 Kopeks** ND (1919). Dark blue on orange underprint.	5.00	15.00	45.00
S514	**1 Ruble** 1919.	5.00	15.00	45.00

		Good	Fine	XF
S515	**3 Rubles** 1919.	5.00	15.00	45.00
S516	**5 Rubles** 1919.	5.00	15.00	45.00
S517	**10 Rubles** 1919.	10.00	30.00	90.00
S518	**25 Rubles** 1919. Brown and yellow.	10.00	30.00	90.00
S519	**50 Rubles** 1919.	10.00	30.00	90.00
S520	**100 Rubles** 1919.	30.00	90.00	270.

ГОСУДАРСТВЕННЫЙ БАНКЪ

Government Bank

СТАВРОПОЛЬСКОЕ ОТДЂЛ ЕНІЕ

Stavropol

1918-19 Issue

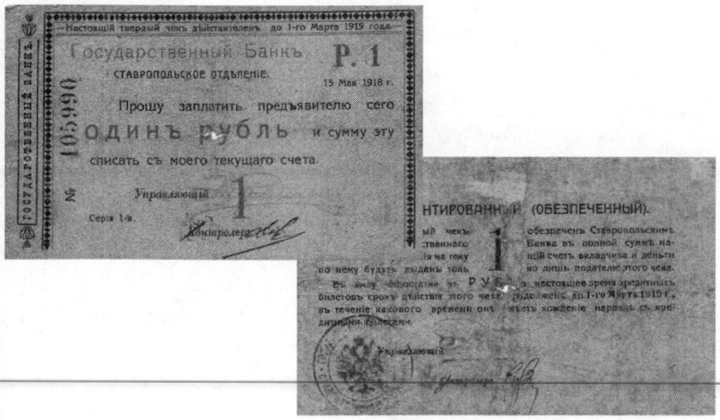

		Good	Fine	XF
S520A	**1 Ruble**			
	1.5.1918.	5.00	15.00	45.00
S520B	**3 Rublya**			
	1.2.1919. Black and green text and numerals on light green underprint.	5.00	15.00	45.00
S520C	**5 Rublei**			
	15.5.1918. Black and red text and numerals on green underprint.	10.00	30.00	90.00

		Good	Fine	XF
S520D	**10 Rublei**			
	15.5.1918. Black and red text and numerals on light red underprint.	10.00	30.00	90.00
S520E	**25 Rublei**			
	1.5.1918.	60.00	180.	550.
S520F	**50 Rublei**			
	1.5.1918.	75.00	225.	675.

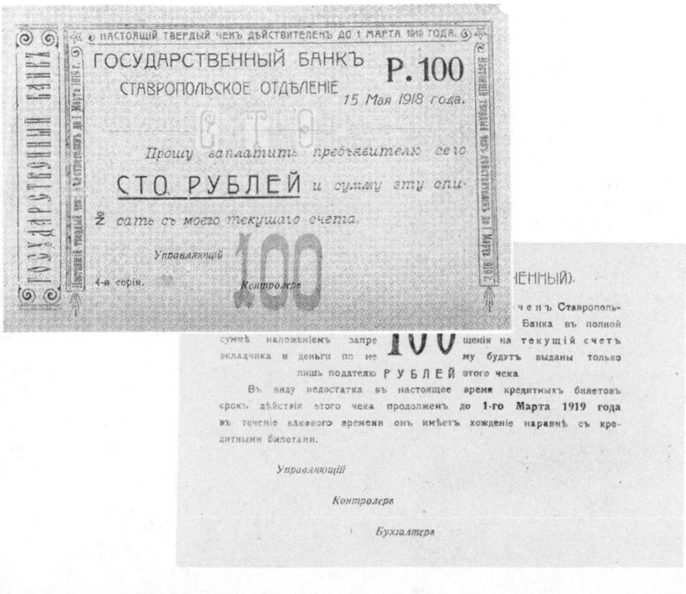

		Good	Fine	XF
S520G	**100 Rublei**			
	1.5.1918. Black on green underprint.	15.00	45.00	135.
S520H	**250 Rublei**			
	1.5.1918.	12.50	35.00	110.

ТЕРСКО-ДАГЕСТАНСКАЯ ОБЛАСТЬ

Terek-Daghestan Territory

1918 Issue

		Good	Fine	XF
S521	**25 Kopeks**			
	25.1.1918.	5.00	15.00	45.00
S522	**50 Kopeks**			
	25.1.1918.	5.00	15.00	45.00
S523	**1 Ruble**			
	25.1.1918. Yellow underprint.	5.00	15.00	45.00
S524	**3 Rubles**			
	25.1.1918. Green underprint.			
	a. Issued note.	7.50	22.50	65.00
	e. Error: БИЛЕТЕМИ.	20.00	60.00	180.
S525	**5 Rubles**			
	25.1.1918.	5.00	15.00	45.00

		Good	Fine	XF
S526	**10 Rubles**			
	25.1.1918. Black on red underprint.	6.00	18.00	55.00
S527	**25 Rubles**			
	25.1.1918. Black on brown underprint.	5.00	15.00	45.00
S528	**100 Rubles**			
	25.1.1918. Black on blue underprint.	10.00	30.00	90.00

ТЕРСКОИ РЕСПУБЛИКИЙ

Terek Republic

1918 РАЗМЂННЫЙ ЗНАКЪ Exchange Tokens Issue

		Good	Fine	XF
S529	**1 Ruble**			
	1918. Black on brown underprint. Double headed eagle within mantle at center. Back: Brown.	5.00	15.00	45.00

		Good	Fine	XF
S530	**3 Rubles**			
	1918. Black on green underprint. Double headed eagle within mantle at center. Like #S529. Back: Brown on green underprint.	7.50	22.50	65.00
S531	**5 Rubles**			
	1918. Blue on gray underprint. Double headed eagle at upper center.			
	a. Printed top on top.	7.50	22.50	65.00
	x. Error with back inverted.	15.00	45.00	135.

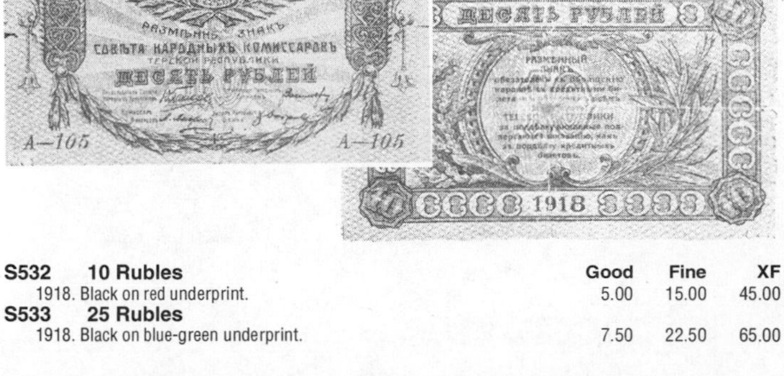

		Good	Fine	XF
S532	**10 Rubles**			
	1918. Black on red underprint.	5.00	15.00	45.00
S533	**25 Rubles**			
	1918. Black on blue-green underprint.	7.50	22.50	65.00

		Good	Fine	XF
S534	**50 Rubles**			
	1918. Black on orange and tan underprint. Sunburst at center. Back: Brown on green underprint.			
	a. Brown printing on face.	7.50	22.50	65.00
	b. Black printing on face.	7.50	22.50	65.00
S535	**100 Rubles**			
	1918.			
	a. Brown on red-brown underprint.	7.50	22.50	65.00
	b. Brown on light yellow-brown underprint.	7.50	22.50	65.00

1918; 1919 ND Postage Stamp Money Issue

		Good	Fine	XF
S536	**10 Kopeks**			
	ND (1918). Blue. Double-headed eagle at center. Back: Text. Paper: Cardboard.	10.00	30.00	90.00

		Good	Fine	XF
S537	**15 Kopeks**			
	ND (1918). Brown. Double-headed eagle at center. Back: Text. Paper: Cardboard.	10.00	30.00	90.00
S538	**20 Kopeks**			
	ND (1919). Green. Double-headed eagle at center. Back: Text. Paper: Cardboard.	10.00	30.00	90.00

Black Sea Peasant Militia

1920 ВРЕМЕНН. РАЗМѢННЫЙ ЗНАКЪ

Provisional Exchange Tokens Issue

		Good	Fine	XF
S539	**10 Rubles**			
	1.4.1920. Rare.	—	—	—
S540	**25 Rubles**			
	1.4.1920. Rare.	—	—	—
S541	**25 Rubles**			
	1920.	15.00	45.00	135.
S542	**100 Rubles**			
	1920. Large numerals.	20.00	60.00	180.
S543	**100 Rubles**			
	1920. Small numerals.	20.00	60.00	180.

		Good	Fine	XF
S544	**250 Rubles**			
	1920. Black. Paper: Light brown. Proof. Rare.	—	—	—

NOTE: Modern forgeries of #S544 are becoming available.

ПИАТИГОРСК-БАТАЛПАЩИНСК КАЗНАЧ

Piatigorsk-Batalpashchinsk Company, Independent Army

1918 ГАРАНТИРОВАННЫЙ ЧЕКЪ Guaranteed Checks Issue

#S551-S558 Stamp on back: БАТАЛПАЩИНСК КАЗНА..

		Good	Fine	XF
S551	**3 Rubles**			
	1918. Double eagle at upper center. Back: Handstamp.	20.00	60.00	180.
S552	**5 Rubles**			
	1918. Double eagle at upper center. Back: Handstamp.	20.00	60.00	180.

		Good	Fine	XF
S553	**10 Rubles**			
	1918. Double eagle at upper center. Back: Handstamp.	40.00	120.	360.

		Good	Fine	XF
S554	**25 Rubles**			
	1918. Double eagle at upper center. Back: Handstamp.	65.00	200.	600.
S555	**50 Rubles**			
	1918. Double eagle at upper center. Back: Handstamp. Rare.	—	—	—

		Good	Fine	XF
S556	**75 Rubles**			
	1918. Double eagle at upper center. Back: Handstamp. Rare.	—	—	—

		Good	Fine	XF
S557	**100 Rubles**			
	1918. Double eagle at upper center. Back: Handstamp. Rare.	—	—	—
S558	**500 Rubles**			
	1918. Double eagle at upper center. Back: Handstamp. Rare.	—	—	—

1918 Issue

		Good	Fine	XF
S559	**3 Rubles**			
	1918. Double eagle at upper center. Back: Stamp: КИСЛОВОДСК ОТД. ГОС. Б.	30.00	90.00	270.
S560	**5 Rubles**			
	1918. Double eagle at upper center. Back: Stamp: КИСЛОВОДСК ОТД. ГОС. Б.	45.00	135.	400.
S561	**50 Rubles**			
	1918. Double eagle at upper center. Back: Stamp: КИСЛОВОДСК ОТД. ГОС. Б. Rare.	—	—	—
S562	**100 Rubles**			
	1918. Double eagle at upper center. Back: Stamp: КИСЛОВОДСК ОТД. ГОС. Б. Rare.	—	—	—

S563	200 Rubles	Good	Fine	XF
	1918. Double eagle at upper center. Back: Stamp: КИСЛОВОДСК ОТД. ГОС. Б. Rare.	—	—	—

1919 Issue

S564	20 Rubles	Good	Fine	XF
	1919. Double eagle at upper center. Back: Stamp: КИСЛОВОДСК ОТД. ГОС. Б. Rare.	—	—	—

S565	40 Rubles	Good	Fine	XF
	1919. Double eagle at upper center. Back: Stamp: КИСЛОВОДСК ОТД. ГОС. Б. Varieties. Rare.	—	—	—

ТЕРСКОЕ КАЗАЧЬЕ ВОИСКО

Terek Cossack Command

1918 Issue

		Good	Fine	XF
S566	100 Rubles 19.7.1918. Rare.	—	—	—
S567	500 Rubles 19.7.1918. Rare.	—	—	—
S568	1000 Rubles 19.7.1918. Rare.	—	—	—

КОМАНДОВАНІЕ КРАСНОЙ АРМІИ

ТЕРСКОЙ ОБЛАСТИ

Terek District Command of the Red Army

1918 Issue

		Good	Fine	XF
S569	100 Rubles 1918. Black hand stamp on Terek note #S528a: КОМ. КРАСН. АРМІЙ ТЕРСК. ОБЛ..	30.00	90.00	270.
S570	100 Rubles 1918. Violet hand stamp on Terek note #S528a: КОМ. КРАСН. АРМІЙ ТЕРСК. ОБЛ.	40.00	120.	360.

ВОЛЖСКО-КАМСКІЙ КОММЕРЧЕСКІЙ БАНКЪ

Volga-Kama Commercial Bank

Grozny

1918 ЧЕКЪ Circulating Bearer Checks Issue

S571	3 Rubles	Good	Fine	XF
	1918. Black.	7.50	22.50	65.00

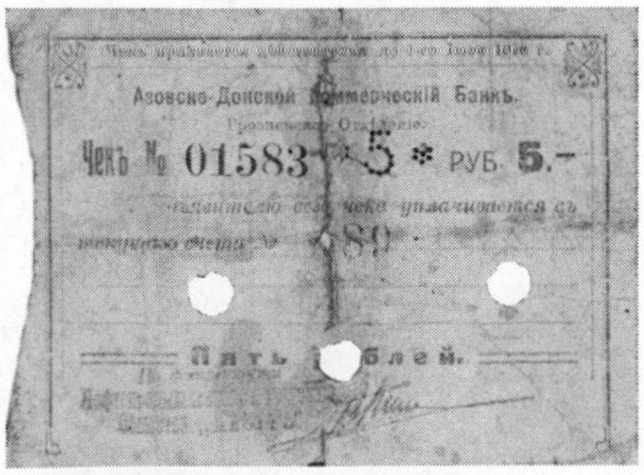

S571A	5 Rubles	Good	Fine	XF
	1918. Black.	10.00	30.00	90.00

		Good	Fine	XF
S572	25 Rubles 1918. Black. Part of legend, validating stamp and signature in purple stampings; black serial #. Paper: Yellowish.	7.50	22.50	65.00
S573	100 Rubles 1918.	7.50	22.50	65.00

РУССКО-АЗІАТСКІЙ БАНКЪ

Russo-Asiatic Bank

1918 ЧЕКЪ Circulating Bearer Checks Issue

#S576-S579 circulating bearer checks 27.1.1918 to 9.3.1918.

		Good	Fine	XF
S576	3 Rubles 1918. Rare.	—	—	—
S577	5 Rubles 1918.	40.00	120.	360.
S578	25 Rubles 1918.	40.00	120.	360.
S579	100 Rubles 1918. Rare.	—	—	—

АЗОВСКО-ДОНСКОЙ КОММЕРЧЕСКІЙ БАНКЪ

Azov-Don Commercial Bank

1918 ЧЕКЪ Circulating Bearer Checks Issue

#S581-S584 circulating bearer checks 5.2.1918 to 8.9.1918. Perforation and ovpt. varieties.

		Good	Fine	XF
S581	3 Rubles 1918.	7.50	22.50	65.00
S582	5 Rubles 1918.	7.50	22.50	65.00
S583	25 Rubles 1918.	7.50	22.50	65.00

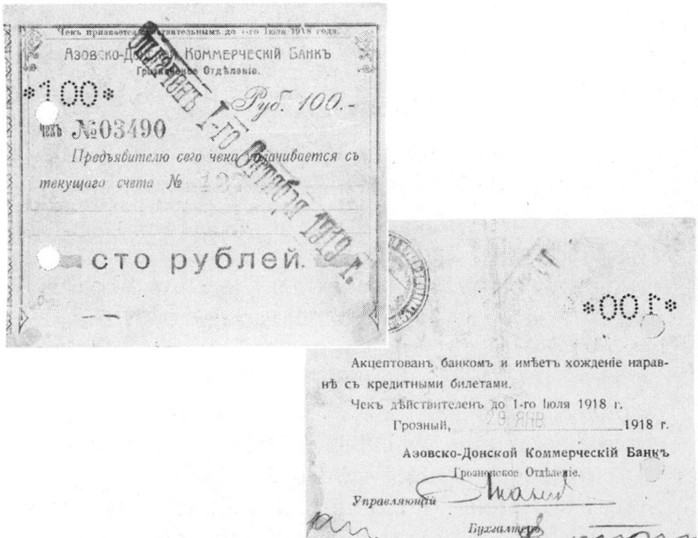

S584	100 Rubles	Good	Fine	XF
	1918.	7.50	22.50	65.00

ВОНЫ СОЧИНСКАГО ГОРОДСКОГО УПРАВЛЕНІЯ

Bons of the Sochi City Administration

1919 ND ВОНЫ Bons (Vouchers) Third Issue

	Good	Fine	XF
S585 1 Ruble ND (1919). Blue on light brown underprint.	15.00	45.00	135.
S585A 3 Rublei 1919. Black on gray-green underprint.	15.00	45.00	135.
S585B 5 Rublei 1919. Blue on gray underprint.	7.50	22.50	65.00
S585C 10 Rublei 1919. Black on light brown underprint.	15.00	45.00	135.

1919 ВОНЫ Bons (Vouchers) Third Issue

	Good	Fine	XF
S585D 25 Rublei 1919. Black on tan underprint.	15.00	45.00	135.
S585E 50 Rublei 1919. Deep blue on blue underprint.	7.50	22.50	65.00
S585F 50 Rublei 1919. Deep blue on gray underprint.	7.50	22.50	65.00
S585G 100 Rublei 1919. Dark brown and orange on light orange-brown underprint.	45.00	135.	400.
S585H 250 Rublei 1919. Blue and orange on olive-gray underprint.	30.00	90.00	270.

ЧЕРНОМОРСКАЯ ЖЕЛЕЗНАЯ ДОРОГА

Black Sea Railroad

1918 ВОНЫ Bons (Vouchers) Issue

	Good	Fine	XF
S586 1 Ruble 1918. Yellow underprint.	40.00	120.	360.
S587 3 Rubles 1918. Green underprint.	40.00	120.	360.
S588 5 Rubles 1918. Blue underprint.	40.00	120.	360.
S589 10 Rubles 1918.	40.00	120.	360.
S590 25 Rubles 1918.	40.00	120.	360.
S591 50 Rubles 1918. Blue on green.	50.00	150.	450.

ОБЩЕСТВА ВЛАДИКАВКАЗСКОЙ ЖЕЛЬЗНОЙ OR КЕАЕЗИОЙ ДОРОГИ

Vladikavkaz Railroad Company

1918 ЗАЕМНЫЙ БИЛЕТЪ

5.4% Interest-bearing Loan Notes Issue

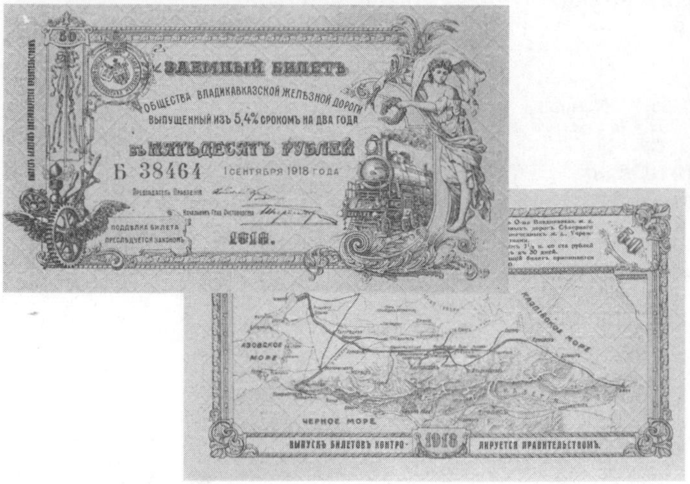

	VG	VF	UNC
S593 50 Rubles 1.9.1918. Black on light blue, buff and light green underprint. Winged gear at lower left, steam locomotive below partly robed woman at right. Back: Caucasus map showing railroad's main line from Rostov-on-the-Don to Petrovsk and Baku.	40.00	120.	360.

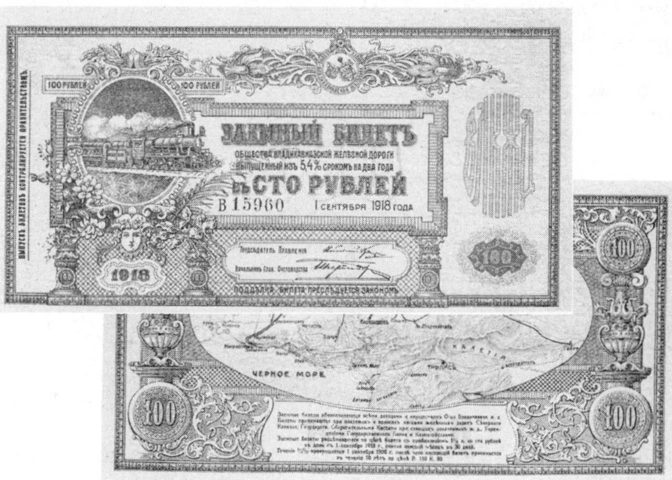

	VG	VF	UNC
S594 100 Rubles 1.9.1918. Black on light blue and light brown underprint. Steam passenger train at upper left. Back: Caucasus map showing railroad's main line from Rostov-on-the-Don to Petrovsk and Baku.	40.00	120.	360.

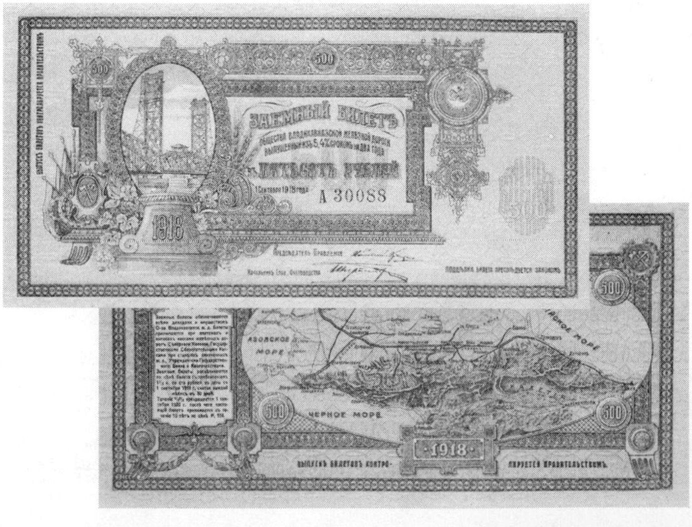

		VG	VF	UNC
S595	**500 Rubles** 1.9.1918. Black on green, gray and light blue underprint. Railroad bridge at upper left. Back: Caucasus map showing railroad's main line from Rostov-on-the-Don to Petrovsk and Baku.	55.00	165.	575.
S596	**1000 Rubles** 1.9.1918. Black on light maroon and light blue underprint. Building atop mountainous scene at lower right. Back: Caucasus map showing railroad's main line from Rostov-on-the-Don to Petrovsk and Baku.	75.00	225.	675.

1919 ЗАЕМНЫЙ БИЛЕТЪ

5.4% Interest-Bearing Loan Notes Issue

		Good	Fine	XF
S597	**1000 Rubles** 1.9.1919. Back: Caucasus map showing railroad's main line from Rostov-on-the-Don to Petrovsk and Baku. Proof only. Rare.	—	Unc	1250.

		Good	Fine	XF
S598	**5000 Rubles** 1.9.1919. Black on blue and salmon underprint. Railroad bridge with central span lifted on uprights at lower left. Back: Caucasus map showing railroad's main line from Rostov-on-the-Don to Petrovsk and Baku.	200.	600.	1800.
S599	**10,000 Rubles** 1.9.1919. Blue-gray on light brown underprint. Steam train at lower center. Back: Caucasus map showing railroad's main line from Rostov-on-the-Don to Petrovsk and Baku.	400.	1200.	3600.

ГОСУДАРСТВЕННАГО БАНКА

Government Bank

ВЛАДИКАВКАЗСКОЕ ОТДѢЛЕНIЙ

Vladikavkaz

1920 ND Issue

#S599A-S600D Perforated w/number and "Т.Б." (for State Bank).

		Good	Fine	XF
S599A	**1 Ruble** ND (1910- old date 191x). Blue underprint. Black text, red denomination. Without filled in date or signature. Back: Black text with 2 signatures.	20.00	60.00	180.
S599B	**3 Rubles** ND (1920- old date 191x). Blue underprint. Black text, red denomination. Without filled in date or signature. Back: Black text with 2 signatures.	25.00	75.00	225.

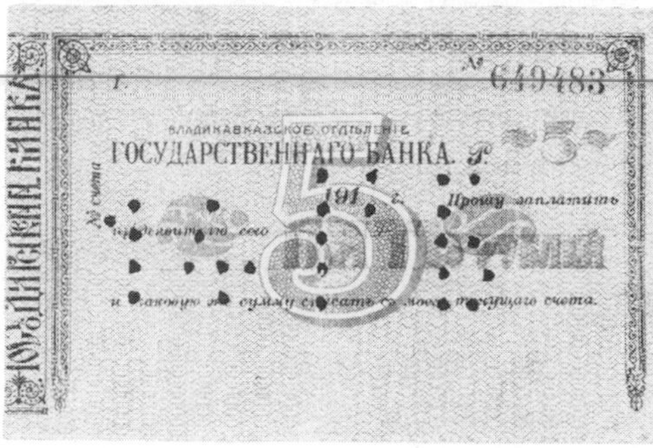

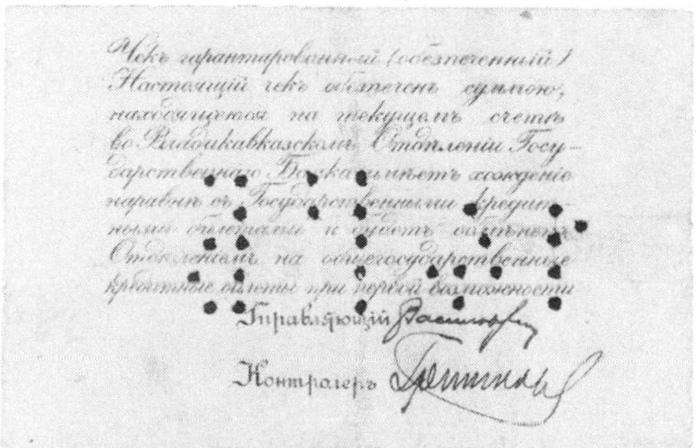

		Good	Fine	XF
S600A	**5 Rubles** ND (1920- old date 191x). Blue underprint. Black text, red denomination. Without filled in date or signature. Back: Black text with 2 signatures.	15.00	45.00	135.
S600B	**10 Rubles** ND (1920- old date 191x). Blue underprint. Black text, red denomination. Without filled in date or signature. Back: Black text with 2 signatures.	20.00	60.00	180.

		Good	Fine	XF
S600C	**25 Rubles** ND (1920- old date 191x). Blue underprint. Black text, red denomination. Without filled in date or signature. Back: Black text with 2 signatures.	25.00	75.00	225.
S600D	**50 Rubles** ND (1920- old date 191x). Blue underprint. Black text, red denomination. Without filled in date or signature. Back: Black text with 2 signatures.	50.00	150.	450.

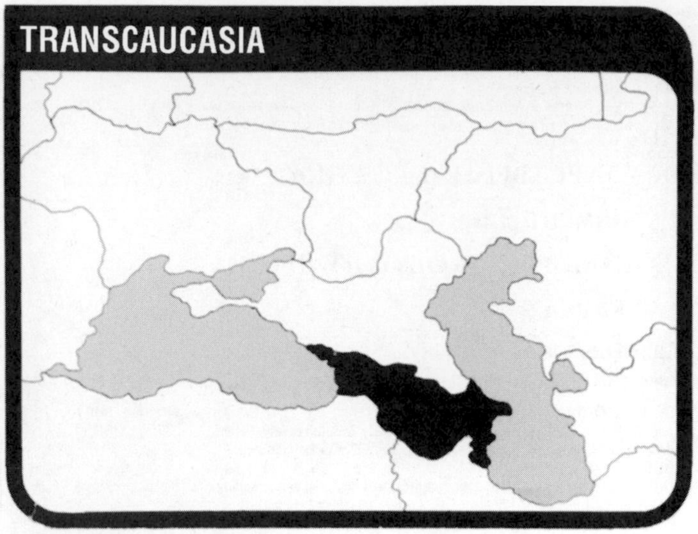

GOVERNMENTS
- Transcaucasian Commissariat
- Federation of Socialist Soviet Republics of Transcaucasia
- Armenian Socialist Soviet Republic
- Alexandropol
- Azerbaijan Socialist Soviet Republic
- Baku
- Batum (British Occupation)
- Georgian Socialist Soviet Republic

RAILROAD
- Transcaucasian S.S.R. Railroad

ЗАКАВКАЗСКАГО КОМИССАРІАТА
TRANSCAUCASIAN COMMISSARIAT

1918 ISSUE

All notes w/ or w/o oil-varnish wetting (patterns in the unpt.). Paper varieties.

		VG	VF	UNC
S601	**1 Ruble**			
	1918. Blue on light tan underprint.	5.00	15.00	45.00

		VG	VF	UNC
S602	**3 Rubles**			
	1918. Black on green underprint.	5.00	15.00	45.00

		VG	VF	UNC
S603	**5 Rubles**			
	1918. Blue on gray underprint.	5.00	15.00	45.00

		VG	VF	UNC
S604	**10 Rubles**			
	1918. Red-brown or maroon on olive underprint.	7.00	22.50	65.00
S605	**50 Rubles**			
	1918. Black on blue-gray underprint.	10.00	30.00	90.00

NOTE: Partial sheets or strips of #S601-S605 are found on occasion.

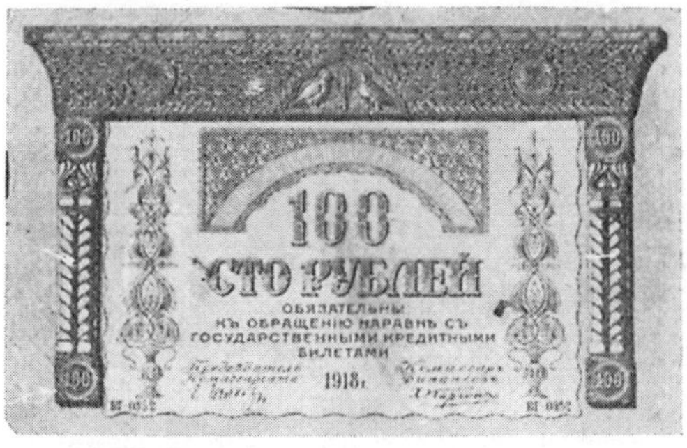

		VG	VF	UNC
S606	**100 Rubles**			
	1918. Black on brown and tan underprint.	10.00	30.00	90.00
S607	**250 Rubles**			
	1918. Gray-olive on pale lilac underprint. Back: Brown and blue.			
	a. Thin paper.	15.00	45.00	135.
	b. Thick paper, crude printing.	15.00	45.00	135.

ФЕД. С. С. Р. ЗАКАВКАЗЬЯ

FEDERATION OF SOCIALIST SOVIET REPUBLICS OF TRANSCAUCASIA

1923 FIRST ДЕНЕЖНЫЙ ЗНАК CURRENCY TOKENS ISSUE

#	Description	VG	VF	UNC
S611	**1000 Rubles**			
	1923. Black-green on yellow-brown underprint. Building with flag at center. Back: Arms at center. Flourishes in frame border face in one direction.	10.00	30.00	90.00
S612	**5000 Rubles**			
	1923. Blue on lilac-brown underprint. Building with flag at center. Back: Arms at center. Flourishes in frame border face in one direction.	15.00	45.00	135.
S613	**10,000 Rubles**			
	1923. Red-brown on gray underprint. Building with flag at center. Back: Arms at center. Flourishes in frame border face in one direction.	15.00	45.00	135.
S614	**10,000 Rubles**			
	1923. Dark purple on red-violet underprint. Building with flag at center. Back: Arms at center. Flourishes in frame border face in one direction.	15.00	45.00	135.
S615	**25,000 Rubles**			
	1923. Black on brown underprint. Building with flag at center. Back: Arms at center. Flourishes in frame border face in one direction.	10.00	30.00	90.00
S616	**50,000 Rubles**			
	1923. Black on green underprint. Building with flag at center. Back: Arms at center. Flourishes in frame border face in one direction.			
	a. Watermark: Stars.	10.00	30.00	90.00
	b. Without watermark.	5.00	15.00	45.00
	s1. Specimen.	FV	FV	500.
	s2. Specimen. Face and back uniface.	FV	FV	750.
S617	**100,000 Rubles**			
	1923. Brown on red-brown underprint. Building with flag at center. Back: Arms at center. Flourishes in frame border face in one direction.			
	a. Watermark: Stars.	10.00	30.00	90.00
	b. Without watermark.	5.00	15.00	45.00
S618	**250,000 Rubles**			
	Black on green underprint. Building with flag at center. Back: Arms at center. Flourishes in frame border face in one direction.			
	a. Normal print.	15.00	45.00	135.
	b. Misprint: back inverted.	10.00	30.00	90.00
S619	**500,000 Rubles**			
	1923. Purple on light blue underprint. Building with flag at center. Back: Arms at center. Flourishes in frame border face in one direction.			
	a. Watermark: Stars.	10.00	30.00	90.00
	b. Without watermark.	10.00	30.00	90.00
S620	**1,000,000 Rubles**			
	1923. Brown on violet underprint. Building with flag at center. Back: Arms at center. Flourishes in frame border face in one direction.			
	a. Watermark: Stars.	10.00	30.00	90.00
	b. Without watermark.	10.00	30.00	90.00
	s. Specimen. Face and back uniface.	—	—	750.
S621	**5,000,000 Rubles**			
	1923. Dark brown on green and lilac underprint. Building with flag at center. Back: Arms at center. Flourishes in frame border face in one direction.	15.00	45.00	135.
S622	**10,000,000 Rubles**			
	1923. Black on blue, green, yellow underprint. Building with flag at center. Back: Arms at center. Flourishes in frame border face in one direction.	20.00	60.00	180.

1923 Second ДЕНЕЖНЫЙ ЗНАК Currency Tokens Issue

#	Description	VG	VF	UNC
S623	**5000 Rubles**			
	1923. Blue on lilac-brown underprint. Building with flag at center. Back: Arms at center. Flourishes in frame border face left and right.	5.00	15.00	45.00
S624	**10,000 Rubles**			
	1923. Red-brown on gray underprint. Building with flag at center. Back: Arms at center. Flourishes in frame border face left and right.	8.00	24.00	75.00
S625	**50,000 Rubles**			
	1923. Black on green underprint. Building with flag at center. Back: Arms at center. Flourishes in frame border face left and right.	10.00	30.00	90.00

#	Description	VG	VF	UNC
S626	**100,000 Rubles**			
	1923. Brown on red-brown underprint. Building with flag at center. Back: Arms at center. Flourishes in frame border face left and right.	10.00	30.00	90.00

#	Description	VG	VF	UNC
S627	**250,000 Rubles**			
	1923. Black on green underprint. Building with flag at center. Back: Arms at center. Flourishes in frame border face left and right.	15.00	45.00	135.

#	Description	VG	VF	UNC
S628	**500,000 Rubles**			
	1923. Purple on light blue underprint. Building with flag at center. Back: Arms at center. Flourishes in frame border face left and right.	15.00	45.00	135.

		VG	VF	UNC
S629	**1,000,000 Rubles**			
	1923. Brown on violet underprint. Building with flag at center. Back: Arms at center. Flourishes in frame border face left and right.	15.00	45.00	135.
S630	**5,000,000 Rubles**			
	1923. Dark brown on green and lilac underprint. Building with flag at center. Back: Arms at center. Flourishes in frame border face left and right.	20.00	60.00	180.
S631	**10,000,000 Rubles**			
	1923. Black on blue, green, yellow underprint. Building with flag at center. Back: Arms at center. Flourishes in frame border face left and right.	20.00	60.00	180.

З.С.Ф.С.Р.

Transcaucasian Socialist Federal Soviet Republic

1924 ДЕНЕЖНЫЙ ЗНАК Currency Tokens Issue

		VG	VF	UNC
S632	**25,000,000 Rubles**			
	1924. Black on gray underprint.			
	a. Watermark: Stars.	10.00	30.00	90.00
	b. Without watermark.	10.00	30.00	90.00
	x. Error: with back inverted.	10.00	30.00	90.00

		VG	VF	UNC
S633	**50,000,000 Rubles**			
	1924. Black on gray-violet underprint.	15.00	45.00	135.
S634	**50,000,000 Rubles**			
	1924. Horizontal format. Printed back only.	100.	300.	900.
S635	**75,000,000 Rubles**			
	1924. Black on brown underprint. Back: Svanetian towers.			
	a. Watermark: Large stars.	30.00	90.00	270.
	b. Without watermark.	30.00	90.00	270.

		VG	VF	UNC
S636	**100,000,000 Rubles**			
	1924. Brown on green underprint. Like #S632.			
	a. Issued note.	20.00	60.00	180.
	s. Specimen. Face and back uniface.	—	—	750.
S637	**250,000,000 Rubles**			
	1924. Brown on tan underprint. Similar to #S635. Back: Green on tan underprint. Svanetian towers.			
	a. Issued note.	50.00	150.	450.
	s. Specimen. Face and back uniface.	—	—	750.
S638	**1 Milliard (= Billion) Rubles**			
	1924. Lilac. Back: Green. Woman seated with fruit and wheat.			
	a. Black-green on green and lilac underprint.	80.00	240.	725.
	b. Brown on tan and lilac underprint.	80.00	240.	725.
	c. Olive on olive and lilac underprint.	80.00	240.	725.
S639	**10 Milliarde Rubles**			
	1924. Black on lilac and green underprint.			
	a. Issued note.	100.	300.	900.
	p. Uniface Proof.	—	—	750.
	ct. Color trial. Black on light brown underprint.	—	—	800.

УПРАВЛЕНИЕ ЖЕЛЕЗНЫХ ДОРОГ С.С.Р. ЗАКАВКАЗЬЯ

Transcaucasian S.S.R.R. Railroad

1920 ND РАСЧЕТНЫЙ ЗНАК Exchange Tokens Issue

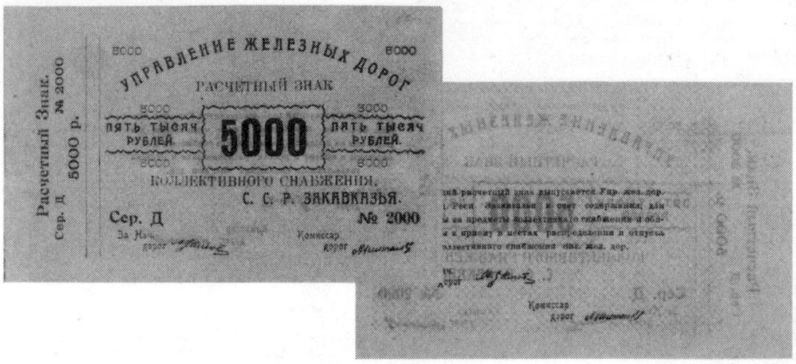

		VG	VF	UNC
S641	**5000 Rubles**			
	ND (1920). Black on yellow underprint.	10.00	30.00	90.00

		VG	VF	UNC
S642	**10,000 Rubles**			
	ND (1920). Black on blue underprint.	10.00	30.00	90.00
S643	**25,000 Rubles**			
	ND (1920). Black on green underprint.	10.00	30.00	90.00
S644	**50,000 Rubles**			
	ND (1920). Black on red underprint.	10.00	30.00	90.00
S645	**100,000 Rubles**			
	ND (1920). Black on purple underprint.	15.00	45.00	135.

РЕСПУБЛйКА АРМЕНйй (or АРМЕНйЯ)

Armenia - Autonomous Republic

NOTE: For previously listed #S646-S677 see Vol. 2, Armenia #1-32.

СОЦИАЛИСТИЧЕСКАЯ СОВЕТСКАЯ РЕСПУБЛИКА АРМЕНИИ

Armenian Socialist Soviet Republic

1919; 1921; 1922 Issues

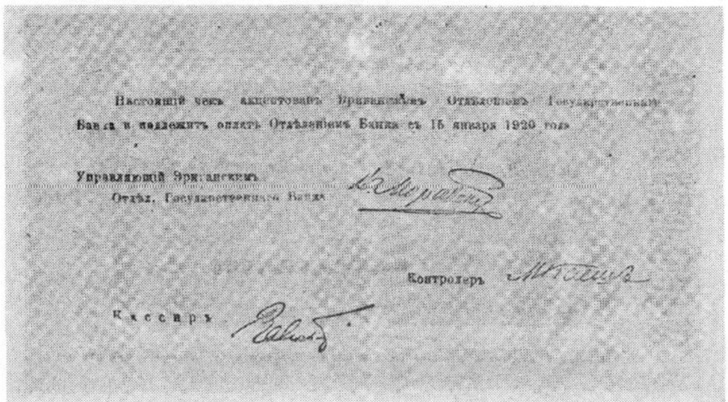

		VG	VF	UNC
S678	**10,000 Rubles**			
	Aug. 1919. Light green. Back: Like #S674 but signature in facsimile print.	20.00	60.00	180.

НОЯБРЯ.

S679 5000 Rubles	VG	VF	UNC
1921. Blue on gray underprint. Back: Arms at center.	15.00	45.00	135.

S680 10,000 Rubles	VG	VF	UNC
1921. Arms at top center.			
a. Rose paper. Watermark.	20.00	60.00	180.
b. Rose to brown paper. Without watermark.	20.00	60.00	180.
c. Lilac paper. Without watermark.	20.00	60.00	180.
d. Trial printing in green.	—	—	450.

S681 25,000 Rubles	VG	VF	UNC
1922. Blue. Arms at center.			
a. Watermark.	20.00	60.00	180.
b. Without watermark.	20.00	60.00	180.

S682 100,000 Rubles	VG	VF	UNC
1922. Gray-green on yellow-brown underprint. Arms at upper right.	15.00	45.00	135.
S683 500,000 Rubles			
1922. Trial printing of back only. Rare.	—	—	—

S684 1,000,000 Rubles	VG	VF	UNC
1922. Red. Back: Arms at center.	40.00	120.	360.

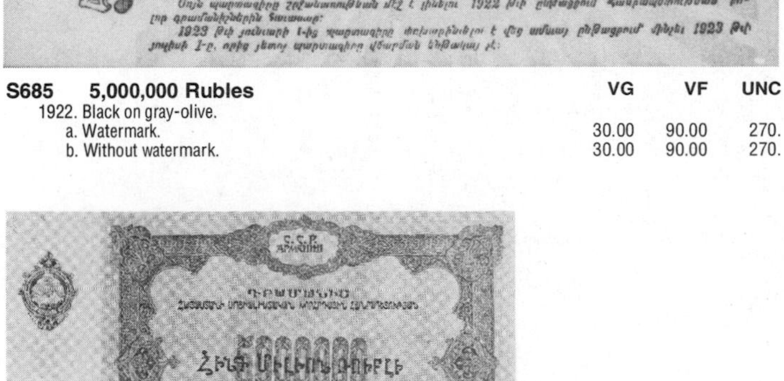

S685 5,000,000 Rubles	VG	VF	UNC
1922. Black on gray-olive.			
a. Watermark.	30.00	90.00	270.
b. Without watermark.	30.00	90.00	270.

S686 5,000,000 Rubles	VG	VF	UNC
1922. Blue-green on light green.	40.00	120.	360.

1923 ДЕНЕЖНЫЙ ЗНАКЪ CURRENCY TOKENS ISSUE

		VG	VF	UNC
S687	**1 Chervonetz** 1923. Blue, light brown and green. Back: Landscape and mountains in background. (Not issued).	150.	450.	1350.

Series letters A; AB and ABG (all Armenian) are known; the illustrated specimen is AB (panels at upper left and right of face side).

ALEXANDROPOL (CITY, ARMENIA)

NOTE: Now called Leninakan. It was in Brivansk Guberniya in Czarist and Independence periods.

АЛЕКСАНДРОПОЛСКІЙ ГОРОДСК.

ОБЖЕСТВЕНН.БАНКЪ

ALEXANDROPOL GOVERNMENT CORPORATION BANK

1919 BEARER ЧЕКЪ CHECKS ISSUE

White regime.

		Good	Fine	XF
S691	**25 Rubles** Oct. to Dec. 1919. Rare.	—	—	—
S692	**50 Rubles** Oct. to Dec. 1919. Rare.	—	—	—

SHIRAK GOVERNMENT CORPORATION BANK

1920-21 ND ISSUE

Soviet regime.

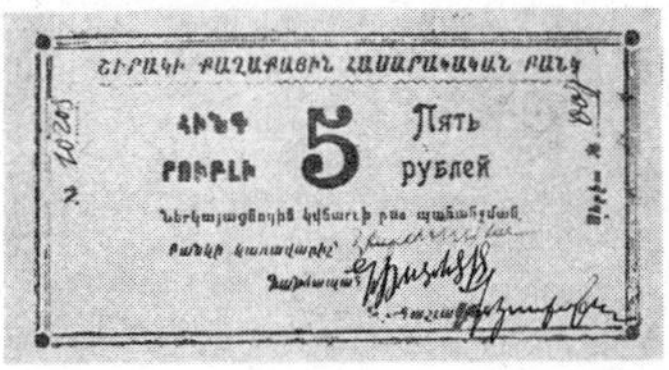

		Good	Fine	XF
S693	**5 Rubles** ND (1920-21). Gray. Text in Armenian. Stamped signature. Back: Purple stamping.	50.00	150.	300.

		Good	Fine	XF
S694	**10 Rubles** ND (1920-21). Gray. Text in Armenian. Stamped signature. Back: Purple stamping.	50.00	150.	300.

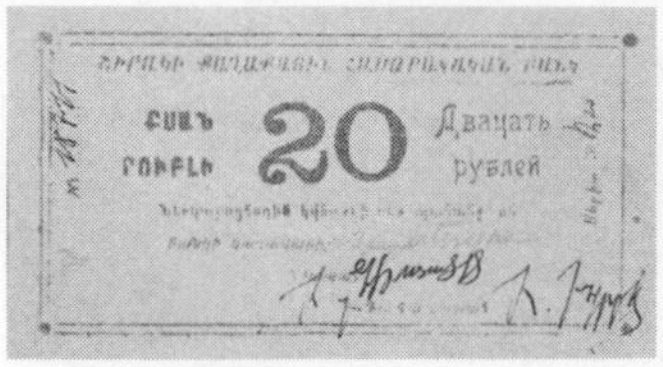
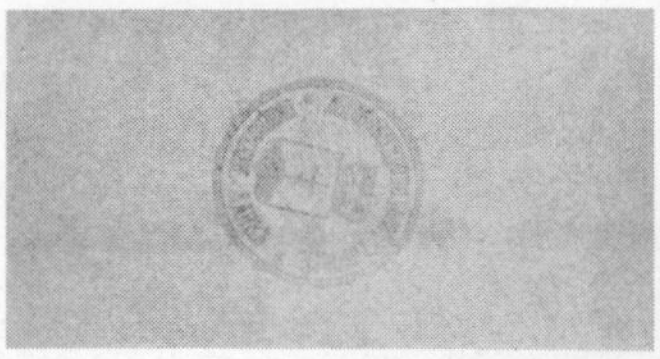

		Good	Fine	XF
S695	**20 Rubles** ND (1920-21). Gray. Text in Armenian. Stamped signature. Back: Purple stamping.	50.00	150.	300.

		Good	Fine	XF
S696	**25 Rubles** ND (1920-21). Gray. Text in Armenian. Stamped signature. Back: Purple stamping.	60.00	180.	550.

		Good	Fine	XF
S697	**50 Rubles** ND (1920-21). Gray. Text in Armenian. Stamped signature. Back: Purple stamping.	60.00	180.	550.

		Good	Fine	XF
S698	**100 Rubles** ND (1920-21). Gray. Text in Armenian. Stamped signature. Back: Purple stamping.	80.00	250.	750.

АЗЕРБАЙДЖАНСКАЯ РЕСПУБЛЙКА

AZERBAIJAN, AUTONOMOUS REPUBLIC

NOTE: For previously listed #S701-S708 see Vol. 2, Azerbaijan #1-8.

АЗЕРБАИДЖАНСКАЯ СОЦИАЛИСТИЧЕСКАЯ

СОБЕТСКАЯ РЕСПУБЛИКА

AZERBAIJAN SOCIALIST SOVIET REPUBLIC

1920 ND ISSUE

		VG	VF	UNC
S709	**5 Rubles** ND (1920). Worker and farmer. Back: Black on purple underprint. Factory.			
	a. Black on yellow underprint.	8.00	24.00	75.00
	b. Black on orange underprint.	12.00	35.00	110.

		VG	VF	UNC
S710	**100 Rubles** ND (1920). Olive and violet. Railway train.	8.00	24.00	75.00

1920-23 Issue

S711 1000 Rubles

1920. Black on green and red underprint. Arms at upper left and right.

	VG	VF	UNC
a. Issued note.	10.00	30.00	90.00
p. Proof print in gray and light blue.	—	—	350.

S712 1000 Rubles

	VG	VF	UNC
1920. Black on green and red underprint. Arms at upper left and right. Like #S711.	10.00	30.00	90.00

S713 5000 Rubles

	VG	VF	UNC
1921. Dark brown on multicolor underprint. Worker at left, arms at center, farmer seated at right. Back: Black on blue and brown underprint.	12.00	35.00	110.

S714 10,000 Rubles

	VG	VF	UNC
1921. Black on rose and green underprint. Worker and farmer standing at center, arms behind. Back: Black on brown underprint. Buildings at left and right.	15.00	45.00	135.

S715 25,000 Rubles

1921. Black on brown and gray underprint.

	VG	VF	UNC
a. Without watermark.	12.00	35.00	110.
b. Watermark.	12.00	35.00	110.

S716 50,000 Rubles

	VG	VF	UNC
1921. Black on gray-green and brown underprint. Standing figures at left and right, arms at center.	15.00	45.00	135.

S717 100,000 Rubles

1922. Black. Back: Arms at center.

	VG	VF	UNC
a. Violet underprint. Without watermark.	12.00	35.00	110.
b. Blue underprint. Without watermark.	12.00	35.00	110.
c. Watermark.	12.00	35.00	110.

S718 250,000 Rubles

	VG	VF	UNC
1922. Brown on blue underprint.	15.00	45.00	135.

S719 1,000,000 Rubles

1922. Red on pink underprint.

	VG	VF	UNC
a. Issued note.	15.00	45.00	135.
b. Without pink underprint on back.	—	—	—
c. Dark red. Watermark: *BANK URANIA.*	—	—	—

S720 5,000,000 Rubles

	VG	VF	UNC
1923. Green on olive and dull red underprint Arms at upper center. Back: Lilac in underprint.	20.00	60.00	180.

БАКУ BAKU

Notes of the city government of Baku, which were accepted all over Azerbaijan. All notes incorporate the city arms of *Three Flames.*

Baku was under Bolshevik control January to July 31, 1918. Then under British to Sept. 14, 1918; Turks to Oct. 30, 1918; British again from Nov. 14, 1918.

БАКИНСКАЯ ГОРОДСКАЯ УПРАВА

BAKU CITY MANAGEMENT

1918 ISSUE

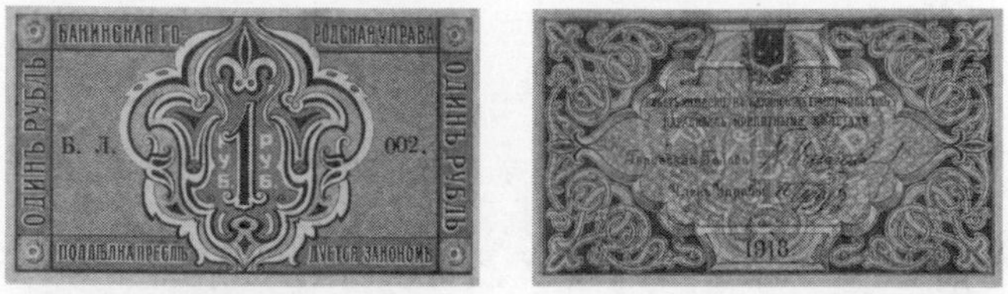

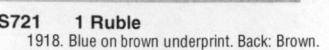

		Good	Fine	XF
S721	**1 Ruble** 1918. Blue on brown underprint. Back: Brown.	10.00	30.00	60.00

		Good	Fine	XF
S722	**3 Rubles** 1918. Brown on orange and light green underprint. Back: Green.	10.00	30.00	60.00

		Good	Fine	XF
S723	**5 Rubles** 1918. Blue on green and red underprint. Back: Blue-gray.	15.00	45.00	135.

		Good	Fine	XF
S724	**10 Rubles** 1918. Dark blue and red on lilac underprint. Back: Pale red.	15.00	45.00	135.

		Good	Fine	XF
S725	**25 Rubles** 1918. Black on purple and light brown underprint. Back: Brown on green underprint.	20.00	60.00	180.

1918 ND POSTAGE STAMP "STYLE" MONEY ISSUE

		Good	Fine	XF
S726	**5 Kopeks** ND (1918). Green. Arms at upper center.	5.00	15.00	45.00

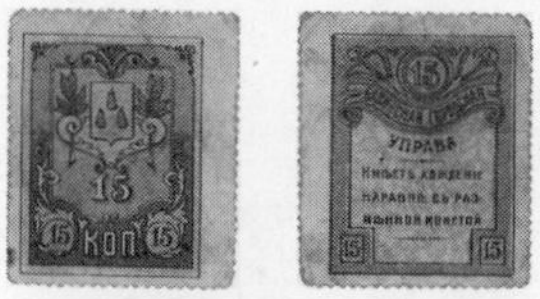

		Good	Fine	XF
S727	**15 Kopeks** ND (1918). Brown. Arms at upper center.	5.00	15.00	45.00

		Good	Fine	XF
S728	**50 Kopeks** ND. Black on reddish brown underprint. Arms at upper center.			
	a. Perforated.	10.00	30.00	90.00
	b. Imperforate.	10.00	30.00	90.00

СОВѢТЪ БАКИНСКАГО ГОРОДСКОГО ХОЗЯЙСТВА

SOVIET BAKU CITY ADMINSTRATION

1918 ISSUE

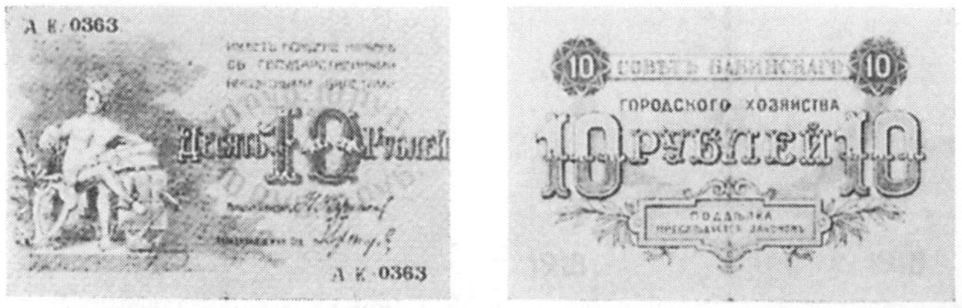

		Good	Fine	XF
S731	**10 Rubles** 1918. Brown on red and light brown underprint. Seated Mercury at left. With or without series IV-VIII. Back: Arms at center in underprint.	20.00	60.00	180.

		Good	Fine	XF
S732	**25 Rubles** 1918. Black and red on violet underprint. Mercury and worker at lower left, arms above. Back: Black on violet underprint.	30.00	90.00	270.

		Good	Fine	XF
S733	**50 Rubles** 1918. Black on light brown and light blue underprint. Arms above oil derricks, sailing ship with anchor, gear, crates and cornucopiae below at left. Serial # and letter on face or on back.			
	a. Without series.	20.00	60.00	180.
	b. Series V-VIII.	20.00	60.00	180.

NOTE: Minor plate and color shade varieties exist between Series V and VI.

ILLUSTRATIONS

Illustrations of bank notes used throughout this catalog are 42% of the actual size.

Batum (British Occupation)

British occupation lasted Dec. 27, 1918 to June 4, 1920.

БАТУМСКАГО КАЗНАЧЕИСТВА

Batum Treasury

1919 ND; 1919 РАЗМЪННЫЙ ДЕНЕЖНЫЙ ЗНАКЪ

Exchange Currency Tokens Issue

S736 1 Ruble	Good	Fine	XF
ND (April 1919). Orange-yellow. Tree. Uniface.	10.00	30.00	90.00

S737 3 Rubles	Good	Fine	XF
ND (April 1919). Green. Tree. Uniface.	10.00	30.00	90.00

S738 5 Rubles	Good	Fine	XF
ND (April 1919). Tree. Back: Signature.	10.00	30.00	90.00
S739 5 Rubles			
1919. Tree. Like #S738 but perforated date *1919* is across center. Back: Signature.	—	Unc	550.

S740 10 Rubles	Good	Fine	XF
ND (April 1919). Tree. Back: Signature.	15.00	45.00	135.
S741 10 Rubles			
1919. Perforated date.	—	Unc	550.

S742 25 Rubles	Good	Fine	XF
ND (April 1919). Brown. Tree. Back: Signature.	10.00	30.00	90.00

S743 25 Rubles	Good	Fine	XF
1919. Brown. Tree. Uniface. Like #S742 but perforated date *1919* is vertically at center.	—	Unc	550.
S744 50 Rubles	VG	VF	UNC
ND (April 1919). Tree. Back: Signature.	10.00	30.00	90.00
S745 50 Rubles			
1919. Perforated date.	—	—	550.

Georgia, Autonomous Republic

ГРУЗИНСКОИ РЕСПУБЛИКИ ОБЯЗАТЕЛЬСТВО КАЗНАЧЕИСТВА

Georgian Republic Treasury Obligations

NOTE: For previously listed #S746-S760 see Vol. 2, Georgia #1-15.

ГРУЗИНСКАЯ СОЦ. СОВЕТСКАЯ РЕСПУБЛИКА

Georgian Socialist Soviet Republic

1921 Issue

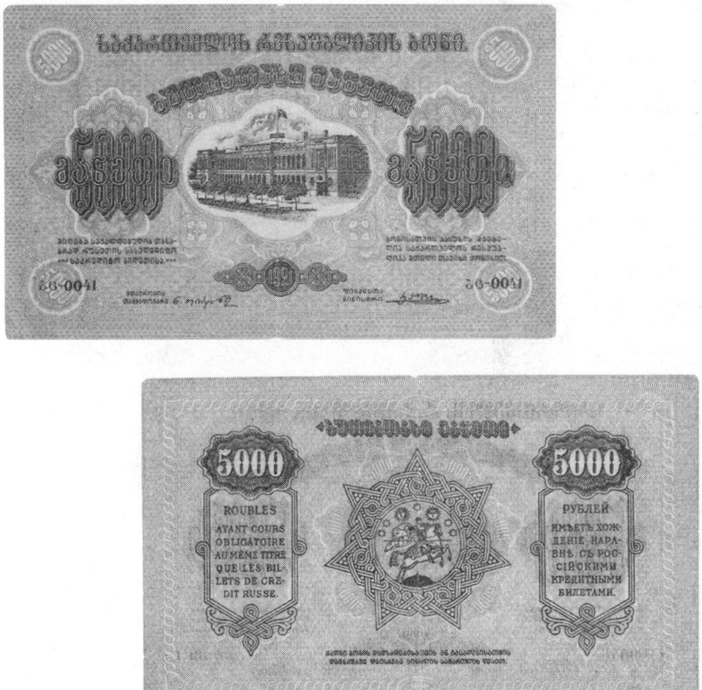

S761 5000 Rubles	VG	VF	UNC
1921. Lilac to brown. Building with flag at center. Like #15, Vol. 2. but margin circles around corner numerals are ringed twice at each side.			
a. Thick paper.	10.00	30.00	90.00
b. Thin paper, black printing.	10.00	30.00	90.00
c. Thin paper, blue printing.	10.00	30.00	90.00
d. Misprint: underprint inverted.	15.00	45.00	135.

		VG	VF	UNC
S762	**10,000 Rubles** 1922. Building with flags. Back: Arms at center.			
	a. Green back.	10.00	30.00	90.00
	b. Light blue back.	10.00	30.00	90.00
	c. Red back.	10.00	30.00	90.00
	d. Misprint: underprint inverted.	10.00	30.00	90.00

1922 ND Accounting Scrip Issue

		VG	VF	UNC
S765	**50,000 Rubles** ND (ca.1922). Red. Same design face and back.	5.00	15.00	45.00

НАРОДНАГО БАНКА С.С.Р. ГРУЗИН

Banque Nationale de Georgie

1922 ОБЯЗАТЕЛЬСТВО БОН Debenture Bonds Issue

		VG	VF	UNC
S766	**100,000 Rubles** 31.5.1922.	25.00	75.00	225.
S767	**500,000 Rubles** 31.5.1922. Black and brown on light green and orange underprint. Back: Light green.	30.00	90.00	270.

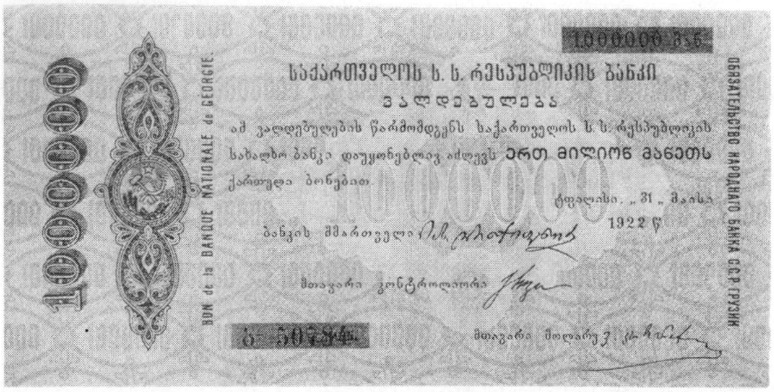

		Good	Fine	XF
S768	**1,000,000 Rubles** 31.5.1922. Black and brown in light green and orange underprint. Like #S767. Back: Gray.	40.00	120.	360.
S769	**5,000,000 Rubles** 31.5.1922.	20.00	60.00	180.

SIBERIA & URALS

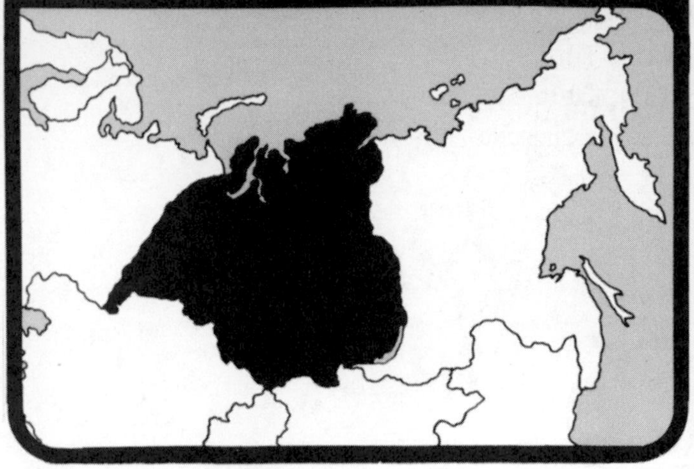

Issues of:

- Samara Directory (Komuch)
- Siberian Provisional Government
- Provisional Russian Government (Kolchak)
- Minister Representative Plenipotentiary for Provisions for Khabarovsk District
- Siberian Revolution Committee
- Urals and Kama Region
- Soviet of the Urals Region
- Urals Cossack Region
- Uralsk Branch, Government Bank
- Government of Central Siberia
- Akmolinsk Region Revolutionary Committee
- Krasnoyarsk
- Orenburg
- Perm

САМАРСКАЯ ДИРЕКТОРИЯ

Samara Directory (Komuch)

1918 ND First ГОСУДАРСТБ. ВНУТРЕНН. 5% ЗАЕМЪ 1905 Г. Provisional Government Loan Obligations Issue

		Good	Fine	XF
S771	**100 Rubles** ND (1918).	12.00	35.00	110.
S772	**1000 Rubles** ND (1918).	17.50	50.00	150.

1918 ND Second ГОСУДАРСТВ. ВТОРОЙ ВНУТР. 5% ЗАЕМЬ 1905 Г. Provisional Government Loan Obligations Issue

		Good	Fine	XF
S773	**100 Rubles** ND (1918).	12.00	35.00	110.
S774	**200 Rubles** ND (1918).	15.00	45.00	135.
S775	**500 Rubles** ND (1918).	17.50	50.00	150.
S776	**1000 Rubles** ND (1918).	25.00	75.00	225.

1918 ND ОБЛИГАЦІЯ ВНУТРЕНН. ЗАЙМА 1914 Г.

Provisional Loan Obligation Issue

		Good	Fine	XF
S777	**100 Rubles** ND (1918).	10.00	30.00	90.00
S778	**1000 Rubles** ND (1918).	20.00	60.00	180.

1914-15 БИЛЕТЪ ГОСУДАРСТВЕННАГО КАЗНАЧЕЙСТВА

Government Treasury Note Issue

		Good	Fine	XF
S779	**50 Rubles** 1914.	8.00	24.00	75.00
S780	**100 Rubles** 1914.	10.00	30.00	90.00
S781	**25 Rubles** 1915.	8.00	24.00	75.00
S782	**50 Rubles** 1915.	8.00	24.00	75.00
S783	**100 Rubles** 1915.	12.00	35.00	110.
S784	**500 Rubles** 1915.	17.50	50.00	150.

1915 ОБЛИГАЦІЯ 5-1/2% ВОЕННАГО КР. ЗАЙМА

Military Debenture Loan Obligation Issue

		Good	Fine	XF
S785	**50 Rubles** 1915.	8.00	24.00	75.00
S786	**100 Rubles** 1915.	8.00	24.00	75.00

		Good	Fine	XF
S787	**500 Rubles** 1915.	12.00	35.00	110.
S788	**1000 Rubles** 1915.	12.00	35.00	110.
S789	**5000 Rubles** 1915.	17.50	50.00	150.
S790	**10,000 Rubles** 1915.	25.00	75.00	225.

1916 ОБЛИГАЦІЯ 5-1/2% ВОЕННАГО КР. ЗАЙМА

Military Debenture Loan Obligation Issue

		Good	Fine	XF
S791	**50 Rubles** 1916.	8.00	24.00	75.00
S792	**100 Rubles** 1916.	8.00	24.00	75.00
S793	**500 Rubles** 1916.	8.00	24.00	75.00
S794	**1000 Rubles** 1916.	10.00	30.00	90.00
S795	**5000 Rubles** 1916.	17.50	50.00	150.
S796	**10,000 Rubles** 1916.	30.00	90.00	270.
S797	**25,000 Rubles** 1916.	50.00	150.	450.

1917 ОБЛИГАЦІЯ ЗАЙМА СВОБОДЫ 1917 Г.

Freedom Loan Obligation Issue

		Good	Fine	XF
S798	**20 Rubles** 1917.	8.00	24.00	75.00
S799	**40 Rubles** 1917.	8.00	24.00	75.00
S800	**50 Rubles** 1917.	8.00	24.00	75.00
S801	**100 Rubles** 1917.	8.00	24.00	75.00
S802	**500 Rubles** 1917.	10.00	30.00	90.00
S803	**1000 Rubles** 1917.	17.50	50.00	150.
S804	**5000 Rubles** 1917.	25.00	75.00	225.
S805	**10,000 Rubles** 1917.	30.00	90.00	270.
S806	**25,000 Rubles** 1917.	40.00	120.	360.

1918 КРАТКОСРОЧНОЕ ОБЯЗАТЕЛЬСТВО

Bills of Exchange Issue

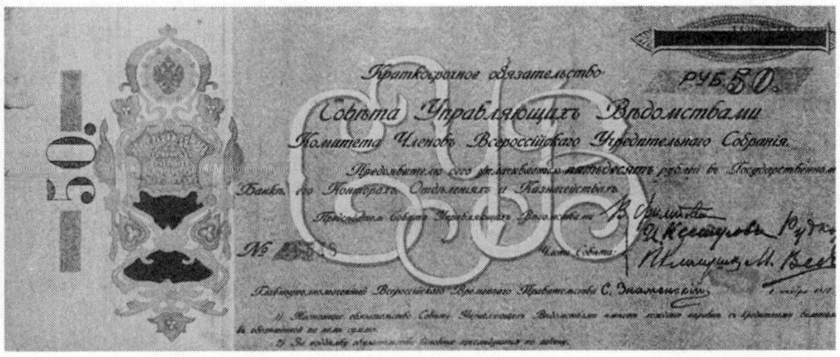

		Good	Fine	XF
S807	**50 Rubles** 1918. Black on green underprint. Multicolor guilloche at left.	15.00	45.00	135.
S808	**100 Rubles** 1918. Black on green underprint. Multicolor guilloche at left.	15.00	45.00	135.
S809	**250 Rubles** 1918. Black on green underprint. Multicolor guilloche at left.	20.00	60.00	180.

		Good	Fine	XF
S810	**500 Rubles** 1918. Black on green underprint. Multicolor guilloche at left.	40.00	120.	360.
S811	**1000 Rubles** 1918. Black on green underprint. Multicolor guilloche at left.	40.00	120.	360.
S812	**5000 Rubles** 1918. Black on green underprint. Multicolor guilloche at left.	50.00	150.	450.

СИБИРСКАГО ВРЕМЕННАГО ПРАВИТЕЛЬСТВА

Siberian Provisional Administration (First)

1918 КАЗНАЧЕЙСКІЙ ЗНАКЪ

Treasury Token Currency Issue

		VG	VF	UNC
S816	**1 Ruble** 1918. Black on light brown underprint. Double headed eagle at left and right. Back: Arms.	3.00	9.00	27.50
S817	**5 Rubles** 1918. Black on blue underprint. Double-headed eagle in wreath between two torches at left and right. Back: Arms.	3.00	9.00	27.50
S818	**10 Rubles** 1918. Black on red underprint. Double-headed eagle in wreath between two torches at left and right. Like #S817. Back: Arms. Thick or thin paper.	3.00	9.00	27.50

1918 ГОСУДАРСТВЕННАГО КАЗНАЧЕЙСТВА СИБИРИ

5% КРАТКОСРОЧНОЕ ОБЯЗАТЕЛЬСТВО

Siberian Government Debenture Obligations Issue

		Good	Fine	XF
S821	**500 Rubles** 1.10.1918. Violet on olive underprint.	10.00	30.00	90.00
S822	**1000 Rubles** 1.10.1918. Red-brown on green underprint.	10.00	60.00	180.
S823	**5000 Rubles** 1.10.1918. Brown on yellow underprint.	20.00	60.00	180.

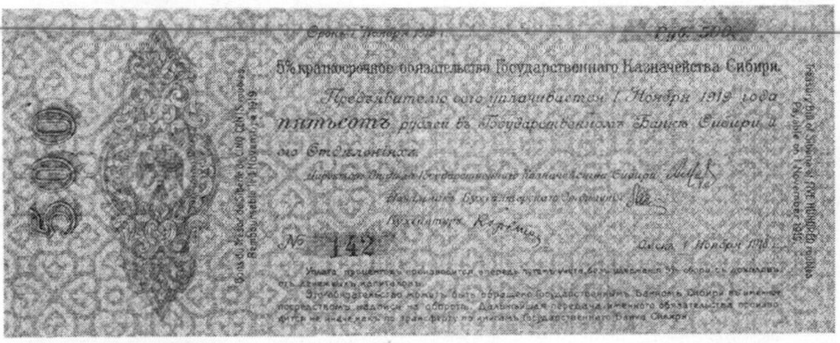

		Good	Fine	XF
S824	**500 Rubles** 1.11.1918. Violet on olive underprint.	10.00	30.00	270.
S825	**5000 Rubles** 1.11.1918. Brown on yellow underprint.	15.00	45.00	135.

СИБИРСКАГО ВРЕМЕННАГО ПРАВИТЕЛЬСТВА

Provisional Siberian Administration (Second)

1918-19; 1919 ND КАЗНАЧЕИСКИЙ ЗНАКЪ

Treasury Token Currency Issue

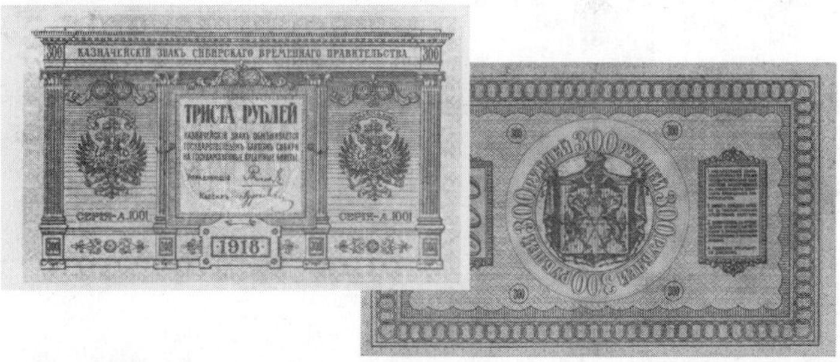

		VG	VF	UNC
S826	**300 Rubles** 1918. Black on blue underprint. Double-headed eagle at left and right. Back: Dark brown on light brown underprint. Arms at center.	10.00	30.00	90.00

		VG	VF	UNC
S827	**3 Rubles** 1919. Black on green underprint. Double-headed eagle at left and right. Back: Green.	4.00	12.50	35.00

		VG	VF	UNC
S828	**50 Kopeks**			
	ND (1919). Orange. No signature. Back: Double-headed eagle. Printer: ABNC (without imprint).	3.00	9.00	27.50

NOTE: For #S828 with signature see #S1244.

1918-20 5% КРАТКОСРОЧНОЕ ОБЯЗАТЕЛЬСТВО ГОСУДАРСТВЕННАГО КАЗНАЧЕЙСТВА

5% Government Debenture Obligations

1. ДЕК. 1918 Issue

Apparently 2 or more printers made this series of notes as there are significant variations in serial #, type style, prefix letter, etc.

		Good	Fine	XF
S831	**500 Rubles**			
	1.12.1918. Violet on olive underprint.	4.00	12.50	35.00
S832	**1000 Rubles**			
	1.12.1918. Light brown on green and orange underprint.	4.00	12.50	35.00

		Good	Fine	XF
S833	**5000 Rubles**			
	1.12.1918. Brown on yellow-brown underprint.	10.00	30.00	90.00

1. ЯНВАРЯ 1919 Issue

		VG	VF	UNC
S834	**25 Rubles**			
	1.1.1919. Black on blue underprint.			
	a. Sixth line: ДИРЕКТОРЪ ОТДѢЛА. **Underprint large flowers.**	5.00	15.00	45.00
	b. Like a., but underprint small flowers.	3.00	9.00	27.50
	c. Sixth line: ДИРЕКУОРЪ ДЕПАРТАМЕНТА.	10.00	30.00	90.00
S835	**50 Rubles**			
	1.1.1919. Black on green underprint.			
	a. Like #S834a.	10.00	30.00	90.00
	b. Like #S834b.	3.00	9.00	27.50
	c. Like #S834c.	10.00	30.00	120.
S836	**100 Rubles**			
	1.1.1919. Blue on blue-violet underprint.			
	a. Second line: 5% КРАТКОС...	10.00	30.00	120.
	b. Second line: КРАТКОС...	10.00	30.00	120.
	c. Error; like a., but *Januari* ЯНБАПЬ **misspelling at right.**	10.00	30.00	120.
S837	**250 Rubles**			
	1.1.1919. Brown on orange underprint.	5.00	15.00	45.00
S838	**500 Rubles**			
	1.1.1919. Gray-violet on green underprint.	5.00	15.00	45.00
S839	**1000 Rubles**			
	1.1.1919. Red-brown on green underprint.	3.00	9.00	27.50

1. ФЕВРАЛЯ 1919 Issue

		VG	VF	UNC
S840	**25 Rubles**			
	1.2.1919. Black on blue underprint.			
	a. Sixth line: ДИРЕКТОРЪ ОТДѢЛА. with or without watermark.	3.00	9.00	27.50
	b. Sixth line: ДИРЕКТОРЪ ДЕПАРТАМЕНТА.	5.00	15.00	45.00
S841	**50 Rubles**			
	1.2.1919. Black on green underprint.			
	a. Like #S840a.	10.00	30.00	90.00
	b. Like #S840b.	3.00	9.00	27.50
S842	**250 Rubles**			
	1.2.1919. Brown on orange underprint.	3.00	9.00	27.50
S843	**500 Rubles**			
	1.2.1919. Gray-violet on olive underprint.	3.00	9.00	27.50
S844	**1000 Rubles**			
	1.2.1919. Red-brown on green underprint.	5.00	15.00	45.00
S845	**5000 Rubles**			
	1.2.1919. Brown on yellow underprint.	10.00	30.00	90.00

1. МАРТА 1919 Issue

		VG	VF	UNC
S846	**25 Rubles**			
	1.3.1919. Black on blue underprint.	3.00	9.00	27.50

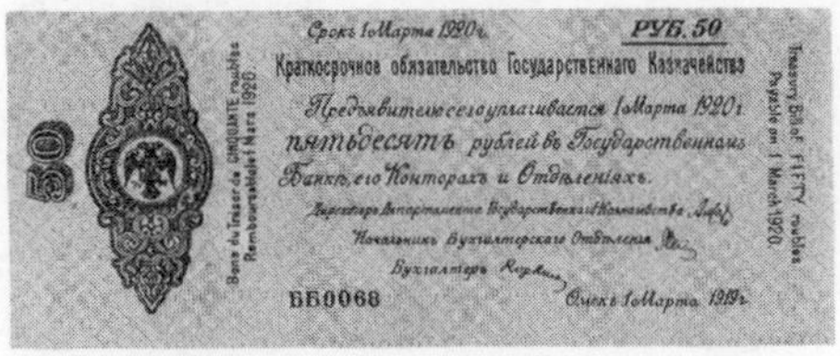

		VG	VF	UNC
S847	**50 Rubles**			
	1.3.1919. Black on green underprint.	3.00	9.00	27.50
S848	**250 Rubles**			
	1.3.1919. Brown on orange underprint.	4.00	12.50	35.00
S849	**500 Rubles**			
	1.3.1919. Gray-violet on olive underprint.			
	a. Sixth line: ДИРЕКТОРЪ ОТДѢЛА.	5.00	15.00	45.00
	b. Sixth line: ДИРЕКТОРЪ ДЕПАРТАМЕНТА.	5.00	15.00	45.00
S850	**1000 Rubles**			
	1.3.1919. Red-brown on green underprint.			
	a. Like #S849a.	5.00	15.00	45.00
	b. Like #S849b.	5.00	15.00	45.00

1. АПРѢЛЯ 1919 Issue

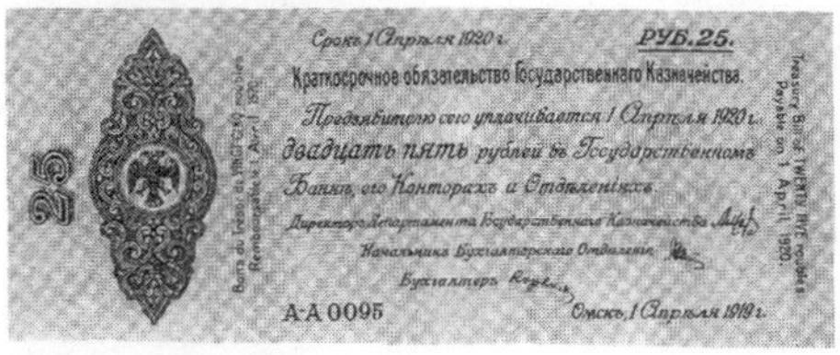

		VG	VF	UNC
S851	**25 Rubles**			
	1.4.1919. Black on blue underprint.	5.00	15.00	45.00
S852	**50 Rubles**			
	1.4.1919. Black on green underprint.	5.00	15.00	45.00
S853	**250 Rubles**			
	1.4.1919. Brown on orange underprint.	5.00	15.00	45.00
S854	**500 Rubles**			
	1.4.1919. Gray-violet on olive underprint.			
	a. Like #S849a.	7.00	22.50	65.00
	b. Like #S849b.	7.00	22.50	65.00

1. МАЯ 1919 Issue

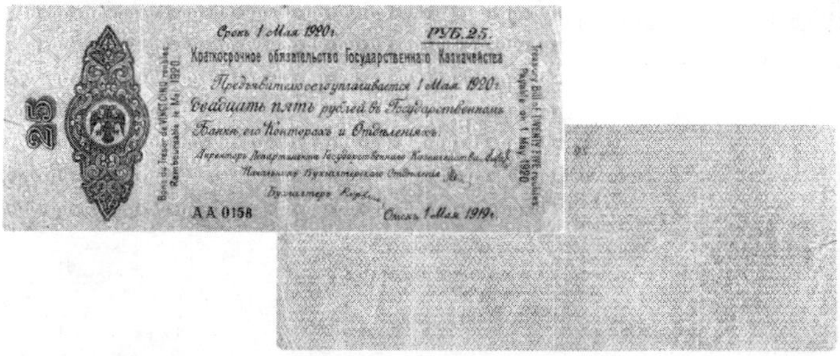

		VG	VF	UNC
S855	**25 Rubles**			
	1.5.1919. Black on blue underprint.			
	a. Vertical format note: *Remboursable le Mai 1920* at left.	4.00	12.50	35.00
	b. Vertical format note: *Remboursable le I. Mai 1920* at left.	5.00	15.00	45.00

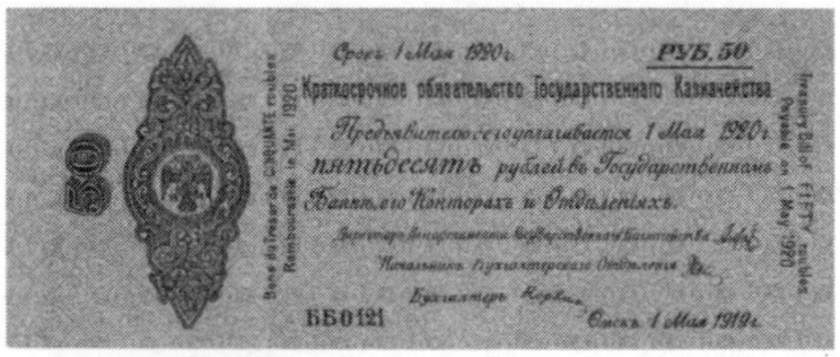

		VG	VF	UNC
S856	**50 Rubles**			
	1.5.1919. Black on green underprint.			
	a. Like #S855a.	3.00	9.00	27.50
	b. Like #S855b, only as a forgery.	10.00	30.00	90.00
S857	**250 Rubles**	VG	VF	UNC
	1.5.1919. Brown on orange underprint.	4.00	12.50	35.00
S858	**500 Rubles**	VG	VF	UNC
	1.5.1919. Gray-violet on green-yellow underprint.	4.00	12.50	35.00

1. ІЮНЯ 1919 Issue

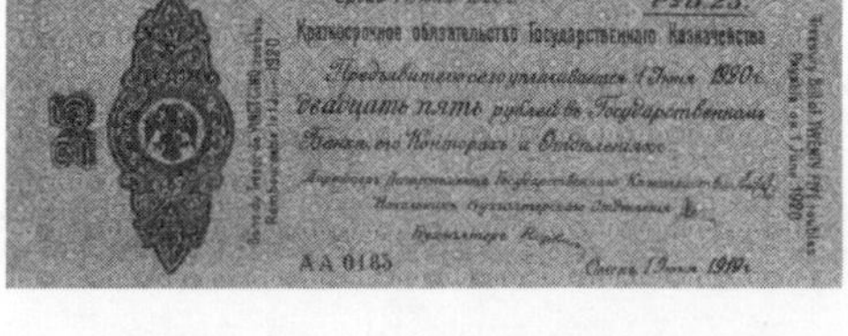

		VG	VF	UNC
S859	**25 Rubles**			
	1.6.1919. Black on blue underprint.			
	a. Sixth line: ГОСУДАРСТВЪ.	4.00	12.50	35.00
	b. Sixth line:. ГОСУДАРСТВЕННАГО.	4.00	12.50	35.00
S860	**50 Rubles**			
	1.6.1919. Black on green underprint.	4.00	12.50	35.00

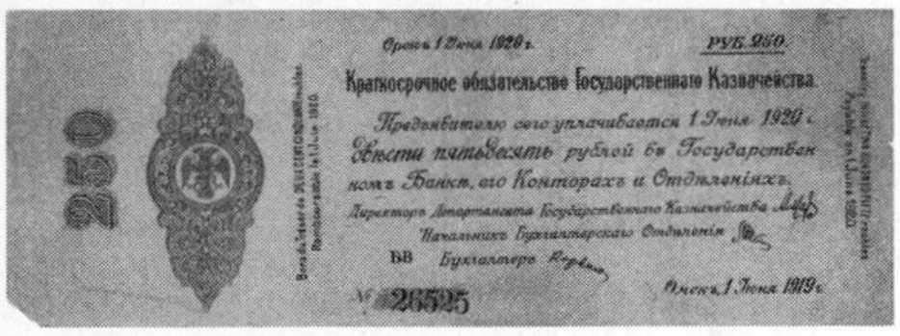

		VG	VF	UNC
S861	**250 Rubles**			
	1.6.1919. Brown on orange underprint.	5.00	15.00	45.00
S862	**500 Rubles**			
	1.6.1919. Gray-violet on green underprint.	4.00	12.50	35.00
S863	**1000 Rubles**			
	1.6.1919. Red-brown on green underprint.	5.00	15.00	45.00

1. ІЮЛЯ 1919 Issue

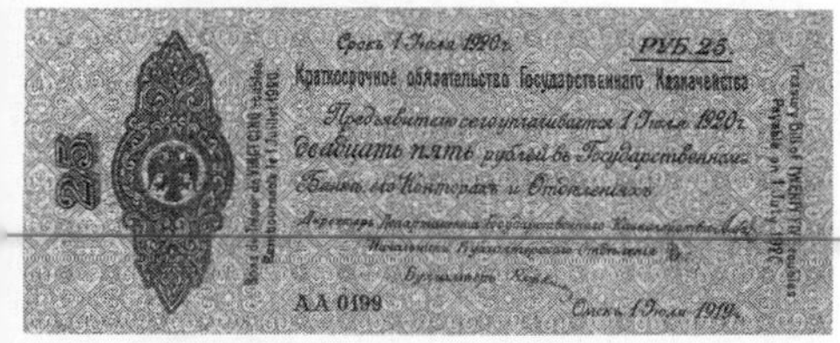

		VG	VF	UNC
S864	**25 Rubles**			
	1.7.1919. Black on blue underprint.	5.00	15.00	45.00

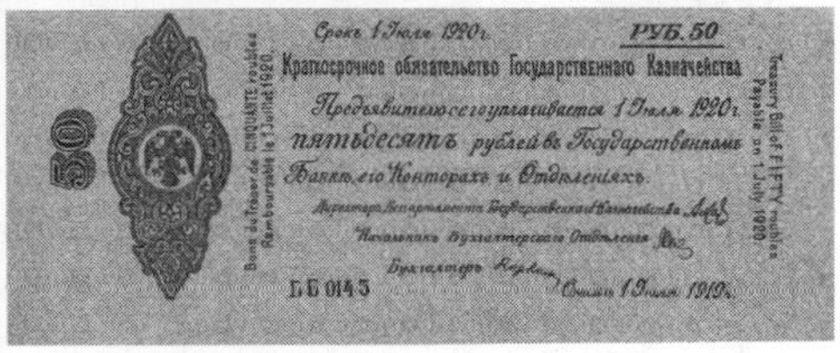

		VG	VF	UNC
S865	**50 Rubles**			
	1.7.1919. Black on green underprint.			
	a. Sixth line like #S859a.	5.00	15.00	45.00
	b. Sixth line like #S859b.	5.00	15.00	45.00
S866	**250 Rubles**			
	1.7.1919. Brown on orange underprint.			
	a. Sixth line 115mm.	5.00	15.00	45.00
	b. Sixth line 85mm.	5.00	15.00	45.00
S867	**500 Rubles**			
	1.7.1919. Gray-violet on green underprint	5.00	15.00	45.00

1. ОКТЯБРЯ 1919 (1920) Issue

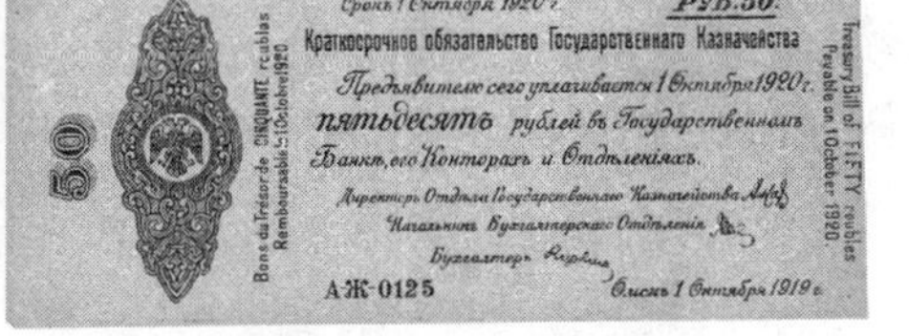

		Good	Fine	XF
S867B	**50 Rubles**			
	1.10.1919 (1920). Black on green underprint. Watermark: Uncrowned double-headed eagle inside diamond pattern.	10.00	30.00	90.00
S868	**250 Rubles**			
	1.10.1919 (1920). Brown on orange underprint. Watermark: Uncrowned double-headed eagle inside diamond pattern.	15.00	45.00	135.
S869	**1000 Rubles**			
	1.10.1919 (1920). Red-brown on yellow underprint. Watermark: Uncrowned double-headed eagle inside diamond pattern.	20.00	60.00	180.
S870	**5000 Rubles**			
	1.10.1919 (1920). Brown on yellow-brown underprint. Watermark: Uncrowned double-headed eagle inside diamond pattern.	15.00	45.00	135.

NOTE: #S867B-S870 on watermark paper.

1. ЯНВАРЯ 1920 Issue

Issued in Vladivostok.

		Good	Fine	XF
S870A	**5000 Rubles**			
	1.1.1920. Black on green underprint. Back: Blue. Without design. Printer: ABNC.			
	a. Issued note. Rare.	—	—	—
	p. Proof.	—	Unc	750.
	s. Specimen.	—	Unc	800.

1919-20 ГОСУДАРСТВЕННЫЙ КРЕДИТНЫЙ БИЛЕТЪ

Government Credit Notes Issue

#S871-S878 different proof-prints w/eagle of the Provisional Government and St. George. (Not issued.)

		Good	Fine	XF
S871	**1 Ruble**			
	1919. Eagle and St. George.	—	Unc	500.
S872	**3 Rubles**			
	1919. Eagle and St. George.	—	Unc	500.
S873	**5 Rubles**			
	1919. Eagle and St. George.	—	Unc	500.
S874	**10 Rubles**			
	1919. Eagle and St. George.	—	Unc	500.
S875	**25 Rubles**			
	1919. Eagle and St. George.	—	Unc	500.
S876	**100 Rubles**			
	1919. Eagle and St. George.	—	Unc	500.
S877	**1000 Rubles**			
	1919. Eagle and St. George.	—	Unc	500.
S878	**5000 Rubles**			
	1920. Eagle and St. George. Rare.	—	—	—

ГОСУДАРСТВЕННИЙ БАНК

Government Bank

IRK. OTD.

Irkutsk

1917 БИЛЕТЪ ГОСУДАРСТВЕННЫЙ ВНУТРЕННІЙ. 4-1/2% ВЫИГРЫШНЫЙ ЗАЕМЪ

Committee Savings Loan Notes Issue

Public bonds and coupons used as currency. Different places of issue are hand stamped at lower l. of bonds, thus: ИРК. ОТД. ГОЧ. Б.

		VG	VF	UNC
S881	**290 Rubles**			
	1917 (1919). Brown and black. Woman with child, sword and shield at top center. Back: Brown. Printer: ABNC. Public loan with 20 coupons.	10.00	30.00	90.00

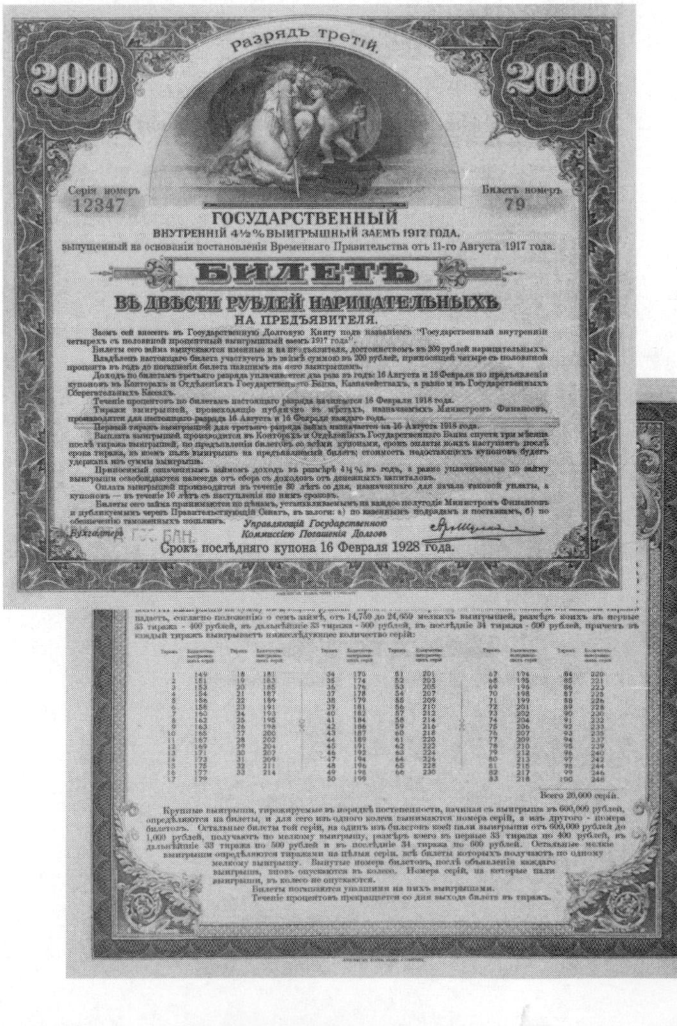

		VG	VF	UNC
S882	**200 Rubles** 1917 (1919). Brown and black. Woman with child, sword and shield at top center. Back: Brown. Printer: ABNC. Like #S881 but without coupons.	15.00	45.00	135.
S883	**90 Rubles** 1917 (1919). Brown and black. Back: Brown. Printer: ABNC. Sheet of 20 coupons from #S881.	10.00	30.00	90.00
S884	**4 Rubles 50 Kopeks** 1917 (1919). Brown and black. Back: Brown. Printer: ABNC. Single coupon of #S881.	2.00	6.00	20.00

		VG	VF	UNC
S885	**290 Rubles** 1917 (1919). Green and black. Woman with child, sword and shield. Back: Green. Printer: ABNC. Public loan with 20 coupons.	20.00	60.00	180.
S885A	**200 Rubles** 1917 (1919). Green and black. Woman with child, sword and shield. Back: Green. Printer: ABNC. Like #S885 but without coupons.	15.00	45.00	135.

		VG	VF	UNC
S886	**200 Rubles** 1917 (1919). Green and black. Woman with child, sword and shield. Back: Green. Printer: ABNC. Like #S885 but without coupons.	10.00	30.00	90.00
S887	**90 Rubles** 1917 (1919). Green and black. Back: Green. Printer: ABNC. Sheet of 20 coupons from #S885.	5.00	15.00	45.00

		VG	VF	UNC
S888	**4 Rubles 50 Kopeks** 1917 (1919). Green and black. Back: Green. Printer: ABNC. Single coupon of #S885.	1.00	3.00	9.00

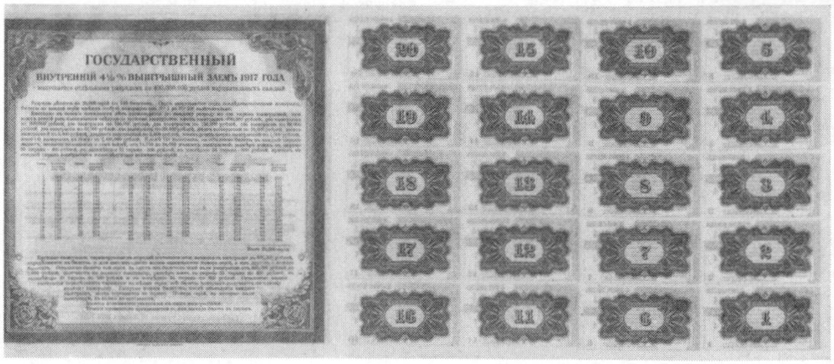

		VG	VF	UNC
S889	**290 Rubles** 1917 (1919). Orange and black. Woman with child, sword and shield at top. Back: Orange. Printer: ABNC. Public loan with 20 coupons.	20.00	60.00	180.

S890 200 Rubles | VG 20.00 | VF 60.00 | UNC 180.
1917 (1919). Orange and black. Woman with child, sword and shield at top. Back: Orange. Printer: ABNC. Like #S889 but without coupons.

S891 90 Rubles | 15.00 | 45.00 | 135.
1917 (1919). Orange and black. Back: Orange. Printer: ABNC. Sheet of 20 coupons from #S889.

S892 4 Rubles 50 Kopeks | VG 1.00 | VF 3.00 | UNC 9.00
1917 (1919). Orange and black. Back: Orange. Printer: ABNC. Single coupon from #S889.

УПОЛНОМОЧЕННЫЙ МИНИСТРА СНАБЖЕНІЯ И ПРОДОВОЛЬСТВІЯ ПО ХАБАРОВСКОМУ РАЙОНУ

MINISTER REPRESENTATIVE PLENIPOTENTIARY FOR PROVISIONS FOR KHABAROVSK DISTRICT

1919 ISSUE

S896 3 Rubles | VG 30.00 | VF 90.00 | UNC 270.
1919. Black on green underprint.

S897 5 Rubles | VG 30.00 | VF 90.00 | UNC 270.
1919. Black on blue underprint.

S898 10 Rubles | 30.00 | 90.00 | 270.
1919.

РОССИЙСКАЯ СОЦИАЛИСТИЧЕСКАЯ ФЕДЕР-АТИВНАЯСОВЕТСКАЯ РЕСПУБЛИКА

SIBERIAN REVOLUTION COMMITTEE

1917 БИЛЕТЪ ГОСУД. ВНУТРЕНН. 4-1/2% ВЫИГР. ЗАЕМЪ

PROVISIONAL GOVERNMENT SAVINGS LOAN NOTES ISSUE

#S899-S904 Kolchak notes w/ovpt. of R.S.F.S.R. text.

S899 200 Rubles | VG 30.00 | VF 90.00 | UNC 270.
1920 (-old date 1917). Brown. Woman with child, sword and shield at top center. Overprint: Blue R.S.F.S.R. text, arms and date on #S882.

S900 90 Rubles | 50.00 | 150. | 450.
ND(1920). Overprint: Blue R.S.F.S.R. text on #S883.

S901 4 Rubles 50 Kopeks | VG 5.00 | VF 15.00 | UNC 45.00
ND(1920). Brown. Overprint: Blue R.S.F.S.R. text on #S884.

S902 200 Rubles | 40.00 | 120. | 360.
1920 (-old date 1917). Blue. Woman with child, sword and shield at top. Overprint: Red R.S.F.S.R. text, arms and date.

S903 90 Rubles | 50.00 | 150. | 450.
ND(1920). Blue. Overprint: Red R.S.F.S.R. text on sheet of 20 coupons from #S902.

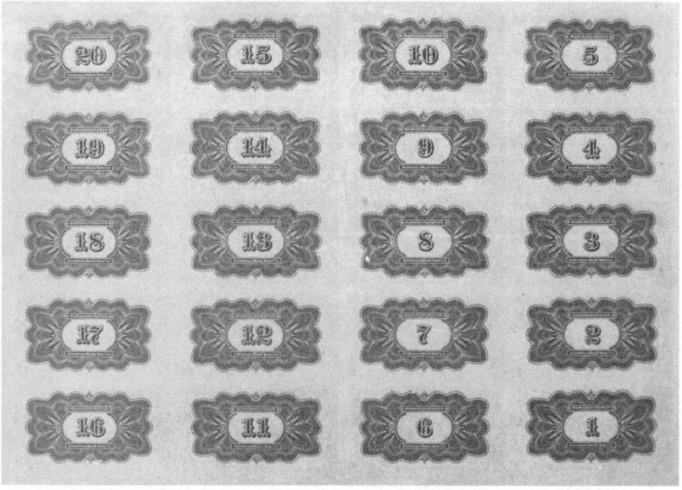

		VG	VF	UNC
S904	**4 Rubles 50 Kopeks** ND(1920). Overprint: Red R.S.F.S.R. text on single coupon from #S903.	5.00	15.00	45.00

ЧРЕЗВЫЧАЙНО-УПОЛНОМОЧЕННЫЙ

ПРИКАМСКАГО РАЙОНА

PLENIPOTENTIARY EXTRAORDINARY FOR THE KAMA REGION

1915 ОБЛ. 5-1/2% ВОЕНН. КР. ЗАЙМОВ.

MILITARY DEBENTURE LOAN OBLIGATION ISSUE

#S906-S915 stamps on Russian public bonds and w/perforation 256 ЧУПР.

		VG	VF	UNC
S906	**50 Rubles** 1915. Stamp on Russian public bond and perforation.	50.00	150.	450.
S907	**100 Rubles** 1915. Stamp on Russian public bond and perforation.	50.00	150.	450.
S908	**500 Rubles** 1915. Stamp on Russian public bond and perforation.	50.00	150.	450.
S909	**1000 Rubles** 1915. Stamp on Russian public bond and perforation.	50.00	150.	450.
S910	**5000 Rubles** 1915. Stamp on Russian public bond and perforation.	50.00	150.	450.

1916 ОБЛ. 5-1/2% ВОЕНН. КР. ЗАЙМОВ.

MILITARY DEBENTURE LOAN OBLIGATION ISSUE

		VG	VF	UNC
S911	**50 Rubles** 1916. Stamp on Russian public bond and perforation.	30.00	90.00	270.
S912	**100 Rubles** 1916. Stamp on Russian public bond and perforation.	30.00	90.00	270.
S913	**500 Rubles** 1916. Stamp on Russian public bond and perforation.	40.00	120.	360.
S914	**1000 Rubles** 1916. Stamp on Russian public bond and perforation.	40.00	120.	360.
S915	**5000 Rubles** 1916. Stamp on Russian public bond and perforation.	40.00	120.	360.

1918 ND ОБЛ. ЗАЙМА СВОБОДЫ 1917

FREEDOM LOAN OBLIGATION ISSUE

		VG	VF	UNC
S916	**500 Rubles** ND (1918).	50.00	150.	450.
S917	**1000 Rubles** ND (1918).	60.00	180.	550.
S918	**5000 Rubles** ND (1918).	100.	300.	900.
S919	**10,000 Rubles** ND (1918).	200.	600.	1800.

SOVIET OF THE URALS REGION

РАБОЧЕЕ Й КРЕСТЬЯНСКОЕ ПРАВЙТЕЛЬСТВО

WORKERS AND CHRISTIANS ADMINISTRATION

РОССИЙСКОЙ СОЦИАЛИСТИЧЕСКОЙ ФЕЛЕРАТИ ВНОЙ РЕСПУБЛИКИ СОВЕТОВ (OR СОВЕТСКОЙ) РЕСПУБЛИКИ

RUSSIAN SOCIALIST FEDERATED SOVIET REPUBLIC

ГОСУДАРСТВЕННЬИЙ БАНК

GOVERNMENT BANK

ЕКАТЕРИНБУРГСКОЕ ОТД ЕЛЕНИЕ

EKATERINBURG

1918 ISSUE

These notes have always held a grim fascination for collectors because their issuers also ordered the murder of Czar Nicholas II and the entire imperial family on July 16, 1918 at the *House of Special Purpose* (home of merchant N. N. Ipatiev) in Ekaterinburg. A combined Czech Legion - White Army force captured the city July 24, 1918, ending the Urals Region Soviet.

		Good	Fine	XF
S920	**50 Kopeks** 21.10.1918. Blue on gold underprint. Double headed eagle at upper center. Back: Black text.	30.00	90.00	270.

		Good	Fine	XF
S921	**1 Ruble** 1918. Blue-black on yellow or orange underprint. Back: Circular ornament with agricultural implements.			
	a. Without stamp.	30.00	90.00	270.
	b. With stamp (different kinds).	30.00	90.00	270.

		Good	Fine	XF
S922	**5 Rubles** 1918. Blue. Back: Arms at upper center, soldier and sailor at bottom center. Vertical format.			
	a. Without stamp.	100.	300.	900.
	b. With stamp (different kinds).	100.	300.	900.
	c. Commemorative overprint in 8 lines of vertical red German and 9 lines of Russian text for German Communist Karl Liebknecht. Rare.	—	—	—
S923	**100 Rubles** 1918. Only printed half-finished face proof. (Not issued.) Rare.	—	—	—

<LOC>Urals Cossack Region

УРАЛЬСКАГО КАЗАЧЬЯГО ВОЙСКА

Urals Cossack Territory

1918 МАРТА Г. 6% ОБЯЗАТЕЛЬСТВО Obligation Issue

	Good	Fine	XF
S926 50 Rubles			
1918. Multicolor guilloche at left. value in one line.	30.00	90.00	270.
S926A 50 Rubles			
1918. Multicolor. Guilloche at left. Denomination in one line.	20.00	60.00	180.

	Good	Fine	XF
S927 100 Rubles			
1918. Multicolor guilloche at left, varieties in the denomination numerals.	30.00	90.00	270.
S928 200 Rubles			
1918. Multicolor guilloche at left, varieties in the denomination numerals.	30.00	90.00	270.
S929 300 Rubles			
1918. Multicolor guilloche at left, varieties in the denomination numerals.	35.00	110.	325.
S930 400 Rubles			
1918. Multicolor guilloche at left, varieties in the denomination numerals.	40.00	120.	360.
S931 500 Rubles			
1918. Multicolor guilloche at left, varieties in the denomination numerals.	35.00	110.	325.
S932 600 Rubles			
1918. Multicolor guilloche at left, varieties in the denomination numerals.	100.	300.	900.
S933 700 Rubles			
1918. Multicolor guilloche at left, varieties in the denomination numerals.	100.	300.	900.
S934 800 Rubles			
1918. Multicolor guilloche at left, varieties in the denomination numerals.	125.	375.	1150.
S935 900 Rubles			
1918. Multicolor guilloche at left, varieties in the denomination numerals.	140.	425.	1275.
S936 1000 Rubles			
1918. Multicolor guilloche at left, varieties in the denomination numerals.	125.	375.	1150.
S937 1500 Rubles			
1918. Multicolor guilloche at left, varieties in the denomination numerals.	140.	425.	1275.
S938 2000 Rubles			
1918. Multicolor guilloche at left, varieties in the denomination numerals.	200.	600.	1800.
S939 3000 Rubles			
1918. Multicolor guilloche at left, varieties in the denomination numerals.	200.	600.	1800.

1918 6% Г. КУПОНЪ 6% ОБЯЗАТЕЛЬСТВА

Coupon Obligation Issue

	Good	Fine	XF
S940 75 Kopeks			
1918.	10.00	30.00	90.00
S941 1 Ruble 50 Kopeks			
1918.	10.00	30.00	90.00
S942 3 Rubles			
1918.	10.00	30.00	90.00
S943 4 Rubles 50 Kopeks			
1918.	10.00	30.00	90.00
S944 6 Rubles			
1918.	12.00	35.00	110.
S945 7 Rubles 50 Kopeks			
1918.	12.00	35.00	110.
S946 9 Rubles			
1918.	15.00	45.00	135.
S947 10 Rubles 50 Kopeks			
1918.	15.00	45.00	135.
S948 12 Rubles			
1918.	20.00	60.00	180.
S949 13 Rubles 50 Kopeks			
1918.	22.00	65.00	195.
S950 15 Rubles			
1918.	25.00	75.00	225.
S951 22 Rubles 50 Kopeks			
1918.	30.00	90.00	360.
S952 30 Rubles			
1918.	40.00	120.	360.
S953 45 Rubles			
1918.	40.00	120.	360.

ГОСУДАРСТВЕННЫЙ БАНК

Government Bank

УРАЛЬСКОЕ ОТД. Г. Б. Uralsk

1918 ND ПОЧТОВАЯ МАРКА Postage Stamp Money Issue

Postage stamps of Czarist Russia on heavy paper, w/printing on back:
ИМѢЕТЬ ХОЖДЕ-
НІЕ НАРАВНѢСЪ
ДЕНЕЖНЫМИ
ЗНАКАМИ
УРАЛЬСКОЕ
ОТД. Г. Б.

	VG	VF	UNC
S956 1 Ruble			
ND (1918). Brown, light brown and orange stamp. Back: Black text.	12.50	35.00	110.

Original size

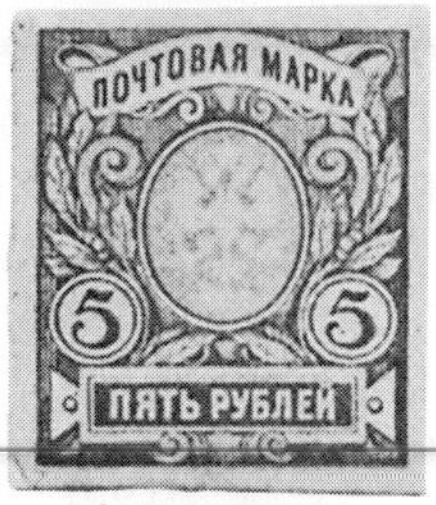

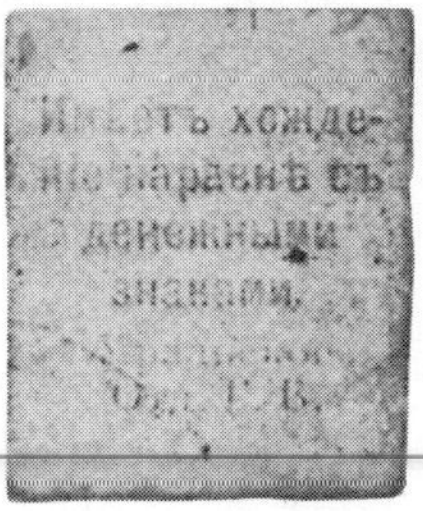

	VG	VF	UNC
S957 5 Rubles			
ND (1918). Blue, light blue and yellow stamp. Back: Black text.	12.50	35.00	110.
S958 10 Rubles			
ND (1918). Red. Back: Black text.	15.00	45.00	135.

ПРАВИТЕЛЬСТВО ЦЕНТРОСИБИРИ.

СИБИРСКИЙ

Government of Central Siberia

1918 КРЕДИТНЫЙ БИЛЕТЪ Credit Notes Issue

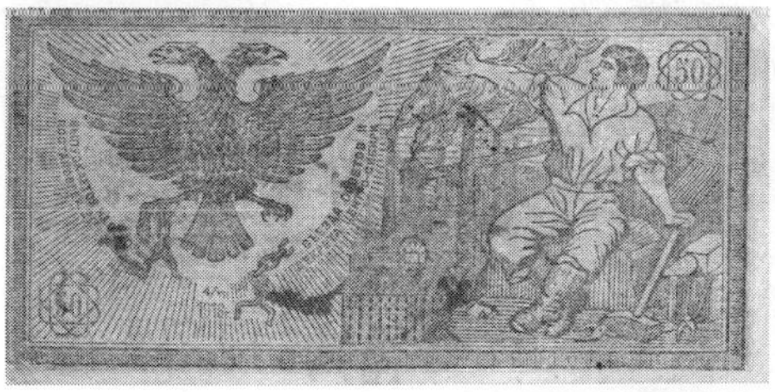

	VG	VF	UNC
S961 50 Rubles			
1918. Blue on pink to brown underprint. Tools under value at left. Back: Double-headed eagle at left, factory and worker at right.			
a. Without stamp.	10.00	30.00	90.00
b. Stamping and overprint from different State Bank branches.	10.00	30.00	90.00

NOTE: Forgeries exist of #S961b.

АКМОЛИНСКОЙ ОБЛАСТИ

Akmolinsk Region

Revolutionary Committee

1919 ND Issue

	VG	VF	UNC
S962 250 Rubles			
ND (1919).	30.00	90.00	270.
S963 500 Rubles			
ND (1919).	30.00	90.00	270.
S964 1000 Rubles			
ND (1919).	30.00	90.00	270.

ГОСУДАРСТВЕННЬИЙ БАНК

Government Bank

КИСЛОБОДСК. ОТДЕЛЕНИЕ

Kislovodsk

ND ЧЕК Checks Issue

	Good	Fine	XF
S965 25 Rubles			
ND.	15.00	45.00	135.
S965A 50 Rubles			
ND.	15.00	45.00	135.
S965B 100 Rubles			
ND.	15.00	45.00	135.

NOTE: #S965-S965B series varieties.

НАРОДНОГО БАНКА Р.С.Ф.С.Р.

National Bank R.S.F.S.R.

КИСЛОВОДСКОЕ ОТДЕЛЕН ИЕ

Kislovodsk

ND ЧЕК Checks Issue

	Good	Fine	XF
S965C 50 Rubles			
ND. Black. 2 hand signatures. Handstamped circular purple seal. Paper: Tan.	15.00	45.00	135.
S965D 100 Rubles			
ND.	15.00	45.00	135.
S965E 250 Rubles			
ND.	20.00	60.00	180.

КРАСНОЯРСК. ЕНИС. Г. О-БО

Krasnoyarsk Territory

1919 РАЗМѢННЫЙ ЧЕКЪ Exchange Checks Issue

	VG	VF	UNC
S966 1 Ruble			
1919. Brown with black text.			
a. Without series.	20.00	60.00	180.
b. Series A.	20.00	60.00	180.
S967 3 Rubles			
1919.			
a. Without series.	25.00	75.00	225.
b. Series A.	25.00	75.00	225.
S968 5 Rubles			
1919.			
a. Without series.	30.00	90.00	270.
b. Series A.	30.00	90.00	270.
S969 10 Rubles			
1919. Red with black text. Back: Red.			
a. Without series.	15.00	45.00	135.
b. Series A.	15.00	45.00	135.
c. Series Ъ, В, or Г.	15.00	45.00	135.

	VG	VF	UNC
S970 25 Rubles			
1919. Black on purple and gray underprint. Back: Purple.			
a. Without series.	30.00	90.00	270.
b. Series A.	20.00	60.00	180.
c. Series Ъ, В, or Г.	20.00	60.00	180.
S971 50 Rubles			
1919. Without series.	30.00	90.00	270.

ГОСУДАРСТВЕННЬИЙ БАНК

Government Bank

ОРЕНБУРГСКАГО ОТДѢЛЕ НІЯ

Orenburg

1917 ДЕНЕЖНЫЙ ЗНАКЪ Currency Tokens Issue

	Good	Fine	XF
S976 5 Rubles			
1917.	30.00	90.00	270.

Varieties exist.

	Good	Fine	XF
S977 25 Rubles			
1917. Black on light red underprint. Arms at upper left.	30.00	90.00	270.

	Good	Fine	XF
S978 100 Rubles			
1917. Black on orange underprint. Arms at center.	40.00	120.	360.

Varieties exist.

1918 ДЕНЕЖНЫЙ ЗНАКЪ Currency Tokens Issue

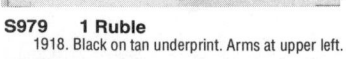

	VG	VF	UNC
S979 1 Ruble			
1918. Black on tan underprint. Arms at upper left.	15.00	45.00	135.

		VG	VF	UNC
S980	**3 Rubles**			
	1918. Black on green underprint. Arms at left. Varieties exist.	15.00	45.00	135.
S981	**25 Rubles**			
	1918.	30.00	90.00	270.
S982	**100 Rubles**			
	1918. Black on rose underprint. Arms.	30.00	90.00	270.

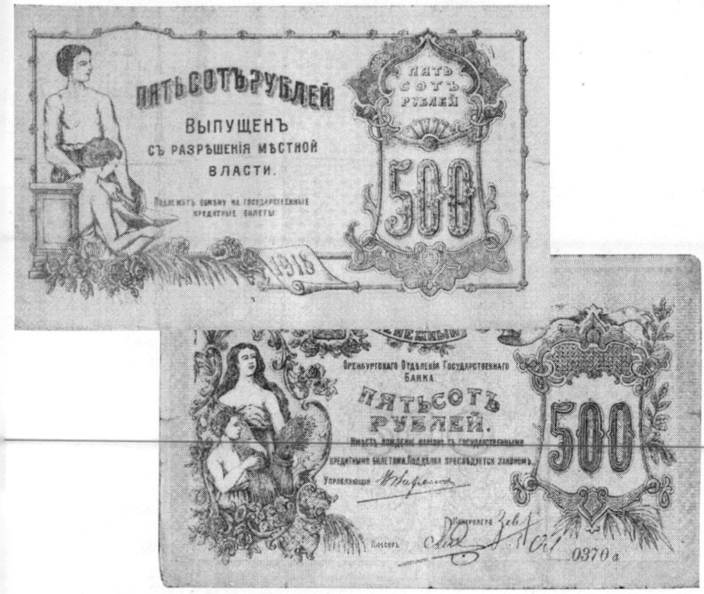

		VG	VF	UNC
S983	**500 Rubles**			
	1918. Black on red underprint. Woman and boy at left. Back: Two youths at left.	40.00	120.	360.

ПЕРМСКАГО ГОРОДСКОГО ОБЩЕСТВА

Perm City Association

1917 Issue

		VG	VF	UNC
S986	**100 Rubles**			
	1917. Dark brown. Ornate flower design with bear in arms at center. Back: Text. Paper: Tan.			
	a. Issued note with signature.	50.00	150.	450.
	r. Remainder.	—	—	250.
S987	**300 Rubles**			
	1917. Blue on light green underprint. Ornate flower design with bear in arms at center. Back: Text.			
	a. Issued note with signature.	60.00	180.	550.
	r. Remainder.	—	—	250.

		VG	VF	UNC
S988	**500 Rubles**			
	1917. Blue on lilac underprint. Ornate flower design with bear in arms at center. Back: Text. Paper: Gray.			
	a. Issued note with signature.	70.00	210.	625.
	r. Remainder.	—	—	250.
S989	**1000 Rubles**			
	1917. Red on light red underprint. Ornate flower design with bear in arms at center. Back: Text. Paper: Pink.			
	a. Issued note with signature.	75.00	225.	675.
	r. Remainder.	—	—	350.
S990	**5000 Rubles**			
	1917. Ornate flower design with bear in arms at center.			
	a. Issued note with signature.	100.	300.	900.
	r. Remainder.	—	—	350.

NOTE: Some authorities believe all supposedly issued notes of #S986-S990 are falsely signed and filled in.

RUSSIAN CENTRAL ASIA

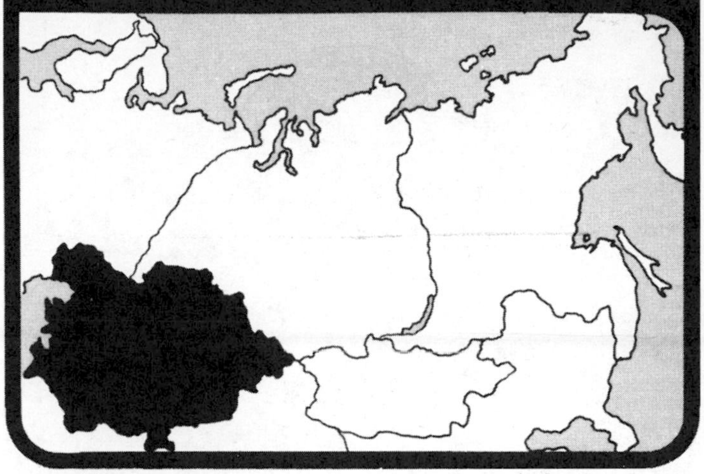

GOVERNMENTS

- Bukhara Soviet Peoples Republic
- Khorezmian Peoples Soviet Republic
- Semireche Region
- Transcaspian Provisional Government

BANKS

- Transcaspian State Bank
- Ashkhabad Branch, State Bank
- Turkestan District (Tashkent)

MILITARY

- Great Britain Government Military Mission (British Maj. Gen. Malleson) Bukhara, Emirate

Bukhara Soviet Peoples Republic

AH1339/1920 Tengas Issue

		Good	Fine	XF
S1026	**50 Tengas**			
	AH 1338 (1920).	50.00	150.	450.
S1027	**100 Tengas**			
	AH 1338 (1920).	50.00	150.	450.
S1028	**200 Tengas**			
	AH 1338 (1920).	60.00	180.	550.

Sign. #S1029-S1034

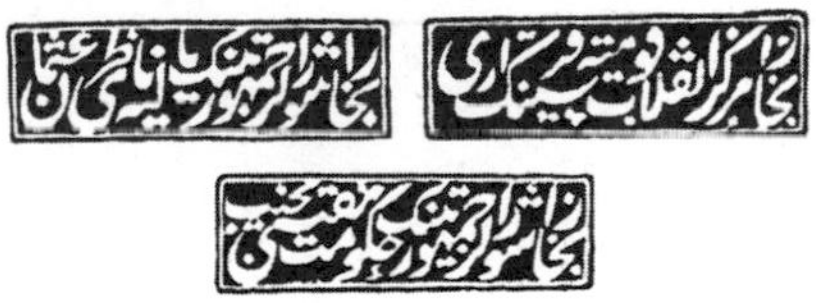

		Good	Fine	XF
S1029	**500 Tengas**			
	AH 1338 (1920).	80.00	240.	725.
S1030	**1000 Tengas**			
	AH 1338 (1920).	80.00	240.	725.
S1031	**2000 Tengas**			
	AH 1339 (1920).	180.	550.	1650.
S1032	**3000 Tengas**			
	AH 1339 (1920).	180.	550.	1650.
S1033	**5000 Tengas**			
	AH 1338-1339 (1920). Blue and green color varieties.			
	a. AH 1337. Without hammer and sickle.	40.00	120.	360.
	b. AH 1339. Hammer and sickle.	50.00	150.	450.

S1034 10,000 Tengas	Good	Fine	XF
AH 1338-1339 (1920).			
a. AH 1338. Without sickle and branch of cotton.	100.	300.	900.
b. AH 1339. Sickle and branch of cotton.	100.	300.	900.

1920-23 Ruble Issues

Sign. #S1035-S1036

S1035 50 Rubles	VG	VF	UNC
AH 1339 (1920). Red-brown to yellow. Paper smooth or ribbed.	30.00	90.00	270.

S1036 100 Rubles	VG	VF	UNC
AH 1339 (1920). Dark brown and blue. Paper smooth or ribbed.	30.00	90.00	270.

Sign. #S1037-S1041A

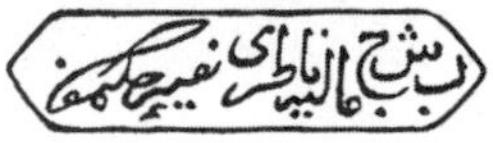

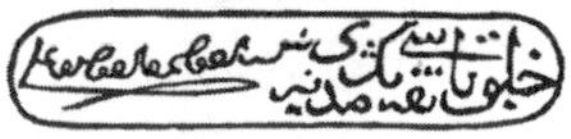

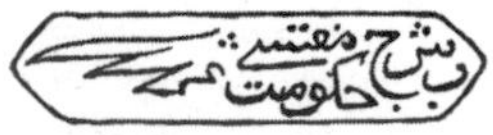

S1037 3000 Rubles	Good	Fine	XF
1920.	40.00	120.	360.

S1038 5000 Rubles	Good	Fine	XF
1920. Red-brown and green.	100.	300.	900.
S1039 10,000 Rubles			
AH 1339 (1920). Paper smooth or ribbed. With or without watermark.	100.	300.	900.

S1040 10,000 Rubles	Good	Fine	XF
AH 1340 (1920). Dark brown. Paper smooth or ribbed. With or without watermark.	100.	300.	900.

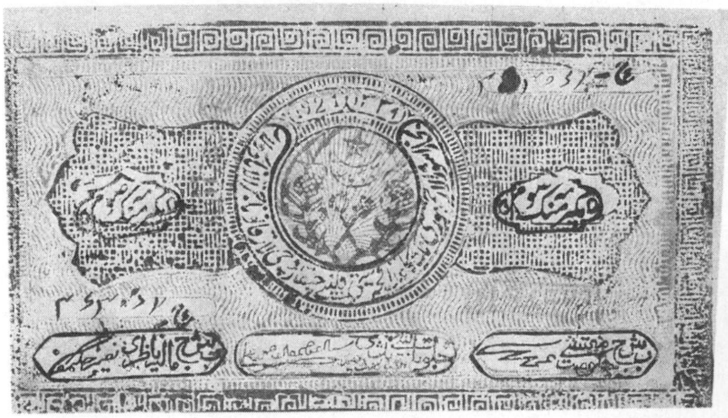

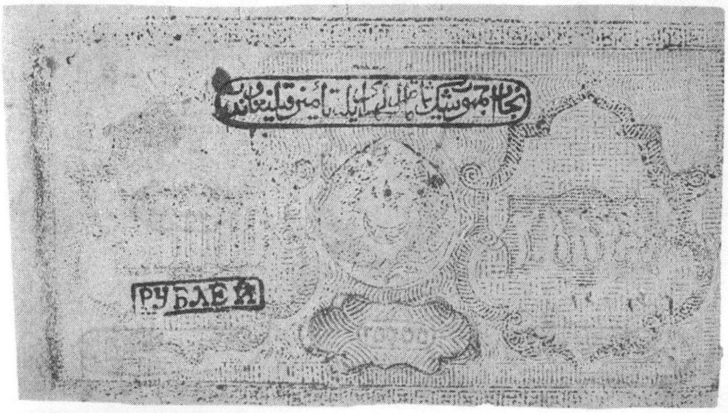

S1041 20,000 Rubles	Good	Fine	XF
1921. Brown and green over orange underprint. Arabic legends, typically primitive printing quality. Signature as on #S1040. Back: Brown and green over orange underprint. Ribbed or plain paper without watermark.	40.00	120.	360.

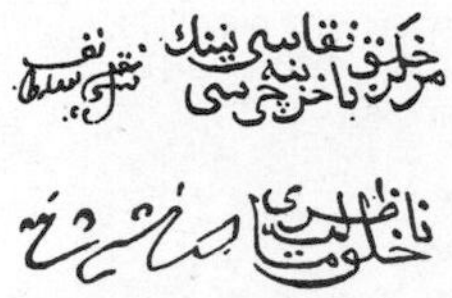

		VG	VF	UNC
S1042	**20,000 Rubles** 1922. Green and pink.	100.	300.	900.

1922 First Ruble Issue

Sign. #S1043-S1050

		VG	VF	UNC
S1043	**10 Rubles** 1922. Green.	50.00	150.	450.

		VG	VF	UNC
S1044	**25 Rubles** 1922. Brown.	25.00	75.00	225.
S1045	**100 Rubles** 1922. Pink.	25.00	75.00	225.

1922 Second Ruble Issue

		VG	VF	UNC
S1046	**1 Ruble** 1922. Yellow-brown.	30.00	90.00	270.

		VG	VF	UNC
S1047	**5 Rubles** 1922. Blue.	30.00	90.00	270.

		VG	VF	UNC
S1048	**10 Rubles** 1922. Green-blue.	30.00	90.00	270.
S1049	**25 Rubles** 1922. Dark brown.	50.00	150.	450.

		VG	VF	UNC
S1050	**100 Rubles** 1922. Red-brown. With or without watermark.	50.00	150.	450.

Sign. #S1051-S1054

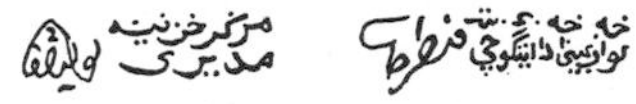

		VG	VF	UNC
S1051	**1000 Rubles** 1922. Violet.	100.	300.	900.
S1052	**2500 Rubles** 1922. Blue. With or without watermark.	40.00	120.	360.

		VG	VF	UNC
S1053	**5000 Rubles** 1922. Red-brown to pink. With or without watermark.	150.	450.	1350.

		VG	VF	UNC
S1054	**5000 Rubles/5 New Rubles** 1922. Red. Paper: White and yellowish.	40.00	120.	360.

Khiva (Khorezm), Khanate of the Padishah

Khorezmian Peoples Soviet Republic

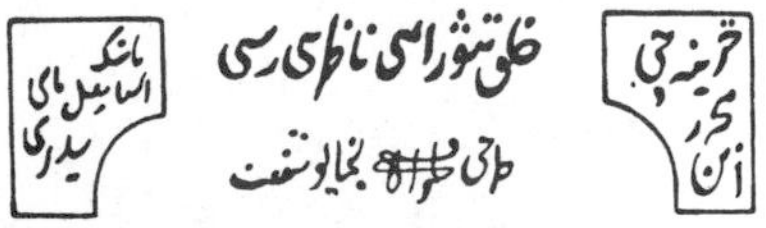

1920 First Issue

		Good	Fine	XF
S1076	**250 Rubles** 1920. Paper ribbed, smooth or lined.	110.	330.	1000.

		VG	VF	UNC
S1077	**500 Rubles** 1920. Red-brown on green. *1920* small or large. Back: Large or small star. Paper: Silk.	250.	750.	2250.

		Good	Fine	XF
S1078	**1000 Rubles** 1920. Violet or blue, red-brown and dark blue on blue. Paper: Silk.	125.	375.	1150.

<AFrame <BRect 0.0 0.0 3.5 0.60><TextLine <TLOrigin 1.5 0.75><TLAlignment Center><String "000.60'>>>

Sign. #S1079-S1081

1920 Second Issue

Sign. #S1079-S1081

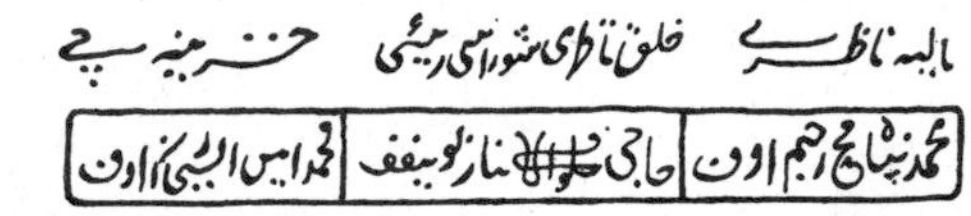

		Good	Fine	XF
S1079	**250 Rubles** 1920. Paper smooth or ribbed.	100.	300.	900.
S1080	**500 Rubles** 1920. Silk note.	100.	300.	900.
S1081	**1000 Rubles** 1920. Red-brown and black on light blue. Silk note.	125.	375.	1150.

Sign. #S1082 similar to #S1076-S1078.

		Good	Fine	XF
S1082	**750 Rubles** 1920. Paper lined or without lines.	100.	300.	900.

Sign. #S1083-S1085 similar to #S1079-S1081.

		Good	Fine	XF
S1083	**750 Rubles** 1920. Paper lined or without lines.	100.	300.	900.

1921 First Issue

		Good	Fine	XF
S1084	**2000 Rubles** 1921. Frame in different colors.	150.	450.	1350.

		Good	Fine	XF
S1085	**5000 Rubles** 1921. Black, red and green. Silk note.	150.	450.	1350.

Sign. #S1086-S1090

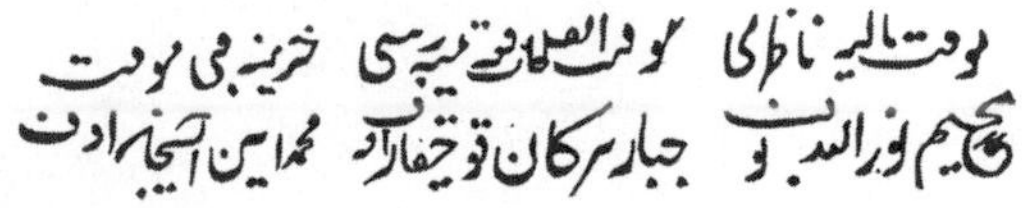

1921 Second Issue

		Good	Fine	XF
S1086	**750 Rubles** 1921. Paper lined, without lines or checkered.	150.	450.	1350.
S1087	**1000 Rubles** 1921. Silk note.	500.	1500.	4500.

		Good	Fine	XF
S1088	**2000 Rubles** 1921. Silk note.	400.	1600.	4800.
S1089	**5000 Rubles** AH 1339 (1921). Red, green and black. Silk note.	200.	600.	1800.
S1090	**10,000 Rubles** 1921. Paper lined or without lines.	200.	600.	1800.

Sign. #S1091-S1092

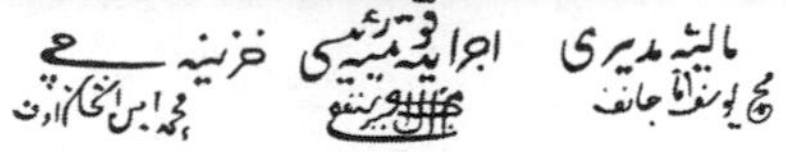

Sign. #S1093-S1094

Individual notes also w/extension stamp.

AH1339/1921 Issue

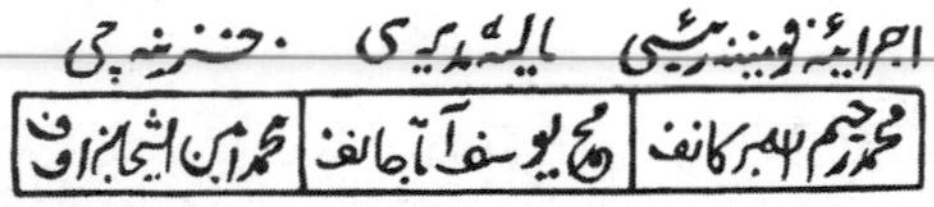

		Good	Fine	XF
S1091	**5000 Rubles** AH 1339 (1921). Silk note.	150.	450.	1350.
S1092	**10,000 Rubles** AH 1339 (1921). Paper lined or without lines.	50.00	150.	450.
S1093	**25,000 Rubles** AH 1339 (1921). Paper note.	70.00	210.	625.

AH1340/1921 Issue

		Good	Fine	XF
S1094	**10,000 Rubles** AH 1340 (1921). Paper lined or without lines.	60.00	180.	550.

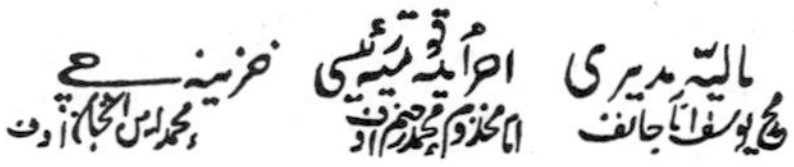

Sign. #S1095

1921 Third Issue

		Good	Fine	XF
S1095	**5000 Rubles** 1921. Paper note.	200.	600.	1800.

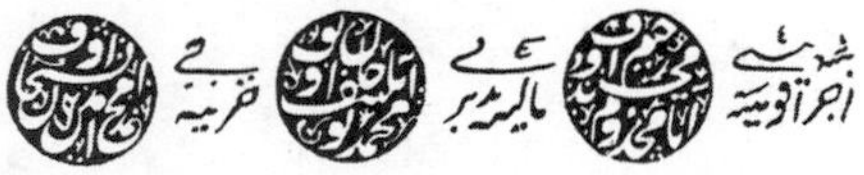

Sign. #S1096-S1097

AH1340/1922 Issue

		Good	Fine	XF
S1096	**10,000 Rubles** AH 1340 (1921).	50.00	150.	450.

		Good	Fine	XF
S1097	**25,000 Rubles** AH 1340 (1921). Paper: White or gray. With or without watermark.			
	a. Issued note. Printed top to top.	50.00	150.	450.
	x. Error with inverted back.	80.00	240.	725.

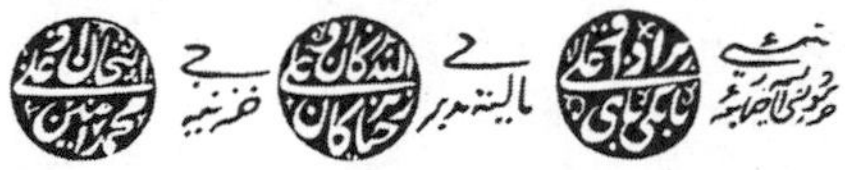

Sign. #S1098

1921 Fourth Issue

		Good	Fine	XF
S1098	**10,000 Rubles** 1921. Paper lined or without lines.	17.50	55.00	165.

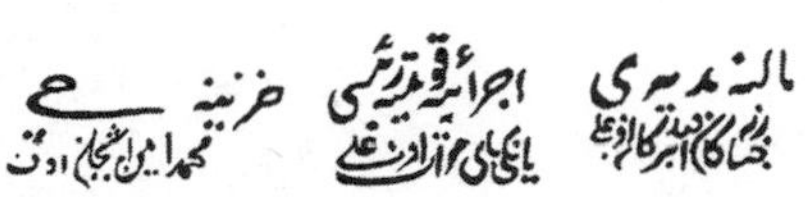

Sign. #S1099

		Good	Fine	XF
S1099	**25,000 Rubles** 1921. Paper: White or gray. With or without watermark.	15.00	45.00	135.

Sign. #S1100

1922 First Issue

		Good	Fine	XF
S1100	**3 = 30,000 Rubles** 1922. Paper lined or without lines, with or without watermark.	40.00	120.	360.

Sign. #S1101

		Good	Fine	XF
S1101	**5 = 50,000 Rubles** 1922. Paper: White or gray. Lined or without lines.	40.00	120.	360.

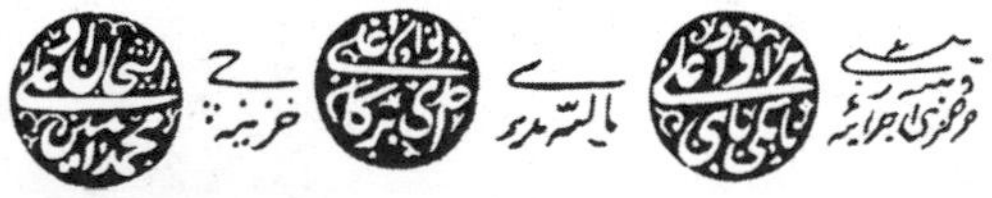

Sign. #S1102

		Good	Fine	XF
S1102	**10 = 100,000 Rubles** 1922. Paper lined or without lines, with or without watermark.	50.00	150.	450.

1922 Second Issue

		Good	Fine	XF
S1103	**3 Rubles** 1922. Paper lined or without lines.	80.00	240.	720.
S1104	**5 Rubles** 1922. Paper lined or without lines.	100.	300.	900.

Sign. #S1105

S1105 1 = 10,000 Rubles

	Good	Fine	XF
1922. Paper smooth, ribbed lines or without lines, with or without watermark.	100.	300.	900.

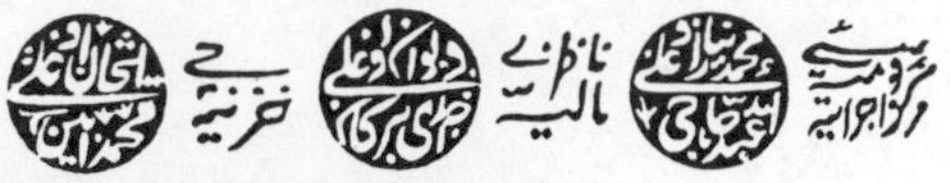

Sign. #S1106

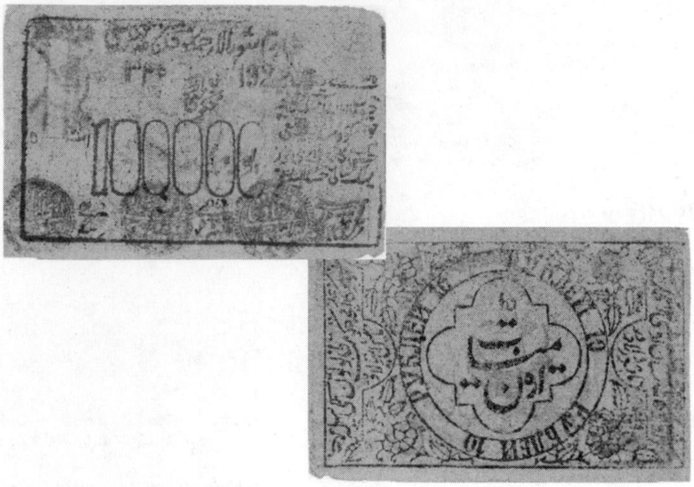

S1106 10 = 100,000 Rubles

	Good	Fine	XF
1922. Paper lined or without lines.	60.00	180.	540.

Sign. #S1107

1922 Third Issue

S1107 25 Rubles

	Good	Fine	XF
1922.	50.00	150.	450.

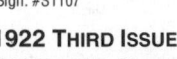

Sign. #S1108

S1108 20 Rubles

	Good	Fine	XF
1922. Blue and green print. Paper lined or without lines.	40.00	120.	360.

Sign. #S1109 similar to #S1107.

S1109 25 Rubles

	Good	Fine	XF
1922. Blue or black print.	40.00	120.	360.

Sign. #S1110

S1110 100 Rubles

	Good	Fine	XF
1922. With or without watermark.	40.00	120.	360.

Sign. #S1111

1923 Issue

S1111 50 Rubles

	Good	Fine	XF
1923. Paper: White or yellowish.	90.00	270.	800.

Sign. #S1112-S1114 similar to #S1110.

S1112 100 Rubles

	Good	Fine	XF
1923. Paper lined or without lines, with or without watermark.	100.	300.	900.

	Good	Fine	XF
S1113 500 Rubles			
1923. With or without watermark.	40.00	120.	360.

	Good	Fine	XF
S1114 1000 Rubles			
1923.	60.00	180.	540.

СЕМИРЕЧЕНСКАЯ ОБЛАСТЬ

Semireche Region

1918 ND ДЕНЕЖНЫЙ ЗНАКЪ-ВРЕМЕНН. РАЗМѢНН. ЗНАКЪ

Currency Tokens - Provisional Exchange Tokens Issue

	Good	Fine	XF
S1116 5 Rubles			
ND (1918). Blue or black print.			
a. Underprint: small crosses.	30.00	90.00	270.
b. Underprint: points.	30.00	90.00	270.

1918 БИЛЕТЪ Note Issue

	Good	Fine	XF
S1117 50 Kopeks			
1918. Yellow or orange.	8.50	25.00	75.00

1918 ND; 1918 КРЕДИТНЫЙ БИЛЕТЪ Credit Notes Issue

Sign. name: ВОЕННЫЙ КОМИССАРЪ

	Good	Fine	XF
S1118 1 Ruble			
ND (1918). Brown.	12.50	35.00	110.

	Good	Fine	XF
S1119 3 Rubles			
1918. Black on green underprint. Worker with hammer at left, opium poppies at center. Back: Differences in text and in numerals.	40.00	120.	360.

	Good	Fine	XF
S1120 5 Rubles			
1918. Black on blue-gray underprint. Woman and child at left, woman and globe at right. With or without serial #.	40.00	120.	360.

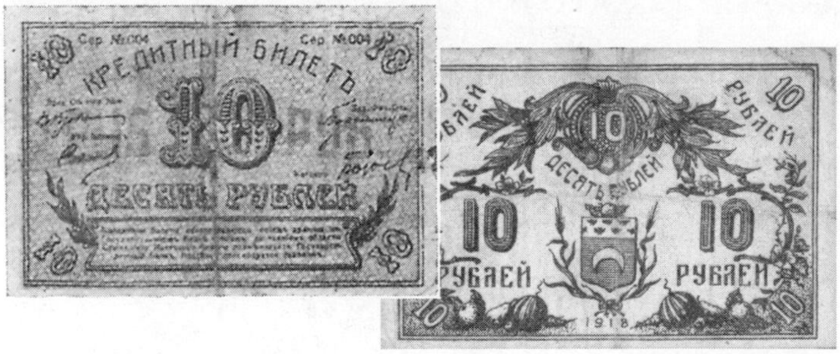

	Good	Fine	XF
S1121 10 Rubles			
ND (1918). Black on light orange underprint.	50.00	150.	450.
S1122 25 Rubles			
ND (1918). Black on brown underprint. Back: Arms.	60.00	180.	540.
S1123 50 Rubles			
ND (1918). Light green.	80.00	240.	725.
S1124 100 Rubles			
ND (1918). Brown on light brown underprint. Back: Brown and dull orange. Seated figure with two winged cherubs at lower center on archway, city scene at left, farm scene at	90.00	270.	800.
S1125 250 Rubles			
ND (1918).	100.	300.	900.

1918 КРЕДИТНЫЙ БИЛЕТЪ Credit Notes Issue

Sign. name: ПРЕД. ОБЛ. or ПРЭД. ОБ. ИСП. КОМ.

	Good	Fine	XF
S1126 10 Rubles			
1918.	30.00	90.00	270.
S1127 25 Rubles			
1918.	40.00	120.	360.
S1128 100 Rubles			
1918.	100.	300.	900.
S1129 250 Rubles			
1918. Brown and green.	80.00	240.	725.

1919 КРЕДИТНЫЙ БИЛЕТЪ Credit Notes Issue

	Good	Fine	XF
S1130 50 Rubles			
1919.	100.	300.	900.
S1131 100 Rubles			
1919.	40.00	120.	360.
S1132 250 Rubles			
1919.			
a. Brown.	40.00	120.	360.
b. dark blue.	40.00	120.	360.
S1133 500 Rubles			
1919.			
a. Brown.	12.00	35.00	110.
b. Black.	7.50	22.50	65.00

Transcaspian Region

ЗАКАСПІЙСКАГО ВРЕМЕННАГО ПРАВЙТЕЛЬСТВА

Transcaspian Provisional Administration.

ГОСУДАРСТВЕННАГО БАНКА

Government Bank

АСХАБАДСКАГО ОТДѢЛЕН ІЯ

Ashkhabad

1919 РАЗМѢННЫЙ ДЕНЕЖНЫЙ ЗНАКЪ

Exchange Currency Tokens Issue

	VG	VF	UNC
S1136 10 Rubles			
1919. Red and brown. Arms at center (tiger), eagle at left and right. (Not issued).	30.00	90.00	270.

ЗАКАСПІЙСКАГО НАРОДНАГО БАНКА

Transcaspian National Bank

1919 ДЕНЕЖНЫЙ ЗНАКЪ Currency Notes Issue

		VG	VF	UNC
S1139	**500 Rubles** 1919. Green on light brown underprint. Back: Arms (tiger) at left, above double headed eagle.	40.00	120.	360.

НАРОДНАГО БАНКА

National Bank

АСХАБАДСКАГО ОТДѢЛЕНІЯ

Ashkhabad

1919 РАЗМѢННЫЙ ДЕНЕЖНЫЙ ЗНАКЪ

Exchange Currency Tokens Issue

		VG	VF	UNC
S1141	**5 Rubles** 1919. Black on green underprint. Arms at center.	20.00	60.00	180.
S1142	**10 Rubles** 1919. Black on red underprint.	20.00	60.00	180.

		VG	VF	UNC
S1143	**25 Rubles** 1919. Black on blue underprint.	20.00	60.00	180.
S1144	**50 Rubles** 1919. Black.			
	a. Green underprint.	25.00	75.00	225.
	b. Blue underprint.	25.00	75.00	225.
S1145	**100 Rubles** 1919. Black on yellow underprint.	25.00	75.00	225.

		VG	VF	UNC
S1146	**250 Rubles** 1919. Black on violet underprint. With or without bank stamp.	20.00	60.00	180.

ОБЯЗАТЕЛЬСТВО ВЕЛИКОБРИТАНСКОЙ ВОЕННОЙ МИССІИ

Great Britain Government Military Mission

1918-19 British Military Intervention Issue

Issued by Major General Malleson. Several major varieties.

		Good	Fine	XF
S1148	**500 Rubles** Dec. 1918. Different hand stamped numerals of the day.			
	a. Dec. 5, 1918. Three months.	300.	900.	2700.
	b. Dec. 14, 1918. Three months. Green background.	300.	900.	2700.
	c. Jan. 14, 1918. Six months. Greenish background.	300.	900.	2700.
	x. Error with *BOUBLES*.	300.	900.	2700.
S1149	**500 Rubles** 14.1.1919. Black. Value in dull red underprint at center. Paper: Green.	300.	900.	2700.

ТУРКЕСТАНСКІЙ КРАЙ

Turkestan District

ГОСУДАРСТВЕННАГО БАНКА

Government Bank

ТАЩКЕНТСКАГО ОТДѢЛЕН ІЯ

Tashkent

1918 РАЗМѢННЫЙ ДЕНЕЖНЫЙ ЗНАКЪ

Exchange Currency Tokens Issue

		VG	VF	UNC
S1151	**1 Ruble** 1918. Blue on brown underprint.	15.00	45.00	135.
S1152	**3 Rubles** 1918. Dark green on green underprint.	20.00	60.00	180.

#S1153-S1155 have bust of woman at upper ctr.

		VG	VF	UNC
S1153	**5 Rubles** 1918. Blue on blue underprint. Bust of woman at upper center.	30.00	90.00	270.
S1154	**10 Rubles** 1918. Black on red and green underprint. Bust of woman at upper center.	20.00	60.00	180.

	VG	VF	UNC
S1155 25 Rubles			
1918. Black on lilac and green underprint. Bust of woman at upper center.	30.00	90.00	270.
S1156 50 Rubles			
1918. Black on blue underprint. Double headed eagle with five arms at center. Back: Town view.	20.00	60.00	180.

	VG	VF	UNC
S1157 100 Rubles			
1918. Black on yellow-brown underprint. Double headed eagle with five arms at center. Like #S1156. Back: Double eagle at left.	30.00	90.00	270.

ТУРКЕСТАНСКАГО КРАЯ TURKESTAN DISTRICT

1918 ДЕНЕЖНЫЙ ЗНАКЪ CURRENCY TOKENS ISSUE

	VG	VF	UNC
S1161 50 Kopeks			
ND (1918). Blue. Arms with hammer and sickle. (Not issued). Also in sheets of 20 pieces.			
a. Issued note. (Not issued).	20.00	60.00	180.
b. Uncut sheet of 20.	—	—	—

1918 ВРЕМЕННЫЙ КРЕДИТНЫЙ БИЛЕТЪ

PROVISIONAL CREDIT NOTES ISSUE

#S1162-S1170 like Tashkent #S1151-S1157.

	VG	VF	UNC
S1162 1 Ruble			
1918. Blue on brown underprint. Signature varieties. Paper and color varieties.	10.00	30.00	90.00

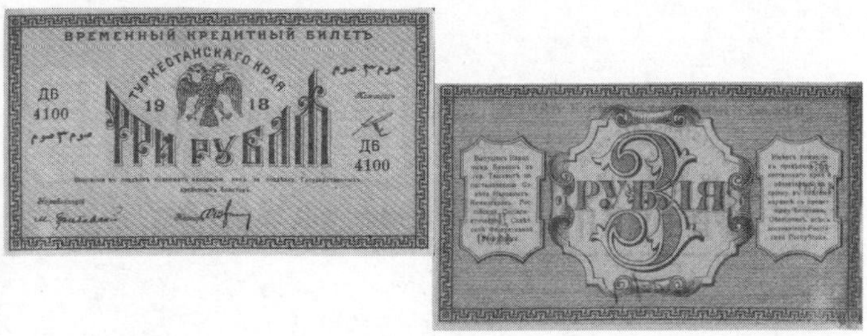

	VG	VF	UNC
S1163 3 Rubles			
1918. Dark green on green underprint. Signature varieties. Paper and color varieties.	10.00	30.00	90.00

	VG	VF	UNC
S1164 5 Rubles			
1918. Blue on blue underprint. Signature varieties. Paper and color varieties.			
a. Black print.	20.00	60.00	180.
b. Dark blue print.	20.00	60.00	180.
S1165 10 Rubles			
1918. Red and green underprint. Signature varieties. Paper and color varieties.			
a. Black print.	30.00	90.00	270.
b. Dark blue print.	30.00	90.00	270.
S1166 25 Rubles			
1918. Black or blue on lilac and green underprint. Signature varieties. Paper and color varieties.	30.00	90.00	270.

	VG	VF	UNC
S1167 50 Rubles			
1918. Black on blue underprint. Signature varieties. Paper and color varieties.	30.00	90.00	270.

	VG	VF	UNC
S1168 100 Rubles			
1918. Black on yellow-brown underprint. Signature varieties. Paper and color varieties.	30.00	90.00	270.
S1169 50 Rubles			
1919. Black on blue underprint. Signature varieties. Like #S1167. Paper and color varieties.	30.00	90.00	270.

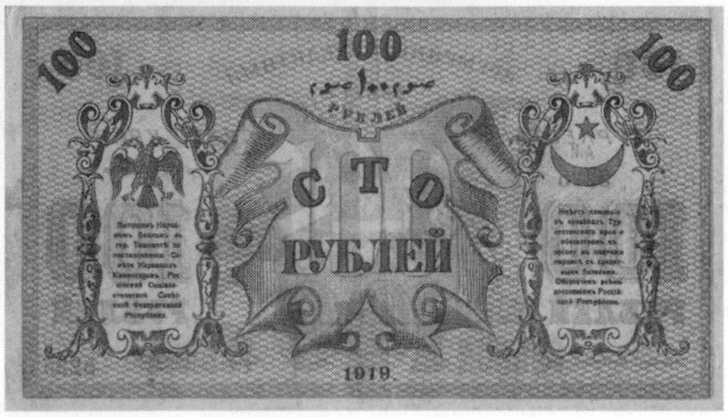

S1170 100 Rubles	**VG**	**VF**	**UNC**
1919. Black or blue on brown to red-brown underprint. Signature varieties. Like #S1168. Paper and color varieties. With or without watermark.	40.00	120.	360.

S1171 250 Rubles	**VG**	**VF**	**UNC**
1919. Brown. Ornament with two torches, gun and hammer at left. Back: Arms at center. With or without watermark. Paper and color varieties.			
a. Green underprint.	50.00	150.	450.
b. Blue underprint.	50.00	150.	450.

S1172 500 Rubles	**VG**	**VF**	**UNC**
1919. Blue on red-brown underprint. Arms with hammer and sickle at upper center. Vertical format. With or without watermark. Paper and color varieties.	80.00	240.	720.
S1173 1000 Rubles			
1920. Black on brown underprint. Back: Arms with hammer and sickle at left. With or without watermark. Paper and color varieties.	50.00	150.	450.
S1174 5000 Rubles			
1920. Blue and red. Back: Arms with hammer and sickle at center.	60.00	180.	550.

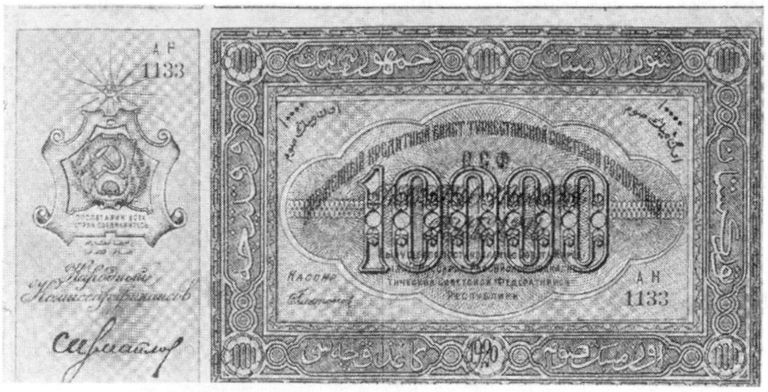

S1175 10,000 Rubles	**VG**	**VF**	**UNC**
1920. Red and green. Arms with hammer and sickle at left. Back: Blacksmith seated with hammer and anvil at left.	180.	550.	1650.

EAST SIBERIA

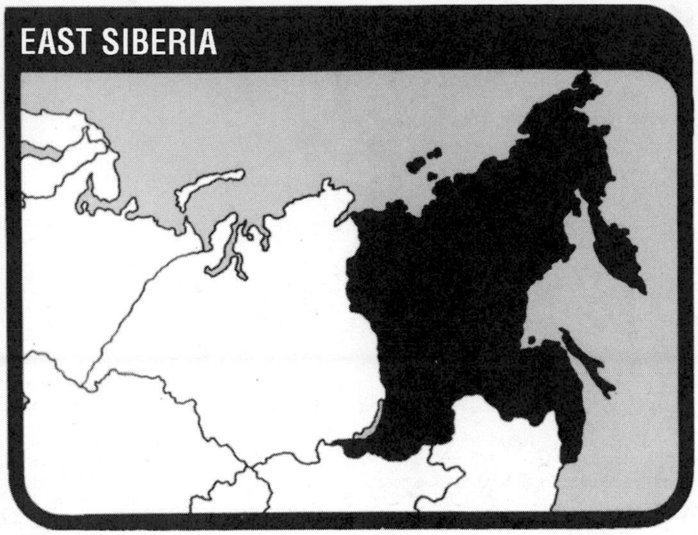

BAIKALIA

- Far Eastern Soviet of People's Commissars
- Government of the Russian Eastern Border Regions
- Provisional Power of the Pribaikal Region
- Far Eastern Republic

MARITIME AREA

- Amur Region Executive Committee
- Amur Region Zemstvo
- Amur Region Credit Union
- Habarovsk Branch Government Bank
- Rural Priamur Province
- Nikolsk-Ussuriisk
- Far East Provisional Government
- Amur Railroad
- Vladivostok
- Vladivostok Office Government Bank
- Vladivos

ДАЛЬНЕВОСТОЧНЫЙ СОВЕТ НАРОДНЫХ КОМИССАРОВ

FAR EASTERN SOVIET OF THE PEOPLES COMMISSARS

1918 ISSUE

	Good	Fine	XF
S1181 10 Rubles			
1918. Black on pink underprint. Globe at center. Back: Green. Workers and farmers.			
a. Without hand stamp.	50.00	150.	450.
b. Hand stamp of Kolchak Government.	50.00	150.	450.
S1182 25 Rubles			
1918. Black on pink underprint. Globe at center. Like #S1181. Back: Workers and farmers.			
a. Without hand stamp.	60.00	180.	540.
b. Hand stamp of Kolchak Government.	60.00	180.	540.
S1183 50 Rubles			
1918. Black on pink underprint. Globe at center. Like #S1181. Back: Workers and farmers.			
a. Without hand stamp.	100.	300.	900.
b. Hand stamp of Kolchak Government.	100.	300.	900.

NOTE: #S1181-S1183 bear sign. of Chairman Krasnoshchekov, commissar of finance T. Kalmanevich, and Fugalevich, director of the Khabarovsk branch of the State Bank. In all, 307,560 R10 notes were issued, 122,639 R25 notes, and 105,101 R50 notes.

ПРАВЙТЕЛЬСТВО РОССИЙСКОЙ ВОСТОЧНОЙ ОКРАЙНЫ

GOVERNMENT OF THE RUSSIAN EASTERN BORDER REGIONS

Ataman Grigori Semenov

ГОСУДАРСТВЕННАГО БАНКА

GOVERNMENT BANK

ЧИТИНСКОЕ ОТДѢЛЕНІЕ

CHITA

1920 ISSUE

	VG	VF	UNC
S1186 50 Rubles			
1920. Blue. Back: Winter landscape. Proof.	—	—	—

	VG	VF	UNC
S1187 100 Rubles			
1920. Black. Flowers below double-headed eagle.			
a. Frame consisting of lines on back. Proof.	—	—	—
b. Frame consisting of small cubes.	20.00	60.00	180.

	VG	VF	UNC
S1188 500 Rubles			
1920. Arms (double-headed eagle) with flowers at center.			
a. Blue.	20.00	60.00	180.
b. Green. (Many shade varieties).	20.00	60.00	180.

СИБИРСКАГО ВРЕМЕННАГО ПРАВИТЕЛЬСТВА

SIBERIAN PROVISIONAL ADMINISTRATION

1920 КАЗНАЧЕЙСКIЙ ЗНАКЪ TREASURY TOKENS ISSUE

	VG	VF	UNC
S1189 25 Rubles			
1920. With or without pink underprint. Watermark: With or without.	150.	450.	1350.
S1190 50 Rubles			
1920. Green. (Many varieties).	150.	450.	1350.
S1191 100 Rubles			
1920.			
a. Brown. With or without watermark.	100.	300.	900.
b. Dark green.	100.	300.	900.

		VG	VF	UNC
S1192	**500 Rubles**			
	1920. Green underprint. Back: Woman with sword at left, with double-headed eagle at center.	50.00	150.	450.
S1193	**1000 Rubles**			
	1920. Woman wearing helmet seated with sword and shield at left.			
	a. Pink and green.	100.	300.	900.
	b. Yellow and brown.	100.	300.	900.
S1194	**5000 Rubles**			
	1920. Green on yellow underprint. Double-headed eagle with maltese cross at center.			
	a. Printed on both sides.	500.	1500.	4500.
	b. Uniface print.	—	—	2500.

ВРЕМЕННАЯ ЗЕМСКАЯ ВЛАСТЬ ПРИБАЙКАЛЬЯ

PROVISIONAL POWER OF THE PRIBAIKAL REGION

1918 (1920) ISSUE

		VG	VF	UNC
S1196	**25 Rubles**			
	1918 (1920). Black on dark blue underprint. Woman seated at center. Without signature. Overprint: Red on back of #S1248.	40.00	120.	360.

		VG	VF	UNC
S1197	**100 Rubles**			
	1918 (1920). Black on brown underprint. Woman seated with fruit at center. Without signature. Overprint: Blue on back of #S1249.	40.00	120.	360.

NOTE: For #S1196 and S1197 issued without Pribaikal overprint see Russia #40 and 42 in Vol. 2.

ДАЛЬНЕ-ВОСТОЧНОЙ РЕСПУБЛИКИ

FAR EASTERN REPUBLIC

1920 FIRST КРЕДИТНЫЙ БИЛЕТ CREDIT NOTES ISSUE

1920 Credit Notes

		VG	VF	UNC
S1201	**1 Ruble**			
	1920. Dark blue on tan underprint. Wheat, pickaxe and anchor at upper center. Back: Brown.	10.00	30.00	90.00

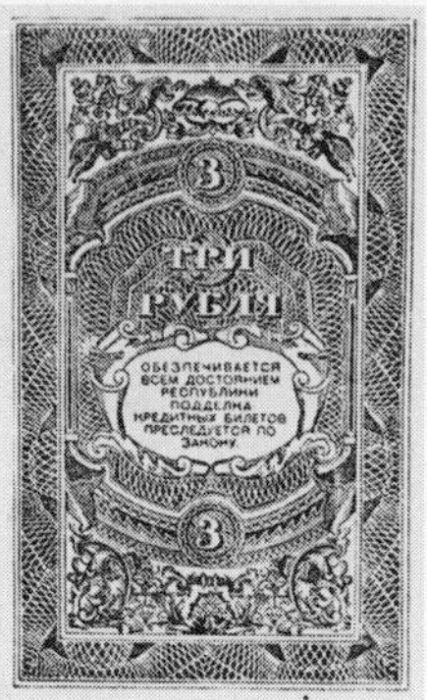

		VG	VF	UNC
S1202	**3 Rubles**			
	1920. Dark green. Wheat, pickaxe and anchor at upper center. Like #S1201.	15.00	45.00	135.
S1203	**5 Rubles**			
	1920. Blue. Wheat, pickaxe and anchor at center.	10.00	30.00	120.
S1204	**10 Rubles**			
	1920. Red. Back: Wheat, pickaxe and anchor at center. Paper: Pink.	10.00	30.00	120.

1920 РАСЧЕТНЫЙ ЗНАК - TOKEN CURRENCY ISSUE

		VG	VF	UNC
S1205	**25 Rubles**			
	1920. Black on green underprint. Back: Violet. Wheat, pickaxe and anchor at center.	10.00	30.00	120.
S1206	**50 Rubles**			
	1920. Black on red-brown underprint. Back: Green.	10.00	30.00	90.00

1920 SECOND КРЕДИТНЫЙ БИЛЕТ CREDIT NOTES ISSUE

		VG	VF	UNC
S1207	**500 Rubles**			
	1920. Brown on tan underprint. Bear and fox at center in outdoor scene with mountains. Back: Blue. Ships and boat.	20.00	60.00	180.

1920 ГОСУДАРСТВЕННЫЙ КРЕДИТИЫЙ БИЛЕТ

GOVERNMENT CREDIT NOTES ISSUE

		VG	VF	UNC
S1208	**1000 Rubles**			
	1920. Black-green on green underprint. Plow at center, sea and mountains in background. Back: Brown. Man with scythe, wheat sheaves and arms at center.	30.00	90.00	270.

1920 THIRD КРЕДИТНЫЙ БИЛЕТ CREDIT NOTES ISSUE

#S1209-S1211 similar to #S1201-S1203 but larger size. Single or double-sided proof prints.

		VG	VF	UNC
S1209	**1 Ruble**			
	1920. Dark blue on tan underprint. Wheat, pickaxe and anchor at upper center. Back: Brown.	—	—	350.
S1210	**3 Rubles**			
	1920. Dark green. Wheat, pickaxe and anchor at upper center.	—	—	350.
S1211	**5 Rubles**			
	1920. Blue. Wheat, pickaxe and anchor at upper center.	—	—	350.
S1212	**10 Rubles**			
	1920.	—	—	350.

1918 ГОСУДАРСТВЕННЫЙ КРЕДИТНЫЙ БИЛЕТЪ

Government Credit Notes Provisional Issue

#S1213 and S1214 overprint: ДАЛЬНЕ-ВОСТОЧНАЯ РЕСПУБЛИКА.

	VG	VF	UNC
S1213 25 Rubles			
1918 (1921). Black on dark blue underprint. Commerce seated at center. Overprint: Red, bronze-colored or red and bronze colored circular on back of #S1248.	50.00	150.	450.
S1214 100 Rubles			
1918 (1921). Black on brown underprint. Agriculture seated with fruit at center. Overprint: Red, bronze-colored or red and bronze-colored on back of #S1249.	60.00	180.	550.

NOTE: It is not known wheather #S1213 or S1214 are official or private issues.

1920 БАНКОВЫЙ БИЛЕТ Gold Kopek Bank Notes Issue

#S1215A-S1215C not issued.

	VG	VF	UNC
S1215A 5 Kopeks			
1922.	—	—	650.

	VG	VF	UNC
S1215B 10 Kopeks			
1922.	—	—	650.

	VG	VF	UNC
S1215C 20 Kopeks			
1922.	—	—	650.

Maritime Area

АМУРСКІЙ ОБЛАСТНОЙ КОММИТЕТ

Amur Region Executive Committee

1918 РАЗМѢННЫЙ БИЛЕТЪ Exchange Notes Issue

	Good	Fine	XF
S1216 5 Rubles			
1918. Blue. Arms with three stars at top.			
a. Without hand stamp.	40.00	120.	360.
b. Various hand stamps of the Kolchak Government.	40.00	120.	360.
S1217 10 Rubles			
1918. Arms with three stars at top.			
a. Without hand stamp.	25.00	75.00	225.
b. Various hand stamps of the Kolchak Government.	15.00	45.00	135.

	Good	Fine	XF
S1218 15 Rubles			
1918. Brown on green. Arms with three stars at top.			
a. Without hand stamp.	50.00	150.	450.
b. Various hand stamps of the Kolchak Government.	40.00	120.	360.
S1219 25 Rubles			
1918. Arms with three stars at top.			
a. Without hand stamp.	80.00	240.	720.
b. Various hand stamps of the Kolchak Government.	50.00	150.	450.
S1220 100 Rubles			
1918. Arms with three stars at top.			
a. Without hand stamp.	40.00	120.	360.
b. Various hand stamps of the Kolchak government.	30.00	90.00	270.

АМУРСКОЕ ОБЛАСТНОЕ ЗЕМСТВО

Amur Region Zemstvo

1917 Stamp "Type" Notes Issue

	VG	VF	UNC
S1221 50 Kopeks			
1917 (1919). Brown and yellow. Arms with three stars at top.	20.00	60.00	180.
S1222 1 Ruble			
1917 (1919). Brown. Arms with three stars at top.	20.00	60.00	180.
S1223 3 Rubles			
1917 (1919). Green. Arms with three stars at top.	20.00	60.00	180.

	VG	VF	UNC
S1224 5 Rubles			
1917 (1919). Blue. Arms with three stars at top.	20.00	60.00	180.

АМУРСКІЙ ОБЛАСТНОЙ КРЕДИТНЫЙ СОЮЗЪ

Amur Region Credit Union

ХАБАРОВСКІЙ КООПЕРАТИВ БАНКЪ

Habarovsk Cooperative Bank

1919 Issue

#S1224-S1224D with or without round bank stamping at left on face or at center on back.

	VG	VF	UNC
S1224A 1 Ruble			
1919. Black on orange underprint. Back: Sunrise over farm scene with trees at upper center, text in ornate oval at center.			
a. Soyuz Bank hand stamp.	20.00	60.00	180.
b. Cooperative Bank hand stamp.	40.00	120.	360.
r. Without stamp. Remainder.	20.00	60.00	180.
S1224B 3 Rublya			
1919. Black on green underprint. Back: Sunrise over farm scene with trees at upper center, text in ornate oval at center.			
a. Soyuz Bank hand stamp.	20.00	60.00	180.
b. Cooperative Bank hand stamp.	20.00	60.00	180.
r. Without stamp. Remainder.	20.00	60.00	180.

S1224C 5 Rublei	VG	VF	UNC
1919. Black on blue underprint. Back: Sunrise over farm scene with trees at upper center, text in ornate oval at center.			
a. Soyuz Bank hand stamp.	20.00	60.00	180.
b. Cooperative Bank hand stamp.	20.00	60.00	180.
r. Without hand stamp. Remainder.	20.00	60.00	180.
S1224D 10 Rublei			
1919. Black on light red underprint. Back: Sunrise over farm scene with trees at upper center, text in ornate oval at center.			
a. Soyuz Bank hand stamp.	20.00	60.00	180.
b. Cooperative Bank hand stamp.	20.00	60.00	180.
r. Without hand stamp. Remainder.	20.00	60.00	180.

ГОСУДАРСТВЕННАГО БАНКА

GOVERNMENT BANK

ХАБАРОВСКОЕ ОТДѢЛЕНІ Е

HABAROVSK

1918 ЯНВАРЬ-МАРТ ISSUE

#S1225A-S1225V combine several issues dated from Jan.-Mar. 1918. Black text on blue frame, or on blue or green unpt. Back stamped w/maroon text and red round seal. All w/hand dating over 190x to 191x.

S1225A 5 Rublei	Good	Fine	XF
1918. Black text on blue frame, or on blue or green underprint. Hand dated. Back: Stamped with maroon text and red round seal.	30.00	90.00	270.
S1225B 10 Rublei			
1918. Black text on blue frame, or on blue or green underprint. Hand dated. Back: Stamped with maroon text and red round seal.	30.00	90.00	270.
S1225C 15 Rublei			
1918. Black text on blue frame, or on blue or green underprint. Hand dated. Back: Stamped with maroon text and red round seal.	30.00	90.00	270.
S1225D 20 Rubeli			
1918. Black text on blue frame, or on blue or green underprint. Hand dated. Back: Stamped with maroon text and red round seal.	30.00	90.00	270.

S1225E 25 Rublei	Good	Fine	XF
1918. Black text on blue frame, or on blue or green underprint. Hand dated. Back: Stamped with maroon text and red round seal.	30.00	90.00	270.
S1225F 30 Rublei			
1918. Black text on blue frame, or on blue or green underprint. Hand dated. Back: Stamped with maroon text and red round seal.	30.00	90.00	270.

S1225G 40 Rublei	Good	Fine	XF
1918. Black text on blue frame, or on blue or green underprint. Hand dated. Back: Stamped with maroon text and red round seal.	30.00	90.00	270.
S1225H 45 Rublei			
1918. Black text on blue frame, or on blue or green underprint. Hand dated. Back: Stamped with maroon text and red round seal.	50.00	150.	450.
S1225I 50 Rublei			
1918. Black text on blue frame, or on blue or green underprint. Hand dated. Back: Stamped with maroon text and red round seal.	30.00	90.00	270.
S1225J 55 Rublei			
1918. Black text on blue frame, or on blue or green underprint. Hand dated. Back: Stamped with maroon text and red round seal.	30.00	90.00	270.
S1225K 60 Rublei			
1918. Black text on blue frame, or on blue or green underprint. Hand dated. Back: Stamped with maroon text and red round seal.	40.00	120.	360.
S1225L 75 Rublei			
1918. Black text on blue frame, or on blue or green underprint. Hand dated. Back: Stamped with maroon text and red round seal.	30.00	90.00	270.

S1225M 80 Rublei	Good	Fine	XF
1918. Black text on blue frame, or on blue or green underprint. Hand dated. Back: Stamped with maroon text and red round seal.	50.00	150.	450.
S1225N 100 Rublei			
1918. Black text on blue frame, or on blue or green underprint. Hand dated. Back: Stamped with maroon text and red round seal.	20.00	60.00	180.
S1225P 125 Rublei			
1918. Black text on blue frame, or on blue or green underprint. Hand dated. Back: Stamped with maroon text and red round seal.	30.00	90.00	270.
S1225Q 140 Rublei			
1918. Black text on blue frame, or on blue or green underprint. Hand dated. Back: Stamped with maroon text and red round seal.	30.00	90.00	270.
S1225R 150 Rublei			
1918. Black text on blue frame, or on blue or green underprint. Hand dated. Back: Stamped with maroon text and red round seal.	30.00	90.00	270.
S1225S 170 Rublei			
1918. Black text on blue frame, or on blue or green underprint. Hand dated. Back: Stamped with maroon text and red round seal. Rare.	—	—	—
S1225T 200 Rublei			
1918. Black text on blue frame, or on blue or green underprint. Hand dated. Back: Stamped with maroon text and red round seal.	50.00	150.	450.
S1225U 250 Rublei			
1918. Black text on blue frame, or on blue or green underprint. Hand dated. Back: Stamped with maroon text and red round seal.	50.00	150.	450.
S1225V 3000 Rubeli			
1918. Black text on blue frame, or on blue or green underprint. Hand dated. Back: Stamped with maroon text and red round seal. Rare.	—	—	—

1918 АВГУСТ-ДЕКАБРЬ ISSUE

S1225W 100 Rublei	Good	Fine	XF
1918. Black text on light green underprint. Denomination stamped diagonally in purple. Back: Like previous issue.	30.00	90.00	270.

PRIAMUR PROVINCE

Gen. Milo K. Dietrichs

This was a monarchist Japanese-supported government established by the Czech General Dietrichs at Nikolaevsk-on-Amur on May 26, 1921. It lasted until mid-1922.

ЗЕМСКИЙ ПРИАМУРСКИЙ КРАЙ

RURAL PRIAMUR PROVINCE

1921 ND РАЗМѢННЫЙ ЗНАКЪ EXCHANGE TOKENS ISSUE

S1226 1 Kopek	Good	Fine	XF
ND (1921). Black on light tan underprint. Back: Blue.	30.00	90.00	270.

	Good	Fine	XF
S1227 5 Kopeks ND (1921). Black on blue underprint. Back: Blue.	30.00	90.00	270.

Nikolsk-Ussuriisk

ОРГАНИЗАЦІЯ КАЗЕННЫХЪ С.-Х. СКЛАДОВЪ

Organization of Farmers Depots

1919 ND Issue

	Good	Fine	XF
S1231 1 Ruble ND (1919). Brown.	50.00	150.	450.
S1232 3 Rubles ND (1919). Green.	50.00	150.	450.

	Good	Fine	XF
S1233 5 Rubles ND (1919). Blue.	50.00	150.	450.
S1234 10 Rubles ND (1919). Red.	50.00	150.	450.
S1235 20 Rubles ND (1919). Orange.	60.00	180.	540.

	Good	Fine	XF
S1236 40 Rubles ND (1919). Violet.	80.00	240.	720.

	Good	Fine	XF
S1237 100 Rubles ND (1919). Brown.	50.00	150.	450.

Far East Provisional Government - Priamur Region

1918-19 РАЗМѢННЫЙ ЗНАКЪ Exchange Tokens Issue

	Good	Fine	XF
S1241 5 Kopeks 1918 (1920). Black on gold underprint. Double-headed eagle at top center.	10.00	30.00	90.00

	Good	Fine	XF
S1242 10 Kopeks 1918 (1920). Brown on orange underprint. Double-headed eagle at center. Back: Orange.	15.00	45.00	135.

	Good	Fine	XF
S1243 30 Kopeks 1918 (1920). Black on green underprint. Double-headed eagle at center. Back: Green.	15.00	45.00	135.

	Good	Fine	XF
S1244 50 Kopeks 1919 (1920). Orange. American printing with 2 black signatures.	5.00	15.00	45.00

NOTE: For #S1244 without signature see #S828.

1920 ГОСДАРСТВЕННЫЙ КРЕДИТНЫЙ БИЛЕТЪ

Government Credit Notes Issue

	Good	Fine	XF
S1245 1 Ruble 1920. Blue on brown underprint. Ship, steam locomotive, houses at center. Back: Brown.	20.00	60.00	180.

	Good	Fine	XF
S1246 5 Rubles 1920. Black on green and pink underprint. Double-headed eagle at left, arms at right. Back: Steam locomotive in front of tunnel entrance at left.	30.00	90.00	270.

S1247 10 Rubles | VG | VF | UNC
1920. Black on green and pink underprint. Sheafs of grain with fruits and shield at center. Back: Red. Double-headed eagle at center. | 20.00 | 60.00 |

S1248 25 Rubles | VG | VF | UNC
1918 (1920). Black on dark blue underprint. Commerce seated at center. With 2 signatures. Back: With 2 signatures. On Russia #39A (in Vol. 2). | 30.00 | 90.00 |

S1249 100 Rubles | VG | VF | UNC
1918 (1920). Black on brown underprint. Agriculture seated with fruit at center. With 2 signatures. Back: With 2 signatures. On Russia #40 (in Vol. 2). | 40.00 | 120. |

NOTE: For #S1248 and S1249 with red or blue circular overprint on back; see #S1196 and S1197. Also see #S1213 and #S1214 for notes with red or bronze overprint on back.

АМУРСКОИ ЖЕЛѢЗНОИ ДОРОГИ

Amur Railroad

1919 General Committee - Cartes d'Avances Issue

	Good	Fine	XF
S1251 1 Ruble 1919. Red-brown.	50.00	150.	450.
S1252 3 Rubles 1919. Blue.	60.00	180.	540.
S1253 5 Rubles 1919. Green.	70.00	200.	600.

ГОСУДАРСТВЕННАГО БАНКА

Government Bank

ВЛАДИВОСТОКСКАГО ОТД ѢЛЕНІЙ

Vladivostok

1920 ЧЕК Checks Issue

	VG	VF	UNC
S1254 1000 Rubles 1.4.1920. Dark blue. Uniface.	50.00	150.	450.

NOTE: See also #S867-S870.

ВЛАДИВОСТОКСКАЯ КОНТОРА

ГОСУДАРСТВЕННАГОБАНКА

Vladivostok Office Government Bank

192x Issue

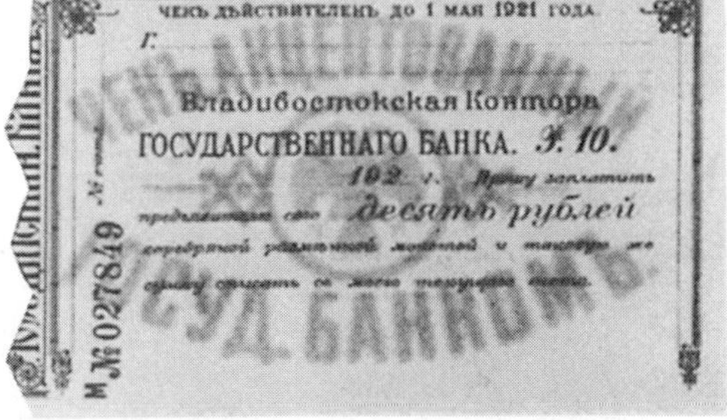

	Good	Fine	XF
S1255A 10 Rublei 192x. Black on green underprint. Not signed, dated or issued. Back: Black text.	40.00	120.	360.
S1255B 25 Rublei 192x. Black text. Not signed, dated or issued. Back: Black text. Paper: Light tan.	40.00	120.	360.
S1255C 100 Rublei 192x. Black text. Not signed, dated or issued. Paper: Light brown.	40.00	120.	360.

ИНДО-КИТАЙСКІЙ БАНКЪ

Banque de L' Indo-Chine

Vladivostok

1919 Issue

#S1256-S1259 proposed Allied issue. The exchange rate on the notes is 1 Ruble = 60 French Centimes. Specimen or proof only. (Not issued).

	VG	VF	UNC
S1256 5 Rubles 12.2.1919. Blue on multicolor underprint. Female head with Liberty cap at center. Text in Russian and French. Series A. Back: Blue. Printer: ABNC.	—	—	—

	VG	VF	UNC
S1257 25 Rubles 12.2.1919. Green on multicolor underprint. Female head with Liberty cap at center. Text in Russian and French. Series A; B. Back: Green. Printer: ABNC.	—	—	—
S1258 100 Rubles 12.2.1919. Brown on multicolor underprint. Female head with Liberty cap at center. Text in Russian and French. Series A. Back: Brown. Printer: ABNC.	—	—	—

	VG	VF	UNC
S1259 500 Rubles 12.2.1919. Dark brown on multicolor underprint. Female head with Liberty cap at center. Text in Russian and French. Series A. Back: Dark brown. Printer: ABNC.	—	—	—

Blagoveshchensk

ГОСУДАРСТВЕННАГО БАНКА

Government Bank

БЛАГОВЪЩЕНСКАГО ОТДЪ ЛЕНІЯ

Blagoveshchensk

1920 ДЕНЕЖНЫЙ ЗНАКЪ Currency Notes Issue

	VG	VF	UNC
S1259A 100 Rubles 1920. Black on orange underprint. Cross over double-headed eagle at center.	30.00	90.00	270.

	VG	VF	UNC
S1259B 500 Rubles 1920. Black on lilac underprint. Cross over double-headed eagle at center.	30.00	90.00	270.

S1259C 1000 Rubles	Good	Fine	XF
1920. Black-brown on green underprint. Cross over double-headed eagle at center. Back: Blue on brown underprint.			
a. Black serial #.	20.00	60.00	180.
b. Seriya 2, red serial #.	20.00	60.00	180.

S1259D 3000 Rubles	Good	Fine	XF
1920. Black on dull orange underprint. Double-headed eagle without cross.			
a. Control # on back.	30.00	90.00	270.
b. Control # and series on face.	20.00	60.00	180.
S1259E 5000 Rubles			
1920. Black on blue underprint. Cross over double-headed eagle at center.	20.00	60.00	180.

1919-20 Issue

S1259F 500 Rublei	Good	Fine	XF
1919. Black text. Back: Purple stamped text with date filled in, also round stamped seal. Paper: Pink.	40.00	120.	360.
S1259G 1000 Rublei			
1919. Black text. Back: Purple stamped text with date filled in, also round stamped seal. Paper: Pink.	40.00	120.	360.

S1259H 5000 Rublei	Good	Fine	XF
1919-20. Black text. Back: Purple stamped text with date filled in, also round stamped seal. Paper: Pink.	50.00	150.	450.

АЛТАЙ Altai

Committee of Nationalities of Altai

1919 Issue

S1260 30 Rubles	VG	VF	UNC
1919. Proof.	—	—	500.

АЛТАЙСКИЙ ГУБЕРНСКИЙ СОЮЗ

Altai Government Union

1920's ND ТАЛОН Talons Issue

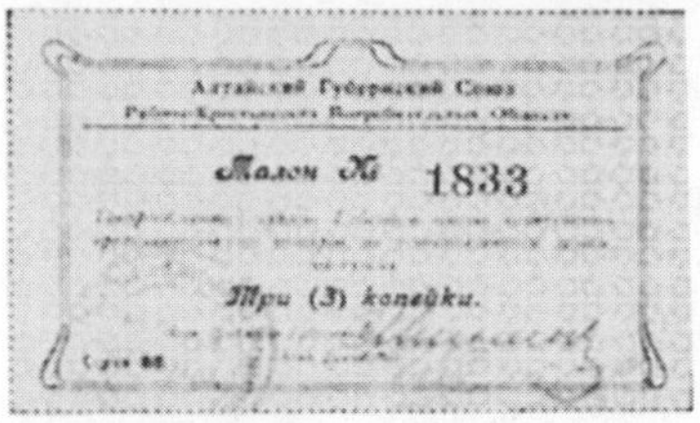

S1261 1 Kopek	VG	VF	UNC
ND (1923?). Black on brown underprint. Circular handstamp at left, 3 or 4 edges perforated. Uniface.	30.00	90.00	270.

S1262 3 Kopeks	VG	VF	UNC
ND. Black on light green underprint. Circular handstamp at left, 3 or 4 edges perforated. Uniface.	30.00	90.00	270.
S1263 5 Kopeks			
ND. Black on green underprint. Circular handstamp at left, 3 or 4 edges perforated. Uniface.	30.00	90.00	270.
S1264 10 Kopeks			
ND. Black on gray underprint. Circular handstamp at left, 3 or 4 edges perforated. Uniface.	30.00	90.00	270.

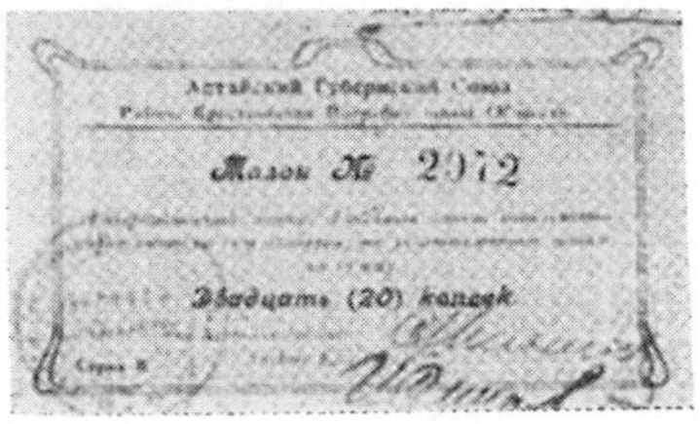

S1265 20 Kopeks	VG	VF	UNC
ND. Black on red underprint. Circular handstamp at left, 3 or 4 edges perforated. Uniface.	30.00	90.00	270.
S1265A 50 Kopeks			
ND. Black on pink underprint. Circular handstamp at left, 3 or 4 edges perforated. Uniface.	30.00	90.00	270.
S1266 1 Ruble			
ND. Circular handstamp at left, 3 or 4 edges perforated. Uniface.	30.00	90.00	270.
S1267 5 Rubles			
ND. Circular handstamp at left, 3 or 4 edges perforated. Uniface.	30.00	90.00	270.
S1268 10 Rubles			
ND. Circular handstamp at left, 3 or 4 edges perforated. Uniface.	30.00	90.00	270.

ГОСУДАРСТВЕННАГО БАНКА

Government Bank

БАРНАУЛЬСКАГО ОТДѢЛЕ НІЯ

Barnaul

1920 ВРЕМЕННОЕ ОБЯЗАТЕЛЬСТВО

Provisional Obligations Issue

S1268A 1000 Rublei	Good	Fine	XF
1.2.1920/191x. Black on gray underprint. Back: Large oval red stamping for branch.	15.00	45.00	135.

НАРОДНАГО БАНКА

National Bank

БАРНАУЛЬСКАГО ОТДѢЛЕНІЯ

Barnaul

1918 ND Issue

	Good	Fine	XF
S1268B 20 Rublei ND (1918).	25.00	75.00	225.
S1268C 40 Rublei ND (1918).	25.00	75.00	225.
S1268D 50 Rublei ND (1918).	25.00	75.00	225.
S1268E 100 Rublei ND (1918).	25.00	75.00	225.
S1268F 500 Rublei ND (1918).	25.00	75.00	225.

ГОСУДАРСТВЕННАГО БАНКА

Government Bank

БІЙСКАГО ОТДѢЛЕНІЯ

Biisk

1920 ND ЧЕКЪ Checks Issue

#S1269A-S1269B w/o red ovpt: РСФСР.

	Good	Fine	XF
S1269A 250 Rublei ND (1920). Dark brown. Back: Dark brown text in 6 lines. Paper: Light tan.	15.00	45.00	135.
S1269B 1000 Rublei ND (1920). Black text on pink underprint. Back: Black text.	15.00	45.00	135.

#S1269C-S1269D as previous issue but w/red ovpt: РСФСРin diagonal rectangle across face.

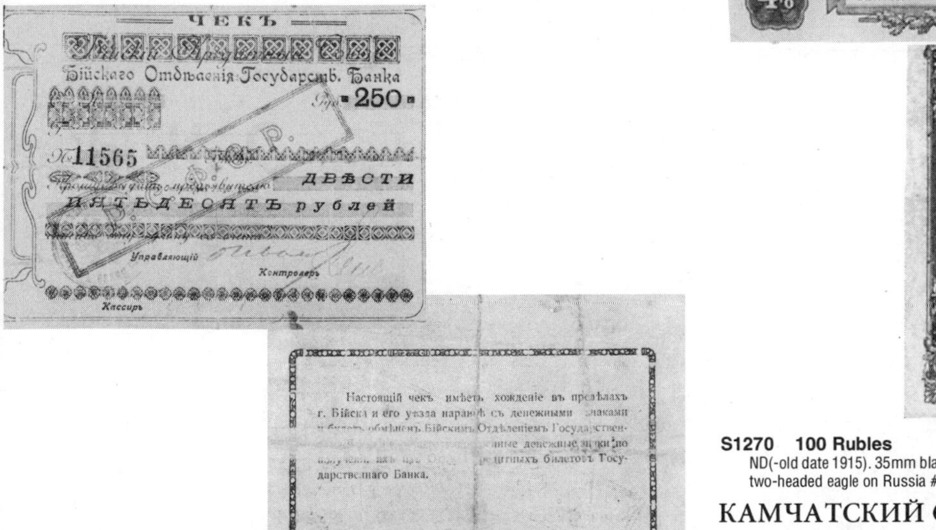

S1269C 250 Rublei	Good	Fine	XF
ND (1920). Overprint: Red RSfSRin diagonal rectangle across face.			
a. Without city and branch bank title across upper center.	20.00	60.00	180.
b. With city and branch bank title across upper center, also other text changes.	20.00	60.00	180.

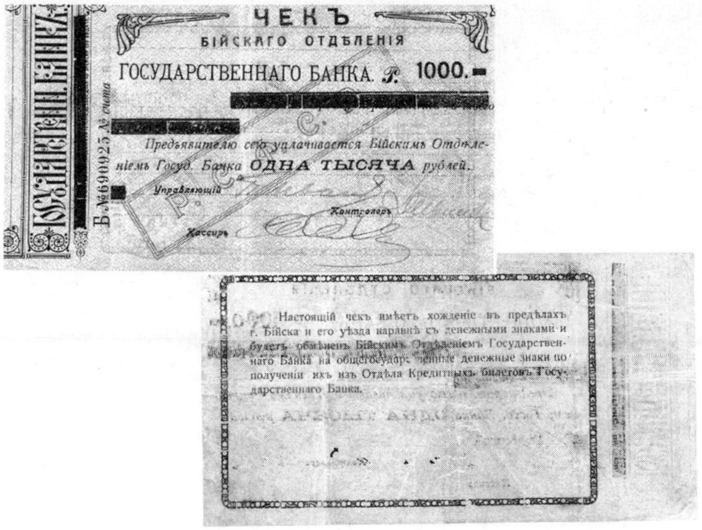

S1269D 1000 Rublei	Good	Fine	XF
ND (1920). Overprint: Red RSfSRin diagonal rectangle across face.	15.00	45.00	135.

Kamchatka

КАМЧАТСКИИ ОБЛАСТНОЙ КОМИТЕТЪ

Kamchatka Region Committee

1915 ND Issue

S1270 100 Rubles	Good	Fine	XF
ND(-old date 1915). 35mm black hand stamp with committee name around two-headed eagle on Russia #58, Vol. 2.	20.00	60.00	180.

КАМЧАТСКИЙ ОБЛАСТНОИ СОВЕТ

НАРОДНАГО ХОЗЯИСТВА

Kamchatka Provincial National Economic (Org.)

1920 КРЕДИТНЫЙ ЗНАК Credit Token Currency Issue

S1271 100 Rubles	Good	Fine	XF
1920. Blue on light brown underprint. Crowned arms at center (three volcanos).	50.00	150.	450.

		Good	Fine	XF
S1272	**250 Rubles**			
	1920. Blue on red underprint. Crowned arms at center.	50.00	150.	450.
S1273	**500 Rubles**			
	1920. Crowned arms at center. Back: Red-brown. Paper: Blue.	50.00	150.	450.
S1274	**1000 Rubles**			
	1920. Black and red on blue underprint.	50.00	150.	450.

САХАЛИНСКОЙ ОБЛАСТИ

Sakhalin Province

1918 КРЕДИТНЫЙ БИЛЕТЪ Credit Notes Issue

		Good	Fine	XF
S1275	**1000 Rubles**			
	1918.			
	a. With *1000* in corners on back.	20.00	60.00	180.
	b. Without *1000* in corners on back.	30.00	90.00	270.

САХАЛИНСКИЙ ОБЛАСТНОЙ НАРОДНО

РЕВОЛЮЦИОННЫЙ КОМИТЕТ

Sakhalin Provincial National Revolutionary

Committee

1920 БОНА Bons Issue

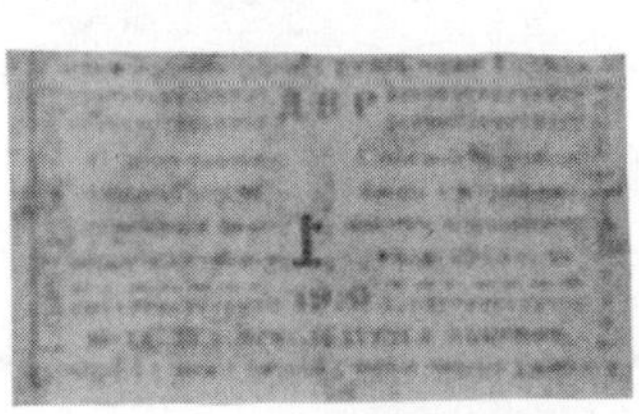

		Good	Fine	XF
S1276	**1 Ruble**			
	1920. Blue.	40.00	120.	360.
S1277	**3 Rubles**			
	1920. Blue.	40.00	120.	360.
S1278	**5 Rubles**			
	1920. Blue.	40.00	120.	360.
S1279	**10 Rubles**			
	1920. Blue.	40.00	120.	360.
S1280	**25 Rubles**			
	1920. Blue.	50.00	150.	450.
S1281	**50 Rubles**			
	1920. Blue.	75.00	225.	675.
S1282	**100 Rubles**			
	1920. Blue.	125.	375.	1150.

ГОСУДАРСТВЕННАГО БАНКА

Government Bank

ТОМСКОЕ ОТДѢЛЕНIЕ

Tomsk

1918 Issue

		Good	Fine	XF
S1283	**100 Rublei**			
	1918. Black on orange-brown underprint. Uniface.	20.00	60.00	180.
S1284	**500 Rublei**			
	1918.	20.00	60.00	180.

Nikolaevsk On Amur

This port city was under Allied occupation beginning in mid-1918, continuing under Japanese bayonets until Oct. 25,1922, long after the Americans and British had pulled out. The city had a large Japanese civilian population in this period.

NIKOLAHVSKOGO NA AMYRH

Nikolaevsk-on-Amur

1918 ЧЕКЪ Checks Issue

		Good	Fine	XF
S1286	**5 Rubles**			
	1918.	80.00	240.	760.
S1287	**25 Rubles**			
	1918.	80.00	240.	760.
S1288	**100 Rubles**			
	1918. Black on brown underprint.	80.00	240.	760.

НИКОЛАЕВСКОГО НА АМУРЕ

ГОСУДАРСТВЭННОГО БАНКА Р.С.Ф.Р. or Р.О.С.Р.

Nikolaevsk-on-Amur Branch Government Bank, R.S.F.R. or R.F.S.R.

1920 РАЗМЕННЫЙ БИЛЕТ Exchange Notes Issue

		VG	VF	UNC
S1291	**250 Rubles**			
	1920. Black on red-brown underprint.	20.00	60.00	180.

		VG	VF	UNC
S1292	**500 Rubles**			
	1920. Black on blue underprint.	30.00	90.00	270.

		VG	VF	UNC
S1293	**1000 Rubles** 1920. Black on green underprint.			
	a. White paper.	30.00	90.00	270.
	b. Light green paper.	10.00	30.00	90.00
	c. Light blue paper.	10.00	30.00	90.00
	d. Yellowish paper.	12.00	35.00	110.

ПЕРЕВОДНОЕ ПИСЬМО ПРИЙСКОВ. УПРАВЛЕН. АМГУНСКАЯ ЗОЛОТО ПРОМЫЩЛЕННАЯ КОМПАНІЯ

Amgun Gold Company

1920 Issue

		VG	VF	UNC
S1296	**50 Rubles** 20.4.1920.	50.00	150.	450.
S1297	**100 Rubles** 20.4.1920.	50.00	150.	450.
S1298	**250 Rubles** 20.4.1920.	50.00	150.	450.
S1299	**500 Rubles** 20.4.1920.	50.00	150.	450.
S1300	**1000 Rubles** 20.4.1920.	50.00	150.	450.

Yakutia

ЯКУТСКАЯ АВТОНОМНАЯ СОЦИАЛ. СОВЕТ РЕСПУБЛИКА

Yakut Autonomous Socialist Soviet Republic

1921 РАСЧЕТНЫЙ ЗНАК Exchange Tokens Issue

		VG	VF	UNC
S1301	**500 Rubles** 1921 (1922). Russia #111 (Vol. 2) with stamp.	—	50.00	150.
S1302	**1000 Rubles** 1921 (1922). Russia #112 (Vol. 2) with stamp.	—	50.00	150.

НАРОДНЫИ КОМИЧЧАРИАТ ТОРГ. И ПРОМЦІШЛЕННОЧТИ

National Commissariat of Commercial Manufacturing

1923 Issue

		VG	VF	UNC
S1306	**3 Rubles** 1923. Black and blue on green underprint.	50.00	150.	—
S1307	**5 Rubles** 1923.	—	—	—
S1308	**10 Rubles** 1923.	—	—	—

NOTE: Market values are for cancelled notes.

1924 Issue

		VG	VF	UNC
S1309	**1 Ruble** 1924.	40.00	120.	360.
S1310	**3 Rubles** 1924.	40.00	120.	360.
S1311	**5 Rubles** 1924.	40.00	120.	360.
S1312	**10 Rubles** 1924.	100.	300.	900.
S1313	**25 Rubles** 1924.	—	—	—

NOTE: Market values are for cancelled notes.

A WORD ON DATE RANGES

Often date ranges or specific dates are listed. These have been observed or reported by our contributors. If a note is outside the published range, it only means that it is a newly reported date, and not necessarily worthy of a premium value.

Foreign Exchange Certificates

Hard Currency Notes

1976 Vneshposyltorg Checks for Military Trade Issue

		VG	VF	UNC
M10	**1 Kopek** 1976. Light orange, brown, blue. Red strip at top and bottom. Back: Light brown, purple.	7.50	16.00	35.00

		VG	VF	UNC
M11	**2 Kopek** 1976. Light orange, red-brown and blue. Red strip at top and bottom. Back: Pink, dark green.	8.00	17.50	40.00
M12	**5 Kopek** 1976. Light orange, dark and light blue. Red strip at top and bottom. Back: Light blue and dark red.	8.00	18.00	40.00
M13	**10 Kopek** 1976. Light orange, dark and light blue. Red strip at top and bottom. Back: Blue and dark green.	10.00	20.00	45.00
M14	**25 Kopek** 1976. Light orange, blue and purple. Red strip at top and bottom. Back: Lilac and dark turquoise.	12.00	25.00	50.00
M15	**50 Kopek** 1976. Light orange, blue and green. Red strip at top and bottom. Back: Green and brown.	15.00	30.00	60.00
M16	**1 Ruble** 1976. Red-brown, green and multicolor. Red strip at top and bottom. Back: Brown and gray.	5.00	15.00	40.00

		VG	VF	UNC
M17	**3 Ruble** 1976. Green, orange and multicolor. Red strip at top and bottom. Back: Blue and green.	5.00	10.00	30.00
M18	**5 Ruble** 1976. Green, dark blue and multicolor. Red strip at top and bottom. Back: Turquoise and blue-gray.	10.00	25.00	50.00
M19	**10 Rubles** 1976. Light blue, red-brown and multicolor. Red strip at top and bottom. Back: Light brown, light red.	10.00	20.00	50.00
M20	**20 Rubles** 1976. Blue-green, dark red and multicolor. Red strip at top and bottom. Back: Dark green and gray-red.	10.00	20.00	50.00

		VG	VF	UNC
M21	**50 Rubles** 1976. Blue-green, green and red. Red strip at top and bottom. Back: Brown-red and gray-green.	—	—	—
M22	**100 Rubles** 1976. Turquoise and brown. Back: Dark blue-green and brown.	15.00	50.00	325.
M23	**250 Rubles** 1976. Pink, brown and multicolor. Back: Olive and pink. Reported not confirmed.	—	—	—
M24	**500 Rubles** 1976. Reported not confirmed.	—	—	—

Foreign Exchange Certificates

Hard Currency Notes

1965-68 Blue Band Issue

	VG	VF	UNC
FX10 1 Kopek			
1965; 1966. Black on light orange underprint in dark green frame. Back: Dark green.			
a. 1965.	.50	3.00	5.00
b. 1966.	.50	3.00	5.00
FX11 2 Kopek			
1965; 1966. Black on light orange underprint in dark green frame. Back: Dark green.			
a. 1965.	.50	3.00	5.00
b. 1966.	.50	3.00	5.00

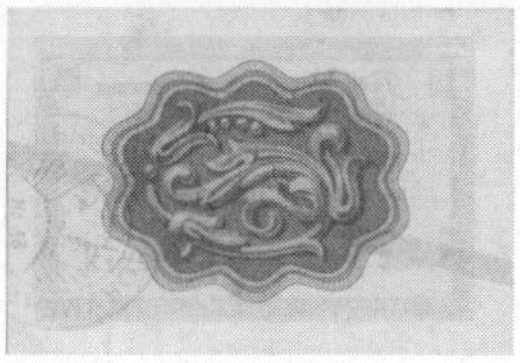

	VG	VF	UNC
FX12 5 Kopek			
1965; 1966. Black on light orange underprint in dark green frame. Back: Dark green.			
a. 1965.	.75	3.00	5.00
b. 1966.	.75	3.00	5.00
FX13 10 Kopek			
1965; 1966. Black on light orange underprint in dark green frame. Back: Dark green.			
a. 1965.	1.00	4.00	8.00
b. 1966.	1.00	4.00	8.00
FX14 25 Kopek			
1965; 1966. Black on light orange underprint in dark green frame. Back: Dark green.			
a. 1965.	2.00	8.00	15.00
b. 1966.	2.00	8.00	15.00
FX15 50 Kopek			
1965; 1966. Black on light orange underprint in dark green frame. Back: Dark green.			
a. 1965.	4.00	15.00	25.00
b. 1966.	4.00	15.00	25.00

	VG	VF	UNC
FX16 1 Ruble			
1965; 1966; 1967; 1968. Black on gray-green underprint in red-brown frame. Back: Red-brown.			
a. 1965.	8.00	15.00	35.00
b. 1966.	8.00	15.00	35.00
c. 1967.	—	—	—
d. 1968.	10.00	18.00	40.00
FX17 3 Ruble			
1966; 1968. Black on gray-green underprint in red-brown frame. Back: Red-brown.			
a. 1965.	10.00	18.00	40.00
b. 1966.	10.00	18.00	40.00
c. 1967.	—	—	—
d. 1968.	15.00	25.00	45.00
FX18 5 Ruble			
1965; 1966; 1967; 1968. Black on gray-green underprint in red-brown frame. Back: Red-brown.			
a. 1965.	10.00	20.00	40.00
b. 1966.	15.00	25.00	45.00
c. 1967.	—	—	—
d. 1968.	20.00	30.00	50.00

	VG	VF	UNC
FX19 10 Rubles			
1965; 1966; 1967; 1968. Black on gray-green underprint in red-brown frame. Back: Red-brown.			
a. 1965.	25.00	40.00	80.00
b. 1966.	25.00	40.00	80.00
c. 1967.	—	—	—
d. 1968.	25.00	40.00	80.00
FX20 20 Rubles			
1965; 1966; 1967; 1968. Black on gray-green underprint in red-brown frame. Back: Red-brown.			
a. 1965.	—	—	—
b. 1966.	—	—	—
c. 1967.	—	—	—
d. 1968.	—	—	—

	VG	VF	UNC
FX21 50 Rubles			
1965; 1966; 1967; 1968.			
a. 1965.	—	—	—
b. 1966.	—	—	—
c. 1967.	—	—	—
d. 1968.	—	—	—
FX22 100 Rubles			
1965; 1966; 1967; 1968.			
a. 1965.	—	—	—
b. 1966.	—	—	—
c. 1967.	—	—	—
d. 1968.	—	—	—
FX23 250 Rubles			
1965; 1966; 1967; 1968.			
a. 1965.	—	—	—
b. 1966.	—	—	—
c. 1967.	—	—	—
d. 1968.	—	—	—

1972 Blue Band Issue

FX25-FX28 like previous issue but for text added to back.

	VG	VF	UNC
FX24 1 Kopek			
1972. Black on light orange underprint in dark green frame. Back: Dark green. Text.	2.00	4.00	8.00
FX25 2 Kopek			
1972. Black on light orange underprint in dark green frame. Back: Dark green. Text.	2.00	4.00	8.00
FX26 5 Kopek			
1972. Black on light orange underprint in dark green frame. Back: Dark green. Text.	2.00	4.00	8.00
FX27 3 Ruble			
1972. Black on gray-green underprint in red-brown frame. Back: Red-brown. Text.	12.50	25.00	45.00
FX28 10 Kopek			
1972. Black on light orange underprint in dark green frame. Back: Dark green. Text.	2.00	4.00	15.00
FX29A 25 Kopek			
1972.	—	—	—
FX29B 50 Kopek			
1972.	—	—	—
FX29C 1 Ruble			
1972.	—	—	—
FX29D 5 Ruble			
1972.	—	—	—
FX29E 10 Rubles			
1972.	—	—	—
FX29F 20 Rubles			
1972.	—	—	—
FX29G 50 Rubles			
1972.	—	—	—
FX29H 100 Rubles			
1972.	—	—	—
FX29I 250 Rubles			
1972.	—	—	—

1965-67 Yellow Band Issue

	VG	VF	UNC
FX30 1 Kopek			
1965; 1966. Black on light orange underprint in dark green frame. Back: Dark green.			
a. 1965.	2.00	4.00	8.00
b. 1966.	2.00	4.00	8.00
FX31 2 Kopek			
1965; 1966. Black on light orange underprint in dark green frame. Back: Dark green.			
a. 1965.	2.00	4.00	8.00
b. 1966.	2.00	4.00	8.00
FX32 5 Kopek			
1965; 1966. Black on light orange underprint in dark green frame. Back: Dark green.			
a. 1965.	2.00	4.00	8.00
b. 1966.	2.00	4.00	8.00
FX33 10 Kopek			
1965; 1966. Black on light orange underprint in dark green frame. Back: Dark green.			
a. 1965.	2.00	5.00	10.00
b. 1966.	2.00	5.00	10.00

	VG	VF	UNC
FX34 25 Kopeks			
1965; 1966. Black on light orange underprint in dark green frame. Back: Dark green.			
a. 1965.	4.00	10.00	15.00
b. 1966.	4.00	10.00	15.00
FX35 50 Kopeks			
1965; 1966.			
a. 1965.	5.00	10.00	20.00
b. 1966.	5.00	10.00	20.00
FX36 1 Ruble			
1965; 1966; 1967. Black on gray-green underprint in red-brown frame. Back: Red-brown.			
a. 1965.	8.00	20.00	30.00
b. 1966.	8.00	20.00	30.00
c. 1967.	8.00	20.00	30.00
FX37 3 Rubles			
1965; 1966; 1967.			
a. 1965.	10.00	30.00	45.00
b. 1966.	10.00	30.00	45.00
c. 1967.	10.00	30.00	45.00
FX38 5 Rubles			
1965; 1966; 1967. Black on gray-green underprint in red-brown frame. Back: Red-brown.			
a. 1965.	10.00	30.00	45.00
b. 1966.	10.00	30.00	45.00
c. 1967.	10.00	30.00	45.00
FX39 10 Rubles			
1965; 1966; 1967.			
a. 1965.	40.00	60.00	100.
b. 1967.	40.00	60.00	100.
c. 1968.	40.00	60.00	100.
FX40 20 Rubles			
1965; 1966; 1967.			
a. 1965.	—	—	—
b. 1966.	—	—	—
c. 1967.	—	—	—
FX41 50 Rubles			
1965; 1966; 1967.			
a. 1965.	—	—	—
b. 1966.	—	—	—
c. 1967.	—	—	—
FX42 100 Rubles			
1965; 1966; 1967.			
a. 1965.	—	—	—
b. 1966.	—	—	—
c. 1967.	—	—	—
FX43 250 Rubles			
1965; 1966; 1967.			
a. 1965.	—	—	—
b. 1966.	—	—	—
c. 1967.	—	—	—

1965-66; 1972 No Band Issue

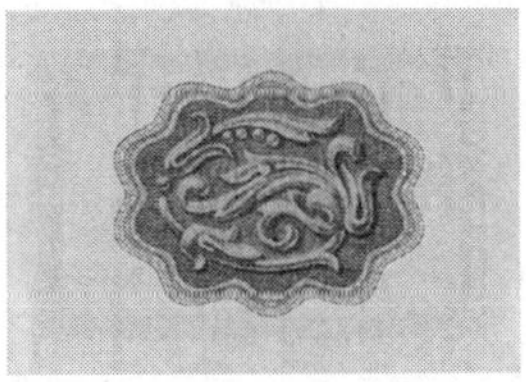

	VG	VF	UNC
FX45 1 Kopek			
1965; 1966; 1972. Black on light orange underprint in dark green frame. Back: Dark green.			
a. 1965.	1.00	3.00	5.00
b. 1966.	1.00	3.00	5.00
c. 1972.	2.00	5.00	8.00
FX46 2 Kopek			
1965; 1966; 1972. Black on light orange underprint in dark green frame. Back: Dark green.			
a. 1965.	1.00	3.00	5.00
b. 1966.	1.00	3.00	5.00
c. 1972.	2.00	5.00	8.00
FX47 5 Kopek			
1965; 1966; 1972. Black on light orange underprint in dark green frame. Back: Dark green.			
a. 1965.	2.00	4.00	8.00
b. 1966.	2.00	4.00	8.00
c. 1972.	3.00	6.00	12.00
FX48 10 Kopek			
1965; 1966; 1972. Black on light orange underprint in dark green frame. Back: Dark green.			
a. 1965.	2.00	4.00	8.00
b. 1966.	2.00	4.00	8.00
c. 1972.	3.00	6.00	12.00
FX49 25 Kopek			
1965; 1966; 1972. Black on light orange underprint in dark green frame. Back: Dark green.			
a. 1965.	2.00	8.00	15.00
b. 1966.	2.00	8.00	15.00
c. 1972.	2.00	8.00	20.00
FX50 50 Kopek			
1965; 1966; 1972. Black on light orange underprint in dark green frame. Back: Dark green.			
a. 1965.	5.00	15.00	25.00
b. 1966.	5.00	15.00	25.00
c. 1972.	10.00	20.00	30.00

	VG	VF	UNC
FX51 1 Ruble			
1965; 1966; 1968; 1972. Black on gray-green underprint in red-brown frame. Back: Red-brown.			
a. 1965.	8.00	15.00	35.00
b. 1966.	8.00	15.00	35.00
c. 1968.	8.00	15.00	35.00
d. 1972.	10.00	20.00	40.00

	VG	VF	UNC
FX52 3 Ruble			
1965; 1966; 1968; 1972. Black on gray-green underprint in red-brown frame. Back: Red-brown.			
a. 1965.	12.00	20.00	35.00
b. 1966.	12.00	20.00	35.00
c. 1968.	15.00	28.00	40.00
d. 1972.	15.00	28.00	40.00
FX53 5 Ruble			
1965; 1966; 1968; 1972. Black on gray-green underprint in red-brown frame. Back: Red-brown.			
a. 1965.	20.00	40.00	60.00
b. 1966.	20.00	40.00	60.00
c. 1968.	20.00	40.00	60.00
d. 1972.	20.00	40.00	60.00
FX54 10 Rubles			
1965; 1966; 1968; 1972.			
a. 1965.	35.00	70.00	100.
b. 1966.	35.00	70.00	100.
c. 1968.	35.00	70.00	100.
d. 1972.	40.00	80.00	120.
FX55 20 Rubles			
1965; 1966; 1968; 1972.			
a. 1965.	—	—	—
b. 1966.	—	—	—
c. 1968.	—	—	—
d. 1972.	—	—	—
FX56 50 Rubles			
1965; 1966; 1968; 1972.			
a. 1965.	—	—	—
b. 1966.	—	—	—
c. 1968.	—	—	—
d. 1972.	—	—	—
FX57 100 Rubles			
1965; 1966; 1968; 1972.			
a. 1965.	—	—	—
b. 1966.	—	—	—
c. 1968.	—	—	—
d. 1972.	—	—	—
fx58 250 Rubles			
1965; 1966; 1968; 1972.			
a. 1965.	—	—	—
b. 1966.	—	—	—
c. 1968.	—	—	—
d. 1972.	—	—	—

1976 Vneshposyltorg Check Issue

	VG	VF	UNC
FX60 1 Kopek			
1976. Light orange, brown, blue. Back: Light brown, purple.	.25	.50	1.50
FX61 2 Kopek			
1976. Light orange, red-brown and blue. Back: Pink, dark green.	.35	.75	1.75
FX62 5 Kopek			
1976. Light orange, dark and light blue. Back: Light blue, dark red.	.50	1.00	2.00
FX63 10 Kopek			
1976. Light orange, dark and light blue. Back: Blue, dark green.	.75	1.50	3.00

	VG	VF	UNC
FX64 25 Kopek			
1976. Light orange, blue and purple. Back: Lilac and dark turquoise.	1.00	2.00	4.50
FX65 50 Kopek			
1976. Light orange, blue and green. Back: Green and brown.	2.00	4.00	8.00

		VG	VF	UNC
FX66	**1 Ruble** 1976. Red-brown, green and multicolor. Back: Brown and gray.	1.00	2.50	5.00
FX67	**3 Ruble** 1976. Green, orange and multicolor. Back: Blue and green.	2.50	5.00	10.00

		VG	VF	UNC
FX68	**5 Ruble** 1976. Green, dark blue and multicolor. Back: Turquoise and blue-gray.	3.50	7.00	15.00
FX69	**10 Rubles** 1976. Light blue, red-brown and multicolor. Back: Light brown, light red.	5.00	12.00	25.00
FX70	**20 Rubles** 1976. Blue-green, dark red and multicolor. Back: Dark green and gray-red.	10.00	18.00	35.00

		VG	VF	UNC
FX71	**50 Rubles** 1976. Blue-green, green and red. Back: Brown-red and gray-green.	10.00	30.00	80.00
FX72	**100 Rubles** 1976. Turquoise and brown. Back: Dark blue-green and brown.	25.00	50.00	160.
FX73	**250 Rubles** 1976. Pink, brown and multicolor. Back: Olive and pink.	40.00	100.	200.

		VG	VF	UNC
FX74	**500 Rubles** 1977.	75.00	200.	500.

Gosbank (ГОСУДАРСТВЕННЫЙ ВАНК СССР)

1961 Issue

#FX80-FX85 issued in booklets. Used on ships to buy food.

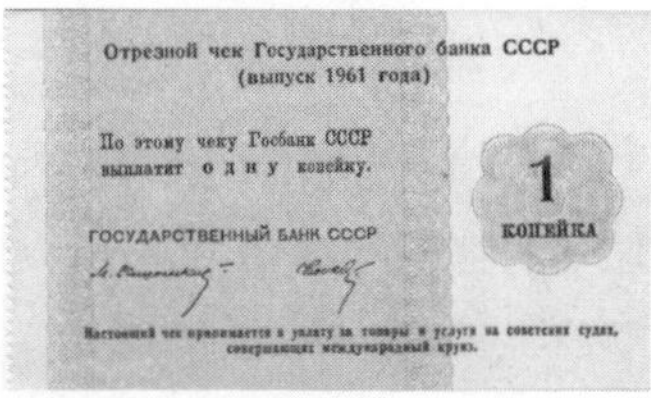

		VG	VF	UNC
FX80	**1 Kopek** 1961. Two signature varieties.	1.00	2.00	4.00

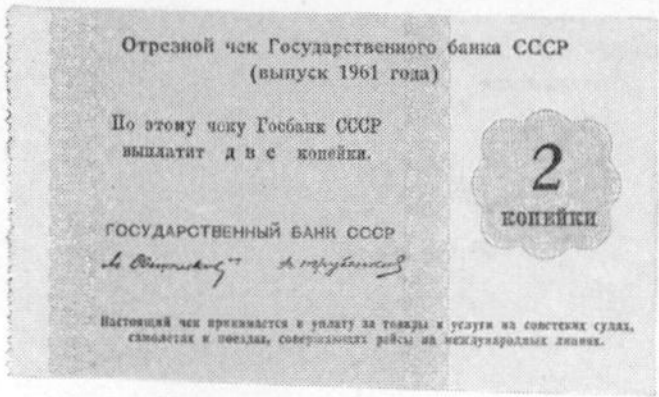

		VG	VF	UNC
FX81	**2 Kopek** 1961. Two signature varieties.	1.00	2.00	4.00
FX82	**5 Kopek** 1961.	2.00	5.00	10.00
FX83	**10 Kopek** 1961. Reported not confirmed.	—	—	—
FX84	**50 Kopek** 1961.	7.50	15.00	30.00
FX85	**1 Ruble** 1961. Reported not confirmed.	—	—	—

1967-74 Series

		VG	VF	UNC
FX90	**1 Kopek** 1970; 1972; 1974.	1.00	2.00	4.00
FX91	**2 Kopek** 1967; 1970.	1.00	2.00	4.00
FX92	**5 Kopek** 1967; 1970.	1.25	2.50	5.00
FX93	**10 Kopek** 1970.	1.50	3.00	6.00

1970-76 Issue

		VG	VF	UNC
FX95	**1 Kopek** 1970; 1974; 1976.	1.25	2.50	5.00
FX96	**2 Kopek** 1970; 1976.	1.25	2.50	5.00
FX97	**5 Kopek** 1976. Reported not confirmed.	—	—	—
FX98	**10 Kopek** 1976.	1.50	3.00	6.00

Vneshtorgbank (БАНКА ДАЯВНЕШНЕЙ ТОРГОВАИ СССР)

1973; 1975 Issue

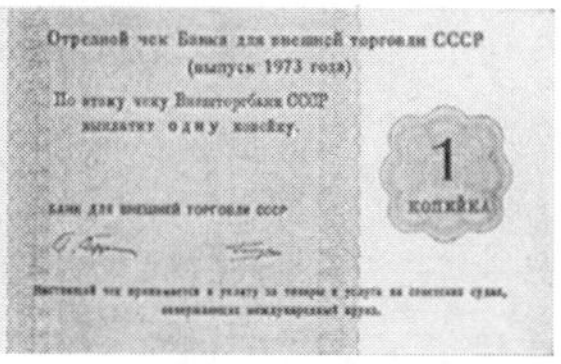

		VG	VF	UNC
FX100	**1 Kopek** 1973; 1975.			
	a. 1973.	1.00	3.00	6.00
	b. 1975.	1.00	3.00	6.00
FX101	**2 Kopek** 1973; 1975.			
	a. 1973.	—	—	—
	b. 1975.	1.50	3.50	7.00
FX102	**5 Kopek** 1973, 1975.			
	a. 1973.	—	—	—
	b. 1975.	2.00	4.00	8.00
FX103	**10 Kopek** 1973, 1975.			
	a. 1973.	—	—	—
	b. 1975.	2.50	4.50	9.00
FX104	**50 Kopek** 1973; 1975.			
	a. 1973.	—	—	—
	b. 1975.	—	—	—
FX105	**1 Ruble** 1973; 1975.			
	a. 1973.	—	—	—
	b. 1975.	—	—	—

1978 Issue

FX120-124 similar to FX95-98 but for new script on note.

		VG	VF	UNC
FX120	**5 Kopek** 1978.	1.00	2.50	5.00
FX121	**10 Kopek** 1978; 1980.	1.50	3.00	7.50

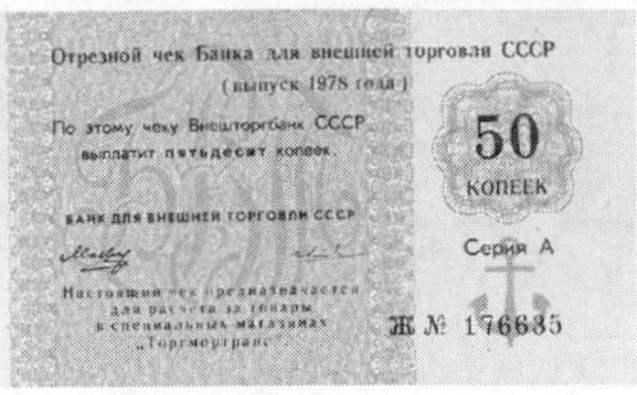

	VG	VF	UNC
FX122 50 Kopek			
1978.	2.00	5.00	9.00
FX123 1 Ruble			
1978.	3.00	8.00	14.00
FX124 5 Ruble			
1978.	5.00	10.00	20.00

Bank of Foreign Trade

1977; 1980 Cruise Ship Series

	VG	VF	UNC
FX135 1 Kopek			
1977; 1980.			
a. 1977; 1980. Without serial #.	1.00	2.00	4.00
b. 1977. With serial #.	1.00	2.00	4.00

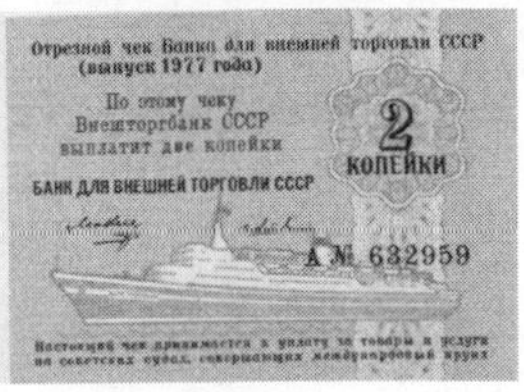

	VG	VF	UNC
FX136 2 Kopek			
1977; 1980.			
a. 1977; 1980. Without serial #.	1.00	2.00	4.00
b. 1977. With serial #.	1.00	2.00	4.00

	VG	VF	UNC
FX137 5 Kopek			
1977; 1980.			
a. 1977; 1980. Without serial #.	1.00	2.00	4.00
b. 1977. With serial #.	1.00	2.00	4.00

	VG	VF	UNC
FX138 10 Kopek			
1977; 1980.			
a. 1977; 1980. Without serial #.	1.00	3.00	5.00
b. 1977. With serial #.	1.00	3.00	5.00
FX139 50 Kopek			
1977; 1980.			
a. 1977; 1980. Without serial #.	2.00	4.00	7.00
b. 1977. With serial #.	2.00	4.00	7.00
FX140 1 Ruble			
1977; 1980.			
a. 1977; 1980. Without serial #.	3.00	6.00	12.00
b. 1977. With serial #.	3.00	6.00	12.00

1985; 1989 Cruise Ship Series

This series has a white border around the printed area, the notes are larger than series 1977 and 1980.

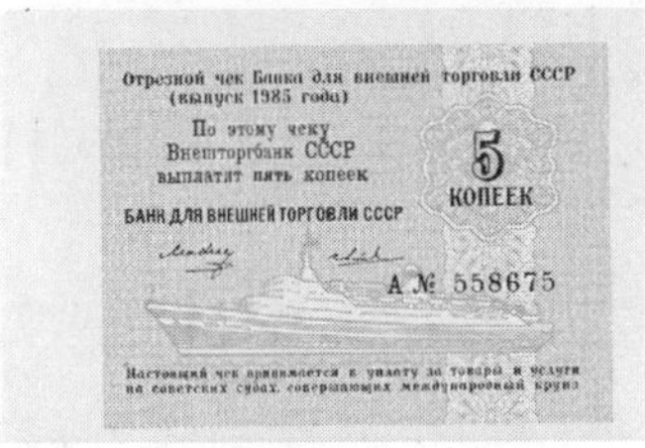

	VG	VF	UNC
FX141 5 Kopek			
1985; 1989.			
a. 1985.	.25	.75	1.50
b. 1989.	.25	.75	1.50

	VG	VF	UNC
FX142 10 Kopek			
1985; 1989.			
a. 1985.	.50	1.00	1.75
b. 1989.	.50	1.00	1.75

	VG	VF	UNC
FX143 50 Kopek			
1985; 1989.			
a. 1985.	.75	1.50	3.00
b. 1989.	.75	1.50	3.00
FX144 1 Ruble			
1985; 1989.			
a. 1985.	1.00	2.00	4.00
b. 1989.	1.00	2.00	4.00

	VG	VF	UNC
FX145 5 Ruble			
1985; 1989.			
a. 1985.	1.25	2.50	5.00
b. 1989.	1.25	2.50	5.00

1965-1985 Diplomatic Series "D"

	VG	VF	UNC
FX146 1 Kopek			
1965-1980.			
a. 1965.	4.00	8.00	12.00
b. 1970.	3.00	6.00	8.00
c. 1973; 1975; 1976; 1977.	2.00	4.00	6.00
d. 1979; 1980.	1.00	2.00	3.00
FX147 2 Kopek			
1965-1980.			
a. 1965.	4.00	8.00	12.00
b. 1970.	3.00	6.00	8.00
c. 1973; 1975; 1976; 1977.	2.00	4.00	6.00
d. 1979; 1980.	1.00	2.00	3.00

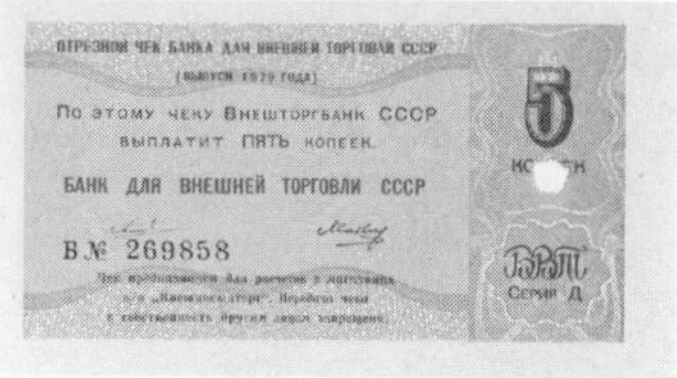

FX148 5 Kopek	VG	VF	UNC
1965-1980.			
a. 1965.	4.00	8.00	12.00
b. 1970.	3.00	6.00	8.00
c. 1973; 1975; 1976; 1977.	2.00	4.00	6.00
d. 1979; 1980.	1.00	2.00	3.00

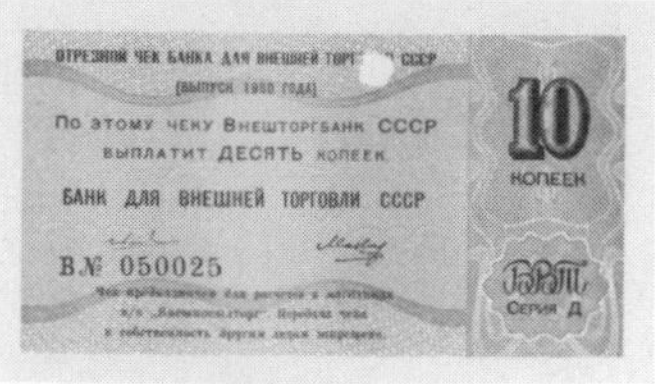

FX149 10 Kopek	VG	VF	UNC
1965-1980.			
a. 1965.	4.00	8.00	12.00
b. 1970.	3.00	6.00	8.00
c. 1973; 1975; 1976; 1977.	2.00	4.00	6.00
d. 1979; 1980.	1.00	2.00	3.00
FX150 20 Kopek			
1965-1980.			
a. 1965.	5.00	10.00	15.00
b. 1970.	5.00	10.00	15.00
c. 1973; 1975; 1976; 1977.	4.00	6.00	10.00
d. 1979; 1980.	1.00	2.00	3.00
FX151 50 Kopek			
1965-1985.			
a. 1965.	5.00	10.00	15.00
b. 1970.	5.00	10.00	15.00
c. 1973; 1975; 1976; 1977.	4.00	6.00	10.00
d. 1979; 1980.	1.00	2.00	3.00
e. 1985.	1.00	2.00	3.00
FX152 1 Ruble			
1965-1985.			
a. 1965.	6.00	12.00	18.00
b. 1970.	6.00	12.00	18.00
c. 1973; 1975; 1976; 1977.	5.00	10.00	15.00
d. 1979; 1980.	2.00	5.00	10.00
e. 1985.	2.00	5.00	10.00
FX153 2 Ruble			
1965-1985.			
a. 1965.	10.00	15.00	30.00
b. 1970.	10.00	15.00	30.00
c. 1973; 1975; 1976; 1977.	8.00	12.00	25.00
d. 1979; 1980.	3.00	6.00	12.00
e. 1985.	3.00	6.00	12.00
FX154 5 Ruble			
1965-1985.			
a. 1965.	15.00	40.00	60.00
b. 1970.	15.00	40.00	60.00
c. 1973; 1975; 1976; 1977.	15.00	40.00	60.00
d. 1979; 1980.	6.00	8.00	10.00
e. 1985.	6.00	8.00	10.00
FX155 10 Rubles			
1965-1985.			
a. 1965.	—	—	—
b. 1970.	—	—	—
c. 1973; 1975; 1976; 1977.	—	—	—
d. 1979; 1980.	10.00	20.00	40.00
e. 1985.	10.00	20.00	40.00
FX156 25 Rubles			
1965-1985.			
a. 1965.	—	—	—
b. 1970.	—	—	—
c. 1973; 1975; 1976; 1977.	—	—	—
d. 1979; 1980.	15.00	30.00	60.00
e. 1985.	15.00	30.00	60.00

Bank for Foreign Economic Activity

1989 Series

FX157 5 Kopek	VG	VF	UNC
1989.	.50	1.00	2.00
FX158 10 Kopek			
1989.	.50	1.00	3.00
FX159 50 Kopek			
1989.	.75	1.50	3.00

FX160 1 Ruble	VG	VF	UNC
1989.	1.00	2.00	4.00
FX161 5 Ruble			
1989.	1.25	2.50	5.00
FX162 10 Rubles			
1989. Rare.	7.50	20.00	40.00
FX163 25 Rubles			
1989. Rare.	10.00	40.00	90.00

SAINT KITTS & NEVIS

St. Kitts (St. Christopher), a West Indian island located in the Leeward Islands southeast of Puerto Rico, is the principal component of a British associated state composed of the islands of St. Kitts, Nevis, and Anguilla. The associated state has an area of 104 sq. mi. (269 sq. km.) Capital: Basseterre, St. Kitts.

St. Kitts was discovered by Columbus in 1493 and was settled by Thomas Warner, an Englishman, in 1623. The island was ceded to the British by the Treaty of Utrecht, 1713. France protested British occupancy, and on three occasions between 1666 and 1782 seized the island and held it for short periods.

RULERS:

British

MONETARY SYSTEM:

1 Dollar = 100 Cents

BRITISH ADMINISTRATION

BARCLAYS BANK (DOMINION, COLONIAL AND OVERSEAS)

1926 PROVISIONAL ISSUE

#S101-S106 original office: Bridgetown, Barbados with overprint: *ISSUED AT ST. KITTS BRANCH* at left and right of center and large *K* at upper right.

S104 5 Dollars	Good	Fine	XF
1.9.1926. Black on pink and blue-green underprint. Crowned supported royal arms at center. Back: Green. Overprint: Large *K* at upper right. Printer: BWC.	900.	2700.	—

1937 ISSUE

S106 5 Dollars	Good	Fine	XF
1937; 1940. Purple on multicolor underprint. Crowned supported royal arms at right. Overprint: Large *K* at upper right. Printer: BWC.			
a. Issued note. 1.3.1937; 1.5.1937.	375.	1150.	3450.
s. Specimen. 1.3.1940.	—	Unc	1250.

COLONIAL BANK

1900'S PROVISIONAL ISSUE

S111 5 Dollars	Good	Fine	XF
To 1926. Black. Arms at upper center. Overprint: *ISSUED AT ST. KITTS BRANCH.*	3500.	10,000.	—

ROYAL BANK OF CANADA

1913 PROVISIONAL ISSUE

#s116 overprint: *ST. KITTS* vertically at left and right, smaller vertical overprint: *PAYABLE AT BASSETERRE, ST. KITTS* at left center on regular Canadian issue.

S116 5 Dollars	Good	Fine	XF
2.1.1913. Black on green underprint. Overprint: On Canada #S1378. Printer: ABNC. Rare.	—	—	—

1920 ISSUE

S121 5 Dollars = 1 Pound 10 Pence	Good	Fine	XF
2.1.1920. Black on green underprint. Steamship at center. Back: Green. Printer: ABNC. Large size note.			
a. Issued note.	1100.	3300.	—
p. Proof.	—	Unc	2000.
s. Specimen.	—	Unc	2000.

1938 ISSUE

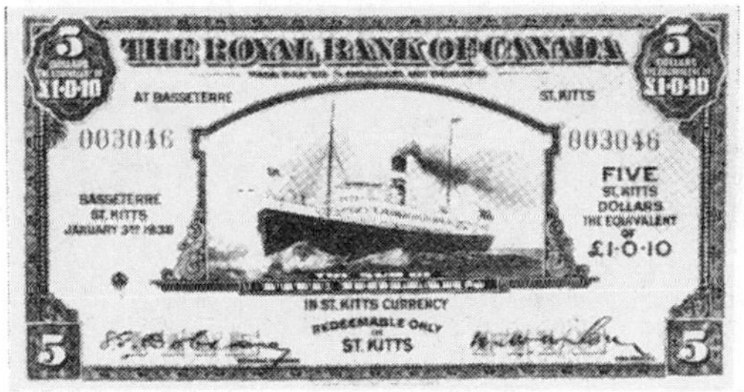

S126 5 Dollars = 1 Pound 10 Pence	Good	Fine	XF
3.1.1938. Black on green underprint. Steamship at center. Similar to #S121 but reduced size. Back: Green. Printer: ABNC.			
a. Issued note.	450.	1350.	4000.
p. Proof.	—	Unc	1400.
s. Specimen.	—	Unc	1400.

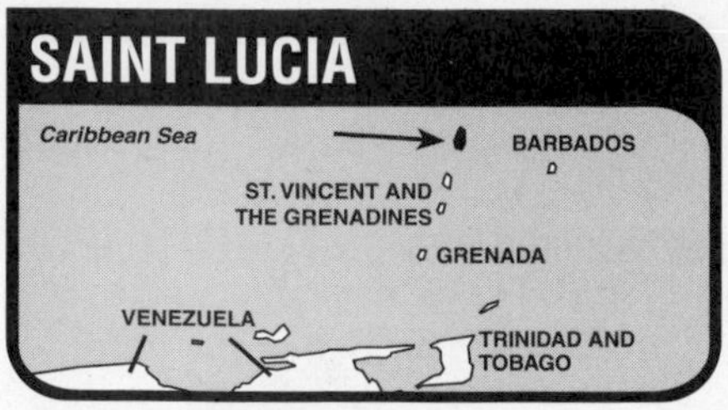

Saint Lucia, an independent island nation located in the Windward Islands of the West Indies between St. Vincent and Martinique, has an area of 616 sq. km. Capital: Castries.<PAR The island, with its fine natural harbor at Castries, was contested between England and France throughout the 17th and early 18th centuries (changing possession 14 times); it was finally ceded to the UK in 1814. Even after the abolition of slavery on its plantations in 1834, Saint Lucia remained an agricultural island, dedicated to producing tropical commodity crops. Self-government was granted in 1967 and independence in 1979.

RULERS:

British

MONETARY SYSTEM:

1 Pound = 20 Shillings until 1948
1 Dollar = 100 Cents, 1949-
1 Pound = 20 Shillings
1 Dollar = 100 Cents
NOTE: For later issues refer to East Caribbean States/British East Caribbean Territories.

British Administration

Barclays Bank (Dominion, Colonial and Overseas)

1926 Provisional Issues

		Good	Fine	XF
S106	**5 Dollars** 1.9.1926. Brown and green. Crowned supported royal arms at center. Overprint: *ISSUED AT ST. LUCIA BRANCH* and Large *L*. Printer: BWC. Office of issue: Bridgetown, Barbados.	1100.	3300.	—
S107	**5 Dollars** 1.9.1926. Brown and green. Crowned supported royal arms at center. Like #S106. Overprint: *ISSUED AT ST. LUCIA BRANCH* and Large *L*. Printer: BWC. Office of issue: Castries, St. Lucia.	1500.	4500.	—

1937 Issue

		Good	Fine	XF
S111	**5 Dollars** 1937-41. Purple on multicolor underprint. Crowned supported royal arms at right. Overprint: *ISSUED AT ST. LUCIA BRANCH* twice at center, and Large *L*. Printer: BWC. Office of issue: Bridgetown, Barbados.			
	a. Issued note. 1.3.1937; 1.5.1937; 1.3.1940; 1.2.1941.	700.	2100.	—
	s. Specimen. 1.2.1941.	—	Unc	1500.

Colonial Bank

1900's Issue

		Good	Fine	XF
S116	**5 Dollars** To 1926. Rare.	—	—	—

Royal Bank of Canada

1900's Issue

		Good	Fine	XF
S121	**5 Dollars = 1 Pound 10 Pence** 2.1.1920. Black on green underprint. Steamship at center. Back: Green. Printer: ABNC.	1500.	4500.	12,500.

SAINT VINCENT

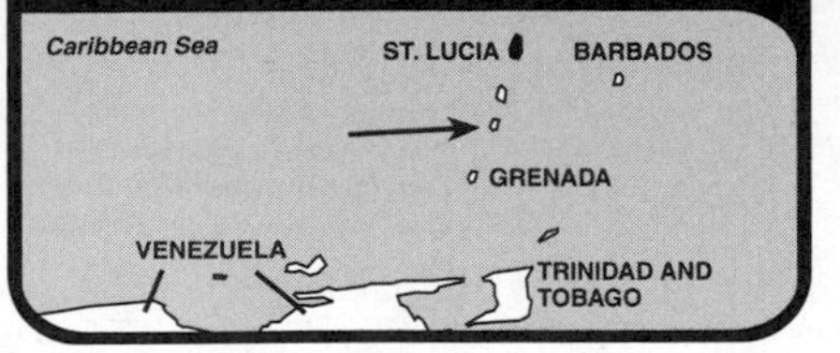

The State of St. Vincent, a British associated state located in the Windward Islands of the West Indies west of Barbados and south of St. Lucia, has an area of 150 sq. mi. (388 sq. km.). Capital: Kingstown.

St. Vincent was discovered by Columbus on Jan. 22, 1498, and was left undisturbed for more than a century. The British began colonization early in the 18th century, against bitter and prolonged Carib resistance. The island was taken by the French in 1779, but restored to the British in 1783, by the Treaty of Paris.

RULERS:
British

MONETARY SYSTEM:
1 Dollar = 100 Cents

British Administration

Barclays Bank (Dominion, Colonial and Overseas)

1926 Provisional Issue

#S101 and S106 overprint: *ISSUED AT ST. VINCENT BRANCH* twice, at left and right of center.

		Good	Fine	XF
S101	**5 Dollars** 1.9.1926; 1.6.1929. Black on pink and blue-green underprint. Crowned supported royal arms at center. Back: Green. Overprint: *ISSUED AT ST. VINCENT BRANCH* at left and right and large *V* at upper right. Printer: BWC. Issuing office: Bridgetown, Barbados.	700.	2100.	—

1939 Issue

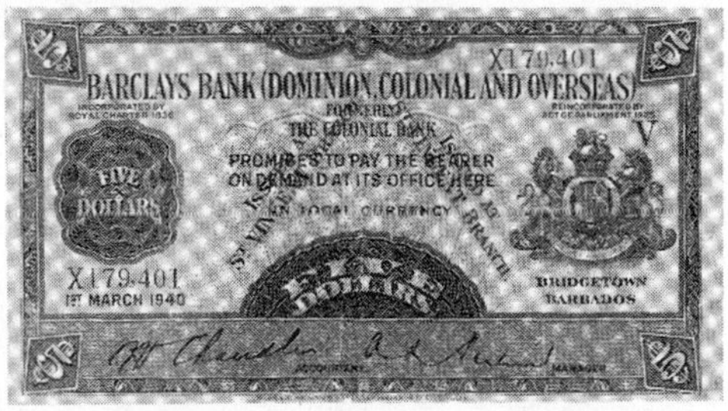

		Good	Fine	XF
S106	**5 Dollars** 1939-41. Purple on multicolor underprint. Crowned supported royal arms at right. Overprint: *ISSUED AT ST. VINCENT BRANCH* at left and right and large *V* at upper right. Printer: BWC.			
	a. Issuing office: Bridgetown, Barbados. 1.3.1940.	450.	1350.	4000.
	b. Issuing office: Port of Spain, Trinidad. Overprint: Large *T* at upper right. 1.3.1939; 1.2.1941.	375.	1100.	3300.

Colonial Bank

1882 Provisional Issue

#S111 Bridgetown, Barbados office. Overprint: *Issued at ST. VINCENT Branch* twice, at left and right of center.

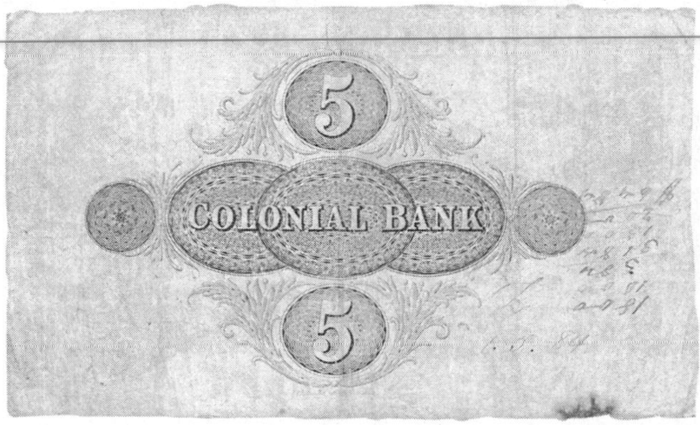

		Good	Fine	XF
S111	**5 Dollars** 1.7.1882. Black. Crowned supported royal arms at upper center. Overprint: *Issued at ST. VINCENT Branch* at left and right. Issuing office: Bridgetown, Barbados.	2400.	7250.	—

1917 Issue

#S115 Bridgetown, Barbados office. Overprint: *Issued at ST. VINCENT Branch* twice, at left and right of center.

		Good	Fine	XF
S115	**5 Dollars** 1.2.1917. Black on orange underprint. Crowned supported royal arms at upper center. Overprint: *Issued at ST. VINCENT Branch* at left and right and large *S V* at upper right. Issuing office: Bridgetown, Barbados. Specimen.	—	Unc	2750.

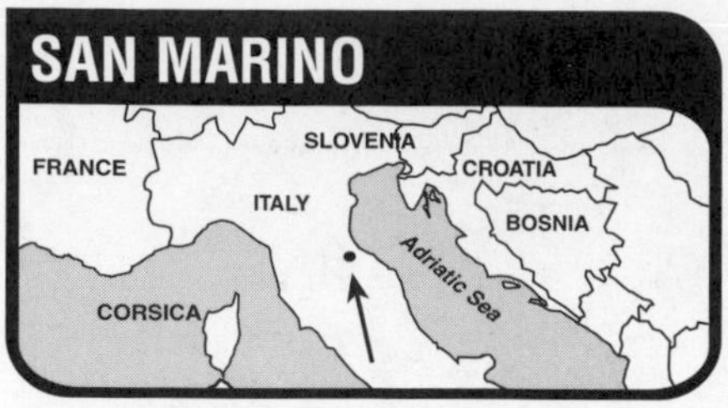

The Republic of San Marino, the oldest and smallest republic in the world, is located in north central Italy entirely surrounded by the Province of Emilia - Romagna. It has an area of 24 sq. mi. (62 sq. km.) Capital: San Marino.

According to tradition, San Marino was founded about 350 A.D. by a Christian stonecutter as a refuge against religious persecution. While gradually acquiring the institutions of an independent state, it avoided the factional fights of the middle ages and except for a brief period in fief to Cesare Borgia, retained its freedom despite attacks on its sovereignty by the Papacy, the lords of Rimini, Napoleon and Mussolini. In 1862 San Marino established a customs union with, and put itself under the protection of, Italy. A Communist - Socialist coalition controlled the government for 12 years after World War II. The Christian Democratic Party has been the core of government since 1957.

San Marino does not issue its own paper money although it has issued coins since 1864. The notes issued in 1976 are emergency small denomination issues prompted by a coin shortage. Similar pieces were issued in 1944 and 1966.

MONETARY SYSTEM:

1 Lira = 100 Centesimi

REPUBLIC

CASSA DI RISPARMIO DELLA REPUBBLICA DI SAN MARINO

1976 EMERGENCY ISSUE

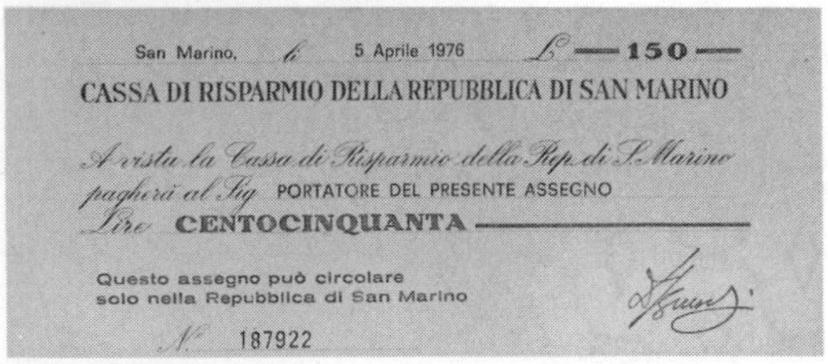
San Marino, 6 5 Aprile 1976 £ 150
CASSA DI RISPARMIO DELLA REPUBBLICA DI SAN MARINO
A vista la Cassa di Risparmio della Rep. di S. Marino
pagherà al Sig PORTATORE DEL PRESENTE ASSEGNO
Lire CENTOCINQUANTA
Questo assegno può circolare solo nella Repubblica di San Marino
N° 187922

		VG	VF	UNC
S101	**150 Lire** 5.4.1976. Arms in light brown underprint.	3.00	9.00	25.00

San Marino, 6 5 Aprile 1976 £ 200
CASSA DI RISPARMIO DELLA REPUBBLICA DI SAN MARINO
A vista la Cassa di Risparmio della Rep. di S. Marino
pagherà al Sig PORTATORE DEL PRESENTE ASSEGNO
Lire DUECENTO
Questo assegno può circolare solo nella Repubblica di San Marino
N° 230759

		VG	VF	UNC
S102	**200 Lire** 5.4.1976. Arms in light green underprint.	3.00	9.00	25.00

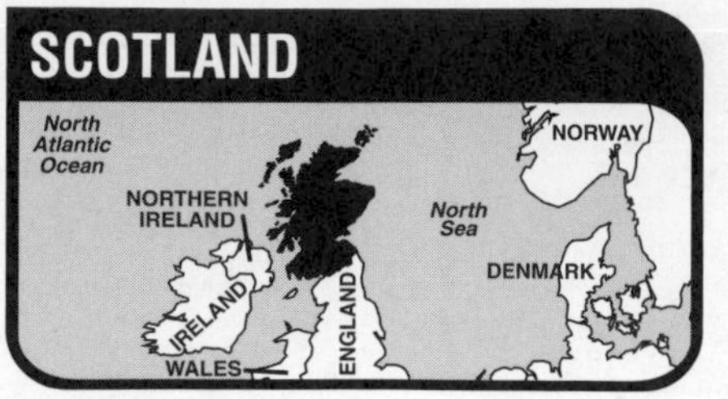

Scotland, a part of the United Kingdom of Great Britain and Northern Ireland, consists of the northern part of the island of Great Britain. It has an area of 30,414 sq. mi. (78,772 sq. km.). Capital: Edinburgh. Principal industries are agriculture, fishing, manufacturing and ship-building.

In the 5th century, Scotland consisted of four kingdoms; that of the Picts, the Scots, Strathclyde, and Northumbria. The Scottish kingdom was united by Malcolm II (1005-34), but its ruler was forced to payo homage to the English crown in 1174. Scotland won independence under Robert Bruce at Bannockburn in 1314 and was ruled by the house of Stuart from 1371 to 1688. The personal union of the kingdoms of England and Scotland was achieved in 1603 by the accession of King James VI of Scotland as James I of England. Scotland was united with England by Parliamentary act in 1707.

RULERS:

British

MONETARY SYSTEM:

1 Shilling = 12 Pence
1 Guinea = 21 Shillings
1 Pound Sterling = 12 Pounds Scots
1 Pound = 20 Shillings to 1971
1 Pound = 100 New Pence, 1971-1981
1 Pound = 100 Pence, 1982-
1 Pound = 20 Shillings to 1971

NOTE ON LISTINGS

Listings for Scotland in Volume I are comprised of selected obsolete bank issues formerly in Volume II, and they go back to the beginning of each bank.

REPLACEMENT NOTES:

#111, Z/1, Z/2 or Z/3 prefix; #112 ZA or ZB prefix; #113 ZB prefix.

COMMERCIAL BANKS:

British Linen Company .... #S141-S179
Commercial Banking Company of Scotland .... #S281-S290
Commercial Bank of Scotland.......... #S291-S309
Commercial Bank of Scotland Ltd.......... #S310-S336
North of Scotland Banking Company .... #S611-S619
North of Scotland Bank Ltd. .... #S620-S624
North of Scotland & Town & County Bank Ltd. .... #S625-S632
North of Scotland Bank Ltd. .... #S633-S647
Union Bank of Scotland .... #S776-S798
Union Bank of Scotland Ltd.......... #S799-S819

PRIVATE BANKS:

The following listing of private banks in Scotland that either issued notes or had notes prepared was furnished by James Douglas, author of *Scottish Banknotes* published in 1975. This catalog was a pioneering effort in reporting what was available, although incomplete, to the author at that time.

Aberdeen Commercial Banking Company, 1778-1833
Arbroath Banking Company, 1825-44
Ayrshire Banking Company, 1830-48
Banking Company in Aberdeen, 1767-1849
Caithness Banking Company, 1812-25
Caledonian Banking Company Limited, 1838-1907
Central Bank of Scotland, 1834-68
City of Glascow Bank, 1839-79
Cupar Banking Company, 1802-11
Douglas Heron & Company, 1769-73
Dumfries Commercial Bank, 1804-08
Dundee Banking Company, 1763-1864
Dundee Commercial Bank, 1825-38
Dundee New Bank, 1802-38
Dundee Union Bank, 1809-44
East Lothian Banking Company, 1810-22
Eastern Bank of Scotland, 1838-63
Edinburgh and Glasgow Bank, 1844-58
Edinburgh and Leith Bank, 1839-44
Falkirk Banking Company, 1782-1825
Falkirk Union Banking Company, 1803-16
Fife Banking Company, 1802-29
William Forbes, James Hunter & Co., 1773-1838
Galloway Banking Company, 1806-21
Glasgow and Ship Bank, 1836-43
Glasgow Arms Bank, 1750-93
Glasgow Bank Company, 1809-36
Glasgow Joint Stock Bank, 1840-44
Glasgow Union Banking Company, 1830-43
Greenock Bank Company, 1785-1843
Greenock Union Bank, 1840-44
Hunters & Company, 1773-1843
Kilmarnock Bank, 1802-21
Leith Banking Company, 1793-1842
Montrose Bank, 1814-29
North British Bank, 1844
North of Scotland Banking Company, 1836-82
Paisley Banking Company, 1783-1836
Paisley Commercial Banking Company, 1838-44
Paisley Union Banking Company, 1788-1838
Perth Banking Company, 1787-1857
Perth Union Bank, 1810-36
Renfrewshire Banking Company, 1802-42
Shetland Bank, 1821-42
Ship Bank, 1750-1836

Southern Bank of Scotland, 1838-40
Stirling Banking Company, 1777-1826
Stirling Merchant Banking Company, 1784-1813
Stornoway Bank (J. Stewart McKenzie), 1823-26
Thistle Bank, 1761-1836
Town and County Bank, 1825-1908
Western Bank of Scotland, 1832-57

Commercial Banks

British Linen Company

1747 Issue

	Good	Fine	XF
S141 5 Pounds (ca.1747). With text: *for value received in goods. Payable without interest.*	—	—	—
S142 10 Pounds (ca.1747). With text: *for value received in goods. Payable without interest.*	—	—	—
S143 20 Pounds (ca.1747). With text: *for value received in goods. Payable without interest.*	—	—	—
S144 100 Pounds (ca.1747). With text: *for value received in goods. Payable without interest.* Interest-bearing, payable after 3 months.	—	—	—

1750 Issue

	Good	Fine	XF
S145 10 Shillings (ca.1750). With text: *for value received in goods.*	—	—	—
S146 1 Pound (ca.1750). With text: *for value received in goods.*	—	—	—

1754 Issue

	Good	Fine	XF
S147 20 Shillings (ca.1754). Seated woman with sailing ship behind at upper left. With text: *for value received in goods.*	—	—	—

1763 Issue

	Good	Fine	XF
S148 5 Pounds (ca.1763). Bank emblem in ornate frame at upper left. With text: *for value received in goods.*	—	—	—

1768 Issue

	Good	Fine	XF
S149 1 Guinea 5.4.1768. Bank emblem at upper center, panel of thistles across top. Words from text: *in goods* deleted.	—	—	—

1770 Issue

	Good	Fine	XF
S150 1 Guinea 6.9.1770. Bank emblem at upper center, panel of thistles across top. Similar to #S149.	—	—	—

1780 Issue

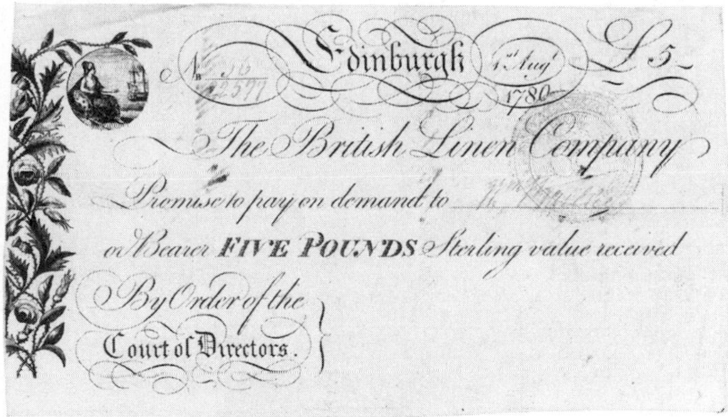

	Good	Fine	XF
S151 5 Pounds 1.8.1780. Emblem of Pallas at upper left, vertical panel of thistles and roses at left. With blind embossed seal.	900.	2700.	—

1797 Issue

	Good	Fine	XF
S152 5 Shillings 31.3.1797. Bank emblem at upper left.	—	—	—

1799 Issue

	Good	Fine	XF
S152A 1 Guinea 2.12.1799. Bank emblem at upper left, panel of thistles across top. With blind embossed seal. Printed date.	1200.	3600.	—

1808 Issue

	Good	Fine	XF
S153 1 Guinea Oct. 1808. Bank emblem at upper left, panel of thistle and rose motif across top. Date in top center oval.	1200.	3600.	—

1811 Issue

	Good	Fine	XF
S154 20 Shillings (ca.1811). Bank emblem at left.			
a. Issued note.	1100.	3300.	—
x. Contemporary forgery. 30.5.1811.	—	—	—

1815 Issue

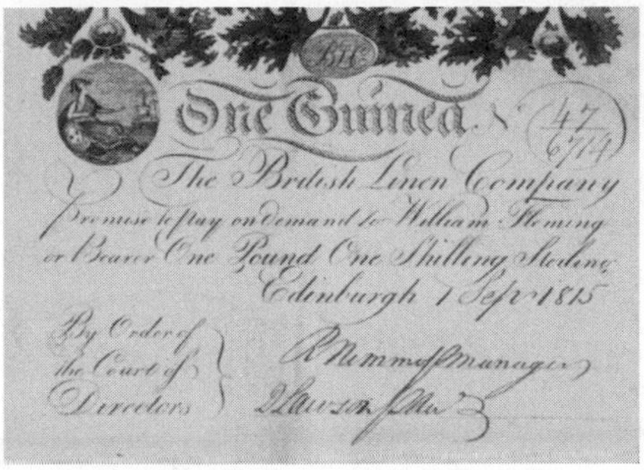

	Good	Fine	XF
S155 1 Guinea 1.9.1815; 1.9.1819. Bank emblem at upper left, panel of thistle and rose motif across top. Similar to #S153 but oval at top center with letters: *BLC* instead of date.			
a. Issued note.	1200.	3600.	—
x. Contemporary forgery. 1.9.1815.	—	—	—

1821 Issue

	Good	Fine	XF
S156 20 Shillings (ca.1821). Bank emblem at upper center.			
a. Issued note.	1150.	3450.	—
x. Contemporary forgery. 18.5.1825.	—	—	—
S157 1 Guinea (ca.1821). Two seated women at upper center, vertical panel of thistles at left.	1200.	3600.	—
S158 5 Pounds (ca.1821). Vertical panel of roses and thistles at left, small vignette of bank emblem at upper left.	1350.	4150.	—
S158A 20 Pounds (ca.1821). Vertical panel of roses and thistles at left, small vignette of bank emblem at upper left. Similar to #S158.	—	—	—
S158B 100 Pounds (ca.1821). Vertical panel of roses and thistles at left, small vignette of bank emblem at upper left. Similar to #S158.	—	—	—

1822 Issue

#S159-S164 Made from steel engraved plates by Perkins Fairman & Heath (later Perkins Bacon & Co.).

	Good	Fine	XF
S159 1 Pound (ca.1822). Black. Crowned supported arms at upper center, seated Britannia with spear, shield and lion in vertical panal at left. Uniface.			
a. Issued note.	1150.	3450.	—
x. Contemporary forgeries. 2.11.1826; 1.5.1828; 1.3.1829.	—	—	—
S160 1 Guinea (ca.1822). Black. Crowned supported arms at upper center, seated Britannia with spear, shield and lion in vertical panal at left. Uniface.	1200.	3600.	—
S161 5 Pounds (ca.1822). Black. Crowned supported arms at upper center, seated Britannia with spear, shield and lion in vertical panal at left. Uniface.	1350.	4150.	—
S162 10 Pounds (ca.1822). Black. Crowned supported arms at upper center, seated Britannia with spear, shield and lion in vertical panal at left. Uniface.	—	—	—
S163 20 Pounds (ca.1822). Black. Crowned supported arms at upper center, seated Britannia with spear, shield and lion in vertical panal at left. Uniface.	—	—	—
S164 100 Pounds (ca.1822). Black. Crowned supported arms at upper center, seated Britannia with spear, shield and lion in vertical panal at left. Uniface.	—	—	—

1861 Issue

#S165-S169 First issue dated 1.9.1860 but not issued until 1861.

	Good	Fine	XF
S165 1 Pound (ca.1861); 1.8.1863; 4.2.1870. Blue and red. Crowned supported arms at upper center, seated Britannia with spear, shield and lion in vertical panal at left. Large red letters: *B.L.Co.* added as underprint. Uniface.	1150.	3450.	—
S166 5 Pounds (ca.1861). Blue and red. Crowned supported arms at upper center, seated Britannia with spear, shield and lion in vertical panal at left. Large red letters: *B.L.Co.* added as underprint. Uniface.	1200.	3600.	—
S167 10 Pounds (ca.1861). Blue and red. Crowned supported arms at upper center, seated Britannia with spear, shield and lion in vertical panal at left. Large red letters: *B.L.Co.* added as underprint. Uniface.	—	—	—
S168 20 Pounds (ca.1861). Blue and red. Crowned supported arms at upper center, seated Britannia with spear, shield and lion in vertical panal at left. Large red letters: *B.L.Co.* added as underprint. Uniface.	—	—	—

	Good	Fine	XF
S169 100 Pounds (ca.1861). Blue and red. Crowned supported arms at upper center, seated Britannia with spear, shield and lion in vertical panal at left. Large red letters: *B.L.Co.* added as underprint. Uniface.	—	—	—

1872 Issue

#S170-S174 Similar to #S165-S169 but different promissory text at ctr.

	Good	Fine	XF
S170 1 Pound 1872-1904. Blue and red. Crowned supported arms at upper center, seated Britannia with spear, shield and lion in vertical panal at left. Large red letters: *B.L.Co.* added as underprint. Uniface.			
a. 2.11.1872-17.10.1885. Two hand signatures on behalf of Manager and Accountant.	1150.	3450.	—
b. 24.5.1886. Printed signature of J.S. Maclean as Manager. Proof only.			
c. 25.1.1887-15.9.1900. Printed signature of P. Martine as Manager.	675.	2000.	—
d. 12.11.1900-6.4.1904. Printed signature of C. Hogg as Manager.	675.	2000.	—
e. 31.5.1904. Printed signature of F. Gordon-Brown as Manager.	900.	2700.	—

	Good	Fine	XF
S171 5 Pounds 2.11.1872-15.8.1904. Blue and red. Crowned supported arms at upper center, seated Britannia with spear, shield and lion in vertical panal at left. Large red letters: *B.L.Co.* added as underprint. Uniface. Unknown in issued form.			
p. Proof.	—	Unc	1150.
s. Specimen. Three punch holes.	—	Unc	2250.
S172 10 Pounds 1.3.1877-2.9.1901. Blue and red. Crowned supported arms at upper center, seated Britannia with spear, shield and lion in vertical panal at left. Large red letters: *B.L.Co.* added as underprint. Uniface. Unknown in issued form.			
p. Proof.	—	Unc	1150.
s. Specimen. Three punch holes.	—	Unc	3750.

	Good	Fine	XF
S173 20 Pounds 1.11.1872-1.11.1904. Blue and red. Crowned supported arms at upper center, seated Britannia with spear, shield and lion in vertical panal at left. Large red letters: *B.L.Co.* added as underprint. Uniface.	900.	2700.	—

	Good	Fine	XF
S174 100 Pounds 7.5.1879-31.8.1904. Blue and red. Crowned supported arms at upper center, seated Britannia with spear, shield and lion in vertical panal at left. Large red letters: *B.L.Co.* added as underprint. Uniface. Unknown in issued form.			
p. Proof.	—	Unc	1150.
s. Specimen.	—	Unc	3750.

1905 Issue

	Good	Fine	XF
S175 1 Pound 28.2.1905; 30.3.1906. Blue. Crowned supported arms at upper center, seated Britannia with spear, shield and lion in vertical panal at left. Large red letters: *B.L.Co.* Uniface. Printer: W&S.	675.	2000.	—
S176 5 Pounds 8.3.1905; 1.6.1905; 14.4.1906; 4.2.1907. Blue. Crowned supported arms at upper center, seated Britannia with spear, shield and lion in vertical panal at left. Large red letters: *B.L.Co.* Uniface. Like #S175. Printer: W&S.	825.	2500.	—
S177 10 Pounds 15.4.1905. Blue. Crowned supported arms at upper center, seated Britannia with spear, shield and lion in vertical panal at left. Large red letters: *B.L.Co.* Uniface. Like #S175. Printer: W&S. Rare.	—	—	—
S178 20 Pounds 7.6.1905; 20.3.1906. Blue. Crowned supported arms at upper center, seated Britannia with spear, shield and lion in vertical panal at left. Large red letters: *B.L.Co.* Uniface. Like #S175. Printer: W&S. Rare.	—	—	—
S179 100 Pounds 14.2.1905; 18.3.1905; 3.8.1905; 30.9.1905; 5.10.1905; 23.11.1905. Blue. Crowned supported arms at upper center, seated Britannia with spear, shield and lion in vertical panal at left. Large red letters: *B.L.Co.* Uniface. Like #S175. Printer: W&S. Rare.	—	—	—

British Linen Bank

For previously listed #S181-S196 refer to Vol. II.
For previously listed #S197-S205 refer to Vol. III.

Commercial Banking Company of Scotland / Commercial Bank of Scotland

1810 Issue

		Good	Fine	XF
S281	**1 Pound**			
	(ca.1810). Small vignette of Edinburgh Castle at upper center, thistle at right.			
	a. Issued note.	900.	2700.	—
	x. Contemporary forgery.	—	—	—

NOTE: 5, 20 and 100 Pounds notes are presumed to have been issued, but no record exists.

		Good	Fine	XF
S285	**1 Guinea**			
	1810-1818. Small vignette of Edinburgh Castle at upper center, thistle at right. Similar to #S281.			
	a. 12.11.1810. *Pay to Hugh Auld* handwritten.	1500.	4500.	—
	b. 1.10.1818. *Pay to Hugh Auld* printed.	1500.	4500.	—

1818 Issue

		Good	Fine	XF
S286	**1 Pound**			
	(ca.1818); 1.5.1826. Larger vignette of Edinburgh Castle at upper left.			
	a. Payable to Edwd. Robertson.	450.	1350.	—
	b. Payable to Robert Paul (from 1823).	450.	1350.	—
	c. Ornamental frame overprint. (1825).	450.	1350.	—
	x. Contemporary forgery.	—	—	300.
S287	**5 Pounds**			
	(ca.1820), 1.7.1823.	750.	2250.	—

NOTE: The 5 Pounds was probably not issued until after 1820. 20 and 100 Pound notes are presumed to have been issued, but no record exists.

1826 Issue

		Good	Fine	XF
S289	**1 Pound**	—	—	—
	(ca.1826). Edinburgh Castle flanked by medallions. Engraved by W. H. Lizars.			

A WORD ON DATE RANGES

Often date ranges or specific dates are listed. These have been observed or reported by our contributors. If a note is outside the published range, it only means that it is a newly reported date, and not necessarily worthy of a premium value.

1827 Issue

		Good	Fine	XF
S290	**1 Pound**	—	—	—
	(ca.1827). Edinburgh Castle flanked by medallions, the left with King George IV and the right with allegorical figure of Caledonia. At bottom is medallion with allegory of Commerce. Back: Printed revenue stamp. Printer: Perkins & Heath (later Perkins Bacon & Co.).			

Commercial Bank of Scotland

1832 Issue

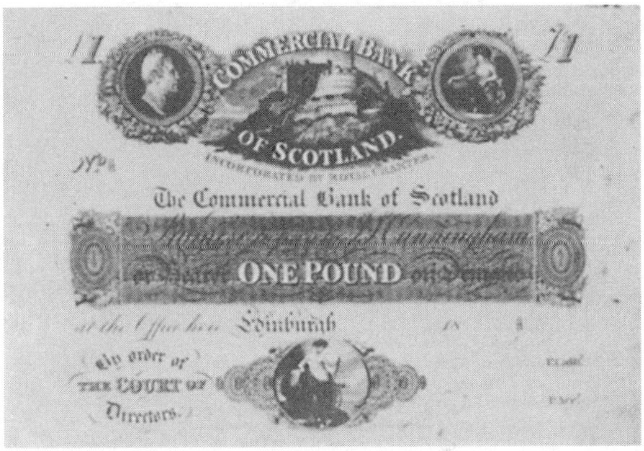

		Good	Fine	XF
S291	**1 Pound**			
	(ca.1832-44). Edinburgh Castle flanked by medallions, the left with King William IV and the right with allegorical figure of Caledonia. At bottom is medallion with allegory of Commerce. Similar to #S290. Back: Printed revenue stamp.			
	a. Payable to Robert Paul (1832).	—	—	—
	b. Payable to J. S. Cunningham; partly printed # (1835).	—	—	—
	c. Entire serial # printed (1844).	—	—	—

1833 Issue

#S292 and S293 from plates by W. H. Lizars.

		Good	Fine	XF
S292	**5 Pounds**			
	2.6.1835. King William IV at left, Edinburgh Castle at upper center. Back: Printed revenue stamp.	1175.	3500.	—
S293	**10 Pounds**			
	(ca.1833). King William IV at left, Edinburgh Castle at upper center. Additional portrait in design. Back: Printed revenue stamp.	—	—	—

1848 Issue

		Good	Fine	XF
S294	**1 Pound**	—	—	—
	(ca.1848). Queen Victoria at left, arms at center, Prince Albert at right. Bank at bottom. Back: Elaborate design with revenue stamp. Plate by W. H. Lizars.			

1850 Issue

#S295-S299 from steel plates by W. H. Lizars.

		Good	Fine	XF
S295	**1 Pound**			
	(ca.1850). Allegorical classic figures at upper center, portrait of Queen Victoria and Prince Albert. Bank at bottom. Printed serial #, hand dated. Back: Printed revenue stamp. Rare.	—	—	—
S296	**5 Pounds**			
	(ca.1850). Allegorical classic figures at upper center, portrait of Queen Victoria and Prince Albert. Bank at bottom. Printed serial #, hand dated. Back: Printed revenue stamp. Rare.	—	—	—

		Good	Fine	XF
S297	**10 Pounds**			
	(ca.1850). Allegorical classic figures at upper center, portrait of Queen Victoria and Prince Albert. Bank at bottom. Printed serial #, hand dated. Back: Printed revenue stamp. Rare.	—	—	—
S298	**20 Pounds**			
	(ca.1850). Allegorical classic figures at upper center, portrait of Queen Victoria and Prince Albert. Bank at bottom. Printed serial #, hand dated. Back: Printed revenue stamp. Rare.	—	—	—
S299	**100 Pounds**			
	(ca.1850). Allegorical classic figures at upper center, portrait of Queen Victoria and Prince Albert. Bank at bottom. Printed serial #, hand dated. Back: Printed revenue stamp.	—	—	—

1854 Issue

#S300-S304 No printed revenue stamp on back.

		Good	Fine	XF
S300	**1 Pound**			
	(ca.1854). Allegorical classic figures at upper center. Bank at bottom. Printer: PBC.	900.	2700.	—
S301	**5 Pounds**			
	(ca.1854). Allegorical classic figures at upper center. Bank at bottom. Printer: PBC.	—	—	—
S302	**10 Pounds**			
	(ca.1854). Allegorical classic figures at upper center. Bank at bottom. Printer: PBC.	—	—	—
S303	**20 Pounds**			
	(ca.1854). Allegorical classic figures at upper center. Bank at bottom. Printer: PBC.	—	—	—
S304	**100 Pounds**			
	(ca.1854). Allegorical classic figures at upper center. Bank at bottom. Printer: PBC.	—	—	—

1860 Issue

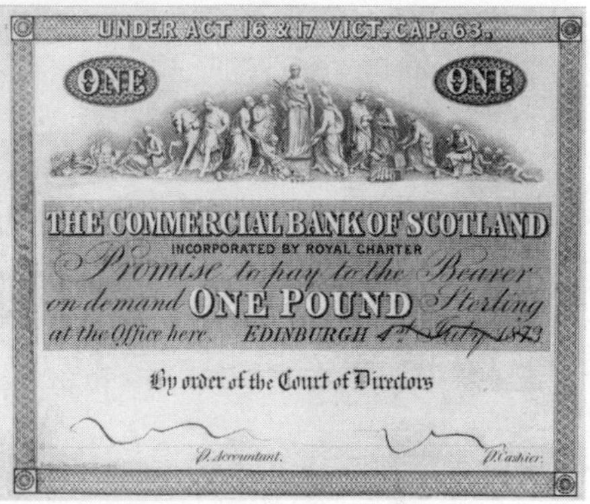

		Good	Fine	XF
S305	**1 Pound**			
	1861-1879. Blue with lithographic overprint in red across center. Allegorical classic figures at upper center. Bank at bottom.			
	a. 1.5.1861; 1.11.1864. Serial # in black.	375.	1125.	—
	b. 1.12.1875; 2.5.1879. Serial # in red.	375.	1125.	—
	p. Proof.	—	—	—
S306	**5 Pounds**			
	(ca.1860). Blue with lithographic overprint in red across center. Allegorical classic figures at upper center. Bank at bottom.	—	—	—
S307	**10 Pounds**			
	(ca.1860). Blue with lithographic overprint in red across center. Allegorical classic figures at upper center. Bank at bottom.	—	—	—
S308	**20 Pounds**			
	(ca.1860). Blue with lithographic overprint in red across center. Allegorical classic figures at upper center. Bank at bottom.	—	—	—
S309	**100 Pounds**			
	(ca.1860). Blue with lithographic overprint in red across center. Allegorical classic figures at upper center. Bank at bottom.	—	—	—

Commercial Bank of Scotland Limited

1882 Issue

		Good	Fine	XF
S310	**1 Pound**			
	(ca.1882). Blue and red.			
	a. Serial # in red.	375.	1125.	—
	b. Serial # in black.	375.	1125.	—
S311	**5 Pounds**			
	(ca.1882). Blue and red.	—	—	—
S312	**10 Pounds**			
	(ca.1882). Blue and red.	—	—	—
S313	**20 Pounds**			
	(ca.1882). Blue and red.	—	—	—

		Good	Fine	XF
S314	**100 Pounds**			
	(ca.1882); 3.1.1887. Blue and red.	—	—	—

1886; 1887 Issue

		Good	Fine	XF
S315	**1 Pound**			
	1886-1906. Blue on buff underprint. Allegorical figures. Back: Green. Bank building at center. Printer: BWC.			
	a. Handsigned. Imprint: Bradbury Wilkinson & Co. 1.7.1886-2.1.1892.	300.	900.	—
	b. Printed signature of Accountant. Imprint: Bradbury Wilkinson & Co. Ltd. 2.1.1892-4.1.1906.	300.	900.	—
S316	**5 Pounds**			
	3.1.1887-2.1.1906. Blue on buff underprint. Allegorical figures. Back: Green. Bank building at center. Printer: BWC.	750.	2250.	—
S317	**20 Pounds**			
	3.1.1887-4.1.1906. Blue on buff underprint. Allegorical figures. Back: Green. Bank building at center. Printer: BWC.	1125.	3375.	—
S318	**100 Pounds**			
	3.1.1887-2.1.1907. Blue on buff underprint. Allegorical figures. Back: Green. Bank building at center. Printer: BWC.	—	—	—

1907; 1908 Issue

		Good	Fine	XF
S319	**1 Pound**			
	2.1.1907; 2.1.1908. Blue on buff underprint. Buildings at left and right, group of allegorical figures at bottom. Printer: BWC.	300.	900.	2700.

	Good	Fine	XF
S320 5 Pounds 2.1.1908. Blue on buff underprint. Buildings at left and right, group of allegorical figures at bottom. Like #S319. Printer: BWC.	600.	1800.	5400.
S321 20 Pounds 2.1.1907. Blue on buff underprint. Buildings at left and right, group of allegorical figures at bottom. Like #S319. Printer: BWC. Rare.	—	—	—
S322 100 Pounds 2.1.1907. Blue on buff underprint. Buildings at left and right, group of allegorical figures at bottom. Like #S319. Printer: BWC. Rare.	—	—	—

1908-10 Issue

ONE
ONE
THE COMMERCIAL BANK OF SCOTLAND
LIMITED
Promise to pay the Bearer on Demand
ONE POUND
STERLING
AT THE OFFICE HERE
EDINBURGH, 22nd Jan. 1915.
BY ORDER OF THE COURT OF DIRECTORS.
Accountant
Cashier

	Good	Fine	XF
S323 1 Pound 1909-23. Blue on buff underprint. Oval frame around buildings at left and right, group of allegorical figures at bottom. Similar to #S319.			
a. Printed signature of *ACCOUNTANT*, handsigned on behalf of the *CASHIER*. 2.1.1909-2.1.1914.	125.	375.	1125.
b. Printed signature of *ACCOUNTANT* and *CASHIER*. *2.1.1914 2.1.1923.*	75.00	225.	675.

FIVE
FIVE
THE COMMERCIAL BANK OF SCOTLAND
LIMITED
FIVE POUNDS
STERLING
AT THE OFFICE HERE
EDINBURGH, 2nd Jan. 1923.

	Good	Fine	XF
S324 5 Pounds 2.1.1909-2.1.1923. Blue on buff underprint. Oval frame around buildings at left and right, group of allegorical figures at bottom. Similar to #S323.	225.	675.	2025.
S325 20 Pounds 3.1.1910-2.1.1923. Blue on buff underprint. Oval frame around buildings at left and right, group of allegorical figures at bottom. Similar to #S323.	350.	1050.	3150.
S326 100 Pounds 2.1.1908-2.1.1923. Blue on buff underprint. Oval frame around buildings at left and right, group of allegorical figures at bottom. Similar to #S323.	900.	2700.	—

ILLUSTRATIONS

Illustrations of bank notes used throughout this catalog are 42% of the actual size.

1924 Issue

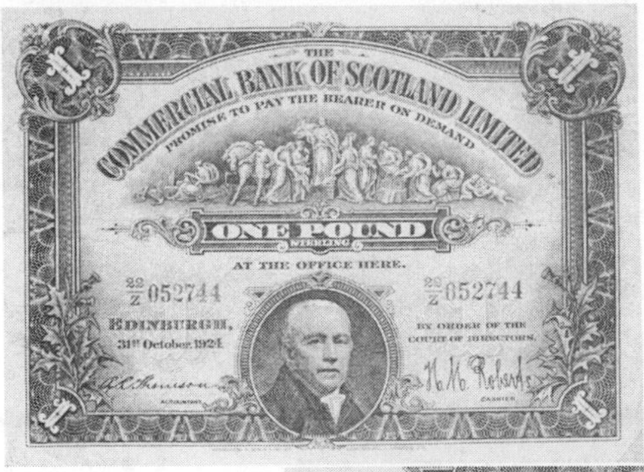
THE
COMMERCIAL BANK OF SCOTLAND LIMITED
PROMISE TO PAY THE BEARER ON DEMAND
ONE POUND
STERLING
AT THE OFFICE HERE.
EDINBURGH,
31st October 1924.
BY ORDER OF THE COURT OF DIRECTORS.

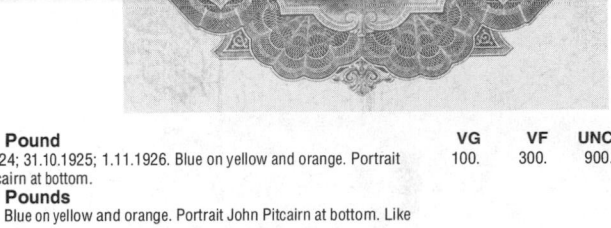

	VG	VF	UNC
S327 1 Pound 31.10.1924; 31.10.1925; 1.11.1926. Blue on yellow and orange. Portrait John Pitcairn at bottom.	100.	300.	900.
S328 5 Pounds 1924-44. Blue on yellow and orange. Portrait John Pitcairn at bottom. Like #S327.			
a. Printed signature of *ACCOUNTANT* and handsigned on behalf of the *MANAGER*. 31.10.1924-1.11.1926.	150.	450.	1350.
b. Printed signature of *CASHIER* and *GENERAL MANAGER*. 1.12.1928-1.12.1944.	60.00	200.	600.

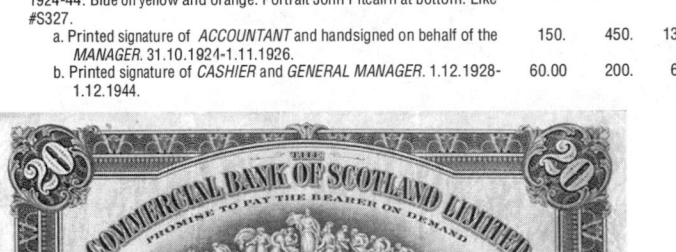

THE
COMMERCIAL BANK OF SCOTLAND LIMITED
PROMISE TO PAY THE BEARER ON DEMAND
TWENTY POUNDS
STERLING
AT THE OFFICE HERE.
EDINBURGH,
2nd March, 1942.
BY ORDER OF THE COURT OF DIRECTORS.

	VG	VF	UNC
S329 20 Pounds 1924-43. Blue on yellow and orange. Portrait John Pitcairn at bottom. Like #S327.			
a. Printed signature of *ACCOUNTANT* and handsigned on behalf of the *MANAGER*. 31.10.1924; 1.5.1925.	225.	675.	2025.
b. Printed signature of *CASHIER* and *GENERAL MANAGER*. 1.5.1928-4.1.1943.	150.	450.	1350.
S330 100 Pounds 1924-43. Blue on yellow and orange. Portrait John Pitcairn at bottom. Like #S327.			
a. Printed signature of *ACCOUNTANT* and handsigned on behalf of the *MANAGER*. 31.10.1924; 1.12.1928.	900.	2700.	7250.
b. Printed signature of *CASHIER* and *GENERAL MANAGER*. 30.9.1937; 1.8.1940; 2.1.1943.	675.	2025.	6000.

1927 Issue

S331 1 Pound	VG	VF	UNC
1.12.1927-2.12.1944. Blue on yellow and orange. Portrait John Pitcairn at bottom. Like #S327. Printer: W&S.			
a. Signature titles: *ACCOUNTANT* and *CASHIER*. 1.12.1927-4.5.1939.	25.00	75.00	225.
b. Signature titles: *CHIEF ACCOUNTANT* and *CASHIER*. 6.8.1940-2.12.1944.	15.00	45.00	135.

1947 Issue

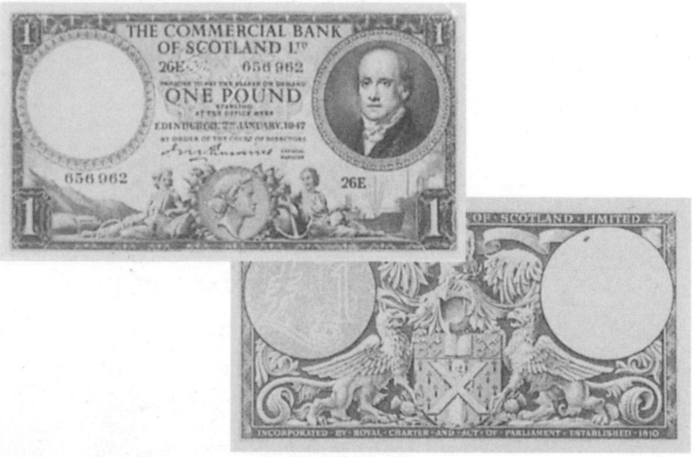

S332 1 Pound	VG	VF	UNC
2.1.1947-2.1.1953. Lilac. Lord Cockburn at right.	15.00	45.00	135.

S333 5 Pounds	VG	VF	UNC
2.1.1947-2.1.1958. Violet. Lord Cockburn at upper center. Back: Bank building at center, people at left and right on back.	40.00	120.	360.

S334 20 Pounds	VG	VF	UNC
2.1.1947-2.1.1958. Blue. Lord Cockburn at upper center. Back: Bank building at center, people at left and right on back. Like #S333.	100.	300.	900.

S335 100 Pounds	VG	VF	UNC
2.1.1947; 3.1.1951; 2.1.1953. Green. Lord Cockburn at upper center. Back: Bank building at center, people at left and right on back. Like #S333.	525.	1575.	4725.

1954 Issue

S336 1 Pound	VG	VF	UNC
2.1.1954-1.7.1958. Blue. Lord Cockburn at right. Like #S332.	15.00	45.00	135.

National Bank of Scotland

Previously listed #S541-S555 are now in Vol. II. National Bank of Scotland Limited

Previously listed #S556-S576 are now in Vol. II. National Commercial Bank of Scotland Limited

Previously listed #S591-S601 are now in Vol. II.

North of Scotland Banking Company

1836 Issue

S611 1 Pound	Good	Fine	XF
(ca.1836). Black. Kings College, Aberdeen, at upper center, seated allegorical woman at left, standing allegorical woman at right. Hand dated and numbered. Uniface. Printer: W. H. Lizars.	1500.	4500.	—

S612 5 Pounds	Good	Fine	XF
(ca.1836). Kings College, Aberdeen, at upper center, seated allegorical woman at left, standing allegorical woman at right. Hand dated and numbered. Uniface. Printer: W. H. Lizars.	—	—	—

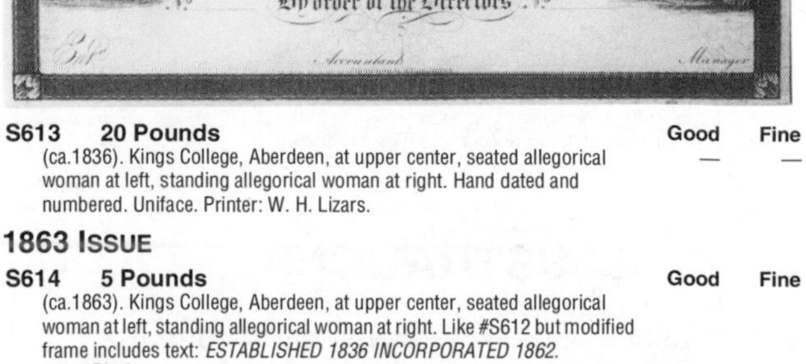

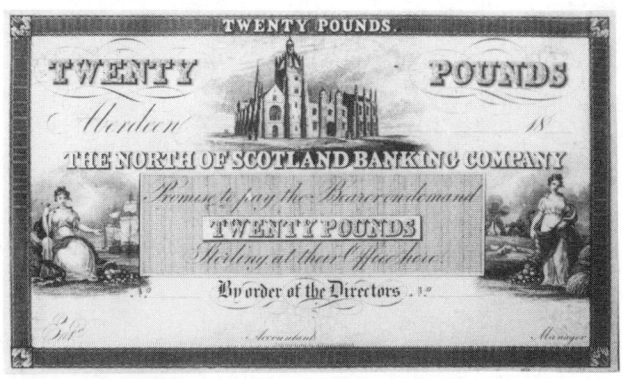

S613 20 Pounds	Good	Fine	XF
(ca.1836). Kings College, Aberdeen, at upper center, seated allegorical woman at left, standing allegorical woman at right. Hand dated and numbered. Uniface. Printer: W. H. Lizars.	—	—	—

1863 Issue

S614 5 Pounds	Good	Fine	XF
(ca.1863). Kings College, Aberdeen, at upper center, seated allegorical woman at left, standing allegorical woman at right. Like #S612 but modified frame includes text: *ESTABLISHED 1836 INCORPORATED 1862*.			
a. Black.	—	—	—
b. Black with red protector: *FIVE* across face.	—	—	—

1865 Issue

		Good	Fine	XF
S615	**1 Pound** (ca.1865). Black with red underprint. Kings College at upper center. Small arms at lower center. Back: Blue. Printer: W. & A.K. Johnston.	1500.	4500.	—
S616	**5 Pounds** (ca.1865). Black with red underprint. Kings College, Aberdeen, at upper center, seated allegorical woman at left, standing allegorical woman at right. Similar to #S614. Back: Blue. Printer: W. & A.K. Johnston.	—	—	—
S617	**20 Pounds** (ca.1865). Black with red underprint. Kings College, Aberdeen, at upper center, seated allegorical woman at left, standing allegorical woman at right. Similar to #S613 with added panel of text like #S616. Back: Blue. Printer: W. & A.K. Johnston.	—	—	—
S618	**100 Pounds** (ca.1865). Black with red underprint. Kings College, Aberdeen, at upper center, seated allegorical woman at left, standing allegorical woman at right. Similar to #S617. Back: Blue. Printer: W. & A.K. Johnston.	—	—	—

1871 Issue

		Good	Fine	XF
S619	**1 Pound** 29.9.1871. Black with green denomination panel across center. Kings College at upper center. Small arms at lower center. Similar to #S615. Printer: PBC.	1500.	4500.	—

North of Scotland Bank Ltd.

1882 Issue

#S620-S624 w/new title.

		Good	Fine	XF
S620	**1 Pound** (ca.1882); 1.10.1903; 1.8.1907. Black with green denomination panel across center. Kings College at upper center. Small arms at lower center. Similar to #S619. Printer: W. & A. K. Johnston.	750.	2250.	—
S621	**5 Pounds** (ca.1882). Black with red protector. Kings College, Aberdeen, at upper center, seated allegorical woman at left, standing allegorical woman at right. Small arms at lower center. Similar to #S616. Back: Blue. Printer: W. & A. K. Johnston.	2250.	675.	—
S622	**10 Pounds** (ca.1882). Black with red protector. Kings College, Aberdeen, at upper center, seated allegorical woman at left, standing allegorical woman at right. Small arms at lower center. Similar to #S616. Back: Blue. Printer: W. & A. K. Johnston.	—	—	—
S623	**20 Pounds** (ca.1882). Black with red protector. Kings College, Aberdeen, at upper center, seated allegorical woman at left, standing allegorical woman at right. Small arms at lower center. Similar to #S617. Back: Blue. Printer: W. & A. K. Johnston.	—	—	—
S624	**100 Pounds** (ca.1882). Black with red protector. Kings College, Aberdeen, at upper center, seated allegorical woman at left, standing allegorical woman at right. Small arms at lower center. Similar to #S618. Back: Blue. Printer: W. & A. K. Johnston.	—	—	—

North of Scotland & Town & County Bank Ltd.

1908 Provisional Issue

New bank name ovpt. on North of Scotland Bank Ltd. notes.

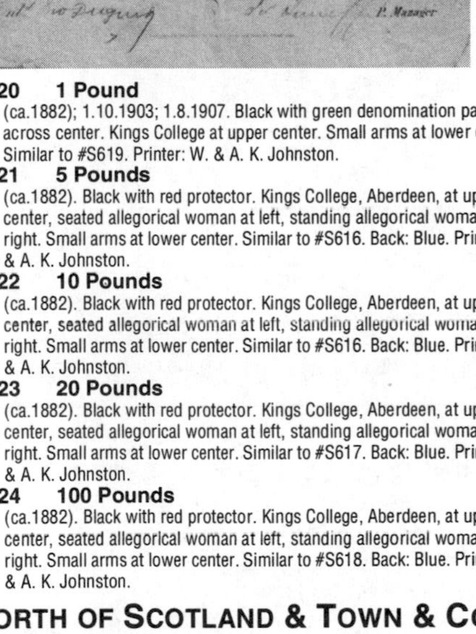

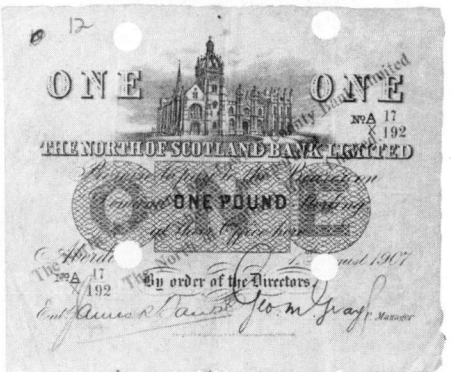

		Good	Fine	XF
S625	**1 Pound** ND (ca.1908-old date 1.8.1907). Overprint: New bank name on North of Scotland Bank Ltd. notes.	525.	1575.	4725.
S626	**5 Pounds** ND (ca.1908). Overprint: New bank name on North of Scotland Bank Ltd. notes. Rare.	—	—	—
S627	**20 Pounds** ND (ca.1908). Overprint: New bank name on North of Scotland Bank Ltd. notes. Rare.	—	—	—
S628	**100 Pounds** ND (ca.1908). Overprint: New bank name on North of Scotland Bank Ltd. notes. Rare.	—	—	—

1909; 1910 Issue

		Good	Fine	XF
S629	**1 Pound** 1.3.1910-1.3.1918. Blue and green on yellow underprint. Marischal College at top center.	150.	450.	1350.

		Good	Fine	XF
S630	**5 Pounds** 1909-18. Blue and green on yellow underprint. Marischal College at top center.	375.	1125.	3375.
S631	**20 Pounds** 1909-18. Purple and green on yellow underprint. Marischal College at top center.	900.	2700.	—

		Good	Fine	XF
S632	**100 Pounds** 1909-18. Brown and green on yellow underprint. Marischal College at top center. Rare.	—	—	—

North of Scotland Bank Limited

1923 Provisional Issue

		Good	Fine	XF
S633	**1 Pound**			
	ND (ca.1923). Blue and green on yellow underprint. Marischal College at top center. Overprint: On #S629.			
	a. Hand stamped overprint.	300.	900.	2700.
	b. Printed overprint.	225.	675.	2025.
S634	**5 Pounds**			
	ND (ca.1923). Blue and green on yellow underprint. Marischal College at top center. Overprint: Hand stamped on #S630.	450.	1350.	4150.
S635	**20 Pounds**			
	ND (ca.1923). Purple and green on yellow underprint. Marischal College at top center. Overprint: Hand stamped on #S631.	750.	2250.	—
S636	**100 Pounds**			
	ND (ca.1923). Brown and green on yellow underprint. Marischal College at top center. Overprint: Hand stamped on #S632. Rare.	—	—	—

1924-35 Issues

		VG	VF	UNC
S638	**1 Pound**			
	1924; 1926. Blue and green on yellow underprint. Reduced size.			
	a. Printed signature of *GENERAL MANAGER* and handsigned on behalf of the *ACCOUNTANT*. 1.3.1924; 1.3.1926.	100.	300.	900.
	b. As a. but printed signature of *ACCOUNTANT*. 1.3.1926.	175.	525.	1575.

		VG	VF	UNC
S639	**1 Pound**			
	1.3.1928; 1.3.1932; 1.3.1935. Blue and green on yellow underprint. *1* instead of £1 at left and right of building at top.	40.00	120.	360.
S639A	**5 Pounds**			
	2.3.1925. Blue and green on yellow underprint. Marischal College at top center. Like #S630 £5 at left and right.	1350.	4150.	—

		VG	VF	UNC
S640	**5 Pounds**			
	1928-34. Brown and green on yellow underprint. *5* rather than £5 at left and right. Reduced size.			
	a. 1.3.1928-1.3.1934. Hand signed on behalf of Accountant.	100.	300.	900.
	b. 1.3.1934. Stamped signature of Thomas Brown on behalf of Accountant.	115.	345.	1050.

		VG	VF	UNC
S641	**20 Pounds**			
	1928-1.3.1930; 1.3.1934. Brown, purple and olive-green on ochre underprint. Marischal College at top center. Like #S631.	175.	525.	1575.

		VG	VF	UNC
S642	**100 Pounds**			
	1928-34 (1.3.1930 confirmed). Brown on light blue, green and orange underprint. Marischal College at top center. Like #S632.	600.	1800.	5400.

#S643 *Deleted.*

1938 Issue

		VG	VF	UNC
S644	**1 Pound** 1.7.1938-1.7.1949. Blue and green on yellow underprint.	15.00	45.00	135.

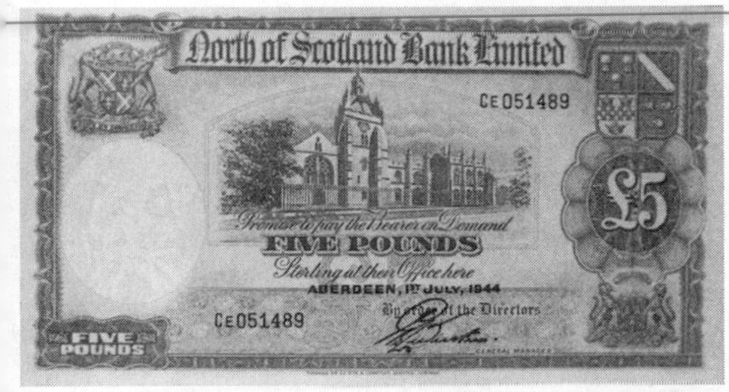

		VG	VF	UNC
S645	**5 Pounds** 1938-1.7.1949. Red.	40.00	120.	360.

		VG	VF	UNC
S646	**20 Pounds** 1938-1.7.1949. Green.	110.	330.	1000.
S647	**100 Pounds** 1938-49.	375.	1125.	3375.

Union Bank of Scotland

Edinburgh Branch

1843 Issue

		Good	Fine	XF
S751	**1 Pound** 1.7.1843. Equestrian statue at upper left and right, allegorical women at lower left and right. Names of four constituent banks in the four borders. Printer: W.H. Lizars (with or without imprint). Proof.	—	Unc	1500.
S752	**5 Pounds** 184x. Equestrian statue at upper left and right, allegorical women at lower left and right. Similar to #S751 but different allegorical figures. Names of four constituent banks in the four borders. Printer: W.H. Lizars (with or without imprint). Proof.	—	Unc	1500.
S753	**10 Pounds** (ca.1843). Three allegorical figures at upper center, equestrian statues at lower left and right. Names of four constituent banks in the four borders. Printer: W.H. Lizars (with or without imprint). Proof.	—	—	—
S754	**20 Pounds** 184x. Front view of two equestrian statues at upper left and right, allegorical figures at lower left and right. Names of four constituent banks in the four borders. Printer: W.H. Lizars (with or without imprint). Proof.	—	Unc	2350.
S755	**100 Pounds** 184x. Small Portrait of Queen Victoria with two allegorical women at center, front view of two equestrian statues at lower left and right. Names of four constituent banks in the four borders. Printer: W.H. Lizars (with or without imprint). Proof.	—	Unc	2700.

1844 Issue

		VG	VF	UNC
S756	**1 Pound** 184x (1844-48). Equestrian statue at upper left and right, allegorical women at lower left and right. Two more bank names added to border, for a total of six. Like #S751. Back: Printed revenue stamp on issued notes. Printer: W.H. Lizars (with or without imprint).		—	
S757	**5 Pounds** 1844-1860. Equestrian statue at upper left and right, allegorical women at lower left and right. Two more bank names added to border, for a total of six. Like #S752. Printer: W.H. Lizars (with or without imprint). Proof.	—	Unc	2000.
S758	**10 Pounds** 184x. Allegorical woman at upper center. Equestrian statue lower left and right. Two more bank names added to border, for a total of six. Printer: W.H. Lizars (with or without imprint). Proof.	—	Unc	2250.
S759	**20 Pounds** 184x. Front view of two equestrian statues at upper left and right, allegorical figures at lower left and right. Two more bank names added to border, for a total of six. Like #S754. Printer: W.H. Lizars (with or without imprint). Proof.	—	Unc	2250.
S760	**100 Pounds** 184x. 100 added at upper left and right. Two more bank names added to border, for a total of six. Printer: W.H. Lizars (with or without imprint). Proof.	—	Unc	2700.

1850 Issue

		Good	Fine	XF
S761	**1 Pound** (ca.1850). Equestrian statue at upper left and right, allegorical women at lower left and right. Additional bank name added to border for total of 7, otherwise similar to #S756. Printer: W.H. Lizars with imprint.	1350.	4100.	—

1857 Issue

		Good	Fine	XF
S762	**1 Pound** 1857. *PURSUANT TO ACT OF PARLIAMENT* added below upper border. *PERTH BANKING CO.* replaces *GLASGOW THISTLE BANK.* Printer: W.H. Lizars with imprint. Proof.	—	—	—

1859 Issue

		Good	Fine	XF
S763	**1 Pound** 1860-61. Seven banks in border. Back: Equestrian statue design in blue. Printer: W. & A.K. Johnston.			
	a. 1.5.1860. Date with 18xx filled in by hand.	1075.	3225.	—
	b. 1.1.1861. Date printed in full.	1075.	3225.	

		Good	Fine	XF
S764	**5 Pounds** 18xx (1861-62). Six banks in border. Printer: W. & A.K. Johnston. Proofs in various colors.	—	Unc	2000.

Glasgow Branch

1846-62 Issue

		Good	Fine	XF
S765	**1 Pound** 1846-1862. Equestrian statue of William of Orange at upper center, allegorical figures at lower left and right. Six constituent banks named within left border. Printer: Perkins, Bacon & Patch with imprint.			
	a. 1.4.1846-2.5.1853. Revenue stamp on back. Accot and Cashier.	—	—	—
	b. 1.4.1854. Without revenue stamp on back. Star hand stamped at upper left on face.	—	—	—
	c. 1.11.1855; 1.10.1856; 1.10.1857. Without revenue stamp on back. Star at upper left on face in printing plate.	—	—	—
	d. 1.11.1860. As c but p Accot and p Cashier.	1500.	4500.	—
	e. 1.1.1861; 2.8.1861; 1.2.1862; 1.8.1862. As d. but date and serial #s printed.	1500.	4500.	—

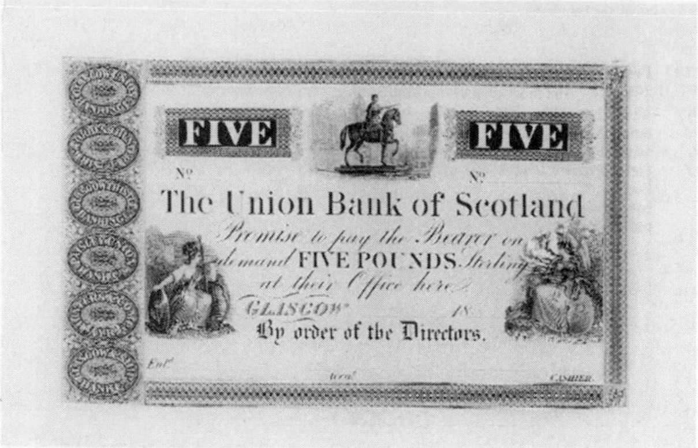

S766 5 Pounds	Good	Fine	XF
1848-62. Equestrian statue of William of Orange at upper center, allegorical figures at lower left and right. Six constituent banks named within left border. Printer: Perkins, Bacon & Patch with imprint.			
a. 1848-1855. Accot and Cashier. Proof.	—	Unc	900.
b. 1860-62. p Accot and p Cashier. Proof.	—	Unc	900.

S767 10 Pounds	Good	Fine	XF
1848-62. Equestrian statue of William of Orange at upper center, allegorical figures at lower left and right. Six constituent banks named within left border. Printer: Perkins, Bacon & Patch with imprint.			
a. 1848-50. Accot and Cashier. Proof.	—	Unc	900.
b. 1860-62. p Accot and p Cashier. Proof.	—	Unc	900.
s. Specimen.	—	—	—

S768 20 Pounds	Good	Fine	XF
1848-62. Equestrian statue of William of Orange at upper center, allegorical figures at lower left and right. Six constituent banks named within left border. Printer: Perkins, Bacon & Patch with imprint.			
a. 1848-50. Accot and Cashier. Proof.	—	Unc	900.
b. 1860-62. p Accot and p Cashier. Proof.	—	—	—

S769 100 Pounds	Good	Fine	XF
1848-62. Equestrian statue of William of Orange at upper center, allegorical figures at lower left and right. Six constituent banks named within left border. Printer: Perkins, Bacon & Patch with imprint.			
a. 1848-50. Accot and Cashier. Proof.	—	—	—
b. 1860-62. p Accot and p Cashier. Proof.	—	—	—

Payable at Glasgow or Edinburgh

1863 Issue

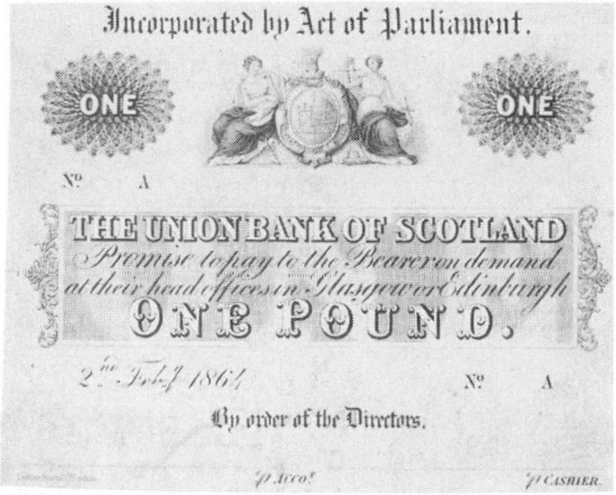

S770 1 Pound	Good	Fine	XF
(ca.1863-65) 2.2.1864. Blue. Two females flank bank arms, panels with value in top corners. *ONE* in large letters across legend panel in green. Added text: *INCORPORATED BY ACT OF PARLIAMENT.* Printer: PBC.			
a. Issued note.	600.	1800.	—
x. Contemporary forgery. 1.11.1865.	—	—	—

S771 5 Pounds	Good	Fine	XF
1.5.1863. Black. Added text: *INCORPORATED BY ACT OF PARLIAMENT.* Printer: PBC. Specimen.	—	—	—

1866 Issue

S772 5 Pounds	Good	Fine	XF
2.11.1866. Black. Two females flank bank arms, panels with value in top corner. *ONE* in large letters across legend panel in green. Added text: *INCORPORATED BY ACT OF PARLIAMENT.* Similar to #S770. Proof.	—	—	—

S773 100 Pounds	Good	Fine	XF
2.11.1866. Black. Two females flank bank arms, panels with value in top corners. *ONE* in large letters across legend panel in green. Added text: *INCORPORATED BY ACT OF PARLIAMENT.* Similar to #S770. Proof.	—	—	—

1867 Issue

S774 1 Pound	Good	Fine	XF
1867-1879.			
a. Issued note.	600.	1800.	—
s. Specimen.	—	Unc	400.

S775 5 Pounds	Good	Fine	XF
1867-79. Specimen.	—	Unc	600.

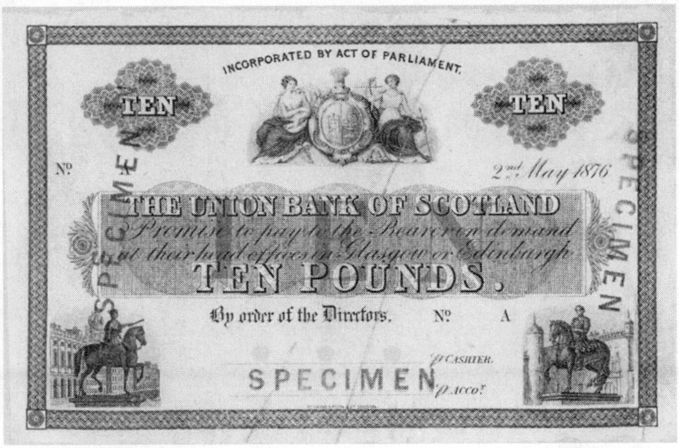

		Good	Fine	XF
S776	**10 Pounds** 1867-79. Specimen.	—	Unc	600.

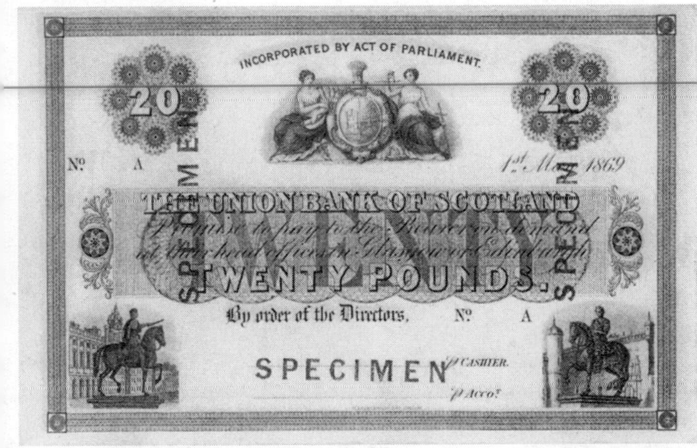

		Good	Fine	XF
S777	**20 Pounds** 2.4.1867; 1.5.1869; 1.5.1877. Specimen.	—	Unc	750.

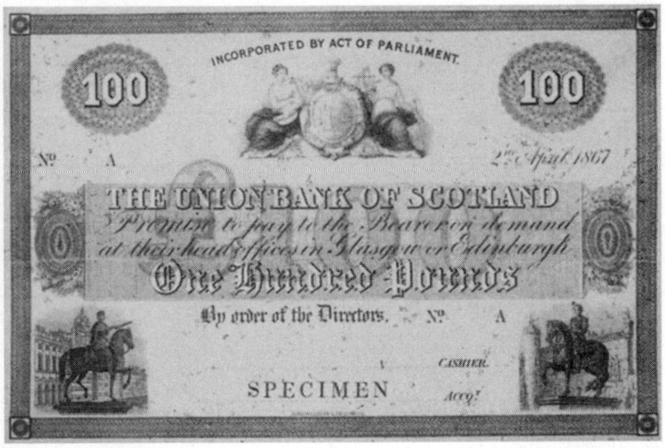

		Good	Fine	XF
S778	**100 Pounds** 1867-71. Specimen.	—	Unc	750.

1872 Issue

		Good	Fine	XF
S779	**100 Pounds** (ca.1872). Similar to #S778 but curved bank title at top, and other small differences in design. Printer: PBC.	—	—	—

NOTICE

Readers with unlisted dates, signature varieties, etc., are invited to submit photocopies or scans of their notes to:
Standard Catalog of World Paper Money,
700 East State St. Iola, WI 54990-0001,
E-Mail: george.cuhaj@fwmedia.com.

1880 Issue

#S780-S784 similar to previous issues but blue w/dark red protector. Minor plate changes.

		Good	Fine	XF
S780	**1 Pound** 2.1.1880. Blue with dark red protector. Two females flank bank arms at top center. Proof.	—	Unc	1250.
S781	**5 Pounds** 2.1.1880. Blue with dark red protector. Two females flank bank arms at top center. Proof.	—	—	—
S782	**10 Pounds** 2.1.1880. Blue with dark red protector. Two females flank bank arms at top center. Proof.	—	—	—
S783	**20 Pounds** 2.1.1880. Blue with dark red protector. Two females flank bank arms at top center. Proof.	—	—	—
S784	**100 Pounds** 2.1.1880. Blue with dark red protector. Two females flank bank arms at top center. Proof.	—	—	—

#S785-798 are held in reserve.

Union Bank of Scotland Ltd.

1882-93 Issue

		Good	Fine	XF
S799	**1 Pound** 15.4.1882-29.8.1902. Similar to previous issue but modified plates for altered bank name. Denomination wording across face in dark redoverprint. Handwritten signature with title: *ACCOUNTANT*. Back: Blue.			
	a. Issued note.	525.	1575.	—
	s. Specimen.	—	Unc	500.

		Good	Fine	XF
S800	**5 Pounds** (ca.1882-1905). Similar to previous issue but modified plates for altered bank name. Denomination wording across face in dark red overprint.			
	a. Issued note.	600.	1800.	—
	s. Specimen. 3.4.1893.	—	Unc	600.
S801	**10 Pounds** 1893. Similar to previous issue but modified plates for altered bank name. Denomination wording across face in dark red overprint. Specimen.	—	Unc	1000.
S802	**20 Pounds** 2.4.1891. Similar to previous issue but modified plates for altered bank name. Denomination wording across face in dark red overprint. Specimen.	—	Unc	1000.

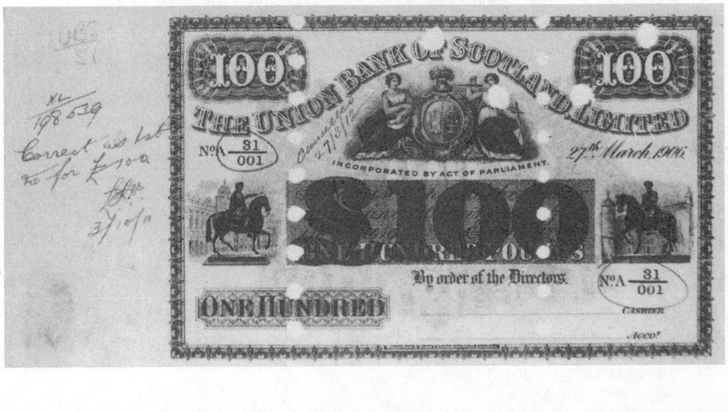

	Good	Fine	XF
S803 100 Pounds 2.4.1891; 7.4.1905. Similar to previous issue but modified plates for altered bank name. Denomination wording across face in dark red overprint. Specimen.	—	Unc	1000.

1903 Issue

	Good	Fine	XF
S804 1 Pound 10.3.1903; 3.5.1904. Like #S799 but printed signature of *ACCOUNTANT.*	450.	1350.	—

1905-06 Issue

	Good	Fine	XF
S805 1 Pound 6.4.1905-10.12.1920. Blue on red underprint. Equestrian statues at lower left and right, arms at top center flanked by two allegorical women at left and right. Value at center. Back: Blue. Printer: W&S.	125.	375.	1150.
S806 5 Pounds 25.2.1905-18.8.1920. Blue on red underprint. Equestrian statues at lower left and right, arms at top center flanked by two allegorical women at left and right. Value at center. Back: Blue. Printer: W&S.	450.	1350.	4250.
S807 10 Pounds 4.4.1905; 15.10.1913; 23.3.1917; 28.2.1918; 6.8.1920. Blue on red underprint. Equestrian statues at lower left and right, arms at top center flanked by two allegorical women at left and right. Value at center. Back: Blue. Printer: W&S.	—	—	—
S808 20 Pounds 31.3.1905-4.6.1920. Blue on red underprint. Equestrian statues at lower left and right, arms at top center flanked by two allegorical women at left and right. Value at center. Back: Blue. Printer: W&S.	—	—	—

	Good	Fine	XF
S809 100 Pounds 7.4.1905; 27.3.1906; 4.11.1913; 9.11.1915; 2.4.1919. Blue on red underprint. Equestrian statues at lower left and right, arms at top center flanked by two allegorical women at left and right. Value at center. Back: Blue. Printer: W&S. Rare.	—	—	—

1921-23 Issue

	VG	VF	UNC
S810 1 Pound 1.10.1921; 2.10.1923. Blue with orange and red sunburst underprint. Equestrian statues at lower left and right, arms at top center flanked by two allegorical women at left and right. Printed signature of *GENERAL MANAGER* and *CASHIER.* Printer: W&S.	200.	600.	1800.

	VG	VF	UNC
S811 5 Pounds 1921-49. Blue with orange and red sunburst underprint. Equestrian statues at lower left and right, arms at top center flanked by two allegorical women at left and right. Printer: W&S.			
a. Printed signature of *GENERAL MANAGER* and handsigned on behalf of the *CASHIER.* 5.4.1921; 4.5.1923.	225.	675.	2000.
b. As a. but with printed signature of the *CASHIER.* 4.8.1923; 5.4.1926; 15.1.1927.	200.	600.	1800.
c. Printed signature of *GENERAL MANAGER* and *CHIEF ACCOUNTANT.* 6.7.1928-18.5.1936	125.	375.	1125.
d. Printed signature of *GENERAL MANAGER* and *CASHIER.* 18.8.1937-3.5.1949.	75.00	225.	675.
S812 10 Pounds 3.8.1923-8.7.1935. Blue with orange and red sunburst underprint. Equestrian statues at lower left and right, arms at top center flanked by two allegorical women at left and right. Printer: W&S.			
a. Printed signature of *GENERAL MANAGER* and handsigned on behalf of the *CASHIER.* 3.8.1923.	600.	1800.	5400.
b. Printed signature of *GENERAL MANAGER* and *CHIEF ACCOUNTANT.* 4.7.1928; 8.12.1933; 8.7.1935.	450.	1350.	4150.
S813 20 Pounds 1923-47. Blue with orange and red sunburst underprint. Equestrian statues at lower left and right, arms at top center flanked by two allegorical women at left and right. Printer: W&S.			
a. Handsigned on behalf of the *GENERAL MANAGER* and the *CASHIER.* 2.8.1923; 3.7.1928; 2.8.1932; 5.9.1933; 2.10.1934; 14.8.1935.	525.	1575.	4650.
b. Handsigned on behalf of the *GENERAL MANAGER* and the *CHIEF ACCOUNTANT.* 31.5.1937; 30.3.1938; 1.6.1940; 2.1.1942.	300.	900.	2700.
c. Printed signature of the *GENERAL MANAGER* and the *CASHIER.* 30.4.1942; 1.2.1943; 10.7.1944; 2.12.1946; 1.9.1947.	225.	675.	2000.

S814 100 Pounds	VG	VF	UNC
1923-47. Blue with orange and red sunburst underprint. Equestrian statues at lower left and right, arms at top center flanked by two allegorical women at left and right. Printer: W&S.			
a. Handsigned on behalf of the *GENERAL MANAGER* and the *CASHIER*. 1.8.1923; 1.3.1939; 2.1.1942.	900.	2700.	5400.
b. Handsigned on behalf of the *GENERAL MANAGER* and the *CHIEF ACCOUNTANT*. 30.6.1928; 10.4.1931; 10.8.1931; 1.12.1933; 20.5.1936.	900.	2700.	5400.
c. Printed signature of the *GENERAL MANAGER* and the *CHIEF ACCOUNTANT*. 18.2.1947.	750.	2250.	6750.

1924 Issue

S815 1 Pound	VG	VF	UNC
1924-48. Blue, red, orange and yellow with orange and red sunburst underprint. Equestrian statues at lower left and right, arms at top center flanked by two allegorical women at left and right. Printer: W&S. Reduced size.			
a. Printed signature of *GENERAL MANAGER* and *CASHIER*. 2.6.1924; 4.1.1926; 3.10.1927.	45.00	135.	400.
b. Printed signature of *GENERAL MANAGER* and *CHIEF ACCOUNTANT*. 2.1.1929-31.3.1936.	30.00	90.00	270.
c. Printed signature of *GENERAL MANAGER* and *CASHIER*. 12.2.1937-1.6.1948.	25.00	75.00	225.

1949-50 Issue

S816 1 Pound	VG	VF	UNC
1949-54. Blue on red, orange and yellow underprint. Arms at left, sailboat at right. Back: Industrial and shipping scene. Printer: W&S.			
a. Signature of J. A. Morrison. 1.3.1949-1.9.1953.	25.00	75.00	225.
b. Signature of Sir W. Watson. 1.6.1954.	45.00	135.	400.

S817 5 Pounds	VG	VF	UNC
1950-54. Blue on red, orange and yellow underprint. Arms at left, sailboat at right. Back: Industrial and shipping scene. Printer: W&S.			
a. Signature of J. A. Morrison. 17.7.1950-1.10.1953.	30.00	90.00	275.
b. Signature of Sir W. Watson. 2.4.1954.	125.	375.	1125.

S818 20 Pounds	VG	VF	UNC
1.9.1950-1.5.1953. Blue on red, orange and yellow underprint. Arms at left, sailboat at right. Back: Industrial and shipping scene. Printer: W&S.	150.	450.	1350.

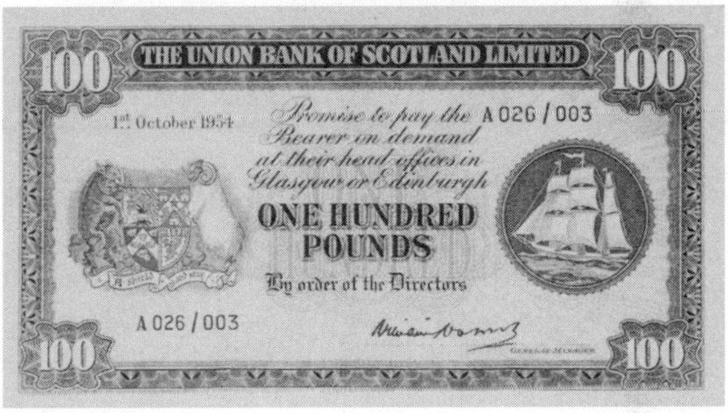

S819 100 Pounds	VG	VF	UNC
1950-54. Blue on red, orange and yellow underprint. Arms at left, sailboat at right. Back: Industrial and shipping scene. Printer: W&S.			
a. Signature of J. A. Morrison. 9.10.1950; 10.3.1952.	450.	1350.	4150.
b. Signature of Sir W. Watson. 1.10.1954.	600.	1800.	5400.

Serbia, a former inland Balkan kingdom (now a federated republic with Montenegro) has an area of 34,116 sq. mi. (88,361 sq. km.) Capital: Belgrade.

The Kingdom of Serbs, Croats, and Slovenes was formed in 1918; its name was changed to Yugoslavia in 1929. Various paramilitary bands resisted Nazi Germany's occupation and division of Yugoslavia from 1941 to 1945, but fought each other and ethnic opponents as much as the invaders. The military and political movement headed by Josip Tito (Partisans) took full control of Yugoslavia when German and Croatian separatist forces were defeated in 1945. Although Communist, Tito's government and his successors (he died in 1980) managed to steer their own path between the Warsaw Pact nations and the West for the next four and a half decades. In 1989, Slobodan Milosevic became president of the Serbian Republic and his ultranationalist calls for Serbian domination led to the violent breakup of Yugoslavia along ethnic lines. In 1991, Croatia, Slovenia, and Macedonia declared independence, followed by Bosnia in 1992. The remaining republics of Serbia and Montenegro declared a new Federal Republic of Yugoslavia in April 1992 and under Milosevic's leadership, Serbia led various military campaigns to unite ethnic Serbs in neighboring republics into a "Greater Serbia." These actions led to Yugoslavia being ousted from the UN in 1992, but Serbia continued its - ultimately unsuccessful - campaign until signing the Dayton Peace Accords in 1995. Milosevic kept tight control over Serbia and eventually became president of the FRY in 1997. In 1998, an ethnic Albanian insurgency in the formerly autonomous Serbian province of Kosovo provoked a Serbian counterinsurgency campaign that resulted in massacres and massive expulsions of ethnic Albanians living in Kosovo. The Milosevic government's rejection of a proposed international settlement led to NATO's bombing of Serbia in the spring of 1999 and to the eventual withdrawal of Serbian military and police forces from Kosovo in June 1999. UNSC Resolution 1244 in June 1999 authorized the stationing of a NATO-led force (KFOR) in Kosovo to provide a safe and secure environment for the region's ethnic communities, created a UN interim Administration Mission in Kosovo (UNMIK) to foster self-governing institutions, and reserved the issue of Kosovo's final status for an unspecified date in the future. In 2001, UNMIK promulgated a constitutional framework that allowed Kosovo to establish institutions of self-government and led to Kosovo's first parliamentary election. FRY elections in September 2000 led to the ouster of Milosevic and installed Vojislav Kostunica as president. A broad coalition of democratic reformist parties known as DOS (the Democratic Opposition of Serbia) was subsequently elected to parliament in December 2000 and took control of the government. DOS arrested Milosevic in 2001 and allowed for him to be tried in The Hague for crimes against humanity. (Milosevic died in March 2006 before the completion of his trial.) In 2001, the country's suspension from the UN was lifted. In 2003, the FRY became Serbia and Montenegro, a loose federation of the two republics with a federal level parliament. Widespread violence predominantly targeting ethnic Serbs in Kosovo in March 2004 caused the international community to open negotiations on the future status of Kosovo in January 2006. In May 2006, Montenegro invoked its right to secede from the federation and - following a successful referendum - it declared itself an independent nation on 3 June 2006. Two days later, Serbia declared that it was the successor state to the union of Serbia and Montenegro. A new Serbian constitution was approved in October 2006 and adopted the following month. After 15 months of inconclusive negotiations mediated by the UN and four months of further inconclusive negotiations mediated by the US, EU, and Russia, on 17 February 2008, the UNMIK-administered province of Kosovo declared itself independent of Serbia.

RULERS:

Milan, Obrenovich IV, as Prince, 1868-1882
Aleksander I, 1889-1902
Petar I, 1903-1918

MONETARY SYSTEM:

1 Dinar DINAR = 100 Para PARA
1 Dinara DINARA = 100 Para PARA
Gold Dinar = Dinar Zlatu = DINAR ZLATY
Silver Dinar = Dinar Srebru = DINAR SRHBRY

Military

Austrian Military Territorial Government

Belgrad

1917 Issue

		Good	Fine	XF
M1	**10 Dinara** 1917.	30.00	60.00	180.
M2	**100 Dinara** 1917.	30.00	100.	250.

Belgrad-Land

1917 Issue

		Good	Fine	XF
M3	**10 Dinara** 1917.	35.00	60.00	90.00
M4	**100 Dinara** 1917.	35.00	60.00	90.00

Cacak

1917 Issue

		Good	Fine	XF
M5	**10 Dinara** 1917.	35.00	60.00	90.00
M6	**100 Dinara** 1917.	35.00	60.00	90.00

Gornji Milanovac

1917 Issue

		Good	Fine	XF
M7	**10 Dinara** 1917.	125.	150.	200.
M8	**100 Dinara** 1917.	125.	150.	200.

Kragujevac

1917 Issue

		Good	Fine	XF
M9	**10 Dinara** 1917.	25.00	50.00	90.00
M9A	**50 Dinara** 1917.	1500.	3000.	6000.
M10	**100 Dinara** 1917.	25.00	50.00	90.00

Krusevac

1917 Issue

		Good	Fine	XF
M11	**10 Dinara** 1917.	35.00	60.00	90.00
M12	**100 Dinara** 1917.	35.00	60.00	90.00

Mitrovica

1917 Issue

		Good	Fine	XF
M13	**10 Dinara** 1917.	125.	150.	200.
M14	**100 Dinara** 1917.	125.	150.	200.

Sabac

1917 Issue

		Good	Fine	XF
M15	**10 Dinara** 1917.	40.00	70.00	100.
M16	**100 Dinara** 1917.	40.00	70.00	100.

Semendria

1917 Issue

		Good	Fine	XF
M17	**10 Dinara** 1917.	45.00	75.00	105.
M18	**100 Dinara** 1917.	45.00	75.00	105.

Smederevo

1917 Issue

		Good	Fine	XF
M19	**10 Dinara** 1917.	30.00	50.00	80.00
M20	**100 Dinara** 1917.	30.00	50.00	80.00

Uzice

1917 Issue

		Good	Fine	XF
M21	**10 Dinara** 1917.	45.00	75.00	120.
M22	**100 Dinara** 1917.	45.00	75.00	120.

Valjevo

1917 Issue

		Good	Fine	XF
M23	**10 Dinara** 1917.	60.00	80.00	120.
M24	**100 Dinara** 1917.	60.00	80.00	120.

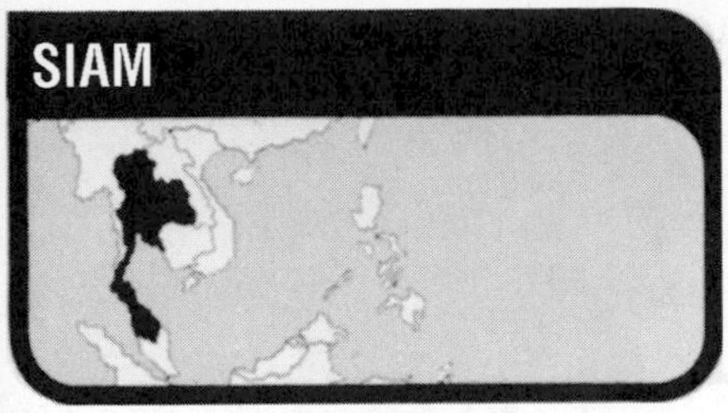

Siam (now the Kingdom of Thailand), a constitutional monarchy located in the center of mainland southeast Asia between Burma and Laos, has an area of 198,457 sq. mi. (514,000 sq. km). Capital: Bangkok.

The history of Siam, the only country in south and southeast Asia that was never colonized by a European power, dates from the 6th century AD when tribes of the Thai stock migrated into the area from the Asiatic continent, a process that accelerated with the Mongol invasion of China in the 13th century. After 400 years of sporadic warfare with the neighboring Burmese, King Taksin won the last battle in 1767. He founded a new capital, Dhonburi, on the west bank of Chao Praya River. King Rama I moved the capital to Bangkok in 1782.

The Thai were introduced to the Western world by the Portuguese, who were followed by the Dutch, British and French. Rama III of the present ruling dynasty negotiated a treaty of friendship and commerce with Britain in 1826, and in 1896 the independece of the kingdom was guaranteed by an Anglo-French accord.

RULERS:

Rama V (Phra Maha Chulalongkorn), 1868-1910
Rama VI (Vajiravudh), 1910-1925
Rama VII (Prajadhipok), 1925-1935
Rama VIII (Ananda Mahidol), 1935-1946
Rama IX (Bhumiphol Adulyadej), 1946-

MONETARY SYSTEM:

1 (Tical) Baht = 100 Satang

KINGDOM

BANQUE DE L'INDOCHINE

BANGKOK

DÉCRETS DES 21.1.1875 ET 20.2.1898

	Good	Fine	XF
S101 5 Ticals 19.12.1898. Blue-green. Oriental woman holding bamboo staff seated below France seated holding caduceus at left. Back: Chinese and Thai text. Specimen. Rare.	—	—	—
S102 20 Ticals 6.12.1898. Brown. Neptune reclining holding trident at lower left. Back: Chinese and Thai text. Specimen. Rare.	—	—	—
S103 80 Ticals 7.11.1898. Blue. Elephant at left and right, two reclining women with animals at lower center. Back: Chinese and Thai text. Specimen. Rare.	—	—	—
S104 100 Ticals 31.2.1898. Red. Vasco da Gama at left, sailing ships at lower center, Polynesian man with paddle by dragon boat at right. Back: Chinese and Thai text. Specimen. Rare.	—	—	—

CHARTERED BANK OF INDIA, AUSTRALIA AND CHINA

1898 ISSUE

	Good	Fine	XF
S111 1 Tical 1.9.1898. Black on purple underprint. Crowned supported royal arms at top center. Stamped date. Back: Green. Thai text. Printer: WWS.	2250.	6750.	—
S112 5 Ticals 1898; 1.9.1899. Blue, pink and red. Crowned supported royal arms at top center. Stamped date. Back: Thai text. Printer: WWS.	—	9500.	—
S113 10 Ticals (ca.1898). Brown, pink and blue. Crowned supported royal arms at top center. Stamped date. Back: Thai text. Printer: WWS. Rare.	—	—	—
S114 20 Ticals (ca.1898). Green, pink and orange. Crowned supported royal arms at top center. Stamped date. Back: Thai text. Printer: WWS. Rare.	—	—	—
S115 40 Ticals (ca.1898). Orange, pink and green. Crowned supported royal arms at top center. Stamped date. Back: Thai text. Printer: WWS. Rare.	—	—	—

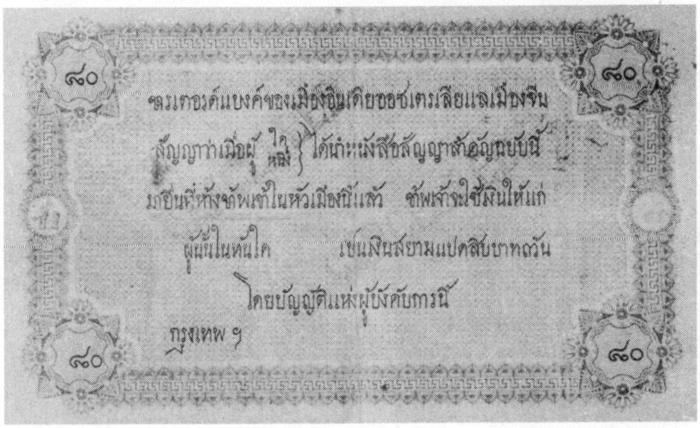

	Good	Fine	XF
S116 80 Ticals 1.5.1898. Gray, pink and brown. Crowned supported royal arms at top center. Stamped date. Back: Thai text. Printer: WWS. Rare.	—	—	—

S117 400 Ticals

(ca.1898). Red, pink and mauve. Crowned supported royal arms at top center. Stamped date. Back: Thai text. Printer: WWS. Rare.

	Good	Fine	XF
S117	—	—	—

HONGKONG AND SHANGHAI BANKING CORPORATION

1889-99 ISSUE

S121 1 Tical

16.5.1889; 1.7.1890; 1.8.1891; 1.8.1901. Orange on gray underprint. Crowned supported royal arms at top center. Hand dated. Back: Thai text. Printer: BFL.

	Good	Fine	XF
S121	3500.	12,500.	—

NOTE: The 1.7.1890 date is known with additional 4 Chinese character overprint of denomination in left and right margins.

S122 5 Ticals

15.11.1897. Green on pink underprint. Crowned supported royal arms at top center. Hand dated. Back: Red-orange. Thai text. Printer: BFL. Perforated: *CANCELLED.*

	Good	Fine	XF
r1. Remainder with 1 signature. Rare.	—	—	—
r2. Remainder with 1 signature with Chinese character overprint. Rare.	—	—	—

S123 10 Ticals

6.2.1899. Blue on light red underrprint. Crowned supported royal arms at top center. Hand dated. Back: Red-orange. Thai text. Printer: BFL. Remainder perforated: *CANCELLED.* Rare.

	Good	Fine	XF
S123	—	—	—

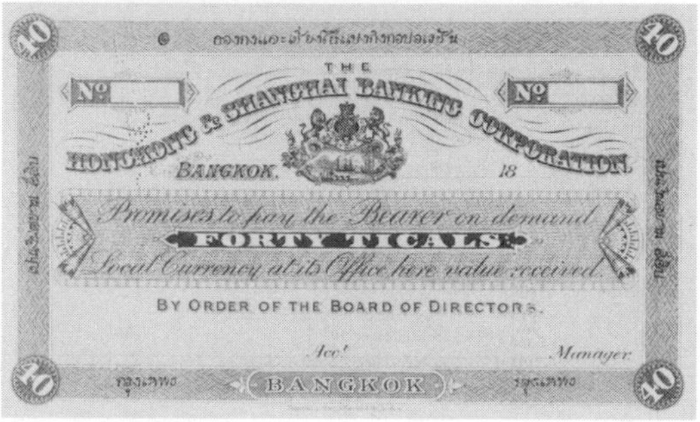

S124 40 Ticals

18xx. Brown on light blue underprint. Crowned supported royal arms at top center. Hand dated. Back: Red-orange. Thai text. Printer: BFL. Remainder perforated: *CANCELLED.* Rare.

	Good	Fine	XF
S124	—	—	—

S125 80 Ticals

18xx. Lilac on yellow-orange underprint. Crowned supported royal arms at top center. Hand dated. Back: Red-orange. Thai text. Printer: BFL. Remainder perforated: *CANCELLED.* Rare.

	Good	Fine	XF
S125	—	—	—

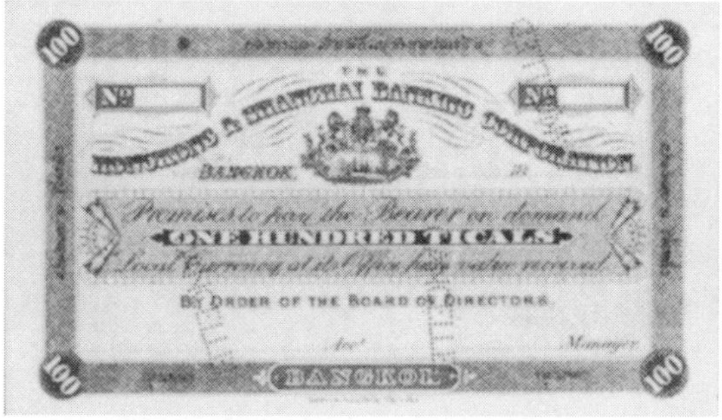

S126 100 Ticals

18xx. Pink-red on light blue underprint. Crowned supported royal arms at top center. Hand dated. Back: Red-orange. Thai text. Printer: BFL. Remainder perforated: *CANCELLED.*

	Good	Fine	XF
r1. Without Chinese character overprint. Rare.	—	—	—
r2. (ca.1891) with Chinese character overprint. Rare.	—	—	—

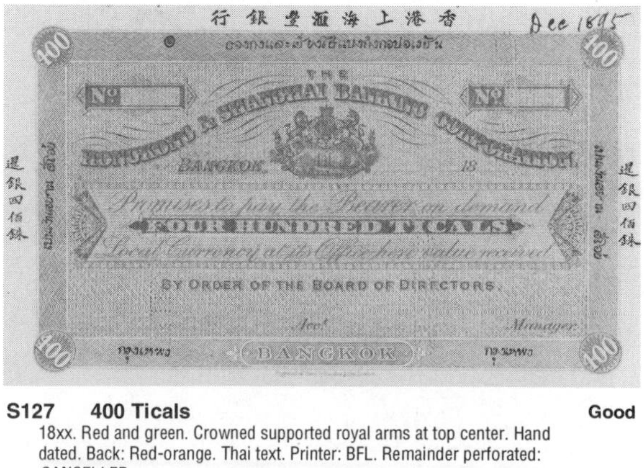

S127 400 Ticals

18xx. Red and green. Crowned supported royal arms at top center. Hand dated. Back: Red-orange. Thai text. Printer: BFL. Remainder perforated: *CANCELLED.*

	Good	Fine	XF
r1. Without Chinese character overprint. Rare.	—	—	—
r2. With Chinese character overprint (ca.1891). Rare.	—	—	—

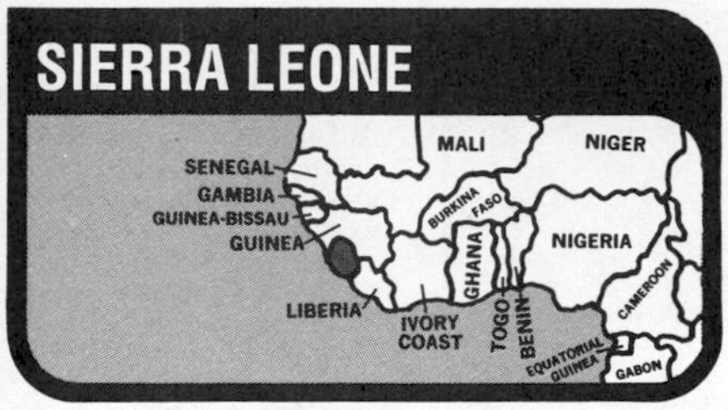

The Republic of Sierra Leone, a British Commonwealth nation located in western Africa between Guinea and Liberia, has an area of 71,740 sq. km. and a population of 6.29 million. Capital: Freetown. The economy is predominantly agricultural but mining contributes significantly to export revenues. Diamonds, iron ore, palm kernels, cocoa and coffee are exported.

Democracy is slowly being reestablished after the civil war from 1991 to 2002 that resulted in tens of thousands of deaths and the displacement of more than 2 million people (about one-third of the population). The military, which took over full responsibility for security following the departure of UN peacekeepers at the end of 2005, is increasingly developing as a guarantor of the country's stability. The armed forces remained on the sideline during the 2007 presidential election, but still look to the UN Integrated Office in Sierra Leone (UNIOSIL) - a civilian UN mission - to support efforts to consolidate peace. The new government's priorities include furthering development, creating jobs, and stamping out endemic corruption.

RULERS:

British to 1971

MONETARY SYSTEM:

1 Leone = 100 Cents
1 Pound = 20 Shillings

REPUBLIC

COMMERCIAL BANK OF SIERRA LEONE

1865 ISSUE

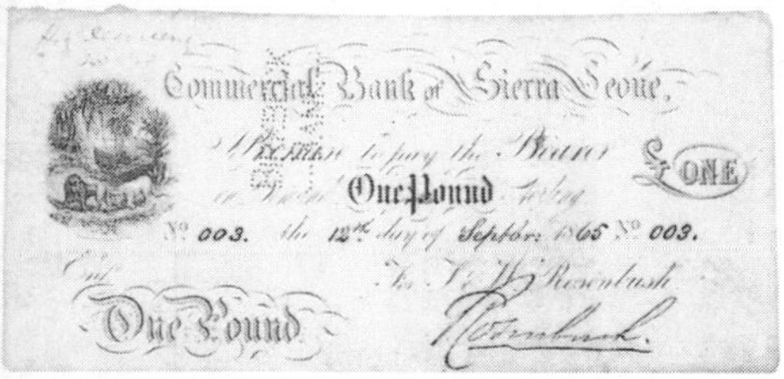

		Good	Fine	XF
S106	**1 Pound** 12.9.1865. Black. Animals, trees at upper left. Uniface.	3750.	10,000.	—

SIERRA LEONE

FREE TOWN

1800'S ISSUE

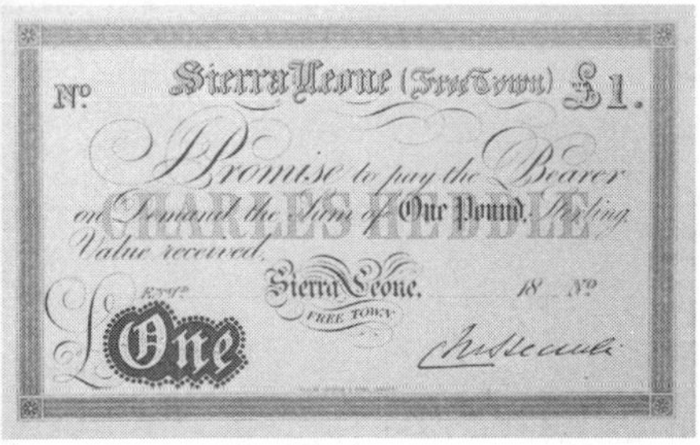

		Good	Fine	XF
S111	**1 Pound** 18xx. Black. *CHARLES HEDDLE* across center. Uniface.			
	a. White paper.	—	Unc	7500.
	b. Green paper.	—	Unc	7500.

The Republic of Slovenia is bounded in the north by Austria, northeast by Hungary, southeast by Croatia and to the west by Italy. It has an area of 20,251 sq. km. and a population of 2.01 million. Capital: Ljubljana. The economy is d on electricity, minerals, forestry, agriculture and fishing. Small industries are being developed during privatization.

The Slovene lands were part of the Austro-Hungarian Empire until the latter's dissolution at the end of World War I. In 1918, the Slovenes joined the Serbs and Croats in forming a new multinational state, which was named Yugoslavia in 1929. After World War II, Slovenia became a republic of the renewed Yugoslavia, which though Communist, distanced itself from Moscow's rule. Dissatisfied with the exercise of power by the majority Serbs, the Slovenes succeeded in establishing their independence in 1991 after a short 10-day war. Historical ties to Western Europe, a strong economy, and a stable democracy have assisted in Slovenia's transformation to a modern state. Slovenia acceded to both NATO and the EU in the spring of 2004.

MONETARY SYSTEM:

1 (Tolar) = 1 Yugoslavian Dinar
1 Tolar = 100 Stotinas

REPLACEMENT NOTES:

#11-19, ZA prefix.

GERMAN OCCUPATION - WWII

HRANILNICA LJUBLJANSKE POKRAJINE / SPARKASSE DER PROVINZ LAIBACH

SAVINGS BANK OF THE PROVINCE OF LJUBLIANA (LAIBACH)

1944 ISSUE

#R1-R9 issued during German occupation. Text in Slovene on one side, German on the other.

		VG	VF	UNC
R1	**1/2 Lira** 28.11.1944. Dark green. Child in national costume at left. Back: Child in national costume at left.	1.50	4.00	10.00
R2	**1 Lira** 28.11.1944.	1.00	3.50	10.00
R3	**2 Lire** 28.11.1944. Brown. Woman with child at left. Back: Woman with child at left.	2.00	6.00	15.00
R4	**5 Lire** 28.11.1944. Brown-red. Man in national costume at right. Series A. Back: Man in national costume at right.	2.00	6.00	15.00
R5	**10 Lire** 28.11.1944. Bluish purple. Woman wearing national costume hat at left. Series D. Back: Woman wearing national costume hat at left.	2.00	6.00	15.00
R6	**50 Lire** 14.9.1944. Red on gold underprint. Farmer's wife at left. Back: Farmer's wife at right.	5.00	20.00	55.00
R7	**100 Lire** 14.9.1944. Blue on gold underprint. Farmer with scythe at left. Back: Farmer with scythe at right.	10.00	30.00	80.00
R8	**500 Lire** 14.9.1944. Blue on green and gray underprint. Man in national costume at left. Back: Man in national costume at right.	12.00	40.00	100.
R9	**1000 Lire** 14.9.1944. Deep purple on pale blue underprint. Woman wearing national costume hat at left. Series A; B; D. Back: Woman wearing national costume hat at right.	15.00	60.00	140.

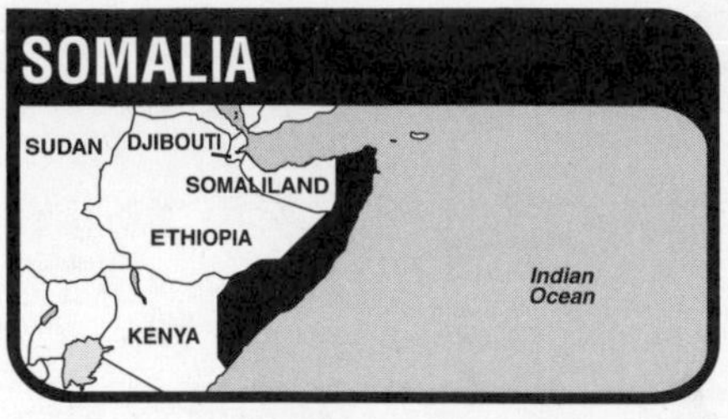

Somalia, the Somali Democratic Republic, comprising the former Italian Somaliland, is located on the coast of the eastern projection of the African continent commonly referred to as the *Horn*. It has an area of 178,201 sq. mi. (461,657 sq. km.) and a population of 11.53 million. Capitol Mogadishu. The economy is pastoral and agricultural. Livestock, bananas and hides are exported. The area of the British Somaliland Protectorate was known to the Egyptians at least 1,500 years B.C., and was occupied by the Arabs and Portuguese before British sea captains obtained trading and anchorage rights in 1827. The land of sandy clay and sporadic rainfall acquired a strategic importance with the opening of the Suez Canal in 1869. After negotiating treaties with the tribes, Britain declared the area a protectorate in 1888. Italy acquired Italian Somaliland in 1895 by purchase from the sultan of Zanzibar. Britain occupied Italian Somaliland in 1941 and administered it until April 1, 1950, when it was returned to Italy as a U.N. trusteeship. The British Somaliland protectorate became independent on June 26, 1960. Five days later it joined with Italian Somaliland to form the Somali Republic. The country was under a revolutionary military regime installed Oct. 21, 1969. After 11 years of civil war rebel forces fought their way into the capital. A. M. Muhammad became president in Aug. 1991 but interfactional fighting continued. A UN-sponsored truce was signed in March 1992 and a peace plan and pact was signed Jan. 15, 1993. The northern Somali National Movements (SNM) declared a secession of the northwestern Somaliland Republic on May 17, 1991 which is not recognized by the Somali Democratic Republic.

MONETARY SYSTEM:

1 Scellino = 1 Shilling = 100 Centesimi
1 Shilin = 1 Shilling = 100 Centi

REGIONAL

MOGADISHU NORTH FORCES

1991 ISSUE

R1	20 N Shilin = 20 N Shillings	VG	VF	UNC
	1991. Purple, red-brown, brown-orange and olive-green on multicolor underprint. Trader leading camel in underprint at left center, arms at top left center. Back: Picking cotton at center right. Watermark: Sayyid Mohammed Aabdullah Hassan.	.50	1.50	7.00

R2	50 N Shilin = 50 N Shillings	VG	VF	UNC
	1991. Brown, green and black on multicolor underprint. Man working loom, arms at top left center. Back: Young person leading a donkey with three children. Watermark: Sayyid Mohammed Aabdullah Hassan.	1.75	5.00	15.00

PUNTLAND REGION

2000 (1999) ISSUE

R10	1000 Shilin = 1000 Shillings	VG	VF	UNC
	1990 (2000). Purple and orange on multicolor underprint. Lithographed copy of #37a.	.50	1.00	5.00

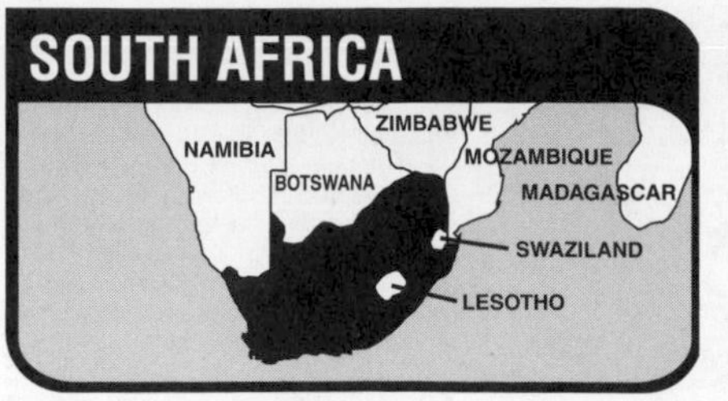

The Republic of South Africa, located at the southern tip of Africa, has an area, including the enclave of Walvis Bay, of 1,219,912 sq. km. and a population of 48.78 million. Capital: Administrative, Pretoria; Legislative, Cape Town; Judicial, Bloemfontein. Manufacturing, mining and agriculture are the principal industries. Exports include wool, diamonds, gold and metallic ores.

Dutch traders landed at the southern tip of modern day South Africa in 1652 and established a stopover point on the spice route between the Netherlands and the East, founding the city of Cape Town. After the British seized the Cape of Good Hope area in 1806, many of the Dutch settlers (the Boers) trekked north to found their own republics. The discovery of diamonds (1867) and gold (1886) spurred wealth and immigration and intensified the subjugation of the native inhabitants. The Boers resisted British encroachments but were defeated in the Boer War (1899-1902); however, the British and the Afrikaners, as the Boers became known, ruled together under the Union of South Africa. In 1948, the National Party was voted into power and instituted a policy of apartheid - the separate development of the races. The first multi-racial elections in 1994 brought an end to apartheid and ushered in black majority rule under the African National Congress (ANC). ANC infighting, which has grown in recent years, came to a head in September 2008 after President Thabo Mneki resigned. Kgalema Motlanthe, the party's General-Secretary, succeeded as interim president until general elections scheduled for 2009.

South African currency carries inscriptions in both Afrikaans and English.

RULERS:

British to 1961

MONETARY SYSTEM:

1 Shilling = 12 Pence
1 Pound = 20 Shillings to 1961
1 Rand = 100 Cents (= 10 Shillings), 1961-

The major areas comprising this section are covered individually according to the following outline:

CAPE OF GOOD HOPE

Many notes issued at Cape Town.

IMPERIAL BANKS:

London and South African Bank . . . . . #S106-S108
Oriental Bank Corporation . . . . . #S110-S115
Standard Bank of British South Africa . . . . . #S116-S117

COMMERCIAL BANKS:

Agricultural Bank of Queenstown . . . . . #S121
Bank of South Africa . . . . . #S131-S146
Beaufort Bank . . . . . #S151
British Kaffrarian Bank . . . . . #S156-S157
Cape Commercial Bank . . . . . #S161-S163
Cape of Good Hope Bank . . . . . #S171-S179
Colesburg Bank . . . . . #S180-S182
Commercial Bank of Port Elizabeth . . . . . #S191
Fort Beaufort & Victoria Bank . . . . . #S196-S198
Frontier Commercial & Agricultural Bank . . . . . #S201-S202
George Divisional Bank . . . . . #S211
Graaf Reinet Bank . . . . . #S216-S217
Kaffrarian Colonial Bank . . . . . #S221
Malmesbury Agricultural & Commercial Bank . . . . . #S226
Montagu Bank . . . . . #S231
Paarl Bank . . . . . #S236
Port Elizabeth Bank . . . . . #S241-S243
Queenstown Bank . . . . . #S251-S253
Somerset East Bank . . . . . #S256-S258
South African Bank . . . . . #S261-S263
South African Central Bank . . . . . #S271
Stellenbosch Bank . . . . . #S276
Stellenbosch District Bank . . . . . #S281
Swellendam Bank . . . . . #S286
Wellington Bank . . . . . #S291
Western Province Bank . . . . . #S296
Worcester Commercial Bank . . . . . #S301

CAPE UNIFORM BANKNOTES:

African Banking Corporation Limited . . . . . #S321-S325
Bank of Africa Limited . . . . . #S331-S335
National Bank of South Africa Limited . . . . . #S341-S345
Standard Bank of South Africa Limited . . . . . #S351-S355

GRIQUALAND

Government of New Griqualand . . . . . #S361

NATAL

Many notes issued at Durban.

IMPERIAL BANKS:

African Banking Corporation Limited . . . . . #S367-S370
Bank of Africa Limited . . . . . #S381-S382
National Bank of South Africa Limited . . . . . #S391-S395
Oriental Bank Corporation . . . . . #S397
Standard Bank of British South Africa Limited . . . . . #S401-S402
Standard Bank of South Africa Limited . . . . . #S406-S425

COMMERCIAL BANKS:

Colonial Bank of Natal . . . . . #S431-S433
Commercial and Agricultural Bank of Natal . . . . . #S436
Durban Bank . . . . . #S440-S444
London and Natal Bank . . . . . #S451-S454
Natal Bank Limited . . . . . #S462-S469

ORANGE RIVER COLONY/ORANGE FREE STATE

Many notes issued at Bloemfontein.

IMPERIAL BANKS:

African Banking Corporation Limited .... #S471-S474
Bank of Africa Limited .... #S482-S485
National Bank of South Africa Limited .... #S491-S495
Standard Bank of South Africa Limited .... #S498-S505

COMMERCIAL BANKS:

Bloemfontein Bank .... #S507-S513
Fauresmith Bank .... #S521-S527
Nationale Bank van den Oranje Vrystaat .... #S531
National Bank of the Orange River Colony Limited .... #S537-S540
Orange Free State Government .... #S541-S549

TRANSVAAL

Many notes issued at Pretoria and Johannesburg.

IMPERIAL BANKS:

African Banking Corporation Limited .... #S551-S556
Bank of Africa Limited .... #S562-S566
National Bank of South Africa Limited .... #S571-S578
Standard Bank of British South Africa Limited .... #S579-S582
Standard Bank of South Africa Limited .... #S583-S589

PRIVATE BANKS:

Cape of Good Hope Bank .... #S597
Cape Commercial Bank .... #S601-S602
Natal Bank Limited .... #S613-S615
Nederlandsche Bank & Crediet Vereeniging voor Zuid-Afrika .... #S621-S624
Nederlandsche Bank voor Zuid-Afrika/Netherlands Bank of South Africa ...... #S625-S636

BOER WAR ISSUES

BECHUANALAND

Siege of Mafeking .... #S651-S655

MATABELELAND

Marshall Hole, Bulawayo .... #S661-S670

NAMAQUALAND

Siege of O'okiep .... #S676-S678

ORANGE FREE STATE

Postal Money Orders .... #S681-S689

ORANGE RIVER COLONY

Siege of Koffyfontein .... #S691

TRANSVAAL (Z.A.R.)

Postal Money Orders .... #S701-S709

UPINGTON

Upington Border Scouts Issue .... #S711-S715

CAPE OF GOOD HOPE

Imperial Banks

LONDON AND SOUTH AFRICAN BANK

1874 ISSUE

		Good	Fine	XF
S106	**5 Pounds** 6.3.1874; 18.3.1874; 28.4.1874; 8.5.1874. Black on purple underprint. Queen Victoria at upper left, arms at center. Back: Black. Valve engraving. Printer: William Brown & Co.			
	a. Issued note.	300.	900.	2700.
	b. Hand stamped: *CANCELLED.*	—	—	—
S107	**10 Pounds** Reported not confirmed.	—	—	—

ORIENTAL BANK CORPORATION

KIMBERLEY - PORT ELIZABETH

1878 PROVISIONAL ISSUE

		Good	Fine	XF
S110	**5 Pounds** 1.7.1878. Black and blue. Arms at upper center. Overprint: Dual: *KIMBERLEY ISSUE PORT ELIZABETH* on face. Printer: PBC. Rare.	—	—	—

CAPE TOWN

1876 ISSUE

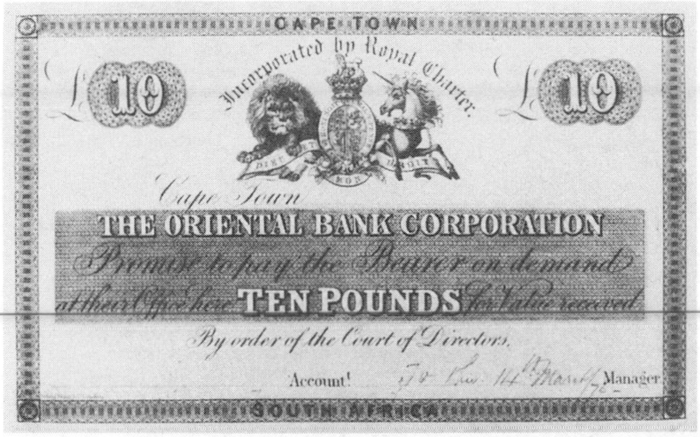

		Good	Fine	XF
S111	**10 Pounds** (ca.1876). Black. Crowned supported royal arms at upper center. Printer: PBC. Proof.	—	—	—

		Good	Fine	XF
S112	**20 Pounds** (ca.1876). Black. Crowned supported royal arms at upper center. Like #S111. Printer: PBC. Proof.	—	—	—

PORT ELIZABETH

1873 ISSUE

		Good	Fine	XF
S113	**5 Pounds** (ca.1873). Black. Crowned supported royal arms at upper center. Like #S112. Proof. Hand stamped: *Specimen.*	—	—	—
S114	**20 Pounds** (ca.1873). Black. Crowned supported royal arms at upper center. Like #S112. Proof. Hand stamped: *Specimen.*	—	—	—

1878 Issue

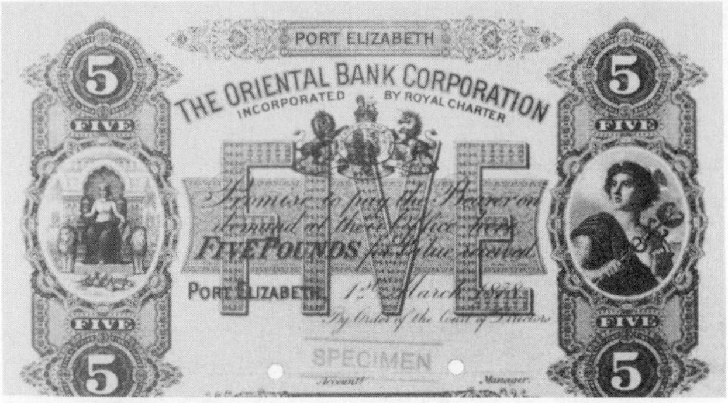

S115 5 Pounds — Good — Fine — XF

1.3.1878. Black on green underprint. Crowned supported royal arms at upper center, seated Britannia at left, Mercury at right. Printer: BWC. Proof. — — —

Standard Bank of British South Africa Limited

Burgersdorp

1864 Issue

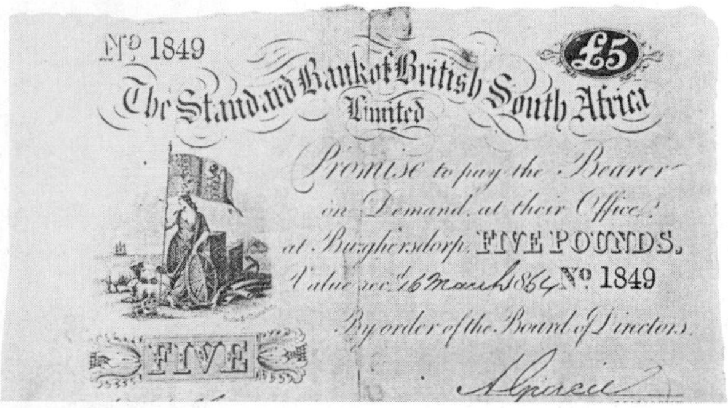

S116 5 Pounds — Good — Fine — XF

16.3.1864. Britannia standing with flag and shield at left. Rare. — — —

Middelburg

1864 Issue

S117 5 Pounds — Good — Fine — XF

4.2.1864. Black. Local print. — — —

Pietermaritzburg

1865 Issue

S119 5 Pounds — Good — Fine — XF

(ca.1865). Blue on light red underprint. Standing Britannia at left with flag by sheep, bales and anchor. Printer: W&S. Perforated: *CANCELLED*. Specimen. — — —

Cape of Good Hope

Commercial Banks

Agricultural Bank of Queenstown

1862 Issue

S121 4 Pounds — Good — Fine — XF

18xx. Rare. — — —

Bank of South Africa

1830's Issue

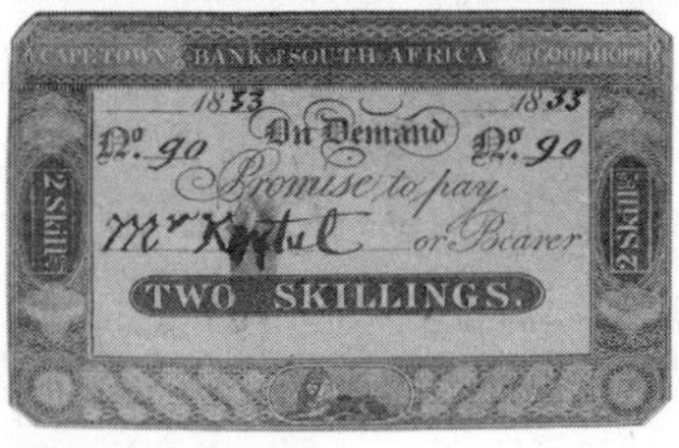

S131 2 Skillings — Good — Fine — XF

18xx. Black and blue. Lion at bottom center. Printer: William Congreve. Rare. — — —

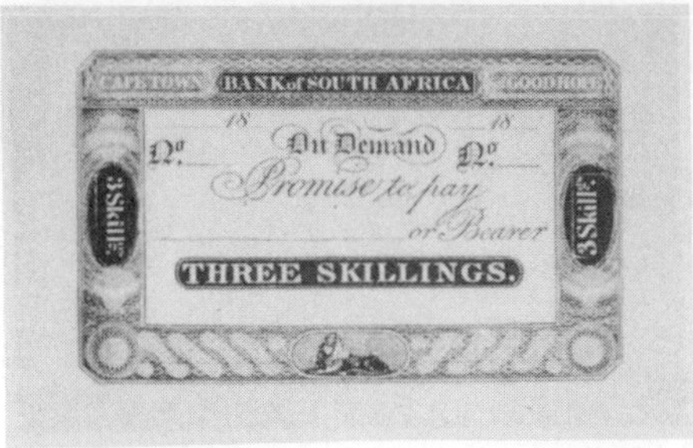

S132 3 Skillings — Good — Fine — XF

18xx. Black and green. Lion at bottom center. Printer: William Congreve. Rare. — — —

S133 4 Skillings

18xx. Black and red. Lion at bottom center. Printer: William Congreve. Rare. — — —

S134 1 Rix Dollar

18xx. Black and orange. Lion at bottom center. Printer: William Congreve. Rare. — — —

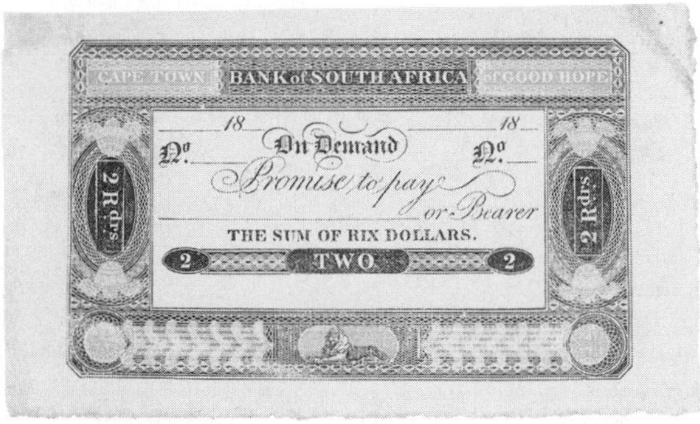

S135 2 Rix Dollars — Good — Fine — XF

18xx. Black and orange. Lion at bottom center. Printer: William Congreve. Rare. — — —

S136 3 Rix Dollars

18xx. Lion at bottom center. Printer: William Congreve. Rare. — — —

S145 400 Rix Dollars

18xx. Red and green. Lion at bottom center. Printer: William Congreve. Rare. — — —

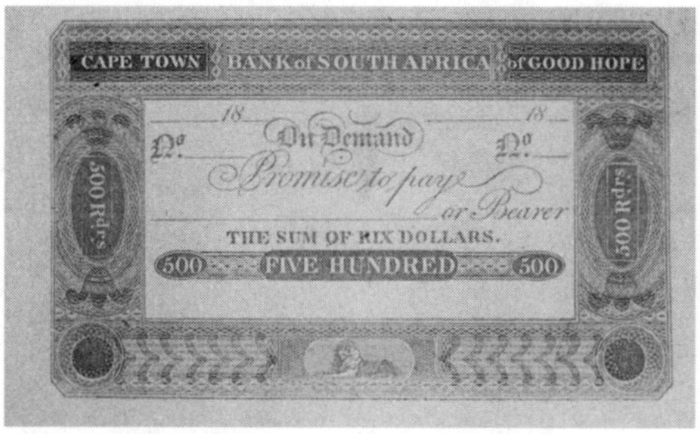

S146 500 Rix Dollars — Good — Fine — XF

18xx. Magenta and orange. Lion at bottom center. Printer: William Congreve. Rare. — — —

Beaufort Bank

1854 Issue

S151 5 Pounds — Good — Fine — XF

18xx. Rare. — — —

British Kaffrarian Bank

1800's Issue

S156 5 Pounds — Good — Fine — XF

18xx. Rare. — —

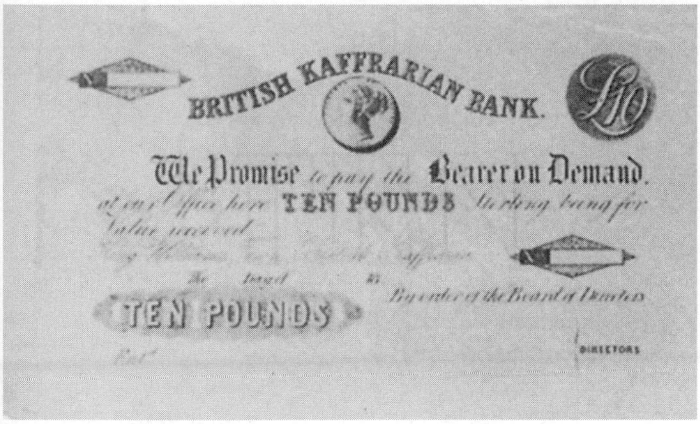

	Good	Fine	XF
S157 10 Pounds 18xx. Queen Victoria medallion at upper center.	300.	900.	2700.

Cape Commercial Bank

1854 Issue

	Good	Fine	XF
S161 5 Pounds 18xx. Rare.	—	—	—
S162 10 Pounds 18xx. Rare.	—	—	—

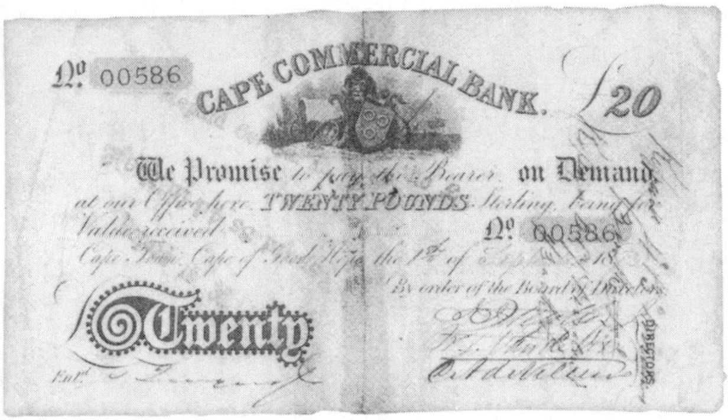

	Good	Fine	XF
S163 20 Pounds 1.9.1873. Black. Arms at upper center. Rare.	—	—	—

Cape of Good Hope Bank (First)

1828 Issue

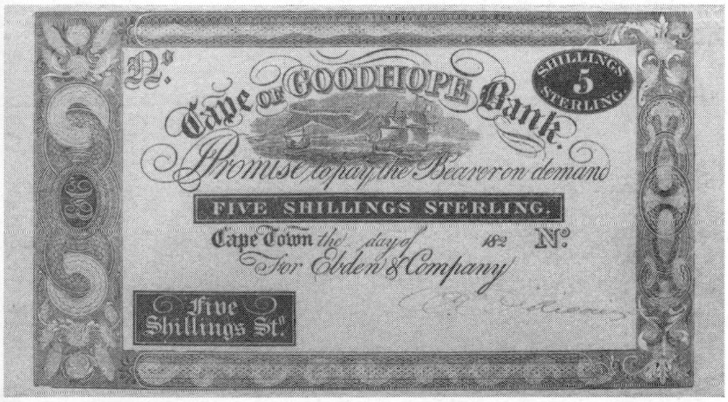

	Good	Fine	XF
S171 5 Shillings 3.6.1828. Black and blue. Sailing ships at upper center. Remainder.	—	Unc	250.

Cape of Good Hope Bank (Second)

Cape Town

1800s Issue

	Good	Fine	XF
S175 1 Pound 18xx. Specimen.	—	—	—

NOTE: For #S175 with overprint: *KLERKSDORP ISSUE* see #S591.

	Good	Fine	XF
S176 5 Pounds 18xx. Specimen.	—	—	—
S177 10 Pounds 18xx. Specimen.	—	—	—

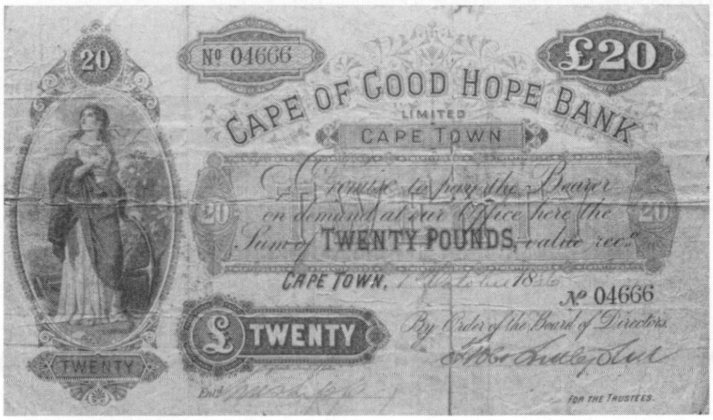

	Good	Fine	XF
S178 20 Pounds 1.10.1886. Black on blue and brown underprint. Woman standing at left. Printer: BWC.			
a. Issued note. Rare.	—	—	—
s. Specimen.	—	—	—

Johannesburg

Provisional Issue

	Good	Fine	XF
S179 5 Pounds 2.12.1889. Like #S176 but *CAPE TOWN* crossed out, *JOHANNESBURG* beneath lower name. *JOHANNESBURG ISSUE* at upper right in red. Rare.	—	—	—

Colesburg Bank

1861-62 Issue

	Good	Fine	XF
S180 5 Pounds 24.10.1861. Black. Arms at upper center. Printer: Saul Solomon & Co. Rare.	—	—	—
S181 4 Pounds 30.1.1862. Black. Horse, hay and cow at center. Printer: William Brown & Co. Rare.	—	—	—
S182 5 Pounds 25.1.1862. Black. Horse, hay and cow at center. Similar to #S181. Rare.	—	—	—

Commercial Bank of Port Elizabeth

1854-60 Issue

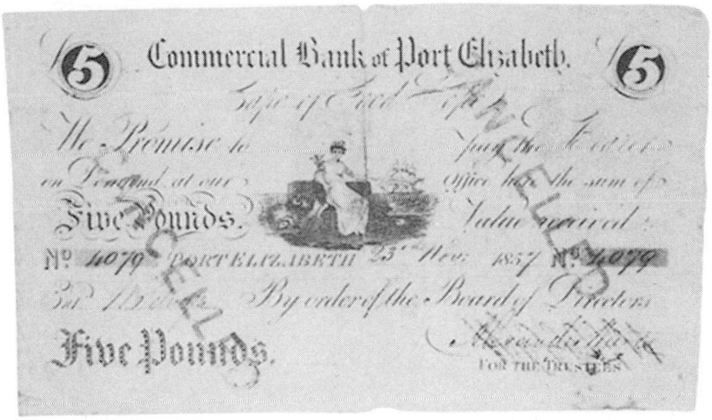

	Good	Fine	XF
S191 5 Pounds 21.12.1854; 23.11.1857; 10.11.1860. Black. Seated woman with bales and sailing ship in background at center. Printer: Rowe, Rentigh & Co., London. Rare.	—	—	—

Fort Beaufort & Victoria Bank

1860's Issue

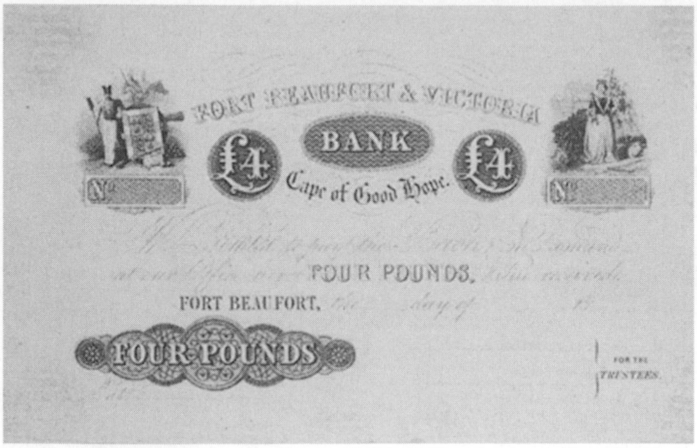

		Good	Fine	XF
S196	**4 Pounds** 18xx. Soldier by large shield at upper left, crowned woman at upper right. Rare.	—	—	—
S197	**5 Pounds** 18xx. Rare.	—	—	—
S198	**10 Pounds** 18xx. Value flanking central bank name. Rare.	—	—	—

Frontier Commercial & Agricultural Bank

1863 Issue

		Good	Fine	XF
S201	**5 Pounds** 18xx. Rare.	—	—	—

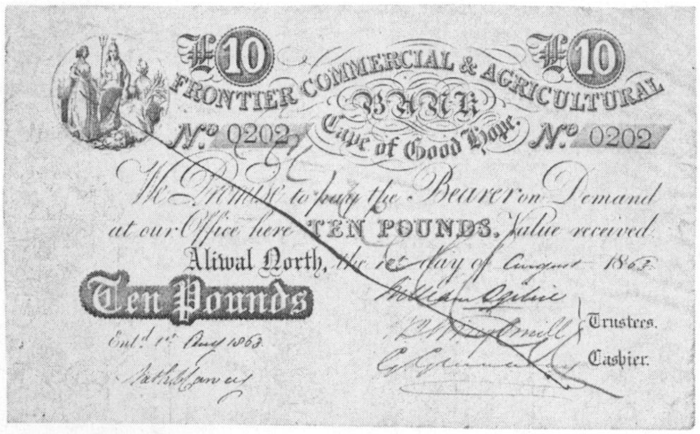

		Good	Fine	XF
S202	**10 Pounds** 1.8.1863. Black. Seated Britannia with two allegorical women at upper left. Printer: William Brown & Co.	450.	1450.	—

George Divisional Bank

1862 Issue

		Good	Fine	XF
S211	**5 Pounds** 1862. Woman's portrait at left and right. Rare.	—	—	—

Graaf Reinet Bank

1860's Issue

		Good	Fine	XF
S216	**5 Pounds** 18xx. Rare.	—	—	—
S217	**10 Pounds** 18xx. Black. Printer: Royston & Brown. Rare.	—	—	—

Kaffrarian Colonial Bank

1800's Issue

		Good	Fine	XF
S221	**5 Pounds** 18xx. Black. Allegorical woman with shield at center. Printer: William Brown & Co. Rare.	—	—	—

Malmesbury Agricultural & Commercial Bank

1860's Issue

		Good	Fine	XF
S226	**5 Pounds** 18xx. Rare.	—	—	—

Montagu Bank

1860's Issue

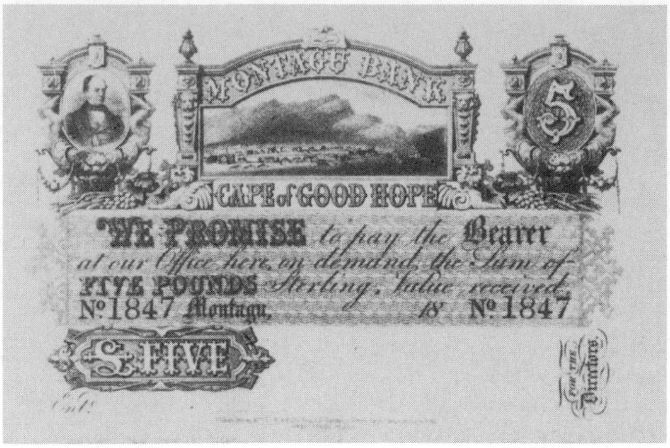

		Good	Fine	XF
S231	**5 Pounds** 18xx. Black on green underprint. Portrait of man at upper left, town and mountains at upper center. Printer: William Brown & Co. Remainder.	—	Unc	100.

Paarl Bank

1873-74 Issue

		Good	Fine	XF
S236	**5 Pounds** 4.8.1873; 27.8.1874. Workers and cherubs at sides, seated Britannia at upper center. Printer: Nissen, Parker & Arnold. Rare.	—	—	—

Port Elizabeth Bank

1850's-70's Issue

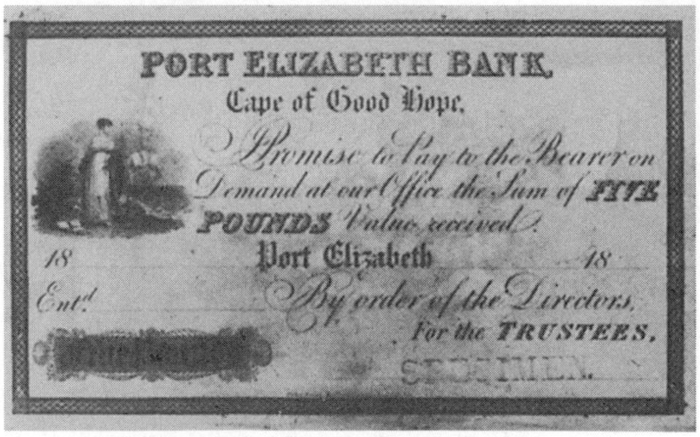

		Good	Fine	XF
S241	**5 Pounds** 18xx; 1872. Black. Woman standing at left.			
	a. 1.1.1872. Rare.	—	—	—
	s. Hand stamped: *SPECIMEN.* 18xx.	—	Unc	1000.

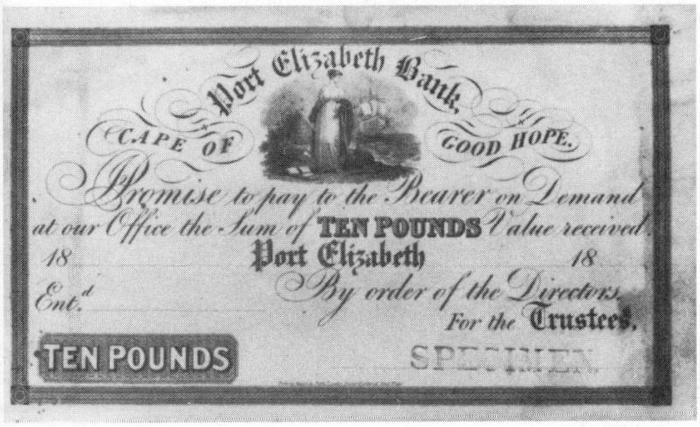

	Good	Fine	XF
S242 10 Pounds			
18xx; 1871. Black. Standing female at upper center.			
a. 19.10.1871. Rare.	—	—	—
s. Hand stamped: *SPECIMEN*. 18xx.	—	Unc	1000.
S243 20 Pounds			
18xx; 1857. Black. Standing Perote at center.			
a. 1857. Rare.	—	—	—
s. Hand stamped: *SPECIMEN*. 18xx.	—	Unc	1000.

Queenstown Bank

1860's Issue

	Good	Fine	XF
S251 4 Pounds			
25.4.1870. Black. Two horseback troopers at center, sheep, cattle and farmers in background. Similar to #S253. Printer: WB&Co. Rare.	—	—	—

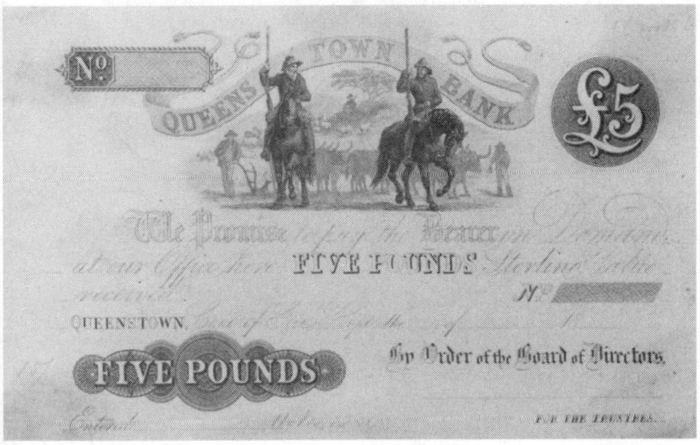

	Good	Fine	XF
S252 5 Pounds			
18xx. Black. Two horseback troopers at center, sheep, cattle and farmers in background. Similar to #S253. Printer: WB&Co. Proof.	—	—	—

	Good	Fine	XF
S253 10 Pounds			
18xx. (ca.1859). Black. Two horseback troopers at center, sheep, cattle and farmers in background. Printer: WB&Co.			
p1. Proof.	—	Unc	750.
p2. Proof. Hand stamped: *CANCELLED*.	—	Unc	750.

Somerset East Bank

1860's Issue

	Good	Fine	XF
S256 4 Pounds			
18xx. Rare.	—	—	—

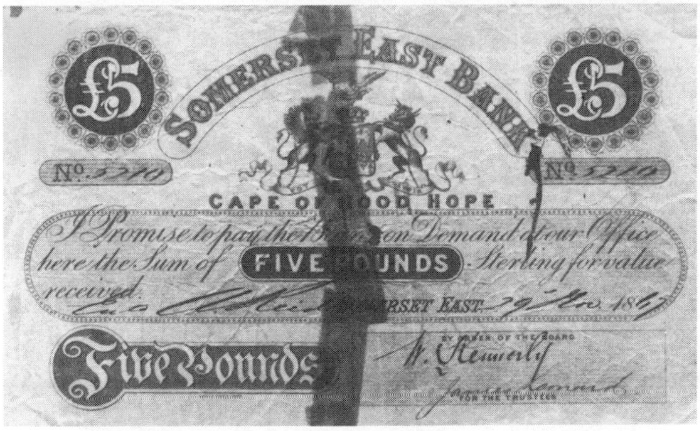

	Good	Fine	XF
S257 5 Pounds			
25.11.1867; 29.11.1867. Black. Crowned supported royal arms at upper center. Printer: Nissen and Parker. Rare.	—	—	—

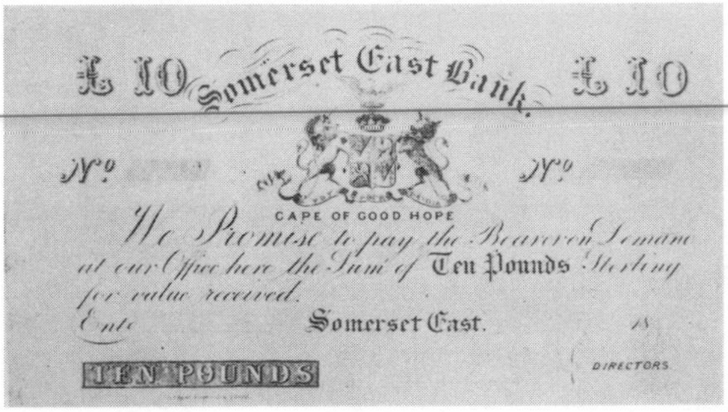

	Good	Fine	XF
S258 10 Pounds			
18xx. Black. Arms at center. Printer: J. A. Crew Engr. Rare.	—	—	—

South African Bank

1881 Issue

	Good	Fine	XF
S261 5 Pounds			
(ca.1881). Rare.	—	—	—

	Good	Fine	XF
S262 10 Pounds			
9.2.1881. Arms at upper center. Printer: William Brown & Co. Rare.	—	—	—
S263 20 Pounds			
7.2.1881. Arms at upper center. Similar to #S262. Rare.	—	—	—

South African Central Bank

1850's Issue

	Good	Fine	XF
S271 5 Pounds			
Black. Printer: Roberts, Cape Town. Rare.	—	—	—

Stellenbosch Bank

1860's Issue

	Good	Fine	XF
S276 5 Pounds			
Allegorical figure at lower left and right, arms at center. Rare.	—	—	—

Stellenbosch District Bank

1860's Issue

	Good	Fine	XF
S281 5 Pounds			
18xx. Black. Allegorical figure at lower left and right, arms at center. Similar to #S276. Printer: Saul Solomon & Co. Rare.	—	—	—

SWELLENDAM BANK

1860's ISSUE

	Good	Fine	XF
S286 5 Pounds			
18xx. Black. Bank arms at upper center. Printer: C. J. Roberts S.C. Rare.	—	—	—

NOTE: #S286 is not to be confused with the commonly seen Barry and Nephews 5 Pound note which also mentions Swellendam as its place of issue. The Barry and Nephews note is a private issue, easily encountered as an uncirculated, unissued remainder at about $50.00 retail.

WELLINGTON BANK

1888 ISSUE

	Good	Fine	XF
S291 5 Pounds			
21.5.1888; 11.9.1888. Black. Anchor at left, Wellington medallion at upper center, rake and shovel at right. Printer: Saul Solomon & Co. Rare.	—	—	—

WESTERN PROVINCE BANK

1880's ISSUE

	Good	Fine	XF
S296 5 Pounds			
188x. Black and green. Building at left, mountain scene at center. Printer: Barry Arnold, Cape Town; William Brown & Co. Rare.	—	—	—

WORCESTER COMMERCIAL BANK

1860's ISSUE

	Good	Fine	XF
S301 5 Pounds			
18xx. Rare.	—	—	—

CAPE UNIFORM BANKNOTES

From 1891 to 1920 a group of four banks used banknotes uniform in design except for the name of the bank. These notes are known as Cape Uniform Banknotes. The four banks are: African Banking Corporation, Bank of Africa Limited, National Bank of South Africa Limited, and Standard Bank of South Africa Limited.

#S321-S355 arms at ctr. An example of the form all banks used is shown:

<AFrame <BRect 0.0 0.0 3.5 1.65><TextLine <TLOrigin 1.5 0.75><TLAlignment Center><String "001.65'>

AFRICAN BANKING CORPORATION LIMITED

1892-1917 UNIFORM ISSUE

	Good	Fine	XF
S321 10 Shillings			
1917-1920. Black and red on yellow underprint. Rare.	—	—	—

	Good	Fine	XF
S322 1 Pound			
1892-1920. Black with orange text on yellow underprint.			
a. Issued note. Rare.	—	—	—
b. Perforated: *CANCELLED*. 27.2.1918.	300.	900.	—
S323 5 Pounds			
1892-1920. Green and red on tan underprint. Back: Green. Rare.	—	—	—
S324 10 Pounds			
1892-1900. Red and green on tan underprint. Back: Red. Rare.	—	—	—
S325 20 Pounds			
1892-1920. Blue and red on tan underprint. Back: Blue. Rare.	—	—	—

BANK OF AFRICA LIMITED

1892-1917 UNIFORM ISSUE

	Good	Fine	XF
S331 10 Shillings			
1917-1920. Rare.	—	—	—
S332 1 Pound			
1892-1920. Rare.	—	—	—

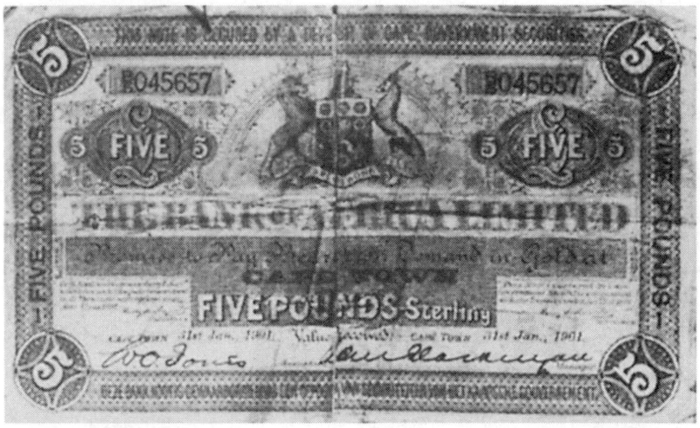

	Good	Fine	XF
S333 5 Pounds			
1892-1920. Green with red text on pink underprint. Rare.	—	—	—
S334 10 Pounds			
1892-1920. Rare.	—	—	—
S335 20 Pounds			
1892-1920. Rare.	—	—	—

NATIONAL BANK OF SOUTH AFRICA LIMITED

1892-1917 UNIFORM ISSUE

	Good	Fine	XF
S341 10 Shillings			
1917-1920. Brown with blue text on green underprint. Back: Brown.			
a. 18.8.1919; 19.3.1920. Rare.	—	—	—
b. Perforated: *CANCELLED*.	—	—	—

S342 1 Pound | Good | Fine | XF

1892-1920. Black, with red and blue text on yellow underprint. Back: Dark gray.

	Good	Fine	XF
a. 5.4.1918. Rare.	—	—	—
b. Perforated: *CANCELLED*. 27.2.1918.	360.	1100.	—

S343 5 Pounds

1892-1920. Green with red text on pink underprint. Back: Green.

	Good	Fine	XF
a. 29.3.1917. Rare.	—	—	—
b. Perforated: *CANCELLED*.	400.	1200.	—

S344 10 Pounds

1892-1920. Red and green on tan underprint. Back: Red.

	Good	Fine	XF
a. Issued note. Rare.	—	—	—
b. Perforated: *CANCELLED*.	500.	1500.	—

S345 20 Pounds

	Good	Fine	XF
1892-1920. Rare.	—	—	—

Standard Bank of South Africa Limited

1892-1917 Uniform Issue

S351 10 Shillings

	Good	Fine	XF
1917-1920. Rare.	—	—	—

S352 1 Pound

	Good	Fine	XF
16.11.1891-1920. Blue and yellow. Rare.	—	—	—

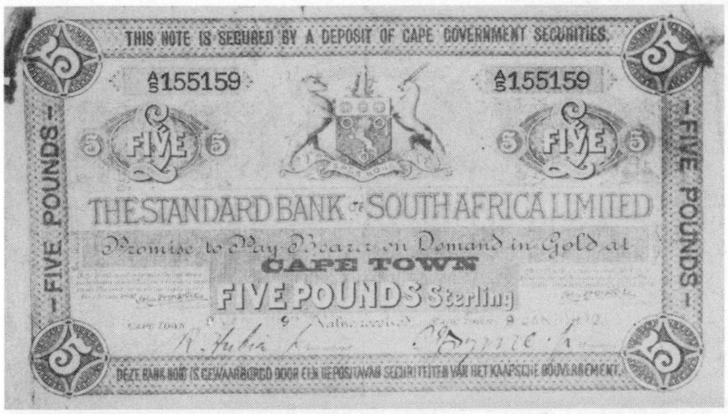

S353 5 Pounds

	Good	Fine	XF
1892-1920. Rare.	—	—	—

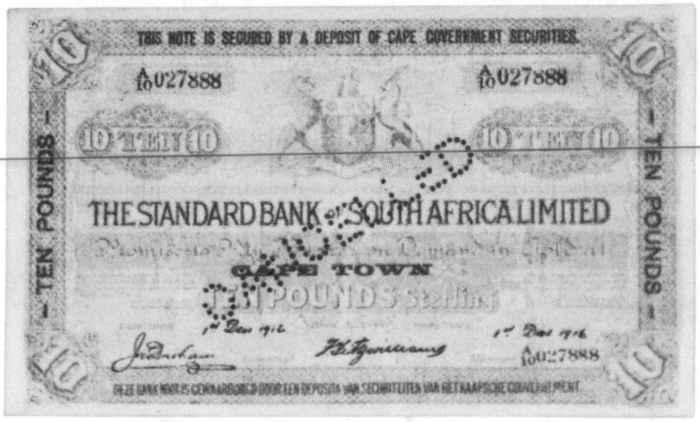

S354 10 Pounds

1892-1920. Red and green on tan underprint. Back: Red.

	Good	Fine	XF
a. Issued note. Rare.	—	—	—
b. Perforated: *CANCELLED*.	450.	1350.	—

S355 20 Pounds

	Good	Fine	XF
1892-1920. Blue and red on tan underprint. Rare.	—	—	—

Griqualand

Government of New Griqualand

1868 Issue

S361 1 Pond (= 1 Pound)

1.1.1868. Black on blue underprint. Arms at upper center. Uniface. Printer: Saul Solomon & Co.

	Good	Fine	XF
r1. Remainder. Rare.	—	—	—
r2. Remainder, cut cancelled.	800.	2400.	—

A WORD ON DATE RANGES

Often date ranges or specific dates are listed. These have been observed or reported by our contributors. If a note is outside the published range, it only means that it is a newly reported date, and not necessarily worthy of a premium value.

NATAL

Imperial Banks

Many notes issued at Durban.

AFRICAN BANKING CORPORATION LIMITED

1890'S ISSUE

#S367-S370 Durban issue.

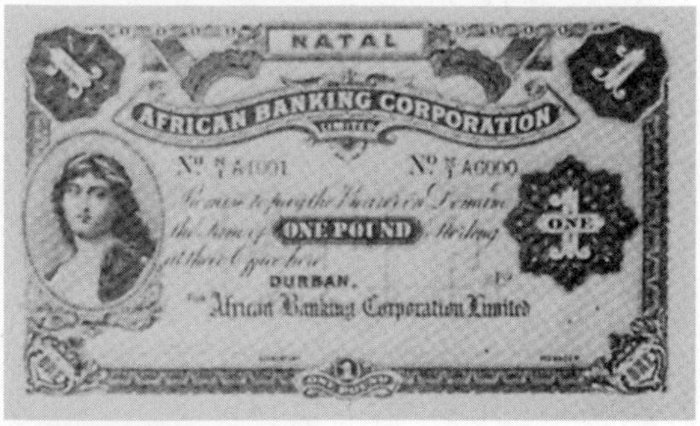

	Good	Fine	XF
S367 1 Pound 189x. Portrait woman at left. Printer: BWC. Specimen.	—	—	—
S368 5 Pounds 189x. Portrait woman at left. Printer: BWC. Specimen.	—	—	—

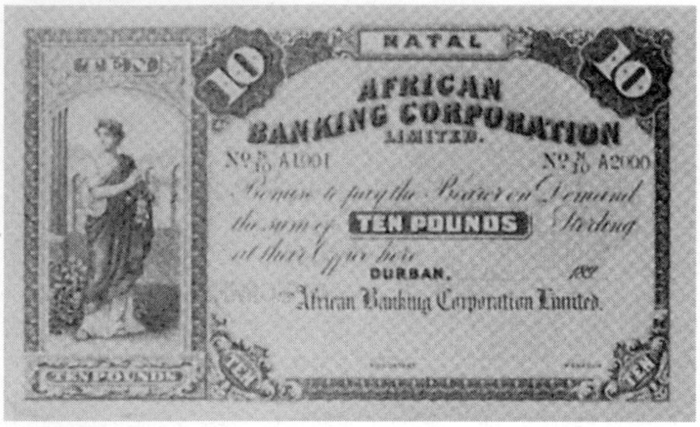

	Good	Fine	XF
S369 10 Pounds 189x. Standing allegorical woman at left. Printer: BWC. Specimen.	—	—	—
S370 20 Pounds 189x. Woman holding shield at left. Printer: BWC. Specimen.	—	—	—

BANK OF AFRICA LIMITED

1890'S ISSUE

	Good	Fine	XF
S381 10 Shillings Before 1900. Reported not confirmed.	—	—	—

1900'S ISSUE

	Good	Fine	XF
S382 10 Shillings After 1900. Black on olive underprint. Map of Africa at left, field workers at right. Back: Purple. Printer: W&S. Rare.	—	—	—

NATIONAL BANK OF SOUTH AFRICA LIMITED

1900-14 ISSUE

#S391-S395 Ovpt: *NATAL ISSUE* at top border.

	Good	Fine	XF
S391 10 Shillings 1900-20. Green and orange. Cherub holding cornucopia at lower left. Back: Springbok at center. Overprint: *NATAL ISSUE* at top border. Printer: W&S.	250.	750.	—

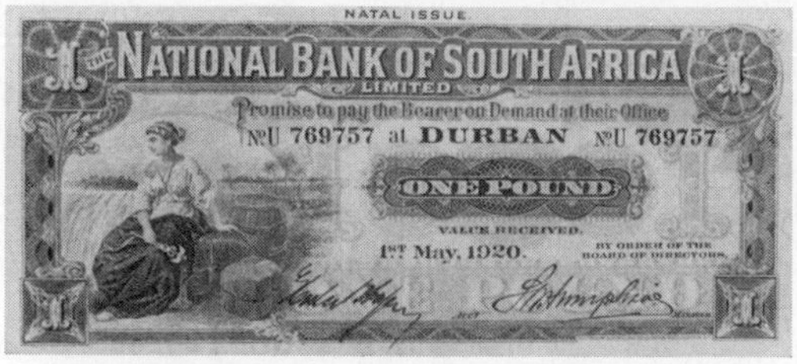

	Good	Fine	XF
S392 1 Pound 1.5.1900; 1.9.1919; 1.5.1920. Black on light red underprint. Seated woman with bale and barrel at left. Back: Dark green. Map of Africa. Overprint: *NATAL ISSUE* at top border. Printer: W&S.	375.	1100.	—

	Good	Fine	XF
S393 5 Pounds 1.9.1914; 1.9.1915; 1.5.1920. Seated woman with cornucopia with Victoria Falls in background at left, cows and wagon at right. Overprint: *NATAL ISSUE* at top border. Printer: W&S.	450.	1350.	—
S395 20 Pounds 1900-20. Overprint: *NATAL ISSUE* at top border. Printer: W&S. Rare.	—	—	—

ORIENTAL BANK CORPORATION

1877 ISSUE

	Good	Fine	XF
S397 1 Pound (ca.1877). Black. Arms at upper center. Punched hole cancelled. Proof.	—	—	—

STANDARD BANK OF BRITISH SOUTH AFRICA LIMITED

1873 ISSUE

S402 1 Pound	Good	Fine	XF
14.4.1873. Blue on red underprint. Underprint of large *ONE*. Standing Britannia with flag and shield at upper center. Printer: WWS.			
a. Issued note. Rare.	—	—	—
b. Issued note. Handwritten: *CANCELLED*.	375.	1100.	—
p. Proof. Perforated: *CANCELLED*.	—	Unc	1750.

Standard Bank of South Africa Limited

Durban

1889 Issue

S406 10 Shillings	Good	Fine	XF
1.5.1889. Orange on blue underprint. Standing Britannia with flag and shield at upper center. Back: Green. Printer: WWS.	300.	900.	—

S407 1 Pound	Good	Fine	XF
1.3.1889. Similar to #S402 but underprint of sunburst in gold and *ONE* twice in red. Standing Britannia with flag and shield at upper center. Back: Green. Bank monogram. Printer: WWS.			
a. Issued note.	300.	900.	—
p1. Black and red underprint. Uniface. Proof.	—	Unc	1500.
p2. Black, gold and red underprint. Uniface. Proof.	—	Unc	1500.
p3. Back uniface. Proof.	—	Unc	1500.

S410 20 Pounds	Good	Fine	XF
18xx. Black. Standing Britannia with flag and shield at upper center. Back: Light brown. Athena head at center Punched hole cancelled.	—	—	—

1896 Issue

S411 10 Shillings	Good	Fine	XF
1.10.1896. Black on orange underprint. Similar to #S412. Back: Green. Printer: William Brown.	175.	550.	1650.

S412 1 Pound	Good	Fine	XF
1.10.1896. Green. Printer: William Brown.	175.	550.	1650.

1900 Issue

#S421-S425 ovpt: *NATAL ISSUE* in top border.

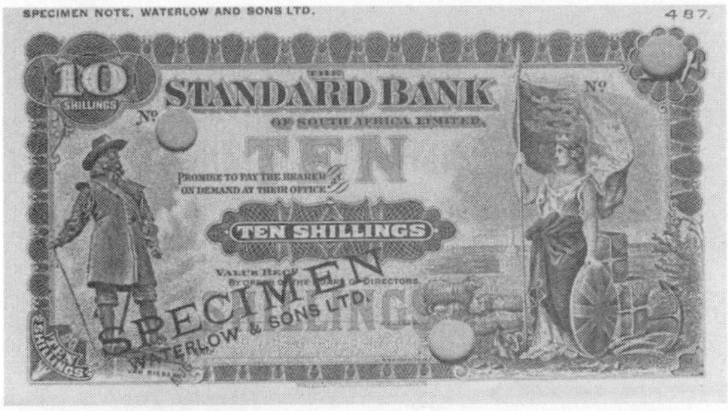

S421 10 Shillings	Good	Fine	XF
1900-20. Overprint: *NATAL ISSUE* in top border. Printer: W&S.	1100.	3300.	—
s. Specimen. Punch hole cancelled.	—	Unc	750.

S422 1 Pound	Good	Fine	XF
1900-20. Black and brown. Standing Britannia with flag and shield at left. Back: Woman at center. Overprint: *NATAL ISSUE* in top border. Printer: W&S.			
a. Issued note. 1.7.1918; 1.5.1920.	150.	450.	—
s. Specimen.	—	Unc	750.

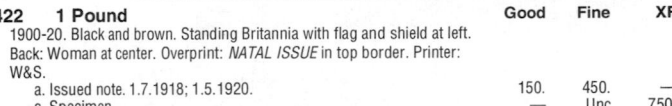

S423 5 Pounds	Good	Fine	XF
1900-20. Statue of Van Riebeeck at left, standing Britannia with flag and shield at right. Overprint: *NATAL ISSUE* in top border. Printer: W&S.			
a. Issued note. 1.7.1918.	225.	675.	—
s. Specimen. Punch hole cancelled.	—	Unc	750.

S425 20 Pounds	Good	Fine	XF
1900-20 (1.1.1919). Black on yellow and green underprint. Statue of Van Riebeeck at left, standing Britannia with flag and shield at right. Similar to #S423. Overprint: *NATAL ISSUE* in top border. Printer: W&S.	400.	1200.	—

NATAL

Commercial Banks

COLONIAL BANK OF NATAL

1862-64 ISSUE

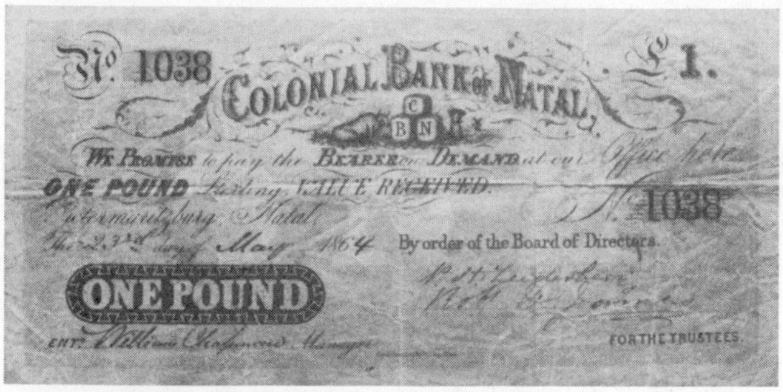

S431 1 Pound — Good / Fine / XF
1.5.1862; 23.5.1864. Black on light blue underprint. Small cow, letters: *CBN* on bales of wool, corn and wheat at top center. Uniface. Printer: Saul Solomon & Co., Cape Town. — 150. / 450. / 1350.

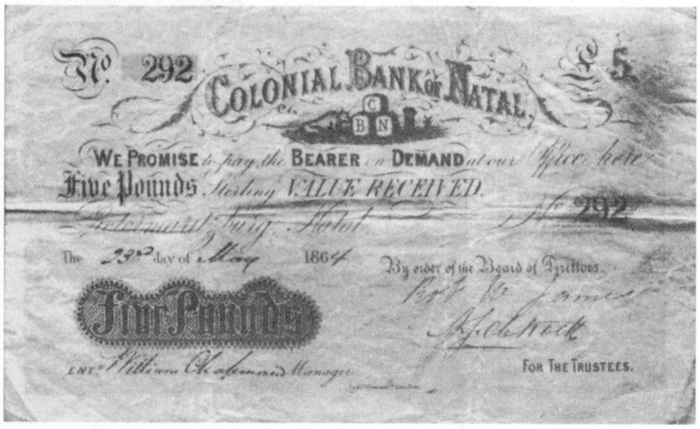

S432 5 Pounds — Good / Fine / XF
9.6.1862; 23.5.1864. Black on light brown underprint. Small cow, letters: *CBN* on bales of wool, corn and wheat at top center. Uniface. Printer: Saul Solomon & Co., Cape Town. — 450. / 1350. / —

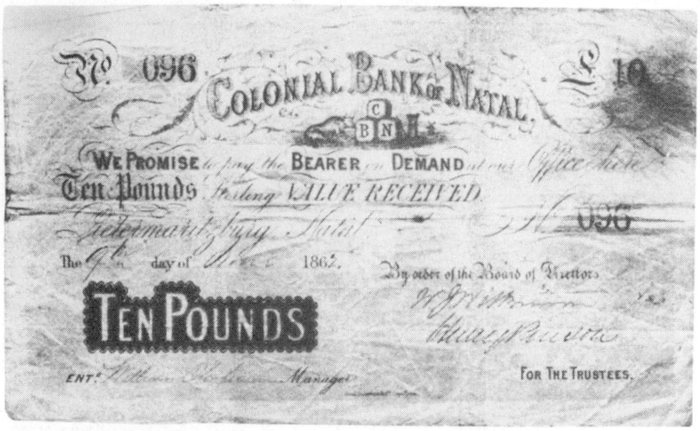

S433 10 Pounds — Good / Fine / XF
9.6.1862. Black on light brown underprint. Small cow, letters: *CBN* on bales of wool, corn and wheat at top center. Uniface. Printer: Saul Solomon & Co., Cape Town. — 300. / 900. / 2700.

COMMERCIAL AND AGRICULTURAL BANK OF NATAL

1860'S ISSUE

S436 1 Pound — Good / Fine / XF
186x. Black and light blue. Coast scene at upper center. Printer: Nissen & Parker, London. Rare. — — / — / —

DURBAN BANK

1860-70'S ISSUE

S440 10 Shillings — Good / Fine / XF
187x. Black. Arms at upper left, animals and shields at upper center. Printer: G. Waterston and Son. — — / — / —

S441 1 Pound — Good / Fine / XF
186x (ca.1864). Blue. Atlas carrying world at upper left, dock scene at the Point Railway Station at upper center. Office: *Durban* or *DURBAN, NATAL* at center. Signature title: *ACCOUNTANT.* Back: Light gray. Value in floral rectangle. Watermark: *DURBAN BANK.* Printer: Nissen & Parker, London. Rare. — — / — / —

S442 5 Pounds
1862; 1864. Atlas carrying world at upper left, dock scene at the Point Railway Station at upper center. Printer: Nissen & Parker, London.

	Good	Fine	XF
a. Signature title: *CHIEF CLERK.* 3.11.1862. Rare.	—	—	—
b. Signature title: *ACCOUNTANT.* 12.4.1864. Rare.	—	—	—

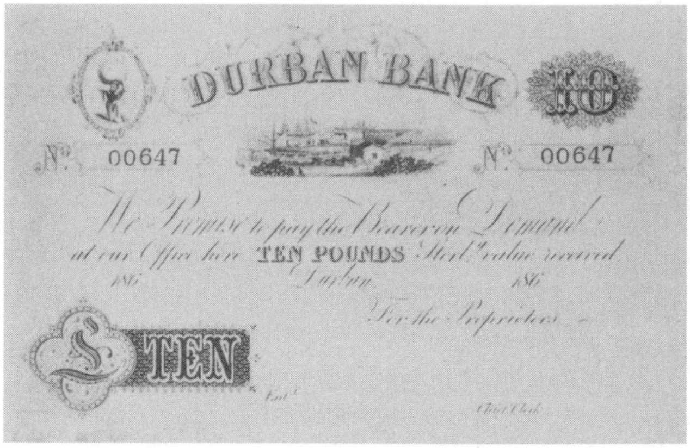

S443 10 Pounds — Good / Fine / XF
186x (ca.1862). Atlas carrying world at upper left, dock scene at the Point Railway Station at upper center. Signature title: *CHIEF CLERK.* Printer: Nissen & Parker, London. Rare. — — / — / —

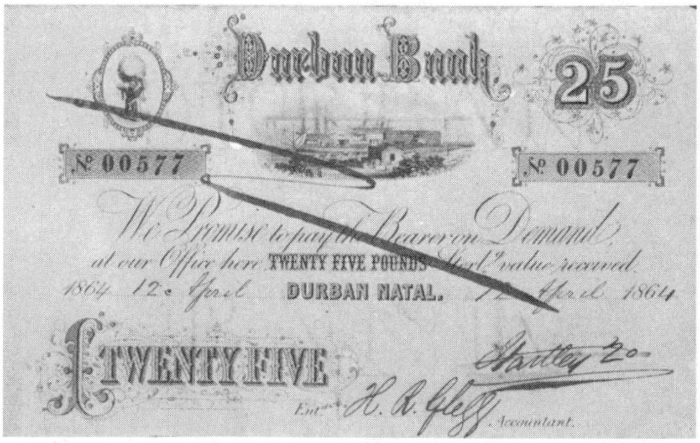

S444 25 Pounds
186x; 1864. Atlas carrying world at upper left, dock scene at the Point Railway Station at upper center. Printer: Nissen & Parker, London.

	Good	Fine	XF
a. Signature title: *CHIEF CLERK.* 186x. Rare.	—	—	—
b. Signature title: *ACCOUNTANT.* Pen cancelled. 12.4.1864.	—	—	600.

London and Natal Bank

1864 Issue

	Good	Fine	XF
S451 10 Shillings			
186x. Black on red underprint. Shield at upper left, shields, produce and animals at center. Remainder with serial #. Printer: Waterston & Son, Edinburgh. Rare.	—	—	—
S452 1 Pound			
186x. Black on green underprint. Shield at upper left, shields, produce and animals at center. Printer: Waterston & Son, Edinburgh. Rare.	—	—	—
S453 5 Pounds			
186x. Black on dark brown underprint. Shield at upper left, shields, produce and animals at center. Printer: Waterston & Son, Edinburgh. Rare.	—	—	—

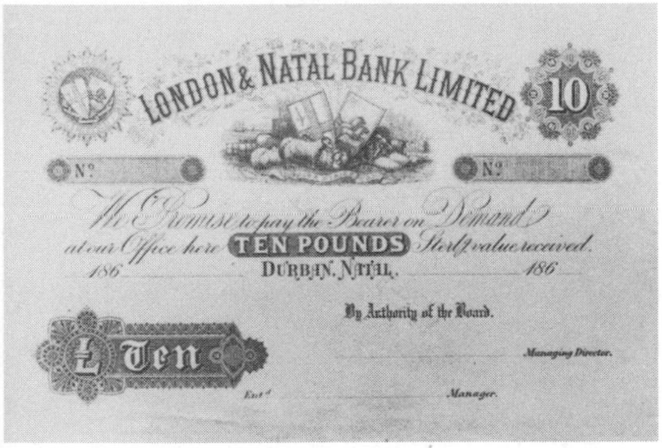

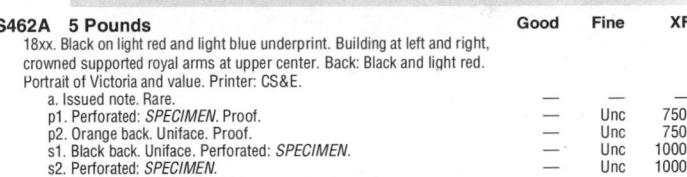

	Good	Fine	XF
S454 10 Pounds			
186x. Black on blue underprint. Shield at upper left, shields, produce and animals at center. Remainder without serial #. Printer: Waterston & Son, Edinburgh. Rare.	—	—	—

Natal Bank Limited

1850's Issue

	Good	Fine	XF
S462 1 Pound			
1852. Black. Arms at upper center. Printer: Jeremiah Cullingworth, Durban.	—	—	—

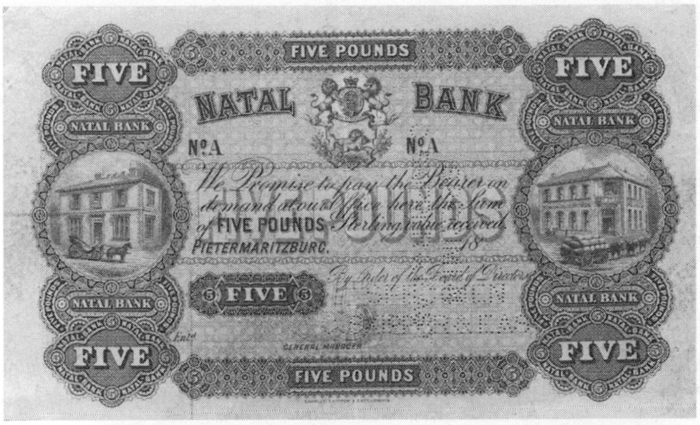

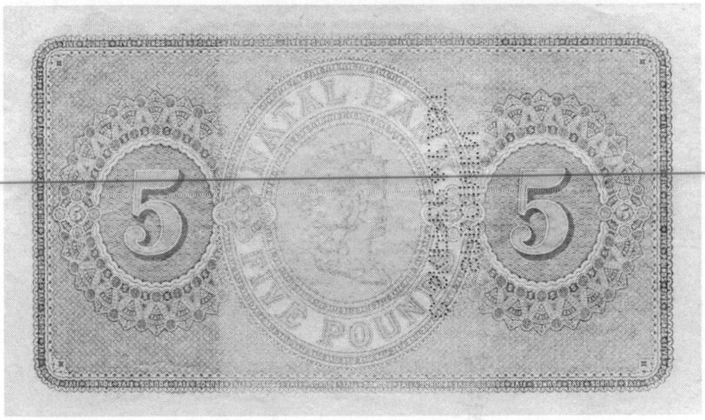

	Good	Fine	XF
S462A 5 Pounds			
18xx. Black on light red and light blue underprint. Building at left and right, crowned supported royal arms at upper center. Back: Black and light red. Portrait of Victoria and value. Printer: CS&E.			
a. Issued note. Rare.	—	—	—
p1. Perforated: *SPECIMEN*. Proof.	—	Unc	750.
p2. Orange back. Uniface. Proof.	—	Unc	750.
s1. Black back. Uniface. Perforated: *SPECIMEN*.	—	Unc	1000.
s2. Perforated: *SPECIMEN*.	—	Unc	1000.

	Good	Fine	XF
S463 10 Pounds			
18xx. Black on orange and yellow underprint. Building at left and right, crowned supported royal arms at upper center. Similar to #S462A. Back: Red and yellow. Two portraits of Queen Victoria and value. Printer: CS&E.			
a. Issued note. Rare.	—	—	—
p. Back uniface. Proof.	—	Unc	750.
s. Perforated: *SPECIMEN*.	—	Unc	1000.

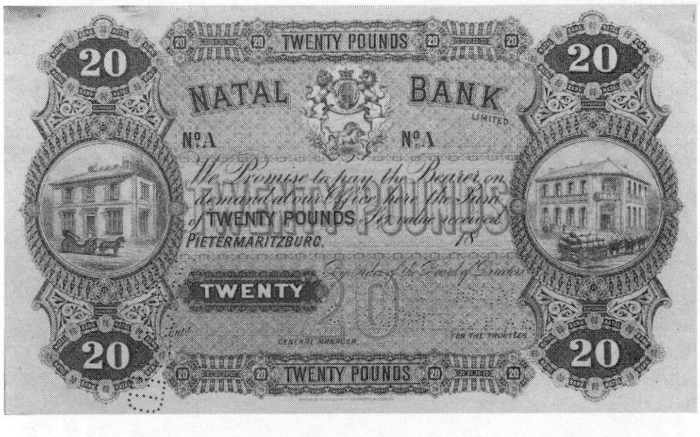

		Good	Fine	XF
S464	**20 Pounds** 18xx. Black on green and orange underprint. Building at left and right, crowned supported royal arms at upper center. Similar to #S462A. Back: Green and orange. Two portraits of Queen Victoria and value. Similar to #S463. Printer: CS&E.			
	a. Issued note. Rare.	—	—	—
	s1. Face without underprint. Uniface. Perforated: *SPECIMEN*.	—	Unc	1000.
	s2. Perforated: *CANCELLED* and *SPECIMEN*.	—	Unc	1000.

18xx; 1906 Issue

		Good	Fine	XF
S466	**1 Pound** 1.11.1906. Black on brownish gray underprint. Two seated women and shield at center. Back: Black. Printer: W&S. Rare.	—	—	—
S467	**5 Pounds** 18xx. Black on brownish gray underprint. Two seated women and shield at center. Similar to #S466. Back: Black.	—	—	—
S468	**10 Pounds** 18xx. Black on brownish gray underprint. Two seated women and shield at center. Similar to #S466. Back: Black. Specimen.	—	Unc	1000.
S469	**20 Pounds** 18xx. Black on brownish gray underprint. Two seated women and shield at center. Similar to #S466. Back: Black. Printer: BWC. Specimen.	—	Unc	1000.

NOTE: A 10 Shillings denomination requires confirmation. 10 and 20 Pound denominations ca.1900-20 require confirmation.

Orange Free State

Imperial Banks

Many notes issued at Bloemfontein.

African Banking Corporation Limited

1900-20 Issue

		Good	Fine	XF
S471	**10 Shillings** 1900-20. Blue on multicolor underprint. Deer grazing at upper center. Back: Green and purple Map of Africa at center. Printer: BWC.	375.	1100.	—
S472	**1 Pound** 12.5.1920. Brown. Arms at left and right, deer grazing at center. Printer: BWC.	375.	1100.	—
S473	**5 Pounds** 191x. Brown. Arms at left and right, deer grazing at center. Rare.	—	—	—
S474	**10 Pounds** 1900-20. Brown. Arms at left and right, deer grazing at center. Rare.	—	—	—

Bank of Africa Limited

1900-20 Issue

		Good	Fine	XF
S482	**1 Pound** 18xx. Winburg branch. Specimen.	—	750.	—
S484	**10 Pounds** 1900-20. Pink and black. Rare.	—	—	—
S485	**20 Pounds** 1900-20. Black and yellow. Rare.	—	—	—

National Bank of South Africa Limited

1900-20 Issue

#S491-S495 ovpt: *ORANGE FREE STATE ISSUE* at top border.

		Good	Fine	XF
S491	**10 Shillings** 1900-20. Green and red. Cherub holding cornucopia at lower left. Like #S391. Back: Springbok at center Overprint: *ORANGE FREE STATE ISSUE* at top border. Printer: W&S. Rare.	—	—	—
S492	**1 Pound** 1900-20. Overprint: *ORANGE FREE STATE ISSUE* at top border. Printer: W&S. Rare.	—	—	—

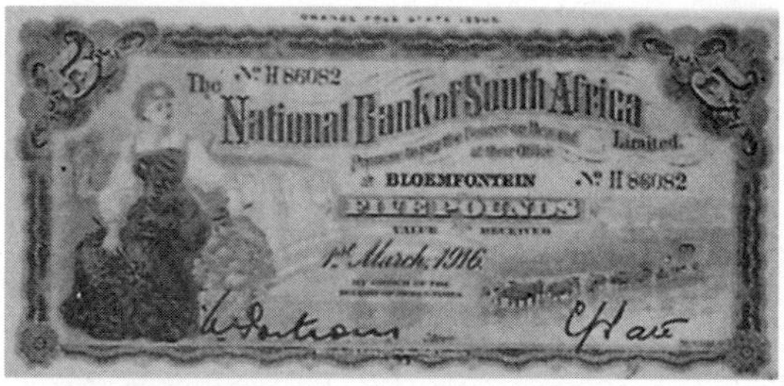

		Good	Fine	XF
S493	**5 Pounds** 1900-20. Seated woman with cornucopia with Victoria Falls in background at left, cows and wagon at right. Overprint: *ORANGE FREE STATE ISSUE* at top border. Printer: W&S. Rare.	—	—	—
S494	**10 Pounds** 3.1.1918. Wagon and cattle at lower left, seated woman with cornucopia at center. Overprint: *ORANGE FREE STATE ISSUE* at top border. Printer: W&S. Perforated: *CANCELLED*.	—	—	—
S495	**20 Pounds** 1900-20. Overprint: *ORANGE FREE STATE ISSUE* at top border. Printer: W&S. Rare.	—	—	—

Standard Bank of South Africa Limited

Bloemfontein

1900s Issue

		Good	Fine	XF
S498	**5 Pounds** 19xx. Orange on tan underprint. Standing Britannia with flag at left. Back: Orange. Specimen.	—	—	—

	Good	Fine	XF
S501 10 Shillings 1900-20. Statue of Van Riebeeck at left, standing Britannia with flag and shield at right. Overprint: *ORANGE FREE STATE ISSUE* at top border. Printer: W&S.			
a. Issued note. Rare.	—	—	—
s. Specimen.	—	Unc	1100.
S502 1 Pound Before 1900. Overprint: *ORANGE FREE STATE ISSUE* at top border. Printer: W&S. Rare.	—	—	—
S503 5 Pounds 1900-20. Overprint: *ORANGE FREE STATE ISSUE* at top border. Printer: W&S. Rare.	—	—	—
S504 10 Pounds 1900-20. Overprint: *ORANGE FREE STATE ISSUE* at top border. Printer: W&S. Rare.	—	—	—

~~#S505 smaller size. Printer: W&S.~~

	Good	Fine	XF
S505 5 Pounds Black on orange underprint. Female seated with foul at left; standing Britannia with flag at center; female seated with wheel and wheat at right. Back: Orange. Female portrait at center. Printer: W&S.	—	—	—

Orange Free State

Commercial Banks

Bloemfontein Bank

1867-74 Issue

<AFrame <BRect 0.0 0.0 3.5 1.30><TextLine <TLOrigin 1.5 0.75><TLAlignment Center><String "001.30'>>>

#S507#S507A#S508

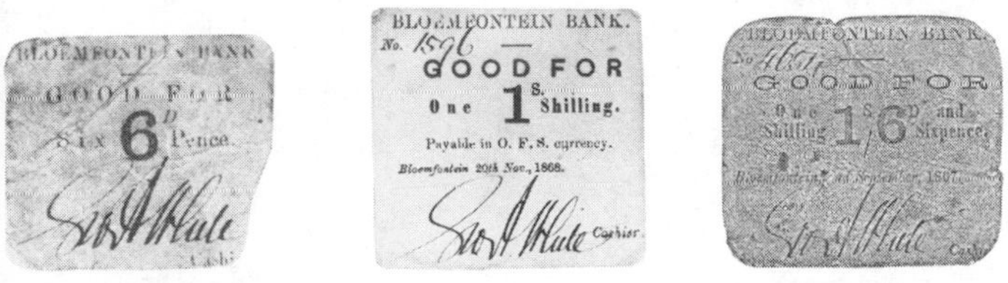

	Good	Fine	XF
S507 6 Pence ND. Black. Paper: Heavy green. Rare.	—	—	—
S507A 1 Shilling 20.11.1868. Black. Paper: Heavy cream. Rare.	—	—	—
S508 1 Shilling - 6 Pence 2.9.1867; 16.4.1874. Printed on heavy paper.	75.00	225.	675.
S509 2 Shillings - 6 Pence 1870.	75.00	225.	675.
S510 5 Shillings (ca.1870).	90.00	270.	800.
S511 1 Pound 18xx. Reported not confirmed.	—	—	—
S512 5 Pounds 1876. Black.	375.	1100.	—
S513 10 Pounds 30.12.1874. Black.	375.	1100.	—

Fauresmith Bank

1863 Issue

	Good	Fine	XF
S521 1 Pound 1863. Red. Printer: Saul Solomon & Co. Rare.	—	—	—

	Good	Fine	XF
S522 5 Pounds 24.8.1863. Black. Sheep at upper center. Printer: Saul Solomon & Co. Hand stamped: *CANCELLED.*	375.	1100.	—

1873-74 Issue

	Good	Fine	XF
S526 1 Pound 18.3.1873. Printer: William Brown & Co. Rare.	—	—	—
S527 5 Pounds 14.10.1874. Printer: William Brown & Co. Rare.	—	—	—

Nationale Bank van den Oranje Vrystaat Beperkt

1860-92 Issue

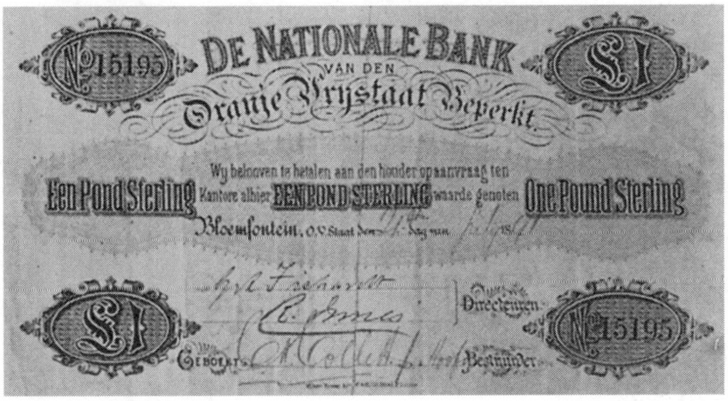

	Good	Fine	XF
S531 1 Pound 9.7.1860; 21.7.1891; 24.6.1892. Black on brown underprint. Uniface. Printer: William Brown Co. Rare.	—	—	—

National Bank of the Orange River Colony Limited

1900-10 Issue

	Good	Fine	XF
S537 1 Pound (ca.1900-1910). Black and yellow. Printer: William Brown & Co. Rare.	—	—	—

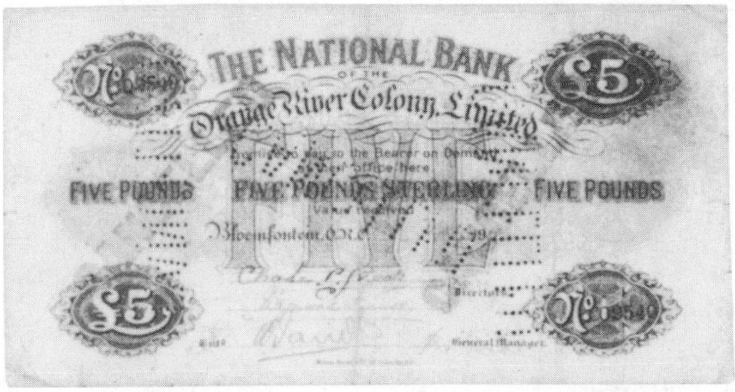

	Good	Fine	XF
S538 5 Pounds 1900-10. Black and blue. Printer: William Brown & Co. Cancelled.	675.	1900.	—

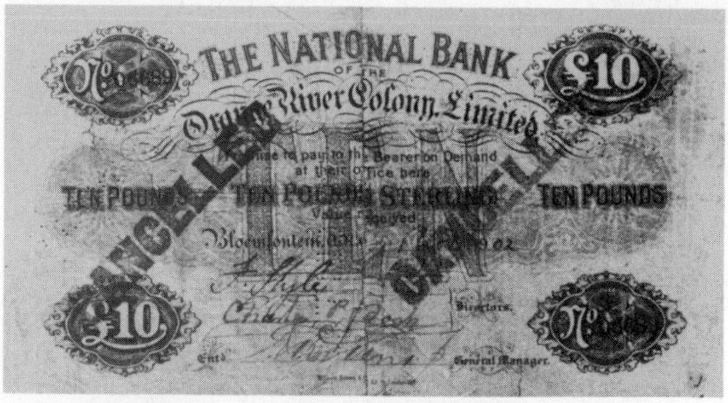

		Good	Fine	XF
S539	**10 Pounds**			
	1900-10. Black on gray and red underprint. Printer: William Brown & Co.			
	a. Issued note. 1.11.1902. Rare.	—	—	—
	b. Hand stamped: *CANCELLED:* perforated: *CANCELLED.*	—	—	—
S540	**20 Pounds**			
	1900-10. Black, blue and green. Printer: William Brown & Co. Rare.	—	—	—

Orange Vrystaat

Orange Free State Government

1865 Issue

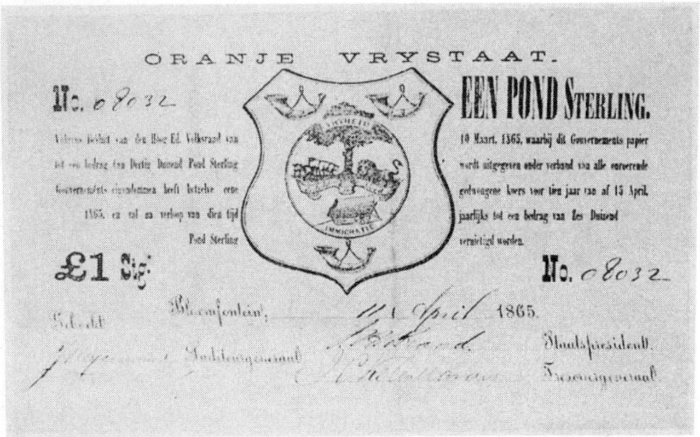

		Good	Fine	XF
S541	**1 Pound**			
	11.4.1865. Arms at center. Rare.	—	—	—
S542	**5 Pounds**			
	1865. Rare.	—	—	—
S543	**10 Pounds**			
	1865. Rare.	—	—	—
S544	**20 Pounds**			
	1865. Rare.	—	—	—

1866 Issue

		Good	Fine	XF
S546	**1 Pound**			
	26.7.1867. Arms at upper center. Printer: William Brown & Co. Rare.	—	—	—
S547	**5 Pounds**			
	1866. Printer: William Brown & Co. Rare.	—	—	—
S548	**10 Pounds**			
	1866. Printer: William Brown & Co. Rare.	—	—	—
S549	**20 Pounds**			
	1866. Printer: William Brown & Co. Rare.	—	—	—

Transvaal

Imperial Banks

Many notes issued in Pretoria or Johannesburg.

African Banking Corporation Limited

1900-20 Issue

		Good	Fine	XF
S551	**10 Shillings**			
	1900-20. Blue on multicolor underprint. Deer grazing at upper center. Like #S471. Back: Map of Africa at center. Printer: BWC. Rare.	—	—	—

		Good	Fine	XF
S552	**1 Pound**			
	1900-19. Green on pink underprint. Portrait woman at left. Back: Map of Africa. Printer: BWC. Rare.	—	—	—

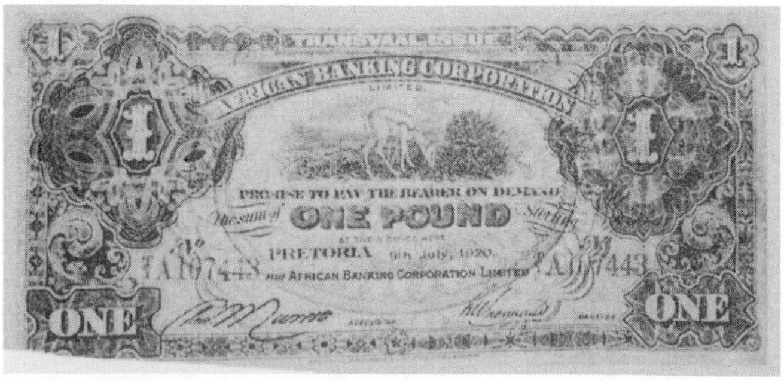

		Good	Fine	XF
S553	**1 Pound**			
	9.7.1920. Violet. Deer grazing at center. Printer: BWC.			
	a. Issued note. Rare.	—	—	—
	s. Specimen.	—	Unc	1000.
S554	**5 Pounds**			
	1900-20. Printer: BWC. Rare.	—	—	—
S555	**10 Pounds**			
	1900-20. Printer: BWC. Rare.	—	—	—
S556	**20 Pounds**			
	189x. Red and black. Woman holding shield at left. Printer: BWC. Rare.	—	—	—

Bank of Africa Limited

1870's-1920 Issue

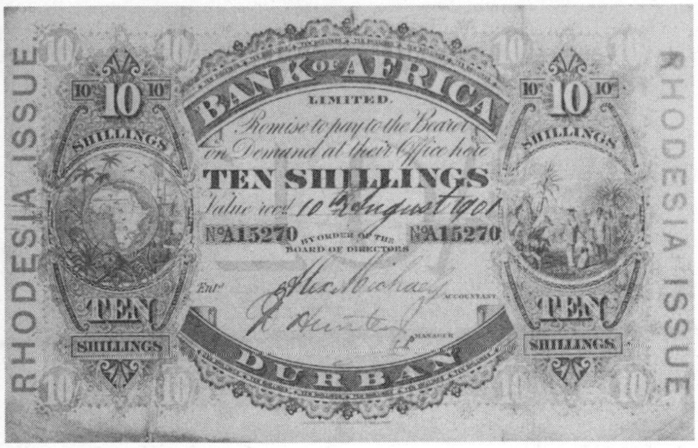

S562 10 Shillings	Good	Fine	XF
18xx. Map of Africa at left. Back: Green. Value in ornate engraving. Printer: W&S. Specimen.	—	—	—

S563 1 Pound	Good	Fine	XF
18xx. Map of Africa at left. Back: Green. Value in ornate engraving. Printer: W&S. Specimen.	—	—	—

S564 5 Pounds	Good	Fine	XF
18xx-1920. Black on blue underprint. Map of Africa at left. Train at right. Printer: W&S.			
a. Issued note. Rare.	—	—	—
b. Issued note. Handstamped: *WITHDRAWN.*	—	—	—
s. Specimen. 18xx.	—	Unc	1000.

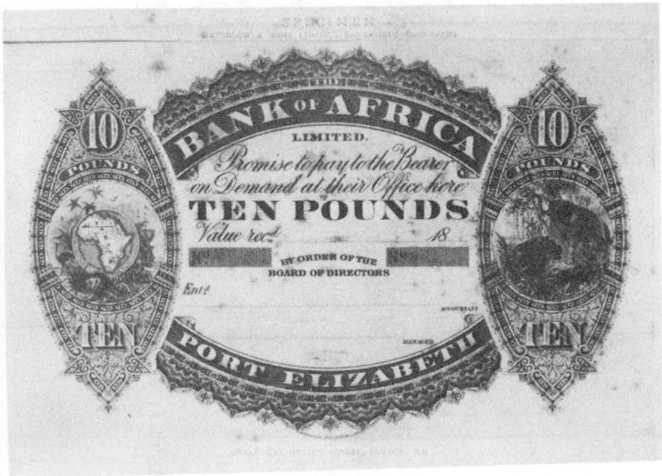

S565 10 Pounds	Good	Fine	XF
18xx-1920. Black and pink. Map of Africa at left. Elephant and hippopotamus at right. Printer: W&S.			
a. Issued note. Rare.	—	—	—
s. Specimen. 18xx.	—	Unc	1000.

S566 20 Pounds	Good	Fine	XF
18xx-1920. Black and yellow. Map of Africa at left. Men and mountain goats at right. Back: Brown. Value in ornate engraving. Printer: W&S.			
a. Issued note. Rare.	—	—	—
s. Specimen. 18xx.	—	Unc	1000.

National Bank of South Africa Limited

1900's Issue

S571 10 Shillings	Good	Fine	XF
1.9.1921. Green and red. Cherub holding cornucopia at lower left. Like #S391. Back: Springbok at center. Overprint: *TRANSVAAL ISSUE* at top margin. Printer: W&S.	375.	1100.	—

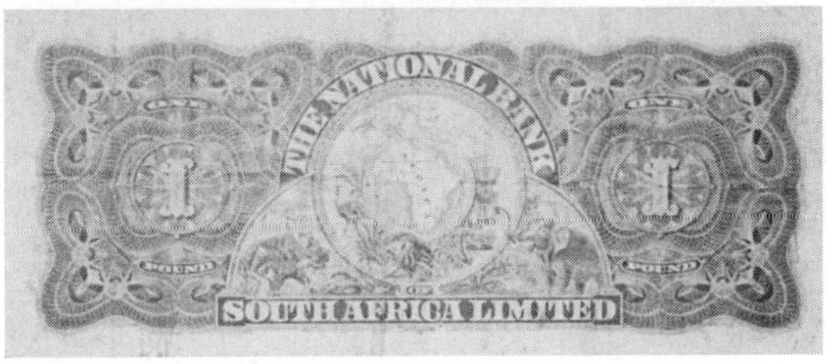

S572 1 Pound	Good	Fine	XF
1.4.1919; 3.1.1920; 1.5.1920. Black on light red underprint. Seated woman with bale and barrel at left. Like #S392. Back: Dark green. Map of Africa. Printer: W&S.	375.	1100.	—

S573 5 Pounds	Good	Fine	XF
1.12.1900. Large denomination at left, bank monogram at upper center. Rare.	—	—	—

#S574 and S575 printer CS&E. Wmk. of value.

S574 5 Pounds	Good	Fine	XF
ND. Black on red underprint. Similar to #S573 but seal at left, *FIVE* in oval at top center, serial # at lower left. Back: Red. Watermark: Value. Printer: CS&E.			
a. Issued note. 1.10.1902. Handstamped *CANCELLED.*	—	—	—
p. Proof. Black only, without underprint.	—	Unc	1000.
r. Remainder.	750.	2250.	—
s. Specimen perforated *SPECIMEN / C. SKIPPER & EAST.*	—	Unc	1250.

S575 5 Pounds	Good	Fine	XF
190x. Black on red and blue underprint. Seal at lower left, serial # at upper left and right. Back: Red. Watermark: Value. Printer: CS&E. Smaller size note. Remainder perforated: *CANCELLED.*	750.	2250.	—

S576 5 Pounds			
1.9.1919. Seated woman with cornucopia with Victoria Falls in background at left, cows and wagon at right. Like #S393. Printer: W&S. Rare.	—	—	—

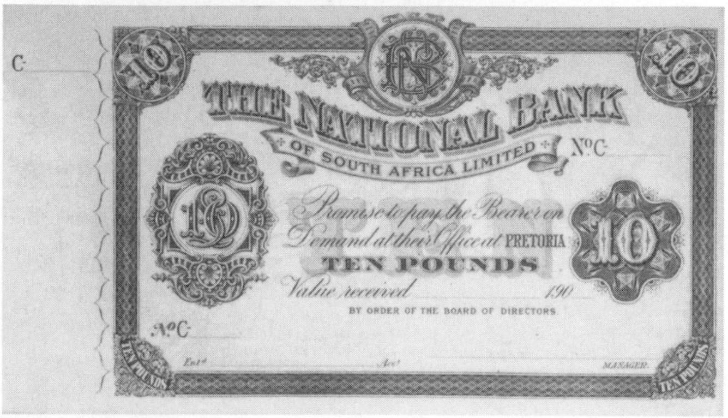

S577 10 Pounds	Good	Fine	XF
1902. Black on green underprint. Monogram at left and top center. Back: Green. Printer: W&S.			
a. Hand stamped: *CANCELLED.* 1.10.1902.	—	—	—
r. Remainder. 190x.	—	—	—

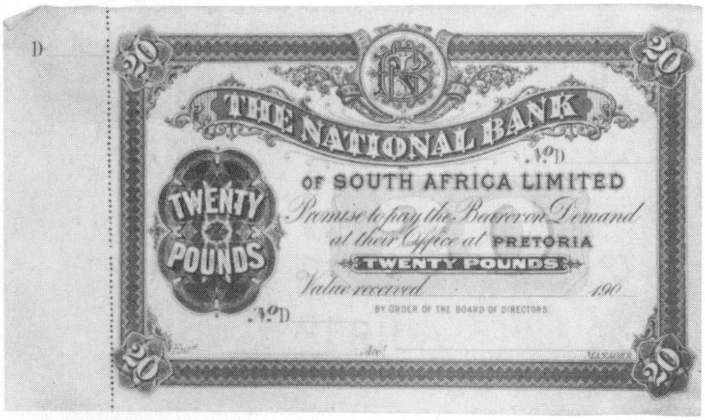

S578 20 Pounds	Good	Fine	XF
1900-1920. Monogram at top center. Printer: W&S. Proof. Rare.	—	—	—

Standard Bank of British South Africa Limited

1870's Issue

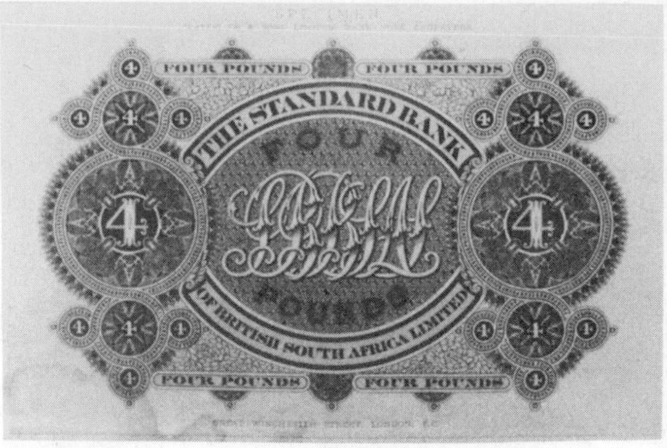

S579 4 Pounds	Good	Fine	XF
18xx. Black. Standing Britannia at left with flag by sheep, bales and anchor. Without office of issue. Engraved border. Printer: W&S (without imprint).			
p1. Face without underprint. Proof.	—	Unc	750.
p2. Back uniface. Proof.	—	Unc	750.

S580 5 Pounds	Good	Fine	XF
18xx. Black on gold underprint. Standing Britannia at left with flag by sheep, bales and anchor. Without office of issue. Engraved border. Similar to #S579. Back: Red. Large value. Printer: W&S (without imprint).			
p1. Black face without underprint. Proof. Perforated: *CANCELLED.*	—	Unc	750.
p2. Red back. Uniface. Proof.	—	Unc	750.

S581 10 Pounds	Good	Fine	XF
18xx. Black. Standing Britannia at left with flag by sheep, bales and anchor. Without office of issue. Engraved border. Similar to #S579. Back: Red. Large value in scroll. Printer: W&S (without imprint).			
p1. Black face without underprint. Uniface. Proof.	—	Unc	750.
p2. Red back. Uniface. Proof.	—	Unc	750.

S582 20 Pounds

18xx. Black. Standing Britannia at center with flag by sheep, bales and anchor. Without office of issue. Engraved border. Similar to #S579 except standing Britannia is at center. Back: Light brown. Athena head at center. Printer: W&S (without imprint).

	Good	Fine	XF
p1. Black face without underprint. Uniface. Proof.	—	Unc	750.
p2. light brown back. Uniface. Proof.	—	Unc	750.

Standard Bank of South Africa Limited

1890's Issue

S583 5 Pounds

18xx. Blue with purple *FIVE*. Seated woman with flag and shield at left. Back: Green. Printer: WWS. Specimen. Rare.

Good	Fine	XF
—	—	—

1896 Issue

S583B 5 Pounds

18xx. Black on gold underprint. Standing Britannia at left with flag by sheep, bales and anchor. Engraved border. Like #S580. Back: Red. Large value.

Good	Fine	XF
—	—	—

S584 20 Pounds

1.1.1896. Black on blue and yellow underprint. Standing Britannia with flag and shield at center. Rare.

Good	Fine	XF
—	—	—

1900 Issue

S585 10 Shillings

1900-20. Statue of Van Riebeeck at left, standing Britannia with flag and shield at right. Like #S501. Overprint: *TRANSVAAL ISSUE* in top border. Printer: W&S.

	Good	Fine	XF
a. Issued note.	375.	1100.	—
s1. overprint: *Specimen*, punched hole cancelled.	—	Unc	1000.
s2. Specimen without markings.	—	Unc	1000.

S586 1 Pound

1900-20. Black and brown. Standing Britannia with flag and shield at left. Like #S422. Back: Woman at center. Overprint: *TRANSVAAL ISSUE* in top border. Printer: W&S.

	Good	Fine	XF
a. Issued note.	300.	900.	—
s. Specimen.	—	Unc	1000.

S587 5 Pounds

1900-20. Red and green. Statue of Van Riebeeck at left, standing Britannia with flag and shield at right center. Similar to #S589. Back: Red and black. Allegorical woman at center between Cape Town and Johannesburg branch bank offices. Overprint: *TRANSVAAL ISSUE* in top border. Printer: W&S. Rare.

Good	Fine	XF
—	—	—

S588 10 Pounds

1900-20. Red and green. Statue of Van Riebeeck at left, standing Britannia with flag and shield at right center. Similar to #S589. Back: Red and black. Allegorical woman at center between Cape Town and Johannesburg branch bank offices. Overprint: *TRANSVAAL ISSUE* in top border. Printer: W&S. Rare.

Good	Fine	XF
—	—	—

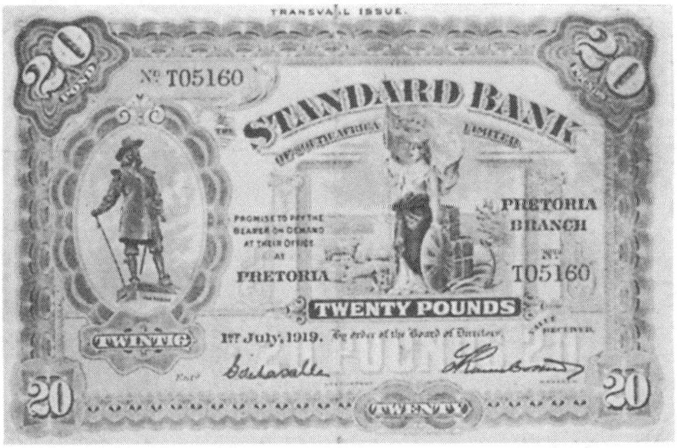

S589 20 Pounds

1900-1.7.1919. Red and green. Statue of Van Riebeeck at left, standing Britannia with flag and shield at right center. Back: Red and black. Allegorical woman at center between Cape Town and Johannesburg branch bank offices. Overprint: *TRANSVAAL ISSUE* in top border. Printer: W&S. Rare.

Good	Fine	XF
—	—	—

Transvaal

Private Banks

Cape of Good Hope Bank

1888 Provisional Issue

		Good	Fine	XF
S597	**1 Pound** 1.9.1888. Standing woman at left. Overprint: *KLERKSDORP ISSUE* at lower left and upper right. Rare.	—	—	—

Cape Commercial Bank

1870's Issue

		Good	Fine	XF
S601	**1 Pound** 18xx. Rare.	—	—	—
S602	**5 Pounds** 18xx. Rare.	—	—	—

Natal Bank Limited

1900-20 Issue

		Good	Fine	XF
S613	**5 Pounds** 1900-20. Rare.	—	—	—
S614	**10 Pounds** 1900-20. Rare.	—	—	—
S615	**20 Pounds** 1900-20. Two seated women and shield at upper center. Rare.	—	—	—

Nederlandsche Bank & Crediet-Vereeniging voor Zuid-Afrika

1890 Issue

		Good	Fine	XF
S621	**1 Pound** 12.4.1890. Black. Man standing with rifle and flag at left. Printer: JEZ. Rare.	—	—	—
S622	**5 Pounds** 14.4.1890. Lilac. Man standing with rifle and flag at left. Similar to #S621. Printer: JEZ. Rare.	—	—	—
S623	**10 Pounds** 18xx. Printer: JEZ. Rare.	—	—	—
S624	**20 Pounds** 26.4.1890. Black. Man standing with rifle and flag at left. Similar to #S621. Printer: JEZ. Rare.	—	—	—

Nederlandsche Bank voor Zuid-Afrika

Netherlands Bank of South-Africa

1888 Issue

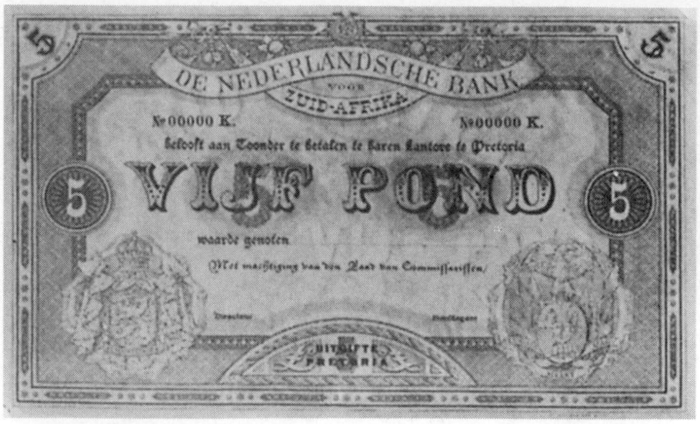

		Good	Fine	XF
S625	**5 Pond** (ca.1888). Orange. Kingdom of the Netherlands arms at lower left, Zuid-Afrikaansche Republiek arms at lower right. Afrikaans text. Back: Orange and brown. Lion supporting Netherlands arms at left center, Zuid-Afrikaansche Republiek arms at center right. Rare.	—	—	—

		Good	Fine	XF
S626	**5 Pounds** (ca.1888). Orange. Kingdom of the Netherlands arms at lower left, Zuid-Afrikaansche Republiek arms at lower right. Similar to #S625 but English text. Back: Orange and brown. Lion supporting Netherlands arms at left center, Zuid-Afrikaansche Republiek arms at center right. Rare.	—	—	—

		Good	Fine	XF
S627	**10 Pond** 1888. Black on blue underprint. Kingdom of the Netherlands arms at lower left, Zuid-Afrikaansche Republiek arms at lower right. Afrikaans text. Back: Lion supporting Netherlands arms at left center, Zuid-Afrikaansche Republiek arms at center right. Rare.	—	—	—

S628 10 Pounds Good Fine XF

(ca.1888). Black on blue underprint. Kingdom of the Netherlands arms at lower left, Zuid-Afrikaansche Republiek arms at lower right. Similar to #S627 but English text. Back: Lion supporting Netherlands arms at left center, Zuid-Afrikaansche Republiek arms at center right. Rare. — — —

S629 10 Shilling Good Fine XF

To 1920. Brown. South African arms at upper center. Afrikaans text. Back: Bank monogram at left and right. Printer: J. H. Bussy, Amsterdam, Holland. Specimen with punched hole cancellation. Rare. — — —

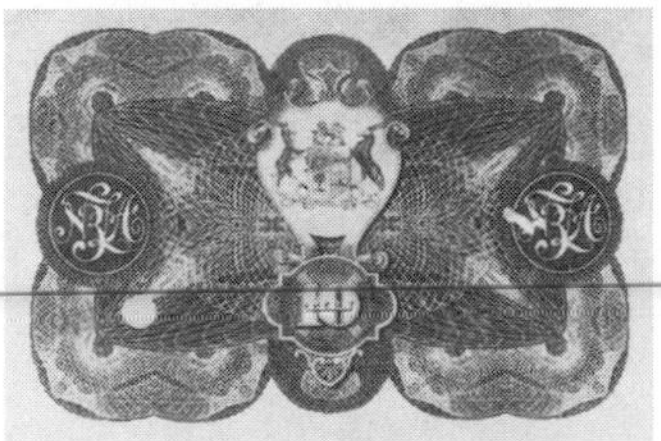

S630 10 Shillings Good Fine XF

14.12.1920. Brown. South African arms at upper center. Similar to #S629 but English text. Back: Bank monogram at left and right. Printer: J. H. Bussy, Amsterdam, Holland. Rare. — — —

S631 1 Pond Good Fine XF

To 1920. South African arms at upper center. Afrikaans text. Printer: J. H. Bussy, Amsterdam, Holland. Rare. — — —

S632 1 Pound Good Fine XF

To 1920. South African arms at upper center. Similar to #S631 but English text. Printer: J. H. Bussy, Amsterdam, Holland. Rare. — — —

#S633-S636 arms at l., bank monogram at r. on back.

S633 5 Pond Good Fine XF

To 1920. Black. South African arms at upper center. Afrikaans text. Back: Arms at left, bank monogram at right. Printer: J. H. Bussy, Amsterdam, Holland. Specimen with punched star hole cancellation. Rare. — — —

S634 5 Pounds Good Fine XF

To 1920. Black. South African arms at upper center. Similar to #S633 but English text. Back: Arms at left, bank monogram at right. Printer: J. H. Bussy, Amsterdam, Holland. Specimen with punched star hole cancellation. Rare. — — —

S635 10 Pond Good Fine XF

To 1920. Brown. Afrikaans text. Back: Arms at left, bank monogram at right. Specimen with punched star hole cancellation. Rare. — — —

S636 10 Pounds Good Fine XF

To 1920. Brown. Similar to #S635 but English text. Back: Arms at left, bank monogram at right. Specimen with punched star hole cancellation. Rare. — — —

Boer War

Siege of Mafeking

1900 Issue

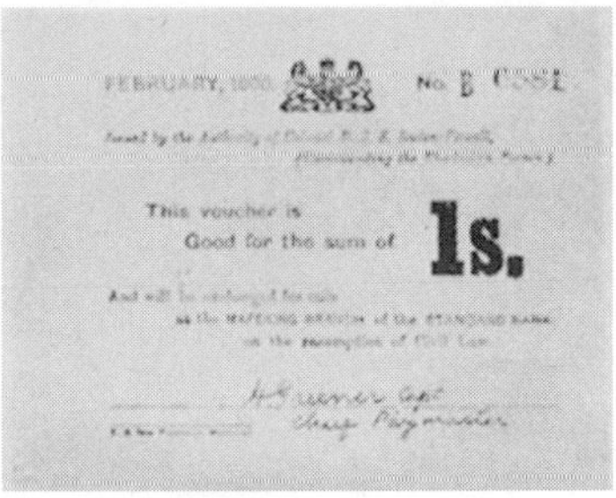

S651 1 Shilling VG VF UNC

1.1900; 2.1900. Blue with green value. Royal arms at top center. Printer: Townshend and Son.

	VG	VF	UNC
a. 1.1900.	175.	525.	1550.
b. 2.1900.	175.	525.	1550.

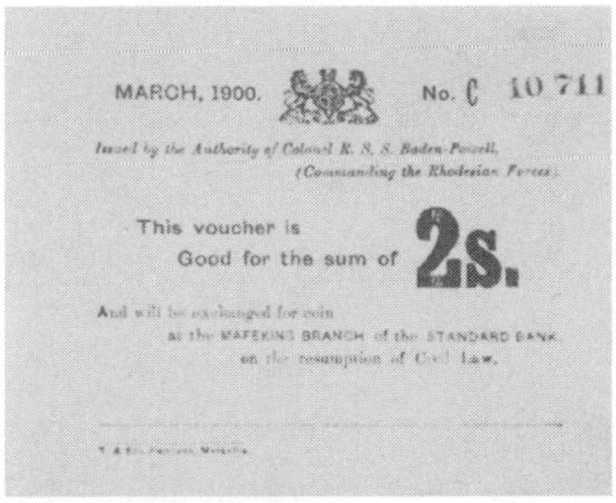

S652 2 Shillings VG VF UNC

1.1900; 2.1900. Blue with brown value. Royal arms at top center. Printer: Townshend and Son.

	VG	VF	UNC
a. 1.1900.	160.	500.	1500.
b. 2.1900.	160.	500.	1500.

NOTE: #S651 and S652 dated 3.1900 were printed but not issued. Several essays and unadopted designs for these notes are known.

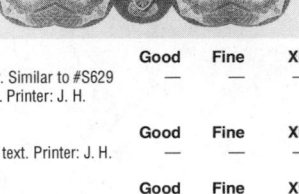

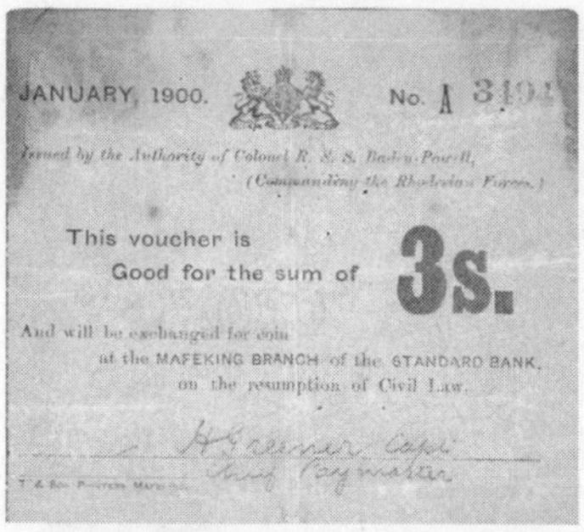

		VG	VF	UNC
S653	**3 Shillings** 1.1900. Blue with red value. Royal arms at top center. Printer: Townshend and Son.	500.	1500.	3000.

		VG	VF	UNC
S654	**10 Shillings** 3.1900. Green. Royal arms at top center. Man with firearms at left, man with cannon at right. Printer: Townshend and Son.			
	a. Misspelled *Commaning* (letter d left out).	250.	750.	2250.
	b. Corrected *Commanding.*	200.	600.	1800.

		VG	VF	UNC
S655	**1 Pound** 3.1900. Dark blue on blue base. Baden-Powell standing by flag, cannon *"WOLF"* with kneeling woman and two soldiers, all at center. Printed by a the "blueprint" process.	650.	1750.	5400.

Marshall Hole

1900 Issue

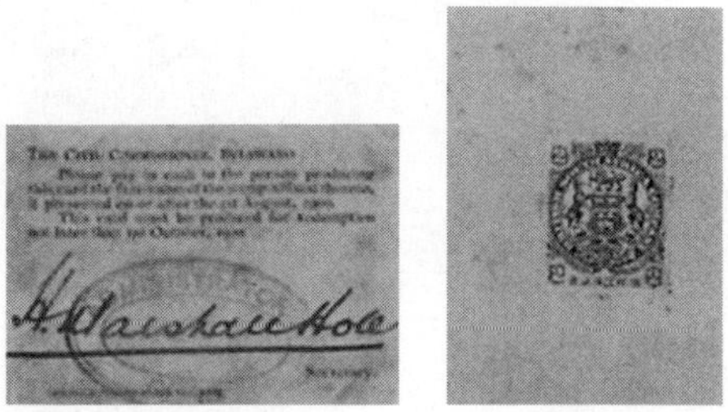

		Good	Fine	XF
S661	**2 Pence** 1.8.1900.			
	a. Adhesive stamp Type A; hand stamp Type I.	50.00	150.	450.
	b. Adhesive stamp Type A; hand stamp Type II.	50.00	150.	450.
	c. Adhesive stamp Type B; hand stamp Type I.	50.00	150.	450.
	d. Adhesive stamp Type B; hand stamp Type II.	50.00	150.	450.
S662	**3 Pence** 1.8.1900.			
	a. Adhesive stamp Type A; hand stamp Type I.	50.00	150.	450.
	b. Adhesive stamp Type A; hand stamp Type II.	50.00	150.	450.
	c. Adhesive stamp Type B; hand stamp Type I.	50.00	150.	450.
	d. Adhesive stamp Type B; hand stamp Type II.	50.00	150.	450.

		Good	Fine	XF
S663	**4 Pence** 1.8.1900.			
	a. Adhesive stamp Type A; hand stamp Type I.	60.00	180.	550.
	b. Adhesive stamp Type A; hand stamp Type II.	60.00	180.	550.
	c. Adhesive stamp Type B; hand stamp Type I.	60.00	180.	550.
	d. Adhesive stamp Type B; hand stamp Type II.	60.00	180.	550.

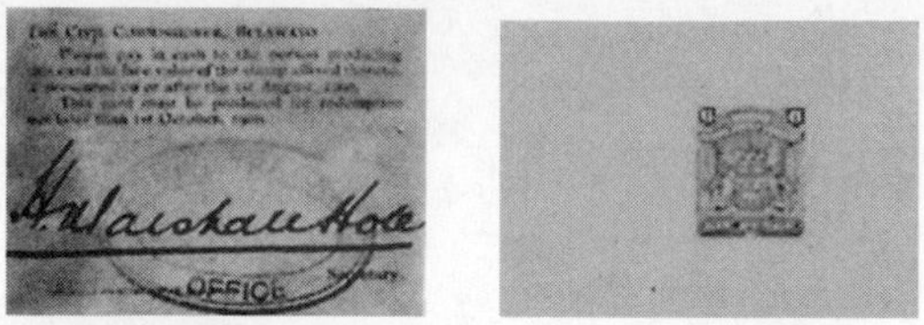

		Good	Fine	XF
S664	**6 Pence** 1.8.1900.			
	a. Adhesive stamp Type A; hand stamp Type I.	60.00	180.	550.
	b. Adhesive stamp Type A; hand stamp Type II.	60.00	180.	550.
	c. Adhesive stamp Type B; hand stamp Type I.	60.00	180.	550.
	d. Adhesive stamp Type B; hand stamp Type II.	60.00	180.	550.
	e. Adhesive stamp Type C; hand stamp Type I.	60.00	180.	550.
	f. Adhesive stamp Type C; hand stamp Type II.	60.00	180.	550.
S665	**1 Shilling** 1.8.1900.			
	a. Adhesive stamp Type A; hand stamp Type I.	75.00	225.	675.
	b. Adhesive stamp Type A; hand stamp Type II.	75.00	225.	675.
	c. Adhesive stamp Type D; hand stamp Type I.	75.00	225.	675.
	d. Adhesive stamp Type D; hand stamp Type II.	75.00	225.	675.
S666	**2 Shillings** 1.8.1900.			
	a. Adhesive stamp Type A; hand stamp Type I.	85.00	255.	770.
	b. Adhesive stamp Type A; hand stamp Type II.	85.00	225.	770.

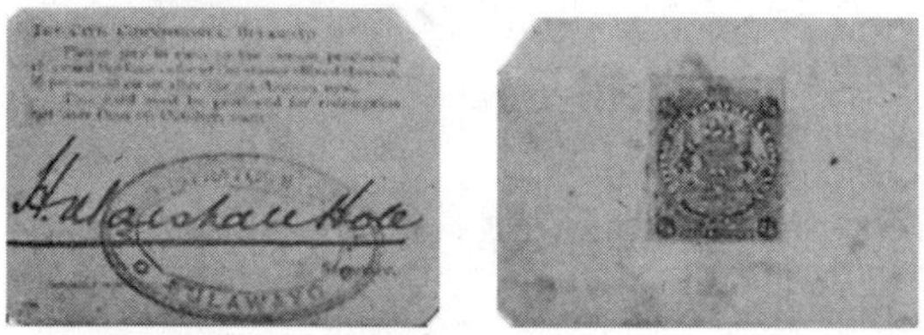

		Good	Fine	XF
S667	**2 Shillings - 6 Pence** 1.8.1900.			
	a. Adhesive stamp Type A; hand stamp Type I.	85.00	225.	770.
	b. Adhesive stamp Type A; hand stamp Type II.	100.	300.	900.
S668	**4 Shillings** 1.8.1900. Adhesive stamp Type A; oval hand stamp Type I.	600.	1800.	5400.
S669	**5 Shillings** 1.8.1900. Adhesive stamp Type A; oval hand stamp Type I.	300.	900.	2700.
S670	**10 Shillings** 1.8.1900.			
	a. Adhesive stamp Type A; hand stamp Type I.	300.	900.	2700.
	b. Adhesive stamp Type A; hand stamp Type II.	300.	900.	2700.

Siege of O'okiep

1902 Issue

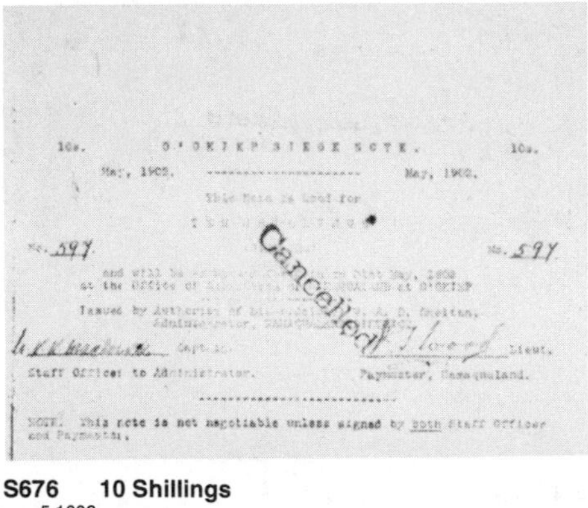

		Good	Fine	XF
S676	**10 Shillings** 5.1902.	900.	2700.	—
S677	**1 Pound** 5.1902.	900.	2700.	—
S678	**5 Pounds** 5.1902.	1100.	3300.	—

Post Office

1900 "Post Noot" Post Notes Issue

#S681-S689 blank postal note forms used as currency during the Boer War.

		Good	Fine	XF
S681	**1 Shilling** 1900.			
	a. Issued note.	25.00	75.00	225.
	b. Cancelled note.	12.50	35.00	115.
S682	**2 Shillings - 6 Pence** 1900.			
	a. Issued note.	25.00	75.00	225.
	b. Cancelled note.	12.50	35.00	115.

		Good	Fine	XF
S683	**5 Shillings**			
	1900.			
	a. Issued note.	25.00	75.00	225.
	b. Cancelled note.	12.50	35.00	115.
S684	**7 Shillings - 6 Pence**			
	1900.			
	a. Issued note.	25.00	75.00	225.
	b. Cancelled note.	12.50	35.00	115.
S685	**10 Shillings**			
	1900.			
	a. Issued note.	30.00	90.00	270.
	b. Cancelled note.	15.00	45.00	135.
S686	**12 Shillings - 6 Pence**			
	1900.			
	a. Issued note.	30.00	90.00	270.
	b. Cancelled note.	15.00	45.00	135.
S687	**15 Shillings**			
	1900.			
	a. Issued note.	30.00	90.00	270.
	b. Cancelled note.	20.00	60.00	180.
S688	**17 Shillings - 6 Pence**			
	1900.			
	a. Issued note.	40.00	120.	360.
	b. Cancelled note.	20.00	60.00	180.

		Good	Fine	XF
S689	**1 Pound**			
	1900.			
	a. Issued note.	45.00	135.	400.
	b. Cancelled note.	25.00	75.00	225.

NOTE: Cancelled postal orders are worth about 1/2 of the values shown.

Siege of Koffyfontein

1901 Issue

		Good	Fine	XF
S691	**5 Pounds**			
	1.1.1901. British flag at left, large numeral at right. Rare.	—	—	—

Post Office

1900 Postal Money Order Issue

#S701-S709 blank postal note forms used as currency during the war.

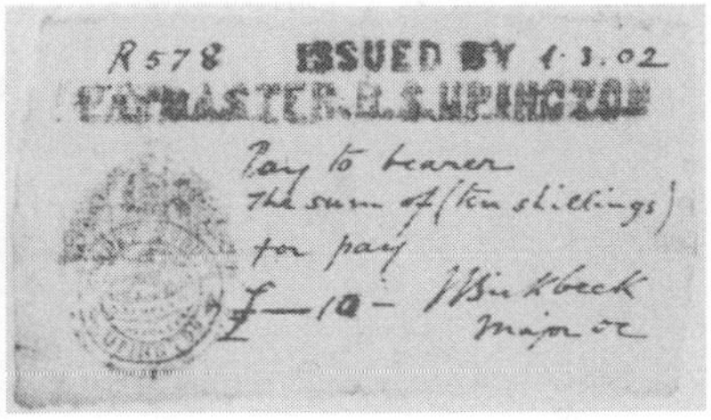

		Good	Fine	XF
S701	**1 Shilling**			
	1900.			
	a. Issued note.	25.00	75.00	225.
	b. Cancelled note.	12.50	35.00	115.
S702	**2 Shillings - 6 Pence**			
	1900.			
	a. Issued note.	25.00	75.00	225.
	b. Cancelled note.	12.50	35.00	115.
S703	**5 Shillings**			
	1900.			
	a. Issued note.	25.00	75.00	225.
	b. Cancelled note.	12.50	35.00	115.
S704	**7 Shillings - 6 Pence**			
	1900.			
	a. Issued note.	25.00	75.00	225.
	b. Cancelled note.	12.50	35.00	115.
S705	**10 Shillings**			
	1900.			
	a. Issued note.	30.00	90.00	270.
	b. Cancelled note.	15.00	45.00	135.
S706	**12 Shillings - 6 Pence**			
	1900.			
	a. Issued note.	30.00	90.00	270.
	b. Cancelled note.	15.00	45.00	135.
S707	**15 Shillings**			
	1900.			
	a. Issued note.	30.00	120.	360.
	b. Cancelled note.	15.00	45.00	135.
S708	**17 Shillings - 6 Pence**			
	1900.			
	a. Issued note.	40.00	120.	360.
	b. Cancelled note.	20.00	60.00	180.
S709	**1 Pound**			
	1900.			
	a. Issued note.	45.00	135.	400.
	b. Cancelled note.	25.00	75.00	225.

Upington Border Scouts

1902 Issue

#S711-S715 are hand dated from the first of February-April 1902.

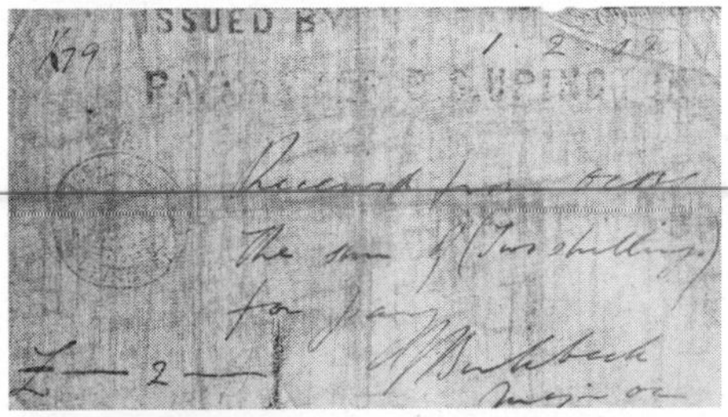

		Good	Fine	XF
S711	**2 Shillings**			
	1.3.1902-4.1902. Emblem of the Border Scouts at left. Hand dated.			
	a. Issued note. Rare.	—	—	—
	b. Hand stamped: *CANCELLED BY PAYMENT*. Rare.	—	—	—
S712	**5 Shillings**			
	1902. Emblem of the Border Scouts at left. Hand dated.			
	a. Issued note. Rare.	—	—	—
	b. Hand stamped: *CANCELLED BY PAYMENT*. Rare.	—	—	—

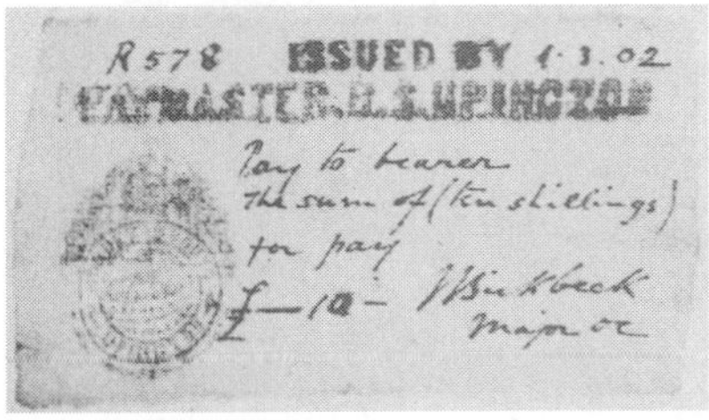

		Good	Fine	XF
S713	**10 Shillings**			
	1902. Emblem of the Border Scouts at left. Hand dated.			
	a. Issued note. Rare.	—	—	—
	b. Hand stamped: *CANCELLED BY PAYMENT*. Rare.	—	—	—

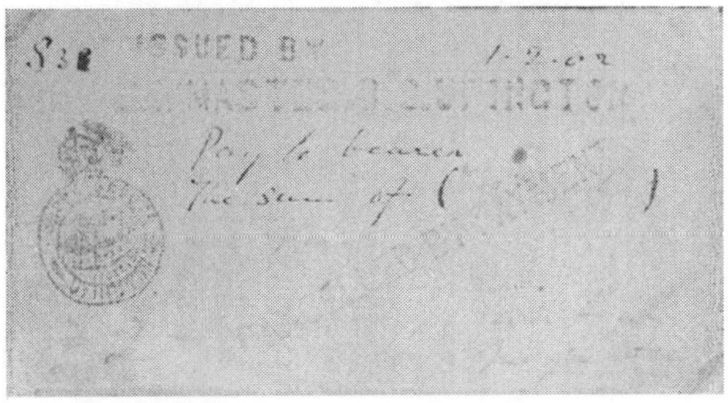

		Good	Fine	XF
S714	**1 Pound**			
	1.2.1902. Emblem of the Border Scouts at left. Hand dated.			
	a. Issued note. Rare.	—	—	—
	b. Hand stamped: *CANCELLED BY PAYMENT*. Rare.	—	—	—

		Good	Fine	XF
S715	**2 Pounds**			
	1902. Emblem of the Border Scouts at left. Hand dated.			
	a. Issued note. Rare.	—	—	—
	b. Hand stamped: *CANCELLED BY PAYMENT*.	750.	2250.	—

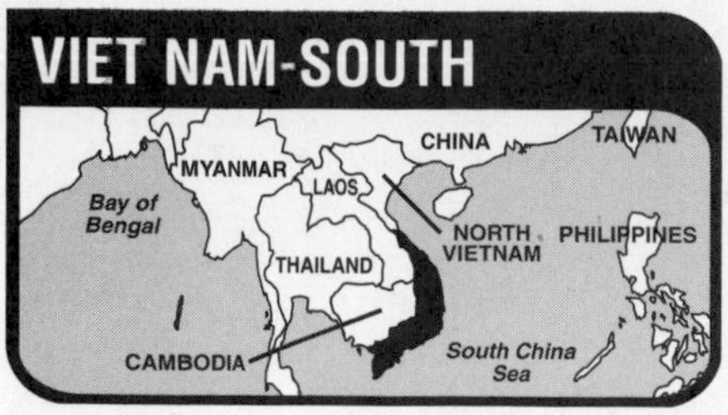

South Viet Nam (the former Republic of Viet Nam), located in Southeast Asia, bounded by North Viet Nam on the north, Laos and Cambodia on the west, and the South China Sea on the east and south, had an area of 66,280 sq. mi. (171,665 sq. km.) and a population of 20 million. Capital: Saigon. The economy of the area is predominantly agricultural.

South Viet Nam, the direct successor to the French-dominated regime (also known as the State of Viet Nam), was created after the first Indochina War (between the French and the Viet-Minh) by the Geneva agreement of 1954 which divided Viet Nam at the 17th parallel of latitude. Elections which would have reunified North and South Viet Nam in 1956 never took place, and the North continued the war for unification of Viet Nam under the the Democratic Republic of (North) Viet Nam. The Republic of Viet Nam surrendered unconditionally on April 30, 1975. There followed a short period of coexistence of the two Viet Namese states, but the South was governed by the North through the Peoples Revolutionary Government (PRG). On July 2, 1976, South and North Viet Nam joined to form the Socialist Republic of Viet Nam.

Also see Viet Nam.

MONETARY SYSTEM

1 Dông = 100 Xu

REGIONAL

ÚY BAN TRUNG U'O'NG

CENTRAL COMMITTEE OF THE NATIONAL FRONT FOR THE LIBERATION OF SOUTH VIETNAM

1963 ND ISSUE

#R1-R8 were printed in China for use in territories under control of the National Liberation Front. They were never issued, but many were captured during a joint US/South Viet Nam military operation into Cambodia. Except for #R2, relatively few survived in uncirculated condition.

		VG	VF	UNC
R1	**10 Xu** ND (1963). Purple and multicolor. Star at center.	.25	1.00	3.00
R2	**20 Xu** ND (1963). Red-brown on aqua and multicolor underprint. Star at center.	.25	1.00	5.00
R3	**50 Xu** ND (1963). Green and multicolor. Star at center.	.50	2.00	8.00

		VG	VF	UNC
R4	**1 Dông** ND (1963). Light brown on multicolor underprint. Harvesting at center. Back: Schoolroom.	1.00	3.00	8.00

		VG	VF	UNC
R5	**2 Dông** ND (1963). Blue on multicolor underprint. Women in convoy at center. Back: Fishermen with boats.	1.00	5.00	25.00
R6	**5 Dông** ND (1963). Lilac on multicolor underprint. Women harvesting at center. Back: Women militia patrol.	1.50	6.00	50.00

		VG	VF	UNC
R7	**10 Dông** ND (1963). Green on multicolor underprint. Harvesting scene at center. Back: War scene.	10.00	60.00	160.

		VG	VF	UNC
R8	**50 Dông** ND (1963). Orange on multicolor underprint. Truck convoy at center. Back: Soldiers shooting down helicopters.	18.00	100.	200.

SENDING SCANNED IMAGES BY E-MAIL

We have been receiving an ever-increasing flow of scanned images from sources world wide. Unfortunately, many of these scans could not be used due to the type of scan, or simple incompatibility with our systems. We appreciate the effort it takes to produce these images and accuracy they add to the catalog listings.

Here are a few simple instructions to follow when producing these scans. We encourage you to continue sending new images or upgrades to those currently illustrated and please do not hesitate to ask questions about this process.

- Scan all images within a resolution of 300 dpi.
- Size setting should be at 100%
- Please include in the e-mail the actual size of the image in millimeters height x width
- Scan in true 4-color
- Save images as jpeg and name in such a way which clearly indentifies the country of the note and catalog number
- Do not compress files
- Please e-mail with a request to confirm receipt of the attachment
- Please send multiple images on a disc if available
- Please send images to: george.cuhaj@fwmedia.com

The Spanish State, forming the greater part of the Iberian Peninsula of southwest Europe, has an area of 504,782 sq. km. and a population of 40.5 million. Capital: Madrid. The economy is d on agriculture, industry and tourism. Machinery, fruit, vegetables and chemicals are exported.

Spain's powerful world empire of the 16th and 17th centuries ultimately yielded command of the seas to England. Subsequent failure to embrace the mercantile and industrial revolutions caused the country to fall behind Britain, France, and Germany in economic and political power. Spain remained neutral in World Wars I and II but suffered through a devastating civil war (1936-39). A peaceful transition to democracy following the death of dictator Francisco Franco in 1975, and rapid economic modernization (Spain joined the EU in 1986) gave Spain a dynamic and rapidly growing economy and made it a global champion of freedom and human rights. The government continues to battle the Basque Fatherland and Liberty (ETA) terrorist organization, but its major focus for the immediate future will be on measures to reverse the severe economic recession that started in mid-2008.

RULERS:

Fernando VII, 1808-1833
Fernando VII, 1808-1833
Isabel II, 1833-1868
Isabel II, 1833-1868
Amadeo I, 1871-1873
Amadeo I, 1871-1873
Regency, 1874
Regency, 1874
Alfonso XII, 1875-1885
Alfonso XII, 1875-1885
Alfonso XIII, 1886-1931
Alfonso XIII, 1886-1931
2nd Republic and Civil War, 1932-1936
2nd Republic and Civil War, 1932-1936
Francisco Franco, regent, 1937-1975
Juan Carlos I, 1975-

MONETARY SYSTEM:

1 Peseta = 100 Centimos 1874-2001
1 Euro = 100 Cents, 2002-

REPLACEMENT NOTES:

#150 and later, *9A, 9B, 9C* type prefix.

COMMERCIAL BANKS:

Aramburu Hermanos	#S151
Banco Balear	#S201-S206
Banco de Barcelona	#S211-S246
Banco de Bilbao	#S251-S256
Banco de Burgos	#S261-S266
Banco de Cádiz	#S271-S296
Banco de la Coruña	#S301-S306
Banco de Emisión de Santiago	#S308
Banco de Jerez de la Frontera	#S311-S316
Banco de Málaga	#S321-S336
Banco de Oviedo	#S341-S346
Banco de Palencia	#S351-S356
Banco de Pamplona	#S361-S366
Banco de Reus	#S371-S380
Banco de San Sebastián	#S381-S386
Banco de Santander	#S391-S396
Banco de Santiago	#S401-S406
Banco de Sevilla	#S411-S416
Banco de Tarragona	#S421-S426
Banco de Valladolid	#S431-S436
Banco de Vitoria	#S441-S446
Banco de Zaragoza	#S451-S456

NOTE: The Assignado Imperial issues are known to be fantasies.

COMMERCIAL BANKS

ARAMBURU HERMANOS

CÁDIZ ISSUE

		Good	Fine	XF
S151	**500 Reales De Vellón** 18xx. Black on brown and green underprint. Allegorical man with lions, two pillars behind, at upper center. Back: Green. Head at left and right. Printer: BWC. Unsigned remainder.	—	Unc	350.

BANCO BALEAR

1864 ISSUE

		Good	Fine	XF
S201	**100 Reales De Vellón** 186x.	—	—	—
S202	**200 Reales De Vellón** 186x.	—	—	—
S203	**500 Reales De Vellón** 186x.	—	—	—
S204	**1000 Reales De Vellón** 186x.	—	—	—

		Good	Fine	XF
S205	**2000 Reales De Vellón** 1864. Two seated allegorical women flanking arms at upper center. Series E.	—	—	—
S206	**4000 Reales De Vellón** 186x.	—	—	—

BANCO DE BARCELONA

1845 ISSUE

		Good	Fine	XF
S211	**250 Pesos** 184x.			
	a. Issued note.	1250.	4000.	—
	b. Reprint. (1894).	—	—	1000.

1840'S ISSUE

		Good	Fine	XF
S221	**5 Pesos** 184x.	1000.	3200.	—
S222	**10 Pesos** 184x.	1000.	3200.	—
S223	**25 Pesos** 184x.	1000.	3200.	—
S224	**50 Pesos** 184x.	1000.	3200.	—
S225	**100 Pesos** 184x.	1000.	3200.	—
S226	**200 Pesos** 184x.			
	a. Issued note.	1000.	3200.	—
	b. Reprint. (1894)	—	—	1000.

1859 ISSUE

		Good	Fine	XF
S231	**5 Pesos** 18xx.	1000.	3200.	—
S232	**10 Pesos** 18xx.	1000.	3200.	—
S233	**25 Pesos** 18xx.	1000.	3200.	—
S234	**50 Pesos** 18xx.	1000.	3200.	—
S235	**100 Pesos** 18xx.	1000.	3250.	—
S236	**200 Pesos** 18xx.			
	a. Issued note.	1000.	3250.	—
	b. Reprint. (1894).	—	—	1000.

1868 ISSUE

		Good	Fine	XF
S241	**5 Pesos** 18xx. Crowned woman at left, woman with shield at right. Series A.			
	a. Issued note.	1000.	3250.	—
	b. Reprint. (1894).	—	—	1000.

		Good	Fine	XF
S242	**10 Pesos** 18xx. Crowned woman at left, woman with shield at right. Series B.	1000.	3250.	—
S243	**25 Pesos** 18xx. Crowned woman at left, woman with shield at right. Series C.	1000.	3250.	—
S244	**50 Pesos** 18xx. Crowned woman at left, woman with shield at right. Series D.	1000.	3250.	—

		Good	Fine	XF
S245	**100 Pesos** 18xx. Crowned woman at left, woman with shield at right. Series E.	1000.	3250.	—
S246	**200 Pesos** 18xx. Crowned woman at left, woman with shield at right. Series F.	1000.	3250.	—

Banco de Bilbao

1859 Issue

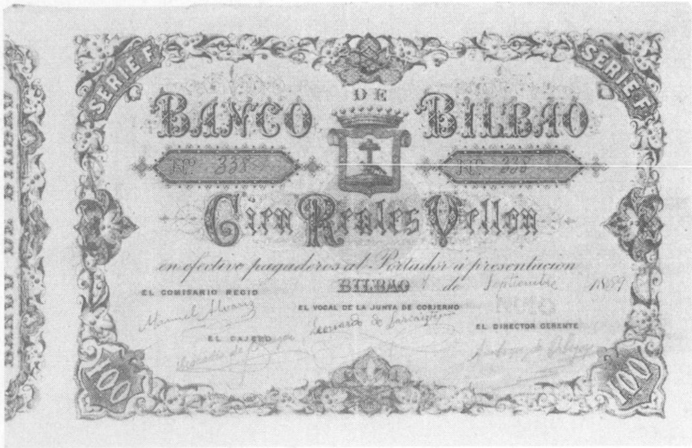

		Good	Fine	XF
S251	**100 Reales De Vellón** 1.9.1859. Crowned arms at upper center. Series F.	650.	2000.	—

NOTE: Facsimiles exist of #S251 and similar designs for denominations of 200, 500, 1000 and 2000 Reales de Vellon produced for stockholder's books in 1932 which were printed on normal paper. Value of $425. for the set of four.

		Good	Fine	XF
S252	**200 Reales De Vellón** 18xx. Series E.	425.	1250.	—

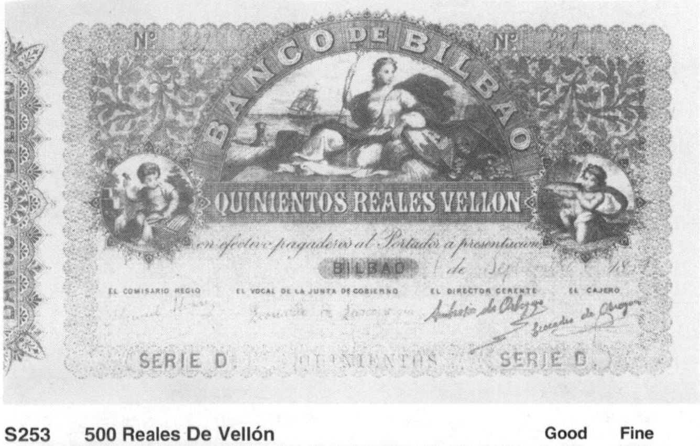

		Good	Fine	XF
S253	**500 Reales De Vellón** 1.9.1859. Cherub at left and right, seated allegorical woman holding staff and shield, sailing ship in background at center. Series D.	425.	1250.	—
S254	**1000 Reales De Vellón** 18xx. Cherub at left and right, seated allegorical woman holding staff and shield, sailing ship in background at center. Series C. Like #S253.	425.	1250.	—

		Good	Fine	XF
S255	**2000 Reales De Vellón** 1.9.1859. Cherub at left and right, seated allegorical woman holding staff and shield, sailing ship in background at center. Series B. Like #S253.	425.	1250.	—
S256	**4000 Reales De Vellón** 18xx. Gateway to mine at left, sailing ship and seated allegorical woman holding staff and shield at center, smelting at right. Series A. Back: Head at left and right.	425.	1250.	—

Banco de Burgos

1864 Issue

		Good	Fine	XF
S261	**100 Reales De Vellón** 1864.	—	—	—
S262	**200 Reales De Vellón** 1864.	—	—	—
S263	**500 Reales De Vellón** 1864.	—	—	—
S264	**1000 Reales De Vellón** 1864.	—	—	—
S265	**2000 Reales De Vellón** 1864.	—	—	—
S266	**4000 Reales De Vellón** 1864.	—	—	—

Banco de Cádiz

1847 Issue

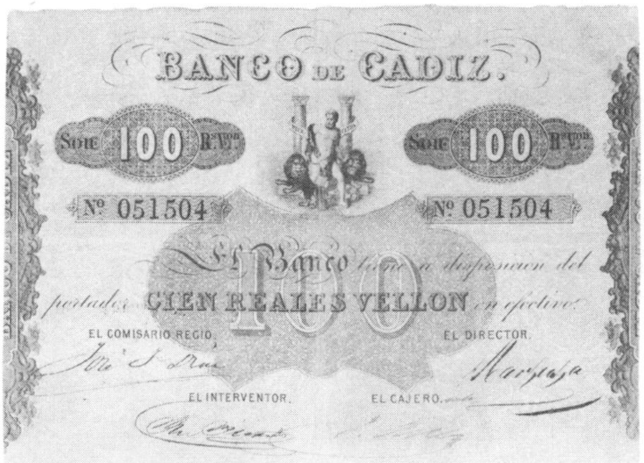

		Good	Fine	XF
S271	**100 Reales De Vellón** 18xx. Black. Without red underprint at center. Hercules with two lions between pillars at top center. Dates filled in by hand. Paper: Green.	50.00	100.	—

		Good	Fine	XF
S272	**200 Reales De Vellón** 18xx. Black. Without red underprint at center. Hercules with two lions between pillars at top center. Dates filled in by hand. Paper: Blue.	200.	650.	—

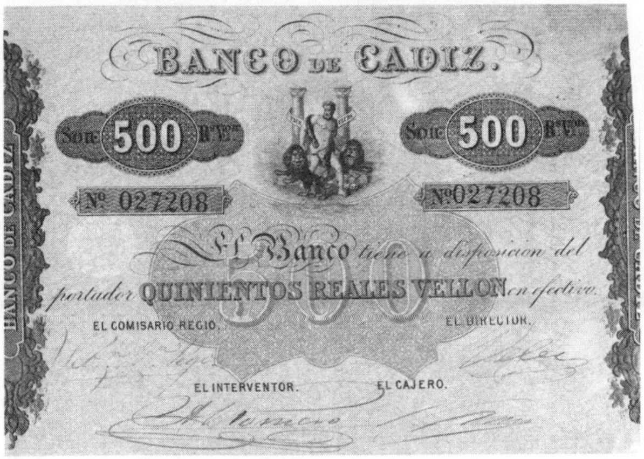

		Good	Fine	XF
S273	**500 Reales De Vellón** 1.8.1851. Black. Without red underprint at center. Hercules with two lions between pillars at top center. Dates filled in by hand. Paper: Brown.	40.00	75.00	—
S274	**1000 Reales De Vellón** 18xx. Black. Without red underprint at center. Hercules with two lions between pillars at top center. Dates filled in by hand. Paper: Yellow.	75.00	200.	—
S275	**2000 Reales De Vellón** 18xx. Black. Without red underprint at center. Hercules with two lions between pillars at top center. Dates filled in by hand. Paper: Rose.	150.	400.	—

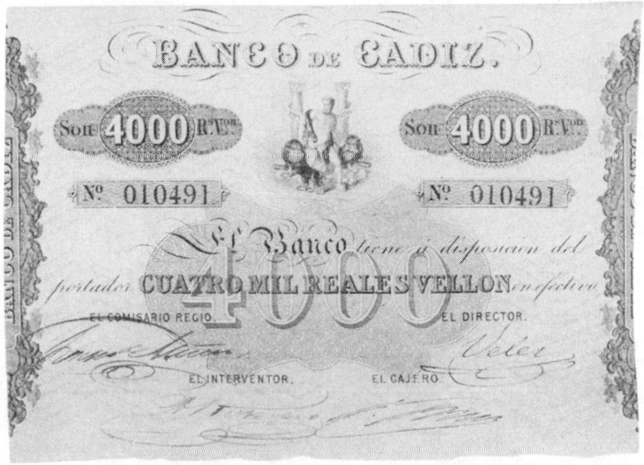

		Good	Fine	XF
S276	**4000 Reales De Vellón** 18xx. Black. Without red underprint at center. Hercules with two lions between pillars at top center. Dates filled in by hand. Paper: White.	125.	350.	—

186x Issue

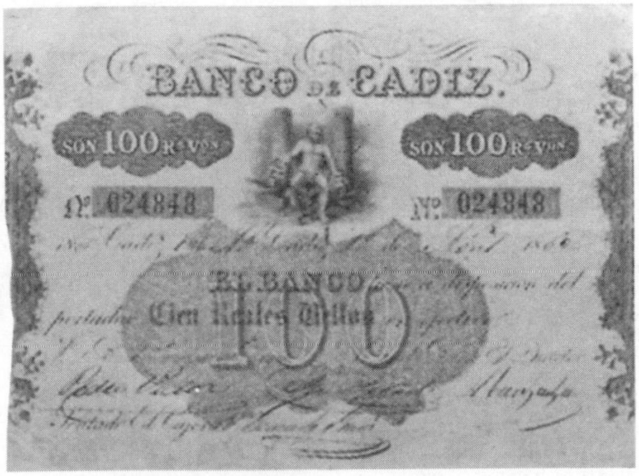

		Good	Fine	XF
S281	**100 Reales De Vellón** 1.8.186x. Black with red underprint at center. Hercules with two lions between pillars at top center. Dates filled in by hand. Paper: Green.	40.00	75.00	—
S282	**200 Reales De Vellón** 18xx. Black with red underprint at center. Hercules with two lions between pillars at top center. Dates filled in by hand. Paper: Blue.	125.	400.	—
S283	**500 Reales De Vellón** 18xx. Black with red underprint at center. Hercules with two lions between pillars at top center. Dates filled in by hand. Paper: Brown.	125.	400.	—
S284	**1000 Reales De Vellón** 18xx. Black with red underprint at center. Hercules with two lions between pillars at top center. Dates filled in by hand. Paper: Yellow.	125.	400.	—
S285	**2000 Reales De Vellón** 18xx. Black with red underprint at center. Hercules with two lions between pillars at top center. Dates filled in by hand. Paper: Rose.	125.	400.	—
S286	**4000 Reales De Vellón** 18xx. Black with red underprint at center. Hercules with two lions between pillars at top center. Dates filled in by hand. Paper: White.	125.	400.	—

1863 ND Issue

		Good	Fine	XF
S291	**100 Reales De Vellón** ND. Black with orange underprint at center. Hercules with two lions between pillars at top center. Paper: Green.	40.00	75.00	—

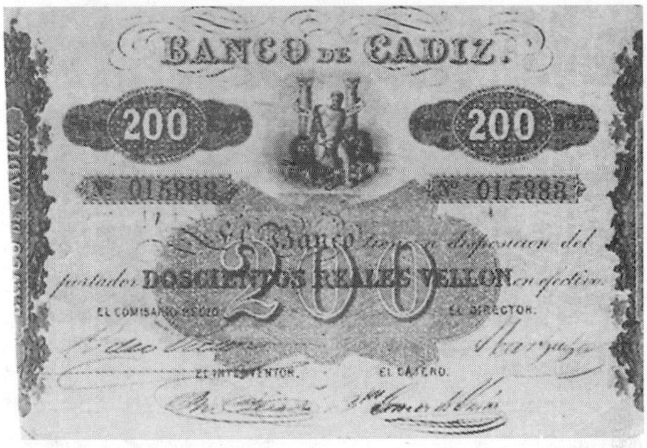

		Good	Fine	XF
S292	**200 Reales De Vellón** ND. Black. Hercules with two lions between pillars at top center. Paper: Blue.	80.00	250.	—
S293	**500 Reales De Vellón** ND. Black. Hercules with two lions between pillars at top center. Paper: Brown.	40.00	75.00	—

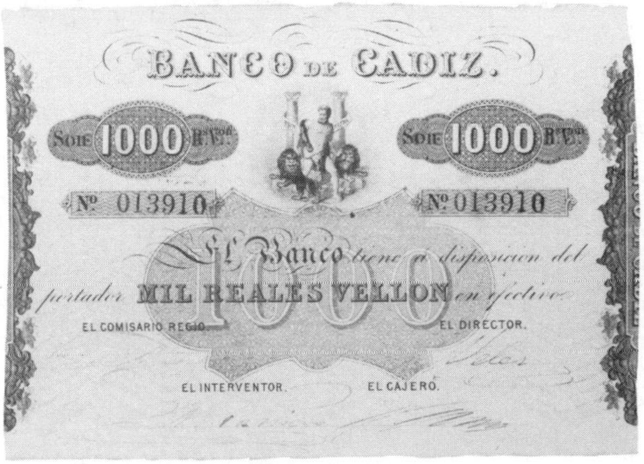

		Good	Fine	XF
S294	**1000 Reales De Vellón** ND. Black. Hercules with two lions between pillars at top center. Paper: Yellow.	60.00	175.	—
S295	**2000 Reales De Vellón** ND. Black. Hercules with two lions between pillars at top center. Paper: Rose.	100.	275.	—

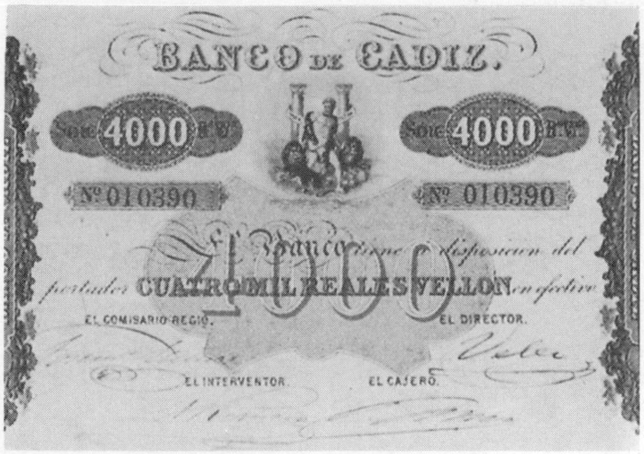

		Good	Fine	XF
S296	**4000 Reales De Vellón** ND. Black with light green underprint at center. Hercules with two lions between pillars at top center. Paper: White.	125.	375.	—

Banco de la Coruña

1857 Issue

		Good	Fine	XF
S301	**100 Reales De Vellón** 18xx.	500.	1500.	—
S302	**200 Reales De Vellón** 18xx.	400.	1250.	—
S303	**500 Reales De Vellón** 18xx.	425.	1300.	—
S304	**1000 Reales De Vellón** 18xx.	425.	1300.	—
S305	**2000 Reales De Vellón** 18xx.	575.	1750.	—
S306	**4000 Reales De Vellón** 18xx.	625.	1900.	—

Banco de Emisión y Descuentos de Santiago

1800's Issue

		Good	Fine	XF
S308	**200 Reales De Vellón** 18xx. Standing allegorical woman holding staff and shield, foliage in background at upper center right. Series B.	—	—	—

Banco de Jerez de la Frontera

1800's Issue

		Good	Fine	XF
S311	**100 Reales De Vellón** 18xx.	—	—	—
S312	**200 Reales De Vellón** 18xx.	—	—	—
S313	**500 Reales De Vellón** 18xx.	—	—	—
S314	**1000 Reales De Vellón** 18xx.	—	—	—

		Good	Fine	XF
S315	**2000 Reales De Vellón** 18xx.	—	—	—
S316	**4000 Reales De Vellón** 18xx.	—	—	—

Banco de Málaga

1860 Issue

		Good	Fine	XF
S321	**100 Reales De Vellón** 18xx. Seated woman with cornucopia at upper center.			
	a. Issued note.	325.	1000.	—
	b. Issued note. Punch hole cancelled.	100.	350.	—
S322	**200 Reales De Vellón** 18xx. Seated woman with cornucopia at upper center.			
	a. Issued note.	350.	1150.	—
	b. Issued note. Punch hole cancelled.	125.	450.	—
S323	**500 Reales De Vellón** 18xx. Seated woman with cornucopia at upper center.			
	a. Issued note.	325.	1000.	—
	b. Issued note.	100.	350.	—
S324	**1000 Reales De Vellón** 18xx. Seated woman with cornucopia at upper center.			
	a. Issued note.	750.	2250.	—
	b. Issued note. Punch hole cancelled.	400.	1250.	—

		Good	Fine	XF
S325	**2000 Reales De Vellón** 18xx. Seated woman with cornucopia at upper center.			
	a. Issued note.	325.	1000.	—
	b. Issued note. Punched hole cancelled.	125.	400.	—
S326	**4000 Reales De Vellón** 18xx. Seated woman with cornucopia at upper center.	500.	1500.	—

1865 ND Issue

		Good	Fine	XF
S331	**100 Reales De Vellón** ND. Multicolor. Seated woman with cornucopia at upper center.	250.	750.	—
S332	**200 Reales De Vellón** ND. Multicolor. Seated woman with cornucopia at upper center.	—	—	—
S333	**500 Reales De Vellón** ND. Multicolor. Seated woman with cornucopia at upper center.	—	—	—
S334	**1000 Reales De Vellón** ND. Multicolor. Seated woman with cornucopia at upper center.	—	—	—
S335	**2000 Reales De Vellón** ND. Multicolor. Seated woman with cornucopia at upper center.	—	—	—
S336	**4000 Reales De Vellón** ND. Multicolor. Seated woman with cornucopia at upper center.	—	—	—

Banco de Oviedo

1864 Issue

		Good	Fine	XF
S341	**100 Reales De Vellón** 186x.	—	—	—
S342	**200 Reales De Vellón** 186x.	—	—	—
S343	**500 Reales De Vellón** 186x.	—	—	—

	Good	Fine	XF
S344 1000 Reales De Vellón 186x.	—	—	—
S345 2000 Reales De Vellón 186x.	—	—	—
S346 4000 Reales De Vellón 186x.	—	—	—

Banco de Palencia

1864 Issue

	Good	Fine	XF
S351 100 Reales De Vellón 186x.	—	—	—
S352 200 Reales De Vellón 186x.	—	—	—
S353 500 Reales De Vellón 186x.	—	—	—
S354 1000 Reales De Vellón 186x.	—	—	—
S355 2000 Reales De Vellón 186x.	—	—	—
S356 4000 Reales De Vellón 186x.	—	—	—

Banco de Pamplona

1863 Issue

	Good	Fine	XF
S361 100 Reales De Vellón 186x.	—	—	—
S362 200 Reales De Vellón 186x.	—	—	—
S363 500 Reales De Vellón 186x.	—	—	—
S364 1000 Reales De Vellón 186x.	—	—	—
S365 2000 Reales De Vellón 186x.	—	—	—
S366 4000 Reales De Vellón 186x.	—	—	—

Banco de Reus

1862 Issue

	Good	Fine	XF
S371 100 Reales De Vellón 186x.	—	—	—
S372 200 Reales De Vellón 186x.	—	—	—
S373 500 Reales De Vellón 186x.	—	—	—
S374 1000 Reales De Vellón 186x.	—	—	—
S375 2000 Reales De Vellón 186x.	—	—	—
S376 4000 Reales De Vellón 186x.	—	—	—

1870s Issue

	Good	Fine	XF
S380 2000 Reales De Vellón 187x. Black. Arms at upper center, standing figures at left and right. Series B.	—	—	—

Banco de San Sebastián

1862 Issue

	Good	Fine	XF
S381 100 Reales De Vellón 186x.	—	—	—
S382 200 Reales De Vellón 186x.	—	—	—

	Good	Fine	XF
S383 500 Reales De Vellón 186x.	—	—	—
S384 1000 Reales De Vellón 186x.	—	—	—
S385 2000 Reales De Vellón 186x.	—	—	—
S386 4000 Reales De Vellón 186x.	—	—	—

Banco de Santander

1857 Issue

	Good	Fine	XF
S391 100 Reales De Vellón 18xx. Flags and sailing ship at upper center.	—	—	—
S392 200 Reales De Vellón 18xx. Flags and sailing ship at upper center.	—	—	—
S393 500 Reales De Vellón 1.5.1861. Black on pink underprint. Flags and sailing ship at upper center. Series C.	425.	1250.	—
S394 1000 Reales De Vellón 18xx. Flags and sailing ship at upper center.	—	—	—
S395 2000 Reales De Vellón 18xx. Flags and sailing ship at upper center.	—	—	—
S396 4000 Reales De Vellón 18xx. Flags and sailing ship at upper center.	—	—	—

Banco de Santiago

1864 Issue

	Good	Fine	XF
S401 100 Reales De Vellón 186x.	—	—	—
S402 200 Reales De Vellón 186x.	—	—	—
S403 500 Reales De Vellón 186x.	—	—	—
S404 1000 Reales De Vellón 186x.	—	—	—
S405 2000 Reales De Vellón 186x.	—	—	—
S406 4000 Reales De Vellón 186x.	—	—	—

Banco de Sevilla

1857 Issue

	Good	Fine	XF
S411 100 Reales De Vellón 185x. Arms at center.	—	—	—
S412 200 Reales De Vellón 185x. Arms at center.	—	—	—

	Good	Fine	XF
S413 500 Reales De Vellón 185x. Arms at center.	—	—	—
S414 1000 Reales De Vellón 185x. Arms at center.	—	—	—

	Good	Fine	XF
S415 2000 Reales De Vellón 185x. Arms at center.	—	—	—
S416 4000 Reales De Vellón 185x. Arms at center.	—	—	—

Banco de Tarragona

1864 Issue

		Good	Fine	XF
S421	**100 Reales De Vellón** 186x.	—	—	—
S422	**200 Reales De Vellón** 186x.	—	—	—
S423	**500 Reales De Vellón** 186x.	—	—	—
S424	**1000 Reales De Vellón** 186x.	—	—	—
S425	**2000 Reales De Vellón** 186x.	—	—	—
S426	**4000 Reales De Vellón** 186x.	—	—	—

Banco de Valladolid

1857 Issue

		Good	Fine	XF
S431	**100 Reales De Vellón** 1.8.1857. Double arms at upper center. Series A.	—	—	—
S432	**200 Reales De Vellón** 1.8.1857. Double arms at upper center. Series B.	750.	2250.	—

		Good	Fine	XF
S433	**500 Reales De Vellón** 1.8.1857. Double arms at upper center. Series C.			
	a. Issued note.	200.	600.	—
	b. With liquidation hand stamp.	150.	450.	—
S434	**1000 Reales De Vellón** 1.8.1857. Lilac and black. Double arms at upper center. Series D.	175.	500.	—
S435	**2000 Reales De Vellón** 1.8.1857. Double arms at upper center. Series E.	200.	600.	—
S436	**4000 Reales De Vellón** 1.8.1857. Double arms at upper center. Series F.	750.	2250.	—

Banco de Vitoria

1860 ND Issue

		Good	Fine	XF
S441	**100 Reales De Vellón** 186x. Arms at upper left, center and right.	—	—	—
S442	**200 Reales De Vellón** 186x. Arms at upper left, center and right.	—	—	—
S443	**500 Reales De Vellón** 186x. Arms at upper left, center and right.	—	—	—
S444	**1000 Reales De Vellón** 186x. Arms at upper left, center and right.	—	—	—
S445	**2000 Reales De Vellón** 186x. Arms at upper left, center and right.	—	—	—
S446	**4000 Reales De Vellón** 186x. Arms at upper left, center and right.	—	—	—

Banco de Zaragoza

1857 Issue

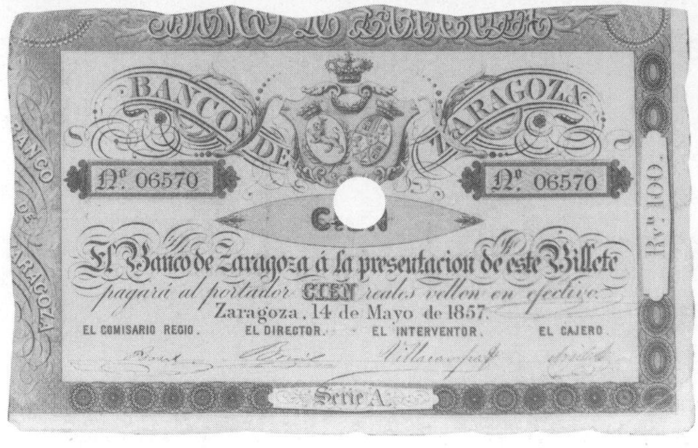

		Good	Fine	XF
S451	**100 Reales De Vellón** 14.5.1857. Crowned double arms at upper center.			
	a. Issued note.	125.	350.	—
	b. Punched hole cancelled.	75.00	225.	—

		Good	Fine	XF
S452	**200 Reales De Vellón** 14.5.1857. Crowned double arms at upper center. Series B.			
	a. Issued note.	125.	375.	—
	b. Punched hole cancelled.	75.00	225.	—

		Good	Fine	XF
S453	**500 Reales De Vellón** 14.5.1857. Crowned double arms at upper center. Series B.			
	a. Issued note.	125.	400.	—
	b. Punched hole cancelled.	75.00	225.	—
S454	**1000 Reales De Vellón** 14.5.1857. Crowned double arms at upper center.	100.	350.	—

		Good	Fine	XF
S455	**2000 Reales De Vellón** 14.5.1857. Crowned double arms at upper center. Series E. Remainder.	125.	400.	—
S456	**4000 Reales De Vellón** 14.5.1857. Crowned double arms at upper center.	500.	1500.	—

Civil War

With the end of the Spanish-American War (1898) and the loss of her empire, Spain drifted into chaotic times. Stung by their defeats in Cuba, the army blamed the socialists for what they considered to be mismanagement at home. Additional political complications were derived from the successful Russian Revolution which gave impetus to an already thriving socialist party and trade union movement. Finally, King Alfonso XIII committed the fatal mistake of encouraging a reckless general to star

MONETARY SYSTEM

1 Peseta = 100 Centimos NOTE: There are primitively produced notes in denominations of 10, 25, 50, 500, 1000 Pesetas, stamped, date hand typewritten and printed heading: *GENERALITAT DE CATALUNYA* which are believed to be forgeries produced for collectors.

Banco de España, Bilbao

1936 Issue

The name of the issuing bank was hand stamped at lower right on the 5 Pesetas notes and imprinted on the 25, 50 and 100 Pesetas notes. The following banks and a bank pawn shop issued notes:

a. Banco de Bilbao
b. Banco Central de Bilbao
c. Banco del Comercio de Bilbao
d. Banco Guipuzcoano
e. Banco Hispano Americano
f. Banco Urquijo Vascongado
g. Banco de Vizcaya (9 varieties of hand stamps)
h. Caja de Ahorros Vizcaína (2 varieties of hand stamps)
i. Caja de Ahorros y Monte de Piedad Municipal de Bilbao

#S551-S554 uniface.

		VG	VF	UNC
S551	**5 Pesetas** 30.8.1936. Red on olive. Hand stamps: a-i.			
	a. Serial # at upper center 2 serial # varieties. Denomination at upper right.	20.00	65.00	135.
	b. Prefix serial letter A at upper right. Denomination at upper center.	20.00	65.00	135.

#S552-S554 various hand stamped dates.

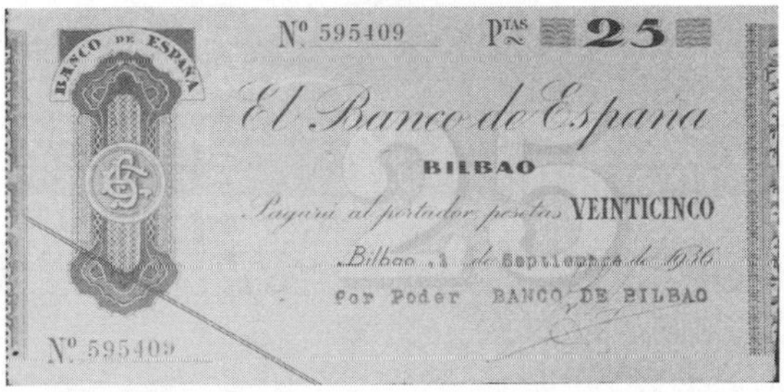

		VG	VF	UNC
S552	**25 Pesetas** 1.9.1936-13.3.1937. Brown-violet. Local bank imprints: a-i. Various hand stamped dates.	20.00	60.00	100.

		VG	VF	UNC
S553	**50 Pesetas** 1.9.1936-17.3.1937. Green on olive. Local bank imprints: a-i. Various hand stamped dates.	20.00	60.00	100.
S554	**100 Pesetas** 1.9.1936; 28.10.1936; 9.1.1937; 6.3.1937. Blue on olive. Local bank imprints: a-i. Various hand stamped dates.	20.00	60.00	100.

1937 Issue

This series has designs on back.

The name of the issuing bank was imprinted at lower right. The following banks and a pawn shop issued notes.

a. Banco de Bilbao
b. Banco del Comercio
c. Banco Guipuzcoano
d. Banco Hispano Americano
e. Banco Urquijo Vascongado
f. Banco de Vizcaya
g. Caja de Ahorros Vizcaína
h. Caja de Ahorros y Monte de Piedad Municipal de Bilbao
I. Banco Central

Market valuations indicated are for the more commonly encountered issues. Some of the scarcer issues are #S561c; S562g; S563d and e, and S564g.

		VG	VF	UNC
S561	**5 Pesetas** 1.1.1937. Green. Local bank imprints: a; c; d; e; f; g; h. Back: Shepherd with herd and tree.	3.00	10.00	17.50

		VG	VF	UNC
S562	**10 Pesetas** 1.1.1937. Brown. Local bank imprints: a; f; g; h. Back: Entrance to a building.	15.00	30.00	65.00

		VG	VF	UNC
S563	**25 Pesetas** 1.1.1937. Brown. Local bank imprints: b; d; e; g. Back: Forge.	7.00	15.00	30.00

		VG	VF	UNC
S564	**50 Pesetas**			
	1.1.1937. Blue. Local bank imprints: a; f; g; h. Back: Worker.	7.00	15.00	30.00

		VG	VF	UNC
S565	**100 Pesetas**			
	1.1.1937. Green. Local bank imprints: a; f; h. Back: Farmer plowing with two oxen.	3.50	7.00	22.50
S566	**500 Pesetas**			
	1.1.1937. Gray-brown. Back: Port.			
	a. Local bank imprints: a-i.	—	—	750.
	b. Without local bank imprint.	—	—	—

		VG	VF	UNC
S567	**1000 Pesetas**			
	1.1.1937. Lilac. Back: Factory plant.			
	a. Local bank imprints: a-i.	—	—	75.00
	b. Without local bank imprint.	—	—	—

Banco de España, Gijón

1936 Issue

		VG	VF	UNC
S571	**5 Pesetas**			
	5.11.1936. Pink with brown. Diagonal stripe.	35.00	120.	250.
S572	**10 Pesetas**			
	5.11.1936. Pink with green. Diagonal stripe.	30.00	100.	200.

		VG	VF	UNC
S573	**25 Pesetas**			
	5.11.1936. Pink with blue. Diagonal stripe.	35.00	90.00	150.
S574	**50 Pesetas**			
	5.11.1936. Green with yellow. Diagonal stripe.	35.00	90.00	160.

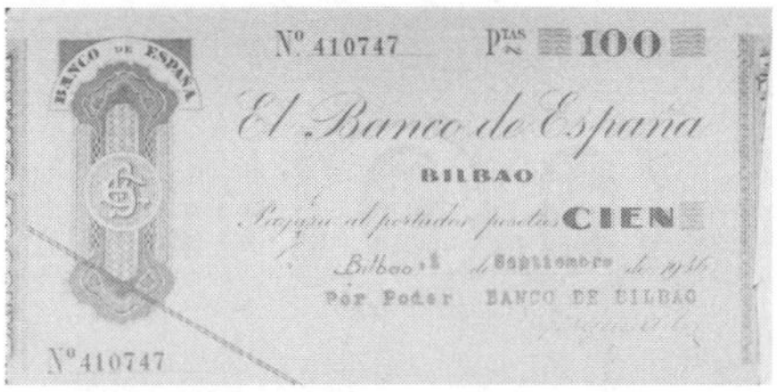

		VG	VF	UNC
S575	**100 Pesetas**			
	5.11.1936. Green with red-brown. Diagonal stripe.	30.00	80.00	150.

1937 Issue

		VG	VF	UNC
S579	**50 Pesetas**			
	Sept., 1937. Blue. Back: Worker in factory plant.	—	—	900.

		VG	VF	UNC
S580	**100 Pesetas**			
	Sept., 1937. Blue on light brown. Back: Two farmers working.	5.00	7.00	15.00

Banco de España, Santander

1936 Issue

Issued by different banks whose name appears imprinted at lower right. The following banks and a pawn shop issued notes:

a. Banco de Bilbao-Santander
b. Banco Español de Crédito
c. Banco Hispano Americano
d. Banco Mercantil
e. Banco de Santander
f. Monte de Piedad

		VG	VF	UNC
S581	**5 Pesetas**			
	1.11.1936. Gray. Local bank or pawn shop imprints: a-f.	25.00	150.	375.
S582	**10 Pesetas**			
	1.11.1936. Gray. Local bank or pawn shop imprints: a-f.	220.	350.	500.
S583	**25 Pesetas**			
	1.11.1936. Gray. Local bank or pawn shop imprints: a-f.	75.00	125.	225.

		VG	VF	UNC
S584	**50 Pesetas** 1.11.1936. Gray. Local bank or pawn shop imprints: a-f.	75.00	120.	175.
S585	**100 Pesetas** 1.11.1936. Gray. Local bank or pawn shop imprints: a-f.	75.00	120.	175.

Generalitat de Catalunya

1936 Issue

NOTE: There are primitively produced notes in denominations of 10, 25, 50, 500, 1000 Pesetas, stamped, date hand typewritten and printed heading: *GENERALITAT DE CATALUNYA* which are believed to be forgeries produced for collectors.

		VG	VF	UNC
S591	**2.50 Pessetes** 25.9.1936. Gray-green. Back: Worker and factory.			
	a. Red serial #.	25.00	100.	300.
	b. Black serial #.	25.00	100.	300.

		VG	VF	UNC
S592	**5 Pessetes** 25.9.1936. Brown. Back: Rifles at center, worker at left, farmer at right.	25.00	150.	375.
S593	**10 Pessetes** 25.9.1936. Green. Back: Fishing boats.	35.00	275.	475.

NOTE: There are primitively produced notes in denominations of 10, 25, 50, 500, 1000 Pesetas, stamped, date hand typewritten and printed heading: *GENERALITAT DE CATALUNYA* which are believed to be forgeries produced for collectors.

Consejo de Asturias y León

1936 Issue

		VG	VF	UNC
S601	**25 Centimos** ND (ca.1936). Gray-violet and blue. Back: Working in the port.	1.50	3.00	5.00
S602	**40 Centimos** ND (ca.1936). Brown-violet and green. Back: Working in the port.	1.50	3.50	6.00
S603	**50 Centimos** ND (ca.1936). Blue and violet. Back: Blacksmith.	20.00	40.00	100.

		VG	VF	UNC
S604	**1 Peseta** ND (ca.1936). Red-brown and yellow. Seated woman with lion at left.	2.00	5.00	15.00
S605	**2 Pesetas** ND (ca.1936). Gray-olive and red. Seated woman with lion at left.	7.50	15.00	27.00

Straits Settlements

Straits Settlements is a former British crown colony on the south and west coast of Malay Peninsula consisting of Malacca, Penang, Singapore, Labuan (Borneo), Cocos Island and Christmas Island. Cocos Island, Christmas Island and Labuan were placed under control of the Governor of Straits Settlements in 1886.

The colony was united under one government as a presidency of India in 1826, was incorporated under Bengal in 1830, and was removed from control of the Indian government and placed under direct British control in 1867. Japanese forces occupied the colony in 1941-45.

RULERS:
British

MONETARY SYSTEM:
1 Dollar = 100 Cents

British Administration

Asiatic Banking Corporation

Singapore

1862 Issue

		Good	Fine	XF
S75	**10 Dollars** 18xx. Pink and black. Arms at center. Printer: Smith Elder & Company, Engravers, London. Unsigned remainder.	—	—	—
S76	**25 Dollars** 18xx. Orange and black. Arms at center. Printer: Smith Elder & Company, Engravers, London. Unsigned remainder.	—	—	—
S77	**50 Dollars** 18xx. Mauve and black. Arms at center. Printer: Smith Elder & Company, Engravers, London. Unsigned remainder.	—	—	—
S78	**100 Dollars** 18xx. Green and black. Arms at center. Printer: Smith Elder & Company, Engravers, London. Unsigned remainder.	—	—	—

		Good	Fine	XF
S79	**500 Dollars** 18xx. Blue and black. Arms at center. Printer: Smith Elder & Company, Engravers, London. Unsigned remainder.	—	—	—

Chartered Bank of India, Australia and China

Penang

1875 Issue

		Good	Fine	XF
S101	**5 Dollars** 18xx. Dark black with deep yellow *FIVE* protector. Crowned supported arms at upper center. Signature varieties. Printer: WWS.	4000.	7500.	15,000.
S102	**10 Dollars** 18xx. Blue with green *TEN* protector. Crowned supported arms at upper center. Signature varieties. Printer: WWS.	5300.	8000.	16,000.
S103	**20 Dollars** 18xx. Orange and blue. Crowned supported arms at upper center. Signature varieties. Printer: WWS.	6750.	9500.	19,000.
S104	**50 Dollars** 18xx. Brown with magenta protector. Crowned supported arms at upper center. Signature varieties. Printer: WWS.	11,500.	16,000.	32,500.
S105	**100 Dollars** 18xx. Green and red-orange. Crowned supported arms at upper center. Signature varieties. Printer: WWS.			
	a. Issued note.	14,500.	24,000.	5000.
	p. Proof. Black.	—	—	17,500.
S106	**500 Dollars** 18xx. Orange and brown. Crowned supported arms at upper center. Signature varieties. Printer: WWS. Rare.	—	—	—

NOTE: A $25 denomination requires confirmation.

Singapore

1861 Issue

		Good	Fine	XF
S111	**5 Dollars** 1.1.1890; 26.3.1890; 1.9.1893. Black on deep yellow *FIVE* protector. Crowned supported arms at upper center. Signature varieties. Printer: WWS.			
	a. Issued note.	4750.	8000.	16,000.
	s. Specimen.	—	—	14,000.

		Good	Fine	XF
S112	**10 Dollars** 25.5.1895. Blue on green *TEN* protector. Crowned supported arms at upper center. Signature varieties. Printer: WWS.	5800.	8500.	17,500.
S113	**20 Dollars** 18xx. Yellow and mauve. Crowned supported arms at upper center. Signature varieties. Printer: WWS.	6500.	9500.	20,000.
S115	**50 Dollars** 18xx. Brown on magenta protector. Crowned supported arms at upper center. Signature varieties. Printer: WWS.	10,500.	13,500.	26,000.
S116	**100 Dollars** 18xx. Green and brown. Crowned supported arms at upper center. Signature varieties. Printer: WWS. Rare.	—	—	—

Chartered Mercantile Bank of India, London and China

Malacca

1881 Issue

		Good	Fine	XF
S121	**5 Dollars** 1.5.1886. Dark blue on light blue underprint. Crowned supported English arms at upper center. Various date and signature varieties. Printer: PBC. Rare.	—	—	—

No.	Description	Good	Fine	XF
S122 10 Dollars	2.1.1882; 2.1.1884. Blue with ornate red *TEN* protector. Crowned supported English arms at upper center. Various date and signature varieties. Printer: PBC. Cancelled. Rare.	—	—	—

#S123 *Deleted.*

No.	Description	Good	Fine	XF
S124 25 Dollars	18xx. Brown and black. Crowned supported English arms at upper center. Various date and signature varieties. Printer: PBC. Rare.	—	—	—
S125 50 Dollars	18xx. Green. Crowned supported English arms at upper center. Various date and signature varieties. Printer: PBC. Rare.	—	—	—
S126 100 Dollars	18xx. Black. Crowned supported English arms at upper center. Various date and signature varieties. Printer: PBC. Rare.	—	—	—
S127 500 Dollars	18xx. Orange and brown. Crowned supported English arms at upper center. Various date and signature varieties. Printer: PBC. Rare.	—	—	—

Penang

1861 Issue

No.	Description	Good	Fine	XF
S131 5 Dollars	2.1.1884; 2.12.1887. Blue on light blue underprint. Crowned supported English arms at upper center. Various date and signature varieties. Printer: PBC. Rare.	—	—	—
S132 10 Dollars	18xx. Blue with ornate red *TEN* protector. Crowned supported English arms at upper center. Various date and signature varieties. Printer: PBC.			
	a. Issued note. Rare.	—	—	—
	b. 4.4.1881. Cut and rejoined.	—	1000.	—

#S133 *Deleted.*

No.	Description	Good	Fine	XF
S134 25 Dollars	18xx. Brown and black. Crowned supported English arms at upper center. Various date and signature varieties. Printer: PBC. Rare.	—	—	—
S135 50 Dollars	18xx. Green. Crowned supported English arms at upper center. Various date and signature varieties. Printer: PBC. Rare.	—	—	—
S136 100 Dollars	18xx. Black. Crowned supported English arms at upper center. Various date and signature varieties. Printer: PBC. Rare.	—	—	—
S137 500 Dollars	18xx. Orange and brown. Crowned supported English arms at upper center. Various date and signature varieties. Printer: PBC. Reported not confirmed.	—	—	—

Singapore

1861 Issue

No.	Description	Good	Fine	XF
S138 50 Dollars	18xx. Seated allegorical woman with lion, crowned shield, tree at center. Proof.	—	—	—
S139 100 Dollars	18xx. Black on red underprint. Proof.	—	—	50,000.
S140 500 Dollars	18xx. Dark brown. Proof.	—	—	—
S141 5 Dollars	19xx. Blue and black. Crowned royal arms at upper center. Printer: WWS. Rare.	—	—	—
S142 10 Dollars	19xx. Blue with red *TEN* protector. Crowned royal arms at upper center. Printer: WWS. Rare.	—	—	—

#S143 *Deleted.*

No.	Description	Good	Fine	XF
S144 25 Dollars	(ca.1862). Brown. Crowned royal arms at upper center. Printer: WWS. Rare.	—	—	—
S145 50 Dollars	18xx. Green. Crowned royal arms at upper center. Printer: WWS. Rare.	—	—	—
S146 100 Dollars	19xx. Crowned royal arms at upper center. Printer: WWS. Rare.	—	—	—
S147 500 Dollars	(ca.1864). Brown with ornate blue *FIVE HUNDRED* protector. Crowned royal arms at upper center. Printer: WWS. Rare.	—	—	—

Hongkong and Shanghai Banking Corporation

Penang

1893 Issue

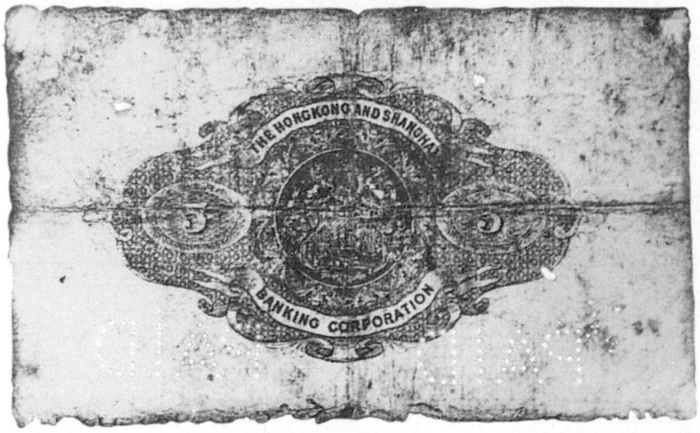

No.	Description	Good	Fine	XF
S151 5 Dollars	1.9.1893. Light green on maroon underprint. Crowned supported arms at upper center, large *PENANG* in underprint. Various date and signature varieties. Back: Ornate arms at center. Printer: Metchim & Son, London.			
	a. Issued note.	4750.	8000.	16,000.
	b. Issued note. Punch hole cancelled: *PAID.*	3000.	7500.	15,000.
S152 10 Dollars	18xx. Blue. Crowned supported arms at upper center, large *PENANG* in underprint. Various date and signature varieties. Back: Ornate arms at center. Printer: Metchim & Son, London.	5500.	8500.	17,500.
S153 20 Dollars	18xx. Blue-green. Crowned supported arms at upper center, large *PENANG* in underprint. Various date and signature varieties. Back: Ornate arms at center. Printer: Metchim & Son, London.	6000.	12,000.	24,000.
S154 25 Dollars	18xx. Brown. Crowned supported arms at upper center, large *PENANG* in underprint. Various date and signature varieties. Back: Ornate arms at center. Printer: Metchim & Son, London.	6500.	13,000.	26,000.
S155 50 Dollars	18xx. Violet. Crowned supported arms at upper center, large *PENANG* in underprint. Various date and signature varieties. Back: Ornate arms at center. Printer: Metchim & Son, London.	9250.	18,000.	36,000.
S156 100 Dollars	18xx. Red-orange. Crowned supported arms at upper center, large *PENANG* in underprint. Various date and signature varieties. Back: Ornate arms at center. Printer: Metchim & Son, London.	11,750.	22,000.	45,000.

		Good	Fine	XF
S157	**500 Dollars** 18xx. Red. Crowned supported arms at upper center, large *PENANG* in underprint. Various date and signature varieties. Back: Ornate arms at center. Printer: Metchim & Son, London. Rare.	—	—	—

SINGAPORE

1881 FIRST ISSUE

		Good	Fine	XF
S161	**5 Dollars** 1.1.1894. Green. Crowned supported arms at upper center with denomination protector. Back: Ornate arms at center. Printer: Metchim & Son, London.	4750.	9000.	18,000.

		Good	Fine	XF
S162	**10 Dollars** 18xx. Blue. Crowned supported arms at upper center with denomination protector. Back: Ornate arms at center. Printer: Metchim & Son, London.	5500.	11,000.	22,500.

#S163 *Deleted.*

		Good	Fine	XF
S164	**25 Dollars** 18xx. Brown. Crowned supported arms at upper center with denomination protector. Back: Ornate arms at center. Printer: Metchim & Son, London.	6500.	13,000.	26,000.
S165	**50 Dollars** 18xx. Violet. Crowned supported arms at upper center with denomination protector. Back: Ornate arms at center. Printer: Metchim & Son, London.	9250.	18,000.	36,000.
S166	**100 Dollars** 18xx. Red-orange with dark blue $100-$100 protector. Crowned supported arms at upper center with denomination protector. Back: Ornate arms at center. Printer: Metchim & Son, London.	11,750.	22,500.	45,000.
S167	**500 Dollars** 18xx. Red. Crowned supported arms at upper center with denomination protector. Back: Ornate arms at center. Printer: Metchim & Son, London. Rare.	—	—	—

1881 SECOND ISSUE

		Good	Fine	XF
S169	**5 Dollars** 18xx. Green. Arms at upper center. Large guilloche as protector.	4750.	9000.	18,000.
S170	**10 Dollars** 18xx. Blue. Arms at upper center. Large guilloche as protector.	5500.	11,000.	23,000.
S171	**25 Dollars** 18xx. Blue-green. Arms at upper center. Large guilloche as protector.	6500.	13,000.	26,000.
S172	**50 Dollars** 18xx. Violet. Arms at upper center. Large guilloche as protector.	9250.	18,500.	37,000.
S173	**100 Dollars** 18xx. Red-orange. Arms at upper center. Large guilloche as protector.	12,000.	24,000.	50,000.
S174	**500 Dollars** 18xx. Red. Arms at upper center. Large guilloche as protector. Rare.	—	—	—

NEW ORIENTAL BANK CORPORATION, LIMITED

1884 ISSUE

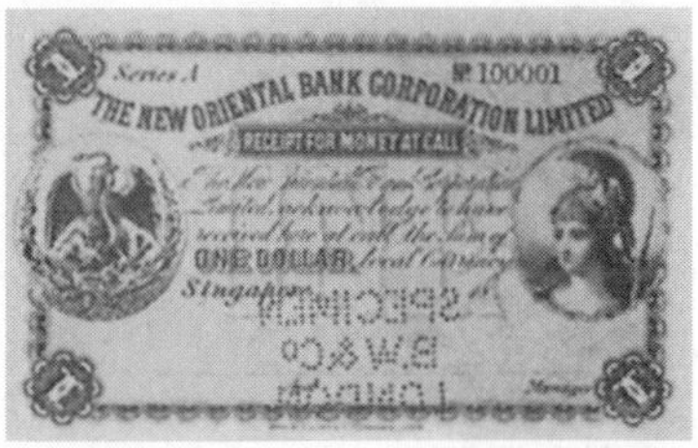

		Good	Fine	XF
S181	**1 Dollar** 18xx. Arms of Mexico at left, woman's head at right. Printer: BWC. Specimen. Rare.	—	—	—

NORTH WESTERN BANK OF INDIA

1830'S ISSUE

		Good	Fine	XF
S196	**100 Dollars** Woman standing by beehive at top center. Specimen. Rare.	—	—	—

NOTE: The single known example of #S196 is unissued. Other denominations are not confirmed.

ORIENTAL BANK

1849 ISSUE

		Good	Fine	XF
S201	**5 Dollars** 31.5.1849. Requires confirmation.	—	—	—
S205	**100 Dollars** 31.5.1849. Requires confirmation.	—	—	—

ORIENTAL BANK CORPORATION

1851 ISSUE

		Good	Fine	XF
S215	**100 Dollars** 1851.	—	—	—

UNION BANK OF CALCUTTA

1840'S ISSUE

		Good	Fine	XF
S225	**100 Spanish Dollars** 184x. Printer: Smith, Elder & Co., Cornhill, London, England. Rare.	—	—	—

NOTE: Additional denominations require confirmation.

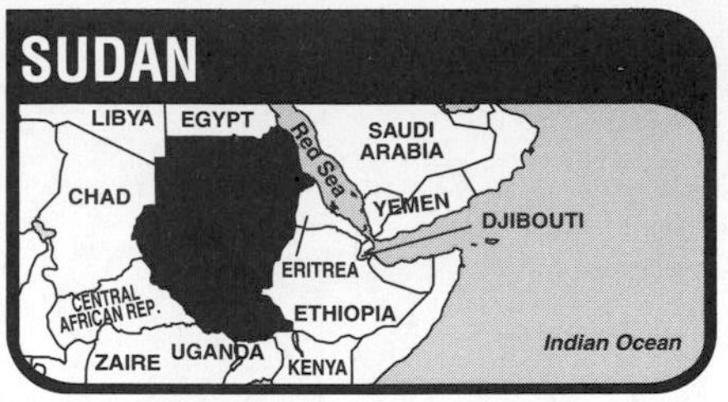

The Democratic Republic of the Sudan, located in northeast Africa on the Red Sea between Egypt and Ethiopia, has an area of 2,505,810 sq. km. and a population of 40.22 million. Capital: Khartoum. Agriculture and livestock raising are the chief occupations. Cotton, gum arabic and peanuts are exported. Military regimes favoring Islamic-oriented governments have dominated national politics since independence from the UK in 1956. Sudan was embroiled in two prolonged civil wars during most of the remainder of the 20th century. These conflicts were rooted in northern economic, political, and social domination of largely non-Muslim, non-Arab southern Sudanese. The first civil war ended in 1972 but broke out again in 1983. The second war and famine-related effects resulted in more than four million people displaced and, according to rebel estimates, more than two million deaths over a period of two decades. Peace talks gained momentum in 2002-04 with the signing of several accords. The final North/South Comprehensive Peace Agreement (CPA), signed in January 2005, granted the southern rebels autonomy for six years. After which, a referendum for independence is scheduled to be held. A separate conflict, which broke out in the western region of Darfur in 2003, has displaced nearly two million people and caused an estimated 200,000 to 400,000 deaths. The UN took command of the Darfur peacekeeping operation from the African Union on 31 December 2007. As of early 2009, peacekeeping troops were struggling to stabilize the situation, which has become increasingly regional in scope, and has brought instability to eastern Chad, and Sudanese incursions into the Central African Republic. Sudan also has faced large refugee influxes from neighboring countries, primarily Ethiopia and Chad. Armed conflict, poor transport infrastructure, and lack of government support have chronically obstructed the provision of humanitarian assistance to affected populations.

RULERS:

British, 1899-1954
Italian, 1940

MONETARY SYSTEM:

1 Ghirsh (Piastre) = 10 Millim (Milliemes)
1 Sudanese Pound = 100 Piastres to 1992
1 Dinar = 10 Old Sudanese Pounds, 1992

British Administration

Siege Of Khartoum, 1884

1884 First Sudan Piastre Issue

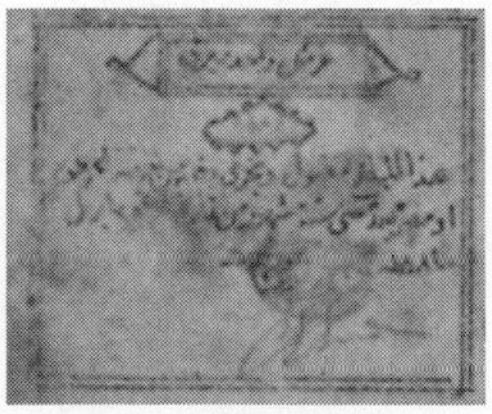

S101 1 Piastre	Good	Fine	XF
25.4.1884. With signature and seal of General Gordon.	3500.	6000.	10,000.

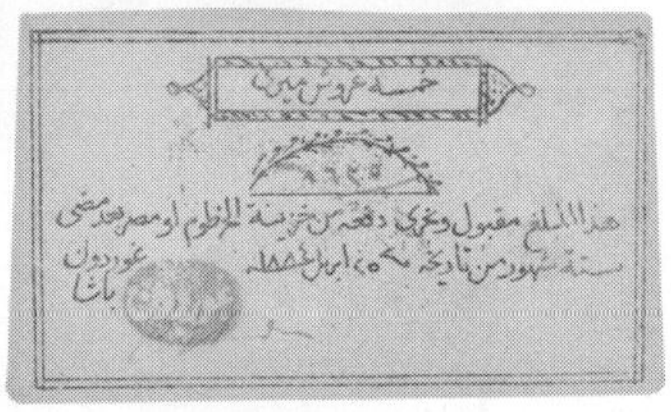

S102 5 Piastres	Good	Fine	XF
25.4.1884. Half-moon design going up at center. With signature and seal of General Gordon. 40 pieces known.			
a. Manuscript signature.	600.	1000.	1600.
b. Hectograph signature.	400.	650.	1200.

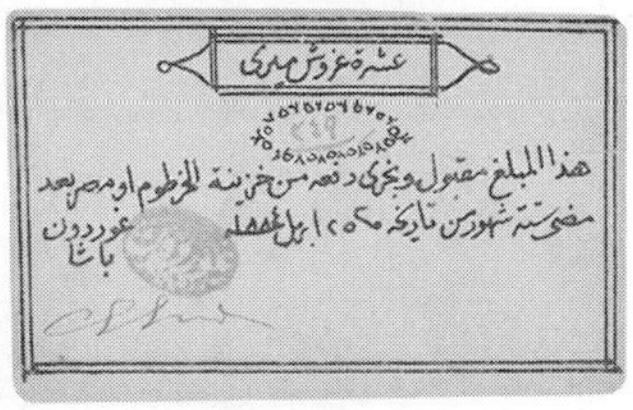

S103 10 Piastres	Good	Fine	XF
25.4.1884. Oval design consisting of circles and angles at center. With signature and seal of General Gordon. 185 pieces known.			
a. Manuscript signature.	450.	750.	1200.
b. Hectograph signature.	250.	375.	650.

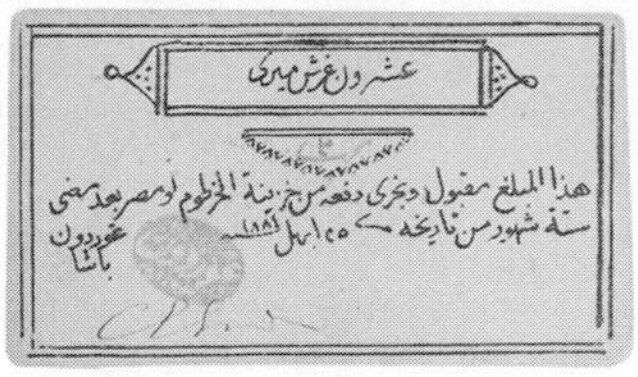

S104 20 Piastres	Good	Fine	XF
25.4.1884. Half-moon design going down at center. With signature and seal of General Gordon. 425 pieces known.			
a. Manuscript signature.	275.	450.	750.
b. Hectograph signature.	160.	250.	400.

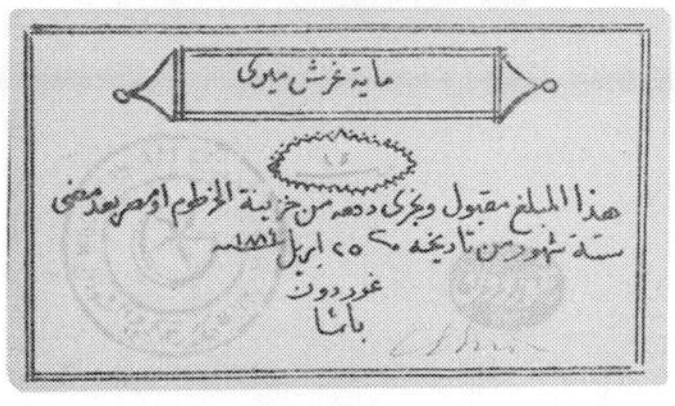

S105 100 Piastres	Good	Fine	XF
25.4.1884. Longer oval design of wavy line and dots at center. With signature and seal of General Gordon. 1,250 pieces known.			
a. Manuscript signature.	275.	400.	675.
b. Hectograph signature.	120.	185.	300.

S106 500 Piastres	Good	Fine	XF
25.4.1884. Circle with sawteeth at center. With signature and seal of General Gordon. 230 pieces known.			
a. Manuscript signature.	375.	600.	1000.
b. Hectograph signature.	240.	375.	600.

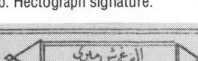

S107 1000 Piastres	Good	Fine	XF
25.4.1884. More evenly oval design of circles and lines at center. With signature and seal of General Gordon. 100 pieces known.			
a. Manuscript signature.	500.	800.	1250.
b. Hectograph signature.	300.	500.	750.

S108 2000 Piastres	Good	Fine	XF
25.4.1884. Rectangle with sawteeth design at center. With signature and seal of General Gordon. 55 pieces known.			
a. Manuscript signature.	600.	950.	1500.
b. Hectograph signature.	400.	650.	1100.

S109 2500 Piastres	Good	Fine	XF
25.4.1884. Plain half-moon going up with a smaller semicircular line coming down through it at center. Hectograph signature only. With signature and seal of General Gordon. 1,050 pieces known.	130.	225.	350.

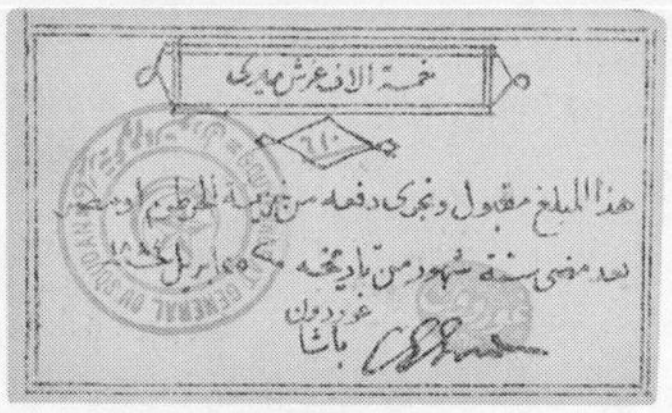

S110	5000 Piastres	Good	Fine	XF
	25.4.1884. Diamond design at center. Hectographic signature only. With signature and seal of General Gordon. 200 pieces known.	225.	350.	600.

1884 Egyptian Pound Issue

S111	50 Egyptian Pounds	Good	Fine	XF
	25.4.1884. Diamond design at center. Hectographic signature only. With signature and seal of General Gordon. 12 pieces known.	2250.	4500.	7000.

1884 British Pound Issue

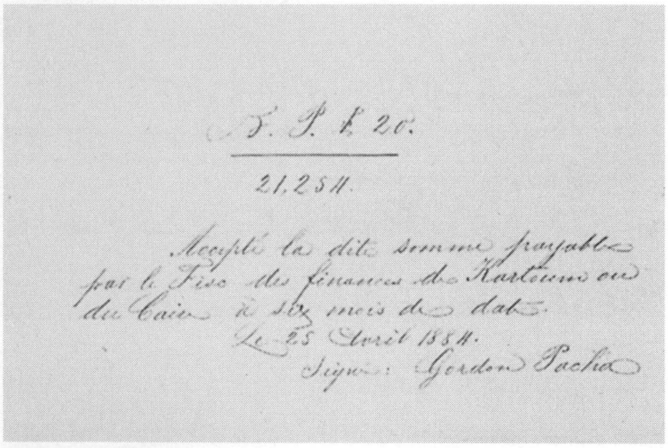

S112	20 Pounds	Good	Fine	XF
	25.4.1884. French text: B.P £20 with serial number 21,254 below. Payable in six months and signed, Gordon Pacha.	—	—	—

1884 Second Sudan Piastre Issue

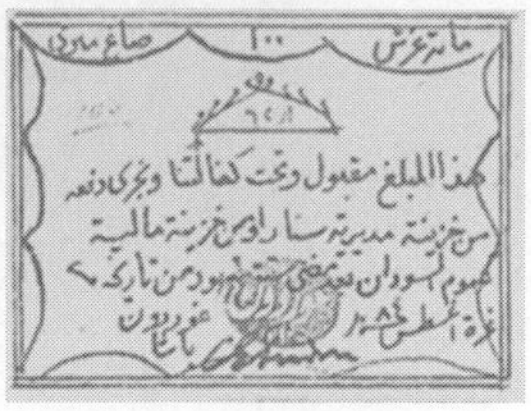

S113	100 Piastres	Good	Fine	XF
	1.8.1884. Similar to earlier issues, but with a later date and with the denomination 100 added to the border design. Regular card stock.	—	—	—

Italian Occupation - WWII

Cassa Mediterranea di Credito per il Sudan

1940 Issue

#M1-M8 Were prepared for the Italian occupation of Sudan during World War II.

M1	5 Piastres	VG	VF	UNC
	ND (1940). Blue and lilac. Apollo at right. Back: Wheat motif. Serial #. Specimen. Rare.	—	—	—

M2	10 Piastres	VG	VF	UNC
	ND (1940). Orange. Apollo at right. Specimen. Rare.	—	—	—
M3	50 Piastres			
	ND (1940). Blue-green. Emperor Augustus at left. Specimen. Rare.	—	—	—
M4	1 Lira			
	ND (1940). Green. Emperor Augustus at left. Specimen. Rare.	—	—	—
M5	5 Lire			
	ND (1940). Brown and yellow. Emperor Augustus at left. Specimen. Rare.	—	—	—
M6	10 Lire			
	ND (1940). Lilac. Emperor Augustus at left. Specimen. Rare.	—	—	—
M7	50 Lire			
	ND. (1940). Green and gray. Michelangelo's *David* at left. Specimen. Rare.	—	—	—

M8	100 Lire	VG	VF	UNC
	ND (1940). Blue. Michelangelo's *David* at left. Specimen. Rare.	—	—	—

Note: Only one specimen set is known. For similar notes with *PER L'EGITTO* see Egypt.

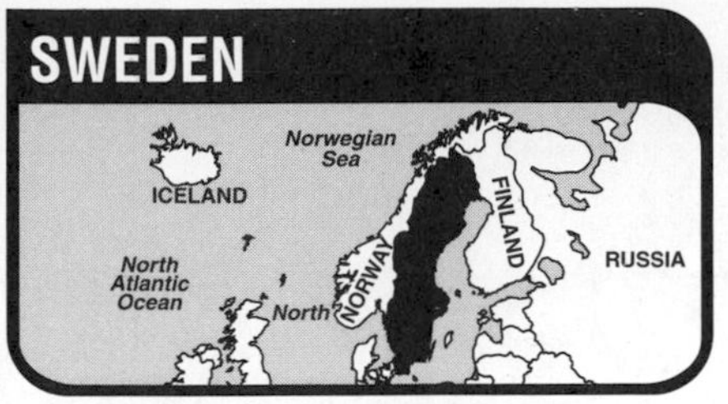

The Kingdom of Sweden, a limited constitutional monarchy located in northern Europe between Norway and Finland, has an area of 449,964 sq. km. and a population of 9.04 million. Capital: Stockholm. Mining, lumbering and a specialized machine industry dominate the economy. Machinery, paper, iron and steel, motor vehicles and wood pulp are exported.

A military power during the 17th century, Sweden has not participated in any war in almost two centuries. An armed neutrality was preserved in both World Wars. Sweden's long-successful economic formula of a capitalist system interlarded with substantial welfare elements was challenged in the 1990s by high unemployment and in 2000-02 by the global economic downturn, but fiscal discipline over the past several years has allowed the country to weather economic vagaries. Sweden joined the EU in 1995, but the public rejected the introduction of the euro in a 2003 referendum.

RULERS:

Carl XI, 1660-1697
Carl XII, 1697-1718
Ulrica Eleonora, 1719-1720
Fredric I, 1720-1751
Adolf Fredric, 1751-1771
Gustaf III, 1771-1792
Gustaf IV Adolf, 1792-1809
Carl XIII, 1809-1818
Carl XIV John, 1818-1844
Oscar I, 1844-1859
Carl XV, 1859-1872
Oscar II, 1872-1907
Gustaf V, 1907-1950
Gustaf VI Adolf, 1950-1973
Carl XVI Gustaf, 1973-

MONETARY SYSTEM:

1 Daler Smt. = 32 Öre Smt. (= 3 Daler Kmt.), 1665
1 Riksdaler = 48 Skilling (= 18 Daler Kmt.), 1777
1 Riksdaler = 1 1/2 Riksdaler Riksgäld, 1803
1 Riksdaler Specie = 2 2/3 Riksdaler Banco = 4 Riksdaler Riksgäld, 1834
1 Riksdaler Riksmynt = 100 Öre (= 1/4 Riksdaler Specie = 1 Riksdaler Riksgäld), 1855
1 Krona = 100 Öre (= 1 Riksdaler Riksmynt), 1873
1 Krona = 100 Öre

MONETARY ABBREVIATIONS

DALER SMT. = Daler Silvermynt
DALER KMT. = Daler Kopparmynt
KOP. SK. = Kopparschillingar
RKD. = Riksdaler
RKD. SP. = Riksdaler Specie
RKD. BC. = Riksdaler Banco
RKD. RMT. = Riksdaler Riksmynt
RKD. RGD. = Riksdaler Riksgäld
SK. = Schillingar
SK. Kop. = Kopparschillingar
SK. SP = Skillingar Specie
SK. BC. = Skillingar Banco
Kr. = Krona (Kronor)

REPLACEMENT NOTES:

Issues since 1956 with asterisk following serial number. Asterisk following the serial number for note issued since 1956.

NOTE ON VALUES: Indicated values apply only to uncancelled examples. Notes with cancellations are worth up to 50% less.

SWEDISH PRINTERS

C. A. Broling .... CAB
AB Jacob Bagges .... JB
Per Axel Nyman .... PAN
Carl Axel Nyman .... CAN

PRIVATE BANKS

Bohus Läns Enskilda Bank .... #S101-S108
Boras Enskilda Bank .... #S111-S120
Christianstads Enskilda Bank .... #S121-S134
Christinehamns Enskilda Bank, see Enskilda Banken i Christinehamn
Enskilda Banken i Christinehamn .... #S141-S149
Enskilda Banken i Wenersborg .... #S151-S159
Enskilda Banken i Orebro, see Privat Banken i Orebro
Enskilda Industribanken i Norrköping .... #S161-S164
Gefleborgs Enskilda Bank, see Gefleborgs Läns Enskilda Bank
Gefleborgs Läns Enskilda Bank .... #S171-S182
Gotlands Enskilda Bank .... #S191-S199
Götheborgs Enskilda Bank, see Götheborgs Privat Bank
Götheborgs Privat Bank .... #S201-S231
Hallands Enskilda Bank .... #S241-S252
Helsinglands Enskilda Bank .... #S261-S267
Hernösands Enskilda Bank .... #S271-S279
Kalmar Enskilda Bank .... #S281-S291
Kopparbergs Enskilda Bank, see Stora Kopparbergs Läns och Bergslags Enskilda Bank
Malmö Enskilda Bank .... #S301-S304
Mälare-Provinsernas Enskilda Bank .... #S311-S333
Norrbottens Enskilda Bank .... #S341-S343
Norrköpings Enskilda Bank .... #S351-S366
Öscarhamns Enskilda Bank .... #S371-S374
Privat Banken i Örebro .... #S381-S404
Skaraborgs Läns Enskilda Bank .... #S411-S421
Skånska Enskilda Bank, see Skånska Priwat-Banken
Skåska Privat-Banken, see Skånska Priwat-Banken
Skånska Priwat-Banken .... #S431-S464
Smalands Enskilda Bank, see Smalands Privat Bank
Smalands Privat Bank .... #S471-S499
Stockholms Enskilda Bank .... #S501-S514
Stora Kopperbergs Läns och Bergslags Enskilda Bank .... #S521-S572
Sundsvalls Enskilda Bank .... #S581-S595
Södermanlands Enskilda Bank .... #S601-S611
Uplands Enskilda Bank .... #S621-S629
Wadstena Enskilda Bank .... #S631-S642
Wermlands Enskilda Bank, see Wermlands Provincial-Bank
Wermlands Provincial-Bank .... #S651-S690
Westerbottens Enskilda Bank .... #S701-S710
Örebro Enskilda Bank, see Privat Banken i Örebro
Öst-Göta Bank .... #S711-S739

NOTE: Numerous deletions and the combining numbering changes in this section from the previous edition.

REPUBLIC

BOHUS LÄNS ENSKILDA BANK

1869-70 ISSUE

		Good	Fine	XF
S101	**5 Riksdaler** 1869. Mercury standing at left. Printer: JB.	150.	300.	900.
S102	**10 Riksdaler** 1869. Mercury standing at left. Printer: JB.	175.	350.	1350.
S103	**50 Riksdaler** 1870. Mercury standing at left. Printer: JB.	—	—	—
S104	**100 Riksdaler** 1870. Mercury standing at left. Printer: JB.	—	—	—

1879 ISSUE

		Good	Fine	XF
S105	**10 Kronor** 1879. Laureated woman at left, crowned arms at right. Printer: JB.	150.	300.	900.

		Good	Fine	XF
S106	**10 Kronor** 1879. Laureated woman at left, crowned arms at right. Printer: BWC.	150.	300.	900.

#S107-S108 printer: BWC.

		Good	Fine	XF
S107	**50 Kronor** 1879. Laureated woman at left, crowned arms at right. Printer: BWC.	—	—	—
S108	**100 Kronor** 1879. Laureated woman at left, crowned arms at right. Printer: BWC.	—	—	—

BORAS ENSKILDA BANK

1866 ISSUE

		Good	Fine	XF
S111	**5 Riksdaler** 1866. Seated allegorical woman with wheels and town in background at upper center. Printer: JB.	125.	250.	500.
S112	**10 Riksdaler** 1866. Seated allegorical woman with wheels and town in background at upper center. Printer: JB.	135.	275.	550.
S113	**50 Riksdaler** 1866. Seated allegorical woman with wheels and town in background at upper center. Printer: JB.	—	—	—

1876 ISSUE

		Good	Fine	XF
S114	**5 Kronor** 1876. Seated allegorical woman with wheels and town in background at upper center. Printer: JB.	90.00	180.	360.
S115	**10 Kronor** 1876. Seated allegorical woman with wheels and town in background at upper center. Printer: JB.	125.	250.	500.
S116	**50 Kronor** 1876. Seated allegorical woman with wheels and town in background at upper center. Printer: JB.	—	—	—
S117	**100 Kronor** 1876. Seated allegorical woman with wheels and town in background at upper center. Printer: JB.	—	—	—

1894 ISSUE

		Good	Fine	XF
S118	**10 Kronor** 1894. King Gustav II Adolf Standing at lower left, seated allegorical woman with wheels and town in background at upper center. Back: Portrait King Gustav II Adolf at center. Printer: JB.	—	—	—
S119	**50 Kronor** 1894. King Gustav II Adolf Standing at lower left, seated allegorical woman with wheels and town in background at upper center. Back: Portrait King Gustav II Adolf at center. Printer: JB.	—	—	—
S120	**100 Kronor** 1894. King Gustav II Adolf Standing at lower left, seated allegorical woman with wheels and town in background at upper center. Back: Portrait King Gustav II Adolf at center. Printer: JB.	—	—	—

Christianstads Enskilda Bank

1865 First Issue

		Good	Fine	XF
S121	**5 Riksdaler** 1865. Arms of King Christian IV at upper center. Printer: PAN.	125.	250.	500.
S122	**10 Riksdaler** 1865. Arms of King Christian IV at upper center. Printer: PAN.	125.	250.	500.
S123	**50 Riksdaler** 1865. Arms of King Christian IV at upper center. Printer: PAN.	135.	275.	550.
S124	**100 Riksdaler** 1865. Arms of King Christian IV at upper center. Printer: PAN.	135.	275.	550.

1865 Second Issue

		Good	Fine	XF
S125	**5 Riksdaler** 1865. Arms of King Christian IV at upper center. Printer: JB.	—	—	—
S126	**10 Riksdaler** 1865. Arms of King Christian IV at upper center. Printer: JB.	—	—	—

1875 First Issue

		Good	Fine	XF
S127	**5 Kronor** 1875. Arms of King Christian IV at upper center. Printer: JB.	90.00	180.	360.
S128	**10 Kronor** 1875. Arms of King Christian IV at upper center. Printer: JB.	125.	250.	500.
S129	**50 Kronor** 1875. Arms of King Christian IV at upper center. Printer: JB.	125.	250.	500.
S130	**100 Kronor** 1875. Arms of King Christian IV at upper center. Printer: JB.	—	—	—

1875 Second Issue

		Good	Fine	XF
S131	**10 Kronor** 1875; 1894. King Christian IV of Denmark at left, arms at right. Printer: BWC.	125.	250.	500.

		Good	Fine	XF
S132	**50 Kronor** 1875; 1894. Portrait King Christian IV at upper center, arms at lower center. Printer: BWC.	—	—	—
S133	**100 Kronor** 1875; 1894. King Christian IV of Denmark at left, arms at right. Printer: BWC.	—	—	—

		Good	Fine	XF
S134	**500 Kronor** 1875; 1894. King Christian IV of Denmark at left, arms at right. Printer: BWC.	—	—	—

Enskilda Banken i Christinehamn

1866 Issue

		Good	Fine	XF
S141	**5 Riksdaler** 1866. City arms at upper center. Printer: PAN.	125.	250.	500.
S142	**10 Riksdaler** 1866. City arms at upper center. Printer: PAN.	135.	275.	550.
S143	**50 Riksdaler** 1866. City arms at upper center. Printer: PAN.	—	—	—
S144	**100 Riksdaler** 1866. City arms at upper center. Printer: PAN.	—	—	—

Christinehamms Enskilda Bank

1876 Issue

		Good	Fine	XF
S145	**5 Kronor** 1876. New bank name. City arms at upper center. Printer: PAN.	90.00	135.	275.
S146	**10 Kronor** 1876. New bank name. City arms at upper center. Printer: PAN.	125.	250.	500.
S147	**50 Kronor** 1876. New bank name. City arms at upper center. Printer: PAN.	—	—	—
S148	**100 Kronor** 1876. New bank name. City arms at upper center. Printer: PAN.	—	—	—

1884 Issue

		Good	Fine	XF
S149	**10 Kronor** 1884. Portrait woman at lower left, city arms at top center, eagle at lower right.	125.	250.	500.

Enskilda Banken i Wenersborg

1865 Issue

		Good	Fine	XF
S151	**5 Riksdaler** 1865. City arms at upper center. Printer: JB.	150.	300.	600.
S152	**10 Riksdaler** 1865. City arms at upper center. Printer: JB.	175.	350.	700.
S153	**50 Riksdaler** 1865. City arms at upper center. Printer: JB.	—	—	—
S154	**100 Riksdaler** 1865. City arms at upper center. Printer: JB.	—	—	—

1874 Issue

		Good	Fine	XF
S155	**5 Kronor** 1874. City arms at upper center. Printer: JB.	125.	250.	500.
S156	**100 Kronor** 1874. City arms at upper center. Printer: JB.	—	—	—

1879 Issue

		Good	Fine	XF
S157	**10 Kronor** 1879. Arms at left and right, woman at center. Printer: BWC.	150.	300.	600.

	Good	Fine	XF
S158 50 Kronor 1879. Arms at left and right, building at top center, woman at bottom center. Printer: BWC.	—	—	—
S159 100 Kronor 1879. Arms at left and right, building at top center, woman at bottom center. Printer: BWC.	—	—	—

Enskilda Industribanken i Norrköping

1865 Issue

	Good	Fine	XF
S161 5 Riksdaler 1865. Ceres at left, Mercury at right. Printer: PAN.	150.	300.	600.
S162 10 Riksdaler 1865. Ceres at left, Mercury at right. Like #S161. Printer: PAN.	175.	325.	650.
S163 50 Riksdaler 1865. Ceres and Mercury at upper left and right center. Printer: PAN.	—	—	—
S164 100 Riksdaler 1865. Ceres and Mercury at upper left and right center. Like #S163. Printer: PAN.	—	—	—

Gefleborgs Läns Enskilda Bank

1865-66 Issue

	Good	Fine	XF
S171 5 Riksdaler 1865. Double arms at upper center. Printer: PAN.	125.	250.	500.
S172 10 Riksdaler 1865. Double arms at upper center. Printer: PAN.	135.	275.	550.
S173 50 Riksdaler 1865. Double arms at upper center. Printer: PAN.	—	—	—
S174 100 Riksdaler 1865. Double arms at upper center. Printer: PAN.	—	—	—
S175 500 Riksdaler 1866. Double arms at upper center. Printer: PAN.	—	—	—

Gefleborgs Enskilda Bank

1875 First Issue

	Good	Fine	XF
S176 5 Kronor 1875. Single arms at upper center. Printer: PAN.	90.00	180.	360.
S177 10 Kronor 1875. Single arms at upper center. Printer: PAN.	125.	250.	500.
S178 50 Kronor 1875. Single arms at upper center. Printer: PAN.	125.	250.	500.
S179 100 Kronor 1875. Single arms at upper center. Printer: PAN.	—	—	—

1875 Second Issue

	Good	Fine	XF
S180 10 Kronor 1875. Allegorical woman at left, arms at right. Printer: BWC.	—	—	—
S181 50 Kronor 1875. Arms at left and right, allegorical woman at upper center. Printer: BWC.	—	—	—
S182 100 Kronor 1875. Arms at left and right, allegorical woman at upper center. Like #S181. Printer: BWC.	—	—	—

Gotlands Enskilda Bank

1869 Issue

	Good	Fine	XF
S191 5 Riksdaler 1869. Arms at upper center. Printer: JB.	125.	250.	500.
S192 10 Riksdaler 1869. Arms at upper center. Printer: JB.	135.	275.	550.
S193 50 Riksdaler 1869. Arms at upper center. Printer: JB.	—	—	—
S194 100 Riksdaler 1869. Arms at upper center. Printer: JB.	—	—	—

1879 Issue

	Good	Fine	XF
S195 5 Kronor 1879. Arms at upper center. Printer: JB.	90.00	180.	360.
S196 10 Kronor 1879. Arms at upper center. Printer: JB.	125.	250.	500.
S197 50 Kronor 1879. Arms at upper center. Printer: JB.	—	—	—
S198 100 Kronor 1879. Arms at upper center. Printer: JB.	—	—	—

1893 Issue

	Good	Fine	XF
S199 10 Kronor 1893. Arms at left, portrait woman at right. Printer: BWC.	125.	250.	500.

Götheborgs Privat Bank

1848 Issue

	Good	Fine	XF
S201 3 1/3 Riksdaler Banco 1848. Arms with two cherubs at upper center. Printer: CAB.	—	—	—
S202 6 2/3 Riksdaler Banco 1848. Arms with two cherubs at upper center. Printer: CAB.	—	—	—
S203 10 Riksdaler Banco 1848. Arms with two cherubs at upper center. Printer: CAB.	—	—	—
S204 50 Riksdaler Banco 1848. Arms with two cherubs at upper center. Printer: CAB.	—	—	—
S205 100 Riksdaler Banco 1848. Arms with two cherubs at upper center. Printer: CAB.	—	—	—

1852 Issue

	Good	Fine	XF
S206 3 1/3 Riksdaler Banco 1852. Arms with two cherubs at upper center. Printer: JB.	—	—	—
S207 10 Riksdaler Banco 1852. Arms with two cherubs at upper center. Printer: JB.	—	—	—

Götheborgs Enskilda Bank

1858 First Issue

	Good	Fine	XF
S208 5 Riksdaler 1858. Two allegorical women and arms at upper center. Printer: BWC.	125.	250.	500.
S209 100 Riksdaler 1858. City scene with arms above at upper center. Printer: BWC.	135.	270.	550.

	Good	Fine	XF
S210 500 Riksdaler 1858. City scene with arms above at upper center. Similar to #S209. Printer: BWC.	—	—	—

1858 Second Issue

	Good	Fine	XF
S211 10 Riksdaler 1858; 1866. Arms at upper center. Printer: JB.	—	—	—
S212 50 Riksdaler 1858. City scene with arms above at upper center. Printer: JB.	—	—	—
S213 100 Riksdaler 1858. City scene with arms above at upper center. Similar to #S212. Printer: JB.			
a. Issued note.	—	—	—
p. Proof.	—	—	—

1868 Issue

	Good	Fine	XF
S215 5 Riksdaler 1868. City scene with arms above at upper center. Printer: PAN.	125.	250.	500.
S216 10 Riksdaler 1868. City scene with arms above at upper center. Printer: PAN.	135.	275.	550.
S217 50 Riksdaler 1868. City scene with arms above at upper center. Printer: PAN.	—	—	—

		Good	Fine	XF
S218	**100 Riksdaler**			
	1868. City scene with arms above at upper center. Printer: PAN.	—	—	—
S219	**500 Riksdaler**			
	1868. City scene with arms above at upper center. Printer: PAN.	—	—	—

1873 Issue

		Good	Fine	XF
S220	**5 Riksdaler**			
	1873. City scene with arms above at upper center. Printer: JB.	125.	250.	500.
S221	**10 Riksdaler**			
	1873. City scene with arms above at upper center. Printer: JB.	135.	270.	550.
S222	**50 Riksdaler**			
	1873. City scene with arms above at upper center. Printer: JB.	—	—	—
S223	**100 Riksdaler**			
	1873. City scene with arms above at upper center. Printer: JB.	—	—	—

1877-78 Issue

		Good	Fine	XF
S224	**5 Kronor**			
	1877. New rendition of arms at upper center. Printer: JB.	90.00	180.	360.
S225	**10 Kronor**			
	1877. New rendition of arms at upper center. Printer: JB.	125.	250.	500.
S226	**50 Kronor**			
	1878. New rendition of arms at upper center. Printer: JB.	—	—	—
S227	**100 Kronor**			
	1878. New rendition of arms at upper center. Printer: JB.	—	—	—

1878-82 Issue

		Good	Fine	XF
S227A	**500 Kronor**			
	1878. King Gustav II Adolf at left, city arms at right. Printer: BWC.	—	—	—
S228	**500 Kronor**			
	1879; 1894. King Gustav II Adolf at left, city arms at right. Printer: BWC.	125.	250.	500.
S229	**50 Kronor**			
	1882. King Gustav II Adolf at left, city arms at right. Printer: BWC.	125.	250.	500.

		Good	Fine	XF
S230	**100 Kronor**			
	1882. King Gustav II Adolf at left, city arms at right. Printer: BWC.	—	—	—

#S231 *Deleted.* See #S227A.

Hallands Enskilda Bank

1857 Issue

		Good	Fine	XF
S241	**5 Riksdaler**			
	1857; 1867. City arms at upper center. Printer: JB.	125.	250.	500.
S242	**10 Riksdaler**			
	1857; 1867. City arms at upper center. Printer: JB.	135.	270.	550.
S243	**50 Riksdaler**			
	1857; 1867. City arms at upper center. Printer: JB.	—	—	—
S244	**100 Riksdaler**			
	1857; 1867. City arms at upper center. Printer: JB.	—	—	—

1877 Issue

		Good	Fine	XF
S249	**5 Kronor**			
	1877. City arms at upper center. Printer: JB.	90.00	180.	360.
S250	**10 Kronor**			
	1877; 1888; 1894. City arms at upper center. Printer: JB.	125.	250.	500.
S251	**50 Kronor**			
	1877; 1888. City arms at upper center. Printer: JB.	—	—	—
S252	**100 Kronor**			
	1877; 1888. City arms at upper center. Printer: JB.	—	—	—

Helsinglands Enskilda Bank

1874 Issue

		Good	Fine	XF
S261	**5 Kronor**			
	1874. City arms at upper center. Printer: JB.	90.00	180.	360.
S262	**10 Kronor**			
	1874. City arms at upper center. Printer: JB.	125.	250.	500.
S263	**50 Kronor**			
	1874. City arms at upper center. Printer: JB.	—	—	—
S264	**100 Kronor**			
	1874. City arms at upper center. Printer: JB.	—	—	—

1879 Issue

		Good	Fine	XF
S265	**10 Kronor**			
	1879. Helmeted Minerva at left, city arms at right. Printer: BWC.	125.	250.	500.

		Good	Fine	XF
S266	**50 Kronor**			
	1879. Helmeted Minerva at left, city arms at right. Printer: BWC.	—	—	—
S267	**100 Kronor**			
	1879. Helmeted Minerva at left, city arms at right. Printer: BWC.	—	—	—

Hernösands Enskilda Bank

1870 Issue

		Good	Fine	XF
S271	**5 Riksdaler**			
	1870. City arms at upper center. Printer: JB.	125.	250.	500.
S272	**10 Riksdaler**			
	1870. City arms at upper center. Printer: JB.	135.	270.	550.
S273	**50 Riksdaler**			
	1870. City arms at upper center. Printer: JB.	—	—	—

1874 Issue

		Good	Fine	XF
S274	**5 Kronor**			
	1874. City arms at upper center. Printer: JB.	90.00	180.	360.
S275	**10 Kronor**			
	1874. City arms at upper center. Printer: JB.	125.	250.	500.

1880 Issue

		Good	Fine	XF
S276	**10 Kronor**			
	1880. Arms at left and right, Mercury at center.	125.	250.	500.
S277	**50 Kronor**			
	1880. Woman at left, arms at upper and lower center, Mercury at right. Square format.	—	—	—

	Good	Fine	XF
S278 100 Kronor 1880. Woman at left, arms at upper and lower center, Mercury at right. Like #S277.	—	—	—

1892 Issue

	Good	Fine	XF
S279 10 Kronor 1892. Portrait woman at left, two arms at right. Printer: BWC.	125.	250.	500.

Kalmar Enskilda Bank

1867 Issue

	Good	Fine	XF
S281 5 Kronor 1867. Double arms at left. Printer: JB.	125.	250.	500.
S282 10 Kronor 1867. Double arms at left. Like #S281. Printer: JB.	135.	270.	550.
S283 50 Kronor 1867. Double arms at upper center. Printer: JB. Square format.	—	—	—
S284 100 Kronor 1867. Double arms at upper center. Like #S283. Printer: JB.	—	—	—

1877 Issue

	Good	Fine	XF
S285 5 Kronor 1877. Mercury at left, double arms at upper center, Ceres at right. Printer: JB.	90.00	180.	360.
S286 10 Kronor 1877. Mercury at left, double arms at upper center, Ceres at right. Printer: JB.	125.	250.	500.
S287 50 Kronor 1877. Mercury at left, double arms at upper center, Ceres at right. Printer: JB.	—	—	—
S288 100 Kronor 1877. Mercury at left, double arms at upper center, Ceres at right. Printer: JB.	—	—	—

1894 Issue

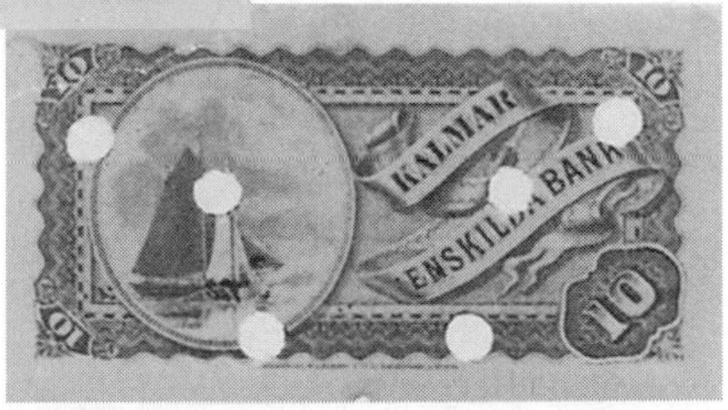

	Good	Fine	XF
S289 10 Kronor 1894; 1898. Queen Margareta at left, castle view at upper center right, arms at right. Back: Sailboat at left. Printer: BWC.	125.	250.	500.
S290 50 Kronor 1894. Queen Margareta at left, castle view at upper center right, arms at right. Printer: BWC.	—	—	—
S291 100 Kronor 1894; 1897. Queen Margareta at left, castle view at upper center right, arms at right. Printer: BWC.	—	—	—

Malmö Enskilda Bank

1865 Issue

	Good	Fine	XF
S301 5 Riksdaler 1865. City arms at upper center. Printer: JB.	125.	250.	500.
S302 10 Riksdaler 1865. City arms at upper center. Printer: JB.	135.	270.	550.
S303 50 Riksdaler 1865. City arms at upper center. Printer: JB.	—	—	—
S304 100 Riksdaler 1865. City arms at upper center. Printer: JB.	—	—	—

Mälare-Provinsernas Enskilda Bank

1847 Issue

	Good	Fine	XF
S311 3 1/3 Riksdaler Banco 1.10.1847. Crowned supported royal arms at top center. Printer: CAB.	—	—	—

	Good	Fine	XF
S312 6 Riksdaler Banco 1.10.1847. Crowned supported royal arms at top center. Printer: CAB.	—	—	—

	Good	Fine	XF
S313 33 1/3 Riksdaler Banco 1.10.1847. Crowned supported royal arms with buildings in background at upper center. Printer: CAB.	—	—	—
S314 50 Riksdaler Banco 1.10.1847. Crowned supported royal arms with buildings in background at upper center. Printer: CAB.	—	—	—

1856 Issue

	Good	Fine	XF
S315 5 Riksdaler 1856. Crowned supported royal arms at top center. Printer: Bradbury & Evans.	125.	250.	500.
S316 10 Riksdaler 1856. Crowned supported royal arms at top center. Printer: Bradbury & Evans.	135.	270.	550.
S317 50 Riksdaler 1856. Crowned supported royal arms at top center. Printer: Bradbury & Evans.	—	—	—
S318 100 Riksdaler 1856. Crowned supported royal arms at top center. Printer: Bradbury & Evans.	—	—	—
S319 500 Riksdaler 1856. Crowned supported royal arms at top center. Printer: Bradbury & Evans.	—	—	—

1863 Issue

	Good	Fine	XF
S320 5 Riksdaler 1863. Crowned supported royal arms at top center. Printer: JB.	125.	250.	500.
S321 10 Riksdaler 1863. Crowned supported royal arms at top center. Printer: JB.	135.	270.	550.

1867 Issue

	Good	Fine	XF
S322 5 Riksdaler 1867. Crowned supported royal arms at top center. Printer: JB.	125.	250.	500.
S323 10 Riksdaler 1867. Crowned supported royal arms at top center. Printer: JB.	135.	270.	550.

		Good	Fine	XF
S324	**50 Riksdaler** 1867. Crowned supported royal arms at top center. Printer: JB.	—	—	—
S325	**100 Riksdaler** 1867. Crowned supported royal arms at top center. Printer: JB.	—	—	—
S326	**500 Riksdaler** 1867. Crowned supported royal arms at top center. Printer: JB.	—	—	—

1875 Issue

		Good	Fine	XF
S327	**5 Kronor** 1875. Crowned supported royal arms at top center. Printer: JB.	90.00	180.	360.

		Good	Fine	XF
S328	**10 Kronor** 1875. Crowned supported royal arms at top center. Printer: JB. Litt. K.	125.	250.	500.
S329	**50 Kronor** 1875. Crowned supported royal arms at top center. Printer: JB.	—	—	—
S330	**100 Kronor** 1875. Crowned supported royal arms at top center.	—	—	—

1894 Issue

		Good	Fine	XF
S331	**10 Kronor** 1894. Ceres and Mercury at left, arms at right. Back: Portrait A. Oxenstierna at center. Printer: BWC.	125.	250.	500.
S332	**50 Kronor** 1894. Ceres and Mercury at left, arms at right. Back: Portrait A. Oxenstierna at center. Printer: BWC.	—	—	—

		Good	Fine	XF
S333	**100 Kronor** 1894. Ceres and Mercury at left, arms at right. Back: Portrait A. Oxenstierna at center. Printer: BWC.	—	—	—

Norrbottens Enskilda Bank

1893 Issue

		Good	Fine	XF
S341	**10 Kronor** 1893. Mercury and arms at right. Printer: BWC.	150.	300.	600.
S342	**50 Kronor** 1893. Cherub with city arms and woman holding sword at left. Printer: BWC.	—	—	—

		Good	Fine	XF
S343	**100 Kronor** 1893. Cherub with city arms and woman holding sword at left. Like #S342. Printer: BWC.	—	—	—

Norrköpings Enskilda Bank

1857 Issue

		Good	Fine	XF
S351	**5 Riksdaler** 1857; 1867. City arms at upper center. Printer: JB.	125.	250.	500.
S352	**10 Riksdaler** 1857. City arms at upper center. Printer: JB.	135.	270.	550.
S353	**50 Riksdaler** 1857. City arms at upper center. Printer: JB.	—	—	—
S354	**100 Riksdaler** 1857. City arms at upper center. Printer: JB.	—	—	—
S355	**500 Riksdaler** 1857. City arms at upper center. Printer: JB.	—	—	—

1867 Issue

		Good	Fine	XF
S357	**5 Riksdaler** 1867. City arms at upper center. Printer: JB.	125.	250.	500.
S358	**10 Riksdaler** 1867. City arms at upper center. Printer: JB.	135.	270.	550.
S359	**50 Riksdaler** 1867. City arms at upper center. Printer: JB.	—	—	—
S360	**100 Riksdaler** 1867. City arms at upper center. Printer: JB.	—	—	—

1877 Issue

		Good	Fine	XF
S361	**5 Kronor** 1877. City arms at upper center. Printer: JB.	90.00	180.	360.
S362	**10 Kronor** 1877. City arms at upper center. Printer: JB.	135.	270.	550.

#S363 and S364 head at l. and r. on back. Printer: BWC.

		Good	Fine	XF
S363	**50 Kronor** 1877. Woman with spool at left, arms at upper center and right. Back: Head at left and right. Printer: BWC.	—	—	—

		Good	Fine	XF
S364	**100 Kronor** 1877. Arms at left and right, woman with spool at upper center. Back: Head at left and right. Printer: BWC.	—	—	—
S365	**500 Kronor** 1877. City arms at upper center. Printer: JB. Rectangular format.	—	—	—

1887 Issue

		Good	Fine	XF
S366	**10 Kronor** 1887. Arms at left and right, woman with spool at center. Printer: BWC.	125.	250.	500.

Oscarshamns Enskilda Bank

1877 Issue

		Good	Fine	XF
S371	**5 Kronor** 1877. Standing woman with arms of King Oscar I in design. Printer: JB.	135.	270.	550.
S372	**10 Kronor** 1877. Standing woman with arms of King Oscar I in design. Like #S371. Printer: JB.	150.	300.	600.
S373	**50 Kronor** 1877. Standing woman with arms of King Oscar I in design at upper center. Printer: JB. Square format.	—	—	—
S374	**100 Kronor** 1877. Standing woman with arms of King Oscar I in design at upper center. Like #S373. Printer: JB. Square format.	—	—	—

Privat Banken i Örebro

1837-47 Issue

		Good	Fine	XF
S381	**2 Riksdaler Schillingar** 1837. Two torches crossed at upper center. Printer: CAB.	—	—	—
S382	**3 Riksdaler Banco** 1837. Two torches crossed at upper center. Printer: CAB.	—	—	—
S383	**3 1/3 Riksdaler Schillingar** 1.12.1847. Two torches crossed at upper center. Printer: CAB.	—	—	—
S384	**10 Riksdaler Schillingar** 1837. Two torches crossed at upper center. Printer: CAB.	—	—	—
S385	**50 Riksdaler Schillingar** 1840. Two torches crossed at upper center. Printer: CAB.	—	—	—

Enskilda Banken Örebro

1847 Issue

		Good	Fine	XF
S386	**3 1/3 Riksdaler Banco** 15.12.1847. Ornate design without vignette. Printer: CAB.	—	—	—

		Good	Fine	XF
S387	**6 2/3 Riksdaler Banco** 1847. Ornate design without vignette. Printer: CAB.	—	—	—
S388	**10 Riksdaler Banco** 1847. Ornate design without vignette. Printer: CAB.	—	—	—
S389	**50 Riksdaler Banco** 1847. Ornate design without vignette. Printer: CAB.	—	—	—

Örebro Enskilda Bank

1857 Issue

		Good	Fine	XF
S390	**5 Riksdaler** 1857; 1867. Staff of Mercury and cornucopia at upper center. Printer: JB.	125.	250.	500.

		Good	Fine	XF
S391	**10 Riksdaler** 1857; 1867. Staff of Mercury and cornucopia at upper center. Like #S390. Printer: JB.	135.	270.	550.
S392	**50 Riksdaler** 1857; 1867. Mercury with produce and industrial implements at upper center. Printer: JB. Square format.	—	—	—
S393	**100 Riksdaler** 1857; 1867. Mercury with produce and industrial implements at upper center. Like #S392. Printer: JB.	—	—	—

1876 Issue

		Good	Fine	XF
S398	**5 Kronor** 1876. Arms with two figures at upper center. Printer: JB.	90.00	180.	360.
S399	**10 Kronor** 1876. Arms with two figures at upper center. Like #S398. Printer: JB.	125.	250.	500.
S400	**50 Kronor** 1876. Arms without figures at upper center. Printer: JB. Square format.	—	—	—

		Good	Fine	XF
S401	**100 Kronor** 1876. Arms without figures at upper center. Like #S400. Printer: JB.	—	—	—

1882-93 Issue

		Good	Fine	XF
S402	**10 Kronor** 1882. Statue of Carl Gustav at left, city arms at right. Printer: W&S. Litt. C.	125.	250.	500.
S403	**10 Kronor** 1893. Statue of Carl Gustav at left, city arms at right. Printer: W&S.	125.	250.	500.

1896 Issue

		Good	Fine	XF
S404	**10 Kronor** 1896. Statue of Carl Gustav at left, city arms at upper center. Back: Castle. Printer: JB.	125.	250.	500.

Skaraborgs Läns Enskilda Bank

1865 Issue

		Good	Fine	XF
S411	**5 Riksdaler** 1865. Single arms at each corner, triple arms at upper center. Printer: PAN.	150.	300.	600.
S412	**10 Riksdaler** 1865. Single arms at each corner, triple arms at upper center. Like #S411. Printer: PAN.	175.	350.	700.
S413	**50 Riksdaler** 1865. Single arms at each corner, triple arms at upper center. Like #S411, but two reclining figures added at lower center. Printer: PAN. Square format.	—	—	—
S414	**100 Riksdaler** 1865. Single arms at each corner, triple arms at upper center. Two reclining figures added at lower center. Like #S413. Printer: PAN.	—	—	—

1875 Issue

		Good	Fine	XF
S415	**5 Kronor** 1875. Mercury with city arms at left. Printer: JB.	125.	250.	500.

		Good	Fine	XF
S416	**10 Kronor** 1875. Mercury with city arms at left. Printer: JB.	150.	300.	600.
S417	**50 Kronor** 1875. Mercury with city arms at left. Printer: JB.	—	—	—
S418	**100 Kronor** 1875. Mercury with city arms at left. Printer: JB.	—	—	—

1888 Issue

		Good	Fine	XF
S419	**10 Kronor** 1888. Standing man at left. Statue at left, arms at right. Printer: BWC. Litt. E.	150.	300.	600.
S420	**50 Kronor** 1888. Statue at left, arms at right. Printer: BWC.	—	—	—
S421	**100 Kronor** 1888. Statue at left, arms at right. Printer: BWC.	—	—	—

Skånska Priwat-Banken

1831 Issue

		Good	Fine	XF
S431	**20 Riksdaler Banco** 1831. Assignationer.	—	—	—

1830's Issue

		Good	Fine	XF
S432	**2 Riksdaler Schillingar** 183x. Arms of Ystad at upper center. Printer: J.O. Osterberg, Ystad.	—	—	—
S433	**3 Riksdaler Banco** 183x. Arms of Ystad at upper center. Printer: J.O. Osterberg, Ystad.	—	—	—
S434	**5 Riksdaler Banco** 183x. Arms of Ystad at upper center. Printer: J.O. Osterberg, Ystad.	—	—	—
S435	**10 Riksdaler Banco** 183x. Arms of Ystad at upper center. Printer: J.O. Osterberg, Ystad.	—	—	—

Skånska Privat-Banken

1841 Issue

		Good	Fine	XF
S436	**2 Riksdaler Schillingar** 1841. Staff of Mercury at left, city arms at right. Printer: CAB.	—	—	—
S437	**3 Riksdaler Banco** 1841. Staff of Mercury at left, city arms at right. Printer: CAB.	—	—	—
S438	**6 2/3 Riksdaler Banco** 1841. Staff of Mercury at left, city arms at right. Printer: CAB.	—	—	—
S439	**10 Riksdaler Banco** 1841. Staff of Mercury at left, city arms at right. Printer: CAB.	—	—	—
S440	**25 Riksdaler Banco** 1841. Staff of Mercury at left, city arms at right. Printer: CAB.	—	—	—
S441	**100 Riksdaler Banco** 1841. Staff of Mercury at left, city arms at right. Printer: CAB.	—	—	—

1847 Issue

		Good	Fine	XF
S442	**3 1/3 Riksdaler Banco** 1847. City arms at upper center. Printer: CAB (to 1851); afterwards, JB.	—	—	—
S443	**6 2/3 Riksdaler Banco** 1847. City arms at upper center. Printer: CAB (to 1851); afterwards, JB.	—	—	—
S444	**10 Riksdaler Banco** 1847. City arms at upper center. Printer: CAB (to 1851); afterwards, JB.	—	—	—
S445	**25 Riksdaler Banco** 1847. City arms at upper center. Printer: CAB (to 1851); afterwards, JB.	—	—	—
S446	**50 Riksdaler Banco** 1847. City arms at upper center. Printer: CAB (to 1851); afterwards, JB.	—	—	—
S447	**100 Riksdaler Banco** 1847. City arms at upper center. Printer: CAB (to 1851); afterwards, JB.	—	—	—

Skånes Enskilda Bank

1857-66 Issue

		Good	Fine	XF
S448	**5 Riksdaler** 1857; 1866. Crowned city arms at upper center. Printer: JB.	125.	250.	500.
S449	**10 Riksdaler** 1857; 1866. Crowned city arms at upper center. Printer: JB.	135.	270.	550.
S450	**50 Riksdaler** 1857; 1866. Crowned city arms at upper center. Printer: JB.	—	—	—
S451	**100 Riksdaler** 1857; 1866. Crowned city arms at upper center. Printer: JB.	—	—	XF —
S452	**500 Riksdaler** 1866. Crowned city arms at upper center. Printer: JB.	—	—	—

1876 First Issue

		Good	Fine	XF
S457	**5 Kronor** 1876. Crowned city arms at upper center. Printer: JB.	90.00	180.	360.
S458	**10 Kronor** 1876. Crowned city arms at upper center. Printer: JB.	125.	250.	500.
S459	**50 Kronor** 1876. Crowned city arms at upper center. Printer: JB.	—	—	—
S460	**100 Kronor** 1876. Crowned city arms at upper center. Printer: JB.	—	—	—

1876 Second Issue

		Good	Fine	XF
S461	**10 Kronor** 1876; 1894. Ceres at left, city arms at right. Printer: BWC.	—	—	—
S462	**50 Kronor** 1876. Mercury at left, Ceres at right, city arms at upper center. Printer: BWC.	—	—	—
S463	**100 Kronor** 1876. Mercury at left, Ceres at right, city arms at upper center. Printer: BWC.	—	—	—

		Good	Fine	XF
S464	**1000 Kronor** 1876. Mercury at left, Ceres at right, city arms at upper center. Printer: BWC.	—	—	—

Smalands Privat Bank

1837 Issue

		Good	Fine	XF
S471	**2 Riksdaler Schillingar** 1837; 1842. Triple arms of three cities at upper center. Printer: CAB.	—	—	—
S472	**2 2/3 Riksdaler Banco** 1837. Triple arms of three cities at upper center. Printer: CAB.	—	—	—
S473	**3 Riksdaler Banco** 1837; 1842. Triple arms of three cities at upper center. Printer: CAB.	—	—	—
S474	**3 1/3 Riksdaler Banco** 1837. Triple arms of three cities at upper center. Printer: CAB.	—	—	—
S475	**10 Riksdaler Banco** 1837. Triple arms of three cities at upper center. Printer: CAB.	—	—	—
S476	**50 Riksdaler Banco** 1837. Triple arms of three cities at upper center. Printer: CAB.	—	—	—

1847-48 Issue

		Good	Fine	XF
S477	**2 Riksdaler Schillingar** 1847. Quadruple arms of four cities at upper center. Printer: CAB.	—	—	—
S478	**3 1/3 Riksdaler Banco** 1847; 1848. Quadruple arms of four cities at upper center. Printer: CAB.	—	—	—
S479	**6 2/3 Riksdaler Banco** 1848. Quadruple arms of four cities at upper center. Printer: CAB.	—	—	
S480	**10 Riksdaler Banco** 1848. Quadruple arms of four cities at upper center. Printer: CAB.	—	—	—
S481	**50 Riksdaler Banco** 1848. Quadruple arms of four cities at upper center. Printer: CAB.	—	—	—

Smalands Enskilda Bank

1857 Issue

		Good	Fine	XF
S485	**5 Riksdaler** 1857. Mercury with implements at upper center. Printer: JB.	125.	250.	500.
S486	**10 Riksdaler** 1857. Mercury with implements at upper center. Printer: JB.	135.	270.	550.
S487	**50 Riksdaler** 1857. Mercury with implements at upper center. Printer: JB.	—	—	—
S488	**100 Riksdaler** 1857. Mercury with implements at upper center. Printer: JB.	—	—	—

1867 Issue

		Good	Fine	XF
S489	**5 Riksdaler** 1867. Triple arms at upper center. Printer: PAN.	125.	250.	500.
S490	**10 Riksdaler** 1867. Triple arms at upper center. Printer: PAN.	135.	270.	550.
S491	**50 Riksdaler** 1867. Single arms at left, upper center, and right. Printer: PAN.	—	—	—
S492	**100 Riksdaler** 1867. Single arms at left, upper center, and right. Printer: PAN.	—	—	—

1877 Issue

		Good	Fine	XF
S493	**5 Kronor** 1877. Crowned arms at upper center. Printer: JB.	125.	250.	500.
S494	**10 Kronor** 1877. Crowned arms at upper center. Printer: JB.	135.	270.	550.
S495	**50 Kronor** 1877. Crowned arms at upper center. Printer: JB.	—	—	—
S496	**100 Kronor** 1877. Crowned arms at upper center. Printer: JB.	—	—	—

1894 Issue

		Good	Fine	XF
S497	**10 Kronor** 1894. Helmeted woman with sword and shield at left, Smaland arms at upper center. Back: Portrait C. van Linne. Printer: BWC.	125.	250.	500.
S498	**50 Kronor** 1894. Helmeted woman with sword and shield at left, Smaland arms at upper center. Back: Portrait C. van Linne. Printer: BWC.	—	—	—

		Good	Fine	XF
S499	**100 Kronor** 1894. Helmeted woman with sword and shield at left, Smaland arms at upper center. Back: Portrait C. van Linne. Printer: BWC.	—	—	—

Stockholms Enskilda Bank

1856 Issue

		Good	Fine	XF
S501	**5 Riksdaler** 1856; 1860. Stockholm arms (with portrait) at upper center. Printer: PAN.	125.	250.	500.
S502	**10 Riksdaler** 1856; 1860. Stockholm arms (with portrait) at upper center. Printer: PAN.	135.	270.	550.
S503	**50 Riksdaler** 1856; 1865. Stockholm arms (with portrait) at upper center. Printer: PAN.	—	—	—

1872 Issue

		Good	Fine	XF
S507	**100 Riksdaler** 1872. Black on dark green underprint. Allegorical woman with shield and lion at lower left, city scene with bridge at upper center, St. Eric at right. *STOCKHOLM* slanted letters. Back: Brown. Printer: NBNC.	—	—	—

1876 First Issue

		Good	Fine	XF
S508	**5 Kronor** 1876. Stockholm arms (with portrait) at upper center. Printer: JB.			
	a. *STOCKHOLM* in tall letters.	90.00	180.	360.
	b. *STOCKHOLM* in slanted letters.	90.00	180.	360.
S509	**10 Kronor** 1876. Stockholm arms (with portrait) at upper center. Printer: JB.			
	a. *STOCKHOLM* in tall letters.	90.00	180.	360.
	b. *STOCKHOLM* in slanted letters.	90.00	180.	360.
S510	**50 Kronor** 1876. Stockholm arms (with portrait) at upper center. Printer: JB.	—	—	—

1876 Second Issue

		Good	Fine	XF
S511	**10 Kronor** 1876. Crowned St. Eric at center. Printer: BWC.	125.	250.	500.

		Good	Fine	XF
S512	**50 Kronor** 1876. Standing woman with sword and lion at left, bridge and buildings at upper center, portait King at right. Printer: BWC.	—	—	—
S513	**100 Kronor** 1876. Standing woman with sword and lion at left, bridge and buildings at upper center, portait King at right. Printer: NBNC.	—	—	—

No.	Denomination / Description	Good	Fine	XF
S514	**1000 Kronor** 1876. Standing woman with sword and lion at left, bridge and buildings at upper center, portait King at right. Printer: BWC.	—	—	—

Stora Kopparbergs Läns och Bergslags Enskilda Bank

1836 Issue

No.	Denomination / Description	Good	Fine	XF
S521	**2 Riksdaler Schillingar** 1836; 1837; 1838; 1839; 1841; 1842; 1845. Latticework design at upper center. Printer: CAB. Square format.	—	—	—
S522	**3 Riksdaler Banco** 1836; 1837; 1838; 1839; 1841; 1842; 1845. Latticework design at upper center. Printer: CAB. Square format.	—	—	—
S523	**6 2/3 Riksdaler Banco** 1836; 1837; 1838; 1839; 1841; 1842; 1845; 1847. Latticework design at upper center. Printer: CAB. Square format.	—	—	—
S524	**10 Riksdaler Banco** 1836; 1837; 1838; 1839; 1841; 1842; 1845; 1847. Latticework design at upper center. Printer: CAB. Square format.	—	—	—

1848 Issue

No.	Denomination / Description	Good	Fine	XF
S551	**4 Riksdaler Banco** 1848; 2.1.1852. Latticework design at upper center. Printer: CAB (to 1851); afterwards, JB.	—	—	—
S552	**6 2/3 Riksdaler Banco** 1848; 1856. Latticework design at upper center. Printer: CAB (to 1851); afterwards, JB.	—	—	—
S553	**10 Riksdaler Banco** 1848. Latticework design at upper center. Printer: CAB (to 1851); afterwards, JB.	—	—	—
S554	**33 1/2 Riksdaler Banco** 1848. Latticework design at upper center. Printer: CAB (to 1851); afterwards, JB.	—	—	—
S555	**50 Riksdaler Banco** 1848. Latticework design at upper center. Printer: CAB (to 1851); afterwards, JB.	—	—	—

Kopparbergs Enskilda Bank

1858 Issue

No.	Denomination / Description	Good	Fine	XF
S558	**5 Riksdaler** 1858; 1868. Latticework design at upper center. Printer: PAN.	125.	250.	500.
S559	**10 Riksdaler** 1858; 1868. Latticework design at upper center. Printer: PAN.	135.	270.	550.
S560	**50 Riksdaler** 1858; 1868. Latticework design at upper center. Printer: PAN.	—	—	—
S561	**100 Riksdaler** 1858; 1868. Latticework design at upper center. Printer: PAN.	—	—	—

1878 Issue

No.	Denomination / Description	Good	Fine	XF
S566	**5 Kronor** 1878. Latticework design in wreath at upper center. Arms at upper center. Printer: JB.	90.00	180.	360.
S567	**10 Kronor** 1878. Latticework design in wreath at upper center. Printer: JB.	125.	250.	500.
S568	**50 Kronor** 1878. Latticework design in wreath at upper center. Printer: JB.	—	—	—
S569	**100 Kronor** 1878. Latticework design in wreath at upper center. Printer: JB.	—	—	—

1894 Issue

No.	Denomination / Description	Good	Fine	XF
S570	**10 Kronor** 1894. King Gustav Vasa at left. Printer: BWC.	125.	250.	500.
S571	**50 Kronor** 1894. King Gustav Vasa at left. Printer: BWC.	—	—	—
S572	**100 Kronor** 1894. King Gustav Vasa at left. Printer: BWC.	—	—	—

Sundsvalls Enskilda Bank

1865 Issue

No.	Denomination / Description	Good	Fine	XF
S581	**5 Riksdaler** 1865. Arms of Sundsvall at upper center. Printer: PAN.	150.	300.	600.
S582	**10 Riksdaler** 1865. Arms of Sundsvall at upper center. Printer: PAN.	175.	350.	700.
S583	**50 Riksdaler** 1865. Standing figures of Mercury and Neptune with arms. Printer: PAN.	—	—	—
S584	**100 Riksdaler** 1865. Standing figures of Mercury and Neptune with arms. Printer: PAN.	—	—	—
S585	**500 Riksdaler** 1865. Standing figures of Mercury and Neptune with arms. Printer: PAN.	—	—	—

1875 First Issue

No.	Denomination / Description	Good	Fine	XF
S586	**5 Kronor** 1875. Seated allegorical woman with helmeted shield and holding wreath at upper center. Printer: JB.	125.	250.	500.
S587	**10 Kronor** 1875. Seated allegorical woman with helmeted shield and holding wreath at upper center. Printer: JB.	150.	300.	600.
S588	**100 Kronor** 1875. Seated allegorical woman with helmeted shield and holding wreath at upper center. Printer: JB.	—	—	—

1875 Second Issue

No.	Denomination / Description	Good	Fine	XF
S589	**10 Kronor** 1875. Woman at center. Printer: BWC.	—	—	—
S590	**50 Kronor** 1875. Woman at left. Printer: BWC.	—	—	—
S591	**100 Kronor** 1875. Woman. Printer: BWC.	—	—	—

1894-1900 Issues

		Good	Fine	XF
S592	**10 Kronor** 1898. Seated allegorical woman with helmeted shield and holding wreath at upper center. Like #S587. Printer: JB.	—	—	—
S593	**10 Kronor** 1900; 1901; 1902. Woman at center. Printer: BWC.	—	—	—
S594	**50 Kronor** 1897. Woman at left. Printer: BWC.	—	—	—
S595	**100 Kronor** 1894; 1898; 1902. Woman. Printer: BWC.	150.	300.	600.

Södermanlands Enskilda Bank

1867 Issue

		Good	Fine	XF
S601	**5 Riksdaler** 1867. Crowned arms of Sodermanland at upper center. Printer: PAN.	125.	250.	500.
S602	**10 Riksdaler** 1867. Crowned arms of Sodermanland at upper center. Printer: PAN.	135.	270.	550.
S603	**50 Riksdaler** 1867. Crowned arms of Sodermanland at upper center. Printer: PAN.	—	—	—
S604	**100 Riksdaler** 1867. Crowned arms of Sodermanland at upper center. Printer: PAN.	—	—	—

1877 Issue

		Good	Fine	XF
S605	**5 Kronor** 1877. Crowned arms of Sodermanland at upper center. Printer: PAN.	90.00	180.	360.
S606	**10 Kronor** 1877. Crowned arms of Sodermanland at upper center. Printer: PAN.	125.	250.	500.
S607	**50 Kronor** 1877. Crowned arms of Sodermanland at upper center. Printer: PAN.	—	—	—
S608	**100 Kronor** 1877. Crowned arms of Sodermanland at upper center. Printer: PAN.	—	—	—

		Good	Fine	XF
S609	**10 Kronor** 1882; 1888; 1898. Crowned arms of Sodermanland at upper center. Printer: JB.	125.	250.	500.

		Good	Fine	XF
S610	**100 Kronor** 1897; 1898. Crowned arms of Sodermanland at upper center. Printer: JB.	—	—	—

Uplands Enskilda Bank

1865 Issue

		Good	Fine	XF
S621	**5 Riksdaler** 1865. Crowned arms at upper center. Printer: JB.	125.	250.	500.
S622	**10 Riksdaler** 1865. Crowned arms at upper center. Printer: JB.	135.	270.	550.
S623	**50 Riksdaler** 1865. Crowned arms at upper center. Printer: JB.	—	—	—
S624	**100 Riksdaler** 1865. Crowned arms at upper center. Printer: JB.	—	—	—

1874 First Issue

		Good	Fine	XF
S625	**5 Kronor** 1874. Crowned arms at upper center. Like #S621. Printer: JB.	90.00	180.	360.
S626	**10 Kronor** 1874. Crowned arms at upper center. Like #S622. Printer: JB.	125.	250.	500.

1874 Second Issue

		Good	Fine	XF
S627	**10 Kronor** 1874. Statue of B. Fogelberg at left. Printer: BWC.			
	a. Without *I Guldmynt* text at center.	125.	250.	500.
	b. With *I Guldmynt* text at center.	—	—	—
S628	**50 Kronor** 1874. Statue of B. Fogelberg at left. Town scene at upper center, arms at right. Printer: BWC. Square format.	—	—	—

		Good	Fine	XF
S629	**100 Kronor** 1874. Statue of B. Fogelberg at left. Town scene at upper center, arms at right. Like #S628. Printer: BWC.	—	—	—

Wadstena Enskilda Bank

1857 Issue

		Good	Fine	XF
S631	**5 Riksdaler** 1857. Crowned arms of Wadstena at upper center. Printer: JB.	150.	300.	600.
S632	**10 Riksdaler** 1857. Crowned arms of Wadstena at upper center. Printer: JB.	175.	350.	700.
S633	**50 Riksdaler** 1857. Crowned arms of Wadstena at upper center. Printer: JB.	—	—	—
S634	**100 Riksdaler** 1857. Crowned arms of Wadstena at upper center. Printer: JB.	—	—	—

1867 Issue

		Good	Fine	XF
S635	**5 Riksdaler** 1867. Crowned arms of Wadstena at upper center. Printer: JB.	150.	300.	600.
S636	**10 Riksdaler** 1867. Crowned arms of Wadstena at upper center. Printer: JB.	175.	350.	700.
S637	**50 Riksdaler** 1867. Crowned arms of Wadstena at upper center. Printer: JB.	—	—	—
S638	**100 Riksdaler** 1867. Crowned arms of Wadstena at upper center. Printer: JB.	—	—	—

1877 Issue

		Good	Fine	XF
S639	**5 Kronor** 1877. Crowned arms of Wadstena at upper center. Printer: JB.	125.	250.	500.
S640	**10 Kronor** 1877. Crowned arms of Wadstena at upper center. Printer: JB.	150.	300.	600.
S641	**50 Kronor** 1877. Crowned arms of Wadstena at upper center. Mercury at left center, woman at right center. Printer: JB. Square format.	—	—	—
S642	**100 Kronor** 1877. Crowned arms of Wadstena at upper center. Mercury at left center, woman at right center. Like #S641. Printer: JB.	—	—	—

Wermlands Provincial-Bank

1833 Issue

		Good	Fine	XF
S651	**2 Riksdaler Schillingar** 18xx (1833-43). Crowned eagle with outstretched wings at upper center. Hand dated. Printer: CAB.	—	—	—
S652	**3 Riksdaler Banco** 18xx (1833-43). Crowned eagle with outstretched wings at upper center. Hand dated. Printer: CAB.	—	—	—
S653	**5 Riksdaler Banco** 18xx (1833-43). Crowned eagle with outstretched wings at upper center. Hand dated. Printer: CAB.	—	—	—
S654	**10 Riksdaler Banco** 18xx (1833-43). Crowned eagle with outstretched wings at upper center. Hand dated. Printer: CAB.	—	—	—

1843-47 Issue

		Good	Fine	XF
S655	**2 Riksdaler Schillingar** 184x (1843-47). City arms at left and right, crowned eagle at upper center. Printer: CAB.	—	—	—
S656	**3 1/3 Riksdaler Banco** 184x (1843-47). City arms at left and right, crowned eagle at upper center. Printer: CAB.	—	—	—
S657	**6 2/3 Riksdaler Banco** 184x (1843-47). City arms at left and right, crowned eagle at upper center. Printer: CAB.	—	—	—

#	Note	Good	Fine	XF
S658	**10 Riksdaler Banco** 184x (1843-47). City arms at left and right, crowned eagle at upper center. Printer: CAB.	—	—	—
S659	**50 Riksdaler Banco** 184x (1843-47). City arms at left and right, crowned eagle at upper center. Printer: CAB.	—	—	—

1848 Issue

#	Note	Good	Fine	XF
S660	**3 1/3 Riksdaler Banco** 1848; 1851. City arms at left and right, crowned eagle at upper center. Printer: CAB.	—	—	—
S661	**5 Riksdaler Banco** 1848; 1951. City arms at left and right, crowned eagle at upper center. Printer: CAB.	—	—	—
S662	**6 2/3 Riksdaler Banco** 1848; 1851. City arms at left and right, crowned eagle at upper center. Printer: CAB.	—	—	—
S663	**10 Riksdaler Banco** 1848; 1851. City arms at left and right, crowned eagle at upper center. Printer: CAB.	—	—	—
S664	**50 Riksdaler Banco** 184x. City arms at left and right, crowned eagle at upper center. Printer: CAB.	—	—	—

1852 Issue

#	Note	Good	Fine	XF
S666	**3 1/3 Riksdaler Banco** 1852; 1853; 1855. City arms at left and right, crowned eagle at upper center. Printer: JB.	—	—	—
S667	**5 Riksdaler Banco** 1852; 1853; 1855. City arms at left and right, crowned eagle at upper center. Printer: JB.	—	—	—
S668	**6 2/3 Riksdaler Banco** 1852; 1853; 1855. City arms at left and right, crowned eagle at upper center. Printer: JB.	—	—	—
S669	**10 Riksdaler Banco** 1852; 1853; 1855. City arms at left and right, crowned eagle at upper center. Printer: JB.	—	—	—

Wermlands Enskilda Bank

1857 Issue

#	Note	Good	Fine	XF
S682	**5 Riksdaler** 1857. New bank name. Crowned eagle with outstretched wings at upper center. Printer: JB.	125.	250.	500.

#	Note	Good	Fine	XF
S683	**10 Riksdaler** 1857. New bank name. Crowned eagle with outstretched wings at upper center. Printer: JB.	135.	270.	550.
S684	**50 Riksdaler** 1857. New bank name. Crowned eagle with outstretched wings at upper center. Printer: JB.	—	—	—
S685	**100 Riksdaler** 1857. New bank name. Crowned eagle with outstretched wings at upper center. Printer: JB.	—	—	—
S686	**500 Riksdaler** 1857. New bank name. Crowned eagle with outstretched wings at upper center. Printer: JB.	—	—	—

1875 Issue

#	Note	Good	Fine	XF
S687	**5 Kronor** 1875. Crowned eagle with outstretched wings at upper center. Printer: JB.	90.00	180.	360.

#	Note	Good	Fine	XF
S688	**10 Kronor** 1875; 1891. Black and pink. Crowned eagle with outstretched wings at upper center. Printer: JB.	125.	250.	500.
S689	**50 Kronor** 1875. Crowned eagle with outstretched wings at upper center. Printer: JB.	—	—	—
S690	**100 Kronor** 1875. Crowned eagle with outstretched wings at upper center. Printer: JB.	—	—	—

Westerbottens Enskilda Bank

1866 Issue

#	Note	Good	Fine	XF
S701	**5 Riksdaler** 1866. Arms of Lappland (wildman) at upper center. Printer: JB.	125.	250.	500.
S702	**10 Riksdaler** 1866. Arms of Lappland (wildman) at upper center. Printer: JB.	135.	270.	550.
S703	**50 Riksdaler** 1866. Arms of Lappland (wildman) at upper center. Printer: JB.	—	—	—

1876 Issue

#	Note	Good	Fine	XF
S704	**5 Kronor** 1876. Arms of Lappland (wildman) at upper center. Printer: JB.	90.00	180.	360.

#	Note	Good	Fine	XF
S705	**10 Kronor** 1876. Arms of Lappland (wildman) at upper center. Printer: JB.	125.	250.	500.
S706	**50 Kronor** 1876. Arms of Lappland (wildman) at upper center. Printer: JB.	—	—	—
S707	**100 Kronor** 1876. Arms of Lappland (wildman) at upper center. Printer: JB.	—	—	—

1881-83 Issue

#	Note	Good	Fine	XF
S708	**10 Kronor** 1881. Portrait Queen Christina at left, arms at right. Back: Head at center. Printer: BWC.	—	—	—
S709	**50 Kronor** 1883. Arms at left and right, Queen Christina at upper center. Printer: BWC.	—	—	—

#	Note	Good	Fine	XF
S710	**100 Kronor** 1883. Arms at left and right, Queen Christina at upper center. Like #S709. Printer: BWC.	—	—	—

Öst-Göta Bank

1837 Issue

#	Note	Good	Fine	XF
S711	**2 Riksdaler Schillingar** 183x (1837-47). Crowned arms of Ostergotland at upper center. Hand dated. Printer: CAB.	—	—	—
S712	**3 Riksdaler Banco** 183x (1837-47). Crowned arms of Ostergotland at upper center. Hand dated. Printer: CAB.	—	—	—
S713	**3 1/3 Riksdaler Banco** 183x (1837-47). Crowned arms of Ostergotland at upper center. Hand dated. Printer: CAB.	—	—	—

S714	**10 Riksdaler Banco** 183x (1837-47); 1839. Black. Crowned arms of Ostergotland at upper center. Hand dated. Paper: Green. Printer: CAB.	—	—	—
S715	**50 Riksdaler Banco** 183x (1837-47). Crowned arms of Ostergotland at upper center. Hand dated. Printer: CAB.	—	—	—
S716	**100 Riksdaler Banco** 183x (1837-47). Crowned arms of Ostergotland at upper center. Hand dated. Printer: CAB.	—	—	—

Östgöta Enskilda Bank

1847 Issue

		Good	Fine	XF
S717	**3 1/3 Riksdaler Banco** 1847. New bank name. Crowned arms of Ostergotland at upper center. Printer: CAB.	—	—	—
S718	**6 2/3 Riksdaler Banco** 1847. New bank name. Crowned arms of Ostergotland at upper center. Printer: CAB.	—	—	—
S719	**10 Riksdaler Banco** 1847. New bank name. Crowned arms of Ostergotland at upper center. Printer: CAB.	—	—	—
S720	**33 1/3 Riksdaler Banco** 18xx or 184x (1847-57). New bank name. Crowned arms of Ostergotland at upper center. Printer: CAB.	—	—	—
S721	**50 Riksdaler Banco** 18xx or 184x (1847-57). New bank name. Crowned arms of Ostergotland at upper center. Printer: CAB.	—	—	—
S722	**66 2/3 Riksdaler Banco** 18xx or 184x (1847-57). New bank name. Crowned arms of Ostergotland at upper center. Printer: CAB.	—	—	—
S723	**100 Riksdaler Banco** 18xx or 184x (1847-57). New bank name. Crowned arms of Ostergotland at upper center. Printer: CAB.	—	—	—

Östergötlands Enskilda Bank

1857 Issue

		Good	Fine	XF
S724	**5 Riksdaler** 1857; 1867. New bank name. Crowned arms of Ostergotland at upper center. Printer: JB.	125.	250.	500.
S725	**10 Riksdaler** 1857; 1867. New bank name. Crowned arms of Ostergotland at upper center. Printer: JB.	135.	270.	550.
S726	**50 Riksdaler** 1857; 1867. New bank name. Crowned arms of Ostergotland at upper center. Printer: JB.	—	—	—
S727	**100 Riksdaler** 1857; 1867. New bank name. Crowned arms of Ostergotland at upper center. Printer: JB.	—	—	—

1877 Issue

		Good	Fine	XF
S732	**5 Kronor** 1877. Crowned arms of Ostergotland at upper center. Printer: JB.	90.00	180.	360.
S733	**10 Kronor** 1877; 1888. Crowned arms of Ostergotland at upper center. Printer: JB.	125.	250.	500.
S734	**50 Kronor** 1877. Crowned arms of Ostergotland at upper center. Printer: JB.	—	—	—
S735	**100 Kronor** 1877. Crowned arms of Ostergotland at upper center. Printer: JB.	—	—	—

1894 Issue

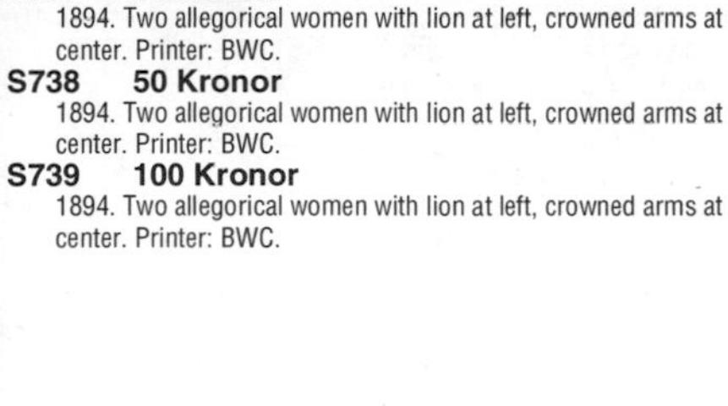

		Good	Fine	XF
S737	**10 Kronor** 1894. Two allegorical women with lion at left, crowned arms at upper center. Printer: BWC.	125.	250.	500.
S738	**50 Kronor** 1894. Two allegorical women with lion at left, crowned arms at upper center. Printer: BWC.	—	—	—
S739	**100 Kronor** 1894. Two allegorical women with lion at left, crowned arms at upper center. Printer: BWC.	—	—	—

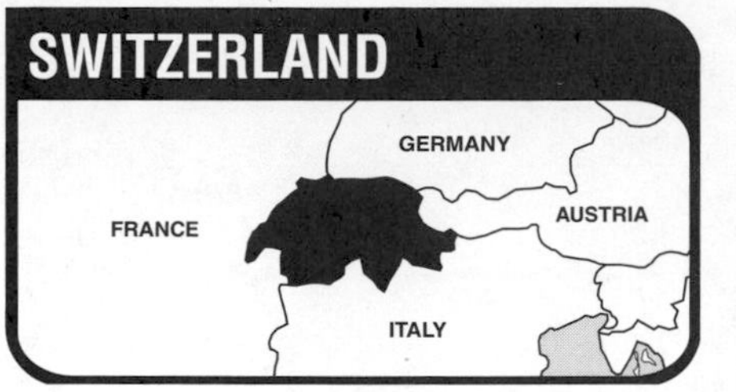

The Swiss Confederation, located in central Europe north of Italy and south of Germany, has an area of 15,941 sq. mi. (41,290 sq. km.) and a population of 7.41 million. Capital: Berne. The economy centers about a well developed manufacturing industry, however the most important economic factor is services (banks and insurance).

Switzerland, the habitat of lake dwellers in prehistoric times, was peopled by the Celtic Helvetians when Julius Caesar made it a part of the Roman Empire in 58 BC. After the decline of Rome, Switzerland was invaded by Teutonic tribes who established small temporal holdings which, in the Middle Ages, became a federation of fiefs of the Holy Roman Empire. As a nation, Switzerland originated in 1291 when the districts of Nidwalden, Schwyz and Uri united to defeat Austria and attain independence as the Swiss Confederation. After acquiring new cantons in the 14th century, Switzerland was made independent from the Holy Roman Empire by the 1648 Treaty of Westphalia. The revolutionary armies of Napoleonic France occupied Switzerland and set up the Helvetian Republic, 1798-1803. After the fall of Napoleon, the Congress of Vienna, 1815, recognized the independence of Switzerland and guaranteed its neutrality. The Swiss Constitutions of 1848, 1874, and 1999 established a union modeled upon that of the United States.

MONETARY SYSTEM:

1 Franc (Franken) = 10 Batzen = 100 Centimes (Rappen)
Plural: Francs, Franchi or Franken.

This section contains listings of cantonal and private banks arranged according to city or area of issue. The following outline indicates where to locate the banks:

AARGAU
- Aargauische Bank .... #S101-S111

APPENZELL
- Appenzell-Ausserhodische Kantonalbank .... #S112-S117
- Innerhodische Kantonalbank .... #S118-S119

BASEL

CANTON
- Basellandschaftliche Kantonalbank .... #S121-S132

CITY
- Bank in Basel .... #S133-S149
- Basler Kantonalbank .... #S150-S153
- Passavant & Co. .... #S154

BERNE
- Deposito-Cassa der Stadt Bern .... #S156-S157
- Eidgenössische Bank .... #S161-S172
- Kantonalbank von Bern .... #S181-S207
- Marcuard & Co. .... #S209

FRIBOURG
- Banque Cantonale Fribourgeoise .... #S210-S227
- Banque de l'Etat de Fribourg .... #S228-S230
- Banque Populaire de la Gruyère .... #S231-S239
- Caisse d'Amortissement de la Dette Publique à Fribourg .... #S241-S249
- Caisse Hypothècaire de Canton de Fribourg .... #S251-S253
- Crèdit Agricole et Industriel de la Broye .... #S261-S266
- Crèdit Gruyèrien .... #S271-S274

GENEVA
- Banque de Genève .... #S281-S289
- Banque du Commerce de Genève .... #S291-S305
- Banque Gènèrale Suisse .... #S307-S308
- B.F. Bonna .... #S309
- Caisse d'Escompte de Genève .... #S311
- Hentsch & Cie. .... #S316
- Lombard, Odier & Cie. .... #S321

GLARUS
- Bank in Glarus .... #S326-S332
- Leih-Cassa Glarus .... #S341-S343
- Glarner Kantonalbank .... #S346-S348

GRAUBÜNDEN
- Bank für Graubünden .... #S351-S357
- Graubündner Kantonalbank .... #S361-S368

LUCERNE
- Bank in Luzern .... #S371-S391
- Luzerner Kantonalbank .... #S392-S395
- Kantonal-Spar-und Leihkasse Luzern .... #S396-S400

NEUCHATEL
- Banque Cantonale Neuchâteloise .... #S401-S412
- Bank Commerciale Neuchâteloise .... #S413-S415
- Banque de Fred: Perret & Co. .... #S416
- Banque de Dépôt et d'Émission .... #S417-S418
- Union Horlogère .... #S419

NIDWALDEN
- Spar-und Leihkasse des Kantons Unterwalden nid dem Wald .... #S421-S424
- Kantonale Spar-und Leihkasse von Nidwalden .... #S425-S426

OBWALDEN
- Obwaldner Kantonalbank .... #S427-S428

ST.GALLEN
- Bank in St. Gallen .... #S431-S453
- Leih-und Sparkasse des Seebezirks .... #S454
- St. Gallische Kantonalbank .... #S455-S462
- Toggenburger Bank .... #S463-S471

SCHAFFHAUSEN
Bank in Schaffhausen .... #S473-S479
Schaffhauser Kantonalbank .... #S480-S482

SCHWYZ
Kantonalbank Schwyz .... #S483-S486

SOLOTHURN
Solothurner Kantonalbank .... #S487-S490
Solothurnische Bank .... #S491-S505

THURGAU
Thurgauische Hypothekenbank .... #S506-S514
Thurgauische Kantonalbank .... #S515-S521

TICINO
Banca Cantonale Ticinese .... #S522-S532
Banca della Svizzera Italiana .... #S533-S542
Banca Popolare di Lugano .... #S543-S545
Credito Ticinese .... #S546-S548

URI
Ersparniss-Cassa des Kantons Uri .... #S549-S552

VAUD
Banque Cantonale Vaudoise .... #S553-S569
Banque Populaire de la Broye .... #S571-S572
Philippe Genton .... #S574
Felix Marcel .... #S576

WALLIS
Banque Cantonale du Valais .... #S581-S585
Caisse Hypothecaire & de Crédit du Valais .... #S586-S586B

ZUG
Zuger Kantonalbank .... #S587-S589

ZÜRICH
Bank in Zürich .... #S591-S610
Zürcher Kantonalbank .... #S611-S625

CONCORDAT NOTE VARIETIES 1883-1906

German language: *in gesezlicher Baarschaft* to 1892 (50-1000 Fr.)
in gesetzlicher Barschaft 1893-1906

Serial #: small, narrow: to 1893 (50, 100 Fr.)
wide: 1894-1906

Series: *SERIE* written out: first issue, 50 Fr. to 1888, 100 Fr. to 1886, 500 Fr. to 1890, 1000 Fr. to 1883.

Ser. abbreviated: later issues, 50 Fr. from 1890, 100 Fr. from 1888, 500 Fr. from 1890, 1000 Fr. from 1892.

Cantons

#S154 was made to replace the former letters of credit.

#S209 was issued to replace checks and letters of credit. #S574 replaced letters of credit issued previously.

The same text was used on #S576 as on #S309 and S316 to circumvent the Banque de France's authority.

#S495-S496 state notes.

Aargauische Bank

1856-57 Issue

		Good	Fine	XF
S101	**20 Fr.** 1856. Castles Lenzburg and Homburg, entrance to a mine, and arms surrounded by children. Paper: Yellow.	—	—	—
S102	**50 Fr.** 1856. Castles Lenzburg and Homburg, entrance to a mine, and arms surrounded by children. Paper: Blue.	—	—	—
S103	**100 Fr.** 1856. Castles Lenzburg and Homburg, entrance to a mine, and arms surrounded by children. Paper: White.	—	—	—
S104	**500 Fr.** 1857. Castles Lenzburg and Homburg, entrance to a mine, and arms surrounded by children. Paper: Pink.	—	—	—

1873 Issue

		Good	Fine	XF
S105	**50 Fr.** 1873. Head of woman and Hermes.	—	—	—
S106	**100 Fr.** 1873. Head of woman and Hermes.	—	—	—
S107	**500 Fr.** 1873. Head of woman and Hermes.	—	—	—

1883-1910 Concordat Issue

		Good	Fine	XF
S108	**50 Fr.** 1883-1910. Helvetia at left leaning on shield, cherub at lower right. Back: Head at left and right.	—	—	—
S109	**100 Fr.** 1883-1910. Helvetia at left leaning on shield, cherub at lower right. Back: Head at left and right.	—	—	—
S110	**500 Fr.** 1883-1910. Helvetia at left leaning on shield, cherub at lower right. Back: Head at left and right.	—	—	—
S111	**1000 Fr.** 1883-1910. Helvetia at left leaning on shield, cherub at lower right. Back: Head at left right.	—	—	—

Ausserhodische Kantonalbank, Herisau

1877 Issue

		Good	Fine	XF
S112	**50 Fr.** 1877. Black on orange underprint. Wagon with cloth in front of factory at left, farm family at farmhouse with trough at right. Back: Cantonal arms. Printer: Dondorf & Naumann, Frankfurt a.M.	—	—	—

		Good	Fine	XF
S113	**100 Fr.** 1.9.1877. Black on blue-green underprint. Wagon with cloth in front of factory at left, farm family at farmhouse with trough at right. Back: Cantonal arms. Printer: Dondorf & Naumann, Frankfurt a.M.	—	—	—
S114	**500 Fr.** 1877. Black on red underprint. Wagon with cloth in front of factory at left, farm family at farmhouse with trough at right. Back: Cantonal arms. Printer: Dondorf & Naumann, Frankfurt a.M.	—	—	—

1883-1910 Concordat Issue

		Good	Fine	XF
S115	**50 Fr.** 1883-1910. Helvetia at left leaning on shield, cherub at lower right. Back: Head at left and right.	—	—	—
S116	**100 Fr.** 1883-1910. Helvetia at left leaning on shield, cherub at lower right. Back: Head at left and right.	—	—	—
S117	**500 Fr.** 1883-1910. Helvetia at left leaning on shield, cherub at lower right. Back: Head at left and right.	—	—	—

Innerhodische Kantonalbank

1901-10 Concordat Issue

		Good	Fine	XF
S118	**50 Fr.** 1901-1910. Helvetia at left leaning on shield, cherub at lower right. Back: Head at left and right.	—	—	—
S119	**100 Fr.** 1901-1910. Helvetia at left leaning on shield, cherub at lower right. Back: Head at left and right.	—	—	—

Basellandschaftliche Kantonalbank, Liestal

1867 Issue

		Good	Fine	XF
S121	**20 Fr.** 1867.	—	—	—
S122	**50 Fr.** 1867.	—	—	—
S123	**100 Fr.** 1867.	—	—	—
S124	**500 Fr.** 1867.	—	—	—

1871 Issue

		Good	Fine	XF
S125	**20 Fr.** 1871. Cantonal arms, mountains and hills with cattle grazing, farm equipment and farm scenes, blacksmith at anvil, train and angel with cornucopia. Back: Text: *Banque Cantonale Liestal.*	—	—	—
S126	**50 Fr.** 1871. Cantonal arms, mountains and hills with cattle grazing, farm equipment and farm scenes, blacksmith at anvil, train and angel with cornucopia. Back: Text: *Banque Cantonale Liestal.*	—	—	—
S127	**100 Fr.** 1871. Cantonal arms, mountains and hills with cattle grazing, farm equipment and farm scenes, blacksmith at anvil, train and angel with cornucopia. Back: Text: *Banque Cantonale Liestal.*	—	—	—
S128	**500 Fr.** 1871. Cantonal arms, mountains and hills with cattle grazing, farm equipment and farm scenes, blacksmith at anvil, train and angel with cornucopia. Back: Text: *Banque Cantonale Liestal.*	—	—	—

1883-1910 Concordat Issue

		Good	Fine	XF
S129	**50 Fr.** 1883-1910. Helvetia at left leaning on shield, cherub at lower right. Back: Head at left and right.	—	—	—
S130	**100 Fr.** 1883-1910. Helvetia at left leaning on shield, cherub at lower right. Back: Head at left and right.	—	—	—
S131	**500 Fr.** 1883-1910. Helvetia at left leaning on shield, cherub at lower right. Back: Head at left and right.	—	—	—
S132	**1000 Fr.** 1883-1910. Helvetia at left leaning on shield, cherub at lower right. Back: Head at left and right.	—	—	—

Bank in Basel

1845 Issue

	Good	Fine	XF
S133 100 Fr. (20 Fünffrankentaler) 1845. River Rhine and woman with Basel arms above. Paper: Yellow.	—	—	—
S134 500 Fr. (100 Fünffrankentaler) 1845. River Rhine and woman with Basel arms above. Paper: White.	—	—	—

1847 Issue

	Good	Fine	XF
S135 100 Fr. 1847. River Rhine and woman with Basel arms above. Similar to #S133 but different paper.	—	—	—
S136 500 Fr. 1847. River Rhine and woman with Basel arms above. Similar to #S134 but different paper.	—	—	—

1852 Issue

	Good	Fine	XF
S137 100 Fr. 1852.	—	—	—
S138 500 Fr. 1852.	—	—	—
S139 1000 Fr. 1854. Printer: OFZ. Interest-bearing state note.	—	—	—

1856 Issue

	Good	Fine	XF
S140 100 Fr. 1856. With stamping: *ODER WERTH IN GOLDSORTEN IM FRANZ. MUNZFUSS.*	—	—	—
S141 500 Fr. 1856. With stamping: *ODER WERTH IN GOLDSORTEN IM FRANZ. MUNZFUSS.*	—	—	—

1873-74 Issue

	Good	Fine	XF
S141C 1000 Fr. 1.12.1873. Swiss cross, woman's head and two boys carrying shields.	—	—	—

	Good	Fine	XF
S142 100 Fr. 1874. Swiss cross, woman's head and two boys carrying shields.	—	—	—
S143 500 Fr. 1874. Swiss cross, woman's head and two boys carrying shields.	—	—	—

	Good	Fine	XF
S144 1000 Fr. 1874. Swiss cross, woman's head and two boys carrying shields.	—	—	—

NOTE: #S144 was issued together with the Bank in Zürich, Bank in St. Gallen and the Kantonalbank von Bern.

1876 Issue

	Good	Fine	XF
S145 50 Fr. 1876. Swiss cross, woman's head and two boys carrying shields.	—	—	—

NOTE: #S145 was issued together with the Kantonalbank von Bern.

	Good	Fine	XF
S145B 500 Fr. 1876. Swiss cross, woman's head and two boys carrying shields.	—	—	—

1883-1907 Concordat Issue

	Good	Fine	XF
S146 50 Fr. 1883-1907. Helvetia at left leaning on shield, cherub at lower right. Back: Head at left and right.	1500.	2500.	—

		Good	Fine	XF
S147	**100 Fr.** 1883-1907. Helvetia at left leaning on shield, cherub at lower right. Back: Head at left and right.	2000.	3250.	—
S148	**500 Fr.** 1883-1907. Helvetia at left leaning on shield, cherub at lower right. Back: Head at left and right	—	—	—
S149	**1000 Fr.** 1883-1907. Helvetia at left leaning on shield, cherub at lower right. Back: Head at left and right.	—	—	—

Basler Kantonalbank

1900-10 Concordat Issue

		Good	Fine	XF
S150	**50 Fr.** 1900-1910. Helvetia at left leaning on shield, cherub at lower right. Back: Head at left and right.	—	—	—
S151	**100 Fr.** 1900-1910. Helvetia at left leaning on shield, cherub at lower right. Back: Head at left and right.	—	—	—
S152	**500 Fr.** 1900-1910. Helvetia at left leaning on shield, cherub at lower right. Back: Head at left and right.	—	—	—
S153	**1000 Fr.** 1900-1910. Helvetia at left leaning on shield, cherub at lower right. Back: Head at left and right.	—	—	—

Passavant & Co., Basel

1840 Issue

#S154 was made to replace the former letters of credit.

		Good	Fine	XF
S154	**100 Fr.** ca.1840.	—	—	—

NOTE: #S154 was made to replace the former letters of credit.

Deposito-Cassa der Stadt Bern

1825-32 Issue

		Good	Fine	XF
S156	**500 Fr.** Paper: Yellow. Alter Währung 1825. Gut-Schein.	—	—	—

		Good	Fine	XF
S157	**100 Fünffrankentaler** 1832.			
	a. Issued note.	—	—	—
	r. Remainder.	—	Unc	1200.

Eidgenössische Bank, Bern

1864 Issue

		Good	Fine	XF
S161	**50 Fr.** 1864. Blue. Allegorical figures of Fortune and Industry, also Swiss cross.	—	—	—
S162	**100 Fr.** 1864. Allegorical figures of Fortune and Industry, also Swiss cross.	—	—	—
S163	**500 Fr.** 1864. Allegorical figures of Fortune and Industry, also Swiss cross.	—	—	—

1873 Issue

		Good	Fine	XF
S164	**50 Fr.** 1873. Blue. Allegorical figures of Fortune and Industry, also Swiss cross. Like #S161 but with hand stamping: *COMPTOIR ZURICH.*	—	—	—
S165	**100 Fr.** 1873. Allegorical figures of Fortune and Industry, also Swiss cross. Like #S162 but with hand stamping: *COMPTOIR ZURICH.*	—	—	—
S166	**500 Fr.** 1873. Allegorical figures of Fortune and Industry, also Swiss cross. Like #S163 but with hand stamping: *COMPTOIR ZURICH.*	—	—	—
S167	**50 Fr.** 19.12.1873.	—	—	—
S168	**100 Fr.** 19.12.1873.	—	—	—
S169	**500 Fr.** 19.12.1873.	—	—	—
S170	**50 Fr.** 19.12.1873. Like #S167 but with hand stamping: *COMPTOIR LUZERN.*	—	—	—
S171	**100 Fr.** 19.12.1873. Like #S168 but with hand stamping: *COMPTOIR LUZERN.*	—	—	—
S172	**500 Fr.** 19.12.1873. Like #S169 but with hand stamping: *COMPTOIR LUZERN.*	—	—	—

Kantonalbank von Bern

1834-47 Issue

		Good	Fine	XF
S181	**10 Fünffrankentaler** 1834. Stub, arms of Bern and vines. Paper: Yellow.	—	—	—
S182	**20 Fünffrankentaler** 1834. Stub, arms of Bern and vines. Paper: Yellow.	—	—	—
S183	**100 Fünffrankentaler** 1838.	—	—	—
S184	**1 Fünffrankentaler** 1847. Issued as welfare assistance for poor watchmakers.	—	—	—

1852 Issue

		Good	Fine	XF
S185	**50 Fr.** 1852.	—	—	—
S186	**100 Fr.** 1852.	—	—	—
S187	**500 Fr.** 1852.	—	—	—

1852-60 Issue

		Good	Fine	XF
S188	**50 Fr.** 1852. With hand stamping: *IN GOLD ODER SILBER.*	—	—	—
S189	**100 Fr.** 1852. With hand stamping: *IN GOLD ODER SILBER.*	—	—	—
S190	**500 Fr.** 1852. With hand stamping: *IN GOLD ODER SILBER.*	—	—	—
S191	**50 Fr.** 1860.	—	—	—
S192	**100 Fr.** 1860.	—	—	—
S193	**500 Fr.** 1860.	—	—	—

1860-62 Issue

		Good	Fine	XF
S194	**50 Fr.** 1860. With hand stamping: *IN GOLD ODER SILBER.*	—	—	—
S195	**100 Fr.** 1860. With hand stamping: *IN GOLD ODER SILBER.*	—	—	—
S196	**500 Fr.** 1860. With hand stamping: *IN GOLD ODER SILBER.*	—	—	—
S197	**20 Fr.** 1862. German text.	—	—	—
S198	**20 Fr.** 1862. French text.	—	—	—

1862-74 Issue

		Good	Fine	XF
S199	**20 Fr.** 1862. German text; with hand stamping: *IN GOLD ODER SILBER.*	—	—	—
S200	**20 Fr.** 1862. French text; with hand stamping: *IN GOLD ODER SILBER.*	—	—	—
S201	**1000 Fr.** 1874.	—	—	—

NOTE: #S201 was issued together with the Bank in Basel, Bank in Zürich, and the Bank in St. Gallen.

1876 Issue

		Good	Fine	XF
S202	**100 Fr.** 1876.	—	—	—

1877 Issue

		Good	Fine	XF
S203	**50 Fr.** 1877. Swiss cross, woman's head and two boys carrying shields.	—	—	—
S204	**500 Fr.** 1877. Swiss cross, woman's head and two boys carrying shields.	—	—	—

1883-1910 Concordat Issue

		Good	Fine	XF
S205	**50 Fr.** 1883-1910. Helvetia at left leaning on shield, cherub at lower right. Back: Head at left and right.	1000.	2000.	—

		Good	Fine	XF
S206	**100 Fr.** 1883-1910. Helvetia at left leaning on shield, cherub at lower right. Back: Head at left and right.	1500.	2500.	—
S207	**500 Fr.** 1883-1910. Helvetia at left leaning on shield, cherub at lower right. Back: Head at left and right.	—	—	—

Marcuard & Co., Bern

1830 Issue

#S209 was issued to replace checks and letters of credit.

		Good	Fine	XF
S209	**50 Fr. Alter Währung** 1830.	—	—	—

Banque Cantonale Fribourgeoise

1851 Issue

#S210-S217 printed on low quality white paper.

		Good	Fine	XF
S210	**5 Fr.** 1851.	—	—	—
S211	**10 Fr.** 1851.	—	—	—
S212	**25 Fr.** 1851.	—	—	—
S213	**50 Fr.** 1851.	—	—	—
S214	**100 Fr.** 1851.	—	—	—
S215	**200 Fr.** 1851.	—	—	—
S216	**500 Fr.** 1851.	—	—	—

1853 Issue

		Good	Fine	XF
S217	**500 Fr.** 1853. Paper: Tinted.	—	—	—

1855-78 Issue

		Good	Fine	XF
S218	**20 Fr.** 1855. Plow drawn by two horses, Alps, bridges over a river, rope bridge near Fribourg and castles of Gruyeres and Estavayer. Paper: Green.	—	—	—
S219	**100 Fr.** 1855. Plow drawn by two horses, Alps, bridges over a river, rope bridge near Fribourg and castles of Gruyeres and Estavayer. Paper: Pink.	—	—	—
S220	**500 Fr.** 1855. Plow drawn by two horses, Alps, bridges over a river, rope bridge near Fribourg and castles of Gruyeres and Estavayer. Paper: White.	—	—	—
S221	**5 Fr.** 1861.	—	—	—
S222	**10 Fr.** 1861. Brown underprint.	—	—	—
S223	**50 Fr.** 1878. Plow drawn by two horses, Alps, bridges over a river, rope bridge near Fribourg and castles of Gruyeres and Estavayer.	—	—	—

1884-1910 Concordat Issue

		Good	Fine	XF
S224	**50 Fr.** 1884-1910. Helvetia at left leaning on shield, cherub at lower right. Back: Head at left and right.	—	—	—
S225	**100 Fr.** 1884-1910. Helvetia at left leaning on shield, cherub at lower right. Back: Head at left and right.	—	—	—
S226	**500 Fr.** 1884-1910. Helvetia at left leaning on shield, cherub at lower right. Back: Head at left and right.	—	—	—
S227	**1000 Fr.** 1884-1910. Helvetia at left leaning on shield, cherub at lower right. Back: Head at left and right.	—	—	—

Banque de l'Etat de Fribourg

1893-1910 Concordat Issue

		Good	Fine	XF
S228	**50 Fr.** 1893-1910. Helvetia at left leaning on shield, cherub at lower right. Back: Head at left and right.	—	—	—
S229	**100 Fr.** 1893-1910. Helvetia at left leaning on shield, cherub at lower right. Back: Head at left and right.	—	—	—
S230	**500 Fr.** 1893-1910. Helvetia at left leaning on shield, cherub at lower right. Back: Head at left and right.	—	—	—

Banque Populaire de la Gruyère, Bulle

1857-66 Issue

		Good	Fine	XF
S231	**10 Fr.** 1857. Beehive with angels, view of Bulle near globe, palette, waterwheel, sheaves and thresher, wine barrel and anchor. Back: Two girls. Paper: Violet. Blurred printing.	—	—	—
S232	**20 Fr.** 1857. Beehive with angels, view of Bulle near globe, palette, waterwheel, sheaves and thresher, wine barrel and anchor. Back: Two girls. Paper: Violet. Blurred printing.	—	—	—
S233	**50 Fr.** 1866. Beehive with angels, view of Bulle near globe, palette, waterwheel, sheaves and thresher, wine barrel and anchor. Back: Two girls. Blurred printing.	—	—	—

1874 Issue

		Good	Fine	XF
S234	**20 Fr.** 1874. Beehive with angels, view of Bulle near globe, palette, waterwheel, sheaves and thresher, wine barrel and anchor. Back: Two girls. Paper: Violet. Finer, sharper printing.	—	—	—
S235	**50 Fr.** 1874. Blue. Beehive with angels, view of Bulle near globe, palette, waterwheel, sheaves and thresher, wine barrel and anchor. Back: Two girls. Paper: White. Finer, sharper printing.	—	—	—
S236	**100 Fr.** 1874. Red. Beehive with angels, view of Bulle near globe, palette, waterwheel, sheaves and thresher, wine barrel and anchor. Back: Two girls. Paper: White. Finer, sharper printing.	—	—	—

1883-90 Concordat Issue

		Good	Fine	XF
S237	**50 Fr.** 1883-1890. Helvetia at left leaning on shield, cherub at lower right. Back: Head at left and right.	—	—	—
S238	**100 Fr.** 1883-1890. Helvetia at left leaning on shield, cherub at lower right. Back: Head at left and right.	—	—	—
S239	**500 Fr.** 1883-1890. Helvetia at left leaning on shield, cherub at lower right. Back: Head at left and right.	—	—	—

Caisse d'Amortissement de la Dette Publique à Fribourg

Decret du 15.5.1874

	Good	Fine	XF
S241 20 Fr. D.1874. Black with red-brown text, border and counterfoil. Seated girl writing on tablet at left, view of Fribourg, the Alps, along bottom, seated girl with sheep at right. Back: Red-brown. Circular bank seal with Fribourg shield at center flanked by value scrolls. Printer: J.J. Hofer, Zurich.	—	—	—

	Good	Fine	XF
S242 50 Fr. D.1874. Black with green text, border and counterfoil. Seated girl writing on tablet at left, view of Fribourg, the Alps, along bottom, seated girl with sheep at right. Back: Green. Circular bank seal with Fribourg shield at center flanked by value scrolls. Printer: J.J. Hofer, Zurich.	—	—	—

	Good	Fine	XF
S243 100 Fr. D.1874. Seated girl writing on tablet at left, view of Fribourg, the Alps, along bottom, seated girl with sheep at right. Back: Circular bank seal with Fribourg shield at center flanked by value scrolls. Printer: J.J. Hofer, Zurich.			
a. Issued note. Black with deep red text, border and counterfoil. Back deep red.	—	—	—
p. Black with brown text, border and counterfoil. Proof.	—	—	—

1877 ND Issue

	Good	Fine	XF
S244 20 Fr. ND (1877). Green underprint. Without vignette.	—	—	—
S245 50 Fr. ND (1877). Blue underprint. Without vignette.	—	—	—

	Good	Fine	XF
S246 100 Fr. ND (1877). Red underprint. Without vignette.	—	—	—

1883-93 Concordat Issue

	Good	Fine	XF
S247 50 Fr. 1883-93. Helvetia at left leaning on shield, cherub at lower right. Back: Head at left and right.	—	—	—
S248 100 Fr. 1883-93. Helvetia at left leaning on shield, cherub at lower right. Back: Head at left and right.	—	—	—
S249 500 Fr. 1883-93. Helvetia at left leaning on shield, cherub at lower right. Back: Head at left and right.	—	—	—

Caisse Hypothécaire du Canton de Fribourg

1856 Issue

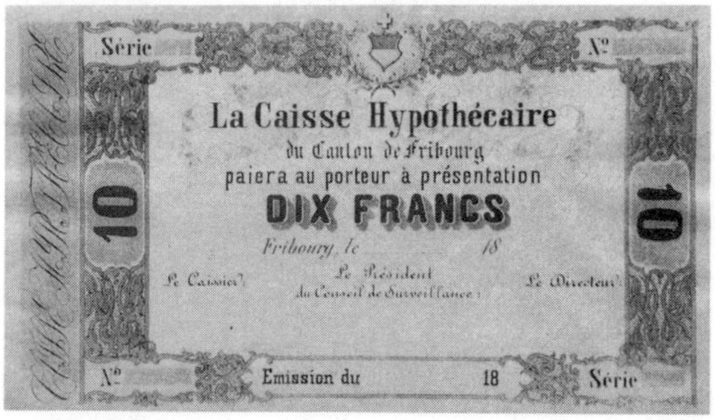

	Good	Fine	XF
S251 10 Fr. 18xx (ca.1856). Black on yellow underprint. Arms at top center, uniface. Remainder with counterfoil.	—	Unc	250.

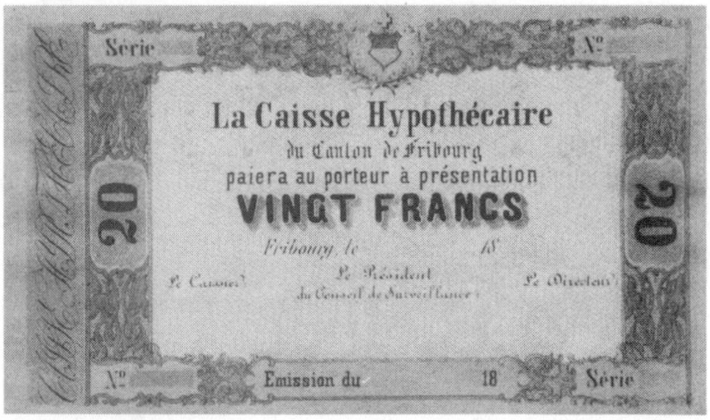

	Good	Fine	XF
S252 20 Fr. 18xx (ca.1856). Black on light red underprint. Arms at top center, uniface. Remainder with counterfoil.	—	Unc	250.

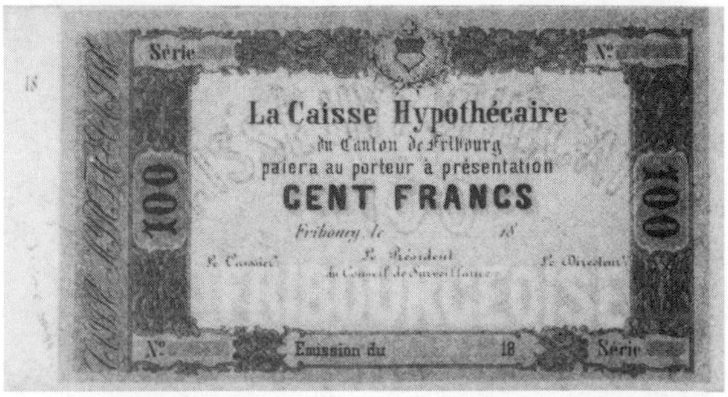

	Good	Fine	XF
S253 100 Fr. 18xx (ca.1856). Green underprint. Arms at top center, uniface.			
a. Issued note.	1000.	1750.	—
r. Remainder with counterfoil.	—	Unc	250.

Crédit Agricole et Industriel de la Broye, Estavayer

1866-77 Issue

S261	**10 Fr.**	**Good**	**Fine**	**XF**
	1.12.1866. Views of Estavayer and surroundings. Paper: Gray. Printer: J.J. Hofer, Zürich. Remainder.	—	Unc	250.

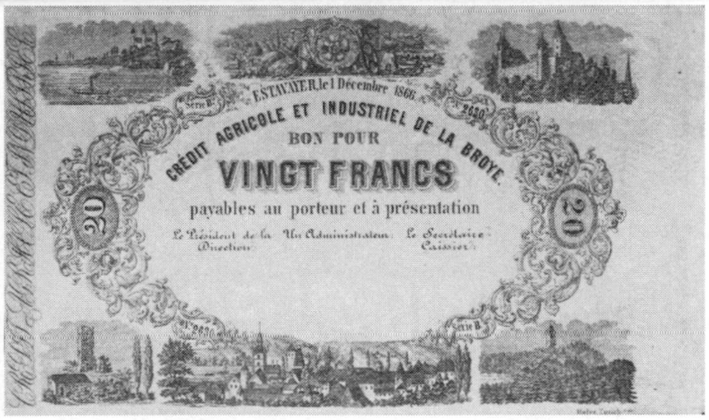

S262	**20 Fr.**	**Good**	**Fine**	**XF**
	1.12.1866. Views of Estavayer and surroundings. Paper: Red. Printer: J.J. Hofer, Zürich. Remainder.	—	Unc	250.

S263	**100 Fr.**	**Good**	**Fine**	**XF**
	28.8.1872. Blue. Views of Estavayer and surroundings. Paper: White. Printer: J.J. Hofer, Zürich. Remainder.	—	Unc	250.

S264	**50 Fr.**	**Good**	**Fine**	**XF**
	28.3.1877. Green. Views of Estavayer and surroundings. Back: Green. Paper: White. Printer: J.J. Hofer, Zürich. Remainder.	—	Unc	200.

1883-1910 Concordat Issue

S265	**50 Fr.**	**Good**	**Fine**	**XF**
	1883-1910. Helvetia at left leaning on shield, cherub at lower right. Back: Head at left and right.	—	—	—
S266	**100 Fr.**			
	1883-1910. Helvetia at left leaning on shield, cherub at lower right. Back: Head at left and right.	—	—	—

Crédit Gruyérien, Bulle

Emission du 1.1.1874

S271	**20 Fr.**	**Good**	**Fine**	**XF**
	D.1874. Green with black text and counterfoil. Arms of *La Gruyère* at top center, vignettes in border of Bulle and Estavayer, a cow herd, woman embroidering, and figures with cornucopias and sheaves. Bank name within frame flanked by cher Back: Green. Black text. Printer: J.J. Hofer, Zürich.	—	—	—

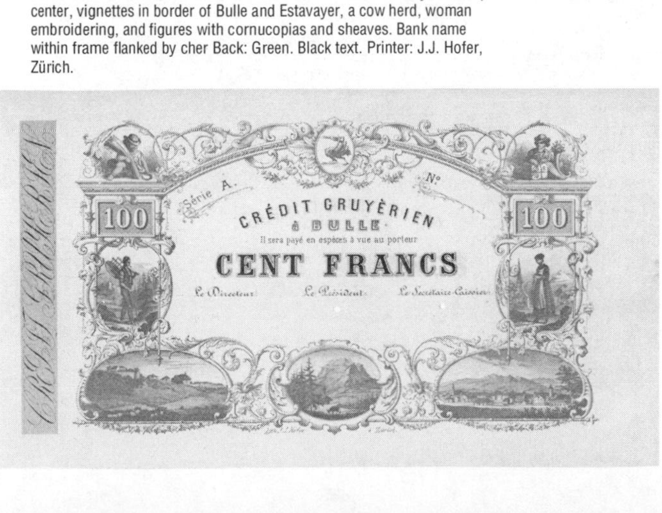

		Good	Fine	XF
S272	**100 Fr.** D.1874. Brown with black text and counterfoil. Arms of *La Gruyère* at top center, vignettes in border of Bulle and Estavayer, a cow herd, woman embroidering, and figures with cornucopias and sheaves. Bank name within frame flanked by cher Back: Brown. Black text. Printer: J.J. Hofer, Zürich.	—	—	—

1883-90 Concordat Issue

		Good	Fine	XF
S273	**50 Fr.** 1883-90. Helvetia at left leaning on shield, cherub at lower right. Back: Head at left and right.	—	—	—
S274	**100 Fr.** 1883-90. Helvetia at left leaning on shield, cherub at lower right. Back: Head at left and right.	—	—	—

Banque de Genève

1848-51 Issue

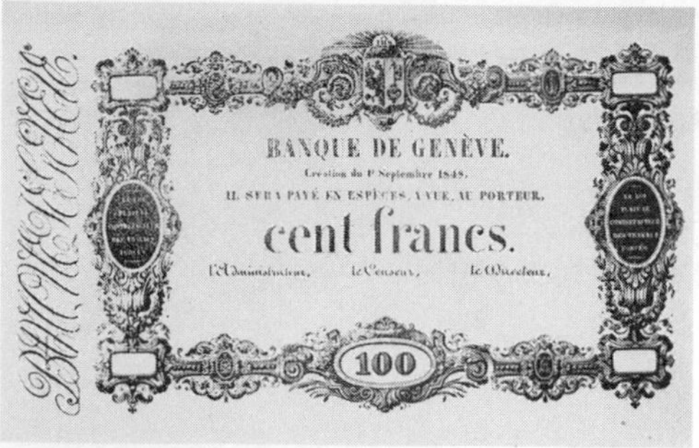

		Good	Fine	XF
S281	**100 Fr.** 1848. Paper: Blue.	—	—	—
S282	**500 Fr.** 1848. Paper: Green.	—	—	—
S283	**1000 Fr.** 1848.	—	—	—
S284	**20 Fr.** 1851. Paper: Red.	—	—	—

1873 Issue

		Good	Fine	XF
S285	**100 Fr.** 1873.	—	—	—

1883-99 Concordat Issue

		Good	Fine	XF
S286	**50 Fr.** 1883-99. Helvetia at left leaning on shield, cherub at lower right. Back: Head at left and right.	—	—	—
S287	**100 Fr.** 1883-99. Helvetia at left leaning on shield, cherub at lower right. Back: Head at left and right.	—	—	—

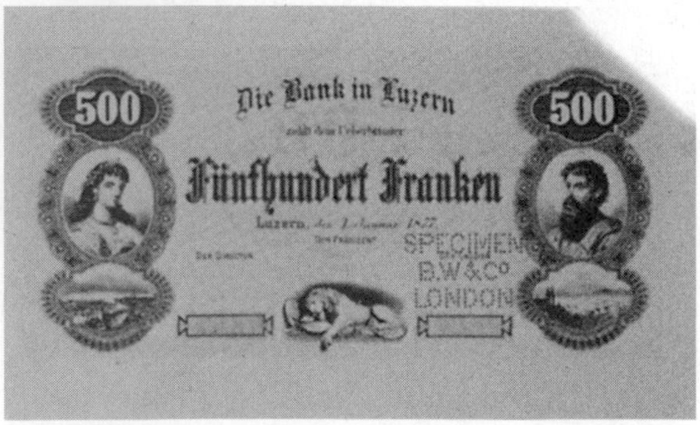

		Good	Fine	XF
S288	**500 Fr.** 1883-99. Helvetia at left leaning on shield, cherub at lower right. Back: Head at left and right.	—	—	—
S289	**1000 Fr.** 1883-99. Helvetia at left leaning on shield, cherub at lower right. Back: Head at left and right.	—	—	—

Banque du Commerce de Genève

1846 Issue

		Good	Fine	XF
S291	**100 Fr.** 1846.	—	—	—
S292	**500 Fr.** 1846.	—	—	—
S293	**1000 Fr.** 1846.	—	—	—

1850 Issue

		Good	Fine	XF
S294	**100 Fr.** 1850.			
	a. Like #S291 but yellow guilloche.	—	—	—
	b. With additional text: *En or ou en argent au cours legal français.*	—	—	—
S295	**500 Fr.** 1850.			
	a. Like #S292 but blue guilloche.	—	—	—
	b. With additional text like #S294b.	—	—	—
S296	**1000 Fr.** 1850.			
	a. Like #S293 but with pink underprint. added.	—	—	—
	b. With additional text like #S294b.	—	—	—

1871 Issue

		Good	Fine	XF
S297	**50 Fr.** 1871.	—	—	—

1874 Issue

		Good	Fine	XF
S298	**50 Fr.** 1874.	—	—	—
S299	**100 Fr.** 1874.	—	—	—

1878 Issue

		Good	Fine	XF
S300	**50 Fr.** 1878.	—	—	—
S301	**100 Fr.** 1878.	—	—	—

1883-1907 Concordat Issue

		Good	Fine	XF
S302	**50 Fr.** 1883-1907. Helvetia at left leaning on shield, cherub at lower right. Back: Head at left and right.	—	—	—
S303	**100 Fr.** 1883-1907. Helvetia at left leaning on shield, cherub at lower right. Back: Head at left and right.	—	—	—
S304	**500 Fr.** 1883-1907. Helvetia at left leaning on shield, cherub at lower right. Back: Head at left and right.	—	—	—
S305	**1000 Fr.** 1883-1907. Helvetia at left leaning on shield, cherub at lower right. Back: Head at left and right.	—	—	—

Banque Générale Suisse

1857 Issue

		Good	Fine	XF
S307	**20 Fr.** 1857.	—	—	—
S308	**50 Fr.** 1857.	—	—	—

B.F. Bonna, Genève

1840 Issue

		Good	Fine	XF
S309	**100 French Fr.** (ca.1840).	—	—	—

NOTE: With text: *1 day after sight* the French banker issuing #S309 wanted to circumvent the monopoly on note issue of the Banque de France.

Caisse d'Escompte de Genève

1856 Issue

		Good	Fine	XF
S311	**10 Fr.** 2.8.1856. Black on green underprint. Arms at upper center. Uniface. Printer: Pilet & Cougnard, Geneva.			
	a. Issued note.	—	—	—
	b. Cancelled, hand stamped: *ANNULÉ* and circular bank stamp.	150.	300.	—

Hentsch & Cie, Genève

1840 Issue

		Good	Fine	XF
S316	**100 French Fr.** (ca.1840).	—	—	—

NOTE: #S316 has the same text as #S309 in hopes of circumventing the Banque de France.

Lombard, Odier & Cie, Genève

1832 Issue

		Good	Fine	XF
S321	**100 Fr.** 1832. *Bon au Porteur.*	—	—	—

Bank in Glarus

1852 Issue

		Good	Fine	XF
S326	**10 Fr.** 1852. Helvetia sitting at left, St. Fridolinus at center, head of Hermes in underprint at right. Printer: OFZ.	—	—	—
S327	**100 Fr.** 1852. Helvetia sitting at left, St. Fridolinus at center, head of Hermes in underprint at right. Printer: OFZ.	—	—	—

1864 Issue

		Good	Fine	XF
S328	**10 Fr.** 1864. Helvetia sitting at left, St. Fridolinus at center, head of Hermes in underprint at right.	—	—	—
S329	**100 Fr.** 1864. Helvetia sitting at left, St. Fridolinus at center, head of Hermes in underprint at right.	—	—	—

1876 Issue

		Good	Fine	XF
S330	**50 Fr.** 1876. Red. Helvetia sitting at left, St. Fridolinus at center, head of Hermes in underprint at right. Printer: Dondorf & Naumann.	—	—	—

		Good	Fine	XF
S331	**100 Fr.** 14.6.1876. Green. Helvetia sitting at left, St. Fridolinus at center, head of Hermes in underprint at right. Printer: Dondorf & Naumann.			
	a. Issued note.	—	—	—
	b. Cancelled, hand stamped: *ANNULE.*	—	—	—
S332	**500 Fr.** 1876. Blue. Helvetia sitting at left, St. Fridolinus at center, head of Hermes in underprint at right. Printer: Dondorf & Naumann.	—	—	—

Leih-Cassa Glarus

1870 Issue

		Good	Fine	XF
S341	**20 Fr.** 1870. Blue. Factory at center, seated Helvetia at right.	—	—	—
S342	**50 Fr.** 1870. Red. Factory at center, seated Helvetia at right.	—	—	—
S343	**100 Fr.** 1870. Green. Factory at center, seated Helvetia at right.	—	—	—

Glarner Kantonalbank

1884-1910 Concordat Issue

		Good	Fine	XF
S346	**50 Fr.** 1884-1910. Helvetia at left leaning on shield, cherub at lower right. Back: Head at left and right.	—	—	—
S347	**100 Fr.** 1884-1910. Helvetia at left leaning on shield, cherub at lower right. Back: Head at left and right.	—	—	—
S348	**500 Fr.** 1884-1910. Helvetia at left leaning on shield, cherub at lower right. Back: Head at left and right.	—	—	—

Bank für Graubünden, Chur

1863 ND Issue

#S351-S353 interest-bearing state notes to the bearer and at sight.

		Good	Fine	XF
S351	**50 Fr.** ND (1863). Three allegorical figures at left and right, arms above. Back: Text.	—	—	—
S352	**100 Fr.** ND (1863). Three allegorical figures at left and right, arms above.	—	—	—
S353	**500 Fr.** ND (1863). Three allegorical figures at left and right, arms above.	—	—	—

1865-67 Issue

		Good	Fine	XF
S354	**50 Fr.** 1865. Industry at left, farm couple symbolizing Agriculture at right. Paper: Brown.	—	—	—
S355	**100 Fr.** 1865. Industry at left, farm couple symbolizing Agriculture at right. Paper: Green.	—	—	—
S356	**500 Fr.** 1865. Industry at left, farm couple symbolizing Agriculture at right. Paper: Brown.	—	—	—
S357	**20 Fr.** 1867. Black on blue and orange underprint. Industry at left, farm couple symbolizing Agriculture at right.	—	—	—

Graubündner Kantonalbank, Chur

1872-73 Issue

		Good	Fine	XF
S361	**10 Fr.** 1872. Yellow. Alps cottage and mountainscape with bears.	—	—	—
S362	**50 Fr.** 1872. Green. Alps cottage and mountainscape with bears.	—	—	—
S363	**100 Fr.** 1872. Blue. Alps cottage and mountainscape with bears.	—	—	—
S364	**500 Fr.** 1872. Brown. Alps cottage and mountainscape with bears.	—	—	—
S365	**20 Fr.** 1873. Red. Alps cottage and mountainscape with bears.	—	—	—

1883-1910 Concordat Issue

		Good	Fine	XF
S366	**50 Fr.** 1883-1910. Helvetia at left leaning on shield, cherub at lower right. Back: Head at left and right.	—	—	—

		Good	Fine	XF
S367	**100 Fr.** 1883-1910. Helvetia at left leaning on shield, cherub at lower right. Back: Head at left and right.	—	—	—
S368	**500 Fr.** 1883-1910. Helvetia at left leaning on shield, cherub at lower right. Back: Head at left and right.	—	—	—

Bank in Luzern

1857 Issue

		Good	Fine	XF
S371	**50 Fr.** 1857. Medallion with steamer at left, view of Lucerne at center, train at right. Uniface. Series A. Paper: Yellow.	—	—	—
S372	**100 Fr.** 1857. Medallion with steamer at left, view of Lucerne at center, train at right. Uniface. Series A. Paper: Blue.	—	—	—
S373	**500 Fr.** 1857. Medallion with steamer at left, view of Lucerne at center, train at right. Uniface. Series A. Paper: White.	—	—	—

1866 Issue

		Good	Fine	XF
S374	**100 Fr.** 1866. Series B.	—	—	—
S375	**500 Fr.** 1866. Series B.	—	—	—

1870-71 Issue

#S376 and S377 interest-bearing state notes.

		Good	Fine	XF
S376	**10 Fr.** 1870.	—	—	—
S377	**100 Fr.** 1870.	—	—	—
S378	**50 Fr.** 1871. Series B.	—	—	—

1872 Issue

		Good	Fine	XF
S379	**50 Fr.** 1872. Series C.	—	—	—
S380	**100 Fr.** 1872. Series C.	—	—	—
S381	**500 Fr.** 1872. Series C.	—	—	—

1873-75 Issue

		Good	Fine	XF
S382	**50 Fr.** 1873. Series D.	—	—	—
S383	**100 Fr.** 1873. Series D.	—	—	—
S384	**500 Fr.** 1873. Series D.	—	—	—
S385	**100 Fr.** 1875. Series E. Back: Text added.	—	—	—

1877 Issue

		Good	Fine	XF
S386	**50 Fr.** 1.1.1877. View of Lucerne, William Tell, girls and lion monument in Lucerne. Back: Woman's head. Printer: BWC.			
	a. Issued note.	—	—	—
	s. Specimen.	—	Unc	800.
S387	**100 Fr.** 1.1.1877. View of Lucerne, William Tell, girls and lion monument in Lucerne. Back: Woman's head. Printer: BWC.			
	a. Issued note.	—	—	—
	s. Specimen.	—	Unc	1000.

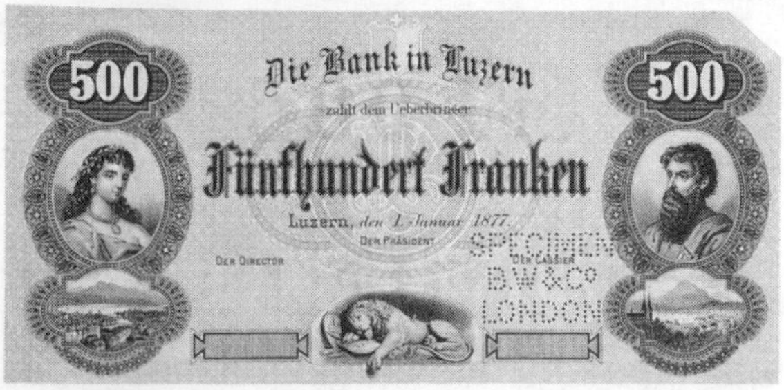

		Good	Fine	XF
S388	**500 Fr.** 1.1.1877. View of Lucerne, William Tell, girls and lion monument in Lucerne. Back: Woman's head. Printer: BWC.			
	a. Issued note.	—	—	—
	s. Specimen.	—	Unc	1200.

1883-1907 Concordat Issue

		Good	Fine	XF
S389	**50 Fr.** 1883-1907. Helvetia at left leaning on shield, cherub at lower right. Back: Head at left and right.	—	—	—
S390	**100 Fr.** 1883-1907. Helvetia at left leaning on shield, cherub at lower right. Back: Head at left and right.	—	—	—
S391	**500 Fr.** 1883-1907. Helvetia at left leaning on shield, cherub at lower right. Back: Head at left and right.	—	—	—

Luzerner Kantonalbank

1892-1910 Concordat Issue

		Good	Fine	XF
S392	**50 Fr.** 1892-1910. Helvetia at left leaning on shield, cherub at lower right. Back: Head at left and right.	—	—	—

		Good	Fine	XF
S393	**100 Fr.** 1892-1910. Helvetia at left leaning on shield, cherub at lower right. Back: Head at left and right.	—	—	—
S394	**500 Fr.** 1892-1910. Helvetia at left leaning on shield, cherub at lower right. Back: Head at left and right.	—	—	—
S395	**1000 Fr.** 1892-1910. Helvetia at left leaning on shield, cherub at lower right. Back: Head at left and right.	—	—	—

Kantonal-Spar- und Leihkasse Luzern

1876-77 Issue

		Good	Fine	XF
S396	**50 Fr.** 31.10.1876. View of Lucerne, William Tell, girls and lion monument in Lucerne. Back: Woman's head.	—	—	—
S397	**100 Fr.** 1877. View of Lucerne, William Tell, girls and lion monument in Lucerne. Back: Woman's head.	—	—	—
S398	**500 Fr.** 1877. View of Lucerne, William Tell, girls and lion monument in Lucerne. Back: Woman's head.	—	—	—

Note: #S396-S398 from the Spar- und Leih-Cassa des Kantons Luzern.

1884-92 Concordat Issue

		Good	Fine	XF
S398A	**50 Fr.** 1884-92. Helvetia at left leaning on shield, cherub at lower right. Back: Head at left and right.	—	—	—
S398B	**100 Fr.** 1884-92. Helvetia at left leaning on shield, cherub at lower right. Back: Head at left and right.	—	—	—
S399	**500 Fr.** 1884-92. Helvetia at left leaning on shield, cherub at lower right. Back: Head at left and right.	—	—	—
S400	**1000 Fr.** 1884-92. Helvetia at left leaning on shield, cherub at lower right. Back: Head at left and right.	—	—	—

Banque Cantonale Neuchâteloise

1855-56 Issue

		Good	Fine	XF
S401	**100 Fr.** 1855. *Billet Provisoire.*	—	—	—
S402	**20 Fr.** 1856. View of Neuchatel, grape harvest and watchmaker's workshop.	—	—	—
S403	**50 Fr.** 1856. View of Neuchatel, grape harvest and watchmaker's workshop.	—	—	—
S404	**100 Fr.** 1856. View of Neuchatel, grape harvest and watchmaker's workshop.	—	—	—
S405	**500 Fr.** 1856. View of Neuchatel, grape harvest and watchmaker's workshop.	—	—	—

1859-74 Issue

		Good	Fine	XF
S406	**20 Fr.** 1859.	—	—	—
S407	**50 Fr.** 1859.	—	—	—
S408	**100 Fr.** 1872.	—	—	—
S409	**500 Fr.** 1874.	—	—	—

1883-1910 Concordat Issue

		Good	Fine	XF
S410	**50 Fr.** 1883-1910. Helvetia at left leaning on shield, cherub at lower right. Back: Head at left and right.	—	—	—
S411	**100 Fr.** 1883-1910. Helvetia at left leaning on shield, cherub at lower right. Back: Head at left and right.	—	—	—
S412	**500 Fr.** 1883-1910. Helvetia at left leaning on shield, cherub at lower right. Back: Head at left and right.	—	—	—

Banque Commerciale Neuchâteloise

1883-1907 Concordat Issue

		Good	Fine	XF
S413	**50 Fr.** 1883-1907. Helvetia at left leaning on shield, cherub at lower right. Back: Head at left and right.	—	—	—
S414	**100 Fr.** 1883-1907. Helvetia at left leaning on shield, cherub at lower right. Back: Head at left and right.	—	—	—
S415	**500 Fr.** 1883-1907. Helvetia at left leaning on shield, cherub at lower right. Back: Head at left and right.	—	—	—

Banque de Fred: Perret & Co., Neuchâtel and Chaux deFonds

(no Release Code)

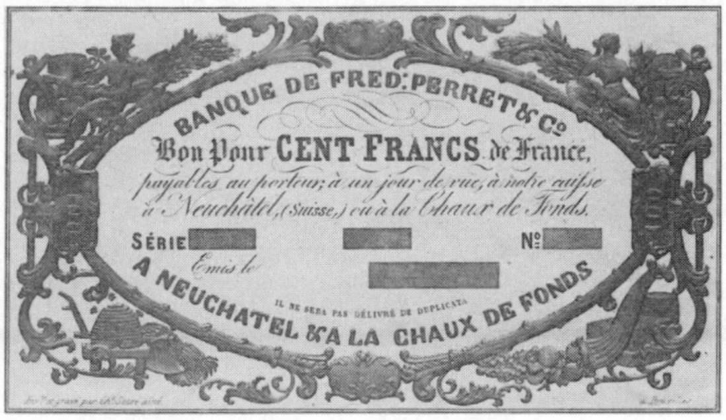

		Good	Fine	XF
S416	**100 Fr.** ND. Allegorical figure and beehive in ornate border.	—	—	—

Banque de Dépôt et d'Émission, Chaux de Fonds

1848 Issue

		Good	Fine	XF
S417	**25 Fr.** 1848. Black and gray. Ornamental octagonal frame.	—	—	—
S418	**50 Fr.** 1848. Ornamental octagonal frame. Similar to #S417. Paper: Red.	—	—	—

Union Horlogère, Le Locle and La Chaux de Fonds

1858 Issue

		Good	Fine	XF
S419	**100 Fr.** (ca.1858). Interest-bearing note.	—	—	—

Spar- und Leihkasse des Kantons Unterwalden nid dem Wald

1879 Issue

		Good	Fine	XF
S421	**50 Fr.** 1879. Cantonal arms, Winkelried monument and woman's head.	—	—	—

		Good	Fine	XF
S422	**100 Fr.** 1879. Cantonal arms, Winkelried monument and woman's head. Lit. A.	—	—	—

1883-91 Concordat Issue

		Good	Fine	XF
S423	**50 Fr.** 1883-91. Helvetia at left leaning on shield, cherub at lower right. Back: Head at left and right.	—	—	—
S424	**100 Fr.** 1883-91. Helvetia at left leaning on shield, cherub at lower right. Back: Head at left and right.	—	—	—

Kantonale Spar- und Leihkasse von Nidwalden, Stans

1891-1904 Concordat Issue

		Good	Fine	XF
S425	**50 Fr.** 1891-1904. Helvetia at left leaning on shield, cherub at lower right. Back: Head at left and right.	—	—	—
S426	**100 Fr.** 1891-1904. Helvetia at left leaning on shield, cherub at lower right. Back: Head at left and right.	—	—	—

Obwaldner Kantonalbank, Sarnen

1887-1910 Concordat Issue

		Good	Fine	XF
S427	**50 Fr.** 1887-1910. Helvetia at left leaning on shield, cherub at lower right. Back: Head at left and right.	—	—	—

		Good	Fine	XF
S428	**100 Fr.** 2.1.1887-1910. Dark blue on tan underprint, black text. Helvetia at left leaning on shield, cherub at lower right. Back: Blue-gray. Head at left and right.	—	—	—

Bank in St. Gallen

1838 Issue

S431	10 Gulden	Good	Fine	XF
	18xx (ca. 1838). Black. Steamship at left, Hermes with dog and key at upper center, steam passenger train at right. Printer: Draper, Toppan, Longacre & Co., N.Y. & Phila. Remainder.	—	Unc	600.

S432	50 Gulden	Good	Fine	XF
	18xx (ca.1838). Black. Newfoundland dog, beehive and rooster at left, steam trains at center, sheaf, plow and farm tools with hills at right. Printer: Draper, Toppan, Longacre & Co., N.Y. & Phila. Remainder.	—	Unc	900.

S433	100 Gulden	Good	Fine	XF
	18xx (ca.1838). Black. Seated allegorical figures at upper center, steam train at left and right. Printer: Draper, Toppan, Longacre & Co., N.Y. & Phila. Remainder.	—	Unc	900.

1852 Gulden Issue

		Good	Fine	XF
S434	10 Gulden			
	18xx (ca.1852). Black. Steamship at left, Hermes with dog and key at upper center, steam passenger train at right. Like #S431. With stamping: *EFFECTIVE GULDEN ODER BRABANTERTHALER ZU FL. 2,42.* Litt. P-W (8 series).	—	—	—
S435	50 Gulden			
	18xx (ca.1852). Black. Dog, beehive and rooster at left, steam trains at center, sheaf, plow and farm tools at right. Like #S432. With stamping: *EFFECTIVE GULDEN ODER BRABANTERTHALER ZU FL. 2,42.* Litt P-W (8 series).	—	—	—
S436	100 Gulden			
	18xx (ca.1852). Black. Seated allegorical figures at upper center, steam train at left and right. Like #S433. With stamping: *EFFECTIVE GULDEN ODER BRABANTERTHALER ZU FL. 2,42.* Litt. P-W (8 series).	—	—	—

1852 Franc Issue

S437	20 Fr.	Good	Fine	XF
	18xx (ca.1852). Black. Seated woman with sheaf next to man with anvil at left, shepherd with sheep at upper center, beehive at bottom, woman with grapes at right. Printer: Toppan, Carpenter, Casilear & Co., N.Y. and Phila. Remainder.	—	Unc	500.

S438	50 Fr.	Good	Fine	XF
	18xx (ca.1852). Seated Justice at left, woman with sheaf at right, train on bridge at upper center. Printer: Toppan, Carpenter, Casilear & Co., N.Y. and Phila. Remainder.	—	Unc	600.

S439	100 Fr.	Good	Fine	XF
	18xx (ca.1852). Woman harvesting at left, man with three horses at trough at top center, seated woman weaving at right. Printer: Toppan, Carpenter, Casilear & Co., N.Y. and Phila. Remainder.	—	Unc	700.

S440	500 Fr.	Good	Fine	XF
	18xx (ca. 1852). Seated woman with hammer and anvil at left, bank at upper center, allegorical Art writing at right. Printer: Toppan, Carpenter, Casilear & Co., N.Y. and Phila. Remainder.	—	Unc	900.

1857 Issue

		Good	Fine	XF
S441	20 Fr.			
	1857. Like #S437. With stamping: *RUCKZAHLBAR IN SILBER ODER GOLD NAP. D'OR A FR. 20,-.*	—	—	—
S442	50 Fr.			
	1857. Like #S438. With stamping: *RUCKZAHLBAR IN SILBER ODER GOLD NAP. D'OR A FR. 20,-.*	—	—	—
S443	100 Fr.			
	1857. Like #S439. With stamping: *RUCKZAHLBAR IN SILBER ODER GOLD NAP. D'OR A FR. 20,-.*	—	—	—
S444	500 Fr.			
	1857. Like #S440. With stamping: *RUCKZAHLBAR IN SILBER ODER GOLD NAP. D'OR A FR. 20,-.*	—	—	—

1873 Issue

	Good	Fine	XF
S445 1000 Fr. 1873. Swiss cross, woman's head, two boys holding shields. Printer: Dondorf & Naumann. Unissued remainder.	—	Unc	3000.

NOTE: #S445 was issued together with the Bank in Zürich, Bank in Basel and Kantonalbank von Bern.

1875 Issue

	Good	Fine	XF
S446 20 Fr. 1875. Seated woman with sheaf next to man with anvil at left, shepherd with sheep at upper center, beehive at bottom, woman with grapes at right. Similar to #S437.	—	—	—
S447 50 Fr. 1875. Seated Justice at left, woman with sheaf at right, train on bridge at upper center. Similar to #S438.	—	—	—
S448 100 Fr. 1875. Woman harvesting at left, man with three horses at trough at top center, seated woman weaving at right. Similar to #S439.	—	—	—
S449 500 Fr. 1875. Seated woman with hammer and anvil at left, bank at upper center, allegorical Art writing at right. Similar to #S440.	—	—	—

1883-1907 Concordat Issue

	Good	Fine	XF
S450 50 Fr. 1883-1907. Helvetia at left leaning on shield, cherub at lower right. Back: Head at left and right.	—	—	—
S451 100 Fr. 1883-1907. Helvetia at left leaning on shield, cherub at lower right. Back: Head at left and right.	—	—	—
S452 500 Fr. 1883-1907. Helvetia at left leaning on shield, cherub at lower right. Back: Head at left and right.	—	—	—
S453 1000 Fr. 1883-1907. Helvetia at left leaning on shield, cherub at lower right. Back: Head at left and right.	—	—	—

Leih- und Sparkasse des Seebezirks, Uznach

1848 Issue

	Good	Fine	XF
S454 10 Gulden 1848. Hermes and Fortune with cornucopia.	—	—	—

St. Gallische Kantonalbank

1868 Issue

	Good	Fine	XF
S455 20 Fr. 1868-82. Woman with sickle near wheat field and apples at left, allegorical woman (Industry) near factory at right. Paper: Green.	—	—	—
S456 50 Fr. 1868-82. Woman with sickle near wheat field and apples at left, allegorical woman (Industry) near factory at right. Paper: Brown.	—	—	—

	Good	Fine	XF
S457 100 Fr. 1868-82. Woman with sickle near wheat field and apples at left, allegorical woman (Industry) near factory at right. Paper: Green.	—	—	—
S458 500 Fr. 1868-82. Woman with sickle near wheat field and apples at left, allegorical woman (Industry) near factory at right. Paper: Green.	—	—	—

1883-1910 Concordat Issue

	Good	Fine	XF
S459 50 Fr. 1883-1910. Helvetia at left leaning on shield, cherub at lower right. Back: Head at left and right.	—	—	—

		Good	Fine	XF
S460	**100 Fr.** 1883-1910. Helvetia at left leaning on shield, cherub at lower right. Back: Head at left and right.	—	—	—
S461	**500 Fr.** 1883-1910. Helvetia at left leaning on shield, cherub at lower right. Back: Head at left and right.	—	—	—
S462	**1000 Fr.** 1883-1910. Helvetia at left leaning on shield, cherub at lower right. Back: Head at left and right.	—	—	—

Toggenburger Bank, Lichtensteig

1864 Issue

		Good	Fine	XF
S463	**10 Fr.** 1864. View of Lichtensteig, woman at cotton machine and Hermes. Uniface. Series A.	—	—	—
S464	**50 Fr.** 1864. View of Lichtensteig, woman at cotton machine and Hermes. Uniface. Series A.	—	—	—
S465	**100 Fr.** 1864. View of Lichtensteig, woman at cotton machine and Hermes. Uniface. Series A.	—	—	—

1865 Issue

		Good	Fine	XF
S466	**10 Fr.** 1865. View of Lichtensteig, woman at cotton machine and Hermes. Back: Value and arms of Lichtensteig.	—	—	—
S467	**50 Fr.** 1865. View of Lichtensteig, woman at cotton machine and Hermes. Back: Value and arms of Lichtensteig.	—	—	—
S468	**100 Fr.** 1865. View of Lichtensteig, woman at cotton machine and Hermes. Back: Value and arms of Lichtensteig.	—	—	—

1883-1907 Concordat Issue

		Good	Fine	XF
S469	**50 Fr.** 1883-1907. Helvetia at left leaning on shield, cherub at lower right. Back: Head at left and right.	—	—	—
S470	**100 Fr.** 1883-1907. Helvetia at left leaning on shield, cherub at lower right. Back: Head at left and right.	—	—	—
S471	**500 Fr.** 1883-1907. Helvetia at left leaning on shield, cherub at lower right. Back: Head at left and right.	—	—	—

Bank in Schaffhausen

1863 Issue

		Good	Fine	XF
S473	**50 Fr.** 1863. Arms of Schaffhausen surrounded by cornucopias with money and flowers. Uniface. Paper: Yellow. Printer: Theofil Beck, Schaffhausen.	—	—	—
S474	**100 Fr.** 1863. Arms of Schaffhausen surrounded by cornucopias with money and flowers. Uniface. Paper: White. Printer: Theofil Beck, Schaffhausen.	—	—	—
S475	**500 Fr.** 1863. Arms of Schaffhausen surrounded by cornucopias with money and flowers. Uniface. Paper: Blue. Printer: Theofil Beck, Schaffhausen.	—	—	—

1875 Issue

		Good	Fine	XF
S476	**50 Fr.** (ca.1875). Allegorical Agriculture at left, arms of Schaffhausen at center, allegorical Industry at right. Paper: Yellow.	—	—	—

ILLUSTRATIONS

Illustrations of bank notes used throughout this catalog are 42% of the actual size.

1883-1908 Concordat Issue

		Good	Fine	XF
S477	**50 Fr.** 1883-1908. Helvetia at left leaning on shield, cherub at lower right. Back: Head at left and right.	—	—	—
S478	**100 Fr.** 1883-1908. Helvetia at left leaning on shield, cherub at lower right. Back: Head at left and right.	—	—	—
S479	**500 Fr.** 1883-1908. Helvetia at left leaning on shield, cherub at lower right. Back: Head at left and right.	—	—	—

Schaffhauser Kantonalbank

1883-1910 Concordat Issue

		Good	Fine	XF
S480	**50 Fr.** 1883-1910. Helvetia at left leaning on shield, cherub at lower right. Back: Head at left and right.	—	—	—
S481	**100 Fr.** 1883-1910. Helvetia at left leaning on shield, cherub at lower right. Back: Head at left and right.	—	—	—
S482	**500 Fr.** 1883-1910. Helvetia at left leaning on shield, cherub at lower right. Back: Head at left and right.	—	—	—

Kantonalbank Schwyz

1890-1910 Concordat Issue

		Good	Fine	XF
S483	**50 Fr.** 1890-1910. Helvetia at left leaning on shield, cherub at lower right. Back: Head at left and right.	—	—	—
S484	**100 Fr.** 1890-1910. Helvetia at left leaning on shield, cherub at lower right. Back: Head at left and right.	—	—	—
S485	**500 Fr.** 1890-1910. Helvetia at left leaning on shield, cherub at lower right. Back: Head at left and right.	—	—	—
S486	**1000 Fr.** 1890-1910. Helvetia at left leaning on shield, cherub at lower right. Back: Head at left and right.	—	—	—

Solothurner Kantonalbank

1886-1910 Concordat Issue

		Good	Fine	XF
S487	**50 Fr.** 1886-1910. Helvetia at left leaning on shield, cherub at lower right. Back: Head at left and right.	—	—	—
S488	**100 Fr.** 1886-1910. Helvetia at left leaning on shield, cherub at lower right. Back: Head at left and right.	—	—	—
S489	**500 Fr.** 1886-1910. Helvetia at left leaning on shield, cherub at lower right. Back: Head at left and right.	—	—	—
S490	**1000 Fr.** 1886-1910. Helvetia at left leaning on shield, cherub at lower right. Back: Head at left and right.	—	—	—

Solothurnische Bank

Bank de Soleure

1858 Issue

		Good	Fine	XF
S491	**20 Fr.** 1858. View of Solothurn. Paper: Green.	—	—	—
S492	**50 Fr.** 1858. View of Solothurn. Paper: Yellow.	—	—	—

		Good	Fine	XF
S493	**100 Fr.** 1858. View of Solothurn. Paper: Pink.	—	—	—
S494	**500 Fr.** 1858. View of Solothurn. Paper: Blue.	—	—	—

1872 Issue

#S495-S496 state notes.

		Good	Fine	XF
S495	**500 Fr.** 1872. Red.	—	—	—
S496	**1000 Fr.** 1872. Blue.	—	—	—

1873 Issue

		Good	Fine	XF
S497	**50 Fr.** 1873. Hermes sitting, woman at spinning wheel near factory chimneys.	—	—	—
S498	**100 Fr.** 1873. Hermes sitting, woman at spinning wheel near factory chimneys.	—	—	—
S499	**500 Fr.** 1873. Hermes sitting, woman at spinning wheel near factory chimneys.	—	—	—

1881 Issue

		Good	Fine	XF
S500	**50 Fr.** 1881. Gray.	—	—	—
S501	**1000 Fr.** 1881. Green.	—	—	—

1883-86 Concordat Issue

		Good	Fine	XF
S502	**50 Fr.** 1883-86. Helvetia at left leaning on shield, cherub at lower right. Back: Head at left and right.	—	—	—
S503	**100 Fr.** 1883-86. Helvetia at left leaning on shield, cherub at lower right. Back: Head at left and right.	—	—	—
S504	**500 Fr.** 1883-86. Helvetia at left leaning on shield, cherub at lower right. Back: Head at left and right.	—	—	—
S505	**1000 Fr.** 1883-86. Helvetia at left leaning on shield, cherub at lower right. Back: Head at left and right.	—	—	—

Thurgauische Hypothekenbank, Frauenfeld

1852-54 Issue

		Good	Fine	XF
S506	**10 Fr.** 1852. Paper: White.	—	—	—
S507	**50 Fr.** 1852. Paper: Yellow.	—	—	—
S508	**100 Fr.** 1854. Paper: Yellow.	—	—	—

1858 Issue

#S509-S511 like previous three notes but ovpt: *IN SILBER UND GOLD.*

		Good	Fine	XF
S509	**10 Fr.** 1858. With overprint. Overprint: *IN SILBER UND GOLD.* Paper: White.	—	—	—
S510	**50 Fr.** 1858. With overprint. Overprint: *IN SILBER UND GOLD.* Paper: Yellow.	—	—	—
S511	**100 Fr.** 1858. With overprint. Overprint: *IN SILBER UND GOLD.* Paper: Yellow.	—	—	—

1883-1908 Concordat Issue

		Good	Fine	XF
S512	**50 Fr.** 1883-1908. Helvetia at left leaning on shield, cherub at lower right. Back: Head at left and right.	—	—	—
S513	**100 Fr.** 1883-1908. Helvetia at left leaning on shield, cherub at lower right. Back: Head at left and right.	—	—	—
S514	**500 Fr.** 1883-1908. Helvetia at left leaning on shield, cherub at lower right. Back: Head at left and right.	—	—	—

Thurgauische Kantonalbank, Weinfelden

1871 Issue

		Good	Fine	XF
S515	**20 Fr.** 1871. Blue guilloche. Fortune with crops, grapes and containers, allegorical Industry with anvil, gear and locomotive at left, cantonal arms at right. Printer: OFZ.	—	—	—
S516	**50 Fr.** 1871. Green guilloche. Fortune with crops, grapes and containers, allegorical Industry with anvil, gear and locomotive at left, cantonal arms at right. Printer: OFZ.	—	—	—
S517	**100 Fr.** 1871. Orange guilloche. Fortune with crops, grapes and containers, allegorical Industry with anvil, gear and locomotive at left, cantonal arms at right. Printer: OFZ.	—	—	—
S518	**500 Fr.** 1871. Red guilloche. Fortune with crops, grapes and containers, allegorical Industry with anvil, gear and locomotive at left, cantonal arms at right. Printer: OFZ.	—	—	—

1883-1910 Concordat Issue

		Good	Fine	XF
S519	**50 Fr.** 1883-1910. Helvetia at left leaning on shield, cherub at lower right. Back: Head at left and right.	—	—	—
S520	**100 Fr.** 1883-1910. Helvetia at left leaning on shield, cherub at lower right. Back: Head at left and right.	—	—	—
S521	**500 Fr.** 1883-1910. Helvetia at left leaning on shield, cherub at lower right. Back: Head at left and right.	—	—	—

Banca Cantonale Ticinese, Bellinzona

1861 Issue

		Good	Fine	XF
S522	**5 Fr.** 1861. Ornamental design.	—	—	—
S523	**20 Fr.** 1861. Ornamental design. Paper: Green.	—	—	—
S524	**50 Fr.** 1861. Head of Hermes and Fortune. Paper: Yellow.	—	—	—
S525	**100 Fr.** 1861. Girl from Ticino at left and right. Paper: Red.	—	—	—

1874-75 Issue

		Good	Fine	XF
S526	**10 Fr.** 1874. Red guilloche. Arms at center. Printer: Carlo Trzaska, Milano.	—	—	—
S527	**20 Fr.** 1874. Green guilloche. Arms at center. Printer: Carlo Trzaska, Milano.	—	—	—
S528	**500 Fr.** 1875. Arms at center. Paper: White. Printer: Carlo Trzaska, Milano.	—	—	—

1884-1908 Concordat Issue

		Good	Fine	XF
S529	**50 Fr.** 1884-1908. Helvetia at left leaning on shield, cherub at lower right. Back: Head at left and right.	—	—	—
S530	**100 Fr.** 1884-1908. Helvetia at left leaning on shield, cherub at lower right. Back: Head at left and right.	—	—	—
S531	**500 Fr.** 1884-1908. Helvetia at left leaning on shield, cherub at lower right. Back: Head at left and right.	—	—	—
S532	**1000 Fr.** 1884-1908. Helvetia at left leaning on shield, cherub at lower right. Back: Head at left and right.	—	—	—

Banca della Svizzera Italiana, Lugano

1874 Issue

#S533-S536 Buoni di Cassa.

		Good	Fine	XF
S533	**5 Fr.** 1874. Green guilloche. Back: Green. Paper: Gray.	—	—	—
S534	**10 Fr.** 1874. Green guilloche. Back: Brown. Paper: Gray.	—	—	—
S535	**20 Fr.** 1874. Brown guilloche. Back: Red. Paper: Gray.	—	—	—
S536	**50 Fr.** 1874. Brown guilloche. Back: Red. Paper: Green.	—	—	—

1877 Issue

		Good	Fine	XF
S537	**50 Fr.** 1877. Black on blue underprint. Boy at left, seated Abundance at center, arms at right. Back: Blue. Printer: ABNC.			
	a. Issued note.	—	—	—
	p. Proof.	—	—	—

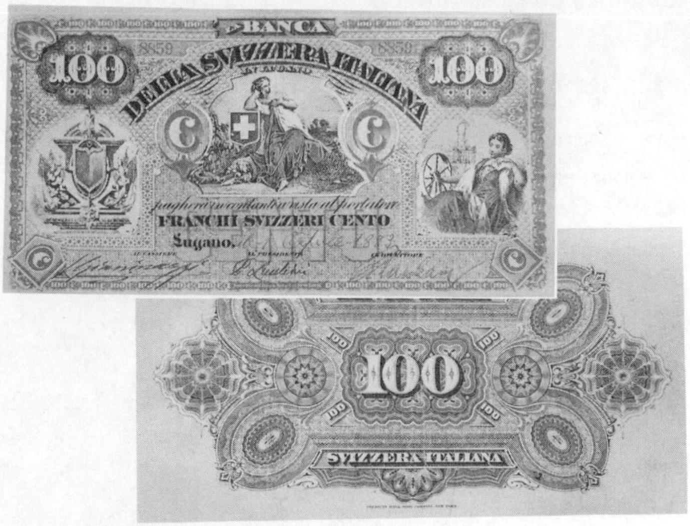

S538 100 Fr. | Good | Fine | XF

1877. Black on green underprint. Arms at left, seated Helvetia at center, Industry at right. Back: Green. Printer: ABNC.

	Good	Fine	XF
a. Issued note.	—	—	—
p. Proof.	—	—	—

S539 500 Fr. | Good | Fine | XF

1877. Black on brown underprint. Arms at left, different portrait of seated Helvetia at center, allegorical woman at right. Back: Dark brown.

	Good	Fine	XF
a. Issued note.	—	—	—
p. Proof.	—	—	—

1883-1907 Concordat Issue

	Good	Fine	XF
S540 50 Fr. 1883-1907. Helvetia at left leaning on shield, cherub at lower right. Back: Head at left and right.	—	—	—
S541 100 Fr. 1883-1907. Helvetia at left leaning on shield, cherub at lower right. Back: Head at left and right.	—	—	—
S542 500 Fr. 1883-1907. Helvetia at left leaning on shield, cherub at lower right. Back: Head at left and right.	—	—	—

NOTE: Facsimile reproductions, often offered as genuine notes, exist of 2 pieces: #S538 with serial #8859 and #S540 with serial #H2-0525. These copies were made to commemorate the centenary of the bank.

Banca Popolare di Lugano

1888-1910 Concordat Issue

	Good	Fine	XF
S543 50 Fr. 1888-1910. Helvetia at left leaning on shield, cherub at lower right. Back: Head at left and right.	—	—	—
S544 100 Fr. 1888-1910. Helvetia at left leaning on shield, cherub at lower right. Back: Head at left and right.	—	—	—
S545 500 Fr. 1888-1910. Helvetia at left leaning on shield, cherub at lower right. Back: Head at left and right.	—	—	—

Credito Ticinese, Locarno

1891-1907 Concordat Issue

	Good	Fine	XF
S546 50 Fr. 1891-1907. Helvetia at left leaning on shield, cherub at lower right. Back: Head at left and right.	—	—	—
S547 100 Fr. 1891-1907. Helvetia at left leaning on shield, cherub at lower right. Back: Head at left and right.	—	—	—
S548 500 Fr. 1891-1907. Helvetia at left leaning on shield, cherub at lower right. Back: Head at left and right.	—	—	—

Ersparniss-Cassa des Kantons Uri, Altdorf

1878 Issue

	Good	Fine	XF
S549 50 Fr. 1.3.1878. Tell's Chapel and Mt. Rütli at left and right, cantonal arms at upper center.	—	—	—

	Good	Fine	XF
S550 100 Fr. 1.3.1878. Tell's Chapel and Mt. Rütli at left and right, cantonal arms at upper center.	—	—	—

1883-1910 Concordat Issue

	Good	Fine	XF
S551 50 Fr. 1883-1910.	—	—	—
S552 100 Fr. 1883-1910.	—	—	—

Banque Cantonale Vaudoise, Lausanne

1846 Issue

	Good	Fine	XF
S553 10 Fünffrankentaler 1846. Cantonal arms, Lake Geneva with ship below, plow at beach, freight and anchor. Paper: White.	—	—	—
S554 100 Fünffrankentaler 1846. Cantonal arms, Lake Geneva with ship below, plow at beach, freight and anchor. Paper: Pink.	—	—	—

NOTE: Facsimiles of #S554 were made for the centenary of the bank.

NOTE: The 20 Fünffrankentaler denomination was printed, but because of the poor quality of paper it was not released.

1847-53 Issue

	Good	Fine	XF
S555 5 Fünffrankentaler 1847.	—	—	—
S556 20 Fünffrankentaler 1853.	—	—	—

1856 Issue

	Good	Fine	XF
S557 5 Fr. 1856. Arms at center.	—	—	—
S558 20 Fr. 1856.	—	—	—
S559 100 Fr. 1856.	—	—	—
S560 500 Fr. 1856.	—	—	—

1864 Issue

	Good	Fine	XF
S561 50 Fr. 1864.	—	—	—
S562 100 Fr. 1864.	—	—	—
S563 500 Fr. 1864.	—	—	—
S564 1000 Fr. 1864.	—	—	—

1879 Issue

	Good	Fine	XF
S565 1000 Fr. 1879.	—	—	—

1883-1910 Concordat Issue

	Good	Fine	XF
S566 50 Fr. 1883-1910. Helvetia at left leaning on shield, cherub at lower right. Back: Head at left and right.	—	—	—
S567 100 Fr. 1883-1910. Helvetia at left leaning on shield, cherub at lower right. Back: Head at left and right.	—	—	—
S568 500 Fr. 1883-1910. Helvetia at left leaning on shield, cherub at lower right. Back: Head at left and right.	—	—	—
S569 1000 Fr. 1883-1910. Helvetia at left leaning on shield, cherub at lower right. Back: Head at left and right.	—	—	—

Banque Populaire de la Broye, Payerne

1865-79 Issue

	Good	Fine	XF
S571 10 Fr. 25.3.1865. Black. Church of Payerne and Queen Berthe de Bourgogne riding, sheaf and agricultural tools. Paper: Pink tint.			
a. Stamping on back: *Mis en circulation le...18...* and handwritten date ca.1870.	—	—	—
b. Handwritten on front: *Annule le 14 Juin 1871.*	200.	400.	—

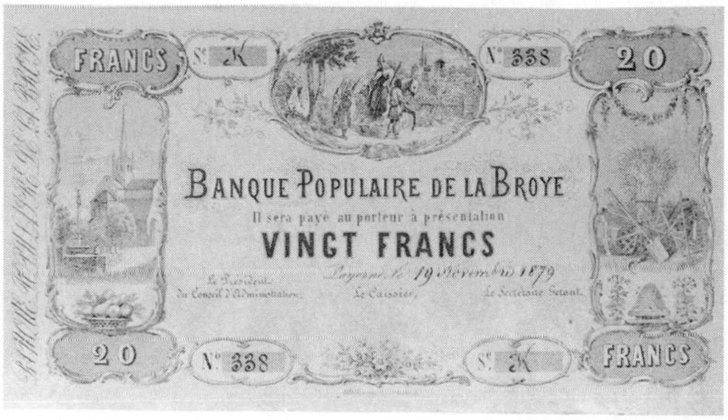

	Good	Fine	XF
S572 20 Fr. 1865; 19.11.1879. Black type. Church of Payerne and Queen Berthe de Bourgogne riding, sheaf and agricultural tools. Paper: Green.			
a. Stamping and date like #S571a.	—	—	—
r. Unsigned remainder. 19.11.1879.	—	Unc	400.

Philippe Genton, Vevey

1840 Issue

#S574 replaced letters of credit issued previously.

	Good	Fine	XF
S574 100 Fr. (ca.1840).	—	—	—

Felix Marcel, Lausanne

1843 Issue

The same text was used on #S576 as on #S309 and S316 to circumvent the Banque de France's authority.

	Good	Fine	XF
S576 100 Fr. 1843.	—	—	—

Banque Cantonale du Valais, Sitten

1858-63 Issue

	Good	Fine	XF
S581 20 Fr. 1858. Cantonal arms. Uniface. Paper: Cream.	—	—	—
S582 50 Fr. 1858. Cantonal arms. Uniface. Paper: Red.	—	—	—
S583 100 Fr. 1858. Cantonal arms. Uniface. Paper: Blue.	—	—	—
S584 200 Fr. 1858. Cantonal arms. Uniface. Paper: White.	—	—	—
S585 10 Fr. 1863.	—	—	—

NOTE: 5 Fr. notes were authorized but none are known to exist.

Caisse Hypothecaire & de Crédit du Valais

1871 Issue

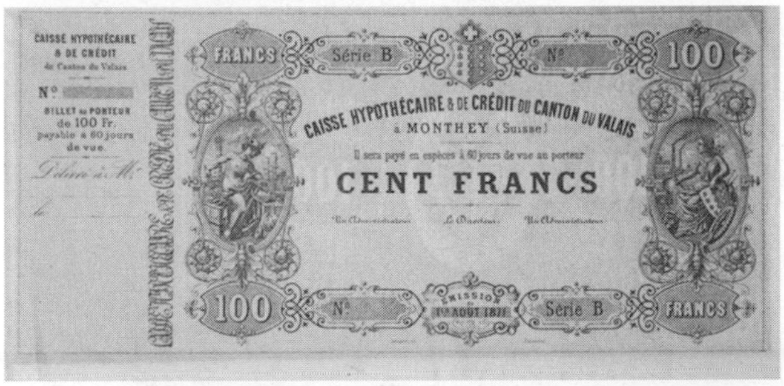

	Good	Fine	XF
S586 50 Fr. 1.8.1871. Black. Mercury seated with anchor, canton shield at top center, Helvetia seated at left. Back: Blue. Canton shield flanked by value scroll. Watermark: Bank name. Printer: Spengler, Lith. Luzanne. Remainder with counterfoil.	—	Unc	400.

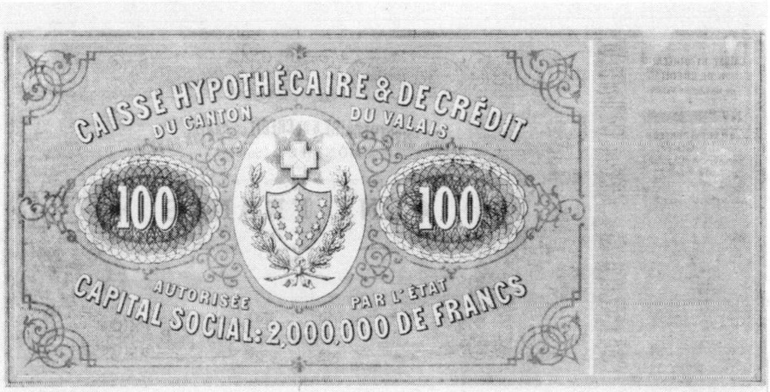

	Good	Fine	XF
S586A 100 Fr. 1.8.1871. Mercury seated with anchor, canton shield at top center, Helvetia seated at left. Back: Canton shield flanked by value scroll. Watermark: Bank name. Printer: Spengler, Lith. Luzanne.	—	Unc	500.

		Good	Fine	XF
S586B	**500 Fr.** 1.8.1871. Red. Mercury seated with anchor, canton shield at top center, Helvetia seated at left. Back: Canton shield flanked by value scroll. Watermark: Bank name. Printer: Spengler, Lith. Luzanne.	—	—	—

Zuger Kantonalbank

1893-1910 Concordat Issue

		Good	Fine	XF
S587	**50 Fr.** 1893-1910. Helvetia at left leaning on shield, cherub at lower right. Back: Head at left and right.	—	—	—
S588	**100 Fr.** 1893-1910. Helvetia at left leaning on shield, cherub at lower right. Back: Head at left and right.	—	—	—
S589	**500 Fr.** 1893-1910. Helvetia at left leaning on shield, cherub at lower right. Back: Head at left and right.	—	—	—

Bank in Zürich

1837 Issue

		Good	Fine	XF
S591	**10 Brabantertaler** 1837. Yellow. Angels' heads and two women with Hermes' staff and cornucopia.	—	—	—
S592	**100 Brabantertaler** 1837. White. Angels' heads and two women with Hermes' staff and cornucopia.	—	—	—

1840-52 Issue

		Good	Fine	XF
S593	**10 Brabantertaler** 1840. Angels' heads and two women with Hermes' staff and cornucopia. Like #S591. Overprint: *ODER DEN WERTH IN WECHSELGELD.*	—	—	—
S594	**100 Brabantertaler** 1840. Angels' heads and two women with Hermes' staff and cornucopia. Like #S592. Overprint: *ODER DEN WERTH IN WECHSELGELD.*	—	—	—
S595	**10 Fünffrankentaler** 1847. (Not issued).	—	—	—
S596	**100 Fünffrankentaler** 1847. (Not issued).	—	—	—
S597	**50 Fr.** 1852. Stamping: *NACH WAHL DER BANK IN EFFEKTIVE FR. ODER DEUTSCHEM GELD ZU OFFIZIELLEM UMRECHNUNGSTARIF EINLÖSBAR.*	—	—	—
S598	**500 Fr.** 1852. Stamping: *NACH WAHL DER BANK IN EFFEKTIVE FR. ODER DEUTSCHEM GELD ZU OFFIZIELLEM UMRECHNUNGSTARIF EINLÖSBAR.* Like #S597.	—	—	—

1853 Issue

		Good	Fine	XF
S599	**50 Fr.** 1853. Without stamping.	—	—	—
S600	**500 Fr.** 1853. Without stamping.	—	—	—

1856-73 Issue

		Good	Fine	XF
S601	**50 Fr.** 1856. Stamping: *EINLOSUNG IN SILBER ODER NAP. D'OR.*	—	—	—
S602	**500 Fr.** 1856. Stamping: *EINLOSUNG IN SILBER ODER NAP. D'OR.*	—	—	—
S603	**1000 Fr.** 1873. Swiss cross, woman's head, two boys holding shields. Printer: Dondorf & Naumann. Remainder.	—	Unc	1500.

NOTE: #S603 was issued together with the Bank in St. Gallen, Bank in Basel and the Kantonalbank von Bern.

1874 Issue

		Good	Fine	XF
S604	**50 Fr.** 1874.	—	—	—
S605	**100 Fr.** 1874.	—	—	—
S606	**500 Fr.** 1874.	—	—	—

1883-92 Concordat Issue

		Good	Fine	XF
S607	**50 Fr.** 1883-92. Helvetia at left leaning on shield, cherub at lower right. Back: Head at left and right.	—	—	—
S608	**100 Fr.** 1883-92. Helvetia at left leaning on shield, cherub at lower right. Back: Head at left and right.	—	—	—
S609	**500 Fr.** 1883-92. Helvetia at left leaning on shield, cherub at lower right. Back: Head at left and right.	—	—	—
S610	**1000 Fr.** 1883-92. Helvetia at left leaning on shield, cherub at lower right. Back: Head at left and right.	—	—	—

Zürcher Kantonalbank, Zürich

1870-72 Issue

		Good	Fine	XF
S611	**20 Fr.** 1870. Orange underprint. Woman's head at left, lion holding shield at upper center, helmeted soldier's head at right.	—	—	—
S612	**50 Fr.** 1870. Green underprint. Woman's head at left, lion holding shield at upper center, helmeted soldier's head at right.	—	—	—
S613	**100 Fr.** 1870. Blue underprint. Woman's head at left, lion holding shield at upper center, helmeted soldier's head at right.	—	—	—
S614	**500 Fr.** 1870. Red underprint. Woman's head at left, lion holding shield at upper center, helmeted soldier's head at right.	—	—	—

#S615-S620 interest-bearing Treasury notes.

		Good	Fine	XF
S615	**10 Fr.** 1870.	—	—	—
S616	**50 Fr.** 1870.	—	—	—
S617	**100 Fr.** 1870.	—	—	—
S618	**500 Fr.** 1870.	—	—	—
S619	**1000 Fr.** 1870.	—	—	—
S620	**5000 Fr.** 1870.	—	—	—
S621	**1000 Fr.** 1872. Dark green underprint. Woman's head at left, lion holding shield at upper center, helmeted soldier's head at right.	—	—	—

1883-1910 Concordat Issue

		Good	Fine	XF
S622	**50 Fr.** 1883-1910. Helvetia at left leaning on shield, cherub at lower right. Back: Head at left and right.	—	—	—
S623	**100 Fr.** 1883-1910. Helvetia at left leaning on shield, cherub at lower right. Back: Head at left and right.	—	—	—
S624	**500 Fr.** 1883-1910. Helvetia at left leaning on shield, cherub at lower right. Back: Head at left and right.	—	—	—
S625	**1000 Fr.** 1883-1910. Helvetia at left leaning on shield, cherub at lower right. Back: Head at left and right.	—	—	—

THAILAND

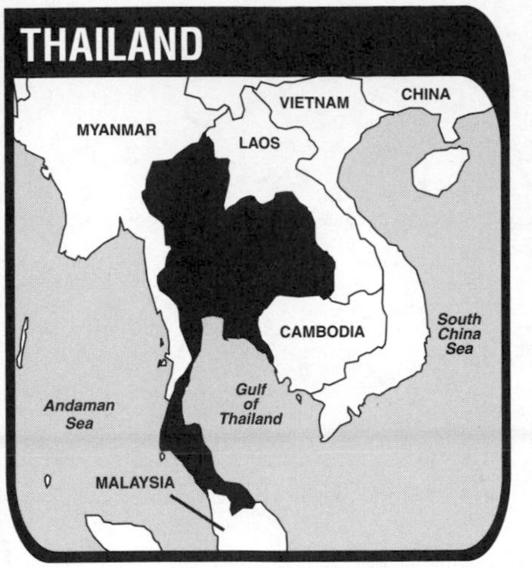

The Kingdom of Thailand, a constitutional monarchy located in the center of mainland southeast Asia between Burma and Lao, has an area of 514,000 sq. km. and a population of 65.49 million. Capital: Bangkok. The economy is d on agriculture and mining. Rubber, rice, teakwood, tin and tungsten are exported.

A unified Thai kingdom was established in the mid-14th century. Known as Siam until 1939, Thailand is the only Southeast Asian country never to have been taken over by a European power. A bloodless revolution in 1932 led to a constitutional monarchy. In alliance with Japan during World War II, Thailand became a US treaty ally following the conflict. A military coup in September 2006 ousted then Prime Minister Thaksin Chinnawat. The interim government held elections in December 2007 that saw the pro-Thaksin People's Power Party (PPP) emerge at the head of a coalition government. The anti-Thaksin People's Alliance for Democracy (PAD) in May 2008 began street demonstrations against the new government, eventually occupying the prime minister's office in August. Clashes in October 2008 between PAD protesters blocking parliament and police resulted in the death of at least two people. The PAD occupied Bangkok's international airports briefly, ending their protests in early December 2008 following a court ruling that dissolved the ruling PPP and two other coalition parties for election violations. The Democrat Party then formed a new coalition government with the support of some of Thaksin's former political allies, and Abhist Wetchachiwa became prime minister. Since January 2004, thousands have been killed as separatists in Thailand's southern ethnic Malay-Muslim provinces increased the violence associated with their cause.

RULERS:

Rama IV (Phra Chom Klao Mongkut), 1851-1868
Rama V (Phra Maha Chulalongkorn), 1868-1910
Rama VI (Vajiravudh), 1910-1925
Rama VII (Prajadhipok), 1925-1935
Rama VIII (Ananda Mahidol), 1935-1946
Rama IX (Bhumiphol Adulyadej), 1946-

MONETARY SYSTEM:

1 Baht (Tical) = 100 Satang
1 Tamlung = 4 Baht, 1853

MILITARY - VIETNAM WAR

AUXILIARY MILITARY PAYMENT CERTIFICATE COUPONS

FIRST SERIES

#M1-M8 issued probably from January to April or May, 1970.

	Good	Fine	XF
M1 5 Cents ND (1970). Black print on check-type security paper. Seahorse shield design at center. Words *Coupon* below below shield or at right. *Non Negotiable* at right. Small Thai symbol only at upper left corner. Denomination at three corners. Back: Seahorse shield design at center. Words *Coupon* below shield or at right. *Non Negotiable<NI* Paper: Yellow.	100.	250.	—
M2 10 Cents ND (1970). Black print on check-type security paper. Shield with leaping panther and *RTAVF*. *Non Negotiable* under shield; *Coupon* deleted. Back: Shield with leaping panther and *RTAVF*. *Non Negotiable* under shield; *Coupon* deleted. Paper: Light gray.	100.	250.	—
M3 25 Cents ND (1970). Black print on check-type security paper. Shield with *Victory Vietnam*. *Coupon* at right. Back: Shield with *Victory Vietnam*. *Coupon* at right. Paper: Pink.	160.	400.	—
M4 50 Cents ND (1970). Black print on check-type security paper. Circle with shaking hands and *Royal Thai Forces Vietnam*. Back: Circle with shaking hands and *Royal Thai Forces Vietnam*. Paper: Light blue.	160.	400.	—
M5 1 Dollar ND (1970). Black print on check-type security paper. Inscription *Victory Vietnam*. *Coupon* at right. Back: Inscription *Victory Vietnam*. *Coupon* at right. Paper: Yellow.	160.	400.	—
M6 5 Dollars ND (1970). Black print on check-type security paper. Seahorse in shield. Back: Seahorse in shield. Paper: Light gray.	200.	500.	—
M7 10 Dollars ND (1970). Black print on check-type security paper. Shield with leaping panther. Back: Shield with leaping panther. Paper: Yellow. .	225.	550.	—
M8 20 Dollars ND (1970). Black print on check-type security paper. Circle with hands shaking. Back: Circle with hands shaking. Paper: Light green.	225.	550.	—

SECOND SERIES

#M9-M16 issued April or May, 1970 to possibly Oct. 7, 1970.

	Good	Fine	XF
M9 5 Cents ND (1970). Black print on check-type security paper. Seahorse shield design at center. Larger shield outline around each shield at left center. Words *Coupon* in margin at lower center. Denomination at all four corners. Back: Seahorse shield design at center. Larger shield outline around each shield at left center. Words Paper: Yellow.	40.00	100.	—
M10 10 Cents ND (1970). Black print on check-type security paper. Shield with leaping panther and *RTAVF. Larger shield outline around each shield at left center. Words Coupon in margin at lower center. Denomination at all 4 corners.* Back: Shield with leaping panther and *RTAVF. Larger shield outline around each shield at left center. W* Paper: Light green.	50.00	125.	—
M11 25 Cents ND (1970). Black print on check-type security paper. Shield with *Victory Vietnam. Larger shield outline around each shield at left center. Words Coupon in margin at lower center. Denomination at all 4 corners.* Back: Shield with *Victory Vietnam. Larger shield outline around each shield at left center. Words Co* Paper: Yellow.	60.00	150.	—
M12 50 Cents ND (1970). Black print on check-type security paper. Circle with shaking hands and *Royal Thai Forces Vietnam*. Larger shield outline around each shield at left center. Words *Coupon* in margin at lower center. Denomination at all 4 corners. Back: Circle with shaking hands and *Royal Thai Forces Vietnam*. Larger shield outline around each sh Paper: Light gray.	60.00	150.	—
M13 1 Dollar ND (1970). Black print on check-type security paper. Inscription *Victory Vietnam. Larger shield outline around each shield at left center. Words Coupon in margin at lower center. Denomination at all 4 corners.* Back: Inscription *Victory Vietnam. Larger shield outline around each shield at left center. Words Co* Paper: Pink.	60.00	150.	—
M14 5 Dollars ND (1970). Black print on check-type security paper. Seahorse in shield. Larger shield outline around each shield at left center. Words *Coupon* in margin at lower center. Denomination at all 4 corners. Back: Seahorse in shield. Larger shield outline around each shield at left center. Words *Coupon* in Paper: Light green.	160.	400.	—
M15 10 Dollars ND (1970). Black print on check-type security paper. Shield with leaping panther. Larger shield outline around each shield at left center. Words *Coupon* in margin at lower center. Denomination at all 4 corners. Back: Shield with leaping panther. Larger shield outline around each shield at left center. Words *Coupo* Paper: Pale yellow.	160.	400.	—

	Good	Fine	XF
M16 20 Dollars ND (1970). Black print on check-type security paper. Circle with hands shaking. Larger shield outline around each shield at left center. Words *Coupon* in margin at lower center. Denomination at all 4 corners. Back: Circle with hands shaking. Larger shield outline around each shield at left center. Words *Coupon<* Paper: Light green.	180.	450.	—

THIRD SERIES

#M17-M23 date of issue not known (Oct., 1970?).

	VG	VF	UNC
M17 5 Cents ND. Light gray, maroon and green. Hands shaking in shield at lower right. More elaborate design. Back: Different shield designs at upper left. More elaborate design.	22.50	75.00	300.

M18 10 Cents
ND. Light yellow and green. Hands shaking in shield at lower right. More elaborate design. Back: Different shield designs at upper left. More elaborate design.

	VG	VF	UNC
M18	22.50	75.00	300.

M19 25 Cents
ND. Green, pink and maroon. Hands shaking in shield at lower right. More elaborate design. Back: Different shield designs at upper left. More elaborate design.

	VG	VF	UNC
M19	40.00	125.	350.

M20 50 Cents
ND. Yellow, green, blue and red. Hands shaking in shield at lower right. More elaborate design. Back: Different shield designs at upper left. More elaborate design.

	VG	VF	UNC
M20	40.00	125.	350.

M21 1 Dollar
ND. Pink, blue and green. Hands shaking in shield at lower right. More elaborate design. Back: Different shield designs at upper left. More elaborate design.

	VG	VF	UNC
a. Issued note.	125.	225.	—
r. Remainder without serial #.	—	—	300.

M22 5 Dollars
ND. Yellow, green, blue and red. Hands shaking in shield at lower right. More elaborate design. Back: Different shield designs at upper left. More elaborate design.

	VG	VF	UNC
a. Issued note.	600.	950.	—
r. Remainder without serial #.	—	—	375.

M23 10 Dollars
ND. Green, maroon and dark red. Hands shaking in shield at lower right. More elaborate design. Back: Different shield designs at upper left. More elaborate design.

	VG	VF	UNC
a. Issued note.	125.	225.	—
r. Remainder without serial #.	—	—	350.

Regional - WW II

#R1 was issued in the northern Malay States of Kedah, Kelantan, Perlis and Trengganu which were ceded to Thailand by Japan during WW II. They were later ovpt: 50 Baht and issued for general circulation; see #62B.

Treasury

1943 Provisional Issue

R1 1 Dollar
ND (1943). Purple and green. Vertical line of Chinese inscription at left, Malay at right. Back: Throne Hall.

	VG	VF	UNC
a. Issued note.	—	—	—
r. Unsigned remainder.	—	100.	350.

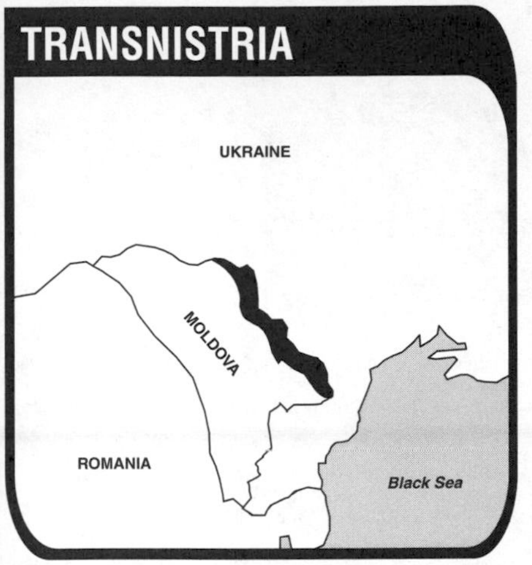

The Transnistria Moldavian Republic was formed in 1990, even before the separation of Moldavia from Russia. It has an area of 11,544 sq. mi. (29,900 sq. km). and a population of 700,000. Capital: Tiraspol.

The area was conquered from the Turks in the last half of the 18th Century, and in 1792 the capital city of Tiraspol was founded. After 1812, the area called Bessarabia (present Moldova and part of the Ukraine) became part of the Russian Empire. During the Russian Revolution, in 1918, the area was taken by Romanian troops, and in 1924 the Moldavian Autonomous SSR was formed on the left bank of the Dniester River. A Romanian occupation area between the Dniester and Bug Rivers called *Transnistria* was established in October 1941. Its center was the port of Odessa. A special issue of notes for use in Transnistria was made by the Romanian government. In 1944 the Russians recaptured Transnistria.

Once the Moldavian SSR declared independence in August 1991. Transnistria did not want to be a part of Moldavia. In 1992, Moldova tried to solve the issue militarily.

Transnistria has a president, parliament, army and police forces, but as yet is lacking international recognition.

1 Ruble = 1,000 old Rubles (August 1994) 1 Ruble = 1,000,000 old Rubles (January 2001)

Romanian Occupation (of U.S.S.R.) - WW II

Institutul de Finantare Externa (Infinex)

1941 ND Bon de Credit Issue

Note: This issue bears unusual denominations because of the exchange rate set by Germany, as follows:

6 Lei = 10 Reichspfennig or 1 Ruble/Karbowanez (Ukrainian German Issue).

1200 Lei = 20 Reichsmark or 200 Rubles/Karbowanez.

	Good	Fine	XF
M1 1 Leu ND (1941-44). Gray.	100.	300.	600.
M2 6 Lei ND (1941-44). Gray-blue.	100.	300.	600.
M3 24 Lei ND (1941-44). Brown.	100.	300.	600.
M4 120 Lei ND (1941-44). Blue. Sunflower at right.	125.	375.	750.
M5 600 Lei ND (1941-44). Gray on brown violet underprint. Cross at center.	125.	375.	750.
M6 1200 Lei ND (1941-44). Gray on tan underprint. Grapes at center. Back: Boat on river at center.	225.	675.	1350.

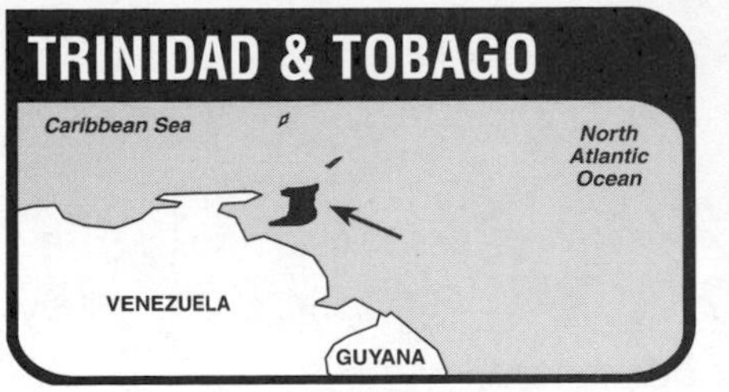

The Republic of Trinidad and Tobago, a member of the British Commonwealth situated 11 km. off the coast of Venezuela, has an area of 5,128 sq. km. and a population of 1.23 million. Capital: Port-of-Spain. The Island of Trinidad contains the world's largest natural asphalt bog. Birds of Paradise live on little Tobago, the only place outside of their native New Guinea where they can be found in a wild state. Petroleum and petroleum products are the mainstay of the economy. Petroleum products, crude oil and sugar are exported.

First colonized by the Spanish, the islands came under British control in the early 19th century. The islands' sugar industry was hurt by the emancipation of the slaves in 1834. Manpower was replaced with the importation of contract laborers from India between 1845 and 1917, which boosted sugar production as well as the cocoa industry. The discovery of oil on Trinidad in 1910 added another important export. Independence was attained in 1962. The country is one of the most prosperous in the Caribbean thanks largely to petroleum and natural gas production and processing. Tourism, mostly in Tobago, is targeted for expansion and is growing.

Notes of the British Caribbean Territories circulated between 1950-1964.

RULERS:

British to 1976

MONETARY SYSTEM:

1 Dollar = 100 Cents

5 Dollars = 1 Pound 10 Pence

Trinidad

Issued at Port of Spain.

Barclays Bank (Dominion, Colonial and Overseas)

1926 Issue

#S101-S104 Ovpt: Lg. *T* at upper r.

	Good	Fine	XF
S101 5 Dollars 1.9.1926; 31.3.1933. Black on pink and blue-green underprint. Crowned supported arms at center. Back: Green. Overprint: Large *T* at upper right. Printer: BWC.	450.	900.	1800.
S101A 20 Dollars 1.9.1926. Crowned supported arms at center. Overprint: Large *T* at upper right. Printer: BWC.	—	—	—

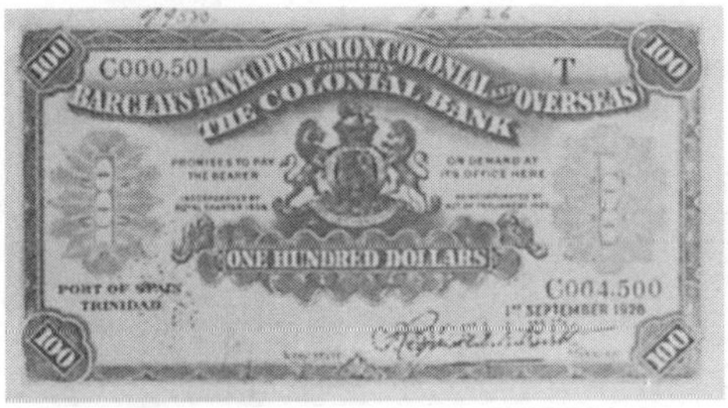

	Good	Fine	XF
S101B 100 Dollars 1.9.1926. Crowned supported arms at center. Overprint: Large *T* at upper right. Printer: BWC.	—	—	—

1937 Issue

#S102-S104 Ovpt: Lg. *T* at upper r.

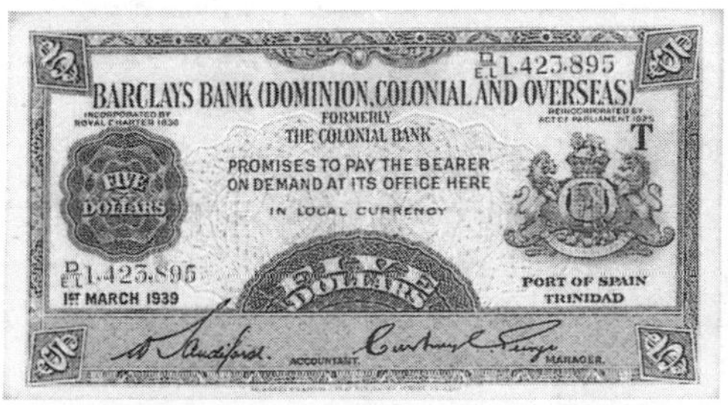

	Good	Fine	XF
S102 5 Dollars 1937-41. Purple on multicolor underprint. Crowned supported royal arms at right. Back: Purple on blue underprint. Overprint: Large *T* at upper right.			
a. 1.5.1937; 1.2.1938; 1.3.1939.	300.	600.	1200.
b. 1.3.1940; 1.2.1941.	225.	450.	900.
s. Specimen. 1.3.1939.	—	Unc	750.
S103 20 Dollars 1937-40. Brown. Crowned supported royal arms at right. Overprint: Large *T* at upper right.			
a. 1937; 1.3.1939; 1.3.1940.	750.	1500.	3000.
s. Specimen. 1.3.1939.	—	Unc	1000.

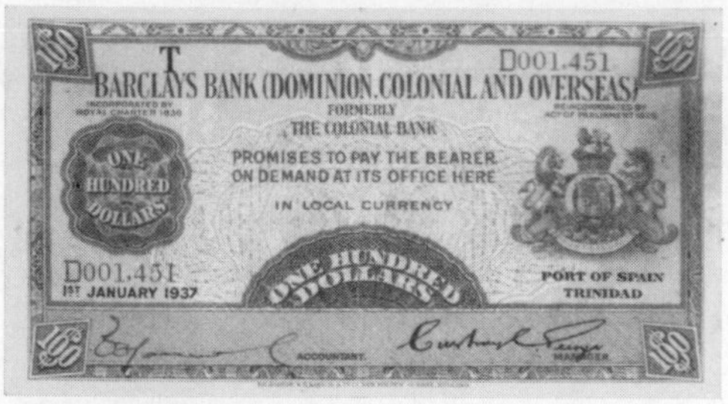

S104 100 Dollars	**Good**	**Fine**	**XF**
1937-40. Green. Crowned supported royal arms at right. Overprint: Large *T* at upper right.			
a. Hand signature at left. 1.1.1937.	800.	1600.	3200.
b. Printed signature at left. 1.3.1939; 1.3.1940.	375.	750.	1550.
s. Specimen. 1.3.1939.	—	Unc	1000.

Canadian Bank of Commerce

1921 Issue

#S111-S113 vertical ovpt: *TRINIDAD* at l. and r. on face.

S111 5 Dollars	**Good**	**Fine**	**XF**
1.3.1921. Black on green and red-orange underprint. Seated woman with rudder and water jug ("Naiad") at center. Back: Green. Mercury at left center, bank arms at center, allegorical woman with sheaf at center right. Overprint: Vertical: *TRINIDAD* at left and right on face.			
a. Issued note.	550.	1100.	2200.
p. Proof. Printer: CBNC.	—	Unc	1000.
s. Specimen.	—	Unc	1250.

S112 20 Dollars	**Good**	**Fine**	**XF**
1.3.1921. Black on green and red underprint. Seated woman and globe ("La Critique") at center. Back: Blue. Mercury at left center, bank arms at center, allegorical woman with sheaf at center right. Like #S11 Overprint: Vertical: *TRINIDAD* at left and right on face.			
a. Issued note.	1400.	2800.	—
p1. Proof. Printer: CBNC.	—	Unc	1000.
p2. Proof. Printer: ABNC.	—	Unc	1000.
s. Specimen.	—	Unc	1250.

S113 100 Dollars	**Good**	**Fine**	**XF**
1.3.1921. Black on olive and red underprint. Seated woman with book ("Literature") and lamp at left. Back: Red. Mercury at left center, bank arms at center, allegorical woman with sheaf at center right. Like #S11 Overprint: Vertical: *TRINIDAD* at left and right on face.			
p1. Proof. Printer: CBNC.	—	Unc	1000.
p2. Proof. Printer: ABNC.	—	Unc	1000.
s. Specimen.	—	Unc	1725.

1939 Issue

S116 5 Dollars	**Good**	**Fine**	**XF**
1.7.1939. Black on ochre and green underprint. Allegorical group at center. Back: Green. Bank emblem at center. Printer: CBNC.	300.	600.	1200.

NOTE: #S116 is similar to a regular Canadian issue made by this bank, although color and wording on the face distinguish it from its Canadian counterpart.

S117 20 Dollars	**Good**	**Fine**	**XF**
1.7.1939. Black on red-orange underprint. Seated Neptune at left, three Naiads at lower center right, Mercury with woman at right.. Back: Blue. Mercury at left center, bank arms at center, allegorical woman with sheaf at center right. Printer: CBNC.			
a. Issued note.	600.	1200.	2400.
p. Proof.	—	Unc	1250.

Colonial Bank

1900's Issue

S119 5 Dollars	**Good**	**Fine**	**XF**
19xx. Curved *COLONIAL BANK* in ornate underprint. Specimen.	—	—	—

S120 5 Dollars	**Good**	**Fine**	**XF**
1.7.1901; 1.5.1903. Black on yellow underprint. Arms at upper center. Printer: PBC.	—	—	—

#S121 *Deleted*. See #S135.

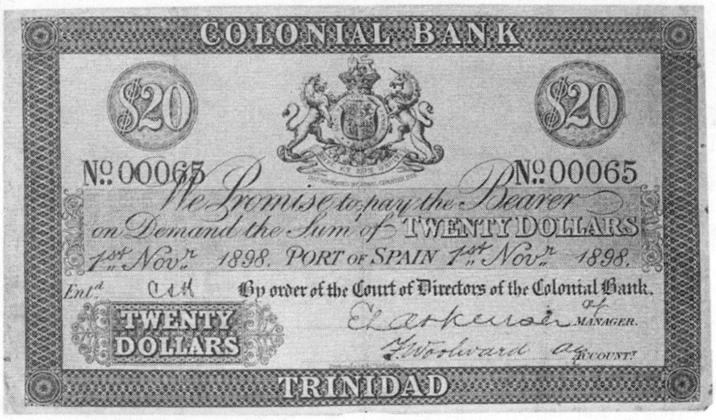

		Good	Fine	XF
S122	**20 Dollars** 1.11.1898. Black on tan underprint. Crowned supported royal arms at center. Back: Blue. Printer: PBC. Rare.	—	—	—
S132	**20 Dollars** 19xx. Black on tan underprint. Crowned supported royal arms at center. Similar to #S122 but large curved *COLONIAL BANK* in ornate underprint. Back: Blue. Printer: PBC. Specimen. Rare.	—	—	—

#S134 *Deleted*. See #S137.

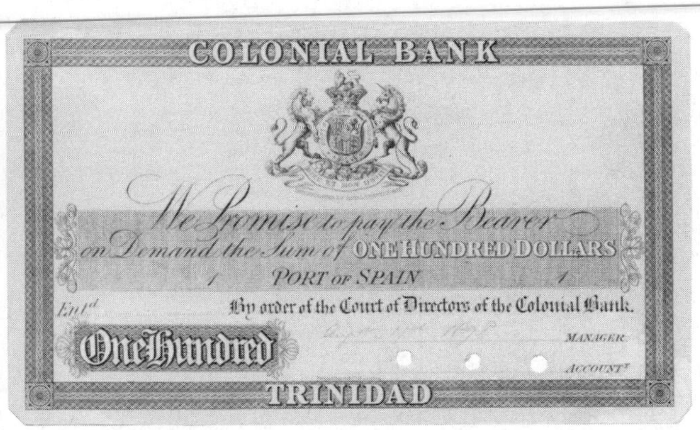

		Good	Fine	XF
S134	**100 Dollars** ND (1898). Black. Royal arms at top center. Printer: PBC. Uniface Proof. Punch hole cancelled.	—	Unc	1000.

1917-20 Issue

#S135-S137 Ovpt: lg. *T* at upper r.

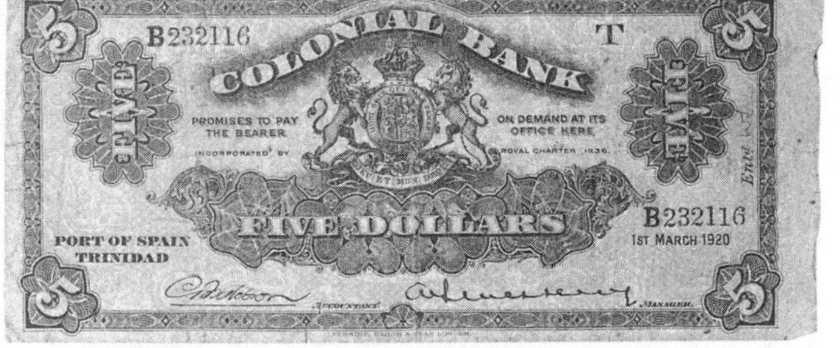

		Good	Fine	XF
S135	**5 Dollars** 1917-20. Black on orange underprint. Crowned supported royal arms at upper center. Back: Green. Overprint: Large *T* at upper right.			
	a. Issued note. 1.1.1918; 1.3.1920.	600.	1200.	2400.
	s. Specimen. 1.2.1917.	—	Unc	1250.

		Good	Fine	XF
S136	**20 Dollars** 1.11.1920. Crowned supported royal arms at upper center. Overprint: Large *T* at upper right. Specimen.	—	Unc	1750.

		Good	Fine	XF
S137	**100 Dollars** 1.11.1920. Crowned supported royal arms at upper center. Overprint: Large *T* at upper right. Specimen.	—	Unc	2500.

Royal Bank of Canada

1909 Provisional Issue

#S141-S143 vertical ovpt: *TRINIDAD* at l. and r., w/smaller vertical text: *PAYABLE AT PORT OF SPAIN, TRINIDAD* in red at l. ctr. Printer: ABNC.

		Good	Fine	XF
S141	**5 Dollars** 2.1.1909. Black on green and yellow underprint. Seated woman with two children ("Peace") at left. Back: Green and yellow. Overprint: Vertical: *TRINIDAD* at left and right, red: *PAYABLE AT PORT OF SPAIN, TRINIDAD* at left. Printer: ABNC.	1100.	2200.	—
S142	**20 Dollars** 2.1.1909. Black on blue and yellow underprint. Seated woman with lion at center. Back: Blue and yellow. Overprint: Vertical: *TRINIDAD* at left and right, red: *PAYABLE AT PORT OF SPAIN, TRINIDAD* at left. Printer: ABNC. Rare.	—	—	—

		Good	Fine	XF
S143	**100 Dollars** 2.1.1909. Black on red-orange underprint. Seated allegory of Commerce at right. Back: Red-orange. Overprint: Vertical: *TRINIDAD* at left and right, red: *PAYABLE AT PORT OF SPAIN, TRINIDAD* at left. Printer: ABNC.			
	a. Issued note. Rare.	—	—	—
	s. Specimen.	—	Unc	1250.

1920 Issue

Notes designed specifically for circulation in the West Indies.

		Good	Fine	XF
S151	**5 Dollars = 1 Pound 10 Pence** 2.1.1920. Black on green underprint. Steamship at center. Back: Green. Printer: ABNC.			
	a. Signature H. S. Holt at right.	500.	1000.	2000.
	b. Signature M. W. Wilson at right.	500.	1000.	2000.

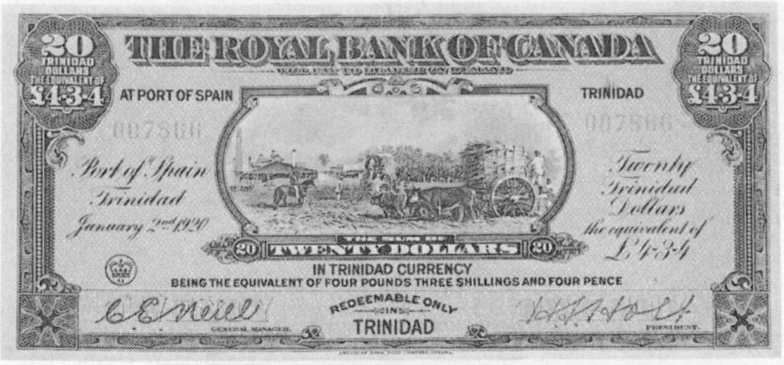

		Good	Fine	XF
S152	**20 Dollars = 4 Pounds 3 Shillings 4 Pence** 2.1.1920. Black on blue underprint. Sugar cane harvesting at center. Back: Blue. Printer: ABNC. Rare.	—	—	—
S153	**100 Dollars = 20 Pounds 16 Shillings 8 Pence** 2.1.1920. Black on orange underprint. Seated woman with island in background. Back: Orange. Printer: ABNC. Specimen. Rare.	—	—	—

1938 Issue

		Good	Fine	XF
S161	**5 Dollars = 1 Pound 10 Pence** 3.1.1938. Steamship at center. Similar to #S151. Printer: CBNC.	250.	500.	1000.
S162	**20 Dollars = 4 Pounds 3 Shillings 4 Pence** 3.1.1938. Black on orange underprint. Sugar cane harvesting at center. Similar to #S152. Back: Rose. Printer: CBNC.	600.	1200.	2400.

Union Bank of Halifax

1904 Issue

#S171-S175 vertical ovpt: *TRINIDAD* at l. and r. and red ovpt: *PAYABLE AT PORT OF SPAIN TRINIDAD* horizontally across the face.

		Good	Fine	XF
S171	**5 Dollars** 1.9.1904. Black on green underprint. Bank building at center. Back: Green. Fishermen on ship. Overprint: Vertical: *TRINIDAD* at left and right, red *PAYABLE AT PORT OF SPAIN, TRINIDAD* across face Printer: BABNC.	—	Unc	1750.

		Good	Fine	XF
S172	**10 Dollars** 1.9.1904. Black on ochre underprint. Crowned, supported royal arms at center. Back: Yellow-orange. Fishermen on ship. Like #S171. Overprint: Vertical: *TRINIDAD* at left and right, red *PAYABLE AT PORT OF SPAIN, TRINIDAD* across face Printer: BABNC.	—	Unc	2000.

		Good	Fine	XF
S173	**20 Dollars** 1.9.1904. Black on blue underprint. Woman with flag sitting on bale at lower left, fishermen on boat at center, anchor and containers at lower right. Back: Blue. Boy and dog on ship. Overprint: Vertical: *TRINIDAD* at left and right, red *PAYABLE AT PORT OF SPAIN, TRINIDAD* across face Printer: BABNC.	—	Unc	2250.

		Good	Fine	XF
S174	**50 Dollars** 1.9.1904. Black on red-brown underprint. Arms with Indian and sailor. Back: Red-brown. Overprint: Vertical: *TRINIDAD* at left and right, red *PAYABLE AT PORT OF SPAIN, TRINIDAD* across face Printer: BABNC.	—	Unc	2250.

		Good	Fine	XF
S175	**100 Dollars** 1.9.1904. Black on red-brown underprint. Coast watcher at left, sailor at center right. Back: Red. Overprint: Vertical: *TRINIDAD* at left and right, red *PAYABLE AT PORT OF SPAIN, TRINIDAD* across face Printer: BABNC.	—	Unc	2500.

West India Bank

1841 Issue

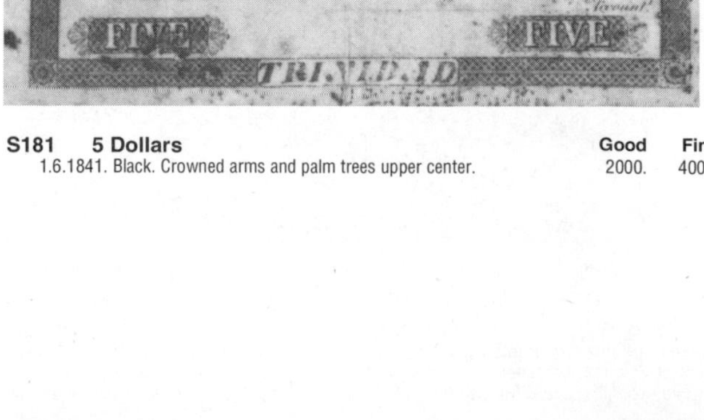

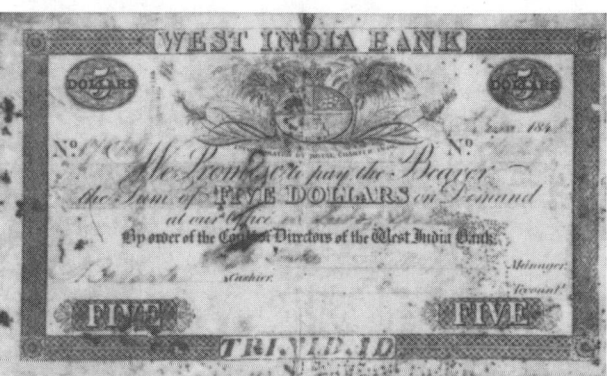

		Good	Fine	XF
S181	**5 Dollars** 1.6.1841. Black. Crowned arms and palm trees upper center.	2000.	4000.	—

UNITED STATES OF AMERICA

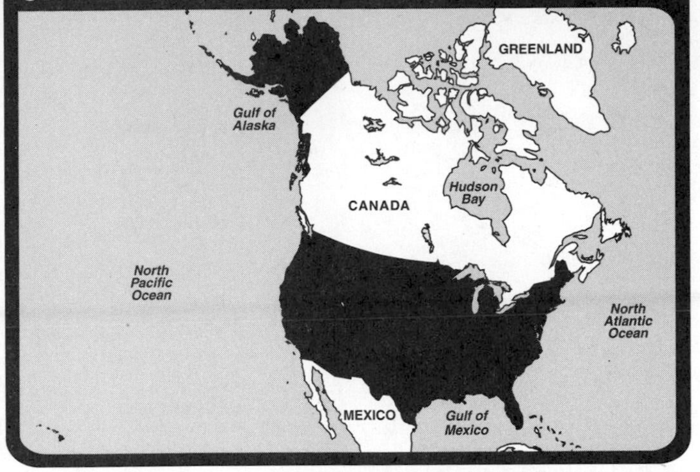

The area of the North American continent currently controlled by the United States of America was originally inhabited by numerous groups of Indian tribes. Some of these groups settled in particular areas, creating permanent settlements, while others were nomadic, traveling great distances and living off the land.

English explorers John and Sebastian Cabot reached Nova Scotia in what is today Canada in 1497; in 1534 the French gained a foothold with the explorations of Jacques Cartier. In 1541 the Spanish explorer Coronado traversed the south central portion of the country in what was to become the states of New Mexico, Texas, Nebraska and Oklahoma. In 1542 another Spaniard, Juan Cabrillo navigated north from Mexico along the Pacific coastline to California. The Spanish set up the first permanent settlement of Europeans in North America at St. Augustine, Florida in 1565. In 1607 the English settled in Jamestown, Virginia, and in 1620 at Plymouth, Massachusetts. This was followed closely by Dutch settlements in Albany and New York in 1624, and in 1638 the Swedes arrived in Delaware. From their foothold in Canada, French explorers pushed inland through the Great Lakes. Jean Nicolet explored what was to become Wisconsin in 1634, and in 1673 explorers Marquette and Joliet reached Iowa. In the 1650s the Dutch won the Swedish lands, and in 1664 the English gained control of the Dutch lands, thus giving the English control all along the Atlantic Coast. The resulting thirteen British colonies; New Hampshire, Vermont, Massachusetts, Rhode Island, Connecticut, New York, Pennsylvania, Delaware, Maryland, Virginia, North Carolina, South Carolina and Georgia formed the nucleus of what would become the United States of America.

From this point on tensions grew between the English, who could not expand westward from their settlements along the Atlantic Coast, and the French who had settled inland into the Ohio river valley. This dispute ended in 1763 after a war with the French loosing control of lands east of the Mississippi river. Manufacturing, textiles and other industry was developing at this time, and by 1775 about one-seventh of the world's production of raw iron came from the colonies. From 1771-1783 the war for American Independence was fought by the colonists against the English, and settled by the Peace of Paris in 1783. Americans gained control of lands south of the St. Lawrence and Great Lakes, and east of the Mississippi, with the exception of Florida which would remain under Spanish control until 1821. At the close of the war, the population was about 3 million, many of whom lived on self-sufficient family farms. Fishing, lumbering and the production of grains for export were becoming major economic endeavors. The newly independent states formed a loose confederation, but in 1787 approved the Constitution of the United States which is the framework for the goverment today. In 1789 it's first president, George Washington was elected, and the capitol was set up in New York City. In 1800 the capitol was moved to a planned city, Washington, D.C. where it remains.

Westward expansion was an inevitability as population grew. French territory west of the Mississippi, stretching to the northern Pacific was purchased in 1804 under the presidency of Thomas Jefferson, who then sent out Lewis and Clark on expedition of discovery. Spain granted independence to Mexico in 1821, which included lands which would become the states of California, New Mexico, Arizona and Texas. From 1836-1845 Texas was an independent republic, not joining the United States until 1845. Upon losing a war with the United States, Mexico ceded California (including most of Arizona and New Mexico) to the United States in 1848. Gold was discovered in California that year, and western migration took off on overland wagon trains or around-the-horn sail and steam ships. Hawaii came under U.S. protection in 1851. As the country developed in the 19th century, the northern states increased in commerce and industry while the southern states developed a vast agricultural through the use of slave labor. Northern political and social threats to slavery lead twelve southern states to secede from the Union in 1860 forming the Confederate States of America. The ensuing Civil War lasted until 1865, at which time slavery was abolished and the States reunited.

In 1867 Alaska was purchased from Russia. The transcontinental railroad was completed in 1869. The central region of the country west of the Mississippi River and east of the Rocky Mountains was the last to be developed, beginning after the Civil War, with the establishment of cattle ranches and farms. Between 1870 and 1891 the nomadic Native American population clashed with settlers and federal troops. By 1891 the Native Americans were confined to reservations.

At the close of the 19th century the United States embarked on a colonial mission of its own, with advances into Cuba, Puerto Rico, Panama, Nicaragua and the Philippines. This resulted in the Spanish-American War which was quickly decided, ending Spanish colonial dominance, and signaling the rise of the United States as a world power. Slow to enter both World Wars of the 20th century, it was a major contributor to the conclusion of both, making it one of the major nations of the 20th century. As the Spanish Milled Dollar achieved widespread acceptance throughout the American colonial period, it was a natural choice on which to a national coinage system. The Spanish Milled Dollar had already been accorded legal tender status in several colonies, notably Massachusetts, Connecticut and Virginia and the others used it. Each colony had its own shilling exchange for a Spanish Milled Dollar ranging from 6 to 32 1/2 shillings. When the Continental Congress issued its first paper money to finance the revolution, the notes themselves promised to pay their face value in *Spanish milled dollars or the Value thereof in Gold or Silver.* The first quasi-official American coinage, the 1776 Continental *Dollar,* while not thus denominated, was struck in the size of the Spanish Milled Dollar.

While the denomination of *One Dollar* may have been a natural choice for a national monetary system, the problem of making change for that dollar was not. In 1782, Robert Morris, superintendent of Finance, proposed a coinage system d on a unit of 1/1440th part of a dollar which, he argued, would reconcile the different *official* values of the Spanish Milled Dollar in all the states. A year later, he submitted a series of copper and silver pattern coinage to Congress d on the basic unit of a quarter-grain of silver. The patterns are known to collectors today as the Nova Constellatio coinage. Other leading financiers saw the traditional division of the Spanish Milled Dollar into *eight reales,* or *bits* as they were familiarly known, as too unwieldy. Gouverneur Morris, assistant financier of the government then operating under the Articles of Confederation, proposed the simple solution of a decimal coinage ratio. With the support of Thomas Jefferson, who remarked, "The most easy ratio of multiplication and division is that of ten," and George Washington, who called it, "indispensably necessary," the decimal coinage proposal won out over more complicated plans. The dollar-decimal system was adopted on July 6, 1785, creating a silver dollar, with fractional coins, also in silver, in denominations of half (50¢), quarter (25¢), tenth (10¢) and twentieth (5¢) parts of a dollar, and copper pieces in denominations of 1/100th (1¢) and 1/200th (1/2¢) of a dollar.

Continental Currency: A total of 11 separate issues of paper currency were authorized by the Continental Congress to finance the war for American independence. The first issue was dated May 10, 1775, the date of the first session of the Continental Congress; the final issue was by Resolution of Jan. 14, 1779. In all, according to early American currency expert Eric P. Newman, a total of $241,552,780 worth of Continental Currency was issued.

Backed only by faith in the success of the Revolution, there was according to a Resolution of Congress a 40-to-1 devaluation by 1780, and in the end the bills were only redeemable at 1/100th of face value in interest-bearing bonds.

MONETARY SYSTEM:

1 Dollar = 100 Cents
1 Dollar = 100 Cents

Colonial & Confederation Period

U.S. Constitutional Period

One Dollar was equal to: . . . . 1 Dollar = 100 Cents
6 New England Shillings . . . . 12 1/2 Cents U.S. = 1 Real (Spanish-American)
8 New York Shillings . . . . 1 Dollar U.S. = 8 Reales (Spanish-American)
7 1/2 Middle States Shillings
6 Virginia Shillings
8 Carolina Shillings
32 1/2 Georgia Shillings

CONTINENTAL CURRENCY

MOTTOS

Various Latin mottos are found on Colonial, Continenal Currency, and early state issues as follows:

ACERVUS E PARVIS GRANDIS (Great accumulation from small things)
ANIMIS OPIBUSQUE PARATI (Prepared in spirit and in resources)
ARMIS CONCURRITE CAMPO (Run together on the field w/arms)
AUSPICIUM SALUTIS (An auspice of well-being)
AUT MORS AUT VICTORIA (Either death or victory)
AUT MORS AUT VICTORIA LAETA (Either death or victory is pleasing)
AUT MORS AUT VITA DECORA (Either death or an honorable life)
AUT NUMQUAM TENTES AUT PERFICE (Either finish or never begin)
CESSANTE VENTO CONQUIESCEMUS (When the wind dies down we rest)
CLARET AB ICTU (It shines from use)
COMMERCITO (Commerce) (Trade)
CONFEDERATION (Confederation)
CONSTANTIA DURISSIMA VINCIT (The firmest constancy will conquer)
CRESCIT SUB PONDERE VIRTUS (Virtue grows under pressure)
DEBELLARE BARBAROS RENOVA ANIMUM (Renew the spirit to fight the Barbarians)
DEPRESSA RESURGIT (Though crushed it comes back)
DEUS NOBISCUM (God be with us)
DEUS REGNAT EXULTET TERRA (God reigns, let the earth rejoice)
DIEU ET MON DROIT (God and my right)
DIVITIAE REIPUBLICAE DANT MIHI PRETIUM (The wealth of the republic gives me value)
DOMINUM GENEROSA RECUSAT (The well born refuses a master)
DULCE PRO PATRIA MORI (It is pleasing to die for one's country)
EN DAT VIRGINIA QUARTAM (Behold Virginia contributes one quarter of the arms)
ET DEUS OMNIPOTENS (And Almighty God)
ET IN SECULA SECULORUM FLORESCEBIT (An it will flourish for ages of ages)
ET SOLI ET MARTI (For the sun and for Mars)
EXITUS IN DUBIO EST (The outcome is in doubt)
FATA VIAM INVENIENT (The fates will find a way)
FIAT JUSTITIA RUAT COELUM (Let justice be done though the heavens fall)
FIDES PUBLICA (Public trust)
FORTIS A FORTE (Strength comes from strength)
FORTIS CADERE CEDERE NON POTEST (A brave man cannot fall)
FUGIO (I fly)
FUNDAMENTUM MIHI AERE PERENNIUS (A foundation for me more enduring than bronze)
GLORIAE FUNDAMENTUM FORTITUDO (Bravery is the foundation of glory)
HANC TUEMUR HAC NITIMUR (This we guard, for this we strive)
HINC OPES (Hence our wealth)
HIS ORNARI AUT MORI (To be decorated with these or to die)
HONI SOIT QUI MAL Y PENSE (Evil to him who evil thinks)
HONOR ET JUSTITIA (Honor and justice)
HORA PACIS & LIBERTATIS APPROPINQUAT (The time for peace and freedom is approaching)
IBI PATRIA UBI LIBERTAS (Our country is there, where is freedom)
ICH DIEN (I serve)
IMPAVIDE (Fearlessly)
INFELIX BRITANNIA (Unhappy England)
INFESTUS TANTUM INFESTIS (Hostile only to the hostile)
INFRACTO FOEDERE (By treaty unbroken)
IN RECTO DECUS (Honor in the right)
IN TE DOMINE SPERAMUS (In you, Lord, we have hope)
IN TE DOMINE SPERAVI (In you, Lord, I have hoped)
JUSTITIA (Justice)
JUSTITIA ADDIT FIDUCIAM (Justice adds trust)
LEX REGIT ARMA TUENTUR (Laws rule, arms guard)
LIBERTAS & NATALE SOLUM (Liberty and our native land)
MAGNIS INTERDUM PARVA NOCENT (Sometimes small things do harm to big ones)
MAJORA MINORIBUS CONSONANT (The large colonies in harmony with the small colonies)
MELIOR RESURGO (I return improved)
MELIOREM LAPSA LOCAVIT (Having fallen, it found a better place)
MINIME VIOLANDA FIDES (Trust by no means is to be violated)
MISERA SERVITUS OMNIS (All slavery is wretched)
MULTORUM SPEC (The hope of many)
MUTARE VEL TIMERE SPERNO (I refuse to change or to fear)

MUTUA DEFENSIO TUTISSIMA (Mutal defense is safest)
NEC ONUS NEC META GRAVABIT (Neither burden nor danger will force me down)
NE IMPROVISO (Not unexpectedly)
NEMO ME IMPUNE LACESSET (No one will provide me with impunity)
NIL DESPERANDUM (Nothing is to be despaired of)
NON DIU (Not for long)
NUSQUAM SUB MOLE FATISCIT (Nowhere does it weaken under weight)
PAR VIRIBUS VIRTUS (Virtue is equal to strength)
PAX REDDITA (Peace restored)
PER ARDUA SURGO (I rise through adversity)
PERENNIS (Everlasting)
PERSEVERANDO (By perseverance)
POSTERITATE (For posterity)
POST NUBILA PHOEBUS (After dark clouds comes the sun)
POST TENEBRAS LUX (After darkness, light)
PRAEMIUM INDUSTRIAE (The reward of industry)
PRO ARIS & FOCIS (For altars and the hearth)
PRO BONO PUBLICO (For the public good)
PRO LIBERTATE (For freedom)
PROVIDENTIA NOSTRIS PRAESIDEAT (Let foresight guide our people)
QUARENDA PECUNIA PRIMUM EST (Money has to be sought first)
QUID NON VIRTUTE EFFICIENDUM (What is not to be accomplished by virtue)
QUIS SEPARABIT (Who will separate)
RESTITUIT REM (He has restored the situation)
SALUTARIS SIBI PARENTIBUS QUE (Fortunate for itself and its parents)
SERENABIT (It will be calm)
SE SUSTULIT IPSA (It raises itself up)
SIC FLORET RESPUBLICA (Thus let the nation flourish)
SIC SEMPER TYRANNIS (Ever thus to tyrants)
SIC TRANSIT GLORIA MUNDI (Thus passes the glory of the world)
SI RECTE FACIES (IF you perform righteously)
SPERANDUM (One must hope)
SPES MENTIS SOLATIO (Hope is the consolation of the mind)
SUB CLYPEO (Under divine protection)
SUB VERTUTE SPERAMUS (With morality we have hope)
SUME EX SCELERATO SANGUINE POENAM (Exact punishment from guilty blood)
SUSTINE VEL ABSTINE (Either survive or refrain)
SUSTINET QUI TRANSTULIT (He who transplants sustains himself)
TERRA LIBERA NOTAM PRAETII IN ME POSUIT (A free land placed a mark of value on me)
THE ACTAEON. IRAM PRUDENTIA VINCIT (The Actaeon. Wisdom overcomes anger)
TRIBULATIO DITAT (Affliction enriches)
TURBAT SED EXTOLLIT (It disturbs but it elevates)
TUTA PEDAMINE VIRTUS (Honor safe in its support)
ULTIMA RATIO (The final reckoning)
UNO EODEMQUE IGNI (With one and the same flame)
UT QUOCUNQUE PARATUS (As prepared in every way)
UTRUM HORUM MAVIS ACCIPE (Accept whichever of these you prefer)
VI CONCITATE (Driven by force)
VIM PROCELLARUM QUADRENNIUM SUSTINUIT (For four years it has withstood the force of storm)
VIM VI REPELLAMUS (By force let us repel force)
VIS UNITATIS (The power of unity)
VOX POPULI (The voice of the people)

CONTINENTAL CONGRESS

FIRST ISSUE, MAY 10, 1775

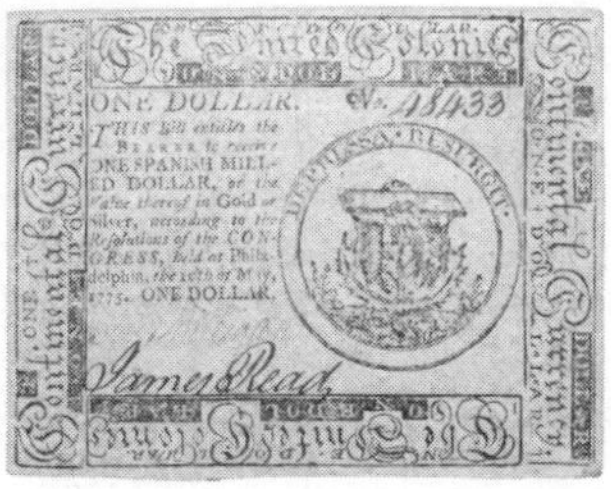

		VG	VF	UNC
S101	**1 Dollar** 10.5.1775. Black. *DEPRESSA RESURGIT* on emblem with weighted bowl on acanthus plant. Back: Ragweed and two willow leaves. Printer: Hall & Sellers, PA. Printed on thick rag paper with blue fibers.	150.	500.	—
S102	**2 Dollars** 10.5.1775. Black. *TRIBULATIO DITAT* on emblem with grain being threshed by a flail. Back: Raspberry and two filbert leaves. Printer: Hall & Sellers, PA. Printed on thick rag paper with blue fibers.	90.00	175.	750.

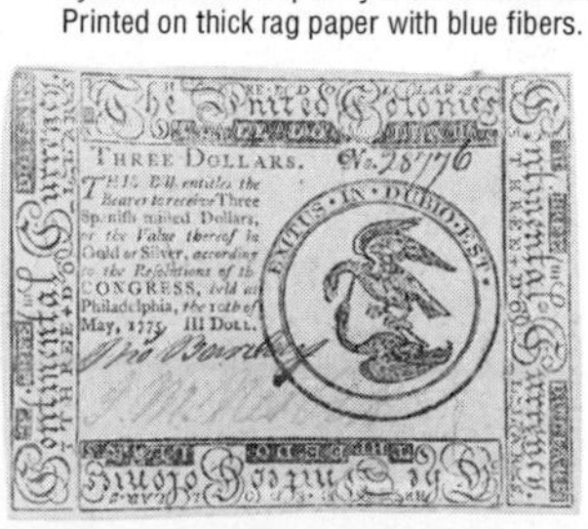

		VG	VF	UNC
S103	**3 Dollars** 10.5.1775. Black. *EXITUS IN DUBIO EST* on emblem with an eagle attacking a heron. Back: Skeletonized elm and maple fruit leaves. Printer: Hall & Sellers, PA. Printed on thick rag paper with blue fibers.	90.00	175.	750.

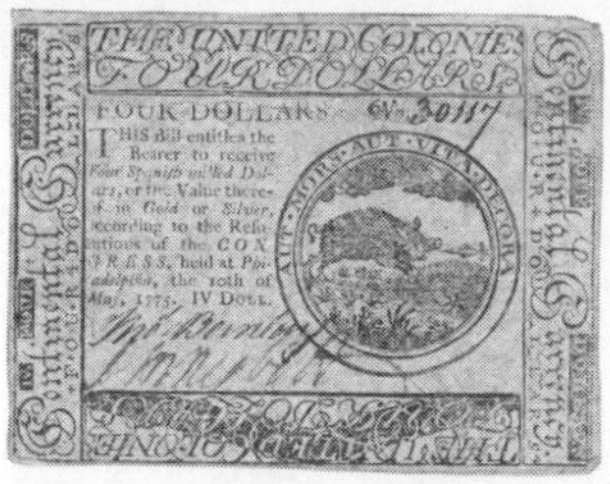

		VG	VF	UNC
S104	**4 Dollars** 10.5.1775. Black. *AUT MORS AUT VITA DECORA* on emblem with wild boar charging into spear. Back: Skeletonized maple fruit leaf. Printer: Hall & Sellers, PA. Printed on thick rag paper with blue fibers.	90.00	175.	750.

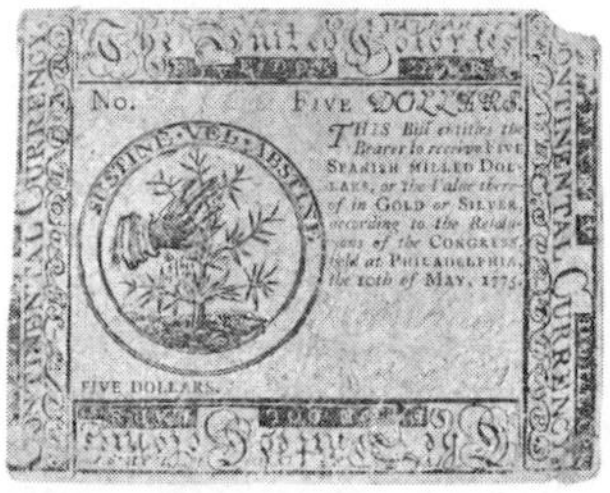

		VG	VF	UNC
S105	**5 Dollars** 10.5.1775. Black. *SUSTINE VEL ABSTINE* on emblem with hand gathering food and bleeding because of pricks from thorns. Back: Betony and sage leaves. Printer: Hall & Sellers, PA. Printed on thick rag paper with blue fibers.	90.00	175.	750.

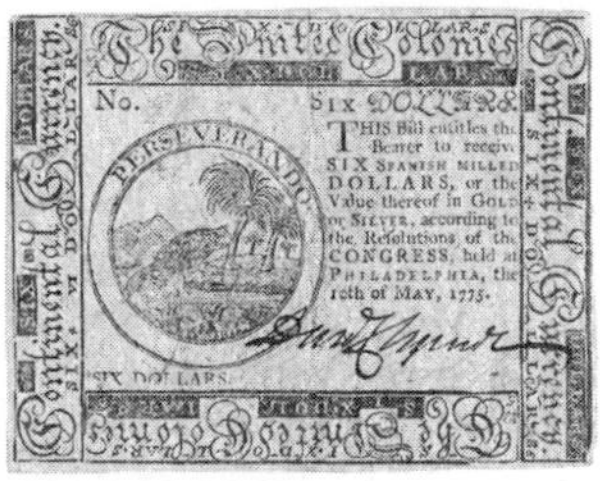

		VG	VF	UNC
S106	**6 Dollars** 10.5.1775. Black. *PERSEVERANDO* on emblem with beaver gnawing down tree. Back: Buttercup leaf. Printer: Hall & Sellers, PA. Printed on thick rag paper with blue fibers.	90.00	175.	750.

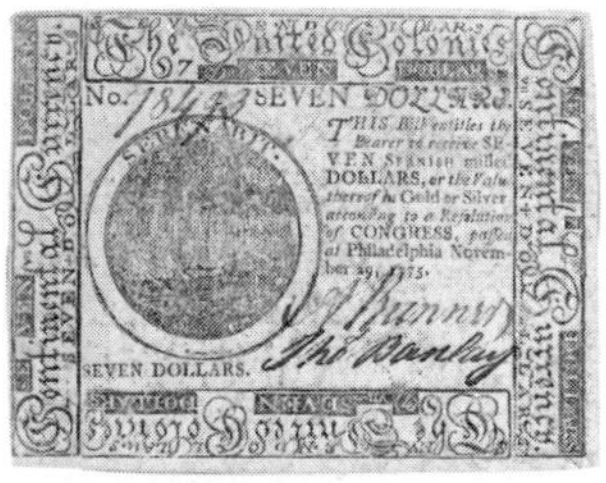

		VG	VF	UNC
S107	**7 Dollars** 10.5.1775. Black. *SERENABIT* on emblem with severe storm at sea. Back: Buttercup leaf. Printer: Hall & Sellers, PA. Printed on thick rag paper with blue fibers.	90.00	175.	750.
S108	**8 Dollars** 10.5.1775. Black. *MAJORA MINORIBUS CONSONANT* on emblem with harp with 13 strings representing the 13 colonies. Back: Henebit and two buttercups leaves. Printer: Hall & Sellers, PA. Printed on thick rag paper with blue fibers.	90.00	175.	750.

S109 20 Dollars

10.5.1775. Black. *VI CONCITATE* on emblem with strong wind blowing. Back: *CESSANTE VENTO CONQUIESCEMUS* on emblem with sun shining on ships at sea. Paper: Thin white. Printer: Hall & Sellers, PA.

VG	VF	UNC
3750.	17,500.	40,000.

S110 30 Dollars

10.5.1775. Black. *SI RECTE FACIES* on emblem with wreath on a tomb. *VI CONCITATE* on left emblem with strong wind blowing, *CESSANTE VENTO CONQUIESCEMUS* on right. Back: Emblem with sun shining on ships at sea. Printer: Hall & Sellers, PA. Printed on thick rag paper with blue fibers.

VG	VF	UNC
150.	300.	1200.

NOTE: The 20 dollar notes were individually printed on thin white paper furnished by Benjamin Franklin. The 30 dollar notes were printed by inserting face and back forms into one position on the double sheet form and removing one of the smaller denominations.

Second Issue, November 29, 1775

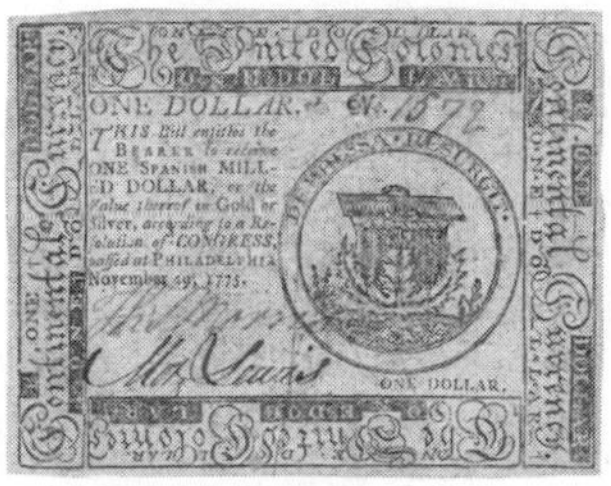

S111 1 Dollar

29.11.1775. Black. *DEPRESSA RESURGIT* on emblem with weighted bowl on acanthus plant. Like #S101. Back: Ragweed and two willow leaves. Printer: Hall & Sellers, PA.

VG	VF	UNC
100.	225.	750.

S112 2 Dollars

29.11.1775. Black. *TRIBULATIO DITAT* on emblem with grain being threshed by a flail. Like #S102. Back: Raspberry and two filbert leaves. Printer: Hall & Sellers, PA.

VG	VF	UNC
75.00	150.	550.

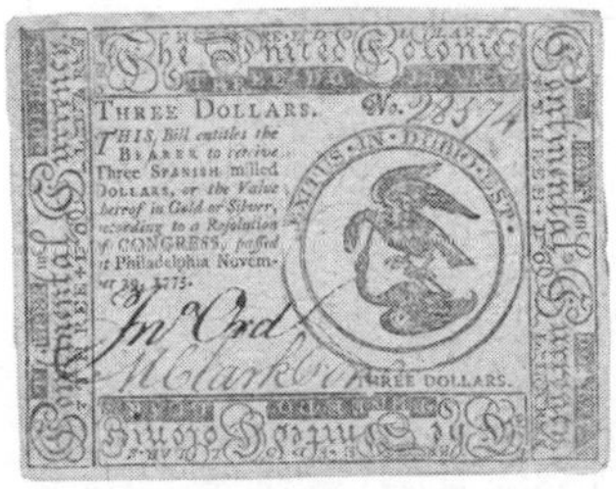

S113 3 Dollars

29.11.1775. Black. *EXITUS IN DUBIO EST* on emblem with an eagle attacking a heron. Like #S103. Back: Skeletonized elm and maple fruit leaves. Printer: Hall & Sellers, PA.

VG	VF	UNC
75.00	150.	550.

S114 4 Dollars

29.11.1775. Black. *AUT MORS AUT VITA DECORA* on emblem with wild boar charging into spear. Like #S104. Back: Skeletonized maple fruit leaf. Printer: Hall & Sellers, PA.

VG	VF	UNC
75.00	150.	550.

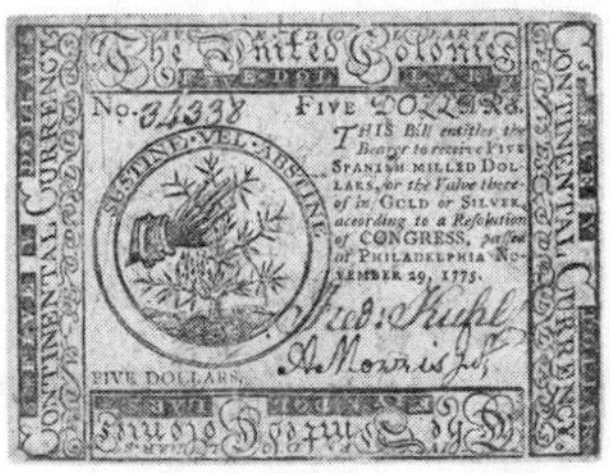
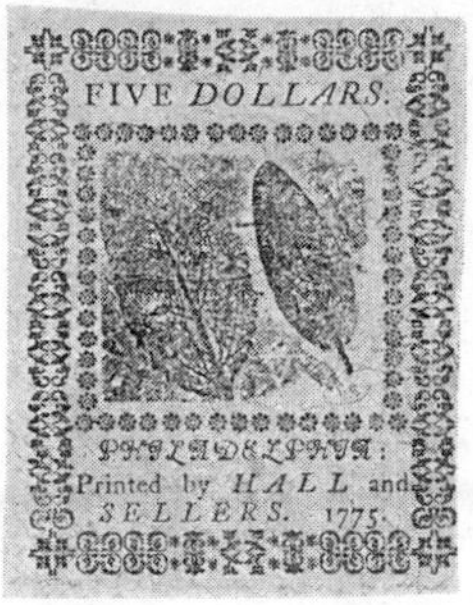

S115 5 Dollars

29.11.1775. Black. *SUSTINE VEL ABSTINE* on emblem with hand gathering food and bleeding because of pricks from thorns. Like #S105. Back: Betony and sage leaves. Printer: Hall & Sellers, PA.

VG	VF	UNC
75.00	150.	550.

S116 6 Dollars

29.11.1775. Black. *PERSEVERANDO* on emblem with beaver gnawing down tree. Like #S106. Back: Buttercup leaf. Printer: Hall & Sellers, PA.

VG	VF	UNC
75.00	150.	550.

S117 7 Dollars

29.11.1775. Black. *SERENABIT* on emblem with severe storm at sea. Like #S107. Back: Buttercup leaf. Printer: Hall & Sellers, PA.

VG	VF	UNC
75.00	150.	550.

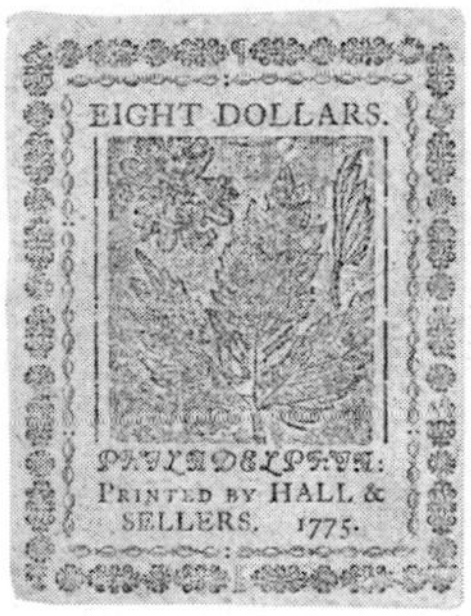

S118 8 Dollars

29.11.1775. Black. *MAJORA MINORIBUS CONSONANT* on emblem with harp with 13 strings representing the 13 colonies. Like #S108. Back: Henebit and two buttercups leaves. Printer: Hall & Sellers, PA.

VG	VF	UNC
75.00	150.	550.

NOTE: Printings on blue paper are counterfeit detectors.

Third Issue, February 17, 1776

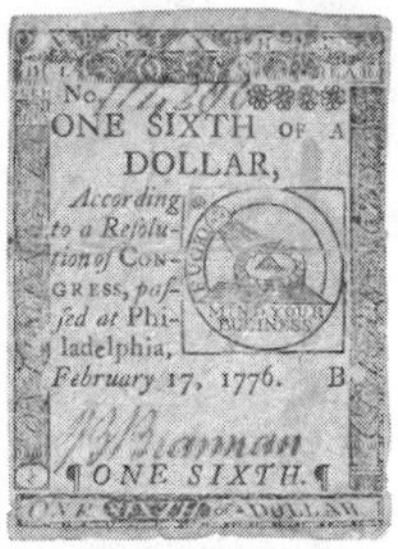

S119 1/6 Dollar

17.2.1776. Black. Sundial rebus at center right. *CURRENCEY* (error) at right. Plate letters: A; B; C. Back: Linked Colonies device. Printer: Hall & Sellers, PA.

VG	VF	UNC
200.	625.	2500.

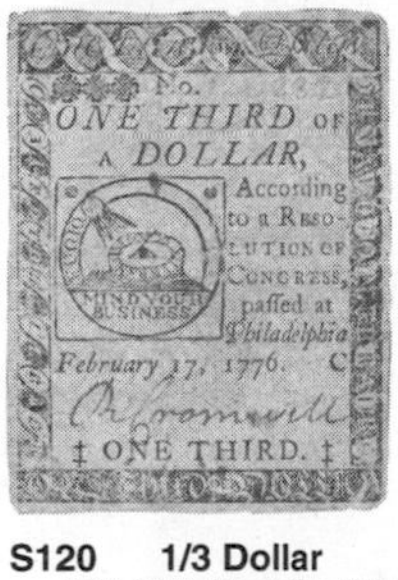

S120 1/3 Dollar

17.2.1776. Black. Sundial rebus at center left. Plate letters: A; B; C. Back: Linked Colonies device. Printer: Hall & Sellers, PA.

VG	VF	UNC
150.	500.	2000.

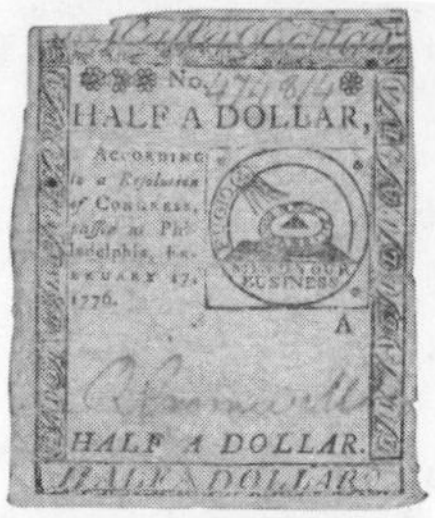

S121 1/2 Dollar

	VG	VF	UNC
17.2.1776. Black. Sundial rebus at center right. Plate letters: A; B; C. Back: Linked Colonies device. Printer: Hall & Sellers, PA.	150.	500.	2000.

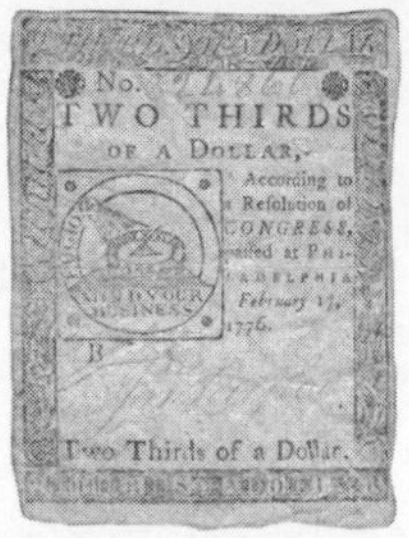

S122 2/3 Dollar

	VG	VF	UNC
17.2.1776. Black. Sundial rebus at center left. Plate letters: A; B; C. Back: Linked Colonies device. Printer: Hall & Sellers, PA.	150.	250.	2000.

S123 1 Dollar
17.2.1776. Black. *DEPRESSA RESURGIT* on emblem with weighted bowl on acanthus plant. Like #S101. Back: Ragweed and two willow leaves. Printer: Hall & Sellers, PA. — 75.00 | 150. | 550.

S124 2 Dollars
17.2.1776. Black. *TRIBULATIO DITAT* on emblem with grain being threshed by, a flail. Like #S102. Back: Raspberry and two filbert leaves. Printer: Hall & Sellers, PA. — 75.00 | 150. | 550.

S125 3 Dollars
17.2.1776. Black. *EXITUS IN DUBIO EST* on emblem with an eagle attacking a heron. Like #S103. Back: Skeletonized elm and maple fruit leaves. Printer: Hall & Sellers, PA. — 75.00 | 150. | 550.

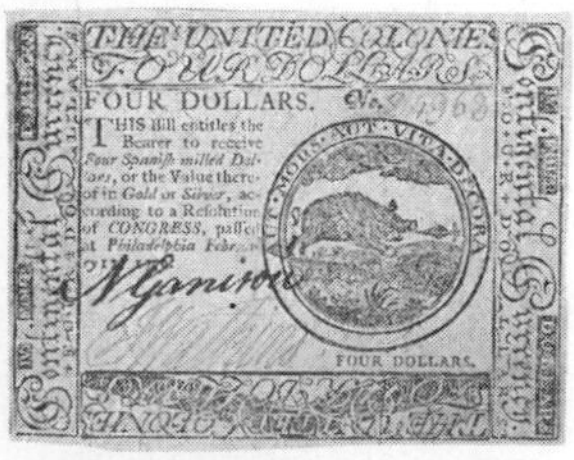

S126 4 Dollars

	VG	VF	UNC
17.2.1776. Black. *AUT MORS AUT VITA DECORA* on emblem with wild boar charging into spear. Like #S104. Back: Skeletonized maple fruit leaf. Printer: Hall & Sellers, PA.	75.00	150.	550.

S127 5 Dollars
17.2.1776. Black. *SUSTINE VEL ABSTINE* on emblem with hand gathering food and bleeding because of pricks from thorns. Like #S105. Back: Betony and sage leaves. Printer: Hall & Sellers, PA. — 75.00 | 150. | 550.

S128 6 Dollars
17.2.1776. Black. *PERSEVERANDO* on emblem with beaver gnawing down tree. Like #S106. Back: Buttercup leaf. Printer: Hall & Sellers, PA. — 75.00 | 150. | 550.

S129 7 Dollars
17.2.1776. Black. *SERENABIT* on emblem with severe storm at sea. Like #S107. Back: Buttercup leaf. Printer: Hall & Sellers, PA. — 75.00 | 150. | 550.

S130 8 Dollars
17.2.1776. Black. *MAJORA MINORIBUS CONSONANT* on emblem with harp with 13 strings representing the 13 colonies. Like #S108. Back: Henebit and two buttercups leaves. Printer: Hall & Sellers, PA. — 75.00 | 150. | 550.

NOTE: Printings on blue paper are counterfeit detectors.

Fourth Issue, May 9, 1776

S131 1 Dollar

	VG	VF	UNC
9.5.1776. Black. *DEPRESSA RESURGIT* on emblem with weighted bowl on acanthus plant. Like #S101. Back: Ragweed and two willow leaves. Printer: Hall & Sellers, PA.	100.	225.	750.

S132 2 Dollars

	VG	VF	UNC
9.5.1776. Black. *TRIBULATIO DITAT* on emblem with grain being threshed by a flail. Like #S102. Back: Raspberry and two filbert leaves. Printer: Hall & Sellers, PA.	75.00	150.	550.

S133 3 Dollars
9.5.1776. Black. *EXITUS IN DUBIO EST* on emblem with an eagle attacking a heron. Like #S103. Back: Skeletonized elm and maple fruit leaves. Printer: Hall & Sellers, PA. — 75.00 | 150. | 550.

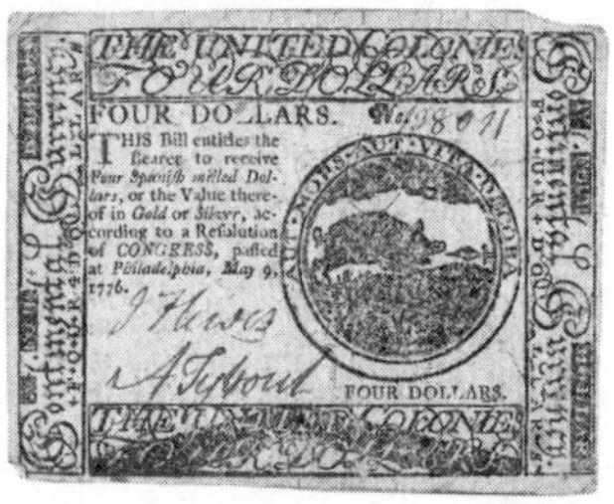

S134 4 Dollars

	VG	VF	UNC
9.5.1776. Black. *AUT MORS AUT VITA DECORA* on emblem with wild boar charging into spear. Like #S104. Back: Skeletonized maple fruit leaf. Printer: Hall & Sellers, PA.	75.00	150.	550.

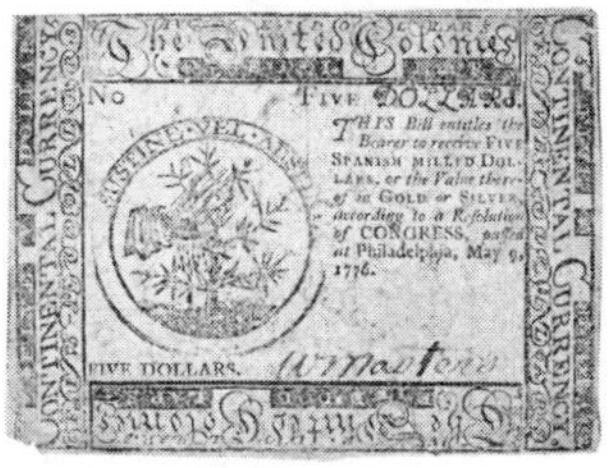
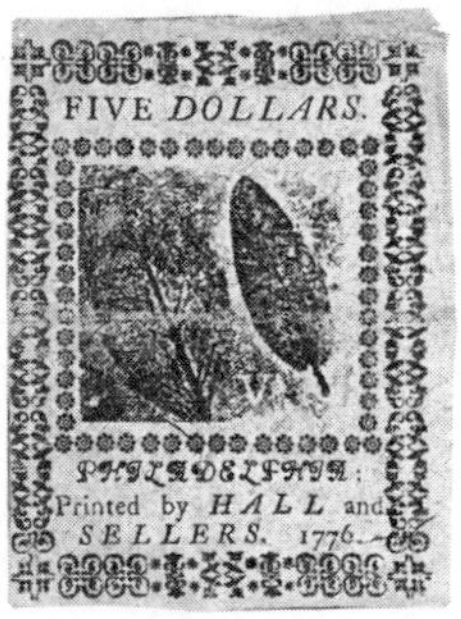

S135 5 Dollars

	VG	VF	UNC
9.5.1776. Black. *SUSTINE VEL ABSTINE* on emblem with hand gathering food and bleeding because of pricks from thorns. Like #S105. Back: Betony and sage leaves. Printer: Hall & Sellers, PA.	75.00	150.	550.

S136 6 Dollars

	VG	VF	UNC
9.5.1776. Black. *PERSEVERANDO* on emblem with beaver gnawing down tree. Like #S106. Back: Buttercup leaf. Printer: Hall & Sellers, PA.	75.00	150.	550.

S137 7 Dollars
9.5.1776. Black. *SERENABIT* on emblem with severe storm at sea. Like #S107. Back: Buttercup leaf. Printer: Hall & Sellers, PA. — 75.00 | 150. | 550.

S138 8 Dollars
9.5.1776. Black. *MAJORA MINORIBUS CONSONANT* on emblem with harp with 13 strings representing the 13 colonies. Like #S108. Back: Henebit and two buttercups leaves. Printer: Hall & Sellers, PA. — 75.00 | 150. | 550.

NOTE: Printings on blue paper are counterfeit detectors.

Fifth Issue, July 22, 1776

S139 2 Dollars

	VG	VF	UNC
22.7.1776. Black. *TRIBULATIO DITAT* on emblem with grain being threshed by a flail. Like #S102. Back: Raspberry and two filbert leaves. Printer: Hall & Sellers, PA.	100.	175.	750.

S140 3 Dollars
22.7.1776. Black. *EXITUS IN DUBIO EST* on emblem with an eagle attacking a heron. Like #S103. Back: Skeletonized elm and maple fruit leaves. Printer: Hall & Sellers, PA.

VG	VF	UNC
100.	175.	750.

S141 4 Dollars
22.7.1776. Black. *AUT MORS AUT VITA DECORA* on emblem with wild boar charging into spear. Like #S104. Back: Skeletonized maple fruit leaf. Printer: Hall & Sellers, PA.

VG	VF	UNC
100.	175.	750.

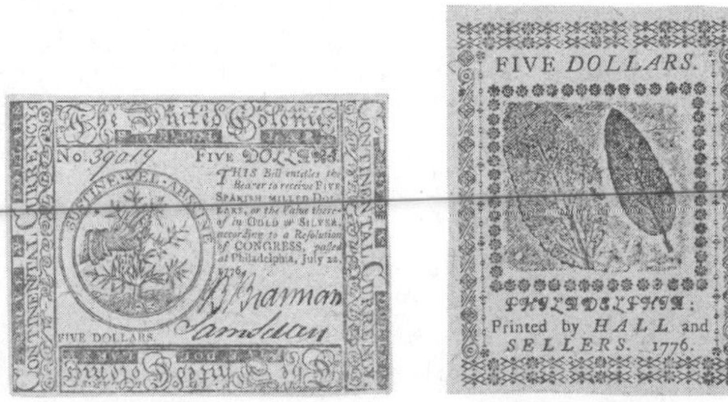

S142 5 Dollars
22.7.1776. Black. *SUSTINE VEL ABSTINE* on emblem with hand gathering food and bleeding because of pricks from thorns. Like #S105, except *B* in motto appears *H*. Back: Betony and sage leaves. Printer: Hall & Sellers, PA.

VG	VF	UNC
100.	175.	750.

S143 6 Dollars
22.7.1776. Black. *PERSEVERANDO* on emblem with beaver gnawing down tree. Like #S106. Back: Buttercup leaf. Printer: Hall & Sellers, PA.

VG	VF	UNC
100.	175.	750.

S144 7 Dollars
22.7.1776. Black. *SERENABIT* on emblem with severe storm at sea. Like #S107. Back: Buttercup leaf. Printer: Hall & Sellers, PA.

VG	VF	UNC
100.	175.	750.

S145 8 Dollars
22.7.1776. Black. *MAJORA MINORIBUS CONSONANT* on emblem with harp with 13 strings representing the 13 colonies. Like #S108. Back: Henebit and two buttercups leaves. Printer: Hall & Sellers, PA.

VG	VF	UNC
100.	175.	750.

S146 30 Dollars
22.7.1776. Black. *SI RECTE FACIES* on emblem with wreath on a tomb. *VI CONCITATE* on left emblem with strong wind blowing, *CESSANTE VENTO CONQUIESCEMUS* on right. Like #S110. Back: Emblem with sun shining on ships at sea. Printer: Hall & Sellers, PA.

VG	VF	UNC
150.	300.	1200.

NOTE: Printings on blue paper are counterfeit detectors.

Sixth Issue, November 2, 1776

S147 2 Dollars
2.11.1776. Black. *TRIBULATIO DITAT* on emblem with grain being threshed by a flail. Like #S102. Back: Raspberry and two filbert leaves. Printer: Hall & Sellers, PA.

VG	VF	UNC
100.	175.	700.

S148 3 Dollars
2.11.1776. Black. *EXITUS IN DUBIO EST* on emblem with an eagle attacking a heron. Like #S103. Back: Skeletonized elm and maple fruit leaves. Printer: Hall & Sellers, PA.

VG	VF	UNC
100.	175.	700.

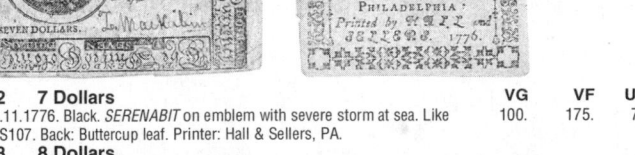

S149 4 Dollars
2.11.1776. Black. *AUT MORS AUT VITA DECORA* on emblem with wild boar charging into spear. Like #S104. Back: Skeletonized maple fruit leaf. Printer: Hall & Sellers, PA.

VG	VF	UNC
100.	175.	700.

S150 5 Dollars
2.11.1776. Black. *SUSTINE VEL ABSTINE* on emblem with hand gathering food and bleeding because of pricks from thorns. Like #S105, except *B* in motto appears as *H*. Back: Betony and sage leaves. Printer: Hall & Sellers, PA.

VG	VF	UNC
100.	175.	700.

S151 6 Dollars
2.11.1776. Black. *PERSEVERANDO* on emblem with beaver gnawing down tree. Like #S106. Back: Buttercup leaf. Printer: Hall & Sellers, PA.

VG	VF	UNC
100.	175.	700.

S152 7 Dollars
2.11.1776. Black. *SERENABIT* on emblem with severe storm at sea. Like #S107. Back: Buttercup leaf. Printer: Hall & Sellers, PA.

VG	VF	UNC
100.	175.	700.

S153 8 Dollars
2.11.1776. Black. *MAJORA MINORIBUS CONSONANT* on emblem with harp with 13 strings representing the 13 colonies. Like #S108. Back: Henebit and two buttercups leaves. Printer: Hall & Sellers, PA.

VG	VF	UNC
100.	175.	700.

S154 30 Dollars
2.11.1776. Black. *SI RECTE FACIES* on emblem with wreath on a tomb. *VI CONCITATE* on left emblem with strong wind blowing, *CESSANTE VENTO CONQUIESCEMUS* on right. Like #S110. Back: Emblem with sun shining on ships at sea. Printer: Hall & Sellers, PA.

VG	VF	UNC
150.	300.	1200.

NOTE: An additional issue of $500,000 in bills of 1/9, 1/6, 1/3, and 2/3 dollars was also authorized by the Nov. 2, 1776 Resolution, but these fractional denominations were never printed because the fractional denominations of the Feb. 17, 1776 issue were still being signed and were in adequate supply through the fall of 1777.

NOTE: Printings on blue paper are counterfeit detectors.

ILLUSTRATIONS

Illustrations of bank notes used throughout this catalog are 42% of the actual size.

Seventh Issue, February 26, 1777

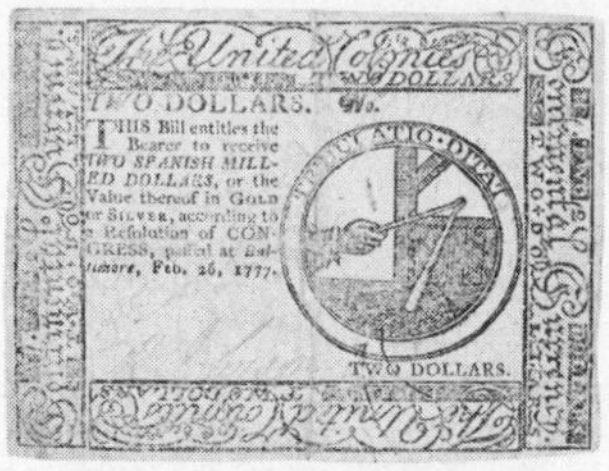

S155 2 Dollars	VG	VF	UNC
26.2.1777. Black. *TRIBULATIO DITAT* on emblem with grain being threshed by a flail. Like #S102. Back: Raspberry and two filbert leaves. Printer: Hall & Sellers, PA.	90.00	160.	650.
S156 3 Dollars			
26.2.1777. Black. *EXITUS IN DUBIO EST* on emblem with an eagle attacking a heron. Like #S103. Back: Skeletonized elm and maple fruit leaves. Printer: Hall & Sellers, PA.	90.00	160.	650.

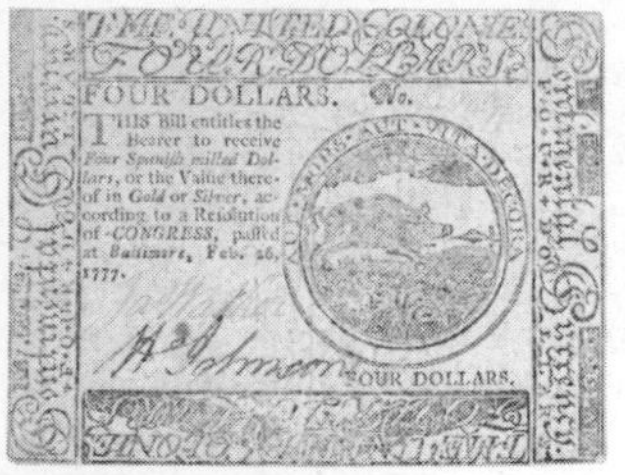
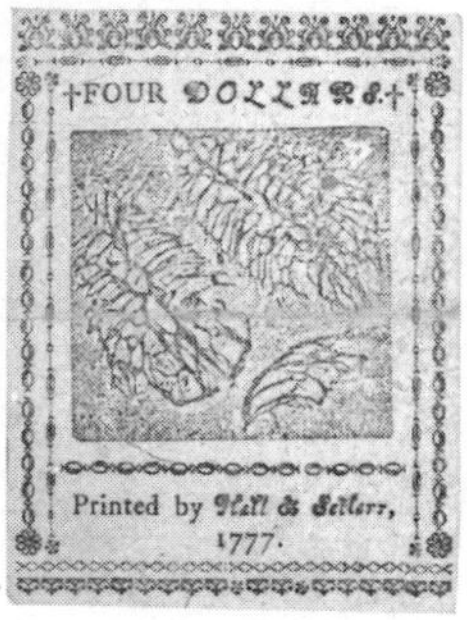

S157 4 Dollars	VG	VF	UNC
26.2.1777. Black. *AUT MORS AUT VITA DECORA* on emblem with wild boar charging into spear. Like #S104. Back: Skeletonized maple fruit leaf. Printer: Hall & Sellers, PA.	90.00	160.	650.
S158 5 Dollars			
26.2.1777. Black. *SUSTINE VEL ABSTINE* on emblem with hand gathering food and bleeding because of pricks from thorns. Like #S105, except *B* in motto appears as *H*. Back: Betony and sage leaves. Printer: Hall & Sellers, PA.	90.00	160.	650.
S159 6 Dollars			
26.2.1777. Black. *PERSEVERANDO* on emblem with beaver gnawing down tree. Like #S106. Back: Buttercup leaf. Printer: Hall & Sellers, PA.	90.00	160.	650.

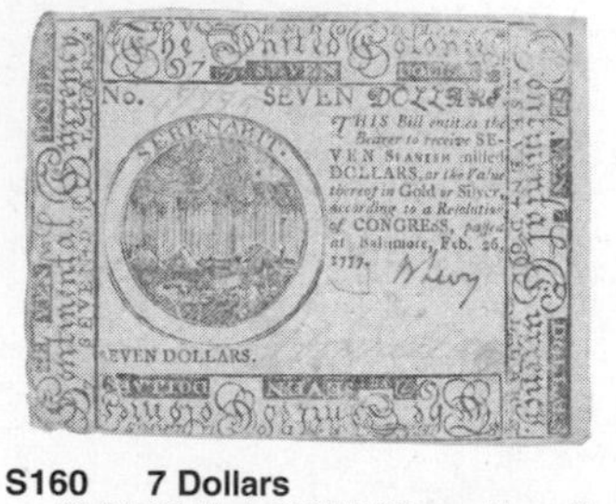

S160 7 Dollars	VG	VF	UNC
26.2.1777. Black. *SERENABIT* on emblem with severe storm at sea. Like #S107. Back: Buttercup leaf. Printer: Hall & Sellers, PA.	90.00	160.	650.

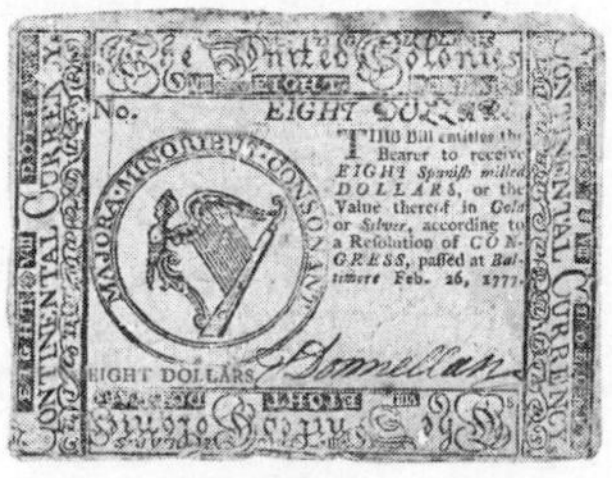

S161 8 Dollars	VG	VF	UNC
26.2.1777. Black. *MAJORA MINORIBUS CONSONANT* on emblem with harp with 13 strings representing the 13 colonies. Like #S108. Back: Henebit and two buttercups leaves. Printer: Hall & Sellers, PA.	90.00	160.	650.

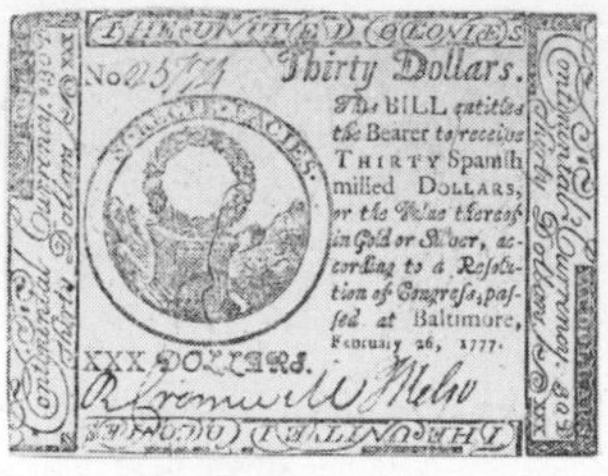
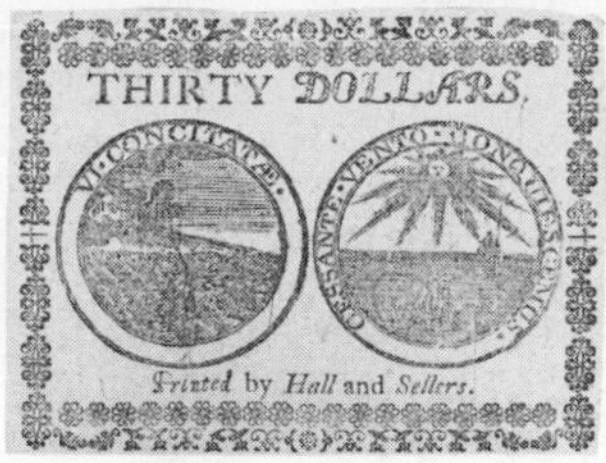

S162 30 Dollars	VG	VF	UNC
26.2.1777. Black. *SI RECTE FACIES* on emblem with wreath on a tomb. *VI CONCITATE* on left emblem with strong wind blowing, *CESSANTE VENTO CONQUIESCEMUS* on right. Like #S110. Back: Emblem with sun shining on ships at sea. Printer: Hall & Sellers, PA.	135.	275.	1000.

Eighth Issue, May 20, 1777

NOTE: #S163-S170 are the same style as the #S155-S162 except that the cuts for the top and bottom borders were modified to *United States* instead of *United Colonies*.

S163 2 Dollars	VG	VF	UNC
20.5.1777. Black. *TRIBULATIO DITAT* on emblem with grain being threshed by a flail. Like #S102. Back: Raspberry and two filbert leaves. Printer: Hall & Sellers, PA.	300.	750.	4000.
S164 3 Dollars			
20.5.1777. Black. *EXITUS IN DUBIO EST* on emblem with an eagle attacking a heron. Like #S103. Back: Skeletonized elm and maple fruit leaves. Printer: Hall & Sellers, PA.	300.	750.	4000.
S165 4 Dollars			
20.5.1777. Black. *AUT MORS AUT VITA DECORA* on emblem with wild boar charging into spear. Like #S104. Back: Skeletonized maple fruit leaf. Printer: Hall & Sellers, PA.	300.	750.	4000.
S166 5 Dollars			
20.5.1777. Black. *SUSTINE VEL ABSTINE* on emblem with hand gathering food and bleeding because of pricks from thorns. Like #S105, except *H* in motto instead of *B*. Back: Betony and sage leaves. Printer: Hall & Sellers, PA.	300.	750.	4000.

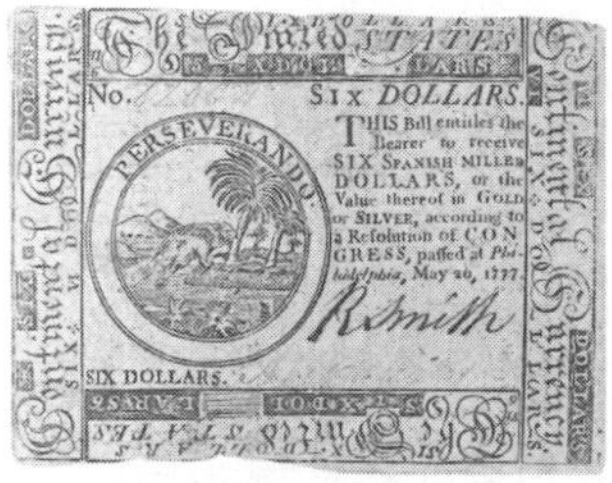

S167 6 Dollars	VG	VF	UNC
20.5.1777. Black. *PERSEVERANDO* on emblem with beaver gnawing down tree. Like #S106. Back: Buttercup leaf. Printer: Hall & Sellers, PA.	300.	750.	4000.
S168 7 Dollars			
20.5.1777. Black. *SERENABIT* on emblem with severe storm at sea. Like #S107. Back: Buttercup leaf. Printer: Hall & Sellers, PA.	300.	750.	4000.
S169 8 Dollars			
20.5.1777. Black. *MAJORA MINORIBUS CONSONANT* on emblem with harp with 13 strings representing the 13 colonies. Like #S108. Back: Henebit and two buttercups leaves. Printer: Hall & Sellers, PA.	300.	750.	4000.
S170 30 Dollars			
20.5.1777. Black. *SI RECTE FACIES* on emblem with wreath on a tomb. *VI CONCITATE* on left emblem with strong wind blowing, *CESSANTE VENTO CONQUIESCEMUS* on right. Like #S110. Back: Emblem with sun shining on ships at sea. Printer: Hall & Sellers, PA.	300.	750.	4000.

NOTE: Printings on blue paper are counterfeit detectors.

Ninth Issue, April 11, 1778

S171 4 Dollars	VG	VF	UNC
11.4.1778. Black. *AUT MORS AUT VITA DECORA* on emblem with wild boar charging into spear. Like #S104. Back: Buttercup leaf. Printer: Hall & Sellers, PA.	325.	1000.	4000.

S172 5 Dollars	VG	VF	UNC
11.4.1778. Black. *SUSTINE VEL ABSTINE* on emblem with hand gathering food and bleeding because of pricks from thorns. Like #S105 with undersigned *S* in motto. Back: Willow leaf. Printer: Hall & Sellers, PA.	325.	1000.	4000.

	VG	VF	UNC
S173 6 Dollars 11.4.1778. Black. *PERSEVERANDO* on emblem with beaver gnawing down tree. Like #S106. Back: Sage leaf. Printer: Hall & Sellers, PA.	325.	1000.	4000.
S174 7 Dollars 11.4.1778. Black. *SERENABIT* on emblem with severe storm at sea. Like #S107. Back: Grape and sage leaf. Printer: Hall & Sellers, PA.	325.	1000.	4000.

	VG	VF	UNC
S175 8 Dollars 11.4.1778. Black. *MAJORA MINORIBUS CONSONANT* on emblem with harp with 13 strings representing the 13 colonies. Like #S108. Back: Three sage leaves. Printer: Hall & Sellers, PA.	300.	900.	3500.
S176 20 Dollars 11.4.1778. Black. *VI CONCITATE* on emblem with strong wind blowing. Like #S109. Back: Buttercup leaf. Printer: Hall & Sellers, PA.	600.	1800.	8000.

	VG	VF	UNC
S177 30 Dollars 11.4.1778. Black. *SI RECTE FACIES* on emblem with wreath on a tomb. *VI CONCITATE* on left emblem with strong wind blowing, *CESSANTE VENTO CONQUIESCEMUS* on right. Like #S110. Back: Three willow leaves. Printer: Hall & Sellers, PA.	325.	1000.	4000.

	VG	VF	UNC
S178 40 Dollars 11.4.1778. Black. *CONFEDERATION* on emblem with rays of an all-seeing eye shining on 13 stars surrounding a flame. Back: Carrot leaf. Printer: Hall & Sellers, PA.	325.	1000.	4000.

NOTE: Denominations below 4 dollars were eliminated, the 20 dollars reinstated, and a 40 dollar denomination added because of inflation.

NOTE: Printings on blue paper are counterfeit detectors.

TENTH ISSUE, SEPTEMBER 26, 1778

	VG	VF	UNC
S179 5 Dollars 26.9.1778. Black. *SUSTINE VEL ABSTINE* on emblem with hand gathering food and bleeding because of pricks from thorns. Like #S105. Back: Willow leaf. Printer: Hall & Sellers, PA.	75.00	150.	500.

	VG	VF	UNC
S180 7 Dollars 26.9.1778. Black. *SERENABIT* on emblem with severe storm at sea. Like #S107. Back: Grape and sage leaf. Printer: Hall & Sellers, PA.	75.00	150.	500.
S181 8 Dollars 26.9.1778. Black. *MAJORA MINORIBUS CONSONANT* on emblem with harp with 13 strings representing the 13 colonies. Like #S108. Back: Three sage leaves. Printer: Hall & Sellers, PA.	75.00	150.	500.

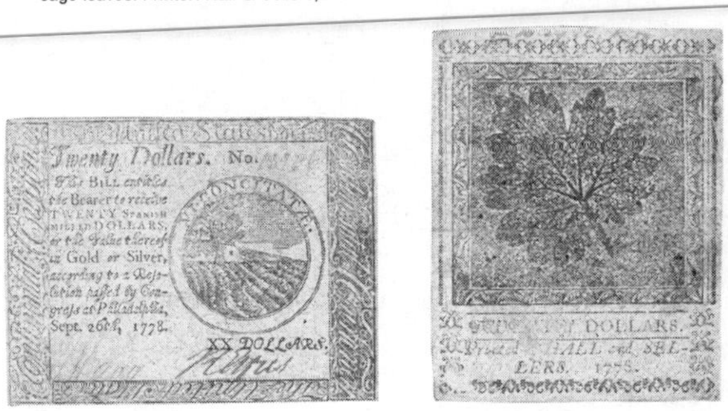

	VG	VF	UNC
S182 20 Dollars 26.9.1778. Black. *VI CONCITATE* on emblem with strong wind blowing. Like #S109. Back: Buttercup leaf. Printer: Hall & Sellers, PA.	75.00	150.	450.

	VG	VF	UNC
S183 30 Dollars 26.9.1778. Black. *SI RECTE FACIES* on emblem with wreath on a tomb. *VI CONCITATE* on left emblem with strong wind blowing, *CESSANTE VENTO CONQUIESCEMUS* on right. Like #S110. Back: Three willow leaves. Printer: Hall & Sellers, PA.	75.00	150.	450.

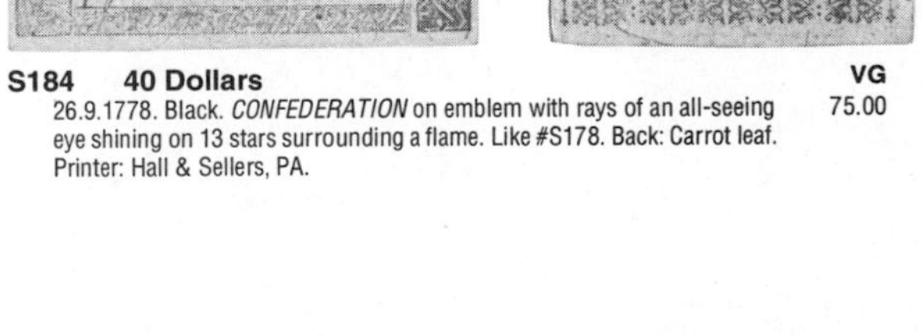

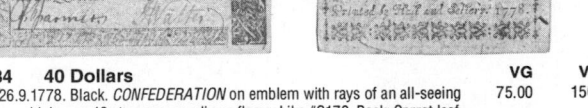

	VG	VF	UNC
S184 40 Dollars 26.9.1778. Black. *CONFEDERATION* on emblem with rays of an all-seeing eye shining on 13 stars surrounding a flame. Like #S178. Back: Carrot leaf. Printer: Hall & Sellers, PA.	75.00	150.	450.

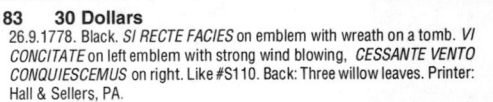

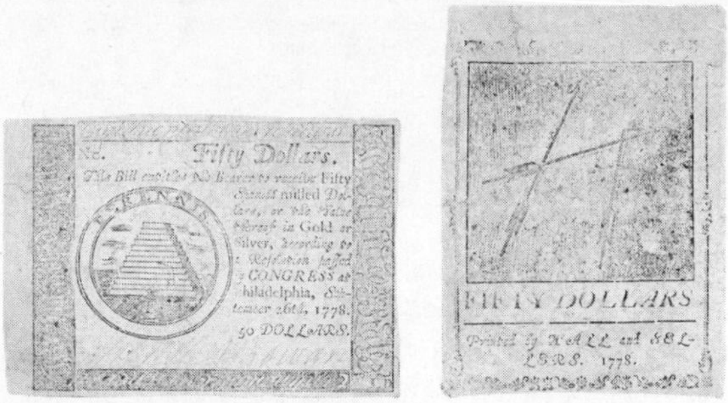

S185 50 Dollars — VG 75.00 | VF 150. | UNC 450.
26.9.1778. Black. *PERENNIS* on emblem with 13-level pyramid. Back: Three arrows. Printer: Hall & Sellers, PA.

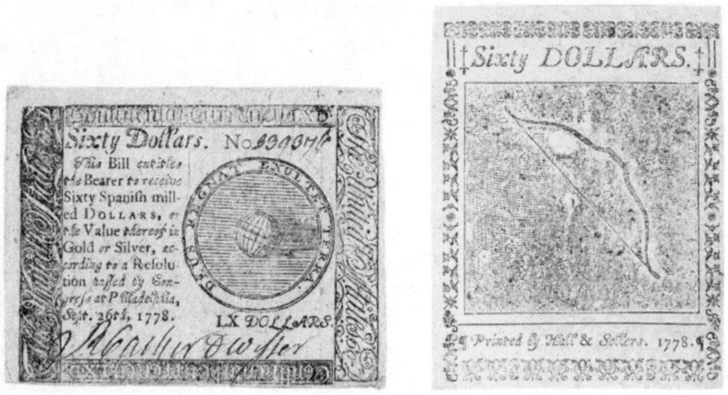

S186 60 Dollars — VG 75.00 | VF 150. | UNC 450.
26.9.1778. Black. *DEUS REGNAT EXULTET TERRA* on emblem with globe. Back: Bow. Printer: Hall & Sellers, PA.

NOTE: Printings on blue paper are counterfeit detectors.

Eleventh Issue, January 14, 1779

S187 1 Dollar — VG 125. | VF 200. | UNC 600.
14.1.1779. Black and red. *DEPRESSA RESURGIT* on emblem with weighted bowl on acanthus plant. Like #S101. Back: Tansy leaf. Printer: Hall & Sellers, PA.

S188 2 Dollars — VG 100. | VF 175. | UNC 550.
14.1.1779. Black and red. *TRIBULATIO DITAT* on emblem with grain being threshed by a flail. Like #S102. Back: Mulberry leaf. Printer: Hall & Sellers, PA.

S189 3 Dollars — VG 100. | VF 175. | UNC 550.
14.1.1779. Black and red. *EXITUS IN DUBIO EST* on emblem with an eagle attacking a heron. Like #S103. Back: Rose leaf. Printer: Hall & Sellers, PA.

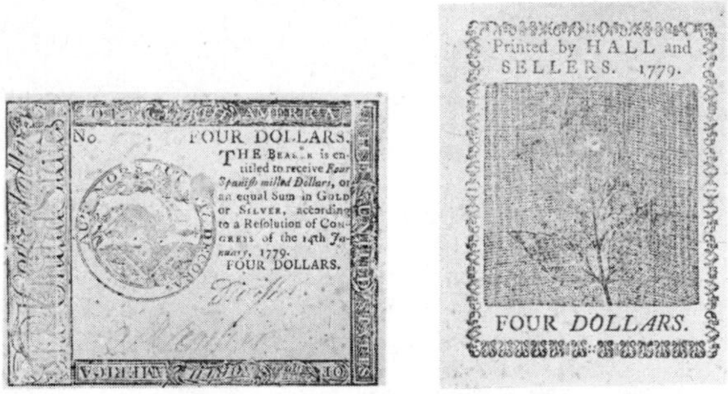

S190 4 Dollars — VG 100. | VF 175. | UNC 550.
14.1.1779. Black and red. *AUT MORS AUT VITA DECORA* on emblem with wild boar charging into spear. Like #S104. Back: Mulberry leaf. Printer: Hall & Sellers, PA.

S191 5 Dollars — VG 100. | VF 175. | UNC 550.
14.1.1779. Black and red. *SUSTINE VEL ABSTINE* on emblem with hand gathering food and bleeding because of pricks from thorns. Like #S105. Back: Fever few leaf. Printer: Hall & Sellers, PA.

S192 20 Dollars — VG 100. | VF 175. | UNC 550.
14.1.1779. Black and red. *VI CONCITATE* on emblem with strong wind blowing. Like #S109. Back: Grape leaf. Printer: Hall & Sellers, PA.

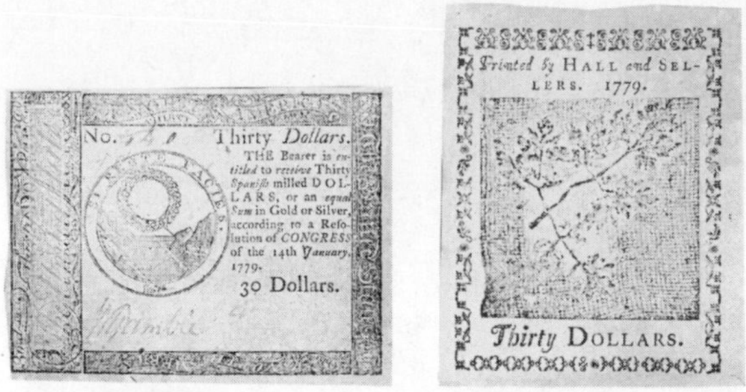

S193 30 Dollars — VG 100. | VF 175. | UNC 500.
14.1.1779. Black and red. *SI RECTE FACIES* on emblem with wreath on a tomb. *VI CONCITATE* on left emblem with strong wind blowing, *CESSANTE VENTO CONQUIESCEMUS* on right. Like #S110. Back: Climbing fumitory leaves. Printer: Hall & Sellers, PA.

S194 35 Dollars — VG 125. | VF 200. | UNC 600.
14.1.1779. Black and red. *HINC OPES* on emblem with plow in a field. Back: Two willow leaves. Printer: Hall & Sellers, PA.

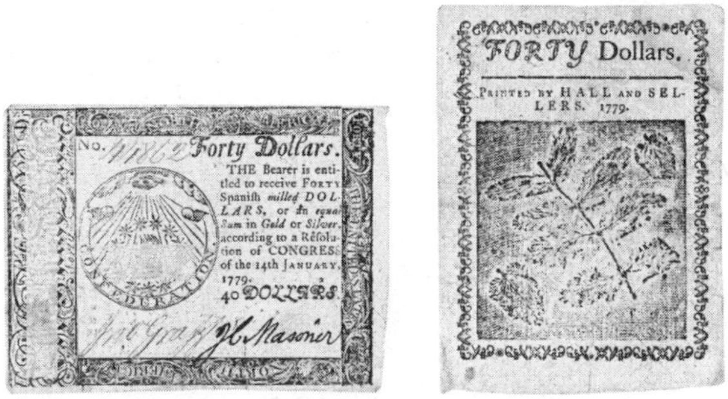

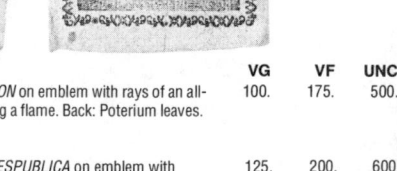

S195 40 Dollars — VG 100. | VF 175. | UNC 500.
14.1.1779. Black and red. *CONFEDERATION* on emblem with rays of an all-seeing eye shining on 13 stars surrounding a flame. Back: Poterium leaves. Printer: Hall & Sellers, PA.

S196 45 Dollars — VG 125. | VF 200. | UNC 600.
14.1.1779. Black and red. *SIC FLORET RESPUBLICA* on emblem with beehives protected by a shed. Back: Ground ivy leaves. Printer: Hall & Sellers, PA.

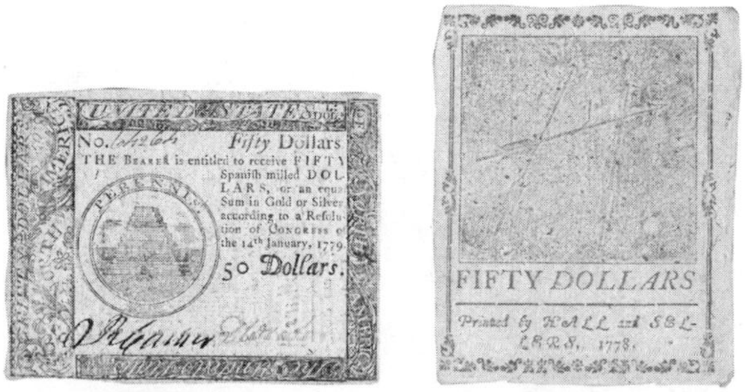

S197 50 Dollars — VG 100. | VF 175. | UNC 500.
14.1.1779. Black and red. *PERENNIS* on emblem with 13-level pyramid. Like #S185. Back: Parsley leaves. Printer: Hall & Sellers, PA.

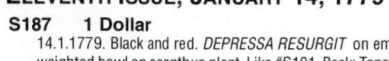

	VG	VF	UNC
S198 55 Dollars 14.1.1779. Black and red. *POST NUBILA PHOEBUS* on emblem with sun coming out after storm. Back: Willow leaf and (?) leaf. Printer: Hall & Sellers, PA.	125.	200.	600.
S199 60 Dollars 14.1.1779. Black and red. *DEUS REGNAT EXULTET TERRA* on emblem with globe. Like #S186. Back: Willow and poison hemlock leaf. Printer: Hall & Sellers, PA.	100.	175.	500.

	VG	VF	UNC
S200 65 Dollars 14.1.1779. Black and red. *FIAT JUSTITIA* on emblem with hand holding balance scale. Back: Parsley leaves. Printer: Hall & Sellers, PA.	125.	200.	600.

	VG	VF	UNC
S201 70 Dollars 14.1.1779. Black and red. *VIM PROCELLARIUM QUADRENNIUM SUSTINUIT* on emblem with tree. Back: Maple leaf. Printer: Hall & Sellers, PA.	125.	225.	750.

	VG	VF	UNC
S202 80 Dollars 14.1.1779. Black and red. *ET IN SECULA SECULORUM FLORESCEBIT* on emblem with diamond superimposed on large tree. Back: Strawberry leaf. Printer: Hall & Sellers, PA.	150.	350.	1000.

NOTE: Printings on blue paper are counterfeit detectors.

1785-1787 Indents Issue

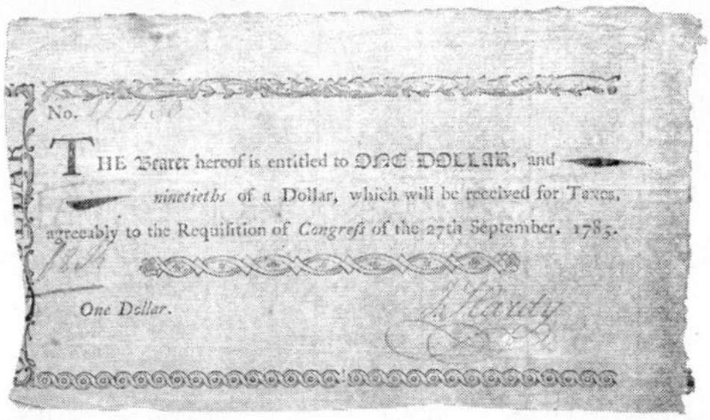

	VG	VF	UNC
S202A 1 Dollar 27.9.1785; 11.10.1787. Black. Signature of J. Hardy or M. Hillegas.	1000.	2250.	—

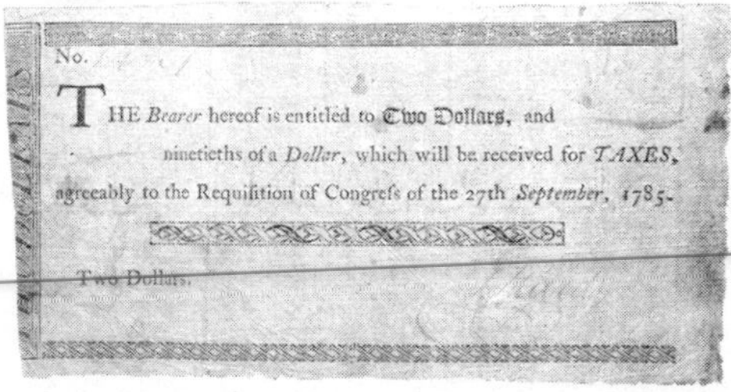

	VG	VF	UNC
S202B 2 Dollars 27.9.1785; 11.10.1787. Black. Signature of J. Hardy or M. Hillegas.	1250.	—	—

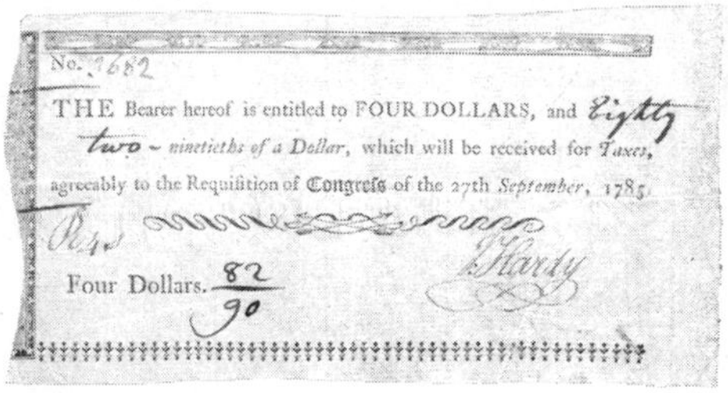

	VG	VF	UNC
S202C 4 Dollars 27.9.1785; 11.10.1787. Black. Signature of J. Hardy or M. Hillegas.	—	2250.	—
S202D 6 Dollars 27.9.1785; 11.10.1787. Black. Signature of J. Hardy or M. Hillegas.	—	2750.	—
S202E 8 Dollars 27.9.1785; 11.10.1787. Black. Signature of J. Hardy or M. Hillegas.	—	3250.	—
S202F 25 Dollars 27.9.1785; 11.10.1787. Black. Signature of J. Hardy or M. Hillegas.	—	—	—

BIBLIOGRAPHY

Newman, Eric P. *The Early Paper Money of America.* Fourth Edition, ©1997, Krause Publications, Inc., Iola, Wisconsin.

State Issues

ISSUES OF THE STATES

COLONIAL CURRENCY:

The colonial governments, continually plagued by the shortage of coins and currency began slowly to issue notes, and by 1730 most were. These early issues are rare. The notes from the revolutionary period are more frequently encountered, and some were signed by the same men who signed the Declaration of Independence. The newly independent states, as well as the Continental Congress, issued currency during the later war years and during

TABLE OF CONTENTS ALABAMA

Territo #S3417-S3448 similar to #S3395-S3416 except the word . *Military* replaces *Civil.* #S231-S235 exist with *ARKANSAS TREASURY WARRANT* printed on back in green, red or blue on white or blue paper and sometimes inverted. Various handwritten dates 1862-63. The terms *ON WAR BOND* and *ON AUDITOR'S WARRANT* (by portrait) were removed from face plates in later issues. Certain notes were printed on the backs of bills of exchange.

Alabama

State

Act of 19.12.1821 Issue

	Good	Fine	XF
S203 6 1/4 Cents 1.6.1822.	—	—	—
S204 12 1/2 Cents 1.6.1822. Stagecoach at top center.	300.	600.	1000.

		Good	Fine	XF
S205	**25 Cents** 1.6.1822. Ox with plow at top center.	500.	800.	1500.
S206	**37 1/2 Cents** 1.6.1822.	—	—	—
S207	**50 Cents** 1.6.1822.	—	—	—
S208	**75 Cents** 1.6.1822.	—	—	—

Alabama

Civil War

1863 Issue

		VG	VF	UNC
S209	**5 Cents** 1.1.1863. Black. Cotton balls at center. Engraved by J.T. Paterson & Co.	12.50	30.00	50.00

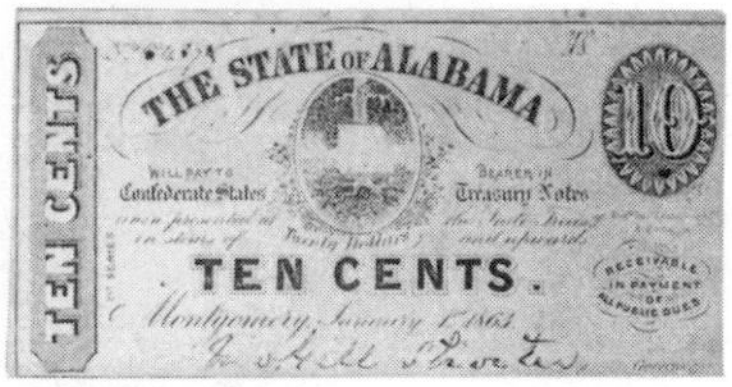

		VG	VF	UNC
S210	**10 Cents** 1.1.1863. Black. Tree with map at center. Engraved by J.T. Paterson & Co.	5.00	25.00	35.00
S211	**25 Cents** 1.1.1863. Black and red. Wagon load of cotton at center. Engraved by J.T. Paterson & Co.			
	a. Without SERIES.	5.00	25.00	35.00
	b. 2nd SERIES.	5.00	25.00	35.00
	c. 3rd SERIES.	5.00	25.00	35.00
S212	**50 Cents** 1.1.1863. Black and blue. Tree with map at center, woman at bottom right. Engraved by J.T. Paterson & Co.			
	a. Without SERIES.	5.00	20.00	30.00
	b. 2nd SERIES.	5.00	25.00	35.00

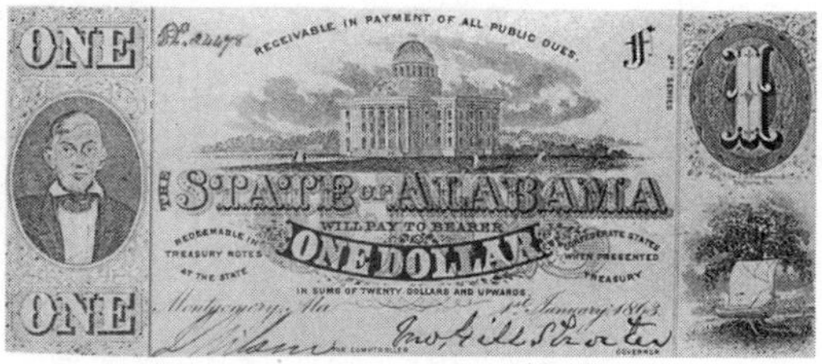

		Good	Fine	XF
S213	**1 Dollar** 1.1.1863. Black and green. Portrait Governor at left, State Capitol at center, tree with map at right. Engraved by J.T. Paterson & Co.			
	a. 1st SERIES.	5.00	20.00	30.00
	b. 2nd SERIES.	5.00	25.00	35.00

1864 Issue

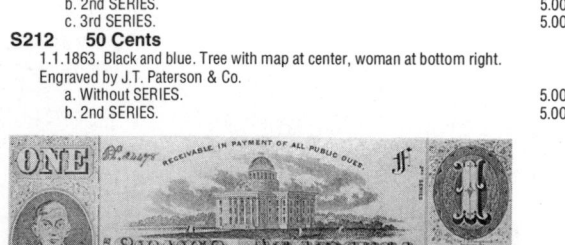

		Good	Fine	XF
S214	**5 Dollars** 1.1.1864. Black and green. Standing Liberty at left, overseer watching slaves at center, tree with map at lower right. Printer: J.T. Paterson & Co. Engraved by W. Keenan & Co.	20.00	75.00	160.
S215	**10 Dollars** 1.1.1864. Black and green. Portrait Gov. Watts at center, tree with map at bottom right. Printer: J.T. Paterson & Co. Engraved by W. Keenan & Co.	25.00	75.00	200.

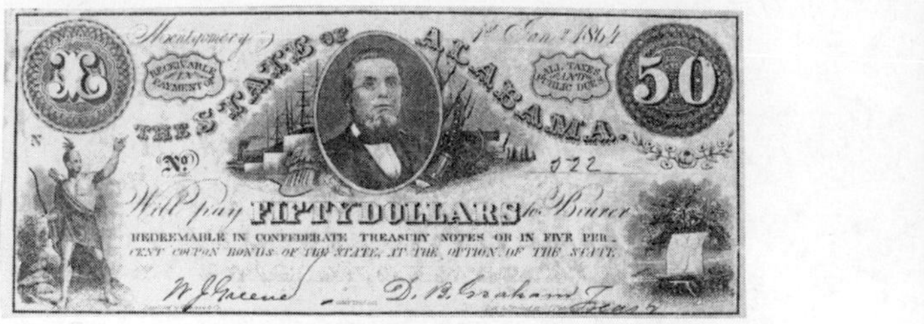

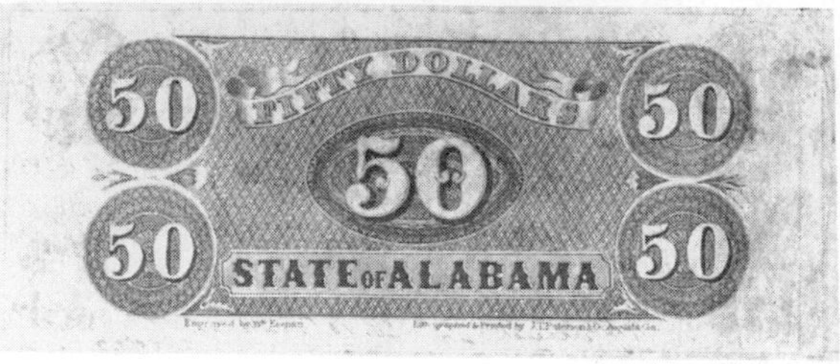

		Good	Fine	XF
S216	**50 Dollars** 1.1.1864. Black. Indian at lower left, portrait Gov. Watts at center, tree with map at lower right. Back: Green. Printer: J.T. Paterson & Co. Engraved by W. Keenan & Co.	35.00	165.	325.
S217	**100 Dollars** 1.1.1864. Black. Tree with map at lower left, group of Indians at center, seated woman by water at lower right. Back: Green. Printer: J.T. Paterson & Co. Engraved by W. Keenan & Co.	50.00	200.	400.
S218	**50 Dollars** 17.2.1864. Black. Indian at lower left, portrait Gov. Watts at center, tree with map at lower right. Similar to #S216. Back: Orange. Printer: J.T. Paterson & Co. Rare.	—	—	—

Arkansas

Civil War

Act of 1861 Issue

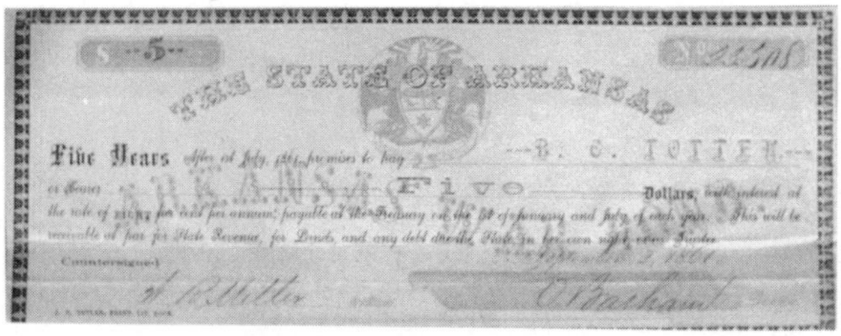

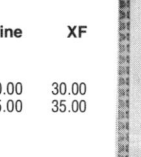

		Good	Fine	XF
S218A	**5 Dollars** 16.9.1861. Blue and red. State coat-of-arms at top center. Handwritten date.	15.00	40.00	80.00

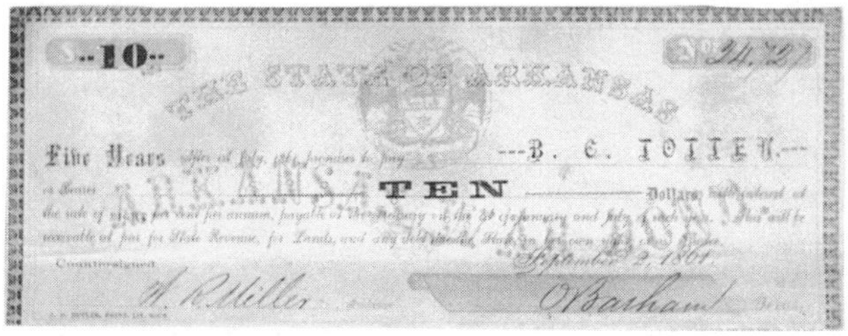

		Good	Fine	XF
S218B	**10 Dollars** 16.9.1861. Blue and red. State coat-of-arms at top center. Handwritten date.	15.00	40.00	80.00

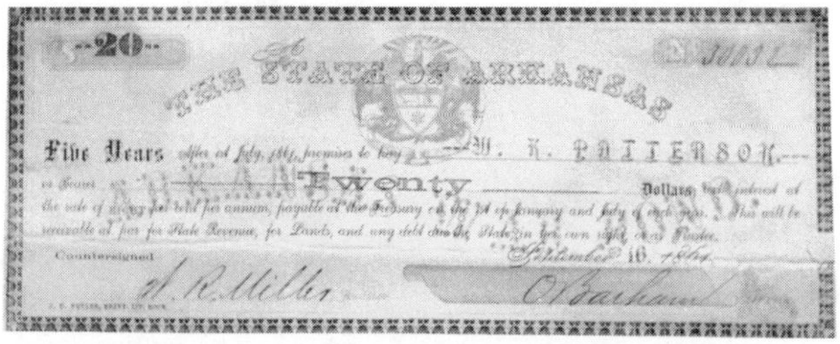

		Good	Fine	XF
S218C	**20 Dollars** 16.9.1861. Blue and red. State coat-of-arms at top center. Handwritten date.	15.00	40.00	80.00

1861 On War Bond Issue

	Good	Fine	XF
S219 1 Dollar			
30.12.1861. Black. Indian maiden at left. Various handwritten dates.			
a. White paper. Rare.	—	—	—
b. Blue paper.	250.	500.	900.
S220 2 Dollars			
1861. Indian maiden at left. Various handwritten dates. Rare.	—	—	—
S221 3 Dollars			
1861. Indian maiden at left. Various handwritten dates. Rare.	—	—	—
S222 10 Dollars			
18.12.1861. Indian maiden at left. Various handwritten dates. Rare.	—	—	—
S222A Various handwritten denominations			
(ca.1861). Indian maiden at left. Various handwritten dates.			
a. White paper.	150.	300.	500.
b. Blue paper. Rare.	—	—	—

1861-62 First On Auditor's Warrant Issue

	Good	Fine	XF
S223 1 Dollar			
9.1.1862. Indian maiden at left. Various handwritten dates. Paper: Blue. Rare.	—	—	—
S224 2 Dollars			
1861-62. Indian maiden at left. Various handwritten dates. Paper: Blue. Rare.	—	—	—
S224A Various handwritten denominations			
(ca.1861). Indian maiden at left. Various handwritten dates.			
a. White paper.	150.	350.	600.
b. Blue paper. Rare.			

1862 First On War Bond Issue

	Good	Fine	XF
S225 1 Dollar			
3.1.1862. Black. Indian brave at left.			
a. White paper.	150.	275.	400.
b. Blue paper.	150.	275.	400.

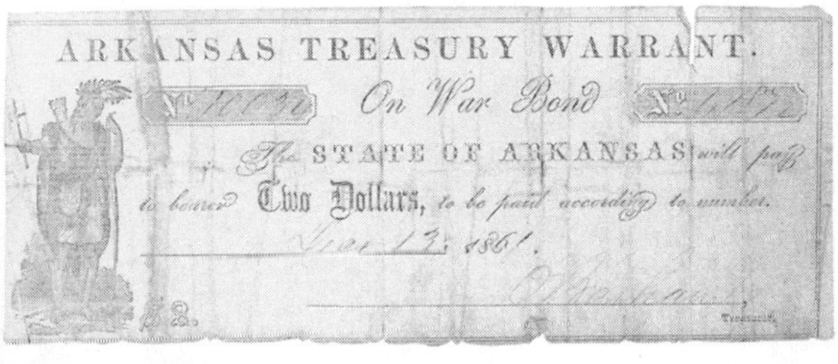

	Good	Fine	XF
S226 2 Dollars			
1861-62. Indian brave at left.	250.	800.	1500.
S227 3 Dollars			
1861-62. Indian brave at left. Rare.	—	—	—

1861-62 Second On Auditor's Warrant Issue

	Good	Fine	XF
S228 1 Dollar			
1861-62. Indian brave at left.	250.	800.	1500.
S229 2 Dollars			
1861-62. Indian brave at left.	200.	800.	1500.
S229A 10 Dollars			
(ca.1861). Indian brave at left.	300.	1000.	2500.
S229B Various handwritten denominations			
(ca.1861). Indian brave at left.			
a. White paper. Rare.	—	—	—
b. Blue paper. Rare.	—	—	—

1862 Second On War Bond Issue

	Good	Fine	XF
S230 1 Dollar			
25.7.1862. Black and white. Bust of maiden at left, state arms at upper center.	150.	300.	500.

1861-62 Third On Auditor's Warrant Issue

#S231-S235 exist with *ARKANSAS TREASURY WARRANT* printed on back in green, red or blue on white or blue paper and sometimes inverted. Various handwritten dates 1862-63. The terms *ON WAR BOND* and *ON AUDITOR'S WARRANT* (by portrait) were removed from face plates in later issues. Certain notes were printed on the backs of bills of exchange.

	Good	Fine	XF
S230A 1 Dollar			
(ca.1861). Paper: White. Rare.	—	—	—
S230B Various handwritten denominations			
(ca.1861). Bust of maiden in oval at left, Arkansas seal at center.			
a. White paper. Rare.	—	—	—
b. Blue paper. Rare.	—	—	—

#S231-S235 exist with *ARKANSAS TREASURY WARRANT* printed on back in green, red or blue on white or blue paper and sometimes inverted. Various handwritten dates 1862-63. The terms *ON WAR BOND* and *ON AUDITOR'S WARRANT* (by portr.) were removed from face plates in later issues. Certain notes were printed on the backs of bills of exchange.

	Good	Fine	XF
S231 1 Dollar			
1862-63. Black. State arms at left, portrait Jefferson Davis at center. Printer: J. D. Butler.			
a. With *ON WAR BOND.*	50.00	140.	225.
b. Without *ON WAR BOND.*	50.00	140.	225.
c. Printed on bills of exchange with *ON WAR BOND.*	50.00	140.	225.
S232 2 Dollars			
1862-63. Black. State arms at left, portrait Jefferson Davis at center. Similar to #S231. All serial letters B. Printer: J. D. Butler.			
a. With *ON WAR BOND.*	60.00	165.	250.
b. Without *ON WAR BOND.*	60.00	165.	250.
S233 3 Dollars			
1862-63. Black. State arms at left, portrait Jefferson Davis at center. Similar to #S231. Printer: J. D. Butler.			
a. With *ON WAR BOND.*	100.	175.	300.
b. Without *ON WAR BOND.*	100.	175.	300.

	Good	Fine	XF
S234 5 Dollars			
1862-63. Black. Black carrying cotton at left, portrait Governor H. M. Rector at top center, dog at bottom center. Printer: J. D. Butler.			
a. With *ON AUDITOR'S WARRANT.*	35.00	100.	165.
b. Without *ON AUDITOR'S WARRANT.*	35.00	100.	165.

	Good	Fine	XF
S235 10 Dollars			
1862-63. Black. Black carrying cotton at left, portrait Samuel Adams at top center, dog at bottom center. Printer: J. D. Butler.			
a. With *ON AUDITOR'S WARRANT.*	35.00	100.	175.
b. Without *ON AUDITOR'S WARRANT.*	35.00	100.	175.

ARKANSAS

POST CIVIL WAR

ACT OF 16.3.1871 ISSUE

	Good	Fine	XF
S236 1 Dollar 1873; 16.1.1874. Basket of corn at lower left, farmer seated with sickle at center, foliage at lower right. Printer: NBNC. Rare.	—	—	—
S237 2 Dollars 1872. Printer: NBNC. Rare.	—	—	—
S238 5 Dollars 1872. Hunter at lower left, woman seated with children at top center, woman walking with girl at lower right. Printer: NBNC. Rare.	—	—	—

	Good	Fine	XF
S239 10 Dollars 187x. Brown and black. Standing Liberty at left, horse drawn load of cotton at top center. Back: Brown. Printer: NBNC.			
a. Issued note. Rare.	—	—	—
b. Punched hole cancelled.	250.	800.	1500.
S240 10 Dollars 187x. Green and black. Back: Green. Printer: NBNC. Rare.	—	—	—

ARKANSAS

TREASURER'S CERTIFICATES

ACT OF 20.1.1875 ISSUE

	Good	Fine	XF
S241 1 Dollar 13.3.1875; 18.8.1875. Black and red on green underprint. Various handwritten dates. Rare.	—	—	—
S242 10 Dollars 18xx. Black on green underprint. Various handwritten dates. Rare.	—	—	—

CALIFORNIA

IMPERIAL GOVERNMENT OF THE U.S.

1872-79 ISSUE

	Good	Fine	XF
S242A 25 Cents ca.1872. Various handwritten dates. Reported not confirmed.	—	—	—

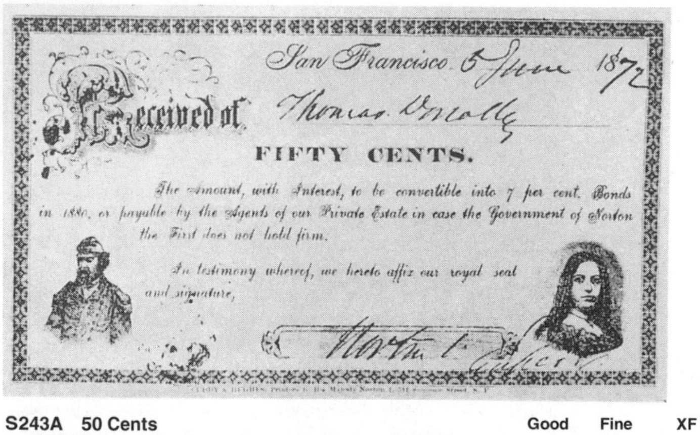

	Good	Fine	XF
S243A 50 Cents 5.6.1872. Red printing. Norton at lower left, girl at lower right with text: *CONVERTIBLE INTO 7% BONDS IN 1880.* Various handwritten dates. Rare.	—	—	—
S243B 50 Cents 30.11.1873. Norton at upper left, girl at upper right. Various handwritten dates. Rare.	—	—	—
S243C 50 Cents 11.3.1876. Standing Liberty with shield and flag at left, Norton at upper right. Various handwritten dates. Rare.	—	—	—

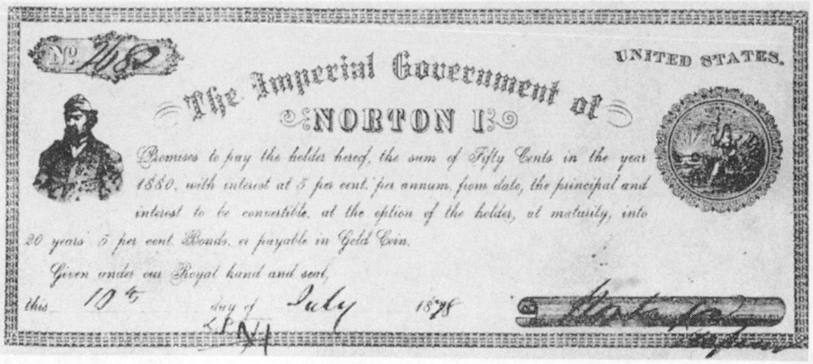

	Good	Fine	XF
S243D 50 Cents 10.7.1878. Norton at left, California seal at right with text: *CONVERTIBLE INTO 5% BONDS IN 1880.* Various handwritten dates. Rare.	—	—	—

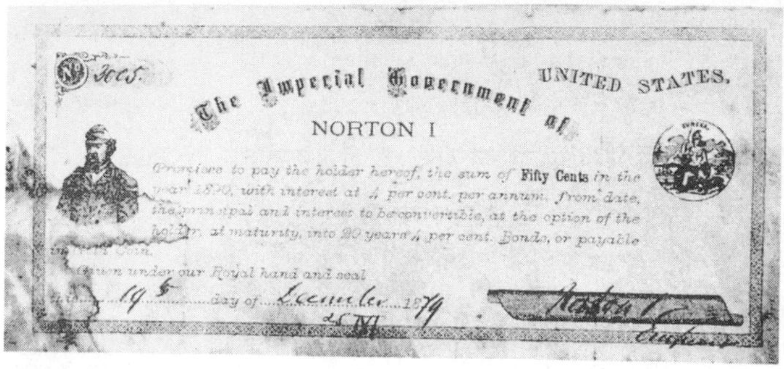

	Good	Fine	XF
S243E 50 Cents 19.12.1879. Norton at left, California seal at right with text: *CONVERTIBLE INTO 4% BONDS IN 1890.* Various handwritten dates. Rare.	—	—	—
S244A 75 Cents ca.1873. Various handwritten dates. Reported not confirmed.	—	—	—
S244B 1 Dollar ca.1873. Various handwritten dates. Reported not confirmed.	—	—	—

CONNECTICUT

COLONIAL

1709 ISSUES

	Good	Fine	XF
S245 2 Shillings 12.7.1709. Black. With motto: *SUSTINET QUI TRANSTULIT.*	—	—	—
S246 2 Shilling 6 Pence 12.7.1709. Black. With motto: *SUSTINET QUI TRANSTULIT.*	—	—	—
S248 5 Shillings 12.7.1709. Black. With motto: *SUSTINET QUI TRANSTULIT.*	—	—	—
S249 10 Shillings 12.7.1709. Black. With motto: *SUSTINET QUI TRANSTULIT.*	—	—	—
S250 20 Shillings 12.7.1709. Black. With motto: *SUSTINET QUI TRANSTULIT.*	—	—	—
S251 40 Shillings 12.7.1709. Black. With motto: *SUSTINET QUI TRANSTULIT.*	—	—	—
S252 5 Pounds 12.7.1709. Black. With motto: *SUSTINET QUI TRANSTULIT.*	—	—	—

1709 MONOGRAMMED *AR* ISSUE

	Good	Fine	XF
S253 2 Shillings 12.7.1709. Black.	—	—	—
S254 2 Shillings 6 Pence 12.7.1709. Black.	—	—	—
S255 3 Shillings 12.7.1709. Black.	—	—	—
S256 5 Shillings 12.7.1709. Black.	—	—	—
S257 10 Shillings 12.7.1709. Black.	—	—	—
S258 20 Shillings 12.7.1709. Black.	—	—	—
S259 40 Shillings 12.7.1709. Black.	—	—	—
S260 5 Pounds 12.7.1709. Black.	—	—	—

1713 FIRST REDATED ISSUE

	Good	Fine	XF
S261 2 Shillings May 1713 (- old date 12.7.1709). Black. Back: Scroll.	—	—	—
S262 2 Shillings 6 Pence May 1713 (- old date 12.7.1709). Black. Back: Scroll.	—	—	—
S263 3 Shillings May 1713 (- old date 12.7.1709). Black. Back: Scroll.	—	—	—
S264 5 Shillings May 1713 (- old date 12.7.1709). Black. Back: Scroll.	—	—	—
S265 10 Shillings May 1713 (- old date 12.7.1709). Black. Lamb. Back: Scroll.	—	—	—
S266 20 Shillings May 1713 (- old date 12.7.1709). Black. Deer. Back: Scroll.	—	—	—

No.	Denomination	Description	Good	Fine	XF
S267	40 Shillings	May 1713. (- old date 12.7.1709). Black. Horse. Back: Scroll.	—	—	—
S268	5 Pounds	May 1713 (- old date 12.7.1709). Black. Lion. Back: Scroll.	—	—	—

1713 Second Redated Issue

No.	Denomination	Description	Good	Fine	XF
S269	2 Shillings	May 1713 (- old date 12.7.1709). Black. Back: Flowers. Printer: Timothy Green.	—	—	—
S270	2 Shillings 6 Pence	May 1713; 12.7.1709. Black. Back: Flowers. Printer: Timothy Green.	—	—	—
S271	3 Shillings	May 1713 (- old date 12.7.1709). Black. Back: Flowers. Printer: Timothy Green.	—	—	—
S272	5 Shillings	May 1713 (- old date 12.7.1709). Black. Back: Flowers. Printer: Timothy Green.	—	—	—
S273	10 Shillings	May 1713 (- old date 12.7.1709). Black. Back: Flowers. Printer: Timothy Green.	—	—	—
S274	20 Shillings	May 1713 (- old date 12.7.1709). Black. Back: Flowers. Printer: Timothy Green.	—	—	—
S275	40 Pounds	May 1713 (- old date 12.7.1709). Black. Back: Flowers. Printer: Timothy Green.	—	—	—
S276	5 Pounds	May 1713 (- old date 12.7.1709). Black. Back: Flowers. Printer: Timothy Green.	—	—	—

1724 Issue

No.	Denomination	Description	Good	Fine	XF
S277	10 Shillings	1.12.1724. Black. Printer: Timothy Green.	—	—	—
S278	20 Shillings	1.12.1724. Black. Printer: Timothy Green.	—	—	—
S279	40 Shillings	1.12.1724. Black. Printer: Timothy Green.	—	—	—
S280	5 Pounds	1.12.1724. Black. Printer: Timothy Green.	—	—	—

1727 Issue

No.	Denomination	Description	Good	Fine	XF
S281	2 Shillings	7.11.1727. Black. Printer: Timothy Green.	—	—	—
S282	2 Shilling 6 Pence	7.11.1727. Black. Printer: Timothy Green.	—	—	—
S283	3 Shillings	7.11.1727. Black. Printer: Timothy Green.	—	—	—
S284	5 Shillings	7.11.1727. Black. Printer: Timothy Green.	—	—	—
S285	10 Shillings	7.11.1727. Black. Printer: Timothy Green.	—	—	—
S286	20 Shillings	7.11.1727. Black. Printer: Timothy Green.	—	—	—
S287	40 Shillings	7.11.1727. Black. Printer: Timothy Green.	—	—	—
S288	5 Pounds	7.11.1727. Black. Printer: Timothy Green.	—	—	—

1728 Issue

No.	Denomination	Description	Good	Fine	XF
S289	10 Shillings	Oct. 1728. Black. Printer: Timothy Green.	—	—	—
S290	20 Shillings	Oct. 1728. Black. Printer: Timothy Green.	—	—	—
S291	40 Shillings	Oct. 1728. Black. Printer: Timothy Green.	—	—	—
S292	5 Pounds	Oct. 1728. Black. Printer: Timothy Green.	—	—	—

1729 Issue

No.	Denomination	Description	Good	Fine	XF
S293	2 Shillings	May 1729. Black. Printer: Timothy Green.	—	—	—
S294	2 Shillings 6 Pence	May 1729. Black. Printer: Timothy Green.	—	—	—
S295	3 Shillings	May 1729. Black. Printer: Timothy Green.	—	—	—
S296	5 Shillings	May 1729. Black. Printer: Timothy Green.	—	—	—
S297	10 Shillings	May 1729. Black. Printer: Timothy Green.	—	—	—
S298	20 Shillings	May 1729. Black. Printer: Timothy Green.	—	—	—
S299	40 Shillings	May 1729. Black. Printer: Timothy Green.	—	—	—
S300	5 Pounds	May 1729. Black. Printer: Timothy Green.	—	—	—

1732 Issue

No.	Denomination	Description	Good	Fine	XF
S301	2 Shillings	Aug. 1732. Black. *AMOR PATRIAE UICIT.* Printer: Timothy Green.	—	—	—
S302	2 Shillings 6 Pence	Aug. 1732. Black. *AMOR PATRIAE UICIT.* Printer: Timothy Green.	—	—	—
S303	3 Shillings	Aug. 1732. Black. *AMOR PATRIAE UICIT.* Printer: Timothy Green.	—	—	—
S304	5 Shillings	Aug. 1732. Black. *AMOR PATRIAE UICIT.* Printer: Timothy Green.	—	—	—
S305	10 Shillings	Aug. 1732. Black. *AMOR PATRIAE UICIT.* Printer: Timothy Green.	—	—	—
S306	20 Shillings	Aug. 1732. Black. *AMOR PATRIAE UICIT.* Printer: Timothy Green.	—	—	—
S307	40 Shillings	Aug. 1732. Black. *AMOR PATRIAE UICIT.* Printer: Timothy Green.	—	—	—
S308	5 Pounds	Aug. 1732. Black. *AMOR PATRIAE UICIT.* Printer: Timothy Green.	—	—	—

1733 Issue

No.	Denomination	Description	Good	Fine	XF
S309	2 Shillings	10.7.1733. Black. Dove. Printer: Timothy Green.	—	—	—
S310	2 Shillings 6 Pence	10.7.1733. Black. Cock. Printer: Timothy Green.	—	—	—
S311	3 Shillings	10.7.1733. Black. Squirrel. Printer: Timothy Green.	—	—	—
S312	5 Shillings	10.7.1733. Black. Fox. Printer: Timothy Green.	—	—	—
S313	10 Shillings	10.7.1733. Black. Lamb. Printer: Timothy Green.	—	—	—
S314	20 Shillings	10.7.1733. Black. Deer. Printer: Timothy Green.	—	—	—
S315	40 Shillings	10.7.1733. Black. Horse. Printer: Timothy Green.	—	—	—
S316	5 Pounds	10.7.1733. Black. Lion. Printer: Timothy Green.	—	—	—

1735 Redated Issue

No.	Denomination	Description	Good	Fine	XF
S317	2 Shillings	1735. (- old date 10.7.1733). Black. Dove. Printer: Timothy Green.	—	—	—
S318	2 Shillings 6 Pence	1735. (- old date 10.7.1733). Black. Cock. Printer: Timothy Green.	—	—	—
S319	3 Shillings	1735 (- old date 10.7.1733). Black. Squirrel. Printer: Timothy Green.	—	—	—
S320	5 Shillings	1735 (- old date 10.7.1733). Black. Fox. Printer: Timothy Green.	—	—	—
S321	10 Shillings	1735 (- old date 10.7.1733). Black. Lamb. Printer: Timothy Green.	—	—	—
S322	20 Shillings	1735 (- old date 10.7.1733). Black. Deer. Printer: Timothy Green.	—	—	—
S323	40 Shillings	1735 (- old date 10.7.1733). Black. Horse. Printer: Timothy Green.	—	—	—
S324	5 Pounds	1735 (- old date 10.7.1733). Black. Lion. Printer: Timothy Green.	—	—	—

1740 First Redated Issue

No.	Denomination	Description	Good	Fine	XF
S325	10 Shillings	May 1740 (- old date 10.7.1733). Black. Printer: Timothy Green.	—	—	—
S326	20 Shillings	May 1740 (- old date 10.7.1733). Black. Printer: Timothy Green.	—	—	—
S327	40 Shillings	May 1740 (- old date 10.7.1733). Black. Printer: Timothy Green.	—	—	—
S328	5 Pounds	May 1740. (- old date 10.7.1733). Black. Printer: Timothy Green.	—	—	—

1740 Issue

No.	Denomination	Description	Good	Fine	XF
S329	1 Shilling	8.5.1740. Black. Printer: Timothy Green.	—	—	—
S330	2 Shillings	8.5.1740. Black. Printer: Timothy Green.	—	—	—
S331	4 Shillings	8.5.1740. Black. Printer: Timothy Green.	—	—	—
S332	7 Shillings	8.5.1740. Black. Printer: Timothy Green.	—	—	—
S333	12 Shillings	8.5.1740. Black. Printer: Timothy Green.	—	—	—
S334	20 Shillings	8.5.1740. Black. Printer: Timothy Green.	—	—	—
S335	40 Shillings	8.5.1740. Black. Printer: Timothy Green.	—	—	—
S336	3 Pounds	8.5.1740. Black. Printer: Timothy Green.	—	—	—

1740 Second Redated Issue

No.	Denomination	Description	Good	Fine	XF
S337	10 Shillings	May, 1740/8.7.1740 (- old date 10.7.1733). Lamb.	—	—	—
S338	20 Shillings	May, 1740/8.7.1740 (- old date 10.7.1733). Deer.	—	—	—
S339	40 Shillings	May, 1740/8.7.1740 (- old date 10.7.1733). Horse.	—	—	—
			VG	VF	UNC
S340	5 Pounds	May, 1740/8.7.1740 (- old date 10.7.1733). Lion.	10,000.	25,000.	

1744 Redated Issues

No.	Denomination	Description	Good	Fine	XF
S341	1 Shilling	10.5.1744 (- old date 8.5.1740). Black. Printer: Timothy Green.	—	—	—
S342	2 Shillings	10.5.1744 (- old date 8.5.1740). Black. Printer: Timothy Green.	—	—	—
S343	4 Shillings	10.5.1744 (- old date 8.5.1740). Black. Printer: Timothy Green.	—	—	—
S344	7 Shillings	10.5.1744 (- old date 8.5.1740). Black. Printer: Timothy Green.	—	—	—
S345	12 Shillings	10.5.1744 (- old date 8.5.1740). Black. Printer: Timothy Green.	—	—	—
S346	20 Shillings	10.5.1744 (- old date 8.5.1740). Black. Printer: Timothy Green.	—	—	—
S347	40 Shillings	10.5.1744 (- old date 8.5.1740). Black. Printer: Timothy Green.	—	—	—
S348	3 Pounds	10.5.1744 (- old date 8.5.1740). Black. Printer: Timothy Green.	—	—	—
S349	1 Shilling	11.10.1744 (- old date 8.5.1740). Black. Printer: Timothy Green.	—	—	—
S350	2 Shillings	11.10.1744 (- old date 8.5.1740). Black. Printer: Timothy Green.	—	—	—

No.	Denomination	Good	Fine	XF
S351	**4 Shillings** 11.10.1744 (- old date 8.5.1740). Black. Printer: Timothy Green.	—	—	—
S352	**7 Shillings** 11.10.1744 (- old date 8.5.1740). Black. Printer: Timothy Green.	—	—	—
S353	**12 Shillings** 11.10.1744 (- old date 8.5.1740). Black. Printer: Timothy Green.	—	—	—
S354	**20 Shillings** 11.10.1744 (- old date 8.5.1740). Black. Printer: Timothy Green.	—	—	—
S355	**40 Shillings** 11.10.1744 (- old date 8.5.1740). Black. Printer: Timothy Green.	—	—	—
S356	**3 Pounds** 11.10.1744 (- old date 8.5.1740). Black. Printer: Timothy Green.	—	—	—

1744/45 Redated Issue

No.	Denomination	Good	Fine	XF
S357	**1 Shilling** 14.3.1744/45 (- old date 8.5.1740). Black. Printer: Timothy Green.	—	—	—
S358	**2 Shillings** 14.3.1744/45 (- old date 8.5.1740). Black. Printer: Timothy Green.	—	—	—
S359	**4 Shillings** 14.3.1744/45 (- old date 8.5.1740). Black. Printer: Timothy Green.	—	—	—
S360	**7 Shillings** 14.3.1744/45 (- old date 8.5.1740). Black. Printer: Timothy Green.	—	—	—
S361	**12 Shillings** 14.3.1744/45 (- old date 8.5.1740). Black. Printer: Timothy Green.	—	—	—
S362	**20 Shillings** 14.3.1744/45 (- old date 8.5.1740). Black. Printer: Timothy Green.	—	—	—
S363	**40 Shillings** 14.3.1744/45 (- old date 8.5.1740). Black. Printer: Timothy Green.	—	—	—
S364	**3 Pounds** 14.3.1744/45 (- old date 8.5.1740). Black. Printer: Timothy Green.	—	—	—

1746 Redated Issues

(Redated May 8, 1746.)

No.	Denomination	Good	Fine	XF
S365	**2 Shillings** 8.5.1746 (- old date 10.7.1733). Black. Dove. Printer: Timothy Green.	—	—	—

No.	Denomination	Good	Fine	XF
S366	**2 Shilling 6 Pence** 8.5.1746 (- old date 10.7.1733). Black. Cock. Printer: Timothy Green.	—	—	—
S367	**3 Shillings** 8.5.1746 (- old date 10.7.1733). Black. Squirrel. Printer: Timothy Green.	—	—	—
S368	**5 Shillings** 8.5.1746 (- old date 10.7.1733). Black. Fox. Printer: Timothy Green.	—	—	—
S369	**1 Shilling** 8.5.1746 (- old date - 8.5.1740). Black. Printer: Timothy Green.	—	—	—
S370	**2 Shillings** (- old date 8.5.1740). Black. Paper: 8.5.1746 Printer: Timothy Green.	—	—	—
S371	**4 Shillings** 8.5.1746 (- old date 8.5.1740). Black. Printer: Timothy Green.	—	—	—
S372	**7 Shillings** 8.5.1746 (- old date 8.5.1740). Black. Printer: Timothy Green.	—	—	—
S373	**12 Shillings** 8.5.1746 (- old date 8.5.1740). Black. Printer: Timothy Green.	—	—	—
S374	**20 Shillings** 8.5.1746 (- old date 8.5.1740). Black. Printer: Timothy Green.	—	—	—
S375	**40 Shillings** 8.5.1746 (- old date 8.5.1740). Black. Printer: Timothy Green.	—	—	—
S376	**3 Pounds** 8.5.1746 (- old date 8.5.1740). Black. Printer: Timothy Green.	—	—	—

1755 Issues

No.	Denomination	Good	Fine	XF
S377	**9 Pence** 8.1.1755. Black. Printer: Timothy Green.	—	—	—
S378	**1 Shilling** 8.1.1755. Black. Printer: Timothy Green.	—	—	—
S379	**2 Shillings 6 Pence** 8.1.1755. Black. Printer: Timothy Green.	—	—	—
S380	**5 Shillings** 8.1.1755. Black. Printer: Timothy Green.	—	—	—
S381	**10 Shillings** 8.1.1755. Black. Printer: Timothy Green.	—	—	—
S382	**20 Shillings** 8.1.1755. Black. Printer: Timothy Green.	—	—	—
S383	**30 Shillings** 8.1.1755. Black. Printer: Timothy Green.	—	—	—
S384	**40 Shillings** 8.1.1755. Black. Printer: Timothy Green.	—	—	—
S385	**9 Pence** 13.3.1755. Black. Printer: Timothy Green.	—	—	—
S386	**1 Shilling** 13.3.1755. Black. Printer: Timothy Green.	—	—	—
S387	**2 Shillings 6 Pence** 13.3.1755. Black. Printer: Timothy Green.	—	—	—

No.	Denomination	Good	Fine	XF
S388	**5 Shillings** 13.3.1755. Black. Printer: Timothy Green.	—	—	—
S389	**10 Shillings** 13.3.1755. Black. Printer: Timothy Green.	—	—	—
S390	**20 Shillings** 13.3.1755. Black. Printer: Timothy Green.	—	—	—
S391	**30 Shillings** 13.3.1755. Black. Printer: Timothy Green.	—	—	—
S392	**40 Shillings** 13.3.1755. Black. Printer: Timothy Green.	—	—	—
S393	**9 Pence** 27.8.1755. Black. Printer: Timothy Green.	—	—	—
S394	**1 Shilling** 27.8.1755. Black. Printer: Timothy Green.	—	—	—
S395	**2 Shillings 6 Pence** 27.8.1755. Black. Printer: Timothy Green.	—	—	—
S396	**5 Shillings** 27.8.1755. Black. Printer: Timothy Green.	—	—	—
S397	**10 Shillings** 27.8.1755. Black. Printer: Timothy Green.	—	—	—
S398	**20 Shillings** 27.8.1755. Black. Printer: Timothy Green.	—	—	—
S399	**30 Shillings** 27.8.1755. Black. Printer: Timothy Green.	—	—	—
S400	**40 Shillings** 27.8.1755. Black. Printer: Timothy Green.	—	—	—
S401	**9 Pence** 9.10.1755. Black. Printer: Timothy Green.	—	—	—
S402	**1 Shilling** 9.10.1755. Black. Printer: Timothy Green.	—	—	—
S403	**2 Shillings 6 Pence** 9.10.1755. Black. Printer: Timothy Green.	—	—	—
S404	**5 Shillings** 9.10.1755. Black. Printer: Timothy Green.	—	—	—
S405	**10 Shillings** 9.10.1755. Black. Printer: Timothy Green.	—	—	—
S406	**20 Shillings** 9.10.1755. Black. Printer: Timothy Green.	—	—	—
S407	**30 Shillings** 9.10.1755. Black. Printer: Timothy Green.	—	—	—
S408	**40 Shillings** 9.10.1755. Black. Printer: Timothy Green.	—	—	—

1758 Issue

No.	Denomination	Good	Fine	XF
S409	**9 Pence** 8.3.1758. Black. Printer: Timothy Green.	—	—	—
S410	**1 Shilling** 8.3.1758. Black. Printer: Timothy Green.	—	—	—
S411	**2 Shillings 6 Pence** 8.3.1758. Black. Printer: Timothy Green.	—	—	—
S412	**5 Shillings** 8.3.1758. Black. Printer: Timothy Green.	—	—	—
S413	**10 Shillings** 8.3.1758. Black. Printer: Timothy Green.	—	—	—
S414	**20 Shillings** 8.3.1758. Black. Printer: Timothy Green.	—	—	—
S415	**30 Shillings** 8.3.1758. Black. Printer: Timothy Green.	—	—	—
S416	**40 Shillings** 8.3.1758. Black. Printer: Timothy Green.	—	—	—

1759 First Issue

No.	Denomination	Good	Fine	XF
S417	**9 Pence** 7.2.1759. Black. Printer: Timothy Green.	—	—	—
S418	**1 Shilling** 7.2.1759. Black. Printer: Timothy Green.	—	—	—
S419	**2 Shillings 6 Pence** 7.2.1759. Black. Printer: Timothy Green.	—	—	—
S420	**5 Shillings** 7.2.1759. Black. Printer: Timothy Green.	—	—	—
S421	**10 Shillings** 7.2.1759. Black. Printer: Timothy Green.	—	—	—
S422	**20 Shillings** 7.2.1759. Black. Printer: Timothy Green.	—	—	—
S423	**30 Shillings** 7.2.1759. Black. Printer: Timothy Green.	—	—	—
S424	**40 Shillings** 7.2.1759. Black. Printer: Timothy Green.	—	—	—

1759 Second Issue

No.	Denomination	Good	Fine	XF
S425	**9 Pence** 8.3.1759. Black. Printer: Timothy Green.	1250.	2750.	—
S426	**1 Shilling** 8.3.1759. Black. Printer: Timothy Green.	1250.	2750.	—
S427	**2 Shillings 6 Pence** 8.3.1759. Black. Printer: Timothy Green.	1250.	2750.	—
S428	**5 Shillings** 8.3.1759. Black. Printer: Timothy Green.	1250.	2750.	—
S429	**10 Shillings** 8.3.1759. Black. Printer: Timothy Green.	1250.	2750.	—
S430	**20 Shillings** 8.3.1759. Black. Printer: Timothy Green.	1250.	2750.	—
S431	**30 Shillings** 8.3.1759. Black. Printer: Timothy Green.	1250.	2750.	—
S432	**40 Shillings** 8.3.1759. Black. Printer: Timothy Green.	1250.	2750.	—

1759 Third Issue

No.	Denomination	Good	Fine	XF
S433	**9 Pence** 10.5.1759. Black. Printer: Timothy Green.	1250.	2750.	—

		Good	Fine	XF
S434	**1 Shilling** 10.5.1759. Black. Printer: Timothy Green.	1250.	2750.	—
S435	**2 Shillings 6 Pence** 10.5.1759. Black. Printer: Timothy Green.	1250.	2750.	—
S436	**5 Shillings** 10.5.1759. Black. Printer: Timothy Green.	1250.	2750.	—
S437	**10 Shillings** 10.5.1759. Black. Printer: Timothy Green.	1250.	2750.	—
S438	**20 Shillings** 10.5.1759. Black. Printer: Timothy Green.	1250.	2750.	—
S439	**30 Shillings** 10.5.1759. Black. Printer: Timothy Green.	1250.	2750.	—
S440	**40 Shillings** 10.5.1759. Black. Printer: Timothy Green.	1250.	2750.	—

1760 Issue

		Good	Fine	XF
S441	**9 Pence** 13.3.1760. Black. Printer: Timothy Green.	1250.	2750.	—
S442	**1 Shilling** 13.3.1760. Black. Printer: Timothy Green.	1250.	2750.	—
S443	**2 Shillings 6 Pence** 13.3.1760. Black. Printer: Timothy Green.	1250.	2750.	—
S444	**5 Shillings** 13.3.1760. Black. Printer: Timothy Green.	1250.	2750.	—
S445	**10 Shillings** 13.3.1760. Black. Printer: Timothy Green.	1250.	2750.	—
S446	**20 Shillings** 13.3.1760. Black. Printer: Timothy Green.	1250.	2750.	—
S447	**30 Shillings** 13.3.1760. Black. Printer: Timothy Green.	1250.	2750.	—
S448	**40 Shillings** 13.3.1760. Black. Printer: Timothy Green.	1250.	2750.	—

1761 Issue

		Good	Fine	XF
S449	**9 Pence** 26.3.1761. Black. Printer: Timothy Green.	—	—	—
S450	**1 Shilling** 26.3.1761. Black. Printer: Timothy Green.	—	—	—
S451	**2 Shillings 6 Pence** 26.3.1761. Black. Printer: Timothy Green.	—	—	—
S452	**5 Shillings** 26.3.1761. Black. Printer: Timothy Green.	—	—	—
S453	**10 Shillings** 26.3.1761. Black. Printer: Timothy Green.	—	—	—
S454	**20 Shillings** 26.3.1761. Black. Printer: Timothy Green.	—	—	—
S455	**30 Shillings** 26.3.1761. Black. Printer: Timothy Green.	—	—	—
S456	**40 Shillings** 26.3.1761. Black. Printer: Timothy Green.	—	—	—

1762 Issue

		Good	Fine	XF
S457	**9 Pence** 4.3.1762. Black. Printer: Timothy Green.	—	—	—
S458	**1 Shilling** 4.3.1762. Black. Printer: Timothy Green.	—	—	—
S459	**2 Shillings 6 Pence** 4.3.1762. Black. Printer: Timothy Green.	—	—	—
S460	**5 Shillings** 4.3.1762. Black. Printer: Timothy Green.	—	—	—
S461	**10 Shillings** 4.3.1762. Black. Printer: Timothy Green.	—	—	—
S462	**20 Shillings** 4.3.1762. Black. Printer: Timothy Green.	—	—	—
S463	**30 Shillings** 4.3.1762. Black. Printer: Timothy Green.	—	—	—
S464	**40 Shillings** 4.3.1762. Black. Printer: Timothy Green.	—	—	—

1763 Issue

		Good	Fine	XF
S465	**5 Shillings** 12.5.1763. Black. Printer: Timothy Green.	1250.	2750.	—
S466	**10 Shillings** 12.5.1763. Black. Printer: Timothy Green.	1250.	2750.	—
S467	**20 Shillings** 12.5.1763. Black. Printer: Timothy Green.	1250.	2750.	—
S468	**30 Shillings** 12.5.1763. Black. Printer: Timothy Green.	1250.	2750.	—
S469	**40 Shillings** 12.5.1763. Black. Printer: Timothy Green.	1250.	2750.	—

1764 Issue

		Good	Fine	XF
S470	**9 Pence** 8.3.1764. Black. Printer: Timothy Green. Rare.	—	—	—
S471	**1 Shilling** 8.3.1764. Black. Printer: Timothy Green. Rare.	—	—	—
S472	**1 Shilling 6 Pence** 8.3.1764. Black. Printer: Timothy Green. Rare.	—	—	—
S473	**2 Shillings** 8.3.1764. Black. Printer: Timothy Green. Rare.	—	—	—
S474	**5 Shillings** 8.3.1764. Black. Printer: Timothy Green. Rare.	—	—	—
S475	**10 Shillings** 8.3.1764. Black. Printer: Timothy Green.	1000.	2500.	—
S476	**20 Shillings** 8.3.1764. Black. Printer: Timothy Green.	1000.	2500.	—
S477	**30 Shillings** 8.3.1764. Black. Printer: Timothy Green.	1000.	2500.	—
S478	**40 Shillings** 8.3.1764. Black. Printer: Timothy Green.	1000.	2500.	—

1770 Issue

		Good	Fine	XF
S479	**2 Shillings 6 Pence** 10.5.1770. Black. Printer: Timothy Green.	250.	1000.	—
S480	**5 Shillings** 10.5.1770. Black. Printer: Timothy Green.	250.	1000.	—
S481	**10 Shillings** 10.5.1770. Black. Printer: Timothy Green. Rare.	—	—	—
S482	**20 Shillings** 10.5.1770. Black. Printer: Timothy Green. Rare.	—	—	—
S483	**40 Shillings** 10.5.1770. Black. Printer: Timothy Green. Rare.	—	—	—

1771 Issue

		VG	VF	UNC
S484	**2 Shillings 6 Pence** 10.10.1771. Black. Printer: Timothy Green.	300.	1000.	—
S485	**5 Shillings** 10.10.1771. Black. Printer: Timothy Green.	300.	1000.	—
S486	**10 Shillings** 10.10.1771. Black. Printer: Timothy Green.	300.	1000.	—
S487	**20 Shillings** 10.10.1771. Black. Printer: Timothy Green.	300.	1000.	—
S488	**40 Shillings** 10.10.1771. Black. Printer: Timothy Green.	300.	1000.	—

1773 Issue

		VG	VF	UNC
S489	**2 Shillings 6 Pence** 1.6.1773. Black. Printer: Timothy Green.	225.	900.	—
S490	**5 Shillings** 1.6.1773. Black. Printer: Timothy Green.	225.	900.	—
S491	**10 Shillings** 1.6.1773. Black. Printer: Timothy Green.	225.	900.	—
S492	**20 Shillings** 1.6.1773. Black. Printer: Timothy Green.	225.	900.	—
S493	**40 Shillings** 1.6.1773. Black. Printer: Timothy Green.	225.	900.	—

1775 First Issue

		VG	VF	UNC
S494	**2 Shillings 6 Pence** 2.1.1775. Black. Printer: Timothy Green.	150.	600.	—
S495	**5 Shillings** 2.1.1775. Black. Printer: Timothy Green.	150.	600.	—
S496	**10 Shillings** 2.1.1775. Black. Printer: Timothy Green.	150.	600.	—
S497	**20 Shillings** 2.1.1775. Black. Printer: Timothy Green.	150.	600.	—
S498	**40 Shillings** 2.1.1775. Black. Printer: Timothy Green.	150.	600.	—

1775 Second Issue

		VG	VF	UNC
S499	**2 Shillings 6 Pence** 10.5.1775. Black. Printer: Timothy Green.	200.	800.	—
S500	**10 Shillings** 10.5.1775. Black. Printer: Timothy Green.	200.	800.	—
S501	**20 Shillings** 10.5.1775. Black. Printer: Timothy Green.	200.	800.	—
S502	**40 Shillings** 10.5.1775. Black. Printer: Timothy Green.	100.	400.	—

1775 Third Issue

		VG	VF	UNC
S503	**2 Shillings 6 Pence** 1.6.1775. Black. Printer: Timothy Green.	125.	250.	—
S504	**6 Shillings** 1.6.1775. Black. Printer: Timothy Green.	125.	250.	—
S505	**10 Shillings** 1.6.1775. Black. Printer: Timothy Green.	125.	250.	—

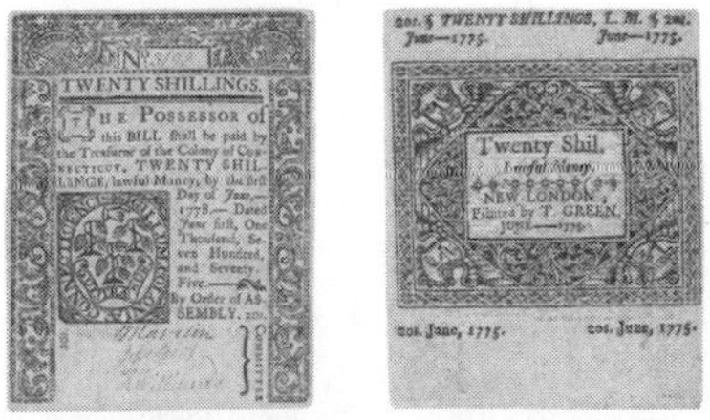

		VG	VF	UNC
S506	**20 Shillings** 1.6.1775. Black. Printer: Timothy Green.	100.	200.	500.

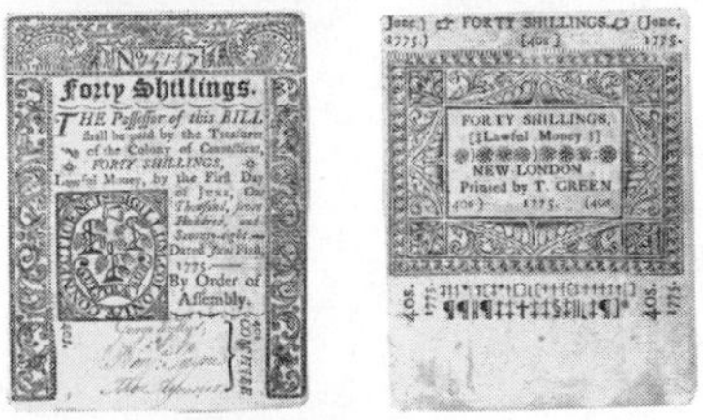

		VG	VF	UNC
S507	**40 Shillings** 1.6.1775. Black. Printer: Timothy Green.	100.	200.	500.

1775 Fourth Issue

		VG	VF	UNC
S508	**2 Shillings** 1.7.1775. Black. Printer: Timothy Green.	200.	600.	—
S509	**2 Shillings 6 Pence** 1.7.1775. Black. Printer: Timothy Green.	200.	600.	—

	VG	VF	UNC
S510 6 Shillings 1.7.1775. Black. Printer: Timothy Green.	200.	600.	—
S511 10 Shillings 1.7.1775. Black. Printer: Timothy Green.	200.	600.	—
S512 20 Shillings 1.7.1775. Black. Printer: Timothy Green.	200.	600.	—
S513 40 Shillings 1.7.1775. Black. Printer: Timothy Green.	100.	250.	500.

CONNECTICUT

STATE

1776 FIRST ISSUE

	VG	VF	UNC
S514 1 Shilling 7.6.1776. Black. Printer: Timothy Green.	100.	150.	400.
S515 1 Shilling 3 Pence 7.6.1776. Black. Printer: Timothy Green.	200.	300.	—
S516 2 Shillings 7.6.1776. Black. Printer: Timothy Green.	200.	300.	—
S517 2 Shillings 6 Pence 7.6.1776. Black. Printer: Timothy Green.	200.	300.	—
S518 3 Shillings 7.6.1776. Black. Printer: Timothy Green.	200.	300.	—

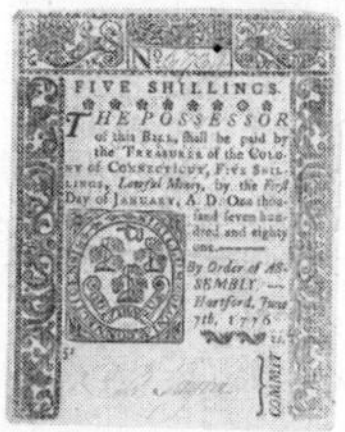
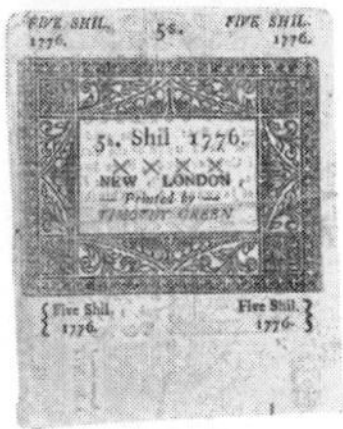

	VG	VF	UNC
S519 5 Shillings 7.6.1776. Black. Printer: Timothy Green.	200.	300.	—
S520 6 Shillings 7.6.1776. Black. Printer: Timothy Green.	—	—	—
S521 10 Shillings 7.6.1776. Black. Printer: Timothy Green.	—	—	—
S522 15 Shillings 7.6.1776. Black. Printer: Timothy Green.	—	—	—
S523 1 Pound 7.6.1776. Black. Printer: Timothy Green.	—	—	—
S524 2 Pounds 7.6.1776. Black. Printer: Timothy Green.	—	—	—

1776 SECOND ISSUE

	VG	VF	UNC
S525 6 Pence 19.6.1776. Black. Printer: Timothy Green.	100.	200.	400.
S526 9 Pence 19.6.1776. Black. Printer: Timothy Green.	100.	200.	400.
S527 1 Shilling 19.6.1776. Black. Printer: Timothy Green.	150.	225.	—

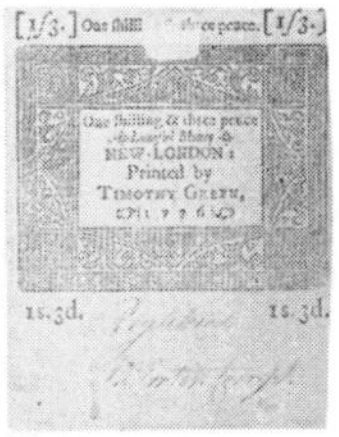

	VG	VF	UNC
S528 1 Shilling 3 Pence 19.6.1776. Black. Printer: Timothy Green.	150.	225.	—
S529 1 Shilling 6 Pence 19.6.1776. Black. Printer: Timothy Green.	150.	225.	—
S530 2 Shillings 19.6.1776. Black. Printer: Timothy Green.	150.	225.	—
S531 2 Shillings 6 Pence 19.6.1776. Black. Printer: Timothy Green.	150.	225.	—
S532 5 Shillings 19.6.1776. Black. Printer: Timothy Green.	150.	225.	—
S532A 20 Shillings 19.6.1776. Black. Printer: Timothy Green.	150.	225.	—
S533 40 Shillings 19.6.1776. Black. Printer: Timothy Green.	150.	225.	—

1777 ISSUE

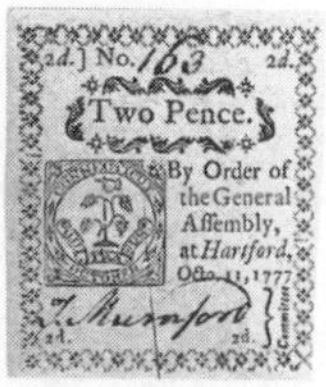

	VG	VF	UNC
S534 2 Pence 11.10.1777. Black. Uniface. White paper.	125.	175.	—
S535 3 Pence 11.10.1777. Black. Uniface.			
a. White paper.	125.	175.	—
b. Blue paper.	125.	175.	—
S536 4 Pence 11.10.1777. Black. Uniface.			
a. White paper.	125.	175.	—
b. Blue paper.	125.	175.	—

	VG	VF	UNC
S537 5 Pence 11.10.1777. Black. Uniface.			
a. White paper.	125.	175.	—
b. Blue paper.	125.	175.	—
S538 7 Pence 11.10.1777. Black. Uniface.			
a. White paper.	125.	175.	—
b. Blue paper.	125.	175.	—

1780 FIRST ISSUE

	VG	VF	UNC
S539 9 Pence 1.3.1780. Black. Printer: Timothy Green.	25.00	50.00	150.
S540 1 Shilling 3 Pence 1.3.1780. Black. Printer: Timothy Green.	25.00	50.00	150.
S541 2 Shillings 6 Pence 1.3.1780. Black. Printer: Timothy Green.	25.00	50.00	150.
S542 5 Shillings 1.3.1780. Black. Printer: Timothy Green.	25.00	50.00	150.

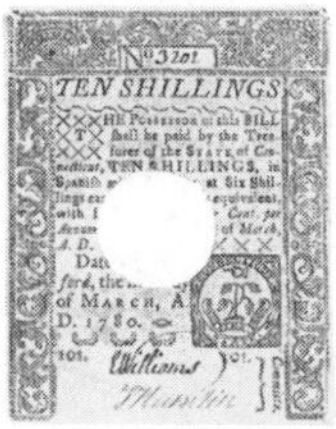
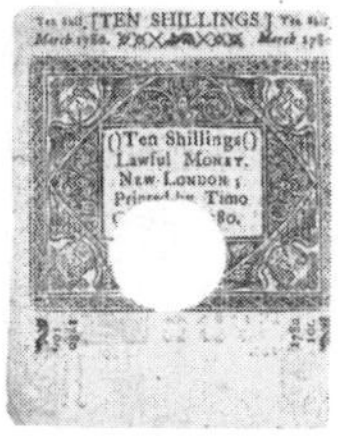

	VG	VF	UNC
S543 10 Shillings 1.3.1780. Black. Printer: Timothy Green.	25.00	50.00	150.
S544 20 Shillings 1.3.1780. Black. Printer: Timothy Green.	25.00	50.00	150.
S545 40 Shillings 1.3.1780. Black. Printer: Timothy Green.	25.00	50.00	150.

1780 SECOND ISSUE

	VG	VF	UNC
S546 9 Pence 1.6.1780. Black. Printer: Timothy Green.	30.00	75.00	200.

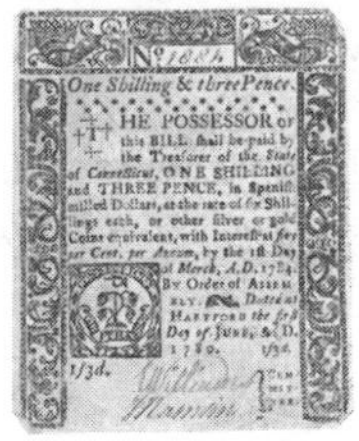

	VG	VF	UNC
S547 1 Shilling 3 Pence 1.6.1780. Black. Printer: Timothy Green.	30.00	75.00	200.
S548 2 Shillings 6 Pence 1.6.1780. Black. Printer: Timothy Green.	30.00	75.00	200.
S549 5 Shillings 1.6.1780. Black. Printer: Timothy Green.	30.00	75.00	200.
S550 10 Shillings 1.6.1780. Black. Printer: Timothy Green.	30.00	75.00	200.
S551 20 Shillings 1.6.1780. Black. Printer: Timothy Green.	30.00	75.00	200.
S552 40 Shillings 1.6.1780. Black. Printer: Timothy Green.	30.00	75.00	200.

1780 THIRD ISSUE

	VG	VF	UNC
S553 9 Pence 1.7.1780. Black. Printer: Timothy Green.	30.00	75.00	200.
S554 1 Shilling 1.7.1780. Black. Printer: Timothy Green.	30.00	75.00	200.
S555 1 Shilling 3 Pence 1.7.1780. Black. Printer: Timothy Green.	30.00	75.00	200.

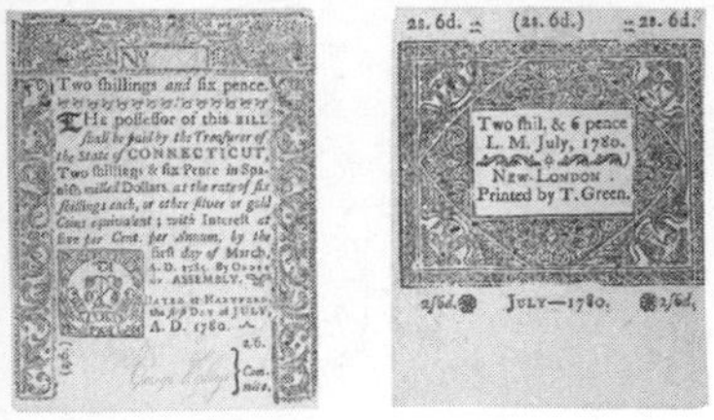

		VG	VF	UNC
S556	**2 Shillings 6 Pence** 1.7.1780. Black. Printer: Timothy Green.	30.00	75.00	200.
S557	**5 Shillings** 1.7.1780. Black. Printer: Timothy Green.	30.00	75.00	200.
S558	**10 Shillings** 1.7.1780. Black. Printer: Timothy Green.	30.00	75.00	200.
S559	**20 Shillings** 1.7.1780. Black. Printer: Timothy Green.	30.00	75.00	200.
S560	**40 Shillings** 1.7.1780. Black. Printer: Timothy Green.	30.00	75.00	200.

Delaware

Colonial

1729 Issue

No.	Denomination / Description	Good	Fine	XF
S561	**1 Shilling** 1729. Black.	—	—	—
S562	**18 Pence** 1729. Black.	—	—	—
S563	**2 Shillings** 1729. Black.	—	—	—
S564	**2 Shillings 6 Pence** 1729. Black.	—	—	—
S565	**5 Shillings** 1729. Black.	—	—	—
S566	**10 Shillings** 1729. Black.	—	—	—
S567	**15 Shillings** 1729. Black.	—	—	—
S568	**20 Shillings** 1729. Black.	—	—	—

1734 Issue

No.	Denomination / Description	Good	Fine	XF
S569	**1 Shilling** 1.3.1734. Black. Uniface. Printer: Benjamin Franklin.	—	—	—
S570	**18 Pence** 1.3.1734. Black. Uniface. Printer: Benjamin Franklin.	—	—	—
S571	**2 Shillings** 1.3.1734. Black. Uniface. Printer: Benjamin Franklin.	—	—	—
S572	**2 Shillings 6 Pence** 1.3.1734. Black. Uniface. Printer: Benjamin Franklin.	—	—	—
S573	**5 Shillings** 1.3.1734. Black. Uniface. Printer: Benjamin Franklin.	—	—	—
S574	**10 Shillings** 1.3.1734. Black. Uniface. Printer: Benjamin Franklin.	—	—	—
		VG	VF	UNC
S575	**15 Shillings** 1.3.1734. Black. Uniface. Printer: Benjamin Franklin.	5000.	—	—
S576	**20 Shillings** 1.3.1734. Black. Uniface. Printer: Benjamin Franklin.	—	—	—

1739 Issue

No.	Denomination / Description	Good	Fine	XF
S577	**1 Shilling** 1.12.1739. Black. Uniface. Printer: Benjamin Franklin.	—	—	—
		VG	VF	UNC
S578	**18 Pence** 1.12.1739. Black. Uniface. Printer: Benjamin Franklin.	1500.	—	—
S579	**2 Shillings** 1.12.1739. Black. Uniface. Printer: Benjamin Franklin.	—	3250.	—
S580	**2 Shillings 6 Pence** 1.12.1739. Black. Uniface. Printer: Benjamin Franklin.	—	—	—
S581	**5 Shillings** 1.12.1739. Black. Uniface. Printer: Benjamin Franklin.	—	—	—
S582	**10 Shillings** 1.12.1739. Black. Uniface. Printer: Benjamin Franklin.	—	—	—

1746 Issue

No.	Denomination / Description	Good	Fine	XF
S583	**1 Shilling** 28.2.1746. Black. Uniface. Printer: Benjamin Franklin.	—	—	—
S584	**18 Pence** 28.2.1746. Black. Uniface. Printer: Benjamin Franklin.	—	—	—
S585	**2 Shillings** 28.2.1746. Black. Uniface. Printer: Benjamin Franklin.	—	—	—
S586	**2 Shillings 6 Pence** 28.2.1746. Black. Uniface. Printer: Benjamin Franklin.	—	—	—
S587	**5 Shillings** 28.2.1746. Black. Back: Sea serpents. Printer: Benjamin Franklin.	—	—	—
S588	**10 Shillings** 28.2.1746. Black. Back: Elephant and leaves. Printer: Benjamin Franklin.	—	—	—
S589	**15 Shillings** 28.2.1746. Black. Back: Horse and sage leaf. Printer: Benjamin Franklin.	—	—	—
S590	**20 Shillings** 28.2.1746. Black. Back: Lion and parsley. Printer: Benjamin Franklin.	—	—	—

1753 Issue

No.	Denomination / Description	Good	Fine	XF
S591	**1 Shilling** 1.1.1753. Black. Uniface. Printer: Benjamin Franklin and David Hall.	—	—	—
S592	**18 Pence** 1.1.1753. Black. Uniface. Printer: Benjamin Franklin and David Hall.	—	—	—
S593	**2 Shillings** 1.1.1753. Black. Uniface. Printer: Benjamin Franklin and David Hall.	—	—	—
S594	**2 Shillings 6 Pence** 1.1.1753. Black. Uniface. Printer: Benjamin Franklin and David Hall.	—	—	—
S595	**5 Shillings** 1.1.1753. Black. Back: Sea serpents and blackberry leaf. Printer: Benjamin Franklin and David Hall.	—	—	—
S596	**10 Shillings** 1.1.1753. Black. Back: Elephant and leaves. Printer: Benjamin Franklin and David Hall.	—	—	—

1756 Issue

No.	Denomination / Description	Good	Fine	XF
S597	**1 Shilling** 1.5.1756. Black. Uniface. Printer: Benjamin Franklin and David Hall.	—	—	—
S598	**18 Pence** 1.5.1756. Black. Uniface. Printer: Benjamin Franklin and David Hall.	—	—	—
S599	**2 Shillings** 1.5.1756. Black. Uniface. Printer: Benjamin Franklin and David Hall.	—	—	—
S600	**2 Shillings 6 Pence** 1.5.1756. Black. Uniface. Printer: Benjamin Franklin and David Hall.	—	—	—
		VG	VF	UNC
S601	**5 Shillings** 1.5.1756. Black. Back: Sea serpents and blackberry leaf. Printer: Benjamin Franklin and David Hall.	750.	—	—
S602	**10 Shillings** 1.5.1756. Black. Back: Elephant and leaves. Printer: Benjamin Franklin and David Hall.	750.	—	—
S603	**15 Shillings** 1.5.1756. Black. Back: Horse and sage leaf. Printer: Benjamin Franklin and David Hall.	750.	—	—
S604	**20 Shillings** 1.5.1756. Black. Back: Lion and parsley. Printer: Benjamin Franklin and David Hall.	750.	—	—

1758 First Issue

No.	Denomination / Description	Good	Fine	XF
S605	**1 Shilling** 1.3.1758. Black. Printer: Benjamin Franklin and David Hall.	—	—	—
S606	**18 Pence** 1.3.1758. Black. Printer: Benjamin Franklin and David Hall.	—	—	—
S607	**2 Shillings** 1.3.1758. Black. Printer: Benjamin Franklin and David Hall.	—	—	—
S608	**2 Shillings 6 Pence** 1.3.1758. Black. Printer: Benjamin Franklin and David Hall.	—	—	—
S609	**5 Shillings** 1.3.1758. Black. Back: Like #S586. Printer: Benjamin Franklin and David Hall.	200.	600.	—
S610	**10 Shillings** 1.3.1758. Black. Back: Elephant and maple leaf. Printer: Benjamin Franklin and David Hall.	200.	600.	—
S611	**15 Shillings** 1.3.1758. Black. Back: Elephant and leaves. Like #S588. Printer: Benjamin Franklin and David Hall.	200.	600.	—
S612	**20 Shillings** 1.3.1758. Black. Back: Lion and assorted leaves. Printer: Benjamin Franklin and David Hall.	200.	600.	—

1758 Second Issue

No.	Denomination / Description	Good	Fine	XF
S613	**1 Shilling** 1.5.1758. Black. Printer: Benjamin Franklin and David Hall.	—	—	—
S614	**1 Shilling 6 Pence** 1.5.1758. Black. Printer: Benjamin Franklin and David Hall.	—	—	—
S615	**2 Shillings** 1.5.1758. Black. Printer: Benjamin Franklin and David Hall.	—	—	—
S616	**2 Shillings 6 Pence** 1.5.1758. Black. Printer: Benjamin Franklin and David Hall.	—	—	—
S617	**5 Shillings** 1.5.1758. Black. Back: Like #S586. Printer: Benjamin Franklin and David Hall.	250.	1000.	—
S618	**10 Shillings** 1.5.1758. Black. Back: Sea serpents and blackberry leaf. Like #S595. Printer: Benjamin Franklin and David Hall.	250.	1000.	—
S619	**15 Shillings** 1.5.1758. Black. Back: Elephant and leaves. Like #S588. Printer: Benjamin Franklin and David Hall.	250.	1000.	—
S620	**20 Shillings** 1.5.1758. Black. Back: Like #S597. Printer: Benjamin Franklin and David Hall.	250.	1000.	—

1759 Issue

No.	Denomination / Description	Good	Fine	XF
S621	**1 Shilling** 1.6.1759. Black. Uniface. Printer: Benjamin Franklin and David Hall. Rare.	—	—	—
S622	**1 Shilling 6 Pence** 1.6.1759. Black. Uniface. Printer: Benjamin Franklin and David Hall. Rare.	—	—	—
S623	**2 Shillings** 1.6.1759. Black. Uniface. Printer: Benjamin Franklin and David Hall. Rare.	—	—	—
S624	**2 Shillings 6 Pence** 1.6.1759. Black. Uniface. Printer: Benjamin Franklin and David Hall. Rare.	—	—	—
S625	**5 Shillings** 1.6.1759. Black. Back: Sea serpents. Printer: Benjamin Franklin and David Hall.	400.	1200.	7000.
S626	**10 Shillings** 1.6.1759. Black. Back: Squirrel, elephant, and bird. Printer: Benjamin Franklin and David Hall.	400.	1200.	7000.

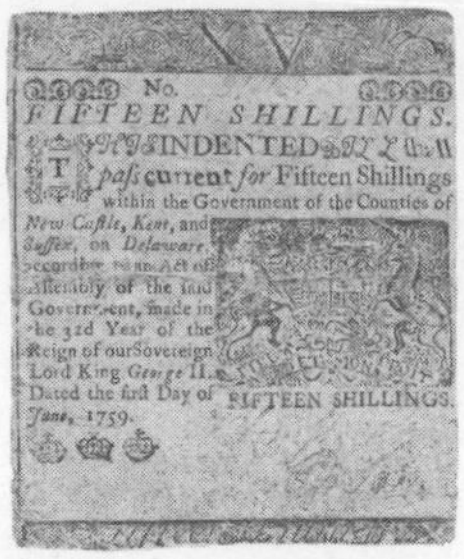

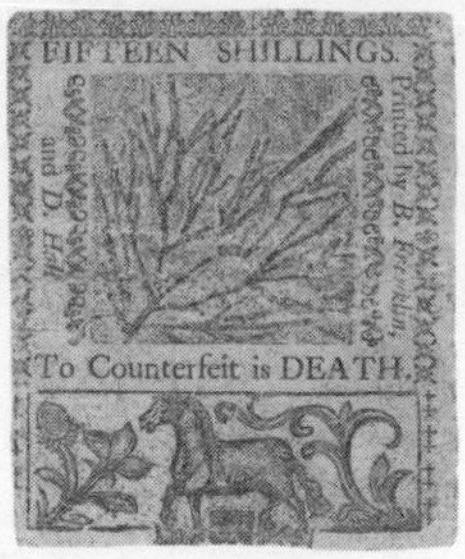

		Good	Fine	XF
S627	**15 Shillings** 1.6.1759. Black. Back: Horse. Printer: Benjamin Franklin and David Hall.	300.	1000.	3000.
S628	**20 Shillings** 1.6.1759. Black. Back: Lion with period over center of *Y*. Printer: Benjamin Franklin and David Hall.	250.	800.	2500.
S629	**20 Shillings** 1.6.1759. Black. Back: Lion with period past right side of *Y*. Printer: Benjamin Franklin and David Hall.	250.	800.	2500.

1760 Issue

		Good	Fine	XF
S630	**20 Shillings** 31.5.1760. Black and red. Printer: Benjamin Franklin and David Hall.	300.	1500.	7000.
S631	**30 Shillings** 31.5.1760. Black and red. *I* omitted in each *THRTY*. Printer: Benjamin Franklin and David Hall.	300.	1500.	7000.
S632	**40 Shillings** 31.5.1760. Black and red. *D* reversed in borders. Printer: Benjamin Franklin and David Hall.	300.	1500.	7000.
S633	**50 Shillings** 31.5.1760. Black and red. Printer: Benjamin Franklin and David Hall.	300.	1500.	7000.

1776 Issue

		VG	VF	UNC
S634	**1 Shilling** 1.1.1776. Black. Back: With cuts of a sheaf of wheat. Printer: James Adams. Thick paper containing blue fibres and mica flakes.	75.00	150.	500.
S635	**18 Pence** 1.1.1776. Black. Back: With cuts of a sheaf of wheat. Printer: James Adams. Thick paper containing blue fibres and mica flakes.	75.00	150.	500.
S636	**2 Shillings 6 Pence** 1.1.1776. Black. Back: With cuts of a sheaf of wheat. Printer: James Adams. Thick paper containing blue fibres and mica flakes.	75.00	150.	500.
S637	**4 Shillings** 1.1.1776. Black. Back: With cuts of a sheaf of wheat. Printer: James Adams. Thick paper containing blue fibres and mica flakes.	75.00	150.	500.
S638	**5 Shillings** 1.1.1776. Black. Back: With cuts of a sheaf of wheat. Printer: James Adams. Thick paper containing blue fibres and mica flakes.	75.00	150.	500.

		VG	VF	UNC
S639	**6 Shillings** 1.1.1776. Black. Back: With cuts of a sheaf of wheat. Printer: James Adams. Thick paper containing blue fibres and mica flakes.	75.00	150.	500.

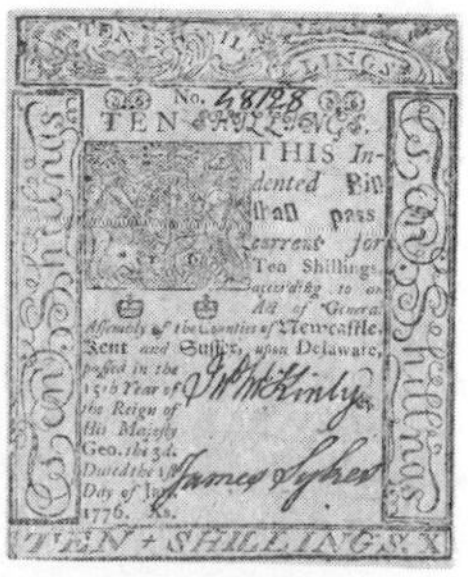

		VG	VF	UNC
S640	**10 Shillings** 1.1.1776. Black. Back: With cuts of a sheaf of wheat. Printer: James Adams. Thick paper containing blue fibres and mica flakes.	75.00	150.	500.

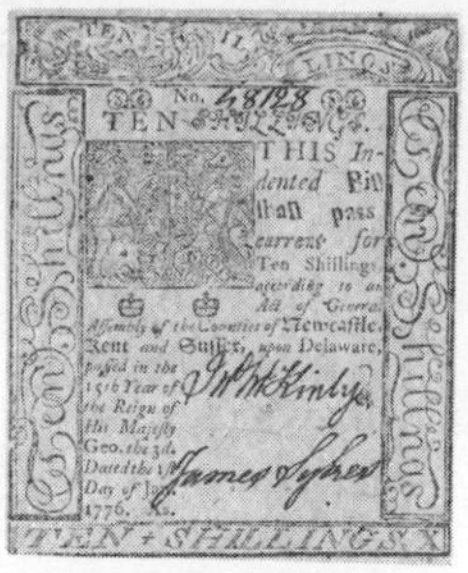

		VG	VF	UNC
S641	**20 Shillings** 1.1.1776. Black. Back: With cuts of a sheaf of wheat. Printer: James Adams. Thick paper containing blue fibres and mica flakes.	75.00	150.	500.

Delaware

State

1777 Issue

		VG	VF	UNC
S642	**3 Pence** 1.5.1777. Black. Back: With cuts of a sheaf of wheat. Printer: James Adams. Thick paper containing blue fibres and mica flakes.	125.	250.	750.
S643	**4 Pence** 1.5.1777. Black. Back: With cuts of a sheaf of wheat. Printer: James Adams. Thick paper containing blue fibres and mica flakes.	125.	250.	750.
S644	**6 Pence** 1.5.1777. Black. Back: With cuts of a sheaf of wheat. Printer: James Adams. Thick paper containing blue fibres and mica flakes.	125.	250.	750.
S645	**9 Pence** 1.5.1777. Black. Back: With cuts of a sheaf of wheat. Printer: James Adams. Thick paper containing blue fibres and mica flakes.	125.	250.	750.
S646	**1 Shilling** 1.5.1777. Black. Back: With cuts of a sheaf of wheat. Printer: James Adams. Thick paper containing blue fibres and mica flakes.	150.	325.	1000.
S647	**1 Shilling 6 Pence** 1.5.1777. Black. Back: With cuts of a sheaf of wheat. Printer: James Adams. Thick paper containing blue fibres and mica flakes.	150.	325.	1000.
S648	**2 Shillings 6 Pence** 1.5.1777. Black. Back: With cuts of a sheaf of wheat. Printer: James Adams. Thick paper containing blue fibres and mica flakes.	150.	325.	1000.
S649	**4 Shillings** 1.5.1777. Black. Back: With cuts of a sheaf of wheat. Printer: James Adams. Thick paper containing blue fibres and mica flakes.	150.	325.	1000.
S650	**5 Shillings** 1.5.1777. Black. Back: With cuts of a sheaf of wheat. Printer: James Adams. Thick paper containing blue fibres and mica flakes.	150.	325.	1000.
S651	**6 Shillings** 1.5.1777. Black. Back: With cuts of a sheaf of wheat. Printer: James Adams. Thick paper containing blue fibres and mica flakes.	150.	325.	1000.
S652	**10 Shillings** 1.5.1777. Black. Back: With cuts of a sheaf of wheat. Printer: James Adams. Thick paper containing blue fibres and mica flakes.	150.	325.	1000.
S653	**20 Shillings** 1.5.1777. Black. Back: With cuts of a sheaf of wheat. Printer: James Adams. Thick paper containing blue fibres and mica flakes.	150.	325.	1000.

Florida

Amelia Island

Custom House Issue

		Good	Fine	XF
S655	**6 1/4 Cents** 19.8.1817. Fernandina. Rare.	—	—	—

Florida

Territory

1829 Treasury Issue

		Good	Fine	XF
S656	**50 Cents** 16.1.1829. Date handwritten. Without vignettes. Rare.	—	—	—
S657	**1 Dollar** 15.2.1829. Date handwritten. Without vignettes. Rare.	—	—	—
S658	**2 Dollars** 17.2.1829. Date handwritten. Without vignettes. Rare.	—	—	—
S659	**3 Dollars** 15.1.1829. Date handwritten. Without vignettes. Rare.	—	—	—
S660	**5 Dollars** 18.2.1829. Date handwritten. Without vignettes. Rare.	—	—	—

1829-30 Issue

		Good	Fine	XF
S661	**1 Dollar** 1829; 24.5.1831. Black. Portrait George Washington at left, Ceres with eagle at top center. Date handwritten. Uniface. Printer: N.& S.S. Jocelyn, New Haven.			
	a. Issued note.	450.	950.	
	b. Remainder without signature.	400.	850.	
S662	**2 Dollars** 12.6.1830. Black. Seated Ceres at left, Hope reclining at top center. Date handwritten. Uniface. Printer: N.& S.S. Jocelyn, New Haven.			
	a. Issued note.	450.	950.	
	b. Remainder without signature.	400.	850.	

		Good	Fine	XF
S663	**3 Dollars**			
	15.7.1830. Black. Justice at left, George Washington at top center. Date handwritten. Uniface. Printer: N.& S.S. Jocelyn, New Haven.			
	a. Issued note.	450.	950.	
	b. Remainder without signature.	400.	850.	
S664	**5 Dollars**			
	15.7.1829; 1830. Black. Standing Liberty at left, Sir W. Raleigh at left of Mercury at top center. Date handwritten. Uniface. Printer: N.& S.S. Jocelyn, New Haven.			
	a. Issued note.	450.	1000.	
	b. Remainder without signature.	400.	900.	

FLORIDA

CIVIL WAR

1861 ISSUES

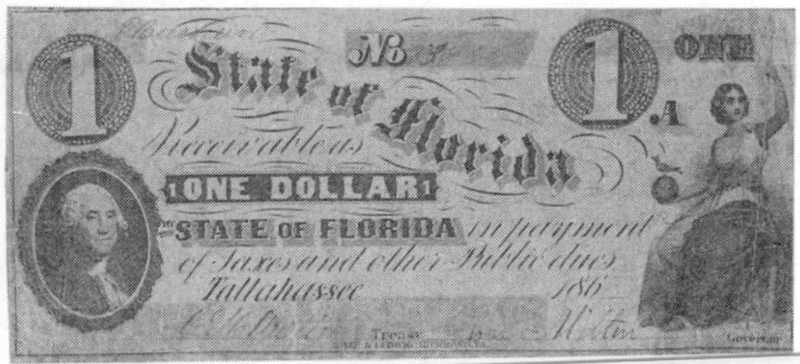

		VG	VF	UNC
S665	**1 Dollar**			
	10.10.1861; 6.12.1861. George Washington at lower left, seated Tellus holding globe and spear at right. Black *ONE* above seated Tellus at right. Various handwritten dates. Uniface. Printer: Hoyer & Ludwig.	125.	225.	500.

		VG	VF	UNC
S666	**1 Dollar**			
	1.12.1861; 6.12.1861. George Washington at lower left, seated Tellus holding globe and spear at right. Similar to #S665 but without *ONE* above Tellus at right. Various handwritten dates. Uniface. Printer: Hoyer & Ludwig.	135.	250.	550.
S667	**2 Dollars**			
	16.9.1861; 6.12.1861. George Washington at lower left, seated Tellus holding globe and spear at right. *TWO* above Tellus at right. Various handwritten dates. Uniface. Printer: Hoyer & Ludwig.	125.	225.	500.
S668	**2 Dollars**			
	10.10.1861. George Washington at lower left, seated Tellus holding globe and spear at right. Similar to #S667 but without *TWO* above Tellus and large 2's at right. Various handwritten dates. Uniface. Printer: Hoyer & Ludwig.	135.	225.	550.
S669	**3 Dollars**			
	9.10.1861. George Washington at lower left, seated Tellus holding globe and spear at right. *THREE* above Tellus at right. Various handwritten dates. Uniface. Printer: Hoyer & Ludwig.	125.	225.	550.
S670	**3 Dollars**			
	10.10.1861; 6.12.1861. George Washington at lower left, seated Tellus holding globe and spear at right. Similar to #S669 but without *THREE* above Tellus at right. Various handwritten dates. Uniface. Printer: Hoyer & Ludwig.	135.	250.	550.
S671	**5 Dollars**			
	10.10.1861. Black. Seated Ceres at center. Engraved date.	125.	225.	500.
S672	**10 Dollars**			
	10.10.1861. Black. Seated Ceres at center. Engraved date.	135.	250.	500.
S673	**20 Dollars**			
	10.10.1861. Black. Seated Ceres at center. Engraved date.	125.	225.	375.

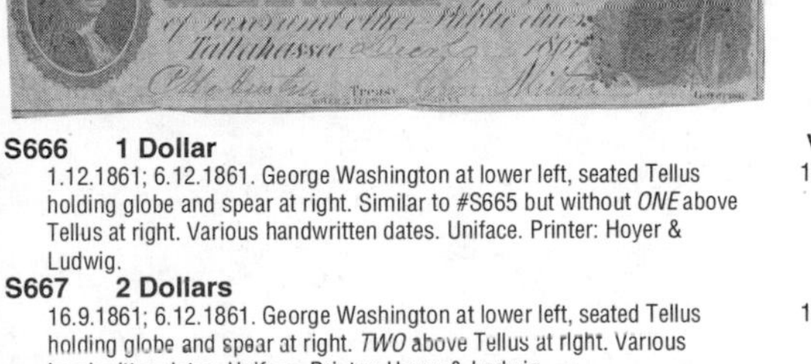

		VG	VF	UNC
S674	**50 Dollars**			
	10.10.1861. Black. Seated Ceres at center. Engraved date.	200.	325.	500.
S675	**50 Dollars**			
	10.10.1861. Black. Seated Ceres at center. Engraved date. Similar to #S674 but inverted *FIFTY* below *FLORIDA*.	160.	275.	435.
S676	**50 Dollars**			
	10.10.1861. Black. Seated Ceres at center. Engraved date. Similar to #S674 but *50* above *L* at left.	160.	275.	475.

		VG	VF	UNC
S677	**100 Dollars**			
	10.10.1861. Black. Seated Ceres at center. Engraved date.	140.	200.	375.

1862 ISSUE

		VG	VF	UNC
S678	**5 Dollars**			
	1.1.1862. Black. Blacks picking cotton at left, seated Ceres, Commerce and Navigation at center. Printer: Hoyer & Ludwig.	100.	275.	550.
S679	**10 Dollars**			
	1.1.1862. Black. Blacks picking cotton at left, seated Ceres, Commerce and Navigation at center. Printer: Hoyer & Ludwig.	100.	275.	500.
S680	**20 Dollars**			
	1.1.1862. Black. Blacks picking cotton at left, seated Ceres, Commerce and Navigation at center. Printer: Hoyer & Ludwig.	135.	250.	425.
S681	**50 Dollars**			
	1.1.1862. Black. Blacks picking cotton at left, seated Ceres, Commerce and Navigation at center. Printer: Hoyer & Ludwig.	200.	325.	525.
S682	**100 Dollars**			
	1.1.1862. Black. Blacks picking cotton at left, seated Ceres, Commerce and Navigation at center. Printer: Hoyer & Ludwig.	200.	325.	525.

1863 FIRST ISSUE

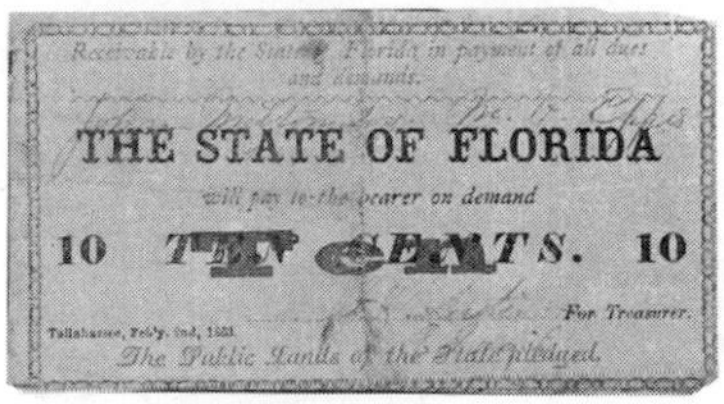

		VG	VF	UNC
S683	**10 Cents**			
	2.2.1863. Black, red, and blue. 1 signature with title: *For Treasurer.*			
	a. Uniface.	25.00	40.00	60.00
	b. Printed on Florida notes.	25.00	40.00	60.00
	c. Printed on Florida bonds.	25.00	40.00	60.00

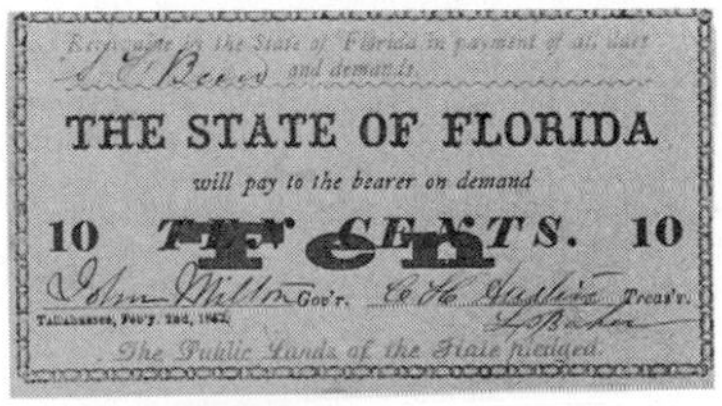

		VG	VF	UNC
S684	**10 Cents**			
	2.2.1863. Black, red and blue. Similar to #S683 but 2 signatures with titles: *Gov'r.* and *Treas'r.*			
	a. Uniface.	25.00	40.00	60.00
	b. Printed on Florida notes. Rare.	—	—	—
	c. Printed on Florida bonds.	25.00	40.00	60.00

		VG	VF	UNC
S685	**25 Cents**			
	2.2.1863. Black, red, and blue. 1 signature with title: *For Treasurer.*			
	a. Uniface.	40.00	65.00	120.
	b. Printed on Florida notes.	40.00	65.00	120.
	c. Printed on Florida bonds.	40.00	65.00	120.

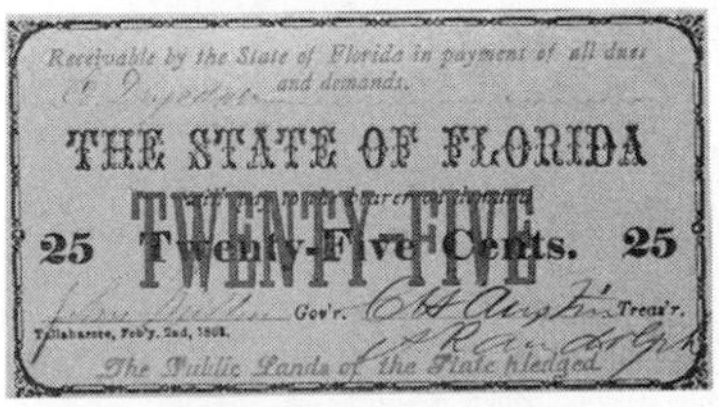

		VG	VF	UNC
S686	**25 Cents**			
	2.2.1863. Black, red, and blue. 2 signatures with titles: *Gov'r* and *Treas'r.*			
	a. Uniface.	25.00	40.00	60.00
	b. Printed on Florida notes. Rare.	—	—	—
	c. Printed on Florida bonds.	25.00	40.00	60.00

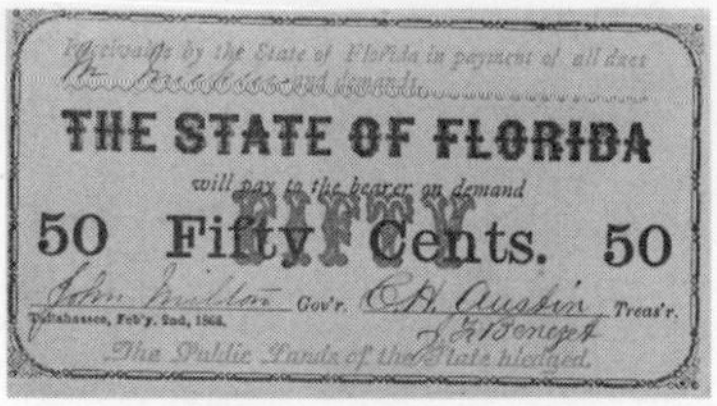

S687 50 Cents	VG	VF	UNC
2.2.1863. Black, red, and blue. 1 signature with titles: *For Treasurer.*			
a. Uniface.	40.00	65.00	120.
b. Printed on Florida notes.	40.00	65.00	120.
c. Printed on Florida bonds.	40.00	65.00	120.

S688 50 Cents	VG	VF	UNC
2.2.1863. Black, red, and blue. 2 signatures with titles: *Gov'r.* and *Treas'r.*			
a. Uniface.	25.00	40.00	60.00
b. Printed on Florida notes. Rare.	—	—	—
c. Printed on Florida bonds. Rare.	—	—	—

1863 Second Issue

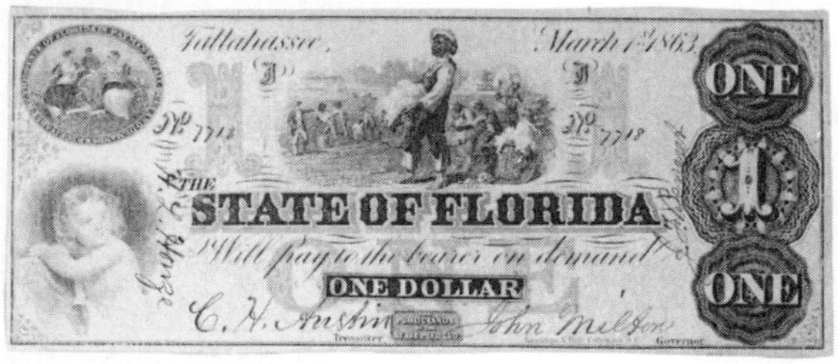

	VG	VF	UNC
S689 1 Dollar 1.3.1863; 1.1.1864. Black on red underprint. Two allegorical figures in seal at upper left. Child at lower left, black carrying cotton at upper center. Printer: Keatinge & Ball.	25.00	40.00	60.00
S690 2 Dollars 1.3.1863; 1.1.1864. Black on red underprint. Two allegorical figures in seal at upper left. Ceres at lower left, steam passenger train at upper center, Indian maiden at lower right. Printer: Keatinge & Ball.	160.	300.	550.

S691 3 Dollars	VG	VF	UNC
1.3.1863; 1.1.1864. Black on red underprint. Two allegorical figures in seal at upper left. Buck at lower left, sailing ship at upper center, Hope at lower right. Printer: Keatinge & Ball.	25.00	40.00	60.00

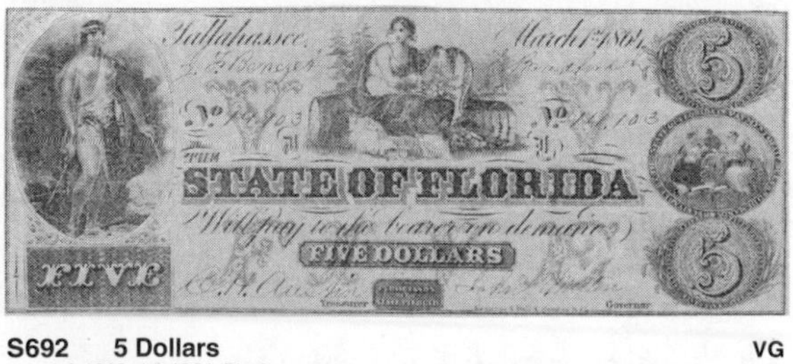

S692 5 Dollars	VG	VF	UNC
1.3.1863; 1.3.1864. Black on red underprint. Two allegorical figures in seal at right. Indian at left, seated Moneta at upper center. Printer: Keatinge & Ball.	120.	275.	500.

S693 10 Dollars	VG	VF	UNC
1.3.1863; 1.3.1864. Black on red underprint. Two allegorical figures in seal at upper left. Ship at lower left, seated Ceres at upper center, black with cotton at lower right. Printer: Keatinge & Ball.	120.	275.	500.

1865 Issue

	Good	Fine	XF
S694 50 Dollars 1.1.1865.	600.	2000.	4500.
S695 100 Dollars 1.1.1865.	1000.	3000.	5500.
S696 500 Dollars 1.1.1865. Rare.	—	—	—

Florida

Post Civil War

1860's Issue

	Good	Fine	XF
S697 1 Dollar 186x. Black and red. Washington at upper left. Rare.	2500.	6000.	—
S698 20 Dollars 186x. Black on green underprint. Bust of Andrew Jackson on pedestal with maiden seated holding shields at center, woman's head at upper right. Rare.	—	—	—

1870 Issue

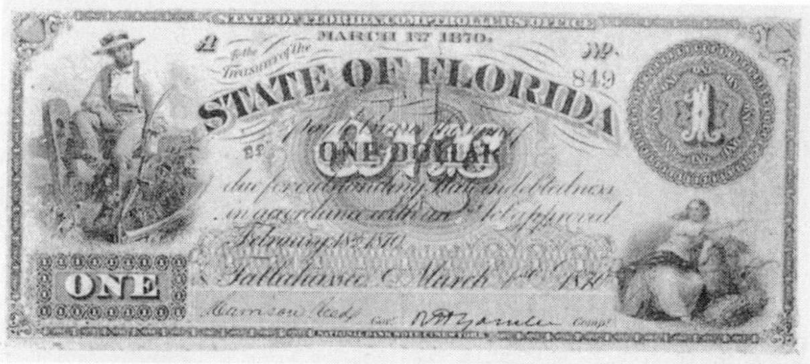

S699 1 Dollar	Good	Fine	XF
1.3.1870. Black and green. Farmer seated on fence holding scythe at upper left, seated Ceres on barrels at lower right. Printer: NBNC.	700.	1250.	2000.

Georgia

Colonial

1755 Issue

	Good	Fine	XF
S710 2 Pence 1755. Black.	—	—	—
S711 3 Pence 1755. Black.	—	—	—
S712 4 Pence 1755. Black.	—	—	—
S713 6 Pence 1755. Black.	—	—	—
S714 9 Pence 1755. Black.	—	—	—
S715 1 Shilling 1755. Black.	—	—	—
S716 1 Shilling 3 Pence 1755. Black.	—	—	—
S717 1 Shilling 6 Pence 1755. Black.	—	—	—
S718 2 Shillings 1755. Black.	—	—	—
S719 2 Shillings 6 Pence 1755. Black.	1500.	—	—
S720 3 Shillings 1755. Black.	—	—	—
S721 3 Shillings 6 Pence 1755. Black.	—	—	—
S722 4 Shillings 1755. Black.	—	—	—
S723 5 Shillings 1755. Black. Bee.	1350.	—	—
S724 10 Shillings 1755. Black. Bush and sickle.	2500.	—	—
S725 20 Shillings 1755. Black. Woman operating thread winder.	3000.	—	—

1762 Issue

No.	Denomination / Description	Good	Fine	XF
S726	**2 Pence** 1762. Black.	—	—	—
S727	**3 Pence** 1762. Black.	—	—	—
S728	**4 Pence** 1762. Black.	—	—	—
S729	**6 Pence** 1762. Black.	—	1750.	—
S730	**9 Pence** 1762. Black.	—	—	—
S731	**1 Shilling** 1762. Black.	—	—	—
S732	**1 Shilling 3 Pence** 1762. Black.	—	—	—
S733	**1 Shilling 6 Pence** 1762. Black.	—	—	3500.
S734	**2 Shillings** 1762. Black.	—	1750.	—
S735	**2 Shillings 6 Pence** 1762. Black.	750.	—	—
S736	**3 Shillings** 1762. Black.	—	—	—
S737	**3 Shillings 6 Pence** 1762. Black.	—	—	—
S738	**4 Shillings** 1762. Black.	—	—	—
S739	**5 Shillings** 1762. Black. Bee. Engraved.	—	—	—
S740	**5 Shillings** 1762. Black. Native American. Typeset.	—	3500.	—

No.	Denomination / Description	Good	Fine	XF
S741	**10 Shillings** 1762. Black. Bush and sickle. Engraved.	1000.	—	—

No.	Denomination / Description	Good	Fine	XF
S742	**10 Shillings** 1762. Black. Ship. Typeset.	—	2500.	—

No.	Denomination / Description	Good	Fine	XF
S743	**20 Shillings** 1762. Black. Woman operating thread winder. Like #S725. Engraved.	1000.	—	—

No.	Denomination / Description	Good	Fine	XF
S744	**20 Shillings** 1762. Red. Horse. Typeset.	—	3000.	—

1774 Issue

No.	Denomination / Description	Good	Fine	XF
S745	**1 Shilling** 1774. Black.	—	—	—
S746	**2 Shillings** 1774. Black.	—	—	—
S747	**2 Shillings 6 Pence** 1774. Black.	—	—	—
S748	**5 Shillings** 1774. Black.	—	—	—

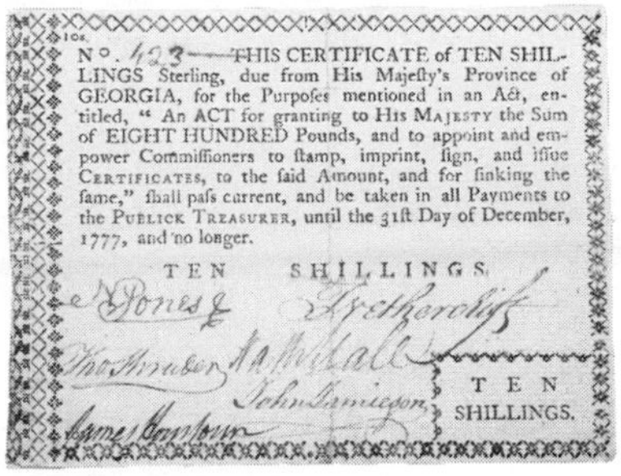

No.	Denomination / Description	Good	Fine	XF
S749	**10 Shillings** 1774. Black.	—	—	—

1775 Issue

No.	Denomination / Description	Good	Fine	XF
S750	**1 Shilling 6 Pence** 1775. Black. Sheaf of wheat.	—	—	—
S751	**2 Shillings 6 Pence** 1775. Black.	—	—	—
S752	**5 Shillings** 1775. Black and red. 1 crown.	—	—	—
S753	**10 Shillings** 1775. Black and red. 2 crowns.	—	—	—
S754	**20 Shillings** 1775. Black and red.	—	—	—
S755	**60 Shillings** 1775. Black and red.	—	—	—
S756	**5 Pounds** 1775. Black and red.	—	—	—

Georgia

State

1776 Pound Sterling Issue

No.	Denomination / Description	Good	Fine	XF
S757	**3 Pence** 1776. Black. 6 border varieties.	300.	600.	1500.
S758	**6 Pence** 1776. Black. 7 border varieties.	300.	600.	1500.
S759	**1 Shilling** 1776. Black. 3 border varieties.	300.	600.	1500.
S760	**1 Shilling 6 Pence** 1776. Black. 5 border varieties.	300.	600.	1500.
S761	**2 Shillings 6 Pence** 1776. Black. Horse. Denomination at left and right.	350.	750.	3000.
S762	**2 Shillings 6 Pence** 1776. Black. Horse. Ornaments at right.	350.	750.	3000.
S763	**5 Shillings** 1776. Black. Crown. 2 border varieties.	350.	750.	3000.
S764	**5 Shillings** 1776. Black. Crown. *SPERANDUM* on blue seal.	750.	6000.	12,000.
S765	**10 Shillings** 1776. Black and red. 3 border varieties.	500.	2250.	4500.
S766	**1 Pound** 1776. Black and red.	500.	2500.	5000.

1776 Dollar Issue

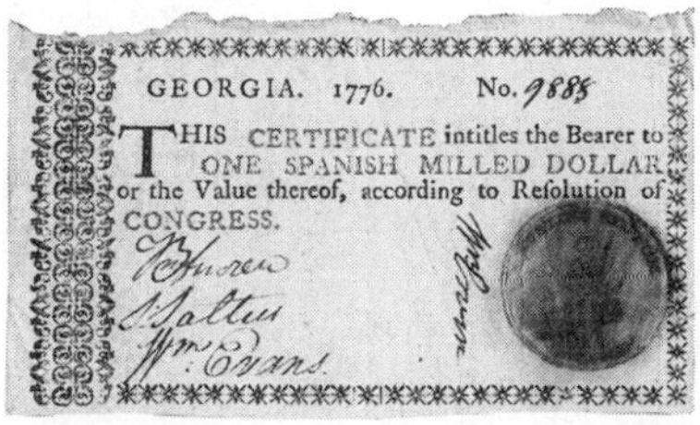

No.	Denomination / Description	Good	Fine	XF
S767	**1 Dollar** 1776. Black and red. Justice. *SUSTINE RECTUM* on light blue circular seal. 2 border varieties.	300.	1000.	5000.
S768	**2 Dollars** 1776. Black and red. Floating jugs. *SI COLLIGIMUS FRANGIMUR* on light blue circular seal. 2 border varieties.	300.	1000.	5000.
S769	**2 Dollars** 1776. Black and red. Liberty cap. *LIBERTAS CARIOR AURO* on light blue circular seal.	400.	1250.	5500.

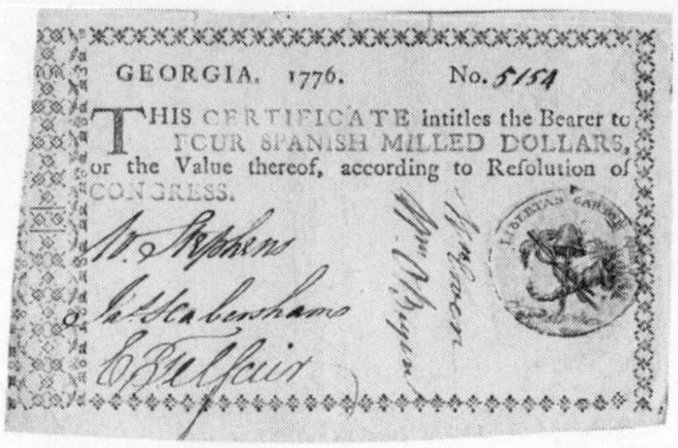

		Good	Fine	XF
S770 4 Dollars	1776. Black and red. Liberty cap. *LIBERTAS CARIOR AURO* on light blue circular seal. 4 border varieties.	300.	1000.	5000.
S771 4 Dollars	1776. Black and red. Floating jugs. *SI COLLIGIMUS FRANGIMUR* on light blue circular seal.	500.	1250.	5500.
S772 10 Dollars	1776. Black and red. Millstone on palm tree. *OPPRESSA SURGIT* on light blue circular seal. 2 border varieties.	500.	1500.	6000.
S773 20 Dollars	1776. Black and red. Rattlesnake. *NEMO ME IMPUNE LACESSET* on light blue circular seal.	750.	2000.	8000.
S774 2 Dollars	1776. Black and red. Floating jugs. *SI COLLIGIMUS FRANGIMUR* on maroon circular seal.	500.	1500.	7500.
S775 4 Dollars	1776. Black and red. Liberty cap. *LIBERTAS CARIOR AURO* on maroon circular seal.	500.	1500.	7500.
S776 10 Dollars	1776. Black and red. Millstone on palm tree. *OPPRESSA SURGIT* on maroon circular seal.	500.	1500.	7500.
S777 20 Dollars	1776. Black and red. Rattlesnake. *NEMO ME IMPUNE LACESSET* on maroon circular seal.	500.	2250.	10,000.

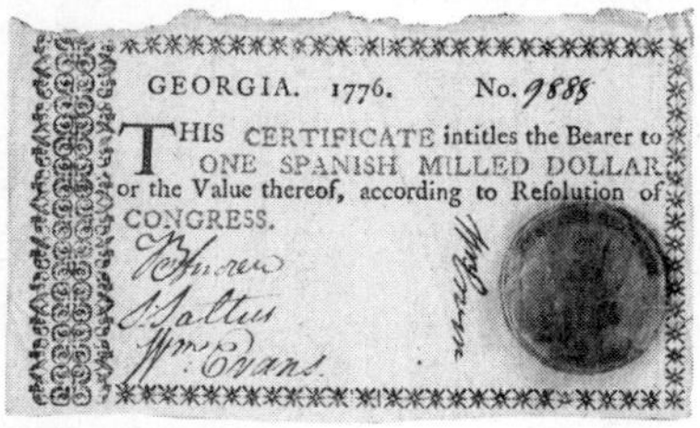

		Good	Fine	XF
S778 1 Dollar	1776. Black and red. Justice. *SUSTINE RECTUM* on orange seal. 9 border varieties.	400.	800.	3500.
S779 1 Dollar	1776. Black and red. Justice. *SUSTINE RECTUM* on green seal. 9 border varieties. Like #S778.	600.	1200.	5250.
S780 2 Dollars	1776. Black and red. Floating jugs. *SI COLLIGIMUS FRANGIMUR* on orange seal. 4 or more border varieties.	450.	900.	4000.
S781 2 Dollars	1776. Black and red. Floating jugs. *SI COLLIGIMUS FRANGIMUR* on green seal. 5 or more border varieties. Like #S780.	900.	1800.	7500.

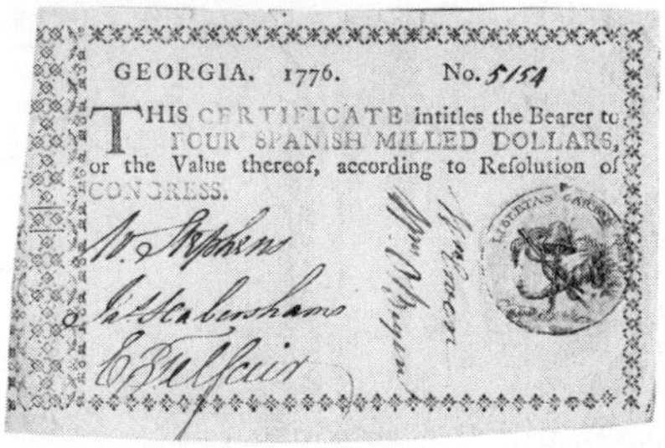

		Good	Fine	XF
S782 4 Dollars	1776. Black and red. Liberty cap. *LIBERTAS CARIOR AURO* on orange seal. 3 border varieties.	450.	900.	4000.
S783 4 Dollars	1776. Black and red. Liberty cap. *LIBERTAS CARIOR AURO* on green seal. 3 border varieties. Like #S782.	600.	1200.	5000.
S784 10 Dollars	1776. Black and red. Millstone on palm tree. *OPPRESSA SURGIT* on orange seal. 3 border varieties.	600.	1200.	6000.
S785 20 Dollars	1776. Black and red. Rattlesnake. *NEMO ME IMPUNE LACESSET* on orange seal. 3 border varieties.	850.	1750.	7500.
S786 1/4 Dollar	1776. Black. 8 border varieties.	225.	450.	1500.
S787 1/2 Dollar	1776. Black. 4 border varieties.	225.	450.	1500.
S788 1 Dollar	1776. Black and red. Justice. *SUSTINE RECTUM* on blue-green seal. 8 border varieties.	750.	1500.	—
S789 4 Dollars	1776. Black and red. Liberty cap. *LIBERTAS CARIOR AURO* on blue-green seal. 2 border varieties.	—	—	—

		VG	VF	UNC
S790 2 Dollars	1776. Black and red. Flag, drum, gun and sword.	2000.	5000.	20,000.
S791 3 Dollars	ND (1776). Black and red. Crossed cannon.	2000.	7500.	—
S792 4 Dollars	ND (1776). Black and red. Frontiersman. 2 border varieties.	1250.	4500.	—
S793 5 Dollars	ND (1776). Black and red. Beehive. 2 border varieties.	1500.	5000.	7000.
S794 8 Dollars	ND (1776). Black and red. Man holding a cane at right. 2 border varieties.	1500.	5000.	7500.
S795 10 Dollars	ND (1776). Black and red. Cannon.	2000.	7500.	—

1777 Issue

		VG	VF	UNC
S796 2 Dollars	1777. Black and red. Floating jugs. *SI COLLIGIMUS FRANGIMUR* on blue-green seal. 4 border varieties.	600.	2500.	—
S797 3 Dollars	1777. Black and red. 9 border varieties with typeset denomination design.	400.	1200.	—
S798 4 Dollars	1777. Black and red. Liberty cap. *LIBERTAS CARIOR AURO* on blue-green seal.	600.	2500.	—
S799 5 Dollars	1777. Black and red. Cannon. *ET DEUS OMNIPOTINCE* on blue-green seal. 9 border varieties.	900.	3750.	—

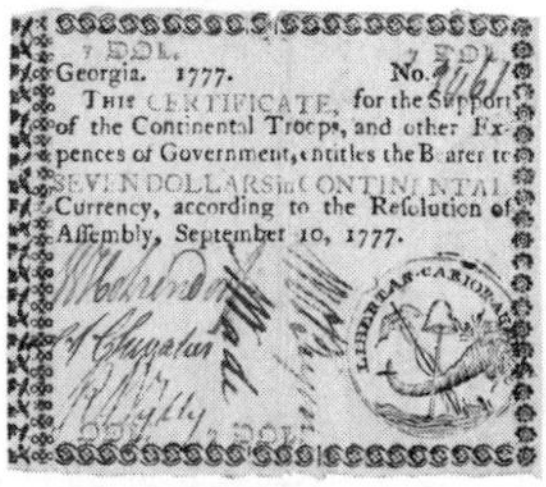

		VG	VF	UNC
S800 7 Dollars	1777. Black and red. Hand. *ULTIMA RADIO* on blue-green seal. 4 border varieties.	900.	3750.	—
S801 9 Dollars	1777. Black and red. Justice. *SUSTINE RECTUM* on blue-green seal. 4 border varieties.	900.	3750.	—
S802 11 Dollars	1777. Black and red. *SI COLLIGIMUS FRANGIMUR* on blue-green seal. 8 or more border varieties.	900.	3750.	—
S803 13 Dollars	1777. Black and red. Liberty cap. *LIBERTAS CARIOR AURO* on blue-green seal. 6 border varieties.	900.	3750.	—
S804 15 Dollars	1777. Black and red. Millstone on palm tree. *OPPRESSA SURGIT* on blue-green seal. 9 border varieties.	900.	3750.	—
S805 17 Dollars	1777. Black and red. Rattlesnake. *NEMO ME IMPUNE LACESSET* on blue-green seal. 6 border varieties.	1200.	5000.	—

Resolution of June 8, 1777

		VG	VF	UNC
S806 1/10 Dollar	1777. Black. Ship.	400.	1250.	—
S807 1/5 Dollar	1777. Black. Fenced house.	350.	1000.	—
S808 1/4 Dollar	1777. Black.	350.	1000.	—
S809 1/3 Dollar	1777. Black.	350.	1000.	—
S810 2/5 Dollar	1777. Black.	350.	1000.	—
S811 1/2 Dollar	1777. Black.	350.	1000.	—
S812 2/3 Dollar	1777. Black.	350.	1000.	—
S813 3/4 Dollar	1777. Black.	350.	1000.	—
S814 4/5 Dollar	1777. Black. 5 border varieties.	350.	1000.	—
S815 1 Dollar	1777. Black and red. Black *in*. Justice. *SUSTINE RECTUM* on red seal.	675.	3000.	—
S816 1 Dollar	1777. Black and red. Justice. *SUSTINE RECTUM* on red seal. Like #S815 but red *in*. 2 border varieties.	450.	2000.	—
S817 2 Dollars	1777. Black and red. Black *in*. Ship.	675.	3000.	—
S818 2 Dollars	1777. Black and red. Red *in*. Ship.	450.	2000.	—
S819 3 Dollars	1777. Black and red. Black *in*. Frontiersman.	675.	3000.	—
S820 3 Dollars	1777. Black and red. Red *in*. Frontiersman.	450.	2000.	—
S821 4 Dollars	1777. Black and red. Black *in*. Stag.	675.	3000.	—
S822 4 Dollars	1777. Black and red. Red *in*. Stag.	450.	2000.	—
S823 5 Dollars	1777. Black and red. Black *in*. Rattlesnake. *NEMO ME IMPUNE LACESSET* on dark blue seal.	850.	3750.	—

		VG	VF	UNC
S824	**5 Dollars** 1777. Black and red. Rattlesnake. *NEMO ME IMPUNE LACESSET* on dark blue seal. Like #S823 but red *in.*	750.	3000.	—
S825	**6 Dollars** 1777. Black and red. Black *in.* Millstone on palm tree. *OPPRESSA SURGIT* on dark blue seal.	675.	3000.	—
S826	**6 Dollars** 1777. Black and red. Millstone on palm tree. *OPPRESSA SURGIT* on dark blue seal. Like #S825 but red *in.*	450.	2000.	—
S827	**7 Dollars** 1777. Black and red. Black *in.* Liberty cap. *LIBERTAS CARIOR AURO* on dark blue seal.	675.	3000.	—
S828	**7 Dollars** 1777. Black and red. Liberty cap. *LIBERTAS CARIOR AURO* on dark blue seal. Like #S827 but red *in.*	450.	2000.	—
S829	**8 Dollars** 1777. Black and red. Black *in.* Thirteen links. *C CONGRESS* on dark blue seal.	1350.	6000.	—
S830	**8 Dollars** 1777. Black and red. Thirteen links. *C CONGRESS* on dark blue seal. Like #S829 but red *in.*	1000.	4500.	—

Resolution of September 10, 1777

		VG	VF	UNC
S831	**1/5 Dollar** 1777. Black. 4 border varieties.	—	—	—
S832	**1/2 Dollar** 1777. Black. 3 border varieties.	300.	675.	—
S833	**4/5 Dollar** 1777. Black. 7 border varieties.	300.	675.	—
S834	**1 Dollar** 1777. Black and red. Justice. *SUSTINE RECTUM* on red seal.	450.	2000.	—
S835	**2 Dollars** 1777. Black and red. Ship. Red seal.	450.	2000.	—
S836	**3 Dollars** 1777. Black and red. Frontiersman. Red seal.	450.	2000.	—
S837	**4 Dollars** 1777. Black and red. Stag. Red seal.	450.	2000.	—
S838	**5 Dollars** 1777. Black and red. Rattlesnake. *NEMO ME IMPUNE LACESSET* on dark blue seal.	750.	3000.	—
S839	**6 Dollars** 1777. Black and red. Millstone on palm tree. *OPPRESSA SURGIT* on dark blue seal.	450.	2000.	—
S840	**7 Dollars** 1777. Black and red. Liberty cap. *LIBERTAS CARIOR AURO* on dark blue seal.	450.	2000.	—
S841	**8 Dollars** 1777. Black and red. Thirteen links. *C CONGRESS* on dark blue seal.	1000.	4500.	—

1778 Issue

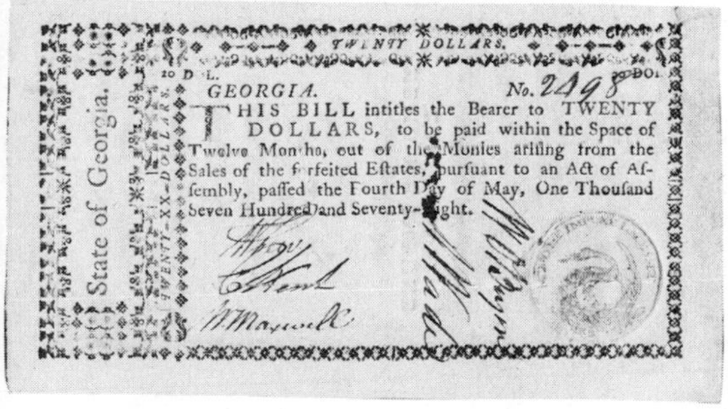

		Good	Fine	XF
S842	**20 Dollars** 1778. Black and red. Rattlesnake. *NEMO ME IMPUNE LACESSET* on greenish blue seal. 4 border varieties. Printer: W. Lancaster, Savannah.	425.	850.	2500.

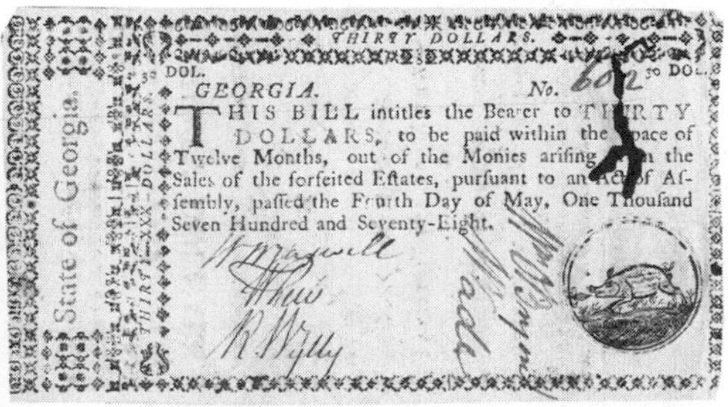

		Good	Fine	XF
S843	**30 Dollars** 1778. Black and red. Wild boar. *AUT MORS, AUT VICTORIA, LAETA* on greenish blue seal. 2 border varieties. Printer: W. Lancaster, Savannah.	425.	850.	2500.
S844	**40 Dollars** 1778. Black and red. Dove and sword. *AUT PAX, AUT BELLUM, IN UTROQUE PARATUS* on greenish blue seal. 2 border varieties. Printer: W. Lancaster, Savannah.	500.	1000.	3000.

January 9, 1782 Resolve

		Good	Fine	XF
S845	**Various Amounts** 1782. Black. First *C* in *confiscated* lower case.	—	—	—

NOTE: No examples of #S845 are known with official signatures.

NOTE: Denominations in pounds were inserted by hand.

1786 Issue

		Good	Fine	XF
S846	**6 Pence** 16.10.1786. Black. Watermark: *HONIG & ZOONEN*. Printer: John E. Smith, Augusta. Printed on Dutch paper.	550.	1750.	3500.
S847	**1 Shilling** 16.10.1786. Black. Watermark: *HONIG & ZOONEN*. Printer: John E. Smith, Augusta. Printed on Dutch paper.	375.	1750.	3500.
S848	**2 Shillings 6 Pence** 16.10.1786. Black. Watermark: *HONIG & ZOONEN*. Printer: John E. Smith, Augusta. Printed on Dutch paper.	250.	1000.	2250.
S849	**5 Shillings** 16.10.1786. Black. Watermark: *HONIG & ZOONEN*. Printer: John E. Smith, Augusta. Printed on Dutch paper.	350.	1200.	2250.
S850	**10 Shillings** 16.10.1786. Black. Watermark: *HONIG & ZOONEN*. Printer: John E. Smith, Augusta. Printed on Dutch paper.	300.	1200.	2250.
S851	**20 Shillings** 16.10.1786. Black. Watermark: *HONIG & ZOONEN*. Printer: John E. Smith, Augusta. Printed on Dutch paper.	350.	1500.	3000.

Georgia

Civil War

1862 Issue

		VG	VF	UNC
S852	**5 Dollars** 15.1.1862. Black and red. J. Oglethorpe in military dress at upper center. Treasury Seal. Back: Black. Printer: H. Engr. Engraved by Douglas.	15.00	25.00	45.00

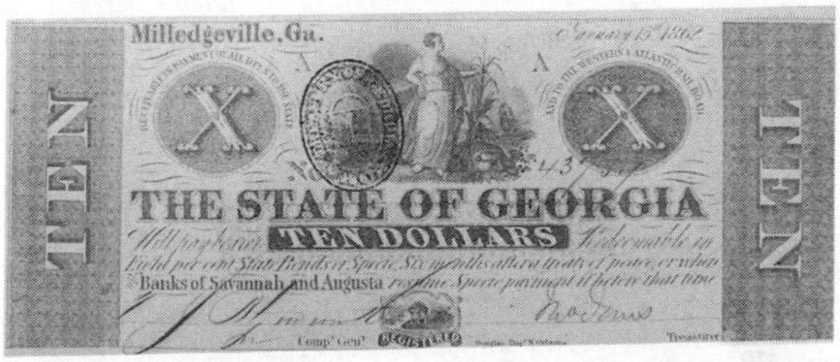

		VG	VF	UNC
S853	**10 Dollars** 15.1.1862. Black and red. Ceres holding grain at upper center, black Treasury Seal. Engraved by Douglas.	15.00	30.00	60.00
S854	**20 Dollars** 15.1.1862. Black and red. Ceres holding grain at center, black Treasury Seal. Engraved by Douglas.	20.00	40.00	90.00

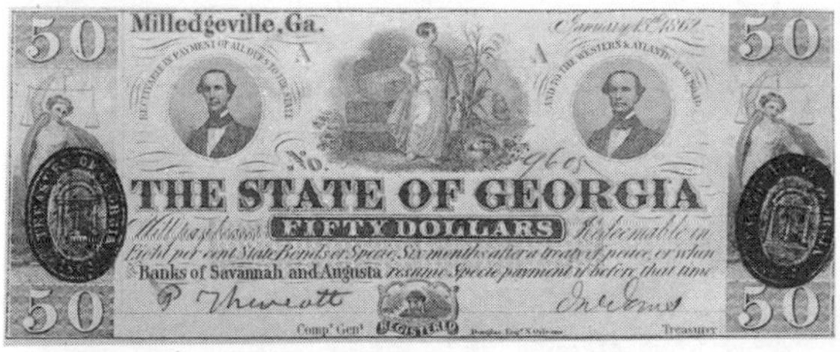

		VG	VF	UNC
S855	**50 Dollars** 15.1.1862. Black and red. Justice at left and right, Gov. Joseph E. Brown at left and center right, Ceres holding grain at center. Two Treasury Seals. Engraved by Douglas.	30.00	55.00	100.

		VG	VF	UNC
S856	**100 Dollars** 15.1.1862. Black and red. Sailor at left and right, Ceres holding grain at center. Two Treasury Seals. Engraved by Douglas.	40.00	60.00	135.

1863-64 Issues

S857 5 Cents	VG	VF	UNC
1.1.1863. Black. Back: Red or green Treasury Seal. Engraved by R.H. Howell.	10.00	17.50	25.00

S858 10 Cents	VG	VF	UNC
1.1.1863. Black. Back: Red or green Treasury Seal. Engraved by R.H. Howell.	10.00	17.50	25.00
S859 15 Cents			
1.1.1863. Black. Back: Red or green Treasury Seal. Engraved by R.H. Howell.	20.00	40.00	90.00
S860 20 Cents			
1.1.1863. Black. Back: Red or green Treasury Seal. Engraved by R.H. Howell.	120.	225.	500.

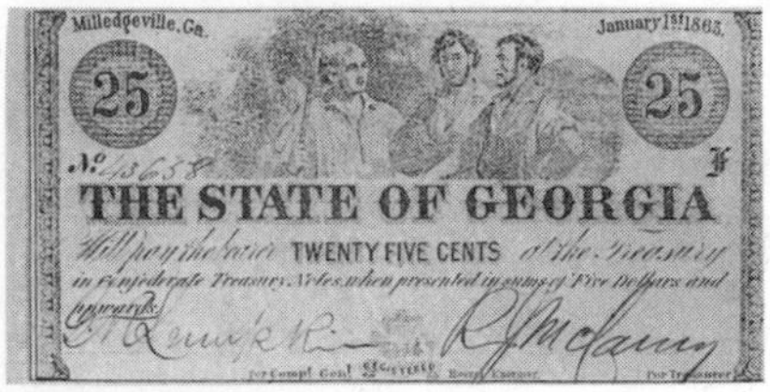

S861 25 Cents	VG	VF	UNC
1.1.1863. Black. Back: Red or green Treasury Seal. Engraved by Howell.	10.00	20.00	40.00
S862 50 Cents			
1863-64. Black. Three workmen at upper center. Back: Red Treasury Seal. Engraved by Howell.			
a. 1.1.1863.	10.00	20.00	35.00
b. 1.1.1864	10.00	20.00	35.00

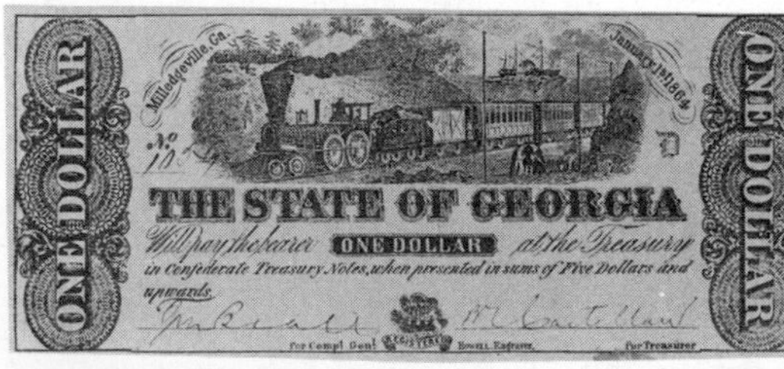

S863 1 Dollar	VG	VF	UNC
1.1.1863; 1.1.1864. Black. Steam passenger train at upper center. Back: Green Treasury Seal. Engraved by Howell.	35.00	65.00	135.

S864 2 Dollars	VG	VF	UNC
1.1.1863; 1.1.1864. Black. Steamship at upper center. Back: Green Treasury Seal. Engraved by Howell.	35.00	65.00	135.
S865 3 Dollars			
1863-64. Black. Standing Minerva at left, horses drinking at upper center, Justice holding scales at lower right. Back: Red or green Treasury Seal. Engraved by Howell.			
a. 1.1.1863.	1200.	3200.	6000.
b. 1.1.1864.	1200.	3200.	6000.
S866 4 Dollars			
1863-64. Black. Blacks picking cotton at lower left, Moneta reclining on chest at top center, black carrying sheaf at lower right. Back: Red or green Treasury Seal. Engraved by Howell.			
a. 1.1.1863.	3000.	—	—
b. 1.1.1864.	3000.	—	—

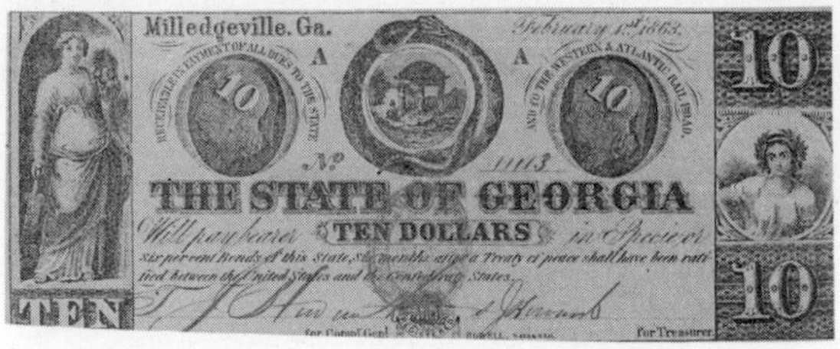

S867 10 Dollars	VG	VF	UNC
1.2.1863. Black. Red Treasury Seal. Minerva at left, state arms within coil of rattlesnake at center, Ceres at right. "Payable to State and Western & Atlantic Railroad." Engraved by Howell, Savannah.	15.00	30.00	60.00
S868 50 Dollars			
2.2.1863. Black and red. State arms at left, *L* at center within coil of rattlesnake. "Payable to State and Western & Atlantic Railroad." Back: Black Treasury Seal. Engraved by Howell, Savannah.	20.00	40.00	85.00

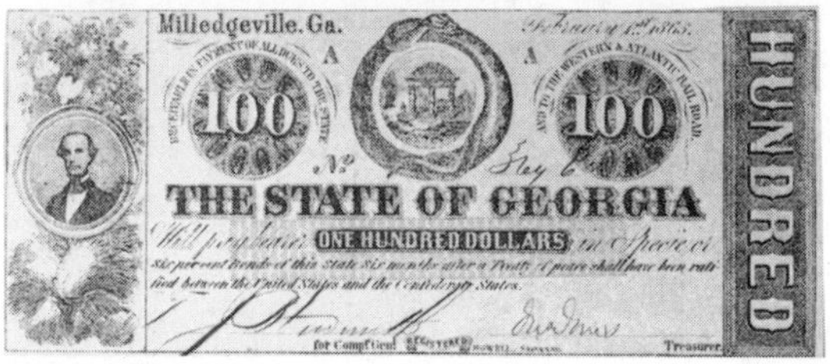

S869 100 Dollars	VG	VF	UNC
2.1.1863. Black and red. Portrait Gov. J. E. Brown at left, state arms within coil of rattlesnake at center. "Payable to State and Western & Atlantic Railroad." Back: Black Treasury Seal. Engraved by Howell, Savannah.	35.00	70.00	120.

Act of 25.12.1863; 1864 Issue

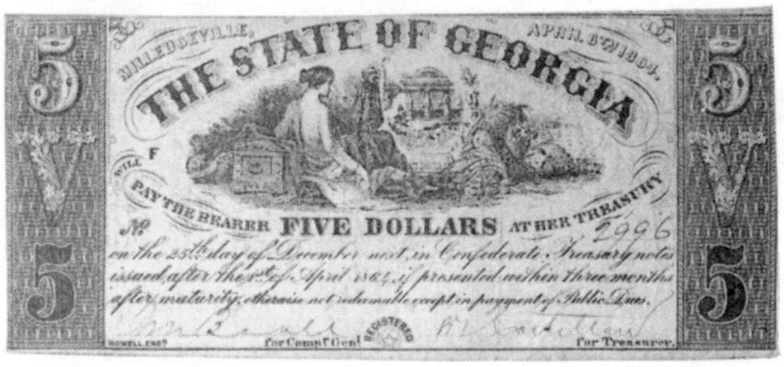

S870 5 Dollars	VG	VF	UNC
6.4.1864. Black. Moneta reclining on chest at top center. Green Treasury Seal. Engraved by Howell.	12.50	30.00	50.00
S871 10 Dollars			
6.4.1864. Black. Moneta reclining on chest at top center. Green Treasury Seal. Engraved by Howell.	15.00	35.00	70.00
S872 20 Dollars			
6.4.1864. Black. Moneta reclining on chest at top center. Green Treasury Seal. Engraved by Howell.	20.00	45.00	90.00
S873 50 Dollars			
6.4.1864. Black and red. Moneta reclining on chest at top center. Engraved by Howell.	30.00	65.00	135.
S874 100 Dollars			
6.4.1864. Black and red. Moneta reclining on chest at top center. Engraved by Howell.	35.00	90.00	180.
S875 500 Dollars			
6.4.1864. Black and red. Moneta reclining on chest at top center. Similar to #S870 but with standing Minerva at left. Engraved by Howell.	400.	1250.	3000.

1865 Issue

S876 5 Dollars	VG	VF	UNC
15.1.1865. Black and red. J. Oglethorpe in military dress at upper center. Similar to #S852. "Payable to State and Western & Atlantic Railroad." Engraved by Howell.	40.00	80.00	140.

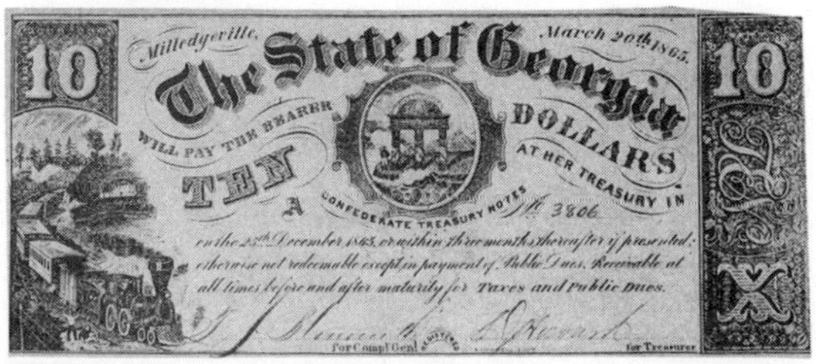

S877 10 Dollars	VG	VF	UNC
20.3.1865. Black. Steam train at lower left, state arms at center. "Payable to State and Western & Atlantic Railroad." Back: Black Treasury Seal. Engraved by Howell.	30.00	60.00	90.00

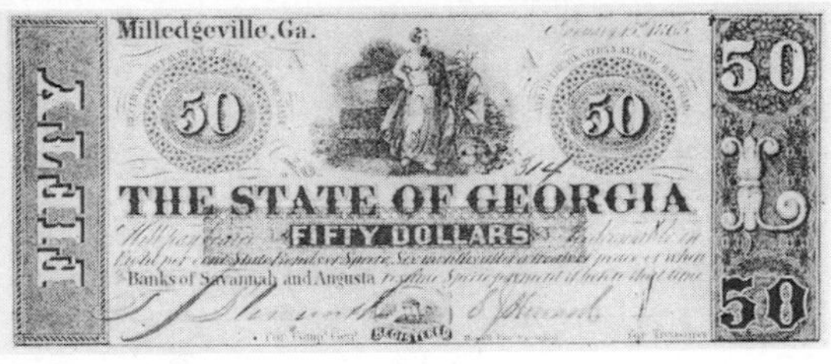

		VG	VF	UNC
S878	**50 Dollars** 15.1.1865. Black and red. Ceres holding grain at top center. "Payable to State and Western & Atlantic Railroad." Back: Black Treasury Seal. Engraved by Howell.	40.00	80.00	140.

Kansas

Post Civil War

1867 Union Military Scrip Issue

		Good	Fine	XF
S881	**1 Dollar** 1.6.1867. Black. Farmer plowing with horses at upper left, allegorical Peace with doves at center. Uniface. Printer: CBNC.	50.00	75.00	125.
S882	**5 Dollars** 1.6.1867. Black. Union soldier with horse talking with blacksmiths at upper left. Uniface. Printer: CBNC.	50.00	75.00	125.
S883	**10 Dollars** 1.6.1867. Black. Farmer plowing with horses at upper left, soldiers in action at lower right. Uniface. Printer: CBNC.	50.00	75.00	125.
S884	**20 Dollars** 1.6.1867. Black. Farmer plowing with horses at upper left, Liberty holding flag at center. Uniface. Printer: CBNC.	75.00	100.	200.
S885	**50 Dollars** 1.6.1867. Black. Farmer plowing with horses at upper left, Indian on horseback hunting buffalo at lower left. Uniface. Printer: CBNC.	75.00	100.	250.
S886	**100 Dollars** 1.6.1867. Black. Portrait George Washington at upper left, farmer plowing with horses at top center, portrait Abraham Lincoln at right. Uniface. Printer: CBNC.	75.00	110.	250.

Louisiana

Spanish Administration

1790s Issue

		Good	Fine	XF
S886A	**25 Pesos** 24.6.1795. Black. Arms at upper center. Figures in 4 corners. Unsigned remainder. Rare.	—	—	—

Louisiana

Civil War

Act of January 23, 1862 Issue

#S887, S889 printed on the backs of notes of The Commercial & Agricultural Bank of Texas.

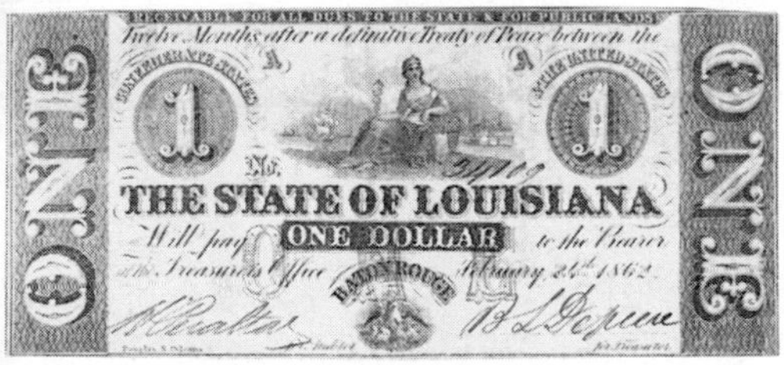

		VG	VF	UNC
S887	**1 Dollar** 24.2.1862. Black. Seated Ceres at top center. Red protector: *ONE*. Printed on backs of various peso or dollar notes. Engraved by Douglas, New Orleans.	30.00	75.00	120.
S888	**1 Dollar** 24.2.1862. Black. Seated Ceres at top center. Similar to #S887 but blue protector: *ONE*. Printed on backs of New Orleans notes. Engraved by Douglas, New Orleans.	50.00	100.	250.

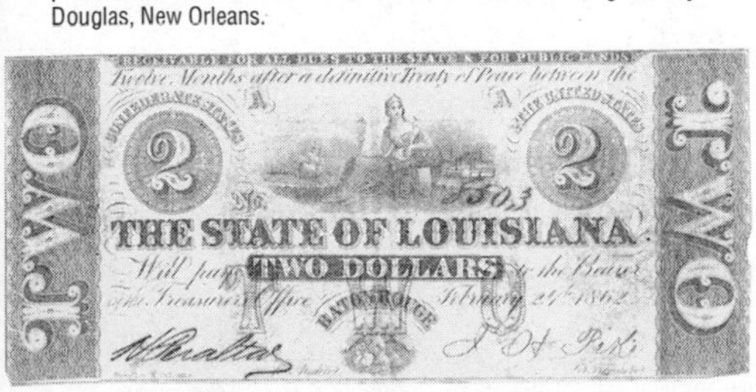

		VG	VF	UNC
S889	**2 Dollars** 24.2.1862. Black. Seated Ceres at top center. Red protector: *TWO*. Printer: B. Duncan, Columbia, S.C. Printed on backs of various peso or dollar notes. Engraved by Douglas, New Orleans.	30.00	75.00	135.
S890	**2 Dollars** 24.2.1862. Black. Seated Ceres at top center. Similar to #S889 but blue protector: *TWO*. Printer: B. Duncan, Columbia, S.C. Printed on backs of New Orleans notes. Engraved by Douglas, New Orleans.	70.00	140.	250.

Act of February 8, 1863 Issue

#S891-S893 w/o vignettes. Printed on the backs of The Exchange Office of Holly Springs, Mississippi Notes.

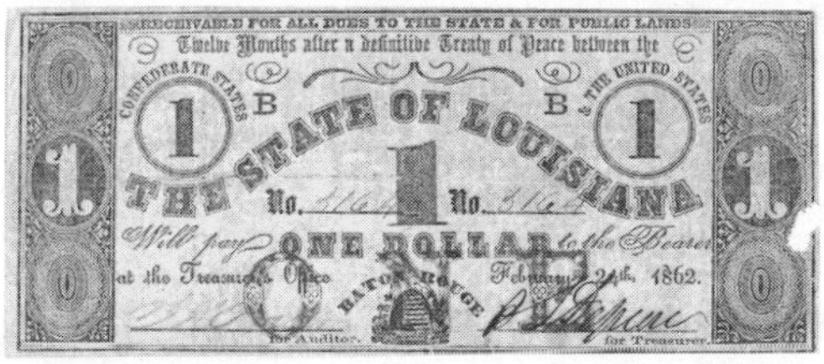

		VG	VF	UNC
S891	**1 Dollar** 24.2.1862. Black and green. Printer: B. Duncan, Columbia, S.C. Printed on backs of 5 dollar notes.	25.00	50.00	80.00
S892	**2 Dollars** 24.2.1862. Black and green. Printer: B. Duncan, Columbia, S.C. Printed on backs of 10 or 20 dollar notes.	30.00	60.00	100.
S893	**3 Dollars** 24.2.1862. Black and green. Printed on backs of 10 or 20 dollar notes.	70.00	140.	250.

		VG	VF	UNC
S894	**5 Dollars** 10.10.1862. Black. Vignette of the Confederacy striking down the Union above lazy *5* at center. Back: Green. Printer: B. Duncan, Columbia, S.C. Baton Rouge.	25.00	55.00	100.

		VG	VF	UNC
S895	**5 Dollars** 10.3.1863. Black. Vignette of the Confederacy striking down the Union. Similar to #S894 but without lazy *5* at bottom center. Back: Green. Shreveport.	25.00	50.00	100.

		VG	VF	UNC
S896	**20 Dollars** 10.3.1863. Red and black. Gen. P. G. T. Beauregard at center, wild man at right. Back: Blue.	75.00	150.	250.

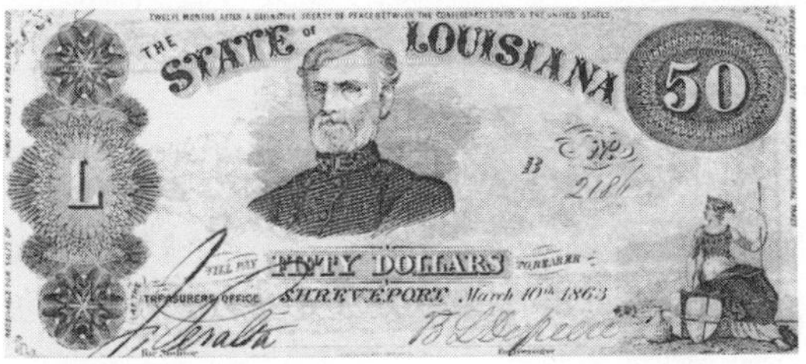

		VG	VF	UNC
S897	**50 Dollars** 10.3.1863. Black. Gen. L. Polk at center, seated Liberty at lower right. Back: Green.	65.00	130.	275.

	VG	VF	UNC
S898 100 Dollars 10.3.1863. Black. Portrait Gov. T. Moore at upper left, State Capitol building at top center, seated Liberty at lower right. Back: Woman seated at center.	75.00	150.	400.

1864 Issues

	VG	VF	UNC
S899 25 Cents 1.3.1864. Black.			
a. Uniface.	50.00	100.	200.
b. Printed on backs of New Orleans notes.	50.00	100.	200.
c. Printed on backs of bills of exchange.	50.00	100.	200.
S900 50 Cents 1.3.1864. Black. Uniface.	40.00	80.00	140.

	VG	VF	UNC
S901 50 Cents 1.3.1864. Seated Liberty at left, three ships at center. Uniface. Printer: South Western Print.	10.00	25.00	50.00
S902 50 Cents 1.3.1864. Black. Eagle at left, three ships at center. Uniface. Printer: South Western Print.	10.00	25.00	50.00
S903 1 Dollar 1.3.1864. Black. Ship in oval at left. Uniface. Printer: South Western Print.	60.00	115.	160.
S904 1 Dollar 1.3.1864. Black. Standing Minerva at left, steamship at upper center. Uniface. Printer: South Western Print.	12.00	25.00	55.00
S905 1 Dollar 1.3.1864. Black. Ship at left, Commerce leaning on bales of cotton at upper center. Uniface. Printer: South Western Print.	12.00	25.00	55.00
S906 1 Dollar 1.3.1864. Black. Statue of Washington at left, Commerce leaning on bales of cotton at center. Uniface. Printer: South Western Print.	12.00	25.00	55.00
S907 1 Dollar 1.3.1864. Black. Steam locomotive at left, sailing vessel at center. Uniface. Printer: South Western Print.	12.00	25.00	55.00
S907A 1 Dollar 1.3.1864. Black. Passenger train in oval at left. Uniface. Printer: South Western Print.	60.00	115.	160.

Louisiana

Post Civil War

1866 Issue

	VG	VF	UNC
S908 5 Dollars 20.12.1866. Black on green underprint. Maiden's head at left and right, Governor at right. Various handwritten dates 1866. Back: Green. Printer: ABNC.	100.	225.	400.
S909 10 Dollars 1.5.1866. Black on green underprint. George Washington at left, dog on chest at top center, cotton ball at lower right. Various handwritten dates. Printer: ABNC.	200.	400.	800.
S910 20 Dollars 20.4.1866; 26.11.1866. Black on green underprint. Ships at dockside at upper left center, portrait Thomas Jefferson at lower right. Various handwritten dates 1866. Back: Green. Printer: ABNC.			
a. Issued note.	180.	350.	700.
b. Punched hole cancelled.	180.	350.	700.

Maryland

Colonial

1733 Issue

	Good	Fine	XF
S911 1 Shilling 1733. Black. Handwritten date. Watermark: *MARYLAND.*	—	—	—
S912 1 Shilling 6 Pence 1733. Black. Handwritten date. Watermark: *MARYLAND.*	—	—	—
S913 2 Shillings 6 Pence 1733. Black. Handwritten date. Watermark: *MARYLAND.*	—	—	—
S914 5 Shillings 1733. Black. Handwritten date. Watermark: *MARYLAND.*	—	—	—
S915 10 Shillings 1733. Black. Handwritten date. Watermark: *MARYLAND.*	—	—	—
S916 15 Shillings 1733. Black. Handwritten date. Watermark: *MARYLAND.*	—	—	—
S917 20 Shillings 1733. Black. Handwritten date. Watermark: *MARYLAND.*	—	—	—

NOTE: Signed notes of #S911-S917 are extremely rare. Unissued remainders are valued at 350 in VF and 550 in Unc.

1740 Issue

	Good	Fine	XF
S918 1 Shilling 2.6.1740. Black.	—	—	—
S919 1 Shilling 6 Pence 2.6.1740. Black.	—	—	—
S920 2 Shillings 6 Pence 2.6.1740. Black.	—	—	—
S921 5 Shillings 2.6.1740. Black.	—	—	—
S922 10 Shillings 2.6.1740. Black.	—	—	—
S923 15 Shillings 2.6.1740. Black.	—	—	—
S924 20 Shillings 2.6.1740. Black.	—	—	—

1748 Issue

	Good	Fine	XF
S925 1 Shilling 1.10.1748. Black. With handwritten *NEW BILL.*	—	—	—
S926 1 Shilling 6 Pence 1.10.1748. Black. With handwritten *NEW BILL.*	—	—	—
S927 2 Shillings 6 Pence 1.10.1748. Black. With handwritten *NEW BILL.*	—	—	—
S928 5 Shillings 1.10.1748. Black. With handwritten *NEW BILL.*	—	—	—
S929 10 Shillings 1.10.1748. Black. With handwritten *NEW BILL.*	—	—	—
S930 15 Shillings 1.10.1748. Black. With handwritten *NEW BILL.*	—	—	—
S931 20 Shillings 1.10.1748. Black. With handwritten *NEW BILL.*	—	—	—

1751 Issue

	Good	Fine	XF
S932 1 Shilling 6.4.1751. Black. With handwritten *NEW BILL* and handwritten date.	—	—	—
S933 1 Shilling 6 Pence 6.4.1751. Black. With handwritten *NEW BILL* and handwritten date.	—	—	—
S934 2 Shillings 6 Pence 6.4.1751. Black. With handwritten *NEW BILL* and handwritten date.	—	—	—
S935 5 Shillings 6.4.1751. Black. With handwritten *NEW BILL* and handwritten date.	—	—	—
S936 10 Shillings 6.4.1751. Black. With handwritten *NEW BILL* and handwritten date.	—	—	—
S937 15 Shillings 6.4.1751. Black. With handwritten *NEW BILL* and handwritten date.	—	—	—
S938 20 Shillings 6.4.1751. Black. With handwritten *NEW BILL* and handwritten date.	—	—	—

1756 Issue

	Good	Fine	XF
S939 6 Pence 14.7.1756. Black. Printer: Jonas Green, Annapolis.	—	—	—
S940 1 Shilling 14.7.1756. Black. Printer: Jonas Green, Annapolis.	—	—	—
S941 1 Shilling 6 Pence 14.7.1756. Black. Printer: Jonas Green, Annapolis.	—	—	—
S942 2 Shillings 14.7.1756. Black. Printer: Jonas Green, Annapolis.	—	—	—
S943 2 Shillings 6 Pence 14.7.1756. Black. Printer: Jonas Green, Annapolis.	—	—	—
S945 10 Shillings 14.7.1756. Black. Printer: Jonas Green, Annapolis.	—	—	—
S946 15 Shillings 14.7.1756. Black. Printer: Jonas Green, Annapolis.	—	—	—
S947 20 Shillings 14.7.1756. Black. Printer: Jonas Green, Annapolis.	—	—	—

1767 Issue

	VG	VF	UNC
S948 1/9 Dollar 1.1.1767. Black. Printer: Jonas Green. Printed on thick paper.	300.	900.	—
S949 1/6 Dollar 1.1.1767. Black. Printer: Jonas Green. Printed on thick paper.	300.	900.	—
S950 2/9 Dollar 1.1.1767. Black. Printer: Jonas Green. Printed on thick paper.	300.	900.	—
S951 1/3 Dollar 1.1.1767. Black. Printer: Jonas Green. Printed on thick paper.	300.	900.	—
S952 1/2 Dollar 1.1.1767. Black. Printer: Jonas Green. Printed on thick paper.	200.	600.	—
S953 2/3 Dollar 1.1.1767. Black. Printer: Jonas Green. Printed on thick paper.	200.	600.	—
S954 1 Dollar 1.1.1767. Black. Printer: Jonas Green. Printed on thick paper.	200.	600.	—
S955 2 Dollars 1.1.1767. Black. Printer: Jonas Green. Printed on thick paper.	200.	600.	—
S956 4 Dollars 1.1.1767. Black. Printer: Jonas Green. Printed on thick paper.	200.	600.	—
S957 6 Dollars 1.1.1767. Black. Printer: Jonas Green. Printed on thick paper.	200.	600.	—
S958 8 Dollars 1.1.1767. Black. Printer: Jonas Green. Printed on thick paper.	200.	600.	—

1770 Issue

	Good	Fine	XF
S959 1/9 Dollar 1.3.1770. Black. Printer: Anne Catherine Green and William Green.	100.	225.	700.
S960 1/6 Dollar 1.3.1770. Black. Printer: Anne Catherine Green and William Green.	100.	225.	700.
S961 2/9 Dollar 1.3.1770. Black. Printer: Anne Catherine Green and William Green.	100.	225.	700.

		Good	Fine	XF
S962	**1/3 Dollar** 1.3.1770. Black. Printer: Anne Catherine Green and William Green.	100.	225.	700.
S963	**1/2 Dollar** 1.3.1770. Black. Printer: Anne Catherine Green and William Green.	100.	225.	700.
S964	**2/3 Dollar** 1.3.1770. Black. Printer: Anne Catherine Green and William Green.	100.	225.	700.
S965	**1 Dollar** 1.3.1770. Black. Printer: Anne Catherine Green and William Green.	75.00	150.	450.
S966	**2 Dollars** 1.3.1770. Black. Printer: Anne Catherine Green and William Green.	75.00	150.	450.
S967	**4 Dollars** 1.3.1770. Black. Printer: Anne Catherine Green and William Green.	75.00	150.	450.
S968	**6 Dollars** 1.3.1770. Black. Printer: Anne Catherine Green and William Green.	75.00	150.	450.
S969	**8 Dollars** 1.3.1770. Black. Printer: Anne Catherine Green and William Green.	75.00	150.	450.

1774 Issue

		Good	Fine	XF
S970	**1/9 Dollar** 10.4.1774. Black. Printer: Anne Catherine Green and Frederick Green. Thin paper containing mica flakes.	60.00	125.	350.
S971	**1/6 Dollar** 10.4.1774. Black. Printer: Anne Catherine Green and Frederick Green. Thin paper containing mica flakes.	60.00	125.	350.
S972	**2/9 Dollar** 10.4.1774. Black. Printer: Anne Catherine Green and Frederick Green. Thin paper containing mica flakes.	60.00	125.	350.

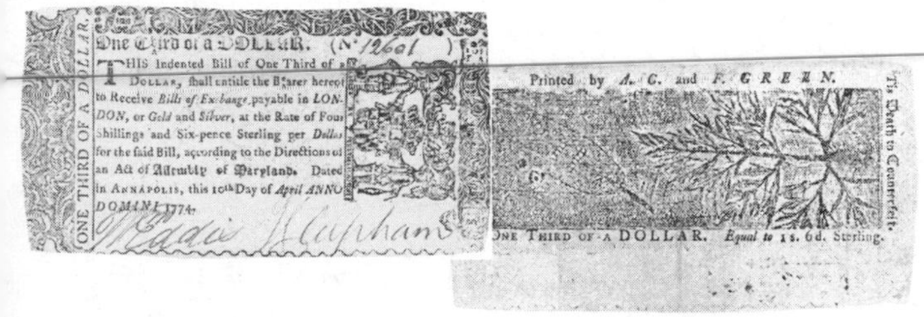

		Good	Fine	XF
S973	**1/3 Dollar** 10.4.1774. Black. Printer: Anne Catherine Green and Frederick Green. Thin paper containing mica flakes.	60.00	125.	350.
S974	**1/2 Dollar** 10.4.1774. Black. Printer: Anne Catherine Green and Frederick Green. Thin paper containing mica flakes.	60.00	125.	350.
S975	**2/3 Dollar** 10.4.1774. Black. Printer: Anne Catherine Green and Frederick Green. Thin paper containing mica flakes.	60.00	125.	350.
S976	**1 Dollar** 10.4.1774. Black. Printer: Anne Catherine Green and Frederick Green. Thin paper containing mica flakes.	35.00	75.00	250.
S977	**2 Dollars** 10.4.1774. Black. Printer: Anne Catherine Green and Frederick Green. Thin paper containing mica flakes.	35.00	75.00	250.
S978	**4 Dollars** 10.4.1774. Black. Printer: Anne Catherine Green and Frederick Green. Thin paper containing mica flakes.	35.00	75.00	250.

		Good	Fine	XF
S979	**6 Dollars** 10.4.1774. Black. Printer: Anne Catherine Green and Frederick Green. Thin paper containing mica flakes.	35.00	75.00	250.

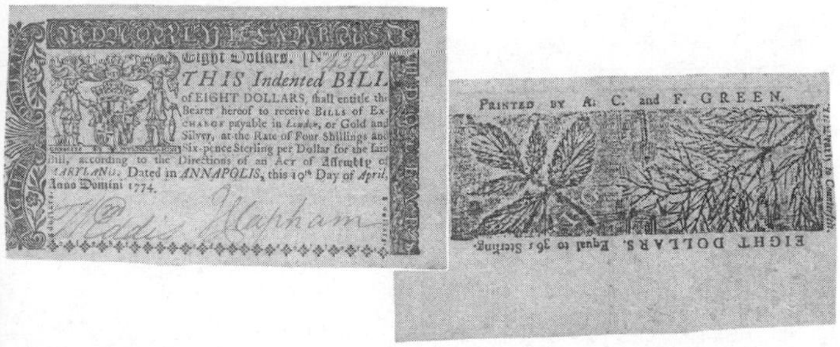

		Good	Fine	XF
S980	**8 Dollars** 10.4.1774. Black. Printer: Anne Catherine Green and Frederick Green. Thin paper containing mica flakes.	35.00	75.00	250.

1775 First Issue

		VG	VF	UNC
S981	**2/3 Dollar** 26.7.1775. Black. Printer: Frederick Green.	7500.	15,000.	
S982	**1 Dollar** 26.7.1775. Black. Printer: Frederick Green.	7500.	15,000.	
S983	**1 1/3 Dollars** 26.7.1775. Black. Printer: Frederick Green.	7500.	15,000.	
S984	**1 2/3 Dollars** 26.7.1775. Black. Printer: Frederick Green.	7500.	15,000.	
S985	**2 2/3 Dollars** 26.7.1775. Black. Printer: Frederick Green.	7500.	15,000.	
S986	**4 Dollars** 26.7.1775. Black. Printer: Frederick Green.	7500.	15,000.	

		VG	VF	UNC
S987	**8 Dollars** 26.7.1775. Black. Printer: Frederick Green.	7500.	15,000.	
S988	**16 Dollars** 26.7.1775. Black. Printer: Frederick Green.	7500.	15,000.	

1775 Second Issue

		Good	Fine	XF
S989	**1/9 Dollar** 7.12.1775. Black. Back: *SUB CLYPEO* on emblem with shield at center. Printer: Frederick Green.	200.	500.	1000.
S990	**1/6 Dollar** 7.12.1775. Black. Back: *SUB CLYPEO* on emblem with shield at center. Printer: Frederick Green.	200.	500.	1000.
S991	**1/3 Dollar** 7.12.1775. Black. Back: *SUB CLYPEO* on emblem with shield at center. Printer: Frederick Green.	200.	500.	1000.
S992	**1/2 Dollar** 7.12.1775. Black. Back: *SUB CLYPEO* on emblem with shield at center. Printer: Frederick Green.	200.	500.	1000.
S993	**2/3 Dollar** 7.12.1775. Black. Back: *SUB CLYPEO* on emblem with shield at center. Printer: Frederick Green.	200.	500.	1000.
S994	**1 Dollar** 7.12.1775. Black. Back: *SUB CLYPEO* on emblem with shield at center. Printer: Frederick Green.	200.	500.	1000.
S995	**1 1/3 Dollars** 7.12.1775. Black. Back: *SUB CLYPEO* on emblem with shield at center. Printer: Frederick Green.	200.	500.	1000.
S996	**2 Dollars** 7.12.1775. Black. Back: *SUB CLYPEO* on emblem with shield at center. Printer: Frederick Green.	200.	500.	1000.
S997	**2 2/3 Dollars** 7.12.1775. Black. Back: *SUB CLYPEO* on emblem with shield at center. Printer: Frederick Green.	200.	500.	1000.
S998	**4 Dollars** 7.12.1775. Black. Back: *SUB CLYPEO* on emblem with shield at center. Printer: Frederick Green.	200.	500.	1000.

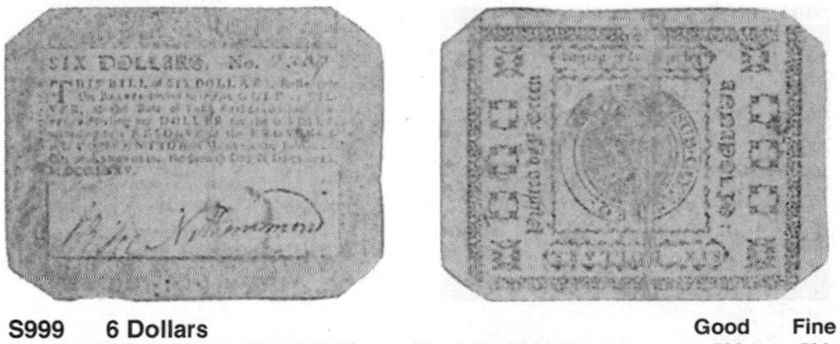

		Good	Fine	XF
S999	**6 Dollars** 7.12.1775. Black. Back: *SUB CLYPEO* on emblem with shield at center. Printer: Frederick Green.	200.	500.	1000.

		Good	Fine	XF
S1000	**8 Dollars** 7.12.1775. Black. Back: *SUB CLYPEO* on emblem with shield at center. Printer: Frederick Green.	200.	500.	1000.

Maryland

State

1776 Issue

		Good	Fine	XF
S1001	**1/9 Dollar** 14.8.1776. Black.	100.	200.	800.

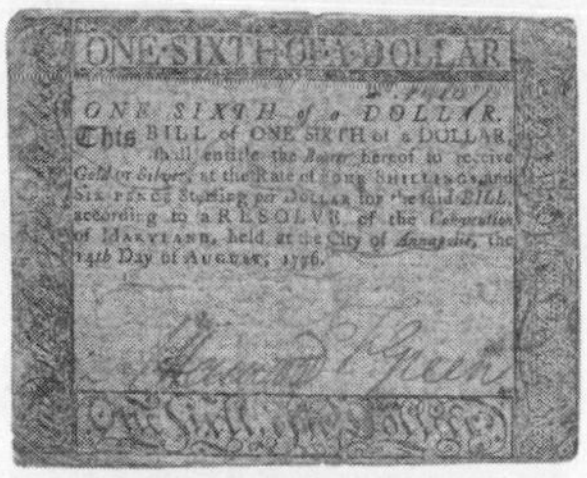

		Good	Fine	XF
S1002	**1/6 Dollar** 14.8.1776. Black.	100.	200.	800.
S1003	**1/3 Dollar** 14.8.1776. Black.	100.	200.	800.

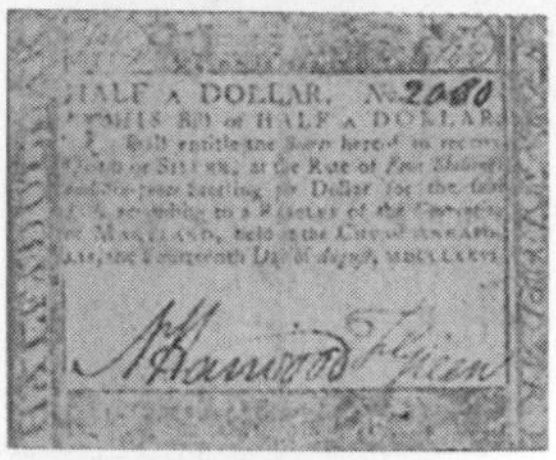

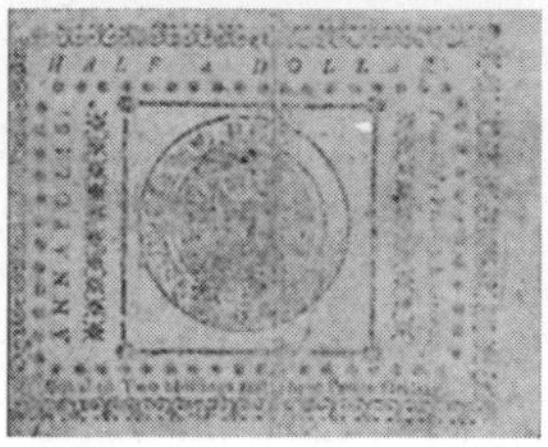

		Good	Fine	XF
S1004	**1/2 Dollar** 14.8.1776. Black.	100.	200.	800.
S1005	**2/3 Dollar** 14.8.1776. Black.	100.	200.	800.
S1006	**1 Dollar** 14.8.1776. Black.	100.	200.	800.
S1007	**1 1/3 Dollars** 14.8.1776. Black.	100.	200.	800.
S1008	**2 Dollars** 14.8.1776. Black.	100.	200.	800.
S1009	**2 2/3 Dollars** 14.8.1776. Black.	100.	200.	800.
S1010	**4 Dollars** 14.8.1776. Black.	100.	200.	800.
S1011	**6 Dollars** 14.8.1776. Black.	100.	200.	800.
S1012	**8 Dollars** 14.8.1776. Black.	100.	200.	800.

1780 First Issue

		VG	VF	UNC
S1013	**1/9 Dollar** 8.6.1780. Black. Back: State arms. Printer: Frederick Green.	1500.	3750.	—
S1014	**1/6 Dollar** 8.6.1780. Black. Back: State arms. Printer: Frederick Green.	1500.	3750.	—
S1015	**1/3 Dollar** 8.6.1780. Black. Back: State arms. Printer: Frederick Green.	1500.	3750.	—
S1016	**1/2 Dollar** 8.6.1780. Black. Back: State arms. Printer: Frederick Green.	1500.	3750.	—
S1017	**2/3 Dollar** 8.6.1780. Black. Back: State arms. Printer: Frederick Green.	1500.	3750.	—
S1018	**1 Dollar** 8.6.1780. Black. Back: State arms. Printer: Frederick Green.	1500.	3750.	—
S1019	**1 1/3 Dollars** 8.6.1780. Black. Back: State arms. Printer: Frederick Green.	1500.	3750.	—
S1020	**2 Dollars** 8.6.1780. Black. Back: State arms. Printer: Frederick Green.	1500.	3750.	—
S1021	**2 2/3 Dollars** 8.6.1780. Black. Back: State arms. Printer: Frederick Green.	1500.	3750.	—
S1022	**4 Dollars** 8.6.1780. Black. Back: State arms. Printer: Frederick Green.	1500.	3750.	—
S1023	**6 Dollars** 8.6.1780. Black. Back: State arms. Printer: Frederick Green.	1500.	3750.	—
S1024	**8 Dollars** 8.6.1780. Black. Back: State arms. Printer: Frederick Green.	1500.	3750.	—

1780 Second Issue

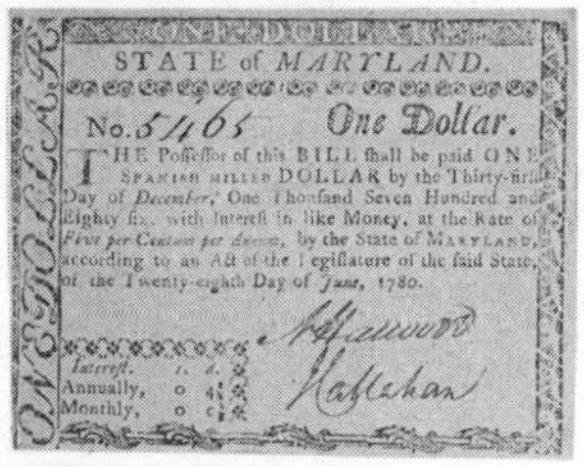

		VG	VF	UNC
S1025	**1 Dollar** 28.6.1780. Black. Back: Black and red. Watermark: *UNITED STATES.* Printer: Hall and Sellers, PA. Mica flaked paper.	300.	600.	1800.
S1026	**2 Dollars** 28.6.1780. Black. Back: Black and red. Watermark: *UNITED STATES.* Printer: Hall and Sellers, PA. Mica flaked paper.	300.	600.	1800.
S1027	**3 Dollars** 28.6.1780. Black. Back: Black and red. Watermark: *UNITED STATES.* Printer: Hall and Sellers, PA. Mica flaked paper.	300.	600.	1800.
S1028	**4 Dollars** 28.6.1780. Black. Back: Black and red. Watermark: *UNITED STATES.* Printer: Hall and Sellers, PA. Mica flaked paper.	300.	600.	1800.
S1029	**5 Dollars** 28.6.1780. Black. Back: Black and red. Watermark: *UNITED STATES.* Printer: Hall and Sellers, PA. Mica flaked paper.	300.	600.	1800.
S1030	**7 Dollars** 28.6.1780. Black. Back: Black and red. Watermark: *UNITED STATES.* Printer: Hall and Sellers, PA. Mica flaked paper.	300.	600.	1800.

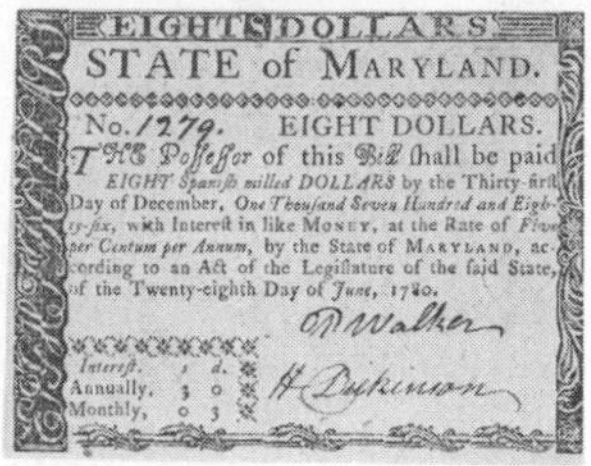

		VG	VF	UNC
S1031	**8 Dollars** 28.6.1780. Black. Back: Black and red. Watermark: *UNITED STATES.* Printer: Hall and Sellers, PA. Mica flaked paper.	300.	600.	1800.
S1032	**20 Dollars** 28.6.1780. Black. Back: Black and red. Watermark: *UNITED STATES.* Printer: Hall and Sellers, PA. Mica flaked paper.	300.	600.	1800.

1780 Third Issue

		Good	Fine	XF
S1033	**1/15 Dollar** 17.10.1780. Black. Printer: Frederick Green.	2500.	5000.	—
S1034	**1/10 Dollar** 17.10.1780. Black. Printer: Frederick Green.	2500.	5000.	—
S1035	**1/6 Dollar** 17.10.1780. Black. Printer: Frederick Green.	2500.	5000.	—
S1036	**1/5 Dollar** 17.10.1780. Black. Printer: Frederick Green.	2500.	5000.	—

1781 First Issue

		VG	VF	UNC
S1037	**1 Shilling** 10.5.1781. Black and red. Printer: Frederick Green.	3000.	7500.	—

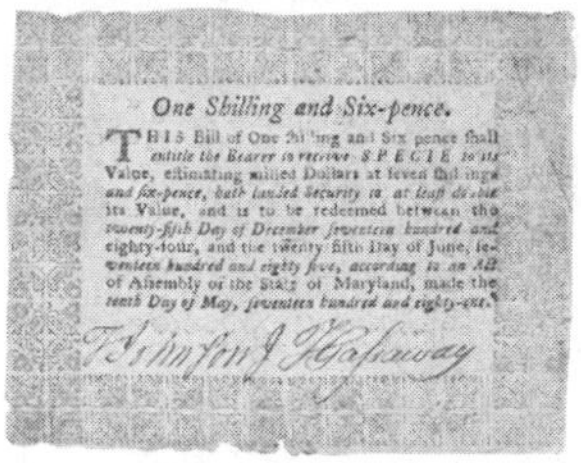

		VG	VF	UNC
S1038	**1 Shilling 6 Pence** 10.5.1781. Black and red. Printer: Frederick Green.	3000.	7500.	—
S1039	**2 Shillings 6 Pence** 10.5.1781. Black and red. Printer: Frederick Green.	3000.	7500.	—
S1040	**5 Shillings** 10.5.1781. Black and red. Printer: Frederick Green.	3000.	7500.	—
S1041	**7 Shillings 6 Pence - 1 Dollar** 10.5.1781. Black and red. Printer: Frederick Green.	3000.	7500.	—
S1042	**15 Shillings** 10.5.1781. Black and red. Printer: Frederick Green.	3000.	7500.	—
S1043	**30 Shillings** 10.5.1781. Black and red. Printer: Frederick Green.	3000.	7500.	—
S1044	**3 Pounds** 10.5.1781. Black and red. Printer: Frederick Green.	3000.	7500.	—

1781 Second Issue

		Good	Fine	XF
S1045	**3 Pence** 8.8.1781. Black.	—	—	—

		VG	VF	UNC
S1046	**4 Pence** 8.8.1781. Black.		5250.	
S1047	**6 Pence** 8.8.1781. Black.	—	—	—
S1048	**9 Pence** 8.8.1781. Black.	—	—	—

Massachusetts

Colonial

1690 Issue

		Good	Fine	XF
S1051	**5 Shillings** 10.12.1690. Black. Colony seal with indian.	—	—	—
S1052	**10 Shillings** 10.12.1690. Black. Colony seal with indian.	—	—	—
S1053	**20 Shillings** 10.12.1690. Black. Colony seal with indian.	—	—	—
S1054	**5 Pounds** 10.12.1690. Black. Colony seal with indian.	—	—	—
S1055	**2 Shillings** 3.2.1690.	—	—	—
S1056	**2 Shillings 6 Pence** 3.2.1690.	—	—	—

			Good	Fine	XF
S1057	3 Pounds	3.2.1690.	—	—	—
S1058	10 Pounds	3.2.1690.	—	—	—

NOTE: 20 SHILLINGS notes are altered 2 SHILLINGS 6 PENCE notes.

1702 Issue

			Good	Fine	XF
S1059	2 Shillings	21.11.1702. Black. 2 varieties. Back: Red scroll. Printer: John Allen.	—	—	—
S1060	2 Shillings 6 Pence	21.11.1702. Black. 2 varieties. Back: Red scroll. Printer: John Allen.	—	—	—
S1061	5 Shillings	21.11.1702. Black. Back: Red scroll. Printer: John Allen.	—	—	—
S1062	10 Shillings	21.11.1702. Black. Back: Red scroll. Printer: John Allen.	—	—	—
S1063	20 Shillings	21.11.1702. Black. 3 varieties. Back: Red scroll. Printer: John Allen.	—	—	—
S1064	40 Shillings	21.11.1702. Black. Back: Red scroll. Printer: John Allen.	—	—	—
S1065	3 Pounds	21.11.1702. Black. Back: Red scroll. Printer: John Allen.	—	—	—
S1066	5 Pounds	21.11.1702. Black. Back: Red scroll. Printer: John Allen.	—	—	—

1708 Issue

			Good	Fine	XF
S1067	2 Shillings	21.11.1708. Black. Back: Red scroll. Overprint: Red *AR* (Anna Regina).	—	—	—
S1068	2 Shillings 6 Pence	21.11.1708. Black. Back: Red scroll. Overprint: Red *AR* (Anna Regina).	—	—	—
S1069	3 Shillings	21.11.1708. Black. Back: Red scroll. Overprint: Red *AR* (Anna Regina).	—	—	—
S1070	3 Shillings 6 Pence	21.11.1708. Black. Back: Red scroll. Overprint: Red *AR* (Anna Regina).	—	—	—
S1071	5 Shillings	21.11.1708. Black. Back: Red scroll. Overprint: Red *AR* (Anna Regina).	—	—	—
S1072	10 Shillings	21.11.1708. Black. Back: Red scroll. Overprint: Red *AR* (Anna Regina).	—	—	—
S1073	20 Shillings	21.11.1708. Black. Back: Red scroll. Overprint: Red *AR* (Anna Regina).	—	—	—
S1074	40 Shillings	21.11.1708. Black. Back: Red scroll. Overprint: Red *AR* (Anna Regina).	—	—	—
S1075	3 Pounds	21.11.1708. Black. Back: Red scroll. Overprint: Red *AR* (Anna Regina).	—	—	—
S1076	5 Pounds	21.11.1708. Black. Back: Red scroll. Overprint: Red *AR* (Anna Regina).	—	—	—

1710 Issue

			Good	Fine	XF
S1077	2 Shillings	31.5.1710. Black. Overprint: Red *AR* mirrored monogram.	—	—	—
S1078	2 Shillings 6 Pence	31.5.1710. Black. Overprint: Red *AR* mirrored monogram.	—	—	—
S1079	3 Shillings	31.5.1710. Black. Overprint: Red *AR* mirrored monogram.	—	—	—
S1080	3 Shillings 6 Pence	31.5.1710. Black. Overprint: Red *AR* mirrored monogram.	—	—	—
S1081	4 Shillings	31.5.1710. Black. Back: Red scroll. Overprint: Red *AR* mirrored monogram.	—	—	—
S1082	5 Shillings	31.5.1710. Black. Back: Red scroll. Overprint: Red *AR* mirrored monogram.	—	—	—
S1083	10 Shillings	31.5.1710. Black. Back: Red scroll. Overprint: Red *AR* mirrored monogram.	—	—	—
S1084	20 Shillings	31.5.1710. Black. Back: Red scroll. Overprint: Red *AR* mirrored monogram.	—	—	—
S1085	40 Shillings	31.5.1710. Black. Back: Red scroll. Overprint: Red *AR* mirrored monogram.	—	—	—
S1086	50 Shillings	31.5.1710. Black. Back: Red scroll. Overprint: Red *AR* mirrored monogram.	—	—	—
S1087	3 Pounds	31.5.1710. Black. Back: Red scroll. Overprint: Red *AR* mirrored monogram.	—	—	—
S1088	5 Pounds	31.5.1710. Black. Back: Red scroll. Overprint: Red *AR* mirrored monogram.	—	—	—

1711 Redated Issue

			Good	Fine	XF
S1089	4 Shillings	1711 (- old date 31.5.1710). Black. *1711* engraved at right of signature. Overprint: Red *AR* mirrored monogram.	—	—	—
S1090	5 Shillings	1711 (- old date 31.5.1710). Black. *1711* engraved at right of signature. Overprint: Red *AR* mirrored monogram.	—	—	—
S1091	10 Shillings	1711 (- old date 31.5.1710). Black. *1711* engraved at right of signature. Overprint: Red *AR* mirrored monogram.	—	—	—
S1092	20 Shillings	1711 (- old date 31.5.1710). Black. *1711* engraved at right of signature. Overprint: Red *AR* mirrored monogram.	—	—	—
S1093	40 Shillings	1711 (- old date 31.5.1710). Black. *1711* engraved at right of signature. Overprint: Red *AR* mirrored monogram.	—	—	—
S1094	50 Shillings	1711 (- old date 31.5.1710). Black. *1711* engraved at right of signature. Overprint: Red *AR* mirrored monogram.	—	—	—
S1095	3 Pounds	1711 (- old date 31.5.1710). Black. *1711* engraved at right of signature. Overprint: Red *AR* mirrored monogram.	—	—	—
S1096	5 Pounds	1711 (- old date 31.5.1710). Black. *1711* engraved at right of signature. Overprint: Red *AR* mirrored monogram.	—	—	—

1713 Issue

			Good	Fine	XF
S1097	1 Shilling	14.10.1713. Black. Back: Nature leaf print.	—	—	—
S1098	1 Shilling 6 Pence	14.10.1713. Black. Back: Nature leaf print.	—	—	—
S1099	2 Shillings	14.10.1713. Black. Back: Nature leaf print.	—	—	—
S1100	2 Shillings 6 Pence	14.10.1713. Black. Back: Nature leaf print.	—	—	—
S1101	3 Shillings	14.10.1713. Black. Back: Nature leaf print.	—	—	—
S1102	5 Shillings	14.10.1713. Black. Back: Nature leaf print.	—	—	—
S1103	10 Shillings	14.10.1713. Black. Back: Nature leaf print.	—	—	—
S1104	20 Shillings	14.10.1713. Black. Back: Nature leaf print.	—	—	—

1714 Issue

			Good	Fine	XF
S1105	30 Shillings	26.5.1714. Black. Back: Nature leaf print.	—	—	—
S1106	40 Shillings	26.5.1714. Black. Back: Nature leaf print.	—	—	—
S1107	60 Shillings	26.5.1714. Black. Back: Nature leaf print.	—	—	—
S1108	100 Shillings	26.5.1714. Black. Back: Nature leaf print.	—	—	—

1714-40 Redated Low Denomination Plate Issue

#S1109-S1112 Redated successively: 1714, 1718, 1719, 1721, 1722, 1723, 1725 ,1727, 1731, 1733, 1735, 1736, and 1740.

			Good	Fine	XF
S1109	12 Pence	1714/40 (- old date 14.10.1713). Black.	—	5000.	—
S1110	1 Shilling 6 Pence	1714/40 (- old date 14.10.1713). Black.	—	5000.	—
S1111	24 Pence	1714/40 (- old date 14.10.1713) Black.	—	500.	—
S1112	2 Shillings 6 Pence	1714/40 (- old date 14.10.1713). Black.	—	—	—

1714-40 Redated Middle Denomination Plate Issue

#S1113-S116 Redated successively: 1714, 1716, 1716 w/star, 1718, 1719, 1721, 1722, 1723, 1724, 1725, 1725 w/cross, 1727, 1728, 1731, 1733, 1735, 1736, and 1740. The insignia following the 1716 and 1725 dates were added to identify the second issue of each of those years.

			Good	Fine	XF
S1113	3 Shillings	1714/40 (- old date 14.10.1713). Black.	—	—	—
S1114	5 Shillings	1714/40 (- old date 14.10.1713). Black.	—	—	—
S1115	10 Shillings	1714/40 (- old date 14.10.1713). Black.	—	—	—
S1116	20 Shillings	1714/40 (- old date 14.10.1713). Black.	—	—	—

1716-40 Redated High Denomination Plate Issue

#S1117-S1120 Redated successively: 1716, 1716 w/star, 1718, 1721, 1722, 1723, 1724, 1725, 1725 w/cross, 1727, 1733, 1735, 1736, and 1740.

			Good	Fine	XF
S1117	30 Shillings	1716/40 (- old date 26.5.1714). Black.	—	—	—
S1118	40 Shillings	1716/40 (- old date 26.5.1714). Black.	—	—	—
S1119	60 Shillings	1716/40 (- old date 26.5.1714). Black.	—	—	—
S1120	100 Shillings	1716/40 (- old date 26.5.1714). Black.	—	—	—

1722 Issue

			VG	VF	UNC
S1121	1 Penny	June 1722. Black. Round shape.	—	—	37,500.
S1122	2 Pence	June 1722. Black. Rectangular shape.	—	—	32,500.
S1123	3 Pence	June 1722. Black. Hexagonal shape.	—	—	35,000.

1736 Issue

			Good	Fine	XF
S1124	10 Pence	4.2.1736. Black.	—	—	—
S1125	1 Shilling 8 Pence	4.2.1736. Black.	—	—	—
S1126	3 Shillings 4 Pence	4.2.1736. Black.	—	—	—
S1127	6 Shillings 8 Pence	4.2.1736. Black.	—	—	—
S1128	10 Shillings	4.2.1736. Black.	—	—	—
S1129	20 Shillings	4.2.1736. Black.	—	—	—
S1130	30 Shillings	4.2.1736. Black.	—	—	—
S1131	40 Shillings	4.2.1736. Black.	—	—	—

1737 Redated Issue

			Good	Fine	XF
S1132	10 Pence	1737 (- old date 4.2.1736). Black.	—	—	—
S1133	1 Shilling 8 Pence	1737 (- old date 4.2.1736). Black.	—	—	—

	Good	Fine	XF
S1134 3 Shillings 4 Pence 1737 (- old date 4.2.1736). Black.	—	—	—
S1135 6 Shillings 8 Pence 1737 (- old date 4.2.1736). Black.	—	—	—
S1136 10 Shillings 1737 (- old date 4.2.1736). Black.	—	—	—
S1137 20 Shillings 1737 (- old date 4.2.1736). Black.	—	—	—
S1138 30 Shillings 1737 (- old date 4.2.1736). Black.	—	—	—
S1139 40 Shillings 1737 (- old date 4.2.1736). Black.	—	—	—

Number / Description	VG	VF	UNC
S1140 1 Pence 1737. Black. Winged figures. Printer: John Draper.	—	7250.	—
S1141 2 Pence 1737. Black. Angels with fruit. Printer: John Draper.	—	7250.	—
S1142 3 Pence 1737. Black. Lion. Printer: John Draper.	3500.	—	—
S1143 4 Pence 1737. Black. Squirrel & turtle. Printer: John Draper.	2250.	—	—
S1144 5 Pence 1737. Black. Circular frame. Printer: John Draper.	2250.	—	—
S1145 6 Pence 1737. Black. Tree and Indian. Printer: John Draper.	—	—	—

1741 Issue

	Good	Fine	XF
S1146 2 Pence 15.1.1741. Black. English and Massachusetts arms. Circle.	—	—	—
S1147 4 Pence 15.1.1741. Black. English and Massachusetts arms. Square.	—	—	—
S1148 6 Pence 15.1.1741. Black. English and Massachusetts arms. Hexagon.	—	—	—
S1149 8 Pence 15.1.1741. Black. English and Massachusetts arms. Octagon.	—	—	—
S1150 1 Shilling 15.1.1741. Black. English and Massachusetts arms. Oval.	—	—	—
S1151 2 Shillings 15.1.1741. Black. English and Massachusetts arms. Square with concave corners.	—	—	—
S1152 3 Shillings 15.1.1741. Black. English and Massachusetts arms.	—	—	—
S1153 4 Shillings 15.1.1741. Black. English and Massachusetts arms.	—	—	—
S1154 5 Shillings 15.1.1741. Black. English and Massachusetts arms.	—	—	—
S1155 10 Shillings 15.1.1741. Black. English and Massachusetts arms.	—	—	—
S1156 15 Shillings 15.1.1741. Black. English and Massachusetts arms.	—	—	—
S1157 20 Shillings 15.1.1741. Black. English and Massachusetts arms.	—	—	—
S1158 30 Shillings 15.1.1741. Black. English and Massachusetts arms.	—	—	—
S1159 40 Shillings 15.1.1741. Black. English and Massachusetts arms.	—	—	—

1742 Redated Issue

Number / Description	VG	VF	UNC
S1160 2 Pence 1742 (- old date 15.1.1741). Black. English and Massachusetts arms.	—	14,000.	—
S1161 4 Pence 1742 (- old date 15.1.1741). Black. English and Massachusetts arms.	—	—	—
S1162 6 Pence 1742 (- old date 15.1.1741). Black. English and Massachusetts arms.	—	—	—
S1163 8 Pence 1742 (- old date 15.1.1741). Black. English and Massachusetts arms.	—	—	—
S1164 1 Shilling 1742 (- old date 15.1.1741). Black. English and Massachusetts arms.	—	—	—
S1165 2 Shillings 1742 (- old date 15.1.1741). Black. English and Massachusetts arms.	—	—	—
S1166 3 Shillings 1742 (- old date 15.1.1741). Black. English and Massachusetts arms.	—	—	—
S1167 4 Shillings 1742 (- old date 15.1.1741). Black. English and Massachusetts arms.	—	—	—
S1168 5 Shillings 1742 (- old date 15.1.1741). Black. English and Massachusetts arms.	—	—	—
S1169 10 Shillings 1742 (- old date 15.1.1741). Black. English and Massachusetts arms.	—	—	—
S1170 15 Shillings 1742 (- old date 15.1.1741). Black. English and Massachusetts arms.	—	—	—
S1171 20 Shillings 1742 (- old date 15.1.1741). Black. English and Massachusetts arms.	—	—	—
S1172 30 Shillings 1742 (- old date 15.1.1741). Black. English and Massachusetts arms.	—	—	—
S1173 40 Shillings 1742 (- old date 15.1.1741). Black. English and Massachusetts arms.	—	—	—

#S1174-S1177 Denominations from changed plates.

Number / Description	VG	VF	UNC
S1174 3 Pence 15.1.1741. Black. English and Massachusetts arms.	—	—	—
S1175 9 Pence 15.1.1741. Black. English and Massachusetts arms.	—	—	—
S1176 15 Pence 15.1.1741. Black. English and Massachusetts arms.	—	—	—
S1177 2 Shillings 6 Pence 15.1.1741. Black. English and Massachusetts arms.	—	—	—

1744 Issue

Number / Description	VG	VF	UNC
S1178 2 Pence 20.6.1744. Black. Circle.	7500.	25,000.	—
S1179 3 Pence 20.6.1744. Black. Octagon.	7500.	25,000.	—
S1180 4 Pence 20.6.1744. Black. Square.	7500.	25,000.	—
S1181 6 Pence 20.6.1744. Black. Hexagon.	7500.	25,000.	—
S1182 9 Pence 20.6.1744. Black. Square with concave corners.	7500.	25,000.	—
S1183 1 Shilling 20.6.1744. Black. *44* in date reversed. Oval.	7500.	25,000.	—
S1184 15 Pence 20.6.1744. Black.	—	—	—
S1185 2 Shillings 6 Pence 20.6.1744. Black.	—	—	—
S1186 5 Shillings 20.6.1744. Black.	—	—	—
S1187 10 Shillings 20.6.1744. Black.	—	—	—
S1188 15 Shillings 20.6.1744. Black.	—	—	—
S1189 20 Shillings 20.6.1744. Black.	—	—	—
S1190 30 Shillings 20.6.1744. Black.	—	—	—
S1191 40 Shillings 20.6.1744. Black.	—	—	—

1750 Issue

Number / Description	VG	VF	UNC
S1192 1/72 Dollar 1750. Black. Codfish at left, balancing scales at center, and pine tree at right with motto: *RESTITUIT REM.*	—	—	—
S1193 1/24 Dollar 1750. Black. Codfish at left, balancing scales at center, and pine tree at right with motto: *RESTITUIT REM.*	—	—	—

	Good	Fine	XF
S1194 1/16 Dollar 1750. Black. Codfish at left, balancing scales at center, and pine tree at right with motto: *RESTITUIT REM.*	—	—	14,000.
S1195 1/12 Dollar 1750. Black. Codfish at left, balancing scales at center, and pine tree at right with motto: *RESTITUIT REM.*	—	—	—
S1196 1/8 Dollar 1750. Black. Codfish at left, balancing scales at center, and pine tree at right with motto: *RESTITUIT REM.*	—	—	—
S1197 1/4 Dollar 1750. Black. Codfish at left, balancing scales at center, and pine tree at right with motto: *RESTITUIT REM.*	—	—	—

1775 First Issue

Number / Description	VG	VF	UNC
S1198 6 Shillings 25.5.1775. Black. Watermark: Crown over *GR* (Georgius Rex). Printer: Paul Revere. Printed on laid paper.	3000.	7500.	—
S1199 9 Shillings 25.5.1775. Black. Watermark: Crown over *GR* (Georgius Rex). Printer: Paul Revere. Printed on laid paper.	3000.	7500.	—
S1200 10 Shillings 25.5.1775. Black. Watermark: Crown over *GR* (Georgius Rex). Printer: Paul Revere. Printed on laid paper.	3000.	7500.	—
S1201 12 Shillings 25.5.1775. Black. Watermark: Crown over *GR* (Georgius Rex). Printer: Paul Revere. Printed on laid paper.	3000.	7500.	—
S1202 14 Shillings 25.5.1775. Black. Watermark: Crown over *GR* (Georgius Rex). Printer: Paul Revere. Printed on laid paper.	3000.	7500.	—
S1203 15 Shillings 25.5.1775. Black. Watermark: Crown over *GR* (Georgius Rex). Printer: Paul Revere. Printed on laid paper.	3000.	7500.	—
S1204 16 Shillings 25.5.1775. Black. Watermark: Crown over *GR* (Georgius Rex). Printer: Paul Revere. Printed on laid paper.	3000.	7500.	—
S1205 18 Shillings 25.5.1775. Black. Watermark: Crown over *GR* (Georgius Rex). Printer: Paul Revere. Printed on laid paper.	3000.	7500.	—
S1206 20 Shillings 25.5.1775. Black. Watermark: Crown over *GR* (Georgius Rex). Printer: Paul Revere. Printed on laid paper.	3000.	7500.	—

1775 Second Issue

Number / Description	VG	VF	UNC
S1207 6 Shillings 8.7.1775. Black. Printer: Paul Revere.	4000.	6000.	
S1208 9 Shillings 8.7.1775. Black. Back: Rev. Samuel Willard. Printer: Paul Revere.	4000.	6000.	
S1209 10 Shillings 8.7.1775. Black. Back: Boston Mascare. Printer: Paul Revere.	4000.	6000.	
S1210 12 Shillings 8.7.1775. Black. Back: Boston Mascare. Printer: Paul Revere.	4000.	6000.	
S1211 14 Shillings 8.7.1775. Black. Back: Harvard College. Printer: Paul Revere.	4000.	6000.	
S1212 15 Shillings 8.7.1775. Black. Back: Rev. Samuel Willard. Printer: Paul Revere.	4000.	6000.	
S1213 16 Shillings 8.7.1775. Black. Back: Rev. Samuel Willard. Printer: Paul Revere.	4000.	6000.	
S1214 18 Shillings 8.7.1775. Black. Back: Boston Mascare. Printer: Paul Revere.	4000.	6000.	
S1215 20 Shillings 8.7.1775. Black. Back: Harvard College. Printer: Paul Revere.	4000.	6000.	

1775 Third Issue

Number / Description	VG	VF	UNC
S1216 1 Shilling 18.8.1775. Black. With three due dates. Back: Man holding a sword in one hand and the Magna Charta in the other.	5000.	—	—

No.	Denomination / Description	VG	VF	UNC
S1217	**2 Shillings** 18.8.1775. Black. With three due dates. Back: Man holding a sword in one hand and the Magna Charta in the other.	2500.	7500.	—
S1218	**2 Shillings 6 Pence** 18.8.1775. Black. With three due dates. Back: Man holding a sword in one hand and the Magna Charta in the other.	2500.	7500.	—
S1219	**4 Shillings** 18.8.1775. Black. With three due dates. Back: Man holding a sword in one hand and the Magna Charta in the other.	2500.	7500.	—
S1220	**5 Shillings** 18.8.1775. Black. With three due dates. Back: Man holding a sword in one hand and the Magna Charta in the other.	2500.	7500.	—
S1221	**6 Shillings** 18.8.1775. Black. With three due dates. Back: Man holding a sword in one hand and the Magna Charta in the other.	2500.	7500.	—
S1222	**7 Shillings 6 Pence - 1 Dollar** 18.8.1775. Black. With three due dates. Back: Man holding a sword in one hand and the Magna Charta in the other.	2500.	7500.	—
S1223	**8 Shillings** 18.8.1775. Black. With three due dates. Back: Man holding a sword in one hand and the Magna Charta in the other.	2500.	7500.	—
S1224	**10 Shillings** 18.8.1775. Black. With three due dates. Back: Man holding a sword in one hand and the Magna Charta in the other.	2500.	7500.	—
S1225	**11 Shillings** 18.8.1775. Black. With three due dates. Back: Man holding a sword in one hand and the Magna Charta in the other.	2500.	7500.	—
S1226	**12 Shillings** 18.8.1775. Black. With three due dates. Back: Man holding a sword in one hand and the Magna Charta in the other.	2500.	7500.	—
S1227	**17 Shillings** 18.8.1775. Black. With three due dates. Back: Man holding a sword in one hand and the Magna Charta in the other.	2500.	7500.	—
S1228	**20 Shillings** 18.8.1775. Black. With three due dates. Back: Man holding a sword in one hand and the Magna Charta in the other.	2500.	7500.	—
S1229	**24 Shillings** 18.8.1775. Black. With three due dates. Back: Man holding a sword in one hand and the Magna Charta in the other.	2500.	7500.	—
S1230	**30 Shillings** 18.8.1775.	2750.	8500.	—
S1231	**40 Shillings** 18.8.1775.	2750.	8500.	—

1775 Fourth Issue

No.	Denomination / Description	VG	VF	UNC
S1232	**8 Pence** 7.12.1775. Black. With three due dates. Back: Man holding a sword in one hand and the Magna Charta in the other. Printer: Paul Revere.	3000.	8750.	—
S1233	**1 Shilling 4 Pence** 7.12.1775. Black. With three due dates. Back: Man holding a sword in one hand and the Magna Charta in the other. Printer: Paul Revere.	3000.	8750.	—
S1234	**1 Shilling 6 Pence** 7.12.1775. Black. With three due dates. Back: Man holding a sword in one hand and the Magna Charta in the other. Printer: Paul Revere.	3000.	8750.	—
S1235	**2 Shillings 8 Pence** 7.12.1775. Black. With three due dates. Back: Man holding a sword in one hand and the Magna Charta in the other. Printer: Paul Revere.	3000.	8750.	—

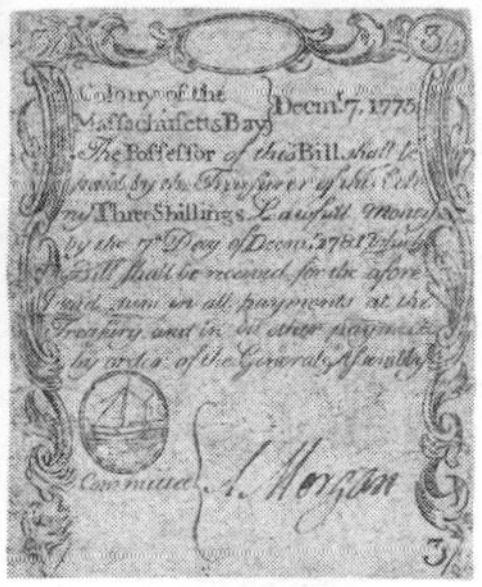

No.	Denomination / Description	VG	VF	UNC
S1236	**3 Shillings** 7.12.1775. Black. With three due dates. Back: Man holding a sword in one hand and the Magna Charta in the other. Printer: Paul Revere.	3000.	8750.	—
S1237	**3 Shillings 4 Pence** 7.12.1775. Black. With three due dates. Back: Man holding a sword in one hand and the Magna Charta in the other. Printer: Paul Revere.	3000.	8750.	—
S1238	**4 Shillings 6 Pence** 7.12.1775. Black. With three due dates. Back: Man holding a sword in one hand and the Magna Charta in the other. Printer: Paul Revere.	3000.	8750.	—
S1239	**7 Shillings** 7.12.1775. Black. With three due dates. Back: Man holding a sword in one hand and the Magna Charta in the other. Printer: Paul Revere.	3000.	8750.	—
S1240	**10 Shillings** 7.12.1775. Black. With three due dates. Back: Man holding a sword in one hand and the Magna Charta in the other. Printer: Paul Revere.	3000.	8750.	—
S1241	**14 Shillings** 7.12.1775. Black. With three due dates. Back: Man holding a sword in one hand and the Magna Charta in the other. Printer: Paul Revere.	3000.	8750.	—
S1242	**16 Shillings** 7.12.1775. Black. With three due dates. Back: Man holding a sword in one hand and the Magna Charta in the other. Printer: Paul Revere.	3000.	8750.	—
S1243	**22 Shillings** 7.12.1775. Black. With three due dates. Back: Man holding a sword in one hand and the Magna Charta in the other. Printer: Paul Revere.	3000.	8750.	—
S1244	**28 Shillings** 7.12.1775. Black. With three due dates. Back: Man holding a sword in one hand and the Magna Charta in the other. Printer: Paul Revere.	3000.	8750.	—
S1245	**36 Shillings** 7.12.1775. Black. With three due dates. Back: Man holding a sword in one hand and the Magna Charta in the other. Printer: Paul Revere.	3500.	10,000.	—
S1246	**42 Shillings** 7.12.1775. Black. With three due dates. Back: Man holding a sword in one hand and the Magna Charta in the other. Printer: Paul Revere.	3500.	10,000.	—
S1247	**48 Shillings** 7.12.1775. Black. With three due dates. Back: Man holding a sword in one hand and the Magna Charta in the other. Printer: Paul Revere.	3500.	10,000.	—

Massachusetts

State

1776 First Issue

No.	Denomination / Description	VG	VF	UNC
S1248	**3 Pence** 18.6.1776. Black. With two due dates. Printer: Benjamin Edes. Coarse paper.	250.	650.	—
S1249	**4 Pence** 18.6.1776. Black. With two due dates. Printer: Benjamin Edes. Coarse paper.	250.	650.	—
S1250	**5 Pence** 18.6.1776. Black. With two due dates. Printer: Benjamin Edes. Coarse paper.	250.	650.	—
S1251	**6 Pence** 18.6.1776. Black. With two due dates. Printer: Benjamin Edes. Coarse paper.	250.	650.	—
S1252	**9 Pence** 18.6.1776. Black. With two due dates. Printer: Benjamin Edes. Coarse paper.	250.	650.	—
S1253	**10 Pence** 18.6.1776. Black. With two due dates. Printer: Benjamin Edes. Coarse paper.	250.	650.	—
S1254	**1 Shilling** 18.6.1776. Black. With two due dates. Printer: Benjamin Edes. Coarse paper.	250.	650.	—
S1255	**1 Shilling 3 Pence** 18.6.1776. Black. With two due dates. Printer: Benjamin Edes. Coarse paper.	250.	650.	—
S1256	**1 Shilling 8 Pence** 18.6.1776. Black. With two due dates. Printer: Benjamin Edes. Coarse paper.	250.	650.	—
S1257	**2 Shillings 4 Pence** 18.6.1776. Black. With two due dates. Printer: Benjamin Edes. Coarse paper.	250.	650.	—
S1258	**2 Shillings 6 Pence** 18.6.1776. Black. With two due dates. Printer: Benjamin Edes. Coarse paper.	250.	650.	—
S1259	**3 Shillings 6 Pence** 18.6.1776. Black. With two due dates. Printer: Benjamin Edes. Coarse paper.	250.	650.	—
S1260	**4 Shillings** 18.6.1776. Black. With two due dates. Printer: Benjamin Edes. Coarse paper.	250.	650.	—
S1261	**4 Pence** 18.6.1776. Black. With two due dates. Printer: Benjamin Edes. Coarse paper.	250.	650.	—
S1262	**5 Shillings** 18.6.1776. Black. With two due dates. Printer: Benjamin Edes. Coarse paper.	250.	650.	—
S1263	**5 Shillings 4 Pence** 18.6.1776. Black. With two due dates. Printer: Benjamin Edes. Coarse paper.	250.	650.	—
S1264	**6 Shillings** 18.6.1776. Black. With two due dates. Printer: Benjamin Edes. Coarse paper.	2000.	5000.	—

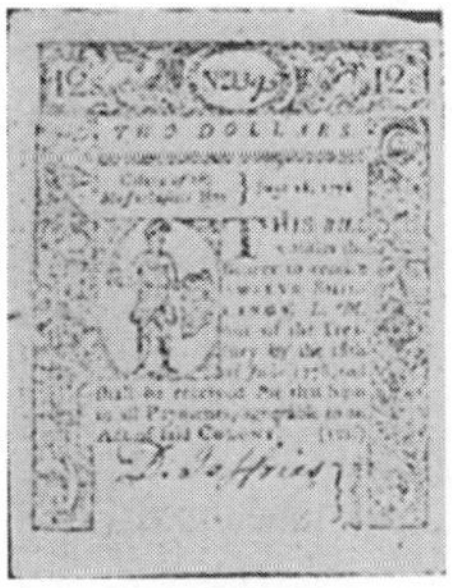

No.	Denomination / Description	VG	VF	UNC
S1265	**12 Shillings** 18.6.1776. Black. With two due dates. Printer: Benjamin Edes. Coarse paper.	2000.	5000.	—
S1266	**18 Shillings** 18.6.1776. Black. With two due dates. Printer: Benjamin Edes. Coarse paper.	2000.	5000.	—
S1267	**24 Shillings** 18.6.1776. Black. With two due dates. Printer: Benjamin Edes. Coarse paper.	2000.	5000.	—
S1268	**30 Shillings** 18.6.1776. Black. With two due dates. Printer: Benjamin Edes. Coarse paper.	2000.	5000.	—
S1269	**36 Shillings** 18.6.1776. Black. With two due dates. Printer: Benjamin Edes. Coarse paper.	2000.	5000.	—

	VG	VF	UNC
S1270 42 Shillings 18.6.1776. Black. With two due dates. Printer: Benjamin Edes. Coarse paper.	2000.	5000.	—
S1271 48 Shillings 18.6.1776. Black. With two due dates. Printer: Benjamin Edes. Coarse paper.	2000.	5000.	—

1776 Second Issue

	Good	Fine	XF
S1272 10 Shillings 17.9.1776. Black. *COLONY* changed to *STATE*.	—	—	—

	VG	VF	UNC
S1273 14 Shillings 17.9.1776. Black. *COLONY* changed to *STATE*.	—	8250.	—
S1274 16 Shillings 17.9.1776. Black. *COLONY* changed to *STATE*.	—	—	—
S1275 22 Shillings 17.9.1776. Black. *COLONY* changed to *STATE*.	3500.	—	—
S1276 28 Shillings 17.9.1776. Black. *COLONY* changed to *STATE*.	—	—	—
S1277 36 Shillings 17.9.1776. Black. *COLONY* changed to *STATE*.	—	—	—
S1278 42 Shillings 17.9.1776. Black. *COLONY* changed to *STATE*.	—	—	—
S1279 48 Shillings 17.9.1776. Black. *COLONY* changed to *STATE*.	—	—	—

1776 Third Issue

	VG	VF	UNC
S1280 2 Pence 18.10.1776. Black. Back: Pine tree. Printer: Paul Revere and John Gill.	250.	600.	2500.
S1281 3 Pence 18.10.1776. Black. Back: Pine tree. Printer: Paul Revere and John Gill.	250.	600.	2500.
S1282 4 Pence 18.10.1776. Black. Back: Pine tree. Printer: Paul Revere and John Gill.	250.	600.	2500.
S1283 6 Pence 18.10.1776. Black. Back: Pine tree. Printer: Paul Revere and John Gill.	250.	600.	2500.
S1284 8 Pence 18.10.1776. Black. Back: Pine tree. Printer: Paul Revere and John Gill.	250.	600.	2500.
S1285 9 Pence 18.10.1776. Black. Back: Pine tree. Printer: Paul Revere and John Gill.	250.	600.	2500.
S1286 1 Shilling 18.10.1776. Black. Back: Pine tree. Printer: Paul Revere and John Gill.	250.	600.	2500.
S1287 1 Shilling 6 Pence 18.10.1776. Black. Back: Pine tree. Printer: Paul Revere and John Gill.	250.	600.	2500.
S1288 2 Shillings 18.10.1776. Black. Back: Pine tree. Printer: Paul Revere and John Gill.	250.	600.	2500.
S1289 3 Shillings 18.10.1776. Black. Back: Pine tree. Printer: Paul Revere and John Gill.	250.	600.	2500.
S1290 4 Shillings 18.10.1776. Black. Back: Pine tree. Printer: Paul Revere and John Gill.	250.	600.	2500.
S1291 4 Shillings 6 Pence 18.10.1776. Black. Back: Pine tree. Printer: Paul Revere and John Gill.	250.	600.	2500.
S1292 6 Shillings 18.10.1776. Black. Back: Pine tree. Printer: Paul Revere and John Gill.	—	—	—
S1293 12 Shillings 18.10.1776. Black. Back: Pine tree. Printer: Paul Revere and John Gill.	—	—	—
S1294 18 Shillings 18.10.1776. Black. Back: Pine tree. Printer: Paul Revere and John Gill.	—	7500.	—
S1295 24 Shillings 18.10.1776. Black. Back: Pine tree. Printer: Paul Revere and John Gill.	—	—	—
S1296 30 Shillings 18.10.1776. Black. Back: Pine tree. Printer: Paul Revere and John Gill.	—	—	25,000.
S1297 36 Shillings 18.10.1776. Black. Back: Pine tree. Printer: Paul Revere and John Gill.	—	—	—
S1298 42 Shillings 18.10.1776. Black. Back: Pine tree. Printer: Paul Revere and John Gill.	—	—	—
S1299 48 Shillings 18.10.1776. Black. Back: Pine tree. Printer: Paul Revere and John Gill.	—	—	—
S1300 54 Shillings 18.10.1776. Black. Back: Pine tree. Printer: Paul Revere and John Gill.	—	—	—
S1301 60 Shillings 18.10.1776. Black. Back: Pine tree. Printer: Paul Revere and John Gill.	—	—	—
S1302 66 Shillings 18.10.1776. Black. Back: Pine tree. Printer: Paul Revere and John Gill.	—	—	—
S1303 72 Shillings 18.10.1776. Black. Back: Pine tree. Printer: Paul Revere and John Gill.	—	8000.	—

1776 Fourth Issue

	VG	VF	UNC
S1304 10 Shillings 17.11.1776. Black. Back: *MAGNA CHARTA* changed to *INDEPENDENCE*.	—	8250.	—
S1305 14 Shillings 17.11.1776. Black. Back: *MAGNA CHARTA* changed to *INDEPENDENCE*.	—	7500.	—
S1306 16 Shillings 17.11.1776. Black. Back: *MAGNA CHARTA* changed to *INDEPENDENCE*.	—	—	—
S1307 22 Shillings 17.11.1776. Black. Back: *MAGNA CHARTA* changed to *INDEPENDENCE*.	—	—	—
S1308 28 Shillings 17.11.1776. Black. Back: *MAGNA CHARTA* changed to *INDEPENDENCE*.	—	—	—
S1309 36 Shillings 17.11.1776. Black. Back: *MAGNA CHARTA* changed to *INDEPENDENCE*.	—	—	—
S1310 42 Shillings 17.11.1776. Black. Back: *MAGNA CHARTA* changed to *INDEPENDENCE*.	—	—	—
S1311 48 Shillings 17.11.1776. Black. Back: *MAGNA CHARTA* changed to *INDEPENDENCE*.	—	—	—

1778 Issue

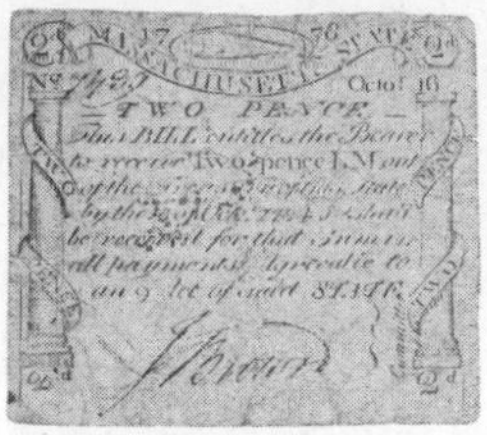

	VG	VF	UNC
S1312 2 Pence 16.10.1778. Black. Printer: Paul Revere and Thomas Fleet.	200.	450.	1500.
S1313 3 Pence 16.10.1778. Black. Printer: Paul Revere and Thomas Fleet.	200.	450.	1500.
S1314 4 Pence 16.10.1778. Black. Printer: Paul Revere and Thomas Fleet.	200.	450.	1500.

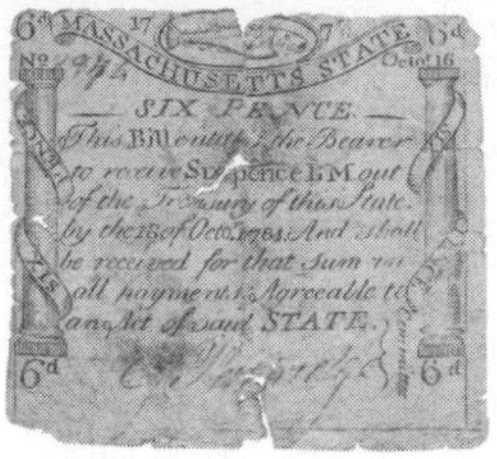

	VG	VF	UNC
S1315 6 Pence 16.10.1778. Black. Printer: Paul Revere and Thomas Fleet.	200.	450.	1500.
S1316 8 Pence 16.10.1778. Black. Printer: Paul Revere and Thomas Fleet.	200.	450.	1500.
S1317 9 Pence 16.10.1778. Black. Printer: Paul Revere and Thomas Fleet.	200.	450.	1500.
S1318 12 Pence 16.10.1778. Black. Printer: Paul Revere and Thomas Fleet.	200.	450.	1500.
S1319 1 Shilling 6 Pence 16.10.1778. Black. Printer: Paul Revere and Thomas Fleet.	200.	450.	1500.
S1320 2 Shillings 16.10.1778. Black. Printer: Paul Revere and Thomas Fleet.	200.	450.	1500.
S1321 3 Shillings 16.10.1778. Black. Printer: Paul Revere and Thomas Fleet.	200.	450.	1500.
S1322 4 Shillings 16.10.1778. Black. Printer: Paul Revere and Thomas Fleet.	200.	450.	1500.
S1323 4 Shillings 6 Pence 16.10.1778. Black. Printer: Paul Revere and Thomas Fleet.	200.	450.	1500.

1779 Issue

	VG	VF	UNC
S1324 1 Shilling 1779. Printer: Paul Revere and Thomas Fleet.	350.	750.	3000.
S1325 1 Shilling 6 Pence 1779. Printer: Paul Revere and Thomas Fleet.	350.	750.	3000.
S1326 2 Shillings 1779. Printer: Paul Revere and Thomas Fleet.	350.	750.	3000.
S1327 2 Shillings 6 Pence 1779. Printer: Paul Revere and Thomas Fleet.	350.	750.	3000.
S1328 3 Shillings 1779. Printer: Paul Revere and Thomas Fleet.	350.	750.	3000.
S1329 3 Shillings 6 Pence 1779. Printer: Paul Revere and Thomas Fleet.	350.	750.	3000.
S1330 4 Shillings 1779. Printer: Paul Revere and Thomas Fleet.	350.	750.	3000.
S1331 4 Shillings 6 Pence 1779. Printer: Paul Revere and Thomas Fleet.	350.	750.	3000.
S1332 4 Shillings 8 Pence 1779. Printer: Paul Revere and Thomas Fleet.	350.	750.	3000.
S1333 5 Shillings 1779. Printer: Paul Revere and Thomas Fleet.	350.	750.	3000.
S1334 5 Shillings 4 Pence 1779. Printer: Paul Revere and Thomas Fleet.	500.	1000.	4000.

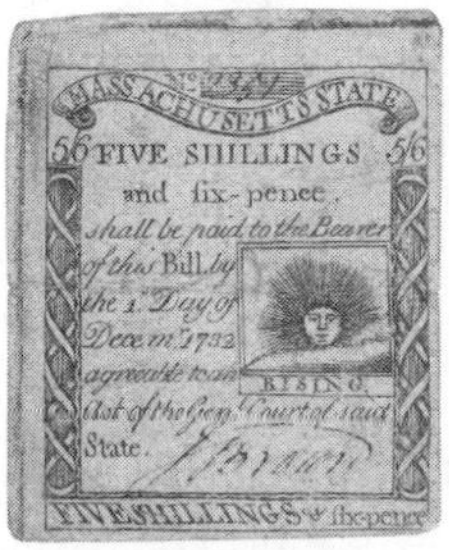

	VG	VF	UNC
S1335 5 Shillings 6 Pence 1779. Printer: Paul Revere and Thomas Fleet.	500.	1000.	4000.

1780 Issue

	VG	VF	UNC
S1336 1 Dollar 5.5.1780. Black. Back: Red and black. Watermark: *UNITED STATES*. Printer: Hall and Sellers, PA.	100.	225.	750.

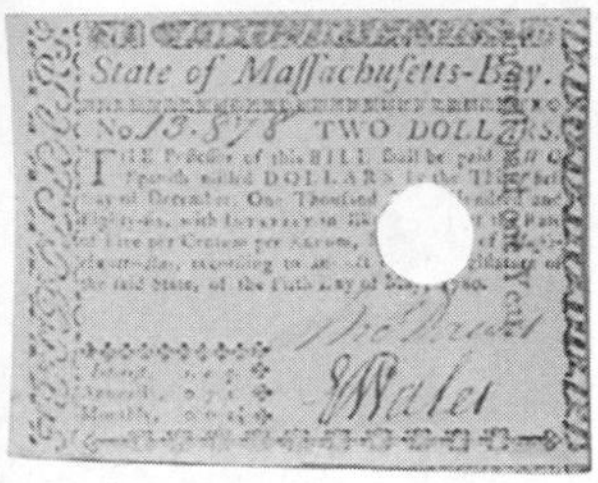

	VG	VF	UNC
S1337 2 Dollars 5.5.1780. Black. Back: Red and black. Watermark: *UNITED STATES.* Printer: Hall and Sellers, PA.	100.	225.	750.
S1338 3 Dollars 5.5.1780. Black. Back: Red and black. Watermark: *UNITED STATES.* Printer: Hall and Sellers, PA.	100.	225.	750.
S1339 4 Dollars 5.5.1780. Black. Back: Red and black. Watermark: *UNITED STATES.* Printer: Hall and Sellers, PA.	100.	225.	750.

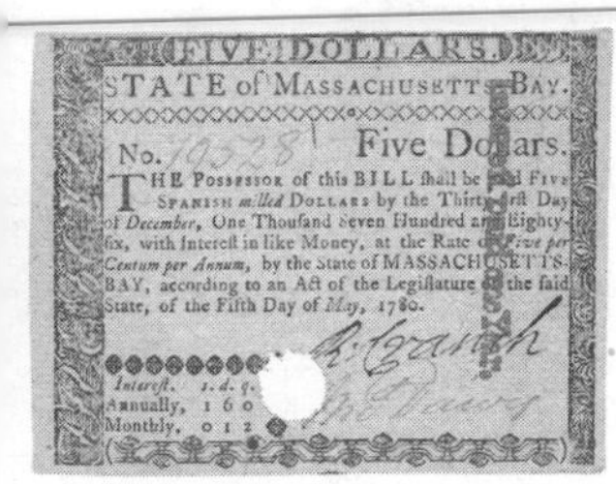

	VG	VF	UNC
S1340 5 Dollars 5.5.1780. Black. Back: Red and black. Watermark: *UNITED STATES.* Printer: Hall and Sellers, PA.	100.	225.	750.
S1341 7 Dollars 5.5.1780. Black. Back: Red and black. Watermark: *UNITED STATES.* Printer: Hall and Sellers, PA.	100.	225.	750.

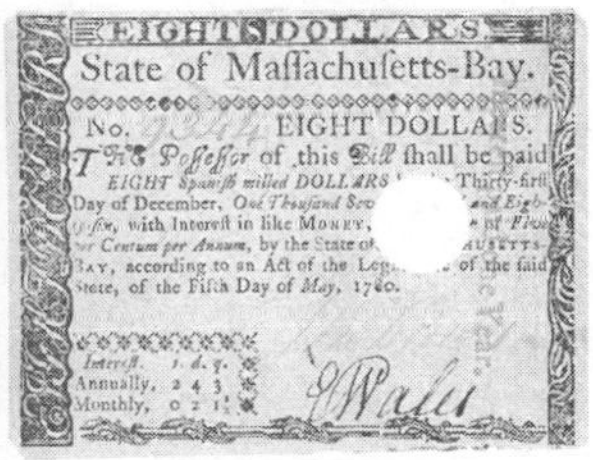

	VG	VF	UNC
S1342 8 Dollars 5.5.1780. Black. Back: Red and black. Watermark: *UNITED STATES.* Printer: Hall and Sellers, PA.	100.	225.	750.
S1343 20 Dollars 5.5.1780. Black. Back: Red and black. Watermark: *UNITED STATES.* Printer: Hall and Sellers, PA.	100.	225.	750.

Commonwealth

1781 Treasury Certificates Issue

	VG	VF	UNC
S1344 4 Dollars 1781. Black. Text in top border: *COMMONWEALTH OF MASSACHUSETTS.* Various handwritten dates.	2250.	4750.	—

	Good	Fine	XF
S1345 6 Dollars 10.12.1781. Black. Text in top border: *COMMONWEALTH OF MASSACHUSETTS.* Various handwritten dates.	—	—	—
S1346 8 Dollars 1781. Black. Text in top border: *COMMONWEALTH OF MASSACHUSETTS.* Various handwritten dates.	—	—	—
S1347 16 Dollars 1781. Black. Text in top border: *COMMONWEALTH OF MASSACHUSETTS.* Various handwritten dates.	—	—	—

Michigan

British Occupation - War of 1812

1815 Fort Michilmackinac Issue

The fort on Michilmackinac Island, located in the Straits of Mackinac, was captured by the British and later restored to U.S.A. forces after the war ended.

	Good	Fine	XF
S1347A 4 Dollars 1.5.1815. Rare.	—	—	—

Minnesota

State

1855 Auditor's Office Treasury Issue

	Good	Fine	XF
S1348 10 Dollars 7.7.1855. Woman standing by another kneeling at left, farmer plowing by Indian on horseback at upper right.	85.00	175.	—

January 29, 1858 Authorized Issue

	Good	Fine	XF
S1349 1 Dollar 1858. Black. Various handwritten dates. Printer: Lith. by Louis Buechner, St. Paul, Minnesota.	42.50	85.00	—
S1350 3 Dollars 20.3.1858. Black. Various handwritten dates. Printer: Lith. by Louis Buechner, St. Paul, Minnesota.	65.00	175.	—
S1351 5 Dollars 1858. Black. Various handwritten dates. Printer: Lith. by Louis Buechner, St. Paul, Minnesota.	65.00	150.	—
S1352 10 Dollars 1858. Black. Various handwritten dates. Printer: Lith. by Louis Buechner, St. Paul, Minnesota.	85.00	175.	—
S1353 20 Dollars 20.3.1858. Black. Various handwritten dates. Printer: Lith. by Louis Buechner, St. Paul, Minnesota.	100.	200.	—

Mississippi

Civil War

1861 Issue

	VG	VF	UNC
S1360 10 Dollars 1861-62; 19.1.1863. Black on red underprint. Portrait Gov. J. J. Pettus at lower left, black with horses at top center, portrait woman at lower right. Various handwritten dates and "payable" dates of a year later. Printer: ABNC, New York and New Orleans.	300.	750.	1600.
S1361 20 Dollars 1861-62; 19.1.1863. Black on red underprint. Woman at lower right, mules pulling wagon load of cotton at top center, portrait Gov. J. J. Pettus at lower right. Various handwritten dates and "payable" dates of a year later. Printer: ABNC, New York and New Orleans.	300.	800.	1800.

	VG	VF	UNC
S1362 50 Dollars 1861-62; 19.1.1863. Black on red underprint. Portrait Gov. J. J. Pettus at upper left, mules pulling wagon at top center, black picking cotton at right. Uniface. Various handwritten dates and "payable" dates of a year later. Printer: ABNC, New York and New Orleans.	300.	800.	1800.
S1363 100 Dollars 1861-62; 19.1.1863. Black on red-orange underprint. Seated female with child ("History") at upper left, blacks gathering cotton at top center, portrait Gov. J. J. Pettus at lower right. Uniface.	300.	700.	1300.

1862 Cotton Pledged Issues

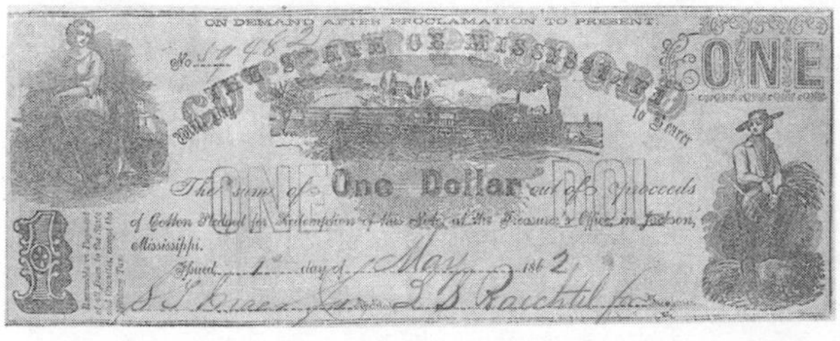

	VG	VF	UNC
S1364 1 Dollar			
1862. Black on red underprint. Seated woman at upper left, steam passenger train at upper center, farmer holding sheaf at lower right. Green text: *COTTON PLEDGED.*			
a. 1.4.1862.	30.00	75.00	175.
b. 1.5.1862.	30.00	75.00	175.
S1365 1 Dollar			
1.5.1862; 1.11.1862. Black on red underprint. Seated woman at upper left, steam passenger train at upper center, farmer holding sheaf at lower right. Similar to #S1364 but blue text: *COTTON PLEDGED.*	30.00	75.00	175.
S1366 2 1/2 Dollars			
1.4.1862; 1.5.1862. Black on red underprint. Farmer standing with sheaf at upper left, standing Indian with tomahawk at lower right. Green text: *COTTON PLEDGED.*	40.00	100.	225.

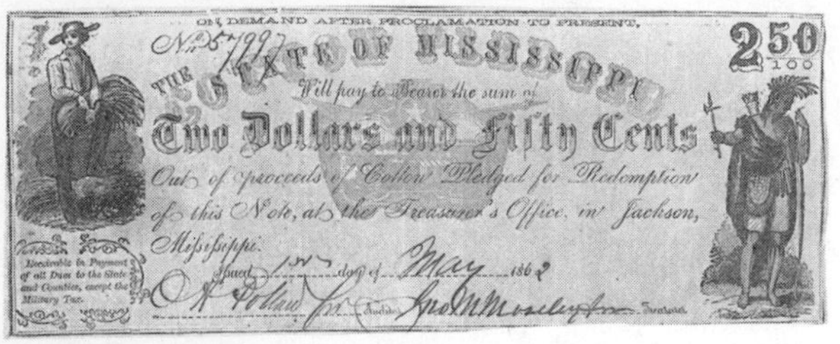

	VG	VF	UNC
S1367 2 1/2 Dollars			
1.5.1862; 1.11.1862. Back on red underprint. Farmer standing with sheaf at upper left, standing Indian with tomahawk at lower right. Similar to #S1366 but with blue text: *COTTON PLEDGED* in underprint.	45.00	120.	265.

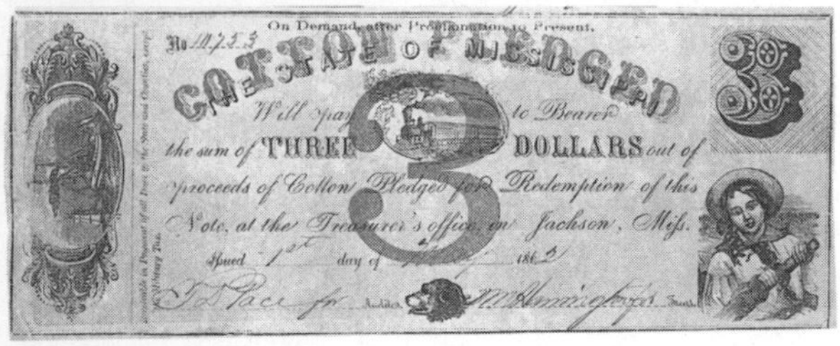

	VG	VF	UNC
S1368 3 Dollars			
1.4.1862; 1.5.1862. Black on green underprint. Landscape in oval at left, steam passenger train at center, young boy at lower right. Green text: *COTTON PLEDGED.*	40.00	125.	275.
S1369 3 Dollars			
1.5.1862; 1.11.1862. Black on green underprint. Landscape in oval at left, steam passenger train at center, young boy at lower right. Similar to #S1368 but blue text: *COTTON PLEDGED.*	45.00	65.00	200.

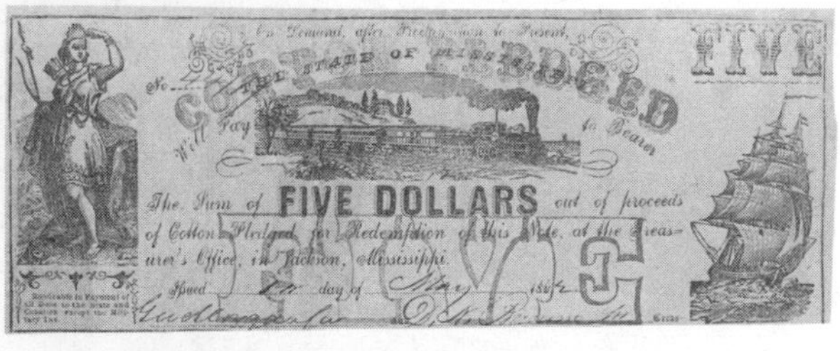

	VG	VF	UNC
S1370 5 Dollars			
7.3.1862. Black on light green underprint. Woman at left, steam passenger train at center, sailing ship at lower right. Olive text: *COTTON PLEDGED.*	75.00	175.	375.
S1371 5 Dollars			
7.3.1862. Black on pink underprint. Woman at left, steam passenger train at center, sailing ship at lower right. Olive text: *COTTON PLEDGED.* Similar to #S1370.	40.00	100.	225.
S1372 5 Dollars			
1862. Black without underprint. Woman at left, steam passenger train at center, sailing ship at lower right. Similar to #S1370 but green text: *COTTON PLEDGED.*			
a. 1.4.1862.	30.00	75.00	185.
b. Printed on backs of auditor's bills. 1.4.1862.	30.00	75.00	185.
c. 1.5.1862.	30.00	75.00	185.
d. Printed on backs of bills of exchange. 1.5.1862.	30.00	75.00	185
S1373 10 Dollars			
7.3.1862. Black on light gray underprint. Woman with balancing scales and sword at left, building behind trees at right. Olive text: *COTTON PLEDGED.*	75.00	200.	475.
S1374 10 Dollars			
7.3.1862. Black on pink underprint. Woman with balancing scales and sword at left, building behind trees at right. Olive text: *COTTON PLEDGED.* Similar to #S1373.	50.00	125.	275.

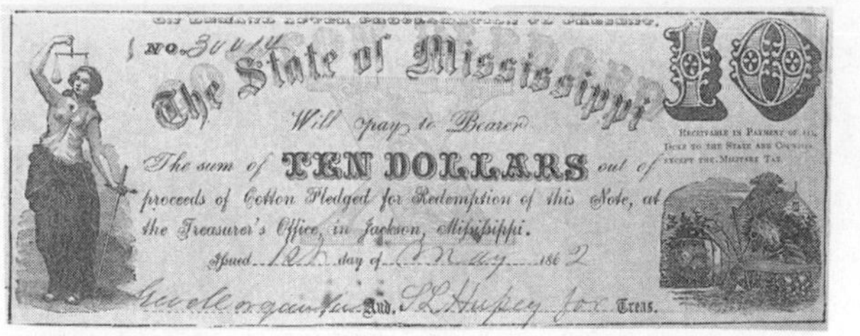

	VG	VF	UNC
S1375 10 Dollars			
1862. Black without underprint. Woman with balancing scales and sword at left, building behind trees at right. Similar to #S1373 but green text: *COTTON PLEDGED.*			
a. 1.4.1862.	50.00	125.	275.
b. Printed on backs of auditor's bills. 1.4.1862.	50.00	125.	275.
c. 1.5.1862.	50.00	125.	275.
d. Printed on backs of bills of exchange. 1.5.1862.	50.00	125.	275.

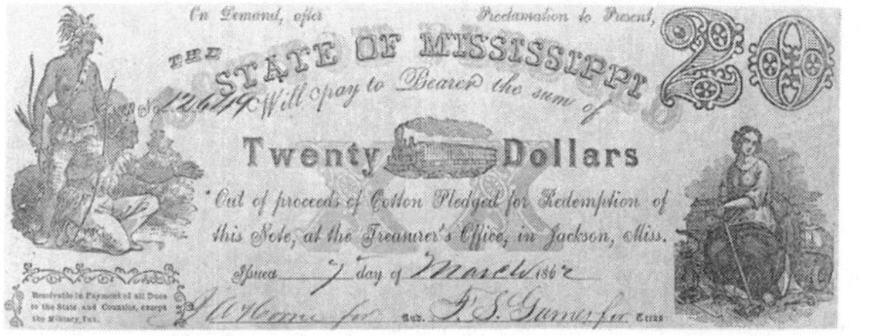

	VG	VF	UNC
S1376 20 Dollars			
7.3.1862. Black on light gray underprint. Two Indian braves at left, steam passenger train at center, seated woman at right. Olive text: *COTTON PLEDGED.*	140.	275.	600.
S1377 20 Dollars			
7.3.1862. Black on pink underprint. Two Indian braves at left, steam passenger train at center, seated woman at right. Olive text: *COTTON PLEDGED.* Similar to #S1376.	70.00	150.	300.

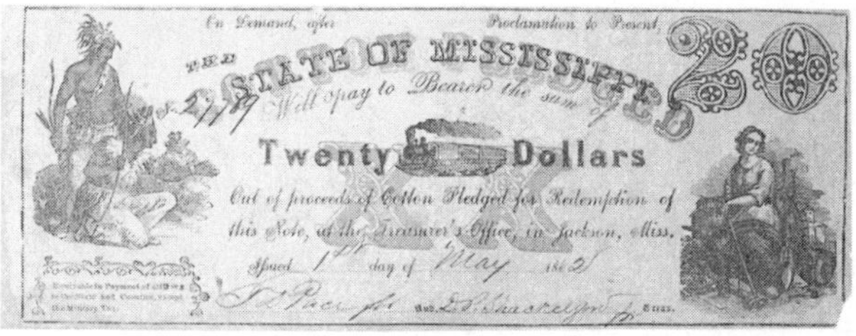

	VG	VF	UNC
S1378 20 Dollars			
1862. Black without underprint. Two Indian braves at left, steam passenger train at center, seated woman at right. Similar to #S1376 but green text: *COTTON PLEDGED.*			
a. 1.4.1862.	50.00	100.	200.
b. Printed on backs of auditor's bills. 1.4.1862.	50.00	100.	200.
c. 1.5.1862.	50.00	100.	200.
d. Printed on backs of bills of exchange. 1.5.1862.	50.00	100.	200.
S1379 50 Dollars			
7.3.1862. Black on light gray underprint. Indian brave at left, blacks picking cotton at right. Olive text: *COTTON PLEDGED.*	175.	350.	625.
S1380 50 Dollars			
7.3.1862. Black on pink underprint. Indian brave at left, blacks picking cotton at right. Olive text: *COTTON PLEDGED.* Similar to #S1379.	85.00	200.	400.

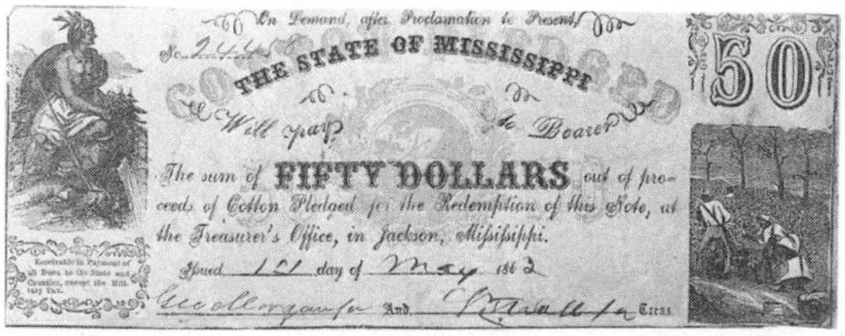

	VG	VF	UNC
S1381 50 Dollars			
1862. Black without underprint. Indian brave at left, blacks picking cotton at right. Similar to #S1379 but green text: *COTTON PLEDGED.*			
a. 1.4.1862.	300.	500.	800.
b. Printed on backs of auditor's bills.	300.	500.	800.
c. 1.5.1862.	300.	500.	800.
d. Printed on backs of bills of exchange. 1.5.1862.	300.	500.	800.
S1382 100 Dollars			
7.3.1862. Black on light gray underprint. Woman standing at left and right, steam train at center. Olive text: *COTTON PLEDGED.*	300.	500.	800.
S1383 100 Dollars			
7.3.1862. Black on pink underprint. Woman standing at left and right, steam train at center. Olive text: *COTTON PLEDGED.* Similar to #S1382. Rare.	—	—	—

S1384 100 Dollars

1862. Black without underprint. Woman standing at left and right, steam train at center. Similar to #S1382 but green text: *COTTON PLEDGED.*

	VG	VF	UNC
a. 1.4.1862.	90.00	250.	500.
b. 1.5.1862.	90.00	250.	500.
c. Printed on backs of bills of exchange. 1.5.1862.	90.00	250.	500.

1862 Faith of the State Pledged Issues

S1385 5 Dollars

1862. Black. Plow at left, steam passenger train at top center, farmer holding sheaf of grain at lower right. Red text: *Faith of the State Pledged.*

	VG	VF	UNC
a. 1.7.1862.	35.00	75.00	200.
b. Overprint: *Re-Issue.* 1.7.1862.	35.00	75.00	200.
c. 1.11.1862.	35.00	75.00	200.
d. Overprint: *Re-Issue..* 1.11.1862.	35.00	75.00	200.
e. Printed on the backs of Mississippi Cotton Company notes. 1.11.1862.	35.00	75.00	200.
f. Overprint: *Re-Issue* on #S1385e.	35.00	75.00	200.

S1386 5 Dollars

1.11.1862. Black. Plow at left, steam passenger train at top center, farmer holding sheaf of grain at lower right. Similar to #S1385 but blue text: *Faith of the State Pledged.*

	VG	VF	UNC
a. Issued note.	40.00	100.	235.
b. Overprint: *Re-Issue.*	40.00	100.	235.

S1387 10 Dollars

1862. Black on red underprint. Seated woman at lower left, train at center, farmer at right. Red text: *Faith of the State Pledged.*

	VG	VF	UNC
a. 1.7.1862.	35.00	75.00	200.
b. Overprint: *Re-Issue.* 1.7.1862.	35.00	75.00	200.
c. 1.11.1862.	35.00	75.00	200.
d. Overprint: *Re-Issue.* 1.11.1862.	35.00	75.00	200.
e. Printed on backs of Mississippi Cotton Company notes. 1.11.1862.	35.00	75.00	200.
f. Overprint: *Re-Issue* on #S1387e.	35.00	75.00	200.

S1388 10 Dollars

1.11.1862. Black on red underprint. Seated woman at lower left, train at center, farmer at right. Similar to #S1387 but blue text: *Faith of the State Pledged.*

	VG	VF	UNC
a. Issued note.	50.00	175.	325.
b. Overprint: *Re-Issue.*	50.00	175.	325.
c. Printed on the backs of Mississippi Cotton Company notes.	50.00	175.	325.

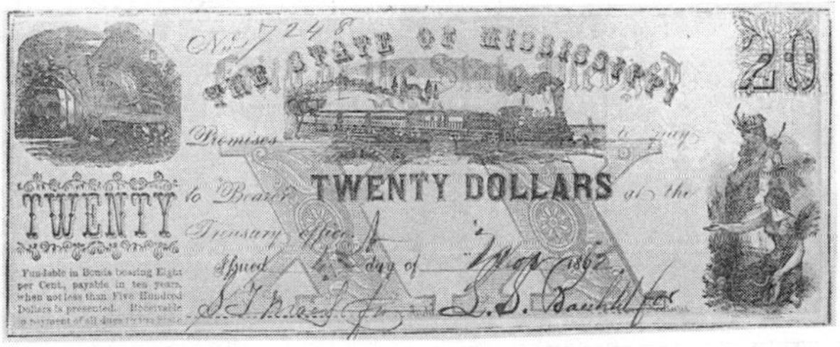

S1389 20 Dollars

1862. Black on green underprint. Plow at upper left, steam passenger train at upper center, woman kneeling beside Indian maiden at lower right. Red text: *Faith of the State Pledged.*

	VG	VF	UNC
a. 1.7.1862.	40.00	90.00	215.
b. Overprint: *Re-Issue.* 1.7.1862.	40.00	90.00	215.
c. 1.11.1862.	40.00	90.00	215.
d. Overprint: *Re-Issue.* 1.11.1862.	40.00	90.00	215.
e. Printed on backs of Mississippi Cotton Company notes 1.11.1862.	40.00	90.00	215.
f. Overprint: *Re-Issue* on #S1389e.	40.00	90.00	215.

S1390 20 Dollars

1.11.1862. Black on green underprint. Plow at upper left, steam passenger train at upper center, woman kneeling beside Indian maiden at lower right. Similar to #S1389 but blue text: *Faith of the State Pledged.*

	VG	VF	UNC
a. Issued note.	65.00	165.	385.
b. Overprint: *Re-Issue.*	65.00	165.	385.

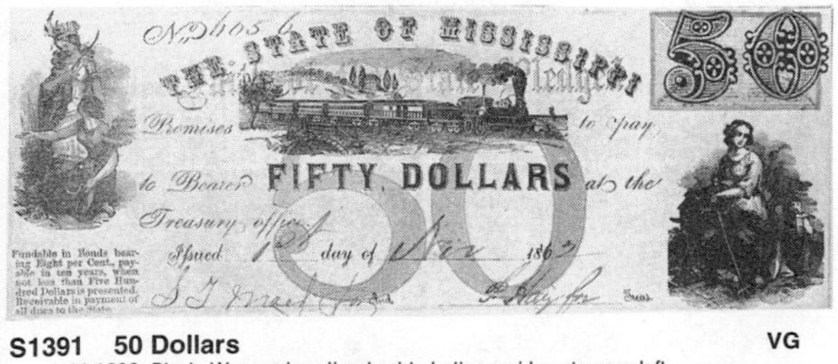

S1391 50 Dollars

1.11.1862. Black. Woman kneeling beside Indian maiden at upper left, steam passenger train at upper center, woman seated at lower right. Red text: *Faith of the State Pledged.*

	VG	VF	UNC
a. Issued note.	60.00	150.	300.
b. Overprint: *Re-Issue.*	60.00	150.	300.

S1392 50 Dollars

1.11.1862. Black. Woman kneeling beside Indian maiden at upper left, steam passenger train at upper center, woman seated at lower right. Similar to #S1391 but blue text: *Faith of the State Pledged.*

	VG	VF	UNC
a. Issued note.	65.00	165.	385.
b. Overprint: *Re-Issue.*	65.00	165.	385.

S1393 100 Dollars

1.11.1862. Black on light gray underprint. Woman standing at left and right, steam train at center. Similar to #S1382 but red text: *Faith of the Sate Pledged.*

	VG	VF	UNC
a. Issued note. Rare.	—	—	—
b. Overprint: *Re-Issue.* Rare.	—	—	—

S1394 100 Dollars

1.11.1862. Black on light gray underprint. Woman standing at left and right, steam train at center. Similar to #S1393 but blue text: *Faith of the State Pledged.*

	VG	VF	UNC
a. Issued note. Rare.	—	—	—
b. Overprint: *Re-Issue.* Rare.	—	—	—

1864 Issue

S1395 25 Cents

	VG	VF	UNC
1.5.1864. Black on red underprint. Cotton bolls at lower left. Printer: J.T. Paterson & Co.	60.00	150.	300.

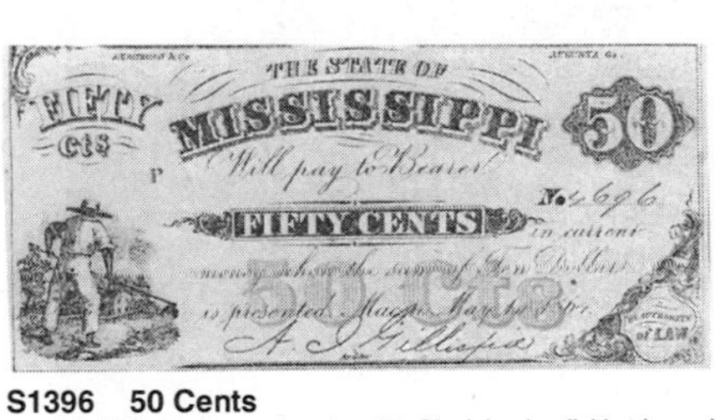

S1396 50 Cents

	VG	VF	UNC
1.5.1864. Black on red underprint. Black hoeing field at lower left. Printer: J.T. Paterson & Co.	20.00	40.00	80.00

S1397 1 Dollar

1.5.1864. Black on red underprint. Ceres at lower left, steam passenger train at top center. Printer: J.T. Paterson & Co.

	VG	VF	UNC
a. With imprint.	25.00	50.00	100.
b. Without imprint.	25.00	50.00	100.

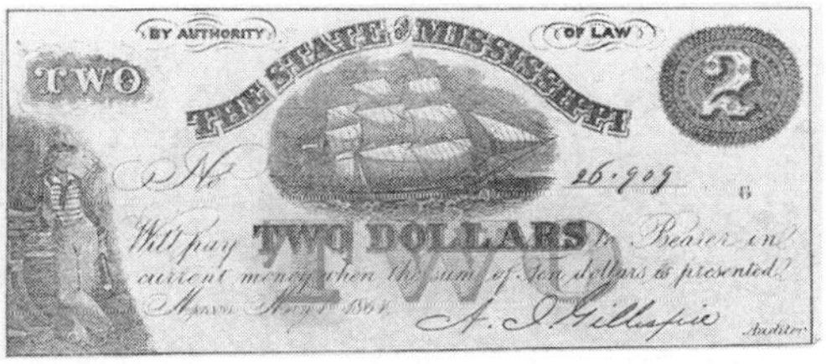

S1398 2 Dollars

1.5.1864. Black on red underprint. Sailor at lower left, sailing ship at top center. Printer: J.T. Paterson & Co.

	VG	VF	UNC
a. With imprint.	25.00	50.00	100.
b. Without imprint.	25.00	50.00	100.

	VG	VF	UNC
S1399 3 Dollars			
1.5.1864. Black on red underprint. Indian at lower left, Sentinel on duty at upper center. Printer: J.T. Paterson & Co.	40.00	80.00	135.
S1400 20 Dollars			
186x. Black on red and green underprint. Eagle with shield at left, seated Indian at right along bottom. Back: Green. Printer: J.T. Paterson & Co.			
a. With green protector: *XX*.	200.	300.	550.
b. Without green protector: *XX* between eagle and seated Indian.	200.	300.	550.
S1401 50 Dollars			
186x. Black on red underprint. Eagle with shield at left, seated Indian at right along bottom. Similar to #S1400. Back: Green. Printer: J.T. Paterson & Co. Rare.	—	—	—

1865 Issue

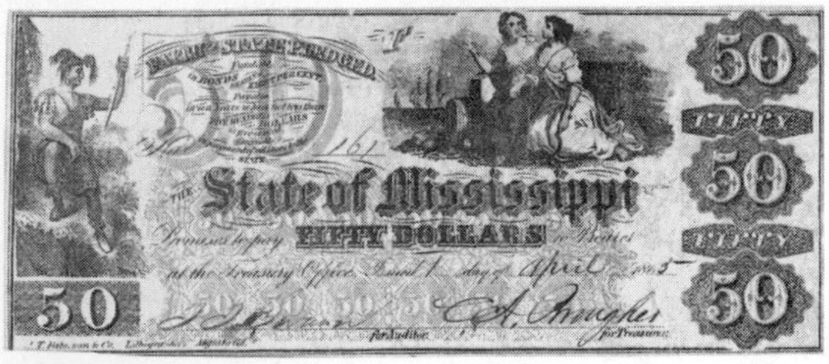

	VG	VF	UNC
S1402 50 Dollars			
1.4.1865. Black on green underprint. Indian at left, seated Commerce and Ceres at upper center right. Back: Orange.	175.	300.	500.

Mississippi

Post Civil War

1867 Issue

	VG	VF	UNC
S1403 100 Dollars			
21.7.1867. Black and orange. Harbor scene at top center. Various handwritten dates. Back: Green.	600.	1000.	1600.

1870 Issue

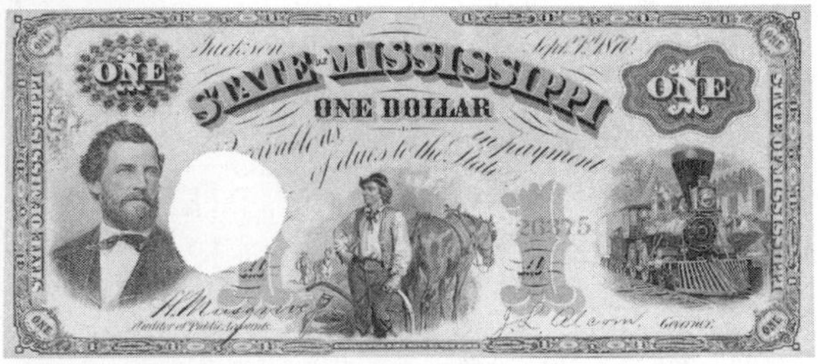

	VG	VF	UNC
S1404 1 Dollar			
1.9.1870. Black and green. Gov. J. L. Alcorn at left, man with horse and plow at lower center, steam locomotive at right. Back: Green. Printer: CBNC.			
a. Issued note.	30.00	65.00	120.
b. Punched hole cancelled.	30.00	65.00	120.
S1405 2 Dollars			
1.9.1870. Green and black. Gov. J. L. Alcorn at left, blacks loading cotton at lower center, steam train at lower right. Back: Green. Printer: CBNC.			
a. Issued note.	30.00	65.00	120.
b. Punched hole cancelled.	30.00	65.00	120.

	VG	VF	UNC
S1406 3 Dollars			
1.9.1870. Green and black. Gov. J. L. Alcorn at left, steamship in rough seas at center, eagle with shield at right. Back: Green. Printer: CBNC.			
a. Issued note.	50.00	100.	160.
b. Punched hole cancelled.	50.00	100.	160.

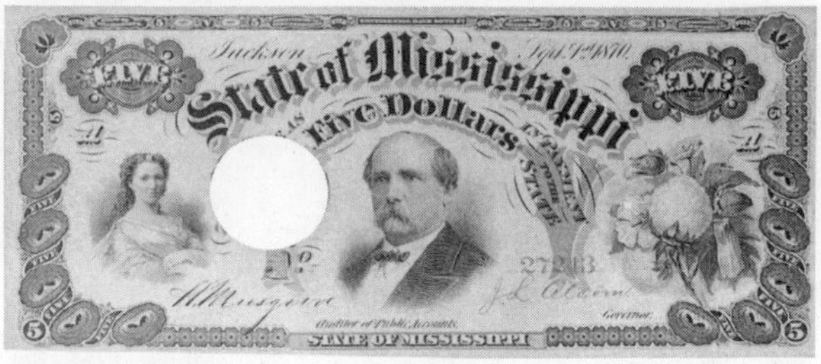

	VG	VF	UNC
S1407 5 Dollars			
1.9.1870. Green and black. Woman at left, Gov. J. L. Alcorn at center, cotton boll at right. Back: Green. Printer: CBNC.			
a. Issued note.	30.00	65.00	120.
b. Punched hole cancelled.	30.00	65.00	120.

Act of 10.2.1894 Special Auditor's Issue

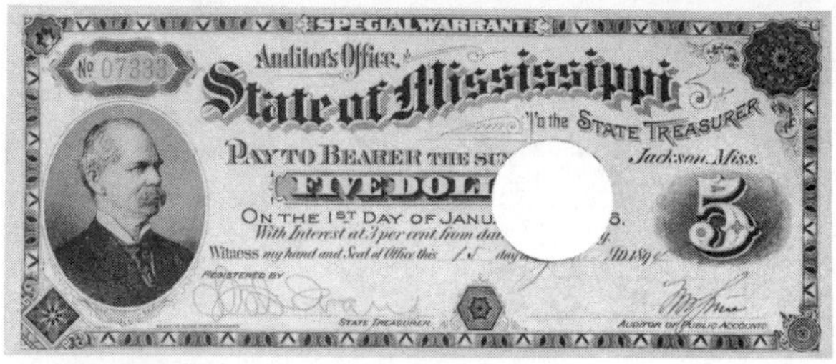

	VG	VF	UNC
S1411 5 Dollars			
1894. Black. Portrait man at left. Various handwritten dates, payable 1.1.1896. Back: Green. Printer: St. Louis Bank Note Co.			
a. Issued note.	75.00	150.	300.
b. Punched hole cancelled.	75.00	150.	300.
S1412 10 Dollars			
1894. Black. Portrait man at left. Various handwritten dates, payable 1.1.1896. Back: Brown. Printer: St. Louis Bank Note Co.			
a. Issued note.	120.	300.	500.
b. Punched hole cancelled.	120.	300.	500.
S1413 20 Dollars			
1894. Black. Portrait man at left. Various handwritten dates, payable 1.1.1896. Printer: St. Louis Bank Note Co.			
a. Issued note.	125.	300.	500.
b. Punched hole cancelled.	125.	300.	500.

Act of February 10, 1895 Issue

	VG	VF	UNC
S1415 10 Dollars			
15.6.1895. Eagle at left. Back: Brown.			
a. Issued note.	50.00	100.	200.
b. Punched hole cancelled.	50.00	100.	200.

Missouri

State

1821 Loan Office Certificates Issue

	Good	Fine	XF
S1421 50 Cents			
1.10.1821. Black. Eagle at top center.	—	2000.	—
S1422 1 Dollar			
1.10.1821. Black. Woman seated at top center. Rare.	—	—	—
S1423 3 Dollars			
1.10.1821. Reported not confirmed.	—	—	—
S1424 5 Dollars			
1.10.1821. Black. Reported not confirmed.	—	—	—
S1425 10 Dollars			
1.10.1821. Black. Woman seated at top center. Rare.	—	—	—

Missouri

Civil War

1862 Issue

	VG	VF	UNC
S1431 1 Dollar			
1.1.1862. Black on red underprint. Liberty at left, Jefferson Davis at upper center, frontiersman at lower right. Engraver: A. Malus, New Orleans.			
a. White paper.	100.	200.	350.
b. Printed on backs of bills of exchange.	100.	200.	350.
c. Blue paper.	100.	200.	350.
d. Printed on backs of bills of exchange, blue paper.	100.	200.	350.

S1432 2 Dollars

1.1.1862. Black on green underprint. Young girl at left, farmer with horses and plow at top center, State arms at right. Engraver: A. Malus, New Orleans.

	VG	VF	UNC
a. White paper.	100.	200.	350.
b. Printed on backs of bills of exchange.	100.	200.	350.
c. Blue paper. Rare.	100.	200.	350.
d. Printed on backs of bills of exchange, blue paper. Rare.	100.	200.	350.

S1433 3 Dollars

1.1.1862. Black on green underprint. Liberty at left, Gov. C. F. Jackson at top center, frontiersman at lower right. Engraver: A. Malus, New Orleans.

	VG	VF	UNC
a. White paper.	250.	500.	800.
b. Printed on backs of bills of exchange.	250.	500.	800.
c. Blue paper.	250.	500.	800.
d. Printed on backs of bills of exchange, blue paper.	250.	500.	800.

S1434 5 Dollars

1.1.1862. Black. Seated Commerce on bale of cotton at top center. Engraver: D. Weil (without imprint).

	VG	VF	UNC
a. Without imprint.	80.00	175.	300.
b. Blue paper with imprint.	80.00	175.	300.
c. Blue paper without imprint.	80.00	175.	300.
d. With text: *Prior to 1st, Nov'br 1861* rubberstamped or handwritten on back.	80.00	175.	300.

S1435 10 Dollars

1.1.1862. Black. Seated Ceres on horn of plenty with sailing ship in left background at top center. Engraver: D. Weil (without imprint).

	VG	VF	UNC
a. Without imprint.	80.00	160.	250.
b. Blue paper with imprint.	80.00	160.	250.
c. Blue paper without imprint.	80.00	160.	250.
d. With text: *Prior to 1st, Nov'br 1861* rubberstamped or handwritten on back.	80.00	160.	250.

S1436 20 Dollars

1862-63. Black. Liberty at left, Ceres Volant at top center. Payable text: *Three Years after Date.* Engraver: A. Malus, New Orleans.

	VG	VF	UNC
a. 1.11.1862.	110.	180.	285.
b. Blue paper. 1.11.1862.	110.	180.	285.
c. 1.11.1863/62.	110.	180.	285.
d. With text: *Prior to 1st, Nov'br 1861* rubberstamped or handwritten on back.	110.	180.	285.

S1437 20 Dollars

1862.63. Black. Liberty at left, Ceres Volant at top center. Similar to #S1436 but payable text: *Five Years after Date.*

	VG	VF	UNC
a. 1.11.1862.	65.00	140.	240.
b. Blue paper. 1.11.1862.	65.00	140.	240.
c. 1.11.1863/62. Rare.	65.00	140.	240.
d. With text: *Prior to 1st, Nov'br 1861* rubberstamped or handwritten on back.	65.00	140.	240.

Missouri

Defence Bond

Act of 5.11.1861 Issue

NOTE: Apparently no examples are known with genuine sign.

S1438 1 Dollar

186x. Black on red underprint. State arms at lower left, cattle in pasture at center, seated woman at lower right. Printer: Keatinge & Ball.

	VG	VF	UNC
a. Issued note.	40.00	80.00	160.
r. Remainder without signature.	40.00	80.00	160.

S1439 3 Dollars

186x. Black on red underprint. State arms at upper left, Ceres Volante at center right, woman at lower right. Printer: Keatinge & Ball.

	VG	VF	UNC
a. Issued note.	50.00	100.	200.
r. Remainder without signature.	50.00	100.	200.

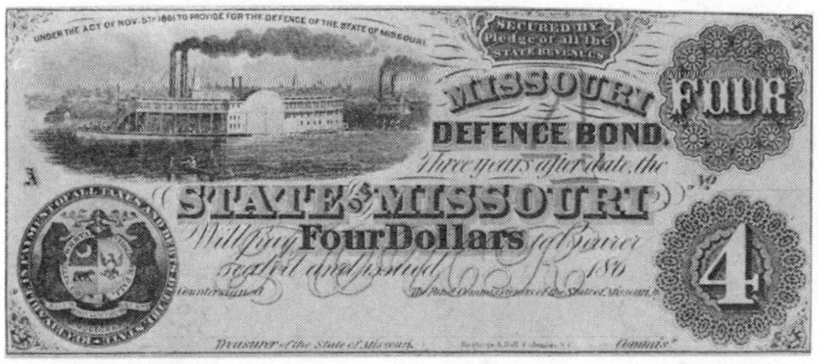

S1440 4 Dollars

186x. Black on red underprint. Mississippi riverboat at upper left center above state arms. Printer: Keatinge & Ball.

	VG	VF	UNC
a. Issued note.	25.00	50.00	100.
r. Remainder without signature.	25.00	50.00	100.

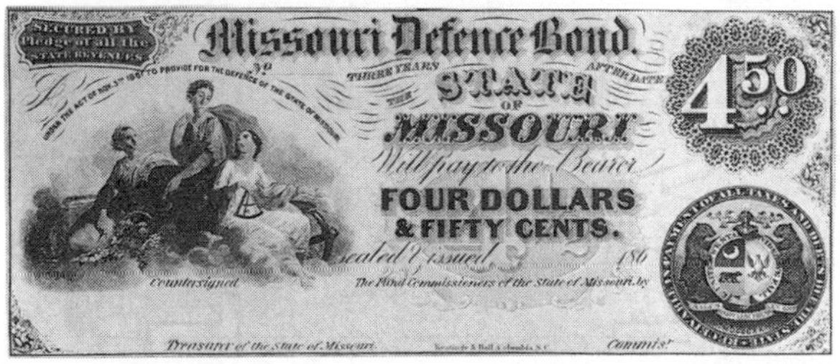

S1441 4 Dollars 50 Cents

186x. Black on red underprint. Ceres seated between Commerce and Navigation at left, state arms at lower right. Printer: Keatinge & Ball.

	VG	VF	UNC
a. Issued note.	110.	235.	450.
r. Remainder without signature.	110.	235.	450.

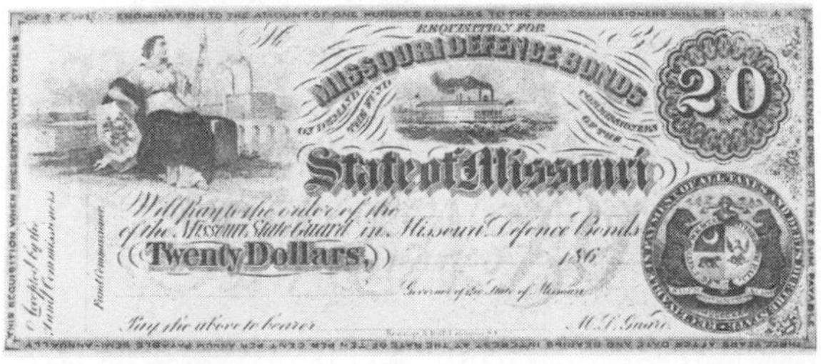

S1442 20 Dollars

186x. Black on red underprint. Seated Liberty at upper left, riverboat at upper center, state arms at lower right. Back: Green. Printer: Keatinge & Ball.

	VG	VF	UNC
a. Issued note.	50.00	125.	275.
r. Remainder without signature.	50.00	125.	275.

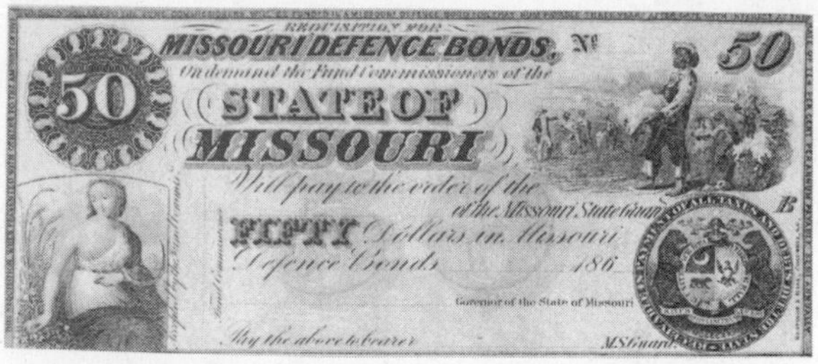

S1443 50 Dollars	VG	VF	UNC
186x. Black on red underprint. Ceres at lower left, blacks gathering cotton at upper right, state arms at lower right. Back: Green. Printer: Keatinge & Ball.			
a. Issued note.	80.00	175.	350.
r. Remainder without signature.	80.00	175.	350.

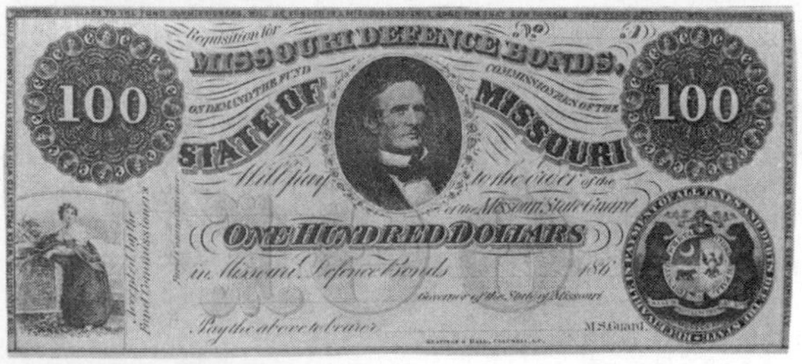

S1444 100 Dollars	VG	VF	UNC
186x. Black on red underprint. Woman standing at lower left, portrait Jefferson Davis at upper center, state arms at lower right. Back: Green. Printer: Keatinge & Ball.			
a. Issued note.	100.	200.	450.
r. Remainder without signature.	50.00	100.	150.

Missouri

Defence Warrant

1862 Issue

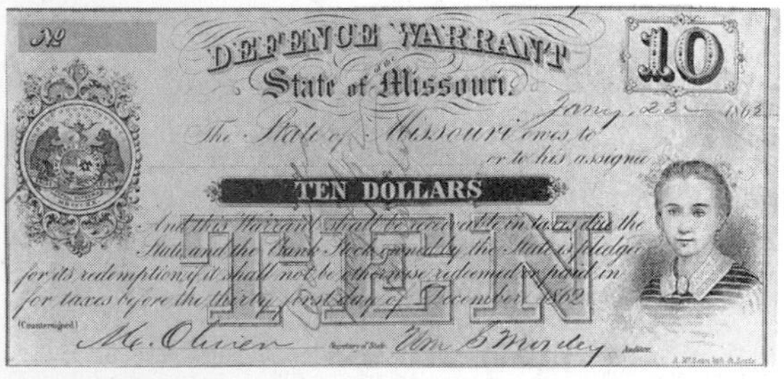

S1445 10 Dollars	Good	Fine	XF
23.2.1862. Black on green underprint. State seal at upper left, girl at lower right. Plain green protector: *TEN*. Handwritten date. Printer: A. McLean. Rare.	—	—	—
S1446 10 Dollars 28.2.1862. Black on green underprint. State seal at upper left, girl at lower right. Similar to #S1445 but with fancy green protector: *TEN*. Printed or stamped date. Printer: A. McLean. Rare.	—	—	—

1864 Issue

S1447 5 Dollars	Good	Fine	XF
25.6.1864. Black. State arms at left. Gen. F. Sigel at lower right. Printer: R.P. Studley & Co. Rare.	—	—	—
S1448 10 Dollars 25.6.1864. Black. State arms at left. Gen. I. Shepard at lower right. Printer: R.P. Studley & Co. Rare.	—	—	—

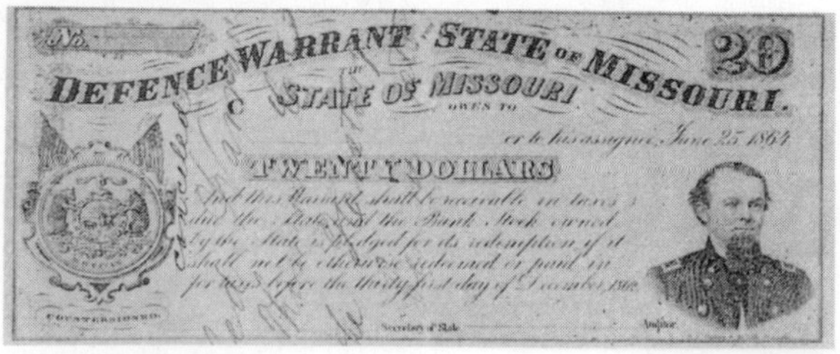

S1449 20 Dollars	Good	Fine	XF
25.6.1864. Black. State arms at left. Gen. J. Pope at lower right. Printer: R.P. Studley & Co. Rare.	—	—	—

S1450 50 Dollars	Good	Fine	XF
25.6.1864. Black. State arms at left. Gov. W. P. Hall at lower right. Printer: R.P. Studley & Co. Rare.	—	—	—

Missouri

Union Military Bond

Act of 9.3.1863 and 20.2.1865 Issue

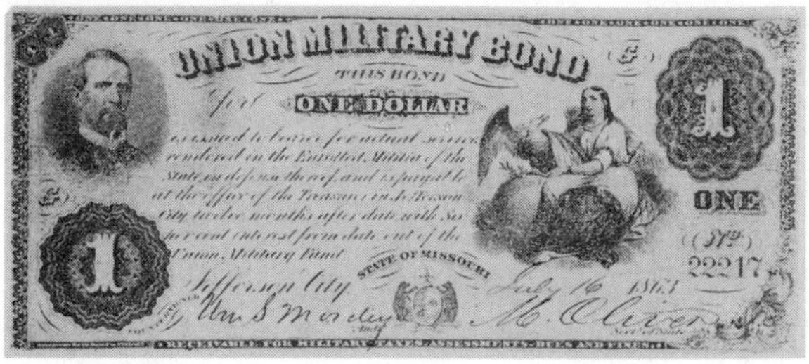

S1451 1 Dollar	VG	VF	UNC
1863-66. Black. Union officer at upper left, seated Liberty with globe and eagle at right. Various handwritten dates. Back: Green. Printer: ABNC.	300.	750.	—
S1452 3 Dollars 1863-66. Black. Man at upper left, Liberty at center, state arms at lower right. Various handwritten dates. Back: Green. Printer: ABNC. Rare.	—	—	—
S1453 5 Dollars 1863.66. Black. Man with horse at upper left, man at center right. Various handwritten dates. Back: Green. Printer: ABNC. Rare.	—	—	—

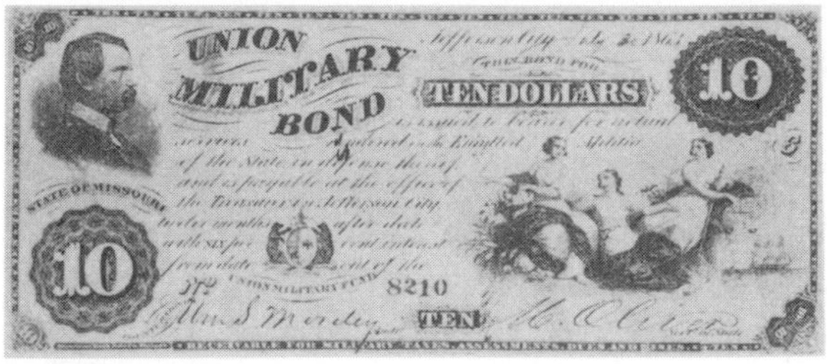

S1454 10 Dollars	Good	Fine	XF
1863-66. Black. Gen. F. Blair at upper left, three reclining allegorical women at lower right. Various handwritten dates. Back: Green. Printer: ABNC. Rare.	—	—	—
S1455 20 Dollars 1863-66. Mountain at upper left, man at lower center. Various handwritten dates. Printer: ABNC. Proof. Rare.	—	—	—
S1456 50 Dollars 1863-66. Various handwritten dates. Printer: ABNC. Reported not confirmed.	—	—	—

New Hampshire

Colonial

1709 Issue

S1461 15 Shillings	Good	Fine	XF
1709. Black and red. Uniface. Printer: Jeremiah Dummer.	—	—	—
S1462 50 Shillings 1709. Black and red. Uniface. Printer: Jeremiah Dummer.	—	—	—

1717 Issue

S1463 1 Shilling	Good	Fine	XF
20.5.1717. Black. Printer: Jeremiah Dummer.	—	—	—
S1464 1 Shilling 6 Pence 20.5.1717. Black. Printer: Jeremiah Dummer.	—	—	—
S1465 4 Shillings 6 Pence 20.5.1717. Black. Printer: Jeremiah Dummer.	—	—	—
S1466 15 Shillings 20.5.1717. Black. Printer: Jeremiah Dummer.	—	—	—
S1467 25 Shillings 20.5.1717. Black. Printer: Jeremiah Dummer.	—	—	—
S1468 30 Shillings 20.5.1717. Black. Printer: Jeremiah Dummer.	—	—	—
S1469 3 Pounds 10 Shillings 20.5.1717. Black. Printer: Jeremiah Dummer.	—	—	—
S1470 4 Pounds 20.5.1717. Black. Printer: Jeremiah Dummer.	—	—	—

1714/17 Redated Issue

No.	Description	Good	Fine	XF
S1471	**1 Shilling** 1714 (- old date 20.5.1717). Black.	—	—	—
S1472	**1 Shilling 6 Pence** 1714 (- old date 20.5.1717). Black.	—	—	—
S1473	**4 Shillings 6 Pence** 1714 (- old date 20.5.1717). Black.	—	—	—
S1474	**25 Shillings** 1714 (- old date 20.5.1717). Black.	—	—	—

1717/17 Redated Issue

No.	Description	Good	Fine	XF
S1475	**1 Shilling** 1717 (- old date 20.5.1717). Black.	—	—	—
S1476	**1 Shilling 6 Pence** 1717 (- old date 20.5.1717). Black.	—	—	—
S1477	**4 Shillings 6 Pence** 1717 (- old date 20.5.1717). Black.	—	—	—
S1478	**25 Shillings** 1717 (- old date 20.5.1717). Black.	—	—	—

1722 Redated Issue

No.	Description	Good	Fine	XF
S1479	**1 Shilling** 1722 (- old date 20.5.1717). Black. Back: *CNH* (Colony of New Hampshire) monogram.	—	—	—
S1480	**1 Shilling 6 Pence** 1722 (- old date 20.5.1717). Black. Back: *CNH* (Colony of New Hampshire) monogram.	—	—	—
S1481	**4 Shillings 6 Pence** 1722 (- old date 20.5.1717). Black. Back: *CNH* (Colony of New Hampshire) monogram.	—	—	—
S1482	**15 Shillings** 1722 (- old date 20.5.1717). Black. Back: *CNH* (Colony of New Hampshire) monogram.	—	—	—
S1483	**25 Shillings** 1722 (- old date 20.5.1717). Black. Back: *CNH* (Colony of New Hampshire) monogram.	—	—	—
S1484	**30 Shillings** 1722 (- old date 20.5.1717). Black. Back: *CNH* (Colony of New Hampshire) monogram.	—	—	—
S1485	**3 Pounds 10 Shillings** 1722 (- old date 20.5.1717). Black. Back: *CNH* (Colony of New Hampshire) monogram.	—	—	—
S1486	**4 Pounds** 1722 (- old date 20.5.1717). Black. Back: *CNH* (Colony of New Hampshire) monogram.	11,000.	—	—

1726/27 Redated Issue

No.	Description	Good	Fine	XF
S1487	**1 Shilling** 1724/27 (- old date 20.5.1717). Black. Boar.	—	—	—
S1488	**1 Shilling 6 Pence** 1724/27 (- old date 20.5.1717). Black. Bear.	—	—	—
S1489	**4 Shillings 6 Pence** 1724/27 (- old date 20.5.1717). Black. Camel.	—	—	—
S1490	**15 Shillings** 1724/17 (- old date 20.5.1717). Black. Cod.	—	—	—
S1491	**25 Shillings** 1724/27 (- old date 20.5.1717). Black. Double headed eagle.	—	—	—
S1492	**30 Shillings** 1724/27 (- old date 20.5.1717). Black. Stag.	—	—	—
S1493	**3 Pounds 10 Shillings** 1724/27 (- old date 20.5.1717). Black. Pine tree.	—	—	—
S1494	**4 Pounds** 1724/27 (- old date 20.5.1717). Black. Indian.	—	—	—

1729 Redated Issue

No.	Description	Good	Fine	XF
S1495	**1 Shilling** 1729. (- old date 20.5.1717). Black. Boar.	—	—	—
S1496	**1 Shilling 6 Pence** 1729 (- old date 20.5.1717). Black. Bear.	—	—	—
S1497	**4 Shillings 6 Pence** 1729. (- old date 20.5.1717). Black. Camel.	—	—	—
S1498	**15 Shillings** 1729. (- old date 20.5.1717). Black. Cod	—	—	—
S1499	**25 Shillings** 1729 (- old date 20.5.1717). Black. Double headed eagle.	—	—	—
S1500	**30 Shillings** 1729 (- old date 20.5.1717). Black. Stag.	—	—	—
S1501	**3 Pounds 10 Shillings** 1729 (- old date 20.5.1717). Black. Pine tree.	—	—	—
S1502	**4 Pounds** 1729 (- old date 20.5.1717). Black. Indian.	—	—	—

1737 Issue

No.	Description	Good	Fine	XF
S1503	**2 Shillings** 1.4.1737. Black.			
	a. Issued note.	—	—	—
	rp. Reprint.	—	—	—
S1504	**3 Shillings** 1.4.1737. Black.			
	a. Issued note.	—	—	—
	rp. Reprint.	—	—	—
S1505	**5 Shillings** 1.4.1737. Black. Crown.			
	a. Issued note.	—	—	—
	rp. Reprint.	—	—	—
S1506	**10 Shillings** 1.4.1737. Black. Angel.			
	a. Issued note.	—	—	—
	rp. Reprint.	—	—	—
S1507	**20 Shillings** 1.4.1737. Black.	—	—	—
S1508	**40 Shillings** 1.4.1737. Black.	—	—	—
S1509	**60 Shillings** 1.4.1737. Black.	—	—	—
S1510	**100 Shillings** 1.4.1737. Black.	—	—	—

1740 Redated Issue

No.	Description	Good	Fine	XF
S1511	**20 Shillings** 7.8.1740 (- old date 1.4.1737). Black.	—	—	—
S1512	**40 Shillings** 7.8.1740 (- old date 1.4.1737). Black.	—	—	—
S1513	**60 Shillings** 7.8.1740 (- old date 1.4.1737). Black.	—	—	—
S1514	**100 Shillings** 7.8.1740 (- old date 1.4.1737). Black.	—	—	—

1742 Issue

No.	Description	Good	Fine	XF
S1515	**6 Pence** 3.4.1742. Black. Motto: *DIEU ET MON DROIT* on state arms. Uniface.	—	—	—
S1516	**1 Shilling** 3.4.1742. Black. Motto: *DIEU ET MON DROIT* on state arms. Uniface.	—	—	—
S1517	**2 Shillings 6 Pence** 3.4.1742. Black. Motto: *DIEU ET MON DROIT* on state arms. Uniface.	—	—	—
S1518	**6 Shillings** 3.4.1742. Black. Motto: *DIEU ET MON DROIT* on state arms. Uniface.	—	—	—
S1519	**7 Shillings 6 Pence - 1 Dollar** 3.4.1742. Black. Motto: *DIEU ET MON DROIT* on state arms. Uniface.			
	a. Issued note.	—	—	—
	rp. Reprint.	—	—	—
S1520	**10 Shillings** 3.4.1742. Black. Motto: *DIEU ET MON DROIT* on state arms. Uniface.			
	a. Issued note.	—	—	—
	rp. Reprint.	—	—	—
S1521	**20 Shillings** 3.4.1742. Black. Motto: *DIEU ET MON DROIT* on state arms. Uniface.			
	a. Issued note.	—	—	—
	rp. Reprint.	—	—	—
S1522	**40 Shillings** 3.4.1742. Black. Motto: *DIEU ET MON DROIT* on state arms. Uniface.			
	a. Issued note.	—	—	—
	rp. Reprint.	—	—	—

1743 Redated Issue

No.	Description	Good	Fine	XF
S1523	**6 Pence** 1743 (- old date 3.4.1742). Black.	—	—	—
S1524	**1 Shilling** 1743 (- old date 3.4.1742). Black.	—	—	—
S1525	**2 Shillings 6 Pence** 1743 (- old date 3.4.1742). Black.	—	—	—
S1526	**6 Shillings** 1743 (- old date 3.4.1742). Black.	—	—	—
S1527	**7 Shillings 6 Pence - 1 Dollar** 1743 (- old date 3.4.1742). Black.	—	—	—
S1528	**10 Shillings** 1743 (- old date 3.4.1742). Black.	—	—	—
S1529	**20 Shillings** 1743 (- old date 3.4.1742). Black.	—	—	—
S1530	**40 Shillings** 1743 (- old date 3.4.1742). Black.	—	—	—

1744 Redated Issue

#S1531-S1538 black. Redated Feb. 1744(5).

No.	Description	Good	Fine	XF
S1531	**6 Pence** 1744 (- old date 3.4.1742). Black.	—	—	—
		VG	**VF**	**UNC**
S1532	**1 Shilling** 1744 (- old date 3.4.1742). Black.	—	16,250.	—
S1533	**2 Shillings 6 Pence** 1744 (- old date 3.4.1742). Black.	—	—	—
S1534	**6 Shillings** 1744 (- old date 3.4.1742). Black.	—	9000.	—
S1535	**7 Shillings 6 Pence - 1 Dollar** 1744 (- old date 3.4.1742). Black.	—	—	—
S1536	**10 Shillings** 1744 (- old date 3.4.1742). Black.	—	—	—
S1537	**20 Shillings** 1744 (- old date 3.4.1742). Black.	—	—	—
S1538	**40 Shillings** 1744 (- old date 3.4.1742). Black.	—	—	—

1755 Issue

Monetary System

15 Shillings = 60 Shillings O.T. = 8 Spanish Reales

		VG	VF	UNC
S1539	**6 Pence** 3.4.1755. Black. Squirrel in tree. Motto: *PRO ARIS & FOCIS* and expedition name of *Crown Point.*	—	18,500.	—
S1540	**1 Shilling** 3.4.1755. Black. Rabbit. Motto: *PRO ARIS & FOCIS* and expedition name of *Crown Point.*	—	—	—
S1541	**3 Shillings** 3.4.1755. Black. Rooster. Motto: *PRO ARIS & FOCIS* and expedition name of *Crown Point.*	—	—	—
S1542	**3 Shillings 9 Pence** 3.4.1755. Black. Bird in flight. Motto: *PRO ARIS & FOCIS* and expedition name of *Crown Point.*	—	—	—

		Good	Fine	XF
S1543	**5 Shillings** 3.4.1755. Black. Bird in tree. Motto: *PRO ARIS & FOCIS* and expedition name of *Crown Point.*	—	—	—
S1544	**7 Shillings 6 Pence - 1 Dollar** 3.4.1755. Black. Bird on ground. Motto: *PRO ARIS & FOCIS* and expedition name of *Crown Point.*	—	—	—
S1545	**10 Shillings** 3.4.1755. Black. Fox. Motto: *PRO ARIS & FOCIS* and expedition name of *Crown Point.*	—	—	—
S1546	**15 Shillings** 3.4.1755. Black. Squirrel. Motto: *PRO ARIS & FOCIS* and expedition name of *Crown Point.*	—	—	—
S1547	**30 Shillings** 3.4.1755. Black. Stag. Motto: *PRO ARIS & FOCIS* and expedition name of *Crown Point.*	—	—	—
S1548	**3 Pounds** 3.4.1755. Black. Wings. Motto: *PRO ARIS & FOCIS* and expedition name of *Crown Point.*	—	—	—

1756 First Redated Issue

		Good	Fine	XF
S1549	**10 Shillings** 1.1.1756 (- old date 3.4.1755). Black. Fox.	—	—	—
S1550	**15 Shillings** 1.1.1756 (- old date 3.4.1755). Black. Squirrel.	—	—	—
S1551	**30 Shillings** 1.1.1756 (- old date 3.4.1755). Black. Stag.	—	—	—
S1552	**3 Pounds** 1.1.1756 (- old date 3.4.1755). Black. Wings.	—	—	—

1756 Second Redated Issue

		Good	Fine	XF
S1553	**6 Pence** 1.6.1756 (- old date 3.4.1755). Black.	—	—	—
S1554	**1 Shilling** 1.6.1756 (- old date 3.4.1755). Black.	—	—	—
S1555	**3 Shillings** 1.6.1756 (- old date 3.4.1755). Black.	—	—	—
S1556	**3 Shillings 9 Pence** 1.6.1756 (- old date 3.4.1755). Black.	—	—	—
S1557	**5 Shillings** 1.6.1756 (- old date 3.4.1755). Black.	—	—	—
S1558	**7 Shillings 6 Pence - 1 Dollar** 1.6.1756 (- old date 3.4.1755). Black.	—	—	—
S1559	**10 Shillings** 1.6.1756 (- old date 3.4.1755). Black.	—	—	—
S1560	**15 Shillings** 1.6.1756 (- old date 3.4.1755). Black.	—	—	—
S1561	**30 Shillings** 1.6.1756 (- old date 3.4.1755). Black.	—	—	—
S1562	**3 Pounds** 1.6.1756 (- old date 3.4.1755). Black.	—	—	—

1759 Issue

		Good	Fine	XF
S1563	**6 Pence** 1759. Black.	—	—	—
S1564	**1 Shilling** 1759. Black.	—	—	—
S1565	**2 Shillings 6 Pence** 1759. Black.	—	—	—
S1566	**10 Shillings** 1759. Black.	—	—	—

1760 Issue

		Good	Fine	XF
S1567	**6 Pence** 1.3.1760. Black.	—	—	—
S1568	**1 Shilling** 1.3.1760. Black.	—	—	—
S1569	**2 Shillings 6 Pence** 1.3.1760. Black. (Not issued).	—	—	—
S1570	**10 Shillings** 1.3.1760. Black.	—	—	—

1761 First Issue

		Good	Fine	XF
S1571	**6 Pence** 1.1.1761. Black. (Not issued).	—	—	—
S1572	**1 Shilling** 1.1.1761. Black.	—	—	—
S1573	**2 Shillings 6 Pence** 1.1.1761. Black.	—	—	—
S1574	**10 Shillings** 1.1.1761. Black.	—	—	—

1761 Second Issue

		Good	Fine	XF
S1575	**6 Pence** 1.5.1761. Black.	—	—	—
S1576	**1 Shilling** 1.5.1761. Black.	—	—	—
S1577	**2 Shillings 6 Pence** 1.5.1761. Black.	—	—	—
S1578	**10 Shillings** 1.5.1761. Black.	—	—	—

1762 First Issue

		Good	Fine	XF
S1579	**6 Pence** 1.1.1762. Black.	—	—	—
S1580	**1 Shilling** 1.1.1762. Black.	—	—	—
S1581	**2 Shillings 6 Pence** 1.1.1762. Black.	—	—	—
S1582	**10 Shillings** 1.1.1762. Black.	—	—	—

1762 Second Issue

		Good	Fine	XF
S1583	**6 Pence** (1.7.) 1762. Black.	—	—	—
S1584	**1 Shilling** (1.7.) 1762. Black.	—	—	—
S1585	**2 Shillings 6 Pence** (1.7.) 1762. Black.	—	—	—
S1586	**10 Shillings** (1.7.) 1762. Black.	—	—	—

1763 Issue

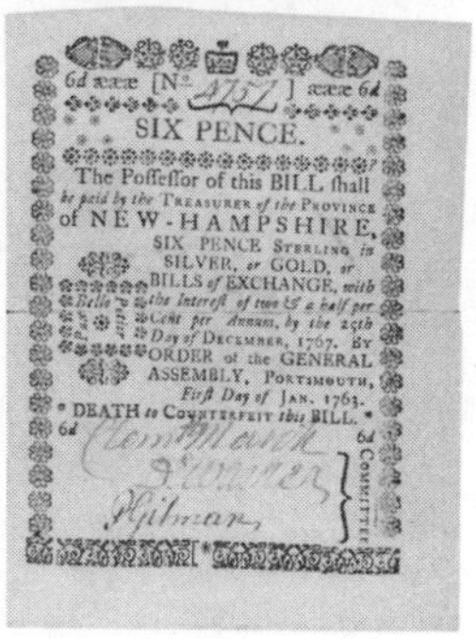

		Good	Fine	XF
S1587	**6 Pence** 1.1.1763. Black.	—	—	—
S1588	**1 Shilling** 1.1.1763. Black.	—	—	—
S1589	**2 Shillings 6 Pence** 1.1.1763. Black.	—	—	—
S1590	**10 Shillings** 1.1.1763. Black.	—	—	—

1775 First Issue

		VG	VF	UNC
S1591	**1 Shilling** 20.6.1775. Black. Large tree. Three due date varieties. Printer: Paul Revere.	5000.	10,000.	—
S1592	**6 Shillings** 20.6.1775. Black. Squirrel in tree. Three due date varieties. Printer: Paul Revere.	5000.	10,000.	—
S1593	**20 Shillings** 20.6.1775. Black. Two leaves. Three due date varieties. Printer: Paul Revere.	5000.	10,000.	—
S1594	**40 Shillings** 20.6.1775. Black. Tree with crossed trunks. Three due date varieties. Printer: Paul Revere.	5000.	10,000.	—

1775 Second Issue

		VG	VF	UNC
S1595	**6 Pence** 25.7.1775. Black.	750.	2250.	—
S1596	**9 Pence** 25.7.1775. Black.	750.	2250.	—
S1597	**1 Shilling 6 Pence** 25.7.1775. Black.	750.	2250.	—
S1598	**1 Shilling 9 Pence** 25.7.1775. Black.	750.	2250.	—
S1599	**2 Shillings 6 Pence** 25.7.1775. Black.	750.	2250.	—
S1600	**3 Pounds** 25.7.1775. Black.	750.	2250.	—

1775 Third Issue

		VG	VF	UNC
S1601	**5 Shillings** 24.8.1775. Black. Three due date varieties.	1250.	—	—
S1602	**10 Shillings** 24.8.1775. Black. Three due date varieties.	1250.	—	—
S1603	**15 Shillings** 24.8.1775. Black. Three due date varieties.	1250.	—	—
S1604	**30 Shillings** 24.8.1775. Black. Three due date varieties.	1250.	—	—
S1605	**3 Pounds** 24.8.1775. Black. Three due date varieties.	750.	1750.	—

1775 Fourth Issue

		VG	VF	UNC
S1606	**6 Pence** 3.11.1775. Black. Four due date varieties.	—	—	—
S1607	**9 Pence** 3.11.1775. Black. Four due date varieties.	1500.	—	—
S1608	**1 Shilling 6 Pence** 3.11.1775. Black. Four due date varieties.	1500.	—	—
S1609	**1 Shilling 9 Pence** 3.11.1775. Black. Four due date varieties.	1500.	—	—
S1610	**2 Shillings 6 Pence** 3.11.1775. Black. Four due date varieties.	1500.	—	—
S1611	**3 Shillings** 3.11.1775. Black. Four due date varieties.	1500.	—	—
S1612	**5 Shillings** 3.11.1775. Black. Four due date varieties.	1250.	—	—
S1613	**10 Shillings** 3.11.1775. Black. Four due date varieties.	1250.	—	—
S1614	**15 Shillings** 3.11.1775. Black. Four due date varieties.	1250.	—	—
S1615	**30 Shillings** 3.11.1775. Black. Four due date varieties.	600.	1200.	—

No.	Description	VG	VF	UNC
S1616	**40 Shillings** 3.11.1775. Black. Four due date varieties.	600.	1200.	—

1776 First Issue

		Good	Fine	XF
S1617	**1 Dollar** 26.1.1776. Black. Four due date varieties. Printer: Daniel Fowle, Portsmouth.	—	—	—
S1618	**2 Dollars** 26.1.1776. Black. Four due date varieties. Printer: Daniel Fowle, Portsmouth.	—	—	5750.
S1619	**3 Dollars** 26.1.1776. Black. Mottos: *SUB VERTUTE SPERAMUS* and *FOR LIBERTY*. Four due date varieties. Printer: Daniel Fowle, Portsmouth.	—	—	8750.
S1620	**4 Dollars** 26.1.1776. Black. Mottos: *NIL DESPERANDUM* and *FOR LIBERTY*. Four due date varieties. Printer: Daniel Fowle, Portsmouth.	—	—	—
S1621	**5 Dollars** 26.1.1776. Black. Mottos: *PRO BONO PUBLICO* and *LIBERTY & PROPERTY*. Four due date varieties. Printer: Daniel Fowle, Portsmouth.	—	—	11,500.
S1622	**6 Dollars** 26.1.1776. Black. Motto: *FOR DEFENCE OF AMERICAN LIBERTY* and name of committee members *MESHECH WEARE* and *LEVI DEARBORN* between ornaments. Four due date varieties. Printer: Daniel Fowle, Portsmouth.	—	8750.	—

1776 Second Issue

No.	Description	VG	VF	UNC
S1623	**3 Pence** 28.6.1776. Black. Two due date varieties. Uniface.	1000.	2000.	—
S1624	**4 Pence** 28.6.1776. Black. Two due date varieties. Uniface.	1000.	2000.	—
S1625	**5 Pence** 28.6.1776. Black. Two due date varieties. Uniface.	1000.	2000.	—
S1626	**7 Pence** 28.6.1776. Black. Two due date varieties. Uniface.	1000.	2000.	—
S1627	**8 Pence** 28.6.1776. Black. Two due date varieties. Uniface.	1000.	2000.	—
S1628	**10 Pence** 28.6.1776. Black. Two due date varieties. Uniface.	1000.	2000.	—

No.	Description	VG	VF	UNC
S1629	**1 Shilling** 28.6.1776. Black. Two due date varieties. Uniface.	1000.	2000.	—
S1630	**15 Pence** 28.6.1776. Black. Two due date varieties. Uniface.	1000.	2000.	—
S1631	**2 Shillings** 28.6.1776. Black. Two due date varieties. Uniface.	1000.	2000.	—
S1632	**4 Shillings** 28.6.1776. Black. Two due date varieties. Uniface.	1000.	2000.	—

1776 Third Issue

No.	Description	VG	VF	UNC
S1633	**1 Dollar** 3.7.1776. Black. Four due date varieties. Printer: Daniel Fowle, Portsmouth.	—	—	—
S1634	**2 Dollars** 3.7.1776. Black. Four due date varieties. Printer: Daniel Fowle, Portsmouth.	—	10,500.	—
S1635	**3 Dollars** 3.7.1776. Black. Four due date varieties. Like #S1619. Printer: Daniel Fowle, Portsmouth.	4000.	—	—
S1636	**4 Dollars** 3.7.1776. Black. Four due date varieties. Like #S1620. Printer: Daniel Fowle, Portsmouth.	—	—	25,000.
S1637	**5 Dollars** 3.7.1776. Black. Four due date varieties. Like #S1621. Printer: Daniel Fowle, Portsmouth.	—	—	—
S1638	**6 Dollars** 3.7.1776. Black. Four due date varieties. Like #S1622. Printer: Daniel Fowle, Portsmouth.	—	12,500.	—

New Hampshire

State

1777 Issue

No.	Description	VG	VF	UNC
S1639	**5 Pounds** 1777. Black. *U-N-I-ON* in border. Various handwritten dates.	—	—	—
S1640	**10 Pounds** 1777. Black. Various handwritten dates.	—	—	—

1780 Issue

No.	Description	VG	VF	UNC
S1641	**1 Dollar** 29.4.1780. Black. Back: Red and black. Watermark: *Confederation* in 2 lines. Printer: Hall & Sellers, PA.	750.	1750.	4000.
S1642	**2 Dollars** 29.4.1780. Black. Back: Red and black. Watermark: *Confederation* in 2 lines. Printer: Hall & Sellers, PA.	750.	1750.	4000.

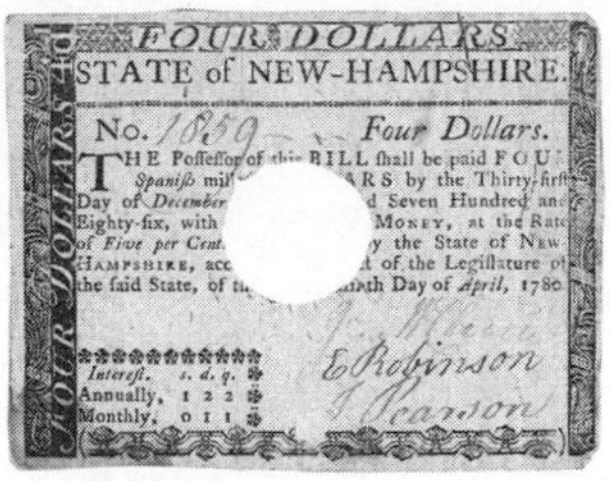

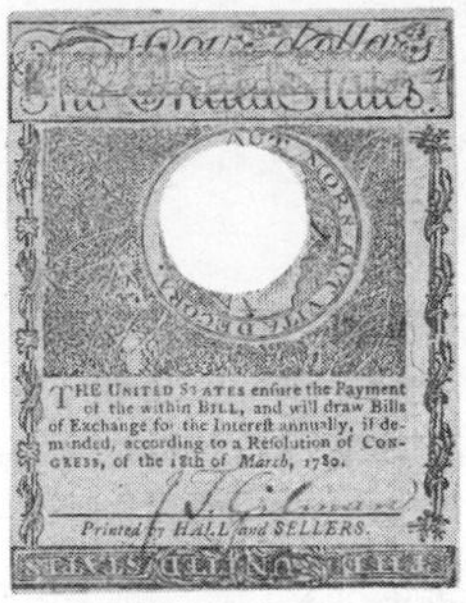

No.	Description	VG	VF	UNC
S1643	**4 Dollars** 29.4.1780. Black. Back: Red and black. Watermark: *Confederation* in 2 lines. Printer: Hall & Sellers, PA.	750.	1750.	4000.
S1644	**5 Dollars** 29.4.1780. Black. Back: Red and black. Watermark: *Confederation* in 2 lines. Printer: Hall & Sellers, PA.	750.	1750.	4000.
S1645	**7 Dollars** 29.4.1780. Black. Back: Red and black. Watermark: *Confederation* in 2 lines. Printer: Hall & Sellers, PA.	750.	1750.	4000.
S1646	**8 Dollars** 29.4.1780. Black. Back: Red and black. Watermark: *Confederation* in 2 lines. Printer: Hall & Sellers, PA.	750.	1750.	4000.
S1647	**20 Dollars** 29.4.1780. Black. Back: Red and black. Watermark: *Confederation* in 2 lines. Printer: Hall & Sellers, PA.	750.	1750.	4000.

New Jersey

Colonial

1709 Issue

By mistake a design of the stub for identification was left out and English arms (3 lions) were used instead of British arms (shield).

		Good	Fine	XF
S1648	**5 Shillings** 1.7.1709. Black.	—	—	—
S1649	**10 Shillings** 1.7.1709. Black.	—	—	—
S1650	**20 Shillings** 1.7.1709. Black.	—	—	—
S1651	**40 Shillings** 1.7.1709. Black.	—	—	—
S1652	**5 Pounds** 1.7.1709. Black.	—	—	—

1711 Issue

		Good	Fine	XF
S1653	**2 Shillings 6 Pence** 14.7.1711. Black.	—	—	—
S1654	**5 Shillings** 14.7.1711. Black.	—	—	—
S1655	**10 Shillings** 14.7.1711. Black.	—	—	—
S1656	**20 Shillings** 14.7.1711. Black.	—	—	—
S1657	**40 Shillings** 14.7.1711. Black.	—	—	—
S1658	**5 Pounds** 14.7.1711. Black.	—	—	—

1716 Issue

		Good	Fine	XF
S1659	**2 Shillings** 24.1.1716 (7). Black. Printer: William Bradford.	—	—	—
S1660	**4 Shillings** 24.1.1716 (7). Black. Printer: William Bradford.	—	—	—
S1661	**5 Shillings** 24.1.1716 (7). Black. Printer: William Bradford.	—	—	—
S1662	**8 Shillings** 24.1.1716 (7). Black. Printer: William Bradford.	—	—	—
S1663	**10 Shillings** 24.1.1716 (7). Black. Printer: William Bradford.	—	—	—
S1664	**16 Shillings** 24.1.1716 (7). Black. Printer: William Bradford.	—	—	—
S1665	**20 Shillings** 24.1.1716 (7). Black. Printer: William Bradford.	—	—	—
S1666	**30 Shillings** 24.1.1716 (7). Black. Printer: William Bradford.	—	—	—
S1667	**40 Shillings** 24.1.1716 (7). Black. Printer: William Bradford.	—	—	—

1724 Issue

		Good	Fine	XF
S1668	**1 Shilling** 25.3.1724. Black. Printer: William Bradford.	—	—	—
S1669	**1 Shilling 6 Pence** 25.3.1724. Black. Printer: William Bradford.	—	—	—
S1670	**3 Shillings** 25.3.1724. Black. Printer: William Bradford.	—	—	—
S1671	**6 Shillings** 25.3.1724. Black. Printer: William Bradford.	—	—	—
S1672	**12 Shillings** 25.3.1724. Black. Printer: William Bradford.	—	—	—
S1673	**15 Shillings** 25.3.1724. Black. Printer: William Bradford.	—	—	—

	Good	Fine	XF
S1674 30 Shillings 25.3.1724. Black. Printer: William Bradford.	—	—	—
S1675 3 Pounds 25.3.1724. Black. Printer: William Bradford.	—	—	—

1728 Issue

	Good	Fine	XF
S1676 1 Shilling 25.3.1728. Black. Printer: Samuel Keimer.	—	—	—
S1677 1 Shilling 6 Pence 25.3.1728. Black. Printer: Samuel Keimer.	—	—	—
S1678 3 Shillings 25.3.1728. Black. Printer: Samuel Keimer.	—	—	—
S1679 6 Shillings 25.3.1728. Black. Printer: Samuel Keimer.	—	—	—
S1680 12 Shillings 25.3.1728. Black. Printer: Samuel Keimer.	—	—	—
S1681 15 Shillings 25.3.1728. Black. Printer: Samuel Keimer.	—	—	—
S1682 30 Shillings 25.3.1728. Black. Printer: Samuel Keimer.	—	—	—
S1683 3 Pounds 25.3.1728. Black. Printer: Samuel Keimer.	—	—	—
S1684 6 Pounds 25.3.1728. Black. Printer: Samuel Keimer.	—	—	—

1733 Issue

	Good	Fine	XF
S1685 1 Shilling 25.3.1733. Black. Mottos: *DIEU ET MON DROIT* and *HONI SOIT QUI MAL Y PENSE*. Printer: Andrew Bradford.	—	—	—
S1686 1 Shilling 6 Pence 25.3.1733. Black. Mottos: *DIEU ET MON DROIT* and *HONI SOIT QUI MAL Y PENSE*. Printer: Andrew Bradford.	—	—	—
S1687 3 Shillings 25.3.1733. Black. Mottos: *DIEU ET MON DROIT* and *HONI SOIT QUI MAL Y PENSE*. Printer: Andrew Bradford.	—	—	—
S1688 6 Shillings 25.3.1733. Black. Mottos: *DIEU ET MON DROIT* and *HONI SOIT QUI MAL Y PENSE*. Printer: Andrew Bradford.	—	—	—
S1689 12 Shillings 25.3.1733. Black. Mottos: *DIEU ET MON DROIT* and *HONI SOIT QUI MAL Y PENSE*. Printer: Andrew Bradford.	—	—	—
S1690 15 Shillings 25.3.1733. Black. Mottos: *DIEU ET MON DROIT* and *HONI SOIT QUI MAL Y PENSE*. Printer: Andrew Bradford.	—	—	—
S1691 30 Shillings 25.3.1733. Black. Mottos: *DIEU ET MON DROIT* and *HONI SOIT QUI MAL Y PENSE*. Printer: Andrew Bradford.	—	—	—
S1692 3 Pounds 25.3.1733. Black. Mottos: *DIEU ET MON DROIT* and *HONI SOIT QUI MAL Y PENSE*. Printer: Andrew Bradford.	—	—	—
S1693 6 Pounds 25.3.1733. Black. Mottos: *DIEU ET MON DROIT* and *HONI SOIT QUI MAL Y PENSE*. Printer: Andrew Bradford.	—	—	—

1737 Issue

	Good	Fine	XF
S1694 1 Shilling 25.3.1737. Black. Printer: Benjamin Franklin.	—	—	—
S1695 1 Shilling 6 Pence 25.3.1737. Black. Printer: Benjamin Franklin.	—	—	—
S1696 3 Shillings 25.3.1737. Black. Printer: Benjamin Franklin.	—	—	—
S1697 6 Shillings 25.3.1737. Black. Printer: Benjamin Franklin.	—	—	—
S1698 12 Shillings 25.3.1737. Black. Printer: Benjamin Franklin.	—	—	—
S1699 15 Shillings 25.3.1737. Black. Printer: Benjamin Franklin.	—	—	—
S1700 30 Shillings 25.3.1737. Black. Printer: Benjamin Franklin.	—	—	—
S1701 3 Pounds 25.3.1737. Black. Printer: Benjamin Franklin.	—	—	—
S1702 6 Pounds 25.3.1737. Black. Printer: Benjamin Franklin.	—	—	—

1746 Issue

	Good	Fine	XF
S1703 1 Shilling 2.7.1746. Back: Sage leaf. Printer: Benjamin Franklin.	—	—	—
S1704 1 Shilling 6 Pence 2.7.1746. Back: Sage leaf. Printer: Benjamin Franklin.	—	—	—
S1705 3 Shillings 2.7.1746. Back: Sage leaf. Printer: Benjamin Franklin.	—	—	—
S1706 6 Shillings 2.7.1746. Back: Sage leaf. Printer: Benjamin Franklin.	—	—	—
S1707 12 Shillings 2.7.1746. Back: Sage leaf. Printer: Benjamin Franklin.	—	—	—

	Good	Fine	XF
S1708 15 Shillings 2.7.1746. Back: Sage leaf. Printer: Benjamin Franklin.	—	—	—
S1709 30 Shillings 2.7.1746. Back: Sage leaf. Printer: Benjamin Franklin.	—	—	—
S1710 3 Pounds 2.7.1746. Black and red. Back: Sage leaf. Printer: Benjamin Franklin.	—	—	—
S1711 6 Pounds 2.7.1746. Black and red. Back: Sage leaf. Printer: Benjamin Franklin.	—	—	—

1755 First Issue

	Good	Fine	XF
S1712 1 Shilling 15.5.1755. Black. Back: Sage leaf. Printer: James Parker.	—	—	—
S1713 1 Shilling 6 Pence 15.5.1755. Black. Back: Sage leaf. Printer: James Parker.	—	—	—
S1714 3 Shillings 15.5.1755. Black. Back: Sage leaf. Printer: James Parker.	—	—	—
S1715 6 Shillings 15.5.1755. Black. Back: Sage leaf. Printer: James Parker.	—	—	—
S1716 12 Shillings 15.5.1755. Black. Back: Sage leaf. Printer: James Parker.	—	—	—
S1717 15 Shillings 15.5.1755. Black. Back: Sage leaf. Printer: James Parker.	—	—	—
S1718 30 Shillings 15.5.1755. Black. Back: Sage leaf. Printer: James Parker.	—	—	—
	VG	**VF**	**UNC**
S1719 3 Pounds 15.5.1755. Black. Back: Sage leaf. Printer: James Parker.	—	4250.	—
S1720 6 Pounds 15.5.1755. Black. Back: Sage leaf. Printer: James Parker.	—	—	—

1755 Second Issue

	Good	Fine	XF
S1721 1 Shilling 8.9.1755. Back: Sage leaf. Printer: James Parker, Woodbridge.	—	—	—
S1722 1 Shilling 6 Pence 8.9.1755. Back: Sage leaf. Printer: James Parker, Woodbridge.	—	—	—
S1723 3 Shillings 8.9.1755. Back: Sage leaf. Printer: James Parker, Woodbridge.	—	—	—
S1724 6 Shillings 8.9.1755. Back: Sage leaf. Printer: James Parker, Woodbridge.	—	—	—
S1725 12 Shillings 8.9.1755. Back: Sage leaf. Printer: James Parker, Woodbridge.	—	—	—
S1726 15 Shillings 8.9.1755. Back: Sage leaf. Printer: James Parker, Woodbridge.	—	—	—
S1727 30 Shillings 8.9.1755. Back: Sage leaf. Printer: James Parker, Woodbridge.	—	—	—
S1728 3 Pounds 8.9.1755. Black and red. Back: Sage leaf. Printer: James Parker, Woodbridge.	—	—	—
S1729 6 Pounds 8.9.1755. Black and red. Back: Sage leaf. Printer: James Parker, Woodbridge.	—	—	—

1756 First Issue

	Good	Fine	XF
S1730 1 Shilling 26.1.1756. Black. Back: Sage leaf. Printer: James Parker.	—	—	—
S1731 18 Pence 26.1.1756. Black. Back: Sage leaf. Printer: James Parker.	—	—	—
S1732 3 Shillings 26.1.1756. Black. Back: Sage leaf. Printer: James Parker.	—	—	—
S1733 6 Shillings 26.1.1756. Black. Back: Sage leaf. Printer: James Parker.	—	—	—
S1734 12 Shillings 26.1.1756. Black. Back: Sage leaf. Printer: James Parker.	—	—	—
S1735 15 Shillings 26.1.1756. Black. Back: Sage leaf. Printer: James Parker.	—	—	—
S1736 30 Shillings 26.1.1756. Red. Back: Sage leaf. Printer: James Parker.	—	—	—
S1737 3 Pounds 26.1.1756. Red. Back: Sage leaf. Printer: James Parker.	—	—	—

	Good	Fine	XF
S1738 6 Pounds 26.1.1756. Red and black. Back: Sage leaf. Printer: James Parker.	—	—	—

1756 Second Issue

No.	Denomination / Description	VG	VF	UNC
S1739	**1 Shilling** 22.6.1756. Black. Back: Sage leaf. Printer: James Parker.	100.	200.	500.
S1740	**18 Pence** 22.6.1756. Black. Back: Sage leaf. Printer: James Parker.	100.	200.	500.
S1741	**3 Shillings** 22.6.1756. Black. Back: Sage leaf. Printer: James Parker.	100.	200.	500.

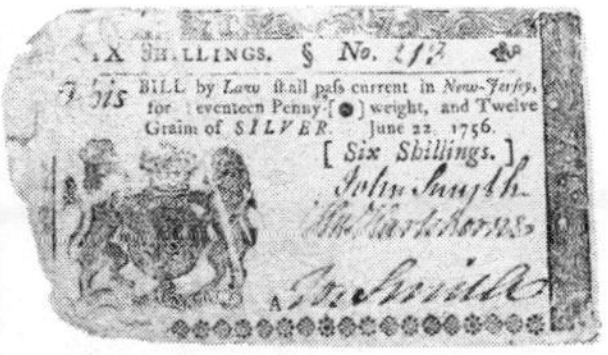

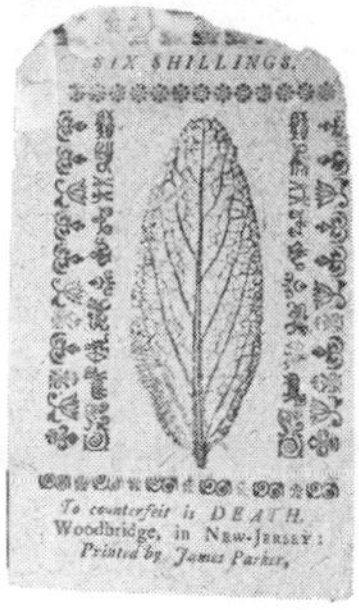

No.	Denomination / Description	VG	VF	UNC
S1742	**6 Shillings** 22.6.1756. Black. Back: Sage leaf. Printer: James Parker.	100.	200.	500.

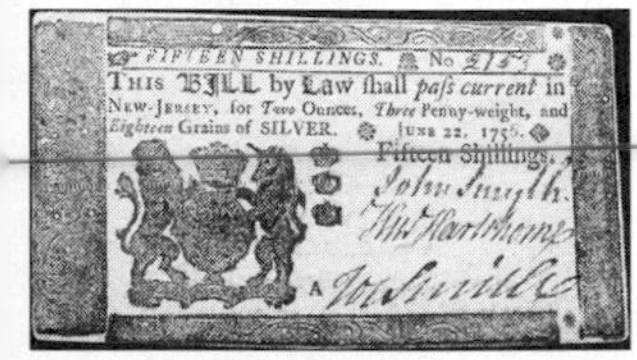

No.	Denomination / Description	VG	VF	UNC
S1743	**12 Shillings** 22.6.1756. Black. Back: Sage leaf. Printer: James Parker.	100.	200.	500.

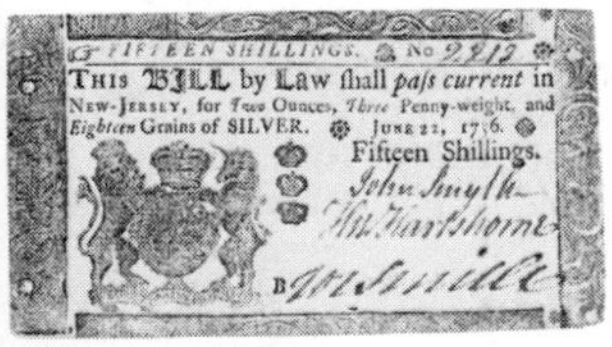

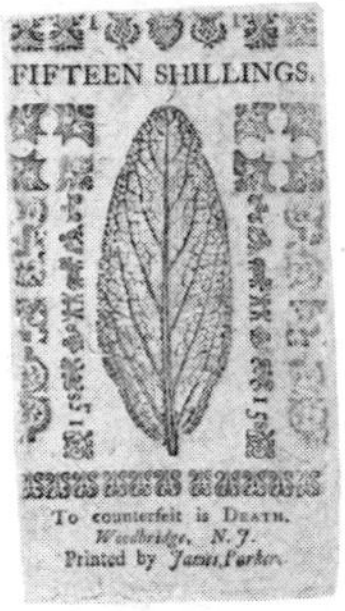

No.	Denomination / Description	VG	VF	UNC
S1744	**15 Shillings** 22.6.1756. Black. Back: Sage leaf. Printer: James Parker.	100.	200.	500.
S1745	**30 Shillings** 22.6.1756. Black and red. Back: Sage leaf. Printer: James Parker.	325.	750.	—
S1746	**3 Pounds** 22.6.1756. Black and red. Back: Sage leaf. Printer: James Parker.	325.	750.	—
S1747	**6 Pounds** 22.6.1756. Black and red. Back: Green. Sage leaf. Printer: James Parker.	400.	—	—

1757 First Issue

No.	Denomination / Description	VG	VF	UNC
S1748	**15 Shillings** 12.4.1757. Red. Back: Black. Sage leaf. Printer: James Parker.	200.	500.	—
S1749	**30 Shillings** 12.4.1757. Red. Back: Black. Sage leaf. Printer: James Parker.	200.	500.	—
S1750	**3 Pounds** 12.4.1757. Red. Back. Black. Sage leaf. Printer: James Parker.	350.	800.	—
S1751	**6 Pounds** 12.4.1757. Red and black. Back: Green. Sage leaf. Printer: James Parker.	600.	2000.	—

1757 Second Issue

No.	Denomination / Description	VG	VF	UNC
S1752	**15 Shillings** 14.6.1757. Black. Back: Sage leaf. Printer: James Parker.	300.	750.	—
S1753	**30 Shillings** 14.6.1757. Black. Back: Sage leaf. Printer: James Parker.	300.	750.	—
S1754	**3 Pounds** 14.6.1757. Black. Back: Sage leaf. Printer: James Parker.	300.	750.	—
S1755	**6 Pounds** 14.6.1757. Red and black. Back: Black. Sage leaf. Printer: James Parker.	1000.	3000.	—

1757 Third Issue

No.	Denomination / Description	VG	VF	UNC
S1756	**6 Shillings** 20.11.1757. Red and black. Back: Black.	150.	500.	—
S1757	**15 Shillings** 20.11.1757. Red and black. Back: Black.	150.	500.	—
S1758	**30 Shillings** 20.11.1757. Red and black. Back: Black.	150.	500.	—
S1759	**3 Pounds** 20.11.1757. Red and black. Back: Black.	150.	750.	—
S1760	**6 Pounds** 20.11.1757. Red and black. Back: Black.	300.	1000.	—

1758 First Issue

No.	Denomination / Description	VG	VF	UNC
S1761	**6 Shillings** 1.5.1758. Red and black. Back: Black. Sage leaf. Printer: James Parker.	100.	150.	250.
S1762	**15 Shillings** 1.5.1758. Red and black. Back: Black. Sage leaf. Printer: James Parker.	100.	150.	250.
S1763	**30 Shillings** 1.5.1758. Red and black. Back: Black. Sage leaf. Printer: James Parker.	100.	150.	250.
S1764	**3 Pounds** 1.5.1758. Red and black. Back: Black. Sage leaf. Printer: James Parker.	150.	225.	375.
S1765	**6 Pounds** 1.5.1758. Red and black. Back: Black. Sage leaf. Printer: James Parker.	300.	450.	750.

1758 Second Issue

No.	Denomination / Description	VG	VF	UNC
S1766	**1 Shilling** 20.10.1758. Black. Back: Sage leaf. Printer: James Parker.	300.	900.	—
S1767	**18 Pence** 20.10.1758. Black. Back: Sage leaf. Printer: James Parker.	300.	900.	—
S1768	**3 Shillings** 20.10.1758. Black. Back: Sage leaf. Printer: James Parker.	300.	900.	—
S1769	**6 Shillings** 20.10.1758. Black. Back: Sage leaf. Printer: James Parker.	300.	900.	—
S1770	**12 Shillings** 20.10.1758. Black. Back: Sage leaf. Printer: James Parker.	300.	900.	—
S1771	**15 Shillings** 20.10.1758. Black. Back: Sage leaf. Printer: James Parker.	300.	900.	—
S1772	**30 Shillings** 20.10.1758. Red and black. Back: Black. Sage leaf. Printer: James Parker.	350.	1000.	—
S1773	**3 Pounds** 20.10.1758. Red and black. Back: Black. Sage leaf. Printer: James Parker.	700.	2000.	—
S1774	**6 Pounds** 20.10.1758. Red and brown. Back: Brown. Sage leaf. Printer: James Parker.	1000.	3000.	—

1759 Issues

No.	Denomination / Description	VG	VF	UNC
S1775	**6 Shillings** 10.4.1759. Red and black. Back: Black. Sage leaf. Printer: James Parker.	150.	350.	—
S1776	**15 Shillings** 10.4.1759. Red and black. Back: Sage leaf. Printer: James Parker.	150.	350.	—
S1777	**30 Shillings** 10.4.1759. Red and black. Back: Sage leaf. Printer: James Parker.	150.	350.	—
S1778	**3 Pounds** 10.4.1759. Red and black. Plate letter "A". O in Ounces is sometimes broken as to resemble C. Back: Black. Sage leaf. Printer: James Parker.	225.	500.	—
S1779	**3 Pounds** 10.4.1759. Red and black. Plate letter "B". Back: Black. Sage leaf. Printer: James Parker.	225.	500.	—
S1780	**6 Pounds** 10.4.1759. Red and black. Back: Black. Sage leaf. Printer: James Parker.	300.	700.	—

1760 Issue

No.	Denomination / Description	VG	VF	UNC
S1781	**1 Shilling** 12.4.1760. Red and black. Back: Black. Sage leaf. Printer: James Parker.	300.	750.	—
S1782	**18 Pence** 12.4.1760. Red and black. Back: Black. Sage leaf. Printer: James Parker.	300.	750.	—
S1783	**3 Shillings** 12.4.1760. Red and black. Back: Black. Sage leaf. Printer: James Parker.	300.	750.	—
S1784	**6 Shillings** 12.4.1760. Red and black. Back: Black. Sage leaf. Printer: James Parker.	300.	750.	—
S1785	**12 Shillings** 12.4.1760. Red and black. Back: Black. Sage leaf. Printer: James Parker.	300.	750.	—
S1786	**15 Shillings** 12.4.1760. Red and black. Back: Black. Sage leaf. Printer: James Parker.	300	750.	—
S1787	**30 Shillings** 12.4.1760. Red and black. Back: Black. Sage leaf. Printer: James Parker.	400.	1000.	—
S1788	**3 Pounds** 12.4.1760. Black. Back: Black. Sage leaf. Printer: James Parker.	500.	1250.	—
S1789	**6 Pounds** 12.4.1760. Black. Back: Black. Sage leaf. Printer: James Parker.	600.	1500.	—

1761 Issue

No.	Denomination / Description	VG	VF	UNC
S1790	**12 Shillings** 23.4.1761. Red and black. Back: Black. Sage leaf. Printer: James Parker.	150.	500.	—
S1791	**15 Shillings** 23.4.1761. Red and black. Back: Black. Sage leaf. Printer: James Parker.	150.	500.	—
S1792	**30 Shillings** 23.4.1761. Red and black. Back: Black. Sage leaf. Printer: James Parker.	150.	500.	—
S1793	**3 Pounds** 23.4.1761. Red and black. Back: Black. Sage leaf. Printer: James Parker.	225.	750.	—
S1794	**6 Pounds** 23.4.1761. Red and black. Back: Black. Sage leaf. Printer: James Parker.	450.	1250.	—

1762 Issue

No.	Denomination / Description	VG	VF	UNC
S1795	**12 Shillings** 8.4.1762. Red and black. Back: Black. Sage leaf. Printer: James Parker.	150.	500.	—
S1796	**15 Shillings** 8.4.1762. Red and black. Back: Black. Sage leaf. Printer: James Parker.	150.	500.	—
S1797	**30 Shillings** 8.4.1762. Red and black. Back: Black. Sage leaf. Printer: James Parker.	150.	500.	—
S1798	**3 Pounds** 8.4.1762. Red and black. Back: Black. Sage leaf. Printer: James Parker.	225.	750.	—
S1799	**6 Pounds** 8.4.1762. Red and black. Back: Black. Sage leaf. Printer: James Parker.	450.	1250.	—

1763 Issue

No.	Denomination / Description	VG	VF	UNC
S1800	**1 Shilling** 31.12.1763. Black. Back: Black. Sage leaf. Printer: James Parker.	40.00	150.	375.
S1801	**18 Pence** 31.12.1763. Back: Black. Sage leaf. Printer: James Parker.			
	a. Plate letters A; C.	40.00	150.	375.
	b. Plate letter B. *t* in *Penny-weight* is in italics instead of upright.	40.00	150.	375.
	c. Plate letter *D. PLATE* misspelled *PTATE.*	40.00	150.	375.

	VG	VF	UNC
S1802 3 Shillings 31.12.1763. Black. Back: Black. Sage leaf. Printer: James Parker.	40.00	150.	375.
S1803 6 Shillings 31.12.1763. Black. Back: Black. Sage leaf. Printer: James Parker.	40.00	150.	375.

	VG	VF	UNC
S1804 12 Shillings 31.12.1763. Black. Back: Black. Sage leaf. Printer: James Parker.	40.00	150.	375.
S1805 15 Shillings 31.12.1763. Black. Back: Black. Sage leaf. Printer: James Parker.	40.00	150.	375.
S1806 30 Shillings 31.12.1763. Red and black. Back: Black. Sage leaf. Printer: James Parker.	150.	450.	—
S1807 3 Pounds 31.12.1763. Red and black. Back: Black. Sage leaf. Printer: James Parker.	200.	600.	—
S1808 6 Pounds 31.12.1763. Red and blue. Back: Black. Sage leaf. Printer: James Parker.	750.	2000.	—

1764 Issue

	VG	VF	UNC
S1809 12 Shillings 16.4.1764. Red and black. Back: Black. Sage leaf. Printer: James Parker.	500.	—	—
S1810 15 Shillings 16.4.1764. Red and black. Back: Black. Sage leaf. Printer: James Parker.	75.00	300.	—
S1811 30 Shillings 16.4.1764. Red and black. Back: Black. Sage leaf. Printer: James Parker.	75.00	300.	—
S1812 3 Pounds 16.4.1764. Red and black. Back: Black. Sage leaf. Printer: James Parker.			
a. Plate letters A; B; D.	75.00	300.	—
b. Without plate letter. Solid sun.	75.00	300.	—
c. Without plate letter. Split sun.	75.00	300.	—

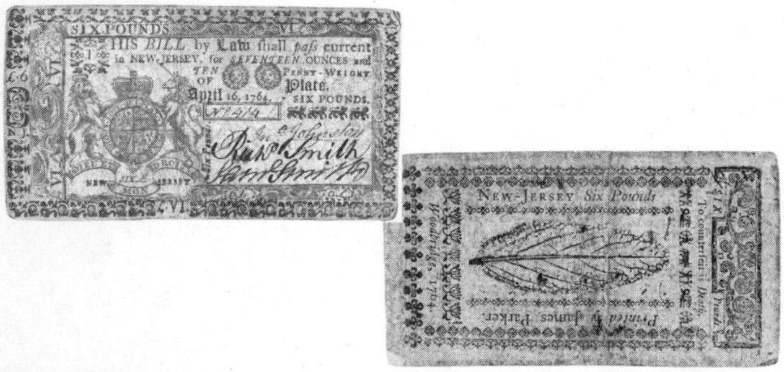

	VG	VF	UNC
S1813 6 Pounds 16.4.1764. Red and black. Back: Black. Sage leaf. Printer: James Parker.	500.	1250.	—

1776 First Issue

	VG	VF	UNC
S1814 6 Shillings 20.2.1776. Red and black. Back: Black. Cut of leaf. Watermark: *NEW JERSEY*. Printer: Isaac Collins, Burlington. Mica flaked paper.	90.00	225.	—
S1815 15 Shillings 20.2.1776. Red and black. Back: Black. Cut of leaf. Watermark: *NEW JERSEY*. Printer: Isaac Collins, Burlington. Mica flaked paper.	90.00	225.	—

	VG	VF	UNC
S1816 30 Shillings 20.2.1776. Red and black. Back: Black. Cut of leaf. Watermark: *NEW JERSEY*. Printer: Isaac Collins, Burlington. Mica flaked paper.	90.00	225.	—
S1817 3 Pounds 20.2.1776. Red and black. Back: Black. Cut of leaf. Watermark: *NEW JERSEY*. Printer: Isaac Collins, Burlington. Mica flaked paper.	90.00	225.	—

1776 Second Issue

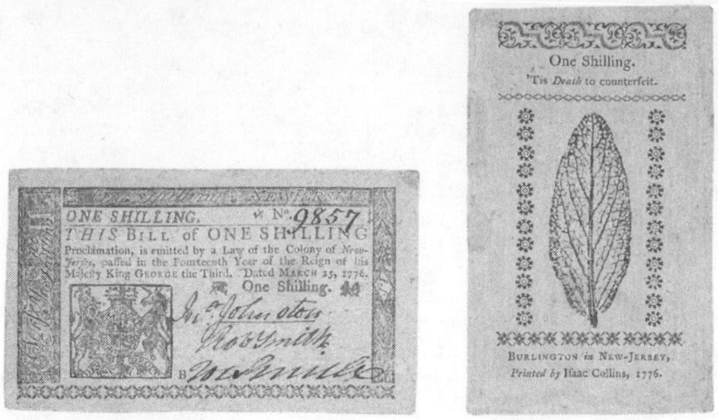

	VG	VF	UNC
S1818 1 Shilling 25.3.1776. Red and black. Back: Black. Leaf. Watermark: *NEW JERSEY*. Printer: Isaac Collins. Mica flaked paper.	50.00	125.	250.
S1819 18 Pence 25.3.1776. Red and black. Back: Black. Leaf. Watermark: *NEW JERSEY*. Printer: Isaac Collins. Mica flaked paper.	50.00	125.	250.
S1820 3 Shillings 25.3.1776. Red and black. Back: Black. Leaf. Watermark: *NEW JERSEY*. Printer: Isaac Collins. Mica flaked paper.	50.00	125.	250.
S1821 6 Shillings 25.3.1776. Red and black. Back: Black. Leaf. Watermark: *NEW JERSEY*. Printer: Isaac Collins. Mica flaked paper.			
a. Plate letter A. Small coat-of-arms.	50.00	125.	250.
b. Plate letter B. Large coat-of-arms.	50.00	125.	250.

	VG	VF	UNC
S1822 12 Shillings 25.3.1776. Red and black. Back: Black. Leaf. Watermark: *NEW JERSEY*. Printer: Isaac Collins. Mica flaked paper.	50.00	125.	250.
S1823 15 Shillings 25.3.1776. Red and black. Back: Black. Leaf. Watermark: *NEW JERSEY*. Printer: Isaac Collins. Mica flaked paper.	50.00	125.	250.
S1824 30 Shillings 25.3.1776. Red and black. Back: Black. Leaf. Watermark: *NEW JERSEY*. Printer: Isaac Collins. Mica flaked paper.	50.00	125.	250.

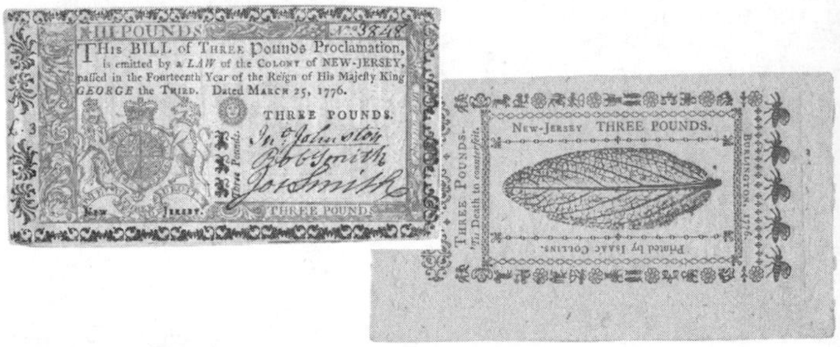

	VG	VF	UNC
S1825 3 Pounds 25.3.1776. Red and blue. Back: Black. Sage leaf and bees. Watermark: *NEW JERSEY*. Printer: Isaac Collins. Mica flaked paper.	200.	450.	1500.

	VG	VF	UNC
S1826 6 Pounds 25.3.1776. Red and blue. *RITTENHOUSE* in center ornament at left. Back: Black. Leaf. Watermark: *NEW JERSEY*. Printer: Isaac Collins. Mica flaked paper.	300.	600.	2000.

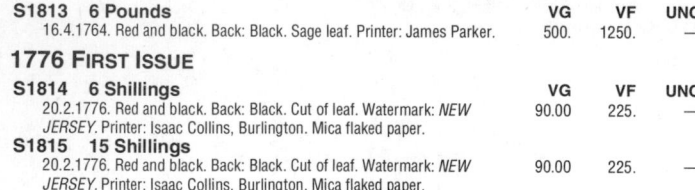

New Jersey

State

1780 Issue

	VG	VF	UNC
S1827 1 Dollar 9.6.1780. Black. Back: Red and black. Watermark: *UNITED STATES.* Printer: Hall & Sellers, PA.	100.	300.	750.
S1828 2 Dollars 9.6.1780. Black. Back: Red and black. Watermark: *UNITED STATES.* Printer: Hall & Sellers, PA.	100.	300.	750.
S1829 3 Dollars 9.6.1780. Black. Back: Red and black. Watermark: *UNITED STATES.* Printer: Hall & Sellers, PA.	100.	300.	750.

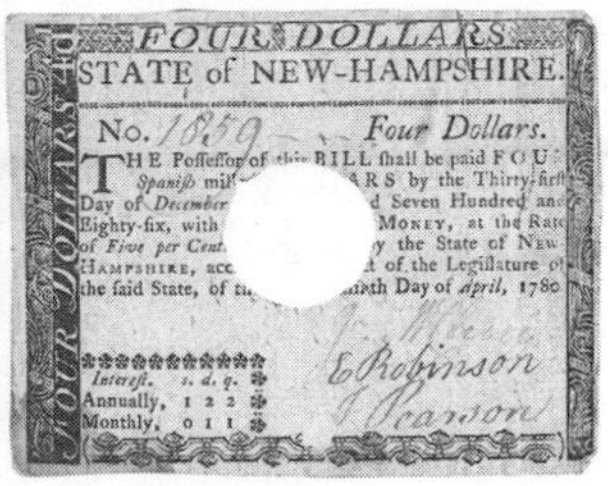

	VG	VF	UNC
S1830 4 Dollars 9.6.1780. Black. Back: Red and black. Watermark: *UNITED STATES.* Printer: Hall & Sellers, PA.	100.	300.	750.
S1831 5 Dollars 9.6.1780. Black. Back: Red and black. Watermark: *UNITED STATES.* Printer: Hall & Sellers, PA.	100.	300.	750.
S1832 7 Dollars 9.6.1780. Black. Back: Red and black. Watermark: *UNITED STATES.* Printer: Hall & Sellers, PA.	100.	300.	750.
S1833 8 Dollars 9.6.1780. Black. Back: Red and black. Watermark: *UNITED STATES.* Printer: Hall & Sellers, PA.	100.	300.	750.
S1834 20 Dollars 9.6.1780. Black. Back: Red and black. Watermark: *UNITED STATES.* Printer: Hall & Sellers, PA.	100.	300.	750.

Act of 9.1.1781; 1781 Issue

	VG	VF	UNC
S1835 6 Pence 1781. Black. N.J. state seal. Back: Sage leaf stem. Printer: Isaac Collins, Trenton.	200.	500.	2000.
S1836 9 Pence 1781. Black. N.J. state seal. Back: Sage leaf stem. Printer: Isaac Collins, Trenton.	200.	500.	2000.

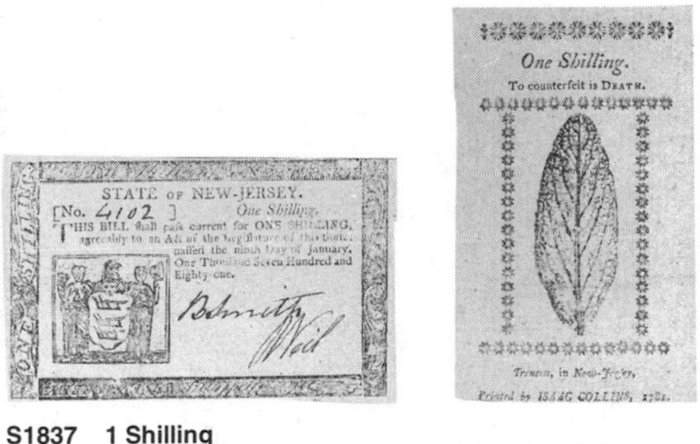

	VG	VF	UNC
S1837 1 Shilling 1781. Black. N.J. state seal. Back: Sage leaf stem. Printer: Isaac Collins, Trenton.	200.	500.	2000.
S1838 1 Shilling 6 Pence 1781. Black. N.J. state seal. Back: Sage leaf stem. Printer: Isaac Collins, Trenton.	200.	500.	2000.
S1839 2 Shillings 6 Pence 1781. Black. N.J. state seal. Back: Sage leaf stem. Printer: Isaac Collins, Trenton.	200.	500.	2000.
S1840 3 Shillings 6 Pence 1781. Black. N.J. state seal. Back: Sage leaf stem. Printer: Isaac Collins, Trenton.	200.	500.	2000.
S1841 3 Shillings 9 Pence 1781. Black. N.J. state seal. Back: Sage leaf stem. Printer: Isaac Collins, Trenton.	200.	500.	2000.
S1842 4 Shillings 1781. Black. N.J. state seal. Back: Sage leaf stem. Printer: Isaac Collins, Trenton.	200.	500.	2000.
S1843 5 Shillings 1781. Black. N.J. state seal. Back: Sage leaf stem. Printer: Isaac Collins, Trenton.	200.	500.	2000.

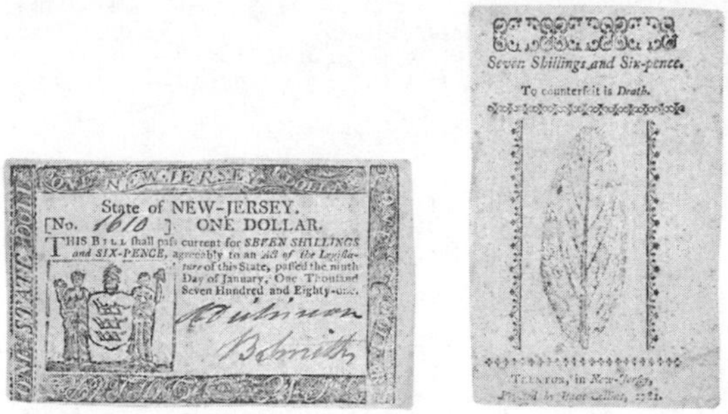

	VG	VF	UNC
S1844 7 Shillings 6 Pence - 1 Dollar 1781. Black. N.J. state seal. Back: Sage leaf stem. Printer: Isaac Collins, Trenton.	200.	500.	2000.

Act of Dec. 20, 1783; 1784 Issue

	Good	Fine	XF
S1845 2 Shillings 6 Pence 1784. Black. N.J. state seal. Back: Sage leaf stem. Watermark: *NEW JERSEY.* Printer: Isaac Collins.	1000.	3000.	—
S1846 3 Shillings 9 Pence 1784. Black. N.J. state seal. Back: Sage leaf stem. Watermark: *NEW JERSEY.* Printer: Isaac Collins.	1000.	3000.	—
S1847 5 Shillings 1784. Black. N.J. state seal. Back: Sage leaf stem. Watermark: *NEW JERSEY.* Printer: Isaac Collins.	1000.	3000.	—
S1848 7 Shillings 1784. Black. N.J. state seal. Back: Sage leaf stem. Watermark: *NEW JERSEY.* Printer: Isaac Collins.	1500.	3500.	—
S1849 12 Shillings 1784. Black. N.J. state seal. Back: Sage leaf stem. Watermark: *NEW JERSEY.* Printer: Isaac Collins.	1000.	3000.	—
S1850 15 Shillings 1784. Black. N.J. state seal. Back: Sage leaf stem. Watermark: *NEW JERSEY.* Printer: Isaac Collins.	1000.	3000.	—
S1851 30 Shillings 1784. Black. N.J. state seal. Back: Sage leaf stem. Watermark: *NEW JERSEY.* Printer: Isaac Collins.	1000.	3000.	—
S1852 3 Pounds 1784. Black. N.J. state seal. Back: Sage leaf stem. Watermark: *NEW JERSEY.* Printer: Isaac Collins.	—	—	—
S1853 6 Pounds 1784. Black. N.J. state seal. Back: Sage leaf stem. Watermark: *NEW JERSEY.* Printer: Isaac Collins.	—	—	—

1786 Issue

	VG	VF	UNC
S1854 1 Shilling 1786. Red and black. Plate letters A; B; C. Back: Black. Sage leaf stem printed opposite the right side of face with SIC which means Sculpist Isaac Collins. Watermark: *NEW JERSEY.* Printer: Isaac Collins.	1000.	3500.	—
S1855 3 Shillings 1786. Red and black. Plate letters A; B; C; D. Back: Black. Sage leaf stem printed opposite the right side of face with SIC which means Sculpist Isaac Collins. Watermark: *NEW JERSEY.* Printer: Isaac Collins.	1000.	3500.	—

	VG	VF	UNC
S1856 6 Shillings 1786. Red and black. Back: Black. Sage leaf stem printed opposite the right side of face with SIC which means Sculpist Isaac Collins. Watermark: *NEW JERSEY.* Printer: Isaac Collins.			
a. Plate letter A. Bees.	1250.	4000.	—
b. Without plate letter. Bees.	1250.	4000.	—
S1857 12 Shillings 1786. Red and black. Back: Black. Sage leaf stem printed opposite the right side of face with SIC which means Sculpist Isaac Collins. Watermark: *NEW JERSEY.* Printer: Isaac Collins.	1250.	4000.	—
S1858 15 Shillings 1786. Red and black. Back: Black. Sage leaf stem printed opposite the right side of face with SIC which means Sculpist Isaac Collins. Watermark: *NEW JERSEY.* Printer: Isaac Collins.	1500.	4500.	—
S1859 30 Shillings 1786. Red and black. Back: Black. Sage leaf stem printed opposite the right side of face with SIC which means Sculpist Isaac Collins. Watermark: *NEW JERSEY.* Printer: Isaac Collins.	1750.	5000.	—
S1860 3 Pounds 1786. Red and black. Back: Black. Sage leaf stem printed opposite the right side of face with SIC which means Sculpist Isaac Collins. Watermark: *NEW JERSEY.* Printer: Isaac Collins.	—	—	—

		VG	VF	UNC
S1861	**6 Pounds** 1786. Red and black. Back: Black. Sage leaf stem printed opposite the right side of face with SIC which means Sculpist Isaac Collins. Watermark: *NEW JERSEY*. Printer: Isaac Collins.	—	—	—

New York

Colonial

1709 Issues

		VG	VF	UNC
S1862	**5 Shillings** 31.5.1709. Black. *&* in fourth line of text. Uniface. Printer: William Bradford.	3000.	6000.	13,500.
S1863	**5 Shillings** 31.5.1709. *d* in first, *and* is inverted.	3000.	6000.	13,500.
S1864	**10 Shillings** 31.5.1709. Black. Uniface. Printer: William Bradford.			
	a. Text: with *Lieut. Governor.*	3000.	6000.	13,500.
	b. Text: with *Lieut. Governour.*	3000.	6000.	13,500.

#S1865 *Deleted*. See #S1846b.

		VG	VF	UNC
S1866	**20 Shillings** 31.5.1709. Black. Uniface. Printer: William Bradford.	3000.	6000.	13,500.
S1867	**40 Shillings** 31.5.1709. Black. Uniface. Printer: William Bradford.	3000.	6000.	13,500.
S1868	**5 Pounds** 31.5.1709. Black. Uniface. Printer: William Bradford.	3000.	6000.	13,500.
S1869	**25 Shillings** 1.11.1709. Black. Uniface. Printer: William Bradford.	4500.	10,000.	—
S1870	**50 Shillings** 1.11.1709. Black. Uniface. Printer: William Bradford.	4500.	10,000.	—
S1871	**5 Pounds** 1.11.1709. Black. Uniface. Printer: William Bradford.	—	—	—

1709 Silver Plate Issue

		Good	Fine	XF
S1872	**4 Lyon Dollars** 1.11.1709.			
	a. Text: with *Lieut. GOVERNOR.*	—	—	—
	b. Text: with *Lieut. GOVERNOUR.*	—	—	—
S1874	**8 Lyon Dollars** 1.11.1709.	—	—	—
S1875	**16 Lyon Dollars** 1.11.1709.	—	—	—
S1876	**20 Lyon Dollars** 1.11.1709.	—	—	—

1711 Silver Plate Issue

		Good	Fine	XF
S1877	**2 Shillings** 20.6.1711. Black. *Fund* spelled *Fond.* Printer: William Bradford.	—	—	—
S1878	**4 Shillings** 20.6.1711. Black. *Fund* spelled *Fond.* Printer: William Bradford.	—	—	—
S1879	**8 Shillings** 20.6.1711. Black. *Fund* spelled *Fond.* Printer: William Bradford.	—	—	—
S1880	**16 Shillings** 20.6.1711. Black. *Fund* spelled *Fond.* Printer: William Bradford.	—	—	—
S1881	**20 Shillings** 20.6.1711. Black. *Fund* spelled *Fond.* Printer: William Bradford.	—	—	—
S1882	**40 Shillings** 20.6.1711. Black. *Fund* spelled *Fond.* Printer: William Bradford.	—	—	—
S1883	**4 Pounds** 20.6.1711. Black. *Fund* spelled *Fond.* Printer: William Bradford.	—	—	—
S1884	**8 Pounds** 20.6.1711. Black. *Fund* spelled *Fond. C* is a different size in the 3rd *COLONY.* Printer: William Bradford.	—	—	—
S1885	**8 Pounds** 20.6.1711. Black. *Fund* spelled *Fond.* First and last use of *COLONY; C* is the same size. Printer: William Bradford.	—	—	—

1714 Silver Plate Issue

		Good	Fine	XF
S1886	**3 Shillings** 1.7.1714. Black. Printer: William Bradford.	—	—	—
S1887	**6 Shillings** 1.7.1714. Black. Printer: William Bradford.	—	—	—
S1888	**12 Shillings** 1.7.1714. Black. Printer: William Bradford.	—	—	—
S1889	**15 Shillings** 1.7.1714. Black. Printer: William Bradford.	—	—	—
S1890	**1 Pound 5 Shillings** 1.7.1714. Black. Printer: William Bradford.	—	—	—
S1891	**1 Pound 10 Shillings** 1.7.1714. Black. Printer: William Bradford.	—	—	—
S1892	**2 Pounds 10 Shillings** 1.7.1714. Black. Printer: William Bradford.	—	—	—
S1893	**3 Pounds** 1.7.1714. Black. Printer: William Bradford.	—	—	—
S1894	**5 Pounds** 1.7.1714. Black. Printer: William Bradford.	—	—	—
S1895	**6 Pounds** 1.7.1714. Black. Printer: William Bradford.	—	—	—
S1896	**7 Pounds 10 Shillings** 1.7.1714. Black. Printer: William Bradford.	—	—	—
S1897	**10 Pounds** 1.7.1714. Black. Printer: William Bradford.	—	—	—

1715 Silver Plate Issue

		Good	Fine	XF
S1898	**5 Shillings** 5.7.1715. Black. Printer: William Bradford.	—	—	—
S1899	**10 Shillings** 5.7.1715. Black. Printer: William Bradford.	—	—	—
S1900	**20 Shillings** 5.7.1715. Black. Printer: William Bradford.	—	—	—
S1901	**40 Shillings** 5.7.1715. Black. Printer: William Bradford.	—	—	—
S1902	**4 Pounds** 5.7.1715. Black. Printer: William Bradford.	—	—	—
S1903	**5 Pounds** 5.7.1715. Black. Printer: William Bradford.	—	—	—
S1904	**10 Pounds** 5.7.1715. Black. Printer: William Bradford.	—	—	—

1717 Spanish Silver Issue

		Good	Fine	XF
S1905	**2 Shillings** 28.11.1717. Black. Crowned arms of New York City. Printer: William Bradford.	—	—	—
S1906	**4 Shillings** 28.11.1717. Black. Crowned arms of New York City. Printer: William Bradford.	—	—	—
S1907	**6 Shillings** 28.11.1717. Black. Crowned arms of New York City. Printer: William Bradford.	—	—	—
S1908	**8 Shillings** 28.11.1717. Black. Crowned arms of New York City. Printer: William Bradford.	—	—	—
S1909	**10 Shillings** 28.11.1717. Black. Crowned arms of New York City. Printer: William Bradford.	—	—	—
S1910	**12 Shillings** 28.11.1717. Black. Crowned arms of New York City. Printer: William Bradford.	—	—	—
S1911	**16 Shillings** 28.11.1717. Black. Crowned arms of New York City. Printer: William Bradford.	—	—	—
S1912	**20 Shillings** 28.11.1717. Black. Crowned arms of New York City. Printer: William Bradford.	—	—	—
S1913	**40 Shillings** 28.11.1717. Black. Crowned arms of New York City. Printer: William Bradford.	—	—	—
S1914	**3 Pounds** 28.11.1717. Black. Crowned arms of New York City. Printer: William Bradford.	—	—	—
S1915	**4 Pounds** 28.11.1717. Black. Crowned arms of New York City. Printer: William Bradford.	—	—	—

1720 Silver Plate Issue

		Good	Fine	XF
S1916	**1 Shilling** 10.11.1720. Black. Crowned arms of New York City. Printer: William Bradford.	—	—	—
S1917	**1 Shilling 6 Pence** 10.11.1720. Black. Crowned arms of New York City. Printer: William Bradford.	—	—	—
S1918	**2 Shillings 6 Pence** 10.11.1720. Black. Crowned arms of New York City. Printer: William Bradford.	—	—	—
S1919	**3 Shillings** 10.11.1720. Black. Crowned arms of New York City. Printer: William Bradford.	—	—	—
S1920	**3 Shillings 6 Pence** 10.11.1720. Black. Crowned arms of New York City. Printer: William Bradford.	—	—	—

1723 Silver Plate Issue

		Good	Fine	XF
S1921	**3 Pounds 10 Shillings** 2.7.1723. Black. Printer: William Bradford.	—	—	—
S1922	**4 Pounds 10 Shillings** 2.7.1723. Black. Printer: William Bradford.	—	—	—

1724 First Issue

		Good	Fine	XF
S1923	**1 Shilling 3 Pence** 10.7.1724. Black. Crowned arms of New York City. Printer: William Bradford.	—	—	—
S1924	**3 Shillings 9 Pence** 10.7.1724. Black. Crowned arms of New York City. Printer: William Bradford.	—	—	—
S1925	**7 Shillings 6 Pence - 1 Dollar** 10.7.1724. Black. Crowned arms of New York City. Printer: William Bradford.	—	—	—
S1926	**14 Shillings** 10.7.1724. Black. Crowned arms of New York City. Printer: William Bradford.	—	—	—
S1927	**1 Pound 12 Shillings** 10.7.1724. Black. Crowned arms of New York City. Printer: William Bradford.	—	—	—
S1928	**3 Pounds 4 Shillings** 10.7.1724. Black. Crowned arms of New York City. Printer: William Bradford.	—	—	—
S1929	**3 Pounds 12 Shillings** 10.7.1724. Black. Crowned arms of New York City. Printer: William Bradford.	—	—	—

1724 Second Issue

		Good	Fine	XF
S1930	**1 Shilling** 22.7.1724. Black. Crowned arms of New York City. Printer: William Bradford.	—	—	—
S1931	**1 Shilling 6 Pence** 22.7.1724. Black. Crowned arms of New York City. Printer: William Bradford.	—	—	—
S1932	**2 Shillings** 22.7.1724. Black. Crowned arms of New York City. Printer: William Bradford.	—	—	—

Cat. #	Denomination / Description	Good	Fine	XF
S1933	**2 Shillings 6 Pence** 22.7.1724. Black. Crowned arms of New York City. Printer: William Bradford.	—	—	—
S1934	**3 Shillings** 22.7.1724. Black. Crowned arms of New York City. Printer: William Bradford.	—	—	—
S1935	**3 Shillings 6 Pence** 22.7.1724. Black. Crowned arms of New York City. Printer: William Bradford.	—	—	—
S1936	**4 Shillings** 22.7.1724. Black. Crowned arms of New York City. Printer: William Bradford.	—	—	—
S1937	**6 Shillings** 22.7.1724. Black. Crowned arms of New York City. Printer: William Bradford.	—	—	—
S1938	**8 Shillings** 22.7.1724. Black. Crowned arms of New York City. Printer: William Bradford.	—	—	—
S1939	**12 Shillings** 22.7.1724. Black. Crowned arms of New York City. Printer: William Bradford.	—	—	—

1726 Replacement Issue

Cat. #	Denomination / Description	Good	Fine	XF
S1940	**1 Shilling** 16.11.1726. Black. Crowned arms of New York City. The year of the note replaced is handwritten near top center.	—	—	—
S1941	**1 Shilling 3 Pence** 16.11.1726. Black. Crowned arms of New York City. The year of the note replaced is handwritten near top center.	—	—	—
S1942	**1 Shilling 6 Pence** 16.11.1726. Black. Crowned arms of New York City. The year of the note replaced is handwritten near top center.	—	—	—
S1943	**2 Shillings** 16.11.1726. Black. Crowned arms of New York City. The year of the note replaced is handwritten near top center.	—	—	—
S1944	**2 Shillings 6 Pence** 16.11.1726. Black. Crowned arms of New York City. The year of the note replaced is handwritten near top center.	—	—	—
S1945	**3 Shillings** 16.11.1726. Black. Crowned arms of New York City. The year of the note replaced is handwritten near top center.	—	—	—
S1946	**3 Shillings 6 Pence** 16.11.1726. Black. Crowned arms of New York City. The year of the note replaced is handwritten near top center.	—	—	—
S1947	**4 Shillings** 16.11.1726. Black. Crowned arms of New York City. The year of the note replaced is handwritten near top center.	—	—	—
S1948	**6 Shillings** 16.11.1726. Black. Crowned arms of New York City. The year of the note replaced is handwritten near top center.	—	—	—
S1949	**8 Shillings** 16.11.1726. Black. Crowned arms of New York City. The year of the note replaced is handwritten near top center.	—	—	—
S1950	**12 Shillings** 16.11.1726. Black. Crowned arms of New York City. The year of the note replaced is handwritten near top center.	—	—	—

1730 Replacement Issue

Cat. #	Denomination / Description	Good	Fine	XF
S1951	**2 Shillings** 20.10.1730. Black. Crowned arms of New York City. The year of the note replaced is handwritten near top center. Printer: William Bradford.	—	—	—
S1952	**5 Shillings** 20.10.1730. Black. Crowned arms of New York City. The year of the note replaced is handwritten near top center. Printer: William Bradford.	—	—	—
S1953	**10 Shillings** 20.10.1730. Black. Crowned arms of New York City. The year of the note replaced is handwritten near top center. Printer: William Bradford.	—	—	—
S1954	**20 Shillings** 20.10.1730. Black. Crowned arms of New York City. The year of the note replaced is handwritten near top center. Printer: William Bradford.	—	—	—

1734 Issue

Cat. #	Denomination / Description	Good	Fine	XF
S1955	**5 Shillings** 15.11.1734. Black. Crowned arms of New York City. Printer: William Bradford.	—	—	—
S1956	**10 Shillings** 15.11.1734. Black. Crowned arms of New York City. Printer: William Bradford.	—	—	—
S1957	**20 Shillings** 15.11.1734. Black. Crowned arms of New York City. Printer: William Bradford.	—	—	—
S1958	**2 Pounds** 15.11.1734. Black. Crowned arms of New York City. Printer: William Bradford.	—	—	—
S1959	**3 Pounds** 15.11.1734. Black. Crowned arms of New York City. Printer: William Bradford.	—	—	—
S1960	**5 Pounds** 15.11.1734. Black. Crowned arms of New York City. Printer: William Bradford.	—	—	—
S1961	**10 Pounds** 15.11.1734. Black. Crowned arms of New York City. Printer: William Bradford.	—	—	—

1737 Issue

Cat. #	Denomination / Description	Good	Fine	XF
S1962	**5 Shillings** 10.12.1737. Black. Crowned arms of New York City. Uniface. Printer: John Peter Zenger.	—	—	—
S1963	**10 Shillings** 10.12.1737. Black. Crowned arms of New York City. Uniface. Printer: John Peter Zenger.	—	—	—
S1964	**20 Shillings** 10.12.1737. Black. Crowned arms of New York City. Uniface. Printer: John Peter Zenger.	—	—	—
S1965	**2 Pounds** 10.12.1737. Black. Crowned arms of New York City. Uniface. Printer: John Peter Zenger.	—	—	—
S1966	**3 Pounds** 10.12.1737. Black. Crowned arms of New York City. Uniface. Printer: John Peter Zenger.	—	3000.	—
S1967	**5 Pounds** 10.12.1737. Black. Crowned arms of New York City. Uniface. Printer: John Peter Zenger.	—	3000.	—

Cat. #	Denomination / Description	Good	Fine	XF
S1968	**10 Pounds** 10.12.1737. Black. Crowned arms of New York City. Uniface. Printer: John Peter Zenger.	—	3000.	—

1739 Replacement Issue

Cat. #	Denomination / Description	Good	Fine	XF
S1969	**5 Shillings** 20.11.1739. Black. Crowned arms of New York City. Printer: William Bradford.	—	—	—
S1970	**10 Shillings** 20.11.1739. Black. Crowned arms of New York City. Printer: William Bradford.	—	—	—
S1971	**20 Shillings** 20.11.1739. Black. Crowned arms of New York City. Printer: William Bradford.	—	—	—
S1972	**2 Pounds** 20.11.1739. Black. Crowned arms of New York City. Printer: William Bradford.	—	—	—
S1973	**3 Pounds** 20.11.1739. Black. Crowned arms of New York City. Printer: William Bradford.	—	—	—

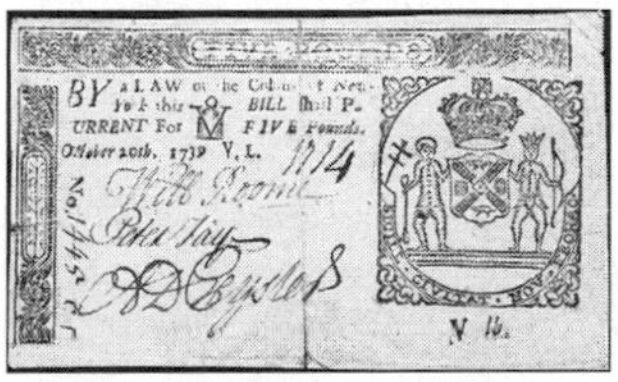

		VG	VF	UNC
S1974	**5 Pounds** 20.11.1739. Black. Crowned arms of New York City. Printer: William Bradford.	—	2000.	—
S1975	**10 Pounds** 20.11.1739. Black. Crowned arms of New York City. Printer: William Bradford.	—	—	—

1746 Defence Issues

Cat. #	Denomination / Description	Good	Fine	XF
S1976	**2 Pounds** 10.5.1746. Black. Crowned arms of New York City at right. Printer: James Parker.	—	—	—
S1977	**3 Pounds** 10.5.1746. Black. Crowned arms of New York City at right. Printer: James Parker.	—	—	—

Cat. #	Denomination / Description	Good	Fine	XF
S1978	**5 Pounds** 10.5.1746. Black. Crowned arms of New York City at right. Printer: James Parker.	—	—	7000.

		VG	VF	UNC
S1979	**10 Pounds** 10.5.1746. Black. Crowned arms of New York City at right. Printer: James Parker.	1400.	—	—
S1980	**10 Shillings** 21.7.1746. Black. Crowned arms of New York City at right. Printer: James Parker.	—	—	—

	Good	Fine	XF
S1981 20 Shillings 21.7.1746. Black. Crowned arms of New York City at right. Printer: James Parker.	—	—	—
S1982 2 Pounds 21.7.1746. Black. Crowned arms of New York City at right. Printer: James Parker.	—	—	—

	VG	VF	UNC
S1983 3 Pounds 21.7.1746. Black. Crowned arms of New York City at right. Printer: James Parker.	—	2500.	—

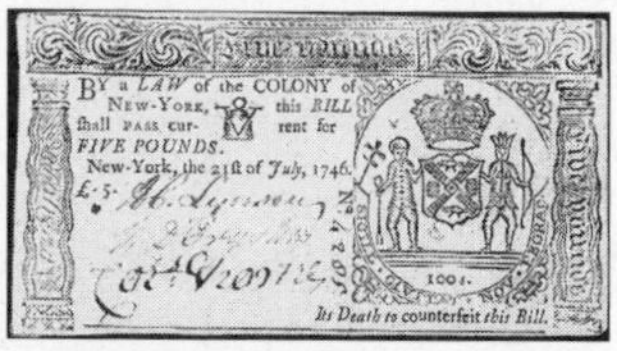

	VG	VF	UNC
S1984 5 Pounds 21.7.1746. Black. Crowned arms of New York City at right. Printer: James Parker.	—	—	4250.
S1985 10 Pounds 21.7.1746. Black. Crowned arms of New York City at right. Printer: James Parker.	—	—	—

1747 Defence Issue

	Good	Fine	XF
S1986 20 Shillings 25.11.1747. Black. Crowned arms of New York City at left. Printer: James Parker.	—	—	—

	VG	VF	UNC
S1987 2 Pounds 25.11.1747. Black. Crowned arms of New York City at left. Printer: James Parker.	1000.	—	—
S1988 3 Pounds 25.11.1747. Black. Crowned arms of New York City at left. Printer: James Parker.	—	—	—
S1989 5 Pounds 25.11.1747. Black. Crowned arms of New York City at left. Printer: James Parker.	—	—	—

	VG	VF	UNC
S1990 10 Pounds 25.11.1747. Black. Crowned arms of New York City at left. Printer: James Parker.	—	2250.	—

1755 First Issue

	Good	Fine	XF
S1991 10 Shillings 25.3.1755. Black. Crowned arms of New York City at right. Paper: White. Printer: James Parker. Uniface with dark coarse paper backs.	—	—	—
S1992 20 Shillings 25.3.1755. Black. Crowned arms of New York City at right. Paper: White. Printer: James Parker. Uniface with dark coarse paper back.	—	—	—
S1993 2 Pounds 25.3.1755. Black. Crowned arms of New York City at right. Paper: White. Printer: James Parker. Uniface with dark coarse paper back.	—	—	—
S1994 3 Pounds 25.3.1755. Black. Crowned arms of New York City at right. Paper: White. Printer: James Parker. Uniface with dark coarse paper back.	—	—	—

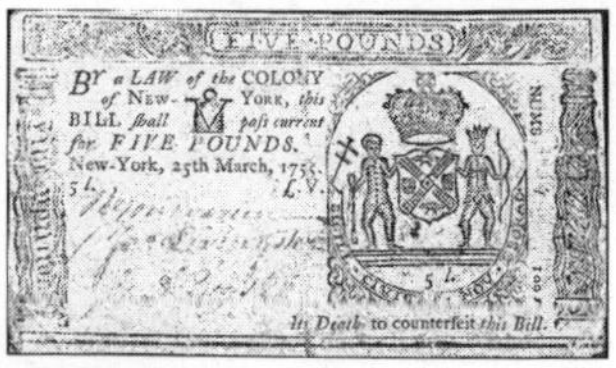

	Good	Fine	XF
S1995 5 Pounds 25.3.1755. Black. Crowned arms of New York City at right. Paper: White. Printer: James Parker. Uniface with dark coarse paper back.	—	1750.	—

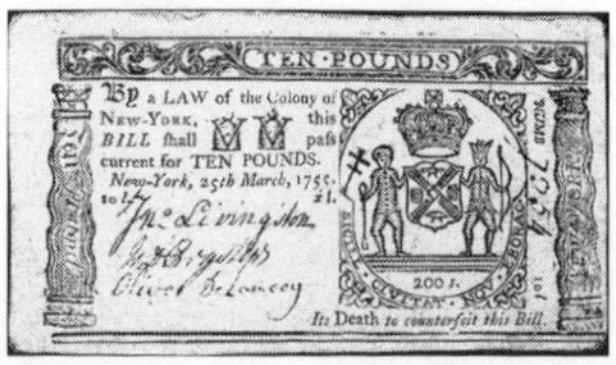

	VG	VF	UNC
S1996 10 Pounds 25.3.1755. Black. Crowned arms of New York City at right. Paper: White. Printer: James Parker. Uniface with dark coarse paper back.	—	—	8000.

1755 Second Issue

	Good	Fine	XF
S1997 5 Shillings 12.5.1755. Black. Crowned arms of New York City at left. Paper: White. Printer: James Parker. Uniface with dark coarse paper back.	—	—	—
S1998 10 Shillings 12.5.1755. Black. Crowned arms of New York City at left. Paper: White. Printer: James Parker. Uniface with dark coarse paper back.	—	—	—
S1999 20 Shillings 12.5.1755. Black. Crowned arms of New York City at left. Paper: White. Printer: James Parker. Uniface with dark coarse paper back.	—	—	—
S2000 2 Pounds 12.5.1755. Black. Crowned arms of New York City at left. Paper: White. Printer: James Parker. Uniface with dark coarse paper back.	—	—	—
S2001 3 Pounds 12.5.1755. Black. Crowned arms of New York City at left. Paper: White. Printer: James Parker. Uniface with dark coarse paper back.	—	—	—
S2002 4 Pounds 12.5.1755. Black. Crowned arms of New York City at left. Paper: White. Printer: James Parker. Uniface with dark coarse paper back.	—	—	—

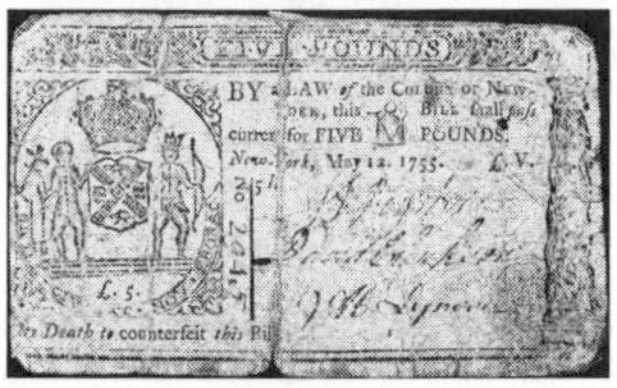

	Good	Fine	XF
S2003 5 Pounds 12.5.1755. Black. Crowned arms of New York City at left. Paper: White. Printer: James Parker. Uniface with dark coarse paper back.	900.	—	—
S2004 10 Pounds 12.5.1755. Black. Crowned arms of New York City at left. Paper: White. Printer: James Parker. Uniface with dark coarse paper back.	—	—	6750.

1755 Third Issue

	Good	Fine	XF
S2005 5 Shillings 15.9.1755. Black. Crowned arms of New York City at left. Paper: White. Printer: James Parker. Uniface with dark coarse paper back.	—	—	—
S2006 10 Shillings 15.9.1755. Black. Crowned arms of New York City at left. Paper: White. Printer: James Parker. Uniface with dark coarse paper back.	—	—	—
S2007 20 Shillings 15.9.1755. Black. Crowned arms of New York City at left. Paper: White. Printer: James Parker. Uniface with dark coarse paper back.	—	—	—
S2008 2 Pounds 15.9.1755. Black. Crowned arms of New York City at left. Paper: White. Printer: James Parker. Uniface with dark coarse paper back.	—	—	—
S2009 3 Pounds 15.9.1755. Black. Crowned arms of New York City at left. Paper: White. Printer: James Parker. Uniface with dark coarse paper back.	—	—	—
S2010 4 Pounds 15.9.1755. Black. Crowned arms of New York City at left. Paper: White. Printer: James Parker. Uniface with dark coarse paper back.	—	—	—
S2011 5 Pounds 15.9.1755. Black. Crowned arms of New York City at left. Paper: White. Printer: James Parker. Uniface with dark coarse paper back.	—	—	—

	VG	VF	UNC
S2012 10 Pounds 15.9.1755. Black. Crowned arms of New York City at left. Paper: White. Printer: James Parker. Uniface with dark coarse paper back.	—	—	9500.

1756 First Issue

	Good	Fine	XF
S2013 10 Pounds 16.2.1756. Black. Crowned arms of New York City at right. Paper: White. Printer: James Parker. Uniface with dark coarse paper back.	—	—	—

1756 Second Issue

	VG	VF	UNC
S2014 20 Shillings 20.4.1756. Black. Crowned arms of New York City at right. Paper: White. Printer: James Parker. Uniface with dark coarse paper back.	250.	—	—
S2015 2 Pounds 20.4.1756. Black. Crowned arms of New York City at right. Paper: White. Printer: James Parker. Uniface with dark coarse paper back.	400.	—	—
S2016 3 Pounds 20.4.1756. Black. Crowned arms of New York City at right. Paper: White. Printer: James Parker. Uniface with dark coarse paper back.	250.	—	—
S2017 5 Pounds 20.4.1756. Black. Crowned arms of New York City at right. Paper: White. Printer: James Parker. Uniface with dark coarse paper back.	225.	—	—
S2018 10 Pounds 20.4.1756. Black. Crowned arms of New York City at right. Paper: White. Printer: James Parker. Uniface with dark coarse paper back.	250.	—	—

1758 Issue

	VG	VF	UNC
S2019 5 Pounds 15.4.1758. Black. Crowned arms of New York City at right. Paper: White. Printer: James Parker. Uniface with dark coarse paper back.	225.	450.	—
S2020 10 Pounds 15.4.1758. Black. Crowned arms of New York City at right. Paper: White. Printer: James Parker. Uniface with dark coarse paper back.	175.	350.	—

1759 Issue

	Good	Fine	XF
S2021 2 Pounds 2.4.1759. Black. Crowned arms of New York City at right. Paper: Thin white. Printer: William Weyman.	40.00	125.	—
S2022 5 Pounds 2.4.1759. Black. Crowned arms of New York City at right. Paper: Thin white. Printer: William Weyman.	125.	350.	—
S2023 10 Pounds 2.4.1759. Black. Crowned arms of New York City at right. Paper: Thin white. Printer: William Weyman.	125.	350.	—

1760 Issue

	VG	VF	UNC
S2024 2 Pounds 21.4.1760. Black. Crowned arms of New York City at right. Printer: William Weyman.	125.	250.	—
S2025 5 Pounds 21.4.1760. Black. Crowned arms of New York City at right. Printer: William Weyman.	125.	250.	—
S2026 10 Pounds 21.4.1760. Black. Crowned arms of New York City at right. Printer: William Weyman.	125.	250.	—

1771 Issue

	VG	VF	UNC
S2027 5 Shillings 16.2.1771. Black. Ornamental upper border, crowned arms of New York City. Printer: Hugh Gaine. Thin laid paper.	225.	900.	—
S2028 10 Shillings 16.2.1771. Black. Ornamental upper border, crowned arms of New York City. Printer: Hugh Gaine. Thin laid paper.	225.	900.	—
S2029 1 Pound 16.2.1771. Black. Ornamental upper border, crowned arms of New York City. Printer: Hugh Gaine. Thin laid paper.	225.	900.	—
S2030 2 Pounds 16.2.1771. Black. Ornamental upper border, crowned arms of New York City. Printer: Hugh Gaine. Thin laid paper.			
a. Comma after February. Stars on bottom border have 12 points.	225.	900.	—
b. Without comma after February. Stars on bottom border have 12 points.	225.	900.	—
c. Stars on bottom border have 12 points except 7th from right.	225.	900.	—
d. Stars on bottom border have 8 points.	225.	900.	—
S2031 3 Pounds 16.2.1771. Black. Ornamental upper border, crowned arms of New York City. Printer: Hugh Gaine. Thin laid paper.	225.	900.	—
S2032 5 Pounds 16.2.1771. Black. Ornamental upper border, crowned arms of New York City. Printer: Hugh Gaine. Thin laid paper.	125.	500.	—
S2033 10 Pounds 16.2.1771. Black. Ornamental upper border, crowned arms of New York City. Printer: Hugh Gaine. Thin laid paper.	125.	500.	—

1775 Spanish Silver Issue

	VG	VF	UNC
S2034 1/2 Dollar 2.9.1775. Black. Crowned arms of New York City. Back: Planting of tree, *POSTERITATE*. Printer: John Holt. Thick paper.	125.	500.	2000.
S2035 1 Dollar 2.9.1775. Black. Crowned arms of New York City. Back: Sheaf of wheat, *ACERVUS E PARVIS GRANDIS*. Printer: John Holt. Thick paper.	125.	500.	2000.
S2036 2 Dollars 2.9.1775. Black. Crowned arms of New York City. Back: Two storks, *SALUTARIS SIBI PARENTIBUSQUE*. Printer: John Holt. Thick paper.	125.	500.	2000.
S2037 3 Dollars 2.9.1775. Black. Crowned arms of New York City. Back: Ten Commandments, *LEX REGIT ARMA TUENTUR*. Printer: John Holt. Thick paper.	125.	500.	2000.
S2038 5 Dollars 2.9.1775. Black. Crowned arms of New York City. Back: Candelabrum, *UNO EODEMQUE IGNI*. Printer: John Holt. Thick paper.	125.	500.	2000.

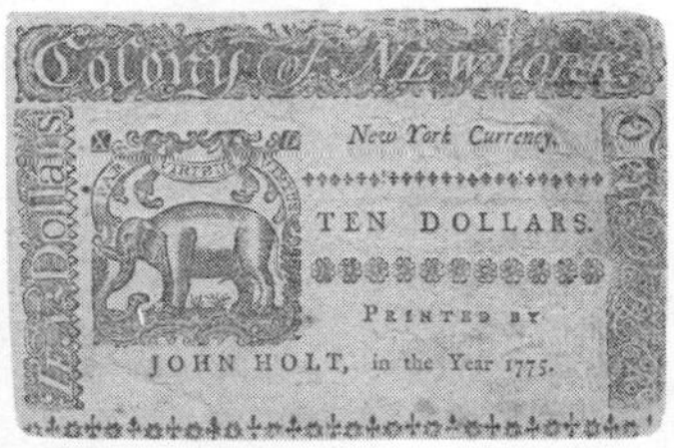

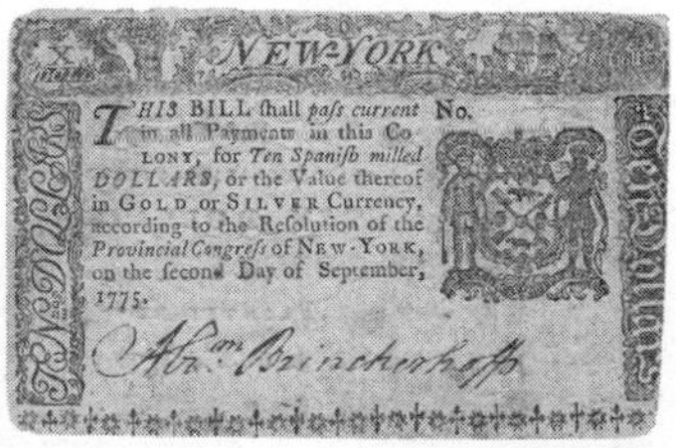

	VG	VF	UNC
S2039 10 Dollars 2.9.1775. Black. Crowned arms of New York City. Back: Elephant, *PAR VIRIBUS VIRTUS*. Printer: John Holt. Thick paper.	125.	500.	2000.

1776 Issue

	VG	VF	UNC
S2040 1/8 Dollar 5.3.1776. Black. Back: Fire, *NON DIU*. Printer: Samuel Loudon. Thick paper.	100.	400.	1750.
S2041 1/6 Dollar 5.3.1776. Black. Back: Stork, *NE IMPROVISO*. Printer: Samuel Loudon. Thick paper.	100.	400.	1750.
S2042 1/4 Dollar 5.3.1776. Black. Back: Book and candle, *CLARET AB ICTU*. Printer: Samuel Loudon. Thick paper.	100.	400.	1750.
S2043 1/3 Dollar 5.3.1776. Black. Back: Three wreaths, *HIS ORNARI AUT MORI*. Printer: Samuel Loudon. Thick paper.	100.	400.	1750.
S2044 1/2 Dollar 5.3.1776. Black. Back: Planting of tree, *POSTERITATE*. Printer: Samuel Loudon. Thick paper.	100.	400.	1750.
S2045 2/3 Dollar 5.3.1776. Black. Back: Eagle, *FORTIS A FORTE*. Printer: Samuel Loudon. Thick paper.	100.	400.	1750.
S2046 1 Dollar 5.3.1776. Black. Back: Sheaf of wheat, *ACERVUS E PARVIS GRANDIS*. Printer: Samuel Loudon. Thick paper.	100.	400.	1750.
S2047 2 Dollars 5.3.1776. Black. Back: Two storks, *SALUTARIS SIBI PARENTIBUSQUE*. Printer: Samuel Loudon. Thick paper.	100.	650.	2500.
S2048 3 Dollars 5.3.1776. Black. Back: Ten Commandments, *LEX REGIT ARMA TUENTUR*. Printer: Samuel Loudon. Thick paper.	100.	650.	2500.
S2049 5 Dollars 5.3.1776. Black. Back: Candelabrum, *UNO EODEMQUE IGNI*. Printer: Samuel Loudon. Thick paper.	100.	650.	2500.
S2050 10 Dollars 5.3.1776. Black. Back: Elephant, *PAR VIRIBUS VIRTUS*. Printer: Samuel Loudon. Thick paper.	100.	650.	2500.

New York

State

1776 Issue

	VG	VF	UNC
S2051 1/16 Dollar 13.8.1776. Black. Printer: Samuel Loudon. Thick paper.	75.00	300.	1600.
S2052 1/8 Dollar 13.8.1776. Black. Back: Fire, *NON DIU*. Printer: Samuel Loudon. Thick paper.	75.00	300.	1600.
S2053 1/4 Dollar 13.8.1776. Black. Back: Book and candle, *CLARET AB ICTU*. Printer: Samuel Loudon. Thick paper.	75.00	300.	1600.
S2054 1/2 Dollar 13.8.1776. Back: Planting of tree, *POSTERITATE*.	75.00	300.	1600.
S2055 2 Dollars 13.8.1776. Back: Two storks, *SALUTARIS SIBI PARENTIBUSQUE*.	75.00	500.	2000.
S2056 3 Dollars 13.8.1776. Back: Ten Commandments, *LEX REGIT ARMA TUENTUR*.	75.00	500.	2000.
S2057 5 Dollars 13.8.1776. Back: Candelabrum, *UNO EODEMQUE IGNI*.	75.00	500.	2000.
S2058 10 Dollars 13.8.1776. Back: Elephant, *PAR VIRIBUS VIRTUS*.	75.00	500.	2000.

1780 Issue

	VG	VF	UNC
S2059 1 Dollar 15.6.1780. Black. Back: Red and black. Watermark: *CONFED / ERATION*. Printer: Hall & Sellers, PA. Mica flaked paper.	250.	500.	—
S2060 2 Dollars 15.6.1780. Black. Back: Red and black. Watermark: *CONFED / ERATION*. Printer: Hall & Sellers, PA. Mica flaked paper.	250.	500.	—
S2061 3 Dollars 15.6.1780. Black. Back: Red and black. Watermark: *CONFED / ERATION*. Printer: Hall & Sellers, PA. Mica flaked paper.	250.	500.	—
S2062 4 Dollars 15.6.1780. Black. Back: Red and black. Watermark: *CONFED / ERATION*. Printer: Hall & Sellers, PA. Mica flaked paper.	250.	500.	—
S2063 5 Dollars 15.6.1780. Black. Back: Red and black. Watermark: *CONFED / ERATION*. Printer: Hall & Sellers, PA. Mica flaked paper.	250.	500.	—
S2064 7 Dollars 15.6.1780. Black. Back: Red and black. Watermark: *CONFED / ERATION*. Printer: Hall & Sellers, PA. Mica flaked paper.	250.	500.	—
S2065 8 Dollars 15.6.1780. Black. Back: Red and black. Watermark: *CONFED / ERATION*. Printer: Hall & Sellers, PA. Mica flaked paper.	250.	500.	—
S2066 20 Dollars 15.6.1780. Black. Back: Red and black. Watermark: *CONFED / ERATION*. Printer: Hall & Sellers, PA. Mica flaked paper.	250.	500.	—

1781 Issue

	Good	Fine	XF
S2067 1 Dollar 27.3.1781. Black. Liberty Cap. Printer: John Holt.	—	—	32,250.
S2068 2 Dollars 27.3.1781. Black. Sword. Printer: John Holt.	—	—	40,500.
S2069 3 Dollars 27.3.1781. Black. Printer: John Holt.	—	—	—
S2070 4 Dollars 27.3.1781. Black. Printer: John Holt.	—	—	—
S2071 5 Dollars 27.3.1781. Black. Printer: John Holt.	—	—	—
S2072 7 Dollars 27.3.1781. Black. Printer: John Holt.	—	—	—
S2073 8 Dollars 27.3.1781. Black. Justice. Printer: John Holt.	—	—	52,000.
S2074 20 Dollars 27.3.1781. Black. Printer: John Holt.	—	—	—

1786 Issue

	Good	Fine	XF
S2075 5 Shillings 18.4.1786. Black. Arms of New York State. Printer: Samuel Loudon.			
a. *EXCELSIOR* in white.	—	—	—
b. *EXCELSIOR* in black.	—	—	—
S2076 10 Shillings 18.4.1786. Black. Arms of New York State. Printer: Samuel Loudon.	—	—	—

		Good	Fine	XF
S2077	**1 Pound** 18.4.1786. Black. Arms of New York State. Printer: Samuel Loudon.	—	—	—
S2078	**2 Pounds** 18.4.1786. Black. Arms of New York State. Printer: Samuel Loudon.	—	—	—

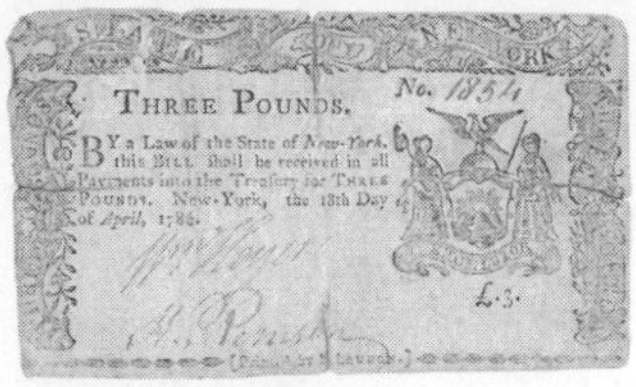

		Good	Fine	XF
S2079	**3 Pounds** 18.4.1786. Black. Arms of New York State. Printer: Samuel Loudon.	—	—	—
S2080	**4 Pounds** 18.4.1786. Black. Arms of New York State. Printer: Samuel Loudon.	—	—	—
S2081	**5 Pounds** 18.4.1786. Black. Arms of New York State. Printer: Samuel Loudon.	—	—	—
S2082	**10 Pounds** 18.4.1786. Black. Arms of New York State. Printer: Samuel Loudon.	—	—	—

1788 Issue

		VG	VF	UNC
S2083	**5 Shillings** 8.2.1788. Black and red. Back: Black. Printer: Hugh Gaine. Thick paper.	—	12,750.	—
S2084	**10 Shillings** 8.2.1788. Black and red. Back: Black. Printer: Hugh Gaine. Thick paper.	—	—	—
S2085	**1 Pound** 8.2.1788. Black and red. Back: Black. Printer: Hugh Gaine. Thick paper.	—	12,750.	—
S2086	**2 Pounds** 8.2.1788. Black and red. Back: Black. Printer: Hugh Gaine. Thick paper.	—	—	—
S2087	**3 Pounds** 8.2.1788. Black and red. Back: Black. Printer: Hugh Gaine. Thick paper.	—	—	—
S2088	**4 Pounds** 8.2.1788. Black and red. Back: Black. Printer: Hugh Gaine. Thick paper.	—	—	—
S2089	**5 Pounds** 8.2.1788. Black and red. Back: Black. Printer: Hugh Gaine. Thick paper.	—	—	—
S2090	**10 Pounds** 8.2.1788. Black and red. Back: Black. Printer: Hugh Gaine. Thick paper.	—	—	—

North Carolina

Colonial

1722 Issue

		Good	Fine	XF
S2091	**12 Pence** 19.10.1722. Black.	—	—	—
S2092	**2 Shillings** 19.10.1722. Black.	—	—	—
S2093	**2 Shillings 6 Pence** 19.10.1722. Black.	—	—	—
S2094	**5 Shillings** 19.10.1722. Black.	—	—	—
S2095	**7 Shillings 6 Pence - 1 Dollar** 19.10.1722. Black.	—	—	—
S2096	**10 Shillings** 19.10.1722. Black.	—	—	—
S2097	**20 Shillings** 19.10.1722. Black.	—	—	—
S2098	**40 Shillings** 19.10.1722. Black.	—	—	—
S2099	**3 Pounds** 19.10.1722. Black.	—	—	—
S2100	**5 Pounds** 19.10.1722. Black.	—	—	—

1729 Issue

		Good	Fine	XF
S2101	**12 Pence** 27.11.1729. Black.	—	—	—
S2102	**2 Shillings** 27.11.1729. Black.	—	—	—
S2103	**2 Shillings 6 Pence** 27.11.1729. Black.	—	—	—
S2104	**5 Shillings** 27.11.1729. Black.	—	—	—
S2105	**7 Shillings 6 Pence - 1 Dollar** 27.11.1729. Black.	—	—	—
S2106	**10 Shillings** 27.11.1729. Black.	—	—	—
S2107	**20 Shillings** 27.11.1729. Black.	—	—	—
S2108	**40 Shillings** 27.11.1729. Black.	—	—	—
S2109	**3 Pounds** 27.11.1729. Black.	—	—	—
S2110	**5 Pounds** 27.11.1729. Black. Denomination in red.	—	—	—
S2111	**10 Pounds** 27.11.1729. Black.	—	—	—

1734 Issue

		Good	Fine	XF
S2112	**1 Shilling** 1734(5). Black.	—	—	—
S2113	**2 Shillings 6 Pence** 1734(5). Black.	—	—	—
S2114	**5 Shillings** 1734(5). Black.	—	—	—
S2115	**10 Shillings** 1734(5). Black.	—	—	—
S2116	**20 Shillings** 1734(5). Black. Crowned lion.	—	—	—
S2117	**40 Shillings** 1734(5). Black.	—	—	—
S2118	**3 Pounds** 1734(5). Black.	—	—	—
S2119	**5 Pounds** 1734(5). Black.	—	—	—
S2120	**10 Pounds** 1734(5). Black. Winged stirrup.	—	—	—

1735 Issue

		Good	Fine	XF
S2121	**1 Shilling** 1735. Black.	—	—	—
S2122	**2 Shillings 6 Pence** 1735. Black.	—	—	—
S2123	**5 Shillings** 1735. Black.	—	—	—
S2124	**10 Shillings** 1735. Black.	—	—	—
S2125	**20 Shillings** 1735. Black. Crowned lion.	—	—	—
S2126	**40 Shillings** 1735. Black. Horse rearing.	—	—	—
S2127	**3 Pounds** 1735. Black.	—	—	—
S2128	**5 Pounds** 1735. Black. Pegasus.	—	—	—
S2129	**10 Pounds** 1735. Black. Winged stirrup.	—	—	—

1748 Issue

		VG	VF	UNC
S2130	**4 Pence** 4.4.1748. Black. Denomination in circle.	400.	1900.	—
S2131	**8 Pence** 4.4.1748. Black. Denomination in circle.	400.	1900.	—
S2132	**1 Shilling** 4.4.1748. Black. Denomination in circle.	400.	1900.	—
S2133	**1 Shilling** 4.4.1748. Black. Denomination in circle.	400.	1900.	—
S2134	**2 Shillings** 4.4.1748. Black. Thistle.	400.	1900.	—
S2135	**2 Shillings 6 Pence** 4.4.1748. Black. Crowned rose.	400.	1900.	—
S2136	**3 Shillings** 4.4.1748. Black. Plumes.	400.	1900.	—
S2137	**5 Shillings** 4.4.1748. Black. Crown.	400.	1900.	—
S2138	**6 Shillings** 4.4.1748. Black. Fleur-de-lys.	400.	1900.	—
S2139	**7 Shillings 6 Pence - 1 Dollar** 4.4.1748. Black. Harp.	400.	1900.	—
S2140	**9 Shillings** 4.4.1748. Black. Crowned lion.	400.	1900.	—
S2141	**10 Shillings** 4.4.1748. Black. Horse.	400.	1900.	—
S2142	**15 Shillings** 4.4.1748. Black. Rampant lion.	400.	1900.	—

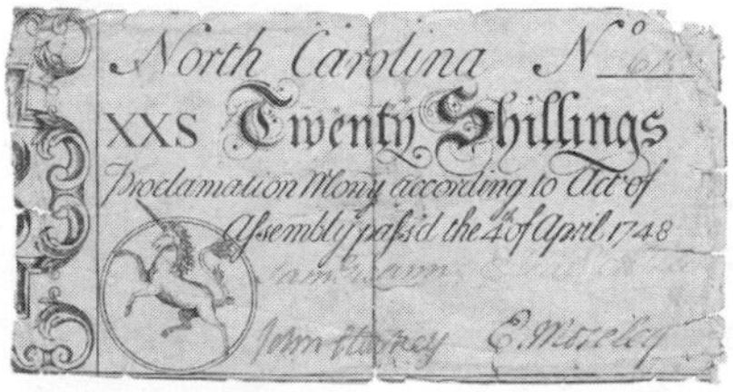

		VG	VF	UNC
S2143	**20 Shillings** 4.4.1748. Black. Unicorn	300.	1500.	—
S2144	**30 Shillings** 4.4.1748. Black. Winged stirrup.	300.	1500.	—
S2145	**40 Shillings** 4.4.1748. Black. Drum, cannon and flags.	300.	1500.	—
S2146	**3 Pounds** 4.4.1748. Black. Fort Johnson and Union Jack.	300.	1500.	—

1754 Issue

		VG	VF	UNC
S2147	**4 Pence** 9.3.1754. Black.			
	a. Key.	300.	1000.	—
	b. Mountain lion.	300.	1000.	—
	c. Monogram.	300.	1000.	—

	VG	VF	UNC
S2148 8 Pence			
9.3.1754. Black.			
a. Butterfly.	300.	1000.	—
b. Boar.	300.	1000.	—
S2149 1 Shilling			
9.3.1754. Black.			
a. Swan.	300.	1000.	—
b. Bear.	300.	1000.	—
c. *NC* monogram.	300.	1000.	—
S2150 2 Shillings 8 Pence			
9.3.1754. Black. Snail.	300.	1000.	—
S2151 4 Shillings			
9.3.1754. Black. Monogram.	300.	1000.	—
S2152 5 Shillings			
9.3.1754. Black. Squirrel.	300.	1000.	—
S2153 10 Shillings			
9.3.1754. Black. Bird.	200.	750.	—
S2154 15 Shillings			
9.3.1754. Black. Armor.	200.	750.	—

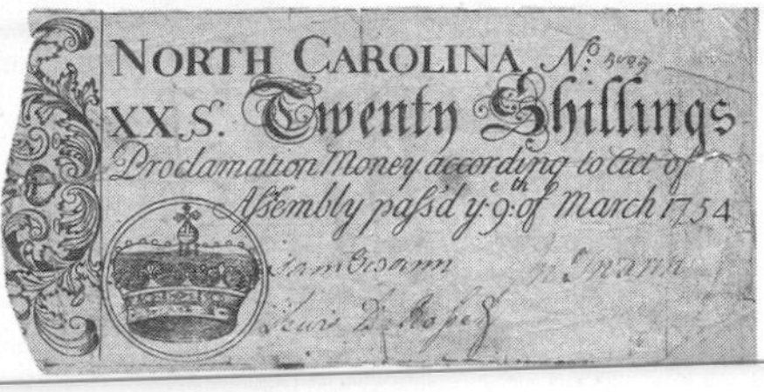

	VG	VF	UNC
S2155 20 Shillings			
9.3.1754. Black. Crown.	200.	750.	—
S2156 26 Shillings 8 Pence			
9.3.1754. Black. Bible.	200.	750.	—
S2157 30 Shillings			
9.3.1754. Black. House.	200.	750.	—
S2158 40 Shillings			
9.3.1754. Black. Christ Church at Newbern.	200.	750.	—

1756-57 Issue

	Good	Fine	XF
S2159 5 Pounds			
1756-57. Black.	—	1500.	—
S2160 10 Pounds			
1756-57. Black.	—	—	—
S2161 20 Pounds			
1756-57. Black.	—	—	—
S2162 50 Pounds			
1756-57. Black.	—	—	—

1757 Issue

	Good	Fine	XF
S2163 10 Shillings			
28.5.1757. Black.			
a. With text: *per Cent.*	—	—	—
b. With text: *per Centum.*	—	—	—
S2164 20 Shillings			
28.5.1757. Black.			
a. With text: *per Cent.*	—	—	—
b. With text: *per Centum.*	—	—	—
S2165 40 Shillings			
28.5.1757. Black.			
a. With text: *per Cent.*	—	—	—
b. With text: *per Centum.*	—	—	—
S2166 5 Pounds			
28.5.1757. Black.			
a. With text: *per Cent.*	—	—	—
b. With text: *per Centum.*	—	—	—

1757 Session Act Issue

	Good	Fine	XF
S2167 10 Shillings			
21.11.1757. Black.	—	—	—
S2168 20 Shillings			
21.11.1757. Black.	—	—	—
S2169 40 Shillings			
21.11.1757. Black.	—	—	—

	VG	VF	UNC
S2170 5 Pounds			
21.11.1757. Black.			
a. With text: *in Pay-ment of Taxes.*	250.	1000.	—
b. With text: *in Payment of Taxes.*	—	—	—

1758 First Issue

	Good	Fine	XF
S2171 10 Shillings			
4.5.1758. Black.	—	—	—
S2172 20 Shillings			
4.5.1758. Black.	—	—	—
S2173 40 Shillings			
4.5.1758. Black.	1250.	—	—

1758 Second Issue

	Good	Fine	XF
S2174 10 Shillings			
22.12.1758. Black.	—	—	—
S2175 20 Shillings			
22.12.1758. Black.	—	—	—
S2176 40 Shillings			
22.12.1758. Black.	—	—	—

1760 Issue

	Good	Fine	XF
S2177 4 Pence			
14.7.1760. Black.	—	—	—
S2178 6 Pence			
14.7.1760. Black.	—	—	—
S2179 8 Pence			
14.7.1760. Black.	—	—	—
S2180 1 Shilling			
14.7.1760. Black.	—	—	—
S2181 2 Shillings			
14.7.1760. Black.	—	—	—
S2182 2 Shillings 8 Pence			
14.7.1760. Black.	—	—	—
S2183 5 Shillings			
14.7.1760. Black.	175.	500.	—
S2184 10 Shillings			
14.7.1760. Black.	175.	500.	—
S2185 20 Shillings			
14.7.1760. Black.	150.	400.	—
S2186 30 Shillings			
14.7.1760. Black.	150.	400.	—
S2187 40 Shillings			
14.7.1760. Black.	150.	400.	—
S2188 3 Pounds			
14.7.1760. Black.	150.	400.	—

1761 Issue

	VG	VF	UNC
S2189 4 Pence			
23.4.1761. Black.	250.	—	—
S2190 6 Pence			
23.4.1761. Black.	250.	—	—
S2191 8 Pence			
23.4.1761. Black.	250.	—	—
S2192 1 Shilling			
23.4.1761. Black.	250.	—	—
S2193 2 Shillings			
23.4.1761. Black.	250.	—	—
S2194 2 Shillings 6 Pence			
23.4.1761. Black.	250.	—	—
S2195 3 Shillings			
23.4.1761. Black.	250.	—	—
S2196 4 Shillings			
23.4.1761. Black.	250.	—	—
S2197 5 Shillings			
23.4.1761. Black.	250.	—	—
S2198 10 Shillings			
23.4.1761. Black.	150.	400.	—
S2199 15 Shillings			
23.4.1761. Black.	150.	400.	—
S2200 20 Shillings			
23.4.1761. Black.	150.	400.	—
S2201 30 Shillings			
23.4.1761. Black.	150.	400.	—
S2202 40 Shillings			
23.4.1761. Black.	150.	400.	—
S2203 3 Pounds			
23.4.1761. Black.	250.	800.	—

1768 Issue

	VG	VF	UNC
S2204 2 Shillings			
Dec. 1768. Black.			
a. *1768* on 6th line.	200.	600.	
b. *1768* on 7th line.	200.	600.	
S2205 5 Shillings			
Dec. 1768. Black.	200.	600.	—
S2206 10 Shillings			
Dec. 1768. Black.	200.	600.	—
S2207 20 Shillings			
Dec. 1768. Black.	150.	400.	—
S2208 40 Shillings			
Dec. 1768. Black.	150.	400.	—
S2209 3 Pounds			
Dec. 1768. Black.	150.	400.	—
S2210 5 Pounds			
Dec. 1768. Black.	150.	400.	—

1771 Issue

	VG	VF	UNC
S2211 1 Shilling			
Dec. 1771. Black.	100.	175.	500.

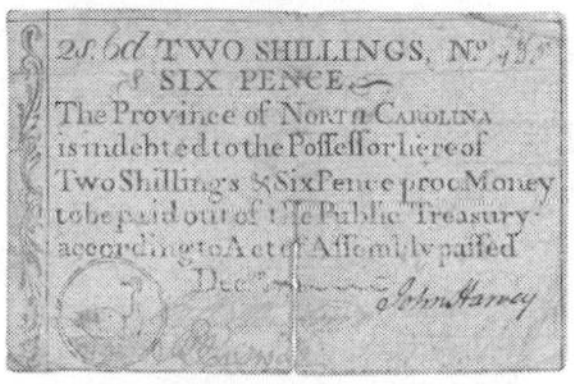

	VG	VF	UNC
S2212 2 Shillings 6 Pence			
Dec. 1771. Black.			
a. Duck.	100.	175.	500.
b. House.	100.	175.	500.

NOTE: Shading on house strengthened in late printing.

	VG	VF	UNC
S2213 5 Shillings			
Dec. 1771. Black. Quill pens.	100.	175.	500.
S2214 10 Shillings			
Dec. 1771. Black. Ship.	80.00	175.	500.

NOTE: Shading on ship strengthened in late printing.

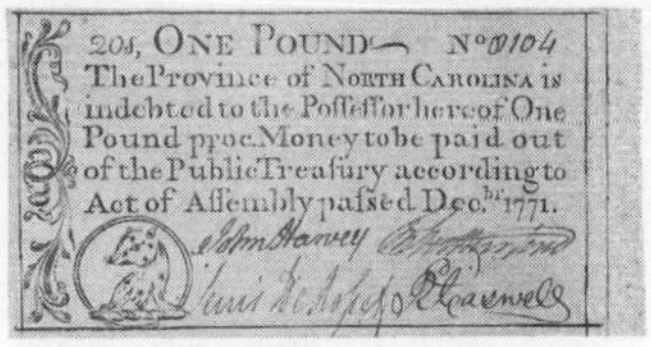

S2215 1 Pound	VG	VF	UNC
Dec. 1771. Black. Bear representing the constellation Ursa Minor.	80.00	150.	400.

NOTE: Shading on bear strengthened on late printing.

S2216 30 Shillings	VG	VF	UNC
Dec. 1771. Black. Hand holding dragger.	125.	175.	500.

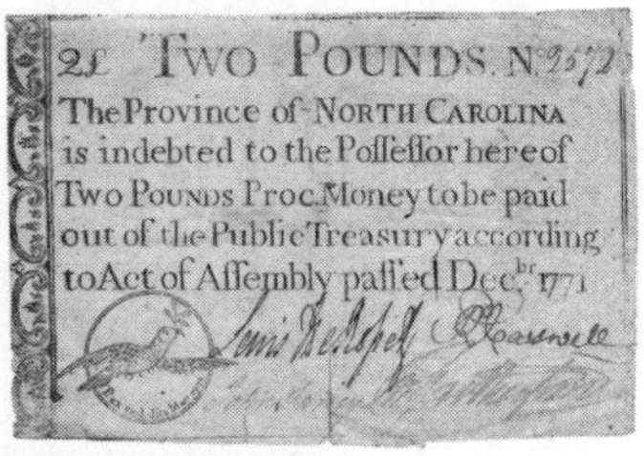

S2217 2 Pounds	VG	VF	UNC
Dec. 1771. Black. Dove with olive branch, *PAX REDDITA MAY 1771.*	100.	200.	600.
S2218 3 Pounds			
Dec. 1771. Black. *MAGNA CHARTA.*	100.	200.	600.

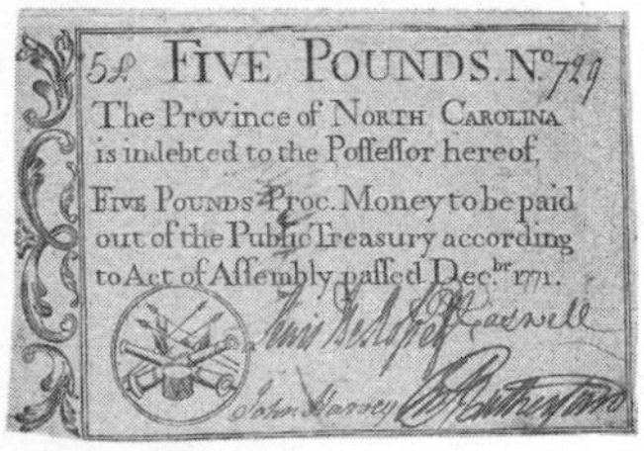

S2219 5 Pounds	VG	VF	UNC
Dec. 1771. Black. Drum, cannon, and flags.	125.	250.	1000.

1775 Issue

S2220 1/4 Dollar	VG	VF	UNC
21.8.1775. Black. Key.	1500.	—	—
S2221 1/2 Dollar			
21.8.1775. Black. Drum, cannon, and flags.	1500.	—	—
S2222 1 Dollar			
21.8.1775. Black. Hermes, *12 UNITED COLONIES.*	1500.	—	—
S2223 2 Dollars			
21.8.1775. Black.	1500.	—	—
S2224 3 Dollars			
21.8.1775. Black. Masonic emblems.	1500.	—	—
S2225 4 Dollars			
21.8.1775. Black. Masonic emblems, *AERA OF MASONRY 1775.*	1500.	—	—
S2226 5 Dollars			
21.8.1775. Black. State House.	1500.	—	—
S2227 8 Dollars			
21.8.1775. Black. Britannia stabbing herself, *INFELIX BRITANNIA.*	1500.	—	—
S2228 10 Dollars			
21.8.1775. Black. 12 arms supporting Liberty cap, *HANC TUEMUR HAC NITIMUR.*	1500.	—	—

1776 Issue

S2229 1/16 Dollar	VG	VF	UNC
2.4.1776. Black. Thin laid paper.			
a. Beetle.	650.	2000.	—
b. Butterfly.	650.	2000.	—
c. Cornucopia.	650.	2000.	—
d. Griffin.	650.	2000.	—
e. Nautilus.	650.	2000.	—
f. Vase of flowers.	650.	2000.	—
S2230 1/8 Dollar			
2.4.1776. Black. Thin laid paper.			
a. Dog.	500.	1500.	—
b. Heron.	500.	1500.	—
c. Lion.	500.	1500.	—
d. Monogram with mirrored *H.*	500.	1500.	—
e. Monogram *JM.*	500.	1500.	—
f. Sculpin.	500.	1500.	—
g. Snake biting sword in scabbard.	500.	1500.	—
h. Steer.	500.	1500.	—

S2231 1/4 Dollar	VG	VF	UNC
2.4.1776. Black. Thin laid paper.			
a. Bird flying.	450.	1250.	—
b. 3 fish.	450.	1250.	—
c. Hare.	450.	1250.	—
d. Monogram: *FB* in black script.	450.	1250.	—
e. Monogram: *NCSN* (State of North Carolina) in white script.	450.	1250.	—
f. Sea urchin.	450.	1250.	—
g. Shark.	450.	1250.	—
h. Tuna.	450.	1250.	—
S2232 1/2 Dollar			
2.4.1776. Black. Thin laid paper.			
a. North American bear.	450.	1250.	—
b. Cock fight.	450.	1250.	—
c. Crown and pitcher.	450.	1250.	—
d. Hunter, dog and target. *HIT OR MISS.* without day in date.	450.	1250.	—
e. Monogram with toothed border of triangles.	450.	1250.	—
f. Monogram with toothed border of radial lines.	450.	1250.	—
g. Owl.	450.	1250.	—
h. Ship.	400.	1000.	—
S2233 1 Dollar			
2.4.1776. Black. Thin laid paper.			
a. Duck.	400.	1000.	—
b. Raccoon.	400.	1000.	—
c. Justice.	400.	1000.	—
d. Scroll with denomination in black.	400.	1000.	—
e. Scroll with denomination in white.	400.	1000.	—
f. Shaking encoiling bird.	400.	1000.	—
S2234 2 Dollars			
2.4.1776. Black. Thin laid paper.			
a. Deer.	400.	1000.	—
b. Fox.	400.	1000.	—
S2235 2 1/2 Dollars			
2.4.1776. Black. Thin laid paper.			
a. Hand holding 13 arrows. Motto: *VIS UNITATIS.*	500.	1500.	—
b. Liberty cap over altar. Motto: *LIBERTAS & NATALE SOLUM.*	500.	1500.	—
S2236 3 Dollars			
2.4.1776. Black. Thin laid paper.			
a. Alligator at top, beaver at left.	400.	1000.	—
b. Beehive.	400.	1000.	—
S2237 4 Dollars			
2.4.1776. Black. Thin laid paper.			
a. Bee.	400.	1000.	—
b. Sheaf of wheat.	400.	1000.	—

S2238 5 Dollars	VG	VF	UNC
2.4.1776. Black. Thin laid paper.			
a. Thrush.	400.	1000.	—
b. Triton. Error *d2* instead of *2d.*	400.	1000.	—
S2239 6 Dollars			
2.4.1776. Black. Thin laid paper.			
a. Goat.	400.	1000.	—
b. Squirrel eating nut.	400.	1000.	—
S2240 7 1/2 Dollars			
2.4.1776. Black. U.S. flag with three stripes and Union Jack. Thin laid paper.	500.	1500.	—
S2241 8 Dollars			
2.4.1776. Black. Thin laid paper.			
a. Leopard.	400.	1000.	—
b. Rooster.	400.	1000.	—
S2242 10 Dollars			
2.4.1776. Black. Thin laid paper.			
a. Cupid.	400.	1000.	—
b. Peacock.	400.	1000.	—
S2243 12 1/2 Dollars			
2.4.1776. Black. Bald eagle carrying broken arrows, *DEUS NOBISCUM.* Thin laid paper.	500.	1500.	—
S2244 15 Dollars			
2.4.1776. Black. Boar. Thin laid paper.	400.	1000.	—
S2245 20 Dollars			
2.4.1776. Black. Rattlesnake, *DON'T TREAD ON ME.* Thin laid paper.	1000.	3000.	—

North Carolina

State

Act of August 8, 1778; 1778 Issue

S2246 1/8 Dollar	VG	VF	UNC
1778. Black. *UNION HEARTS THE STRENGTH OF INTEREST.* Printer: James Davis. Dark coarse mica flaked and thin unsized paper.	150.	400.	—
S2247 1/4 Dollar			
1778. Black. *INDEPENDENCE.* Printer: James Davis. Dark coarse mica flaked and thin unsized paper.	125.	300.	—
S2248 1/2 Dollar			
1778. Black. *BEHOLD! A NEW WORLD.* Printer: James Davis. Dark coarse mica flaked and thin unsized paper.	125.	300.	—
S2249 1 Dollar			
1778. Black. Printer: James Davis. Dark coarse mica flaked and thin unsized paper.			
a. With motto: *LIBERTY AND PEACE, THE REWARD OF VIRTUOUS RESISTANCE.*	125.	300.	—
b. With motto: *VIRTUOUS COUNCILS THE CEMENT OF STATES.*	125.	300.	—

		VG	VF	UNC
S2250	**2 Dollars** 1778. Black. *VIRTUOUS COUNCILS THE CEMENT OF STATES.* Printer: James Davis. Dark coarse mica flaked and thin unsized paper.	125.	300.	—
S2251	**4 Dollars** 1778. Black. *A LESSON TO ARBITRARY KINGS, AND WICKED MINISTERS.* Printer: James Davis. Dark coarse mica flaked and thin unsized paper.	125.	300.	—
S2252	**5 Dollars** 1778. Black. Printer: James Davis. Dark coarse mica flaked and thin unsized paper.			
	a. With motto: *BEHOLD! A NEW WORLD.*	125.	300.	—
	b. With motto: *INDEPENDENCE.*	125.	300.	—
	c. With motto: *A LESSON TO ARBITARY KINGS, AND WICKED MINISTERS.*	125.	300.	—
	d. With motto: *THE RISING STATES.*	125.	300.	—
S2253	**10 Dollars** 1778. Black. Printer: James Davis. Dark coarse mica flaked and thin unsized paper.			
	a. With motto: *INDEPENDENCE.*	125.	300.	—
	b. With motto: *PERSECUTION THE RUIN OF EMPIRES.*	125.	300.	—
	c. With motto: *UNION OF HEARTS THE STRENGTH OF INTERESTS.*	125.	300.	—
S2254	**20 Dollars** 1778. Black. *AMERICAN VIRTUE TRIUMPHANT.* Printer: James Davis. Dark coarse mica flaked and thin unsized paper.	125.	300.	—
S2255	**25 Dollars** 1778. Black. *SIC TRANSIT GLORIA MUNDI.* Printer: James Davis. Dark coarse mica flaked and thin unsized paper.	150.	400.	—
S2256	**40 Dollars** 1778. Black. *FREEDOM OF SPEECH AND THE LIBERTY OF THE PRESS.* Printer: James Davis. Dark coarse mica flaked and thin unsized paper.	350.	1000.	—
S2257	**50 Dollars** 1778. Black. *THE RISING STATES.* Printer: James Davis. Dark coarse mica flaked and thin unsized paper.	200.	500.	—
S2258	**100 Dollars** 1778. Black. *FREEDOM OR AN HONORABLE DEATH.* Printer: James Davis. Dark coarse mica flaked and thin unsized paper.	500.	2000.	—

1779 Issue

		VG	VF	UNC
S2259	**5 Dollars** 15.5.1779. Black. Printer: Hugh Walker. Light coarse paper.			
	a. Small *u* over *y* in *May.* Motto: *BE FREEDOM AND INDEPENDENCE STEADILY PURSUED.*	150.	650.	—
	b. Umlaut over *e* in *Silver. Motto: GOOD GOVERNMENT ALWAYS REVERE.*	150.	650.	—
S2260	**10 Dollars** 15.5.1779. Black. Printer: Hugh Walker. Light coarse paper.			
	a. Small *u* over *y* in *May.* Motto: *AMERICAN UNION FOR EVER.*	150.	650.	—
	b. Dash over *y* of *Assembly.* Motto: *VIRTUE EXCELS RICHES.*	150.	650.	—
S2261	**20 Dollars** 15.5.1779. Black. Umlaut over *e* of 2nd *the.* Motto: *PEACE ON HONOURABLE TERMS.* Printer: Hugh Walker. Light coarse paper.	150.	650.	—
S2262	**25 Dollars** 15.5.1779. Black. Printer: Hugh Walker. Light coarse paper.			
	a. *Q* instead of *O* in right border. Motto: *A FREE COMMERCE.*	150.	650.	—
	b. Top border lettering is mirrored image. Period after *No* is missing. Motto: *AMERICAN FORTITUDE DISPLAYED.*	150.	650.	—
S2263	**50 Dollars** 15.5.1779. Black. Circumflex over *e* in *Silver.* Motto: *A RIGHTEOUS CAUSE THE PROTECTION OF PROVIDENCE.* Printer: Hugh Walker. Light coarse paper.	200.	750.	—
S2264	**100 Dollars** 15.5.1779. Black. *Q* instead of *O* in right border. Motto: *A FREE COMMERCE.* Printer: Hugh Walker. Light coarse paper.	250.	850.	—
S2265	**250 Dollars** 15.5.1779. Black. Circumflex over *e* in *Silver,* dash over first *i* in *Smithfield.* Motto: *A RIGHTEOUS CAUSE THE PROTECTION OF PROVIDENCE.* Printer: Hugh Walker. Light coarse paper.	300.	1000.	—

Session Act of April 17, 1780; 1780 Issue

		VG	VF	UNC
S2266	**50 Dollars** 1780.			
	a. Motto: *INDEPENDENCE.*	—	8250.	—
	b. Motto: *LIBERTY AND PEACE, THE REWARD OF VIRTUOUS RESISTANCE.*	—	—	—
	c. Motto: *PERSECUTION THE RUIN OF EMPIRES.*	—	—	—
S2267	**25 Dollars** 10.5.1780. Black. Printer: James Davis.			
	a. Motto: *DULCE PRO PATRIA MORI.*	150.	300.	—
	b. *S* is omitted from *DOLLARS* in text. Motto: *HORA PACIS & LIBERTATIS APPROPINQUAT.*	150.	300.	—
	c. Motto: *JUSTITIA ADDIT FIDUCIAM.*	150.	300.	—
	d. Motto: *QUID NON VIRTUTE EFFICIENDUM.*	150.	300.	—
	e. Center bar of *F* in *FIVE* is missing. Motto: *TERRA LIBERA NOTAM PRAEII IN ME POSUIT.*	150.	300.	—
	f. Motto: *VIM VI REPELLAMUS.*	150.	300.	—
S2268	**50 Dollars** 10.5.1780. Black. Motto: *FUNDAMENTUM MIHI AERE PERENNIUS.* Printer: James Davis.	150.	350.	—
S2269	**100 Dollars** 10.5.1780. Black. Motto: *FORTIS CADERE CEDERE NON POTEST.* Printer: James Davis.	175.	450.	—
S2270	**200 Dollars** 10.5.1780. Black. Motto: *UT QUOCUNQUE PARATUS.* Printer: James Davis.	200.	450.	—
S2271	**250 Dollars** 10.5.1780. Black. Printer: James Davis.			
	a. *T* in *This* in ornamented box. Motto: *QUAERENDA PECUNIA PRIMUM EST.*	185.	450.	—
	b. *T* in *This* without box. Motto as a.	185.	450.	—
S2272	**300 Dollars** 10.5.1780. Black. Motto: *AUT UMQUAM TENTES AUT PERFICE.* Printer: James Davis.	200.	450.	—
S2273	**400 Dollars** 10.5.1780. Black. Motto: *MUTARE VEL TIMERE SPERNO.* Printer: James Davis.	200.	450.	—
S2274	**500 Dollars** 10.5.1780. Black. Printer: James Davis.			
	a. *T* in *This* in ornamented box. Motto: *DIVITIAE REIPUBLICAE DANT MIHI PRETIUM.*	200.	450.	—
	b. *T* in *This* without box. Motto as a.	200.	450.	—
S2275	**600 Dollars** 10.5.1780. Black. Motto: *CRESIT SUB PONDERE VIRTUS.* Printer: James Davis.	225.	600.	—

#S2276 Deleted.

1783 Issue

		VG	VF	UNC
S2277	**6 Pence** 17.5.1783. Black. Bird. Printer: Thomas Davis, Halifax.	400.	—	—
S2278	**1 Shilling** 17.5.1783. Black. Printer: Thomas Davis, Halifax.	400.	—	—
S2279	**2 Shillings** 17.5.1783. Black. Corinthian column, motto: *IN RECTO DECUS.* Printer: Thomas Davis, Halifax.	400.	—	—
S2280	**5 Shillings** 17.5.1783. Black. Printer: Thomas Davis, Halifax.	400.	—	—

		Good	Fine	XF
S2281	**10 Shillings** 17.5.1783. Black. Ships, motto: *COMMERCIO.* Printer: Thomas Davis, Halifax.	—	—	5250.
S2282	**20 Shillings** 17.5.1783. Black. Printer: Thomas Davis, Halifax.			
	a. Justice, motto: *DO AS YOU WOULD BE DONE BY.*	—	—	—
	b. Crown and book.	—	—	—
S2283	**40 Shillings** 17.5.1783. Black. Angel Gabriel and church. Printer: Thomas Davis, Halifax.	—	—	—

1785 Issue

		Good	Fine	XF
S2284	**6 Pence** 29.12.1785. Black. 13 stars. Watermark: *NORTH CAROLINA.* Printer: Thomas Davis. Thick paper.	—	3250.	—
S2285	**1 Shilling** 29.12.1785. Black. Wreath. Watermark: *NORTH CAROLINA.* Printer: Thomas Davis. Thick paper.	—	—	7500.
S2286	**2 Shillings** 29.12.1785. Black. Plough. Watermark: *NORTH CAROLINA.* Printer: Thomas Davis. Thick paper.	2000.	—	—
S2287	**2 Shillings 6 Pence** 29.12.1785. Black. Phoenix, motto: *MELIOR RESURGO.* Watermark: *NORTH CAROLINA.* Printer: Thomas Davis. Thick paper.	—	—	—
S2288	**5 Shillings** 29.12.1785. Black. Ship near fort. Watermark: *NORTH CAROLINA.* Printer: Thomas Davis. Thick paper.	—	—	—
S2289	**10 Shillings** 29.12.1785. Black. Crown and book. Watermark: *NORTH CAROLINA.* Printer: Thomas Davis. Thick paper.	1500.	—	—
S2290	**20 Shillings** 29.12.1785. Black. Angel Gabriel and church. Watermark: *NORTH CAROLINA.* Printer: Thomas Davis. Thick paper.	—	2750.	—
S2291	**40 Shillings** 29.12.1785. Black. Justice. Watermark: *NORTH CAROLINA.* Printer: Thomas Davis. Thick paper.	—	3250.	—

NOTE: Test specimens printed on blue paper.

Act of 1814; 1815 Issue

		Good	Fine	XF
S2292	**5 Cents** 1815. Printed date 1815, with various handwritten day, month and 1816/1815.	—	—	—
S2293	**10 Cents** 1815. Printed date 1815, with various handwritten day, month and 1816/1815.	—	—	—
S2294	**20 Cents** 4.1.1816/15. Printed date 1815, with various handwritten day, month and 1816/1815.	—	—	—
S2295	**25 Cents** 4.10.1815. Allegorical female with spear at top center. Printed date 1815, with various handwritten day, month and 1816/1815.	—	—	—
S2296	**30 Cents** 1815. Printed date 1815, with various handwritten day, month and 1816/1815.	—	—	—
S2297	**40 Cents** 1815. Printed date 1815, with various handwritten day, month and 1816/1815.	—	—	—
S2298	**50 Cents** 1815. Printed date 1815, with various handwritten day, month and 1816/1815.	—	—	—

Act of 1816; 1817 Issue

		Good	Fine	XF
S2299	**5 Cents** 1817. Printed date 1817, with various handwritten day and month.	—	—	—
S2300	**6 1/4 Cents** 1817. Printed date 1817, with various handwritten day and month.	—	—	—
S2301	**10 Cents** 1817. Printed date 1817, with various handwritten day and month.	—	—	—
S2302	**12 1/2 Cents** 1817. Printed date 1817, with various handwritten day and month.	—	—	—
S2303	**20 Cents** 1817. Printed date 1817, with various handwritten day and month.	—	—	—
S2304	**25 Cents** 1817. Printed date 1817, with various handwritten day and month.	—	—	—
S2305	**30 Cents** 1817. Printed date 1817, with various handwritten day and month.	—	—	—
S2306	**40 Cents** 1817. Printed date 1817, with various handwritten day and month.	—	—	—

	Good	Fine	XF
S2307 50 Cents			
1817.	—	—	—
S2308 75 Cents			
1817.	—	—	—

Act of 1823; 1824 Issue

	Good	Fine	XF
S2309 5 Cents			
1824.	—	—	—
S2310 10 Cents			
1824.	—	—	—
S2311 20 Cents			
1824.	—	—	—
S2312 25 Cents			
1824.	—	—	—
S2313 30 Cents			
1824. Two cherubs at top center.	—	—	—
S2314 40 Cents			
1824. Sir W. Raleigh at top center.	—	—	—
S2315 50 Cents			
1824.	—	—	—
S2316 75 Cents			
1824.	—	—	—

North Carolina

Civil War

Act of 28.6.1861; 1861 Issue

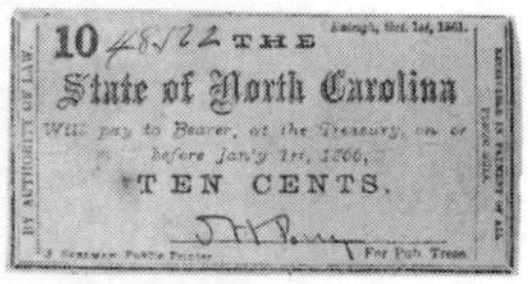

	VG	VF	UNC
S2321 5 Cents			
1.10.1861. Black.			
a. Without watermark.	10.00	30.00	70.00
b. Printed on backs of North Carolina bonds.	10.00	30.00	70.00
c. Watermark: *FIVE.*	10.00	30.00	70.00
d. Watermark: *TEN.*	10.00	30.00	70.00
e. Watermark: *T.C. & Co.*	10.00	30.00	50.00

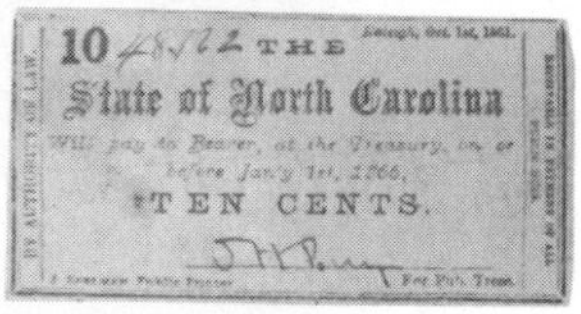

	VG	VF	UNC
S2322 10 Cents			
1.10.1861.			
a. Without watermark.	15.00	35.00	70.00
b. Watermark: *FIVE.*	15.00	35.00	70.00
c. Watermark: *TEN.*	15.00	35.00	70.00
d. Watermark: *T.C. & Co.* Rare.	15.00	35.00	70.00
S2323 20 Cents			
1.10.1861. Black.			
a. Watermark: *FIVE.*	40.00	90.00	160.
b. Watermark: *TEN.*	40.00	90.00	160.
c. Watermark: *T.C. & Co.* Rare.	40.00	90.00	160.
d. Without watermark.	40.00	90.00	160.
e. Printed on backs of North Carolina bonds.	40.00	90.00	160.
S2324 25 Cents			
1.10.1861. Black.			
a. Without watermark.	20.00	40.00	70.00
b. Watermark: *FIVE.*	20.00	40.00	70.00
c. Watermark: *TEN.*	20.00	40.00	70.00
d. Watermark: *T.C. & Co.* Rare.	20.00	40.00	70.00

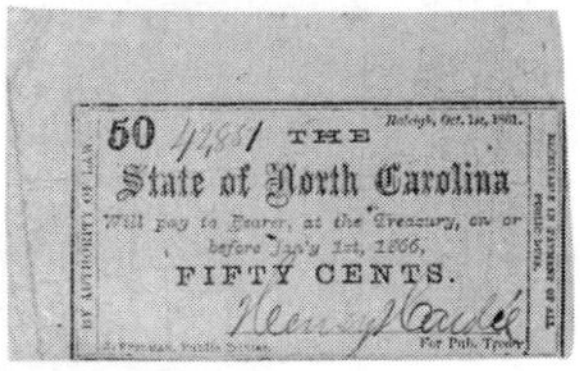

	VG	VF	UNC
S2325 50 Cents			
1.10.1861. Black.			
a. Without watermark	20.00	40.00	70.00
b. Watermark: *FIVE.*	20.00	40.00	70.00
c. Watermark: *TEN.*	20.00	40.00	70.00
d. Watermark: *T.C. & Co.* Rare.	20.00	40.00	70.00
S2326 2 Dollars			
1.10.1861; 2.10.1861; 4.10.1861; 6.10.1861. Black. Printer: F. W. Bornemann.			
a. Without watermark.	20.00	40.00	70.00
b. Red protector: *TWO DOLLARS* on back. 1.10.1861.	20.00	40.00	70.00
c. Printed on backs of North Carolina bank notes.	20.00	40.00	70.00
d. Printed on backs of North Carolina 1000 Dollar bonds.	20.00	40.00	70.00
e. Watermark: *FIVE.* 4.10.1861.	20.00	40.00	70.00

	VG	VF	UNC
S2327 1 Dollar			
1-5.10.1861. Black. Standing Minerva at left, dog lying by strongbox at lower center. Printer: N. C. Inst. Deaf and Dumb Print.			
a. Red protector: *ONE DOLLAR* on back.	40.00	100.	200.
b. Printed on backs of North Carolina bank notes.	40.00	100.	200.
c. Printed on backs of North Carolina bonds. 5.10.1861.	40.00	100.	200.
S2328 2 Dollars			
3.10.1861. Black. Standing Minerva at left, dog lying by strongbox at lower center. Back: Red protector: *TWO DOLLARS.* Printer: N. C. Inst. Deaf and Dumb Print. Printed on backs of North Carolina bank notes. 12-20 known.	1000.	1500.	—

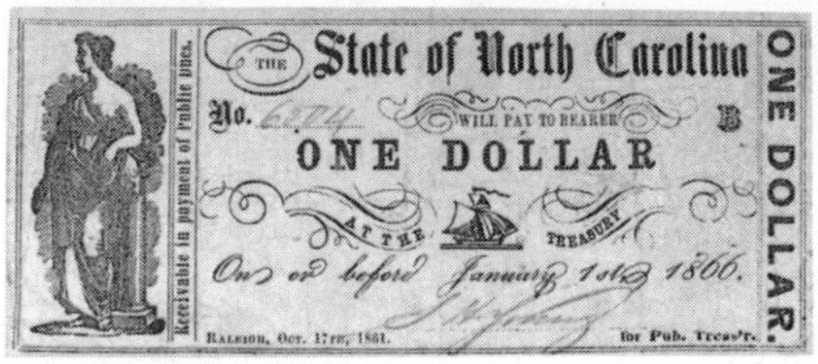

	VG	VF	UNC
S2329 1 Dollar			
10-21.10.1861. Black. Standing Minerva at left, ship at center. Series A; B. Without imprint. Back: Light brownish pink.			
a. Without watermark.	10.00	35.00	70.00
b. Watermark: *FIVE.*	10.00	35.00	70.00
c. Watermark: *TEN.*	10.00	35.00	70.00
d. Watermark: *T.C. & Co.*	10.00	35.00	70.00
S2330 100 Dollars			
1.12.1861. Black. Agricultural tools at top center, seated Commerce at lower right. Various handwritten dates. Printer: J. Manouvrier.	600.	1500.	3000.

NOTE: Interest bearing at six percent per annum.

1862 Issues

	VG	VF	UNC
S2331 20 Dollars			
1862. Black. Ceres Volant at top center. Various handwritten dates. Printer: J. Manouvrier.			
a. With text: *FUNDABLE IN SIX PERCENT COUPON BONDS* in upper and lower borders.	65.00	135.	240.
b. Printed on backs of bills of exchange.	65.00	135.	240.
c. Printed on backs of North Carolina bonds.	65.00	135.	240.
S2332 20 Dollars			
1862. Black. Ceres Volant at top center. Various handwritten dates. Like #S2331. Printer: J. Manouvrier.			
a. Red overprint: *FUNDABLE / ONLY / IN SIX PERCENT BONDS* on #S2331a.	65.00	135.	240.
b. Overprint on #S2331b.	65.00	135.	240.
c. Overprint on #S2331c.	65.00	135.	240.

	VG	VF	UNC
S2333 50 Dollars			
1862. Black. Standing Liberty next to seated Ceres at top center. Various handwritten dates. Overprint: Red *FIFTY DOLLARS* on back. Printer: J. Manouvrier.	600.	1500.	3000.
S2334 50 Dollars			
1862. Black. Standing Liberty next to seated Ceres at top center. Various handwritten dates. Overprint: Red *FUNDABLE/ONLY/IN SIX PERCENT BONDS* on #S2333. Printer: J. Manouvrier.	1000.	2000.	—
S2335 100 Dollars			
1862. Black. Agricultural tools at top center, seated Commerce at lower right. Various handwritten dates. Similar to #S2330 but without *Bearing Interest at Six percent . . .* at right. Printer: J. Manouvrier. Rare.	—	—	—
S2336 20 Dollars			
1862. Black. Ceres Volant at top center. Various handwritten dates. Similar to #S2331. Printer: J. Manouvrier.			
a. With text: *FUNDABLE IN EIGHT PERCENT COUPON BONDS* in top border and *RECEIVABLE IN PAYMENT OF ALL PUBLIC DEBTS* in lower border.	35.00	65.00	150.
b. Printed on backs of bills of exchange.	30.00	60.00	150.
S2337 20 Dollars			
1862. Black. Ceres Volant at top center. Various handwritten dates. Similar to #S2331. Printer: J. Manouvrier.			
a. Red overprint: *FUNDABLE / ONLY / IN SIX PERCENT BONDS* on #S2336a.	30.00	60.00	150.
b. Overprint on #S2336b.	30.00	60.00	150.

S2338 20 Dollars — VG | VF | UNC

1862. Black. Ceres Volant at top center. Various handwritten dates. Overprint: Red vertical *FUNDABLE* in 2 lines on #S2336a. Printer: J. Manouvrier. — 40.00 | 65.00 | 165.

S2338A 20 Dollars

1862. Black. Ceres Volant at top center. Various handwritten dates. Similar to #S2331. With text: *FUNDABLE . . .* in upper border but blocked out in lower border. Printed on backs of bills of exchange. — 30.00 | 50.00 | 100.

S2339 10 Dollars

1862. Black. Steam passenger train at center. Interest bearing at the rate of *SIX PERCENT* per annum in oval at right. Various handwritten dates. Printer: J. Manouvrier. Printed on backs of North Carolina bonds. — 30.00 | 65.00 | 125.

S2340 5 Dollars

1862. Black. Seated Ceres with produce, sailing ship in background, steam train vertically at right. Various handwritten dates. Printer: J. Manouvrier.
- a. Issued note. — 75.00 | 175. | 400.
- b. Printed on backs of bills of exchange. — 75.00 | 175. | 400.

S2341 5 Dollars

1862. Black. Seated Ceres with produce, sailing ship in background, steam train vertically at right. Various handwritten dates. Printer: J. Manouvrier.
- a. Red overprint: *FUNDABLE / ONLY / IN SIX PERCENT BONDS* on #S2340a. — 75.00 | 175. | 400.
- b. Red overprint on #S2340b. — 75.00 | 175. | 400.

S2342 10 Dollars — VG | VF | UNC

1862. Black. Steam passenger train at center. Various handwritten dates. Similar to #S2339 but with *FUNDABLE IN SIX PERCENT COUPON BONDS* in oval at right. Printer: J. Manouvrier.
- a. Issued note. — 75.00 | 150. | 320.
- b. Printed on backs of bills of exchange. — 75.00 | 150. | 320.
- c. Printed on backs of North Carolina bonds. — 75.00 | 150. | 320.

S2343 10 Dollars

1862. Black. Steam passenger train at center. Various handwritten dates. With *FUNDABLE IN SIX PERCENT COUPON BONDS* in oval at right. Overprint: Oval *FUNDABLE. . .* at right on #S2342. Printer: J. Manouvrier. — 45.00 | 75.00 | 140.

S2344 5 Dollars

1862. Black. Standing Liberty with seated Ceres at top center, steam passenger train vertical at right. Various handwritten dates. Printer: J. Manouvrier. — 35.00 | 65.00 | 125.

S2345 5 Dollars

1862. Black. Standing Liberty with seated Ceres at top center, steam passenger train vertical at right. Various handwritten dates. Overprint: Red *FUNDABLE / ONLY / IN SIX PERCENT BONDS* on #S2344. Printer: J. Manouvrier. — 40.00 | 65.00 | 150.

S2346 10 Dollars

1862. Black. Steam passenger train at center. Various handwritten dates. Similar to #S2342 but with *FUNDABLE IN EIGHT PERCENT BONDS* at right. Printer: J. Manouvrier.
- a. Without watermark. — 40.00 | 55.00 | 125.
- b. Watermark: *TEN.* — 45.00 | 70.00 | 135.

S2347 10 Dollars

1862. Black. Steam passenger train at center. Various handwritten dates. With *FUNDABLE IN EIGHT PERCENT BONDS* at right. Overprint: Red *FUNDABLE / ONLY / IN SIX PERCENT BONDS* on #S2346. Printer: J. Manouvrier. — 40.00 | 65.00 | 135.

S2348 20 Dollars

1862. Black. Grain at left, steam passenger train at center. *FUNDABLE IN EIGHT PERCENT COUPON BONDS* in top border. Various handwritten dates. Printer: J. Manouvrier. — — | — | —

S2349 20 Dollars

1862. Black. Grain at left, steam passenger train at center. *FUNDABLE IN EIGHT PERCENT COUPON BONDS* in top border. Various handwritten dates. Overprint: Red *FUNDABLE/ONLY/IN SIX PERCENT BONDS* on #S2348. Printer: J. Manouvrier. — 50.00 | 65.00 | 150.

NOTE: #S2348 and S2349 with full upper and lower borders command a considerable premium.

S2350 3 Dollars

1.5.1862. Black. Without vignette or imprint. Rare. — — | — | —

S2351 3 Dollars

8.6.1862. Black. Without vignette or imprint. Rare. — — | — | —

S2352 5 Dollars — Good | Fine | XF

1.7.1862. Black. Standing Ceres at left, steamship at upper center. — — | — | —

S2353 5 Dollars — VG | VF | UNC

1862. Black. Standing Ceres at left, steamship at upper center. Overprint: Red *FUNDABLE / ONLY / IN SIX PERCENT BONDS* on #S2352. — 25.00 | 45.00 | 80.00

S2354 4 Dollars — Good | Fine | XF

1.8.1862. Black. Without vignette. Rare. — — | — | —

NOTE: #S2352-S2354 full upper and lower borders command a considerable premium.

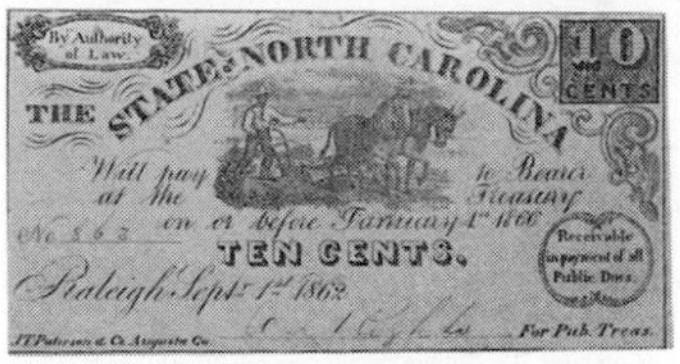

S2355 10 Cents — VG | VF | UNC

1.9.1862. Black. Black plowing at center. — 9.00 | 16.00 | 25.00

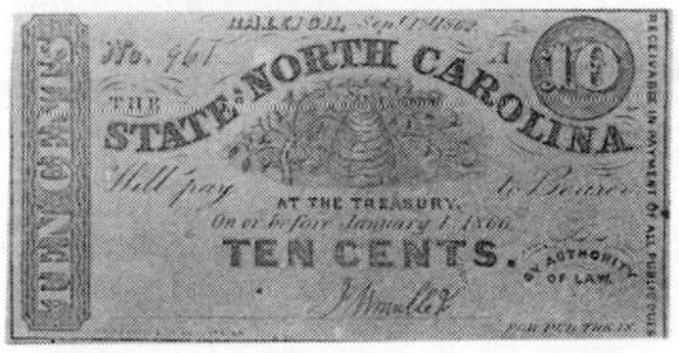

S2356 10 Cents — VG | VF | UNC

1.9.1862. Black. Hornet's nest at center. — 9.00 | 12.00 | 20.00

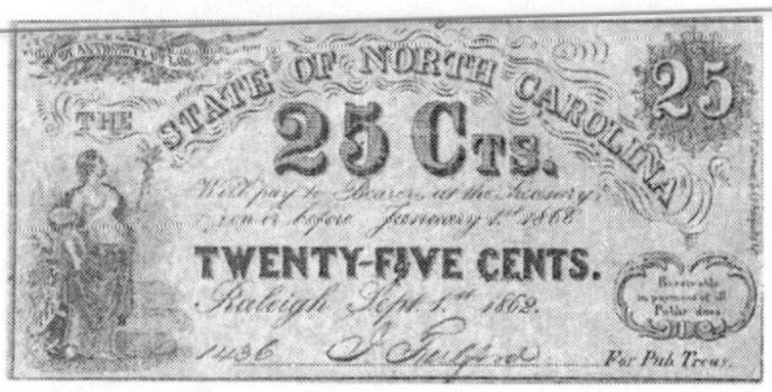

S2357 25 Cents — VG | VF | UNC

1.9.1862. Black. Ceres at lower left.
- a. Issued note. — 8.00 | 10.00 | 20.00
- b. Printed on backs of North Carolina bonds. — 12.00 | 20.00 | 30.00
- c. Printed on backs of North Carolina banknotes. — 12.00 | 20.00 | 30.00

S2358 50 Cents

1.9.1862. Black. Sailing ship at left center.
- a. Issued note. — 8.00 | 10.00 | 20.00
- b. Printed on backs of North Carolina bonds. — 9.00 | 15.00 | 25.00

S2359 1 Dollar — VG | VF | UNC

1.9.1862. Black.
- a. Without watermark. — 7.00 | 10.00 | 20.00
- b. Watermark: *FIVE.* — 25.00 | 50.00 | 100.

1863 Issue

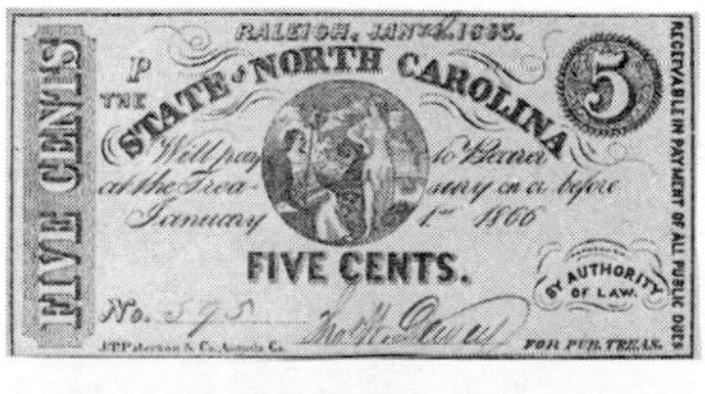

S2360 5 Cents — VG | VF | UNC

1.1.1863. Black. Liberty and Peace at center. — 10.00 | 20.00 | 40.00

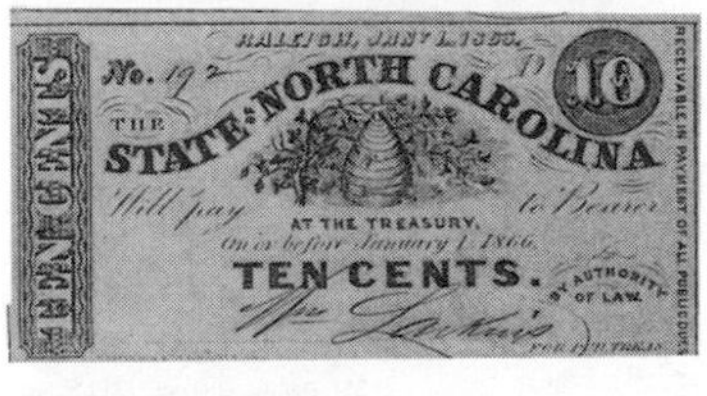

S2361 10 Cents — VG | VF | UNC

1.1.1863. Black. Hornet's nest at center. — 10.00 | 20.00 | 40.00

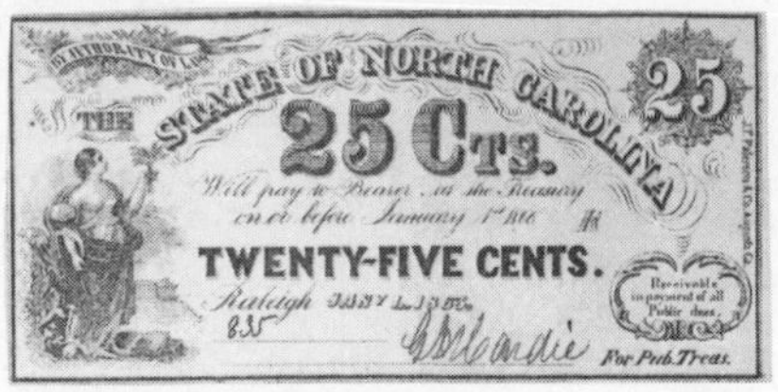

S2362 25 Cents	VG	VF	UNC
1.1.1863. Black. Ceres at left.			
a. Without watermark.	15.00	30.00	50.00
b. Watermark: *WHATMAN.*	15.00	30.00	50.00
c. Printed on the backs of Georgia notes.	15.00	30.00	50.00
d. Printed on the backs of North Carolina notes.	15.00	30.00	50.00

S2363 50 Cents	VG	VF	UNC
1.1.1863. Black. Sailing ship at center.	20.00	45.00	80.00

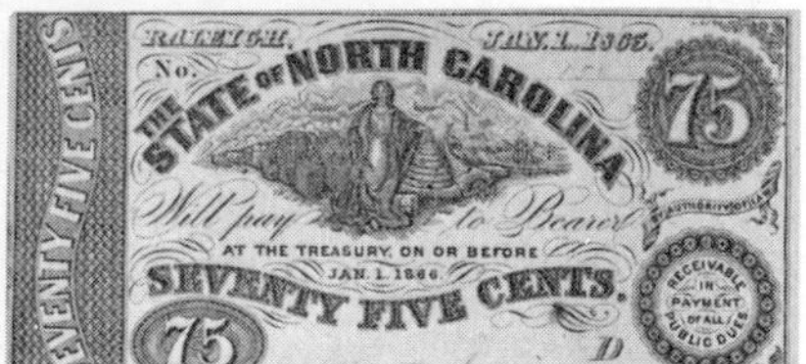

S2364 75 Cents	VG	VF	UNC
1.1.1863. Black. Standing Industry by beehive at center.	20.00	45.00	80.00

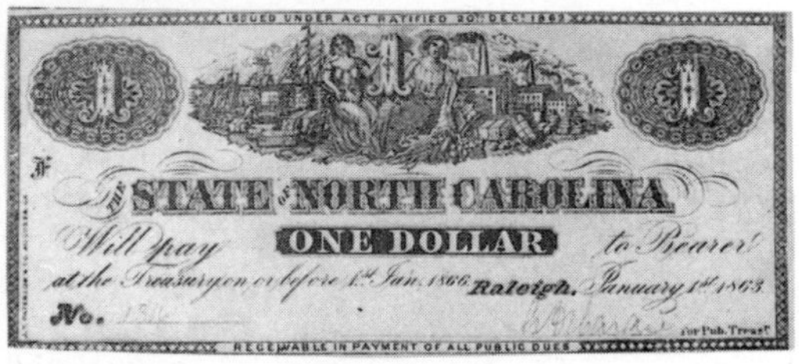

S2365 1 Dollar	VG	VF	UNC
1.1.1863. Black. Commerce and Industry holding figure *1*.	15.00	25.00	40.00

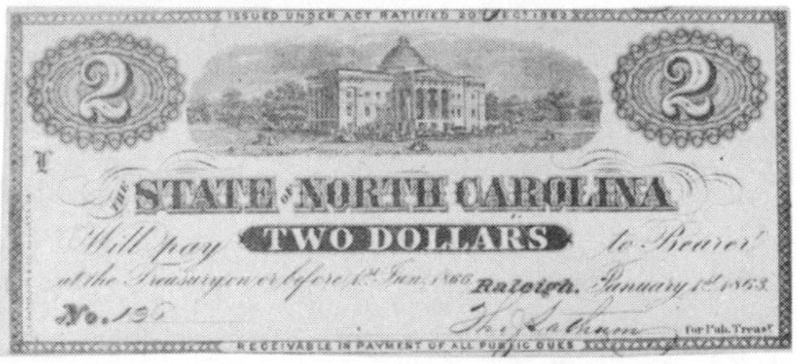

S2366 2 Dollars	VG	VF	UNC
1.1.1863. Black. State Capitol in Raleigh at center.	20.00	35.00	55.00

S2367 3 Dollars	VG	VF	UNC
1.1.1863. Black. Standing Liberty by seated Ceres at top center.			
a. Without watermark.	30.00	50.00	80.00
b. Watermark: *FIVE.*	30.00	50.00	80.00
c. Watermark: *TEN.*	30.00	50.00	80.00
d. Watermark: *T.C. & Co.*	30.00	50.00	80.00
S2368 5 Dollars			
1.1.1863. Black. Ceres at left, sailing steamship at center.			
a. Issued note.	30.00	50.00	80.00
b. With red handwritten text: *Fundable in six ...*	35.00	70.00	125.

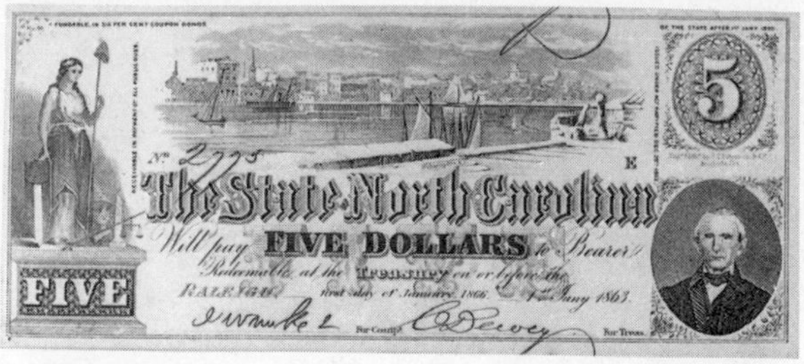

S2369 5 Dollars	VG	VF	UNC
1.1.1863. Black. N.C. standing Liberty at left, harbor and City of Wilmington at upper center, portrait D. W. Courts at lower right.	40.00	100.	165.
S2370 10 Dollars			
1.1.1863. Black on red underprint. State Capitol in Raleigh at center, portrait D. W. Courts at right.	40.00	100.	165.
S2371 20 Dollars			
1.1.1863. Black. Grain at left, steam passenger train at center. Like #S2348.	25.00	50.00	100.

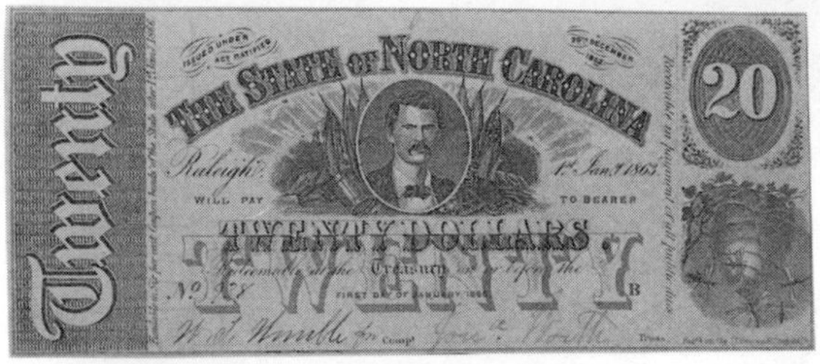

S2372 20 Dollars	VG	VF	UNC
1.1.1863. Black and red. Portrait Gov. Z. Vance at center.			
a. Plain paper.	75.00	150.	275.
b. Watermark: *J. Whatman. 1861* horizontal lines, arms or parts thereof.	75.00	150.	275.

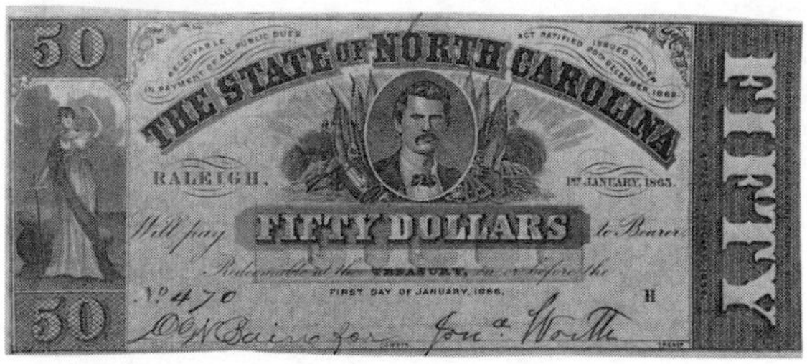

S2373 50 Dollars	VG	VF	UNC
1.1.1863. Black and red. Portrait Gov. Z. Vance at center.			
a. Plain paper. Rare.	200.	400.	700.
b. Watermark. Like #S2372b.	200.	400.	700.

1864 Issue

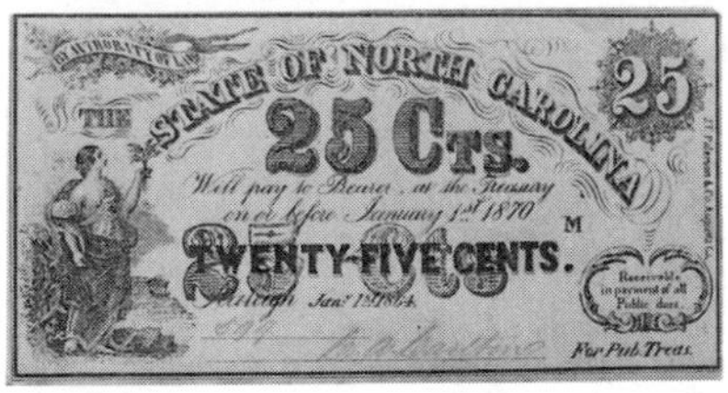

S2374 25 Cents	VG	VF	UNC
1.1.1864. Black. Standing Ceres at lower left. Blue protector: *25 Cts./Twenty-Five Cents.*	30.00	60.00	100.

S2375 50 Cents	VG	VF	UNC
1.1.1864. Black. Sailing ship at center. Red protector: *50 Cts.*	20.00	45.00	80.00

Pennsylvania

Colonial

1723 First Issue

No.	Note	Good	Fine	XF
S2384	**1 Shilling** 17.1.1723. Black. Arms of the Penn family. Uniface.	—	—	—
S2385	**1 Shilling 6 Pence** 17.1.1723. Black. Arms of the Penn family. Uniface.	—	—	—
S2386	**2 Shillings** 17.1.1723. Black. Arms of the Penn family. Uniface.	—	—	—
S2387	**2 Shillings 6 Pence** 17.1.1723. Black. Arms of the Penn family. Uniface.	—	—	—
S2388	**5 Shillings** 17.1.1723. Black. Arms of the Penn family. Uniface.	—	—	—
S2389	**10 Shillings** 17.1.1723. Black. Arms of the Penn family. Uniface.	—	—	—
S2390	**15 Shillings** 17.1.1723. Black. Arms of the Penn family. Uniface.	—	—	—
		VG	**VF**	**UNC**
S2391	**20 Shillings** 17.1.1723. Black. Arms of the Penn family. Uniface.	—	17,250.	—

1723 Second Issue

No.	Note	Good	Fine	XF
S2392	**1 Shilling** 2.4.1723. Black. Arms of the Penn family. Uniface.	—	—	—
S2393	**2 Shillings** 2.4.1723. Black. Arms of the Penn family. Uniface.	—	—	—
S2394	**2 Shillings 6 Pence** 2.4.1723. Black. Arms of the Penn family. Uniface.	—	—	—
S2395	**5 Shillings** 2.4.1723. Black. Arms of the Penn family. Uniface.	—	—	—
S2396	**10 Shillings** 2.4.1723. Black. Arms of the Penn family. Uniface.	—	—	—
S2397	**15 Shillings** 2.4.1723. Black. Arms of the Penn family. Uniface.	—	—	—
S2398	**20 Shillings** 2.4.1723. Black. Arms of the Penn family. Uniface.	—	—	—

1726 Replacement Issue

No.	Note	Good	Fine	XF
S2399	**1 Shilling** 25.3.1726. Black.	—	—	—
S2400	**1 Shilling 6 Pence** 25.3.1726. Black.	—	—	—
S2401	**2 Shillings** 25.3.1726. Black.	—	—	—
S2402	**2 Shillings 6 Pence** 25.3.1726. Black.	—	—	—
S2403	**5 Shillings** 25.3.1726. Black.	—	—	—
S2404	**10 Shillings** 25.3.1726. Black.	—	—	—

1729 Issue

No.	Note	Good	Fine	XF
S2405	**1 Shilling** 15.9.1729. Black. Arms of the Penn family. Uniface. Printer: Andrew Bradford.	—	—	—
S2406	**1 Shilling 6 Pence** 15.9.1729. Black. Arms of the Penn family. Uniface. Printer: Andrew Bradford.	—	—	—
S2407	**2 Shillings** 15.9.1729. Black. Arms of the Penn family. Uniface. Printer: Andrew Bradford.	—	7250.	—
S2408	**2 Shillings 6 Pence** 15.9.1729. Black. Arms of the Penn family. Uniface. Printer: Andrew Bradford.	—	—	—
S2409	**5 Shillings** 15.9.1729. Black. Arms of the Penn family. Uniface. Printer: Andrew Bradford.	—	—	—
S2410	**10 Shillings** 15.9.1729. Black. Arms of the Penn family. Uniface. Printer: Andrew Bradford.	—	—	—
S2411	**15 Shillings** 15.9.1729. Black. Arms of the Penn family. Uniface. Printer: Andrew Bradford.	—	—	—
S2412	**20 Shillings** 15.9.1729. Black. Arms of the Penn family. Uniface. Printer: Andrew Bradford.	—	—	—

1731 Issue

No.	Note	Good	Fine	XF
S2413	**1 Shilling** 10.4.1731. Black. Printer: B. Franklin.	—	—	—
S2414	**1 Shilling 6 Pence** 10.4.1731. Black. Printer: B. Franklin.	—	—	—
S2415	**2 Shillings** 10.4.1731. Black. Printer: B. Franklin.	—	—	—
S2416	**2 Shillings 6 Pence** 10.4.1731. Black. Printer: B. Franklin.	—	—	—
S2417	**5 Shillings** 10.4.1731. Black. Printer: B. Franklin.	—	—	—
S2418	**10 Shillings** 10.4.1731. Black. Printer: B. Franklin.	—	—	—
S2419	**15 Shillings** 10.4.1731. Black. Printer: B. Franklin.	—	—	—
S2420	**20 Shillings** 10.4.1731. Black. Printer: B. Franklin.	—	—	—

1739 Issue

No.	Note	Good	Fine	XF
S2421	**1 Shilling** 10.8.1739. Black. Arms of the Penn family. Uniface. Printer: B. Franklin.	—	—	—
S2422	**18 Pence** 10.8.1739. Black. Arms of the Penn family. Uniface. Printer: B. Franklin.	—	—	—
S2423	**2 Shillings** 10.8.1739. Black. Arms of the Penn family. Uniface. Printer: B. Franklin.	—	—	—
S2424	**2 Shillings 6 Pence** 10.8.1739. Black. Arms of the Penn family. *Pensilvania.* Uniface. Printer: B. Franklin.	—	—	—
S2425	**5 Shillings** 10.8.1739. Black. Arms of the Penn family. *Pensilvania.* Plate letter A; B. Back: Nature print of leaves. Printer: B. Franklin.	—	—	—
S2426	**10 Shillings** 10.8.1739. Black. Arms of the Penn family. *Pensilvania.* Plate letter A; B; C; D. Back: Nature print of leaves. Printer: B. Franklin.	—	—	—
S2427	**15 Shillings** 10.8.1739. Black. Arms of the Penn family. *Pensilvania.* Plate letter A; B. Back: Nature print of leaves. Printer: B. Franklin.	—	—	—
		VG	**VF**	**UNC**
S2428	**20 Shillings** 10.8.1739. Black. Arms of the Penn family. *Pensilvania.* Plate letter A; B. Back: Nature print of leaves. Printer: B. Franklin.	—	5750.	—

NOTE: The 4 highest denominations have *Pensilvania* deliberately misspelled to act as a secret check to detect alterations from the lower denominations.

1744 Issue

No.	Note	Good	Fine	XF
S2429	**1 Shilling** 1.8.1744. Black. Arms of the Penn family. Uniface. Printer: B. Franklin.	—	—	—
S2430	**18 Pence** 1.8.1744. Black. Arms of the Penn family. Uniface. Printer: B. Franklin.	—	—	—
S2431	**2 Shillings** 1.8.1744. Black. Arms of the Penn family. Uniface. Printer: B. Franklin.	—	—	—
S2432	**2 Shillings 6 Pence** 1.8.1744. Black. Arms of the Penn family. Uniface. Printer: B. Franklin.	—	—	—
S2433	**5 Shillings** 1.8.1744. Black. Arms of the Penn family. Uniface. Printer: B. Franklin.	—	—	—

1746 Issue

		VG	VF	UNC
S2434	**4 Pence** 1.8.1746. Black. Printer: B. Franklin.	7250.	—	—
S2435	**6 Pence** 1.8.1746. Black. Printer: B. Franklin.	—	—	—
S2436	**9 Pence** 1.8.1746. Black. Printer: B. Franklin.	—	—	—
S2437	**20 Shillings** 1.8.1746. Black. Arms of the Penn family. Plate letter A; B; C; D. Back: Nature print of leaves. Printer: B. Franklin.	—	—	—

1749 Issue

No.	Note	Good	Fine	XF
S2438	**3 Pence** 16.5.1749. Black. Arms of the Penn family. Uniface. Printer: B. Franklin and D. Hall.	—	—	—
S2439	**4 Pence** 16.5.1749. Black. Arms of the Penn family. Uniface. Printer: B. Franklin and D. Hall.	—	—	—
S2440	**6 Pence** 16.5.1749. Black. Arms of the Penn family. Uniface. Printer: B. Franklin and D. Hall.	—	5000.	—
S2441	**9 Pence** 16.5.1749. Black. Arms of the Penn family. Uniface. Printer: B. Franklin and D. Hall.	—	—	—

1755 Issue

No.	Note	Good	Fine	XF
S2442	**3 Pence** 1.10.1755. Black. Arms of the Penn family. Uniface. Printer: B. Franklin and D. Hall.	—	—	—
S2443	**4 Pence** 1.10.1755. Black. Arms of the Penn family. Uniface. Printer: B. Franklin and D. Hall.	—	—	—
S2444	**6 Pence** 1.10.1755. Black. Arms of the Penn family. Uniface. Printer: B. Franklin and D. Hall.	—	—	—
S2445	**9 Pence** 1.10.1755. Black. Arms of the Penn family. Uniface. Printer: B. Franklin and D. Hall.	—	—	—
S2446	**1 Shilling** 1.10.1755. Black. Arms of the Penn family. Uniface. Printer: B. Franklin and D. Hall.	—	—	2500.
S2447	**18 Pence** 1.10.1755. Black. Arms of the Penn family. Uniface. Printer: B. Franklin and D. Hall.	—	—	—
S2448	**2 Shillings** 1.10.1755. Black. Arms of the Penn family. Uniface. Printer: B. Franklin and D. Hall.	—	—	—
S2449	**2 Shillings 6 Pence** 1.10.1755. Black. Arms of the Penn family. Uniface. Printer: B. Franklin and D. Hall.	—	—	—
S2450	**5 Shillings** 1.10.1755. Black. Arms of the Penn family. Back: Complex nature print of leaves. Printer: B. Franklin and D. Hall.	400.	1500.	3750.
S2451	**10 Shillings** 1.10.1755. Black. Arms of the Penn family. Back: Complex nature print of leaves. Printer: B. Franklin and D. Hall.	350.	1750.	—

1756 Issue

		VG	VF	UNC
S2452	**1 Shilling** 1.1.1756. Black. Arms of the Penn family. *Pennsilvania.* Plate letter: A; B. Back: Nature print of leaf. Printer: B. Franklin and D. Hall.	750.	3000.	—
S2453	**18 Pence** 1.1.1756. Black. Arms of the Penn family. *Pensilvania.* Plate letter: A; B. Back: Nature print of leaf. Printer: B. Franklin and D. Hall.	750.	3000.	—

		VG	VF	UNC
S2454	**2 Shillings** 1.1.1756. Black. Arms of the Penn family. *Pensilvania.* Plate letter: A; B. Back: Nature print of leaf. Printer: B. Franklin and D. Hall.	750.	3000.	—
S2455	**2 Shillings 6 Pence** 1.1.1756. Black. Arms of the Penn family. *Pennsylvania.* Plate letter: A; B. Back: Nature print of leaf. Printer: B. Franklin and D. Hall.	750.	3000.	—
S2456	**5 Shillings** 1.1.1756. Black. Arms of the Penn family. *Pensilvania.* Plate letter: A; B. Back: Nature print of leaf. Printer: B. Franklin and D. Hall.	750.	3000.	—
S2457	**10 Shillings** 1.1.1756. Black. Arms of the Penn family. *Pennsilvania.* Plate letter: A; B. Back: Nature print of leaf. Printer: B. Franklin and D. Hall.	750.	3000.	—
S2458	**15 Shillings** 1.1.1756. Black. Arms of the Penn family. *Pennsylvania.* Plate letter: A; B. Back: Nature print of leaf. Printer: B. Franklin and D. Hall.	750.	3000.	—
S2459	**20 Shillings** 1.1.1756. Black. Arms of the Penn family. *Pensylvania.* Plate letter: A; B. Back: Nature print of leaf. Printer: B. Franklin and D. Hall.	750.	3000.	—
S2460	**5 Shillings** 1.10.1756. *Pensilvania.*	750.	3000.	—
S2461	**10 Shillings** 1.10.1756. *Pennsilvania.*	750.	3000.	—
S2462	**15 Shillings** 1.10.1756. *Pennsylvania.*	750.	3000.	—
S2463	**20 Shillings** 1.10.1756. *Pensylvania.*	750.	3000.	—

1757 First Issue

		VG	VF	UNC
S2464	**5 Shillings** 10.3.1757. Black. Arms of the Penn family. Plate letter A;B. *Pensilvania.* Back: Nature print of leaf. Printer: B. Franklin and D. Hall.	750.	3000.	—
S2465	**10 Shillings** 10.3.1757. Black. Arms of the Penn family. Plate letter A;B. *Pennsilvania.* Back: Nature print of leaf. Printer: B. Franklin and D. Hall.	750.	3000.	—
S2466	**15 Shillings** 10.3.1757. Black. Arms of the Penn family. Plate letter A;B. *Pennsylvania.* Back: Nature print of leaf. Printer: B. Franklin and D. Hall.	750.	3000.	—
S2467	**20 Shillings** 10.3.1757. Black. Arms of the Penn family. Plate letter A;B. *Pensylvania.* Back: Nature print of leaf. Printer: B. Franklin and D. Hall.	750.	3000.	—

1757 Second Issue

		VG	VF	UNC
S2468	**5 Shillings** 1.7.1757. Black. Arms of the Penn family. Plate letter A;B. *Pensilvania.* Back: Nature print of leaf. Printer: B. Franklin and D. Hall.	500.	2500.	—
S2469	**10 Shillings** 1.7.1757. Black. Arms of the Penn family. Plate letter A;B. *Pensilvania.* Back: Nature print of leaf. Printer: B. Franklin and D. Hall.	500.	2500.	—
S2470	**15 Shillings** 1.7.1757. Black. Arms of the Penn family. Plate letter A;B. *Pennsylvania.* Back: Nature print of leaf. Printer: B. Franklin and D. Hall.	500.	2500.	—
S2471	**20 Shillings** 1.7.1757. Black. Arms of the Penn family. Plate letter A;B. *Pensylvania.* Back: Nature print of leaf. Printer: B. Franklin and D. Hall.	500.	2500.	—

1758 Issue

		Good	Fine	XF
S2472	**1 Shilling** 20.5.1758. Black. Arms of the Penn family. Uniface. Printer: B. Franklin and D. Hall.	—	—	—
S2473	**18 Pence** 20.5.1758. Black. Arms of the Penn family. Uniface. Printer: B. Franklin and D. Hall.	—	—	—
S2474	**2 Shillings** 20.5.1758. Black. Arms of the Penn family. Uniface. Printer: B. Franklin and D. Hall.	—	—	—
S2475	**2 Shillings 6 Pence** 20.5.1758. Black. Arms of the Penn family. Uniface. Printer: B. Franklin and D. Hall.	—	—	—

		VG	VF	UNC
S2476	**5 Shillings** 20.5.1757. Black. Arms of the Penn family. Plate letter A; B. *Pensilvania.* Back: Nature print of leaf. Printer: B. Franklin and D. Hall.	—	—	6000.
S2477	**10 Shillings** 20.5.1758. Black. Arms of the Penn family. Plate letter A; B. *Pennsilvania.* Back: Nature print of leaf. Printer: B. Franklin and D. Hall.	450.	—	—
S2478	**15 Shillings** 20.5.1758. Black. Arms of the Penn family. Plate letter A; B. *Pennsylvania.* Back: Nature print of leaf. Printer: B. Franklin and D. Hall.	450.	—	—
S2479	**20 Shillings** 20.5.1758. Black. Arms of the Penn family. Plate letter A; B. *Pensylvania.* Back: Nature print of leaf. Printer: B. Franklin and D. Hall.	450.	2000.	—

1759 First Issue

		VG	VF	UNC
S2480	**5 Shillings** 25.4.1759. Black. *Pensilvania.* Printer: B. Franklin and D. Hall.	—	—	—
S2481	**10 Shillings** 25.4.1759. Black. *Pennsilvania.*. Printer: B. Franklin and D. Hall.	—	—	—
S2482	**15 Shillings** 25.4.1759. Black. *Pennsylvania.* Printer: B. Franklin and D. Hall.	450.	2000.	—
S2483	**20 Shillings** 25.4.1759. Black. *Pensylvania.* Printer: B. Franklin and D. Hall.	450.	2000.	—
S2484	**50 Shillings** 25.4.1759. Black and red. *Pensylvania.* Back: Black and red. Nature print of leaves. Printer: B. Franklin and D. Hall.	900.	4000.	—

		VG	VF	UNC
S2485	**5 Pounds** 25.4.1759. Black and red. *Pennsylvania.* Back: Black and red. Nature print of leaves. Printer: B. Franklin and D. Hall.	900.	4000.	—

1759 Second Issue

		Good	Fine	XF
S2486	**50 Shillings** 21.6.1759. Black and red. Nature print of leaves. *Pensylvania.* Plate letter C; D.	1000.	—	—

		VG	VF	UNC
S2487	**5 Pounds** 21.6.1759. Black and red. Nature print of leaves. *Pennsylvania.* Plate letter A; B.	—	2750.	—

1760 Issue

		Good	Fine	XF
S2488	**3 Pence** 1.5.1760. Black. Arms of the Penn family. Plate letter A; B. Printer: B. Franklin and D. Hall.	—	—	—
S2489	**4 Pence** 1.5.1760. Black. Arms of the Penn family. Plate letter A; B. Printer: B. Franklin and D. Hall.	—	—	—
S2490	**6 Pence** 1.5.1760. Black. Arms of the Penn family. Plate letter A; B. Printer: B. Franklin and D. Hall.	—	—	—
S2491	**9 Pence** 1.5.1760. Black. Arms of the Penn family. Plate letter A; B. Printer: B. Franklin and D. Hall.	—	—	—

		VG	VF	UNC
S2492	**5 Shillings** 1.5.1760. Black. Arms of the Penn family. Plate letter A; B. *Pensilvania.* Back: Nature print of leaves. Printer: B. Franklin and D. Hall.	400.	1500.	—
S2493	**10 Shillings** 1.5.1760. Black. Arms of the Penn family. Plate letter A; B. *Pennsilvania.* Back: Nature print of leaves. Printer: B. Franklin and D. Hall.	400.	1500.	—
S2494	**15 Shillings** 1.5.1760. Black. Arms of the Penn family. Plate letter A; B. *Pennsylvania.* Back: Nature print of leaves. Printer: B. Franklin and D. Hall.	400.	1500.	—
S2495	**20 Shillings** 1.5.1760. Black. Arms of the Penn family. Plate letter A; B. *Pennsylvania.* Printer: B. Franklin and D. Hall.	400.	1500.	—
S2496	**50 Shillings** 1.5.1760. Black and red. *Pensylvania.* Plate letter C; D. Back: Black and red. Nature print of leaves. Printer: B. Franklin and D. Hall.	800.	3000.	—

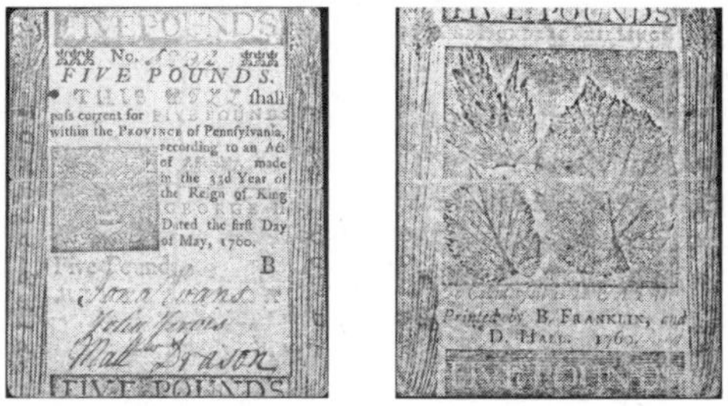

		VG	VF	UNC
S2497	**5 Pounds** 1.5.1760. Black and red. Plate letter A; B. *Pennsylvania.* Printer: B. Franklin and D. Hall.	800.	3000.	—

NOTE: Notes printed on blue paper are counterfeit detectors.

1764 Issue

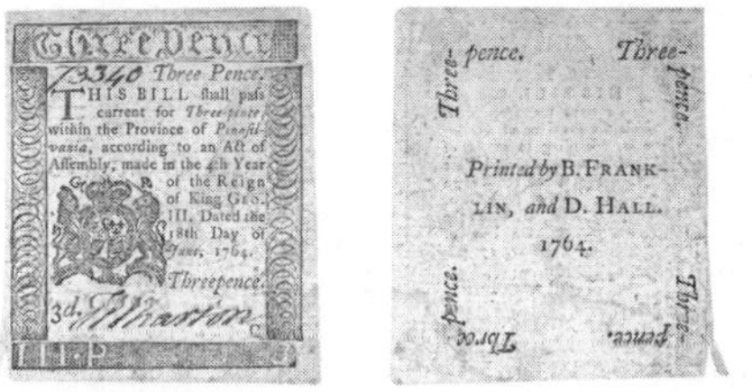

		VG	VF	UNC
S2498	**3 Pence** 18.6.1764. Black. Crowned supported British arms. Plate letter A; B. *Pennsilvania.* Printer: B. Franklin and D. Hall.	225.	500.	2000.
S2499	**4 Pence** 18.6.1764. Black. Crowned supported British arms. Plate letter A; B. *Pensylvania.* Printer: B. Franklin and D. Hall.	250.	500.	2000.
S2500	**6 Pence** 18.6.1764. Black. Crowned supported British arms. Plate letter A; B. *Pennsylvania.* Printer: B. Franklin and D. Hall.	200.	500.	2000.
S2501	**9 Pence** 18.6.1764. Black. Crowned supported British arms. Plate letter A; B. *Pennsylvania.* Printer: B. Franklin and D. Hall.	200.	500.	2000.

Cat. No.	Denomination / Description	VG	VF	UNC
S2502	**1 Shilling** 18.6.1764. Black. Crowned supported British arms. Plate letter A; B. *Pennsilvania.* Back: Nature print: leaf or leaves. Printer: B. Franklin and D. Hall.	200.	750.	—
S2503	**1 Shilling 6 Pence** 18.6.1764. Black. Crowned supported British arms. Plate letter A; B. Back: Nature print: leaf or leaves. Printer: B. Franklin and D. Hall.	200.	750.	—
S2504	**2 Shillings** 18.6.1764. Black. Crowned supported British arms. Plate letter A; B. Back: Nature print: leaf or leaves. Printer: B. Franklin and D. Hall.	200.	750.	—
S2505	**2 Shillings 6 Pence** 18.6.1764. Black. Crowned supported British arms. Plate letter A; B. Back: Nature print: leaf or leaves. Printer: B. Franklin and D. Hall.	200.	750.	—
S2506	**5 Shillings** 18.6.1764. Black. Crowned supported British arms. Plate letter A; B; C; D. *Pensylvania.* Back: Nature print: leaf or leaves. Printer: B. Franklin and D. Hall.	200.	750.	—
S2507	**10 Shillings** 18.6.1764. Black. Crowned supported British arms. Plate letter A; B. *Pennsilvania.* Back: Nature print: leaf or leaves. Printer: B. Franklin and D. Hall.	200.	750.	—
S2508	**20 Shillings** 18.6.1764. Black. Crowned supported British arms. Plate letter A; B. *Pennsylvania.* Printer: B. Franklin and D. Hall.	200.	750.	—

1767 Issue

		Good	Fine	XF
S2509	**40 Shillings** 15.6.1767. Black. Arms of the Penn family. Plate letter A; B; C; D. Back: Nature print of leaves. Printer: David Hall and William Sellers.	—	—	—
S2510	**4 Pounds** 15.6.1767. Black. Arms of the Penn family. Plate letter A; B. Back: Nature print of leaves. Printer: David Hall and William Sellers.	—	—	—
S2511	**6 Pounds** 15.6.1767. Black. Arms of the Penn family. Plate letter A; B; C; D. Back: Nature print of leaves. Printer: David Hall and William Sellers.	—	5750.	—

NOTE: Notes printed on blue paper are Test Notes.

1769 First Issue

		Good	Fine	XF
S2512	**8 Shillings** 1.3.1769. Black. Arms of the Penn family. *Pensilvania.* Back: Nature print of leaves. Printer: David Hall and William Sellers.	150.	1500.	—
S2513	**12 Shillings** 1.3.1769. Black. Arms of the Penn family. *Pensylvania.* Back: Nature print of leaves. Printer: David Hall and William Sellers.	150.	1500.	—
S2514	**1 Pound 10 Shillings** 1.3.1769. Black. Arms of the Penn family. *Pennsylvania.* Plate letter A; B; C. Back: Nature print of leaves. Printer: David Hall and William Sellers.	125.	1500.	—
S2515	**3 Pounds** 1.3.1769. Black. Arms of the Penn family. *Pennsilvania.* Plate letter A; B. Back: Nature print of leaves. Printer: David Hall and William Sellers.	125.	1500.	—

1769 Second Issue

Cat. No.	Denomination / Description	VG	VF	UNC
S2516	**3 Pence** 10.3.1769. Black. Arms of the Penn family. *Pensilvania.* Plate letter A; B; C. Uniface. Printer: David Hall and William Sellers.	—	—	—
S2517	**4 Pence** 10.3.1769. Black. Arms of the Penn family. *Pennsilvania.* Plate letter A; B; C. Uniface. Printer: David Hall and William Sellers.	—	—	—
S2518	**6 Pence** 10.3.1769. Black. Arms of the Penn family. *Pensylvania.* Plate letter A; B; C. Uniface. Printer: David Hall and William Sellers.	—	—	—
S2519	**9 Pence** 10.3.1769. Black. Arms of the Penn family. *Pensylvania.* Plate letter A; B; C. Uniface. Printer: David Hall and William Sellers.	—	—	—
S2520	**1 Shilling** 10.3.1769. Black. Arms of the Penn family. *Pennsilvania.* Plate letter A; B; C; D. Uniface. Printer: David Hall and William Sellers.	500.	2000.	6000.
S2521	**18 Pence** 10.3.1769. Black. Arms of the Penn family. *Pennsylvania.* Plate letter A; B; C; D. Uniface. Printer: David Hall and William Sellers.	500.	2000.	6000.

Cat. No.	Denomination / Description	VG	VF	UNC
S2522	**2 Shillings** 10.3.1769. Black. Arms of the Penn family. *Pensilvania.* Plate letter A; B; C; D. Uniface. Printer: David Hall and William Sellers.	500.	2000.	6000.
S2523	**2 Shillings 6 Pence** 10.3.1769. Black. Arms of the Penn family. *Pensylvania.* Plate letter A; B. Uniface. Printer: David Hall and William Sellers.	500.	2000.	6000.
S2524	**5 Shillings** 10.3.1769. Black. Arms of the Penn family. *Pennsylvania.* Plate letter A; B; C; D. Back: Nature print of leaves. Printer: David Hall and William Sellers.	750.	—	—
S2525	**10 Shillings** 10.3.1769. Black. Arms of the Penn family. *Pensylvania.* Back: Nature print of leaves. Printer: David Hall and William Sellers.			
	a. Asterisk follows date on face. Twelve identical ornaments to right of colon on lower border.	750.	—	—
	b. Without asterisk after date. Eleven identical ornaments to right of colon on lower border.	750.	—	—
S2526	**15 Shillings** 10.3.1769. Black. Arms of the Penn family. *Pennsylvania.* Back: Nature print of leaves. Printer: David Hall and William Sellers.	1000.	—	—
S2527	**20 Shillings** 10.3.1769. Black. Arms of the Penn family. *Pennsylvania.* Back: Nature print of leaves. Printer: David Hall and William Sellers.	1000.	—	—

1771 Issue

Cat. No.	Denomination / Description	VG	VF	UNC
S2528	**5 Shillings** 20.3.1771. Black and red. Arms of the Penn family. Plate letter A; B. *Pensilvania.* Back: Nature print of leaves. Printer: David Hall and William Sellers. Paper with mica flakes.	125.	350.	—
S2529	**10 Shillings** 20.3.1771. Black and red. Arms of the Penn family. Plate letter A; B. *Pensylvania.* Back: Nature print of leaves. Printer: David Hall and William Sellers. Paper with mica flakes.	125.	350.	—

Cat. No.	Denomination / Description	VG	VF	UNC
S2530	**15 Shillings** 20.3.1771. Black and red. Arms of the Penn family. Plate letter A; B. *Pennsilvania.* Back: Nature print of leaves. Printer: David Hall and William Sellers. Paper with mica flakes.	125.	350.	—

Cat. No.	Denomination / Description	VG	VF	UNC
S2531	**20 Shillings** 20.3.1771. Black and red. Arms of the Penn family. Plate letter A; B. *Pennsylvania.* Back: Nature print of leaves. Printer: David Hall and William Sellers. Paper with mica flakes.	125.	350.	—

1772 Issue

Cat. No.	Denomination / Description	VG	VF	UNC
S2532	**3 Pence** 3.4.1772. Black. Arms of the Penn family. *Pennsylvania.* Plate letter A; B; C. Printer: David Hall and William Sellers.	150.	250.	—
S2533	**4 Pence** 3.4.1772. Black. Arms of the Penn family *Pennsilvania.* Plate letter A, B; C. Printer: David Hall and William Sellers.	150.	250.	—
S2534	**6 Pence** 3.4.1772. Black. Arms of the Penn family. *Pensylvania.* Plate letter A; B; C. Printer: David Hall and William Sellers.	150.	250.	—
S2535	**9 Pence** 3.4.1772. Black. Arms of the Penn family. *Pensilvania.* Plate letter A; B; C. Printer: David Hall and William Sellers.	150.	250.	—

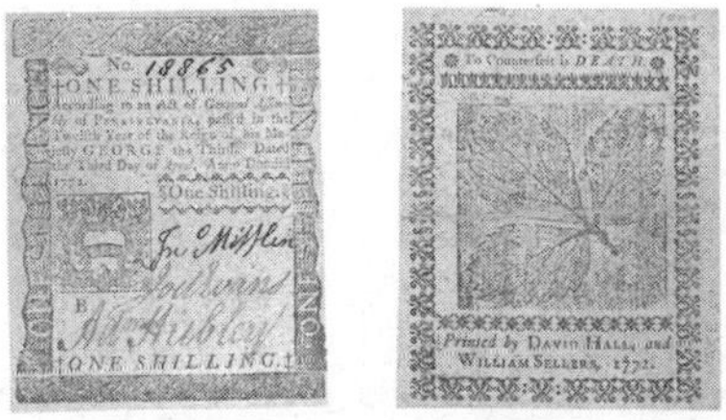

Cat. No.	Denomination / Description	VG	VF	UNC
S2536	**1 Shilling** 3.4.1772. Black. Arms of the Penn family. *Pennsylvania.* Plate letter A; B. Back: Nature print of leaf. Printer: David Hall and William Sellers.	80.00	175.	1000.
S2537	**18 Pence** 3.4.1772. Black. Arms of the Penn family. *Pennsilvania.* Plate letter A; B. Back: Nature print of leaf. Printer: David Hall and William Sellers.	80.00	175.	1000.

S2538 2 Shillings | VG 80.00 | VF 175. | UNC 1000.

3.4.1772. Black. Arms of the Penn family. *Pensylvania.* Plate letter A; B. Back: Nature print of leaf. Printer: David Hall and William Sellers.

S2539 2 Shillings 6 Pence | VG 80.00 | VF 175. | UNC 1000.

3.4.1772. Black. Arms of the Penn family. *Pensilvania.* Plate letter A; B. Printer: David Hall and William Sellers.

S2540 40 Shillings | VG 250. | VF 750. | UNC —

3.4.1772. Black and red. Arms of the Penn family. *Pennsylvania.* Plate letter A; B; C; D. Printer: David Hall and William Sellers.

1773 Issue

S2540A 18 Pence | VG 75.00 | VF 150. | UNC 400.

1.10.1773. Black and red. Arms of the Penn family. *Pennsilvania.* Back: Landscape. Paper with mica flakes and blue fibres.

S2540B 2 Shillings | VG 75.00 | VF 150. | UNC 400.

1.10.1773. Black and red. Arms of the Penn family. *Pennsylvania.* Back: Landscape. Paper with mica flakes and blue fibres.

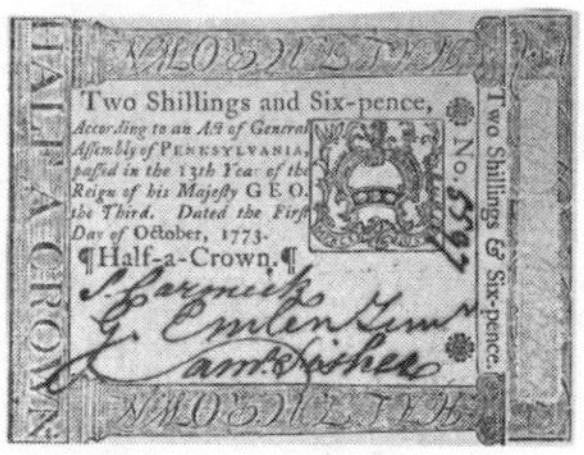

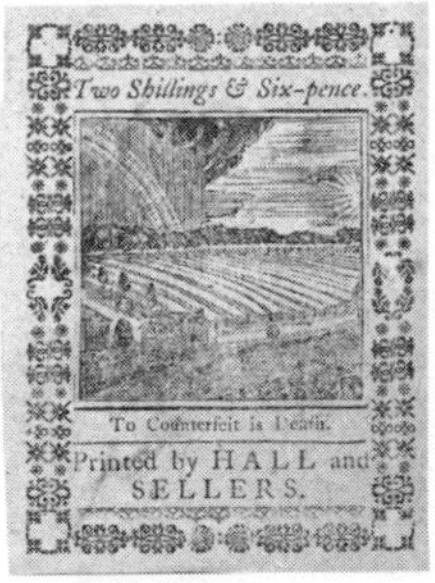

S2540C 2 Shillings 6 Pence | VG 75.00 | VF 150. | UNC 400.

1.10.1773. Black and red. Arms of the Penn family. *Pennsylvania.* Back: Landscape. Paper with mica flakes and blue fibres.

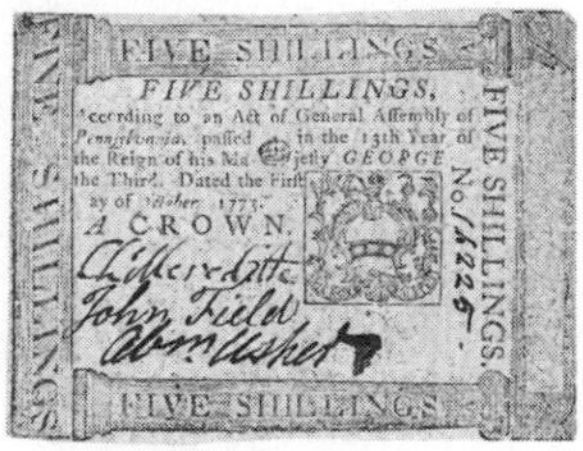

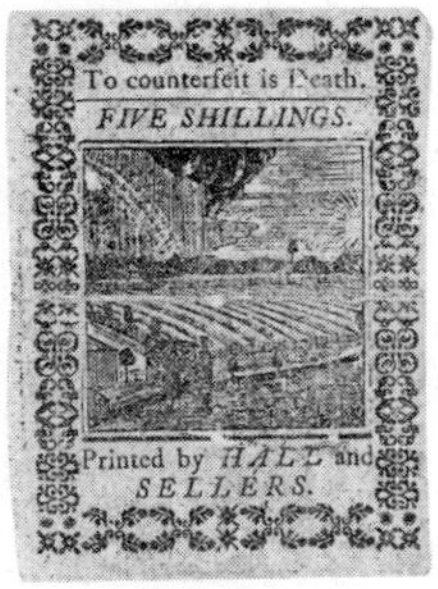

S2540D 5 Shillings | VG 75.00 | VF 150. | UNC 400.

1.10.1773. Black and red. Arms of the Penn family. *Pennsylvania.* Back: Landscape. Paper with mica flakes and blue fibres.

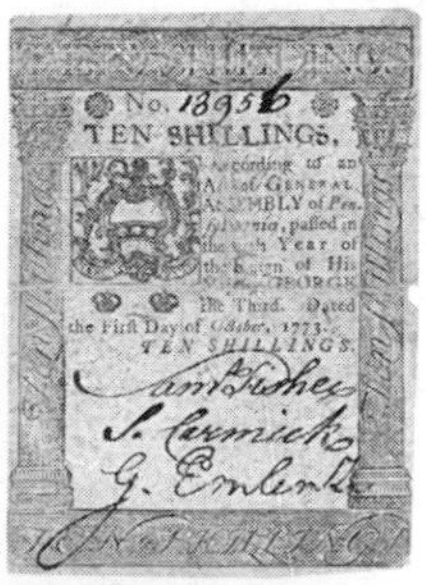

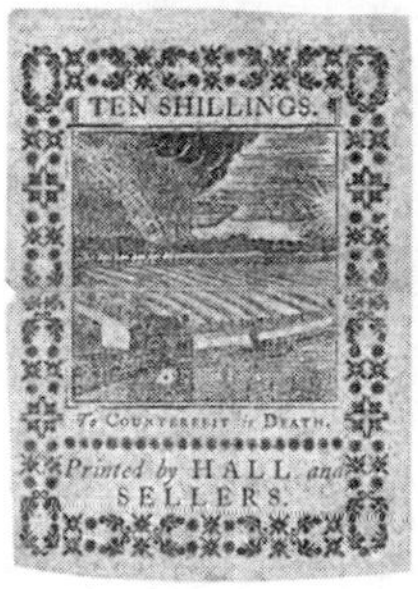

S2540E 10 Shillings | VG 75.00 | VF 150. | UNC 400.

1.10.1773. Black and red. Arms of the Penn family. *Pensylvania.* Red *X.* Back: Landscape. Paper with mica flakes and blue fibres.

S2540F 15 Shillings | VG 75.00 | VF 150. | UNC 400.

1.10.1773. Black and red. Arms of the Penn family. *Pensylvania.* Red *XV.* Back: Landscape. Paper with mica flakes and blue fibres.

S2540G 20 Shillings | VG 75.00 | VF 150. | UNC 400.

1.10.1773. Black and red. Arms of the Penn family. *Pennsylvania.* Red *1* (pound). Back: Landscape. Paper with mica flakes and blue fibres.

S2540H 50 Shillings | VG 75.00 | VF 150. | UNC 400.

1.10.1773. Black and red. Arms of the Penn family. *Pennsilvania.* Red *L.* Back: Landscape. Paper with mica flakes and blue fibres.

1773 Lighthouse Construction Issue

S2540I 4 Shillings | VG 125. | VF 250. | UNC 1000.

20.3.1773. Black. Arms of the Penn family. Plate letter A; B. Back: Lighthouse, sailing ship. Printer: David Hall and William Sellers. Paper with mica flakes.

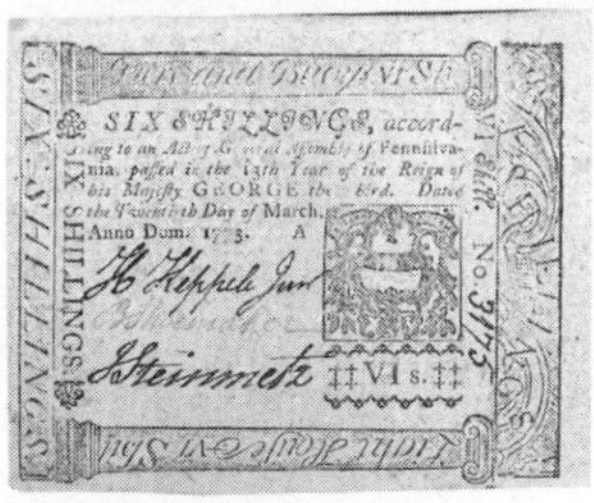

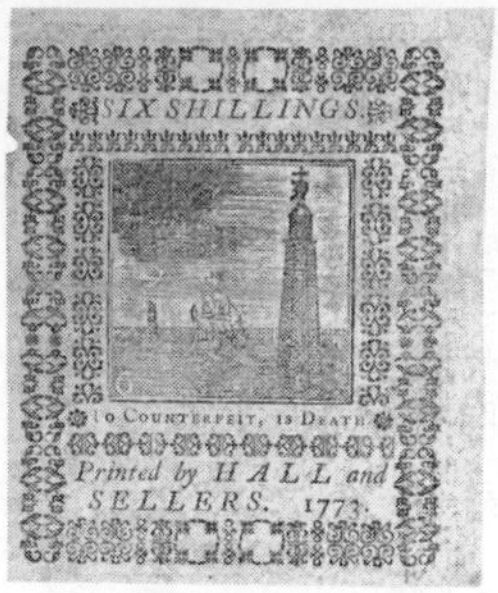

S2540J 6 Shillings | VG 125. | VF 250. | UNC 1000.

20.3.1773. Black. Arms of the Penn family. Arms upside down. Plate letter A. Back: Lighthouse, sailing ship. Printer: David Hall and William Sellers. Paper with mica flakes.

S2540K 6 Shillings | VG 125. | VF 250. | UNC 1000.

20.3.1773. Black. Arms of the Penn family. Arms corrected. Plate letter B. Back: Lighthouse, sailing ship. Printer: David Hall and William Sellers. Paper with mica flakes.

S2540L 14 Shillings | VG 125. | VF 250. | UNC 1000.

20.3.1773. Black. Arms of the Penn family. Plate letter A; B. Back: Lighthouse, sailing ship. Printer: David Hall and William Sellers. Paper with mica flakes.

S2540M 16 Shillings | VG 125. | VF 250. | UNC 1000.

20.3.1773. Black. Arms of the Penn family. Plate letter A; B. Back: Lighthouse, sailing ship. Printer: David Hall and William Sellers. Paper with mica flakes.

NOTE: Notes printed on blue paper are counterfeit detectors.

1775 Lighthouse Construction Issue

#S2540N-S2540Q black. Similar to #S2540I-S2540M. Plate letter A; B.

S2540N 4 Shillings | VG 125. | VF 250. | UNC 1000.

25.3.1775. Black. Arms of the Penn family. Plate letter A; B. Back: Lighthouse, sailing ship. Printer: David Hall and William Sellers. Paper with mica flakes.

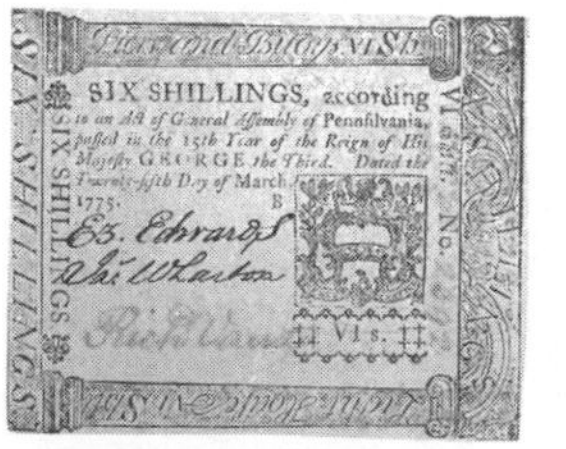

S2540O 6 Shillings | VG 125. | VF 250. | UNC 1000.

25.3.1775. Black. Arms of the Penn family. Plate letter A; B. Back: Lighthouse, sailing ship. Printer: David Hall and William Sellers. Paper with mica flakes.

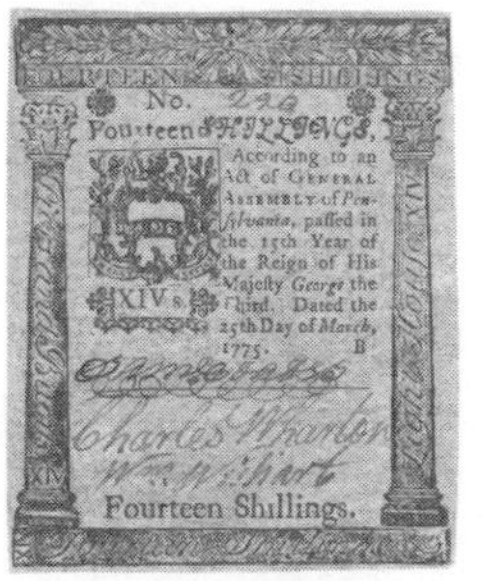

S2540P 14 Shillings | VG 125. | VF 250. | UNC 1000.

25.3.1775. Black. Arms of the Penn family. Plate letter A; B. Back: Lighthouse, sailing ship. Printer: David Hall and William Sellers. Paper with mica flakes.

S2540Q 16 Shillings | VG 125. | VF 250. | UNC 1000.

25.3.1775. Black. Arms of the Penn family. Plate letter A; B. Back: Lighthouse, sailing ship. Printer: David Hall and William Sellers. Paper with mica flakes.

1775 First Jail and Correctional Institution Construction Issue

S2540R 50 Shillings | VG 100. | VF 200. | UNC 700.

10.4.1775. Red and black. *Pennsilvania.* Plate letter C. Back: Workhouse (Philadelphia City jail). Printer: David Hall and William Sellers. Paper with mica flakes.

	VG	VF	UNC
S2540S 50 Shillings			
10.4.1775. Red and black. *Pennsylvania.* Plate letter D. Back: Workhouse (Philadelphia City jail). Printer: David Hall and William Sellers. Paper with mica flakes.	100.	200.	700.
S2540T 5 Pounds			
10.4.1775. Red and black. *Pensylvania.* Plate letter A. Back: Workhouse (Philadelphia City jail). Printer: David Hall and William Sellers. Paper with mica flakes.	100.	200.	700.
S2540U 5 Pounds			
10.4.1775. Red and black. *Pensilvania.* Plate letter B. Back: Workhouse (Philadelphia City jail). Printer: David Hall and William Sellers. Paper with mica flakes.	100.	200.	700.

1775 Second Jail and Correctional Institution Construction Issue

	VG	VF	UNC
S2541 10 Shillings			
20.7.1775. Black. Back: Nature print of leaves. Paper with mica flakes and blue fibres.			
a. Plate letter A. Reversed *S* on left column. *Pennsilvania.*	100.	225.	900.
b. Plate letter B. Reversed *S* on right column. *Pennsylvania.*	100.	225.	900.
S2542 20 Shillings			
20.7.1775. Black. Back: Nature print of leaves. Paper with mica flakes and blue fibres.			
a. Plate letter A. Capital letters on right column. *Pennsylvania.*	100.	225.	900.
b. Plate letter B. Capital letters on left column. *Pennsilvania.*	100.	225.	900.
S2543 30 Shillings			
20.7.1775. Black. Back: Nature print of leaves. Paper with mica flakes and blue fibres.			
a. Plate letter A. *Pensylvania.*	100.	225.	900.
b. Plate letter B. *Pensilvania.*	100.	225.	900.
S2544 40 Shillings			
20.7.1775. Black. Back: Nature print of leaves. Paper with mica flakes and blue fibres.			
a. Plate letter A. *Pensilvania.*	100.	225.	900.
b. Plate letter B. *Pensylvania.*	100.	225.	900.

1775 Third Jail and Correctional Institution Construction Issue

	VG	VF	UNC
S2545 3 Pence			
25.10.1775. Black. Arms of the Penn family. *Pennsylvania.* Back: Nature print of leaf or leaves. Printer: David Hall and William Sellers.	90.00	175.	500.
S2546 4 Pence			
25.10.1775. Black. Arms of the Penn family. *Pennsilvania.* Back: Nature print of leaf or leaves. Printer: David Hall and William Sellers.	90.00	175.	500.

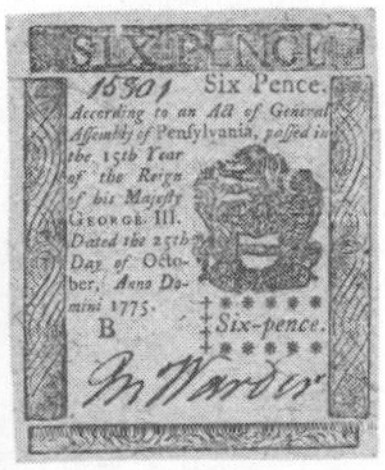

	VG	VF	UNC
S2547 6 Pence			
25.10.1775. Black. Arms of the Penn family. *Pensylvania.* Back: Nature print of leaf or leaves. Printer: David Hall and William Sellers.	90.00	175.	500.
S2548 9 Pence			
25.10.1775. Black. Arms of the Penn family. *Pensilvania.* Back: Nature print of leaf or leaves. Printer: David Hall and William Sellers.	90.00	175.	500.
S2549 1 Shilling			
25.10.1775. Black. Arms of the Penn family. *S* for Smither in top border. *Pensylvania.* Back: Nature print of leaf or leaves. Printer: David Hall and William Sellers.	75.00	150.	400.

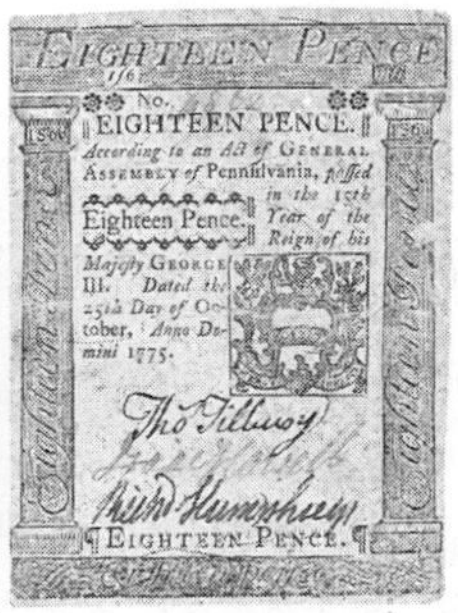

	VG	VF	UNC
S2550 18 Pence			
25.10.1775. Black. Arms of the Penn family. *Pennsilvania.* Back: Nature print of leaf or leaves. Printer: David Hall and William Sellers.	75.00	150.	400.

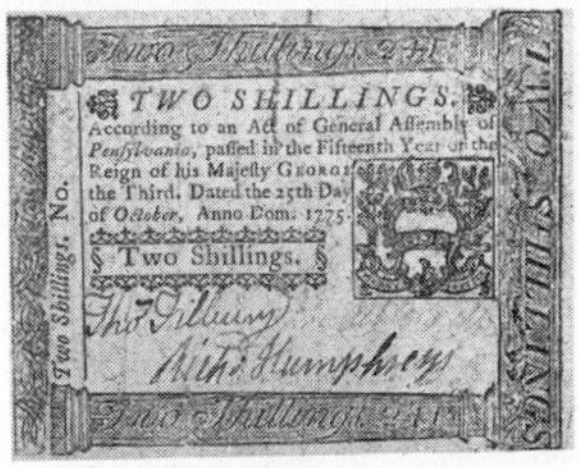

	VG	VF	UNC
S2551 2 Shillings			
25.10.1775. Black. Arms of the Penn family. *Pensylvania.* Back: Nature print of leaf or leaves. Printer: David Hall and William Sellers.	75.00	150.	400.
S2552 2 Shillings 6 Pence = 1/2 Crown			
25.10.1775. Black. Arms of the Penn family. *Pennsylvania.* Back: Chevron designs. Printer: David Hall and William Sellers.	75.00	150.	400.
S2553 5 Shillings = 1 Crown			
25.10.1775. Black. Arms of the Penn family. *Pennsylvania.* Back: Nature print of leaf or leaves. Printer: David Hall and William Sellers.	90.00	175.	500.
S2554 10 Shillings = 2 Crowns			
25.10.1775. Black. Arms of the Penn family. *Pennsylvania.* Back: Nature print of leaf or leaves. Printer: David Hall and William Sellers.	90.00	175.	500.
S2555 15 Shillings = 3 Crowns			
25.10.1775. Black. Arms of the Penn family. *Pensilvania.* Back: Nature print of leaf or leaves. Printer: David Hall and William Sellers.	90.00	175.	500.
S2556 20 Shillings = 4 Crowns			
25.10.1775. Black. Arms of the Penn family. *Pensylvania.* Back: Nature print of leaf or leaves. Printer: David Hall and William Sellers.	90.00	175.	500.

1775 Fourth Jail and Correctional Institution Construction Issue

	VG	VF	UNC
S2557 10 Shillings			
8.12.1775. Black. Crowned supported British arms. Back: Nature print of leaf or leaves. Printer: David Hall and William Sellers. Paper with blue fibres.			
a. Plate letter A. Reversed *S* on left column.	90.00	175.	500.
b. Plate letter B. Reversed *S* on right column.	90.00	175.	500.
S2558 20 Shillings			
8.12.1775. Black. Crowned supported British arms. Back: Nature print of leaf or leaves. Printer: David Hall and William Sellers. Paper with blue fibres.			
a. Plate letter A. Capital letters on right column.	90.00	175.	500.
b. Plate letter B. Capital letters on left column.	90.00	175.	500.
S2559 30 Shillings			
8.12.1775. Black. Crowned supported British arms. *Pensilvania.* Back: Nature print of leaf or leaves. Printer: David Hall and William Sellers. Paper with blue fibres.	75.00	150.	450.

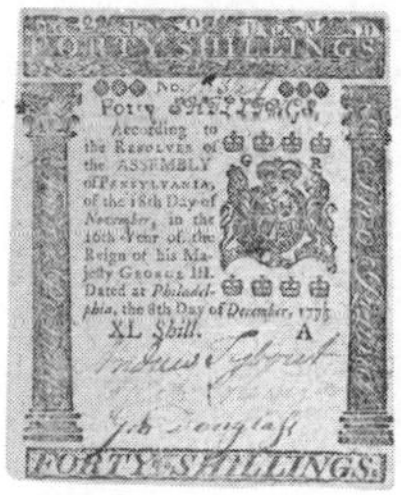

	VG	VF	UNC
S2560 40 Shillings			
8.12.1775. Black. Crowned supported British arms. *Pensylvania.* Back: Nature print of leaf or leaves. Printer: David Hall and William Sellers. Paper with blue fibres.	75.00	150.	450.

1776 Jail and Correctional Institution Construction Issue

	VG	VF	UNC
S2561 3 Pence			
25.4.1776. Black. Arms of the Penn family. *Pennsylvania.* Printer: David Hall and William Sellers. Paper with Mica flakes and blue fibres.	65.00	125.	300.

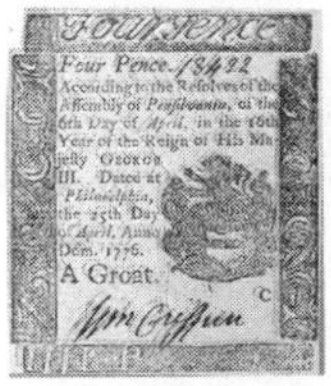

	VG	VF	UNC
S2562 4 Pence			
25.4.1776. Black. Arms of the Penn family. *Pensilvania.* Printer: David Hall and William Sellers. Paper with Mica flakes and blue fibres.	65.00	125.	300.
S2563 6 Pence			
25.4.1776. Black. Arms of the Penn family. *Pensylvania.* Printer: David Hall and William Sellers. Paper with Mica flakes and blue fibres.	65.00	125.	300.
S2564 9 Pence			
25.4.1776. Black. Arms of the Penn family. *Pensylvania.* Printer: David Hall and William Sellers. Paper with Mica flakes and blue fibres.	65.00	125.	300.
S2565 1 Shilling			
25.4.1776. Black. Crowned supported British arms. *Pennsylvania.* Back: Nature print of leaf or leaves. Printer: David Hall and William Sellers. Paper with Mica flakes and blue fibres.	75.00	150.	400.

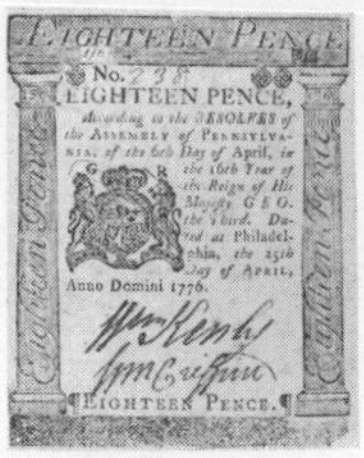

S2566 18 Pence

25.4.1776. Black. Crowned supported British arms. *Pennsylvania.* Back: Nature print of leaf or leaves. Printer: David Hall and William Sellers. Paper with Mica flakes and blue fibres.

	VG	VF	UNC
S2566	75.00	150.	400.

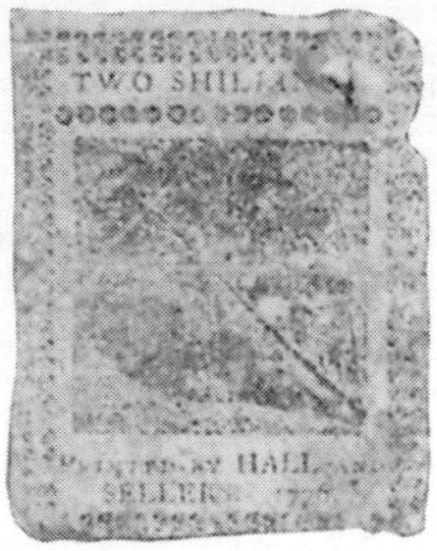

S2567 2 Shillings

25.4.1776. Black. Crowned supported British arms. *Pennsilvania.* Back: Nature print of leaf or leaves. Printer: David Hall and William Sellers. Paper with Mica flakes and blue fibres.

	VG	VF	UNC
S2567	75.00	150.	400.

S2568 2 Shillings 6 Pence

25.4.1776. Black. Crowned supported British arms. *Pennsylvania.* Back: Nature print of leaf or leaves. Printer: David Hall and William Sellers. Paper with Mica flakes and blue fibres.

	VG	VF	UNC
S2568	75.00	150.	400.

S2569 10 Shillings

25.4.1776. Black. Crowned supported British arms. Back: Nature print of leaf or leaves. Printer: David Hall and William Sellers. Paper with Mica flakes and blue fibres.

	VG	VF	UNC
a. Plate letter A. Reversed *S* on right column. *Pennsylvania.*	80.00	175.	500.
b. Plate letter B. Reversed *S* on left column. *Pennsilvania.*	80.00	175.	500.

S2570 20 Shillings

25.4.1776. Black. Crowned supported British arms. Back: Nature print of leaf or leaves. Printer: David Hall and William Sellers. Paper with Mica flakes and blue fibres.

	VG	VF	UNC
a. Plate letter A. Capital letters on right column. *Pennsilvania.*	80.00	175.	500.
b. Plate letter B. Capital letters on left column. *Pennsylvania.*	80.00	175.	500.

S2571 30 Shillings

25.4.1776. Black. Crowned supported British arms. Back: Nature print of leaf or leaves. Printer: David Hall and William Sellers. Paper with Mica flakes and blue fibres.

	VG	VF	UNC
a. Plate letter A. *Pensylvania.*	80.00	175.	500.
b. Plate letter B. *Pensilvania.*	80.00	175.	500.

S2572 40 Shillings

25.4.1776. Black. Crowned supported British arms. Back: Nature print of leaf or leaves. Printer: David Hall and William Sellers. Paper with Mica flakes and blue fibres.

	VG	VF	UNC
a. Plate letter A. *Pensylvania.*	80.00	175.	500.
b. Plate letter B. *Pensilvania.*	75.00	150.	350.

Pennsylvania

Commonwealth

1777 First Issue

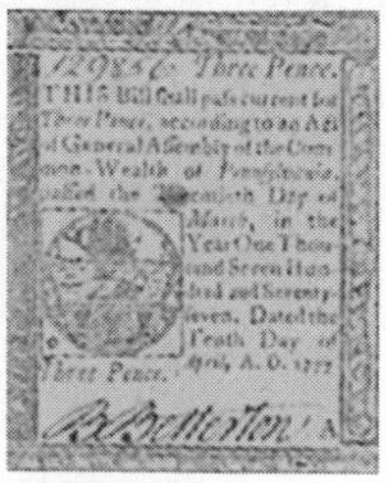
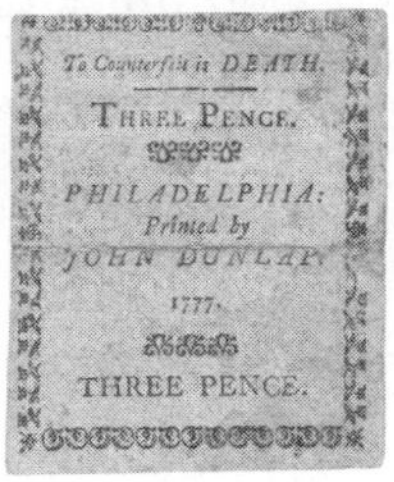

S2573 3 Pence

10.4.1777. Black. Arms of the Commonwealth of Pennsylvania. Red serial numbers. Plate letter A; B; C. Watermark: *PENSYL / VANIA.* Printer: John Dunlap.

	VG	VF	UNC
S2573	75.00	150.	350.

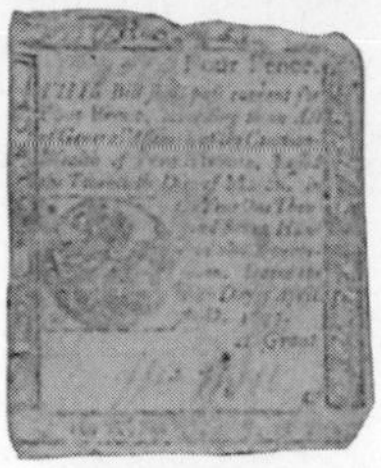
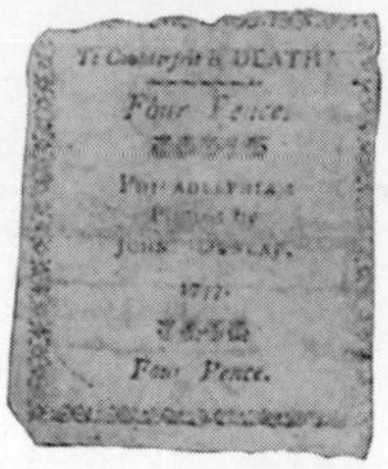

S2574 4 Pence

10.4.1777. Black. Arms of the Commonwealth of Pennsylvania. Red serial numbers. Plate letter A; B; C. Watermark: *PENSYL / VANIA.* Printer: John Dunlap.

	VG	VF	UNC
S2574	75.00	150.	350.

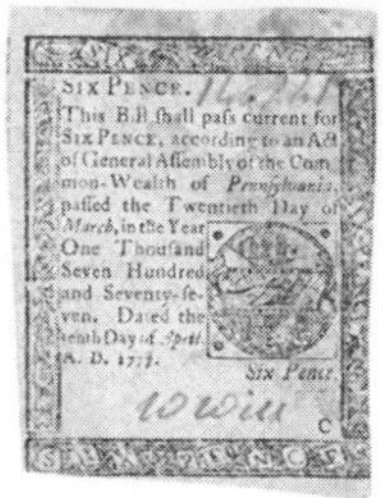

S2575 6 Pence

10.4.1777. Black. Arms of the Commonwealth of Pennsylvania. Red serial numbers. Plate letter A; B; C. Watermark: *PENSYL / VANIA.* Printer: John Dunlap.

	VG	VF	UNC
S2575	75.00	150.	350.

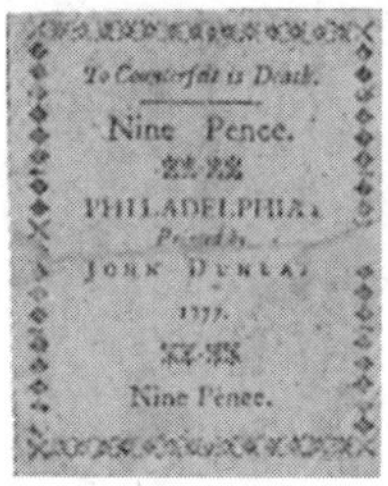

S2576 9 Pence

10.4.1777. Black. Arms of the Commonwealth of Pennsylvania. Red serial numbers. Plate letter A; B; C. Watermark: *PENSYL / VANIA.* Printer: John Dunlap.

	VG	VF	UNC
S2576	75.00	150.	350.

S2577 1 Shilling

10.4.1777. Black. Arms of the Commonwealth of Pennsylvania. Red serial numbers. Plate letter A; B; C. Back: Farm landscape. Watermark: *PENSYL / VANIA.* Printer: John Dunlap.

	VG	VF	UNC
S2577	90.00	175.	500.

S2578 1 Shilling 6 Pence

10.4.1777. Black. Arms of the Commonwealth of Pennsylvania. Red serial numbers. Plate letter A; B; C. Back: Farm landscape. Watermark: *PENSYL / VANIA.* Printer: John Dunlap.

	VG	VF	UNC
S2578	90.00	175.	500.

S2579 2 Shillings

10.4.1777. Black. Arms of the Commonwealth of Pennsylvania. Red serial numbers. Plate letter A; B; C. Back: Farm landscape. Watermark: *PENSYL / VANIA.* Printer: John Dunlap.

	VG	VF	UNC
S2579	90.00	175.	500.

S2580 3 Shillings

10.4.1777. Black. Arms of the Commonwealth of Pennsylvania. Red serial numbers. Plate letter A; B; C. Back: Farm landscape. Watermark: *PENSYL / VANIA.* Printer: John Dunlap.

	VG	VF	UNC
S2580	90.00	175.	500.

S2581 4 Shillings

10.4.1777. Black. Arms of the Commonwealth of Pennsylvania. Red serial numbers. Plate letter A; B; C. Back: Farm landscape. Watermark: *PENSYL / VANIA.* Printer: John Dunlap.

	VG	VF	UNC
S2581	90.00	175.	500.

S2582 6 Shillings

10.4.1777. Black. Arms of the Commonwealth of Pennsylvania. Red serial numbers. Plate letter A; B; C. Back: Farm landscape. Watermark: *PENSYL / VANIA.* Printer: John Dunlap.

	VG	VF	UNC
S2582	90.00	175.	500.

S2583 8 Shillings

10.4.1777. Black. Arms of the Commonwealth of Pennsylvania. Red serial numbers. Plate letter A; B; C. Back: Farm landscape. Watermark: *PENSYL / VANIA.* Printer: John Dunlap.

	VG	VF	UNC
S2583	90.00	175.	500.

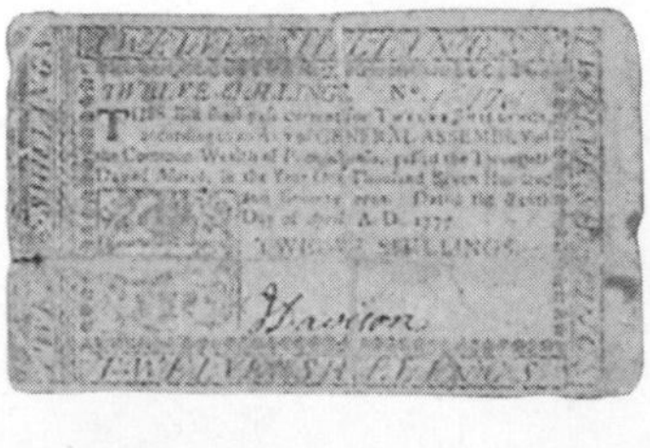
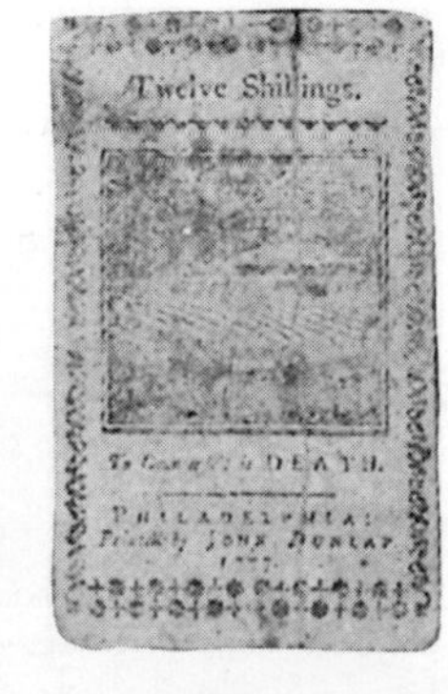

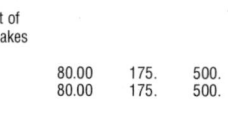

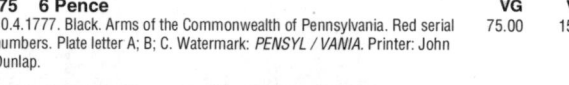

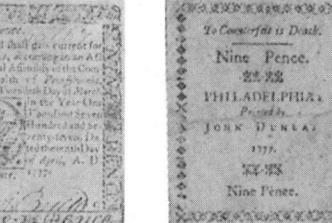

	VG	VF	UNC
S2584 12 Shillings 10.4.1777. Black. Arms of the Commonwealth of Pennsylvania. Red serial numbers. Plate letter A; B; C. Back: Farm landscape. Watermark: *PENSYL / VANIA*. Printer: John Dunlap.	90.00	175.	500.
S2585 16 Shillings 10.4.1777. Black. Arms of the Commonwealth of Pennsylvania. Red serial numbers. Plate letter A; B; C. Back: Farm landscape. Watermark: *PENSYL / VANIA*. Printer: John Dunlap.	90.00	175.	500.

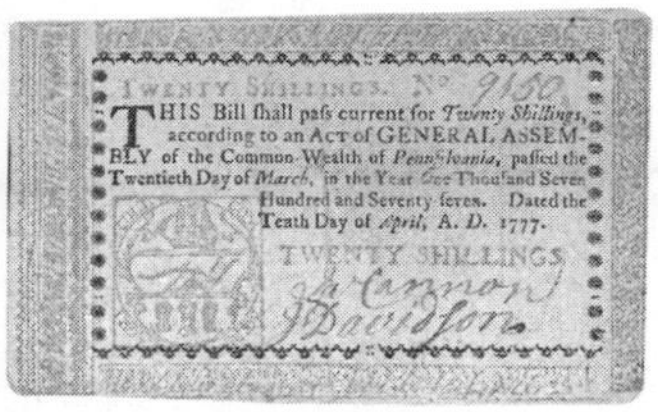

	VG	VF	UNC
S2586 20 Shillings 10.4.1777. Black. Arms of the Commonwealth of Pennsylvania. Red serial numbers. Plate letter A; B; C. Back: Farm landscape. Watermark: *PENSYL / VANIA*. Printer: John Dunlap.	90.00	175.	500.
S2587 40 Shillings 10.4.1777. Black. Arms of the Commonwealth of Pennsylvania. Red serial numbers. Plate letter A; B; C. Back: Farm landscape. Watermark: *PENSYL / VANIA*. Printer: John Dunlap. Issued note.	150.	300.	—
S2588 4 Pounds 10.4.1777. Black. Arms of the Commonwealth of Pennsylvania. Red serial numbers. Plate letter A; B; C. Back: Farm landscape. Watermark: *PENSYL / VANIA*. Printer: John Dunlap. Issued note.	150.	300.	—

1777 Second Issue

	VG	VF	UNC
S2589 1 Shilling 10.4.1777. Red and black. Arms of the Commonwealth of Pennsylvania. Back: Red and black. Farm landscape.	150.	375.	1250.
S2590 1 Shilling 6 Pence 10.4.1777. Red and black. Arms of the Commonwealth of Pennsylvania. Back: Red and black. Farm landscape.	150.	375.	1250.
S2591 2 Shillings 10.4.1777. Red and black. Arms of the Commonwealth of Pennsylvania. Back: Red and black. Farm landscape.	150.	375.	1250.
S2592 3 Shillings 10.4.1777. Red and black. Arms of the Commonwealth of Pennsylvania. Back: Red and black. Farm landscape.	150.	375.	1250.
S2593 4 Shillings 10.4.1777. Red and black. Arms of the Commonwealth of Pennsylvania. Back: Red and black. Farm landscape.	150.	375.	1250.
S2594 6 Shillings 10.4.1777. Red and black. Arms of the Commonwealth of Pennsylvania. Back: Red and black. Farm landscape.	150.	375.	1250.
S2595 8 Shillings 10.4.1777. Red and black. Arms of the Commonwealth of Pennsylvania. Back: Red and black. Farm landscape.	150.	375.	1250.
S2596 12 Shillings 10.4.1777. Red and black. Arms of the Commonwealth of Pennsylvania. Back: Red and black. Farm landscape.	150.	375.	1250.
S2597 16 Shillings 10.4.1777. Red and black. Arms of the Commonwealth of Pennsylvania. Back: Red and black. Farm landscape.	150.	375.	1250.
S2598 20 Shillings 10.4.1777. Red and black. Arms of the Commonwealth of Pennsylvania. Back: Red and black. Farm landscape.	150.	375.	1250.
S2599 40 Shillings 10.4.1777. Red and black. Arms of the Commonwealth of Pennsylvania. Back: Black. Farm landscape.	200.	500.	—
S2600 4 Pounds 10.4.1777. Red and black. Arms of the Commonwealth of Pennsylvania. Back: Black. Farm landscape.	200.	500.	—

1780 First Issue

	VG	VF	UNC
S2601 5 Shillings 29.4.1780. Black. Back: New set of nature prints with leaf or leaves. Watermark: *PENSYL / VANIA*. Printer: John Dunlap.	3500.	—	—
S2602 10 Shillings 29.4.1780. Black. Back: New set of nature prints with leaf or leaves. Watermark: *PENSYL / VANIA*. Printer: John Dunlap.	3500.	—	—
S2603 15 Shillings 29.4.1780. Black. Back: New set of nature prints with leaf or leaves. Watermark: *PENSYL / VANIA*. Printer: John Dunlap.	3500.	—	—
S2604 20 Shillings 29.4.1780. Black. Back: New set of nature prints with leaf or leaves. Watermark: *PENSYL / VANIA*. Printer: John Dunlap.	3500.	—	—
S2605 30 Shillings 29.4.1780. Black. Back: New set of nature prints with leaf or leaves. Watermark: *PENSYL / VANIA*. Printer: John Dunlap.	3500.	—	—
S2606 40 Shillings 29.4.1780. Black. Back: New set of nature prints with leaf or leaves. Watermark: *PENSYL / VANIA*. Printer: John Dunlap.	3500.	—	—
S2607 50 Shillings 29.4.1780. Black. Back: New set of nature prints with leaf or leaves. Watermark: *PENSYL / VANIA*. Printer: John Dunlap.	3500.	—	—
S2608 60 Shillings 29.4.1780. Black. Back: New set of nature prints with leaf or leaves. Watermark: *PENSYL / VANIA*. Printer: John Dunlap.	3500.	—	—

1780 Second Issue

	VG	VF	UNC
S2609 1 Dollar 1.6.1780. Black. Back: Red and black. Watermark: *CONFEDE / RATION*. Printer: David Hall and William Sellers.	1500.	3750.	—
S2610 2 Dollars 1.6.1780. Black. Back: Red and black. Watermark: *CONFEDE / RATION*. Printer: David Hall and William Sellers.	1500.	3750.	—
S2611 3 Dollars 1.6.1780. Black. Back: Red and black. Watermark: *CONFEDE / RATION*. Printer: David Hall and William Sellers.	1500.	3750.	—

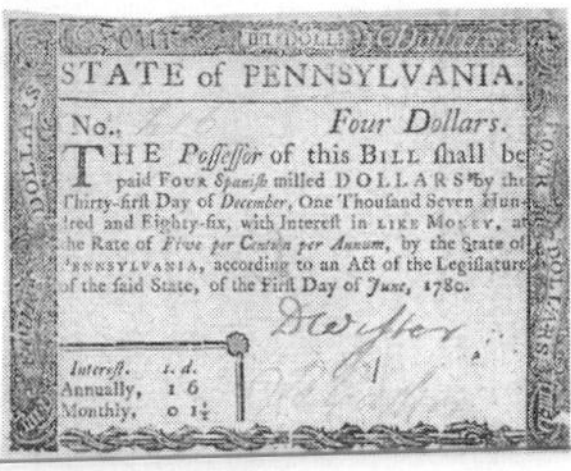

	VG	VF	UNC
S2612 4 Dollars 1.6.1780. Black. Back: Red and black. Watermark: *CONFEDE / RATION*. Printer: David Hall and William Sellers.	1500.	3750.	—
S2613 5 Dollars 1.6.1780. Black. Back: Red and black. Watermark: *CONFEDE / RATION*. Printer: David Hall and William Sellers.	1500.	3750.	—
S2614 7 Dollars 1.6.1780. Black. *DOLLARS* misspelled *DOLLRAS* in upper right border. Back: Red and black. Watermark: *CONFEDE / RATION*. Printer: David Hall and William Sellers.	1500.	3750.	—
S2615 8 Dollars 1.6.1780. Black. Back: Red and black. Watermark: *CONFEDE / RATION*. Printer: David Hall and William Sellers.	1500.	3750.	—

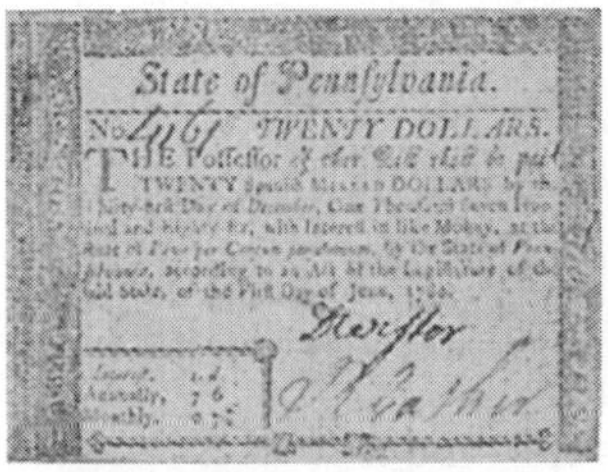

	VG	VF	UNC
S2616 20 Dollars 1.6.1780. Black. Back: Red and black. Watermark: *CONFEDE / RATION*. Printer: David Hall and William Sellers.	1500.	3750.	—

1781 Issue

	VG	VF	UNC
S2617 3 Pence 20.4.1781. Black. Watermark: *PENSYL / VANIA*. Printer: John Dunlap.			
a. Plate letter A. *Pence* misspelled *PENEE* at end of text.	100.	200.	800.
b. Plate letter B.	100.	200.	800.
S2618 6 Pence 20.4.1781. Black. Watermark. *PENSYL / VANIA*. Printer: John Dunlap.			
a. Plate letter A. Lower border words separated.	100.	200.	800.
b. Plate letter B. Lower border words too close.	100.	200.	800.
S2619 9 Pence 20.4.1781. Black. Watermark: *PENSYL / VANIA*. Printer: John Dunlap.			
a. Plate letter A. Lower border letters are black.	100.	200.	800.
b. Plate letter B. Lower border letters are white.	100.	200.	800.
S2620 1 Shilling 6 Pence 20.4.1781. Black. Watermark: *PENSYL / VANIA*. Printer: John Dunlap.	400.	1000.	3000.
S2621 2 Shillings 20.4.1781. Black. Back: Leaves. Watermark: *PENSYL / VANIA*. Printer: John Dunlap.	400.	1000.	3000.
S2622 2 Shillings 6 Pence 20.4.1781. Black. Back: Chevron designs. Watermark: *PENSYL / VANIA*. Printer: John Dunlap.	400.	1000.	3000.
S2623 5 Shillings 20.4.1781. Black. Back: Leaves. Watermark: *PENSYL / VANIA*. Printer: John Dunlap.	400.	1000.	3000.
S2624 10 Shillings 20.4.1781. Black. Back: Leaves. Watermark: *PENSYL / VANIA*. Printer: John Dunlap.	400.	1000.	3000.
S2625 15 Shillings 20.4.1781. Black. Back: Leaves. Watermark: *PENSYL / VANIA*. Printer: John Dunlap.	400.	1000.	3000.
S2626 20 Shillings 20.4.1781. Black. Back: Leaves. Watermark: *PENSYL / VANIA*. Printer: John Dunlap.	400.	1000.	3000.
S2627 30 Shillings 20.4.1781. Black. Back: Leaves, *Dunlap* misspelled *DNNLAP*. Watermark: *PENSYL / VANIA*. Printer: John Dunlap.	400.	1000.	3000.

	VG	VF	UNC
S2628 40 Shillings 20.4.1781. Black. Back: Leaves. Watermark: *PENSYL / VANIA*. Printer: John Dunlap.	400.	1000.	3000.
S2629 50 Shillings 20.4.1781. Black. Back: Leaves. Watermark: *PENSYL / VANIA*. Printer: John Dunlap.	400.	1000.	3000.
S2630 60 Shillings 20.4.1781. Black. Back: Leaves. Watermark: *PENSYL / VANIA*. Printer: John Dunlap.	400.	1000.	3000.
S2631 5 Pounds 20.4.1781. Black. Back: Farm landscape. Watermark: *PENSYL / VANIA*. Printer: John Dunlap.	650.	150.	5000.

1783 Treasury Issue

	Good	Fine	XF
S2632 1/4 Dollar 21.3.1783. Black.	—	14,000.	—
S2633 1 Dollar 21.3.1783. Black.	—	—	—
S2634 2 Dollars 21.3.1783. Black.	—	—	—
S2635 3 Dollars 21.3.1783. Black.	—	—	—
S2636 6 Dollars 21.3.1783. Black.	—	—	—
S2637 12 Dollars 21.3.1783. Black.	—	—	—
S2638 15 Dollars 21.3.1783. Black.	—	—	—
S2639 20 Dollars 21.3.1783. Black.	—	—	—

1785 Issue

	VG	VF	UNC
S2640 3 Pence 16.3.1785. Black. Commonwealth seal in various shapes. Back: Nature and cloth design. Watermark: *PENSYL / VANIA*. Printer: Francis Bailey.	500.	1250.	4000.
S2641 9 Pence 16.3.1785. Black. Commonwealth Seal in various shapes. Back: Nature and cloth design. Watermark: *PENSYL / VANIA*. Printer: Francis Bailey.	500.	1250.	4000.
S2642 1 Shilling 6 Pence 16.3.1785. Black. Commonwealth Seal in various shapes. Back: Nature and cloth design. Watermark: *PENSYL / VANIA*. Printer: Francis Bailey.	500.	1250.	4000.
S2643 2 Shillings 6 Pence 16.3.1785. Black. Commonwealth Seal in various shapes. Back: Nature and cloth design. *Bailey* misspelled *BAILLY*. Watermark: *PENSYL / VANIA*. Printer: Francis Bailey.	500.	1250.	4000.
S2644 5 Shillings 16.3.1785. Black. Commonwealth Seal in various shapes. Back: Nature and cloth design. Watermark: *PENSYL / VANIA*. Printer: Francis Bailey.	500.	1250.	4000.
S2645 10 Shillings 16.3.1785. Black. Commonwealth Seal in various shapes. Back: Nature and cloth design. Watermark: *PENSYL / VANIA*. Printer: Francis Bailey.	500.	1250.	4000.

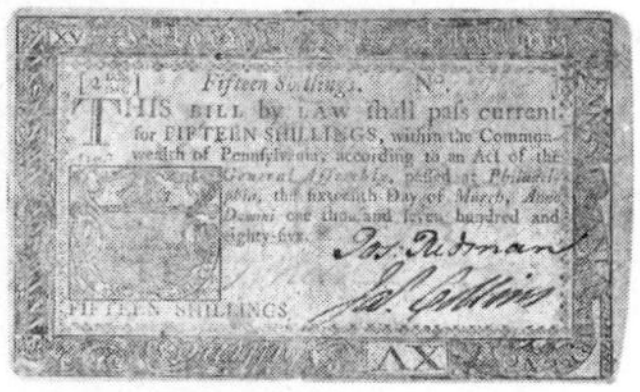

	VG	VF	UNC
S2646 15 Shillings 16.3.1785. Black. Commonwealth Seal in various shapes. Back: Nature and cloth design. Watermark: *PENSYL / VANIA*. Printer: Francis Bailey.	500.	1250.	4000.
S2647 20 Shillings 16.3.1785. Black. Commonwealth Seal in various shapes. Back: Nature and cloth design. Watermark: *PENSYL / VANIA*. Printer: Francis Bailey.	500.	1250.	4000.

Rhode Island

Colonial

1710 Issue

	Good	Fine	XF
S2651 2 Shillings 16.8.1710. Black. Arms of Rhode Island. Uniface.	25,500.	—	—
S2652 2 Shillings 6 Pence 16.8.1710. Black. Arms of Rhode Island. Uniface.	—	—	—
S2653 5 Shillings 16.8.1710. Black. Arms of Rhode Island. Uniface.	—	—	—
S2654 10 Shillings 16.8.1710. Black. Arms of Rhode Island. Uniface.	—	—	—
S2655 20 Shillings 16.8.1710. Black. Arms of Rhode Island. Uniface.	—	—	—
S2656 40 Shillings 16.8.1710. Black. Arms of Rhode Island. Uniface.	—	—	—
S2657 3 Pounds 16.8.1710. Black. Arms of Rhode Island. Uniface.	—	—	—
S2658 5 Pounds 16.8.1710. Black. Arms of Rhode Island. Uniface.	—	—	—

1715 Issue

	Good	Fine	XF
S2659 12 Pence 5.7.1715. Black. Arms with motto: *IN TE DOMINE SPERAMUS*. Back: Ornamental designs. Printer: Samuel Vernon.	—	—	—
S2660 2 Shillings 6 Pence 5.7.1715. Black. Arms with motto: *IN TE DOMINE SPERAMUS*. Back: Ornamental designs. Printer: Samuel Vernon.	—	—	—
S2661 3 Shillings 5.7.1715. Black. Arms with motto: *IN TE DOMINE SPERAMUS*. Back: Ornamental designs. Printer: Samuel Vernon.	—	—	—
S2662 4 Shillings 6 Pence 5.7.1715. Black. Arms with motto: *IN TE DOMINE SPERAMUS*. Back: Ornamental designs. Printer: Samuel Vernon.	—	—	—
S2663 5 Shillings 5.7.1715. Black. Arms with motto: *IN TE DOMINE SPERAMUS*. Back: Ornamental designs. Printer: Samuel Vernon.	—	—	—
S2664 10 Shillings 5.7.1715. Black. Arms with motto: *IN TE DOMINE SPERAMUS*. Back: Ornamental designs. Printer: Samuel Vernon.	—	—	—
S2665 20 Shillings 5.7.1715. Black. Arms with motto: *IN TE DOMINE SPERAMUS*. Back: Ornamental designs. Printer: Samuel Vernon.	—	—	—
S2666 40 Shillings 5.7.1715. Black. Arms with motto: *IN TE DOMINE SPERAMUS*. Back: Ornamental designs. Printer: Samuel Vernon.	—	—	—
S2667 3 Pounds 5.7.1715. Black. Arms with motto: *IN TE DOMINE SPERAMUS*. Back: Ornamental designs. Printer: Samuel Vernon.	—	—	—
S2668 5 Pounds 5.7.1715. Black. Arms with motto: *IN TE DOMINE SPERAMUS*. Back: Ornamental designs. Printer: Samuel Vernon.	—	—	—

1721 Redated Issue

	Good	Fine	XF
S2669 12 Pence 1721 (- old date 5.7.1715). Black.	—	—	—
S2670 2 Shillings 6 Pence 1721 (- old date 5.7.1715). Black.	—	—	—
S2671 3 Shillings 1721 (- old date 5.7.1715). Black.	—	—	—
S2672 4 Shillings 6 Pence 1721 (- old date 5.7.1715). Black.	—	—	—
S2673 5 Shillings 1721 (- old date 5.7.1715). Black.	—	—	—
S2674 10 Shillings 1721 (- old date 5.7.1715). Black.	—	—	—
S2675 20 Shillings 1721 (- old date 5.7.1715). Black.	—	—	—
S2676 40 Shillings 1721 (- old date 5.7.1715). Black.	—	—	—
S2677 3 Pounds 1721 (- old date 5.7.1715). Black.	—	—	—
	VG	**VF**	**UNC**
S2678 5 Pounds 1721 (- old date 5.7.1715). Black.	15,000.	—	—

1724 Redated Issue

	Good	Fine	XF
S2679 12 Pence 1724 (- old date 1721/5.7.1715). Black.	—	—	—
S2680 2 Shillings 6 Pence 1724. (- old date 1721/5.7.1715). Black.	—	—	—
S2681 3 Shillings 1724. (- old date 1721/5.7.1715). Black.	—	—	—
S2682 4 Shillings 6 Pence 1724. (- old date 1721/5.7.1715). Black.	—	—	—
S2683 5 Shillings 1724. (- old date 1721/5.7.1715). Black.	—	—	—
S2684 10 Shillings 1724. (- old date 1721/5.7.1715). Black.	—	—	—
S2685 20 Shillings 1724. (- old date 1721/5.7.1715). Black.	—	—	—
S2686 40 Shillings 1724. (- old date 1721/5.7.1715). Black.	—	—	—
S2687 3 Pounds 1724. (- old date 1721/5.7.1715). Black.	—	—	—
S2688 5 Pounds 1724. (- old date 1721/5.7.1715). Black.	—	—	—

1726 Redated Issue

	Good	Fine	XF
S2689 12 Pence 1726 (- old date 1724/21/5.7.1715). Black.	—	—	—
S2690 2 Shillings 1726 (- old date 1724/21/5.7.1715). Black.	—	—	—
S2691 3 Shillings 1726 (- old date 1724/21/5.7.1715). Black.	—	—	—
S2692 4 Shillings 6 Pence 1726 (- old date 1724/21/5.7.1715). Black.	—	—	—

1726 Issue

	Good	Fine	XF
S2693 5 Shillings 14.6.1726. Black. Back: Leaf and bird design.	—	—	—
S2694 10 Shillings 14.6.1726. Black. Back: Leaf and bird design.	—	—	—
S2695 20 Shillings 14.6.1726. Black. Back: Leaf and bird design.	—	—	—
S2696 40 Shillings 14.6.1726. Black. Back: Leaf and bird design.	—	—	—
S2697 3 Pounds 14.6.1726. Black. Back: Leaf and bird design.	—	—	—
S2698 5 Pounds 14.6.1726. Black. Back: Leaf and bird design.	—	—	—

1728 Redated Issue

Cat.	Denomination / Description	Good	Fine	XF
S2699	**12 Pence** 1728 (- old date 1726/24/21/5.7.1715). Black. Printer: Samuel Vernon.	—	—	—
S2700	**2 Shillings 6 Pence** 1728 (- old date 1726/24/21/5.7.1715). Black. Printer: Samuel Vernon.	—	—	—
		VG	VF	UNC
S2701	**3 Shillings** 1728 (- old date 1726/24/21/5.7.1715). Black. Printer: Samuel Vernon.	11,000.	—	—
S2702	**4 Shillings 6 Pence** 1728 (- old date 1726/24/21/5.7.1715). Black. Printer: Samuel Vernon.	—	—	—
S2703	**5 Shillings** 1728 (- old date 14.6.1726). Black. Printer: Samuel Vernon.	—	—	—
S2704	**10 Shillings** 1728 (- old date 14.6.1726). Black. Printer: Samuel Vernon.	—	—	—
S2705	**20 Shillings** 1728 (- old date 14.6.1726). Black. Printer: Samuel Vernon.	—	—	—
S2706	**40 Shillings** 1728 (- old date 14.6.1726). Black. Printer: Samuel Vernon.	—	—	—
S2707	**3 Pounds** 1728 (- old date 14.6.1726). Black. Printer: Samuel Vernon.	—	—	—
S2708	**5 Pounds** 1728 (- old date 14.6.1726). Black. Printer: Samuel Vernon.	—	—	—

1731 Redated Issue

Cat.	Denomination / Description	Good	Fine	XF
S2709	**12 Pence** 1731 (- old date 1728/26/24/21/5.7.1715). Black. Printer: Samuel Vernon.	—	—	—
S2710	**2 Shillings 6 Pence** 1731 (- old date 1728/26/24/21/5.7.1715). Black. Printer: Samuel Vernon.	—	—	—
S2711	**3 Shillings** 1731 (- old date 1728/26/24/21/5.7.1715). Black. Printer: Samuel Vernon.	—	—	—
S2712	**4 Shillings 6 Pence** 1731 (- old date 1728/26/24/21/5.7.1715). Black. Printer: Samuel Vernon.	—	—	—
S2713	**5 Shillings** 1731 (- old date 1728/14.6.1726). Black. Printer: Samuel Vernon.	—	—	—
S2714	**10 Shillings** 1731 (- old date 1728/14.6.1726). Black. Printer: Samuel Vernon.	—	—	—
S2715	**20 Shillings** 1731 (- old date 1728/14.6.1726). Black. Printer: Samuel Vernon.	—	—	—
S2716	**40 Shillings** 1731 (- old date 1728/14.6.1726). Black. Printer: Samuel Vernon.	—	—	—
S2717	**3 Pounds** 1731 (- old date 1728/14.6.1726). Black. Printer: Samuel Vernon.	—	—	—
S2718	**5 Pounds** 1731 (- old date 1728/14.6.1726). Black. Printer: Samuel Vernon.	—	—	—

1733 Redated Issue

Cat.	Denomination / Description	Good	Fine	XF
S2719	**12 Pence** 1733 (- old date 1731/28/26/24/21/5.7.1715). Black.	—	—	—
S2720	**2 Shillings 6 Pence** 1733 (- old date 1731/28/26/24/21/5.7.1715). Black.	—	—	—
S2721	**3 Shillings** 1733 (- old date 1731/28/26/24/21/5.7.1715). Black.	—	—	—
S2722	**4 Shillings 6 Pence** 1733 (- old date 1731/28/26/24/21/5.7.1715). Black.	—	—	—
S2723	**5 Shillings** 1733 (- old date 1731/28/14.6.1726). Black.	—	—	—
S2724	**10 Shillings** 1733 (- old date 1731/28/14.6.1726). Black.	—	—	—
S2725	**20 Shillings** 1733 (- old date 1731/28/14.6.1726). Black.	—	—	—
S2726	**40 Shillings** 1733 (- old date 1731/28/14.6.1726). Black.	—	—	—
S2727	**3 Pounds** 1733 (- old date 1731/28/14.6.1726). Black.	—	—	—
S2728	**5 Pounds** 1733 (- old date 1731/28/14.6.1726). Black.	—	—	—

1737 Redated Issue

Cat.	Denomination / Description	Good	Fine	XF
S2729	**12 Pence** 1737 (- old date 1733/11/5.7.1715). Black. Printer: Samuel Vernon.	—	—	—
S2730	**12 Shillings 6 Pence** 1737 (- old date 1733/11/5.7.1715). Black. Printer: Samuel Vernon.	—	13,000.	—
S2731	**3 Shillings** 1737 (- old date 1733/11/5.7.1715). Black. Printer: Samuel Vernon.	—	—	—
S2732	**4 Shillings 6 Pence** 1737 (- old date 1733/11/5.7.1715). Black. Printer: Samuel Vernon.	—	—	—

1737 Issue

Cat.	Denomination / Description	Good	Fine	XF
S2733	**1 Pound** 15.8.1737. Black. Printer: Samuel Vernon, Jr.	—	—	—
S2734	**2 Pounds** 15.8.1737. Black. Printer: Samuel Vernon, Jr.	—	—	—
		VG	VF	UNC
S2735	**3 Pounds** 15.8.1737. Black. Printer: Samuel Vernon, Jr.	8750.	—	—
S2736	**50 Pounds** 15.8.1737. Black. Printer: Samuel Vernon, Jr.	—	—	—

1738 Redated Issue

Cat.	Denomination / Description	Good	Fine	XF
S2737	**1 Pound** 1738 (- old date 15.8.1737). Black. Printer: William Claggett.	—	—	—
S2738	**2 Pounds** 1738 (- old date 15.8.1737). Black. Printer: William Claggett.	—	—	—
S2739	**3 Pounds** 1738 (- old date 15.8.1737). Black. Printer: William Claggett.	—	—	—
S2740	**5 Pounds** 1738 (- old date 15.8.1737). Black. Printer: William Claggett.	—	—	—

1738 Issue

Cat.	Denomination / Description	Good	Fine	XF
S2741	**1 Shilling** 22.8.1738. Black. Printer: William Claggett.	—	—	—
S2742	**2 Shillings 6 Pence** 22.8.1738. Black. Printer: William Claggett.	—	—	—
S2743	**3 Shillings** 22.8.1738. Black. Printer: William Claggett.	—	—	—
S2744	**5 Shillings 6 Pence** 22.8.1738. Black. Printer: William Claggett.	—	—	—
S2745	**7 Shillings 6 Pence - 1 Dollar** (Seaven) 22.8.1738. Black. Printer: William Claggett.	—	—	—
S2746	**10 Shillings** 22.8.1738. Black. Printer: William Claggett.	—	—	—

1740 Issue

Cat.	Denomination / Description	Good	Fine	XF
S2747	**6 Pence** 2.12.1740. Black. Printer: John Coddington.	—	—	—
S2748	**1 Shilling** 2.12.1740. Black. Printer: John Coddington.	—	—	—
S2749	**1 Shilling 6 Pence** 2.12.1740. Black. Printer: John Coddington.	—	—	—
		VG	VF	UNC
S2750	**2 Shilling 6 Pence** 2.12.1740. Black. Printer: John Coddington.	—	—	—
S2751	**5 Shillings** 2.12.1740. Black. Printer: John Coddington.	—	—	—
		Good	Fine	XF
S2752	**10 Shillings** 2.12.1740. Black. Printer: John Coddington.	5000.	—	—
S2753	**20 Shillings** 2.12.1740. Black. Printer: John Coddington.	—	—	—
S2754	**40 Shillings** 2.12.1740. Black. Printer: John Coddington.	—	—	—

1741-42 Issue

Cat.	Denomination / Description	Good	Fine	XF
S2755	**6 Pence** 2.2.1741/42. Black. Arms with motto: *IN TE DOMINE SPERAMUS.* Printer: William Claggett.	—	—	17,250.
S2756	**1 Shilling** 2.2.1741/42. Black. Arms with motto: *IN TE DOMINE SPERAMUS.* Printer: William Claggett.	—	—	—
S2757	**1 Shilling 6 Pence** 2.2.1741/42. Black. Arms with motto: *IN TE DOMINE SPERAMUS.* Printer: William Claggett.	—	—	—
		VG	VF	UNC
S2758	**2 Shillings 6 Pence** 2.2.1741/42. Black. Arms with motto: *IN TE DOMINE SPERAMUS.* Printer: William Claggett.	6250.	—	—
S2759	**5 Shillings** 2.2.1741/42. Black. Arms with motto: *IN TE DOMINE SPERAMUS.* Printer: William Claggett	—	—	—
S2760	**10 Shillings** 2.2.1741/42. Black. Arms with motto: *IN TE DOMINE SPERAMUS.* Printer: William Claggett.	—	—	—
S2761	**20 Shillings** 2.2.1741/42. Black. Arms with motto: *IN TE DOMINE SPERAMUS.* Two angels. Printer: William Claggett.	—	—	—
S2762	**40 Shillings** 2.2.1741/42. Black. Arms with motto: *IN TE DOMINE SPERAMUS.* Printer: William Claggett.	—	—	—

1743-44 Issue

Cat.	Denomination / Description	Good	Fine	XF
S2763	**4 Pence** 14.2.1743/44. Black.	—	—	—
S2764	**6 Pence** 14.2.1743/44. Black. *SPERAMUS* misspelled *SPEARMUS.*	—	—	—
S2765	**1 Shilling** 14.2.1743/44. Black.	—	7250.	—

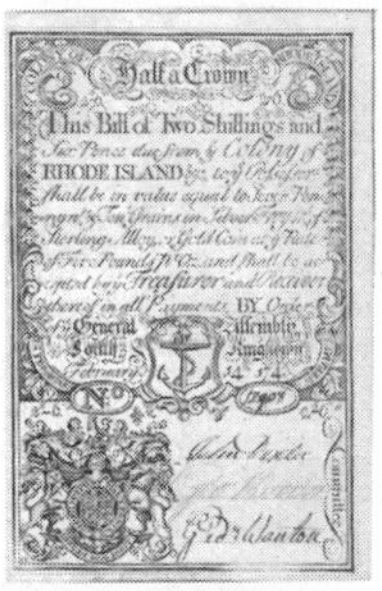

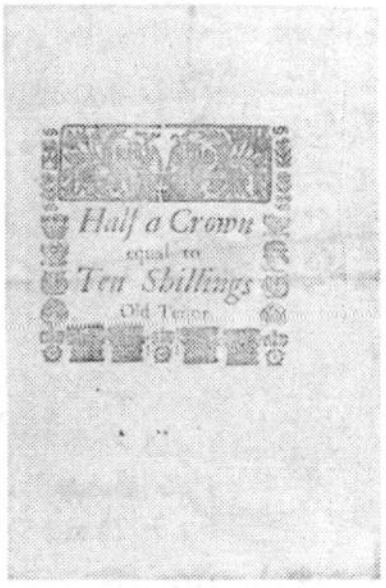

Cat.	Denomination / Description	Good	Fine	XF
S2766	**2 Shillings 6 Pence** 14.2.1743/44. Black.	—	—	—
S2767	**5 Shillings** 14.2.1743/44. Black.	—	—	—
S2768	**10 Shillings** 14.2.1743/44. Black.	—	—	—
S2769	**20 Shillings** 14.2.1743/44. Black.	—	—	—
S2770	**40 Shillings** 14.2.1743/44. Black.	—	—	—

1743/44 Redated Issues

Cat.	Denomination / Description	Good	Fine	XF
S2771	**5 Shillings** 1744/45 (- old date 14./2.1743/44). Black.	—	—	—
S2772	**10 Shillings** 1744/45 (- old date 14./2.1743/44). Black.	—	—	—
S2773	**20 Shillings** 1744/45 (- old date 14./2.1743/44). Black.	—	—	—
S2774	**40 Shillings** 1744/45 (- old date 14./2.1743/44). Black.	—	—	—
S2775	**5 Shillings** 1745 (- old date 14./2.1743/44). Black.	—	—	—

Catalog #	Description	Good	Fine	XF
S2776	**10 Shillings** 1745 (- old date 14./2.1743/44). Black.	—	—	—
S2777	**20 Shillings** 1745 (- old date 14./2.1743/44). Black.	—	—	—
S2778	**40 Shillings** 1745 (- old date 14./2.1743/44). Black.	—	—	—
S2779	**4 Pence** 1746 (- old date 14./2.1743/44). Black.	—	—	—
S2780	**6 Pence** 1746 (- old date 14./2.1743/44). Black.	—	—	—
		VG	**VF**	**UNC**
S2781	**1 Shilling** 1746 (- old date 14./2.1743/44). Black.	—	11,000.	—
S2782	**2 Shillings 6 Pence** 1746 (- old date 14./2.1743/44). Black.	—	—	—
S2783	**5 Shillings** 1746 (- old date 14./2.1743/44). Black.	—	—	—
S2784	**10 Shillings** 1746 (- old date 14./2.1743/44). Black.	—	—	—
S2785M	**20 Shillings** 1746 (- old date 14./2.1743/44). Black.	—	—	—
S2786	**40 Shillings** 1746 (- old date 14./2.1743/44). Black.	—	—	—
S2787	**4 Pence** 1746/47 (- old date 14./2.1743/44). Black.	—	—	—
S2788	**6 Pence** 1746/47 (- old date 14./2.1743/44). Black.	—	—	—
S2789	**1 Shilling** 1746/47 (- old date 14./2.1743/44). Black.	—	—	—
S2790	**2 Shillings 6 Pence** 1746/47 (- old date 14./2.1743/44). Black.	—	—	—
S2791	**5 Shillings** 1746/47 (- old date 14./2.1743/44). Black.	—	16,250.	—
S2792	**10 Shillings** 1746/47 (- old date 14./2.1743/44). Black.	—	—	—
S2793	**20 Shillings** 1746/47 (- old date 14./2.1743/44). Black.	—	—	—
S2794	**40 Shillings** 1746/47 (- old date 14./2.1743/44). Black.	—	—	—
S2795	**4 Pence** 1747/48 (- old date 14./2.1743/44). Black.	—	—	—
S2796	**6 Pence** 1747/48 (- old date 14./2.1743/14./2.1743/44). Black. *SPEARAMUS* spelling corrected.	—	—	—
S2797	**1 Shilling** 1747/48 (- old date 14./2.1743/44). Black.	—	—	—
S2798	**2 Shillings 6 Pence** 1747/48 (- old date 14./2.1743/44). Black.	—	—	—
S2799	**5 Shillings** 1747/48 (- old date 14./2.1743/44). Black.	—	—	—
S2800	**10 Shillings** 1747/48 (- old date 14./2.1743/44). Black.	—	—	—
S2801	**20 Shillings** 1747/48 (- old date 14./2.1743/44). Black.	—	—	—
S2802	**30 Shillings** 1747/48 (- old date 14./2.1743/44). Black.	—	—	—

1750-51 Sterling Silver Coin Issue

Catalog #	Description	Good	Fine	XF
S2803	**2 Shillings O.T.** 18.3.1750/51. Black. Back: Value in "Old Tenor."	—	5000.	—
S2804	**5 Shillings O.T.** 18.3.1750/51. Black. Back: Value in "Old Tenor."	—	—	—
S2805	**8 Shillings O.T.** 18.3.1750/51. Black. Back: Value in "Old Tenor."	—	—	—
		VG	**VF**	**UNC**
S2806	**1 Pound O.T.** 18.3.1750/51. Black. Back: Value in "Old Tenor."	7750.	—	—
		Good	**Fine**	**XF**
S2807	**2 Pounds O.T.** 18.3.1750/51. Black. Back: Value in "Old Tenor."	—	7750.	—
		VG	**VF**	**UNC**
S2808	**4 Pounds O.T.** 18.3.1750/51. Black. Back: Value in "Old Tenor."	—	1300.	—
S2809	**8 Pounds O.T.** 18.3.1750/51. Black. Back: Value in "Old Tenor."	—	—	—
S2810	**16 Pounds O.T.** 18.3.1750/51. Black. Back: Value in "Old Tenor."	—	—	—

1750/51 Redated Sterling Silver Coin Issue

Catalog #	Description	Good	Fine	XF
S2811	**2 Shillings O.T.** 1755 (- old date 18.3.1750/51). Black. Back: Value in "Old Tenor."	—	—	—
S2812	**5 Shillings O.T.** 1755 (- old date 18.3.1750/51). Black. Back: Value in "Old Tenor."	—	—	—
S2813	**8 Shillings O.T.** 1755 (- old date 18.3.1750/51). Black. Back: Value in "Old Tenor."	—	—	—
S2814	**1 Pound O.T.** 1755 (- old date 18.3.1750/51). Black. Back: Value in "Old Tenor."	—	—	—
S2815	**2 Pounds O.T.** 1755 (- old date 18.3.1750/51). Black. Back: Value in "Old Tenor."	—	—	—
S2816	**4 Pounds O.T.** 1755 (- old date 18.3.1750/51). 1755 redating omitted. Black. Back: Value in "Old Tenor."	—	—	—
S2817	**8 Pounds O.T.** 1755 (- old date 18.3.1750/51). Black. Back: Value in "Old Tenor."	—	—	—
S2818	**16 Pounds O.T.** 1755 (- old date 18.3.1750/51). Black. Back: Value in "Old Tenor."	—	—	—

1756 Issues

Catalog #	Description	Good	Fine	XF
S2819	**6 Pence** 27.2.1756. Black.	—	—	—
S2820	**9 Pence** 27.2.1756. Black.	—	—	—
S2821	**1 Shilling** 27.2.1756. Black.	—	—	—
S2822	**2 Shillings** 27.2.1756. Black.	—	—	—
S2823	**3 Shillings** 27.2.1756. Black.	—	—	—
S2824	**5 Shillings** 27.2.1756. Black.	—	—	—
S2825	**10 Shillings** 27.2.1756. Black.	—	—	—
S2826	**20 Shillings** 27.2.1756. Black.	—	—	—
S2827	**25 Shillings** 27.2.1756. Black.	—	—	—
S2828	**6 Pence** 8.1756. Black.	—	—	—
S2829	**9 Pence** 8.1756. Black.	—	—	—
S2830	**1 Shilling** 8.1756. Black.	—	—	—
S2831	**2 Shillings** 8.1756. Black.	—	—	—
S2832	**3 Shillings** 8.1756. Black.	—	—	—
S2833	**5 Shillings** 8.1756. Black.	—	—	—
S2834	**10 Shillings** 8.1756. Black.	—	—	—
S2835	**20 Shillings** 8.1756. Black.	—	—	—
S2836	**25 Shillings** 8.1756. Black.	—	—	—

1758 First Issue

Catalog #	Description	Good	Fine	XF
S2837	**6 Pence** 8.5.1758. Black.	—	—	—
S2838	**1 Shilling** 8.5.1758. Black.	—	—	—
S2839	**2 Shillings** 8.5.1758. Black.	—	—	—
S2840	**5 Shillings** 8.5.1758. Black.	—	—	—
S2841	**10 Shillings** 8.5.1758. Black.	—	—	—
S2842	**20 Shillings** 8.5.1758. Black.	—	—	—
S2843	**30 Shillings** 8.5.1758. Black.	—	—	—

1758 Second Issue Probably same denominations as 8.5.1758. Dated 23.12.1758.

#S2844-S2850 *Reserved.*

1759 Issues Probably same denominations as 8.5.1758. Dated 15.3.1759; 4.4.1759; 23.6.1759.

#S2851-S2858 *Reserved.*

1760 First Issue

Catalog #	Description	Good	Fine	XF
S2859	**6 Pence** 10.3.1760. Black.	—	—	—
S2860	**9 Pence** 10.3.1760. Black.	—	—	—
S2861	**1 Shilling** 10.3.1760. Black.	—	—	—
S2862	**2 Shillings** 10.3.1760. Black.	—	—	—
S2863	**5 Shillings** 10.3.1760. Black.	—	—	—
S2864	**10 Shillings** 10.3.1760. Black.	—	—	—
S2865	**20 Shillings** 10.3.1760. Black.	—	—	—
S2866	**30 Shillings** 10.3.1760. Black.	—	—	—

1760 Second Issue

Catalog #	Description	Good	Fine	XF
S2867	**5 Shillings** 12.5.1760. Black.	—	—	—
S2868	**10 Shillings** 12.5.1760. Black.	—	—	—
S2869	**20 Shillings** 12.5.1760. Black.	—	—	—
S2870	**30 Shillings** 12.5.1760. Black.	—	—	—

1762 First Issue

Catalog #	Description	Good	Fine	XF
S2871	**3 Pence** 20.3.1762. Black.	—	—	—
S2872	**6 Pence** 20.3.1762. Black.	—	—	—
S2873	**9 Pence** 20.3.1762. Black.	—	—	—
S2874	**1 Shilling** 20.3.1762. Black.	—	—	—
S2875	**2 Shillings** 20.3.1762. Black.	—	—	—
S2876	**5 Shillings** 20.3.1762. Black.	—	—	—
S2877	**10 Shillings** 20.3.1762. Black.	—	—	—
S2878	**20 Shillings** 20.3.1762. Black.	—	—	—
S2879	**30 Shillings** 20.3.1762. Black.	—	—	—

1762 Second Issue

		Good	Fine	XF
S2880	**5 Shillings** 10.4.1762. Black.	—	—	—
S2881	**10 Shillings** 10.4.1762. Black.	—	—	—
S2882	**20 Shillings** 10.4.1762. Black.	—	—	—
S2883	**30 Shillings** 10.4.1762. Black.	—	—	—

1762 Third Issue

		Good	Fine	XF
S2884	**5 Shillings** 8.5.1762. Black.	—	—	—
S2885	**10 Shillings** 8.5.1762. Black.	—	—	—
S2886	**20 Shillings** 8.5.1762. Black.	—	—	—
S2887	**30 Shillings** 8.5.1762. Black.	—	—	—

1762 Fourth Issue

		Good	Fine	XF
S2888	**3 Pence** 1.11.1762. Black.	—	—	—
S2889	**6 Pence** 1.11.1762. Black.	—	—	—
S2890	**9 Pence** 1.11.1762. Black.	—	—	—
S2891	**1 Shilling** 1.11.1762. Black.	—	—	—
S2892	**2 Shillings** 1.11.1762. Black.	—	—	—
S2893	**3 Shillings** 1.11.1762. Black.	—	—	—
S2894	**4 Shillings** 1.11.1762. Black.	—	—	—
S2895	**5 Shillings** 1.11.1762. Black.	—	—	—
S2896	**10 Shillings** 1.11.1762. Black.	—	—	—
S2897	**20 Shillings** 1.11.1762. Black.	—	—	—

1766 Issue

		Good	Fine	XF
S2898	**3 Pence** 1.3.1766. Black.	—	—	—
S2899	**6 Pence** 1.3.1766. Black.	—	—	—
S2900	**9 Pence** 1.3.1766. Black.	—	—	—
S2901	**1 Shilling** 1.3.1766. Black.	—	—	—
S2902	**2 Shillings** 1.3.1766. Black.	—	—	—
S2903	**3 Shillings** 1.3.1766. Black.	—	—	—
S2904	**5 Shillings** 1.3.1766. Black.	—	—	—

1767 Issue

		Good	Fine	XF
S2905	**4 Pence** 28.2.1767. Black.	—	—	15,000.
S2906	**8 Pence** 28.2.1767. Black.	—	—	—
S2907	**1 Shilling** 28.2.1767. Black.	—	—	—
S2908	**2 Shillings** 28.2.1767. Black.	—	—	—
S2909	**3 Shillings** 28.2.1767. Black.	—	—	—
S2910	**4 Shillings** 28.2.1767. Black.	—	—	—
S2911	**6 Shillings** 28.2.1767. Black.	—	—	—
S2912	**10 Shillings** 28.2.1767. Black.	—	—	—
S2913	**20 Shillings** 28.2.1767. Black.	—	—	—

1775 First Issue

No.	Denomination	VG	VF	UNC
S2914	**6 Pence** 3.5.1775. Black. Printer: John Carter.	1000.	2500.	—
S2915	**9 Pence** 3.5.1775. Black. Printer: John Carter.	1000.	2500.	—
S2916	**1 Shilling** 3.5.1775. Black. Printer: John Carter.	1000.	2500.	—
S2917	**2 Shillings** 3.5.1775. Black. Printer: John Carter.	1000.	2500.	—
S2918	**3 Shillings** 3.5.1775. Black. Printer: John Carter.	1000.	2500.	—
S2919	**4 Shillings** 3.5.1775. Black. Printer: John Carter.	1000.	2500.	—
S2920	**5 Shillings** 3.5.1775. Black. Printer: John Carter.	1000.	2500.	—
S2921	**10 Shillings** 3.5.1775. Black. Printer: John Carter.	1000.	2500.	—
S2922	**20 Shillings** 3.5.1775. Black. Printer: John Carter.	1000.	2500.	—
S2923	**30 Shillings** 3.5.1775. Black. Printer: John Carter.	1000.	2500.	—
S2924	**40 Shillings** 3.5.1775. Black. Printer: John Carter.	1000.	2500.	—

1775 Second Issue

No.	Denomination	VG	VF	UNC
S2925	**6 Pence** 16.6.1775. Black.	1000.	2500.	—
S2926	**9 Pence** 16.6.1775. Black.	1000.	2500.	—
S2927	**1 Shilling** 16.6.1775. Black.	1000.	2500.	—
S2928	**2 Shillings** 16.6.1775. Black.	1000.	2500.	—
S2929	**3 Shillings** 16.6.1775. Black.	1000.	2500.	—
S2930	**4 Shillings** 16.6.1775. Black.	1000.	2500.	—
S2931	**5 Shillings** 16.6.1775. Black.	1000.	2500.	—
S2932	**10 Shillings** 16.6.1775. Black.	1000.	2500.	—
S2933	**20 Shillings** 16.6.1775. Black.	1000.	2500.	—
S2934	**30 Shillings** 16.6.1775. Black.	1000.	2500.	—
S2935	**40 Shillings** 16.6.1775. Black.	1000.	2500.	—

1775 Third Issue

No.	Denomination	VG	VF	UNC
S2936	**6 Pence** 29.6.1775. Black.	1000.	2500.	—
S2937	**9 Pence** 29.6.1775. Black.	1000.	2500.	—
S2938	**1 Shilling** 29.6.1775. Black.	1000.	2500.	—
S2939	**2 Shillings** 29.6.1775. Black.	1000.	2500.	—
S2940	**3 Shillings** 29.6.1775. Black.	1000.	2500.	—
S2941	**4 Shillings** 29.6.1775. Black.	1000.	2500.	—
S2942	**5 Shillings** 29.6.1775. Black.	1000.	2500.	—
S2943	**10 Shillings** 29.6.1775. Black.	1000.	2500.	—
S2944	**20 Shillings** 29.6.1775. Black.	1000.	2500.	—
S2945	**30 Shillings** 29.6.1775. Black.	1000.	2500.	—
S2946	**40 Shillings** 29.6.1775. Black.	1000.	2500.	—

1775 Fourth Issue

No.	Denomination	VG	VF	UNC
S2947	**6 Pence** 6.11.1775. Black.	1000.	2500.	—
S2948	**9 Pence** 6.11.1775. Black.	1000.	2500.	—
S2949	**1 Shilling** 6.11.1775. Black.	1000.	2500.	—
S2950	**2 Shillings** 6.11.1775. Black.	1000.	2500.	—
S2951	**3 Shillings** 6.11.1775. Black.	1000.	2500.	—
S2952	**5 Shillings** 6.11.1775. Black.	1000.	2500.	—
S2953	**10 Shillings** 6.11.1775. Black.	1000.	2500.	—
S2954	**20 Shillings** 6.11.1775. Black.	1000.	2500.	—
S2955	**30 Shillings** 6.11.1775. Black.	1000.	2500.	—
S2956	**40 Shillings** 6.11.1775. Black.	1500.	3000.	—

1776 Issue

No.	Denomination	VG	VF	UNC
S2957	**6 Pence** 15.1.1776. Black. Printer: John Carter.	1000.	2500.	—
S2958	**9 Pence** 15.1.1776. Black. Printer: John Carter.	1000.	2500.	—
S2959	**1 Shilling** 15.1.1776. Black. Printer: John Carter.	1000.	2500.	—
S2960	**2 Shillings** 15.1.1776. Black. Printer: John Carter.	1000.	2500.	—
S2961	**3 Shillings** 15.1.1776. Black. Printer: John Carter.	1000.	2500.	—
S2962	**4 Shillings** 15.1.1776. Black. Printer: John Carter.	1000.	2500.	—
S2963	**5 Shillings** 15.1.1776. Black. Printer: John Carter.	1000.	2500.	—
S2964	**10 Shillings** 15.1.1776. Black. Printer: John Carter.	1000.	2500.	—
S2965	**20 Shillings** 15.1.1776. Black. Printer: John Carter.	1000.	2500.	—
S2966	**30 Shillings** 15.1.1776. Black. Printer: John Carter.	1000.	2500.	—
S2967	**40 Shillings** 15.1.1776. Black. Printer: John Carter.	1000.	2500.	—
S2968	**60 Shillings** 15.1.1776. Black. Printer: John Carter.	—	—	—

Rhode Island

State

1776 First Issue

	VG	VF	UNC
S2969 9 Pence 18.3.1776. Black. Printer: John Carter.	1000.	2250.	—
S2970 1 Shilling 18.3.1776. Black. Printer: John Carter.	1000.	2250.	—
S2971 2 Shillings 18.3.1776. Black. Printer: John Carter.	1000.	2250.	—
S2972 3 Shillings 18.3.1776. Black. Printer: John Carter.	1000.	2250.	—
S2973 4 Shillings 18.3.1776. Black. Printer: John Carter.	1000.	2250.	—
S2974 5 Shillings 18.3.1776. Black. Printer: John Carter.	1000.	2250.	—
S2975 10 Shillings 18.3.1776. Black. Printer: John Carter.	1000.	2250.	—
S2976 20 Shillings 18.3.1776. Black. Printer: John Carter.	1000.	2250.	—
S2977 30 Shillings 18.3.1776. Black. Printer: John Carter.	1000.	2250.	—
S2978 40 Shillings 18.3.1776. Black. Uniface. Printer: John Carter.	1000.	2250.	—
S2979 60 Shillings 18.3.1776. Black. Uniface. Printer: John Carter.	—	—	—

1776 Second Issue

	VG	VF	UNC
S2980 1/16 Dollar 5.9.1776. Black. Uniface. Printer: John Carter.	500.	1500.	—
S2981 1/8 Dollar 5.9.1776. Black. Uniface. Printer: John Carter.	500.	1500.	—

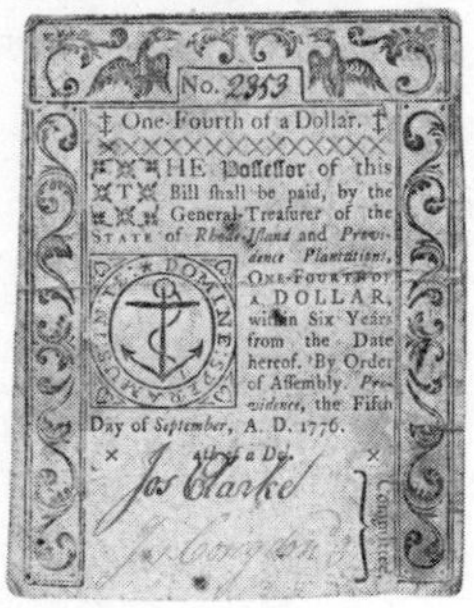

	VG	VF	UNC
S2982 1/4 Dollar 5.9.1776. Black. Printer: John Carter.	500.	1500.	—
S2983 1/2 Dollar 5.9.1776. Black. Printer: John Carter.	500.	1500.	—
S2984 1 Dollar 5.9.1776. Black. Printer: John Carter.	1000.	2500.	—
S2985 2 Dollars 5.9.1776. Black. Printer: John Carter.	1000.	2500.	—
S2986 3 Dollars 5.9.1776. Black. Printer: John Carter.	1000.	2500.	—
S2987 4 Dollars 5.9.1776. Black. Printer: John Carter.	1000.	2500.	—
S2988 5 Dollars 5.9.1776. Black. Printer: John Carter.	1000.	2500.	—
S2989 6 Dollars 5.9.1776. Black. Printer: John Carter.	1000.	2500.	—
S2990 7 Dollars 5.9.1776. Black. Printer: John Carter.	1000.	2500.	—
S2991 8 Dollars 5.9.1776. Black. Printer: John Carter.	1000.	2500.	—
S2992 10 Dollars 5.9.1776. Black. Printer: John Carter.	1000.	2500.	—
S2993 20 Dollars 5.9.1776. Black. Printer: John Carter.	1000.	2500.	—

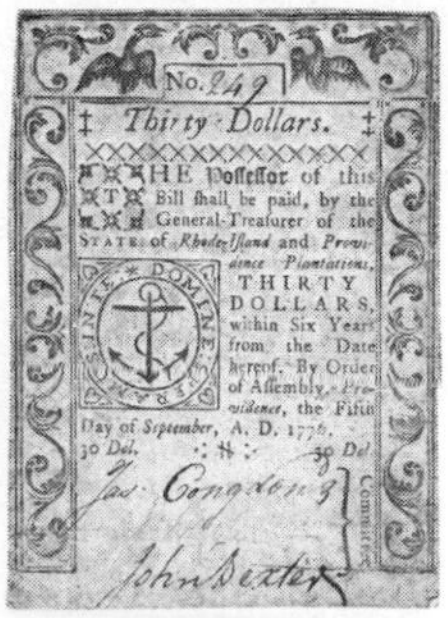

	VG	VF	UNC
S2994 30 Dollars 5.9.1776. Black. Printer: John Carter.	1000.	2500.	—

1777 First Issue

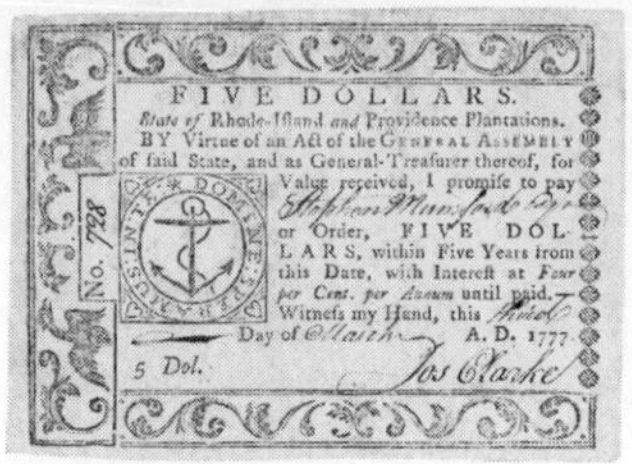

	Good	Fine	XF
S2995 5 Dollars 1777. Black. Handwritten date.	—	—	—
S2996 6 Dollars 1777. Black. Handwritten date.	—	—	—
S2997 7 Dollars 1777. Black. Handwritten date.	—	—	—

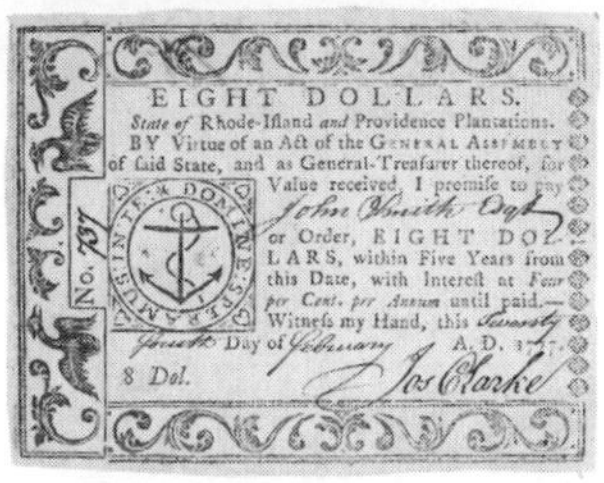

	Good	Fine	XF
S2998 8 Dollars 1777. Black. Handwritten date.	—	—	—

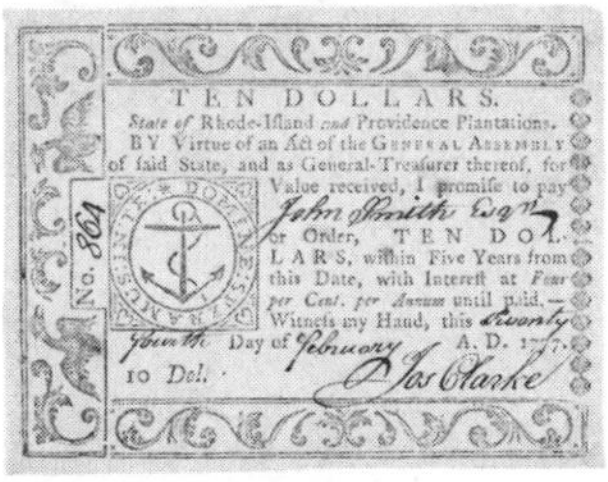

	Good	Fine	XF
S2999 10 Dollars 1777. Black. Handwritten date.	—	—	—
S3000 20 Dollars 1777. Black. Handwritten date.	—	—	—
S3001 30 Dollars 1777. Black. Handwritten date.	—	—	—

1777 Second Issue

	VG	VF	UNC
S3002 1/36 Dollar 1777. Black.	200.	750.	—
S3003 1/24 Dollar 1777. Black.	200.	750.	—
S3004 1/18 Dollar 1777. Black.	200.	750.	—
S3005 1/12 Dollar 1777. Black.	200.	750.	—
S3006 1/9 Dollar 1777. Black.	200.	750.	—
S3007 1/8 Dollar 1777. Black.	200.	750.	—
S3008 1/6 Dollar 1777. Black.	200.	750.	—
S3009 1/4 Dollar 1777. Black.	200.	750.	—
S3010 1/3 Dollar 1777. Black.	250.	1000.	—

1778-79 Issue

	Good	Fine	XF
S3011 10 Pounds Black. Handwritten date.	—	3250.	—

1780 First Issue

	Good	Fine	XF
S3012 6 Pence 6.1780. Black. Printer: B. Wheeler.	—	—	—
S3013 9 Pence 6.1780. Black. Printer: B. Wheeler.	—	—	—
S3014 1 Shilling 6.1780. Black. Printer: B. Wheeler.	—	—	—
S3015 2 Shillings 6.1780. Black. Printer: B. Wheeler.	—	—	—
S3016 3 Shillings 6.1780. Black. Printer: B. Wheeler.	—	—	—
S3017 4 Shillings 6.1780. Black. Printer: B. Wheeler.	—	—	—
S3018 6 Shillings 6.1780. Black. Printer: B. Wheeler.	—	—	—

	VG	VF	UNC
S3019 9 Shillings 6.1780. Black. Printer: B. Wheeler. Issued but not authorized.	—	14,000.	—

	Good	Fine	XF
S3020 10 Shillings 6.1780. Black. Printer: B. Wheeler.	—	—	—

	VG	VF	UNC
S3021 20 Shillings 6.1780. Black. Printer: B. Wheeler.	—	13,000.	—
S3022 30 Shillings 6.1780. Black. Printer: B. Wheeler.	—	—	—
S3023 40 Shillings 6.1780. Black. Printer: B. Wheeler.	—	—	—

1780 Second Issue

	VG	VF	UNC
S3024 1 Dollar 2.7.1780. Black. Back: Red and black. Printer: David Hall and William Sellers.	125.	150.	250.
S3025 2 Dollars 2.7.1780. Black. Back: Red and black. Printer: David Hall and William Sellers.	125.	150.	250.
S3026 3 Dollars 2.7.1780. Black. Back: Red and black. Printer: David Hall and William Sellers.	125.	150.	250.

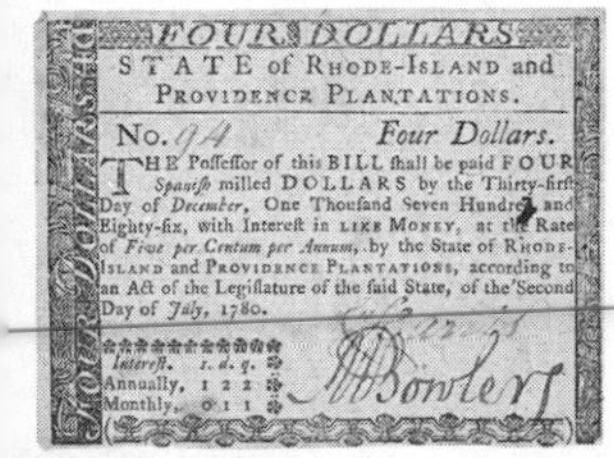

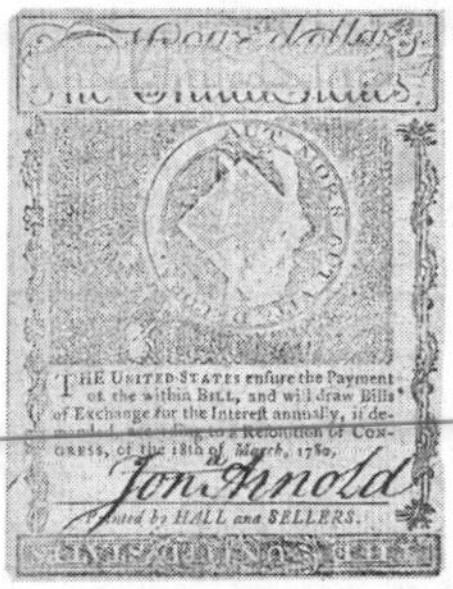

	VG	VF	UNC
S3027 4 Dollars 2.7.1780. Black. Back: Red and black. Printer: David Hall and William Sellers.	125.	150.	250.
S3028 5 Dollars 2.7.1780. Black. Back: Red and black. Printer: David Hall and William Sellers.	125.	150.	250.
S3029 7 Dollars 2.7.1780. Black. Back: Red and black. Printer: David Hall and William Sellers.	125.	150.	250.

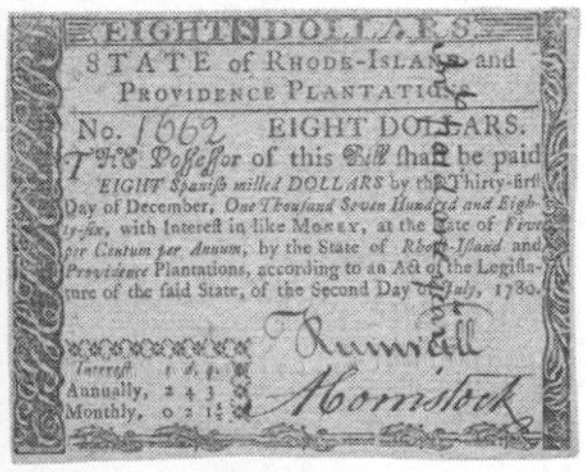

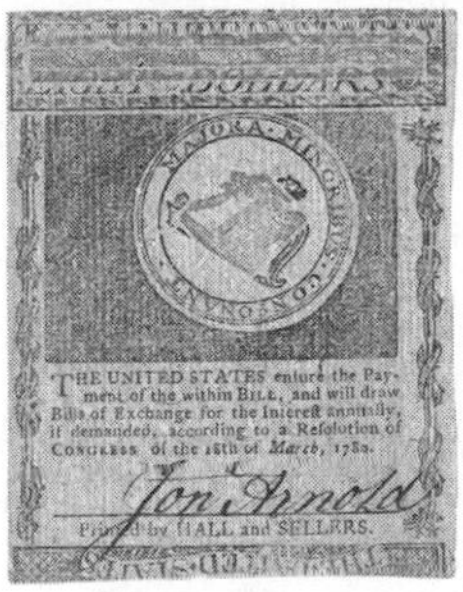

	VG	VF	UNC
S3030 8 Dollars 2.7.1780. Black. Back: Red and black. Printer: David Hall and William Sellers.	125.	150.	250.
S3031 20 Dollars 2.7.1780. Black. Back: Red and black. Printer: David Hall and William Sellers.	135.	180.	300.

1786 Issue

	VG	VF	UNC
S3032 6 Pence 5.1786. Black. Printer: Southwick and Barber.	50.00	75.00	125.
S3033 9 Pence 5.1786. Black. Printer: Southwick and Barber.	50.00	75.00	125.
S3034 1 Shilling 5.1786. Black. Printer: Southwick and Barber.	50.00	75.00	125.
S3035 2 Shillings 6 Pence 5.1786. Black. Printer: Southwick and Barber.	50.00	75.00	125.

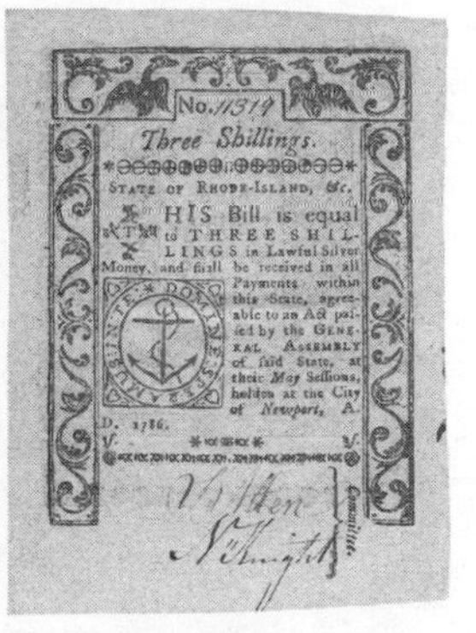

	VG	VF	UNC
S3036 3 Shillings 5.1786. Black. Printer: Southwick and Barber.	50.00	75.00	125.
S3037 5 Shillings 5.1786. Black. Printer: Southwick and Barber.	60.00	80.00	225.
S3038 6 Shillings 5.1786. Black. Printer: Southwick and Barber.	60.00	80.00	225.
S3039 10 Shillings 5.1786. Black. Printer: Southwick and Barber.	60.00	80.00	225.
S3040 20 Shillings 5.1786. Black. Printer: Southwick and Barber.	60.00	80.00	225.
S3041 30 Shillings 5.1786. Black. Printer: Southwick and Barber.	60.00	80.00	225.

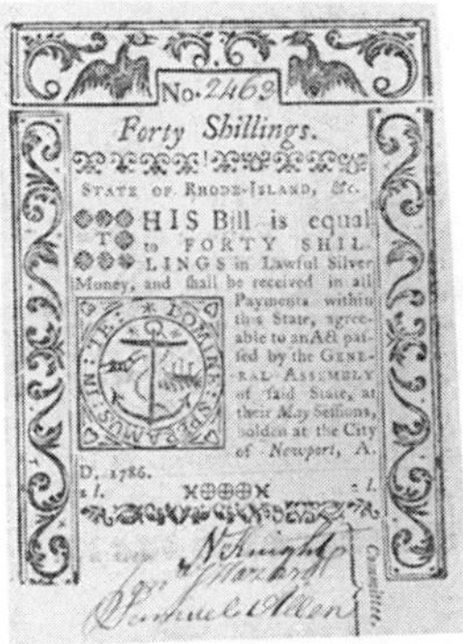

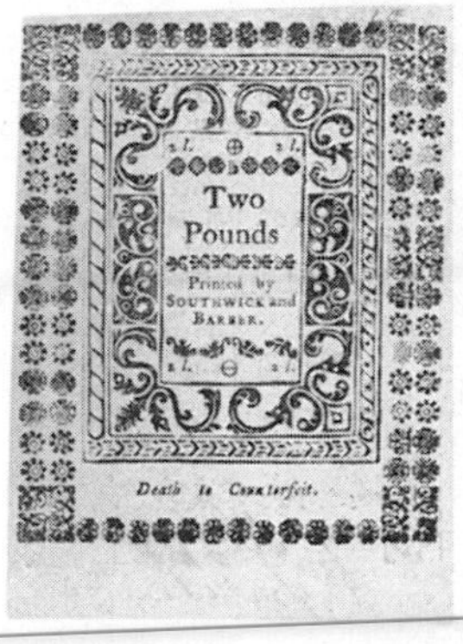

	VG	VF	UNC
S3042 40 Shillings 5.1786. Black. Printer: Southwick and Barber. Vertical format.	60.00	80.00	225.

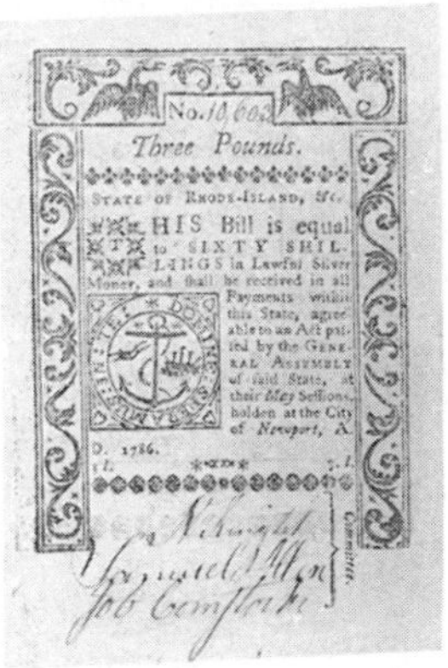

	VG	VF	UNC
S3043 3 Pounds 5.1786. Black. Printer: Southwick and Barber. Vertical format.	70.00	100.	200.

South Carolina

Colonial

1703 Issue

	Good	Fine	XF
S3101 50 Shillings 8.5.1703. Black. Engraver: Joseph Massey.	—	—	—
S3110 20 Pounds 8.5.1703. Black. Engraver: Joseph Massey.	—	—	—

1707 Issue

	Good	Fine	XF
S3111 20 Shillings 5.7.1707. Black.	—	—	—
S3112 40 Shillings 5.7.1707. Black.	—	—	—
S3116 4 Pounds 5.7.1707. Black.	—	—	—
S3120 10 Pounds 5.7.1707. Black.	—	—	—
S3121 20 Pounds 5.7.1707. Black.	—	—	—
S3122 20 Shillings 14.2.1707. Black.	—	—	—

1708 Issue

	Good	Fine	XF
S3123 20 Shillings 24.4.1708. Black.	—	—	—
S3124 40 Shillings 24.4.1708. Black.	—	—	—

1710 Issue

	Good	Fine	XF
S3125 5 Shillings 1.3.1710. Black.	—	—	—
S3126 10 Shillings 1.3.1710. Black.	—	—	—

Act of 10.11.1711; 1712 Issue

	Good	Fine	XF
S3131 5 Shillings 7.6.1712. Black.	—	—	—
S3135 20 Pounds 7.6.1712. Black.	—	—	—

1715 Issue

No.	Denomination	Good	Fine	XF
S3140	**4 Pounds** 27.8.1715. Black.	—	—	—

1716 Issue

No.	Denomination	Good	Fine	XF
S3145	**5 Pounds** 30.6.1716. Black.	—	—	—
S3147	**20 Pounds** 30.6.1716. Black.	—	—	—

1723 Issue

No.	Denomination	Good	Fine	XF
S3161	**5 Shillings** 1723. Black. Crown above rose. Printer: Joseph Massey.	—	—	—
S3162	**6 Shillings 6 Pence** 1723. Black. Crown above plume. Printer: Joseph Massey.	—	—	—
S3163	**7 Shillings 6 Pence - 1 Dollar** 1723. Black. Printer: Joseph Massey.	—	—	—
S3164	**10 Shillings** 1723. Black. Plum with motto: *ICH DIEN.* Printer: Joseph Massey.	—	—	—
S3165	**1 Pound** 1723. Black. Printer: Joseph Massey.	—	—	—
S3166	**2 Pounds** 1723. Black. Printer: Joseph Massey.	—	—	—
S3167	**4 Pounds** 1723. Black. Printer: Joseph Massey.	—	—	—
S3168	**6 Pounds** 1723. Black. Printer: Joseph Massey.	—	—	—
S3169	**8 Pounds** 1723. Black. Printer: Joseph Massey.	—	—	—
S3170	**12 Pounds** 1723. Black. Printer: Joseph Massey.	—	—	—
S3171	**15 Pounds** 1723. Black. Printer: Joseph Massey.	—	—	—
S3172	**20 Pounds** 1723. Black. Printer: Joseph Massey.	—	—	—

1731 Issues

No.	Denomination	Good	Fine	XF
S3173	**4 Shillings 6 Pence** 1731. Black.	—	—	—
S3174	**5 Shillings** 1731. Black.	—	—	—
S3175	**7 Shillings 6 Pence - 1 Dollar** 1731. Black. Thistle.	—	—	—
S3176	**20 Shillings** 1731. Black.	—	—	—
S3177	**2 Pounds** 1731. Black.	—	—	—
S3178	**3 Pounds** 1731. Black.	—	—	—
S3179	**4 Pounds** 1731. Black.	—	—	—
S3180	**6 Pounds 5 Shillings** 1731. Black.	—	—	—
S3181	**10 Pounds** 1731. Black. Deer.	—	—	50,000.
S3182	**12 Pounds 10 Shillings** 1731. Black.	—	—	—
S3183	**15 Pounds** 1731. Black.	—	—	—
S3184	**20 Pounds** 1731. Black.	—	—	—
S3185	**5 Pounds** 20.8.1731. Black.	—	—	—
S3186	**6 Pounds 5 Shillings** 20.8.1731. Black.	—	—	—
S3187	**12 Pounds 10 Shillings** 20.8.1731. Black.	—	—	—
S3188	**25 Pounds** 20.8.1731. Black.	—	—	—
S3189	**50 Pounds** 20.8.1731. Black.	—	—	—

1736 Issue

No.	Denomination	Good	Fine	XF
S3190	**6 Pounds** 5.3.1736. Black.	—	—	—
S3191	**12 Pounds** 5.3.1736. Black.	—	—	—

1740 First Issue

No.	Denomination	Good	Fine	XF
S3192	**4 Pounds** 5.4.1740. Black.	—	—	—
S3193	**8 Pounds** 5.4.1740. Black.	—	—	—

1740 Second Issue

No.	Denomination	Good	Fine	XF
S3194	**4 Pounds** 19.9.1740. Black.	—	—	—
S3195	**8 Pounds** 19.9.1740. Black.	—	—	—

1748 Issue

No.	Denomination	Good	Fine	XF
S3196	**2 Shillings 6 Pence** 30.6.1748. Black.	—	—	—
S3197	**5 Shillings** 30.6.1748. Black.	—	—	—
S3198	**6 Shillings 3 Pence** 30.6.1748. Black.	—	—	—
S3199	**7 Shillings 6 Pence - 1 Dollar** 30.6.1748. Black.	—	—	—
S3200	**10 Shillings** 30.6.1748. Black.	—	—	—
S3201	**1 Pound** 30.6.1748. Black. Horse.	—	—	—
S3202	**2 Pounds** 30.6.1748. Black.	—	—	—

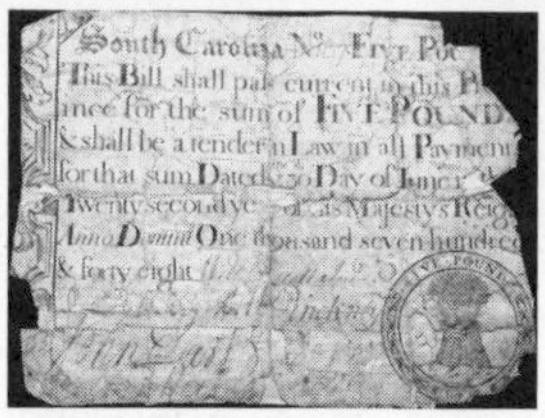

No.	Denomination	Good	Fine	XF
S3203	**5 Pounds** 30.6.1748. Black. Sheaf.	—	—	—
S3204	**10 Pounds** 30.6.1748. Black. Deer.	—	—	—
S3205	**20 Pounds** 30.6.1748. Black. Lion on crown.	—	—	—

NOTE: Illustration of #S3201 is that of a reprint.

1750-69 Issue

No.	Denomination	Good	Fine	XF
S3206	**5 Pounds** 1750-69. Black. Various handwritten dates. Back: Elaborately engraved with *JACOB MOTTE P. TREASURER.*	—	—	—
S3207	**10 Pounds** 1750-69. Black. Various handwritten dates. Back: Elaborately engraved with *JACOB MOTTE P. TREASURER.*	—	—	—
S3208	**20 Pounds** 1750-69. Black. Various handwritten dates. Back: Elaborately engraved with *JACOB MOTTE P. TREASURER.*	—	—	—
S3209	**30 Pounds** 1750-69. Black. Various handwritten dates. Back: Elaborately engraved with *JACOB MOTTE P. TREASURER.*	—	—	—
		VG	**VF**	**UNC**
S3210	**50 Pounds** 1750-69. Black. Various handwritten dates. Back: Elaborately engraved with *JACOB MOTTE P. TREASURER.*	3250.	—	—

1752 Issue

No.	Denomination	Good	Fine	XF
S3211	**5 Shillings** 16.5.1752. Black.	—	—	—
S3212	**6 Shillings 3 Pence** 16.5.1752. Black.	—	—	—
S3213	**1 Pound** 16.5.1752. Black.	—	—	—
S3214	**2 Pounds** 16.5.1752. Black.	—	—	—
S3215	**5 Pounds** 16.5.1752. Black.	—	—	—
S3216	**10 Pounds** 16.5.1752. Black.	—	—	—

1757 Issue

No.	Denomination	Good	Fine	XF
S3217	**10 Pounds** 6.7.1757. Black.	—	—	—
		VG	**VF**	**UNC**
S3218	**20 Pounds** 6.7.1757. Black.	7500.	—	—

1760 Issue

No.	Denomination	Good	Fine	XF
S3219	**25 Pounds** 1760. *DEBELLARE BARBAROS RENOVA ANIMUM* around seal.	—	—	—
S3220	**50 Pounds** 1760.	—	—	—
S3221	**20 Pounds** 1760. Black. *SUME EX SCELERATO SANGUINE POENAM* around and *INFRACTO FOEDERE* within seal. Issued primarily for expenses of Middleton's Regiment.	—	—	—

1761 Issue

No.	Denomination	Good	Fine	XF
S3222	**2 Shillings 6 Pence** 25.7.1761. Black.	—	—	—
S3223	**5 Shillings** 25.7.1761. Black.	—	—	—
S3224	**7 Shillings 6 Pence - 1 Dollar** 25.7.1761. Black.	—	—	—
S3225	**10 Shillings** 25.7.1761. Black.	—	—	—
S3226	**1 Pound** 25.7.1761. Black.	—	—	—

1762 Issue

No.	Denomination	Good	Fine	XF
S3227	**2 Pounds** 29.5.1762. Black.	—	—	—

1770 Issue

No.	Denomination	Good	Fine	XF
S3228	**2 Shillings 6 Pence** 1.1.1770. Black.	—	—	—
S3229	**5 Shillings** 1.1.1770. Black.	—	—	—
		VG	**VF**	**UNC**
S3230	**6 Shillings 3 Pence** 1.1.1770. Black.	—	4750.	—
S3231	**7 Shillings 6 Pence - 1 Dollar** 1.1.1770. Black.	—	—	—

	Good	Fine	XF
S3232 10 Shillings 1.1.1770. Black.	—	—	—
S3233 1 Pound 1.1.1770. Black.	—	—	—
S3234 2 Pounds 1.1.1770. Black.	—	—	—
S3235 5 Pounds 1.1.1770. Black.	1750.	—	—
S3236 10 Pounds 1.1.1770. Black. Stag.	1500.	—	—
S3237 20 Pounds 1.1.1770. Black. Lion on crown.	—	—	—

1775 Issue

	VG	VF	UNC
S3238 2 Shillings 6 Pence 15.11.1775. Black. Printer: James Oliphant.	500.	1500.	—
S3239 5 Shillings 15.11.1775. Black. Printer: James Oliphant.	500.	1500.	—
S3240 7 Shillings 6 Pence - 1 Dollar 15.11.1775. Black. Printer: James Oliphant.	500.	1500.	—
S3241 10 Shillings 15.11.1775. Black. Printer: James Oliphant.	500.	1500.	—
S3242 15 Shillings 15.11.1775. Black. Printer: James Oliphant.	500.	1500.	—
S3243 20 Shillings 15.11.1775. Black. Printer: James Oliphant.	500.	1500.	—
S3244 30 Shillings 15.11.1775. Black. Printer: James Oliphant.	500.	1500.	—
S3245 2 Pounds 15.11.1775. Black. *UTRUM HORUM MAVIS ACCIPE.* Printer: James Oliphant.	750.	2250.	—

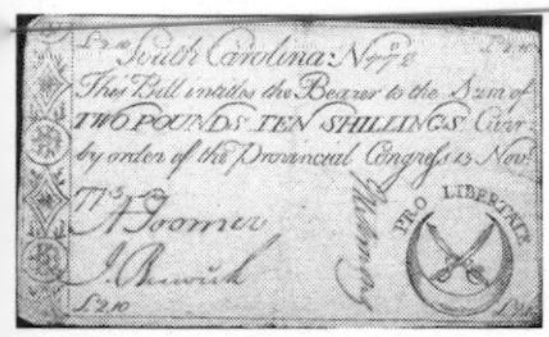

	VG	VF	UNC
S3246 2 Pounds 10 Shillings 15.11.1775. Black. *PRO LIBERTATE.* Printer: James Oliphant.	1000.	3000.	—
S3247 3 Pounds 15.11.1775. Black. *ULTIMA RATIO.* Printer: James Oliphant.	1000.	3000.	—

1776 Issue

	VG	VF	UNC
S3248 1 Shilling 3 Pence 6.3.1776. Red and black. Printer: Peter Timothy.	1000.	3500.	—
S3249 2 Shillings 6 Pence 6.3.1776. Red and black. Printer: Peter Timothy.	1000.	3500.	—
S3250 3 Shillings 9 Pence 6.3.1776. Red and black. Printer: Peter Timothy.	1000.	3500.	—
S3251 5 Shillings 6.3.1776. Red and black. Printer: Peter Timothy.	1000.	3500.	—
S3252 6 Shillings 3 Pence 6.3.1776. Red and black. Printer: Peter Timothy.	1000.	3500.	—
S3253 12 Shillings 6 Pence 6.3.1776. Red and black. Printer: Peter Timothy.	1000.	3500.	—
S3254 17 Shillings 6 Pence 6.3.1776. Red and black. Printer: Peter Timothy.	1000.	3500.	—
S3255 1 Pound 6.3.1776. Red and black. Printer: Peter Timothy.	1000.	3500.	—
S3256 1 Pound 15 Shillings 6.3.1776. Red and black. Printer: Peter Timothy.	1000.	3500.	—
S3257 2 Pounds 6.3.1776. Red and black. Printer: Peter Timothy.	1000.	3500.	—
S3258 2 Pounds 5 Shillings 6.3.1776. Red and black. Printer: Peter Timothy.	1000.	3500.	—
S3259 3 Pounds 6.3.1776. Red and black. Printer: Peter Timothy.	1000.	3500.	—
S3260 15 Pounds 6.3.1776. Black. Rattlesnake attacking British lion. *MAGNIS INTERDUM PARVA NOCENT* and *hite.* Paper: Bluish. Printer: Peter Timothy.	750.	2500.	—
S3261 25 Pounds 6.3.1776. Black. Flourishing tree and fallen tree. *MELIOREM LAPSA LOCAVIT* and *hite.* Paper: Bluish. Printer: Peter Timothy.	1000.	—	—
S3262 50 Pounds 6.3.1776. Black. Trophies. *ANIMIS OPIBUSQUE PARATI* and *hite.* Paper: Bluish. Printer: Peter Timothy.	1000.	—	—
S3263 100 Pounds 6.3.1776. Black. 13 hearts. *QUIS SEPARABIT* and *hite.* Paper: Bluish. Printer: Peter Timothy.	4000.	—	—

South Carolina

State

1776 First Issue

	VG	VF	UNC
S3264 1 Dollar 19.10.1776. Black. Palm tree. *NUSQUAM SUB MOLE FATISCIT.* Paper: Thick brownish. Printer: Peter Timothy.	250.	1000.	—
S3265 2 Dollars 19.10.1776. Black. Tree. *SE SUSTULIT IPSA.* Paper: Thick brownish. Printer: Peter Timothy.	250.	1000.	—
S3266 4 Dollars 19.10.1776. Black. Elephant. *INFESTUS TANTUM INFESTIS.* Paper: Thick brownish. Printer: Peter Timothy.	250.	1000.	—

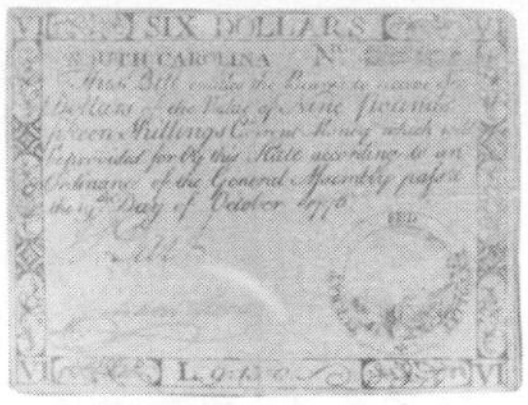

	VG	VF	UNC
S3267 6 Dollars 19.10.1776. Black. Wind and waves. *TURBAT SED EXTOLLIT.* Paper: Thick brownish. Printer: Peter Timothy.	250.	1000.	—
S3268 8 Dollars 19.10.1776. Black. Wind on rock. *IMPAVIDE.* Paper: Thick brownish. Printer: Peter Timothy.	250.	1000.	—
S3269 10 Dollars 19.10.1776. Black. Drums and flags. *TUTA PEDAMINE VIRTUS.* Paper: Thick brownish. Printer: Peter Timothy.	250.	1000.	—

1776 Second Issue

	VG	VF	UNC
S3270 1 Dollar 23.12.1776. Black. Tree. *PER ARDUA SURGO.* Paper: Thick brownish. Printer: Peter Timothy.	100.	375.	1500.
S3271 2 Dollars 23.12.1776. Black. Rooster. *ET SOLIET MARTI.* Paper: Thick brownish. Printer: Peter Timothy.			
a. Regular date.	90.00	375.	1500.
b. Text on face is misdated December 23, 1777.	90.00	375.	1500.
S3272 3 Dollars 23.12.1776. Black. Oracle. *FATA VIAM INVENIENT.* Paper: Thick brownish. Printer: Peter Timothy.	90.00	375.	1500.
S3273 4 Dollars 23.12.1776. Black. Ship. *THE ACTAEON. IRAM PRUDENTIA VINCIT.* Paper: Thick brownish. Printer: Peter Timothy.			
a. Regular date.	90.00	375.	1500.
b. Text on face is misdated December 23, 1777.	90.00	375.	1500.

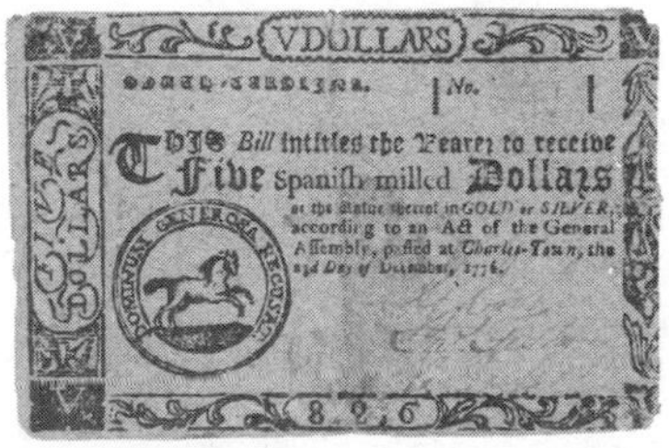

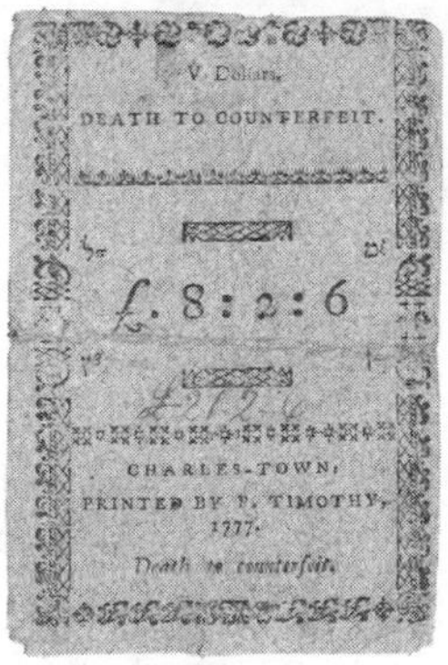

	VG	VF	UNC
S3274 5 Dollars 23.12.1776. Black. Horse. *DOMINUM GENEROSA RECUSAT.* Paper: Thick brownish. Printer: Peter Timothy	120.	375.	1500.
S3275 6 Dollars 23.12.1776. Black. Camel. *NEC ONUS NEC META GRAVABIT.* Paper: Thick brownish. Printer: Peter Timothy.	90.00	375.	1500.

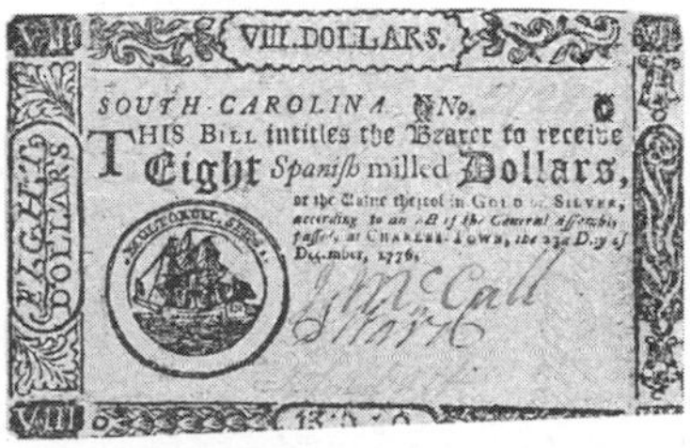

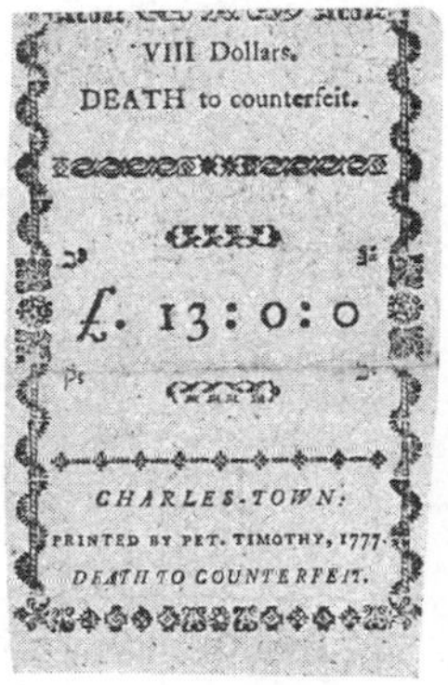

	VG	VF	UNC
S3276 8 Dollars 23.12.1776. Black. Sailing ship . *MULTORUM SPES.* Paper: Thick brownish. Printer: Peter Timothy.	90.00	375.	1500.
S3277 20 Dollars 23.12.1776. Black. Bull. *AUT MORS AUT VICTORIA.* Paper: Thick brownish. Printer: Peter Timothy.	250.	1500.	—

1777 Issue

	VG	VF	UNC
S3278 20 Dollars 14.2.1777. Black. Bird escaping from cage. *IBI PATRIA UBI LIBERTAS.* Paper: Dark brownish.	200.	1000.	—

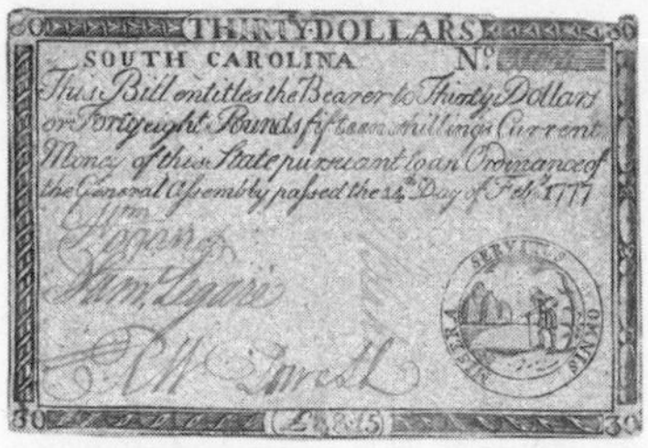

		VG	VF	UNC
S3279	**30 Dollars** 14.2.1777. Black. Man with pack. *MISERA SERVITUS OMNIS.* Paper: Dark brownish.	250.	1000.	—

1778 Issue

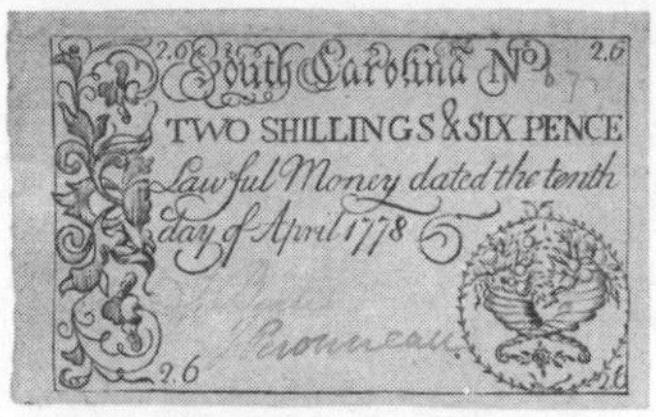

		VG	VF	UNC
S3280	**2 Shillings 6 Pence** 10.4.1778. Black. Cornucopiae. Thin paper.	75.00	200.	500.
S3281	**3 Shillings 9 Pence** 10.4.1778. Black. Beaver. Thin paper.	75.00	200.	500.

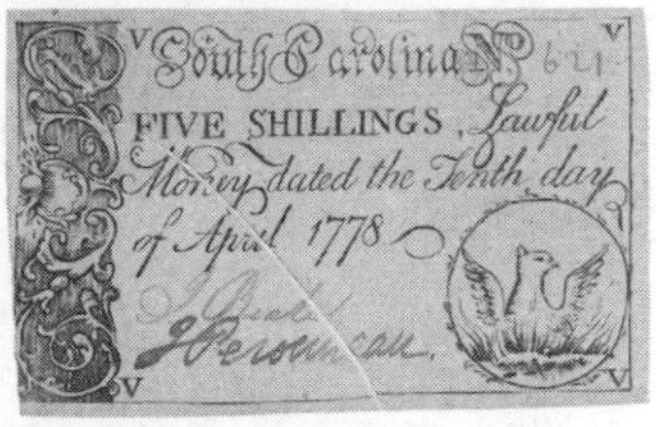

		VG	VF	UNC
S3282	**5 Shillings** 10.4.1778. Black. Phoenix. Thin paper.	75.00	200.	500.
S3283	**7 Shillings 6 Pence - 1 Dollar** 10.4.1778. Black. Beehive. Thin paper.	100.	200.	550.
S3284	**10 Shillings** 10.4.1778. Black. Palmetto. Thin paper.	100.	200.	550.
S3285	**15 Shillings** 10.4.1778. Black. Sun. Thin paper.	100.	200.	550.
S3286	**20 Shillings** 10.4.1778. Black. Horse. Thin paper.	100.	200.	550.
S3287	**30 Shillings** 10.4.1778. Black. Hope and anchor. Thin paper.	100.	200.	550.

1779 Issue

		VG	VF	UNC
S3288	**40 Dollars** 8.2.1779. Black. Ceres. *MINIME VIOLANDA FIDES.* Back: Angel blowing trumpet and holding book. Paper: White or blue.	300.	1000.	4500.
S3289	**50 Dollars** 8.2.1779. Black. Providence and globe. *PROVIDENTIA NOSTRIS PRAESIDEAT.* Back: Atlas holding a boulder. Paper: White or blue.	250.	750.	3500.

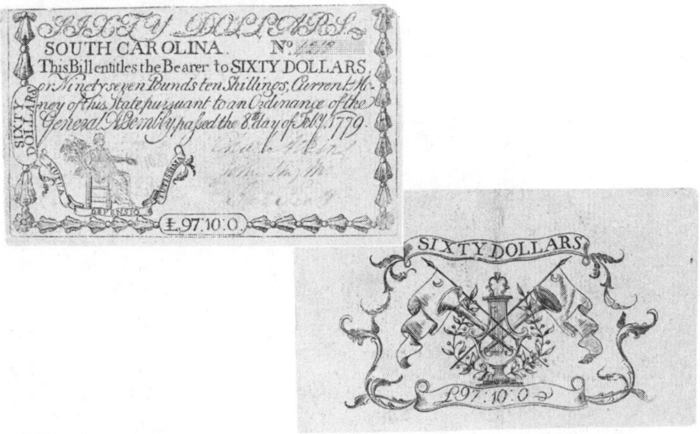

		Good	Fine	XF
S3290	**60 Dollars** 8.2.1779. Black. Figure and cornucopia. *MUTUA DEFENSIO TUTISSIMA.* Back: Lyre, horns and flags. Paper: White or blue.	300.	1000.	4500.

		Good	Fine	XF
S3291	**70 Dollars** 8.2.1779. Black. Hope with anchor. *SPES MENTIS SOLATIO.* Back: Prometheus bound and attacked by vulture. Paper: White or blue.	225.	750.	3500.
S3292	**80 Dollars** 8.2.1779. Black. Man with sword. *CONSTANTIA DURISSIMA VINCIT.* Back: Shield and Liberty cap. Paper: White or blue.	350.	1250.	5000.

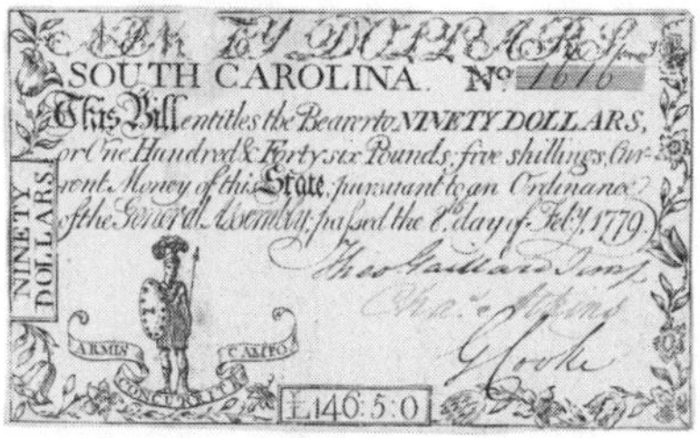

		Good	Fine	XF
S3293	**90 Dollars** 8.2.1779. Black. Warrior. *ARMIS CONCURRITE CAMPO.* Back: Hercules strangling a lion. Paper: White or blue.	225.	750.	3500.
S3294	**100 Dollars** 8.2.1779. Black. Athena. *GLORIAE FUNDAMENTUM FORTITUDO.* Back: Palmetto, drum and flags. Paper: White or blue.	375.	1500.	5500.

1786 First Issue

		Good	Fine	XF
S3295	**2 Shillings 6 Pence** 1786. Black. *FIDES PUBLICA.*	—	—	—
S3296	**5 Shillings** 1786. Black.	—	—	—
S3297	**10 Shillings** 1786. Black.	—	—	—
S3298	**1 Pound** 1786. Black.	—	—	—
S3299	**1 Pound 10 Shillings** 1786. Black.	—	—	—
S3300	**3 Pounds** 1786. Black.	—	—	—
S3301	**5 Pounds** 1786. Black.	—	—	—
S3302	**10 Pounds** 1786. Black.	—	—	—
S3303	**20 Pounds** 1786. Black.	—	—	—

1786 Second Issue

		Good	Fine	XF
S3304	**1 Pound** 1.5.1786. *HONOR ET JUSTITIA.* Engraver: Abernethie of Charleston.	—	—	—
S3305	**2 Pounds** 1.5.1786. *PRAEMIUM INDUSTRIAE.* Engraver: Abernethie of Charleston.	—	—	—
S3306	**3 Pounds** 1.5.1786. *HINC OPES.* Engraver: Abernethie of Charleston.	—	3500.	—
S3307	**10 Pounds** 1.5.1786. *VOX POPULI.* Engraver: Abernethie of Charleston.	—	—	—

South Carolina

Post Civil War

1866 Issue

		Good	Fine	XF
S3311	**1 Dollar** 1.1.1866. Black and green. Oxen pulling cart at upper left center, two children in oval at upper center right, maiden seated at lower right. Similar to #S3321. Back: Green. Printer: ABNC. Rare.	—	—	—
S3312	**2 Dollars** 1.1.1866. Black and green. Two young girls with sheaves of grain at lower left, harbor scene ("Propeller Loading") at center right, woman's head ("Star of Empire") at lower right. Similar to #S3322. Back: Green. Printer: ABNC. Rare.	—	—	—
S3313	**5 Dollars** 1.1.1866. Black and green. Gen. T. Sumter at lower left, Gen. F. Marion's *Sweet Potato Dinner* at top center, Gen. W. Moultrie at lower right. Similar to #S3323. Back: Green. Printer: ABNC. Rare.	—	—	—

		Good	Fine	XF
S3314	**10 Dollars** 1.1.1866. Black and green. Revolutionary Gen. at lower left, Revolutionary scene of an Indian being captured ("The Rescue") at upper center, young girl at lower right. Similar to #S3324. Back: Green. Printer: ABNC. Rare.	—	—	—

Act 2.3.1872 Revenue Bond First Issue

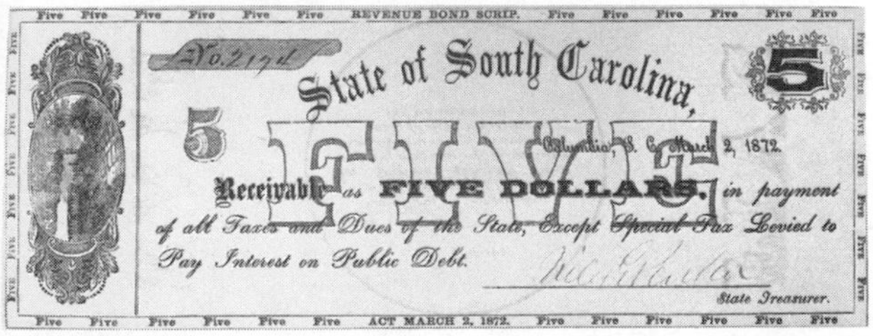

		VG	VF	UNC
S3318	**5 Dollars** 2.3.1872. Black on green underprint. Steam train in vertical at left.	30.00	40.00	70.00

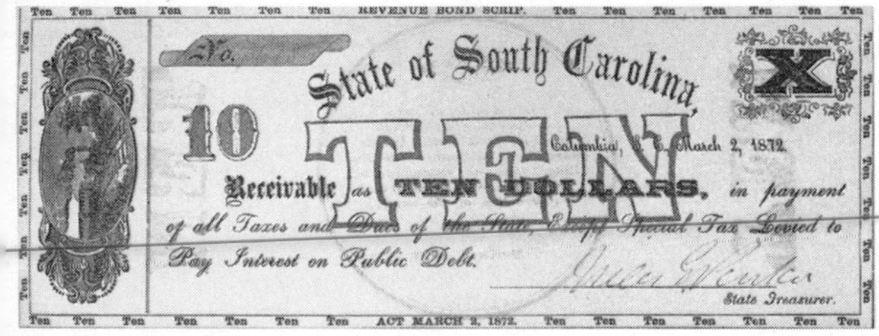

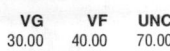

		VG	VF	UNC
S3319	**10 Dollars** 2.3.1872. Black on green underprint. Steam train in vertical at left.	20.00	30.00	60.00
S3319A	**100 Dollars** 2.3.1872. Palmetto tree at center, small dog and safe at lower right.	100.	200.	400.
S3320	**1000 Dollars** 1872. Black. Palmetto tree within circle at upper center, dog and safe at lower left. Handwritten dates. Rare.	—	—	—
S3320A	**5000 Dollars** 2.3.1872. Black. Palmetto tree within circle at upper center, dog and safe at lower left. Similar to #S3320. Rare.	—	—	—

Act 2.3.1872 Revenue Bond Second Issue

		VG	VF	UNC
S3321	**1 Dollar** 2.3.1872. Green and black. Oxen pulling cart at upper left center, two children in oval at upper center right, maiden seated at lower right. *REVENUE BOND SCRIP.* Back: Green. Printer: ABNC.	75.00	150.	—

		VG	VF	UNC
S3322	**2 Dollars** 2.3.1872. Green and black. Two young girls with sheaves of grain at lower left, harbor scene ("Propeller Loading") at center right, woman's head ("Star of Empire") at lower right. *REVENUE BOND SCRIP.* Back: Green. Printer: ABNC.	75.00	150.	—

		VG	VF	UNC
S3323	**5 Dollars** 2.3.1872. Green and black. Gen. T. Sumter at lower left, Gen. F. Marion's *Sweet Potato Dinner* at top center, Gen. W. Moultrie at lower right. *REVENUE BOND SCRIP.* Back: Green. Printer: ABNC.	65.00	140.	—

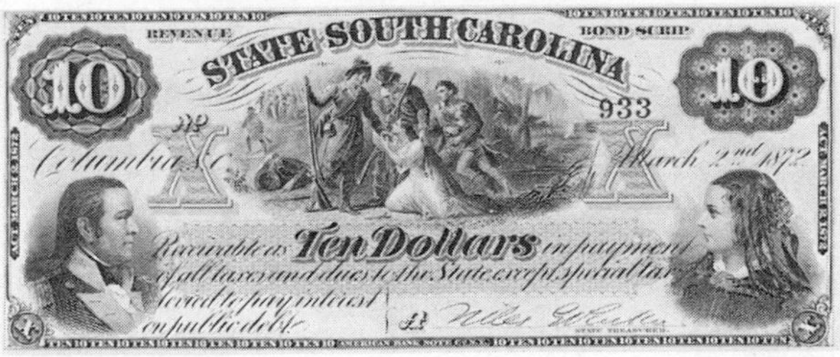

		VG	VF	UNC
S3324	**10 Dollars** 2.3.1872. Green and black. Revolutionary Gen. at lower left, Revolutionary scene of an Indian being captured ("The Rescue") at upper center, young girl at lower right. *REVENUE BOND SCRIP.* Back: Green. Printer: ABNC.	65.00	135.	—

		VG	VF	UNC
S3325	**20 Dollars** 2.3.1872. Green and black. Liberty, soldier, and angel guarding state seals at upper center, young girl at lower right. *REVENUE BOND SCRIP.* Back: Green. Printer: ABNC.	65.00	135.	—

		VG	VF	UNC
S3326	**50 Dollars** 2.3.1872. Black. Horse drawn cart at left, portrait George Washington at center, black carrying cotton at right. *REVENUE BOND SCRIP.* Printer: ABNC.	75.00	150.	—

#S3327 *Deleted.* See #S3320.

Tennessee

Post Civil War

1875 Payable Warrant Issue

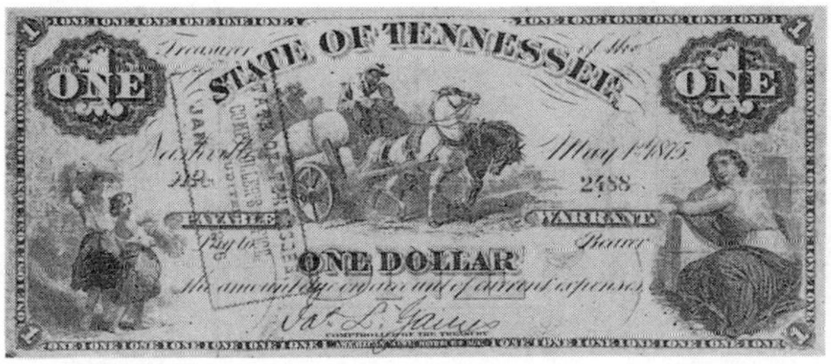

		VG	VF	UNC
S3334	**1 Dollar** 1.5.1875. Black on green underprint. Two young girls with sheaves of grain at lower left, horsedrawn cart at center, seated Ceres at lower right. Back: Green. Printer: ABNC.			
	a. Issued note.	200.	500.	1100.
	b. Punched hole cancelled.	200.	500.	1100.

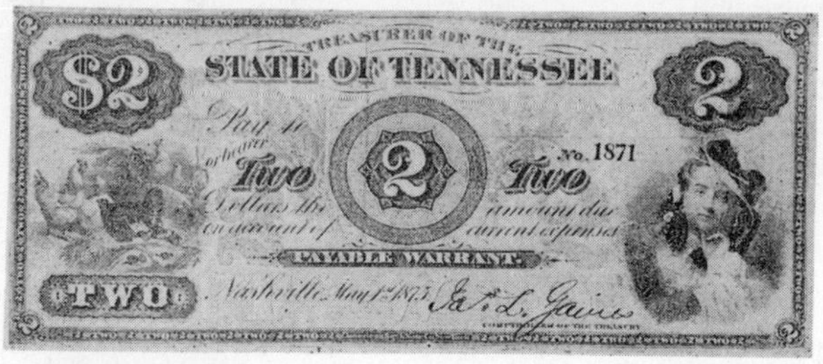

S3335 2 Dollars	VG	VF	UNC
1.5.1875. Black on green underprint. Chickens at left, woman's head ("Nathalie") at lower right. Back: Green. Printer: ABNC.			
a. Issued note.	200.	500.	1100.
b. Punched hole cancelled.	200.	500.	1100.

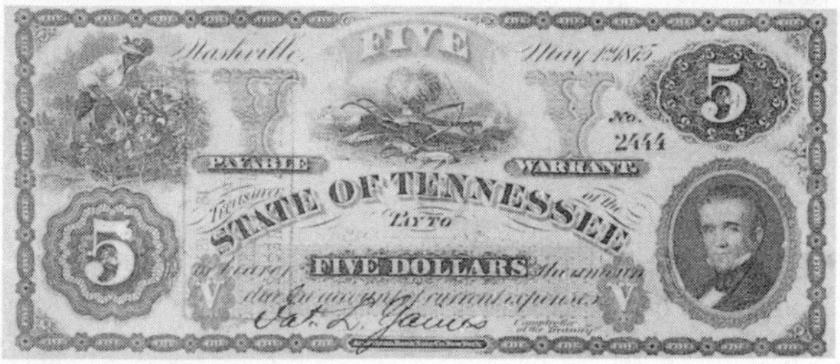

S3336 5 Dollars	VG	VF	UNC
1.5.1875. Black on green underprint. Black picking cotton at upper left, portrait man at lower right. Back: Green. Printer: ABNC.			
a. Issued note.	300.	700.	1400.
b. Punched hole cancelled.	200.	500.	1100.

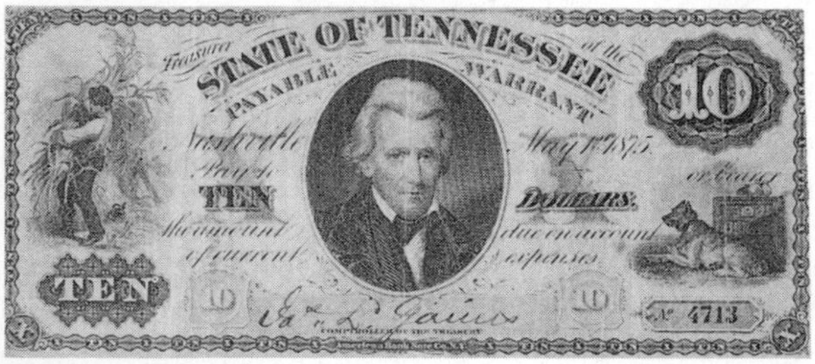

S3337 10 Dollars	VG	VF	UNC
1.5.1875. Black on green underprint. Boy gathering corn stalks at left, portrait A. Jackson at center dog lying by safe at lower right. Back: Green. Printer: ABNC.			
a. Issued note.	—	—	—
b. Punched hole cancelled.	200.	500.	1100.
S3338 20 Dollars			
1.5.1875. Black on green underprint. Black picking cotton at upper left, young woman reclining at lower right. Back: Green. Printer: ABNC.			
a. Issued note.	300.	700.	1400.
b. Punched hole cancelled.	300.	700.	1400.
S3339 50 Dollars			
1.5.1875. Black on green underprint. Young girl with puppy at left, man and horses with plow at center, girl with quill pen at lower right. Back: Green. Printer: ABNC.			
a. Issued note.	200.	500.	1100.
b. Punched hole cancelled.	—	—	—

1883 Issue

S3340 1 Dollar	VG	VF	UNC
1.7.1883. Portrait of man at left. Series D. Back: Building at center.			
a. Issued note.	50.00	85.00	120.
b. Punched hole cancelled.	—	—	—

Texas

State

Civil War

1860-64 Treasury Warrant Civil Service Issues

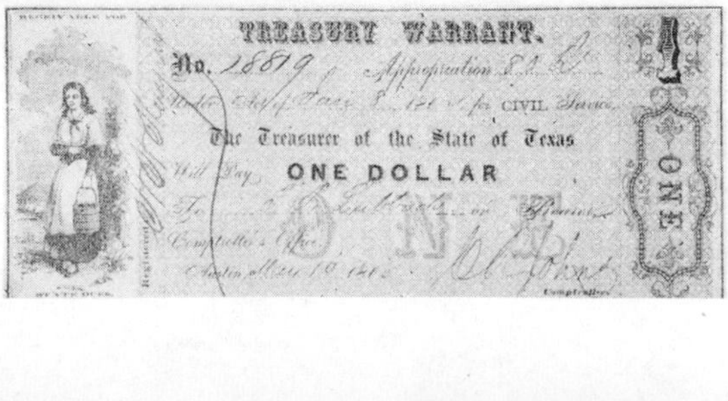

S3395 1 Dollar	VG	VF	UNC
1860-64. Black on orange underprint. Milkmaid at left. Various handwritten dates.	50.00	85.00	120.
S3396 1 Dollar			
1860-64. Green and black. Ornate *ONE* vertically at left. Various handwritten dates.	60.00	100.	150.
S3397 1 Dollar			
1860-64. Black. Signature vertical at left. Various handwritten dates.	75.00	125.	200.
S3398 2 1/2 Dollars			
1860-64. Black. Various handwritten dates. Paper: Light brown.	50.00	125.	240.

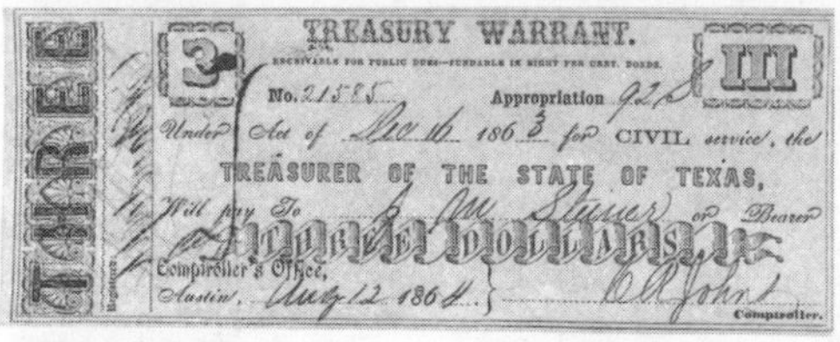

S3399 3 Dollars	VG	VF	UNC
1860-64. Green and black. Various handwritten dates.	50.00	100.	200.

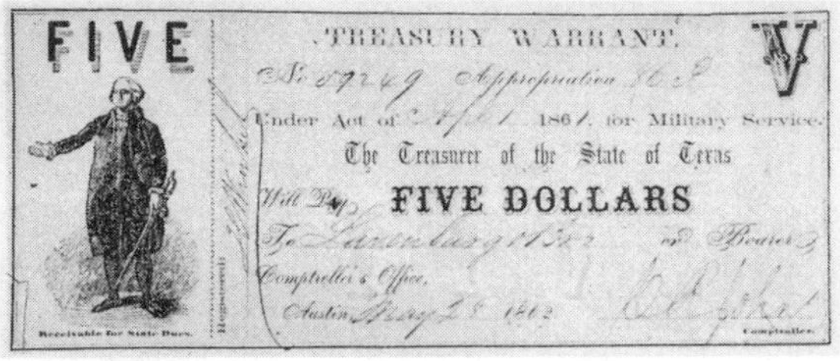

S3400 5 Dollars	VG	VF	UNC
1860-64. Black on green underprint. Standing George Washington at left. Various handwritten dates.	50.00	100.	200.
S3400A 5 Dollars			
1860-64. Green and black. Similar to #S3399 with ornate *FIVE* vertically at left. Various handwritten dates.	50.00	100.	2000.
S3401 5 Dollars			
1860-64. Black. Signature vertical at left. Various handwritten dates. Similar to #S3397.	50.00	100.	200.
S3402 10 Dollars			
1860-64. Black on red underprint. Sailing ship at left. Various handwritten dates.	75.00	150.	265.
S3403 10 Dollars			
1860-64. Green and black. Similar to #S3399 with ornate *TEN* vertically at left. Various handwritten dates.	50.00	100.	200.
S3404 10 Dollars			
1860-64. Black. Signature vertical at left. Various handwritten dates. Similar to #S3397.	60.00	125.	250.
S3405 20 Dollars			
1860-64. Black on red underprint. Standing Ceres at left, steamboat at upper right. Various handwritten dates.	100.	235.	400.
S3406 20 Dollars			
1860-64. Green and black. Similar to #S3399 with ornate *TWENTY* vertically at left. Various handwritten dates.	85.00	175.	300.
S3407 20 Dollars			
1860-64. Black. Signature vertical at left. Various handwritten dates. Similar to #S3397.	80.00	175.	325.
S3408 50 Dollars			
1860-64. Black and green on yellow underprint. Steam passenger train vertically at left, ships at upper right. Various handwritten dates.	150.	300.	500.
S3409 50 Dollars			
1860-64. Black. *FIFTY* vertically at left and right. Various handwritten dates. Back: Green.	75.00	150.	275.
S3410 50 Dollars			
1860-64. Black. Signature vertical at left. Various handwritten dates. Similar to #S3397.	800.	1000.	
S3411 100 Dollars			
1860-64. Black on red underprint. Sailing ship at upper center right. Various handwritten dates.	175.	350.	650.
S3412 100 Dollars			
1860-64. Black. Similar to #S3409 w/*ONE HUNDRED* vertically at left and right. Various handwritten dates. Back: Green.	75.00	150.	275.
S3413 100 Dollars			
1860-64. Black. Various handwritten dates.	—	—	—
S3414 Written Denominations			
1860-64. Black on blue underprint. Liberty at left, beehive at upper right. Various handwritten dates.	60.00	125.	225.
S3415 Written Denominations			
1860-64. Black on green underprint. Indian maiden at left, seated Ceres at center right. Various handwritten dates.	85.00	175.	300.
S3416 Written Denominations			
1860-64. Black. Signature vertical at left. Various handwritten dates. Similar to #S3397.	100.	200.	400.

1860-64 Military Service Issues

#S3417-S3448 similar to #S3395-S3416 except the word . *Military* replaces *Civil.*

S3417 1 Dollar	VG	VF	UNC
1860-64. Black on orange underprint. Milkmaid at left. Various handwritten dates. Like #S3395. *Military* replaces *Civil.*	60.00	100.	150.
S3418 1 Dollar			
1860-64. Green and black. Ornate *ONE* vertically at left. Various handwritten dates. Like #S3396. *Military* replaces *Civil.*	60.00	100.	150.

	Good	Fine	XF
S3419 1 Dollar 1860-64. Black. Signature vertical at left. Various handwritten dates. Like #S3397. *Military* replaces *Civil*.	75.00	125.	200.

	VG	VF	UNC
S3420 2 1/2 Dollars 1860-64. Black. Various handwritten dates. Like #S3398. *Military* replaces *Civil*. Paper: Light brown.	40.00	90.00	165.
S3421 3 Dollars 1860-64. Green and black. Various handwritten dates. Like #S3399. *Military* replaces *Civil*.	40.00	90.00	165.
S3422 5 Dollars 1860-64. Black on green underprint. Standing George Washington at left. Various handwritten dates. Like #S3400. *Military* replaces *Civil*.	40.00	90.00	165.
S3423 5 Dollars 1860-64. Black. Signature vertical at left. Various handwritten dates. Similar to #S3401. *Military* replaces *Civil*.	50.00	100.	200.
S3424 10 Dollars 1860-64. Black on red underprint. Sailing ship at left. Various handwritten dates. Like #S3402. *Military* replaces *Civil*.	50.00	100.	200.
S3425 10 Dollars 1860-64. Green and black. Ornate *TEN* vertically at left. Various handwritten dates. Like #S3403. *Military* replaces *Civil*.	50.00	100.	200.
S3426 10 Dollars 1860-64. Black. Signature vertical at left. Various handwritten dates. Like #S3404. *Military* replaces *Civil*.	80.00	165.	300.
S3427 20 Dollars 1860-64. Black on red underprint. Standing Ceres at left, steamboat at upper right. Various handwritten dates. Like #S3405. *Military* replaces *Civil*.	80.00	175.	325.
S3428 20 Dollars 1860-64. Green and black. Ornate *TWENTY* vertically at left. Various handwritten dates. Like #S3406. *Military* replaces *Civil*.	85.00	175.	300.
S3429 20 Dollars 1860-64. Black. Signature vertical at left. Various handwritten dates. Like #S3407. *Military* replaces *Civil*.	80.00	175.	300.
S3430 50 Dollars 1860-64. Black and green on yellow underprint. Steam passenger train vertically at left, ships at upper right. Various handwritten dates. Like #S3408. *Military* replaces *Civil*.	150.	300.	500.
S3431 50 Dollars 1860-64. Black. *FIFTY* vertically at left and right. Various handwritten dates. Like #S3409. *Military* replaces *Civil*.	75.00	150.	275.
S3432 50 Dollars 1860-64. Black. Signature vertical at left. Various handwritten dates. Like #S3410. *Military* replaces *Civil*.	800.	1000.	—
S3433 100 Dollars 1860-64. Black on red underprint. Sailing ship at upper center right. Various handwritten dates. Like #S3411. *Military* replaces *Civil*.	175.	350.	650.
S3434 100 Dollars 1860-64. Black. *ONE HUNDRED* vertically at left and right. Various handwritten dates. Like #S3412. *Military* replaces *Civil*.	75.00	150.	275.
S3435 100 Dollars 1860-64. Black. Various handwritten dates. Like #S3413. *Military* replaces *Civil*.	—	—	—
S3436 Various handwritten denominations 1860-64. Black on blue underprint. Liberty at left, beehive at upper right. Various handwritten dates. Like #S3414. *Military* replaces *Civil*.	60.00	125.	225.
S3437 Various handwritten denominations 1860-64. Black on green underprint. Indian maiden at left, seated Ceres at center right. Various handwritten dates. Like #S3415. *Military* replaces *Civil*.	60.00	135.	250.
S3438 Various handwritten denominations 1860-64. Black. Signature vertical at left. Various handwritten dates. Like #S3416. *Military* replaces *Civil*.	100.	200.	400.

Provisional Issues

Note: #S3395-S3416 are known with *Military* handwritten over *Civil* while #S3417-S3438 are known with *Civil* handwritten over *Military*.

Vermont

State

1781 Treasury Issue

#S3441-S3448 Seal that has 13 joined links and 1 loose link exemplifying Vermont's objection from being excluded from being one of the original colonies attaining statehood. W/motto: *VERMONT CALLS FOR JUSTICE*.

	Good	Fine	XF
S3441 1 Shilling February 1781. Black. Seal with 13 joined links and 1 loose link. *VERMONT CALLS FOR JUSTICE*. Printer: Spooner and Green. Thin weak paper.	9000.	20,000.	—
S3442 1 Shilling 3 Pence February 1781. Black. Seal with 13 joined links and 1 loose link. *VERMONT CALLS FOR JUSTICE*. Printer: Spooner and Green. Thin weak paper.	9000.	20,000.	—
S3443 2 Shillings 6 Pence February 1781. Black. Seal with 13 joined links and 1 loose link. *VERMONT CALLS FOR JUSTICE*. Printer: Spooner and Green. Thin weak paper.	7500.	17,500.	—
S3444 5 Shillings February 1781. Black. Seal with 13 joined links and 1 loose link. *VERMONT CALLS FOR JUSTICE*. Printer: Spooner and Green. Thin weak paper.	10,000.	25,000.	—
S3445 10 Shillings February 1781. Black. Seal with 13 joined links and 1 loose link. *VERMONT CALLS FOR JUSTICE*. Printer: Spooner and Green. Thin weak paper.	10,000.	25,000.	—
S3446 20 Shillings February 1781. Black. Seal with 13 joined links and 1 loose link. *VERMONT CALLS FOR JUSTICE*. Printer: Spooner and Green. Thin weak paper.	10,000.	25,000.	—
S3447 40 Shillings February 1781. Black. Seal with 13 joined links and 1 loose link. *VERMONT CALLS FOR JUSTICE*. Printer: Spooner and Green. Thin weak paper.	10,000.	25,000.	—
S3448 3 Pounds February 1781. Black. Seal with 13 joined links and 1 loose link. *VERMONT CALLS FOR JUSTICE*. Printer: Spooner and Green. Thin weak paper.	12,500.	40,000.	—

Virginia - Colonial

1755 Second Issue

	Good	Fine	XF
S3451 10 Shillings 11.12.1755.	—	—	—
S3454 5 Pounds 11.12.1755.	—	—	—

NOTE: Several additional denominations apparently existed. #S3451 and S3454 are known only as counterfeits.

1757 Issue

	Good	Fine	XF
S3461 1 Shilling 8.6.1757. Black. Virginia Colony seal with motto: *EN DAT VIRGINIA QUARTAM*. Printer: William Hunter. Thin laid paper.	—	—	—
S3462 1 Shilling 3 Pence 8.6.1757. Black. Virginia Colony seal with motto: *EN DAT VIRGINIA QUARTAM*. Printer: William Hunter. Thin laid paper.	—	—	—
S3463 2 Shillings 6 Pence 8.6.1757. Black. Virginia Colony seal with motto: *EN DAT VIRGINIA QUARTAM*. Printer: William Hunter. Thin laid paper.	—	—	—
S3464 5 Shillings 8.6.1757. Black. Virginia Colony seal with motto: *EN DAT VIRGINIA QUARTAM*. Printer: William Hunter. Thin laid paper.	—	—	—
S3465 10 Shillings 8.6.1757. Black. Virginia Colony seal with motto: *EN DAT VIRGINIA QUARTAM*. Printer: William Hunter. Thin laid paper.	—	—	—
S3466 20 Shillings 8.6.1757. Black. Virginia Colony seal with motto: *EN DAT VIRGINIA QUARTAM*. Printer: William Hunter. Thin laid paper.	1000.	—	—
S3467 2 Pounds 8.6.1757. Black. Virginia Colony seal with motto: *EN DAT VIRGINIA QUARTAM*. Printer: William Hunter. Thin laid paper.	—	—	—
S3468 3 Pounds 8.6.1757. Black. Virginia Colony seal with motto: *EN DAT VIRGINIA QUARTAM*. Printer: William Hunter. Thin laid paper.	—	—	—
S3469 5 Pounds 8.6.1757. Black. Virginia Colony seal with motto: *EN DAT VIRGINIA QUARTAM*. Printer: William Hunter. Thin laid paper.	—	—	—
S3470 10 Pounds 8.6.1757. Black. Virginia Colony seal with motto: *EN DAT VIRGINIA QUARTAM*. Printer: William Hunter. Thin laid paper.	—	—	—

1758 Issue

	Good	Fine	XF
S3470C 10 Pounds 12.4.1758. Black. Virginia Colony seal at left. Rare.	—	—	—
S3471 1 Shilling 12.10.1758. Black. Larger Virginia Colony seal. Printer: William Hunter.	—	2750.	—
S3472 1 Shilling 3 Pence 12.10.1758. Black. Larger Virginia Colony seal. Printer: William Hunter.	—	—	—
S3473 2 Shillings 6 Pence 12.10.1758. Black. Larger Virginia Colony seal. Printer: William Hunter.	—	—	—
S3474 5 Shillings 12.10.1758. Black. Larger Virginia Colony seal. Printer: William Hunter.	—	—	—
S3475 10 Shillings 12.10.1758. Black. Larger Virginia Colony seal. Printer: William Hunter.	—	—	—
S3476 20 Shillings 12.10.1758. Black. Larger Virginia Colony seal. Printer: William Hunter.	—	—	—
S3477 2 Pounds 12.10.1758. Black. Larger Virginia Colony seal. Printer: William Hunter.	—	—	—
S3478 3 Pounds 12.10.1758. Black. Larger Virginia Colony seal. Printer: William Hunter.	—	—	—

	VG	VF	UNC
S3479 5 Pounds 12.10.1758. Black. Larger Virginia Colony seal. Printer: William Hunter.	—	3250.	—

1759 First Issue

	Good	Fine	XF
S3480 1 Shilling 5.4.1759. Black. Virginia Colony seal.	—	—	—
S3481 1 Shilling 3 Pence 5.4.1759. Black. Virginia Colony seal.	—	—	—
S3482 2 Shillings 6 Pence 5.4.1759. Black. Virginia Colony seal.	—	—	—
S3483 5 Shillings 5.4.1759. Black. Virginia Colony seal.	—	—	—
S3484 10 Shillings 5.4.1759. Black. Virginia Colony seal.	—	—	—
S3485 20 Shillings 5.4.1759. Black. Virginia Colony seal.	—	—	—
S3486 2 Pounds 5.4.1759. Black. Virginia Colony seal.	—	—	—
S3487 3 Pounds 5.4.1759. Black. Virginia Colony seal.	—	—	—
S3488 5 Pounds 5.4.1759. Black. Virginia Colony seal.	—	—	—

1759 Second Issue

	Good	Fine	XF
S3490 3 Pounds 21.11.1759. Black. Virginia Colony seal.	—	—	—
S3491 5 Pounds 21.11.1759. Black. Virginia Colony seal.	—	—	—

NOTE: Additional denominations may have been issued.

1760 First Issue

	Good	Fine	XF
S3492 2 Shillings 6 Pence 11.3.1760. Black. Virginia Colony seal.	—	—	—
S3493 5 Shillings 11.3.1760. Black. Virginia Colony seal.	—	—	—

	VG	VF	UNC
S3494 2 Pounds 11.3.1760. Black. Virginia Colony seal.	1750.	—	—
S3495 3 Pounds 11.3.1760. Black. Virginia Colony seal.	—	—	—
S3496 5 Pounds 11.3.1760. Black. Virginia Colony seal.	—	—	—

1760 Second Issue

	Good	Fine	XF
S3497 1 Shilling 24.5.1760. Black. Virginia Colony seal.	—	—	—
S3498 1 Shilling 3 Pence 24.5.1760. Black. Virginia Colony seal.	—	—	—
S3499 2 Shillings 6 Pence 24.5.1760. Black. Virginia Colony seal.	—	—	—
S3500 5 Shillings 24.5.1760. Black. Virginia Colony seal.	—	—	—

	VG	VF	UNC
S3501 10 Shillings 24.5.1760. Black. Virginia Colony seal.	750.	—	—

	Good	Fine	XF
S3502 20 Shillings 24.5.1760. Black. Virginia Colony seal.	850.	—	—
S3503 2 Pounds 24.5.1760. Black. Virginia Colony seal.	—	—	—
S3504 3 Pounds 24.5.1760. Black. Virginia Colony seal.	—	—	—
S3505 5 Pounds 24.5.1760. Black. Virginia Colony seal.	—	—	—

1762 Issue

	Good	Fine	XF
S3506 2 Shillings 6 Pence 7.4.1762. Black. Virginia Colony seal.	—	—	—
S3507 5 Shillings 7.4.1762. Black. Virginia Colony seal.	—	—	—
S3508 10 Shillings 7.4.1762. Black. Virginia Colony seal.	—	—	—
S3509 20 Shillings 7.4.1762. Black. Virginia Colony seal.	—	—	—
S3510 2 Pounds 7.4.1762. Black. Virginia Colony seal.	—	—	—
S3511 3 Pounds 7.4.1762. Black. Virginia Colony seal.	—	—	—
S3512 5 Pounds 7.4.1762. Black. Virginia Colony seal.	—	—	—

Act of Nov. 7, 1769; 1770 Issue

	Good	Fine	XF
S3513 20 Shillings 1770. Black. Virginia Colony seal. Printer: William Rind.	—	—	—
S3514 2 Pounds 1770. Black. Virginia Colony seal. Printer: William Rind.	—	—	—
S3515 5 Pounds 1770. Black. Virginia Colony seal. Printer: William Rind.	—	—	—

1771 Tobacco Issue

	Good	Fine	XF
S3516 2 Pounds 11.7.1771. Black. Virginia Colony seal. *TOBACCO*. Printer: William Rind.	—	—	—
S3517 3 Pounds 11.7.1771. Black. Virginia Colony seal. *TOBACCO*. Printer: William Rind.	—	—	—
S3518 5 Pounds 11.7.1771. Black. Virginia Colony seal. *TOBACCO*. Printer: William Rind.	—	—	—

1773 Issue

	Good	Fine	XF
S3519 20 Shillings 4.3.1773. Black. Virginia Colony seal.	600.	2000.	—
S3520 2 Pounds 4.3.1773. Black. Virginia Colony seal.	600.	2000.	—
S3521 3 Pounds 4.3.1773. Black. Virginia Colony seal.	600.	2000.	—
S3522 5 Pounds 4.3.1773. Black. Virginia Colony seal.	600.	2000.	—

1775 Small Size Issue

	VG	VF	UNC
S3523 1 Shilling 3 Pence 17.7.1775. Black. Virginia Colony seal. Small sized note. Heavy rag paper with blue fibres.			
a. *And* in denomination in text.	150.	500.	
b. *&* in denomination in text.	150.	500.	
c. Proof of border cuts and arms only.	—	—	—
S3524 2 Shillings 6 Pence 17.7.1775. Black. Virginia Colony seal. Small sized note. Heavy rag paper with blue fibres.			
a. *SIXPENCE* as one word.	125.	350.	—
b. *Six Pence* as two words.	125.	350.	—
c. Proof of border cuts and arms only.	—	—	—
S3525 5 Shillings 17.7.1775. Black. Virginia Colony seal. Small sized note. Heavy rag paper with blue fibres.	125.	350.	—
S3526 7 Shillings 6 Pence - 1 Dollar 17.7.1775. Black. Virginia Colony seal. Small sized note. Heavy rag paper with blue fibres.	125.	350.	—
S3527 10 Shillings 17.7.1775. Black. Virginia Colony seal. Small sized note. Heavy rag paper with blue fibres.	125.	350.	—
S3528 12 Shillings 6 Pence 17.7.1775. Black. Virginia Colony seal. Small sized note. Heavy rag paper with blue fibres.	125.	350.	—
S3529 20 Shillings 17.7.1775. Black. Virginia Colony seal. *FOUR CROWNS* spelled *FOWR CROWNS* in right border. Small sized note. Heavy rag paper with blue fibres.	150.	400.	—
S3530 2 Pounds 17.7.1775. Black. Virginia Colony seal. Small sized note. Heavy rag paper with blue fibres.	150.	400.	—

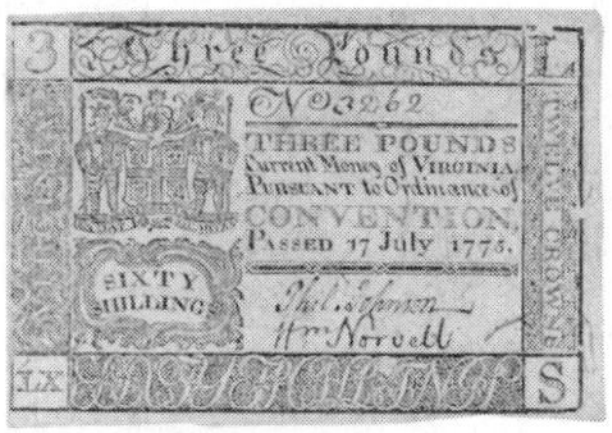

	VG	VF	UNC
S3531 3 Pounds 17.7.1775. Black. Virginia Colony seal. Small sized note. Heavy rag paper with blue fibres.	150.	400.	—

1775 Large Size Issue

	VG	VF	UNC
S3532 20 Shillings = 1 Pound 17.7.1775. Black. Virginia Colony seal. Large sized note with counterfoil at left.	450.	1500.	—

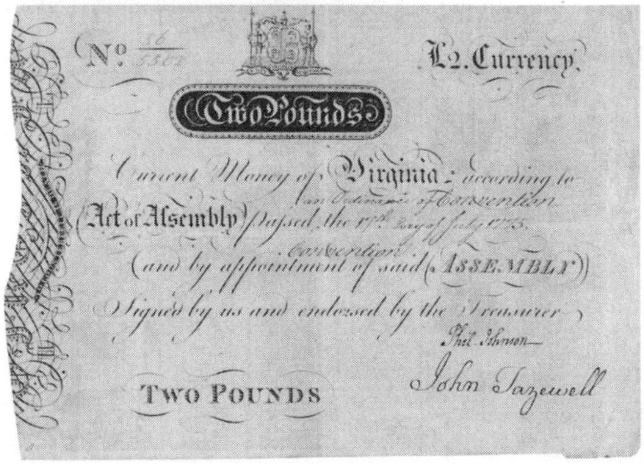

	VG	VF	UNC
S3533 2 Pounds 17.7.1775. Black. Virginia Colony seal. Large sized note with counterfoil at left.	450.	1500.	—
S3534 3 Pounds 17.7.1775. Black. Virginia Colony seal. Large sized note with counterfoil at left.	450.	1500.	—
S3535 5 Pounds 17.7.1775. Black. Virginia Colony seal. Large sized note with counterfoil at left.	450.	1500.	—

Virginia

State

1776 First Issue

	Good	Fine	XF
S3536 1/6 Dollar = 1 Shilling			
6.5.1776. Black. State arms. Heavy rag paper with blue fibers.	90.00	250.	—
S3537 1 Shilling 3 Pence			
6.5.1776. Black. Virginia Colony seal. Heavy rag paper with blue fibers.			
a. *And* in denomination in text.	100.	350.	—
b. *&* in denomination in text.	100.	350.	—
S3538 1/3 Dollar = 2 Shillings			
6.5.1776. Black. State arms. Heavy rag paper with blue fibers.	90.00	250.	—
S3539 2 Shillings 6 Pence			
6.5.1776. Black. Virginia Colony seal. Heavy rag paper with blue fibers.			
a. *SIXPENCE* as one word.	100.	350.	—
b. *Six Pence* as two words.	100.	350.	—
S3540 5 Shillings			
6.5.1776. Black. Virginia Colony seal. Heavy rag paper with blue fibers.	90.00	250.	—
S3541 7 Shillings 6 Pence - 1 Dollar			
6.5.1776. Black. Virginia Colony seal. Heavy rag paper with blue fibers.	90.00	250.	—
S3542 10 Shillings			
6.5.1776. Black. Virginia Colony seal. Heavy rag paper with blue fibers.	90.00	250.	—
S3543 12 Shillings 6 Pence			
6.5.1776. Black. Virginia Colony seal. Heavy rag paper with blue fibers.	90.00	250.	—
S3544 20 Shillings			
6.5.1776. Black. Virginia Colony seal. *FOUR CROWNS* spelled *FOWR CROWNS.* Heavy rag paper with blue fibers.	—	—	—
S3545 4 Dollars = 24 Shillings			
6.5.1776. Black. State arms. Heavy rag paper with blue fibers.	90.00	250.	—
S3546 5 Dollars = 30 Shillings			
6.5.1776. Black. State arms. Spanish 8 Reales. Heavy rag paper with blue fibers.	90.00	250.	—
S3547 2 Pounds			
6.5.1776. Black. Virginia Colony seal. Heavy rag paper with blue fibers.	—	—	—

	Good	Fine	XF
S3548 3 Pounds			
6.5.1776. Black. Virginia Colony seal. Heavy rag paper with blue fibers.	—	—	—
S3549 4 Pounds			
6.5.1776. Black. Virginia Colony seal. Heavy rag paper with blue fibers.	—	—	—

1776 Second Issue

	VG	VF	UNC
S3550 1/6 Dollar			
7.10.1776. Black. State arms. Heavy rag paper with blue fibers.	100.	300.	—
S3551 1/3 Dollar			
7.10.1776. Black. State arms. Heavy rag paper with blue fibers.	100.	300.	—
S3552 2/3 Dollar			
7.10.1776. Black. State arms. Heavy rag paper with blue fibers.	100.	300.	—
S3553 1 Dollar			
7.10.1776. Black. State arms. Spanish 8 Reales. Heavy rag paper with blue fibers.	100.	300.	—
S3554 4 Dollars			
7.10.1776. Black. State arms. *SIC SEMPER TYRANNIS* spelled *TYRANNUS.* Heavy rag paper with blue fibers.	100.	300.	—
S3555 5 Dollars			
7.10.1776. Black. State arms. *SIC SEMPER TYRANNIS* spelled *TYRANNUS.* Heavy rag paper with blue fibers.	100.	300.	—
S3556 6 Dollars			
7.10.1776. Black. State arms. *SIC SEMPER TYRANNIS* spelled *TYRANNUS.* Heavy rag paper with blue fibers.	100.	300.	—
S3557 8 Dollars			
7.10.1776. Black. State arms. *SIC SEMPER TYRANNIS* spelled *TYRANNUS.* Heavy rag paper with blue fibers.	—	—	—
S3558 10 Dollars			
7.10.1776. Black. State arms. *SIC SEMPER TYRANNIS* spelled *TYRANNUS.* Heavy rag paper with blue fibers.	150.	450.	—

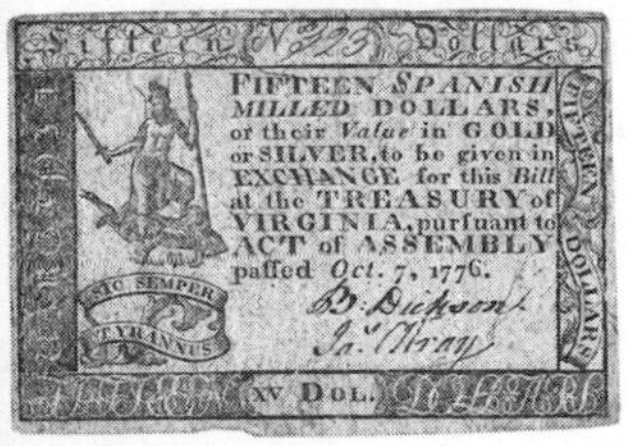

	VG	VF	UNC
S3559 15 Dollars			
7.10.1776. Black. State arms. *SIC SEMPER TYRANNIS* spelled *TYRANNUS.* Heavy rag paper with blue fibers.	150.	450.	—

1777 First Issue

	VG	VF	UNC
S3560 1/6 Dollar			
5.5.1777. Black. State arms. Heavy rag paper with blue fibers and mica flakes.	100.	300.	—
S3561 1/3 Dollar			
5.5.1777. Black. State arms. Heavy rag paper with blue fibers and mica flakes.	100.	300.	—
S3562 2/3 Dollar			
5.5.1777. Black. State arms. Heavy rag paper with blue fibers and mica flakes.	100.	300.	—
S3563 1 Dollar			
5.5.1777. Black. State arms. Spanish 8 Reales. Heavy rag paper with blue fibers and mica flakes.	100.	300.	—
S3564 4 Dollars			
5.5.1777. Black. State arms. Heavy rag paper with blue fibers and mica flakes.	100.	300.	—
S3565 5 Dollars			
5.5.1777. Black. State arms. Heavy rag paper with blue fibers and mica flakes.	100.	300.	—
S3566 6 Dollars			
5.5.1777. Black. State arms. Heavy rag paper with blue fibers and mica flakes.	100.	300.	—
S3567 8 Dollars			
5.5.1777. Black. State arms. Heavy rag paper with blue fibers and mica flakes.	100.	300.	—
S3568 10 Dollars			
5.5.1777. Black. State arms. Heavy rag paper with blue fibers and mica flakes.	100.	300.	—
S3569 15 Dollars			
5.5.1777. Black. State arms. Heavy rag paper with blue fibers and mica flakes.	100.	300.	—

1777 Second Issue

	VG	VF	UNC
S3570 1/6 Dollar			
20.10.1777. Black. State arms. Uniface. Heavy rag paper with blue fibers.	100.	300.	900.
S3571 1/3 Dollar			
20.10.1777. Black. State arms. Heavy rag paper with blue fibers.	100.	300.	900.
S3572 2/3 Dollar			
20.10.1777. Black. State arms. Heavy rag paper with blue fibers.	100.	300.	900.
S3573 1 Dollar			
20.10.1777. Black. State arms. Spanish 8 Reales. Heavy rag paper with blue fibers.	100.	300.	900.
S3574 4 Dollars			
20.10.1777. Black. State arms. Heavy rag paper with blue fibers.	100.	300.	900.
S3575 5 Dollars			
20.10.1777. Black. State arms. Heavy rag paper with blue fibers.	100.	300.	900.
S3576 6 Dollars			
20.10.1777. Black. State arms. Heavy rag paper with blue fibers.	100.	300.	900.
S3577 8 Dollars			
20.10.1777. Black. State arms. Heavy rag paper with blue fibers.	100.	300.	900.
S3578 10 Dollars			
20.10.1777. Black. State arms. Heavy rag paper with blue fibers.	100.	300.	900.

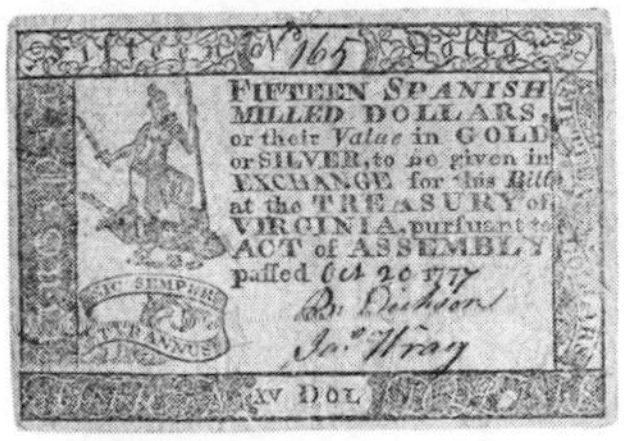

	VG	VF	UNC
S3579 15 Dollars			
20.10.1777. Black. State arms. Heavy rag paper with blue fibers.	100.	300.	900.

1778 First Issue

	VG	VF	UNC
S3580 1/6 Dollar			
4.5.1778. Black. State arms. Various handwritten dates.	450.	2000.	—
S3581 1/3 Dollar			
4.5.1778. Black. State arms. Various handwritten dates.	450.	2000.	—
S3582 2/3 Dollar			
4.5.1778. Black. State arms. Various handwritten dates.	450.	2000.	—
S3583 1 Dollar			
4.5.1778. Black. State arms. Various handwritten dates. Spanish 8 Reales.	450.	2000.	—
S3584 4 Dollars			
4.5.1778. Black. State arms. Various handwritten dates.	450.	2000.	—
S3585 5 Dollars			
4.5.1778. Black. State arms. Various handwritten dates.	450.	2000.	—
S3586 6 Dollars			
4.5.1778. Black. State arms. Various handwritten dates.	450.	2000.	—
S3587 8 Dollars			
4.5.1778. Black. State arms. Various handwritten dates.	450.	2000.	—

1778 Second Issue

	VG	VF	UNC
S3588 1/6 Dollar			
4.5.1778. Black. New borders and state arms. *TYRANNIS* corrected. Thick paper.	225.	675.	—
S3589 1/4 Dollar			
4.5.1778. Black. New borders and state arms. *TYRANNIS* corrected. Thick paper.	225.	675.	—
S3590 1/3 Dollar			
4.5.1778. Black. New borders and state arms. *TYRANNIS* corrected. Thick paper.	225.	675.	—
S3591 2/3 Dollar			
4.5.1778. Black. New borders and state arms. *TYRANNIS* corrected. Thick paper.	225.	675.	—
S3592 1 Dollar			
4.5.1778. Black. New borders and state arms. *TYRANNIS* corrected. Thick paper.	225.	675.	—
S3593 3 Dollars			
4.5.1778. Black. New borders and state arms. *TYRANNIS* corrected. Thick paper.	225.	675.	—
S3594 4 Dollars			
4.5.1778. Black. New borders and state arms. *TYRANNIS* corrected. Thick paper.	225.	675.	—
S3595 5 Dollars			
4.5.1778. Black. New borders and state arms. *TYRANNIS* corrected. Thick paper.	225.	675.	—
S3596 6 Dollars			
4.5.1778. Black. New borders and state arms. *TYRANNIS* corrected. Thick paper.	225.	675.	—

		VG	VF	UNC
S3597	**7 Dollars** 4.5.1778. Black. New borders and state arms. *TYRANNIS* corrected. Thick paper.	225.	675.	—
S3598	**10 Dollars** 4.5.1778. Black. New borders and state arms. *TYRANNIS* corrected. Thick paper.	225.	675.	—
S3599	**15 Dollars** 4.5.1778. Black. New borders and state arms. *TYRANNIS* corrected. Thick paper.	225.	675.	—

1778 Third Issue

		VG	VF	UNC
S3600	**1/6 Dollar** 5.10.1778. Black. State arms. Thin laid paper.	225.	675.	—
S3601	**1/4 Dollar** 5.10.1778. Black. State arms. Thin laid paper.	225.	675.	—
S3602	**1/3 Dollar** 5.10.1778. Black. State arms. Thin laid paper.	225.	675.	—
S3603	**2/3 Dollar** 5.10.1778. Black. State arms. Thin laid paper.	225.	675.	—
S3604	**1 Dollar** 5.10.1778. Black. State arms. Thin laid paper.	225.	675.	—
S3605	**3 Dollars** 5.10.1778. Black. State arms. Thin laid paper.	225.	675.	—
S3606	**5 Dollars** 5.10.1778. Black. State arms. Thin laid paper.	225.	675.	—
S3607	**7 Dollars** 5.10.1778. Black. State arms. Thin laid paper.	225.	675.	—
S3608	**10 Dollars** 5.10.1778. Black. State arms. Thin laid paper.	225.	675.	—
S3609	**15 Dollars** 5.10.1778. Black. State arms. Thin laid paper.	225.	675.	—
S3610	**50 Dollars = 15 Pounds** 5.10.1778. Black. Thin laid paper.	1000.	—	—
S3611	**100 Dollars = 30 Pounds** 5.10.1778. Black. Thin laid paper.	1000.	—	—

1779 Issue

		VG	VF	UNC
S3612	**3 Dollars** 3.5.1779. Black. State arms. Thin laid paper.	225.	675.	—
S3613	**5 Dollars** 3.5.1779. Black. State arms. Thin laid paper.	225.	675.	—
S3614	**7 Dollars** 3.5.1779. Black. State arms. Thin laid paper.	225.	675.	—
S3615	**10 Dollars** 3.5.1779. Black. State arms. Thin laid paper.	225.	675.	—
S3616	**15 Dollars** 3.5.1779. Black. State arms. Thin laid paper.	225.	675.	—
S3617	**50 Dollars = 15 Pounds** 3.5.1779. Black. Ship in left border. Thin laid paper.	500.	3000.	—
S3618	**100 Dollars = 30 Pounds** 3.5.1779. Black. Ship in left border. Thin laid paper.	500.	3000.	—

1780 First Issue

		VG	VF	UNC
S3619	**1 Dollar** 1.5.1780. Black. Various handwritten dates. Back: Red and black. Watermark: *CONFEDERATION* in 2 lines. Printer: David Hall and William Sellers.	200.	250.	1000.
S3620	**2 Dollars** 1.5.1780. Black. Various handwritten dates. Back: Red and black. Watermark: *CONFEDERATION* in 2 lines. Printer: David Hall and William Sellers.	200.	250.	1000.
S3621	**3 Dollars** 1.5.1780. Black. Various handwritten dates. Back: Red and black. Watermark: *CONFEDERATION* in 2 lines. Printer: David Hall and William Sellers.	200.	250.	1000.
S3622	**4 Dollars** 1.5.1780. Black. Various handwritten dates. Back: Red and black. Watermark: *CONFEDERATION* in 2 lines. Printer: David Hall and William Sellers.	200.	250.	1000.
S3623	**5 Dollars** 1.5.1780. Black. Various handwritten dates. Back: Red and black. Watermark: *CONFEDERATION* in 2 lines. Printer: David Hall and William Sellers.	200.	250.	1000.
S3624	**7 Dollars** 1.5.1780. Black. Various handwritten dates. Back: Red and black. Watermark: *CONFEDERATION* in 2 lines. Printer: David Hall and William Sellers.	200.	250.	1000.
S3625	**8 Dollars** 1.5.1780. Black. Various handwritten dates. Back: Red and black. Watermark: *CONFEDERATION* in 2 lines. Printer: David Hall and William Sellers.	200.	250.	1000.
S3626	**20 Dollars** 1.5.1780. Black. Various handwritten dates. Back: Red and black. Watermark: *CONFEDERATION* in 2 lines. Printer: David Hall and William Sellers.	200.	250.	1000.

1780 Second Issue

		VG	VF	UNC
S3627	**3 1/3 Dollars = 20 Shillings** 14.7.1780. Black. Back: Denomination. Very thin paper.	90.00	250.	1200.
S3628	**6 2/3 Dollars = 2 Pounds** 14.7.1780. Black. Back: Denomination. Very thin paper.	90.00	250.	1200.
S3629	**10 Dollars = 3 Pounds** 14.7.1780. Black. *Bill* spelled *Qill*. Back: Denomination. Very thin paper.	90.00	250.	1200.
S3630	**13 1/3 Dollars = 4 Pounds** 14.7.1780. Black. Back: Denomination. Very thin paper.	90.00	250.	1200.
S3631	**15 Dollars = 4 Pounds** 14.7.1780. Black. Back: Denomination. Very thin paper.	90.00	250.	1200.
S3632	**20 Dollars = 6 Pounds** 14.7.1780. Black. Back: Denomination. Very thin paper.	90.00	250.	1200.
S3633	**35 Dollars = 10 Pounds 10 Shillings** 14.7.1780. Black. Back: Denomination. Very thin paper.	90.00	250.	1200.
S3634	**45 Dollars = 13 Pounds 10 Shillings** 14.7.1780. Black. Back: Denomination. Very thin paper.	90.00	250.	1200.
S3635	**55 Dollars = 15 Pounds 10 Shillings** 14.7.1780. Black. *DOLLARS* spelled *DOLLANS*. Back: Denomination. Very thin paper.	90.00	250.	1200.
S3636	**60 Dollars = 18 Pounds** 14.7.1780. Black. *Bill* spelled *DILL*. Back: Denomination. Very thin paper.	90.00	250.	1200.
S3637	**80 Dollars** 14.7.1780. Black. Lower border text inverted. Back: Denomination. Very thin paper.	90.00	250.	1200.
S3638	**100 Dollars = 30 Pounds** 14.7.1780. Black. Back: Denomination. Very thin paper.	90.00	250.	1200.

1780 Third Issue

		VG	VF	UNC
S3639	**50 Dollars = 15 Pounds** 16.10.1780. Black. Back: Denomination. Very thin paper.	100.	250.	1000.
S3640	**100 Dollars = 30 Pounds** 16.10.1780. Black. *This* spelled *Tnis*. Back: Denomination. Very thin paper.	100.	250.	1000.
S3641	**200 Dollars = 60 Pounds** 16.10.1780. Black. Back: Denomination. Very thin paper.	100.	250.	1000.
S3642	**300 Dollars = 90 Pounds** 16.10.1780. Black. Back: Denomination. Very thin paper.	100.	250.	1000.
S3643	**400 Dollars = 120 Pounds** 16.10.1780. Black. *HUNDRED* spelled *HUNDNED*. Back: Denomination. Very thin paper.	100.	250.	1000.

		VG	VF	UNC
S3644	**500 Dollars = 150 Pounds** 16.10.1780. Black. *Bill* spelled *Qill*. Back: Denomination. Very thin paper.	100.	250.	1000.

1780 Act for Clothing the Army Issue

		VG	VF	UNC
S3645	**100 Dollars = 30 Pounds** 16.10.1780. Black. Uniface. Without control letters. Very thin laid paper.	1500.	5000.	—
S3646	**200 Dollars = 60 Pounds** 16.10.1780. Black. Uniface. Without control letters. Very thin laid paper.	1500.	5000.	—
S3647	**300 Dollars = 90 Pounds** 16.10.1780. Black. Uniface. Without control letters. Very thin laid paper.	1500.	5000.	—
S3648	**400 Dollars = 120 Pounds** 16.10.1780. Black. Uniface. Without control letters. *HUNDRED* spelled *HUNDNED*. Very thin laid paper.	1500.	5000.	—
S3649	**500 Dollars = 150 Pounds** 16.10.1780. Black. Uniface. Without control letters. *Bill* spelled *Qill*. Very thin laid paper.	1500.	5000.	—
S3650	**1000 Dollars = 300 Pounds** 16.10.1780. Black. Uniface. Without control letters. Very thin laid paper.	1500.	5000.	—

1781 First Issue

		VG	VF	UNC
S3651	**20 Dollars = 6 Pounds** 1.3.1781. Black. Both very thin laid paper and thick laid paper.	125.	325.	—
S3652	**50 Dollars = 15 Pounds** 1.3.1781. Black. Both very thin laid paper and thick laid paper.	125.	325.	—
S3653	**80 Dollars = 24 Pounds** 1.3.1781. Black. Both very thin laid paper and thick laid paper.	125.	325.	—

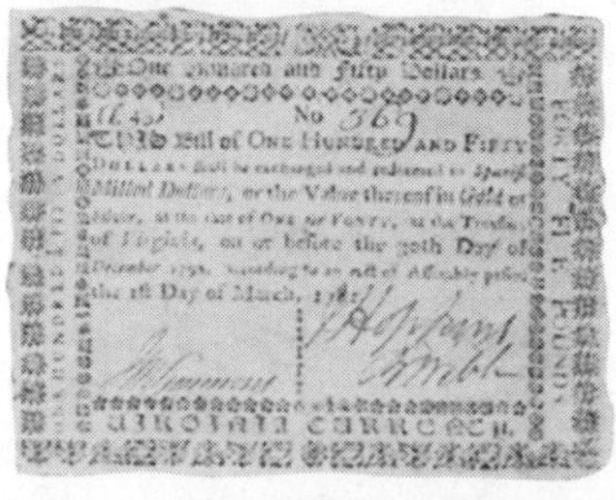

		VG	VF	UNC
S3654	**150 Dollars = 45 Pounds** 1.3.1781. Black. *DOLLARS* spelled *DOLLARAE*. Both very thin laid paper and thick laid paper.	125.	325.	—

		VG	VF	UNC
S3655	**250 Dollars = 75 Pounds** 1.3.1781. Black. *DOLLARS* spelled *DOLLAR8.* Both very thin laid paper and thick laid paper.	125.	325.	—
S3656	**500 Dollars = 150 Pounds** 1.3.1781. Black. *FIVE* spelled *OIVE.* Both very thin laid paper and thick laid paper.	125.	325.	—
S3657	**750 Dollars = 225 Pounds** 1.3.1781. Black. POUN(D)S, *Bill* spelled *Qill.* Both very thin laid paper and thick laid paper.	125.	325.	—
S3658	**1000 Dollars = 300 Pounds** 1.3.1781. Black. Both very thin laid paper and thick laid paper.	125.	325.	—

1781 Second Issue

		VG	VF	UNC
S3659	**10 Dollars = 3 Pounds** 7.5.1781. Black. Printer: John Dunlap, Philadelphia.	125.	325.	—
S3660	**15 Dollars = 4 Pounds 10 Shillings** 7.5.1781. Black. Printer: John Dunlap, Philadelphia.	125.	325.	—
S3661	**25 Dollars = 7 Pounds 10 Shillings** 7.5.1781. Black. Printer: John Dunlap, Philadelphia.	125.	325.	—
S3662	**30 Dollars = 9 Pounds** 7.5.1781. Black. Printer: John Dunlap, Philadelphia.	125.	325.	—
S3663	**35 Dollars = 10 Pounds 10 Shillings** 7.5.1781. Black. Printer: John Dunlap, Philadelphia.	125.	325.	—
S3664	**40 Dollars = 12 Pounds** 7.5.1781. Black. Printer: John Dunlap, Philadelphia.	125.	325.	—
S3665	**50 Dollars = 15 Pounds** 7.5.1781. Black. Printer: John Dunlap, Philadelphia.	125.	325.	—
S3666	**70 Dollars = 21 Pounds** 7.5.1781. Black. Printer: John Dunlap, Philadelphia.	125.	325.	—
S3667	**75 Dollars = 22 Pounds 15 Shillings** 7.5.1781. Black. Printer: John Dunlap, Philadelphia.	125.	325.	—
S3668	**100 Dollars = 30 Pounds** 7.5.1781. Black. Printer: John Dunlap, Philadelphia.	125.	325.	—
S3669	**200 Dollars = 60 Pounds** 7.5.1781. Black. *WF* in lower border. Printer: John Dunlap, Philadelphia.	125.	325.	—
S3670	**500 Dollars = 150 Pounds** 7.5.1781. Black. Printer: John Dunlap, Philadelphia.	150.	350.	—
S3671	**1000 Dollars = 300 Pounds** 7.5.1781. Black. Printer: John Dunlap, Philadelphia.	150.	350.	—
S3672	**1200 Dollars = 360 Pounds** 7.5.1781. Black. Printer: John Dunlap, Philadelphia.	150.	350.	—

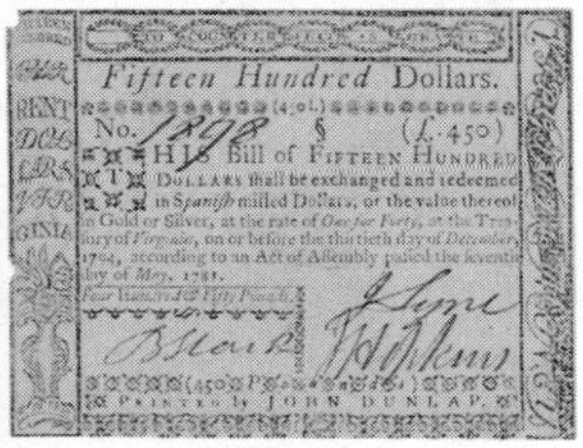

		VG	VF	UNC
S3673	**1500 Dollars = 450 Pounds** 7.5.1781. Black. Printer: John Dunlap, Philadelphia.	175.	375.	—
S3674	**2000 Dollars = 600 Pounds** 7.5.1781. Black. Printer: John Dunlap, Philadelphia.	250.	650.	—

Virginia

Civil War

1861 Treasury Issue

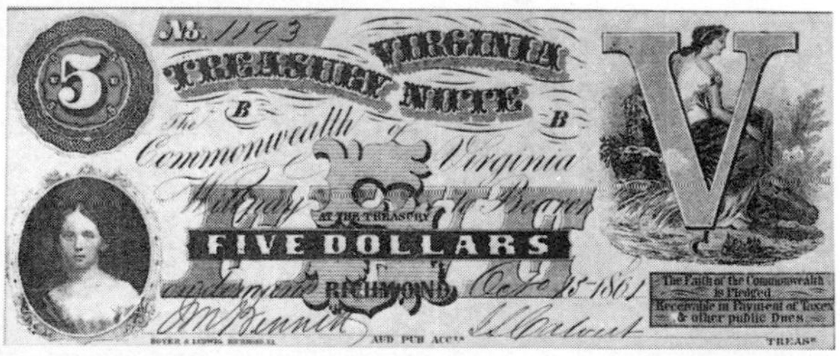

		VG	VF	UNC
S3675	**5 Dollars** 15.10.1861. Girl at lower left, seated Ceres in large *V* at right. Various handwritten dates. Engraver: Hoyer and Ludwig.	75.00	200.	400.
S3676	**10 Dollars** 15.10.1861. Standing Liberty with shield at left. Various handwritten dates. Engraver: Hoyer and Ludwig.	75.00	200.	400.

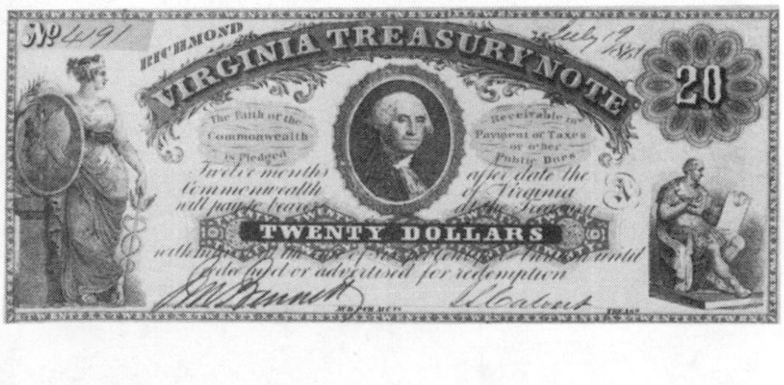

		VG	VF	UNC
S3677	**20 Dollars** 1.8.1861. Black on green underprint. Standing Minerva at left, portrait George Washington at center, seated man reading script at right. Various handwritten dates. Engraver: Hoyer and Ludwig.	150.	400.	750.

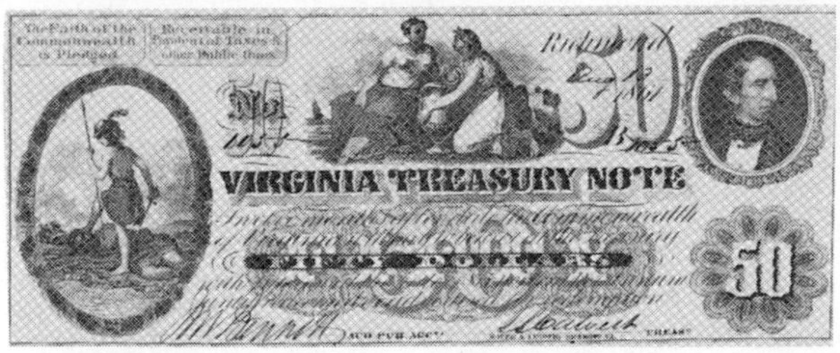

		VG	VF	UNC
S3678	**50 Dollars** 13.8.1861. Black on red underprint. Gladiator at left, Ceres and Commerce with urn at top center, J. Tyler at right. Various handwritten dates. Engraver: Hoyer and Ludwig.	2500.	5000.	8500.
S3679	**100 Dollars** 13.8.1861. Black on red underprint. Woman reclining at left, portrait George Washington between seated woman and man in underprint at center. Various handwritten dates. Engraver: Hoyer and Ludwig.	3500.	6000.	10,000.
S3680	**500 Dollars** 25.9.1861. Three women seated at left, portrait George Washington at upper right. Various handwritten dates. Engraver: Hoyer and Ludwig. Rare.	—	—	—

1862 Treasury Issue

		VG	VF	UNC
S3681	**1 Dollar** 1862. Black on red underprint. Portrait Gov. J. Letcher at left, seated Ceres at center. Engraver: Keatinge & Ball.			
	a. 15.5.1862.	20.00	45.00	80.00
	b. 21.7.1862.	20.00	45.00	80.00
	c. 21.10.1862.	20.00	45.00	80.00

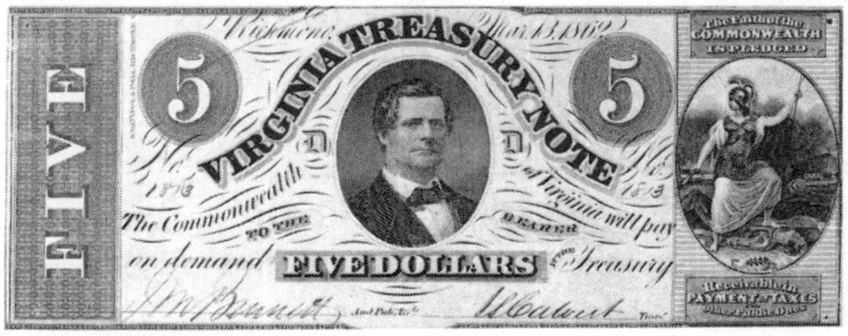

		VG	VF	UNC
S3682	**5 Dollars** 13.3.1862. Black on green underprint. Portrait Gov. J. M. Bennett at center, Gladiatorial figure at right. Plain paper. Engraver: Keatinge & Ball.			
	a. Watermark: *Hodgkinson & Co. Wookey Hole Mill.*	150.	250.	500.
	b. Watermark: *CSA.*	150.	250.	500.
	c. Watermark: *J. Whatman.*	150.	250.	500.
S3683	**10 Dollars** 15.10.1862. Black on green underprint. Hercules in cartouche at left, seated Ceres at center, Gov. J. B. Floyd at right. Plain paper. Engraver: Keatinge & Ball.			
	a. Watermark: *FIVE.*	50.00	90.00	135.
	b. Watermark: *W.T.C.C. & Co.*	50.00	90.00	135.
	c. Watermark: *J. Green & Sons 1862.*	50.00	90.00	135.

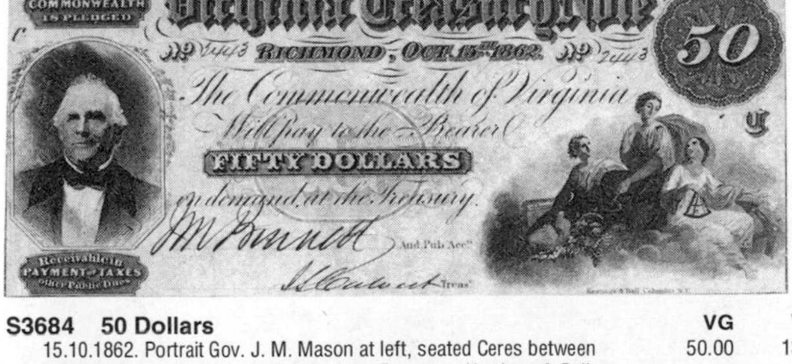

		VG	VF	UNC
S3684	**50 Dollars** 15.10.1862. Portrait Gov. J. M. Mason at left, seated Ceres between Commerce and Navigation at lower right. Engraver: Keatinge & Ball.	50.00	135.	275.

		VG	VF	UNC
S3685	**100 Dollars** 15.10.1862. Black on orange underprint. Portrait George Washington at left, portrait Gov. Letcher left. Washington at center, Indian girl at right. Engraver: Keatinge & Ball.	75.00	175.	375.

Military Payment Certificates

Series 461

16.9.1946 to 10.3.1947.

		FINE	XF	CU
M1	**5 Cents**			
	ND (1946). Blue underprint. Back: Seal of the United States at lower center.	4.00	20.00	65.00
M1r	**5 Cents**			
	Replacement A-	—	Unc	1000.

		FINE	XF	CU
M2	**10 Cents**			
	ND (1946). Blue underprint. Like #M1. Back: Seal of the United States at lower center.	4.00	20.00	65.00
M2r	**10 Cents**			
	Replacement A-	—	Unc	1000.

		FINE	XF	CU
M3	**25 Cents**			
	ND (1946). Blue underprint. Like #M1. Back: Seal of the United States at lower center.	13.00	95.00	250.
M3r	**25 Cents**			
	Replacement A-	—	—	—

		FINE	XF	CU
M4	**50 Cents**			
	ND (1946). Blue underprint. Like #M1. Back: Seal of the United States at lower center.	14.00	70.00	250.
M4r	**50 Cents**			
	Replacement A-	—	—	—

		FINE	XF	CU
M5	**1 Dollar**			
	ND (1946). Blue underprint. Back: Seal of the United States at lower center.	6.00	30.00	185.
M5r	**1 Dollar**			
	Replacement A-	—	Unc	1300.

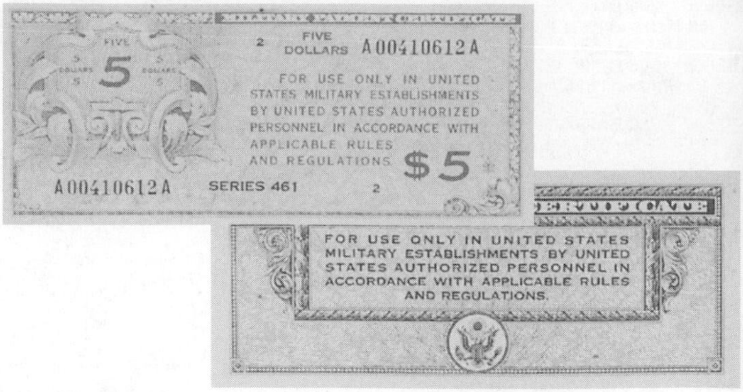

		FINE	XF	CU
M6	**5 Dollars**			
	ND (1946). Blue underprint. Like #M7. Back: Seal of the United States at lower center.	32.50	125.	325.
M6r	**5 Dollars**			
	Replacement A-	—	—	—

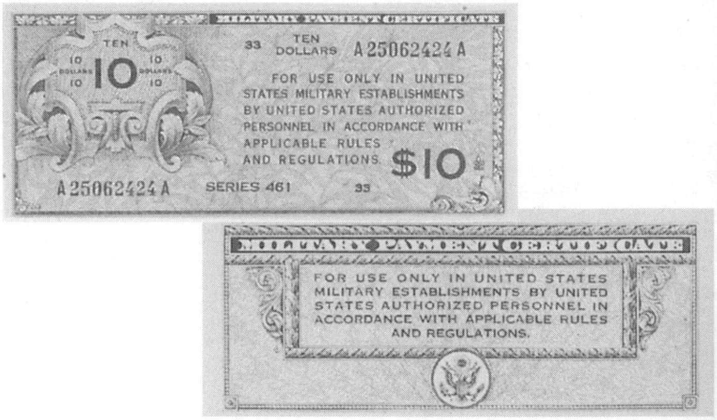

		FINE	XF	CU
M7	**10 Dollars**			
	ND (1946). Blue underprint. Back: Seal of the United States at lower center.	25.00	75.00	300.
M7r	**10 Dollars**			
	Replacement A-	—	—	—

Series 471

10.3.1947 to 22.3.1948.

		FINE	XF	CU
M8	**5 Cents**			
	ND (1947). Red and blue. Back: Seal of the United States at lower center.	7.50	30.00	90.00
M8r	**5 Cents**			
	Replacement B-	—	—	—

		FINE	XF	CU
M9	**10 Cents**			
	ND (1947). Red and blue. Back: Seal of the United States at lower center.	6.00	30.00	90.00
M9r	**10 Cents**			
	Replacement B-	—	—	—

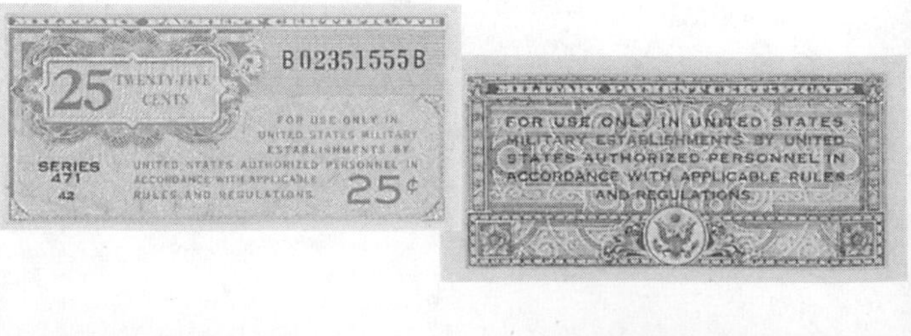

		FINE	XF	CU
M10	**25 Cents** ND (1947). Red and blue. Back: Seal of the United States at lower center.	15.00	75.00	300.
M10r	**25 Cents** Replacement B-	—	—	—

		FINE	XF	CU
M11	**50 Cents** ND (1947). Red and blue. Back: Seal of the United States at lower center.	20.00	110.	325.
M11r	**50 Cents** Replacement B-	—	—	—

		FINE	XF	CU
M12	**1 Dollar** ND (1947). Red and blue. Back: Seal of the United States at lower center.	15.00	85.00	275.
M12r	**1 Dollar** Replacement B-	—	—	—
M13	**5 Dollars** ND (1947). Red and blue. Back: Seal of the United States at lower center.	775.	2375.	20,000.
M13r	**5 Dollars** Replacement B-	—	—	—

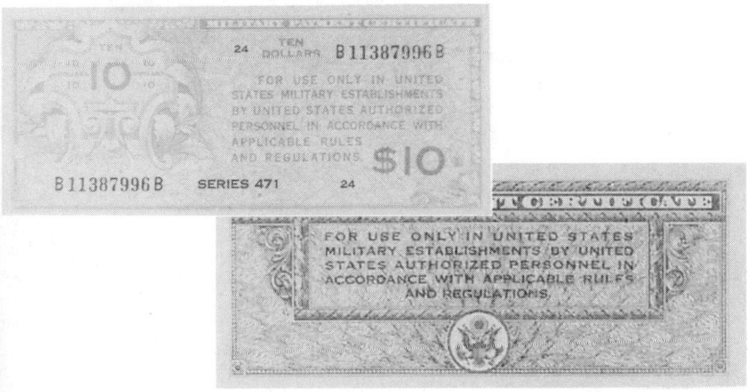

		FINE	XF	CU
M14	**10 Dollars** ND (1947). Red and blue. Back: Seal of the United States at lower center.	200.	600.	2400.
M14r	**10 Dollars** Replacement B-	—	—	—

SERIES 472

		FINE	XF	CU
M15	**5 Cents** ND (1948). Blue underprint. Seal of the United States at center. Back: Seal of the United States at center.	1.00	4.00	12.50
M15r	**5 Cents** Replacement C-	—	Unc	750.
M16	**10 Cents** ND (1948). Blue underprint. Seal of the United States at center. Like #M15. Back: Seal of the United States at center.	2.25	18.00	70.00
M16r	**10 Cents** Replacement C-	—	Unc	675.

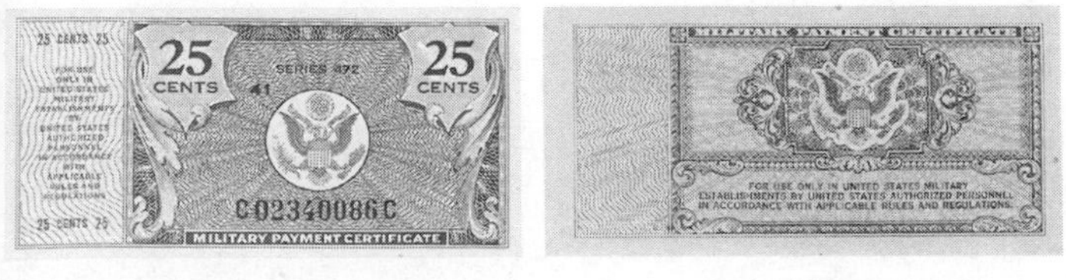

		FINE	XF	CU
M17	**25 Cents** ND (1948). Blue underprint. Seal of the United States at center. Like #M15. Back: Seal of the United States at center.	8.00	65.00	225.
M17r	**25 Cents** Replacement C-	—	—	—

		FINE	XF	CU
M18	**50 Cents** ND (1948). Blue underprint. Seal of the United States at center. Like #M15. Back: Seal of the United States at center.	10.00	75.00	275.
M18r	**50 Cents** Replacement C-	—	—	—

		FINE	XF	CU
M19	**1 Dollar** ND (1948). Blue underprint. Seal of the United States at center. Back: Seal of the United States at center.	12.00	85.00	250.
M19r	**1 Dollar** Replacement C-	—	Unc	2400.

		FINE	XF	CU
M20	**5 Dollars** ND (1948). Blue underprint. Seal of the United States at center. Back: Seal of the United States at center.	125.	900.	2750.
M20r	**5 Dollars** Replacement C-	—	—	—

		FINE	XF	CU
M21	**10 Dollars** ND (1948). Blue underprint. Seal of the United States at center. Like #M20. Back: Seal of the United States at center.	50.00	275.	2000.
M21r	**10 Dollars** Replacement C-	—	—	—

Series 481

20.6.1951 to 25.5.1954.

M22 5 Cents

	FINE	XF	CU
ND (1951). Light blue and brown underprint. Seated woman with compasses and sphere at left. Back: Seal of the United States at center.	2.00	9.00	27.50

M22r 5 Cents

Replacement D-	—	Unc	600.

M23 10 Cents

	FINE	XF	CU
ND (1951). Light blue and brown underprint. Seated woman with compasses and sphere at left. Like #M22. Back: Seal of the United States at center.	2.50	15.00	35.00

M23r 10 Cents

Replacement D-	—	Unc	450.

M24 25 Cents

	FINE	XF	CU
ND (1951). Light blue and brown underprint. Seated woman with compasses and sphere at left. Like #M22. Back: Seal of the United States at center.	10.00	25.00	60.00

M24r 25 Cents

Replacement D-	—	Unc	800.

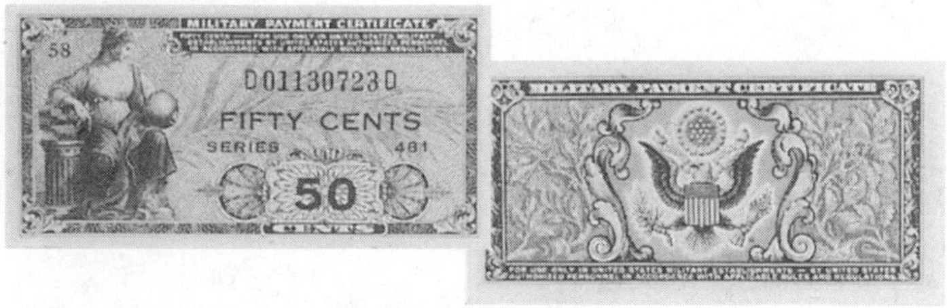

M25 50 Cents

	FINE	XF	CU
ND (1951). Light blue and brown underprint. Seated woman with compasses and sphere at left. Like #M22. Back: Seal of the United States at center.	10.00	55.00	275.

M25r 50 Cents

Replacement D-	—	—	—

M26 1 Dollar

	FINE	XF	CU
ND (1951). Light blue and brown underprint. Women at upper left and right.	20.00	95.00	295.

NOTE: #M26 exists with position # at right or left; the left variety is worth 10 percent more.

M26r 1 Dollar

Replacement D-	—	Unc	1000.

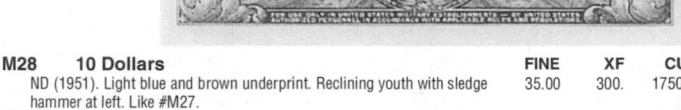

M27 5 Dollars

	FINE	XF	CU
ND (1951). Light blue and brown underprint. Reclining youth with sledge hammer at left.	80.00	550.	3000.

M27r 5 Dollars

Replacement D-	—	—	—

M28 10 Dollars

	FINE	XF	CU
ND (1951). Light blue and brown underprint. Reclining youth with sledge hammer at left. Like #M27.	35.00	300.	1750.

M28r 10 Dollars

Replacement D-	—	—	—

Series 521

25.5.1954 to 27.5.1958.

M29 5 Cents

	FINE	XF	CU
ND (1954). Blue on green and yellow underprint. Woman with helmet at left. Back: Woman at center.	2.00	9.00	30.00

M29r 5 Cents

Replacement E-	—	Unc	1500.

M30 10 Cents

	FINE	XF	CU
ND (1954). Lilac on green and blue underprint. Woman with helmet at left. Like #M29. Back: Woman at center.	3.00	12.50	32.50

M30r 10 Cents

Replacement E-	—	Unc	2000.

M31 25 Cents

	FINE	XF	CU
ND (1954). Brown on green underprint. Woman with helmet at left. Like #M29. Back: Woman at center.	8.00	27.50	85.00

M31r 25 Cents

Replacement E-	—	Unc	2250.

M32 50 Cents

	FINE	XF	CU
ND (1954). Green on lilac and blue underprint. Woman with helmet at left. Like #M29. Back: Woman at center.	10.00	75.00	150.

		FINE	XF	CU
M32r	**50 Cents** Replacement E-	—	Unc	2500.

		FINE	XF	CU
M33	**1 Dollar** ND (1954). Brown. Woman with Liberty Cap at left. Back: Woman at center.	9.50	50.00	175.
M33r	**1 Dollar** Replacement E-	—	Unc	2250.

		FINE	XF	CU
M34	**5 Dollars** ND (1954). Blue. Woman with flower basket at center. Back: Woman at center.	300.	1300.	3000.
M34r	**5 Dollars** Replacement E-	—	—	—

		FINE	XF	CU
M35	**10 Dollars** ND (1954). Brown-violet. Woman with wreath at right.	100.	650.	1800.
M35r	**10 Dollars** Replacement E-	—	—	—

Series 541

27.5.1958 to 26.5.1961.

		FINE	XF	CU
M36	**5 Cents** ND (1958). Violet on green and yellow-green underprint. Woman with wreath at left. Back: Woman at center.	1.50	6.00	17.50
M36r	**5 Cents** Replacement E-	—	Unc	350.

		FINE	XF	CU
M37	**10 Cents** ND (1958). Green on orange underprint. Woman with wreath at left. Like #M36. Back: Woman at center.	5.00	20.00	50.00
M37r	**10 Cents** Replacement F-	—	Unc	350.
M38	**25 Cents** ND (1958). Blue on lilac underprint. Woman with wreath at left. Like #M36. Back: Woman at center.	9.00	30.00	80.00
M38r	**25 Cents** Replacement F-	—	Unc	600.

		FINE	XF	CU
M39	**50 Cents** ND (1958). Brown on green and yellow underprint. Woman with wreath at left. Like #M36. Back: Woman at center.	30.00	100.	325.
M39r	**50 Cents** Replacement F-	—	Unc	300.

		FINE	XF	CU
M40	**1 Dollar** ND (1958). Blue. Woman with cap at center. Back: Woman with fasces and jug at center.	30.00	100.	400.
M40r	**1 Dollar** Replacement F-	—	Unc	1500.

		FINE	XF	CU
M41	**5 Dollars** ND (1958). Lilac. Woman with wreath at left. Back: Woman at center.	1250.	3750.	15,000.
M41r	**5 Dollars** Replacement F-	—	—	—

		FINE	XF	CU
M42	**10 Dollars** ND (1958). Brown. Woman at center. Back: Woman at center.	300.	1500.	3500.
M42r	**10 Dollars** Replacement F-	—	—	—

Series 591

26.5.1961 to 6.1.1964.

		VG	VF	UNC
M43	**5 Cents** ND (1961). Lilac on green and yellow underprint. Head of Statue of Liberty at right. Back: Value.		3.50	55.00
M43r	**5 Cents** Replacement G-	—	Unc	1250.

		VG	VF	UNC
M44	**10 Cents** ND (1961). Blue on lilac underprint. Head of Statue of Liberty at right. Back: Value.		4.00	65.00
M44r	**10 Cents** Replacement G-	—	Unc	2500.
M45	**25 Cents** ND (1961). Green on purple underprint. Head of Statue of Liberty at right. Back: Value.		17.50	140.
M45r	**25 Cents** Replacement G-	—	—	—

		VG	VF	UNC
M46	**50 Cents** ND (1961). Brown on aqua underprint. Head of Statue of Liberty at right. Back: Value.		35.00	240.
M46r	**50 Cents** Replacement G-	—	Unc	1200.

		VG	VF	UNC
M47	**1 Dollar** ND (1961). Red on purple and multicolor underprint. Portrait of a woman facing left at right. Back: Value.		25.00	275.
M47r	**1 Dollar** Replacement G-	—	Unc	2500.

		VG	VF	UNC
M48	**5 Dollars** ND (1961). Blue on multicolor underprint. Woman at left. Back: Value.		550.	4500.
M48r	**5 Dollars** Replacement G-	—	—	—

		VG	VF	UNC
M49	**10 Dollars** ND (1961). Green on multicolor underprint. Portrait of a woman 3/4 facing left at right. Back: Value.		200.	2000.
M49r	**10 Dollars** Replacement G-	—	—	—

Series 611

6.1.1964 to 28.4.1969.

		VG	VF	UNC
M50	**5 Cents** ND (1964). Blue on multicolor underprint. Liberty head profile facing right at left. Back: Value.		5.00	40.00
M50r	**5 Cents** Replacement H-	—	Unc	125.

		VG	VF	UNC
M51	**10 Cents** ND (1964). Green on multicolor underprint. Liberty head profile facing right at left. Back: Value.		5.00	45.00
M51r	**10 Cents** Replacement H-	—	Unc	125.
M52	**25 Cents** ND (1964). Brown on multicolor underprint. Liberty head profile facing right at left. Back: Value.		30.00	275.
M52r	**25 Cents** Replacement H-	—	—	—
M53	**50 Cents** ND (1964). Lilac on multicolor underprint. Liberty head profile facing right at left. Back: Value.		30.00	275.
M53r	**50 Cents** Replacement H-	—	—	—

		VG	VF	UNC
M54	**1 Dollar** ND (1964). Green on multicolor underprint. Portrait of a woman with tiara facing at left. Back: Value.		5.00	100.
M54r	**1 Dollar** Replacement H-	—	Unc	250.
M55	**5 Dollars** ND (1964). Red on multicolor underprint. Woman facing at center. Back: Value.		125.	2000.
M55r	**5 Dollars** Replacement H-	—	Unc	3000.

		VG	VF	UNC
M56	**10 Dollars** ND (1964). Blue on violet and multicolor underprint. Portrait of a woman facing left at center. Back: Value.		130.	1400.
M56r	**10 Dollars** Replacement H-	—	Unc	2100.

Series 641

31.8.1965 to 21.10.1968.

		VG	VF	UNC
M57	**5 Cents** ND (1965). Purple on blue underprint. Woman at left. Back: Eagle with outstretched wings clasping fasces at center. Value.		1.00	13.50
M57r	**5 Cents** Replacement J-	—	Unc	300.
M58	**10 Cents** ND (1965). Green on dark red underprint. Woman at left. Back: Eagle with outstretched wings clasping fasces at center. Value.		1.00	18.50

	VG	VF	UNC
M58r 10 Cents Replacement J-	—	Unc	450.
M59 25 Cents ND (1965). Red on blue-green underprint. Woman at left. Back: Eagle with outstretched wings clasping fasces at center. Value.		2.50	24.00
M59r 25 Cents Replacemetn J-	—	Unc	450.
M60 50 Cents ND (1965). Orange on multicolor underprint. Woman at left. Back: Eagle with outstretched wings clasping fasces at center. Value.		3.50	35.00
M60r 50 Cents Replacement J-	—	Unc	750.

	VG	VF	UNC
M61 1 Dollar ND (1965). Light red on multicolor underprint. Woman at right. Back: Value.		4.00	45.00
M61r 1 Dollar Replacement J-	—	Unc	1250.

	VG	VF	UNC
M62 5 Dollars ND (1965). Green on multicolor underprint. Woman with wreath of flowers at center. Back: Woman facing right at center. Value.		17.50	250.
M62r 5 Dollars Replacement J-	—	Unc	3750.

	VG	VF	UNC
M63 10 Dollars ND (1965). Brown on orange and multicolor underprint. Portrait of a woman facing right at center. Back: Liberty head facing at center. Value.		10.00	250.
M63r 10 Dollars Replacement J-	—	Unc	1500.

Series 661

21.10.1968 to 11.8.1969.

	VG	VF	UNC
M64 5 Cents ND (1968). Light green and lilac on multicolor underprint. Woman wearing scarf at left. Back: Value.		1.00	10.00
M64r 5 Cents Replacement B-	—	Unc	800.

	VG	VF	UNC
M65 10 Cents ND (1968). Blue and violet on multicolor underprint. Woman wearing scarf at left. Back: Value.		1.00	10.00
M65r 10 Cents Replacement B-	—	Unc	375.
M66 25 Cents ND (1968). Brown and orange on multicolor underprint. Woman wearing scarf at left. Back: Value.		2.00	27.50
M66r 50 Cents Replacement B-	—	Unc	600.
M67 50 Cents ND (1968). Red and green on multicolor underprint. Woman wearing scarf at left. Back: Value.		2.00	22.50
M67r 50 Cents Replacement B-	—	—	—

	VG	VF	UNC
M68 1 Dollar ND (1968). Blue on multicolor underprint. Portrait of a woman 3/4 facing left at right. Back: Mountain scene. Value.		5.00	24.00
M68r 1 Dollar Replacement B-	—	Unc	750.
M69 5 Dollars ND (1968). Dark brown on red and multicolor underprint. Woman holding flowers at center. Back: Girl's head at center. Value.		5.00	30.00
M69r 5 Dollars Replacement B-	—	Unc	800.
M70 10 Dollars ND (1968). Red and orange on multicolor underprint. Woman holding fasces at left. Back: Woman facing left at center right. Value.		200.	1850.
M70r 10 Dollars Replacement B-	—	Unc	5000.

	VG	VF	UNC
M71 20 Dollars ND (1968). Black, brown and blue on multicolor underprint. Woman at center. Back: Standing woman at left. Value.		125.	1450.
M71r 20 Dollars Replacement B-	—	Unc	3000.

Series 651

28.4.1969 to 19.11.1973.

	VG	VF	UNC
M72A 5 Cents ND (1969). Dark blue on multicolor underprint. Woman at left. "Minuteman statue" at left. Back: Eagle with outstretched wings clasping fasces at center. Value. Not issued.		—	700.
M72B 10 Cents ND (1969). Red-violet on multicolor underprint. Woman at left. "Minuteman statue" at left. Back: Eagle with outstretched wings clasping fasces at center. Value. Not issued.		—	700.
M72C 25 Cents ND (1969). Aqua blue on multicolor underprint. Woman at left. "Minuteman statue" at left. Back: Eagle with outstretched wings clasping fasces at center. Value. Not issued.		—	700.

	VG	VF	UNC
M72D 50 Cents ND (1969). Dark brown on multicolor underprint. Woman at left. "Minuteman statue" at left. Back: Eagle with outstretched wings clasping fasces at center. Value. Not issued.		—	275.

	VG	VF	UNC
M72E 1 Dollar ND (1969). Green on violet and multicolor underprint. Portrait of a woman facing left at right. "Minuteman statue" at left.		6.00	45.00
M72Er One Dollar Replacement A-	—	—	—

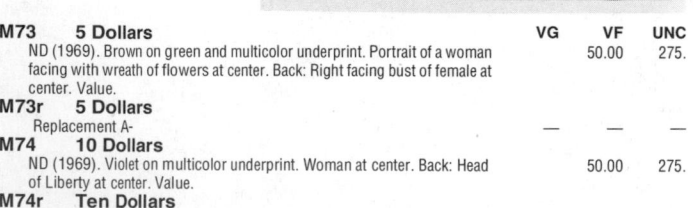

	VG	VF	UNC
M73 5 Dollars ND (1969). Brown on green and multicolor underprint. Portrait of a woman facing with wreath of flowers at center. Back: Right facing bust of female at center. Value.		50.00	275.
M73r 5 Dollars Replacement A-	—	—	—
M74 10 Dollars ND (1969). Violet on multicolor underprint. Woman at center. Back: Head of Liberty at center. Value.		50.00	275.
M74r Ten Dollars Replacement A-	—	—	—

SERIES 681

11.8.1969 to 7.10.1970.

	VG	VF	UNC
M75 5 Cents ND (1969). Green and blue. Submarine at right. Back: Astronaut in spacewalk at center. Value.		1.00	12.50
M75r 5 Cents Replacement C-	—	Unc	250.
M76 10 Cents ND (1969). Violet and blue. Submarine at right. Back: Astronaut in spacewalk at center. Value.		1.00	16.00
M76r 10 Cents Replacement C-	—	Unc	250.
M77 25 Cents ND (1969). Red and blue. Submarine at right. Back: Astronaut in spacewalk at center. Value.		2.00	27.50
M77r 25 Cents Replacement C-	—	—	—

	VG	VF	UNC
M78 50 Cents ND (1969). Brown and blue. Submarine at right. Back: Astronaut in spacewalk at center. Value.		3.00	25.00
M78r 50 Cents Replacement C-	—	Unc	450.
M79 1 Dollar ND (1969). Violet on multicolor underprint. Air Force pilot at right. Back: FourThunderbirds in formation at center. Value.		3.00	25.00
M79r 1 Dollar Replacement C-	—	Unc	400.

	VG	VF	UNC
M80 5 Dollars ND (1969). Purple and green. Sailor at center. Back: Eagle at center. Value.		10.00	125.
M80r 5 Dollars Replacement C-	—	Unc	2250.

	VG	VF	UNC
M81 10 Dollars ND (1969). Blue-green and black. Infantryman (Green Beret) at center. Back: Tank at center. Value.		30.00	300.
M81r 5 Dollars Replacement C-	—	—	—

	VG	VF	UNC
M82 20 Dollars ND (1969). Brown, pink and blue. Portrait of a soldier facing wearing helmet at center. Back: B-52 bomber at center. Value.		30.00	1100
M82r 20 Dollars Replacement C-	—	—	—

SERIES 691

#M83-M85 not assigned.

	VG	VF	UNC
M83 5 Cents ND (1969). (Not issued).	—	—	—
M83r 5 Cents Replacement E-	—	Unc	200.

	VG	VF	UNC
M84 10 Cents ND (1969). (Not issued).	—	—	—
M84r 10 Cents Replacement E-	—	Unc	250.
M85 25 Cents ND (1969). (Not issued).	—	—	—
M85r 25 Cents Replacement E-	—	Unc	750.
M86 50 Cents ND (1969). (Not issued).	—	—	—
M86r 50 Cents Replacement E-	—	Unc	750.

	VG	VF	UNC
M87 1 Dollar ND (1969). Slate gray on light blue underprint. Woman's portrait at center. Back: Allegorical female seated at center. Not issued.		—	250.
M87 1 Dollar	—	Unc	95.00
M87r 1 Dollar Replacement E-	—	Unc	450.

	VG	VF	UNC
M88 5 Dollars ND (1969). Brown on light blue underprint. Woman's head at left looking right. Back: Woman's head at center. Not issued.		—	1000.

	VG	VF	UNC
M89 10 Dollars ND (1969). Turquoise on light blue and red underprint. Bust of a woman at center. Back: Young girl's head at center. Not issued.		—	1000.

	VG	VF	UNC
M90 20 Dollars ND (1969). Purple on blue and light blue underprint. Veiled woman's head at center. Back: Eagle perched on rock at center. Not issued.		—	300.

Series 692

7.10.1970 to 15.3.1973.

	VG	VF	UNC
M91 5 Cents ND (1970). Red-brown and lilac on multicolor underprint. Sculpture of seated Roman warrior at left. (National Archives, Washington DC facade). Back: Eagle at center.		1.00	16.50
M92 10 Cents ND (1970). Green and blue on multicolor underprint. Sculpture of seated Roman warrior at left. (National Archives, Washington DC facade). Back: Eagle at center.		1.00	17.50
M92r 5 Dollars Replacement E-	—	—	—
M93 25 Cents ND (1970). Dark blue on yellow and multicolor underprint. Sculpture of seated Roman warrior at left. (National Archives, Washington DC facade). Back: Eagle at center.		3.00	30.00
M93 10 Dollars	—	—	—
M93r 10 Dollars Replacement E-	—	—	—
M94 50 Cents ND (1970). Purple on yellow and multicolor underprint. Sculpture of seated Roman warrior at left. (National Archives, Washington DC facade). Back: Eagle at center.		4.00	40.00
M94r 20 Dollars Replacement E-	—	Unc	1800.

	VG	VF	UNC
M95 1 Dollar ND (1970). Blue-green on multicolor underprint. Portrait of a woman facing right at left, flowers at bottom center. Back: Buffalo at center.		8.00	95.00
M96 5 Dollars ND (1970). Brown on orange and multicolor underprint. Girl and flowers at center. Back: Elk family at left center.		50.00	1000.
M97 10 Dollars ND (1970). Blue on pink and multicolor underprint. Chief Hollow Horn Bear at center. Back: Eagle at left center.		75.00	1150.
M98 20 Dollars ND (1970). Violet on orange and multicolor underprint. Chief Ouray at center. Back: Dam.		30.00	1200.

Series 701

#M99-M102 not assigned.

	VG	VF	UNC
M99 5 Cents ND (1970). (Not issued).	—	—	—
M100 10 Cents ND (1970). (Not issued).	—	—	—
M101 25 Cents ND (1970). (Not issued).	—	—	—
M102 50 Cents ND (1970). (Not issued).	—	—	—

	VG	VF	UNC
M103 1 Dollar ND (1970). Light green on brown and orange underprint. Washington Irving and open books. Back: Hay harvesting.		—	750.

	VG	VF	UNC
M104 5 Dollars ND (1970). Purple on green underprint. Thomas Edison at right, light bulb at center, Benjamin Franklin and kite/key at left. Back: Rocky Mountain vista at left center.		—	750.

		VG	VF	UNC
M105	**10 Dollars** ND (1970). Red-brown on tan underprint. Mt. Vernon at center, George Washington at right. Back: Mountain vista at left.		—	750.

		VG	VF	UNC
M106	**20 Dollars** ND (1970). Brown on light blue-green underprint. Steamboat *Clermont* at left, Robert Fulton at right. Back: Coastline vista at center right.		—	750.

AAFES (Army and Air Force Exchange Service)

First Issue

		VG	VF	UNC
M121	**5 Cents** Large value in red. (1A51). Back: Large value in red.	FV	FV	.25

		VG	VF	UNC
M122	**10 Cents** Large vlaue in blue. (1A101). Back: Large value in blue.	FV	FV	.50

		VG	VF	UNC
M123	**25 Cents** Large value in white. (1A251). Back: Large value in white.	FV	FV	.75

Second Issue

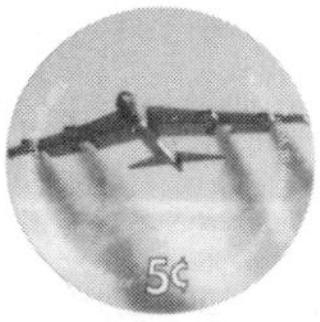

		VG	VF	UNC
M124	**5 Cents** A-10 Thunderbolt II. (2A51).	FV	FV	.25
M125	**5 Cents** B-2 Spirit. (2B51).	FV	FV	.25
M126	**5 Cents** Patriot missile truck. (2C51).	FV	FV	.25
M127	**5 Cents** Paratroopers skyjumping. (2D51).	FV	FV	.25
M128	**5 Cents** B-52 Stratofortress. (2E51).	FV	FV	.25

		VG	VF	UNC
M129	**5 Cents** A-7 Corsair II. (2F51).	FV	FV	.25
M130	**5 Cents** AH-64 Apache helicopter. (2G51).	FV	FV	.25
M131	**5 Cents** *Operation Iraqi Freedom* legend in clouds from a Patriot missle launching. (2H51).	FV	FV	.25

		VG	VF	UNC
M132	**5 Cents** Two F-15 Eagles, sun in background. (2J51).	FV	FV	.25
M133	**5 Cents** Two F-15 Eagles, one banking. (2K51).	FV	FV	.25
M134	**5 Cents** *K-Dog*, Navy's bottle-nose dolphin jumping upwards. (2L51).	FV	FV	.25
M135	**5 Cents** CH-47 Chinook helicopter transporting tank. (2M51).	FV	FV	.25
M136	**10 Cents** AC-130 Spectre front view. (2A101).	FV	FV	.50

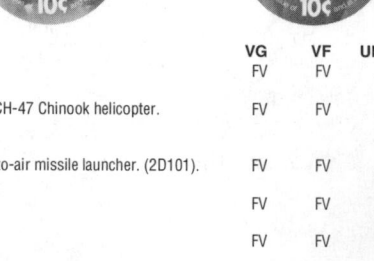

		VG	VF	UNC
M137	**10 Cents** Two F-16 Fighting Falcons. (2B101).	FV	FV	.50
M138	**10 Cents** Two H-60 Black Hawk helicopters and a CH-47 Chinook helicopter. (2C101).	FV	FV	.50
M139	**10 Cents** *Operation Iraqi Freedom* legend, surface-to-air missile launcher. (2D101).	FV	FV	.50
M140	**10 Cents** F-15 Eagle in banking turn. (2E101).	FV	FV	.50
M141	**10 Cents** Warheads on bombs. (2F101).	FV	FV	.50
M142	**10 Cents** Two soldiers in protective masks and MOPP gear. (2G101).	FV	FV	.50

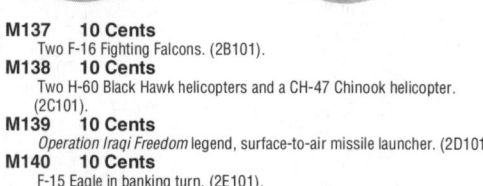

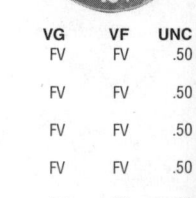

		VG	VF	UNC
M143	**10 Cents** Troops around an artillery piece. (2H101).	FV	FV	.50
M144	**10 Cents** Battleship firing. (2J101).	FV	FV	.50
M145	**10 Cents** Four pilots being assisted into four F-15 Eagles. (2K101).	FV	FV	.50
M146	**10 Cents** Soldier aiming a machine gun. (2L101).	FV	FV	.50
M147	**10 Cents** M1A1Tank advancing right. (2M101).	FV	FV	.50

		VG	VF	UNC
M148	**25 Cents** CH-46 Sea Knight helicopter. (2A251).	FV	FV	.75
M149	**25 Cents** F-16 Fighting Falcon diving. (2B251).	FV	FV	.75
M150	**25 Cents** Close-up of soldier wearing protective mask. (2C251).	FV	FV	.75
M151	**25 Cents** Two UH-1Iroquois helicopters advancing forward. (2D251).	FV	FV	.75

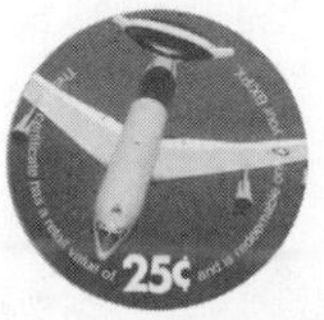

		VG	VF	UNC
M152	**25 Cents** E-3 Sentry AWACS. (2E251).	FV	FV	.75
M153	**25 Cents** Pilot in cockpit of F-16 Fighting Falcon as seen from above. (2F251).	FV	FV	.75

	VG	VF	UNC
M154 25 Cents			
Operation Iraqi Freedom legend, top of tank. (2G251).	FV	FV	.75
M155 25 Cents			
Hovercraft. (2H251).	FV	FV	.75

	VG	VF	UNC
M156 25 Cents			
F/A-18 Hornet in a banking turn. (2J251).	FV	FV	.75
M157 25 Cents			
Mother of all Bombs MOAB, in flight. (2K251).	FV	FV	.75
M158 25 Cents			
H-60 helicopter with soldier on ladder. (2L251).	FV	FV	.75
M159 25 Cents			
Humvee. (2M251).	FV	FV	.75

Third Issue

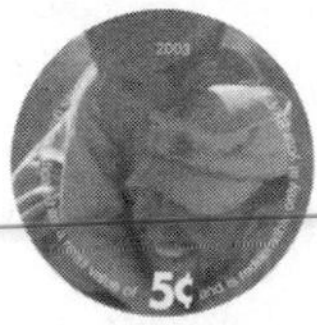

	VG	VF	UNC
M160 5 Cents			
2003. Soldier inspecting mouth of child. (3A51).	FV	FV	.25
M161 5 Cents			
2003. Soldier seated in vehicle, flag in background. (3B51).	FV	FV	.25
M162 5 Cents			
2003. Soldier standing by flag. (3C51).	FV	FV	.25
M163 5 Cents			
2003. Child on shoulders of soldier. (3D51).	FV	FV	.25

	VG	VF	UNC
M164 5 Cents			
2003. Soldier wearing firefighter's protective MOPP gear. (3E51).	FV	FV	.25
M165 5 Cents			
2003. *Operation Iraqi Freedom* legend. H-3 Sea King helicopter and soldier. (3F51).	FV	FV	.25
M166 5 Cents			
2003. SWIFT hight speed vessel, HSV 2. Wave piercing catamaran. (3G51).	FV	FV	.25

	VG	VF	UNC
M167 5 Cents			
2003. Statue of Liberty and HH-65 Dolphin helicopter. (3H51).	FV	FV	.25
M168 5 Cents			
2003. *We go where you go* legend. Soldier at BX/PX store. (3J51).	FV	FV	.25
M169 5 Cents			
2003. *Proudly serving those who serve* legend, flag background. (3K51).	FV	FV	.25
M170 5 Cents			
2003. KC-Extender refueling F/A-22 Raptor. (3L51).	FV	FV	.25

	VG	VF	UNC
M171 5 Cents			
2003. F/A-18 Hornet. (3M51).	FV	FV	.25
M172 10 Cents			
2003. AH-640 Apache-Longbow helicopter. (3A101).	FV	FV	.50
M173 10 Cents			
2003. Child's face and flag. (3B101).	FV	FV	.50

	VG	VF	UNC
M174 10 Cents			
2003. Soldier and flag. (3C101).	FV	FV	.50
M175 10 Cents			
2003. *Operation Iraqi Freedom* legend. Flight deck crewmember in red/white helmet. (3D101).	FV	FV	.50
M176 10 Cents			
F-16 Fighting Falcon, view over pilot's shoulder. (3E101).	FV	FV	.50

	VG	VF	UNC
M177 10 Cents			
2003. Soldier left, rock pile in background. (3F101).	FV	FV	.50
M178 10 Cents			
2003. Flair of a rocket. (3G101).	FV	FV	.50
M179 10 Cents			
2003. Seated soldier with shoulder missile launcher. (3H101).	FV	FV	.50

	VG	VF	UNC
M180 10 Cents			
2003. Soldier looking over barrel of weapon. (3J101).	FV	FV	.50
M181 10 Cents			
2003. Soldier with machine gun on H-60 Black Hawk helicopter. (3K101).	FV	FV	.50
M182 10 Cents			
2003. Amphibious tank. (3L101).	FV	FV	.50

	VG	VF	UNC
M183 10 Cents			
2003. C-130 Hercules dumping red fire retardent liquid during flight. (3M101).	FV	FV	.50
M184 25 Cents			
2003. Silhouette of soldier with machine gun facing right. (3A251).	FV	FV	.75
M185 25 Cents			
2003. Silhouette of soldier with mounted machine gun facing left. (3B251).	FV	FV	.75
M186 25 Cents			
2003. *Operation Iraqi Freedom* legend. Soldier saluting flag. (3C251).	FV	FV	.75
M187 25 Cents			
2003. Two AV-8B Harrier jets on approach. (3D251).	FV	FV	.75

	VG	VF	UNC
M188 25 Cents			
2003. Silhouette of soldier on vehicle. (3E251).	FV	FV	.75
M189 25 Cents			
2003. V-22 Osprey lifting off from carrier deck. (3F251).	FV	FV	.75
M190 25 Cents			
2003. Soldier inspecting child's ear. (3G251).	FV	FV	.75
M191 25 Cents			
2003. Lineup of C-130 Hercules cargo planes on runway. (3H251).	FV	FV	.75
M192 25 Cents			
2003. U.S. Coast Guard Barque *Eagle*, the Academy's training vessel based in New London, Connecticut. (3J251).	FV	FV	.75
M193 25 Cents			
2003. *Operation Enduring Freedom* legend. Soldier at console. (3K251).	FV	FV	.75
M194 25 Cents			
2003. American flag on deck of an Aircraft carrier. (3L251).	FV	FV	.75
M195 25 Cents			
2003. Three Marines in dress uniform. (3M251).	FV	FV	.75

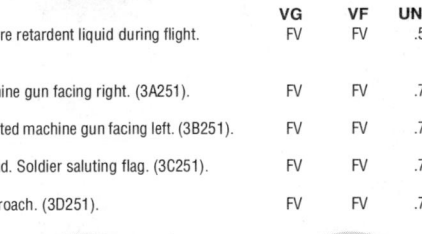

Fourth Issue

	VG	VF	UNC
M196 5 Cents 2004. F-35 flying right. (4A51).	FV	FV	.25
M197 5 Cents 2004. Sailor holding child. (4B51).	FV	FV	.25
M198 5 Cents 2004. Soldier and child. (4C51).	FV	FV	.25

	VG	VF	UNC
M199 5 Cents 2004. CH-47 Chinook helicopter transporting cargo in net. (4D51).	FV	FV	.25
M200 5 Cents 2004. Patrial view, B-17 Flying Fortress. (4E51).	FV	FV	.25
M201 5 Cents 2004. *Operation Iraqi Freedom* legend. Soldier with machine gun. (4F51).	FV	FV	.25

	VG	VF	UNC
M202 5 Cents 2004. Sailor walking away, toward row of flags. (4G51).	FV	FV	.25
M203 5 Cents 2004. Female soldier facing, looking thru gun. (4H51).	FV	FV	.25
M204 5 Cents 2004. *We go where you go!* legend. Female soldier. (4J51).	FV	FV	.25

	VG	VF	UNC
M205 5 Cents 2004. *Proudly serving those who serve* legend. Three female soldiers. (4K51).	FV	FV	.25
M206 5 Cents 2004. WWII era troops landing off on an amphibious craft. (4L51).	FV	FV	.25
M207 5 Cents 2004. Lookout tower silhouette. (4M51).	FV	FV	.25

	VG	VF	UNC
M208 10 Cents 2004. Soldier standing left, holding rifle. (4A101).	FV	FV	.50
M209 10 Cents 2004. WWII era female assembling an aircraft. (4B101).	FV	FV	.50
M210 10 Cents 2004. Soldier holding an object. (4C101).	FV	FV	.50
M211 10 Cents 2004. *Operation Iraqi Freedom* legend. Two soldiers in desert. (4D101).	FV	FV	.50

	VG	VF	UNC
M212 10 Cents 2004. Navy ship number 3 superstructure and flag. (4E101).	FV	FV	.50
M213 10 Cents 2004. H-60 Black Hawk helicopter approaching. (4F101).	FV	FV	.50
M214 10 Cents 2004. *Operation Enduring Freedom* legend. Oil well smoke. (4G101).	FV	FV	.50

	VG	VF	UNC
M215 10 Cents 2004. Bradley fighting vehicle profile left. (4H101).	FV	FV	.50
M216 10 Cents 2004. Eight WWII crewmembers by plane. (4J101).	FV	FV	.50
M217 10 Cents 2004. Two soldiers near burning item. (4K101).	FV	FV	.50

	VG	VF	UNC
M218 10 Cents 2004. B-1B Lancer cockpit. (4L101).	FV	FV	.50
M219 10 Cents 2004. H-60 Black Hawk helicopter on aircraft carrier. (4M101).	FV	FV	.50
M220 25 Cents 2004. Two soldiers helping another get into a deep-sea diving suit. (4A251).	FV	FV	.75

	VG	VF	UNC
M221 25 Cents 2004. U.S. Coast Guard craft with men standing under deck canopy. (4B251).	FV	FV	.75
M222 25 Cents 2004. Vietnam era soldier with purchase from PX. (4C251).	FV	FV	.75
M223 25 Cents 2004. Child with small flag. (4D251).	FV	FV	.75
M224 25 Cents 2004. Five WWII era pilots. (4E251).	FV	FV	.75

	VG	VF	UNC
M225 25 Cents 2004. WWII era submarine officer looking thru periscope. (4F251).	FV	FV	.75
M226 25 Cents 2004. AV-BB Harrier lifting off from carrier deck. (4G251).	FV	FV	.75
M227 25 Cents 2004. WWII era aircraft #63 approaching aircraft carrier. (4H251).	FV	FV	.75
M228 25 Cents 2004. Machine gunner atop Humvee. (4J251).	FV	FV	.75
M229 25 Cents 2004. *Operation Enduring Freedom* legend. C-130 Hercules cargo plane. (4K251).	FV	FV	.75

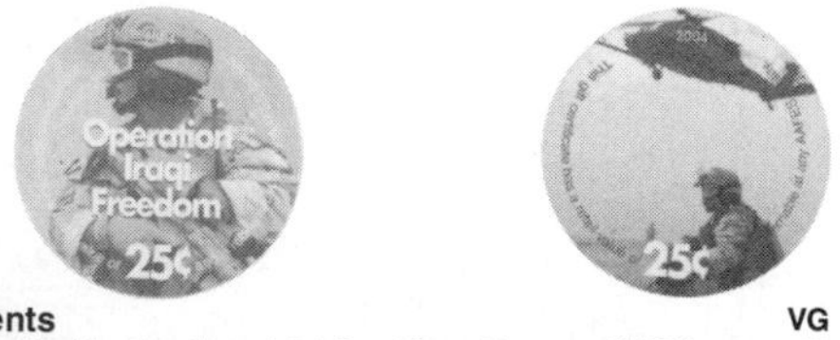

	VG	VF	UNC
M230 25 Cents 2004. *Operation Iraqi Freedom* legend. Soldier with machine gun. (4L251).	FV	FV	.75
M231 25 Cents 2004. H-60 Black Hawk helicopter above soldier in the desert. (4M251).	FV	FV	.75

Fifth Issue

	VG	VF	UNC
M232 5 Cents 2004. *Proudly serving those who serve* legend. Burger King ad on deplaning truck. (5A51).	FV	FV	.25

	VG	VF	UNC
M233 5 Cents			
2004. Soldiers lined up at a BX/PX grand opening. (5B51).	FV	FV	.25
M234 5 Cents			
2004. BX/PX sign, soldiers around. (5C51).	FV	FV	.25

	VG	VF	UNC
M235 5 Cents			
2004. Flight deck officer sending off P-51 Mustang. (5D51).	FV	FV	.25
M236 5 Cents			
2004. HH-53 Jolly Green Giant helicopter in flight. (5E51).	FV	FV	.25
M237 5 Cents			
2004. F-86 Sabre accending skyward. (5F51).	FV	FV	.25

	VG	VF	UNC
M238 5 Cents			
2004. Soldier with Iraqi blue topped building in background. (5G51).	FV	FV	.25
M239 5 Cents			
2004. H-60 Black Hawk helicopter and sunset. (5H51).			
a. *Operation Iraqi Freedom* legend.	FV	FV	.40
b. Without legend.	FV	FV	.40
M240 5 Cents			
2004. Six TBM Avenger bombers in formation. (5J51).	FV	FV	.25
M241 5 Cents			
2004. Five jets comprised of: F-15E Strike Eagles, F-15 Eagle and F-16 Fighting Falcon in formation. Burning oil wells in distance. (5K51).	FV	FV	.25

	VG	VF	UNC
M242 5 Cents			
2004. Coast Guard vessel. (5L51).	FV	FV	.25
M243 5 Cents			
2004. Captain Charles "Chuck" Yeager with Bell XS-1. (5M51).	FV	FV	.25
M244 10 Cents			
2004. Six crewmembers of the B-29 Super Fortress *Enola Gay*. (5A101).	FV	FV	.50

	VG	VF	UNC
M245 10 Cents			
2004. Soldier with infant, wife, flag behind. (5B101).	FV	FV	.50
M246 10 Cents			
2004. *Operation Enduring Freedom* legend. F-14 Tomcat and crew member on flight deck. (5C101).	FV	FV	.50
M247 10 Cents			
2004. Guard tower and razor wire. (5D101).	FV	FV	.50

	VG	VF	UNC
M248 10 Cents			
2004. Humvee in flood waters in Djibouti. (5E101).	FV	FV	.50
M249 10 Cents			
2004. Soldier silhouette with night vision scope. (5F101).	FV	FV	.50
M250 10 Cents			
2004. 4B-24 Liberator in flight. (5G101).	FV	FV	.50

	VG	VF	UNC
M251 10 Cents			
2004. Soldiers boarding rear of C-130 Hercules cargo transport. (5H101).	FV	FV	.50
M252 10 Cents			
2004. Pilot standing before F-4 Phantom II. (5J101).	FV	FV	.50
M253 10 Cents			
2004. Soldier with goggles and chains. (5K101).	FV	FV	.50

	VG	VF	UNC
M254 10 Cents			
2004. Sailor greeting young daughter. *Bassett* on denomination side. (5L101).	FV	FV	.50
M255 10 Cents			
2004. Soldier seated with rifle in field. (5M101).	FV	FV	.50
M256 25 Cents			
2004. KC-B5 Stratotanker refueling F-16 Fighting Falcon. (5A251).	FV	FV	.75

	VG	VF	UNC
M257 25 Cents			
2004. B-1B Lancer flying away. (5B251).	FV	FV	.75
M258 25 Cents			
2004. Soldier standing next to flag reading letter. (5C251).	FV	FV	.75
M259 25 Cents			
2004. Six F-16 Falcons, USAF *Thunderbirds* in formation. (5D251).	FV	FV	.75

	VG	VF	UNC
M260 25 Cents			
2004. Four airmen under wing. WWII Tuskeegee airmen. (5E251).	FV	FV	.75
M261 25 Cents			
2004. F/A Hornet crossing the sound barrier. (5F251).	FV	FV	.75
M262 25 Cents			
2004. Humvee in rearview mirror. (5G251).			
a. With *Operation Enduring Freedom* legend.	FV	FV	1.00
b. Without legend.	FV	FV	1.00
M263 25 Cents			
2004. WACS in front of B-17 Flying Fortress. (5H251).	FV	FV	.75

	VG	VF	UNC
M264 25 Cents			
2004. Flag raising on Iwo Jima. (5J251).	FV	FV	.75
M265 25 Cents			
2004. *Operation Iraqi Freedom* legend. Man and german shepard. (5K251).	FV	FV	.75
M266 25 Cents			
2004. B-17 Flying fortress and crew. (5L251).	FV	FV	.75
M267 25 Cents			
2004. *Operation Iraqi Freedom* legend. Crew member performing maintenance on plane nose. (5M251).	FV	FV	.75

Sixth Issue

Due to the use of selected Elvis Presley images, this issue was limited to 50,000 pieces of each design.

	VG	VF	UNC
M268 5 Cents			
2005. P-51 Mustang. GG. (6A51).	FV	FV	.75
M269 5 Cents			
2005. Two soldiers; one seated and one kneeling. GG. (6B51).	FV	FV	.75
M270 5 Cents			
2005. B-17 Flying Fortress *Our Mom* and crew. GG. (6C51).	FV	FV	.75

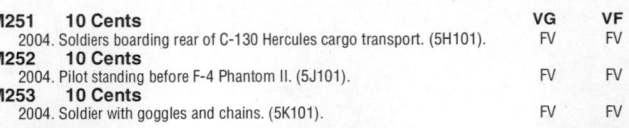

	VG	VF	UNC
M271 5 Cents 2005. A-10 Thunderbolt II in the sky, seen from below. (6D51).	FV	FV	.75
M272 5 Cents 2005. Soldier looking in hillside cave. (6E51).	FV	FV	.75
M273 5 Cents 2005. Air Force One, VC-25 in flight. (6F51).	FV	FV	.75

	VG	VF	UNC
M274 5 Cents 2005. OH-58 Kiowa Warrior helicopter, sun behind. (6G51).	FV	FV	.75
M275 5 Cents 2005. *Operation Iraqi Freedom* legend. Soldier kneeling with gun. (6H51).	FV	FV	.75
M276 5 Cents 2005. *Operation Enduring Freedom* legend. Two soldiers walking, white domed building in background. (6J51).	FV	FV	.75

	VG	VF	UNC
M277 5 Cents 2005. CH-46 Sea Knight helicopter, soldiers jumping out back. (6K51).	FV	FV	.75
M278 5 Cents 2005. Two soldiers launching mortar. (6L51).	FV	FV	.75
M279 5 Cents 2005. Elvis Presley in fatigues leaning against barrack wall. (6M51).	FV	FV	3.00
M280 10 Cents 2005. CH-47 Chinook helicopter in desert, soldier with gun. (6A101).	FV	FV	1.00
M281 10 Cents 2005. Six soldiers outside large tent, rainbow in background. (6B101).	FV	FV	1.00
M282 10 Cents 2005. HH-60 Dolphin helicopter in flight. (6C101).	FV	FV	1.00
M283 10 Cents 2005. Elvis Presley in dress uniform standing on river bridge. (6D101).	FV	FV	3.00
M284 10 Cents 2005. Elvis Presley advancing between vertical opening. (6E101).	FV	FV	3.00
M285 10 Cents 2005. Elvis Presley leaning against building wall. (6F101).	FV	FV	3.00
M286 10 Cents 2005. Navy football player - Midshipman. (6G101).	FV	FV	1.00
M287 10 Cents 2005. Air Force football player - Falcons. (6H101).	FV	FV	1.00
M288 10 Cents 2005. Army football player - Black Knights. (6J101).	FV	FV	1.00
M289 10 Cents 2005. Soldier sitting with child. (6K101).	FV	FV	1.00
M290 10 Cents 2005. Soldier walking amongst confiscated weapons. (6L101).	FV	FV	1.00
M291 10 Cents 2005. Three sholdiers advancing with weapons pointed. (6M101).			
a. with *Operation Enduring Freedom* legend.	FV	FV	1.50
b. Without legend.	FV	FV	1.50

	VG	VF	UNC
M292 25 Cents 2005. Female sailor and young child. (6A251).	FV	FV	1.50
M293 25 Cents 2005. Soldier profile clutching rifle. Image from number M81. (6B251).	FV	FV	1.50
M294 25 Cents 2005. Submarine conning tower. (6C251).	FV	FV	1.50

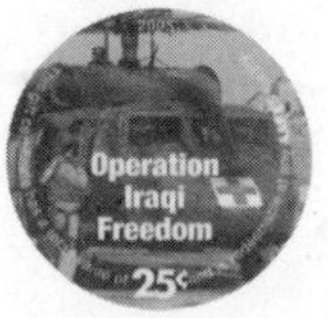

	VG	VF	UNC
M295 25 Cents 2005. Tank with explosions in background. (6D251).	FV	FV	1.50
M296 25 Cents 2005. B-1B Lancer flying before pyramids. (6E251).	FV	FV	1.50
M297 25 Cents 2005. *Operation Iraqi Freedom* legend. Red Cross H-60 Black Hawk helicopter. (6F251).	FV	FV	1.50
M298 25 Cents 2005. Soldier standing before Humvee. (6G251).			
a. With *Operation Enduring Freedom,* legend.	FV	FV	2.00
b. Without legend.	FV	FV	2.00

	VG	VF	UNC
M299 25 Cents 2005. SR-71 Black Bird as seen from above. (6H251).	FV	FV	1.50
M300 25 Cents 2005. Army NASCAR. (6J251).	FV	FV	1.50
M301 25 Cents 2005. F/A-18 Hornet takeoff from aircraft carrier. (6K251).	FV	FV	1.50

	VG	VF	UNC
M302 25 Cents 2005. Flag montage of the Allies: United States, Australia and Great Britain. (6L251).	FV	FV	1.50
M303 25 Cents 2005. *Proudly serving those who serve* legend. Soldiers with banner. (6M251).	FV	FV	1.50

SEVENTH ISSUE

	VG	VF	UNC
M304 5 Cents 2005 B. General Eisenhower talking to 101st Airborne troops before the Normandy invasion. GG. (7A51).	FV	FV	.25
M305 5 Cents 2005 B. Five soldiers before AAFES store. (7B51).	FV	FV	.25
M306 5 Cents 2005 B. Soldier and Medal of Honor. (7C51).	FV	FV	.25

	VG	VF	UNC
M307 5 Cents 2005 B. Pilot close-up. Vignette from MPC number M79. (7D51).	FV	FV	.25
M308 5 Cents 2005 B. Ronald Reagan in tie close-up. GG. (7E51).	FV	FV	.25
M309 5 Cents 2005 B. Two soldiers with guns beside Humvee. (7F51).	FV	FV	.25

	VG	VF	UNC
M310 5 Cents 2005 B. Soldier giving kid candy in street. (7G51).	FV	FV	.25
M311 5 Cents 2005 B. *Operation Iraqi Freedom* legend. Plane in flight right. (7H51).	FV	FV	.25
M312 5 Cents 2005 B. Four WWII planes above aircraft carrier. (7J51).	FV	FV	.25

	VG	VF	UNC
M313 5 Cents 2005 B. Soldier holding Purple Heart. (7K51).	FV	FV	.25
M314 5 Cents 2005 B. *Operation Enduring Freedom* legend. Tank. (7L51).	FV	FV	.25
M315 5 Cents 2005 B. Four soldiers around artillery piece. (7M51).	FV	FV	.25

	VG	VF	UNC
M316 10 Cents 2005 B. Mom holding child, soldier inspecting child's mouth. (7A101). *Operation Enduring Freedom* legend.	FV	FV	.75
M317 10 Cents 2005 B. John F. Kennedy, shirtless in PT boat. GG. (7B101).	FV	FV	.50
M318 10 Cents 2005 B. George H. W. Bush close-up portrait as WWII pilot. GG. (7C101).	FV	FV	.50

	VG	VF	UNC
M319 10 Cents 2005 B. Gerald Ford in uniform wearing necktie. GG. (7D101).	FV	FV	.50
M320 10 Cents 2005 B. Soldier holding silver star. (7E101).	FV	FV	.50
M321 10 Cents 2005 B. Two soldiers with guns behind sandbag line. (7F101).	FV	FV	.50

	VG	VF	UNC
M322 10 Cents 2005 B. *Operation Iraqi Freedom* legend. Amphibious tank. (7G101).	FV	FV	.50
M323 10 Cents 2005 B. Air Force NASCAR number 21. (7H101).	FV	FV	.50
M324 10 Cents 2005 B. Coast Guard NASCAR number 44. (7J101).	FV	FV	.50

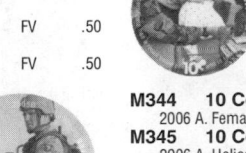

	VG	VF	UNC
M325 10 Cents 2005 B. Marines NASCAR. (7K101).	FV	FV	.50
M326 10 Cents 2005 B. Navy NASCAR number 14. (7L101).	FV	FV	.50
M327 10 Cents 2005 B. National Guard NASCAR number 16. (7M101).	FV	FV	.50

	VG	VF	UNC
M328 25 Cents 2005 B. Jet from the front and above. (7A251).	FV	FV	.75
M329 25 Cents 2005 B. George H. W. Bush standing before WWII era plane. (7B251).	FV	FV	.75
M330 25 Cents 2005. Soldier standing with rifle. (7C251).	FV	FV	.75

	VG	VF	UNC
M331 25 Cents 2005 B. *Operation Iraqi Freedom* legend. Three soldiers standing in line advancing forward. (7D251).	FV	FV	.75
M332 25 Cents 2005 B. Two soldiers atop tank. (7E251).	FV	FV	.75
M333 25 Cents 2005 B. Two soldiers by BX/PX sign superimposed on Iraq Campaign Medal. (7F251).	FV	FV	.75

	VG	VF	UNC
M334 25 Cents 2005 B. Soldier directing excavator. (7G251).	FV	FV	.75
M335 25 Cents 2005 B. Soldier standing with British and American Flags atop vehicle. (7H251).	FV	FV	.75
M336 25 Cents 2005 B. Soldier playing bagpipes, flanked by flags. (7J251).	FV	FV	.75

	VG	VF	UNC
M337 25 Cents 2005. Helicopter superimpsed on Afghanistan Campaign medal design. (7K251).	FV	FV	.75
M338 25 Cents 2005 B. Two soldiers walking in street with machine guns. (7L251). *Operation Enduring Freedom,* legend.	FV	FV	1.00
M339 25 Cents 2005 B. Army NHRA dragster. (7M251).	FV	FV	.75

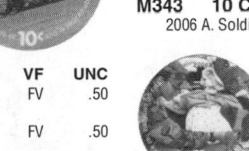

Eighth Issue

	VG	VF	UNC
M340 10 Cents 2006 A. Soldier walking with German shepard on patrol. (8A101).			
a. *Operation Enduring Freedom* legend.	FV	FV	.50
b. Without legend.	FV	FV	.50
M341 10 Cents 2006 A. Richard M. Nixon as Naval officer. GG. (8B101).	—	Unc	.50
M342 10 Cents 2006 A. James E. Carter as Naval officer. (8C101).	FV	FV	.50
M343 10 Cents 2006 A. Soldiers in a vehicle in a flooded New Orleans street. (8D101).	FV	FV	.50

	VG	VF	UNC
M344 10 Cents 2006 A. Female soldier attending to a child lying down. (8E101).	FV	FV	.50
M345 10 Cents 2006 A. Helicopter aerial refuling from a tanker. (8F101).	FV	FV	.50
M346 10 Cents 2006 A. Army soldier boxing. (8G101).	FV	FV	.50

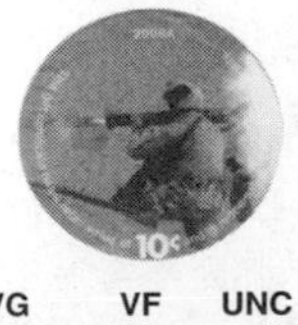

	VG	VF	UNC
M347 10 Cents 2006 A. Army motorcycle racer. (8H101).	FV	FV	.50
M348 10 Cents 2006 A. Rodeo rider. (8J101).	FV	FV	.50

		VG	VF	UNC
M349	**10 Cents**			
	2006 A. Soldier firing rocket launcher. (8K101).	FV	FV	.50

		VG	VF	UNC
M350	**10 Cents**			
	2006 A. *Operation Iraqi Freedom* legend. Soldier loading bomb. (8L101).	FV	FV	.50
M351	**10 Cents**			
	2006 A. Iraqi citizen placing paper ballot in voting box. (8M101).	FV	FV	.50
M352	**25 Cents**			
	2006 A. Soldier with rifle amongst sandbag enclosure. (8A251).	FV	FV	.75

		VG	VF	UNC
M353	**25 Cents**			
	2006 A. U.S. flag flying above base. (8B251).	FV	FV	.75
M354	**25 Cents**			
	2006 A. M1A1Tank firing left. (8C251).	FV	FV	.75
M355	**25 Cents**			
	2006 A. *Operation Iraqi Freedom* legend. Soldiers in double line walking toward rear of a helicopter. (8D251).	FV	FV	.75

		VG	VF	UNC
M356	**25 Cents**			
	2006 A. Humvee with soldier manning weapons. (8E251).	FV	FV	.75
M357	**25 Cents**			
	2006 A. WWII era sailor portrait vignette from MPC #M80. (8F251).	FV	FV	.75
M358	**25 Cents**			
	2006 A. Two prone soldiers firing weapons. GG. (8F251).	FV	FV	.75

		VG	VF	UNC
M359	**25 Cents**			
	2006 A. Soldier charging left in full gear with rifle. GG. (8H251).	FV	FV	.75
M360	**25 Cents**			
	2006 A. Soldier with head set holding child. (8J251).	FV	FV	.75
M361	**25 Cents**			
	2006 A. Soldier kneeling shaking hand of child. (8K251).	FV	FV	.75

		VG	VF	UNC
M362	**25 Cents**			
	2006 A. Soldier flying in a helicopter manning a machine gun. (8L251).			
	a. With *Operation Enduring Freedom* legend.	FV	FV	.75
	b. Without legend.	FV	FV	.75
M363	**25 Cents**			
	2006 A. Ink-stained fingers of Iraqi citizens after placing their votes. (8M251).	FV	FV	.75

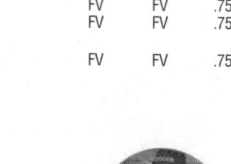

Ninth Issue

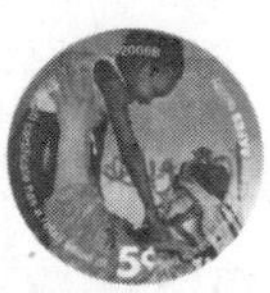

		VG	VF	UNC
M364	**5 Cents**			
	2006 B. Paratroopers in the sky. (9A51).	FV	FV	.25
M365	**5 Cents**			
	2006 B. Four armed soldiers in silhouette. (9B51).	FV	FV	.25
M366	**5 Cents**			
	2006 B. Soldier holding a child. (9C51).	FV	FV	.25

		VG	VF	UNC
M367	**5 Cents**			
	2006 B. Post Exchange, Fort Mills, 5 centavos token. (9D51).	FV	FV	.25
M368	**5 Cents**			
	2006 B. *Operation Enduring Freedom* legend, Silhouette of a gunner. (9E51).	FV	FV	.25
M369	**5 Cents**			
	2006 B. Soldier running, helicopter in background. (9F51).	FV	FV	.25

		VG	VF	UNC
M370	**5 Cents**			
	2006 B. Troops in formation with American flag. (9G51).	FV	FV	.25
M371	**5 Cents**			
	2006 B. *Operation Iraqi Freedom* legend, Soldier ready to parachute jump. (9H51).	FV	FV	.25
M372	**5 Cents**			
	2006 B. Thumb touching a Purple Heart Medal on a uniform. (9J51).	FV	FV	.25

		VG	VF	UNC
M373	**5 Cents**			
	2006 B. Soldier kissing a baby, *Father and Son* photo by Tracy Olson. (9K51).	FV	FV	.25
M374	**5 Cents**			
	2006 B. Baby in helmet, *Baby Colin in helmet* photo by SFC Chad Johnson. (9L51).	FV	FV	.25
M375	**5 Cents**			
	2006 B. Soldier holding a picture and letter, *Letter from Home* photo by SSgt. Xavier Goco. (9M51).	FV	FV	.25

		VG	VF	UNC
M376	**10 Cents**			
	2006 B. Two soldiers with minesweeper. (9A101).	FV	FV	.50
M377	**10 Cents**			
	2006 B. Four soldiers sitting in helicopter doorway. (9B101).	FV	FV	.50
M378	**10 Cents**			
	2006 B. Fireman with hose. (9C101).			
	a. With *Operation Iraqi Freedom* legend.	FV	FV	.50
	b. Without legend.	FV	FV	.50

		VG	VF	UNC
M379	**10 Cents**			
	2006 B. Soldier with binoculars next to U.S. flag on a guard tower. (9D101).	FV	FV	.50
M380	**10 Cents**			
	2006 B. *Operation Enduring Freedom* legend, tank. (9E101).	FV	FV	.50
M381	**10 Cents**			
	2006 B. Helicopter flying, viewed from gun hatch of another helicopter. (9F101).	FV	FV	.50

		VG	VF	UNC
M382	**10 Cents**			
	2006 B. Navy racing truck. (9G101).	FV	FV	.50
M383	**10 Cents**			
	2006 B. Aircraft carrier. (9H101).	FV	FV	.50
M384	**10 Cents**			
	2006 B. Child holding hand of adult, *Father and Son holding hands* photo by Deanna Seto. (9J101).	FV	FV	.50

		VG	VF	UNC
M385	**10 Cents**			
	2006 B. Two soldiers, *Soldiers competing for EMFB* photo by Sgt. Tal Wick. (9K101).	FV	FV	.50

		VG	VF	UNC
M386	**10 Cents**			
	2006 B. Soldier holding a baby, *Father and Daughter* photo by Ashleigh Collins. (9L101).	FV	FV	.50
M387	**10 Cents**			
	2006 B. Soldier with children, *Soldier with Iraqi Children* photo by Kamel Saad. (9M101).	FV	FV	.50

		VG	VF	UNC
M388	**25 Cents**			
	2006 B. President Theodore Roosevelt. (9A251).	FV	FV	.75
M389	**25 Cents**			
	2006 B. Airman with Anthony's Pizza boxes. (9B251).	FV	FV	.75
M390	**25 Cents**			
	2006 B. *Operation Iraqi Freedom* legend, Bradley Fighting Vehicle. (9C251).	FV	FV	.75

		VG	VF	UNC
M391	**25 Cents**			
	2006 B. Aircraft taking off. (9D251).	FV	FV	.75
M392	**25 Cents**			
	2006 B. Soldier on one knee in front of a Blackhawk helicopter. (9E251).	FV	FV	.75
M393	**25 Cents**			
	2006 B. Female soldier with a boy. (9F251).			
	a. With *Operation Enduring Freedom* legend.	FV	FV	.75
	b. Without legend.	FV	FV	.75

		VG	VF	UNC
M394	**25 Cents**			
	2006 B. Antiaircraft weapon firing on a ship. *GG* overprint. (9G251).	FV	FV	.75
M395	**25 Cents**			
	2006 B. Maj. General Kathryn G. Frost, AAFES Commander, August 2002-April 2006. (9H251).	FV	FV	.75
M396	**25 Cents**			
	2006 B. Boy in uniform saluting. *Son Saluting* photo by Cpt. Dennis A. Christian. (9J251).	FV	FV	.75

		VG	VF	UNC
M397	**25 Cents**			
	2006 B. Soldier in front of burning car. *Route Irish, Bagdad Car Bomb* photo by CSM James Ross. (9K251).	FV	FV	.75
M398	**25 Cents**			
	2006 B. Silhouette of a soldier and a dog. *Summer Sunset of a soldier with a dog.* photo by PFC Timothy J. Viera. (9L251).	FV	FV	.75
M399	**25 Cents**			
	2006 B. Soldier with sand covered face. *Dusted Marine* photo by Jim Vandenberg. (9M251)	FV	FV	.75

TENTH ISSUE

		VG	VF	UNC
M400	**5 Cents**			
	2007. Airman walking across two aircraft engines. (10A51).	FV	FV	.25
M401	**5 Cents**			
	2007. Four bomb handlers with three bombs. (10B51).	FV	FV	.25
M402	**5 Cents**			
	2007. Lenticular images of a B-2 bomber swooping under the Gateway Arch. (10C51).	.25	.50	1.00

		VG	VF	UNC
M403	**5 Cents**			
	2007. Armored HMMWV stuck in mud. (10D51).	FV	FV	.25

		VG	VF	UNC
M404	**5 Cents**			
	2007. *Operation Enduring Freedom* legend, Soldier and a group of children giving thumbs up. (10E51).	FV	FV	.25
M405	**5 Cents**			
	2007. Two Air Force mechanics confering under an aircraft. (10F51).	FV	FV	.25

		VG	VF	UNC
M406	**5 Cents**			
	2007. *Operation Iraqi Freedom* legend. A child watching an airman write. (10G51).	FV	FV	.25
M407	**5 Cents**			
	2007. Skin diver with head and mask above the water. (10H51).	FV	FV	.25
M408	**5 Cents**			
	2007. Five airmen infront of a BX/PX. (10J51).	FV	FV	.25

		VG	VF	UNC
M409	**5 Cents**			
	2007. Fuel handler working. (10K51).	FV	FV	.25
M410	**5 Cents**			
	2007. Soldier walking by a man sitting in front of his store. (10L51).	FV	FV	.25
M411	**5 Cents**			
	2007. Soldiers standing around an armored HMMWV in the desert. (10M51).	FV	FV	.25

		VG	VF	UNC
M412	**10 Cents**			
	2007. Soldier training a dog. (10A101).	FV	FV	.50
M413	**10 Cents**			
	2007. Soldiers walking past a sheet herder and sheep. (10B101).	FV	FV	.50
M414	**10 Cents**			
	2007. Three airmen walking past a BX/PX. (10C101).	FV	FV	.50

		VG	VF	UNC
M415	**10 Cents**			
	2007. Mother holding a child in a doorway, Soldier kicks a soccer ball. (10D101).			
	a. With *Operation Iraqi Freedom* legend.	FV	FV	.50
	b. Without legend.	FV	FV	.50
M416	**10 Cents**			
	2007. *Operation Enduring Freedom* legend. Female soldier in full gear. (10E101).	FV	FV	.50
M417	**10 Cents**			
	2007. Soldier looking into a child's mouth (10F101).	FV	FV	.50

		VG	VF	UNC
M418	**10 Cents**			
	2007. Lenticular image of three soldiers on patrol that advance. (10G101).	.50	.75	1.25
M419	**10 Cents**			
	2007. Soldier in battle stance in front of an aircraft nosecone. (10H101).	FV	FV	.50
M420	**10 Cents**			
	2007. Soldier standing guard. (10J101).	FV	FV	.50

		VG	VF	UNC
M421	**10 Cents**			
	2007. Two soldiers exploring an area of exposed pipes. (10K101).	FV	FV	.50
M422	**10 Cents**			
	2007. Soldier in full gear in front of a C-130 aircraft. (10L101).	FV	FV	.50
M423	**10 Cents**			
	2007. Two soldiers standing on the back of a truck with merchandise from AAFES. (10M101).	FV	FV	.50

	VG	VF	UNC
M424 25 Cents 2007. Soldiers standing in formation. (10A251).	FV	FV	.75
M425 25 Cents 2007. Sailors pulling an aircraft away during the attack on Pearl Harbor. GG (10B251).	FV	FV	.75
M426 25 Cents 2007. Female soldier looking between racks of M-16 rifles. (10C251).	FV	FV	.75

	VG	VF	UNC
M427 25 Cents 2007. Sailor hugging a child. (10D251).	FV	FV	.75
M428 25 Cents 2007. Stryker vehicle on a beach. (10E251).	FV	FV	.75
M429 25 Cents 2007. Sitting Camel with Navy Ship in background. (10F251).	FV	FV	.75

	VG	VF	UNC
M430 25 Cents 2007. Spiraling U.S. Flag. (10G251).	FV	FV	.75
M431 25 Cents 2007. *Operation Enduring Freedom*, legend. Soldier in battle gear next to vehicle. (10H251).	FV	FV	.75
M432 25 Cents 2007. 3rd ID soldier preparing to heat his MRE meal. (10J251).	FV	FV	.75

	VG	VF	UNC
M433 25 Cents 2007. Boy observing a soldier in battle gear kneeling. (10K251).	FV	FV	.75
M434 25 Cents 2007. Lenticular imagea of New York City with twin beams of light from the site of the World Trade Center. (10L251).	.75	1.00	1.50
M435 25 Cents 2007. Two soldiers standing in front of burning wreckage from an explosion. (10M251).			
a. With *Operation Iraqi Freedom* legend.	FV	FV	.75
b. Without legend.	FV	FV	.75

Eleventh Issue

	VG	VF	UNC
M436 5 Cents 2008. Helicopter flying over Baghdad Crossed Swords Monument. (11A51).	FV	FV	25.00
M437 5 Cents 2008. Soldier and female standing on rear door of Striker vehicle. (11B51).	FV	FV	.25
M438 5 Cents 2008. Close-up of uniformed man on a porch. (11C51).	FV	FV	.25

	VG	VF	UNC
M439 5 Cents 2008. Baby under a flag. Photo by Maj. Brent and Amy Waring. (11D51).	FV	FV	.25
M440 5 Cents 2008. Marvel's She Hulk. (11E51).	FV	FV	
M441 5 Cents 2008. *Operation Iraqi Freedom* legend. Soldier in front of US and Iraqi flag. (11F51).	FV	FV	.25

	VG	VF	UNC
M442 5 Cents 2008. Apache helicopter flying over Light Attack Vehicle. (11G51).			
a. With *Operation Enduring Freedom* legend.	FV	FV	.25
b. Without legend.	FV	FV	.25
M443 5 Cents 2008. Open 24 Hours sign infront of PX. (11H51).	FV	FV	.25
M444 5 Cents 2008. Soldier and female child walking on a street. (11J51).	FV	FV	.25

	VG	VF	UNC
M445 5 Cents 2008. Four soldiers with Armor patch. (11K51).	FV	FV	.25
M446 5 Cents 2008. Soldier and working dog on armored vehicle (11L51).	FV	FV	.25
M447 5 Cents 2008. Lenticular images of Coast Guard helicopter and boat. (11M51).	FV	FV	.25

	VG	VF	UNC
M448 10 Cents 2008. *Operation Enduring Freedom* legend. Soldier facing a camel in the desert. (11A101).	FV	FV	.50
M449 10 Cents 2008. Standing soldier with rifle. (11B101).	FV	FV	.50
M450 10 Cents 2008. Soldier giving candy to three boys. (11C101).	FV	FV	.50
M451 10 Cents 2008. Apache helicopter flying by the sun. (11D101).	FV	FV	.50

	VG	VF	UNC
M452 10 Cents 2008. Child with angel wings pushing a wheelchair. Photo by Tawny Campbell. (11E101).	FV	FV	.50
M453 10 Cents 2008. Five airmen standing with bombs in front of aircraft. (11F101).	FV	FV	.50
M454 10 Cents 2008. Two soldiers with a working dog. (11G101).	FV	FV	.50

	VG	VF	UNC
M455 10 Cents 2008. Soldier praying with a bible. Photo by Sr. Airman David Gregg. (11H101).	FV	FV	.50
M456 10 Cents 2008. Marine insignia framed by the soles of two boots. (11J101).	FV	FV	.50
M457 10 Cents 2008. Marvel's Ironman. (11K101).	FV	FV	.50

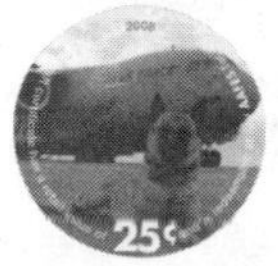

	VG	VF	UNC
M458 10 Cents 2008. Two soldiers kneeking on a street. (11L101).			
a. With *Operation Iraqi Freedom* legend.	FV	FV	.50
b. Without legend.	FV	FV	.50
M459 10 Cents 2008. Lenticular images Navy fleet moving through the ocean. (11M101).	FV	FV	.50
M460 25 Cents 2008. Dog in front of C-17 aircraft. (11A251).	FV	FV	.75

	VG	VF	UNC
M461 25 Cents 2008. Marvel's Captain America. (11B251).	FV	FV	.75
M462 25 Cents 2008. Three Boy Scouts in front of War Memorial. Photo by Deborah Thomas. *Taco Bell* under denomination.	FV	FV	.75

	VG	VF	UNC
M463 25 Cents 2008. US and Iraqi flags. Photo by 1st Lt. Steven Pugh. *Pizza Hut* under denomination.	FV	FV	.75
M464 25 Cents 2008. Smoke in front of MRAP vehicles. (11E251).	FV	FV	.75
M465 25 Cents 2008. *Operation Enduring Freedom* legend. Two air Force women in the desert. (11F251).	FV	FV	.75

	VG	VF	UNC
M466 25 Cents 2008. Chinook helicopter flying over damaged Chinook. (11G251).	FV	FV	.75
M467 25 Cents 2008. Soldier with arms raised in front of US flag. (11H251).	FV	FV	.75
M468 25 Cents 2008. Soldier with weapon in helicopter doorway. (11J251).	FV	FV	.75

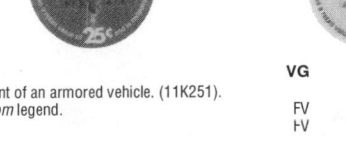

	VG	VF	UNC
M469 25 Cents 2008. Three soldiers walking in front of an armored vehicle. (11K251).			
a. With *Operation Iraqui Freedom* legend.	FV	FV	.75
b. Without legend.	FV	FV	.75
M470 25 Cents 2008. Lenticular image of C-130s deploying infrared counter measures (11L251).	.75	1.00	1.50
M471 25 Cents 2008. Lenticular image of AAFES logo and *We go where you go!*. (11M251).	.75	1.00	1.50

URUGUAY

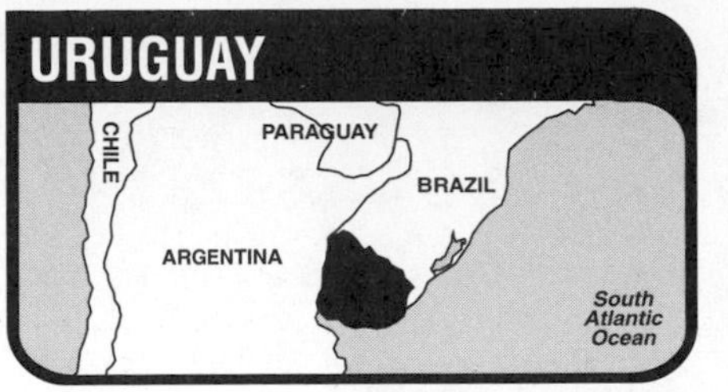

The Oriental Republic of Uruguay (so called because of its location on the east bank of the Uruguay River) is situated on the Atlantic coast of South America between Argentina and Brazil. This most advanced of South American countries has an area of 176,220 sq. km. and a population of 3.48 million. Capital: Montevideo. Uruguay's chief economic asset is its rich, rolling grassy plains. Meat, wool, hides and skins are exported.

Montevideo, founded by the Spanish in 1726 as a military stronghold, soon took advantage of its natural harbor to become an important commercial center. Claimed by Argentina but annexed by Brazil in 1821, Uruguay declared its independence four years later and secured its freedom in 1828 after a three-year struggle. The administrations of President Jose Battle in the early 20th century established widespread political, social, and economic reforms that established a statist tradition. A violent Marxist urban guerrilla movement named the Tupamaros, launched in the late 1960s, led Uruguay's president to cede control of the government to the military in 1973. By year end, the rebels had been crushed, but the military continued to expand its hold over the government. Civilian rule was not restored until 1985. In 2004, the left-of-center Frente Amplio Coalition won national elections that effectively ended 170 years of political control previously held by the Colorado and Blanco parties. Uruguay's political and labor conditions are among the freest on the continent.

MONETARY SYSTEM:

1 Patacón = 960 Reis
1 Peso = 8 Reales to 1860
1 Peso = 100 Centésimos
1 Doblon = 10 Pesos, 1860-1875
1 Peso = 100 Centésimos, 1860-1975
1 Doblon = 10 Pesos, 1860-1875
1 Nuevo Peso = 1000 Old Pesos, 1975-1993
1 Peso Uruguayo = 1000 Nuevos Pesos, 1993-

BANK ISSUES

Banco Comercial . . . . . #S95-S130
Banco Comercial de Paysondú . . . . . #S131-S149
Banco Comercial del Salto. . . . . . #S152-S159
Banco de Crédito Auxiliar . . . . . #S161-S168
Banco de España y Rio de la Plata . . . . . #S169-S170
Banco Franco-Platense . . . . . #S171-S173
Banco Herrera, Eastman & Ca. . . . . . #S181
Banco Inglés del Rio de la Plata . . . . . #S191-S194
Banco Italiano . . . . . #S201-S209
Banco Italiano del Uruguay . . . . . #S212-S215
Banco Italo-Oriental. . . . . . #S222-S225
Banco de Londres y Rio de la Plata. . . . . . #S231-S245
Banco Mauá & Cia., Montevideo . . . . . #S251-S321
Banco Mercantil del Rio de la Plata. . . . . . #S333-S336
Banco Montevideano . . . . . #S341-S359
Banco Navia y Ca. . . . . . #S361-S379
Banco Oriental. . . . . . #S381-S387
Banco de Paysandú. . . . . . #S388-S391
Banco Popular. . . . . . #S395
Banco del Salto . . . . . #S401-S415
Banco Villaamil & Ca. . . . . . #S417
Cambio de Monedas de Viñas y Ca. . . . . . #S418
Comercio de Tacuarembo . . . . . #S418D
Progreso Oriental. . . . . . #S419-S423
Sociedád Auxiliar de Crédito y Alquileres . . . . . #S426
Sociedád de Cambios . . . . . #S431-S437
Sociedád de Cambios, Montevideo . . . . . #S438-S440D
Sociedád de Cambios Carmelo y Na Palmira . . . . . #S441-S447
Sociedád de Cambios de Cerro Largo. . . . . . #S451
Sociedád de Cambios de Pay-Sandú . . . . . #S461-S469
Sociedád de Crédito Hipotecario . . . . . #S471-S478
Sociedád Fomento Territorial. . . . . . #S480-S482

STATE ISSUE

Departamento de Artigas. . . . . . #S491-S492

Note: Certain listings encompassing issues circulated by various bank and regional authorities are contained in Volume 1.

BANKS

BANCO COMERCIAL, MONTEVIDEO

1857 ISSUE

	Good	Fine	XF
S95 240 Centésimos 21.9.1857. Black. Beehives at upper center.	—	—	—

1858 ISSUES

S101 120 Centésimos — Good 600. · Fine — · XF —
1.10.1858. Brown. Printer: Lit. Mege.

S106 240 Centésimos — Good 750. · Fine — · XF —
1.10.1858. Black. Lion at upper center. Printer: Lit. Mege.

S107 480 Centésimos — Good 750. · Fine — · XF —
1.10.1858. Swan at top center. Uniface.

S107A 960 Centésimos — Good — · Fine — · XF —
1.10.1858. Sailing ships at upper center.

S107B 1 Onza De Oro — Good — · Fine — · XF —
1.10.1858. Horse at upper center.

S108 1 Onza De Oro — Good 1500. · Fine — · XF —
1.10.1858. Wagon at center, city in background. Printer: H. Bradbury & Co.

1860 Issue

S111 240 Centésimos — Good 600. · Fine — · XF —
1.1.1860. Black. Paper: Orange. Printer: H. Bradbury & Co.

S112 480 Centésimos — Good 1050. · Fine — · XF —
1.1.1860. Black. Paper: Blue. Printer: H. Bradbury & Co.

S113 960 Centésimos — Good 1500. · Fine — · XF —
1.1.1860. Printer: H. Bradbury & Co.

Law of 23.6.1862; 1863 Issue

S121 10 Centésimos — Good 450. · Fine — · XF —
3.1.1863. Medallic woman portrait at center. Printer: Lit. A. Hequet y Cohas Hnos.

S122 20 Centésimos — Good 225. · Fine — · XF —
2.1.1863. Black. Uniface. Paper: Yellow. Printer: BWC.

S123 50 Centésimos — Good 450. · Fine — · XF —
2.1.1863. Black on brown underprint. Uniface. Printer: BWC.

S124 1 Peso	Good	Fine	XF
2.1.1863. Black and light brown-orange. Paper: Green. Printer: BWC.	1200.	—	—

S125 1 Doblon	Good	Fine	XF
2.1.1863. Woman at top center. Printer: BWC.			
a. Issued note.	1500.	—	—
p. Proof.	—	Unc	1500.
S125A 2 Doblones			
2.1.1863. Woman at top center. Similar to #S125. Printer: BWC.	—	—	—

Law of 23.6.1862; 1872 Issues

Law of 23.6.1862

S126 10 Pesos	Good	Fine	XF
1.4.1872. Black, brown, green and salmon. Seated allegorical woman with two children at top center; woman's head at left and right.	1500.	—	—
S128 100 Pesos			
1.10.1872. Woman at left and right. Payable text: *(en billetes de curso legal).*	—	—	—
S129 100 Pesos			
1.10.1872. Two women at center.	—	—	—

1886 Issue

S130 10 Pesos = 1 Doblon	Good	Fine	XF
1.10.1886. Standing allegorical figure at left, woman with train and farm scene at center, woman at right. Printer: W&S.	—	—	—

Banco Comercial de Paysandú, Paysandú

1863 Issue

S131 5 Centésimos	Good	Fine	XF
4.1.1863. Black. Dog running at center. Printer: Lit. A. Hequet y Cohas Hnos, Montevideo.			
a. Issued note.	—	—	—
b. Black oval handstamp: *BANCO COMERCIAL PAYSANDU / AGENCIA DE MERCEDES* at right.	—	—	—
S133 20 Centésimos			
4.1.1863. Black. Mountain with sailboat at center. Paper: Blue. Printer: Lit. A. Hequet y Cohas Hnos, Montevideo.	—	—	—

S133A 25 Centésimos	Good	Fine	XF
4.1.1863 printed date, 30.6.1865 hand dated. Black. Ostrich at center. Printer: Lit. A. Hequet y Cohas Hnos, Montevideo.	—	—	—
S134 50 Centésimos			
4.1.1863. Printer: Lit. A. Hequet y Cohas Hnos, Montevideo.	—	—	—

S135 1 Peso	Good	Fine	XF
4.1.1863; 28.2.1863. Black on blue underprint. Standing woman at left and right, galloping stallion at center. Printer: Lit. A. Hequet y Cohas Hnos, Montevideo.			
a. Issued note.	—	—	—
b. Black oval handstamp: *BANCO COMERCIAL DE PAYSANDU / AGENCIA DE MERCEDES* at right. 4.1.1863.	—	—	—
S136 2 Pesos			
4.1.1863. Green and black. Bull at center. Paper: Pink. Printer: Lit. A. Hequet y Cohas Hnos, Montevideo.	—	—	—

1866 Issue

S141 20 Centésimos	Good	Fine	XF
30.6.1866. Black on red underprint. Dog at lower left, plow and farm implements at upper center, allegorical women flanking shield at lower right. Uniface. Printer: ABNC.			
a. Issued note.	—	—	—
p. Proof.	—	Unc	1500.
S142 25 Centésimos			
30.6.1866. Black on blue underprint. Cherub at lower left and right, girl's head at upper center. Printer: ABNC.			
a. Issued note.	—	—	—
b. Blue oval handstamp: *AGENCIA DEL BANCO COMERCIAL DE PAYSANDU / MERCEDES* at right.	—	—	—
p. Proof.	—	Unc	1500.
S143 50 Centésimos			
30.6.1866. Black on blue-green underprint. Dog at upper left, young girl at lower right. Printer: ABNC. Proof.	—	Unc	1750.
S144 1 Peso			
30.6.1866. Black on brown underprint. Two cherubs holding fruit at left, three farmers with sheep at upper center, woman with produce at right. Printer: ABNC. Proof.	—	—	—

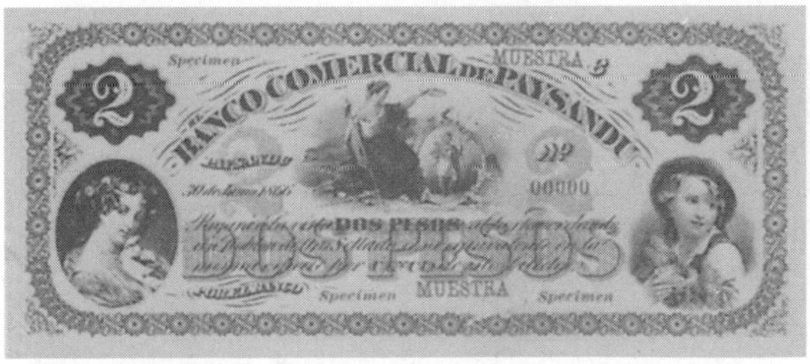

S145 2 Pesos	Good	Fine	XF
30.6.1866. Black on green underprint. Portrait young woman at lower left, seated allegorical woman at upper center, young girl at lower right. Printer: ABNC. Uniface.	—	—	—

		Good	Fine	XF
S148	**10 Pesos = 1 Doblon** 30.6.1866. Black on red-orange underprint. Seated woman at lower left, vaqueros with cattle at upper center, woman at lower right. Back: Brown. Printer: ABNC.	—	—	—
S149	**20 Pesos = 2 Doblones** 30.6.1866. Black on orange underprint. Woman at left, horse's head between Indian woman and allegorical woman at center, shield at right. Back: Green. Printer: ABNC. Proof.	—	—	—

NOTE: Some issues of this bank have oval overprint at right for *Agencia de Mercedes*.

Banco Comercial del Salto, Salto

1866 Issue

		Good	Fine	XF
S152	**20 Centésimos** 1.4.1866. Black on olive underprint. Beehive at lower left and right, steamship at upper center. Printer: ABNC. Proof.	—	—	—

		Good	Fine	XF
S153	**50 Centésimos** 1.4.1866. Black on green underprint. Dog on top of safe at upper center. Printer: ABNC. Proof.	—	—	—
S154	**1 Peso** 1.4.1866. Black on orange underprint. Young girl at lower left, galloping stallion at upper center, bull's head at lower right. Printer: ABNC.	—	—	—

		Good	Fine	XF
S157	**10 Pesos = 1 Doblon** 1.4.1866. Black on green underprint. Seated woman with sheaf and sickle at lower left, vaquero chasing bull at upper center, young girl with puppies at lower right. Printer: ABNC.			
	a. Issued note.	—	—	—
	p. Proof.	—	Unc	1250.
S158	**20 Pesos = 2 Doblones** 1.4.1866. Black on orange underprint. Woman at lower left, seated allegorical woman holding sword with child in wharf scene at upper center, eagle on cliff at lower right. Printer: ABNC. Proof.	—	—	—

		Good	Fine	XF
S159	**50 Pesos = 5 Doblones** 1.4.1866. Black on green underprint. Man and dog at lower left, village scene at upper center, cow at lower right. Uniface. Printer: ABNC.	—	—	—

Banco de Crédito Auxiliar, Montevideo

Law of 25.10.1887

		Good	Fine	XF
S161	**4 Centésimos** L.1887. Blue. Series A. Printer: CSABB, Buenos Aires.			
	a. Signed and dated. 29.9.1888.	50.00	100.	—
	r. Unsigned remainder.	—	Unc	15.00

		Good	Fine	XF
S162	**50 Centésimos** 1.10.1888. Black on rose or brown underprint. Series A. Printer: CSABB, Buenos Aires.			
	a. Signed and dated.	—	—	—
	r. Unsigned remainder.	—	Unc	15.00

		Good	Fine	XF
S163	**10 Pesos** L.1887. Black on blue underprint. Shoreline at right. Series A. Back: Blue. Printer: CSABB, Buenos Aires.			
	a. Signed and dated.	—	—	—
	r. Unsigned remainder.	—	Unc	15.00

		Good	Fine	XF
S164	**20 Pesos** L.1887. Black on green underprint. Harvest scene at center. Series B. Back: Green. Printer: CSABB, Buenos Aires.			
	a. Signed and dated.	5.00	10.00	20.00
	r. Unsigned remainder.	—	Unc	15.00

S165 50 Pesos

	Good	Fine	XF
L.1887. Black on tan underprint. Two horses at left. Series C. Back: Orange. Printer: CSABB, Buenos Aires.			
a. Signed and dated. 1.1.1888-1.1.1889.	7.50	15.00	30.00
r. Unsigned remainder.	—	Unc	15.00

NOTE: #S165a also has rectangular or round stamping on back for 8% interest paid, and a rectangular revenue adhesive stamp affixed to the back.

S168 1000 Pesos

	Good	Fine	XF
L.1887. Two allegorical figures standing at left. Series E. Back: Cows at water. Printer: CSABB, Buenos Aires.			
a. Issued note.	—	—	—
r. Unsigned remainder.	—	Unc	150.

NOTE: Additional denominations require confirmation.

Banco de España y Río de la Plata, Montevideo

1888 Issue

S169 10 Pesos

	Good	Fine	XF
1.1.1888. Black on orange and green underprint. Two allegorical women ("The Reapers") at left, sailors sighting land at center, cattle at right. Back: Orange. Steam passenger train, allegorical woman with shield and implements, and sailing ship at center. Printer: ABNC.			
a. Issued note.	—	—	—
p. Proof.	—	Unc	750.

S170 100 Pesos

	Good	Fine	XF
1.1.1888. Black on blue and brown underprint. Christopher Columbus, Indian woman and crowned shield at left, eagle at center, seated allegorical woman with shield at right. Back: Dark brown. Girl at left, sailing ships at center right. Printer: ABNC. Proof.	—	—	—

Banco Franco-Platense, Montevideo

Law of 1.5.1870; 1871 Issues

S171 10 Pesos = 1 Doblon

	Good	Fine	XF
1.5.1871. Black on orange and green underprint. Liberty with caduceus and shields at left. Back: Brown. Printer: A. Hequet y Cohas Hos.			
a. Signed.	30.00	60.00	120.
b. Without signature	7.50	15.00	30.00

S172 10 Pesos = 1 Doblon

1.8.1871. Black on orange underprint. Three shields at left, reclining woman at dockside with sailing ship at center, two young girls at right. Back: Orange. Printer: ABNC.

	Good	Fine	XF
a. Signed.	7.50	15.00	30.00
b. Without signature.	5.00	10.00	20.00

S173 20 Pesos = 2 Doblones

1.8.1871. Black on orange underprint. Three shields at left, ship on stormy sea at center, two young girls at right. Back: Orange. Printer: ABNC.

	Good	Fine	XF
a. Signed.	7.50	15.00	30.00
b. Without signature.	5.00	10.00	20.00

Banco Herrera, Eastman & Ca., Montevideo

1873 Issue

S181 10 Pesos

1.1.1873. Black and blue. Portrait Mercury at upper left, portrait woman below, building at right. Back: Light violet. Head at left and right. Printer: BWC. Rare.

Good	Fine	XF
—	—	—

Banco Inglés del Rio de la Plata, Montevideo

1885 Issue

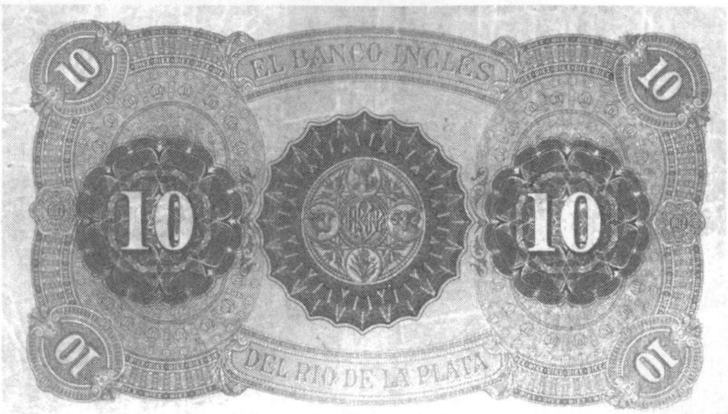

S191 10 Pesos

1.5.1885. Black on blue and yellow underprint. Allegorical woman at left and right. Back: Black, blue, green and brown. Cow, sheaf, ram and plant at center. Printer: BWC.

	Good	Fine	XF
a. Issued note.	150.	300.	—
b. Branch overprint: *PAYSANDU.*	225.	450.	—
c. Branch overprint: *SALTO.*	225.	450.	—

S194 100 Pesos

1.5.1885. Black on pink underprint. Standing Minerva with shield and staff at left, animals around oval center with arms at top, woman at right. Back: Black on red and green underprint. Two horses pulling man in small cart at center. Printer: BWC.

Good	Fine	XF
900.	—	—

Banco Italiano, Montevideo

1867 Issue

S201 20 Centésimos	Good	Fine	XF
2.1.1867. Black on orange underprint. Boy with cows at center. Back: Brown. Printer: ABNC.			
a. Issued note. Rare.	—	—	—
b. 3-line black handstamp: *SUCURSAL DEL BANCO ITALIANO SAN CARLOS.*	—	—	—
p. Proof.	—	Unc	750.

S202 50 Centésimos	Good	Fine	XF
2.1.1867. Black on green underprint. Gaucho on horse with cattle and sheep at center. Back: Orange. Printer: ABNC.			
a. Issued note. Rare.	—	—	—
p. Proof.	—	Unc	750.

S203 1 Peso	Good	Fine	XF
2.1.1867; 2.1.1869. Black on orange underprint. Four cherubs with numeral *1* at left, girl at top center right. Back: Green. Printer: ABNC.			
a. Issued note. Rare.	—	—	—
b. Square 3-line blue handstamp: *SUCURSAL DEL BANCO ITALIANO MERCEDES.*	—	—	—
s. Specimen.	—	Unc	750.

S204 1 Peso	Good	Fine	XF
2.1.1867. Black on green underprint. Four cherubs with numeral *1* at left, girl at top center right. Like #S203. Overprint: Blue: *SUCURSAL DEL BANCO ITALIANO MERCEDES* in square. Printer: ABNC. Rare.	—	—	—

S206 10 Pesos = 1 Doblon	Good	Fine	XF
2.1.1867. Black on brown underprint. Justice at left, cherub at upper left center and center right, allegorical woman with barrels at right. Back: Orange. Arms at center. Printer: ABNC. Proof.	—	—	—

S207 20 Pesos = 2 Doblones	Good	Fine	XF
2.1.1867. Black on dark orange underprint. Young girl's head at lower left, winged allegorical woman blowing horn with globe and condor at left center, arms at lower right. Back: Blue. Printer: ABNC. Proof.	—	—	—

S208 50 Pesos = 5 Doblones	Good	Fine	XF
2.1.1867. Black on green underprint. Christopher Columbus sighting land ("First Land") at left, allegorical woman ("Science") at upper center, cherub with flowers at right. Back: Brownish purple. Printer: ABNC. Proof.	—	—	—

S209 100 Pesos = 10 Doblones	Good	Fine	XF
2.1.1867. Black on blue underprint. Allegorical woman leaning on anchor ("Hope") at left, sailor holding horn ("The Hail") at upper center right, cherub with sheaf and sickle at lower right. Back: Dark brown. Printer: ABNC. Proof.	—	—	—

Banco Italiano del Uruguay, Montevideo

1887 Issues

S212 10 Pesos	Good	Fine	XF
20.9.1887. Black on blue and brown-violet underprint. Portrait Cavour at lower left, two allegorical women standing with two flags and arms at center, portrait Garibaldi at lower right. Back: Blue on yellow underprint. Seated woman with gear and bales at center. Printer: ABNC.			
a. Issued note. Rare.	—	—	—
b. Branch overprint: *MERCEDES.*	—	—	—
r. Unsigned remainder.	—	Unc	20.00

S214 100 Pesos	Good	Fine	XF
20.9.1887. Black on green and orange underprint. Portrait King Vittorio Emanuele II at left, portrait Christopher Columbus at right. Back: Brown on yellow underprint. Cow at left, vaqueros with cows at right. Printer: ABNC.			
a. Issued note with signature titles: *PRESIDENTE/DIRECTOR GERENTE.* Rare.	—	—	—
b. Issued note without signature titles.	—	—	—
p. Proof.	—	Unc	750.
s. Specimen.	—	Unc	1000.

NOTE: Virtually all signed and issued notes of #S212 and S214 are cancelled. Remainders range generally from 30,000 to 50,000 for #S212 and above 7,000 for #S214.

S215 100 Pesos	Good	Fine	XF
20.9.1887. Black on green and orange underprint. Portrait King Vittorio Emanuele II at left, portrait Christopher Columbus at right. Like #S214. Back: Green on yellow underprint. Cow at left, vaqueros with cows at right. Printer: ABNC. Remainder.	—	Unc	20.00

Banco Italo-Oriental, Montevideo

1889 Issue

S222 10 Pesos	Good	Fine	XF
10.6.1889. Printer: W&S.	—	—	—

S225 100 Pesos	Good	Fine	XF
10.6.1889. Three allegorical women with sheaves and other implements at center. Printer: W&S. Specimen.	—	Unc	750.

Banco de Londres y Rio de la Plata, Montevideo

Law of 23.6.1862; 1865 Issue

S231 20 Centésimos	Good	Fine	XF
1.7.1865. Black and olive-gray. Galloping stallion at left, English arms at right. Printer: BWC.	—	—	—

S232 50 Centésimos	Good	Fine	XF
1.7.1865. Liberty standing at left, British shield at right. Printer: BWC.	—	—	—

S233 1 Peso	Good	Fine	XF
1.7.1865. Black and blue-gray. Arms at left and right. Printer: BWC.	—	—	—

1867 Issue

S234 20 Centésimos	Good	Fine	XF
1.1.1867. Galloping stallion at left. Printer: BWC.	—	—	—

S235 50 Centésimos	Good	Fine	XF
1.1.1867. Bull at left. Printer: BWC.	—	—	—

1872 Issue

S237 20 Pesos = 2 Doblones	Good	Fine	XF
1.1.1872. Black on light green and light brown underprint. Liberty standing with sword, shield and flag at left. Similar to #S238 but English arms at upper right. Printer: BWC.	—	—	—

S238 50 Pesos = 5 Doblones	Good	Fine	XF
1.1.1872. Green and brown. Liberty standing with sword, shield and flag at left, British shield at right. Printer: BWC.			
a. Issued note.	—	—	—
r. Unsigned remainder.	—	Unc	25.00

1870's Issue

	Good	Fine	XF
S239 10 Pesos 187-. Black on green and orange underprint. Portrait Christopher Columbus at left, boy planting seeds at right. Like #S242. Back: Green. Head at left and right. Printer: BWC. Unsigned remainder.	—	—	—
S240 20 Pesos 187-. Black on blue and orange underprint. Portrait Christopher Columbus at left. Similar to #S239 but different figure at right. Back: Blue. Head at left and right. Printer: BWC. Unsigned remainder.	—	—	—

1883 Issue

	Good	Fine	XF
S242 10 Pesos 1.1.1883. Black on blue and brown underprint. Portrait Christopher Columbus at left, boy planting seeds at right. Back: Brown. Head at left and right. Printer: BWC.			
a. Issued note.	—	—	—
r. Unsigned remainder.	—	Unc	15.00

	Good	Fine	XF
S245 100 Pesos (date filled in). Black on yellow underprint. Portrait Christopher Columbus at left, boy running with rope at right. Back: Woman's head at center. Printer: BWC.			
a. Issued note.	—	—	—
r. Unsigned remainder.	—	Unc	15.00

NOTE: Beware of notes falsely signed with serial # over 415000 ($10.) (see #S245 illustration) or 60000 ($100.). Original Issued notes must have a scalloped cutting line at left margin.

Banco Mauá & Cia., Montevideo

1857 Issue

	Good	Fine	XF
S251 240 Centésimos 1.8.1857. Printer: BWC.	—	—	—

	Good	Fine	XF
S252 480 Centésimos 1.9.1857. Black. Uniface. Paper: Gray.	300.	600.	—
S253 960 Centésimos 10.8.1857. Overprint: Branch: *AGENCIA DEL BANCO MAUA PAYSANDU.* Printer: BWC.	—	—	—

1860-62 Issue

	Good	Fine	XF
S255 240 Centésimos 2.1.1861. Printer: Bradbury and Evans.	—	—	—
S256 480 Centésimos 2.1.1861.	—	—	—

	Good	Fine	XF
S257 960 Centésimos 1.8.1861. Printer: BWC.	—	—	—

	Good	Fine	XF
S258 1 Onza De Oro 1860; 1862. Printer: BWC.	—	—	—

1863-65 Issue

	Good	Fine	XF
S261 20 Centésimos 2.1.1863. Black and green. Paper: Rose. Printer: BWC.	60.00	125.	—

	Good	Fine	XF
S262 50 Centésimos 2.1.1863. Orange and black. Paper: Yellow. Printer: BWC.			
a. Issued note.	60.00	125.	—
b. Branch overprint: *AGENCIA DEL ... PAYSANDU.*	—	—	—
c. Blue branch overprint: *AGENCIA DEL ... SALTO.*	—	—	—

S263 1 Peso	Good	Fine	XF
2.1.1863. Black on red underprint. Uniface. Printer: BWC.			
a. Issued note.	75.00	200.	—
b. Branch overprint: *AGENCIA DEL ... SALTO.*	—	—	—

S265 10 Pesos			
1865. Black and brownish-red. Oval branch stamping: *PAYSANDU.* Uniface.	—	—	—

S266 20 Pesos			
2.1.1863. Blue and red. Woman reclining at center. Paper: Violet.	—	—	—

1865 Issue

S271 20 Centésimos	Good	Fine	XF
1.7.1865. Black on green underprint. Portrait Irineo Evangelista de Souza, Vizconde de Maua at left. Child at top center. Printer: BWC.	75.00	200.	—

S272 50 Centésimos	Good	Fine	XF
1.7.1865. Black on red underprint. Portrait Irineo Evangelista de Souza, Vizconde de Maua at left. Two children with anvil at upper center. Paper: Pale rose. Printer: BWC.	75.00	200.	—

S273 1 Peso	Good	Fine	XF
1.7.1865. Black on green underprint. Portrait Irineo Evangelista de Souza, Vizconde de Maua at left. Child at top center. Paper: Pale yellow. Printer: BWC.	75.00	200.	—

#S276-S279 portr. V. Mauá at upper ctr.

S276 10 Pesos	Good	Fine	XF
1.7.1865. Portrait V. Mauá at upper center. Child at left. Printer: BWC.	—	—	—

S277 20 Pesos			
1.7.1865. Black on green and red underprint. Portrait V. Mauá at upper center. Boy at left. Back: Like face, but inverted without black print. Printer: BWC.	—	—	—

S279 100 Pesos	Good	Fine	XF
1.7.1865. Blue and multicolor. Portrait V. Mauá at upper center. Cherub in boat at left, gaucho on galloping stallion at right. Uniface. Printer: BWC.	—	—	—

1869-70 Issue

S281 100 Pesos	Good	Fine	XF
1.7.1869. Black, grayish blue and salmon. Portrait V. Mauá at center. Back: Retrograde printing of frame but with bust of Minerva at center. Printer: BWC.	—	—	—

S283 10 Pesos = 1 Doblon	Good	Fine	XF
1.9.1870. Liberty standing with shield and anchor at left. Printer: Hequet y Cohas Hos.	—	—	—

A WORD ON DATE RANGES

Often date ranges or specific dates are listed. These have been observed or reported by our contributors. If a note is outside the published range, it only means that it is a newly reported date, and not necessarily worthy of a premium value.

S284 20 Pesos = 2 Doblones — Good: — Fine: — XF: —
1.9.1870. Black on yellow and red underprint. Mercury and lion at left. Back: Green.

Law of 4.5.1870; 1871 Issue

S291 10 Pesos = 1 Doblon — Good: 60.00 Fine: 180. XF: —
1.3.1871. Green. Portrait young girl at right.

S292 20 Pesos = 2 Doblones — Good: 5.00 Fine: 15.00 XF: 45.00
1.3.1871. Black on red and green. Portrait woman at top center. Paper: Rose.

1875 Issue

S301 20 Centésimos — Good: 75.00 Fine: 225. XF: —
26.10.1875. Black on orange underprint. Portrait woman at left. Printer: BWC.

S302 50 Centésimos — Good: 75.00 Fine: 225. XF: —
26.10.1875. Green. Woman with sickle and sheaf at left. Paper: Rose. Printer: BWC.

S303 1 Peso — Good: 125. Fine: 375. XF: —
26.10.1875. Black on orange underprint. Portrait Liberty at left, young bird at right. Back: Light brown. Paper: Yellow. Printer: BWC.

S304 2 Pesos — Good: 75.00 Fine: 225. XF: —
26.10.1875. Black on red underprint. Portrait Mauá at left, portrait woman at right. Back: Red. Printer: BWC.

S305 5 Pesos — Good: — Fine: — XF: —
26.10.1875. Black on blue and red underprint. Barón Mauá at left, bull at upper center, Liberty at right. Back: Blue. Two cameo heads. Paper: Pink. Printer: BWC.

S309 100 Pesos	Good	Fine	XF
1.7.1869. Altered date. *75* written over *69*. Black, grayish blue and salmon. Portrait V. Mauá at center. Overprint: *ORO SELLADO* on #S281. Printer: BWC. Rare.	—	—	—

1876 Issue

S311 20 Centésimos	Good	Fine	XF
3.1.1876. Black on orange underprint. Portrait woman at left. Like #S301.	—	—	—
S312 50 Centésimos			
3.1.1876. Green. Woman with sickle and sheaf at left. Like #S302.	—	—	—
S313 1 Peso			
3.1.1876. Black and orange. Portrait Liberty at left, young bird at right. Like #S303. Paper: Yellow.	—	—	—
S314 2 Pesos			
3.1.1876. Black on red underprint. Portrait Mauá at left, portrait woman at right. Like #S304.	—	—	—
S315 5 Pesos			
3.1.1876. Black on blue and red underprint. Barón Mauá at left, bull at upper center, Liberty at right. Like #S305. Back: Blue. Two cameo heads.	—	—	—

S320 50 Pesos	Good	Fine	XF
1.1.1876. Farm implements at center, horse ("My Horse") at right. Printer: NBNC.			
p. Proof.	—	Unc	750.
r. Remainder without signature.	—	Unc	500.

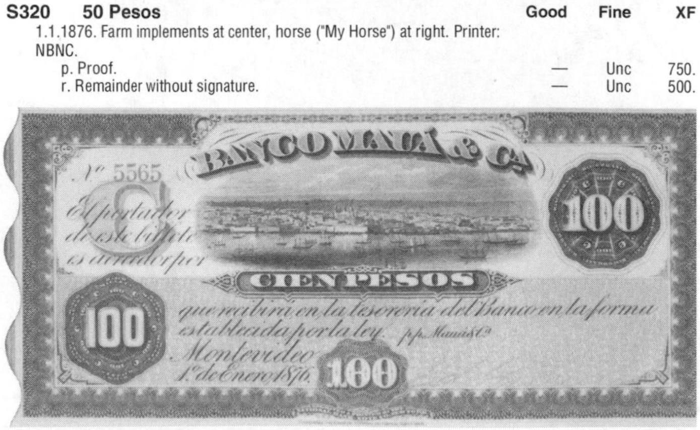

S321 100 Pesos	Good	Fine	XF
1.1.1876. Black and blue. Harbor and city view of Montevideo at center. Back: Brown. Printer: NBNC.			
a. Hand signed issued note. Scalloped cutting line at left.	—	—	—
p. Proof.	—	Unc	750.
r. Remainder without signature, straight cutting line at left.	—	Unc	500.

Banco Mercantil del Rio de la Plata, Montevideo

1873 Issue

S333 10 Pesos	Good	Fine	XF
1.9.1873. Black and green. Minerva at center. Back: Green and red. Printer: BWC. Rare.	—	—	—
S334 20 Pesos			
1.9.1873. Minerva at center. Printer: BWC.	—	—	—
S335 50 Pesos			
1.9.1873. Minerva at center. Printer: BWC.	—	—	—
S336 100 Pesos			
1.9.1873. Minerva at center. Printer: BWC.	—	—	—

Banco Montevideano, Montevideo

1865 Issue

S341 20 Centésimos	Good	Fine	XF
1.8.1865. Black. Large denomination in underprint at center. Printer: Litog. Wiegeland, Montevideo.	—	—	—

S346 10 Pesos = 1 Doblon	Good	Fine	XF
1.8.1865. Brown. Standing woman at left in numeral *1*. Back: Blue. Printer: Litog. Wiegeland, Montevideo.	—	—	—

1866 Issue

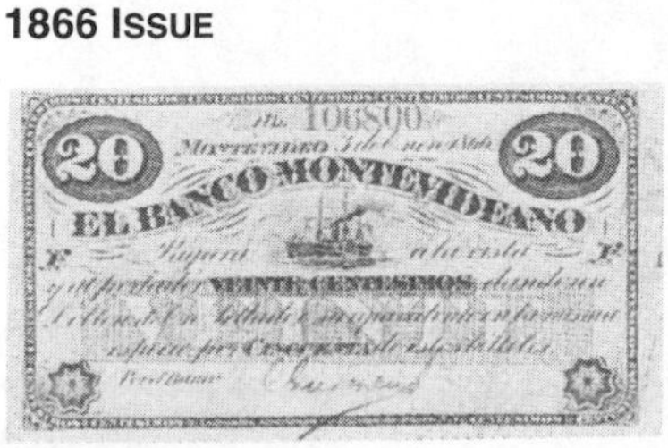

S351 20 Centésimos	Good	Fine	XF
3.1.1866. Black on green underprint. Steamship at center. Back: Green. Printer: ABNC.			
a. Issued note.	—	—	—
p. Proof.	—	Unc	1750.

S352 50 Centésimos	Good	Fine	XF
3.1.1866. Black on green underprint. Cherub at lower left and right, young girl's head ("Autumn") at upper center. Printer: ABNC.			
a. Issued note.	—	—	—
b. Branch overprint: *SUCURSAL. . . DOLORES.*	—	—	—
p. Proof.	—	Unc	1750.

S353 1 Peso	Good	Fine	XF
3.1.1866. Black on green underprint. Two children at lower left, galloping stallion at top center, bull's head at right. Uniface. Printer: ABNC.	225.	500.	—

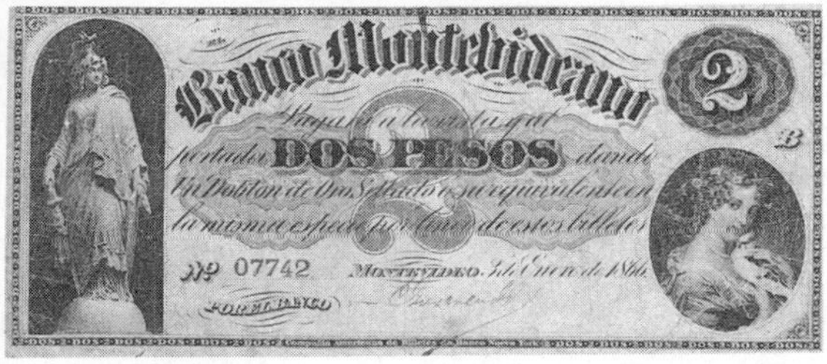

S354 2 Pesos	Good	Fine	XF
3.1.1866. Black on green and red underprint. Statue of Freedom at left, woman with bird at lower right. Large *2* in underprint at center. Printer: ABNC.	450.	900.	—

S356 10 Pesos = 1 Doblon	Good	Fine	XF
3.1.1866. Black on green underprint. Woman at lower left, woman reclining with globe at top center, arms at right. Printer: ABNC.	—	—	—

S357 20 Pesos = 2 Doblones	Good	Fine	XF
3.1.1866. Black on green underprint. Sheep at upper left, man at lower right. Printer: ABNC. Rare.	—	—	—

S358 50 Pesos = 5 Doblones	Good	Fine	XF
3.1.1866. Black on green underprint. Justice with barrels and boxes at left, landing of Columbus at center, Columbus at right. Printer: ABNC. Archive copy.	—	—	—

S359 100 Pesos = 10 Doblones	Good	Fine	XF
3.1.1866. Black on green underprint. Dog on top of safe at lower left, cattle watering in pond at upper center, horse at bottom center, man at lower right. Printer: ABNC. Archive copy.	—	—	—

Banco Navia y Ca., Montevideo

1865 First Issue

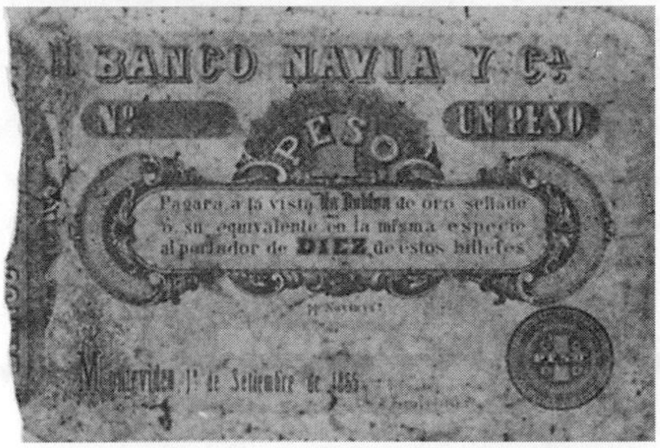

S361 1 Peso	Good	Fine	XF
1.9.1865. Red. Printer: A. Hequet y Cohas Hos. Rare.	—	—	—

S362 1 Doblon	Good	Fine	XF
1.9.1865. Black and red. Boy at top center. Back: Brown. Ornate design. Paper: Pink. Printer: A. Hequet y Cohas Hos. Rare.	—	—	—

1865 Second Issue

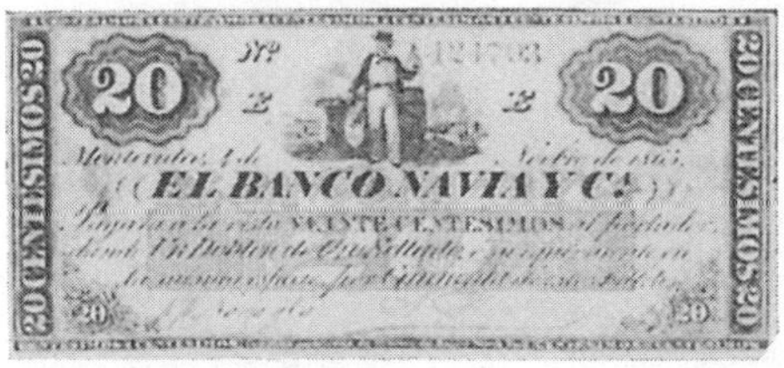

S371 20 Centésimos	Good	Fine	XF
4.11.1865. Black on red-brown underprint. Sailor standing at top center. Back: Red-brown. Printer: ABNC.	—	—	—

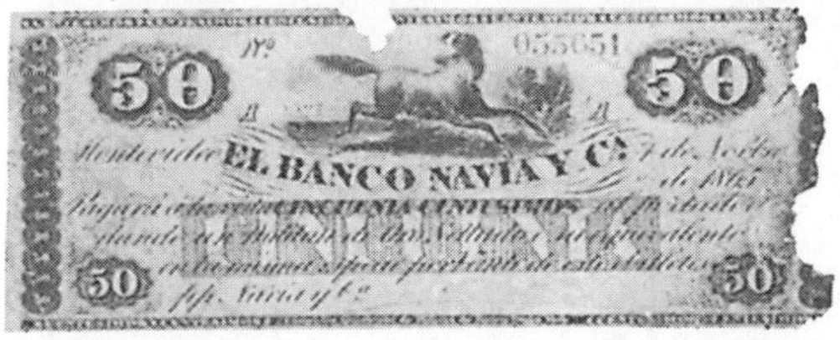

S372 50 Centésimos	Good	Fine	XF
4.11.1865. Black on brown underprint. Galloping stallion at center. Printer: ABNC.			
a. Issued note.	—	—	—
p. Proof.	—	Unc	1750.

S373 1 Peso

	Good	Fine	XF
4.11.1865. Black on orange underprint. Girl's bust at lower left, cows at upper center, dog and safe at lower right. Printer: ABNC.	—	—	—

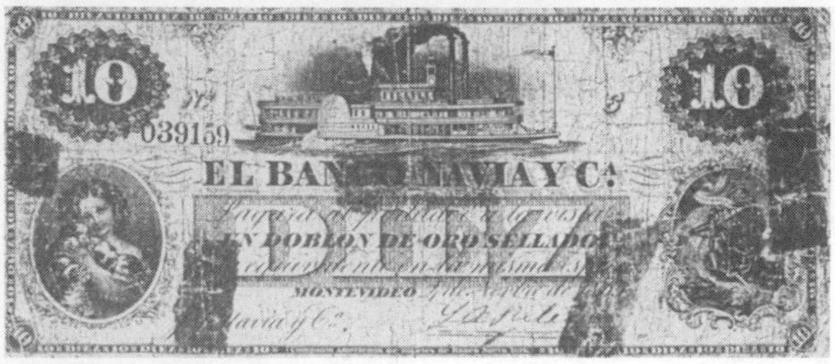

S376 10 Pesos = 1 Doblon

	Good	Fine	XF
4.11.1865. Black on green underprint. Girl and puppies at left, paddlewheel steamship *MONTEVIDEO* at upper center, anchor at right. Back: Green. Printer: ABNC. Rare.	—	—	—

S377 20 Pesos = 2 Doblones

	Good	Fine	XF
4.11.1865. Black on green underprint. Seated Justice at lower left, two seated allegorical women with shield at upper center, seated woman at lower right. Back: Lilac-brown. Printer: ABNC. Rare.	—	—	—

S378 50 Pesos = 5 Doblones

	Good	Fine	XF
4.11.1865. Black on green underprint. Cow at left, steamship, globe and train at center, Indian woman holding arrow at right. Back: Blue. Printer: ABNC. Archive copy.	—	—	—

S379 100 Pesos = 10 Doblones

	Good	Fine	XF
4.11.1865. Black on green underprint. Two sailors with ship at lower left, seated woman with sheaf at upper center, two children at lower right. Back: Brown. Printer: ABNC. Rare.	—	—	—

Banco Oriental, Montevideo

1867-69 Issue

S381 20 Centésimos

	Good	Fine	XF
1.8.1867; 1.8.1869. Black on brown underprint. Gaucho pouring drink at left, gaucho smoking at right. Printer: ABNC. Rare.	—	—	—

S382 50 Centésimos

	Good	Fine	XF
1.8.1867. Black on red-brown underprint. Allegorical figure with cornucopia at left, steam/sailing ship at right. Uniface. Printer: ABNC.			
a. Issued note. Rare.	—	—	—
p. Proof.	—	—	—

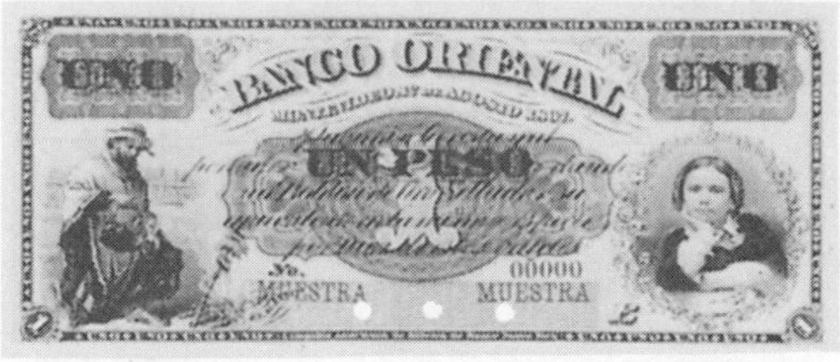

S383 1 Peso

	Good	Fine	XF
1.8.1867. Black on green underprint. Gaucho pouring drink at left, woman at right. Uniface. Printer: ABNC.			
a. Issued note.	180.	360.	—
r. Remainder.	—	Unc	200.
s. Specimen.	—	Unc	1000.

S384 5 Pesos

	Good	Fine	XF
1.8.1867. Black on orange underprint. Allegorical woman holding sword seated by child on wharf at left, young girl ("Chloe") at center right. Back: Green. Printer: ABNC.			
a. Issued note. Rare.	—	—	—
p. Proof.	—	Unc	1000.

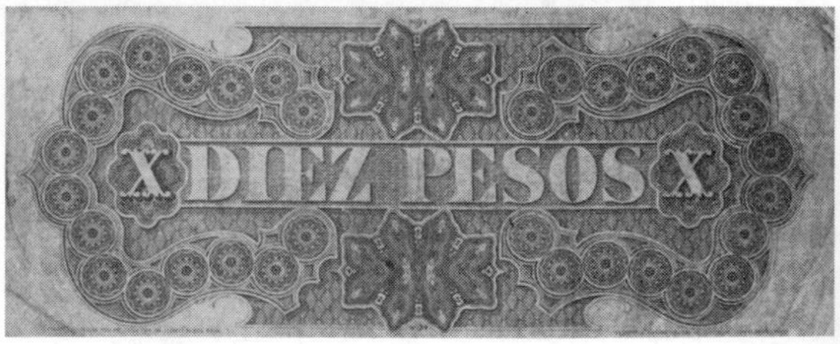

S385 10 Pesos = 1 Doblon

	Good	Fine	XF
1.8.1867. Black on orange underprint. Two standing allegorical women ("North and South") at left, arms at lower right. Back: Orange. Printer: ABNC.			
a. Issued note.	10.00	20.00	60.00
p. Proof.	—	Unc	1000.

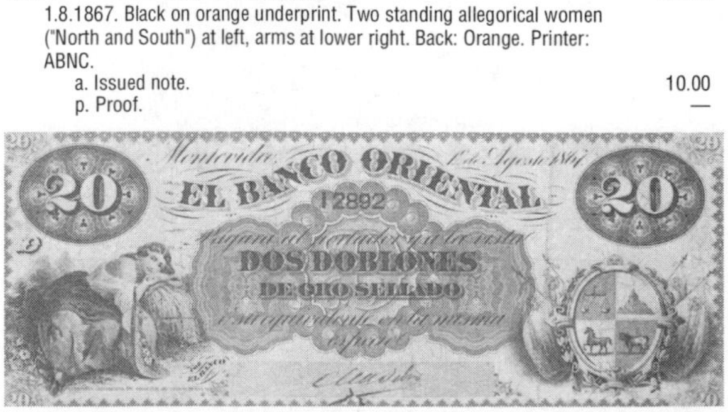

S386 20 Pesos = 2 Doblones

	Good	Fine	XF
1.8.1867. Black on dark orange underprint. Allegorical woman leaning on sheaf at left, arms at right. Back: Blue. Printer: ABNC.	10.00	20.00	60.00

S387 **50 Pesos = 5 Doblones**	Good	Fine	XF
1.8.1867. Black on blue underprint. Seated woman beneath trees at left, arms at lower right. Back: Orange. Printer: ABNC.	10.00	20.00	60.00

Banco de Paysandú

1862 Issue

S388 **120 Centésimos**	Good	Fine	XF
27.9.1862. Black. Sailing ship at upper center. Paper: Cream. Printer: Lit. de Mege y Willems, Montevideo.	—	—	—
S389 **240 Centésimos** 27.9.1862. Black. Printer: Lit. de Mege y Willems, Montevideo.	—	—	—

S390 **480 Centésimos**	Good	Fine	XF
27.9.1862. Black. Two cows at upper center. Paper: Blue. Printer: Lit. de Mege y Willems, Montevideo.	—	—	—

S391 **960 Centésimos = 1 Patacon**	Good	Fine	XF
27.9.1862. Black. Two standing allegorical women at left. Paper: Blue-green. Printer: Lit. de Mege y Willems, Montevideo. Rare.	—	—	—

Banco Popular, Montevideo

Law of 23.6.1862; 1888 Issue

S395 **10 Pesos**	Good	Fine	XF
5.11.1888. Black on light green underprint. Man in chariot with bow and arrow at left. Back: Green. Woman at center. Printer: A. Godel.			
a. Issued note.	45.00	135.	270.
r. Remainder.	7.50	22.50	65.00

Banco del Salto, Salto

1858 Issue

S401 **120 Centésimos**	Good	Fine	XF
1.10.1858. Brown. Tree at upper center.			
a. Issued note.		—	—
r. Remainder.	—	Unc	125.

S403 **480 Centésimos**	Good	Fine	XF
1.10.1858. Black. Sheep at center. Remainder.	—	—	—

S404 **960 Centésimos = 1 Patacon**	Good	Fine	XF
1.10.1858. Black. Ostrich at center. Paper: Cream.	—	—	—

1863 Issue

	Good	Fine	XF
S411 5 Centésimos 2.1.1863. Black. Tree at upper center. Uniface. Paper: Yellow. Printer: BWC.	—	—	—
S412 10 Centésimos 2.1.1863. Black. Tiger at center. Uniface. Paper: Tan. Printer: BWC.	—	—	—
S413 20 Centésimos 2.1.1863. Black. Rooster at center. Paper: Yellow. Printer: BWC.	—	—	—
S414 50 Centésimos 2.1.1863. Black. Deer at center. Paper: Blue. Printer: BWC.	—	—	—
S415 1 Peso 2.1.1863. Black. Sheep at upper center. Paper: Orange. Printer: BWC.	—	—	—

Banco Villaamil & Ca., Montevideo

Decreto 12.10.1876

	Good	Fine	XF
S417 10 Pesos D.1876. Black on tan and light blue underprint. Justice at left, allegorical woman with beehive at right. Uniface. Printer: BWC.	—	—	—

Cambio de Monedas de Viñas y Ca., Montevideo

1873 Issue

	Good	Fine	XF
S418 1 Peso 1.8.1873. Black on orange underprint. Cherub with numeral *1* at left. Without signature. Printer: A. Hequet y Ca.	—	—	—

Comercio de Tacuarembo

1861 Issue

	Good	Fine	XF
S418D 480 Centésimos Feb. 1, 1861. Black. Sheep at upper center right. Oval seal: *COMERCIO DE TACUAREMBO/480 CENTÉSIMOS* at left. Uniface.	—	—	—

Progreso Oriental, Montevideo

1868 Issue

	Good	Fine	XF
S419 1 Peso 18xx (ca.1868). Black on orange underprint. Anchor at upper center. Back: Orange. Authorization date of 14.2.1868 and guarantee text. Printer: ABNC. Proof.	—	—	—

	Good	Fine	XF
S419A 5 Pesos 18xx (ca.1868). Black on blue underprint. Dog with safe at upper center. Back: Blue. Authorization date of 14.2.1868 and guarantee text. Printer: ABNC. Proof.	—	—	—

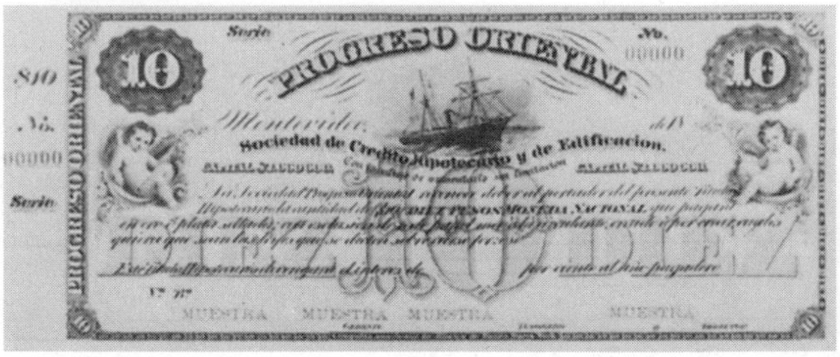

	Good	Fine	XF
S420 10 Pesos 18xx (ca.1868). Black on green underprint. Cherubs at left and right, sailing ship at center. Back: Green. Authorization date of 14.2.1868 and guarantee text. Printer: ABNC. Proof.	—	—	—
S420A 50 Pesos 18xx (ca.1868). Black on brown underprint. Sailor at upper left, three allegorical women holding denomination numeral at right. Back: Brown. Authorization date of 14.2.1868 and guarantee text. Printer: ABNC. Proof.	—	—	—

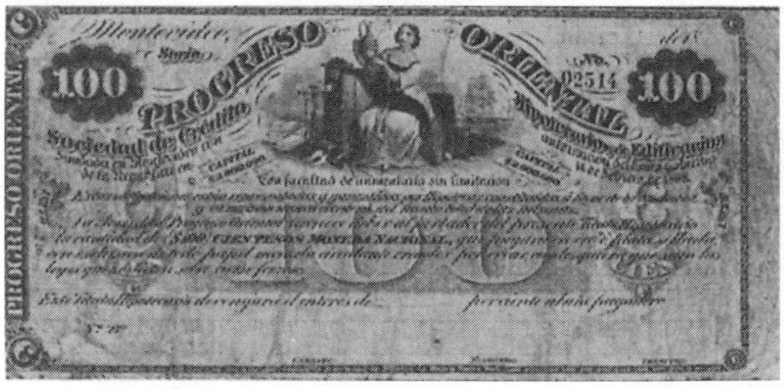

	Good	Fine	XF
S421 100 Pesos 18xx (ca.1868). Black on red-orange underprint. Seated allegorical woman holding vase with barrels, boxes and other implements, ships behind, at center. Authorization date of 14.2.1868 and guarantee text. Back: Red-orange. Printer: ABNC. Remainder.	150.	450.	—
S422 100 Pesos 18xx (ca.1868). Black on green underprint. Reclining allegorical woman with coins, anchor and other marine implements at center. Authorization date of 14.2.1868 and guarantee text. Back: Green. Printer: ABNC. Proof.	—	—	—
S423 1000 Pesos 18xx (ca.1868). Black on brown underprint. Seated woman at left, sailor at right. Authorization date of 14.2.1868 and guarantee text. Back: Brown. Printer: ABNC.	—	—	—

Sociedád Auxiliar de Crédito y Alquileres, Montevideo

Law of 18.9.1889

		Good	Fine	XF
S426	**100 Pesos** L.1889. Lion at left. Printer: A. Godel, Montevideo. Remainder.	—	—	—

Sociedád de Cambios

1856 Issue

		Good	Fine	XF
S431	**120 Reis** 5.1856. Red. Rooster at upper center.	—	—	—

		Good	Fine	XF
S432	**240 Reis** 5.1856. Blue. Ostrich at upper center.	—	—	—

		Good	Fine	XF
S433	**320 Reis** 5.1856. Brown. Buggy pulled by four horses at upper center.	—	—	—

		Good	Fine	XF
S434	**480 Reis** 5.1856. Orange. Ewe at upper center.	—	—	—

		Good	Fine	XF
S435	**640 Reis** 5.1856. Bridge at upper center.	—	—	—

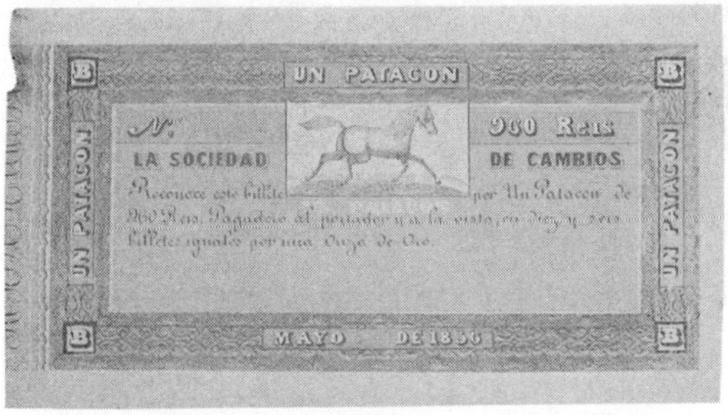

		Good	Fine	XF
S436	**960 Reis = 1 Patacón** 5.1856. Trotting horse at upper center.	—	—	—

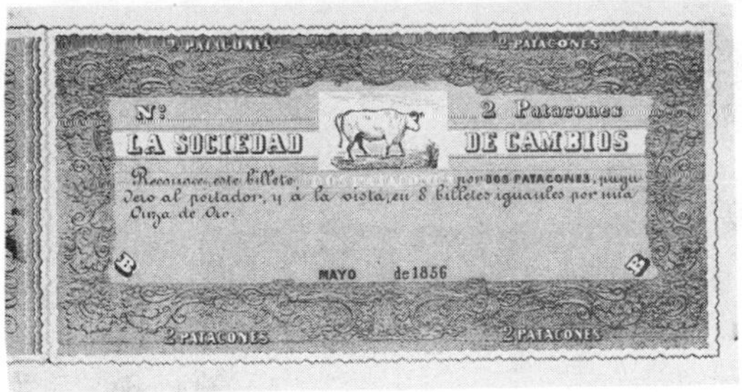

		Good	Fine	XF
S437	**2 Patacónes** 5.1856. Bull at upper center.	—	—	—

Sociedád de Cambios, Montevideo

1856 Issue

		Good	Fine	XF
S438	**120 Reis** 1.7.1856. Black. Sailing ships at upper center. Uniface.	—	—	—
S439	**240 Reis** 1.7.1856. Black.	—	—	—

		Good	Fine	XF
S440	**480 Reis** 1.7.1856. Black.	—	—	—
S440A	**640 Reis** 1.7.1856. Black.	—	—	—
S440B	**960 Reis** 1.7.1856. Black.	—	—	—
S440C	**1920 Reis** 1.7.1856. Black.	—	—	—
S440D	**3840 Reis** 1.7.1856. Black.	—	—	—

Sociedád de Cambios Carmelo y Na (Nueva) Palmira

1856 Issue

		Good	Fine	XF
S441	**120 Reis** 5.1856. Red. Rooster at upper center. Similar to #S431.	—	—	—

		Good	Fine	XF
S444	**480 Reis** 5.1856. Orange. Ewe at upper center. Similar to #S434.	—	—	—

		Good	Fine	XF
S445	**640 Reis** 5.1856. Brown. Bridge at upper center. Similar to #S435.	—	—	—

		Good	Fine	XF
S447	**2 Patacónes** 5.1856. Black. Bull at upper center. Similar to #S437.	—	—	—

Sociedád de Cambios de Cerro Largo

ND Issue

		Good	Fine	XF
S451	**480 Reis** ND.	—	—	—

Sociedád de Cambios de Paysandú

1856 Issue

		Good	Fine	XF
S461	**2 Patacónes** 1856. Printer: Lit. Mege. Specimen.	—	—	—

1840's Issue

		Good	Fine	XF
S465	**120 Reis** 184x.	—	—	—

1864 Issue

		Good	Fine	XF
S466	**240 Reis** 1864. Printer: Hequet y Cohas Hnos.	—	—	—
S467	**480 Reis** 1864. Printer: Hequet y Cohas Hnos.	—	—	—
S468	**1 Patacón** 1864. Printer: Hequet y Cohas Hnos.	—	—	—

1865 Issue

		Good	Fine	XF
S469	**2 Patacónes = 1920 Reis** 4.1.1865. Allegorical figures left and right, bull at center. Printer: Hequet y Cohas Hnos.	—	—	—

Sociedád de Crédito Hipotecario

1868 Issue

		Good	Fine	XF
S471	**2 Centésimos** 30.9.1868. Black and green. Back: Oval hand stamp. Printer: A. Hequet y Cia.	45.00	135.	—

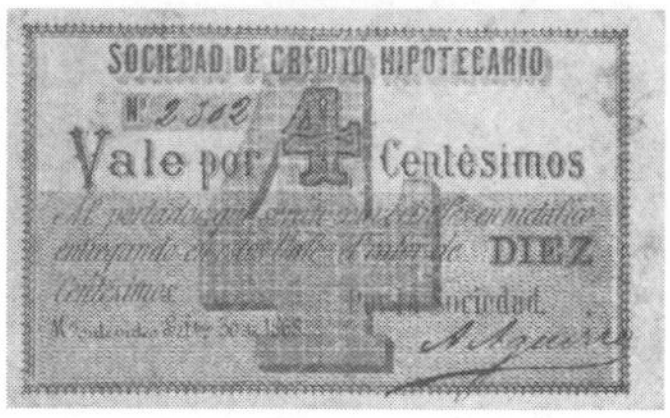

		Good	Fine	XF
S472	**4 Centésimos** 30.9.1868. Black and orange. Like #S471. Back: Oval hand stamp. Printer: A. Hequet y Cia.	45.00	135.	—
S472A	**5 Centésimos** 30.9.1868. Black on orange underprint. Like #S471. Back: Oval hand stamp. Printer: A. Hequet y Cia.	—	—	—

		Good	Fine	XF
S473	**8 Centésimos** 30.9.1868. Black and orange. Like #S471. Back: Oval hand stamp. Printer: A. Hequet y Cia.	45.00	135.	—

S478 10 Pesos

	Good	Fine	XF
1.11.1868. Black on gray underprint. Standing woman holding caduceus at left. Printer: A. Hequet y Cia.	—	—	—

Sociedád Fomento Territorial, Montevideo

1868 Issue

S480 1 Peso

	Good	Fine	XF
1.7.1868. Black on orange underprint. Boy with torch and arms at left, value beneath. Printer: Lit. A. Hequet y Cohas Hnos.	60.00	180.	—

S481 10 Pesos

	Good	Fine	XF
1.6.1868. Black on green underprint. Boy with torch, map of Uruguay and shield at left. Back: Gold. Printer: Lit. A. Hequet y Cohas Hnos.	10.00	30.00	90.00

S482 20 Pesos

	Good	Fine	XF
1.6.1868. Black on orange underprint. Boy with torch, map of Uruguay and shield at left. Like #S481. Back: Blue. Printer: Lit. A. Hequet y Cohas Hnos.	10.00	30.00	90.00

Departamento de Artigas

1907 Provisional Billetes de Canje (Bills of Exchange) Issue

S491 1 Peso

	Good	Fine	XF
1907. Original receipt is black and gray. Series 1.	—	—	—

S492 5 Pesos

	Good	Fine	XF
1907. Original receipt is blue and gray. Series 1.	—	—	—

NOTE: #S491 and S492 without text on back as shown are not believed to be items that could have circulated.

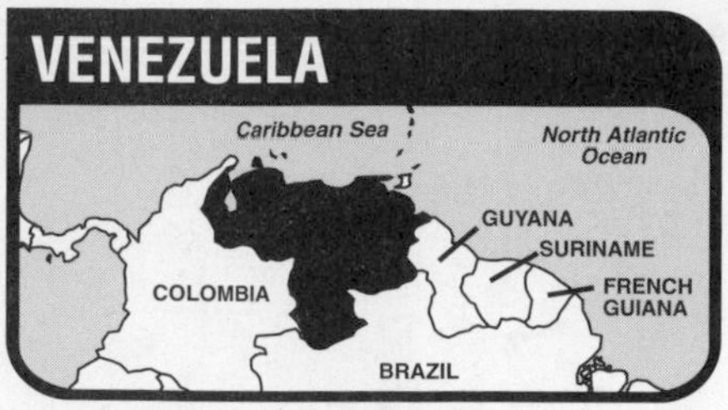

The Republic of Venezuela, located on the northern coast of South America between Colombia and Guyana, has an area of 912,050 sq. km. and a population of 26.41 million. Capital: Caracas. Petroleum and mining provide 90 percent of Venezuela's exports although they employ less than 2 percent of the work force. Coffee, grown on 60,000 plantations, is the chief crop.

Venezuela was one of three countries that emerged from the collapse of Gran Colombia in 1830 (the others being Ecuador and New Granada, which became Colombia). For most of the first half of the 20th century, Venezuela was ruled by generally benevolent military strongmen, who promoted the oil industry and allowed for some social reforms. Democratically elected governments have held sway since 1959. Hugo Chavez, president since 1999, seeks to implement his "21st Century Socialism," which purports to alleviate social ills while at the same time attacking globalization and undermining regional stability. Current concerns include: a weakening of democratic institutions, political polarization, a politicized military, drug-related violence along the Colombian border, increasing internal drug consumption, overdependence on the petroleum industry with its price fluctuations, and irresponsible mining operations that are endangering the rain forest and indigenous peoples.

MONETARY SYSTEM:

1 Bolívar = 100 Centimos, 1879-

BANKS

Banco de Carabobo, 188x .... #S101-S104
Banco de Carácas, ca.1876-79 .... #S111-S124
Banco Carácas, 189x-1928 .... #S131-S157
Banco Colonial Britanico, 18xx .... #S161
Banco Comercial, 188x .... #S166-S170
Banco Comercial de Maracaibo, ca.1916-33 .... #S171-S183
Banco de Londres y Venezuela, Limitado, 1865 .... #S185
Banco de Maracaibo, 188x-1935 .... #S190-S229
Banco Mercantil y Agrícola, 1934-35 .... #S231-S233
Banco Nacional de Venezuela, 1841 .... #S236
Banco Venezolano de Crédito, 1925-39 .... #S241-S248

Banco de Venezuela

First Bank Issue, 1862 .... #S251-S256
Second Bank Issue, 189x-1939 .... #S261-S315

GOVERNMENT

Compañía de Accionistas, 1856 .... #S321-S324
Compañía de Crédito, ca.1873 .... #S325-S329

STATE

Estado de Guayana, 1878-79 .... #S332-S354

LEPROSARIUM

Isla de Providencia, Leprosarios Nacionales, ca.1940 .... #S361-S370

Banks

Banco de Carabobo

1880's Issue

S101 20 Bolívares Good Fine XF
188x. Black on blue underprint. State arms at left, seated allegorical woman with globe ("La Critique") at center, national arms at right. Back: Blue. Printer: ABNC. Proof. — — —

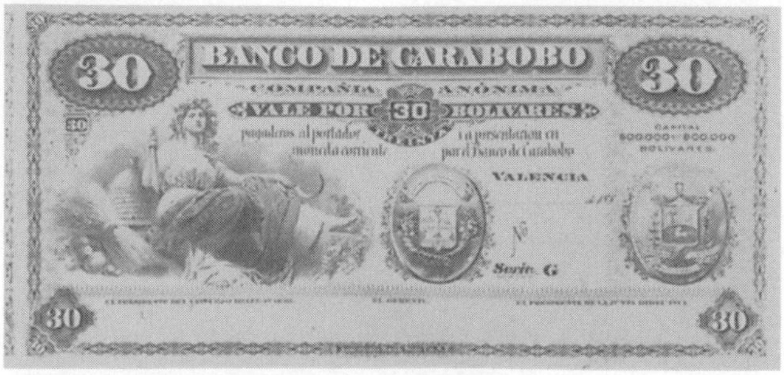

S102 30 Bolívares Good Fine XF
188x. Black on orange underprint. Allegorical woman with beehive and sickle ("Agriculture") at left, state arms at center, national arms at right. Back: Orange. Printer: ABNC. Proof. — — —

S103 100 Bolívares Good Fine XF
188x. Black on yellow underprint. State arms at left, allegorical woman with plants ("Tropics No. 2") at center, national arms at right. Back: Yellow. Printer: ABNC. Proof. — — —

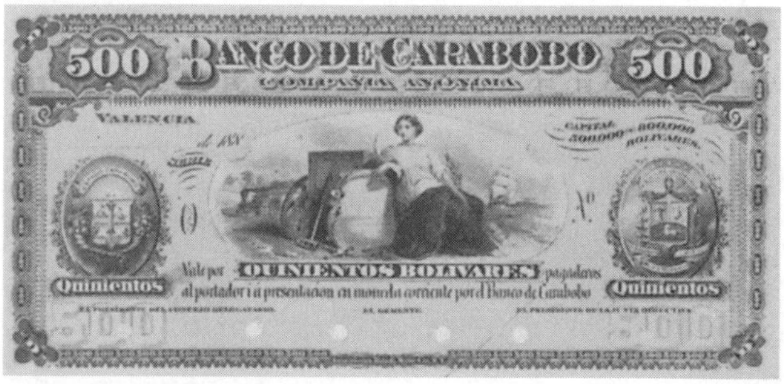

S104 500 Bolívares Good Fine XF
188x. Black on green underprint. State arms at left, allegorical woman with implements, shield, train and sailing ship at center, national arms at right. Back: Green. Printer: ABNC. Proof. — — —

Banco de Carácas

1876 Issue

S111 5 Venezolanos Good Fine XF
18xx (ca.1876). Black on brown underprint. Allegorical woman with boxes, globe and marine implements at center. Printer: CABB. Proof. — — —

S112 20 Venezolanos Good Fine XF
18xx (ca.1876). Black on brown underprint. Columbus sighting land at center. Printer: CABB. Proof. — — —

		Good	Fine	XF
S113	**100 Venezolanos** 20.11.1876. Black on brown underprint. Explorer landing at center. Printer: CABB. Proof.	—	—	—

1877 Issue

#S116-S118 *CAPITAL V. 200,000.*

		Good	Fine	XF
S116	**5 Venezolanos** 18xx (ca.1877). Black on brown underprint. Printer: CABB. Proof.	—	—	—

		Good	Fine	XF
S117	**20 Venezolanos** 18xx (ca.1877). Black on brown underprint. Printer: CABB. Proof.	—	—	—

		Good	Fine	XF
S118	**100 Venezolanos** 18xx (ca.1877). Black on brown underprint. Printer: CABB. Proof.	—	—	—

1879 Issue

#S121-S124 *CAPITAL B. 1,300,000.*

		Good	Fine	XF
S121	**20 Bolívares** 18xx (ca.1879). Black on brown underprint. Printer: CABB. Proof.	—	—	—

		Good	Fine	XF
S122	**100 Bolívares** 18xx (ca.1879). Black on green underprint. Griffins at bottom center. Printer: CABB. Proof.	—	—	—

		Good	Fine	XF
S123	**500 Bolívares** 18xx (ca.1879). Black on blue underprint. Horse at bottom center. Printer: CABB. Proof.	—	—	—
S124	**1000 Bolívares** 18xx (ca.1879). Black on salmon underprint. Printer: CABB. Proof.	—	—	—

Banco Carácas

189x First Issue

		Good	Fine	XF
S131	**20 Bolívares** 189x. Black on purple and lilac underprint. Liberty at left, cherub at lower right. Center signature title: *PRESIDENTE DEL DIRECTORIO.* Back: Red. Allegorical woman with sword and scale. Printer: HLBNC. Proof.	—	—	—
S132	**100 Bolívares** 189x. Black on blue and tan underprint. Seated allegorical woman with anchor and sailing ships at left, young girl at right. Center signature title: *PRESIDENTE DEL DIRECTORIO.* Back: Brown. Allegorical woman with sword and scale. Printer: HLBNC. Proof.	—	—	—
S134	**800 Bolívares** 189x. Black on blue and orange orange underprint. Two allegorical women with cornucopias and other implements in harbor scene ("Prosperity") at left. Center signature title: *PRESIDENTE DEL DIRECTORIO.* Back: Blue. Allegorical woman with sword and scale. Printer: HLBNC. Proof.	—	—	—

189x Second Issue

		Good	Fine	XF
S136	**20 Bolívares** 189x. Black on purple and lilac underprint. Liberty at left, cherub at lower right. Like #S131. Center signature title: *DIRECTOR.* Back: Red. Allegorical woman with sword and scale. Printer: HLBNC.			
	p1. Back blue. Proof.	—	—	—
	p2. Back green. Proof.	—	—	—
	s1. Back blue. Specimen.	—	—	—
	s2. Back green. Specimen.	—	—	—

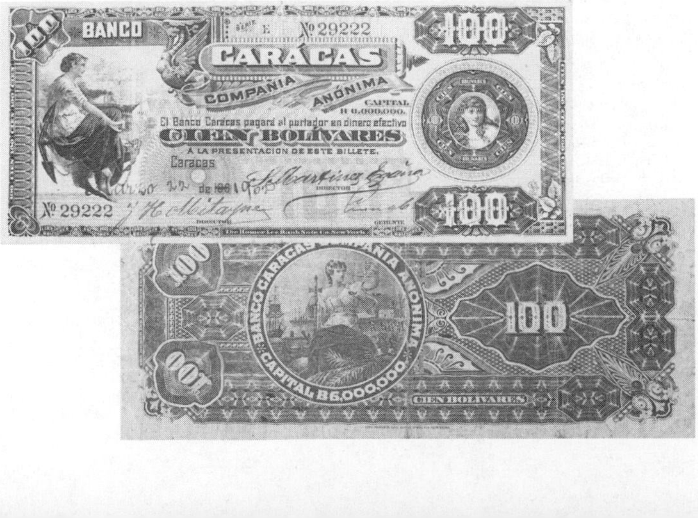

S137 100 Bolívares — Good — Fine — XF
189x; 22.3.1902/189x. Black on blue and tan underprint. Seated allegorical woman with anchor and sailing ships at left, young girl at right. Like #S132. Center signature title: *DIRECTOR*. Back: Brown. Allegorical woman with sword and scale. Printer: HLBNC. — — —

S138 400 Bolívares — Good — Fine — XF
189x; 1910. Black on blue and orange underprint. Seated allegorical woman with globe at left. Center signature title: *DIRECTOR*. Back: Allegorical woman with sword and scale. Printer: HLBNC.
- a. Back orange. 189x; 29.8.1910/189x. — — —
- p. Back green. Proof. 189x. — — —

S139 800 Bolívares — Good — Fine — XF
189x; 1.12.1910/189x. Black on blue and orange orange underprint. Two allegorical women with cornucopias and other implements in harbor scene ("Prosperity") at left. Series C. Like #S134. Center signature title: *DIRECTOR*. Back: Blue. Allegorical woman with sword and scale. Printer: HLBNC. Proof. — — —

1907 Issue

S141 20 Bolívares — Good — Fine — XF
19xx (ca.1907). Black on green and yellow underprint. Liberty at left, cherub at lower right. Like #S136. Series F. Back: Allegorical woman with sword and scale. Printer: HLBNC.
- p. Proof. — — —
- s. Specimen. — — —

S142 100 Bolívares
19xx (ca.1907). Black on green and lilac underprint. Seated allegorical woman with anchor and sailing ships at left, young girl at right. Like #S137. Series F. Back: Allegorical woman with sword and scale. Printer: HLBNC.
- p. Proof. — — —
- s. Specimen. — — —

19xx; 1914 Issue

S146 10 Bolívares — Good — Fine — XF
24.7.1914. Black on gold underprint. Ornate building at center. Series H. Short text: *A LA PRESENTACION DE ESTE BILLETE* beneath denomination words at center. Back: Red. Arms at center. Printer: ABNC.
- a. Issued note. — — —
- p. Proof. — Unc 1250.

S147 20 Bolívares
19xx. Black on green and yellow underprint. Liberty at left, cherub at lower right. Like #S141. Series G. Short text: *A LA PRESENTACION DE ESTE BILLETE* beneath denomination words at center. Back: Allegorical woman with sword and scale. Printer: HLBNC.
- p. Proof. — Unc 1750.
- s. Specimen. — — —

S149 100 Bolívares
19xx. Black on green and lilac underprint. Seated allegorical woman with anchor and sailing ships at left, young girl at right. Like #S142. Series G. Short text: *A LA PRESENTACION DE ESTE BILLETE* beneath denomination words at center. Back: Allegorical woman with sword and scale. Printer: HLBNC.
- p. Proof. — Unc 2250.
- s. Specimen. — — —

S150 400 Bolívares — Good — Fine — XF
19xx. Black on blue and orange underprint. Seated allegorical woman with globe at left. Like #S138. Short text: *A LA PRESENTACION DE ESTE BILLETE* beneath denomination words at center. Back: Allegorical woman with sword and scale. Printer: HLBNC. — — —

S151 800 Bolívares
19xx. Black on blue and orange orange underprint. Two allegorical women with cornucopias and other implements in harbor scene ("Prosperity") at left. Like #S139. Short text: *A LA PRESENTACION DE ESTE BILLETE* beneath denomination words at cente Back: Allegorical woman with sword and scale. Printer: HLBNC. — — —

1925 Provisional Issue

S153 20 Bolívares — Good — Fine — XF
30.1.1925; 1.12.1928. Black on green and yellow underprint. Liberty at left, cherub at lower right. *A LA PRESENTACION DE ESTE BILLETE* beneath denomination words at center. Back: Allegorical woman with sword and scale. Overprint: Red *PAGADERO EN LAS OFICINAS DEL BANCO* at left on #S147. Printer: HLBNC. — — —

S155 100 Bolívares
ND (old date- 21.3.1911). Black on green and lilac underprint. Seated allegorical woman with anchor and sailing ships at left, young girl at right. Short text: *A LA PRESENTACION DE ESTE BILLETE* beneath denomination words at center. Back: Allegorical woman with sword and scale. Overprint: Red *PAGADERO EN LAS OFICINAS DEL BANCO* at left on #S149. Printer: HLBNC. — — —

1926-28 Regular Issue

S157 10 Bolívares — Good — Fine — XF
26.3.1928. Black on gold underprint. Ornate building at center. Series J. Like #S146. Text: *A LA PRESENTACION DE ESTE BILLETE EN LAS OFICINAS DEL BANCO* beneath denominaion words at center. Back: Red. Arms at center. — — —

S158 20 Bolívares — Good — Fine — XF
19xx. Black on green and yellow underprint. Liberty at left, cherub at lower right. Series J. Like #S147. Text: *A LA PRESENTACION DE ESTE BILLETE EN LAS OFICINAS DEL BANCO* beneath denominaion words at center. Back: Allegorical woman with sword and scale. Printer: HLBNC. Proof. — — —

S159 100 Bolívares
9.4.1926. Black on green and lilac underprint. Seated allegorical woman with anchor and sailing ships at left, young girl at right. Series I. Like #S149. Text: *A LA PRESENTACION DE ESTE BILLETE EN LAS OFICINAS DEL BANCO*. Back: Allegorical woman with sword and scale. Printer: HLBNC. — — —

NOTE: The following dates were listed in the fifth edition: 20 Bolívares, 30.3.1928; 100 Bolívares, 4.9.1922; 400 Bolívares, 30.3.1925; 800 Bolívares, 30.3.1925. Confirmation is needed to assign these dates to their proper variety listings.

Banco Colonial Britanico

1839 Issue

S161 50 Pesos — Good — Fine — XF
18xx. Black. English arms at upper center. Printer: PB&P. Specimen. — — —

NOTE: Denominations of 5, 10, 20, and 100 Pesos require confirmation.

Banco Comercial

1880's Issue

S166 20 Bolívares — Good — Fine — XF
188x. Black on red-orange underprint. Seated allegorical woman with marine implements at left. Back: Red-orange. Printer: ABNC. Proof. — — —

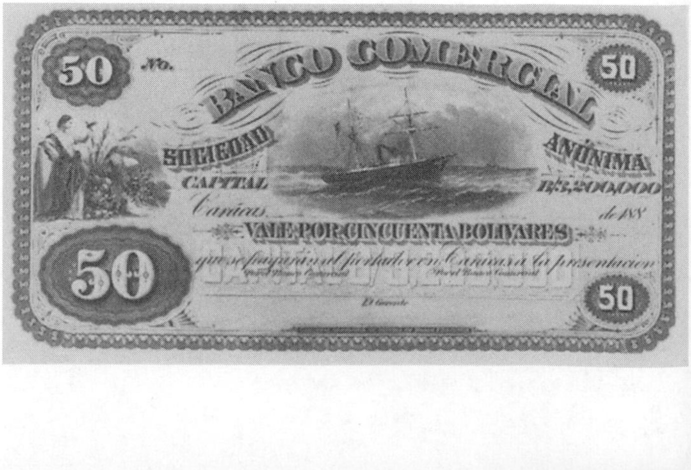

	Good	Fine	XF
S167 50 Bolívares 188x. Black on gold underprint. Allegorical woman with plants at left, ships at center. Back: Gold. Printer: ABNC. Proof.	—	—	—

	Good	Fine	XF
S168 100 Bolívares 188x. Black on blue underprint. Allegorical woman seated with produce and plants ("Tropics No. 2") at left, Christopher Columbus and Indian woman at right. Back: Blue. Arms at center. Printer: ABNC. Proof.	—	—	—

	Good	Fine	XF
S169 500 Bolívares 188x. Black on salmon underprint. Christopher Columbus sighting land ("First Land") at left. Back: Salmon. Two sailors at center. Printer: ABNC. Proof.	—	—	—

	Good	Fine	XF
S170 1000 Bolívares 188x. Black on green underprint. National arms at left, horse at upper center, Christopher Columbus sighting land at right. Back: Green. Steam passenger train at center. Printer: ABNC. Proof.	—	—	—

Banco Comercial (de Maracaibo)

1916 Issue

	Good	Fine	XF
S171 10 Bolívares 19xx. Black on olive underprint. Portrait Gen. R. Urdaneta at center. Back: Olive. Vaquero roping cattle at center. Printer: ABNC.			
p. Proof.	—	Unc	2250.
s. Series A. Specimen.	—	—	—

Banco Comercial de Maracaibo

1921 Issue

#S173 and S174 *CAPITAL Bs 400,000.*

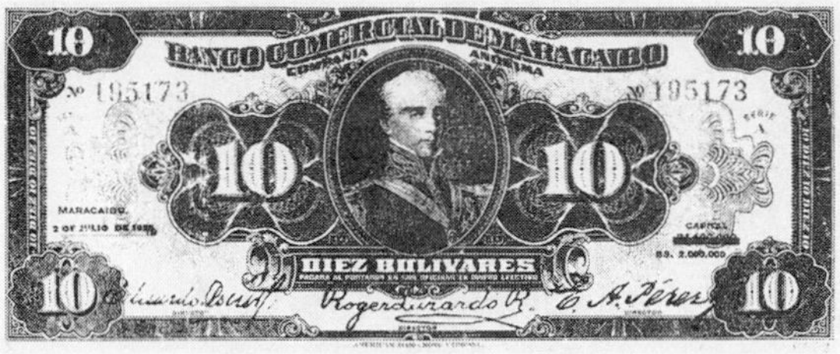

	Good	Fine	XF
S173 10 Bolívares 1.5.1921; 1.2.1922. Black on olive underprint. Portrait Gen. R. Urdaneta at center. Similar to #S171. Back: Olive. Vaquero roping cattle at center. Printer: ABNC.			
a. Issued note.	—	—	—
p. Proof.	—	Unc	2000.

	Good	Fine	XF
S174 10 Bolívares 19xx. Black on multicolor underprint. Portrait Gen. R. Urdaneta at center. Similar to #S173. Back: Vaquero roping cattle at center. Printer: ABNC. Proof.	—	Unc	2000.

1929 Issue

#S176-S179 *CAPITAL Bs 2,000,000.*

	Good	Fine	XF
S176 10 Bolívares 9.3.1929. Black on multicolor underprint. Portrait Gen. R. Urdaneta at center. Like #S174, but different capitalization amount. Back: Vaquero roping cattle at center. Printer: ABNC.			
a. Issued note.	—	—	—
p. Proof.	—	Unc	2250.

	Good	Fine	XF
S177 20 Bolívares 9.3.1929. Blue on multicolor underprint. Oil field and steam passenger train at center. Back: Blue. Dock scene with ship, steam passenger train and truck at center. Printer: ABNC.			
a. Issued note.	—	—	—
p. Proof.	—	Unc	1000.

	Good	Fine	XF
S179 100 Bolívares 1.3.1929. Red on multicolor underprint. Woman at left. Back: Red. Market scene at center. Printer: ABNC.			
a. Issued note.	—	—	—
p. Proof.	—	Unc	1500.

1933 Issue

#S181-S183 CAPITAL Bs 2,000,000.

		Good	Fine	XF
S181	**10 Bolívares** 19xx (ca.1933). Red on multicolor underprint. Portrait Gen. R. Urdaneta at center. Like #S176. Back: Vaquero roping cattle at center. Printer: ABNC.	—	—	—
S182	**20 Bolívares** 19xx (ca.1933). Green on multicolor underprint. Oil field and steam passenger train at center. Like #S177. Back: Dock scene with ship, steam passenger train and truck at center. Printer: ABNC.	—	—	—
S183	**100 Bolívares** 19xx (ca.1933). Olive on multicolor underprint. Woman at left. Like #S179. Back: Market scene at center. Printer: ABNC.	—	—	—

NOTE: A 10 Bolívares dated 2.7.1925 was previously listed. Confirmation is needed to assign this date to the proper variety listing.

Banco de Londres y Venezuela, Limitado

1865 Issue

		Good	Fine	XF
S185	**5 Pesos** 23.1.1865. Black on green underprint. Oval arms of City of London and of Venezuela at top center. Back: *FIVE DOLLARS CURRENCY*. Rare.	—	—	—

Banco de Maracaibo

1882 Issue

#S190-S192 CAPITAL B 160,000.

		Good	Fine	XF
S190	**20 Bolívares** 188x (ca.1882). Black on gold underprint. Sailing ships at left, seated allegorical woman with bales ("Commerce") at center, arms at right. Signature title: *PRESIDENTE DE LA ASEMBLEA DELAGATORIA.* Back: Gold. Printer: ABNC. Proof.	—	—	—

		Good	Fine	XF
S191	**50 Bolívares** 188x (ca.1882). Black on green underprint. Sailor at left, woman pouring water ("Rebecca") at center, arms at right. Signature title: *PRESIDENTE DE LA ASEMBLEA DELAGATORIA.* Back: Green. Printer: ABNC. Proof.	—	—	—

		Good	Fine	XF
S192	**100 Bolívares** 188x (ca.1882). Black on blue underprint. Arms and seated allegorical woman with ship at left, seated allegorical woman with bales, wheel and train at right. Signature title: *PRESIDENTE DE LA ASEMBLEA DELAGATORIA.* Back: Blue. Printer: ABNC. Proof.	—	—	—

1885 Issue

#S195-S197 CAPITAL B 320,000. Sign. title: *PRESIDENTE DE LA ASEMBLEA DELAGATORIA.*

		Good	Fine	XF
S195	**20 Bolívares** 188x (ca.1885). Black on gold underprint. Sailing ships at left, seated allegorical woman with bales ("Commerce") at center, arms at right. Like #S190. Signature title: *PRESIDENTE DE LA ASEMBLEA DELAGATORIA.* Back: Gold. Printer: ABNC. Proof.	—	—	—

		Good	Fine	XF
S196	**50 Bolívares** 188x (ca.1885). Black on green underprint. Sailor at left, woman pouring water ("Rebecca") at center, arms at right. Like #S191. Signature title: *PRESIDENTE DE LA ASEMBLEA DELAGATORIA.* Back: Green. Printer: ABNC. Proof.	—	—	—

		Good	Fine	XF
S197	**100 Bolívares** 188x (ca.1885). Black on blue underprint. Arms and seated allegorical woman with ship at left, seated allegorical woman with bales, wheel and train at right. Like #S192. Signature title: *PRESIDENTE DE LA ASEMBLEA DELAGATORIA.* Back: Blue. Printer: ABNC. Proof.	—	—	—

1889 Issue

#S200-S202 CAPITAL B 800,000.

		Good	Fine	XF
S200	**20 Bolívares** 188x (ca.1889). Black on gold underprint. Sailing ships at left, seated allegorical woman with bales ("Commerce") at center, arms at right. Signature title: *PRESIDENTE DE LA ASEMBLEA DELAGATORIA.* Like #S190. Back: Gold. Printer: ABNC. Proof.	—	—	—
S201	**50 Bolívares** 188x (ca.1889). Black on green underprint. Sailor at left, woman pouring water ("Rebecca") at center, arms at right. Signature title: *PRESIDENTE DE LA ASEMBLEA DELAGATORIA.* Like #S191. Back: Green. Printer: ABNC. Proof.	—	—	—
S202	**100 Bolívares** 188x (ca.1889). Black on blue underprint. Arms and seated allegorical woman with ship at left, seated allegorical woman with bales, wheel and train at right. Signature title: *PRESIDENTE DE LA ASEMBLEA DELAGATORIA.* Like #S192. Back: Blue. Printer: ABNC. Proof.	—	—	—
S203	**200 Bolívares** 188x (ca.1889). Black on red-orange underprint. Helmeted Athena and allegorical woman at left, reclining woman ("Literature No. 2") at center, two allegorical women and arms at right. Signature title: *PRESIDENTE DE LA ASEMBLEA DELAGATORIA.* Back: Red-orange. Printer: ABNC. Proof.	—	—	—

1897 Issue

S207-S208 *CAPITAL B 1,250,000.*

		Good	Fine	XF
S205	**20 Bolívares** 1.1.1897. Black on gold underprint. Sailing ships at left, seated allegorical woman with bales ("Commerce") at center, arms at right. Signature title: *PRESIDENTE DE LA ASEMBLEA DELAGATORIA.* Like #S200. Back: Gold. Printer: ABNC.			
	a. Issued note.	1500.	3000.	—
	p. Proof.	—	—	—
S206	**40 Bolívares** 189x (ca.1897). Black on green underprint. Sailor at left, woman pouring water ("Rebecca") at center, arms at right. Signature title: *PRESIDENTE DE LA ASEMBLEA DELAGATORIA.* Similar to #S201, but minor plate differences. Back: Green. Printer: ABNC. Proof.	—	—	—
S207	**100 Bolívares** 18xx (ca.1897). Black on blue underprint. Arms and seated allegorical woman with ship at left, seated allegorical woman with bales, wheel and train at right. Signature title: *PRESIDENTE DE LA ASEMBLEA DELAGATORIA.* Like #S202. Back: Blue. Printer: ABNC. Proof.	—	—	—

		Good	Fine	XF
S208	**200 Bolívares** 18xx (ca.1897). Black on red-orange underprint. Helmeted Athena and allegorical woman at left, reclining woman ("Literature No. 2") at center, two allegorical women and arms at right. Signature title: *PRESIDENTE DE LA ASEMBLEA DELAGATORIA.* Back: Red-orange. Printer: ABNC. Proof.	—	—	—

		Good	Fine	XF
S209	**400 Bolívares** 189x (ca.1897). Black on yellow underprint. Arms at lower left, standing allegorical woman with book and plant at left, female portrait ("Haidee") at center right. Signature title: *PRESIDENTE DE LA ASEMBLEA DELAGATORIA.* Back: Yellow. Printer: ABNC. Proof.	—	—	—

1908-09 Issue

#S211 and S212 partially engraved date: *19xx.*

		Good	Fine	XF
S211	**20 Bolívares** 19xx; 1908. Black on gold underprint. Sailing ships at left, seated allegorical woman with bales ("Commerce") at center, arms at right. Signature title: *PRESIDENTE DE LA ASEMBLEA DELAGATORIA.* Like #S190. Back: Gold. Printer: ABNC.			
	a. Overprint: *RESELLADO* at left. 1.5.1908.	—	—	—
	s. Specimen. 19xx (ca.1907).	—	—	—

		Good	Fine	XF
S212	**40 Bolívares** 1.4.1909. Black on green underprint. Sailor at left, woman pouring water ("Rebecca") at center, arms at right. Signature title: *PRESIDENTE DE LA ASEMBLEA DELAGATORIA.* Like #S206. Back: Green. Printer: ABNC. Specimen.	—	—	—

1915-17 Issue

		Good	Fine	XF
S216	**10 Bolívares** 1.1.1917/19xx. Black on purple underprint. Seated allegorical man with scythe at left, arms at center, seated allegorical woman holding ship at right. Right signature title: *SEGUNDO DIRECTOR PRINCIPAL.* Back: Purple. Printer: ABNC.			
	a. Issued note.	—	—	—
	p. Proof.	—	Unc	1250.

#S217 *Deleted.* See #S223.

		Good	Fine	XF
S218	**20 Bolívares** 1917/19xx. Black on gold underprint. Sailing ships at left, seated allegorical woman with bales ("Commerce") at center, arms at right. Right signature title: *SEGUNDO DIRECTOR PRINCIPAL.* Like #S190. Back: Gold. Printer: ABNC.			
	a. 1.1.1917/19xx.	—	—	—
	p. Proof. 19xx (ca.1916).	—	Unc	1500.

		Good	Fine	XF
S219	**40 Bolívares** 1917/19xx. Black on green underprint. Sailor at left, woman pouring water ("Rebecca") at center, arms at right. Right signature title: *SEGUNDO DIRECTOR PRINCIPAL.* Like #S206. Back: Green. Printer: ABNC.			
	a. 1.1.1917/19xx.	—	—	—
	p. Proof. 19xx (ca.1916).	—	Unc	1500.

		Good	Fine	XF
S220	**100 Bolívares** 1915/19xx. Black on blue underprint. Arms and seated allegorical woman with ship at left, seated allegorical woman with bales, wheel and train at right. Right signature title: *SEGUNDO DIRECTOR PRINCIPAL.* Like #S192. Back: Blue. Printer: ABNC.			
	a. Overprint near bottom: *EN LAS OFICINAS DEL BANCO* and 2 signature titles, black bar below. 15.1.1915/19xx.	—	—	—
	p. Proof. 19xx (ca.1916).	—	Unc	2750.

S221 200 Bolívares	Good	Fine	XF
15.3.1915/19xx. Black on red-orange underprint. Helmeted Athena and allegorical woman at left, reclining woman ("Literature No. 2") at center, two allegorical women and arms at right. Right signature title: *SEGUNDO DIRECTOR PRINCIPAL.* Back: Red-orange. Overprint: *PAGADERO/EN LAS/OFICINAS DEL BANCO,* 2 signature titles and black bar like #S220. Printer: ABNC.	—	—	—

S222 400 Bolívares	Good	Fine	XF
1.1.1917/19xx. Black on yellow underprint. Arms at lower left, standing allegorical woman with book and plant at left, female portrait ("Haidee") at center right. Right signature title: *SEGUNDO DIRECTOR PRINCIPAL.* Like #S209. Back: Yellow. Printer: ABNC.			
a. Issued note.	—	—	—
p. Proof.	—	Unc	2750.

1924 Issue

S223 10 Bolívares	Good	Fine	XF
19xx (ca.1924). Black on purple underprint. Seated allegorical man with scythe at left, arms at center, seated allegorical woman holding ship at right. Similar to #S216. Capitalization at lower left, date area upper right. Series A.			
a. Issued note.	—	—	—
p. Proof.	—	Unc	1250.

NOTE: #S223 is a transitional issue as it has close similarities to #S226.

1925-26 Issue

#S226-S229 reduced size: *CAPITAL B 2,500,000.*

S226 10 Bolívares	Good	Fine	XF
10.9.1925; 27.4.1933; 2.8.1934; 1.9.1935. Black on purple underprint. Seated allegorical man with scythe at left, arms at center, seated allegorical woman holding ship at right. Similar to #S223, but different capitalization. Printer: ABNC.			
a. Issued note.	250.	750.	—
p. Proof.	—	Unc	1250.

NOTE: #S226 dated 1.7.1923 and 3.3.1925 were formerly listed in the fifth edition. Confirmation is needed to ensure their proper inclusion in this listing.

S227 20 Bolívares	Good	Fine	XF
19xx. Black on gold underprint. Sailing ships at left, seated allegorical woman with bales ("Commerce") at center, arms at right. Similar to #S190. Back: Gold. Printer: ABNC. Proof.	—	Unc	1800.

S228 100 Bolívares	Good	Fine	XF
20.5.1926. Black on blue underprint. Arms and seated allegorical woman with ship at left, seated allegorical woman with bales, wheel and train at right. Similar to #S192. Back: Blue. Printer: ABNC.	—	—	—

S229 500 Bolívares	Good	Fine	XF
20.5.1926. Black on yellow and multicolor underprint. Arms at lower left, allegorical woman at left, female portrait ("Haidee") at center right. Similar to #S222 but different allegorical woman at left. Printer: ABNC.			
a. Issued note.	—	—	—
p. Proof.	—	Unc	2750.

Banco Mercantil y Agrícola

1929-35 Issue

S231 10 Bolívares	Good	Fine	XF
20.3.1934; 8.11.1935. Orange on multicolor underprint. Cattle under trees at center. Back: Bank arms at center, reclining allegorical figures supporting shield with bank monogram at center. Printer: ABNC.			
a. Issued note with date.	150.	450.	1350.
r. Remainder, without date but with 2 hand signatures.	—	—	75.00

S232 20 Bolívares	Good	Fine	XF
21.2.1927. Dark green on multicolor underprint. Ships and steam passenger train at loading area. Back: Bank arms at center, reclining allegorical figures supporting shield with bank monogram at center. Printer: ABNC.			
a. Issued note with date.	175.	525.	1650.
r1. Remainder, without date but with 2 hand signatures.	—	—	75.00
r2. Remainder, without date or signature.	—	—	75.00

S233 100 Bolívares	Good	Fine	XF
6.1.1929. Purple on multicolor underprint. Reclining allegorical woman with globe at center. Back: Bank arms at center, reclining allegorical figures supporting shield with bank monogram at center. Printer: ABNC.			
a. Issued note with date.	180.	540.	1650.
r1. Remainder, without date but with 2 hand signatures.	—	—	125.
r2. Remainder, without date or signature.	—	—	125.

Banco Nacional de Venezuela

1841 Issue

S236 5 Pesos	Good	Fine	XF
6.12.1841. Black. Sailing ship at left, arms at upper center, woman standing at right. Printer: NEBNC.	—	—	—

NOTE: A 20 Pesos denomination is reported, not confirmed.

Banco Venezolano de Crédito

1925-26 Issue

S241 10 Bolívares	Good	Fine	XF
27.7.1926; 28.12.1927; 28.6.1929. Red on yellow and multicolor underprint. Woman with basket on head at center. Back: Red. Workers picking cotton at center. Printer: ABNC.			
a. Issued note.	450.	1350.	—
p. Proof.	—	Unc	750.
s. Specimen.	—	—	—

S242 20 Bolívares	Good	Fine	XF
2.11.1925; 24.5.1928; 4.12.1928. Green on multicolor underprint. Vaqueros roping cattle at center. Back: Green. Cows watering at center. Printer: ABNC.			
a. Issued note. Rare.	—	—	—
p. Proof.	—	Unc	850.
s. Specimen.	—	—	—

S243 100 Bolívares	Good	Fine	XF
18.11.1925; 2.6.1926; 16.3.1928; 21.9.1928. Brown on multicolor underprint. Reclining allegorical woman at left. Back: Brown. Seated allegorical man on crate at center. Printer: ABNC.			
a. Issued note. Rare.	—	—	—
p. Proof.	—	—	—
s. Specimen.	—	—	—

1931 Issue

S247 20 Bolívares	Good	Fine	XF
31.8.1931; 31.10.1933; 11.4.1934; 28.8.1935; 14.1.1939. Green. Coffee pickers at center. Back: Cattle at center. Printer: W&S.			
a. Issued note.	—	—	—
s. Specimen.	—	—	—

S248 100 Bolívares	Good	Fine	XF
31.1.1931; 3.2.1933; 14.1.1939. Brown on multicolor underprint. Allegorical woman with tablet held by cherub at left. Back: Mercury with Cupid at center. Printer: W&S.			
a. Issued note.	—	—	—
s. Specimen.	—	—	—

NOTE: Specimen notes (from salesman's sample books) have different colors than issued notes.

Banco de Venezuela (since 1860's)

1862 Issue

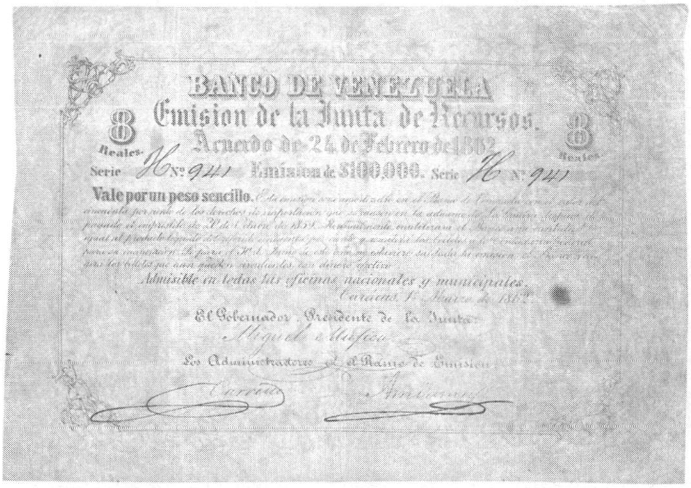

S251 8 Reales = 1 Peso	Good	Fine	XF
1.3.1862. Black. Uniface.	—	—	—

S256 50 Pesos	Good	Fine	XF
1.2.1862. Black. Red seal stamped at lower left center. Uniface.	—	—	—

NOTE: A 5 Pesos of this issue is reported, not confirmed.

Banco de Venezuela (since 1890)

1890's Issue

#S261-S265 CAPITAL B/8,000,000.

S261 20 Bolívares — Good / Fine / XF
189x (ca.1890). Black on yellow and brown underprint. Plowman and two horses at left. Portrait Simon Bolívar at right. Back: Dark brown. Arms at center. Printer: ABNC.

	Good	Fine	XF
p. Proof.	—	Unc	2000.
s. Specimen.	—	—	—

S262 40 Bolívares — Good / Fine / XF
18xx (ca.1890). Black on green and yellow underprint. Portrait Simon Bolívar at left, cowboys roping cattle at center right. Back: Green. Arms at left. Printer: ABNC.

	Good	Fine	XF
p. Proof.	—	Unc	2250.
s. Specimen.	—	—	—

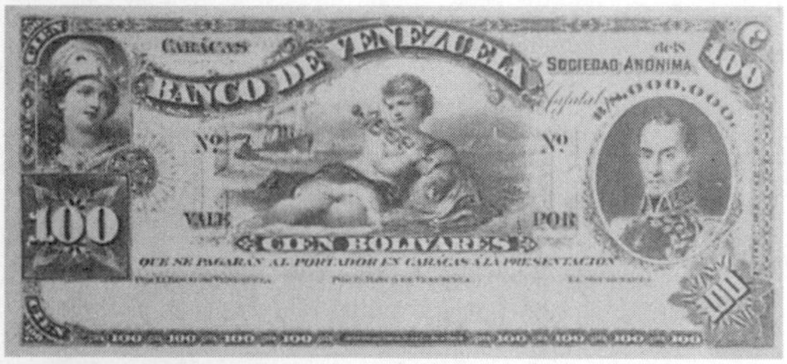

S263 100 Bolívares — Good / Fine / XF
18xx (ca.1890). Black on yellow and red-orange underprint. Helmeted Minerva at upper left, cherub with fish ("Off Shady Hook") at center, portrait Simon Bolívar at right. Back: Red-orange. Arms at center. Printer: ABNC.

	Good	Fine	XF
p. Proof.	—	Unc	2500.
s. Specimen.	—	—	—

S264 500 Bolívares
18xx (ca.1890). Black on blue and yellow underprint. Miners at left center, Simon Bolívar at right. Back: Blue. Arms at left. Printer: ABNC.

	Good	Fine	XF
p. Proof.	—	—	—
s. Specimen.	—	—	—

S265 1000 Bolívares — Good / Fine / XF
18xx (ca.1890). Black on orange and yellow underprint. Portrait Simon Bolívar at left, allegorical woman with industrial implements ("Mechanics") at center right. Back: Orange. Arms at center. Printer: ABNC.

	Good	Fine	XF
p. Proof.	—	—	—
s. Specimen.	—	—	—

1897 Issue

#S271-S273 CAPITAL B/15,000,000.

S271 20 Bolívares — Good / Fine / XF
189x (ca.1897). Black on green and yellow underprint. Vaquero and cattle at center right. Back: Green. Arms at center. Printer: ABNC. Proof. — Unc 2000.

S272 50 Bolívares — Good / Fine / XF
189x (ca.1897). Black on blue and yellow underprint. Seated allegorical woman with pallette ("Arts") at right. Back: Blue. Arms at center. Printer: ABNC.

	Good	Fine	XF
p. Proof.	—	—	—
s. Specimen.	—	—	—

S273 100 Bolívares — Good / Fine / XF
19xx (ca.1900). Black on rose and yellow underprint. Allegorical woman kneeling at left, value at center, seated allegorical woman at right. Back: Red-orange. Arms at center. Printer: ABNC.

	Good	Fine	XF
p. Proof.	—	Unc	2000.
s. Specimen.	—	—	—

S274 500 Bolívares — Good / Fine / XF
19xx (ca.1900). Black on orange and rose underprint. Portrait Simon Bolívar at left, reclining allegorical woman with water vase and rudder ("Naiad") at right. Back: Orange. Proof. — — —

S275 1000 Bolívares — Good / Fine / XF
189x (ca.1897). Black on green and blue underprint. Horses and handlers at left and right, portrait Simon Bolívar at center. Back: Blue. Proof. — — —

NOTE: Later notes (1900's) have minor plate and color differences from earlier (1890's) issues.

1910 PROVISIONAL ISSUE

S281 20 Bolívares	Good	Fine	XF
19xx (ca.1910). Black on green and yellow underprint. Vaquero and cattle at center right. Back: Green. Arms at center. Overprint: *CAPITAL Bs 12,000,000* and text: *PAGADERO EN LAS/OFICINAS DEL BANCO.* on #S271.			
a. Issued note.	—	—	—
p. Proof.	—	Unc	1000.
r. Remainder.	—	Unc	50.00

NOTE: Additional denominations require confirmation.

1910 ISSUE

#S286-S289 *CAPITAL Bs 12,000,000.*

S286 20 Bolívares	Good	Fine	XF
19xx (ca.1910). Black on green and multicolor underprint. Vaqueros herding cattle towards left at center. Text: *QUE SE PAGARAN AL PORTADOR EN CARACAS A LA PRESENTACION.* Back: Green. Printer: ABNC. Proof.	—	—	—

#S287 Held in reserve.

S288 100 Bolívares	Good	Fine	XF
19xx (ca.1910). Black on brown and multicolor underprint. Vaqueros and cattle towards right at center. Text: *QUE SE PAGARAN AL PORTADOR EN CARACAS A LA PRESENTACION.* Back: Brown. Printer: ABNC. Proof.	—	Unc	2000.

S289 500 Bolívares	Good	Fine	XF
19xx (ca.1910). Black on blue and multicolor underprint. Portrait Simon Bolívar at left. Text: *QUE SE PAGARAN AL PORTADOR EN CARACAS A LA PRESENTACION.* Back: Blue. Printer: ABNC.			
a. Issued note.	—	—	—
p. Proof.	—	Unc	1750.

1919 PROVISIONAL ISSUE

#S291 and S292 w/text: *PAGADERO EN LAS OFICINAS DEL BANCO* (payable in the offices of the bank) ovpt. near upper ctr. on face. Also wording: *EN CARÁCAS* blacked out in text line across ctr.

S291 20 Bolívares	Good	Fine	XF
29.1.1919. Black on green and multicolor underprint. Vaqueros herding cattle towards left at center. Like #S286 but with alterations. Back: Green. Arms at center. Overprint: Text: *PAGADERO EN LAS OFICINAS DEL BANCO* near upper center. *EN CARACAS* blacked out. Printer: ABNC.	375.	1100.	—

S292 100 Bolívares	Good	Fine	XF
(ca.1919). Black on brown and multicolor underprint. Vaqueros and cattle towards right at center. Like #S288 but with alterations. Back: Brown. Overprint: Text: *PAGADERO EN LAS OFICINAS DEL BANCO* near upper center. *EN CARACAS* blacked out. Printer: ABNC. Rare.	—	—	—

NOTE: Additional denominations require confirmation.

1916-21 ISSUE

#S293 and S294 w/text: *PAGADEROS AL PORTADOR EN LAS OFICINAS DEL BANCO* (payable to bearer in the offices of the bank).

S293 100 Bolívares	Good	Fine	XF
19xx (ca.1916-21). 15.6.1918. Black on brown and multicolor underprint. Vaqueros and cattle towards right at center. Text: *PAGADEROS AL PORTADOR EN LAS OFICINAS DEL BANCO.* Three signatures and titles. Similar to #S288, but different payable clause. Back: Brown. Printer: ABNC.			
a. Issued note.	—	—	—
p. Proof.	—	Unc	1950.

S294 500 Bolívares	Good	Fine	XF
19xx (ca.1916-21). Black on blue and multicolor underprint. Portrait Simon Bolívar at left. Text: *PAGADEROS AL PORTADOR EN LAS OFICINAS DEL BANCO.* Three signatures and titles. Similar to #S289, but different payable clause. Back: Blue. Printer: ABNC.	—	—	—

1921 ISSUE

#S297 and S298 *CAPITAL Bs 24,000,000.*

S297 100 Bolívares	Good	Fine	XF
19xx (ca.1921). Black on brown and multicolor underprint. Vaqueros and cattle towards right at center. Three signature titles. Similar to #S288, but different capitalization amount. Back: Brown. Printer: ABNC. Proof.			
a. Issued note.	225.	675.	—
p. Proof.	—	—	—

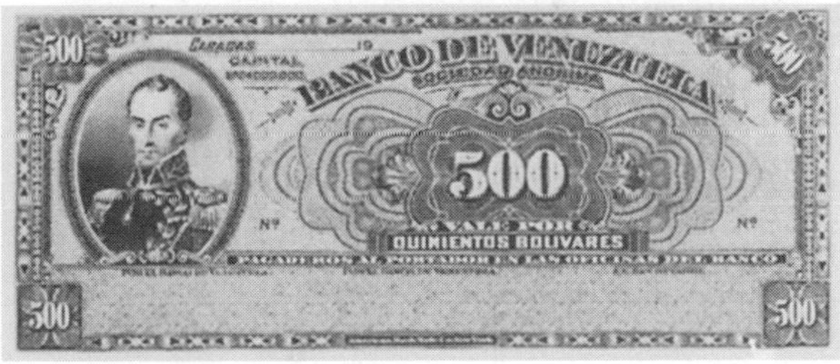

S298 500 Bolívares	Good	Fine	XF
Aug. 1921. Black on blue and multicolor underprint. Portrait Simon Bolívar at left. Three signature titles. Similar to #S289, but different capitalization amount. Back: Blue. Printer: ABNC. Proof.	—	—	—

1924-26 ISSUE

#S301-S305 *CAPITAL Bs 24,000,000.*

S301 20 Bolívares	Good	Fine	XF
5.7.1925; 27.10.1926. Black on green and multicolor underprint. Vaqueros herding cattle towards left at center. Two signature titles: *POR EL BANCO DE VENEZUELA* at left and right. Similar to #S286, but plate differences. Printer: ABNC.	—	—	—

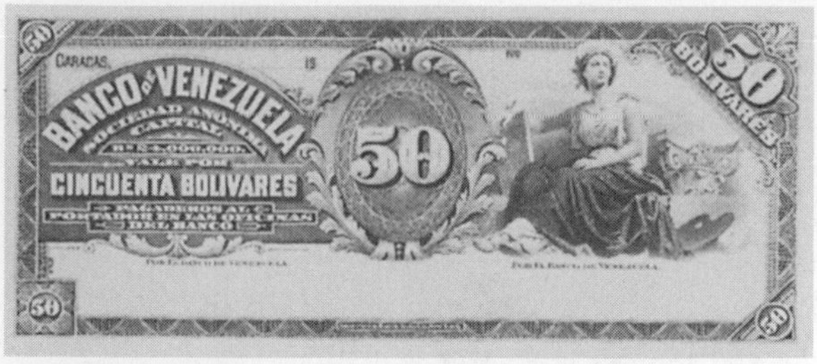

S302 50 Bolívares	Good	Fine	XF
19xx (ca.1924). Black on orange and salmon underprint. Seated allegorical woman with pallette ("Arts") at right. Two signature titles: *POR EL BANCO DE VENEZUELA* at left and right. Similar to #S272, but some plate differences. Back: Orange. Printer: ABNC.			
a. Issued note.	—	—	—
p. Proof.	—	Unc	1750.

S303 100 Bolívares	Good	Fine	XF
19xx (ca.1926). Black on brown and multicolor underprint. Vaqueros and cattle towards right at center. Two signature titles: *POR EL BANCO DE VENEZUELA* at left and right. Similar to #S288. Printer: ABNC.	—	—	—

S304 500 Bolívares	Good	Fine	XF
19xx (ca.1924). Black on blue and multicolor underprint. Portrait Simon Bolívar at left. Two signature titles: *POR EL BANCO DE VENEZUELA* at left and right. Similar to #S289. Printer: ABNC.	—	—	—

S305 1000 Bolívares	Good	Fine	XF
19xx (ca.1926). Black on brown and yellow underprint. Horses and handlers at left and right, portrait Simon Bolívar at center. Two signature titles: *POR EL BANCO DE VENEZUELA* at left and right. Similar to #S275, but some plate differences. Back: Gold. Printer: ABNC.			
p. Proof.	—	—	—
s. Specimen.	—	—	—

1930-36 Issue

#S311-S315 *CAPITAL Bs 24,000,000.*

S311 20 Bolívares	Good	Fine	XF
1.6.1930; 29.2.1931; 30.10.1933; 29.4.1934; 29.11.1938. Black on multicolor underprint. Vaqueros herding cattle towards left at center. Two signature titles. Changed guilloches. Similar to #S286. Printer: ABNC.	225.	675.	—

S312 50 Bolívares	Good	Fine	XF
27.9.1935-26.9.1939. Black on multicolor underprint. Seated allegorical woman with pallette ("Arts") at right. Two signature titles. Changed guilloches. Similar to #S272. Printer: ABNC.	375.	1500.	—

S313 100 Bolívares	Good	Fine	XF
4.9.1931-9.11.1939. Black on multicolor underprint. Vaqueros and cattle towards right at center. Two signature titles. Changed guilloches. Similar to #S288. Printer: ABNC.	—	—	—
S314 500 Bolívares			
27.9.1935; 26.10.1935. Black on multicolor underprint. Portrait Simon Bolívar at left. Two signature titles. Changed guilloches. Similar to #S289. Printer: ABNC.	—	—	—

S315 1000 Bolívares	Good	Fine	XF
31.1.1936. Black on green and blue underprint. Horses and handlers at left and right, portrait Simon Bolívar at center. Two signature titles. Changed guilloches. Similar to #S275. Printer: ABNC.	—	—	—

Government

Compañía de Accionistas

1856 Issue

S321 5 Pesos	Good	Fine	XF
18.2.1856. Black on red denomination in underprint at center. Justice at left, reclining allegorical woman at upper center, seated woman at right. Uniface. Printer: Baldwin, Adams & Co., New York.	—	—	—
S322 10 Pesos			
(ca.1855). Printer: Baldwin, Adams & Co., New York.	—	—	—
#S323 Not assigned.			
S324 100 Pesos			
(ca.1855). Printer: Baldwin, Adams & Co., New York.	—	—	—

Compañía de Crédito

1870 Issue

S325 5 Venezolanos	Good	Fine	XF
12.12.1870. Seated navigation at deckside at upper center.	—	—	—

1800's Issue

	Good	Fine	XF
S326 5 Venezolanos 18xx (ca.1873). Black. Arms at center. Uniface. Printer: ABNC. Proof.	—	—	—

	Good	Fine	XF
S327 10 Venezolanos 18xx (ca.1873). Black. Arms at center. Uniface. Printer: ABNC. Proof.	—	—	—
S328 50 Venezolanos 18xx (ca.1873). Black. Arms at center. Uniface. Printer: ABNC. Proof.	—	—	—

	Good	Fine	XF
S329 100 Venezolanos 18xx (ca.1873). Black. Arms at center. Uniface. Printer: ABNC. Proof.	—	—	—

State

Estado de Guayana

1878 First Issue

	Good	Fine	XF
S331 50 Centésimos 31.8.1878. Purple. Arms of Guayana at left, standing allegorical woman at right. Uniface. Printer: Lith. Sedille & Cie., Paris. Rare.	—	—	—

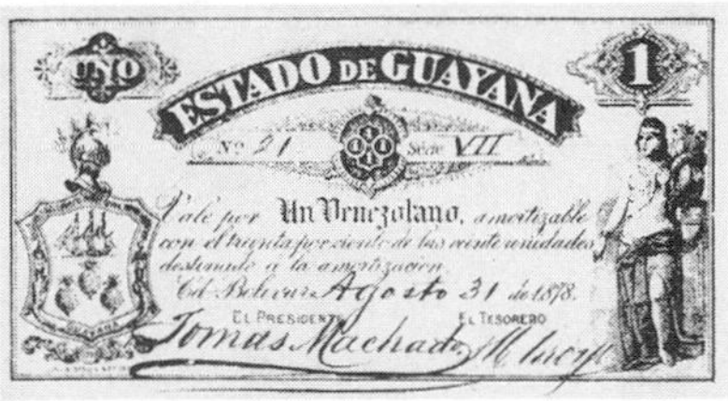

	Good	Fine	XF
S332 1 Venezolano 31.8.1878. Black. Arms of Guayana at left, standing allegorical woman at right. Uniface. Similar to #S331. Printer: Lith. Sedille & Cie., Paris. Rare.	—	—	—

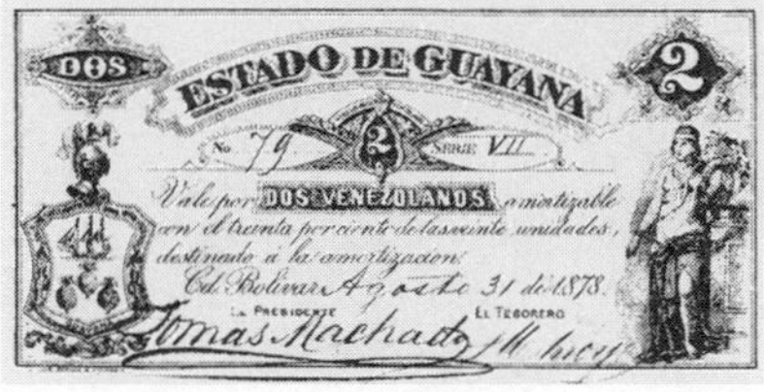

	Good	Fine	XF
S333 2 Venezolanos 31.8.1878. Black on light red underprint. Arms of Guayana at left, standing allegorical woman at right. Uniface. Similar to #S331. Printer: Lith. Sedille & Cie., Paris. Rare.	—	—	—
S334 4 Venezolanos 1878. Blue. Arms of Guayana at left, standing allegorical woman at right. Uniface. Similar to #S331. Printer: Lith. Sedille & Cie., Paris. Rare.	—	—	—
S335 8 Venezolanos 1878. Brown. Arms of Guayana at left, standing allegorical woman at right. Uniface. Similar to #S331. Printer: Lith. Sedille & Cie., Paris. Rare.	—	—	—
S337 20 Venezolanos 1878. Black. Arms of Guayana at left, standing allegorical woman at right. Uniface. Similar to #S331. Printer: Lith. Sedille & Cie., Paris. Rare.	—	—	—

NOTE: Issued notes may have a circular state stamping on back.

1878 Second Issue

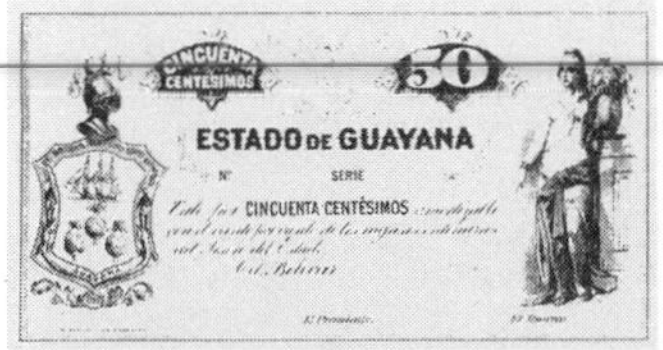

	Good	Fine	XF
S341 50 Centésimos ND (1878). Black. Arms of Guayana at left, standing allegorical woman at right. Uniface. Printer: The Hatch Lith. Co., N.Y.			
a. Green underprint. Rare.	—	—	—
b. Pale purple underprint. Rare.	—	—	—
S342 1 Venezolano 1878. Arms of Guayana at left, standing allegorical woman at right. Uniface. Printer: The Hatch Lith. Co., N.Y. Reported not confirmed.			

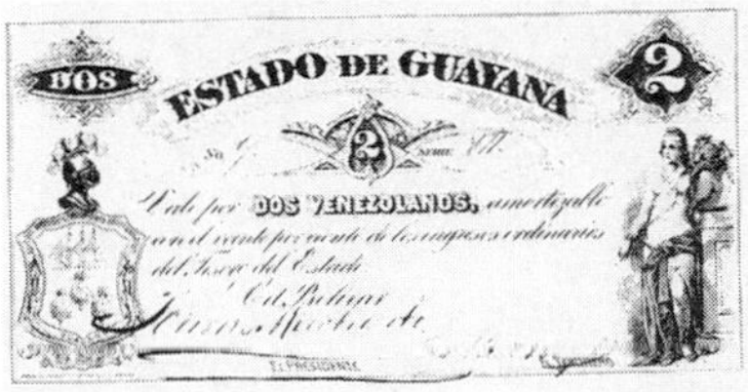

	Good	Fine	XF
S343 2 Venezolanos 1878. Black on dark red underprint. Arms of Guayana at left, standing allegorical woman at right. Uniface. Printer: The Hatch Lith. Co., N.Y. Rare.	—	—	—
S344 4 Venezolanos 1878. Black and green. Arms of Guayana at left, standing allegorical woman at right. Uniface. Printer: The Hatch Lith. Co., N.Y. Rare.	—	—	—
S345 8 Venezolanos 1878. Brown. Arms of Guayana at left, standing allegorical woman at right. Uniface. Printer: The Hatch Lith. Co., N.Y. Rare.	—	—	—

1879 Issue

	Good	Fine	XF
S351 5 Bolívares = 1 Venezolano 31.12.1879. Green. Arms at left, Simon Bolivar in underprint at center. Heading: *ESTADO GUAYANA*. Dates filled in by hand. Printer: Hatch Lith. Co. (without imprint). Rare.	—	—	—
S352 10 Bolívares = 2 Venezolanos 31.12.1879. Black on brown underprint. Arms at left, Simon Bolivar in underprint at center. Heading: *ESTADO GUAYANA*. Dates filled in by hand. Back: Brown. Printer: Hatch Lith. Co. (without imprint). Rare.	—	—	—

		Good	Fine	XF
S353	**20 Bolívares = 4 Venezolanos** 31.12.1879. Black on blue underprint. Arms at left, Simon Bolivar in underprint at center. Heading: *ESTADO GUAYANA*. Dates filled in by hand. Back: Blue. Printer: Hatch Lith. Co. (without imprint). Rare.	—	—	—
S354	**40 Bolívares = 8 Venezolanos** 31.12.1879. Black on yellow underprint. Arms at left, Simon Bolivar in underprint at center. Heading: *ESTADO GUAYANA*. Dates filled in by hand. Printer: Hatch Lith. Co. (without imprint). Rare.	—	—	—

Leprosarium

Leproserias Nacionales - Ministerio de Sanidad y Asistencia Social

1940 ND Series B Issue

		Good	Fine	XF
S361	**.25 Bolívar** ND(1940). Green. Sailboat with island in background at center. Serial #. Back: Sailboat with island in background at center. Printer: Tip (ografia) Del Comercio-Caracas. Reported not confirmed.	—	—	—
S362	**.50 Bolívar** ND(1940). Orange. Sailboat with island in background at center. Serial #. Back: Sailboat with island in background at center. Printer: Tip (ografia) Del Comercio-Caracas. Reported not confirmed.	—	—	—
S363	**1 Bolívar** ND(1940). Red-orange. Sailboat with island in background at center. Serial #. With hand stamp variety Type I. Back: Sailboat with island in background at center. Printer: Tip (ografia) Del Comercio-Caracas.	—	—	—

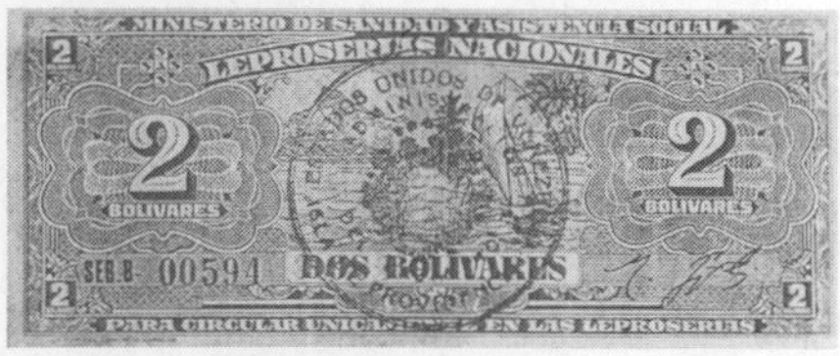

		Good	Fine	XF
S364	**2 Bolívares** ND(1940). Purple. Sailboat with island in background at center. Serial #. With hand stamp variety Type I. Back: Sailboat with island in background at center. Printer: Tip (ografia) Del Comercio-Caracas.	50.00	100.	200.

		Good	Fine	XF
S365	**5 Bolívares** ND(1940). Grayish blue. Sailboat with island in background at center. Serial #. With hand stamp variety Type I. Back: Sailboat with island in background at center. Printer: Tip (ografia) Del Comercio-Caracas.	50.00	100.	200.

1940 ND Series C Issue

		Good	Fine	XF
S366	**.25 Bolívar** ND(1940). Green. Sailboat with island in background at center. Serial #. Back: Sailboat with island in background at center. Serial #. Printer: Edit (orial) Bellas Artes. Reported not confirmed.	—	—	—
S367	**.50 Bolívar** ND(1940). Orange. Sailboat with island in background at center. Serial #. Back: Sailboat with island in background at center. Serial #. Printer: Edit (orial) Bellas Artes. Reported not confirmed.	—	—	—

		Good	Fine	XF
S368	**1 Bolívar** ND(1940). Pale orange. Sailboat with island in background at center. Serial #. With hand stamp varieties Type I and II. Back: Sailboat with island in background at center. Serial #. Printer: Edit (orial) Bellas Artes.	20.00	40.00	80.00
S369	**2 Bolívares** ND(1940). Purple. Sailboat with island in background at center. Serial #. With hand stamp varieties Type I and II. Back: Sailboat with island in background at center. Serial #. Printer: Edit (orial) Bellas Artes.	30.00	60.00	120.
S370	**5 Bolívares** ND(1940). Light blue. Sailboat with island in background at center. Serial #. With hand stamp varieties Type I and II. Back: Sailboat with island in background at center. Serial #. Printer: Edit (orial) Bellas Artes.	75.00	150.	300.

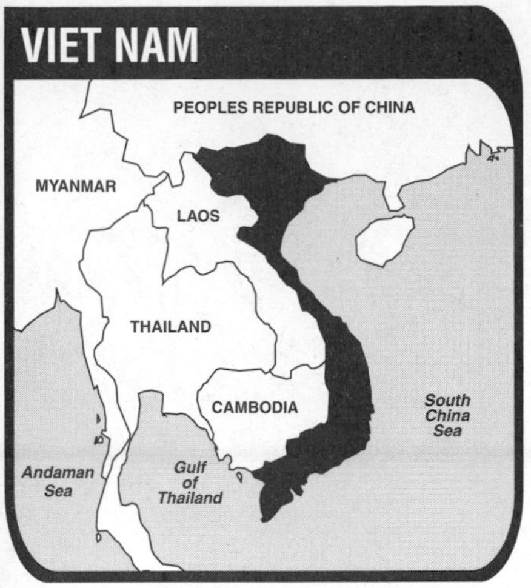

The Socialist Republic of Viet Nam, located in Southeast Asia west of the South China Sea, has an area of 329,560 sq. km. and a population of 86.12 million. Capital: Hanoi. Agricultural products, saltwater fish, shellfish, coal, mineral ores and electronic products are exported.

The conquest of Vietnam by France began in 1858 and was completed by 1884. It became part of French Indochina in 1887. Vietnam declared independence after World War II, but France continued to rule until its 1954 defeat by Communist forces under Ho Chi Minh. Under the Geneva Accords of 1954, Vietnam was divided into the Communist North and anti-Communist South. US economic and military aid to South Vietnam grew through the 1960s in an attempt to bolster the government, but US armed forces were withdrawn following a cease-fire agreement in 1973. Two years later, North Vietnamese forces overran the South reuniting the country under Communist rule. Despite the return of peace, for over a decade the country experienced little economic growth because of conservative leadership policies, the persecution and mass exodus of individuals - many of them successful South Vietnamese merchants - and growing international isolation. However, since the enactment of Vietnam's "doi moi" (renovation) policy in 1986, Vietnamese authorities have committed to increased economic liberalization and enacted structural reforms needed to modernize the economy and to produce more competitive, export-driven industries. The country continues to experience small-scale protests from various groups, the vast majority connected to land-use issues and the lack of equitable mechanisms for resolving disputes. Various ethnic minorities, such as the Montagnards of the Central Highlands and the Khmer Krom in the southern delta region, have also held protests.

MONETARY SYSTEM:

1 Hao = 10 Xu
1 Dông = 100 Xu
1 Dông = 100 "Old" Dong, 1951
1 Dong = 100 Xu = 100 Su to 1975
1 New Dong = 500 Old Dong, 1975-76

FOREIGN EXCHANGE CERTIFICATES

NGÂN HANG NGOAI THUONG VIET NAM

BANK FOR FOREIGN TRADE

1987 ND DÔNG B ISSUE

#FX1-FX5 green on pale blue and yellow unpt. Back pale blue.

FX1 10 Dông B	VG	VF	UNC
ND (1987). Green on pale blue and yellow underprint. Back: Pale blue.			
a. Unissued.	—	—	5.00
s. Specimen.	—	—	10.00

FX2 50 Dông B	VG	VF	UNC
ND (1987). Green on pale blue and yellow underprint. Back: Pale blue.			
a. Unissued.	—	—	5.00
s. Specimen.	—	—	10.00

FX3 100 Dông B	VG	VF	UNC
ND (1987). Green on pale blue and yellow underprint. Back: Pale blue.			
a. Unissued.	—	—	5.00
s. Specimen.	—	—	10.00

FX4 200 Dông B	VG	VF	UNC
ND (1987). Green on pale blue and yellow underprint. Back: Pale blue.			
a. Unissued.	—	—	5.00
s. Specimen.	—	—	10.00

FX5 500 Dông B	VG	VF	UNC
ND (1987). Green on pale blue and yellow underprint. Back: Pale blue.			
a. Unissued.	—	—	5.00
s. Specimen.	—	—	10.00

FX6 1000 Dông B	VG	VF	UNC
ND (1987). Red-violet on pink and pale orange underprint. Back: Pink.			
a. Unissued.	—	—	5.00
s1. Specimen. Overprinted. Series AA, EE.	—	—	10.00
s2. Specimen. Perforated. Series EE.	—	—	25.00

FX7 5000 Dông B	VG	VF	UNC
ND (1987). Brown on ochre underprint. Back: Ochre.			
a. Unissued.	—	—	5.00
s1. Specimen. Overprinted. Series AA, EE.	—	—	10.00
s2. Specimen. Perforated. Series EE.	—	—	25.00

PHIÊU' THAY NGOAI TÊ

1981 US DOLLAR A ISSUE

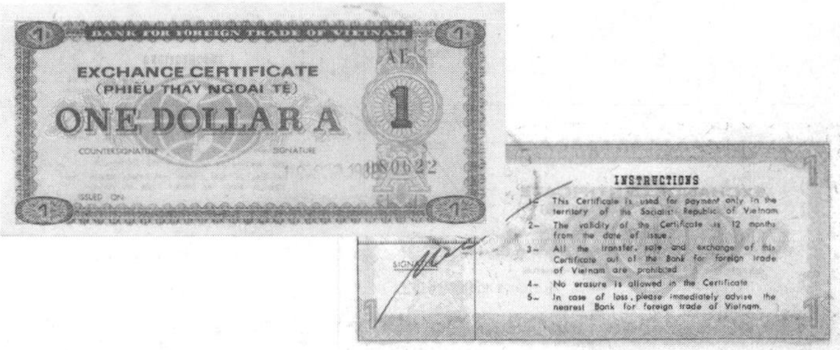

FX8 1 Dollar	VG	VF	UNC
1981-84. Green on peach and light blue underprint.			
a. Issued note with validation overprint.	1000.	1250.	1500.
b. Unissued note without validation overprint.	—	1000.	1250.

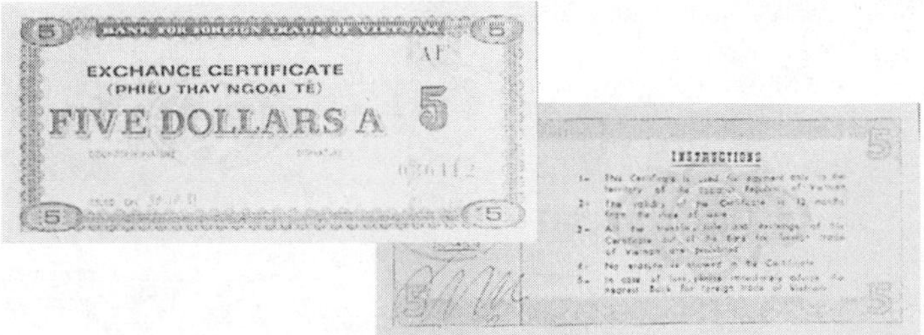

FX9 5 Dollars	VG	VF	UNC
1981-84. Purple on peach and light blue underprint.			
a. Issued note with validation overprint.	1250.	1500.	1750.
b. Unissued note without validation overprint.	—	1750.	2000.

		VG	VF	UNC
FX10	**10 Dollars** 1981-84. Reported not confirmed.	—	—	—
FX11	**20 Dollars** 1981-84. Reported not confirmed.	—	—	—

Regional

Phieu Tiep Te

1949-50 ND Emergency Issues

Issued by the various local (provincial and lower) administrations.

		Good	Fine	XF
R1	**5 Cac** ND (1949-50). Dark blue. Farmers and oxen at left center. Back: Metal working.	15.00	30.00	60.00
R2	**5 Cac** ND (1949-50). Red-brown. HCM at center in oval wreath of corn. Back: Soldier at left, seated man at right. (Soc-Trang).	25.00	50.00	100.

		Good	Fine	XF
R3	**1 Dông** ND (1949-50). Blue on brown. HCM at center in oval formed of Laurel wreath. Back: Soldier at left, star at right. (Soc-Trang).	20.00	40.00	100.

		Good	Fine	XF
R4	**1 Dông** ND (1949-50). Red and yellow. Man and woman. Back: Five soldiers. (Thu Dau Mot).			
	a. Back with text: *TINH-THU-DAU-MOT.*	40.00	75.00	150.
	b. Back with text: *TINH THUDAUMOT.*	40.00	75.00	150.
	c. Back without either style of above legend.	40.00	75.00	150.

		Good	Fine	XF
R5	**1 Dông** ND (1949-50). Red. Five stars at left and right. Back: Woman carrying load on shoulder. (Tay Ninh).	25.00	75.00	150.
R6	**1 Dông** ND (1949-50). Blue. HCM in rectangular frame. Back: Man carrying load on head at left, man holding spear at right. (Soc Trang).	20.00	50.00	100.

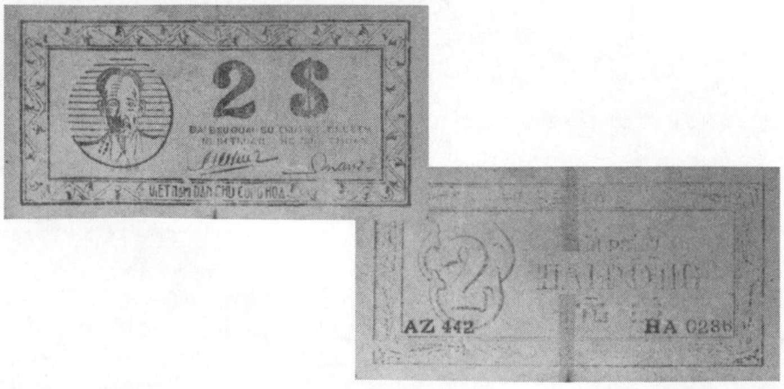

		Good	Fine	XF
R7	**2 Dông** ND (1949-50). Dark red. HCM at left. Back: Large *2* at left, *HAI DONG* at right.	40.00	75.00	150.

		Good	Fine	XF
R8	**2 Dông** ND (1949-50). Brown. Mountains at right. Back: Green. Man digging at left, blacksmith at right. (Ha Tien).	30.00	100.	175.
R10	**2 Dông** 23.12.1949. Blue. Soldiers at left attacking burning village at right. Back: Woman with baskets. (Can Tho).			
	a. Back with text: *Tat Ca De.*	30.00	100.	175.
	b. Back with text: *Chuan Bi De.*	30.00	100.	175.

		Good	Fine	XF
R10A	**5 Dông** ND. HCM in spray at left.	20.00	50.00	125.

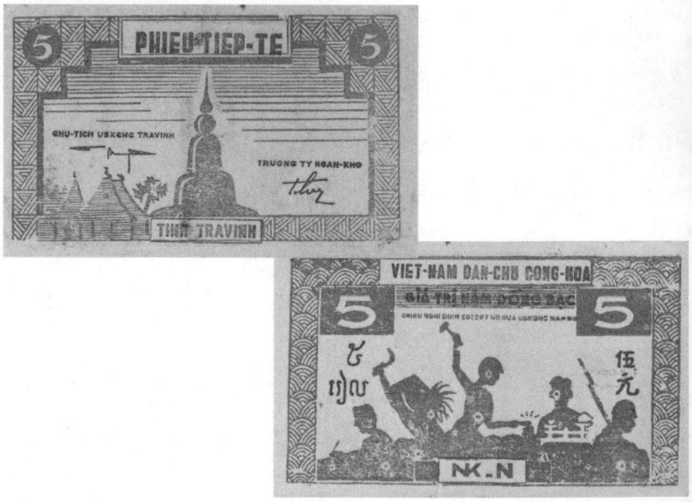

		Good	Fine	XF
r10b	**5 Dông** ND. Tower at center. Back: Farmers and laborers.			
	a. Without printer imprint.	20.00	40.00	75.00
	b. With printer imprint at lower left on both sides.	20.00	40.00	75.00

Viet-Minh Administrative Committees

1945 ND Provisional Issues

Beginning in 1945, various Viet-Minh administrative committees (provincial, city, village and military) handstamped notes of the Banque de l'Indochine and Nam Bo. These overstamps were intended to control the use of French issued notes within the Viet-Minh liberated zones. Nam Bo notes were overstamped to assure the people who were unfamiliar with them that these newly Democratic Republic notes were authentic. These overstamps appear on numerous French Indochina issues, particularly #48, 54, 55, 66, 67 and 73. They also appear on many Nam Bo issues, particularly #17 and 50. The overstamps are found in red, black and purple ink; some are handsigned by a local Viet-Minh official, and others are either stamp signed or not signed. The Following

		Good	Fine	XF
R11	**1 Piastre** ND. Red circular handstamp: *BIEN HOA* on French Indochina #54c.	5.00	15.00	—

	Good	Fine	XF
R11A 1 Piastre			
ND. Red rectangular handstamp: *LONG CHAU TIEN* on French Indochina #54e for Long Xuyen, Chau Doc and Tien Giang provinces.	5.00	15.00	—
R11B 1 Piastre			
ND. Large circular handstamp: *THU BIEN* on French Indochina #48b. Back: 2 small handstamps with star in center	5.00	15.00	—
R11C 1 Piastre			
ND. Large circular handstamp: *CHAO DOC* on French Indochina #105.	5.00	15.00	—
R12 5 Piastres			
ND. Red circular and rectangular handstamps: *BEN TRE* on French Indochina #55.	5.00	15.00	—
R13 5 Piastres			
ND. Red circular handstamp: *CHO LON* on French Indochina #49.	5.00	15.00	—
R14 5 Piastres			
ND. Red circular handstamp: *CHO LON* on French Indochina #55.	5.00	15.00	—
R15 10 Piastres			
ND. Black circular handstamps: *LONG PHUOC* on French Indochina #80.	5.00	15.00	—
R16 20 Piastres			
ND. Red circular handstamp: *CHO LON* on French Indochina #81.	5.00	15.00	—
R17 100 Piastres			
ND. Red circular handstamp: *RACH-GIA*.			
a. On French Indochina #66.	5.00	15.00	—
b. On French Indochina #67.	5.00	15.00	—
c. On French Indochina #73.	5.00	15.00	—
R18 100 Piastres			
ND. Red rectangular handstamp: *LONG CHAU HA* on French Indochina #66.	5.00	15.00	—

Note: No doubt virtually all of the Banque de l'Indochine notes in circulation at the time were overstamped by various Viet-Minh agencies. Only reported complete notes are listed above. Many more must exist.

	Good	Fine	XF
R19 100 Piastres			
ND. Red circular handstamp: *BEN-TRE* on French Indochina #66.	5.00	15.00	—

Tra Vinh Province

1951 Provisional Issue

	Good	Fine	XF
R31 100 Dông			
18.3.1951. Control ticket added with red-violet handstamp: *TRA VINH* on #28.	150.	300.	—
R32 100 Dông			
18.3.1951. Control ticket with added black handstamp: *VINH LONG* on #28.	125.	—	—

The Federal Republic of Yugoslavia is a Balkan country located on the east shore of the Adriatic Sea bordering Bosnia-Herzegovina and Croatia to the west, Hungary and Romania to the north, Bulgaria to the east, and Albania and Macedonia to the south. It has an area of 39,449 sq. mi. (102,173 sq. km.) and a population of 10.5 million. Capital: Belgrade. The chief industries are agriculture, mining, manufacturing and tourism. Machinery, nonferrous metals, meat and fabrics are exported.

The first South-Slavian State - Yugoslavia - was proclaimed on Dec. 1, 1918, after the union of the Kingdom of Serbia, Montenegro and the South Slav territories of Austria-Hungary; it then changed its official name from the Kingdom of the Serbs, Croats, and Slovenes to the Kingdom of Yugoslavia on Oct. 3, 1929. The Royal government of Yugoslavia attempted to remain neutral in World War II but, yielding to German pressure, aligned itself with the Axis powers in March of 1941; a few days later it was overthrown by a military-led coup and its neutrality reasserted. The Nazis occupied the country on April 17, and throughout the remaining years were resisted by a number of guerrilla armies, notably that of Marshal Josip Broz known as Tito. After the defeat of the Axis powers, a leftist coalition headed by Tito abolished the monarchy and, on Jan. 31, 1946, established a "People's Republic". Tito's rival General Draza Mihajlovic, who led the Chetniks against the Germans and Tito's forces, was arrested on March 13, 1946 and executed the following day after having been convicted by a partisan court.

The Federal Republic of Yugoslavia was composed of six autonomous republics: Serbia, Croatia, Slovenia, Bosnia-Herzegovina, Macedonia and Montenegro with two autonomous provinces within Serbia: Kosovo-Metohija and Vojvodina. The collapse of the Socialist Federal Republic of Yugoslavia during 1991-92 has resulted in the autonomous republics of Croatia, Slovenia, Bosnia-Herzegovina and Macedonia declaring their respective independence.

The Federal Republic of Yugoslavia was proclaimed in 1992; it consists of the former Republics of Serbia and Montenegro.

RULERS:

Peter I, 1918-1921
Alexander I, 1921-1934
Peter II, 1934-1945

MONETARY SYSTEM:

1 Dinar = 100 Para
1 Dinar = 100 *Old* Dinara, 1965
1 Dinar = 10,000 *Old* Dinara, 1990-91
1 Dinar = 10 *Old* Dinara, 1992
1 Dinar = 1 Million *Old* Dinara, 1.10.1993
1 Dinar = 1 Milliard *Old* Dinara, 1.1.1994

Regional - WWII

ФЕДЕРАЛНА ЦРНА ГОРА У ФЕДЕРАТИВНОЈ ДЕМОКРАТСКОЈ ЈУГОСЛАВИИИ ЦЕТИЊЕ

Federal Regime of the Yugoslav Democratic Federation Cetinje, Montenegro

1945 Issue

	Good	Fine	XF
S101 10 Dinara			
1.1.1945. Blue. People with hands raised at left, burning house at right. Back: Monthly depreciating redemption values.	120.	360.	950.
S102 100 Dinara			
1.2.1945. Blue-green and yellow. Woman offering bearded man a drink. Back: Monthly depreciating redemption values.	225.	675.	1950.

S103 1000 Dinara — Good | Fine | XF
1.2.1945. Light brown and brown. Horseman with arm in sling. Back: Monthly depreciating redemption values. — 200. | 600. | 1800.

Regional Military - WWII

Gospodarsko Financni Odbor Osvobodilne Fronte

State Finance Department Liberation Front

1944 ND Issue

S104 50 Lit — Good | Fine | XF
ND. Orange with dark red text. Partisan family in woods at center. Blue or black serial #. Back: State seal at center.
a. Issued note. — 2.50 | 7.50 | 22.50
b. Hand stamp (cancelled). — 1.50 | 4.50 | 12.50

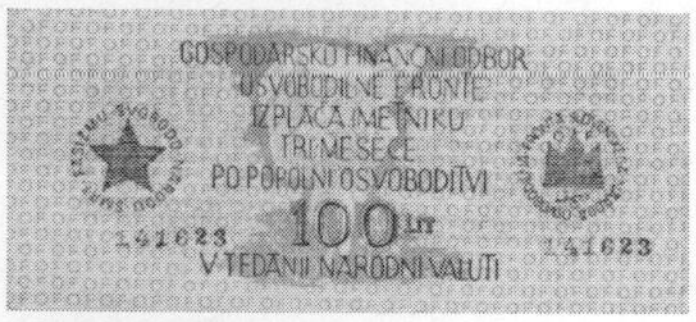

S105 100 Lit — Good | Fine | XF
ND. Lilac, brown and blue. Partisan carrying flag at center. Back: Partisan carrying flag at center.
a. Hand stamp, serial # and hand signature. — — | — | —
b. Without hand stamp or signature. — 1.50 | 4.50 | 12.50
c. Without serial #. — 1.50 | 4.50 | 12.50

S106 500 Lit — Good | Fine | XF
ND. Red-brown and gray-olive. (Not issued). — 22.50 | 65.00 | 200.

S107 1000 Lit — Good | Fine | XF
ND. Red-brown and gray-olive. Soldiers at center. — 30.00 | 90.00 | 270.

S108 5000 Lit — Good | Fine | XF
ND. Red-brown and gray-olive. — 60.00 | 180. | 540.

S109 10,000 Lit
ND. Red-brown and gray-olive. Partisans at center. Back: Seal at center. — 75.00 | 225. | 675.

Denarni Zavod Slovenije

Monetary Bank of Slovenia

1944 First Issue

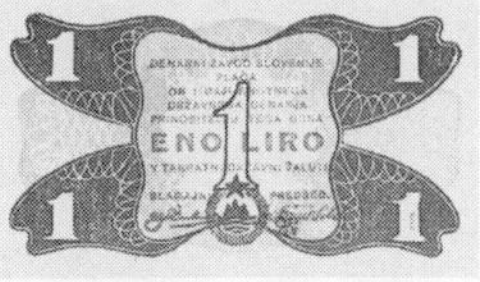

S110 1 Liro — VG | VF | UNC
20.2.1944-12.3.1944. Blue-green. *No.* or letters with serial #. Back: Brown. — 3.00 | 9.00 | 27.50

S111 5 Lir — VG | VF | UNC
20.2.1944-12.3.1944. Blue and light blue. 2 serial # varieties. — 4.00 | 12.50 | 35.00

S112 10 Lir — VG | VF | UNC
20.2.1944-12.3.1944. Red. 2 serial # varieties. — 4.00 | 12.50 | 35.00

NOTE: German propaganda issue face like #S112, back with *Ra denar je prau. . .* Value $60 in XF.

1944 Second Issue

#S113-S118 various date and sign. varieties. Wmk. paper.

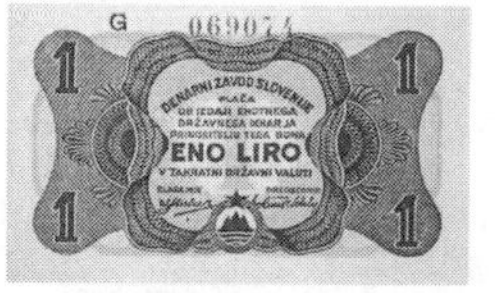

S113 1 Liro — VG | VF | UNC
20.2.1944-12.3.1944. Blue on olive underprint. Red serial #. Various date and signature varieties. — 3.00 | 9.00 | 27.50

S114 5 Lir — VG | VF | UNC
20.2.1944-12.3.1944. Blue on gray-olive underprint. Red serial #. Various date and signature varieties. — 3.00 | 9.00 | 27.50

S115 10 Lir — VG | VF | UNC
20.2.1944-12.3.1944. Brown on gray-violet underprint. Black serial #. Various date and signature varieties. — 3.00 | 9.00 | 27.50

S116 50 Lir — VG | VF | UNC
20.2.1944-12.3.1944. Green. Various date and signature varieties. — 9.00 | 36.00 | 100.

S117 100 Lir — VG | VF | UNC

20.2.1944-12.3.1944. Brown on light brown underprint. Black serial #. Various date and signature varieties. — 9.00 | 36.00 | 100.

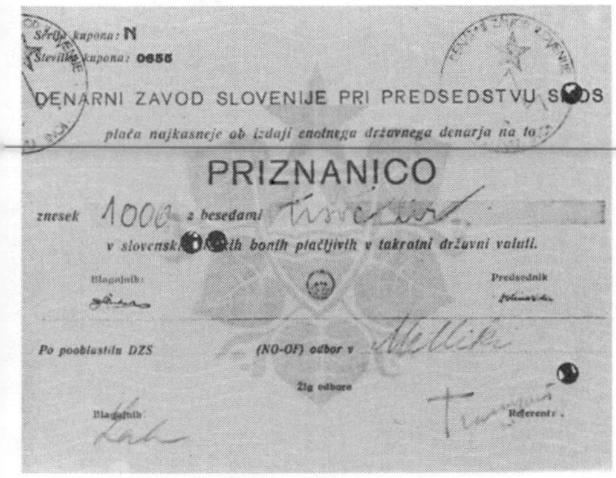

S118 Various Denominations — Good | Fine | XF

Green. Various date and signature varieties. — 25.00 | 75.00 | 225.

NOTE: #S118 recorded in handwritten denominations of 1000, 1500, 3000 and 5000 Lir.

Izvreni Odbor Osvobodilne Fronte Slovenskega Naroda

Committee of the Slovenian Government Liberty Front

1943 RM Issue

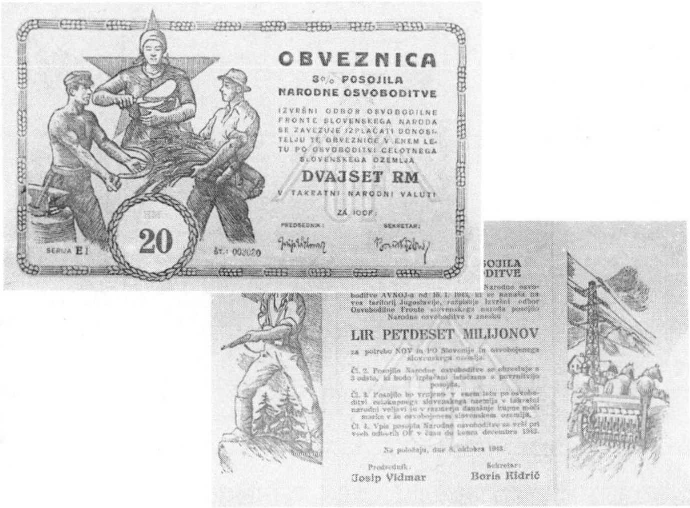

S119 20 Rm — Good | Fine | XF

8.10.1943. Blue and red. Star behind woman with loaf between farmer and blacksmith at right. 3% obligations. — 45.00 | 135. | 400.

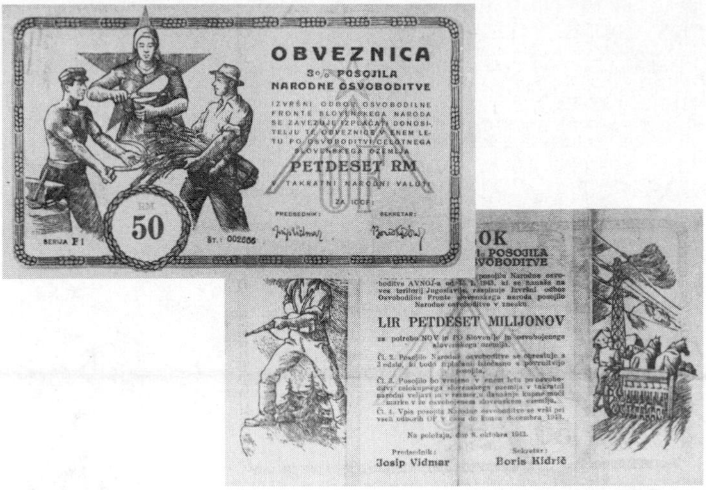

S120 50 Rm — Good | Fine | XF

8.10.1943. Green and red. Star behind woman with loaf between farmer and blacksmith at right. 3% obligations. — 45.00 | 135. | 400.

S121 100 Rm

8.10.1943. Green and red. Star behind woman with loaf between farmer and blacksmith at right. 3% obligations. — 75.00 | 225. | 675.

S122 500 Rm — Good | Fine | XF

8.10.1943. Lilac and red. Star behind woman with loaf between farmer and blacksmith at right. 3% obligations. — 90.00 | 270. | 750.

1943 Lir Issue

S123 100 Lir — Good | Fine | XF

8.10.1943. Blue and red. Star behind woman with loaf between farmer and blacksmith at right. 3% obligations. — 90.00 | 270. | 750.

S124 500 Lir

8.10.1943. Blue and red. Star behind woman with loaf between farmer and blacksmith at right. 3% obligations. — 90.00 | 270. | 750.

1943 ND Lit Issue

		Good	Fine	XF
S125	**100 Lit** ND (1943). Brown. Agricultural work at left and right. Star behind woman with loaf between farmer and blacksmith at right. 3% obligations. Similar to #S127.	45.00	125.	375.
S126	**1000 Lit** ND (1943). Brown. Agricultural work at left and right. Star behind woman with loaf between farmer and blacksmith at right. 3% obligations. Similar to #S127.	60.00	180.	540.

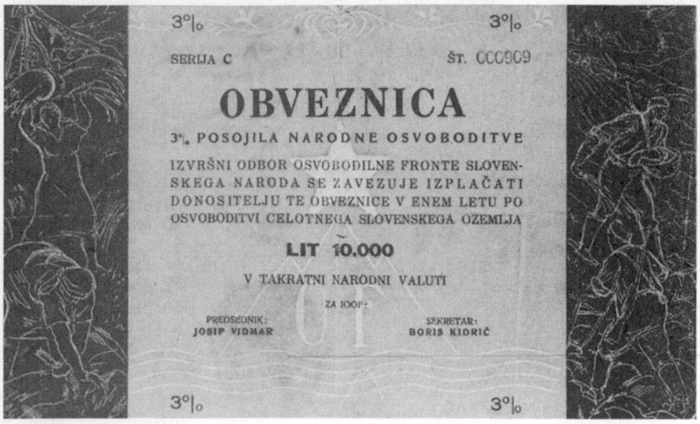

		Good	Fine	XF
S127	**10,000 Lit** ND (1943). Brown. Agricultural work at left and right. Star behind woman with loaf between farmer and blacksmith at right. 3% obligations.	100.	300.	900.

Partisan Certificates "Potrdilo" WWII

Glavno Poveljstvo Slovenskih Partizanskih Cet Ljubljana

1942-45 Issue

#S128 crudely printed or duplicated.

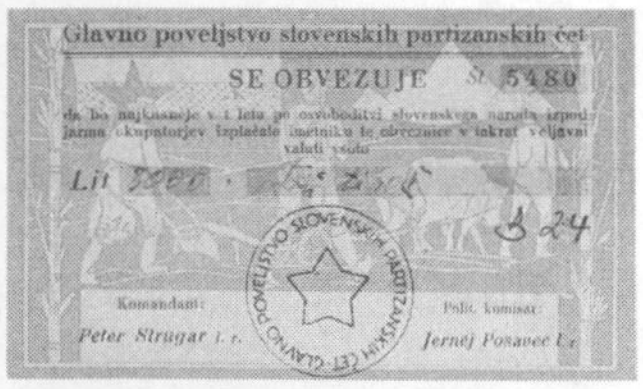

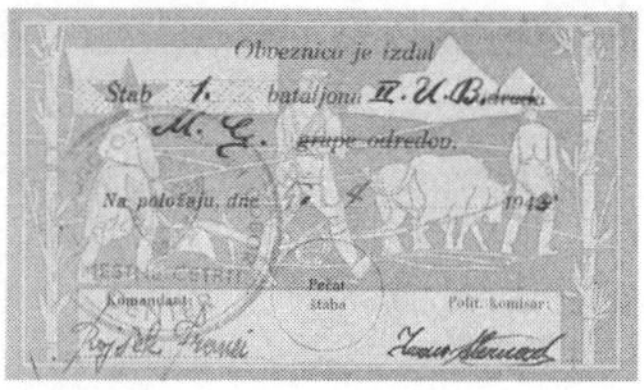

		Good	Fine	XF
S128	**Various Denominations** 1942-45. Blue with red text. Farmer and partisan plowing. Various handwritten denominations and dated.	25.00	75.00	225.

Kanalski O.N. OO. (O.F.)

District National Committee of the Liberation Front for Kanal

1944-45 Issue

		Good	Fine	XF
S129	**100 Lir** 1944-45. Lilac. Tito at right. Various handwritten dates.	75.00	225.	675.

		Good	Fine	XF
S130	**600 Lir** 1944-45. Lilac. Tito at right. Various handwritten dates.	75.00	225.	675.

Narodni Osvobodilni Svet Za Primorsko Slovenijo

National Liberation Committee for the Slovenian Coast

1944-45 Issue

		Good	Fine	XF
S131	**100 Lir** 1944-45. Blue.	75.00	225.	675.
S132	**300 Lir** 1944-45. Blue.	75.00	225.	675.
S133	**400 Lir** 1944-45. Blue.	75.00	225.	675.

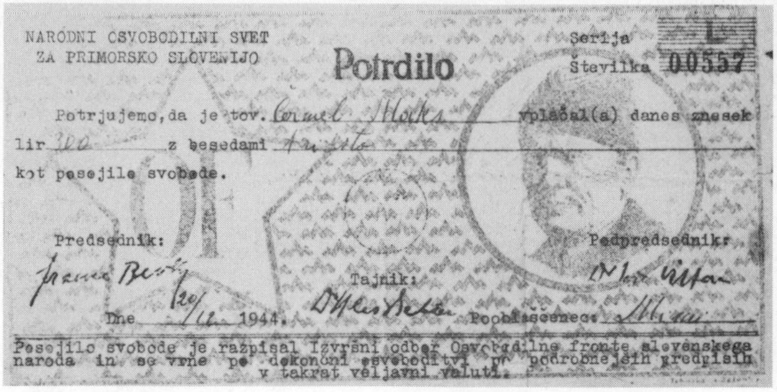

		Good	Fine	XF
S134	**1000 Lir** 1944-45. Purple. Tito at right.	75.00	225.	675.
S135	**2000 Lir** 1944-45. Blue.	75.00	225.	675.

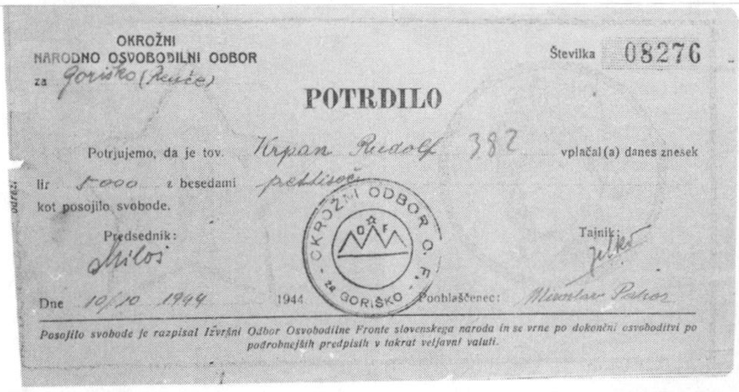

		Good	Fine	XF
S136	**5000 Lir** 1944-45.	75.00	225.	675.
S137	**7000 Lir** 1944-45. Purple. Tito at right.	75.00	225.	675.
S138	**10,000 Lir** 1944-45. Green.	75.00	225.	675.

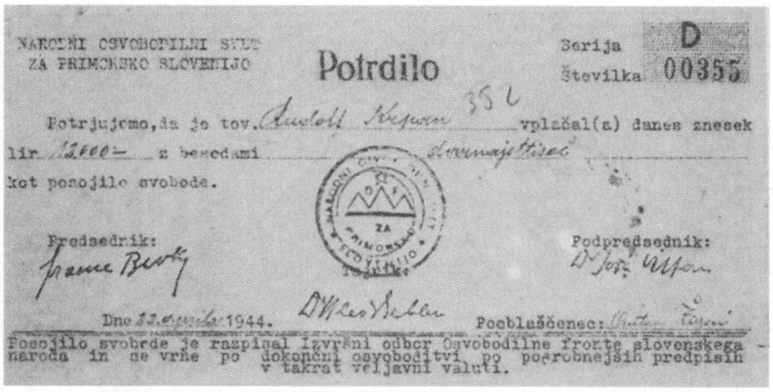

		Good	Fine	XF
S139	**12,000 Lir** 1944-45. Green. Tito at right.	75.00	225.	675.

Okrozni Odbor O.F. za Pivko

District Committee of the Liberation Front for Pivko

1940's Issue

		Good	Fine	XF
S140	**500 Lir** 194x. Red. Without underprint.	75.00	225.	675.

Okrozni Odbor O.F. za Juzno Primorsko

District Committee of the Liberation Front for Primorsko District

1940's Issue

		Good	Fine	XF
S141	**200 Rm** 194x. Without underprint. Various dates.	75.00	225.	675.
S142	**250 Rm** 194x. Without underprint. Various dates.	75.00	225.	675.

Okrozni Odbor O.F. za Zapadno Primorsko

District Committee of Liberation Front for Primorsko District

1940's Issue

		Good	Fine	XF
S143	128 Lir 194x. Blue. Tito at right. Various dates.	75.00	225.	675.
S144	200 Lir 194x. Blue. Tito at right. Various dates. Similar to #S143.	75.00	225.	675.

Okrozni Odbor O.F. za Slov. Istro

District Committee of the Liberation Front for Slovenian Istria

1945 Issue

		Good	Fine	XF
S145	100 Lir 1945. Blue-gray. Various dates.	75.00	225.	675.
S146	400 Lir 1945. Blue-gray. Various dates.	75.00	225.	675.
S147	500 Lir 1945. Blue-gray. Various dates.	75.00	225.	675.
S148	1000 Lir 1945. Blue-gray. Various dates.	180.	540.	—

OOOF (Okrozni Odbor O.F.) za Brkine

District Committee of the Liberation Front for Brkine

1944 Issue

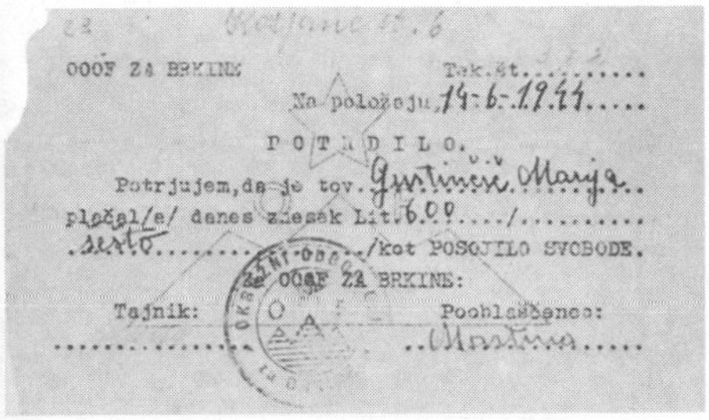

		Good	Fine	XF
S149	600 Lit 1944. Black. Outline of star and mountains at center. Hand dated.	75.00	225.	675.
S150	1000 Lit 1944. Black. Outline of star and mountains at center. Hand dated. Similar to #S149.	75.00	225.	675.

Okrozni N.O.O. za Brkine

District National Committee of the Liberation Front for Brkine

1940's Issue

		Good	Fine	XF
S151	1000 Lir 194x. Green. Tito at right. Various dates.	75.00	225.	675.

Okrozni N.O.O. (Odbor O.F.) za Viparsko Okrozje

District National Committee of the Liberation Front Viparsko

1940's Issue

		Good	Fine	XF
S152	500 Lir 194x. Black. Various dates.	75.00	225.	675.

Okrozni Narodno Osvobodilni Odbor za Brda

District National Liberation Committee for Brda

1944 Issue

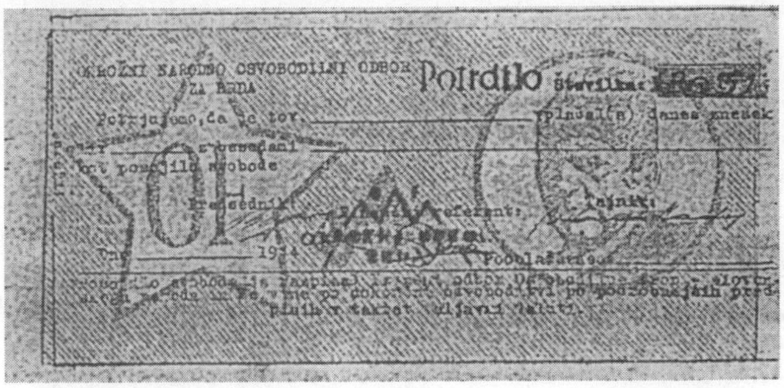

		Good	Fine	XF
S153	50 Lir 1944. Lilac. Tito at right. Various dates.	75.00	225.	675.
S154	300 Lir 1944. Red-brown. Tito at right. Various dates.	75.00	225.	675.
S155	600 Lir 1944. Brown. Various dates.	75.00	225.	675.
S156	2000 Lir 1944. Gray. Tito at right. Various dates. Similar to #S154.	75.00	225.	675.
S157	10,000 Lir 1944. Gray. Tito at right. Various dates.	75.00	225.	675.

Okrozni N.O.O. za Kras

District National Liberation Committee for Kras

1944 Issue

		Good	Fine	XF
S158	100 Lir 1944. Various dates.	75.00	225.	675.
S159	200 Lir 1944. Gray. Star at center. Various dates.	75.00	225.	675.

		Good	Fine	XF
S160	500 Lir 1944. Gray. Various dates.	75.00	225.	675.

Okrozni N.O.O. za Gorisko

District National Liberation Committee for Gorisko

1940's Issue

		Good	Fine	XF
S161	250 Lir 194x. Green. Tito at right. Various dates.	75.00	225.	675.
S162	500 Lir 194x. Brown. Tito at right. Various dates.	75.00	225.	675.
S163	1000 Lir 194x. Green. Tito at right, with or without Italian text. Various dates.	75.00	225.	675.
S164	5000 Lir 194x. Green. Various dates.	75.00	225.	675.

NOTICE

Readers with unlisted dates, signature varieties, etc.,
are invited to submit photocopies or scans of their notes to:
Standard Catalog of World Paper Money,
700 East State St. Iola, WI 54990-0001,
E-Mail: george.cuhaj@fwmedia.com.

Okrozni N.O.O. za Idrijsko

District National Liberation Committee for Idrijsko

1940's Issue

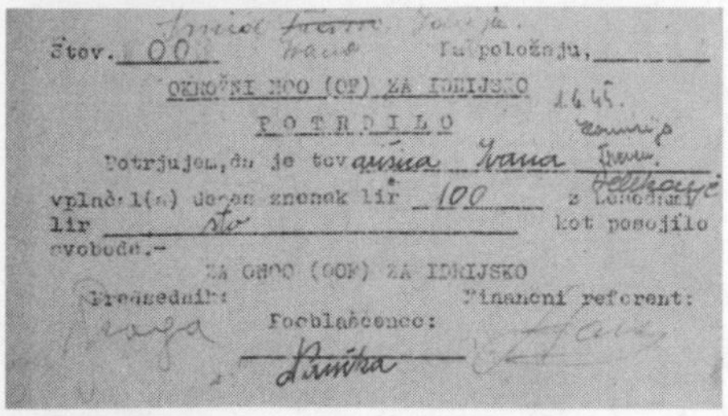
Štev. ... Na položaju,
OKROŽNI NOO (OF) ZA IDRIJSKO
POTRDILO
Potrjujemo, da je tov. ... vplačal(a) danes znesek lir ... lir ... kot posojilo svobode.-
ZA OKNOO (OOF) ZA IDRIJSKO
Predsednik: Finančni referent:
Pooblaščenec:

		Good	Fine	XF
S165	100 Lir 194x. Gray. Various dates.	75.00	225.	675.
S166	200 Lir 194x. Black. Various dates.	75.00	225.	675.
S167	500 Lir 194x. Black. Various dates.	75.00	225.	675.

Okrozni N.O.O. za Basko

District National Liberation Committee for Basko

1944-45 Issue

		Good	Fine	XF
S168	50 Lir (ca.1944-45). Hand dated.	75.00	225.	675.
S169	100 Lir (ca.1944-45). Red star at right. Hand dated.	75.00	225.	675.
S170	200 Lir (ca.1944-45). Red star at right. Hand dated.	75.00	225.	675.
S171	400 Lir (ca.1944-45). Gray. Red star at right. Hand dated.	75.00	225.	675.

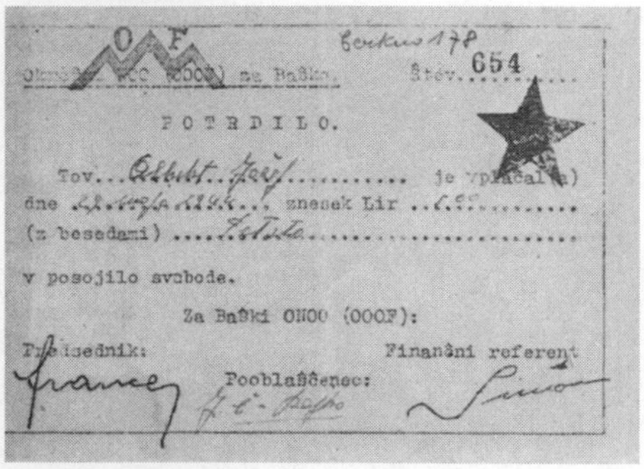
Okrožni NOO (OOOF) za Baško Štev. 654
POTRDILO.
Tov. ... je vplačal(a) dne ... znesek Lir ...
(z besedami) ...
v posojilo svobode.
Za Baški ONOO (OOOF):
Predsednik: Finančni referent
Pooblaščenec:

		Good	Fine	XF
S172	500 Lir (ca.1944-45). Gray. Red star at right. Hand dated.	75.00	225.	675.
S173	1000 Lir (ca.1944-45). Hand dated.	75.00	225.	675.
S174	2000 Lir (ca.1944-45). Gray. Red star at right. Hand dated. Similar to #S172.	75.00	225.	675.
S175	5000 Lir (ca.1944-45). Hand dated.	75.00	225.	675.

Okrozni N.O.O. za Tolminsko

District National Liberation Committee for Tolminsko

1940's Issue

		Good	Fine	XF
S176	100 Lir 194x. Blue. Tito at right. Various dates.	75.00	225.	675.

Okrozni N.O.O. za Vipavsko

District National Liberation Committee for Vipavsko

1940's Issue

		Good	Fine	XF
S177	10 Lir ND. Gray.	75.00	225.	675.

Pokrajinski Odbor O.F. za Stajersko

Committee of the Liberation Front for Stajersko

1940's Issue

		Good	Fine	XF
S178	50 Rm 194x. Various dates.	75.00	225.	675.
S179	75 Rm 194x. Various dates.	75.00	225.	675.

Pokrajinski Odbor O.F. za Gorenjsko

Committee of the Liberation Front for Gorenjsko

1940's Issue

		Good	Fine	XF
S180	200 Rm 194x. Blue-gray. Tito at right.	75.00	225.	675.

Regional

Gospodarska Banka za Istru, Rijeku i Slovensko Primorje

State Bank for Istria, Fiume and Slovene Coastal Area

1945 Issue

		VG	VF	UNC
R1	1 Lira 1945. Brown. Back: Sailboat. Female soldier at left.	2.00	5.00	40.00

		VG	VF	UNC
R2	5 Lire 1945. Green. Back: Sailboat.	2.00	5.00	15.00
R3	10 Lire 1945. Brown on green underprint. Back: Sailboat.	2.00	5.00	15.00

		VG	VF	UNC
R4	20 Lire 1945. Purple on light green underprint. Back: Sailboat.			
	a. With serial #.	2.00	5.00	20.00
	b. Without serial #.	3.00	7.50	30.00
R5	50 Lire 1945. Red-brown. Back: Sailboat.			
	a. Red serial #.	3.00	7.50	30.00
	b. Black serial #.	15.00	50.00	175.
	c. Without serial #.	20.00	60.00	225.

		VG	VF	UNC
R6	100 Lire 1945. Brown and blue. Back: Sailboat.			
	a. With serial #.	5.00	25.00	75.00
	b. Without serial #.	3.00	20.00	60.00

R7 500 Lire	VG	VF	UNC
1945. Gray on green underprint. Back: Brown on green underprint. Sailboat.	12.00	30.00	90.00
R8 1000 Lire			
1945. Purple and light brown. Back: Sailboat. Farmer plowing with ox.	8.00	25.00	75.00

Hungarian Occupation of Backa - WW II

Hungarian Armed Forces

1941 Issue

R9A 1000 Dinara	VG	VF	UNC
ND (1941). Blue-gray and brown. Queen Marie at left, bird at right. Back: Standing women at left and right. Revalidation adhesive stamp affixed to #29.	—	—	—

Italian Occupation of Montenegro - WW II

Italian Armed Forces

1941 Issue

#R10-R15 *VERIFICATO* handstamp on Yugoslav notes.

R10 10 Dinara	Good	Fine	XF
ND (1941 - old date 22.9.1939). Green. King Peter II at left, bridge at center. Back: Woman in national costume at right. Watermark: Older man in uniform. Handstamp on #35.	1.00	4.50	15.00

R11 20 Dinara	Good	Fine	XF
ND (1941 - old date 6.9.1936). Multicolor. Group of six people with three horses and lion. Handstamp on #33.	1.00	4.50	15.00

R12 50 Dinara	Good	Fine	XF
ND (1941 - old date 1.12.1931). Brown and multicolor. Portrait King Alexander I at left. Back: Equestrian statue. Handstamp on #28.	1.00	3.50	12.50

		Good	Fine	XF
R13	**100 Dinara**			
	ND (1941 - old date 1.12.1929). Purple on yellow underprint. Boats in water at center, seated woman with sword at right. Back: Violet and multicolor. Sailboats at center, man with fruit leaning on shield with arms at right. Handstamp on #27.			
	a. Watermark: Karageorge.	2.00	8.00	20.00
	b. Watermark: Alexander.	.50	2.00	6.00
R13A	**100 Dinara**			
	ND (1941 - old date 30.11.1920). Purple on yellow underprint. Boats in water at center, seated woman with sword at right. Back: Violet and multicolor. Sailboats at center, man with fruit leaning on shield with arms at right. Watermark: Karageorge. Handstamp on #22 in error. Rare.	—	—	—
R14	**500 Dinara**			
	ND (1941 - old date 3.9.1935). Blue and multicolor. Woman seated with boy at right center. Back: Shield with arms and two seated women. Handstamp on #31.	10.00	20.00	50.00

		Good	Fine	XF
R15	**1000 Dinara**			
	ND (1941 - old date 1.12.1931). Blue-gray and brown. Queen Marie at left, bird at right. Back: Standing women at left and right. Handstamp on #29.	10.00	20.00	50.00

German Occupation - WWII

Hranilnica Ljubljanske Pokrajine

Sparkasse der Provinz Laibach

1944 Issue

#R16-R24 issued during German occupation.

		VG	VF	UNC
R16	**50 Cent. = 1/2 (Lira)**			
	28.11.1944. Dark green. Child in national costume at left. Slovene text. Back: Child in national costume at left. German text.	2.00	7.50	20.00
R17	**1 Lira**			
	28.11.1944. Dark brown. Tower with dragon at right. Slovene text. Back: Tower with dragon at right. German text.	1.50	6.00	17.50
R18	**2 Liri**			
	28.11.1944. Brown. Woman with child at left. Slovene text. Back: Woman with child at left. German text.	2.50	10.00	25.00

		VG	VF	UNC
R19	**5 Lir**			
	28.11.1944. Brown-red. Man in national costume at right. Slovene text. Series A. Back: Man in national costume at right. German text.	2.50	10.00	25.00

		VG	VF	UNC
R20	**10 Lir**			
	28.11.1944. Bluish-purple. Woman wearing national costume hat at left. Slovene text. Series D. Back: Woman wearing national costume hat at left. German text.	2.50	10.00	25.00
R21	**50 Lir**			
	14.9.1944. Red on gold underprint. Farmer's wife at left. Slovene text. Back: Farmer's wife at right. German text.	2.50	12.50	30.00
R22	**100 Lir**			
	14.9.1944. Blue on gold underprint. Farmer with scythe at left. Slovene text. Back: Farmer with scythe at right. German text.	4.00	15.00	45.00

		VG	VF	UNC
R23	**500 Lir**			
	14.9.1944. Blue on green and gray underprint. Man in national costume at left. Slovene text. Back: Man in national costume at right. German text.	5.00	25.00	70.00

		VG	VF	UNC
R24	**1000 Lir**			
	14.9.1944. Brown on tan underprint. Woman wearing national costume hat at left. Slovene text. Back: Woman wearing national costume hat at right. German text.	10.00	50.00	125.

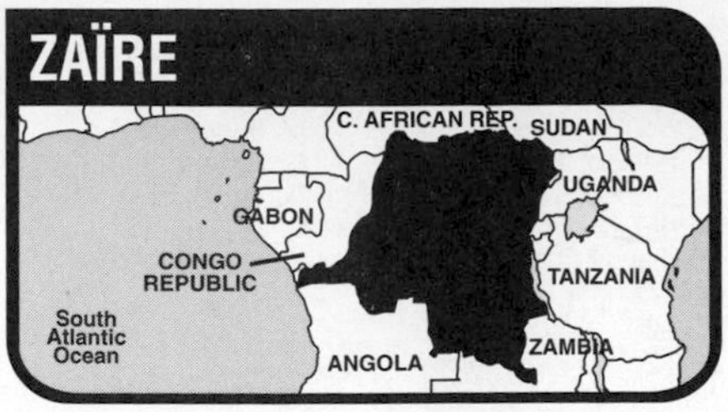

The Republic of Zaïre (formerly the Congo Democratic Republic) located in the south-central part of Africa, has an area of 905,568 sq. mi. (2,345,409 sq. km.) and a population of 43.81 million. Capital: Kinshasa. The mineral-rich country produces copper, tin, diamonds, gold, zinc, cobalt and uranium.

In ancient times the territory comprising Zaïre was occupied by Negrito peoples (Pygmies) pushed into the mountains by Bantu and Nilotic invaders. The interior was first explored by the American correspondent Henry Stanley, who was subsequently commissioned by King Leopold II of Belgium to conclude development treaties with the local chiefs. The Berlin conference of 1885 awarded the area to Leopold, who administered and exploited it as his private property until it was annexed to Belgium in 1908. Following the eruption of bloody independence riots in 1959, Belgium granted the Belgian Congo independence as the Republic of the Congo on June 30, 1960. The Belgian Congo attained independence with the distinction of being the most ill-prepared country to ever undertake self-government. Without a single doctor, lawyer or engineer, with no organized unit capable of maintaining law and order, independence disintegrated into an orgy of anarchy. Provinces seceded. Intertribal warfare erupted. Belgian troops intervened to protect Belgian citizens from retributive massacre. By 1961, four groups were fighting for political dominance. The most serious threat to the viability of the country was posed by the secession of mineral-rich Katanga province on July 11, 1960.

After two and one-half years of sporadic warfare with a U.N. military force, Katanga's leaders capitulated, Jan. 14, 1963 and the rebellious province was partioned into three provinces. The nation officially changed its name to Zaïre on Oct. 27, 1971. In May 1997, the dictator was overthrown after a three-year rebellion. The country changed its name to the Democratic Republic of the Congo.

See also Rwanda, Rwanda-Burundi or Congo Democratic Republic.

MONETARY SYSTEM:

1 Franc = 100 Centimes to 1967
1 Zaïre = 100 Makuta, 1967-1993

1 Nouveau Zaïre = 100 N Makuta = 3 million "old" Zaïres, 1993-1998

Banque du Zaïre GovernorGovernor

J. Sambwa Mbagui	Bofossa W. Amba
Emony	J. Sambwa Mbagui
Pay Pay wa Syakassighe	Nyembo Shabanga
B. Mushaba	Ndiang Kabul
L. O. Djamboleka	

REGIONAL

Validation Ovpt:

Type I: Circular handstamp: *REPUBLIQUE DU ZAÏRE-REGION DU BAS-ZAÏRE; GARAGE - STA/BANANA* around arms.

BANQUE DU ZAÏRE BRANCHES

1980'S ND PROVISIONAL ISSUE

	Good	Fine	XF
R3 5 Zaïres			
1980's ND (- old date 1972-77). Overprint: Handstamp on #21b.			
a. 1972.	5.00	15.00	60.00
b. 1974-76.	3.00	7.00	30.00
c. 1977.	1.00	3.00	7.50
R4 10 Zaïres			
1980's ND (-old date various). Overprint: Handstamp on #23b.			
a. 1975-76.	4.00	7.00	30.00
b. 1977.	1.00	3.00	10.00

HEJIRA DATE CONVERSION CHART

HEJIRA (Hijira, Hegira), the name of the Muslim era (A.H. = Anno Heglrae) dates back to the Christian year 622 when Mohammed "fled" from Mecca, escaping to Medina to avoid persecution from the Koreish tribemen. Based on a lunar year the Muslim year is 11 days shorter.

*=Leap Year (Christian Calendar)

AH Hejira	AD Christian Date
1010	1601, July 2
1011	1602, June 21
1012	1603, June 11
1013	1604, May 30
1014	1605, May 19
1015	1606, May 9
1016	1607, April 28
1017	1608, April 17
1018	1609, April 6
1017	1608, April 28
1018	1609, April 6
1019	1610, March 26
1020	1611, March 16
1021	1612, March 4
1022	1613, February 21
1023	1614, February 11
1024	1615, January 31
1025	1616, January 20
1026	1617, January 9
1027	1617, December 29
1028	1618, December 19
1029	1619, December 8
1030	1620, November 26
1031	1621, November 16
1032	1622, November 5
1033	1623, October 25
1034	1624, October 14
1035	1625, October 3
1036	1626, September 22
1037	1627, September 12
1038	1628, August 31
1039	1629, August 21
1040	1630, August 10
1041	1631, July 30
1042	1632, July 19
1043	1633, July 8
1044	1634, June 27
1045	1635, June 17
1046	1636, June 5
1047	1637, May 26
1048	1638, May 15
1049	1639, May 4
1050	1640, April 23
1051	1641, April 12
1052	1642, April 1
1053	1643, March 22
1054	1644, March 10
1055	1645, February 27
1056	1646, February 17
1057	1647, February 6
1058	1648, January 27
1059	1649, January 15
1060	1650, January 4
1061	1650, December 25
1062	1651, December 14
1063	1652, December 2
1064	1653, November 22
1065	1654, November 11
1066	1655, October 31
1067	1656, October 20
1068	1657, October 9
1069	1658, September 29
1070	1659, September 18
1071	1660, September 6
1072	1661, August 27
1073	1662, August 16
1074	1663, August 5
1075	1664, July 25
1076	1665, July 14
1077	1666, July 4
1078	1667, June 23
1079	1668, June 11
1080	1669, June 1
1081	1670, May 21
1082	1671, May 10
1083	1672, April 29
1084	1673, April 18
1085	1674, April 7

AH Hejira	AD Christian Date
1086	1675, March 28
1087	1676, March 16*
1088	1677, March 6
1089	1678, February 23
1090	1679, February 12
1091	1680, February 2*
1092	1681, January 21
1093	1682, January 10
1094	1682, December 31
1095	1683, December 20
1096	1684, December 8*
1097	1685, November 28
1098	1686, November 17
1099	1687, November 7
1100	1688, October 26*
1101	1689, October 15
1102	1690, October 5
1103	1691, September 24
1104	1692, September 12*
1105	1693, September 2
1106	1694, August 22
1107	1695, August 12
1108	1696, July 31*
1109	1697, July 20
1110	1698, July 10
1111	1699, June 29
1112	1700, June 18
1113	1701, June 8
1114	1702, May 28
1115	1703, May 17
1116	1704, May 6*
1117	1705, April 25
1118	1706, April 15
1119	1707, April 4
1120	1708, March 23*
1121	1709, March 13
1122	1710, March 2
1123	1711, February 19
1124	1712, February 9*
1125	1713, January 28
1126	1714, January 17
1127	1715, January 7
1128	1715, December 27
1129	1716, December 16*
1130	1717, December 5
1131	1718, November 24
1132	1719, November 14
1133	1720, November 2*
1134	1721, October 22
1135	1722, October 12
1136	1723, October 1
1137	1724, September 19
1138	1725, September 9
1139	1726, August 29
1140	1727, August 19
1141	1728, August 7*
1142	1729, July 27
1143	1730, July 17
1144	1731, July 6
1145	1732, June 24*
1146	1733, June 14
1147	1734, June 3
1148	1735, May 24
1149	1736, May 12*
1150	1737, May 1
1151	1738, April 21
1152	1739, April 10
1153	1740, March 29*
1154	1741, March 19
1155	1742, March 8
1156	1743, February 25
1157	1744, February 15*
1158	1745, February 3
1159	1746, January 24
1160	1747, January 13
1161	1748, January 2
1162	1748, December 22*
1163	1749, December 11
1164	1750, November 30
1165	1751, November 20
1166	1752, November 8*
1167	1753, October 29
1168	1754, October 18
1169	1755, October 7
1170	1756, September 26*
1171	1757, September 15
1172	1758, September 4
1173	1759, August 25
1174	1760, August 13*
1175	1761, August 2
1176	1762, July 23

AH Hejira	AD Christian Date
1177	1763, July 12
1178	1764, July 1*
1179	1765, June 20
1180	1766, June 9
1181	1767, May 30
1182	1768, May 18*
1183	1769, May 7
1184	1770, April 27
1185	1771, April 16
1186	1772, April 4*
1187	1773, March 25
1188	1774, March 14
1189	1775, March 4
1190	1776, February 21*
1191	1777, February 1
1192	1778, January 30
1193	1779, January 19
1194	1780, January 8*
1195	1780, December 28*
1196	1781, December 17
1197	1782, December 7
1198	1783, November 26
1199	1784, November 14*
1200	1785, November 4
1201	1786, October 24
1202	1787, October 13
1203	1788, October 2*
1204	1789, September 21
1205	1790, September 10
1206	1791, August 31
1207	1792, August 19*
1208	1793, August 9
1209	1794, July 29
1210	1795, July 18
1211	1796, July 7*
1212	1797, June 26
1213	1798, June 15
1214	1799, June 5
1215	1800, May 25
1216	1801, May 14
1217	1802, May 4
1218	1803, April 23
1219	1804, April 12*
1220	1805, April 1
1221	1806, March 21
1222	1807, March 11
1223	1808, February 28*
1224	1809, February 16
1225	1810, February 6
1226	1811, January 26
1227	1812, January 16*
1228	1813, January 6
1229	1813, December 24
1230	1814, December 14
1231	1815, December 3
1232	1816, November 21*
1233	1817, November 11
1234	1818, October 31
1235	1819, October 20
1236	1820, October 9*
1237	1821, September 28
1238	1822, September 18
1239	1823, September 8
1240	1824, August 26*
1241	1825, August 16
1242	1826, August 5
1243	1827, July 25
1244	1828, July 14*
1245	1829, July 3
1246	1830, June 22
1247	1831, June 12
1248	1832, May 31*
1249	1833, May 21
1250	1834, May 10
1251	1835, April 29
1252	1836, April 18*
1253	1837, April 7
1254	1838, March 27
1255	1839, March 17
1256	1840, March 5*
1257	1841, February 23
1258	1842, February 12
1259	1843, February 1
1260	1844, January 22*
1261	1845, January 10
1262	1845, December 30
1263	1846, December 20
1264	1847, December 9
1265	1848, November 27*
1266	1849, November 17
1267	1850, November 6

AH Hejira	AD Christian Date
1268	1851, October 27
1269	1852, October 15*
1270	1853, October 4
1271	1854, September 24
1272	1855, September 13
1273	1856, September 1*
1274	1857, August 22
1275	1858, August 11
1276	1859, July 31
1277	1860, July 20*
1278	1861, July 9
1279	1862, June 29
1280	1863, June 18
1281	1864, June 6*
1282	1865, May 27
1283	1866, May 16
1284	1867, May 5
1285	1868, April 24*
1286	1869, April 13
1287	1870, April 3
1288	1871, March 23
1289	1872, March 11*
1290	1873, March 1
1291	1874, February 18
1292	1875, February 7
1293	1876, January 28*
1294	1877, January 16
1295	1878, January 5
1296	1878, December 26
1297	1879, December 15
1298	1880, December 4*
1299	1881, November 23
1300	1882, November 12
1301	1883, November 2
1302	1884, October 21*
1303	1885, October 10
1304	1886, September 30
1305	1887, September 19
1306	1888, September 7*
1307	1889, August 28
1308	1890, August 17
1309	1891, August 7
1310	1892, July 26*
1311	1893, July 15
1312	1894, July 5
1313	1895, June 24
1314	1896, June 12*
1315	1897, June 2
1316	1898, May 22
1317	1899, May 12
1318	1900, May 1
1319	1901, April 20
1320	1902, April 10
1321	1903, March 30
1322	1904, March 18*
1323	1905, March 8
1324	1906, February 25
1325	1907, February 14
1326	1908, February 4*
1327	1909, January 23
1328	1910, January 13
1329	1911, January 2
1330	1911, December 22
1332	1913, November 30
1333	1914, November 19
1334	1915, November 9
1335	1916, October 28*
1336	1917, October 17
1337	1918, October 7
1338	1919, September 26
1339	1920, September 15*
1340	1921, September 4
1341	1922, August 24
1342	1923, August 14
1343	1924, August 2*
1344	1925, July 22
1345	1926, July 12
1346	1927, July 1
1347	1928, June 20*
1348	1929, June 9
1349	1930, May 29
1350	1931, May 19
1351	1932, May 7*
1352	1933, April 26
1353	1934, April 16
1354	1935, April 5
1355	1936, March 24*
1356	1937, March 14
1357	1938, March 3
1358	1939, February 21
1359	1940, February 10*

AH Hejira	AD Christian Date
1360	1941, January 29
1361	1942, January 19
1362	1943, January 8
1363	1943, December 28
1364	1944, December 17*
1365	1945, December 6
1366	1946, November 25
1367	1947, November 15
1368	1948, November 3*
1369	1949, October 24
1370	1950, October 13
1371	1951, October 2
1372	1952, September 21*
1373	1953, September 10
1374	1954, August 30
1375	1955, August 20
1376	1956, August 8*
1377	1957, July 29
1378	1958, July 18
1379	1959, July 7
1380	1960, June 25*
1381	1961, June 14
1382	1962, June 4
1383	1963, May 25
1384	1964, May 13*
1385	1965, May 2
1386	1966, April 22
1387	1967, April 11
1388	1968, March 31*
1389	1969, March 20
1390	1970, March 9
1391	1971, February 27
1392	1972, February 16*
1393	1973, February 4
1394	1974, January 25
1395	1975, January 14
1396	1976, January 3*
1397	1976, December 23*
1398	1977, December 12
1399	1978, December 2
1400	1979, November 21
1401	1980, November 9*
1402	1981, October 30
1403	1982, October 19
1404	1984, October 8
1405	1984, September 27*
1406	1985, September 16
1407	1986, September 6
1409	1987, August 26
1409	1988, August 14*
1410	1989, August 3
1411	1990, July 24
1412	1991, July 13
1413	1992, July 2*
1414	1993, June 21
1415	1994, June 10
1416	1995, May 31
1417	1996, May 19*
1418	1997, May 9
1419	1998, April 28
1420	1999, April 17
1421	2000, April 6*
1422	2001, March 26
1423	2002, March 15
1424	2003, March 5
1425	2004, February 22*
1426	2005, February 10
1427	2006, January 31
1428	2007, January 20
1429	2008, January 10*
1430	2008, December 29
1431	2009, December 18
1432	2010, December 8
1433	2011, November 27*
1434	2012, November 15
1435	2013, November 5
1436	2014, October 25
1437	2015, October 15*
1438	2016, October 3
1439	2017, September 22
1440	2018, September 12
1441	2019, September 1*
1442	2020, August 20
1443	2021, August 10
1444	2022, July 30
1445	2023, July 19*
1446	2024, July 8
1447	2025, June 27
1448	2026, June 17
1449	2027, June 6*
1450	2028, May25

Experience. Knowledge. Integrity.

Backed by the Ponterio Family Name

Kent Ponterio

Kyle Ponterio

Richard Ponterio

When Richard Ponterio opened his new auction house in 1982 he knew he wanted to become the premier auctioneer of ancient and world coins and paper money, in honor of his lifelong passion. He felt so confident in their capabilities that he put his own name on the door, and more than 25 years later, two generations of Ponterios have made the family business stronger than ever. Now a division of Bowers and Merena Auctions, the two together create an auction powerhouse that covers the collecting interests of U.S. and world enthusiasts.

Call today to speak with Kent, Kyle, or Rick Ponterio about how you can maximize your consignment potential in an upcoming Ponterio & Associates auction of ancient and world coins and paper money.

Of Particular Interest:

Rare U.S. and World Coins • American Coins • Mexican Coins • Spain and All Spanish Colonial Coins • South and Central American Coins • Germany, Austria and Switzerland • British and British Colonial • Japan, Korea and Philippines • Ancient Coins • Rare World Banknotes

We also buy and sell direct – please call for information.

For more information on consigning to a future Ponterio & Associates auction, please contact us at the Bowers and Merena offices.

800.458.4646

Ponterio
& associates, inc.
a division of
BOWERS AND MERENA AUCTIONS

P·N·G
Knowledge · Integrity · Responsibility
RICHARD H. PONTERIO
PNG #308

18061 Fitch, Irvine, CA 92614
TOLL FREE: 800.458.4646 • Fax: 949.253.4091
Email: auction@bowersandmerena.com • www.bowersandmerena.com

ANA 1891
RICHARD H. PONTERIO
LM-2163